PEARS

CYCLOPAEDIA

1977–78

A BOOK OF BACKGROUND INFORMATION AND REFERENCE FOR EVERYDAY USE

ANNIVERSARY EDITION
1897–1977

EDITED BY

L. MARY BARKER
B.Sc. Lond.

AND

CHRISTOPHER COOK
M.A. Cantab., D.Phil. Oxon., F.R.Hist.S.

Eighty-sixth edition

The Editors desire to express their gratitude to readers for their criticisms and suggestions and to all those who in one way or another have contributed to the making of this edition. Correspondence is welcomed and should be addressed to Dr. Christopher Cook, "Pears Cyclopaedia", Pelham Books Ltd., 52 Bedford Square, London, WC1B 3EF.

First published 1897

ISBN 0 7207 1004 9

Printed and Bound in Great Britain by Richard Clay (The Chaucer Press) Ltd, Bungay, Suffolk

CONTENTS

Sections are arranged alphabetically, or chronologically, or have a detailed Table of Contents.

HISTORICAL EVENTS

Chronicle of events from the earliest times to the present day. For events in pre-history the reader may also like to consult the Geological Time Scale in Part IV and the sub-section "Man's Primate Ancestry" in Part V of the Science Section.

CHRONICLE OF EVENTS

Note.—*For classical history and for the past millennium most dates are well established. For other periods there is sometimes considerable uncertainty. Many of the dates in ancient history are either dubious or approximate, sometimes both.*

B.C. **PREHISTORY**

4,600,000,000 Age of Earth.

3,300,000,000 Earliest known rocks (found in Greenland).

2,000,000,000 Life appears.

600,000,000 First large-scale occurrence of fossils.

30,000,000 Earliest ape fossils (Oligocene period—Fayum, Egypt).

20,000,000 Early ape fossils (Miocene period—*Proconsul*, E. Africa).

1,700,000 Earliest known hominids (Lower Pleistocene—*Australopithecus*, and *Homo habilis* S. Africa, E. Africa.) Oldowan culture—first stage of Palaeolithic or Old Stone Age (hunting and food-gathering) which persisted until end of Ice Age, *c.* 8,000 B.C.

400,000 *Homo erectus* stage (Java, China, Africa) with crude chopping tools and early hand-axes. Heidelberg jaw, Vertezöllös remains (Europe).

180,000 Ancestors of Neanderthalers and *Homo sapiens*, with advanced hand-axes (Europe: Steinheim and Swanscombe).

70,000 Neanderthalers (Europe, Asia, N. Africa). Rhodesian Man (S. Africa). Solo Man (Java). Flake tools.

40,000 First cold phase ends. Neanderthal race becoming extinct.

30,000 Second cold phase. *Homo sapiens* (modern man). Implements show significant advances: small knife-blades, engraving tools. Paintings and sculpture; magic rites and ceremonies. Cro-Magnons with Aurignacian culture.

18,000 Final culmination of last ice age. Aurignacian culture dying out to be replaced by Solutrean and then by the Magdalenian cultures. Great flowering of Palaeolithic art.

15,000 First immigrants from Asia to cross Behring Straits?

8,000 Last glaciers in Britain disappeared. Proto-Neolithic in Middle East. Agricultural settlements (*e.g.*, Jericho). Settled way of life leading eventually to such skills as weaving, metallurgy; inventions as ox-drawn plough, wheeled cart.

5,000 Britain becomes an island (land connection with continent severed by melting ice-sheets).

B.C. **CIVILISATION IN THE MIDDLE EAST**

4000 Susa founded.

3500 Sumerian civilisation flourishes. Cuneiform writing.

3100 First Egyptian Dynasty. Hieratic writing already perfected.
Early Minoan Age (Crete). Pictorial writing, copper, silver, gold in use. Early Mycenaean civilisation begins.

2980 Memphis capital of Egypt.

B.C.

2870 First settlements at Troy.

2850 Golden Age of China begins (legendary).

2700 Great Pyramid age in Egypt begins.

2400 Aryan migrations.

2371 Sargon founds Akkad: Akkadian empire.

2205 Hsia Dynasty begins in China (legendary).

2200 Middle Minoan Age: pottery, linear writing in pen and ink.

2100–1600 Building and rebuilding of Stonehenge.

1720–1550 Hyksos in Egypt. War chariots introduced. Hebrews entered Egypt (Joseph) *c.* 1600.

1751 Code of Hammurabi at Babylon.

1600 Late Minoan Age: Linear B script.

1600–1027 Shang Dynasty in China.

1546 18th Dynasty in Egypt commences. Civilisation at peak (under Tuthmosis III, 1490). Chronology more certain.

1500 Powerful Mitanni (Aryan) kingdom in Asia Minor. Phoenicia thriving—trade with Egypt and Babylonia. Vedic literature in India.

1450 Zenith of Minoan civilisation.

1400 Ugarit (N. Syria) culture at its zenith. Cretan civilisation ends: Knossos burnt. Temple at Luxor built.

1379 Amenhotep IV (Akhnaten), the "heretic" Pharaoh.

1350 Zenith of Hittite civilisation.

1300 Israelite oppression (Rameses II): Exodus from Egypt (Moses). Phoenician settlements—Hellas and Spain (Cadiz). Tyre flourishing.

1250 Israelites invade Palestine (Joshua).

1200 Attacks on Egypt by "Peoples of the Sea". Downfall of Hittite kingdom. Siege of Troy (Homeric). Beginning of sea-power of independent Phoenician cities. Probably all these are connected with Achaean and other migrations in Aegean area.

1115 Magnetic needle reputed in China.

1027–249 Chou Dynasty in China.

1005–925 Kingdom of David and Solomon: Jerusalem as Sanctuary.

1000 *Rig Veda* (India).

925–722 Israel and Judah divided.

900 Probably period of writing of Homer's epics.

893 Assyrian chronological records begin.

850 Foundation of Carthage (traditional).

781 Chinese record of an eclipse.

776 First Olympiad to be used for chronological purposes.

753 Foundation of Rome (traditional).

750 Greek colonists settling in Southern Italy.

745 Accession of Tiglath-Pileser III; Assyrian Power at its height.

722 Capture of Samaria by Sargon II: Israel deported to Nineveh.

683 Kingship abolished in Athens.

625 Neo-Babylonian (Chaldean) Empire (Nineveh destroyed 612).

B.C.

621 Publication of Athenian laws by Draco.

610 Spartan constitution, made rigid after Messenian Wars: later attributed to Lycurgus.

594 Athenian constitution reformed by Solon.

586 Capture of Jerusalem: Judah deported to Babylon (partial return 538).

561 Pisistratus tyrant of Athens.

560 Accession of Croesus—great prosperity of Lydia.

538 Babylon taken by Persians: Empire founded by Cyrus, soon covers almost all of civilised Middle East.

509 Foundation of Roman Republic (traditional).

508 Democratic constitution proclaimed in Athens.

500 Etruscans at height of their power in Northern Italy. Iron age beginning in Britain.

GREAT AGE OF GREECE

499 Revolt of Ionian Greek cities against Persian king Darius.

494 Secession of Plebeians from Rome. Tribunes established.

490 Battle of Marathon: Athenian repulse of Persian attack.

480 Death of Buddha. Battle of Thermopylae: Spartans under Leonidas wiped out by Persians. Battle of Salamis: Persian fleet defeated by Athenians under Themistocles; Persian invasion of Greece halted.

479 Battles of Plataea and Mycale: Greek victories by land and sea respectively destroy Persian invasion force. Death of Confucius.

477 League of Delos founded by Athens for defence against Persia; soon becomes Athenian Empire. (467 Naxos kept in by force.)

461 Pericles comes to power in Athens.

458 Cincinnatus saves Rome (traditional).

456 Death of Aeschylus.

447 Building of Parthenon begun.

431 Death of Phidias. Outbreak of Great Peloponnesian War between Athens and Sparta. Pericles "Funeral Oration" (according to Thucydides).

425 Death of Herodotus.

416 Massacre of Melos by Athenians.

415 Sicilian Expedition: flight of Alcibiades from Athens to Sparta.

413 Loss of entire Athenian expeditionary force at Syracuse.

406 Death of Euripides and Sophocles.

405 Battle of Aegospotami: Athenian navy destroyed by Sparta.

404 Athenian surrender to Sparta: beginning of Spartan hegemony in Greece.

403 Beginning of epoch of Warring States in China.

400 Death of Thucydides, Greek historian (?).

399 Execution of Socrates.

390 Occupation of Rome by Gauls under Brennus.

371 Battle of Leuctra: Spartans defeated by Thebans: beginning of Theban hegemony in Greece.

370 Death of Hippocrates of Cos (?).

347 Death of Plato.

338 Battle of Chaeronea: Greek city-states defeated by Philip II of Macedon, who becomes supreme in Greece.

336 Assassination of Philip of Macedon: accession of Alexander.

334 Alexander's invasion of Persian Empire. Battle of Granicus, first victory.

333 Battle of Issus: Alexander defeats Darius of Persia.

332 Alexander's siege and capture of Tyre, occupation of Egypt.

B.C.

331 Battle of Arbela (Gaugamela)—final defeat of Darius.

330 Death of Darius and end of Persian Empire. Alexander heir to civilisations of Middle East.

326 Battle of Hydaspes: Alexander conquers the Punjab.

323 Death of Alexander at Babylon. Beginning of Hellenistic Age in Middle East and Eastern Mediterranean. Ptolemy I founds dynasty in Egypt. Alexandria becomes intellectual centre of Hellenic world.

322 Death of Demosthenes.

321 Death of Aristotle. Maurya dynasty unites N. India.

312 Seleucus I founds dynasty in Asia.

300 Zeno the Stoic, Epicurus and Euclid flourishing.

ROME: CONQUESTS AND DECAY OF REPUBLICAN INSTITUTIONS

290 End of Third Samnite War. Rome dominates Central Italy.

280 Translation of Pentateuch into Greek.

275 Battle of Beneventum: Rome finally defeats Pyrrhus and the Greek cities of Southern Italy. Rome dominates all Italy.

274 Asoka becomes ruler of two-thirds of Indian sub-continent.

264 Beginning of First Punic War (Rome *v.* Carthage).

260 Battle of Mylae: first great Roman naval victory.

255 Defeat and capture of Regulus by Carthaginians.

250 "La Tène" Iron Age people invade Britain.

241 End of First Punic War. Sicily becomes first Province of Rome.

221 Kingdom of Ch'in completes conquest of all Chinese states under Shih Huang-ti.

218 Outbreak of Second Punic War: Hannibal crosses Alps.

216 Battle of Cannae: Hannibal wipes out great Roman army.

214 Great Wall of China constructed (by linking existing walls).

213 Burning of Chinese classics.

212 Capture of Syracuse by Romans and death of Archimedes.

207 Battle of Metaurus: defeat and death of Hasdrubal. End of Hannibal's hopes of overcoming Rome.

205 Roman provinces organised in Spain.

202 Battle of Zama: Hannibal defeated by Scipio Africanus. 202–A.D. 220 Han Dynasty in China.

201 End of Second Punic War. Rome dominates Western Mediterranean.

196 After defeating Macedon, Rome proclaims independence of Greek city-states. Death of Eratosthenes the geographer (?).

160 Death in battle of Judas Maccabaeus: Jewish revolt against Seleucids continues successfully.

149 Outbreak of Third Punic War.

146 Carthage destroyed. Roman province of Africa formed. Roman provinces of Macedonia and Achaea formed, and most of remainder of Greece reduced to vassal status.

134 First Servile War: Revolt of slaves in Sicily under Eunus. Suppressed 132.

133 Siege and destruction of Numantia by Romans. Tiberius Gracchus Tribune. Attempted land reforms. Murdered 132.

129 Roman province of Asia formed from lands bequeathed by Attalus of Pergamum.

124 Chinese Grand College to train Civil Service officials.

123 Caius Gracchus Tribune. Attempted land reforms. Murdered 121.

110 Chinese expansion to include most of south-east of modern China, under Emperor Wu Ti. Commercial activity in Indian Ocean.

B.C.

106 Jugurtha captured by Marius and Sulla.

104 Second Servile War: revolt of slaves in Sicily under Tryphon and Athenion. Suppressed 101.

102 Chinese expedition to Ferghana and possible knowledge of West.

101 Battle of Vercellae: Marius ends threat of Cimbri to Rome.

91 Social War: revolt of Italian cities against Rome. Suppressed 88. Roman franchise granted to most Italians.

88 Civil Wars of Marius and Sulla begin.

87 Massacre in Rome by Marius.

82 Proscriptions in Rome by Sulla.

75 Belgic invasion of south-eastern Britain.

73 Third Servile War: revolt of slaves in southern Italy under Spartacus the gladiator. Suppressed 71.

63 Conspiracy of Catiline exposed by Cicero.

60 First Triumvirate: Pompey, Caesar, Crassus.

58 Beginning of Caesar's conquest of Gaul.

55 Caesar's first British expedition: second, 54.

53 Battle of Carrhae: destruction of Roman army under Crassus by Persians.

52 Revolt of Vercingetorix against Caesar.

50 Migration to Britain of Commius and his followers.

49 Caesar crosses the Rubicon. Beginning of war against Pompey and the Senate.

48 Battle of Pharsalus: defeat of Pompey by Caesar.

46 Caesar's calendar reforms.

44 Murder of Caesar.

43 Second Triumvirate: Antony, Octavian, Lepidus.

42 Battle of Philippi: defeat and death of Brutus and his associates.

31 Battle of Actium: naval victory of Octavian over Antony and Cleopatra. Octavian unchallenged master of the Roman world.

THE ROMAN EMPIRE

27 Octavian given the title of Augustus by the Senate.

19 Death of Virgil.

8 Death of Horace

4 Assumed birth of Jesus.

A.D.

6 Civil Service Examination system in China.

9 Radical reforms by Wang Mang (short Hsin dynasty 9–23). Annihilation of Roman army under Varus by Teutonic tribesman under Arminius.

10 Cunobelinus reigning over much of south-east Britain from Colchester.

14 Death of Augustus.

17 Death of Livy.

18 Death of Ovid.

30 Crucifixion of Jesus.

43 Roman invasion of Britain under Aulus Plautius.

51 Caractacus taken to Rome as prisoner.

60 Revolt of Boudicca.

63 Death of St. Paul.

64 Great Fire of Rome.

65 Death of Seneca.

66 Jews of Palestine rebelled against Roman rule.

68 Death of Nero—end of Julio-Claudian line of Roman Emperors.

70 Jerusalem taken and Jewish revolt suppressed by Titus.

79 Destruction of Pompeii and Herculaneum by eruption of Vesuvius.

A.D.

80 Completion of Colosseum (Flavian Amphitheatre).

83 Battle of Mons Graupius: Agricola crushes Caledonians.

96 Accession of Nerva: first of the "Five Good Emperors."

97 Chinese expedition under Kang Yin (lieutenant of Pan Ch'ao) penetrates to Persian Gulf.

117 Death of Trajan, accession of Hadrian. Roman Empire at its greatest extent.

122 Beginning of Hadrian's Wall (Tyne–Solway) by Aulus Platorius Nepos.

135 Suppression of Bar-Cochba's revolt and Dispersion of Jews.

142 Construction of Antonine Wall (Forth–Clyde) by Quintus Lollius Urbicus.

180 Death of Marcus Aurelius, last of the "Five Good Emperors." Beginning of the "Decline" of the Roman Empire (Gibbon).

193 Praetorian guards murder Emperor Pertinax, sell Empire to highest bidder (Didius Julianus).

196 Clodius Albinus, governor, withdraws forces from Britain to support his attempt to become Emperor. Northern Britain overrun by barbarians.

208 Septimius Severus visits Britain to punish Caledonians (death at York 211).

212 Edict of Caracalla. Roman citizenship conferred on all free inhabitants of Empire.

220 End of Han Dynasty: China divided and frequently invaded for next three centuries.

227 Sassanid Empire in Persia.

230 Emperor Sujin—Japanese history emerging from legendary stage.

251 Goths defeat and kill Emperor Decius.

259 Break-away "Gallic Empire" set up: suppressed 273.

273 Defeat of Zenobia and destruction of Palmyra by Emperor Aurelian.

284 Accession of Diocletian, who reorganises Roman Empire (293) with rigid social laws and heavy taxation.

287 Carausius attempts to found independent "Empire of Britain": suppressed 297.

306 Constantine proclaimed Emperor at York.

313 Edict of Milan. Christianity tolerated in Roman Empire.

320 Gupta dynasty reunites India.

325 Council of Nicaea: first general Council of the Church.

367 Successful attack on Britain by Picts, Scots, Saxons.

369 Restoration of Roman authority in Britain by Theodosius.

378 Battle of Adrianople: Goths defeat and kill Eastern Roman Emperor Valens.

383 Magnus Maximus withdraws forces from Britain to support his attempt to conquer north-western part of Empire.

388 Magnus Maximus defeated and killed in Italy.

395 Death of Emperor Theodosius the Great: the division of the Empire into East and West at his death proves eventually to be the final one.

406 Usurper Constantine III withdraws forces from Britain to support his claims: probable end of Roman military occupation of Britain.

410 Sack of Rome by Alaric the Goth. Emperor Honorius tells Britons to arrange for their own defence.

THE BARBARIAN INVASIONS

415 Visigoths begin conquest of Spain.

419 Visigothic kingdom of Toulouse recognised by Roman government.

429 Vandals begin conquest of North Africa.

432 St. Patrick begins mission in Ireland.

A.D.
446 "Groans of the Britons"—last appeal to Rome (traditional).

451 Châlons: Attila the Hun repelled from Gaul by mixed Roman–Barbarian forces.

452 Attila's raid into Italy: destruction of Aquilea and foundation of Venice by refugees.

455 Rome pillaged by Vandals.

476 Romulus Augustulus, last Western Roman Emperor, deposed by Odovacar: conventionally the end of the Western Roman Empire.

481 Clovis becomes King of the Franks, who eventually conquer Gaul (d. 511).

493 Theodoric founds Ostrogothic Kingdom in Italy (d. 526).

515 Battle of Mount Badon: West Saxon advance halted by Britons, perhaps led by Arthur (?).

BYZANTIUM AND ISLAM

527 Accession of Justinian I (d. 565).

529 Code of Civil Law published by Justinian. Rule of St. Benedict put into practice at Monte Cassino (traditional).

534 Byzantines under Belisarius reconquer North Africa from Vandals.

552 Byzantine reconquest of Italy complete.

563 St. Columba founds mission in Iona.

568 Lombard Kingdom founded in Italy.

570 Birth of Mohammed.

577 Battle of Deorham: West Saxon advance resumed.

581–618 Sui Dynasty in China.

590 Gregory the Great becomes Pope.

597 St. Augustine lands in Kent.

605 Grand Canal of China constructed.

618–907 T'ang Dynasty in China: their administrative system lasts in essentials for 1,300 years.

622 Hejira or flight from Mecca to Medina of Mohammed: beginning of Mohammedan era.

627 Battle of Nineveh: Persians crushed by Byzantines under Heraclius.

632 Death of Mohammed: all Arabia now Moslem. Accession of Abu Bakr, the first Caliph.

634 Battle of Heavenfield: Oswald becomes king of Northumbria, brings in Celtic Christianity.

638 Jerusalem captured by Moslems.

641 Battle of Mehawand: Persia conquered by Moslems.

643 Alexandria taken by Moslems.

645 Downfall of Soga clan in Japan, after establishing Buddhism: beginning of period of imitation of Chinese culture.

650 Slav occupation of Balkans now complete.

663 Synod of Whitby: Roman Christianity triumphs over Celtic Christianity in England.

685 Nectansmere: end of Northumbrian dominance in England.

698 Carthage taken by Moslems.

711 Tarik leads successful Moslem invasion of Spain.

718 Failure of second and greatest Moslem attack on Constantinople. Pelayo founds Christian kingdom of Asturias in Northern Spain.

726 Byzantine Emperor Leo III begins Iconoclast movement: opposed by Pope Gregory II, and an important cause of difference between Roman and Byzantine churches.

THE HOLY ROMAN EMPIRE AND THE TRIUMPH OF CHRISTIANITY IN EUROPE: NORSEMEN AND NORMANS

732 Tours: Moslem western advance halted by Charles Martel.

735 Death of Bede.

750 Beginning of Abbasid Caliphate (replacing Omayyads).

A.D.
751 Pepin King of the Franks: founds Carolingian dynasty. Ravenna taken by Lombards: end of Byzantine power in the West.

754 Pepin promises central Italy to Pope: beginning of temporal power of the Papacy.

778 Roncesvalles: defeat and death of Roland.

786 Accession of Haroun-al-Rashid in Baghdad.

793 Sack of Lindisfarne: Viking attacks on Britain begin.

795 Death of Offa: end of Mercian dominance in England.

800 Coronation of Charlemagne as Holy Roman Emperor.

814 Death of Charlemagne: division of empire.

825 Ellandun: Egbert defeats Mercians and Wessex becomes leading kingdom in England.

827 Moslem invasion of Sicily.

840 Moslems capture Bari and occupy much of Southern Italy.

843 Treaty of Verdun: final division of Carolingian Empire, and beginning of France and Germany as separate states.

844 Kenneth MacAlpin becomes king of Picts as well as Scots: the kingdom of Alban.

862 Rurik founds Viking state in Russia: first at Novgorod, later at Kiev.

866 Fujiwara period begins in Japan. Viking "Great Army" in England: Northumbria, East Anglia and Mercia subsequently overwhelmed.

868 Earliest dated printed book in China.

872 Harold Fairhair King of Norway.

874 Iceland settled by Norsemen.

885–6 Viking attack on Paris.

893 Simeon founds first Bulgar Empire in Balkans.

896 Arpad and the Magyars in Hungary.

899 Death of Alfred the Great.

900 Ghana at the height of its power in North West Africa.

907–960 Five Dynasties in China: partition.

910 Abbey of Cluny founded: monastic reforms spread from here.

911 Rolf (or Rollo) becomes ruler of Normandy.

912 Accession of Abderrahman III: the most splendid period of the Omayyad Caliphate of Cordova (d. 961).

928 Brandenburg taken from the Slavs by Henry the Fowler, first of the Saxon Holy Roman Emperors.

929 Death of Wenceslas, Christian King of Bohemia.

937 Battle of Brunanburh: crowning victory of Athelstan. West Saxon kings now masters of England.

955 Battle of Lechfeld: Magyars finally defeated by Otto the Great and settle in Hungary.

960–1279 Sung Dynasty in China.

965 Harold Bluetooth, king of Denmark, accepts Christianity.

966 Mieszko I, king of Poland, accepts Christianity.

968 Fatimids begin their rule in Egypt.

982 Discovery of Greenland by Norsemen.

987 Hugh Capet king of France: founder of Capetian dynasty.

988 Vladimir of Kiev accepts Christianity.

991 Battle of Maldon: defeat of Byrhtnoth of Essex by Vikings—renewed Viking raids on England.

993 Olof Skutkonung, king of Sweden, accepts Christianity.

1000 Leif Ericsson discovers North America.

1001 Coronation of St. Stephen of Hungary with crown sent by the Pope.

1002 Massacre of St. Brice's Day: attempt by Ethelred to exterminate Danes in England.

A.D.
1014 Battle of Clontarf: victory of Irish under Brian Boru over Vikings.

1016 Canute becomes king of England; builds short-lived Danish "empire."

1018 Byzantines under Basil II complete subjection of Bulgars.

1040 Attempts to implement Truce of God from about this time.

1046 Normans under Robert Guiscard in southern Italy.

1054 Beginning of Almoravid (Moslem) conquests in West Africa.

1060 Normans invade Sicily.

1066 Norman conquest of England under William I.

1069 Reforms of Wang An-Shih in China.

THE CRUSADES

1071 Manzikert: Seljuk Turks destroy Byzantine army and overrun Anatolia.

1073 Hildebrand (Gregory VII) becomes Pope. Church discipline and Papal authority enforced.

1075 Seljuk Turks capture Jerusalem.

1076 Kumbi, capital of Ghana, sacked by Almoravids: subsequent break-up of Ghana Empire.

1084 Carthusians founded by St. Bruno at Chartreuse.

1086 Compilation of Domesday Book.

1094 El Cid takes Valencia.

1095 Council of Clermont: Urban II preaches First Crusade.

1098 Cistercians founded by St. Robert at Cîteaux.

1099 First Crusade under Godfrey of Bouillon takes Jerusalem.

1100 Death of William Rufus in the New Forest. Baldwin I: Latin Kingdom of Jerusalem founded.

1106 Tinchebrai: Henry I of England acquires Normandy, captures his brother Robert.

1115 Abelard teaching at Paris. St. Bernard founds monastery at Clairvaux.

1119 Order of Knights Templars founded.

1120 Loss of the White Ship and heir to English throne.

1122 Concordat of Worms: Pope and Emperor compromise on the Investiture Controversy, but continue to quarrel over other matters (Guelfs and Ghibellines).

1135 Stephen takes English crown: civil wars with Matilda and anarchy ensue.

1143 Alfonso Henriques proclaimed first king of Portugal.

1144 Moslems take Christian stronghold of Edessa.

1148 Second Crusade fails to capture Damascus.

1150 Carmelites founded about this time by Berthold.

1152 Accession of Emperor Frederick Barbarossa.

1154 Henry of Anjou succeeds Stephen: first of Plantagenet kings of England.

1161 Explosives used in warfare in China.

1169 Strongbow invades Ireland: beginning of Anglo-Norman rule. Saladin ruling in Egypt.

1170 Murder of Thomas Becket in Canterbury cathedral.

1171 Spanish knightly Order of Santiago founded.

1176 Battle of Legnano: Frederick Barbarossa defeated by the Lombard League. Italian autonomy established.

1185 Kamakura Period in Japan: epoch of feudalism: until 1333.

1187 Hattin: destruction of Latin kingdom of Jerusalem by Saladin.

A.D.
1189 Third Crusade launched: leaders—Frederick Barbarossa, Philip Augustus of France, Richard Lionheart of England.

1191 Capture of Acre by Crusaders.

1192 End of Third Crusade without regaining Jerusalem. Richard I seized and held to ransom in Austria on return journey.

1198 Innocent III becomes Pope.

1202 Fourth Crusade, diverted by Venetians, takes Zara from Byzantines.

1204 Fourth Crusade captures Constantinople, founds Latin Empire. King John of England loses Normandy to France.

1206 Temujin proclaimed Gengiz Khan (Very Mighty King) of all the Mongols: soon controls all of Central Asia.

1208 Albigensian Crusade launched: the first against Christians.

1212 Battle of Las Navas de Tolosa: decisive victory of Spaniards over Moors. The Children's Crusade.

THE CULMINATION OF THE MIDDLE AGES

1215 Fourth Lateran Council: the authority of the mediaeval Church and Papacy at its zenith. Dominicans recognised by the Pope. Magna Carta extorted by barons from John.

1223 Franciscans recognised by the Pope.

1229 Emperor Frederick II, through diplomacy, recognised by Moslems as King of Jerusalem.

1230 Teutonic Knights established in Prussia.

1237 Golden Horde (Mongols) begin subjugation of Russia.

1241 Mongol incursions into Central Europe.

1250 St. Louis of France captured on his Crusade in Egypt. Mamelukes become rulers of Egypt. Mandingo king declares his independence of Ghana and embraces Islam.

1256 Conference of Baltic ports; the first form of the Hanseatic League.

1258 Provisions of Oxford: barons under Simon de Montfort force reforms on Henry III of England. Baghdad destroyed by Mongols.

1264 Battle of Lewes: Montfort's party become rulers of England.

1265 Simon de Montfort's Parliament. Battle of Evesham: defeat and death of de Montfort.

1274 Death of Thomas Aquinas.

1279–1368 Mongol Dynasty in China (Kublai Khan).

1281 Repulse of Mongol attack on Japan.

1282 Sicilian Vespers: rising of Sicilians against French ruler.

1284 Completion of Edward I of England's conquest of Wales.

1290 Expulsion of Jews from England. Death of Maid of Norway: Edward I begins attempts to rule Scotland.

1291 Fall of Acre: end of Crusading in Holy Land. Everlasting League of Uri: beginnings of Swiss Confederation.

1294 Death of Roger Bacon, the founder of experimental science.

1295 "Model Parliament" of Edward I (anticipated in 1275).

1308 Death of Duns Scotus.

THE DECLINE OF THE MIDDLE AGES

1309 Papacy moves to Avignon: beginning of the Babylonish Captivity.

1312 Suppression of Templars by king of France and Pope.

1314 Battle of Bannockburn: victory of Robert Bruce secures Scottish independence.

1321 Death of Dante.

1325 Zenith of Mandingo Empire of Mali (North West Africa) under Mansa Musa; superseded at end of 15th century by Songhai empire.

1327 Deposition of Edward II; subsequently murdered.

A.D.

1336 Ashikaga Period in Japan: great feudal lords semi-independent of authority of Shogun.

1337 Death of Giotto.

1338 Beginning of Hundred Years' War between England and France.

1340 Battle of Sluys: English capture French fleet.

1344 Swabian League: weakness of Imperial authority in Germany obliges towns to form leagues for mutual protection.

1346 Battles of Crecy and Neville's Cross: spectacular English victories over French and Scots.

1347 Calais taken by Edward III of England. Cola di Rienzi attempts to reform government of Rome: killed 1354.

1348 Black Death reaches Europe (England 1349, Scotland 1350).

1351 Statute of Labourers: attempt by English Parliament to freeze wages.

1353 Statute of Praemunire: restraints placed on Papal intervention in England.

1354 Ottoman Turks make first settlement in Europe, at Gallipoli.

1355 Death of Stephen Dushan: collapse of Serbian Empire which he had built.

1356 Battle of Poitiers: capture of King John of France by Black Prince. "Golden Bull" regulates Imperial elections in such a way as to place power in the hands of the German princes: valid until 1806.

1358 The Jacquerie: rising of French peasants.

1360 Peace of Bretigny: Edward III makes great territorial gains in France.

1362 English becomes the official language in Parliament and the Law Courts.

1363 Timur (Tamerlane) begins his career of conquest in Asia.

1368–1644 Ming Dynasty in China.

1370 Bertrand du Guesclin Constable of France: regains much territory from the English. Peace of Stralsund: Hansa in complete control of Baltic Sea.

1377 Pope returns to Rome: End of Babylonish Captivity.

1378 Disputed Papal Election: Beginning of Great Schism.

1380 Battle of Chioggia: decisive victory of Venice over Genoa. Battle of Kulikovo: Dmitri Donskoi of Moscow wins first major Russian victory over Golden Horde.

1381 Peasants' Revolt in England under Wat Tyler.

1384 Death of John Wyclif.

1385 Battle of Aljubarotta: Portugal safeguards independence from Castile.

1386 Battle of Sempach: Swiss safeguard independence from Habsburgs. Jagiello (Vladislav V) unites Lithuania and Poland.

1389 Battle of Kossovo: crushing defeat of Serbs and neighbouring nations by Turks.

1396 Battle of Nicopolis: "the last crusade" annihilated by Turks.

1397 Union of Kalmar: Denmark, Norway and Sweden united under one crown: dissolved 1448.

1398 Timur invades and pillages Northern India.

1399 Richard II deposed by Henry IV: first of the Lancastrian kings of England.

1400 Owen Glendower revolts in Wales. Death of Chaucer.

1401 De Haeretico Comburendo: the burning of heretics made legal in England.

1410 Battle of Tannenberg: Poles and Lithuanians break power of Teutonic Knights.

1415 Battle of Agincourt: great success of Henry V of England in France. Council of Constance ends Great Schism, burns John Hus.

1420 Treaty of Troyes: English claims to French throne recognised. Hussite Wars begin: Bohemian heretics defend themselves successfully.

A.D.

1429 Relief of Orleans by Joan of Arc.

1431 Burning of Joan of Arc.

1433 Rounding of Cape Bojador: first great achievement in exploration ordered by Henry the Navigator.

1434 Cosimo dei Medici begins his family's control of Florence.

1435 Congress of Arras: Burgundians withdraw support from England, in favour of France.

1438 Albert I becomes Emperor—the first Habsburg Emperor.

1440 Death of Jan van Eyck.

1450 Rebellion of Jack Cade against government of Henry VI of England.

1453 Battle of Castillon: final English defeat and end of Hundred Years' War. Constantinople taken by Turks: end of Byzantine or Eastern Roman Empire.

RENAISSANCE, DISCOVERIES, "NEW MONARCHIES"

1454 First dated printing from movable types in Europe: Papal indulgence printed at Mainz.

1455 First battle of St. Albans: beginning of Wars of the Roses.

1458 Mathias Corvinus becomes king of Hungary. George of Podiebrad becomes king of Bohemia.

1461 Battle of Towton: Yorkist victory in a particularly bloody battle. Louis XI becomes king of France.

1467 Charles the Bold becomes Duke of Burgundy.

1469 Marriage of Ferdinand of Aragon with Isabella of Castile: union of the main kingdoms of Spain. Lorenzo the Magnificent becomes ruler of Florence.

1470 Warwick ("The Kingmaker") turns Lancastrian, dethrones Edward IV.

1471 Return of Edward IV: Lancastrians crushed at Barnet and Tewkesbury. Ivan III of Moscow takes Novgorod: Muscovy rising to supremacy in Russia.

1476 Caxton sets up his press at Westminster.

1477 Battle of Nancy: defeat and death of Charles the Bold: end of the greatness of Burgundy.

1479 Pazzi conspiracy against the Medici in Florence.

1481 Inquisition becomes active in Castile (1484 in Aragon).

1485 Battle of Bosworth Field: beginning of Tudor period in England.

1487 Lambert Simnel's rising fails.

1488 Bartholomew Diaz rounds Cape of Good Hope.

1491 Brittany acquired by King of France (by marriage).

1492 Rodrigo Borgia becomes Pope Alexander VI. Granada, last Moorish foothold in Western Europe, conquered by Spain. Christopher Columbus discovers the West Indies.

1493 Sonni Ali brings Songhai Empire to height of its prestige: Timbuktu renowned centre of literary culture.

1494 Italy invaded by French led by Charles VIII: beginning of Italian Wars and "modern" European diplomacy and international relations. Treaty of Tordesillas: Spain and Portugal agree to divide unexplored part of world; subsequently approved by Pope.

1496 Hapsburg–Spanish marriages: foundation of later empires.

1497 Perkin Warbeck captured by Henry VII (hanged 1499). John Cabot discovers Newfoundland.

1498 Savonarola burned. Vasco da Gama at Calicut: the sea route to India found.

1499 Amerigo Vespucci charts part of the South American coast.

A.D.

1500 Brazil discovered by Pedro Cabral.

1503 Casa de Contratación established at Seville; beginnings of Spanish colonial government. Fall of Caesar Borgia.

1507 Affonso de Albuquerque becomes Viceroy of Portuguese Empire in the East.

1513 Accession of Pope Leo X, zenith of Renaissance Papacy. Machiavelli writes *The Prince*. Balboa discovers the Pacific (South Sea). Battle of Flodden: James IV of Scotland defeated and killed by English.

1514 Battle of Chaldiran: Turkish victory begins long series of wars between Turkish and Persian Empires.

REFORMATION, HAPSBURG–VALOIS WARS

1515 Francis I becomes king of France: victory of Marignano ends legend of Swiss invincibility. Thomas Wolsey becomes Lord Chancellor of England and Cardinal.

1516 Algiers taken by Barbarossa; beginning of the Corsairs.

1517 Martin Luther nails up his Ninety-five Theses: beginning of the Reformation. Turks conquer Egypt.

1519 Charles V inherits Hapsburg lands and elected emperor. Magellan begins first circumnavigation of the world. Death of Leonardo da Vinci.

1520 Suleiman the Magnificent becomes Sultan; Turkish power at its height. Field of Cloth of Gold; celebrated diplomatic meeting, spectacular but with no results.

1521 Mexico conquered by Hernando Cortes. Belgrade taken by the Turks. Diet of Worms; Luther commits himself irrevocably. Charles V divides his dominions: Austrian and Spanish Hapsburgs.

1522 Rhodes taken by the Turks; Knights of St. John move to Malta. Election of Adrian VI, last non-Italian Pope.

1523 Swedes expel Danish overlords, elect Gustavus Vasa King. [(1525).

1524 Peasants' War in Germany (suppressed

1525 Battle of Pavia: defeat and capture of Francis I by Imperialists.

1526 Battle of Mohács: Turkish victory ends Hungarian independence. Foundation of Danubian Hapsburg Monarchy (Hungarian and Bohemian crowns united with Austrian patrimony of Hapsburgs): Holy Roman Empire prolonged for 300 years. Battle of Panipat: Babar begins Moslem conquest of India, founds Mogul Empire.

1527 Sack of Rome by Imperialists. Italy under control of Charles V.

1529 Siege of Vienna by the Turks. Peace of Cambrai; pause in Hapsburg–Valois struggle, end of serious French intervention in Italy. Diet of Speyer: origin of the name Protestant.

1532 Peru conquered by Francisco Pizarro.

1533 Ivan IV (the Terrible) becomes Tsar. Marriage of Henry VIII and Catherine of Aragon declared null.

1534 Act of Supremacy: Henry VIII asserts control over English Church.

1535 Coverdale's English Bible printed. Execution of Thomas More and John Fisher.

1536 Execution of Anne Boleyn. Dissolution of smaller Monasteries by Henry VIII and Thomas Cromwell (remainder dissolved 1539). Pilgrimage of Grace: Northern rising because of religious grievances. [de Quesada.

1538 Chibchas of Bogota conquered by Gonzalo

1540 Francisco de Coronado begins explorations in North America. Society of Jesus recognised by Pope.

1541 John Calvin regains authority in Geneva.

1542 First Portuguese reach Japan. New Laws of the Indies: first attempt to legislate for welfare of colonial natives, by Spanish government.

1543 Death of Copernicus. [Reformation.

1545 Opening of Council of Trent: the Counter-

A.D.

1547 Death of Henry VIII: Somerset Protector in the name of the boy king, Edward VI.

1549 First English Book of Common Prayer. Kett's Rebellion in Norfolk, because of economic grievances.

1550 Deposition of Protector Somerset: Northumberland rules England.

1553 Lady Jane Grey proclaimed Queen by Northumberland on death of Edward VI: Mary I succeeds. Servetus burned by Calvin.

1555 Latimer and Ridley burned by Mary. Religious Peace of Augsburg: policy of *cuius regio, eius religio* accepted in Germany.

1556 Charles V abdicates imperial powers in favour of brother Ferdinand. Cranmer burned. Akbar becomes Mogul Emperor (d. 1605).

1557 Macao becomes permanent Portuguese port in China.

1558 Calais lost by English to French. Elizabeth I becomes Queen of England.

1559 Peace of Cateau-Cambrésis: end of Hapsburg–Valois duel.

RELIGIOUS WARS

1561 Mary, Queen of Scots, returns to Scotland.

1562 First War of Religion in France: wars continue intermittently until 1598.

1563 Thirty-nine Articles define Elizabethan Church settlement.

1564 Birth of Shakespeare; death of Michelangelo.

1565 Malta beats off Turks.

1567 Deposition of Mary, Queen of Scots. Alva in the Netherlands: severe rule.

1568 Flight of Mary, Queen of Scots, to England: imprisonment. San Juan de Ulua: defeat of Hawkins, and end of his slave-trading voyages. Beginning of Anglo-Spanish maritime feud. Revolt of Moriscos of Granada (suppressed 1570). [England.

1569 Rebellion of Northern Earls (Catholic) in

1570 Elizabeth I anathematised by Pope.

1571 Battle of Lepanto: spectacular defeat of Turkish sea-power by Don John of Austria. Bornu (or Kanem) in Central Sudan at its zenith under Idris III.

1572 Dutch "Sea Beggars" take Brill. Massacre of St. Bartholomew in France. Polish Crown elective again, on death of Sigismund II.

1576 Catholic League formed in France, led by Guise family. [1580).

1577 Drake begins voyage round world (returns

1578 Battle of Alcazar-Quivir: death of King Sebastian of Portugal. Parma re-establishes Spanish rule in Southern Netherlands.

1579 Union of Utrecht: seven northern provinces of Netherlands form what becomes Dutch Republic. Death of Grand Vizier Sokolli: decline of Turkish power begins.

1580 Philip II of Spain becomes king of Portugal.

1582 Gregorian Calendar (or New Style) introduced by Pope Gregory XIII.

1584 Assassination of William the Silent.

1585 Hidéyoshi Dictator of Japan: unification of the country. English intervention in Spanish–Dutch War.

1587 Execution of Mary, Queen of Scots. Drake "singes King of Spain's beard." Shah Abbas I (the Great) becomes ruler of Persia (d. 1629).

1588 Spanish Armada defeated.

1589 Death of Catherine de' Medici, Queen-Mother of France.

1591 Songhai Empire destroyed by troops from Morocco.

1593 Henry IV of France becomes Catholic.

1598 Edict of Nantes: French Protestants guaranteed liberty of worship. End of French Wars of Religion.

1600 English East India Company founded. Tokugawa Period begins in Japan (Ieyasu takes title of Shogun, 1603): lasts until 1868.

A.D.

1601 Rebellion and execution of Earl of Essex. Elizabethan Poor Law.

1602 Dutch East India Company founded.

1603 Irish revolts finally suppressed by Mountjoy. Accession of James VI of Scotland as James I of England: Union of English and Scottish Crowns.

1604 Hampton Court Conference: James I disappoints Puritans.

1605 Gunpowder Plot.

1607 Virginia colonised by London company: Jamestown founded.

1608 Quebec founded by Champlain.

1609 Twelve Years' Truce between Spain and United Provinces: Dutch independence in fact secured. Expulsion of Moriscos from Spain.

1610 Assassination of Henry IV of France.

1611 Plantation of Ulster with English and Scottish colonists. Authorised Version of the Bible in England.

1613 Michael Romanov becomes Czar: the first of the dynasty.

1614 Napier publishes his explanation of logarithms.

1616 Death of Shakespeare and Cervantes. Edict of Inquisition against Galileo's astronomy.

1618 "Defenestration of Prague": Bohemian assertion of independence begins Thirty Years' War.

1620 Pilgrim Fathers settle in New England.

1624 "Massacre of Amboina": English driven out of spice islands by Dutch. Richelieu becomes Chief Minister in France.

1628 Murder of Duke of Buckingham. Petition of Right by Commons to Charles I. Fall of La Rochelle: French Protestants lose political power. Harvey publishes his work on the circulation of blood.

1629 Charles I begins Personal Rule.

1630 Gustavus Adolphus of Sweden enters Thirty Years' War, turns tide against Imperialists.

1631 Sack of Magdeburg, one of the worst incidents of the Thirty Years' War.

1632 Battle of Lützen: death of Gustavus Adolphus.

1633 William Laud appointed Archbishop of Canterbury. Thomas Wentworth takes up his post as Lord Deputy of Ireland.

1634 Dismissal and murder of Imperialist general Wallenstein.

1635 John Hampden refuses to pay Ship Money.

1636 Japanese forbidden to go abroad.

1637 Russian pioneers reach shores of Pacific.

1638 Covenant widely signed in Scotland.

1639 First Bishops' War: Charles I comes to terms with Scots.

1640 Second Bishops' War: Charles I defeated by Scots. Long Parliament begins: abolition of Royal prerogatives. Great Elector (Frederick William) becomes ruler of Brandenburg. Revolt of Catalonia (finally suppressed 1659). Revolt of Portugal: Duke of Braganza proclaimed king.

1641 Japanese exclude all foreigners (except for small Dutch trading fleet). Massacre of Protestants in Ireland. Wentworth (Earl of Strafford) executed. Grand Remonstrance of Commons to Charles I.

1642 Charles I attempts to arrest the Five Members. Outbreak of English Civil War: first general engagement, Edgehill. Death of Richelieu.

1643 Mazarin becomes Chief Minister of France. Battle of Rocroi: French victory, end of Spanish reputation for invincibility. English Parliament agrees to Solemn League and Covenant, secures services of Scots army.

1644 Marston Moor: decisive battle of English Civil War. North lost to Charles I. Tippemuir: Montrose begins victorious Royalist campaign in Scotland. 1644–1911 Manchu Dynasty in China.

1645 Formation of New Model Army. Naseby: main Royalist army crushed. Battle of Philiphaugh: Montrose's army destroyed.

1646 Charles I surrenders to Scots.

1647 Charles I handed over to Parliament. Charles I seized by Army. Charles I flees to Carisbrooke Castle.

1648 Second Civil War: New Model Army defeats Scots and Royalists. "Pride's Purge": Parliament refashioned by Army. Peace of Westphalia ends Thirty Years' War.

ASCENDANCY OF FRANCE

1649 Charles I executed. England governed as Commonwealth. Cromwell in Ireland. New Code of Laws in Russia completes establishment of serfdom.

1651 Battle of Worcester: Cromwell's final victory, now master of all Britain. First English Navigation Act. Hobbes' *Leviathan* published.

1652 Foundation of Cape Colony by Dutch under Van Riebeek. First Anglo-Dutch War begins (ends 1654).

1653 Cromwell dissolves Rump, becomes Protector.

1655 Major-Generals appointed to supervise districts of England. Jamaica seized by English.

1656 Grand Vizier Kiuprili: revival of Turkish government.

1658 Death of Cromwell.

1659 Peace of the Pyrenees: France replaces Spain as greatest power in Western Europe.

1660 Restoration of monarchy in Britain: Charles II. Royal Society founded.

1661 Death of Mazarin: Louis XIV now rules in person. "Clarendon Code": beginning of persecution of Non-conformists in England.

1664 New York taken by English: Second Anglo-Dutch War ensues (ends 1667).

1665 Great Plague of London.

1666 Great Fire of London. Newton's discovery of law of gravitation.

1667 Dutch fleet in the Medway. War of Devolution begins: first of Louis XIV's aggressions.

1668 Portuguese Independence recognised by Spain.

1669 Death of Rembrandt.

1670 Secret Treaty of Dover between Charles II and Louis XIV. Revolt of peasants and Don Cossacks under Stenka Razin (suppressed 1671).

1672 Third Anglo-Dutch War begins (ends 1674). Murder of De Witt brothers: William of Orange becomes leader of Dutch against French invasion.

1673 Test Act deprives English Catholics and Non-conformists of public offices. Death of Molière.

1675 Battle of Fehrbellin: Swedes defeated by Great Elector; rise of Prussian military power. Greenwich Royal Observatory founded.

1678 "Popish Plot" of Titus Oates utilised by Shaftesbury and the Whigs to bring pressure on Charles II.

1679 Bothwell Brig: suppression of Scottish Covenanters. Habeas Corpus Act passed.

1680 Chambers of Reunion: Louis XIV uses legal arguments to complete annexation of Alsace.

1681 Oxford Parliament: Charles II overcomes his opponents, begins to rule without Parliament.

1683 Rye House Plot. Siege of Vienna by the Turks: last major Turkish attack on Europe.

1685 Sedgemoor: Monmouth's rebellion crushed by James II. Revocation of Edict of Nantes: persecution of French Protestants by Louis XIV.

A.D.

1688 Seven Bishops protest against James II's policy of toleration, and are acquitted. William of Orange lands in England: flight of James II. "The Glorious Revolution."

1689 Derry relieved: failure of James II to subdue Irish Protestants. Killiecrankie: death of Dundee and collapse of Highland rising. Bill of Rights defines liberties established by "Glorious Revolution."

1690 Locke's *Two Treatises on Government* published. Beachy Head: French victory over Anglo-Dutch fleet. Boyne: defeat of James II by William III.

1691 Capitulation of Limerick: surrender of Irish supporters of James II on conditions which are not fulfilled.

1692 Massacre of Glencoe: Government's "lesson" to Highlanders. La Hogue: Anglo-Dutch fleet regains command of the sea.

1693 National Debt of England begun.

1694 Bank of England founded.

1695 Press licensing abandoned: freedom of the press in England.

1696 Peter the Great sole Czar.

1697 Peace of Ryswyck between Louis XIV and William III. Peter journeys "incognito" to the West.

1699 Treaty of Karlowitz: great Turkish concessions to Austrians. Death of Racine.

1700 Great Northern War, involving all Baltic powers, begins (ends 1721). Battle of Narva: Russians defeated by Charles XII of Sweden. Death of Charles II of Spain: under French influence Louis XIV's grandson Philip of Anjou named successor.

1701 War of the Spanish Succession begins. Hungarian revolt led by Francis Rakoczi against Austrians. Elector of Brandenburg receives title of King of Prussia. Act of Settlement establishes Protestant Hanoverian Succession in England.

1703 Methuen Treaty between England and Portugal. St. Petersburg founded.

1704 Gibraltar taken by Rooke. Blenheim: Marlborough stops France from winning war.

1706 Ramillies: Marlborough's second great victory. Turin: Eugene defeats French in Italy.

1707 Almanza: Anglo-Austrian forces in Spain defeated by French under Berwick. Act of Union: English and Scottish Parliaments united. Death of Aurungzib, last powerful Mogul.

1708 Oudenarde: Marlborough's third great victory.

1709 Pultava: Charles XII's invasion of Russia smashed by Peter the Great. Malplaquet: Marlborough's fourth great victory—at great cost in lives.

1710 Tory government in England.

1711 Dismissal of Marlborough.

1713 Peace of Utrecht: England makes advantageous peace with Louis XIV. Bourbon king of Spain grants Asiento (monopoly of Spanish American slave trade) to England.

1714 Peace of Rastatt between France and Austria. Death of Queen Anne: accession of George I. Beginning of Hanoverian Dynasty in Britain. Whig oligarchy rules.

1715 Jacobite Rising defeated at Preston and Sheriffmuir. Death of Louis XIV. France under Regent Orleans.

ENLIGHTENED DESPOTS: FIRST BRITISH EMPIRE

1716 Septennial Act: English Parliament prolongs its life from three to seven years. Prince Eugène of Savoy defeated Turks at Petrovaradin (Yugoslavia).

1720 Collapse of Law's system of banking ("Mississippi Bubble") in France. "South Sea Bubble" in England.

1721 Robert Walpole becomes first Prime Minister. Peace of Nystad: Sweden no longer a major power at end of Great Northern War. Russian gains.

1723 Death of Christopher Wren.

1727 First Indemnity Act for Non-conformists.

1729 Methodists begin at Oxford.

1730 Resignation from government of Townshend, who becomes agricultural pioneer.

1733 First Family Compact between Bourbon kings of France and Spain. Withdrawal of Walpole's Excise Bill. John Kay invents flying shuttle, first of the great textile inventions. Jethro Tull publishes *The Horse-Hoing Husbandry*, advocating new agricultural methods.

1738 Lorraine ceded to France.

1739 Nadir Shah with Persian army sacks Delhi, ruins Mogul power. War of Jenkins' Ear begins between Spain and Britain.

1740 Frederick II (the Great) becomes king of Prussia. Maria Theresa succeeds to Austrian dominions. Frederick seizes Silesia, begins War of the Austrian Succession.

1742 Fall of Walpole.

1743 Dettingen: George II, last British king to command his army in the field, defeats French.

1745 Fontenoy: Duke of Cumberland defeated by Marshal Saxe. Jacobite Rebellion under Prince Charles Edward: initial success, victory of Prestonpans, march to Derby.

1746 Culloden: Jacobites destroyed by Cumberland.

1748 Treaty of Aix-la-Chapelle: Frederick retains Silesia, elsewhere status quo.

1750 Death of J. S. Bach.

1751 First volume of the *Encyclopédie* published in France. Clive takes and holds Arcot: checks plans of Dupleix in Southern India. Chinese conquest of Tibet.

1752 Britain adopts New Style calendar.

1753 British Museum begun by government purchase of Sloane's collection.

1755 Lisbon earthquake. Braddock's defeat and death at the hands of French and Indians.

1756 Diplomatic Revolution (alliance of Austria with France) achieved by Kaunitz; Britain and Prussia perforce became allies. Seven Years' War begins. Minorca taken from British by French (Byng executed 1757). Black Hole of Calcutta: suffocation of many British prisoners.

1757 Pitt Secretary of State, main influence in British government. Rossbach: one of Frederick II's numerous victories against heavy odds. Plassey: Clive conquers Bengal.

1759 "Year of Victories" for Britain: Quebec, Minden, Lagos, Quiberon Bay. James Brindley designs Worsley–Manchester Canal: the beginning of this form of transport in Britain. Voltaire publishes *Candide*. Death of Handel.

1760 Wandewash: decisive defeat of French in India, by Coote.

1761 Panipat: Mahrattas heavily defeated by Afghans. Fall of Pitt.

1762 Catherine II (the Great) becomes Czarina. Rousseau's *Social Contract* and *Emile* published.

1763 Peace of Paris: British colonial gains, First British Empire at its height. Peace of Hubertusburg: Frederick II retains his gains. Pontiac's Conspiracy: failure of Red Indian attempt to destroy British power.

1764 John Wilkes expelled from Commons. James Hargreaves invents spinning jenny.

1766 Henry Cavendish proves hydrogen to be an element.

1768 Royal Academy of Arts founded.

1769 Richard Arkwright erects spinning mill (invention of water frame).

1770 Struensee comes to power in Denmark (executed 1772). "Boston Massacre." James Cook discovers New South Wales.

1772 First Partition of Poland between Russia, Prussia, and Austria.

A.D.

1773 Society of Jesus suppressed by Pope (restored 1814). Revolt led by Pugachov in Russia (suppressed 1775). "Boston Tea Party."

1774 Warren Hastings appointed first Governor-General of India. Treaty of Kutchuk Kainarji: great Turkish concessions to Russia. Karl Scheele discovers chlorine. Joseph Priestley's discovery of oxygen.

1775 Watt and Boulton in partnership at Soho Engineering Works, Birmingham. Lexington: first action in American War of Independence.

1776 American Declaration of Independence. Adam Smith's *Wealth of Nations* published.

1777 Saratoga: surrender of British army under Burgoyne to Americans.

1779 Beginning of great Franco-Spanish siege of Gibraltar (raised finally, 1783). Samuel Crompton invents spinning mule.

1780 Joseph II assumes sole power in Austria. Armed neutrality of maritime nations to restrain British interference with shipping.

1781 Joseph II introduces religious toleration, abolishes serfdom in Austria. Yorktown: surrender of British under Cornwallis to American and French forces.

1782 Battle of the Saints: Rodney's victory saves British West Indies.

1783 Treaty of Versailles: American independence recognised. Pitt the Younger becomes Prime Minister of Britain. First flights in hot-air (Montgolfier) and hydrogen (Charles) balloons.

1784 Death of Dr. Samuel Johnson.

1785 Edmund Cartwright invents the power loom.

1787 American Constitution drafted.

1788 Impeachment of Warren Hastings begins (ends 1795).

FRENCH REVOLUTION AND NAPOLEON

1789 Washington first President of U.S.A. French Revolution begins. Storming of the Bastille (July 14).

1790 Civil constitution of the Clergy in France.

1791 Flight of Louis XVI and Marie Antoinette to Varennes.

1792 Battle of Valmy: French Revolution saved from intervention of European kings. Denmark becomes first country to prohibit slave trade. France becomes a Republic.

1793 Louis XVI beheaded. Second partition of Poland.

1794 "Glorious First of June." Fall of Robespierre and end of Jacobin Republic. Negro revolt in Haiti led by Toussaint L'Ouverture.

1795 The Directory established. "Whiff of Grapeshot": Napoleon Bonaparte disperses Paris mob, Oct. 5. Batavian Republic set up by France.

1796 First Italian campaign of Bonaparte: victories of Lodi, Arcola.

1797 Treaty of Campo Formio: Bonaparte compels Austria to make peace. Britain left to fight France alone.

1798 Bonaparte goes to Egypt. Battle of the Nile. Vinegar Hill rebellion in Ireland suppressed.

1799 New coalition against France: Suvorov and Russians victorious in Italy. Bonaparte returns to France. *Coup d'état* of Brumaire, Nov. 9. Consulate set up.

1800 Parliamentary Union of Great Britain and Ireland.

1801 Treaty of Lunéville: Austria makes peace; great French gains in Germany.

1802 Peace of Amiens between Britain and France. *Charlotte Dundas*, first practical steamship, on Clyde.

1803 Insurrection in Ireland under Robert Emmet. Britain again at war with France.

1804 Bonaparte becomes Emperor. Spain declares war against Great Britain. Serbian revolt against Turks under Kara George.

1805 Battle of Trafalgar, Nelson's great victory and death, Oct. 21. Battle of Austerlitz, Dec. 2.

1806 Death of Pitt, Jan. 23. Confederation of the Rhine: Napoleon's reorganisation of Germany, July 12. End of Holy Roman Empire, Aug. 6. Prussia overthrown at Jena. Napoleon declares Great Britain in a state of blockade—"Continental System."

1807 Slave trade abolished in British Empire. Treaty of Tilsit: with Alexander of Russia his friend, Napoleon controls all of Europe. Occupation of Portugal by French, to enforce Continental Blockade.

1808 Occupation of Spain by French. Spanish rising: guerrilla warfare. Peninsular War begins. Battle of Vimeiro (defeat of French by Wellington), Aug. 21.

1809 Battle of Corunna and death of Sir John Moore, Jan. 16. Attempted risings in Germany against Napoleon: Austria renews war. Treaty of Schönbrunn, Oct. 14.

1810 Self-government established in Argentina: first South American state to become independent of Spain.

1811 Massacre of Mamelukes at Cairo. Luddite riots.

1812 Retreat from Moscow: destruction of Napoleon's Grand Army.

1813 War of Liberation starts in Germany. Defeat of French by Wellington at Vitoria, June 21.

1814 Soult defeated by Wellington at Toulouse, April 10. Abdication of Napoleon, April 11; Louis XVIII king of France. Congress of Vienna (concluded June 1815) under guidance of Metternich. Resettlement of Europe, usually by restoration of kings. Germanic Confederation under Austrian supervision. Poland ruled by Czar. Kingdom of Netherlands to include Belgium.

THE OLD ORDER RESTORED

1815 Escape of Napoleon from Elba. Battle of Waterloo, June 18. Corn Law in Britain to safeguard agricultural interests by keeping up prices. Quadruple Alliance (Austria, Russia, Prussia, Britain) to maintain Vienna settlement and hold regular meetings ("Congress System")—frequently confused with Holy Alliance, which was simply a declaration of Christian principles. Napoleon sent to St. Helena, Oct. 16.

1818 Bernadotte made king of Sweden (Charles XIV), Feb. 6.

1819 Singapore founded by Stamford Raffles. Beginnings of Zollverein (Customs Union) in Germany under Prussian influence. Parliamentary reform meeting at Manchester dispersed by military ("Peterloo"), Aug. 16.

1820 Death of George III, Jan. 29.

1821 Death of Napoleon at St. Helena, May 5.

1822 Congress of Verona: congress system breaks down with refusal of Britain (Canning) to intervene against revolutions.

1823 "Monroe Doctrine" announced by U.S.A. President, Dec. 2.

1824 Repeal of Combination Acts in Britain which had forbidden Trades Unions. Charles X king of France.

1825 Independence of all Spanish American mainland now achieved. Nicholas I Czar of Russia. First railway, Stockton to Darlington, opened.

1826 First crossing of Atlantic under steam by Dutch ship *Curaçao*. Menai suspension bridge opened.

1827 Battle of Navarino, Turkish and Egyptian fleet destroyed. Death of Beethoven.

1828 Death of Chaka, great Zulu conqueror.

1829 Greece independent. Catholic Emancipation Act in Britain. Metropolitan Police established.

A.D.

1830 Death of George IV, June 26. Louis Philippe ousts Charles X. Belgium breaks away from Holland. Russian Poland revolts ineffectually.

1831 First Reform Bill introduced by Lord John Russell. Leopold of Saxe-Coburg becomes king of independent Belgium. British Association founded. Faraday discovers electromagnetic induction.

1832 Reform Bill passed, June 7. Walter Scott, Jeremy Bentham, and Goethe die. Electric telegraph invented by Morse.

1833 Beginning of "Oxford Movement" in English Church. First government grant made to English schools. First British Factory Act.

1834 Poor Law Amendment Act: tightening up of relief in Britain. "Tolpuddle Martyrs" victimised to discourage British working-class movement. Carlist wars begin in Spain.

1835 Municipal Reform Act revises British local government. The word "socialism" first used. "Tamworth Manifesto" of Peel defines aims of Conservative Party.

1836 People's Charter states programme of Chartists. Great Trek of Boers from British South African territory. Texas achieves independence of Mexico.

1837 Queen Victoria succeeds to the throne.

1838 National Gallery opened.

1839 First Afghan war begins. Chartist riots at Birmingham and Newport. Anti-Corn Law League founded. Aden annexed by Britain.

1840 Penny postage instituted. Queen Victoria marries Prince Albert of Saxe-Coburg-Gotha. "Opium War" with China begins. Union Act gives Canada responsible government. Last convicts landed in New South Wales.

1841 Hong Kong acquired by Britain.

1842 Chartists present second national petition and put themselves at the head of strikes.

1846 Repeal of the Corn Laws. Peel resigns.

1847 British Museum opened.

REVOLUTIONS AND NEW NATIONS

1848 Monster meeting of Chartists on Kennington Common, procession abandoned, Apr. 10. General revolutionary movement throughout the Continent. Louis Philippe abdicates: French Republic proclaimed. Swiss Federal Constitution established after defeat of Sonderbund (Catholic secession movement). Rising in Vienna: flight of Metternich, accession of Francis Joseph. Nationalist risings in Bohemia and Hungary. Frankfurt Parliament: attempt to unite Germany on liberal principles. Communist Manifesto produced by Marx and Engels. U.S.A. makes great territorial gains from Mexico. Gold discovered in California.

1849 Collapse of revolutionary movements. Rome republic besieged by French (June 3), defended by Garibaldi, holds out until July 2. Austrians take Venice, Aug. 22. Repeal of old Navigation Laws. Punjab annexed by Britain.

1850 Cavour becomes Prime Minister of Piedmont. Don Pacifico affair; privileges of British citizenship at their highest defended by Palmerston.

1851 Great Exhibition in Hyde Park. First satisfactory submarine telegraph cable between Dover and Calais laid. Gold discovered in Australia.

1852 Independence of Transvaal recognised by Britain. Napoleon III Emperor of the French.

1853 Perry lands in Japan: beginning of Western influence. Russia and Turkey at war.

1854 War declared against Russia by France and Britain. Allied armies land in Crimea, Sept. 14 (Alma, Siege of Sevastopol, Balaklava, Inkerman). Orange Free State set up.

1855 Sardinia joins Britain and France against Russia. Fall of Sevastopol and end of Crimean War. Alexander II Czar of Russia.

A.D.

1856 Peace Treaty signed at Paris. Bessemer invents process for large-scale production of steel. Livingstone completes journey across Africa.

1857 Indian Mutiny. Relief of Lucknow. Canton captured by English and French.

1858 *Great Eastern* launched. Crown assumes government of India. Treaty of Aigun, by which China cedes Amur region to Russia.

1859 Darwin publishes *Origin of Species*. French support for Piedmont in war with Austria (Magenta, Solferino). Piedmont receives Lombardy. Harper's Ferry raid: John Brown hanged, Dec. 2.

1860 Garibaldi and the Thousand Redshirts in Sicily and Naples; most of Italy united to Piedmont. Vladivostok founded; Russia strongly established on N.W. Pacific.

1861 Abraham Lincoln takes office as Pres. of U.S. American Civil War commences with 11 states breaking away to form Southern Confederacy. Bull Run (July 21) Confederate success ends Federal hopes of easy victory. Victor Emmanuel proclaimed by first Italian Parliament as king of Italy. Emancipation of Serfs in Russia. Death of Prince Albert, Dec. 14.

1862 Bismarck becomes leading minister in Prussia. Garibaldi attempts to seize Rome but wounded at Aspromonte, Aug. 29. Cotton famine in Lancashire.

1863 Polish rising against Russia (suppressed 1864). French in Mexico. Battle of Gettysburg, July 1–3. Maximilian of Austria made emperor of Mexico.

1864 Cession of Schleswig-Holstein to Prussia and Austria. First Socialist International formed. Taiping rebellion in China ended. Federal army enters Atlanta, Sept. 2: General Sherman captures Savannah ("From Atlanta to the sea"), Dec. 22. Geneva Convention originated.

1865 Death of Cobden, Apr. 2. General Lee surrenders to Grant, Apr. 9. Lincoln assassinated, Apr. 14. Thirteenth Amendment to Constitution: slavery abolished in U.S. Death of Palmerston, Oct. 18. Lister introduces antiseptic surgery in Glasgow. Tashkent becomes centre of Russian expansion in Central Asia. Mendel experiments on heredity. William Booth founds Salvation Army.

1866 Austro-Prussian War over Schleswig-Holstein ("Seven Weeks War"). Prussian victory at Sadowa (July 3). Venice secured for Italy, who had, however, been defeated by Austrians at Custozza (June 24) and Lissa (July 20). Treaty of Prague, Aug. 23.

1867 North German Confederation founded. Emperor Maximilian of Mexico shot. Dominion of Canada established. Russia sells Alaska to America for $7 million. Garibaldi makes second attempt to seize Rome, but defeated by Pope with French support at Mentana, Nov. 3. Second Parliamentary Reform Bill passed (Disraeli "dished the Whigs").

1868 Shogunate abolished in Japan: Meiji period of rapid Westernisation under Imperial leadership begins. Ten Years' War (1868–78); struggle for Cuban independence from Spain. Disraeli succeeds Derby as Prime Minister but defeated in general election by Gladstone, Nov.

1869 General Grant, Pres. of U.S. Irish Church disestablished. Suez Canal formally opened.

1870 Napoleon III declares war against Prussia. French defeated at Woerth, Gravelotte, and Sedan. Paris besieged. Rome and Papal states annexed to kingdom of Italy. Irish Land Act passed. Forster's Education Act puts elementary education within reach of all British children. Papal Infallibility announced.

1871 William I of Prussia proclaimed emperor of Germany at Versailles, Jan. 18. Paris capitulates, Jan. 28. Commune of Paris proclaimed, Mar. 28. Peace signed at Frankfurt-on-Main, May 10. Government troops enter Paris and

A.D.

crush Communards, May 28. Thiers President of the Republic, Aug. 31. Mont Cenis tunnel opened. Trade Unions in Britain legalised

RIVAL IMPERIAL POWERS

1872 Ballot introduced in Britain. Death of Mazzini, Mar. 10.

1873 Death of Livingstone, May 4. Ashanti war.

1874 Disraeli succeeds Gladstone as Prime Minister.

1875 England purchases Khedive's shares in Suez Canal, Nov.

1876 Bulgarian massacres. Serbo-Turkish war. Bell invents the telephone. Custer defeated and killed in last large-scale Red Indian success. Porfirio Diaz in power in Mexico (until 1911).

1877 Victoria declared Empress of India. Transvaal annexed to British Empire. War between Russia and Turkey. Satsuma rebellion in Japan: final unsuccessful attempt to halt new ideas.

1878 Congress of Berlin: general Balkan settlement. Cyprus ceded to Britain. Second war with Afghanistan (ended 1880). Edison and Swan produce first successful incandescent electric light.

1879 Dual control (Britain and France) in Egypt. Zulu War. Gladstone's Midlothian Campaign. Tay Bridge destroyed, Dec. 28.

1880 Beaconsfield ministry succeeded by second Gladstone ministry. Transvaal declared a republic.

1881 British defeat at Majuba: independence of Transvaal recognised. France occupies Tunis. Gambetta becomes Prime Minister of France. Revolt of the Mahdi in the Sudan. Pasteur's famous immunisation experiment to show that inoculated animals can survive anthrax.

1882 Lord Frederick Cavendish, Irish Secretary, assassinated in Phoenix Park, Dublin, May 6. Triple Alliance (Germany, Austria, Italy) first formed. Alexandria bombarded, July 11. Cairo occupied by British troops, Sept. 14.

1883 National Insurance begun in Germany. Death of Wagner.

1884 Wolseley heads expedition to Khartoum to rescue Gordon. French establish complete protectorate in Indo-China. Evelyn Baring takes over administration of Egypt. Russians capture Merv. Berlin Conference defines rights of European Powers in Africa. Third Parliamentary Reform Bill. Parsons invents his turbine. Greenwich meridian internationally recognised as prime meridian. Fabian Society founded.

1885 Khartoum captured; Gordon slain, Jan. 26.

1886 Upper Burma annexed by Britain. Home Rule Bill defeated in Commons. All Indians in U.S.A. now in Reservations. Daimler produces his first motor car. Completion of Canadian Pacific Railway. Gold discovered in the Transvaal.

1887 Queen Victoria's Jubilee celebration, June 21.

1888 William II German Emperor. County Councils set up in Britain.

1889 Mayerling: tragic death of Prince Rudolf of Austria, Jan. 30. Flight of General Boulanger, after attempting to become master of France. Second Socialist International set up. Great London dock strike, Aug. 15–Sept. 16. Parnell Commission concludes sittings, Nov. 23 (129th day).

1890 Parnell ruined by divorce case: Irish politicians split. Sherman Anti-Trust Law: first attempt in U.S.A. to break cartels. Opening of Forth Bridge, Mar. 4. Bismarck resigns, Mar. 17, Caprivi succeeds. Heligoland ceded to Germany.

1891 The United States of Brazil formed.

1892 Panama Canal financial scandals in France.

1893 Home Rule Bill passes third reading in Commons, Sept. 1: Lords reject Bill, Sept. 8.

1894 Opening of Manchester Ship Canal, Jan. 1. Gladstone resigns, Mar. 3, Lord Rosebery succeeds. Armenian massacres by Turks: repeated at intervals for next quarter of century. Japan declares war against China. Dreyfus convicted of treason.

1895 Opening of Kiel canal, June 21. Rosebery resigns, June 22; Salisbury Ministry succeeds. Treaty of Shimonoseki: Japan gets Formosa, free hand in Korea. New Cuban revolution breaks out against Spanish. Marconi sends message over a mile by wireless. Röntgen discovers X-rays. Freud publishes his first work on psycho-analysis. Jameson Raid, Dec. 29.

1896 Jameson raiders defeated by Boers, Jan. 1. Adowa: Italian disaster at hands of Abyssinians, the first major defeat of a white colonising power by "natives." Gold discovered in the Klondike.

1897 Cretan revolt leads to Greek–Turkish War. Hawaii annexed by U.S.A. Queen Victoria's Diamond Jubilee, June 22. Great Gold Rush began.

1898 Port Arthur ceded to Russia. Spanish-American War. *Maine*, U.S. warship blown up in Havana harbour. Treaty of Paris, Dec. 10: Cuba freed, Puerto Rico and Guam ceded to U.S.A., Philippines surrendered for $20 million. Death of Gladstone, May 19. Battle of Omdurman, decisive defeat of Mahdists, Sept. 2. Empress of Austria assassinated, Sept. 10. The Curies discover Radium.

1899 Boer War begins, Oct. 10.

1900 Boers attack Ladysmith, Jan. 6. Battle of Spion Kop, Buller repulsed with severe losses, Jan. 24. Relief of Kimberley, Feb. 15. Ladysmith relieved, Feb. 28. Mafeking relieved May 17. Boxer outbreak in China, May. Annexation of Orange Free State, May 26. Roberts occupies Johannesburg, May 31. "Khaki Election." Annexation of the Transvaal, Oct. 25. Australian Commonwealth proclaimed, Dec. 30.

1901 Queen Victoria dies, Jan. 22. Trans-Siberian Railway opened for single-track traffic.

1902 Anglo-Japanese Alliance, Jan. 30. Death of Cecil Rhodes, Mar. 26. Treaty of Vereeniging ends Boer War, May 31.

1903 Congo scandal: celebrated case of misrule and exploitation. Royal family of Serbia assassinated, May 29. First controlled flight in heavier-than-air machine—Orville and Wilbur Wright at Kitty Hawk, U.S.A., Dec. 17.

1904 Russo-Japanese War begins, Feb. 8. Japanese victory at Yalu River, May 1. British forces under Younghusband reach Lhasa, Aug. 3. Treaty with Tibet signed at Lhasa, Sept. 7.

1905 Port Arthur falls to Japanese, Jan. 3. "Bloody Sunday" massacre at St. Petersburg, Jan. 22. Destruction of Russian fleet under Rozhdestvenski at Tsushima by Admiral Togo (May). Treaty of Portsmouth (U.S.A.) ends Russo-Japanese war. Separation of Church and State in France. Norway separates itself from Sweden.

1906 General strike in Russia. San Francisco destroyed by earthquake and fire, Apr. 18. Simplon tunnel opened for railway traffic, June 1. First Duma (Parliament with limited powers) in Russia. Liberal "landslide" majority in Britain: Labour M.P.s appear. Movement for Women's Suffrage becomes active in Britain. Algeciras Conference: Franco-German crisis resolved in favour of France. Death of Ibsen. Vitamins discovered by F. G. Hopkins.

1907 New Zealand becomes a dominion.

1908 Annexation of Congo by Belgium. Young Turk revolution. Annexation of Bosnia and Herzegovina by Austria: severe rebuff for Russia. Asquith becomes Prime Minister of Britain.

1909 Old Age Pensions in Britain. Peary reaches North Pole. Blériot makes first cross-Channel flight. House of Lords rejects Lloyd George's budget. Union of South Africa formed. Henry Ford concentrates on producing Model T chassis: beginnings of cheap motors.

A.D.

1910 Accession of George V on death of Edward VII, May 6. Liberals win two General Elections. Labour Exchanges established in Britain. Death of Tolstoy and Florence Nightingale.

1911 Parliament Act: power of Lords decisively reduced. British M.P.s paid for first time. National Insurance in Britain. Great British rail strike. Tripoli taken from Turkey by Italy. Chinese Revolution. Amundsen reaches South Pole, Dec. 14.

1912 China becomes a Republic under Sun Yat Sen. *Titanic* disaster off Cape Race, Apr. 14–15. Great British coal strike. Scott's last expedition. Outbreak of Balkan Wars.

1913 Treaty of Bucharest: most of Turkey-in-Europe divided among Balkan states.

FIRST WORLD WAR

1914 Archduke Francis Ferdinand, heir to the Hapsburg thrones, assassinated at Sarajevo, June 28. Austria–Hungary declares war against Serbia, July 28. Germany declares war against Russia, Aug. 1. Germany declares war against France, Aug. 3. German invasion of Belgium: Great Britain declares war against Germany, Aug. 4. Great Britain declares war on Austria–Hungary, Aug. 12. British Expeditionary Force concentrated before Mauberge, Aug. 20. Battle of Mons; Japan declared war on Germany, Aug. 23. Battle of the Marne, Sept. 5–9. Trench warfare began on Aisne salient, Sept. 16. Three British cruisers (*Aboukir*, *Hogue*, and *Cressy*) sunk by one U-boat, Sept. 22. First Battle of Ypres, Oct. 12–Nov. 11. Raiding of German cruiser *Emden* until destroyed, Nov. 9. Battle of Coronel: German cruisers *Scharnhorst* and *Gneisenau* sink British cruisers *Good Hope* and *Monmouth*, Nov. 1. Great Britain declares war against Turkey, Nov. 5. Destruction of German squadron off Falkland Is., Dec. 8. British protectorate over Egypt proclaimed, Dec. 17. First Zeppelin appeared over British coast, Dec. 29.

1915 Turkish army defeated in Caucasus, Jan 5. Great Britain declared blockade of Germany, Mar. 1. Battle of Neuve Chapelle, Mar. 10–13. Naval attack on Dardanelles called off, Mar. 22. First landing of British, Australian, New Zealand troops on Gallipoli Peninsula, Apr. 25. Second Battle of Ypres, Apr. 22–May 25: Germans first used gas. Sinking of *Lusitania*, May 7. Battle of Aubers Ridge, May 9–25. Italy declares war on Austria, May 22. British Coalition Government formed, May 26. Italian army crosses Isonzo, June 2. Zeppelin destroyed by R. A. J. Warneford, June 7. Second landing of Allied troops at Suvla Bay. Italy declares war on Turkey, Aug. 20. Turks defeated at Kut-el-Amara, Sept 28. Serbia conquered by Austria and Bulgaria, Nov. 28. French and British troops occupy Salonika, Dec. 13. British troops withdraw from Anzac and Suvla, Dec. 20.

1916 Evacuation of Gallipoli completed, Jan 8. Opening of Battle of Verdun, Feb. 21. Sinn Fein rising in Ireland, Apr. 24. First Daylight Saving Bill passed. Fall of Kut, Apr. 29. Battle of Jutland, May 31. Brusilov's offensive in Galicia begins, June 4. Kitchener drowned when *Hampshire* struck mine, June 5. Battle of the Somme, July 1–Nov. 13: British losses: 420,000. Italians capture Gorizia, Aug. 10. Hindenburg and Ludendorff chiefs of German staff, Aug. 27. Rumania declares war against Austria and Germany, Aug. 27. Tanks first used by British, Sept. 15. Death of Francis Joseph of Austria, Nov. 21. Lloyd George forms War Cabinet, Dec. 6. Joffre replaced by Nivelle, early Dec.

1917 Unrestricted submarine warfare begins, Feb. 1. British troops occupy Baghdad, Mar. 11. Revolution in Russia, Mar. 12. U.S.A. declares war on Germany, April 6. Battle of Arras, Apr. 9–14: Vimy Ridge taken by Canadians, Apr. 10. Pétain replaced Nivelle, May 15. Messines Ridge taken by British, June 7. First American contingents arrive in France, June 26. Allenby assumes Palestine command, June 29. Third Battle of Ypres opened, July 31. Russia proclaimed a Republic, Sept. 15. British victory on Passchendaele Ridge, Oct. 4. French victory on the Aisne, Oct. 23. Caporetto: Italians severely defeated by Austrians, Oct. 24. Bolshevik Revolution, Nov. 7 (Oct. 25 O.S.). Passchendaele captured by British, Nov. 6. Balfour declaration recognised Palestine as "a national home" for the Jews, Nov. 8. Hindenburg Lines smashed on 10-mile front, Nov. 20. Fall of Jerusalem, Dec. 9. Russo-German armistice signed, Dec. 15.

1918 Treaty of Brest-Litovsk, Mar. 3. German offensive against British opened on Somme, Mar. 21. Battle of Arras, Mar. 21–Apr. 4. Second German offensive against British, Apr. 9–25. British naval raid on Zeebrugge and Ostend, Apr. 23. Foch appointed C.-in-C. Allied armies, Apr. 14. Peace signed between Rumania and Central Powers, May 7. *Vindictive* sunk in Ostend harbour, May 9. Last German offensive against French, July 15. British, Canadians, and Australians attack in front of Amiens, Aug. 8. Allenby destroyed last Turkish army at Megiddo, Sept. 19. Bulgarians signed armistice Sept. 29. General Allied offensive in West began, Sept. 26. Germans accepted Wilson's Fourteen Points, Oct. 23. Great Italian advance, Oct. 24. Turkey surrenders, Oct 30. Austria accepts imposed terms, Nov. 3. Popular government in Poland (Lubin), Nov. 7. Revolutionary movement begins in Germany, Nov. 8. Kaiser abdicates and escapes to Holland, Nov. 9. Armistice signed by Germans, Nov. 11. Proclamation of Kingdom of Serbs, Croats and Slovenes in Belgrade, Dec. 1.

THE TWENTIES AND THIRTIES

1919 Peace Conference in Paris, Jan. 18. Total eclipse of the sun, as predicted by Einstein March 29. First direct flight across Atlantic by Sir J. Alcock and Sir A. W. Brown, June 15. Interned German fleet scuttled at Scapa Flow, June 19. Treaty of Peace with Germany signed at Versailles, June 28. Treaty of St. Germain: break-up of Austrian Empire, Sept. 10.

1920 Peace Treaty ratified in Paris. First meeting of League of Nations, from which Germany, Austria, Russia, and Turkey are excluded, and at which the U.S.A. is not represented. Prohibition in U.S.A. Peace Treaty with Turkey signed at Sèvres: Ottoman Empire broken up, Aug. 10. Degrees first open to women at Oxford Univ., Oct. 14.

1921 Riots in Egypt, May 23. In complete disregard of the League of Nations, Greece makes war on Turkey. Heligoland fortresses demolished, Oct. 14. Irish Free State set up by Peace Treaty with Britain, Dec. 6.

1922 Four-Power Pacific Treaty ratified by U.S. Senate, Mar. 24. Heavy fighting in Dublin, the Four Courts blown up, July 2. Defeat of Greek armies by the Turks, Aug.–Sept. Mussolini's Fascist "March on Rome," Oct. 28.

1923 French troops despatched to Ruhr, Jan. 11. Treaty of Lausanne, July 24. Earthquake in Japan, Tokio and Yokohama in ruins, Sept. 1. Rhine Republic proclaimed, Bavaria defies the Reich, Oct. 20. Turkish Republic proclaimed; Kemal Pasha, first President, Oct. 29.

1924 Lenin dies, Jan. 21. First Labour Ministry in Britain under MacDonald, Jan. 22; lasts 9 months. George II of Greece deposed and a Republic declared, Mar. 25. Dawes Plan accepted by London conference; Ruhr evacuation agreed to, Aug. 16.

1925 Hindenburg elected German President, Mar. 26. Treaty of Locarno signed in London, Dec. 1. Summer Time Act made permanent.

1926 Ibn Saud proclaimed king of the Hedjaz in Jeddah, Jan. 11. Evacuation of Cologne by British forces, Jan. 31. General strike in Britain.

1927 Lindbergh flies Atlantic alone, May 21.

1928 Earthquake in Greece, Corinth destroyed, Apr. 23. Capt. Kingsford-Smith flies the

A.D.

Pacific, June 9. General Nobile rescued by aeroplane from Arctic one month after disaster, June 24. Kellogg Pact accepted by Gt. Britain, July 18. German airship with 60 persons crosses Atlantic, Oct. 15. Women in Britain enfranchised.

1929 Second Labour Ministry under MacDonald. Graf Zeppelin makes numerous successful intercontinental flights. Commander Byrd flies over South Pole, Nov. 30. American slump and Wall Street crash.

1930 *R.101* destroyed in France on first flight to India, 48 lives lost, Oct. 5—end of British interest in airships.

1931 Great floods in China. Resignation of Labour Government and formation of Coalition under MacDonald.

1932 Manchuria erected into Japanese puppet state of Manchukuo, Feb. 18. Sydney Harbour Bridge opened, Mar. 19. Ottawa Imperial Conference.

1933 Hitler appointed Chancellor by Hindenburg, Jan. 30, and step by step gains supreme control. German Reichstag set on fire, Feb. 27.

1934 Dollfuss, Austrian Chancellor, murdered by Austrian Nazis, July 25. Death of Hindenburg, Aug. 2. Hitler becomes Dictator. Alexander of Yugoslavia assassinated in Marseilles, Oct. 9.

1935 Saar plebiscite for return to Germany, Jan. 13. Baldwin succeeds MacDonald as Prime Minister, June 7. War begins between Italy and Abyssinia, Oct. 3. Ineffectual economic "sanctions" by League of Nations against Italy, Nov. 18.

1936 Accession of King Edward VIII, Jan. 20. Repudiation of Locarno Treaty by Germany, Mar. 7. Remilitarisation of Rhineland, Mar. 8. Italian troops occupy Addis Ababa, May 5. Civil War breaks out in Spain, July 18. King Edward VIII abdicates after a reign of 325 days, Dec. 10. The Duke of York succeeds his brother as King George VI, Dec. 12.

1937 Coalition Ministry under Chamberlain, May 28. Japanese begin attempted conquest of China—"China incident," July 7.

1938 Austria annexed by Germany, Mar. 13. British navy mobilised, Sept. 28. Munich Agreement between Chamberlain, Daladier, Hitler, and Mussolini, Sept. 29.

1939

February 27 Great Britain recognises General Franco's Government.

March 16 Bohemia and Moravia annexed by Hitler and proclaimed a German Protectorate. 22 Memel ceded to Germany by Lithuania. 28 Anti-Polish press campaign begun by Germany.

April 1 Spanish War ends. 7 Italy seizes Albania. 14 First British talks with Russia. 27 Conscription introduced in Great Britain. 28 Hitler denounces Anglo-German Naval agreement and the Polish Non-Aggression Treaty.

May 12 Great Britain signs defensive agreement with Turkey. 22 Italy and Germany sign pact. 23 France and Turkey sign defensive agreement. 25 Anglo-Polish treaty signed in London.

July 10 Chamberlain re-affirms British pledge to Poland.

August 23 German-Soviet Pact signed by von Ribbentrop. 25 Japan breaks away from the Anti-Comintern Pact. 28 Holland mobilises. 31 British fleet mobilised.

SECOND WORLD WAR

September 1 Poland invaded by German forces. Great Britain and France mobilise. 1–4 Evacuation schemes put in motion in England and Wales: 1,200,000 persons moved. 2 Compulsory military service for all men in Britain aged 18 to 41. 3 War declared (11 a.m.) between Britain and Germany as from 5 p.m. 4 British liner *Athenia* sunk by submarine. R.A.F. raid the Kiel Canal entrance and bomb German warships. 6 First enemy air raid on Britain. 8 Russia mobilises. Russian troops on Polish border. 11 British troops on French soil. 17 Russian troops cross the Polish frontier along its entire length. Russian and German troops meet near Brest Litovsk. 27 Capitulation of Warsaw. 29 Nazi–Soviet pact signed in Moscow approving partition of Poland.

October 14 *Royal Oak* sunk in Scapa Flow with a loss of 810 lives.

November 8 Bomb explosion in the Bürgerbräukeller at Munich after Hitler's speech. Germans using magnetic mines. 29 Diplomatic relations between Russia and Finland severed. 30 Finland attacked by Russia.

December 11 Italy leaves the League of Nations. 13 Battle of the River Plate: engagement of German warship *Admiral Graf Spee* by H.M. cruisers *Exeter*, *Ajax*, and *Achilles*. 14 Rejection by Russia of the League of Nations' offer of mediation in the Russo-Finnish war. Russia expelled from the League of Nations. 18 *Admiral Graf Spee* scuttles herself in the entrance of Montevideo harbour.

1940

February 14 Finnish advanced posts captured by Russians. 16 299 British prisoners taken off the German Naval Auxiliary *Altmark* in Norwegian waters. 26 Finns lose the island fortress of Koivisto. Finns retreat from Petsamo.

March 12 British ships to be fitted with a protective device against magnetic mines. Finland concludes a peace treaty whereby she cedes to Russia the Karelian Isthmus, the town of Vipuri and a military base on Hango Peninsula.

April 9 Invasion of Denmark and Norway by Germany. 15 British troops arrive in Norway. 19 British soldiers land in the Faroes.

May 2 British troops withdrawn from Norway. 10 Holland, Belgium and Luxembourg invaded by German forces. Parachute troops landed near Rotterdam. British troops cross the Belgian border. British troops land in Iceland. Rotterdam bombed. 11 National Government formed under Churchill. 13 Queen Wilhelmina arrives in London. 14 Rotterdam captured. Holland ceases fighting. Allied troops land near Narvik. 17 Belgian Government moves to Ostend. 24 German forces enter Boulogne. 27 Belgian army capitulates on the order of King Leopold. British forces to be withdrawn from Flanders. Narvik captured by Allied forces. 29 Ostend, Ypres, Lille and other Belgian and French towns lost to the Germans.

June Evacuation of British army from Dunkirk (May 27–June 4): 299 British warships and 420 other vessels under constant attack evacuate 335,490 officers and men. 5 Hitler proclaims a war of total annihilation against his enemies. 8 German armoured forces penetrate French defences in the West near Rouen. 10 Italy declares war on Great Britain and France. 14 Paris captured by German forces. 15 Soviet troops occupy Lithuania, Latvia and Estonia. 22 French delegates accept terms for an Armistice. 25 Hostilities in France cease at 12.35 a.m.

July 1 Channel Islands occupied by Germany. 3 French naval squadron at Oran immobilised. 10 Battle of Britain began.

August 19 British withdrew from British Somaliland. 25 British began night bombing of Germany.

September 6 King Carol of Rumania abdicates in favour of his son Michael. 7 London sustains severe damage in the largest aerial attack since war commenced. 15 Battle of Britain ends with British victory: German aeroplanes destroyed, 1,733; R.A.F. losses, 915. 23 Japanese troops enter Indo-China.

October 7 German troops enter Rumania. 28 Greece rejects an Italian ultimatum.

November 1 Greeks repel Italian attacks. 5 H.M.S. *Jervis Bay* lost defending Atlantic convoy from German warship *Admiral Scheer*. 11 Italian fleet at Taranto crippled by Fleet Air Arm. 14 Coventry heavily attacked, the Cathedral destroyed. 22 Albanian town of Koritza captured by the Greeks.

December 2 Bristol heavily bombed. 11 Sidi Barrani captured by British forces: beginning

A.D.

of Wavell's destruction of Italian forces in Cyrenaica. 29 City of London severely burned by incendiary bombs: Guildhall and eight Wren Churches destroyed.

1941

January 5 Bardia captured. 22 Tobruk captured by Australian troops.

February 7 Benghazi captured. 26 Mogadishu, capital of Italian Somaliland, occupied by Imperial troops. German mechanised troops in Libya.

March 4 British raid Lofoten Islands. 11 U.S. Lease and Lend Bill signed by Roosevelt. 27 Keren—main battle in British conquest of Abyssinia and Somaliland. 28 Cape Matapan: Italian fleet routed by British. 30 Rommel opens attack in N. Africa.

April 4 Addis Ababa entered by Imperial troops. 6 Greece and Yugoslavia invaded by German troops. 8 Massawa capitulates. 11 Belgrade occupied by German forces. 13 Bardia given up by British. Tobruk holds out. 24 Empire forces withdrawing from Greece. 27 Athens captured by the Germans.

May 2 Evacuation from Greece completed. 10 Rudolf Hess descends by parachute in Scotland. 20 Crete invaded by German air-borne troops. 24 H.M.S. *Hood* sunk. 27 German battleship *Bismarck* sunk; British forces withdraw from Crete.

June 2 Clothes rationing commences. 4 William II (ex-Kaiser of Germany) dies. 18 Treaty of friendship between Turkey and Germany signed. 22 Germany attacks Russia. 24 Russia loses Brest Litovsk.

July 3 Palmyra (Syria) surrenders to Allied forces. 7 U.S. forces arrive in Iceland. 9 General Dentz, the French High Commissioner in Syria, asks for Armistice terms. 25 Fighting round Smolensk.

August 25 British and Russian troops enter Persia. 27 The Dnepropetrovsk dam blown up by the Russians.

September 18 Crimea cut off from mainland. 19 Kiev entered by Germans.

October 6 German attack on Moscow. 16 Soviet Government leaves Moscow. Odessa occupied by German and Rumanian troops. 19 Taganrog on Sea of Azov captured by Germans. 26 Kharkov captured by the Germans.

November 14 *Ark Royal* sunk. 18 Libyan battle opens: Eighth Army's first offensive. 23 Bardia and Fort Capuzzo captured by British. 24 H.M.S. *Dunedin* torpedoed. 25 H.M.S. *Barham* sunk. 30 Russians re-take Rostov.

December 1 Points rationing scheme in force in Britain. 4 German attack on Moscow halted. 7 Japanese attack on Pearl Harbor. 8 Japanese forces land in Malaya. 9 British forces in Tobruk relieved. 10 H.M.S. *Repulse* and *Prince of Wales* sunk off Malaya by Japanese. Phillippines invaded by Japanese. 25 Hongkong surrenders to Japanese.

1942

January 2 Manila and Cavite taken by Japanese. 23 Japanese forces land in New Guinea and the Solomon Islands.

February 9 Soap rationed. 12 Escape through English Channel of German ships *Scharnhorst*, *Gneisenau*, and *Prinz Eugen*. 15 Singapore surrenders to Japanese. 27 Battle of Java Sea.

March 9 Surrender of Java to Japanese.

April 15 George Cross awarded to the island of Malta.

May 4–8 Battle of Coral Sea. 7 Madagascar invaded by British forces. 7 U.S. forces sink 11 Japanese warships off the Solomon Islands. 30 Over 1,000 bombers raid Cologne. Canterbury bombed.

June 3–7 Midway Island: U.S. naval victory turns tide in Pacific. 20 Tobruk captured by the Germans.

July 16 R.A.F. make first daylight raid on the Ruhr.

August 6 Germans advancing towards the Caucasus. 10 American forces land in the Solomon Islands. 11 Malta convoy action (loss of H.M.S. *Eagle*, *Manchester*, *Cairo*, and one destroyer). 19 Raid on Dieppe. 23–25 Battle of Solomons.

September 6 Germans halted at Stalingrad.

October 23 El Alamein: Allied offensive opens in Egypt.

November 4 Rommel's army in full retreat. 5 Red Army holding firm at Stalingrad. 7 Allied invasion of N. Africa. 27 German forces enter Toulon. French Fleet scuttled.

December 2 First self-sustained, controlled nuclear chain reaction in uranium achieved by group working under Enrico Fermi at Chicago. 24 Admiral Darlan assassinated.

1943

January 6 German armies in the Caucasus and the Don elbow in retreat. 18 Leningrad 16-month siege ended. 23 Tripoli occupied by the Eighth Army. 27 American bombers make their first attack on Germany. 31 Remnants of the German army outside Stalingrad surrender.

February 9 Guadalcanal Island cleared of Japanese troops. 16 Kharkov retaken by the Russians.

March 1–3 Battle of Bismarck Sea. 23 8th Army penetrates the Mareth Line.

May 7 Tunis and Bizerta captured by Allies. 12 All organised German resistance in Tunisia ceases. 16 Dams in the Ruhr breached by the R.A.F. 22 Moscow dissolves the Comintern.

June 3 French Committee for National Liberation formed in Algiers.

July 10 Allied invasion of Sicily. 25 Mussolini overthrown. 28 Fascist Party in Italy dissolved.

August 17 Sicily in Allied hands.

September 3 Italian mainland invaded. 7 Italy surrenders. 9 British and American troops land near Naples. 10 Rome seized by the Germans. 14 Salamaua captured from the Japanese. 23 *Tirpitz* severely damaged (sunk Nov. 12, 1944). 25 Smolensk taken by the Russians.

October 1 Naples taken. 25 Russians capture Dnepropetrovsk and Dneprodzerzhinck.

November 6 Kiev taken by the Russians. 26 Second Battle of Solomons. 28 Churchill, Roosevelt, and Stalin meet in Teheran.

December 2 Men between 18 and 25 to be directed to the mining industry by ballot in Britain. 26 Sinking of German battleship *Scharnhorst*.

1944

January 22 Allied landings at Anzio. 28 Argentina breaks with the Axis Powers.

February 1 American forces land on the Marshall Islands. 2 Russians penetrate Estonia.

March 15 Cassino (Italy) destroyed by Allied bombers.

May 9 Sevastopol captured by Russians. 18 Capture of Cassino and Abbey by Allies. 19 50 Allied officers shot after escaping from a German prison camp. 30 Battle for Rome commences.

June 4 Allied forces enter Rome. King of Italy signs decree transferring his powers to Prince Umberto, his son. 6 *D-Day*: invasion of Europe (over 4,000 ships in invasion fleet). 7 Defeat of Japanese thrust at India, outside Imphal. 9 Heavy fighting near Caen. 12 First V-1 falls on England. 18 Cherbourg peninsula cut by the Americans. Russians break through the Mannerheim Line.

July 3 Minsk captured by Russians. 9 Caen captured by Allies. 20 "Bomb plot" on Hitler's life. 21 Guam captured by Americans.

August 1 Uprising in Warsaw. 4 Myitkyina falls to Allied forces. 15 Allied forces land in southern France. 23 Paris liberated. Marseilles taken. Rumania surrenders. 25 Rumania declares war on Germany.

September 3 Allies in Belgium. 4 Antwerp and Brussels taken by Allies. Holland entered. Finland "ceases fire." 6 Bulgaria asks for an armistice. 7 Boulogne entered by Allies. Bulgaria declares war on Germany. 8 First V-2 falls on England. 11 Allied forces fighting on

A.D.

Reich territory. 17 Allied air-borne troops land near Arnhem. 22 First Battle of Philippines.

October 3 Warsaw rising crushed by the Germans. 5 British troops land on the mainland of Greece. 14 Athens occupied by Allies. 15 Hungary asks for armistice terms. 20 Aachen captured by the Americans. 25 Battle of Leyte Gulf: end of Japanese sea-power. 28 Second Battle of Philippines.

December 6 Civil war breaks out in Athens. 16 German forces counter-attack in the Ardennes: last German offensive in the West. 26 Budapest encircled by Russians.

1945

January 5 Organized fighting in Athens ceases. 11 U.S. forces land on Island of Luzon. 17 Warsaw captured by the Russians. 21 Russian troops in Silesia. 23 Burma road to China reopened.

February 4 Yalta conference. 14 Bombing of Dresden. 19 Americans land on Iwojima Island.

March 6 Cologne captured by Allies.

April 1 U.S. Invasion of Okinawa. 5 Russian Government denounces the Soviet-Japan neutrality pact. Japanese Cabinet resigns. 11 Russian Army enters Vienna after 7-day battle. 12 Death of President Roosevelt. 25 Berlin surrounded by Russian troops. 27 Russians and Americans link up in Germany. 28 Mussolini and his mistress shot by Italian partisans. 30 Hitler killed himself and his mistress.

May 2 German armies in Italy surrender. Berlin captured by the Russians. 3 Rangoon captured by British. 4 German forces in N.W. Germany, Holland and Denmark surrender. 8 End of World War II against Germany officially declared to be one minute past midnight (Tuesday). 28 Naval air attacks on Japan.

June 26 United Nations Charter signed at San Francisco.

July 5 Polish Government in Warsaw recognised by Allies. 26 Striking Labour victory in general election; Attlee became Prime Minister.

August 6 Atomic bomb first used against Japan: Hiroshima laid waste. 8 Russia declares war against Japan. 9 Russia advances into Manchuria. Nagasaki target for atomic bomb No. 2. 14 Japan surrenders unconditionally to the Allies. 17 Lend-Lease terminated.

September 2 Victory over Japan celebrated: end of Second World War.

"COLD WAR": AFRO-ASIAN INDEPENDENCE

October 9 U.S.A. to keep secret of manufacture of atomic bomb. 15 Laval executed.

November 20 Trial of major war criminals opens at Nuremberg.

1946

February 1 Mr. Trygve Lie elected Secretary-General of UNO.

April 19 League of Nations formally wound up.

June 5 Italy votes for Republic. 30 United States atom bomb tests at Bikini.

July 13 United States House of Representatives approves loan to Britain. 22 Bread rationing in Britain. British H.Q. in Jerusalem blown up. 24 Underwater atom bomb test at Bikini.

August 1 Peace Conference opens in Paris.

September 6 United Nations F.A.O. considers establishment of World Food Board.

October 16 Nuremberg sentences on Nazis carried out, Goering commits suicide. 23 General Assembly of the United Nations opens in New York.

November 10 Communists head poll in French General Elections.

December 2 Agreement signed for economic fusion of British and American zones in Germany.

A.D.

1947

January 1 British coal industry nationalised. 14 M. Vincent-Auriol elected first President of Fourth Republic.

March 15 Floods in England worst recorded. 24 Netherlands Government and Indonesian Cabinet sign agreement in Batavia for a United States of Indonesia.

April 1 School leaving age raised to 15 in Great Britain.

June 5 Inauguration of "Marshall Aid".

August 3 Dutch military action in Indonesia ends. 15 India and Pakistan assume Dominion Status. Viscount Mountbatten appointed Governor-General of India and Mr. Jinnah Governor-General of Pakistan. 29 Palestine Committee agrees British Mandate should end, majority report recommends partition.

September 22 First Atlantic automatic flight by U.S. pilotless aircraft.

October 6 Cominform, new international Communist organization, set up in Belgrade.

November 20 Marriage of Princess Elizabeth. 29 Palestine Committee of U.N. Assembly votes in favour of partition of Palestine into Jewish and Arab States.

December 15 Breakdown of 4-Power Conference on Germany. 30 King Michael of Rumania abdicates; Rumania becomes a People's Republic.

1948

January 1 British Railways nationalised. 4 Burma becomes independent Republic. 30 Mahatma Gandhi assassinated in New Delhi.

February 1 New Malayan federal constitution comes into force. 4 Ceylon Independence Act. 25 New Czechoslovak Government formed under Communist leadership.

March 10 Death of Jan Masaryk.

April 1 British electricity industry nationalised. 5 First European Aid shipments sail from America. 16 O.E.E.C. established.

May 3 Mr. Rajagopalachari appointed Gov.-Gen. of India in succession to Earl Mountbatten. 14 British Mandate for Palestine ended at midnight. Jews proclaim new State of Israel.

June 28 Yugoslavia expelled from Cominform; "Titoism" denounced.

July 1 "Berlin Airlift": American, British and French zones of Berlin supplied by air. 23 Malayan Communist party outlawed. 29 Bread rationing in Great Britain ends.

August 15 Republic of Korea proclaimed.

September 3 Death of Dr. Benes. 11 Death of Mohammed Ali Jinnah. 17 Count Bernadotte, U.N. Mediator for Palestine, assassinated.

October 30 Chinese Communist forces capture Mukden.

November 3 Mr. Truman elected U.S. President. 14 Birth of a son to Princess Elizabeth.

December 21 Republic of Ireland Bill signed in Dublin.

1949

March 15 Clothes rationing ends in Great Britain. 31 Russia protests against Atlantic Pact.

April 1 Newfoundland becomes part of Canada.

May 1 Gas Industry nationalised. 3 Ten-power conference in London establishes Council of Europe. 12 Berlin blockade lifted.

August 24 North Atlantic Treaty comes into force.

September 12 Professor Theodor Heuss elected first President of West German Republic. 21 General Mao Tse-Tung proclaims People's Republic of China.

October 2 Russia recognises newly-established Chinese People's Republic. 11 Herr Wilhelm Pieck elected first President of East German Republic.

December 8 Chinese Nationalist Government leaves mainland and sets up H.Q. in Formosa. 27 United States of Indonesia come into being.

1950

January 6 Britain recognises Communist Government of China; 24 Dr. Rajendra Prasad elected

A.D.

first President of Indian Republic; 26 New Constitution of Indian Republic comes into force.

February 14 30-year treaty of alliance between Russia and China signed in Moscow; 23 Labour Party wins General Election with narrow majority.

March 5 Lord Boyd Orr warns world that communism spreads where hunger prevails; 22 First of U.S. super-fortresses arrives in Norfolk.

April 1 Italy takes over from Britain administration of Somaliland; 13 First shipment of military aid to France under N.A. Pact unloaded at Cherbourg.

May 1 New Chinese marriage law abolishes polygamy and child marriages and gives both sexes equal rights; 19 Points rationing ends in Britain after 8 years; 25 Middle East Tripartite Declaration by Britain, France, and U.S.A.; 26 Petrol rationing ends in Britain.

June 25 N. Korean troops advance into S. Korea; Security Council calls for cease fire; 27 Pres. Truman orders U.S. air, and sea forces to support S. Korea and protect Formosa; U.N. Commission in Korea proposes neutral mediator; military assistance to S. Korea endorsed by Security Council; 30 Pres. Truman authorizes use of American ground troops in Korea.

July 2 American troops land in S. Korea; 8 Gen. MacArthur designated C.-in-C. of U.N. forces in Korea.

August 1 Security Council meets under chairmanship of M. Malik, the Soviet delegate; 7 American forces in Korea open offensive and halt drive on Pusan; 15 Princess Elizabeth gives birth to a daughter; severe earthquake in Assam; 17 independence Day in Indonesia.

September 6 British troops in action in Korea; 9 Soap rationing ends in Britain.

October 9 U.N. forces across the 38th parallel in strength; 19 Sir Stafford Cripps retires from public life on account of illness; Pyongyang, N. Korean capital, captured by U.N. forces; 21 Princess Anne Elizabeth Alice Louise christened; 26 New Chamber of House of Commons opened at Westminster; 29 King Gustav V of Sweden dies.

November 2 Death of George Bernard Shaw aged 94; 6 Chinese forces from Manchuria reported fighting in Korea.

December 3 Mr. Attlee flies to Washington for talks with Pres. Truman; 4 Pyongyang occupied by Chinese; 19 Gen. Eisenhower appointed Supreme Commander of West European Defence Forces set up by Atlantic Powers; 25 Stone of Scone stolen from Westminster Abbey.

1951

January 30 U.N. Assembly rejects resolution of 12 Asian and Arab nations calling for 7-nation conference for peaceful settlement of Korean question; 31 Decree confiscating property of Alfred Krupp cancelled.

February 15 Vesting date for Iron and Steel.

April 11 Gen. MacArthur relieved of all his commands by Pres. Truman and replaced by Lt.-Gen. Ridgway; 13 Coronation Stone returned to Westminster Abbey.

May 2 Persian oil industry nationalized; Germany admitted to Council of Europe; 3 H.M. the King opens Festival of Britain from steps of St. Paul's.

June 23 M. Malik, Russian delegate to the U.N., appeals for settlement of Korean war.

July 1 Colombo plan comes into force; 9 State of war between Britain and Germany officially ended; 10 Armistice negotiations open at Kaesong; 17 King Leopold abdicates in favour of his son Baudouin, who becomes fifth King of the Belgians; 20 King Abdullah of Jordan assassinated.

September 1 Tripartite Security Treaty between U.S.A., Australia, and New Zealand signed in San Francisco; 8 Japanese Peace Treaty—to which Russia, China, and India are not parties—signed at San Francisco; Security Pact between Japan and U.S.A., providing for retention of American forces in Japan, also signed; 23 H.M. the King undergoes successful operation; 30 Festival of Britain ends.

October 8 Princess Elizabeth and Duke of Edinburgh leave for Canadian tour; 15 Egyptian Parliament passes unanimously Bills abrogating Anglo-Egyptian treaty of 1936 and 1899 Sudan Condominion Agreement; 16 Assassination of Liaquat Ali Khan; 25 General Election won by Conservatives with small majority.

November 5 Mr. Attlee receives the Order of Merit.

December 17 London foreign-exchange market reopens after 12 years; 24 Libya becomes independent state; 31 I.R.O. closes down.

1952

January 2 Mutual Security Agency replaces Economic Co-operation Administration; 31 Princess Elizabeth and Duke of Edinburgh leave London on first stage of Commonwealth tour.

February 6 King George VI died at Sandringham aged 56; 7 Queen Elizabeth II and the Duke of Edinburgh arrive home by air from Kenya; 15 Funeral of King George VI at Windsor; 21 Identity cards abolished.

March 20 South African Supreme Court rules invalid Dr. Malan's Act which places Cape coloured voters on separate electoral register.

April 11 H.M. the Queen declares that she wishes her children and descendants to bear the name of Windsor; 21 Death of Sir Stafford Cripps in Switzerland; 28 Japan regains status as sovereign and independent power.

May 5 H.M. the Queen takes up residence at Buckingham Palace; 27 Treaty setting up European Defence Community signed in Paris.

June 23 Power plants along Yalu River attacked by U.S. aircraft in biggest raid of Korean war.

July 7 American ship *United States* wins Atlantic Blue Riband; 19 Fifteenth Olympic Games held in Helsinki; 23 Military *coup d'état* takes place in Cairo.

August 1 Ratification of Bonn Agreement, by which W. Germany again becomes independent nation, and Treaty of Paris, which sets up the European Defence Community, approved by Government against Labour opposition; 16 Severe thunderstorms in Somerset and N. Devon cause rivers to flood; W. Lyn changes course bringing devastation to Lynmouth; 26 Passive resistance campaign against racial laws in S. Africa gains momentum.

September 2 Sir William Slim appointed Gov.-Gen. of Australia (from 1953); 8 New Egyptian Cabinet appoints Gen. Neguib military Gov.-Gen. of Egypt and approves land reforms.

October 3 Britain's first atomic weapon exploded in Monte Bello Islands, off N.W. Australia; 5 Tea derationed and decontrolled; 20 State of emergency declared in Kenya as a result of Mau Mau activities.

November 1 Reported explosion of U.S. hydrogen bomb at Eniwetok atoll in mid-Pacific; 4 Gen. Eisenhower, Republican Candidate, wins sweeping victory in American Presidential election.

December 29 Fish recently caught off Madagascar confirmed as species of the prehistoric Cœlacanth.

1953

January 20 Inauguration of General Eisenhower as 34th President of the United States; 31 Violent N.E. gales combined with surging high tides caused extensive flooding with loss of life along coasts of eastern England, the Netherlands, and Belgium.

February 4 Sweet rationing ended; 23 War-time deserters in Britain granted amnesty.

March 6 Marshal Stalin died, aged 74; 24 Death of Queen Mary at Marlborough House, aged 85; 31 Mr. Dag Hammarskjöld elected U.N. Sec.-Gen. in succession to Mr. Trygve Lie.

April 15 Dr. Malan's National Party again returned to power in S. Africa with increased

A.D.

majority; 24 Mr. Churchill created a Knight of the Garter by the Queen.

May 4 Duke of Edinburgh received his pilot's "wings"; 29 E. P. Hillary and Sherpa Tenzing of the Everest Expedition led by Colonel John Hunt reached summit of Everest (29,002 ft.).

June 2 Coronation of H.M. Elizabeth II in Westminster Abbey amid scenes of magnificent pageantry; ceremony televised; 26 Republic of Egypt accorded *de facto* recognition by Britain.

July 4 German–Austrian Expedition reached summit of Nanga Parbat in the Himalayas; 13 De-nationalisation of British steel industry; 14 Royal Assent given to Central African Federation Bill; 27 Korean Armistice signed at Panmunjom.

August 9–12 Disastrous earthquakes in Greek Ionian Islands; 12 Explosion of Russian hydrogen bomb reported.

September 17 Bank rate reduced from 4 to 3½ per cent; 23 Royal Commission on Capital Punishment recommended that juries should decide whether death sentence or life imprisonment should be imposed on prisoners found guilty of murder, and that the M'Naghten Rules on insanity should be abrogated or amended; 26 Sugar rationing ended after nearly 14 years; 30 Professor Piccard in his bathyscaphe dived 10,000 ft. off Italian coast.

October 15 Sir Winston Churchill awarded 1953 Nobel Prize for Literature.

November 11 Great bell at Notre Dame rung by electricity for first time; 21 Piltdown skull, discovered in Sussex in 1911, found by anthropologists to be partial hoax; 23 The Queen and Duke of Edinburgh left in stratocruiser *Canopus* on first stage of 6-months' tour of Commonwealth.

December 1 Agreement signed for laying first transatlantic telephone cable; 23 M. René Coty elected Pres. of France at the 13th ballot; L. P. Beria, former chief of Soviet Secret Police, and six associates sentenced to death and shot; 25 The Queen gave her Christmas broadcast from Auckland; 31 Mildest December for 20 years, and before that for over 200 years.

1954

January 9 Self-government began in the Sudan; 12 M. Le Trouquer (Socialist) elected President of French National Assembly on retirement of M. Herriot; 16 M. René Coty became President of France in succession to M. Vincent Auriol; 31 Intense cold covered most of Europe.

February 3 The Queen and the Duke of Edinburgh arrived in Australia; First Parliament of newly formed Federation of Rhodesia and Nyasaland opened in Salisbury; 5 Britain's first "breeder" pile in operation at Harwell.

March 1 American hydrogen bomb exploded at Bikini; 22 London gold market reopened after 15 years.

April 1 The Queen and the Duke of Edinburgh left Australia; 3 Oxford won 100th Boat Race; 21 Russia joined UNESCO; 26 Conference on Far East opened in Palais des Nations, Geneva, Mr. Chou En-lai representing China; Russia joined I.L.O.

May 6 Roger Bannister ran the mile in under 4 min., the first man in the world to do so; 7 Fortress of Dien Bien Phu fell to Viet-Minh after siege of 8 weeks and final battle of 20 hours; 11 Bank rate reduced from 3½ to 3 per cent; 15 The Queen and the Duke of Edinburgh returned from their six-months' tour of the Commonwealth; 18 Liverpool Cotton Exchange reopened

June 1 Television licence fee raised from £2 to £3 a year; 2 Mr. John A. Costello (Fine Gael) elected Prime Minister of Ireland; 17 Indo-Chinese crisis brought M. Mendès-France to power in France; 22 First all-African Cabinet in British Africa appointed in the Gold Coast; 27 First electric power station using atomic energy began working in Soviet Union; 30 Eclipse of the sun.

July 3 All food rationing ended in Britain; 8 Mr. Nehru opened the world's longest canal (Bhakra–Nangal hydro-electric project); 27 Agreement reached in Cairo for withdrawal of British troops from Suez Canal Zone; 31 K2 (Mount Godwin Austen), second highest peak in the world, climbed by Italian team led by Prof. Ardito Desio of Milan Univ.

August 5 Persian oil dispute settled; 11 Cessation of hostilities in Indo-China after 8 years of fighting.

September 14 Sheffield–Manchester electrified railway opened.

October 14 Mr. Anthony Eden created a Knight of the Garter by the Queen; 19 Anglo-Egyptian Suez Canal Agreement.

November 1 French settlements in India passed under Indian control; 22 Death of Andrei Vyshinsky; 30 Sir Winston Churchill celebrated his 80th birthday and was presented by both Houses of Parliament with a portrait of himself by Graham Sutherland.

1955

January 27 Bank rate increased from 3 to 3½ per cent; 31 Princess Margaret left for tour of W. Indies.

February 8 Marshal Bulganin succeeded Mr. Malenkov as chairman of the Soviet Council of Ministers; 15 Plans to build 12 atomic power stations in Britain during next 10 years announced; 17 Britain to proceed with manufacture of hydrogen bombs; 24 Bank rate raised to 4½ per cent and restrictions on hire purchase announced; Dr. Albert Schweitzer appointed honorary member of the Order of Merit; Turco–Iraqi pact signed at Baghdad (Britain, Pakistan, and Persia acceded later).

April 5 Sir Winston Churchill resigned as Prime Minister; 6 Sir Anthony Eden succeeded as Prime Minister; 18 Afro-Asian conference (29 nations) opened at Bandung; Death of Dr. Albert Einstein; 29 Signor Gronchi elected President of Italy.

May 5 Ratification of London and Paris agreements completed; Germany attained full sovereignty and Western European Union came into being; 26 British general election resulted in Conservative majority of 59.

June 15 U.S. and Britain agreed to co-operate on atomic energy; 16 Revolt against the Perón government in Argentina.

July 9 Leading world scientists issued appeal for renunciation of war because of possible effects of hydrogen bomb; 18 Four-Power conference opened in Geneva (Pres. Eisenhower, Sir Anthony Eden, M. Faure, Marshal Bulganin), the first meeting between heads of Government since Potsdam, 1945; 27 Austrian State Treaty came into force.

August 8 International conference on peaceful uses of atomic energy opened in Geneva (1200 scientists from 72 countries attended).

September 16 Universal Copyright convention came into force, bringing U.S. into agreement with European countries; 19 General Perón resigned after rebels threatened to bombard Buenos Aires; 22 Independent television service began.

October 2 City of London became a "smokeless zone"; 12 British and Soviet warships exchanged courtesy visits; 20 Syria and Egypt signed mutual defence treaty; 23 Referendum on Saar European Statute gave victory to pro-German parties.

November 5 Vienna State Opera House re-opened; 23 *Hamlet* played on Russian stage by British company, the first since Tsarist times.

December 7 Mr. Attlee announced his retirement and was created an earl; 12 Completion of 830-mile pipeline through Urals, crossing 6 rivers; 14 Mr. Hugh Gaitskell elected leader of the Parl. Labour Party; 18 Anglo–American offer of financial assistance to Egypt in building Aswan High Dam; 24 In Christmas broadcast the Pope spoke of need to suspend nuclear test explosions.

1956

January 1 Sudan proclaimed an independent republic; 27 The Queen and the Duke of Edin-

A.D.

burgh left by air for 3 weeks' tour of Nigeria; 200th anniversary of birth of Mozart celebrated; Terrorist activity in Cyprus increasing.

February 1 Britain had coldest day since 1895; 13 Referendum in Malta resulted in vote in favour of integration with Britain; 16 House of Commons rejected by majority of 31 Government motion to retain death penalty; Bank rate increased from 4½ to 5½ per cent. (highest since 1932); 23 Remarkable sunflare caused increased cosmic radiation and long-wave radio disturbances; 25 M. Khrushchev in speech to Congress of Russian Communist Party denounced Stalin.

March 2 King Hussein of Jordan discharged Lieut.-Gen. J. B. Glubb; 5 Telephone weather forecast began; 9 Archbishop Makarios with leaders of Enosis movement in Cyprus deported to the Seychelles; 23 The Queen laid foundation stone of new Coventry Cathedral; Pakistan proclaimed an Islamic Republic within the Commonwealth.

April 6 Earl Attlee created Knight of the Garter; 11 Five-day week for Civil Servants announced; 18 Cease-fire between Israel and Egypt came into force; 29 French occupation of Indo-China ended after 80 years.

May 23 First atomic power station in Britain started working at Calder Hall; 24 2,500th anniversary of the death of Buddha celebrated in India; 31 May was the sunniest month at Kew since 1922 and the driest since 1896.

June 3 Third-class travel abolished on British Railways to conform to continental practice; 13 Last British troops left Suez; 24 Col. Nasser elected Pres. of Egypt.

July 20 Britain joined U.S.A. in withdrawing offer to help Egypt finance Aswan High Dam; 26 Pres. Nasser announced nationalisation of Suez Canal Company.

August 30 French troops arrived in Cyprus.

September 25 Newly-laid submarine telephone cable linking Britain and America opened to public service.

October 3 Bolshoi Ballet danced at Covent Garden; 15 Duke of Edinburgh left on world tour; 16 Prime Minister left with For. Sec. for Paris meeting; 17 The Queen opened Calder Hall, the world's first nuclear power station for commercial use; 19–21 New liberalised policy adopted by Central Committee of Polish United Workers' Party; M. Gomulka elected first secretary; 23 Insurrection broke out in Budapest and spread throughout country; 28 Pres. Eisenhower called upon Israel not to "endanger the peace"; 29 Israeli forces invaded Egypt and after 5 days' fighting had control of Sinai peninsula, heavy fighting at Abu Aweigila; 30 Britain and France issued 12-hour ultimatum to Israel and Egypt to cease fighting; Britain and France vetoed US resolution in Security Council calling upon Israel to withdraw behind armistice line; 31 Anglo-French offensive launched against military targets in Egypt.

November 2 UN Gen. Assembly called for immediate cease fire in Egypt; 4 Canadian resolution calling for international UN force for Middle East adopted; Soviet forces launched attack on Budapest to crush uprising; 5 Anglo-French airborne troops landed at Port Said; 6 Seaborne troops landed at Port Said; Pres. Eisenhower re-elected President with Congress controlled by Democrats; Anglo-French forces ceased fire at midnight; 7 Egypt accepted cease fire on UN conditions; 15 UN Emergency Force left Naples for Suez; 16 Suez Canal blocked by 49 ships; 17 First refugees from Hungary arrived in Britain; 22 Duke of Edinburgh opened 16th Olympic Games in Melbourne; 23 Sir Anthony Eden flew to Jamaica for rest cure; 24 UN for third time called upon Britain, France, and Israel to withdraw troops from Egypt.

December 5 140 people arrested in S. Africa for alleged treason; Anglo-French forces began to leave Port Said; 19 Lord Radcliffe's proposals for a constitution for Cyprus published; 29 Suez Canal clearing operation by UN salvage fleet began.

A.D.

1957

January 1 Anglo-Egyptian treaty of 1954 abrogated by Pres. Nasser as from October 31, 1956; Saar became tenth *Land* of German Federal Republic; Road Traffic Act came into force; 5 Eisenhower Doctrine for Middle East announced; 9 Resignation of Sir Anthony Eden as Prime Minister; 10 Mr. Harold Macmillan appointed Prime Minister; 16 Sadlers Wells Ballet group combined to form The Royal Ballet; Death of Signor Toscanini; 20 Mr. Gomulka's National Unity Front overwhelmingly returned in Polish general election; India's first atomic reactor, *Apsara*, inaugurated; 31 Trans-Iranian oil pipeline from Abadan to Teheran (600 m.) completed.

February 7 Bank Rate reduced from 5½ to 5 per cent; 15 Mr. Gromyko replaced Mr. Shepilov as Soviet Foreign Minister; 16 The Queen flew to Portugal on State visit and joined Duke of Edinburgh there who had just completed World tour; 22 Duke of Edinburgh granted title of Prince of the United Kingdom; 26 Indian resolution adopted by UN for "peaceful, democratic, and just solution" of Cyprus problem.

March 1 Mass protest in Tokio against nuclear weapon tests in Pacific; 5 Fianna Fail party under Mr. de Valera secured absolute majority in general election; 6 Ghana celebrated independence; Israeli withdrawal from Sinai completed; 11 Warning by WHO of genetic effects of radiation; 13 Anglo-Jordanian treaty of 1948 ended; 21 Homicide Act in force (death penalty retained only for five categories of "capital murder"); 25 European Common Market and Euratom treaties signed by France, Germany, Italy, and Benelux countries.

April 3 British Labour Party called for abolition of H-bomb tests; 4 No further call-ups for National Service after 1960; 8 The Queen and Prince Philip arrived in France on State visit; 9 Suez Canal cleared and opened to all shipping; 11 Agreement signed in London granting full internal self-government to Singapore from Jan. 1, 1958; 17 Archbishop Makarios arrived in Athens from exile; During the month appeals were made by the Pope, Dr. Schweitzer and Mr. Nehru for the banning of nuclear tests and weapons.

May 14 Petrol rationing (imposed 17.12.56) ended; 15 First British H-bomb exploded in Central Pacific near Christmas I.; 16 M. Spaak succeeded Lord Ismay as NATO Sec. Gen.; 18 The Queen and Prince Philip left for State visit to Denmark; 20 Death of Dr. Gilbert Murray.

June 1 New Copyright Act came into force; First drawing of Premium Bond prizes; 17 Historic decisions taken by US Supreme Court on matters relating to civil liberties; 19 Completion of British H-bomb tests in Pacific; 30 The IGY opened at midnight.

July 1 Women voted for the first time in Egypt's first general election since revolution of 1952; 17 Electricity Bill enacted appointing new Central Electricity Generating Board and Electricity Council in place of Central Electricity Authority; 18 President Mao Tse-tung's famous "Let 100 flowers blossom and 100 schools of thought contend" speech published; 25 Tunisia declared a republic; 31 Federation of Malaya Independence Act received Royal Assent.

August 1 Sir Christopher Hinton appointed chairman of new C.E.G.B., responsible for new nuclear power stations; 31 Royal Charter granted to Tangier by King of Morocco.

September 6 Disarmament discussions in London ended without agreement; 15 German general election (Dr. Adenauer re-elected Chancellor Oct. 22); 19 Bank Rate raised from 5 to 7 per cent.; 20 Death of Jean Sibelius, the Finnish composer; 30 Network Three introduced by B.B.C.

October 4 First earth satellite launched by Russia (180 lb. sphere, 23 in. diameter); 10 U.S.A. abolished fingerprinting for foreign visitors staying less than a year; 11 Largest radio tele-

A.D.

scope in world went into operation at Jodrell Bank for Manchester University; 14 The Queen opened Canadian Parliament in Ottawa; New road–rail double-decker bridge over Yangtse, one of largest in world, opened to traffic; 17 Endorsement of cheques no longer necessary save when negotiated.

November 3 Second earth satellite weighing half a ton launched into space by Russia with dog on board; 16 Russia announced construction of "scientific city" of 12 research institutes in Siberia; 20 Britain's first export order for nuclear power station for Northern Italy announced.

December 1 Latin 26-letter alphabet to be adopted in China; 4 Ninety people killed in railway accident in fog at Lewisham; 6 Attempt to launch earth satellite in the U.S.A. failed; *Sputnik I* completed its thousandth circuit of the Earth; 25 The Queen's Christmas broadcast televised for the first time; 31 The *Sputniks* were still circling the Earth, the first being expected to fall in the first days of January.

CO-EXISTENCE AND REALIGNMENT: THE NEW EUROPE

1958

January 1 Treaties establishing EEC (Common Market) and EAEC (Euratom) came into force; Metric system adopted throughout Japan; 3 Inauguration of West Indian Federation; Sir Edmund Hillary and New Zealand party reached South Pole; 4 *Sputnik I* disintegrated after completing 1,367 circuits of the Earth and travelling 43 million miles; 6 Mr. Thorneycroft resigned from Government after disagreement in Cabinet over pruning Budget estimates; 7 Mr. Macmillan left for six-week tour of Commonwealth; 8 Summit talks proposed by Marshal Bulganin and Notes sent to 19 States; 13 Over 9,000 scientists from 44 countries petition UN Sec. Gen. to end nuclear weapons tests; 20 Dr. Vivian Fuchs, leader of Commonwealth expedition, reached South Pole; 28 Abolition of licensed prostitution in Italy; 31 First American earth satellite *Explorer I* launched.

February 1 Union of Egypt and Syria in the United Arab Republic; 5 Continuation of Antarctic research for at least 5 years after end of IGY announced; 8 French aircraft bombed Tunisian frontier village of Sakhiet; 14 Merger of Iraq and Jordan under name of Arab Federation; 19 Worst colliery disaster in Indian history in West Bengal; 25 Campaign for Nuclear Disarmament launched under presidency of Lord Russell.

March 2 IGY Commonwealth Trans-Antarctic Expedition, led by Dr. Vivian Fuchs, completed first crossing of Antarctic (2,200 miles in 99 days); 8 Federal union between UAR and Yemen established; 14 Small test satellite, *Beta 1958*, successfully launched by US Navy; 20 Bank rate reduced to 6 per cent; 21 Opening of London planetarium, the first of its kind in Britain; 26 Third US earth satellite, *Explorer III*, successfully launched; 27 Mr. Khrushchev elected Prime Minister in succession to Mr. Bulganin; 31 Russian resolution to suspend nuclear tests; other powers invited to follow suit.

April 1 Abolition of legalised prostitution in Japan; 4 Campaign for Nuclear Disarmament organised 50-mile protest march from London to Atomic Weapons Research Establishment at Aldermaston, Berkshire; 17 Nationalist Party of S. Africa returned with increased majority.

May 1 Intense radiation belt in outer space discovered by US *Explorer* earth satellite; 10 Anti-government disturbances in Lebanon; 13 Military and colonist insurrection in Algeria; President of Italy paid state visit to Britain; 15 *Sputnik III* launched; New college to be built at Cambridge University (Churchill College); 22 Further reduction in Bank Rate to 5½ per cent.; 24 Nuclear reactor at Dounreay began working; 29 General de Gaulle accepted invitation to form a "Government of national safety."

June 1 General de Gaulle became Prime Minister of France; Clean Air Act banning emission of dark smoke came into force; 9 Gatwick Airport opened by the Queen; 19 Further cut in Bank Rate to 5 per cent.; New British plan for Cyprus announced; 20 London bus strike ended after 7 weeks; 21 Greek Government rejected British plan for Cyprus; 23 Ghana to be a republic.

July 1 Conference of scientists, including Russian delegation, met at Geneva to discuss ways of detecting nuclear tests; 14 Iraq monarchy overthrown, King Faisal assassinated; establishment of Republic; 15 US marines landed in Lebanon; 17 British troops flown to Amman in response to King Hussein's appeal; 24 First life barons and baronesses under Life Peerages Act named; 26 H.M. the Queen created her son, Charles, Prince of Wales.

August 1 British Government recognised Republic of Iraq; 5 U.S. nuclear submarine *Nautilus* surfaced after having passed under North Pole; 7 Litter Act came into force in Britain; 14 Bank Rate reduced to 4½ per cent.; 17 First attempt by America to launch moon rocket failed; Britain to resume nuclear tests on Christmas Island; 23 Bombardment by Chinese of Quemoy (Formosa Strait); 29 More American warships join Seventh Fleet in Formosa Strait.

September 1 International conference on peaceful uses of atomic energy opened in Geneva; 7 Britain successfully fired its first ballistic rocket (Black Knight) from Woomera; 15 Ambassadors of America and China met in Warsaw for discussions on Formosa crisis; 16 Relaxations in hire-purchase; 29 Referendum resulted in overwhelming victory for General de Gaulle; Lord Goddard retired as Lord Chief Justice; succeeded by Lord Justice Parker.

October 1 India began change to metric system; 2 French Guinea proclaimed Republic of Guinea after overwhelming vote for independence in French referendum; 8 Martial law in Pakistan; 9 Death of Pope Pius XII; 11 The London weeklies *John Bull* and *Illustrated* merged; US *Pioneer* space-rocket successfully launched (but failed to reach moon); 21 First women peers introduced to House of Lords; 28 State opening of Parliament and Queen's Speech televised; Cardinal Roncalli, Patriarch of Venice, elected as Pope John XXIII at age of 76; 31 Conference opened in Geneva (Russia, Britain, and the US) on suspension of nuclear tests.

November 20 Bank Rate reduced to 4 per cent.; 21 Work started on Forth road bridge, the largest suspension bridge in Europe; 27 Russian plan for withdrawal of troops and demilitarised free Berlin.

December 8 Last of four nuclear reactors at Calder Hall brought into operation; 17 Chinese leader, Mao Tse-tung, to resign as chairman of Republic but to retain party office; 18 US 4-ton missile fired into orbit; Empire Day to be known as Commonwealth Day; 21 General de Gaulle elected President of France; 27 Partial convertibility between £ and $ announced; UAR and Russia signed agreement on Russian co-operation in Aswan high dam project; 28 General de Gaulle announced devaluation of the franc.

1959

January 1 Batista Government in Cuba overthrown by revolutionary movement under Dr. Fidel Castro; 2 Russia launched planet round the sun (*Lunik I*); 3 Alaska became 49th state of American Union; 4 Mr. Mikoyan, Soviet Dep. Prime Min., arrived in Washington on 16-day visit; Rioting in Leopoldville; 7 Britain recognised new Cuban Government; 8 Gen. de Gaulle installed as first Pres. of Fifth French Republic; 10 Russian proposal for conference of 28 nations to draw up German Peace Treaty; 25 Oecumenical Council, the first since 1870, convened by Pope John XXIII.

A.D.

February 1 Votes for women rejected by Swiss national poll; 11 M. Vincent Auriol resigned from French Socialist Party; 21 Mr. Macmillan arrived in Moscow on official visit; 23 Archbishop Makarios returned to Cyprus after 3-year exile; Cyprus to become a republic with Greek Pres. and Turkish Vice-Pres.; 26 State of emergency declared in Southern Rhodesia; 27 Riots in Malta dockyard due to dismissal of workers.

March 3 American *Pioneer IV* went into planetary orbit round sun; State of emergency declared in Nyasaland; British scientists isolated basic molecule of penicillin; 17 Uprising in Lhasa against Chinese rule; Flight of Dalai Lama to India; 24 Iraq withdrew from Baghdad Pact.

April 5 Panchen Lama arrived in Lhasa to take over local government of Tibet; 8 Chair of Criminology founded at Cambridge; 14–16 Worst flood disaster of century in S. America; 27 Liu Shao-ch'i succeeded Mao Tse-tung as Chairman (President) of Chinese People's Republic.

May 1 Opening of Rajendra Bridge (6,074 ft.) over Ganges at Hathidah; 2 First Scottish nuclear power-station opened at Chapelcross; 15 Jodrell Bank radioed message to United States via moon; 28 Opening of Mermaid Theatre in City of London; 30 Auckland Harbour Bridge officially opened; 31 World's population (2,800 millions) increasing at rate of 45 millions a year.

June 8 U.S. Post Office made first successful delivery of mail by guided missile; 17 Mr. de Valera elected Pres. of Rep. of Ireland; Serious riots in African townships in Durban; 18 Five-year plan for Scottish Highlands announced; 24 World record price (£275,000) paid at Sotheby's for Rubens' *The Adoration of the Magi*; 26 St. Lawrence Seaway formally opened by the Queen and Pres. Eisenhower; 29 Norwegian Halden nuclear reactor in operation.

July 3 Tancarville road bridge near Le Havre, longest suspension bridge in Europe, opened; 4 Transatlantic record flight set up by Vickers *Vanguard* turbo-prop airliner (2,500 m. in 5½ hrs.); 5 Recovery in good condition of 3 animals from outer space; 7 Litter Act passed making it an offence to drop litter; 21 Launching of first nuclear merchant ship *Savannah* by Mrs. Eisenhower.

August 16 The Street Offences Act came into force; 21 Baghdad Pact renamed Central Treaty Organisation; 22 First round-the-world service by British airliners inaugurated; 23 Announcement of plan for oil-pipeline network between Soviet Union and East European countries (completion 1963).

September 11 British loan made available for Malta dockyard. 13 Russian launched *Lunik II* which landed on moon; 15 Soviet atomic ice-breaker *Lenin* made maiden voyage into Baltic; 25 Mr. Bandaranaike, Prime Min. of Ceylon, assassinated; 27 Typhoon in W. Japan (5,000 killed and missing, 1,000,000 homeless).

October 4 Russia fired *Lunik III*, which took photographs of back of moon; 8 General Election returned Conservatives with 100 overall majority; 10 End of one of longest droughts ever recorded in Britain; 24 Opening of new airport for Wellington, N.Z.; 29 Dublin's famous Abbey Theatre to be rebuilt (destroyed by fire 1951).

November 1 Basic travel allowance for British tourists ended; 2 First section of London-Yorkshire motorway (M1) opened to traffic; 5 Philip Noel-Baker awarded Nobel Peace Prize; 8 Sudan and U.A.R. signed agreement on distribution of Nile waters; 14 Dounreay fast breeder reactor went into operation; 17 Announcement of discovery by American scientists of submarine plateau in Arctic Ocean; 19 Bank of England announced introduction of new series of bank notes (10s. £1, £5, £10); 21 British book exhibition opened in Moscow; 24 CERN's proton synchrotron at Geneva went into full operation; 27 Duke of Edinburgh opened Ghana's Academy of Learning in Accra; 28 Naval dockyard at Hong Kong closed after 80 years; 30 Inauguration of Italy's first nuclear research reactor.

December 1 Anglo-Russian cultural agreement signed in London; 12-power treaty on Antarctica signed in Washington; State of emergency in Cyprus ended; Bursting of dam at Fréjus killed 384 people; Pres. Eisenhower began tour of Europe, Asia, and Middle East; 5 Opening of 400-mile Sahara pipeline by French Prime Minister; 6 Inauguration of Panchet Hill Dam on Damodar R., Bihar; 10 Raising of school-leaving age to 16 recommended by Crowther Report; 14 Archbhisop Makarios elected first Pres. of Cyprus; 15 New world speed record of 1,520 m.p.h. set up by U.S. Air Force pilot; 21 Marriage of Shah of Persia to Miss Farah Diba; 26 Soviet Antarctic expedition reached South Pole; 28 Yugoslavia's first nuclear reactor.

1960

January 1 Republic of Cameroun (formerly French Cameroons) became independent. 4 Albert Camus, French writer, killed in car crash. 7 Hirfanli Dam in Turkey opened, largest in Europe. 9 Work begun on Aswan High Dam. 12 State of emergency ended in Kenya after 8 years; 13 Nr. Aleksander Soldatov appointed to succeed Mr. J. Malik as Soviet Ambassador to Britain. 21 Bank rate increased to 5%. 23 M. Jacques Piccard and an American naval Officer descended 7 miles under Pacific in Marianas Trench. 24 Army rising in Algeria. 29 Broadcast of Pres. de Gaulle to nation contributed to collapse of military revolt.

February 3 Mr. Macmillan addressed S. African Parliament ("wind of change" speech). 13 First French atomic test in Sahara. 17 British agreement to U.S. ballistic missile early-warning system at Fylingdales Moor, Yorkshire. 19 Prince Andrew born. 29 Agadir destroyed by earthquake.

March 17 New £1 notes issued in Britain. 18 Last steam locomotive of British Railways named. 21 Sharpeville shooting in S. Africa when police fired on African gathering. 23 Mr. Khrushchev in Paris. 30 State of emergency in S. Africa.

April 1 U.N. Security Council adopted resolution deploring shootings in S. Africa. Dr. Hastings Banda, Pres. of proscribed Nyasaland African Congress, released from detention in S. Rhodesia. 5 Pres. de. Gaulle on state visit to Britain. 9 Attempt on life of Dr. Verwoerd. 13 *Blue Streak* as military weapon abandoned. 27 Rep. of Togo (former Togoland) came into being as independent state.

May 1 U.S. aircraft engaged in military reconnaissance flight over Soviet territory shot down. 6 Wedding of Princess Margaret and Mr. A. Armstrong-Jones in Westminster Abbey. 7 U.S. to resume underground nuclear tests; Mr. Leonid Brezhnev succeeded Marshal Voroshilov as Pres. of Soviet Union. 16 Opening and breakdown of Summit conference in Paris. 17 The Queen Mother officially opened Kariba Dam. 21 Earthquake disaster in Chile. 25 Everest climbed by 3 Chinese. Army seized control in Turkey. End of U.S. foreign aid to Cuba. 30 Death of Boris Pasternak.

June 10 Britain's first guided-missile destroyer *Devonshire* launched. Britain's nuclear power programme to be slowed down. 23 Bank rate raised to 6%. 25 Completion of second Saharan oil pipe-line (Edjelé to La Skirra on Tunisian coast). 26 British rule in Somaliland ended; Madagascar became independent state within French Community. 29 House of Commons rejected Wolfenden Committee's recommendations on homosexuality. 30 Belgian Congo

A.D.

became independent as the Congo Republic (Pres. M. Kasavubu, Prime Min. M. Lumumba).

July 1 Ghana proclaimed a Republic; Somali Republic came into being (merging of former British Somaliland and Italian Somaliland). 6 Army mutiny in Congo. Death of Aneurin Bevan. 11 Ivory Coast, Dahomey, Niger, and Upper Volta became independent. M. Tshombe, Congolese privincial leader, declared Katanga independent. M. Lumumba asked for U.N. help. 12 Congo (French), Chad and Central African Rep. became independent. 14 Sec. Council called for withdrawal of Belgian troops from Congo. 19–26 Royal Society Tercentenary celebrations.

August 2 Rawalpindi capital of Pakistan instead of Karachi. 8 Military *coup d'état* in Laos 9 Sec. Council called on Belgium to withdraw troops from Katanga and authorised U.N. troops to replace them. 16 End of British rule in Cyprus which becomes independent Republic. 25 Olympic Games opened in Rome. 29 Prime Minister of Jordan assassinated.

September 5 Announcement by Pres. Kasavubu that he had dismissed M. Lumumba as Prime Minister of Congo. 14 M. Lumumba appealed to U.N. for protection. 19 India and Pakistan signed Indus Waters Treaty. 23 Mr. Khrushchev led Soviet delegation to U.N. General Assembly in New York and criticised U.N. operations in Congo.

October 1 Federation of Nigeria became independent Member of the Commonwealth. 5 Labour Party Conference voted against Party's official defence policy. 14 Turkish trials of members of Menderes régime began. 21 Royal Navy's first nuclear submarine *Dreadnought* launched by the Queen. 27 Bank rate reduced to 5½%.

November 1 U.S. *Polaris* missile submarines to have base on Clyde. 3 Mr. Gaitskell re-elected leader of Parliamentary Labour Party 9 Senator John Kennedy elected Pres. of United States. 28 Islamic Republic of Mauritania proclaimed its independence.

December 1 Capture of M. Lumumba by Col. Mobutu's forces. 2 Archbishop of Canterbury visited the Pope at the Vatican. 8 Bank rate reduced to 5%. 14 Fighting in Vientiane, cap. of Laos, between right-wing and left-wing forces. 15 Marriage of King Baudouin of Belgium. 17 Revolt in Ethiopia crushed. 21 Strikes in Belgium. 27 Union of Ghana, Guinea, and Mali. 31 Farthing ceased to be legal tender.

1961

January 18 M. Lumumba, first Prime Min. of the independent Congo, sent to Katanga for imprisonment. 20 The Queen and the Duke of Edinburgh left for tour of India, Pakistan, Nepal and Iran; Mr. John Kennedy took office as 35th Pres. of the United States. 23 Portuguese liner *Santa Maria* seized in Caribbean by insurgents as protest against Salazar dictatorship. 26 Full diplomatic relations resumed between Britain and United Arab Republic. 31 M. Spaak resigned as Sec.-Gen. of Nato.

February 1 Increased National Health Service prescription charges announced. 3 Capt. Galvão hands over *Santa Maria* to Commander of Brazilian Navy in Recife. 5 Riots in Angola. 13 Death of M. Lumumba announced (violent demonstrations in many countries). 15 Total eclipse of the sun visible from Europe. 21 U.N. authorised the use of force "if necessary, in the last resort" to prevent civil war in Congo; measures also for withdrawal of foreign military personnel and mercenaries. 26 Death of King Mohammed V of Morocco; succeeded by elder son who becomes King Hassan II.

March 8 First of American nuclear-powered submarines carrying Polaris missiles arrived at Holy Loch; Death of Sir Thomas Beecham. 12 First winter ascent of the Eiger. 14 The New English Bible (New Testament) published. 15 Uprising of tribal groups in Angola, brutal retaliation of Portuguese by burning and bombing. 25 Russian satellite with dog aboard launched and brought safely back to earth. 29 Four-year South African treason trial ended with acquittal of accused.

April 9 Death of former King Zog of Albania. 11 Opening of trial of Adolf Eichmann in Jerusalem. 12 Major Yuri Gagarin made first flight into space and back. 17 Unsuccessful invasion of Cuba by rebel forces. 22 Insurrection of part of French army in Algeria; State of emergency declared in France. 23 Census held in Great Britain. 24 Gen. de Gaulle ordered blockade of Algeria. 25 Both sides in Laos agreed to cease-fire. 26 Collapse of mutiny in Algeria. 27 Independence of Sierra Leone.

May 1 Betting and Gaming Act came into force in Britain: betting shops opened. 5 Commander Alan Shepard made first American flight into space; The Queen and the Duke of Edinburgh visited Pope John XXIII at the Vatican. 12 Botvinnik regained world chess championship. 16 International conference on Laos opened in Geneva; Army in South Korea seized power. 17 Guildford Cathedral consecrated. 20 Talks opened at Evian between French government and Algerian provincial government (broke down July 18). 31 Gen. Trujillo, dictator of Dominican Republic, assassinated; South Africa became a Republic and withdrew from British Commonwealth.

June 1 N. Cameroons became part of Nigeria. 3 Meeting of Pres. Kennedy and M. Khrushchev in Vienna. 9 Security Council voted for Afro-Asian resolution calling upon Portugal to end repressive measures in Angola. 27 Enthronement of Dr. Ramsey as Archbishop of Canterbury in Canterbury Cathedral. 30 Portuguese refused to stop repressive measures in Angola.

July 1 British forces landed in Kuwait following appeal from ruler. 2 Death of Ernest Hemingway. 7 Soviet Trade Exhibition opened in London. 11 Major Yuri Gagarin, Russian pioneer of space travel, welcomed in London. 18 Over £9 million raised in Britain for 1960 World Refugee Year. 19 Fighting began between French and Tunisian forces over Bizerta naval base; U.K.–U.S. agreement to establish Missile Defence Alarm Station at Kirkbride, Cumberland. 21 U.S. launched its second space traveller (Capt. V. Grissom) 118 m. high, flight time 16 mins.; New Runcorn–Widnes Bridge opened over Mersey and Manchester Ship Canal (the largest span arch in Europe). 24 Bank rate rose to 7%. 30 Israel began construction of deep-sea port at Asdod.

August 4 International Monetary Fund placed £714 million at Britain's disposal. 6 Major Titov, Russia's second space man, circled earth 17 times before landing back near Moscow 13 Soviet sector of Berlin sealed off from Western sectors. 14 Jomo Kenyatta became a free man again. 15 U.N. recognised M. Adoula's government as the central government of the Congo. 16 Dr. Hastings Banda's Malawi Congress Party won control in the Nyasaland Legislative Assembly. 30 No agreement reached at Geneva on banning of nuclear tests. 31 Soviet announcement of resumption of nuclear weapons tests.

September 5 International conference on preservation of wild life opened at Arusha, Tanganyika; U.S. to resume underground nuclear tests. 18 Mr. Hammarskjöld killed in plane crash when flying from Leopoldville, to Ndola, to arrange cease-fire between U.N. and Katanga forces. 28 Syria seceded from the United Arab Republic.

October 1 S. Cameroons gained independence as part of Cameroun. 3 Mr. A. Armstrong-Jones created Earl of Snowdon. 4 Labour Party Conference voted against Polaris bases and German

A.D.

troops in Britain 5 Bank rate reduced to 6½%. 10 Volcanic eruption on Tristan da Cunha; whole population evacuated to Britain. 14 Death of Chico Marx. 21 U.S. put into space, amid world-wide protest, 350 million copper needles for reflecting radio signals (they failed to disperse into orbit). 23 Nobel Peace Prize for 1960 awarded to South African, Albert Luthuli; that for 1961 posthumously to Dag Hammarskjöld. 30 Russia tested a bomb of over 60 megatons amid world-wide protest. 31 Hurricane struck British Honduras, Belize devastated; Stalin's body removed from the Lenin Mausoleum in Red Square.

November 2 Bank rate reduced to 6%. 3 U Thant, Burma's chief representative at U.N., elected Acting Sec.-Gen. of U.N.; Birth of son to Princess Margaret and Lord Snowdon; 7 Dr. Adenauer re-elected Chancellor of Fed. German Rep. for fourth time. 8 Official negotiations for entry of Britain into Common Market opened in Brussels; Wales votes for Sunday opening. 9 The Queen and the Duke of Edinburgh left for tour of Ghana, Liberia, and Sierra Leone. 20 Admission of Russian Orthodox Church to World Council of churches. 28 South Africa's apartheid policy condemned by U.N.

December 8 Cross-Channel submarine cable linking electricity systems of England and France officially inaugurated. 9 Tanganyika became independent sovereign state; Russia broke off diplomatic relations with Albania. 15 Adolf Eichmann sentenced to death by Israeli court for crimes against the Jewish people and against humanity; Mr. Macmillan and Pres. Kennedy met in Bermuda. 17 Indian troops took over Portuguese colony of Goa. 19 Decimal coinage accepted in principle by British government. 20 Mr. Adoula and Mr. Tshombe agreed on Katanga's subordinate status. 27 Belgium and the Congo resumed diplomatic relations.

1962

January 1 Western Samoa became independent. 10 Avalanche disaster in Peru. 11 Smallpox outbreak in Britain. 15 Centigrade first used in weather forecasts. 16 Death of R. H. Tawney. 24 T.U.C. decided to join "Neddy". 27 New world record for mile by New Zealander Peter Snell (3 min. 54·4 secs.).

February 11 Death of Lord Birkett. 20 American first manned orbital flight.

March 7 Franco-Algerian negotiations began at Evian; Publication of Royal College of Physician's Report on dangers to health from cigarette smoking. 8 Bank rate reduced to 5½%. 14 Opening of 17-nation disarmament conference at Geneva. 19 End of Algerian war. 28 Inauguration of Marlborough House built by Wren, as Commonwealth Centre.

April 1 Government's "pay pause" ended. 5 Completion of Gt. St. Bernard road tunnel. 7 Strike in Asturias—first of many throughout Spain. 8 French people voted in referendum approving Algerian peace settlement. 11 Pres. Kennedy condemned U.S. steel industry for raising prices. 13 International agreement (40 countries) to stop oil pollution of seas and beaches. 20 Gen. Salan, O.A.S. leader, arrested by French in Algiers. 25 U.S. began new series of atmospheric nuclear tests in Pacific. 26 Britain's first satellite, *Ariel*, launched from Cape Canaveral; Bank rate down to 4½%. 30 Norway applied to join Common Market.

May 6 Signor Segni elected Pres. of Italy; Canonisation of St. Martin de Porres of Lima (d. 1639), first mulatto saint of the R.C. church. 8 Trolleybuses ran for last time in London. 13 Dr. Radhakrishnan elected Pres. of India. 25 Consecration of new Coventry Cathedral. 31 Eichmann executed in Israel; Dissolution of The West Indies Federation.

June 5 Creation of University of Lagos. 14 Creation of European Space Research Organisation (ESRO). 15 Nuclear power station at Berkeley, Glos., began electricity supply to national grid. 18 The *Flying Scotsman* made centenary journey; Conservatives (Mr. Diefenbaker) won Canadian general election by small majority. 23 Cease-fire in Laos. 24 Opening of Punjabi University, India. 28 U.N. called for more liberal constitution for S. Rhodesia.

July 1 Burundi and Rwanda became independent; French colonial rule in Algeria ended; Commonwealth Immigrants Act came into force. 3 Plan for British national theatre and opera house accepted by L.C.C. and Government. 8 Pres. de Gaulle and Chan. Adenauer attended Mass in Rheims cathedral. 10 *Telstar*, first experimental satellite in space communications, launched—first live television between U.S. and Europe. 20 Death of G. M. Trevelyan, the historian. 26 Government announce setting up of "Nicky". 30 Archbishop of Canterbury visited Moscow. 31 Rendezvous of U.S. nuclear submarines at North Pole.

August 5 Russia began series of atmospheric nuclear tests; Death of Marilyn Monroe, at age 36. 6 Jamaica became independent. 10 Abandonment of *Blue Water* missile. 11 British mountaineers scaled Russia's highest peak (Mt. Communism). 11 and 12 Russia launched two men into orbit (64 orbits and 48 orbits). 14 Completion of Mont Blanc tunnel (7¼ m.). 17 Pres. Kennedy's Bill on medical care rejected by Senate. 20 Government approval for construction of new underground railway between Victoria and Walthamstow. 21 Maiden voyage of *Savannah*, world's first nuclear-powered merchant ship. 27 U.S. *Mariner II* launched towards Venus. 31 Trinidad and Tobago became independent.

September 3 Opening of Trans-Canada highway (4,800 m. from St. John's, Newfoundland, to Victoria, B.C.). 7 Life Presidency for Dr. Nkrumah. 15 Iran assured Russia that no foreign rocket bases would be permitted. 20 Zimbabwe African People's Union banned in S. Rhodesia; Fighting between Chinese and Indian troops on disputed N.E. frontier. 27 Overthrow of Imamate and republic proclaimed in Yemen. 29 Canada launched her first satellite, the *Alouette*, into orbit. 30 U.S. troops enforced Fed. Government's order that Negro student should enrol at Mississippi State University.

October 3 6-orbit flight of U.S. astronaut. 9 Uganda became independent. 11 21st Oecumenical Council opened at Rome. 17 Opening of Hyde Park Corner underpass; Electricity for national grid generated at Dounreay reactor. 24 Commencement of U.S. naval quarantine of Cuba. 28 Dismantling of missile base in Cuba agreed by Russia; Gen. de Gaulle won referendum for direct election of President.

November 1 Russia sent spacecraft on 7-month journey to Mars. 6 Admiralty announced record ocean depth by H.M.S. *Cook* in Mindanao trench (37,782 ft.); Opening of Commonwealth Institute (replaces Imperial Institute, S. Kensington). 18 Death of Niels Bohr. 20 Cuba blockade ended. 21 Cease-fire declaration by China on Sino-Indian border dispute (no further hostilities occurred). 29 Announcement of new Indo-Pakistan negotiations on Kashmir. 30 U Thant unanimously elected Sec.-Gen. of U.N.

December 5 Soviet-American space research cooperation agreement; Uprising in British prot. of Brunei in protest to joining Fed. of Malaysia; British nuclear device exploded underground in Nevada. 9 Tanganyika became republic and Dr. Julius Nyerere its first president. 12 British troops in control of Brunei uprising. 14 Signals from *Mariner II* as it passed within 21,000 miles of Venus; Eritrea became province of Ethiopia; N. Rhodesia's first African dominated government formed. 15 Sir Edgar Whitehead's party lost to right-wing party in S. Rhodesian general election. 17 Mr. Macmillan left for meeting with Pres. Kennedy at Nassau, Bahamas. 21 U.S. decision to abandon *Sky*

A.D.

bolt; offer of *Polaris* missiles for British submarines to form part of multilateral Nato nuclear force. 25 Europe snowbound with freezing temperatures. 28 Agreement in principle reached between China and Pakistan defining mutual boundary. 30 Worst snowstorms in England since 1881. 31 British Transport Commission replaced by British Railways Board (created by Transport Act, 1962), with Dr. Beeching as chairman.

1963

January 2 Gen. Lemnitzer succeeded Gen. Norstad as Supreme Allied Commander, Europe. 3 Bank rate reduced to 4 per cent. 14 Gen. de Gaulle's press conference repulsing Britain's entry to EEC and rejecting U.S. Polaris offer. 15 Official ending of Katanga secession. 18 Death of Hugh Gaitskell; Aden acceded to Fed. of S. Arabia. 29 Britain was refused entry to EEC; Death of Robert Frost, the American poet.

February 1 Nyasaland became self-governing protectorate. 6 Shipping restrictions on Cuba announced by U.S. Government. 8 Overthrow of Iraq government and execution of Gen. Kassim. 12 Seventeen-nation disarmament conference resumed in Geneva. 14 Harold Wilson elected leader of Labour Party. 19 Earthquake in Barce, Libya. 22 Unemployment figures showed 878,356, highest since 1947.

March 5–6 First frost-free night in Britain since Dec. 22. 8 Syrian government overthrown by military coup. 17 Typhoid broke out in Zermatt; First of Tristan de Cunha islanders returned home. 27 Publication of Beeching Report on British Railways.

April 5 Opening of Berkeley and Bradwell civil nuclear power stations. 6 Polaris missile agreement signed between U.S. and Britain. 8 Mr. Diefenbaker's Conservative Party defeated by Liberals in Canadian general election. 10 Pope John XXIII published his encyclical *Pacem in Terris*; New Zealand to change to decimal coinage in 1967; Loss of U.S. nuclear submarine *Thresher* with 129 lives. 17 Commissioning of Royal Navy's first nuclear-powered submarine, H.M.S. *Dreadnought*. 20 Execution of Julian Grimau, Spanish communist leader.

May 1 End of Dutch East Indies; New Guinea (West Irian) handed to Indonesia. 15 Twenty-two-orbit flight of Major Cooper of U.S. Air Force. 20 Petrosian won world chess title from Botvinnik; Life presidency for Pres. Sukarno of Indonesia.

June 1 New internal self-government constitution for Kenya came into force with Jomo Kenyatta as Kenya's first Prime Minister. 3 Death of Pope John XXIII. 11 Iraq resumed war against Kurds. 12 Rioting on big scale in Georgetown, British Guiana. 14–19 Bykovsky-Tereshkova space flights (first woman astronaut). 16 Resignation of Mr. Ben-Gurion. 20 House of Commons censure on Mr. John Profumo, former Sec. of State for War. 24 Zanzibar achieved internal self-government. 28 Inauguration in Nairobi of Univ. of East Africa. 30 Pope Paul VI crowned.

July 2 Franco-German Treaty of Co-operation came into force. 5 Sino-Soviet ideological talks began. 9 State visit of King and Queen of Greece to Britain. 26 Skopje destroyed by earthquake. 29 Pres. de Gaulle rejected Moscow test-ban treaty. 31 The Peerage Bill received Royal Assent; Security Council called on member states to impose partial arms embargo on Portugal.

August 1 Under Criminal Justice Act, 1961, minimum prison age raised to 17. 3 First successful solo climb on north wall of Eiger by Michel Darbellay. 5 Partial nuclear-test ban treaty signed in Moscow by America, Russia, and Britain. 7 Security Council resolution to stop sale and shipment of arms to S. Africa.

A.D.

8 Glasgow–London mail train robbery (£2·5 million). 16 Announcement of American-Soviet weather- and communications-satellite programme. 20 Mr. Khrushchev visited Yugoslavia. 21 Buddhists arrested and martial law imposed in South Vietnam. 28 Great Negro "freedom march" on Washington. 31 Death of George Braque, the French painter; The "hot-line" linking Kremlin with White House went into service.

September 5 Soviet-American co-operation in cosmic ray research in Antarctica announced. 15 Ben Bella elected first President of Algeria. 16 New state of Malaysia (Malaya, Singapore, North Borneo and Sarawak) came into being. 17 Malaysia broke off diplomatic relations with Indonesia; Fylingdales ballistic missile early warning station came into operation. 18 New Australian decimal currency to be introduced Feb. 1966. 19 Anglo-French report recommended rail tunnel as Channel link. 21 Reform of Roman Catholic Curia announced by Pope Paul VI. 23 Report on decimal currency advocated division of £1 into 100 units. 25 Denning report on Profumo affair published. 29 Reopening of Vatican Council; First buildings of University of East Anglia opened at Norwich.

October 1 Nigeria became a republic within the Commonwealth with Dr. Azikiwe its first President. 3 Honduras government overthrown by Army. 4 Hurricane Flora struck the Caribbean. 9 Vaiont dam disaster (N. Italy); the Kubaka of Buganda became first President of Uganda. 15 Dr. Adenauer retired after 14 years as Chancellor of Fed. German Republic; succeeded by Prof. Ludwig Erhard. 18 Mr. Macmillan resigned as Prime Minister; succeeded by the Earl of Home. 23 Robbins report on higher education published.

November 1 Diem oligarchy of S. Vietnam overthrown by military coup; First executions in S. Africa under the Sabotage Act of 1963. 7 Eleven German miners rescued after a fortnight underground; Sir Alec Douglas-Home elected at Kinross and W. Perthshire. 9 Train and mine disasters in Japan. 16 Greece began to release Communist prisoners taken during last war. 17 Temples of Abu Simbel to be removed and re-sited. 18 Opening of Dartford–Purfleet tunnel, linking Kent and Essex under Thames. 22 Assassination of President Kennedy in Dallas, Texas; Vice-President Lyndon Johnson sworn in as new President. 27 Publication of Buchanan report.

December 3 Britain's second nuclear submarine, the *Valiant*, launched. 4 Second session of Vatican Council ended. 10 Zanzibar became independent within the Commonwealth. 12 Kenya became independent within the Commonwealth. 22 Greek liner *Lakonia* caught fire and sank on cruise, off Gibraltar. 31 Dissolution of Federation of Rhodesia and Nyasaland.

1964

January 4–6 Pope Paul made pilgrimage to Holy Land; meeting between Pope and Patriarch of Constantinople. 9 Rioting in Panama. 12 Republican régime in Zanzibar. 20 Army mutiny in Tanganyika. 27 France recognized China; School-leaving age to be raised to 16 in 1970–71. 28 Riots in Salisbury, S. Rhodesia, after trial of Joshua Nkomo.

February 6 Anglo-French agreement on rail Channel tunnel announced. 11 Fighting between Greeks and Turks at Limassol, Cyprus. 27 Bank rate raised to 5%.

March 4 August Bank holiday to be moved to last Monday in month. 6 Death of King Paul of the Hellenes; son proclaimed King Constantine XIII. 10 Birth of Prince Edward. 11 S. Africa withdrew from I.L.O. 19 Opening of Great St. Bernard tunnel. 24 Stansted, Essex, provisionally chosen as site of London's

A.D.

third airport. 27 U.N. peacekeeping force in Cyprus operational; Severe earthquake and tidal wave in Alaska.

April 4 Dr. Leakey confirmed discovery in Tanganyika of *Homo habilis*; heavy fighting in Cyprus between Greek and Turkish communities. 5 Death of General MacArthur. 8 Shaikh Abdullah, former Prime Minister of Kashmir, released by Indian Government. 9 First Greater London Council election; Labour 64, Conservatives 36. 10 Mr. Macmillan declined earldom and Order of the Garter. 13 Mr. Ian Smith became Prime Minister of S. Rhodesia on resignation of Mr. Winston Field. 16 Sentences passed on 12 men found guilty in mail train robbery trial (two subsequently escaped from prison). 21 Opening of BBC-2. 23 Shakespeare quatercentenary celebrations. 27 Tanganyika and Zanzibar united (United Republic of Tanzania).

May 1 Birth of a daughter to Princess Margaret and Lord Snowdon. 9 Mr. Khrushchev's first visit to Egypt (completion of first stage Aswan High Dam). 22 State of emergency declared in British Guiana. 26 Typhoid outbreak in Aberdeen. 27 Death of Jawaharlal Nehru.

June 2 Mr. Lal Bahadur Shastri elected Prime Minister of India. 3 Senator Barry Goldwater defeated Mr. Nelson Rockefeller, in Republican Party's primary in California. 5 First flight into space of Britain's *Blue Streak* rocket (fired) from Woomera). 9 Death of Lord Beaverbrook. 12 Life imprisonment imposed on Nelson Mandela and others in Rivonia trial, Pretoria; 20-year treaty of friendship signed between Soviet Union and E. Germany. 30 Last U.N. troops left Congo.

July 2 Enactment of U.S. Civil Rights Bill. 3–4 Foreign ministers of Iran, Pakistan and Turkey agreed to form Regional Co-operation for Development (R.C.D.) group. 6 Nyasaland became independent state of Malawi. 10 M. Tshombe succeeded M. Adoula as Prime Minister of the Congo. 15 Mr. Mikoyan succeeded Mr. Brezhnev as President of the Soviet Union. 17 Mr. Donald Campbell broke land-speed record on Lake Eyre with 403·1 m.p.h. 27 Last appearance of Sir Winston Churchill in House of Commons. 31 American *Ranger* 7 hit moon after sending back over 4,000 pictures of surface.

August 2 U.S. destroyer attacked by N. Vietnam torpedo boats off N. Vietnam. 4 Nine French miners rescued after being trapped underground at Champagnole for 8 days; Bodies of three murdered civil rights workers found near Philadelphia, Mississippi. 5 Congolese rebels captured Stanleyville; U.S. air raid on N. Vietnam. 13 General Grivas, former EOKA leader took over supreme command of Cypriot National Guard. 13 Common Market set up by Arab League (Iraq, Jordan, Kuwait, Syria and U.A.R.) to come into force Jan. 1965.

September 2 Indonesian landings in Malaya. 4 Opening of new Forth bridge (largest suspension bridge in Europe). 7 People's Republic of the Congo declared by Congolese rebels. 14 Third session of Vatican Council opened (closed 21 Nov.). 20 Gen. de Gaulle began his tour of S. America. 21 Malta became independent within the Commonwealth after 164 years of British rule. 28 Maiden flight of supersonic TSR 2; Death of Harpo Marx, the comedian.

October 5 The Queen and the Duke of Edinburgh in Canada on week's visit. 10 Opening of Olympic Games in Tokyo. 12 Soviet 3-man spaceship launched on 24-hour flight. 14 1964 Nobel Peace Prize awarded to Dr. Martin Luther King. 15 Mr. Khrushchev replaced in posts of First Secretary of the CPSU and Prime Minister by Mr. Brezhnev and Mr. Kosygin respectively; General election in Britain: Labour won with overall majority of five. 16 Mr. Harold Wilson became Prime Minister; China exploded an atomic device. 22 M. Jean-Paul Sartre declined Nobel Prize for Literature. 24 Northern Rhodesia achieved independence as Republic of Zambia with Kenneth Kaunda as its first President; S. Rhodesia became officially known as Rhodesia. 26 Government proposed 15% import surcharge and export tax rebate to deal with balance of payments crisis. 29 Nobel Prize for Chemistry awarded to Prof. Dorothy Hodgkin.

November 2 Deposition of King Saud of Saudi Arabia and accession of his brother Faisal. 3 U.S. Presidential election: sweeping victory for President Johnson over Senator Goldwater. 5 Mr. Chou En-lai in Moscow for 47th anniversary of October revolution; Cease-fire in Yemen after two years of civil strife. 10 Australia to introduce selective compulsory service for military service overseas. 12 Grand Duchess Charlotte of Luxembourg abdicated in favour of her son. 17 Government to ban export of arms to S. Africa. 21 Opening of Verrazano-Narrows bridge spanning mouth of New York harbour, the world's longest bridge. 23 Bank rate rose to 7%. 24 Belgian paratroops landed at Stanleyville to rescue rebel-held hostages.

December 2 The Pope welcomed in Bombay. 5 Bishopsgate railway goods depot destroyed by fire. 12 Kenya became Republic within Commonwealth with Mr. Kenyatta as first President. 16 Statement of Intent on productivity, prices and incomes signed by Government, T.U.C. and Employers' organisations. 17 Free prescriptions from 1 February 1965. 28 Signor Saragat elected President of Italy. 31 Mr. Donald Campbell broke world water-speed record with speed of 276·33 m.p.h. on Lake Dumbleyung in W. Australia.

1965

January 7 Indonesia withdrew from U.N. 15 Child's body found (Dec. 11, 1964) in coffin in Stepney identified as that of Lady Anne Mowbray (1472–81), remains reinterred in Westminster Abbey; Prime Minister of Burundi assassinated. 20 Lyndon Baines Johnson inaugurated as 36th President of U.S. 21 Prime Minister of Iran assassinated. 24 Death of Sir Winston Churchill. 26 Hindi became official language of India with English an additional official tongue. 31 National Health prescription charges ended.

February 1 The Queen and Duke of Edinburgh in Ethiopia on state visit. 7 First U.S. retaliatory raids against N. Vietnam. 17 Pres. Johnson announced U.S. would continue "actions that are justified as necessary for defence of S. Vietnam." 18 Gambia became independent as 21st member of the Commonwealth. 24 U.S. jets bombed Vietcong in S. Vietnam. 25 Dr. Heenan, Archbishop of Westminster, created a cardinal.

March 3 Remains of Roger Casement, from Pentonville Prison, reburied in Dublin; Seretse Khama became Bechuanaland's first Prime Minister. 7 First of 3,500 American marines landed in S. Vietnam. 18 Alexei Leonov became first man to leave a spaceship and float in space. 19 Record price of 760,000 guineas paid at Christie's for Rembrandt's *Titus*. 23 First successful two-man manœuvrable flight by Grissom and Young in *Gemini III*; Dr. Dorothy Hodgkin awarded Order of Merit. 24 Successful completion of U.S. *Ranger* moon shot programme. 25 Defeat of Mrs. Bandaranaike in Ceylon elections; Mr. Senanayake became Prime Minister. 28 Earthquake in Chile.

April 1 Younger brother of King Hussein made heir to Jordan throne in place of his 3-year-old son. 6 Launching of *Early Bird* commercial communication satellite; Cancellation of TSR 2. 9 Fighting broke out between Indian and Pakistan forces in Rann of Kutch. 11 Tornadoes in mid-western U.S. 23 Opening of 250-mile Pennine Way, Britain's first long-distance foot-

A.D.

path from Edale in Derbyshire to Kirk Yetholm in Roxburghshire. 29 Australian troops to be sent to S. Vietnam.

May 8 Arrest of Sheikh Abdullah. 11 Cyclone and tidal wave disaster in E. Pakistan killing 16,000 people. 13 Conservatives made big gains in U.K. local government elections. 14 Inaguration of Kennedy memorial at Runnymede; China exploded second atomic bomb. 17 31 miners killed in Welsh colliery disaster. 18 The Queen and the Duke of Edinburgh on 10-day state visit to Fed. German Republic. 20–29 Indian ascents of Everest. 28 267 miners killed in Indian colliery disaster.

June 1 237 miners killed in Japanese colliery explosion. 3 Bank rate reduced to 6 per cent: Launching of U.S. *Gemini IV* with McDivitt and White. 4–7 Visit of Mr. Chou En-lai to Tanzania. 7 128 miners killed in Yugoslav mine disaster. 19 Pres. Ben Bella of Algeria deposed by Revolutionary Council under Col. Boumedienne. 22 700th anniversary of Parliament celebrated. 30 Cease-fire agreement in Rann of Kutch signed.

July 14 Adlai Stevenson died. 15 U.S. *Mariner IV* transmitted first close-up pictures of Mars; King Constantine of Greece dismissed his Prime Minister, Mr. Papandreou. 16 Opening of Mont Blanc tunnel. 19 Death of Syngman Rhee, former Pres. of S. Korea. 22 Sir Alec Douglas-Home resigned as leader of the Conservative Party; succeeded by Mr. Edward Heath (July 28). 26 Maldive Islands became independent. 30 U.S. Medical Care for the Aged Bill passed.

August 1 Radio and television licence fees increased; Television ban on cigarette advertising. 3 Creation of "The Queen's Award to Industry" for export and technological achievement. 5 Clashes on Kashmir border. 6 U.S. Voting Rights Bill passed. 9 Singapore seceded from Malaysia; 11 Negro riots in Los Angeles. 12 Appointment of first woman High Court judge. 21 U.S. *Gemini V* (Cooper and Conrad) launched. 24 Pres. Nasser and King Faisal signed cease-fire agreement in Yemen.

September 1 Pakistan forces crossed Kashmir cease-fire line. 2 Death of Sir Harry Hylton-Foster, Speaker of the House of Commons. 5 Death of Dr. Albert Schweitzer. 6 Indian forces invaded W. Pakistan and bombed Lahore. 12 American division 20,000 strong landed in S. Vietnam: General election in Norway: Labour Government defeated. 14 Second Vatican Council reconvened for 4th session. 21 British Petroleum struck oil in North Sea. 22 Cease-fire in Indo-Pakistan war.

October 1 Attempt to overthrow Pres. Sukarno of Indonesia: reprisals against communists. 4 The Pope addressed the U.N. Assembly. 8 Rhodesian independence talks failed. 11 Publication of Vinland Map, the only known example of mediæval Norse cartography. 13 Pres. Kasavubu of the Congo dismissed Mr. Tshombe. 17 Demonstrations throughout U.S. and in London against war in Vietnam. 19 Dr. Erhard re-elected Chancellor of Fed. Rep. of Germany. 22 Pakistan and India accept cease-fire call of Security Council. 26 Dr. Horace King elected Speaker of House of Commons. 28 Parliament passed Bill abolishing death penalty for murder.

November 8 New British colony of British Indian Ocean Territory set up. 11 UDI in Rhodesia: Britain declared régime illegal and introduced economic sanctions. 15 New land speed record of 600·6 m.p.h. set up in Utah by jet-powered car. 20 Security Council called on all states to sever economic relations with Rhodesia, and urged oil embargo. 25 General Mobuto deposed Pres. Kasavubu: France launched her first earth satellite.

December 1 R.A.F. Javelins arrived in Zambia. 4 *Gemini VII* (Borman and Lovell) launched. 8 The Second Vatican Council closed. 9 Mr. Mikoyan retired as President of the Soviet Union; replaced by Mr. Nikolai Podgorny. 15 Rendezvous in orbit between *Geminis VI* and *VII*. 17 Britain imposed oil embargo on Rhodesia; New forms of service for Anglican Church published. 19 General de Gaulle re-elected French President. 22 Death of Richard Dimbleby; 70 m.p.h. speed limit on British roads came into force. 27 Oil rig *Sea Gem* collapsed in North Sea. 28 900th anniversary of Westminster Abbey celebrated.

1966

January 3 Indo-Pakistani summit talks in Tashkent with Mr. Kosygin as host. 9 Violent rioting in Nigeria. 10 Sudden death of Mr. Shastri in Tashkent. 11 Opening of Lagos Commonwealth Conference. 15 Army coup in Nigeria; Fed Prime Min. killed. 16 General Ironsi, C.-in-C. of Nigerian army, took over command to restore law and order; Death of Sergei Korolyov, Russian space scientist. 21 Smith régime in Rhodesia rejected Royal Prerogative commuting death sentences on two Africans. 22 Opening of Volta River project in Ghana. 24 Air India *Boeing* crashed into Mont Blanc; 177 killed. 31 U.S. bombing of N. Vietnam resumed after 37 days; British Government banned all trade with Rhodesia; Russia launched *Luna 9*.

February 3 Successful soft landing on moon by *Luna 9*. 17 Britain protested to S. Africa over petrol supplies to Rhodesia. 23 Death of Vicky, political cartoonist. 24 Army coup in Ghana while Dr. Nkrumah absent in Far East.

March 1 Russian rocket landed on Venus. 4 Britain recognised new régime in Ghana; Canadian *DC 9* crashed near Tokyo: 64 killed. 5 BOAC *Boeing* crashed near Tokyo: 124 killed; Nelson pillar in O'Connell Street, Dublin, blown up. 8 Severe earthquake in Hopeh, N. China. 11 Chi-Chi, the London Zoo's giant panda, flew to Moscow for union with An-An of the Moscow Zoo. 23 Historic meeting in Rome of Archbishop of Canterbury and the Pope. 25 Two of the team climbing north face of the Eiger reached summit. 31 British General Election: Labour victory with overall majority of 97.

April 3 Soviet *Luna 10* became the first lunar orbiter. 7 Recovery of U.S. hydrogen bomb lost off coast of Spain. 10 British Forces in Middle East instructed to stop any ship going to Beira with oil for Rhodesia: *Manuela* intercepted and boarded by British naval party and escorted away from Beira; Death of Evelyn Waugh, the novelist. 11 Students and militant Buddhists intensified campaign for return to civilian rule in S. Vietnam. 21 Opening of Parliament televised for first time. 30 Official support from Chou En-lai for "cultural revolution" to wipe out "bourgeois ideology" in all fields of culture.

May 9 China exploded third nuclear device. 16 Seaman's strike began (ended 1 July—biggest strike in England since the war and the first of its kind since 1911). 18 Talks between Britain and Spain opened over Gibraltar. 26 British Guiana became independent state of Guyana.

June 1 Peace talks between Malaysia, and Indonesia. 2 American *Surveyor I* made soft landing on moon; De Valera re-elected President of Irish Republic. 6 *Gemini 9*, manned by two astronauts, recovered after 45 orbits. 11 Commonwealth Day (the Queen's official birthday) to be observed on this date in future. 27 Death of Arthur Waley, translator.

July 3 Resignation of Mr. Frank Cousins as Minister of Technology over prices and incomes policy. 6 Malawi became a Republic within Commonwealth with Dr. Banda as its first President. 7 Sino-Tanzanian co-operation in joint shipping line. 14 Bank rate raised to 7 per cent; In by-election, Labour lost Carmarthen to Welsh Nationalist. 16 Prime Minister in Moscow for talks with Mr. Kosygin. 18 International Court of Justice ruled in favour of S.

A.D.

Africa; no violation of mandate of S.W. Africa. 20 Prime Minister announced six-month freeze on wages, salaries, and prices. 21 Successful landing of *Gemini 10*: docking manœuvre and space walk. 24 Common Market completed its agricultural policy; 25 Report that Mao Tse-tung had swum 9 miles in Yangtze R. 27 Retirement of M. Spaak from political life. 29 Mutiny by section of Nigerian army; General Ironsi killed; U.S. aircraft attacked oil depots near Hanoi and Haiphong. 30 World Cup won by England.

August 1–2 Plenary session of Central Committee of Chinese Communist Party: Marshal Lin Piao officially recognised as Mao Tse-tung's successor. 3 Post Office to become public corporation. 4 Sir Edmund Compton named Britain's first Parliamentary Commissioner (Ombudsman). 7 Opening of Salazar Bridge spanning Tagus River (longest suspension bridge in Europe). 10 American *Orbiter I* launched—first U.S. moon satellite; Public inspection of Cabinet and other official documents to be allowed after 30 years instead of present 50; Cabinet reshuffle: Mr. George Brown became Foreign Secretary. 11 Indonesian–Malaysian peace agreement signed in Djakarta. 18 Mass rally of Chinese Red Guards in Peking celebrating the "cultural revolution," attended by Mao Tse-tung, Lin Piao, and Chou En-lai; Tay road bridge opened (longest road bridge in Britain). Earthquake in E. Turkey: over 2,000 killed. 27 Francis Chichester set sail round world. 31 Decree restoring federal system of government to Nigeria announced.

September 1 Britannia airliner crashed at Ljubljana in Yugoslavia: 95 killed. 5 Selective Employment Tax came into force. 6 Dr. Verwoerd assassinated in Parliament, Cape Town. 8 Opening of new Severn road bridge. 11 Dr. Immanuel Jakobovits elected Chief Rabbi of Commonwealth; Fourth French nuclear device exploded over Mururoa. 13 Mr. John Vorster chosen as S. Africa's new Prime Minister. 15 German submarine *Hai* sank off Dogger Bank. 16 Opening of new Metropolitan Opera House at Lincoln Centre, New York: Launching of Britain's first Polaris submarine. 19 Inauguration of Paris–Shanghai air service: Civil Rights Bill providing housing integration defeated in U.S. Senate. 28 Indonesia resumed U.N. membership. 30 Sir Seretse Khama became first President of Botswana.

October 1 Release of Speer and von Schirach from Spandau, leaving only Rudolf Hess there. 2 Heavy casualties after cyclone and tidal wave struck E. Pakistan; hurricane Inez in Caribbean. 4 Basutoland became independent kingdom of Lesotho. 5 Part 4 of 1966 Prices and Incomes Act came into effect, giving Government power to freeze wages and prices. 21 Aberfan disaster avalanche from coal tip slid down upon mining village killing 144, including 116 children. 26 Brussels chosen as new headquarters of NATO Council. 27 China's fourth nuclear test. 28 Channel Tunnel announced; Indonesia re-admitted to U.N.

November 4 Italian floods: torrential rain caused Arno to burst its banks into city of Florence; 9 "Hot line" between Paris and Moscow. 22 Organic Law of Spanish State provided for appointment of Prime Minister. 23 Red Guards demanded dismissal of Liu Shao-Ch'i, China's Head of State. 26 Opening of the Rance barrage; Australian General Election: Liberal–Country Party Coalition Government led by Mr. Harold Holt returned; New Zealand General Election: Mr. Keith Holyoake's National Party returned. 29 King Ntare of Burundi overthrown. 30 Resignation of Dr. Erhard, Western German Chancellor; Barbados became independent.

December 1 Mr. Kosygin in France; Dr. Kiesinger (Christian Democratic Union) took office as Chancellor of German Federal Republic. 2 Meeting of Prime Minister and Mr. Ian Smith of Rhodesia on board H.M.S. *Tiger* off Gibraltar: working document prepared; U Thant re-elected U.N. Sec.-Gen. for further five years. 5 Mr. Ian Smith and colleagues rejected working document. 10 Opening of first stage of Roseires dam on Blue Nile, Sudan. 16 U.N. Security Council voted for British resolution for mandatory sanctions (including oil) against Rhodesia. 28 China exploded her fifth nuclear bomb. 31 Death of Mr. Christian Herter, former U.S. Sec. of State.

1967

January 4 Donald Campbell killed at Coniston while trying to break own water speed record. 10 General Election in Bahamas (first all-Negro Cabinet took office Jan. 16 under Mr. Lynden O. Pindling). 11 Last detachment of British troops left Sarawak. 13 Army took over power in Togo. 15 Prime Minister and Foreign Secretary in Rome for Common Market talks. 18 Mr. Jeremy Thorpe, elected Leader of Liberal Party following resignation of Mr. Grimond. 20 Agreement on Soviet–Japanese air service between Moscow and Tokyo via Siberia. 26 Bank rate reduced to 6½ per cent. 27 Death of Marshal Juin; Three American astronauts killed in fire during ground test at Cape Kennedy.

February 6 Mr. Kosygin arrived in London. 7 Bush fire in Tasmania: 62 lives lost and heavy damage. 9 Historic meeting between the Queen and Mr. Kosygin at Buckingham Palace. 13 Agreement on a "hot line" between Kremlin and 10 Downing Street. 15 Chinese authorities ordered dissolution of all "revolutionary organisations" and return of their members to their own provinces. 19 Death of Robert Oppenheimer, the American physicist. 22 Pres. Sukarno of Indonesia surrendered rule to Gen. Suharto. 23 Trinidad and Tobago first Commonwealth member to join Organisation of American States. 26 Congress Party returned to power in Indian elections but lost 8 states. 27 International treaty banning nuclear weapons from outer space and prohibiting use of Moon and other celestial bodies signed in London, Moscow, and Washington.

March 6 Death of Zoltán Kodály, composer. 12 Mrs. Indira Gandhi re-elected Prime Minister of India. 13 Gaullists gained bare majority in French National Assembly. 16 Bank rate reduced to 6 per cent. 18 *Torrey Canyon* ran aground off Land's End with 120,000 tons of crude oil aboard. 22 Army in Sierra Leone seized power. 28 *Torrey Canyon* bombed and oil released and set on fire; Pope Paul issued encyclical on duties of rich nations towards poor nations. 29 Launching of France's first nuclear submarine, *Le Redoutable*; Last link of South-East Asia Commonwealth cable system, inaugurated. 31 Death of Marshal Malinovsky, defender of Stalingrad.

April 13 Conservatives gained landslide victory in GLC elections. 19 Death of Konrad Adenauer. 21 Army coup in Greece. 23 Col. Vladimir Komarov, Soviet cosmonaut, killed after parachute failure. 27 Opening in Montreal of Expo 67—Canada's 100th birthday international fair.

May 4 Bank rate reduced to 5½%. 8 Dr. Zakir Hussain elected President of India. 11 Britain presented application to join Common Market. 14 Opening of Liverpool's new R.C. cathedral. 19 U.N. peace forces removed from Egypt–Israel border after request from Pres. Nasser. 22 Egypt closed Straits of Tiran to Israeli shipping; Japan joined European Nuclear Energy Agency's Reactor Programme. 23 J. Ryun (U.S.A.) broke his own world mile record—3 min. 51·1 sec. 28 Francis Chichester arrived in Plymouth. 30 Secession of Eastern Region (Biafra) from Nigerian Federation; Egypt and Jordan concluded five-year defence agreement.

June 1 Gen. Moshe Dayan appointed Israeli Defence Minister. 3–4 166 people killed in two British air crashes, at Perpignan and Stockport. 5 Outbreak of six-day war in Middle East;

A.D.

lightning attack by Israel caused severe Arab losses and capture of territory, mainly from Egypt and Jordan. 6 E. African Economic Community formed by Kenya, Uganda and Tanzania. 8 U.N. called for immediate Middle East cease fire. 8–9 Riots in Hong Kong. 9 France's fishing limits extended to 12 miles. 10 Middle East fighting ceased; Soviet Union broke off diplomatic relations with Israel. 12 Soviet Union launched Venus spacecraft. 17 China exploded her first H-bomb. 19 Pres. Nasser took over as P.M. 23 Meetings between Pres. Johnson and Mr. Kosygin in Glassboro. New Jersey. 23–24 More violence in Hong Kong. 26 EEC Council of Ministers to refer British application for membership to EEC Commission: Mr. Kosygin visited Cuba; U.S.A. and Panama agreed treaty concerning Panama Canal. 28 Israel took over control of the Old City of Jerusalem. 30 End of period of severe economic restraint in Britain.

July 1 Mr. Tshombe kidnapped in mid-flight and arrested in Algeria; Colour television began in Britain on BBC-2. 2 Third French nuclear test at Muratoa atoll in Pacific. 7 Francis Chichester knighted by the Queen at Greenwich. 8 Police post in Hong Kong attacked by demonstrators from China. 10 Last use of steam engines on British Rail Southern Region; New Zealand changed to decimal currency. 12 Negro riots in Newark, N.J. 13 Public Record Act passed: public records now closed for only 30 years (from Jan. 1968). 14 Decimal Currency Act became law, providing for decimal currency in Britain in 1971. 15 *Lake Palourde*, sister ship of *Torrey Canyon*, arrested at Singapore as surety for oil pollution damage. 17 U.N. observers began operating on Arab-Israeli cease-fire line; London's first supersonic boom test. 18 Defence cuts announced: withdrawal from East of Suez by mid-1970s. 20 Latey Commission recommended that 18 should be legal age of majority. 21 Albert Luthuli killed in railway accident in S. Africa. 22 Earthquake in N.W. Turkey. 23 Negro riot in Detroit. 25 Pope Paul visited Istanbul, Izmir and Ephesus. 28 Vesting day of British Steel Corporation.

August 3 Aberfan tribunal report blamed N.C.B. for the disaster; Lord Robens' resignation not accepted. 13 U.S. bombed N. Vietnam 10 miles from Chinese border. 21 Britain began phased withdrawal of forces from Aden and S. Arabia.

September 3 Chinese Red Guards ordered to cease violence; Sweden's traffic changed from left to right. 10 Gibraltar referendum: overwhelming vote to stay with Britain. 13 U.S. announced an anti-ballistic missile system against China. 20 Launching on Clydebank of Cunard Liner *Queen Elizabeth II*. 27 *Queen Mary* arrived at Southampton at end of her last transatlantic voyage.

October 2 H.M.S. *Resolution*, Britain's first Polaris submarine, commissioned. 8 Death of Lord Attlee. 9 Road Safety Act dealing with drink and driving came into force; Che Guevara, Cuban revolutionary leader, killed in guerrilla fighting in Bolivia. 10 Outer Space Treaty ratified by 93 countries. 13 Tyne toll tunnel opened by the Queen. 16 Opening of new NATO H.Q. at Evère, Brussels. 18 Russian *Venus 4* made first soft-landing on Venus. 19 American *Mariner 5* passed within 2,000 miles of Venus; Bank Rate increased to 6%. 22 Big demonstrations against Vietnam war in Washington, London and other capitals. 24 Israel bombarded Egypt's Suez oil refineries. 25 Foot-and-mouth epidemic began at Oswestry. 26 Coronation of Shah of Iran; Anglo-French agreement on joint production of helicopters. 30 End of Canadian Expo 67; Old age pensions and other benefits increased in Britain; Russians performed first automatic link-up and separation of unmanned spacecraft.

November 9 Bank rate increased to 6½%; launching of U.S. giant *Saturn 5* rocket. 14 State visit to Malta by the Queen. 18 Devaluation of Sterling by 14·3% to $2·40 to the £; Bank rate increased to 8%. 20 Professor Blackett and Sir William Walton awarded the O.M. 22 Security Council unanimously adopted British resolution requiring Israeli forces to withdraw from occupied Arab territory. 23 Indus water project inaugurated at Mangla Dam in W. Pakistan. 26 Lisbon area floods—464 dead. 27 End of eight-week unoffi ial London dock strike. 29 Aden independent as Republic of South Yemen.

December 3 First human heart transplant operation at Cape Town. 13 King Constantine attempted unsuccessfully to overthrow the Greek military junta. 17 Mr. Harold Holt, Australian P.M., drowned in swimming accident. 19 France voted against negotiations for Britain's entry to EEC—Britain not to withdraw application. 20 Diplomatic relations resumed between Britain and Egypt.

1968

January 9 U.S. *Surveyor* spacecraft soft-landed on moon; Senator John G. Gorton elected P.M. of Australia. 14–15 Violent earth tremors in W. Sicily. 16 Prime Minister announced cuts in public spending. 23 Seizure by N. Korea of *USS Pueblo* off N. Korean coast.

February 11–12 U Thant in Moscow and London for talks on Vietnam. 13 U.S. planes bombed outskirts of Saigon. 18 Second Communist offensive in Vietnam; Introduction of British Standard Time. 19 Decision of Rann of Kutch Tribunal: nine-tenths to India and rest to Pakistan. 24 End of 25-day defence of Hué by Vietcong.

March 6 Africans in Rhodesia hanged in defiance of the Queen's reprieve. 12 Mauritius became independent. 14 Rush for gold in leading financial centres: U.S. Bank rate raised. Stock Exchange and Banks closed in Britain; Resignation of Mr. George Brown as Foreign Secretary. 17–18 Summit Meeting of Western Central Bankers: two-tier system for gold agreed. 21 Bank rate reduced to 7½%. 22 Resignation of Pres. Novotny of Czechoslovakia; Gen. Westmoreland, U.S. Commander in Vietnam, recalled to be Army Chief of Staff in Washington. 27 Yuri Gagarin killed in air crash. 30 Monetary Conference in Stockholm: special drawing rights scheme agreed, despite French non-co-operation.

April 4 Assassination of Martin Luther King at Memphis, Tennessee. 8 N. Vietnam agreed to direct talks with U.S. 16 Britain to withdraw from ELDO. 20 Pierre Trudeau became Liberal P.M. of Canada. 28 Extreme right-wing N.P.D. party won 12 seats in Baden-Württemberg state elections.

May 10 Violent clashes between students and security police in Paris. 13 Vietnam peace talks began in Paris. 17 French workers occupied factories. 18 Pres. de Gaulle cut short Romanian tour. 22 French National Assembly adopted amnesty after trade unions had agreed to negotiate with employers and Government. 29 U.N. Security Council adopted resolution imposing comprehensive mandatory sanctions against Rhodesia.

June 5–6 Senator Robert Kennedy shot and died in Los Angeles. 10 National Health prescription charge introduced. 14 Restrictions on entry into Britain by anyone connected with the Rhodesian régime. 15 Warsaw Pact manœuvres in Czechoslovakia. 26 Pierre Trudeau's Liberal Party won Canadian election. 30 Gaullists increased their majority in French election.

July 1 EEC abolished last internal industrial tariffs and common external tariff came into effect. 4 Fourth assembly of World Council of Churches; Mr. Alec Rose landed at Portsmouth after sailing single-handed round the world. 10 M. Couve de Murville replaced M. Pompidou as French P.M. 26 Government to

A.D.

remove Aberfan tips. 28 Serious riots in Mexico City. 29 Pope issued encyclical condemning all forms of artificial birth control; Summit Conference between Czech and Soviet leaders at Cierna.

August 3 Meeting at Bratislava between leaders of Czechoslovakia and other Warsaw Pact countries; death of Marshal Rokossovsky, Russian Second World War hero. 20 Soviet and Warsaw Pact forces entered Czechoslovakia. 22 The Pope visited Colombia, first papal visit to Latin America. 27 Death of Princess Marina, Duchess of Kent. 28 Chicago riots at National Democratic Convention. 31 Major earthquake in N.E. Iran.

September 6 Swaziland independent. 11 Departure of Soviet troops from Prague. 13 High Court of Rhodesia ruled that the 1965 Constitution was legal. 15 Worst flooding in England since 1953. 16 Two-tier postal system began in Britain. 19 Bank rate reduced to 7%. 21–22 Clashes between students and police in Mexico City. 22 Successful recovery of Soviet *Zond 5* spacecraft after voyage round the moon. 26 Theatres Act, abolishing censorship, in force; Professor Marcelio Caetano appointed P.M. of Portugal (Dr. Salazar ill). 27 French again vetoed British entry into Common Market.

October 1 Federal Nigerian troops captured Okigwi in Biafra. 5 Clashes between police and crowds in Londonderry (beginning of disturbances in N. Ireland). 9 H.M.S. *Fearless* talks on Rhodesia failed. 11 U.S. successfully launched *Apollo* 7 3-man moon rocket. 12 Olympic Games in Mexico City. 14 Queen opened new Euston Station. 16 Treaty signed providing for stationing of Soviet troops in Czechoslovakia. 27 Czechoslovakia became a two-state federation; Massive demonstration march in London against Vietnam war. 31 Pres. Johnson ordered halt to bombing of N. Vietnam.

November 1 Pres. Liu Shao-Chi expelled from Chinese Communist Party. 4 N.L.F. delegation in Paris. 5 Mr. Richard Nixon won U.S. presidential elections. 12 Credit restrictions in France; Major policy statement by Mr. Brezhnev at Polish Party Congress—"a threat to a Socialist country is a threat to all Socialist countries." 15 New Greek Constitution came into force. 22 Stringent economy measures in France and higher taxation in Britain. 29 Rioting in Rawalpindi. 30 Civil rights disturbances in Armagh.

December 1 Pres. Ayub Khan agreed to students' educational demands. 2 Two pipelines blown up which carry water over Welsh border. 8 Royal Naval Dockyard in Singapore formally handed over to Singapore Government. 21–27 *Apollo* 8 mission—Borman, Lovell and Anders made first lunar orbits. 27 China tested thermonuclear weapon. 28 Israeli commandos destroyed 13 Arab aircraft at Beirut after two Israeli airliners attacked by Arabs at Athens. 31 Maiden flight of Soviet TU-144 supersonic airliner.

1969

January 1–4 People's Democracy march from Belfast to Londonderry. 5 Soviet Venus probe launched. 7 Commonwealth Prime Ministers' Conference in London. 16 First manned docking operation in orbit by Soviet *Soyuz 4* and *5*. 20 Spain extended her territorial waters to 12 miles.

February 3 Assassination of Dr. Mondlane, Mozambique nationalist leader. 13 Arab attack on Israeli airliner at Zurich: Lisbon-Cape Town submarine cable opened. 22 Vietnam Tet offensive began. 23 Pres. Nixon began series of visits to European capitals. 24 U.S. *Mariner* Mars spacecraft launched. 26 Death of Israeli P.M., Mr. Eshkal. 28 Bank rate raised to 8%.

A.D.

March 2 Maiden flight of French-built *Concorde*; Mrs. Golda Meir chosen as Israel's P.M.; Sino-Soviet clash on Ussuri River. 3 *Apollo 9* launched on 10-day test mission. 5 Dr. Gustav Heinemann became President of W. Germany. 7 Opening of London's Victoria Line. 9 Gen. Riad Egypt's Chief of Staff killed in artillery battle with Israel along Suez Canal. 13 B.P. found Alaskan oil deposits. 18 U.S. offensive in S. Vietnam. 19 British troops landed with no opposition on Anguilla. 25 Resignation of Pres. Ayub Khan—succeeded by Gen. Yahya Khan.

April 1 Opening of China's ninth Communist Party Congress. 9 Maiden flight of British built *Concorde*. 14 Lin Piao declared Mao's successor. 17 Mr. Dubcek replaced as first Secretary of Czechoslovak Communist Party by Dr. Husak. 21 British Army units to guard key points in N. Ireland. 23 Biafran capital of Umuahia captured by Federal forces. 28 Gen. de Gaulle resigned as President of France after defeat on referendum; Anglo-Italian declaration of policy on Europe.

May 1 Maj. James Chichester-Clark became P.M. of N. Ireland after resignation of Mr Terence O'Neill. 2 *Queen Elizabeth 2*'s maiden voyage began. 3 Death of Dr. Husain, India's President (succeeded by Mr. V. V. Giri, 23 Aug. 1969) 12 Conservatives gained 957 seats in Borough elections in England and Wales. Voting age became 18. 16–17 Landing of Soviet spacecraft on Venus. 18–26 U.S. *Apollo 10* moon flight (Stafford, Young and Cernan). 27 Hungary ratified Nuclear Non-Proliferation Treaty.

June 5 World Communist Conference in Moscow. 8 Spain closed frontier with Gibraltar; Conference between Pres. Nixon and Pres. Thieu and withdrawal of 25,000 U.S. troops announced. 15 M. Georges Pompidou elected President of France. 17 Boris Spassky became World Chess Champion. 18 Government dropped plans to put legal restraints on unofficial strikers in return for T.U.C. pledge to deal with disputes. 24 Resignation of Sir Humphrey Gibbs as Governor of Rhodesia. 29 Death of Mr. Tshombe.

July 1 Investiture of Prince Charles as 21st Prince of Wales at Caernarvon Castle. 3 Security Council censured measures taken by Israel to change status of Jerusalem. 5 Assassination in Nairobi of Tom Mboya. 8 Church of England rejected scheme for unity with Methodists, Methodists accepted it. 13 Launching of Soviet unmanned *Luna 15*; Renewed violence in Londonderry. 14 First major contingent of U.S. troops withdrawn from Vietnam. 21 Armstrong and Aldrin first men to land on the Moon at 3·56 a.m. (B.S.T.). 22 Prince Juan Carlos named future King of Spain by Gen. Franco. 23 Commissioner Erick Wickberg elected General of Salvation Army. 24 Splashdown in Pacific of *Apollo 11*. 31 U.S. *Mariner 6* took photos of Mars; Pope Paul visited Kampala; Halfpennies ceased to be legal tender in Britain.

August 8 French franc devalued by 12½%. 12 Three-day street battle in Londonderry after apprentice boys march. 14 British troops on duty in Ulster. 18 Hurricane Camille swept across Mississippi Gulf. 19 Army took over security and police in N. Ireland. 29 General Election in Ghana: Dr. Busia (Progress Party) became P.M.

September 1 King Idris of Libya deposed by military junta. 3 Death of Ho Chi-minh, President of N. Vietnam. 10 Barricades dismantled in Belfast and Army's "peace line" erected; Cameron Report *Disturbances in Northern Ireland*. 11 Meeting in Peking of Soviet and Chinese P.M.s. 16 Pres. Nixon announced withdrawal of further 35,000 troops from S. Vietnam by mid-December. 23 Ton Duc Thang elected President of N. Vietnam; China carried out her first nuclear test underground. 28 Herr Brandt became

A.D.

Chancellor of W. Germany. 29 China exploded H-bomb.

October 1 Vesting day for new Post Office Corporation. 10 Hunt Committee report on N. Ireland recommended disarming police and disbanding B specials. 11–13 Group flight by Soviet *Soyuz* spacecraft and first experiment in space welding. 13 Vatican international synod of bishops in Rome. 14 50p (10s.) piece introduced. 15 Mr. Dubcek resigned as President of Czechoslovak Federal Assembly; Peaceful demonstrations by millions of Americans against Vietnam war. 20 Talks in Peking on Soviet–China border dispute. 24 Deutsche Mark revalued upwards to 3·66 to the $.

November 11 Owners of *Torrey Canyon* agreed to pay £1·5 million each to Britain and France for oil damage. 14 Launching of *Apollo 14* (Conrad, Gordon and Bean); Colour programmes began on BBC-1 and ITV. 15 Tanzania, Zambia and China agreed on construction of railway from Dar es Salaam to Zambia's copperbelt. 17 Strategic Arms Limitation talks between U.S. and Soviet Union at Helsinki. 24 Soviet Union and U.S. ratified Nuclear Non-Proliferation Treaty. 25 U.S. renounced use of biological warfare.

December 1–2 EEC Summit Meeting at The Hague agreed on negotiations for British entry by June 1970. 2 Death of Marshal Voroshilov, former Soviet President 11 European Conservation Year began. 12 Greece withdrew from Council of Europe. 15 Pres. Nixon announced withdrawal of 50,000 more troops from Vietnam by April 1970. 16–18 Houses of Commons and Lords voted for permanent abolition of the death penalty. 19 Relaxation of U.S. trading restrictions with China. 27 Ruling Liberal Democratic Party won sweeping victory in Japanese General Election.

1970

January 11 Federal Nigerian troops captured Owerri; flight of Gen. Ojukwu from Biafra. 12 Gen. Effiong proclaimed end of Biafran secession. 30 Demonstrations in Indian state of Haryana against proposals for future of Chandigarh.

February 1 Pope reaffirmed celibacy as a fundamental law of the Latin church; Serious clash on Golan Heights between Israel and Syria. 3 Bertrand Russell died. 5 Special Public Order Act for N. Ireland passed. 11 Japan launched her first earth satellite. 15 Opening of Eilat to Ashkelon oil pipeline to by-pass Suez Canal. 17 Mrs. Meir, Israeli P.M. offered to halt attacks if Egypt agreed to respect the cease-fire. 21 Israel-bound Swiss airliner exploded killing 47 people.

March 2 The Queen began tour of Australasia; Rhodesia proclaimed a republic. 4 French submarine *Eurydice* lost off Toulon. 5 Nuclear Non-Proliferation Treaty in force; Bank rate reduced to 7½%. 6 German Bank rate reduced; Teachers' strike ended with pay settlement. 7 Total solar eclipse in Mexico. 15 Expo-70 opened near Osaka, Japan; Assassination of Mr. Georgadis, Cypriot Minister of the Interior. 16 Publication of the complete *New English Bible*. 18 Prince Sihanouk overthrown in right-wing coup; Security Council resolution calling for an end to all relations between Rhodesia and U.N. member states. 19 Meeting of Federal Chancellor and E. German P.M. at Erfurt. 22 Publication of Rhodesian Church's *Crisis for Conscience* criticising recent Rhodesian legislation. 23 S. Africa banned from 1970 Davis Cup. 24 House of Commons rejected bill to impose sentences of at least 30 years for murders of policemen. 28 Earthquake in Turkish town of Gediz.

April 1 Murder of Count von Spreti, W. German Ambassador to Guatemala, by guerrillas. 8 Chinese–North Korean communiqué on America's new Asian policy; Israel bombed Nile delta. 9 County Council Elections: Conservatives made net gain of 74 seats and held control of GLC, but Labour gained control of ILEA. 10 U.S. Senate Foreign Relations Committee repealed Tonking Bay resolutions of 1964, used by Pres. Johnson to justify involvement in Vietnam. 15 Bank rate reduced to 7%; Greece condemned at Council of Europe meeting for repeated violations of human rights. 18 Splashdown of *Apollo 13* after complex rescue operation (Lovell, Halse and Swigert). 21 Pres. Nixon announced withdrawal of another 150,000 U.S. troops from Vietnam in next year. 24 China launched her first satellite. 25 Russia launched eight Cosmos research satellites from one rocket. 28 ELDO decided to abandon British *Blue Streak* in favour of French rocket. 30 U.S. combat troops entered Cambodia.

May 1 Pres. Obote of Uganda nationalised all important export businesses. 4 Four students shot dead during demonstration at Kent State University, U.S.A.; Royal Family returned from Commonwealth tour. 6 20-year treaty of friendship between Soviet Union and Czechoslovakia. 8 Borough Elections in England and Wales: 433 Labour net gains. 12 Security Council resolution condemning Israeli military action in Lebanon; Danube floods in Romania. 15 S. Africa expelled from International Olympic Committee. 22 Britain cancelled S. African cricket tour. 25 Foreign banks in Sudan nationalised. 31 Earthquake in N. Peru; France carried out nuclear test in Pacific.

June 4 Tonga independent. 7 Fighting for many days between Jordan troops and Palestinian guerrillas. 11 Drought of over 8 weeks in Borrowdale; warmest night in Britain for a century. 15 Pres. Kaunda banned coal imports from Rhodesia. 18 General Election in Britain: Conservative overall majority of 30. 19 Orbital space flight by Soviet cosmonauts in *Soyuz 9*. 21 Brazil won World Cup (Soccer). 23 Arrival of steamship *Great Britain* at Bristol from Falklands. 26 Mr. Dubcek expelled from Czechoslovak Communist Party. 27–28 Violent disturbances in Belfast and Londonderry, additional troops flown in. 29 British Government to end restrictions on sale of Council houses; Britain made third application to join EEC; Circular 10/70 issued, with Conservative policy on secondary education.

July 1 Division of W. Pakistan into four provinces. 5–10 Royal visit to Canada. 6 Sir Alec Douglas-Home told Commons of Government's intention to resume arms sales to S. Africa. 20 Death of Mr. Iain Macleod, Chancellor of the Exchequer. 23 Bill enacted to give pensions to people over 80 not entitled in present scheme, CS gas canisters thrown into Commons Chamber from Gallery. 30 Damages awarded to 28 deformed thalidomide children and their parents.

August 2 Inter-island ferry sank off Nevis; Army fired rubber bullets during Belfast disturbances. 7 Cease-fire in force along Suez Canal. 12 German-Soviet non-aggression treaty signed by Herr Brandt and Mr. Kosygin. 14 End of second round of arms limitation talks between U.S.A. and Soviet Union in Vienna. 19 Sino-Soviet trade talks began in Khabarovsk. 23 All marches in N. Ireland banned until Jan. 1971. 25 Indirect talks between Egypt, Israel and Jordan in New York, with U.N. mediator, Dr. Jarring. 26 Sudan Government announced nationalisation of the Press. 31 Mr. Edward Akufo-Addo elected Pres. of Ghana.

September 2 Britain's Black Arrow rocket failed at Woomera. 4 World Council of Churches proposed financial aid to African guerrillas. 6–12 Four planes hijacked by Arab guerrillas. 17 Civil War in Jordan between King Hussein's army and Palestinian guerrillas. 19 Syrian Army units intervened in Jordan. 22 Resumption of U.S. arms aid to Greece; Tunku Abdul Rahman resigned as Malaysian P.M. (succeeded by Tun Abdul Razak). 24 Soviet unmanned *Luna 16* brought back moon rock samples.

A.D.

27 Agreement to end Jordan Civil War signed in Cairo by King Hussein, guerrilla leaders and leaders of eight Arab states. 29 Death of Pres. Nasser (later succeeded by Mr. Anwar Sadat).

October 5 Mr. James Cross and M. Laporte kidnapped by Quebec separatists. 13 China and Canada established diplomatic relations. 15 Canonisation of 40 English and Welsh martyrs. 17 Murder of M. Laporte. 24 Dr. Salvador Allende, Marxist Socialist, elected President of Chile.

November 9 Death of Gen. de Gaulle. 13 Cyclone and tidal wave struck Brahmaputra-Ganges delta area of E. Pakistan. 17 Russia's *Luna 17* landed on moon with moon-walker which moved on surface. 20 U.N. voted to admit China but without necessary two-thirds majority. 21 U.S. bombed N. Vietnam after two-year halt.

December 3 Release of Mr. James Cross. 7 Poland and W. Germany signed treaty recognising Oder-Neisse boundary; Elections in Pakistan. 8 Earthquakes in N. Peru. 15 Soviet *Venus 7* spacecraft transmitted scientific information from surface of Venus. 18 Divorce became legal in Italy. 20 Mr. Gomulka resigned and was succeeded by Mr. Edward Gierek. 30 Gen. Franco commuted death penalties on six Basque nationalists.

1971

January 1 Divorce Reform Act (1969) came into force; Kentucky mine disaster. 2 Ibrox Park disaster in Glasgow. 3 Open University on the air. 5 Resignation of Lord Robens as Chairman of the N.C.B. 10 Highest ever January temperatures recorded in London. 14 Commonwealth Conference opened in Singapore. 15 Opening of Aswan High Dam. 19 Postal workers' strike began. 25 Pres. Obote of Uganda deposed by Maj. Gen. Amin, Army Commander. 28 Indian Ocean cyclone caused severe flooding in Mozambique. 31 Launching of *Apollo 14* to moon (Shepard, Roosa, Mitchell).

February 4 Troop reinforcements sent to Belfast, after further violence; Financial collapse of Rolls Royce Ltd. 7 Male referendum in Switzerland gave women right to vote in national elections. 8 S. Vietnamese troops with U.S. air and artillery support crossed into Laos. 9 Earthquake in San Fernando valley, California. 14 Agreement in Tehran between Western oil companies and six Gulf oil-producing countries, to increase prices. 15 Decimal Day in Britain. 21 March of over 100,000 trade unionists in London against Industrial Relations Bill. 22 Tornadoes hit Southern states of U.S.; British Government approved sale of seven helicopters to S. Africa against Security Council embargo. 24 Immigration Bill published, placing Commonwealth and alien immigrants under one system of control. 25 S. Vietnamese drive in Laos halted.

March 1 One-day strike by 1·5 million engineers against Industrial Relations Bill. 4 Mr. Maudling, Home Secretary, addressed joint session of N. Ireland Parliament. 10 Mr. Gorton resigned as Australian P.M., replaced by Mr. William McMahon. 11 Landslide victory for Mrs. Gandhi in Indian General Election. 18 More troops to N. Ireland bringing total to 9,700. 19 S. Vietnam began withdrawal from Laos; Landslide near Lima. 20 Resignation of Maj. Chichester-Clark as N. Ireland's P.M. (succeeded by Mr. Brian Faulkner). 26 Civil war erupted in E. Pakistan after arrest of Sheikh Mujibar Rahman. 29 Lieut. Calley convicted of murder of 22 people in My Lai massacre in S. Vietnam. 30 Soviet Union agreed to outlaw germ warfare.

April 1 Bank rate reduced to 6%. 6 Death of Igor Stravinsky. 13 Table Tennis teams from U.S., Canada, Colombia, Nigeria and Britain in Peking. 14 Direct telephone link between Britain and China opened after 22 years. 17 Egypt, Syria and Libya formed new Federation of Arab republics. 23 Launching of *Soyuz 10* (with three cosmonauts) to dock with Salyut space station in technical experiment to develop permanent base above Earth.

May 3 Resignation of Herr Ulbricht as First Secretary of East German Communist Party, in favour of Herr Erich Honecker. 6 Greece and Albania agreed to establish diplomatic relations, broken off in 1940. 10 Flotation of Deutsche Mark and Dutch guilder following Common Market currency crisis. Swiss franc and Austrian Schilling revalued upwards. 11 Vote for unity by Congregational and Presbyterian churches in England and Wales. 13 Sweeping Labour gains (2,801 seats) in municipal elections in England and Wales; Britain, France, Belgium and Holland agreed on plan to control Channel shipping traffic; Eruption of Mount Etna threatened villages on lower slopes. 20–21 Heath–Pompidou talks on Common Market in Paris. 22 Earthquake in E. Turkey. 27 15-year treaty of friendship and co-operation signed by Egypt and Russia: Labour gained Bromsgrove seat from Conservatives in by-election. 31 Dissolution of Industrial Reorganisation Corporation, set up in 1966.

June 8 Famine among refugees in West Bengal (India) and in East Pakistan. 10 Lifting of 21-year embargo on trade with China by U.S. 21 Labour Party victory in Malta General Election, Mr. Dom Mintoff Prime Minister. 25 Death of Lord Boyd-Orr. 30 Russian space tragedy; Patsayev, Dobrovolsky and Volkov killed just before touchdown after 24 days in space.

July 1 Death of Sir Lawrence Bragg. 3 Opening of Erskine Bridge over Clyde. 5 Selective Employment Tax halved. 6 Death of Louis Armstrong, jazz musician. 7 Publication of Government's *The United Kingdom and the European Communities* setting out terms for entry. 15 Chilean Government nationalised mining industry. 26 Launch of *Apollo 15* (Scott, Irwin and Worden). 30 Workers at Upper Clyde Shipbuilders took control of shipyard.

August 2 Lockheed Aircraft Corporation saved from bankruptcy by single Senate vote. 9 Internment without trial introduced in Northern Ireland; India signed treaty of friendship with Russia. 11 Trial in secret of Sheikh Mujibar Rahman, by Pakistan military court. 22 Right wing coup in Bolivia: Juan Torres replaced as President by Col. Hanzer. 23 Foreign Exchange markets reopened: sterling allowed to float upwards to new parity against the U.S. dollar. 24 U.S. imposed special 10% surcharge on all import duties to meet balance of trade crisis.

September 2 Belfast explosions injured 40 people; Bank rate reduced to 5%. 4 Monsoons caused major floods in Bengal. 8 Australia cancelled S. African cricket tour after protests. 9 Parliament recalled for special debate on Northern Ireland. 11 Khrushchev died. 13 Attica prison stormed by U.S. police after riots; 40 killed. 20 Lord Goodman in Salisbury for talks with Smith régime on behalf of the Government. 24 Britain expelled 105 Russian diplomats for espionage. 27 Meeting of Prime Ministers Heath, Lynch and Faulkner at Chequers.

October 2 BEA Vanguard crashed near Ghent with no survivors. 4 Labour Party Conference voted against Common Market terms by large majority. 8 Mortgage rates in Britain reduced by ½%. 9 Emperor Hirohito, on visit to Europe, given hostile reception at Amsterdam. 13 Conservative Party Conference voted overwhelmingly in favour of Common Market entry terms. 18 Prime Minister announced free vote for Conservatives on Common Market terms (Labour decided on a three-line whip on October 20); Queen on state visit to Turkey. 23 India called up army reservists after further border friction with Pakistan. 26 U.N. General Assembly voted to admit China and expel Taiwan. 28 House of Commons (and Lords)

A.D.

voted in favour of joining Common Market on terms presented by Government: 69 Labour M.P.s voted with the Government. 31 Explosion at Post Office tower in London wrecked three floors.

November 1 Tidal wave disasters on Bay of Bengal coast. 13 U.S. *Mariner 9* went into orbit round Mars. 16 Compton Report on Interrogation in Northern Ireland found "some ill-treatment but no brutality." 24 Pakistan mobilised reserves for war. 25 Terms of Rhodesia settlement announced in London and Salisbury and at U.N.

December 3 Outbreak of Indo-Pakistan war after prolonged friction and many border disputes. 7 Libya nationalised B.P. oil investments in retaliation for British policy in Persian Gulf. 11 Mr. Geoffrey Rippon agreed terms with EEC for protection of fishing limits after Britain's entry. 16 Indian forces occupied Dacca. 17 End of Indo-Pakistan War. 18 Pres. Yahya Khan of Pakistan ousted and succeeded by Mr. Ali Bhutto; Group of Ten agreed on terms for re-alignment of currencies. 20–21 Heath–Nixon talks in Bermuda. 24 Signor Leone elected new President of Italy after 24 ballots. 29 British troops began withdrawal from Malta after breakdown of talks.

1972

January 1 Death of Maurice Chevalier. 9 *Queen Elizabeth* destroyed by fire in Hong Kong harbour; Miners' strike began with widespread power cuts and industrial disruption. 12 Sheikh Mujibar Rahman appointed Prime Minister of Bangladesh; Pearce Commission began work in Rhodesia. 13 Dr. Busia's government in Ghana overthrown. 14 Death of Frederick IX, King of Denmark; succession of Queen Margrethe II. 20 Unemployment in Britain reached over a million. 22 Britain, Ireland, Norway and Denmark signed European Economic Community treaty. 30 "Bloody Sunday" in Londonderry: 13 civilians killed.

February 3 Winter Olympic Games opened in Sapporo, Japan. 4 Britain recognised Bangladesh. 9 State of emergency in power crisis declared and large-scale power cuts began. 10 The Queen began state visits to South-East Asia and India. 15 Over 1·5 million workers laid off at height of power crisis. 17 Second reading of European Communities Bill carried by only eight votes. 18 Wilberforce Enquiry's terms for settling the miners' dispute published. 21 President Nixon in Peking for talks. 22 Seven killed in IRA bomb explosion at Aldershot. 24 £2m paid to hijackers to release crew of an aircraft in Aden. 25 Miners voted to return to work.

March 4 Belfast restaurant explosion killed two and injured 136; Hovercraft capsized in Solent, killing five. 20 Dr. Sicco Mansholt appointed President of the European Commission; Six killed and 47 injured in bomb explosion in Donegall Street, Belfast. 26 New defence agreement signed between Britain and Malta. 29 Tutankhamun exhibition opened at the British Museum; Berlin Wall opened for the first time in six years; Transport and General Workers' Union fined for contempt by National Industrial Relations Court. 30 Direct rule came into force in Northern Ireland: Mr. William Whitelaw appointed Secretary of State.

April 2 North Vietnamese troops mounted big offensive. 5 Senator McGovern won Wisconsin primary. 6 Scarman Tribunal reported on 1969 riots in Ulster. 7 73 internees released in Northern Ireland. 10 46 countries signed a convention outlawing biological weapons; 5,000 killed in earthquake in southern Iran. 16 Launch of *Apollo 16* (Young, Mattingley and Duke). 17 Work-to-rule began on British Rail over pay claim. 18 Bangladesh admitted to the Commonwealth. 19 National Industrial Relations Court ordered 14-day cooling-off period in rail dispute; Widgery Report on "Bloody Sunday" published. 20 Transport and General Workers' Union fined further by National Industrial Relations Court for contempt. 23 French referendum showed majority in favour of the enlargement of the EEC. 25 More internees released in Northern Ireland. 27 Ban on marches in Northern Ireland lifted; death of ex-President Kwame Nkrumah of Ghana.

May 1 Quang Tri captured by North Vietnamese. 2 60 miners trapped in silver mine in Idaho. 3 Church of England Synod failed to reach required vote in favour of Anglican-Methodist union. 4 Labour gained over 1,500 seats in local elections. 9 Black September hijackers killed at Lydda airport by Israeli soldiers. 11 73 killed in collision between two ships in the River Plate. 13 Work-to-rule caused complete weekend shut-down of British Rai; 15 The Queen began state visit to Francel Governor George Wallace of Alabama shot and wounded in Maryland. 18 Bomb disposal experts parachuted in mid-Atlantic to *Queen Elizabeth II* following bomb threat. 22 President Nixon arrived in Moscow for talks; Ceylon became the republic of Sri Lanka; Poet Laureate, Mr. C. Day Lewis, died. 23 Pearce Commission reported that the Rhodesians were not generally in favour of settlement proposals. 28 Duke of Windsor died in Paris. 30 Three Japanese terrorists killed 20 people at Lydda airport.

June 4 Miss Angela Davis, a United States black militant, was acquitted after trial for murder, kidnapping and conspiracy. 5 Stockholm conference on the human environment opened. 6 430 killed in Wankie Colliery explosion in Rhodesia. 11 In Eltham rail crash four were killed and 115 injured. 12 Settlement of rail dispute. 16 A National Industrial Relations Court order against three London dockers was set aside by the Court of Appeal; 120 killed in tunnel rail crash near Soissons, France. Five burglars caught in Watergate building, Democratic Party's campaign H.Q. 18 BEA Trident crashed near Staines with loss of 118 lives. 20 Dr. Henry Kissinger in Peking for talks on Vietnam. 22 Bank rate rose from 5% to 6%. 23 Government decision to "float" the pound. 26 Mr. William Whitelaw accepted an IRA cease-fire proposal.

July 5 M. Pierre Messmer became French Prime Minister after resignation of M. Chaban-Delmas; 30 patients killed in a fire at Coldharbour Hospital, Sherborne. 9 Ceasefire in Northern Ireland ended and six people were shot dead in Belfast. 12 Younger Report on privacy published. 18 Mr. Robert Carr became Home Secretary; Tripartite talks on combating inflation began. 21 Eleven people were killed and 130 injured in a series of bomb explosions in Northern Ireland; Five dockers committed to prison for contempt by National Industrial Relations Court. 22–28 Industrial action in support of dockers prevented publication of national newspapers. 28 Start of national dock strike following rejection of Jones–Aldington proposals for the modernisation of the docks. 31 "Operation Motorman" removed all barricades in Northern Ireland.

August 4 President Amin ordered expulsion of 40,000 British Asians in Uganda. 10 Housing Finance Act, 1972, came into operation. 22 International Olympic Committee expelled Rhodesia from the Olympic Games. 23 Sir Charles Cunningham appointed chairman of the Uganda Resettlement Board. 26 XXth Olympic Games opened in Munich; Sir Francis Chichester died. 28 Prince William of Gloucester killed in air race crash.

September 1 Iceland extended fishing limits from 12 to 50 miles. 4 32 unions suspended by Trades Union Congress for registering under Industrial Relations Act. 5 Arab guerrillas held Israeli athletes hostage in Munich: the hostages, five guerrillas and a policeman were killed in gun battle at Fürstenfeldbruk airport. 8 Israeli aircraft struck at guerrilla bases in

A.D.

Syria and Lebanon. 17 First British Asian refugees arrived in England. 25 Darlington conference on the future of Northern Ireland opened. 26 Norway voted in a referendum against joining the European Economic Community. 29 Franks Committee report on secrecy published.

October 2 Denmark voted to join European Economic Community. 5 Peace agreement between Uganda and Tanzania signed; Congregational Church in England and Wales and Presbyterian Church of England combined to form the United Reformed Church. 10 Sir John Betjeman appointed Poet Laureate. 13 Bank rate abolished (now called minimum lending rate); 176 killed in air crash in Moscow. 17 The Queen began state visit to Yugoslavia. 19 European summit conference opened in Paris. 24 President Heinemann of West Germany began state visit to England. 27 Mr. Cyril Smith won Rochdale by-election for the Liberal Party. 29 Three Olympic Games terrorists released by West Germany following a hijacking by Palestine guerrillas near Beirut.

November 6 Government imposed immediate 90-day freeze on prices pay, rent and dividend increases. 7 President Nixon elected for a further term of office. 14 British Everest expedition turned back. 19 Herr Brandt re-elected in West German poll; Mr. Sean MacStiofan, Chief of Staff of the Provisional IRA, arrested in Dublin and began hunger strike. 20 Silver Wedding anniversary of the Queen and Duke of Edinburgh. 22 Government defeated on new immigration rules; United States made biggest raids ever in Vietnam war. 25 Mr. Sean MacStiofan sentenced to six months' imprisonment. 26 Armed men attempted to release him from hospital where he was continuing hunger strike. 30 £10 million loan to Uganda cancelled.

December 2 Mr. G. Whitlam became first Labour Prime Minister in Australia since 1946. 4 Army seized power in Honduras. 5 Committee on Liquor Licensing published report suggesting lowering of minimum drinking age and more flexibility in opening hours. 6 End of Angry Brigade trial: four found guilty. 7 Mr. Graham Tope won Sutton and Cheam by-election for the Liberals; Launch of *Apollo 17*; Ireland voted to remove special position of the Roman Catholic Church from the constitution. 12 President Thieu rejected Vietnam peace terms. 18 United States resumed bombing of North Vietnam. 21 Treaty signed between West and East Germany. 22 Survivors found ten weeks after an air crash in the Andes; Bank of England raised minimum lending rate to 9%. 23 Earthquake in Nicaragua devastated the capital Managua. 26 Mr. Harry S. Truman died. 27 Mr. Lester Pearson, formerly Prime Minister of Canada, died. 30 Tutankhamun exhibition in British Museum closed: 1,600,000 visitors.

1973

January 1 Britain, Ireland and Denmark became members of the European Economic Community. 9 Rhodesia closed border with Zambia because of terrorist attacks. 15 Australian government announced its intention to end legal and judicial ties with Britain. 22 Ex-President Lyndon B. Johnson died in Texas; Major volcanic eruption in Iceland began; 180 people killed in Kano air crash. 27 Vietnam cease-fire agreement signed. 31 Pan Am and T.W.A. cancelled delivery options on Concorde.

February 1 The Common Agricultural Policy of the EEC came into operation. 5 First Protestant loyalists detained without trial in Northern Ireland. 7 One-day strike of loyalists in Northern Ireland: widespread violence in the province. 8 Start of foreign exchange crisis. 12 First group of American prisoners released from North Vietnam; Dollar devalued by 10%. 14 Industrial action in the gas industry began. 20 Two Pakistani youths shot by police at India House. 21 Israeli fighters brought down a Libyan Boeing 727 with the loss of 104 lives. 23 Government granted heavy increases in food prices. 27 One-day strike of Civil servants. 28 One-day strike of ASLEF caused cancellation of all passenger train services.

March 1 Fine Gael and Labour Party coalition won Irish General Election: Mr. Liam Cosgrave became Prime Minister; Strike of hospital ancillary workers began; Mr. Dick Taverne won Lincoln by-election as a Democratic Labour candidate: Labour held seats at Dundee and Chester-le-Street; Guerrillas raided Saudi-Arabian embassy in Khartoum and seized five diplomats as hostages. 2 Guerrillas executed two of their hostages, both American diplomats; Further murders in Belfast brought total for the year to 27. 4 Guerrillas surrendered to Sudanese Forces. 5 68 people died in mid-air collision over Western France: many world airlines suspended flights over France until end of strike of French air traffic controllers; EEC foreign exchange markets closed as a result of currency crisis. 6 Budget Day in Britain: VAT to be levied at 10%, pensions to go up in October, unified tax rate to be introduced in April. 8 One killed and 238 injured in two bomb blasts in central London. 9 Result of Northern Ireland referendum showed 591,820 in favour of retaining links with Britain, and 6,463 for links with the Republic. 10 Governor of Bermuda and his aide-de-camp murdered. 11 Gaullists and their allies won an absolute majority of seats in the French General Election. 16 ASLEF suspended industrial action. 18 Icelandic patrol vessel fired live shots across bow of a British trawler. 19 Boy of 16 sentenced to 20 years for a mugging offence. 20 White Paper on future of Northern Ireland published: Northern Ireland Assembly to be elected by proportional representation. 21 Seven miners killed by floodwater at Lofthouse colliery. 23 Gas workers' ballot showed majority in favour of return to work. 26 Sir Noel Coward died. 29 Last American soldier left Vietnam; Irish defence forces seized large haul of arms aboard the *Claudia*.

April 1 VAT introduced in Britain; Phase 2 of counter-inflation policy came into operation. 3 National Union of Mineworkers voted against a national stoppage. 4 Building societies raised mortage rates to 9½%: Government announced a subsidy of £15m to prevent rate rising to 10%. 6 Mr. Peter Niesewand, correspondent of the *Guardian* and B.B.C., was gaoled in Rhodesia for an alleged breach of the Official Secrets Act (on appeal he was cleared of charges and released on 3 May). 8 Pablo Picasso died. 9 Arab guerrillas in Nicosia attacked the residence of the Israeli ambassador and an El Al airliner. 10 Israeli Forces raided guerrilla bases in Beirut and Southern Lebanon in reprisal; 104 killed in Vanguard crash near Basle. 12 Labour won control of the Greater London Council and the six other big conurbations. 13 Leaders of hospital ancillary workers recommended a return to work. 15 *Queen Elizabeth 2* sailed for Israel with unprecedented security precautions. 16 Sean MacStiofain released from gaol. 17 Letter bombs received by policemen in Londonderry. 26 Acting head of the FBI resigned over his part in the Watergate affair.

May 1 TUC day of protest against Government pay and prices policy. 7 President Nixon denied all knowledge of Watergate. 10 Elections held for 36 new metropolitan district councils; Seven miners killed in pit collapse at Seafield colliery, Kirkcaldy. 11 Charges dismissed in Pentagon papers case in Washington. 14 Skylab space station launched. 15 Zambian troops shoot two Canadian tourists at Victoria Falls. 17 Senate Select Committee hearings on Watergate opened. 18 Royal Navy frigates sent to protect British trawlers in disputed 50-mile limit off Iceland. 21 Government announced cuts in public spending of £500m. in 1974/5; Lord Lambton, Under-Secretary for Defence (RAF) resigned after admitting a relationship with a call-girl. 24

A.D.

Lord Jellicoe resigned too as Lord Privy Seal and Leader of the House of Lords; Labour held West Bromwich and Westhoughton in by-elections. 25 Three American astronauts docked with crippled Skylab. 31 Northern Ireland local elections; Mr. Erskine Childers succeeded Mr. de Valera as President of Ireland.

June 1 Greece declared a republic. 3 Russian Tupolev 144 crashed at Paris Air Show. 7 Skylab astronauts freed solar panels and saved mission. 9 Admiral Carrero Blanco became Prime Minister of Spain. 11 House of Lords ruled that 1971 Immigration Act was retrospective. 12 Car bomb killed six civilians in Coleraine. 15 Lord Melchett died. 18 Two men died in American midget submarine. 21 Treaty between East and West Germany came into force; Mr. Brezhnev and President Nixon signed agreement on arms limitation. 26 SDLP election agent in Belfast murdered. 27 Labour held Manchester Exchange in by-election. 29 New Northern Ireland Assembly elected.

July 4 Rioting at Long Kesh prison in N. Ireland. 10 Reports of Portuguese military atrocities in Mozambique published in *The Times*. 11 122 killed in Paris Boeing 707 crash. 16 Portuguese Prime Minister, Dr. Caetano, in Britain. 20 Japanese airliner hijacked near Amsterdam and blown up at Benghazi after release of passengers. 21 French exploded nuclear device at Mururoa atoll. 24 Nine died in hotel fire in Oban. 26 Liberals won by-elections at Ripon and Ely. 27 Bank of England minimum lending rate rose to 11½%. 28 Second team of astronauts docked with Skylab. 30 18 miners killed in pit cage accident at Markham colliery in Derbyshire. 31 First sitting of Ulster Assembly ended in chaos.

August 2 Fifty killed in Summerland fire at Douglas, Isle of Man; Commonwealth Prime Ministers' Conference opened in Ottawa. 3 Littlejohn brothers, gaoled in Ireland, claimed they were working for Ministry of Defence. 5 Three killed and 55 injured by Arab gunmen at Athens airport. 7 Vice-President Agnew under investigation concerning possible criminal offences. 9 Explosions and demonstrations marked second anniversary of internment in Northern Ireland. 14 Mortgage interest rate rose to 10%; U.S. ceased bombing Cambodia. 19 Mr. George Papadopoulos became first President of Greece. 20 Bomb attacks on London began with a bomb in Hampstead. 21 Six letter bombs and nine fire bombs found in London. 24 Two injured by letter bombs at Stock Exchange.

September 2 Men rescued from midget submarine after 76 hours; Professor J. R. R. Tolkien died; Death toll in Naples cholera outbreak rose to 11. 3 Dr. Henry Kissinger became U.S. Secretary of State. 7 Mr. Len Murray succeeded Mr. Vic Feather as TUC General Secretary. 10 Bombs in London stations injured 13 people. 11 Allende government overthrown in Chile: President Allende committed suicide when army took over; Lending restrictions imposed on banks; 12 Africans killed by police during riot in South African mine. 13 Air battle between Israeli and Syrian fighters over Mediterranean. 14 Mortgage rates rose to 11%. 15 Death of King Gustav of Sweden. 16 Mr. Tommy Herron, vice-chairman of UDA, found shot dead at Lisburn near Belfast. 17 Mr. Heath arrived in Irish Republic for talks on Ulster. 19 33,000 car workers were on strike or laid off. 20 Bomb exploded in Chelsea barracks. 25 Skylab astronauts returned after 59 days in space. 29 Arab terrorists released three Soviet Jews held hostage at Vienna after government agreed to close transit camp.

October 6 Start of Arab–Israeli war: Israel attacked by Egypt across Suez Canal and by Syria on Golan Heights. 8 Mr. Heath launched Phase 3 of counter-inflation policy; Britain's first commercial radio station opened. 10 Mr. Spiro Agnew resigned as Vice-President of U.S.A. 12 General Peron became President of Argentina and his wife Vice-President. 16 Israeli tanks crossed Suez Canal; Government placed embargo on arms sales to Middle East. 17 Arab oil producers announced cut in oil supplies until Israel withdrew from occupied territories. 22 UN proposal for ceasefire agreed by Israel, Egypt and Jordan (marred by subsequent clashes). 26 Firemen began series of unofficial strikes. 31 Kilbrandon Report on the Constitution published; Three Provisional IRA leaders freed from Mountjoy prison by hijacked helicopter.

November 1 Electrical Power Engineers' Association began ban on out-of-hours work (called off Dec. 28). 4 Sunday driving banned in Netherlands and Belgium. 8 End of "cod war" between Britain and Iceland: Britain to fish within 50-mile limit but with reduced annual catch; Conservatives held Hove and Edinburgh North in by-elections, Scottish Nationalists won Govan and Liberals Berwick. 12 Miners started overtime ban and ambulance drivers began selective strikes; Mr. Whitelaw outlawed two Protestant extremist groups. 13 Bank minimum lending rate increased to 13%. 14 Eight found guilty at Winchester in London car bombs trial; Six killed in explosion at ammunition factory in Birmingham; Wedding of Princess Anne and Captain Mark Phillips. 16 Three more astronauts docked with Skylab. 17 Riots in Athens resulted in 11 deaths. 22 New 11-man Executive announced for Northern Ireland. 25 Army coup in Greece deposed President Papadopoulos: new Cabinet formed under Mr. Androutsopoulos.

December 1 Death of David Ben-Gurion. 2 Cabinet reshuffle: Mr. Pym to Northern Ireland, Mr. Whitelaw to Employment Secretary, Mr. Macmillan to Paymaster General. 5 50 mile/h speed limit imposed to conserve fuel. 6 Mr. Gerald Ford became Vice-President of U.S.A. 9 Tripartite talks on Northern Ireland ended in sufficient agreement to set up Council of Ireland in 1974. 11 Treaty normalising relations between W. Germany and Czechoslovakia signed in Prague. Resignation of Nelson Rockefeller as Governor of New York. 12 Rail drivers' union ASLEF began ban on overtime. 13 Further series of measures to conserve fuel announced: three-day working week from 31 December; cuts in electricity consumption. 17 Emergency budget included cuts in consumer credit and reduction in public expenditure; 32 killed by Arab guerrillas at Rome airport. 18 Bombs in London injured 60 people. 19 Nine killed in train crash at Ealing. 20 Admiral Carrero Blanco, Prime Minister of Spain, assassinated in Madrid. 21 Geneva conference on Middle East opened. 22 105 people killed in Morocco plane crash. 23 Iran announced doubling of price of Persian Gulf oil. 26 Member of UDA beaten to death in Maze prison; Two more bombs in London. 27 Honorary West German consul in Belfast abducted. 28 Power engineers called off ban on out-of-hours working. Social Democratic Labour Party (SDLP) withdrew support for rent and rates strike in N. Ireland. 30 249 people killed in N. Ireland in 1973: 170 civilians, 66 Army or UDR personnel, 13 policemen of RUC. Since beginning of troubles 927 people killed (241 of whom were soldiers and men of the UDR).

1974

January 1 Direct rule by U.K. Govt. in N. Ireland ended: New Ulster Executive took office; Mrs. Golda Meir won narrow victory in Israeli General Election. 4 Bank minimum rate reduced to 12¾%. 5 Three charged with conspiracy relating to the possession of firearms at Heathrow. 6 Anti-terrorist security operation mounted at Heathrow; Further bomb attacks in London. 7 Mr. Brian Faulkner resigned as leader of the Unionist Party. 8 Lord Carrington became Secretary for Energy at head of new department. 9 Parliament recalled for two-day debate on energy crisis. 11 ASLEF policy of non-cooperation lifted, but ban on Sunday and

A.D.

rest day working continued. **15** One-day strike of ASLEF halted all rail services. **18** Israel and Egypt signed agreement on separation of forces. **19** Naval battle between China and S. Vietnam led to occupation of Paracel Is. by China. **22** Loyalists expelled from N. Ireland Assembly after angry scenes. **24** Publication of Pay Board's Report on Relativities (Cmnd. 5535); Commonwealth Games opened in Christchurch. **27** Death of General Grivas, leader of Greek Cypriot movement for *enosis* (Union with Greece). **30** Non-stop air service between Peking and Moscow introduced.

February 4 12 killed in army coach explosion on M62 in Yorkshire; Miner's strike ballot showed 81% in favour of strike action. **7** Prime Minister called for General Election on 28 February. Island of Grenada achieved independence. **8** Skylab astronauts returned after record 84 days in space. **10** Miners' strike began. **11** ASLEF suspended industrial action. **12** Bomb attack on National Defence College. **13** Alexander Solzhenitsyn deported to the West; Washington energy conference agreed to set up co-ordinating body to deal with energy crisis. **15** Search for trawler *Gaul* called off. **24** £2 million Vermeer painting stolen from Kenwood House. **27** Mutiny by armed forces in Ethiopia (widespread unrest caused by famine). **28** Election in Britain resulted in no clear majority.

March 3 Turkish Airlines DC10 crashed with loss of 345 lives. **4** Mr. Edward Heath resigned and a minority Labour Government took office. **8** Inauguration of third Paris airport—the Charles de Gaulle. **9** Britain returned to five-day week. **11** Miners returned to work; Kenneth Littlejohn escaped from Mountjoy Prison, Dublin; Archbishop of Canterbury announced his retirement on 15 November; Senator Billy Fox shot dead in County Monaghan. **20** Gunmen injured four in attempt to kidnap Princess Anne; Two soldiers accidentally shot by RUC; Government announced £21 million subsidy on bread. **22** Sir Alec Douglas-Home announced his retirement from politics. **26** Budget Day in Britain: increased pensions, extra food subsidies, higher income tax rates, indirect taxes on sweets, crisps, soft drinks, petrol, diesel fuel; gift tax to be introduced later in year, green paper on an annual wealth tax to be published. **29** Admission charges to museums and galleries in U.K. (in operation since 2 Jan.) abolished.

April 1 Mr. Callaghan (Foreign Secretary) at his first EEC meeting in Luxembourg. **2** Death of M. Pompidou. **3** Channel Tunnel Bill to be reintroduced: reassessment of project. **5** Death of Richard Crossman. **7** Colonel Gaddafi of Libya relieved of most of his state duties. **10** Resignation of Mrs. Golda Meir and her Cabinet after 5 years as Prime Minister. **11** Arab suicide squad in massacre attack on Israeli border community. **14** Heaviest fighting on Golan Heights and Mount Hermon since ceasefire in Oct. 1973. **15** President of Niger (since independence 1960) removed by Army coup. **18** Mr. Wilson visited N. Ireland. **20** Death of Ayub Khan. **23** Pan-Am air crash in Bali: 107 killed. **23** Chair of peace to be created at London University to begin operating Sept. 1976. **24** General election in S. Africa: Nationalist Party returned for seventh successive time; Progressive Party won 6 seats. **25** Army uprising in Portugal: authoritarian régime in power since 1926 overthrown.

May 2 London borough elections: Labour control 19, Conservative control 12, no overall control 1. **6** Resignation of Herr Brandt on discovery of chancellery aide spying for E. Germany; Portuguese junta offered ceasefire to African guerrillas. **8** Nurses began series of strikes in protest against low pay; In new Scottish regional and district councils, Labour won control of all major cities except Edinburgh where control shared with Liberals. **10** Defeat of former world chess champion, Boris Spassky, by Anatoly Karpov. **12** In referendum Italy voted to keep 3-year-old law legalising divorce (59·1% in favour, 40·9% against). **14** Dr. Donald Coggan, Archbishop of York, to succeed Dr. Ramsey as Archbishop of Canterbury in Nov; Dr. David Pitt (b. in Grenada) became first black GLC chairman; In N. Ireland Assembly the executive won vote in favour of Sunningdale agreement by 44 votes to 28. **15** General Spinola became President of Portugal; In Israeli village of Ma'alot schoolchildren killed when Israeli troops stormed school where children held hostage by Arab terrorists. **16** Herr Schmidt became Chancellor of West Germany. **16–17** Israeli reprisal air raids on Palestinian refugee camp in Lebanon. **17** Car bombs in Dublin and Monaghan killed 28 people and injured over 100. **19** State of emergency declared in N. Ireland because of Protestant general strike in protest against Sunningdale agreement; victory for M. Giscard d'Estaing in French general election: 13,214,648 votes (50·7%) to 12, 842, 833 (40·3%) for M. Mitterand; bomb exploded in car park at Heathrow airport. **22** Plan to establish a Council of Ireland postponed. **23** Labour held Newham South in by-election; Entry into service of European Airbus. **24** Death of Duke Ellington, jazz musician. **27** Inauguration of M. Giscard d'Estaing as President of France; M. Jacques Chirac Prime Minister; Army in N.I. took over power stations. **28** Collapse of N.I. executive. **29** Ulster Workers' Council called off strike; Assembly suspended: direct rule from Westminster resumed; Syria and Israel agreed to disengage forces on Golan Heights following 32-day mission of Dr. Kissinger.

June 1 Biggest explosion in Britain since war at Flixborough Nypro chemical works: 29 dead. **3** Mr. Callaghan's second speech at Luxembourg on renegotiation of terms of British membership of EEC; Mr. Rabin became Prime Minister of Israel; Michael Gaughan, Irish hunger striker, died at Parkhurst. **6** Exchange of prisoners between Israel and Syria. **7** Price sisters ended their fast after 206 days; Valery and Galina Panov granted exit visas from Soviet Union. **10** Death of Duke of Gloucester. **15** Rival groups of left and right clashed in Red Lion Square, London: a university student died. **16** France exploded nuclear device in Pacific; Full diplomatic relations to be restored (after 7 years of hostility) between U.S. and Syria. **17** Bomb exploded beside Westminster Hall, injuring 11 people. **27** Foreign husbands and fiancés of British women to be allowed to live in Britain; Press and public to be excluded from wide range of matrimonial cases from 1 Oct. **27–3 July** Brezhnev-Nixon Moscow summit meeting. **30** Martin Luther King's mother assassinated.

July 1 Death of General Peron of Argentina, aged 78. **3** Launch of Soyuz-14 which docked (5 July) with space station Salyut-3 (manned by Popovich and Artyukhin). **4** Swahili adopted as official language in Kenya in place of English. **9** Canadian general election gave Trudeau overall majority of 18. **10** Government announced choice of British-designed nuclear reactor for third stage of programme in 1980s. **12** Repeal of 1971 Industrial Relations Act. **13** Final Report of Ervin Senate Watergate Committee published. **14** Bombs in Birmingham and Manchester. **15** Coup d'état in Cyprus by National Guard officers: President Makarios overthrown and replaced by Nicos Sampson. **17** Bomb exploded with no warning in Tower of London: one killed, 41 injured. **18** Maplin airport project cancelled; Abolition of Pay Board and end of statutory incomes policy. **20** Turkish invasion of Cyprus. **22** Ceasefire in Cyprus declared; Mini-Budget cut VAT to 8%, doubled regional employment premium, extended rate relief and food subsidies and partially relaxed dividend controls. **23** Junta in Greece collapsed: Mr. Karamanlis returned to power; Glafkos Clerides interim-acting President of Cyprus. **24** Supreme Court ordered surrender of 64 White House tape recordings subpoenaed by Mr. Leon Jaworski, the Special Watergate prosecutor. **25** International Court of Justice in The Hague ruled that Britain not bound by Iceland's unilateral decision in 1972 to extend its rights from 12 to 50 miles. **26** Bomb exploded at Heathrow

A.D.
European terminal car park; French made official language of province of Quebec. 27–30 Three articles of impeachment adopted by Judiciary Committee of the House of Representatives against President Nixon. 30 British, Greek and Turkish foreign ministers signed a peace agreement in Geneva. 31 Abolition of the National Industrial Relations Court (NIRC); Enactment of: 1974 Trade Union and Labour Relations Bill; 1974 Rent Bill (which abolished distinction between furnished and unfurnished accommodation); 1974 Health and Safety at Work Bill; 1974 Housing Bill (which provided *inter alia* for increased assistance to voluntary housing movement and for changed criteria for improvement grants).

August 3 Portugal to grant independence to her 3 African colonies: Angola, Mozambique, Guinea-Bissau. 5 President Nixon admitted he had withheld information on Watergate. 8 President Nixon resigned; Chancellor outlined proposals for new wealth tax and capital transfer tax; BBC cameraman killed by mines in Cyprus. 9 Mr Gerald Ford sworn in as 38th President of USA; Extension of Italy's sea limits from 6 to 12 miles. 11 Half Bangladesh under water following monsoon floods: followed by famine and cholera epidemic. 12 President Ford addressed Congress: first priority to control inflation. 14 Greek Prime Minister announced withdrawal of Greek armed forces from NATO. Failure of peace talks on Cyprus: Turks renewed offensive and took control of most of north-east third of island. 15 Collapse of Court Line left many holidaymakers stranded; White Paper published on Government plans for greater state intervention in industry. 16 Fresh ceasefire in Cyprus; Cyclone in north-east India added to havoc caused by floods. 18 19 leading Provisionals broke out of Portlaoise top security prison. Egyptian girl of 13 swam English Channel, the youngest to do so. 19 U.S. Ambassador shot dead in Nicosia. 20 President Ford named Mr. Nelson Rockefeller as Vice-President; Mr. F. A. Ahmed elected President of the Indian Union. 24 Youth killed at football match. 26 Death of Charles Lindbergh; Guinea-Bissau became independent, ending 4 centuries of Portuguese rule. 29 Police broke up pop festival in Windsor Great Park. 30 Explosion of time-bomb in Tokio: 8 killed, 300 injured. 31 Express overturned at speed at Zagreb station: 150 dead.

September 1 U.S. Lockheed SR-71 crossed from New York to London in 1 h 55 m (3,490 miles). 2 New Conciliation and Arbitration Service (CAS) started work. 3 Two crew drowned when Mr. Heath's *Morning Cloud* was hit in Channel by huge waves; Enoch Powell adopted as Unionist candidate for South Down. 4 Sikkim's status changed from Indian protectorate to associated state; Opening of Bulgaria's first nuclear power station (at Kozlodui). 6 Wallace Rowling became Prime Minister of New Zealand following death of Norman Kirk. 8 President Ford granted full pardon to Richard Nixon. 12 Emperor Haile Selassie deposed by military command. 13 Bishop Blanch, Bishop of Liverpool, appointed Archbishop of York. 15 Dominant role for Frelimo in caretaker government in Mozambique (independence June 1975). 16 Judge and magistrate assassinated in N.I. 17 Nurses' pay rises of up to 30% approved. 19 Hurricane Fifi struck Honduras: 8,000 dead; 600,000 homeless. 24 Portugal and India re-established diplomatic relations with Portugal recognising Indian sovereignty over Portuguese territories seized in 1961; Devaluation of currencies of Australia (12%) and New Zealand (9%). 30 General Spínola resigned as President of Portuguese Republic; succeeded by General Francisco da Costa Gomes.

October 5 Death of Miguel Enriques, Chilean revolutionary, shot in battle with police; Two bombs in Guildford public houses killed five people and injured 70; Salazar Bridge over R. Tagus in Lisbon renamed April 25 Bridge. 10 General Election in Britain: Labour returned with overall majority of 3. 15 Rioting in the Maze prison: fire destroyed many of the buildings; British space satellite UK5 launched off coast of Kenya. 16 Governor and three women prison officers held hostage in Armagh gaols House of Lords ruled that working men's club; can operate colour bar. 18 Unit in Whitehall set up to prepare for devolution of power to Scotland and Wales. 22 Bomb exploded in Brooks's Club, St. James's Street. 23 Mr. Vorster announced that South Africa wished to develop peaceful relations and co-operation with Black African states. 24 Death of David Oistrakh, Russian violinist and conductor. 26 Mr. Vorster's initiative welcomed by Pres. Kaunda of Zambia. 26–29 Rabat summit meeting of Arab heads of state: PLO recognised as representative of Palestinians. 30 Muhammad Ali regained world heavyweight boxing title by knocking out George Foreman at Kinshasa. 31 Hostages held for six days at Scheveningen gaol freed by Dutch commandos. After five years of famine and drought torrential rains in Sahel region (Chad, Mali, Niger, Upper Volta), Aug.–Oct.

November 2–3 Summit meeting between President Ford and Mr. Brezhnev at Vladivostok. 3 Strong reaction by hospital consultants to proposed phasing out of pay beds in National Health hospitals. 4 Judith Ward given 12 life sentences for causing M62 bomb blast deaths. 5 World Food Conference opened in Rome; President Amin ordered Britain to reduce embassy staff to five. 7 Two killed in bomb attack on Woolwich pubs. 8 After 300 years in Central London Covent Garden market moved to new site at Nine Elms. 8 Ronald Milhench gaoled for forging Mr. Harold Wilson's signature in land deals affair. 12 Budget day: increase in pensions; 25% VAT on petrol; £1,500 million relief to industry; UN General Assembly voted to exclude South Africa from meetings this session; Wolfson College, Oxford, opened by Mr. Harold Macmillan. 13 Yassir Arafat of the Palestine Liberation Organisation addressed UN General Assembly. 14 IRA bombs in Midlands: member of IRA James McDaid killed while placing bomb. 15 Dr. Donald Coggan succeeded Dr. Michael Ramsey as Archbishop of Canterbury. 17 Greece held first general elections since 1967: victory for Mr. Constantine Karamanlis; Mr. Erskine Childers, President of the Irish Republic, died. 20 Jumbo jet crashed on take-off from Nairobi killing 59 people. 21 21 killed and 120 injured in bomb blasts in two Birmingham bars; British Airways VC10 hijacked in Persian Gulf; Mr. John Stonehouse MP disappeared after going for a swim at Miami Beach. 24 Six charged with Birmingham bomb murders; Ethiopian military government announced execution of 60 former ministers. 25 Death of U Thant. 26 Plan for high-speed rail link between Folkestone and London abandoned for economy reasons. 27 Two bombs exploded in Chelsea. 29 Anti-Terrorism Bill proscribing the IRA and giving police wider powers received Royal Assent; Mr. Ceabhall O Dalaigh appointed to succeed the late Mr. Erskine Childers as President of the Irish Republic.

December 1 Two Irishmen charged with Guildford pub bomb outrage; Trans World Boeing 727 crashed near Washington killing 93. 2 Start of bakers' strike. 3 Defence cuts announced: £4,700 million over next 10 years. 5 Sir Don Ryder, Chief Executive of Reed International appointed Industrial Adviser to the Government; Appeal for £3·5 million to save fabric of Canterbury Cathedral; 90 people killed in Tehran when roof of Mehrabad airport terminal collapsed. 6 Government announced aid to British Leyland. 7 Archbishop Makarios returned to Cyprus; Talks in Lusaka on constitutional settlement for Rhodesia. 8 Greeks voted against return of the monarchy and for a republic. 9 Energy saving programme announced: speed restrictions and reduced heating levels; Mr. Tanaka resigned as Prime Minister of Japan. 11 Mr. Ian Smith announced cease-fire with nationalist guerrillas and release of political prisoners in Rhodesia; House of Commons voted against restoration of capital

A.D.

punishment for terrorism. 15 18 Residents died in fire at old people's home outside Nottingham. 18–22 New wave of bombs in London: outside Selfridges; at Harrods; and at the home of Mr. Edward Heath. 19 Petrol prices went up by 10p a gallon; Compensation to relatives of those killed on "Bloody Sunday" (1972) announced. 22 Ceasefire ordered by IRA over Christmas. 24 Mr. John Stonehouse found in Australia. 25 Devastation of Darwin, Australia, by cyclone Tracy. 27 41 miners died in explosion in Liévin, France. 28 Many killed in Pakistan earthquake; State of emergency declared in Bangladesh. 31 Resumption of diplomatic relations between Portugal and India: Indian sovereignty recognised over former Portuguese territories of Goa, Daman, Diu, Dadra and Nagar Haveli; Completion of Liuchiahsia hydroelectric station, highest and largest in China, supplying electrical power to Kansu, Shensi and Chinghai.

1975

January 1 Watergate defendants Mitchell, Haldeman, Ehrlichman and Mardian found guilty of conspiracy and of obstruction of justice. 2 IRA announced 14-day extension of ceasefire; Mr. Mishra, Indian cabinet minister, and two others killed by bomb attack at Samastipur in Bihar. 6 London Stock market index at lowest point of 146. 7 EEC finance ministers agreed on London scheme to recycle 12 billion petro-dollars through IMF; Fall of provincial capital Phuoc Binh to N. Vietnamese forces. 9 Mr. Elliot Richardson appointed Ambassador to UK. 13 In nationwide broadcast Pres. Ford proposed to reduce unemployment by increased spending. 13–17 China's Fourth National People's Congress: new state constitution adopted: post of Chairman (President) abolished; Mao Tse-tung named as Head of Forces. 20 Evacuation of some 9,000 Turkish Cypriot refugees from British base at Akrotiri. 23 Unemployment in UK: 770,000; Bomb attack on Europa hotel in Belfast; Referendum to be held on British Common Market membership before end of June; First heavy snow in Britain this winter (in Scotland). 24 Minimum lending rate reduced to 11%; Dr. Coggan enthroned 101st Archbishop of Canterbury; Pope represented at ceremony. 25 End of democracy in Bangladesh: Shaikh Mujibur Rahman became President of one-party state. 27 24 hurt in terrorist bomb attacks in Manchester and London; President Sadat in Paris on arms deal; Government to introduce low-start mortgages for first-time home buyers; US Senate to set up Select Committee to investigate activities of CIA, FBI and other spying organisations; Khmer Rouge major offensive in Cambodia. 29 Government defeat on the earnings rule (tax-free earning allowance for old people); 24-hour strike by crews of London buses in tribute to their workmate who died after attack on him. 30 Wilson–Ford meeting in White House. 31 Death of Duke of Norfolk.

February 1 Death of Um Kalthoum, Egypt's popular singer. 4 Mr. Heath withdrew as leader of the Conservative Party after defeat by Mrs. Thatcher in first ballot for Tory leadership. 6 The Queen abandoned plan to spend £200,000 on modernising Sandringham; Lady Plowden appointed chairman of IBA; Seventh day of fighting in northern Ethiopia between government soldiers and secessionist rebels. 7 Minimum lending rate reduced to 10¾%; Unemployment in US up to 8.2%, highest since 1941. 11 Mrs. Thatcher elected leader of the Conservative Party; Assassination of President of Malagasy. 12 Queen's Civil List to be increased by £420,000 to £1.4 million. 13 Wilson–Brezhnev summit meeting in Moscow began; Declaration by Turkish Cypriots of separate state in Cyprus. 14 Sir Julian Huxley and P. G. Wodehouse died; Minimum lending rate reduced to 10½%. 17 Dr. Kissinger met Shah of Iran in Zurich; Reginald Maudling appointed Shadow Foreign Secretary. 18 Industry Bill given Second Reading (313 votes to 299); Big nuclear power programme planned for Sweden. 20 Unemployment in UK: 790,892. 23 Khmer Rouge in control of both sides of Mekong River. 25 Death of Nikolai Bulgarin, former Russian Prime Minister. 26 Government White Paper on organisation of Britain's EEC referendum published: result to be judged by simple majority. 28 Train at speed crashed into blind tunnel at Moorgate station, London Underground: 41 dead. Mildest winter in Britain since 1869.

March 2 The Queen arrived back in England after Caribbean tour. 4 Charles Chaplin knighted by the Queen. 5 Seaborne attack by Arab guerrillas on Tel-Aviv: 13 died including 7 terrorists; Phnom Penh airport under artillery attack from Khmer Rouge. 6 End of OPEC meeting in Algiers: oil prices to be linked to inflation: agreement between Iran and Iraq. 7 Minimum lending rate reduced to 10¼%. 10 South Africa ordered police units in Rhodesia to withdraw from anti-guerrilla activities; Workers' motorcycle cooperative at Meriden began work. 11 Agreement reached at EEC summit meeting at Dublin on renegotiation terms for Britain; Unsuccessful counter-coup in Portugal: General Spinola fled first to Spain, then to Brazil. 13 Portugal's new Supreme Revolutionary Council headed by President Gomes took power. 17 Retreat of S. Vietnamese forces from Central Highlands after fall of Ban Me Thuot: flight of refugees from northern provinces began. 18 Mr. Wilson told Parliament of Cabinet's majority decision to recommend acceptance of renegotiation terms of Common Market membership (Cabinet vote 16–7 in favour); Herbert Chitepo, Rhodesian nationalist leader in exile (ZANU) assassinated in Lusaka; Lady Donaldson became first woman to be admitted to the Court of Aldermen of the City of London. 19 Dolours and Marion Price transferred to Armagh jail in Ulster; Eight Irishmen sentenced to 20 years' imprisonment for bomb plot offences in London and Home Counties. 20 Unemployment in UK: 802,630. 21 Minimum lending rate reduced to 10%. 22 Collapse of Kurdish uprisings in northern Iraq after Iranian withdrawal of support. 23 N. Vietnamese closed coast road between Hué and Da Nang; Breakdown of Dr. Kissinger's Middle East talks by failure to reach a new Egyptian–Israel accord. 25 Assassination of King Faisal of Saudi Arabia. 26 Evacuation of Hué by S. Vietnamese forces: Biological Weapons Convention came into force. 27 Death of Sir Arthur Bliss. 30 Da Nang abandoned by S. Vietnamese forces after panic and confusion; Suez Canal to be reopened 5 June 1975 but not yet to Israeli shipping. 31 Qui Nhon captured by N. Vietnamese.

April 1 Departure of Marshal Lon Nol from besieged capital Phnom Penh; Nha Trang evacuated by S. Vietnamese forces. 3 Death of Tung Pi-su, founder member of Chinese Communist Party; Britain's inshore fishermen protesting against cheap imports called off blockade of 48 ports. 5 Death of Chiang Kai-shek, aged 87. 9 Motion to approve EEC renegotiation White Paper carried by majority of 226 votes. 12 Death of Josephine Baker, aged 69. 16 Mr. Alexander Shelepin dropped from Soviet Politburo. 17 Phnom Penh government surrendered to Khmer Rouge: end of 5 years of civil war in Cambodia. 18 Death of Dr. Sarvepalli Radhakrishnan, second President of India, aged 86; minimum lending rate reduced to 9¾%. 19 Fall of Phan Thiet to N. Vietnamese. 21 President Thieu resigned as N. Vietnamese forces encircled Saigon. 21–25 First European Nuclear Energy Conference held in Paris (47 countries represented). 23 Massive airlift of refugees from Vietnam to USA. 24 Unemployment in UK 939,767 (inc. students and school-leavers); Government statement to Commons on British Leyland: Government to invest £1400 million over 8 years. 25 Elections in Portugal the first for 50 years: Socialist Party (PSP) 38% of votes, the largest single party; 29 Commonwealth Conference opened in Jamaica; Evacuation of remaining Americans in Saigon. 30 End of Vietnamese war, the longest conflict of the 20th century, when Saigon surrendered to Communist forces.

May 2 Minimum lending rate raised to 10%. 5 *Scottish Daily News* published, the first workers' cooperative national newspaper. 7 Communication links between Saigon and outside world reopened. 12 US merchant vessel *Mayaguez* forced by Cambodian forces to anchor in Gulf of Thailand; Laos fell to Communists. 13 Britain recognised Provisional Revolutionary Government in S. Vietnam; Sterling sank to all-time low of 25·2% below Dec. 1971 levels; French franc to rejoin EEC's currency "snake" (arrangement for narrowing margin of fluctuation between participating currencies) after 16 months of floating by itself. 14 President Ford authorised air attacks on Cambodian patrol boats. 15 *Mayaguez* and crew rescued by US marines. 16 Entry into force of new local government structure in Scotland: 9 regional, 13 district and 3 island councils. 18 Filbert Bayi of Tanzania broke J. Ryun's 8-year-old world mile record in Jamaica: 3 min 51 s. 21 Death of Barbara Hepworth, English sculptor. 29 Dr. Gustav Husak elected President of Czechoslovakia. 30 European Space Agency (ESA) set up (supersedes ELDO). 30–31 Coldest May night in Britain since records began.

June 1 Police killed 13 Africans in Salisbury, Rhodesia. 2 Israeli decision to pull back further from Suez Canal; Snow fell in London for first time (in June) since reliable records began. 5 UK voted "Yes" by 2 to 1 majority in EEC referendum:

Yes	17,378,581	(67·2%)
No	8,470,073	(32·8%)
Turnout:	64·5%	
Electorate:	40,086,677	

5 Reopening of Suez Canal to international shipping after 8 years of closure. 9 First live radio broadcast of House of Commons sitting. 13 Second Reading of Hare Coursing Bill to make competitive matches illegal. 12 Mrs. Gandhi convicted of illegally using Government officials in her campaign for Parliament in 1971. 15 Significant left-wing surge in Italian regional elections: Rome, Naples, Turin, Venice went Communist. 16 UK ended Simonstown Defence Agreement with S. Africa. 19 UK unemployment 869,822 (3·7% (including students and school-leavers)—the highest June figure since records began in 1948). 24 Plane crash at New York Kennedy airport: 110 killed. 26 State of emergency declared by Mrs. Gandhi: 676 people arrested including 100 top political figures; British Government announced ending of Beira patrol now that Mozambique can itself impose sanctions against Smith regime. 30 £ fell to 29% of its Jan. 1971 value; Zambian economy put under state control: freehold land titles abolished. Sunniest June in London since records began.

July 1 Mr. S. S. Ramphal (Guyana's Minister of Justice) succeeded Mr Arnold Smith (appointed 1965) as Commonwealth Secretary-General. 3 Watergate grand jury (in existence for 3 years) dissolved. 4 New Kurdish nationalist party formed in Iraq. 5 Cape Verde Islands achieved independence from Portugal. 6 Record wheat yield in China; Unilateral Declaration of Independence from France declared by Comoro Islands. 7 British Labour Party MPs attended European Parliament at Strasbourg. 8 Formal declaration by President Ford that he would be presidential candidate in 1976; School leaving date in England and Wales to be changed from end of summer term to Friday before Spring bank holiday. 11 Mr. Healey's statement of anti-inflation policy: £6 a week limit on pay increases till 1 Aug. 1976; Withdrawal of Socialist Party from Portuguese government; Independence of Portuguese São Tomé and Principe. 15 Launch of *Apollo-Soyuz* spacecraft for first international link-up; Fifth day of fighting between rival nationalist forces in Angola; British signed treaty of friendly relations with Poland; First-class letter post (7p) fell 26·2% (March 23–June 28) and second-class (5½p) rose by 11·4% compared with same period 1974. 16 £85,000 paid for Turner's "The Dark Rigi" at Sotheby's. 17 First link up of US astronauts and Soyuz cosmonauts in space when *Apollo* and *Soyuz* spacecraft successfully docked; 4 British soldiers in explosion in border area of N. Ireland—second such incident since cease-fire. Mineworkers' national executive committee gave support (14 to 10) to Government's anti-inflation policy; Fall of Portuguese coalition government; Portugal to receive no aid from EEC until democracy restored. 23 Approval of Mrs. Gandhi's emergency powers passed by both Houses of Parliament. 24 Plan to release all detainees in N. Ireland by Xmas. 25 Minimum lending rate raised 1% to 11%. 26 *Salyut 4* space station landed after record time (63 days) in space; Turkish decision to close US air bases in protest against arms embargo. 28 Organisation of African Unity (OAU) under chairmanship of Pres. Amin met in Kampala (boycotted by Tanzania, Zambia, Mozambique and Botswana because of Uganda killings); Britain's coal and steel industries to receive £74 million from Europe in loans and grants. 29 Military coup in Nigeria deposed Gen. Gowon while he was in Kampala: new head of state Brigadier Mustaia Mohammed; Lord Kearton head of new state oil combine (British National Oil Corporation); Expansion of British Rail's main line electrification programme under threat because of economic crisis. 30 Helsinki 35-nation summit conference on European security and cooperation; Gen. Gowon accepted defeat and pledged loyalty to new Government. 31 Britain recognised new Nigerian Government; Cabinda declared itself independent.

August 7 Hottest August day in London since records began in 1940 (32·3°C); Government plans to abolish tied cottages on farms and give 70,000 farmworkers protection of Rent Acts against eviction; Indian constitution amended to give Mrs. Gandhi fresh powers. 8 Pres. Costa Gomez swore in new Government in Portugal led by Prime Minister Gen. Goncalves; Fierce fighting between two independence groups in Angola; Death of Shostakovich, aged 68. 10 Weekend violence in N. Ireland. 12 John Walker of New Zealand set world record for mile at 3 min 49.4 s. 15 Assassination of Muzibur Rahman of Bangladesh. 20 Mr. Wilson made television broadcast on inflation. 22 Opening of South Africa's Orange-Fish tunnel (50 miles long). 26 Collapse of constitutional talks between Rhodesian Government and African National Council (held at Victoria Falls). 26–28 Meeting of Commonwealth Finance Ministers in Georgetown (Guyana). 27 Death of Haile Selassie, former Emperor of Ethiopia. 27–28 Bombs at Caterham and London. 28 Miners voted for Government/TUC counter-inflation measures (pay increase limit of £6 a week). 29 Death of De Valera.

September 3 At Blackpool TUC Congress backed Government's £6 flat-rate pay policy. 4 Disengagement agreement negotiated by Dr. Kissinger signed between Egypt and Israel at Geneva: Israel to evacuate 2590 sq. miles of occupied Sinai, inc. Abu Rudeis and Ras Sudar oilfields and strategic Mitla and Giddi passes; Egypt committed to 3½ years without a war; US undertook to post 200 civilian technicians to man early-warning station for both sides. 5 Gen. Goncalves, Portugal's pro-Communist former Prime Minister, abandoned attempt to become commander-in-chief of armed forces; Two people killed and 62 injured in bomb explosion in London's West End Hilton Hotel; Covent Garden to house proposed Theatre Museum. 6 Severe earthquake (Anatolian fault) in E. Turkey: over 2000 killed. 9 Return after 5½ years of exile of Prince Sihanouk to Cambodia as titular head of state. 11 Soviet Union proposed international treaty banning all nuclear weapons tests. 14 Rembrandt's *The Nightwatch* severely slashed but not irreparably; The Pope canonised America's first native-born saint—Elizabeth Bayley Seton (1774–1821). **16** Independence of Papua New Guinea as 35th member of the Commonwealth. **24** Government announced £175m package of measures to check unemployment, including payment of £5 a head to companies recruiting young people. Dougal Haston and Doug Scott climbed Everest by south-west face, the first ever successful assault by this route. **27** Execution of five political activists in Spain: 12 countries recalled their ambassadors in protest. **28** Gunmen took seven Italians as hostages in the Spaghetti House restaurant in London; 10 Territorials drowned during exercise on the Trent, near Littleborough, Lincs.

October 1 Three policemen shot dead in Madrid; Attorney General refused injuction by High Court to prevent publication of Crossman diaries. **2** Widespread sectarian violence in N. Ireland resulted in 11 deaths: Ulster Volunteer Force claimed responsibility. **3** End of the Spaghetti House siege: hostages released unharmed and captors surrendered; Dr. Herrema a Dutch industrialist, kidnapped in Limerick, held captive at Monasterevin, near Dublin; minimum lending rate rose 1% to 12%. **6** EEC broke off trade negotiations with Spain; In Argentina's guerrilla war, 30 people killed when troops fought guerrillas attacking army base and airport. **9** 1975 Nobel peace prize awarded to Dr. Andrei Sakharov; bomb explosion at Green Park London killed one man. **15** Iceland unilaterally extended its fishing rights from 50 to 200 miles; Archbishop of Canterbury launched campaign urging British people to rise to new sense of moral purpose. **17** "Cod war" talks between Britain and Iceland broke down. **20** Appointment of a Royal Commission to investigate the Health Service. **21** In Britain, unemployment rose to over one million for first time since the war; Inauguration at Teesside of first pipeline from Norwegian Ekofisk field. **22** Life sentences passed on three IRA men and an English girl found guilty of murder in explosions in public houses in Guildford and Woolwich in 1974; Agreement on economic cooperation signed by Britain and Saudi Arabia. **23** Ceremony marking completion of track-laying of Tanzam railway (in full operation 1976) with tribute by Pres. Kaunda to Chinese assistance; Bomb placed under car of Mr. Hugh Fraser MP in London killed Professor Fairley, leading cancer expert; Nobel prize for literature awarded to Signor E. Montale. **25** Soviet *Venus 10* soft-landed on Venus (*Venus 9* landed on 22nd); **26** In Beirut, clashes between right-wing Christian Phalangists and left-wing Muslims developed into full-scale battles. **27** Alfred Herbert, the machine tool group, taken over by the Government.

November 3 Major changes at top level in American government: dismissal of Dr. J. Schlesinger (Defence) and Mr. W. Colby (Director CIA); At Dyce, Aberdeenshire, the Queen formally inaugurated the flow of North Sea oil from the BP Forties field. **4** Five men killed in explosion at British Steel Corporation's plant at Scunthorpe. **5** Chequers Meeting: Government, TUC, CBI and NEDC met to discuss strategy for regeneration of British industry; Reinforcement of Belize garrison in face of Guatemalan militancy. **6** Visit of President Sadat to England. **7** Death of Cardinal Heenan; Mrs. Gandhi won her appeal in Supreme Court against corrupt electoral practice. Dr. Herrema released by kidnappers; IMF approached for £975 loan by Britain; *Scottish Daily News* closed down. **10** Independence of Angola after 500 years of Portuguese rule; UN General Assembly attacked Zionism as "a form of racism": bitter Israeli reaction to accusation. **11** Australia's Labour Government, led by Gough Whitlam, dismissed by the Governor-General, Sir John Kerr: Opposition leader, Malcolm Fraser, appointed acting Prime Minister and general election called for 13 December; Number of civilians killed in N. Ireland since 1969 reached 1000. **12** One man killed and 15 injured when bomb exploded at Scott's Restaurant in Mount Street, London; HMS *Achilles* and *Olympia Alliance* (a Liberian oil tanker) collided in thick fog in English Channel; Merlyn Rees, Secretary of State for N. Ireland, closed all Government's incident centres (set up to monitor the provisional IRA's ceasefire). **13** WHO announced eradication of smallpox in Asia. **14** Spain agreed to give up sovereignty of the Spanish Sahara by end of February 1976; minimum lending rate reduced from 12% to 11¾%. **15** Leaders from Britain, United States, France, West Germany, Japan and Italy met at Rambouillet, near Paris, for 3-day summit conference on economic matters; Incidents with Iceland gunboats: arrival in Iceland of British minister. **18** Two people killed and 20 injured when bomb thrown into Waltons Restaurant in Chelsea. President Nyerere on state visit to England: first official visit since he led Tanzania to independence in 1961. **19** Queen's Speech promised Bills to devolve some powers to new assemblies in Scotland and Wales, to nationalise the aircraft and shipbuilding industries, to remove the remaining "unsatisfactory features" of the 1971 Industrial Relations Act, to safeguard dockers' employment, to abolish agricultural tied cottages, to introduce a development land tax, to phase out private practice from National Health Service hospitals and to abolish selection in secondary education. **20** Death of General Franco, aged 82; Ronald Reagan, former Governor of California, announced his candidature for Republican Party's nomination for the Presidency. **21** Anthony Crosland, Secretary for the Environment, announced 1% cut in Government grant towards councils' total expenditure in 1976. **22** Prince Juan Carlos crowned King of Spain. **25** British Government authorised the sending of three Royal Navy frigates to protect British trawlers fishing off Iceland; Surinam (Dutch Guiana) became independent. **27** Publication of White Paper on devolution for Scotland and Wales. Ross McWhirter, writer and publisher, shot dead by two gunmen at his home in north London. **28** Minimum lending rate reduced to 11½%. Fretilin military forces in East Timor unilaterally declared the Portuguese colony independent, renaming it the People's Republic of East Timor. **29** New Zealand general election: Labour Party defeated by National Party. **30** UN Security Council agreed to renew for six months the mandate of UN peacekeeping force on Golan Heights; Republic of Dahomey, former French West African colony, changed name to People's Republic of Benin.

December 1 Over 11,000 hospital consultants treated only emergency cases in protest at Government's proposals for separation of private practice from National Health Service; President Ford arrived in Peking for five-day visit; EEC heads of government met in Rome. **2** British Aircraft Corporation signed contract worth £186 million to supply Iran with Rapier anti-aircraft missile system. Five South Moluccan terrorists held passengers hostage in train hijacked in isolated part of Dutch countryside; Israeli attack on refugee camps in Lebanon: 77 killed. **3** Soviet Union's grain harvest of 137 million tonnes lowest for 10 years; King Savang Vatthana of Laos abdicated and the Government resigned. **4** End of detention without trial in N. Ireland after 4½ years. **10** First shots fired in "cod war". **11** House of Commons voted 361–232 not to restore death penalty; End of Balcombe Street siege in London: Mr. and Mrs. Matthews held in flat by IRA terrorists since 6 Dec. **12** Estate of Picasso valued at £650 million. **14** End of Dutch train siege at Beilen; Landslide victory in Australia for Malcolm Fraser's Liberal Country Party over Gough Whitlam's Labour Party. **16** Government announced measures costing £162.5 million to save Chrysler; World's energy and raw materials conference in Paris. **18** Announcement that 7 June 1977 would be Bank Holiday to mark 25th anniversary of the Queen's accession; Education Bill compelling comprehensive school education published.

19 US Senate voted (against President Ford) to cut off aid to Angola. 24 Minimum lending rate reduced to 11¼%. 26 Russia's supersonic Tupolov 144 began its first regular service. 27 Mine disaster in Bihar, India: 372 trapped by floodwater. 29 Sex Discrimination and Equal Pay Acts came into force; Bomb explosion at La Guardia airport, New York: at least 12 people killed. Britain in 1975 had one of the six driest years of the century.

1976

January 3 Weekend tidal wave and gales caused severe flood damage to east coast of England and northern Europe: sea defences after 1953 flood disaster held. 4 Five Roman Catholics killed in ambush by Protestant terrorists. 5 Machine-gun massacre of 10 Protestant textile workers at Whitecross, Armagh, by Catholic terror group—worst sectarian murder since 1969; police reservist killed in IRA ambush 6 MPLA offensive in Angolan civil war; British Army's "Spearhead Battalion" flown to S. Armagh as reinforcement. 7 Death of Sir Thomas Monnington, Pres. of Royal Academy; Strike of metro-workers in Madrid: other workers struck in sympathy; Troops of Special Air Service (anti-insurgency unit) ordered into Armagh; Signor Moro's Christian Democratic Government resigned after Socialist Party withdrew support. 8 Death of Chou En-lai, aged 77, for 26 years senior leader of China; Indian Government suspended freedom of speech, assembly and movement, the fourth suspension since emergency began. 10 Meeting in Addis Ababa of heads of state of Organisation for African Unity: deadlock over Angolan issue. 11 Iceland asked Dr. Luns, Sec. Gen. of NATO to mediate in "cod war". 12 Death of Agatha Christie, aged 85; Government to reconvene N. Ireland Convention from 3 Feb. (for 4 weeks). 13 Agreement signed between Zambia and Mozambique for construction of road and rail links. 14 Death of Tun Abdul Razak, Prime Minister of Malaysia; Mrs. Anne Armstrong to succeed Mr. Elliot Richardson as American Ambassador to Britain; British Airways took possession of their first Concorde. 15 Further limitations (part voluntary, part statutory) announced by Government for reducing health hazards of cigarette smoking. 19 Icelandic Prime Minister invited to London for talks; Government majority of 158 at end of 4-day devolution debate. 20 UK unemployment 1,430,369 (inc. students): 6·1% of work force; Dr. Kissinger in Moscow for détente talks with Mr. Brezhnev. 21 Concorde entered supersonic passenger service after 14 years' Anglo-French co-operation: simultaneous take-offs from London (to Bahrein) and Paris (to Rio de Janerio). 22 Cease-fire announcement in Lebanon: Syrian peace plan; Seychelles to become independent 28 June; Government accepted Radcliffe Report on ministerial memoirs: author must (1) not reveal anything that contravenes the requirements of national security; (2) make no disclosures injurious to the country's relations with other nations; (3) refrain from publishing information destructive of the confidential relationships on which British system of government is based (to apply for 15 years). 23 Sir Idwal Pugh to succeed Sir Alan Marre as Parliamentary Commissioner for Administration (Ombudsman); British Steel Corporation and unions agreed on compromise solution to planned economy measures; Minimum lending rate reduced to 10½%; Death of Paul Robeson, aged 77. 27 Mr. Whitlam re-elected leader of Australian Labour Party; Clash in Spanish Sahara between Algerian and Moroccan forces; China to send official delegation to Brussels to negotiate trade agreement with EEC. 29 Soviet Government reported to favour OAU playing decisive role in reaching an Angolan settlement. 30 Minimum lending rate reduced to 10%. 31 Most violent month in N. Ireland since 1969: 50 killed.

February 1 Death of Werner Heisenberg, German physicist, whose name is associated with the uncertainty principle. 2 Opening by the Queen of 310-acre National Exhibition Centre at Bickenhill, Birmingham. Mr. Selwyn Lloyd retired as Speaker of the House of Commons: succeeded by Mr. George Thomas. Iceland rejected Britain's proposals to end "cod war"; Attempt on life of President Bokassa of the Central African Republic. 4 Licence granted for Concorde to land at Washington and New York for 16-month trial period; British trawlers in disputed waters off Iceland to have naval protection; Earthquake in Guatemala: over 20,000 dead. 6 Minimum lending rate reduced to 9½%. 11 Recognition of MPLA as legal government of Angola by OAU. 12 Workmen discovered a rose perfectly preserved, hidden in wall of Romsey Abbey in 1120, thought to be oldest botanical specimen found in Europe (the oldest was a posy recovered from Tutankhamun's tomb). 13 Assassination of General Murtala Mohammed, Nigerian head of state, in unsuccessful coup. 17 France first of Western countries to recognise MPLA as legal government of Angola; Sir Hugh Casson elected new President of Royal Academy; Abbot Basil Hume of Ampleforth to be next Archbishop of Westminster. 19 Iceland broke off diplomatic relations with Britain over fishing dispute. 23 Death of L. S. Lowry, Salford artist, aged 88. 24 Opening in Moscow of 25th Soviet Party Congress. 27 Minimum lending rate reduced to 9¼%.

March 3 Mozambique closed border with Rhodesia and implemented sanctions; Mr. William Scranton to succeed Mr. Daniel Moynihan as US Ambassador to United Nations. 5 Mr. Dmitry Ustinov and Mr. Grigory Romanov to be full members of Soviet Politburo; Ulster Convention dissolved: direct rule from Westminster continued. 16 Resignation of Mr. Wilson as Prime Minister. 19 Official announcement of separation of Princess Margaret and Lord Snowdon; Collapse of Mr. Ian Smith's talks with Mr. Nkomo. 23 Rejection by Mr. Smith of Britain's conditions for bringing about a constitutional settlement in Rhodesia. 24 Death of Lord Montgomery of Alamein; Senora Perón of Argentina deposed; Summit meeting in Lusaka of Presidents of Zambia, Tanzania, Botswana and Mozambique. 30 As from 1978 May Day to be a Bank Holiday.

April 5 Mr. James Callaghan became Prime Minister: defeated Mr. Michael Foot by 176 votes to 137 in final ballot for leadership of the Labour Party; Demonstrations and rioting by thousands of people in Peking. 6 Community Land Act (passed 12 Nov. 1975) became effective. 9 Syrian regular forces advanced in Lebanon. 16 India raised minimum marriage ages from 18 to 21 (men) and 15 to 18 (women). 22 Mr. Harold Wilson appointed Knight of the Garter. 24 Dr. Kissinger began visit to Kenya, Tanzania, Zambia, Zaïre, Liberia and Senegal. 25 Portuguese parliamentary elections gave Dr. Mario Soares and his Socialist Party decisive lead: Socialists 35·14%, Popular Democrats 23·80%, Centre Democrats 15·76%, Communists 14·73%. 26 Death of Marshal Grechko, Soviet Defence Minister. 27 Britain began exporting North Sea oil (from B.P.'s Forties field).

May 4 Mr. Anthony Crosland left for visit to China and Japan. 5 Fourth Unctad conference opened in Nairobi: Dr. Kissinger put forward constructive proposals for consumer-producer co-operation on commodities; TUC general council endorsed Chancellor's pay policy. 6 Severe earthquake in N.E. Italy; Tory gains in local council elections. 8 Mr. Brezhnev named a marshal of the army, the Soviet Union's highest military rank. 10 Resignation of Mr. Jeremy Thorpe as leader of the Liberal Party; Visit of Mr. Lee Kuan Yew, Prime Minister of Singapore, to China. 11 Suicide in prison of Frau Ulrike Meinhof, German anarchist leader. 12 Mr. Jo Grimond agreed to resume leadership of the Liberal Party for a temporary period. 17 Violent earthquake in Tashkent area of Soviet Central Asia. 21 Minimum Lending Rate raised to 11½%. 24 Concordes from England

and France flew to Washington for first time. 25 State visit of the Queen to Finland. 28 Soviet–American treaty controlling underground nuclear explosions for non-military purposes signed, providing for on-site verification. 29 South Africa to buy two nuclear power stations from France; Opening of first direct railway line from Belgrade to Adriatic.

June 1 Interim agreement signed in Oslo ending "cod war" between Britain and Iceland; Intervention by Syrian troops in Lebanon to restore law and order. 5 Release of former Rhodesian Prime Minister, Mr. Garfield Todd, from house arrest. 7 Chancellor secured £3 billion stand-by credit from central banks of Europe and America. 8 Visit of Mrs. Gandhi to Moscow. 9 Death of Dame Sybil Thorndike. 16 Riots began in African township of Soweto near Johannesburg against compulsory teaching of Afrikaans, exacerbated by pent-up grievances. 20–21 Italian general election:

	%	*Seats*
Christian Democrats	38·7	262
Socialists	9·6	57
Communists	34·4	228

(Signor Andreotti formed minority Christian Dem. Government July 29). 21 OECD adopted code of conduct on bribery and disclosure of information for multinational companies. 24 Vietnam reunified: recognition by Britain; Talks in W. Germany between Dr. Kissinger and South African Prime Minister, Mr. Vorster. 26 Pictures from Mars *Viking 1* gave rich geological data. 25 President Amin made life-president of Uganda. 25–28 Hottest consecutive four days in London with temperatures reaching 35°C (96°F). 26 Severe earthquake in Indonesian New Guinea: over 9,000 killed. 27 Leaders from Britain, France, W. Germany, Italy, Canada, US and Japan met in Puerto Rico for second "economic summit" conference; Gen. Antonio Ramalho Eanes, Army Chief of Staff, elected President of Portugal. 29 Independence of Seychelles as republic within Commonwealth. 30 Mr. Dmitry Ustinov (who succeeded the late Marshal Grechko as Minister of Defence) promoted Marshal of the Soviet Union.

July 2 Government emergency powers to control water shortage in Britain. 4 Israeli attack on Entebbe airport to free 100 Israeli hostages from Air France Flight 139 from Tel Aviv hijacked by Palestinian extremists. 7 The Queen arrived in Washington for bicentennial celebrations; Death of Dr. Gustav Heinemman, President of W. Germany 1969–74; Death of Marshal Chu Teh, Grand Old Man of the Chinese Army; Mr. David Steel elected leader of the Liberal Party by party workers. 10 Explosion at Hoffman-La Roche's Seveso plant near Milan; poisonous chemical contaminated area of 7 km radius. 13 Mr. Roy Jenkins to be President of EEC Commission from Jan. 1977. 14 Official handing over to Tanzania and Zambia of Chinese-built Tanzam railway (1,860 km). 15 Governor Jimmy Carter of Georgia nominated presidential candidate by Democratic Convention; Senator Walter Mondale from Minnesota Mr. Carter's vice-presidential nominee. 16 Dr. Soares asked by Portuguese President Eanes to form government. 18 Fortieth anniversary of Spanish Civil War: bombs in Madrid. 21 Mr. Christopher Ewart-Biggs, British Ambassador to Irish Republic, and a member of his staff, assassinated by landmine. 22 Death of archaeologist Sir Mortimer Wheeler. 28 Major earthquake (8·2 Richter scale), the worst since 1556, destroyed Chinese mining town of Tangshan: very heavy death toll; Britain broke off diplomatic relations with Uganda. 30 Partial amnesty granted by King Juan to Spanish political prisoners (about 650). 31 Bomb incidents in Spanish cities.

August 1 Trinidad and Tobago became independent republic within Commonwealth. 2 China reported another 15 earthquakes and over 100 earth tremors. 4 Death of Lord Thomson of Fleet, owner of *The Times*; Renewed violence in South African township of Soweto. 6 Drought Act 1976 came into force: water authorities given power to limit or cut off supplies. 7 *Viking 2* went into orbit round Mars. 8 Sortie by Rhodesian troops across Mozambique border. 10 Return of former President Spinola to Portugal after 17-month exile in Brazil. 12 Embattled Palestinian refugee camp of Tel al-Zaatar fell to right-wing Christian forces: over 200 dead found there. 14 First mass rally of Women's Peace Movement in N. Ireland, formed by Mrs. Betty Williams and Miss Maireaed Corrigan. 16 Two powerful earthquakes in E. Asia: at Changtu, central China, and in S. Philippines where many people were drowned in tidal waves; Opening in Colombo of non-aligned nations' summit meeting: own monetary system sought; Spread of Black unrest in Cape Town's townships. 18 Soviet *Luna 24* made soft landing on surface of moon (S.E. part of Sea of Crises) to take soil samples with automatic scoop; Mr. Brian Faulkner, leader of the Unionist Party of N. Ireland, to retire from politics. 19 N. and S. Korea on war footing. 22 According to historical evidence drought in Britain worst for 500 years. 25 Hong Kong had heaviest rainfall (16 in.) for 15 years; Resignation of M. Chirac, Prime Minister of France; Unemployment figure (crude) in Britain rose above 1·5 million. 26 Death of Lotte Lehmann, operatic soprano.

September 2 European Commission on Human Rights reported on charges against Britain brought by Irish Government: Britain guilty of torturing detainees in Ulster after introduction of internment in 1971 but cleared of charge of discrimination between Republican and Protestant extremists; Official reception in Peking for earthquake relief workers. 3 Second day of rioting in Cape Town with mounting death toll and arrests; End of 67-hour prison riot in Hull prison. 4 Meeting of Mr. Vorster and Dr. Kissinger in Zurich to find political solution to problems of Southern Africa. 6 Meeting of five African states around Rhodesia in Dar-es-Salaam. 8 High pressure system over Britain came to an end. 9 Death of China's great leader Mao Tse-tung, aged 82. 10 Mid-air collision of 2 airliners near Zagreb (one British, one Yugoslav), all 176 aboard killed; Minimum Lending Rate lifted to 13%. 11 Mourning ceremony in Peking began for Mao Tse-tung in the Great Hall of the People. 13 Riots in Basque region of Spain. 14 Meeting of Mr. Vorster and Mr. Smith in Pretoria to discuss Dr. Kissinger's proposals relating to Southern Africa. 19 Dr. Kissinger held week-end talks in Pretoria with Mr. Vorster and Mr. Ian Smith; India relaxed censorship of foreign journalists. 20 Convention signed by EEC members in Brussels for election of a 410-member European Parliament; Electoral defeat of Sweden's Social Democratic Party after 44 years in power; British minesweeper *Fittleton* sank after collision with frigate *Mermaid* on NATO exercise off Dutch coast: 12 dead; Mr. Dom Mintoff (Labour) won Malta's general election with majority of 3 seats. 22 Portugal became 19th member of Council of Europe. 23 Demonstration by African students in Johannesburg violently countered by riot police. 24 Mr. Ian Smith announced acceptance of British and American proposals for majority rule in Rhodesia in two years. 29 Following two days of exceptional pressure on £, Chancellor applied to IMF for stand-by of £2·3 billion.

October 1 Roman Catholic Bishop of Umtali sentenced by Rhodesian court to 10 years' imprisonment for failing to report presence of guerrillas. 3 Welcome in Salisbury, Rhodesia, for nationalist leader, Bishop Muzorewe, who returned from exile; W. German Bundestag elections: ruling coalition of Social Democrats and Free Democrats (SPD–FDP) gained narrow victory over Christian Democrats (CDM) and Christian Social Union (CSU). 4 British Rail's high-speed train came into service on London–

Bristol route. **6** MLR raised to 15%; Military coup in Thailand and the end of civilian rule after 3 years. **7** Sir Harold Wilson to head committee to investigate functioning of the City. **8** Building Societies put up mortgage rate to 12¼%. **12** Official announcement of appointment of Hua Kuo-feng as Chairman of the Chinese Communist Party. **14** Death of Dame Edith Evans. **18** Revaluation of the Deutsche Mark took pressure off £. **19** Meeting of six Arab leaders in Saudi Arabian capital of Riyadh to draw up plans for ending civil war in Lebanon. **21** Mr. Michael Foot elected deputy leader of the Parliamentary Labour Party. **25** Official opening of the National Theatre by the Queen; Independence of the Transkei (international recognition withheld because seen as part of S. Africa's apartheid policy); New coalfield with 50 million tons of reserves located under Firth of Forth; **28** Conference on future of Rhodesia, chaired by Mr. Ivor Richard, opened in Geneva; State Opening of Parliament delayed from 17 to 24 November on account of slow progress of legislation through House of Lords. **29** Opening of world's largest mining complex at Selby, Yorks. **30** EEC agreement on introduction of 200-mile Community fishing zone as from 1 Jan. 1977.

November 1 Top Premium Savings Bond increased from £75,000 to £100,000; President Micombero of Burundi overthrown in bloodless military coup. Mr. Jimmy Carter elected President of the USA with Democratic majorities in both Houses. **4** By-elections at Newcastle Central (held by Lab.), Workington (Con. win), Walsall, North (Con. win). **7** Another earthquake in S.E. China near Kunming; Planting in Belfast of crosses for lives lost since 1969—a total of 1,662. **12** General strike in Spain; **15** Earth tremor near Peking; Formal end of civil war in Lebanon as Syrian troops (as part of Arab peacekeeping force) moved into heart of Beirut; US vetoed Vietnam's application for UN membership. **23** Tangshan (destroyed by earthquakes 28 July and 15 November) to be rebuilt in another location. **24** Earthquake in E. Turkey: at least 4,000 killed with injured survivors dying of exposure in freezing temperatures; Mr. Robert Anderson's American oil group, Atlantic Richfield, to take control of the *Observer*. **26** The Children Act 1976 came into force. **27** Rally in Trafalgar Square in support of N. Ireland Peace People. **30** Publication of Bill setting up Scottish and Welsh assemblies.

December 1 Angola admitted to UN as 146th member; Death of Marshal Ivan Yakubovsky, Soviet C.-in-C. of Warsaw Pact military alliance, aged 64. **4** Death of Benjamin Britten. **5** M. Jacques Chirac, former French Prime Minister, elected leader of new Gaullist movement, the Rassemblement pour la République, against alliance of socialists and communists. **13** First oil from Brent North Sea oilfield taken by tanker to Fawley for refining. **15** Government's Mini-budget: fresh constraints on public spending. **14** Geneva Conference on Rhodesia adjourned for a month. **16** Scotland and Wales to have referendum on devolution; Landslide victory for Mr. Michael Manley in Jamaica's general election; 11 OPEC members voted to increase oil prices by 10% on 1 Jan. 1977 and by a further 5% on 1 July 1977, Saudi Arabia to raise prices by only 5%. **17** MLR reduced to 14½%. Exchange of Vladimir Bukovsky, Soviet dissident, and Señor Corvalán, veteran leader of Chilean Communist Party; Mr. Ian Trethowan to succeed Sir Charles Curran as Director-General of BBC. **22** Death toll in N. Ireland in 1976 totalled 296.

EVENTS

1977

January 1 Britain together with EEC countries extended fishing limits to 200 miles offshore (with effect from 1 April). **5** Figures released from International Wheat Council showed bumper crops in Soviet Union, N. America, India, China and Argentina (while world population increased by 67%, wheat production increased by 155%). **6** MLR reduced to 14%. **11** Chancellor announced agreement on safety net to solve problem of Britain's sterling balances; Mr. Roy Jenkins, first British President of EEC Commission, made his inaugural speech in European Parliament in Luxembourg. **12** Volcanic eruption in E. Zaïre: lava flow moved at 7 km/h on surrounding countryside; Executive of National Union of Mineworkers voted for Coal Board's retirement scheme: miners with 20 years' underground service to retire at 62. **13** Britain had heaviest snowfall for a decade. **14** Death of Lord Avon. **15** Opening of Festival of Arts and Culture (FESTAC 1977) in Lagos. **17** Britain tabled new proposals for second round of Rhodesian talks. **18** Overhead bridge collapsed on commuter train in suburb of Sydney: 80 killed. **18** Mrs. Gandhi announced holding of general election in March; Mr. Ivor Richard arrived in Cape Town from Nairobi on second round of talks to find solution to Rhodesian problem. **19** Food riots in Egypt. **20** Inauguration of Mr. Jimmy Carter as 39th President of USA; Relaxation of emergency powers imposed by Mrs. Gandhi in 1975: censorship lifted and release of political prisoners. **21** MLR reduced by ¾% to 13¼%; President Carter pardoned "draft dodgers". **24** Collapse of second round of Rhodesian talks: Mr. Ian Smith rejected British proposals for transition to black majority rule. **26** Publication of Bullock Report on industrial democracy. **28** Despite Government ban on demonstrations in Spain, renewed violence; MLR reduced to 12¼%. **29** Bomb explosions in Central London, no casualties. **31** Mr. Ivor Richard returned to London after end of his tour of Southern Africa; Earthquake in Soviet Central Asia near Tashkent; One of worst winters this century in Eastern States of USA.

February 2 Important NEDC meeting on industrial strategy; Britain had lowest strike record in 1975 for 9 years; Defection of Mr. Ram, senior member of Mrs. Gandhi's cabinet. **2** MLR reduced to 12%. **8** Diplomatic relations between Soviet Union and Spain resumed (for first time since Civil War); Soviet *Soyuz 24* docked with orbiting *Salyut 5* space laboratory one day after launch. **9** Meeting between Mr. Smith and Mr. Vorster about what to do in Rhodesia. **15** Deaths in England and Wales exceeded number of live births in 1976 (for first time since records began in 1837). **17** Uganda's Anglican archbishop and two cabinet ministers killed in mysterious circumstances while under arrest; Government to spend £6 million during next 4 years on solar energy research and development. **19** Death of Anthony Crosland, aged 58. **21** Dr. David Owen (aged 38) became Foreign Secretary. **22** British Government pressed for UN investigation into deaths in Uganda; Government defeated on guillotine motion to cut short debate on Devolution Bill. **23** Reports of large-scale massacres in Uganda of the Christian Achole and Lango tribes. **24** Rhodesian Government reduced Bishop Lamont's 10-year sentence to loss of citizenship and deportation; USA to cut aid to Ethiopia, Argentina and Uruguay because of human rights violations.

March 1 Mr. Callaghan's Government went into minority; Government to drop ship repairing section from aircraft and shipbuilding nationalisation Bill. **3** Death of Lord Faulkner, former N. Ireland Prime Minister. **4** Major earthquake in Transylvania, north of Bucharest (7·2 Richter scale: death toll estimated 1500, over 11,000 injured). **7** The Queen arrived in Australia on her Jubilee tour; Landslide victory for Mr. Bhutto in Pakistan's national assembly election. **10** Astronomers observed (for first time) rings around Uranus as planet passed in front of a star; MLR reduced to 11%; Mr. Callaghan in Washington for talks with President Carter. **13** French municipal elections: Alliance of left (Socialists and Communists) gained ground. **14** David McNee became Commissioner of the Metropolitan Police on retirement of Sir Robert Mark. **15** Sorin Crainic, aged 19, survived 252 hours under earthquake rubble in Bucharest.

16 Assassination of Lebanese left-wing leader, Kamal Jumblatt; 16–25 Dr. Castro's visit to Tanzania, Mozambique and Angola. 18 Assassination of President Ngouabi of Congo Rep. 18 MLR reduced to 10½%. 22 Resignation of Mrs. Indira Gandhi after loss of seat in general election and defeat of Congress Party after 30 years in power; Earthquake in Iran (6·7 Richter scale) around Bandar Abbas. 23 Labour Government and Liberal Party's consultation agreement: Conservative motion of no-confidence defeated by 322 to 298. 24 Janata Government sworn in with Mr. Moraji Desai as Prime Minister of India; Publication of Annan Committee's Report on future of broadcasting in Britain; 25 World's worst aircraft disaster: collision on runway of two jumbo-jets (Pan Am and KLM) at Tenerife's Los Rodeos airport: 577 killed; Summit meeting in Rome of EEC countries chaired by Mr. Callaghan. 26 Mr. Podgorny began visit to southern Africa. 27–30 American Secretary of State, Mr. Cyrus Vance, in Moscow: rejection by Soviet Union of US proposals on arms control. 31 The Queen and Prince Philip arrived back home after 7-week tour of Australia and New Zealand; Stechford by-election won by Conservatives on swing of 17·4%; Britain to go ahead with Hawker Siddeley *Nimrod* aircraft to police waters around Britain as a result of no agreement by NATO countries on US Awacs project; MLR reduced by 1% to 9½%.

April 7 President Carter's nuclear energy policy statement: production of plutonium to end; reprocessing techniques and fast-breeder programme to slow down; Mrs. Margaret Thatcher began her visit to China. 11 Report of French air transport for Moroccan troops to Zaïre. 12 New British initiative on Rhodesia: Dr. David Owen, Foreign Secretary, arrived in Tanzania on his diplomatic tour of southern Africa to gain consensus for a negotiated transfer of power in Rhodesia in 1978.

CALENDAR 1978

January

S	M	T	W	T	F	S
1	2	3	4	5	6	7
8	9	10	11	12	13	14
15	16	17	18	19	20	21
22	23	24	25	26	27	28
29	30	31				

February

S	M	T	W	T	F	S
			1	2	3	4
5	6	7	8	9	10	11
12	13	14	15	16	17	18
19	20	21	22	23	24	25
26	27	28				

March

S	M	T	W	T	F	S
			1	2	3	4
5	6	7	8	9	10	11
12	13	14	15	16	17	18
19	20	21	22	23	24	25
26	27	28	29	30	31	

April

S	M	T	W	T	F	S
						1
2	3	4	5	6	7	8
9	10	11	12	13	14	15
16	17	18	19	20	21	22
23	24	25	26	27	28	29
30						

May

S	M	T	W	T	F	S
	1	2	3	4	5	6
7	8	9	10	11	12	13
14	15	16	17	18	19	20
21	22	23	24	25	26	27
28	29	30	31			

June

S	M	T	W	T	F	S
				1	2	3
4	5	6	7	8	9	10
11	12	13	14	15	16	17
18	19	20	21	22	23	24
25	26	27	28	29	30	

July

S	M	T	W	T	F	S
						1
2	3	4	5	6	7	8
9	10	11	12	13	14	15
16	17	18	19	20	21	22
23	24	25	26	27	28	29
30	31					

August

S	M	T	W	T	F	S
		1	2	3	4	5
6	7	8	9	10	11	12
13	14	15	16	17	18	19
20	21	22	23	24	25	26
27	28	29	30	31		

September

S	M	T	W	T	F	S
					1	2
3	4	5	6	7	8	9
10	11	12	13	14	15	16
17	18	19	20	21	22	23
24	25	26	27	28	29	30

October

S	M	T	W	T	F	S
1	2	3	4	5	6	7
8	9	10	11	12	13	14
15	16	17	18	19	20	21
22	23	24	25	26	27	28
29	30	31				

November

S	M	T	W	T	F	S
			1	2	3	4
5	6	7	8	9	10	11
12	13	14	15	16	17	18
19	20	21	22	23	24	25
26	27	28	29	30		

December

S	M	T	W	T	F	S
					1	2
3	4	5	6	7	8	9
10	11	12	13	14	15	16
17	18	19	20	21	22	23
24	25	26	27	28	29	30
31						

RELIGIOUS CALENDAR

Epiphany	Jan. 6
Septuagesima Sunday	Jan. 22
Quinquagesima Sunday	Feb. 5
Ash Wednesday	Feb. 8
Quadragesima Sunday	Feb. 12
Palm Sunday	Mar. 19
Good Friday	Mar. 24
Easter Day	Mar. 26
Mohammedan New Year (1399)	Dec. 2
Passover, First day of (Pesach)	Apr. 22
Feast of Weeks (Shebuoth)	June 11
Jewish New Year 5739 (Rosh Hashanah)	Oct. 2
Low Sunday	Apr. 2
Rogation Sunday	Apr. 30
Ascension Day – Holy Thursday	May 4
Whit Sunday – Pentecost	May 14
Trinity Sunday	May 21
Corpus Christi	May 25
First Sunday in Advent	Dec. 3
Christmas Day	Dec. 25
Ramadan, First day of (tabular)	Aug. 5
Day of Atonement (Yom Kippur)	Oct. 11
Tabernacles, First day of (Succoth)	Oct. 16

CIVIL CALENDAR – THE COMMONWEALTH

Australia Day	Jan. 26
Republic Day (India)	Jan. 26
Independence Commemoration Day (Sri Lanka)	Feb. 4
Accession of Queen Elizabeth II	Feb. 6
National Day (New Zealand)	Feb. 6
St. David (Wales)	Mar. 1
St. Patrick (Ireland)	Mar. 17
Birthday of Queen Elizabeth II	Apr. 21
St. George (England)	Apr. 23
Commonwealth Day	May 24
Birthday of Prince Philip, Duke of Edinburgh	June 10
Dominion Day (Canada)	July 1
Remembrance Sunday	Nov. 12
Birthday of the Prince of Wales	Nov. 14
St. Andrew (Scotland)	Nov. 30

Commonwealth Day may be observed in Great Britain on June 10

Reproduced, with permission, from data supplied by the Science Research Council.

PROMINENT PEOPLE

Glimpses of some of the famous people in the history of the world. See also Section E for composers; Section I for contemporary dramatists; Section M for novelists and poets of the twentieth century.

PROMINENT PEOPLE

A

Abel, Sir Frederick (1826–1902), English military chemist, an authority on explosives. He and his friend James Dewar patented the propellant cordite (*see* **Section L**).

Abelard, Peter (1079–1142), one of the founders of scholastic moral theology, b. at Pallet (Palais) near Nantes. He lectured in Paris, where he was sought by students, though persecuted for alleged heresy. His main achievement was to discuss where others asserted. His love for Héloïse, a woman of learning, ended in tragic separation and in a famous correspondence.

Abercrombie, Sir Patrick (1879–1957), architect and town-planner. He was consulted on the re-planning of Plymouth, Hull, Bath and other cities and produced a plan for Greater London, 1943.

Acton, 1st Baron (John Emerich Edward Dalberg Acton) (1834–1902), English historian. He planned the *Cambridge Modern History*.

Adam, Robert (1728–92), architect, one of four Scottish brothers. He developed a characteristic style in planning and decoration and his achievements in interior design include Harewood House, Yorks.; Osterley Park, Middlesex; Syon House, Middlesex; Kedleston Hall, Derbyshire; Luton Hoo, Bedfordshire; and Kenwood. *See* **Neo-Classical Style, Section L.**

Adams, John (1735–1826), succeeded Washington as president of the U.S.A. He was the first of the republic's ambassadors to England.

Adams, John Couch (1819–92), English mathematician and astronomer. He shared credit for the discovery of the planet Neptune (1846) with the French astonomer Leverrier, working independently.

Adams, Samuel (1722–1803), American revolutionary statesman, b. Boston. He advocated "no taxation without representation" as early as 1765; promoted the "Boston tea-party"; and in 1776 signed the Declaration of Independence.

Adams, William (*c.* 1564–1620), navigator, b. Gillingham, Kent; the first Englishman to visit Japan. He found favour with the emperor Ieyasu, and an English and Dutch trading settlement was established till 1616.

Addams, Jane (1860–1935), American sociologist who founded Hull House, Chicago, in 1889.

Addison, Joseph (1672–1719), writer and Whig politician. He contributed to the *Tatler*, and was co-founder with Steele of the *Spectator*.

Adelard of Bath (*c.* 1090–*c.* 1150), English mathematician who translated into Latin the *Arithmetic* of Al-Kwarizmi and so introduced the Arabic numerals to the West (*see* **L7**).

Adenauer, Konrad (1876–1967), chancellor of the West German Federal Republic, 1949–63; founder and chairman of the Christian Democratic Party, 1945–66. To a defeated Germany he gave stable constitutional government and a place in the Western alliance. He promoted reconciliation with France but resisted accommodation with Russia.

Adler, Alfred (1870–1937), Austrian psychiatrist, founder of the school of individual psychology. An earlier pupil of Freud, he broke away in 1911, rejecting the emphasis on sex, regarding man's main problem as a struggle for power to compensate for feelings of inferiority. *See* **Adlerian psychology, Section J.**

Adrian, 1st Baron (Edgar Douglas Adrian) (b. 1889), English physiologist. He shared with Sherrington the 1932 Nobel prize for medicine for work on the electrical nature of the nerve impulse. Pres. Royal Society 1950–5; Pres. British Association 1954; Chancellor Leicester Univ. 1958–71; Chancellor Cambridge Univ. 1967–75; O.M. 1942.

Adrian IV (Nicholas Breakspear) (d. 1159), pope 1154–59, the only English pope, b. near St. Albans. He crowned Frederick Barbarossa Holy Roman Emperor. Granted overlordship of Ireland to Henry II.

Aeschylus (525–456 B.C.), founder of Greek tragic drama. Of the many plays he wrote, only seven have come down to us, including *The Seven against Thebes*, *Prometheus Bound*, and a trilogy on Orestes.

Aesop (? 6th cent. B.C.), semi-legendary fabulist, originally a slave. The fables attributed to him probably have many origins.

Agassiz, Louis (1807–73), Swiss-American embryologist, author of *Lectures on Comparative Embryology*, intended for laymen, *Researches on Fossil Fishes*, and *Studies on Glaciers*. He was an opponent of Darwinian evolution.

Agricola, Gnaeus Julius (37–93), Roman governor of Britain, who subdued the country except for the Scottish highlands. His son-in-law Tacitus wrote his life.

Agrippa, Marcus Vipsanius (63–12 B.C.), Roman general.

Ahmad Khan, Sir Syed (1817–98), Indian educationist and social reformer who founded what is now the Aligarh Muslim University.

Airy, Sir George Biddell (1801–92), English mathematician who was astronomer royal for over 40 years, 1835–81. He set up a magnetic observatory at Greenwich.

Akbar, Jalal-ud-din Mohammed (1542–1605), Mogul emperor of India, son of Humayun. He extended the imperial power over much of India, stabilised the administration, promoted commerce and learning; and, though a Muslim, respected Hindu culture and tolerated Christian missions. His reign saw a flowering of Mogul culture.

Akhenaten, the name adopted by the heretic pharaoh, **Amenhotep IV** (d. 1362 B.C.), who introduced a short-lived, but influential religious and artistic reformation. He sought to convert his people from their polytheistic beliefs to a more compassionate religion based on the one supreme sun-god Aten (hence his name). His pacifism caused the temporary loss of most of Egypt's overseas territories. His wife was Nefertiti and he was succeeded by Tutankhamun, who gave in to the conservative forces of the priesthood.

Alanbrooke, 1st Viscount (Alan Francis Brooke) (1883–1963), British field-marshal; chief of the imperial general staff 1941–46. Sir Arthur Bryant's *The Turn of the Tide* and *Triumph in the West* are based on his war diaries.

Alarcón, Pedro Antonio de (1833–91), Spanish novelist. His short story, *El Sombrero de tres picos* (The Three-Cornered Hat) became the subject of Falla's ballet and of Hugo Wolf's opera *Der Corregidor*.

Alaric I (376–410), Visigothic chief who, as first auxiliary to the Roman emperor Theodosius, later attacked the empire and sacked Rome in 410.

Alban, St. (d. *c.* 303), proto-martyr of Britain, converted by a priest to whom he had given shelter. He suffered under Diocletian at Verulam (now St. Albans), where in the 8th cent. King Offa of Mercia founded the abbey of that name.

Albert, Prince Consort (1819–61), son of the Duke of Saxe-Coburg-Gotha, married Queen Victoria in 1840. He helped the queen with political duties, projected the international exhibition of 1851, and in 1861 in a dispute with the United States advised a conciliatory attitude which averted war. He died of typhoid fever and is commemorated by the Albert Memorial in Kensington Gardens.

Albertus Magnus (Albert the Great) (1206–80), Dominican scholastic philosopher, b. Swabia. His interest in nature as an independent observer marked the awakening of the scientific spirit. Among his pupils was Thomas Aquinas.

Alcibiades (*c.* 450–404 B.C.), Athenian general and statesman. Pupil and friend of Socrates, he was an egoist whose career brought Athens disaster. He was murdered in Phrygia.

Alcott, Louisa May (1832–88), American author of books for girls, notably *Little Women*.

Alcuin (735–804), English scholar, who settled on the continent and helped Charlemagne with the promotion of education. *See* Monasticism, Section J.

Aldred (d. 1069), Saxon archbishop of York who crowned William the Conqueror.

Aldrich, Henry (1647–1710), English composer of church music, theologian and architect. He designed Peckwater quadrangle at Christ Church, the chapel of Trinity College, and All Saint's Church, Oxford, and wrote the "Bonny Christ Church bells."

Alekhine, Alexander (1892–1946), world chess champion, 1927–35, 1937–46. He was born in Moscow and became a French citizen after the Russian revolution.

Alembert, Jean le Rond d' (1717–83), French mathematician and philosopher, one of the encyclopaedists, a leading representative of the Enlightenment.

Alexander of Tunis, Earl of (Harold Leofric George Alexander) (1891–1969), British field-marshal, b. Ireland. Directed retreat at Dunkirk 1940, and Burma 1942; C.-in-C. Allied Armies in Italy 1943–4; Supreme Allied Commander, Mediterranean 1944–5. Governor-general of Canada 1946–52.

Alexander II (1818–81), reforming Tsar of Russia, succeeded his father Nicholas in 1855. In 1861 he emancipated the serfs and in 1865 established provincial elective assemblies. Later his government became reactionary; he was assassinated by Nihilists; the pogroms followed.

Alexander the Great (356–323 B.C.), Greek conqueror. Educated by Aristotle, he succeeded his father Philip as king of Macedon in 336 B.C. He led the Greek states against Persia; and, crossing the Hellespont, he defeated Darius and sacked Persepolis. He captured Egypt and founded Alexandria. He penetrated to India. D. at Babylon. Centuries later legends formed round him.

Alexandra, Queen (1844–1925), daughter of Christian IX of Denmark, married the Prince of Wales (afterwards Edward VII) 1863.

Alfieri, Vittorio, Count (1749–1803), Italian poet and dramatist.

Alfonso the Wise (1221–84), king of León and Castile, known for his code of laws and his planetary tables. He caused the first general history of Spain to be written. Dethroned 1282.

Alfred the Great (849–99), king of Wessex who became a national figure. From the outset he had to repel Danish invaders. After years of effort he won the battle of Ethandun (Edington), and subsequently, probably in 886, made peace with Guthrum, leaving to the Danes the north and east. He built ships, was an able administrator, and promoted education, his own translations from the Latin being part of the earliest English literature.

Al-Kwarizimi (fl. *c.* 830), Persian mathematician said to have given algebra its name.

Allenby, 1st Viscount (Edmund Henry Hynman Allenby) (1861–1936), British general. He served on the Western front 1914–16, commanded in Palestine 1917–18, capturing Jerusalem on 9 December 1917.

Allende, Salvador (1908–73), Chilean radical leader, a Marxist democrat, who won the presidency 1970. He tried to bring social reform by democratic means but met his death resisting the military coup in which it is alleged the American CIA played a role.

Alleyne, Edward (1566–1626), actor and founder of Dulwich College.

Al-Mamun (813–33), caliph of Baghdad, son of Harun-al-Rashid. He built an observatory at Baghdad where observations were long recorded.

Ampère, André Marie (1775–1836), French physicist who propounded the theory that magnetism is the result of molecular electric currents. The unit of electric current is named after him.

Amundsen, Roald (1872–1928), Norwegian explorer, the first to navigate the north-west passage and to reach the south pole. Sailing in the fishing smack *Gjoa*, he made the north-west passage in 3 years, 1903–6, and in 1911 sailed to the antarctic in the *Fram*, reaching the pole on 14 December 1911, a month before his English rival Scott. His attempt to rescue Nobile after his crash in the airship *Italia* cost him his life.

Anacreon (*c.* 560–475 B.C.), Greek lyric poet.

Anaxagoras (488–428 B.C.), Ionian philosopher who came to Athens 464 B.C. and inspired Pericles and the poet Euripides with his love of science. His rational theories outraged religious opinion, and, like Socrates (who differed from him) he was indicted for impiety.

Anaximander (611–547 B.C.), Miletan philosopher, pupil of Thales, the first among the Greeks to make geographical maps, and to speculate on the origin of the heavenly bodies. He introduced the sun-dial from Babylon or Egypt.

Anaximenes (b. *c.* 570 B.C.), the last of the Milesian school founded by Thales. For him the primal substance was air and he was the first to see the differences between substances in quantitative terms.

Andersen, Hans Christian (1805–75), Danish writer, especially of fairy tales such as *The Little Mermaid* and *The Ugly Duckling*, which are still widely read. He also wrote an autobiography *Mit Livs Eventyr*.

Anderson, Elizabeth Garrett (1836–1917), one of the first English women to enter the medical profession. She practised in London for many years and later became mayor of Aldeburgh, her native town, the first woman to hold the office of mayor.

Andrea del Sarto (1487–1531), Italian painter, b. Florence, the son of a tailor. Known as the "faultless painter," his chief works are the frescoes of the Annunziata at Florence and his Holy Families. He died of the plague.

Andrée, Salomon August (1854–97), Swedish explorer who attempted in 1897 to reach the north pole by balloon. In 1930 a Norwegian scientific expedition discovered the remains of the Andrée expedition on White Island, including a log-book, sketch maps, and diaries.

Andrew, St., one of the apostles of Jesus, brother of Simon Peter, whose festival is observed on 30 November. He became the patron saint of Scotland in the 8th cent.

Angelico, Fra (1387–1455), Italian painter. An exquisite colourist, Fra Giovanni (his Dominican name) painted especially religious frescoes, mainly at Florence and Rome.

Ångström, Anders Jöns (1814–74), Swedish physicist who studied heat, magnetism, and spectroscopy; hence the angstrom unit used for measuring the wavelength of light.

Anne, Queen (1665–1714), Queen of Gt. Britain and Ireland. A daughter of James II, she succeeded William III in 1702. The act of union with Scotland was passed in 1707. A well-intentioned woman without marked ability, she was influenced by favourites, at first by the Duchess of Marlborough, but in the main she was guided by Tory and high church principles (she established Queen Anne's Bounty to improve church finances). Her reign was notable for literary output (Swift, Pope, Addison, Steele, Defoe), developments in science (Newton), architecture (Wren, Vanbrugh), and for the Duke of Marlborough's victories in war.

Anouilh, Jean (b. 1910), French playwright. *See* Section I.

Anselm, St. (1033–1109), Italian scholar who succeeded Lanfranc as archbishop of Canterbury. He resisted William II, but was able to work with the latter's successor, Henry I.

Anson, 1st Baron (George Anson) (1697–1762), English admiral who sailed round the world 1740–44, his squadron being reduced during the voyage from seven ships to one. An account was compiled by his chaplain.

Antoninus Pius (86–161), Roman emperor, successor of Hadrian. In his reign, which was peaceful, the Antonine wall between the Forth and the Clyde was built to protect Britain from northern attack.

Antonius Marcus (Mark Antony) (*c.* 83–30 B.C.), Roman triumvir. He supported Caesar, and after the latter's death was opposed by Brutus and Cassius, and defeated by Octavian; committed suicide. His association with the Egyptian queen Cleopatra is the subject of Shakespeare's play.

Antony, St. (*c.* 251–356), early promoter of the monastic life. B. in Upper Egypt, he retired into the desert, where he was tempted, but attracted disciples and founded a monastery. Took part in the Council of Nicaea 325. (From his supposed help against erysipelas derives its name of St. Antony's fire.)

Apelles, 4th cent. B.C., Greek painter whose chief paintings, which have not survived, were of Alexander the Great holding a thunderbolt and of Aphrodite rising from the sea.

Apollinaire, Guillaume (Wilhelm Apollinaris Kostrowitzi) (1880–1918), French poet representative of the restless and experimental period in the arts before the first world war. He invented the term *surrealism* (*see* **Section L**). B. Rome of Polish extraction.

Apollonius of Perga (fl. 220 B.C.), Greek mathematician of the Alexandrian school, remembered for his conic sections; introduced the terms *ellipse, parabola*, and *hyperbola*.

Apollonius Rhodius (fl. 250 B.C.), scholar and poet of Alexandria and Rhodes, librarian at Alexandria. His epic *Argonautica* is about the Argonaut heroes.

Appert, Nicholas (1752–1841), sometimes known as François Appert, invented the method of preserving animal and vegetable foods by means of hermetically sealed cans or tins, and paved the way for the creation of a vast world industry.

Appleton, Sir Edward Victor (1892–1965), English physicist, best known as the discoverer of the ionised region of the upper atmosphere which became known as the Appleton layer. His researches led to the development of radar. Nobel prizewinner 1947.

Aquinas, Thomas, St. (*c.* 1225–74), scholastic philosopher and Dominican friar of Italian birth, whose philosophico-theological system (called Thomism) is still accepted by Catholic ecclesiastics. He understood Aristotle well and interpreted his thought in accord with Christian teaching. His most important works are *Summa contra Gentiles* and *Summa theologica*. *See also* **God and Man, Section J.**

Arago, Dominique François Jean (1786–1853), French astronomer and physicist, remembered for his discoveries in electromagnetism and optics.

Archimedes (287–212 B.C.), Greek mathematician, b. Syracuse, son of an astronomer; remembered for his contributions to pure mathematics, mechanics, and hydrostatics, notably the Archimedean screw for raising water, the conception of specific gravity, the doctrine of levers, and the measurement of curved areas. Not less than his scientific knowledge was his practical skill. He was killed by the Romans in the siege of Syracuse.

Argand, Aimé (1755–1803), Swiss physician, inventor of the lamp bearing his name, which was the first to admit a current of air to increase the power of the flame, by use of a chimney glass and circular wick.

Ariosto, Ludovico (1474–1533), Italian poet, author of *Orlando Furioso*.

Aristides (d. *c.* 468 B.C.), Athenian general and statesman, called "the just"; fought at Marathon.

Aristippus (*c.* 435–356 B.C.), founder of the Cyrenaic school of philosophy. He taught that man should aim at pleasure, but held that the pleasant was identical with the good.

Aristophanes (*c.* 444– *c.* 385 B.C.), Greek dramatist and comic poet, who satirised Athenian life. Among his plays are *The Clouds* and *The Birds*.

Aristotle (384–322 B.C.), Greek philosopher, pupil of Plato, after whose death in 347 he left Athens to become tutor to the young prince Alexander of Macedon. Subsequently at Athens he established his famous school in the garden known as the *Lyceum*, where he lectured in the *peripatos* (cloister) which gave his school of philosophy its name *Peripatetic*. He took the whole field of knowledge as his subject, giving it unity, and providing a philosophy which held its own for 2,000 years.

Arkwright, Sir Richard (1732–92), English inventor. A native of Preston, and originally a barber, he experimented with cotton-spinning machines. His "water frame" (run by water power), patented in 1769, was an early step in the industrial revolution. In 1790 he made use of Boulton and Watt's steam-engine. Rioters sacked one of his mills in 1779.

Armstrong, Neil (b. 1930), American astronaut, the first man to set foot on the moon, 20 July 1969.

Arne, Thomas Augustine (1710–78), English composer, remembered for *Rule, Britannia!* (from a masque called *Alfred*), and for Shakespearean songs such as *Where the Bee sucks*. He also wrote operas (women singers appeared in *Judith* in 1761) and oratorios.

Arnold, Matthew (1822–88), English poet, critic, and educational reformer; son of Thomas. Among his poems is *The Scholar-Gipsy*.

Arnold, Thomas (1795–1842), English headmaster, whose influence at Rugby gave it a high position among public schools.

Arrhenius, Svante August (1859–1927), Swedish chemist, one of the founders of modern physical chemistry. Received 1903 Nobel prize for originating the theory of electrolytic dissociation (ionisation).

Artaxerxes, the name borne by several ancient Persian kings. The first Artaxerxes, son of Xerxes, reigned 464–424 B.C.; he was succeeded by Darius II 424–404 B.C., who was followed by Artaxerxes II, who reigned until 358 B.C. Artaxerxes III, the last to bear the name, was a cruel and treacherous man and was poisoned in 338 B.C.

Arthur (*c.* 600), fabled Celtic warrior, whose feats, although referred to in passing in early Celtic writings, were first narrated in Geoffrey of Monmouth's *Historia* (*c.* 1135). In mediaeval times his legend developed an extensive literature, woven together by Sir Thomas Malory in his *Morte Darthur*, printed in 1485. Excavations are currently proceeding at South Cadbury, Somerset, the supposed site of his seat, Camelot.

Arundel, Thomas (1353–1414), archbishop of Canterbury 1396, and for a time lord chancellor. An enemy of heresy, he persecuted the Lollards.

Aske, Robert, leader of the Pilgrimage of Grace 1536, directed against the Henrician Reformation; executed 1537.

Asoka (c. 269–232 B.C.), Indian emperor and upholder of Buddhism. At first he expanded his empire by conquest, but on being converted to Buddhism rejected war and aimed at the good of his people. He sent Buddhist missionaries as far as Sri Lanka and Syria. Art flourished, and many rock inscriptions commemorate his doings.

Asquith, Herbert Henry, 1st Earl of Oxford and Asquith (1852–1928), Liberal prime minister 1908–16, having previously served under Gladstone. His government enacted social reforms including old-age pensions (1908) and unemployment insurance (1911), but as a war minister he had to give way to Lloyd George. He resigned leadership of his party in 1926. His daughter Violet (1887–1969), an eloquent speaker, was created a life peeress in 1964.

Asser, a Welsh monk of the 9th cent., traditionally author of a life of King Alfred.

Astor, John Jacob (1763–1848), founder of the millionaire family, was a native of Heidelberg, emigrated to America, and made a fortune by trading in fur.

Astor, Viscountess (Nancy Witcher Astor, *née* Langhorne) (1879–1964), the first woman M.P. to take her seat in the House of Commons, an American by birth, wife of the 2nd Viscount Astor.

Atatürk, Kemal (1881–1938), builder of modern Turkey. A fine soldier, he defended the Dardanelles against the British in 1915 and drove the Greeks out of Turkey in 1922. President of the Turkish Republic, and virtually dictator, 1923–38.

Athanasius, St. (296–373), upholder of the doctrine of the Trinity against Arius, who denied the divinity of Christ. He was bishop of Alexandria. He is not now thought the author of the creed which bears his name.

Athelstan (895–940), grandson of Alfred the Great, was crowned king of England in 925, and was the first ruler of all England.

Attila (406–53), invading king of the Huns from Asia. He defeated the Roman emperor Theodosius, and entered Gaul, but was defeated in 451 near Châlons-sur-Marne.

Attlee, 1st Earl (Clement Richard Attlee) (1883–1967), Labour prime minister 1945–51, having served as deputy to Churchill 1942–5. Called to the Bar in 1905, he lectured at the London

School of Economics 1913–23, was mayor of Stepney 1919, and parliamentary leader of his party 1935–55. His government helped to create a welfare society and granted independence to India. His writings include an autobiography, *As it Happened*, and *Empire into Commonwealth*.

Auchinleck, Sir Claude John Eyre (b. 1884), British field-marshal; G.O.C. North Norway 1940; C.-in-C. India 1941, 1943–7; Middle East 1941–2.

Auden, Wystan Hugh (1907–73), poet, b. in England and naturalised an American. Succeeded C. Day Lewis as professor of poetry at Oxford 1956–61. *See* **Section M, Part III.**

Auer, Leopold (1845–1930), Hungarian violinist and teacher; Mischa Elman and Jascha Heifetz were among his pupils.

Augustine of Canterbury, St. (d. *c.* 605), first archbishop of Canterbury. He was sent from Rome in 597 by Gregory the Great to convert the English peoples.

Augustus, Caius Octavianus (63 B.C.–A.D. 14), first Roman emperor. Nephew of Julius Caesar, he was for 12 years triumvir with Mark Antony and Lepidus; then reigned alone. His reign was notable for peace, and for writers like Horace and Virgil; hence Augustan age for a great period in literature (the title Augustus was given him by the Senate).

Aurelius, Marcus Antonius. *See* **Marcus Aurelius Antoninus.**

Auriol, Vincent (1884–1966), French politician. He voted against surrender in 1940, was interned and escaped to London in 1943. President of the Fourth Republic 1947–54.

Aurangzeb (1618–1707), Mogul emperor of India. Son of Shah Jehan, he obtained power by acting against his father and brothers. In his long reign the Mogul empire reached its fullest extent; but he estranged Hindus and Sikhs; and when he died his authority was in dispute and the Mogul empire broke up.

Austen, Jane (1775–1817), author of *Emma, Mansfield Park, Northanger Abbey, Persuasion, Pride and Prejudice*, and *Sense and Sensibility*. Though confining herself to the personal relations of the English middle classes, she combined artistry, accuracy, imaginative power, satiric humour, sense, and genuine feeling with the ability to create a range of living characters. She spent the first 25 years of her life at her father's Hampshire vicarage. She was un-married.

Austin, 1st Baron (Herbert Austin) (1866–1941), English motor manufacturer, pioneer of the small car—the 7-horsepower car—which he put on the market in 1921.

Avenzoar (Ibn Zuhr) (*c.* 1090–1162), Arab physician, b. Seville. His chief work was the *Tasir*.

Averroës (Ibn Rushd) (1126–98), Arab philosopher, b. Córdova. He believed in the eternity of the world (not as a single act of creation as demanded by the current theology of Islam, Christianity and Judaism, but as a continuous process) and in the eternity of a universal intelligence, indivisible but shared in by all. He expounded Aristotle to his countrymen, but his teaching was modified by Neoplatonism. He was a friend of Avenzoar.

Avicenna (Ali ibn-Sina) (980–1037), Arab philosopher and physician, of Bokhara, whose influence on mediaeval Europe was chiefly through his *Canon of Medicine*, in which he attempted to systematise all the medical knowledge up to his time.

Avogadro, Amedeo (1776–1856), Italian physicist, remembered for his hypothesis, since known as Avogadro's Law, that equal volumes of gases under identical conditions of temperature and pressure contain the same number of molecules.

Avon, Earl of. *See* **Eden, Anthony.**

Ayrton, William Edward (1847–1908), English electrical engineer, inventor of a number of electrical measuring instruments. His first wife, **Matilda Chaplin Ayrton** (1846–83), was one of the first woman doctors, and his second wife, **Hertha Ayrton** (1854–1923), became known for her scientific work on the electric arc and sand ripples and for her work for woman suffrage.

Ayub Khan, Mohammed (b. 1907–74), Pakistani military leader; president of Pakistan, 1958–69.

Azikiwe, Nnamdi (b. 1904), Nigerian statesman; president of Nigeria, 1963–6.

B

Baber, Babar or Babur (Zahir ud-din Mohammed) (1483–1530), founder of the Mogul dynasty which ruled northern India for nearly three centuries; a descendant of Tamerlane.

Bach, Johann Sebastian (1685–1750), composer. B. at Eisenach, Germany, he was successively violinist, church organist, and chief court musician. It was as organist at the Thomaskirche, Leipzig, that he composed the St. Matthew and the St. John Passion and the B minor Mass. His work was in the school of the contrapuntal style (especially the fugue and the chorale); after his day it lost favour, but during the last century it has gained ground continually. Personally he was contented and unwordly; latterly he became blind. His family was connected with music for seven generations. *See* **Section E.**

Bach, Karl Philipp Emmanuel (1714–88), 3rd son of the above, and one of the first experimenters in the symphonic and sonata forms.

Backhaus, Wilhelm (1884–1969), German pianist, gifted in interpreting classical and romantic concertos.

Bacon, Francis, Lord Verulam (1561–1626), English philosopher. He threw over Aristotelian deductive logic for the inductive method (*see* **Baconian method, Section J**); remembered for the impulse his writings gave to the foundation of the Royal Society (*c.* 1662). His chief work is the *Novum Organum*. His career as statesman under Elizabeth and James I was brought to an end by charges of corruption.

Bacon, Roger (*c.* 1219/20–1294), founder of English philosophy, advocate of the value of observation and experiment in science. He first studied arts at Oxford but when he returned from lecturing in Paris he devoted himself to experimental science, especially alchemy and optics. He became a Franciscan friar in 1257. After his death he acquired a reputation for necromancy which was undeserved.

Baden-Powell, 1st Baron (Robert Stephenson Smyth Baden-Powell) (1857–1941), founder of Boy Scouts (1908) and Girl Guides (1910) to promote good citizenship in the rising generation; Chief Scout of the World 1921–41. As a young cavalry officer in the South African war he defended Mafeking.

Baer, Karl Ernst von (1792–1876), German naturalist, b. Estonia, founder of the science of embryology. He discovered the mammalian ovum (1827). An opponent of Darwin's theory.

Baffin, William (1584–1622), British navigator and explorer who in 1616 discovered the bay which separates the north-east coast of Canada from Greenland, which bears his name.

Bagehot, Walter (1826–77), English economist and journalist, editor of *The Economist*. Among his works are *The English Constitution, Physics and Politics*, and *Lombard Street*.

Baird, John Logie (1888–1946), Scottish television pioneer, inventor of the televisor and the noctovisor.

Baker, Sir Benjamin (1840–1907), English civil engineer. With Sir John Fowler he built the Forth bridge and the London Metropolitan railway. He designed the vessel which brought Cleopatra's Needle to London. In Egypt he was consulting engineer for the Aswan dam.

Baker, Sir Herbert (1862–1946), English architect who designed the Bank of England, Rhodes house, Oxford, and, with Sir E. Lutyens, New Delhi.

Bakst, Léon (1868–1924), Russian painter who designed scenery and costumes for Diaghilev's ballets.

Baldwin of Bewdley, 1st Earl (Stanley Baldwin) (1867–1947), Conservative prime minister, 1923–4, 1924–9, and 1935–7. His handling of the crisis over Edward VIII's proposed marriage ended with the king's abdication.

Balewa, Sir Abubakar Tafawa (1912–66), federal prime minister of Nigeria, 1960–6; murdered during the crisis of January 1966.

Balfour, 1st Earl (Arthur James Balfour) (1848–1930), statesman and writer. He was Conservative prime minister 1902–5. As foreign secretary under Lloyd George, he was responsible for a declaration on Palestine.

Balliol, John de (d. 1269), founder of Balliol College, Oxford; a regent for Scotland; sided with Henry III against his barons.

Balliol, John de (1249–1315), king of Scotland. Son of the above, he claimed the throne against Robert Bruce and was chosen by the arbitrator, Edward I of England, whose overlordship he acknowledged. Later, on renouncing homage, he was taken captive and d. in retirement. His son **Edward Balliol** (d. 1363) obtained the kingdom for a time, acknowledging Edward III of England and surrendering Lothian; but retired on an annuity, 1356.

Ball, John (d. 1381), English priest and a leader of the Peasants' Revolt, after which he was executed. The couplet *When Adam delved, and Eve span, Who was then the gentleman?* is attributed to him.

Balzac, Honoré de (1799–1850), French novelist of wide influence, and author of over eighty novels to which he gave the covering title of *La Comédie Humaine*, depicting the appetites and passions of the new social class born of the revolution and Napoleon.

Bancroft, Sir Squire (1841–1926), Victorian actor-manager.

Bandaranaike, Solomon West Ridgway Dias (1899–1959), socialist prime minister of Ceylon from 1956 until his assassination in 1959. His widow, **Mrs. Sirimavo Bandaranaike**, became the world's first woman prime minister, 1960–5, 1970–.

Banks, Sir Joseph (1743–1820), an amateur scientist of wealth who accompanied Captain Cook on his expedition to the Pacific 1768–76. He left botanical collections to the British Museum.

Banting, Sir Frederick Grant (1891–1941), Canadian physician who with C. H. Best discovered insulin.

Bantock, Sir Granville (1868–1946), composer of songs, orchestral and choral music.

Barbarossa (Ital. = red beard), surname of two brothers who were Barbary pirates: **Uruz** (*c.* 1474–1518), was killed by Spaniards, and **Khaireddin** (*c.* 1483–1546) conquered Tunis for the Turks and died in Constantinople.

Barbirolli, Sir John (1899–1970), conductor of the Hallé Orchestra 1943–70; succeeded Toscanini as conductor of the New York Philharmonic Symphony Orchestra 1937–42.

Barbusse, Henri (1874–1935), French writer, author of the war novel *Le Feu*, which portrays in a starkly vivid way the experience of the common soldier.

Barham, Richard Harris (1788–1845), English humorist, author of *The Ingoldsby Legends*, written under his pen-name of Thomas Ingoldsby. His best-known poem is *The Jackdaw of Rheims*.

Barnardo, Thomas John (1845–1905), founder of homes for orphan-waifs; devoted himself to the protection, education, and advancement of destitute children.

Barrie, Sir James Matthew (1860–1937), Scottish author and dramatist. His novels include *A Window in Thrums*. Among his plays are *Dear Brutus*, *The Admirable Crichton*, and *Peter Pan* which gained great popularity with children.

Barrow, Isaac (1630–77), divine and mathematician, tutor of Sir Isaac Newton.

Barry, Sir Charles (1795–1860), architect of the houses of parliament at Westminster, the details of which were contributed by his assistant A. W. Pugin.

Barth, Karl (1886–1968), Swiss theologian, described by the late Pope John as a Protestant St. Thomas Aquinas.

Bartók, Bela (1881–1945), Hungarian composer. From an early age he was deeply interested in folk-song which inspired his researches into Hungarian and Rumanian peasant music. He left for America in 1940, where he lived precariously and apparently unhappily until the end of the war made a return possible, regrettably too late. *See* **Section E.**

Bartolommeo, Fra (di Paolo) (1475–1517), Italian painter. At first influenced by Savonarola, he later resumed painting. Some of his best work is at Lucca.

Bartolozzi, Francesco (1725–1815), Italian engraver, who settled in England and became a founder-member of the Royal Academy; noted for his stipple engravings.

Bashkirtseff, Marie (1860–84), a Russian girl, b. Poltava, in the Ukraine, writer of a famous diary.

Bassi, Agostino (1773–1856), Italian amateur microscopist who first suggested that infectious diseases might be caused by the invasion of the body by micro-organisms.

Batten, Jean Gardner (b. 1909), New Zealand airwoman who flew solo from England to Australia in 1934.

Baudelaire, Charles Pierre (1821–67), French poet of originality and sensitivity, best known for his *Les Fleurs du Mal*. His life was darkened by poverty and ill-health. He was also a talented draughtsman.

Bax, Sir Arnold (1883–1953), composer of numerous piano compositions, songs, and chamber works.

Baxter, Richard (1615–91), presbyterian divine and author; imprisoned after the Restoration. He wrote an autobiography.

Bayard, Pierre de Terrail, Seigneur de (*c.* 1474–1524), French knight, known as the "chevalier sans peur et sans reproche." He fought in campaigns against Italy and fell at the battle of Romagnano.

Bayle, Pierre (1647–1706), French philosopher, author of the *Dictionnaire historique et critique* (1697). His sceptical views influenced Voltaire and the encyclopedists of the 18th cent.

Baylis, Lilian Mary (1874–1937), manager of the Old Vic theatre from 1898 and of Sadler's Wells from 1931. Promoter of Shakespeare and of opera in English.

Beaconsfield. *See* Disraeli.

Beardsley, Aubrey Vincent (1872–98), black-and-white artist, who in a brief life published much work, some of it controversial (as in the *Yellow Book*).

Beatles, The (Paul McCartney (b. 1942), John Lennon (b. 1940), George Harrison (b. 1943), Ringo Starr (b. 1940)), a Liverpool pop group whose highly original and melodic songs held the attention of youth all over the world, especially during the period 1963–5 when they were in their prime.

Beatty, 1st Earl (David Beatty) (1871–1936), British admiral; succeeded Jellicoe as commander of the Grand Fleet 1916–19. Commanding the British battlecruisers, he fought the German fleet on 28 August 1914 in the Heligoland Bight, and on 31 May 1916 off Jutland.

Beaufort, Sir Francis (1774–1857), hydrographer of the navy, who introduced the wind scale (1805) which bears his name. *See* **Section N.**

Beaumont, Francis (1584–1616), and **Fletcher, John** (1579–1625), joint authors of many plays, including *The Maid's Tragedy* and *Philaster*.

Beaverbrook, 1st Baron (William Maxwell Aitken) (1879–1964), British newspaper owner and politician, a Canadian by birth. He gave energetic service as minister of aircraft production 1940–1. He controlled the *Daily Express*, *Sunday Express*, and *Evening Standard*, which sponsored his political campaigns.

Becket, Thomas (1118?–70), saint and martyr. An able chancellor, 1155–62, on becoming archbishop of Canterbury he made the position of the church his first care; and, coming into conflict with Henry II, was murdered in Canterbury cathedral. His shrine became a place of pilgrimage.

Beckett, Samuel (b. 1906), Anglo-Irish dramatist and novelist. Nobel prizewinner 1969. *See* **Sections I and M.**

Becquerel, Antoine Henri (1852–1908), French physicist who in 1896 discovered radioactivity in uranium. Shared with the Curies the 1903 Nobel prize in physics.

Bede, the Venerable (673–735), English historian and scholar; lived at Jarrow. His chief work is his *Ecclesiastical History* to 731.

Beecham, Sir Thomas (1879–1961), English conductor and impresario. Founded the London Philharmonic Orchestra in 1931; introduced into England the operas of Richard Strauss, Russian operas, and the Diaghilev ballet; championed the music of Delius.

Beecher, Henry Ward (1813–87), American preacher and lecturer, whose church was at Brooklyn.

Beerbohm, Sir Max (1872–1956), critic and caricaturist, master of irony and satire. His works include *Zuleika Dobson* and *A Christmas Garland*, and he contributed to the *Saturday Review*.

Beethoven, Ludwig van (1770–1827), composer. B. at Bonn (his father being a tenor singer at the Elector's court), at 17 he went to Vienna, was recognised by Mozart, and eventually settled there; he never married; gradually he became deaf. In the development from simplicity to complexity of musical treatment, he stands midway between Mozart and Wagner; but in him were uniquely combined the power to feel and the mastery of musical resources necessary to express his feelings. Between the years 1805 and 1808 he composed some of his greatest works: the oratorio *Mount of Olives*, the opera *Fidelio*, and the *Pastoral* and *Eroica* symphonies besides a number of concertos, sonatas, and songs. The symphonies, nine in number, rank as the greatest ever written and the pianoforte sonatas and string quartets are unequalled in beauty. He died in Vienna at the age of 56. *See* **Section E.**

Behring, Emil von (1854–1917), German bacteriologist, founder of the science of immunology. Nobel prizewinner 1901.

Behring, Vitus (1680–1741), Danish navigator who entered the Russian service and in 1728 discovered the strait which bears his name.

Belisarius (505–65), Roman general under Justinian who fought against the Vandals, Ostrogoths, and Persians.

Bell, Alexander Graham (1847–1922), inventor, b. Edinburgh, emigrated to Canada in 1870, later becoming an American citizen. In 1876 he exhibited an invention which was developed into the telephone. He devoted attention to the education of deaf-mutes.

Bell, Gertrude Margaret Lowthian (1868–1926), the "uncrowned queen of Arabia," was a traveller in the Middle East; her knowledge proved of service to the British government in the first world war.

Bellamy, Edward (1850–98), American author of *Looking Backward*, a prophetic utopian novel.

Bellini, family of Venetian painters: **Jacopo** (*c.* 1400–70) and his two sons, **Gentile** (1429–1507), whose works include the *Adoration of the Magi* (National Gallery); and **Giovanni** (*c.* 1429–1516), brother-in-law of Mantegna, and teacher of Giorgione and Titian, who continued his tradition of light and colour.

Bellini, Vincenzo (1801–35), Italian operatic composer; b. Sicily. His melodies were admired by Chopin. His best-known operas are *I Capuleti ed i Montecchi, La Sonnambula, Norma* and *I Puritani*. *See* **Section E.**

Belloc, Hilaire (1870–1953), versatile writer whose works include *The Bad Child's Book of Beasts, The Path to Rome, Hills and the Sea, Cautionary Tales*, and historical studies of Danton, Robespierre, and Richelieu. B. in France, he became a British subject in 1902.

Bellow, Saul (b. 1915), American novelist. Nobel prizewinner 1976. *See* **Section M, Part I.**

Belzoni, Giovanni Battista (1778–1823), Egyptologist. B. at Padua, he settled in England in 1803. His first interest was in hydraulics, and for this purpose he went to Egypt to Mehemet Ali. There he explored Thebes, Abu Simbel, and one of the pyramids, sending some sculptures to the British Museum.

Benavente y Martinez, Jacinto (1866–1954), Spanish dramatist, whose plays include *Los Intereses Creados* (Bonds of Interest). Nobel prizewinner 1922.

Benedict, St. (*c.* 480–*c.* 550), patriarch of western monasticism. B. at Nursia, and at first a hermit at Subiaco, he attracted numerous followers and grouped them in twelve monasteries. Later he went to Monte Cassino, where he formulated the Benedictine rule, of wide application in Western Christendom. *See* **Monasticism, Section J.**

Benes, Eduard (1884–1948), Czechoslovak statesman; co-founder with Thomas Masaryk of the Czech Republic after the break-up of the Austro-Hungarian monarchy (1918).

Ben Gurion, David (1886–1973), Zionist leader. He helped organise the Jewish Legion in 1918, and was prominently connected with the Labour movement in Palestine in between the world wars. Prime minister of Israel 1948–63.

Bennett, Enoch Arnold (1867–1931), English author, who wrote of the pottery towns where he was brought up. His novels include *The Old Wives' Tale, Clayhanger*, and *Hilda Lessways*.

Bennett, James Gordon (1841–1918), proprietor of the *New York Herald*. He sent out Stanley on an expedition to find Livingstone.

Bentham, Jeremy (1748–1832), utilitarian philosopher and writer on jurisprudence. His main works are *Government* and *Principles of Morals and Legislation*.

Bentley, Richard (1662–1742), classical scholar who did pioneer work in textual criticism.

Benz, Karl (1844–1929), German engineer whose motor car produced in 1885 was one of the first to be driven by an internal combustion engine.

Beresford, 1st Viscount (William Carr Beresford) (1768–1854), British general. He fought under Wellington in the Peninsular War and reorganised the Portuguese army.

Berg, Alban (1885–1935), Austrian composer whose best-known work is the three-act opera *Wozzeck*, based upon a drama by Buchner, which has become a modern classic.

Bergson, Henri Louis (1859–1941), French philosopher, exponent of the theory of creative evolution and the life force. Nobel prizewinner 1927. *See* **Vitalism, Section J.**

Bériot, Charles Auguste de (1802–70), Belgian violinist, whose wife was the operatic contralto Malibran. His son, **Charles Wilfrid de Bériot** (1833–1914) was a pianist and the teacher of Ravel.

Berkeley, George (1685–1753), idealist philosopher and critic of Locke. His spiritual outlook led him to believe that reality exists only in the eye of God, that it is undiscoverable by science, though it can be revealed by religion. His chief work is *Alciphron*. He was a master of prose. Of Irish birth, he became bishop of Cloyne.

Berlin, Irving (b. 1888), American composer of popular songs, b. Russia; pioneer of both ragtime and jazz music. His songs include *Alexander's Rag-time Band, Always, What'll I do?*; his musicals include *Annie Get your Gun* and *Call me Madam*.

Berlin, Sir Isaiah (b. 1909), British philosopher, b. Riga; Chichele Prof. of Social and Political Theory at Oxford 1957–67. His works include *Karl Marx, The Hedgehog and the Fox*, and *The Age of Enlightenment*. O.M. (1971).

Berlioz, Hector (1803–69), composer. B. near Grenoble, the son of a doctor, his romantic sensibility, taste for the grand (as in his *Requiem*), and response to literary influence made him a prime figure in the French romantic movement. His works include the symphony *Romeo and Juliet*, and the operas *Benvenuto Cellini* and *Beatrice and Benedict*. *See* **Section E.**

Bernadotte, Count Folke (1895–1948), nephew of the late King Gustav of Sweden. U.N. mediator for Palestine 1947. Assassinated by Jewish terrorists.

Bernadotte, Jean Baptiste (1764–1844), a French commander who served under Napoleon, and in 1810 was chosen heir to the throne of Sweden. In 1818 he succeeded as Charles XIV.

Bernal, John Desmond (1901–71), physicist, b. Ireland. Prof. of Physics, Birkbeck College, Univ. of London, 1937–63, Prof. of Crystallography, 1963–8. Author of *The Social Functions of Science, Science in History, The Origin of Life*. Lenin peace prize 1953.

Bernard, Claude (1813–78), French physiologist whose discoveries though not of immediate application paved the way for the work of Pavlov and Hopkins.

Bernard of Menthon (923–1008), patron saint of mountaineers. He founded Alpine hospices in the passes that bear his name.

Bernard, St. (1090–1153), abbot of Clairvaux, which became a chief centre of the Cistercian order. This order aimed at seclusion and austerity, and practised manual work. His writings had wide influence in Europe.

Bernhardt, Sarah (1844–1923), French tragedienne, b. Paris, daughter of a Dutch jewess. She became a member of the Comédie Française after the siege of Paris. Her first performance in London was in 1879. Her successes included *Phèdre, La Dame aux Camélias, Fédora, Thédora*, and *La Tosca*, and she produced and played in Racine and Molière.

Best, Charles Herbert (b. 1899), Canadian physiologist, who with F. G. Banting discovered the use of insulin in the treatment of diabetes.

Berthelot, Marcellin Pierre Eugène (1827–1907), French chemist and politician. He was the first to produce organic compounds synthetically.

Berzelius, Jöns Jakob (1779–1848), Swedish chemist, founder of electrochemical theory. His work was mainly concerned with the exact determination of atomic and molecular weights and he devised the system of chemical symbols in use today.

Bessemer, Sir Henry (1813–98), inventor of the process of converting cast-iron direct into steel. This revolutionised steel manufacture, reducing the cost of production and extending its use.

Betjeman, Sir John (b. 1906), English poet, author and broadcaster; succeeded C. Day Lewis as poet laureate 1972.

Bevan, Aneurin (1897–1960), British socialist politician, architect of the National Health Service which came into operation in 1948.

Beveridge, 1st Baron (William Henry Beveridge) (1879–1963), British economist who drew up the Beveridge Plan (1942), which formed the basis of the present social security services.

Bevin, Ernest (1881–1951), British trade union leader, who later became a forceful foreign secretary. He was assistant general secretary of the Dockers Union (his masterly advocacy of the London dockers' case in 1920 earned him the title of "the dockers' K.C."), later general secretary of the Transport and General Workers Union; Minister of Labour 1940–5, and Foreign Secretary 1945–51.

Beyle, Marie Henri. *See* **Stendhal.**

Bhave, Vinova (b. 1895), Indian reformer, leader of the Sarvodaya movement. A follower of Gandhi, in 1951 he began a walking mission to persuade landlords to help landless peasants.

Bichat, Marie François Xavier (1771–1802), French physiologist whose study of tissues founded modern histology. His theory was that life is "the sum of the forces that restrict death."

Biddle, John (1615–62), unitarian. He taught in Gloucester; was several times imprisoned for his controversial writings; and died of fever contracted in prison.

Binyon, Laurence (1869–1943), poet, art critic, and orientalist, who worked at the British Museum 1893–1933.

Birch, Samuel John Lamorna (1869–1955), English landscape painter in watercolour, known for his Cornish and Australian studies.

Birkbeck, George (1776–1841), founder of mechanics' institutes, first at Glasgow, later in London (the Birkbeck Institution developed into Birkbeck College, London University).

Birkenhead, 1st Earl of (Frederick Edwin Smith) (1872–1930), English lawyer and politician; lord chancellor 1919–22; secretary for India 1924–8.

Bishop, Sir Henry Rowley (1786–1855), English composer who wrote *Home, sweet Home*, glees, and operas.

Bismarck, Otto Eduard Leopold von, Prince Bismarck, Duke of Lauenburg (1815–98), Prusso-German diplomat and statesman, chief architect of the German empire. He was of Junker family. As Prussian ambassador at St. Petersburg (1859–62) and at Paris (1862), he learned to assess the European situation. He was recalled to Berlin by the king to become chief Prussian minister; and when the house of representatives would not pass a military bill he closed the house. He used a dispute over Schleswig-Holstein to bring about the defeat of Austria at Königgratz in 1866; and he provoked the Franco-Prussian war of 1870–1 when France was defeated at Sedan. Germany then became united under the military leadership of Prussia, with the king as emperor, instead of by the slower processes of democracy. He presided over the Berlin Congress of European powers in 1878. In 1884 he began a colonial policy. His authoritarian system, in spite of its inherent defects, was at least based on cautious and accurate assessment of power politics. This factor was not understood by William II, who succeeded as emperor in 1888, and dismissed the "iron chancellor" in 1890.

Bizet, Georges (1838–75), properly **Alexandre César Léopold**, French composer, chiefly remembered for his opera *Carmen* from the story by Merimée.

Björnson, Björnstjerne (1832–1910), Norwegian poet, dramatist and novelist. His work provides an image of Norwegian life from the period of the sagas (*Kong Sverre*) to contemporary problems (*Over Aevne*), and he wrote the national anthem.

Black, Joseph (1728–90), Scottish chemist. A professor first at Glasgow, later at Edinburgh, he was the first to undertake a detailed study of a chemical reaction. He laid the foundation of the quantitative science of heat and his discovery of latent heat was applied by Watt in improving his steam-engine.

Blackett of Chelsea, Baron (Patrick Maynard Stuart Blackett) (1897–1974), British physicist whose work on nuclear and cosmic ray physics gained him a Nobel prize in 1948; author of *Military and Political Consequences of Atomic Energy* (1948), *Lectures on Rock Magnetism* (1956), *Studies of War* (1962). Pres. British Assoc. 1956; Pres. Royal Society 1966–70; O.M. 1967.

Blackmore, Richard Doddridge (1825–1900), English novelist and author of *Lorna Doone.*

Blackstone, Sir William (1723–80), English judge. His *Commentaries on the Laws of England* is a classic.

Blackwood, Algernon (1869–1951), English novelist and writer of short stories.

Blackwood, William (1776–1834), originator of *Blackwood's Magazine.*

Blair, Robert (1699–1746), Scottish poet, author of *The Grave.*

Blake, Robert (1599–1657), Parliamentary general and an admiral in the Cromwellian navy in the Dutch and Spanish wars.

Blake, William (1757–1827), English poet, mystic, and artist, son of a hosier in Carnaby market, Soho. A solitary and deeply religious man, he had a hatred of materialism. He produced his own books, engraving on copper plates both the text of his poems and the illustrations. His *Book of Job* is a masterpiece in line-engraving in metal, his poems range from the mystical and almost incomprehensible to the delightfully simple *Songs of Innocence*. He has been called "the great teacher of the modern western world." His art is in many ways reminiscent of that of another rebel of the same day, the Spanish painter Goya.

Blanqui, Louis Auguste (1805–81), French revolutionary leader, master of insurrection. He invented the term "dictatorship of the proletariat," and his social theories, stressing the class struggle, influenced Marx. Active in 1830, 1848, and 1871, he spent 37 years in prison.

Blériot, Louis (1872–1936), French airman; the first to fly the English Channel from Calais to Dover, on 25 July 1909.

Bligh, William (1754–1817), sailor, b. Plymouth. He accompanied Cook 1772–4, and discovered bread-fruit; but was in 1789 cast adrift from *The Bounty* by his mutinous crew. As governor of New South Wales (1806) he fought to suppress the rum traffic.

Blind, Karl (1826–1907), German agitator, b. Mannheim. He was active in the German risings of 1848, and imprisoned; but escaped and settled in England, remaining in touch with men like Mazzini and Louis Blanc.

Bliss, Sir Arthur (1891–1975), English composer; succeeded Sir Arnold Bax as Master of the Queen's Musick 1953.

Bloch, Ernest (1880–1959), composer, whose music is characterised by Jewish and oriental themes. B. in Geneva, he became a naturalised American.

Blondin, Charles (1824–97), French rope performer, who crossed the Niagara Falls on a tight-rope.

Blücher, Gebhard Leberecht von (1742–1819), Prussian general. He fought against Napoleon, especially at Lützen and Leipzig; and he completed Wellington's victory at Waterloo by his timely arrival.

Blum, Léon (1872–1950), French statesman, leader of the French Socialist Party. His efforts strengthened the growth of the Popular Front and the campaign against appeasement of Hitler. He held office only briefly and was interned in Germany 1940–5.

Blunden, Edmund Charles (1896-1974), English poet and critic; professor of poetry at Oxford 1966–8.

Blunt, Wilfrid Scawan (1840–1922), English poet and political writer who championed Egyptian, Indian, and Irish independence.

Boadicea (Boudicca), queen of the Iceni in eastern Britain, who fought against the Roman invaders, but was defeated in A.D. 61 and killed herself.

Boccaccio, Giovanni (1313–75), Italian author, father of the novel. He is chiefly known for his *Decameron* (set in the neighbourhood of Florence during the plague), and for his life of Dante.

Boccherini, Luigi (1743–1805), Italian cellist and composer of chamber music. He settled in Madrid.

Bode, Johann Ehlert (1747–1826), German astronomer remembered for his theoretical calculation (known as Bode's law) of the proportionate distances of the planets from the sun. *See* **L16.**

Boethius (480–524) Roman scientific writer who translated the logical works of Aristotle and provided the dark ages with some elementary mathematical treatises.

Bohr, Niels Henrik David (1885–1962), Danish nuclear physicist whose researches into the structure of the atom gave him great authority in the world of theoretical physics. With Rutherford he applied the quantum theory to the study of atomic processes. Nobel prizewinner 1922.

Boieldieu, François Adrien (1775–1834), French composer especially of operas, including *La Dame blanche.*

Boileau-Despréaux, Nicolas (1636–1711), French literary critic and poet, best known for his *Satires.*

Boito, Arrigo (1842–1918), Italian poet and composer; he wrote the libretti of *Otello* and *Falstaff* for Verdi.

Boleyn, Anne (1507–36), queen of Henry VIII and mother of Queen Elizabeth. She was maid-in-waiting to Catherine of Aragon and her successor when Catherine's marriage was annulled. She failed to produce a male heir and was beheaded on a charge of adultery.

Bolivar, Simón (1783–1830), South American revolutionist, called the Liberator, b. Carácas. He led independence movements in the north-west of South America against Spanish rule, aiming at a South American federation. He founded Grand Colombia (now Venezuela, Colombia, Panama, Ecuador). He died poor, of tuberculosis, but is revered as a Latin-American hero.

Bonaventura, St. (1221–74), Franciscan theologian, b. Orvieto. His mystical theory of knowledge was in the Augustinian tradition.

Bondfield, Margaret Grace (1873–1953), as minister of Labour, 1929–31, she was the first woman to enter the cabinet and to be a member of the privy council.

Bondi, Sir Hermann (b. 1919), British mathematician and astronomer, b. Vienna; chief scientist to the Min. of Defence, 1971–; associated with the steady state theory of the universe. *See* **F5.**

Bone, Sir Muirhead (1876–1953), architectural draughtsman and etcher, b. Glasgow; excelled in dry-point and drawings of intricate scaffolding; official war artist in both world wars.

Bonheur, Rose (1822-99), French painter of animals.

Boniface, St. (680–754), apostle of Germany. B. at Credition, Devon, his name being Wynfrith, he became a Benedictine monk, and went as missionary to Friesland, securing papal approval. He founded Fulda Abbey and became archbishop of Mainz, but was martyred.

Bonnard, Pierre (1867–1947), French painter of landscapes, still life, and nudes, a colourist and skilled draughtsman.

Booth, Edwin Thomas (1833–93), American Shakespearean actor, brother of John Wilkes Booth who assassinated President Lincoln.

Booth, William (1829–1912), founder and first general of the Salvation Army, b. Nottingham. In 1865, with the help of his wife, Catherine Booth, he began mission work in the East End of London, which led to the creation in 1878 of the Salvation Army on military lines. It developed branches in many parts of the world. His son Bramwell (d. 1929) and his daughter Evangeline were among his successors. *See also* **Salvation Army, Section J.**

Borges, Jorge Luis (b. 1899), Argentine poet, critic, and short story writer. Some of his work has been translated into English, including *A Personal Anthology* and *Labyrinths.*

Borgia, Caesar (1476–1507), Italian general. The son of Pope Alexander VI, at 17 he was suspected of murdering his brother. He became captain-general of the church, and made himself master of Romagna, the Marches, and Umbria. Banished by Pope Julius II, he met his death fighting in Spain.

Borlaug, Norman Ernest (b. 1914), American wheat scientist, responsible for the "green revolution" (*see* **Section L**) which is transforming the agricultural prospects of the less-developed countries of the world. Nobel prize for peace 1970.

Borodin, Alexander Porfyrievich (1833–87), Russian composer who taught chemistry and founded a school of medicine for women. In a busy professional life he wrote two symphonies, two string quartets, the symphonic sketch *In the Steppes of Central Asia* and the opera *Prince Igor. See* **Section E.**

Borrow, George Henry (1803–81), English author, for many years agent for the British and Foreign Bible Society; in the course of his wanderings he studied gypsy life and wrote of his experiences in *Lavengro, Romany Rye, Bible in Spain.*

Bose, Subhas Chandra (1897–1945), Indian nationalist leader; killed in a plane crash.

Boswell, James (1740–95), Scottish author of *The Life of Dr. Johnson*, with whom he spent some years in intimacy. His own journals and letters recently published form an extensive literary collection.

Botha, Louis (1862–1919), South African soldier and statesman. In command of Transvaal forces 1899–1902 in the Boer war, he became prime minister of the Transvaal in 1907, and first premier of the Union of South Africa in 1910. In the 1914–18 war he conquered territory then under German rule.

Bottesini, Giovanni (1821–89) Italian double-bass player.

Botticelli, Sandro (*c.* 1445–1510), Italian painter. He worked under Fra Lippo Lippi, and was influenced by Savonarola. His art is delicate and poetic. His *Birth of Venus* is in the Uffizi Gallery, Florence, and his *Mars and Venus* in the National Gallery. He illustrated Dante's *Inferno.*

Bottomley, Horatio (1860–1933), English politician, journalist, and notorious financier, who died in poverty after serving a prison sentence for fraud.

Botvinnik, Mikhail (b. 1911), Russian chess player; world champion 1948–57, 1958–60, 1961–3. Retired 1965.

Boughton, Rutland (1878–1960), English composer of the opera *The Immortal Hour*, and writer on the history and philosophy of music.

Boult, Sir Adrian (b. 1889), conductor of the London Philharmonic Orchestra 1950–7, and of the B.B.C. Symphony Orchestra 1930–50. Musical Director B.B.C. 1930–42.

Boulton, Matthew (1728–1809), engineer who in partnership with James Watt manufactured steam-engines at his Soho works near Birmingham. He also minted a new copper coinage for Great Britain.

Bowdler, Thomas (1754–1825), issued for family reading expurgated editions of Shakespeare and Gibbon hence the term "bowdlerise."

Boyce, William (1710–79), London organist and composer, who also collected the works of English church composers. He was master of the orchestra of George III.

Boyd Orr, 1st Baron (John Boyd Orr) (1880–1971), British physiologist and nutritional expert. Director-general World Food and Agricultural Organisation 1945–8. Chancellor Glasgow Univ. 1946. Nobel prizewinner 1949.

Boyle, Robert (1627–91), English scientist who with Robert Hooke laid the foundations of the modern sciences of chemistry and physics. He established the law which states that the volume of a gas varies inversely as the pressure upon it, provided temperature is constant. His chief work is the *Sceptical Chymist* (1661).

Bradley, Omar Nelson (b. 1893), American general. In the second world war he commanded in Tunis, Sicily, and Normandy, and was made chief of staff in 1948. Retired 1953.

Bradman, Sir Donald George (b. 1908), Australian cricketer who captained Australia in test matches against England 1936–48.

Bragg, Sir William Henry (1862–1942), English physicist. He held the chair of physics at Adelaide, Leeds, and London, and was professor of chemistry at the Royal Institution 1923–42. Pres. Royal Society 1935–40.

Bragg, Sir William Lawrence (1890–1971), son of the above. He succeeded Rutherford at the Cavendish laboratory, Cambridge, 1938–53. Dir. Royal Institution 1954–66. Shared with his father the 1915 Nobel prize for their fundamental work on X-rays and crystal structure.

Brahe, Tycho (1546–1601), Danish astronomer. At his island observatory at Uraniborg, provided by his sovereign, he carried out systematic observations which enabled Kepler to work out his planetary laws.

Brahms, Johannes (1833–97), composer. B. in Hamburg (son of a double-bass player), he did not marry, and led a simple life devoted to music; latterly he lived in Vienna. He was a friend of the Schumanns. *See* **Section E.**

Braille, Louis (1809–52), French educationist, who, as teacher of the blind, perfected his system of reading and writing for the blind. As the result of an accident when he was three years old he was himself blind.

Bramah, Joseph (1749–1814), English inventor of the safety-lock and hydraulic press which bear his name. He also invented the water-closet (1778) and a machine for printing the serial numbers on bank-notes.

Brandes, Georg Morris Cohen (1842–1927), Danish literary critic who exerted a vitalising influence on literature and art.

Brandt, Willy (b. 1913), first social democratic chancellor of the Federal Republic of Germany, 1969–74. His main achievements have been the Moscow and Warsaw treaties (1972) and the treaty between E. and W. Germany (1973) which recognised their sovereign existence.

Brangwyn, Sir Frank (1867–1956), artist of Welsh extraction, b. Bruges; first worked for William Morris making cartoons for textiles; he excelled in murals and in etching.

Breakspear, Nicholas. *See* **Adrian IV.**

Brecht, Bertold (1898–1956), German dramatist and poet, whose brilliant experimental theatre was characteristic of the period in Germany between the two world wars. Being a Marxist, he left Germany in 1933 for Russia, went to the U.S.A. in 1941, and returned to East Germany after the war. His plays include *The Threepenny Opera* (with music by Kurt Weill), *Mother Courage* and *The Caucasian Chalk Circle.* *See* **Section I.**

Brennan, Louis (1853–1932), inventor, b. Ireland. His inventions include a gyro-directed torpedo and a mono-rail locomotive on the gyroscope principle.

Breton, Andrée (1896–1966), French poet, founder of the surrealist literary movement in France and a close friend of Apollinaire.

Brewster, Sir David (1781–1868), Scottish physicist, noted for his research into the polarisation of light; invented the kaleidoscope. He helped to found the British Association for the Advancement of Science.

Brezhnev, Leonid Ilyich (b. 1906), succeeded Khrushchev as First Secretary of the Soviet Communist Party in 1964. In the Brezhnev decade the Soviet Union has achieved strategic parity with the United States, society has become more stable and education and living standards have steadily improved.

Bridges, Robert (1844–1930), poet laureate 1913–30. His *Testament of Beauty* (1929) has been called " a compendium of the wisdom, learning and experience of an artistic spirit." His son Edward (d. 1969) was the head of the civil service from 1945.

Bridgewater, 3rd Duke of (Francis Egerton) (1736–1803), founder of British inland navigation by his canal, to the design of James Brindley (*q.v.*) from Manchester to his coal mines at Worsley, later extended to join the Mersey at Runcorn.

Bridie, James (pseudonym of Osborne Henry Mavor) (1888–1951), Scottish author and dramatist. The first of his many successful plays was *The Anatomist*, produced in 1931. Other plays include *Tobias and the Angel, Jonah and the Whale, Mr. Bolfrey, Dr. Angelus.*

Bright, Sir Charles Tilston (1832–88), English telegraph engineer who supervised the laying of the British telegraph network and the Atlantic cables (1856–8).

Bright, John (1811–89), radical Quaker statesman and orator, b. Rochdale: friend of Cobden, with whom he promoted the movement for free trade.

Brindley, James (1716–72), English canal builder, b. Derbyshire, of poor parents, apprenticed as a millwright. He was employed by the Duke of Bridgewater (*q.v.*) and designed and constructed the Bridgewater canal, carrying it over the R. Irwell by an aqueduct, the first of its kind. He also built the Grand Trunk canal linking the Mersey with the Trent.

Britten, Baron (Edward Benjamin Britten) (1913–76), English composer, closely associated with the Aldeburgh festival. O.M. 1965. *See* **Section E.**

Broca, Paul (1824–80), French pathologist, anthropologist and pioneer in neuro-surgery. He localised the seat of speech in the brain and originated methods for measuring brain and skull ratios.

Broch, Hermann (1886–1951), Austrian novelist, author of the trilogy *The Sleepwalkers.* Lived in U.S.A. after 1938.

Broglie, prominent family of Piedmontese origin; **Victor Maurice** (1647–1727), and **François Marie** (1671–1745) were marshals of France; **Louis Victor, Prince de Broglie** (b. 1892) received the Nobel prize for his work on quantum mechanics, and his brother **Maurice, Duc de Broglie** (1875–1960), also a physicist, is noted for his work on the ionisation of gases, radioactivity, and X-rays.

Brontë, Charlotte (1816–55), forceful novelist, daughter of an Anglican clergyman of Irish descent, incumbent of Haworth, Yorkshire. She published under a pseudonym *Jane Eyre*, which was at once successful, and was followed by *Shirley* and *Villette.* Her sister **Emily** (1818–48) wrote poetry and also *Wuthering Heights*; and **Anne** (1820–49) wrote *Agnes Grey.*

Brooke, Rupert (1887–1915), English poet who died during the first world war, whose works, though few, showed promise and include the poems *Grantchester* and *If I Should Die.*

Brougham and Vaux, 1st Baron (Henry Peter Brougham) (1778–1868), English legal reformer; advocate of Queen Caroline against George IV; helped to found London university.

Brown, Sir Arthur Whitten (1886–1948), together with Sir John Alcock (d. 1919) in 1919 made the first transatlantic flight, crossing from Newfoundland to Ireland in 16 hr. 12 min.

Brown, John (1800–59), American abolitionist. His action in inciting Negro slaves to rebel in 1859 led to the civil war. He was hanged after failing to hold the U.S. arsenal at Harper's Ferry which he had captured. Known as " Old Brown of Osawatomie " and regarded as a martyr.

Browne, Charles Farrer (1834–67), American humorist who wrote under the pseudonym of Artemus Ward.

Browne, Hablot Knight (1815–82), English artist, the " Phiz " of many book illustrations, including Dickens's *Pickwick Papers.*

Browne, Sir Thomas (1605–82), author of *Religio Medici* and *Urne-Buriall* was born in London and practised in Norwich as a physician.

Browning, Elizabeth Barrett (1806–61), English poet. Owing to an injury in childhood, she spent her youth lying on her back, but her meeting with Robert Browning, whom she married, brought a remarkable recovery. In her lifetime her works were more read than those of her husband. They include *Cry of the Children, Sonnets from the Portuguese*, and *Aurora Leigh.*

Browning, Robert (1812–89), English poet. Because of his involved style his reputation grew only slowly. In *Strafford* and *The Blot on the 'Scutcheon* he attempted drama also. He married Elizabeth Barrett and lived mainly abroad. His works include *Dramatis Personae* and *The Ring and The Book.*

Bruce, Robert (1274–1329), Scottish national leader against Edward I and Edward II of England. Crowned king in 1306, after years of struggle he defeated Edward II at Bannockburn in 1314.

Bruce, William Spiers (1867–1921), Scottish polar explorer who led the Scottish national antarctic expedition in the *Scotia* 1902–4 and set up a meteorological station on the South Orkneys.

Bruch, Max (1838–1920), German composer and conductor, best known for his G minor violin concerto.

Bruckner, Anton (1824–96), Austrian composer and organist. *See* **Section E.**

Brummell, George Bryan (1778–1840), "Beau Brummell," fashion leader and friend of the Prince Regent (George IV).

Brunel, Isambard Kingdom (1806–59), English civil engineer, son of **Sir Marc Isambard Brunel** (1769–1849), whom he assisted in building the Thames (Rotherhithe) tunnel. He was engineer of the Great Western Railway and built the ocean liners, the *Great Western*, the *Great Britain* (brought back from the Falkland Is. to Bristol in 1970), and the *Great Eastern*. His other works include the Clifton suspension bridge over the R. Avon at Bristol and the Royal Albert bridge over the R. Tamar at Saltash.

Brunelleschi, Filippo (1377–1446), Italian architect, b. Florence; he adapted the ideals of the Roman period. Examples of his work in Florence include the Pitti Palace, the churches of San Lorenzo and San Spirito, and the cathedral dome (the biggest in Europe).

Bruno, Giordano (1548–1600), Italian philosopher. A Dominican friar, he came to favour the astronomical views of Copernicus and was burnt at the stake.

Bruno, St. (*c.* 1032–1101), German monk, founder in 1084 of the Carthusian order at La Grande Chartreuse in the French Alps.

Brutus, Marcus Junius (85–42 B.C.), conspirator against Julius Caesar; later committed suicide.

Buchanan, George (1506–82), Scottish humanist who spent most of his life in France lecturing and writing Latin poems, plays, and treatises. Montaigne, Mary Queen of Scots, and James VI of Scotland were his pupils at various times.

Buchner, Eduard (1860–1917), German chemist, remembered for his work on the chemistry of fermentation. Nobel prizewinner 1907.

Büchner, Georg (1813–37), German dramatist. Dying at 24, his limited output (principally *Dantons Tod* and the fragment *Wozzeck*) is marked by power and maturity.

Buckle, Henry Thomas (1821–62), author of *The History of Civilisation in England.*

Buddha. *See* **Gautama, Siddhartha.**

Budge, Sir Ernest Alfred Wallis (1857–1934), archaeologist who conducted excavations in Mesopotamia and Egypt.

Buffon, Georges-Louis Leclerc, Comte de (1707–88), French naturalist, author of the *Histoire naturelle* (44 vols., 1749–1804).

Bulganin, Nikolai Alexandrovich (1895–1975), Soviet prime minister 1955–8; defence minister 1947–9, 1953–5. Retired 1960.

Bull, John (*c.* 1562–1628), English composer; possibly composer of *God save the Queen.*

Bülow, Hans Guido von (1830–94), German pianist and conductor. He married Liszt's daughter Cosima, who later left him to marry Wagner.

Bunsen, Robert Wilhelm (1811–99), German chemist, discoverer of the metals caesium and rubidium, and inventor of the Bunsen burner, battery, and pump. Made important observations in spectrum analysis.

Bunyan, John (1628–88), was originally a travelling tinker and is believed to have served in the Parliamentary army. He joined an Independent church in Bedford in 1655 and became a popular preacher. After the Restoration he was thrown into prison, and there wrote *The Pilgrim's Progress.* Of his 60 works, the best known after *Pilgrim's Progress* are *The Holy War*, *Grace Abounding*, and *Mr. Badman*. *See also* **Allegory, Section M, Part VI.**

Burckhardt, Jacob Christoph (1818–97), Swiss historian, author of *The Civilisation of the Renaissance in Italy.*

Burghley, 1st Baron (William Cecil) (1520–98), English statesman. After holding office under her two predecessors, he was Queen Elizabeth I's secretary of state, 1558–72, and lord high treasurer, 1572–98.

Burke, Edmund (1729–97), Whig writer and political philosopher. B. in Dublin, he became secretary to Lord Rockingham and entered parliament in 1765. He advocated the emancipation (though not the independence) of the American colonies; and better administration in India; but was against the French revolution.

Burnet, Gilbert (1643–1715) bishop of Salisbury, b. Edinburgh. He wrote a *History of his Own Times*, which deals with many events of which he had personal knowledge.

Burnet, Sir John James (1859–1938), architect, b. Glasgow. The north front of the British Museum (King Edward's galleries) is his most important work in London.

Burney, Fanny (Madame D'Arblay) (1752–1840), originator of the simple novel of home life. Daughter of the organist, Dr. Burney, she published *Evelina* in 1778, and this brought her into court and literary society. She also wrote *Cecilia* and *Camilla.*

Burns, Robert (1759–96), Scottish poet. The son of a cottar, his first poems published in 1786 were at once successful, and he bought a farm. The farm failed, but he had a post as exciseman, and continued to write simply with tenderness and humour. Among his best known poems are *Auld Lang Syne*, *Scots wa hae*, *Comin' through the rye*, and *The Banks of Doon.*

Burton, Sir Richard Francis (1821–90), British explorer and orientalist, who made a pilgrimage to Mecca and Medina in 1853 disguised as a Moslem. He explored Central Africa and translated the *Arabian Nights* (16 vols.).

Burton, Robert (1577–1640), English clergyman and scholar, author of *The Anatomy of Melancholy.*

Busoni, Ferruccio Benvenuto (1866–1920), pianist and composer of three operas (the last *Dr. Faust*, unfinished at his death), much orchestral and chamber music, and works for the piano. B. in Empoli, he lived in Germany. *See* **Section E.**

Butler, Joseph (1692–1752), English bishop, remembered for his *Analogy of Religion*, published in 1736 in reply to deistic attacks.

Butler, Nicholas Murray (1862–1947), American educationist who shared with the sociologist Jane Addams the 1931 Nobel peace prize.

Butler, Baron (Richard Austen Butler) (b. 1902), Conservative politician who brought in the Education Act of 1944 and helped secure Conservative acceptance of the welfare state. He took a leading part in drafting the *Industrial Charter* of 1947. "Butskellism" was the term applied to Conservative social and economic policies of the early fifties. Master of Trinity College, Cambridge, 1965. Life peer 1965.

Butler, Samuel (1612–80), English verse-satirist, author of the poem *Hudibras* against the Puritans.

Butler, Samuel (1835–1902), English novelist and satirist, author of *Erewhon* and its sequel *Erewhon Revisited.* Other works include *The Fair Haven*, *Life and Habit*, and *Evolution Old and New*, in which he attacked Darwinism. His autobiographical novel *The Way of All Flesh* and his *Notebooks* were published after his death. He exhibited regularly at the Academy and was also a musician.

Butt, Clara (1872–1936), English contralto; made her début in London in 1892. She married Kennerly Rumford in 1900.

Buxton, Sir Thomas Fowell (1786–1845), English social reformer; succeeded Wilberforce as leader of the anti-slavery group in parliament.

Buys Ballot, Christoph Henrich Diedrich (1817–90), Dutch meteorologist who formulated the law which bears his name (an observer with back to wind in northern hemisphere has lower pressure to left; in southern hemisphere to right).

Byrd, Richard Evelyn (1888–1957), American rear-admiral, explorer and aviator. He flew over the north pole, 1926; and in 1929 made the first flight over the south pole. He made other polar expeditions in 1925, 1933–5, 1939 and 1946.

Byrd, William (1543–1623), English composer of church music, sacred choral music, string music, vocal and instrumental music; and a founder of the school of English madrigalists. He was organist of Lincoln cathedral at 20 and later of Queen Elizabeth's chapel royal. *See* **Section E.**

Byron, 6th Baron (George Gordon Byron) (1788–1824), English romantic poet who influenced European literature and thought. At 20 he published *Hours of Idleness*, which was violently attacked by the *Edinburgh Review*. This provoked his retaliatory *English Bards and Scotch Reviewers*, which caused a sensation. His *Childe Harold's Pilgrimage* appeared in 1812. His married life was unhappy. He went to help the Greeks in their struggle for independence and died at Missolonghi.

C

Cable, George Washington (1844–1925), American author and social critic, b. New Orleans, whose writings reflect the colour problems of his day: *Ole Creol Days, The Silent South.*

Cabot, John (1425–*c.* 1500), Genoese explorer who settled in Bristol and sailed westwards under letters-patent from Henry VII of England in 1497. Discovered Newfoundland and Nova Scotia, believing them to be part of Asia, and may have reached the mainland of America before Columbus did. His son:

Cabot, Sebastian (1474–1557), was born in Venice, and in 1509 in search of a north-west passage to Asia sailed as far as Hudson Bay. Entered Spanish service in 1512, and spent several years exploring the Plate and Paraná rivers. Re-entered English service in 1548 and organised expedition to seek a north-east passage to India, which resulted in trade with Russia. English claim to North America is founded on the voyages of the Cabots.

Cabral, Pedro Alvarez (*c.* 1467–*c.* 1520), Portuguese navigator, friend of Vasco da Gama, discovered Brazil, which he named "Terra da Santa Cruz."

Cadbury, George (1839–1922), liberal Quaker philanthropist of Cadbury Bros., mainly responsible for the pioneer garden city of Bournville.

Cadogan, Sir Alexander (1884–1968), English diplomat. He helped to draft the charter of the United Nations organisation and became Gt. Britain's representative on the Security Council.

Caedmon, the first English Christian poet, lived in the 7th cent. and, according to Bede, was first a cowherd and later a monk at Whitby. His poetry was based on the scriptures.

Caesar, Caius Julius (*c.* 101–44 B.C.), Roman general and writer. Under the declining republic, he was assigned in 61 the province of Gaul; in the course of pacifying it he invaded Britain (55 B.C.). Opposition in Rome to his career, mainly from Pompey, provoked him in 49 to the defiance of crossing the Rubicon with his army. He defeated Pompey, whom he pursued to Egypt, where he established Cleopatra as queen. At Rome he became dictator, and his reforms include the Julian calendar. He was murdered in 44. His career paved the way for Rome becoming an empire under his nephew Octavian. His writings are masterly accounts of his wars.

Calderón de la Barca, Pedro (1600–81), Spanish dramatist, representative of contemporary Spanish thought, who also wrote court spectacles for Philip IV. Among his best-known works are *La Vida es Sueño* and *El divino Orfeo.*

Callaghan, James (b. 1912), Labour's fourth prime minister; elected leader of the Labour Party, April 1976, following Sir Harold Wilson's resignation; elected for South Cardiff 1950; served as Chancellor of the Exchequer, Home Secretary, and Foreign Secretary in the Labour administrations, 1964–70, 1974–76.

Calvin, John (1509–64), French Protestant reformer and theologian. B. in Picardy, he broke with the Roman Catholic church about 1533, and subsequently settled in Geneva, where from 1541 he established a theocratic regime of strict morality. His theology was published in his *Institutes*; while, like Luther, he accepted justification by faith without works, he also believed in predestination. His doctrines spread on the continent, in Scotland and to some extent in England. *See* **Calvinism, Section J.**

Câmara, Helder Pessoa (b. 1909), Brazilian archbishop of Recife; critic of the economic imperialism of multinational companies and courageous campaigner for social reform in Latin America.

Camden, William (1551–1623), English antiquary and historian. His *Britannia* appeared in 1586.

Cameron, Sir David Young (1865–1945), Scottish etcher and landscape painter.

Cameron, Richard (1648–80), Scottish preacher who revolted in defence of the Solemn League and Covenant and was killed at Airds Moss (Ayrshire).

Cameron, Verney Lovett (1844–94), English explorer, the first to cross the African continent from east to west. He surveyed Lake Tanganyika and in 1872 went out to find Livingstone.

Camillus, Marcus Furius (4th cent. B.C.), Roman general. When the Gauls attacked in 387 B.C., he was made dictator and defeated them.

Camões, Luis Vaz de (1624–80), Portuguese poet, author of *Os Lusiadas*, an epic of Portuguese history and discovery.

Campbell, Colin, 1st Baron Clyde (1792–1863), Scottish general who was commander-in-chief in India during the Mutiny.

Campbell, Sir Malcolm (1885–1948), racing driver who held the land-speed record of 301 mile/h (1935) and water-speed record of 141·7 mile/h (1939). His son, **Donald** held the water-speed record of 276·33 mile/h (1964); killed in 1967 at Coniston.

Campbell, Mrs. Patrick (Beatrice Stella Tanner) (1865–1940), English actress of beauty and wit, friend of G. B. Shaw.

Campbell, Thomas (1777–1844) Scottish poet, who at 22 published *The Pleasures of Hope*. His war poems include *Ye Mariners of England* and *The Battle of the Baltic*. He was one of the founders of University College, London.

Campbell-Bannerman, Sir Henry (1836–1908), Liberal statesman, prime minister 1905–8. His ministry included Asquith, Lloyd George, and Churchill.

Camus, Albert (1913–60), French writer native of Algeria. Preoccupied with the themes of the Stranger and the Absurd, the works for which he is particularly remembered are the philosophical essay *Le Mythe de Sisyphe*, the play *Caligula*, and the novel *L'Etranger*. Nobel prize for literature 1957. Killed in car crash. *See* **Section I.**

Canaletto (Antonio Canal) (1697–1768), Italian artist. B. at Venice, he painted views of his city. From 1746 to 1756 he worked mainly in London. Some of his work is in the National Gallery, and there is a collection at Windsor.

Canning, George (1770–1827), English statesman. He was an advocate of Catholic emancipation, and was the first to recognise the free states of South America.

Cannizzaro, Stanislao (1826–1910), Italian chemist who carried forward the work of Avogadro in distinguishing between molecular and atomic weights.

Canova, Antonio (1757–1822), Italian sculptor. B. at Venice, he infused grace into the classical style.

Canton, John (1718–72), English physicist and schoolmaster, the first to verify in England Franklin's experiments on the identity of lightning with electricity. He was the first to demonstrate that water is compressible and produced a new phosphorescent body (Canton's phosphorus) by calcining oyster shells with sulphur.

Canute (*c.* 994–1035), king of the English, Danes and Norwegians. The son of a Danish king, after some years of fighting he established himself as king of England and ruled with wisdom and firmness.

Capablanca, José Raoul (1888–1942), Cuban chess player, world champion from 1921 to 1927 when he was beaten by Alekhine.

Caractacus or **Caradoc**, a king in west Britain, who resisted the Romans in the first century. After capture he was freed by the emperor Claudius.

Carey, William (1761–1834), first Baptist missionary to India. An Oriental scholar, he published 24 translations of the scriptures.

Carissimi, Giacomo (1604–74), Italian composer, b. near Rome. He introduced more instrumental variety into the cantata and oratorio, and brought the recitative to perfection. His *Jephtha* is still in print, and there are collections of his works at Paris and Oxford. *See* **Sec. E.**

Carlyle, Thomas (1795–1881), Scottish author. Of peasant stock, he went to Edinburgh university, but later lived mainly in England where he lectured. He married Jane Welsh. His individual views pervade his historical writing. His best known works include *Sartor Resartus*, *Heroes and Hero Worship*, *Cromwell's Letters and Speeches*, and the *French Revolution*.

Carnegie, Andrew (1835–1919), philanthropist b. Dunfermline; emigrated to America 1848; after early struggles established the Carnegie iron works. He made munificent gifts to Free Libraries and other educational work.

Carnot, Lazare Nicolas Marguerite (1753–1823), French military engineer, prominent in the French revolutionary wars, 1792–1802. His son, **Sadi Carnot** (1796–1832), was a physicist and engineer who worked on the motive power of heat, establishing the principle that heat and work are reversible conditions. *See* **F17.**

Caroline, Queen (1768–1821), was married to George IV when he was Prince of Wales. They soon separated, but when he became king in 1820, she tried to assert her position. The question came before parliament. In spite of some public sympathy she was unsuccessful.

Carrel, Alexis (1873–1944), American surgeon who won the Nobel prize in 1912 for his success in suturing blood vessels in transfusion and in transplantation of organs. A Frenchman by birth, he returned to France in 1939.

Carroll, Lewis. *See* **Dodgson, Charles Lutwidge.**

Carson, Baron (Edward Henry Carson) (1854–1935), Irish barrister, solicitor-general for Ireland 1892; attorney general 1915; first lord of the admiralty 1916–17; member of the war cabinet 1917–18. He led a semi-militant organisation against Home Rule.

Carson, Rachel (d. 1964), American biologist, remembered for *The Silent Spring*.

Carter, Howard (1873–1939), Egyptologist who was associated with Lord Carnarvon in discovering in 1922 the Tomb of Tutankhamun.

Carter, James Earl (b. 1924), American Democratic President 1977–; former Governor of Georgia.

Carter, Jacques (1494–1557), French navigator, b. St. Malo, who explored Canada, especially the gulf and river of St. Lawrence.

Cartwright, Edmund (1743–1823), English inventor of the power-loom, and also of a wool-combing machine, important steps in the weaving side of the textile revolution.

Cartwright, John (1740–1824), brother of the above: reformer and agitator against slavery.

Caruso, Enrico (1873–1921), Italian tenor, b. Naples.

Carver, George Washington (1864–1943), American Negro agricultural chemist of world repute.

Casabianca, Louis de (*c.* 1752–98), captain of the French flagship *L'Orient* at the Battle of the Nile. He and his ten-year-old son died together in the burning ship.

Casals, Pablo (1876–1973), Spanish cellist and conductor, son of an organist, b. Vendrell, Tarragona. He exiled himself from Spain in 1938 as a protest against dictatorship.

Casanova de Seingalt, Giacomo (1725–98), Italian adventurer, author of licentious memoirs.

Cassini, French family of Italian origin, distinguished for work in astronomy and geography. Through four generations (1671–1793) they were heads of the Paris Observatory.

Cassius, Caius Longinus, Roman general who opposed the dictatorship of Julius Caesar, and took part in his murder. He died in 42 B.C. after being defeated by Mark Antony.

Castlereagh, Viscount (Robert Stewart Castlereagh) (1769–1822), British minister of war and foreign secretary, who took a leading part in the Napoleonic wars. He was however unpopular and committed suicide.

Castro, Fidel (b. 1927), Cuban revolutionary. After two unsuccessful attempts he succeeded in 1959 in overthrowing a police-state. He has initiated reforms in agriculture, industry, and education, and repulsed American economic dominance. His acceptance of Russian support led to the " missiles crisis " of 1962.

Catchpool, E. St. John (b. 1890), first secretary of the English Youth Hostels Association, 1930–50; president of the International Federation, 1938–50.

Catherine, St. (4th cent.). Traditionally a virgin martyr in Alexandria, though not mentioned before the 10th cent. Legend represents her as tied to a wheel.

Catherine de' Medici (1519–89), Italian-born wife of Henry II and mother of three French kings (she was regent for Charles IX). Her antagonism to the Protestants may have led to the massacre of St. Bartholomew's day. She was able, and appreciated art and literature, but was unscrupulous and cruel.

Catherine of Aragon (1485–1536), first wife of Henry VIII of England, was daughter of Ferdinand and Isabella of Spain, and mother of Mary Tudor. When Henry VIII attempted to obtain papal dissolution of their marriage, and subsequently obtained an English declaration of its nullity (thus precipitating a movement towards the Reformation) she bore herself with dignity during her retirement.

Catherine the Great (1729–96), Empress Catherine II of Russia. Daughter of a German prince, she married in 1745 the future Peter III, a weakling, later deposed and murdered. Intelligent, cultivated, autocratic, she proved a capable ruler for a time but was hampered and opposed by the landed interests and, despite plans for reform, her reign was marked by imperialist expansion and extension of serfdom.

Cato, Marcus Porcius (234–149 B.C.), Roman statesman and writer. His tenure of office as censor was characterised by austerity and conservatism. He advocated opposition to Carthage. His writings deal with agriculture and history.

Catullus, Caius Valerius (*c.* 84–54 B.C.), Roman poet who wrote lyrics to Lesbia. His poems show sincere feeling and also Greek influence.

Cavell, Edith Louisa (1865–1915), English nurse who cared for friend and foe in Brussels in 1914–15 but was executed by the Germans for helping Allied fugitives to escape.

Cavendish, Henry (1731–1810), English scientist, a contemporary of Black, Priestley, Scheele, and Lavoisier, remembered for his investigations into the nature of gases. He discovered hydrogen and the chemical composition of water. He was the first to determine the weights of equal volumes of gases.

Cavour, Camillo Benso di (1810–61), Italian statesman, who, as premier of Piedmont, helped to bring about the unification of Italy.

Caxton, William (1422–91), the first English printer and publisher, a man of wide-ranging abilities. He probably learnt the art of printing at Cologne (1471–2), setting up his own printing press at Westminster (1476). He printed Chaucer's *Canterbury Tales*, Malory's *Le Morte Darthur* and Aesop's *Fables*. He was an accomplished linguist.

Cecil of Chelwood, 1st Viscount (Robert Cecil) (1864–1958), English politician who helped draft the Charter of the League of Nations. Nobel prize for peace 1937.

Cecilia, St. (2nd or 3rd cent.), patron saint of music. She is often represented playing the organ.

Cellini, Benvenuto (1500–71), Italian sculptor and goldsmith. B. at Florence, he worked for some years in Rome. His bronze statue *Perseus with the head of Medusa* is at Florence. His life was adventurous and he wrote an *Autobiography* which is revealing of himself and his time.

Celsius, Anders (1701–44), Swedish physicist and astronomer who invented the centigrade thermometer.

Ceresole, Pierre (1879–1945), Swiss founder of International Voluntary Service. He was by profession a teacher of engineering, and his pacifism led him to become a Quaker.

Cervantes, Saavedra Miguel de (1547–1616), Spanish novelist and dramatist, b. at Alcalá de Henares. He was injured at the battle of Lepanto, and thereafter struggled to earn a livelihood from literature. His *Don Quixote* describes the adventures of a poor gentleman, confused in mind, who on his horse Rosinante with his squire Sancho Panza seeks adventures; it satirised chivalry, but is also a permanent criticism of life. Of his plays only two survive.

Cézanne, Paul (1839–1906), French painter, b. in Aix-en-Provence, the son of a wealthy banker and tradesman. He developed a highly original style, using colour and tone in such a way as to increase the impression of depth. He said that he wanted "to make of Impressionism something solid and durable, like the art of the Museums." Like Giotto, six hundred years before, he more than any other artist determined the course European painting was to take. *La Vielle au Chapelet* and *Les Grandes Baigneuses* are in the National Gallery. He was a friend of Zola.

Chadwick, Sir James (b. 1891), English physicist, one of Rutherford's collaborators in the field of atomic research. Discovered the neutron in 1932, one of the main steps in the discovery of the fission process which led to the production of the atom bomb.

Chagall, Marc (b. 1889), Russian painter, b. at Vitebsk of Jewish parents, the forerunner of surrealism. He lives in Paris.

Chaliapin, Fedor Ivanovich (1873–1938), Russian opera singer, a bass with dramatic gifts.

Chamberlain, Joseph (1836–1914), English statesman. He began with municipal work in Birmingham. At first a Liberal under Gladstone, he became Conservative. He opposed Home Rule for Ireland, and was the first advocate of a partial return to protection.

Chamberlain, Neville (1869–1940), son of Joseph. He was prime minister 1937–40, when he appeased Hitler by the Munich agreement of 1938.

Chambers, Sir William (1726–96) British architect, b. Stockholm. He rebuilt Somerset House and designed the pagoda in Kew Gardens.

Chaminade, Cécile (1857–1944), French pianist and composer.

Champlain, Samuel de (1567–1635), French navigator who founded Quebec (1608), and discovered the lake known by his name.

Chantrey, Sir Francis Legatt (1781–1841), English sculptor who contributed statues to Westminster Abbey and St. Paul's. He left a fortune to the Royal Academy for the purchase of works of British art. The collection is in the Tate Gallery.

Chaplin, Sir Charles Spencer (b. 1889), first international screen star, with more than 50 years' achievement. B. in London, his mother was a music-hall singer and he made his début at five. In 1910 he went to the United States; and with the Keystone Company in Los Angeles (1914–15) he made films in which his early hardships are reflected in humour and sadness. His films include *Shoulder Arms*, *The Kid*, *The Gold Rush*, *City Lights*, *The Great Dictator*, *Modern Times*, and *Limelight*. In 1953 he went to live in Switzerland. *Autobiography* (1964).

Chapman, George (1559–1634), Elizabethan poet, dramatist, and translator of the *Iliad* and *Odyssey*. His best-known play is *Bussy d'Ambois*.

Chapman, Sydney (1888–1970), English mathematician and geophysicist, noted for his work on the kinetic theory of gases, geomagnetism, and solar and ionospheric physics. He was president of the special committee of the I.G.Y., 1957–8. An upper layer of the atmosphere and a crater on the far side of the moon are named after him.

Charcot, Jean Baptiste (1867–1936), French explorer, who in 1903–5 and 1908–10 commanded expeditions to the south polar regions. Charcot Island in the Antarctic is named after him.

Chardin, Jean Baptiste Siméon (1699–1779), French painter of still life and interior domestic scenes.

Chares (*c.* 300 B.C.), Greek worker in bronze from Rhodes, sculptor of the Colossus of Rhodes, one of the seven wonders of the world, which was destroyed in the earthquake of 225 B.C.

Charlemagne (742–814), Charles the Great. From being King of the Franks, he came to govern an empire comprising Gaul, Italy, and large parts of Spain and Germany, and was crowned Holy Roman Emperor.

Charles, Jacques Alexandre César (1746–1823), French physicist, the first to use hydrogen gas in balloons and who anticipated Gay-Lussac's law on the expansion of gases.

Charles Edward (Stuart) (1720–88), the Young Pretender (*i.e.*, claimant of the English throne), grandson of James II, led an unsuccessful rising in 1745 and died in exile.

Charles I (1600–49), King of England, Scotland, and Ireland, succeeded his father James I in 1625. Personally sincere, and having an appreciation of art, he was yet ill-fitted to cope with the political problems of his time. His marriage with the French princess Henrietta Maria was unpopular. He supported Archbishop Laud's strict Anglicanism, and he also attempted to rule without parliament. Defeated in the Civil War which broke out in 1642, he spun out negotiations for a settlement till he was beheaded in 1649.

Charles II (1630–85), King of England, Scotland, and Ireland, son of Charles I; after the Civil War escaped to France, and returned in 1660 when the monarchy was restored. His religious sympathies were Roman Catholic and his personal life was amorous; but in political matters he was shrewd and realistic, and contrived not to "go on his travels" again. He promoted the development of the navy, but had to accept the laws enforcing religious conformity imposed by parliament.

Charles V (1500–58), Hapsburg ruler, succeeded his grandfather, Maximilian I, as emperor of the Holy Roman Empire, and as heir to Ferdinand and Isabella succeeded to the Spanish crown. His rivalry with Francis I of France led to prolonged war. He crushed a revolt of peasants in 1525. He presided in 1521 at the Diet before which Luther appeared, after which religious struggle continued in Germany till the Augsburg settlement of 1555. In that year he retired to a monastery in Spain.

Charles XII of Sweden (1682–1718), a brave but rash and ambitious general. He repelled Russian attacks at Narva in 1700, but subsequently pursuing military adventure he was defeated by Peter the Great at Poltava in 1709; and on invading Norway was killed at a siege.

Chateaubriand, François René, Vicomte de (1768–1848), French writer and diplomat. In a varied career he was at first an emigré, and later served as diplomat under both Napoleon and Louis XVIII. He was a friend of Mme. Recamier. His writings include *Mémoires d'outre-tombe*.

Chatham, 1st Earl of (William Pitt) (1708–78), English statesman and orator. His energetic conduct of the Seven Years War was an important contribution to English victory and to acquisitions in Canada and India at the peace (1763), though by then he was out of office. In the dispute with the American colonies he upheld their right to resist imposed taxation, and collapsed while making a last speech on this dispute.

Chatterton, Thomas (1752–70), English poet who tried to pass off his writings as newly discovered ancient manuscripts and killed himself at the age of 17.

Chaucer, Geoffrey (1340?–1400), English poet. His main work, *The Canterbury Tales*, gives a vivid picture of contemporary life.

Chekov, Anton (1860–1904), Russian dramatist and short-story writer, whose plays include *The Cherry Orchard*, *Uncle Vanya*, and *The Three Sisters*. His stories include *The Steppe*, *The Sleepyhead*, *The Post*, *The Student*, and *The Bishop*. He was of humble origin and while a student at Moscow supported his family by writing humorous sketches and tales.

Cherubini, Luigi (1760–1842), Italian-born musician, for many years director of the Paris Conservatoire and composer of operas and church music.

Chesterfield, 4th Earl of (Philip Dormer Stanhope) (1694–1773), English statesman, whose *Letters* to his natural son, Philip Stanhope, are full of grace, wit, and worldly wisdom.

Chesterton, Gilbert Keith (1874–1936), English essayist, novelist and poet, who also wrote studies of Charles Dickens and Robert Browning. His best-known works include *The Napoleon of Notting Hill* and *The Ballad of the White Horse*.

Chevalier, Albert (1861–1923), English music-hall comedian known for his coster sketches.

Chevalier, Maurice (1889–1972), French stage and film actor.

Chiang Kai-shek (1887–1975), Chinese general. He at first fought for Sun Yat-sen. After the latter's death (1925), as commander of the

Kuomintang army, he attempted to unite China; but (involved as he was with business interests) he was more anxious to defeat the Communists than to repel the Japanese adventure in Manchuria in 1931. He was unable to establish peace and a stable, progressive régime; and in 1949 retired to Formosa after military defeat by the Communists. His widow is Mayling Soong.

Chichester, Sir Francis (1902–72), English seaman, who sailed his *Gipsy Moth IV* into Sydney harbour in 1966 after a 107-day voyage from Plymouth, and back again round the Horn.

Chippendale, Thomas (1718–79), designer of furniture, b. Otley, Yorks., son of a joiner. His designs are shown in *The Gentleman and Cabinet Maker's Director*, 1754. *See* **D13.**

Chirico, Giorgio de (b. 1888), painter associated with the surrealist school, born in Greece of Italian parents.

Chomsky, Noam (b. 1908), American theoretical linguist, professor of Linguistics, Massachusetts Institute of Technology; inventor of transformational grammar.

Chopin, Frédéric François (1810–49), Polish pianist and composer, son of a French father and Polish mother. He has been called "the poet of the piano" because of the originality and delicacy of his playing. He enjoyed Paris intellectual and musical society, was a friend of George Sand, and played in numerous concerts all over Europe. He died of consumption. *See* **Section E.**

Chou En-lai (1898–1976), Chinese revolutionary statesman, administrator and diplomat. He organised revolt in Shanghai 1927, later formed close partnership with Mao Tse-tung, took part in the "long march" 1934–5, becoming prime minister of the new China in 1949. Headed the Chinese delegation to the Geneva Conference of 1954.

Chrysostom, St. John (*c.* 347–407), preacher. Chrysostom means golden-mouthed. First at Antioch, and later as patriarch of Constantinople, he was an eloquent teacher; but by outspokenness he lost the Empress Eudoxia's favour and died from ill-treatment.

Chulalongkorn, Phra Paramindr Maha (1853–1910), Siamese reforming monarch.

Churchill, Lord Randolph Henry Spencer (1849–95), Conservative politician, who held brief office only. He was father of Winston Churchill.

Churchill, Sir Winston Leonard Spencer (1874–1965), British statesman and author, son of the last-named. He entered parliament in 1900. He served as a junior officer with the British forces abroad; and during the Boer War he acted as war correspondent. He held the following ministerial posts: Under-Secretary for the Colonies 1905–8; President of the Board of Trade 1908–10; Home Secretary 1910–11; First Lord of the Admiralty 1911–15, 1939–40; Chancellor of the Duchy of Lancaster 1915; Minister of Munitions 1917; Minister of War 1918–21; Minister of Air 1919–21; Secretary of State for the Colonies 1921–2; Chancellor of the Exchequer 1924–9; Prime Minister and Minister of Defence 1940–5; Prime Minister 1951–5. He was rector or chancellor of three universities. Cast in the heroic mould, he lived a full life. His main achievement was as leader of the British people in the second world war. His writings include a biography of his ancestor, Marlborough, and histories of the first and second world wars. He exhibited at the Royal Academy. Hon. American citizenship conferred 1963.

Cibber, Colley (1671–1757), a London actor and dramatist. His best comedies are *The Careless Husband* and *Love's Last Shift*. He wrote an autobiography.

Cicero, Marcus Tullius (106–43 B.C.), Roman orator and philosopher, many of whose letters and speeches survive. He held political office but was killed by the troops of the triumvirate.

Cid (El Campeador) (*c.* 1035–99), name given to the Spanish knight Rodrigo Diaz, a soldier of fortune who fought against Moors and Christians alike. Myth made him a national hero of knightly and Christian virtue.

Cierva, Juan de la (1895–1936), Spanish engineer who invented the autogiro.

Cimabue, Giovanni (Cenni di Pepo) (1240–1302), early Florentine painter. His only certain work is the St. John in Pisa cathedral.

Cimarosa, Domenico (1749–1801), Italian composer. His best-known opera is *Il Matrimonio Segreto*. He held revolutionary views.

Cimon (*c.* 512–449 B.C.), Athenian statesman and general, son of Miltiades. He defeated the Persian fleet at the mouth of the Eurymedon in 468. He worked for cooperation with other states, including Sparta.

Cipriani, Giambattista (1727–85), Italian painter of historical subjects who worked in London; a founder member of the Royal Academy.

Clair, René (b. 1898), French film producer, whose early films, full of wit and satire, include *Sous les Toits de Paris* and *A Nous la Liberté*.

Clare, John (1793–1864), Northamptonshire labourer who became a poet. *Poems Descriptive of Rural Life and Scenery*, and *The Village Minstrel* were among his publications. He died in the county lunatic asylum.

Clarendon, 1st Earl of (Edward Hyde) (1609–74), English statesman and historian. He was for some years chancellor to Charles II, and his daughter married the future James II, but he fell and died in exile. He wrote a *History of the Rebellion*.

Clark, Baron (Kenneth McKenzie Clark) (b. 1903), English art historian. He was director of the National Gallery 1934–45, Slade professor of fine arts at Oxford 1946–50, and chairman of the Arts Council 1953–60. Life peer 1969. Chanc. York University 1969. O.M. 1976.

Clarkson, Thomas (1760–1846) devoted his life to the abolition of slavery and shares with Wilberforce credit for the passing of the Act of 1807 abolishing the British slave trade.

Claude Lorrain (Gellée) (1600–82), French landscape painter. B. near Nancy, he settled in Rome. A close student of nature, he excelled in depicting sunrise or sunset, and founded a "picturesque" tradition.

Claudius (10 B.C.–A.D. 54), Roman emperor. After the murder of Caligula, he was proclaimed emperor almost accidentally by the Praetorian Guard. He was a sensible administrator. In his time the empire was extended to include Britain, Thrace, and Mauretania. He was probably poisoned by his wife Agrippina.

Clausewitz, Karl von (1780–1831), German military expert whose *Vom Kriege*, expounding his theories on war, dominated Prussia in the 19th cent.

Clemenceau, Georges (1841–1929), French statesman of radical views; twice premier, 1906–9, 1917–20. He was a defender of Dreyfus. In old age he presided at the peace conference of 1919, where he was hostile to Germany ("the Tiger").

Cleopatra (69–30 B.C.), daughter of Ptolemy XI, the sixth queen of Egypt by that name, a brilliant, ambitious woman. In 51 she became joint sovereign with her younger brother Ptolemy XII. She was banished to Syria, but, obtaining the help of Caesar regained the kingdom. She and Caesar became lovers, and in 47 she bore him a son Caesarion (later Ptolemy XIV). After Caesar's murder she returned to Egypt. She met the triumvir Mark Antony and bore him twins; he deserted his wife and broke with his brother-in-law Octavian (later Augustus). Antony and Cleopatra were, however defeated in 31 B.C.; Antony fell upon his sword, and Cleopatra killed herself with an asp bite. Her life inspired Shakespeare's *Antony and Cleopatra* and Shaw's *Caesar and Cleopatra*.

Clive, 1st Baron (Robert Clive) (1725–74), English general who helped to lay the foundations of English power in India. B. near Market Drayton, he entered the service of the East India Company. He contemplated suicide, but Anglo-French rivalry, culminating in the Seven Years War, gave scope for his military powers in the siege of Arcot and the battle of Plassey. As a governor he showed administrative capacity. In his later life he was poor and unpopular.

Clovis (*c.* 465–511), Merovingian king of the Franks and a convert to Christianity. He defeated the Burgundians and West Goths, and fixed his court at Paris.

Clyde, Lord. *See* **Campbell, Colin.**

Cobbett, William (1763–1835), English controversialist. He is chiefly known for his *Rural Rides*, but also published a weekly *Political Register* from 1802.

Cobden, Richard (1804–65), English advocate of free trade. The son of a Sussex farmer, he led agitation against the laws restricting import of corn, and they were repealed in 1846. He was impoverished by his public work and was helped by subscription.

Cochrane, Thomas, 10th Earl of Dundonald (1775–1860), British seaman, who crippled a French fleet in Biscay (1809), aided the liberation of Chile and Peru from Spanish rule (1819–22), of Brazil from Portuguese rule (1823–5), and assisted the Greeks in their struggle to throw off the Turkish yoke (1827).

Cockcroft, Sir John Douglas (1897–1967), Cambridge nuclear physicist who shared with E.T.S. Walton the 1951 Nobel prize. They had worked together at Cambridge in the historic "atom-splitting" experiments beginning with the transmutation of lithium into boron. He was directly involved in Britain's first nuclear power programmes.

Cockerell, Christopher (b. 1910), English inventor of the hovercraft, which works on the aircushioning principle. *See* **Hovercraft, Section L.**

Cocteau, Jean (1891–1963), French writer and artist in widely varied forms of art.

Cody, Samuel Franklin (1861–1913), American aviator, the first man to fly in Britain (1,390 ft. on 16 Oct. 1908). He became a British subject in 1909. Killed while flying.

Cody, William Frederick (1846–1917), American showman, known as "Buffalo Bill," whose Wild West Show toured America and Europe.

Coggan, Donald (b. 1909), enthroned 101st archbishop of Canterbury, January 1975; archbishop of York 1961–74.

Cohn, Ferdinand Julius (1828–98) German botanist, founder of the science of bacteriology.

Coke, Sir Edward (1552–1634), English legal author, judge, and rival of Francis Bacon. His legal works are his *Reports* and *Institutes*.

Colbert, Jean Baptiste (1619–83), French statesman under Louis XIV, who fostered new industries, encouraged commerce, reformed the finances and established the navy on a sound basis. A patron of literature, science, and art.

Cole, George Douglas Howard (1889–1959), English economist and political journalist, professor of social and political theory at Oxford, 1944–57. Among his writings are *The Intelligent Man's Guide through World Chaos*, and *A History of Socialist Thought* (5 vols.).

Coleridge, Samuel Taylor (1772–1834), English poet, critic, and friend of Wordsworth, with whom he published *Lyrical Ballads*. His poems include *The Ancient Mariner, Christabel*, and *Kubla Khan*. His literary criticism is still valuable.

Coleridge-Taylor, Samuel (1875–1912), English composer, the son of a West African doctor practising in London and an Englishwoman. He is best known for his Hiawatha trilogy.

Colet, John (*c.* 1467–1519), English humanist and divine, founded St. Paul's School (1512). As scholar and friend of Erasmus he helped to bring the new learning to England.

Colette (Sidonie Gabrielle Claudine Colette) (1873–1954), French author of the *Claudine* stories, *Chéri* and *La Fin de Chéri*.

Collier, John (1850–1934), English painter noted for his "problem" pictures.

Collingwood, 1st Baron (Cuthbert Collingwood) (1750–1810), British admiral whose ship, the *Royal Sovereign*, led the fleet to battle at Trafalgar, and who on Nelson's death assumed command.

Collingwood, Robin George (1889–1943), English philosopher, historian, and archaeologist, associated with Oxford from 1908 to 1941. His philosophical thought is best studied in *Speculum Mentis, Essay on Philosophical Method, Idea of Nature*, and *Idea of History*.

Collins, Michael (1890–1922), Irish politician and Sinn Fein leader. He successfully organised guerrilla warfare, and mainly negotiated the treaty with Britain in 1921, but was killed in a Republican ambush on his return.

Collins, William (1788–1847), English landscape and figure painter.

Collins, William Wilkie (1824–89), son of the above; practically the first English novelist to deal with the detection of crime. *The Woman in White* appeared in 1860.

Colt, Samuel (1814–62), of Hartford, Connecticut, invented the revolver in 1835. It was used in the war with Mexico.

Columba, St. (521–97), founder of the monastery of Iona, b. Ireland. From his island shrine he made missionary journeys to the Highlands of Scotland.

Columbanus, St. (*c.* 540–615), Irish abbot who founded a number of monasteries in continental Europe. *See* **Monasticism, Section J.**

Columbus, Christopher (*c.* 1451–1506), Italian navigator, b. Genoa, who, prevailing upon Ferdinand and Isabella of Spain to bear the expense of an expedition, in 1492 discovered the Bahamas, Cuba, and other West Indian islands. In 1498 he landed on the lowlands of S. America.

Comenius, John Amos (1592–1670), Czech educationist and pastor, advocate of the "direct" method of teaching languages, of the use of pictures in education, and of equality of educational opportunity for girls.

Compton, Arthur Holly (1892–1962), American physicist whose work on X-rays established what is known as the Compton effect (1923). While professor of physics at the university of Chicago (1923–45) he helped to develop the atomic bomb. Nobel prizewinner 1927.

Compton, Karl Taylor (1887–1954), scientist-administrator, brother of the above. Pres. Massachusetts Institute of Technology 1930–48.

Compton-Burnett, Dame Ivy (1884–1969), English novelist whose books deal with family relationships and include *Pastors and Masters, Men and Wives, A House and Its Head, Manservant and Maidservant*. *See* **Section M, Part I.**

Comte, August (1798–1857), French philosopher, founder of positivism. *See* **Positivism, Section J.**

Condé, Louis, Prince de (1621–86), French general who defeated Spain at Rocroi in 1643.

Confucius or **K'ung Fu-tse** (*c.* 551–478 B.C.), Chinese philosopher, founder of the system of cosmology, politics, and ethics known as Confucianism. He was not concerned with the supernatural, but appealed to reason and taught love and respect of one's fellows, superiority to ambition, charity, forgiveness, and repentance. *See* **Confucianism, Section J.**

Congreve, William (1670–1729), Restoration dramatist, whose witty plays include *The Way of the World* and *Love for Love*.

Conrad, Joseph (1857–1924), English novelist of Polish birth, whose parents were exiled to France for political reasons. He became master mariner in the British merchant service, and began to write novels after he left the sea in 1884. His novels include *Almayer's Folly, Lord Jim, Nostromo*. *See* **Section M, Part I.**

Conscience, Hendrik Henri (1812–83), Flemish novelist who wrote *The Lion of Flanders*.

Constable, John (1776–1837), English landscape painter, b. East Bergholt, Suffolk. Unlike his contemporary Turner, who journeyed over the continent with his sketchbook, he found his scenes within a few miles of his home. His work was more popular in France than in England at the time and affected the Barbizon school and Delacroix. Examples of his work are in the National Gallery (including *The Hay Wain, Flatford Mill*, and *The Cornfield*), the Victoria and Albert, and the Tate (*The Valley Farm*).

Constant, Jean Joseph Benjamin (1845–1902), French painter of portraits and Oriental subjects.

Constantine (274–338), called "the Great", the first Christian Roman emperor. He was proclaimed at York by the army in 306. He stabilised the empire after a period of decline, and founded a new capital at Constantinople. A Christian council was held under his auspices at Nicaea in 325, and he was baptised on his death-bed.

Cook, James (1728–79), English navigator, son of an agricultural labourer. He entered the Royal Navy and gained a high reputation for his scientific skill. He made voyages of discovery to New Zealand and Australia in the ships under his command, *Endeavour, Resolution*, and *Adventure*. He anchored at Botany Bay in 1770 on his first voyage and gave it that name because of the interesting plants found on its shores. He also surveyed the Newfoundland coast. In an attempt to find the north-west passage he was murdered at Hawaii.

Cooper, Sir Astley Paston (1768–1841), English surgeon and author of medical textbooks.

Cooper, James Fenimore (1789–1851), American novelist, who produced stirring stories of adventure, among them *The Spy*, *The Last of the Mohicans*, *The Pathfinder*, and *The Deer Slayer*.

Cooper, Samuel (1609–72), English miniaturist, represented with his brother **Alexander** (d. 1660) in the Victoria and Albert Museum. Among his miniatures is a portrait of Cromwell.

Copernicus, Nicolas (1473–1543), founder of modern astronomy, b. at Torun in Poland. He studied at Cracow and at a number of Italian universities before settling at Frauenburg in 1512 where he became canon of the cathedral. More of a student than a practical astronomer, he spent most of his private life seeking a new theory of the heavenly bodies. In his *On the Revolution of the Celestial Orbs*, published after his death, he broke with the past and put forward the novel theory that the planets, including the earth, revolve round the sun.

Coppée, François Joachim (1842–1908), French poet, novelist and dramatist.

Coquelin, Benoit Constant (1841–1909), and **Coquelin, Ernest** (1848–1909), (Coquelin aîné et cadet), brothers, were leading lights of the French theatre.

Corelli, Arcangelo (1653–1713), Italian composer and violinist, who established the form of the concerto grosso. *See* **Section E.**

Corneille, Pierre (1606–84), French dramatist, who ranks with Racine as a master of classical tragedy. *Le Cid*, *Polyeucte*, and *Le Menteur* marked a new era in French dramatic production.

Cornwallis, 1st Marquess (Charles Cornwallis) (1738–1805), British general who commanded the British forces which surrendered to the Americans at Yorktown in 1781, thus ending the war of independence. He was twice governor-general of India.

Corot, Jean Baptiste (1796–1875), French landscape painter.

Correggio, Antonio Allegri da (1494–1534), Italian painter, b. Correggio. His style anticipates the baroque. His *Ecce Homo* is in the National Gallery.

Cortés, Hernando (1488–1547), Spanish adventurer, b. Medellín, Estremadura, who captured Mexico for Spain, crushing an ancient civilisation.

Coulton, George Gordon (1858–1947), scholar and historian of the Middle Ages. In his *Five Centuries of Religion* he sets forth his interpretation of monastic history in England from the Conquest to the Reformation.

Couperin, a family of French musicians who were organists at St. Gervais, Paris, from about 1650 till 1826. **François Couperin** (1668–1733), called "Couperin the Great," is the best known today for his harpsichord music.

Cousin, Victor (1792–1867), French educationist and philosopher, founder of the eclectic school.

Cousins, Samuel (1801–87), English mezzotint engraver of plates after Reynolds, Millais, Landseer, and Hogarth.

Cousteau, Jacques-Yves (b. 1910), French underwater explorer, pioneer of aqualung diving.

Couve de Murville, Maurice (b. 1900), French diplomat; General de Gaulle's foreign minister 1958–68.

Coverdale, Miles (1488–1568), one of the early English reformers, b. Yorkshire, later to become bishop of Exeter. He assisted Tyndale in translating the Pentateuch and completed his own translation of the Bible in 1535. The Psalms still used in the Prayer Book and many of the phrases in the authorised version of 1611 are from his translation.

Cowper, William (1731–1800), English religious poet. His work is characterised by simplicity and tenderness. His best-known poems are *John Gilpin* and *The Task*.

Cox, David (1783–1859), English landscape painter. A collection of his works is in the Birmingham Gallery and the Tate Gallery.

Crabbe, George (1754–1832), English narrative poet of grim humour; author of *The Village* and *The Borough*.

Craig, Edward Gordon (1872–1966), son of Ellen Terry, producer and author of books on stagecraft.

Cranmer, Thomas (1489–1556), archbishop of Canterbury under Henry VIII, and Edward VI; an ardent promoter of the Reformation. On Mary's accession he at first consented to return to the old faith, but when called upon to make public avowal of his recantation, refused, and was burnt at the stake. His contributions were the English Bible and Book of Common Prayer.

Crichton, James (1560–82), Scottish adventurer who for his scholarly accomplishments was called "the admirable Crichton." He was killed in a brawl.

Cripps, Sir Stafford (1889–1952), British Labour statesman. A successful barrister, he relinquished practice for public work. As chancellor of the exchequer in post-war Britain, his programme was one of austerity, but his able exposition and single-minded purpose won him general support. Ill-health terminated his career.

Crispi, Francesco (1819–1901), Italian statesman, who aided Garibaldi and was later premier.

Crispin, St. (*c.* 285), martyr with his brother. By tradition they were Roman and became shoemakers, hence patron saints of shoemaking.

Croce, Benedetto (1866–1952), Italian philosopher and critic. His philosophy is expounded in the four volumes of *Filosofia dello Spirito* (which has been translated into English). He founded and edited *La Critica* in 1903, a review of literature, history, and philosophy. He was strongly opposed to fascism.

Croesus (d. *c.* 546 B.C.), last king of Lydia, reputed to be of immense wealth. Conquered and condemned to death by Cyrus, he was reprieved when Cyrus heard him recall Solon's saying "Call no man happy till he is dead."

Crome, John (1769–1821), English landscape painter, b. Norwich.

Cromer, 1st Earl of (Evelyn Baring) (1841–1917), British diplomat who, as British comptroller-general in Egypt from 1883 to 1907, did much to maintain order, improve the finances, and promote development. His *Modern Egypt* appeared in 1908.

Crompton, Samuel (1753–1827), English inventor of the spinning-mule (1779), which substituted machinery for hand work. He was b. near Bolton, a farmer's son, and benefited little by his invention.

Cromwell, Oliver (1599–1658), Protector of the commonwealth of England, Scotland, and Ireland. B. at Huntingdon, he represented Huntingdon in parliament. When civil war broke out, he served under the Earl of Essex; and then reorganised the parliamentary army, winning victories at Marston Moor and Naseby. Tortuous negotiations with Charles I could not be brought to an end, and he promoted the king's trial and execution in 1649. He defeated the Scots at Dunbar. When continued difficulties beset government he became Protector in 1653, but was soon obliged to govern by major-generals. His handling of Ireland enhanced the difficulties of that country. An able general and a strong character, he was personally tolerant (an Independent), sincere and devout; but he found himself in the revolutionary's dilemma—that there is no easy exit from a revolutionary situation; thus paradoxically he provoked English aversion to military rule.

Cromwell, Richard (1626–1712), son of the above, and his successor in the protectorate.

Cromwell, Thomas (1485–1540), English statesman, who succeeded Wolsey in the service of Henry VIII, and carried out the dissolution of the monasteries, but on his fall from favour he was executed.

Crookes, Sir William (1832–1919), English physicist who discovered the element thallium (1861) and invented the Crookes tube (1874) which was used by J. J. Thomson and others in their researches into the conduction of electricity in gases. He was also an authority on sanitation.

Cruikshank, George (1792–1878), caricaturist and book illustrator, whose work includes illustrations to *Grimm's Fairy Tales*, and *Oliver Twist*. Collections of his work are in the British Museum and the Victoria and Albert Museum.

Cummings, Bruce Frederick (1889–1919), English

zoologist and author of *Journal of a Disappointed Man.*

Cunard, Sir Samuel (1787–1865), founder of the Cunard line of steam ships. He was born in Nova Scotia, of a Welsh family of Quakers.

Cunningham of Hyndhope, 1st Viscount (Andrew Browne Cunningham) (1883–1963), British admiral in two world wars, b. Edinburgh. He served as commander-in-chief, Mediterranean, 1939–42 and Feb.–Oct. 1943; naval commander-in-chief for the Allied assault on North Africa 1942; first sea lord 1943–6.

Curie, Marie Sklodowska (1867–1934), first great woman scientist, b. Poland. Her father was a professor of physics at Warsaw. She came to Paris to study at the Sorbonne and married **Pierre Curie** (1859–1906), professor of physics. Thus began a fruitful collaborative career that led to the discovery of radium for which they shared the 1903 Nobel prize for physics. In 1911 Mme. Curie received the Nobel prize for chemistry. Pierre Curie was killed in an accident. *See also* **Joliot-Curie.**

Curzon of Kedleston, 1st Marquess (George Nathaniel Curzon) (1859–1925), statesman and administrator; viceroy of India 1898–1905; member of Lloyd George's war cabinet 1916–18; foreign secretary 1919–24.

Cuthbert, St. (*c.* 635–87), Celtic monk who became prior of Old Melrose (on the Tweed) and later of Lindisfarne. For a time he lived in seclusion on one of the Farne islands. The story of his life we owe to Bede.

Cuvier, Georges (1769–1832), French naturalist, noted for his system of classification of animals and his studies in comparative anatomy. His *Le Règne Animal* (1819) was a standard work for many years.

Cuyp, Albert (1620–91), Dutch landscape painter of sea and river views.

Cyprian, St. (d. 258), bishop of Carthage, and early Christian writer who was martyred.

Cyrus (559–529 B.C.), Persian emperor. He founded the Achaemenid line, having defeated the Medes. By conquering Lydia and Babylonia, he controlled Asia Minor. He was a wise and tolerant ruler, allowing the Jews to rebuild their temple.

D

Daguerre, Louis Jacques Mandé (1789–1851), French photographic pioneer, who invented the daguerrotype process. *See* **Section L.**

Daimler, Gottlieb (1834–1900), German inventor, with N. A. Otto of Cologne, of the Otto gas engine. The Mercédès car, exhibited at Paris in 1900, was named after the daughter of Emile Jellinek, Austrian banker and car enthusiast.

Dale, Sir Henry Hallett (1875–1968), English physiologist. He shared the 1936 Nobel prize for medicine for his work on the chemical transmission of nerve impulses.

Dalhousie, 1st Marquess of (James Andrew Broun Ramsay) (1812–60), governor-general of India. He annexed the Punjab and later other states; opened the civil service to Indians and acted against suttee.

Dalton, John (1766–1844), English chemist and mathematician, a Quaker teacher of Manchester. In 1808 in the first number of his *New System of Chemical Philosophy* (1808–27) the modern chemical atomic theory was first propounded by him. According to this the atoms of the chemical elements are qualitatively different from one another. *See* **Section F, Part II.**

Damien, Father (1840–89), Belgian missionary priest, originally named Joseph de Veuster, who, witnessing the sufferings of the lepers confined on the Hawaiian island of Molokai, obtained permission to take charge, and remained there until he himself died of leprosy.

Damocles, 5th cent. B.C., Syracusan flatterer who pronounced the tyrant Dionysius the happiest of men. To illustrate the uncertainty of life, Dionysius invited him to a banquet, where a naked sword hung over his head by a hair. Hence the expression " Sword of Damocles " to mean impending danger or threat.

Damrosch, Walter Johannes (1862–1950), American conductor and composer, b. Breslau, Prussia. He promoted musical development in the U.S., especially while conductor of the New York Symphony Society which his father, **Leopold Damrosch** (1832–1885) had founded in 1878.

D'Annunzio, Gabriele (1863–1938), Italian poet, dramatist and nationalist. In 1919 he led a raid on Fiume and seized it, but was eventually forced to surrender. His bodyguard wore the black shirt which was to be the uniform of the Fascists.

Dante Alighieri (1265–1321), Italian poet, a figure of world literature. He was b. at Florence in a troubled period. Though he saw her but once or twice, he loved a lady whom he called Beatrice, who is believed to have been Bice Portinari who married Simone di Bardi; she died in 1290, after which Dante wrote his *Vita Nuova*. His next work *Convivio* was philosophical. He joined the party of the Bianchi, attained municipal office, but was imprisoned and in 1301 fled. His *Divina Commedia* is a description of hell, purgatory, and heaven, a work of moral edification, replete with symbolism. He d. at Ravenna.

Danton, Georges Jacques (1759–94), French revolutionary. To his eloquent lead in 1792 was largely due the defeat of the foreign forces attempting to quell the revolution. He was a member of the committee of public safety, and sought to modify the extremists, but was displaced by Robespierre and was subsequently executed.

D'Arblay. *See* **Burney.**

Darby, Abraham (1677–1717), member of the Quaker family of ironmasters of Coalbrookdale, Salop, who paved the way for the industrial revolution by developing iron metallurgy. His grandson Abraham (1750–91) built the first cast-iron bridge (1779) over the Severn at Coalbrookdale.

Darius I (548–486 B.C.), Persian king and founder of Persepolis. He extended the borders of the Persian empire beyond the Indus, and reorganised it into satrapies. He declared " God's plan for the earth is not turmoil but peace, prosperity and good government." On clashing with the Greeks, however, he was defeated at Marathon. **Darius II** was a natural son of Artaxerxes I and d. 405 B.C. **Darius III** (d. 331 B.C.) was the last of the Persian kings, and was defeated by Alexander and assassinated.

Darling, Grace Horsley (1815–42), English heroine who by putting off in a small boat from the lighthouse on one of the Farne islands, of which her father was keeper, saved the shipwrecked crew of the *Forfarshire.*

Darnley, Henry Stewart, Lord (1545–67), second husband of Mary, Queen of Scots (1565). He plotted the murder of her secretary, Rizzio, and was subsequently himself murdered. Through his son James I he is the ancestor of the Stuart monarchs.

Darwin, Charles Robert (1809–82), English naturalist, b. Shrewsbury, one of the pioneers of experimental biology. After returning from his formative voyage round the world as naturalist on the *Beagle* (1831–6), he spent nearly twenty years building up evidence for his theory of evolution before publishing it in *The Origin of Species* (1859). In it he argued that the evolution of present-day morphology had been built up by the gradual and opportunistic mechanism of natural selection. His ideas though welcomed by biologists aroused bitter controversy. *See* **Section F, Part IV.**

Daudet, Alphonse (1840–97), French writer who covered a wide range and whose works include *Lettres de mon Moulin, Robert Helmont,* and *Tartarin de Tarascon.*

David I (1084–1153), King of Scotland. As uncle of Matilda, daughter of Henry I of England, he supported her claim to the English crown, but was defeated. In Scotland he promoted unity and development.

David II (1324–71), King of Scotland. He was son of Robert Bruce. In invading England he was captured at Neville's Cross, 1346.

David, Sir Edgeworth (1858–1934), Australian geologist who accompanied Shackleton's antarctic expedition, 1907–9, leading the party that reached the south magnetic pole.

David, Jacques Louis (1748–1825), French painter of classical subjects and an ardent republican.

David, St., patron saint of Wales who lived in south Wales in the 6th cent.

Davidson, 1st Baron (Randall Thomas Davidson) (1848–1930), archbishop of Canterbury, 1903–28.

Davies, Sir Walford (1869–1941), English organist, composer, and broadcaster on music.

Davies, William Henry (1871–1940), Welsh poet. He spent some years tramping, both in England and America, and his work shows knowledge of and love for nature. He wrote *Autobiography of a Super Tramp*.

Da Vinci. *See* **Leonardo.**

Davis, Jefferson (1808–89), American civil war leader. B. in Kentucky, he was made president of the Confederate States when the civil war broke out. After the war he was tried for treason, but discharged. He wrote *The Rise and Fall of the Confederate Government*.

Davis, John (*c.* 1550–1605), Elizabethan explorer and discoverer of Davis's Strait, the channel between the Atlantic and Arctic oceans on the west of Greenland. Invented the backstaff, or Davis's quadrant.

Davitt, Michael (1846–1906), Irish nationalist. The son of a peasant who later came to England, he joined the Fenians, and in 1870 was sentenced to penal servitude. On his release he helped to found the Land League in 1879; was again imprisoned; and wrote *Leaves from a Prison Diary*. He was subsequently returned to parliament.

Davy, Sir Humphry (1778–1829), English chemist, b. Penzance. Much of his work found practical application, *e.g.*, the miner's safety lamp which still bears his name. His *Elements of Agricultural Chemistry* (1813) contains the first use in English of the word "element." He took Michael Faraday as his assistant at the Royal Institution.

Dawber, Sir Guy (1861–1938), English architect. As chairman of the Council for the Preservation of Rural England, he did much to bring about the restoration of buildings throughout the country.

Day Lewis, Cecil (1904–72), poet and critic; professor of poetry at Oxford 1951–6. He succeeded Masefield as poet laureate in 1968. *See* **Section M, Part III.**

Debussy, Claude Achille (1862–1918), composer and leader of the French Impressionist school in music. Among his works are *Suite bergamasque*, containing the popular *Clair de lune*; *L'Après-midi d'un Faune*, inspired by the poem of Mallarmé, and *La Mer*. He also wrote an opera *Pelléas et Mélisande* based on Maeterlinck's drama. *See also* **Section E.**

Defoe, Daniel (1660–1731), English political writer; also author of *Robinson Crusoe*, *Moll Flanders*, and a *Tour of Gt. Britain*. His *Shortest Way with Dissenters* brought him imprisonment.

De Forest, Lee (1873–1961), American inventor who was the first to use alternating-current transmission, and improved the thermionic valve detector by which wireless and sound films were made possible.

Degas, Edgar (1834–1917), French Impressionist painter and sculptor, son of a banker. He painted subjects from everyday life—dancers, café life, the racecourse.

De Gasperi, Alcide (1881–1954), Italian politician who founded the Christian Democrat Party and worked for European federation; prime minister 1945–53.

de Gaulle. *See* **Gaulle, Charles de.**

De Havilland, Sir Geoffrey (1882–1965), pioneer of civil and military aviation in Britain; designer of the famous Moth machines. His son was killed in 1946 while testing a plane.

Delacroix, Ferdinand Victor Eugène (1798–1863), French painter of the Romantic school.

De la Mare, Walter John (1873–1956), English poet and novelist whose work has a characteristic charm. Much of it was written for children.

Delane, John Thadeus (1817–79), editor of *The Times*, 1841–77, who did much to establish that paper's standing.

Delaroche, Paul (1797–1856), French historical painter.

Delibes, Clément Philibert Léo (1836–91), French composer of much graceful music, including operas, of which *Lakmé* is the best known, and ballets, among them *Coppélia*.

Delius, Frederick (1862–1934), English composer of German parentage. His music, highly idiosyncratic in idiom, was more readily received in Germany than in England until promoted by Sir Thomas Beecham. *See* **Section E.**

Democritus (*c.* 470–*c.* 400 B.C.), one of the first scientific thinkers, pupil of Leucippus (fl. *c.* 440 B.C.). He took an atomic view of matter, denied the existence of mind as a separate entity, and counted happiness and inner tranquillity as important moral principles. His attitude was not shared by his contemporary, Socrates, nor by Plato and Aristotle, but was accepted by Epicurus. The atomic theory thus passed into the background for many centuries.

Demosthenes (385–322 B.C.), Greek orator who, by his *Philippics*, roused the Athenians to resist the growing power of Philip of Macedon.

De Quincey, Thomas (1785–1859), English essayist and critic; friend of Wordsworth and Southey. He wrote *Confessions of an Opium-eater*.

De Reszke, Jean (1853–1925) and **De Reszke, Edouard** (1856–1917), Polish operatic singers, the first a tenor, the second a baritone.

Derwentwater, 3rd Earl of (James Radcliffe) (1689–1716), leader of the English Jacobite movement for placing the pretender on the throne. He was defeated at Preston in 1715 and beheaded.

Descartes, René (1596–1650), French mathematician, pioneer of modern philosophy. Unconvinced by scholastic tradition and theological dogma, he sought to get back to why anything can be said to be true, which turned out to be a fruitful line of thought. The basis of his Cartesian philosophy is summed up in his own words, *cogito, ergo sum* (I think, therefore I am).

Desmoulins, Camille (1760–94), French revolutionary. He represented Paris in the National Convention, and wrote witty and sarcastic pamphlets and periodicals. He was an ally of Danton, and when Robespierre came to power he was arrested and executed on the same day as Danton.

Deutscher, Isaac (1907–67), Marxist historian, biographer of Stalin and Trotsky. B. in Poland, he joined the outlawed Polish Communist Party but was expelled for his anti-Stalinist views. In 1939 he came to London.

De Valéra, Eamon (1882–1975), Irish statesman, b. New York, son of a Spanish father and an Irish mother. He was imprisoned for his part in the Easter rising of 1916. He opposed the treaty of 1921; and in 1926, when the republican Fianna Fáil was founded, he became its president. Fianna Fáil won the election of 1932, and he then became president of the Executive Council, 1932–7; prime minister, 1937–48, 1951–4, 1957–9; president of the republic, 1959–73. He promoted Irish neutrality in the second world war, encouraged the use of the Irish language, and in spite of early intransigence his leadership was moderate.

de Valois, Dame Ninette (b. 1898), Irish-born ballet dancer and choreographer. She toured Europe with Diaghilev, 1923–5, and in 1931 founded the Sadlers Wells Ballet School (now Royal Ballet School), of which she became director. *Autobiography* (1957).

Dewar, Sir James (1842–1923), chemist and physicist, a native of Kincardine. He succeeded in liquefying hydrogen, and invented the vacuum flask. The explosive cordite was the joint invention of himself and Sir Frederick Abel.

Dewey, John (1859–1952), American philosopher, psychologist, and educationist. A follower of William James, he was an exponent of pragmatism.

De Wit, Jan (1625–72), Dutch republican statesman, who carried on war with England and later negotiated the Triple Alliance, but was overthrown by the Orange Party and murdered.

Diaghilev, Sergei Pavlovich (1872–1929), Russian ballet impressario and founder of the Russian ballet. Among those associated with him are Anna Pavlova, Vaslav Nijinsky, Tamara Karsavina, Leonide Massine, Michel Fokine, the choreographer, L. N. Bakst, the painter, and Igor Stravinsky, the composer.

Dickens, Charles (1812–70), popular English novelist of the 19th cent., with enormous output and capacity for vivid story-telling. Of humble origin, he was extremely successful.

His best-known works are perhaps *Pickwick Papers*, *Oliver Twist*, *A Christmas Carol* (this influenced the observance of Christmas), *Dombey and Son*, *David Copperfield*, *Little Dorrit*, and *Great Expectations*. He gave public readings from his works.

Dickinson, Emily (1830–86), American poet whose writing has a mystic quality. She lived a cloistered life and published almost nothing in her lifetime.

Dickinson, Goldworthy Lowes (1863–1932), English author, an interpreter and upholder of the Greek view of life.

Diderot, Denis (1713–84), French man of letters, critic of art and literature, and editor of the *Encyclopédie* (1713–84) to which many writers of the Enlightenment contributed.

Diemen, Anthony van (1593–1645), Dutch promoter of exploration. As governor-general in the Far East, he promoted Dutch trade and influence; and despatched Abel Tasman, who in 1642 discovered New Zealand and Van Diemen's Land (now Tasmania).

Diesel, Rudolf (1858–1913), German engineer, inventor of an internal combustion engine which he patented in 1893. *See also* **L31.**

Diocletian (245–313), Roman emperor and persecutor of Christianity. He divided the empire under a system of joint rule; later abdicated; and built a palace in Dalmatia.

Diogenes (412–322 B.C.), Greek cynic philosopher who lived in a tub and told Alexander to get out of his sunshine. He sought virtue and moral freedom in liberation from desire.

Dionysius the elder and younger, tyrants of Syracuse in the 4th cent. B.C.

Dirac, Paul Adrien Maurice (b. 1902), English physicist who shared with Erwin Schrödinger the 1933 Nobel prize for their work in developing Heisenberg's theory of quantum mechanics. Order of Merit (1973). *See* **Section F, Part II.**

Disney, Walter Elias (1901–66), American film cartoonist, creator of Mickey Mouse. He is known for his *Silly Symphonies*, *Snow White and the Seven Dwarfs*, and *Pinocchio*.

Disraeli, Benjamin, Earl of Beaconsfield (1804–81), British statesman and novelist who helped to form modern Conservatism in England. The son of Isaac (*q.v.*), he published his first novel at 21, and later *Coningsby* and *Sibyl*, which helped to rouse the social conscience. He entered parliament in 1837 and was prime minister 1868 and 1874–80, when he arranged the purchase of shares in the Suez canal. He was rival of Gladstone and friend of Queen Victoria.

D'Israeli, Isaac (1766–1848), father of Benjamin (*q.v.*) and author of *Curiosities of Literature*.

Dobson, Austin (1840–1921), English writer of light verse and of 18th cent. biography.

Dodgson, Charles Lutwidge (1832–98), English writer. Under the pseudonym Lewis Carroll, he wrote poems and books for children, including *Alice in Wonderland*. In private life he was a lecturer in mathematics at Oxford.

Dolci, Carlo (1616–86), one of the last Florentine painters.

Dolci, Danilo (b. 1925), Italian architect who since 1952 has dedicated himself to the rehabilitation of the people of Sicily in their desperate poverty.

Dominic, St. (1170–1221), founder of the Friars Preachers or Black Friars. B. in Castile, he and his followers sought to teach the ignorant. In 1216 they were formed into an order and vowed to poverty. The order spread through Europe.

Domitian (Titus Flavius Domitianus) (A.D. 51–96), Roman emperor, son of Vespasian. He ruled despotically, aroused the hatred of the senate, and was assassinated as a result of a palace conspiracy.

Donatello (Donato di Niccolò) (*c.* 1386–1466), Italian sculptor, b. Florence, son of Niccolò di Betto di Bardo. He was the founder of modern sculpture, producing statues independent of a background, designed to stand in the open to be viewed from all angles. Among his masterpieces are the statues of *St. George* and *David* (in the Bargello, Florence) and his equestrian *Gattamelata* in Padua, the first bronze horse to be cast in the Renaissance.

Donizetti, Gaetano (1797–1848), Italian composer. The best-known of his sixty operas are *Lucia di Lammermoor*, *La Fille du Régiment*, and *Don Pasquale*. *See* **Section E.**

Donne, John (1572–1631), English metaphysical poet and preacher (dean of St. Paul's). His poems and sermons, marked by passion, wit, and profundity of thought have received full publicity only in the present century. His writings include *Elegies*, *Satires*, *Songs and Sonnets*, *Problems and Paradoxes* and the *Holy Sonnets*.

Doré, Gustave (1833–83), French artist who painted scriptural subjects and illustrated Dante, Milton, and Tennyson.

Dostoyevsky, Feodor Mikhailovich (1821–81), Russian novelist, b. Moscow. As a result of his revolutionary activity he was sent to hard labour in Siberia. In his books, which include *Crime and Punishment*, *The Brothers Karamazov*, *The Idiot*, and *The Possessed*, he explored the dark places of the human spirit to a degree not previously attempted.

Douglas of Kirtleside, 1st Baron (William Sholto Douglas) (1893–1969), British airman; commanded Fighter command, 1940–2, Coastal command, 1944–5. A Labour peer.

Douglas, Norman (1868–1952), novelist and travel writer. A Scot, born in Austria, he made his home on the Mediterranean. His works include *South Wind*.

Doulton, Sir Henry (1820–97), English potter and the inventor of Doulton ware.

Dowden, Edward (1843–1913), English literary critic and Shakespearean scholar.

Dowding, 1st Baron (Hugh Caswell Tremenheere Dowding) (1882–1970), British airman; commanded Fighter command during the Battle of Britain period (1940).

Dowland, John (*c.* 1563–1626), English composer of songs with lute accompaniment. His son Robert succeeded him as Court lutanist to Charles I.

Doyle, Sir Arthur Conan (1859–1930), British writer, b. Edinburgh, creator of the detective Sherlock Holmes and of his friend and foil, Dr. Watson. He was trained as a doctor but gave up his medical practice in 1890 to devote himself to writing.

Doyle, Richard (1824–83), humorous artist on the staff of *Punch*.

D'Oyly Carte, Richard (1844–1901), English theatrical manager, who built the Savoy theatre and there produced Gilbert and Sullivan operas.

Drake, Sir Francis (*c.* 1540–96), English seaman. In 1577–80 he sailed round the world in the *Golden Hind*. In 1587 he destroyed a number of Spanish ships in Cadiz harbour; and under Lord Howard he helped to defeat the Spanish Armada in 1588.

Draper, John William (1811–82), American chemist, b. near Liverpool. He was the first, using Daguerre's process, to take a successful photograph of the human face (1840) and of the moon.

Dreiser, Theodore (1871–1935), American novelist of austere realism, author of *An American Tragedy*.

Dreyfus, Alfred (1859–1935), French victim of injustice. Of Jewish parentage, in 1894 he was accused of divulging secrets to a foreign power, and was sentenced by a military secret tribunal to imprisonment for life on Devil's Island in French Guiana. At a new trial in 1899 he was again found guilty. Efforts continued to be made on his behalf, and in 1906 he was entirely exonerated, restored to his rank in the army, and made a Chevalier of the Legion of Honour.

Drinkwater, John (1882–1937), English poet and playwright. His plays include *Abraham Lincoln* and *Oliver Cromwell*.

Drummond, William (1585–1649), Scottish poet and Royalist pamphleteer. He was laird of Hawthornden.

Drury, Alfred (1857–1944), English sculptor, especially of statues of Queen Victoria at Bradford and Portsmouth.

Dryden, John (1631–1700), prolific English poet and dramatist, who also wrote political satire (*Absalom and Achitophel*). He was hostile to the revolution of 1688, and thereafter mainly translated classical writers, including Virgil.

Du Barry, Marie Jeanne Bécu, Comtesse (1746–93), mistress of Louis XV of France and guillotined by the revolutionary tribunal.

Du Chaillu, Paul Belloni (1835–1903), traveller in Africa, who in 1861 and 1867 published accounts of his explorations. A French-American.

Dufferin and Ava, 1st Marquess of (Frederick Temple Hamilton-Temple Blackwood) (1826–1902), British diplomat, writer, and governor-general of Canada and viceroy of India.

Dulles, John Foster (1888–1959), U.S. Secretary of State in the Republican administration 1953–9. His foreign policy was inflexibly opposed to negotiation with Russia and to U.S. recognition of China.

Dumas, Alexandre (1802–70), French romantic novelist, among whose many works are *The Three Musketeers*, *The Count of Monte Cristo*, and *The Black Tulip*.

Dumas, Alexandre (1824–95), French dramatist, son of the above; author of *La Dame aux Camélias*.

Du Maurier, George (1834–96), contributor to *Punch* and author of *Trilby*.

Dundee, 1st Viscount (John Graham of Claverhouse), (1648–89), Scottish soldier ("Bonnie Dundee"). Employed to suppress the covenanters, he was defeated at Drumclog, but victorious at Bothwell Brig. At the revolution of 1688 he supported James II, and was killed in the (victorious) battle of Killiecrankie.

Dundonald, Earl of. *See* **Cochrane, Thomas.**

Duns Scotus, John (*c.* 1265–1308), Scottish scholastic philosopher, b. at Maxton near Roxburgh, opponent of Thomas Aquinas. He joined the Franciscans, studied and taught at Oxford and Paris, and probably d. at Cologne. He challenged the harmony of faith and reason.

Dunstable, John (*c.* 1380–1453), the earliest English composer known by name. He was a contemporary of the Netherlands composers Dufay and Binchois. *See* **Section E.**

Dunstan, St. (908–88), reforming archbishop of Canterbury. He lived through seven reigns from Athelstan to Ethelred, and was adviser especially to Edgar. Under him Glastonbury Abbey became a centre of religious teaching.

Dupleix, Joseph François (1697–1763), French governor in India. He extended French influence and power in the Carnatic, but his plans were frustrated by his English opponent, Clive. He was recalled in 1754 and died in poverty.

Dürer, Albrecht (1471–1528), German painter and engraver. B. at Nuremberg, he was (like his Italian contemporary, Leonardo) a man of intellectual curiosity and scientific insight. His best work is in his copper engravings, woodcuts, and drawings; the former include *The Knight*, *Melancholia*, and *St. Jerome in his Study*. He may be regarded as the founder of the German school and a pioneer of etching. Examples of his work are in the British Museum. He was the friend of Luther and Melancthon.

Durham, Earl of (John George Lambton) (1792–1840), served as governor-general of Canada after the disturbances of 1837, and in 1839 presented to parliament the *Durham Report*, which laid down the principle of colonial self-government.

Duse, Elenora (1861–1924) Italian tragedienne.

Duval, Claude (1643–70), notorious highwayman who came to England from Normandy and was eventually hanged at Tyburn.

Dvořák, Antonin (1841–1904), Czech composer whose music is rich in folk-song melodies of his native Bohemia. In 1884 he conducted his *Stabat Mater* in London. His *New World* symphony was composed in New York, where he was head of the National Conservatoire (1892–5). *See* **Section E.**

Dyson, Sir Frank Watson (1868–1939), English astronomer who was astronomer royal 1910–33, and astronomer royal for Scotland 1905–10.

Dyson, Sir George (1883–1964), English composer and writer. In *The New Music* he analyses the technique of modern schools of composition. He composed several choral works such as *The Canterbury Pilgrims* and *Nebuchadnezzar*.

E

Eastlake, Sir Charles Lock (1793–1865), English painter of historical and religious works.

Eastman, George (1854–1932), American inventor of the roll photographic film and the Kodak camera. His philanthropies were estimated at over $100 million.

Eck, Johann von (1486–1543), German Catholic theologian and opponent of Luther.

Eddington, Sir Arthur Stanley (1882–1944), English astronomer (Greenwich observatory 1906–13; Cambridge observatory 1914–44). His works include *The Nature of the Physical World*.

Eddy, Mrs. Mary Baker (1821–1910), American founder of the Church of Christ Scientist. Her *Science and Health with Key to the Scriptures* was published in 1875. *See* **Christian Science, Section J.**

Edelinck, Gerard (1640–1707), Flemish engraver, b. Antwerp, the first to reproduce in print the colour, as well as the form, of a picture.

Eden, Robert Anthony, 1st Earl of Avon (1897–1977), British statesman. He entered parliament in 1923; became foreign secretary in 1935 (resigning in 1938 over Chamberlain's negotiation with Mussolini and rebuff to President Roosevelt); deputy prime minister in 1951; succeeded Sir Winston Churchill in 1955. His Suez policy divided the country. He resigned for health reasons in 1957. Memoirs, *Facing the Dictators; The Reckoning;* and *Full Circle*. Earldom conferred 1961.

Edgar (943–75), King of England 959–75. He was advised by Archbishop Dunstan.

Edgar Atheling (*c.* 1060–*c.* 1130), was the lawful heir of Edward the Confessor, but in the Norman invasion he was unable to maintain his claim.

Edgeworth, Maria (1767–1849), Irish novelist, whose stories include *Castle Rackrent*, *The Absentee*, and *Belinda*.

Edinburgh, Duke of (Philip Mountbatten) (b. 1921), consort of Queen Elizabeth II. He relinquished his right of accession to the thrones of Greece and Denmark on his naturalisation in 1947 when he took the name of Mountbatten. He is the great-great-grandson of Queen Victoria, grandson of Admiral Prince Louis of Battenberg, and nephew of Earl Mountbatten of Burma. Pres. British Association 1951–2. Chancellor, Universities of Edinburgh, Wales, and Salford.

Edison, Thomas Alva (1847–1931), American inventor of the transmitter and receiver for the automatic telegraph; the phonograph; the first practical incandescent lamp; and many devices for the electrical distribution of light and power. From being a newsboy on the railway and later a telegraph clerk, he became a master at applying scientific principles to practical ends. He set up a research laboratory (originally a barn) at Menlo Park, New Jersey, where his inventions were tested out.

Edmund II (Ironside) (980–1016), the son of Ethelred, king of the English, made a compact with Canute to divide England, but soon afterwards died.

Edward the Confessor (*c.* 1004–1066), English king who preceded the Norman Conquest and founded Westminster Abbey. He was canonised in 1161.

Edward the Elder (*c.* 870–*c.* 924), son of Alfred, succeeded him as king of the West Saxons in 899. He overcame the Danes and reoccupied the northern counties.

Edward I (1239–1307), King of England, succeeded his father Henry in 1272. Able and energetic, his legislation influenced the development of the land law, and he summoned parliamentary assemblies. A soldier, he conquered Wales, building castles, but could not maintain his hold on Scotland.

Edward II (1284–1327), succeeded his father Edward I as king of England in 1307 and was defeated by the Scots at Bannockburn. Weak and inept, he was murdered in 1327.

Edward III (1312–77), succeeded his father Edward II as king of England in 1327. Popular and ambitious for military glory, he began the Hundred Years War with France. He fostered the woollen industry. Latterly he became senile.

Edward IV (1442–83), able but dissolute Yorkist leader whose reign brought about a revival in the power of the monarchy, in English sea power, and in foreign trade (in which he himself took part). Spent 1470–71 in exile. Began rebuilding of St. George's chapel, Windsor. Patron of Caxton.

Edward V (1470–83), succeeded his father Edward IV at the age of 12 and was a pawn in the quarrels of baronial relatives. He and his brother were shut up in the Tower by his uncle, Richard, Duke of Gloucester, and there probably murdered, though exact proof has not been establisned.

Edward VI (1537–53), succeeded his father, Henry VIII, as king of England when in his tenth year. He was delicate and studious, and his government was carried on successively by the Dukes of Somerset and Northumberland; while under Archbishop Cranmer the prayer book was issued. He was induced to name Lady Jane Grey his successor.

Edward VII (1841–1910), King of Gt. Britain and Ireland. The son of Queen Victoria, he married Princess Alexandra of Denmark in 1863, and succeeded his mother in 1901. Interested mainly in social life and in international contacts, he visited India in 1875 and travelled much in Europe.

Edward VIII (1894–1972), King of Gt. Britain, succeeded his father George V 1936, and abdicated later that year because of disagreement over his proposed marriage. He was created Duke of Windsor, and was governor of the Bahamas 1940–45.

Ehrlich, Paul (1854–1915), German bacteriologist, who at Frankfurt-on-Main carried out work in immunology. He discovered salvarsan for the treatment of syphilis. Nobel prizewinner 1908.

Eiffel, Alexandre Gustave (1832–1923), French engineer, one of the first to employ compressed air caissons in bridge building. Among his works are the Eiffel Tower (1887–9) and the Panama Canal locks.

Einstein, Albert (1879–1955), mathematical physicist whose theory of relativity superseded Newton's theory of gravitation. He was born in Ulm of Jewish parents, lived for many years in Switzerland, and held a succession of professorial chairs at Zurich, Prague, and Berlin. In 1921 he was awarded the Nobel prize for his work in quantum theory. He was driven by the Nazis to seek asylum in America and became professor at the Institute for Advanced Study at Princeton 1933–45. In August 1939 at the request of a group of scientists he wrote to President Roosevelt warning of the danger of uranium research in Germany and stressing the urgency of investigating the possible use of atomic energy in bombs. *See* **Relativity, Section F, Part II.**

Eisenhower, Dwight David (1890–1969), American general and statesman. He was C.-in-C. Allied Forces, N. Africa, 1942–3; and in the European theatre of operations, 1943–5; and was Republican President, 1953–61.

Eisenstein, Sergei Mikhailovich (1898–1948), Russian film director of *The Battleship Potemkin*, *Alexander Nevsky*, and *Ivan the Terrible*.

Eleanor, Queen of Edward I. After her death in 1290 the king had memorial crosses erected at the twelve places where her body rested on its way from Grantham to Westminster.

Elgar, Sir Edward (1857–1934), English composer, especially of choral-orchestral works for festivals. His oratorios include *The Kingdom*, *The Apostles*, and *The Dream of Gerontius*; he also wrote the *Enigma Variations*, and the tone-poem *Falstaff*. *See* **Section E.**

Elgin, 7th Earl of (Thomas Bruce) (1766–1841), British diplomat who, with the object of saving them, conveyed some sculptures from the Parthenon in Athens to the British Museum.

Eliot, George (1819–80), pen-name of Mary Anne (later Marion) Evans, b. Warwickshire. Her novels include *Adam Bede*, *The Mill on the Floss*, *Silas Marner*, *Middlemarch*, and *Daniel Deronda*. Her works show deep insight. She lived with the writer George Lewes from 1854 until his death 25 years later. (Although Lewes had been deserted by his wife it was then not possible to obtain a divorce.) She brought up his three children.

Eliot, Thomas Stearns (1888–1965), poet and critic. He was born in St. Louis, Missouri, and became a British subject in 1927. His poems include *Prufrock and Other Observations*, *The Waste Land*, *The Hollow Men*, *Ash Wednesday*, *Four Quartets*; his verse dramas *Murder in the Cathedral* and *The Family Reunion*. He described himself as "classicist in literature, royalist in politics, and Anglo-Catholic in religion". Nobel prizewinner 1948. *See* **Sections I and M (Part III).**

Elizabeth (b. 1900), Queen Consort of George VI, daughter of the 14th Earl of Strathmore. Before her marriage in 1923 she was Lady Elizabeth Angela Marquerite Bowes-Lyon. Chancellor, Universities of London and Dundee.

Elizabeth I (1533–1603), Queen of England, daughter of Henry VIII, succeeded her sister Mary in 1558. Politically and intellectually able and firm, though personally vain and capricious, she chose to serve her able men such as William Cecil; and her long reign was one of stability, victory over the Spanish, and adventure in the New World; while the Church of England was established, and literary output prepared the way for Shakespeare; it was however marred by the execution of Mary, Queen of Scots.

Elizabeth II (Elizabeth Alexandra Mary of Windsor) (b. 1926), Queen of Gt. Britain and N. Ireland, ascended the throne Feb. 1952 on the death of her father George VI. Her Consort, Prince Philip, Duke of Edinburgh, is the son of Prince Andrew of Greece and a descendant of the Danish royal family. They have four children: Charles, Prince of Wales (b. 1948), Princess Anne (b. 1950), Prince Andrew (b. 1960), and Prince Edward (b. 1964).

Ellis, Havelock (1859–1939), English writer whose *Studies in the Psychology of Sex* was influential in changing the public attitude towards sex. His books were published in America long before they were in England.

Emerson, Ralph Waldo (1803–82), American poet and essayist, b. Boston, member of the transcendentalist group of thinkers. Among his best-known poems are *Woodnotes*, *Threnody*, *Terminus*, *Brahma*, *The Problem*.

Emin Pasha, the name adopted by **Eduard Schnitzer** (1840–92), a German explorer associated with Gen. Charles Gordon in the Sudan as a medical officer; and governor of the Equatorial Province 1878–89, when he was menaced by the Mahdi and rescued by Stanley. He has contributed greatly to African studies.

Emmet, Robert (1778–1803), Irish patriot, led the rising of 1803, was betrayed, and executed.

Empedocles (*c.* 500–*c.* 430 B.C.), Greek philosopher, b. Agrigentum in Sicily, founder of a school of medicine which regarded the heart as the seat of life, an idea which passed to Aristotle, as did his idea that all matter was composed of four elements: earth, air, fire, and water.

Engels, Friedrich (1820–95), German socialist, son of a wealthy textile manufacturer, lifelong friend of Karl Marx, with whom he collaborated in writing the *Communist Manifesto* of 1848. Through him Marx acquired his knowledge of English labour conditions.

Epicurus of Samos (342–270 B.C.), refounded the atomic view of matter put forward by Democritus, and held that peace of mind comes through freedom from fear, the two main sources of which he regarded as religion and fear of death. The Epicureans were a rival sect to the Peripatetics and Stoics.

Epstein, Sir Jacob (1880–1959), sculptor, b. New York of Russian-Polish parents. His work includes *Rima*, in Hyde Park; *Day* and *Night* on the building of London Underground headquarters; *Genesis*, exhibited in 1931; *Lazarus*, in New College, Oxford; the *Madonna and Child* group in Cavendish Square, London; the figure of *Christ in Majesty* in aluminium in Llandaff cathedral; a sculpture for the T.U.C. headquarters in London; and a bronze group for Coventry cathedral.

Erasmus, Desiderius (1466–1536), Dutch Renaissance humanist, who spent several years in England and was the friend of Dean Colet and Sir Thomas More. He aimed at ecclesiastical reform from within and scorned the old scholastic teaching. He thus prepared the way for Luther. His *Praise of Folly* is still read.

Erhard, Ludwig (b. 1897), German economist and politician; succeeded Adenauer as Chancellor of the West German Federal Republic, 1963–7.

Essex, 2nd Earl of (Robert Devereux) (1566–1601), favourite of Queen Elizabeth I in her old age. Unsuccessful as governor-general of Ireland, he returned to England against the Queen's wish; plotted; and was executed.

Ethelbert, King of Kent at the close of the 6th cent., accepted Christianity on the mission of St. Augustine.

Ethelred II (*c.* 968–1016), King of England. Unable to organise resistance against the Danish raids, he was called the Unready (from Old Eng. uraed = without counsel).

Etty, William (1787–1849), English artist of historical and classical subjects.

Eucken, Rudolf Christoph (1846–1926), German philosopher of activism, which puts personal ethical effort above intellectual idealism. Nobel prizewinner 1908.

Euler, Leonhard (1707–83), Swiss mathematician, remembered especially for his work in optics and on the calculus of variations. He was called by Catherine I to St. Petersburg, where he was professor, 1730–41, and by Frederick the Great to Berlin, where he remained from 1741 till 1766. He became blind but continued his work.

Euripides (480–406 B.C.), Greek tragic dramatist, who is known to have written about 80 plays, of which 18 are preserved, including *Alcestis, Medea, Iphigenia,* and *Orestes.* He displayed a sceptical attitude towards the myths.

Eusebius (264–340), ecclesiastical historian. His *Ecclesiastical History* gives the history of the Christian church to 324. He also wrote a general history, *Chronicon.*

Evans, Sir Arthur John (1851–1941), English archaeologist, known for his excavations at Knossos in Crete and his discovery of the pre-Phoenician script.

Evans, Dame Edith Mary (1888–1976), versatile English actress who made her first appearance as Cressida in *Troilus and Cressida* in 1912.

Evelyn, John (1620–1706), cultured English diarist who gives brilliant portraits of contemporaries. He also wrote *Sylva,* a manual of arboriculture.

Eyck, Jan van (*c.* 1389–1441), Flemish painter, whose best-known work is the altarpiece in Ghent cathedral. His brother **Hubert** (*c.* 1370–1426) is associated with him.

F

Fabius, the name of an ancient Roman family who over many generations played an important part in early Roman history. **Quintus Fabius Maximus Verrucosus** (d. 203 B.C.) saved Rome from Hannibal by strategic evasion of battle; hence his name *Cunctator* (delayer), and the term Fabian policy.

Fabre, Jean Henri Casimir (1823–1915), French naturalist, whose study of the habits of insects were delightfully recorded in his *Souvenirs entomologiques.*

Faed, name of two Scottish genre painters, **Thomas** (1826–1900), and **John** (1819–1902). A third brother, James, engraved their works.

Fahrenheit, Gabriel Daniel (1686–1736), German physicist, b. Danzig. He introduced *c.* 1715 the mercury thermometer and fixed thermometric standards.

Fairbairn, Sir William (1789–1874), Scottish engineer. In 1817 he took the lead in using iron in shipbuilding.

Fairfax, 3rd Baron (Thomas Fairfax) (1612–71), parliamentary general in the English civil war, and victor of Marston Moor. In 1650 he withdrew into private life.

Falconer, Hugh (1808–65), British botanist and palaeontologist, b. Forres, Scot.; physician to East India Co.; introduced tea into India.

Falla, Manuel (1876–1946), Spanish composer whose music is highly individual with a strong folk-song element. *See* **Section E.**

Faraday, Michael (1791–1867), English experimental physicist, founder of the science of electromagnetism. He was the son of a Yorkshire blacksmith and at 13 became apprenticed to a bookseller in London. In 1813 he became laboratory assistant to Sir Humphry Davy at the Royal Institution, succeeding him as professor of chemistry in 1833. He set himself the problem of finding the connections between the forces of light, heat, electricity, and magnetism and his discoveries, translated by Maxwell (*q.v.*) into a single mathematical theory of electromagnetism, led to the modern developments in physics and electronics. He inaugurated the Christmas lectures for juvenile audiences at the Royal Institution.

Farman, Henri (1874–1958) French aviator, one of the pioneers of aviation, and a designer and builder of aeroplanes.

Farouk I (1920–65), King of Egypt, 1936–52. He was forced to abdicate as a result of the military coup of 1952.

Farrar, Frederick William (1831–1903), English clergyman, author of the schoolboy story *Eric.*

Faulkner, William (1897–1962), American novelist, whose series of novels, *The Sound and the Fury, As I Lay Dying, Light in August, Sanctuary* depict the American South. Nobel prizewinner 1949. *See* **Section M, Part I.**

Fauré, Gabriel Urbain (1845–1924), French composer and teacher. His works include chamber music, nocturnes, and barcarolles for piano, an opera *Pénélope,* some exquisite songs, and *Requiem.* Ravel was among his pupils. *See* **Section E.**

Fawcett, Millicent Garrett (1847–1929), educational reformer and leader of the movement for women's suffrage; one of the founders of Newnham College, Cambridge. She was the wife of the blind Liberal politician and economist, **Henry Fawcett** (1833–84).

Fawkes, Guy (1570–1606), a Yorkshire catholic, who with Catesby and other conspirators planned the Gunpowder Plot. Although warned, he persisted and was captured and hanged.

Fénelon, François de Salignac de la Mothe (1651–1715), archbishop of Cambrai and author of *Telemachus.*

Ferdinand V of Aragon (1452–1516), who married Isabella of Castile, and with her reigned over Spain, saw the Moors expelled from Spain, equipped Columbus for the discoveries that led to Spain's vast colonial possessions, and instituted the Inquisition.

Ferguson, James (1710–76), Scottish astronomer who, from being a shepherd-boy, educated himself in astronomy, mathematics, and portrait painting.

Fermi, Enrico (1901–54), Italian nuclear physicist whose research contributed to the harnessing of atomic energy and the development of the atomic bomb. Nobel prizewinner 1938.

Fichte, Johann Gottlieb (1762–1814), German philosopher of the nationalistic Romantic school who prepared the way for modern totalitarianism.

Field, John (1782–1837), Irish composer of nocturnes, pupil of Clementi and teacher of Glinka. His work served as a model for Chopin.

Fielding, Henry (1707–54), English novelist, author of *Tom Jones, Joseph Andrews,* and *Amelia,* as well as plays.

Fildes, Sir Luke (1844–1927), English painter and woodcut-designer.

Finsen, Niels Ryberg (1860–1904), Danish physician who established an institute for light therapy and invented the Finsen ultra-violet lamp. Nobel prizewinner 1903.

Firdausi, pen-name of **Abu'l Kasim Mansur** (940–1020), Persian poet, author of the epic *Shah-Nama* or Book of Kings.

Fisher of Lambeth, Baron (Geoffrey Francis Fisher) (1887–1972), archbishop of Canterbury, 1945–61; Headmaster of Repton School, 1914–32.

Fisher, Herbert Albert Laurens (1865–1940), English historian and educational reformer; author of *A History of Europe.*

Fisher, Sir Ronald Aylmer (1890–1962), British scientist who revolutionised both genetics and the philosophy of experimentation by founding the modern corpus of mathematical statistics.

FitzGerald, Edward (1809–83), English poet who translated the *Rubaiyát* of Omar Khayyam (1859).

Fitzroy, Robert (1805–65), British meteorologist who introduced the system of storm warnings which were the beginning of weather forecasts.

Flammarion, Camille (1842–1925), French astronomer, noted for his popular lectures and books which include *L'Astronomie Populaire*.

Flamsteed, John (1646–1719), the first English astronomer royal, for whom Charles II built an observatory at Greenwich (1675) where he worked for 44 years.

Flaubert, Gustave (1821–80), French novelist, and creator of *Madame Bovary*. His perfection of style was attained through unremitting effort. Other works were *Salammbô*, *L'Education sentimentale*, and *Bouvard et Pécuchet*.

Flaxman, John (1755–1826), English sculptor, b. York, employed as modeller by Josiah Wedgwood. He then took to monumental sculpture.

Flecker, James Elroy (1884–1915), English poet whose works include *Golden Journey to Samarkand*, *Hassan* (staged in London, 1923), and *Don Juan*, as well as many lyrics.

Fleming, Sir Alexander (1881–1955), Scottish bacteriologist who discovered the antibacterial enzyme lysozyme in 1922 and penicillin in 1928. Full recognition came during the war when Florey separated the drug now used for treatment from the original penicillin. Awarded Nobel prize for medicine jointly with Florey and Chain, 1945.

Fleming, Sir Ambrose (1849–1945), British scientist whose invention of the radio valve in 1904 revolutionised radio telegraphy and solved problems of radio-telephony. This eventually made possible high quality sound transmission, and thus led to broadcasting and television.

Fletcher, John (1579–1625), English dramatist who collaborated with Francis Beaumont (*q.v.*) in writing many pieces for the stage.

Flinders, Matthew (1774–1814), English navigator and explorer who made discoveries in and around Australia. He sailed through Bass Strait, so called in honour of his surgeon.

Florey, Baron (Howard Walter Florey) (1898–1968), British pathologist, b. Australia. Shared 1945 Nobel prize with Fleming and Chain for work on penicillin.

Foch, Ferdinand (1851–1929), French general, b. Tarbes. In the first world war he halted the German advance at the Marne (1914), and was engaged in the battles of Ypres (1914 and 1915) and the Somme (1916). In 1918 he became supreme commander of the British, French, and American armies and dictated the terms of Allied victory.

Fokine, Michel (1880–1944), Russian dancer, choreographer to Diaghilev's company, and creator of *Les Sylphides*, *Prince Igor*, *Scheherazade*, *Firebird*, and *The Spectre of the Rose*.

Fokker, Anthony (1890–1939), Dutch aircraft engineer, b. Java. The Fokker factory in Germany made warplanes for the Germans in the first world war.

Fonteyn, Dame Margot (Mme. Roberto de Arias) (b. 1919), prima ballerina of the Royal Ballet and acclaimed foremost English dancer.

Ford, Gerald R. (b. 1913), American Republican President 1974–7; automatically succeeded Richard Nixon when he resigned.

Ford, Henry (1863–1947), founder of Ford Motor Company (1903), of which he was president until 1919, when he was succeeded by his son, Edsel B. Ford (1893–1943). He was the pioneer of the cheap motor car.

Forester, Cecil Scott (b. 1899), English novelist, author of the *Captain Hornblower* series.

Forster, Edward Morgan (1879–1970), English novelist, author of *The Longest Journey*, *A Room with a View*, *Howards End*, *A Passage to India*. O.M. 1969. *See* **Section M, Part I.**

Foscari, Francesco (*c.* 1372–1457), Doge of Venice and victor over Milan.

Fourier, Charles (1772–1837), French socialist who propounded a system of associated enterprise which although utopian stimulated social reform.

Fourier, Jean Baptiste Joseph (1768–1830), French mathematical physicist. He played an active part in politics, holding administrative posts in Egypt and Isère, yet finding time for his own research, especially on the flow of heat along a conductor.

Fowler, Sir John (1817–98), was the engineer of the first underground railway (the London Metropolitan) and with his partner, Sir Benjamin Baker, of the Forth bridge.

Fox, Charles James (1749–1806), English Whig statesman. Son of the 1st Lord Holland, he entered parliament at 19. He held office only for brief periods between 1770 and 1806, but he upheld the liberal causes of the day (American independence, the French revolution, and parliamentary reform), and was one of the impeachers of Warren Hastings. During a period of war and reaction his leadership inspired younger men.

Fox, George (1624–91), founder of the Society of Friends, son of a weaver of Fenny Drayton, Leicestershire.

Foxe, John (1516–87), English martyrologist, author of *History of the Acts and Monuments of the Church* (better known as *Foxe's Book of Martyrs*).

Frampton, Sir George James (1860–1928), English sculptor of the Peter Pan statue in Kensington Gardens and the Edith Cavell memorial.

France, Anatole (1844–1924), French writer, especially of short stories. Nobel prize 1921.

Francis I (1494–1547), King of France. Brilliant but ambitious and adventurous, he fostered learning and art, and met Henry VIII at the Field of the Cloth of Gold. His rivalry with the Emperor Charles V involved France in prolonged war, especially in Italy (he was captured at Pavia, 1525). He persecuted the Protestants.

Francis of Assisi, St. (1181/2–1226), founder of the Franciscan Order. Son of a wealthy cloth merchant, in 1208 he turned from a life of pleasure to poverty and the complete observance of Christ's teaching. He and his friars went about preaching the gospel by word and example, and the brotherhood increased rapidly. He was canonised in 1228.

Francis, Sir Philip (1740–1818), English politician, reputed author of the *Letters of Junius*.

Franck, César Auguste (1822–90), composer and organist, b. at Liège in Belgium. His music is romantic, mystical, and personal in idiom. Much of his composition is for the organ. *See* **Section E.**

Franco, Francisco (1892–1975), Spanish general and dictator. He led the Fascist rebellion against the Republican government (1936) and with German and Italian help ended the civil war (1939), since when he ruled Spain with utter ruthlessness.

Franklin, Benjamin (1706–90), American statesman. B. at Boston, he was at first a printer and journalist. He then took an interest in electricity, explained lightning as of electrical origin, and invented the lightning conductor. He was active in promoting the Declaration of Independence in 1773; he negotiated French support; and helped to frame the American constitution.

Franklin, Sir John (1786–1847), English Arctic explorer. His expedition in the *Erebus* and the *Terror* to find the north-west passage ended disastrously, and all attempts to find survivors failed.

Fraunhofer, Joseph von (1787–1826), optical instrument-maker of Munich, the first to map the dark lines of the solar spectrum named after him.

Frazer, Sir James George (1854–1941), Scottish anthropologist, b. Glasgow; author of *The Golden Bough*.

Frederick I (*c.* 1123–90), Holy Roman Emperor, nicknamed Barbarossa. A strong personality, he sought to impose his will on the city-states of northern Italy and the papacy, and was defeated at Legnano in 1176 but was more successful with a conciliatory policy (1183). He had also to contend with opposition at home. He died on the third crusade.

Frederick II (1194–1250), Holy Roman Emperor, grandson of the above, and son of the heiress of Sicily. Brilliant and enlightened, he attracted to his court in Sicily Jewish, Mohammedan, and Christian scholars; founded the university of Naples; was a patron of the medical school of Salerno; wrote a treatise on falconry; and commissioned a code of laws. Politically he was less successful, having trouble with the Lombard cities, and being involved with the papacy especially as regards his delay in going on crusade; but after negotiations with the sultan of Egypt he actually was crowned king of Jerusalem.

Frederick II (the Great) (1712–86), King of Prussia. Having inherited from his father a well-drilled army, in 1740 he seized Silesia from Austria, and retained it through the resulting war and the Seven Years war. He also took part in the partition of Poland. An able administrator and an outstanding general, he made Prussia powerful and strengthened its military tradition. He corresponded with Voltaire and he also played the flute.

French, Sir John, Ist Earl of Ypres (1852–1925), first British commander-in-chief in the first world war; replaced by Sir Douglas Haig in 1915.

Freud, Sigmund (1856–1939), psychiatrist and founder of psychoanalysis; b. Moravia, studied medicine in Vienna, where he lived until 1938 when the Nazi invasion of Austria sent him into exile in London where he died. His theories of the mind, based on years of investigation, illumined the way we think about ourselves, and had immense influence upon modern thought. *See* Psychoanalysis, Section J.

Friese-Greene, William (1855–1921), English inventor of the cinematograph. His first film was shown in 1890. He died in poverty.

Frobisher, Sir Martin (1535–94), first British navigator to seek the north-west passage from the Atlantic to the Pacific through the Arctic seas. He is commemorated in Frobisher's Strait. He also fought against the Spanish Armada.

Froebel, Friedrich Wilhelm August (1782–1852), German educational reformer, founder of the Kindergarten system.

Froissart, Jean (1337–1410), French author of *Chronicles* covering the history of Western Europe from 1307 to 1400, one of the chief sources for the history of the first half of the Hundred Years war.

Frost, Robert (1874–1963), American poet, author of *Stopping by Woods on a Snowy Evening, Birches, The Death of the Hired Man, After Apple-Picking.*

Froude, James Anthony (1818–94), English historian and biographer of Carlyle.

Fry, Christopher (b. 1907), English poet and dramatist of Quaker family; author of *The Lady's Not for Burning, Venus Observed, The Dark is Light Enough, Curtmantle*, and *A Yard of Sun. See* Section I.

Fry, Elizabeth (1780–1845), English prison reformer. She lived at Norwich and belonged to the Society of Friends.

Fry, Roger (1866–1934), English art critic and painter; introduced the work of Cézanne and the post-impressionists into England; author of *Vision and Design.*

Fuchs, Leonard (1501–66), German naturalist whose compendium of medicinal plants was for long a standard work. He was professor of medicine at Tübingen and the genus *Fuchsia* is named after him.

Fuchs, Sir Vivian Ernest (b. 1908), British geologist and explorer; leader of the British Commonwealth Trans-Antarctic Expedition 1957–8, the first to cross the Antarctic continent.

Fuller, Thomas (1608–61), English antiquarian and divine, author of *Worthies of England* and a *Church History of Britain.*

Fulton, Robert (1765–1815), American engineer who experimented in the application of steam to navigation, and in 1807 launched the *Clermont* on the Hudson.

Furniss, Harry (1854–1925), caricaturist, b. Wexford. He came to London as a young man, served on the staff of *Punch* and illustrated the works of Dickens and Thackeray.

G

Gade, Niels Vilhelm (1817–90), Danish composer. While studying at Leipzig he met Mendelssohn, whom he succeeded as conductor of the Gewandhaus orchestra.

Gagarin, Yuri Alexeyevich (1934–68), Soviet cosmonaut, the first man to be launched into space and brought safely back (12 April 1961). His flight was made in the front portion of a multi-stage rocket which made a single circuit of the earth in 108 min. Killed in an air crash.

Gainsborough, Thomas (1727–88), English landscape and portrait painter, b. at Sudbury in Suffolk. His portraits are marked by informality and grace; examples are in the Tate Gallery.

Gaiseric or Genseric (*c.* 390–477), king of the Vandals, the ablest of the barbarian invaders of the Roman empire. He led his people from Spain into Africa, took Carthage, gained control of the Mediterranean by his pirate fleets, and sacked Rome in 455. He was a bigoted Arian.

Gaitskell, Hugh Todd Naylor (1906–63), Labour politician and economist. He represented Leeds South from 1945; was chancellor of the exchequer 1950–1; and leader of the Labour opposition 1955–63.

Galbraith, John Kenneth (b. 1908), American university professor of economics, b. Canada; author of *The Affluent Society* (1958), *The Liberal Hour* (1960), *The New Industrial State* (1967), *The Age of Uncertainty* (1977). He was ambassador to India 1961–3.

Galdós, Benito Pérez. *See* Pérez Galdós.

Galen, Claudius (131–201), physician, b. Pergamum (Asia Minor) of Greek parents. He systematised medical knowledge with his idea of purposive creation by the will of God; and thus discouraged original investigation. Many of his treatises survive, and his influence lasted for more than a thousand years.

Galileo (1564–1642), Italian scientist whose experimental-mathematical methods in the pursuit of scientific truth laid the foundations of modern science. He became professor of mathematics at Pisa university when he was 25 and lectured at Padua for 18 years. He made a number of fundamental discoveries, *e.g.*, in regard to the hydrostatic balance, thermometer, magnet, telescope, and foreshadowed Newton's laws of motion. He detected the four major satellites of Jupiter, the ring of Saturn, and the spots of the sun. He proved the superiority of the Copernican over the Ptolemaic theory, and was imprisoned for so doing. He died the year Newton was born.

Galsworthy, John (1867–1933), English novelist and playwright, author of *The Forsyte Saga*, a series of novels dealing with the history of an upper middle-class family. Nobel prizewinner 1932.

Galton, Sir Francis (1822–1911), founder of eugenics, cousin of Darwin. His early work, *Meteorographica* (1863), contains the basis of the modern weather chart. He devised fingerprint identification, and was one of the first to apply mathematics to biological problems.

Galvani, Luigi (1737–98), Italian physician and physiologist, whose experiments at Bologna demonstrated the principle of animal electricity.

Gama, Vasco da (*c.* 1460–1524), Portuguese navigator who discovered the sea route to India in 1498 by doubling the Cape of Good Hope.

Gandhi, Indira (b. 1917), daughter of Nehru, succeeded Shastri in 1966 to become India's first woman prime minister. *See* **Section C, Part I.**

Gandhi, Mohandas Kamamchand (Mahatma) (1869–1948), Indian patriot, social reformer and moral teacher. From 1893 to 1914 he lived in South Africa opposing discrimination against Indians. In the movement for Indian independence after 1914 he dominated Congress, instituted civil disobedience, and advocated non-violence; and he sought to free India from caste. After independence he strove to promote the co-operation of all Indians but was assassinated on his way to a prayer meeting. His teaching of non-violence has had influence outside India.

Garbo, Greta (b. 1905), Swedish film actress of poetical quality. Her films included *Queen Christina* and *Ninotchka.*

Garcia, Manuel de Popolo Vicente (1775–1832), Spanish tenor, composer, and singing master. His son **Manuel Patricio Rodriguez** (1805–1906) was tutor to Jenny Lind. Both his daughters (Mme. Malibran and Mme. Viardot) were operatic singers, and his grandson and great-grandson baritones.

Garcia Lorca, Federico. *See* **Lorca.**

Gardiner, Samuel Rawson (1829–1902), English historian of the Stuart period.

Garibaldi, Giuseppe (1807–82), Italian soldier and patriot, who with Mazzini and Cavour created a united Italy. In 1834 he was condemned to death for helping in a republican plot to seize Genoa, but escaped to S. America. He returned in 1848 to fight for Mazzini but was again forced to flee. In 1851 he returned and gave his support to Cavour, taking part in the Austrian war of 1859. In 1860 with a thousand volunteers he freed Sicily, took Naples, and handed over the Two Sicilies to Victor Emmanuel who was proclaimed king.

Garrick, David (1717–79), English actor and theatrical manager. Brought up at Lichfield, he was taught by Samuel Johnson.

Garrison, William Lloyd (1805–79), American philanthropist who worked to end slavery.

Gaskell, Mrs. Elizabeth Cleghorn (1810–65), English novelist, author of *Mary Barton*, *Cranford*, and a *Life of Charlotte Brontë*. She was brought up by an aunt in the little Cheshire town of Knutsford.

Gaulle, Charles de (1890–1970), French general and statesman, son of a headmaster of a Jesuit school; first president of the Fifth Republic 1959–69. He fought in the first world war until his capture in 1916. In the second world war he refused to surrender (1940) and raised and led the Free French forces, with headquarters in England. He came to political power in 1958; allowed Algerian independence in 1962 in face of an army and civilian revolt, initiated closer ties with West Germany (Franco-German treaty 1963), recognised Communist China, withdrew from NATO, building his own nuclear force, vetoed Britain's entry into the Common Market (1963 and 1967); and based his government on personal prestige and use of the referendum in place of parliamentary approval. He was taken by surprise by the rising of students and workers in 1968 and resigned after losing the referendum in 1969.

Gauss, Karl Friedrich (1777–1855), German mathematician. He spent most of his life at the university of Göttingen where he set up the first special observatory for terrestrial magnetism. He made major contributions to astronomy, mathematics, and physics. The unit of magnetic induction is named after him.

Gautama, Siddhartha (Buddha, the enlightened) (*c.* 563–*c.* 483 B.C.). B. near Benares, a rajah's son, he gave himself up to the religious life and attracted many disciples. Concerned with man's sorrow and suffering, he planned a movement which could be universally shared, in which kindness to others, including animals, took a leading part. His teaching is summarised in the "four noble truths" and the "eightfold path" (*see* **Buddhism, Section J**). After his death his teaching spread (with the help of the King Asoka) over much of India and through eastern Asia as far as Japan, and developed varying schools of thought. Buddhism is tolerant and also maintains that the good of the part is that of the whole; hence it is wrong to harm another or take life.

Gautier, Théophile (1811–72), French poet and novelist, author of *Mademoiselle de Maupin*.

Gay, John (1685–1732), English poet, author of *The Beggar's Opera* (set to music by Pepusch) and *Polly*.

Gay-Lussac, Joseph Louis (1778–1850), French chemist, who showed that when gases combine their relative volumes bear a simple numerical relation to each other and to the volume of their product, if gaseous (1808), *e.g.*, one volume of oxygen combines with two volumes of hydrogen to form two volumes of water vapour.

Ged, William (1690–1749), Scottish printer who patented stereotyping.

Geddes, Sir Patrick (1854–1932), Scottish biologist and a pioneer in town and regional planning, who invented the term conurbation.

Geikie, Sir Archibald (1835–1924), Scottish geologist. His brother James specialised in glacial geology.

Genghiz Khan (1162–1227), Mongol conqueror. After years of struggle to make good his succession to his father, he overran the greater part of Asia bringing devastation wherever he went.

Geoffrey of Monmouth (1100–54), chronicler, b. Monmouth, later bishop of St. Asaph. His chronicle drew on his creative imagination.

George I (1660–1727), became King of Great Britain in 1714 as descendant of James I. His chief minister was Sir Robert Walpole. Himself personally undistinguished, his reign saw political development; and in spite of the Jacobite threat (rising in 1715) it began a period of dynastic stability.

George II (1685–1760), son of the above, succeeded in 1727, and survived a more serious Jacobite rising in 1745. His long reign helped the development of constitutional government, for he kept within the limitations of his powers and capacity; and it saw the extension of English power in India and North America.

George III (1738–1820), grandson of George II, reigned 1760–1820. Sincere and well-intentioned, but not politically able, he suffered from mental illness due to intermittent porphyria. His reign saw a clash with John Wilkes, the rise of Methodism, and agrarian and industrial revolution; also the loss of the American colonies, the extension and the questioning of English power in India (Warren Hastings), and prolonged French wars.

George IV (1762–1830), eldest son of George III, reigned 1820–30, having become Prince Regent in 1812. Styled "the first gentleman of Europe," he is remembered for his interest in art and architecture. His married life was unfortunate, and the monarchy was at a low ebb; while his reign was a time of distress and of demand for reform.

George V (1865–1936), was the second son of Edward VII and Queen Alexandra, but became heir to the English throne on the death of his elder brother in 1892. He joined the Navy as a cadet in 1877. In 1893 he married Princess Mary of Teck. He succeeded in 1910 and discharged his office conscientiously. In 1932 he began the royal broadcast on Christmas Day and in 1935 celebrated his silver jubilee. His reign included the Kaiser's war, the emergence of the Irish Free State, and the first Labour government.

George VI (1895–1952), second son of George V, was called to the throne in 1936 on the abdication of his elder brother, Edward VIII. His personal qualities gained wide respect. His reign was marked by Hitler's war and rapid social change.

George, Henry (1839–97), American political economist whose "single tax" on land values as a means of solving economic problems is expounded in his *Progress and Poverty* (1879).

George, St., patron saint of England, adopted by Edward III. He is believed to have been martyred by Diocletian at Nicomedia in 303 (and not, as believed by Gibbon, to be confused with George of Cappadocia). The story of his fight with the dragon is of late date.

Gershwin, George (1898–1937), American jazz pianist and song-writer, composer of *Rhapsody in Blue* and the Negro folk-opera *Porgy and Bess*.

Gesner, Conrad (1516–65), Swiss naturalist, b. Zurich. In a series of magnificently illustrated volumes he gave a complete description of the animal and vegetable kingdoms.

Ghiberti, Lorenzo (1378–1455), Florentine sculptor whose bronze doors, beautifying the baptistery in Florence, were described by Michelangelo as fit for the gates of paradise.

Ghirlandaio, Domenico (1449–94), Florentine painter. Most of his frescoes are in Florence, including the cycle of the life of the Virgin and the Baptist in S. Maria Novella. Michelangelo began his apprenticeship in his workshop.

Giacometti, Alberto (1901–66), Swiss sculptor and painter, who worked mainly in Paris and produced abstract symbolic constructions.

Giap, Vo Nguyen (b. 1912), Vietnamese general who defeated the French at Dien Bien Phu (1954) and withstood American intervention in the Vietnam war which followed; deputy prime minister and commander-in-chief, North Vietnam.

Gibbon, Edward (1737–94), English historian of the *Decline and Fall of the Roman Empire*.

Gibbons, Grinling (1648–1720), English wood-carver and sculptor, b. Rotterdam, was brought to the notice of Charles II by Evelyn, the diarist. The choir stalls of St. Paul's and the carving in the Wren library at Trinity College, Cambridge, are his work.

Gibbons, Orlando (1583–1625), English composer

of church music, organist at the chapel royal. *See also* Section E.

Gide, André (1869–1951), French writer of many short novels in which he gives expression to his struggle to escape from his protestant upbringing (*Strait is the Gate, The Counterfeiters*). In his memoir *Si le grain ne meurt* he tells the story of his life up to his marriage. The narratives of his journeys in Africa led to a reform in French colonial policy. Nobel prizewinner 1947.

Gielgud, Sir John (b. 1904), English actor and producer, member of the Terry family, to whom the present popularity of Shakespeare is largely due. *See* Section I, Part I.

Gigli, Beniamino (1890–1957), Italian operatic tenor.

Gilbert, Sir Alfred (1854–1934), English sculptor and goldsmith. His sculptures include *Eros* in Piccadilly Circus.

Gilbert, Sir Humphrey (1537–83), English navigator. He was knighted by Queen Elizabeth for service in Ireland. In 1583 he discovered Newfoundland, but was drowned the same year.

Gilbert, William (1540–1603), English physician to Queen Elizabeth. His book *On the Magnet*, published in Latin in 1600, was the first major original contribution to science published in England.

Gilbert, Sir William Schwenck (1836–1911), English humorist and librettist of the Gilbert and Sullivan light operas. First known as author of the *Bab Ballads*, from 1871 he collaborated with Sir Arthur Sullivan, his wit and satire finding appropriate accompaniment in Sullivan's music. Their operas include *H.M.S. Pinafore, Patience, Iolanthe, The Mikado, The Gondoliers*, and *The Yeoman of the Guard*.

Gill, Eric (1881–1940), English sculptor and engraver, whose works include the *Stations of the Cross* (Westminster Cathedral), *Prospero and Ariel* (Broadcasting House), *Christ Driving the Money-changers from the Temple* (Leeds University). He also worked as a designer for printing (Gill Sans type), and the George VI stamps were his designs.

Gillray, James (1757–1815), English caricaturist who produced upwards of a thousand political cartoons.

Giotto di Bondone (1267–1337), Florentine artist. A pupil of Cimabue, he continued the development away from Byzantine tradition towards greater naturalism. His frescoes survive in the churches of Assisi, Padua, and Florence. He designed the western front of the cathedral at Florence and the campanile.

Gissing, George Robert (1857–1903), English novelist whose works deal with the degrading effect of poverty. The best known is *New Grub Street*.

Giulio Romano or **Giulio Pippi** (*c.* 1492–1546), Italian artist, was a pupil of Raphael. He was also an engineer and architect.

Gladstone, William Ewart (1809–98), English Liberal statesman. B. at Liverpool, he entered parliament in 1832 as a Tory and held office under Peel. From 1852 he served several terms as chancellor of the exchequer and was Liberal prime minister 1868–74, when his legislation included the education act of 1870, the ballot act, the disestablishment of the Church of Ireland and an Irish land act. In 1874 when Disraeli came to power, he temporarily withdrew, but made a come-back in 1876 with his Mid-Lothian campaign. He was again prime minister 1880–5, 1886 and 1892–4; he carried a parliamentary reform act, and advocated home rule for Ireland but was not able to carry it. His long life was one of moral stature and increasing advocacy of liberal causes. He was also a classical scholar and a writer on church matters.

Glazunov, Alexander Constantinovich (1865–1936), Russian composer, pupil of Rimsky-Korsakov. The first of his eight symphonies was composed when he was 16.

Glendower, Owen (*c.* 1350–*c.* 1416), Welsh chief, who conducted guerrilla warfare on the English border, and figures in Shakespeare's *Henry IV*.

Glinka, Mikhail Ivanovich (1804–57), Russian composer, first of the national school, best known for his operas, *A Life for the Tsar*, and *Russlan and Ludmilla*, based on a poem by Pushkin. *See* Section E.

Gluck, Christoph Wilibald (1714–87), German composer, important in the development of opera. He studied in Prague, Vienna and Italy, and his first operas were in the Italian tradition; but with *Orfeo ed Euridice* (1762) his style became more dramatic. There followed *Alceste, Armide*, and *Iphigénie en Tauride* (his best-known work). *See* Section E.

Goddard of Aldbourne, Baron (Rayner Goddard) (1877–1971), Lord Chief Justice of England, 1946–58.

Godfrey of Bouillon (*c.* 1061–1100), Crusader on the first crusade, was proclaimed King of Jerusalem, but declined the title for that of Protector of the Holy Sepulchre.

Godiva, Lady (1040–80), English benefactress. According to tradition, she obtained from her husband Leofric, Earl of Chester, concessions for the people of Coventry by riding naked through the town.

Godwin, Earl of the West Saxons (d. 1053), was the father of Edith, wife of King Edward the Confessor, and of Harold, last Saxon king.

Godwin, William (1756–1836), English political writer and philosoper, author of *Political Justice* (which criticised many contemporary institutions) and a novel *Caleb Williams*. He married Mary Wollstonecraft (1759–97), author of *A Vindication of the Rights of Women*; and their daughter, Mary Wollstonecraft Godwin (1797–1851) wrote *Frankenstein* and married Shelley.

Goethe, Johann Wolfgang von (1749–1832), German poet and thinker. B. at Frankfurt-on-Main, his first notable work was a romantic play, *Götz von Berlichingen*, followed by a novel *Werthers Leiden*. In 1776 he became privy councillor to the Duke of Weimar, whom he served for many years. He had wide-ranging interests, and made discoveries in anatomy and in botany. Among his later writings are the play *Iphigenie* and the novel *Wilhelm Meister*, and he wrote many lyrics. His best-known work however is *Faust*, which was composed over many years; its theme is man's search for happiness. In later life he was a friend of Schiller.

Gogol, Nikolai Vasilievich (1809–52), Russian novelist and dramatist. His comedy, *The Government Inspector*, satirised provincial bureaucracy; and his novel, *Dead Souls*, deals with malpractice in the supposed purchase of dead serfs.

Goldsmith, Oliver (1728–74), Irish poet, dramatist and novelist. The son of a poor curate, he came to London in 1756, and eventually joined the circle of Dr. Johnson. He is best known for his novel *The Vicar of Wakefield* and his play *She Stoops to Conquer*.

Goncourt, Edmond Louis Antoine Huot de (1822–96) and **Jules Alfred Huot de** (1830–70), French brothers, remembered for their *Journal des Goncourts*, an intimate account of Parisian society spanning 40 years, and of documentary interest.

Góngora y Argote, Luis de (1561–1627), Spanish poet, b. Córdova. In *Polifemo* and *Soledades* he attempted to express the core of poetry in new experimental forms.

Goodyear, Charles (1800–60), American inventor who discovered the art of vulcanising rubber.

Goossens, Sir Eugene (1893–1962), English conductor and composer of Belgian descent. His compositions include the operas *Judith* and *Don Juan de Mañara*; brother of Léon, oboe virtuoso, and of Sidonie and Marie Goossens, harpists.

Gordon, Charles George (1833–85), Scottish soldier. After service in the Crimea and China, in 1873 he was made governor of the Equatorial provinces of Egypt; and he was a notable governor of the Sudan, 1877–80. When a rising was led by the Mahdi, he was sent out in 1884 to the garrisons in rebel territory and was killed at Khartoum.

Gordon, Lord George (1751–93), agitator, led No-Popery riots in London in 1780.

Gorky, Maxim (Alexey Maximovich Peshkov) (1868–1936), Russian writer. From the age of ten he worked at many trades from scullion on a Volga steamboat to railway guard, while learning to write: see *My Childhood*. His early work was romantic. He spent many years abroad, but returned in 1928, a supporter of the Soviet regime. His later work is marked by social realism.

Gosse, Sir Edmund (1849–1928), English poet and critic, known for his literary studies of the 17th and 18th centuries; and for his memoir *Father and Son.*

Gounod, Charles François (1818–93), French composer, known for his operas *Faust* and *Roméo et Juliette*, though his lyrical gifts are shown in earlier works, such as *Le Médicin malgré lui* and *Mireille.*

Gower, John (1325–1408), English poet of the time of Chaucer, author of *Confessio Amantis.*

Goya y Lucientes, Francisco José (1746–1828), Spanish painter and etcher, b. nr. Saragossa. He became court painter to Charles III in 1786. His portraits are painted with ruthless realism; his series of satirical etchings (*Los Caprichos* and the *Disasters of War*) expose man's inhumanity and express his hatred of the cruelty and reaction of his day. His work can best be seen in Madrid.

Grace, William Gilbert (1848–1915), English cricketer who scored 54,896 runs, including 126 centuries, and took 2,876 wickets. Scored 1,000 runs in May 1895; and three times made over 300 runs in an innings.

Grahame, Kenneth (1859–1932), Scottish writer of books for children, including *The Golden Age, Dream Days*, and *Wind in the Willows.*

Grahame-White, Claude (1879–1959), aviator and engineer, the first Englishman to gain an aviator's certificate, 1909.

Grant, Ulysses Simpson (1822–85), American general of the civil war, and president of the United States from 1869 to 1876.

Granville-Barker, Harley (1877–1946), English dramatist, actor, and producer, who promoted the plays of Ibsen, Shaw, and other serious writers. His own works include *The Voysey Inheritance.*

Grattan, Henry (1746–1820), Irish statesman, who struggled for Irish legislative independence and for Catholic emancipation (though himself a Protestant) and parliamentary reform; but unsuccessfully.

Graves, Robert Ranke (b. 1895), English writer, author of *Goodbye to All That*, written after the first world war; and of *I Claudius* and *Claudius the God*; besides poetry.

Gray, Thomas (1716–71), English poet, author of *Elegy written in a Country Churchyard* and *Ode on a Distant Prospect of Eton College.*

Greeley, Horace (1811–72), American newspaper editor, founder of the New York *Tribune* (1841).

Green, John Richard (1837–83), English historian, author of *Short History of the English People.*

Greenaway, Kate (1846–1901), English artist of children, especially for book illustrations.

Greene, Graham (b. 1904), English novelist and journalist, whose novels (*The Heart of the Matter, Brighton Rock, The Quiet American, Our Man in Havana, A Burnt-out Case*), like his plays (*The Complaisant Lover*) and films (*Fallen Idol, The Third Man*) deal with moral problems in a modern setting from a Catholic standpoint. *See also* **Section M, Part I.**

Gregory, St. (*c.* 240–332), converted King Tiridates of Armenia and was thus founder of the Armenian church.

Gregory I (the Great), St. (*c.* 540–604), Pope 590–604, was the last great Latin Father and the forerunner of scholasticism. The main founder of the temporal power and the political influence of the papacy, he also maintained the spiritual claims of Rome, enforcing discipline, encouraging monasticism, defining doctrine, and adding to the music, liturgy, and canons of the Church. It was he who sent Augustine on a mission to England.

Gregory VII (Hildebrand) (*c.* 1020–85), Pope 1073–85. He strove for papal omnipotence within the church and for a high standard in the priesthood (especially by stamping out simony and clerical marriage). He also upheld the papacy against the Holy Roman Empire, and the emperor Henry IV did penance for three days in the snow at Canossa; but he had not quite the vision of Gregory I of an ideal theocracy embracing all states.

Gregory XIII (1502–85), Pope 1572–85; introduced the Gregorian calendar.

Gregory, James (1638–75), Scottish mathematician. He invented a reflecting telescope and was the first to show how the distance of the sun could be deduced by observations of the passage of Venus across the disc of the sun. Successive generations of the family reached distinction.

Grenville, Sir Richard (1541–91), English sea captain, who with his one ship engaged a fleet of Spanish war vessels off Flores in 1591, an exploit celebrated in Tennyson's ballad *The Revenge.*

Gresham, Sir Thomas (1519–79), English financier and founder of the Royal Exchange. Son of a Lord Mayor of London, he was an astute moneyfinder for four successive sovereigns, including Queen Elizabeth I. "Gresham's Law" is the statement that bad money drives out good.

Greuze, Jean Baptiste (1725–1805), French artist, known especially for his studies of girls. His *Girl with Doves* is in the Wallace Collection.

Grey, 2nd Earl (Charles Grey) (1764–1845), British Whig statesman under whose premiership were passed the Reform Bill of 1832, a bill abolishing slavery throughout the British Empire (1833), and the Poor Law Amendment Act, 1834.

Grey, Lady Jane (1537–54), Queen of England for a few days. The daughter of the Duke of Suffolk, she was put forward as queen by Protestant leaders on the death of her cousin, Edward VI; but overcome by the legal claimant, Mary Tudor, and executed.

Grieg, Edvard Hagerup (1843–1907), Norwegian composer, b. Bergen. He presented the characteristics of his country's music with strong accentuation. He is best known for his incidental music to *Peer Gynt.*

Griffin, Bernard William (1899–1956), Roman catholic archbishop of Westminster from 1944 until his death.

Griffith, Arthur (1872–1922), the first president of the Irish Free State, 1921; founder of the *Sinn Fein* movement.

Griffith, David Wark (1880–1948), American film producer, who introduced the close-up, the flash-back, and developed leading actors. His films include *Birth of a Nation*, and *Broken Blossoms.*

Grimm, the brothers **Jakob Ludwig Karl** (1785–1863), and **Wilhelm Karl** (1786–1859), German philologists and folk-lorists, best known for their *Fairy Tales.* Jakob published a notable philological dictionary, *Deutsche Grammatik.* The brothers also projected the vast *Deutsches Wörterbuch* which was completed by German scholars in 1961.

Grimthorpe, 1st Baron (Edmund Beckett Denison) (1816–1905), horologist who invented the double three-legged escapement for Big Ben (1854). For long known as Sir Edmund Beckett.

Gromyko, Andrei Andreevich (b. 1908), Russian diplomat who has served as foreign minister since 1957. He was ambassador to Britain 1952–3.

Grossmith, George (1847–1912), English actor. With his brother, **Weedon Grossmith**, he wrote *Diary of a Nobody.* His son, George Grossmith (1874–1935) was a comedian and introduced revue and cabaret entertainment into England.

Grote, George (1794–1871), English historian, author of a *History of Greece.*

Grotius (Huig van Groot) (1583–1645), Dutch jurist, the founder of international law. He was condemned to life imprisonment for religious reasons, but escaped to Paris, where he wrote *De Jure Belli et Pacis.*

Grouchy, Emmanuel, Marquis de (1766–1847), French general, who served under Napoleon; and after Waterloo led the defeated army back to Paris.

Grove, Sir George (1820–1900), English musicologist, author of *Dictionary of Music and Musicians.* By profession he was a civil engineer.

Guedalla, Philip (1889–1944), English historian, author of *The Second Empire, Palmerston*, and *The Hundred Days.*

Guevara, Ernesto "Che" (1928–67), revolutionary hero, b. Argentina. He took part in the Cuban guerrilla war and became a minister in the Cuban government 1959–65. He was killed while leading a band of guerrillas against American-trained Bolivian troops. ("Che" is Argentine for "chum".)

Guido Reni (1575–1642), Italian painter of the Bolognese school whose works are characteristic of the Italian baroque of his period and include the *Aurora* fresco in the Rospigliosi palace at Rome, and *Crucifixion of St. Peter* (Vatican).

Gustavus Adolphus (1594–1632), King of Sweden, the " Lion of the North." After a campaign in Poland he entered the Thirty Years' war in support of Swedish interests and Protestant distress, won the battle of Breitenfeld in 1631 and was killed in action the next year.

Gutenberg, Johann (*c.* 1400–68), German printer, b. Mainz, the first European to print with movable types cast in moulds. The earliest book printed by him was the Mazarin Bible (*see* **L76**).

Guy, Thomas (1644–1724), English philanthropist. A printer, he made money by speculation; and in 1722 founded Guy's Hospital in Southwark.

Gwynne, Nell (*c.* 1650–87), mistress of Charles II of England. Of Hereford origin, she sold oranges in London and became a comedienne at Drury Lane.

H

Haakon VII (1872–1957), King of Norway, was a Danish prince and elected on the separation of Norway from Sweden in 1905. He resisted the Nazi occupation.

Hadley, George (1685–1768). He developed Halley's theory of the trade winds by taking into account the effect of the earth's rotation and the displacement of air by tropical heat (1735).

Hadrian (76–138), Roman emperor. An able general, he suppressed revolts, and he was also a lover of the arts. He visited Britain *c.* A.D. 121 and built a protective wall between Wallsend-on-Tyne and Bowness-on-Solway.

Hafiz, pseudonym of **Shams ad-Din Mohammed** (d. *c.* 1388), Persian lyrical poet. His principal work is the *Divan*, a collection of short sonnets called *ghazals*. The sobriquet *Hafiz*, meaning one who remembers, is applied to anyone who has learned the Koran by heart.

Hahn, Otto (1879–1968), German chemist and physicist, chief discoverer of uranium fission, the phenomenon on which nuclear power and the atom bomb are based.

Hahnemann, Samuel Christian Friedrich (1755–1843), German physician who founded homoeopathy (treatment of disease by small doses of drugs that in health produce similar symptoms).

Haig, Douglas, 1st Earl of Bermersyde (1861–1928), British field-marshal, b. Edinburgh. He replaced French as commander-in-chief in France, 1915–19, leading the offensive in August 1918; and after the war presided over the British Legion.

Haile Selassie I (1891–1975), Emperor of Ethiopia 1930–74. He spent the years of the Italian occupation 1936–41 in England. Deposed 1974.

Hakluyt, Richard (1553–1616), English writer on maritime discovery. B. in Herefordshire, he spent some time in Paris. From 1582 (when *Divers Voyages* appeared), he devoted his life to collection and publishing accounts of English navigators, thus giving further impetus to discovery.

Haldane, John Burdon Sanderson (1892–1964), biologist and geneticist, noted not only for his work in mathematical evolutionary theory but for explaining science to the layman. He emigrated to India in 1957. He was the son of **John Scott Haldane** (1860–1936), b. Edinburgh, who studied the effect of industrial occupations upon health.

Haldane, 1st Viscount (Richard Burdon Haldane) (1856–1928), British Liberal statesman. As war minister in 1905 he reorganised the army and founded the Territorials.

Halévy, Ludovic (1834–1903) French playwright, who collaborated with Henri Meilhac in writing libretti for Offenbach and Bizet.

Halifax, 1st Earl of (Edward Frederick Lindley Wood) (1881–1959), British Conservative politician; foreign secretary during the period of appeasement of Germany; as Lord Irwin, viceroy of India 1926–31.

Halifax, 1st Marquess of (George Savile) (1633–95), English politician of changeable views, who wrote *Character of a Trimmer*.

Hallam, Henry (1777–1859), English historian, best known for his *Constitutional History*. He was father of Arthur Hallam, friend of Tennyson.

Hallé, Sir Charles (1819–95), German-born pianist and conductor, who settled in Manchester and organised an orchestra of high-class talent. He married the violinist Wilhelmine Neruda.

Halley, Edmond (1656–1742), English astronomer royal 1720–42. He published observations on the planets and comets, being the first to predict the return of a comet (*see* **Section L**). He furthered Newton's work on gravitation, setting aside his own researches. He made the first magnetic survey of the oceans from the naval vessel *Paramour*, 1698–1700. His meteorological observations led to his publication of the first map of the winds of the globe (1686).

Hale, George Ellery (1868–1935), American astronomer, after whom is named the 200-inch reflecting telescope on Mount Palomar.

Hals, Frans (*c.* 1580–1666), Dutch portrait painter, b. at Mechlin. He is best known for his *Laughing Cavalier* in the Wallace Collection, and for other portraits in the Louvre and at Amsterdam.

Hamilton, Alexander (1755–1804), American statesman and economist. With Madison and Jay he wrote the *Federalist* (1787). As secretary of the Treasury (1789–95) he put Washington's government on a firm financial footing and planned a national bank. He was the leader of the Federalists, a party hostile to Jefferson. He was killed in a duel.

Hamilton, Emma, Lady (*née* **Lyon**) (*c.* 1765–1815), a beauty of humble birth who, after several liaisons, was married in 1791 to Sir William Hamilton, British ambassador at Naples. There she met Nelson, and later bore him a child, Horatia.

Hammarskjöld, Dag (1905–61), world statesman. After an academic and political career in Sweden, in 1953 he became secretary-general of the United Nations, and aimed at extending its influence for peace, especially by initiating a U.N. emergency force in the Middle East. He was killed in an air crash while attempting to mediate in a dispute between the Congo and the secessionist province of Katanga. Posthumous Nobel peace prize.

Hammond, John Lawrence (1872–1949), English historian of social and industrial history, whose works (with his wife Barbara) include *The Town Labourer* and *The Village Labourer*.

Hampden, John (1594–1643), English parliamentarian and civil war leader. He refused to pay Charles I's illegal ship money in 1636. When civil war broke out, he raised a regiment and was killed on Chalgrove Field.

Hamsun, Knut, pen-name of Knut Pedersen (1859–1952), Norwegian author who in his youth struggled for existence, visited America twice and earned his living by casual labour. *The Growth of the Soil* won him the Nobel prize in 1920. Other great novels are *Hunger* and *Mysteries*.

Handel, George Frederick (1685–1759), German composer, son of a barber-surgeon to the Duke of Saxony; b. Halle, the same year as Bach; spent much of his life in England composing operas and oratorios. His operas, of which there are over 40, include *Atalanta, Berenice* and *Serse*, and his oratorios, of which there are 32, include *Saul, Israel in Egypt, Samson, Messiah, Judas Maccabaeus*, and *Jephtha*. Eight years before he died he became blind and relied upon his old friend and copyist John Christopher Smith to commit his music to paper. *See* **Section E.**

Hannibal (247–182 B.C.), Carthaginian general. He fought two wars against Rome. In the first he conquered southern Spain. In the second he overran Gaul, crossed the Alps, and defeated the Romans in successive battles, especially at Cannae. Thereafter his forces were worn down by Roman delaying tactics; he was defeated by Scipio at Zama and later poisoned himself.

Harcourt, Sir William Vernon (1827–1904), Liberal politician who revised death duties.

Hardicanute (1019–42), son of Canute, and last Danish king of England.

Hardie, James Keir (1856–1915), Scottish Labour leader, one of the founders of the Labour party. He first worked in a coal-pit; in 1882 became a journalist; and in 1892 was the first socialist to be elected to the House of Commons (for

(West Ham – South). He edited the *Labour Leader* 1887–1904. He was the first chairman of the parliamentary Labour party, 1906. A pacifist, he opposed the Boer war.

Hardy, Thomas (1840–1928), English novelist and poet, was trained as an architect and practised for some time, but became known in 1871 with *Desperate Remedies*. In 1874 his *Far from the Madding Crowd* was published. Following that came a series of novels, including *The Trumpet-Major*, *The Mayor of Casterbridge*, *Tess of the D'Urbervilles*, and *Jude the Obscure*. In 1908 he completed a dramatic poem, *The Dynasts*, whose central figure is Napoleon. His underlying theme is man's struggle against neutral forces, and he depicts the Wessex countryside.

Hargreaves, James (1720–78), English inventor, b. Blackburn. His spinning-jenny was invented in 1764 and became widely used, though his own was broken by spinners in 1768 and his invention brought him no profit.

Harkness, Edward Stephen (1874–1940), American banker and philanthropist, who in 1930 founded the Pilgrim Trust in Gt. Britain.

Harley, Robert, 1st Earl of Oxford and Mortimer (1661–1724), English statesman and collector of MSS. He held office under Queen Anne, and brought a European war to an end with the treaty of Utrecht. After the Hanoverian succession he lived in retirement, and formed the MSS. collection, now in the British Museum, which bears his name.

Harold II (1022–66), last Saxon king of England, was son of Earl Godwin. He was chosen king in succession to Edward the Confessor. He had at once to meet a dual invasion. He defeated the Norwegian king at Stamford Bridge; but was himself defeated by William of Normandy at the battle of Hastings (fought at Battle 1066).

Harriman, William Averell (b. 1891), American public official. He was adviser to President Roosevelt and later presidents especially on Marshall Aid and in connection with foreign affairs generally.

Harris, Joel Chandler (1848–1908), American author, creator of Uncle Remus and Brer Rabbit in Negro folk-tales.

Harrison, Frederick (1831–1923), English philosopher and lawyer, author of *The Meaning of History* and *The Philosophy of Common Sense*. He was president of the Positivist committee. *See* **Positivism, Section J.**

Harrison, John (1692–1776)—"Longitude Harrison," English inventor of the chronometer.

Harty, Sir Hamilton (1880–1941), composer and for some years conductor of the Hallé orchestra; b. County Down.

Harun al-Rashid (Aaron the Upright) (763–809), 5th Abbasid caliph of Baghdad. His court was a centre for art and learning, but he governed mainly through his vizier until the latter lost favour and was executed in 803. The *Arabian Nights* associated with him are stories collected several centuries later.

Harvey, William (1578–1657), English physician and discoverer of the circulation of the blood. B. at Folkestone, he studied at Padua while Galileo was there, and was physician to James I and Charles I. His treatise on circulation was published in Latin in 1628.

Hastings, Warren (1732–1818), English administrator in India. As governor-general for the East India Company he revised the finances, improved administration and put down disorder. On his return to England he was impeached for alleged corruption, and, though acquitted, lost his fortune in his own defence. Later however he received a grant from the company. Though he suffered unduly, his trial was important for the future as setting a high standard for Indian administration.

Hauptmann, Gerhart (1862–1946), German dramatist and novelist. B. in Silesia, he lived at first in Berlin and later abroad. His play *The Weavers* deals with a revolt of 1844 and has a collective hero. Other works include *Die versunkene Glocke*, *Der arme Heinrich*, and *Rose Bernd*. Nobel prizewinner 1912.

Havelock, Sir Henry (1795–1857), British general who helped to put down the Indian mutiny.

Hawke, 1st Baron (Edward Hawke) (1705–81), English admiral, who in 1759 defeated the French at Quiberon in a tremendous storm.

Hawkins, Sir John (1532–95), English sailor and slave-trader. In 1562 he was the first Englishman to traffic in slaves. He helped to defeat the Spanish Armada in 1588.

Hawthorne, Nathaniel (1804–64), American author. His works include *The Marble Faun*, *The Scarlet Letter*, *The House of the Seven Gables*.

Haydn, Franz Joseph (1732–1809), Austrian composer, belongs to the classical period of Bach, Handel, and Mozart. He has been given the title "father of the symphony." Much of his life was spent as musical director to the princely Hungarian house of Esterhazy. In 1791 and again in 1794 he visited London, where he conducted his Salomon symphonies. His two great oratorios, *The Creation* and *The Seasons*, were written in his old age. *See* **Section E.**

Hazlitt, William (1778–1830), English essayist and critic. His writings include *The Characters of Shakespeare's Plays*, *Table Talk*, and *The Spirit of the Age*. His grandson William Carew Hazlitt (1834–1913) was a bibliographer and writer.

Hearst, William Randolph (1863–1951), American newspaper proprietor who built up a large newspaper empire.

Heath, Edward (b. 1916), British statesman, leader of the Conservative Party 1965–75; prime minister 1970–4; leader of the opposition 1974–5.His unwavering faith in European unity was rewarded in 1972 by Britain's successful application for entry into the European Economic Community. In the contest for the leadership held in February 1975 he was defeated in the first ballot by Mrs. Thatcher and did not contest the second.

Hedin, Sven Anders (1865–1952), Swedish explorer of Central Asia; wrote *My Life as Explorer*.

Heenan, John Carmel (1905–76). English Roman Catholic prelate, archbishop of Westminster 1963–76; member of Sacred College (1965).

Hegel, Georg Wilhelm Friedrich (1770–1831), German idealist philosopher, b. Stuttgart, whose name is associated with the dialectic method of reasoning with its sequence of thesis –antitheses—synthesis. He studied theology at Tübingen with his friend Schelling. He taught philosophy at Jena, Nuremberg, Heidelberg, and Berlin. He produced an abstract philosophical system which was influenced by his early interest in mysticism and his Prussian patriotism. His doctrines were very influential in the 19th cent. and led to modern totalitarianism. He died of cholera. *See* **Dialectical Materialism, Section J.**

Heidenstam, Verner von (1859–1940), Swedish author and poet, leader of a new romantic movement. Nobel prizewinner 1916.

Heifetz, Jascha (b. 1901), Russian-born violinist, a U.S. citizen. He was the first musician to win a reputation in England by gramophone records before a personal appearance.

Heine, Heinrich (1797–1856), German lyric poet, b. Düsseldorf of Jewish parents. He lived mostly in Paris. His poems show profound beauty and subtlety of thought, but the satire and sometimes bitterness of his writings excited antagonism.

Heisenberg, Werner (1901–76), German physicist, noted for his theory of quantum mechanics and the Uncertainty Principle (*see* **F15(1)**. Nobel Prizewinner 1932.

Helmholtz, Hermann von (1821–94), German physicist and physiologist. He published his *Erhaltung der Kraft* (Conservation of Energy) in 1847, the same year that Joule gave the first clear exposition of the principle of energy. His pupil Heinrich Hertz discovered electromagnetic radiation in accordance with Maxwell's theory.

Héloïse (*c.* 1101–64), beloved of Abelard (*q.v.*). Her letters to him are extant.

Hemingway, Ernest (1898–1961), American novelist of new technique and wide influence. His works include *A Farewell to Arms*, *Death in the Afternoon*, *For Whom the Bell Tolls*, *The Old Man and the Sea*. He committed suicide. Nobel prizewinner 1954. *See* **Section M, Part I.**

Henderson, Arthur (1863–1935), British Labour politician, b. Glasgow. He worked mainly for disarmament, and was president of the World Disarmament Conference, 1932–5. Nobel peace prize 1934.

Henrietta Maria (1609–69), the daughter of Henry IV of France and wife of Charles I.

Henry, Joseph (1797–1878), American physicist and schoolteacher who independently of Faraday discovered the principle of the induced current. The weather-reporting system he set up at the Smithsonian Institution led to the creation of the U.S. Weather Bureau.

Henry I (1068–1135), King of England. The youngest son of William the Conqueror, he ascended the throne during the absence on crusade of his elder brother Robert of Normandy. His long reign brought order and progress, not entirely destroyed by the anarchy under his successor Stephen.

Henry II (1133–89), King of England. He was son of Matilda, daughter of Henry I, and Geoffrey Plantagenet, count of Anjou; and his lands stretched to the Pyrenees. He was a strong ruler to whom we largely owe the establishment of the common law system and permanent administrative reforms. His conflict with the Church brought about the murder of his archbishop Becket, a man of resolute character; and his later life was troubled by his unruly sons.

Henry III (1207–72), King of England, succeeded his father John in 1216. Himself devout and simple, his long reign was troubled by a partly factious baronial opposition.

Henry IV (1367–1413), grandson of Edward III and heir to the Duchy of Lancaster, became king of England in 1399. More solid and practical than his cousin Richard II, whom he had supplanted, he consolidated the government.

Henry V (1387–1422), son of Henry IV, succeeded his father as king of England in 1413. A successful commander, he renewed the French war and won the battle of Agincourt, but died young.

Henry VI (1421–71), son of Henry V, succeeded his father as king of England in 1422 as a baby. Gentle and retiring, he inherited a losing war with France. He founded Eton, and King's College, Cambridge. The Yorkist line claimed the crown from his (the Lancastrian) line, and the Wars of the Roses led to his deposition and death.

Henry VII (1457–1509) succeeded Richard III as king of England after defeating him in 1485. The first Tudor king, he was firm and shrewd, even avaricious; he built Henry VII's Chapel in Westminster Abbey, and encouraged John Cabot to sail to North America.

Henry VIII (1491–1547), King of England, succeeded his father Henry VII in 1509. A prince of the Renaissance, skilled in music and sports, he loved the sea and built up the navy. His minister Cardinal Wolsey fell when Henry, seeking divorce to obtain a legal heir, rejected papal supremacy and dissolved the monasteries. Ruthless and ostentatious, he executed Sir Thomas More, spent his father's accumulation, and in spite of six marriages left a delicate son to succeed.

Henry IV of France (Henry of Navarre) (1553–1610). Prior to becoming king, he was the leader of the Huguenots; and although on being crowned he became a Catholic, he protected the Protestants by the Edict of Nantes. He then became a national king, but was later assassinated by Ravaillac, a religious fanatic.

Henry the Navigator (1394–1460), Portuguese promoter of discovery, son of John I. His sailors discovered Madeira and the Azores.

Henschel, Sir George (1850–1934), singer, composer, and conductor. B. in Breslau, he became a naturalised Englishman in 1890. Founder and conductor of the London Symphony Concerts (1886).

Hepplewhite, George (d. 1786), English cabinet-maker whose name is identified with the style which followed the Chippendale period. **D13.**

Heraclitus of Ephesus (*c.* 540–475 B.C.), Greek philosopher. His discovery of a changing world (he lived in an age of social revolution when the ancient tribal aristocracy was beginning to give way to democracy) influenced the philosophies of Parmenides, Democritus, Plato, and Aristotle, and later, of Hegel.

Herbert, George (1593–1633), the most purely devotional of English poets.

Hereward the Wake, the last Saxon leader to hold out against the Normans. His base in the fens was captured in 1071 but he escaped. His exploits were written up by Kingsley.

Herod the Great (*c.* 73–4 B.C.). At first governor of Galilee under the Romans, he obtained the title of king of Judaea in 31 B.C. The massacre of the Innocents reported in the New Testament is in keeping with his historical character.

Herodotus (*c.* 485–425 B.C.), Greek historian, called by Cicero the father of history. He travelled widely collecting historical evidence.

Herrick, Robert (1591–1674), English lyric poet. His poems include *Gather ye Rose Buds*, *Cherry Ripe*, and *Oberon's Feast*.

Herriot, Edouard (1872–1957), French Radical-Socialist statesman. A scholar, mayor of Lyons for more than a generation, three times prime minister, he resisted the German occupation, and was president of the National Assembly 1947–54.

Herschel, Sir John (1792–1871), British astronomer who continued his father's researches and also pioneered photography, a term introduced by him. One of his twelve children introduced fingerprints into criminology.

Herschel, Sir William (1738–1822), German-born astronomer who came to England from Hanover as a musician; father of the above. Unrivalled as an observer, and with telescopes of his own making he investigated the distribution of stars in the Milky Way and concluded that some of the nebulae he could see were separate star systems outside our own. He discovered the planet Uranus in 1781. His sister, Caroline Lucretia (1750–1848), compiled a catalogue of the clusters and nebulae discovered by him.

Hertz, Heinrich Rudolf (1857–95), German physicist, whose laboratory experiments confirmed Maxwell's electromagnetic theory of waves and yielded information about their behaviour.

Herzl, Theodor (1860–1904), founder of modern political Zionism, was b. Budapest. He convened a congress at Basle in 1897.

Hesiod (fl. *c.* 735 B.C.) Greek poet, author of *Work and Days*, which tells of life in the country.

Hill, Octavia (1838–1912), English social reformer concerned with the housing conditions of the poor, a pioneer in slum clearance in London; founder (with Sir Robert Hunter and Canon Rawnsley) of the National Trust.

Hill, Sir Rowland (1795–1879), originator of the penny postal system. He was secretary to the Postmaster-General 1846–54, then chief secretary to the Post Office until 1864.

Hindemith, Paul (1895–1963), German composer and viola player. He is associated with the movement for *Gebrauchsmusik*, which regarded music as a social expression. He incurred Nazi hostility and his later life was spent abroad. His numerous works include chamber works, songs, operas, ballet music, symphonies, and the oratorio *Das Unaufhörliche*. *See* **Section E.**

Hindenburg, Paul von (1847–1934), German field-marshal. In 1914 he defeated the Russians at Tannenberg. In his old age a national hero, he was president of the German Reich, 1925–34.

Hinshelwood, Sir Cyril Norman (1897–1967), English chemist. He shared with Prof. Semenov of Russia the 1956 Nobel prize for chemistry for researches into the mechanism of chemical reactions. Pres. Royal Society, 1955–60.

Hinton of Bankside, Baron (Christopher Hinton) (b. 1901), as managing director of the industrial group of the U.K. Atomic Energy Authority he played an important part in the building of Calder Hall. Chancellor University of Bath. O.M. 1976.

Hippocrates of Chios (fl. *c.* 430 B.C.), Greek mathematician, the first to compile a work on the elements of geometry.

Hippocrates of Cos (fl. *c.* 430 B.C.), Greek physician, whose writings are lost, but who is believed to have established medical schools in Athens and elsewhere, and to have contributed towards a scientific separation of medicine from superstition. Traditionally he is the embodiment of the ideal physician.

Hirohito, Emperor of Japan (b. 1901), acceded to the throne in 1926. In 1946 he renounced his legendary divinity. In 1971 he visited Europe.

Hitler, Adolf (1889–1945), German dictator, founder of National Socialism, b. in Austria, son of a customs official. He was in Vienna for 5 years with no regular work before going to Münich in

1913; enlisted in Bavarian infantry at outbreak of the Kaiser's war. At the end of the war conditions in Germany favoured the growth of a fascist movement and under his leadership the National Socialist (Nazi) party climbed to power. He became Reich chancellor in 1933 and on the death of Hindenburg in 1934 Führer; and commander-in-chief Wehrmacht 1935. Under his regime working class movements were ruthlessly destroyed; all opponents—communists, socialists, Jews—were persecuted and murdered. By terrorism and propaganda the German state was welded into a powerful machine for aggression. There followed the occupation of the Rhineland (1936), the annexation of Austria and Czechoslovakia (1938–9), the invasion of Poland and declaration of war by Great Britain and France (1939), the invasion of Russia (1941). Final defeat came in 1945; on 30 April he committed suicide as the Russian troops closed in on Berlin.

Hobbes, Thomas (1588–1679), English philosopher who published *Leviathan* in 1651. He favoured strong government and supported the supremacy of the state, but his arguments aroused antagonism even among royalists. He was a child of his age in his enthusiasm for scientific enquiry.

Hobhouse, Leonard Trelawney (1864–1929), English sociologist. His books include *The Theory of Knowledge, Morals in Evolution*, and *Development and Purpose*.

Ho Chi-minh (1892–1969), leader of the Vietnam revolutionary nationalist party of Indo-China, which struggled for independence from France during and after the second world war. His main purpose was to weld together the nationalistic and communistic elements in Vietnam. As president of North Vietnam he fought to extend his control over South Vietnam, defying the United States.

Hodgkin, Alan Lloyd (b. 1914), British biophysicist working in the field of nerve impulse conduction. During the second world war he worked on the development of radar. Pres. Royal Society, 1970–75. Nobel prizewinner, 1970; O.M., 1973.

Hodgkin, Dorothy Crowfoot (b. 1910), the third woman to win the Nobel prize in chemistry, awarded in 1964 for her X-ray analysis to elucidate the structure of complex molecules, notably penicillin and vitamin B-12. She and her team at the Dept. of Molecular Biophysics at Oxford succeeded in 1969 in determining the crystalline structure of insulin. Chancellor Bristol Univ.; Order of Merit (1965).

Hogarth, William (1697–1764), English engraver and painter, who satirised his time with character, humour, and power, especially in his *Harlot's Progress, Rake's Progress, Marriage à la Mode, Industry and Idleness*, and *The March to Finchley*.

Hogg, Quintin (1845–1903), educationist and philanthropist who purchased the old Polytechnic Institution in 1882 and turned it into a popular college providing education at moderate rates. His grandson, Lord Hailsham, was lord chancellor in the 1970–4 Conservative administration.

Hokusai, Katsushika (1760–1849), Japanese artist of the Ukiyo-e (popular school). He excelled in landscapes.

Holbein, Hans, the elder (*c.* 1465–1524), German painter, b. Augsburg, father of:

Holbein, Hans, the younger (1497–1543), German painter, b. Augsburg; settled in London 1532. He won the favour of Henry VIII, for whom he painted many portraits. He is also known for his series *The Dance of Death*.

Holden, Charles (1875–1960), British architect, designer of public buildings, including British Medical Asscn. Building, London; Underground Head Offices; Univ. of London Senate House.

Holden, Sir Isaac (1807–97), British inventor of woolcombing machinery.

Hölderlin, Johann Christian Friedrich (1770–1843), German poet, friend of Hegel. His works include the novel *Hyperion* and the elegy *Menon's Laments for Diotima*. In his middle years his mind became unhinged.

Holford, Baron (William Graham Holford) (1907–75). British architect and town-planner; planned post-war redevelopment of City of London, including precincts of St. Pauls.

Holmes, Oliver Wendell (1809–94), American author. His writings include *Autocrat of the Breakfast Table, The Professor at the Breakfast Table*, and *The Poet at the Breakfast Table*.

Holst, Gustav Theodore (1874–1934), British composer of Swedish descent whose compositions include *The Planets* suite, *The Hymn of Jesus*, an opera *The Perfect Fool*, and a choral symphony. He was outstanding as a teacher. *See* Section E.

Holyoake, George Jacob (1817–1906), English social reformer and secularist. He wrote a history of the co-operative movement.

Holyoake, Keith Jacka (b. 1904), New Zealand politician and farmer; prime minister 1960–72.

Homer, (*c.* 700 B.C.), epic poet. He is supposed to have been a Greek who lived at Chios or Smyrna, and has been regarded as the author of the *Iliad* and the *Odyssey*, though this is tradition rather than ascertained fact.

Hood, 1st Viscount (Samuel Hood) (1724–1816), British admiral who in 1793 was in command of the Mediterranean fleet and occupied Toulon.

Hood, Thomas (1799–1845), English poet. His poems include *The Song of the Shirt, The Dream of Eugene Aram* and *The Bridge of Sighs*. He was also a humorist and punster.

Hooke, Robert (1635–1703), English physicist. His inventions include the balance spring of watches. He was also an architect and drew up a plan for rebuilding London after the Great Fire. His *Diary* is published.

Hooker, Richard (1554–1600), English theologian, author of *Ecclesiastical Polity*. He was Master of the Temple, 1585–91. For his choice of words he was known as "Judicious Hooker ".

Hopkins, Sir Frederick Gowland (1861–1947), English biochemist, pioneer in biochemical and nutritional research. He first drew attention to the substances later known as vitamins. Pres. Royal Society 1930–5. Nobel prize 1929.

Hopkins, Gerard Manley (1844–89), English poet of religious experience and of a style new in his day.

Hopkins, Harry (1890–1946), Franklin Roosevelt's personal assistant at foreign conferences, and in the New Deal and Lend-Lease.

Hopkinson, John (1849–98), English engineer. By developing the theory of alternating current and of the magnetic current in dynamos he paved the way to the common use of electricity.

Hoppner, John (1758–1810), English portrait painter, b. Whitechapel, of German parents.

Horace (Quintus Horatius Flaccus) (65–8 B.C.), Roman satirist and poet, son of a Greek freedman. He wrote *Satires, Epodes, Odes*, and *Epistles*. He fought on the republican side at Philippi, but lived to become poet laureate to Augustus.

Horniman, Annie Elizabeth Fredericka (1830–1937), founder of the modern repertory system in England. Her father F. J. Horniman founded the Horniman Museum.

Houdini, Harry (Erich Weiss) (1874–1926), American illusionist, son of a Hungarian rabbi. Famed for his escapes from handcuffs.

Housman, Alfred Edward (1859–1936), English poet, author of *A Shropshire Lad*; he was also a classical scholar. His brother Laurence (1865–1959) was a playwright and wrote *Little Plays of St. Francis* and *Victoria Regina*.

Howard, John (1726–90), English prison reformer. Imprisoned in France in wartime, he subsequently investigated English prisons, securing reforms; and later also continental prisons, dying in Russia of gaol fever.

Howard of Effingham, 2nd Baron (Charles Howard) (1536–1624), afterwards Earl of Nottingham; commanded the fleet which defeated the Spanish Armada (1588), and took part in the capture of Cadiz (1596).

Howe, Elias (1819–67), American inventor of the sewing machine.

Howe, Julia Ward (1819–1910), American suffragette, author of *Mine eyes have seen the glory*.

Howe, 1st Earl (Richard Howe) (1726–99), British admiral whose victories over the French in two wars included that off Ushant on 1 June 1794 (" the glorious first of June ").

Hua Kuo-feng (b. 1922), b. Hunan, succeeded Mao tse-Tung as Chairman of the Chinese Communist Party and leader of China, 1976. *See* **Section C, Part II.**

Hubble, Edwin Powell (1889–1953), American astronomer, noted for his work on extragalactic nebulae. With the 100-inch telescope on Mount Wilson he detected the Cepheid variables in Andromeda. *See also* **F5(1).**

Hudson, Henry (d. 1611), English navigator credited with the discovery of the Hudson river and Hudson Bay, where mutineers turned him adrift to die. He was on a voyage to find a passage by the north pole to Japan and China. Nothing is known of his life before 1607.

Hudson, William Henry (1841–1922), naturalist, b. Buenos Aires of American parents, naturalised in England (1900). His books include *The Purple Land, Green Mansions*, and *Far Away and Long Ago*. Hyde Park bird sanctuary, containing *Rima* by Epstein, was established in his memory.

Huggins, Sir William (1824–1910), British astronomer who pioneered in spectroscopic photography, and was helped by his wife, Margaret Lindsay Murray (1848–1915).

Hughes, Thomas (1822–96), English novelist, author of *Tom Brown's Schooldays*, which is based on Rugby school.

Hugo, Victor Marie (1802–85), French poet, dramatist, and novelist, who headed the Romantic movement in France in the early 19th cent. His dramas include *Hernani, Lucrèce Borgia, Ruy Blas*, and *Le Roi s'amuse*. Of his novels *Notre Dame* belongs to his early period, *Les Misérables, Les Travailleurs de la mer*, and *L'Homme qui rit* were written while he was living in exile in Guernsey. Less well known is his skill as a graphic artist.

Humboldt, Friedrich Heinrich Alexander, Baron von (1769–1859), German naturalist and explorer whose researches are recorded in *Voyage de Humboldt et Bonpland* (23 vols., 1805–34), and *Kosmos* (5 vols., 1845–62).

Hume, David (1711–76), Scottish philosopher who developed the empiricism of Locke into the scepticism inherent in it. His main works are *Treatise of Human Nature* and *Dialogues Concerning Natural Religion*. He also wrote a *History of England*.

Hunt, Holman (1827–1910), English artist, one of the founders of the Pre-Raphaelite movement. His best-known picture is *The Light of the World*.

Hunt, Baron (John Hunt) (b. 1910), leader of the 1953 British Everest Expedition when Tenzing and Hillary reached the summit.

Hunt, Leigh (1784–1859), English poet and essayist. In 1813 he was fined and imprisoned for libelling the Prince Regent in *The Examiner*. He was a friend of Keats and Shelley.

Hutton, James (1726–97), an Edinburgh doctor who founded modern geological theory. *See* **The Evolution of Organisms, Section F, Part IV.**

Huxley, Aldous (1894–1963) English author. *See* **Section M, Part I.**

Huxley, Sir Julian (1887–1975), biologist and writer, grandson of T. H. Huxley and brother of Aldous; director of the London Zoo 1935–42; first director general of Unesco 1946–8; one of the founders of the International Union for the Conservation of Nature and of the World Wild Life Fund.

Huxley, Thomas Henry (1825–95), English biologist, b. Ealing. He started life as assistant-surgeon on H.M.S. *Rattlesnake* and during the voyage (1846–50) studied marine organisms. After the publication of Darwin's *Origin of Species* he became an ardent evolutionist and gave the first recognisably modern lecture on the origin of life to the British Association in 1870. He coined the term " agnostic " to distinguish a person who does not know whether God exists or not from the atheist who asserts there is no God. By his popular lectures and vigorous writings, *e.g., Man's Place in Nature*, he made a real attempt to interest the public in the importance of science.

Huygens, Christian (1629–95), Dutch mathematician, physicist, and astronomer, son of the poet **Constantijn Huygens** (1596–1687); discovered the rings of Saturn, invented the pendulum clock, and developed the wave theory of light in opposition to the corpuscular theory of Newton.

Hyde, Douglas (1860–1949), Irish scholar, historian, poet, and folk-lorist; first president of Eire in the 1937 constitution, 1938–45.

Hypatia of Alexandria, the only woman mathematician of antiquity. She excited the enmity of Christian fanatics, who raised an agitation against her, and she was murdered in A.D. 415.

I

Ibsen, Henrik Johan (1828–1906), Norwegian playwright and poet, who dealt with social and psychological problems and revolutionised the European theatre. His chief works are *Ghosts, The Wild Duck, The Master Builder, A Doll's House, Hedda Gabler* and the poetic drama, *Peer Gynt*.

Ingres, Jean Auguste Dominique (1780–1867), French historical and classical painter. His paintings include *La grande odalisque* in the Louvre.

Innocent III (*c.* 1160–1216), Pope 1198–1216. He asserted the power and moral force of the papacy over the Emperor Otto IV, Philip II of France, and John of England. He launched the fourth crusade, encouraged the crusade against the Albigensian heretics, and held the 4th Lateran council. His pontificate marks the zenith of the mediaeval papacy.

Inönü, Ismet (1884–1973), Turkish soldier and statesman; leader of the Republican People's Party founded by Kemal Atatürk; premier, 1923–38; president 1938–50 and 1961–5.

Ionesco, Eugene (b. 1912), French playwright of the Absurd, b. Romania, whose influential plays include *The Bald Prima Donna, The Chairs*, and *Rhinoceros*. *See* **Section I.**

Iqbal, Sir Muhammad (1875–1938), poet-philosopher, b. Sialkot (Pakistan). He wrote both poetry and prose in Urdu, Persian, and English, and his work is marked by mystic nationalism.

Ireland, John (1879–1962), English composer, popularly known for his setting of Masefield's *Sea Fever*, but also a composer of chamber music and sonatas for pianoforte and violin.

Irving, Sir Henry (1838–1905), English actor. At the Lyceum theatre from 1871, later with Ellen Terry, he gave notable Shakespearean performances, especially as Shylock and Malvolio.

Irving, Washington (1783–1859), American essayist, whose works include *Tales of a Traveller* and *The Sketch Book*, also biographies.

Isabella of Castile (1451–1504), reigned jointly with her husband, Ferdinand V of Aragon, over a united Spain, from which the Moors and the Jews were expelled. During their reign the New World was discovered.

Ismail Pasha (1830–95), grandson of Mehemet Ali, was Khedive of Egypt, and became virtually independent of the Sultan. Under him the Suez canal was made, but his financial recklessness led to Anglo-French control and to his own abdication.

Ismay, 1st Baron (Hastings Lionel Ismay) (1887–1965), British general who was chief of staff to Sir Winston Churchill in the second world war, and later the first secretary-general of NATO.

Ito, Hirobumi, Prince (1841–1909), Japanese statesman, four times premier, who helped to modernise his country. He was assassinated by a Korean.

Ivan the Great (1440–1505) brought the scattered provinces of Muscovy under one control and put an end to Tartar rule.

Ivan the Terrible (1530–84), crowned as first Tsar of Russia in 1547, was an autocratic ruler who consolidated and expanded Russia and entered into trading relations with Queen Elizabeth. He killed his own son.

J

Jackson, Andrew (1767–1845), American general who was twice president of the United States.

Jackson, Thomas Jonathan (1824–63), " Stonewall Jackson," was general on the Southern side in the American Civil War; killed at Chancellorsville.

Jacobs, William Wymark (1863–1943), English novelist, b. London, author of humorous sea and other stories.

Jacquard, Joseph Marie (1752–1834), French inventor whose loom provided an effective method of weaving designs.

Jagellons, Lithuanian–Polish dynasty, which ruled Poland 1386–1572.

Jahangir (1569–1627), 3rd Mogul emperor and patron of art.

James I (1566–1625), King of England (1603–25) and, as James VI, King of Scotland (1567–1625). He was the son of Mary Stuart and succeeded to the English throne on the death of Elizabeth I. His reign saw the Gunpowder Plot of 1605 and the publication of the Authorised Version of the Bible, but it also marked an increasingly critical attitude of the Puritans towards the established church. Personally more of a scholar than a man of action, he was described as " the wisest fool in Christendom."

James II (1633–1701), King of England and, as James VII, King of Scotland (1685–88), was the younger son of Charles I. Personally honest, and an able admiral, he lacked political understanding; and when, having put down Monmouth's rebellion, he tried and failed to obtain better conditions for his fellow Roman Catholics, he was obliged in 1688 to flee the country.

James, Henry (1843–1916), American novelist, brother of William. He lived mainly in England. His work is noted for intellectual subtlety and characterisation, and includes *The American, Daisy Miller, The Portrait of a Lady, What Maisie Knew*, and *The Spoils of Poynton*. *See also* **Section M, Part I.**

James, William (1842–1910), American psychologist and philosopher, brother of Henry. He was a protagonist of the theory of pragmatism developed by his friend C. S. Peirce, and invented the doctrine which he called "radical empiricism." His major works are *The Principles of Psychology, The Will to Believe*, and *The Meaning of Truth*.

Janácek, Leos (1854–1928), Czech composer and conductor, and student of folk music, b. in Moravia, son of a village schoolmaster, creator of a national style. His best-known opera is *Jenufa*. *See* **Section E.**

Jefferies, Richard (1848–87), English naturalist of poetic perception, b. in Wiltshire, author of *Gamekeeper at Home* and *The Life of the Fields*.

Jefferson, Thomas (1743–1826), American president, 1801–9. He created the Republican Party, by which the federalists, led by Hamilton, were overthrown, and helped to draft the Declaration of Independence. He tried unsuccessfully to bring an end to slavery.

Jeffreys, 1st Baron (George Jeffreys) (1648–89), English judge who held the " bloody assize " after Monmouth's unsuccessful rebellion. In 1688 he was sent to the Tower and there died.

Jellicoe, 1st Earl (John Rushworth Jellicoe) (1859–1935), British admiral. He fought the uncertain battle of Jutland in 1916, after which the German fleet remained in harbour. He was later governor-general of New Zealand.

Jenkins, Roy (b. 1920), British policitian, b. Wales; Pres. EEC Commission 1977; served as Labour's Home Sec. 1965–7; Chanc. of Exchequer 1967–70.

Jenner, Edward (1749–1823), English physician, b. in Gloucs., pupil of John Hunter. His discovery of vaccination against smallpox (1798) helped to lay the foundations of modern immunology.

Jerome, Jerome Klapka (1859–1927), English humorous writer, author of *Three Men in a Boat*.

Jerome, St. (*c.* 331–420), scholar, whose translation of the Bible into Latin (the Vulgate) became for centuries the standard use.

Jesus Christ (*c.* 4 B.C.–A.D. 30), founder of Christianity, was born at Bethlehem in Judaea in a critical period of Jewish history. The firstborn of his mother Mary, he was said to be miraculously conceived, Joseph being his fosterfather. His home was at Nazareth in Galilee, but when he was about 30 he began a 3-year mission. His teaching is summarised in the Sermon on the Mount, and its main theme is love, especially for the poor and downtrodden. He was later crucified. The main source of his life is the New Testament. The title " Christ " comes from the Greek word *christos* = anointed, which is the Greek translation of the Hebrew title *Messiah*. Modern dating has amended the probable year of his birth.

Jiménez, Juan Ramón (1881–1958), Spanish lyric poet, author of *Platero y Yo*. Nobel prizewinner 1956.

Jinnah, Mohammed Ali (1876–1948), Pakistani statesman. B. at Karachi, he became president of the Muslim League, and succeeded in 1947 in establishing the Dominion of Pakistan, becoming its first governor-general.

Joachim, Joseph (1831–1907), Hungarian violinist and composer.

Joan of Arc, St. (Jeanne d'Arc) (1412–31), French patriot, called the Maid of Orlèans; of peasant parentage (she was b. at Domrémy), she believed herself called to save France from English domination; and by her efforts Charles VII was crowned at Rheims in 1429. Captured by the English, she was burned as a heretic; but canonised in 1920.

Joffre, Joseph Jacques Césaire (1852–1931), French general. He was commander-in-chief of the French army in the 1914–18 war.

John, St., the Baptist (executed A.D. 28), the forerunner of Jesus Christ.

John, St., the Evangelist, one of the twelve apostles of Jesus Christ, a Galilean fisherman, son of Zebedee and brother of James; traditionally author of the fourth Gospel.

John (1167–1216), youngest son of Henry II, was King of England from 1199. Able but erratic and arbitrary, he lost Normandy. Baronial opposition to him, under the influence of Archbishop Stephen Langton, acquired a national character, and in 1215 he was obliged to seal Magna Carta (*see* **Section L**).

John of Gaunt (1340–99), Duke of Lancaster, son of Edward III and father of Henry IV.

John XXIII (1881–1963), elected Pope in 1958, succeeding Pius XII, was formerly Cardinal Angelo Giuseppe Roncalli, patriarch of Venice. He sought to bring the Church closer to modern needs and to promote Christian unity. His teaching is given in his encyclicals, *Mater et Magistra* and *Pacem in Terris*. He held an Ecumenical Council in 1962.

John, Augustus (1878–1961), British painter and etcher, b. in Wales; noted for his portraits, *e.g.*, Lloyd George, Bernard Shaw, T. E. Lawrence.

Johnson, Amy (1904–41), was the first woman aviator to fly solo from England to Australia. She lost her life serving in the Air Transport Auxiliary in the second world war.

Johnson, Lyndon Baines (1908–73), President of the United States, 1963–9. He became president on Kennedy's assassination and followed a progressive policy at home, but his achievements were clouded by the war in Vietnam.

Johnson, Samuel (1709–84), English lexicographer and man of letters, b. at Lichfield. His *Dictionary* was published in 1755, and was followed by *Rasselas, The Idler* (a periodical), and *Lives of the Poets*. He was a focus of London literary life of his day, and his biographer, James Boswell, has vividly portrayed his circle.

Johnston, Sir Harry (1858–1927), British explorer who led an expedition to Kilimanjaro.

Jókai, Mór (1825–1904), Hungarian novelist, author of *Black Diamonds*.

Joliot-Curie, Jean Frédéric (1900–58), and his wife **Irène** (1896–1956), French scientists who discovered artificial radioactivity. Nobel prizewinners 1935. Joliot-Curie was one of the discoverers of nuclear fission. Irène was the daughter of Pierre and Marie Curie. Both were communists, and both died from cancer caused by their work.

Jones, Ernest Charles (1819–69), English Chartist leader and poet.

Jones, Sir Harold Spencer (1890–1960), British astronomer royal, 1933–55. His major research was to determine the mean distance of the earth from the sun, 93,004,000 miles.

Jones, Inigo (1573–1652), architect of the English renaissance who studied in Italy and inspired the use of Palladian forms in England. His buildings include the banqueting hall in Whitehall and the queen's house at Greenwich. He also designed furniture and introduced the proscenium arch and movable scenery on the English stage.

Jonson, Ben (1573–1637), English poet and dramatist. His plays include *Every Man in his Humour*, *Volpone*, and *The Alchemist*; and his poems *Drink to me only with thine Eyes*. He also produced court masques.

Josephine, Empress (1763–1814), wife of Napoleon I, *née* de la Pagerie, she was previously married to the Vicomte de Beauharnais. She was divorced from Napoleon in 1809.

Josephus, Flavius (38–*c*.100), Jewish historian, author of *History of the Jewish War*.

Joule, James Prescott (1818–89), English physicist, pupil of Dalton, who researched on electromagnetism and determined the mechanical equivalent of heat. *See* **Section L.**

Jowett, Benjamin (1817–93), English scholar. He translated Plato's *Dialogues*, and he was an influential Master of Balliol College, Oxford.

Jowitt, Earl (William Allen Jowitt) (1885–1957), British Labour politician and lord chancellor. He wrote *The Strange Case of Alger Hiss*.

Joyce, James (1882–1941), Irish author, b. Dublin. His *Ulysses* gives a microscopic picture of a day in the life of two Irishmen, and flouted the conventions of his day. Other works include *Portrait of the Artist* and *Finnegans Wake*. *See* **Section M, Part I.**

Juin, Alphonse (1888–1967), French general who took part in the Allied invasion of Tunisia and the Italian campaign in the second world war.

Julian the Apostate (331–63), Roman emperor who tried to restore paganism in the empire. He was killed in war against Persia.

Jung, Carl Gustav (1875–1961), Swiss psychiatrist. A former pupil of Freud, he later formulated his own system of analytical psychology. *See* **Section J.**

Junot, Andoche (1771–1813), French general defeated by Wellington in the Peninsular War.

Jusserand, Jean Jules (1855–1932), French author and diplomat, who wrote on English literature and wayfaring life in the Middle Ages.

Justinian I (483–565), Roman emperor in the East. He and his wife Theodora beautified Constantinople, and his general Belisarius was successful in war. He codified Roman law.

Juvenal (60–140), Roman poet and Stoic, remembered for his *Satires*.

K

Kafka, Franz (1883–1924), German-speaking Jewish writer, b. Prague, whose introspective work, the bulk of which was not published till after his early death from tuberculosis, has had a notable influence on later schools, especially the surrealists. It includes the three novels *The Trial*, *The Castle*, and *America*, and some short stories. *See* **Section M, Part I.**

Kālidāsa (*c.* A.D. 400), chief figure in classic Sanskrit literature. No facts are known about his life and date, but certain evidence places him in the 5th cent. Seven of his works survive: two lyrics, *Ritu-samhara* (The Seasons), and *Megha-dūta* (Cloud Messenger); two epics, *Raghu-vamśa* (Dynasty of Raghu) and *Kumara-sambhava* (Birth of the War-god); and three dramas, *Śakūntalā*, *Mālavikāgnimitra*, and *Vikramorvaśīya*.

Kant, Immanuel (1724–1804), German philosopher, author of *Critique of Pure Reason* (1781), *Critique of Practical Reason* (1788), and *Critique of Judgement* (1790). He came from a Pietist family of Königsberg, where he lectured, but the Prussian government forbade his lectures as anti-Lutheran. He was influenced by the writings of his neighbour Hamann (*see* **Romanticism, Section J**) and by Rousseau and Hume, and his own work was of immense influence in shaping future liberal thought. He believed in the freedom of man to make his own decisions and considered the exploitation of man as the worst evil. In *Perpetual Peace* he advocated a world federation of states.

Kapitza, Pyotr (b. 1894), Russian physicist who worked on atomic research with Rutherford at the Cavendish Laboratory, Cambridge, and returned to Russia in 1935. Member of the Soviet Academy of Sciences and Fellow of the Royal Society.

Kauffmann, Angelica (1741–1807), Anglo-Swiss painter, a foundation member of the Royal Academy and the first woman R.A.

Kaulbach, Wilhelm von (1805–74), German painter who illustrated the works of Goethe and Schiller.

Kaunda, Kenneth (b. 1924), African leader of international standing, son of Christian missionaries. He has been president of Zambia since independence in 1964.

Kean, Edmund (1787–1833), English tragic actor. He made his name as Shylock.

Kean, Charles John (1811–68), English actor-manager, son of Edmund. He married Ellen Tree and in the 1850s played with her in spectacular revivals at the Princess's Theatre, London.

Keats, John (1795–1821), English poet who in his short life produced poems notable for richness of imagination and beauty of thought. They include *Odes*, *Isabella*, and *The Eve of St. Agnes*.

Keble, John (1792–1866), English clergyman associated with the Tractarian movement and author of *The Christian Year*. *See* **Tractarianism, Section J.**

Keller, Helen Adams (1880–1968), American author and lecturer who overcame great physical handicaps (blind and deaf before the age of two) to live an active and useful life.

Kelvin of Largs, 1st Baron (William Thomson) (1824–1907), British mathematician and physicist, b. Belfast, known for his work on heat and thermodynamics, and contributions to electrical science and submarine telegraphy. In the domain of heat he stands to Joule as Maxwell stands to Faraday in the history of electrical science, both bringing pre-eminently mathematical minds to bear on the results of experimental discoveries. He introduced the Kelvin or Absolute scale of temperature and was one of the original members of the Order of Merit.

Kemble, Fanny (1809–93), English actress. She came of a noted theatrical family, her father and uncle respectively being the actors Charles Kemble and John Philip Kemble, and her aunt, Mrs. Siddons.

Kempenfelt, Richard (1718–82), English admiral, who sank with his ship the *Royal George* together with 600 of the ship's company off Spithead through a shifting of the guns which caused it to capsize.

Kempis, Thomas à (1380–1471), name by which the German mystic Thomas Hammerken was known, was a monk of the Augustinian order, whose life was mainly spent at a monastery near Zwolle. He was the author of *The Imitation of Christ*.

Kennedy, John Fitzgerald (1917–63), President of the U.S.A., 1961–3, the youngest and the first Roman Catholic to be elected; son of a financier. He had world-wide pre-eminence and gave the American people a sense of purpose to meet the challenges of a scientific age. He opposed racial discrimination and initiated a new era in East–West relations; but his foreign policy sowed the seeds of the Vietnam war. He and his brother Robert were assassinated, the latter while campaigning for the presidency in 1968.

Kent, William (1684–1748), English painter, furniture designer, landscape gardener, and architect, protégé of Lord Burlington, whose buildings include the great hall at Holkham and the Horse Guards, Whitehall.

Kenyatta, Jomo (b. 1893), African leader who became president of Kenya in 1964.

Kepler, Johann (1571–1630), German astronomer and mystic, for a short time assistant to Tycho Brahe whose measurements he used in working out his laws of planetary motion, which are: 1. Planets move round the sun not in circles, but in ellipses, the sun being one of the foci. 2. A planet moves not uniformly but in such a way that a line drawn from it to the sun sweeps out equal areas of the ellipse in equal times. 3. The squares of the period of revolution round the sun are proportional to the cubes of the distances. The explanation of these laws was given by Newton; they dealt a death-blow to Aristotelian cosmology.

Keyes, 1st Baron (Roger John Brownlow Keyes) (1872–1945), British admiral who led the raid on Zeebrugge in 1918.

Keynes, 1st Baron (John Maynard Keynes) (1883–1946), British economist, who was a Treasury representative at the Versailles peace conference, and published his views in *The Economic Consequences of the Peace*. His *Treatise on Money* (1930) and *The General Theory of Employment, Interest and Money* (1936) influenced economic thought all over the world.

Khrushchev, Nikita Sergeyevich (1894–1971), Russian statesman who became leader of the Soviet Union soon after the death of Stalin; first secretary of the Soviet Communist Party, 1953–64; prime minister, 1958–64. After the harsh years of the Stalinist régime he pursued a policy of relaxation both in home and foreign affairs. Relations with America improved but those with China became strained. Advances were made in scientific achievement, notably in the field of space research. In 1964 his posts were taken over by Leonid Brezhnev (first secretary) and Alexei Kosygin (prime minister).

Kierkegaard, Sören (1813–55), Danish philosopher and religious thinker, whose views have influenced contemporary existentialism. His main work is *Either–Or*.

King, Martin Luther (1929–68), American clergyman and Negro integration leader; awarded the 1964 Nobel peace prize for his consistent support of the principle of non-violence in the coloured people's struggle for civil rights. Assassinated at Memphis, Tennessee.

King, Mackenzie (1874–1950), prime minister of Canada, 1921–5, 1926–30, and 1935–48.

Kingsley, Charles (1819–75), English clergyman and novelist, author of *Hypatia*, *Westward Ho!*, *Hereward the Wake* and *The Water Babies*.

Kipling, Rudyard (1865–1936), British writer, b. Bombay. His vivid work portrays contemporary British rule in India and includes *The Light that Failed*, *Stalky and Co.*, *Kim*, and the *Barrack Room Ballads*. Among his books for children are the *Just So Stories*, *Puck of Pook's Hill* and the *Jungle Books*. Nobel prize 1907.

Kirchhoff, Gustav Robert (1824–87), German mathematical physicist, who with R. W. Bunsen discovered that in the gaseous state each chemical substance emits its own characteristic spectrum (1859). He was able to explain Fraunhofer's map of the solar spectrum. Using the spectroscope, he and Bunsen discovered the elements caesium and rubidium.

Kissinger, Henry (b. 1923), American Secretary of State 1973–7 and special adviser on national security affairs to Richard Nixon; inventor of shuttle-service diplomacy. Played active role in peace missions to the Middle East, Vietnam and Southern Africa and in SALT negotiations with the Soviet Union. Nobel Peace Prize 1973. *See* **Section C, Part II.**

Kitchener of Khartoum, 1st Earl (Horatio Herbert Kitchener) (1850–1916), English general. In 1898 he won back the Sudan for Egypt by his victory at Omdurman. He served in the South African war; and in the first world war he was secretary of war, 1914–16. He was drowned on his way to Russia.

Klee, Paul (1879–1940), Swiss artist, whose paintings, in a restless, experimental period, are small-scale, delicate dream-world fantasies of poetical content.

Klemperer, Otto (1885–1973), German-born conductor, renowned as interpreter of the Beethoven symphonies. Expelled by the Nazis he became an American citizen and returned to Europe in 1946. He had been principal conductor of the Philharmonic Orchestra since 1959.

Kneller, Sir Godfrey (1646–1723), portrait painter, b. at Lübeck, who settled in England and was patronised by English sovereigns from Charles II to George I.

Knox, John (1505–72), Scottish reformer, b. near Haddington. While in exile at Geneva he was influenced by Calvin. On return to Scotland he was a leader of the reforming party against Mary, Queen of Scots. He wrote a *History of the Reformation in Scotland*.

Koch, Robert (1843–1910), German bacteriologist who discovered the bacillus of tuberculosis, and worked on cholera and cattle diseases.

Kodály, Zoltán (1882–1967), Hungarian composer and teacher. He worked with Bartok in the collection of folk-tunes. *See* **Section E.**

Kokoschka, Oskar (b. 1886), Austrian portrait and landscape painter, a rare interpretative artist, who, after teaching in Dresden, in 1938 settled in England.

Koniev, Ivan Stepanovich (b. 1897), Russian general of the second world war and commander of the Warsaw Pact forces in the 1950s.

Korolyov, Sergei (1907–66), Russian space scientist, who designed the world's first earth satellite, the first manned spaceship and the first moon rocket.

Kosciusko, Tadeusz (1746–1817), Polish patriot. After experience gained in America in the War of Independence, he led his countrymen against Russia in 1792 and 1794 in opposition to the partition of Poland and was temporarily successful.

Kossuth, Louis (1802–94), Hungarian patriot, who in 1848 led a rising of his countrymen against the Hapsburg dynasty, but had to flee to Turkey and later to England.

Kosygin, Alexei Nikolayevich (b. 1904), succeeded Nikita Khrushchev as chairman of the Council of Ministers of the U.S.S.R. (prime minister) in 1964; formerly a deputy chairman of the State Economic Planning Commission, Gosplan.

Kreisler, Fritz (1875–1962), Austrian violinist, who composed violin music and an operetta. He became an American citizen in 1943.

Krenek, Ernst (b. 1900), Austrian composer of partly Czech descent, whose compositions cover a wide range, including the jazz opera *Jonny spielt auf*. He settled in America in 1938.

Kropotkin, Peter, Prince (1842–1921), Russian anarchist, geographer and explorer, who was imprisoned for favouring the political action of a working men's association, but escaped to England. He wrote on socialistic and geographical subjects. Returned to Russia in 1917.

Kruger, Stephanus Johannes Paulus (1825–1904), Boer leader, who in 1881 was appointed head of the provisional government against Britain, and later president. When the war of 1899–1902 turned against the Boers, he vainly sought help in Europe.

Krupp, Alfred (1812–87), founder of the German gun factories at Essen. He installed in a disused factory left him by his father a new steam-engine from England, began to make cast steel, and from 1844 specialised in armaments. The firm's factories made the Big Bertha guns which shelled Paris in 1918. His great-grandson Alfried (b. 1907) was tried as a war criminal in 1948.

Krylov, Ivan Andreyevich (1768–1844), Russian writer of fables who has been called the Russian La Fontaine.

Kubelik, Jan (1880–1940), Czech violinist, son of a gardener at Michle, near Prague, who at the age of 12 played in public. His son Rafael (b. 1914), a conductor of international repute, was musical director of the Royal Opera House, Covent Garden, 1955–8.

Kublai Khan (1216–94), grandson of Genghiz Khan, was the first Mongol emperor of China. He extended the Mongol empire by conquest, and lived in unparalleled splendour. His court was described by Marco Polo and is the subject of a poem by Coleridge.

L

La Fayette, Marie Joseph Paul Roch Yves Gilbert du Motier, Marquis de (1757–1834), French soldier and statesman. He fought for the colonists in the American War of Independence; and in the 1789 French revolution he proposed a declaration of rights and was commander of the National Guard till his moderation made him unpopular. When the monarchy was restored he was an opposition leader, and took part in the revolution of 1830.

La Fontaine, Jean de (1621–95), French poet and fabulist, b. in Champagne, a friend of Molière, Boileau, and Racine, all brilliant writers of the reign of Louis XIV.

Lagerlöf, Selma (1858–1940), Swedish novelist and first woman member of the Swedish Academy. Nobel prizewinner 1909.

Lagrange, Joseph Louis, Comte (1736–1813),

French mathematician, of Turin and Paris, whose interest in astronomy led him to distinguish two types of disturbance of members of the solar system, the periodic and the secular. He was called by Frederick the Great to Berlin to succeed Euler.

Lalande, Joseph Jerome LeFrançais de (1732–1807), French astronomer, author of *Traité d'astronomie*.

Lamarck, Jean Baptiste Pierre Antoine de Monet de (1744–1829), French biologist whose explanation of evolution was that new organs are brought into being by the needs of the organism in adapting to its environment and that the new facilities can be passed on to the offspring through heredity. *See* **The Evolution of Organisms, Section F, Part IV.**

Lamb, Charles (1775–1834), English essayist, b. London. A clerk in the East India Office, he devoted his life to his sister Mary, who was of unstable mind. He is chiefly known for his *Essays of Elia*, and his letters, which have a blend of humour and tenderness.

Lambert, Constant (1905–51), English composer and critic, and conductor of Sadler's Wells ballet. His *Rio Grande* is in jazz idiom.

Landor, Walter Savage (1775–1864), English writer, b. Warwick, remembered for his *Imaginery Conversations* and poems.

Landseer, Sir Edwin (1802–73), English animal painter, b. London. He painted the *Monarch of the Glen* and designed the lions in Trafalgar Square.

Lane, Edward William (1801–76), English Arabic scholar, translator of the *Arabian Nights*.

Lanfranc (*c*. 1005–89), ecclesiastic. B. at Pavia, he became a prior in Normandy, and in 1070 archbishop of Canterbury, in which office he was energetic.

Lang, Andrew (1844–1912), Scottish man of letters, whose output includes *Myth, Ritual and Religion*, poems, fairy-tales, and fiction.

Lang, 1st Baron (Cosmo Gordon Lang) (1864–1945), was archbishop of Canterbury, 1928–42,

Langland, William (1330?–1400?), English poet. probably educated at Malvern, author of *Piers the Plowman*.

Langton, Stephen (1151–1228), archbishop of Canterbury, and adviser to the insurgent barons who induced King John to sign Magna Carta.

Lansbury, George (1859–1940), British Labour politician, founder of the *Daily Herald*. He improved London's amenities.

Lâo-Tsze (old philosopher) (*c*. 600 B.C.), traditional founder of Taoism in China. *See* **Section J.**

Laplace, Pierre Simon, Marquis de (1749–1827), French mathematician and astronomer, author of *Celestial Mechanics* (1799–1825). He advanced the hypothesis that the solar system had condensed out of a vast rotating gaseous nebula.

La Rochefoucauld, François, Duc de (1613–80), French writer, author of *Reflections and Moral Maxims*.

Lasker, Emanuel (1868–1941), German chess player, world champion, 1894–1921.

Lassalle, Ferdinand (1825–64), German socialist who took part in the revolutionary movement of 1848 and organised workers to press for political rights.

Lassus, Orlandus (Lasso, Orlando di). (*c*. 1532–94), Flemish composer and choirmaster, contemporary of Palestrina, writer of *chansons*, madrigals, and sacred music. *See* **Section E.**

Latimer, Hugh (*c*. 1485–1555), English Protestant martyr, became bishop of Worcester in 1535, and was executed under Queen Mary.

Laud, William (1573–1645), archbishop of Canterbury and adviser to Charles I. His attempts to get conformity for his high church policy made him unpopular and he was impeached and beheaded.

Lauder, Sir Harry (1870–1950), Scottish comic singer of wide popularity. He also wrote *Roamin' in the Gloamin'*.

Laval, Pierre (1883–1945), French politician who collaborated with the German occupation in the second world war and was subsequently tried and executed.

Lavery, Sir John (1856–1941), Irish portrait painter.

Lavoisier, Antoine Laurent (1743–94), French chemist, b. Paris, was the first to establish the fact that combustion is a form of chemical action. We owe the word *oxygen* to him. He perished in the French Revolution.

Law, Andrew Bonar (1858–1923), Conservative politician, prime minister 1922–3.

Lawrence, David Herbert (1885–1930), English poet and novelist, b. Notts., a miner's son. He tried to interpret emotion on a deeper level of consciousness. His works, which have had wide influence, include *The White Peacock, Sons and Lovers, The Rainbow, Women in Love*, and *Lady Chatterley's Lover*; also plays. *See* **Sections I and M (Part I).**

Lawrence, Sir Thomas (1769–1830), English portrait painter.

Lawrence, Thomas Edward (1888–1935) (Lawrence of Arabia), British soldier who led the Arabs against the Turks in the war of 1914–18, and wrote *The Seven Pillars of Wisdom*.

Leacock, Stephen (1869–1944), Canadian humorist.

Leavis, Frank Raymond (b. 1895), British critic, who edited *Scrutiny*, 1932–63, and whose works include *The Great Tradition, D. H. Lawrence, Novelist*, and *"Anna Karenina" and Other Essays*.

Lecky, William Edward Hartpole (1838–1903), Irish historian, author of *England in the Eighteenth Century*.

Leclerc, Jacques Philippe (Philippe, Comte de Hauteclocque) (1902–47), French general. He led a Free French force in Africa in the second world war and liberated Paris in 1944. He died in a plane crash.

Le Corbusier (1887–1965), pseudonym of Charles Édouard Jeanneret, Swiss architect, whose books and work (especially his Unité d'Habitation at Marseilles and the new Punjab capital at Chandigarh) have widely influenced town-planning.

Le Duc Tho (b. 1911), member of the Politburo of the N. Vietnamese Workers' Party who was his country's chief negotiator at the Vietnam truce talks 1970–3. He would not accept the 1973 Nobel peace prize awarded jointly with Dr. Kissinger until peace had "really been restored in S. Vietnam."

Lee of Fareham, 1st Viscount (Arthur Hamilton Lee) (1868–1947), British politician who presented Chequers Court to the nation as prime minister's residence.

Lee, Robert Edward (1807–70), American Confederate general in the Civil War, who made the surrender at Appomattox.

Lee, Sir Sidney (1859–1926), English critic, and joint editor of the *Dictionary of National Biography*.

Leech, John (1817–64), humorist artist, b. London, of Irish descent, contributed to *Punch*.

Leibnitz, Gottfried Wilhelm (1646–1716), German philosopher and mathematician, who invented the differential and integral calculus (1684) independently of Newton whose previous work on the same subject was not published until 1687. It was Leibnitz's nomenclature that was universally adopted.

Leicester, Earl of (Robert Dudley) (1538–88), English soldier, commanded English troops in the Netherlands, 1585–7, without much success, and in 1588 commanded forces assembled against the Armada. He was husband of Amy Robsart.

Leif Ericsson (fl. 1000), discoverer of Vinland on the north-east coast of America; b. Iceland, son of the Norse explorer, Eric the Red, who colonised Greenland.

Leighton, 1st Baron (Robert Leighton) (1830–96), English painter of wide popularity, whose works include *Paolo and Francesca*. He was also a sculptor.

Lely, Sir Peter (Pieter van der Faes) (1618–80), Dutch painter who settled in London and painted court portraits.

Lenin (Vladimir Ilyich Ulyanov) (1870–1924), Russian revolutionary leader and statesman. From 1893 to 1917 he worked underground in Russia and abroad for the revolutionary cause. During this time the Social-Democratic party was formed; within it developed an uncompromising revolutionary group, the Bolsheviks, and of this group Lenin was the leading spirit. In April 1917 he and his fellow exiles returned; after the November revolution he headed the new government having to face both war and anarchy. In 1921 his "new economic policy" somewhat modified the intensive drive towards planned industrial development. He was born in Simbirsk (now Ulyanovsk) on the middle Volga, the son of the local inspector of education. His body lies embalmed in Red Square, Moscow.

Leonardo da Vinci (1452–1519), Italian artist and man of science, son of a Florentine lawyer and a peasant. He described himself (when applying to Lodovico Sforza, Duke of Milan, for the post of city planner) as painter, architect, philosopher, poet, composer, sculptor, athlete, mathematician, inventor, and anatomist. His artistic output is small in quantity, and he is best known for his *Last Supper* in the refectory of Santa Maria delle Grazie in Milan and his *Mona Lisa* in the Louvre. He recorded his scientific work in unpublished notebooks written from right to left in mirror writing. The anatomy of the body (himself carrying out dissections), the growth of the child in the womb, the laws of waves and currents, and the laws of flight, all were studied by this astonishing man who believed nothing but had to see for himself. Although he was much admired, few people in his time had any notion of his universal genius.

Leoncavallo, Ruggiero (1858–1919), Italian composer of the opera *Pagliacci.*

Leonidas was king of Sparta at the time of the invasion of Greece by Xerxes (480 B.C.), and led the defence of the pass of Thermopylae, where he fell.

Lermontov, Mikhail Yurevich (1814–41), Russian poet and novelist, exiled to the Caucasus for a revolutionary poem addressed to Tsar Nicholas I on the death of Pushkin. He has been called the poet of the Caucasus. His novel *A Hero of Our Time* was written at St. Petersburg. He lost his life in a duel.

Le Sage, Alain René (1668–1747), French author, b. in Brittany, who wrote *Gil Blas* and *Le Diable Boiteux.* He was also a dramatist and his plays include *Turcaret.*

Lesseps, Ferdinand, Vicomte de (1805–94), French engineer who while serving as vice-consul at Alexandria conceived a scheme for a canal across the Suez isthmus; the work was completed in 1869. He also projected the original Panama canal scheme, which failed.

Lessing, Gotthold Ephraim (1729–81), German philosopher, dramatist, and critic, noted for his critical work *Laokoon* and his play *Minna von Barnhelm.*

Leucippus (fl. 440 B.C.), Greek philosopher, founder with Democritus of atomism, a theory of matter more nearly that of modern science than any put forward in ancient times. One of his sayings survives: "Naught occurs at random, but everything for a reason and of necessity."

Leverhulme, 1st Viscount (William Hesketh Lever) (1851–1925), British industrialist and philanthropist. He founded Lever Bros. which later became Unilever Ltd., and was a practical exponent of industrial partnership. He gave Lancaster House to the nation.

Leverrier, Urbain Jean Joseph (1811–77), French astronomer who, working independently of J. C. Adams of Cambridge, anticipated the existence of the planet Neptune which was later revealed by telescopic search.

Lévi-Strauss, Claude (b. 1908), French social anthropologist, b. Belgium, exponent of the theory of symbolic structures. He has written works on anthropology, religion, myths and language: *Les structures élémentaires de la parenté* (1949), *Tristes tropiques* (1955), *La Pensée Sauvage* (1963).

Lewis, Sinclair (1885–1951), American writer of novels satirising small-town life and philistinism. His works include *Main Street, Babbitt* (hence the term Babbitry), and *Elmer Gantry.* Nobel prizewinner 1931.

Liaquat Ali Khan (1895–1951), leader of the Moslem League (1946) and first premier of Pakistan in 1947. He was assassinated.

Lie, Trygve (1896–1968), Norwegian politician who became secretary-general of the United Nations, 1946–52.

Li Hung Chang (1823–1901), Chinese statesman, who though enlightened, was unable to secure much modernisation and had to cede Formosa to Japan in 1895.

Lilburne, John (1614–57), English agitator and pamphleteer, leader of the Levellers in the Civil War period.

Linacre, Thomas (*c.* 1460–1524), English humanist and physician, who translated Galen's works and founded the College of Physicians.

Lincoln, Abraham (1809–65), American president. B. in Kentucky, he became a lawyer and was returned to Congress from Illinois in 1846. He was a leader of the Republican party which was formed in 1856 to oppose slavery. He became president in 1861, in which year the Confederate States proposed to withdraw from the Union, and war broke out. The phrase "government of the people, by the people, for the people" comes from his Gettysburg speech of 1863. He was assassinated in 1865.

Lind, Jenny (1820–87), Swedish singer, popular in Europe, and known as the Swedish nightingale. She founded musical scholarships.

Linnaeus (1707–78), Swedish botanist, remembered for his system of defining living things by two Latin names, the first being its *genus*, and the second its *species*. His method is expounded in *Philosophia Botanica* (1751). In 1757 he was ennobled as Karl von Linné. He studied, taught and died at Uppsala.

Lippi, Fra Filippo (1406–69), Italian artist, b. Florence. Frescoes in Prato cathedral are his main work. His son **Filippino** (1457–1504) finished Masaccio's frescoes in the Carmine, Florence, and executed others, for instance in Santa Maria Novella.

Lippmann, Gabriel (1845–1921), French physicist who invented a capillary electrometer and was a pioneer in colour photography. Nobel prizewinner 1908.

Lippmann, Walter (1889–1974), American journalist of influence, writing for the New York *Herald Tribune*, 1931–62.

Lipton, Sir Thomas Johnstone (1850–1931), Scottish business man and philanthropist. B. Glasgow, he emigrated to America, but returned to Scotland and established extensive chainstores for groceries. He unsuccessfully competed in yachting for the America's Cup.

Lister, Baron (Joseph Lister) (1827–1912), English surgeon, son of **J. J. Lister** (1786–1869), an amateur microscopist. He founded antiseptic surgery (1865) which greatly reduced mortality in hospitals.

Liszt, Franz (1811–86), Hungarian pianist and composer. His daughter Cosima became the wife of Hans von Bülow and later of Wagner. *See* **Section E.**

Litvinov, Maxim (1876–1952), Russian diplomat, of revolutionary origin, who first as ambassador in London, then as commissar for foreign affairs, and 1941–3 ambassador to the U.S., gained respect and understanding for his country.

Livingstone, David (1813–73), Scottish explorer in Africa. He discovered the course of the Zambesi, the Victoria Falls and Lake Nyasa (now Lake Malawi), and roused opinion against the slave trade. At one time believed lost, he was found by Stanley (*q.v.*) on 10 Nov. 1871.

Lloyd-George of Dwyfor, 1st Earl (David Lloyd George) (1863–1945), Liberal statesman of Welsh origin. He was M.P. for Caernarvon, 1890–1944; and as chancellor of the exchequer he introduced social insurance, 1908–11. The war of 1914–18 obliged him to become a war premier (superseding Asquith), and he was subsequently one of the main figures at the peace conference. In 1921 he conceded the Irish Free State. His daughter, Lady Megan Lloyd George, was M.P. for many years, latterly for the Labour Party.

Locke, John (1632–1704), English liberal philosopher and founder of empiricism, the doctrine that all knowledge is derived from experience. His chief work in theoretical philosophy, *Essay Concerning Human Understanding*, was written just before the revolution of 1688 and published in 1690. Other writings include *Letters on Toleration, Treatises on Government*, and *Education.*

Lombroso, Cesare (1836–1909), Italian criminologist, whose *L'uomo delinquente* maintained the existence of a criminal type distinguishable from the normal.

Lomonosov, Mikhail Vasilievich (1711–65),

Russian philologist and poet who systematised Russian grammar and orthography.

London, Jack (1876–1916), American author of adventure tales such as *Call of the Wild*.

Longfellow, Henry Wadsworth (1807–82), American poet, popular in his lifetime, author of *The Golden Legend* and *Hiawatha*.

Lope de Vega Carpio, Félix (1562–1635), Spanish writer of immense output. First a ballad-writer, he took to play-writing and founded the Spanish drama. The number of his plays is said to have been 1,500, the earlier ones historical, the later ones dealing with everyday life; but most are lost.

Lorca, Federico Garcia (1899–1936), Spanish poet and dramatist of Andalusia. Among his works are *Llanto por Ignacio Sánchez Mejías*, an unforgettable lament on the death of a bullfighter, and *Canción de Jinete* with its haunting refrain, "Cordoba, far away and alone." He was brutally murdered by Franco sympathisers at the outbreak of the civil war.

Louis IX (1214–70), St. Louis, King of France. Of saintly character (as described in Joinville's *Memoirs*), he also carried out practical reforms. He died on crusade.

Louis XIV (1638–1715), King of France. A despotic ruler, builder of Versailles, he also dominated the Europe of his day; but he sowed the seeds of future trouble for France by his exhausting wars. He revoked the Edict of Nantes which had given religious freedom to the Huguenots since 1598. His reign, however, was a great period for literature.

Louis XV (1710–74), King of France. Extravagant and self-indulgent, his reign marked a declining period for the monarchy, but produced some fine art.

Louis XVI (1754–93), King of France. Well-meaning but incapable, this king saw the outbreak of the French revolution of 1789, in which he and his queen Marie Antoinette were executed.

Louis, Joe (Joseph Louis Barrow) (b. 1914), American Negro boxer, who became world heavyweight champion in 1936, successfully defending his title 25 times.

Low, Archibald Montgomery (1888–1956), British scientist who worked in varied fields, including wireless, television, and anti-aircraft and anti-tank apparatus.

Low, Sir David (1891–1963), British cartoonist, b. New Zealand, associated with the *Evening Standard* and later the *Guardian*; creator of Colonel Blimp.

Lowell, Robert (b. 1917), American poet, author of the verse play *The Old Glory*, and *Life Studies*, an autobiographical volume in verse and prose. *See* **Section M, Part III.**

Loyola, St. Ignatius (1491–1556), Spanish founder of the Jesuits, a missionary order working directly under the Pope.

Lucretius (99–55 B.C.), Roman poet, author of *De rerum natura*, a long philosophical poem advocating moral truth without religious belief.

Ludendorff, Erich (1865-1937), German general who directed German strategy in the first world war.

Lugard, 1st Baron (Frederick John Dealtry Lugard) (1858–1945), British colonial administrator in Africa, especially Nigeria, and exponent of the system of indirect rule through native chiefs.

Lukács, Georg (1885–1971), Hungarian writer, Marxist thinker and literary critic. His ideas are expounded in *History and Class Consciousness* (1923), *Studies in European Realism* (1946, Eng. tr. 1950), *The Historical Novel* (1955; Eng. tr. 1962).

Luther, Martin (1483–1546), German Protestant reformer. After spending time in a monastery, he was ordained priest (1507), and lectured at Wittenberg university. In 1517 he protested against the sale of indulgences; and when summoned before the Diet of Worms made a memorable defence. He was protected by the Elector of Saxony, and translated the Bible. German Protestantism culminated in the Augsburg confession (1530). *See also* **Lutheranism, Section J.**

Luthuli, Albert (1899–1967), African non-violent resistance leader, an ex-Zulu chief. Killed in train accident. Nobel prize for peace 1960.

Lutyens, Sir Edwin Landseer (1869–1944), English architect both of country houses and public buildings; designed the cenotaph, Whitehall, and Liverpool Roman catholic cathedral.

Lyell, Sir Charles (1797–1875), Scottish geologist, whose *Principles of Geology* (1830–33) postulated gradual geological change and helped to shape Darwin's ideas. His terminology—Pliocene (*Greek* = more recent), Miocene (less recent) and Eocene (dawn)—is still in use.

Lysenko, Trofim (1898–1976), Russian biologist who maintained that environmental experiences can change heredity somewhat in the manner suggested by Lamarck. After the death of Stalin his novel theories were severely criticised.

Lytton, 1st Baron (Edward George Earle Lytton Bulwer-Lytton) (1803–73), English novelist and playwright, author of *The Last Days of Pompeii*.

M

Macadam, John Loudon (1756–1836), Scottish inventor of the "macadamising" system of road repair.

MacArthur, Douglas (1880–1964), American general. He defended the Philippines against the Japanese in the second world war, and was relieved of his command in 1951 in the Korean war.

Macaulay of Rothley, 1st Baron (Thomas Babington Macaulay) (1800–59), English historian, poet and Indian civil servant. His poems include *Lays of Ancient Rome*. In India he was mainly responsible for education being given in English.

Macaulay, Zachary (1768–1838), anti-slavery agitator, father of the above.

Macbeth (d. 1057), Scottish king, married Gruoch, granddaughter of Kenneth, king of Alban. He was mormaer of Moray, succeeding Duncan in 1040 after killing him in fair fight. His reign of seventeen years was prosperous, but he was killed by Duncan's son, Malcolm, in 1057. Shakespeare's play is based on the inaccurate *Chronicle* of Holinshed.

MacDiarmid, Hugh (b. 1892), pseudonym of Christopher Murray Grieve, Scottish poet, leader of the Scottish literary renaissance; author of *A Drunk Man Looks at the Thistle*.

Macdonald, Flora (1722–90), Scottish Jacobite heroine who saved the life of Prince Charles Edward after the defeat at Culloden Moor in 1746.

Macdonald, Sir John Alexander (1815–91), Canadian statesman, first prime minister of the Dominion of Canada.

Macdonald, James Ramsay (1866–1937), Labour politician of Scottish origin, premier 1924 and 1929–31; also of a coalition 1931–5. His action over the financial crisis of 1931 divided his party.

Macdonald, Malcolm (b. 1901), son of above, has held positions overseas in the Commonwealth, the last as special representative in Africa.

Machiavelli, Niccolò (1467–1527), Florentine Renaissance diplomat and theorist of the modern state. His book *The Prince* (1513), dedicated to Lorenzo the Magnificent, is concerned with the reality of politics—what rulers must do to retain power. His *Discourses* is more republican and liberal.

Mackail, John William (1859–1945), British classical scholar, translator of the *Odyssey*.

Mackenzie, Sir Compton (1883–1972), British writer, whose works include *Carnival*, *Sinister Street*, and a monumental autobiography.

McLuhan, Herbert Marshall (b. 1911), Canadian author of a number of books on contemporary communications, including *The Gutenberg Galaxy*, *The Mechanical Bride*. *See* **Section J.**

Macmillan, Harold (b. 1894), British Conservative statesman, prime minister 1957–63; During his premiership came the crises of the Berlin Wall and the Cuban missiles (in which his personal diplomacy played an influential role), de Gaulle's veto to our entry into Europe, the signing of the Partial Test-Ban Treaty and his "wind of change" speech which hailed African independence. The final vol. of his memoirs was pub. 1973. Chancellor of Oxford University (1960). O.M. 1976.

McMillan, Margaret (1860–1931), Scottish educational reformer, b. New York, and pioneer (with her sister Rachel) of child welfare work in London and of open-air nursery schools.

Macneice, Louis (1907–63), British poet, playwright, and translator. *See* **Section M, Part III.**

Macready, William Charles (1793–1873), British actor and manager, especially associated with Shakespearean roles.

Maeterlinck, Maurice (1862–1949), Belgian man of letters, whose plays include *La Princesse Maleine, Pelléas et Mélisande,* and *L'Oiseau Bleu.* Nobel prizewinner 1911. He also did scientific work on bees.

Magellan, Ferdinand (c. 1480–1521), Portuguese navigator, and commander of the first expedition (1519) to sail round the world.

Mahler, Gustav (1860–1911), Austrian composer and conductor; a writer of symphonies and songs, a classical romantic, much influenced by Anton Bruckner and Wagner. *See* **Section E.**

Mahavira, Vardhamana Jnatriputra (6th cent. B.C.), Indian historical (as opposed to legendary) founder of Jainism, which teaches the sacredness of all life. *See* **Jainism, Section J.**

Maintenon, Françoise d'Aubigne, Marquise de (1635–1719), second wife of Louis XIV. Her first husband was the poet Scarron. On the king's death she retired to a home for poor girls which she had founded.

Makarios III (b. 1913), Greek Orthodox archbishop and Cypriot national leader. Deported by the British to the Seychelles in 1956, he returned in 1957 to become president of the newly independent republic in 1960.

Malibran, Marie Félicité (1808–36), Spanish mezzo-soprano.

Malik, Yakov Alexandrovich (b. 1906), Soviet diplomat; permanent representative at U.N. 1949–52, 1967– ; ambassador to Britain 1953–60; deputy foreign minister 1960–7.

Malory, Sir Thomas (c. 1430–71), English writer. From earlier sources and legends of King Arthur and the Knights of the Round Table, he compiled the *Morte Darthur* printed by Caxton in 1485.

Malraux, André (1895–1976), French novelist and politician. His works include *La Condition humaine, L'Espoir,* and *Psychologie de l'art* (tr. in 2 vols., *Museum without Walls,* and *The Creative Act*). Served under de Gaulle.

Malthus, Thomas Robert (1766–1834), English clergyman and economist who in his gloomy essay *The Principle of Population* contended that population tends to increase faster than the means of subsistence and that its growth could only be checked by moral restraint or by disease and war. *See* **Malthusianism, Section J.**

Manet, Edouard (1832–83), French painter. His Impressionist pictures include *Olympia* and *Un bar aux Folies-Bergère* (the latter at the Courtauld).

Mann, Thomas (1875–1955), German writer who won world recognition at the age of 25 with his novel *Buddenbrooks.* His liberal humanistic outlook had developed sufficiently by 1930 for him to expose national socialism. He left Germany in 1933 to live in Switzerland, then settled in the U.S. Other works are *The Magic Mountain,* and the *Joseph* tetralogy. Nobel prizewinner 1929.

Mann, Tom (1856–1941), British Labour leader for more than fifty years.

Manning, Henry Edward (1808–92), English cardinal; archbishop of Westminster 1865–92. He was an Anglican churchman before he entered the church of Rome.

Mansfield, Katherine (1890–1923), short-story writer, b. Wellington, New Zealand, whose work was influenced by the short stories of Chekov. Her second husband was John Middleton Murry, literary critic.

Manson, Sir Patrick (1844–1922), Scottish physician, the first to formulate the hypothesis that the malarial parasite was transmitted by the mosquito. His joint work with Sir Ronald Ross rendered habitable vast areas of the earth hitherto closed.

Manuzio, Aldo Pio (1450–1515), Italian printer, founder of the Aldine press in Venice, which for just over a century issued books famed for their beautiful type and bindings.

Manzoni, Alessandro (1785–1873), Italian novelist and poet, b. Milan, whose historical novel *I Promessi Sposi* (The Betrothed) won European reputation.

Mao Tse-tung (1893–1976), Chinese national and Communist leader. B. in Hunan, of rural origin but university training, he understood how to win peasant support for a national and progressive movement. Attacked by Chiang Kai-shek, he led his followers by the "long march" to N.W. China, whence later they issued to defeat both Japanese and Chiang and proclaim a People's Republic in 1949, and later to promote the "great leap forward" of 1958–9 (the commune movement). He stood for an egalitarian democratic society, unbureaucratic, with revolutionary momentum. He was much to the fore in the "cultural revolution" which lasted from 1965 to 1969. See **Section C, Part II,** and **Maoism, Section J.**

Marat, Jean Paul (1743–93), French revolution leader, largely responsible for the reign of terror, and assassinated by Charlotte Corday.

Marconi, Guglielmo, Marchese (1874–1937), Italian inventor and electrical engineer who developed the use of radio waves as a practical means of communication. In 1895 he sent long-wave signals over a distance of a mile, and in 1901 received in Newfoundland the first transatlantic signals sent out by his station in Cornwall, thus making the discovery that radio waves can bend around the spherically-shaped earth. Nobel prizewinner 1909.

Marcus Aurelius Antoninus (121–80), Roman emperor and Stoic philosopher of lofty character, whose *Meditations* are still read.

Marcuse, Herbert (b. 1898), political philosopher. B. Berlin, he emigrated to the U.S. during the Nazi regime. A critic of Western industrial society, he sees the international student protest movement as the agent of revolutionary change.

Maria Theresa (1717–80), Empress, daughter of the Hapsburg Charles VI. Able and of strong character, she fought unsuccessfully to save Silesia from Prussian annexation. She promoted reforms in her dominions. She married the Duke of Lorraine and had 16 children.

Marie Antoinette (1755–93), Queen of France, was daughter of the above and wife of Louis XVI; accused of treason, she and her husband were beheaded in the French revolution.

Marie Louise (1791–1847), daughter of Francis I of Austria, became the wife of Napoleon and bore him a son (Napoleon II).

Marius, Caius (157–86 B.C.), Roman general who defended Gaul from invasion; later civil war forced him to flee from Rome, and on his return he took terrible revenge.

Mark Antony. *See* **Antonius, Marcus.**

Marlborough, 1st Duke of (John Churchill) (1650–1722), English general, victor of Blenheim, Ramillies, Oudenarde and Malplaquet. His wife, Sarah Jennings, was a favourite of Queen Anne.

Marlowe, Christopher (1564–93), English dramatist and precursor of Shakespeare. His plays include *Dr. Faustus, Tamburlaine the Great, Edward II,* and *The Jew of Malta.* His early death was due to a tavern brawl.

Marryat, Frederick (1792–1848), English author of sea and adventure stories, including *Peter Simple, Mr. Midshipman Easy,* and *Masterman Ready.* He was a captain in the Royal Navy.

Marshall, George Catlett (1880–1959), American general. He was U.S. chief of staff 1939–45, and originated the Marshall Aid plan for European reconstruction. Nobel prize for peace 1953.

Martial, Marcus Valerius (c. 40–104), Roman poet, b. in Spain, remembered for his epigrams.

Marvell, Andrew (1620–78), English poet and political writer. He was Milton's assistant and wrote mainly during the commonwealth.

Marx, Karl (1818–83), German founder of modern international communism, b. Trier of Jewish parentage. He studied law, philosophy and history at the universities of Bonn and Berlin, and later took up the study of economics. In conjunction with his friend Engels he wrote the *Communist Manifesto* of 1848 for the Communist League of which he was the leader. Because of his revolutionary activities he was forced to leave the continent and in 1849 settled in London. Here, mainly while living at 28 Dean Street, Soho, he wrote *Das Kapital,* a deep analysis of the economic laws that govern modern society. In 1864 he helped to found the first International. He ranks as one of the most original and influential thinkers of modern times. He was buried at Highgate cemetery. *See* **Marxism, Section J.**

Mary I (1516–58), Queen of England, was daughter of Henry VIII and Catherine of Aragon. A Roman Catholic, she reversed the religious changes made by her father and brother, and about 300 Protestants were put to death. She married Philip of Spain.

Mary II (1662–94), Queen of England with her husband the Dutch William III. As daughter of James II, she was invited to succeed after the revolution of 1688 and expelied her father.

Mary Stuart, Queen of Scots (1542–87), daughter of James V of Scotland and Mary of Guise, she laid claim to the English succession. She was imprisoned in England by Elizabeth and beheaded. Her husbands were the dauphin of France (d. 1560), Lord Darnley (murdered 1566) and Bothwell.

Masaryk, Jan Garrigue (1886–1948), Czech diplomat. The son of Thomas, he was Czech minister in London 1925–38, and foreign secretary while his government was in exile in London and after it returned to Prague, 1940–8.

Masaryk, Thomas Garrigue (1850–1937), Czech statesman and independence leader. He was the first president of Czechoslovakia, 1918–35.

Mascagni, Pietro (1863–1945), Italian composer of *Cavalleria Rusticana*.

Masefield, John (1878–1967), English poet. His best-known works are *Salt-Water Ballads* (as a boy he ran away to sea), and *Reynard the Fox*. He became poet laureate in 1930.

Maskelyne, John Nevil (1839–1917), English illusionist. He also exposed spiritualistic frauds.

Massenet, Jules Emile Frédéric (1842–1912), French composer of songs, orchestral suites, oratorios, and operas, among them *Manon* and *Thaïs*.

Massine, Léonide (b. 1896), Russian dancer, one of Diaghilev's choreographers. In 1944 he became a U.S. citizen.

Masters, Edgar Lee (1869–1950), American poet remembered for his *Spoon River Anthology*.

Matisse, Henri (1869–1954), French painter, member of a group known as *Les Fauves* (the wild beasts) for their use of violent colour and colour variation to express form and relief. A number of his paintings are in the Moscow Museum of Western Art.

Matsys (Massys), Quentin (1466–1530), Flemish painter, b. Louvain, settled Antwerp; he worked at a time when Italian influence was gaining ground. His *Money-changer and his Wife* is in the Louvre.

Maugham, William Somerset (1874–1965), British writer, b. Paris. He practised as a doctor till the success of *Liza of Lambeth* (1897), followed by *Of Human Bondage*. He was a master of the short story and his work reflects his travels in the East. In both world wars he served as a British agent.

Maupassant, Guy de (1850–93), French writer whose novels and short stories show penetrating realism. His stories include *Boule de Suif*, *La Maison Tellier*, and *La Parure* (The Necklace).

Mauriac, François (1885–1970), French writer whose novels deal with moral problems and include *Le Baiser au Lépreux* and the play *Asmodée*. Nobel prizewinner 1952.

Maurois, André (Emile Herzog) (1885–1967), French writer whose works include lives of Shelley and Disraeli.

Maxim, Sir Hiram Stevens (1840–1916), American inventor of the automatic quick-firing gun, perfected in London.

Maxton, James (1885–1946), Scottish Labour politician and pacifist; entered parliament 1922; chairman of I.L.P. 1926–31, 1934–9.

Maxwell, James Clerk (1831–79), Scottish physicist. He wrote his first scientific paper at 15, and after teaching in Aberdeen and London became first Cavendish professor of experimental physics at Cambridge. His mathematical mind, working on the discoveries of Faraday and others, gave physics a celebrated set of equations for the basic laws of electricity and magnetism. His work revolutionised fundamental physics. *See* **Section F, Part II.**

Mazarin, Jules (1602–61), cardinal and minister of France was b. in Italy. In spite of opposition from the nobles, he continued Richelieu's work of building up a strong centralised monarchy.

Mazeppa, Ivan Stepanovich (1644–1709), Cossack nobleman, b. Ukraine (then part of Poland, before E. Ukraine passed to Russia, 1667). He fought unsuccessfully for independence allying himself with Charles XII of Sweden against Peter I of Russia (Poltava, 1709). According to legend he was punished for intrigue by being tied to the back of a wild horse and sent into the steppes. Byron wrote a poem about him.

Mazzini, Giuseppe (1805–72), Italian patriot. B. Genoa, he advocated a free and united Italy, and from Marseilles he published a journal, *Young Italy*. Expelled from the Continent, he took refuge in London in 1837. In 1848 he returned to Italy, and became dictator of the short-lived Roman republic, which was put down by French forces. His contribution to Italian unity was that of preparing the way.

Medawar, Sir Peter Brien (b. 1915), British zoologist, author of *The Art of the Soluble* and *The Future of Man*; president of the British Association 1969. Nobel prizewinner 1960.

Medici, Florentine family of merchants and bankers who were politically powerful and who patronised the arts. **Cosimo the Elder** (1389–1464) was for over 30 years virtual ruler of Florence. His grandson, **Lorenzo the Magnificent** (1449–92), poet, friend of artists and scholars, governed with munificence. His grandson, **Lorenzo**, was father of **Catherine de' Medici**, Queen of France (*q.v.*). A later **Cosimo** (1519–74) was an able Duke of Florence and then Grand-Duke of Tuscany, which title the Medicis held until 1737.

Méhul, Etienne Nicolas (1763–1817), French operatic composer. *Joseph* is his masterpiece.

Meitner, Lise (1878–1969), co-worker of Otto Hahn (*q.v.*) who interpreted his results (1939) as a fission process. A Jewish refugee scientist from Germany, she became a Swedish citizen in 1949.

Melanchthon, Philip (1497–1560), German religious reformer, who assisted Luther, and wrote the first Protestant theological work, *Loci communes*. He drew up the Augsburg confession (1530).

Melba, Nellie (Helen Porter Mitchell) (1861–1931), Australian soprano of international repute, b. near Melbourne.

Melbourne, 2nd Viscount (William Lamb) (1779–1848), English Whig statesman, was premier at the accession of Queen Victoria.

Mendel, Gregor Johann (1822–84), Austrian botanist. After entering the Augustinian monastery at Brünn he became abbot and taught natural history in the school. His main interest was the study of inheritance, and his elaborate observations of the common garden pea resulted in the law of heredity which bears his name. His hypothesis was published in 1866 but no attention was given to it until 1900. *See* **Section F, Part IV.**

Mendeleyev, Dmitri Ivanovich (1834–1907), Russian chemist, first to discover the critical temperatures. He formulated the periodic law of atomic weights (1869) and drew up the periodic table (*see* **Section F**), predicting the properties of elements which might fill the gaps. Element 101 is named after him.

Mendelssohn-Bartholdy, Felix (1809–47), German composer, grandson of Moses Mendelssohn, philosopher. He belongs with Chopin and Schumann to the early 19th cent. classic-romantic school, and his music has delicacy and melodic beauty. He was conductor of the Gewandhaus concerts at Leipzig for a time and often visited England. *See* **Section E.**

Mendès-France, Pierre (b. 1907), French politician, premier 1954–5, but defeated on his North African policy. He was a critic of de Gaulle.

Menuhin, Yehudi (b. 1916), American violinist, b. New York of Jewish parentage. He first appeared as soloist at the age of seven and has international repute.

Menzies, Sir Robert Gordon (b. 1894), Australian Liberal statesman, premier 1939–41, 1949–66.

Mercator, Gerhardus (Gerhard Kremer) (1512–94), Flemish geographer who pioneered the making of accurate navigational maps. He worked out the map which bears his name in which meridians and parallels of latitude cross each other at right angles, enabling compass bearings to be drawn as straight lines.

Meredith, George (1828–1909), English writer, b. Portsmouth. His novels include *The Ordeal of Richard Feverel*, *The Egoist*, *Evan Harrington*, *Diana of the Crossways*, and *The Amazing Marriage*. His poetry has had renewed attention; the main works are *Modern Love* and *Poems and Lyrics of the Joy of Earth*.

Mesmer, Friedrich Anton (1733–1815), Austrian founder of mesmerism, or animal magnetism. *See* **Mesmerism, Section J.**

Mestrovic, Ivan (1883–1962), Yugoslav sculptor of international repute. He designed the temple at Kossovo. He later lived in England, and examples of his work are in London museums.

Metastasio, Pietro (Pietro Bonaventura Trapassi) (1698–1782), Italian librettist who lived in Vienna and provided texts for Gluck, Handel, Haydn, and Mozart.

Mechnikov, Ilya (1845–1916), Russian biologist who discovered that by "phagocytosis" certain white blood cells are capable of ingesting harmful substances such as bacteria (*see* **Diseases of the Blood, Section P**). For his work on immunity he shared the 1908 Nobel prize for medicine.

Michelangelo (Michelagniolo Buonarroti) (1475–1564), Italian painter, sculptor and poet. Of a poor but genteel Tuscan family, his first interest in sculpture came through his nurse, wife of a stone-cutter. He was apprenticed to Domenico Ghirlandaio. Like Leonardo, he studied anatomy, but instead of spreading his talents over a wide field, he became obsessed with the problem of how to represent the human body. In him, classical idealism, mediaeval religious belief, and renaissance energy met. Perhaps his most impressive work is the ceiling of the Sistine Chapel (a surface of about 6,000 square feet), the *Last Judgement* behind the chapel altar, his marble *Pieta* (St. Peter's), the statue of *David* (Academy, Florence), the great figure of *Moses* (San Pietro in Vincoli, Rome), and the four allegorical figures *Day*, *Night*, *Dawn*, *Twilight* (intended for the tombs of the Medici family at San Lorenzo, Florence).

Michelet, Jules (1798–1874), French historian who wrote a history of France in 24 vols. and of the revolution in 7 vols.

Michelson, Albert Abraham (1852–1931), American physicist, b. Poland. He collaborated with E. W. Morley in an experiment to determine ether drift, the negative result of which was important for Einstein. Nobel prizewinner 1907. *See* **Relativity, Section F, Part II.**

Mickiewicz, Adam (1798–1855), Polish revolutionary poet, author of *The Ancestors* and *Pan Tadeusz*.

Mill, John Stuart (1806–73), English philosopher. A member of Bentham's utilitarian school, he later modified some of its tenets. His main work is *On Liberty*, which advocates social as well as political freedom and warns against the tyranny of the majority. *The Subjection of Women* supported women's rights. He also wrote *Principles of Political Economy*. He was godfather to Bertrand Russell.

Millais, Sir John Everett (1829–96), English artist, b. Southampton; in his earlier years a pre-Raphaelite (*Ophelia*). Later works include *The Boyhood of Raleigh* and *Bubbles*. He married Mrs. Ruskin after the annulment of her marriage.

Millet, Jean François (1814–75), French painter of rural life, sometimes in sombre mood; his works include *The Angelus*.

Millikan, Robert Andrews (1868–1954), American physicist, who determined the charge on the electron and discovered cosmic rays. Nobel prizewinner 1923.

Milne, Alan Alexander (1882–1956), English humorist and poet whose work for children is still widely read.

Milner, 1st Viscount (Alfred Milner) (1854–1925), British administrator, especially in South Africa; author of *England in Egypt*.

Miltiades (d. 489 B.C.), one of the leaders of the Athenian army against the Persians at Marathon.

Milton, John (1608–74), English poet, author of *Paradise Lost*. B. in London, he wrote while still at Cambridge *L'Allegro*, *Il Penseroso*, *Comus*, and *Lycidas*. The Civil War diverted his energies for years to the parliamentary and political struggle, but during this period he defended in *Areopagitica* the freedom of the press. After he had become blind he wrote *Paradise Lost* and a sonnet *On His Blindness*.

Minot, George Richards (1885–1950), who with W. P. Murphy discovered the curative properties of liver in pernicious anaemia. Shared Nobel prize 1934.

Mirabeau, Gabriel, Honoré Victor Riquetti, Comte de (1749–91), French revolutionary leader. His writings and speeches contributed to the revolution of 1789.

Mistral, Frédéric (1830–1914), French poet, and founder of a Provençal renaissance. His works include *Lou Trésor dóu Félibrige* and a Provençal dictionary. Nobel prizewinner 1904.

Mithridates (*c.* 132–63 B.C.), King of Pontus, in Asia Minor; after early successes against the Romans was defeated by Pompey.

Modigliani, Amedeo (1884–1920), Italian painter and sculptor, b. Livorno. His portraits and figure studies tend to elongation and simplification. He lived mainly in Paris, in poverty, illness and disillusionment.

Moffat, James (1870–1944), Scottish divine who translated the Bible into modern English.

Mohammed (570–632), the founder of Islam, the religion of the Moslems, fled from Mecca to Medina in 622, from which date the Mohammedan era opens. By his constant preaching and proclaiming of the one and only deity Allah, he gathered round him a small and loyal, hard-fighting band of followers and was able to return to Mecca eight years later, an acknowledged conqueror. The sacred book of Islam, the *Koran*—though presented by him as an original revelation from the angel Gabriel—may in the main be traced to biblical and rabbinical sources. *See* **Islam, Section J.**

Molière (Jean Baptiste Poquelin) (1622–73), French playwright. B. in Paris, he gained experience as a strolling player, and subsequently in Paris, partly in the king's service, he wrote an unsurpassed series of plays varying from farce as in *Les Précieuses ridicules* to high comedy. Among his plays are *Tartuffe*, *Le Misanthrope*, *Le Bourgeois gentilhomme*, *Le Malade imaginaire*, and *Le Médecin malgré lui*.

Molotov, Vyacheslav Mikhailovich (b. 1890), Russian diplomat. He succeeded Litvinov as commissar for foreign affairs, 1939–49, and was chief representative of the Soviet Union at numerous post-war conferences. Expelled from the Communist Party 1964. He changed his name from Scriabin to Molotov (the hammer) early in his career to escape the imperial police.

Moltke, Helmuth, Count von (1800–91), Prussian general and chief of staff (1858–88) during the period when Prussia used success in three wars to unite Germany.

Mond, Ludwig (1838–1909), German chemist who in 1867 settled in England as an alkali manufacturer and in partnership with John Brunner successfully manufactured soda by the Solvay process.

Monet, Claude (1840–1926), French painter, leader of the Impressionists, the term being derived in 1874 from his landscape *Impression soleil levant*. He liked painting a subject in the open air at different times of day to show variation in light.

Monier-Williams, Sir Monier (1819–99), English Sanskrit scholar whose works include grammars, dictionaries, and editions of the *Sákuntalá*.

Monk, George, 1st Duke of Albemarle (1608–69), English general and admiral, whose reputation and moderation were mainly responsible for the return of Charles II in 1660.

Monmouth, Duke of (James Scott) (1649–85), English pretender, natural son of Charles II; centre of anti-Catholic feeling against succession of Duke of York (later James II). His troops, mostly peasants, were routed at Sedgemoor (1685) by John Churchill (later Duke of Marlborough). Beheaded on Tower Hill.

Monnet, Jean (b. 1888), French political economist, "father of the Common Market." He drafted the Monnet plan for French economic recovery (1947) and the plan for the establishment of the European Coal and Steel Community, of which he was president 1952–5.

Monroe, James (1758–1831), president of the U.S. He negotiated the purchase of Louisiana from France in 1803, and propounded the doctrine that the American continent should not be colonised by a European power. (At that time however the U.S. could not have enforced it.)

Montagu, Lady Mary Wortley (1689–1762), English writer. From Constantinople where her husband was ambassador she wrote *Letters* of which a complete edition was published 1965–7. She introduced England to the idea of inoculation against smallpox.

Montaigne, Michel de (1533–92), French essayist of enquiring, sceptical, and tolerant mind.

Montcalm, Louis Joseph, Marquis de (1712–59), French general, who unsuccessfully commanded the French at Quebec against Wolfe.

Montesquieu, Charles de Secondat, Baron de la Brède et de (1689–1755), French philosopher. His works include *Lettres persanes*, a satire on contemporary life; and *L'Esprit des Lois*, giving his political philosophy. The latter was based largely, but to some extent mistakenly, on English practice, and its influence led the U.S. constitution to separate the executive (President) from the legislature (Congress).

Montessori, Maria (1860–1952), Italian educationist, who developed an educational system based on spontaneity.

Monteverdi, Claudio (1567–1643), Italian composer who pioneered in opera. His chief dramatic work is *Orfeo* (1608). *See* **Section E.**

Montezuma II (1466–1520), last emperor of Mexico when the Spanish under Cortes invaded.

Montfort, Simon de, Earl of Leicester (*c.* 1208–65), English statesman. He led the barons in revolt against the ineffective rule of Henry III, but he differed from other rebels in that he summoned a parliamentary assembly to which for the first time representatives came from the towns. He was killed at Evesham.

Montgolfier, the name of two brothers, **Joseph Michel** (1740–1810) and **Jacques Etienne** (1745–99), French aeronauts who constructed the first practical balloon, which flew 6 miles.

Montgomery of Alamein, 1st Viscount (Bernard Law Montgomery) (1887–1976), British field-marshal; commanded 8th Army in North Africa, Sicily, and Italy, 1942–4; commander-in-chief, British Group of Armies and Allied Armies in Northern France, 1944. He served as Deputy Supreme Allied Commander Europe (NATO), 1951–8. His memoirs were published in 1958.

Montrose, Marquess of (James Graham) (1612–50), Scottish general. In the Civil War he raised the Highland clansmen for Charles I and won the battles of Tippermuir, Inverlochy, and Kilsyth; but was finally defeated and executed. He was also a poet.

Moody, Dwight Lyman (1837–99), American revivalist preacher, associated with Ira D. Sankey, the "American singing pilgrim."

Moore, George (1852–1933), Irish novelist, author of *Confessions of a Young Man*, *Esther Waters*, and *Evelyn Innes*.

Moore, Henry (b. 1898), English sculptor in semi-abstract style, son of a Yorkshire coalminer. Examples of his work are to be seen in the Tate Gallery, St. Matthew's Church, Northampton, the Unesco building in Paris, and on an outside site opposite the House of Lords. O.M. 1963.

Moore, Sir John (1761–1809), British general, who trained the infantry for the Spanish Peninsular campaigns and conducted a brilliant retreat to Corunna, where he was mortally wounded after defeating the French under Soult.

Moore, Thomas (1779–1852), Irish poet, author of *Irish Melodies*, *Lalla Rookh* (oriental stories), and *The Epicurean* (novel). He also wrote a life of Byron.

More, Sir Thomas (1478–1535), English writer and statesman. In 1529 he succeeded Wolsey as lord chancellor, but on his refusal to recognise Henry VIII as head of the church he was executed. His *Utopia* describes an ideal state. He was canonised 1935.

Morgan, Sir Henry (*c.* 1635–88), Welsh buccaneer who operated in the Caribbean against the Spaniards, capturing and plundering Panama in 1671. Knighted by Charles II and made deputy-governor of Jamaica.

Morgan, John Pierpont (1837–1913), American financier who built the family fortunes into a vast industrial empire.

Morland, George (1763–1804), English painter of rural life. His *Inside of a Stable* is in the National Gallery

Morley, 1st Viscount (John Morley) (1838–1923), English biographer and Liberal politician. He held political office, but is mainly remembered for his life of Gladstone. He also wrote on Voltaire, Rousseau, Burke, and Cobden.

Morley, Thomas (*c.* 1557–1603), English composer of madrigals, noted also for his settings of some of Shakespeare's songs. He was a pupil of Byrd, organist of St. Paul's cathedral, and wrote *Plaine and Easie Introduction to Practicall Music* (1597) which was used for 200 years.

Morris, William (1834–96), English poet and craftsman. His hatred of 19th-cent. ugliness, his belief in human equality, and in freedom and happiness for all, combined to make him a socialist, and he accomplished much for the improvement of domestic decoration. He was a popular lecturer, founded the Socialist League and the Kelmscott Press.

Morrison of Lambeth, Baron (Herbert Morrison) (1888–1965), British Labour statesman. From being an errand-boy, he rose to become leader of the London County Council. During the war he was home secretary, and he was deputy prime minister in a period of notable legislation, 1945–51.

Morse, Samuel Finley Breese (1791–1872), American pioneer in electromagnetic telegraphy and inventor of the dot-and-dash code that bears his name. He was originally an artist.

Mountbatten of Burma, 1st Earl (Louis Mountbatten) (b. 1900), British admiral and statesman. In the second world war he became chief of combined operations in 1942. As last viceroy of India, he carried through the transfer of power to Indian hands in 1947 and was the first governor-general of the dominion. He became first sea lord in 1955 and was chief of defence staff 1959–65.

Mozart, Wolfgang Amadeus (1756–91), Austrian composer. B. Salzburg, he began his career at four and toured Europe at six. In 1781 he settled in Vienna, where he became a friend of Haydn and where his best music was written. His genius lies in the effortless outpouring of all forms of music, in the ever-flowing melodies, in the consistent beauty and symmetry of his compositions, and in the exactness of his method. Among the loveliest and grandest works in instrumental music are his three great symphonies in E flat, G minor, and C (called the "Jupiter"), all written in six weeks in 1788. Three of the greatest operas in musical history are his *Marriage of Figaro* (1786), *Don Giovanni* (1787), and *The Magic Flute* (1791). His last composition, written under the shadow of death, was the *Requiem Mass*, a work of tragic beauty. *See* **Section E.**

Müller, Sir Ferdinand (1825–96), German-born botanist who emigrated to Australia, where he was director of the Melbourne Botanical Gardens, 1857–73, and whence he introduced the eucalyptus into Europe.

Mumford, Lewis (b. 1895), American writer on town-planning and social problems. His works include a tetralogy: *Technics and Civilisation*, *The Culture of Cities*, *The Condition of Man*, and *The Conduct of Life; The Myth of the Machine*, and *The Urban Prospect*.

Munkacsy, Michael von (1844–1900), Hungarian painter of historical subjects.

Munnings, Sir Alfred (1878–1959), English painter, especially of horses and sporting subjects.

Murdock, William (1754–1839), Scottish engineer and inventor, the first to make practical use of coal gas as an illuminating agent (introduced at the Soho works, Birmingham, 1800).

Murillo, Bartolomé Esteban (1617–82), Spanish painter, b. Seville, where he founded an Academy. His early works, such as *Two Peasant Boys* (Dulwich) show peasant and street life; his later paintings are religious, *e.g.*, the *Immaculate Conception* in the Prado.

Murray, Gilbert (1866–1957), classical scholar of Australian birth who settled in England. A teacher of Greek at the universities of Glasgow and Oxford, he translated Greek drama so as to bring it within the reach of the general public. His interest in the classics was begun by an English master's enthusiasm at his country school at Mittagong, New South Wales. He was a strong supporter of the League of Nations and the United Nations.

Mussolini, Benito (1883–1945), Fascist dictator of Italy 1922–43. From 1935 an aggressive foreign policy (Abyssinia and Spain) was at first successful, and in June 1940 he entered the war on the side of Hitler. Defeat in North Africa and the invasion of Sicily caused the collapse of his government. He was shot dead by partisans while attempting to escape to Switzerland.

Mussorgsky, Modest Petrovich (1839–81), Russian composer whose masterpiece is the opera *Boris Godunov* after the play by Pushkin. His piano suite *Pictures at an Exhibition* was orchestrated by Ravel. *See* **Section E.**

N

Nanak (1469–1538), Indian guru or teacher, who tried to put an end to religious strife, teaching that "God is one, whether he be Allah or Rama." His followers are the Sikhs. *See* **Sikhism, Section J.**

Nansen, Fridtjof (1861–1930), Norwegian explorer. In 1893 his north polar expedition reached the highest latitude till then attained—86° 14′. He published an account called *Farthest North*. He was active in Russian famine relief, 1921. Nobel peace prize 1922.

Napier, John (1550–1617), Scottish mathematician, b. Edinburgh, invented logarithms (published 1614) and the modern notation of fractions, improvements in the methods of mathematical expression which helped to advance cosmology and physics.

Napoleon I (Bonaparte) (1769–1821), French emperor and general, of Corsican birth (Ajaccio). Trained in French military schools, he became prominent in the early years of the revolution, with uncertainty at home and war abroad. In 1796 he became commander of the army in Italy and defeated the Austrians, so that France obtained control of Lombardy. He then led an expedition to Egypt but Nelson destroyed his fleet. After further Italian victories, he made a *coup d'état* in 1799, and in 1804 became emperor. Against continuing European opposition, he defeated the Austrians at Austerlitz, and his power in Europe was such that he made his brothers Joseph, Louis, and Jerome kings of Naples, Holland, and Westphalia; but in Spain he provoked the Peninsular War, and his armies were gradually driven back by the Spanish, helped by Wellington; while his invasion of Russia in 1812 ended in a disastrous retreat from Moscow; and in 1814 the Allies forced him to abdicate and retire to Elba. He emerged again in 1815 to be defeated at Waterloo and exiled to St. Helena. His government at home was firm and promoted some reforms (*e.g.*, legal codification), but the country was weakened by his wars. In Europe, in spite of the suffering caused by war, there was some spread of French revolutionary ideas, and equally a reaction against them on the part of authority. The imperial idea lingered in France, and Napoleon's remains were brought to Paris in 1840. He married first Josephine Beauharnais and second Marie Louise of Austria.

Napoleon II (1811–32), son of Napoleon I and Marie Louise.

Napoleon III (1808–73), son of Napoleon I's brother Louis. He returned to France in the revolution of 1848, and in 1851 came to power by a *coup d'etat*. In his reign Paris was remodelled. His foreign policy was adventurous (the Crimean war, intervention in Mexico, war against Austria and Italy); but when he was manoeuvred by Bismarck into the Franco-Prussian war and defeated at Sedan he lost his throne and retired to England. His wife was the Spanish Eugénie de Montijo.

Nash, John (1752–1835), English architect who planned Regent Street, laid out Regent's Park, enlarged Buckingham Palace, and designed Marble Arch and the Brighton Pavilion.

Nash, Paul (1889–1946), English painter and designer, official war artist in both world wars. Best-known pictures are *The Menin Road* of 1918 and *Totes Meer* of 1941.

Nash, Walter (1882–1968), New Zealand Labour politician; prime minister 1957–60.

Nasmyth, James (1808–90), Scottish inventor of the steam-hammer, which became indispensable in all large iron and engineering works.

Nasser, Gamal Abdel (1918–70), leader of modern Egypt and of the Arab world. He led the 1952 army coup that deposed King Farouk, becoming president of the first Egyptian Republic in 1956 and of the United Arab Republic in 1958. His nationalisation of the Suez Canal in 1956 precipitated a short-lived attack by Britain and France. Israeli-Arab hostility led to the June war of 1967. He carried out reforms to bring his people out of feudal backwardness, including the building (with Russian help and finance) of the Aswan High Dam.

Needham, Joseph (b. 1900), British biochemist, historian of science, orientalist, author of the monumental work of scholarship *Science and Civilisation in China* (7 vols., 1954–).

Nehru, Pandit Jawaharlal (1889–1964), Indian national leader and statesman, first prime minister and minister of foreign affairs when India became independent in 1947. He studied at Harrow and Cambridge, and was for many years a leading member of the Congress Party, during which time he was frequently imprisoned for political activity. He played a part in the final negotiations for independence. Under his leadership India made technical, industrial, and social advances. In world affairs his influence was for peace and non-alignment. His daughter Indira became India's first woman prime minister in 1966.

Nelson, 1st Viscount (Horatio Nelson) (1758–1805), English admiral. Son of a Norfolk clergyman, he went to sea at 12 and became a captain in 1793. In the French revolutionary wars he lost his right eye in 1794 and his right arm in 1797. Rear-admiral in 1797, he defeated the French at Aboukir Bay in 1798. He was also at the bombardment of Copenhagen in 1801. In 1805 he destroyed the French fleet at Trafalgar, in which battle he was killed. His daring and decision made him a notable commander. He loved Emma Hamilton.

Nenni, Pietro (b. 1891), Italian socialist politician. He became secretary-general of his party in 1944, and was deputy prime minister, 1963–8.

Nernst, Walther Hermann (1864–1941), German scientist who established the third law of thermodynamics that dealt with the behaviour of matter at temperatures approaching absolute zero. Nobel prizewinner 1920.

Nero, Claudius Caesar (A.D. 37–68), Roman emperor, the adopted son of Claudius. He was weak and licentious and persecuted Christians. In his reign occurred the fire of Rome.

Newcomen, Thomas (1663–1729), English inventor, one of the first to put a steam-engine into practical operation. In 1705 he patented his invention, which was the pumping-engine used in Cornish mines until the adoption of Watt's engine.

Newman, Ernest (1868–1959), English music critic, whose chief work is the *Life of Richard Wagner*.

Newman, John Henry (1801–90), English priest and writer, who became a cardinal of the Roman church in 1879, and was a founder of the Oxford Movement. He is best remembered by his *Apologia pro Vita Sua* in which he described the development of his religious thought. He wrote *Lead, kindly Light*, set to music 30 years later by J. B. Dykes, and *The Dream of Gerontius*, set to music of Elgar. *See* **J52.**

Newton, Sir Isaac (1642–1727), English scientist, b. Woolsthorpe, Lincs. (the year Galileo died). He studied at Cambridge but was at home during the plague years 1665 and 1666 when he busied himself with problems concerned with optics and gravitation. Through his tutor Isaac Barrow he was appointed to the Lucasian chair of mathematics at Cambridge in 1669 and remained there until 1696 when he was appointed Warden, and later Master of the Mint. He was a secret Unitarian and did not marry. His three great discoveries were to show that white light could be separated into a sequence of coloured components forming the visible spectrum; to use the calculus (invented by him independently of Leibnitz) to investigate the forces of nature in a quantitative way; and to show by his theory of gravitation (for which Copernicus, Kepler and Galileo had prepared the way) that the universe was regulated by simple mathematical laws. His vision was set forth in the *Philosophiae Naturalis Principia Mathematica* of 1687, usually called the *Principia*. It was not until 200 years later that Einstein showed there could be another theory of celestial mechanics.

Ney, Michel (1769–1815), French general who served under Napoleon, especially at Jena, Borodino, and Waterloo.

Nicholas II (1868–1918), last emperor and Tsar of Russia, son of Alexander III. His reign was marked by an unsuccessful war with Japan (1904–5), and by the 1914–18 war. Ineffective and lacking ability, he set up a Duma in 1906 too late for real reform. Revolution broke out in 1917 and he and his family were shot in July 1918.

Nicholson, Sir William (1872–1949), English artist known for his portraits and woodcuts. His son, **Ben Nicholson, O.M.**, (b. 1894) is noted for his abstract paintings.

Nicolson, Sir Harold (1886–1968), English diplomat, author, and critic. His works include *King George V*; and *Diaries and Letters*. His wife was the novelist **Victoria Sackville-West** (1892–1962).

Niemöller, Martin (b. 1892), German Lutheran pastor who opposed the Nazi regime and was confined in a concentration camp. He was president of the World Council of Churches in 1961.

Nietzsche, Friedrich Wilhelm (1844–1900), German philosopher, in his younger years influenced by Wagner and Schopenhauer. His teaching that only the strong ought to survive and his doctrine of the superman are expounded in *Thus spake Zarathustra, Beyond Good and Evil*, and *The Will to Power*.

Nightingale, Florence (1820–1910), English nurse and pioneer of hospital reform, who during the Crimean war organised in face of considerable official opposition a nursing service to relieve the sufferings of the British soldiers, who called her " the lady with the lamp." Her system was adopted and developed in all parts of the world.

Nijinsky, Vaslav (1892–1950), Russian dancer, one of the company which included Pavlova, Karsavina and Fokine, brought by Diaghilev to Paris and London before the 1914–18 war. In *Les Sylphides, Spectre de la Rose* and *L'Après-midi d'un Faune* he won a supreme place among male dancers.

Nikisch, Arthur (1855–1922), Hungarian conductor of the Boston Symphony Orchestra, 1889–93. He was piano-accompanist to the Lieder singer, Elena Gerhardt.

Nimitz, Chester William (1885–1966), American admiral, commanded in the Pacific 1941–5; chief of naval operations 1945–7.

Nixon, Richard Milhous (b. 1913), Republican president (for two terms) of the U.S., 1969–74. In foreign affairs he negotiated the withdrawal of American troops from S. Vietnam and began a process of reconciliation with China and détente with the Soviet Union. But at home the Watergate conspiracies brought disgrace and an end to his presidency. His resignation in August 1974 rendered the impeachment process unnecessary; he accepted the pardon offered by his successor, President Ford. *See* **The United States, Section C, Part II.**

Nkrumah, Kwame (1909–72), Ghanaian leader, first premier of Ghana when his country achieved independence in 1957 and president in 1960. His government was spectacular and he promoted the Pan-African movement; but unsound finance and dictatorial methods led to his overthrow in 1966.

Nobel, Alfred Bernhard (1833–96), Swedish inventor and philanthropist. An engineer and chemist who discovered dynamite, he amassed a fortune from the manufacture of explosives; and bequeathed a fund for annual prizes to those who had contributed most to the benefit of mankind in the fields of physics, chemistry, medicine, literature and peace. *See* **L126–8.**

North, Frederick (1732–92), favourite minister of George III who held the premiership from 1770 to 1782. (He held the courtesy title of Lord North from 1752.) His incompetent foreign policy led to the American war of independence.

Northcliffe, 1st Viscount (Alfred Charles Harmsworth) (1865–1922), British journalist and newspaper proprietor, b. near Dublin. He began *Answers* in 1888 with his brother Harold, (later Lord Rothermere). In 1894 they bought the *Evening News*, and in 1896 the *Daily Mail*. In 1908 he took over *The Times*.

Northumberland, John Dudley, Duke of (1502–53), English politician who attempted to secure for his daughter-in-law Lady Jane Grey the succession to the throne after Edward VI.

Nostradamus or **Michel de Notre Dame** (1503–66), French astrologer and physician, known for his prophecies in *Centuries*.

Novalis, the pseudonym of Baron Friedrich von Hardenberg (1772–1801), German romantic poet and novelist, whose chief work is the unfinished *Heinrich von Ofterdingen*.

Nuffield, 1st Viscount (William Richard Morris) (1877–1963), British motor-car manufacturer and philanthropist, and until he retired in 1952 chairman of Morris Motors Ltd. He provided large sums for the advancement of medicine in the university of Oxford, for Nuffield College, and in 1943 established the Nuffield Foundation, endowing it with £10 million.

Nyerere, Julius (b. 1922), Tanzanian leader. He became first premier of Tanganyika when it became independent in 1961; and president in 1962. In 1964 he negotiated its union with Zanzibar.

O

Oates, Lawrence Edward (1880–1912), English antarctic explorer. He joined Scott's expedition of 1910, and was one of the five to reach the south pole; but on the return journey, being crippled by frost-bite, he walked out into the blizzard to die.

Oates, Titus (1649–1705), English informer and agitator against Roman catholics.

O'Casey, Sean (1884–1964), Irish dramatist whose plays include *Juno and the Paycock, The Silver Tassie, Red Roses for Me*, and *Oak Leaves and Lavender*.

Occam (Ockham), William of (c. 1270–1349), English scholar and philosopher and one of the most original thinkers of all time. He belonged to the Order of Franciscans, violently opposed the temporal power of the Pope, espoused the cause of nominalism and laid the foundations of modern theories of government and theological scepticism. *See* **Occam's razor, Section J.**

O'Connell, Daniel (1775–1847), Irish national leader. A barrister, he formed the Catholic Association in 1823 to fight elections; his followers aimed at the repeal of the Act of Union with England, and formed a Repeal Association in 1840; but the formation of the Young Ireland party, the potato famine, and ill-health undermined his position and he died in exile.

O'Connor, Feargus (1794–1855), working-class leader in England, of Irish birth. He presented the Chartist petition in 1848.

O'Connor, Thomas Power (1848–1929), Irish nationalist and journalist, sat in parliament 1880–1929 and founded the *Star*.

Oersted, Hans Christian (1777–1851), Danish physicist who discovered the connection between electricity and magnetism.

Offa (d. 796), king of Mercia (mid-England), was the leading English king of his day, and built a defensive dyke from the Dee to the Wye.

Offenbach, Jacques (1819–80), German-Jewish composer, b. Cologne, settled at Paris, and is mainly known for his light operas, especially *Tales of Hoffmann*.

Ohm, Georg Simon (1787–1854), German physicist, professor at Munich, who in 1826 formulated the law of electric current, known as Ohm's law, one of the foundation stones in electrical science. *See* **L86.**

Olivier, Baron (Laurence Kerr Olivier) (b. 1907), British actor and director, especially in Shakespearean roles. He has also produced, directed, and played in films, including *Henry V, Hamlet*, and *Richard III*, and in television drama. In 1962 he was appointed director of the National Theatre (*see* **Section I, Part II**), and in 1970 received a life peerage.

Oman, Sir Charles William (1860–1946), English historian, especially of mediaeval warfare and of the Peninsular War. He also wrote memoirs.

Omar ibn al Khattab (581–644), adviser to Mahomet, succeeded Abu Bakr as 2nd caliph. In his reign Islam became an imperial power. He died at the hands of a foreign slave.

Omar Khayyám (*c*. 1050–1123), Persian poet and mathematician, called Khayyám (tent-maker) because of his father's occupation. His fame as a scientist has been eclipsed by his *Rubaiyat*, made known to English readers by Edward FitzGerald in 1859.

O'Neill, Eugene Gladstone (1888–1953), American playwright who, after spending his adventurous youth in sailing, gold-prospecting, and journalism, first won success in 1914 with the one-act play, *Thirst*. His later plays include *Anna Christie*, *Strange Interlude*, *Mourning Becomes Electra*, *The Iceman Cometh*. Nobel prizewinner 1936. *See also* **Section I.**

Orchardson, Sir William Quiller (1835–1910), Scottish painter, b. Edinburgh, best known for his *Napoleon I on board H.M.S. Bellerophon* and *Ophelia*.

Origen (*c*. 185–254), Christian philosopher and Biblical scholar, who taught at Alexandria and Caesarea, and was imprisoned and tortured in the persecution of Decius, 250. He drew on Greek philosophy as well as on the Hebrew scriptures in his exposition of Christian doctrine.

Orpen, Sir William (1878–1931), British painter of portraits, conversation pieces, and pictures of the 1914–18 war.

Ortega y Gasset, José (1883–1955), Spanish philosopher and essayist, known for his *Tema de Nuestro Tiempo* and *La Rebelión de Las Masas*.

Orwell, George (Eric Arthur Blair) (1903–50), English satirist, b. India, author of *Animal Farm* and *Nineteen Eighty-Four*.

Osler, Sir William (1849–1919), Canadian physician and medical historian, authority on diseases of the blood and spleen.

Ossietzky, Carl von (1889–1938), German pacifist leader after the first world war; sent by Hitler to a concentration camp. Nobel peace prize 1935.

Oswald, St. (*c*. 605–42), won the Northumbrian throne by battle in 633 and introduced Christianity there.

Otto I (the Great) (912–73), founder of the Holy Roman Empire (he was crowned king of the Germans in 936 and emperor at Rome in 962). The son of Henry I of Germany, he built up a strong position in Italy (as regards the papacy) and in Germany where he established the East Mark (Austria).

Otto, Nikolaus August (1832–91), German engineer who built a gas engine (1878) using the four-stroke cycle that bears his name.

Ouida (Maria Louise Ramé) (1939–1908), English novelist of French extraction, whose romantic stories include *Under Two Flags*.

Ovid (43 B.C.–A.D. 18), Latin poet (Publius Ovidius Naso), chiefly remembered for his *Art of Love* and *Metamorphoses*. He died in exile.

Owen, Robert (1771–1858), Welsh pioneer socialist, b. Montgomeryshire. As manager, and later owner, of New Lanark cotton mills he tried to put his philanthropic views into effect; other communities on co-operative lines were founded in Hampshire and in America (New Harmony, Indiana) but although unsuccessful they were influential in many directions. He challenged the doctrine of *laissez-faire*, inaugurated socialism and the co-operative movement, and foresaw the problems of industrial development.

P

Pachmann, Vladimir de (1848–1933), Russian pianist gifted in the playing of Chopin.

Paderewski, Ignace Jan (1860–1941), Polish pianist and nationalist. He represented his country at Versailles and was the first premier of a reconstituted Poland. He died in exile in the second world war.

Paganini, Niccolo (1782–1840), Italian violinist and virtuoso who revolutionised violin technique.

Paine, Thomas (1737–1809)k English-born radical political writer, champion of agrarian reform. He spent the years 1774–87 in America helping the American revolutionary cause. On his return to England he wrote *The Rights of Man*, was condemned for treason, and had to flee to France. There he entered French politics, was sent to prison, and wrote *The Age of Reason*, advocating deism. His last years were spent in poverty in America.

Palestrina, Giovanni Pierluigi da (*c*. 1525–94), Italian composer of unaccompanied church music and madrigals. *See* **Section E.**

Palgrave, Sir Francis (1788–1861), English historian and archivist, an early editor of record series. His son **Francis Turner Palgrave** (1824–97) was a poet and critic and edited *The Golden Treasury*; while another son, **William Gifford Palgrave** (1826–88) was a traveller and diplomat.

Palissy, Bernard (*c*. 1510–89), French potter who discovered the art of producing white enamel, after which he set up a porcelain factory in Paris which was patronised by royalty.

Palladio, Andrea (1508–80), Italian architect, b. Padua, whose style was modelled on ancient Roman architecture (symmetrical planning and harmonic proportions) and had wide influence; author of *I Quattro Libri dell' Architettura*.

Palmer, Samuel (1805–81), English landscape painter and etcher, follower of Blake whom he met in 1824. *Bright Cloud* and *In a Shoreham Garden* are in the Victoria and Albert Museum.

Palmerston, 3rd Viscount (Henry John Temple) (1784–1865), English Whig statesman. At first a Tory, he was later Whig foreign secretary for many years, and prime minister 1855 and 1859–65. His vigorous foreign policy wherever possible took the lead and bluntly asserted English rights.

Pancras, St. (d. 304), patron saint of children, was (according to tradition) baptised in Rome where he was put to death at the age of fourteen in the persecution under Diocletian.

Pandit, Vijaya Lakshmi (b. 1900), sister of Nehru, was India's first ambassador to the Soviet Union (1947–9), and to the U.S. (1949–51), and the first woman to be elected president of the U.N. General Assembly (1954).

Panizzi, Sir Anthony (1797–1879), Italian bibliographer and nationalist. Taking refuge in England after 1821, he became in 1856 chief libarian of the British Museum, undertook a new catalogue and designed the reading room.

Pankhurst, Emmeline (1858–1928), English suffragette who, with her daughters Christabel and Sylvia, worked for women's suffrage, organising the Women's Social and Political Union.

Papin, Denis (1647–1714), French physicist and inventor. He invented the condensing pump, and was a pioneer in the development of the steam-engine. Not being a mechanic, he made all his experiments by means of models.

Paracelsus (Theophrastus Bombastus von Hohenheim) (1493–1541), Swiss physician whose speculations though muddled served to reform medical thought. He criticised the established authorities, Galen and Aristotle, and experimented and made new chemical compounds. His earliest printed work was *Practica* (1529).

Park, Mungo (1771–1806), Scottish explorer in west Africa, where he lost his life. He wrote *Travels in the Interior of Africa* (1799).

Parker of Waddington, Baron (Hubert Lister Parker) (1900–72) Lord Chief Justice of England 1958–70.

Parker, Joseph (1830–1902), English Congregational preacher, especially at what later became the City Temple.

Parnell, Charles Stewart (1846–91), Irish national leader. To draw attention to Ireland's problems, he used obstruction in parliament. He was president of the Land League but was not implicated in crimes committed by some members. His party supported Gladstone, who became converted to Home Rule. His citation in divorce proceedings brought his political career to an end.

Parry, Sir William Edward (1790–1855), English explorer and naval commander in the Arctic, where he was sent to protect fisheries and also tried to reach the north pole.

Parsons, Sir Charles Algernon (1854–1931),

English inventor of the steam-turbine, who built the first turbine-driven steamship in 1897.

Pascal, Blaise (1623–62), Frenchman of varied gifts, b. at Clermont-Ferrand. At first a mathematician, he patented a calculating machine. His *Lettres provinciales* influenced Voltaire. In 1654 he turned to religion, and his incomplete religious writings were published posthumously as *Pensées*. *See also* **Jansenism, Section J.**

Pasternak, Boris Leonidovich (1890–1960), Russian poet and writer. B. Moscow, he published his first poems in 1931. For some years his time was spent in translating foreign literature, but in 1958 his novel *Dr. Zhivago*, which describes the Russian revolution and is in the Russian narrative tradition, was published abroad, though banned in the Soviet Union. He was awarded a Nobel prize but obliged to decline it.

Pasteur, Louis (1822–95), French chemist, b. at Dôle in the Jura, whose work was inspired by an interest in the chemistry of life. His researches on fermentation led to the science of bacteriology and his investigations into infectious diseases and their prevention to the science of immunology. The pathological-bacteriological import of his researches came about mainly through his disciples (Lister, Roux, and others) and not directly, though all founded on his early non-medical investigations on organisms of fermentation, etc., which were of great importance in industry, and fundamentally. He spent most of his life as director of scientific studies at the Ecole Normale at Paris. The Institute Pasteur was founded in 1888.

Patmore, Coventry (1823–96), English poet. *The Angel in the House* deals with domesticity. Later he became a Roman catholic, and *The Unknown Eros* is characterised by erotic mysticism.

Patrick, St. (*c.* 389–*c.* 461), apostle of Ireland, was born in Britain or Gaul, and after some time on the continent (taken thither after his capture by pirates) went as missionary to Ireland, where after years of teaching and a visit to Rome he fixed his see at Armagh. He wrote *Confessions*.

Patti, Adelina (1843–1919), coloratura soprano, b. in Madrid of Italian parents, and of international repute.

Paul, St. (*c.* A.D. 10–*c.* 67), Jew to whom was mainly due the extension of Christianity in Europe. B. Tarsus (in Asia Minor), he was a Pharisee, and became converted about A.D. 37. His missionary journeys took him to the Roman provinces of Asia, Macedonia, and Greece (Rome had already had Christian teaching); and his epistles form nearly half the New Testament and were written before the gospels. He helped to develop both the organisation of the early church and its teaching. The date order of his epistles is to some extent conjectural. It is believed that he was executed in Rome. His Hebrew name was Saul.

Paul VI (Giovanni Battista Montini) (b. 1897), elected Pope in 1963 on the death of John XXIII. He was formerly archbishop of Milan. He visited the Holy Land in 1964.

Pauli, Wolfgang (1900–58), Austrian-born physicist who first predicted theoretically the existence of neutrinos (*see* **F14**). Nobel prizewinner 1945.

Pavlov, Ivan Petrovich (1849–1936), Russian physiologist, known for his scientific experimental work on animal behaviour, particularly conditioned reflexes and the relation between psychological stress and brain function. Nobel prizewinner 1904. *See* **Q17–18.**

Pavlova, Anna (1882–1931), Russian ballerina, b. St. Petersburg, excelling in the roles of *Giselle* and the *Dying Swan*.

Peabody, George (1795–1869), American philanthropist, a successful merchant who lived mainly in London. He supported exploration and education.

Peacock, Thomas Love (1785–1866), English novelist, b. Weymouth. His work, which is mainly satirical, includes *Headlong Hall* and *Nightmare Abbey*.

Pearson, Lester Bowles (1897–1972), Canadian politician, served as minister for external affairs 1948–57, and prime minister 1963–8. He supported the United Nations. Nobel peace prize 1957.

Peary, Robert Edwin (1856–1920), American arctic explorer, discoverer of the north pole (1909).

Peel, Sir Robert (1788–1850), English Conservative statesman, b. in Lancashire, son of a manufacturer. He first held office in 1811. With Wellington he enacted toleration for Roman catholics in 1829. As home secretary he reorganised London police. He developed a new policy of Conservatism, and in 1846, largely as a result of the Irish famine, he repealed the corn laws which protected English agriculture. He died from a riding accident.

Peirce, Charles Sanders (1839–1914), American physicist and philosopher of original mind, founder of the theory of pragmatism which was later developed by his friend William James. *See* **Pragmatism, Section J.**

Penfield, Wilder Graves (1891–1976), Canadian brain surgeon, author of *The Cerebral Cortex of Man, Epilepsy and the Functional Anatomy of the Human Brain*. O.M.

Penn, William (1644–1718), English Quaker and founder of Pennsylvania. The son of Admiral William Penn, he persisted in becoming a Quaker, and on receiving for his father's services a crown grant in North America he founded there Pennsylvania. He wrote *No Cross, No Crown*.

Penney, Baron (William George Penney) (b. 1909), British scientist. His nuclear research team at A.E.A. developed the advanced gas-cooled reactor (A.G.R.) chosen for the Dungeness "B" and Hinkley Point "B" power stations.

Pepys, Samuel (1633–1703), English diarist and naval administrator. His diary, 1660–69, was kept in cipher and not deciphered till 1825. It gives vivid personal details and covers the plague and fire of London. (The first complete and unexpurgated version of the diary was issued in 1970.)

Pereda, José María de (1833–1906), Spanish regional novelist (around his native Santander).

Pérez Galdós, Benito (1843–1920), Spanish novelist and dramatist, who has been compared to Balzac for his close study and portrayal of all social classes, especially in the series of 46 short historical novels *Episodios nacionales*. His longer novels, *Novelas españolas contemporáneas*, some of which are translated, number 31.

Pergolesi, Giovanni Battista (1710–36), Italian composer, best known for his humorous opera *La Serva Padrona* and his *Stabat Mater*.

Pericles (*c.* 490–429 B.C.), Athenian statesman, general, and orator, who raised Athens to the point of its fullest prosperity, and greatest beauty, with the Parthenon, Erechtheum, and other buildings; but he died in the plague which followed the outbreak of the Peloponnesian war.

Perkin, Sir William Henry (1838–1907), English chemist, b. London, who while seeking to make a substitute for quinine discovered in 1856 the first artificial aniline dye, mauve. His son, **W. H. Perkin** (1860–1929) was an organic chemist of note.

Perrin, Francis (b. 1901), French scientist and socialist; succeeded Joliot-Curie as High Commr. of Atomic Energy, 1951–; professor of Atomic Physics, Collège de France, 1946–. Nobel prizewinner 1926.

Persius Flaccus Aulus (A.D. 34–62), Roman satirist and Stoic philosopher.

Perugino, Pietro (1446–1524), Italian artist. He worked in the Sistine Chapel at Rome and he taught Raphael.

Pestalozzi, Johann Heinrich (1746–1827), Swiss educational reformer whose theories laid the foundation of modern primary education. His teaching methods were far in advance of his time. He wrote *How Gertrude Educates Her Children*.

Pétain, Henri Philippe (1856–1951), French general and later collaborator. In the first world war he was in command at Verdun, and between the wars he sponsored the Maginot line. In the second world war, when French resistance collapsed, he came to terms with Germany and headed an administration at Vichy. After the war he was sentenced to life imprisonment.

Peter I, the Great (1672–1725), emperor of Russia. Son of Alexei, he succeeded his brother after some difficulty. He reorganised the army, and, after coming to Deptford to learn shipbuilding, he created a navy. To some extent he westernised Russian social life, and created a new capital at St. Petersburg (1703). In war with Charles XII of Sweden he was at first defeated, but later victorious at Poltava (1709). He married a peasant, Catherine, who succeeded him.

Peter the Hermit (*c.* 1050–1115), French monk who preached the First Crusade, originated by pope Urban II at the council of Clermont. He went on the crusade himself, but gave up at Antioch.

Petrarch, Francesco (1304–74), Italian poet, son of a Florentine exile. He is chiefly remembered for his poems *To Laura*, but he was also a scholar who paved the way for the Renaissance.

Petrie, Sir Flinders (1853–1942), British egyptologist. He excavated in Britain (1875–90), Egypt (1880–1924), and Palestine 1927–38). See his *Seventy Years of Archaeology*.

Phidias (5th cent. B.C.), Greek sculptor especially in gold, ivory and bronze, worked at Athens for Pericles. No certain examples of his work are extant, but the Elgin marbles in the British Museum may be from his designs.

Philip II of France (1165–1223), son of Louis VII. He went on the Third Crusade with Richard I of England, but in France is mainly remembered for firm government, the recovery of Normandy from England, and the beautifying of Paris.

Philip II of Macedonia (382–336 B.C.), a successful commander, made his the leading military kingdom in Greece and was father of Alexander the Great.

Philip II of Spain (1527–98), succeeded his father Charles V in Spain and the Netherlands, also in Spanish interests overseas. In the Netherlands his strict Roman catholic policy provoked a revolt which ended in 1579 in the independence of the United Provinces. He married Mary Tudor of England; and after her death sent the ill-fated Armada against Elizabeth in 1588.

Philip V of Spain (1683–1746), first Bourbon king, succeeded his uncle Charles II and was grandson of Louis XIV. His accession provoked European war.

Phillip, Arthur (1738–1814), first governor of New South Wales. Under his command the first fleet of 717 convicts set sail from Britain to Australia, and with the founding of Sydney in 1788 colonisation of the whole country began.

Phillips, Stephen (1868–1915), English poet who wrote verse dramas, including *Paolo and Francesca*.

Piast, first Polish dynasty in Poland until the 14th cent. and until the 17th cent. in Silesia.

Piazzi, Giuseppe (1746–1826), Italian astronomer who discovered Ceres, the first of the asteroids to be seen by man.

Picasso, Pablo Ruiz (1881–1973) Spanish painter, b. Málaga; received his early training in Catalonia and settled in Paris in 1903. He and Braque were the originators of Cubism (*c.* 1909). His influence over contemporary art is comparable with that exercised by Cézanne (*q.v.*) over the artists of his time. Perhaps the best-known single work is his mural *Guernica*, painted at the time of the Spanish civil war, expressing the artist's loathing of fascism and the horrors of war. His genius also found scope in sculpture, ceramics, and the graphic arts, and he designed décor costumes for the ballet.

Piccard, Auguste (1884–1962), Swiss physicist, noted for balloon ascents into the stratosphere and for submarine research. In 1960 his son Jacques made a descent of over 7 miles in the Marianas trench in the western Pacific in a bathyscaphe designed and built by his father.

Pilsudski, Joseph (1867–1935), Polish soldier and statesman who in 1919 attempted by force to restore Poland's 1772 frontiers but was driven back. From 1926 he was dictator.

Pindar (522–443 B.C.), Greek lyric poet.

Pinero, Sir Arthur Wing (1855–1934), English dramatist whose plays include *Dandy Dick*, *The Second Mrs. Tanqueray* and *Mid-Channel*.

Pirandello, Luigi (1867–1936), Italian dramatist and novelist whose plays include *Six Characters in Search of an Author*. Nobel prizewinner 1934.

Pissarro, Camille (1830–1903), French impressionist painter of landscapes; studied under Corot.

Pitman, Sir Isaac (1813–97) b. Trowbridge, English inventor of a system of phonographic shorthand.

Pitt, William (1759–1806), English statesman. Younger son of the Earl of Chatham, he entered parliament at 21 and became prime minister at 24 in 1783 when parties were divided and the American war had been lost. He rose to the position, and held office with scarcely a break till his death. An able finance minister, he introduced reforms, and would have gone further, but Napoleon's meteoric rise obliged him to lead European allies in a long struggle against France. He died worn out by his efforts.

Pius XII (1876–1958), elected Pope 1939. As Eugenio Pacelli, he was papal nuncio in Germany and later papal secretary of state. It has been argued that, as Pope in wartime, he could have taken a stronger line against Nazi war crimes.

Pizarro, Francisco (*c.* 1478–1541), Spanish adventurer, b. Trujillo. After Columbus's discoveries, he conquered Peru for Spain, overthrowing the Inca empire. He was murdered by his men.

Planck, Max (1857–1947), German mathematical physicist, b. Kiel, whose main work was on thermodynamics. In 1900 he invented a mathematical formula to account for some properties of the thermal radiation from a hot body which has since played an important role in physics. Nobel prizewinner 1918. *See* **Quantum theory, F13.**

Plato (427–347 B.C.), Athenian philosopher, pupil of Socrates, teacher of Aristotle. He founded a school at Athens under the name of the Academy, where he taught philosophy and mathematics. His great work is his *Dialogues*, which includes the *Republic*, the longest and most celebrated. His known writings have come down to us and constitute one of the most influential bodies of work in history. *See also* **Mind and Matter, Section J.**

Playfair, 1st Baron (Lyon Playfair) (1818–98), a far-sighted Victorian who stood for the greater recognition of science in national life. He forsook his profession as professor of chemistry at Edinburgh to enter parliament. Pres. British Association 1885.

Plimsoll, Samuel (1824–98), English social reformer, b. Bristol. He realised the evil of overloading unseaworthy ships, and as M.P. for Derby he procured the passing of the Merchant Shipping Act, 1876 which imposed a line (the Plimsoll Mark) above which no ship must sink while loading.

Pliny the Elder (A.D. 23–79), Roman naturalist, author of a *Natural History*. He died of fumes and exhaustion while investigating the eruption of Vesuvius. His nephew, **Pliny the Younger** (A.D. 62–113), wrote *Letters* notable for their charm and the insight they give into Roman life.

Plotinus (*c.* 203–*c.* 262), Greek philosopher, was the founder of Neoplatonism, which had considerable influence on early Christian thought. *See also* **God and Man, Section J.**

Plutarch (*c.* 46–120), Greek biographer, whose *Lives* portray 46 leading historical figures (in pairs, a Greek and a Roman whose careers were similar). Although based on myth his *Life of Lycurgus* about life in Sparta had a profound influence on later writers, *e.g.*, Rousseau and the romantic philosophers. He was educated at Athens but visited Rome.

Poe, Edgar Allan (1809–49), American poet and story-writer, b. Boston, Mass. His poems include *The Raven*, *To Helen*, and *Annabel Lee*, and his stories, often weird and fantastic, include *Tales of the Grotesque and Arabesque*.

Poincaré, Raymond Nicolas (1860–1934), French statesman. He was president 1913–20, and as prime minister occupied the Ruhr in 1923.

Pole, Reginald (1500–58), archbishop of Canterbury, cardinal of the Roman church and antagonist of the reformation. He opposed Henry VIII's divorce and went abroad in 1532, writing *De Unitate Ecclesiastica*; as a result of which his mother, Countess of Salisbury, and other relatives were executed. Under Queen Mary Tudor he became archbishop and died the year she did.

Pollard, Albert Frederick (1869–1948), English historian, especially of the Tudor period, and first director of the Institute of Historical Research.

Polo, Marco (1256–1323), Venetian traveller, who made journeys through China, India, and other eastern countries, visiting the court of Kubla Khan, and publishing an account of his travels.

Pompadour, Jeanne Antoine Poisson, Marquise de (1721–64), mistress of Louis XV of France, who exercised disastrous political influence.

Pompey (106–48 B.C.), Roman commander, who cleared the Mediterranean of pirates, and became triumvir with Caesar and Crassus.

Pompidou, Georges Jean Raymond (1911–74), French administrator and politician who succeeded de Gaulle as president 1969.

Pope, Alexander (1688–1744), English poet, b. London, of a Roman catholic family, and largely self-educated. His brilliant satire was frequently directed against his contemporaries. He is especially remembered for *The Rape of the Locke*, *The Dunciad*, *Essay on Criticism*, and *Essay on Man*.

Popper, Sir Karl (b. 1902), British philosopher of science, b. Vienna; author of *The Open Society and Its Enemies* (1945), *Conjectures and Refutations* (1963), *Objective Knowledge* (1972). He rejects the doctrine that all knowledge starts from perception or sensation and holds that it grows through conjecture and refutation.

Pound, Ezra Loomis (1885–1972), American poet and writer on varied subjects, a controversial figure. He is noted for his translations of Provençal, Latin, Chinese, French, and Italian poets.

Poussin, Nicolas (1593–1665), French painter. He lived in Rome 1624–40, 1642–65. His *Golden Calf* is in the National Gallery.

Powys, John Cowper (1872–1964), English writer, best known for his novel *Wolf Solent* and his essays *The Meaning of Culture* and *A Philosophy of Solitude*. His brothers, **Theodore Francis** (1875–1953) and **Llewelyn** (1884–1939) were also original writers.

Prasad, Rajendra (1884–1963), Indian statesman, first president of the Republic of India, 1950–62.

Praxiteles (4th cent. B.C.), Greek sculptor, whose main surviving work is *Hermes carrying Dionysus*.

Preece, Sir William Henry (1834–1913), Welsh electrical engineer, associated with the expansion of wireless telegraphy and telephony in the United Kingdom. He was connected with Marconi and introduced the block system.

Prichard, James Cowles (1786–1848), English ethnologist who perceived that people should be studied as a whole. His works include *Researches into the Physical History of Mankind* and *The Natural History of Man*. He practised medicine.

Priestley, John Boynton (b. 1894), English critic, novelist, and playwright, b. Bradford. His works include the novels *The Good Companions*, *Angel Pavement*, and the plays *Dangerous Corner*, *Time and the Conways*, *I Have Been Here Before*, and *The Linden Tree*.

Priestley, Joseph (1733–1804), English chemist who worked on gases, and shared with Scheele the discovery of oxygen. A presbyterian minister, he was for his time an advanced thinker. In 1794 he settled in America.

Prior, Matthew (1664–1721), English poet. In early life he was a diplomat. He was a neat epigrammatist and writer of occasional pieces. His works include *The City Mouse and Country Mouse* and *Four Dialogues of the Dead*.

Prokofiev, Serge Sergeyevich (1891–1953), Russian composer, whose music has a strong folk-song element, rich in melody and invention. He has written operas: *The Love of Three Oranges*, *The Betrothal in a Nunnery*, *War and Peace*; ballets: *Romeo and Juliet*, *Cinderella*; symphonies, chamber music, and the music for Eisenstein's films *Alexander Nevsky*, *Ivan the Terrible*.

Protagoras (c. 480–411 B.C.), Greek philosopher, chief of the Sophists, noted for his scepticism and disbelief in objective truth, and for his doctrine that "man is the measure of all things."

Proudhon, Pierre Joseph (1809–65), French socialist. In 1840 he propounded the view that property is theft. His main work is *Système des contradictions économiques* (1846). He was frequently in prison.

Proust, Marcel (1871–1922), French psychological novelist, author of a series of novels known under the title of *A la recherche du temps perdu*. His works have been admirably translated into English by C. K. Scott Moncrieff.

Ptolemy of Alexandria (Claudius Ptolemaeus) (fl. A.D. 140), astronomer and founder of scientific cartography. In the *Almagest* he attempted a mathematical presentation of the paths along which the planets appear to move in the heavens. His other great work was his *Geographical Outline*.

Puccini, Giacomo (1858–1924), Italian composer, b. Lucca, whose operas include *Manon Lescaut*, *La Bohême*, *Tosca*, *Madam Butterfly*, and *Turandot* (completed by a friend).

Pupin, Michael Idvorsky (1858–1935), physicist and inventor (telephony and X-rays), b. Idvor, Hungary (now in Yugoslavia); went to America penniless 1874 to become professor of electromechanics at Columbia University.

Purcell, Henry (1658–95), English composer, b. Westminster, son of a court musician. He became organist of the chapel royal and composer to Charles II. His best works are vocal and choral. He also wrote for the stage. *See* **Section E.**

Pusey, Edward Bouverie (1800–82), English theologian, a leader of the Oxford or Tractarian movement with Keble and at first also with Newman, till the latter became Roman catholic. The movement aimed at revival. *See* **Tractarianism, Section J.**

Pushkin, Alexander (1799–1837), Russian writer, b. Moscow, whose place in Russian literature ranks with Shakespeare's in English. He wrote in many forms—lyrical poetry and narrative verse, drama, folk-tales and short stories. Musicians have used his works as plots for operas—the fairy romance *Russlan and Ludmilla* was dramatised by Glinka; the verse novel *Eugene Onegin* and the short story *The Queen of Spades* were adapted by Tchaikovsky, and the tragic drama *Boris Godunov* formed the subject of Mussorgsky's opera. Like Lermontov, who too was exiled, he was inspired by the wild beauty of the Caucasus. He was killed in a duel defending his wife's honour.

Pym, John (1584–1643), English parliamentary leader in opposition to Charles I. He promoted the impeachment of the king's advisers, Strafford and Laud.

Pythagoras (c. 582–500 B.C.), Greek philosopher, b. on the island of Samos, off the Turkish mainland, which he left c. 530 to settle at Croton, a Greek city in southern Italy. He was a mystic and mathematician, and founded a brotherhood who saw in numbers the key to the understanding of the universe.

Q

Quasimodo, Salvatore (1901–68), Italian poet of humanity and liberal views whose works include *La vita non e sogno*. Nobel prizewinner 1959.

Quesnay, François (1694–1774), French economist, founder of the physiocratic school who believed in *laizzez-faire* and influenced the thought of Adam Smith. *See* **Physiocrats, Section J.**

Quiller-Couch, Sir Arthur Thomas (1863–1944), English man of letters, b. Bodmin, known as "Q." He edited the *Oxford Book of English Verse* and his works include *From a Cornish Window*.

R

Rabelais, François (c. 1495–1553), French satirist. At first in religious orders, he late studied medicine and practised at Lyons. His works, mainly published under a pseudonym, are full of riotous mirth, wit and wisdom. The main ones are *Gargantua* and *Pantagruel*.

Rachel, Élisa (Élisa Felix) (1821–58), Alsatian-Jewish tragic actress. Her chief triumph was in Racine's *Phèdre*.

Rachmaninov, Sergey Vasilyevich (1873–1943), Russian composer and pianist, b. Nijni-Novgorod (now Gorki), best known for his piano music, especially his *Prelude*. After the Russian revolution he settled in America. *See* **Section E.**

Racine, Jean (1639–99), French tragic poet whose dramas include *Andromaque*, *Iphigénie* and *Phèdre*. An orphan, he was brought up by grandparents who sent him to Port Royal school where he acquired a love of the classics. In Paris he became a friend of Molière, whose company acted his first play, and of Boileau, with whom he became joint historiographer to Louis XIV. *Esther* and *Athalie* were written for Madame de Maintenon's schoolgirls.

Rackham, Arthur (1867–1939), English artist and book-illustrator, especially of fairy tales.

Radhakrishnan, Sir Sarvepalli (1888–1975), Indian philosopher and statesman, vice-president of India 1952–62, president 1962–7. He was at one time a professor at Oxford, and was chairman of Unesco in 1949.

Raffles, Sir Thomas Stamford (1781–1826), English colonial administrator who founded a settlement at Singapore in 1819. He was also a naturalist, and founded the London Zoo, being first president.

Raikes, Robert (1735–1811), English educational pioneer, whose lead in the teaching of children at Gloucester on Sundays led to an extensive Sunday School movement.

Raleigh, Sir Walter (1552–1618), adventurer and writer. He found favour at the court of Elizabeth I, helped to put down the Irish rebellion of 1580, and in 1584 began the colonisation of Virginia, introducing potatoes and tobacco to the British Isles. At the accession of James I he lost favour and was sent to the Tower, where he wrote his *History of the World*. Released in 1615 to lead an expedition to the Orinoco, he was executed when it failed.

Raman, Sir Chandrasekhara Venkata (1888–1970), Indian physicist whose main work has been in spectroscopy. For his research on the diffusion of light and discovery of the "Raman effect" (a phenomenon of scattered light rays) he was awarded the 1930 Nobel prize.

Rameau, Jean Philippe (1683–1764), French composer and church organist whose works on musical theory influenced musical development in the 18th cent.

Ramón y Cajal, Santiago (1852–1934), Spanish histologist who made discoveries in the structure of the nervous system. Shared 1906 Nobel prize.

Ramsay, Sir William (1852–1916), Scottish chemist, and discoverer with Lord Rayleigh of argon. Later he discovered helium and other inert gases, which he called neon, krypton, and xenon. Nobel prizewinner 1904.

Ramsey, Arthur Michael (b. 1904), archbishop of Canterbury, 1961–74. His previous career was: professor of divinity at Cambridge 1950–2; bishop of Durham 1952–6; archbishop of York 1956–61. Widely travelled, he worked hard for church unity; in 1970 he preached in South Africa.

Ranke, Leopold von (1795–1886), German historian, one of the first to base his work on methodical research. His chief work is a *History of the Popes*.

Raphael (Raffaello Santi) (1483–1520) of Urbino was the youngest of the three great artists of the High Renaissance. He was taught at Perugia by Perugino, and then at Florence he came under the influence of Leonardo and Michelangelo. Raphael's Madonnas, remarkable for their simplicity and grace, include the *Madonna of the Grand Duke* (Palazzo Pitti), the *Sistine Madonna* (Dresden) the *Madonna with the Goldfinch* (Uffizi) the *Madonna of Foligno* (Vatican), and the *Ansidei Madonna* (National Gallery). He painted the frescoes on the walls of the Stanza della Segnatura in the Vatican, and designed 10 cartoons for tapestries for the Sistine Chapel, 7 of which are on loan from the Royal Collection at the V. and A. After the death of Bramante he was appointed architect in charge of the rebuilding of St. Peter's.

Rasputin, Grigori Yefimovich (1871–1916), Russian peasant monk, who at the court of Nicholas II exerted a malign influence over the Tsarina through his apparent ability to improve the health of the sickly Tsarevich Alexis. He was murdered by a group of nobles.

Rathbone, Eleanor (1872–1946), social reformer who championed women's pensions and in her book *The Disinherited Family* set out the case for family allowances.

Ravel, Maurice (1875–1937), French composer, pupil of Fauré, one of the leaders of the impressionist movement. He wrote chamber music, piano pieces, songs, and ballet music, including *Daphnis et Chloé*, specially commissioned by Diaghilev. *See* **Section E.**

Rawlinson, Sir Henry Creswicke (1810–95), English diplomat and archaeologist. He made Assyrian collections now in the British Museum and translated the Behistun inscription of the Persian king Darius. He also wrote on cuneiform inscriptions and on Assyrian history.

Ray, John (1627–1705), English naturalist. A blacksmith's son, he went to Cambridge, travelled in Europe, and produced a classification of plants. He also wrote on zoology.

Rayleigh, 3rd Baron (John William Strutt) (1842–1919), English mathematician and physicist. He studied sound and the wave theory of light; and with Sir William Ramsay discovered argon. Nobel prizewinner 1904.

Read, Sir Herbert (1893–1968), English poet and art critic. His writings include *Collected Poems*, *The Meaning of Art*, and an autobiography, *Annals of Innocence and Experience*.

Reade, Charles (1814–84), English novelist. His chief work is *The Cloister and the Hearth*. He also wrote *Peg Woffington*, *It is Never too Late to Mend*, and *Griffith Gaunt*, aimed at social abuses. He tried unsuccessfully to write plays.

Réaumur, René Antoine Ferchault de (1683–1757), French naturalist who invented a thermometer of eighty degrees, using alcohol.

Récamier, Jeanne Françoise (*née* Bernard) (1777–1849), French beauty and holder of a noted salon. Her husband was a banker.

Regnault, Henri Victor (1810–78), French chemist and physicist, who worked on gases, latent heat, and steam-engines.

Reith, 1st Baron (John Charles Walsham Reith) (1889–1971), Scottish civil engineer, first director-general of the British Broadcasting Corporation 1927–38.

Rembrandt (Rembrandt Harmenszoon van Rijn) (1606–69), Dutch painter and etcher, b. Leiden, a miller's son, one of the most individual and prolific artists of any period. His output includes portraits, landscapes, large groups, etchings, and drawings. He settled in Amsterdam establishing his reputation with *The Anatomy Lesson*, painted in 1632. In 1634 he married Saskia, a burgomaster's daughter. *The Night Watch* was painted in 1642; it was not well received and Saskia died the same year, leaving the infant Titus. The path from relative wealth to lonely old age is depicted in his self-portraits. Caring little for convention or formal beauty, his work is characterised by bold realism and spiritual beauty, by vitality and simplicity. His understanding of the play of colour and the effects of light can give his pictures a mystical beauty, as in the atmospheric painting *The Mill*. His figures, even for religious pictures, were taken from real life, the Jews in the etching *Christ Healing* from the Jewish quarter where he lived. He met the misfortunes of later life by withdrawing from society and it was during this period of detachment that he produced his greatest works in portraiture, landscape, and biblical story.

Renan, Ernest (1823–92), French writer who, though unable to accept the orthodox viewpoint, wrote much on religious themes, especially a *Life of Jesus*.

Reni, Guido. *See* **Guido Reni.**

Rennie, John (1761–1821), Scottish civil engineer who built the old Waterloo and Southwark bridges and designed the granite London bridge which stood until recently. He also designed docks at London, Liverpool, Leith, Dublin, and Hull; constructed Plymouth breakwater; made canals and drained fens.

Renoir, Pierre Auguste (1841–1919), French impressionist painter, b. Limoges. His works include portraits, still-life, landscapes, and groups, including *La Loge*, *Les Parapluies*, *La première Sortie*, *La Place Pigalle*. He was later crippled with arthritis.

Reuter, Paul Julius, Freiherr von (1816–99), German pioneer of telegraphic press service, who in 1851 fixed his headquarters in London.

Reymont, Vladislav Stanislav (1868–1925), Polish novelist, author of *The Peasants*. Nobel prizewinner 1924.

Reynolds, Sir Joshua (1723–92), English portrait painter, b. Plympton, Devon. His portraits, which include *Mrs. Siddons*, are remarkable for expressiveness and colour and he was a sympathetic painter of children. He was first president of the R.A. from 1768 till his death.

Rhodes, Cecil John (1853–1902), English empire-builder. B. at Bishop's Stortford, he went to South Africa for health reasons and there prospered at the diamond mines. He became prime minister of what was then Cape Colony and secured British extension in what is now Rhodesia. He withdrew from politics after the failure of the ill-advised Jameson Raid of 1896 into the Transvaal. He bequeathed large sums to found scholarships at Oxford for overseas students.

Ricardo, David (1772–1823), English political economist of Jewish descent. By occupation a London stockbroker, he wrote a useful work, *Principles of Political Economy*.

Richard I (1157–99), succeeded his father Henry II as king of England in 1189. A patron of troubadours and a soldier (Lion-heart), he went on the third Crusade and took Acre, but could not recover Jerusalem from Saladin. On his return journey across Europe he was imprisoned and ransomed. He was killed in war with France.

Richard II (1367–1400), son of the Black Prince, succeeded his grandfather Edward III as king of England in 1377. Artistic and able, but erratic and egocentric, he personally at the age of fourteen met the Peasants' Revolt in 1381, making untenable promises. Latterly his rule became increasingly arbitrary, and he was deposed and imprisoned in 1399.

Richard III (1452–85), King of England, succeeded his brother, the Yorkist, Edward IV, in 1483, and is believed to have murdered his two nephews in the Tower. Shortly afterwards he was defeated and killed at Bosworth by the invading Earl of Richmond, who as Henry VII brought to an end the Wars of the Roses. Richard's character is disputed, but he was able and might have been a successful ruler.

Richardson, Sir Albert Edward (1880–1964), British architect, author of *Georgian Architecture*.

Richardson, Sir Owen Willans (1879–1959), English physicist who worked on thermionics, or emission of electricity from hot bodies. Nobel prizewinner 1928.

Richardson, Sir Ralph David (b. 1902), English actor who has worked at the old Vic, on the West End stage, and at Stratford-on-Avon, and appeared in films, including *South Riding*, *Anna Karenina*, and *The Fallen Idol*.

Richardson, Samuel (1689–1761), English author of *Pamela*, *Clarissa*, and *The History of Sir Charles Grandison*, exercised considerable influence on the development of the novel.

Richelieu, Armand Jean du Plessis, Duc de (1585–1642), French statesman, cardinal of the Roman church. As minister to Louis XIII from 1624 till his death, he built up the power of the French crown at home in central government, and by his military preparedness and active foreign policy gave France a lead in Europe.

Ridley, Nicholas (1500–55), English Protestant martyr, bishop of Rochester and later of London, was burnt with Latimer under Queen Mary Tudor.

Rienzi, Cola di (1313–54), Italian patriot, b. Rome, led a popular rising in 1347 and for seven months reigned as tribune, but had to flee, was imprisoned, and eventually murdered.

Rilke, Rainer Maria (1872–1926), German lyric poet, b. Prague. His work, marked by beauty of style, culminated in the *Duino Elegies* and *Sonnets to Orpheus*, both written in 1922, which gave a new musicality to German verse. His visits to Russia in 1899 and 1900 and his admiration for Rodin (who had been his wife's teacher) influenced his artistic career.

Rimbaud, Jean Nicolas Arthur (1854–91), French poet, b. Charleville, on the Meuse. In his brief poetic career (4 years from about the age of 16) he prepared the way for symbolism (*Bateau ivre*, *Les Illuminations*) and anticipated Freud (*Les déserts de l'amour*). He became intimate with Verlaine and at 18 had completed his memoirs, *Une saison en enfer*. He died at Marseilles.

Rimsky-Korsakov, Nikolai Andreyevich (1844–1908), Russian composer whose works include the operas *The Maid of Pskov*, *The Snow Maiden*, *Le Coq d'or*, and the symbolic suite *Scheherezade*. He was a brilliant orchestrator and rescored many works, including Borodin's *Prince Igor*.

Rizzio, David (1533?–66), Italian musician and secretary of Mary, Queen of Scots. He was murdered in her presence at Holyrood by her jealous husband, Darnley.

Robbia, Luca Della (1400–82), Florentine sculptor who introduced enamelled terra-cotta work.

Roberts of Kandahar, 1st Earl (Frederick Sleigh Roberts) (1832–1914), British general. He took part in the suppression of the Indian Mutiny, in the Afghan war (relieving Kandahar), and when put in command in South Africa in the Boer War he relieved Kimberley and advanced to Pretoria.

Robertson, Sir William (1860–1933), the only British soldier to rise from private to field-marshal. His son, **Brian Hubert, 1st Baron** (b. 1896) served in both world wars and was chairman of the British Transport Commission, 1953–61.

Robeson, Paul (1898–1976), American Negro singer, b. Princeton, especially remembered for his singing of Negro spirituals, and his appearance in works ranging from *Showboat* to *Othello*.

Robespierre, Maximilien Marie Isidoire de (1758–94), French revolutionary. A country advocate, b. Arras, he was in 1789 elected to the States General and in 1792 to the Convention. He became a leader of the Jacobins, the more extreme party which came to power under stress of war and after the king's execution in 1793. In this crisis, the Committee of Public Safety, of which he was a member and which used his reputation as a cloak, sent many to the guillotine. He opposed the cult of Reason and inaugurated the worship of the Supreme Being. In the reaction from the reign of terror he was denounced, tried to escape, but was guillotined.

Robinson, William Heath (1872–1944), English cartoonist and book-illustrator, especially known for his fantastically humorous drawings of machines.

Rob Roy (Robert McGregor) (1671–1734), Scottish freebooter who helped the poor at the expense of the rich, and played a lone hand in the troubled times of the Jacobite rising of 1715.

Robsart, Amy (1532–60), English victim (it is believed) of murder. The wife of Robert Dudley, Earl of Leicester, she was found dead at Cumnor Place. Her death was used by Scott in *Kenilworth*.

Rockefeller, John Davison (1839–1937), American philanthropist, b. Richford, N.Y. He settled in Cleveland, Ohio, and with his brother William founded the Standard Oil Company, making a fortune. His philanthropic enterprises are carried on by the Rockefeller Foundation. Nelson Rockefeller, Gov. of New York 1958–73, Vice-Pres. of the United States 1974–7, is his grandson.

Rodin, Auguste (1841–1917), French sculptor, b. Paris. His best-known works include *Le Penseur*, *Les Bourgeois de Calais*, the statues of Balzac and Victor Hugo, and *La Porte d'Enfer*, a huge bronze door for the Musée des Arts Décoratifs, which was unfinished at his death.

Rodney, 1st Baron (George Rodney) (1719–92), English admiral, who served in the Seven Years War and the War of American Independence; in the latter war he defeated the French fleet under de Grasse.

Roland de la Platière, Manon Jeanne (1754–93), a leading figure in the French revolution. Her husband Jean Marie (1734–93), belonged to the more moderate or Girondist party, and when threatened escaped; but she was imprisoned and executed. She wrote *Letters* and *Memoirs*.

Rolland, Romain (1866–1944), French author, whose main work is a ten-volume novel, *Jean-Christophe*, the biography of a German musician, based on the life of Beethoven, and a study of contemporary French and German civilisation. Nobel prizewinner 1915.

Romilly, Sir Samuel (1757–1818), English lawyer

and law-reformer, who aimed at mitigating the severity of the criminal law.

Rommel, Erwin (1891–1944), German general. He took part in the 1940 invasion of France, and was later successful in commanding the Afrika Korps till 1944. He committed suicide.

Romney, George (1734–1802), English artist, b. in Lancashire. He painted chiefly portraits, especially of Lady Hamilton, and lived mainly in London, but returned to Kendal to die.

Röntgen, Wilhelm Konrad von (1845–1923), German scientist who in 1895 discovered X-rays. Nobel prizewinner 1901.

Roosevelt, Franklin Delano (1882–1945), American statesman, a distant cousin of Theodore Roosevelt. During the first world war he held office under Wilson, and though stricken with poliomyelitis in 1921 continued his political career, becoming governor of New York in 1929 and U.S. president in 1933 (the first to hold office for more than two terms), till his death. A Democrat, he met the economic crisis of 1933 with a policy for a "New Deal" (*see* **Sec. L**). He strove in vain to ward off war. Towards other American countries his attitude was that of "good neighbour." After Pearl Harbor, he energetically prosecuted the war, holding meetings with Churchill and Stalin, and adopting a "lend-lease" policy for arms. He kept contact with his people by "fireside talks." His wife **Eleanor** (1884–1962) was a public figure in her own right, and was chairman of the U.N. Human Rights Commission 1947–51.

Roosevelt, Theodore (1858–1919), American president. Popular because of his exploits in the Spanish-American war, he was appointed Republican vice-president in 1900, becoming president when McKinley was assassinated, and was re-elected 1905. He promoted the regulation of trusts; and his promotion of peace between Russia and Japan gained the Nobel prize, 1906.

Rops, Félicien (1833–98), Belgian artist, known for his often satirical lithographs and etchings.

Ross, Sir James Clark (1800–62), Scottish explorer of polar regions, who accompanied his uncle Sir John, and himself discovered the north magnetic pole in 1831. He commanded the *Erebus* and *Terror* to the antarctic (1839–43), where his discoveries included the Ross ice barrier.

Ross, Sir John (1777–1856), Scottish explorer of polar regions, uncle of the above. He searched for the north-west passage and discovered Boothia peninsula.

Ross, Sir Ronald (1857–1932), British physician, b. India, who discovered the malaria parasite. He was in the Indian medical service, and later taught tropical medicine in England. Nobel prizewinner 1902.

Rossetti, Dante Gabriel (1828–82), English poet and painter, son of **Gabriele** (1783–1852), an exiled Italian author who settled in London in 1842. With Millais, Holman Hunt and others he formed the Pre-Raphaelite brotherhood which returned to pre-Renaissance art forms. His model was often his wife, Elizabeth Siddal. His poems include *The Blessed Damozel.* His sister **Christina Georgina** (1830–94) wrote poetry, including *Goblin Market.*

Rossini, Gioacchino Antonio (1792–1868), Italian operatic composer. *See* **Section E.**

Rostand, Edmond (1868–1918), French dramatist, whose *Cyrano de Bergerac* created a sensation in 1898.

Rothenstein, Sir William (1872–1945), English portrait painter. His son, **Sir John** (b. 1901), is an art historian and until 1964 was director of the Tate Gallery; he has written an autobiography.

Rothschild, Meyer Amschel (1743–1812), German financier, founder of a banking family, b. Frankfurt. His five sons controlled branches at Frankfurt, Vienna, Naples, Paris and London (Nathan Meyer, 1777–1836). Nathan's son, Lionel (1808–79), was the first Jewish member of the House of Commons.

Roubiliac, Louis François (1695–1762), French sculptor who settled in London and carved a statue of Handel for Vauxhall gardens and one of Newton for Trinity College, Cambridge.

Rouget de Lisle, Claude Joseph (1760–1836), French poet, author of words and music of the *Marseillaise*, revolutionary and national anthem.

Rousseau, Henri (1844–1910), influential French "Sunday" painter, called "Le Douanier" because he was a customs official; self-taught, he was for long unrecognised as an artist of considerable talent and originality; he used the botanical gardens for his jungle scenes.

Rousseau, Jean-Jacques (1712–78), French political philosopher and educationist, b. Geneva, herald of the romantic movement. After a hard childhood he met Mme de Warens who for some years befriended him. In 1741 he went to Paris where he met Diderot and contributed articles on music and political economy to the *Encyclopédie. La nouvelle Héloïse* appeared in 1760, *Emile*, and *Le Contrat Social* in 1762. *Emile* is a treatise on education according to "natural" principles and *Le Contrat Social*, his main work, sets forth his political theory. It begins, "Man is born free and everywhere he is in chains." Both books offended the authorities and he had to flee, spending some time in England. Later he was able to return to France. His views on conduct and government did much to stimulate the movement leading to the French Revolution. *See also* **Education, Section J.**

Rubens, Sir Peter Paul (1577–1640), Flemish painter. B. in exile, his family returned to Antwerp in 1587. He studied in Italy and visited Spain. His range was wide, his compositions vigorous, and he was a remarkable colourist. *Peace and War, The Rape of the Sabines,* and *The Felt Hat* are in the National Gallery. He was knighted by Charles I.

Rubenstein, Anton Grigorovich (1829–94). Russian pianist and composer, who helped to found the conservatoire at St. Petersburg (Leningrad); as did his brother Nicholas (1835–81) at Moscow.

Rücker, Sir Arthur (1848–1915), English physicist, who made two magnetic surveys of the British Isles, 1886, and 1891.

Ruisdael, Jacob van (*c.* 1628–82), Dutch painter of landscapes, b. Haarlem. Several of his works are in the National Gallery, including *Coast of Scheveningen* and *Landscape with ruins.* He was also a fine etcher.

Rupert, Prince (1619–82), general, son of Frederick of Bohemia and his wife Elizabeth, daughter of James I of England. He commanded the Royalist cavalry in the English civil war, but was too impetuous for lasting success. At sea he was defeated by Blake. He improved the art of mezzotinting and was the first governor of the Hudson's Bay Company.

Rusk, Dean (b. 1909), American politician, who has held various posts especially in connection with foreign affairs; a former Rhodes scholar.

Ruskin, John (1819–1900), English author and art critic, b. London. His *Modern Painters* in 5 volumes was issued over a period of years, the first volume having a strong defence of Turner. He helped to establish the Pre-Raphaelites. Other notable works include *The Seven Lamps of Architecture, The Stones of Venice* and *Praeterita. Unto this Last* develops his views on social problems, and he tried to use his wealth for education and for non-profitmaking enterprises. Ruskin College at Oxford, the first residential college for working people, is named after him. In 1848 he married Euphemia Gray, but in 1854 she obtained a decree of nullity and later married Millais.

Russell, 3rd Earl (Bertrand Arthur William Russell) (1872–1970), English philosopher, mathematician, and essayist, celebrated for his work in the field of logic and the theory of knowledge, and remembered for his moral courage, belief in human reason and his championship of liberal ideas. He published more than 60 books, including *The Principles of Mathematics* (1903), *Principia Mathematica* (in collaboration with A. N. Whitehead; 3 vols., 1910–13), *The Problem of Philosophy* (1912), *Mysticism and Logic* (1918), *The Analysis of Mind* (1921), *An Inquiry into Meaning and Truth* (1940), *History of Western Philosophy* (1945), and a number on ethics and social questions. His *Autobiography* (3 vols.) appeared 1967–9. He was the grandson of Lord John Russell and John Stuart Mill was his godfather. Nobel prize for literature 1950; O.M. 1949.

Russell, 1st Earl (John Russell), (1792–1878), English statesman, third son of the 6th Duke of Bedford. He had a large share in carrying the parliamentary reform bill of 1832. He was Whig prime minister 1846–52 and 1865–6. He was also a historian and biographer.

Russell of Killowen, 1st Baron (Charles Russell), British lawyer, b. Ireland; lord chief justice 1894–1900. He defended Parnell.

Rutherford, 1st Baron (Ernest Rutherford) (1871–1937), British physicist, b. New Zealand, eminent in the field of atomic research. His experiments were conducted at Manchester and Cambridge and attracted young scientists from all over the world. In 1911 he announced his nuclear theory of the atom and in 1918 succeeded in splitting the atom. His work prepared the way for future nuclear research.

Ruysdael, Jacob van. *See* **Ruisdael.**

Ruyter, Michiel Adrianszoon de (1607–76), Dutch admiral who ranks with Nelson. He fought against England and in 1667 caused alarm by sailing up the Medway as far as Rochester and up the Thames as far as Gravesend. He was mortally wounded at Messina.

S

Sachs, Hans (1494–1576), German poet, b. Nuremberg. A shoemaker, he wrote over 6,000 pieces, some dealing with everyday life, many (including *Die Wittenbergische Nachtigall*) inspired by the Reformation.

Sachs, Julius von (1832–97), German botanist, founder of experimental plant physiology. He demonstrated that chlorophyll is formed in chloroplasts only in light (*see* **F28**).

Sadi or Saadi (Muslih Addin) (*c.* 1184–1292), Persian poet, b. Shiraz, best known for his *Gulistan* (Flower Garden), which has been translated into English.

Sainte-Beuve, Charles Augustin (1804–69), French critic, b. Boulogne. He studied medicine, abandoning it for journalism, and after attempting to write poetry, turned to literary criticism. His work reveals the wide range of his intellectual experience and includes *Causeries du lundi* and *Histoire de Port-Royal*. He was sometimes in political trouble for upholding freedom of thought.

Saint-Just, Antoine (1767–94), French revolutionary, a follower of Robespierre and executed with him.

St. Laurent, Louis Stephen (b. 1882), Canadian politician, prime minister 1948–57.

Saint-Saëns, Charles Camile (1835–1921), French composer, for 20 years organist at the Madeleine. His compositions include symphonic and chamber music and the opera *Samson et Dalila*, which was produced by Liszt at Weimar in 1877. *See* **Section E.**

Saint-Simon, Claude, Comte de (1760–1825), French socialist, who in his *L'Industrie* and *Nouveau christianisme* prepared the way for much later thought.

Saintsbury, George Edward (1845–1933), English critic and literary historian.

Sakharov, Andrei Dimitrievich (b. 1921), Soviet nuclear physicist and human rights campaigner. Nobel prizewinner 1975.

Sala, George Augustus (1828–95), English journalist who contributed to *Household Words* and was a notable foreign correspondent.

Saladin (Salah-ad-din) (1137–93), sultan of Egypt and Syria and founder of a dynasty, who in 1187 defeated the Christians near Tiberias and took Jerusalem. This gave rise to the unsuccessful Third Crusade, in which Richard I of England joined. His great qualities were admired by his opponents, and his administration left many tangible signs in such matters as roads and canals.

Salazar, Antonio d'Oliveira (1889–1970), Portuguese dictator, having first been premier in 1932, a new constitution being adopted in 1933. He gave Portugal stability, but refused to bow to nationalism in Portuguese Africa and India.

Salda, František (1867–1937), Czech critic, essayist and poet.

Salimbene de Adamo (1221–*c.*1228), mediaeval chronicler, b. Parma, whose vivid description of life in the 13th cent. is embodied in his *Cronica*.

Salisbury, 3rd Marquess (Robert Arthur Salisbury) (1830–1903), English Conservative statesman, prime minister 1885–6, 1886–92, 1895–1902, mainly remembered for his conduct of foreign affairs during a critical period, culminating in the Boer War. His grandson, **Robert Arthur, 5th Marquess** (1893–1972), led the Conservative opposition in the House of Lords.

Samuel, 1st Viscount (Herbert Samuel) (1870–1963), British Liberal statesman of Jewish parentage. He published philosophical works, including *Practical Ethics*.

Sand, George (1804–76), pseudonym of the French writer Armandine Lucie Dupin. Her publications are extensive and varied, and include the novel *Mauprat*, rural studies, and an autobiography *Histoire de ma vie*. She was associated with Alfred de Musset and Chopin.

Sandow, Eugene (1867–1925), German "strong man" who opened an Institute of Health in London.

Sanger, Frederick (b. 1918), British scientist noted for his work on the chemical structure of the protein insulin. Nobel prizewinner 1958.

Sankey, Ira David (1840–1908), American evangelist and composer, associated with Moody.

San Martin, José de (1778–1850), South American national leader in securing independence from Spanish rule to his native Argentina, Chile and Peru.

Santayana, George (1863–1952), American philosopher and poet, b. Madrid, of Spanish parentage. He was professor of philosophy at Harvard, 1907–12. His books include *The Sense of Beauty*, *The Life of Reason*, and *The Realms of Being*.

Santos-Dumont, Alberto (1873–1932), Brazilian aeronaut who in 1898 flew a cylindrical balloon with a gasoline engine. In 1909 he built a monoplane.

Sappho of Lesbos (fl. early 6th cent. B.C.), Greek poetess, of whose love poems few remain.

Sardou, Victorien (1831–1908), French dramatist popular in his day. Sarah Bernhardt created famous parts in *Fédora*, *Théodora* and *La Tosca*; *Robespierre* and *Dante* were written for Irving.

Sargent, John Singer (1856–1922), American painter, b. Florence, who worked mainly in England, especially on portraits.

Sargent, Sir Malcolm (1895–1967), British conductor, b. Stamford, who conducted the Promenade Concerts from 1950 till his death, and succeeded Sir Adrian Boult as conductor of the B.B.C. Symphony Orchestra, 1950–7.

Sartre, Jean-Paul (b. 1905), French existentialist philosopher, left-wing intellectual, dramatist, essayist and novelist. His major philosophical work is *L'Etre et le Néant* and his plays include *Les Mouches*, *Huis Clos*, *Crime passionel*, *La Putain respectueuse*, and *Les Séquestrés d'Altona*. He was awarded (though he declined it) the 1964 Nobel prize. *See* **Section I.**

Sassoon, Siegfried (1886–1967), English poet and writer with a hatred of war. He is mainly known for *The Memoirs of a Foxhunting Man*, the first part of the *Memoirs of George Sherston*.

Savonarola, Girolamo (1452–98), Florentine preacher and reformer, a Dominican friar, who denounced vice and corruption not only in society but also in the Church itself, especially attacking Pope Alexander VI. He was excommunicated, imprisoned, and with two of his companions hanged and burned. His passion for reform made him impatient of opposition and incapable of compromise, yet he was a notable figure and commands the respect of later ages. George Eliot's *Romola* portrays him.

Scarlatti, Allessandro (1659–1725), Italian musician who founded the Neopolitan school of opera. He composed over 100 operas, 200 masses, and over 700 cantatas and oratorios. His son **Domenico** (1685–1757) was a harpsichord virtuoso whose work influenced the evolution of the sonata. The chief years of his life were spent at the Spanish court in Madrid. *See* **Section E.**

Scheele, Carl Wilhelm (1742–86), Swedish chemist, discoverer of many chemical substances, including oxygen (*c.* 1773—but published in 1777 after the publication of Priestley's studies).

Schiaparelli, Giovanni Virginio (1835–1910), Italian astronomer, noted for having detected certain dark markings on the surface of the planet Mars which he called canals.

Schiller, Johann Christoph Friedrich von (1759–1805), German dramatist and poet, b. Marbach in Württemberg, began life as a military surgeon. His play *The Robbers* with a revolutionary theme was successful in 1782 in Mannheim After a stay at Dresden, where he wrote *Don Carlos*, and at Jena, where he wrote a history of the Thirty Years War, he became the friend of Goethe and removed to Weimar, where he wrote *Wallenstein*, *Mary Stuart*, *The Maid of Orleans* and *William Tell*, but died young. He is a leading figure in the European romantic movement.

Schirrmann, Richard (1874–1961), German originator of youth hostels. A schoolmaster, in 1907 he converted his schoolroom during holidays to a dormitory. The Verband für deutsche Jugendherbergen was founded in 1913, and the International Youth Hostels Federation in 1932, with Schirrmann as first president.

Schlegel, Friedrich von (1772–1829), German critic, b. Hanover, prominent among the founders of German romanticism, whose revolutionary and germinating ideas influenced early 19th cent. thought. His brother, **August Wilhelm** (1767–1845), made remarkable translations of Shakespeare (which established Shakespeare in Germany), Dante, Calderón, and Camões.

Schliemann, Heinrich (1822–90), German archaeologist, who discovered Troy and excavated Mycenae.

Schnabel, Artur (1882–1951), American pianist of Austrian birth, regarded as a leading exponent of Beethoven's pianoforte sonatas.

Schoenberg, Arnold (1874–1951), Austrian composer of Jewish parentage who in 1933 was exiled by the Nazi regime and settled in America, teaching at Boston and Los Angeles. Among his works are the choral orchestral *Gurre-Lieder* and *Pierrot Lunaire*, a cycle of 21 poems for voice and chamber music. *See* **Section E.**

Schopenhauer, Arthur (1788–1860), German philosopher, b. Danzig, important historically for his pessimism, and his doctrine that will is superior to knowledge. His chief work is *The World as Will and Idea*. He regarded his contemporary Hegel as a charlatan.

Schubert, Franz Peter (1797–1828), Austrian composer, b. Vienna, the son of a schoolmaster, and a contemporary of Beethoven. He wrote not only symphonies, sonatas, string quartets, choral music and masses, but also over 600 songs of unsurpassed lyrical beauty. He might almost be called the creator of the German *Lied* as known today. He died in poverty in Vienna at 31 before his musical genius could reach its full flowering. *See* **Section E.**

Schumann, Robert Alexander (1810–56), composer of the early 19th cent. German romantic school. He wrote much chamber music, four symphonies, a piano concerto, and choral music, but it is his early piano pieces and songs that give constant delight. His wife **Clara** (1819–96) was one of the outstanding pianists of her time, especially as interpreter of Chopin. *See* **Section E.**

Schweitzer, Albert (1875–1965), Alsatian medical missionary, theologian, musician and philosopher, b. at Kaysersberg. After publishing learned works, he resigned a promising European career to found at Lambaréné in French Equatorial Africa a hospital to fight leprosy and sleeping sickness and made it a centre of service to Africans. His funds were raised by periodic organ recitals in Europe. His motivation was not patronage but atonement. Nobel peace prize 1952. O.M. 1955.

Scipio, Publius Cornelius (237–183 B.C.), Roman general in the second Punic War, known as Scipio Africanus the elder. **Scipio Africanus the younger** (185–129 B.C.) was an adoptive relative and an implacable opponent of Carthage (destroyed 146).

Scott, Charles Prestwich (1846–1931), English newspaper editor. Under his editorship (1872–1929) the *Manchester Guardian* (now *The Guardian*) became a leading journal.

Scott, Sir George Gilbert (1811–78), English architect in the Gothic revival. He restored many churches and designed the Albert Memorial and the Martyrs' Memorial at Oxford.

Scott, Sir Giles Gilbert (1880–1960), English architect, grandson of above, designed the Anglican cathedral at Liverpool and planned the new Waterloo bridge.

Scott, Robert Falcon (1868–1912), English antarctic explorer. He led two expeditions; one 1901–4 which discovered King Edward VII Land; and another 1910–12 which reached the south pole and found the Amundsen records; but while returning the party was overtaken by blizzards and perished 11 miles from their base. *See also* **Antarctic exploration, Sec. L.** His son, **Sir Peter Scott** (b. 1909), is an artist and ornithologist, founder of the Severn Wild Fowl Trust; Chancellor Birmingham University.

Scott, Sir Walter (1771–1832), Scottish novelist and poet, b. Edinburgh. He was educated for the law, but came to know and love the Border country and his interests were literary; and in 1802–3 he issued a collection of ballads, *Border Minstrelsy*. Poems such as *Marmion* and *The Lady of the Lake* followed. His novels appeared anonymously, beginning with *Waverley* in 1814; and continuing with *Guy Mannering*, *The Antiquary*, *Old Mortality*, *Rob Roy*, and the *Heart of Midlothian*. From 1819 he turned also to English history, with *Ivanhoe* and *Kenilworth*. In 1826 he became bankrupt, largely as the fault of his publishing partner, and worked heroically to clear off debts.

Scott-Paine, Hubert (1891–1954), pioneer in the design and construction of aircraft and sea-craft.

Scriabin, Alexander (1872–1915), Russian composer and pianist, who relied to some extent on extra-musical factors such as religion, and in *Prometheus* tried to unite music and philosophy. *See* **Section E.**

Seeley, Sir John Robert (1834–95), English historian, author of a life of Christ, *Ecce Homo*.

Segovia, Andrés (b. 1894), Spanish concert-guitarist. He has adapted works by Bach, Haydn, Mozart, and other classical composers to the guitar.

Selfridge, Harry Gordon (1858–1947), American-born merchant who in 1909 opened a new style of department store in Oxford Street.

Semmelweis, Ignaz Philipp (1818–65), Hungarian obstetrician, a pioneer in the use of antiseptic methods, thus reducing the incidence of puerperal fever.

Seneca, Lucius Annaeus (*c.* 4 B.C.–A.D. 65), Roman stoic philosopher who was tutor to Nero, but lost favour and was sentenced to take his own life.

Senefelder, Alois (1772–1834), Bavarian inventor of lithography about 1796.

Severus, Lucius Septimius (146–211), Roman emperor, and a successful general. On a visit to Britain he suppressed a revolt, repaired Hadrian's Wall, and died at York.

Sévigné, Marie de Rabutin-Chantal, Marquise de (1626–96), French woman of letters. Her letters to her daughter Françoise written in an unaffected elegance of style give a moving picture of fashionable society in 17th cent. France.

Sgambati, Giovanni (1841–1914), Italian pianist (pupil of Liszt), composer and teacher, who revived interest in classical instrumental music in an age of opera.

Shackleton, Sir Ernest Henry (1874–1922), British explorer, who made four antarctic expeditions; that of 1909 reached within 100 miles of the south pole. He died on his last expedition.

Shaftesbury, 7th Earl of (**Anthony Ashley Cooper**) (1801–85), English philanthropist largely responsible for legislation reducing the misery of the industrial revolution. He was for 40 years chairman of the Ragged Schools Union.

Shakespeare, William (1564–1616), England's greatest poet and dramatist, b. Stratford-on-Avon. Little is known of his career up to his eighteenth year, when he married Anne Hathaway. He came to London at the height of the English renaissance and soon became connected with the Globe theatre as actor and playwright. Thirty-eight plays comprise the Shakespeare canon. Thirty-six were printed in the First Folio of 1623 (the first collected edition of his dramatic works), of which eighteen had been published during his lifetime in the so-called Quartos. *Love's Labour's Lost* and *The Comedy of Errors* seem to have been among the earliest, being followed by *The Two Gentlemen of Verona*, and *Romeo and Juliet*. Then followed *Henry VI*, *Richard III*, *Richard II*, *Titus Andronicus*, *The Taming of the Shrew*, *King John*, *The*

Merchant of Venice, *A Midsummer Night's Dream*, *All's Well that Ends Well*, *Henry IV*, *The Merry Wives of Windsor*, *Henry V*, *Much Ado about Nothing*, *As You Like It*, *Twelfth Night*. Then came some of his greatest plays, *Julius Caesar*, *Hamlet*, *Troilus and Cressida*, *Othello*, *Measure for Measure*, *Macbeth*, *King Lear*, *Timon of Athens*, *Pericles*, *Antony and Cleopatra*, *Coriolanus*, *Cymbeline*, *A Winter's Tale*, *The Tempest*, *Henry VIII*, and *The Two Noble Kinsmen*. In mastery of language, in understanding of character, and in dramatic perception, he has never been surpassed. Fresh interpretation of his work continues. *See* **Section I.**

Sharp, Granville (1735–1813), English abolitionist of slavery, and founder of the colony of Sierra Leone.

Shastri, Shri Lal Bahadur (1904–66), Indian politician who became prime minister of India after the death of Nehru in 1964. He died of a heart attack at the end of the Soviet-sponsored Tashkent talks.

Shaw, George Bernard (1856–1950), Irish dramatist who conquered England by his wit and exposure of hypocrisy, cant, and national weaknesses, and whose individual opinions found expression in musical criticism, socialist pamphlets and plays. His plays include *Man and Superman*, *Heartbreak House*, *Back to Methuselah*, *Saint Joan*, *The Apple Cart*, and *Buoyant Billions*, and most have important prefaces. In 1884 he joined the newly-born Fabian Society. Nobel prizewinner 1925.

Shelley, Percy Bysshe (1792–1822), English poet, b. Horsham. He was a master of language and of literary form, and a passionate advocate of freedom and of new thought. Sent down from Oxford for his pamphlet *The Necessity of Atheism*, he came under the influence of William Godwin; and, after his first marriage came to an unhappy end, married the latter's daughter, Mary Wollstonecraft, herself a writer. In the same year began his friendship with Byron. His works include *The Revolt of Islam*, the *Masque of Anarchy* (an indictment of Castlereagh), *The Cenci* (a play on evil), and *Prometheus Unbound*, besides lyrics such as *To a Skylark* and *Ode to the West Wind*. He was accidentally drowned while sailing near Spezzia.

Sheppard, Hugh Richard (Dick) (1880–1937), Anglican divine and pacifist. He made St. Martin-in-the-Fields a centre of social service and also founded the Peace Pledge Union.

Sheraton, Thomas (1751–1806), English cabinet-maker, b. Stockton, whose *Cabinetmaker's Book* promoted neo-classical designs. *See* **D13.**

Sheridan, Richard Brinsley (1751–1816), British dramatist, b. Dublin. He was a brilliant writer of comedies, especially *The Rivals*, *The Duenna*, *The School for Scandal*, and *The Critic*. He acquired and rebuilt Drury Lane theatre, which reopened in 1794, but was burnt down in 1809; and this, with his lack of business sense, brought him to poverty, in spite of his friends' efforts to help him. He was also in parliament where he made some notable speeches.

Sherman, William Tecumseh (1820–91), American general, who served especially in the Civil War. He took part in the battles of Bull Run and Shiloh, was appointed in 1864 to the command of the southwest, and with 65,000 men marched across Georgia to the sea. In 1865 he accepted Johnston's surrender.

Sherrington, Sir Charles Scott (1875–1952), English scientist, an authority on the physiology of the nervous system. His research led to advances in brain surgery. His principal work is *Integrative Action of the Nervous System* (1906). Shared with E. D. Adrian the 1932 Nobel prize.

Shirley, James (1596–1666), English dramatist. His tragedies include *The Traitor*, and his comedies *Hyde Park*. His death was hastened by the Great Fire.

Sholokhov, Mikhail Aleksandrovich (b. 1905), Russian novelist, author of *And Quiet Flows the Don*. Nobel prizewinner 1965.

Shostakovich, Dimitri (1906–75), Russian composer whose music is complex, profound, and deeply significant of the Soviet age in which he lived. His works include operas, ballets, symphonies, chamber music, and music for films. Hero of Soviet Labour 1966. *See* **Section E.**

Sibelius, Jean (1865–1957), Finnish composer, imbued with national feeling. His works include seven symphonies, a violin concerto, and several tone poems, notably *Finlandia*, and some based on the Finnish poem *Kalevala*. *See* **Section E.**

Sickert, Walter Richard (1860–1942), British artist, b. Munich. He was influenced by Degas, and has himself influenced later painters. His *Ennui* is in the Tate Gallery.

Siddons, Sarah (1755–1831), English actress especially in tragic parts. She was daughter of the manager Roger Kemble and her reputation was almost unbounded.

Sidgwick, Henry (1838–1900), English philosopher who wrote *Methods of Ethics*, and who also promoted women's education, especially in the foundation of Newnham and Girton colleges.

Sidney, Sir Philip (1554–86), English poet and writer, best remembered for his *Arcadia*, *Apologie for Poetrie*, and *Astrophel and Stella*, all published after his death. He was killed at the battle of Zutphen, where he passed a cup of water to another, saying "Thy necessity is greater than mine."

Siemens, Sir William (1823–83), German-born electrical engineer who settled in England and constructed many overland and submarine telegraphs. He was brother of Werner von Siemens, founder of the firm of Siemens-Halske.

Sienkiewicz, Henryk (1846–1916), Polish novelist and short-story writer; best known of his historical novels is *Quo Vadis?*. Nobel prizewinner 1905.

Sikorski, Vladislav (1881–1943), Polish general and statesman, prime minister of the Polish government in exile (1939) and commander-in-chief of the Polish forces. Killed in an aircraft accident at Gibraltar.

Simpson, Sir James Young (1811–70), Scottish obstetrician who initiated the use of chloroform in childbirth.

Sinclair, Upton (1878–1968), American novelist whose documentary novel *The Jungle* on the Chicago slaughter yards caused a sensation in 1906.

Singer, Isaac Merritt (1811–75), American mechanical engineer who improved early forms of the sewing-machine and patented a single-thread and chain-stitch machine.

Sisley, Alfred (1839–99), French impressionist painter of English origin, who painted some enchanting landscapes, such as *Meadows in Spring* in the Tate Gallery. He was influenced by Corot and Manet.

Sitwell, Edith (1887–1964), English poet, a great experimenter in verse forms. *Gold Coast Customs*, *Façade* (set to music by William Walton) and *Still Falls the Rain* are probably best known. She had two brothers, **Osbert** (1892–1969) and **Sacheverell** (b. 1897), both poets and critics. *See also* **Section M, Part III.**

Slim, 1st Viscount (William Slim) (1891–1970), British general. He commanded the 14th Army in Burma, was chief of the Imperial General Staff 1948–52, and governor-general of Australia 1953–60.

Sloane, Sir Hans (1660–1753), British collector, b. Ireland. He practised in London as a physician. His library of 50,000 volumes and his collection of MSS. and botanical specimens were offered under his will to the nation and formed the beginning of the British Museum.

Slowacki, Julius (1809–49), Polish romantic poet, a revolutionary, he lived in exile in Paris. His work includes the poetic drama *Kordian*, *Balladyna* and *Lilli Weneda*, written in the style of Shakespeare; and the unfinished poem *King Spirit* which reveals his later mystical tendencies.

Smeaton, John (1724–92), English engineer; he rebuilt Eddystone lighthouse (1756–59), improved Newcomen's steam-engine, and did important work on bridges, harbours, and canals. He also invented an improved blowing apparatus for iron-smelting.

Smetana, Bedřich (1824–84), Czech composer, creator of a national style. He was principal conductor of the Prague National Theatre, for which he wrote most of his operas, including *The Bartered Bride* and *The Kiss*. Best known of his other compositions are the cycle of symphonic poems *My Country* and the string quartets *From My Life*. He became totally deaf in 1874, suffered a mental breakdown, and died in an asylum. *See* **Section E.**

Smiles, Samuel (1812–1904), Scottish writer, b. Haddington, in early life a medical practitioner, remembered for *Self Help* (1859), and his biographies of engineers of the industrial revolution.

Smith, Adam (1723–90), Scottish economist, b. Kirkcaldy. In Edinburgh he published *Moral Sentiments*. Later he moved to London, and his *Wealth of Nations* (1776) is the first serious work in political economy.

Smith, Sir Grafton Elliot (1871–1937), Australian anatomist who did research on the structure of the mammalian brain. His works include *The Evolution of Man*.

Smith, John (1580–1631), English adventurer who in 1605 went on a colonising expedition to Virginia and was saved from death by the Red Indian Pocahontas.

Smith, Joseph (1805–44), American founder of the Mormons. He claimed that the *Book of Mormon* was revealed to him. In 1838 feeling against the Mormons culminated in a rising and Smith was murdered. He was succeeded by Brigham Young. *See* **Mormonism, Section J.**

Smith, Sydney (1771–1845), Anglican divine and journalist, who founded the *Edinburgh Review* and supported Catholic emancipation.

Smith, William (1769–1839), English surveyor and canal-maker, the first to map the rock strata of England and to identify the fossils peculiar to each layer.

Smith, Sir William Alexander (1854–1914), Scottish founder of the Boys' Brigade (1883), the oldest national organisation for boys in Britain.

Smith, William Robertson (1846–94), Scottish biblical scholar whose " Bible " contribution to the 9th edition of *The Encyclopaedia Britannica* resulted in an unsuccessful prosecution for heresy.

Smollett, Tobias George (1721–71), Scottish novelist whose work is characterised by satire and coarse humour. His main novels are *Roderick Random*, *Peregrine Pickle*, and *Humphrey Clinker*.

Smuts, Jan Christian (1870–1950), South African statesman and soldier. B. in Cape Colony, during the Boer War he fought on the Boer side. He was premier of the Union 1919–24, 1939–48, and worked for cooperation within the Commonwealth and in the world, but his party was defeated in 1948 by the Nationalists under Malan.

Smyth, Ethel Mary (1858–1944), English composer and suffragette. Her main works are operas (*The Wreckers* and *The Boatswain's Mate*) and a *Mass in D*. She studied at the Leipzig Conservatory.

Snow, Baron (Charles Percy Snow) (b. 1905), English physicist and novelist, author of the essay *The Two Cultures of the Scientific Revolution*, and a sequence of novels *Strangers and Brothers* (11 vols.). *See* **Section M, Part I.**

Snyders, Frans (1597–1657), Flemish still-life and animal painter who studied under Breughel.

Soane, Sir John (1753–1837), English architect who designed the Bank of England. He left the nation his house and library in Lincoln's Inn Fields (Soane Museum).

Sobers, Sir Garfield (b. 1936), West Indies and Nottinghamshire cricketer who ranks as one of the greatest all-rounders. Knighted 1975.

Socinus or Sozzini, Laelius (1525–62), Italian founder of the sect of Socinians, with his nephew **Faustus** (1539–1604). Their teachings resemble those of Unitarians.

Socrates (470–399 B.C.), Greek philosopher and intellectual leader, was the son of a sculptor of Athens. He distinguished himself in three campaigns (Potidaea, Delium, and Amphipolis). Returning to Athens, he devoted himself to study and intellectual enquiry, attracting many followers; through these, especially Xenophon and Plato, we know of his teachings, for he wrote nothing. In 399 B.C. he was charged with impiety and with corrupting the young, found guilty, and accordingly died by drinking hemlock; see Plato's *Apology*, *Crito*, and *Phaedo*.

Soddy, Frederick (1877–1956), English chemist, who in Glasgow about 1912 laid the foundation of the isotope theory, before the physicists became prominent in that field. Nobel prizewinner 1921.

Solon (638–558 B.C.), Athenian lawgiver, who in a time of economic distress cancelled outstanding debts, and introduced some democratic changes.

Solzhenitsyn, Alexander Isayevich (b. 1918), Russian novelist, b. Rostov-on-Don; author of *One Day in the Life of Ivan Denisovich*, a documentary novel depicting life in one of Stalin's prison camps where he spent many years of his life. He was expelled from the Soviet Writers' Union in 1969, and from his country in 1974. Nobel prizewinner 1970.

Somerset, Duke of (Edward Seymour) (1506–52), lord protector of England in the time of the young Edward VI, but he fell from power and was executed.

Sophocles (495–406 B.C.), Athenian dramatist, who was awarded the prize over Aeschylus in 468. Of over a hundred plays of his, the only extant ones are *Oedipus the King*, *Oedipus at Colonus Antigone*, *Electra*, *Trachiniae*, *Ajax*, *Philoctetes*.

Sorel, Georges (1847–1922), French advocate of revolutionary syndicalism, author of *Reflections on Violence* (1905). The irrational aspects of his philosophy (derived from Bergson) appealed to Mussolini and the Fascists.

Soult, Nicolas Jean de Dieu (1769–1851), French general who fought under Napoleon in Switzerland and Italy, at Austerlitz, and in the Peninsular War.

Sousa, John Philip (1854–1932), American bandmaster and composer of some stirring marches.

Southey, Robert (1774–1843), English poet and historian. In 1803 he settled near Coleridge at Keswick, and in 1813 became poet laureate. His best work was in prose: histories of Brazil and of the Peninsular War; lives of Nelson, Wesley, and others.

Southwell, Robert (1561–95), English poet and Jesuit martyr, beatified 1929. His poems include *The Burning Babe*.

Spaak, Paul Henri (1899–1972), Belgian statesman, first president of the U.N. General Assembly in 1946 and of the Assembly of the Council of Europe, 1949–51; secretary-general of NATO, 1957–61.

Spartacus (d. 71 B.C.), Thracian rebel. A Roman slave and gladiator in Capua, he escaped and headed a slave insurrection, routing several Roman armies, but was defeated and killed by Crassus.

Speke, John Hanning (1827–64), British explorer. In 1858 he discovered the Victoria Nyanza; and in 1860 with J. A. Grant traced the Nile flowing out of it.

Spence, Sir Basil Urwin (1907–76), Scottish architect, mainly known for the new Coventry cathedral, and for Hampstead civic centre. He also brought a new approach to university buildings. O.M. 1962.

Spencer, Herbert (1820–1903), English philosopher. B. Derby, he was at first a civil engineer, then a journalist (sub-editor of the *Economist*), when he wrote *Social Statics*. He coined the phrase (1852) " the survival of the fittest " and his *Principles of Psychology* (1855), published four years before Darwin's *Origin of Species*, expounded doctrines of evolution. His ten-volume *Synthetic Philosophy* was issued over a period of thirty years.

Spencer, Sir Stanley (1891–1959), English artist of visionary power. His two pictures of the *Resurrection* are in the Tate Gallery. He also painted Cookham regatta.

Spengler, Oswald (1880–1936), German historicist who held that every culture is destined to a waxing and waning life cycle and that the West European culture was entering its period of decline. His principal work is *The Decline of the West*. His views prepared the way for national socialism.

Spenser, Edmund (1552–99), English poet, b. London and educated at Cambridge. His *Shepheards Calender* appeared in 1579. In 1580 he went to Ireland as the lord deputy's secretary, and later acquired Kilcolman castle, where he wrote most of his main work, *The Faerie Queene*. His castle was burnt in an insurrection in 1598, when he returned to London. He is called " the poet's poet."

Spinoza, Baruch (1632–77), Dutch philosopher, b. Amsterdam, whose parents came to Holland from Portugal to escape the Inquisition. An independent thinker, his criticism of the Scriptures led to his being excommunicated from the synagogue. He supported himself by grinding and polishing lenses. He owed much to Descartes but was mainly concerned with religion and virtue. His philosophical theories are set out in the *Ethics* which was published posthumously. In the light of modern science his metaphysic cannot be accepted but his moral teaching has enduring validity.

Spofforth, Reginald (1770–1827), English writer of glees, including *Hail, Smiling Morn.*

Spurgeon, Charles Haddon (1834–92), English Baptist who preached at the vast Metropolitan Tabernacle, London, from 1861 (burnt down 1898).

Staël, Anne Louise, Baronne de Staël-Holstein (1766–1817), French writer. Daughter of the finance minister, Necker, she married the Swedish ambassador, and kept a salon. Her *Lettres sur Rousseau* appeared in 1788. After the revolution she lived partly abroad, partly in France, and after a visit to Italy wrote her novel *Corinne* (1807).

Stalin (Joseph Vissarionovich Djugashvili) (1879–1953), Soviet statesman who for nearly 30 years was leader of the Russian people. He originally studied at Tiflis for the priesthood, but became an active revolutionary and took part in the civil war after 1917. After Lenin's death, he ousted Trotsky and became the outstanding figure. He modernised agriculture on socialist lines by ruthless means, and his series of five-year plans from 1929 made Russia an industrial power. On the German invasion in 1941 he assumed military leadership; and later attended Allied war conferences. After his death some of his methods and the "personality cult" were denounced by Khrushchev, and this had far-reaching results in other Communist countries. In his attack on "official" Marxism, George Lukács says Stalin "turned Marxism on its head" by making it into theories and strategies which fitted his own tactics of the day.

Stanford, Sir Charles Villiers (1852–1924), Irish composer of instrumental, choral, operatic, and other music.

Stanley, Sir Henry Morton (1841–1904), British explorer, b. Denbigh. He fought for the Confederates in the American Civil War. He then became a correspondent for the *New York Herald*, was commissioned to find Livingstone, and did so in 1871 at Ujiji, and with him explored Lake Tanganyika. In 1879 he founded the Congo Free State under the Belgian king. His works include *Through the Dark Continent* and an *Autobiography*.

Steele, Sir Richard (1672–1729), British essayist, b. Dublin. He founded the *Tatler* (1709–11), to which Addison also contributed, and later the *Spectator* (1711–12) and the *Guardian* (1713). He also wrote plays and had a minor political career.

Steen, Jan (1626–79), Dutch genre painter, b. Leiden, son of a brewer. *The Music Lesson* and *Skittle Alley* are in the National Gallery, the *Lute Player* in the Wallace collection.

Steer, Philip Wilson (1860–1942), English painter, especially of landscapes and of portraits.

Stefansson, Vilhjalmur (1879–1962), Canadian arctic explorer of Icelandic parentage; his publications include *Unsolved Mysteries of the Arctic.*

Stein, Sir Aurel (1862–1943), British archaeologist, b. Budapest. He held archaeological posts under the Indian government and explored Chinese Turkestan.

Stendhal, pseudonym of Marie Henri Beyle (1783–1842), French novelist, b. Grenoble. He was with Napoleon's army in the Russian campaign of 1812, spent several years in Italy, and after the revolution of 1830 was appointed consul at Trieste, and afterwards at Civitavecchia. In his plots he recreates historical and social events with imaginative realism and delineates character with searching psychological insight. His main works are *Le Rouge et le Noir*, and *La Chartreuse de Parme.*

Stephen (1105–54), usurped the crown of England from Henry I's daughter in 1135; and, after anarchy, retained it till his death.

Stephen, Sir Leslie (1832–1904), English writer, critic, and biographer. He edited the *Cornhill Magazine* (1871–82), and the *Dictionary of National Biography* (1882–91), and was the father of Virginia Woolf.

Stephenson, George (1781–1848), English engineer; a locomotive designer, b. at Wylam near Newcastle, a colliery fireman's son. As enginewright at Killingworth colliery he made his first locomotive in 1814 to haul coal from mines. He and his son Robert built the *Locomotion* for the Stockton and Darlington Railway (1825), the first locomotive for a public railway. His *Rocket* at 30 miles an hour won the prize of £500 in 1829 offered by the Liverpool and Manchester Railway. He also discovered the principle on which the miners' safety lamp was based. He was the first president of the Institution of Mechanical Engineers.

Stephenson, Robert (1803–59), English engineer, son of the above, engineered railway lines in England and abroad, and built many bridges including the Menai and Conway tubular bridges and others overseas.

Sterne, Laurence (1713–68), English novelist and humorist. His main works are *Tristram Shandy* and *A Sentimental Journey.* He led a wandering and unconventional life, dying in poverty. His work helped to develop the novel.

Stevenson, Adlai (1900–65), American politician, an efficient governor of Illinois, 1949–1953; ambassador to the U.N., 1960–5, and unsuccessful presidential challenger to Eisenhower 1952 and 1956.

Stevenson, Robert (1772–1850), Scottish engineer and builder of lighthouses, who invented "intermittent" and "flashing" lights.

Stevenson, Robert Louis (1850–94), Scottish author, b. Edinburgh. He suffered from ill-health and eventually settled in Samoa. His main works are *Travels with a Donkey, Treasure Island, Kidnapped, Dr. Jekyll and Mr. Hyde,* and *The Master of Ballantrae.*

Stinnes, Hugo (1870–1924), German industrialist who built up a huge coalmining, iron and steel, and transport business, and later entered politics.

Stoker, Bram (Abraham Stoker) (1847–1912), Irish author of the horror story *Dracula* and *Personal Reminiscences of Henry Irving.*

Stokes, Sir George Gabriel (1819–1903), Irish mathematician and physicist to whom is due the modern theory of viscous fluids and the discovery that rays beyond the violet end of the spectrum (the ultra-violet rays) produce fluorescence in certain substances.

Stopes, Marie Carmichael (1880–1958), English pioneer advocate of birth control. Her *Married Love* appeared in 1918, and she pioneered birth control clinics.

Stowe, Harriet Beecher (1811–96), American author of *Uncle Tom's Cabin* (1852), written to expose slavery.

Strachey, John St. Loe (1901–63), English Labour politician and writer. He held office under Attlee, 1945–51.

Stradivari, Antonio (1644–1737), Italian maker of violins, b. Cremona, first in his art.

Strafford, 1st Earl of (Thomas Wentworth) (1593–1641), English statesman. He supported Charles I with a "thorough" policy, both as president of the north and as lord deputy in Ireland, where he introduced flax. His efficiency made him a special target when parliament met, and he was impeached and executed.

Strauss, David Friedrich (1808–74), German theologian, whose *Life of Jesus* attempted to prove that the gospels are based on myths.

Strauss, family of Viennese musicians. **Johann Strauss** (1804–49), the elder, was a composer of dance music, who with Joseph Lanner established the Viennese waltz tradition. His son, **Johann Strauss** (1825–99), the younger, although not so good a violinist or conductor as his father, was the composer of over 400 waltzes, which include *The Blue Danube* and *Tales from the Vienna Woods.* Two of his brothers, **Josef Strauss** (1827–70) and **Eduard Strauss** (1835–1916) were also composers and conductors.

Strauss, Richard (1864–1949), German composer and conductor, the son of a horn player in the opera orchestra at Munich. He succeeded von Bülow as court musical director at Meiningen. His works include the operas *Salome, Elektra,* and *Der Rosenkavalier* the symphonic poems *Don Juan, Till Eulenspiegel,* and *Don Quixote,* and many songs. *See* Section E.

Stravinsky, Igor (1882–1971), Russian composer and conductor, pupil of Rimsky-Korsakov.

His ballets, *The Fire Bird* (1910), *Petrushka* (1911), representative of his early romantic style, and the revolutionary *The Rite of Spring*, which caused a furore in 1913, were written for the ballet impresario Diaghilev. He adopted a neo-classical style in later works, for example, in the ballets *Pulcinella* and *Apollo Musagetes* and the opera-oratorio *Oedipus Rex*. He brought new vigour and freedom to rhythm and younger composers have been much influenced by his music. He became a French citizen in 1934 and a U.S. citizen in 1945. *See* **Section E.**

Strindberg, Johan August (1849–1912), Swedish writer of intense creative energy. His work is subjective and reflects his personal conflicts. He married three times but never happily. He produced some 55 plays as well as novels, stories, poems, and critical essays. *Lucky Peter*, *Gustav Adolf*, *Till Damascus*, *The Father*, *Miss Julie* are some of his plays.

Suckling, Sir John (1609–42), English poet, author of *Why so pale and wan?* He invented cribbage.

Sudermann, Hermann (1857–1928), German writer of plays and novels, including *Frau Sorge* (translated as Dame Care).

Sulaiman the Magnificent (1494–1566), sultan of Turkey, conquerer, and patron of art and learning, who dominated the eastern Mediterranean but failed to capture Malta.

Sullivan, Sir Arthur Seymour (1842–1900), Irish composer, mainly known for the music he wrote for light operas with W. S. Gilbert as librettist, especially *The Pirates of Penzance*, *Patience*, *The Mikado*, *The Yeomen of the Guard* and *The Gondoliers*. He also wrote sacred music which was popular at the time. He and a friend discovered Schubert's lost *Rosamunde* music.

Sully, Maximilien de Béthune, Duc de (1560–1641), French statesman, finance minister to Henry IV. He also left *Memoirs*.

Sun Yat Sen (1867–1925), Chinese revolutionary, idealist and humanitarian. He graduated in medicine at Hong Kong, but after a rising failed in 1895 he lived abroad, planning further attempts, which succeeded in 1911 when the Manchus were overthrown and he became president. He soon resigned in favour of Yuan Shih-kai. His "Three Principles" were nationalism, democracy, and livelihood.

Sutherland, Graham Vivian (b. 1903), British artist. He painted the 80th birthday portrait of Sir Winston Churchill for parliament, and designed the tapestry for Coventry cathedral. O.M. 1960.

Swedenborg, Emanuel (1689–1772), Swedish author of *Arcana Coelestia*, *The Apocalypse Revealed*, *Four Preliminary Doctrines*, and *The True Christian Religion*. He claimed that his soul had been permitted to travel into hell, purgatory, and heaven. His works became the scriptures of the sect named Swedenborgians.

Sweelinck, Jan Pieterszoon (1562–1621), Dutch organist and composer of sacred music. In his fugues he made independent use of the pedals, and prepared the way for Bach. *See* **Section E.**

Swift, Jonathan (1667–1745), English satirist, b. Dublin of English parents. He crossed to England in 1688 to become secretary to Sir William Temple, and took Anglican orders, but did not obtain promotion. His *Tale of a Tub* and *The Battle of the Books* appeared in 1704. At first active in Whig politics, he became Tory in 1710, writing powerful tracts such as *Conduct of the Allies* (1711). In 1714 he retired to Ireland as Dean of St. Patrick's. His devoted women friends followed him—Hester Johnson (d. 1728), the Stella of his *Journal*, and Esther Vanhomrigh (d. 1723), the Vanessa of his poetry. Here he wrote his best work, including *Gulliver's Travels* (1726) and *The Drapier's Letters*.

Swinburne, Algernon Charles (1837–1909), English poet and critic. He first won attention with a play, *Atalanta in Calydon*, in 1865, followed by *Poems and Ballads*. Later followed *Songs before Sunrise*, *Bothwell*, and *Mary Stuart*. His criticism includes an essay on Blake.

Swithin, St. (d. 862), English saint, bishop of Winchester. Violent rain for 40 days fell in 971 when his body was to be removed to the new cathedral; hence the superstition as to rain on 15 July.

Syme, Sir Ronald (b. 1903), Camden Professor of Ancient History at Oxford, 1949–70; an authority on Tacitus. O.M. 1976.

Symonds, John Addington (1840–93), English author who wrote on the Italian Renaissance.

Synge, John Millington (1871–1909), Irish poet and playwright, author of *Riders to the Sea* and *The Playboy of the Western World*. He was a director of the Abbey Theatre.

T

Tacitus, Gaius Cornelius (*c.* 55–120), Roman historian. His chief works are a life of his father-in-law Agricola, and his *Histories* and *Annals*.

Taft, William Howard (1857–1930), United States president, 1909–13.

Tagore, Sir Rabindranath (1861–1941), Indian poet and philosopher who tried to blend east and west. His works include the play *Chitra*. Nobel prize 1913 (first Asian recipient).

Talbot, William Henry Fox (1800–77), English pioneer of photography which he developed independently of Daguerre. He also deciphered the cuneiform inscriptions at Nineveh.

Talleyrand-Périgord, Charles Maurice de (1754–1838), French politician and diplomat, led a mission to England in 1792 and was foreign minister from 1797 until 1807. He represented France at the Congress of Vienna.

Tallis, Thomas (*c.* 1510–85), English musician, with Byrd joint organist to the chapel royal under Elizabeth. He composed some of the finest of our church music.

Tamerlane (Timur the Lame) (1336–1405), Mongol conqueror. Ruler of Samarkand, he conquered Iran, Transcaucasia, Iraq, Armenia, and Georgia, and invaded India and Syria. He defeated the Turks at Angora, but died marching towards China. A ruthless conqueror, he was also a patron of literature and the arts. The line of rulers descended from him are the Timurids. He is the subject of a play by Marlowe.

Tarkington, Booth (1869–1946), American author of *Monsieur Beaucaire*.

Tarquinius: two kings of Rome came from this Etruscan family; **Lucius the Elder** (d. 578 B.C.); and **Lucius Superbus**, or the proud, (d. 510 B.C.) whose tyranny provoked a successful rising and brought an end to the monarchy.

Tartini, Giuseppe (1692–1770), Italian violinist, who wrote *Trillo del Diavolo*. He discovered the "third sound" resulting from two notes sounded together, a scientific explanation of which was later given by Helmholtz.

Tasman, Abel Janszoon (1603–59), Dutch navigator despatched by Van Diemen. He discovered Tasmania or Van Diemen's Land, and New Zealand, in 1642.

Tasso, Torquato (1544–95), Italian epic poet, b. Sorrento, author of *Gerusalemme Liberata*. He also wrote plays, *Aminta* and *Torrismondo*.

Tawney, Richard Henry (1880–1962), British historian, b. Calcutta, pioneer of adult education, and leader of socialist thought—the first critic of the affluent society. His works include *The Acquisitive Society*, *Equality*, *Religion and the Rise of Capitalism*.

Taylor, Sir Geoffrey Ingram (b. 1886), British scientist, noted for his work on aerodynamics, hydrodynamics, and the structure of metals. O.M. 1969.

Taylor, Jeremy (1613–67), English divine, b. Cambridge, author of many religious works, of which the chief are *Holy Living* and *Holy Dying*.

Tchaikovsky, Peter Ilyich (1840–93), Russian composer. His music is melodious and emotional and he excelled in several branches of composition. Among his works are the operas *Eugene Onegin* and *The Queen of Spades* (both from stories by Pushkin), symphonies, including the *Little Russian* and the *Pathétique*, ballets, including *Swan Lake*, *The Sleeping Beauty*, and *The Nutcracker*, the fantasies *Romeo and Juliet*, and *Francesca da Rimini*, the piano concerto in B flat minor, the violin concerto in D, and numerous songs. *See* **Section E.**

Tedder, 1st Baron (Arthur William Tedder) (1890–1967), British air marshal. From 1940 he reorganised the Middle East Air Force and later became deputy supreme commander under

Eisenhower for the invasion of Europe. He wrote an autobiography.

Teilhard de Chardin, Pierre (1881–1955), French palæontologist and religious philosopher. He went on palæontological expeditions in Asia, but his research did not conform to Jesuit orthodoxy, and his main works were published posthumously, *The Phenomenon of Man* and *Le Milieu Divin*.

Telemann, Georg Philipp (1681–1767), German composer, b. Magdeburg. His vitality and originality of form are appreciated today after a long period of neglect.

Telford, Thomas (1757–1834), Scottish engineer, originally a stonemason. He built bridges (two over the Severn and the Menai suspension bridge), canals (the Ellesmere and Caledonian canals), roads, and docks.

Tell, William, legendary Swiss patriot, reputedly required by the Austrian governor Gessler to shoot an apple from his son's head, and the subject of a play by Schiller. The story is late, but the Swiss confederation did first arise in the 14th cent. with Schwyz, Uri, and Unterwalden.

Temple, Frederick (1821–1902), English divine. He was headmaster of Rugby, 1857–69, and archbishop of Canterbury, 1897–1902.

Temple, William (1881–1944), English ecclesiastic, son of above, was a leading moral force in social matters and a worker for ecumenism. He was headmaster of Repton, 1910–14, and became archbishop of Canterbury in 1942.

Temple, Sir William (1628–99), English diplomat and writer, was instrumental in bringing about the marriage of Princess Mary with William of Orange. Swift was his secretary.

Templewood, 1st Viscount (Samuel John Gurney Hoare) (1880–1959), British Conservative politician. He piloted the India Act through the Commons while secretary for India, 1931–5; and as foreign secretary he negotiated an abortive pact with Laval.

Teniers, David, the elder (1582–1649), **and the younger** (1610–94), Flemish painters of rural life and landscape. The elder lived at Antwerp and the younger at Brussels.

Tenniel, Sir John (1820–1914), English book illustrator, especially for *Alice in Wonderland* and *Punch*.

Tennyson, 1st Baron (Alfred Tennyson) (1809–92), English poet-laureate, b. Somersby, Lincs. A master of language, his publications extended over 60 years, mirroring much of his age. *In Memoriam* reflects his grief for his friend Arthur Hallam. Apart from his lyrics, his longer works include *The Princess*, *Maud*, *Idylls of the King*, and *Enoch Arden*. Interest in his work is returning.

Terence, Publius Terentius Afer (*c.* 184–159 B.C.), a Latin poet and dramatist, an African (Berber), who rose from the position of a slave.

Teresa, St. (1515–82), influential Spanish religious reformer and writer, b. Avila, a woman of boundless energy and spiritual strength. She entered the Carmelite order about 1534, established a reformed order in 1562 (St. Joseph's, Avila), and also founded, with the help of St. John of the Cross, houses for friars. Her writings which rank high in mystical literature include *The Way of Perfection* and *The Interior Castle*.

Terry, Ellen Alice (Mrs. James Carew) (1848–1928), English actress, especially in Shakespearean parts with Sir Henry Irving, and in the plays of her friend Bernard Shaw.

Tertullian, Quintus (*c.* 160–220), Carthaginian theologian whose works, especially *Apologeticum*, have profoundly influenced Christian thought.

Tesla, Nikola (1856–1943), Yugoslav physicist and inventor; went to America 1883; pioneer in high-tension electricity.

Tettrazzini, Luisa (1871–1940), Italian soprano, especially successful in *Lucia di Lammermoor*.

Tetzel, John (*c.* 1465–1519), German Dominican preacher, whose sale of indulgences for St. Peter's building fund provoked Luther.

Thackeray, William Makepeace (1811–63), English novelist, b. Calcutta, author of *Vanity Fair*, *Pendennis*, *Esmond*, *The Newcomes*, *The Virginians*, *Philip*, and *Lovel the Widower*. He edited the *Cornhill Magazine* from the first number in 1860, his most notable contributions being *RoundaboutPapers*. He also wrote *Yellowplush Papers*, *The Book of Snobs*, and *The Four Georges* (lectures given in the United States).

Thales of Miletus (*c.* 624–565 B.C.), earliest of the Greek scientists, he created a sensation by his prediction of an eclipse of the sun, which was visible at Miletus in 585 B.C. He looked upon water as the basis of all material things, and in his mathematical work was the first to enunciate natural laws. *See also* **God and Man, Section J.**

Thant, Sithu U (1909–74), Burmese diplomat; secretary-general of the United Nations 1962–1972.

Thatcher, Margaret Hilda (b. 1925), leader of the Conservative Party 1975–; the first woman in Europe to lead a political party; entered parliament as member for Finchley 1959.

Themistocles (*c.* 523–458 B.C.), Athenian soldier and statesman. He fortified the harbour of Piraeus and created a navy, defeating the Persians at Salamis in 480 B.C. He prepared the way for later greatness, but fell from power and died in exile.

Theocritus (*c.* 310–250 B.C.), Greek poet, especially of pastoral subjects. His short poems came to be called *Idylls*.

Theodoric the Great (455–526), King of the East Goths, who conquered Italy. Himself an Arian, he practised toleration, and his long reign was peaceful and prosperous.

Theodosius the Great (346–95), Roman emperor of the East (the Empire being divided in 364). He was baptised as a Trinitarian, issuing edicts against the Arians, and after a judicial massacre at Thessalonica he did penance to (St.) Ambrose.

Theophrastus (*c.* 372–287 B.C.), Greek philosopher, who succeeded Aristotle as teacher at Athens and inherited his library. He is best known for his botanical works and his *Characters* (moral studies).

Thibaud, Jacques (1880–1953), French violinist, killed in an air crash.

Thierry, Augustin (1795–1856), French historian, known for his *History of the Norman Conquest*.

Thiers, Louis Adolphe (1797–1877), French statesman and historian. After a varied political career, he became president in 1871, helping to revive France after defeat. He wrote a history of the Revolution.

Thomas, Dylan (1914–53), Welsh poet, whose highly individual *Eighteen Poems* (1934) brought him instant recognition. There followed *Twenty-five Poems* and *Deaths and Entrances*. *Under Milk Wood*, a play for voices, has more general appeal. *See* **Section M, Part III.**

Thompson, Sir D'Arcy Wentworth (1860–1948), Scottish zoologist whose *On Growth and Form* (1917), written in lucid and elegant style, has influenced biological science. He was also a classical scholar.

Thomson, Sir George Paget (1892–1975), English physicist, son of Sir J. J. Thomson; author of *The Atom*, *Theory and Practice of Electron Deffraction*, *The Inspiration of Science*. Nobel prizewinner 1937.

Thomson, James (1700–48), Scottish poet who wrote *The Seasons* and *The Castle of Indolence*.

Thomson, James (1834–82), poet and essayist, b. near Glasgow, who wrote *The City of Dreadful Night*.

Thomson, Sir Joseph John (1856–1940), English physicist and mathematician, leader of a group of researchers at the Cavendish laboratory, Cambridge. He established in 1897 that cathode-rays were moving particles whose speed and specific charge could be measured. He called them corpuscles but the name was changed to electrons. This work was followed up by the study of positive rays which led to the discovery of isotopes, the existence of which had earlier been suggested by Soddy. Nobel prizewinner 1906. *See also* **Section F, Part II.**

Thoreau, Henry David (1817–62), American essayist and nature-lover, who rebelled against society and lived for a time in a solitary hut. His chief work is *Walden*. He was a friend of Emerson.

Thorez, Maurice (1900–64), French communist leader from 1930 and especially after the second world war.

Thorndike, Dame Sybil (1882–1976), English actress. She made her début in 1904, and played in Greek tragedies, in the plays of Shakespeare and Shaw, and in Grand Guignol. Her husband was Sir Lewis Casson.

Thornycroft, Sir William Hamo (1850–1925), English sculptor, whose works include a statue of General Gordon in Trafalgar Square.

Thorpe, Sir Thomas Edward (1845–1925), English chemist who researched in inorganic chemistry and with his friend Arthur Rücker made a magnetic survey of the British Isles.

Thorwaldsen, Bertel (1770–1844), Danish sculptor whose works include the Cambridge statue of Byron.

Thucydides (*c.* 460–399 B.C.), Greek historian, especially of the Peloponnesian War in which he himself fought. He was not merely a chronicler, but saw the significance of events and tried to give an impartial account. The speeches attributed by him to leaders include the beautiful funeral oration of Pericles.

Tiberius, Claudius (42 B.C.–A.D. 37), Roman emperor who succeeded Augustus. His early reign was successful but his later years were marked by tragedy and perhaps insanity. He is the Tiberius of Luke 3.1.

Tillett, Benjamin (1860–1943), English trade-union leader, especially of a dockers' strike in 1889 and a transport-workers' strike in 1911.

Tillotson, John (1630–94), English divine, a noted preacher who became archbishop of Canterbury in 1691.

Tindal, Matthew (1655–1733), English deist, author of *Christianity as old as the Creation.*

Tintoretto (1518–94), Venetian painter whose aim it was to unite the colouring of Titian with the drawing of Michelangelo. His numerous paintings, mostly of religious subjects, were executed with great speed, some of them on enormous canvasses. His *Origin of the Milky Way* is in the National Gallery. His name was Jacopo Robusti, and he was called Il Tintoretto (little dyer) after his father's trade.

Tippett, Sir Michael Kemp (b. 1905), English composer whose works include the operas *The Midsummer Marriage, King Priam,* and *Knot Garden,* and the song-cycles *Boyhood's End* and *The Heart's Assurance.* *See* Section E.

Titian (Tiziano Vecelli) (*c.* 1487–1576), Venetian painter. He studied under the Bellinis and was influenced by Giorgione, for example, in his frescoes at Padua. His mature style is one of dynamic composition and full colour, as in his *Bacchus and Ariadne* (National Gallery). Among his principal works are *Sacred and Profane Love* (Borghese Gallery, Rome), and some in the Prado, Madrid.

Tito (Josip Broz) (b. 1892), Yugoslav leader, b. Kumrovec. In 1941 he organised partisan forces against the Axis invaders, liberated his country, and carried through a communist revolution. In 1945 he became the first communist prime minister and in 1953 president. He has successfully pursued an independent line for his country. Order of Lenin (1972).

Titus (A.D. 39–81), Roman emperor, son of Vespasian, brought the Jewish war to a close with the capture of Jerusalem. He completed the Colosseum.

Tizard, Sir Henry Thomas (1885–1959), English scientist and administrator. He was chairman of the Scientific Survey of Air Defence (later known as the Tizard Committee) that encouraged the birth of radar before the second world war and turned it into a successful defence weapon. He was chief scientific adviser to the government, 1947–52.

Tocqueville, Alexis, Comte de (1805–59), French liberal politician and historian, author of *Democracy in America,* still relevant reading.

Todd, 1st Baron (Alexander Robertus Todd) (b. 1907), Scottish biochemist, noted for his work on the structure of nucleic acids. Nobel prizewinner 1957; Pres. Royal Society 1975. Chancellor Univ. of Strathclyde.

Tolstoy, Leo Nikolayevich, Count (1828–1910), Russian writer and philosopher, b. Yasnaya Polyana. Of noble family, he entered the army and fought in the Crimean War. Beginning with simple, natural accounts of his early life (*Childhood* and *Boyhood*), he proceeded to articles on the war, and so eventually to perhaps his best work, the long novel *War and Peace,* followed by *Anna Karenina.* Increasingly preoccupied with social problems, he freed his serfs before this was done officially, and refused to take advantage of his wealth. His later works include *The Kreutzer Sonata* and *Resurrection.* By many he was regarded as a moral teacher.

Tooke, John Horne (1736–1812), English politician and pamphleteer, was a supporter of Wilkes and later of Pitt. He was tried for high treason, but was acquitted.

Torquemada, Tomas de (1420–98), first inquisitor-general of Spain.

Torricelli, Evangelista (1608–47), Italian physicist, pupil of Galileo. He invented the barometer and improved both microscope and telescope.

Toscanini, Arturo (1867–1957), Italian conductor, b. Parma. He had a remarkable musical memory, and was at the same time exacting and self-effacing. He spent the second world war in exile.

Toulouse-Lautrec, Henri de (1864–1901), French painter, whose pictures portray with stark realism certain aspects of Parisian life in the nineties, especially the *Moulin Rouge* series. Many are in the Musée Lautrec at Albi.

Tovey, Sir Donald Francis (1875–1940), English pianist and composer. His compositions include chamber music, a piano concerto, and an opera *The Bride of Dionysus;* and his writings *Essays in Musical Analysis.*

Toynbee, Arnold (1852–83), English historian and social reformer. The settlement Toynbee Hall was founded in his memory.

Toynbee, Arnold Joseph (1889–1975), nephew of above, English historian, known mainly for his 10-volume *A Study of History,* an analysis of many civilisations. He was for 30 years director of the Institute of International Affairs.

Traherne, Thomas (*c.* 1636–74), English religious poet, b. Hereford; author also of *Centuries of Meditations.*

Trajan (*c.* 53–117), Roman emperor, was a successful general and firm administrator. He was born in Spain.

Tree, Sir Herbert Beerbohm (1853–1917), English actor-manager of the Haymarket theatre until 1897 when he built His Majesty's theatre. Sir Max Beerbohm was his half-brother.

Trenchard, 1st Viscount (Hugh Montague Trenchard) (1873–1956), British air-marshal. He served with the Royal Flying Corps in the first world war and became the first air marshal of the R.A.F. He was largely responsible for the R.A.F. college at Cranwell and was also concerned in establishing Hendon police college.

Trent, 1st Baron (Jesse Boot) (1850–1931), British drug manufacturer, b. Nottingham. He built up the largest pharmaceutical retail trade in the world, and was a benefactor of Nottingham and its university.

Trevelyan, George Macaulay (1876–1962), English historian, known for his *History of England* and *English Social History.*

Trevelyan, Sir George Otto (1838–1928), English liberal politician, father of above. He wrote a life of his uncle Lord Macaulay.

Trevithick, Richard (1771–1833), English mining engineer and inventor, b. near Redruth, Cornwall. His most important invention was a high-pressure steam-engine (1801) and he is commonly acknowledged as the inventor of the steam locomotive for railways.

Trollope, Anthony (1815–82), English novelist. His early life was a struggle, the family being supported by his mother's writings. His own career was in the post office, but by strict industry he produced many novels especially portraying clerical life (the *Barchester* series) and political life (the *Phineas Finn* series).

Trotsky, Leo (Lev Davidovich Bronstein) (1879–1940), Russian revolutionary, b. of Jewish parents in the Ukraine, one of the leaders of the Bolshevik revolution. As commissar of foreign affairs under Lenin he led the Russian delegation at the Brest-Litovsk conference. He differed from Stalin on policy, believing in "permanent revolution," according to which socialism could not be achieved in Russia without revolutions elsewhere, and was dismissed from office in 1925 and expelled from the Communist party in 1927. In 1929 he took up exile in Mexico where he was assassinated.

Trudeau, Pierre Eliott (b. 1919), Liberal prime minister of Canada since 1968.

Truman, Harry S. (1884–1972), U.S. President, 1945–53. He inherited the presidency on Roosevelt's death in 1945 when he took the decision to drop the first atom bomb, and he won the election of 1948. He intervened in Korea, dismissed General MacArthur, and aimed at raising standards in underdeveloped countries.

Tulsi Das (1532–1623), Indian poet whose masterpiece *Ram-Charit-Mânas* (popularly known as the *Râmayana* and based on the Sanskrit epic of Vālmiki) is venerated by all Hindus as the Bible is in the West.

Turenne, Henri de la Tour d'Auvergne, Vicomte de (1611–75), French commander who was successful in the Thirty Years' War.

Turgenev, Ivan Sergeyvich (1818–83), Russian novelist, friend of Gogol and Tolstoy, who spent part of his life in exile. His works include *Fathers and Children*, *Smoke*, and *Virgin Soil*.

Turner, Joseph Mallord William (1775–1851), English landscape painter, b. London, a barber's son. He entered the Royal Academy and was at first a topographical watercolourist. Later he turned to oil and became a master of light and colour, achieving magical effects, especially in depicting the reflection of light in water. His works include *Crossing the Brook*, *Dido building Carthage*, *The Fighting Temeraire*, *Rain, Steam and Speed*. He also made thousands of colour studies. He encountered violent criticism as his style became more abstract which led to Ruskin's passionate defence of him in *Modern Painters*. He bequeathed his work to the nation (National and Tate Galleries, and the British Museum).

Tussaud, Marie (1760–1850), Swiss modeller in wax who learnt from her uncle in Paris, married a Frenchman, and later came to England where she set up a permanent exhibition.

Tutankhamun (d. *c.* 1340 B.C), Egyptian pharaoh of the 18th dynasty, son-in-law of Akhenaten, whose tomb was discovered by Howard Carter in 1922, with the mummy and gold sarcophagus intact. He died when he was 18.

Twain, Mark (Samuel Langhorne Clemens) (1835–1910), American humorist. His *Innocents Abroad* was the result of a trip to Europe. His works include *A Tramp Abroad*, *Tom Sawyer*, *Huckleberry Finn*, and *Pudd'nhead Wilson*.

Tweedsmuir, 1st Baron (John Buchan) (1875–1940), Scottish author of biographies, historical novels, and adventure stories, including *Montrose* and *Thirty-nine Steps*. He was governor-general of Canada 1935–40.

Tyler, Wat (d. 1381), English peasant leader. He was chosen leader of the Peasants' Revolt of 1381 (due to various causes), and parleyed at Smithfield with the young king Richard II, but was killed.

Tyndale, William (*c.* 1494–1536), English religious reformer, translator of the Bible. He had to go abroad, where he visited Luther and his New Testament was printed at Worms. When copies entered England they were suppressed by the bishops (1526). His Pentateuch was printed at Antwerp, but he did not complete the Old Testament. He was betrayed, arrested, and executed. Unlike Wyclif, who worked from Latin texts, he translated mainly from the original Hebrew and Greek and his work was later to become the basis of the Authorised Version of the Bible.

Tyndall, John (1829–93), Irish physicist whose wide interests led him to research on heat, light, and sound, and on bacteria-free air and sterilisation. He discovered why the sky is blue (Tyndall effect) and pioneered popular scientific writing, *e.g.*, *Heat as a Mode of Motion*. A mountaineer, one of the peaks of the Matterhorn is named after him.

U

Unamuno, Miguel de (1864–1936), Spanish philosopher, poet, essayist, and novelist, author of *El Sentimiento Trágico de la Vida* (The Tragic Sense of Life).

Ulanova, Galina (b. 1910), Russian ballerina, who made her début in 1928.

Undset, Sigrid (1882–1949), Norwegian novelist, daughter of an antiquary, author of *Jenny*, *Kristin Lavransdatter*, and *Olav Audunsson*. Nobel prizewinner 1928.

Unwin, Sir Raymond (1863–1940), English architect of the first garden city at Letchworth.

Ursula, St., said in late legend to have been killed by Huns at Cologne with many companions while on pilgrimage. It took rise from a 4th cent. inscription which simply referred to virgin martyrs.

Usher or Ussher, James (1581–1656), Irish divine who in 1625 became archbishop of Armagh, and whose writings include a long-accepted chronology, which placed the creation at 4004 B.C.

V

Valentine, St., was a Christian martyr of the reign of the emperor Claudius II (d. A.D. 270). The custom of sending valentines may be connected with the pagan festival of Lupercalia.

Valéry, Paul (1871–1945), French poet and essayist, strongly influenced by the symbolist leader, Mallarmé. His poems include *La jeune Parque*, *Charmes*, and *Le cimetière marin*.

Vanbrugh, Sir John (1664–1726), English architect and playwright. His buildings include Blenheim Palace and his plays *The Provok'd Wife*.

Vancouver, George (1758–98), British navigator who served under Captain Cook, also doing survey work, and who sailed round Vancouver island.

Vanderbilt, Cornelius (1794–1877), American merchant and railway speculator who amassed a fortune and founded a university at Nashville. His son, **William Henry Vanderbilt** (1821–85), inherited and added to it.

Van Dyck, Sir Anthony (1599–1641), Flemish painter, b. Antwerp. He studied under Rubens, travelled in Italy, and then settled in England with an annuity from Charles I. He excelled in portraits, especially of Charles I and Henrietta Maria, and of their court.

Vane, Sir Henry (1613–62), English parliamentary leader during the civil war period, though not involved in the execution of Charles I. He was executed in 1662.

Van Gogh, Vincent (1853–90), Dutch painter of some of the most colourful pictures ever created. With passionate intensity of feeling he painted without pause whatever he found around him—landscapes, still life, portraits; his was a truly personal art. His life was one of pain, sorrow, and often despair, and in the end he committed suicide.

Vauban, Sebastien de Prestre de (1633–1707), French military engineer, whose skill in siege works (*e.g.*, at Maestrict 1673) was a factor in the expansive wars of Louis XIV. He protected France with fortresses and also invented the socket bayonet.

Vaughan Williams, Ralph (1872–1958), English composer, b. Gloucestershire. After Charterhouse and Cambridge he studied music in Berlin under Max Bruch and, later in Paris, under Ravel. He wrote nine symphonies besides a number of choral and orchestral works, operas (including *Hugh the Drover*, *Riders to the Sea*), ballets, chamber music, and songs. He showed great interest in folk tunes. *See* Section E.

Velasquez, Diego (*c.* 1460–1524), Spanish conquistador, first governor of Cuba.

Velasquez, Diego Rodriguez de Silva y (1599–1660), Spanish painter, b. Seville, especially of portraits at the court of Philip IV, and also of classical and historical subjects. He made two visits to Italy (1629–31, 1649–51), studying the Venetian painters, especially Titian, which hastened the development of his style. Among his masterpieces are *The Maids of Honour*, *The Tapestry Weavers* (both in the Prado), the Rokeby Venus and a portrait of Philip IV (both in the National Gallery), the landscape views from the Villa Medici (Prado) and *Juan de Pareja* (sold in London in 1970 for £2·25 million).

Venizelos, Eleutherios (1864–1936), Greek statesman, b. Crete. He became prime minister in 1910 and held this office intermittently. He promoted the Balkan League (1912), forced the king's abdication (1917), and brought Greece into the war on the Allied side, securing territorial concessions at the peace conference, but his expansionist policy in Turkish Asia failed.

Verdi, Giuseppe (1813–1901), Italian composer, b. near Busseto in the province of Parma. His early works include *Nabucco*, *Ernani*, *I Due Foscani*, and *Macbeth*; a middle period is represented by *Rigoletto*, *Il Trovatore*, *La Traviata*, *Un Ballo in Maschera*, and *Don Carlos*; to the last period of his life belong *Aïda*, *Otello*, and *Falstaff* (produced when he was 80). *See* Section E.

Verlaine, Paul (1844–96), French poet, one of the first of the symbolists, also known for his memoirs and confessions. His works include *Poèmes saturniens*, *Fêtes galantes*, *Sagesse*, and *Romances sans paroles*. He was imprisoned for two years in Belgium for shooting and wounding his friend Rimbaud. He died in poverty in Paris.

Vermeer, Jan (1632–75), Dutch painter, b. Delft. His main paintings are of domestic interiors, which he makes into works of art, as in *Lady at the Virginals* (National Gallery). His reputation has grown during the last century.

Verne, Jules (1828–1905), French writer of science fiction, including *Five Weeks in a Balloon*, *Twenty Thousand Leagues Under the Sea*, *Round the World in Eighty Days*.

Vernier, Pierre (1580–1637), French inventor of the small sliding scale which enables readings on a graduated scale to be taken to a fraction of a division.

Veronese, Paolo (1528–88), Italian painter of the Venetian school, whose works include *Marriage Feast at Cana in Galilee*, *The Feast in the House of Simon*, and *The Presentation of the Family of Darius to Alexander. His Adoration of the Magi* is in the National Gallery.

Veronica, St., legendary woman who was said to hand her kerchief to Christ on the way to Calvary, to wipe his brow, and his impression was left on the kerchief. In its present form her legend dates from the 14th cent.

Verwoerd, Hendrik Frensch (1901–66), South African politician, b. Amsterdam, exponent of the policy of apartheid; prime minister 1958–66. He was assassinated.

Vespasian, Titus Flavius (A.D. 9–79), Roman emperor. He was sent by Nero to put down the Jews and was proclaimed by the legions. He began the Colosseum.

Vespucci, Amerigo (1451–1512), Florentine explorer, naturalised in Spain, contractor at Seville for Columbus. He later explored Venezuela. The use of his name for the continent arose through a mistake.

Vico, Giambattista (1688–1744), Italian philosopher of history and of culture, b. Naples. His ideas were developed in his *Scienza nuova* (science of history) but it was not until our own day that his originality as a thinker was fully recognised.

Victor Emmanuel II (1820–78), first king of Italy. King of Sardinia, he was proclaimed king of Italy in 1861 after the Austrians had been defeated and Garibaldi had succeeded in the south. Rome was added in 1870.

Victoria (1819–1901), Queen of the United Kingdom of Gt. Britain and Ireland and Empress of India, was granddaughter of George III and succeeded an uncle in 1837. In 1840 she married Prince Albert of Saxe-Coburg-Gotha, who died in 1861. Conscientious, hard-working, and of strict moral standards, she had by the end of a long life (jubilees 1887 and 1897) won the affection and respect of her subjects in a unique degree. Her reign saw industrial expansion, growing humanitarianism, literary output, and in the main prolonged peace; and by its close the British empire and British world power had reached their highest point.

Villeneuve, Pierre de (1763–1806), French admiral defeated by Nelson at Trafalgar and captured along with his ship, the *Bucentaure*.

Villon, François (1431–?1463), French poet, b. Paris, who lived at a turbulent time at the close of the Hundred Years War. After fatally stabbing a man in 1455 he joined the *Conquillards*, a criminal organisation. They had a secret language (the *jargon*) and it was for them that he composed his ballads. His extant works consist of the *Petit Testament* (1456), originally called *Le Lais*, and the *Grand Testament* (1461), masterpieces of mediaeval verse.

Virgil (Publius Vergilius Maro) (70–19 B.C.), Roman epic poet, b. at Andes near Mantua, he went to Rome to obtain redress for the military confiscation of his farm. He was patronised by Maecenas, and wrote his pastoral *Eclogues*, followed by his *Georgics*. His best-known work, the *Aeneid*, deals with the wanderings of Aeneas after the fall of Troy till his establishment of a kingdom in Italy.

Vivaldi, Antonio (*c.* 1675–1743), Venetian composer, violin master at the Ospedal della Pieta. His output of orchestral works was prolific and Bach arranged some of his violin pieces for the harpsichord. *See* Section E.

Volta, Alessandro (1745–1827), Italian physicist of Pavia, who, working on the results of Galvani, invented the voltaic pile, the first instrument for producing an electric current. It provided a new means for the decomposition of certain substances. His name was given to the volt, the unit of electrical potential difference.

Voltaire (François Marie Arouet) (1694–1778), French philosopher and writer. His first essays offended the authorities, and he spent the years 1726–9 in England, where he wrote some of his dramas. Returning to France, he published his *Philosophical Letters*, which aroused the enmity of the priesthood. At this juncture, the Marquise du Châtelet offered him the asylum of her castle of Cirey, and for the next 15 years he made this his home, writing there his *Discources of Man*, *Essay on the Morals and Spirit of Nations*, *Age of Louis XIV*, etc. The marquise was a mathematician and taught him some science, thus helping him in his interpretation of Newton's *Principia*. To Voltaire we owe the story of the falling apple, also the dictum that Admiral Byng was shot "pour encourager les autres." He spent the years 1750–3 in Berlin at the invitation of Frederick the Great. In challenging accepted beliefs and traditions he prepared the way for the French revolution.

Vondel, Joost van den (1587–1679), Dutch poet who lived at Amsterdam. Most of his dramas are on biblical subjects, and the two most famous are *Jephtha* and *Lucifer*.

Voroshilov, Klimentiv Efremovich (1881–1969), Soviet general who commanded the Leningrad defences in 1941, and was U.S.S.R. president, 1953–60.

Vyshinsky, Andrei Yanuarievich (1883–1954), Soviet jurist and diplomat; conducted the prosecution of the Moscow treason trials, 1936–8; represented Russian interests at the U.N.

W

Wade, George (1673–1748), English general and military engineer who, after the rising of 1715, pacified the Scottish highlands, constructing military roads and bridges. In the 1745 rising Prince Charles' forces evaded him.

Wagner, Richard (1813–83), German composer, b. Leipzig. He achieved a new type of musical expression in his operas by the complete union of music and drama. He made use of the *Leitmotif* and was his own librettist. His originality and modernism aroused a good deal of opposition, and he was exiled for some years. But he was supported by loyal friends, including Liszt, the young King Ludwig of Bavaria, and the philosopher Nietzsche. He began the music of the *Ring des Nibelungen* in 1853, but it was not until 1876 that the whole of the drama (Rheingold, Valkyrie, Siegfried, Götterdämmerung) was performed at Bayreuth under the conductor Hans Richter. Other operas are *The Flying Dutchman*, *Rienzi*, *Tannhäuser*, *Lohengrin*, *Tristan und Isolde*, *Die Meistersinger von Nürnberg*, and *Parsifal*, a religious drama. He married Liszt's daughter Cosima, formerly wife of his friend Hans von Bülow. *See* Section E.

Waldheim, Kurt (b. 1918), Austrian diplomat; succeeded U Thant as secretary-general of the United Nations in 1972.

Waley, Arthur (1889–1966), English orientalist, known for his translations of Chinese and Japanese poetry and prose, being the first to bring the literature of those countries to the western world.

Walker, George (1618–90), hero of the siege of Londonderry in 1688, who kept the besiegers at bay for 105 days.

Wallace, Alfred Russel (1823–1913), British naturalist, b. Usk, Monmouth, joint author with Darwin of the theory of natural selection. In 1858, while down with illness in the Moluccas, he sent a draft of his theory to Darwin in England who was amazed to find that it closely agreed with his own theory of evolution which he was on the point of publishing. The result was a reading of a joint paper to the Linnaean Society.

Wallace, Edgar (1875–1932), English novelist and playwright, known for his detective thrillers.

Wallace, Sir Richard (1818–90), English art collector and philanthropist, whose widow bequeathed his collection to the nation (Wallace Collection, Manchester Square, London).

Wallace, Sir William (*c.* 1274–1305), Scottish patriot. He withstood Edward I, at first successfully, but was defeated at Falkirk and executed.

Wallenstein, Albrecht von (1583–1634), German soldier and statesman during the Thirty Years War. An able administrator of his own estates, he sought the unity of Germany, but was distrusted and eventually assassinated.

Waller, Edmund (1606–87), English poet of polished simplicity, author of *Go, lovely rose*. He was able to agree with both parliamentarians and royalists.

Wallis, Sir Barnes Neville (b. 1887), British scientist and inventor whose many designs include the R100 airship, the Wellington bomber, the swing-wing aircraft, and the " bouncing bomb " that breached the Ruhr Dams in 1943.

Walpole, Horace, 4th Earl of Orford (1717–97), younger son of Sir Robert Walpole, English writer, chiefly remembered for his *Letters*, his *Castle of Otranto*, and his " Gothic " house at Strawberry Hill.

Walpole, Sir Hugh Seymour (1884–1941), English novelist, b. New Zealand. His works include *Fortitude*, *The Dark Forest*, and *The Herries Chronicle*.

Walpole, Sir Robert, 1st Earl of Orford (1676–1745), English Whig statesman, who came to office soon after the Hanoverian succession and is considered the first prime minister—a good finance minister, a peace minister, and a "house of commons man."

Walter, Bruno (1876–1962), German–American conductor, especially of Haydn, Mozart, and Mahler.

Walter, John (1776–1847), English newspaper editor. Under him *The Times*, founded by his father John Walter (1739–1812), attained a leading position.

Walton, Izaak (1593–1683), English writer, especially remembered for *The Compleat Angler*. He also wrote biographies of Donne, Hooker, and George Herbert.

Walton, Sir William Turner (b. 1902), English composer, whose works include concertos for string instruments, two symphonies, two coronation marches, *Façade* (setting to Edith Sitwell's poem), and an oratorio, *Belshazzar's Feast*. O.M. 1967.

Warbeck, Perkin (1474–99), Flemish impostor, b. Tournai, who claimed to be the younger son of Edward IV with French and Scottish backing, but failed and was executed.

Warwick, Earl of (Richard Neville) (*c.* 1428–71), " the kingmaker." At first on the Yorkist side in the Wars of the Roses, he proclaimed Edward IV king; but later changed sides and restored the Lancastrian Henry VI. He was killed at Barnet.

Washington, Booker Taliaferro (1858–1915), American Negro educationist, author of *Up from Slavery*. He became principal of Tuskegee Institute, Alabama.

Washington, George (1732–99), first U.S. president. B. in Virginia, of a family which originated from Northamptonshire, he served against the French in the Seven Years War. When the dispute between the British government and the Americans over taxation came to a head, he proved a successful general, and Cornwallis's surrender to him at Yorktown in 1781 virtually ended the war. In 1787 he presided over the Philadelphia convention which formulated the constitution, and was president 1789–97.

Watson, John Broadus (1878–1958), American psychologist, an exponent of behaviourism. *See* **Behaviourism, Section J.**

Watson-Watt, Sir Robert (1892–1973), Scottish physicist, who played a major part in the development of radar.

Watt, James (1736–1819), Scottish engineer and inventor, b. Greenock. He made important improvements to Newcomen's steam-engine by inventing a separate condenser (applying Black's discoveries (1761–4) on latent heat) and other devices based on scientific knowledge of the properties of steam. He was given support by Matthew Boulton, a capitalist, and settled down in Birmingham with him. He defined one horse-power as the rate at which work is done when 33,000 lb are raised one foot in one minute. He also constructed a press for copying manuscripts. The watt as a unit of power is named after him.

Watteau, Jean Antoine (1684–1721), French painter. He painted pastoral idylls in court dress. His works include *Embarquement pour Cythère* in the Louvre.

Watts, Isaac (1674–1748), English hymn-writer, author of *O God, our help in ages past*.

Watts-Dunton, Walter Theodore (1836–1914), English poet and critic, friend of Swinburne whom he looked after until his death in 1909. His works include *The Coming of Love* and *Aylwin*.

Waugh, Evelyn (1902–66), English satirical writer, author of *Vile Bodies*, *The Loved One*, *Brideshead Revisited*, *Life of Edmund Campion*, *The Ordeal of Gilbert Pinfold*, and an autobiography, *A Little Learning*. *See* **Section M, Part I.**

Wavell, 1st Earl (Archibald Percival Wavell) (1883–1950), British general. He served in the first great war on Allenby's staff and in the second he commanded in the Middle East 1939–41, defeating the Italians; and in India 1941–3. He was viceroy of India 1943–7.

Webb, Matthew (1848–83), English swimmer, the first to swim the English Channel (1875).

Webb, Sidney James, Baron Passfield (1859–1947), and his wife **Beatrice**, *née* Potter (1858–1943), English social reformers and historians. They combined careful investigation of social problems (their books include *History of Trade Unionism* and *English Local Government*) with work for the future; they were members of the Fabian Society, launched the *New Statesman*, and helped to set up the London School of Economics. He held office in Labour governments.

Weber, Carl Maria Friedrich Ernst von (1786–1826), German composer, who laid the foundation of German romantic opera. His reputation rests principally on his three operas, *Der Freischütz*, *Euryanthe*, and *Oberon*. He was also an able pianist, conductor, and musical director. *See* **Section E.**

Webster, Daniel (1782–1852), American statesman and orator. He held office more than once and negotiated the Ashburton Treaty which settled the Maine–Canada boundary.

Webster, Noah (1758–1843), American lexicographer, who published an *American dictionary of the English language*.

Wedgwood, Dame Cicely Veronica (b. 1910), English historian, author of *William the Silent*, *Thomas Wentworth*, *The Thirty Years' War*, *The King's Peace*, *The Trial of Charles I*; a member of the Staffordshire pottery family. O.M. 1969.

Wedgwood, Josiah (1730–95), English potter, who at his Etruria works near Hanley produced from a new ware (patented 1763) pottery to classical designs by Flaxman, and gave pottery a new impetus.

Weill, Kurt (1900–50), German composer of satirical, surrealist operas, including *Die Dreigroschenoper* (librettist Brecht), and musical comedies, including *Lady in the Dark* and *One Touch of Venus*. In 1936 he settled in the United States. *See* **Section E.**

Weingartner, Felix (1863–1942), Austrian conductor, also a composer and writer of a text book on conducting.

Weismann, August (1834–1914), German biologist. He worked on the question of individual variability in evolution, stressing the continuity of the germ plasm and rejecting the idea of inheritance of acquired characteristics.

Weizmann, Chaim (1874–1952), Israeli leader, b. Pinsk. He came to England in 1903 and taught biochemistry at Manchester. He helped to secure the Balfour Declaration (1917), promising a Jewish national home, and was for many years president of the Zionists. In 1948 he became first president of Israel.

Wellesley, Marquess (Richard Colley Wellesley) (1760–1842), British administrator. He was a successful governor-general of India, and was brother of the Duke of Wellington.

Wellington, 1st Duke of (Arthur Wellesley) (1769–1852), British general. B. in Ireland, he joined the army and gained experience in India. In the Peninsular War he successfully wore down and drove out the invading French. When Napoleon escaped from Elba, Wellington defeated him at Waterloo. Thereafter he took some part in politics as a Tory, but in the last resort was capable of accepting change.

Wells, Herbert George (1866–1946), English author. B. London, he was at first a teacher. He believed in progress through science, and became one of the most influential writers of his time. His long series of books includes romances of the Jules Verne variety (*The Time Machine*, *The Island of Dr. Moreau*, *The Invisible Man*), sociological autobiography (*Love and Mr. Lewisham*, *Kipps*, *Tono-Bungay*, *The History of Mr. Polly*, *Mr. Britling Sees it Through*), and popular education (*Outline of History*, *The Science of Life*, *The Work, Wealth and Happiness of Mankind*, *The Shape of Things to Come*, *The Fate of Homo Sapiens*). He was an early and successful educator of the common man. He was also a founder member of the Fabian Society.

Wesley, Charles (1707–88), English hymnwriter. He was the companion of his brother John, and wrote over 5,500 hymns, including *Love divine* and *Jesu, lover of my soul*.

Wesley, John (1703–91), English evangelist and founder of Methodism (at first a nickname applied to friends of himself and his brother), b. at Epworth. After a trip to Georgia and after encountering Moravian influence, he began to teach on tour, covering in over 50 years more than 200,000 miles and preaching over 40,000 sermons. He made religion a live force to many ignorant folk of humble station who could only be reached by a new and direct challenge. He made a feature of the Sunday school and increased the use of music (the brothers' first hymnbook appeared in 1739). He did not plan separation from the Anglican church, though it was implicit in his ordination of a missionary, and it took place after his death. *See also* **Methodism, Section J.**

Westermarck, Edward Alexander (1862–1939), Finnish sociologist. His works include *History of Human Marriage*, *Origin and Development of the Moral Ideas*, and *The Oedipus Complex*.

Westinghouse, George (1846–1914), American engineer who invented an air-brake for railways (1868) called by his name, and pioneered the use of high tension alternating current for the transmission of electric power.

Westmacott, Sir Richard (1775–1856), English sculptor of Achilles in Hyde Park.

Wharton, Edith (1862–1937), American novelist and friend of Henry James. Her works include *House of Mirth* and *Custom of the Country*.

Whately, Richard (1787–1863), English archbishop of Dublin. He wrote treatises on *Rhetoric* and *Logic*.

Wheatstone, Sir Charles (1802–75), English physicist, one of the first to recognise Ohm's law. In 1837 he (with W. F. Cooke) patented an electric telegraph. He also introduced the microphone.

Wheeler, Sir Charles (1892–1974), English sculptor, especially on buildings. His autobiography is *High Relief*. P.R.A., 1956–66.

Whistler, James Abbott McNeill (1834–1903), American artist. B. at Lowell, he studied in Paris and settled in England. He reacted against the conventions of his day, and Ruskin's uncomprehending criticism of his work resulted in a lawsuit. Among his main works are studies of the Thames, and a portrait of his mother, now in the Louvre.

White, Sir George Stuart (1835–1912), British general who defended Ladysmith in the South African War.

White, Patrick (b. 1912), Australian novelist. Nobel prizeman 1973. *See* **Section M, Part I.**

Whitefield, George (1714–70), English evangelist, b. Gloucester. He was at first associated with the Wesleys, but differed from them on predestination. His supporters built him a "Tabernacle" in London, and he had other chapels elsewhere, but founded no lasting sect.

Whitgift, John (1530–1604), archbishop of Canterbury in the time of Elizabeth I (from 1583). His policy helped to clarify and strengthen the Anglican church.

Whitman, Walt (1819–92), American poet, b. Long Island. He led a wandering life and did hospital work in the Civil War. He aimed at forming a new and free American outlook. His works include *Leaves of Grass*, *Drum Taps*, and *Democratic Vistas*.

Whittier, John Greenleaf (1807–92), American Quaker poet, b. Haverhill, Mass. He wrote against slavery (*Justice and Expediency*), turning to poetry after the Civil War, especially remembered for *Snow-bound*. His religious poems have become hymns, including *Dear Lord and Father of Mankind*.

Whittington, Richard (*c.* 1358–1423), English merchant. Son of a Gloucestershire knight, he became a London mercer and was mayor of London 1398, 1406, 1419. He left his fortune to charity. The cat legend is part of European folklore.

Whittle, Sir Frank (b. 1907), pioneer in the field of jet propulsion. The first flights of Gloster jet propelled aeroplanes with Whittle engine took place in May 1941.

Whymper, Edward (1840–1911), English wood-engraver and mountaineer. He was the first to climb the Matterhorn. His books include *Scrambles amongst the Alps*.

Wilberforce, William (1759–1833), English philanthropist, b. Hull. He was the parliamentary leader of the campaign against the slave trade, abolished in 1807. He then worked against slavery itself, but that further step was only taken in the year of his death.

Wilcox, Ella Wheeler (1855–1919), American writer of romantic sentimental verse.

Wilde, Oscar Fingall (1854–1900), Irish author and dramatist, son of a Dublin surgeon and leader of the cult of art for art's sake. His works include poems, fairy-tales, short stories, and witty comedies—*Lady Windermere's Fan*, *A Woman of No Importance*, *An Ideal Husband*, and *The Importance of Being Earnest*. In a libel action he was convicted of homosexual practices and imprisoned for two years, when he wrote *The Ballad of Reading Gaol*.

Wilder, Thornton Niven (1897–1975), American author and playwright. Among his books are *The Bridge of San Luis Rey* and *Ides of March*.

Wilkes, John (1727–97), English politician. A Whig, he violently attacked George III in his paper the *North Briton*, and as a result of unsuccessful proceedings against him, general warrants were determined illegal. He was again in trouble for obscene libel; his defiance of authority brought him popularity, and he was four times re-elected to parliament but refused his seat, until his opponents gave way. His motives were mixed, but he helped to establish freedom of the press.

Willcocks, Sir William (1852–1932), British engineer, b. India, who carried out irrigation works in India, Egypt, South Africa, and Mesopotamia. He built the Aswan dam (1898–1902).

Willett, William (1856–1915), English advocate of "daylight savings," adopted after his death.

William I of England (1027–87), the "Conqueror," Duke of Normandy, claimed the English throne as successor to Edward the Confessor, and defeated Harold II at Hastings in 1066. An able commander and a firm ruler, he crushed Saxon resistance, especially in the north, transferred most of the land to his Norman followers, and drew England into closer relations with the continent, as did his archbishop Lanfranc. He ordered the Domesday survey (*see* **Section L**).

William II of England (1056–1100), the Conqueror's son, surnamed Rufus, succeeded in 1187. Capricious and self-indulgent, his reign was troubled, and he was shot (by accident or design) while hunting in the New Forest.

William III of England (1650–1702), King of England, Scotland, and Ireland (1689–1702), son of William II of Orange and Mary, daughter of Charles I. He married Mary, daughter of the Duke of York (later James II) while stadtholder of Holland. In 1688, when James had abdicated and fled the country, he was invited to succeed and he and Mary became joint king and queen. The revolution of 1688 brought to England tolerance of Protestant worship, but William was mainly concerned with war against France, brought to an end in 1697.

William IV of England (1765–1837), third son of George III, succeeded his brother George IV in 1830; called the " sailor king." The reform bill of 1832 and other reform measures were carried without obstruction from him.

William I of Germany (1797–1888), King of Prussia and first German emperor. He succeeded to the throne in 1861 and continued resistance to reform, appointing Bismarck as chief minister, and supporting him through the Austro-Prussian and Franco-Prussian wars. His personal character was simple and unassuming.

William II of Germany, the Kaiser (1859–1941), King of Prussia and German emperor from 1888, was grandson of William I and of Queen Victoria. He was intelligent but impetuous, and believed in military power. He dismissed Bismarck. In 1914 his support of Austria helped to precipitate European war, and the resulting defeat brought his abdication, after which he lived in retirement at Doorn in Holland.

William the Silent (1533–1584), Dutch national leader. Prince of Orange, he led the revolt of the Protestant Netherlands against the rule of the Spanish Philip II. The union of the northern provinces was accomplished in 1579, and Spanish rule was renounced by 1584, in which year William was assassinated.

Williams, Sir George (1821–1905), founder of the Young Men's Christian Association.

Williamson, Malcolm (b. 1931), Australian composer, pianist and organist; succeeded Sir Arthur Bliss as Master of the Queen's Musick.

Wilson, Edmund (1895–1972), American critic, author of *Axel's Castle* (1931), *The Triple Thinkers* (1938), *The Wound and the Bow* (1941), *To the Finland Station* (1940), *The Shores of Light* (1952), *The Dead Sea Scrolls* (1955).

Wilson, Harold, Sir (b. 1916), British statesman, leader of the Labour Party 1963–76; prime minister 1964–70, 1974–6. Entered parliament 1945 as member for Ormskirk; elected for Huyton 1950. Returned twice, in 1964 and a decade later, to head a government facing a formidable balance-of-payments deficit. In Feb. 1974 returned to power at head of first minority government since 1929; in subsequent election Oct. 1974 secured narrowest overall majority in any election in recent history. Resigned March 1976. Founder of the Open University. Chancellor of Bradford University.

Wilson, Richard (1714–82), British landscape painter, b. Montgomeryshire. Admired by Turner and Constable.

Wilson, Thomas Woodrow (1856–1924), American statesman. He was U.S. president 1913–21, brought America into the first world war and advocated the League of Nations, but was not a successful negotiator at the peace conference and could not carry his country into the League. His administration introduced prohibition and women's suffrage.

Wingate, Orde Charles (1903–44), leader of the Chindit forces engaged behind the Japanese lines in Burma during the second world war.

Winifred, St., the 7th cent. patron saint of North Wales, said in late legend to have been killed by her rejected suitor, Prince Caradoc, but restored by her uncle.

Wiseman, Nicholas Patrick (1802–65), cardinal, b. in Spain of an Irish family. In 1850 on the restoration in England of the Roman Catholic hierarchy he became first archbishop of Westminster, and reorganised and developed his church in Great Britain.

Wittgenstein, Ludwig Josef Johann (1889–1951), Austrian linguistic philosopher whose main works were the *Tractatus Logico-Philosophicus* of his early period, much admirred by Russell, and the *Philosophical Investigations*.

Wodehouse, Pelham Grenville (1881–1975), English humorist, creator of Jeeves in the Bertie Wooster stories. He became a U.S. citizen.

Wolf, Friedrich August (1759–1824), German classical scholar, a founder of scientific classical philology.

Wolf, Hugo (1860–1903), Austrian song-writer. In his settings of over 300 German lyrics, including many of Mörike and Goethe, he achieved complete union of poetry and music. *See* **Section E.**

Wolfe, James (1727–59), British general, b. Westerham. He showed early promise in the Seven Years' War, and was given command of the expedition against Quebec, which in spite of its strong position he captured, but lost his life.

Wolsey, Thomas (*c.* 1475–1530), English cardinal. A butcher's son at Ipswich, he entered the church, becoming archbishop of York and cardinal, while in the same year (1515) he became Henry VIII's lord chancellor. But in spite of his ability he was unable to secure papal sanction for the king's divorce from Catherine of Aragon, and fell from power and died. He was the last of the great ecclesiastical statesmen of the Middle Ages.

Wood, Sir Henry Joseph (1869–1944), English conductor, founder of the Promenade Concerts which he conducted from 1895 till his death.

Woodcock, George (b. 1904), English trade union leader, T.U.C. general secretary 1960–69; first chairman of the Commission on Industrial Relations set up by the Labour government, 1969–71.

Woodville, Elizabeth (1437–91), wife of Edward IV. Her daughter Elizabeth married Henry VII.

Woolf, Virginia (1882–1941), English writer, daughter of Sir Leslie Stephen and wife of Leonard Woolf with whom she founded the Hogarth Press. Her works develop the stream-of-consciousness technique and include *To the Lighthouse*, *Mrs. Dalloway*, *The Waves*, *A Room of One's Own*. *See* **Section M, Part I.**

Woolley, Sir Richard van der Riet (b. 1906), succeeded Sir Harold Spencer Jones as astronomer royal (England), 1956–72.

Wootton of Abinger, Baroness (Barbara Frances Wootton) (b. 1897), English social scientist; chairman Metropolitan Juvenile Courts 1946–62; deputy speaker of the House of Lords 1966–70. Her works include *Social Science and Social Pathology*, *Crime and the Criminal Law*, and an autobiography *In a world I never made*.

Wordsworth, William (1770–1850), English poet, b. Cockermouth. He went to Cambridge, and in 1798 with Coleridge issued *Lyrical Ballads*, a return to simplicity in English poetry. He settled at Grasmere with his sister Dorothy (1771–1855), to whose insight his poems owe much. Among his best works are his sonnets and his *Ode on the Intimations of Immortality*, besides his *Prelude*.

Wren, Sir Christopher (1632–1723), English architect, b. Wiltshire. After the great fire (1666) he prepared an abortive plan for rebuilding London, but did in fact rebuild St. Paul's and more than fifty other city churches, including St. Stephen, Walbrook, and St. Mary-le-Bow. Other works include Chelsea Hospital, portions of Greenwich Hospital, the Sheldonian theatre, Oxford, and Queen's College library, Oxford. He had wide scientific interests (he was professor of mathematics at Gresham College, London, and professor of astronomy at Oxford) and helped to found the Royal Society.

Wright, Frank Lloyd (1869–1959), American architect, initiator of horizontal strip and all-glass design. His influence has spread over the world. His buildings include the Imperial Hotel, Tokio, and the Guggenheim Museum, New York.

Wright, Orville (1871–1948), American airman who with his brother Wilbur (1867–1912) in 1903 was the first to make a controlled sustained flight in a powered heavier-than-air machine, flying a length of 852 ft. at Kitty Hawk, N.C.

Wyatt, James (1746–1813), English architect who built Fonthill Abbey.

Wyatt, Sir Thomas (1503–42), English poet who introduced the sonnet from Italy. He was also a diplomat.

Wyatt, Sir Thomas the younger (*c.* 1520–54), son of above, unsuccessfully led a revolt against Queen Mary on behalf of Lady Jane Grey.

Wycherley, William (1640–1715), English dramatist of the Restoration period. A master of satiric comedy, his plays include *Love in a Wood*, *The Plain Dealer*, and (the best-known) *The Country Wife*.

Wyclif, John (*c.* 1320–84), English religious reformer. He taught at Oxford, later becoming rector of Lutterworth. He insisted on inward religion and attacked those practices which he thought had become mechanical. His followers, called Lollards, were suppressed, partly for political reasons. The Wyclif Bible, the first and literal translation of the Latin Vulgate into English, was mainly the work of his academic followers at Oxford.

Wykeham, William of (1324–1404), English churchman. He held office under Edward III and became bishop of Winchester in 1367. He founded New College, Oxford, and Winchester School, and improved Winchester cathedral.

Wyllie, William Lionel (1851–1931), English marine painter of *The Thames Below London Bridge*.

Wyspianski, Stanislav (1869–1907), Polish poet, dramatist and painter. His plays *The Wedding*, *Liberation*, and *November Night* treat of national themes.

X

Xavier, St. Francis (1506–52), "apostle of the Indies," b. at Xavero in the Basque country. He was associated with Loyola in founding the Jesuits, and undertook missionary journeys to Goa, Ceylon, and Japan. He died while planning another to China.

Xenophon (444–359 B.C.), Athenian general and historian. He commanded Greek mercenaries under the Persian Cyrus, and on the latter's death safely marched the Ten Thousand home through hostile country. His chief works are the *Anabasis*, the *Hellenica*, and *Cyropaedia*.

Xerxes (*c.* 519–465 B.C.), King of Persia, was son of the first Darius. In 481 B.C. he started on an expedition against Greece when, according to Herodotus, he had a combined army and navy of over two and a half million men. He defeated the Spartans at Thermopylae, but his fleet was overcome at Salamis. He reigned from 485 to 465 B.C. and met his death by assassination.

Ximénes de Cisneros, Francisco (1436–1517), Spanish statesman and churchman. He became cardinal in 1507; carried out monastic reforms; and directed preparation of a polyglot bible, the *Complutensian*; but as inquisitor-general he was fanatical against heresy. He was adviser to Queen Isabella; in 1506 regent for Queen Juana; and himself directed an expedition to conquer Oran and extirpate piracy.

Y

Yeats, William Butler (1865–1939), Irish lyric poet and playwright, b. near Dublin, a leader of the Irish literary revival. His plays were performed in the Abbey Theatre (which with Lady Gregory (1852–1932) he helped to found), and include *Cathleen Ni Houlihan*, *The Hour Glass*, and *Deidre*. His poetry is discussed in **Section M, Part III.** A complete edition of the *Collected Poems* appeared in 1950.

Yonge, Charlotte Mary (1823–1901), English novelist. Influenced by Keble, she wrote novels which faithfully reflect some aspects of Victorian life; one such is *The Daisy Chain*. She also wrote historical fiction such as *The Dove in the Eagle's Nest*.

Young, Brigham (1801–77), American Mormon leader, and president in 1844 after the founder's death. He was a main founder of Salt Lake City. He practised polygamy. *See also* **Mormonism, Section J.**

Young, Francis Brett (1884–1954), English novelist, author of *My Brother Jonathan* and *Dr. Bradley remembers*.

Young, James (1811–83), Scottish chemist, b. Glasgow, whose experiments led to the manufacture of paraffin oil and solid paraffin on a large scale.

Young, Thomas (1773–1829), English physicist, physician and egyptologist, b. Somerset, of Quaker family. He established the wave theory of light and its essential principle of interference, put forward a theory of colour vision, and was the first to describe astigmatism of the eye. He was also largely responsible for deciphering the inscriptions on the Rosetta stone.

Younghusband, Sir Francis Edward (1863–1942), English explorer and religious leader. He explored Manchuria and Tibet, and wrote on India and Central Asia. He founded the World Congress of Faiths in 1936 (*see* **Section J**).

Ypres, 1st Earl of. *See* **French.**

Ysayë, Eugène (1858–1929), Belgian violinist and conductor, noted chiefly for his playing of the works of Bach and César Franck.

Yukawa, Hideki (b. 1907), Japanese physicist, who received the 1949 Nobel prize for predicting (1935) the existence of the meson.

Z

Zadkiel (angel in rabbinical lore), pseudonym of two astrologers: **William Lilly** (1602–81) and **Richard James Morrison** (1794–1874).

Zadkine, Ossip (b. 1890), Russian sculptor in France, who makes play with light on concave surfaces. His works include *Orpheus* and the public monument *The Destruction of Rotterdam*.

Zaharoff, Sir Basil (1849–1936), armaments magnate and financier, b. Anatolia of Greek parents. He was influential in the first world war.

Zamenhof, Ludwig Lazarus (1859–1917), Polish-Jew who invented Esperanto. He was by profession an oculist.

Zeno of Citium (?342–270 B.C.), philosopher, founder of the Stoic system. He left Cyprus to teach in Athens.

Zeppelin, Ferdinand, Count von (1838–1917), German inventor of the dirigible airship, 1897–1900. It was used in the first world war.

Zeromski, Stefan (1864–1925), Polish novelist, author of *The Homeless*, *The Ashes*, *The Fight with Satan*.

Zhukov, Georgi Konstantinovich (1896–1974), Soviet general, who led the defence of Moscow and Stalingrad and lifted the siege of Leningrad in the second world war, and accepted the German surrender in 1945. He continued to be active till 1957.

Zhukovsky, Vasily Andreyevich (1783–1852), Russian poet and translator of German and English poets. For many years he was tutor to the future Tsar Alexander II.

Zola, Emile Edouard (1840–1902), French novelist, b. Paris, of Italian descent. His series, *Les Rougon-Macquart*, portrays in a score of volumes (the best known of which are perhaps *L'Assommoir*, *Nana* and *Germinal*) the fortunes of one family in many aspects and in realistic manner. He had the moral courage to champion Dreyfus.

Zorn, Anders Leonhard (1860–1920), Swedish sculptor, etcher, and painter.

Zoroaster (Zarathustra) (fl. 6th cent. B.C.), Persian founder of the Parsee religion. He was a monotheist, and saw the world as a struggle between good (Ahura Mazda) and evil (Ahriman). *See* **Zoroastrianism, Section J.**

Zoshchenko, Mikhail (1895–1958), Russian writer of humorous short stories, which include *The Woman who could not Read and other Tales* and *The Wonderful Dog and other Stories*.

Zosimus (fl. *c.* 300), the first known alchemist. He lived in Alexandria.

Zuccarelli, Francesco (1702–88), Italian artist of fanciful landscapes. He spent many years in London and was elected a founder member of the R.A. (1768).

Zuckermann, Baron (Solly Zuckermann) (b. 1904), British biologist; chief scientific adviser to British governments; 1940–71. His publications include *Scientists and War* and *The Frontiers of Public and Private Science*. O.M. 1968.

Zwingli, Ulrich (1484–1531), Swiss religious reformer. He taught mainly at Zurich, where he issued a list of reformed doctrines, less extreme than those of Calvin.

Zwirner, Ernst Friedrich (1802–61), German architect who restored Cologne cathedral.

BACKGROUND TO PUBLIC AFFAIRS

This section is in two parts. The first provides an up-to-date chronicle and analysis of recent changes in Britain and describes the political system and institutions under which we are governed. The second part provides a wide-ranging guide to events and movements elsewhere in the world.

TABLE OF CONTENTS

BACKGROUND TO PUBLIC AFFAIRS

This section is in two parts. The first describes some major events in Britain since 1945 and looks at the political system and institutions under which we are governed. The second part provides a wide-ranging guide to events elsewhere in the world and takes stock of the changing patterns in international relations.

I. SURVEY OF THE BRITISH POLITICAL SCENE

I. NARRATIVE OF EVENTS 1945–77

The Labour Government 1945–51.

In July 1945 the Labour Party, led by Clement Attlee, was elected into office with an overall majority of 146. Although the Government had to cope with a very difficult economic situation as a result of the strains of the War, it undertook a major programme of reform. Domestically, important developments included the nationalisation of coal, electricity, gas, most of inland transport and the iron and steel industry and the creation of the National Health Service. Abroad, Britain played a major part in the creation of the North Atlantic Treaty Organisation and the Council of Europe.

The Conservatives Regain Power.

In 1950 the Labour Government was re-elected but with an overall majority of only six. It lasted for just 20 months as, weakened by the death and retirement of some of its senior members and by the resignation of two Cabinet ministers, Aneurin Bevan and Harold Wilson, Attlee decided to call another election in October 1951. Although the Labour Party secured the largest number of votes ever cast for a party, the Conservatives won a small majority of seats. Sir Winston Churchill thus became Prime Minister for the second time, remaining in office until April 1955. He was succeeded by Sir Anthony Eden who led the Conservatives to victory in the general election of 1955. At the end of 1955 Hugh Gaitskell replaced Attlee as leader of the Labour Party.

The Suez Crisis.

Increasing prosperity, which was one of the reasons for the Conservatives' electoral success, should have ensured a long tenure of office for Eden. However, in 1956 his reputation suffered seriously as a result of the Suez crisis. Following the nationalisation of the Suez Canal by the Egyptians, Britain intervened with France to occupy the canal zone but, under great pressure from the United States, the Government was compelled to withdraw the troops. Early in 1957, Eden was forced to resign due to ill-health and he was succeeded by Harold Macmillan.

The Macmillan Years.

Although Macmillan was confronted with serious problems on both the domestic and foreign fronts, he succeeded in turning the tide such that when the country went to the polls in 1959 the Conservatives won for a third time with a handsome overall majority of 100 seats. There was despair in the Labour camp and swift recriminations took place. Gaitskell believed that the Party's image was outmoded, and in 1960 decided to fight for the abandonment of Clause 4, the nationalisation clause of the Party's constitution. This led to a fierce internal struggle between right and left, which was followed by a further campaign to get Conference to adopt a motion making unilateral nuclear disarmament the official policy of the Labour Party. Gaitskell promised to "fight, fight and fight again" to secure the reversal of this decision, and succeeded the following year.

In July 1961 the Chancellor of the Exchequer, Selwyn Lloyd, introduced a pay pause in response to further balance of payments difficulties. This was unpopular and started the Government's decline. From the middle of 1962 it seemed dogged by misfortune. Quickly following the failure of Britian's application to enter the European Economic Community came the hardships of a severe winter and a sudden increase in unemployment. When the spring came the Government was caught in another misfortune, the Profumo affair, involving the resignation of its War Minister.

Changes in Leadership.

These troubles led to a growing feeling that Macmillan should make way for a younger man. However he determined to lead his party into the next election and probably would have done so but for an illness which led to his resignation on the day before the opening of the annual party conference in 1963. As a result the conference became an election convention in which the candidates for the leadership attempted to advance their cause. At the end of the processes of selection, however, it was Lord Home, the Foreign Secretary, who emerged as leader. He renounced his peerage and was elected to the House of Commons in a by-election. During 1963 the Labour Party was also compelled to find a new leader, following the death of Hugh Gaitskell at the age of 57. In his place the Parliamentary Labour Party elected Harold Wilson, who had stood unsuccessfully against Gaitskell in 1960.

Election Year 1964.

Most of 1964 was dominated by electoral activity as the election was not held until almost the last possible date, in October. The result was a photo-finish. The large Conservative majority was wiped out but the Labour Party only had a majority of five over all the other parties. However, after thirteen years in opposition, the Labour Party returned to office with Harold Wilson as Prime Minister. Although there was considerable doubt as to how long the new government could survive, it immediately started to take action to correct the serious economic situation it inherited.

New Conservative Leader.

The loss of the 1964 election and the popular appeal of the new Prime Minister convinced many Conservatives that a change of leader was necessary. Before tendering his resignation in 1965, Sir Alec Douglas-Home introduced a new procedure for the election of his successor by Conservative M.P.s. In the ensuing election Edward Heath was chosen to take his place.

1966 Election.

Harold Wilson succeeded in exploiting his Party's position in Parliament to the full. As a result he was able to choose the date of the next election. This he did at the end of March 1966 and his tactical skill was rewarded by a convincing victory which gave Labour an overall majority of almost 100. However, the Government's fortunes soon changed with a serious deterioration in the economic situation. These problems and the harsh measures needed to deal with them dominated the life of the Government for the next three years. In July 1966 a severe deflationary package and a freeze on prices and incomes were introduced. These measures, however, failed to cure the problems and in November 1967 the Government was compelled to devalue the pound. This in itself necessitated further deflation. Economic policy thus produced tension between the trade unions and the Government and their relationship was further exacerbated by the attempt by the Government to introduce legislation to reform industrial relations. After long and bitter negotiations, the Government agreed to withdraw its proposals in favour of an undertaking by the trade unions to introduce reforms themselves. All these difficulties were reflected in great unpopularity for the Government as its record in by-elections testifies (C17).

A Reforming Government.

Despite these traumatic experiences in the economic field, the Labour Government succeeded in implementing a substantial programme of reform. In housing, education and the social services important changes were introduced; a start was made with reforming the institutions of government; and major developments occurred in industrial and regional policy. The Government also provided parliamentary time for the passage of private members' legislation to abolish capital punishment, to reform the divorce laws and to legalise abortion and homosexuality.

Foreign Affairs.

Three principal problems in foreign affairs confronted the Government. First, in 1965 Rhodesia declared independence unilaterally. Economic sanctions were introduced against the regime and Mr. Wilson made two unsuccessful attempts to negotiate with the rebel Prime Minister, Mr. Ian Smith. Secondly, the Government had to take decisions on Britain's relations with the European Economic Community. Although the Labour Party had opposed the Conservative Government's application, its attitude began to change after 1964 and, in May 1967, a second application was made to see what terms could be obtained. When France voted in December 1967 against the opening of negotiations, the application was left on the table. Thirdly, largely as a result of the pressing need to reduce defence expenditure, the Government decided to withdraw from our traditional role East of Suez.

The 1970 General Election.

By 1970 the Government had succeeded in restoring the balance of payments position. This was reflected in an increase in its popularity in the opinion polls. The local election results were also encouraging, with Labour regaining some of the ground it had lost in earlier years when its representation had been decimated. In this favourable climate, the Prime Minister decided to hold the election on 18 June.

On the eve of the poll, a Labour victory seemed certain. The opinion polls, with one exception (Opinion Research Centre), were predicting a Labour victory. The eventual result, however, was a 4·7 per cent swing to the Conservatives and their return to power with an overall majority of 30 over all other parties. The reasons for what appears to have been a last-minute change are complex, but the most accepted argument is that the publication of unfavourable trade figures just 3 days before polling day enabled the Conservatives to stir up anxiety about the cost of living and the economy.

A New Style of Government.

Right from the start, Mr. Heath made it clear that he intended his Government to be substantially different from Mr. Wilson's both in style and policies. Mr. Heath determined to shun the publicity and personal initiatives which had characterised Mr. Wilson's tenure of 10 Downing Street. For instance, he refused initially to intervene personally in industrial disputes. The Government's new policies had been outlined in the Conservative election manifesto and it used the parliamentary recess over the summer to prepare the details of its plans.

The New Policies.

In October 1970 the Government announced a number of major developments:

(1) Reorganisation of the machinery of government—including the creation of two new giant departments (Environment and Trade and Industry).

(2) **Cuts in Public Expenditure.**—The Conservatives believed that government was intervening too much in the life of the nation and that too high a proportion of the nation's resources were committed to public expenditure. Following a major review of government activities, the Chancellor of the Exchequer announced that the Government planned to be more selective in its approach to the social services and to withdraw generally in its relations with private industry. A number of decisions were announced which were mostly implemented during 1970 and 1971.

(3) **Reform of Industrial Relations.**—One of the major issues of the Conservatives' election campaign had been the need to take stronger action to reform industrial relations. The Government published its proposals in October 1970 and, after a long and bitter parliamentary battle, the Industrial Relations Act became law in 1971.

Industrial Unrest.

The first two and a half years of the Government's life were marked by widespread industrial unrest. This was the result of a number of factors. First, the Government's policy of confrontation as a means of limiting wage inflation led to a number of prolonged disputes, for instance, in the docks, in the electricity power industry and by local authority manual workers. Trade union opposition to the Industrial Relations Act produced a number of one-day stoppages and unofficial strikes of longer duration. These problems were aggravated by persistently high levels of unemployment especially in certain regions. Finally, after 1972, there was industrial action in protest against the Government's prices and incomes policy.

The Government's About-Turn.

1972 was not a happy year for the Government. We have already seen that it was a year of confrontation with the trade unions over the operation of the Industrial Relations Act. It was also a year in which the pressure of circumstances, especially the problems of unemployment and inflation, forced the Government to abandon many of the initiatives it had started in 1970 and to adopt policies similar to those which it had attacked so vehemently when it had been in Opposition. This was particularly the case in the fields of regional policy, consumer protection, and prices and incomes policy.

Government assistance to private industry was increased especially in the development areas; new legislation was enacted to regulate commercial practice; and in November 1972 a 90-day standstill was imposed upon wages and salaries, dividends, rates and rents and on all prices other than imports and fresh foods. In April 1973 this was replaced by a more flexible form of restraint, known as Stage Two, designed to last for six months. *See* Section G, Part IV.

Entry into Europe.

Negotiations with the EEC started immediately after the General Election of 1970. After a long series of talks in Brussels and a summit meeting between President Pompidou and Mr. Heath in Paris in May 1971, a formula was found to which Britain and the Six could agree. On this basis the House of Commons took the decision in principle to join the EEC on 18 October 1971, when the Conservative Government, opposed by some of its own back-benchers but supported by 69 Labour pro-marketeers and five of the Liberals, had a majority of 112. Legislation to give effect to this decision was passed after a long parliamentary struggle in September 1972. Thus, twelve years after the first application had been made, Britain joined the Common Market on 1 January 1973.

The Oil Crisis.

In the autumn of 1973 the Government announced Stage Three of the counter-inflation policy, designed to last twelve months. Its implementation, however, took place against a rapidly changing economic situation. In the aftermath of the Arab-Israeli war of October 1973, problems arose in the supply of oil, on which Britain depends for 50% of her energy. First, the Arab oil producers decided to boycott some countries and to restrict supplies to most others. British imports were cut by 15%. Second, all the oil exporting countries decided to increase the price of crude oil dramatically. Shortage of petrol produced panic among many motorists leading to long queues and even violent scenes at some garages. The Government took the precaution of issuing ration coupons but managed to avoid introducing rationing, relying instead on voluntary restraint.

Deepening Economic Crisis.

The increased cost of oil imports and the reduction in supplies adversely affected both the balance of payments and industrial output. The economic situation was further weakened by the decision of the National Union of Mineworkers (NUM) in November 1973 to implement a ban on overtime and weekend working in support of a pay claim in excess of Stage Three. The rapidly deteriorating fuel situation was aggravated by an out-of-hours working ban by electricity power engineers which limited the ability of the Central Electricity Generating Board to cope with shortages at various power stations. Consequently on 13 November the Government declared a State of Emergency. Orders were enacted restricting space heating by electricity, except in the home and certain other places, and prohibiting the use of electricity for advertising, displays or floodlighting. The position worsened still further following the decision of the Amalgamated Society of Locomotive Engineers and Firemen (ASLEF) to ban Sunday, overtime and rest-day working. This had the effect of disrupting the delivery of coal to power stations as well as causing a considerable amount of inconvenience to passengers, especially in the South-East. The Government refused to make an offer to the miners outside the terms of Stage Three and was therefore compelled to introduce a package of tougher measures to deal with the crisis. Most important, as from 1 January, electricity was only provided to industry on three specified days per week. In addition a 50 mile/h speed limit was introduced on all roads, a maximum heating limit was imposed on all commercial premises and offices and television was required to close down at 10.30 p.m. each evening. The Chancellor of the Exchequer also announced large cuts in public expenditure and tighter controls on consumer credit.

Miners' Strike and the February 1974 Election.

Following an overwhelming vote in a pithead ballot, the NUM decided to intensify its industrial action by calling a national strike as from 10 February. Before the strike began, however, the Prime Minister announced that he had asked the Queen to dissolve Parliament so as to hold a general election on 28 February. For the Government, the main issue of the election was the attempt by a trade union to use its industrial strength to defeat the policy of the elected government. The Labour Party, however, attempted to widen the campaign to include the Government's general record since 1970. There was also general interest in the performance of the Liberals following a series of dramatic by-election successes in 1972 and 1973.

Minority Labour Government.

At the dissolution, Mr. Heath had had an overall majority of 16 in the House of Commons. As the results came in on election night it was clear that he was going to lose this and that the result was going to be very close. Eventually the result was as follows:

Labour	301
Conservative	296
Liberal	14
Others	24

In this situation Mr. Heath did not offer his resignation immediately but entered into discussions with Mr. Jeremy Thorpe, the Leader of the Liberals, to see if the basis existed for the formation of a coalition. Accommodation could not be reached on proportional representation and Mr Heath resigned on 4 March. The Queen then asked Mr. Wilson to form a government which he agreed to do without obtaining the support of any other parties. Immediate steps were taken to settle the miners' dispute and to end the three-day working week.

The Social Contract.

Although leading a minority government, Mr. Wilson knew that the other parties would be reluctant to force another election immediately. The Government was therefore able to make a start in implementing its programme. Most of its domestic policies were included in the *Social Contract*, a package of measures agreed between the Labour Party and the Trades Union Congress in 1973. Most important were the measures to control inflation. In return for the abolition of the Pay Board and all associated statutory controls on pay, which occurred in July 1974, the trade unions agreed voluntarily to restrain wage increases. Other measures included the repeal of the Industrial Relations Act 1971, the introduction of food subsidies, the strengthening of price controls and increased payments to old-age pensioners. *See also* **Section G, Part IV.**

October 1974 Election.

Despite the Government's success in exploiting its parliamentary position, it was clear that it would seek a new mandate from the electorate at an early opportunity. Following the publication of a large number of statements of policy during the summer, the Prime Minister sought a dissolution of Parliament for polling to take place on 10 October. The Labour Party remained ahead in the opinion polls throughout the campaign and this was confirmed in the results but its margin was rather smaller than predicted. Labour only obtained a majority of three over all other parties. However its position was in fact considerably stronger than this because of the fragmented nature of the Opposition. (*See* **C16**).

Conservative Leadership.

Although many Conservatives were critical of Mr. Heath's leadership, his support was not tested immediately after the February election because of the proximity of another general election. However, after the October election, Mr. Heath decided to establish a committee, under the chairmanship of Lord Home, to review the procedure for electing the leader of the Conservative Party. It proposed a number of changes which were adopted for the election, held in February 1975. In the first ballot, Mrs Margaret Thatcher defeated Mr. Heath but failed to win the required majority. Mr. Heath then withdrew, announcing his intention of returning to the backbenches, and in the second ballot Mrs. Thatcher secured an overall majority.

European Renegotiation.

The Government was committed to seek a fundamental renegotiation of the terms of entry into the European Economic Community and to consult the British people as to whether the new terms should be accepted. In April 1974 Mr. Callaghan outlined to the Council of Ministers the terms which Britain wished to change, the most important of which were the contribution to the Community budget, the effect of the Common Agricultural Policy, the need to safeguard the interests of the Commonwealth and developing countries and the promotion of regional development. After concluding successful negotiations on most of these points the Cabinet voted to recommend continued membership and this view was endorsed by 67·2% of those who voted in a referendum held in June 1975.

Counter-Inflation Programme.

Despite the agreement of the trade unions voluntarily to restrain wage increases, the rate of inflation accelerated so much that by the middle of 1975 it had reached 25% per annum. In July 1975, the Government was therefore compelled to introduce a limit of £6 a week on pay settlements for people earning up to £8,500 a year, with no increase for those earning more. This policy remained voluntary but the Government announced that employers who increased pay by more than the limit would have not only the excess but the whole pay increase disallowed for the approval of price increases under the Price Code and it warned that if the limits were exceeded it would have to seek statutory powers of enforcement. The Government also undertook to maintain strict price controls and to continue and extend the payment of food subsidies.

Rising Unemployment.

The measures taken by the Government to reduce the rate of inflation, implemented during a serious world-wide recession, led to a sharp rise in unemployment such that in January 1977 1·5 million were out of work. Various steps were taken to provide additional employment but, short of major reflationary measures which were ruled out on other grounds, there was little that the Government could do. Preparations were made, however, to facilitate the development of the economy when conditions permitted. In November 1975 the Government published a new industrial strategy designed to ensure that assistance was given to those sectors of the economy with good prospects. Its difficulties, however, were highlighted in the following month when it had to launch a major rescue to avert the closure of Chrysler car production in Great Britain.

Pay and Prices.

Although the £6 limit, which was observed without exception, succeeded in reducing the rate of inflation, it was clear that further pay restraint was needed. In his Budget the Chancellor announced various tax reliefs conditional upon agreement being reached on a voluntary pay limit for another year. Such an agreement was made in May with a new limit curbing average wage increases to 4½% in the year starting in August 1976. Price controls were also maintained, but there was some relaxation to encourage industrial investment.

Cuts in Public Expenditure.

During 1976 a vigorous campaign was mounted in favour of cuts in public expenditure. Concern that the Government was borrowing excessively to finance this spending also led to weakness of sterling on the foreign exchange markets. In July, to avert a further fall in the value of sterling, substantial cuts were announced in the Government's spending plans for 1977–8 and interest rates were raised to record levels. These measures were not sufficient, however, to prevent a dramatic slide in the £ during the autumn which forced the Government to seek a $3,900 million loan from the International Monetary Fund. To obtain this assistance, further cuts in public expenditure, amounting to £3,000 m. over the next two years, and increases in taxation were imposed in December. At the beginning of 1977 there was some brighter economic news, including the announcement that 25% of Britain's oil needs were being met from the North Sea.

Lords v. Commons.

Despite these economic problems, the Government proceeded with one of the largest legislative programmes ever introduced in a single session. Most of it was also controversial, and strong opposition was encountered in the House of Commons, where the Government's small majority was frequently threatened, and in the House of Lords. The Lords attempted to make major changes in six bills, but the conflict eventually centred around two bills: the Dock Work Regulation Bill and the Aircraft and Shipbuilding Industries Bill. The former was returned to the Commons with its main provision transformed by the Lords, but the defection of two of its own backbenchers prevented the Government restoring its original proposal. Disagreement over the latter was not resolved by the time Parliament was prorogued and the bill to nationalise the aerospace and shipbuilding industries has therefore had to be reintroduced at the beginning of the 1976–7 session. It became law in March 1977 but only after the Government had made substantial concessions.

Devolution.

In October 1974 the Scottish National Party secured 30·4% of the Scottish vote, winning 11 seats, and Plaid Cymru won 10·8% of the Welsh vote, winning 3 seats. The SNP also came second in 42 constituencies, 35 of them held by Labour. These successes brought the question of devolution to the centre of political debate and the Government announced its intention of setting up assemblies in Scotland and Wales. Both parties are split on this issue. Traditionally the Labour Party, and particularly its Scottish members, have opposed devolution, but with a few prominent exceptions in both Scotland and Wales, the Party supports the Government's proposals. The Conservatives have supported the creation of a Scottish assembly since the late 1960s, but in 1976 decided officially to oppose the Government's plans. A number of senior Conservatives, however, dissented from this apparent change of policy. In December 1976 the Scotland and Wales Bill was given a Second Reading by a majority of 45, the Government having secured the votes of most Labour MPs by promising to hold referenda before bringing the assemblies into existence. The Committee Stage which is being taken on the floor of the House of Commons and is to occupy a record number of sittings, is fraught with difficulties for the Government, and it is likely that substantial concessions will have to be made if the Bill is to be enacted. The difficulties facing the Government were demonstrated when a "guillotine" motion on the Bill was lost on 22 February by 312 votes to 289, with back-bench Labour rebels joining Conservatives and Liberals.

Wilson's Resignation.

The resignation of Harold Wilson, announced on 16 March 1976, came as a political bombshell. In the fight for the succession, it soon became a race between James Callaghan and Michael Foot. The other contenders—Denis Healey, Roy Jenkins and Anthony Crosland polled poorly, although Tony Benn on the left-wing made a creditable showing. On 5 April, Callaghan was the victor, by 176 votes to the 137 of Michael Foot. Callaghan inherited a weak parliamentary position, as the by-elections went against the Government.

The Parliamentary Position in 1977.

In May 1977 following the loss of Ashfield the House of Commons was composed as follows:

	Seats
Labour	310
Conservative	279
Liberal	13
Scottish Nationalists	11
United Ulster Unionist	10
Plaid Cymru	3
Scottish Labour	2
Social Democratic and Labour	1
Independent	1
Vacant	1 (Saffron Walden)

Excluding the Speaker and his three Deputies, the Government's overall majority had now disappeared. Labour was thus in a minority if all the opposition parties united. However, the Liberal–Labour pact ensured that the Government would survive, at least for several months.

Major Legislation 1976.

Major legislation enacted during 1976 included:

Trade Union and Labour Relations (Amendment) Act 1976, required the newspaper publishing industry to draw up a charter containing practical guidance on matters relating to the freedom of the Press.

Drought Act 1976, gave the Government additional powers to deal with the consequences of a prolonged period of drought, including the limitation of non-essential supplies and the rationing of supplies.

Police Act 1976, set up a Police Complaints Board to take part, with the police, in the investigation and determination of complaints by the public against the police.

Dock Work Regulation Act 1976, reconstituted the National Dock Labour Board and provided for a new National Dock Labour Scheme based on a new definition of "dock work." The Government sought to extend the scheme to a zone five miles from the sea, but this was amended by Parliament to ½ mile.

Health Services Act 1976, provided for the progressive withdrawal from NHS hospitals of facilities for private medical and dental practice, under the supervision of a Health Services Board, and seeks to control the development of large private hospitals.

Education Act 1976, empowers the Secretary of State for Education and Science to require local education authorities to submit proposals to abolish selection in secondary education.

Race Relations Act 1976, strengthens the laws against racial discrimination and amalgamates the Race Relations Board and the Community Relations Commission into a new Commission for Racial Equality.

Rent (Agriculture) Act 1976, provides greater security of tenure for agricultural workers living in "tied cottages."

Northern Ireland in Crisis.

Violence has erupted in Northern Ireland on various occasions since the implementation of the Government of Ireland Act of 1920. The latest troubles started in 1968. A new civil rights movement organised a number of marches which, although peaceful in intent, tended to become violent because of the involvement of extremists on both sides. During the summer of 1969 serious rioting in Belfast and Londonderry led the Government of Northern Ireland to ask for the assistance of British troops to prevent a breakdown of law and order. Although the arrival of the troops and the acceleration of the programme of reforms produced a temporary lull, the situation continued to deteriorate during 1970 and 1971. As a result, in March 1972 the UK Government decided to suspend the Government of Ireland Act and to impose "direct rule" from Westminster.

The table below sets out the main political events since the imposition of direct rule:

1973 March	Plebiscite held on the border. Boycotted by Catholic parties; 57·4% of electorate voted in favour of union with UK.
June	Election for new Assembly to replace Stormont Parliament. Discussions start on formation of a power-sharing executive.
December	Tripartite conference (UK Government, Northern Ireland Executive-designate and Irish Government) agrees to establish a Council of Ireland.
1974 January	Establishment of Executive comprising members of the Official Unionists, Social Democratic and Labour Party and Alliance Party.
February	UK General Election in which 11 out of the 12 seats were won by candidates opposed to the Executive.
May	Resignation of Executive following strike action initiated by Ulster Workers' Council. Direct rule resumed.
1975 May	Election for a Constitutional Convention, established to put forward recommendations on the future government of Northern Ireland.
1976 March	Following the failure of the Convention to produce a unanimous report and the rejection of the majority report by the UK Government, the Convention was dissolved.
August	Formation of Peace Movement which during the autumn held rallies and meetings in Northern Ireland, in Britain and overseas.

Terrorism.

Since 1968–9 terrorist activity has persisted in Northern Ireland, and it has sporadically broken out in other parts of the United Kingdom. Over 1500 people have been killed in Northern Ireland and almost 20,000 injured. In Northern Ireland in 1975–6 there were fewer bombings, but there was a marked increase in the number of sectarian and inter-factional killings. Less violence occurred in Britain during 1976 than during the previous two years. In the Republic of Ireland the UK Ambassador and a member of his staff were killed in July 1976 when a bomb exploded under their car.

II. HOW BRITAIN GOVERNS HERSELF

1. THE BRITISH CONSTITUTION

Strictly there is no British Constitution. There is no single document which contains all the rules regulating the operation of our system of government. Indeed many of these rules have not been written down. But this is not to say that there are no constitutional rules. Some are to be found in Acts of Parliament, such as the Representation of the People Acts, but these have no special validity which distinguishes them from Acts which relate to less important aspects of our national life. Even those which have never been written down can be fairly clearly delineated at any particular time. It is thus possible to outline with some precision the working of our system of government, although there is always room for controversy especially during a constitutional crisis such as that produced by the general election of February 1974.

One consequence of the lack of a written constitution has been the gradual evolution of the system over the centuries without any sharp breaks in continuity. Thus, although there have been fundamental changes, for instance in the role of the monarch, many of these changes have not been recorded in any formal manner. Survivals from past ages remain to confuse the student so that it is necessary to distinguish between those parts which are important in the actual running of the country and those parts which remain in existence but only have a symbolic role.

It is not possible to attach a single label to our system of government which serves to distinguish it from others. A number of labels—monarchical, parliamentary, unitary, and democratic—provide a reasonably accurate short description: monarchical in the sense that the Queen is Head of State although she now only plays a formal part in the conduct of the government, acting always on the advice of her ministers; parliamentary both in the sense that Parliament is the sovereign law-making body and that the government is formed out of Parliament and dependent upon its continuing support; unitary in the sense that Parliament is ultimately responsible for all parts of the United Kingdom although it may have chosen to delegate some of its powers to other institutions; and democratic in the sense that the House of Commons is elected on the basis of universal adult suffrage.

In the absence of the safeguard of a written constitution, democracy is preserved by the ordinary law, by the political organisation of the people and by customs and rights which depend on the capacity of the people to sustain them. It is manifested in universal adult suffrage, the rule of the majority and the right to oppose. Thus all citizens, male and female, over the age of eighteen have the right to elect their own member of Parliament and to vote in local elections. Secondly, it is accepted that the majority has the right to rule subject to a number of safeguards, in particular the right of the minority to oppose. This consideration is vital to a true democracy and opposition is so essentially a part of our system that the Leader of the Opposition is paid a salary by the government.

Although their functions overlap, the three organs of government are easily distinguishable:

(i) The legislature, consisting of the Queen in Parliament.

(ii) The executive, consisting of the Cabinet and other ministers in charge of government departments staffed by civil servants; local authorities; and a number of statutory boards, such as the National Coal Board and the Post Office, responsible for the administration of particular services.

(iii) The judiciary.

2. CENTRAL GOVERNMENT

A. STRUCTURE

I. THE QUEEN.

The Queen's tenure of the Crown holds for life (unless she abdicates), it is hereditary and it is held by statutory right. The Queen is a constitutional monarch; she took an oath at her Coronation to rule according to the laws and customs of the people. In law, she is head of the executive, an integral part of the legislature and the head of the judiciary as well as being commander-in-chief of the armed forces and temporal head of the Church of England. Thus the Queen appoints the prime minister and legally other ministers only assume office on receiving their seals of office from the Queen. Equally, her assent is necessary before a bill, passed by the House of Commons and the House of Lords, becomes an Act of Parliament. In practice, however, the Queen's role is now purely formal. She reigns but she does not rule. If one party has an overall majority in the House of Commons, she has no freedom of choice in the selection of a prime minister, summoning the leader of that party to form the government. Even when no party has an overall majority it is unlikely that the Queen would play an active role in the formation of a government. Rather she would leave it to the leaders of the parties in the House of Commons to reach an agreement and then appoint whoever they had selected. The power of veto is never exercised. In all important respects she acts only on the advice of her ministers. In effect the United Kingdom is governed by Her Majesty's Government in the name of the Queen. However, the Queen still plays an important role socially and symbolically as the Head of State. All members of the Commonwealth recognise the Queen as Head of the Commonwealth and in 12 of the 36 member countries she is also Head of State.

II. PARLIAMENT.

Parliament consists of the Queen, the House of Lords and the House of Commons. Collectively they form the legislature. Over the centuries the balance between the three elements has changed such that the Queen only remains a part of the legislature in a formal sense and that the House of Commons, as the popularly elected lower House, has established its paramountcy over the House of Lords, composed of lords spiritual and lords temporal. The maximum life of a Parliament is five years but, on the advice of the prime minister, the Queen may dissolve Parliament at any time and issue a proclamation calling for the election of a new Parliament. Parliament is adjourned from day to day while in session. At the end of a session (usually 12 months in length) it is prorogued. At the expiry of its life it is dissolved.

(a) The Parties.

To understand the operation of our system of government it is essential to appreciate the importance of the party system. The party system emerged in the latter half of the seventeenth century as Parliament gained the right to be the law-making body. Since then two parties have usually been predominant, at different times Tories and Whigs, Conservatives and Liberals and, since the 1930s, Conservatives and Labour. This fact has had an important effect upon both the nature of the parties and upon the organisation of Parliament. Parties exist to form governments and the path to this goal lies in the House of Commons, for the party which obtains a majority of seats has the right to have its leaders form the government. The other party forms Her Majesty's Opposition. To this end parties in this century have been highly disciplined and coherent organisations. Once elected the majority's main function is to sustain the government in office. The minority accepts that, because of the rigidity of the party system, it is unlikely to defeat the government in the Commons and it therefore sees its rôle as one of criticising government policy and setting forth an alternative programme which it hopes will win the support of the electorate at the next election. However, on a few occasions, no party has had an overall majority in the House of Commons. In this situation a coalition may be formed consisting of the members of two or more parties whose combined strength commands a majority. Alternatively the party with the largest number of seats may decide to form a government on its own but it will only be able to remain in office if the other parties do not combine to defeat it. If such a government was defeated on an important question which it regarded as an issue of confidence it would have to resign. Following its resignation there would either be a general election or, if it was clear that an alternative government could be formed which would be able to command a majority in the Commons, the Queen would summon the leader of one of the other parties as prime minister.

(b) The House of Lords.

The House of Lords is the oldest second chamber in the world and the most hereditary in its character. It is composed of lords temporal and lords spiritual. The former include all peers who inherited their titles and who have not disclaimed their peerages under the Peerage Act 1963, all peers created for their own life-times under the provisions of the Life Peerages Act 1958 and the Lords of Appeal appointed to assist the House in its judicial duties. The lords spiritual are the 26 most senior bishops. The hereditary element is still large but of declining importance especially as a result of the more frequent attendance of the life peers and peeresses. This has tended to reduce the overwhelming majority which the Conservative Party used to enjoy and which constitutes a threat to legislation in the final year of a Labour government (*see* Legislation below). However, the unrepresentative character of the House of Lords has limited its usefulness. Its rôle is to ease the work-load of an over-burdened House of Commons but not to thwart its will. It still performs a useful function in the legislative process by examining some bills in detail and initiating bills on non-controversial subjects but its part is limited by the Parliament Acts of 1911 and 1949 (*see* Legislation below). It also serves as the highest Court of Appeal. Finally the House of Lords is a forum where men and women, distinguished in all fields of national life, can discuss issues of importance free from the reins of party discipline.

(c) The House of Commons.

The House of Commons is a representative assembly consisting of 635 M.P.s elected by simple majority in single-member constituencies. Although our system of government is rightly described as parliamentary, this does not mean that Parliament governs. Because of the party system the initiative in government lies elsewhere—in the Cabinet. But Parliament, and especially the Commons, has important functions to play not only as the assembly to which the government is ultimately responsible but also in legitimising legislation, in voting money and in acting as a body in which complaints may be raised.

1. Legislation.—The law of the United Kingdom consists of common law and case law, statute law and equity. Statute law is that part which is made by Parliament and enshrined in Acts of Parliament. Any member of Parliament may present a bill after giving formal notice, provided that it does not propose the expenditure of public money, but the principal bills are introduced by the government based upon its programme outlined at the beginning of each session in the Queen's Speech.

Usually the government consults affected interests before a bill is presented to Parliament. One means of doing this is to publish documents known as Green and White Papers. A Green Paper sets out proposals which are at a formative stage and to which the government is not committed. A White Paper contains the government's decisions and its justification for them but often it indicates areas in which the government is still open to persuasion. Where legislation is complex and affects many people and interests, this pre-legislative process can be very important.

Bills may originate in either House, unless they deal with finance or representation when they are always introduced in the Commons. The First Reading is just a formality. The House begins its examination at the Second Reading when the general principles are debated and voted. If they are approved, the bill is then referred for detailed clause-by-clause examination either to a standing committee or to a committee of the Whole House. (*see* **Committees of the House** below). After the Committee Stage comes the Report Stage when the House considers the bill as reported to it by the committee and decides whether any further changes in individual clauses should be made. The final stage is the Third Reading when the House considers the bill as a whole and votes whether, as amended, it should become law. If passed, it is sent to the Lords where it must go through the same stages. Once passed by both Houses the bill is sent to the Queen for Royal Assent.

The Lords cannot require the Commons to agree to amendments; nor can they delay a bill indefinitely. They have no power in respect of money bills; and, since the passing of the Parliament Act of 1949, any other public bill which has been passed in the Commons in two successive sessions may be presented for Royal Assent without the consent of the Lords provided that a year has elapsed between the date of the Second Reading of the bill in the Commons and the date on which it was finally passed in that House. Thus the House of Lords was able to prevent the enactment of the Aircraft and Shipbuilding Industries Bill in the 1975–6 session but, even if the Government had not agreed to drop the shiprepairing section from the Bill it would eventually, under the 1911 and 1949 Parliament Acts, have received the Royal Assent (*see* **C6**).

2. Money Functions of the Commons.—The second function of the Commons (and one of its earliest in history) is to provide the State with money. The government cannot raise money by taxation (or in any other way) or spend money without the authority of Parliament; and this power of authority belongs exclusively to the Commons. The House can vote money only on the demand and on the responsibility of a minister of the Crown. Traditionally the House considers expenditure on an annual cash basis, its procedure being centred around the annual voting of Supply based upon Estimates provided by the government. Since 1969, however, it has also had the opportunity of considering expenditure in more general terms. The government has published an annual White Paper in the late autumn or early in the New Year setting out its plans for public expenditure for the next three financial years and its provisional allocations for the following two years, which is debated in the House. The most recent **White Paper**, *The Government's Expenditure Plans* (Cmnd. 6721) was published in January 1977. In its work in this area, the House is assisted by the Select Committee on Expenditure (*see* **Specialised Committees C11(2)**).

On the revenue side, the highlight of the year is the Chancellor of the Exchequer's Budget Statement, announced in the House during March or April. Many of his proposals have to be implemented immediately under a special procedure but they are all embodied in the finance bill which has to be enacted before the summer recess. Traditionally, the committee stage of this bill was taken in the committee of the Whole House but, following an experiment of sending the whole bill upstairs to a standing committee, it is now divided, the main clauses being considered on the floor of the House, the rest being committed upstairs. Recently economic pressures have forced Chancellors to introduce supplementary budgets at other times of the year. *See* **Section G, Part IV.**

3. Critical Functions of the Commons.—There are a number of opportunities for the opposition and the government's own back-benchers to criticise government policy. They can question ministers on the floor of the House and have the right to ask a supplementary question to the reply. They can table motions for debate which may help to mould public opinion. They can speak in debates and can raise issues which do not involve public expenditure on the adjournment, or under the 10-minute rule, or by promoting private members' bills (subject to success in the ballot for places).

To assist it in its critical rôle Parliament has, since 1967, had a new officer, the Parliamentary Commissioner for Administration, commonly known as the Ombudsman. His function is to investigate complaints of maladministration which are referred to him by MPs on behalf of members of the public. (*See* **Complaints Procedures, C12(2).**)

4. Committees of the House.—The House of Commons uses committees to assist it in its work in a number of different ways:

(1) **Standing Committees.**—A standing committee is a miniature of the House itself, reflecting its party composition, and consists of between 20 and 50 MPs. Its function is to examine the Committee Stage of legislation. Some bills are not sent to a standing committee but are examined by a committee of the Whole House which consists of all MPs but working under special rules of procedure, for instance enabling an MP to speak more than once to the same question.

(2) **Select Committees.**—A select committee is a body with special powers and privileges to which the House has delegated its authority in a special way for the purpose of discovering information, examining witnesses, sifting evidence and drawing up conclusions which are reported to the House. There are a number of sessional select committees which are almost permanent bodies (such as the Committee of Public Accounts and the Committee of Privileges). There are also a number of *ad hoc* select committees. For instance in November 1976 a committee was appointed to investigate the conduct of MPs in connection with the activities of the architect, Mr. J. Poulson. (*See* **Specialised Committees, C11(2).**)

(3) **Joint Committees.**—A joint committee consists of members of both Houses. It is really a select committee of the Commons deliberating with a select committee of the Lords and is used to save duplication of effort, usually on uncontentious matters.

(4) **Private Bill Committees.**—A private bill is a special kind of legislation conferring particular powers on any person or body of persons, such as local authorities, in excess of the general law. Private bill committees deal with the Committee Stage of such bills.

III. THE EXECUTIVE.

The executive work of central government is performed by the prime minister and the other ministers of the Crown. The power of executive action is not given to a government department as a corporate body but to the minister individually who is responsible for the exercise of his duties legally to the Queen and politically to Parliament. All ministers must be members of either the Commons or the Lords.

1. The Cabinet and The Prime Minister.

At the head of the government structure is the Cabinet which is responsible for defining the broad lines of policy of the government and for coordinating its work in different fields. It consists of the leading members of the majority party in the Commons, selected by the prime minister, most of whom are heads of government departments which are staffed by civil servants and responsible for the implementation of government policy in particular fields. In addition there are usually a number of ministers without departmental responsibilities. Its normal size is about 20. Although legally the Cabinet has no corporate constitutional existence, ministers being individually responsible for the exercise of governmental powers, politically it is accepted that the Cabinet is collectively responsible for government policy. Thus the Cabinet acts as one man and a minister who disagrees with the Cabinet must either resign or remain silent.

The head of the government is the prime minister. He is the leader of the majority party in the House of Commons and is responsible for choosing the other members of the government. He takes the chair at meetings of the Cabinet and, while he has few specific responsibilities, not having a department of his own (although the present Prime Minister is also Minister for the Civil Service), he takes a lead on the most important aspects of government policy.

Although both the Cabinet and the office of prime minister have long histories it is only recently that they have been given formal recognition in law. The fundamental rules of the working of the executive remain informal and within limits they vary according to political circumstances.

2. The Civil Service.

The Civil Service is the body of permanent officials who, working in the different departments and ministries, administer the policy of the central government. It consists of some 746,000 people (2·9 per cent of the working population) of whom 569,000 are non-industrial civil servants and the rest industrial workers in places such as the Royal Ordnance Factories and the Royal Naval Dockyards. It is important to realise that seven out of every ten civil servants work outside London, mainly in the regional and local offices of departments such as Health and Social Security, Employment, and Inland Revenue.

The political head of each department is a minister. Very often the minister has no special knowledge or experience in the field to which he is appointed and his tenure of office may be fairly short-lived. Great responsibility therefore falls on the shoulders of the permanent civil servants in his department. They have to ensure that he receives all the relevant facts on which to base decisions and usually he will seek their advice before reaching a decision. The precise relationship between a minister and his senior civil service advisers is a complex and subtle one. On the one hand they are entirely his servants in that he alone is responsible for everything that goes on in the department and he alone can be called to account in Parliament. Civil servants remain largely anonymous and their relationship with their minister is a confidential one. On the other hand the expertise and experience of senior civil servants is such that he depends on them and they can dominate a minister who is not sure of his own mind and who is not backed by the Cabinet as a whole. However, the distinguishing feature of the British Civil Service is that at all levels it is non-political in the sense that it serves both political parties impartially. In recent years ministers have also tended to bring in personal advisers, whose appointments lapse when the government's term of office ends. In November 1976 there were 23 such advisers.

The Civil Service has undergone a period of substantial reform, following the report of the Fulton Committee on the Civil Service (Cmnd. 3638, 1968). Although the Committee accepted that the Civil Service had many strengths, it felt that in a number of ways there were important shortcomings. In particular, it criticised the fragmentation of the Service into a large number of classes, the lack of adequate training and professionalism and the absence of modern personnel management. Most of its main recommendations were accepted by the Labour Government and the Conservative Government proceeded with their implementation. With the steps already taken to put them into practice, they are outlined below:

(1) The establishment of a new Civil Service Department to absorb the recruitment functions of the Civil Service Commisssion and to take over the responsibilities for central management of the Service exercised by the Pay and Management Divisions of the Treasury. The CSD was established in November 1968. It is headed by the Prime Minister but day-to-day responsibility is delegated to a non-departmental minister of Cabinet rank. The official head of the CSD is also designated Head of the Home Civil Service. The Civil Service Commission retains its independence in relation to individual appointments.

(2) The abolition of the class system and its replacement by a unified grading structure throughout the entire service, each post being graded by the technique of job evaluation. This recommendation is not being implemented in full. However the largest classes have been merged into groups. For instance, the former Administrative, Executive and Clerical Classes (comprising about 274,000 administrative civil servants) now form the Administration Group and similar mergers have taken place on the scientific and works sides. At the top of the service a new open structure has taken effect, so that posts of Under Secretary and above (carrying salaries of £12,000 and upwards) will be filled with the most suitable people without regard to academic background or previous employment.

(3) The development of greater professionalism, particularly by providing more training. The Civil Service College started running courses in autumn 1970 in London and at two residential centres at Sunningdale Park and Edinburgh. The closure of the Edinburgh Centre was announced in 1976.

(4) Improvements in personnel management. The CSD, in conjunction with the departments, has devoted a considerable amount of effort to securing improvements in this area.

3. Semi-autonomous Executive Bodies.

Particularly in recent years, a large number of semi-autonomous agencies have been established to carry out functions on behalf of the government. Some have been created because a particular function is considered to be unsuitable for a normal government department. In this category would be quasi-judicial bodies such as the Supplementary Benefits Commission, and bodies, such as the British Broadcasting Corporation, which need to be insulated from the political process. A second distinct group are the public corporations which run the nationalised industries, such as the British Railways Board, the National Coal Board, and the Post Office. These boards operate commercial enterprises in which a high degree of managerial flexibility is essential, but some public control over their activities is maintained by means of various general powers which ministers possess. Finally there is a large and diverse group of administrative bodies carrying out a wide variety of functions and subject to widely differing degrees of control by the government. Examples include the Countryside Commission, the Price Commission, the Research Councils, the British Museum and the Agricultural Marketing Boards.

IV. THE JUDICIARY.

The judiciary is responsible for the interpretation of statutes and the determination of the common law. Judicial functions are exercised quite separately from legislative or executive functions. However there are some links in personnel. Judges are appointed by the Queen acting on the advice of ministers but to safeguard their independence all senior judges can only be removed by the Sovereign on an address presented by both Houses of Parliament. The Lord Chancellor, the head of the judiciary, is the only political appointment who, as a member of the Cabinet, resigns his position with a change of government. He also serves as Speaker of the House of Lords. The Lords of Appeal are members of the House of Lords.

V. BRITAIN'S MEMBERSHIP OF THE EEC.

Britain's membership of the EEC, confirmed in the referendum of June 1975, has important implications for the system of government. In particular decisions and regulations emanate from the institutions of the EEC which are binding upon member countries. The structure of the EEC is discussed elsewhere (C52). In this section reference is made only to the effects which membership has had upon British government.

Council of Ministers.—The Secretary of State for Foreign and Commonwealth Affairs is Britain's principal representative on the Council of Ministers. In 1973 it was decided that, instead of creating a European Ministry, individual ministers should deal with European affairs as they affect their departments. They therefore attend meetings of the Council where appropriate. One of the ministers of state in the Foreign Office works full-time on European affairs. There is also a European Unit in the Cabinet Office.

European Parliament.—Britain is entitled to send a delegation of 36 MPs and peers to the European Parliament in Strasbourg. These seats are allocated according to the strength of the parties in the House of Commons, at present Labour 18, Conservative 16, Liberal 1 and Scottish National Party 1. The powers of the European Parliament are very limited but it is expected that they will be increased after direct election of its members has been introduced. The first such elections are scheduled for 1978 but it is likely that they will have to be postponed.

EEC Regulations.—EEC regulations, made by the Council of Ministers and the Commission, come into force in member countries without being ratified by each national Parliament. In 1974 a Select Committee was established to help MPs identify important proposals which might affect matters of principle or policy or which would involve changes in UK law before final decisions were taken upon them. The Government has also agreed to provide MPs with greater opportunities for questioning ministers and for debating Community matters.

B. REFORM OF GOVERNMENT

1. Machinery of Government.

All governments have to take decisions about the number of departments and the division of responsibility between them. Usually these decisions are taken *ad hoc*. In October 1970, however, the then Conservative Government published a White Paper entitled *The Reorganisation of Central Government* (Cmnd. 4506), the first official publication on the machinery of government since the Report of the Haldane Committee in 1918. It proposed a number of changes in the division of functions between departments and the establishment of a new central policy review staff. Continuing the developments of recent years towards the unification of functions within single departments, as seen, for instance, in the Ministry of Defence and the Department of Health and Social Security, the White Paper proposed the merging of the Ministry of Technology and the Board of Trade in a new Department of Trade and Industry and the creation of a new Department of the Environment by integrating the Ministry of Housing and Local Government, the Ministry of Transport and the Ministry of Public Building and Works. A number of other minor changes in ministerial responsibilities and departmental organisation were also proposed. By the end of 1970 all these changes had been effected.

Between 1970 and 1974 few additional changes were made apart from the transfer of the functions of the Northern Ireland Government and of the Northern Ireland Department of the Home Office to the new Secretary of State for Northern Ireland following the decision to suspend the Government of Ireland Act in 1972. Some of these functions were vested in the Northern Ireland Executive in January 1974 but had to be returned to the Northern Ireland Office on the collapse of the Executive in May 1974 (*see* C7(2)). During 1974 the Department of Trade and Industry was divided into four separate ministries. In January, as a result of the oil crisis, a new Department of Energy was created. In March, the Labour Government divided the rest of the Department into three. Industry, Trade, and Prices and Consumer Protection. In 1976 transport was taken out of the Department of the Environment and a separate department re-established.

The other most important feature of the 1970 White Paper was the establishment of a small multi-disciplinary central policy review staff within the Cabinet Office. Under the supervision of the Prime Minister it works for ministers collectively outlining for the Cabinet as a whole the wider implications of government programmes, thus acting as a counter-balancing force for members of the Cabinet when considering the proposals of individual ministers who have the backing of their departmental staffs. The head of the unit is Sir Kenneth Berrill and it consists of a staff of about 15, drawn from both within and outside the Civil Service. In March 1974 a policy advisory unit was also created in 10 Downing Street working for the Prime Minister on day-to-day questions of domestic policy.

2. Specialised Committees.

In 1966, as one of the procedural reforms introduced by the late Richard Crossman, then Leader of the House, the Government proposed the establishment of a number of specialised select committees to investigate particular areas of policy or the activities of particular departments. Between 1966 and 1970 six such committees were appointed and they produced a large number of reports. On taking office, the Conservative Government announced that it would review this experiment, especially in the light of the Report of the Select Committee on Procedure which recommended the establishment of a Select Committee on Expenditure to replace the Estimates Committee.

In October 1970 the results of this review were published as a Green Paper *Select Committees of the House of Commons* (Cmnd. 4507). It proposed a dual system of some specialised committees and an expenditure committee. On the one hand the Select Committee on Nationalised Industries was to be retained along with a number of specialised committees dealing with particular subjects but not with individual departments. The Estimates Committee was also to be enlarged and transformed into an Expenditure Committee which would focus not on the Supply Estimates but on the longer-term and wider implications of public expenditure as a whole and which would not be barred from considering the policies behind the figures. The Expenditure Committee, consisting of 49 MPs, was established in 1971. It is divided into six sub-committees, one considering public expenditure in general, the other five specialising in different areas of government activity. Select committees on Nationalised Industries, Race Relations and Immigration, Science and Technology and Overseas Development have also been appointed.

3. Reorganisation of the National Health Service.

Until 1974, the administrative structure of health and welfare services had not been substantially changed since 1948, when the National Health

Service was established. Basically there was a tripartite structure. Hospitals were managed by regional hospital boards appointed by the Secretary of State for Social Services, and by their subordinate hospital management committees, which were appointed by the boards. Responsibility for health care in the local community was divided. Doctors, dentists, opticians, and pharmacists were in contract with executive councils which were appointed by the Secretary of State, local authorities and by the professions themselves. The remaining health services, such as ante-natal clinics, health visiting, vaccination and other preventive services, and welfare services such as the provision of residential homes for the elderly and the handicapped, were the responsibility of local authorities. Over this fragmented structure the Department of Health and Social Security had a number of important supervisory functions.

For some time it had generally been agreed that a greater degree of unification was essential to ensure that all the different kinds of care and treatment that an individual might need at different times should be readily available. Difficulties were encountered in devising a new structure, but eventually legislation was enacted in 1973 and the new authorities took over in April 1974.

Management Structure.—The principal result of reorganisation in England and Wales is the drawing together of the administration of the family practitioner services, community health services and the hospitals. In England the new structure consists of two levels—area and regional—in addition to the central Department of Health and Social Security (DHSS). The operational bodies, responsible for assessing needs in their areas and for planning, organising and administering services to meet them, are called Area Health Authorities (AHAs). 72 AHAs have been created in England outside London, their boundaries coinciding with those of the new non-metropolitan counties and metropolitan districts (*see* C14). This facilitates cooperation as local authorities continue to be responsible for the personal social services. In London the 32 boroughs have been grouped to form a smaller number of health areas. Above the AHAs, 14 Regional Health Authorities (RHAs) have been created with responsibility for allocating resources to the AHAs, for coordinating their activities and for monitoring their performance. The RHAs are also the building authorities for major projects. At the apex of this structure, the DHSS retains responsibility for determining national objectives and priorities and for allocating resources to the RHAs.

In Wales 8 AHAs have been established, again corresponding to the new counties. No special regional authority has been created, the remaining responsibilities being shared between the DHSS and the Secretary of State for Wales.

Composition.—The members of the new authorities are not elected but have been appointed on grounds of their ability and experience. The members of the RHAs have been appointed by the Secretary of State for Social Services after consulting bodies such as the universities, the main local authorities and the health professions. Each AHA comprises about 15 members. The chairman is appointed by the Secretary of State after consulting the chairman of the appropriate RHA, 4 members are appointed by the corresponding local authority, 1 or 2 are nominated by the university which provides teaching facilities and the rest are appointed by the RHA. In June 1974 the Labour Government published a consultative paper on methods of introducing greater democracy into this structure, which included plans for district councillors to serve on AHAs.

Community Health Councils.—In each area a number of community health councils have been established to represent the views of the consumer to the AHA. Half the members of each CHC are appointed by local government district councils and the rest by the RHA, mainly on the nomination of voluntary bodies concerned locally with the NHS.

Health Service Commissioner.—In the first instance complaints are handled by the AHAs. However, two new offices, Health Service Commissioner for England and for Wales, have been created. Complainants have direct access to the commissioners who are empowered to investigate any questions other than those which in their opinion relate to the exercise of clinical judgment or for which other statutory procedures exist. Initially the Parliamentary Commissioner for Administration (*see* Critical Functions of Commons (C9) and Complaints Procedures (below)) has been appointed Health Service Commissioner for both England and Wales.

NHS Reorganisation in Scotland.—The aim of reorganisation in Scotland was the same as in the rest of the country. However, the structure is rather different. 14 health boards have been created, each one having responsibility for the organisation and management of all the services. The remaining health service functions are performed by the Secretary of State for Scotland. A Health Service Commissioner has also been established, at present the office being held by the Parliamentary Commissioner for Administration.

Royal Commission on the NHS.—In October 1975 the Prime Minister announced the establishment of a Royal Commission on the NHS "to consider in the interests both of the patients and of those who work in the NHS the best use and management of the financial and manpower resources of the NHS".

4. Complaints Procedures.

Reference is made elsewhere to the office of Parliamentary Commissioner for Administration, created in 1967, and to the new offices of Health Service Commissioner and the Commission for Local Administration, established in 1973 and 1974 respectively (*see* C9(2) and C15). In addition in Northern Ireland a Commissioner for Complaints was appointed in 1969 to consider complaints against public bodies outside the field of central government. These developments mark the introduction into the United Kingdom of a modified version of he ombudsman concept, pioneered in Scandinavia. Unlike their overseas counterparts, the commissioners, with the exception of the Health Service Commissioners and the Commissioner for Complaints, may only investigate complaints transmitted through elected representatives, either MPs or local councillors. All of them investigate complaints of injustice through maladministration and then report their findings to the responsible authority which can decide whether to accept or to reject them. When the office of Parliamentary Commissioner was created criticism was voiced at the large areas of government excluded from its terms of reference. Subsequent developments have remedied some of these complaints. In 1976 a Police Complaints Board was created to take part, with the police, in the investigation and determination of complaints by the public against the police.

5. Water Services in England and Wales.

In April 1974 a new structure for administering water services, such as conservation, supply, sewerage, drainage and river control came into force. In place of the large number of river authorities, water undertakings and sewerage authorities, nine all-purpose regional water authorities, composed of members appointed by the Secretary of State for the Environment, the Minister of Agriculture, Fisheries and Food and local authorities, have been created. Under the control of the regional authorities, statutory water companies will continue to supply water.

6. Devolution.

Royal Commission on the Constitution.—In April 1969 the Labour Government appointed a Royal Commission on the Constitution, under the chairmanship of Lord Crowther, to examine "the present functions of the central legislature and government in relation to the several countries, nations and regions of the United Kingdom" and to consider "whether any changes were desirable in these functions or otherwise in present constitutional and economic relationships". Following the death of Lord Crowther in February 1972, Lord Kilbrandon, a Lord of Appeal in Ordinary and a member of the Commission since its inception, was appointed chairman. The Commission's findings were published in October 1973 (Cmnd. 5460). Initially the Report was not received very favourably. However, the successes of the Nationalist parties in both the general elections of 1974 (C6(1)) brought devolution to the centre of political debate. In June 1974 the Government published a consultative document which set out seven possible schemes for greater devolution. In September 1974 a White Paper was published and, following further discussions, a second White Paper, *Our Changing Democracy: Devolution to Scotland and Wales*, (Cmnd. 6348), was produced in November 1975. After further consultations legislation was introduced at the start of the 1976–7 session.

Scotland and Wales Bill.—The Bill provides for the establishment of assemblies in Scotland and Wales, to be elected initially by simple majority on the basis of existing Parliamentary constituencies.

In *Scotland* the assembly is to have law-making powers on such matters as local government, health, social services, education, housing, physical planning, the environment and roads. Executive powers on these questions will be exercised by a Scottish Executive, a team drawn wholly or mainly from the assembly, headed by a Chief Executive, who will normally be the leader of the majority party in the assembly.

In *Wales* the assembly will not have legislative powers but will have certain powers in relation to delegated legislation and will be given responsibility for many of the executive functions at present carried out by nominated bodies and by the Secretary of State for Wales. Executive powers will be vested in the assembly itself, operating through committees whose members will reflect the political balance in the assembly.

Over-riding responsibility will continue to lie with the UK Parliament and government and for this reason Scotland and Wales will retain their existing number of MPs at Westminster and Secretaries of State for Scotland and Wales will continue to serve in the UK Cabinet.

The Bill received a Second Reading in December 1976. The Committee Stage was taken on the floor of the House but after the defeat of the Government on a guillotine motion to cut short debate, it is unlikely to become law in its present form.

3. LOCAL GOVERNMENT

Local government in the United Kingdom is the creation of Parliament. Its structure is laid down by Parliament and local authorities may only exercise those powers which Parliament either commands or permits them to exercise. Their functions include responsibility for all education services, except the universities, most personal health and welfare services (*see* **Reorganisation of the National Health Service, C11**), housing, public health, environmental planning, traffic management and transport, in each case subject to some central government control.

Since 1958 the structure of local government has been under almost continuous review. Following the report of the Herbert Commission in 1960, Greater London was reorganised under the terms of the London Government Act 1963. In 1966 the restricted Local Government Commission was replaced by two Royal Commissions with wider terms of reference, one for England, chaired by Lord Redcliffe-Maud, the other for Scotland, chaired by Lord Wheatley. Both Commissions reported during 1969. Although the Conservative Government, elected in June 1970, did not accept the Redcliffe-Maud Commission's recommendations, it proceeded with its own proposals for reform in England and Wales which received the Royal Assent in October 1972 and came into operation on 1 April 1974. Legislation, broadly conforming to the Wheatley Commission's recommendations for Scotland, was enacted in 1973 and the new structure came into force in May 1975.

1. Local Government in Greater London.

The London Government Act 1963 created a new two-tier system of local government for Greater London, consisting of the Greater London Council and 32 London boroughs, which came fully into operation on 1 April 1965. These authorities replaced the London County Council and the Middlesex County Council, with their second-tier councils, and three county boroughs. Parts of Essex, Surrey, Kent, and Hertfordshire were also incorporated in Greater London, thereby enlarging it to include 7·2 million people and to cover the whole of the continuously developed area within the green belt. The independent position of the City of London Corporation was unaffected and it was given the powers of a borough.

The Greater London Council.—The GLC, the first-tier authority, at present consists of 92 councillors and 15 aldermen. Elections have been held every third year. For the first three elections (1964, 1967, 1970) each of the London boroughs was an electoral area returning two, three or four councillors, according to the size of the electorate. The elections held in April 1973 took place under different arrangements. Each parliamentary constituency in Greater London now forms an electoral division returning a single councillor and the number of GLC councillors has therefore been reduced from 100 to 92. The term of office was also increased to four years. Elections were thus held in 1977 and the next elections will be in 1981.

The result of the 1977 GLC election was as follows (1973 figures in brackets):

Conservative	64 (33)
Labour	28 (57)
Liberal	0 (2)

The London Boroughs.—The 32 London boroughs have populations varying between 136,500 and 329,300. Elections have been held every fourth year (one year after the GLC elections), all the councillors retiring together. Following the elections of May 1974 Labour controls 19 boroughs, the Conservatives 12 and there is no overall control in one.

Powers of the GLC.—The GLC carries out those functions which need to be planned and administered over Greater London as a whole. Its main responsibilities are as follows:

(1) Strategic Planning—The GLC was responsible for the preparation of the Greater London Development Plan which was the subject of a lengthy public inquiry between 1970 and 1972. It is also involved in a number of major development schemes, including the replanning of the Covent Garden Area and the Thamesmead project which will provide homes for 60,000 people.

(2) Traffic and transport—The Transport (London) Act 1969 gave the GLC responsibility for preparing detailed transport plans and transferred overall responsibility for London Transport to it, although the services are run by a public corporation, the London Transport Executive, which it appoints. The GLC constructs, improves and maintains "metropolitan roads" and is the traffic authority for the whole of Greater London.

(3) Housing—The London boroughs are the main housing authorities but the GLC inherited the London County Council's large stock of houses. It is in process of transferring these to the borough councils. It retains some responsibility for house-building and is the sole authority for providing new houses outside Greater London.

(4) Main drainage and sewage disposal, refuse disposal.

(5) Fire and ambulance services.

(6) Other responsibilities include licensing, parks, and the ownership of the Royal Festival Hall, Crystal Palace, various museums, and other buildings of historic interest.

Education in Greater London.—In the 20 outer London boroughs education is the responsibility of the borough council. In inner London, however, a special arrangement was made to preserve the continuity of the service which formerly had been provided by the London County Council. A special committee of the GLC was created, the Inner London Education Authority (ILEA), consisting of the members of the GLC elected for the inner boroughs together with a representative of each inner London borough council and of the City of London. The Authority is virtually autonomous, running the education service and charging its expenditure to the inner London borough councils. Since 1970 it has been under Labour control.

Powers of the London Boroughs.—Within the framework of the GLC's overall development plan, the boroughs prepare their own plans and are responsible for determining applications for planning permission. They are the primary housing authorities and are wholly responsible for a wide range of personal health and welfare services for the sick, the elderly and the handicapped, and for children's services.

2. The New Local Government Structure.

ENGLAND.

Under the terms of the Local Government Act 1972, a new local government structure came into operation in England in April 1974.

Structure.—The former dual framework of county councils and their district councils and of all-purpose county borough councils has been replaced by a two-tier system throughout England, outside Greater London, based upon 45 counties (one additional county, the Isle of Wight, was created during the passage of the Bill through Parliament).

(i) In 6 predominantly urban areas (Greater Manchester, Merseyside, South Yorkshire, Tyne and Wear, West Midlands, West Yorkshire), new authorities, called metropolitan counties have been created. Large metropolitan district authorities, whose boundaries are laid down in the Act and with a minimum size of about 200,000, form the second-tier of local government.

(ii) In the rest of England existing county boundaries have been retained wherever possible, although the number of counties has been reduced to 39, and the new county councils have authority over the whole county including those areas formerly within the boundaries of county boroughs. Former borough councils and district councils have been rationalised to form second-tier, non-metropolitan district councils, with sufficient resources to carry out their responsibilities effectively (minimum size about 40,000).

The Act also provides for the continued existence of parish meetings and, where they are already constituted, parish councils. Parish councils may also be created in those areas where former borough councils and urban district councils were too small to form district authorities on their own. Parish councils do not have any powers other than those which they previously possessed and their main responsibility is to represent the views of their electorate to the principal authorities.

Constitution.—All members of the new county and district councils are directly elected. There are no aldermen on the new councils and those serving on the GLC and the London borough councils will be phased out by 1977 and 1978 respectively. After the initial period all councillors will serve for four years. The first elections—of complete county and district councils—were held in 1973. County councillors are elected on the basis of electoral divisions and retire together every fourth year. Elections were therefore held in 1977 and the next ones will be in 1981. **Metropolitan district councillors** are elected on the basis of wards, each returning three or a multiple of three members, according to the size of the electorate. One third retire at a time and elections will be held in three years out of every four, in each year in which there are not county elections. The first such elections were held in May 1975. **Non-metropolitan district councils** have been able to choose whether all councillors should retire together or whether one third should retire each year. In either case elections were held in 1976.

As a result of the elections held in 1977, Labour controls only two metropolitan counties. Control of the non-metropolitan counties is divided as follows:

Conservative	35
Labour	1
Conservative with Independent support	1
Independent	2

All councillors, including elected members in Greater London, are entitled to receive a flat-rate attendance allowance to cover time spent on council business as well as the travelling and subsistence allowances which they already receive. The amount is determined by each local authority, within maxima laid down by the Secretary of State. This system has given rise to much public controversy and, after an internal review, the Government appointed an independent inquiry in November 1976.

The Act also contains sections relating to the internal organisation of councils. Within certain limits, they give local authorities greater freedom to organise their own affairs although the basic committee structure is to be preserved. In 1971 the local authority associations and the Secretary of State for the Environment appointed a working party under the chairmanship of Mr. M. Bains to examine management in local government at both the elected member and officer levels. Its report, *The New Local Authorities: Management and Structure*, published in 1972, has been generally welcomed.

Functions.—Non-metropolitan county authorities are responsible for broad planning functions, for education, personal social services, traffic management, transport co-ordination, major highways, police and fire services and they have certain reserve housing powers. Their district councils are the main housing authorities and they are also responsible for the preparation of local plans within the county's framework, for the operation of municipal transport undertakings, for the maintenance of "urban" roads (those with speed limits not exceeding 40 mile/h which are neither trunk nor classified roads), for the enforcement of building regulations and for the provision of local amenities. They are also the new rating authorities. With certain major exceptions, the division of functions in the metropolitan areas is similar. Firstly, the districts are large enough in population and resources and sufficiently compact in size to assume responsibility for education and the personal social services. Secondly, the operation of public transport, in some areas already being organised on a conurbation basis by passenger transport authorities established under the Transport Act 1968, is a county and not a district responsibility.

WALES.

The Local Government Act 1972 also reformed local government in Wales, the new structure coming into force in April 1974.

Local government functions are divided between eight counties and thirty-seven district authorities. Broadly, the division of functions between the two tiers is the same as that in English non-metropolitan counties but the county councils do not have even reserve housing powers and a number of additional responsibilities, such as libraries, weights and measures, and refuse disposal, may be conferred upon district authorities.

New community meetings and community councils have been created throughout Wales except in the most heavily populated areas. Their main responsibility is to represent the views of their electorate to the principal authorities but they may also continue to perform those functions formerly the responsibility of parish councils.

As a result of the elections held in 1977, the Welsh counties are controlled as follows:

Labour	2
Independent	3
No overall control	2
Conservative	1

SCOTLAND.

Under the terms of the Local Government (Scotland) Act 1973 a new structure came into force in May 1975.

Structure.—In mainland Scotland, there is a two-tier structure consisting of:

(i) 9 regional councils (Highland, Grampian, Tayside, Fife, Lothian, Borders, Central, Strathclyde, Dumfries and Galloway).

(ii) 53 district councils.

By 1976 each district council was required to submit a scheme for the creation of community councils in its area. These councils which will be set up in 1976–7 are intended to ascertain and to express the views of the local community to local and other public authorities.

Regional councils are responsible for major and strategic services, including economic and physical planning, roads and transport, education, social services, police and fire services. District councils are responsible for local services, including housing, local planning, environmental health, licensing and amenity services. The more rural regional councils perform some of the functions allocated elsewhere to district councils.

Special " most-purpose " island authorities have been created for Orkney, Shetland and the Western Isles, performing all local government functions apart from police and fire services.

Constitution.—Eventually the members of each authority will be elected for four years with the elections for regions and island authorities and for the districts alternating at two-year intervals. The next regional elections will be held in 1978. District elections were held in 1974 and 1977. Those elected in 1977 will all retire in 1980, the last transitional elections. As a result of the elections held in 1977, Labour lost control of such citadels as Glasgow, Aberdeen, and Dundee.

3. Local Government Finance.

Expenditure by local authorities amounts to about one-third of total public expenditure. Its scale and the methods by which it is financed are therefore of great importance to the Chancellor of the Exchequer in his management of the national economy. Central government is also concerned to ensure that its national policies are implemented by local authorities. On the other hand, the objective of a healthy local democracy demands that local authorities should enjoy a genuine degree of financial independence.

At present local government current expenditure is financed from three sources:

(i) Rates—rates are a poundage tax levied on the rateable value of property in the local authority's area. Although subject to some central government control, the level of rates is fixed annually by the local authority itself.

(ii) Grants from central government—local authorities receive a number of grants for specific services they provide and a general grant, the rate support grant, which is calculated on the basis of the needs of the area (*e.g.*, its rate resources in relation to the national average, the number of children and old people, etc.).

(iii) Charges for services rendered—consisting of rents from council houses and income from services such as public transport, swimming baths, etc.

Over the years local authorities have become progressively more dependent on central government grants, so that on average 60 per cent of their current expenditure in 1970 was financed in this way. The Redcliffe-Maud Commission expressed concern at this situation, arguing that the reorganisation of local government structure provided a unique opportunity for financial reform and that, unless substantial changes were implemented, the new authorities it proposed would be severely handicapped. In July 1971 the Conservative Government published a Green Paper, *The Future Shape of Local Government Finance* (Cmnd. 4741), and in 1974 a number of minor changes were made. A new rate rebate scheme came into force on 1 April 1974, designed to make rates more responsive to the ability of the householder to pay and to extend relief to those higher up the income scale, and alterations were also made in the rate support grants which central government pays to local authorities. However, no fundamental reforms were introduced and during 1974 the financing of local government and the burden of rates in particular became a matter of political controversy. As a result the Government appointed a committee of inquiry, under the chairmanship of Mr. Frank Layfield QC, to review this question. Its report, published in May 1976, advocated a system of local income tax. At the end of 1976 no decision had been announced on its recommendations.

4. Complaints System for Local Government.

New machinery has been created for the investigation of complaints of maladministration by local authorities, police and water authorities. Three Commissions for Local Administration have been created, for England, Wales and Scotland. The English Commission consists of three Local Commissioners, each investigating complaints in a particular part of the country, and the Parliamentary Commissioner. In Wales and in Scotland there is a single Local Commissioner.

The commissioners work in the same manner as the Parliamentary Commissioner. They investigate complaints which are submitted to them, on behalf of a member of the public, by a member of the authority concerned although they are empowered to deal with a matter directly if they are satisfied that a member of an authority has failed to refer it to them. Once an investigation is completed, a report is submitted to the complainant, to the member concerned and to the authority against whom the complaint was made. It is also normally published. Responsibility for taking action on the basis of such a report rests with the authority concerned, the commissioner having no powers of compulsion at his disposal. The commissioners cannot investigate matters for which other statutory remedies exist or those relating to contractual or commercial transactions, to personnel matters or to the conduct, curricula, internal organisation and discipline of schools and colleges.

NORTHERN IRELAND.

From 1921 until 1972 Northern Ireland was governed under the scheme of devolution embodied in the Government of Ireland Act, 1920. This created the Northern Ireland Parliament (generally known as Stormont after its eventual location) consisting of a House of Commons of 52 members elected on the basis of single-member constituencies and a Senate of 2 ex-officio members and 24 others elected by the members of the Northern Ireland House of Commons. Executive powers were formally vested in the Governor of Northern Ireland but were in effect performed by a prime minister and a small cabinet. The Act conferred upon Stormont extensive powers for regulating the affairs of Northern Ireland but excluded certain matters from its jurisdiction, such as foreign relations and defence, customs and excise and income tax, which remained the responsibility of the United Kingdom Parliament. Largely because of these reserved powers, 12 MPs continued to be returned to Westminster from Northern Ireland constituencies. The Act however saved the sovereign authority of the UK Parliament over all matters.

The continuation of the troubles in the province, which led to the presence of over 20,000 British soldiers there, and the withdrawal of the principal opposition parties from Stormont, forced the UK Government, in March 1972, to the conclusion that responsibility for law and order should be removed from the Parliament and Government of Northern Ireland. The Northern Ireland Government having indicated their refusal to accept this transfer of functions, it was decided to suspend the Government of Ireland Act and to impose direct rule for a period of twelve months.

The Northern Ireland (Temporary Provisions) Act, which received the Royal Assent at the end of March 1972, prorogued Stormont and transferred all legislative and executive functions to London. In March 1973 the Government published a White Paper, *Northern Ireland: Constitutional Proposals* (Cmnd. 5259) setting out its plans for the replacement of the Government of Ireland Act by a new system of devolution. During the summer of 1973 legislative effect was given to these proposals.

The Northern Ireland Assembly Act provided for the election of an Assembly on the basis of the twelve Westminster constituencies by means of the single transferable vote system. It consisted of 78 members elected for a term of four years. The Northern Ireland Constitution Act abolished the Northern Ireland Parliament and replaced it by the Assembly and it provided for the creation of an executive consisting of a chief executive and a number of members, formed out of the Assembly, to whom the Secretary of State for Northern Ireland could devolve powers.

As we have already seen (C7(1)), direct rule from Westminster ended on 1 January 1974 but in May, following ratification by the Assembly of the Sunningdale Agreement, strike action led to the resignation of the Chief Executive and his Unionist colleagues. The Assembly was prorogued and direct rule resumed. The UK Government accepted the failure of the attempt to create a power-sharing executive and proposed the election of a Northern Ireland constitutional convention, elected by proportional representation.

General Elections 1945–74

1. *Party strengths*

	1945	1950	1951	1955	1959	1964	1966	1970	Feb. 1974	Oct. 1974
Conservative	213	298	321	345	365	303	253	330	296	276
Labour	393	315	295	277	258	317	363	287	301	319
Liberal	12	9	6	6	9	9	12	6	14	13
SNP	—	—	—	—	—	—	—	1	7	11
Others	22	3	3	2	—	2*	2*	6*†	17*†	16*†
Total	640	625	625	630	630	630	630	630	635	635

* Includes The Speaker.
† Includes all Northern Ireland MPs.

2. *Votes cast*

	Electorate and turnout %	*Conservative* %	*Labour* %	*Liberal* %	*Nationalist* %	*Communist* %	*Others* %	*Votes cast* %
1945	72·7 33,240,391	39·8 9.988,306	47·8 11,995,152	9·0 2,248,226	0·6 138,415	0·4 102.760	1·8 433,688	100 25,085.978
1950	84·0 33,269,770	43·5 12,502,567	46·1 13,266,592	9·1 2,621,548	0·6 173,161	0·3 91,746	0·4 117,057	100 28.772,671
1951	82·5 34,645,573	48·0 13,717,538	48·8 13,948.605	2·5 730,556	0·5 145,521	0·1 21,640	0·1 31,808	100 28,595,668
1955	76·7 34,858,263	49·7 13,286,569	46·4 12,404,970	2·7 722,405	0·9 225,591	0·1 33,144	0·2 62,447	100 26,760,498
1959	78·8 35,397,080	49·4 13,749.830	43·8 12,215,538	5·9 1,638,571	0·6 182,788	0·1 30,897	0·2 61,619	100 27,859,241
1964	77·1 35,892,572	43·4 12,001,396	44·1 12,205,814	11·2 3,092,878	0·9 249.866	0·2 45,932	0·2 53,116	100 27,655,374
1966	75·8 35,964,684	41·9 11,418,433	47·9 13,064 951	8·5 2,327,533	1·2 315,431	0·2 62,112	0·3 75.146	100 27,263,606
1970	72·0 39,384,364	46·4 13,144,692	42·9 12,179,166	7·5 2,117,638	1·7 481,812	0·1 38,431	1·4 383,068	100 28,344,807
Feb. 1974	78·7 39,798,899	38·2 11,963,207	37·2 11,654,726	19·3 6,063,470	2·6 803,396	0·1 32,741	2·6 815,686	100 31,333,226
Oct. 1974	72·8 40,072,971	35·8 10,462,583	39·2 11,457,079	18·3 5,346,754	3·5 1,005,938	0·1 17.426	3·1 899,398	100 29,189,178

The Convention, elected in May 1975, failed to produce a unanimous report although there was a considerable measure of agreement among all the parties. At the heart of their disagreement was the refusal of the United Ulster Unionist Council, the majority party, to recommend the inclusion of members of the mainly Catholic Social and Democratic Labour Party in a future cabinet. The UUUC did, however, propose the creation of a powerful committee system with opposition members serving on, and in some cases chairing, committees. In the vain hope that some compromise could be found, the Government reconvened the Convention for one month at the beginning of February 1976. As we have seen (C7(1)), the Convention was finally dissolved and direct rule from Westminster continued.

Local Government.—The deficiencies of the local government structure were similar to those in the rest of UK and between 1966 and 1969 plans were agreed for reorganisation. Their implementation however was overtaken by the disturbances of summer 1969 and by the decision to transfer all responsibility for public house-building, management and allocation from local government to a regional body, the Northern Ireland Housing Executive.

Consequently an independent review body was appointed to prepare a new scheme. Its report, published in May 1970, proposed a two-tier structure similar to that adopted by the Wheatley Commission, with Stormont acting as the top-tier authority and 26 district councils performing more local functions. These recommendations were accepted by the NI Government and have been re-affirmed by the Secretary of State.

Elections for the district councils, originally scheduled for December 1972, had to be postponed until 1973 and the new authorities started to operate in October 1973.

By-Elections 1945–77

	Total by-elections	*Changes*	*Con.* +	*Con.* −	*Lib.* +	*Lib.* −	*Lab.* +	*Lab.* −	*Others* +	*Others* −
1945–50	52	3	3	—	—	—	—	—	—	3
1950–51	16	—	—	—	—	—	—	—	—	—
1951–55	48	1	1	—	—	—	—	1	—	—
1955–59	52	6	1	4	1	1	4	—	—	1
1959–64	62	9	2	7	1	—	6	2	—	—
1964–66	13	2	1	1	1	—	—	1	—	—
1966–70	38	16	12	1	1	—	—	15	2	—
1970–74	30	9	—	5	5	—	2	3	2	1
1974	1	—	—	—	—	—	—	—	—	—
1975	1	1	1	—	—	—	—	1	—	—
1976	9	2	2	—	—	—	—	2	—	—
1977 (Jan–May)	4	2	2	—	—	—	—	2	—	—

PRINCIPAL MINISTERS 1945–77

	Prime Minister	Chancellor of the Exchequer	Foreign Secretary	Home Secretary
1945–51	C. Attlee	H. Dalton Sir S. Cripps H. Gaitskell	E. Bevin H. Morrison	C. Ede
1951–55	Sir W. Churchill	R. Butler	Sir. A. Eden	Sir D. Maxwell-Fyfe G. Lloyd George
1955–57	Sir A. Eden	R. Butler H. Macmillan	H. Macmillan S. Lloyd	G. Lloyd George
1957–63	H. Macmillan	P. Thorneycroft D. Heathcoat Amory S. Lloyd R. Maudling	S. Lloyd Earl of Home	R. Butler H. Brooke
1963–64	Sir A. Douglas-Home	R. Maudling	R. Butler	H. Brooke
1964–70	H. Wilson	J. Callaghan R. Jenkins	P. Gordon Walker M. Stewart G. Brown M. Stewart	Sir F. Soskice R. Jenkins J. Callaghan
1970–74	E. Heath	A. Barber	Sir A. Douglas-Home	R. Maudling R. Carr
1974–76	H. Wilson	D. Healey	J. Callaghan	R. Jenkins
1976–	J. Callaghan	D. Healey	A. Crosland D. Owen	R. Jenkins M. Rees

HER MAJESTY'S GOVERNMENT

The Cabinet

Prime Minister, First Lord of the Treasury and Minister for the Civil Service	Mr. James Callaghan
Lord President of the Council and Leader of the House of Commons	Mr. Michael Foot
Lord Chancellor	Lord Elwyn-Jones
Chancellor of the Exchequer	Mr. Denis Healey
Secretary of State for the Home Department	Mr. Merlyn Rees
Secretary of State for Foreign and Commonwealth Affairs	Dr. David Owen
Secretary of State for Education and Science and Paymaster General	Mrs. Shirley Williams
Secretary of State for Energy	Mr. Anthony Wedgwood Benn
Secretary of State for Industry	Mr. Eric Varley
Secretary of State for the Environment	Mr. Peter Shore
Secretary of State for Northern Ireland	Mr. Roy Mason
Secretary of State for Scotland	Mr. Bruce Millan
Secretary of State for Wales	Mr. John Morris
Secretary of State for Defence	Mr. Frederick Mulley
Secretary of State for Employment	Mr. Albert Booth
Secretary of State for Social Services	Mr. David Ennals
Secretary of State for Trade	Mr. Edmund Dell
Lord Privy Seal and Leader of the House of Lords	Lord Peart
Minister of Agriculture, Fisheries and Food	Mr. John Silkin
Secretary of State for Prices and Consumer Protection	Mr. Roy Hattersley
Secretary of State for Transport	Mr. William Rodgers
Minister for Social Security	Mr. Stanley Orme
Chancellor of the Duchy of Lancaster	Mr. Harold Lever
Chief Secretary to the Treasury	Mr. Joel Barnett

Ministers not in the Cabinet

Minister of State, Ministry of Agriculture	Mr. Edward Bishop
Minister of State, Civil Service Department	Mr. Charles Morris
Minister of State, Ministry of Defence	Dr. John Gilbert
Ministers of State, Department of Education and Science	Mr. Gordon Oakes
	Lord Donaldson
Minister of State, Department of Employment	Mr. Harold Walker
Minister of State, Department of Energy	Dr. J. Dickson Mabon
Minister for Housing and Construction	Mr. Reginald Freeson
Minister of State for Sport and Recreation	Mr. Denis Howell
Ministers of State, Foreign and Commonwealth Office	Mr. Frank Judd
	Lord Goronwy-Roberts
	Mr Edward Rowlands
Minister of State, Department of Health and Social Security	Mr. Roland Moyle
Ministers of State, Home Office	Lord Harris
	Mr. Brynmor John
Ministers of State, Department of Industry	Mr. Gerald Kaufman
	Mr. Alan Williams
Ministers of State, Northern Ireland Office	Lord Melchett
	Mr. Don Concannon
Minister of State for Overseas Development	Mrs. Judith Hart
Minister of State, Department of Prices and Consumer Protection	Mr. John Fraser
Minister of State, Privy Council Office	Mr. John Smith
Ministers of State, Scottish Office	Mr. Gregor Mackenzie
	Lord Kirkhill
Parliamentary Secretary, Treasury	Mr. Michael Cocks
Financial Secretary to the Treasury	Mr. Robert Sheldon
Minister of State, Treasury	Mr. Denzil Davies
Attorney General	Mr. Samuel Silkin
Solicitor General	Mr. Peter Archer

HER MAJESTY'S OPPOSITION

The Shadow Cabinet

Leader of the Opposition	Mrs. Margaret Thatcher
Deputy Leader and shadow Home Secretary	Mr. William Whitelaw
Overall responsibility for policy and research	Sir Keith Joseph
Agriculture	Mr. John Peyton
Consumer Affairs and Prices	Mrs. Sally Oppenheim
Defence	Mr. Ian Gilmour
Devolution and House of Commons Affairs	Mr. Francis Pym
Education and Arts	Mr. Norman St. John-Stevas
Employment	Mr. James Prior
Energy	Mr. Tom King

Environment	Mr. Michael Heseltine
Foreign and Commonwealth Affairs	Mr. John Davies
Industry	Sir Keith Joseph
Northern Ireland	Mr. Airey Neave
Scotland	Mr. Edward Taylor
Social Services	Mr. Patrick Jenkin
Trade	Mr. John Nott
Treasury	Sir Geoffrey Howe
Wales	Mr. Nicholas Edwards
Leader of the Opposition, House of Lords	Lord Carrington
Without specific duties	Lord Hailsham
Chairman of the Party	Lord Thorneycroft
Chairman of Research Department	Mr. Angus Maude
Opposition Chief Whip	Mr. Humphrey Atkins

HOLDERS OF IMPORTANT PUBLIC OFFICE

PARTIES

Conservative Party.

Chairman of the Party Organisation	Lord Thorneycroft
Director of Organisation	Mr. Anthony Garner
Chairman of the Conservative (Private) Members' Committee ("1922 Committee")	Mr. Edward du Cann

Labour Party.

Chairman of the Labour Party	Joan Lestor
General Secretary	Mr. Ron Hayward
Chairman of the Parliamentary Labour Party	Mr. Cledwyn Hughes

Liberal Party.

Leader of Parliamentary Party	Mr. David Steel
Liberal Chief Whip	Mr. Alan Beith

Scottish National Party.

Leader of Parliamentary Group	Mr. Donald Stewart

United Ulster Unionist Council.

Leader of Parliamentary Group	Mr. James Molyneaux

Plaid Cymru.

Leader of Parliamentary Group	Mr. Gwynfor Evans

SENIOR CIVIL SERVANTS

Head of the Home Civil Service and Permanent Secretary to the Civil Service Department	Sir Douglas Allen
Head of the Diplomatic Service and Permanent Under-Secretary to the Foreign Office	Sir Michael Palliser
Secretary to the Cabinet	Sir John Hunt

CHAIRMEN OF IMPORTANT PUBLIC BODIES

British Airports Authority	Mr. Norman Payne
British Airways Board	Sir Frank McFadzean
British Broadcasting Corporation	Sir Michael Swann
British Gas Corporation	Sir Denis Rooke
British National Oil Corporation	Lord Kearton
British Railways Board	Mr. Peter Parker
British Steel Corporation	Sir Charles Villiers
Civil Aviation Authority	Mr. Nigel Foulkes
Electricity Council	Mr. Francis Tombs
Independent Broadcasting Authority	Lady Plowden
London Transport Executive	Sir Kenneth Robinson
National Coal Board	Sir Derek Ezra
National Enterprise Board	Lord Ryder
Post Office Corporation	Sir William Ryland
Price Commission	Sir Arthur Cockcroft

II. THE CHANGING WORLD SCENE

WESTERN EUROPE

FRANCE.

Gaullism without de Gaulle.

General de Gaulle died on 11 November 1970 at his home at Colombey-les-Deux-Eglises. He was 79. A somewhat Olympian figure, his main achievement had been to restore prestige and self-respect to France. Moreover the constitutional system which he introduced has survived the departure of the central figure about whom it was created (although the problem of what would happen if the President were faced with a hostile majority in the National Assembly remains unresolved). So has the party which he created to assist him in maintaining power. Part of the credit for this must go to the late President Pompidou, who while adhering to Gaullist traditions and stubbornly insisting on French interests revealed a cautious and pragmatic approach, shunning his predecessor's obsession with French grandeur. With this came a much needed revival of interest in economic and social matters. The most significant change was the ending of French hostility to Britain's entry to the EEC, culminating in the highly successful summit conference between M. Pompidou and Mr. Heath in May 1971—although this reversal was in fact initiated by de Gaulle himself. However as the parliamentary elections due in March 1973 approached the position of the Gaullists looked insecure. A referendum on expansion of the EEC gave only lukewarm endorsement to M. Pompidou's new policy, and the Gaullists were shaken by a series of scandals which led to the replacement of M. Chaban-Delmas by M. Messmer as Prime Minister. Moreover the Communist Party and the Socialists agreed on a common programme of government, thus forming the first Popular Front since 1934.

In fact the French electors came close in the first ballot to electing a Socialist-Communist coalition. However, in the second round, the Gaullists, and their Reformist allies led by M. Lecanuet, achieved a remarkable comeback. Although the left-wing parties almost doubled their parliamentary representation and the Gaullists suffered the heaviest losses, the Government parties retained an overall majority of 58 seats.

France under Giscard d'Estaing.

After a period of speculation about his failing health, President Pompidou died in April 1974. In the election to find his successor the official Gaullist candidate and former Prime Minister M. Chaban-Delmas was eliminated on the first ballot with a humiliating 15% of the vote. On the second ballot Valéry Giscard d'Estaing, leader of the centre-right Independent Republicans, only just defeated the candidate of the Left, M. Mitterand, by 50·8% to 49·2% of the vote. He appointed M. Chirac, who had been Gaullist Minister of the Interior under President Pompidou, as Prime Minister in a coalition widened to include all centre groupings. The President's programme included social reform and comprehensive anti-inflation measures. In January 1976 the first major reorganisation of government was carried out since M. Chirac's appointment as Premier. The coalition continued to be the basis for the President's support.

In August 1976, M. Chirac resigned as Premier and was replaced by M. Raymond Barre, one of the President's non-party supporters. M. Chirac had become frustrated by the policies pursued by the President and in December he announced a grand reform of the Gaullist Party, now to be known as the Assembly for the Republic. Together with right-wing disillusion, left-wing opposition to the government increased. M. Mitterand's near success in the Presidential election increased support for his socialist party and following gains for the Socialists and Communists in departmental elections M. Mitterand and the Communist Party leader, M. Marchais, resolved some differences and agreed on joint left-wing lists of candidates for the municipal elections held in March 1977. The alliance gained ground, capturing 58 major cities and towns. In early 1977 M. Chirac announced his candidacy for the recreated post of Mayor of Paris, presenting further problems for the President who, was already under criticism for his handling of the Daoud affair. President Giscard d'Estaing's decision in April 1977 to transport military supplies from Morocco to Zaïre met with a mixed reaction.

THE TWO GERMANYS.

Adenauer and West Germany.

The Federal Republic of Germany, founded in 1949, had as its first Chancellor Dr. Konrad Adenauer until his retirement in 1963 at the age of 86. His Christian Democrat government produced conditions of stability and confidence in which Germany rebuilt her shattered prosperity and a viable parliamentary democracy. His work in building a special relationship with France, culminating in a treaty of friendship, was a dramatic contrast to the long tradition of enmity towards France. But while he succeeded in building his country into the Western community he remained intransigent over German reunification within the boundaries of 1937, stressing West Germany's right to speak for the whole of Germany, including the Soviet Zone. The two states drifted steadily apart, and a seal was set on their division by East Germany's building of the Berlin Wall in 1961.

Erhard and Kiesinger.

Adenauer's successor Dr. Erhard had the prestige of having as economics minister been the main architect of West Germany's "economic miracle." As Chancellor from 1963 to 1966 he was a loyal supporter of the Atlantic Alliance—indeed it was held that he encouraged ties with the United States at the expense of the Franco-German friendship treaty, which had not lived up to the hopes reposed in it. This partly accounted for the enmity of the Bavarian wing of the Christian Democrats called the Christian Social Union (CSU), the party of Franz-Josef Strauss.

In 1966 a governmental crisis caused by the resignation of the junior partners in the coalition, the Free Democrats (FDP), led to the formation under Dr. Kiesinger of a Grand Coalition in which the Social Democrats (SDP) joined the CDU and so had their first taste of government on the national level since the Federal Republic's foundation. This helped to establish the SPD in the eyes of the electorate as a potential governing party.

The End of Christian Democratic Rule, 1969.

In the general election of September 1969 the SPD made significant gains in both votes and seats. Despite widespread publicity the extreme right-wing NPD (often referred to as Neo-Nazis) failed to qualify for any seats since it polled less than the necessary 5 per cent of the total votes. It is now virtually defunct. Thus the three-party system remained. Although the CDU was still the largest party, the SPD and FDP leaders agreed to form a coalition government with Herr Brandt, the SPD leader, as Chancellor and Herr Scheel, the FDP leader, as Foreign Minister.

Herr Brandt's achievement in reaching the Chancellorship was considerable, in view of his unpopularity in some quarters for having fled to Norway during the war and taken out Norwegian citizenship. However he had built up his reputation as Mayor of West Berlin.

Efforts to Improve Relations Between the Two Germanys.

The Brandt Government's main achievements were in the field of foreign policy. A radical development in 1970 was the two meetings between Chancellor Brandt and the East German Prime Minister, Herr Stoph. These showed that Herr Brandt had accepted the existence of two separate states within the German nation (although this fell short of East Germany's demand for complete recognition by Bonn). A treaty signed by West Germany and the Soviet Union in Moscow on 12 August stated that the borders of all European countries are inviolable, including that between the Federal and the Democratic Republics. Bonn implies that frontiers can still be changed by mutual agreement.

Bonn insisted that the ratification of the Moscow treaty and of the Warsaw treaty recognising the Oder–Neisse Line and normalising relations between West Germany and Poland depended on a satisfactory outcome of the Four-Power talks on Berlin. At last in September 1971 an agreement was signed by which the Soviet Union in turn accepted the realities which matter to the West. It recognised the rights of the Allies in Berlin and the city's special relations with the Federal Republic, which had been constantly disputed, especially by the East Germans. The free flow of traffic to and from Berlin, formerly unregulated and therefore a favourite object of disruption and escalation of tension, is now covered by an agreement for which the Soviet Union, rather than East Germany, can be held responsible. The representation abroad of West Berlin by the Federal Republic is now legally based. West Berliners can again visit the eastern part of the city and the GDR. The details of transit were left to be filled in by East and West Germany, and after the Russians had overcome East German recalcitrance the first treaty between the two German states was signed on 20 December 1971. The Brandt Government immediately initiated the ratification of the Moscow and Warsaw treaties, which was eventually achieved in May 1972 after prolonged antagonism from the opposition CDU and some former government supporters. Bonn stressed that the treaties were not an anticipation of a Peace Treaty and formed no legal basis for the existing frontiers, but this view was rejected by the USSR and Poland.

The way was now open for general agreements on traffic and for a general treaty between East and West Germany signed on 21 December 1972, which recognised the existence of two virtually sovereign German states. Though a shock for those who clung to the illusion of German unity, the treaty marked a new realism which promised greater contact between the two states and was therefore welcomed by a majority of Germans. The concessions extorted from the East Germans as a condition of signing the treaty considerably increased the numbers of West Germans and Berliners able to visit the East. The advantages gained by the GDR in terms of confirmation of its statehood and of the division of Germany for the foreseeable future are evident from the flood of countries (including Britain and France) which have recognised it since the signature of the treaty. Despite an attempt to have it declared unconstitutional, the treaty came into force in the summer of 1973. This was quickly followed by the admission of the two German states to the United Nations on 18 September. However the limits of détente were shown up by highly restrictive interpretations of the agreements by East Germany and by the latter's doubling of the sum visitors from West Germany and Berlin were required to exchange per day to 20 Marks, though it was later reduced. In pursuance of the Basic Treaty, Permanent Missions were opened in Bonn and East Berlin in May 1974.

1973 also saw the conclusion of a treaty normalising relations between West Germany and Czechoslovakia, long delayed by the Czech attempt to have the Munich Agreement of 1938 declared invalid "ab initio". In 1975 agreements were signed between West Germany and Poland on the granting of credits to Poland, the payment of claims arising from the Second World War and the resettlement of ethnic Germans living in Poland. This was criticised as paying for emigration by the Opposition, who blocked it with their majority in the Upper house.

The SPD/FDP Coalition

In April 1972 a government crisis was brought about by defections from the government coalition mainly on the question of its Ostpolitik. This led to an early election in November 1972 as a result of which Chancellor Brandt's government was triumphantly returned to power. For the first time, the SPD became the largest party in the Bundestag and their position was strengthened by their coalition colleagues, FDP. However relations between them became strained as a result of demands from the left wing of the SPD.

In May 1974, following the arrest of Günther Guillaume, a Chancellery aide, who admitted spying for E. Germany, political responsibility for negligence was accepted by Chancellor Brandt who then resigned. His successor was the former finance minister Helmut Schmidt whose approach is marked by realism and pragmatism.

During 1974 the CDU made significant gains in elections in the Länder. Helmut Kohl, chairman of CDU, was accepted as its candidate for Federal Chancellor. In October 1976 federal elections to the Bundestag were held. The SPD–FDP coalition lost ground (see Table below) and based upon the fact that the CDU–CSU alliance was now the largest party in the Bundestag, Kohl attempted to claim the Chancellorship. However, with assurances from Hans Dietrich Genscher that the FDP would continue to support the SPD in a governing coalition, President Scheel was persuaded by Genscher and Brandt to ask Schmidt to continue as Chancellor. After the elections the CSU–CDU alliance was temporarily split by the actions of Franz Joseph Strauss (the Bavarian leader of CSU), but their differences have since been resolved.

Table: German election results for the Bundestag

	1972			1976	
	Seats	%		Seats	%
SPD .	214	42·6		230	45·9
CDU .	190	38·0	}243, 48·6	224	44·8
CSU .	53	10·6			
FDP. .	39	7·9		42	8·4
NPD .	—	0·3		—	0·6
Others .	—	0·6		—	0·3

East German Developments.

In October 1975 a wide-ranging 25-year Treaty of Friendship, Cooperation and Mutual Assistance was signed in Moscow. In May 1976 at the Ninth Congress of the Socialist Unity Party, the E. German leader Herr Honecker presented the General Committee report which reaffirmed close ties with the Soviet Union, reviewed economic and social developments and produced a new 5-year economic plan. The aims of the plan include increased national productivity and investment and closer economic integration with the Soviet Union and other COMECON countries. Following elections to the Volkskammer in October, the 5-year plan was endorsed and unanimous approval was given to the appointments of Herr Honecker as Chairman of the Council of State, Willi Stoph as Chairman of the Council of Ministers and Horst Sindermann as president of the Volkskammer.

Although an amendment was made to the new party programme allowing references to equality of religious beliefs, the position regarding religious and intellectual freedom remains unsatisfactory. Recent examples of this include the suicide of 2 clerics and the effective exiling of folksinger Wolf Biermann.

ITALY.

The centre-left coalition which has dominated recent Italian politics was formed in 1963 in an "opening to the Left" which brought Pietro Nenni's Socialists out of the wilderness with the Communists and into government. It was born of frustration with the inertia of the previous centre-right coalition. But it too had a long list of social reforms which it had failed to accomplish, though its problems came as much from dis sensions within the Christian Democratic Party as between it and the Socialists. A major cause of the governmental crises which have afflicted postwar governments in Italy has been the increasing strength of the Communist Party and, until the 1976 elections, that of the Neo-fascists (MSI). The room for manoeuvre of the other parties was thus reduced. The elections of May 1972 were followed by the formation by Signor Andreotti of Italy's 34th post-war government, a coalition of the Christian Democrats (DC) Social Democrats (PSDI) and Liberals supported by the Republicans (PRI). In this " Government of the Centre " the Liberals were represented after a 15-year break and the Socialists (PSI) excluded for the first time since 1963.

The holding of the election had the effect of postponing the referendum on the law of 1970 which had legalised divorce in Italy. It had been passed despite bitter opposition from the Roman Catholic Church and the reluctance of the Christian Democrats, the senior party in the governing coalition, but the opposition to it was still powerful. This ideological issue complicated the political scene by ranging Christian Democrats and Neo-fascists on one side, Liberals, Socialists and Communists on the other.

After a series of parliamentary defeats and the withdrawal of Republican support, the Andreotti Government resigned in June 1973. Signor Rumor, the outgoing Minister of the Interior and former Prime Minister, was able to re-establish the Centre-Left coalition of Christian Democrats, Socialists, Social Democrats and Republicans. When the divorce referendum became inevitable in May 1974, the result was a surprisingly substantial majority in favour of retaining the divorce laws, to the discredit of the Christian Democrats.

In the economic sphere Italy continues to be plagued by numerous strikes and by the seemingly intractable problems of the economically deprived south (Mezzogiorno). Particularly since the oil crisis there have been massive balance of payments deficits, rampant inflation, falling production and continuing bureaucratic paralysis. These economic problems and political unrest, manifested in bomb explosions and attacks on persons and property by extreme groups, on the left and especially the right, led to a further government crisis in late 1974. Signor Moro emerged as Prime Minister because he alone, among the DCs, retained some degree of credibility with parties of the left. A minority coalition of DCs and Republicans resulted.

In January 1976, the Socialists withdrew their support from the Government but reached an agreement with the DCs that they would abstain from voting against the Government. In April, faced with opposition to its abortion legislation, the falling value of the lira, increasing political violence and the exposition of bribery and corruption, the Moro government resigned. Elections were held in June, the main issue being the future pattern of government in Italy. The Communist Party, which had long demonstrated its independence from Moscow, had made significant gains in the regional, provincial and municipal elections in 1975 and had indicated its willingness to respect party pluralism and the transfer of power through elections. This position, together with the lowering of the voting age for the Chamber of Deputies, resulted in their share of the votes being increased from 27·1% in 1972 to 34·4% in the Chamber and from 28·3% in 1972 to 33·8% in the Senate. The strength of the DCs remained almost the same at about 38% in both Chambers. The full results compared to 1972 were:

Chamber of Deputies

	1976		1972	
	Seats	%	Seats	%
DC .	262	38·7	266	38·7
PCI.	228	34·4	179	27·1
PSI.	57	9·6	61	9·6
PSDI	15	3·4	29	5·1
PRI	14	3·1	15	2·9
PLI.	5	1·3	20	3·9
MSI.	35	6·1	56	8·7
Others	14	3·4	4	4·0

Senate

	1976		1972	
	Seats	%	Seats	%
DC .	135	38·9	135	38·1
PCI.	116	33·8	94	28·3
PSI.	29	10·2	33	10·7
PSDI	6	3·1	11	5·4
PRI	6	2·7	5	3·0
PLI.	2	1·4	8	4·4
MSI.	15	6·6	26	9·2
Others	6	3·3	3	0·9

In July 1976, Signor Andreotti agreed to form a new minority government. Measures have been taken to alleviate the economic crisis and protect the lira, including loans from the IMF and the EEC. The Communists provide tacit support for the Government, but are faced with the dilemma of either supporting measures with which they disagree or opposing them with the clear risk of economic and political collapse. The proposed solution is to formally involve the PCI in policy-making by allowing them to enter government in a coalition.

PORTUGAL.

A military take-over in 1926 which brought Antonio Salazar to power inaugurated nearly fifty years of authoritarian rule. In 1968 Salazar was succeeded by Marcello Caetano who, despite slightly more liberal sympathies, maintained the instruments of oppression, including the hated Political Police (PIDE).

However, the dictatorship was overthrown by an almost bloodless military coup on 25 April 1974. Although the leadership of the seven-man " Junta of National Salvation " belonged to General Spínola, who became President, the coup was largely the work of middle-ranking officers whose experience in the long struggle against Nationalist forces in Portuguese Angola, Mozambique and Guinea had brought about profound dissatisfaction with the aims and methods of the Caetano government.

The new government initiated an impressive series of liberal measures, including the abolition of press censorship (later partially restored), the lifting of the ban on political parties, the abolition of the secret police, release of political prisoners and the promise of free elections. The right to strike and right of assembly were secured in August. Rapid progress was also made towards granting independence to Portugal's large African Territories. However after so many years of dictatorship it was not surprising that the preparations for democracy and the competition for power brought about a very unsettled situation. In September, after a split between left- and right-wing factions of the Junta and an alleged attempt at a counter-coup by General Spínola to reverse Portugal's leftward drift, the latter was replaced by General Costa Gomes and other conservatives were dismissed. Under pressure from the leftist Movement of the Armed Forces, impatient with the pace of reform, the officers of the Junta took over exceptional powers in February 1975.

The failure of an attempted *coup d'état* on 11 March 1975 resulted in General Spínola fleeing the country and the Armed Forces Movement's Revolutionary Council taking supreme power. A ban was imposed on three political parties, including the right-wing Christian Democrats, and the activities of the Popular Democrats were disrupted by left-wing elements.

In elections to a Constituent Assembly held in April 1975 (the first for fifty years) the Socialists under Dr. Soares emerged as the strongest party with 37% of the vote, while the Popular Democrats received 26% and the Communists only 12%. But there were no corresponding cabinet changes and the government continued with a programme of extensive nationalisation. Tension developed between the increasingly pro-Communist Armed Forces Movement and the Socialists and Popular Democrats, with both parties temporarily withdrawing from the coalition government. There was mounting indiscipline in the armed forces and in November 1975 some extreme leftist army units unsuccessfully attempted a putsch. In its wake the government under Pinheiro de Azevedo was able increasingly to promote law and order and in February 1976 a constitutional pact was reached between the army and the main political parties to reduce the powers of the former in the Supreme Revolutionary Council. After elections to the legislative assembly in April 1976, the Socialists remained the largest party and a new constitution was promulgated. On 27 June General Antonio dos Santos Ramalho Eanes, backed by the leading parties, was elected President with 61·5% of the vote. A new government was formed by Dr. Soares and a programme of economic measures was initiated to fight rampant inflation and high unemployment. The local election results at the end of 1976 indicate that a strong division still exists between the conservative north and the Communists in the south. Despite continuing support from Western Europe and a massive loan from the U.S., the position of Dr. Soares and the Socialists will remain tenuous because of the virtually intractable economic problems.

SPAIN.

The extremely bitter Civil War from 1936 to 1939, between, on the one hand, the republican forces which had been coming under increasingly left-wing influence and, on the other, the Catholic and conservative National Front and the army which revolted under General Franco's leadership, resulted in a victory for the latter with the help of fascist Germany and Italy, which enabled Franco to dominate Spanish political life for three and a half decades. After remaining neutral during the Second World War Franco, despite cosmetic liberalisation measures and the temporary pushing into the background of the Falangist Party (Spanish Fascist Party), was ostracised by the United Nations and received no Marshall Aid. Even relations with the Vatican were strained (though the régime was certainly preferred to the anti-clerical Republicans), at least until a new Concordat was signed in 1953. However it became clear that the ostracism of Spain was having the unintended effect of helping to promote a defiant Spanish solidarity, and in 1953 the United States concluded bilateral agreements on defence and economic aid with Franco's government and two years later Spain was admitted to membership of the United Nations. Meanwhile the domestic scene in Spain was marked by political apathy, despite economic and other problems, and by a desire to avoid another civil war at all costs.

Franco had been grooming Prince Juan Carlos of the Spanish House of Bourbon-Parma to be his successor, despite Falangist opposition, and in 1966 an Organic Law declared Spain a monarchy though with a reigning monarch only after Franco's departure. At the same time provision was made for direct election of part of the Cortes, or parliament of estates of the realm, but on a restricted franchise and with candidates vetted by the Falangist movement. The Succession Law of July 1969 finally named Prince Juan Carlos as eventual successor of General Franco as Head of the Spanish State and King of Spain.

During the early 1970s Spain experienced increasing social and industrial unrest despite government repression; as well as terrorist activity by the Basque separatist movement ETA. This culminated in the assassination of the Prime Minister, Admiral Luis Carrero Blanco, in December 1973. He was succeeded by Sr. Arias Navarro. There followed a mixture of cautious attempts at liberalisation and retreat into repression. In December 1974 "political associations" (not parties) were legalised under certain conditions. But after industrial unrest and strikes, especially in the Basque provinces, to demand an amnesty for political prisioners, press censorship was intensified. In April 1975 after shootings of policemen a state of emergency was declared in two Basque provinces. The following month there came some liberalisation of local government as well as the introduction of a limited right to strike and labour legislation. However in August a new anti-terrorism law was followed by the execution of Basque and Communist extremists, an action which provoked strong international protests.

In November 1975 the long dictatorship of General Franco finally came to an end when he died after a prolonged illness. However it soon became clear that the new king, Juan Carlos, was not going to make any sharp break with the past. Hence his confirmation of Sr. Arias Navarro as Prime Minister. He had to try to carry the intransigent Right with him in his reform plans, since they had a majority in the Cortes, the communes and the ministries and were determined not to give up their power. Only long-term plans were announced for repeal of the anti-terrorist law, amnesty for political prisoners and changes in the electoral law. Despite increasing toleration in practice of the activities at least of the Christian Democratic parties, the government lacked credibility with the rest of the population because of its desire not to provoke the right-wing opposition from the so-called "Bunker." It was faced with the dilemma of either suppressing strikes (such as the Madrid Metro Strike of January 1976) and so disavowing its democratisation programme, or permitting them and endangering the recession-bound economy.

Early in 1976 there were only vague indications of where and how elections would take place. However, in July Sr. Navarro was replaced by Sr. Adolfo Suárez Gonzáles who promised that the Government would be a "lawful promoter of a political process which is open to all" and an amnesty was offered for all political prisoners, excluding those concerned with terrorist offences. In November the Cortes approved plans for political reform which would replace the Cortes with a two-chamber parliament and in December, a referendum gave 94·2% support to the proposals. This was the first free vote in Spain since 1936. Unrest in the Basque regions continued as did discontent with the political situation evidenced by the assassination of Juan Villar and the kidnapping of Antonio Oriol, the Chief of the Council of State. In February Sr. Oriol was freed; responsibility for the kidnapping being claimed by GRAPO, an anti-fascist resistance group. In April 1977 the Communist Party was officially recognised thus raising the possibility of further right-wing violence and reaction. At the time of writing (April 1977) an election was scheduled for 15 June 1977.

EASTERN MEDITERRANEAN

GREECE.

On 21 April 1967 dictatorial power was seized in Greece by right-wing army colonels. They did so out of fear of the expected electoral victory of the Centre Union, under Mr. George Papandreou, which had increasing support from the Left. Many politicians, journalists and others were arrested, often without charges being preferred. A rigid press censorship was imposed. The critical position of the 26-year-old King Constantine came to a head in December 1967 when after an abortive attempt to free himself of the military junta he went into exile in Rome.

In 1969 Greece withdrew from the Council of Europe when it became clear that a majority would vote for her suspension on the grounds of her repudiation of the values which the Council exists to uphold. The attitude of the United States, Greece's major protector, was crucial, but Mr. Papadopoulos managed to get the supply of heavy arms from the United States resumed in 1970 without naming a date for elections. In 1972 the régime's external position was strengthened by an agreement that Piraeus should become the home port of part of the US Sixth Fleet.

But the internal position was less secure. The foiling of an attempted naval mutiny in May 1973 was followed by the abolition of the monarchy and its replacement by a Presidential Republic. A referendum approved the change and elected Mr. Papadopoulos President. He then announced the abolition of martial law and of the Athens Special Military tribunal and an amnesty for all political crimes. But further trials of political opponents of the régime continued. In October 1973 President Papadopoulos appointed Mr. Spyros Markezinis, leader of the Progressive Party in the former Parliament, to form a civilian government. But bloody clashes between students and police in Athens led to the reimposition of martial law and mass arrests. On 25 November a bloodless military coup led by Brigadier Ioannides overthrew President Papadopoulos and Lieut.-General Gizikis replaced him as head of state. However the new régime commanded an even narrower basis of support than its predecessor and, in a fatal attempt to increase its popularity inside Greece, it moved steadily into a confrontation with Turkey.

The first dispute arose out of the discovery of oil in the Aegean near the island of Thasos and stirred old animosities as to the rights of the two countries over the Aegean. Turkey granted drilling rights outside Greek territorial waters but though Turkey maintained a conciliatory position the Greek Government became belligerent and uncompromising.

The Cyprus problem had been an even more emotive issue between Greece and Turkey. Yet Brigadier Ioannides decided to use the officers of the Greek National Guard on Cyprus in July 1975 in a coup to replace President Makarios with a régime controlled from Athens. This grossly unrealistic move was swiftly followed by the Turkish invasion of the island, and it transpired that Greece's military rulers had allowed the army to deteriorate to a point where it was unable to go to war. In this situation the President and the Armed Forces Commanders turned to the civilian politicians.

It was decided to call back the former premier, Mr. Constantine Karamanlis, to head a government of national unity. Mr. Karamanlis, who had been living in self-imposed exile in Paris since his defeat in the 1963 elections, returned to be greeted by tumultuous crowds celebrating the downfall of the junta.

The Restoration of Democracy in Greece.

Mr. Karamanlis's emergency coalition was no more capable than its predecessor of a military response to the Turkish challenge. However it was able to blame its impotence on the incompetence of the military régime whose apparatus it now began to dismantle.

Political detainees were freed. Greek citizenship was restored to those who had been stripped of it. The junta's constitution was scrapped and the 1952 Greek Constitution reintroduced. By mid-December more than 120,000 supporters of the junta had been removed from the state services. In October, ex-President Papadopoulos and his closest associates were banished to the island of Kea. Subsequently it was announced they they, along with Brigadier Ioannidis, would be charged with treason and with responsibility for the deaths at the Athens Polytechnic in November 1973.

Political parties—including the two Greek Communist parties—were allowed to operate freely again. Mr. Karamanlis set up his own New Democracy Party, while Mr. Mavros continued to lead the Centre-Union Party. The leftward leaning and volatile Mr. Andreas Papandreou, son of the now dead George Papandreou, formed PASOK—the Pan-Hellenic Socialist Union.

Only Colonel Papadopoulos was prevented from participating in the general elections which followed on 17 November 1974.

Mr. Karamanlis won a crushing victory, with the New Democracy Party taking more than 54% of the votes. Mr. Mavros's Centre Union received 20%, the Pan-Hellenic Socialist Union 13% and the Communists 8%.

Three weeks later in a referendum on the future of the monarchy the Greek people overwhelmingly rejected "crowned democracy" in favour of a presidential republic.

In January 1975 the Greek parliament ruled that the army's seizure of power on 21 April 1967 was a coup d'état and therefore illegal. The original coup leaders Ioannides and Papadopoulos and four other members of the junta were charged with revolt and high treason. Major trials began in the summer of 1975 and convictions soon followed.

A new republican constitution was adopted by the Greek parliament in June 1975 with the opposition abstaining. In ensuing Presidential elections Mr. Tsatsos, a friend of Mr. Karamanlis, was elected. Mr. Karamanlis is due to retire in 1979 and it is expected that he will then seek the presidency.

Greek Foreign Policy since the Junta.

Throughout the seven years of army rule, many Greeks regarded the United States as being responsible for the junta's survival. The invasion of Cyprus by Turkey generated a further upsurge in anti-American feeling and, on 15 August 1974, Mr. Karamanlis announced that Greece would withdraw from the military side of NATO in protest at the second Turkish military operation on the island. In December American bases and installations in the country, not belonging to NATO, were brought under "national control" though they continued to operate.

In contrast the new regime made determined efforts to restore its links with Western Europe, pressing for early acceptance as a full member of the Common Market and readmission to the Council of Europe. Despite the serious gap in NATO's southern flank which the departure of Greece created, it seemed likely that the country would maintain its pro-Western stance. In July 1976, formal negotiations were commenced for full membership of the EEC. Relations with neighbouring Balkan states were improved following a meeting on Balkan co-operation early in 1976.

TURKEY.

The military coup of 1960 and the liberal constitution promulgated under the caretaker junta in 1961 were followed by ten years of trying to reconcile democracy with rapid development—an increasingly difficult operation with the growth of extremists on the left and right. But in 1971 the army threw out the civilian government of Mr Demirel's Justice Party. Many arrests were made and constitutional reforms reduced civil liberties. After two years of disguised military rule, Parliament reasserted its initiative in 1973 by refusing to elect the Chief of Staff as President. Mr. Demirel was expected to return to power after the general elections in October, but a shock result produced major gains for Mr. Ecevit's Republican People's Party (approximately social democrat). After a period of deadlock Mr. Ecevit reached agreement to form a coalition with the Muslim-traditionalist National Salvation Party in January 1974. In the face of grave economic problems they maintained an increasingly shaky alliance until Mr. Ecevit resigned in September. Despite the national euphoria caused by the successes in Cyprus, Turkey's politics sank once more into a seemingly unbreakable deadlock. The right-wing parties could agree neither on the formation of a government nor on a date for early elections. They feared that Mr. Ecevit's success in Cyprus, which had reinvigorated his public popularity, would sweep him back to power. There followed several months without normal government but with rising political tension and pitched battles between leftist and rightist university students in an atmosphere reminiscent of the eve of the military coup in 1971. However in March 1975 a minority Nationalist Front cabinet of right-wing parties was formed under the leadership of Mr. Demirel. It faced a worsening economic crisis with inflation at 30%, high unemployment, reduced exports and a fall in the vital remittances from Turks working abroad, especially in West Germany.

Turkish Invasion of Cyprus.

After the Greek-inspired coup of 15 July 1974 which deposed, but failed to kill, President Makarios of Cyprus and replaced him with Nicos Sampson, a former gunman of the EOKA organisation which had fought for union of Cyprus with Greece, Mr. Ecevit tried in vain to persuade Britain to help restore the status quo under its obligations as a guarantor of the treaty setting up an independent Cypriot republic. Then on 20 July Turkish forces landed at Kyrenia in the north of Cyprus and after tough fighting established a secure foothold on the island.

The Turkish invasion triggered the rapid collapse of the Sampson regime in Nicosia and of the Colonels' dictatorship in Athens. Initially therefore it was greeted with support and approval by world opinion. But as events were to show, nationalist passions in both countries ruled out a speedy and peaceful settlement to the island's problems and as Turkey tightened her grip on the north of Cyprus, sympathy passed to the new governments in Athens and Nicosia.

Turkey's announced aim in Cyprus was the establishment of a bi-regional federation with a degree of geographical separation between the two communities. However, Mr. Karamanlis's first speech after his triumphant return to Athens rejected a federal solution for Cyprus, and Turkey thus went to the August peace talks in Geneva convinced that the Greeks did not seriously desire a settlement.

The early breakdown of the talks was thus more or less inevitable. Turkey immediately launched a second offensive to secure the 30% of the territory of the island which she claimed for its Turkish community, advancing along a line stretching from Lefka in the West to Famagusta in the east.

Behind this Attila Line, as it became known, had lain 70% of the economic wealth of Cyprus and 40% of the Greek population. 180,000 Greek Cypriots fled before the Turkish army to the south of the island where they lived as refugees in the Troodos mountains. Under these circumstances it was difficult to imagine any Greek Cypriot Government accepting the new boundaries as the basis for a " bi-cantonal federation ".

In September 1975, talks were resumed between Mr. Denktash, the Turkish Cypriot leader and Mr. Glafkos Clerides, who was acting as President of Cyprus until the return of Archbishop Makarios. Several interruptions occurred after the discovery of mass graves of Turkish Cypriots murdered apparently by the Greeks, soon after the invasion. Nevertheless prisoners of war were exchanged and the diplomatic atmosphere eased.

Mr. Clerides had come to agree that the future of Cyprus must be settled in federal terms and a package deal was thought to have been agreed. When Archbishop Makarios returned to Cyprus in December 1975 a final political solution had not been reached and the Archbishop rejected any proposals which might lead to a partitioning of the island. Britain eventually allowed Turkish refugees living in British military bases in the Greek part of Cyprus to depart for the north of the island. The overwhelming majority of Turkish Cypriots were now concentrated in the Turkish-held sector of the island. Yet 8,000 Greek Cypriots were not allowed to return home despite assurances from Mr. Denktash that they would be able to do so. As a result of a decision of the US Congress to cut off aid to Turkey on 5 February 1975, the Turkish attitude became more intransigent leading to a proclamation eight days later by Mr. Denktash that the Turkish-held zone would be a federal state of the future Federal Republic of Cyprus. The Greeks, regarding this as an indication that there would be no prospect of returning refugees to their homes and that outright partition was near at hand, refused to negotiate with the Turks. Talks were in fact resumed although little progress was made during 1976. In April Mr. Clerides resigned his post as negotiator after the revelation of a secret agreement with Mr. Denktash of which Archbishop Makarios had not been informed. Mr. Denktash also resigned and was elected President of the Turkish Cypriot state. In January 1977 a major breakthrough occurred when Archbishop Makarios met Mr. Denktash in Nicosia, their first meeting in 13 years. Details of the talks have not been disclosed but both leaders commented afterwards that the talks had been a success.

Relations with Greece had not been improved when in July and August 1976 a Turkish oil-prospecting vessel began operations in the disputed area of the Aegean sea. Greek warships were sent to patrol the area and border troops were mobilized. A Greek application to the International Court of Justice for an injunction to prevent Turkish exploration was refused and attempts were made to negotiate a settlement of the dispute.

THE SOVIET UNION

A Turning Point in Soviet History.

Stalin died in 1953 and the struggle for succession then continued for five years. A triumvirate of successors, Malenkov, Molotov, and Beria had decided to give the post of party chief—First Secretary—to Khrushchev, then a relatively harmless outsider, or so he was deemed by them. Beria, the all powerful police chief, was executed as a spy in 1953, Malenkov was forced to give up the premiership in 1954 and three years later both he and Molotov were expelled from the Central Committee. Khrushchev thereupon emerged with supreme powers.

In 1961 Khrushchev publicly and dramatically completed the process which he had begun in 1956, of finally rejecting the cult of Stalin. Stalin had made the Soviet Union a modern industrial society and a great armed power. But the arbitrary bureaucracy through which this had been achieved had, in Khrushchev's view, overrun itself. Radical changes became essential and Khrushchev attempted various steps—the scaling down of the secret police; the rebuilding of the administrative apparatus; the opening up of virgin lands; and a new theory that war was not inevitable. The legacy of the Stalinist era had been the concept of the " monolithic " party, which, however torn by internal conflict, must never allow any open division of opinion and free debate, much less the formation of any groups expounding distinctive views. But here de-Stalinisation brought little change.

Khrushchev was abruptly removed from power in October 1964 and replaced by Brezhnev and Kosygin.

The New Leadership.

A meeting of the Supreme Soviet in 1965 confirmed the principle of collective leadership, with Kosygin as Premier and Brezhnev First Secretary. At the 23rd Soviet Party Congress held in April 1966 it was decided that the Praesidium of the Central Committee should go back to being the Politburo and the First Secretary should revert to General Secretary. The Brezhnev era has seen no re-Stalinisation as originally forecast, but there has been a retrenchment of the restrictive power of the establishment which had been disturbed by Khrushchev. The new balancing and compromising leadership style has strengthened both collective leadership and centralism. Critics of Brezhnev, including the conservative Pyotr Shelest and Voronov, were dropped from the Politburo and subsequently all the most important ministers including Andrei Gromyko (Foreign Secretary) and Marshal Grechko (Defence Minister) were brought into the Politburo. Tension between the party and state machinery was thus eased. In April 1975 Shelepin, at 56 the youngest member of the Politburo, was ousted. At the 25th Party Congress in February 1976, Brezhnev appeared fully in control and in May he was promoted to Marshal of the Soviet Union following the death of Marshal Grechko. The 5-year plan for the Soviet economy was presented in December 1975 and the disastrous agricultural situation is to be remedied by massive investment and better planning. Priority is to be given to heavy industry with the overall aim of raising the standard of living. The plan was endorsed in November by the Central Committee.

Foreign Relations.

The historic rapprochement between the United States and China in 1971–2 met with a sharp condemnation of Chinese intentions by the Russians. Yet Soviet–American negotiations over Berlin and the limitation of strategic armaments were speeded up and in May 1972, the first visit to Moscow of a US President (President Nixon) took place. A 12 point statement of principles to guide the future relationship between the two countries resulted and co-operation agreements were signed. Above all, agreements on the limitation of strategic nuclear weapons were also signed. Russia's declared eagerness for the holding of the European Security Conference indicated a new willingness to discuss mutual balanced force reductions in Europe with the West.

In June 1973 Mr. Brezhnev and other Soviet ministers visited the US. Co-operation agreements were signed and principles for further arms limitation and measures for the prevention of nuclear war were discussed. In the latter, they undertook to enter into urgent consultations if relations between them or between either and another country appeared to involve the risk of nuclear conflict.

The general policy of détente continued during 1974–5 with the visits of President Nixon in the summer of 1974 and of President Ford in November and trade agreements with Western European countries. Dr. Kissinger attempted to continue negotiations on the limitation of strategic weapons during the early months of 1976, but little progress was made due partly to the Presidential election campaign, but also to the development by both countries of weapons which had not been included in previous negotiations. Since the election of President Carter in November 1976, Mr. Brezhnev has met Mr. Vance, US Secretary of State, and although the American proposals for limiting strategic nuclear arms were turned down, further steps were to be taken to reach agreement before the current SALT agreement expires in October 1977.

Apart from relations with the United States, the Russians have tried to consolidate their position elsewhere by tying formerly non-aligned powers to themselves *e.g.*, Egypt and India. However, in March 1976 the Treaty of Friendship and Co-operation with Egypt was abrogated following the Russians' refusal to supply arms and their demand for repayment of Egypt's debts. Later in the year relations were improved with the signing of a bilateral trade agreement.

Despite trade agreements with W. European countries, the new line taken by communist parties in those countries in support of democratic socialism and party pluralism, has been a blow to the Soviet claim to ideological leadership: renunciation of the principle of "proletarian internationalism" was severely condemned at the Party Congress in February. Efforts were made to strengthen relations with E. European countries. Mr. Brezhnev visited President Tito in Yugoslavia and the Warsaw Pact summit was held in Bucharest, Rumania.

Support for national liberation movements was reiterated at the Party Congress and President Neto of Angola visited the Soviet Union to express his thanks for Russian support of the MPLA during the civil war.

Dissidents.

Despite the agreement of the Soviet Union to the statement of the Conference on Security and Co-operation in Europe, concerning "respect for human rights and fundamental freedoms", there have been persistent complaints about the treatment of the so-called "dissidents" and the restrictions on the right to emigrate. Prior to the Helsinki agreement, the famous writer and dissident Alexander Solzhenitsyn was expelled from the Soviet Union.

During 1976 several appeals were made by groups of dissidents for amnesty for those imprisoned for their political, religious or ideological views. In December 1976 Vladimir Bukovsky was released from prison in central Russia and was allowed to go to the West in return for the release of a Chilean, Luis Corvalán. Shortly afterwards the dissidents were blamed for a bomb explosion in the Moscow underground which killed several people. The most prominent of the remaining dissidents is Andrei Sakharov, a nuclear physicist who suffers continuous harassment and has recently been warned of possible prosecution for his activities.

EASTERN EUROPE

(For East Germany see The Two Germanys)

Background.

During the Second World War Czechoslovakia, Poland, Yugoslavia and Albania were occupied by Axis forces. Hungary, Romania and Bulgaria fought initially with the Axis powers. When they attempted to withdraw from the war they too underwent German occupation. Resistance movements of varying degrees of effectiveness developed in all the East European countries: the Yugoslav and Albanian movements succeeded in liberating their countries substantially by their own efforts. Elsewhere liberation was achieved by the Soviet army, as a result of which Communist regimes were established. The diplomatic prehistory of this takeover took place at the Moscow meeting of Stalin and Churchill in October 1944, which resulted in the "percentages" agreement on postwar spheres of interest, and the Yalta Conference of February 1945. Stalin's motives in extending Soviet power into East Europe were to create a buffer zone between the USSR and the West and to establish a system of economic exploitation under which allies fared little better than former enemies. However, the exercise was presented by the Communists as the consequence of genuine popular uprisings, and the constitutional label of "People's Democracies" was attached to the new regimes. Czechoslovakia, Romania and Yugoslavia have since taken the title of "Socialist Republics".

The monolithic unity which Stalin imposed upon Eastern Europe was breached in July 1948 by the expulsion of Yugoslavia from the Communist camp, a manoeuvre to unseat Tito which developed into a permanent rupture. Since then the Soviet Union has been unable to stem a movement towards "polycentrism", the desire of each Communist government to follow its "own road to socialism". This was demonstrated yet again at the Conference of European Communist Parties in July 1976. The USSR, however, has always been ready to resort to force to repress fellow Communist regimes if it fears they might move out of the Communist orbit altogether, as in Hungary in 1956 and Czechoslovakia in 1968.

With the exception of Czechoslovakia, which inherited an industrial base from the Austro-Hungarian Empire, these countries had underdeveloped agrarian economies before the Second World War and as suppliers of raw materials were dangerously susceptible to fluctuations in world trade and pressure from powerful neighbours. After the war, therefore, each country hastened to embark on a Stalinist course of collectivising agriculture and creating a heavy industry. Soviet aid facilitated this development, but also increased these countries' dependence on the USSR. Although a Communist international economic organisation (the Council for Mutual Economic Assistance, or "Comecon") was created as early as 1949, Stalin preferred to see each satellite economically autarkic and linked to the USSR by bilateral agreements, and only since the sixties have genuinely integrative economic policies been implemented. These have met with some resistance, notably from Romania.

The East European Communist countries (except Albania and Yugoslavia) have been linked to the USSR in the Warsaw Pact military alliance since 1955.

Poland.

During the Second World War two rival claimants to postwar government existed: the prewar government was in exile in London, while in Moscow the National Home Council headed by Bolestaw Bierut was formed in December 1943. An important section of the Polish resistance was wiped out in the abortive Warsaw rising of 1944 while the Soviet army was halted in the suburbs. It remains a matter of dispute whether this was a deliberate move by Stalin to ensure the preponderance of "Moscow Poles" after the war. The National Home Council established the Polish Committee of National Liberation in Lublin in July 1944, and this claimed the status of provisional government in January 1945. In June 1945 a Provisional Government of National Unity was set up in Warsaw which the Western Allies recognised instead of the "London" government. It was during this period that the foundations were laid for Poland's transformation into a People's Democracy, although there was vigorous armed resistance lasting into 1947. Poland's frontiers were redrawn by the Potsdam Agreement along the Curzon Line (thus losing territory to the USSR) and the Oder–Neisse Line (thus gaining territory from Germany). At the elections of January 1947 9 million votes out of 12·7 million were cast for the Communist-dominated "Democratic Bloc". Opposition came only from the Polish Peasant Party, whose leader was subsequently forced into exile. In 1948 the Socialist Party was merged into the Communist Party.

With Bierut as President and Party Secretary the way was clear for full Communisation. The constitution of 22 July 1952 set the seal on this. During the wave of purges at the end of the forties of "rightests, nationalists and Titoists" Wladyslaw Gomulka (then deputy premier) and other high-ranking leaders received prison sentences. But after Khrushchev's revelations to the Soviet Communist Party's 20th Congress in February 1956 and the death of Bierut in March a process of de-Stalinisation set in hastened by workers' riots in Poznań in June. In October Gomulka became Party leader and inaugurated a regime which granted considerable concessions. Collectivisation of agriculture was abandoned and more tolerance shown towards the Catholic Church, which commands a very wide adherence in Poland. In foreign affairs Poland in 1957 advanced the Rapacki Plan for an armaments-free zone in Central Europe which after the 1968 Nuclear Test Ban Treaty and the SALT talks remained a basis for negotiation of a European security system. Poland's efforts to obtain recognition for her Western border culminated in success in December 1970 when the West German Chancellor Willy Brandt signed a treaty affirming its inviolability.

At home the early promise of Gomulka's regime was not maintained into the sixties. There were attacks on the government from the right and the Moczar led his "Partisans" faction in a bid for power in the Communist Party. This faction was not definitively dislodged until 1971. In 1968 a wave of student unrest was followed by an official campaign of anti-Zionism with strong undertones of anti-Semitism, and this led to the exodus of a number of intellectuals. Both attacks were repressed by Gomulka with an increasing insensitivity to the mood of the country. His government was finally toppled by the direct action of workers striking and rioting in the Baltic ports in December 1970, the immediate cause of which had been an increase in consumer prices. Gomulka was succeeded as Party leader by Edward Gierek, a popular trade unionist from the coal mining district of Silesia. Prices were frozen with the aid of Soviet subventions, but a second attempt to increase them in June 1976 led to more strikes and sabotage. Several workers received heavy prison sentences, some intellectuals formed a committee of protest and most price rises were temporarily withdrawn.

Czechoslovakia.

Czechoslovakia functioned as a constitutional democracy between the wars, but her path to Communism was facilitated by the large number of Communist supporters (at the 1935 elections Communists had polled 10% of the vote), traditional pro-Russian sentiment dating from the Pan-Slavist movement, Beneš's inclination to rely on Soviet support in the bitterness following the 1938 Munich Agreement and the *fait accompli* of the Soviet prior presence as a liberation army. In July 1941 Beneš secured British and Soviet recognition for his government in exile in London, and in December 1943 he signed a 20-year treaty of friendship with the USSR. In October 1945 a provisional National Assembly was set up. The multiplicity of prewar parties was reduced by the expulsion of the Sudeten Germans under the Potsdam Agreement and the banning of collaborationist parties. In May 1946 the Communists gained 38% of the electoral vote, more than twice as many as any other party, and their leader, Klement Gottwald, became prime minister of a coalition government. In February 1948 12 non-Communist ministers resigned in protest at the replacement of non-Communist members of the security forces. In an atmosphere of Communist-inspired workers' militancy Beneš was pressured into dropping the resigning ministers and approving a new cabinet of Communists and fellow-travellers. Jan Masaryk, veteran foreign minister since the government in exile, died in a fall from his window a few days later in suspicious circumstances. Communist-style elections were held in May 1948 resulting in an 89% majority for the government. Beneš resigned as president and was replaced by Gottwald. Antonín Zapotocký became prime minister. Under a new constitution of June 1948 Czechoslovakia became a People's Republic. The Gottwald government pursued a policy of ruthless repression. Party purges which began in 1950 resulted in the execution of Clementis and Slánský and the imprisonment of the Slovak Gustáv Husák among others, and paved the way for the emergence of Antonín Novotný as Party Secretary (1954) and President (1957). Even after the Khrushchev revelations the Party persisted in a hard Stalinist line, but by the sixties opposition was appearing in its own ranks, triggered by a serious deterioration in the economy. The 1961–5 Plan was abandoned and a more flexible system of planning and management was introduced in January 1967. Economic liberalisation led to an increasing pressure generally for political liberalisation and from Slovakia for more autonomy. In January 1968 a Slovak, Alexander Dubček, was elected to replace Novotný as Party Secretary (Novotný was later replaced as President by General Svoboda), and the era opened which has since been dubbed "the Prague Spring", when an attempt was made to give Socialism "a human face". Wide-ranging reforms were mooted in the Action Programme issued in April, but the Communist Party did not envisage relinquishing its commanding position in society. Fears that this was happening, however, led the USSR first to press for the abandonment of the Programme in a number of talks with the Czechoslovak leadership between May and August, and ultimately, in concert with the other Warsaw Pact powers except Romania, to occupy Czechoslovakia on 21 August in accordance with the "Brezhnev Doctrine" of "limited sovereignty". Soviet efforts to set up a puppet government at first met without success. The projected federalisation of the country into the twin republics of the Czech Lands and Slovakia went ahead in October, although plans for a similar federalisation of the Party were vetoed. Gradually, however, Dubček and his team were ousted from positions of influence, and Gustáv Husák, a partisan of "normalisation", took over as Party Secretary in April 1969. Czechoslovakia repudiated its condemnation of the Warsaw Pact invasion in October 1969 and consented to the stationing of Soviet troops. Pro-Dubček personnel were hounded from the Party and their jobs (Dubček himself becoming a forestry official) and most of the reforms were abandoned. In May 1970 Czechoslovakia signed a 20-year treaty of friendship with the USSR. In December 1973 West Germany and Czechoslovakia signed a treaty annulling the Munich Agreement, thus normalising their relations.

Hungary.

When in October 1944 the Regent Horthy attempted to conclude an armistice with the Soviet Union Hitler replaced him with a fanatical pro-Nazi. By April 1945 German forces had been driven out of the country by the Red Army. The peace treaty of February 1947 restored the frontiers established by the Treaty of Trianon (1920). At the elections of November 1945 the Smallholder Party won an absolute majority, but at Soviet insistence a Communist was appointed to the key post of Minister of the Interior. As a result of a purge of allegedly fascist Smallholders and the enforced unification of the Social Democrats with the Communist Party the Communists increased their membership in the government at the 1947 and 1949 elections. The constitution of August 1949 made Hungary a People's Republic, and all power passed to the Communists under Mátyás Rákosi. Executions of "Titoist" Communists, notably Lászlo Rajk, took place in 1949. Cardinal Mindszenty, who refused to collaborate with the Communist authorities in their anti-church measures, was imprisoned (in 1956 he took refuge in the US legation, where he stayed until 1971). In July 1953 Rákosi was replaced by Imre Nagy as prime minister. The latter attempted to follow a "new course" but aroused the misgivings of Moscow and was expelled from office in April 1955. Rákosi took over again but was himself dismissed in July 1956, this time as a move in Khrushchev's game of wooing Tito. It was under his successor Gerö that the 1956 uprising flared up. On 23 October a vast procession of protest, initiated by students and originally peaceful, was roughly handled by Gerö and the police, and met force with force. The army joined the revolutionaries and Soviet forces were expelled from Budapest. A coalition government was formed under Nagy, and Soviet forces withdrew to the borders. However, on 1 November, after Nagy had proclaimed Hungary's withdrawal from the Warsaw Pact and asked for UN protection, Soviet forces re-entered the country. János Kádár, who had been imprisoned under Rákosi, formed a pro-Soviet alternative government on 3 November. On 4 November Soviet forces reached Budapest and Nagy took refuge in the Yugoslav embassy, whence he was subsequently abducted and murdered. Fighting continued for a fortnight before the uprising was suppressed, and there was a substantial exodus of refugees. The inaction of the Western powers, who were simultaneously preoccupied with the Suez crisis, definitively dispelled East European notions that the West might intervene in situations of this sort.

In its early days the Kádár regime promised many concessions, few of which were carried out. Kádár's achievement, however, has been in striking the right balance between reforming enough to satisfy the people without going far enough to arouse the anxieties of Moscow. In 1968 a "New Economic Mechanism" was introduced, and Kádár has eased political repression by reversing the militant Marxist maxim to form the less discriminatory "He who is not against us is for us".

Romania.

Support for Romania's participation in the war on Hitler's side (except for the recovery of Bessarabia) was never wholehearted, and opposition to it was by no means confined to the left. In June 1944 the National Liberal Party and the National Peasant Party joined with the Social Democrats and Communists in a National Democratic Front which toppled Antonescu's government on 23 August 1944 and brought Romania into the war against Germany. An armistice with the USSR was signed on 12 September 1944. Although the Communist Party had only a little over 1,000 members at this time, the presence of Soviet occupation troops ensured that it and the Social Democrats received representation out of proportion to their numbers in the first postwar administration. In March 1945 a government was set up (excluding the National Liberals and National Peasants) headed by the Soviet fellow-traveller Petru Groza. The National Democratic Front claimed 79% of the votes cast at the November 1946 election, but its validity has been disputed. There followed the arrest of non-Communist politicians, the banning of the National Peasant Party and in December 1947 the abdication of King Michael and the proclamation of a People's Republic. Elections were held in March 1948 from a single list of candidates. A Soviet-type constitution was introduced in April. At the close of the forties a purge of Communists accused of "Titoism" opened. In 1952 Gheorghe Gheorghiu-Dej, Party leader since 1944, achieved supreme power in the government as well by engineering the removal of three ministers closely identified with Soviet interests. On his death in 1965 he was succeeded by Nicolae Ceausescu, who has pursued a steady path of self-aggrandisement, becoming in 1974 President of the State Council and the first holder of the newly created Presidency of the Republic.

In internal affairs rigid and orthodox, Romania began to develop an independent foreign policy in Gheorghiu-Dej's last years, and Ceausescu has continued this trend, maintaining friendly relations with China and Israel, becoming the first Soviet bloc country to recognise West Germany, and objecting to the Soviet invasion of Czechoslovakia. There are no Soviet troops in Romania. Although a full member of Comecon, Romania has blocked plans to integrate the Communist countries' economies for fear of becoming a second-class supplier of raw materials to the more industrialised members. Instead the Romanians are aiming for economic independence by pushing ahead with a massive industrialisation programme of their own. Another point at issue with the USSR is the latter's incorporation of Bessarabia, with its two-thirds Romanian population, as the Moldavian SSR. A high-point in this dispute was reached in May 1976: senior Soviet officials visited Romania and the Romanian army was "mobilised for manoeuvres". Shortly after, Ceausescu stated that Romania had no territorial or other problems with the Soviet Union, and after a meeting with Brezhnev in August it was announced that there was a "growing identity of views" between the two leaders. This rapprochement is probably attributable to Romania's need for closer economic cooperation with the USSR as a result of economic difficulties at home and increasing indebtedness to the West.

Yugoslavia.

In their political and economic development' religion and culture the South Slav peoples (Slovenes, Croats, Serbs and Macedonians) have had separate and differing histories, and their unification since 1918 in one state has always been at risk. Prewar politics were dominated by the efforts of the centralising monarchy to Serbianise the whole country. Croat resistance to this reached its apogee in the establishment of a quasi-independent fascist state in 1941 under Ante Pavelic. Internecine atrocities rivalled the excesses of the Axis occupiers. Two resistance movements developed: the predominantly Serbian Chetniks under Draža Mihailovič, who supported King Peter's government in exile, and the Partisans, under the Moscow-trained Communist Josip Broz (Tito). The two movements frequently fought each other, and Mihailovič at times collaborated with the Nazis. His wait-and-see methods also made him militarily less effective than Tito, which caused the Allies, following a British initiative of mid-1943, to shift their support from him to Tito. By the middle of 1944 Tito had succeeded in liberating a large part of the country by his own efforts, and in October he assisted the advancing Soviet troops in the capture of Belgrade. In November 1942 the Partisans had formed a soi-disant legislative body called the Antifascist Council of National Liberation. This formed the nucleus for a postwar provisional government under Tito. At the elections of November 1945 the Communist-dominated People's Front gained 90% of the vote. Although opposition parties were handicapped in the election campaign, foreign observers declared these elections to be fair, and Tito commanded a lot of support from non-Communists as a Croat who would not embark on another round of Serbianisation, and as a successful and popular wartime leader. The new government proclaimed a federal People's Republic, adopted an intransigent attitude to the West and embarked upon a programme of Communisation which soon made Yugoslavia to all appearances the most Soviet-like of the satellites. Stalin, however, found Tito not subservient enough, and attempted to get him replaced as Party leader by expelling the Yugoslav Party from the Communist Information Bureau (Cominform), successor in all but name to the Communist International. This shocked the Yugoslav Communists as much as it surprised the West: Yugoslavia continued to protest its loyalty to Stalin and support the Soviet line in foreign affairs. Few Yugoslavs took a pro-Soviet position, however, in fact the unparalleled advantage of being able to identify the Communist Party with anti-Russian sentiment rallied people closer round Tito. In August 1949 the USSR broke off state relations with Yugoslavia, and Yugoslavia launched out on a course of independent Communism, surviving by securing economic aid from the West and abolishing the command economy at home. The institution of "workers' self-management" has transformed Yugoslavia's economy into a unique "market socialism" and has led to changes in the political structure embodied in the constitutions of 1963 and 1974.

In May 1955 Khrushchev made a visit to Belgrade in an attempt to win Yugoslavia back into the Soviet camp. Inter-government relations were re-established, but very much on Tito's terms: the joint "Belgrade Declaration" promised "non-interference in other countries' affairs for any reason whatever". Tito's return visit the following June re-established Party relations, and the "Moscow Declaration" issued then conceded that countries should be allowed to follow "their own roads to Socialism". Khrushchev and Tito, however, failed to reach agreement on Yugoslavia's place in the Communist community, and a growing division between them began to emerge against a background of "Titoist" nationalist disturbances in Poland and Hungary, hardening with the publication of a new Yugoslav Party Programme in April 1958, which the Soviets considered "revisionist". This hostile episode was terminated when the Soviet Union was looking around for allies at the outbreak of its dispute with China. A further inducement to the Soviet Union to mend its fences with Yugoslavia was the latter's influence among Third World countries as one of the founders of the non-alignment movement at the Belgrade Conference in September 1961. In 1965 Yugoslavia gained observer status in Comecon, and in 1967 Tito joined other Communist leaders in condemning Israel's alleged aggression against the Arabs. The drift towards closer relations with the USSR was temporarily halted by the Soviet invasion of Czechoslovakia in 1968. In the period of tension which followed there were some fears that Yugoslavia might be the next to be invaded. A territorial defence law was hurried through, and on 15 October 1968 US Secretary of State Dean Rusk reminded the USSR that the US considered Yugoslavia to be in a "grey zone" under NATO protection. These fears were shortlived: Brezhnev and Tito exchanged visits in 1971 and 1972, and in June 1976 Yugoslavia broke a long tradition by taking part in the Conference of European Communist Parties, albeit reiterating her independent stance. Soviet toleration of Yugoslavia has been made easier by the latter's recent adoption of a harder line at home. For all its democratisation of the state structure, the League of Communists retains a monopolistic grip on the levers of power. Challenging that has led to the persecution of intellectuals like Djilas, Mihajlov and the "Praxis" group of philosophers. An upsurge of Croat nationalism in the early seventies led to a widespread purge of Party and government officials. In a Yugoslavia split by ethnic dissensions after Tito's death it would be easy for the Soviet Union to re-establish its control over the area and gain access to the Adriatic, and there are some grounds for believing that discreet Soviet support has been offered to émigré Croat terrorist organisations. In 1974 and 1975 a number of groups of "Cominformists" (Yugoslav pro-Soviet Communists) were arrested, and in September 1974 a Soviet official was asked to leave. In November 1975 Yugoslav Party Secretary Dolanc complained to the Soviets about their interference, since when the anti-Cominformist campaign has been muted.

Albania.

Communism was imposed on feudal Albania by a handful of intellectuals acting in a long tradition of élitist rule. King Zog was deposed in absentia in January 1945. The wartime resistance movement had been captured by the Communists because of the support of Yugoslavia's Partisans, and Albania became a satellite of Yugoslavia until the latter's rupture with Stalin in 1948. Albania's security and economic development depend on having the favour of a more powerful ally, and in 1948 the Albanian leadership split into a pro-Yugoslav faction led by Koci Xoxe and a Stalinist faction under Party Secretary Enver Hoxha. The latter triumphed, Xoxe was executed and relations with Yugoslavia broken off. Privately the Albanian leaders considered Khrushchev's debunking of Stalin and particularly his wooing of Tito as a danger to their security, and when the Soviet–Chinese quarrel broke out in 1960 they made this view public and supported the Chinese position. Relations with the Soviet Union were broken off in 1961 and Albania became a client of China. Since 1971 there have seen some signs of dissension with China and of pro-Soviet activity at home. The remarkable stability of the leadership came to an end in 1974 with the sacking of the Minister of Defence Balluku, and in April 1976 two more ministers were sacked and Hoxha announced that an "anti-China group" had been smashed.

THE MIDDLE EAST

The Middle East War of 1967.

The third Arab–Israeli war began on 5 June 1967. In a pre-emptive strike Israel destroyed the air forces of Egypt, Jordan, and Syria in a few hours. She then destroyed their three armies in six days, occupying all Sinai to the banks of the Suez Canal (which was therefore closed, and remained so for 8 years), the west bank of the Jordan, and the Syrian hills above Galilee. The toll of human misery was immense: at least 300,000 refugees fled the occupied territories. As a consequence of the war, the Russians moved permanently into the Middle East, backing the Arabs.

The members of the Security Council in November 1967 reached unanimous agreement to send a special emissary to the Middle East, Mr. Gunnar Jarring, a Swedish diplomat. But he could achieve little.

The Israeli case remained that peace could only be achieved through a negotiated settlement between the parties directly affected, which involves recognition of Israel as a nation-state. Furthermore, since neither the UN nor the four Powers could of themselves guarantee a settlement, Israel, in the interim period, must rely on her own resources to maintain her existence. The Arab governments continued to insist that Israel must first withdraw from the occupied areas before a settlement, or even recognition, could be considered. The Palestinian fedayeen organisation went further and refused to accept the state of Israel under any circumstances.

Obstacles to Peace.

The fighting continued in 1970, until the United States produced a peace initiative which led to a cease-fire between Egypt, Jordan and Israel. On 28 September the Arabs and Egypt lost their leader, President Nasser, who died of a heart attack. His successor, President Sadat, issued a warning that Israel must produce a timetable for withdrawal from the occupied territories.

Palestinian guerrillas were predictably hostile to peace initiatives, which they feared would frustrate their plan to establish a democratic state of Palestine in place of Israel. Their extreme line led to conflict with King Hussein's army, the guerrillas having used Jordan as their base for attacks on Israel. During 1970 King Hussein's position appeared to be very precarious, but after a major offensive Jordan was able to announce the total defeat of the guerrillas by July 1971.

Early in 1971 President Sadat indicated for the first time that Egypt would be prepared to sign a contractual peace treaty with Israel guaranteeing her inviolability and independence within secure and recognised boundaries. Israel in turn accepted the principle of withdrawal to "secure, recognised and agreed boundaries" to be established by a peace agreement, but rejected a retreat to the borders before the Six-day War. Mrs. Meir insisted on the retention of the Gaza strip, a united Jerusalem and the Golan Heights overlooking Syria. But 1971 also reaffirmed the willingness of the Great Powers to stand by their respective protégés. In May at the end of the visit of President Podgorny of the Soviet Union to Cairo, a 15-year treaty of friendship was signed in which the USSR undertook to continue to supply arms and training to the Egyptians. Later the United States agreed to resume deliveries of Phantom bombers to Israel, without the latter making far-reaching concessions to the Egyptians.

In June 1972 in a show of strength President Sadat announced the expulsion of all Soviet military experts from Egypt. The reasons he gave were disagreements about the type of Soviet armaments supplied to Egypt and delays in their delivery. The removal of the Russians should have made it easier for Israel to make concessions.

The Fourth Arab–Israeli War.

War suddenly broke out again on 6 October 1973 with simultaneous powerful Egyptian and Syrian offensives across the Suez Canal and on the Golan Heights. The Israelis were taken by surprise by the attack which came on the Day of Atonement, the holiest day of the Jewish year. The fighting was fierce and featured in Sinai one of the biggest tank battles in history. The Egyptians consolidated their position along much of the east bank of the Suez Canal and advanced some miles into Sinai. But a dramatic Israeli counter-attack established a major bridge-head on the west bank of the Canal, pushing well inland, destroying or capturing most of the Soviet

SAM missile sites and re-establishing total air superiority. As the tide was turning in Israel's favour and the Egyptian Third Army of some 20,000 had been virtually caught in a pincer movement at the southern end of the front, a cease-fire was agreed in response to UN Security Council resolutions. On the northern front the Syrians also had considerable initial success, regaining most of the Golan Heights. But having contained the Egyptian assault the Israelis threw their weight against the Syrians and advanced to within 20 miles of Damascus before a cease-fire was agreed.

The Israelis thus more than overcame the paper situation by which their forces were vastly outnumbered and outgunned by the Egyptians and Syrians alone. During the war the USA began an "appreciable" airlift of military supplies to Israel to offset what was claimed had become a "massive" Soviet airlift to Egypt and Syria.

A third UN Security Council resolution approved the despatch of a UN peace-keeping force which would exclude military contingents from any of the permanent members. This defused the critical situation caused by American information that large Soviet forces might be sent to the Middle East, which had led to a world-wide alert of US forces. In November the mission of Dr. Kissinger to the Middle East worked out a cease-fire agreement—the first major agreement between Israel and an Arab country since 1949.

The Search for a Settlement.

This time the consequence of war was not new hostilities but on Kissinger's insistence and with Moscow's consent a peace conference, which was opened in Geneva by UN General Secretary Dr. Waldheim in December 1973, though the Syrians refused to take part. Both sides still have the means to attack again. But the war showed Israel that borders pushed forward by force give no absolute security and the Arabs that even a surprise attack with advanced Soviet weapons cannot wipe Israel off the map.

Despite advances for the right-wing Likud opposition in the elections at the beginning of 1974, making Mrs. Meir's Labour Alignment more dependent on the religious groups, Israel did make major concessions when on 18 January it signed with Egypt an agreement for the disengagement of their forces (negotiated by Dr. Kissinger commuting between the two countries). In return for the withdrawal of most of the Egyptian forces from the east bank of the Suez Canal, Israel undertook to evacuate the west bank (thus releasing the Egyptian Third Army) and withdraw from the east bank. Israel appeared to have departed from her insistence that there would be no withdrawal unless Egyptians undertook publicly to end the state of belligerency; Egypt from her insistence that there could be no partial agreement with Israel without a prior Israeli undertaking to evacuate all territory captured in the Six-Day War. Prisoners of war were exchanged between Egypt and Israel and the process of disengagement was completed by 4 March. A similar agreement between Syria and Israel was not achieved until 31 May after renewed heavy fighting. A UN Disengagement Observation Force was established and prisoners were repatriated.

Meanwhile full diplomatic relations had been restored between the United States and Egypt, and in June 1974 during President Nixon's visit to five Middle-East countries he was given a very enthusiastic reception in Cairo and agreements were signed for substantial economic aid to Egypt including the area of nuclear energy.

A summit meeting of Arab Heads of State and representatives of the Palestine Liberation Organisation (PLO) in October 1974 was dominated by the dispute between Jordan and the PLO over which should be the legitimate representative of the Palestinian people of the Israeli-occupied West Bank of the Jordan. It resulted in a political victory for the PLO and in effect a commitment to the establishment of a separate Palestinian state after Israel withdrew. This inevitably complicated the search for a settlement. The following month the UN General Assembly, which had invited Yassir Arafat, leader of the PLO, to take part in its Middle East debate, gave him a hero's welcome and recognised the PLO as representing the Palestinians. This was accompanied by unrest among the Arab population of Israeli-occupied territory.

Meanwhile an escalation of tension in late 1974 brought Israel and Syria to the verge of active hostilities again and there was an intensification of the arms race with both sides seeking to replace losses in the 1973 war from traditional suppliers (which led to some improvement in Soviet–Egyptian relations). The breakdown of a further peace mission by Dr. Kissinger in March followed by the assassination of King Faisal of Saudi Arabia once again threw the long-term prospects for peace in the Middle East into serious doubt. Nevertheless June 1975 saw the reopening of the Suez Canal and in September a further limited agreement was signed by Israel and Egypt on military disengagement in the Sinai Peninsula, providing for Israeli withdrawal from some occupied territory in return for American commitment to Israel. The implementation of this agreement was completed in February 1976, and meanwhile Israeli ships were also allowed through the Suez Canal.

Terrorist Activities.

Since 1972 the Palestinian terrorists had resorted to desperate methods against Israelis including the attack on the Israeli Olympic team in Munich. During 1974 attacks within Israel intensified with the massacre of 20 Israeli children in a school at Ma'alot. Israeli reprisals included raids on Palestinian guerrilla bases in Lebanon. Some of the more extreme terrorists began to turn their anger on other Arabs. In December 1975 members of a group known as the Arm of the Arab Revolution seized 11 leading representatives in an attack on OPEC headquarters in Vienna. A statement was broadcast condemning Egypt and Iran and demanding sovereignty over oil resources for the benefit of the Arab people and the Third World. The hostages were eventually released, but the action was condemned by other Palestinian organisations. Among the terrorists involved was Carlos Martinez, one of the most sought after activists.

In 1976 an Air France airbus was hijacked by members of the Haifa section of the Popular Front for the Liberation of Palestine, and made to fly to Entebbe, Uganda. The drama ended with an Israeli rescue raid to free the Israeli hostages after demands had been made for the release of "freedom fighters" imprisoned in Europe and Israel.

In January 1977 France suffered international criticism after detaining and then releasing the terrorist Abu Daoud alleged to have been one of the organisers of the massacre of Israeli athletes at the Munich Olympics.

The Oil Crisis 1973–4.

During and after the war the Arabs began to make serious use of the dependence of much of the Western world on oil from the Middle East as a weapon to weaken support for Israel. The Organisation of Arab Petroleum Exporting Countries (OAPEC) decided to reduce production progressively until Israeli forces had withdrawn completely from territories occupied in June 1967 and the legal rights of the Palestinians had been restored. Several Arab countries also imposed a total ban on shipments to the USA and the Netherlands because of their support for Israel. The former ban affected some 6 per cent of American consumption: the latter also seriously affected other Western European countries whose oil normally came through Rotterdam.

In November the OAPEC countries decided to exempt EEC members except the Netherlands from the December cuts in appreciation of their communiqué of 6 November calling on Israel to end the territorial occupation which it had maintained since 1967, and recognising that any settlement must take account of the "legitimate rights of the Palestinians". This resolution aroused strong criticism in Israel. But Holland's subscription to it did not alter her position in Arab eyes. The Dutch Government expressed resentment at the lack of support from other Community countries, which because of their own shortages and fears of Arab reprisals had withheld their oil reserves from a European "pool".

Following a 70% price increase in October, the petroleum exporting countries (OPEC) in conference at Teheran in December decided to double the crude oil price. However on 25 December OAPEC agreed on a 10 per cent raising of production, leaving them 15 per cent under their October production level. Meanwhile in most oil-importing countries measures were introduced to restrict oil consumption, including reductions in heating levels, lower speed limits and bans on Sunday driving.

Confronted by this challenge, a conference of 13 major oil-consuming countries in Washington in February agreed (with France dissenting) on provisions for co-operation on energy policy. After the disengagement agreement between Israel and Egypt supplies to the USA and the Netherlands were resumed during 1974. The easing of supplies generally, though not of price, caused many of the restrictions on the use of oil to be lifted. But the non-oil-producing developing countries were far more vulnerable, and both the International Monetary Fund and the World Bank organised funds to aid them. In November, on the initiative of Dr. Kissinger, a working-party was set up to examine the question of recycling the massive surplus revenues of the OPEC countries, which had given them crucial economic power. An International Energy Agency was established in Paris under the auspices of the OECD by 16 oil-consuming countries to co-ordinate policy, especially by an oil-sharing scheme in times of supply difficulties. A meeting of the American and French Presidents on Martinique in December 1974 ironed out disagreements on a French initiative for a conference of oil exporting and importing countries as soon as possible. Although there is no shortage of oil, its vastly inflated price has seriously distorted the Western economies.

The conference was eventually held in Paris in December 1975, its agenda having been extended, despite American reluctance, to cover not only energy but other raw materials, development and financial questions. There were 27 participants—8 from developed industrial nations, including the EEC acting as a single unit (Britain having eventually given up her claim to a separate seat on the basis of her special oil interests), 4 oil-exporting countries and 15 other developing countries. It was decided to establish four commissions which would report in a year's time.

In December 1976 at the OPEC meeting in Qatar, the first split appeared in OPEC ranks led by Saudi Arabia. 11 members voted to raise prices by 10·4% on 1 January and by a further 5% on 1 July 1977. Saudi Arabia and the United Arab Emirates announced that they would raise their prices only 5% for the whole year. Whether this position will be maintained by the Saudis will depend on progress at the North-South dialogue to be continued in Paris in the spring.

Civil War in Lebanon.

From April 1975 internal conflict between left-wing Moslems (including Lebanon-based Palestinian groups) and the Christian Phalangist Party escalated to full-scale civil war. The basic cause of the conflict appeared to be the inadequate representation of the Moslem community in government and resentment of the political and economic ascendancy of the Christians. As the fighting intensified, the Lebanese army was involved for the first time in September 1975. President Frangie's calls for a cessation of hostilities resulted in a series of abortive cease-fires. His failure to secure the agreement of Moslem leaders to his proposals for their involvement in government increased demands for his resignation which eventually took place in April 1976. In May, the Syrian-backed Mr. Elias Sarkis was elected in his place.

Throughout the war Syria backed the moderate groups and attempted in 1976 to involve other Arab States in a peace-keeping force. In July the "Damascus agreement" proposed Arab involvement through the calling and policing of a cease-fire and the regulation of Palestinian activities in Lebanon. After an initial set-back, the Arabs deterrent force increased and an effective cease-fire continues. Meanwhile President Sarkis has taken steps to reform the existing system of government and also to restore economic order. Further unrest was caused when Kamal Jumblatt, leader of the Muslim left was assassinated in March 1977.

Prospects for Peace

By the end of 1976 prospects for an overall Middle East settlement had improved. With the Lebanese civil war tenuously settled, and the US elections over, President Sadat and other Arab leaders began to talk of peace initiatives. President Carter announced that Secretary Vance would visit the area and the UN Secretary-General Kurt Waldheim planned steps to re-convene the Geneva conference.

However, in January 1977 following the announcement of price rises, food riots occurred in Cairo and the Government's ability to deal decisively with foreign affairs was curbed. This, together with forthcoming elections in Israel which will provide a period of uncertainty there, cast doubt upon the prospects for progress in 1977.

SOUTH ASIA

Background.

In 1947 the British Empire in India was divided into 2 new states, broadly along communal lines—India and Pakistan. India is predominantly Hindu in religion, but the constitution of 1950 asserted its secularist, democratic republican nature. Pakistan resulted from the demand of the Muslim minority for its own separate state. The establishments of the two new states was marred by the slaughter of over 250,000 people as Hindus and Moslems struggled to transfer their homes. Disputes arose over the resources of the Raj and also as a result of the failure of some of the Princely states to accede to either of the new states. The strategically important state of Kashmir has remained a source of dissension.

India.

In January 1948 India's spiritual leader Mahatma Gandhi was assassinated. Jawaharlal Nehru, India's first prime minister, shared many of Gandhi's ideals. Unlike Gandhi, Nehru believed that economic progress would be achieved through western-style industrialisation and introduced five-year economic plans. India's economic problems also dictated a foreign policy of neutrality and nonalignment with the major powers.

In 1965 Mrs. Indira Gandhi (daughter of Jawaharlal Nehru) became Prime Minister. After a close election victory for the ruling Congress Party in 1967, Mrs. Gandhi faced the problems of opposition from the old guard of the Party in 1969 and terrorist activities in 1970. However, in 1971, the Party won a landslide election victory and plans for Socialist reforms were launched. Since the monsoon failure of 1972 and governmental attempts to remedy the severe food crisis, opposition to the Government increased. An anti-corruption campaign led by Jayaprakash Narayan was in part to blame for election losses in 1974–5 and a further setback was experienced when in June 1975, the Allahabad High Court declared Mrs. Gandhi's election null and void on the grounds that government officials had been involved in electioneering; she was debarred from office for six years. Mrs. Gandhi's appeal against the decision was subsequently upheld by the Supreme Court, but meanwhile a state of emergency was declared in June 1975. Opposition both inside and outside the government increased. Fundamental rights were suspended during the early months of 1976. In November wide powers were given to the Prime Minister. Mrs. Gandhi called elections for March 1977. She and her Congress party suffered a resounding defeat at the hands of the opposition Janata coalition led by Mr. Morarji Desai who subsequently became Prime Minister. Mr. Desai faced problems in forming a government as the Janata coalition appeared to be united only by their opposition to Mrs. Gandhi.

Pakistan and Bangladesh.

After independence, Pakistan was beset by internal and external problems. India provided a constant external threat and there was resentment by East Pakistan of the political and economic domination by the western wing. Violent struggles resulted from the attempt to impose Urdu as the national language. Moreover, disunity among the western provinces provided continuing problems for the Government. Thirteen months after independence, Mohammed Ali Jinnah, Pakistan's leader died, and during the next decade there were many changes of government. The chaos was finally ended in October 1958 by a bloodless army coup resulting in the army dictatorship of General Ayub Khan. In 1960 he was formally elected President, and with the strong powers conferred on him by a new constitution in 1962 he instituted a series of reforms. After increasing opposition to Ayub Khan's leadership during the late 1960s, promises were made for a return to democracy. Elections were finally held in 1970 but not before the country had experienced martial law under General Yahya Khan who took over from Ayub Khan in March 1969.

Civil War.

As a result of the elections in December 1970, Sheikh Mujibur Rahman of the Awami League obtained a majority in the East and Mr. Bhutto of the People's Party triumphed in the west. Due to the greater population of the East, the Awami League commanded an overall majority, and insisted on a constitution which would give East Pakistan wide-ranging autonomy. Mr Bhutto opposed this and Civil War erupted on 26 March 1971 following the outlawing of the Awami League and the declaration of E. Pakistan as the independent republic of Bangladesh. The opposition was quickly suppressed, but involved the loss of thousands of innocent lives and created a severe refugee problem as many fled to India. Widespread disease and the cyclone disaster of November 1970 threatened a major famine in E. Pakistan.

War between India and Pakistan 1971.

Support for the Bangladesh guerrillas (Mukti Bahini) was provided by India and after charges and counter charges and incidents on the border between E. Pakistan and India in November 1971, a general offensive was launched. On 3 December India was put on a war footing following Mrs. Gandhi's demand for the withdrawal of Pakistani troops from Bangladesh. Bitter fighting occurred in both E. and W. Pakistan which was ended by Yahya Khan's acceptance of India's unilateral offer of a cease-fire.

The Aftermath.

On 20 December 1971 President Yahya Khan resigned and was replaced by Mr. Bhutto who released Sheikh Mujibur Rahman the following January. At the same time Pakistan left the Commonwealth as other members were about to recognise Bangladesh. (In April 1972 Bangladesh was admitted in place of Pakistan.) Peace negotiations with India were initiated to deal mainly with withdrawal from areas conquered in 1971 and the exchange of prisoners. The latter was only achieved after Pakistani recognition of Bangladesh. Diplomatic relations with India were finally re-established in May 1976. Internal problems within Pakistan arose with conflict in the provinces of Sindh and Baluchistan and have continued since then. Mr. Bhutto has gradually introduced economic reform but throughout 1975 and 1976 unrest in the provinces and the outlawing of the Awami League led to approval of a declaration of a state of emergency. Elections were held in March 1977. Amid accusations of election malpractice, Mr. Bhutto claimed victory. Widespread unrest followed.

Bangladesh.

After the release of Sheikh Mujibur Rahman in 1972, plans were announced to make Bangladesh a parliamentary democracy and to carry out large-scale nationalisation. In March 1973 the Awami League won all but 7 seats in the general elections. However, rising food prices, corruption among leading members of the Awami League and national disasters created widespread unrest. In 1975 a state of emergency was declared, fundamental civil rights were suspended and the parliamentary government was replaced by a presidential one party system under President Mujib. A series of radical reforms ensued causing resentment and opposition particularly from the army and in August 1975 the President and his family were killed in a military coup. Mr. Khandaker Moshtaque Ahmed succeeded to the presidency and began to reverse President Mujib's policies. In November 1975 a series of coups upset President Ahmed's government and that which replaced it under Brigadier Khalid Musharaf. Power passed to the hands of President Sayem and the chiefs of the armed services. Steps have since been taken to restore normal conditions to Bangladesh and the Government is committed to early elections.

THE FAR EAST

CHINA.

On 1 October 1949, after the Communists had gained complete control of the Chinese mainland and the Nationalist forces of Chiang Kai-shek had retreated to Taiwan, the Chinese People's Republic was proclaimed under Chairman Mao Tse-tung. It claims sovereignty over one fifth of mankind, with a population of about 800 million.

The Cultural Revolution.

In 1966 Mao instigated China's remarkable "Cultural Revolution." Slogans and portraits of Mao Tse-tung appeared everywhere. Huge crowds of young people with red armbands thronged the streets in general excitement. Red Guards took a prominent part. Mao's essential teaching was disseminated by millions of copies of a little 300-page book of his selected writings, in a red plastic cover, carried by almost everyone and universally quoted, discussed, and preached. An objective of the movement was to stimulate the young who might otherwise take for granted the achievements of their elders made possible only by their past suffering and hunger. The revolution must be uninterrupted; the class strugge continued. This revolution emphasised rejectioln both of western capitalist technological society exemplified by Japan, and of "revisionism" leading to "bourgeois decay" as, it was claimed, had happened in Russia. But it developed into violent struggles between revolutionaries and reactionaries and then between the revolutionaries themselves. Chou En-lai warned that industrial production was being seriously affected. The situation remained very confused until 1968 when there was a gradual return to moderation. Of the 17 surviving members of the Politburo elected at the eighth Communist Party congress of 1956, 13 were declared "bourgeois reactionaries" during the cultural revolution. President Liu Shao-chi who had been Mao's right-hand man, was among those expelled from the party and was portrayed thereafter as the arch-villain at work in Chinese society.

Reconstruction.

The end of the Cultural Revolution was marked formally by the Ninth Congress of the Chinese Communist Party, which took place in Peking during April 1969 in conditions of great secrecy. The following years were devoted to restoring normal conditions. Disturbances caused by ultra-leftist organisations were firmly repressed; reorganisation was carried out of the Communist Party, whose structure had virtually disintegrated except in the army, and of the Communist Youth League, which had been supplanted by the Red Guards; a campaign was launched to increase production.

China and the World Powers.

Relations between China and the Soviet Union, already embittered by major ideological differences, were not improved when in 1969 serious clashes took place between Russian and Chinese troops on the Ussuri river boundary for control of the river islands. Relations mellowed in 1970 with exchanges of ambassadors and the signature of a new trade pact. However, in January 1974 the Chinese expelled Soviet diplomats accused of spying and the Russians responded in kind. Meanwhile relations with the West improved. In 1971 the 21-year embargo on the export of non-strategic goods by the US to the Chinese mainland was lifted and telephone links between London and Shanghai were resumed. In October 1971 the UN voted to admit the People's Republic of China and the Republic of China (Taiwan) was expelled. Shortly afterwards President Nixon visited China where he was received by Mao Tse-tung and had many talks with Chou En-lai. In the final communiqué the common desire for understanding, peace and an increase in trade was stressed, but differences remained about the solution to current political and military problems, especially Taiwan. A further visit by an American president was made in December 1975 when President Ford and Dr. Kissinger had talks with Mr. Teng Hsiao-p'ing and Chairman Mao. In September 1975 official relations were established with the EEC.

In 1966 China announced that she had tested a guided missile with a nuclear warhead and further activities have taken place including underground tests and the explosion of a hydrogen bomb in 1969. These developments underline the need for China to be brought into arms control discussions.

Internal Political Developments.

In 1969 Defence Minister Marshal Lin Piao was formally named as Mao's successor, however, he was subsequently discredited and died in a plane crash in 1972 while trying to escape to the Soviet Union. Campaigns against Lin Piao and the philosopher Confucius began just before the Tenth Party Congress in 1973 and local political and military leaders were condemned. The Congress produced the election of 5 vice-chairmen by the Central Committee, whereas Lin Piao alone had been elected in 1969. Teng Hsiao-p'ing increasingly took over public duties from the ailing Chou En-lai. In January 1975 the National People's Congress adopted a new constitution which emphasised the role of the Communist Party and, among other things, abolished the office of President of the Republic. Command of the armed forces was transferred to the party chairman and the president's other prerogatives to the standing committee of the National People's Congress. Chou En-lai was appointed head of the new State's council, but in January 1976 he died.

He was succeeded by Hua Kuo-feng and not Teng Hsiao-p'ing as had been expected. It was suggested that Hua (later appointed by the Politburo to the Vice-Chairmanship of the Party in April 1976) was chosen as a compromise between the moderates and the radicals led by Chang Chun chiao and Chiang Ching (Mao's wife), on a question of priorities. The latter stress ideological purity and permanent revolution at the expense of internal development, while the moderates aim at political advancement through economic progress. During the early months of 1976 rioting occurred and campaigns were directed against the " capitalist roaders " despite Mao's directive that " stability and unity do not mean writing off class struggle ".

On 9 September 1976 after leading China since 1949, Chairman Mao died at the age of 82. Many tributes were paid from all corners of the world and the Chinese people observed a period of mourning. Mao's body lay in state and is to be preserved.

China after Mao.

Mao has been succeeded by Hua Kuo-feng, who before he replaced Chou En-lai had been a security minister for one year and had previously only been known as an agricultural specialist in the southern province of Hunan. In the months after Mao's death, a vicious poster campaign was mounted against Chiang Ching (Mao's wife) and three others, Wang Hung-wen, Chang Chun-chiao and Yao Wen-yuan—known as the " gang of four ". All four were arrested and the allegations against them included their planning to persuade the armed militia to take over the army and causing unrest by their backing of the Shanghai radicals. In their turn they were attacked as the real " capitalist roaders ".

Meanwhile Hua's image was built up through films and other propaganda. His colleagues were close associates of Chou En-lai and he appears to have the support of the army. In a speech at the beginning of January 1977, he promised massive " purification " and said the task for 1977 was to " expose and repudiate " the followers of Chiang Ching and to " move towards the goal of the great order ". Moves have been made to rehabilitate Teng Hsiao-p'ing who had been dismissed from government and party posts in April 1976.

Given the general focus on internal matters little change has been indicated in attitudes towards the outside world especially the US.

JAPAN.

The new Japanese constitution of 1946 retained the emperor (who had renounced his claim to divinity) as " symbol of the state and of the unity of the people ", but provided for government by ministers responsible to a parliament elected by universal adult suffrage. It thus gave Japan fully representative institutions for the first time. Reforms were passed to achieve the growth of trade unions, the equality of women and a non-authoritarian educational system. The former rightist and militarist elements were deprived of much influence. On the other hand recognition of the need for economic recovery made the occupation authorities moderate in their reparations policy and in the deconcentration of the great zaibatsu monopoly firms.

Despite the prohibition of armed forces in the new constitution, the Korean War made the occupation authorities keen for limited Japanese rearmament. The result was the peace treaty signed by 48 nations at San Francisco in 1951 and a defence agreement with the USA providing for the continued maintenance of American bases in Japan. The new army, navy and air force were known as " self-defence forces ".

Economic and National Resurgence.

Relations were gradually resumed with Asian countries on the conclusion of treaties covering reparations, and full international recognition came with admission to the United Nations in 1956. Meanwhile Japan enjoyed rapid economic recovery. She has had a consistently high growth rate and sustained prosperity, while population control successfully reduced the undesirably high birth-rate.

This economic resurgence brought a new self-confidence and indeed nationalism, and some internal dissent. The attempts of successive conservative governments to water down the reforms carried out under the occupation produced protests and violence from left-wing groups. The latter were also critical of the defence agreement with the United States, and here they found much public support on nationalist grounds. In 1960 the Kishi Government extracted some concessions in a revised agreement. But there were violent student demonstrations in Tokyo against the bases remaining at all. As a result the American President cancelled a planned visit and the Kishi Government resigned. This showed that Japan was no longer under US tutelage, but also that it had failed to achieve a consensus on its new role. Nevertheless when Japan acted as host to the Olympic Games in 1964 it symbolised her return to international status and to a sense of national identity and pride. Then in 1971 Emperor Hirohito visited seven Western European countries—the first Japanese sovereign ever to leave Japan during his reign.

By the peace treaty of 1951 Japan had given up her claims to her former colonies of Korea and Formosa, to the Kurile Islands (which went to the USSR), and to the Pacific islands mandated to it by the League of Nations. Okinawa and the neighbouring islands, which had been administered as integral parts of Japan, were taken over by the United States, though recognising Japan's residual sovereignty. In the 1960s Japan pressed for restoration, but the Americans regarded Okinawa as too important for their defence commitments. Finally, however, a treaty was signed in June 1971 providing for the return of Okinawa and the other Ryukyu Islands in 1972, with the retention of the use of some bases by US forces.

Japan's close ties with the United States made it difficult to achieve better relations with the Soviet Union and Communist China. However in the wake of President Nixon's initiatives Mr. Tanaka was able to make a historic visit to Peking and to achieve a rapprochement with the Soviet Union as well; though the problem of the Kurile Islands delayed the conclusion of a peace treaty.

The Soviet Union warned Japan without success against concluding a peace treaty with China which included a clause against attempts by any country to establish hegemony in the Asian-Pacific region. In January 1976 Mr. Gromyko visited Tokyo and a peace treaty is to be completed as soon as possible although a temporary setback occurred when a Soviet pilot landed a Mig jet in Japan and the Russian demand for the immediate return of the plane was only eventually complied with.

Internal Problems.

In 1969 Japan experienced the world-wide phenomenon of left-wing student demonstrations in a particularly violent form. They were directed especially against the United States. Then followed a dramatic indication that not all Japanese accept the increasing Westernisation of their country. This was the forcible occupation of an army headquarters by Yukio Mushima, one of Japan's foremost writers and a member of a small group dedicated to the revival of the old Samurai tradition and its martial spirit. He tried to incite an army coup in favour of the Emperor and then committed hara-kiri (ritual suicide by self-disembowelment).

Elections were held for the Lower House of the Diet in December 1972, soon after Mr. Tanaka had succeeded Mr. Sato as Prime Minister. The premature dissolution was probably prompted by the success of Mr. Tanaka's overtures to China and his desire for a mandate for his plan to overcome overcrowding and pollution by spreading industry and the population more evenly throughout the country by the building of modest new cities in less developed areas. The main opposition parties were the Japan Socialist Party (JSP), the Democratic Socialist Party (an offshoot from the JSP), the Japan Communist Party and Komeito (" Clean Government Party "). The JSP and the Communists strongly attacked increasing defence expenditure and the mutual security treaty with the USA; all called for greater emphasis on welfare policies. In the event Mr. Tanaka's Liberal Democratic Party, which had had 25 years of uninterrupted power, retained a large overall majority with 271 of the 491 seats. But significant gains were made by the left-wing parties, JSP increasing its share from 87 to 118 and the Communists from 14 to 38.

When Mr. Tanaka visited several South-East Asian countries in 1974 Japanese " economic imperialism " was bitterly attacked. Mr. Tanaka resigned in December 1974 after allegations of corrupt business and political activities. He was replaced by Mr. Takeo Miki who also resigned at the end of December 1976 following internal party disagreements and an election defeat which split the Liberal Democratic party. His successor is Mr. Takeo Fukuda whose main task will be to put new life into the Japanese economy. The other major cause of political turmoil in Japan during 1976 was the revelation of large-scale bribery of leading Japanese politicians by American firms, particularly Lockheed, in order to promote the sale of their products. Mr. Tanaka's trial began at the end of January 1977 and could last several years.

VIETNAM.

When Japan collapsed in 1945, the only organised troops in Vietnam were controlled by Ho Chi-minh, a Communist, who set up a Democratic Republic in the northern part of Vietnam. France was bent upon restoring her colonial empire in the south and the next year war broke out between the French and Ho Chi-minh, culminating in the dramatic siege and capture by Ho's forces of the fort of Dien Bien Phu in 1954. As a result of a 14-nation conference on Indo-China at Geneva in the same year Vietnam was partitioned after a cease-fire, the country to be united after free elections. Laos and Cambodia became independent.

Unfortunately the United States refused to sign the agreement and South Vietnam refused to hold elections, but both affirmed that they would not use force to upset the agreement. There was thus a crystallisation into two Vietnams—Ho Chi-minh's Hanoi régime in the North and that of the Catholic nationalist Ngo Dinh Diem at Saigon in the South. By 1960 the Communist guerrillas in the South, known as the Vietcong, had set up a National Liberation Front. For eight or nine years a civil war was waged in South Vietnam against a very unpopular dictatorship. All that time it received United States military support while the North helped the rebels in the South. The position became increasingly untenable, and in 1963 the Buddhists rioted against the ruling Roman Catholic minority. The Diem régime which had savagely persecuted the Buddhists was overthrown by the military. In August 1964 two vessels of the US fleet were alleged to have been attacked in the Gulf of Tonking (off the North Vietnam coast) and American planes bombed North Vietnam installations as retaliation. This was the first of a series of bombing raids. In June 1965 the State Department gave authority to the American military commander to use troops in offensive operations against the Vietcong. An inquiry conducted by the US Senate Foreign Relations Committee in 1968 made it doubtful whether the alleged attacks on the two US destroyers in the Gulf of Tonking had ever taken place. This put a question mark against the constitutional legality of the war, as Congress had never declared war on North Vietnam.

After being advised by his officials that a military solution was impossible and that the only possible political solution was a negotiated settlement, President Johnson in March 1968 announced his partial bombing pause. Peace talks began in Paris in May, and by January 1969 the US, South Vietnam, North Vietnam, and the National Liberation Front (NLF) were sitting round a table. But little progress was made.

On 3 September 1969 Ho Chi-minh died after 24 years in power. His special achievement was the welding together of the two elements of nationalism and communism in Vietnam.

Growing opposition and disillusionment at home with the American rôle in the war, and the advent of Mr. Nixon to the Presidency brought an increased determination to reduce and eventually end the US military commitment in S.E. Asia. To this end a programme of " Vietnamisation " was launched by which the South Vietnamese were given the means to take on progressively a greater share of the burden.

On 26 January 1972 President Nixon revealed 2½ years of secret negotiations with the North Vietnamese and American concessions, including an offer of a massive reconstruction programme for the whole of Indo-China including N. Vietnam. He made a new 8-point peace offer which proposed total withdrawal of troops, simultaneous release of prisoners and neutrally organised elections in S. Vietnam. The plan was flatly rejected by N. Vietnam, mainly because it failed to provide for the discarding of President Thieu.

North Vietnamese Offensive 1972.

On 30 March the North Vietnamese began a new offensive in which for the first time North Vietnamese forces fought conventionally in South Vietnam. They succeeded in taking the provincial capital Quang Tri and endangered the former imperial capital of Hué. The United States replied with ever heavier bombing of targets in N. Vietnam, supply routes and North Vietnamese units in the Demilitarised Zone and S. Vietnam. In May President Nixon announced the mining of Haiphong and other North Vietnamese ports. This brought a sharp denunciation by the Soviet Union (and China), but significantly none of the current bilateral negotiations was broken off.

Vegotiations and Truce.

During the summer of 1972 the N. Vietnamese offensive failed: no major towns fell and the morale of the S. Vietnamese army held. This, combined with devastating American bombing, produced a more accommodating attitude from the Vietcong and the N. Vietnamese negotiators after many fruitless meetings between President Nixon's special adviser Dr. Kissinger and the leader of the N. Vietnamese delegation at the Paris peace talks, Le Duc Tho. But the talks dragged on, with the United States apparently trying to secure President Thieu's position, and finally broke down on 13 December. To put pressure on N. Vietnam the United States then resumed full-scale bombing (which they had suspended in October), thus unleashing a world-wide storm of protest.

However the negotiations did at last lead to the signature of a cease-fire agreement on 27 January 1973. By its terms US forces were to leave Vietnam within 60 days and there would be an exchange of prisoners of war. Vietnamese forces on both sides were to remain within their present territory. An international commission would supervise the observance of the agreement. Only vague outlines of a political settlement were included: principles for the reunification and neutrality of North and South and provisions for the people of S. Vietnam to exercise self-determination in supervised elections. The agreement did give a non-Communist S. Vietnam a chance of existence. Its most serious omissions were its failure to mention any withdrawal of the N. Vietnamese forces in S. Vietnam, or even to define what territory was controlled by whom, and the fact that it applied only to S. Vietnam, not to Cambodia or Laos. But President Nixon claimed "peace with honour" and promised S. Vietnam continued support.

Both Vietnamese governments claimed the agreement as a victory. President Thieu gave up his objections and expressed satisfaction that Hanoi had been forced to recognise North and South Vietnam as two independent sovereign states. But he warned that the political struggle ahead could be even more dangerous than the war. Le Duc Tho commented that it could not be denied that there now existed in S. Vietnam "two administrations, two armies, two areas of control, and three political forces."

Vietnam was now a totally devastated country. The military casualties amounted to about 1,100,000 dead Vietnamese (and an unknown number of civilians) and 46,000 Americans. The United States had poured some $120 billion into Indo-China and suffered immense damage to its international authority. Yet the basic issue of the war remained unsettled: who has the right to govern S. Vietnam?

Neither War nor Peace.

Despite frequent and major infringements of the cease-fire the USA began withdrawal of its 23,000 soldiers still in Vietnam. An ultimatum to Hanoi was needed to procure the release of the remaining American prisoners, but finally 29 March 1973 marked the end of an era of US military presence in Vietnam. The agreements of the third international Vietnam conference in three decades meeting in Paris in March had little significance, as Saigon was alleging large-scale infiltration of troops and munitions into S. Vietnam. The attempts of the International Commission of Control and Supervision to enforce the cease-fire were proving largely ineffective. An agreement in June between Dr. Kissinger and Le Duc Tho in Paris on measures to ensure implementation of the ceasefire achieved a temporary sharp drop in the level of fighting. But talks between the S. Vietnamese Government and the Provisional Revolutionary Government on a political settlement remained fruitless: President Thieu would have no truck with anything approaching coalition government, and the Communists therefore refused to agree to elections. Then in January 1974 the increasingly offensive role of the Communist forces prompted President Thieu to put his troops on a war footing again.

Communist Victory.

In March and April 1975 as a result of increasing Vietcong pressure, South Vietnamese forces were withdrawn from the Central Highlands in order to strengthen the defence of more strategic towns. After the decisive battle of Xuan Loc in April 1975 and with Saigon encircled, President Thieu resigned. By the beginning of May the Communists had triumphed. During the latter half of 1975 an estimated 230,000 refugees left S. Vietnam. On 21 January 1976 the Military Management Committee handed over government to the People's Revolutionary Committee. Following the elections in April of a National Assembly for all Vietnam, the reunification of the country was proclaimed for the first time since 1859. A government for the Socialist Republic of Vietnam was formed by Mr. Phan van Dong and in December 1976 the first congress of the Vietnamese Communist party since 1960 was held.

LAOS AND CAMBODIA.

The war in Laos officially ended on 21 February 1973 with a standstill cease-fire agreement (leaving the Pathet Lao in control of two-thirds of the country). The formation of a coalition government was agreed after some US pressure on the rightists in the Vientiane Government.

In May 1975 after local fighting and left-wing demonstrations in Vientiane the right-wing ministers resigned and fled. Army units mutinied against right-wing officers and southern Laos was occupied by Pathet Lao forces. The American protégé Souvanna Phouma remained at the head of the coalition government until December when his half-brother Prince Souphanouvong proclaimed the existence of a People's Democratic republic with a government headed by Mr. Kaysone Phomvihan. A complete takeover by the Pathet Lao had not been expected until April 1976. In August 1976 a delegation from Thailand visited Vientiane and a 5-point communiqué for peaceful co-existence was signed.

In Cambodia President Lon Nol proclaimed a state of emergency in March 1973: Prince Sihanouk's predominantly Communist forces had virtually cut off all supply routes to the capital Phnom Penh. The Republican Government was saved only by greatly intensified US bombing. However by dramatically cutting off all funds the US Congress forced an end to bombing raids on Cambodia by 15 August. Heavy fighting followed with the Sihanoukists just failing to take Kompong Cham.

During 1974 the military situation in Cambodia continued to deteriorate as the authority of the Lon Nol régime ceased to extend beyond Phnom Penh, Battambang and a few other centres. By January 1975 Khmer Rouge pressure had virtually isolated Phnom Penh, and the Mekong supply route had been cut. Increasing diplomatic recognition of the exiled Sihanouk régime followed. As Cambodia's plight became desperate, Lon Nol left the country in March 1975 and in April came surrender to the victorious Khmer Rouge Army.

All foreigners were swiftly expelled from Cambodia, and although information was scanty apparently the whole population of Phnom Penh was sent to work in the fields to increase food production.

The victors were an uneasy alliance between the royalist followers of the exiled Prince Sihanouk and the Marxist Khmer Rouges.

Prince Sihanouk remained as head of state with Penn Nouth as Prime Minister. After returning to Cambodia from Peking in September 1975 Sihanouk left soon afterwards on extensive travels. Elections were held on 30 March 1976 and the Prince resigned in April. He was replaced by Mr. Khieu Samphan and Penn Nouth's Government resigned to be followed by a new Cabinet under Mr. Pol Pot. In the early months of 1976 the entire population was mobilised in order to reconstruct the economy, but since then reports have reached the West of massive killings verging on genocide.

The pro-Chinese guerrilla movements in Thailand and Malaysia were naturally encouraged by these developments. Most countries in South-East Asia hastened to improve their relations with China and the other Communist countries of the area. The withdrawal of US forces from Thailand was accelerated at the behest of the Thais.

AFRICA

NIGERIA.

Tension between the main tribal groups (Hausa and Yoruba and Ibo) led to the assassination in 1966 by Ibo officers of the Hausa Prime Minister,

Sir Abubakar Tafawa Balewa. General Ironsi, an Ibo soldier, tried to impose a unitary system of government but was murdered by non-Ibo soldiers.

Civil war broke out in July 1967 after the secession of the Eastern Region under its Ibo leader, Colonel Ojukwu. This region became known as Biafra. Federal troops under the head of the new Federal Military Government, General Gowon, advanced into Biafra, cut the secessionists off from the sea and confined them to the Ibo heartland.

The Federal Military Government said that military operations would cease immediately if Colonel Ojukwu and his associates would agree to remain part of Nigeria and accept the new structure of the Federation based on the 12 states, including the South Eastern and Rivers States.

The end of the civil war after a period of apparent stalemate came at the beginning of 1970. Federal troops captured Owerri, headquarters of the secessionist régime, together with Uli airstrip through which relief supplies had reached Biafra. Colonel Ojukwu departed, leaving Colonel Effiong in charge of affairs. Colonel Effiong called on his troops to stop fighting and sued for peace.

Although he had promised a return to civilian rule, General Gowon announced its deferment in 1974. The first half of 1975 saw serious industrial unrest and highly inflationary pay increases, though Nigeria had a steadily increasing trade surplus because of her oil exports. In July 1975 General Gowon was deposed in a bloodless coup. The new head of state and commander-in-chief of the armed forces was Brigadier Murtala Mohammed. All former members of the Government and all state governors were dismissed. The plans of the new government included a timetable for return to civilian rule, the drafting of a new constitution, an anti-corruption drive and reduction of the armed forces. Steps were also taken to relieve the congestion in the port of Lagos. In February 1976 an attempted coup by officers was crushed but General Mohammed was killed. He was succeeded by General Olusegun Obasanjo who proceeded with his predecessor's policies. Port congestion was reduced and a strict economic programme placing emphasis on housing, health and agriculture was mounted. A new constitution was published in October 1976 and October 1979 is the projected date for the re-establishment of full democratic government.

UGANDA.

In August 1972 the President of Uganda, General Amin, announced that all Asians who held British passports (whose numbers were estimated at 57,000) must leave the country within 3 months. He accused them of sabotaging the economy and corruption and insisted that the economy must be in the hands of black Ugandans. Britain condemned this move as irresponsible and racist and reacted by suspending economic aid to Uganda. But she recognised her responsibility towards Asians with British passports and organised an air-lift. The expulsions were soon extended to Asians with Indian, Pakistani or Bangladesh passports, but these countries refused to accept the expellees. The Asians had played an indispensable rôle in the Ugandan economy, which must suffer from their departure, despite aid from Colonel Gaddafi in Libya. Favourable reactions by Australia, Canada, the United States and other countries to the British appeal to accept some of the Asians helped reduce the influx into Britain.

General Amin had been strongly condemned by Presidents Nyerere of Tanzania and Kaunda of Zambia for racism of just the kind Africans deplore. There were actually brief military clashes on the Uganda–Tanzanian border in September 1972, and further allegations by Amin in 1974 that Tanzania and Zambia were planning an invasion of Uganda and supporting conspiracies by ex-President Obote.

Relations with Britain deteriorated when following British press reports of attempts to assassinate Amin and of brutal murders of prominent Ugandans, action was taken against British interests and all but 5 British diplomats were expelled in November 1974. In April 1975, General Amin said that he was ready to lift restrictions on the British High Commission. But relations were soured by the trial and sentence to death of Mr. Dennis Hills, a British lecturer, for treason and sedition. Only intense diplomatic activity including the mediation of President Mobutu of Zaïre and a visit to Kampala by Mr. Callaghan, then the British Foreign Secretary, secured a reprieve. In July 1976 a further dispute arose over the disappearance of Mrs. Dora Block, one of the hostages in the hijacked Air France airbus which landed at Entebbe airport. On 28 July Britain broke off diplomatic relations with Uganda, the first time this had been done with a Commonwealth country.

The Entebbe incident also caused friction with Kenya who had allowed Israel to use Kenyan facilities during the rescue operation.

Early in 1977 came reports of mass arrests and killings in Uganda.

SOUTH AFRICA.

In South Africa Africans have no civil rights except in the "Bantustans". These are some 200 pieces of land, making up about 13 per cent of the country's land area, specifically designated for African use. Elsewhere in South Africa, Africans may not vote, and they have no representatives in the South African Parliament or on any of the Provincial or Local Authorities. They may form Trades Unions but these are not recognised in law and take no part in industrial negotiations. Their right to strike is severely limited and they have no freehold rights of land or house ownership. Freedom of movement is restricted by influx-control laws governing movement between towns and between town and country. Regulations require them to carry a pass at all times. African industrial wages average a sixth of those of Whites, and foreign firms have also been blameworthy in this respect.

The Afrikaans-led Nationalist Party has been in power since 1948. In 1961 after a referendum they made South Africa a republic, fulfilling a Nationalist aspiration of fifty years standing.

The theory of the government's policy of "apartheid", which owes much to the late Prime Minister, Dr. Verwoerd, looks forward to the eventual partition of South Africa as the only viable alternative to integration, which most Afrikaners regard as racial suicide. In practice, however, the government's policies are adapted to making a rigid caste system based on colour compatible with industrialisation and economic growth. Hence the increasing emphasis on the migrant labour system described by government ministers as "the cornerstone of our labour policy". Africans are brought to work in industry and returned to the Reserves at the end of their contracts.

The government is unable to impose the taxes on White voters that genuine separate development would require. The Bantustans are therefore likely to remain overcrowded Labour reserves, and millions of Africans will always live and work in the "White areas".

The implementation of apartheid legislation covering employment, housing and education after 1948 led to increasing African unrest, organised especially by the African National Congress (ANC). In 1959 the Pan Africanist Congress (PAC) broke from the ANC, and began to organise anti-pass law demonstrations. In March 1960 such a demonstration took place at the police station in the African township of Sharpeville. The police opened fire, killing 69 Africans and wounding over 180. The government declared a state of emergency and began mass arrests of African leaders. Strikes and mass marches of Africans continued for another week and the government then banned the ANC and PAC under the Suppression of Communism Act. Some African leaders went underground and organised a campaign of sabotage. But the security forces were able to infiltrate the organisations and in 1963 Nelson Mandela, the outstanding African leader, was captured with others and brought to trial. He was sentenced to life imprisonment.

Unrest among the Africans broke out again in 1973 with widespread strikes in Natal. In 1976 the worst riots since Sharpeville occurred in Soweto. The immediate cause was opposition to the compulsory use of Afrikaans as the medium of instruction in schools. The riots continued throughout the summer and spread to other areas.

Student protest was reinforced by political strikes and despite conciliatory moves by the Government, discontent continues.

In 1974 the Transkei, a Bantu homeland, took up the Government's offer of independence negotiations. In October independence was declared, but the state has not received international recognition.

Despite apparently growing African self-confidence, the White minority, overwhelmingly powerful and controlling the military and state machinery, remains determined to hold its privileged position. In 1974 there were some signs of change in South African attitudes both externally as well as internally. Mr. Vorster initiated talks with African nationalist leaders. With the significantly increasing involvement of Russian and Cuban forces in Angola, South African concern about the possibility of a Communist take-over led to the entry of South African troops from Namibia into Angola. The troops were withdrawn in 1976 following the MPLA victory. Mr. Vorster played a key role during Dr. Kissinger's visit to Africa and it appears that in the future South Africa's position will continue to be crucial to developments in Southern Africa.

NAMIBIA.

Namibia (South West Africa) has been under South African control since it was wrested from Germany in the First World War. In 1920 the League of Nations mandated the territory to South Africa.

In 1964 the Odendaal Commission, set up by the SA government, recommended the effective integration of South West and South Africa with the mandated territory being divided into ten tribal Bantustans having home rule, and a White homeland consisting of 70 per cent of the land area. The response of the United Nations was a 1966 General Assembly resolution revoking South Africa's mandate on the grounds that she was extending apartheid to the territory and therefore not administering it in the interests of all its inhabitants. SA legislation in 1969 largely put the Odendaal recommendations into effect and it has not yet relented in the face of an advisory judgment of the International Court or Security Council resolutions that it withdraw its "illegal administration" and "transfer power to the people of Namibia."

During the 1960s nationalist sentiment began to grow among the majority Ovambo tribe and a number of political parties were formed including the South West Africa People's Organisation (SWAPO). This party was banned and its leaders in exile have organised guerrilla infiltration of the territory. In December 1973 negotiations between the South African government and the UN Secretary-General Kurt Waldheim were broken off when it became apparent that the UN demand for independence for the whole territory under universal adult suffrage was irreconcilable with the South African plan of "independence" for a number of tribal Bantustans. In September 1974 the South African government declared itself ready to discuss the future of S.W. Africa and at a constitutional conference at the end of 1975 a declaration was signed promising independence in 3 years. SWAPO boycotted the conference and carried out intermittent guerrilla attacks during 1976, despite some attempt to facilitate their participation in a series of negotiations held during 1976. The UN continued to condemn S. African action and during his visit to Africa, Dr. Kissinger proposed that a constitutional conference be convened at a neutral location, under the auspices of the UN so that all parties including SWAPO could participate.

RHODESIA (ZIMBABWE).

In Rhodesia over five million Africans remain subordinate to 250,000 Whites. The 1961 Constitution provided for progressively increasing African representation in the Rhodesian Parliament. But a new White political party, the Rhodesian Front gained power at the 1963 elections on a platform of independence from Britain, opposition to the 1961 Constitution as too liberal, and opposition to proposals to repeal the Land Apportionment Act. The dissolution in December 1963 of the Federation of Rhodesia and Nyasaland led to the independence of Northern Rhodesia (as Zambia) and of Nyasaland (as Malawi) under majority governments and left Southern Rhodesia, renamed Rhodesia, as a self-governing colony with a White minority government. The Rhodesian Front leader, Winston Field, was replaced by Ian Smith after failing to obtain independence.

Unilateral Declaration of Independence.

Protracted negotiations took place between Mr. Smith and Mr. Wilson to reach a settlement in 1965. The latter took his stand on "five principles", including the stipulation that an agreed independence constitution should guarantee unimpeded progress to majority rule. But after winning all 50 White seats at the 1965 election, Mr. Smith made the unilateral declaration of independence from Britain on 11 November 1965. The British Government was thus confronted by an act of rebellion. However, it ruled out from the start the use of force. Mr. Wilson embarked on a policy of graduated economic sanctions, including an oil embargo; the objective being the emergence, under economic hardship, of a liberal alternative to the Smith régime. In December 1966 on board H.M.S. *Tiger* Mr. Wilson and Mr. Smith prepared a working document. But after the Rhodesian cabinet had rejected these terms, the UN Security Council passed a British resolution for mandatory sanctions including oil. Further talks on H.M.S. *Fearless* in October 1968 ended in fundamental disagreement. The white minority had found themselves unready to give the African majority reasonable prospects of education, jobs, political and civil rights. It was clear that what Mr. Smith objected to was majority rule in Rhodesia at any time. In 1969 a referendum led to Rhodesia being declared a republic. Under the republican Constitution, Whites were assured of a perpetual majority in the Senate and Africans could not hope for more than parity of representation in the lower House, and that in the indefinite future.

Stalemate and African Resistance.

Meanwhile exiled supporters of the banned African Nationalist organisations, Zimbabwe African People's Union (ZAPU) and Zimbabwe African National Union (ZANU), whose leaders Joshua Nkomo and Ndabaningi Sithole were imprisoned in Rhodesia, began armed incursions into Rhodesia from bases in Zambia in 1967 in co-operation with the South African ANC. As a result South African police were drawn in to help the security forces.

The Conservative Government came to power in Britain in 1970 committed to make another attempt to reach a settlement in Rhodesia. Sanctions were succeeding only in increasing rural unemployment and a shortage of foreign exchange and because of "leaks" through South Africa and the Portuguese territories, they were seen more as a bargaining counter than a solution. In 1971 agreement on a settlement was reached between Mr. Smith and Sir Alec Douglas-Home conditional upon the British Government being satisfied that it was acceptable to most Rhodesians. African parliamentary representation was to rise to parity with the whites and following a referendum and a Commission inquiry majority rule was expected to follow. However, a British Commission found the settlement unacceptable to the Africans. Sanctions therefore continued and guerrilla activity increased.

Further secret negotiations were held between Mr. Smith and Bishop Muzorewa, leader of the African National Council (ANC), but the proposals of the Government were rejected. In July 1974 the Rhodesia Front again won all European seats in the elections. Early in 1976 talks between Smith and Nkomo which proposed British involvement in a settlement reached impasse. The majority African faction under Bishop Muzorewa was not in favour of the proposal and guerrilla activity continued. Hopes for a solution to Rhodesia's problems were raised when Dr. Kissinger held a series of talks with African leaders and Mr. Vorster between April and September 1976. On 19 September Dr. Kissinger met Mr. Smith and on 24 September Mr. Smith broadcast his agreement to the "Kissinger package". He made it clear that he had no option but to accept. In essence the package provided for the establishment of an interim government, composed of a white-headed council of state and a black-led council of ministers, which would pave the way for majority rule within 2 years. In return steps would be taken to lift sanctions and end the guerrilla war. Black African leaders, including the so-called "front-line" presidents rejected Smith's version of the agreement, but eventually a constitutional conference began in Geneva under the British chairmanship of Mr. Ivor Richard. The Africans were represented by the different nationalist leaders, Bishop Muzorewa (ANC), Joshua Nkomo (ZAPU), Robert Mugabe (ZANU) and Rev. Ndabaningi Sithole (ZANU). The talks foundered on the question of a date for majority rule and by December 1976 hopes for agreement on details had faded. Over Christmas, the "front line" presidents recognised Nkomo and Mugabe (now united as the Patriotic Front) as the representatives of Zimbabwe and Mr. Richard began a series of visits to African capitals in an attempt to negotiate a basis for the resumption of talks. His proposals which envisaged majority rule within 14 months with an interim government headed by a British "commissioner" were rejected by Mr. Smith who maintained adherence to his version of the Kissinger package.

New British Initiative.

At the time of writing (May 1977) the British Foreign Secretary, Dr. David Owen, had just completed a visit to Southern Africa. Britain was seeking (with American support) to convene a new Constitutional Conference.

MOZAMBIQUE AND ANGOLA.

Rebellion broke out in Mozambique in 1963 and intensified in Angola after 1966 forcing the Portuguese to pour in more troops. In 1973 their army in Africa numbered some 180,000 men of whom over a third were African (Portugal's population is some 9 million). Over half Portugal's annual budget went on defence, and conscription was lengthened to four years for all able-bodied men.

In countering guerrillas the Portuguese moved African villagers into fortified settlements so insulating them from insurgents. Non-Portuguese Catholic missionaries reported a series of atrocities in Tete when Africans were herded against their will and whole hamlets sympathetic to Frelimo (Front for the Liberation of Mozambique) were wiped out. Portugal denied these charges but following an international outcry in 1973, the civilian governor of Tete province was replaced.

Fighting in Mozambique and Angola intensified during 1973 and 1974, but cease-fires were called after an appeal by the new Portuguese government to the liberation movements for a cessation of hostilities. Agreements were reached for the independence of Guinea Bissau and Mozambique after President Spinola's statement in July on the independence of Portugal's African territories.

A transitional government was installed in Mozambique in September made up of Frelimo and Portuguese elements and full independence was scheduled for July 1975. However, the agreement led to serious racial unrest with white extremists attempting to proclaim UDI and thereby provoking a Black backlash. Nevertheless independence was granted on schedule. The Marxist-oriented government under President Machel produced plans to revolutionise the state machine and improve the economy. In December an attempt to overthrow President Machel was crushed. Relations with Portugal deteriorated and in February 1976 the capital Lourenço Marques was renamed Maputo.

Civil War in Angola.

Negotiations on Angola were held up because it had three rival liberation movements torn by dissension and because of serious racial violence in this the richest of the colonies, with great mineral wealth and hundreds of thousands of Portuguese settlers. However after the formation of a common front between the three liberation movements (MPLA, FNLA and UNITA) in January 1975, agreement was reached on independence in November 1975 and until then the establishment of a transitional government of all three plus representatives of the Portuguese Government.

But fighting continued, particularly between the FNLA and the Marxist MPLA, despite a truce agreement in March and became increasingly intense. During the summer of 1975 the MPLA gradually took over sole control of the capital Luanda, and UNITA joined the FNLA in operations against the MPLA. The latter held a central strip from the coast to the border with Zaïre, while UNITA held most of the South and FNLA the rest of the South and the northern provinces.

In the months before independence there was a massive departure of European settlers, leaving appalling economic problems for Angola. Meanwhile there was increasing evidence of the Soviet Union supplying the MPLA with tanks and artillery and of Soviet transport planes flying arms in to them. Several thousand Cuban soldiers also appeared on the MPLA side. The FNLA received support from China and some from the USA via Zaïre, though Congress soon put a stop to this by refusing further appropriations. South African troops were initially deployed to protect the Cunene River Dam project. In November the FNLA and UNITA formally established a joint military and political command, and two separate Angolan Republics were proclaimed, with rival governments being set up, by the MPLA in Luanda and by FNLA and UNITA in Huambo (formerly Nova Lisboa).

Full-scale civil war now developed. With Soviet and Cuban support, the MPLA first brought the North under control pushing the FNLA back into Zaïre. UNITA forces in the South were attacked and the South African forces which had advanced several hundred miles into Angola withdrew to patrol a 30 mile-wide strip along the border. In February 1976, following the capture of Huambo, an MPLA victory was declared. UNITA forces under Dr. Jonas Savimbi and the FNLA under Mr. Holden Roberto continued guerrilla activities throughout 1976 while the MPLA attempted to bring the country back to normal.

In June 1976 foreign mercenaries who had fought against the MPLA were tried and, despite appeals for clemency, four were executed—Costas Georgiou (Colonel Callan), Andrew McKenzie, John Baker and Daniel Gearhart.

THE UNITED STATES

The Cuban Crisis.

In 1961 the United States broke off diplomatic relations with Cuba with whom relations had been strained since the Castro revolution of 1959. Shortly afterwards two US aeroplanes, but manned by Cubans, attacked the principal military bases near Havana, the capital. Two days later 1,500 invaders, Cuban exiles—armed, trained and largely controlled by US agencies—landed on the island but were driven back. The United States intelligence service had wrongly assumed that the Cuban people would rise against Dr. Castro. Controversy broke out in the States. Confidence in the new Kennedy administration was shaken.

The world came to the brink of war in October 1962. President Kennedy had pledged the United States to resist the creation of offensive military power in Cuba. On 22 October, upon alleged evidence of offensive Soviet missile sites there, he announced a quarantine of ships carrying weapons to Cuba. Some Soviet ships altered course thus avoiding a direct confrontation; and shortly afterwards Khrushchev decided to dismantle Soviet missile bases in Cuba and ship "offensive weapons" back to the Soviet Union, the United States agreeing to give assurances against an invasion of Cuba which had been threatened.

Assassination of Kennedy.

The assassination of President Kennedy in November 1963 at Dallas, Texas, shocked the entire world. The youngest ever elected American President (43) when he succeeded Eisenhower, he had during his three years of office asserted his leadership and commitment to policies which promised increasing conciliation among nations. Lyndon B. Johnson, as Vice-President, automatically succeeded him.

The Presidential Election, 1968.

With memories of the rout of Goldwater in 1964, the Republican Party chose as its Presidential candidate Richard Nixon (who had once been Vice-President and a Presidential candidate). On the Democratic side the presidential race was thrown into confusion when President Johnson announced that he would initiate peace moves in Vietnam and lay down the presidency. Vice-President Humphrey entered the lists to become the chosen candidate for the Democratic Party. It was one of the most closely contested presidential elections in American history. But although securing only a small majority of the popular vote Nixon obtained 301 votes in the Electoral College against Humphrey's 191 and became the 37th President of the United States.

The Presidential Election 1972.

President Nixon's Democratic rival in the 1972 election was Mr. George McGovern, a "populist" with simple radical promises: an abrupt end to the Vietnam War, a radical reduction of the American military presence in Europe, and a better deal for Blacks and other disadvantaged minorities. His chief contender for the nomination, Governor George Wallace of Alabama, an advocate of strict segregation of the races, was severely wounded at an election meeting in May by an apparently deranged young white man. Mr. McGovern's programme was probably too radical and too vague for the electorate. Despite the scandal of the bugging of the Democratic Party Headquarters by men employed by the President's re-election committee, President Nixon was helped by an improving economy, by his decisive and adventurous diplomacy, and by progressive disengagement from Vietnam. The result on 7 November was the worst-ever defeat of a Democratic candidate: Nixon won in 49 of the 50 states. However the gains of the Republican Party in the simultaneous election for the House of Representatives were far from enough to give it a majority.

	No. of votes	%	No. of electors
Nixon .	45,861,690	61	521
McGovern .	28,402,465	38	17

The Nixon Administration.

The American commitment in Vietnam was finally ended early in 1973.

Despite his aggressive commitment on taking office to promotion of laissez-faire free enterprise, President Nixon swung round in 1971 in favour of control of prices and incomes, which, maintained in 1972, proved quite successful. However, in the first months of 1973 prices again surged ahead. Nearly all controls were lifted in May 1974.

The Watergate Affair.

The Watergate scandal which burst fully upon the United States during 1973, not merely shattered the credibility of President Nixon but caused a crisis in the whole American governmental system. Its effect was enhanced by Nixon's admission that he paid virtually no taxes in 1970–1 and by accusations that he granted favours to milk producers and the International Telephone and Telegraph (ITT) Corporation in return for election campaign contributions.

Two of those who had broken into and attempted to "bug" the offices of the Democratic Party in the Watergate Building in Washington in June 1972 were convicted in January 1973. The US Senate then set up a seven-man commission of enquiry under the chairmanship of Senator Ervin into what appeared to be a programme of illegal political espionage aimed at manipulating the democratic election process. Accusations and disclosures followed and the four main figures who emerged in the investigation of what became known as the "coverup" were among Nixon's closest associates. They were: Bob Haldeman (White House chief of staff), John Ehrlichman (Domestic Affairs adviser), John Mitchell (the Attorney-General), and John Dean (White House Counsel). Haldeman and Ehrlichman resigned in April, 1973, and John Dean was dismissed. He soon accused the President of having had full knowledge of the Watergate exploit in September 1972, three months after the break-in, and of having approved the cover-up attempts. Nixon maintained that he had first learned of it in March 1973 and denied having ever done anything towards covering up the affair.

In July 1973, it was revealed to the Senate Watergate Committee that Nixon had secretly been tape recording almost all of his White House conversations and telephone calls since before the break-in. If the tapes could be heard, they would indicate one way or the other the complicity of the President in the "coverup" which, rather than the break-in at Watergate itself, had become the central issue. A mammoth legal and political struggle over the tapes then ensued which was to last just over a year. The legal struggle centred on Federal Judge John Sirica who was presiding over the Federal Grand Jury. President Nixon resisted giving up the tapes on the grounds of confidentiality of staff deliberations and national security.

In the midst of the continuing crisis over Nixon's role, Vice-President Spiro Agnew resigned on 10 October 1973, shortly before pleading "no contest" to an income tax evasion charge. This incident led to the eventual appointment of Congressman Gerald R. Ford as Vice-President.

Events continued to work against the President. On 20 October, Attorney-General Elliot Richardson (Mitchell had resigned much earlier) and his deputy resigned after refusing to follow President Nixon's order to fire the Watergate Prosecutor, Archibald Cox. This incident became known as the "Saturday Night Massacre". Controversy over the tapes and documents continued, including the revelation by the White House that an 18 minute gap existed in one of the most crucial tapes. These events culminated in July 1974, when the House Judiciary Committee adopted three articles of impeachment against President Nixon (only the second time that impeachment of a President had been recommended). These alleged that the President, in violation of his constitutional oath to uphold the law

(1) "engaged personally or through his subordinates or agents in a course of conduct or plan designed to delay, impede and obstruct the investigation" into the burglary at the Watergate building;

(2) "repeatedly engaged in conduct violating the constitutional rights of citizens" and impaired "the due and proper administration of justice and the conduct of lawful inquiries".

(3) "failed without lawful cause or excuse to produce papers and things as directed by duly authorised subpoenas issued by the Committee".

This was followed by an admission by President Nixon that it was "clear that portions of the tapes of these June 23 conversations (with Haldeman, six days after the Watergate break-in in 1972) are at variance with certain of my previous statements." Though he remained committed not to resign, this statement unleashed demands for resignation or impeachment even among formerly staunch Republican supporters. Three days later, on 8 August, President Nixon finally announced in a televised broadcast his decision to resign (the first President ever to do so). But his statement did not include the expected confession of guilt. It was not the many breaches of the law by his subordinates but the affair of the tapes and his own abuse of executive privilege that destroyed Richard Nixon's credibility. By the end of his stubborn attempt to cling to power the nation was convinced of his complicity. He left America a legacy of shocked disillusionment with the sordid abuse of power by its political leaders and impaired respect for the highest office in the land.

America after Nixon.

On 9 August Vice-President Gerald Ford was sworn in as 38th President of the United States.

He granted a controversial pardon to Mr. Nixon for "all offences against the United States" in order to spare the ex-President further suffering and the nation further divisive debate, but insisted there had been no "deal" involved. In January 1975 the Watergate cover-up trial resulted in the conviction of Ehrlichman, Haldeman and Mitchell for obstruction of justice and perjury.

President Ford had committed himself above all to combating inflation ("public enemy number one") as well as to continuing the foreign policy of President Nixon. But in January 1975 he declared that the emphasis must be shifted because of the serious rise in unemployment (which was to reach 8 million in April 1975).

To many observers, the failure of American policy in Indo-China, the reverses suffered to Kissinger's attempts at Middle East peace and the trauma of Nixon's resignation seemed to indicate that a watershed in post-war American history had arrived—that America now needed a drastic reappraisal of her role in the world. In the wake of Watergate Congress began increasingly to challenge Presidential foreign policy, as with the "Jackson Amendment" to the Trade Treaty with the Soviet Union and the cutting off of military aid to Turkey. Its refusal to provide aid for Angola was clear evidence of the United States' new reluctance to become involved in foreign ventures. The increasing obstructionism of Congress was causing problems for President Ford with the Presidential election due in November 1976.

Revelation of Malpractices.

The CIA (Central Intelligence Agency) had been frequently accused of implication in operations to bring about a change in the political balance of some foreign countries (including the overthrow of President Allende in Chile in 1973) and of planning the assassination of political leaders to whose policies the United States strongly objected. Then in December 1974 allegations were made in the *New York Times* that the CIA in violation of its charter had conducted a vast illegal intelligence operation against adherents of the anti-war movement and other dissident groups inside the USA. President Ford established a commission headed by Vice-President Rockefeller to examine these allegations and recommend future safeguards. Both houses of Congress set up special committees to investigate the operations of the CIA, FBI and other intelligence and law enforcement agencies. The report of the Rockefeller Commission in June confirmed the allegations of large-scale spying on American citizens in the United States, including the opening of private mail, wire-tapping, room-bugging and infiltration of political groups (though generally with the aim of discovering foreign influence).

A further indirect result of Watergate was the discovery by a Senate Committee early in 1976 that many major American firms and particularly the Lockheed Aircraft Corporation had paid many millions of dollars in bribes to foreign officials, politicians and political parties to promote the sale of their products. This caused a sensation around the world, especially in those developed countries most affected, notably Japan, Italy and also the Netherlands in so far as the Queen's husband, Prince Bernhard, was alleged to be implicated. President Ford announced that he would establish a commission to investigate the practices of US firms in foreign countries.

However the question began to be raised whether the national, and especially the Congressional, mood of self-flagellation was not going too far, whether for the sake of a new political morality after Watergate all the sins whether of the CIA or of top American companies should be blazoned abroad, or whether the damage to American interests might be too great. Early in 1976 President Ford persuaded the House of Representatives not to publish the report of its committee on the activities of the CIA (though much had previously been leaked concerning such matters as CIA support of the Kurds in Iraq at the request of the Shah of Iran and on the orders of President Nixon and the payment of money to politicians and parties, particularly in Italy).

1976 Elections.

1976 became the year in which the country finally put Watergate and associated traumas behind it. With the election of a new President, the nation ended the year in a more positive mood than it had been since Nixon's re-election. Much of this spirit was symbolised by the nation's celebration of 200 years of independence which reached a climax on 4 July.

The year was dominated by the Presidential elections. President Ford had announced his intention to seek election to the office he then held by appointment, but was strongly challenged by Ronald Reagan, former Governor of California. The Democrats had no single, obvious candidate and a free-for-all emerged among the possible challengers. At the beginning of the long primary election procedure to select the eventual candidate, Jimmy Carter, former Governor of Georgia, was a relative unknown outside the South. By late Spring he had become a front-runner, and in July he captured the Democratic Presidential nomination with only token oppositions at the convention in New York City. He chose Senator Walter Mondale of Minnesota as his Vice-Presidential running mate. After a bitter contest before and during the Republican convention, President Ford barely won the nomination over Governor Reagan and selected Senator Robert Dole of Kansas as his running mate.

After the exciting primary and convention activity, the election proved to be a rather dull affair. The main feature was a series of three televised "debates" in which Carter and Ford faced each other to answer journalists' questions. Starting with a massive early lead in the polls, Carter's lead gradually dwindled until the outcome was called a "toss-up" by the pollsters. At the end, the result was close, although Carter had a larger popular majority than either Kennedy in 1960 or Nixon in 1968. In the electoral college, which constitutionally elects the President, the result was a margin of 56 votes for Carter.

President Carter.

Carter's election was both unusual and symbolic in a number of ways. The first President from the "deep South" since before the Civil War, some view Carter's election as the final act of reconciliation between North and South. Rising out of obscurity and possessing relatively little political experience, and having based much of his campaign on an attack on the Washington establishment, Carter is seen by some as a genuine Washington "outsider" not tied to any entrenched group. He is thus in a position to symbolise the "new beginning" he has spoken about.

In picking his Cabinet, however, Carter disappointed many of his supporters while reassuring the "establishment". He did not pick as many women or blacks as many had hoped, but chose several former associates and many others who had served as officials in previous Democratic administrations. In domestic affairs he is expected to be a more activist President than his predecessor and acted immediately after his January 20 inauguration to propose measures to stimulate the US economy. He is expected to concentrate heavily on domestic affairs during the first two years of his term, including his plans to reorganise the executive branch and deal with the worsening energy situation.

In foreign affairs his approach is expected to differ from the previous two Republican administrations more in tone than in substance. He has strong views on nuclear weapons control and has proposed a halt to all nuclear testing and eventual reductions in Soviet and US nuclear arsenals. His commitment to Europe is strong and was emphasised by his sending of Mondale on a trip to Europe and Japan only a few days after the inauguration. Secretary of State Cyrus Vance, who replaced Dr. Kissinger, travelled to Moscow in March 1977 to reinvigorate détente and the SALT talks. Although the latter were adjourned, both sides saw the need for future understandings.

CANADA

The relationship between the English and French speaking communities remains Canada's principal political problem. In 1970 the Quebec liberal party committed to federalism gained a clear majority in the elections, but the separatist Parti Quebecois took 25 per cent of the vote. The

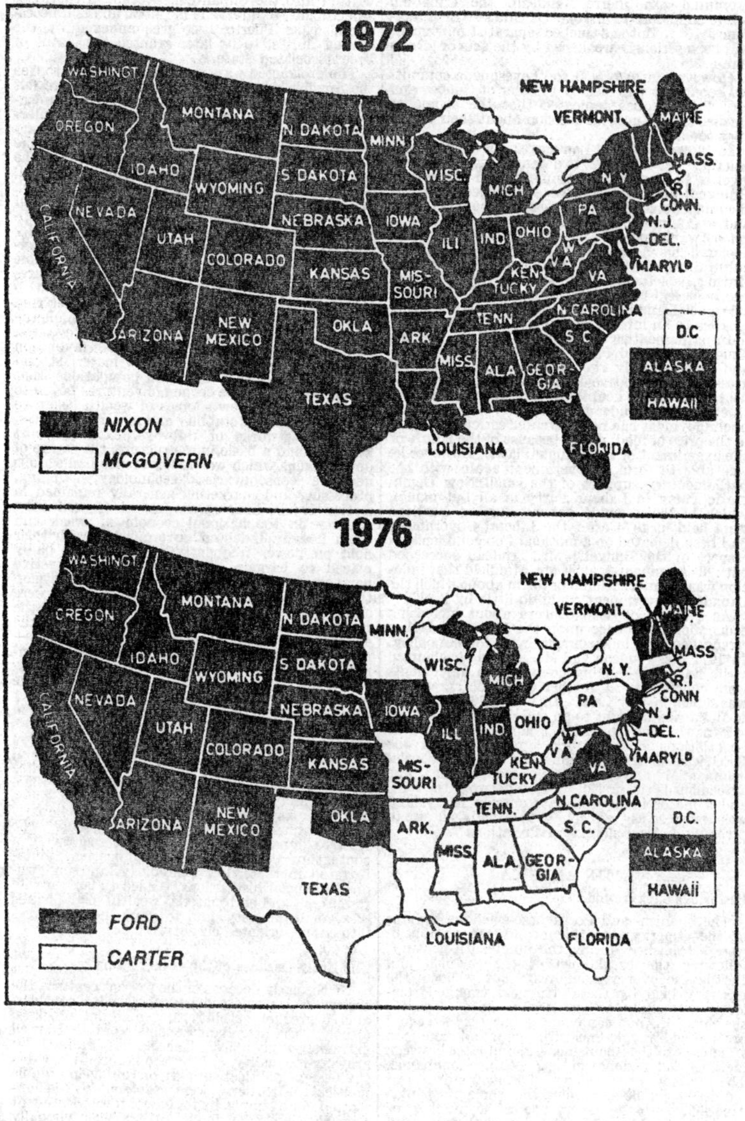

	Popular Vote	Per cent	Electoral Votes
Carter	40,249,963	50·4	297
Ford	38,498,494	48·3	241
Margin	1,751,467	2·1	56

separatist movement lost some impact as the economic situation improved under the Liberal government. The kidnapping by the Front de Liberation du Québec of a British trade commissioner and the Quebec minister of Labour, Mr. Pierre Laporte (who was later found dead), prompted Mr. Pierre Trudeau, the Canadian prime minister, to invoke Canada's War Emergency Act But the Quebec separatist movement had been seriously weakened by the acts of terrorism.

However, in 1976 M. Réné Levesque, a committed separatist was elected Premier of Quebec and Mr. Trudeau has indicated that the people of Quebec should make a decision about their future very soon.

In 1969 the Official Languages Act provided for equality between the two languages at federal level in parliament, government, and the courts. Bilingual districts could be established wherever the minority reached 10 per cent of the population and a Commission of Official Languages was to act as watchdog. In October 1971 Mr. Trudeau declared his allegiance to a policy of " multiculturalism within a bi-lingual framework." During 1974 there was great controversy in Quebec over legislation seeking to make French the sole official language of the Province and relegating English to an inferior position.

In parliamentary elections in October 1972 Mr. Trudeau's Liberal Party lost its overall majority and obtained only two seats more than the Progressive Conservative Party under Robert Stanfield, although it held its own in its stronghold of Quebec. Mr. Trudeau failed partly because rising unemployment had not prevented serious increases in the price of food, partly because of the failure of the experiment of the bilingual law. However he was able to form a government again with the parliamentary support of the small New Democratic Party (a Labour Party in all but name), which had also made gains. Further elections were held in 1974 after the Liberal Government had been defeated on a motion of no confidence in respect of the Budget. Mr. Trudeau succeeded with his argument against Mr. Stanfield that inflation was an international problem about which the Canadian Government could do little by itself.

As a result of deep concern about increasing economic dependence upon the US, Canada has strengthened its independent line in foreign policy. In 1971 Mr. Trudeau and Mr. Kosygin exchanged visits and wide-ranging co-operation agreements were concluded. A further economic agreement was signed in July 1976. In May 1976 nuclear aid to India was brought to an end due to the lack of safeguards over its use. Following 2 years of negotiations a framework agreement with the EEC was signed providing for non-preferential commercial and economic co-operation. The agreement is the first of its kind between the EEC and a major industrial state outside EFTA and was described as " a response to Canada's desire to diversify and extend external relations ".

LATIN AMERICA

Historical Background.

The Spanish- and Portuguese-speaking nations of the American continent and the Caribbean were established during the nineteenth century, following the breakdown of the Spanish and Portuguese overseas empires. But whereas the territory held by the Portuguese emerged relatively peacefully as one nation state—Brazil—the Spanish American colonies faced a bitter and protracted struggle first with Spain and American adherents to the Spanish cause, and later between factions and regional groups seeking dominance. The result was the collapse of Bolivar's dream of a united republic embracing the whole of Spanish America, and the emergence of a number of separate republics wracked by civil wars and burdened by poverty and debt. By 1840 the four original Spanish vice-royalties (New Spain, New Granada, Peru, and La Plata) had spawned sixteen separate and independent states, while Cuba and Puerto Rico remained under Spanish rule. To these were added the Dominican Republic in 1944, and the Republic of Panama, founded in 1903 after a breakaway revolt inspired by the USA in the face of Colombian hostility to ceding of territory for the building of a canal to link the Pacific and Atlantic Oceans. The Spanish–American War of 1899 finally wrested Cuba and Puerto Rico from Spanish control, with Cuba becoming an independent republic in 1902 (although the United States retained the right, written into the Cuban constitution in the Platt amendment, to intervene in Cuban affairs if necessary), while Puerto Rico was annexed by the United States, to be later granted the status of Free Associated State.

The protracted wars that were necessary to free the Spanish dominions had effects that were felt for many decades; fragile systems of communications broke down, mining and agricultural enterprises fell into decay, reserves were exhausted and debts incurred in the purchase of arms and the maintenance of armies. The majority of the nations which emerged were highly militarised, and in many cases struggles for control between armed factions extended well into the second half of the nineteenth century. A significant exception occurred however in Chile, which rapidly emerged as a stable nation with a civilian government and a prosperous economy. On the whole though, the decadence of the mining ventures which had brought wealth to Spain, coupled with the chronic instability which prevailed, deterred attempts, both native and foreign, to exploit the vast natural resources of the former vice-royalties, and it was not until the industrial revolution stimulated world demand for raw materials, and for food for growing industrial populations, that significant large-scale economic ventures began to develop. While new sources of wealth began to develop a basis for stability and material progress, bringing networks of railways, extended port facilities, and a basic infrastructure, the course of development which was followed also had serious negative consequences. Technology, shipping, processing and marketing generally remained in foreign hands, limiting the impact of productive activity on the national economies; weak and often heavily indebted governments, with their hold on power frequently tenuous, were badly placed to bargain effectively with prospective partners, and were generally eager to develop their natural resources on whatever terms were available. Added to these difficulties were the recognised weaknesses of an economy based on the export of raw materials or agricultural products—there was a tendency to depend upon a single commodity, prices were generally unstable, fluctuating widely in response to booms and slumps in the world economy, and the discovery of cheaper sources or synthetic substitutes could bring sudden and devasting ruin. Typically then, these factors created economies dominated by a sector exporting foodstuffs or industrial raw materials (meat and grain from Argentina, tin from Bolivia, coffee from Colombia, sugar from Cuba and Puerto Rico, nitrates and then copper from Chile, and coffee and bananas from Central America), and importing manufactures and industrial goods. The relative dynamism of such export sectors in a context of poor overall communications, unintegrated markets, low technology, and undeveloped financial institutions, tended to concentrate resources (land and material wealth) in the hands of a small minority, and to draw such resources into export-oriented activity.

The Early Decades of the 20th Century.

By the early decades of the present century, the society which emerged had achieved a considerable degree of stability and material progress, although the attendant benefits were distributed extremely unequally. The strains created by growing inequality, and by the failure to broaden the base of political support or to develop viable political institutions, were spectacularly demonstrated, for example, by the overthrow of President Porfirio Diaz of Mexico in 1911, after a virtually uninterrupted rule of thirty-four years. What began as an attempt to establish a reformist constitutional government developed into a bloody revolution which dragged on for twenty years, cost the lives of hundreds of thousands of Mexicans, and finally resulted in the establishment of a stable civilian regime in which power has been held by the same party (now called the Institutional Party of the Revolution) since 1928. Elsewhere in Latin America, the unsettling effects of the Mexican and Russian revolutions were added to the social tensions produced by the pattern of development pursued until 1914, and to the dislocation caused by the First World War. The latter brought an end to a period of steady and sustained export-oriented growth, and the following decades revealed some of the weaknesses of the development that had taken place. The bulk of the population still lived in landless poverty, while the modern sector of the economy remained highly dependent on stimuli from outside, lacking as it did a thriving domestic market. While the First World War cut off sources of manufactured and industrial goods from Western Europe, thus stimulating a degree of industrialisation, and also led to increases in the prices of strategic materials, the Latin American nations were frequently unable to respond sufficiently quickly to maintain former levels of production, or to prevent shortages causing severe domestic inflation. The disruption to the world economic order occasioned by the war and subsequent developments led to a marked decline in foreign investment, a catastrophic recession in the early 1920s, and increasing difficulty in finding export markets due to competition from Africa and Asia, and to the general adoption of tariffs and controls in the developed world. The intensification of these pressures, and the general collapse of commodity prices, during the great depression of the early thirties, threatened the viability of the export economies still further, and provoked a number of attempts to follow different paths to economic development.

Emergence from Colonialism and Slavery.

While Brazil had experienced development prior to 1930 upon lines largely similar to Spanish America, emerging in the second half of the nineteenth century as the dominant world producer of coffee, its prosperity reflected its achievement in passing relatively peacefully from colony to empire in 1822, and from empire to republic in 1889. The Portuguese court, in flight from Napoleon, had come to Brazil in 1807, and when King Joao VI left for Portugal in 1821, he left his son Pedro behind as regent. He in turn declared the independence of Brazil in 1822, becoming Pedro I. He was himself sent into exile in 1831, but after a decade of political uncertainty and sporadic regional revolts his son Pedro II was invited to assume the throne; he ruled until deposed by the army, without opposition, in 1889. Within five years Brazil had a stable civilian government once more. The social, political and economic development of Brazil was particularly shaped, after the decline of the sugar plantations and of gold-mining, by the spread of coffee cultivation and by two successive forces, slavery and immigration. For most of the nineteenth century the sugar and coffee plantations were worked by slave labour, and a total of over three and a half million slaves were imported from Africa, nearly ten times as many as ever went to the United States. Slavery was not finally abolished until 1888, a generation after British naval activity had put a stop to the slave trade itself. The abolition of slavery was followed by a flood of immigration, principally from Italy and Portugal, which changed the face of the country. From 1884 to 1914, an annual average of practically 50,000 people entered the state of São Paulo alone, and during the same period native migrants poured into the state from the devastated drought area of the north-east. Only Argentina and Uruguay in the rest of Latin America experienced such a flow of European immigration.

From the turn of the century, however, Brazil's coffee economy was continuously threatened with over-production, and a succession of measures were necessary in the following decades to keep up the price on the world market. Fortuitously, it was the coffee protection policy of the Vargas government (which came to power after the revolution of 1930) which boosted internal demand, and allowed Brazil to emerge almost unscathed from the depression, with a growing industrial base.

Search for Paths to Economic Development.

The crisis of the export economies led to a search for alternative development strategies, and it is this search which has dominated Latin American political debate and activity in recent decades. A number of factors have added urgency to the task. The first of these is the "population explosion"; the population of Latin America has grown from 30 million in 1850 to 300 million at the present day (mid-1974 UN estimate), and it is expected to reach 600 million some time before the end of the century. The strain on resources due to such explosive growth is increased by the general trend of migration to the cities—while population growth has averaged 2·8 per cent per year over recent years, the urban population has grown twice as fast as migrants have flooded in from the countryside. As a result there was by 1970 a total of 36 cities in the area with populations of over 500,000: the lack of facilities condemns thousands of new migrants to live in makeshift shanty towns without sewage, electricity, transport or schools. This wave of migration reflects two important phenomena. Firstly, the countryside is unable to support the population it produces. Rates of expansion of agricultural production have failed to match the growth in population, and thousands of rural workers have been driven to the cities in search of work; secondly, a revolution of rising expectations has taken place, fuelled by improved mass communications, and in particular by the impact of patterns of consumption prevalent in the developed world and spread through radio, television, advertising and example. Along with demands for increased material well-being have gone demands for greater participation in political life, resulting in sustained challenges to the land-based oligarchies which had generally held power before. The kind of challenge which emerged varied; in a number of the more advanced countries of the region, radical or reformist governments, largely with middle-class backing, appeared early in the century; this was particularly the case in Uruguay, where Batlle, who became President in 1903, presided over a programme of reforms which built a progressive welfare state by 1920, in Argentina where the Radical Party came to power in 1916, and in Chile, where Alessandri, the candidate of the Liberal Alliance, was elected in 1920. The possibility of a gradual move towards truly democratic institutions, threatened by the faltering export economies, was further undermined by the general collapse of prices following the Wall Street crash of 1929; a wave of coups, revolutions, and unrest swept the area. Chile saw its dollar receipts drop by 80 per cent in three years, and experienced a short-lived socialist revolution and a return to conservative economic policy; in Argentina, the military came to power in September 1930, and in the same year Vargas seized power in Brazil, with the support of some state militias and sectors of the military, after losing a closely fought election. In the same period, Peru, Cuba, Guatemala, El Salvador, Nicaragua, and the Dominican Republic experienced similar upheavals. In the last four named, Ubico, Martinez, Somoza and Trujillo respectively established harsh and extremely conservative dictatorships, marked by extreme degrees of repression; in Cuba and Brazil the regimes which emerged blended authoritarian control with measures aimed at building support among the middle and working classes. Bolivia also emerged with a "military socialist" government, after the disastrous Chaco War (1932–5), in which the incompetence of the Bolivian High Command, and the unfamiliarity of their highland Indian troops with the tropical lowlands and swamps where the war was fought, allowed the Paraguayans to make substantial territorial gains, though at a disastrous human cost. In Mexico, President Cardenas (1934–40) initiated a programme of reforms marked by massive redistribution of land to the landless peasantry.

The complexity and diversity of subsequent events preclude easy generalisations; competing social groups and competing ideologies, set against a changing international background, produced a variety of developments. The rise of fascism in Europe inspired a number of Latin American emulators, influencing some aspects of the Estado Novo created by Vargas in Brazil in 1937; such influence was most noticeable in the rise of Juan Domingo Perón in Argentina. The markedly pro-axis position taken by Perón during his rise to power (1943–6), and the fascist trappings with which he sometimes surrounded himself, gave way however to the somewhat confused doctrine of "Justicialismo", which combined ideas of nationalism, social justice, economic independence and non-alignment. While wartime prosperity allowed massive redistribution of income in favour of urban workers, organised into powerful but closely controlled unions, and courted by Perón's remarkable first wife, Evita, the increasingly critical economic situation after 1951, marked by inflation and balance-of-payments difficulties, led to increasingly coercive policies; when the army revolted in 1955, Peron chose exile rather than a direct appeal to the working classes to rise in his support.

The Post-War Years.

Throughout the sub-continent, the early post-war years were however marked by a growing commitment to schemes of rapid industrialisation. The case for policies of forced industrialisation was put forward strongly by economists concerned with the founding of the Economic Commission for Latin America (ECLA) in 1949, in Santiago, Chile, under the auspices of the United Nations' Economic and Social Council, and particularly by Raul Prebisch and Celso Furtado. The argument was that governments should adopt policies aimed at protecting domestic industry, allowing it to produce those goods previously imported, and thus to reduce the need for foreign exchange. They could thus build an industrial base, and escape the consequences of steadily declining terms of trade. More radical reformists argued that development would be impossible without the expropriation of large and inefficiently run estates (or latifundios), and the nationalisation of foreign monopolies. Such policies as were adopted along these lines gave rise to fears that widespread Communist infiltration was taking place, although with hindsight it might be argued that gross inequality and poverty were far more important factors in precipitating violent change than subversion from outside. In Guatemala, the ousting of the authoritarian Jorge Ubico in 1944 led after a brief interlude to a period of six years constitutional rule by Juan Jose Arevalo. The process of democratic reform which he initiated was continued by his successor, Colonel Jacobo Arbenz, backed by left-wing forces, including the Communist Party: his policy of development of road, harbour and energy facilities, in competition with foreign-owned monopolies, and of wide-ranging land reform, involving the compulsory purchase of large and uncultivated estates, aroused the opposition of native and foreign owners of property, including the dominant United Fruit Company, which had vast banana interests in the Republic. The process of reform was cut short in June 1954, when an invasion from neighbouring Honduras and Nicaragua, led by Colonel Carlos Castillo Armas, succeeded in overthrowing the Government. This followed a resolution obtained by US Secretary of State Dulles at the Inter-American Conference at Caracas in March 1954 condemning "the domination or control of the political institutions of any American State by the International Communist Movement", and the invasion itself was organised and supported by the Central Intelligence Agency of the United States. The pattern of American intervention was not however repeated throughout the sub-continent. In Bolivia in 1952 the MNR seized power under Victor Paz Estenssoro in a dramatic coup in which the army was defeated by a makeshift force of miners, peasants and workers. The revolutionary government under considerable pressure from the militant miners and peasants, nationalised the large tin-mining companies (owned by the Bolivians Aramayo, Hochschild and Patino), and initiated a land reform programme which effectively destroyed the latifundio. A breakneck programme of economic diversion, based on development of oil resources and of the almost unpopulated eastern lowlands, and backed by a complex system of exchange controls, led to hyperinflation and the disappearance of foreign currency reserves. Food aid from the United States, from 1953 onwards, saved the urban population from starvation, and the handing over of oil deposits to foreign companies in 1955 and the acceptance of a US stabilisation mission in 1956 marked the end of the Bolivian "revolution", although the MNR itself remained in power until 1964 and its major achievements were not reversed.

The 1950s and '60s.

The optimism that had characterised the early post-war years was considerably modified as the foreign exchange built up during the war dwindled, and the situation was made more difficult by the circumstances created by the sudden collapse of commodity prices after the sharp rises provoked by the outbreak of the Korean War. As the fifties drew to a close, however, there was some cause for renewed optimism. Democratic regimes had replaced dictatorships in Peru, Colombia and Venezuela, Brazil was experiencing a boom under the inflationary development-oriented policies of President Kubitschek, Mexico appeared to be coping well with the strains of sustained growth, and the creation of the Central American Common Market in 1958 seemed to promise a degree of economic development there.

The promise of development and prosperity was, however, not carried over into the 1970s. Increasingly severe problems of inflation, faltering growth rates and critical balance of payments difficulties beset the economies of Brazil and Argentina, provoking pessimistic forecasts that import substituting industrialisation itself simply shifted the demand for imports from consumer goods to the raw material inputs and machinery needed to produce them, while domestic markets remained small, so that stagnation was an inherent and permanent condition, given the status of the Latin American economies in the Western capitalist system.

Effects of the Cuban Revolution.

The debate over the possible paths of development during the sixties was however most strongly influenced by the Cuban revolution, which brought Latin America to the notice of the world, significantly affected United States' policy towards the area, and had dramatic effects upon the internal politics of other countries in Latin America and elsewhere.

The Cuban economy, organised around the production of sugar for the world market, had reached its peaks in the 1920s, and the disastrous effects of the depression added to increasing problems of over-supply in the world market, inefficient production techniques, the failure to diversify the economy, and rapid increases in the population of the island, led to prolonged stagnation, marked by declining per capita right up to 1958, and low rates of national investment. Furthermore, the extreme dependence on sugar, and the proximity and economic power of the United States, created an economy marked by an extreme concentration of land and wealth, high remittances of profits and interest payments to the United States, and extreme dependence on imported manufactures and technology. These problems co-existed with high average per capita incomes, and led to high social tensions, in a society marked by a sophisticated urban middle class, a long history of student radicalism, and a labour force in the countryside subjected to seasonal rates of unemployment of over twenty per cent. To this was added the corruption, opulent lifestyle, and harsh repressive policies of the Batista regime. In the circumstances, the victory of Fidel Castro and his followers, welcomed enthusiastically in Cuba itself, was at first greeted with some sympathy in the United States. The subsequent developments are related elsewhere, and the dramatic events of the mismanaged and miscalculated Bay of Pigs invasion, the Missile Crisis, and the US-imposed blockade of Cuba, all paralleling the radicalisation of the revolutionary process in Cuba, and the rise to dominance of the Communist Party, are well known. The Cuban revolution, however, coincided with, and in some ways provoked, a number of changes in Latin America. President Kennedy, attempting to remedy decades of neglect or support for conservative dictatorial regimes, launched the Alliance for Progress in 1961. While it captured the imagination of democrats in Latin America and in the United States, it was perceived and planned largely as a holding operation against international communism. The death of Kennedy himself certainly spelt the end of any US vocation to foster "democratic" government and to push for land reform and the strengthening of progressive forces, as President Johnson's precipitate recognition of the military government installed in Brazil in 1964, and the subsequent US marine invasion of Santo Domingo in 1965 were to witness.

Recent Pattern of Events.

Events since the early sixties in the major Latin American states are detailed individually below; perhaps the three most generalised phenomena are the trend towards industrialisation promoted locally by multi-national corporations, the emergence of a number of socialist experiments and of Cuban-style guerrilla movements, and the proliferation of military governments.

ARGENTINA.

The recent political history of Argentina has been dominated, even in his absence and after his death, by Juan Domingo Perón. During his eighteen years of exile (1955–1973) a succession of civilian and military regimes failed to break the loyalty of his followers, or to solve the problems posed by a series of worsening economic crises; his return, and death while in office, provoked a further crisis which led to a military intervention early in 1976.

The ousting of Perón in 1955 was followed by three years of military rule, but 1958 saw the installation of a civilian President, Dr. Arturo Frondizi. His attempt to introduce a stabilisation programme and to attract foreign capital into the country provoked an economic crisis in 1961, and his tolerance of Perónist politicians (who had supported his election, and who in 1962 won a majority of the seats contested in Congressional elections), led the military to depose him, rather than see Perón return. Senate chairman Dr. Guido ruled until Dr. Arturo Illia was elected to the Presidency in 1963, with the Perónists proscribed and Frondizi under arrest; but Illia's weakness (he had received less than a quarter of the votes cast) and his equivocating policies, led to a further military intervention, on 28 June 1966, after a series of Perónist by-election victories. The new President, General Ongania, reverted to policies of devaluation, wage control, and cuts in public spending, and his harsh suppression of labour and student opposition led to serious confrontations and the outbreak of guerrilla activity. He was deposed by Brigadier General Levingston on 8 June 1970. With the military increasingly divided, and unable to cope with civil unrest, and with the mounting guerrilla campaigns, Levingston was himself replaced by General Lanusse in March 1971. Convinced that the military could no longer rule the country, Lanusse called elections for early 1973, and in those elections the representative of the Perónist Justicualist Party, Dr. Hector Campora, emerged triumphant. Events thereafter moved swiftly. Perón returned permanently to Argentina in June, and less than a month later Campora resigned, and called new elections, while Lastiri remained as Provisional President. On 23 September, Perón was elected to the presidency with a vote of 62 per cent, and with absolute majorities in both houses of Congress, and on 12 October he was sworn in as President with his wife, Maria Estela Perón, as Vice-President. Rapidly approaching eighty, and in poor and failing health, Perón was no longer able to govern with vigour, or to control the widely disparate elements backing him. He suffered a heart attack on 29 June 1974, and after handing the Presidency on to his wife, he died on 1 July. Without political experience, and relying heavily on a close circle of personal advisers, Sra. Perón rapidly lost control of the political and economic situation. In early 1975 she gave wide-ranging responsibility to Lopez Rega, but was forced to dismiss him in July. When the new Economics Minister Celestino Rodrigo refused to grant a promised wage rise, a major crisis broke out. Sra. Perón departed briefly from office in September and October 1975, but returned amid rumours of an impending military coup. As inflation approached and passed 600 per cent per annum, and Sra. Perón's political support evaporated, the military reluctantly intervened, with General Jorge Videla taking power on 24 March 1976. Videla's attempts to follow a moderate line were undermined by guerrilla activity by the ERP (People's Revolutionary Army) and the Montoneros (although this abated significantly after a series of successes by the security forces, culminating in the death of ERP leader Roberto Santucho in July 1976), by the constant assassinations by right-wing terrorist groups (particularly the Argentinian Anti-Communist Alliance and the Liberation of America Commando), and by the hostility aroused by the very harsh economic measures taken to eliminate the balance of payments deficit and reduce inflation. By the end of 1976, Videla was faced with growing pressure from the right wing within the army, increasing combattiveness from the once dominant trade unions, and continuing inflationary pressure. Measures were taken in January 1977 to control the labour unions, but there was little reason to believe that Argentina was at last emerging from the troubles of previous years.

BRAZIL.

Since 1964 Brazil has been governed by a series of military Presidents, and civilian political activity has been severely limited. Attempts by successive Presidents to liberalise the regime, whether sincerely intended or not, have so far failed, despite the considerable economic growth that has been achieved particularly since 1967; with the rapid growth rate now faltering, and a number of weaknesses becoming apparent in the "Brazilian economic model", the prospects for a return to any form of civilian government in the near future must be slight.

The military seized power with remarkable ease in April 1964, closing a period of civilian rule which had lasted practically uninterrupted for seventy years, and a period of nearly twenty years of democratic politics. The ease with which the military established themselves in power owed much to the disarray of civilian politics, and the weakness of the Goulart regime, for Goulart's attempt to mobilise the masses in his favour upset not only his traditional opponents, but the more conservative members of his own fragile coalition. Once in power, Marshal Castelo Branco attempted to construct a stable regime with a degree of democratic accountability, but found himself caught between a vociferous "hard-line" sector in the armed forces and among civilian politicians, demanding wide-ranging repression of dissidents and the total destruction of the previous political system, and a shifting coalition of leading politicians seeking to capitalise on the discontent created by harshly deflationary economic policies by seeking more popular measures, and guarantees that the traditional electoral system would be respected. The harsh economic policies which Castelo Branco felt were necessary to solve the crisis inherited from previous regimes led to three years of recession and falling wages, and to a massive inflow of foreign capital into Brazil on favourable terms. The lack of popularity of the regime made electoral success improbable, and the hardliners insisted that political rights be withdrawn from an increasing number of politicians. After the gubernatorial elections of 1965, seen as a defeat for the government, all existing political parties were dissolved, and in their place ARENA, the government party, and MDB the "official" opposition party, were created by decree; state governors and the President were to be elected indirectly. While the Chamber of Deputies and the Senate continued to function, their role in government was practically eliminated. The dominance of the hard-line faction was confirmed by the succession to the presidency in 1967 of Marshal Arturo Costa e Silva, Castelo Branco's Minister of War, and while his presidency saw a shift in economic policy and the start of the "boom", the political situation deteriorated steadily. In July 1967 former Presidents Goulart and Kubitschek joined dissident rightist Carlos Lacerda (former governor of Guanabara state, and an enthusiastic supporter of the 1964 coup) in an opposition Broad Front, which was banned in April 1968. Increasing problems with a weakened but hostile Congress led to its suspension in December 1968. Costa e Silva suffered a stroke in

August 1969, and the military hierarchy, bypassing the civilian vice-President, installed a triumvirate which gave way in October to General Garrastazu Médici. Carefully controlled elections in 1970 created a new Congress, with ARENA winning substantial majorities in both houses, and claiming 21 of 22 governorships (with governors nominated by Médici, and "elected" by state assemblies). However, the declining economic situation, particularly after the spectacular increases in the price of oil, led to increasing opposition, and the MDB began to gain popularity. When General Ernesto Geisel, who succeeded Médici in 1974, allowed elections to take place with a greater degree of freedom, ARENA suffered considerable setbacks, and the project of liberalisation was halted. By 1976 inflation was mounting, the promises that wages would be allowed to rise substantially were brusquely withdrawn. Nationalist sectors within the army were annoyed by the opening of oil-fields to foreign companies; lack of finance threatened important development projects in steel and hydro-electric power, and the gains in export earnings due to significant diversification in the production of basic commodities, and the steady expansion of manufactured exports, were increasingly outstripped by the increased cost of oil and capital goods imports, and the growing burden of foreign debt, which by 1977 was absorbing an estimated 50 per cent of Brazil's export earnings. By early 1977 conflicts within the government led to the resignation of Trade and Industry Minister Severo Gomes, and pressure from industrialists for more open government and an expansion of the severely restricted domestic economy; meanwhile pressure was building up for further modifications to the already practically emasculated political system, as the question of the presidential succession in 1978 became a matter of public debate.

CHILE.

The trend towards military rule, and from constitutional government to dictatorship has been nowhere more marked and more tragic than in Chile; the Junta which seized power so bloodily in September 1973 still held power in 1977, but showed no sign of restoring the liberties it had destroyed when it came to power.

As long ago as 1958 Allende, the leader of the Chilean Socialist Party, narrowly failed to defeat the Conservative candidate, Jorge Alessandri in the Presidential elections; the subsequent rapid rise of the Christian Democrat Party, led by Eduardo Frei (and heavily backed by the CIA and American State Department) changed the face of Chilean politics. When the Conservative alliance collapsed in 1964, Frei was elected to the Presidency, and his young party gained control of Congress. Proclaiming a "revolution in liberty", Frei however failed to push his ambitious reform programme through, and popular disenchantment led to rapidly declining support for his government, and to serious splits within the party, with a sector pledging alliance to the leftist opposition. In elections of historic importance in 1970, Socialist leader Allende, the candidate of the Popular Unity coalition (Unidad Popular) won a narrow victory over Alessandri in a bitterly contested three-way fight. Conspiratorial attempts to prevent his taking office, organised by conservative forces within Chile and within the Chilean military, and backed by the CIA, the United States Ambassador in Santiago, Korry, the ITT organisation (which stood to lose considerable holdings in Chile if planned nationalisation programmes went ahead), and by President Nixon himself, led to the assassination of Army Commander-in-Chief General Schneider, but failed to prevent Christian Democrats in Congress voting with Popular Unity representatives to vote Allende into the Presidency on 4 November 1970, in accordance with the constitutional requirement that the President be elected by Congress if no candidate receives more than half the vote in the national elections. Throughout 1971 Allende enjoyed considerable popularity as he moved ahead with a land reform programme, the nationalisation of the US-owned copper companies, and of strategic sectors of the Chilean economy, and an expansionist economic programme based on rapidly growing real wages. But despite these apparent successes, several major problems were unresolved. Deep divisions within Allende's coalition were carried over into administration and government, popular initiatives consistently outran the willingness or capacity of the government to respond, foreign hostility exacerbated problems of finance and the supply of imports and highlighted the dependence of the Chilean economy on external sources; most seriously, Allende's commitment to a "peaceful road to Socialism", combined with his inability to command a majority in Congress, and thus to enact legislation, led remorselessly to a position of stalemate and growing frustration. By 1972 growth was faltering and inflation soaring; a wave of strikes, co-ordinated by the opposition, late in 1972, led to the introduction of representatives of the armed forces into the cabinet. In March 1973, the Popular Unity coalition gained 44 per cent of the vote in the Congressional elections, but plans for the violent overthrow of the government were already underway. A failed coup in June was followed by an increasingly violent campaign of sedition and sabotage, and a further co-ordinated wave of strikes, particularly in the crucial transport sector; the Commander-in-Chief of the Armed Forces, General Prats, was forced to resign, and on 11 September 1973, the new High Command moved to overthrow Allende. He himself died besieged in the bombed Presidential Palace, and a military Junta took power, headed by General Augusto Pinochet. It is now officially recognised that thousands of Chileans died in the aftermath of the coup; many thousands more have passed through the hands of the security forces, with hundreds dying as a result of summary executions or prolonged torture. While an international campaign has drawn attention to the horrific human rights record of the Junta, the implacable pursuit of an orthodox monetarist policy has had only relative success in slowing inflation (still nearly 200 per cent in 1976), while inflicting irreparable damage on the economy. The depression was at its worst in 1975, with the GNP falling by a staggering 15 per cent; real wages have been drastically cut, investment has slumped, and unemployment reached 20 per cent during 1976. Agricultural production has steadily declined, although falling domestic consumption has made some exports possible. Early 1977 saw the beginning of an acute financial crisis, as the high cost of borrowing and the desperate need for credit combined to provoke a series of bankruptcies among financial institutions. Prospects for economic recovery seemed poor, but despite regular forecasts that he would be deposed, Pinochet continued to cling to power.

COLOMBIA.

Colombia's history of violence and instability notwithstanding, it has enjoyed until recently a brief period of relatively orderly if somewhat fragile civilian government, resulting from the Liberal–Conservative National Front coalition formed in 1958. Threatened from the start by slender electoral majorities, intra-party factionalism, and the activity of left-wing guerrilla movements, as well as by the intransigence of traditional conservatives, the coalition has nevertheless managed to elect Liberal President Alberto Lleras Camargo in 1958 Conservative Guillermo Leon Valencia in 1962, Liberal Carlos Lleras Restrepo in 1966, Conservative Dr. Misael Pastrana Borrero in 1970 and Liberal Alfonso Lopez Michelson in 1974.

The narrow victory of Dr. Pastrana over ANAPO (the National Popular Front) led by ex-dictator turned populist General Rojas Pinilla (1953–7) in 1970 provoked widespread protest and disorder, while in concurrent Congressional elections the coalition National Front lost its majority, dropping 53 of its 142 seats to the opposition groups. The army, brought back to prominence by its long campaigns against guerrillas, began to play an increasingly important role, particularly in the breaking of the general strike called in early 1971 to protest against rising unemployment. By May there were serious splits in both Conservative and Liberal parties, and in June Pastrana dismissed his cabinet, forming another from the right of each party. The atmosphere remained tense throughout the year, with troops occupying the National University in September. However, as the economy recovered from the mild recession of 1971 the political situation also eased, and in April 1972 the National Front emerged with considerable success from departmental and municipal elections. The coalition was able to approach the 1974 elections with some confidence; they turned out to be a particular triumph for the Liberals, for with Alfonso López Michelson assuming the Presidency, his party achieved considerable majorities in the Senate and Chamber of Deputies. Cabinet posts were then shared between Liberal and Conservative politicians. However, despite the advantages accruing from an increasingly successful diversification into non-traditional exports, and from the rapid rise in the price of coffee (Colombia's major export) after the 1975 frost destroyed trees in Brazil, the political situation remained difficult through 1975 and 1976. A bank strike in early 1975 was followed by considerable disturbances in the National University, particularly in the Medical Faculty; these led to a doctors' strike in May, and to the dismissal of the radical Rector of the National University, Luis Carlos Pérez. A state of siege was declared on 6 June 1975. With Congressional and Municipal elections due to take place in April 1976, Lopez Michelson planned to discontinue the state of siege by the beginning of the year, but in the event splits in his own party over the choice of a candidate for the 1978 elections for the Presidency combined with a scandal within the military arising from the conducting of a trial after the assassination of a senior General, and a wave of strikes and civil unrest, made this inadvisable. As the elections approached, public servants, bank workers, and teachers were again on strike, and the military occupation of the University in March was followed by a number of student deaths, while the dismissed Rector, Luis Carlos Pérez, emerged as the leftist candidate for 1978. The April elections were a defeat for the system as a whole, as only 25 per cent of those eligible to vote actually did so, and for Alfonso López Michelson himself, for while the Liberal Party as a whole gained 50 per cent of the vote (to 40 per cent by the Conservatives), both López Michelson's faction within the party, and that of former President Lleras Restrepo, lost out to the "Group of Ninety" of Julio Cesar Turbay, the Colombian Ambassador in Washington, who had dominated the January convention of the Liberal Party. However, the state of siege was lifted on 22 June; in August and September medical workers were again on strike, and the dispute was not settled until 27 October, by which time a state of siege had again been declared, Labour Minister Maria Elena de Crovo had resigned, the cabinet had been reorganised, and the University had again been closed. It remains to be seen whether Colombia's recent economic prosperity will be translated into political peace.

CUBA.

Cuba, since the coming to power of Fidel Castro in the 1959 revolution, has caught the headlines when its impact on international politics has been most marked—with the Bay of Pigs invasion, the Missile Crisis, Che Guevara's disappearance from Cuba in 1965, his subsequent Bolivian campaign and his death at the hands of the Bolivian military, and, more recently, with the sending of Cuban troops to aid the MPLA in Angola; but in the meantime, significant developments have taken place within Cuba itself. While Cuba has moved firmly into the Socialist camp, there are indications that the relaxations in its isolation from the West may proceed further; meanwhile, however, despite ambitious plans for diversification, and despite considerable achievements in social policy, it remains heavily dependent on the production of sugar as its major export crop.

Cuba's alignment with the Soviet bloc was complete by the early sixties, although Castro continued to insist on supporting Latin-American guerrilla movements not supported by orthodox Communist parties in the region; in 1965 the PURS (United Party of the Socialist Revolution), created in 1962, was renamed the Cuban Communist Party. During the same period, economic dependence on the USSR was enforced by the US blockade, and by the 1962 expulsion of Cuba from the Organisation of American States (OAS). The achievements of the revolution in health, education and housing are no longer a matter for dispute; and while some food rationing continues, starvation and abject poverty have disappeared. However, ambitious plans for vast programmes of public spending and social welfare have forced reliance on sugar to earn foreign exchange or trade goods from Russia, and after early denigrations of sugar, increasing efforts have been made to boost production. The policy of concentration of resources on the production of sugar reached its peak in 1970, with the promotion of a national campaign to produce a harvest of ten million tons—over three million tons more than had ever been produced before during the revolutionary period—when it was by no means clear that the international market could absorb such quantities. The scheme called for vast investments, and the massive deployment of labour, which was withdrawn from other productive areas. Despite this, the target was not reached, and although the harvest—possibly over eight million tons—was the highest ever recorded, the damage to other sectors of the economy was considerable. In the wake of the crisis, the USSR was able to demand a fuller implementation of Soviet-aided central planning, and one result of this was the modification of earlier schemes of "moral incentives" and ruthlessly egalitarian wage structures, and their replacement by a system of material incentives for increases in labour productivity. Helped by these moves, by the rising price of sugar on world markets, and by a 1972 agreement that debts to the Soviet Union would be paid off only after 1986, the Cuban economy recovered well, recording a small trade surplus in 1974, and attracting a number of foreign loans in 1975. However, the rapid decline in the world price of sugar to extremely low levels by 1977, with little immediate prospect for improvement as substantial surpluses were still being produced, threatened steady growth once more, and caused a cutback in investment planned for the 1976–80 period.

During recent years, Cuba has moved towards the development of a system of popular government within a constitutional framework, though always in the context of a single party state. In 1973, a new system of local courts was set up with lay judges acting with legal guidance, and in 1974 an experiment in "popular power" took place in Matanzas province, with the election in June and July of a 68-member provincial assembly. The experiment was declared a success, and in 1975 a draft constitution was produced for discussion at local level. On 17 December 1975, 3,000 delegates gathered for the First Congress of the Cuban Communist Party, and heard Castro describe in detail various CIA plots to assassinate him, then announce that the new constitution would be submitted to a national plebiscite. It was thus tested in February 1976, and went into effect on the 24th of that month. In October 1976 indirect elections took place to provincial and national assemblies, as a prelude to the election of a council of state.

There were suggestions that the Carter administration would seek a rapprochement with Cuba, following up US acceptance of the 1975 OAS decision to leave the question of relations with Cuba to individual states to decide, as many Latin American states had already resumed relations despite the 1962 ban. But while Cuban troops remained in Angola there seemed no question of a settlement; there remains a substantial lobby in Congress opposed to any change in relations.

MEXICO.

Mexico has for many years enjoyed a reputation for political stability and steady economic growth, and if the first of these seemed under threat when Luis Echeverria Alvarez inherited the presidency in 1970, the second seemed more in danger when he left it in 1976. However, the changes introduced by his successor, together with the huge oil deposits revealed early in 1977, may ensure the stability and prosperity of the Institutional Revolutionary Party (PRI) and of the country for the foreseeable future.

Echeverria came to the Presidency in 1970 in difficult circumstances, in the wake of the student massacre which preceded the 1968 Olympic Games, held in Mexico; he himself, as Minister of the Interior in the Diaz Ordaz government (1964–

1970) had been partially responsible for the incident, and had to face considerable initial hostility, despite his being elected with 84 per cent of the popular vote. The complete dominance of the PRI itself was confirmed, with all sixty seats in the Senate, and practically ninety per cent of all seats in the Chamber of Deputies. In the first years of his administration however Echeverria presided over a period of rapid economic expansion, and inaugurated a political style marked by conciliation, liberalisation, and radical rhetoric. Countering the steady trend to the right of the PRI in the latter sixties, Echeverria gained considerable support. However, he antagonised the strong and conservative group of industrialists based on Monterrey, and failed to convince the student left of his sincerity in proposing reform. The price of his ambitious programme was a growing balance of payments deficit, and rates of inflation which while low by Latin American and even by recent British standards, were unusual in Mexico. 1972 saw a reform aimed at strengthening the small opposition parties in Mexico, by granting them a sliding quota of seats in the Chamber of Deputies if they obtained nationally a minimum share of the vote, and in 1973 Echeverria turned his attention to the international arena, promoting his "Third World" manifesto, the "Charter of Economic Rights and Duties of States", engaging in prolonged overseas tours, and, on 31 May, calling jointly with the President of Guatemala for a "New Economic Order" to protect the legitimate interests of the Third World bloc. Meanwhile the domestic economy was suffering, shaken both by US inflation after the oil price rise and by the demands of Echeverria's expansionist programme, which called for heavy state investment. Inflation in 1973 reached 18 per cent, and it was argued that the Mexican peso (unchanged at 12·5 to the dollar since 1954) was over-valued, and that exports were suffering as a result. Echeverria was confronted with a dual problem in the closing years of his administration – a deteriorating economic situation, and growing hostility from conservatives to his increasingly radical pronouncements and his statist policies.

Despite the problems, the PRI had no difficulty in choosing its candidate for the 1976 elections, or in winning them handsomely, and the surprise choice, Treasury Secretary José López Portillo, a man with little organised political support, but a close and long-standing friend of Echeverria himself, was duly elected on 4 July to take office on 1 December 1976. In the event, his was the only name on the ballot, as the largest opposition party, the National Action Party (PAN), failed to agree on a candidate.

The economic situation was, however, rapidly becoming more critical. In the wake of a Mexican vote in the United Nations equating Zionism with racism, Jewish associations in the United States declared a boycott on tourism in Mexico, and although it was short-lived, Mexico's income from tourism began to fall. A growing trade deficit, and heavy speculation against the peso, provoked what was at the time an unexpectedly early devaluation in August 1976. The political costs of devaluation are such that there was some doubt whether Echeverria would take the decision upon himself, or whether he would leave it to his successor. By the time López Portillo took power, the peso had lost more than half its international value. Echeverria's parting gesture was to hand over to landless peasants 100.000 hectares of prime agricultural land in Northern Mexico. However, López Portillo came to office proclaiming that he would look more to the interests of private enterprise, and in the same month a federal court ruled that the land transfer was illegal. The peso made a slight recovery, but it remained to be seen whether Mexico could emerge from its pressing economic problems, or whether López Portillo could handle the political problems with which he had been presented. The first signs were that he was winning from the conservative labour unions some support for his policies.

PERU.

Until 1975 it seemed that the military regime which seized power in Peru in 1968 might be, in contrast to the regimes in power in 1975 in Argentina, Bolivia, Brazil, Chile and Uruguay, a genuinely progressive and reforming force; these hopes were somewhat dashed by the replacement in 1975 of President Velasco by Morales Bermúdez, and by an economic crisis which forced harsh policies in 1976. While many of the reforms of the revolutionary period, including the major nationalisations and the programme of land reform, remained largely untouched, it appeared at the beginning of 1977 that the Government might be embarking on a policy of open repression.

The military intervention of October 1968 came after a troubled period in which the reforms promised by civilian President Fernando Belaúnde were soon blocked by a hostile Congress; as the economic situation worsened, the Government coalition (formed by the Popular Action Party and the Christian Democrats) collapsed in 1967. A substantial and unpopular devaluation in the same year was followed by the announcement late in 1968 of an agreement with the International Petroleum Company over ownership of disputed deposits and the pricing of crude oil; this provoked nationalists within the military, already dissatisfied with Belaúnde's inability to achieve reforms, to remove him from power and send him into exile. The government of General Juan Velasco immediately repudiated the agreements, and expropriated the IPC oil interests, then embarked on an ambitious programme of social and economic reform. The Government went on to establish state control over fishmeal, fish oil and minerals, and to set limits to the role foreign capital could play in Peru; it also developed a scheme of workers' participation in industry based on the concept of "industrial communities", which were intended, over a period of years, to transfer the ownership of the enterprise to the workers themselves. It also set up SINAMOS (Office for Social Mobilisation), under General Leonidas Rodriguez, to organise and rally political support for the regime. By 1971 foreign oil companies were allowed into Peru again, and pressing debt problems led to attempts, unsuccessful until 1972, to obtain from major creditors a rescheduling agreement. Despite these problems, and the ecological crisis which caused, in 1972 and 1973, the practical disappearance of the rich anchovy shoals on which the lucrative and expanding fishmeal industry depends, Velasco moved ahead with his programme of reforms, nationalising the fishmeal and fish oil industries in 1973, placing newspapers under government control in 1974, and nationalising the American Cerro de Pasco mining company at the end of that year. 1975 opened with the announcement that the agrarian reform programme, which had already placed the rich coastal sugar plantations under co-operative ownership, was to be extended; but a police strike, and possible coup attempt in February, followed by riots and widespread unrest, led to the declaration of a state of emergency. It came, however, as a surprise when Velasco, admittedly already seriously ill at the time, was replaced in a bloodless coup on 29 August 1975 by Prime Minister Morales Bermúdez, and despite initial claims that the continuity of the revolution was assured, it gradually became clear that a substantial shift to the right was taking place, and that *velasquistas* were being removed from positions of influence, although the retirement of Prime Minister General Oscar Vargas Prieto in February 1976 was followed by the elevation to the post of the leading pro-Velasco progressive left in the Cabinet, General Jorge Fernández Maldonado. An apparent attempt to seize power from the right by General Briceño on 13 February was foiled, but at the same time Morales Bermúdez was moving to strengthen private enterprise, to impose a programme of austerity in the face of threatened international insolvency, and to tempt back national and foreign investment. On 31 March, he announced that the Peruvian revolution had entered a "second phase" of consolidation; he offered an amnesty to former dissidents, but his attempt at rapprochement with the conservative forces of APRA (American Popular Revolutionary Alliance) was blocked by sectors of the army still hostile to their traditional opponents. By May it was apparent that the financial crisis was acute, and that Peru's only recourse was to seek an accomodation with her creditors on the terms available. On 28 June the sol was devalued by 31 per cent, and on 1 July a national state of emergency was declared. A further attempt at a coup from the right (this time by General Bobbio) was also foiled, but was followed on 16 July by the resignation of Prime Minister Fernández Maldonado; this signified the elimination of the *velasquistas* from positions of major influence. He was replaced as Prime Minister, War Minister and Commander-in-Chief of the Army by General Guillermo Arbulu Galliani. In November 1976 the announcement of the formation of a Socialist Revolutionary Party by Velasco supporters was announced; but in January 1977 founders of the party, including General Leonidas Rodriguez, were exiled.

URUGUAY.

After a long history of democracy, prosperity, and advanced social welfare, Uruguay has become the victim of one of the most repressive and totalitarian regimes in Latin America, with its essentially pastoral economy in a state of extreme crisis.

The process of militarisation is relatively recent; total domination of the Government by the Colorado (Liberal) party only ended in 1958, when the Blanco (National) party, led by Luis Alberto de Herrera, came to power. It held power narrowly in the 1962 elections, but 1966 saw the return of the Colorados, and the reintroduction of the Presidential system, which had been abandoned in 1951 for a National Council of Government. General Oscar Gestido embarked on a five-year term of office in 1967, but died on 6 December of the same year, and was replaced by Vice-President Jorge Pacheco Areco. He sought throughout his term of office to retain the presidency beyond 1971, but a referendum conducted simultaneously with the November 1971 elections failed to win popular acceptance for the idea; he had been involved throughout 1971 in attempts to gain special powers, largely to deal with the challenge presented by the Tupamaros, the urban guerrilla movement which had scored a number of spectacular successes in 1970 and 1971, culminating in the mass escape from Punta Carretas prison of 109 detainees, including the guerrilla leader Raúl Sendic himself. Pacheco's attempt to extend his own powers were blocked by Congress, and he narrowly escaped being impeached and removed from office. The November 1971 elections saw the emergence as President of the Colorado candidate, Juan Maria Bordaberry, confirmed by the Supreme Court in February 1972 and installed on 1 March. His first act in office was to order a massive devaluation of the currency, causing considerable discontent among the urban population. As Bordaberry sought to co-ordinate army and police activity to contain the threat from the Tupamaros (and succeeded in destroying the guerrilla group almost completely) the army began to play a more prominent role. In February 1973 the Army itself demanded an officially recognised role in government, and the National Security Council was formed, despite opposition from Congress and from the traditional political parties. Increasing tension between Congress and the military led to demands from the military that immunity should be lifted from two Senators accused of contacts with the guerrilla movement. On 27 June 1973, with the support of the army, Bordaberry dissolved Congress, declared a state of emergency, and continued to govern by decree and increasingly as a representative of the Armed Forces. On 29 October, the National University was closed. An atmosphere of increasing repression was made more difficult by rapid inflation throughout 1974, reaching over 100 per cent by the end of the year, while EEC regulations suspending imports of beef from outside the community threatened Uruguay's beef industry with disaster. Opposition grew throughout 1975, and detention and torture by the omnipresent security forces became more common; in November, these forces began a massive operation against suspected Communists, in which dozens of army officers were arrested, and as many again sought refuge in foreign embassies. On 28 November 1975 plans for elections were dropped and Bordaberry sought support from the army for his continuance in power beyond his constitutional term. Despite pressures from the marginalised political parties and from the United States Embassy for a return to a limited form of constitutionalism, perhaps along the lines of the Brazilian "two-party" system, the Army Commander-in-Chief announced on 18 May 1976 that Bordaberry would remain in the Presidency. However, in a remarkable *volte face*, the armed forces withdrew their support from Bordaberry a month later, and he was forced to resign. He was temporarily replaced by the 79-year-old head of the Council of State, Alberto Demichelli. On 14 July 1976, Dr. Aparicio Mendez, who had replaced Demichelli as the head of the Council of State, and was himself 71 years old, was chosen to succeed to the Presidency; he duly took office on 1 September. His first acts were to withdraw political rights from hundreds of Uruguayan citizens, and to dissolve the Supreme Court, announcing that its functions would henceforth be carried out by the Ministry of Justice. Subsequently the pro-US Minister of the Economy, Vegh Villegas, was forced to resign.

At the end of the year the United States Congress, annoyed at the course taken by the Uruguayan armed forces, voted to cut off military aid to Uruguay, and in February 1977 the Secretary of State of the new Carter administration, Cyrus Vance, told a Senate Committee that foreign aid to Uruguay had been cut by President Carter because of Uruguay's record of persistent human rights violations. With 3 million dollars of military credits already cut off, economic assistance to Uruguay fell from 220,000 to 25,000 dollars. It seems over-optimistic, however, to believe that Uruguay will enjoy democratic government again in the near future.

VENEZUELA.

The sub-continental trend towards military dictatorship has been reversed in Venezuela, which has been ruled by constitutionally elected civilian Presidents since the elections of 1959, which followed the overthrow in 1958 of the dictator Marcos Pérez Jiménez. Since then, Venezuela's increasing oil wealth has brought it considerable prosperity, and a surge of industrial development.

Two parties have dominated recent Venezuelan politics. The first is the Democratic Action party (AD) which maintains a nationalistic stance but has moved steadily to the centre right after its founding as a radical alternative in 1941; the second is the Social Christian Party (COPEI) founded in 1946 to promote reformist policies favoured by currents within the Catholic Church. It is essentially a Christian Democrat party. Each of the parties has been dominated since its foundation by one man – the Democratic Action party by Romulo Betancourt, COPEI by Dr. Rafael Caldera.

During the first years of constitutional government, Venezuela was governed by coalitions. The winner of the 1959 Presidential elections, Romulo Betancourt, formed a coalition with COPEI, but his successor, Dr. Raúl Leoni, also of AD, when he came to power in 1964, governed in coalition not with COPEI, but with two smaller parties, the URD (Democratic and Republican Union Party), and the FND (National Democratic Front). In December 1968 the elections were won by Dr. Rafael Caldera, but although COPEI gained the Presidency, it had only a minority in Congress, and formed a working coalition with AD. Caldera attempted to put a stop to guerrilla activity which had been spreading through the country particularly after the Cuban Revolution; he legalised the Communist Party, and invited dissidents to express their views through the system, but was unsuccessful in achieving an end to guerrilla activity. The run of coalitions was ended by the spectacular success of AD in the elections of December 1973; its candidate, Carlos Andrés Pérez, won the Presidency with practically 50 per cent of the vote, and the party won commanding majorities in Congress, with 183 seats in the Chamber of Deputies, and 42 in the Senate.

Oil has sustained and developed Venezuela's economy throughout most of the twentieth century (the first discoveries were made in 1922). During recent years, the position of the Venezuelan government has been increasingly nationalistic. Venezuela was one of the founder members of OPEC, which was formed in January 1961 in the Venezuelan capital, Caracas, and measures were taken during the sixties to boost Venezuela's income from the operation of foreign-owned oil companies operating in Venezuela. The 1970 OPEC conference held in Caracas in December 1970 enforced a minimum tax level of 55 per cent, and Venezuela raised its own tax levels from 52 to 60 per cent. A year later the state assumed a monopoly of sales of oil products within Venezuela, and the Oil Reversion Bill stipulated that all installations would be nationalised when existing contracts ran out in 1983. With the growing strength of OPEC, and the spectacular rise in the price of crude oil, stronger policies were however adopted; on 16 April 1974 the Government announced its intention of nationalising the industry in the near future, and on 29 August 1975, the year in which iron ore deposits and mining operations were also nationalised, a decree was published declaring that all installations and oil-fields would become the property of the state on 1 January 1976. Over the same period, the increasingly nationalistic stance of the Government was shown in the growing international prominence of President Pérez as a spokesman for the interests of the Third World. Nationalisation went ahead smoothly as planned, with the new state corporation, Petroven, headed by retired General Rafael Alonzo Rimard. This maintained production at over 2 million barrels per day, exporting an average of 2·15 million barrels per day; of 8·84 billion dollars earned from sales, nearly 7 billion accrued directly to the state treasury. Venezuela has proven reserves of 18 billion barrels, and enormous reserves of heavy crude oils in the Orinoco region, although these are not immediately commercially viable.

Venezuela has recently abandoned its cautious policy of spending only from its own reserves, and announced plans early in 1976 to invest 14 billion dollars by 1978; this will require considerable borrowing on international markets, but there is unlikely to be any major problem in attracting loans.

Early in 1977 it was reported in the United States that in the past the CIA had made considerable personal payments to President Pérez, but such reports were unanimously denounced in Venezuela as an attempt to besmirch his considerable reputation as a nationalist, and to damage a leading opponent of United States policy.

AUSTRALIA AND NEW ZEALAND

In the sixties, the Liberal–Country coalition in Australia and the National Party in New Zealand were able to consolidate and extend their power at the expense of the Labour Party in each country. During 1968 and 1969 Labour opposition to participation in the Vietnam war increased in strength; this feeling combined with new leadership within each Labour party and, in Australia in particular, a feeling that the ruling party had "lost its steam." But in the 1969 elections the ruling parties just maintained their leads.

With Britain joining the European Community, both Australia and New Zealand sought closer relations with their neighbours. New Zealand began a search for new markets for her agricultural products, especially in Japan and Latin America. Australia made an agreement with Japan on the peaceful use of atomic energy and one with Indonesia on the provision of defence and economic aid. Both countries have established diplomatic relations with China. On 1 November 1972 Mr. McMahon announced that the Australian High Commission in Britain would no longer be the responsibility of the Prime Minister's office but of the Foreign Office. This announcement came a day after publication of the new immigration regulations in Britain as a consequence of EEC entry: Australia pointed out that EEC citizens would now have easier entry to Britain than citizens of Commonwealth countries.

Elections in 1972 brought the long expected victories of the Labour Parties, under Mr. Gough Whitlam in Australia (who thus became the first Labour Prime Minister since 1949), and Mr. Kirk in New Zealand (succeeded by Mr. Rowling in 1974). Apart from a vote for new faces these victories perhaps contained some nationalist elements: old alliances were no longer found so useful. Both victors promised the end of conscription. Mr. Whitlam's government was returned with a reduced majority in 1974.

Both countries were foremost in the world-wide protests at the French nuclear tests carried out in the atmosphere on Mururoa Atoll in the South Pacific during the summer of 1973. Only after France announced in 1974 that in future tests would only be carried out underground did relations improve.

The greater participation in Asian affairs appears slowly to be moderating Australia's traditional immigration policies. Since 1945 some three million people have settled in the country of which almost half have had assisted passages. Over half have come from Britain and more than 100,000 from each of Italy, Greece, the Netherlands, and Germany. But more than 50,000 have been admitted from Asian and African countries including 16,000 Chinese and Japanese. From 1973 non-white racial characteristics no longer constitute an obstacle to immigration though in general immigration is permitted only for those with relations in Australia and for skilled workers. As from January 1975 white citizens of Britain, Ireland, Canada and Fiji require visas before visiting or settling in Australia, thus ending long-standing preferential treatment. (New Zealand had also introduced restrictions on British and Irish immigrants.)

During 1975 the opposition Liberal–Country majority in the Australian Senate blocked approval of the budget for months, thus condemning the Whitlam government to impotence. The deadlock was eventually broken by a very controversial decision of the Governor to dismiss the Prime Minister. The constitutional conflict which thus flared up, added to economic problems and dissension about the Government's socialist measures, poisoned the atmosphere of the ensuing election campaign. The election in December 1975 was won by the conservative opposition led by Mr. Malcolm Fraser. The Liberal–Country coalition won their largest majority in Australian political history. A new inner cabinet was created and to deal with economic problems a new Department of Productivity was established in November 1976 taking over the functions of other departments. A similar trend was experienced in New Zealand with the decisive defeat of the Labour government by the Nationalist party led by Robert Muldoon.

During February and March 1977 the Queen and Prince Philip visited Australia and New Zealand on a Jubilee tour.

DÉTENTE

The Partial Nuclear Test-Ban Treaty.

This important treaty was signed in Moscow in August 1963 between Britain, the USA, and the USSR who undertook not to conduct nuclear tests in three out of four possible spheres—in the atmosphere, in outer space and under water. The fourth possibility—underground tests—was not touched by the Treaty (but see below). The USA and Britain insist that since no foolproof method of identifying underground explosions has been devised, a ban would require a limited number of on-the-spot inspections. But Russia rejects this on the grounds that it would amount to espionage.

Treaty to Prevent Spread of Nuclear Weapons.

At the 18-power Conference at Geneva in 1967 a draft treaty was tabled by the US and USSR, which was then amended to meet some of the demands of the non-nuclear powers. In the UN General Assembly it was adopted by 95 votes to 4, with 21 abstentions. One of the countries that voted against was India which was dissatisfied with the guarantees against China. The Nuclear Non-Proliferation Treaty was signed in London, Moscow, and Washington on 1 July 1968. It came into force on 5 March 1970. In May 1975 a conference was held in Geneva to review the treaty. A large majority of countries have ratified or at least signed it. But of existing nuclear powers China and France have not signed, in common with several countries which are thought to have nuclear potential, such as Israel, Pakistan, Saudi Arabia, Spain and some South American countries.

Seabed Treaty.

A treaty was signed in February 1971 by the three nuclear powers, Britain, the US, and Russia, and by 64 other countries, banning nuclear weapons from the seabed. France and China did not sign.

Biological Weapons Convention 1972.

A treaty outlawing biological warfare was signed on 10 April 1972 by Britain, the US and Russia, banning the future production and requiring the destruction of stockpiles of agents of biological warfare. It came into force in March 1975.

Nuclear Arms and SALT.

A desire to attempt control of the burgeoning strategic arms stockpiles of the two superpowers has been an urgent goal ever since the Cuban missile crisis when the horrific possibility of nuclear war was brought to the forefront of men's fears. In 1969, formal bilateral negotiations began in Helsinki between the United States and Soviet Union. These Strategic Arms Limitation Talks (SALT) culminated in 1972 when President Nixon visited Moscow and with Mr. Brezhnev signed two important documents. The first, the ABM Treaty, limited the number of anti-ballistic missile defence systems that the two countries could construct. A 1974 protocol has further limited each side to one system each, and the US has now abandoned the one it had defending an ICBM (intercontinental ballistic missile) field. The Soviet Union maintains one, early technology ABM system around Moscow. The two countries were motivated to achieve these agreements not only by the enormous cost of the systems themselves, but also by the further offensive developments they would provoke in an attempt to overcome their defensive capabilities.

The second part of SALT I was an interim agreement on limiting strategic offensive weapons, which expires in October 1977. The Soviets were allowed a numerical superiority which was offset by US technological superiority, especially in the area of MIRV's (multiple independently targetable re-entry vehicles), which allow as many as 12 targets to be attacked with one missile. At a meeting between Mr. Brezhnev and President Ford at Vladivostok in November 1974, an agreement was reached that a ceiling of 2400 strategic nuclear delivery vehicles should be the basis of a SALT II accord which would run until 1985, and would have to be reached before the interim agreement expired.

Progress has largely been stalled since that time for two reasons: technology and politics. One of the major difficulties in SALT is the inability of negotiators and politicians to keep up with technological developments. The current sticking point is the US development of the B-1 bomber and, more importantly, the cruise missile which is extremely accurate, cheap to build and small and therefore difficult to detect. On the Soviet side, the Backfire bomber worries US analysts.

The second obstacle was the US Presidential election campaign which in effect blocked progress throughout 1976. Despite adjournment of the March 1977 Moscow talks, both sides have given signals that they wish to move to an agreement before the October 1977 deadline.

WESTERN EUROPEAN ORGANISATIONS

The North Atlantic Treaty Organisation.

The founder members of the Pact in 1949 were Great Britain, the USA, Canada, France, Holland, Belgium, Luxembourg, Italy, Denmark, Norway, Iceland, and Portugal. The parties agreed that an armed attack against one or more of them in Europe or North America shall be considered an attack against them all and consequently they agreed that if such an armed attack occurs, each of them in exercise of the right of individual or collective self-defence recognised by the Charter of the UN, will assist the party so attacked. Greece and Turkey joined NATO in 1952. In 1966 France withdrew from NATO military organisations, though not from the Alliance.

The conflict over Cyprus between two of its members in 1974 was acutely embarrassing for NATO. Greece withdrew its armed forces from NATO in 1974, and during 1974–5 relations between the United States and Turkey deteriorated, particularly with the cutting off of US defence-aid and "nationalisation" of US bases in Turkey. NATO's south-eastern flank looked in considerable disarray.

With a gradual easing of tensions between Greece and Turkey over both the Aegean Sea and the Cyprus dispute, the situation improved, but still remains a crucial NATO problem.

The Search for Détente.

Force levels continue to be a major worry for the Alliance, whose conventional strength is so inferior to that of the Soviet bloc as to lead to a dangerous, and sometimes not very credible, reliance on nuclear weapons. Reductions of defence expenditure by Britain and other members create difficulties for NATO. There is also a wasteful reduplication of effort and resources and an impaired capacity for working together caused by the failure of the Alliance (unlike the Warsaw Pact) to co-ordinate arms production and procurement, since national interests predominate.

NATO policies continue to be based, sometimes rather uneasily, on the twin concepts of deterrence and détente. The latter aim prompted acceptance of a Conference on Security and Co-operation in Europe (CSCE), long campaigned for by the Soviet Union. NATO's preconditions for such a conference were met by the Berlin settlement and by the required progress in the talks between East and West Germany (*see* **C21**) and the SALT negotiations (*see* above). Above all the USSR agreed to parallel talks on mutual and balanced force reductions in Europe (MBFR), as frequently proposed by NATO (an urgent subject in view of the threats by some countries to reduce unilaterally their commitment to NATO).

The CSCE finally opened in Helsinki in July 1973 with 35 foreign ministers taking part (representing all the European countries except Albania, plus the USA and Canada). The agenda concluded by the preparatory consultations was grouped under four heads: (1) Questions relating to security in Europe; (2) Co-operation in the fields of science and technology and of the environment; (3) Co-operation in humanitarian and other fields (the result of the insistence of the West and the neutral countries on the inclusion of self-determination and human rights in the catalogue of principles); (4) Follow-up to the Conference. In October the MBFR talks began in Vienna between NATO and the Warsaw Pact states.

The stage thus seemed set for decisive steps on multilateral détente. But the momentum was halted in a mass of detail. At the CSCE the West demanded 60 days' notice for manoeuvres and sizeable troop movements; the USSR refused to look more than 5 days ahead or to talk about troop movements at all. Moscow tried to turn "inviolability" of borders into "unchangeability", and raised the old barriers against proposals for the free movement of persons and information. The third and final stage of the Conference ended in August 1975. The MBFR talks (like SALT II: see above) were held up by Soviet insistence on superiority. The East European countries consider the present power relations in Central Europe with 770,000 NATO ground troops facing 925,000 of the Warsaw Pact (excluding Hungary) as balanced already. Moscow wants to stabilise this ratio at a lower level and proposes a 17% reduction on both sides between 1975 and 1977. The West demands 700,000 on each side, amounting to a 20% reduction for the Warsaw Pact, 10% for NATO. By December 1975 the West had shown willingness to include a reduction of their tactical nuclear weapons and air force strengths in exchange for reduced Warsaw Pact tank contingents.

As with SALT, talks came to a standstill in 1976 due largely to the US Presidential elections. President Ford even dropped the word "détente" from his vocabulary.

The Council of Europe.

This body was formed in 1949 and now has 19 member nations. It has a Committee of Ministers and a Consultative Assembly. Headquarters are at Strasbourg. The Consultative Assembly is empowered to debate and make recommendations upon any matter which (i) is referred to it by the Committee of Ministers with a request for its opinion, or (ii) has been approved by the Committee. It consists of 147 members elected by their national parliaments, who sit grouped in political parties irrespective of their nationality. The Committee of Ministers is the Council's executive organ and is not responsible to the Assembly, but merely reports to it.

Future Role of the Council.—The Council remains in doubt about its future rôle, particularly now that Britain and the other candidates for Common Market entry have been admitted. Its condemnation of Greece in 1970 demonstrated that it has a claim to be the collective voice of European democratic opinion. (Greece had withdrawn when it became clear that a majority would vote for her suspension for repudiating the values which the Council exists to uphold. She was readmitted in 1974 after the return to democratic government.) But criticisms that it is no more than a talk shop and that the EEC and even NATO can better discharge many of the tasks it has attempted continue. It has a reasonably impressive record in encouragement of reciprocal social service arrangements, co-ordination of medical standards, harmonisation of law, and youth exchanges. It can also hope to act as a bridge between the EEC countries and the other members.

Meanwhile the most important achievements of the Council have been in the implementation of the Human Rights Convention under which the member states guarantee the recognition of fundamental rights within their territories.

The European Free Trade Association.

In November 1958 France rejected the British proposals for linking the six European common-market nations with the eleven other OEEC countries in a free-trade area.

Thereupon seven countries outside the area of the Six formed a European Free Trade Association. They were Great Britain, Austria, Denmark, Norway, Portugal, Sweden, and Switzerland. Between them tariffs on industrial goods were actually abolished faster than in the EEC, but member states retained separate external systems. The Seven were later joined by Finland as an associate member and Iceland as a full member. When EFTA was formed, its member nations confidently expected that the EEC would soon see the error of its ways and agree to the creation of a vast European free trade zone. In the event, EFTA members saw their error first, with three members of the original seven starting negotiations with the EEC in 1961. The same three once again began negotiations with the EEC in June 1970. In the event a national referendum in Norway decided against entry, but in joining the EEC Britain and Denmark left EFTA. However the others decided on maintaining co-operation in the EFTA framework, although they have all also concluded agreements with the EEC on the phased establishment of a free trade area.

Organisation for Economic Co-operation and Development.

This body took the place of OEEC in 1961. Canada and the United States, who were associated members of OEEC, joined with the eighteen member countries of that body to set it up. Its broader objectives were to achieve in Europe the highest sustainable economic growth, employment, and standard of living; to contribute to economic development; and to expand world trade on a multilateral and non-discriminatory basis. Japan has also joined. It has recently been concerned with co-ordinating the responses of the oil-consuming countries to the world energy situation (*see* **C31**) and in April 1975 it established a $25,000 million "safety net" fund for the mutual support of members in case of severe balance of payments difficulties arising from increased oil prices.

In January 1977 reports from the OECD warned of further energy crises for its members as a result of the continual growth in energy consumption.

The European Economic Community.

The EEC was formed in 1958, growing out of the European Coal and Steel Community, a supranational body set up in 1952 for the co-ordination of coal and steel production in West Germany, Belgium, Holland, Luxembourg, France, and Italy. The EEC is unquestionably the strongest and most significant of all European organisations and the only one which provides any sort of basis for West European unity. Other bodies, such as the Council of Europe and the European Free Trade Area (EFTA) as well as regional associations like the Nordic Council and the Benelux Economic Union now stand outside the mainstream of European political and economic development. Others still, like the Organisation for Economic Co-operation and Development, the successor to the Organisation for European Economic Co-operation (OEEC), have so expanded their terms of reference as to have ceased to be solely European organisations.

The Treaty of Rome, 1957, which had established the European Economic Community defined (in Articles 2 and 3) the principles and objects for which the Community is to work. Those articles specify in detail the steps for creating a Common Market, for approximating the economic policies of member States, the promotion of harmonious development of economic activities, and raising the standard of living. But the aim of "closer relations between its member States" is stated without elaboration. It is into this gap that speculation is poured. No limit is set in the Treaty to the process of integration; on the other hand there is no commitment to join a Federation of Europe. While member States commit themselves to a common policy on a number of economic issues there will be co-ordination of national policies designed to take account of the needs of the rest of the Community.

The Organs of EEC.

The machinery of government of the European Economic Community consists of:

1. The Council of Ministers
2. The Commission
3. The Court
4. The Parliament or Assembly

The Council of Ministers issues regulations and decisions which are binding in law on all member States. It consists of one minister from each member State. Although the treaties provide for many decisions to be taken by an ordinary or qualified majority (the latter protecting the interests of the smaller states), in practice almost all decisions require unanimity.

The Council represents national interests. "If federation is unity in diversity, the Commission represents the unity and the Council the diversity. The balancing of individual interests and Community interests is accomplished by discussions between these institutions, culminating in the meetings of the Council of Ministers" (the words of Walter Hallstein, former President of the European Community).

The Commission.—Whereas the Council consists of politicians the Commission consists of permanent officials. It has 13 members—2 each from Britain, France, Germany and Italy, one from each of the other countries. They are the custodians of the supranational idea and are pledged to complete independence from national control. The business of the Commission is to further the general purposes of the treaties of the Communities and decisions are by majority vote. From the Commission flow two streams:

(*a*) Proposals, which it sends to the Council.

(*b*) Under powers of its own:

1. Decisions to named countries and binding on them.

2. Directives to named countries to achieve certain results, without specifying the means.

3. Recommendations and Opinions, which are not binding.

4. Authorisations without which many things are forbidden.

The Court, whose procedure is wholly Continental, consists of nine Judges appointed by Governments for a maximum of six years. Its word is final on the interpretation of the Treaty, on the rules made under the Treaty, and on the legality of all the actions of the organs of the Community.

European Parliament.—The Parliament or Assembly consists of nominated representatives of the national Parliaments, sitting according to party affiliation and not nationality. There are at present 198 representatives in all—36 members each from Britain, France, Italy, and the German Federal Republic; 14 each from Belgium and the Netherlands; 10 from Ireland and Denmark; six from Luxembourg. The European Parliament has no legislative or executive powers, but it debates all major policy issues, scrutinises legislation and has recently been granted control over a limited part of the Community's budget. Its members may question the Council and Commission. It can, by a two-thirds majority, enforce the resignation of the entire Commission, but the power to reappoint lies with the Council of Ministers. Plans have recently been agreed for the doubling of members of the Parliament through direct elections in 1978. Disagreement persists on the method of direct suffrage and it is unlikely that the deadline will be met.

Expansion of the EEC.

After a summit meeting of the Six in the Hague in December 1969 had agreed on the principle of enlargement of the Communities, Britain opened negotiations in June 1970 on its third attempt to join the Common Market. The application had been made by the Labour Government, but it fell to the new Conservative Government actually to begin the talks. Denmark, Norway, and the Rep. of Ireland had applied at the same time.

Progress in the negotiations was laborious until the Paris summit conference between Mr. Heath and President Pompidou in May 1971, which opened the way for British entry to the European Community. The two men declared themselves in agreement on the future shape of the Community—loose confederation (*not* a federal structure), respect for national interests, and the special position of the French language—as well as on Europe's relationship with the outside world and especially with the United States always a crucial point for the French. They also agreed on the phasing out of the rôle of sterling as a reserve currency and on safeguarding the interests of New Zealand and the Commonwealth sugar producers. The misjudgements and bitterness of the British "No" to the Coal and Steel Community and the EEC and the French "Non" to British entry in 1963 and 1967 had now been exorcised. The communiqué emphasised that British entry was not only "desirable" but "possible."

However it was not until 23 June 1971 in Luxembourg that M. Schumann, the French Foreign Minister and Mr. Rippon, the chief British negotiator officially announced agreement on the detailed terms of entry. These were set out in a White Paper published on 7 July. They were largely concerned with transitional arrangements for Britain's adaptation to the rules of the Common Market. They were accompanied by the Government's enthusiastic recommendation of this acceptance. On 28 October the House of Commons voted in favour of the principle of entry on these terms with a majority of 112, the Lords with a majority of 393. Some details remained to be worked out. Of the eventual terms of accession, apart from provisions for the representation of new members on the various Community bodies and arrangements for Commonwealth countries, the most important elements were provisions for adaptation to the Common Agricultural Policy, for adjustment to the customs union, for implementing the free movement of capital, and for contributions to the Community budget. On these terms the Treaty of Accession was signed in Brussels on 22 January 1972.

Referenda in Ireland and Denmark ratified their accession, but in Norway the voters decided against joining. In Britain, according to tradition, Parliament's decision was final, but the European Communities Bill, bringing existing EEC legislation into effect in Britain, was passed only after a bitter struggle. Britain, Denmark and the Irish Republic finally became members on 1 January 1973.

The Community in Crisis.

The first anniversary of the enlargement of the EEC found it in a serious state of crisis. The selfish refusal by Britain and France of solidarity with the Dutch in the oil crisis (*see* **C30**(2)) was a shock to their partners. Both countries rushed off to make bilateral deals with oil-producing countries, leaving West Germany and others no choice but reluctantly to follow suit. This made a nonsense of the simultaneous solemn commitment of the heads of government of the Nine in Copenhagen to work out a common energy policy and a common approach to the oil producing countries.

The ambitious Paris summit conference of 1972 had also committed the EEC to a regional policy, including the establishment of a Regional Development Fund by the end of 1973. But a disillusioned West Germany, tired of being the "milch cow" of the Community, insisted on restricting the fund to one-fifth of the £1,250 million demanded by Britain. An unnecessary row developed between the two at the end of 1973, especially after Britain vetoed progress on the energy question until Bonn would offer more. However both later modified their positions, and the Regional Development Fund finally came into being in 1975.

The serious balance of payments problems caused by the soaring oil prices, which called for increased EEC co-operation, in fact produced further disarray. Despite their frequent criticism of the failure of Britain, Ireland, and Italy to tie their currencies to the EEC joint float, the French acted blatantly to protect their national interests in January 1974 by letting their own currency float independently. This caused further dislocation of the Common Agricultural Policy and was a blow to hopes of economic and monetary union. Thus although unspectacular progress had continued, morale in the Community had reached a low ebb. The Nine were unable to agree on a joint mandate for the Washington oil-consumers' conference in February, France alone rejecting collaboration by oil-consuming industrialised countries independent of the oil producers (*see* **C31**(**1**)). This caused delay in working out a common energy policy, to which the Community was committed. France also refused to join the International Energy Agency formed in November. However in October the Council of Ministers did agree that the EEC should raise a substantial loan from the oil-producing countries to finance member states' balance-of-payments deficits due to increased oil prices.

British Renegotiation.

Worst of all, the new British Labour Government in the spring of 1974 demanded major renegotiation of the terms of British membership and threatened to leave the Community if not given satisfaction. The four main areas concerned were the Common Agricultural Policy; the level of contributions to the Community budget; the Community's trade and aid policies towards Commonwealth and other developing countries; and how far the existing rules interfered with the British Government's ability to pursue independent regional and industrial policies. Increasing concentration by the EEC on the renegotiation issue brought most progress in other areas (including the fundamental aspects of agricultural and regional policy) to a halt. However by early 1975 arrangements had been worked out in most of the areas of renegotiation, including intermediate exemptions for Britain on sugar and beef; a plan whereby members would be eligible for reimbursements on their contributions to the EEC budget on the basis of their gross national product and economic growth; and generous terms for developing countries as described below. Although the concessions would probably have been obtained without dramatising them as renegotiation the Community appeared to be prepared to go along with the British Government for British domestic consumption. In March 1975 a meeting of the European Council in Dublin settled the two outstanding renegotiation issues, contributions to the Community budget and continued access after 1977 for New Zealand dairy produce. On the former, a "correcting mechanism" was agreed on to prevent the development of situations unacceptable for a member state. For New Zealand there were improved provisions on prices, on quantities of butter and the possibility of some continuing imports of New Zealand cheese. In the light of the renegotiation the British Government decided, with a minority dissenting, to recommend that the British people should vote for remaining in the European Community. The result of the referendum, held in 1975 was a 67·2% "Yes" vote.

The EEC and Developing Countries.

The first major Community achievement for some time was the conclusion in February 1975 of the Lomé Convention on trade, economic cooperation and development between the EEC and 46 developing countries in Africa, the Caribbean and the Pacific (ACP), replacing the Yaoundé and Arusha Conventions. The agreement is unexampled in relations between industrial and developing countries and was described by the spokesman of the ACP countries as "revolutionary". It guarantees them unrestricted access to Europe's markets for all their industrial and 84% of their agricultural produce and special terms for sugar. It also offers financial support from a European Development Fund trebled in volume, and guarantees to developing countries dependent on the export of a few primary products equalisation payments (repayable only by the richer) when export earnings suffer from price fluctuations on the world market. All that is asked in return is "most favoured nation" treatment under GATT, i.e. that the ACP countries should not treat the EEC worse than other trading partners. This agreement was a great achievement of the European Commission, and the generous treatment of mainly former colonies will further raise the Community's standing in the world (which is in any case higher than within its own borders).

The Future of the EEC.

At the summit meeting of the heads of government of the Nine in Paris in October 1972 a statement of objectives was agreed. This included a programme, based on the previous Werner Plan, for achieving economic and monetary union, and affirmation of their "intention to transform before the end of the present decade . . . the whole complex of their relations into a European Union." Major issues remain unresolved. Thus there are sharp differences between France (and Denmark) and Germany (and Benelux) on the question of ultimately conferring supranational powers on community institutions, and the member nations are unready to undertake the pooling of political power which alone would make possible the fulfilment of their declarations. Reform of the confessedly unsatisfactory Common Agricultural Policy has continually been postponed, largely because both France and the German farmers gain so much from the present system. However Britain and Germany are pushing for major structural changes. *See also* Section G, Part IV.

Recently thought has been given to some issues not covered by the Treaty of Rome, such as the harmonisation of European foreign policies and defence. As a first step machinery was set up in 1971 for regular consultations on foreign policy matters. 1974 saw the beginnings of co-operation on the field of education and the adoption of a Community action programme on scientific and technological policy, with projects to be coordinated by a committee for scientific and technical research (CREST).

An institutional step forward was taken when the summit conference of heads of government in Paris in December 1974 agreed that the heads of government of member nations would in future meet at least three times a year to further political co-operation and co-ordinate diplomatic action. These meetings have been institutionalised as the "European Council". At the same time there was a commitment to give up the practice of making agreement on all questions conditional upon unanimous consent, and a working party was to study the possibility of introducing a uniform Community passport. Meanwhile the European Parliament in 1975 received increased powers over the EEC's budget and direct elections are planned for 1978, though with a notable lack of enthusiasm in some countries including Britain.

The report by the Belgian Prime Minister, Mr. Tindemans, which had been commissioned by the EEC heads of government on the development of the EEC into a European Union, was published in January 1976. In line with the current mood it was sober and pragmatic, proposing that the European Council should be developed into a real decision-making centre with a parliament worthy of the name as counterweight. Much more controversial was the suggestion of a two-tier participation in the proposed economic and monetary union, allowing the weaker members to wait until their economics were capable of further integration. This inevitably raised again the bogy of "second class" membership of the Community.

The question of Greece's membership of the European Community had been revived after its return to democratic government, and early in 1976 the Commission argued that Greece should be accepted as a member only after a period of adjustment. However the Council of Ministers decided to accept Greece's full membership without preconditions and start negotiations forthwith. This appeared to be a key decision (even if not an explicit one) on the Community's future: enlargement was being given priority over integration, since the wider and more heterogeneous the Community, the more complicated will be the process of co-ordination and compromise and the prospects of working towards economic and monetary union between countries of widely differing economic strength.

During 1976 the Community announced a new fisheries policy which is based on a 200-mile economic zone around all member states' coasts known as the Community "pond". Limits have been set on the amount of fish which can be caught by vessels from non-member states. Arrangements have still to be made for those member states particularly Ireland and the United Kingdom who have important fishing interests, and the major problem of policing any regulations remains unsolved.

Euratom.

Euratom is the short title of the European Atomic Energy Community formed in 1957 to further the use of nuclear energy in Europe for peaceful purposes and to ensure that Europe does not lag behind in the atomic revolution. The UK, Denmark and Ireland joined the Six in Euratom on 1 January 1973.

Co-ordination on Scientific and Technological Policies.

The Six encouraged co-operation in the fields of data processing, transport, oceanography, the environment and meteorology, participation being extended to many European countries outside the EEC. This was in addition to co-operation in international organisations such as ELDO (European Rocket Launcher Development Organisation), ESRO (European Space Research Organisation), and CERN (European Nuclear Research Centre) in all of which the Six were associated with Britain, until Britain withdrew from ELDO at the end of 1972. The urgency of co-operation has been sharpened by growing anxiety in Europe generally about the consequences of a technological gap, the difficulties actually encountered in *ad hoc* co-operation—in the aero-space sector, for example—and the extensive overlapping of effort and expenditure.

In August 1973 it was agreed to set up a European Space Agency precipitated by a US offer for Europe to build a scientists' space laboratory as part of the post-Apollo research programme. Other projects are a marine satellite and a European rocket. The European Space Agency was formally inaugurated in May 1975 with ten countries as full members: the EEC countries except Ireland and Luxembourg, plus Spain, Sweden, and Switzerland. It officially superseded ELDO and ESRO.

COLLECTING ANTIQUES

This section tells of the pleasures of antique-collecting and of the wide range of opportunities for learning about antiques. Practical advice is given about how antiques are bought and sold and their value and price determined. The text is accompanied by line-drawings of some interesting chairs of the past 300 years, together with tables of silver and pottery marks. A collectors' glossary completes the section.

TABLE OF CONTENTS

COLLECTING ANTIQUES

1. Introduction.

Until recently it was mainly the prosperous and the rich who could indulge in collecting. During the 17th and 18th centuries the English aristocracy acquired antiques with passion and avidity, or rather antiquities, for their interests were almost exclusively concentrated upon marble statues, vases and coins from the classical world. The 19th century saw an ever increasing interest in highly decorated *objets d'art*, Venetian glass, Pallissy pottery, French 18th century furniture, Dresden porcelain, elaborate clocks, arms and armour, and rich people built up vast collections. We can mention men like Felix Slade (1790–1868) and George Salting (1836–1909), who spent most of their leisure time and considerable fortunes on antique-collecting, and who have left hundreds of thousands of precious objects to our museums. Or the Fourth Marquess of Hertford (1800–70) and John Bowes (1811–85) and his wife, whose collections have been preserved in museums of their own—the Wallace Collection in London and the Bowes Museum at Barnard Castle. The early 20th century saw a great widening in the public interest in antiques, but it would still be fair to say that until recently antique-collecting was a somewhat sedate pastime for middle-aged people of comfortable means.

It was during the post-war period, and especially from the early 1960s onwards that the interest in antiques spread to every section of society. There is today a nostalgia for the past, especially among the young, for its fashions in dress, its interiors, its household goods and ornaments. In a world which changes with such confusing rapidity people find themselves turning towards the past to find some kind of continuity in life, to preserve what is so quickly disappearing and to get a feeling of stability—for the past has a way of looking stable when seen from an unstable present. The love of antiques is one expression of these needs.

What is an Antique?

As collectors have become so very much more numerous, the ideas of what is collectable have widened correspondingly. Chronological definitions have been immensely widened. The old definition of an antique as "something made before 1830" (i.e., before industrialisation began seriously to change our physical surroundings), is no longer generally accepted. The official definition of an antique, when Government has to decide for instance on questions of import and export is "what is more than a hundred years old". But for the general public, all kinds of Victoriana and objects in the styles of Art Nouveau (*c.* 1880–1914) and Art Deco (*c.* 1920–40) are eagerly and sometimes expensively collected, and even post-war objects begin to make their appearance in shops and sale-rooms. In fact, the immediate past is to many people of more absorbing interest than any period of history.

Likewise, the whole concept of objects worth collecting has expanded out of all recognition. Antiques no longer include only the old classic genres of furniture, pottery and porcelain, glass, silver, coins, ethnographica. Today, people collect everything under the sun, and the aesthetic appeal is no longer of primary importance. To mention only a few examples: grandmother's ball-dress and fur coat, old dolls, medicine-bottles, postcards, typewriters and cameras of twenty or fifty or a hundred years ago, all these and many more things are now treasured, labelled and systematised, bought and sold through the regular channels of the antique trade. Other significant additions to the world of antiques are veteran cars, boats and railway-engines, and for those who cannot handle these bulky objects in the original, pictures, old or new, will do. They, are all messengers from the past, and as such they charm, amuse and fascinate.

Why we love our Heirlooms.

Objects which have come down to us from parents, grandparents or even earlier links in the family chain are, of course, prized with special affection. Many serve us as well in daily life as they did our forbears. A mahogany chair of 18th-century design effortlessly takes its place in a modern interior as a useful piece of furniture, while at the same time it pleases us as a thing of beauty. Grandmother's tea-set is as serviceable today as when it was made, and so is what may remain of a Victorian flint dinner-service. If all that survives of it is a colourful plate or a tureen too capacious for modern family needs, they look pretty when hung on the wall or displayed on a sideboard. And even things without intrinsic beauty or modern usefulness, like a washstand with marble top, a set of tools made of brass with turned wooden handles, or a pair of old-fashioned scales, thrill us by their natural materials, the quality of their craftmanship and the simplicity of their mechanisms. Family "heirlooms", however modest, may suffer from infirmities, but we put up with them and look after them as we do our aged relatives.

Collecting—Casual or Systematic.

Many people will, however, want to add to what they may already possess by acquiring old things. Perhaps they want to cheer up a drab corner of a room with let us say "something blue", and find that an old-fashioned blue and white milk jug of Staffordshire pottery just fills the bill. A small Oriental rug, perhaps of no very great antiquity, but warm and delicious in colour and texture, will add a new charm to an interior. A bronze lion of modest size thrills us by the elegance of its lines and the energy of its movements, and we "fall for it". Perhaps we approach the antique shop or market with some purely practical purpose in mind: we go in search of a set of cut glass tumblers to match what we already have from the parental home, or we need a new armchair, and we discover that it is actually cheaper to buy an old than a new one. Living with the "new old" chair, we discover that its capriciously curved lines give a welcome element of variety to an otherwise austerely modern interior. If it needs repair and upholstery, this may be an added attraction for those with do-it-yourself talents (*see* **D17**).

Most of us are content to wander about among the welter of antiques now being offered for sale, to enjoy looking at so many things curious or beautiful (or with some luck, both), and occasionally perhaps purchase something that takes our fancy and suits our purse. But from this casual kind of buying, one is easily led on to more systematic and purposeful collecting. Having acquired something that thrills and fascinates, one's eye becomes sharpened, and one begins to look for something similar when browsing in shops and markets. One starts looking at marks on pottery signatures on old prints, and the next purchase and perhaps the one after that again is done with greater discernment. And one day one discovers that one has become a real and keen collector—of brass candlesticks, or pestles and mortars, or old sewing-box accessories, or views of London or Norwich or Cheltenham, or memories of Queen Victoria, or whatever one finds truly fascinating among the myriads of items that are available. Having once found a subject with appeal, one is happily caught up in a hobby that will provide great enjoyment, concentrate a restless mind, and give occasion for absorbing detective work in museums and libraries.

It is a natural desire to want to create order out of what may at first look like chaos, to arrange thoughts, ideas or concrete objects in groups and series, and to want to see things, once begun, completed. Systematic collecting satisfies many of these desires. Classic examples are of course the collecting of coins and stamps. Here every item can be fairly easily identified and its date and place determined, and it is possible with application to build up complete series—whether one goes in for English postage-stamps from the Edwardian era, pennies from all ages or coins from the reign of William IV. Each item has interesting historical associations, and many are things of beauty. But people with tidy minds may find it satisfying to collect less ambitious objects, matchboxes, or figures of swans or elephants in wood or pottery or any other material, or Penguin books from before decimalisation, or eggcups or eyebaths —the possibilities are virtually endless.

Collectors who concentrate for long periods, perhaps for a lifetime, on one speciality, will have the chance to build up a solid knowledge within their particular field of interest. They will find their way to dealers who are knowledgeable within their speciality and can assist in making significant additions to their collections; they will become increasingly able to distinguish between excellent, good, less good and trash, and to spot the odd fake. They will read ever bigger and better books on their chosen subject, and in time perhaps themselves contribute to a greater understanding of it: some of the most learned books on special groups of antiques have been written by impassioned and experienced amateur collectors. And they will get in touch with people who nurse the same interest, and spend enjoyable hours exchanging views and experiences, comparing and perhaps "swapping". Today collectors in a large number of fields have organised themselves into societies that hold regular meetings, read papers, arrange excursions and publish transactions.

Some Collectors' Clubs and Societies.

The Antique Collectors' Club.
Founded 1966.
Secretariat: Clopton, Woodbridge, Suffolk.
(With *c.* 70 affiliated regional clubs all over Britain.)

The Arms and Armour Society.
Founded 1950.
Hon. Sec.: R. J. Whittaker,
30 Alderney Street, London S.W.1.

The British Bottle Collectors' Club.
Hon. Sec.: Gregory Payne,
Greenacres, Church Road,
Black Notley,
Braintree, Essex.

The Society of Caddy Spoon Collectors.
Founded 1963.
Hon. Sec.: Edward Kramer.
5 Verulam Buildings, Gray's Inn, London W.C.1.

The English Ceramic Circle.
Founded in 1927 as The English Porcelain Circle.
Reorganised under its present name in 1931.
Hon. Sec.: Mrs. E. Adams,
26 St. Paul's Place, London N.1.

The Oriental Ceramic Society.
Founded 1921.
Secretariat;
31b Torrington Square, London W.C.1.

The Commemorative Collectors' Society.
Founded 1970s.
Hon. Sec.: Steven Jackson,
25 Farndale Close, off Wilsthorpe Road,
Long Eaton, Nr. Nottingham.

The Costume Society.
Founded 1965.
Hon. Sec.: Mrs. Anne Thomas,
251, Popes Lane, London W.5.

The Decorative Arts Society 1890–1940.
Founded 1975.
Secretariat: The Royal Pavilion,
Art Gallery and Museums,
Brighton, Sussex.

The Doll Club of Great Britain.
Hon. Sec.: Mrs. Jean Palmer
2 Broomfield Road,
Oxshott,
Leatherhead, Surrey.

The Fan Circle.
Founded 1975.
Hon. Sec.: Mrs. G. Hardy,
8/8 The Paragon, Blackheath, London S.E.3.

The Fire Mark Circle.
Hon. Sec.: James Williamson
21 Winston Drive,
Bexhill-on-Sea,
Sussex.

The Friends of Blue (transfer printed earthenware)
Hon. Sec.: Robin Gurnett,
367 Liverpool Road,
London, N.1.

The Furniture History Society. Founded 1964.
Secretariat: The Department of
Furniture and Woodwork,
Victoria and Albert Museum, London S.W.7.

The Glass Circle.
Founded 1937.
Hon. Sec.: Mrs C. G. Benson,
The Old Rectory, Waldershare, nr. Dover, Kent.

Goss Collectors' Club.
Hon. Sec.: Roland Ward,
21 St. Anne's Drive,
Fonce, Nr. Burnley,
Lancs.

The Heraldry Society
Hon Sec.: Mrs. Linda Biermann,
28 Museum Street,
London W.C.1.

The Antiquarian Horological Society.
Founded 1953.
Hon. Sec.: Commander D. Clarke,
New House, High Street, Ticehurst, Wadhurst,
Sussex.

The National Horse Brass Society.
Founded 1975.
Hon. Sec.: J. E. C. Armitage,
Longstone Grange. Nr. Bakewell, Derbyshire.

The Islamic Art Circle.
Founded 1956.
Hon. Sec.: Mrs. P. L. Baker,
2 Tower Mansions, 134 West End Lane,
London N.W.6.

The Map Collectors' Circle.
Founded 1963.
Hon. Sec.: R. V. Tooley,
30 Baker Street.
London W.1.

The British Matchbox Label and Booklet Society.
Founded 1945.
Hon. Sec.: J. H. Luker,
The Bungalow, Pine Ridge School,
Esher Road,
Old Dean Estate,
Camberley, Surrey.

The Musical Box Society of Great Britain.
Founded 1962.
Hon. Sec.: A. R. Waylett,
"Bylands", Crockham Hill, Edenbridge Kent.

The Northern Ceramic Society.
Hon. Sec.: Michael Parkinson,
The Athenaeum,
81 Princess Street
Manchester, 1.

The Royal Numismatic Society.
Founded 1836.
Secretariat: The Department of Coins and Medals,
British Museum, London W.C.1.

The British Numismatic Society.
Founded 1903.
(for collectors of British coins).
Hon. Sec.: Mr. W. Slayter,
63 West Way, Edgware, Middlesex.

The Pewter Society.
Founded 1918.
Hon. Sec.: C. A. Peal, The Wold, 12 Stratford Crescent, Cringleford, Norwich, Norfolk.

The Royal Philatelic Society.
Founded 1869.
Secretariat: 41 Devonshire Place, London W.1.

The Pot Lid Circle.
Hon. Sec.: A. Ball,
Garthside,
15 Arden Road,
Nuneaton,
Warwickshire.

The Scottish Pottery Society.
Secretariat: The Art Gallery and Museum,
Kelvingrove,
Glasgow, 3.

The Vintage Transport Enthusiasts' Club
(Veteran Cars and Motorcycles).
Founded 1971.
Secretariat: 14 Broadway, London S.W.1.

The Wedgwood Society.
Founded 1954.
Hon. Sec.: Miss G. T. B. Brixie Jarvis,
The Roman Villa, Rockbourne, Fordingbridge, Hants.

The Wine Label Society.
Founded 1968.
Dr. Bernard Watney,
32 Upper Park Road, London N.W.3.

2. Values and Valuations.

There is also an important financial aspect. As stocks and shares are increasingly considered risky, many people invest what money they may have to spare in antiques, believing—sometimes rightly and sometimes not—that they will keep their value even when other commodities may lose theirs. Serious investors in antiques usually go in search of items of accepted excellence: silver plate from the 17th and 18th centuries, Oriental carpets, Chinese porcelain of pre-Ming vintage, good mahogany furniture of two hundred years ago or more. Sometimes such treasures are too precious and too fragile to keep on show, and they are put away in bank vaults, while their owners wait for their value to increase, so that they can be sold at a profit when the market prices are particularly favourable. This kind of speculative handling of precious and beautiful things may seem cynical to genuine lovers of what is old and excellent. But the phenomenon is not new; there have always been people to whom the monetary value of their possessions is of overriding interest, and who treat them primarily as investments. And if we are honest with ourselves, whoever owns something old will wonder about its possible monetary value. At some stage thoughts like these will cross our minds: Could the silver spoons with the sculptured heads be genuinely old Apostle spoons and something truly precious, or could the quaint porcelain figure brought home from the East by mother's grandfather be a rare Chinese piece? We find comfort in the thought that if we were ever in serious financial trouble, they might help us out.

Apart from the investment and profit motives, there are several good and sensible reasons why we should know the value of whatever we possess. For insurance purposes it is useful to know if anything old in one's possession is particularly valuable and should be separately insured. And when making a Will, everyone should see to it that one's possessions are shared out between friends and relatives with fairness, so that squabbles and disputes are avoided when the time comes. For such purposes, reputable antique dealers and auctioneers take on valuations at reasonable charges.

Below are set out rates which are currently used as a guide by members of BADA (*see* **D9**(2)) and by the big London auctioneers for these services. The exact scale of fees should of course be agreed upon between valuer and client before the work is undertaken.

1½ per cent up to	£ 10,000
1 per cent from	£ 10,000 to £100,000
½ per cent from	£100,000 to £200,000
¼ per cent above	£200,000

(with a minimum fee of £10 plus travelling expenses).

What Determines Prices?

In the world of antiques there are no fixed standards or criteria of value, and prices are determined almost exclusively according to demand. An item made of precious metal and set with rare stones will of course have some intrinsic value, but even so this may be trifling compared to what beauty, age and style have invested it with in the eyes of a collector. Generally speaking, it is the capricious taste of the great public which determines what antiques are worth in terms of money at any given moment. And taste, as we all know, can change from love to indifference and back again, almost overnight, for reasons which are often inexplicable in rational terms. The rise and fall in the value of glass paperweights can serve as a good example of what demand can do to prices.

Glass paperweights are pretty and colourful things, and they are clever glassmakers' products. But they are not staggeringly interesting when seen in the greater perspective of the history of the art of glass, and they are not very old, the first ones having been made during the 1840s. During their time of fashion in the 19th century they became very popular and many different categories of patterns were evolved—many-coloured spirals and dots, figures of flowers and insects inlaid into the massive crystal clear glass—and some factories began to sign their best examples. Then they were forgotten for many decades, until suddenly rediscovered by collectors in a sale at Sotheby's in the early 1950s. In no time the interest exploded into wild enthusiasm, and soon a large and learned literature grew up around them: the different genres were listed and systemised into divisions and subdivisions, signatures were studied, records quoted, and for several years collectors were fighting over rare examples and paying truly fantastic prices for them. Then in 1968 came the crash. The market had been flooded, collectors' interest suddenly appeared to have been exhausted; and prices dropped sharply, the dealers who had invested heavily in paperweights finding themselves in some trouble. Glass paperweights are still very much on the collectors' map, and regular sales are still devoted to paperweights only, but prices have now found levels which are more attuned to the "real" value of these pretty baubles.

However unpredictable the value of an antique may be, and will remain, certain guidelines can be drawn up.

Generally speaking, one can say that the older an object is the greater its value will be. But the principle operates within watertight compartments: a piece of European porcelain is old at 1750, while a piece of silver of the same age is comparatively trivial, and 18th-century Chinese porcelain is young and vulgar when seen in the light of the long, long history of this most aristocratic group among antiques: it is ceramics from the T'ang and Sung dynasties (A.D. 618–1280) and bronzes from even more distant ages that hold the interest of the truly serious collectors. There are also many exceptions to the rule. Anything mediaeval will be of great interest and value, for the period is remote and its output of artefacts comparatively small. Some Roman objects—glass jars and red *terra sigillata* pottery—are on the other hand not so rare, as the period was a productive one in industrial goods, and though several hundred years older than an example of mediaeval craftsmanship, modest examples of Roman glass and pottery can be acquired fairly easily and at comparatively low prices, while almost anything mediaeval will be rare—and consequently expensive.

For rarity is a great price-raiser, in antique-dealing as in every other kind of trade. In March 1975 a chair designed by Charles Rennie Mackintosh (1868–1928) came up for sale at Sotheby Belgravia where it fetched £9,200. Why this truly staggering price for one single chair, made a mere 70 years ago? Partly because Mackintosh was a great designer, and the chair is very beautiful, with long elegant lines in an unusual rhythm and with mauve oval glass insets into the back. But also, and perhaps mainly, because Mackintosh's work is at the moment much admired, and things designed by him only rarely come on the market. This particular chair was designed for an individual patron in Glasgow, and it is believed to be unique.

Other categories of antiques, which are very attractive in themselves, but not so hard to come by, have a way of finding a kind of price level, though this will also be subject to fluctuations, some explicable, some not. An experienced dealer or collector will be able to forecast with some accuracy what the price will be at the next auction sale of an English 18th-century wineglass with a spiral stem, a piece of *famille rose* porcelain from China, a Continental silver tankard of the Baroque period or an English 17th-century silver spoon, for there are plenty of things like these about, and they regularly come on the market.

Very important in the assessment of the value of an antique is its physical condition, but here again, standards change from one group to another. Even a hair-thin beginning of a crack on a piece of pottery may reduce its value as a commercial object quite considerably, while legitimate signs of wear on an old chair may actually add to its attractiveness: the shiny surface on the ends of the arm-rest, polished by generations of users, does not detract from the beauty or solidity of the thing, but gives a charming feeling of constant use by those who came before us. In another area, that of numismatics, signs of wear are nothing but detracting. A coin in mint condition can fetch more than double the price of another example of the very same piece where the details have been blurred by wear or perhaps by polishing—for the serious coin-collector abrasive polishing materials are taboo.

Marks Add to Value.

This seems to be one rule that has no exception. But the marks themselves must be studied carefully; some are of more interest than others, and sometimes they do not mean what they may seem to at the first rapid glance.

The assaying and consequent marking of silver and gold has been a matter of law from mediaeval times to this day. Only certain objects of very small size could be sold without marks. The rules have been enforced with greater or lesser energy at different times and in different places, but a piece of unmarked silver should always be looked at with some scepticism. And marks on silver have sometimes been tampered with, at the time when they were new, or recently. Silver marks should therefore be scrutinised with great care before they are accepted for what they at first appear to tell us. But a piece of good old silver (or even better, of gold) with clear and unproblematical marks will fetch a much bigger price among dealers and collectors than a very similar piece with questionable marks or no marks at all. *See* D20–22, and Hallmarks, L52.

From 1784 onwards, the marking of Sheffield plate (plate of silver on a copper base and made not only in Sheffield), was a right, not a duty, and the marks were put on by the makers as trade-marks or advertisement. The meaning of them all has not yet been fully worked out, but even so marks will add greatly to the interest and value of an item. Indeed, unidentified marks may pose the collector with an intriguing problem. If the name in the marks has not yet been registered in printed books, one can sometimes solve the question of identity by a simple search in easily accessible records like directories or newspapers.

On ceramic wares of all kinds, marks have been put on by the makers in the great majority of cases, not because any laws told them to do so, but because they wanted to advertise their names. Here again, marks should be looked at with care, for very famous marks, like the crossed swords of Meissen or the name of Wedgwood, have been copied, perhaps with minute alterations, imitated or downright faked by other, less famous producers (*see* D19(2)). Sometimes the factory mark is accompanied by figures, emblems or letters, which to those who know, can reveal details about dating, or about the identity of individual craftsmen and painters. And, of course, the more telling the mark, the more valuable the piece. (For more details, see table of ceramic marks D23–28).

Pewter marks have been well studied and have their own characteristics and rules. One or two on each piece normally signify the quality of the metal, others show the pewterer's name and the date when he became master of his guild. A date in a pewter mark does not therefore give the date of the piece itself, which can be several decades later than the date in the maker's mark. Apart from quality and maker's marks, pewter sometimes carries several other marks, whose meaning we do not always know. But old pewter marks have been much copied on later pieces and should be studied with great care before accepted as really being what they look like, and priced accordingly.

Until about a hundred years ago, glass was hardly ever marked, and an old glass can normally be assigned to a particular place or period only approximately, by a study of style and technique alone. Occasionally during the 17th and 18th centuries, good engravers signed their pictures, and such pieces are of course of the greatest interest and take high prices. *c.* 1880 the French glass-maker, Emile Gallé, began to sign every piece that left his factory with his full name. This turned out to be an enormous commercial success, and since then it has been normal practice for makers of art glass to put signatures on their works. Since the 1930s even serially produced table ware has sometimes been signed with the name of the factory and perhaps engraved or acid-etched with the initials of the designer. Glass from the last hundred years or so can at times be identified if the producer's paper label is still intact. The great interest in the glass of the 19th and 20th centuries which has recently developed must surely to a large extent be attributed to the wide use of makers' marks.

From 1751 onwards, the best Paris furniture-makers (*ébénistes*) were bound by the rules of their guild to mark their products with a stamp bearing the master's name or initials, and many Swedish furniture makers of the same period followed their example. Apart from these two groups, furniture is only rarely signed. But if a piece is found to bear the stamp of a maker, or a trade-card or maker's label is discovered glued inside it, this of course adds enormously to its value.

No scholar, collector or dealer, however learned or experienced, can have all marks within one particular area of antiques in his head; everybody is dependent on printed lists in books. When using such books it is important to find up-to-date editions, for the study of marks goes on unendingly, new marks are drawn into the world of antiques as new periods catch collectors' interest, more marks are being identified, new interpretations are constantly made possible, and monetary values fluctuate accordingly.

Look for Quality!

In the final analysis, what will give an antique, whether old or not so old, its lasting value is quality. The public's interest in certain curiosities and oddities, its preference for particular periods and names, may come and go from week to week, month to month or year to year, soon to fade away again without trace. But a thing well made of good design and of attractive materials, truly representative of its period, will always retain its value, even though it may pass through short phases of neglect within the trade. Most of all, things of quality will continue to give their owner deep and genuine pleasure, unaffected by superficial changes in taste and fashion. The best advice one can give to those who want to buy antiques must therefore be: buy what you *really* like and feel a genuine desire to possess. For behind such likes and desires usually lies a true sense of the quality of the object chosen.

3. The Antique Trade in Britain.

For two centuries Britain, especially London, has held a central position in the world's antique trade. There are many reasons why this should be so.

First of all, there is in Britain an enormous stock of antiques. The British have themselves produced things of great beauty and originality—we can think of Chippendale and Hepplewhite furniture, Wedgwood table services and ornamental ware, wine glasses of lead crystal, Sheffield plate and much else. But this stock of home products has been constantly added to by British collectors, who have been active for several hundred years (*see* **D3(1)**). First royalty and the aristocracy, later also the prosperous middle classes, travelled widely in Europe, in the classic lands round the Mediterranean, and eventually all over the globe, and wherever they went, they bought whatever products of excellence and originality each country had to offer, be it old or new—French furniture, German porcelain, Venetian glass, Italian majolica, Chinese bronzes and porcelain vases, African masks and weapons, Japanese lacquer ware and ivory carvings and many many other things.

Secondly, over the years, British dealers have gained a world-wide reputation for being well stocked, experienced, knowledgeable and fair as businessmen, and collectors and fellow dealers from all over the world have come and continue to come, to buy from their shops and bid at their auctions. Apart from the commercial apparatus working smoothly and pleasantly, the British art market also offers certain advantages within the field of tax and commissions, which one must hope will be retained in spite of the present-day financial climate, for it is undoubtedly a main attraction for both buyers and vendors from abroad.

Auctioneers.

The cornerstones of the antique trade in Britain, perhaps in the world, are the two famous London auctioneers, Christie's and Sotheby's. The firm of Christie, Manson & Woods was founded by James Christie in 1766, and it has from the very beginning worked purely within the field of antiques and works of art. Its catalogues, which have been preserved from the start, have always been of a very high standard, containing much useful information, and they are today not only major sources in the history of art dealing but of art history. Christie's has been at its present address, 8 King Street, St. James's, since 1823. Sotheby's was founded in 1794, at first specialising in old books. Since 1909 the firm has been handling antiques and works of art of all kinds, and it has operated from its present address in 34–35 New Bond Street since 1917.

Both Christie's and Sotheby's hold auctions five days a week all the year round, except during the months of August and January. The number of auctions per week for each firm works out at about ten, as frequently several sales run concurrently in different rooms on the same day. It is estimated that altogether some 100,000 items pass through each of these two establishments every year. Each sale is devoted to one particular category of works of art or antiques: Furniture, silver, coins, ceramics, glass etc., often with subdivisions within each category: English silver, oak chests of Tudor times, inlaid French 18th-century furniture, Oriental or Continental or English porcelain, Staffordshire figures or the like.

Apart from traditional kinds of antiques, both firms now have regular sales of old wines, photographic and scientific instruments, ethnographica, toys, musical instruments, fans and costumes. Even vintage cars and steam railway engines are being sold through the two major London auctioneers.

Catalogues are published for each sale about three weeks in advance. One can buy them singly over the counter from the firm, or one can put in an annual subscription for all catalogues for the sales of one or several categories of antiques (silver and plate, Oriental ceramics, glass etc.) and receive them by post. Most of them are illustrated, and contain much learned information: the reading of potters' and goldsmiths' marks, attributions based on careful research, the detailed pedigree of single items. The high standard of the catalogues makes them much sought after, not only by prospective buyers, but by anyone interested in a particular kind of antique. In every catalogue, conditions of sale are carefully set out, and certain terms used for identification and attribution are explained in detail. Prospective clients should read it all with attention.

Some very spectacular prices are being paid for single items in the " rooms " of these two firms. In the spring of 1975 a very rare ewer of French Renaissance pottery fetched £40,000 at Sotheby's, while later the same year silver price records were broken, when a pair of *jardinières* on stands, made by a famous Paris goldsmith of the period of Louis XV, were sold for more than £400,000 in a Christie sale at Geneva.

With present-day inflated prices, good examples of silver or pottery go into price ranges which ten years ago were reserved for major paintings by Rubens and Velasquez. For specially interesting sales there is admission by ticket only, and on exceptional occasions the TV cameras move in, so that millions can watch the bidding as it climbs rapidly at first, a little more slowly in the later stages, the competitors needing a few more moments for reflection as really staggering sums of money are set at risk. And when at last the auctioneer's hammer falls: " So many hundred thousand pounds to Mr. X "—viewers all over the country gasp with astonishment and excitement in company with the couple of hundred people actually present.

But the great majority of items that pass through the great auction rooms take much lower prices. It is estimated that *c.* 60% of those sold go for less than £100. Until recently, the firm's commission on the sale of each item was higher for the cheaper things than for those fetching the bigger sums. The sinking scale in commission was reasonable enough: an 18th-century chair of anonymous make and not of the highest quality needs as much storage space and almost as much paper and print in the catalogue as a most exquisite ormolu mounted chest, made of precious woods in rich inlaid work, and signed by some famous 18th-century French *ébéniste*. The commission used to be paid exclusively by the vendor, but since September 1975 the two big auctioneers, Sotheby's and Christie's, have changed that system. Under the pressure of inflation and the complexities of modern accountancy, they now charge a commission from the vendor of 10% of the final bid price (except for wines, coins and medals, where the charge is 15%) and a buyer's premium of 10% (except for wines, coins and medals, which are exempt from this premium). The new arrangement caused much dismay among the many dealers who acquire much of their stock from the great sale-rooms, but it has now been generally accepted, and other firms have followed suit.

The auctioneers do not insure things to be sold while they are in their care, but they take great security precautions. From the time of delivery of an object by the vendor, until it comes up for sale, from three to six months may pass. But the time may be shorter for silver, for instance which is being sold at quite frequent sales, than for say, Russian icons, for which there are sales only once or twice a year.

In recent years, both Christie's and Sotheby's have expanded far beyond their traditional premises in London's West End. They frequently arrange sales in the British regions; and most importantly, they have established themselves widely abroad. Christie's now organise regular sales in Geneva, Rome and Florence, in Laren in Holland and in Melbourne, while Sotheby's have a close connection with Parke Bernet in New York. Both firms have agents in many other foreign centres. A most interesting initiative from Sotheby's side was the setting up in 1971 of a branch in Motcomb Street in London's Belgravia, exclusively devoted to the sale of art and antiques from after 1830. Sotheby Belgravia have three to four sales per week, where pictures, furniture, silver, pottery, glass and Oriental goods, all dating from the Victorian and Edwardian ages or Art Deco items from the 1920s and 1930s, are sold and bought. Even things from the early post-war times are now being offered for sale at Sotheby Belgravia. The establishment issues learned catalogues with many illustrations of objects that only ten or twenty years ago were spurned as "old-fashioned" and second-rate. Prices here are apt to be lower than those paid in the Bond Street mother firm, but at times they go into four figures, as when a glass vase by Emile Gallé in November 1971 fetched £2300. The works of the famous French glassmaker are very numerous, and frequently come on the market in London and elsewhere. Until the auction in 1971, the best pieces by Gallé had easily fetched quite high three-figure prices, but the sum paid on that occasion represented a sensational leap forward in the Gallé prices, and gave them a lasting boost.

Sotheby Belgravia was the first of the London auctioneers to publish advance prices in their catalogues, thus giving prospective buyers some idea of what sort of sums could be expected to be paid for each item. These forecasts are frequently found to tally quite well with the prices actually paid at the auction, but at times they are, of course, way out—as when the maximum estimated price for the famous Mackintosh chair, which fetched £9,200 in the spring of 1975 (*see* **D6**) was £3,000! The custom of publishing advance price estimates has now been taken up by most of the major art auctioneers in Britain.

In January 1975 Christie's opened a branch in Brompton Road in South Kensington, with a slightly different programme from Sotheby Belgravia. Good quality antiques of Victorian and later date are still being sold at Christie's auction rooms in King Street, while the aim of the Kensington branch is to try and sell antiques in the lower price ranges as quickly as possible and with the minimum overhead expenses. Here are no soft carpets, no glossy and scholarly catalogues; the whole machinery of selling has been cut down to a utilitarian minimum, and the time from delivery of an item until it comes up for sale, has been reduced to three weeks. There are five sales a week, devoted to pictures, furniture, jewellery, silver and pottery, as well as to toys, dresses, gramophones and much else.

There are several other auctioneers in London who handle antiques. Of almost equally venerable age as Christie's and Sotheby's are W. & F. C. Bonham's (founded 1793) of Montpelier Street, South Kensington, and King's Road, Chelsea, and Phillips Son & Neale (now Phillips for short) at Blenheim Street, off Oxford Street (founded 1796). They are smaller establishments than the two most famous firms, and the very greatest treasures do not easily find their way to their rooms, but they are excellent and reliable auctioneers, and Phillips has taken an original line in sticking to the old system of commission, and charging no buyer's premium (*see* **D7**(2). It now sometimes operates outside London and at times abroad.

There are many auctioneers outside London who handle antiques, exclusively or partly. Most of them arrange occasional sales, usually concentrating three or four in a couple of days to suit people who have to travel in order to attend. In 1973 The Society of Fine Art Auctioneers (SOFAA) was founded; in 1975 it had 25 members from all over Britain (Christie's and Sotheby's are not among them), and membership should vouch for the standards of expertise among the staff of each firm. Many collectors will also find great attraction in attending general country sales, which are not organised as "art sales" but where among masses of trivial household goods the odd antique can be spotted by a perspicacious buyer.

Attending an Auction.

Before a sale, the auctioneers and their staff willingly give advice to a client about how to go about an auction, whether as vendor or buyer. A vendor can set a reserve (minimum) price on the object he wants to sell. This protects him from seeing his treasure go at a price he considers not worth his while, but he runs the risk that if the reserve price is not reached the object is not sold at all. And the buyer who cannot or does not want to bid at a sale can arrange for the auctioneer to have bids made on his behalf, with an upper price limit agreed beforehand.

Anybody who wants to can walk in and watch an auction in progress without taking an active part, and a sale, especially at one of the great London houses, can be a fascinating spectacle. The seats immediately below the auctioneer's rostrum are usually reserved, by tacit agreement, for the dealers who regularly attend particular kinds of sales and get most of their stock from the auction rooms. Round about are rows of chairs, and as particularly interesting sales attract quite a crowd, many people may have to stand. On the fringe of the crowd there is a constant coming and going, and much whispered talk goes on, in a babel of foreign languages. But round the rostrum, at the heart of the sale, there is deep silence, broken only by the voice of the auctioneer, as he (or, since 1976, she) in an almost rhythmical sing-song calls out the bids as they fall. By tradition these are rarely cried out in so many words and figures; the client who is "in the bidding" signifies with only a nod or a wink or a slight wave with the pencil or catalogue that he is following up with a new bid. These go in "jumps", directed by the auctioneer. For small and modest items the price may go up by only two or five pounds at a time, but when rare and coveted pieces are up for sale, and perhaps very few people, in the end two only, are left to fight it out, they may be overbidding each other by a thousand pounds a time or more. As each item comes up for bidding, it is carried round to those nearest the rostrum by the saleroom staff, so that prospective buyers can have a last chance to look at it, check the mark, and finally make up their minds about how far to go to acquire it. Large and unwieldy pieces are held up at the back of the room and pointed out by the auctioneer as they come up for sale.

The job of the auctioneer needs intense concentration. He must have an eye on every finger to make sure that all interested get their chance, and he must be absolutely sure exactly where the bidding is standing at each precise moment—a slip may lead to disagreements, complaints and even litigation. There is a tempo and a drive about the whole procedure, a tenseness in the atmosphere, which must affect anybody present. Sometimes over 200 items are sold within the traditional hours between 11 and 1 o'clock, while some sales go on from 2.30 in the afternoon for another two hours. For those not used to the sale-room, it is easy to be carried away, and make higher bids than one had planned for, when competition becomes sharp and decisions have to be taken within split seconds.

The auction-rooms themselves have their own, very special aspect and appearance. On the walls of the room where a sale is in progress hang pictures and mirrors, and from the ceilings chandeliers are suspended, which are to be sold at some later occasion, and in the adjoining rooms people are busy inspecting what is to come up for sale in the next few days, pictures, pieces of furniture or smaller items of silver, porcelain or the like, displayed in showcases. Members of the staff go around giving assistance, answering questions and giving customers access to the locked showcases to hold and inspect items they are interested in. There is a unique atmosphere of museum-cum-salon-cum-warehouse, which has a fascination all of its own.

After the sale is over, the great auctioneers' firms give ready help and advice to people who have been buying, about packing and dispatch, payment in foreign currencies, insurance of goods in transit etc. Immediately after a sale, the prices paid are published in printed lists, which are sent out to subscribers to the catalogues.

Auction Prices.

Sales at auction are influenced by all sorts of factors, which change from place to place, from one season to another, and from day to day, even hour to hour within the particular sale. During the spring and the "London season", when customers from the country and from abroad flock to London, prices are generally higher than during the late autumn and the early part of the winter. The weather, good or bad news in the papers, the energy of the auctioneer or the intangible mood of the buying public may all influence the sale. It may be a stimulating occasion where people feel encouraged to buy at good prices, or a dull couple of hours which fail to inspire anyone to spectacular action. One sensational item in the sale catalogue may attract a larger audience than would otherwise have turned up, and have a stimulating effect on the whole auction, and one impassioned buyer in the audience, set on getting what he or she wants "at any price", can lift the price level beyond all expectations. There is, however, also much routine selling and buying going on in the auction rooms, where well-known and frequently recurring categories of antiques—English wine-glasses of the 18th century, Staffordshire pottery, certain well-established types of Chinese porcelain or Turkish Isnik plates—change hands at prices which most of those present expect and accept as reasonable.

Auction rooms, especially those of the two big London auctioneers, have a way of acting as price-setters. The prices are widely publicised through the price-lists published after every sale, and in spectacular cases through the press and even television, so that everybody involved in the trade of the particular commodity takes note of what happens at Christie's and Sotheby's, and adjusts his own prices and ideas accordingly.

Antique Shops.

It is estimated that there are some 6,500 antique shops in Britain today, and to categorise and map them out with any accuracy is an impossible task, not only because the picture is so large and complex, but also because it is constantly changing. Antique shops are to be found in considerable numbers in practically every town and city, frequently in the older quarters, and they line the High Streets of market towns and villages, where their position is often marked by attractive hanging signs with the magic word ANTIQUES in period style letting. At the top of the quality and price range are the spacious, softly carpeted establishments of London's Mayfair and South Kensington, and their equivalents in other major cities. Many of them are old establishments, perhaps family firms, who have worked for generations in the same line of business. Here things of venerable age and of museum quality are beautifully displayed, the staff is experienced and knowledgeable to the highest degree, and they cater for an international *clientèle*. At the other end of the scale are the small, dusty shops which fade into secondhand and junk shops, mostly to be found in back streets in unfashionable areas of towns and villages. Many people find them more interesting than the big, elegant ones, partly because their prices are lower, but especially because here there may be chances of finding surprises and bargains: among the broken-down bedroom furniture, chairs and kitchen utensils, one *might* with luck come across a shimmering glass vase by Tiffany, which the owner may not have identified for what it is, and will sell at a reasonable price. Or one might see a little wooden box, offered cheaply as an anonymous "bygone", recognise it as a good example of Victorian Tonbridge work of inlaid wood, and be able to buy it "for a song". But today the chances of making such finds are small indeed, as experienced dealers early in the day comb these small and unpretentious shops for stock, and knowledge of what is sought after is spreading very widely.

In between these two extremes of elegance and shoddiness are large numbers of pleasant, middle-sized shops with a varied stock of pleasant, middle-range priced goods, where many people can enter happily, spend a fascinating half-hour, and come out with a purchase that will grace one's home or please a friend without having broken one's budget.

Within the immensely wide and varied field, there is a great deal of specialisation. Some categories of antiques like Oriental carpets, coins and stamps, books and maps, arms and armour, are to a very large extent to be found in shops which trade in these things only. And particularly in London's West End are many important antique shops, which trade exclusively in silver and plate, or in porcelain (English or Continental, Chinese or Islamic), in furniture or glass. Other dealers again concentrate on even rarer objects—long-case clocks of the 17th and 18th centuries, glass chandeliers, fireplace furnishings, Russian icons, brass locks and mounts—to mention but a few in an almost endless range.

In 1918 a group of antique dealers organised themselves into the British Antique Dealers' Association (BADA). This is not a "closed shop", many dealers operate outside the organisation, but it is considered an asset to one's reputation to be a member, and be able to display the badge of the Association in one's shop window. New members are accepted on application only. Every applicant has to obtain a proposer and a seconder among the existing membership, and at the Council meeting where an application is being considered, he or she will be accepted only if a 75% majority of the votes is obtained. When applications are considered, the main qualifications are integrity and expert knowledge, while quality of stock is also taken into account. Every membership is reviewed annually by the Council.

Today BADA has *c.* 500 members from all over England, Scotland and Wales and a few also in more distant English-speaking countries. It works in close cooperation with similar organisations in other countries, and all of them are affiliated to the International Federation of Antique Dealers' Associations (CINOA). Since 1958 BADA has operated with a full-time staff from its own premises in 20 Rutland Gate, London S.W.7. This makes it possible for the organisation to provide all the facilities which it wants to give to its membership and to meet the problems that face the trade in a rapidly changing world. Representations made to successive Governments by BADA have resulted in legislation which has helped to maintain London as the principal centre of the world's trade in art and antiques. If a dispute arises between a member and one of his customers, Council members of BADA will hear the case from both sides, and try and settle the argument. In serious cases a tribunal of three to five members will be set up, all experts within the field in question, to look carefully into the problem and make a final decision.

BADA publishes a neat little handbook, which contains much useful information for members as well as for the general public. Most valuable is the list of members, where the name and address of each is given twice, first according to where they operate, and then according to what particular kind of antiques they handle. The book is brought up to date at regular intervals. Since 1975 they have also distributed two useful little folders, with lists of London and country members and their specialities.

Shop Prices.

The antique shop provides an atmosphere of peace and quiet, which is very different from the auction room with its hustle and bustle. In the shop one can browse and look around, ask questions and discuss problems with the proprietor and the staff, take one's time, perhaps go home and sleep on the question of whether to buy or not, having reserved the object in question for a day or two. The dealer will have set a price on it, which may be subject to discussion, but which provides a *point de départ* for negotiations.

When the honest dealer adds a new object to his stock and has no firm lead as to the price he should ask, he will start from what he himself paid, take into account its probable age and physical condition, use his experience and discretion and feeling for quality and set his price accordingly.

The collector who goes shopping in London's West End will most likely pay a little extra for the good name and expertise of the shop, its pleasant situation and its comfortable, even luxurious premises. But it is a fallacy to believe that the prices in London are always higher than those demanded elsewhere in the country. Prices may be just as high—and dealers just as knowledgeable and experienced—in the elegant streets of Brighton or Bath, or in the High Street of any picturesque village, where the thoughts of visitors naturally turn towards the past and their hearts are easily filled with a desire to buy something old.

Markets—Indoor and Outdoor.

Markets, whether under cover or in the open air, are becoming increasingly important meeting-places for those who want to sell antiques, and those who desire to acquire them.

The **outdoor market** has a long tradition in this country and some of those in modern London go quite far back in time. The Sunday morning market in Petticoat Lane in the traditionally Jewish part of East London is more than a hundred years old. The Caledonian market began its life in 1855, as a cattle-market in Highbury in North London. Eventually a more general public market grew up in parts of its grounds, much of it devoted to secondhand goods and antiques. During the second world war it was closed down and afterwards it was reopened in Bermondsey Square, near London Bridge, under its famous old name. The Caledonian market is open on Friday mornings. Portobello Road in the more bohemian part of London's West End is lined with antique shops, and on Wednesdays and Saturdays the pavements outside are invaded by stallholders, some belonging to the dealers of the area, others to people coming in from outside, many from far beyond the boundaries of London. In these and many other areas of London and other towns and cities, the municipal authorities hire out stalls and market space in certain streets on special days to anyone who wishes to sell, and who can pay the modest fees charged, and dealers queue up to get the stalls, for this is a simple and cheap way of contacting the buying public. In some street markets, the stalls containing antiques are appendages to those where food and vegetables, clothing and household wares are sold, and antiques and secondhand goods merge imperceptibly into each other.

There is an informality and directness about antique dealing in the outdoor markets, which has great appeal to both sides, and as expenses are kept down to a minimum, prices can also be kept within reasonable limits—though those days are definitely gone when one could pick up good antiques for almost nothing at the markets. Many of the stallholders have great expertise, and much of the most interesting stock is acquired early in the morning by other representatives of the trade. Especially the London markets have become important tourist attractions, and on a Saturday morning in Portobello Road and at the Bermondsey market, all the languages of the world can be heard among the clients who collect in their thousands. Bargaining is permitted, even expected, and especially towards the end of the day, stallholders may sell off some of their stock at bargain prices. On the other hand, the customer has less assurance about what he buys than if he had gone to a shop. He cannot "go back and complain" if the clock he bought in a moment of enthusiasm was sold without a key to wind it with, or if there is a crack in the Staffordshire plate that was hidden from view until the plate was brought home and examined with care.

The **indoor market** is a fairly recent phenomenon in the world of antique dealing in Britain. It works like this: a large number of people wishing to sell, jointly rent some large indoor space, which they pack with individual stalls, each one usually quite small. The first to adopt this kind of sharing arrangement were the London dealers in silver and plate. In order to protect their valuable stock, they hired armoured premises in the basements in Chancery Lane, which are now popularly known as the Silver Vaults. Here the public, not least foreign tourists, crowd in to look and to buy during business hours every day of the week, while at night armoured doors protect the goods under joint security arrangements.

The first general indoor antique market in London was The Antique Supermarket, situated just behind Selfridge's, on the corner of Barrett Street and St. Christopher's Place. This charming old passage-way for pedestrians only was already lined with antique shops, and the Supermarket with its mass of stalls and its show of stock under awnings on the pavement provides a natural continuation for the prospective buyer after a walk down St. Christopher's Place. Similar markets have since sprung up all over London, and in many places up and down the country. The markets in Chelsea are cheerfully young and "with it" in atmosphere. Those in South Kensington have a slightly more traditional air, while the Bond Street Antique Centre has caught some of the glamour of this famous street for elegant shopping. And of course there is an indoor market or "Antique Centre" in Camden Passage in Islington, where antique dealers of all kinds have been congregating for many years.

At the time of writing (January 1976) markets are also to be found in South London, at Greenwich, in several places in the Home Counties as well as in the West Country, in the Midlands and in the North. By the time this appears in print, the picture may have changed—probably several more markets will have sprung up in yet more areas of Britain.

The indoor market offers great and obvious advantages to both buyers and sellers of antiques. Those with things to sell find an easy and inexpensive outlet for their stock by sharing accommodation in this way, while those interested in buying can see an enormous mass of varied antiques within a limited area. The indoor markets are attractive places to visit, with an easy camaraderie between stallholders, cups of coffee being passed around among dealers and customers alike and an informal atmosphere which must appeal to everyone.

Fairs.

To complete the picture of antique dealing in Britain, a mention should be made of the fairs, which are being arranged more widely and more frequently every year. The fair can be defined as a short-term market, and the most spectacular of them is the great Antiques' Fair, which has been organised in June every year (with a few exceptions) since 1934 to date, in the resplendent setting of the great ballroom in Grosvenor House Hotel, Park Lane, London. It lasts for two weeks, and all the *c.* ten thousand exhibits are carefully vetted by committees of experts within each field (most of them members of BADA, *see* **D9**(2)), to assure, as far as is humanly possible, that every item is genuine. The *c.* 80 exhibitors try to build up the finest of stock for the occasion, and go to great lengths to show their goods attractively and to the greatest advantage. The main fair still adheres to the old definition of antiques as being made before 1830, but in 1975 an annexe was set up in an adjoining room, where *c.* 30 exhibitors showed first-quality goods from the period up to 1930. Apart from the dealers, restorers and packers also have their stalls at the Antiques' Fair and so have booksellers specialising in books on antiques and the major antique magazines.

Since the war, antique fairs on a smaller and less ambitious scale than the one in Grosvenor House, but on the same general pattern, are being arranged with increasing frequency in all kinds of contexts all over the country. Some last for a week or more and have become annual events, and some are devoted to one particular category of antiques, be it coins or military effects or clocks or whatever. But most fairs produce a general showing and are informal and improvised occasions, where a handful of dealers hire premises for a couple of days and make a local event of it.

With the present hunger for antiques, they collect a good public and business is brisk.

4. How to Learn about Antiques.

The enjoyment of antiques is greatly increased the more one knows about one's possession. Indeed, one of the fascinating aspects of antique-collecting is the way it has of making one first look at things, then speculate and eventually try and find answers to at least some of the questions that have begun to pose themselves. If the contemplation of music boxes gives one a genuine thrill, the collector will soon begin to wonder why music boxes were invented, and where, and why the invention happened just then and there, and little by little one small corner of the history of human skill and endeavour will reveal itself to one's fascinated eyes.

It is not too difficult to acquire quite a detailed knowledge within some limited field, to master the history of glass paperwieghts or Goss pottery, or thimbles or dolls, without troubling too much about the wider historical context. But few people will become collectors at all unless they already possess some feeling for the passing of time and some knowledge of a few fixed points in the great flow of history. In order to enlarge and deepen one's understanding of history, it is not necessary, perhaps not even desirable, to read thick books on political events, wars and conquests. One can gain an easier access to the past, and acquire more relevant historical knowledge by reading biographies and books on social customs and on technology.

Very useful, in fact indispensable to anyone who wants to try and identify things old, is some familiarity with the period styles.

Some Knowledge of Period Styles is Usefu

The existence of period styles is a strange phenomenon within the great framework of history.

Any artefact of the past will tell us something about the practical needs of its time, about the technical ability of its people and the tools and materials available to them. What is extraordinary is that the shape of the artefact—if it goes at all beyond the most sober, utilitarian functional form—in many cases reflects, not only the superficial fashions of the day, but the deeper thoughts and mental attitudes of its time.

Innumerable works have been written on the history of styles, and it is not too hard to acquire a basic knowledge of the chief characteristics of each, and how they follow one another in a historical sequence. The logical Renaissance and the exuberant Baroque cover the 16th and 17th centuries, while the styles of Queen Anne, of Chippendale and Adam (*Régence*, Rococo and Neo-Classicism, to mention the corresponding Continental styles) dominate the 18th century in turn. The English Regency style is a variant and a close relation of French Empire, and covers a period which goes somewhat beyond the regency of Prince George, who became King in 1820. (It should always be kept in mind that the period of a style named after a reigning monarch (Queen Anne) or an individual person (Chippendale), never coincides *exactly* with the dates of that person.)

From the early years of the 19th century industrialisation had widened its impact on the methods of production of most European artefacts. One result of this was a great confusion of stylistic ideas with a revival of all the historic styles of the past, Neo-Gothic, Neo-Rococo, Neo-Renaissance and all the others. It is hard to map out the revival styles with exactitude, and modern art historians now discuss the whole period under the general name of Historicism.

With the ideas of John Ruskin (1819–1900) and William Morris (1834–96) as guiding stars, reformers began to see the futility of much of this often clumsy copying of styles created for people of times long past, and began to try and find their way back to basic principles of form and ornament in the light of the capacities of modern production methods and the real needs of modern people.

The Art Nouveau of the *fin-de-siècle* (or Jugend-Stil as it was called in many parts of the Continent) reflected the spirit of the age in applying to the products of craftsmen and industry alike the principles of natural growth and organic form. The style reached its climax at the Paris Exhibition of 1900 and lingered on in the design of many commercial goods until the outbreak of the first world war.

Earlier in the 19th century a few pioneers had propagated ideas of pure construction and sober, functional form, especially for industrial goods. After the end of the first world war these ideas were generally accepted as suitable for the brave new world of speed, jazz and efficiency that was rapidly taking form.

Functionalism and its somewhat more mondaine and coquettish sister, Art Deco, remained the dominating styles in progressive circles between the two wars. So much for the bare bones of the history of styles.

But the history of styles must not be accepted as a simple " grammar " but should be used with discretion. It must always be remembered that there is no clear division between each style. The one grew naturally and gradually out of the one that went before, and in time merged imperceptibly into the next. Another point to keep in mind is that styles took on new faces under differing circumstances. The great period styles first emerged in the important cultural centres of their time, in Florence and Rome, Venice and Augsburg, Paris and London. But as the ideas and impulses moved from the places of origin to other countries, the style often changed its character quite fundamentally: the Baroque style of Italy is very different from that of France, and this again differs in an easily recognisable way from the English equivalents of Stuart and Jacobean. And as the great styles reached provincial centres and remote country districts, there was sometimes a considerable time-lag, and in these outlying areas styles survived perhaps for decades after their original inception.

Finally, period styles have constantly been repeated and revived by men of later times. The great example of a recurring style is of course that of classical Greek and Roman antiquity, with its columns and pediments and the rest. It has been revived over and over again for over 2000 years and always in slightly varying versions. Classical forms have been used not only in architecture, but in furniture, silver and many other products of crafts and industry.

We have already mentioned how the Victorian age saw a welter of revivals of all the historic styles of Europe. During that period, some of them came back several times, and it needs experience and sensitivity to distinguish the Neo-Rococo of the 1830s from that of the 1890s, and both from the 18th century originals.

These are just some indications of how the history of styles is more complex and subtle than would appear at first approach, and has to be applied with care and perspicacity by anyone who is trying to identify the date and place of origin of his or her antiques by its criteria.

Chairs in Different Styles.

Among all things old the chair is our most sensitive barometer of the changing period styles. Its dimensions have remained the same from its invention hundreds of years ago to this day, dictated as they are by the proportions of the human frame, and its basic function, to support a sitting person, is the same today as at any time in its long history. The following diagrams of chairs from the last 300 years should give some idea of how access to new materials and techniques and the changes in mental climate of differing periods have altered its appearance and construction.

Baroque, c. 1680

This chair is made of walnut, a favourite kind of wood for the richly carved types that became fashionable in England after the Restoration. The cane-work of the seat and the panel back is another novelty of the age. The arm-rests make it a truly luxurious example, a fitting seat for some high-ranking servant of the King and Court, for armchairs were until then somewhat rare. With its majestic contours and splendid carving, the chair reflects the new prosperity of the age and its love of grandeur and extravagance.

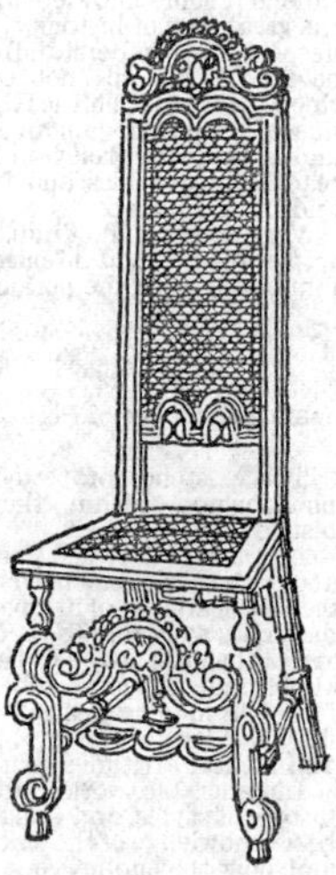

Queen Anne, c. 1700

A direct descendant of the previous chair, this example is also made of walnut, richly carved, with cane-work for the seat and back. Standing tall, it retains some of the dignity of the Baroque style, but there is a restraint about it that makes it representative of the austere and logical Queen Anne style in its early stages. Carved ornamentation is sparingly used and concentrated on important points of the construction, top and bottom of the back, legs and stretcher, the latter member being particularly fine. Considerable areas have been left plain and unadorned.

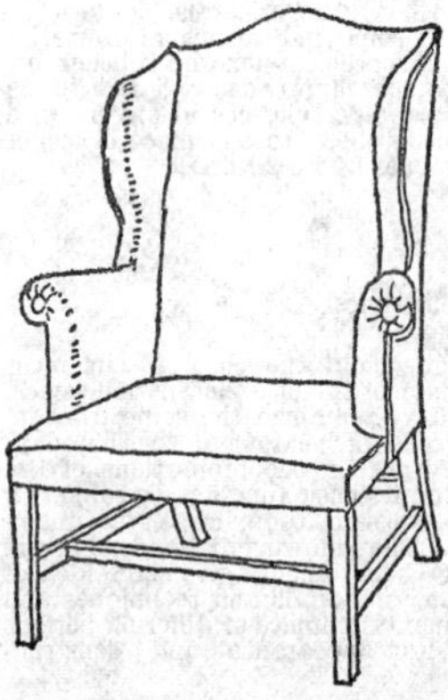

Wing-chair, c. 1720

An English invention of the late 17th century, the wing-chair became a favoured piece of furniture in prosperous homes during the early part of the 18th century. It is the earliest fully upholstered chair in history, the first real easy-chair. Its solid sides and back gave protection against draught, and in its capacious interior one could lean back, even curl up, be alone and take a nap. No wonder the type has remained popular and been in constant production in versions almost unchanged from the original ones to this day.

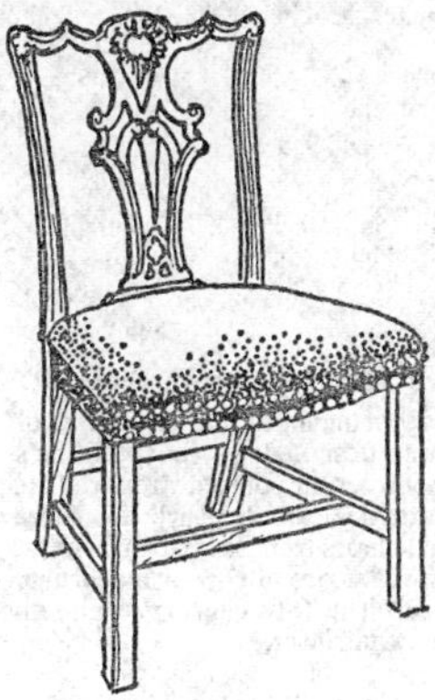

Chippendale, c. 1760

One of a set of six, this chair is made of mahogany which from c. 1720 became the most sought-after material for fine furniture. The chair is simple, sturdy and practical, all ornamentation being concentrated on the back with its gently curving outline and its finely carved splat. When chairs of this type are called " Chippendale ", it does not of course mean that they are known to have been made in the workshops of Thomas Chippendale (1718–79), merely that they are in the style which became popularised through his famous book of furniture designs, *The Gentleman and Cabinet Makers' Director*, first published in 1762.

Hepplewhite, c. 1775

With its simple closed outlines and its neat gracefulness, this chair has caught much that is essential in the Neo-Classical style. It is more subtly elegant than the Chippendale example, having tapering legs that make it look as if it stands on tip-toe, and a shield back with exquisitely carved splat. A special refinement is provided by the curved supports that attach the back to the seat. The name Hepplewhite also needs comment. No piece of extant furniture can be ascribed to George Hepplewhite (d. 1786), but his design-book, *The Cabinet Maker and Upholsterer's Guide* (2nd ed., publ. 1794, after his death) is so representative of the Neo-Classical style in English furniture that the whole stylistic phase has become associated with his name.

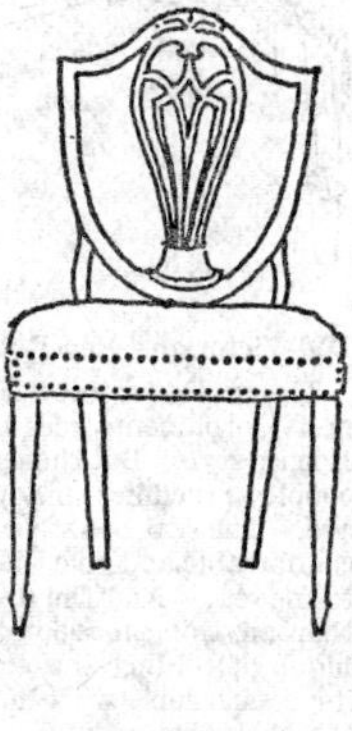

Sheraton, c. 1810

With its pleasantly flowing lines, the Sheraton chair is somewhat more relaxed than the Hepplewhite example. It has obviously been made for comfort as well as for beauty. It is made of beechwood that has been painted and gilded. Thomas Sheraton (1751–1806) is the last in the great triumvirate of English furniture-makers and his fame, like his predecessors', is based not on any important body of extant furniture, but on a book of designs *The Cabinet-Maker and Upholsterer's Drawing-Book*, publ. between 1791 and 1794. It is doubtful whether Sheraton ever made furniture at all, but his book seems to epitomise the general taste in furniture of the Regency style.

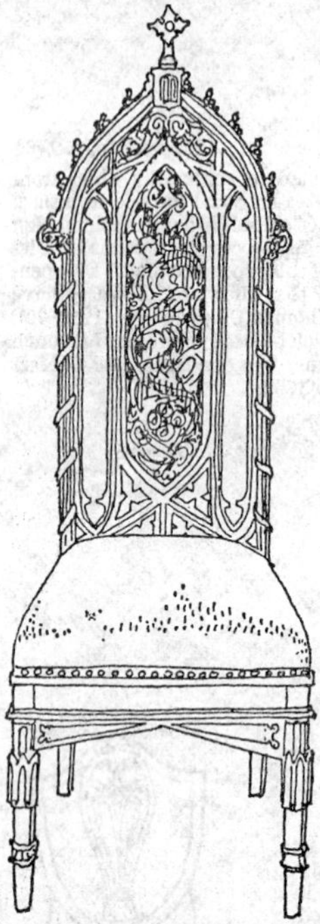

Early Victorian—Neo-Gothic, 1847

When in 1847 a royal lodge was being built for the King of Sweden and Norway, this chair was designed by the building's Danish architect. The Gothic features, the pointed arch and its decoration, were borrowed from cathedral architecture, for there were no direct models for upholstered chairs from real Gothic times. Neo-Gothic was the first of the revival styles of the 19th century. In England it can be traced back into the 18th century, while on the Continent its vogue began somewhat later.

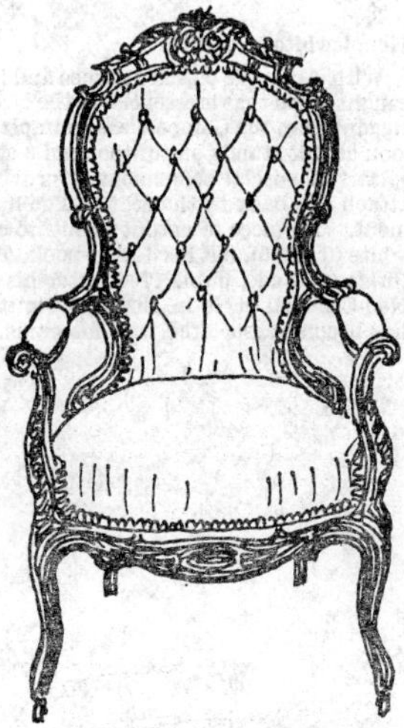

Mid-Victorian—Neo-Rococo, c. 1850–60

The wooden framework of this chair with its curves and pretty ornaments goes back to the original 18th-century Rococo style. But though traditional in form, it contains a couple of technical innovations that are very much of the age. The seat has steel springs that make the chair more comfortable and give the characteristic domed appearance to the seat. And the upholstery is much more elaborate than anything made in the 18th century. The new technique of folding the covering material and fixing it to its background with buttons, made it possible to cover the back firmly, solidly and with beautiful precision despite its complicated curvature.

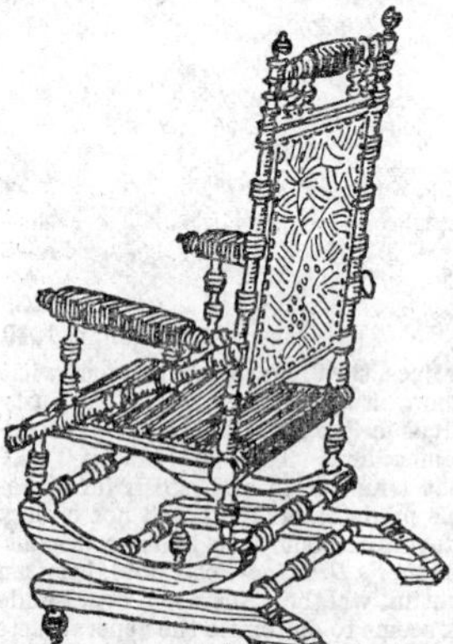

Rocking-chair, c. 1890

The rocking-chair is an American invention, the earliest examples dating from c. 1840. They are simple wooden chairs with four legs put on rockers, and the type became popular all over the world. This chair, also American, was invented c. 1890 and remained popular for a couple of decades. It has the advantage of saving the floorboards, as the rockers rest upon a construction of firm legs. Its mechanism is fairly complex, with steel springs holding the rockers in place and regulating their movements. The chair itself has a seat with steel springs, it is covered with plush, and the woodwork is elaborately turned and polished.

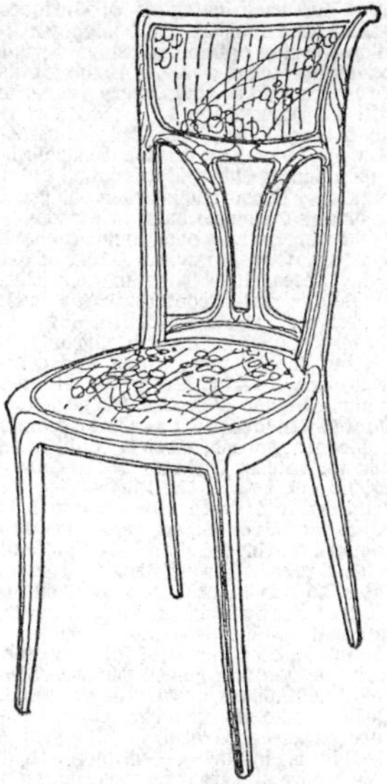

Art Nouveau, c. 1900

With its subtly curved lines, its exquisite materials (palisander and silk), its fine detail and gentle and sweet appearance, this chair is typical of the *fin de siècle* in Paris. Tired of the pomp and over-decoration of many 19th-century products, artists in many countries had begun to grope their way back to basic principles of design and decoration, simplicity of line, good workmanship and a close marriage between form and ornamentation. The designer of this chair, Eugène Gaillard (1862–1933), was among the finest furniture-makers of his time, and one of a circle of young artists who collected round the fashionable shop, " L'Art Nouveau " of Samuel Bing (opened in 1896). It became such a centre for the promotion and sale of fashionable articles of quality that its name came to be given to the whole style.

Bent-wood furniture, 1860

When this chair was made in 1860 it represented something revolutionary in construction. It was the work of a German carpenter, Michael Thonet (1796–1871), who shortly before had invented a completely new method for making chairs. Instead of joining rigid pieces of wood together in complex constructions strengthened with glue and pegs, he bent specially prepared pieces of beechwood into the desired curves and angles, thus saving much work and complicated craftsmanship. His chairs became cheap to buy, light in weight and handsome to look at. From his factory in Vienna (which was active until after the first world war) millions of chairs went out all over the world. His rocking-chair is the most exciting of his models. It remained in production for a long time after its invention.

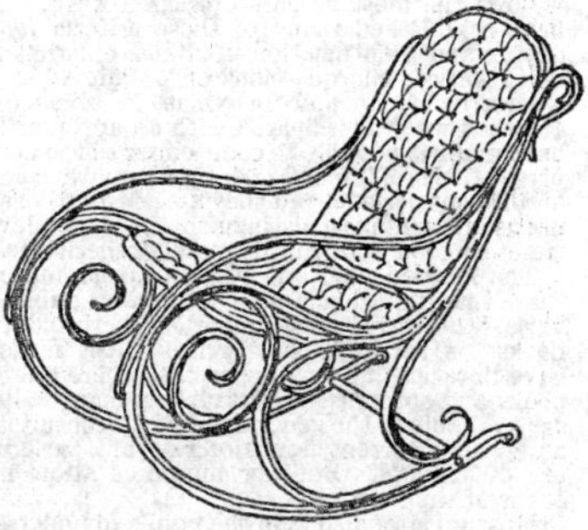

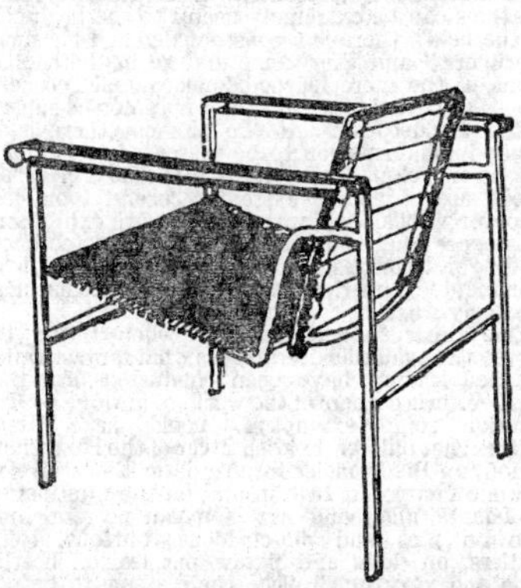

Functionalism, 1928

When cold hard shiny steel was first introduced into furniture-making it represented an almost brutal break with tradition. This chair is one of the earliest of its kind. It is made of chromium-plated steel tube, and is covered with calf's skin. The designer is the famous French architect Le Corbusier (1887–1965), who produced it for a villa he built for a private client in 1928–29. It is a real luxury product, with a clear, intellectual construction that has not been camouflaged in any way, and it is also comfortable to sit in. In 1965 it was put into production again in Britain and in Italy.

Line-drawings by courtesy of H. Aschehoug & Co. (W. Nygaard), Oslo, Norway.

Facilities Offered by Museums.

Those interested in increasing their understanding of antiques have many aids and facilities at their disposal.

Of primary importance are our museums. Here we can walk in, without paying any entrance fee, and look at things old, usually of good quality and frequently well documented, for museums of repute try to admit nothing else to their collections. Where finance and staffing make it possible, the objects are attractively displayed, in their contexts, either together with other things of the same period or as part of systematical series of silver, pottery or whatever it may be. Usually the objects are accompanied by labels, which give basic information about date, place of origin and the reading of marks. The visitor who wants to pursue his quest into a particular subject beyond what he can gather from the display, may ask for further information from the museum offices, where detailed catalogues and original documents are kept, containing all available knowledge about each object in the museum's care.

In the professional staff of museums is lodged an enormous body of learning, based on a wide experience in handling and analysing things old, and backed by general academic training. Many curators have done extremely valuable original research into particular subjects. A generation or two back, much of the research into antiques in Britain was done by amateurs: it is to the patient and imaginative work by non-professionals that we owe our basic understanding of what marks on English silver and pewter mean, and many old books, still useful and valuable, on subjects like Oriental pottery and English glass, were written by collectors. But today, as art history has become a regular subject in our universities and as the museum services have become more highly organised. It is largely to the men and women working inside these institutions that we owe the most valuable research work. They have established many of those criteria for the dating and identification of things old that help us to answer the questions of "Made when and where, by whom and for whom?", asked by us all when we get fascinated with an antique. They have made it possible to come closer to the artistic personalities of important designers and decorators of different periods, and they are constantly assisting us in learning to distinguish what is good, what is not so good and what is merely repetitious.

The learned men and women of our museums share their knowledge with the greater public in a variety of ways, most importantly through the books and articles they write. Most museums have libraries and reading-rooms, where reference books and specialised literature on many subjects are available to the general public for consultation, and where current issues of relevant periodicals are on display. But few museums allow home loans of their books.

Museum staff also help the public to understand the objects in their care by demonstrations in the collections. The larger institutions have people who work on education only, giving lectures in front of the objects, guiding schoolchildren in their first approach to museums, and assisting teachers in understanding how to interpret the collections to their pupils as part of history courses within the normal school curriculum. To art students, the museum collections and libraries are of course treasure houses for visual inspiration.

Members of the public can also bring their own antiques to museums, where the staff will inspect them and to the best of their abilities give opinions on date, origin and quality. Most of the larger public museums provide this kind of service, and it has become so popular that in many places it has become necessary to limit the times for such visits to certain hours of certain days of the week.

Museum staff will give opinions on objects brought in by the public free of charge, but they cannot take any legal or other responsibility for what they say on these occasions, and they will not discuss monetary values.

Facilities Offered by Auctioneers and Dealers.

The great auctioneers in London now have a highly organised service for giving opinions on things brought in to them in advance of sales. As special counters for each category of antiques members of their staff look at what is shown to them, give an on-the-spot opinion and suggest what price the thing might fetch in a sale. As thousands of objects are brought in to them every year, the inspection will at times have to be somewhat summary, but if there is any possibility of something of real value or rarety having turned up higher grade members of the staff are called in for closer examination. For at the heart of the great auctioneering firms sit a small band of extremely learned men and women, who over the years have built up a vast experience, and who keep abreast of whatever new research is being made within their special field; some contribute to such research themselves. These specialists are of course of vital importance to the firm, not only to their prestige, but in the most direct and commercial way: a piece of enamelled glass will fetch a very very much higher price if a perspicacious member of the staff can identify it as a fine example of Islamic 13th-century work, when it could have been presented for sale as a pretty 19th-century ornament and no one to tell the difference. Or suppose a drinking horn with silver mounts is brought in, and the silver expert remembers to have seen the mark on the rim on a dated piece of Bergen silver that passed through the firm years ago. From this he can identify the horn as an undoubted piece of Norwegian Renaissance silver, and its interest and value are greatly enhanced.

Whoever is in doubt about the identity and value of an antique can find good assistance also from a dealer—if he finds his way to the right one. Specialised dealers, like the members of auction-room staff, are experienced and knowledgeable people, and—this is important—through their hands pass many more objects than most museum curators normally handle, and the dealers get an experience in eye and fingertip that is of inestimable value. Naturally, the serious dealer will also keep himself informed on what scholarly research is going on within his chosen field—and, most importantly, he will be able to set a price to the object brought in for his inspection.

The collector who wants to get as close as possible to a true identification of his treasure and find out its monetary value, should first ask for the impartial opinion of a museum curator. Then, with what he has been told in mind, he should approach a good dealer, ask for *his* opinion—and if this doesn't precisely coincide with what the museum has said an interesting discussion may arise, before the dealer finally estimates the price.

Books and Periodicals.

There is today available an enormous literature in English on every possible aspect of antiques, from the most learned treatise containing original scholarly discoveries, to the simplest compendium of what is known, or some of what is known, on any general or particular subject. If well written and attractively presented, these simpler publications can be extremely useful to the beginner in the field: there is a constant demand for such "primers" and they come and go in the shops. Some of the more learned books remain cornerstones of basic knowledge, and may not be superseded for decades. At the moment there is a vogue for information to be presented in dictionary or encyclopaedia form, and the best of these books are of course extremely useful tools for whoever works with antiques. So are exhibition catalogues and sale catalogues, where sometimes leading authorities in their special fields have documented and described important items in a scholarly way.

One thing that strikes one when trying to survey the available literature is what fantastically detailed studies have been conducted into the most esoteric corners of the world of antiques. To mention some examples: books have been written, not only on English silver of the Huguenot period, on Biedermeier furniture, on almost every ceramic factory in Britain and on the Continent, on Islamic glass and Art Nouveau posters, but also on pins and pin-cushions, buttons, toy-soldiers, on dolls and jigsaw puzzles on bottle seals and very much else—there seems to be no limit to the specialisation, and there is a public for it all.

Whoever wants to keep up to date with what goes on in the world of antiques should keep an eye on at least some of the periodicals devoted to the subject that are being published in Britain. The periodicals contain articles on antiques, some written for beginners, some presenting original research of great interest to those really advanced within the special field. Added to this, most periodicals also comment on current exhibitions and fairs, and publish reviews of new books and reports on recent sales, with prices. Not the least valuable are the advertisements, many beautifully illustrated, giving details about forthcoming auction sales, and about specially fine objects that specific dealers have to offer at this particular moment.

Here is a list of some of the most useful and well-established periodicals on antiques:

The Connoisseur. Monthly.
Chestergate House, Vauxhall Bridge Road
London S.W.1.

Apollo. Monthly.
22 Davies Street, London W.1.

The Antique Collector. Monthly.
Chestergate House, Vauxhall Bridge Road
London S.W.1.

The Antique Collector's Guide. Monthly.
1–3 Wine Office Court, Fleet Street,
London E.C.4.

More informal publications act as direct links between buyers and sellers of antiques, advertising specific antiques to be bought or sold, and listing current fairs of interest to dealers and collectors alike:

Antique Collecting. Monthly.
Founded 1966.
5 Church Street, Woodbridge, Suffolk.

The Antiques and Art Weekly.
Founded 1961.
181 Queen Victoria Street, London E.C.4.

Collectors' Bazaar. Monthly.
Founded 1975.
14 Broadway, London S.W.1.

5. Upkeep and Repairs.

To keep one's antiques in good condition demands constant vigilance and attention, and the problems one meets are as extensive and varied as the world of antiques itself. Let it be said at once and emphatically: for the handling of things of some age and technical complexity, one should seek the advice and assistance of professional restorers, for much damage can be done if an amateur tackles the finer points of upkeep and repair in enthusiastic ignorance. The mechanism of an old clock is to the serious clock collector as valuable an antique as the handsomest clockcase, and these fine examples of old skill and craftsmanship may be seriously and irreparably damaged by clumsy repairs by someone who takes one in hand with the only purpose of "making it go". The beautiful joints of a drawer of an 18th-century chest can be masterpieces of traditional cabinet-making, and should not be touched except by those who really know the old methods by which they were made, and can repeat them. And, of course, one should never apply modern chemicals (perhaps camouflaged in detergents or paints) to fragile old materials without first conferring with a restorer, who will know exactly what does which to what, whether beneficial of destructive. Most antique dealers are in regular touch with professional restorers, and will advise their clients on where to get the best assistance when questions of repair arise—and this goes for specialised areas like musical instruments, book-bindings, carpets and chair covers, as well as for the more conventional categories of antiques.

All we can do here is to touch upon some of the problems most frequently met with by those who own antique furniture, silver, pewter, glass and pottery.

Looking after Furniture.

Old furniture will always need quite regular repair, for much of it still has to stand the wear and tear of daily use. Many pieces are complex constructions, and the problems faced here are more manifold than those of almost any other category of antique.

It is a well-known fact that old furniture often responds unhappily to modern home-heating methods. The high, even temperatures in centrally heated rooms have made old glues dry up and crack, and old woods contract and expand in unexpected ways. Fine veneers and inlaid work have often suffered particularly badly, and here one should always consult experts if one wants to obtain good and lasting improvements.

All pre-19th century furniture and many things of later make will need regular polishing to preserve the beautiful texture of the old "naked" wood, and today special polishes suitable for antique furniture are easily available, if not in one's household shop, then at good dealers in old furniture. French polishing was an invention of the early 19th century, and consists in layers of fine shellac lacquers applied to the surface and producing a brilliant gloss. Good French polishing is long and patient work, and should not easily be undertaken by the amateur. It should of course not be applied to furniture of earlier periods than is correct. The removal of old paint or polish should also be tackled with great care, and preferably under the guidance of an expert. Valuable information about what the original paint really was can be lost for ever by heavy-handed removal work, and it will be impossible to bring the piece back to its original appearance.

Locks, hinges and handles are subjected to heavy wear, and will often need replacement or repair. It is very important to the appearance of an old piece of furniture that these details be correct in period-style materials and techniques. Today many firms specialise in selling old locks, hinges and handles, or good reproductions, suitable for replacements on furniture in any period style.

Upholstery on seating furniture in regular use will frequently need renewal, and here it is very important that one should follow the style of the relevant historical period as closely as possible. There is now a big choice of materials available in all period styles, both as to texture and pattern; real horsehair is still being produced, but it is very costly. It is worth remembering that in the development of upholstery, quite a revolution happened at the beginning of the 19th century. It is important that chairs made before the invention of interior springs (or, of course, of foam rubber) should be given the hard flat seats that were used up till then. The restoration of 19th-century upholstery may be quite complicated and expensive to undertake, for it is a difficult process to cover a Victorian chair or a sofa neatly with all the necessary folds and buttons, the correct interior springing (or at least the appearance of it, to give the right curves and angles to the seats), and finish off with adding the full and rich set of trimmings, fringes and tassles in the materials and colours right for the period.

Chair seats and backs with cane-work or rush-work should be cleaned gently with warm soapy water on a soft sponge, then carefully dried and left for twenty-four hours before use. Most antique shops will be able to advise on how to get such work professionally repaired, when that is needed.

Old leather covers on chairs and tables or indeed on books need constant "feeding" not to dry up and crack. Saddle-soap will do for pieces that are not too old or precious, but in the case of things of truly venerable age or with rich decorations one should seek the advice of a museum or responsible dealer for a more subtle polish. The cleaning of really old leather and its repair when torn should also be done on expert advice only.

Looking after Gold and Silver.

Gold presents few problems to its owner for it neither rusts nor tarnishes. Any visitor to our museums will have seen gold objects made hundreds of years ago appearing as bright and shiny as if they were made yesterday. But their silver neighbours may show signs of tarnish, if the museum staffs have not very recently been doing their polishing round, and the same goes for Sheffield plate.

For centuries the only way of removing tarnish was by polishing with abrasive, and much old silver has suffered badly at the hands of overzealous housewives and their maids: engraved ornaments have all but disappeared, the profiles of chased ornaments have lost their precision and marks have been worn away and become undecipherable. Undecorated silver can take a lot of cleaning with soft modern abrasives and soft modern silver cloths. Some of these silver cloths are impregnated with cleaning-material, and are fine for day-to-day upkeep. And now we have the fluid " dips " that remove tarnish by chemical means and work miraculously, though a few seconds in the dip is enough. Longer immersion will remove some of the real silver surface, and produce a dead and unattractive appearance. The dip method is particularly useful for objects of filigree or silver with other kinds of rich and detailed decoration. Dipped objects should be rinsed afterwards in warm water; soap or detergent is unnecessary. It is very important that silver should be meticulously dried after washing, for moisture is one of the enemies of silver. The tarnish it produces is particularly hard to remove.

In the old days, green baize was the standard protective material for storing away cleaned and polished silver. Today plastic provides perfect protection.

Looking after Pewter.

Rule one concerning the upkeep of old pewter is that it should not be over-polished. A certain matting of the surface is part of its natural ageing-process, indeed this patina represents some of the charm of this popular kind of antique. Pewter is easily contaminated by contact with salts and other chemicals, and if left for a long time in very cold surroundings, the surface will develop dark spots and bubbles; if this process is left to develop, the surface will eventually dissolve into a sort of powder. Day-by-day cleaning should be done with a soft polishing cloth, and if something stronger is needed, an oily rag with a gentle abrasive can be applied, but not too often or for too long. Pewter is very soft and the surface highly susceptible to scratches and knocks. Dents and other accidental imperfections should preferably be corrected by experts. A clumsy amateur can do much damage by well-meaning efforts to try and " do it oneself ", just because the material is so soft. Engraved ornaments should of course be polished with particular care, so that the sharpness of the lines is not destroyed.

Looking after Glass.

To keep old glass is not difficult, for it is corrupted neither by rust nor moths. Undecorated glass can take a lot of cleaning in strong soapy warm (not hot!) water, and spots and impurities can be attacked with abrasives, but the fragility of the glass itself must of course always be kept in mind. Glass with cut or engraved decoration should be handled more gently, and here one can try and remove obstinate spots or marks by soaking the object concerned in a strong solution of household detergent for some hours. But glass decorated with enamelling or gilding should of course not be submitted to cleaning with abrasives nor to very strong soapy solutions. In all cases careful drying is essential to a good result.

If glass should break, which it does all too easily, it is hard to repair in a way that looks well, especially where the glass is colourless and transparent. In most cases the best one can do is to try and make the repairs look as neat and tidy as one can, for to make them invisible is very rarely possible. The broken stem of a precious wineglass may be joined again with silver, and in such cases care should be taken that the original proportions of the glass are not unduly disturbed. Work like this should of course be entrusted only to specialists. In many cases one must resign oneself to the fact that a glass is broken beyond repair and write it off as lost, however reluctantly. Only when glass of great age or rarety is at stake is it worth trying to save it by joins and repairs with glues and rivets.

To repair old glass by replacing decayed or missing parts with new glass, is to all intents and purposes not possible. Glass is made by melting its various ingredients in furnaces at extremely high temperatures, and then submitting it to a long and gradual cooling process. Any contact between the old " cold " glass and the new hot one will involve the greatest risks of breaks and bursts in the old glass, and the method, though it has been tried with some success in a few cases, is not to be recommended

Decanters are among the most popular types of antique glass. They were normally made with stoppers. and when acquiring an old decanter, it is important to see that the original stopper is still there. Usually, a wrong stopper is easily recognised: it will differ from the decanter in the colour and consistency of the glass, as well as in patterns of decoration, and the proportions of decanter and stopper may not harmonise. A decanter which has lost its stopper is a better antique than a decanter with a wrong one added. Naturally, similar problems pose themselves with glass goblets and other glasses with covers. To clean a decanter that has become stained inside, fine silver sand and water should be swilled around the inside to act as a gentle abrasive, or one can use a mixture of tea leaves and vinegar in the same way. The decanter should then be rinsed and drained by inverting it in a vase or jug until absolutely dry.

Glass sometimes suffers from what is called " glass disease ". The symptoms are, first, the appearance of shades of matting, which look like dirt or impurities, but cannot be removed by rubbing. They occur most frequently where there are natural marks of use, for instance round the inner rim of a wineglass. For the weakness inherent in the glass is affected by contact with moisture of every kind, first of all by the contents which it has been filled with. But the ordinary moisture of the air will also have its effect. The disease usually develops slowly, but inexorably. In the later stages the glass will take on a " crizzled " aspect like cracked ice, and if unchecked, the process will end in total collapse.

Glass disease is caused by an imbalance in the original mixture of the ingredients that make up the glass, and it cannot be cured. All one can do is to try and stop its progress, by insulating the glass from any moisture of the air by putting it in an airtight case, or by covering the surface with some protective and invisible kind of lacquer; expert advice is necessary for the application of such remedies. Venetian glass of the 18th century, Potsdam and Bohemian glass and English glass of the late 17th century are particularly prone to glass disease. But even some 19th- and 20th-century glass can be found to suffer from glass disease. It is of course not infectious.

Looking after Pottery.

Generally speaking, glazed pottery (which of course includes porcelain), is fairly resistant to cleaning, even scrubbing with abrasives—that is, if the decorations, whether printed or enamel-painted, were properly fixed to the surface by firing when the things were first made. " Cold " (i.e., unfired) paint is very fragile, but fortunately also very rare. But gilding should be handled with some care when submitted to cleaning.

Simple, clean breaks in ceramic wares can usually be repaired at home with the help of the excellent modern glues now available. The instructions printed on the packing should be followed meticulously But when it comes to more complicated breaks and cracks, where perhaps some of the original ware has been broken " into smithereens " and has to be repaired with replacement material then expert hands and experience are needed.

It is only a generation or two since modern glues

came on to the market, and in many cases old, heavily repaired examples of ceramic ware can with advantage be re-repaired. Old, discoloured glues and ugly rivets can be removed, and the necessary repairs done much more neatly.

6. Fakes.

What ever kind of antique one takes an interest in, one stands in danger of meeting fakes, and anyone can fall into a trap. Even learned academics and experienced dealers will at some time or another have been deceived by a skilful fake. Books and articles have been written on the subject, unveiling famous examples of fakes in the past, and many others are undoubtedly at this moment on the market. But when one handles antiques, one soon discovers that there is no neat dividing line between good honest things on the one hand, and wicked fakes on the other. The world of fakes is a complex one, full of gliding values and transitional cases.

Let us first define what we mean by a " genuine fake "—it is an object made to look like something much older and rarer than it really is, a counterfeit offered for sale as the genuine article, with the express purpose to deceive. A flagrant example is the case of the " Billies and Charlies ". They were lead figures, crudely and " primitively " made by two illiterate labourers, at the middle of the last century. They had invented these figures with their own hands and out of their own heads, and distributed them generously into various sites under excavation. For a short time the figures were accepted as products of mediaeval craftsmanship, but they were fairly soon recognised by specialists as the naïve fakes they were—though they have continued to puzzle less sophisticated diggers until quite recent times.

But let us consider some less clear-cut cases.

What is a " real " Chippendale chair?

If one want to be pedantic, one must say that no such thing exists, for none have been preserved which are known for certain to have been made by Thomas Chippendale himself. The nearest we can come to " real " Chippendale are chairs made during his period and in his style as we know it from his pattern-book (*see* line drawing **D13**), in solid mahogany and of first-class workmanship. What makes the problem really knotty is that chairs in the style of Chippendale have been made continuously through long periods during the Victorian age, not as fake antiques, but in order to satisfy a never-ending demand for these neat and handsome chairs, and it needs a trained eye to distinguish Victorian from 18th-century Chippendale. And then we have the frank copies, made as " period furniture " from late Victorian into modern times, when the Chippendale style had become historical and attractive as such. None of these varieties are wicked fakes, but if inexperienced people are asked to pay " real " Chippendale prices for these later versions, the element of faking must be laid at the door of the vendor whose aim it has been to deceive for personal monetary gain.

Honest copies, made in admiration for the craftsmanship of past ages, may lead to misunderstanding. Philippe-Joseph Brocard (d. 1896) of Paris went to enormous trouble to learn to master the difficult technique of enamelling on glass, practised in such a masterly way by Islamic decorators of the 13th–16th centuries. He succeeded so well that some of his works can only with difficulty be distinguished from the Islamic masterpieces, especially the copies of mosque lamps with Cufic inscriptions. Fortunately he signed much of his work, and to the sharp observer the smoother quality of the 19th-century glass he used will reveal even his unsigned works as modern copies. Brocard was a fine craftsman, who surely never worked with any intention of faking.

Repairs are of course perfectly legitimate means of keeping valuable and much-loved antiques from the natural decay brought on by heavy use and the passing of time (*see* **D17**). But sometimes restorations may be so extensive that they take us into the borderland of faking.

Tudor furniture has for long been greatly admired by collectors, but it is, oh!, so easily counterfeited, wholly or partly. It is constructed by a rich combination of framed panels, supported by bulbous feet and columns, and it is fairly easy to substitute one or two—or five or ten—parts with " restorations ". If in the end one is left with only one or two original pieces of carving, combined with a multiplicity of modern copies and variations of old carved work and with new supports added, there is not really much left of the original Tudor piece. One also finds old parts of such furniture combined with new in ways that were never dreamt of by our Tudor forefathers; the very constructions are fruits of the modern restorer's—or faker's—imagination.

All porcelain figures are made from moulds. A clever person can reproduce things moulded, like coins and certain kinds of jewellery, without too much difficulty: he can make a cast from the original and then a new mould, from which he can draw as many copies as he likes. Such copies can usually be recognised for what they are from a certain crudity of detail. But porcelain figures can pose more difficult problems than that. In some cases old moulds from one or two hundred years back have been preserved and used again. These later copies will usually be painted in a different and more varied colour-scale than those of the original period, and it may have been necessary to make small repairs to the moulds which will show in the finished product. If figures made in modern times from 18th-century moulds are presented as 18th-century work and sold at correspondingly high prices, faking is taking place. But if they are being offered for what they are—repeats, reproductions—and sold at suitably lower prices, this is of course perfectly honest—and incidentally, the figures can still give great pleasure, preserving as they do the major sculptural qualities of the original models.

Finally a word about the faking of marks. This has been done extensively on silver and pewter as well as on pottery. The famous mark of two crossed swords has from 1724 to this day been the mark of Meissen porcelain, and over the centuries a number of less exalted factories have been tempted to adopt marks so similar to the Meissen one, that at a quick glance they could be mistaken for it. Apart from these imitations, there has been quite a lot of downright faking of the Meissen mark. The most famous of English potteries is that founded by Josiah Wedgwood during the 1750s and still, of course, very much alive and active. From 1771 to this day every piece of pottery that has left the Wedgwood factory has been marked with the name WEDGWOOD, sometimes in solitary grandeur, sometimes accompanied by emblems or names of individual decorators, and from 1860 onwards often with a date-mark in the form of a single letter, that changes from one year to another. All these details can easily be checked in any up-to-date book on pottery marks, or on the firm of Josiah Wedgwood & Sons Ltd., which is the correct trade-name of the firm. But c. 1825 an indifferent producer of pottery in Stockton, called Willam Smith, began to put the word **Wedgwood**, or more frequently **Wedgewood**, after his own name or initials, on his products. In 1848 the real Wedgwood firm fought a lawsuit to prevent this misuse of their name, and the practice was stopped. But from c. 1860 until quite recently, a firm in Tunstall has been calling itself Wedgwood & Co. and marked its ware with this name, sometimes combined with the figure of a unicorn. Only a sharp observer will notice the difference between " & Co " and " & Sons "—at a quick glance. More details on the faking of ceramic marks can be found adjoining the tables of marks on **D23–28**.

These brief remarks will give the reader some indication of what kind of problems face the unwary, or for that matter even the most vigilant, when moving about the world of antiques.

How can one protect oneself? Absolute guarantees against fakes and counterfeits do not exist, as fakers and irresponsible traders use their imagination and wicked skills in ever new ways. But one can guard against being taken in by being constantly sceptical, by acquiring whatever knowledge there is about known fakes, and by using one's imagination about what can technically and financially be worthwhile for anyone to try and counterfeit.

THE LONDON

A	1598	a	1618	a	1638	A	1658	a	1678	a	1697
B	9	b	19	b	39	B	59	b	79	b	97
C	1600	c	20	c	40	C	Chas. II. 60	c	80	c	98
D	1	d	21	d	41	D	61	d	81	d	99
E	2	e	22	e	42	E	62	e	82	e	1700
F	Jas. I. 3	f	23	f	43	F	63	f	83	f	1
G	4	g	24	g	44	G	64	g	84	g	Anne. 2
H	5	h	Chas. I. 25	h	45	H	65	h	Jas. II. 85	h	3
I	6	i	26	i	46	I	66	i	86	i	4
K	7	k	27	k	47	K	67	k	87	k	5
L	8	l	28	l	48	L	68	l	88	l	6
M	9	m	29	m	Cmwth. 49	M	69	m	W. & M. 89	m	7
N	10	n	30	n	50	N	70	n	90	n	8
O	11	o	31	o	51	O	71	o	91	o	9
P	12	p	32	p	52	P	72	p	92	p	10
Q	13	q	33	q	53	Q	73	q	93	q	11
R	14	r	34	r	54	R	74	r	94	r	12
S	15	s	35	s	55	S	75	s	Wm. III. 95	s	13
T	16	t	36	t	56	T	76	t	96	t	Geo. I. 14
V	17	v	37	v	57	V	77			v	15

PROVINCIAL SILVER MARKS

BIRMINGHAM . . 1800  1900 

CHESTER . 1701  1800 

EXETER . . 1601  1800 

See also Hall-mark, Gen. Information.

SILVER MARKS

A	Geo. I. 1716	a	1736	A	1756	a	1776	A	1796	a	1816
B	17	b	37	B	57	b	77	B	97	b	17
C	18	c	38	C	58	c	78	C	98	c	18
D	19	dd	39	D	59	d	79	D	99	d	19
E	20	e	40	E	Geo. III 60	e	80	E	1800	e	Geo. IV. 20
F	21	f	41	F	61	f	81	F	1	f	21
G	22	g	42	G	62	g	82	G	2	g	22
H	23	h	43	H	63	h	83	H	3	h	23
I	24	i	44	I	64	i	84	I	4	i	24
K	25	k	45	K	65	k	85	K	5	k	25
L	26	l	46	L	66	l	86	L	6	l	26
M	Geo. II 27	m	47	M	67	m	87	M	7	m	27
N	28	n	48	N	68	n	88	N	8	n	28
O	29	o	49	O	69	o	89	O	9	o	29
P	30	p	50	P	70	p	90	P	10	p	Will. IV. 30
Q	31	q	51	Q	71	q	91	Q	11	q	31
R	32	r	52	R	72	r	92	R	12	r	32
S	33	ſ	53	S	73	s	93	S	13	s	33
T	34	t	54	T	74	t	94	T	14	t	34
V	35	u	55	U	75	u	95	U	15	u	35

PROVINCIAL SILVER MARKS

NEWCASTLE 1702  1800 

SHEFFIELD 1800  1900 

YORK 1700  1800 

THE LONDON SILVER MARKS

A	1836	a	1856	A	1876	a	1896	a	1916	A	Ed. VIII. 1936
B	Vic. 37	b	57	B	77	b	97	b	17	B	Geo. VI 37
C	38	c	58	C	78	c	98	c	18	C	38
D	39	d	59	D	79	d	99	d	19	D	39
E	40	e	60	E	80	e	1900	e	20	E	40
F	41	f	61	F	81	f	Ed. VII. 1	f	21	F	41
G	42	g	62	G	82	g	2	g	22	G	42
H	43	h	63	H	83	h	3	h	23	H	43
I	44	i	64	I	84	i	4	i	24	I	44
K	45	k	65	K	85	k	5	k	25	K	45
L	46	l	66	L	86	l	6	l	26	L	46
M	47	m	67	M	87	m	7	m	27	M	47
N	48	n	68	N	88	n	8	n	28	N	48
O	49	o	69	O	89	o	9	o	29	O	49
P	50	p	70	P	90	p	Geo. V. 10	p	30	P	50
Q	51	q	71	Q	91	q	11	q	31	Q	51
R	52	r	72	R	92	r	12	r	32	R	Eliz. II. 52
S	53	s	73	S	93	s	13	s	33	S	53
T	54	t	74	T	94	t	14	t	34	T	54
U	55	u	75	U	95	u	15	u	35	U	55

SCOTTISH AND IRISH SILVER MARKS

EDINBURGH . 1700  1800 

GLASGOW . . 1700  1800 

DUBLIN . . 1700  1800 

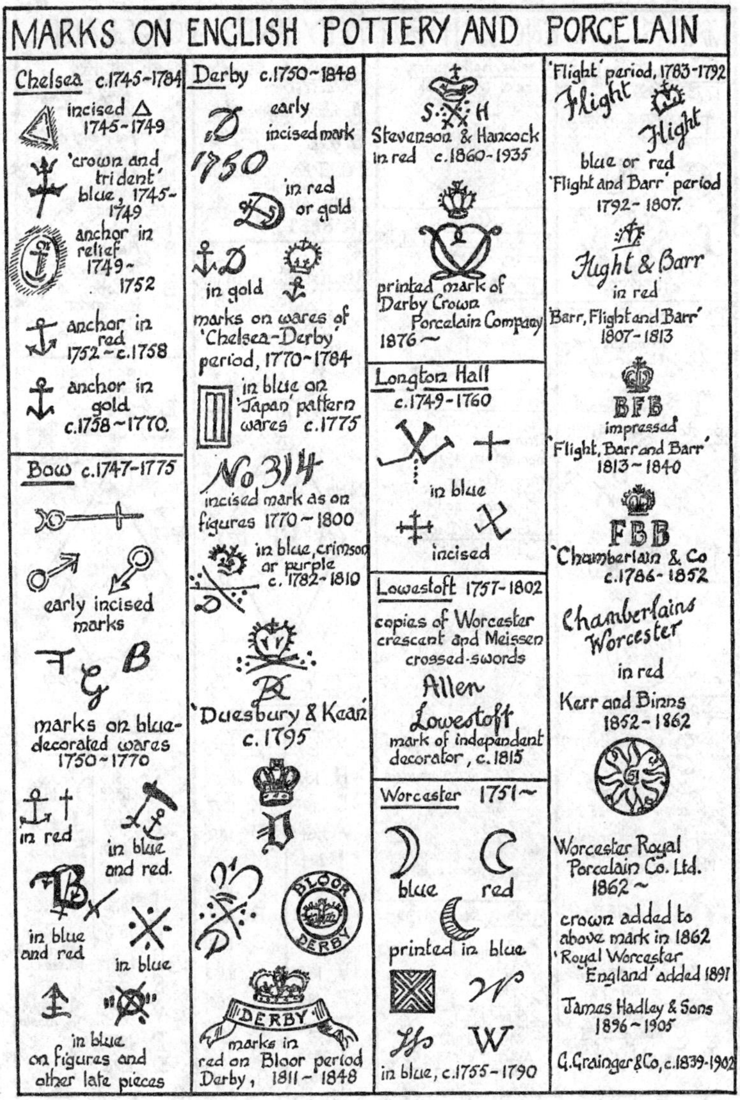

Many of the marks found on ceramics are merely the marks of painters and workman. Even when identified, they are not a sure guide to the place of manufacture, as these people would work in many different factories in the course of their careers. The throwers or "repairers" (the workers who assembled the various parts of figures, etc.) invariably used a mark scratched in the body of the ware prior to the biscuit-firing. These marks when *under* the glaze can safely be treated as genuine. A mark which has been ground in after firing, in order to deceive, will not have the characteristic burr or raised edge produced when soft clay is scratched.

Painters and gilders would generally use one of the colours in their palette or gilt to mark the wares upon which they worked. This was probably for the benefit of the management as payment was often on a piecework basis.

The marks used on English wares were applied in several different ways—by incising, impressing, painting, or by transfer-printing *under* the glaze

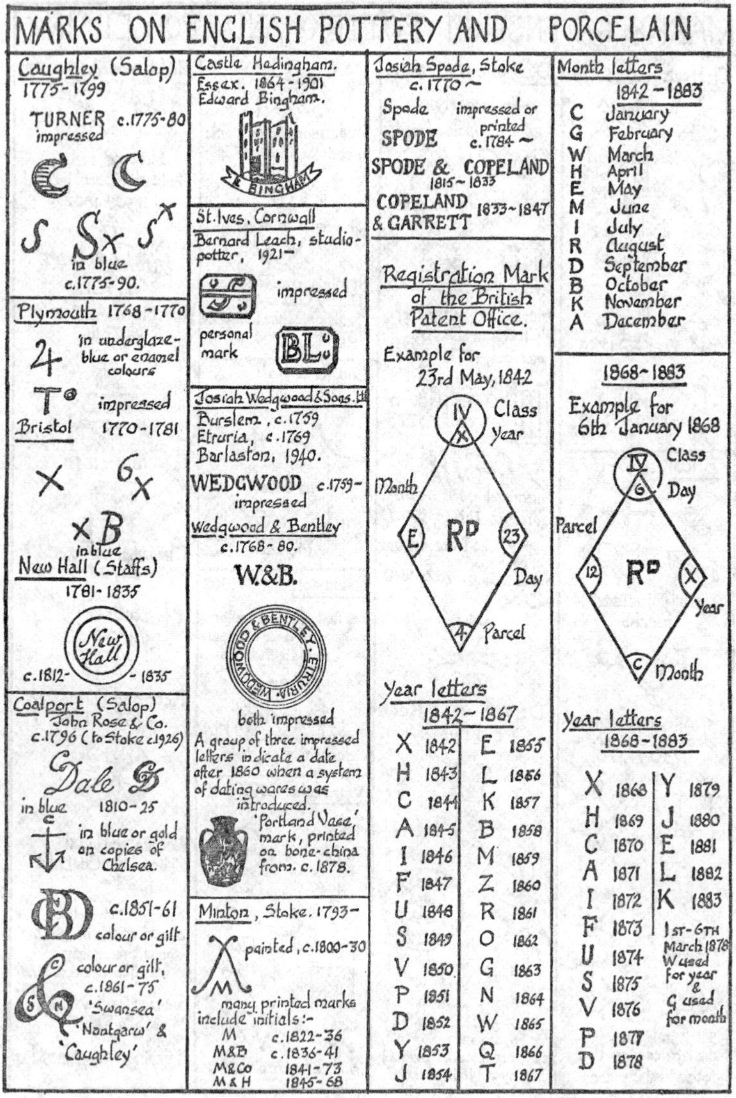

in blue (also in green after 1850). Marking by painting, transfer-printing, or stencilling *over* the glaze in enamel colours is always liable to be fraudulent as these types of mark can be added at any time after the piece has been made.

From 1842–83 many manufacturers' wares were marked with the "diamond-mark", illustrated above. This was an indication that the design had been registered with the British Patent Office. Ceramics was Class IV, indicated in the topmost section of the mark. This gave copyright protection for three years. After 1883 the mark was written as a number, *e.g.*, Rd. No. 12345.

A further indication of late wares is the inclusion of the word "England" in the mark. This was necessary to comply with the American McKinley Tariff Act of 1891. The full term "Made in England" is an indication of 20th century manufacture.

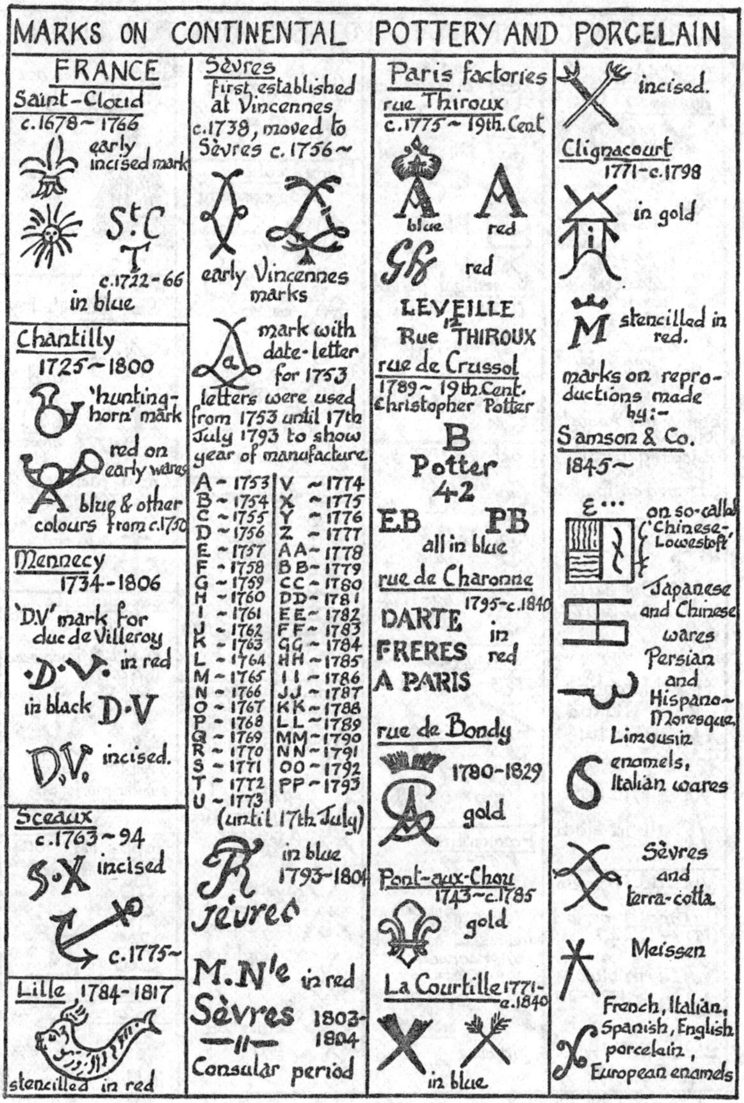

It was not until the adoption on Meissen porcelain in 1723 of the " K.P.M." and in 1724 of the cross-swords (from the arms of Saxony) that marks began to be used at all regularly in Europe. The placing of the mark underneath and the use of blue are clear indications that the Chinese model was being followed. The Meissen practice was then adopted by other German and, indeed, by most porcelain factories of repute.

Throughout the 18th century the practice was never regularised, and except for a brief period in France from 1766, and two years later in the Dutch town of Delft, there was no compulsory marking of wares. The factories of repute, proud of their productions, added a recognised mark and even used it, as at Nymphenburg, as part of the decoration. Their imitators left their wares unmarked or employed a mark likely to be mistaken for a more famous one: Weesp and Tournay both adopted a version of the Meissen crossed-swords;

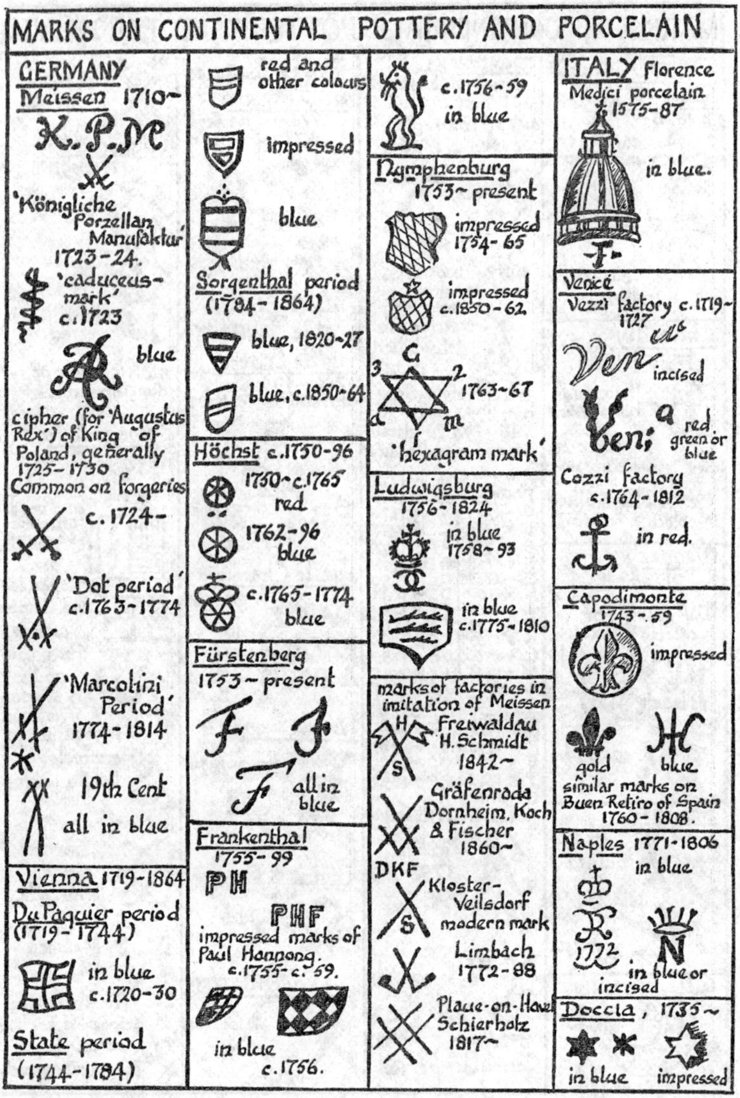

the torches of La Courtille, the hooks of Rauenstein, the hayforks of Rudolstadt, the "L"s of Limbach, and the "W" of Wallendorf, were all drawn in such a way as to resemble the Meissen mark.

The firm of Samson & Co. was established in Paris in 1845, claiming to make " Reproductions of Ancient Works emanating from the Museums and from Private Collections ". When imitating the true hard-paste porcelain of the Far East or the Continent, Samson's wares are difficult to detect, due to their being made from similar materials, whereas his reproductions of such English factories as Bow, Chelsea, and Derby are more easily recognised as fakes. Unfortunately the range of Samson's marks, illustrated above, do not appear to have been regularly used, or, as is sometimes the case, the original mark has been removed by grinding or by etching away with acid, and a replica of a known genuine mark added.

Factory marks in the Western sense are practically unknown on Chinese porcelain wares, while those purporting to record the period of manufacture are so liable to be "commemorative", or even deliberately fraudulent, as to be a frequent cause of dispute among students. Marks of the Ming Chinese Emperors, Hsüan Tê, Ch'êng Hua and Chia Ching are commonly found on wares of the reign of the Ch'ing Emperor K'ang Hsi, while the reign name of K'ang Hsi himself, rare on the abundant porcelain of his period, is chiefly found on 19th- and 20th-century wares.

Under the rule of the Ming Emperors (1368-1644) the Sung ideals in pottery were largely rejected in favour of the vogue for fine-grained white porcelain heralding the beginning of a new period in Chinese ceramic history with its centre in the town of Ching-tê Chên in Kiangsi province where a new Imperial factory was started in 1369 with a prolific output of early Ming blue-and-white

Drawn by J. P. Cushion, Victoria and Albert Museum.

and fine enamel-painted porcelain both for the court and later for general use and export.

Following the fall of the Ming Dynasty in 1644 their declining culture was revived by the Ch'ing Emperor K'ang Hsi (1662—1722) who was a great patron of the arts. The European influence of the French and Netherlandish Jesuits at his courts is seen in the Baroque character of the early Ch'ing porcelain.

There was a backward-looking tendency during the reigns of Yung-Chêng (1723–35) and Ch'ien Lung (1736–95) when exact copies of the classical Sung wares and the early Ming painted porcelain were made.

The Imperial porcelain of the 19th century was as a rule carefully and weakly correct in following earlier styles and models. The factory was burnt in 1853 by the T'ai-ping rebels and hardly recovered before the 1911 revolution ended the Dynasty.

Arabesque in black and white marble, from the floor of the Cathedral at Siena, dated 1372.

COLLECTORS' GLOSSARY

Animaliers (Fr. = "animal makers"), term used to describe the group of French 19th cent. sculptors who specialised in the modelling of animals. They made them singly or in pairs to form a group, and the animals are described in much naturalistic detail and always in vigorous movement, leaping, running, fighting. They are cast in bronze, in dimensions small enough for them to be used as table ornaments. The originator of the genre was Antoine-Louis Barye (1796–1875). The quality of the works of *les animaliers* can vary greatly, and there has been much recasting of good models, with results which are inevitably imperfect.

Arabesque, a decorative motif consisting of curved and interlacing lines, symmetrically arranged; a stylised interpretation of branches, tendrils and leaves as seen in nature. As the name suggests, the motif was invented by the Arabs, who used it for hundreds of years, partly because the representation of beings, animal or human, were not permitted by their culture. Arabesques were used most impressively to cover large areas, like tiled walls and carpets. From the Renaissance onwards, the Europeans adapted the arabesque to decorate inlaid furniture, ceramic plates and tiles and textiles.

Arita, see **Imari**.

Automobile mascots, sculptured ornaments affixed to the bonnet of motor-cars. They came into fashion immediately after the first world war, when fast cars became symbols of the modern age of streamlined speed. The mascots have been made in a variety of materials, silver or silver plate, brass and bronze, cast glass. The figures usually suggest speed (girls' heads or figures facing the oncoming wind with ecstatic joy) or power (prancing horses, falcons' heads). Today they are becoming increasingly collectable.

Blanc-de-Chine, a kind of Chinese porcelain, made into vessels or figures, covered with a fine, milky-white glaze and otherwise unornamented. Within the great ceramic history of China, *blanc-de-Chine* represents a distinctive and strictly limited group. It was made during the 18th, 19th and 20th centuries in Te-Hua in Fukien province. Much of it was exported to Europe. The serene figure of the female deity Kuan-Yin has always been very popular in the West, and many models have been made, varying from the exquisite to the clumsy and angular. Of great interest are also the groups of Europeans with their Chinese servants, made in Te-Hua for the Western market.

Boulle (Buhl) furniture, a luxurious kind of case furniture, first made in Paris by the Court cabinetmaker André-Charles Boulle (Buhl is the Germanised form) (1642–1732). Cupboards, chests, clocks, etc. are veneered with tortoiseshell and inlaid with patterns in bronze. The technique was practised in Paris throughout the 18th cent. by the sons and successors of André-Charles Boulle, and later by imitators in many countries. Boulle furniture has been made right up to recent times.

Bullet teapot, a modern collectors' term for silver teapots, as first made by Huguenot goldsmiths in London at the time of Queen Anne, with the body and its cover made in the form of a sphere, with a low foot and a spout of silver and a black wooden handle. Bullet teapots were also made after the reign of Queen Anne, and the shape was eventually translated into porcelain and earthenware, in England and on the Continent.

Cased glass, a technique whereby clear or coloured glass is covered by a layer of glass in a different shade; when patterns are cut through the top layer the inner core will be revealed and interesting colour effects and contrasts result. The most famous piece of cased glass in history is the Portland Vase, of Roman make (1st cent. A.D.), now in the British Museum (*see* **Section L**).

Celadon, a soft greyish-green coloured glaze, widely used on Chinese pottery and porcelain from the Sung period (960–1279) and well into the 19th cent. The name was given it by the Europeans: in Honoré d'Urfé's 17th cent. pastoral romance "L'Astreé" a shepherd called Celadon wore a costume of this subtle and beautiful colour. The French imported a lot of Celadon ware from China during the 18th cent., and the best pieces were mounted in elaborate bronze.

Creamware, a ceramic material which has a cream-coloured glaze over a solid and resistant body the clay usually containing calcined flint. Creamware was developed in Staffordshire during the middle years of the 18th cent., and brought to perfection in the course of the 1760s by Josiah Wedgwood. He formed the new ware into shapes which were at the same time practical and handsome, suitable for every household, and with a distinctive touch of the Neo-Classical style which was just coming into fashion. When his product was complete and perfect, he appealed to Royalty for patronage and received permission to call his invention Queen's Ware.

Soon creamware was put into production by most Staffordshire firms, and, most importantly, by the factory at Leeds, who became a major producer. Because of its excellent ceramic qualities, its elegant appearance and reasonable price, creamware became the standard material for plates, dishes and the like all over the world and by the beginning of the 19th cent. it was being widely produced on the Continent. The rise of creamware meant the decline of faience (*q.v.*). Until quite recently, English creamware was still the basis for most of the ceramic tableware used in the world.

Davenport, a special type of writing desk, originally made for travelling, small in size, with a sloping top and three or four drawers opening to the side. According to tradition, it got its name from one Captain Davenport, who ordered such a desk from Gillow's in Lancaster in the early 19th cent. This is, however, apparently apocryphal, for the type has now been traced back to the late 18th cent. The early examples are compact in shape and devoid of ornamentation. But as the 19th cent. proceeded, the type became popular as a lady's desk, and it was provided with pigeon-holes on top and richly ornamented in Neo-Rococo. Most of the extant examples are veneered with mahogany. Davenports remained in regular use until the end of the Victorian age.

Etagère, *see* **Whatnot**.

Faience, a ceramic ware of porous, lightweight, fired clay covered with a milky-white, non-transparent tin glaze. It began as an imitation of Chinese porcelain, and was usually decorated with coloured ornamentation. As the painted motifs have to be applied directly on to the wet glaze to be fired with it, the colours are absorbed into the damp surface as if it were blotting-paper, and the painter has to work fast, without changing his mind or correcting his work. This gives to faience painting an imminence, at times a nonchalance, which is its greatest charm.

The name faience is derived from Faenza, the name of a north Italian town, which has had a large and important output from the 15th cent. to this day. But Faenza was only one of many centres in Italy to produce this kind of ware during the Renaissance, which in some contexts is described as Maiolica (*q.v.*). The word faience is applied more specifically to tin-glazed ceramic ware made in northern Europe during post-Renaissance times.

Friggers, objects made by glassblowers outside working hours. Some were made by apprentices in training, others by highly-skilled and experienced men, who could display their personal fancies and idiosyncracies more freely when "friggering" than when working on instructions to produce commercial goods.

Imari, a port on the Japanese island of Kyushu, whence porcelain made at the nearby production centre of Arita was exported in large quantities. The name applies particularly to the wares made from the 17th cent. and until recently, with red and dark blue ornaments on a white ground, accompanied by plenty of gilding; in essence the style changed little over the long period when Imari porcelain enjoyed its great popularity in the West. The best examples are very fine, while other pieces made in the later stages can be somewhat crude.

Mahogany, a very hard wood with a fine grain and distinctive markings. Because it is so hard, carved work retains its precision even after years of wear. Mahogany can also be polished to a wonderfully high gloss and sparkle. Because of these qualities it has been widely used for fine furniture ever since it was first imported into Europe early in the 18th cent. The dark Cuban mahogany (Swietenia) was first used most widely, later much fine mahogany (Khaya) from Africa was in demand. The English were the first to use mahogany for furniture, and it gave distinctive character to many of their finest 18th cent. products, like the chairs in the styles of Chippendale and Hepplewhite (*see* **D13**) and, as veneers, to innumerable chests and cupboards.

Maiolica, a ceramic ware with a white tin glaze and decorated with painted figures, often with a metallic lustre sheen. The name itself appears to have been derived from Majorca because ware of this kind by Hispano-Moresque potters was largely imported into Italy, the ships arriving by way of this island. The name has been retained for tin-glazed ware with painted decoration, made in various Italian centres during the Renaissance, but it can also be defined as Faience (*q.v.*).

Majolica, a ceramic ware of the 19th cent., invented at the Minton factory in 1849, and imitated all over Europe within a short time. It is a kind of earthenware, suitable for bold modelling on a large scale, and when covered with colourful glazes in greens and browns, particularly well suited for outdoor goods, *jardinières* on tall stands or decorative sculptures. Majolica tiles became extremely popular for covering halls, kitchens, etc. Some of them are handsomely provided with relief decoration, while the fact that they could easily be washed down with water added to their popularity.

Marquetry, inlaid work of woods in constrasting colours. The patterns can be geometrical (and this is particularly suitable when marquetry is used for floors), but the technique can also be applied to veneered furniture, with delicate motifs of flowers, animals or human figures with lively curves and much fine detail. Marquetry first became fashionable on fine furniture during the Renaissance, but it reached a peak of popularity from the end of the 17th cent. onwards. During the latter part of the 18th and throughout the 19th cent., marquetry was used widely, but sparingly, mostly in the form of small, neat ornaments like stars, shells and the like on large, undecorated surfaces. The Victorian age saw a great revival of elaborate marquetry work.

Netsuke, a clasp or sliding toggle, used on the sash of the Japanese kimono, to carry a small bag or box for the little necessities of daily life. Netsuke can be made in a variety of materials, wood, horn, ivory, bamboo, etc.; and carved into sculptured form or covered with black lacquer ornamented with pictures in gold. The subjecst of the decorations are usually taken from Japanese folklore or mythology. Netsuke have been collectors' items for many decades.

Niello, a method for decorating silver. A line pattern is engraved into the silver surface, and the lines are filled with an alloy of metals, which produces a black colour. The black makes a handsome contrast to the whiteness of the silver, and niello has been one of the most ancient ways of ornamenting the precious metal, having been used in classical antiquity as well as in pre-Christian and medieval Europe. Later, it gave way to more sophisticated methods of decoration.

Opaline, modern collectors' word used to describe an important group of French 19th cent. ornamental glass. *Opaline* is made of opaque, usually milky-white glass with an opalescent sheen. The best *opaline* is the earliest, which dates from the Napoleonic period and the Restoration. It comes in vases, urns, ewers and the like, severely Neo-Classical in shape and frequently mounted in brass or bronze. After *c.*1830, the shapes become less austere, and the glass is sometimes tinted into pastel shades. *Opaline* became widely used for dainty flacons for ladies' boudoirs and decorated with gilding and pretty painted flowers. After *c.*1860 the whole genre degenerated; the opalescent glass was replaced by a grey and dull kind of material, and decorations in relief were produced by machine-pressing. *Opaline* with painted decorations was also made in England.

Papier maché (French literally: "chewed paper"), one of the earliest man-made materials, produced from pulped paper, rags, chalk, sand and glues. After mixing and preparation, it becomes plastic and can be pressed and formed into any variety of shapes. When covered in black varnish, inlaid with mother-of-pearl, gilt and painted, it becomes very attractive. *Papier-maché* was invented in England in the late 18th cent., and Birmingham become an important centre of production. It was particularly well suited for trays, covered boxes and other small and medium-sized objects, but by the middle of the 19th cent. whole pieces of furniture of *papier-maché* were also being made. By this time, the taste for it had spread to the Continent, and it was soon being widely produced in Europe. The fashion for *papier-maché* declined towards the end of the century, when the market was being flooded by so many new inventions of materials and processes.

Parian ware, a kind of opaque white porcelain with a surface that gives an illusion of marble. It was invented in England *c.*1845, and used by many porcelain factories for the production of statuettes, groups and busts in sculptured forms for use as ornaments for parlours; it was sometimes called "statuary porcelain". Parian ware was imitated, name and all, in many European countries and in the USA.

The name is derived from Paros, a Greek island which in classical antiquity provided a particularly fine marble, much sought after by sculptors.

Porcelain, *see* **Section L.**

Prayer carpet, a small portable rug, used by Mohammedans when they perform the five daily prayers demanded by Islam of its adherents. The carpet, usually knotted in several colours, is rectangular with the figure of a niche woven in. When the carpet is rolled out for use, the niche is made to point towards Mecca. Above it is an ornamental strip where the praying man should touch his forehead, while a pair of small ornamental panels on either side are provided for supporting the palms of his hands. The individual prayer carpets are the most usual, but there are bigger ones, with five or more niches, for use in family prayers.

Roemer, the wineglass with the most ancient history. It has a rounded bowl, a broad hollow stem with "strawberries" or prunts, and a tall foot made of coiled-up glass thread. The basic shape is known from classical antiquity as well as from southern and eastern Europe during the mediaeval period. During the Renaissance it was revived in the Rhine area and became the classic vessel for the drinking of Rhenish wines, a role it has retained to this day. The early examples are made of rough green glass, but during the 17th cent., *Roemers* were sometimes made from fine, crystal-clear glass or from glass purposedly tinted into a bright green. The tradition of the green glass for German wines dates from this period. The 19th cent. saw a revival of the ancient form, in a number of new varieties. Modern *Roemers* have the rounded bowl, the prunts and the tall stem with horizontal lines. They are usually made of tinted glass in green or mauve or brown, and sometimes vine-leaves are engraved on the bowl.

Satinwood, an exotic kind of wood, blond in colour, with a fine grain and a silky sheen. From *c.*1770 until *c.*1800 it was widely used for small and exquisite pieces of furniture in the Adam Style (*see* **D11**). Rarer than mahogany, satinwood was used mainly for veneering, and throughout the 19th cent. for small inlaid motifs on less expensive woods. During the 18th cent. satinwood was imported mainly from the West and East Indies, though it has also been found in Tasmania and Florida. During the Edwardian period satinwood furniture enjoyed a brief revival.

Ship-bowls, made of faience (*q.v.*) in sea-ports like Bristol, Liverpool and Hamburg, were made for sale to visiting sea-captains. The bowls are usually decorated in blue with the picture of a sailing-ship in the centre, and with the name of the captain and his vessel on the rim. The ship pictures are conventional, and should not be accepted as "portraits" of the ship named. The genre belongs mainly to the 18th cent.

Wedgwood, Josiah, *see* **Creamware**, *also* **B63**.

Whatnot, a piece of furniture made of three to five shelves or trays, placed one above the other between four corner-supports. The whatnot, which in France is called an *etagère*, became fashionable during the early part of the 19th cent. for the display of ornaments. Today it seems to epitomise one aspect of Victorian life, the love of fancy objects.

THE WORLD OF MUSIC

The art of music as it has developed in the Western world, with a glossary of musical terms and an index to composers. Special topics discussed include Festivals and Music Clubs and Societies.

TABLE OF CONTENTS

THE WORLD OF MUSIC

In writing this section no special knowledge on the part of the reader is assumed: it is for those who want to know about the history of music, how different styles evolved, and how one composer influenced another. It is a background to music as the science section is a background to science, and just as the latter cannot show the reader the colours of the spectrum but only tell of Newton's experiments and of the relationship between colour and wavelength, so in this section we can only describe man's achievements in the world of sound. But knowing something about a composer, his work, and when he lived can help to bring fuller understanding and enjoyment when listening to his music.

The section is in four parts:

I. Historical Narrative and Discussion
II. Glossary of Musical Terms
III. Index to Composers
IV. Special Topics

I. HISTORICAL NARRATIVE AND DISCUSSION

The history of music, like that of any people or art, is not one of uninterrupted progress towards some ideal perfection. For five centuries or more music in the West has achieved peaks of accomplishment in one style or another before society has dictated or composers have felt the need for something new and different. Thus Wagner's music-drama *Parsifal*, lasting five hours, is not necessarily a more rewarding work than what Monteverdi achieved in *Orfeo* 250 years earlier. More complex yes, more rewarding—well, that is for the listener to judge.

We must keep this in mind when considering the development of music from a starting point of, say, Gregorian chant down to the complicated structures of a Schoenberg in our own day. In this development there is no true dividing line between one period and another, nor must simplifying terms such as "classical" or "romantic" be taken too literally.

The earliest history of Western music as we know it today is closely bound up with the Church, for music had to be provided for services. The earliest Christian music was influenced by Greek songs, few of which unfortunately have survived, and by the music of synagogues, where the art of chanting originated. The modal system of the ancient Greeks was highly organised. The earliest Greek scale was from A to A and the four descending notes A,G,F,E became the basis of their musical theory, and it is from them that Western music learned to call notes after the letters of the alphabet. A scale can begin on any note and always includes two semitones upon which much of the character of a melody depends.

The Greek modes were based on the white notes only; the Dorian, Phrygian, Lydian, and Mixolydian began respectively on E,D,C, and B. Their character was thus decided by the position of the semitones, and they formed the basis, often corrupted, of the mediaeval modes. This system was transmitted through Latin writers such as Boethius and Cassiodorus, and through Arabic writers. The eight Church modes were not established until the 8th or 9th cent. These plagal modes, as they are called, started in each case, for technical reasons, a fourth below the authentic modes.

By the end of the 6th cent. Gregorian chant had developed so far that some sort of permanent record was required. *Neumes*, signs placed over the Latin text, were the earliest attempt at musical notation. Gradually lines came into use until a four-line stave was established, probably in the 11th and 12th cent., and with them clef signs, although the treble clef as we know it today did not appear until the 13th cent.

And what is this music—plainchant—like? It is an unaccompanied, single line of melody, which, when we have become used to its "antique" flavour is heard to have a wide range of spiritual and emotional expression, not excluding word painting. The texts used came from the Liturgy. These beautiful, extended lines of flowing, flexible melody can still be heard on Sundays in Roman Catholic cathedrals and churches.

Polyphony is Born.

The 10th cent. saw the appearance of a book called *Musica Enchiriadis* (whose authorship is disputed) which introduced theories about unison singing in which the melody is doubled at the fourth or fifth. Organum, or diaphony, is used to describe this method of writing, a term which confusingly could also be used for a kind of singing where melismatic melody was heard over a drone note on the organ. Rules came into fashion defining which intervals were allowed and which parts of the church services could be sung in more than one part. By the time of Guido d'Arezzo (*c.* 990–1050), a Benedictine monk who helped advance notation, contrary motion was permitted as the cadence was approached, another technical advance. Gradually the voices became more and more independent, and the third, so long considered a discord, came into use. Pérotin, of Notre Dame, was the first composer to write for three and four voices, and he and his great predecessor Léonin were the great masters of early polyphony. The proximity and spikiness of Pérotin's harmony is almost modern-sounding, and as with Gregorian chant, once we have adjusted ourselves to the sound, this music can be a rewarding experience.

Early Secular Music.

In mediaeval France, towards the end of the 11th cent., there developed what has become known as the age of the troubadours, poet-musicians. They were the successors to the *jongleurs*, or jugglers, and minstrels about whom we know little as practically none of their music has survived. The troubadours hymned the beauty of spring and of ladies. Contemporary with them in Germany were the Minnesingers. Their songs were mostly set in three modes. Adam de la Halle (d. 1287), because so much of his music survives, is perhaps the best-known of the troubadours. He was a notable composer of *rondels*, an early form of round, of which the English *Sumer is icumen in*, written by a monk of Reading *c.* 1226, is a fine example. In that modes were used, the troubadours' music remained definitely akin to that of ecclesiastical hymns, although there is an undoubted feeling of our modern major scale in some of the songs.

Ars Nova.

The term *ars nova* derives partly from writings of Philippe de Vitry (1291–1361) who codified the rules of the old and the new music in a valuable treatise. This *new art* represented a freeing of music from organum and rhythmic modes, and an increase in the shape and form of melodic line. France was the centre of music during the 14th cent. and apart from Philippe de Vitry the leading composer was Guillaume de Machaut (1300–77), who wrote many secular works as well as a polyphonic setting of the Mass. His music is notable for its vigour and tenderness as well as for its technical expertise. Meanwhile in 14th-cent. Italy a quite separate branch of *ars nova* was developing. Imitation and canon were to be noted in the music of Italian composers, and choral forms such as the Ballata, Madrigal (which often included instrumental accompaniment) and Caccia (a two-voice hunting song in canon) were common. The greatest Italian composer of this period was the blind organist and lutenist Francesco di Landini (*c.* 1325–97). Italian pieces of the time, as compared with their French counterparts, are notable for their sensual rather than their intellectual qualities, a difference—it has been noted—between The Southern and The Northern New Art.

England was less affected by *ars nova*, but surviving music shows the influence of the Continent. Not until the 15th cent. did she begin to make a significant contribution to the history of music. Both John Dunstable (*c.* 1380–1453), who was no less eminent as a mathematician and an astronomer than as a musician, and his contemporary Lionel Power advanced the technique of music by their method of composition (use of the triad, for instance) and mellifluous style. Their musicianship was much appreciated on the Continent. Dunstable did away with the use of *cantus firmus*—a fixed melody—and increased the use of free composition.

After Dunstable the next great figure in European music was Guillaume Dufay (*c.* 1400–74), the most celebrated composer of the Burgundian school. His music is distinguished for its blend of flowing melody, cleverly wrought counterpoint and tender expressiveness. Much travelled, Dufay was a man of catholic outlook. Together with Dunstable and the Burgundian Gilles Binchois he bridged the gap between 14th cent. *ars nova* and the fully developed polyphony of the 15th cent.

Ars nova composers also showed an interest in secular music and many of their *rondeaux* and *chansons* (those of Binchois particularly) have been preserved. Personality began to play a distinguishing part in composition.

The results of Dufay's good work can be heard in the flowering of the Franco-Netherland school later in the 15th cent. Its two most notable representatives are Ockeghem (*c.* 1420–95) and his pupil Josquin des Prés (*c.* 1450–1521), who carried musical expressiveness even further than Dufay; their work can also be grand and majestic. Indeed Josquin's wide range, from the humorous to the dignified, partially accounts for his justly deserved high reputation. He was a master of counterpoint but tempered his mechanical ingenuity with imaginative insight.

Throughout the Renaissance choral music was breaking away, as we have seen, from its earlier bonds. The mediaeval tradition of having the *cantus firmus* in the tenor went by the board; the use of dissonance, when only two voices were used in mediaeval times, was abandoned in favour of euphony; and all the voices, democratically, came to share the musical lines. Composers also began to respect their texts; where words were previously fitted to the music, the reverse was now the case. In Josquin's music, indeed, we have the first attempts at symbolism: matching verbal ideas with musical ones. The importance of this musical renaissance has been realised only over the past twenty years. At last the Renaissance composers are coming to be seen not merely as historical figures relevant only in so far as their work culminated in the great classical composers, but as masters in their own right, whose music should be nearly as familiar to us as is that of a Mozart or a Beethoven.

With the exception of Dufay, little is known of the lives of the musicians so far mentioned. Most of them were in the service of royal or ducal households where they were in charge of the chapel choir, or else they worked in or around the great cathedrals, teaching at choir-schools. They were well rewarded for their services and their social position was probably high.

During recent years there has been an appreciable revival of interest in mediaeval music. Arguments continue about how much of it should be performed, but that is just one of the many indications that it is alive and not just part of the history of music. It can communicate, as the late David Munrow showed, just as well as music of later eras.

The Sixteenth Century.

By the 16th cent. music in England was a steadily expanding art and much encouraged. Music-making in the home was becoming quite the fashion in social circles. The Chapels Royal remained the chief musical centres but the music was changing with the development of new secular forms so that it was not so much religious as a part of life. Composers began their lives as choirboys and received a thoroughgoing education, both theoretical and practical.

Carrying on from where Josquin and his contemporaries left off, Palestrina in Italy, Victoria in Spain, Lassus in the Netherlands, and Byrd in England brought the polyphonic style to its zenith. At the same time came the rise of the madrigalists, first in Italy, then in the Netherlands; and then the beginnings of instrumental music as it came to be known in the succeeding centuries.

The vocal composers began to use chordal (homophonic) as well as contrapuntal (polyphonic) methods of writing—examples are Victoria's *Ave Verum Corpus* and Palestrina's *Stabat Mater*—but polyphony was still the fullest most magnificent instrument of composition, as for instance in Byrd's *O Quam Gloriosum* which shows an eager response to the mood and to the inflection of the words in a kind of vocal orchestration. A feature of all these composers' music, bu more especially that of Victoria (*c.* 1535–1611) and Palestrina (1525–94), is its serene simplicity and fervour of utterance. Palestrina was perhaps more spacious in his effects, Victoria the more passionate. How well we can imagine—and sometimes hear—their music resounding down the naves of the great cathedrals of Europe.

The music of Lassus (*c.* 1532–94) is distinguished both in sheer amount and in vitality. His mastery in the field of motets was unrivalled, encompassing a wide range of subject and mood. He and his fellow Flemish composers, Willaert, de Monte and Arcadelt, were also expert in the Madrigal, a form popular in Italy and England as well. The Madrigal was a contrapuntal setting of a poem, usually not longer than twelve lines, in five or six parts. The subject (of the poetry) was usually amorous or pastoral. It was a short-lived, but highly prolific vogue. Orlando Gibbons (1583–1625), Thomas Weelkes (*c.* 1573–1623), and John Wilbye (1574–1638) were the most prominent English exponents.

Instrumental Music.

By the end of the 14th cent. instrumental music began to become something more than mere anonymous dance tunes or primitive organ music. Instruments often accompanied voices, or even replaced them, so that the recorder, lute, viol, and spinet indoors, and sackbuts and shawms outdoors, had already been developed by the time instrumental music came to be written down. Gradually a distinction grew up between what was appropriate to the voice and what was suitable for instruments. Byrd, Gibbons, and Giles Farnaby in England, the great blind keyboard player, Cabezón (1510–66) in Spain, and Frescobaldi (1583–1643) in Italy produced valuable instrumental works. Perhaps the *Parthenia* and the *Fitzwilliam Virginal Book*, collections of Early English Keyboard music, give as fair a representative idea as any of the development of instrumental form at this time.

In chamber music musicians often played collections of dance tunes strung together to make a whole; or they chose fantasies (or "fancies"). where a composer altered a tune as he wished Then there were sets of variations on a ground, that is a simple tune played over and over again on a bass viol.

As far as brass instruments are concerned, they were often used on festive occasions in spacious halls or in cathedrals. The Venetian composer Andrea Gabrieli (*c.* 1510–86) was the first to combine voice and instruments and his nephew Giovanni Gabrieli (1557–1612) carried the process further to produce sacred symphonies, often using antiphonal effects.

Drama in Music.

Not until the end of the 16th cent. did anyone begin to think about combining drama and music, and so "invent" the new art we know today as opera. A group of artistic intelligentsia met together in Florence and conceived the idea of reviving the ancient declamation of Greek tragedy. They took Greek mythological subjects, cast them in dramatic form, and set them to music, not in the choral polyphonic style of the Madrigal, but with single voices declaiming dialogue in music. The earliest examples of what was called *Dramma per Musica* were Peri's *Daphne* in 1597 (now lost) and his *Eurydice*, in which he co-operated with Caccini. The new style came to its full flowering with the appearance of Monteverdi (1567–1643), whose genius would surely have shone in any age.

Monteverdi's first opera, *Orfeo*, produced in 1607, is a landmark of dramatic expression, and it is nothing less than a catastrophe that so many of his later operas have been lost. His *Orfeo* provides the basic ground work for the operas of the next two centuries: recitative, accompanied recitative, and aria. His last opera *L'Incoronazione di Poppaea*, written when he was at the great age (for those days) of 75, succeeds in its aim of creating a free, fluid form, slipping easily from recitative to arioso and even aria without the strict, closed forms that were to be used in the 17th and 18th cent. He focusses attention to an almost unbelievable extent on character rather than situation. He creates real people with all their faults and foibles—the kittenish, sexually attractive Poppaea, the power-drunk, infatuated Nero, the noble Seneca, and the dignified, rejected empress Octavia. As recent productions have shown these characters leap from the musical page as if they had just been created, each unerringly delineated in musical terms. Only the vocal line, the continuo, and the very incomplete instrumental ritornelli parts have been preserved, but in sensitive, knowledgeable hands tonal variety in the shape of wind and string parts can be added, as we know certain instruments were available to the composer.

Monteverdi's successors were Cavalli (1602–76), Cesti (1623–69) and Stradella (1642–82), who gave the solo voice more and more prominence encouraged by the advent of the castrati's brilliant voices. These artificially created singers had a vogue and popularity similar to "pop" singers of today, fêted wherever they appeared. The aria became more extended and ornate, and dramatic verisimilitude gradually but inexorably took second place to vocal display. An aria was nearly always in *da capo* form, the first section being repeated after a contrasting middle one.

Sixteenth- and Seventeenth-century Church Music.

Of course, the invention of a new dramatic style affected church music too. The concentration on the vertical aspect of music (homophony) as opposed to the horizontal (polyphony) led to the increasing importance of the voice in religious music. In Italy, it is true, there was the late-flowering, great madrigalist Carlo Gesualdo (1560–1614), whose harmonic daring still astonishes us today, but by 1600 the cantata was coming to replace older forms in church music. In its simplest form this was a story told in accompanied recitative. Giacomo Carissimi (*c.* 1604–74) was one of the first significant composers of this new form. He too was in on the birth of the oratorio, whose forerunner was the *sacra rappresentazione* (mystery or miracle play) of early 16th-cent Florence. Then in the mid-16th cent. St. Philip Neri brought in elements from popular plays on sacred subjects in his services in Rome, designed to hold the attention of youth—rather as certain parsons have tried with "pop" services today. Emilio del Cavalieri (*c.* 1550–1602) and Carissimi developed the form adding arias and choral movements, omitting actual representation. Alessandro Scarlatti (1660–1725), whose oratorios bear a close resemblance to his operas, brought oratorio to its zenith in Italy.

Heinrich Schütz (1585–1672), Bach's great predecessor, was the founder of German church music. His historical place has never been called into question but only in recent times have the intrinsic merits of his own music come to be recognised. He studied with Giovanni Gabrieli in his youth and later came under the influence of Monteverdi, so it was not surprising that he brought Italian ideas across the Alps to Germany and wrote the first German opera *Daphne*, now sadly lost. He also introduced his country to the Italian declamatory style and to the new kind of concertato instrumental writing. But his dramatic religious works were his greatest contribution to musical development. He wrote with a devout intensity, bringing to life the scriptural texts by closely allying his urgent music to the words. His three settings of the Passions—Matthew, Luke, and John—paved the way for Bach's even more remarkable works in this genre. Two contemporaries of Schütz, Johann Hermann Schein (1586–1630) and Samuel Scheidt (1587–1654), were both important figures in German Reformation music.

Lully, Purcell, and Seventeenth-century Opera.

France resisted the tide of Italian opera, although paradoxically it was an Italian, Jean-Baptiste Lully (*c.* 1632–87), who charted the different course of French opera which was from the beginning associated with the court ballet. His musical monopoly during the reign of Louis XIV was put to good use. In his thirteen operas the libretto, usually on classical, allegorical themes, plays a vital part in the composition, which is therefore less clearly divided between recitative and aria than in Italian opera. The orchestration and the ballets assume greater importance than in the traditional Italian form. It was, in short, a more realistic, less stylised art.

In England, opera developed out of the entertainment known as the Masque, a succession of dances, accompanied by voices and instruments and often incorporated in a drama or spectacle. Henry Lawes's (1596–1662) setting of Milton's *Comus* is probably the most famous of these entertainments. The *Venus and Adonis* of John Blow (1649–1708) can be called the first English opera because here the music is gradually gaining the ascendancy over the spoken word. However, it was Purcell (*c.* 1659–95), Blow's pupil, with *Dido and Aeneas*, who really gave dramatic life to the new medium by giving his characters a true musical personality that was subtler than anything the mere spoken word could achieve. The grief-laden lament of the dying Dido "When I am laid in earth" has an expressive power, achieved by extraordinarily bold harmonic effects, never before and seldom since achieved. The opera was in fact written for a young ladies' boarding school. Purcell followed it with several outstanding semi-operas—such as *The Fairy Queen* (to Dryden's text). His untimely death at the age of 36 probably robbed us of several full-length operas—and perhaps a consequence of this was that English music after him did not develop as it should have done.

His verse anthems and much of his instrumental music, especially the Fantasias, are also rich in imaginative mastery through his original use of harmony and counterpoint. However, a great deal of his pieces were written for a specific occasion and many of the odes are set to impossibly trite texts. At least his genius was partly acknowledged in his own day, and he was appointed organist in Westminster Abbey where he was buried with due pomp. He is said to have died through catching cold when locked out of his own house at night.

Vivaldi and the Rise of Instrumental Music.

Out of the dance suites popular in the 16th cent. and the beginning of the 17th (known in Italy as the *Sonata da Camera*) developed the concerto. This began as two groups of instrumentalists compared and contrasted with each other as in Giovanni Gabrieli's *Sonata piano e forte*. With Arcangelo Corelli (1653–1713) the concerto grosso took a more definite shape, alternating a solo group of instruments with the main body of strings in three or more contrasting movements. Guiseppe Torelli (1658–1709), Francesco Geminiani (1687–1762) and Tommaso Albinoni (1671–1750) were other notable contributors to the form, but none of the composers so far mentioned has today achieved the popularity of the priest Antonio Vivaldi (*c*. 1678–1741), himself a violinist, who had at his disposal the orchestra at the Ospedale della Pieta in Venice. The young women at this music school also contributed the vocal side of the concerts there of which there are many descriptions. One says: "They sing like angels, play the violin, flute, organ, oboe, cello, bassoon—in short no instrument is large enough to frighten them . . . I swear nothing is so charming than to see a young and pretty nun, dressed in white, a sprig of pomegranate blossom behind one ear, leading the orchestra, and beating time with all the grace and precision imaginable." For this body, Vivaldi wrote about 500 concertos which maintain a remarkably even quality, but "The Four Seasons" are perhaps the most felicitous.

Meanwhile organ music was advancing rapidly in technique. Girolamo Frescobaldi (1583–1643) and Jan Pieterszoon Sweelinck (1562–1621) wrote works that provided the foundation of the Italian and Northern German schools of organ music. Their ricercares gradually developed into the fugue, a vein so richly mined by Bach. Among their successors the most notable figure before Bach was Johann Pachelbel (1653–1706).

Other keyboard music, especially for the harpsichord, was the particular province of France; and Jean-Philippe Rameau (1683–1764) and François Couperin (1668–1733) were both masters of keyboard style and harmonic invention. They wrote many pieces of subtle charm and exquisite craftsmanship.

Bach (1685–1750).

The two giant figures of Bach and Handel bestride the first half of the 18th cent. Their differences are perhaps greater than their similarities. Bach wrote essentially for himself (although of course, he had to satisfy his employers at Cöthen and Leipzig) while Handel was composing to please his wide public. Bach was a provincial, always remaining in central Germany; Handel was widely travelled. Bach was devoutly religious, almost ascetic; Handel was more a man of the world. They never met.

To summarise Bach's vast output in a short space is virtually impossible. One can only try to distil the flavour of his music. He brought the art of polyphony to the highest pitch of mastery that has ever been achieved or is ever likely to be achieved. In his famous "Forty-Eight" and "the Art of the Fugue" he explored all the fugal permutations of the major and minor keys. At the same time his music rose above technical brilliance to achieve, especially in his organ music, the two Passions, many of the church cantatas, and the B minor Mass, intense emotional and expressive power. The cantatas, from his Leipzig appointment (1723) onwards, were integrated into the services. They consisted usually of a chorus based on a Lutheran hymn tune, recitatives, several extended arias, and a concluding chorus usually a straightforward version of the hymn tune in which the congregation joined. There are some two hundred of these works and they contain a wealth of comparatively unknown and sometimes even unrecognised beauties. The St. John and the St. Matthew Passion extend these procedures to a grand scale, an Evangelist telling the new Testament story in vivid recitative, the chorus taking the part of the crowd, soloists pondering in arias on the meaning of the Gospel, and Jesus's words being sung by a bass. Anyone who has heard either of these works well performed cannot help but dismiss from his mind any idea of Bach as a mere dry-as-dust musical mathematician. In the St. Matthew Passion, every suggestion in the text that can possibly be illustrated by a musical equivalent is so illustrated. The Old Testament Pharasaic law is represented by strict musical forms such as the canon; Christ's sayings are given noble arioso life; and the arias reflect truly the New Testament's compassionate message. Technically the work is a marvel; expressively it is eloquent. The B minor Mass, although it contains borrowings from many of his own works, still stands as a satisfying monumental whole in which Bach's choral writing achieved a new richness, the adaptations being in accord with their new setting.

Bach's instrumental music, especially the violin concertos and the unaccompanied works for violin and cello, not only show the immense range of his powers but also contain many of his deeper thoughts, whereas the orchestral suites and the Brandenburg concertos are more extrovert, particularly the rhythmically exuberant fast movements.

Bach closes an era—that of the later contrapuntalists—by achieving the *ne plus ultra* in fugal composition; his last, incomplete work, The Art of the Fugue, is evidence of that. In recent years there has been a trend towards playing Bach's music on original instruments of his time (or replicas) and singing it with appropriately sized, all-male choirs.

Handel (1685–1759).

During his lifetime Handel was far more widely recognised as a great composer than Bach, and his music, unlike Bach's, maintained its place in popular esteem until the re-discovery of Bach and the dominance of the symphony placed Handel somewhat in the background.

During the latter part of the 19th cent. Handel's name was mainly associated with mammoth, anachronistic performances of a small sample of his oratorios at the Crystal Palace and elsewhere in England. In his lifetime these works, and all his other pieces in the genre, were sung by a small choir who were outnumbered by the instrumental players. Over the past few years authentic-sized performances of his oratorios and a revival of interest in his operas have revealed the real Handel, unknown to our grandparents.

The operas were neglected partly because the vocal prowess they required—and which the castrati so brilliantly supplied—was no longer available and because their dramatic life, at least according to 19th- and early 20th-cent. tenets, hardly existed. Now it is realised that this neglect has deprived us of an unending stream of glorious melody and of much daring harmony. But perhaps it is in the hitherto disregarded oratorios, such as *Semele*, that Handel's innate dramatic sense and musical range are to be heard gloriously fulfilled, and the pastoral serenade *Acis and Galatea* is surely one of the most delightful scores ever composed.

Handel was a colourful, imaginative orchestrator, and this can be heard both in his accompaniment to vocal music and in his concerti grossi, op. 3 and 6, the earlier set exploiting a diversity of interesting string and wind combination. In his writing he was at home in a polyphonic or homophonic style as his superb choruses show. His organ concertos, of which he was the "inventor" (to quote a contemporary source), were often played between the acts of his oratorios. They are alternately expressive and exuberant pieces calling for some virtuosity from the player. His occasional works, such as the Water Music and Fireworks Music show his ingenuity in extending the range of the typical 17th cent. suite to serve a particular occasion.

Handel's working life was mostly spent in England where his Italian operas were acclaimed. In the years between his arrival here in 1711 and 1729 he wrote nearly thirty operas. It was only when the public tired of these and his reputation slumped that he turned to oratorio with equal success.

Bach and Handel between them crowned the age of polyphony that had lasted for two hundred years or more. After them, it is hardly surprising that composers began looking for a new style, already anticipated in the music of Rameau and particularly Dominico Scarlatti (1685–1737), whose harpsichord sonatas foreshadowed the classical sonata form that was to dominate music for the next two hundred years. The change in musical style about 1750 was partly the result of a change in musical patronage. Bach was the last great composer to earn his living through being employed by the church. The new patrons were the nobility who liked to have a composer on hand to write for the various evening entertainments of the time. For this purpose the princes and dukes had their own orchestras and their own small opera houses. The music required had to be elegant, formal, *galant*. Haydn was exceptionally fortunate in having an employer, Prince Nicholas of Esterhazy, who allowed him to write more of less as he wished so that he was able to develop symphonic form into something more than a pleasing way of passing an evening.

The early symphonists, culminating in Haydn, broke away from Bach's contrapuntal treatment of the orchestra. Instruments now came to be treated in a more colourful manner according to their particular timbre. The court of Mannheim had an orchestra of a standard unheard hitherto, and Johann Stamitz (1717–57) and his son Karl (1745–1801) influenced the great composers who were to follow in their footsteps. The composition of their orchestra was flexible, oboes, flutes, and horns often being added to the standard string section. Bach's son Carl Philipp Emanuel (1714–88) added to and developed symphonic and sonata form, especially as regards keys and subjects.

Haydn and Mozart.

These two figures dominate the second half of the 18th cent. as Bach and Handel did the first. In a brief space only a general picture can be presented of their huge output and influence. Of Haydn's 104 symphonies (there may even be others) nearly all are worthy of study and hearing. The craftsmanship is always remarkable, the invention ever new. Indeed without Haydn's harmonic daring or his melodic ingenuity, the even greater symphonic thought of Beethoven would have been impossible: Haydn laid the groundwork on which his successor built towering edifices. A work such as the 93rd symphony in D is typical of his mature style with its searching introduction, powerfully wrought, earnestly argued first movement, beautiful *Largo* and resourceful bustling finale. Haydn did not fight shy of contrapuntal writing: the development section of this symphony's first movement and the finale are evidence of that, but it was only as an integral part of a predominantly homophonic technique.

Mozart's symphonies are not so different in form from Haydn's but—and this must be a subjective judgment—he put more emotional feeling into his. Nobody could listen to the heart-searching first movement of his 40th symphony without being deeply moved. It was in his final three works in the medium that Mozart brought his symphonic art to perfection, and these obviously had an effect on Haydn's later symphonies written after them. For passion and tenderness contained within a classical form these late symphonies, and many other of Mozart's works, have yet to be surpassed.

Haydn, who has been rightly termed "the Father of the Symphony", was also the founder of the string quartet—perhaps the most perfect, because the most exactly balanced, form of musical expression. The four instruments—two violins, viola, and cello—discuss, argue, commune with each other over the whole gamut of feeling. In his quartets Haydn's mastery of structure is even more amazing than in his symphonies. Mozart's quartets (especially the six devoted to Haydn) and even more his quintets achieve miracles of beauty in sound, nowhere more so than in the first movement of the G minor (his most personal key) quintet. The two late piano quartets show how the piano *can* be ideally combined with strings. His clarinet quintet is also a masterly work.

Haydn did not leave any concertos of consequence. Mozart's, especially those for piano, are among his greatest works. As a brilliant clavier player himself, he showed a consummate skill in writing for the keyboard. Although the instrument he knew was slightly less advanced than the piano today, his concertos call for virtuosity in execution, yet they are as searching in emotional content as the late symphonies and quartets. Indeed the C major concerto (K. 467) and the C minor (K. 491) may be said to hold the quintessential Mozart. As well as twenty (mature) piano concertos, Mozart wrote six for the violin, four for the horn, and eighteen others, but none of these, delightful as they are, can be placed in quite the same class.

Of their church music, Haydn's sixteen masses and his oratorios—*The Creation* and *The Seasons* (both late works)—are perhaps more worthy of attention than Mozart's various masses, but we must not forget Mozart's final work—the Requiem or the serene late Motet *Ave Verum Corpus*.

Eighteenth-century Opera.

Mozart—for many the first great opera composer—did not, of course, create his masterpieces out of nothing. In France, Lully was followed by Rameau (1683–1764), who carried on his tradition of using classical themes but developed a more flexible style of recitative and greatly increased vividness of expression. But it was Gluck (1714–87) who more than anyone broke out of the straitjacket of the now ossified Italian form of opera—dominated by the singer—and showed just what could be achieved in moving human terms. Drama in music really came of age with his *Orfeo e Euridice* (1762), *Alceste* (1767) and *Iphigénie en Tauride* (1779). His simplicity and poignancy of expression were not lost on Mozart.

Meanwhile in Germany a kind of opera called *Singspiel* appeared during the 18th cent. Breaking away from classical themes, mundane stories were told in dialogue and music.

Until quite recently Haydn's operas were dismissed as unworthy representations of his genius but, chiefly through the enlightening efforts of the Haydn scholar, H. C. Robins Landon, some of his fifteen surviving works in the medium have been successfully revived. They have proved to be perfectly viable for the stage and, especially in the ensembles, full of that delightful invention to be found in the rest of his opus, if on a less fully developed scale. Still as musical drama they inevitably fall far short of Mozart's achievements, for the younger composer seems to have had an instinctive feeling for the stage. Into his operas he poured his most intense, personal music. He vividly portrays the foibles, desires, loves, and aspirations of mankind.

The earlier, immature stage pieces of his youth led to such works as *Lucio Silla* (1772) and *La*

Finta Giardiniera (1775) with their first glimpses of the glories to come. His first indubitably great opera is *Idomeneo* (1781). Despite its unpromisingly static plot, *Idomeneo* reveals Mozart's stature through its ability to breathe new life into a conventional *opera seria* form. Though influenced by Gluck it is yet more human and touching in its musical expression. To succeed this Mozart wrote a much more frivolous piece *Die Entführung aus dem Serail.* Stemming from the *Singspiel* tradition, it none the less creates real-life characters who have much charming music to sing.

After three lesser pieces Mozart embarked on his four masterpieces—*Le Nozze di Figaro* (1786), *Don Giovanni* (1787), *Così fan tutte* (1790), and *Die Zauberflöte* (1791).

Figaro, as well as being a delightful comedy, explores more fully than any previous opera situation and character, which find expression in beautiful arias and in two finales of symphonic proportion. In *Don Giovanni*, less satisfactory as a dramatic structure, the range of musical characterisation and insight into human motives is widened still further. *Così* lyrically but humorously expresses the follies of love. Mozart could not help but love his characters and his music for them is at one and the same time amusing and heartfelt. *Die Zauberflöte*—The Magic Flute—displays Mozart's deep-felt sympathy for his fellow men and of truth in an opera of great spiritual strength. Nor has opera any more loveable personality than the birdcatcher Papageno. Mozart's final opera *La Clemenza di Tito*, extolling imperial magnanimity, has never achieved the success or popularity of his other maturer stage works, though it contains much excellent music, and has recently been revived with honour in several opera houses.

Beethoven.

Mozart was the last major composer to depend, to any large extent, on private patronage for his living, and even he left the service of the Archbishop of Salzburg because he could not stand the restrictions imposed on his freedom. Henceforth composers would have to stand on their own two feet with all the advantages (liberty) and disadvantages (lack of security) that implied. Beethoven (1770–1827) was the first such composer of importance.

Although his work is usually divided into three periods, that division is somewhat too arbitrary, for no other composer in history, with the possible exception of Wagner, has shown such a continual development of his genius. Coming at just the right moment in musical history, he crowned the achievements of Haydn and Mozart with music of the utmost profundity of thought and feeling that looks back to its classical heritage and forward to the romantic movement of the 19th cent. His influence on musical thinking and writing is incalculable.

His first period shows his strong melodic gifts and the beginning of his individuality in developing form and structure to suit his own ends and match his particular genius. Unusual keys are explored, unusual harmonic procedures employed. With the "Eroica" (his third symphony) he established his position as a great composer. The unity of purpose he here achieved within a long and diverse structure is truly staggering, even today. In the first movement alone the formal invention and cogency went far beyond what even Mozart had achieved in his "Jupiter" symphony, and the second movement—a vast funeral March—has an overwhelmingly tragic emotional content. But the "Eroica" was followed by six equally great symphonies, each one as varied, as inventive, as unified as the others. The ninth symphony is significant for both its length and its finale. Here Beethoven crowns three superb instrumental movements with a choral movement that, as well as summing up all that has gone before, expresses in music the joy in existence more ecstatically than any other work.

The burning intensity of Beethoven's genius is just as evident in his chamber music. His quartets are the product of a revolutionary age in which the social graces and formal restraint of the 18th cent. were thrown off in a search for a more personal mode of expression. The early op. 18 set, and the Razoumovsky quartets, op. 59, go even beyond the range of Haydn's and Mozart's works in the medium but it was in his late quartets, his final musical testament, that Beethoven refined and distilled his art for posterity. No words can possibly describe their unique quality, but any and every chance should be taken to make their acquaintance: the effort required will be more than amply rewarded.

The early piano concertos do not reach quite that level of attainment, but the last three, together with the violin concerto, are on a par with the finest of the symphonies and quartets, as well as being considerable tests of the performers' technique. The Triple Concerto for piano, violin, and cello is an unusual and rewarding work.

Beethoven's grandest choral work—and one of the most noble in existence—is the Mass in D (*Missa Solemnis*). Its vast scale and sublime utterance often defeat performers, but when it is successfully done there is no more spiritually uplifting experience for the listener, except perhaps Beethoven's only opera, *Fidelio*. This simple escape story was transformed by Beethoven's creative fire into a universal symbol of liberty, the composer identifying himself with the struggle for freedom from tyranny and release from darkness.

Beethoven lived in a period of war and revolution. A passionate believer in the brotherhood of man and in liberty, he was shocked to find his ideals thrown over by revolutionaries-turned-dictators. His own tragedy of deafness, which came upon him at the moment of his triumph, nearly submerged him, but in the end he won through and produced the string of masterpieces from the "Eroica" onwards. Hope springing from despair, love from hatred, victory over defeat, these are the unquenchable legacies left by Beethoven.

The Romantic Movement.

Inevitably, the Romantic movement in literature that burst forth about 1800 was bound to have its counterpart in music. And so it was. Breaking the classical bonds, composers such as Schubert, Schumann, Liszt, and Berlioz sought a new freedom in musical expression. Form became of less importance than content; and that content often had literary connections. For their purposes a larger orchestra was needed and supplied, but the miniature, the song especially, because of its very personal connotation, was also a favourite form.

Schubert (1797–1828)—described by Liszt as "the most poetic of musicians"—is perhaps the greatest lyrical genius in musical history. In him the Viennese tradition and influence of Haydn, Mozart, and Beethoven reached its zenith. The song was always Schubert's starting point, so it is hardly surprising that his reputation as a song writer has never been impaired but in his symphonic and instrumental works too it is always his inexhaustible fund of melody that first calls for attention. Nobody could listen to his "Trout" quintet, for piano and strings, his octet, his fifth symphony, or his song cycle *Die Schöne Müllerin* without being enchanted and invigorated by the sheer tunefulness of the music. But there is much more to Schubert than this: his understanding of the possibilities of harmonic change, his grasp of orchestral coloration (in the great C major symphony, for instance), his free use of sonata structure.

Although Mozart, Haydn, and Beethoven had all contributed to the song as an art form, it was with Schubert that it achieved its first full flowering. If he had written nothing but his songs, his place in the musical firmament would be assured. With his *Erlkönig* in 1815 the German *Lied* came of age and from then until the end of his life he wrote more than six hundred songs, hardly a dud among them. Whether it is the charm of *Heidenröslein*, the drama of *Der Doppelgänger* or the numbed intensity of the *Winterreise* cycle, Schubert unerringly went to the heart of a poet's meaning; indeed he often raised poor verses to an inspired level by his settings. And for the first time the pianist shares a place of equal importance with the singer.

There is only room to mention one or two other composers, some of them wrongly neglected, who were roughly contemporaries of Beethoven and Schubert: the Czech Dussek (1760–1812), who like Beethoven bridges the classical-romantic gulf, Boccherini (1743–1805), the two Italian opera composers Cimarosa (1749–1801) and Paisiello (1740–1816), the Frenchman Méhul (1763–1817) and the German Hummel (1778–1837).

Weber (1786–1826) lacked Beethoven's energy and constructive powers and Schubert's sheer lyrical profundity, but he is an important figure, especially in the field of opera, where his *Der Freischütz* and *Oberon* led the way to a more flexible, dramatically realistic form of opera. His vivid imagination exactly fitted the new romantic mood abroad. The sheer beauty in the melodic shape of his music is also not to be denied. His instrumental works are attractive but insubstantial.

Mendelssohn and Schumann.

Mendelssohn (1809–47) was the civilised craftsman among the Romantic composers. A boy genius—many of his finest works were written before he was twenty—he maintained the importance of classical form while imbuing it with his own affectionate brand of poetic sensibility. His third and fourth symphonies—the "Scottish" and "The Italian"—(and possibly the fifth "The Reformation"), his string quartets (some of which go deeper than the rest of his music), octet, violin concerto, first piano concerto, and of course, the incidental music to "A Midsummer Night's Dream" represent his tidy yet effervescent style at its most winning.

Schumann (1810–56) is less easy to categorise. His early romantic flame was burnt out by some flaw in his intellectual and/or emotional make-up, and his inspiration seems to have declined in later years. No matter, by then he had given us the marvellous song cycles of 1840, an ever fresh piano concerto, many fine piano solos, including the mercurial, popular *Carnaval* and several symphonies, which, if not structurally perfect, contain much lovely music. The joys and sorrows of love and the feeling for natural beauty are all perfectly mirrored in these charming, lyrical works, and in the genial piano quintet.

Romantic Giants.

Berlioz (1803–69) and Liszt (1811–86) are the two most typical representative composers of the Romantic era. Both have always been controversial figures, with ardent advocates and opponents either unduly enthusiastic or unfairly derogatory. Berlioz might be termed the perfect painter in music. With an uncanny mastery of orchestral sound he could conjure up the countryside, the supernatural and the historical with the utmost ease. He based his music on the "direct reaction to feeling" and a desire to illustrate literature by musical means. That his technical expertise was not always the equal of his undoubted genius, can be heard in many of his larger works such as the dramatic cantata *The Damnation of Faust* and the dramatic symphony *Romeo and Juliet*, yet most people are willing to overlook the occasional vulgarity for the ineffable beauty of his many fine pages, but brutal cuts in his music, such as are often made in, for instance, his epic opera *The Trojans* only have the effect of reducing the stature of his works. We must accept him, warts and all. Anyone who has seen the two parts of *The Trojans*, presented complete in one evening at Covent Garden, will realise that Berlioz knew what he was about.

His output is not quantitatively large but includes several monumental works, as well as *The Trojans*. The *Requiem* ("Grand Messe des Morts") requires a tenor solo, huge chorus and orchestra, and brass bands, although Berlioz uses these forces fastidiously. The *Symphonie funèbre et triomphale* calls in its original form, for choir, brass, and strings. But Berlioz was just as happy writing on a smaller scale as his exquisite song cycle, to words of Théophile Gautier, *Nuits d'Été*, shows. Gautier perhaps summed up better than anyone Berlioz's singular talent: "In that renaissance of the 1830s Berlioz represents the romantic musical idea, the breaking up of old moulds, the substitution of new forms for unvaried square rhythms, a complex and competent richness of orchestration, truth of local colour, unexpected effects in sound, tumultuous and Shakespearian depth of passion, amorous or melancholy dreaminess, longings and questionings of the soul, infinite and mysterious sentiments not to be rendered in words, and that something more than all which escapes language but may be divined in music."

During his lifetime Liszt was fêted and honoured not only by his musical colleagues but by the world at large, which idolised him and his piano. Then his reputation took a plunge from which it has only recently recovered. To be sure much of his early music is glitter and gloss, but his symphonies and tone poems—especially the Faust Symphony, the Dante Symphony (both, of course, inspired by literature), and *Orpheus* and *Prometheus*—and his late piano works show that he was an extraordinary harmonic innovator. The piano sonata in B minor brings his romantic, wilful temperament within a reasonably stable, pianistic form, and as such is a landmark in the repertory of the instrument. Liszt's output was prodigious, but the inquiring listener should explore the more original of his compositions already mentioned to form a true picture of his fertile genius.

Chopin.

Chopin (1810–49) was the master of the keyboard, par excellence. His development of the technical and expressive capabilities of the piano is unique in musical history. His inventive powers were poured out with nervous passionate energy and in a highly individual style through twenty astonishing, possibly agonised years of creative activity before his early death. A Chopin melody, limpid, transparent, singing, can be recognised easily by anyone, but his style gradually developed into something more subtle, more satisfying than pure melody. He took the greatest care of every detail so that any alteration, however small, upsets the perfect balance of his work. His poetic sensibility can be found in any of his works; for his constructive ability we must turn to the Ballades, the B minor Sonata, and the Barcarolle, while the Preludes and Studies blend technical powers and emotional expressiveness in ideal proportions.

Nineteenth-century Opera.

After Mozart's operas and Beethoven's *Fidelio* the medium might have been expected to decline. Instead it took on a new, if different, lease of life that culminated in Verdi's extraordinary output.

Rossini (1792–1868) created a world of exuberant high spirits in his operatic works that are as cheerful and heart-warming today as they were a hundred or more years ago.

He always worked in and around the lyric theatres of Italy and between 1810 and 1830 poured out a stream of works, not all of which can be expected to be masterpieces. However, *Il Barbiere di Siviglia*, *L'Italiana in Algieri*, *La Cenerentola* and *Le Comte Ory* will always delight audiences as long as opera houses exist. Although these works are difficult to sing really well, their vitality and charm can never be submerged even by poor voices or indifferent staging.

His German contemporaries were critical of his confidence and frivolity, but his works show a consistency of invention and an irresistible tunefulness that anyone might envy. In recent years, there has also been a renewed interest in his more serious operas—*Otello* (1816), *La Gazza Ladra* (1817), *Semiramide* (1823), *La Siège de Corinthe* (1820), and *Guillaume Tell* (1829)—which were certainly surpassed in dramatic power by his successors but which nevertheless are not to be despised or neglected.

William Tell, to give it its more popular title, was his last work for the stage although he lived on for nearly forty years in retirement in Paris, scene of many of his greatest successes. There he enjoyed good living, dispensing *bons mots*, and occasionally composing trifles. An exception is the unpretentious *Petite Messe Solennelle*, written originally for soloists, chorus, a harmonium, and two pianos. Rossini later orchestrated it, but he would not allow it to be performed during his lifetime. The first public performance was on 28 February 1869, as near as possible to the 78th anniversary of the composer's birth on Leap Year Day 1792.

In contrast to the mercurial Rossini, Vincenzo Bellini (1801–35) was an exquisite, romantic figure dealing with exquisite, romantic stories, an operatic equivalent to Chopin, who much admired him. His delicate, sinuous vocal line (in the arias) and brilliant acrobatics in the final sections (cabalettas) require singers of the utmost accomplishment to do them justice, although his music is never as florid as Rossini's. His most typical and popular works are probably *La Sonnambula* (1831), *Norma* (1831) and *I Puritani* (1835). The first is a tender, homely country story, the second an almost heroic lyrical drama of sacrifice, and the third a rather unsatisfactory historical story redeemed by its appealing music. In the past few years singers of the calibre of Maria Callas, Joan Sutherland, Guiletta Simionato, and Marilyn Horne have brought Bellini's operas a popularity almost equal to that they enjoyed at the time they were written.

Gaetano Donizetti (1797–1848) was an even more prolific operatic composer than Rossini. He wrote at least 75 works, mostly for the Italian stage, several of which, such as *Alfredo il Grande* or *Emilia di Liverpool*, are never likely to be revived, but during the past few years, with the renewed interest in what are called the *Ottocento* operas, many of his serious operas have been resuscitated and found as enjoyable in performance as his more frequently heard comedies.

He was a well-grounded musician and although his invention is often criticised for being too tied to the conventions of his day performances often belie this reputation, his dramatic instinct proving sure. *Lucia di Lammermoor*, because of the chances it offers to a coloratura soprano with tragic pretensions, has always held the stage and of late *Lucrezia Borgia*, *Anna Bolena*, *La Favorita*, and *Poliuto* have all been successfully revived. Of his lighter works, the comedies *L'Elisir d'Amore* and *Don Pasquale* have never declined in popularity. One of his last works was *Linda di Chamounix* (1842) which he wrote for Vienna where it aroused such enthusiasm that the Emperor appointed him Court Composer and Master of the Imperial Chapel.

French Opera.

The taste in Paris was for more and more lavish productions. Following Spontini (1774–1851), whose works were comparatively austere, came Halévy (1799–1862) and Giacomo Meyerbeer (1791–1864) whose operas contain all the ingredients that came to be expected of "Grand Opera"—spectacle, huge ensembles, showpieces for the soloists, and extended, if superfluous ballet. Drawing from Italian, German, and French traditions Meyerbeer's music contained everything the public wanted, yet today they are seldom revived, perhaps because his creative powers were essentially derivative, yet when they *are* given, operas like *Les Huguenots*, *Le Prophète*, and *L'Africaine* still have the power to fascinate and his influence on his successors, notably Wagner, was considerable.

Verdi.

Italian opera in the 19th cent. culminated in the works of Giuseppe Verdi (1813–1901), who rose from a peasant background to become his country's most noted composer, as well as something of a natural hero during the period of the Risorgimento. His earliest works, indeed, often roused his hearers to patriotic fervour. For instance, *Nabucco* (1842), with its theme of an oppressed people seeking deliverance, was treated as a symbol of the Italians' fight for freedom.

Musically, Verdi developed out of all recognition during the course of his long career. The continuously flowing structure of his last two operas *Otello* and *Falstaff* is very far removed from the start–stop formulas, inherited from his predecessors, of his first works, yet even they are touched, in harmonic subtleties, orchestral felicities, and a sense of drama, by a spark of genius, a burning inspiration that sets him apart from all other operatic composers. *Ernani* (1844), *I due Foscari* (1844), and *Luisa Miller* (1849) all have foretastes of glories to come even if as a whole they are flawed dramas, and these "galley years", as Verdi himself later described them, gave him the essential know-how to produce his later, greater operas, as well as establishing him incontrovertibly as the most popular Italian composer of the time.

However, it was with *Rigoletto* (1851), *Il Trovatore* (1853), and *La Traviata* (1853) that Verdi first really staked his claim to immortality. In these pieces his increasing dramatic mastery is married to a wonderful flow of lyrical melody, at the same time controlled by a fine musical sensibility. They were followed by four operas—*Simon Boccanegra* (1857), *Un Ballo in Maschera* (1858), *La Forza del Destino* (1862), and *Macbeth* (revised version, 1865)—in which Verdi overcame complexities of story line by his continually developing musical powers. This period is crowned by *Don Carlos* (written for the Paris Opéra, 1867) a masterly exercise in combining private and public situations in a single, grand, and characterful work. In some respects Verdi never surpassed the subtlety of his writing in this opera. *Aïda* (1871) carried on the process but the characterisation in this ever-popular piece is less refined than in *Don Carlos*, if the grandeur of the design is more spectacular.

The success of *Otello* (1887) owes nearly as much to the skill of Boito whose literary ability combined with musical knowledge (he was himself a composer) presented Verdi with an ideal libretto for his seamless music in which the drama moves inevitably to its tragic end. Recitative, aria, ensemble are fused in a single, swiftly moving music-drama, which in its very different way equals that of Wagner. *Falstaff* (1893) achieves the same success in the field of comic opera, a brilliant, mercurial ending to a distinguished career. If Verdi had written only these two final masterpieces his place in musical history would be assured.

Brahms.

Brahms (1833–97) has justly been described as "a romantic spirit controlled by a classical intellect," for while complying with most of the formal regulations of sonata form he imbued them with an emotional content that accorded with his time. Indeed Schumann declared that he was the "one man who would be singled out to make articulate in an ideal way the highest expression of our time."

Perhaps in his chamber music will be found the quintessence of his art. The piano and clarinet quintets, the two string sextets, the horn trio, and the violin sonatas all are designed on a large scale yet the expression remains intimate, the design and structure clear.

The symphonies and concertos, though, remain his most popular works; they are part of the solid repertory of every orchestra and most piano and violin players in the world. Their high seriousness, constant lyrical beauty, and control of form are deeply satisfying. They do not provide the extremes of passion and excitement provided by his contemporaries, but their study provides continuous absorption and delight. The double concerto for violin and cello deserves a mention as a unique work in music.

Brahms wrote more than two hundred songs in which the desire for melodic beauty takes precedence over the words and meaning. Many are set to poor poetry, but hidden away are still some unexplored treasures, and the Four Serious Songs, at least, are tragic masterpieces. In a lighter vein the two sets of *Liebeslieder Walzer* for four voices are irresistible. The choral Requiem, too, is a fine work.

Bruckner.

In recent years Bruckner's reputation *vis-à-vis* his great contemporary Brahms has been enhanced in England. The old conception of him as a naïve Austrian unable to grasp the fundamentals of symphonic architecture has died hard, and the prevailing popularity of his grandest works is at last gaining him his rightful place in the 19th-cent. firmament. The nine symphonies and the masses are his chief claim to immortality. They contain melodies of unforgettable beauty, symphonic paragraphs of unparalleled grandeur, and an appreciation of formal development that, though different, is as equally valid as that of Brahms. The movements of his symphonies are long and he often pauses, as if for breath and to admire the scenery, before he reaches the climactic peak of his musical journey. His idiom is best approached by a newcomer to his work through the fourth and seventh symphonies as they are perhaps the easiest to understand, but the fifth, sixth, eighth, and ninth (unfinished) are just as beautiful—and cogently argued—once one has acquired the knack, so to speak, of listening to his music. Most of these works are now to be heard in their original form, stripped of the veneer of "improvements" suggested to the diffident composer by his friends.

The masses, which translate Bruckner's symphonic ideas to the choral plain, and Bruckner's delightful string quintet are worth investigating.

Wagner.

Praised only this side of idolatry by his admirers, unmercifully criticised by his detractors, Richard Wagner (1813–83) is perhaps the most controversial composer in musical history. And so it was bound to be with such a revolutionary figure, whose writings, other than his music, contain, to say the least, dubious theories and whose operas, composed to his own libretti, broke the bonds of the form as known until his time. He regarded music-drama as a fusion of all the arts—music, literature, painting—in one unity. With *The Ring of the Nibelungs* he achieved his purpose; no other work of art has ever tried to encompass the whole of existence. Today, and surely forever, musicians, philosophers, and writers will argue over its meaning, and each age will reinterpret it according to its own lights.

But before he reached this pinnacle of achievement, Wagner gradually transformed opera—through *Rienzi*, *The Flying Dutchman*, *Tannhäuser*, and *Lohengrin*—so that a new mould was fashioned to take what he wanted to pour into it. He introduced the *Leitmotiv*, a musical theme that could be associated with a particular person, situation, or idea, each time it occurred. Slowly he developed the musical form so that the drama could unfold continuously without breaks for arias. By the time he began to write *Tristan and Isolde* and *Die Meistersinger*, he had perfected his methods and had he never undertaken *The Ring* that tragedy and that comedy would have assured him his place in the musical firmament. Indeed, *Die Meistersinger* is considered a masterpiece even by those who are not willing or prepared to accept the rest of the Wagnerian ethos.

The length and complexity of these operas, and of *Parsifal*, a work of unique beauty in spite of certain *longueurs*, means that it is almost essential to prepare oneself by homework, with libretti and records, before attempting to assimilate them in the opera house. The added effort is well worth while for the ultimate musical satisfaction they bring because Wagner was more than an operatic reformer: he opened up a new harmonic language (especially in the use of chromaticism) that was logically to develop into the atonality of the 20th cent.

Wolf.

As Wagner was the culmination of the 19th cent. symphonic and operatic tradition, so Hugo Wolf (1860–1903) summed up, if he did not surpass, the achievements in song-writing of Schubert Schumann, and Loewe (1796–1869).

Wolf was a lonely, pathetic man. He lived much of his life in poverty, and eventually lost his reason and died of an incurable disease. These circumstances account perhaps for his almost feverish bursts of creative activity, which were also the outward sign of his burning genius. His greatest contributions to the art of *Lieder* were his extraordinary insight into the poet's meaning and the harmonic means by which he heightened the expression of the words. He raised the importance of the piano part even higher than had Schumann, and in some of his songs the vocal part takes the form of a free declamation over a repeated idea in the piano. However, in the main the vocal and piano parts are interweaved with great subtlety, and he unerringly matched the very varied moods of the poems he chose to set. His greatest creative period was between early 1888 and early 1890 when songs poured from his pen daily—more than 50 settings of the German poet Mörike, 20 of Eichendorff, more than 50 of Goethe, and more than 40 of Heyse and Geibel (the Spanish Song-book). Later he composed songs from Heyse's Italian Song-book and the three Michelangelo sonnets. And the range of his creative understanding was wide, taking in the almost wild passion of the Spanish songs, the humanity and humour of the Italian love-songs, the titanic power of *Prometheus* (Goethe), the varying moods of the Mörike book, and the intangible power of the Michelangelo sonnets. There are almost inexhaustible riches here for the inquiring mind to discover. Outside *Lieder*, Wolf's output is small, but it includes a sadly neglected opera, *Der Corregidor*, the Italian Serenade for string quartet (alternatively for small orchestra) and a tone poem *Penthesilea*.

Ernest Newman, his greatest champion, summed up his work most aptly: "Wolf practically never repeats himself in the songs; every character is drawn from the living model. It is a positively Shakespearian imagination that is at work—Protean in its creativeness, inexhaustibly fecund and always functioning from the inside of the character or the scene, not merely making an inventory from the outside."

National Movements.

During the course of the 19th cent., alongside the emergence of national political identity, came the rise of nationalism in music, fertilising traditional Western—that is basically German—musical forms with folk material. Of these groups the Russian is certainly the most important, if not the most vital.

Glinka (1804–57) was the first important Russian composer of the national school and, although his two operas *A Life for the Tsar* (sometimes called *Ivan Susanin*) and *Russlan and Ludmilla* are strongly influenced by Italian models, they do introduce Russian song and harmony into the texture. He undoubtedly influenced Borodin (1833–87), Cui (1835–1918), Balakireff (1837–1910), Mussorgsky (1839–81) and Rimsky-Korsakov (1844–1908)—the so-called "Five" of 19th-cent. Russian music. However, each was very much of an individualist too. Borodin was a lecturer in chemistry who wrote in his spare time. His two symphonies, two string quartets led up to his most notable work, the opera *Prince Igor*, left incomplete at his death. Balakireff, friend and adviser to the rest of the group, wrote little himself, but his orchestral works and the piano fantasia, *Islamey*, are worthy of investigation.

Modest Mussorgsky (1839–81) is today seen as the most important and inspired of "The Five." More than the others he used Russian song and Russian speech as the basis of his operas in which he portrayed the lives and destinies of his own people. Although his capacities were seriously impaired by an uncongenial job, poverty, and drinking, he produced two great operas, *Boris Godunov* and *Khovanshchina*, and another *Sorochintsy Fair* that is immensely enjoyable. *Boris* should be given in its original, with spare orchestration, but more often than not it is heard in Rimsky-Korsakov's more elaborate revision. In any case the opera exists in various versions, none of them necessarily the right one: what is important is to hear it in one or the other because of its great portrayal of Boris's personality set against the background of the Russian people, unforgettably presented in choral outbursts. *Khovanshchina* was completed by Rimsky-Korsakov, *Sorochintsy Fair* by Tcherepnin (although other versions also exist). Mussorgsky's songs explore a new vein of naturalistic vocal declamation. Each of the four *Songs and Dances of Death* is a miniature drama worthy of Wolf, although of course in a quite other idiom. The *Nursery* songs miraculously conjure up a child's world as seen from a child's point of view. Many of the individual songs, the *Sunless* cycle too, should be investigated.

Rimsky-Korsakov (1844–1908) is perhaps a less attractive figure because so much of his music seems heartless or merely decorative, but this judgment is probably made on the strength of hearing *Shéhérazade* and the *Capriccio Espagnol* a few too many times. Such of his 15 operas as are played evince a (literally) fantastic mind and lyrical vein, and it is a pity that *Sadko*, *The Snow Maiden*, and *The Tsar's Bride*, at least, are not heard more often.

Tchaikovsky.

Peter Ilyich Tchaikovsky (1840–93) is a more universally admired figure than any of "The Five" and his music is indubitably closer to the mainstream than theirs in that it adheres more nearly to Western European forms. His popularity is due to his unhesitating appeal to the emotions and to his tender, often pathetic melodic expression. His lyrical gift is stronger than his sense of architecture, as he himself admitted. Yet his later symphonies—the fourth, fifth, and sixth (the *Pathétique*)—are all cogently enough argued and invigorating, as can be heard in the hands of a conductor willing to emphasise their formal power rather than their tendency towards sentimentality: the orchestral craftsmanship is also superb. The three piano concertos and the violin concerto offer rare opportunities for virtuoso display within a reasonably dramatic structure and his various overtures are always exciting to hear.

The three ballets—*The Sleeping Beauty*, *Swan Lake*, and *Nutcracker* show Tchaikovsky's skill on a smaller and perhaps more congenial scale, but only two of his operas—*Eugene Onegin* and *The Queen of Spades*—survive in regular performance. They demonstrate his ability to delineate character and his always eloquent melodic invention. His songs often felicitously capture a passing mood or emotion.

Bohemia (Czechoslovakia).

The Czech national school is dominated by two composers—Smetana (1824–84) and Dvořák (1841–1904). In his own country Smetana holds a unique position as the father of his country's music—which is remarkable when you consider that he lived in a country that was then under Austrian rule and never spoke the Czech language perfectly. Yet his music is filled with the spirit of Czech history and national life, and many of his operas, his most important contribution, deal purely with national subjects. The reawakening of interest in things national, after Austria's defeat by Italy in 1859, led to the establishment of a Provisional Theatre in 1862 and Smetana's first opera *The Brandenburgers in Bohemia* was produced there in 1866, but its success was eclipsed by the enormous popularity of *The Bartered Bride*, which appeared the same year. Its melodic charm, lively characterisation and cosy humour have carried it round the world and it is the one Smetana opera to be in the repertory of most opera houses. However, his next opera *Dalibor* (1868) is considered by some authorities as his masterpiece. It is conceived on a heroic scale, and frequently rises to great dramatic heights. His later operas include *Libuše* (1872) a solemn festival tableau, *The Two Widows* (1874), a delightful comedy, *The Kiss* (1876), *The Secret* (1878), and *The Devil's Wall* (1882).

His main orchestral work *Má Vlast* (My Country), written between 1874 and 1879, is a cycle of six symphonic poems nobly depicting the life and legends of his country. He composed only three mature chamber works—an elegiac piano trio, written in 1855 in memory of the death of his eldest daughter, and two string quartets, both autobiographical. The first in E minor (1876)—"From My Life"—tells of his youth and aspirations until a terrible, screeching E in *altissimo* describes the onset of deafness; the second in D minor, sadly neglected, was described by the composer as an attempt to explain the "whirlwind of music in the head of one, who has lost his hearing," and was probably influenced by Beethoven's later music.

Dvořák combined a fecund melodic gift with an intelligent grasp of structure. His symphonies and chamber music are mostly written in classical form, yet the works are imbued with a spontaneity and freshness that have not lost one whit of their charm over the years.

He wrote nine symphonies and, although only the last three or four are regularly performed, they are mostly mature works, several of which, for instance No. 7 in D minor (formerly known as No. 2) reach a tragic grandeur at times. They are all orchestrated in a masterly way and are full of delightful detail. Dvořák wanted to show that a Brahms could come out of Bohemia—and he succeeded in doing so while maintaining a definitely individual flavour, strongly influenced by natural rhythms.

He wrote three concertos, one each for piano, violin, and cello. The earlier ones are interesting without being quite in the first flight of the composer's output, but the cello concerto of 1895 is perhaps the composer's crowning achievement—warm, mellifluous, romantic.

He wrote chamber music throughout his long creative life. Some of the early works are weak and derivative, but the later string quartets, the "Dumky" trio, and the piano quartet and quintet are expressive and full of unforced invention. Dvořák felt himself somewhat hampered when setting words, nevertheless his *Stabat Mater* and *Te Deum* are both deeply felt choral works and he wrote songs throughout his career, many of them very fine indeed. He wrote ten operas, but only *Rusalka* (1901) has gained a foothold outside Czechoslavakia.

Janáček.

The Moravian composer Leoš Janáček (1858–1928) spent most of his life in Brno as a working musician. His music has recently come to be recognised as some of the most original written in the past hundred years. His operas, in which he closely followed the inflection of the speech of his native land, are his finest works. Over the score of his last opera, *From the House of the Dead*, he wrote the words "In every human being there is a divine spark", and it is this deep love of humanity that permeates all his works. Of his operas *Kátya Kabanová* (1921) and *The Cunning Little Vixen*

(1924), the *Makropoulos Affair* (1926), and *From the House of the Dead* (adapted from a Dostoyevsky novel, 1928) are the most important and they have all been produced in Britain in recent years. His original genius is self-evident in all of them.

Among his orchestral works *Taras Bulba* and *Sinfonietta* should be noted, and his two string quartets, very difficult to play, should be better known. The song cycle, *Diary of one who has disappeared*, for tenor, contralto, and three female voices with piano, and the Glagolithic Mass contain music of much expressive beauty.

Hungary.

The Hungarian musical outburst came somewhat later than that in other countries. Its great figure is Bela Bartók (1881–1945) who, as well as being a national figure, has proved an influential composer in the whole of 20th-cent. music. His mind was full of folk music, but it was transmuted by his strongly personal style and powerful intellect into something highly original. His music is tense and volatile but this restlessness is sometimes relieved by a kind of other-wordly, ethereal lyricism, as in the lovely slow movements of his quartets.

Bartók was affected as much by the musical innovations of Debussy and Stravinsky (see below) as by East European, notably Magyar, folk music and many of his works are an attempt to meld the two.

The most important part of his output is undoubtedly his string quartets which cover most of his creative life. To this intimate form he confided his personal innermost thoughts and in it conducted his most far-reaching musical experiments, thereby extending its boundaries beyond anything previously known. As with Beethoven's late quartets many of Bartok's rely on organic or cyclic development while remaining just within the laws of classical form. As Mosco Carner puts it, "For profundity of thought, imaginative power, logic of structure, diversity of formal details, and enlargement of the technical scope, they stand unrivalled in the field of modern chamber music."

The most important of his orchestral works are the three piano concertos, of which the first two are harsh and uncompromising, and fiendishly difficult to play, while the third, written in 1945, is mellower and more diatonic. The second violin concerto (1937–8) shows the various elements of Bartók's style in full flower, by turns exuberant, passionate, and brilliant. The *Music for Strings, Percussion and Celesta* (1937) is remarkable for its strange sonorities and its fascinating texture. The *Concerto for Orchestra* (1944) is more immediately appealing and again shows the composer in complete command of a large canvas. Of the piano works *Mikrokosmos* (1935) and the sonata for two pianos and percussion (1937) are worth investigating.

His chief stage pieces are *The Miraculous Mandarin* (1919), a harsh, cruel ballet which drew appropriately dramatic music from the composer, and the opera *Duke Bluebeard's Castle* (1911), a luscious, original score that makes one regret that he wrote no more operas later in his career.

Kodály (1882–1967) was from early years closely associated with Bartók and with him collected Hungarian folk melodies using many of them in his music. He worked in many forms and the more important of his works are the *Peacock Variations* for orchestra, the choral *Psalmus Hungaricus* and *Te Deum*, The *Dances of Galánta*, and the opera *Háry János*, and the sonatas for cello and for unaccompanied cello.

Sibelius, Nielsen and Grieg.

Among Scandinavian composers the Finn Jean Sibelius (1865–1957) and the Dane Carl Nielsen (1865–1931) are outstanding. Sibelius is a lone northern figure ploughing his own furrow oblivious or, at any rate, ignoring the unusual developments that were taking place in Central Europe, yet his seven symphonies are strong as granite, honest, rugged works that will undoubtedly stand the test of time. They are not by any means all similar in mood, or even form. The first is very much influenced by Tchaikovsky and Borodin, the second and third show a more personal style developing, the fourth is terse and tragic, the fifth lyrical, bright, and lucid; the sixth is perhaps most typically Sibelian in its evocation of primeval nature, and the seventh—in one continuous movement—is a more purely abstract piece, notable for its structural logic and the grandness of its themes. The violin concerto is the most easily understood of the composer's main works and has a grateful part for the soloist.

The tone poems *The Swan of Tuonela, Pohjola's Daughter, En Saga, Night Ride and Sunrise, The Bard*, and *Tapiola* uncannily evoke the icy words of the legends of the far north, and the primeval forces of nature. Sibelius's one string quartet *Voces Intimae* and many of his songs are worth hearing too. His music, reviled in some quarters during the 1950s, has now been restored to favour, and seems to be enjoyed again by critics and the general public alike.

Carl Nielsen (1865–1931) is another individualist. His six symphonies, like Sibelius's seven, are the most important part of his output, but whereas Sibelius was dealing with a huge, uninhabited northern landscape, Nielsen is more friendly and serene in his music, which is seldom forbidding, always inventive, throwing a new light, through unusual ideas about harmony, structure and tonality, on traditional forms. He also wrote highly individual concertos for the flute and clarinet, four string quartets and two operas—the dramatic, rather Brahmsian *Saul and David* (1902) and a delightful comedy, *Maskarade* (1906), full of lyrical music.

The Norwegian composer Edvard Grieg (1843–1907) was essentially a miniaturist whose range of feeling was not wide but whose music is always gentle and appealing. His most notable works are the romantic piano concerto, the atmospheric incidental music to Ibsen's play *Peer Gynt*, the charming Lyric Suite, and the small piano pieces. Not an important composer, then, but always an attractive one.

Elgar and the English Revival.

After the death of Purcell there is hardly a name in English music worth speaking of until the 19th cent. when Hubert Parry (1848–1918) and Charles Villiers Stanford (1852–1924), actually an Irishman, led a revival. Their music is seldom heard today, but their pioneer work paved the way for Edward Elgar (1857–1934). Although all were influenced by Brahms they nevertheless managed to establish a new English tradition that has been carried on in our own day. Elgar's symphonies are laid out on a grand, leisurely scale and they are both eloquent and exhilarating. His violin concerto has an elegiac slow movement as has the glorious cello concerto and both contain many fine opportunities for the soloist. The cello concerto is as appealing a work as any by Elgar expressing his innermost thoughts. His *Enigma Variations* are a series of portraits in sound of his friends, but there is another overall theme to go with them that has never been identified. This has not prevented the work from becoming Elgar's most popular, not surprisingly when one considers its charm and melodiousness. Three other orchestral pieces that should not be neglected are his symphonic study *Falstaff*, a many-sided musical picture of the Fat Knight, and the overtures *Cockaigne*, a happy evocation of London, and *In the South*, inspired by a visit to Italy. His three late chamber works, written when he was 61, are reticent, economic pieces that remove any misconception of Elgar as a bombastic composer. His songs are mostly feeble, but the oratorios, notably *The Dream of Gerontius*, show the composer's ability to control a large canvas. The composer himself wrote over the score of *Gerontius*,

"This is the best of me"—a verdict with which we can readily agree.

The French Impressionists.

César Franck (1822–90) was the main figure in mid-19th-cent. musical France and his influence spread even wider than his music of which only the D minor Symphony, the Symphonic Variations for piano and orchestra, the piano quintet, and the violin sonata are likely to be encountered today. The leading French opera composers of that time were Gounod (1818–93), Bizet (1838–75) and Massenet (1842–1912). Gounod's *Faust*, Bizet's *Carmen* (composed just before his untimely death when he caught cold after a swim) and Massenet's *Mamon* all retain a deserved place in the repertory; each is a well-judged mini-drama unafraid of romantic ardour and forceful, histrionic strokes. Some of Massenet's other numerous operas, such as *Werther* and *Don Quichotte*, have enjoyed a revival in recent years.

Concurrently with similar movements in French painting and poetry came the French Impressionist composers at the end of the 19th cent. Their leader—and one of the great seminal forces of modern music—was Claude Debussy (1862–1918). His aim was to capture a mood or sensation, and he did that by more or less inventing a fresh system of harmony using a whole-tone scale, unusual chords, and by creating in the orchestra new, highly personal textures—there is no mistaking the Debussy idiom once you have heard at least one piece by him. His impressionistic style did not lead him, however, to abandon form as some have suggested and his main works are just as closely organised as those by classical German composers. His music is sensuous and poetic yet nearly always structurally satisfying as well.

His reputation, at least with the general musical public, rests largely on his orchestral music, a few piano pieces and his only opera *Pelléas et Mélisande*. *La Mer* is a scintillating evocation of the sea in all its moods; *Nocturnes*, *Images*, and *Prélude à l'Après-midi d'un Faune* exactly suggest different places, times, moods—the "Iberia" and "Gigues" sections of *Images*, calling to mind respectively the spirit of Spain and the flickering light of a rainy English night. *Pelléas*, based on a Symbolist drama by Maeterlinck, tells a story of love, jealousy, and murder in predominantly restrained yet emotionally loaded terms. It is an elusive original work that has no predecessor or successor. Intensely atmospheric, rivetingly beautiful, it weaves an irresistible spell over the listener.

Debussy's chamber music is unjustly neglected. His string quartet (1893) was one of the first works in which he displayed his new and strange world of sound, and the three late sonatas, one for violin, one for cello, and the third for flute, viola, and harp are elliptical, compressed pieces which seem to be questing disjointedly into new regions of sound. His songs too, are worthy of investigation, and his piano music, especially the twenty-four Preludes and some of the shorter pieces, contain some of his most imaginative and original ideas and thoughts.

Gabriel Fauré (1845–1924) is a difficult figure to place. He lived through all kinds of musical revolutions yet they seemed to affect the character of his work very little. He has never been, and is never likely to be, a widely known or popular composer, yet his music has a reticence and delicacy that is very appealing. Despite his dreamy, retiring art he was not a recluse, but a very sociable man.

He was content with forms as he found them, but he imbued them with a very personal, human style. Perhaps his art is best heard in his songs. They are not overtly passionate or dramatic but the long, sinuous melodies and subtle harmonies are exquisitely wrought. Of the song-cycles, *La Bonne Chanson*, *Cinq Mélodies* (Verlaine), *Le Chanson d'Eve*, and *L'Horizon Chimérique* are best known. The last written in 1922, when the composer was seventy-seven, is a beautiful setting of words by a soldier killed in the first World War. There are also many remarkable single songs, many of them settings of poems by Verlaine. His opera *Pénélope*, based on the classical heroine, is unjustly neglected.

He wrote few orchestral pieces, but the *Ballade* for piano and orchestra and the *Pavane* are among his most typical, and delicate compositions, and his outstanding piano music, modelled on Chopin's, includes Nocturnes, Impromptus, and Barcarolles. His chamber music covers more than half a century from the violin sonata of 1876 to the string quartet written the year he died. In that period he composed two piano quartets, two piano quintets, another violin sonata and two cello sonatas, the later works failing to show quite the unforced lyrical grace of the earlier ones. Perhaps Fauré is best approached with the first piano quartet, a charming, easily assimilated work, and the beautiful choral *Requiem*.

Saint-Saëns (1835–1921), an accomplished, cultivated musician, has had a "bad press" but his craftsmanship, as displayed in his symphonies, concertos, and *Samson et Dalila* (one among his 12 operas) is not to be despised.

Henri Duparc (1844–1933), despite a very long life, is known today only for a group of songs he wrote before he was forty. They are among the most emotionally direct yet tasteful melodies ever written. Paul Dukas (1865–1935) is another figure off the beaten track, as it were. He, too, is known only for a handful of compositions. He was strongly influenced by Vincent d'Indy (1851–1931) and the school who strongly opposed Debussy's new ideas, yet he could not help but come under Debussy's spell. Dukas's one great work is his opera *Ariane et Barbe-Bleue*, the text adapted from a Maeterlinck play written with the composer in mind.

Maurice Ravel (1875–1937), a pupil of Fauré, followed in Debussy's footsteps, although his later pieces were more ascetic. Indeed, he was one of the most fastidious of composers, always seeking, and often finding, artistic perfection. The works he wrote before 1918 are definitely of the Impressionist School and it would be difficult to imagine more beautiful sounds than are to be found in the ballet *Daphnis et Chloé*, in the song-cycle *Shéhérazade*, and the piano fantasy *Gaspard de la Nuit*. His first style was summed up in the A minor piano trio (1915). In his later music Ravel was struggling, not always successfully, to keep up with new developments such as jazz and atonality. The piano concerto, for instance, shows very strongly the influence of jazz.

Outstanding orchestral works of his, other than *Daphnis* are *Rapsodie espagnole* (1907), *La Valse* (1920), a sumptuous evocation of the Vienna waltz, and the ever-popular *Boléro*. Two chamber works, besides the trio, are masterpieces—the string quartet (1902–3) and the Introduction and Allegro for Harp, String Quartet, Flute, and Clarinet. This Septet composed in 1906, ravishes the senses with magical sound.

Ravel's piano pieces are perhaps his most notable contribution to music, combining an extraordinary feeling for the instrument's technical possibilities with the sensibility of a Chopin, and in this field *Jeux d'eau*, *Miroirs*, and *Ma Mère l'Oye*, all written just after the turn of the century, come very close to the perfection of *Gaspard de la Nuit*. His songs show his unusual appreciation of the need to fuse poetic and musical values, and he set exotic poems for preference. The song-cycle *Histoires naturelles* (1906) is an acutely observed setting of five poems about birds and animals; *Cinq Mélodies populaires Grecques* (1907) are charming settings of Greek folk songs; *Trois Poèmes de Mallarmé* (1913), *Chansons Medécasses* (1926), are suitably exotic settings of three poems by an 18th-cent. Creole poet called Parny. Finally in 1932 came *Don Quichotte à Dulcinée*, three poems by Paul Morand, Ravel's last composition.

Ravel wrote two operas—the slight but moderately amusing *L'Heure espagnole* (1907), nicely orchestrated in a faintly and appropriately Spanish style and *L'Enfant et les Sortilèges* (1925) to a story by Colette, a delicious fantasy about a naughty child who gets his due punishment for tormenting animals and destroying furniture.

Spain.

Felipe Pedrell (1841–1922) has been aptly described as the midwife of Spanish nationalist music. As a musicologist and teacher he strongly influenced the two main composers of the school, Manuel de Falla (1876–1946) and Enrique Granados (1867–1916). Falla's output was not large and most of it was written about the time of the first World War. He had spent the years before the war in Paris and there he naturally came under the influence of Debussy. Debussy wrote Spanish music without ever having been to Spain but so true was it that even to Falla, born and bred in Andalusia, it had new things to say. He was able to take something from Debussy and blend it with his own highly individual style, evoking in his music all the passion and gaiety of his native land. Perhaps his most typical works are the two ballets *Love the Magician* (1915) full of Spanish atmosphere, and *The Three-Cornered Hat* (1919). The opera *La Vida Breve* (1905), despite its weak libretto, has much appeal, especially when the leading rôle is sung by such a vibrant artist as Victoria de los Angeles. The Seven Popular Spanish Songs (1914) conjure up the vivacity and smouldering passion at the heart of the country's character, as does *Nights in the Garden of Spain* (1916), an evocative piece for piano and orchestra. His later works, especially the harpsichord concerto of 1926, show Falla tending towards a less ebullient, more neo-classical style. His second opera *Master Peter's Puppet Show* (1923) is a miniaturist work, refined and intense. His third opera *Atlantida*, left unfinished at his death, was completed by his pupil Ernesto Halffter and first staged in 1962. It is a long work, more a dramatic cantata than an opera, and as such a rather unwieldy epic.

Granados, who was drowned when his ship was torpedoed by the Germans in 1916, was perhaps a more restrictedly Spanish composer than Falla, but his music is unfailingly attractive, and surely others of his seven operas, besides *Goyescas* (which is heard occasionally), deserve to be rescued from oblivion. *Goyescas* itself is especially famous for the second interlude and opening of Act III—*La Maja y el Ruiseñor* (The lover and the nightingale), a haunting, sinuous melody for soprano, sometimes heard in its original form as a piano solo. He wrote a set of *Tonadillas*. A tonadilla is a type of Spanish song popular in the 18th cent., and Granados's set ably and enchantingly recaptures a lost age of grace and character. His exciting Spanish Dances are heard in both their piano and orchestral form.

The chief claim to fame of Albéniz (1860–1909) is *Ibéria*, masterly descriptive pieces for piano. Turina (1882–1949), not altogether successfully, attempted a more cosmopolitan style, but his most often heard music, especially that for guitar, is typically Spanish.

The Late German Romantics.

While composers such as Debussy, Sibelius, Stravinsky, and Schoenberg (see below for the latter pair) were striking out along new paths, Richard Strauss (1864–1949) continued in the trend of 19th-cent. German composers; he was the tradition's last great figure. At least two of his operas—*Salome* and *Elektra*—were considered shocking at the time, but today we can hear that they are essentially big-scale, romantic works—natural successors to Wagner's—however startling the harmonies may once have seemed.

If Strauss did not achieve the granite intellectual greatness of Beethoven or Wagner, there is no denying his melodic genius and powers of fertile invention which overlaid the streak of vulgarity and inflation in his musical make-up. His first outstanding achievement was in the field of the symphonic poem, where he carried the work of composers such as Liszt and Berlioz to its logical conclusion. Starting with *Don Juan* in 1888 and ending with *Sinfonia Domestica* in 1903 he wrote a series of kaleidoscopic works, full of enormous vitality, endless melody, and fascinating orchestration. The most easily assimilated—and the most popular—are *Don Juan* and *Till Eulenspiegel* but some of the longer works, notably *Also Sprach Zarathustra* (based on Nietzsche's prose poem) and *Don Quixote* (based, of course, on Cervantes's great work) will reward the persistent, inquiring mind with long hours of enthralled listening. Other works sound somewhat dated in their bombastic over-confidence, though Strauss's skill in composition seldom flagged at this stage of his long creative career. The symphonic poems all tell something of a story usually based on a literary source, but it is not essential to the enjoyment of the music to know what this is, although it may be helpful.

Strauss's reputation is even more solidly based on his fifteen operas, the earliest of which *Guntram* was first performed in 1894, the last, *Capriccio*, in 1942. During these years the essentials of Strauss's style changed little, though it became very much more refined as the years passed. His first operatic period ended with the violent, sensual tragedies *Salome* (1905) and *Elektra* (1909), the latter being his first collaboration with his chief librettist Hugo von Hofmannsthal. Then came their unique *Der Rosenkavalier* (1911), which filters the charm and the decadence of 18th-cent. Vienna through early 20th-cent. eyes. This was followed by *Ariadne auf Naxos* (1912). Originally intended to be given after Molière's *Le Bourgeois Gentilhomme*, it was later presented (1916) without the play but with an amusing Prologue, written by von Hofmannsthal. *Die Frau ohne Schatten* is the most grandiose result of the Strauss–Hofmannsthal partnership. It is a complex psychological allegory, but Strauss's contribution is not on as consistently lofty a level as is his librettist's. *Intermezzo* (1924), which has a libretto by Strauss himself, is a largely autobiographical domestic comedy, which has lately gained in reputation as a compact, charming piece. With *Die Aegyptische Helena* (1928), an opera on a mythical theme, and *Arabella* (1933), another sensuous Viennese comedy, the Strauss–Hofmannsthal collaboration ended on account of the librettist's death. Strauss then wrote *Die Schweigsame Frau* (1935) to a libretto by Stefan Zweig, based on a play by Ben Jonson, and *Friedenstag* (1938), *Daphne* (1938)—a beautiful opera—and *Die Liebe der Danae* (written 1938–40) with Josef Gregor as librettist. His swan-song was *Capriccio*, a dramatisation of the old argument about the relative importance of words and music in opera. The libretto is by the conductor Clemens Krauss and the opera, a serene, melodious work, was a fit end to a great operatic career.

However, Strauss went on composing till nearly the end of his life, adding a group of late orchestral pieces to his already large catalogue of works. The *Metamorphosen* for 23 solo string instruments, is probably the best of these. During his long creative career he wrote numerous songs, many of them, such as *Morgen*, *Wiegenlied* and *Ruhe, meine Seele* of surpassing beauty.

Other notable figures in German music at this time were Max Reger (1873–1916), a somewhat ponderous but highly accomplished composer who, in a quarter of a century of creative life, wrote more than 150 works, of which his sets of variations, his piano concerto, and chamber music are probably the most impressive. Hans Pfitzner (1869–1949), another German traditionalist, is chiefly remembered today for his opera *Palestrina*, about events, now known to be spurious, in the life of the 16th-cent. Italian composer.

Twentieth-century Music.

Mahler.

Gustav Mahler (1860–1911), the Austrian Jewish composer, is one of the most important figures in 20th-cent. music. In a sense he bridges the gulf between the late Romantics, who were tending more and more towards chromaticism and away from established key relationships, and the atonalists, who abandoned key signatures entirely. His detractors maintain that his inflation of allegedly banal Viennese beer-house music to unheard-of lengths rules him out of court as a serious writer. His admirers would claim that his music encompasses the whole of life in enormous, valid structures. The truth, if truth there be, perhaps lies somewhere in between: if his material does not always justify the length of his symphonies, and if there are occasional imperfections and *longueurs*, these shortcomings are worth enduring with for the sake of the depth of utterance, the humanity and the poetry of the great pages. He admitted himself that "I cannot do without trivialities," but it is out of these impurities that he forged his titanic victories.

His music is undoubtedly best approached through his songs, where the words force him to discipline his wide-ranging vision. *Lieder eines fahrenden Gesellen* (1884), to his own words, *Kindertotenlieder* (1901–4), to poems by Rückert, and some individual songs perfectly relate words to music, and are all of a poignant loveliness. Similarly *Das Lied von der Erde* (1908), especially the last of the six songs, is a touching farewell to the world, nobly expressed.

The ten symphonies, however, are Mahler's most impressive legacy to posterity. They are almost impossible to characterise briefly so vast are they in terms of both length and variety. The first, fourth and ninth are probably the easiest to grasp but the fifth, sixth and seventh, despite flaws, contain some of his most awe-inspiring conceptions. The second and third, both of which use soloists and chorus, are revolutionary in orchestration and structure; they both try, inevitably without complete success, to carry out the composer's dictum, "a symphony should be like the world—it must contain everything." The eighth is even more gargantuan, but as in all Mahler's work size does not mean loss of clarity or an overloading of the structure. Part one—a mighty choral invocation—is a visionary setting of the mediaeval hymn *Veni Creator Spiritus*. Part two, which incorporates adagio, scherzo, and finale in one, is a setting of the final scene of Goethe's *Faust*. Until recently all of Mahler's unfinished tenth symphony that was ever performed was the Adagio, but the musicologist and Mahler scholar, the late Deryck Cooke, completed the symphony to critical and popular acclaim during the 1960s and thus added a noble, and also optimistic epilogue to the Mahler opus. The debate over the quality of Mahler's music is likely to continue: one fact, however, that cannot be gain-said is his popularity with an ever-increasing audience, largely made up of young people. There must be something in his uncertainty and intense self-inquiry that accords with the mood of the youthful mind.

Schoenberg and the Second Viennese School.

Arnold Schoenberg (1874–1951) revolutionised Western music by his twelve-note theory—a system which uses all the notes of the chromatic scale "and denies the supremacy of a tonal centre," as Schoenberg himself puts it. This serial technique of composition, as it is commonly called, naturally sounds strange to an ear acclimatised to music written, as it were, with a home base, but Schoenberg and his disciples Berg and Webern showed that the system could produce works that were something more than mere intellectual exercises. None of the more recent advances in music would have been possible, even thinkable, without Schoenberg's pioneer work.

Schoenberg always regarded himself as much as a composer as a theorist or teacher, and his works are supposed to appeal as much to the emotions as to the intellect, although to be understood they do, of course, require the listener's concentrated attention. To appreciate how his ideas developed it is necessary to hear first his pre-atonal music, such as the *Gurrelieder* (1900–1) and *Verklärte Nacht* (1899), in which he carried Wagnerian chromaticism to extreme lengths. The *Gurrelieder*, in particular, is a luxuriant, overblown work that shows the Wagnerian idiom in an advanced stage of decay, in spite of many beautiful pages of music. In his succeeding works the feeling of tonality began to disappear until in the Three Piano Pieces (opus 11), of 1909, he finally rejected tonality, although the new 12-note scheme is not yet evident; traces of the old order can still be heard. The succeeding works were mostly short, highly compressed, and very expressive. Schoenberg was reaching out for a new system, which would "justify the dissonant character of these harmonies and determine their successions." By 1923 he had formulated his 12-note system and the Five Piano Pieces (opus 23), and the Serenade (opus 24) of that year, can thus be considered the first works that used a note-row as the fundamental basis of their composition. Between 1910 and 1915, however, the Russian composer Alexander Skryabin (1872–1915) had attempted to define a new method of composition of his own employing the "mystic chord" of ascending fourths, but his scheme proved comparatively abortive when compared with Schoenberg's. Josef Hauer (1883–1959) also developed a 12-note system which he propounded in 1919 and he always considered himself, rather than Schoenberg, as the true founder of the system. He later worked out a system of tropes (*i.e.*, half-series of six notes).

To return to Schoenberg, in later works he shows much more freedom and assurance in the use of his system. The wind quintet (1924), the Variations for Orchestra, opus 31 (1927–8), the third (1926), and fourth (1936) string quartets, and the string trio (1946) are modern classics of their kind: they require concentrated listening and a degree of understanding of the unfamiliar style of composition. The set of songs with piano *Das Buch der hängenden Gärten* (opus 15), written in 1908, *Pierrot Lunaire*, opus 21 (1912) and the Four Songs, opus 22 (1913–14) provide a kind of bridge between tonality and atonality that the adventurous mind should cross. The monodrama *Erwartung* (1909) is another fascinating work, but perhaps the unfinished *Moses and Aaron* (1932) is Schoenberg's masterpiece as its production at Covent Garden in 1965 showed. Here, for certain, the composer matched his obvious intellectual capacities with an evident emotional content and managed to combine *Sprechgesang* (speech-song) and singing with a real degree of success.

It is only in recent years that Schoenberg's music has had a real chance to make its mark through the essential prerequisite of frequent performance. If his idiom now seems approachable, and a reasonably natural outcome of late 19th-cent. developments, it is perhaps because other, more recent composers have extended the boundaries of sound much further.

Schoenberg's two most respected disciples were Anton Webern (1883–1945) and Alban Berg (1885–1935). Webern's output is small, reaching only to opus 31, and many of his works are very brief. They are exquisitely precise, and delicate almost to a fault. He was trying to distil the essence of each note and in so doing carried the 12-note system to its most extreme and cerebral limit. His music has often been described as pointillist in the sense that one note is entirely separated from the next, there being little discernible melody. Beyond Webern's music, there is indeed the sound of nothingness, and he was rightly described during his lifetime as the "composer of the *pianissimo espressivo*". In his later works, Webern tended towards a strict, and often ingenious use of form and the Variations for Orchestra of 1940 are a good example of this and of his delicacy of orchestration. Webern's influence has perhaps been greater than the impact of his own music, even though he has had no direct successor.

Berg's music is much more accessible. Like Webern his total output was not large, but nearly all his works are substantial additions to the repertory. He is also the directest link between Mahler and the second Viennese School, as Mahler's music influenced him strongly. He studied with Schoenberg from 1904 to 1910. His music is more intense, more lyrical, and less attenuated in sound than Schoenberg's or Webern's. His humanity and abiding compassion can be heard most strongly in his finest opera *Wozzeck* (1925) and his violin concerto (1935), written as an elegy on the death of Manon Gropius, a beautiful 18-year-old girl. Both works are very carefully designed yet formal considerations are never allowed to submerge feeling, and the note-row is fully integrated into the structure.

Both *Wozzeck* and the unfinished but rewarding *Lulu* are concerned with society's outcasts who are treated with great tenderness in both operas. The later work is entirely dodecaphonic, all the opera's episodes being based on a theme associated with Lulu. Between these operas Berg wrote the highly complex Chamber Concerto for piano, violin, and thirteen wind instruments (1925) and the expressive Lyric Suite (1926). Among his early works the Seven Early Songs (1908–9) and the concert aria *Der Wein* (1929) are notable.

Stravinsky.

Igor Stravinsky (1882–1971) was another vital figure in 20th-cent. music. If his influence has been in quite another and perhaps less drastic direction than Schoenberg's it is hardly less important. Indeed, future musical historians may consider his achievement the more significant. He has been compared with the painter Picasso in his almost hectic desire to keep up with the times, yet, although he wrote in a number of very different styles over a period of fifty years, every work of his is stamped with his own definitive musical personality. His most revolutionary and seminal work is undoubtedly *The Rite of Spring* (written for the ballet impresario Diaghilev), which caused a furore when it first appeared in 1913, and although it no longer shocks, the rhythmical energy, the fierce angular thematic material, and the sheer virtuosity of the orchestration will always have the power to excite new audiences. Before *The Rite* Stravinsky had written two ballets for Diaghilev—*The Firebird* and *Petrushka*—that are no less filled with vitality and new, albeit not so violent, sounds. During the next thirty years Stravinsky wrote a series of ballet works, gradually becoming more austere and refined in composition. *Apollo* (1928) and *Orpheus* (1947) belong among his most attractive scores.

Stravinsky did not confine himself in stage works to the ballet. *The Nightingale* (1914) is a charming, early opera; *The Soldiers Tale* (1918) is a witty combination of narration, mime, and dance; *Les Noces* (1923) is a concise, original choreographic cantata for soloists and chorus; *Oedipus Rex* (1927) is a dignified version of the Sophocles play, which can be staged or given on the concert platform; either way it is a moving experience. *Perséphone* (1934), a melodrama for reciter, tenor, chorus, and orchestra is an appealing, lucid score. After the war his most important stage work by far was *The Rake's Progress* (1951), with a libretto by W. H. Auden and Chester Kallman. This fascinating opera is deliberately based on 18th-cent. forms and the music itself is neo-classical, always attractive, sometimes haunting.

Stravinsky was no laggard in writing for the concert-platform either. The finest of his orchestral pieces are probably the fervent choral *Symphony of Psalms* (1930), the violin concerto (1931) and the aggressive compact Symphony in three movements (1945). Of his chamber music the octet (1923), a duo concertant (1932), and septet (1952) are probably the most important, but no piece, even the dryest and most pedantic, is without redeeming features.

Stravinsky is often thought of as an aloof, detached figure. He has been castigated for his lack of lyrical warmth. But in spite of his own professed desire to drain his music of specific emotion, craftsmanship and originality, often with a strange other-worldly beauty added, are unmistakably there throughout his many scores. Quirky and annoying he may be, dull never.

Busoni and Puccini.

Italian music in the early part of the century was dominated by two very different composers—Ferruccio Busoni (1866–1924) and Giacomo Puccini (1858–1924). Busoni is a difficult figure to place. His austere, intellectual power is never called in question, but he seldom, if ever, succeeded in translating his technical prowess into altogether successful compositions. We can admire the strength, honesty, and often beauty of such works as his huge piano concerto (1903–4), *Fantasia Contrappuntisca* (1912)—for piano solo—and his unfinished opera *Doktor Faust* without ever capitulating to them entirely. None the less, it has to be admitted that those who have studied his music closely have always fallen completely under his spell. In style his music is anti-Romantic and often neo-Classical yet he was an ardent admirer of Liszt and more especially of Liszt's realisation of the possibilities of the pianoforte. Busoni, himself a great pianist, carried on where Liszt had left off in his own piano music, in which form and expression often find their perfect balance. *Doktor Faust* is undoubtedly his most important opera but *Die Brautwahl* (1908–10) and *Turandot* (1917) have many points of interest too.

Puccini's *Turandot*—his last opera—is a much grander version of the same Gozzi fable and the culmination of this great opera composer's work. His achievement is at an almost directly opposite pole to Busoni's. Not for him the severity or intellectuality of his contemporary. He sought and found an almost ideal fusion of straight-forward lyricism and dramatic truth. His music unerringly follows the pathos and passion of the stories he sets and all his characters "live" as human beings. That, and his abundant flow of easy, soaring melody, are the reasons for his immense popular success, unequalled by any other 20th-cent. composer. Whether it is the pathetic Mimi (*La Bohème*—1896) and Cio-Cio-San, (*Madama Butterfly*—1904), the evil Scarpia, (*Tosca*—1900), the cunning Schicchi (*Gianni Schicchi*—1918), the ardent Rodolfo (*La Bohème*) and Cavaradossi (*Tosca*), or the ice-cold Turandot (*Turandot*—1926), Puccini's musical characterisation is unfailing. And he backs his *verismo* vocal writing with an orchestral tissue that faithfully reflects the milieu of each opera, for instance, Japanese for *Butterfly*, Chinese for *Turandot*, while never losing his particular brand of Italian warmth. His orchestration is always subtle and luminous.

Other Italian composers who wrote operas in the *verismo* style of Puccini were Leoncavallo (1858–1919), Mascagni (1863–1945), and Giordano (1867–1948). Mascagni's *Cavalleria Rusticana* and Leoncavallo's *Pagliacci* have formed an inseparable bill and a regular part of the repertory in most opera houses.

Prokofiev, Shostakovich, and Rachmaninov.

Sergey Prokofiev (1891–1953) spent part of his creative life in his native Russia, part of it (1918–34) abroad, mostly in Paris. His early music, apart from the popular Classical Symphony (1916–17) tended to be acid and harsh, but on his return to Russia his style, though still frequently satirical, became warmer, more Romantic. The third piano concerto (1917) and the second symphony (1924) are good examples of the former period, the ballets *Romeo and Juliet* (1935) and *Cinderella* (1941–4) and the fifth (1944) and sixth (1949) symphonies of the latter. His music gives the impression of immense rhythmical energy, as in the outer movements of several of his nine piano sonatas, but this fierce drive is often leavened by the soft, wistful lights of his slow movements. His second string quartet (1941), perhaps, presents all the elements of his music in the kindest light.

His strong leaning towards fantasy and mordant parody is felt in his earlier operas *The Love of the Three Oranges* (1921) and *The Fiery Angel* (1922–5). *War and Peace* (1941–2), written in the face of strong pressure from the Soviet authorities, is an epic work that catches unerringly the mood of Dostoyevsky's vast novel.

Dmitri Shostakovich (1906–75) also suffered from attacks on his style. He had to conform to Stalin's requirements for writing music, but he survived and continued to produce music of universal appeal, as, for example, his later string quartets. Like Prokofiev, his music falls into two very distinct styles: one humorous and spiky, the other intense, very personal and often large-scale in its implications. Not all his symphonies reach the expressive depths of numbers one, five, six, eight, ten and fourteen, but they all have rewarding passages, and his violin and cello concertos are of high quality. He also wrote fifteen string quartets, a piano quintet (an attractive piece) and two operas: the satirical *The Nose* (1930) and *Katerina Ismailova* (1934, revised 1959), originally known as "Lady Macbeth of Mtensk."

Although Sergey Rachmaninov (1873–1943) was born in Russia, he left his home country in 1918, disliking the Soviet régime, and lived mostly in Switzerland and the United States. His music is chiefly notable for its Romanticism, nostalgic melody, nervous energy and, in the piano works, its opportunities for displays of virtuosity. The first three piano concertos, the third symphony, the piano preludes, and the Rhapsody on a theme of Paganini, are his most typical and attractive works, and many of his songs are touching and beautiful. He wrote three operas.

Modern French Music.

French music after Debussy and Ravel was dominated by the slighter composers known as *Les Six*, the most important of whom were Arthur Honegger (1892–1955, Swiss born), Darius Milhaud (1892-1974) and Francis Poulenc (1899–1963). Each has contributed music of some wit and charm to the repertory. They were influenced by Erik Satie (1866–1925), an eccentric but interesting figure, who wrote works with odd titles such as *Three Pear-Shaped Pieces*. His music is entirely unsentimental, often ironic.

Much more revolutionary has been the work of Olivier Messiaen (b. 1908), who has turned to Indian music and, above all, to bird-song for inspiration. He first came to notice as a composer of organ music. Then his *Quatuor pour la fin de temps*, written in captivity between 1940 and 1942, his long piano pieces, based on bird-song (often literally) and his gigantic *Turangalila* symphony show him experimenting with complex rhythms, strange sonorities (using unusual instruments such as the Ondes Martenot in the symphony), and considerably widening music's horizons. Edgar Varèse (1885–1965) cultivated an even broader spectrum of sound, employing electronic instruments to complement and contrast with traditional ones. Pierre Boulez (b. 1925), a pupil of Messiaen, bases his extremely complex works on mathematical relationships. His music, other than that for the piano, mostly calls for a variety of percussion instruments often combined with the soprano voice in evocations of French poetry (Mallarmé in particular). The resulting timbre and sonorities are intriguing even when the structural basis of the music is but dimly perceived. In recent years, he has devoted most of his time to conducting rather than composing.

Modern German Music.

Kurt Weill (1900–50) is chiefly known for his socio-politically pointed operas, such as *Die Dreigroschenoper* (1929), *Mahagonny* (1929), *Der Jasager* (1930), and *Happy End* (1929), all effective works on the stage, and for his particular brand of brittle, yet fundamentally romantic music. His influence on later composers has been considerable.

Carl Orff (b. 1895) has written chiefly for the stage. His music is rhythmically insistent, avoids counterpoint, and is deliberately, even self-consciously straightforward. Most frequently heard is his *Carmina Burana*, lively, rumbustious choral settings of mediæval poems.

Paul Hindemith (1895–1964) in his later years wrote in a strictly tonal, often neo-classical idiom, after being one of the most advanced intellectuals of his time. As well as many chamber and orchestral works, he wrote three formidable operas: *Die Harmonie der Welt*, *Cardillac* and *Mathis der Maler*.

Karlheinz Stockhausen (b. 1928), a pupil of Messiaen, is another extreme innovator. He more than anyone puts electronics to musical use. His scores are a maze of diagrams and instructions, which really need the composer's presence for their true interpretation. It is too early to say whether his music is evidence of a passing vogue or a real step forward in musical ideas.

Hans Werner Henze (b. 1926) has rebelled against the musical climate in Germany, and now lives in Italy, yet his music combines the intellectuality of the modern German schools with the lyricism of Italian music. He has written five symphonies, though none follow the traditional form, and nine operas, among them three impressive large-scale works, *Konig Hirsch* (1952–5), *The Young Lord* (1965) and *The Bassarids* (1966), to an Auden-Kallman libretto. His more recent work, as exemplified in *The Raft of Medusa* and certain stage works of a non-operatic nature, show him adopting a much more revolutionary style conditioned by his adherence to extreme left-wing views. This culminated in his opera written for Covent Garden, *We Come to the River* (1976), employing several stages and three separate instrumental groups.

American Music.

It was not until the 20th cent. that American music really got under way and an American school came into being. With the possible exception of MacDowell (1861–1908) no earlier composers are remembered or played today. Many composers of the American school have, of course, taken their cue from Europe but the influence of American jazz and folk-song is also recognisable in some of their music. Aaron Copland (b. 1900) is probably the most important figure on the current scene, and such works as *Appalachian Spring*, *Billy the Kid*, and his third symphony have gained a certain amount of international recognition and popularity. Samuel Barber (b. 1910) works along traditional lines and his music, like Copland's, is essentially diatonic. He has contributed to all the usual forms (symphony, concerto, sonata), most recently to opera with *Vanessa* (1958) and *Antony and Cleopatra* (1966), which opened the new Metropolitan Opera House in New York's Lincoln Centre. Roy Harris (b. 1898) has written seven symphonies and several concertos which include folk elements.

Charles Ives (1874–1954) has recently been recognised as the most original American composer. While carrying on a highly successful career in insurance, Ives yet managed to anticipate in his works, all written before 1920, many of the innovations which were later "invented" in Europe. His orchestral music is much influenced by the sounds, such as brass bands, which he heard in his native New England as a boy. His *Three Places in New England* and *The Unanswered Question* have a beautiful, elusive quality about them. In his five symphonies and *Concord* sonata we notice the working of an original mind employing polytonality and polyrhythms in larger and more complex works. An element of improvisation is sometimes introduced, another anticipation of latter-day technique. Ives is unlikely ever to become a popular composer—his music is too complicated and eclectic for that—but his importance as a prophet is surely established.

Modern English School.

The amazing 20th cent. revival of music in England owes much to Ralph Vaughan Williams (1872–1958) and Gustav Holst (1874–1934). Vaughan Williams's music is today suffering a decline in reputation, but the best of his symphonies (one, four, five, and six), his Fantasia on a theme by Tallis, his ballet *Job*, and the best of his choral and chamber music have a sturdiness that will no doubt weather the whim of passing fashion. His music alternates between the forceful and the contemplative and both moods are expressed in a distinctive musical vocabulary, based on modalism and 16th-cent. polyphony.

Holst was a more enigmatic figure, but his influence has undoubtedly been greater. Only his suite *The Planets* and the choral *The Hymn of Jesus* have established themselves as repertory works, but his bold harmonic experiments and the austerity, even mysticism, of his style as heard in the orchestral pieces *Egdon Heath*, *Beni Mora*, and the opera *Savitri* are perhaps more typical of this contemplative original composer. His daughter Imogen, a conductor, has done much to promote understanding of her father's music. Contemporaries who deserve much more than a passing reference are John Ireland (1879–1962) and Sir Arnold Bax (1883–1953), who wrote seven symphonies.

Frederick Delius (1862–1934) was the only important English disciple of the French impressionist school. He lived in France from 1888 onwards. His most important works are the atmospheric tone-poems for orchestra, such as *Brigg Fair*; the vocal and orchestral *A Mass of Life*, *Sea Drift* and *Appalachia*, and the opera *A Village Romeo and Juliet*.

Of the more recent generation of English composers the most important are undoubtedly Benjamin Britten (1913–76) Sir Michael Tippett (b. 1905), Alan Rawsthorne (1905–71), and Sir William Walton (b. 1902). Britten did more than anyone to establish English music on the forefront of the international stage. Much of his music seems to have an immediate appeal to large audiences and certainly his many stage works earned him a quite exceptional prestige both at home and abroad. *Peter Grimes* (1945), *Billy Budd* (1951), *Gloriana* (1953), *A Midsummer Night's Dream* (1960) all, in their very different ways, show his consummate mastery of stage technique and the first two are also moving human documents. His opera for television, *Owen Wingrave*, is a masterly adaptation of the Henry James short story. On a smaller scale he has achieved as much with his chamber operas—*The Rape of Lucretia* (1946), *Albert Herring* (1947), and *The Turn of the Screw* (1954, based on a Henry James novel)—and with the three Parables for Church Performance—*Curlew River* (1964), *The Burning Fiery Furnace* (1966) and *The Prodigal Son* (1968). His operatic output was crowned by *Death in Venice* (1973), also a personal expression of his love for the tenor Peter Pears who sang Aschenbach. If he had written nothing else, those dramatic works would have marked him out as a composer of outstandingly imaginative gifts.

But there is more—the choral works culminating in the *War Requiem* (1962), his various song cycles written for Pears, the *Serenade* for tenor, horn, and strings, *Nocturne* for tenor and orchestra, the three Canticles, and the Spring Symphony are further evidence—in very different media—of both his intense emotional commitment and his technical skill. While being strongly influenced by such composers as Schubert, Verdi, Mahler, and Berg, his style is entirely his own: it is a musical personality that manages to combine, as it has been said, "a deep nostalgia for the innocence of childhood, a mercurial sense of humour and a passionate sympathy with the victims of prejudice and misunderstanding."

This last quality is particularly evident also in Tippett's emotional makeup as expressed in his music, especially in one of his earliest successes, the choral work *A Child of Our Time* (1941), which shows both his compassion and his ability to write on a large scale. But Tippett is as much a mystic and searcher as a composer and he is constantly seeking new and different ways of widening his listeners' horizons, as may be heard in the exceedingly complex *Vision of St. Augustine* (1965), which tellingly sets to music the striving to understand the " beyond " of Augustine's words.

Tippett has also sought new means of musical expression as he has shown in his second opera *King Priam* (1962), very spare and pointed in idiom, and in the concerto for orchestra (1962). These works, his piano concerto (1956) and second symphony (of three)—a luminous work—and his three string quartets, are very difficult to perform—and to get to know—but the effort to understand the composer's wide-spanning mind is always richly rewarded. However, perhaps a newcomer to his music does better to approach him through the more straightforward earlier works, the concerto for double string orchestra (1939), the Fantasia Concertante on a theme of Corelli (1953)—a lyrically poetic piece—or the song cycles *Boyhood's End* (1943) and *Heart's Assurance* (1957). The quality of his allegorical opera *The Midsummer Marriage* (1952), in spite of its involved libretto (by the composer), is now better appreciated since its more recent revival. *The Knot Garden*, also concerned with the inner life of the spirit and the external world, was first performed at Covent Garden in 1970. Tippett is an uncompromising individualist, writing without fear or favour, perhaps considerably in advance of his time in thought and achievement.

Rawsthorne's style is admirably direct and honest. Eschewing the latest fashions in music he ploughed his own furrow of deeply felt writing. His ideas are argued out with considerable lyrical force, and his astute regard for form does not hide the underlying emotional content of his music nor the touch of wit that pervades some of his more lively movements. Among his most important accomplishments are his three string quartets, violin concerto, two piano concertos, and the quintet for piano and wind instruments.

Walton's outstanding contribution was made before the second World War in music that was alternately gay and romantic. The irreverent *Façade* (1923) for speaker and chamber orchestra falls into the former category, the poetic viola concerto (1929) into the second. His first symphony (1934–5) is an arresting, dramatic score, and the oratorio *Belshazzar's Feast* (1931) is a landmark in choral music. Since the war his works have never quite recaptured the same urgency of expression. His sole full-length opera, *Troilus and Cressida* (1954) was revised with success in 1976.

Elisabeth Lutyens (b. 1906) is Britain's leading twelve-note composer. For long shunned by the musical establishment, she has now been accepted as an important and seminal figure in the history of 20th-cent. music. Her output has been large and includes numerous works for unusual, small groups of instruments, often combined with a solo voice. Benjamin Frankel (1906–73), Edmund Rubbra (b. 1901), Sir Arthur Bliss (1891–1975), and Lennox Berkeley (b. 1903) are other composers of note among the senior school of living British composers. Egon Wellesz (1885–1970), Austrian-born, settled in Britain in 1939. He wrote operas, choral works, symphonies, and chamber music, and taught widely. There is a thriving junior school of British composers who have already made their mark, among them Alexander Goehr, Richard Rodney Bennett, Malcolm Williamson, Harrison Birtwistle, and Nicholas Maw, each of whom has written one or more operas. Roger Smalley and John Taverner, still younger, also seem to have promising futures before them. Williamson was created Master of the Queen's Musick, in succession to Bliss, in 1975.

Where Does the Future Lie?

It is anybody's guess which way music will develop during the next few decades. Are older forms quite outmoded, as some recent innovators suggest, and does the future therefore lie with the electronic music and/or percussive sounds—of Boulez, Stockhausen, Luigi Nono (b. 1924), and their disciples? Or will what has been recognised as musical sound for several generations adapt itself to the new mood abroad? Has atonalism still something to offer or was it a passing phase, already dated and out of fashion? Perhaps the only answer that can be given with certainty is that, as with other centuries, a dozen or so composers' music will survive to delight later generations and that these geniuses will be found among composers who do and say what they must in music without regard to fashion, patronage, or fear of what anyone writes about them. May they be worthy of their rich heritage.

II. GLOSSARY OF MUSICAL TERMS

A. Note of scale, commonly used for tuning instruments.

Absolute Music. Music without any literary descriptive or other kind of reference.

A Capella. Literally "in the church style." Unaccompanied.

Accelerando. Quickening of the pace.

Accidental. The sign which alters a note by a semitone, *i.e.*, ♯ (sharp) raises it; ♭ (flat) lowers it; ♮ restores a note to its original position.

Accompaniment. Instrumental or piano part forming background to a solo voice or instrument that has the melody.

Ad. lib. (L. *ad libitum*). Direction on music that strict time need not be observed.

Adagio. A slow movement or piece.

Aeolian mode. One of the scales in mediæval music, represented by the white keys of the piano from A to A.

Air. A simple tune for voice or instrument.

Alberti bass. Rhythmical accompanying figure made up by splitting a chord. Used extensively in 18th-cent. music and associated with the Italian composer Alberti.

Allegretto. Not quite so fast as *Allegro.*

Allegro. Fast, but not too fast.

Alto. An unusually high type of male voice; also the vocal part sung by women and boys with a low range.

Ambrosian Chant. Plainsong introduced into church music by St. Ambrose, bishop of Milan (d. 397), and differing from Gregorian chant.

Andante. At a walking pace, not so slow as *Adagio* nor as fast as *Allegretto.*

Animato. Lively.

Answer. Second entry in a fugue, usually in the dominant.

Anthem. Composition for use in church during a service by a choir with or without soloists.

Antiphonal. Using groups of instruments or singers placed apart.

Appoggiatura. An ornament consisting of a short note just above or below a note forming part of a chord.

Arabesque. Usually a short piece, highly decorated.

Arco. Direction for string instruments to play with bow.

Aria. Vocal solo, usually in opera or oratorio, often in three sections with the third part being a repeat of the first. An *Arietta* is a shorter, lighter kind of aria.

Arioso. In the style of an aria; halfway between aria and recitative.

Arpeggio. Notes of a chord played in a broken, spread-out manner, as on a harp.

Ars antiqua. The old mediæval music, based on organum and plainsong, before the introduction of *Ars nova* in 14th cent.

Ars nova. Musical style current from 14th cent., more independent than the old style in the part-writing and harmony.

Atonal. Not in any key; hence *Atonality.*

Aubade. Morning song.

Augmentation. The enlargement of a melody by lengthening the musical value of its notes.

Ayre. Old spelling of *air.*

B. Note of scale, represented in Germany by *H.*

Bagatelle. A short, generally light piece of music. Beethoven wrote 26 Bagatelles.

Ballad. Either a narrative song or an 18th-cent. drawing-room song.

Ballade. Instrumental piece in story-telling manner. Chopin wrote 4.

Ballet. Stage entertainment requiring instrumental accompaniment; originated at French court in 16th and 17th cent.

Bar. A metrical division of music; the perpendicular line in musical notation to indicate this.

Barcarolle. A boating-song, in particular one associated with Venetian gondoliers.

Baritone. A male voice, between tenor and bass.

Baroque. A term applied, loosely, to music written in the 17th and 18th cent., roughly corresponding to baroque in architecture.

Bass. The lowest male voice; lowest part of a composition.

Bass Drum. Largest of the drum family, placed upright and struck on the side.

Bassoon. The lowest of the woodwind instruments, uses double reed.

Beat. Music's rhythmic pulse.

Bel canto. Literally "beautiful singing"—in the old Italian style with pure tone and exact phrasing.

Berceuse. Cradle song.

Binary. A piece in two sections is said to be binary in form. The balance is obtained by a second phrase (or section) answering the first.

Bitonality. Use of two keys at once.

Bow. Stick with horsehair stretched across it for playing string instruments.

Brass. Used as a collective noun for all brass or metal instruments.

Breve. Note, rarely used nowadays, with tone value of two semibreves.

Bridge. Wood support over which strings are stretched on a violin, cello, guitar, etc.

Buffo(a). Comic, as in *buffo bass* or *opera buffa.*

C. Note of scale.

Cabaletta. Final, quick section of an aria or duet.

Cadence. A closing phrase of a composition or a passage, coming to rest on tonic (key note).

Cadenza. Solo vocal or instrumental passage, either written or improvised, giving soloist chance to display technical skill to audience.

Calando. Becoming quieter and slower.

Canon. Device in contrapuntal composition whereby a melody is introduced by one voice or instrument then repeated by one or more voices or instruments, either at the same pitch (canon at the unison) or at different intervals (canon at the fifth, for example).

Cantabile. Song-like, therefore flowing and expressive.

Cantata. Vocal work for chorus and/or choir.

Cantilena. Sustained, smooth melodic line.

Cantus firmus. Literally "fixed song." Basic melody from 14th to 17th cent., around which other voices wove contrapuntal parts.

Canzonet. Light songs written in England *c.* 1600.

Carillon. A set of bells in tower of church, played from a keyboard below.

Carol. Christmas song.

Castrato. Artificially-created male soprano and alto, fashionable in 17th and 18th cent. (The castration of vocally gifted boys prevailed in Italy until the 19th cent.)

Catch. A part-song like a round, in vogue in England from 16th to 19th cent.

Cavatina. An operatic song in one section, or a slow song-like instrumental movement.

Celesta. Keyboard instrument with metal bars struck by hammers.

Cello. Four-stringed instrument, played with bow, with a bass range. Comes between viola and double bass in string family.

Cembalo. Originally the Italian name for the dulcimer, but sometimes applied to the harpsichord.

Chaconne. Vocal or instrumental piece with unvaried bass.

Chamber Music. Music originally intended to be played in a room for three or more players.

Chanson. Type of part-song current in France from 14th to 16th cent.

Chant. Singing of psalms, masses, etc., in plainsong to Latin words in church.

Choir. Body of singers, used either in church or at concerts.

Chorales. German hymn tunes, often made use of by Bach.

Chord. Any combination of notes heard together *See also* Triad.

Chording. Spacing of intervals in a chord.

Chorus. Substantial body of singers, usually singing in four parts.

Chromatic. Using a scale of nothing but semitones.

Clarinet. Woodwind instrument with single reed in use since mid-18th cent.

Clavichord. Keyboard instrument having strings struck by metal tangents, much in use during 17th and 18th cent. as solo instrument.

Clavier. Used in German (*Klavier*) for piano, in England for any stringed keyboard instrument.

Clef. Sign in stave that fixes place of each note.

Coda. Closing section of movement in Sonata form.

Coloratura. Term to denote florid singing.

Common chord. *See* Triad.

Common Time. Four crotchets to the bar, 4/4 time.

Compass. Range of notes covered by voice or instruments.

Composition. Piece of music, originated by a composer's own imagination; act of writing such a piece.

Compound time. Any musical metric not in simple time.

Con Brio. With dash.

Concert. Public performance of any music.

Concertato. Writing for several solo instruments to be played together.

Concerto. Work for one or more solo instruments and orchestra.

Concerto grosso. Orchestral work common in 17th and 18th cent. with prominent parts for small groups of instruments.

Concord. Opposite of discord, *i.e.*, notes that when sounded together satisfy the ear. (Conventional term in that its application varies according to the age in which one lives.)

Conduct. To direct a concert with a baton.

Consecutive. Progression of harmonic intervals of like kind.

Consonance. Like Concord.

Continuo. Bass line, used in 17th- and 18th-cent. music, for a keyboard instrument, requiring special skill from performer.

Contralto. A woman's voice with a low range.

Counterpoint. Simultaneous combination of two or more melodies to create a satisfying musical texture. Where one melody is added to another, one is called the other's counterpoint. The adjective of counterpoint is contrapuntal.

Counter-tenor. Another name for male alto.

Courante. A dance in triple time.

Crescendo. Getting louder.

Crook. Detachable section of tubing on brass instruments that change the tuning.

Crotchet. Note that equals two quavers in time value.

Cycle. Set of works, especially songs, intended to be sung as group.

Cyclic form. Form of work in two or more movements in which the same musical themes recur.

Cymbal. Percussion instrument; two plates struck against each other.

D. Note of scale.

Da Capo (abbr. D.C.). A *Da Capo* aria is one in which the whole first section is repeated after a contrasting middle section.

Descant. Additional part (sometimes improvised) sung against a melody.

Development. Working-out section of movement in sonata form. *See* Sonata.

Diatonic. Opposite of chromatic; using proper notes of a major or minor scale.

Diminished. Lessened version of perfect interval, e.g., semitone less than a perfect fifth is a diminished fifth.

Diminuendo. Lessening.

Diminution. Reducing a phrase of melody by shortening time value of notes.

Discord. Opposite of concord, *i.e.*, notes that sounded together produce a clash of harmonies.

Dissonance. Like discord.

Divertimento. A piece, usually orchestral, in several movements; like a suite.

Dodecaphonic. Pertaining to 12-note method of composition.

Dominant. Fifth note of major or minor scale above tonic (key) note.

Dorian Mode. One of the scales in mediæval music, represented by the white keys on the piano from D to D.

Dot. Placed over note indicates staccato; placed after note indicates time value to be increased by half.

Double bar. Two upright lines marking the end of a composition or a section of it.

Double bass. Largest and lowest instrument of violin family; played with bow.

Drone bass. Unvarying sustained bass, similar to the permanent bass note of a bagpipe.

Drum. Variety of percussion instruments on which sound is produced by hitting a skin stretched tightly over a hollow cylinder or hemisphere.

Duet. Combination of two performers; composition for such a combination.

Duple time. Time in which main division is two or four.

Dynamics. Gradations of loudness or softness in music.

E. Note of scale.

Electronic. Term used to describe use of electronic sounds in music.

Encore. Request from audience for repeat of work, or extra item in a programme.

English horn (*Cor anglais*). Woodwind instrument with double reed of oboe family.

Enharmonic. Modulation made by means of change of note between sharps and flats, although note remains the same (E flat becomes D sharp, for example).

Ensemble. Teamwork in performance; item in opera for several singers with or without chorus; a group of performers of no fixed number.

Episode. Section in composition usually divorced from main argument.

Exposition. Setting out of thematic material in a sonata-form composition.

Expression marks. Indication by composer of how he wants his music performed.

F. Note of scale.

False relation. A clash of harmony produced when two notes, such as A natural and A flat, are played simultaneously or immediately following one another.

Falsetto. The kind of singing by male voices above normal register and sounding like an unbroken voice.

Fanfare. Flourish of trumpets.

Fantasy. A piece suggesting free play of composer's imagination, or a piece based on known tunes (folk, operatic, etc.).

Fermata. Pause indicated by sign 𝄐 prolonging note beyond its normal length.

Fifth. Interval taking five steps in the scale. A perfect fifth (say, C to G) includes three whole tones and a semitone; a diminished fifth is a semitone less, an augmented fifth a semitone more.

Figure. A short phrase, especially one that is repeated.

Fingering. Use of fingers to play instrument, or the indication above notes to show what fingers should be used.

Flat. Term indicating a lowering of pitch by a semitone, or to describe a performer playing under the note.

Florid. Term used to describe decorative passages.

Flute. Woodwind instrument, blown sideways. It is played through a hole, not a reed. Nowadays, sometimes made of metal.

Folksong. Traditional tune, often in different versions, handed down aurally from generation to generation.

Form. Course or layout of a composition, especially when in various sections.

Fourth. Interval taking four steps in scale. A perfect fourth (say, C to F) includes two whole tones and a semitone. If either note is sharpened or flattened the result is an augmented or a diminished fourth.

Fugato. In the manner of a fugue.

Fugue. Contrapuntal composition for various parts based on one or more subjects treated imitatively but not strictly.

G. Note of scale.

Galant. Used to designate elegant style of 18th-cent. music.

Galliard. Lively dance dating back to 15th cent. or before.

Gavotte. Dance in 4/4 time, beginning on third beat in bar.

Giusto. Strict, proper.

Glee. Short part-song.

Glissando. Rapid sliding scales up and down piano or other instruments.

Glockenspiel. Percussion instrument consisting of tuned steel bars and played with two hammers or keyboard.

Grace note. *See* Ornament.

Grave. In slow tempo.

Grazioso. Gracefully.

Gregorian Chant. Plainsong collected and supervised mainly by Pope Gregory (d. 604).

Ground bass. Figure on theme used as bass in a composition and constantly repeated without change.

Guitar. Plucked string instrument of Spanish origin, having six strings of three-octave compass.

H. German note-symbol for *B.*

Harmony. Simultaneous sounding of notes so as to make musical sense.

Harp. Plucked string instrument of ancient origin, the strings stretched parallel across its frame. The basic scale of C flat major is altered by a set of pedals.

Harpsichord. Keyboard stringed instrument played by means of keyboard similar to a piano but producing its notes by a plucking, rather than a striking action.

Homophonic. Opposite of polyphonic, *i.e.*, indicated parts move together in a composition, a single melody being accompanied by block chords, as distinct from the contrapuntal movement of different melodies.

Horn. Brass instrument with coiled tubes. Valves introduced in 19th cent. made full chromatic use of instrument possible.

Hymn. Song of praise, especially in church.

Imitation. Repetition, exactly, or at least recognisably, of a previously heard figure.

Impromptu. A short, seemingly improvised piece of music, especially by Schubert or Chopin.

Improvise. To perform according to fancy or imagination, sometimes on a given theme.

In alt. The octave above the treble clef; *in altissimo*, octave above that.

Instrumentation. Writing music for particular instruments, using the composer's knowledge of what sounds well on different instruments.

Interlude. Piece played between two sections of a composition.

Intermezzo. Formerly meant interlude, now often used for pieces played between acts of operas.

Interval. Distance in pitch between notes.

Ionian mode. One of the scales in mediæval music, represented on piano by white keys between C and C, identical therefore to modern C major scale.

Isorhythmic. Term applied to motets of 14th and 15th cent. where rhythm remains strict although melody changes.

Jig. Old dance usually in 6/8 or 12/8 time.

Kettledrum (It. pl. *Timpani*). Drum with skin drawn over a cauldron-shaped receptacle, can be tuned to definite pitch by turning handles on rim, thus tightening or relaxing skin.

Key. Lever by means of which piano, organ, etc., produces note; classification, in relatively modern times, of notes of a scale. Any piece of music in major or minor is in the *key* of its tonic or keynote.

Keyboard. Term used to describe instruments with a continuous row of keys.

Key-signature. Indication on written music, usually at the beginning of each line, of the number of flats or sharps in the key of a composition.

Kitchen Department. Humorous term for percussion section of an orchestra.

Lament. Musical piece of sad or deathly significance.

Largamente. Spaciously.

Largo. Slow.

Leading-motive (Ger. *Leitmotiv*). Short theme, suggesting person, idea, or image, quoted throughout composition to indicate that person, etc.

Legato. In a smooth style (of performance, etc.).

Lento. Slow.

Libretto. Text of an opera.

Lied. (pl. *Lieder*). Song, with special reference to songs by Schubert, Schumann, Brahms, and Wolf.

Lute. String instrument plucked with fingers, used in 15th- and 16th-cent. music especially.

Lydian mode. One of the scales in mediæval music, represented by white keys of piano between F and F.

Lyre. Ancient Greek plucked string instrument.

Madrigal. Contrapuntal composition for several voices, especially prominent from 15th to 17th cent.

Maestoso. Stately.

Major. One of the two main scales of the tonal system with semitones between the third and fourth, and the seventh and eighth notes, identical with 16th-cent. Ionian mode.

Mandolin(e). Plucked string instrument of Italian origin.

Manual. A keyboard for the hands, used mostly in connection with the organ.

Master of the King's (or Queen's) Musick. Title of British court appointment, with no precise duties.

Melisma. Group of notes sung to a single syllable.

Mélodie. Literally a melody or tune; has come to mean a French song (cf. German *Lied*).

Metronome. Small machine in use since the beginning of the 18th cent., to determine the pace of any composition by the beats of the music, *e.g.*, ♩ = 60 at the head of the music indicates sixty crotchets to the minute.

Mezzo, Mezza. (It. = "half") *Mezza voce* means using the half voice (a tone between normal singing and whispering). *Mezzo-soprano*, voice between soprano and contralto.

Minim. Note that equals two crotchets in time value.

Minor. One of the two main scales of the tonal system (cf. major), identical with 16th-cent. Aeolian mode. It has two forms—the harmonic and melodic, the former having a sharpened seventh note, the latter having the sixth and seventh note sharpened.

Minuet. Originally French 18th-cent. dance in triple time, then the usual third movement in symphonic form (with a contrasting trio section) until succeeded by scherzo.

Mixolydian mode. One of the mediaeval scales represented by the white keys on the piano from G to G.

Modes. Scales prevalent in the Middle Ages. *See* Aeolian, Dorian, Ionian, Lydian, Mixolydian, Phrygian.

Modulate. Changing from key to key in a composition, not directly but according to musical "grammar".

Molto. Much, very; thus *allegro molto.*

Motet. Sacred, polyphonic vocal composition. More loosely, any choral composition for use in church but not set to words of the liturgy.

Motive, motif. Short, easily recognised melodic figure.

Motto. Short, well-defined theme recurring throughout a composition, cf. *Idée fixe* in Berlioz's *Symphonie Fantastique.*

Movement. Separate sections of a large-scale composition, each in its own form.

Music drama. Term used to describe Wagner's, and sometimes other large-scale operas.

Mutes. Devices used to damp the sound of various instruments.

Natural (of a note or key). Not sharp or flat.

Neo-classical. Term used to describe music written mostly during the 1920s and 30s in the style of Bach or Mozart.

Ninth. Interval taking nine steps, *e.g.*, from C upwards an octave and a whole tone to D.

Nocturne. Literally a "night-piece", hence usually of lyrical character.

Nonet. Composition for nine instruments.

Notation. Act of writing down music.

Note. Single sound of specified pitch and duration; symbol to represent this.

Obbligato. Instrumental part having a special or essential rôle in a piece.

Oboe. Woodwind instrument with double reed, descended from hautboy; as such, in use since 16th cent., in modern form since 18th cent.

Octave. Interval taking eight steps of scale, with top and bottom notes having same "name"; C to C is an octave.

Octet. Composition for eight instruments or voices.

Ondes Martenot. Belongs to a class of melodic instruments in which the tone is produced by electrical vibrations controlled by the movement of the hands not touching the instrument.

Opera. Musical work for the stage with singing characters, originated in early years of 17th cent.

Opera seria. Chief operatic form of 17th and 18th cent., usually set to very formal librettos, concerning gods or heroes of ancient history.

Operetta. Lighter type of opera.

Opus. (abbr. *Op.*) With number following *opus* indicates order of a composer's composition.

Oratorio. Vocal work, usually for soloists and choir with instrumental accompaniment, generally with setting of a religious text.

Orchestra. Term to designate large, or largish, body of instrumentalists, originated in 17th cent.

Orchestration. Art of setting out work for instruments of an orchestra. To be distinguished from *Instrumentation* (*q.v.*).

Organ. Elaborate keyboard instrument in which air is blown through pipes by bellows to sound notes. Tone is altered by selection of various stops and, since the 16th cent., a pedal keyboard has also been incorporated.

Organum. In mediæval music a part sung as an accompaniment below or above the melody or plainsong, usually at the interval of a fourth or fifth; also, loosely, this method of singing in parts.

Ornament. Notes that are added to a given melody by composer or performer as an embellishment.

Overture. Instrumental introduction or prelude to larger work, usually opera. Concert overtures are simply that: *i.e.*, work to be played at start of a concert.

Part. Music of one performer in an ensemble; single strand in a composition.

Part-song. Vocal composition in several parts.

Passacaglia. Composition in which a tune is constantly repeated, usually in the bass.

Passage. Section of a composition.

Passion. Musical setting of the New Testament story of Christ's trial and crucifixion.

Pastiche. Piece deliberately written in another composer's style.

Pavan(e). Moderately paced dance dating from 16th cent. or earlier.

Pedal. Held note in bass of composition.

Pentatonic Scale. Scale of five notes—usually piano's five black keys or other notes in the same relation to each other.

Percussion. Collective title for instruments of the orchestra that are sounded by being struck by hand or stick.

Phrygian Mode. One of the scales of mediæval music, represented by the white keys on piano from E to E.

Piano. Soft, abbr. *p*; *pp* = *pianissimo*, very soft; instrument, invented in 18th cent., having strings struck by hammer, as opposed to the earlier harpsichord where they are plucked. The modern piano has 88 keys and can be either "upright" (vertical) or "grand" (horizontal).

Pianoforte. Almost obsolete full Italian name for the piano.

Pitch. Exact height or depth of a particular musical sound or note.

Pizzicato. Direction for stringed instruments, that the strings should be plucked instead of bowed.

Plainchant, Plainsong. Mediæval church music consisting of single line of melody without harmony or definite rhythm.

Polka. Dance in 2/4 time originating in 19th cent. Bohemia.

Polonaise. Polish dance generally in 3/4 time.

Polyphony. Combination of two or more musical lines as in *counterpoint.*

Polytonality. Simultaneous use of several keys.

Postlude. Closing piece, opposite of Prelude.

Prelude. Introductory piece.

Presto. Very fast. *Prestissimo.* Still faster.

Progression. Movement from one chord to next to make musical sense.

Quartet. Work written for four instruments or voices; group to play or sing such a work.

Quaver. Note that equals two semiquavers or half a crotchet.

Quintet. Work written for five instruments or voices; group to play or sing such a work.

Rallentando. Slowing down.

Recapitulation. Section of composition that repeats original material in something like its original form.

Recitative. Term used for declamation in singing written in ordinary notation but allowing rhythmical licence.

Recorder. Woodwind instrument, forerunner of flute.

Reed. Vibrating tongue of woodwind instruments.

Register. Set of organ pipes controlled by a particular stop; used in reference to different ranges of instrument or voice (*e.g.*, chest register).

Relative. Term used to indicate common key signature of a major and minor key.

Répétiteur. Member of opera house's musical staff who coaches singers in their parts.

Rest. Notation of pauses for instrument in composition, having a definite length like a note.

Retrograde. Term used to describe a melody played backwards.

Rhapsody. Work of no definite kind with a degree of romantic content.

Rhythm. Everything concerned with the time of music (*i.e.*, beats, accent, metre, etc.) as opposed to the pitch side.

Ritornello. Passage, usually instrumental, that recurs in a piece.

Romance, Romanza. Title for piece of vague song-like character.

Romantic. Term used vaguely to describe music of 19th cent. that has other than purely musical source of inspiration.

Rondo. Form in which one section keeps on recurring.

Rubato. Manner of performing a piece without keeping strictly to time.

Sackbut. Early English name for trombone.

Saxophone. Classified as wind instrument, although made of brass, because it uses a reed.

Scale. Progression of adjoining notes upwards or downwards.

Scherzo. One of two middle movements, usually third, in four-movement sonata form. Displaced minuet in this form at beginning of 19th cent.

Score. Copy of any music written in several parts.

Second. Interval taking two steps in scale, *e.g.*, C to D flat, or to D.

Semibreve. Note that equals two minims or half a breve.

Semiquaver. Note that equals half a quaver.

Semitone. Smallest interval commonly used in Western music.

Septet. Composition for seven instruments or voices.

Sequence. Repetition of phrase at a higher or lower pitch.

Serenade. Usually an evening song or instrumental work.

Seventh. Interval taking seven steps in the scale.

Sextet. Composition for six instruments or voices.

Sharp. Term indicating a raising of pitch by a semitone.

Shawm. Primitive woodwind instrument, forerunner of oboe.

Simple time. Division of music into two or four beats.

Sinfonietta. Small symphony.

Sixth. Interval taking six steps in the scale.

Solo. Piece or part of a piece for one performer playing or singing alone.

Sonata. Term to denote a musical form and a type of composition. In *sonata form* a composition is divided into exposition, development and recapitulation. A *sonata* is a piece, usually, for one or more players following that form.

Song. Any short vocal composition.

Soprano. Highest female voice.

Sostenuto. Sustained, broadly.

Sotto voce. Whispered, scarcely audible, applied to vocal as well as instrumental music.

Sprechgesang. (Ger. Speech-song.) Vocal utterance somewhere between speech and song.

Staccato. Perform music in short, detached manner.

Staff. Horizontal lines on which music is usually written.

Stop. Lever by which organ registration can be altered.

String(s). Strands of gut or metal set in vibration to produce musical sounds on string or keyboard instruments. Plural refers to violins, violas, cellos, and basses of orchestra.

Study. Instrumental piece, usually one used for technical exercise or to display technical skill, but often having artistic merits as well (*e.g.* Chopin's).

Subject(s). Theme or group of notes that forms principal idea or ideas in composition.

Suite. Common name for piece in several movements.

Symphony. Orchestral work of serious purpose usually in four movements, occasionally given name (*e.g.*, Beethoven's "Choral" symphony).

Syncopation. Displacement of musical accent.

Tempo. Pace, speed of music.

Tenor. Highest normal male voice.

Ternary. A piece in three sections is said to be in ternary form. The balance is obtained by repeating the first phrase or section (though it need not be exact or complete) after a second of equal importance.

Tessitura. Compass into which voice or instrument comfortably falls.

Theme. Same as *subject* but can also be used for a whole musical statement as in "theme and variations."

Third. Interval taking three steps in scale.

Time. Rhythmical division of music.

Timpani. *See* Kettledrum.

Toccata. Instrumental piece usually needing rapid, brilliant execution.

Tonality. Key, or feeling for a definite key.

Tone. Quality of musical sound; interval of two semitones.

Tonic Sol-fa. System of musical notation to simplify sight-reading.

Transcribe. Arrange piece for different medium, instrument, or voice than that originally intended.

Transition. Passage that joins two themes of sections of a composition.

Transpose. Perform a piece at different pitch from that originally intended.

Treble. Highest part in vocal composition; high boy's voice.

Triad. A chord consisting of a note with the third and fifth above it, *e.g.*, C–E–G. A common chord is a triad of which the 5th is perfect, e.g., C–E–G or C–E flat–G. Thus major and minor triads are common chords.

Trio. Work written for three instruments or voices; group to play or sing such a work.

Trombone. Brass instrument with slide adjusting length of tube.

Trumpet. Metal instrument of considerable antiquity; modern version has three valves to make it into a chromatic instrument.

Tuba. Deepest-toned brass instrument with three or four valves.

Twelve-note. Technique of composition using full chromatic scale with each note having equal importance. Notes are placed in particular order as the thematic basis of works.

Unison. Two notes sung or played together at same pitch.

Valve. Mechanism, invented in early 19th cent. to add to brass instruments allowing them to play full chromatic scale.

Variation. Varied passage of original theme. Such variations may be closely allied to or depart widely from the theme.

Verismo. Term to describe Italian operas written in " realist " style at the turn of this century.

Vibrato. Rapid fluctuation in pitch of voice or instrument. Exaggerated it is referred to as a " wobble " (of singers) or tremolo.

Viol. String instrument of various sizes in vogue until end of 17th cent.

Viola. Tenor instrument of violin family.

Violin. Musical four-string instrument, played with bow, of violin family, which superseded viol at beginning of 18th cent.

Virginals. English keyboard instrument, similar to harpsichord of 17th and 18th cent.

Vivace. Lively.

Voluntary. Organ piece for church use, but not during service.

Waltz. Dance in triple time, fashionable in 19th cent.

Whole-tone scale. Scale progressing by whole tones. Only two are possible, one beginning on C, the other on C sharp.

Xylophone. Percussion instrument with series of wood bars tuned in a chromatic scale and played with sticks.

Zither. String instrument laid on knees and plucked. Common in Central-European folk music.

III. INDEX TO COMPOSERS

IV. SPECIAL TOPICS

Festivals.

The term derives from the Latin *festivitas* (merriment), and was used as early as the Renaissance to describe celebrations with music at royal courts to mark special occasions as, for example, the meeting of Francis I and Pope Leo X at Bologna in 1515. In more recent times the term was employed to describe grand musical occasions, usually dedicated to the greater glory of one particular composer. In Austria there were Haydn Festivals right at the end of the composer's life (1808–11), in Germany a Beethoven Festival in 1845, in England Handel Festivals beginning in 1862. The oldest of festivals still in existence is the Three Choirs, dating back to the first half of the 18th century. Bayreuth, begun by Wagner in 1876, is the most venerable of international events, and has its own purpose-built theatre for the performance of his operas. A year later the first Mozart Festival was held in Salzburg. Munich began its opera festival in 1901. The Florence Maggio Musicale was established in 1933. The Glyndebourne Festival in Sussex, England, started solely with Mozart's operas in 1934. The big expansion in festivals did not start until after the second world war, the first major new festival being in Edinburgh in 1947. Today the coinage has been badly debased, in the sense that any small town will call the most minor musical or theatrical occasion a festival, and many of the major ones have become unduly commercialised.

These are clearly divided between those that are wide-ranging and cosmopolitan in flavour and those that are specialised, either hymning the achievements of a single composer or else reflecting the style of one or two people. Into the first category go Salzburg and Edinburgh the largest events of their kind comprising all the arts. In recent years Salzburg has been dominated by the conductor-producer Herbert von Karajan who has directed most of the operas in the larger of the two main opera houses. He has also established a Salzburg Easter Festival, which is under his sole control, and presents one major production each spring. At the summer festival he has shared the honours with the veteran Karl Böhm, who has specialised in the operas of Mozart and Richard Strauss. Concerts are given by several major world orchestras every summer and by visiting soloists of international repute.

The first Mozart festivals were held at Salzburg between 1877 and 1910. Operas and concerts were conducted by such famous figures of the time as Mahler, Hans Richter, Richard Strauss, Felix Mottl, and Karl Muck. Later the famous director Max Reinhardt was a main influence on the festival. During the 1920s and 1930s, Strauss, Clemens Krauss, and Bruno Walter conducted memorable performances of Mozart and other operas. Toscanini appeared there in 1935 and 1937. The festival was resumed after the war in 1946 with Wilhelm Furtwängler as the leading light. In 1960 the Grosses Festspielhaus was opened. It has one of the largest and widest stages in the world.

Edinburgh was the brainchild of Glyndebourne, which presented the opera there during the first five years of the festival, again from 1953 to 1955. Since then there have been visits from companies from all over the world, augmented in recent years by performances from the Scottish Opera company. All these have to be squeezed on to the small stage of the King's Theatre pending the promised new opera house. As costs have soared that has become something of a mirage. Edinburgh has also played host to almost every orchestra of consequence, and about five of these give concerts there every year in the Usher Hall. Chamber music and recitals appear at the Freemasons' Hall and at Leith Town Hall. Rudolf Bing was the festival's first director and he has been succeeded by, among others, Lord Harewood and Peter Diamand. Various attempts have been made, especially by Harewood, to give the festival a theme or a purpose; none has proved lasting and the festival has continued along its somewhat amorphous way.

Benjamin Britten and his friend, the tenor Peter Pears, started the Aldeburgh Festival on the Suffolk coast in 1948. Their taste dominated the early years of the festival, which also saw the premiers of many Britten works, although by no means to the exclusion of the music of other modern composers. The conversion of the Maltings at Snape into a concert hall greatly increased the possibilities of the festival, and Britten lived long enough to conduct several unforgettable performances in the new building. In latter years he also welcomed several Soviet artists, and wrote works for, as well as playing with, Richter, Rostropovich and Vishnevskaya. The festival has always maintained a pleasingly informal and local atmosphere. This festival with its purpose and profile should be a model for others. Bath, like Aldeburgh, has its surroundings to recommend it, but it has not yet established such a true identity. Directors have included Beecham, Menuhin, Tippett, and most recently Sir William Glock, formerly head of music at the BBC. Cheltenham (for new music) and King's Lynn are other significant English post-war festivals. The Three Choirs and Leeds Triennial Festivals have a much longer history, both based on strong choral traditions. They continue to flourish.

Bayreuth, the oldest and most worthwhile of the German festivals, is a classic example of an event devoted wholly to the works of a single composer and thus having a continuing *raison d'être*. The festival celebrated its centenary in 1976, and could look back on a history of almost uninterrupted activity, apart from the period of the two world wars and of uninterrupted direction by the Wagner family. The composer's widow Cosima was in charge from 1883 until 1908 when her son Siegfried took charge. On his death in 1930 his widow Winfried succeeded him. Her friendship with Hitler threw a cloud over the festival lifted by her sons Wieland and Wolfgang, who revolutionised the staging of their grandfather's music-dramas from 1951 onwards. In the centenary year, a young Frenchman Patrice Chereau altered the pattern of the stagings once again with his modernistic ideas. Both changes caused a furore. The opera house at Bayreuth is an ideal design for seeing and hearing. It was copied at Munich's Prinzregententheater in 1901 when the Munich Festival started with the intention of presenting Wagner's works, but today performances are given in the rebuilt National Theatre and in the renovated 18th-cent. Cuvillies Theatre. The festival tends to concentrate on the works of its native son, Richard Strauss, and on Mozart, with some excursions into the modern repertory. This is a good example of a basically home-orientated festival. The West Berlin Festival in September each year is more internationally based. Wiesbaden, held in May, has a history going back to 1900; it calls on predominantly local talent. In East Germany, the Handel Festivals at the composer's birthplace of Halle have been held steadily since 1951.

In Italy the spectacular yearly seasons in the Verona Arena (July–August), begun in 1913, are not actually called festivals but qualify as such. The repertory consists mainly of large-scale pieces from the Italian repertory sung by leading singers of the day. The Maggio Musicale Fiorentino, held as its title would suggest in May, was originally a biennial event but became annual in 1938, and has continued as such, apart from a wartime break, ever since. Again the repertory has been chiefly Italian, but there have been occasional experiments in other territory. The events are spread through May and the beginning of June. Spoleto, a little like Aldeburgh, is the brainchild of Gian-Carlo Menotti, the Italian American composer, and its performances (since its inception in 1958) take place in the attractive Teatro Nuovo and Teatro Melisso in the little hillside town in Umbria. Newish works and youngish artists are given prominence, and many youthful Americans are always in attendance.

In Austria, besides Salzburg, festivals are regularly held at Vienna (May–June), a kind of extension of the usual season with many extra opera and concert performances, and at Bregenz (July–August), where the lakeside theatre is unique. Operetta is a particular feature of this festival, which was started in 1956.

The attraction of a beautiful site is also one of the advantages of the Aix Festival, held every July in the open-air theatre of the Archbishop's Palace since 1948. Mozart and other 18th-cent. works has been the speciality there, but of late more 19th-cent. works have been given. France also has a number of smaller festivals among them the piano feast at Tours whose mastermind is Richter, and it attracts all the world's leading players to the attractive barn where the recitals take place. Other European festivals of note take place at Lucerne, Montreux, Zurich, Stockholm, Copenhagen, Prague, Athens, Savonlinna (Finland), Helsinki, Dubrovnik, Wexford.

In the United States the main festival is that at Santa Fé, held in the large, partially open-air heatre. Its moving spirit is John Crosby, and his choice of operas is wide-ranging. The festival is steadily gaining in prestige as the seasons go by, and may before long rival some of the best European events. At Caramoor (New York State), a kind of Glyndebourne-like Festival is held. The Marlboro Festival, begun by Rudolf Serkin and friends, is a training as much as a performing event, and it encourages young players, who come to perfect their craft. Other American festivals are held at Tanglewood, Hollywood Bowl, Newport, Ravinia Park (nr. Chicago), and Wolf Trap (nr. Washington DC). In Australia Adelaide now holds a biennial festival of the Arts.

The Gramophone.

Although the beginnings of recording stretch back well into the 19th century, its enormous potential did not begin to be realised until about 1900. In the 1890s some recording was done on cylinder machines, but it was eventually Emil Berliner's disc reproducer that won the day. The Gramophone and Typewriter Company (later HMV) was established in 1898, and by 1902 its roster of artists included besides the already indispensable Caruso (it has been said with truth that "Caruso made the gramophone, and the gramophone Caruso"), Chanliapin, Calvé, Battistini, to whom was soon to be added the legendary Patti, recorded in 1906 in her Welsh castle, Melba, De Luca. Tamagno, indeed most of the reputable operatic artists of the age. In those days of pre-electrical recording, the voice was predominant, as it was impossible to record an orchestra around the horn with any kind of fidelity. In fact, many of the earliest discs were cut with only piano accompaniment.

However, surprisingly early (1906–14), a number of operas were recorded in some kind of complete form. They may sound comic today, but the achievement for its time was considerable. Electrical recording replaced the acoustic process in the middle of the 1920s. Already in the early part of the decade, some symphonies had been recorded, albeit often in abbreviated form. Now, with the new method, recording of the orchestral repertory began in earnest, while several operas were committed to disc for the first time, including sizeable chunks of the Wagnerian works. In the Italian repertory there were often rival versions of the same work made by the two main companies of the time, HMV and Columbia.

The advent of so many records began gradually to change the whole musical climate. Whereas in the past, the public had learnt their music through practical music-making in the home, often in piano reductions of orchestral and operatic scores, they now began to get to know music through the record, and naturally there were losses as well as gains in the process. There is no substitute for practical music-making; on the other hand, the enormous pleasure records have brought to millions is not to be denied. The danger has lain in using records as what has been aptly called "wallpaper music", that is as merely a background to other activities; as such it does an injury to compositions intended to demand wholehearted attention.

With the advent of the long-playing disc in 1950, the possibilities for recording received perhaps an even bigger boost than at the coming of the electrical process. It was now possible to contain most of the works in the symphonic and chamber repertory on one disc and most operas on two or three. Almost immediately the whole range of works was re-recorded for the new medium, and a further, if not quite so drastic, revision was called for with the introduction of the stereo process in 1958–9. Today there is a wider catalogue of music available to the ordinary person in the home than at any previous time. At the same time, the study of past recording achievements is becoming almost a history on its own, as musicians come to realise that in the eighty years of the gramophone styles in singing and playing have changed—and changed more than once. Listening to Melba in opera or Pachmann on the piano is in itself an instruction in performing practices at the beginning of the century.

One of the first benefits from the advent of LP was the recording of much pre-classical (i.e., pre-1700) music. Gradually the music of Monteverdi and his great predecessors became readily accessible and also acceptable to the general public, whereas they had previously been the preserve of specialists. In the classical period the cantatas of Bach, formerly a virtually closed book to all but Bach experts, began to be recorded in large numbers. All the piano sonatas of Haydn, all his symphonies and quartets, all Mozart's piano concertos were projects realised during the 1970s. In the early 1960s the whole of Wagner's *Ring*, always considered an impossible task became available owing to the enterprise of John Culshaw of Decca, which often led the field in widening the recorded repertory. Soon it was followed by three or four other complete sets of the huge work, while all the other Wagnerian operas were also recorded, as were, almost needless to say, the major operas of Mozart, soon succeeded by his early works in the genre. There followed the first recording of many of Verdi's early operas to supplement the already released issues of his mature works. This led to the investigation of other early 19th-cent. opera, in particular the operas of Bellini and Donizetti. If the modern repertory, Britten excepted, received less than its due, that only reflected the comparative lack of interest from the general public in music of its own time. Even so, a good number of *avant-garde* works were recorded, and the 20th cent. as a whole was well treated: not only were the works of such important traditional figures as Sibelius, Elgar, and Nielsen recorded but also all the major works of Stravinsky, Schoenberg, Berg, and Webern, affording in all a comprehensive view of the century's achievements. Britten, while he was alive, supervised the recording of his works, and conducted most of his operas on disc himself, although sadly not *Gloriana*, while after his illness his last opera, *Death in Venice*, was entrusted to Steuart Bedford. Other British music of recent times was almost as generously treated.

The policy of some companies to delete records when they were not selling in sufficient numbers deprived the catalogue of many important issues. At the same time, HMV and Deutsche Grammophon, who hold in their archives the bulk of historic material, began to realise their responsibilities, and issued many successful boxes of classic performances. In this way, Elgar conducting Elgar, Beecham conducting Delius, the ancient records of Patti, Caruso, and Melba, the more recent ones of Maggie Teyte, the discs of Bayreuth singers from 1902 onwards were all issued in large-scale and well-annotated boxes.

Boxes indeed became the order of the day. All Mahler's symphonies, all of Bruckner's, all Mozart's string quarters, all Schubert's piano sonatas and so on were issued in boxes, fulfilling an apparently insatiable demand for comprehensive compilations and the saving in price that went with them. While the number of sets of Beethoven symphonies available surpassed all bounds, each seemed to find its market. The record industry became big business, but at the same time did not neglect its duty as an educational influence.

To accompany the revolution in recording, there has to be a complementary one in equipment, what became known in the record trade as " hardware ". From the primitive horn of the early years of the century to the most complex set-ups, costing hundreds of pounds, of today is a huge step, although the objective, the most lifelike representation of what is enshrined on the records, remains the same. The early days of electrical recording saw the coming of the " radiogram ", large consoles containing radios and gramophones as the name suggests. They were succeeded, in the early days of LP, by separate components of turntable, pick-up, amplifier, and loudspeakers, often unsightly but doing their job efficiently. While the specialist continued to concentrate on individual sections in the days of stereo and then quadrophonic (the invention, not widely disseminated, of the mid-1970s), the ordinary listener was offered what was called " music-centres ", which tried to incorporate some kind of " hi-fi " within a smaller space. The development of small but highly competent loudspeakers was a great gain in space-saving and looks.

A less welcome result of the record revolution has been the search for a spurious perfection. By the use of innumerable tape edits of several " takes " in recording sessions it has been possible to hear more exact performances of any work than would ever be possible in a concert hall or opera house, but such near-perfection has often been achieved at a severe cost to spontaneity and life in recorded interpretations. Another drawback is the following: people who hear near-ideal opera casts or solo–conductor partnerships in their home become disillusioned when they cannot encounter, for financial reasons, similar standards in live performances. The record industry would argue that they are able to give to the public something that they would never otherwise hear, and often at a very reasonable cost, that indeed the home has become the true opera house or concert hall; but it is simply not possible to have such performances if the live side of music-making is in a state of atrophy. An element of artificiality, even falsity, is therefore present in today's developments in the field of the gramophone. However, more live performances are now being recorded, and one must hope that a *modus vivendi* between the needs of record-makers and the existence of full-blooded interpretations will be found.

The most recent development in recorded music has been the arrival of the cassette as a potent rival to the disc. Easier to manage, easier to reproduce, it for long suffered from the disadvantage of more restricted sound, as compared with the record. That difficulty has been largely overcome, and more and more collectors now run a cassette machine in tandem with their record-player, even if they have not entirely replaced the one with the other.

Instruments of the Orchestra.

The standard orchestra for symphonic music consists of four primary sections: strings, woodwind, brass, and percussion. The strings subdivide into violins, firsts and seconds; violas; cellos; double-basses. The wind subdivide into flutes (principal and second); piccolo; oboes (principal and second); clarinet (ditto); bassoon (ditto); bass-clarinet; double-bassoon; cor anglais. Not all compositions contain parts for piccolo and cor anglais, or bass clarinet and double-bassoon nor in 18th-cent. music, for clarinets. Some conductors insist on doubling the number of the main wind parts in tutti passages (i.e., passages where the whole orchestra is playing), in order that there should be a balance between the wind and the (usually large) string departments, consisting of fourteen first violins, fourteen seconds, twelve violas, ten cellos, and eight basses.

The brass subdivides into horns (four); trumpets (three or more); trombones (two tenor, one bass); tuba. For works by Bruckner and Wagner the " Wagner tuba " is used in addition to the other instruments. The percussion section is infinitely variable. Its most common components are the harp, timpani (or kettledrum), xylophone and tubular bell, which define pitch, and the cymbal and triangle, which are of indefinite pitch. To these are added more exotic instruments for many modern scores. Indeed, many of these make a feature of percussion sounds. Most of the main instruments have their attributes defined in the glossary.

A symphony orchestra indicates the full-scale, standard orchestra heard in the big concert halls. A chamber orchestra is a smaller body, sometimes containing strings only, but augmented by outside wind and brass players as pieces demand. Most chamber orchestras sometimes have as few as six first violins, with the remainder of the orchestra reduced accordingly.

Music Clubs and Societies.

There are many ways for the amateur to take part in making music. The oldest established is undoubtedly the choral society. There is hardly a district in Britain that does not have its own amateur choir (they are fully listed in the *British Music Yearbook*), ranging from the major London choruses such as the Royal Choral Society and Bach Choir, the two longest established, the New Philharmonia Choir, the London Philharmonic Choir, and the London Symphony Chorus to the small local groups. Most meet once a week to practise for three or four events through the season. Standards required vary, of course, according to the aspirations and range of each body. Similar organizations exist throughout Britain in the orchestral field. In the United States choirs and orchestras are more likely to be based on universities or on religious organizations, although more widely based groups also exist.

Music Clubs and Societies meet up and down Britain. They promote either live concerts by professionals and/or amateurs, or illustrated lectures by visiting speakers, or a combination of both. They are mostly under the umbrella of the National Federation of Music Societies or the National Federation of Gramophone Societies. There are also operatic societies, which as the name suggests, exist for the promotion of that specific branch of music; they, too, have their national association. Then there are, particulary in Northern Britain, brass bands, many of which compete yearly in major championships.

For young people there are equivalent organisations, the main one being the National Youth Orchestra. That supplements the orchestras of the various music academies throughout the country. For a younger age group there are various schools specialising in musical tuition and the specialised choir schools. Those are supplemented by the various competitions held throughout the country, with prizes given, for all forms of musical attainments. In several cases financial awards are given for further study, often abroad. The most famous among these are the Kathleen Ferrier Memorial Scholarship (for singers), the Leeds Piano Competition (triennial) and the Rupert Foundation (for conductors). In addition, there are many international competitions in Europe and various courses, generalised or specialised, for holiday music study. These are often open to people of all ages as well as to students. Many universities in this country run extra-mural courses, and the Open University runs a degree course from Milton Keynes. Most local authorities have Senior Music officials, and they run courses of adult education in music.

The main music periodicals are *The Musical Times*, *Music and Musicians*, *Opera*, *The Gramophone*, *Records and Recordings*, and *Classical Music*, all except the last (which is weekly) appear monthly. There are many other, more specialised magazines, several of them concerning themselves with particular instruments, or other aspects of music.

THE WORLD OF SCIENCE

A contemporary picture of scientific discovery, designed to explain some of the most important ideas in astronomy, physics, chemistry, biology and to give some account of recent research in various fields. A special section looks at man and his environment.

TABLE OF CONTENTS

THE WORLD OF SCIENCE

I. ASTRONOMY AND COSMOLOGY—THE NATURE OF THE UNIVERSE

The universe includes everything from the smallest sub-atomic particle to the mightiest system of stars. The scientific view of the universe (not the only view but the one we are concerned with here) is a remarkable achievement of the human mind, and it is worth considering at the outset what a "scientific view" is, and what is remarkable about it.

A scientific view of something is always an intimate mixture of theories and observed facts, and not an inert mixture but a seething and growing one. The theories are broad general ideas together with arguments based on them. The arguments are designed to show that, if the general ideas are accepted, then this, that, or the other thing ought to be observed. If this, that, or the other actually are observed, then the theory is a good one; if not, then the theoreticians have to think again. Thus theoretical ideas and arguments are continually subjected to the severe test of comparison with the facts, and scientists are proud of the rigour with which this is done. On the other hand, theories often suggest new things to look for, *i.e.*, theories lead to predictions. These predictions are frequently successful, and scientists are entitled to be proud of that too. But it follows that no theory is immutable; any scientific view of any subject may, in principle, be invalidated at any time by the discovery of new facts, though some theories are so soundly based that overthrow does not seem imminent.

A remarkable aspect of the scientific view of the universe is that same principles are supposed to operate throughout the whole vastness of space. Thus the matter and radiation in stars are not different from the matter and radiation on earth, and their laws of behaviour are the same. Therefore theories hard won by studies in terrestrial physics and chemistry laboratories are applied at once to the whole cosmos. Astronomy and cosmology are spectacular extensions of ordinary mechanics and physics.

LOOKING AT THE UNIVERSE.

The universe is observable because signals from it reach us and some manage to penetrate our atmosphere.

First, there are waves of visible light together with invisible rays of somewhat longer (infra-red) and somewhat shorter (ultra-violet) wavelengths. These waves show us the bright astronomical objects and, to make use of them, astronomers have constructed telescopes of great power and precision backed up with cameras, spectroscopes, and numerous auxiliaries. The most powerful telescope is the 236·2-inch reflector at Mount Semirodriki in the Soviet Union. The earth's atmosphere acts as a distorting and only partially transparent curtain and the erection of telescopes on satellites is beginning to extend optical telescope performance significantly.

Secondly, there are radio waves of much longer wavelength than light. Radiotelescopes are sensitive radio receivers with specialised aerial systems. The scientific stature of modern radioastronomy was emphasised by the award in 1974 of the Nobel Physics Prize to two Cambridge radioastronomers, Ryle and Hewish.

Other types of radiation from outer space impinge on the atmosphere. Cosmic radiation consists of very fast-moving fundamental particles, including protons (F14). Cosmic rays are detected by Geiger counters, by the minute tracks they leave on photographic plates, and by other means. The origin of cosmic rays is still uncertain, but many people think they must have an intimate connection with the nature and evolution of the universe itself.

X-rays and neutrinos (F14) from outer space can also be detected, the former especially by satellite-borne detectors and the latter by apparatus buried in deep mines. X-ray astronomy and neutrino astronomy are being born.

By interpreting the signals that reach us by these various routes, astronomers have formed a remarkably detailed picture of its structure. The merest outline of this will now be given.

Great Distances and Large Numbers.

Let us start with nearby objects. This raises at once the question of what "nearness" and "distance" are in astronomy and how they are to be expressed. A convenient unit of distance is the *light-year*, *i.e.*, the distance that light, travelling at $2{\cdot}997925 \times 10^8$m/s, traverses in one year. Since vast numbers as well as vast distances will enter the question, we need a shorthand for large numbers. Ten times ten times ten will be represented by 10^3; six tens multiplied together (*i.e.*, one million) will be written 10^6, and so on. 10^{14} would mean a hundred million million. One divided by a million (*i.e.*, one-millionth) will be written 10^{-6}; the very small number obtained by dividing one by the product of fourteen tens will be written 10^{-14}. A light-year is $9{\cdot}463 \times 10^{12}$ km; the radius of an atom is about 10^{-8} cm.

PLANETS, STARS, AND GALAXIES.

The Solar System.

The earth is the third, counting outwards, of nine planets revolving in nearly circular orbits round the sun. Their names and some other particulars are given in the table (F7). The sun and its planets are the main bodies of the solar system. Between Mars and Jupiter revolve numerous chunks of rock called the asteroids; the largest of these, Ceres, is 480 miles across. Apart from these, the solar system is tenuously populated with gas, dust, and small particles of stone and iron. Dust continuously settles on the earth, and frequently small fragments enter the atmosphere, glow, and evaporate; these are meteors or shooting stars. Sometimes larger rocks, called meteorites, hit the earth. Comets are relatively compact swarms of particles—containing ice according to one theory—which travel in elongated orbits round the sun. Their spectacular tails form under the sun's influence when they approach it. Not all comets stay indefinitely in the solar system; some visit us and go off into space for ever.

The sun itself is a dense, roughly spherical mass of glowing matter, 1,392,000 km across. Its heat is so intense that the atoms are split into separated electrons and nuclei (*see* F10) and matter in such a state is called plasma. At the sun's centre the temperature has the unimaginable value of about 13 million degrees Centigrade (a coal fire is about 800° C). Under such conditions the atomic nuclei frequently collide with one another at great speeds and reactions occur between them. The sun consists largely of hydrogen and, in the very hot plasma, the nuclei of hydrogen atoms interact by a series of reactions whose net result is to turn hydrogen into helium. This is a process which releases energy just as burning does, only these nuclear processes are incomparably more energetic than ordinary burning. In fact, the energy released is great enough to be the source of all the light and heat which the sun has been pouring into thousands of millions of years.

Emerging from the sun and streaming past the earth is a "solar wind" of fast-moving electrons and protons (*see* F10) whose motion is closely linked with the behaviour of an extensive magnetic field based on the sun. In fact, the region round the sun and extending far into space past the earth is full of complex, fluctuating particle streams and magnetic fields which interact with planetary atmospheres causing, among other things, auroras and magnetic storms.

Stars.

In colour, brightness, age, and size the sun is typical of vast numbers of other stars. Only from the human point of view is there anything special about the sun—it is near enough to give us life. Even the possession of a system of revolving planets is not, according to some modern views, very unusual.

No star can radiate energy at the rate the sun does without undergoing internal changes in the course of time. Consequently stars evolve and old processes in them give rise to new. The exact nature of stellar evolution—so far as it is at present understood—would be too complex to describe here in any detail. It involves expansion and contraction, changes of temperature, changes of colour, and changes in chemical composition as the nuclear processes gradually generate new chemical elements by reactions such as the conversion of hydrogen to helium, helium to neon, neon to magnesium, and so on. The speed of evolution changes from time to time, but is in any case very slow compared with the pace of terrestrial life; nothing very dramatic may occur for hundreds of millions of years. Evidence for the various phases of evolution is therefore obtained by studying many stars, each at a different stage of its life. Thus astronomers recognise many types with charmingly descriptive names, such as blue giants, sub-giants, red and white dwarfs, supergiants.

The path of stellar evolution may be marked by various explosive events. One of these, which occurs in sufficiently large stars, is an enormous explosion in which a substantial amount of the star is blown away into space in the form of high-speed streams of gas. For about a fortnight, such an exploding star will radiate energy 200 million times as fast as the sun. Japanese and Chinese (but not Western) astronomers recorded such an occurrence in A.D. 1054, and the exploding gases, now called the Crab nebula, can still be seen in powerful telescopes and form a cloud six or seven light-years across. While it lasts, the explosion shows up as an abnormally bright star and is called a *supernova.*

Groups of Stars.

It is not surprising that ancient peoples saw pictures in the sky. The constellations, however, are not physically connected groups of stars but just happen to be patterns visible from earth. A conspicuous exception to this is the Milky Way, which a telescope resolves into many millions of separate stars. If we could view the Milky Way from a vast distance and see it as a whole we should observe a rather flat wheel of stars with spiral arms something like the sparks of a rotating Catherine wheel. This system of stars is physically connected by gravitational forces and moves through space as a whole; it is called a *galaxy.*

The galaxy is about 10^5 light-years across and contains roughly 10^{11} stars. An inconspicuous one of these stars near the edge of the wheel is our sun; the prominent stars in our night sky are members of the galaxy that happen to be rather near us. Sirius, the brightest, is only 8·6 light-years away, a trivial distance, astronomically speaking.

The galaxy does not contain stars only, there are also clouds of gas and dust, particularly in the plane of the galaxy. Much of the gas is hydrogen, and its detection is difficult. However, gaseous hydrogen gives out radio waves with a wavelength of 21 cm. Radio telescopes are just the instruments to receive these, and workers in Holland, America, and Australia detected the gas clouds by this means. In 1952 they found that the hydrogen clouds lie in the spiral arms of the galaxy, and this is some of the strongest evidence for the spiral form.

Another important feature of the galactic scene is the weak but enormously extensive magnetic field. This is believed to have an intimate connection with the spiral structure.

Around the spiral arms, and forming part of the galaxy, are numerous globular clusters of stars. These are roughly spherical, abnormally densely packed, collections of stars with many thousands of members. Because of its form and density, a globular cluster may be assumed to have been formed in one process, not star by star. Thus all its stars are the same age. This is of great interest to astronomers, because they can study differences between stars of similar age but different sizes.

Galaxies.

One might be forgiven for assuming that such a vast system as the galaxy is in fact the universe; but this is not so. In the constellation of Andromeda is a famous object which, on close examination, turns out to be another galaxy of size and structure similar to our own. Its distance is given in the table (F7). The Milky Way, the Andromeda nebula, and a few other smaller galaxies form a cluster of galaxies called the Local Group. Obviously it would not be so named except to distinguish it from other distinct groups, and it is indeed a fact that the universe is populated with *groups*, or *clusters*, of *galaxies*. A cluster may contain two or three galaxies, but some contain thousands. So far as the eye of the telescope and camera can see, there are clusters of galaxies.

On a photograph a galaxy is a nebulous blob without the hard outline that a single star produces. Such nebulæ were formerly thought to be inside the Milky Way, but, after controversy, it was established that many of them were separate distant galaxies. By about 1920 it was known that there were at least half a million galaxies, and with the advent of the 100-in. Mt. Wilson telescope this number rose to 10^8 and has been increased further by the 254 cm telescope which can see out to a distance of 7×10^9 light-years. Through the powerful telescopes the nearer galaxies reveal their inner structures. Photographs of galaxies are among the most beautiful and fascinating photographs ever taken, and readers who have never seen one should hasten to the nearest illustrated astrononomy book. Most galaxies have spiral or other roughly regular structures but about 2 per cent have peculiar wisps and appendages. Some galaxies are strong emitters of radio waves.

The Expanding Universe.

Two discoveries about galaxies are of the utmost importance. One is that, by and large, clusters of galaxies are uniformly distributed through the universe. The other is that the distant galaxies are receding from us.

How is this known? Many readers may be familiar with the Doppler effect first discovered in 1842. Suppose a stationary body emits waves of any kind and we measure their wavelength, finding it to be L cm. Now suppose the body approaches us; the waves are thereby crowded together in the intervening space and the wavelength appears less than L; if the body recedes the wavelength appears greater than L. The Austrian physicist, J. Doppler (1803–53), discovered this behaviour in sound waves, and it explains the well-known change of pitch of a train whistle as it approaches and passes us. The same principle applies to the light. Every atom emits light of definite wavelengths which appear in a spectroscope as a series of coloured lines—a different series for each atom. If the atom is in a receding body all the lines have slightly longer wavelengths than usual, and the amount of the change depends uniquely on the speed. Longer wavelengths mean that the light is redder than usual, so that a light from a receding body shows what is called a "red shift." The speed of recession can be calculated from the amount of red shift.

It was the American astronomer, V. M. Slipher, who first showed (in 1914) that some galaxies emitted light with a red shift. In the 1920s and 1930s the famous astronomer E. Hubble (1889–1953) measured both the distances and red shift of many galaxies and proved what is now known as Hubble's Law. This states that the speed of recession of galaxies is proportional to their distance from us. This does not apply to our neighbours in the Local Group, we and they are keeping together. Hubble's Law has been tested and found to hold for the farthest detectable galaxies; they are about 7×10^9 light-years away and are receding with a speed $\frac{2}{5}$ of that of light.

Does this mean that the Local Group is the centre of the universe and that everything else is rushing away from us? No; Hubble's Law would appear just the same from any other cluster of galaxies. Imagine you are in a square on some fabulous chess board which is steadily doubling its size every hour; all other squares double their distances from you in an hour. Therefore the farther squares from you must travel faster than the nearer ones; in fact, Hubble's Law must be obeyed. But anyone standing in any other square would get the same impression.

This extraordinary behaviour of the universe is one of the most exciting discoveries of science. Let us envisage one possible implication. If the galaxies have always been receding, then in the past they must have been closer together. Following this to its conclusion, it seems that all the matter in the universe must have been packed densely together about 10^{10} years ago. Was this really so? The lack of a certain answer to this question is one of the things that makes cosmology so interesting.

Quasars, Pulsars and Black Holes.

In November 1962 Australian radio astronomers located a strong radio emitter with sufficient precision for the Mt. Palomar optical astronomers to identify it on photographs and examine the nature of its light. The red shift was so great that the object must be exceedingly distant; on the other hand it looked star-like, much smaller than a galaxy. By the beginning of 1967 over a hundred of these objects had been discovered and other characteristics established, such as strong ultraviolet radiation and inconstancy, in some cases, of the rate at which radiation is emitted. Not all of these so-called quasars are strong radio emitters; some show all the other characteristics except radio emission. It has been estimated that the "quiet" kind are about a hundred times more numerous than the radio kind. One great problem here is: how can such relatively small objects generate such inconceivably great amounts of energy that they appear bright at such huge distances? So far this is unanswered; these quasi-stellar objects are a great mystery, though they are generally held to be an important pointer towards a deeper understanding of cosmology.

Late in 1967 while investigating quasars, Cambridge radio astronomers discovered pulsars, a new type of heavenly body. Their characteristic is the emission of regular pulses of radio waves every second or so. A pulsar in the Crab nebula has a repetition rate even faster—about 1/30 sec—and it follows that pulsars must be very small bodies little if at all bigger than the Earth.

The existence of such small bodies raises again the problem of the ultimate fate of evolving stars. Much depends on their mass because this determines how strong the inward pull of gravity is. For a star to be at least temporarily stable the inward pull must be balanced by an outward pressure. In the Sun this is the pressure of the burning hydrogen (*see* F4) and the resulting density is about 1·4 times that of water (*see* Table, F7). In some stars the inward pressure is so great that collapse proceeds until it is balanced by a different type of outward pressure that sets in when electrons are forced into proximity. Stars so formed are the "white dwarfs". They are millions of times denser than the Sun—"a matchbox of their matter would weigh a ton"—and they are very small though not small enough to be pulsars. The latter are now generally thought to be a million times denser even than white dwarfs and to consist largely of neutrons (*see* F10). Such bodies are called neutron stars and their gravity is balanced by the outward pressure of tightly packed neutrons.

Could the tendency of a massive star to fall inwards ever be so great that no outward pressure known to physics would suffice to balance it? Apparently it could! Many astrophysicists now hold on theoretical grounds that such a gravitational collapse could create a high density object whose gravitational field would be too strong to allow anything—including light waves—ever to leave the body. Such hypothetical objects are called "black holes" because, light and other signals being unable to emerge from them, their matter has literally disappeared from view. Black holes could be detected by the disturbance their gravitational attraction causes to neighbouring visible stars and also because atoms attracted by the black hole would emit X-rays before falling so far in that they too disappear into the black hole. Both of these detection methods have led some astronomers to conjecture (by 1973) that there is a black hole in the constellation Cygnus. The theory of gravitational collapse raises profound and unresolved problems about our physical concepts. The relation between gravitation and the other forces of nature (*see* F15) is called into question.

THE ORIGIN AND DEVELOPMENT OF THE UNIVERSE.

Errors of observation and interpretation occur of course. But there are many checks and repetitions made, so that, on the whole, the descriptive account of the universe would be generally agreed among astronomers. When it comes to inventing theoretical explanations, however, science is on less sure ground, and indeed the theory of the universe is an arena of controversy at present. In most other sciences experiments can be repeated and the same phenomena observed under differing but controlled conditions. This is very helpful. But, by definition, there is only one universe; one cannot repeat it or do experiments with it. On the other hand, it must be remembered that the light from distant galaxies has taken perhaps 10^9 years to reach us, so it tells us what the galaxies were like that number of years ago. Therefore we are not confined simply to describing the present state of the universe; by looking farther into space we are looking farther into the past as well. How, then, does the state of the universe vary with time?

Evolutionary Theories.

One answer to this can be obtained from Einstein's general theory of relativity. Some slight indication of what this theory is about is given on page F15, and its logical development is, of course, a matter for mathematical specialists. It turns out that, if we assume that matter is distributed uniformly throughout space (as observation strongly suggests), then the solutions of Einstein's equations show how the state of the universe may vary with time. Unfortunately there are many possible solutions corresponding to expanding, static, or contracting universes. As we have already seen, the actual universe is expanding, therefore the static and contracting solutions can be ruled out. There is still a multiplicity of expanding possibilities; some correspond to indefinite expansion from an initially very dense state, others to expansion followed by contraction to a dense state followed by expansion and so on repeatedly, *i.e.*, a *pulsating* universe. The "dense state" is presumably to be identified with the time when the receding galaxies were all concentrated near one another, possibly in some dense conglomeration of atoms. This initia ate is thought by some to be the origin of the universe; they would say it has been expanding and evolving ever since. If the universe is pulsating, then sooner or later, gravitational attractions between galaxies will slow the observed recession down and turn it into a mutual approach and so back to the dense state. A straightforward application of the mathematics makes this dense state *infinitely* dense, and presumably something must happen before this inconceivable situation arises. For example, forces between atomic nuclei may play an important part and determine what the dense state (if any) is actually like.

The Steady-State Theory.

A rival theory was proposed in 1948 by Bondi, Gold, and Hoyle. They suggested that the universe is not changing with time; there was no initial dense state and no pulsations; the universe always has been, and always will be, like it is now. This does not mean that no local changes can be observed—this would clearly be contrary to the facts. But it does mean that, on the large scale, the clusters of galaxies have a distribution which is uniform in space and unchanging in time. If the numbers of clusters of galaxies in a large volume of space were counted every few thousand million years the answer would always be the same.

At first sight this appears to contradict outright the observed expansion of the universe. For if the galaxies are receding from one another how can the number in a given volume remain constant? The situation is saved by a bold proposal. It is that matter, in the form of hydrogen atoms, is being *continuously created* throughout space. This gas accumulates in due course into new galaxies, so that as the old ones move apart the young ones appear to keep the numbers up.

The Formation of Galaxies and Stars.

On any theory of the universe, some explanation has to be found for the existence of clusters of galaxies. In all theories galaxies condense out from dispersed masses of gas, principally hydrogen.

Once a huge gas cloud becomes sufficiently condensed to be separately identifiable as a galaxy, further condensation goes on inside it. It is believed on theoretical grounds that it could not condense into one enormous star but must form many fragments which shrink separately into clusters of stars. In these clusters many stars, perhaps hundreds or thousands or even millions, are born at once. A small cluster, visible to the naked eye, is the Pleiades. The Orion nebula, visible as a hazy blob of glowing gas in the sword of Orion, is the scene of much star-forming activity at present.

According to the evolutionary theory, the "initial dense state" consisted of very hot plasma in a state of overall expansion. The expanding plasma was both cooling and swirling about. The random swirling produces irregularities in the distribution of the hot gas—here it would be rather denser, there rather less dense. If a sufficiently large mass of denser gas happened to occur, then the gravitational attraction between its own particles would hold it together and maintain its permanent identity, even though the rest of the gas continued to swirl and expand. Such a large mass would gradually condense into fragments to become galaxies, the whole mass turning into a cluster of galaxies.

A theoretical proposal allowing for galaxy creation was in fact provided by steady-state cosmologists but will not be outlined here because it now seems that the steady-state theory has lost much ground.

The Changing Scene.

The 1960s witnessed revolutionary developments in both observational and theoretical astronomy. For example, it now seems agreed after some years of uncertainty that remote sources of radio waves are more abundant the weaker their intensity. This strongly suggests that they are more abundant at greater distances. Thus the universe is not *uniform* as the original steady-state theory prescribed. Since greater distances correspond to earlier times, any extra abundance of objects observed at the greater distance means that the universe was denser in its younger days than now. This favours an evolutionary theory of the universe.

The same theory requires that the initial dense state of the universe—aptly christened "the primæval fireball"—should contain intense electromagnetic radiation with a distribution of wavelengths characteristic of the high temperature. As the fireball, *i.e.*, the universe, expanded over a period of about 10^{10} years it cooled, and one feature of this process is that the wavelengths of the radiation increase and their distribution becomes characteristic of a much lower temperature. In fact, the wavelengths should now be concentrated round about 1 mm to 1 cm (corresponding to about —270° C) and the radiation should approach the earth uniformly from all directions. Radiation just like this has recently been detected in several laboratories, first by Penzias and Wilson in America during 1965. They used very sensitive radio receivers originally designed to detect signals from artificial satellites. No plausible terrestrial or galactic origin for the radiation has yet been conceived; the waves appear to have something to do with the universe itself. Neither is there a rational basis for the radiation within the steady-state theory which probably receives here its *coup de grâce.* The evolutionary theory survives so far.

The Formation of the Chemical Elements.

A stable nucleus is one that lasts indefinitely because it is not radioactive. There are 274 known kinds of stable atomic nuclei and little likelihood of any more being found. These nuclei are the isotopes (*see* F10) of 81 different chemical elements; the other elements, including, for example, uranium and radium are always radioactive. Some elements are rare, others abundant. The most common ones on earth are oxygen, silicon, aluminium, and iron. However, the earth is rather atypical. It is especially deficient in hydrogen, because the gravitational attraction of our small planet was not strong enough to prevent this very light gas from escaping into space.

It is possible to examine the chemical constituents of meteorites and to infer the composition of the sun and other stars from the spectrum of the light they emit. By such means, the conclusion has been reached that 93% of the atoms in our galaxy are hydrogen, 7% are helium; all the other elements together account for about one in a thousand atoms. A glance at the Table of Elements (*see* end of Sec.) will show that hydrogen and helium are two of the lightest elements: they are in fact the two simplest. The problem is to explain how the heavier chemical elements appear in the universe at all. It is here that a fascinating combination of astronomy and nuclear physics is required.

We have already referred to the fact that the energy radiated from the sun originates in nuclear reactions which turn hydrogen into helium. Why is energy given out? To answer this question we note that nuclei are made up of protons and neutrons (*see* F10). These particles attract one another strongly—that is why a nucleus holds together. To separate the particles, energy would have to be supplied to overcome the attractive forces. This amount of energy is called *binding energy* and is a definite quantity for every kind of nucleus. Conversely, when the particles are brought together to form a nucleus the binding energy is *released* in the form of radiations and heat. Different nuclei consist of different numbers of particles, therefore the relevant quantity to consider is the *binding energy per particle*. Let us call this B. Then if elements of *high* B are formed out of those of *low* B there is a *release* of energy.

Now B is small (relatively) for light elements like lithium, helium, and carbon; it rises to a maximum for elements of middling atomic weight like iron; it falls again for really heavy elements like lead, bismuth, and uranium. Consequently, energy is released by forming middleweight elements either by splitting up heavy nuclei ("nuclear fission") or by joining up light ones ("nuclear fusion").

It is the latter process, fusion, that is going on in stars. The fusion processes can be studied in physics laboratories by using large accelerating machines to hurl nuclei at one another to make them coalesce. In stars the necessary high velocity of impact occurs because the plasma is so hot. Gradually the hydrogen is turned into helium, and helium into heavier and heavier elements. This supplies the energy that the stars radiate and simultaneously generates the chemical elements.

The very heavy elements present a problem. To form them from middleweight elements, energy has to be *supplied*. Since there is plenty of energy inside a star, a certain small number of heavy nuclei will indeed form, but they will continually undergo fission again under the prevailing intense conditions. How do they ever get away to form cool ordinary elements, like lead and bismuth, in the earth? One view links them with the highly explosive supernovæ, to which we have already referred (F4 (1)). If the heavy elements occur in these stars the force of the explosion disperses them into cool outer space before they have time to undergo the fission that would otherwise have been their fate. The heavy elements are thus seen as the dust and debris of stellar catastrophes. This view is in line with the steady-state theory, because supernovæ are always occurring and keeping up the supply of heavy elements. In the evolutionary theory some of the generation of elements is supposed to go on in the very early stages of the initial dense state and to continue in the stars that evolve in the fullness of time. It cannot be claimed that the origin of the chemical elements is completely known, but we have said enough to show that there are plausible theories. Time and more facts will choose between them.

The Formation of the Planets.

The origin of the planets is still something of a mystery. This is not for lack of thought, indeed there are at present several conflicting theories but rather few firm conclusions or decisive facts. Some of the questions are: did the sun collect its family of planets one by one as a result of chance encounters in the depths of space? Were the planets formed from hot gaseous material which gradually solidified and cooled to the present temperature or are they perhaps accretions of small cold particles of dust and ice that have warmed up since? Was the solar system as a whole, including the sun, made in one process or was the sun there first and the planets "built on"?

We may reasonably reject the "chance collection theory" because observation shows that the planetary orbits all lie in the same plane and the planets except Venus all revolve in the same counter-clockwise direction round the sun. This could hardly have happened if the planets were picked up randomly one by one—indeed it provides almost conclusive evidence that the planets were all made at once.

There are two main schools of thought about how this happened. One thinks that the sun once encountered something else in space and the planets are the debris of the encounter. The "something else" was once held to be another star whose gravitational field drew from the sun an immense jet of gas which condensed into the planets. This version is not now believed but if instead of colliding with a star the sun entered an extensive dust cloud perhaps it dragged some away with it. If this is indeed possible, then the dust particles would gradually fall into the sun and form a disc in which, by their gravitational attraction, the smaller particles would grow bigger and merge, finally becoming planets and asteroids.

However this whole approach may be inferior to the other view which goes back to Kant and Laplace and believes that the sun and planets formed out of some primeval nebula of gas which gradually condensed into a rotating core with a disc of gas stretching out in the equatorial plane. The core then further condensed into the sun while the outer clouds of gas became the planets. Opinions differ as to whether and how this could have happened and it is a complex problem in mechanics involving at least three kinds of force, namely, gravitational attraction, gas pressure and the frictional force of one layer of swirling gas against another and electromagnetic forces present because some moving atoms become ionised and are then influenced by the nebular magnetic field.

The chemical composition of the planets was probably influenced by the temperature prevailing at the time and place when various substances condensed out of the vapour into solid particles and fell on to the growing planets. Planets forming at higher temperatures nearer the centre would therefore differ in composition and density from those further out. This idea agrees with many observations about planetary and meteoric compositions. For example, inner planets have a much higher proportion of chemicals which solidify at high temperatures *e.g.*, metallic compounds, whereas the outer ones are believed to have more volatile materials such as ammonia water and methane which solidify only when the temperature is low.

THE SOLAR SYSTEM.

	Mean distance from Sun (millions of km)	Diameter km	Period of Revolution	Average density (water = 1)	Number of Satellites
Sun	—	1,392,000			—
Mercury	57·9	4,880	88 days	5·4	0
Venus	108·2	12,104	224·7 days	5·2	0
Earth	149·6	12,756	365·26 days	5·5	1
Mars	227·9	6,787	687 days	3·9	2
Jupiter	778·3	142,800	11·86 years	1·3	13
Saturn	1,427	120,000	29·46 years	0·7	10
Uranus	2,869·6	51,800	84·01 years	1·2	5
Neptune	4,496·6	49,500	164·8 years	1·7	2
Pluto	5,900	6,000	247·7 years	?	0

SOME ASTRONOMICAL DISTANCES.

(1 light-year = $5{\cdot}88 \times 10^{12}$ miles).

Object.	Distance from Earth (light-years).	Velocity of recession (km per second).	Object.	Distance from Earth (light-years).	Velocity of recession (km per second).
Sun	$1{\cdot}6 \times 10^{-5}$	—	Andromeda Galaxy	$1{\cdot}5 \times 10^{6}$	—
Nearest star (Proxima Centauri)	4·2	—	Galaxy in Virgo	$7{\cdot}5 \times 10^{7}$	1,200
Brightest star (Sirius)	8·6	—	Galaxy in Gt. Bear	10^{9}	14,900
Pleiades	340	—	Galaxy in Corona Borealis	$1{\cdot}3 \times 10^{9}$	21,600
Centre of Milky Way	$2{\cdot}6 \times 10^{4}$	—	Galaxy in Bootes	$4{\cdot}5 \times 10^{9}$	39,300
Magellanic clouds (the nearest galaxies)	$1{\cdot}6 \times 10^{5}$	—	Very remote quasi-stellar object	$\sim 1{\cdot}5 \times 10^{10}$	~240,000

With space exploration now beginning in earnest, considerable future progress in understanding planetary formation can be anticipated. *See also* Section L, Mars, Venus, Planets.

THE EARTH.

Structure.

The earth has the shape of a slightly flattened sphere, with an equatorial radius of 6378 km and a polar radius 21 km less. Its mass can be calculated from Newton's Law of Gravitation and from measurements of the acceleration due to gravity, and is $5{\cdot}97 \times 10^{24}$ kg. The average density follows from these two figures and is about 5·5 grams per cubic centimetre. This is nearly twice the density of typical rocks at the surface, so there must be very much denser material somewhere inside, and the earth must have a definite internal structure.

This structure can be investigated using shock waves from earthquakes or large explosions. These are received at recording stations at different distances from their source, having penetrated to varying depths within the earth, and their relative times of arrival and characteristic forms enable the deep structure to be worked out. This consists of three main units, a core at the centre with a radius about half that of the earth, the mantle outside this, and the thin crust, about 35 km thick under the continents and 5 km thick under the oceans, forming a skin surrounding the mantle.

The composition of these three units can be deduced by observation and inference. For example, meteorites which arrive at the earth's surface from other parts of the solar system consist of three main types, composed of iron–nickel alloy, stony silicates, and a mixture of iron and silicates. Could these have originated from the break-up of some planet like the earth? If so, then perhaps the core of the earth is made up of iron–nickel alloy and the mantle of magnesium-rich silicates. Experiments on the physical properties of these materials at high pressures show strong similarities with the measured properties of the earth's interior. In addition, rocks composed of magnesium-rich silicates are found at the earth's surface in places where material seems to have come from great depth, such as in the debris from volcanic explosions. These may be direct samples of the earth's mantle.

Core, Mantle, and Crust.

By these arguments, and by many others, a picture can be built up of the internal structure of the earth. The core is composed of iron-nickel alloy. It is liquid at the outside, but contains a solid inner core of radius about one-fifth of that of the earth. Convection currents flowing in the liquid part give rise to the earth's magnetic field. Outside this the mantle is solid, and is made up mainly of magnesium–iron silicates of various kinds. By studying its physical properties through earthquake wave observations, the mantle may be divided into several zones, of which the most important is the asthenosphere. This is the part of the mantle between 70 and 300 km depth in which volcanic lavas are formed. In this region the mantle is everywhere quite near to the temperature at which it begins to melt, and is thus rather soft compared with the rest of the mantle. The presence of a soft asthenosphere accounts for many of the surface features of the earth, mountain belts and ocean basins, that make it so very different from cratered planets such as the Moon and Mars.

The sharp boundary between mantle and crust is called the Mohorovicic Discontinuity. Above it, the crust is different under continents and oceans. The thick continental crust has a composition that can broadly be called granitic, while the thin oceanic crust is poorer in silicon, sodium, and potassium and richer in calcium, iron, and magnesium. The continental crust has been built up over thousands of millions of years by welding together mountain belts of different ages, while the oceanic crust is made up of basalt lavas and is nowhere older than 250 million years.

Rocks.

Rocks are naturally occurring pieces of the solid earth. If you take a rock and break it up into grains, then separate the grains into different heaps of like grains, each heap will consist of grains of the same *mineral.* For example, the kind of rock called granite can be divided into glassy grains of the mineral quartz, milky white or pink grains of the mineral feldspar, shiny black flakes of the mineral biotite, and shiny colourless flakes of the mineral muscovite. Both biotite and muscovite belong to the mica group of minerals. Each different mineral has a well-defined composition or range of composition, and a definite and characteristic arrangement of the atoms that compose it. There are several thousand known kinds of minerals, but only fifty or so are at all common.

There are three main kinds of rock; igneous rocks, formed by the solidification of molten lava; sedimentary rocks, formed from material laid down under gravity on the earth's surface; and metamorphic rocks, formed by heating or reheating of either of the other kind of rock. Each of these broad groups may be further subdivided. When *igneous rocks* solidify deep inside the earth, they cool slowly and large crystals have time to form. Coarse-grained igneous rocks such as granites are known as plutonic igneous rocks. Conversely the rapidly cooled fine-grained igneous rocks that form the volcanic lavas, such as basalts and rhyolites, are called volcanic igneous rocks. *Sedimentary rocks* can be divided into three kinds: Clastic sediments are those formed from mechanically abraded and transported fragments of pre-existing rocks and include sandstone, mudstone, and clay. Organic sediments are those composed, as are most limestones, of fragments of organically produced material such as shells, wood, and bone. Chemical sediments are formed by direct chemical action and include, most typically, salt deposits formed by evaporation of sea water. *Metamorphic rocks* are more difficult to subdivide. They are usually classified on the basis of their original composition and/or the maximum pressure and temperature to which they have been subjected. Chemical reactions in metamorphic rocks give rise to successions of minerals as the pressure and temperature change, so that examination of a metamorphic rock will often allow one to say how deeply it was buried and how hot it was.

Age of Rocks.

There are two distinct ways of estimating the age of rocks. The first gives the *relative age.* It is based on the principle that in a sequence of sediments, older rocks lie underneath and younger ones above, that igneous rocks are younger than the rocks they intrude, and that folded rocks are formed earlier than the earth movements that fold them. Correlation of a sequence of rocks in one place with those in another is made by fossil faunas and floras. Thus a complete scale of relative ages can be built up, stretching back to the first rocks containing fossils (see the table in Part IV). The *age in years* can, on the other hand be measured by using radioactive elements (Part II) contained in rocks. If the amount of a radioactive element present is measured, and the amount of the product of radioactive decay can also be found, then, using the known rates of decay, the time since the product started to accumulate (defined for this purpose as the age in years) can be measured. This method is particularly useful for studying rocks that do not contain fossils (igneous and metamorphic rocks, or those too old to contain fossils). By similar methods, the *age of the earth* can be obtained. This turns out to be about $4{\cdot}6 \times 10^9$ years. The rocks containing the first fossils are $2{\cdot}5$–3×10^9 years old, while organised life in abundance first appeared about $0{\cdot}6 \times 10^9$ years ago.

The Continents and the Ocean Floor.

The outer part of the earth, namely, the asthenosphere and the solid mantle and crust overlying it, the lithosphere, is in a state of restless movement, and it is this movement that gives rise to the formation of oceans, continents, and mountain belts. The surface of the earth can be divided into a number of rigid plates of lithosphere, which move apart, or together, or slide past one another. Some of these plates are very large, such as the one which contains all of North America, all of South America, and about half of the Atlantic Ocean. Others are no more than a few thousand square kilometres in size. But they are all moving about relative to one another like ice floes in pack-ice. Where two plates move apart, hot material rises from the asthenosphere to fill the gap, partly melts, and gives rise to a chain of volcanoes and a thin volcanic crust. This is how ocean basins form and grow larger. In the Atlantic, the Mid-Atlantic Ridge marks the line along which plates are moving apart, and where new ocean is being formed. Long narrow pieces of ocean such as the Red Sea and the Gulf of California mark where a continent has just begun to split apart, and a new ocean is forming. Where two plates slide past one another, a great tear fault results. Such a fault is the San Andreas fault which runs from the Gulf of California to San Francisco. Jerky movement on this fault gave rise to the great San Francisco earthquake of 1906 and could give rise to another earthquake there at any time.

Where two plates move together, the result depends on the nature of the crust forming the plates. If at least one of the plates is oceanic, the oceanic crust dips down into the mantle and slides away to great depths until it eventually merges with the asthenosphere. Along this dipping sheet of crust, strong earthquakes occur and frictional heating of the sheet leads to melting and the production of quantities of lava. Examples of such boundaries are the Andes, where the Pacific Ocean dips beneath South America, and Indonesia, where the Indian Ocean dips below Asia. When both plates are continental, on the other hand, the crust is too thick and buoyant to slide into the mantle, and a collision results, giving rise to a fold mountain chain. Eventually the movement grinds to a halt, the plates weld together, and the fold mountains become dormant. The Himalayas were formed in this way from the recent collision of India and Asia. The evidence that has led to these conclusions is too complex to summarise here. It comes from a study of rock magnetism, earthquakes, the flow of heat from inside the earth and even from the shapes of the continents, that must match across the oceans by which they have been split apart. Confirmation has come from a series of holes drilled in the ocean which has shown how the crust becomes younger towards the centres of the oceans.

Rates of movement of plates have been calculated, ranging from a few millimetres a year to ten centimetres a year. The faster movements can be measured directly on the ground by such simple techniques as looking at the displacement of railway lines, walls, and roads, but the slower ones, and those beneath the oceans must be measured by more indirect geophysical methods. The mechanism by which this movement takes place is still unknown. Are the plates pulled by their sinking edges, or pushed by their rising edges, or moved by some other means? But it cannot be doubted that the movement does happen, and that it holds the key to the development of the earth's crust since the time it was first formed.

The Rest.

There is a lot more to the study of the earth than has been possible to set down here. The oceans, the atmosphere, and the rocks of the crust all interact with one another in their development in a complex way. The surface of the earth has gradually changed as life has evolved over thousands of millions of years and ice ages have come and gone, changing the surface again and again. Just as important is the economic potential of the earth, on which we depend for all of our energy and all raw materials. This section has given the basic framework within which such further investigations are carried out, to help the reader understand as he reads more widely.

II. PHYSICS—THE FUNDAMENTAL SCIENCE OF MATTER

WHAT PHYSICS IS ABOUT.

Anyone compelled by curiosity or professional interest to look into contemporary journals of pure physics research is soon struck by the fact that the old text-book division of physics into "heat, light, sound, electricity, and magnetism" has become very blurred. The indispensable periodical of research summaries, *Physics Abstracts*, contains no less than 7,000 entries a month, under many separate headings. This is daunting even to the experienced physicist and, as a token of the human effort devoted to one single branch of science, it is impressive for variety, for degree of specialisation, and for sheer volume. How can the main features of this great work be presented to the non-specialist?

Two different, though complementary, sections can be distinguished. First, there is the physics concerned with the properties of matter in bulk, with solids, liquids, and gases, and with those odd but very important substances, such as paints, plastic solutions, and jelly-like material, which are neither properly solid nor liquid. In this vast domain of physics questions like this are asked: Why is iron magnetic, copper not? What happens when solids melt? Why do some liquids flow more easily than others? Why do some things conduct electricity well, others badly, some not at all? During the last century, particularly the last few decades, it has become clear that such questions can be answered only by raising and solving others first. In particular, we must ask: (i) Of what nature are the invisible particles of which matter is composed? and (ii) How are those particles arranged in bulk matter?

The first of these two questions has generated the second major category of modern physics: this is the physics of particles and of the forces that particles exert on each other. In this field which represents science at its most fundamental questions like this are asked: If matter is composed of small units or particles, what are they like? How many kinds of particle are there? Do the particles possess mass? electric charge? magnetism? How do the particles influence each other? How can their motion be described and predicted?

Once scientists became convinced that matter did indeed consist of particles, the *arrangement* of the particles in matter became an important question. This is the problem of *structure*. It was discovered, by von Laue in Germany and by W. H. and W. L. Bragg in England, that the structure of solids could be inferred from the way X-rays are reflected. It is well known that X-rays can penetrate solids. In doing so, they encounter successive layers of particles and are reflected from them. The reflections reveal how far apart the layers are and how the particles are arranged in space. This is the technique of X-ray crystallography. By now it has shown that most solid matter is *crystalline*, *i.e.*, it consists of a regular pattern of particles repeated over and over again to fill the volume of the solid—just as a wallpaper is covered by repeated units of design. The units in a crystal are very small, often about 10^{-8} cm across, and the particles in them are very close together.

Liquids, on the other hand, have no repeated pattern, but consist of particles which are jumbled up, though still very closely packed—like marbles in a bag. In gases, the particles are widely separated and moving rapidly about; the average distance between particles in air is about 10 times that in ordinary solids, and air particles have an average speed of 5×10^4 cm per sec. (1,000 mile/h.).

In general, therefore, the structure of matter

is fairly well understood. This does not mean that structure studies are out of date, but only that now they are devoted to elucidating the structure of particular substances, often extremely complex ones such as are found in living matter. We shall therefore say no more about structure, but turn to the major divisions of physics introduced above: (i) particles and their forces; (ii) the properties of matter in bulk.

PARTICLES AND FORCES.

The idea that matter is composed of small particles, or atoms, originated, it is true, in classical times. Nevertheless, the modern views need be traced back no farther than the beginning of the nineteenth century, when Dalton and his contemporaries were studying the laws of chemical combination. By that time the distinctions between elements, compounds, and mixtures were already made. Compounds and mixtures are substances which can be separated into smaller amounts of chemically distinguishable constituents. Elements (*see* end of Sec.) cannot be so divided. In a mixture the components may be mixed in any proportion and sorted out again by non-chemical means. In a compound the elements are combined in fixed proportions by weight. This last fact gives the clue to atomic theory.

Dalton and Atomic Theory.

Dalton pointed out that the fixed combining weights of elements could easily be explained if the elements consisted of atoms which combined in simple numerical ratios, *e.g.*, 1 atom of element A with one of B, or one of B with two of C, and so on. For instance, 35·5 g of chlorine combine with 23·0 g of sodium to make 58·5 g of ordinary salt. If we assume one atom of chlorine links with one of sodium, then the atoms themselves must have weights in the ratio 35·5 to 23·0. This turns out to be consistent with the combining weights of chlorine and sodium in all other compounds in which they both take part. Sometimes two elements combine in several different proportions by weight. But this is easily explained by assuming that the atoms link up in different numbers, *e.g.*, one iron atom with one oxygen, or two irons with three oxygens, or three irons with four oxygens. Then the three different combining proportions arise from the three different numbers of atoms, *using in each case the same ratio of oxygen atom weight to iron atom weight.*

Atomic Weight.

Over the century and a half since Dalton, these ideas have been repeatedly tested by chemical experiments. No one now doubts that every chemical element has atoms of characteristic weight. By convention the number 12·0000 is ascribed to carbon and called its " atomic weight." The atomic weights of other atoms are expressed by giving their ratio to that of carbon, *e.g.*, hydrogen, 1·008; iron, 55·85. These numbers are only ratios; the real weight of one single oxygen atom is $2{\cdot}7 \times 10^{-23}$ g.

J. J. Thomson and the Electron.

Matter is electrically uncharged in its normal state, but there exist many well-known ways of producing electric charges and currents—rubbing amber, or rotating dynamos, for example. It is therefore necessary to have some theory of electricity linked to the theory of matter. The fundamental experiment in this field was made by J. J. Thomson when, in 1897, he discovered the electron.

If you take two metal electrodes sealed inside a glass vessel, and if the air is suitably pumped out and a high voltage applied to the electrodes, then the negative one emits a radiation which causes the walls of the tube to glow. The rays are called *cathode rays*. The discovery of the electron was essentially a clarification of the nature of cathode rays. Thomson showed that they were streams of particles with mass and negative electric charge and a general behaviour unlike any other atomic particle known at that time. The importance of this discovery for the world of science cannot be overestimated, and its technical progeny are in every home and factory in X-ray machines, television tubes, and other devices.

Rutherford-Bohr Atom.

Since the electrons emerge from matter, they are presumably parts of atoms. The relation between the negative electrons and the positively charged constituents of matter was elucidated by the great experimenter Rutherford and the great theoretician Bohr. Their work, just before the First World War, showed that the positive charge, together with almost all the mass, is concentrated in the central core or nucleus of the atom about which the very light-weight electrons revolve. The diameter of an atom is about 10^{-8} cm, roughly one three-hundred-millionth part of an inch. The central nucleus has a diameter about 10,000 times smaller still. The nucleus and the electrons hold together because of the electric attraction between them.

At this stage work could, and did, go on separately along several different lines:

(i) Electrons could be studied on their own. Nowadays the handling of beams of electrons of all sizes and intensities has become a major branch of technology.

(ii) The nucleus could be treated as a special problem, and this led to the mid-century flowering of nuclear physics, to the atomic bomb, and to nuclear power.

(iii) The behaviour of electrons in the atom could be analysed; this is the great domain of atomic physics which spreads into many other sciences as well.

Volumes have been written about each of these three fields, but we can spare only a few lines for each.

The Electron.

Electrons are expelled from solids by light, heat, electric fields, and other influences. It has therefore been possible to study beams of electrons on their own *in vacuo*. Electrons inside matter, either as constituents, or temporarily in transit, can also be observed by their innumerable effects. These observations all show the particles to be indistinguishable one from another; all electrons are the same wherever they come from. They have a definite mass ($9{\cdot}11 \times 10^{-28}$ g), a negative electric charge, a magnetic moment, and a " spin " (intrinsic rotatory motion). No one has ever subdivided an electron or obtained an electric charge smaller than that on one electron. The electronic charge is therefore used as a basic unit of charge in atomic physics. The electron has come to be the best known of all the " fundamental particles."

The Nucleus.

The early research programmes in nuclear physics were greatly facilitated by the occurrence in nature of certain unstable (radioactive) nuclei which emit fast-moving fragments. The latter can be used as projectiles to aim at other nuclei as targets; the resulting impacts yield much valuable information. This technique still dominates nuclear physics, though nowadays the projectiles are artificially accelerated by one or other of the large costly machines designed for the purpose.

The most important early discovery was that the nucleus consists of two types of fundamental particle—the positively charged *proton* and the electrically neutral *neutron*. These two are of nearly equal mass (about 1,800 times that of the electron), and like electrons, have a magnetic moment and spin. The proton charge is equal to the electron charge, though opposite in sign. Consider a moderately complex nucleus like that of iron. This usually has 30 neutrons and 26 protons. Its atomic weight therefore depends on the total number of neutrons plus protons, but the total charge depends only on the number of protons—called the *atomic number*. The latter is denoted by Z while the total number of neutrons plus protons is called *mass number* and denoted by M. A species o nucleus with given values of Z and M is called a *nuclide*. Z is also the number of electrons in the atom, since the atom as a whole is electrically neutral. The atomic number determines the chemical nature of the atom (see below).

so that by altering the number of *neutrons* in a nucleus we do not change the chemical species. It is therefore possible to find—and nowadays to make—nuclei of the same element which nevertheless differ slightly in weight because they have different numbers of neutrons. These are called *isotopes*. Iron isotopes are known with 26, 27, 28, 29, 30, 31, 32, and 33 neutrons, but all have 26 protons. Thus a set of isotopes consists of the various nuclides that have the same Z but different M's.

Stable Nuclides.

The protons and neutrons in a nucleus are bound together by strong forces called *nuclear forces*. In many cases, the forces are so strong that no particles ever escape and the nucleus preserves its identity. There are two hundred and seventy-four different combinations of neutrons and protons of this kind, and they are called the *stable nuclides*. The earth is largely composed of such stable nuclides, because any unstable ones have, in the course of time, spontaneously broken up into stable residues.

Nevertheless, there are some unstable nuclei left on earth. They give rise to the phenomenon of radioactivity which was discovered by Becquerel in 1893.

Unstable Nuclides: Radioactivity.

Becquerel found that certain chemicals containing uranium gave off rays capable of blackening a photographic plate, and shortly afterwards Marie and Pierre Curie discovered more substances, including radium, which produce similar but stronger effects. By now, about fifty chemical elements having radioactive properties are known to exist on earth, some, like radium, being strongly radioactive, others, like potassium, being so weak that the radiations are difficult to detect. These are called the *natural radioactive nuclides*.

The main facts about radioactivity are as follows: it is a *nuclear* phenomenon and (with minor exceptions) proceeds quite independently of whatever the electrons in the atom may be doing. Thus, the radioactivity of an atom is not affected by the chemical combination of the atom with other atoms, nor by ordinary physical influences like temperature and pressure. The radioactivity consists of the emission by the substance of certain kinds of rays. The early workers, Rutherford being the giant among them, distinguished three kinds of rays labelled α, β, and γ. These are described below. Whatever kind of ray is examined, it is found that the radiation from a given sample decreases gradually with time according to a definite law which states that the intensity of radiation decreases by half every T seconds. The number T, called the half-life, is constant for each radioactive material, but varies enormously from substance to substance. For instance, radium decreases its activity by a half every 1,622 years, whereas the half-life of one of the polonium isotopes is about $0{\cdot}3 \times 10^{-6}$ sec.

α-, β-, and γ-rays.

The three most well-known types of radioactive emission are quite distinct from one another.

(i) α-rays or α-particles consist of two protons and two neutrons bound together. They are ejected from the radioactive nucleus with one of several well-defined speeds. These speeds are high, often of the order 10^9 cm per sec. Two protons and two neutrons are the constituents of the nucleus of helium, and α-particles are thus fast-moving helium nuclei.

(ii) β-rays are moving electrons. They may emerge from their parent nucleus with any speed from zero to a definite maximum. The maximum speed often approaches that of light, and is different for each isotope. The electron has a positively charged counterpart, the positron (see below), and β-rays are sometimes positrons. To distinguish the two cases, the symbols $\beta-$ and $\beta+$ are used. The naturally occurring β-radiations are almost all $\beta-$.

(iii) γ-rays travel with the speed of light because they are in fact electromagnetic waves differing from light only in the extreme shortness of their wavelength. They have no electric charge.

It is unusual, though not unheard of, for the same radioactive substance to emit both α- and β-rays. On the other hand, γ-rays frequently accompany either α- or β-rays.

γ-rays pass through matter easily; in fact, they are extra penetrating X-rays. α-rays can be stopped by thin sheets of tissue paper. α-rays brought to rest pick up a pair of electrons from the surrounding matter and become neutral helium atoms, and helium gas from this source is consequently found imprisoned in certain radioactive rocks. β-rays are intermediate in penetrating power between α- and γ-rays.

We must now try to interpret these observations.

Radioactive Disintegration.

A nucleus is a collection of neutrons and protons interacting with each other and possessing collectively a certain amount of energy. Just as some human organisations lose their coherence if they accept too many members, so nuclei can remain stable only if (i) the total number of particles is not too great, and (ii) neutrons and protons are there in suitable proportions. Radioactive nuclei are the ones for which either or both these conditions do not hold. Sooner or later such nuclei eject a fragment, thus getting rid of some energy they cannot contain. This is called a *radioactive disintegration*, and the fragments are the α-, β-, and γ-rays. α-emission relieves a nucleus of two neutrons and two protons and some energy; γ-emission simply carries off excess energy without altering the number or kind of particles left behind. β-emission is more complicated. There are no electrons normally present in a nucleus, but they are suddenly created and explosively emitted if a neutron changes into a proton; positive electrons are similarly generated if a proton changes into a neutron. β-emission is therefore a mechanism for changing the ratio of protons to neutrons without altering the total number of particles.

Both α- and β-emission change the Z of a nucleus, and the product, or daughter nucleus, is a different chemical element. α-emission also changes the M. It might happen that the daughter nucleus is unstable, in which case it too will disintegrate. Successive generations are produced until a stable one is reached. Part of such a family tree is shown below. The symbols above the arrows show the kind of rays emitted at each stage, the figures are the mass numbers, M, and the names and symbols of chemical elements can be found at the end of the Section.

$$U^{238} \xrightarrow{\alpha} Th^{234} \xrightarrow{\beta} Pa^{234} \xrightarrow{\beta} U^{234} \xrightarrow{\alpha} Th^{230} \xrightarrow{\alpha}$$
$$Ra^{226} \xrightarrow{\alpha} Rn^{222} \xrightarrow{\alpha} Po^{218} \xrightarrow{\alpha} Pb^{214} \xrightarrow{\beta} Bi^{214} \xrightarrow{\beta}$$
$$Po^{214} \xrightarrow{\alpha} Pb^{210} \xrightarrow{\beta} Bi^{210} \xrightarrow{\beta} Po^{210} \xrightarrow{\alpha} Pb^{206}$$

(Pb^{206} is stable lead).

This family exists naturally on earth, because the head of the family, U^{238}, has so long a half-life ($4{\cdot}5 \times 10^9$ years) that there has not yet been time enough since its formation for it to have disappeared.

Artificial Radioactivity.

Nowadays many new radioactive isotopes can be man-made. All that is required is to alter the M or Z (or both) of a stable isotope to a value which is incompatible with stability. The means for doing this is *bombardment*, *i.e.*, stable nuclei are exposed to the impacts of atomic particles such as streams of protons from an accelerator, the neutrons in an atomic reactor, or simply the α-particles from another radioactive substance. The new material is called an *artificially radioactive isotope*. Artificial radioactivity is not different in kind from that of the naturally radioactive substances, but the half-lives are usually on the short side. Indeed, the isotopes in question would exist in nature but for the fact that their short half-lives ensured their disappearance from the earth long ago.

Suppose a piece of copper is exposed to the intense neutron radiation in an atomic reactor at Harwell.

The more abundant of the two stable isotopes of ordinary copper has thirty-four neutrons and twenty-nine protons (*i.e.*, $Z = 29$, $M = 63$). In the reactor many (not all) of these nuclei absorb a neutron, giving an unstable copper nucleus with $Z = 29$, $M = 64$. When removed from the reactor the specimen is observed to be radioactive with a half-life of 12·8 hours. It is somewhat unusual in that it gives out both β^- and β^+ rays. Some nuclei emit electrons, leaving a daughter nucleus with one more positive charge than copper, *i.e.*, a zinc nucleus ($Z = 30$, $M = 64$). One neutron has become a proton, and the resulting zinc nucleus is stable. The others emit positrons, leaving behind a nucleus in which a proton has been turned into a neutron ($Z = 28$, $M = 64$); this is a stable nickel nucleus. The overall process is one example of the artificial transmutation of the chemical elements which is now a commonplace of nuclear physics. It was first discovered by Irene and Frederick Joliot-Curie in 1934.

Lack of a Complete Theory.

Consider now a collection of, say, one million radioactive nuclei of the same kind. It is impossible to tell exactly when any one of them will disintegrate; it is a matter of chance which ones break up first. All we know is that, after a time equal to the half-life, only a half a million will survive unchanged. In general, the more excess energy a nucleus has, the more likely it is to break up, and therefore the shorter the half-life of that particular nuclear species. In principle, to calculate the half-life theoretically, one would have to have a reliable theory of nuclear forces and energies. This is still being sought after, so it is probably fair to say that while the laws of behaviour of radioactive isotopes are well and accurately known, the *explanation* of this behaviour in terms of the properties of protons and neutrons is by no means complete.

Nuclear Fission—Chain Reaction.

A discovery important not just for nuclear physics but for the whole of mankind was made by Hahn and Strassman in 1939. This was the discovery of nuclear fission in uranium. One of the natural isotopes of uranium is an unstable one, U^{235}, with 143 neutrons and 92 protons. It normally shows its instability by emitting α- and γ-rays. If uranium is bombarded with neutrons, some U^{235} nuclei temporarily gain an extra neutron, which makes them even less stable. This they show by splitting into two roughly equal parts, called fission fragments, together with two or three neutrons. There are two highly important things about this disintegration. One is that the two or three neutrons can promote further disintegrations in other uranium nuclei, and the process can therefore be self-propagating: it is then called a *chain reaction*. The other is that the total mass of the fission products is less than that of the original nucleus. This mass difference does not disappear without trace; it turns into energy according to a formula referred to in a paragraph below (F15(1).

Application of these New Forces.

The world has found two uses for the energy liberated in nuclear chain reactions: the atomic bomb and nuclear power plants. In the first, conditions are arranged to promote and encourage a tremendous and rapid chain reaction leading to an explosion; in the second, the steady liberation of energy in the form of heat is controlled for use in turbines which can generate electricity or provide propulsion. Both uses represent epoch-making technical achievements, but mankind has yet to show itself capable of bearing sanely the burden of responsibility which nuclear physicists have laid upon it. One thing is certain: the discoveries will not cease. Already, other fissionable elements have been made and used; new chemical elements have been created; nuclear plants ("atomic piles") have stimulated great demands for new materials that will stand the heat and radiation inside the reactor, and this promotes research in other fields of science; irradiation inside an atomic pile gives new and potentially useful properties to old materials; nuclear power drives ships and submarines. It is difficult to write even briefly about contemporary nuclear physics without feeling keenly the ambiguity of its powerful promises.

Although so much is known about the behaviour of nuclei, the theory of the nucleus leaves much to be desired. What holds the neutrons and protons together? Why are some nuclei more stable than others? It is certain that the forces between neutrons and protons in a nucleus are unlike the electrical attractions between the nucleus as a whole and its surrounding electrons. Nor have they anything to do with gravitation. Indeed, the best description and explanation of nuclear forces is the objective of much of the contemporary research effort in nuclear physics.

Atoms.

A nucleus surrounded by its full complement of electrons is an electrically neutral system called an atom. Neither the atom as a whole, nor its nucleus, counts as a "fundamental particle" because either can be subdivided into more elementary parts, thus:

$$\text{atom} \longrightarrow \text{electrons} + \text{nucleus} \longrightarrow \text{electrons} + \text{neutrons} + \text{protons}$$

The chemical identity of the atoms of a given element, which was Dalton's key idea, depends entirely on the number and motion of the electrons. For example, the simplest element, hydrogen, has one proton for a nucleus, and one electron. The latter is comparatively easily detached or disturbed by the electric forces exerted by neighbouring atoms, consequently hydrogen is reactive chemically, *i.e.*, it readily lends its electron to build chemical structures with other equally co-operative elements. The second element, helium, has a nucleus of two protons and two neutrons; outside are two electrons in a particularly stable arrangement. Indeed, this pair of electrons is so difficult to disarrange that a special name has been coined to cover such cases—*closed shells*. Helium, with its closed shell, will not react chemically with anything. As the nuclear charge increases, different electron arrangements of greater or lesser stability succeed one another, with every so often a closed shell corresponding to one of the chemically inert gases neon, argon, xenon, krypton. *See* F20 (1).

Such considerations, pursued in sufficient detail, enable atomic physics to account for all the differences and similarities among the chemical elements and, in principle at least, for the other facts of chemistry as well.

Ions.

It is possible to remove one or more electrons from an atom, leaving it positively charged. The atom is then said to be *ionised* and is called a *positive ion*. Alternatively, some atoms are capable of accepting electrons above their normal complement, thus becoming negative ions. The behaviour of ions is very important in many fields of physics and chemistry, and some of these will be referred to later.

Molecules.

Electrical attractions of various kinds cause atoms and ions to form compound groups. This is the basis of chemical combination, and the smallest conceivable fragment of compound which still preserves the chemical identity of that compound is called a molecule. Molecules have a wide range of complexity, from simple pairs of atoms to highly intricate spirals and chains composed of thousands of atoms. *See* Part III.

Excited Atoms.

Like the nuclei described above, atoms can be given excess energy and will then return to their ground state with the emission of radiation. The excess energy usually resides in one of the electrons which is executing unusually violent motion. The electron returns to normal by releasing its excess energy in the form of light whose colour is characteristic of the atom involved. Herein lies the explanation of innumerable natural and technical phenomena, such as the colours of glowing gases whether they exist in the sun and stars, in auroræ, or in street-lamps and neon signs. Herein also lies the reason for the importance of spectroscopy, which is the study of the characteristic radiation from excited atoms: for spectroscopy is not only a useful tool for the chemical identification of elements ("spectroscopic analysis") but was one of the main routes along which twentieth-century physicists broke through to a knowledge of the inner nature of the atom.

Maxwell and Electromagnetic Waves.

Atoms are held together by the electric attraction of the nucleus for the electrons. Finer details of atomic behaviour depend on the magnetic moments of the particles. Any region of space subject to electric and magnetic influences is called an *electromagnetic field*. Before the discovery of the electron, Maxwell had perfected a general theory of the electromagnetic field, giving to physics a celebrated set of equations which describe satisfactorily almost all electric and magnetic phenomena. *Inter alia*, he proved that disturbances in the electric and magnetic conditions at one place could be propagated to another place through empty space, with a definite velocity, just as sound waves are propagated through air. Such electromagnetic disturbances in transit are called *electromagnetic waves*, and their velocity turned out experimentally to be the same as that of light and radio waves—which was a decisive argument to show that both of these phenomena are themselves electromagnetic waves.

Einstein and Photons.

In the years between about 1900 and 1920 this view was upset by Planck, Einstein, Millikan, and others, who focused attention on phenomena (radiant heat, photoelectricity) in which light behaves like a stream of particles and not at all like waves A wave and a particle are two quite different things, as anyone will admit after a moment's contemplation of, say, the ripples on a pond and a floating tennis ball. The acute question was: is light like waves or particles? This celebrated dilemma soon multiplied its horns. In 1927 electrons were shown to be quite capable of behaving as waves instead of particles, and this is now known to be true of protons, neutrons, and all other fundamental particles as well.

Theoretical physicists have devised means of having it both ways. To say that light behaves as particles means that the waves of the electromagnetic field cannot have their energy subdivided indefinitely. For waves of a given frequency, there is a certain irreducible quantity of energy that must be involved whenever light interacts with anything. This quantity is the product $h\nu$, where ν is the frequency and h is a constant named after Planck. Each such unit is called a *quantum of the electromagnetic field* or a *photon* and is counted as one of the fundamental particles. Frequencies and wavelengths vary widely; typical wavelengths are: radio—hundreds or thousands of metres; radar—a few centimetres; visible light—5×10^{-5} cm; X-rays—10^{-8} cm.

Different Types of Force.

Nature seems to use four different kinds of force to make one particle interact with another. The weakest force is gravity; while this dominates celestial mechanics its effect inside atoms is negligible compared with the other three. The binding forces inside atoms are *electromagnetic*, *e.g.*, the attraction of nuclei for electrons. Considerably stronger still is the nuclear force which holds the nuclei together and this is called the *strong interaction*. The fourth force is called the *weak interaction* and is intermediate in strength between electromagnetic and gravitational forces. It is responsible for a number of phenomena of which the best known is β-radioactivity.

Elementary Particles. Leptons and Hadrons.

Particles may respond to some or all of the forces. Protons are involved with all of them but electrons respond to all except the "strong interaction." When new particles are discovered physicists try to find out their fundamental properties and among these is their response (if any) to each kind of force. Some other basic properties are: electric charge (if any), mass (if any), and the speed with which the particle splits up spontaneously into other types.

A few particles are stable but most decay into products. The lifetimes of unstable particles are extraordinarily short by everyday standards but, even so, some (of about 10^{17} sec. or upwards) are much longer than others (of about 10^{22} sec.). The Table on page F14 contains the stable particles and a *selection* of the moderately unstable ones with brief comments on their properties.

The Table shows a rudimentary classification into four groups: (i) the photon; (ii) leptons—which are particles, lighter than protons, which do not react to the "strong" type of force; (iii) mesons—which are particles, lighter than protons which are subject to all the kinds of force; (iv) baryons—which include protons, neutrons, and heavier particles. All particles sensitive to the strong force—*i.e.* mesons and baryons—are called "hadrons." Many of these particles have been produced for the first time in recent years by bombarding matter with beams of high energy particles. Much of this work is done in the large accelerating machines in Europe, the USA and USSR.

The Riddle of Elementary-ness. Quarks.

Hundreds of particles have now been discovered—so many that their "elementary-ness" has been called into question. Surely, it is asked, some of them are combinations or excited states, of others? The current trend is to form them into groups and this is a significant matter. It is comparable with arranging chemical elements into the Periodic Table. The pattern does not of itself explain anything but it strongly suggests where to look for explanations. The classification of particles currently favoured is based on the very sophisticated mathematical ideas known as *group theory*. Group theory is a branch of mathematics which is finding increasing application in physics and it had a resounding success when, in 1964, a particle, the "omega minus", was discovered with exactly the properties required to complete a family of particles deducible from group theory. However there seems no end to the questions, *e.g.*, why are some groupings of particles found and not others? Efforts to tackle this kind of question led to the idea that there are *really* fundamental particles, called *quarks*, of which all the hadrons are made. There is theoretical debate as to how many kinds of quark there are (3? 9? 12?) and experimental attempts to detect isolated quarks have failed so far. But there is growing confidence about quarks, especially since the discovery in 1974 in the USA of the ψ-particle which elicited much theoretical excitement and speculation and *may* turn out to be a linked pair of quarks, though the matter is by no means settled at the time of writing (early 1977).

It is now accepted that every fundamental particle is a manifestation of the waves of one or other kind of field. Physicists speak of waves, particles, and fields in the same breath or rather the same equation. Little is to be gained by asking if electrons or photons are "really" particles or waves. All one can say is that they are things whose behaviour is predicted and described by certain equations. Those who must visualise can imagine particles in some phenomena and waves in others: neither conception contains the whole truth. Why should the ultimate invisible constituents of matter be forced into one or other category derived from everyday experience? For convenience however, we shall continue to call these things "elementary particles."

SOME MEMBERS OF THE ATOMIC FAMILY

The numbers in brackets after the name denote first the electric charge and second, the mass. The charge on an electron is counted as −1 unit and the electron mass as +1 unit. Thus (+1, 207) means the particle has a positive charge of 1 unit and a mass 207 times that of the electron.

Photon (0, 0)	A quantum of electromagnetic radiation, *e.g.*, light, X-rays, γ-rays. The concept was introduced by M. Planck in 1900 when he described the emission of light as taking place in " packets " rather than in a steady stream. The energy of a photon is proportional to the frequency of the radiation and inversely proportional to the wavelength.
	Leptons
Electron (−1, 1)	Discovered by J. J. Thomson in 1897. The number of orbital electrons in an atom determines its chemical properties. Actual rest mass = $9{\cdot}1 \times 10^{-28}$ g. Emitted as β-rays by some radioactive nuclei. A stable particle.
Positron (+1, 1)	Positive counterpart or, " anti-particle," to the electron. Predicted theoretically by P. A. M. Dirac in 1928 and first discovered in cosmic rays by C. D. Anderson in 1932. Emitted as β-rays by some radioactive nuclei. When positrons and electrons collide they usually annihilate each other and turn into γ-rays; consequently, positrons only last about 10^{-10} sec. within ordinary matter, but are stable in isolation.
Neutrino (0, 0) and Anti-neutrino (0, 0)	These particles travel with the speed of light and are distinguished from one another by the relation of their spin to their direction of motion. A neutrino is emitted with the positron during positive β-decay; and an anti-neutrino with the electron during negative β-decay. Their interaction with matter is extremely slight. First postulated by Pauli in 1933 and detected in 1956. π-meson decay also produces neutrinos and anti-neutrinos but in 1962 it was proved experimentally that these are a different species. Thus there are two kinds of neutrino each with an anti-neutrino. All these particles are distinguished from photons by having different spin.
Muon (±1, 207)	Similar to, but heavier than, the electron and positron; disintegrates into electron (or positron if positive) +neutrino +anti-neutrino.
	Mesons
Pion (±1, 273) or (0, 264)	The π-meson. Charged pions decay either into muons and neutrinos or into electrons and neutrinos. Neutral pions decay into γ-rays, into " positron-electron pairs," or both. Pions are intimately connected with nuclear forces, *i.e.*, with the " strong " interaction.
Kaon (±1, 966) or (0, 974)	The K-mesons. These decay in many different ways producing other mesons, electrons, and neutrinos.
	Baryons
Proton (+1, 1836·1)	The positively-charged constituent of nuclei; the hydrogen nucleus is one proton. Fast-moving protons occur in cosmic rays. Does not spontaneously disintegrate.
Anti-proton (−1, 1836·1)	Negative anti-particle of the proton. Its existence was long suspected. Artificially produced and detected for the first time in 1955. Will react with the proton to produce pions or kaons.
Neutron (0, 1838·6)	Discovered by J. Chadwick in 1932. The neutral constituent of nuclei. When free it spontaneously disintegrates into a proton, an electron, and an anti-neutrino, after an average lifetime of about 18 minutes. Passes through matter much more easily than charged particles.
Anti-neutron (0, 1838·6)	The anti-particle of the neutron from which it is distinguished by properties connected with its magnetic moment and spin. Will react with neutron to produce pions or kaons.
Lambda Particle (0, 2183)	Discovered in 1947. Decays into proton plus pion.
Sigma Particle (0 or ±1; about 2330)	Various modes of disintegration, producing neutrons, protons, mesons and lambda particles.
Omega Particle (±1, 3272)	Predicted by recent theory and discovered at Brookhaven, New York, in 1964.
Psi Particle (0, about 6100)	Discovered independently by two laboratories in the USA 1974. Still under intensive study.

QUANTUM THEORY AND RELATIVITY.

Quantum Theory.

The point of view of the last paragraph is characteristic of quantum theory, which is the currently accepted fundamental theory of matter and motion. One can reasonably ask at what position in space, exactly, is a particle? Or, what, exactly, is the wavelength of a wave? But the first question cannot be reasonably asked of a wave, nor the second of a particle. Since electrons have something in common with both, one question cannot be answered precisely for electrons without ignoring the other; alternatively, both questions can be given an imprecise answer. As the wavelength of electrons is intimately connected with their speed, one has to accept an accurate knowledge of the speed (wavelength) and ignorance of position, or the converse, or *inaccurate* knowledge of both. This is the famous Heisenberg Uncertainty Principle. Quantum theory is a set of mathematical rules for calculating the behaviour of fundamental particles in accordance with the Uncertainty Principle. In spite of its equivocal-sounding name, the principle has led to an enormous increase in the accuracy with which physical phenomena can be described and predicted. Quantum theory includes all that previous theories did and more.

Quantum theory grew up in the same epoch as the Theory of Relativity. Heroic attempts have been made to combine the two, but with only partial success so far. Relativity is concerned with all motion and all physical laws, but its characteristic manifestations occur only when something is moving with nearly the velocity of light. Quantum theory is likewise all-embracing, but its typical phenomena almost always occur when something on the minute atomic scale is in question. Consequently, the vast majority of everyday mechanics needs no more than the classical theory laid down by Newton, which is neither relativistic nor quantum.

Relativity.

Historically, relativity grew out of attempts to measure the speed with which the earth moved through that hypothetical medium, called the ether, which was supposed at that time to be the bearer of light waves. To take a simple analogy: sound waves travel through still air with a certain definite speed, v. If you move through the air with speed v' towards oncoming sound waves, they will pass you at the speed $v + v'$. Michelson and Morley, in their celebrated experiment of 1887, failed to find the corresponding behaviour on the part of light. This is so important an experiment that it has been repeated, and repeatedly discussed, ever since. In October 1958 the latest and most accurate confirmation of the Michelson–Morley result was announced. It seems as if light always travels with the same speed relative to an observer, however fast he moves relative to anything else. Einstein put it this way: two observers moving with any constant velocity relative to each other will always agree that light travels past them at the same speed; this speed is denoted by c, and is approximately 186,000 miles per second.

This postulate, logically developed, leads to remarkable conclusions. For instance: if you walk from tail to nose of an aircraft at 4 m.p.h. and the plane is receding from me at 300 m.p.h., then you recede from me at 304 m.p.h. "Common sense," Newton, and Einstein would all agree on this. But if you could walk at $0{\cdot}25c$ and the plane moved at $0{\cdot}5c$, the Newtonian mechanics would give your recession speed as $0{\cdot}75c$, whereas Einsteinian relativity would give about $0{\cdot}67c$. Although at the everyday speed of 300 m.p.h., the disagreement, though present in principle, is absolutely negligible, at speeds near that of light it becomes very pronounced. Many experiments show that the relativity answer is right.

Equivalence of mass and energy.

Another famous consequence of relativity is the equation $E = mc^2$, connecting energy, E, with mass, m. c is so great that when mass is converted to energy a small mass gives a large energy. The grim demonstration of this was given to the world at Hiroshima; a more hopeful one at Calder Hall, the world's first nuclear power station. The life-giving energy of the sun is derived from nuclear processes which consume mass and deliver energy according to this equation.

Mass and rest mass.

"Mass" is far from being a simple notion. The only complication we shall note here is that the mass of a body is not necessarily constant. A stationary body can be observed to have a mass called its *rest mass*. If the body moves, it has energy of motion and therefore, according to Einstein's mass–energy equation, it increases its mass. Mass thus depends on speed, but in such a way that there is very little change unless the speed approaches that of light. Many experiments on atomic particles demonstrate this. The interesting question now arises: do all fundamental particles have rest mass? or do some have mass derived solely from their energy? The answer appears to be that photons and neutrinos have no rest mass; all other particles have. The Table on F14 gives their rest masses.

Special theory of relativity.

The mathematical development of Einstein's ideas, leading to the conclusions just referred to, constitutes the Special Theory of Relativity. Stated more generally, the theory raises the question whether two observers in uniform relative motion could ever detect, as a result of their relative speed, any difference in the physical laws governing matter, motion, and light. To this, Special Relativity answers: No. The detailed theory involves special consideration of the results the two observers would obtain when measuring (i) the spatial distance, and (ii) the time interval, between the same two events. It turns out that they would not agree on these two points. They would agree, however, on the value of a certain quantity made up jointly of the spatial distance and the time interval in a somewhat complex combination. The intimate mixture of space and time in this quantity has led to the treatment of the three space dimensions and time on an equivalent footing. Hence the frequent references to time as the "fourth dimension." Minkowski devised an extremely elegant presentation of relativity theory by using an extension of ordinary geometry to four dimensions. A line drawn in his four-dimensional space represents the path of a particle in space and time, *i.e.*, the whole history of the particle. Thus the movement of particles in the ordinary world is turned into the geometry of lines in Minkowski's four-dimensional world of "space-time."

Relativity and Gravitation.

The apparently innocuous extension of the preceding ideas to include observers in accelerated relative motion opened up new fields of mathematical complexity, but enabled Einstein to bring gravitation into the argument. In speaking of atoms and particles we have not yet mentioned gravity. This is because the electrical and magnetic forces acting between the particles constituting matter are much stronger than the gravitational; gravity need not enter atomic theory at all. But in the discussion of astronomical problems and the movements of large-scale, electrically uncharged bodies, it has been usual, ever since Newton, to say that two bodies of mass m_1 and m_2, separated by a distance r attract one another with a force proportional to m_1m_2/r^2. This is Newton's inverse square law of gravitation. With this, Newton explained the movements of planets and comets and the falling to earth of the apple from his tree.

The apple's fall is accelerated, and we observe this by noting its position relative to certain marks fixed with respect to us, and by timing it with some sort of clock. This system of location in space and time may be called our "frame of reference." We therefore assert that, in our frame of reference, the apple falls down with an acceleration which Newton saw no alternative but to attribute to a thing called gravitational attraction. Galileo had shown that *all* bodies fall with the same acceleration at all points, and we can now rephrase this by saying that in our frame of reference there is a constant gravitational attraction or *uniform gravitational field*. (This last statement and Galileo's demonstration only refer strictly to points fairly near the earth's surface; at greater distances the gravitational field decreases and is therefore not uniform.)

Now suppose a collection of falling bodies is observed by an intelligent creature, designated C, who inhabits one of them. C has his own frame of reference fixed relative to him. In C's frame neither his own body, nor any of the others, is accelerated, and therefore he has no reason to suppose a gravitational force is acting on them. We have, therefore, the following situation:

(i) in our frame, fixed relative to us, we find all the bodies falling subject to a gravitational pull;

(ii) in *C*'s frame, undergoing accelerated fall relative to us, no gravitational field is apparent.

It looks, therefore, as if one has only to choose the correct frame of reference for the measurements in order to remove the need for any assumptions about the existence of gravitational fields. This is a simple illustration of the connection between gravitation and frames of reference for the measurement of space and time. Einstein's General Theory of Relativity extends this to cover non-uniform gravitational fields and shows that what Newton taught us to call the gravitational field of material bodies is better thought of as a peculiarity of the space and time in the neighbourhood of such bodies. Since space–time, as we mentioned above, can be expressed in geometrical terms, Einstein has transformed the theory of gravitation into an exercise (a difficult one) in the geometry of space-time. Other physicists, in Einstein's tradition, are trying to turn *all* physics into geometry, but no one knows whether this is really feasible.

All this abstruse work is much more than a demonstration of mathematical power and elegance. Observable phenomena which fall outside the scope of Newton's theory of gravitation are accounted for by relativity. One is the small but definite discrepancy between the actual orbit of the planet Mercury and the predictions of Newton's theory. Another is the bending of stellar light rays as they pass close to the sun, an effect which results in the apparent displacement of the position of the star. A third is the effect of a gravitational field on the wavelength of light emitted by atoms. Similar atoms in different places in a gravitational field emit radiations with slightly different wavelengths. For example, the light from an atom in the intense field of a star should have slightly longer wavelength than the corresponding light from an atom on earth. This effect has always proved very difficult to detect with certainty. However, Einstein's prediction was verified with moderate accuracy in 1960 by a very subtle method which was purely terrestrial in its operation. The atoms being compared were placed at the top and bottom of a water tower and the difference in their emission was detected by means that belong rather to nuclear physics than to astronomy.

Quantum Theory and Relativity Combined.

The atomic family table refers to "antiparticles." The theory which first introduced such things in 1934 is due to the Cambridge physicist Dirac and was epoch-making. Dirac conceived an equation to describe the motion of electrons subject to the laws of both quantum theory and relativity. His achievement was thus to synthesise these two great ideas. The spin of the electron was originally a supposition that helped to make sense of spectroscopic observations of light emitted from atoms. Dirac's equation made spin a logical consequence of the union of relativity and quantum theory. Perhaps even more important was the brilliant inference that the equation for the electron implied the existence of another particle having the same mass and spin but with a positive instead of a negative electric charge. This object is called the electron's antiparticle and is now well known as a positron.

A positron and electron can be created simultaneously (" pair production ") and can annihilate each other when they collide.

Every particle is now believed to imply an antiparticle, so it is conceivable that the universe could have been (but isn't) an anti-universe, *i.e.*, all the electrons and protons might have been positrons and antiprotons and so on. The laws of physics would still have been applicable, however.

Not all particles are charged electrically but, when they are, their antiparticles have equal charges of the opposite sign. Whenever charged particles interact the total amount of electric charge is the same before and after whatever events occur. This is called the law of conservation of charge.

Conservation Laws.

Parity. Charge conservation and the conservation of energy (**F 17(2)**) are only two of a considerable number of conservation laws. Readers who have studied mechanics will also be aware of the conservation of momentum and of angular momentum. A conservation law is the proposition that in the course of physical happenings such and such a quantity is " conserved," *i.e.*, maintains a constant value.

The establishment of conservation laws is playing a great part in our growing understanding of elementary particles although the things that are conserved are somewhat abstruse. One of them is called parity.

Any reader who looks in a mirror knows that the left- and right-hand sides of his face are interchanged in the image. Fortunately mirrors do not also turn the image upside down, but, if they did, the face would then have undergone what is called " a parity transformation." A screwdriver driving a right-handed screw downwards becomes, on parity transformation, a screwdriver driving a left-handed screw upwards. The law of conservation of parity is a way of asserting that any physical process that goes on in the world could equally well go on—obeying the same laws—in a parity transformed world. There is nothing left-handed that does not in principle have a right-handed counterpart.

For many years this belief was strongly held. It came as something of a shock when, in 1957, after theoretical proposals by Lee and Yang in America, Wu and co-workers proved that parity was not always conserved. To understand Wu's experiment, we must recall that nuclei can have intrinsic spin. Suppose the axis of spin were downwards into the page and the rotation were suitable for driving an ordinary screw into the page. Then Wu showed that beta-rays from such a nucleus are emitted *preferentially upwards*, *i.e.*, against the direction of travel of the screw. The parity transformed version of this would have the beta-rays preferentially emitted in the same direction as the travel of the screw and, if parity is conserved, this process would happen too. But it does not. If the beta-rays in the experiment had been emitted in equal numbers up and down, then the parity transformed version would have had this feature too, and thus parity would have been conserved.

Of the four types of force referred to on **F 13(1)**, only the weak interaction does not conserve parity. The whole matter is bound up with the antineutrino which is emitted simultaneously with the negative beta-ray. It appears that antineutrinos are always " right-handed " which means that if one could look at an antineutrino receding from us it would be seen to be spinning clockwise.

Modern research on elementary particles is greatly concerned to find out which types of process obey which conservation laws. The parity surprise is only one of the stimulating shocks that this type of work is heir to. It is very much in the tradition of Einstein, part of whose monumental contribution to physics was his demonstration of the need to analyse conservation laws.

Conclusion.

Over a century's development of the atomic ideas has brought a progressive, if jerky, increase in the mathematical precision of the theories. In some fields of particle physics, observations to one part in a million, or even better, can be explained, to that level of accuracy, by the existing theories. At the same time, however, the theories have lost visual definition. An atom as an invisible but none the less solid billiard ball was easy enough; so was a light wave conceived like a sound wave in air. Even after Rutherford, an atom consisting of a miniature solar system merely exchanged the solid billiard ball for a system of revolving billiard balls and was no great obstacle to visualisation. But since quantum theory and the Uncertainty Principle, every unambiguous visualisation of fundamental wave-particles leaves out half the picture, and although the electrons are in the atom, we can no longer represent them in definite orbits. The moral seems to be that visualisation is unnecessary, or at best a partial aid to thought. All the theoretical knowledge is in the equations, and these are very precise. Hence the non-physicists' grumble—that physics is too mathematical these days—has some justification, and hence also the growing distinction in physics between the theoreticians, who are usually mathematically trained, and the experimenters, who can rarely read the papers their theoretical colleagues write, but provide the results for them to write about.

THE PROPERTIES OF MATTER IN BULK.

One of the most obvious and at the same time most wonderful things about the properties of matter is their great variety. Think of air, diamond, mercury, rubber, snow, gold, pitch, asbestos. . . . Even the differences of state of the same chemical substance are remarkable enough, ice, water, and steam, for example. One of the aims of physics is to reach an understanding of all these different properties by explaining them in terms of the behaviour of the particles discussed in the previous section (F9–17). The widespread success with which this imposing programme has been carried out indicates the maturity of physics. It is difficult to think of any major property of matter in bulk for which there is not some attempted theoretical explanation, though future physicists will no doubt regard some present-day theories as rudimentary or incorrect.

Physics, Statistics, and Thermodynamics.

Take a number equal to the population of London, multiply it by itself, and multiply the product by another million. The answer is about the number of molecules in 1 cubic centimetre of ordinary air. They are constantly moving about and colliding with one another. Even if the nature of the molecules and their laws of motion were perfectly understood, it would clearly be impracticable to calculate the exact paths described by each particle of so vast an assembly. This difficulty brought into being a whole branch of physics concerned with calculating the overall or average properties of large numbers of particles. Just as statisticians will provide the average height, income, expectation of life, and so on, of the population of London, without knowing everything about every individual, so statistical physicists can work out average properties of molecules or atoms in large groups. This important branch of physics is called *Statistical Mechanics*. It was founded in the nineteenth century by Maxwell, Boltzmann, and Gibbs and is still being actively developed.

Consider now all the molecules in 1 cubic centimetre of air contained in a small box. They are continually bombarding the walls of the box and bouncing off. This hail of impacts (it is actually about 10^{23} impacts per square centimetre per second) is the cause of the pressure which the gas exerts against the walls of the box. Now suppose we pump air in until there is twice as much as before, though the box is still the same size and at the same temperature. This means that the density of the gas (*i.e.*, the mass of 1 unit of volume) has doubled. We should now expect twice as many impacts per second on the walls as before, and consequently twice the pressure. We therefore arrive at a conclusion that, if the volume and temperature are constant, the pressure of a gas is proportional to its density. This is one of the simplest statistical arguments that can be checked against observation; in fact, it stands the test very well.

Heat, temperature, and energy.

The proviso about the temperature remaining the same is an important one for the following reason. In the nineteenth century there was much discussion about the nature of heat. To Joule we owe the now well-established view that heat is equivalent to mechanical work. In one of his experiments, in the 1840s, the work necessary to rotate paddle wheels against the resistance of water in a tank generated heat that caused a slight rise in the temperature of the water. Joule found out exactly how much work was equivalent to a given quantity of heat. However, one can do other things with work besides generate heat; in particular, work creates motion, as when one pushes a car. Bodies in motion possess a special form of energy, called kinetic energy, which is equal to the work done in accelerating them from a state of rest. We have, then, three closely connected ideas: work, heat, and kinetic energy. Now according to the views of the nineteenth century, which are still accepted, any heat given to a gas simply increases the kinetic energy of its molecules; the hotter the gas, the faster its molecules are moving. If, therefore, the gas in our box is allowed to get hotter, there is an increase in molecular speed, and the impacts on the walls become correspondingly more violent. But this means the pressure increases, so we have another law: if the density remains the same, the pressure increases if the temperature does.

Laws of Thermodynamics.

Such considerations as these have been pursued with great elaboration and subtlety. The notions of heat, temperature, energy, and work—familiar but vague in everyday life—have been given precise definitions, and the relations between them have been enshrined in the Laws of Thermodynamics. Enshrined is perhaps a suitable word, because these laws are so soundly and widely based on experimental results that they have greater prestige than any others in physics. If any proposed physical law comes in conflict with thermodynamics then so much the worse for that law—it has to be revised. It is sometimes asserted that no one is properly educated who does not understand the Second Law of thermodynamics. We cannot, therefore, leave this section without at least stating the two best known thermodynamic laws:

First Law: *If any physical system is given a quantity of heat, and if the system performs some work, then the energy of the system increases by an amount equal to the excess of heat given over work done.* This law asserts that heat, energy, and work are convertible one into the other, and that all such transactions balance exactly. This is one form of a principle accepted as fundamental in all science, *viz.*, the Principle of the Conservation of Energy, according to which energy can never be created or destroyed, but only changed from one form to another.

Second Law: *It is impossible to make an engine which will continuously take heat from a heat source and, by itself turn it all into an equivalent amount of mechanical work.* In fact, all engines which produce work from heat—steam engines for example—always use only a fraction of the heat they take in and give up the rest to some relatively cool part of the machine. The Second Law makes this obligatory on all work-from-heat devices. This statement of the Second Law has an engineering ring about it and, indeed, it arose from the work of the nineteenth-century French engineer Carnot. Nevertheless, it can be rephrased in very abstract terms, and has been applied with unbroken success to all fields of science involving the transfer of heat and allied matters. It sets a definite limit to the kinds of physical process that can be conceived to take place. Nothing has been known to contravene it.

The States of Matter.

The molecular motion in gases has been referred to in the previous section. Tacitly it was assumed that each molecule acted independently of all others, except that collisions occurred between them. In reality, molecules exert attractive forces on one another and if a gas is cooled so that molecular movements become relatively sluggish, a time comes when the attractive forces succeed in drawing the molecules close together to form a liquid. This process is called condensation.

The molecules in a liquid are packed tightly together and they impede each others' movements. On the other hand, movement still persists, and the molecules struggle about like people in a milling crowd. Besides wandering about, the molecules vibrate. These motions represent the energy contained in the liquid.

The fact that the molecules, though irregularly packed, can still slip past one another and move from place to place, explains the essential property of liquids that distinguishes them from solids—ability to flow. As a matter of fact, although the rather vague assertion that in a liquid molecules are irregularly packed would be generally accepted, there is no agreed opinion on what the irregularity is actually like. Indeed, not only the precise structure of liquids, but the theory of liquids in general, is fraught with such considerable mathematical difficulties that the liquid state is much less well understood than the solid or gaseous.

Most solids are crystals. The popular idea of a crystal is of something which has a more or less regular geometrical form with faces that glint in the light—like snowflakes or gems. However, crystallinity really depends on a regular inner pattern of the atoms, and may or may not show itself on the visible surface. A lump of lead, for example, is crystalline, though it may not look it.

The actual arrangement of the atoms in a crystal can be extremely complex. Some are quite simple, however. The largest model of a crystal structure must surely be the 400-ft. "Atomium" building in the 1958 Brussels Exhibition. This consisted of eight balls, representing atoms, situated at the corners of a cube, and one more ball exactly in the middle. Imagine this repeated in all directions so that every ball is the centre of a cube whose corners are the eight neighbouring balls. This is known to crystallographers and physicists as the "body-centred cubic structure"; it is the actual arrangement of atoms in iron, sodium, chromium, and some other metals. If every ball, instead of being the centre of a cube, were the centre of a regular tetrahedron (a solid figure with four equal triangular faces), and had its four neighbours at the corners of the tetrahedron, then we should have the "diamond structure." This is how the carbon atoms are arranged in diamonds.

In crystals the atoms are locked into a regular ordered structure by attractive forces which give the solid its rigidity and prevent it from flowing. The atoms are so close together that any attempt to press them closer involves crushing or distorting the atoms—a process they resist strongly. This explains why solids (and liquids too) are so difficult to compress. Gases can easily be compressed because there is so much space between the molecules.

The distinction between solid and liquid is not so sharp as is commonly supposed. A lump of dough will not bounce, but is plastic; a steel ball-bearing is very elastic and bounces excellently, but one cannot mould it in the fingers. Neither dough nor steel qualifies for description as a liquid. There are, however, substances which can be moulded like plasticine into a ball that will then bounce very well on the floor like an elastic solid, and finally, if left on a flat table, will spread into a pool and drip off the edge like a liquid. There is no point in trying to force such things into rigid categories. One may say instead that for short, sharp impacts the material behaves like an elastic solid, but under long-sustained forces it flows like a liquid. The properties of these, and many other anomalous materials, are increasingly engaging the attention of those who study the science of flow—*rheology*. It is interesting to see how many familiar and important materials exhibit peculiar rheological behaviour—paint, dough, ball-pen ink, cheese, unset cement, and solutions of nylon and other plastics are only a few examples.

Inside a Crystalline Solid.

We now return to our wallpaper analogy of crystal structure and give some free play to our visual imagination.

Suppose we have walls papered with a regular pattern of, say, roses, fuchsias, and green leaves. These represent the different kinds of atoms in the solid. Careful observation shows that the whole pattern is shimmering. The flowers and leaves are not stationary, but are undergoing slight random oscillations about their proper positions. In a crystal these movements are called thermal vibrations, and are never absent. The hotter the crystal, the more the vibration, and at a high enough temperature the vibrations become so great that the atoms get right out of position and the pattern disappears altogether, *i.e.*, the crystal melts. Thermal vibrations are essential to the theory of solids, and are responsible for numerous physical properties.

Next we note something extraordinary about some of the papered walls. On these the paper has been hung in irregular patches fitted together like a not very well-made jig-saw puzzle. Lines of roses which should be vertical are horizontal in some patches, oblique in others. This represents the situation in most ordinary solids, for they consist of many small pieces of crystal irregularly packed together. Such material is called *polycrystalline*, and the small pieces are *crystal grains*. Crystal grains may be almost any size, sometimes visible to the naked eye, as often on galvanised iron.

However, on one wall, we see excellent regularity and no obvious patches at all. The physicist would call this a *single crystal*, and several techniques exist for preparing them. Natural single crystals can be found, and there are some beautiful large single crystals of rock salt. But on examining the single crystal wall closely, we find a number of places where the paperhanger has failed to make adjacent pieces register perfectly—there is a slight disjointedness. This occurs in real single crystals, and the line along which the structure fails to register is called a *dislocation*. These are much studied by physicists because of their bearing on the mechanical properties of solids, on the yielding of metals under strong stress, for instance.

This by no means exhausts the possibilities of the wallpaper analogy; several other phenomena can be found. For example, in a place where there should be a fuchsia there is actually a daffodil—something completely foreign to the pattern. Or perhaps a small wrongly shaped leaf is jammed between the proper leaves in a place that should really be blank. These represent chemical impurity atoms. The first is called *substitutional*, because it occupies the position of an atom that should be there, the second is called *interstitial*, because it does not. Substitutional impurities of indium metal, deliberately added to the semi-conductor silicon, make possible the manufacture of transistors (*see* Section L). Some steels derive their valuable properties from interstitial carbon atoms within the iron pattern.

What physicists call a vacancy would occur if a flower or leaf were simply missing. Remembering that all the atoms are vibrating, we should not be surprised if occasionally an atom jumps into a neighbouring vacancy if there happens to be one, *i.e.*, the atom and the vacancy change places. Later this may occur again. In the course of time, a rose which was near the ceiling may make its way to the floor by jumping into vacant rose positions when they occur near enough. This process, which the physicist calls *diffusion*, is also analogous to the game in which numbers or letters can be moved about in a flat box because there is one vacant space to permit adjustment. The more vacancies there are in a crystal, the faster diffusion occurs. It is, in fact, very slow in solids, but is nevertheless evidence that apparently quiescent materials are really internally active.

Metals, Electricity, and Heat.

There is ample evidence that inside metals there are large numbers of free electrons. To illuminate this statement let us take sodium metal as an example. One single sodium atom has a nucleus with eleven protons; there are therefore eleven electrons in the atom. The outermost one is easily detached, leaving a positively charged sodium ion behind. We may think of these ions arranged in the three-dimensional pattern characteristic of sodium crystals. It is the same as the iron structure previously described. The detached electrons, one per atom, occupy the spaces in between. The usual metaphor is that the structure of ions is permeated by a "gas" of electrons. Like all visualisations of fundamental particles, this must be taken as a rough approximation. The important point is that the electrons in the gas are not bound to individual atoms but may wander freely about the crystal, hindered only by the collisions they make with the vibrating ions.

This is the picture as it appeared to physicists of the first decade of this century, and we can explain many properties of metals with it. Naturally the theory has developed greatly since then, thanks to the great work of Lorentz, Sommerfeld, and Bloch; it now relies heavily on quantum theory, but it is surprising how little violence is done to modern ideas by the simple picture we are using.

The free electrons move randomly in all directions at thousands of miles per hour. If the metal is connected across a battery it experiences an electric field. Electrons are negatively charged particles, and are therefore attracted to the electrically positive end of the metal. They can move through the metal because they are free; this flow is not possible to those electrons which remain bound to the ions. The function of the battery is to keep the flow going and, for as long as it is going, it is the electric current.

The flow of electrons is not unimpeded. They constantly collide with the ions and are deflected from the path of flow. This hindrance is what the electrician calls *electrical resistance*. The electric force, due to the battery or a dynamo, accelerates the electrons, thus giving them extra energy; but they lose this to the ions at collisions because the ions recoil and vibrate more than before. The net effect of innumerable collisions is to increase the thermal vibrations of the ions, *i.e.*, to make the metal hotter. This is the explanation of the fact well known to every user of electric irons; that electric current heats the conductor. If a strong current is passed through a wire, the heating is so great the wire glows, as in electric-light bulbs, or melts and breaks, as in blown fuses.

If one end of a metal rod is heated we soon feel the heat at the other end; metals are excellent thermal conductors. This is because the mobile free electrons carry the heat energy down the rod, passing it on to the ions by colliding with them. Substances without free electrons cannot do this, nor can they conduct electricity well; so we have, in the free electrons, an explanation of the fact that the good electrical conductors are the good heat conductors. For technical purposes, it would be useful to have electrical insulators that would conduct heat well, and *vice versa*; but this is almost a contradiction in terms, and one can only compromise.

Non-conductors and Semi-conductors.

There are some elements, and numerous compounds, in which all the electrons are so tightly bound to their parent atoms that free electron flow is impossible. These materials are electrical and thermal insulators.

Let us return to our sodium atom. It readily loses its outer electron, forming a positive ion. The ion is very stable; indeed, its electron arrangement resembles the "closed shell" belonging to the inert gas neon. The chlorine atom, on the other hand, would have a very stable structure, resembling the inert gas argon, if only it could be given one extra electron to complete the closed shell. If the outer sodium electron were given to a chlorine atom we should have two stable ions, one positive and one negative. These would then attract each other and form a compound. This is just how common salt, sodium chloride, is formed, and its crystals consist of a regular network of alternate sodium and chlorine ions. As all the electrons are bound to ions, it is not surprising that salt will not conduct electricity or heat to any appreciable extent. Not all insulating compounds are built on this pattern, but all have structures which bind the electrons tightly.

We have seen (F18) that Nature does not permit a hard-and-fast distinction between solids and liquids; nor does she between conductors and insulators. Over a hundred years ago, Faraday knew of substances which would conduct electricity, but rather badly. A common one is the graphite in pencils. Others are the elements selenium, germanium, and silicon, and a considerable number of compounds. Such substances are called semi-conductors.

Semi-conductors conduct badly because they have so few free electrons, many thousands of times fewer than metals. In very cold germanium—say, 200 degrees below freezing—all the electrons are tightly bound to atoms and the substance is an insulator. It differs from normal insulators in that, on warming it, the gradually increasing thermal vibration of the crystal detaches some of the electrons, for they are only moderately tightly bound. The warmer the crystal becomes, the more of its electrons become detached and the better it conducts electricity. By about the temperature of boiling water, there are so many freed electrons that conduction is moderately good, though less good than in metals. This is basic semi-conductor behaviour. Because transistors were made of germanium, and because they are of such great technical importance, more knowledge has accumulated about germanium than about any other material. *See also* **Transistor, Section L.**

Magnetism.

The most important thing about magnetism is that it is inseparably connected with electricity. Oersted showed this in July 1820, when he deflected a magnetic compass needle by passing an electric current through a wire near it. Since then, many experiments have shown that wherever a current flows there will certainly be a magnetic field in the surrounding space. The laws of this are very well known now—they are the Maxwell equations previously referred to (F13). However, most people first meet magnetism when, as children, they pick up pins with a magnet. Where is the electricity here? and what is a magnet?

The explanation of magnetism exemplifies beautifully the technique of explaining the bulk properties of matter in terms of fundamental particles. In the atoms the electrons are moving, and a moving electric charge constitutes an electric current. Therefore each moving electron is a tiny source of magnetism. It does not immediately follow that every atom is a source of magnetism because it might—and often does—happen that the magnetic effect of different electrons in the atom cancel out. In helium atoms, for example, the two electrons have equal but opposed magnetic effects. Nevertheless, some atoms and ions have a net effect called their *magnetic moment*. This simply means they behave like tiny magnets. Crystals containing such atoms will be magnetic, though the magnetism is much weaker than in ordinary magnets because the different atoms largely annul one another's effects. In a very limited number of crystals, however, the magnetic ions act on one another in a special way which forces all the atomic magnets to point in the same direction. The total effect of many co-operating atoms is very strong and the crystal becomes what we normally call a magnet. Iron acts like this, so do cobalt and nickel, the rarer elements gadolinium and dysprosium, and a fair number of alloys. On the whole, this behaviour, which is called *ferromagnetism*, is very rare. The reason for the co-operation of all the atomic magnets is not explained to everyone's satisfaction yet, though the key idea was given by Heisenberg in 1928.

In the section dealing with the electron it was pointed out that every electron has an *intrinsic* magnetic moment. This is in addition to any effect simply due to the electron's motion round a nucleus. The net effects of ions are therefore partly due to the intrinsic magnetism of electrons. In the ferromagnetic metals the latter is by far the most important contribution. Thus we pick up pins, and benefit from magnets in other ways, because innumerable fundamental particles act in co-operation for reasons that are still somewhat obscure. It is interesting to ask whether the electrons responsible for magnetism are the same free electrons that allow the metals to conduct electricity. It is thought not.

We are accustomed to think of magnets as metallic. Actually the magnet originally discovered by the Chinese was the mineral lodestone, which is a non-metallic oxide of iron. Nowadays a number of non-metallic magnets are made. They are called *ferrites*, and some are insulators and some are semi-conductors. The combination of magnetism and insulation is technically very valuable in radio, radar, and other applications. The explanation of ferrite behaviour is related to that of metallic ferromagnetism, but is not the same.

Conclusion.

The aim of the second part of this account of physics is to show how our conception of fundamental particles allows us to build theories of the properties of matter. This very aim shows that the two "major divisions" of physics referred to at the beginning (F9) are divided only in the way that labour is divided by co-operating workers to lighten the task. For the task of physics is a very great one—no less than to explain the behaviour of matter; and since the universe, living and inanimate, is made of matter, physics must necessarily underlie all the other sciences.

III. THE WORLD OF THE CHEMISTS

WHAT CHEMISTRY IS ABOUT.

The science of chemistry is concerned with the properties of atoms, the laws governing their combination to form molecules, and, more generally, with the behaviour of materials composed of large numbers of molecules. Thus chemistry borders on or, rather, interpenetrates physics—a fact illustrated by the existence of professional journals devoted to "chemical physics" and "physical chemistry." Physics is more concerned with the fundamental nature of matter and radiation; chemistry concentrates on the ways in which atoms combine, or can be made to combine, with each other to form innumerable compounds. Chemistry also merges with the life sciences where it deals, as in biochemistry, with the properties of the complex molecular building blocks of living organisms, *e.g.*, proteins, carbohydrates, nucleic acids. Because of its comprehensiveness, the science of chemistry has been subdivided into what were at one time convenient sub-sciences, *e.g.*, organic chemistry, electrochemistry, but here too the borderlines are becoming progressively blurred. Our task here will be to outline some of the ideas in use by present-day chemists.

ELEMENTS AND COMPOUNDS.

Electron Shells and Stability.

The reader will find in Part II a brief description of the atom and definitions of atomic number, atomic weight, isotope, and other terms. The simplest atom is hydrogen (H) with atomic number 1. Some common elements with their chemical symbols and atomic numbers are:—carbon (C) 6; oxygen (O) 8; sodium (Na) 11; chlorine (Cl) 17; calcium (Ca) 20; silver (Ag) 47; and uranium (U) 92. Let us now consider atoms in more detail.

The electrons in atoms move in well-defined *orbits* and the orbits fall into well-defined groups called *shells*. If all the orbits in a shell have electrons actually present in them the shell is *filled* or *closed* and this confers on the shell an unusual stability or inertness. Conversely, unfilled shells lead to activity and the electrons in the incompletely filled shells largely determine the chemical and physical properties of the element and are responsible for the combination of atoms to form molecules. The inner shell, *i.e.*, the one nearest the nucleus, can accommodate only two electrons (the element helium has just that number) and the next two shells can hold eight each. Large atoms, *e.g.*, lead, radium, have many filled shells and, subject to special exceptions, the general rule is that the inner shells are the filled ones and the outer shell may be incomplete. Elements which have equal numbers of electrons in their outer shell resemble each other. Thus the elements with complete electronic shells are chemically unreactive gases, *e.g.*, argon and neon (minor constituents of the atmosphere). Elements with just one electron in the outer shell are highly reactive metals, *e.g.*, sodium and potassium, whereas those with just one electron too few are also reactive but are not metals, *e.g.*, chlorine, bromine, iodine.

Molecules, Ions, and Bonds.

The general tendency of matter is for those changes that are possible to go on happening until a lasting arrangement or *stable state* is reached. Atoms with closed shells are stable but atoms with unfilled shells can achieve stability in several ways, of which two are as follows:

(*i*) *Electron sharing.*

When atoms share electrons, the resulting structure, composed of several atoms, is known as a molecule. The simplest case is the molecule of hydrogen, composed of two atoms each contributing one electron. Thus each atom will have a share of two electrons which is the number required to fill completely the inner shell. The shared electrons constitute a *chemical bond* and confer stability on the resulting hydrogen molecule.

A more complex molecule is carbon tetrachloride, CCl_4. Here the carbon atom with four electrons in its outer shell is bonded to four chlorine atoms each of which needs one electron to complete a set of eight. Thus by sharing the electrons each of the five atoms can form a complete shell of eight electrons. The properties of the resulting molecular species do not usually bear any resemblance to the constituent atoms. Whereas molecular chlorine is a gas and carbon is a solid, carbon tetrachloride is a liquid which finds application as a dry cleaning fluid.

(*ii*) *Electron transfer.*

Another method of completing electron shells is by transfer of one or more electrons from an atom with one or two electrons in its outer shell to one with that number too few. Thus sodium, with one electron in its outer shell, will combine with chlorine, deficient in one electron. This results in two electronically stable species (ions), both of which carry electric charges. Thus the sodium will now have a net positive charge of 1 unit (11 protons, 10 electrons), whereas the chlorine has an excess negative charge (17 protons, 18 electrons). Because of these electric charges, solutions of ionic substances conduct electricity and this property is utilised in industrial processes such as electroplating and in the extraction of metals from their ores.

Thus the electrons which participate in the formation of chemical bonds are those in partly-filled shells (valence electrons), and the simplest and most stable type of bonds are those in which two electrons are shared (a covalent bond) and those in which there is a net transfer of electrons (an ionic bond). Sometimes, in order to attain a complete electronic shell, a chemical bond will require the sharing of four or even six electrons. The resulting molecules are highly reactive and will readily, and sometimes violently, combine with other molecules or atoms to achieve the greater stability associated with the two-electron covalent bond.

Molecules must not be envisaged as rigid assemblies of atoms with electrons uniformly distributed around the various nuclei. The properties of molecules are best acccounted for by imagining the atomic nuclei to be vibrating about mean positions the bonds acting like spiral springs, holding the nuclei together. The electrons form a mobile cloud of negative charge which sorrounds the nuclei. The valence electrons, constituting the bond between pairs of atoms, also have no fixed location but fluctuate about mean positions, more or less along the line joining the atoms. Although the electrons are shared, their mean position is not usually halfway between the two atoms but depends on the relative atomic sizes and charges. In the carbon–chlorine bond of carbon tetrachloride the valence electrons are subjected to electrical attractions due to 17 positive charges on the chlorine nucleus and 6 positive charges on the carbon nucleus. Although the forces due to the chlorine nucleus are partially compensated by the intervening negative charges of the complete electronic shells, they are stronger than the forces from the carbon nucleus, and the valence electrons are therefore pulled towards the chlorine atom which thus attains a net negative charge, leaving the carbon with a corresponding positive charge. The magnitude of this charge is less than that of an ion, and the carbon–chlorine bond should be symbolised $\overset{+}{C}-\overset{-}{Cl}$ to emphasise that separate positive and negative charges of equal magnitude are embodied in the structure, and are attracting each other as well as causing an electric field outside the molecule.

A pair of equal and opposite charges like this is called a *dipole* and is the electrical analogue of the ordinary magnet which has north and south *poles* instead of charges. Chemical bonds made with dipoles are called *polar bonds.* Most molecules, both simple and complex, are bound with polar bonds, but in the case of CCl_4 the four bonds are symmetrically arranged in space so that the electric effects of the dipoles cancel each other outside the molecule which therefore does not, as a whole, act like a dipole. On the other hand, the bond dipoles in a molecule may not cancel in this way (Fig. 1) in which case the whole molecule will possess the properties of a dipole *e.g.,* when subjected to an electric field it will rotate to align itself with the field just as a compass needle will line up with a magnetic field.

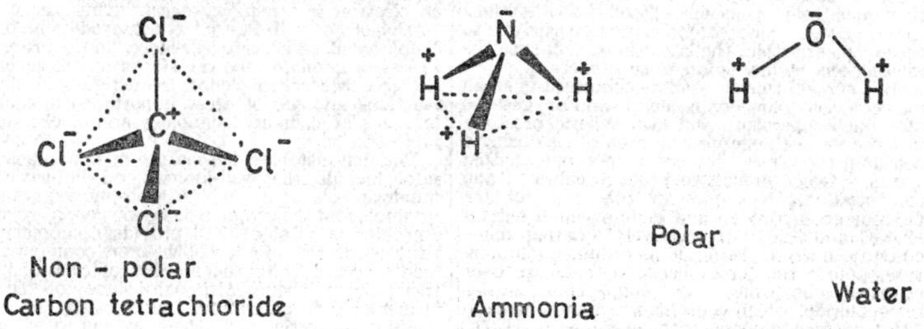

Fig. 1. The arrangement in space of molecules CCl_4, NH_3, and H_2O.

Atomic and Molecular Weights.

The masses of the electron and proton were determined early in the 20th century by ingenious experiments. The electronic mass is extremely small, about 9×10^{-28}g and the mass of a hydrogen atom is $1{\cdot}7 \times 10^{-24}$g, which indicates that the proton is 1,837 times heavier than the electron and that the mass of the atom is almost completely confined to the nucleus.

The molecular weight of a compound is the sum of the atomic weights (F10) of all the constituent atoms, *e.g.,* water (H_2O) and ethyl alcohol (C_2H_5OH) have molecular weights 18 and 46 respectively. This means that the alcohol molecule weighs more than the water molecule in the ratio 46 to 18. If therefore we take 18 g of water and 46 g of alcohol, both quantities will contain the same number of molecules. Similarly, 1 litre of water with 342 g of sugar dissolved in it, and 1 litre with 58·5 g of salt, will again contain the same number of dissolved molecules because the molecular weights of sugar ($C_{12}H_{22}O_{11}$) and salt (NaCl) are 342 and 58·5 respectively. In each case the number of grams taken is numerically equal to the molecular weight and this amount is called 1 *mole* of a substance or the *gram molecular weight.*

The word mole may also be used for atoms or ions and means, in general, that amount of molecules (or atoms or ions, as the case may be) such that the total number of them is equal to the number of atoms in 12 g of carbon (F10). This number, called Avogadro's number, is approximately 6×10^{23}. Thus one mole of any substance contains 6×10^{23} molecules of that substance and this fact makes the mole a very useful unit both in theory and practice.

Forces between Molecules.

Something has already been said (F17, 18) about the differences between solids, liquids, and gases and we may now put the question: what forces are responsible for the organisation of molecules in liquids or solids and their disorganisation in the gaseous state? Questions of this kind are of profound interest to chemists, physicists, and biologists.

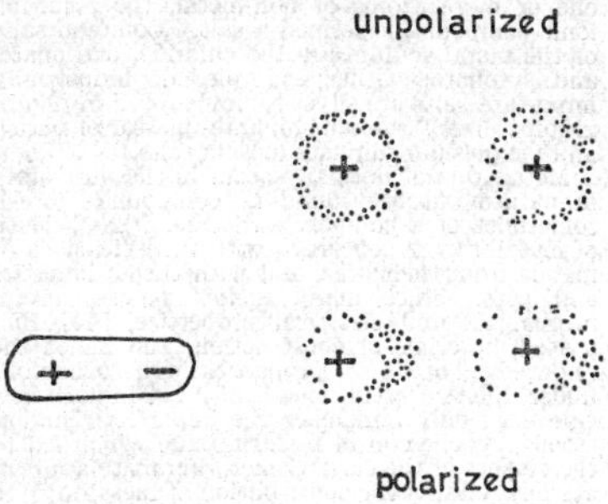

FIG. 2. Mutual polarisation of molecules by distortion of their electron clouds.

The forces which act between molecules depend mainly on the fact that the electrons orbiting a molecule form a mobile cloud of negative charge. If a polar molecule is brought up to another molecule, then the latter will become polarised, *i.e.,* its electronic cloud will be displaced with respect to the nucleus. This is shown in Fig. 2 and it is apparent that the formerly non-polar molecule has acquired a temporary polar character. In this state it will be able to polarise other nearby molecules, and the ease with which molecules are polarised depends on how strongly the electrons are held in position by the nuclear charge, and this in turn depends on the mean distance between the nucleus and the electronic cloud. Thus, the larger the molecule, the more easily the electron cloud can be distorted by a nearby dipole and hence the stronger are the intermolecular forces. These forces are attractions or *binding forces*. They can be disrupted by violent vibratory or other motions whose source is heat, as when a solid is first melted and then boiled and its molecules fly off in all directions to form a gas. Since strong attractions are due to ease of polarisation, the latter must influence the melting and boiling points of substances.

As a general rule substances composed of small molecules have low boiling points and are gaseous at room temperature and atmospheric pressure, because when they approach each other during a collision, the forces they exert upon one another are not strong enough to produce cohesion and condensation. Examples of this type of behaviour are hydrogen and helium which boil at −253°C and −269°C respectively. Larger molecules are likely to be liquid at ordinary temperature, and if the forces between them are even stronger, they may be solid. Thus carbon tetrachloride, which contains five atoms, boils at 77°C, whereas glucose, with 24 atoms ($C_6H_{12}O_6$) is a solid, melting at 146°C. Chemical compounds which are ionic in character are usually crystalline solids with high melting points (*e.g.*, common salt, quicklime) because ions, possessing permanent charges, exert stronger forces on one another than do molecules.

Metals and Salts.

It has already been explained that chemical elements are conveniently classified according to the number of electrons in the outer shell, because it is mainly those electrons which participate in chemical reactions and make bonds. Thus elements with 1, 2, or at most 3 electrons in the outer shell (*e.g.*, sodium, calcium, aluminium respectively) will undergo reactions which enable them to lose those electrons, *i.e.*, they will attempt to form ionic compounds. These elements are metallic, and when solid or liquid, conduct heat and electricity. On the other hand, elements which need 1 or 2 electrons to form a complete shell (*e.g.*, chlorine, oxygen respectively) can also form ionic compounds by reacting with a metal, though these elements are themselves classed as nonmetals and can be gases, liquids, or solids at room temperature. When a metal atom combines with one or more atoms of non-metal, the resulting ionic compound is termed a salt. Common salts of the metal sodium are the chloride, carbonate, and sulphate. Other examples of industrially important salts are silver bromide (used in photographic films), calcium sulphate (plaster of paris), and magnesium sulphate (epsom salts.)

Metals do not normally occur in the pure state in nature but are found as compounds (ores), sometimes of a complex structure. The science of metallurgy is concerned with the extraction of metals from their ores, and with their properties and uses. Since many metals possess useful mechanical and electrical properties, they find use as materials of construction, and hence the knowledge of their properties and behaviour under different conditions is of great importance. One need only remember the imperfectly understood phenomenon of metal fatigue which led to the crashes of the early Comet aircraft to appreciate how vital is the contribution of metallurgy to the process of engineering.

Although metals can be mixed with other metals to form alloys, the large majority of metallic compounds are the salts in which the metal is present as positive ion (*cation*), and the negative ion (*anion*) is composed of one or several non-metallic elements. Common anions are the chloride, bromide, iodide, nitrate, sulphate, phosphate, and carbonate. Metals with simple electron structures can form only one type of ion. Thus sodium, with one outer shell electron forms Na^+ and 1 electron; calcium with two outershell electrons forms Ca^{++} and 2 electrons. There are, however, a number of metals with more complex electronic structures, involving partially filled inner electronic shells and these can exist in a variety of ionic forms. They include many metals which find application as structural materials, *e.g.*, iron, copper, gold, platinum, nickel, chromium. For instance, iron can exist as Fe^{++} or Fe^{+++} and the process of removing a further electron from Fe^{++} is termed *oxidation*, and any chemical reagent which is capable of bringing about such a process is an *oxidising agent*. Conversely the addition of an electron is called *reduction* and the reagent which can give up an electron is a *reducing agent*. Thus the conversion of Fe^{++} to Fe^{+++} is achieved by an oxidising agent which is itself reduced in the process. Processes involving the transfer of one or several electrons are called Redox (reduction-oxidation) reactions and are of great importance in many branches of chemical technology and biochemical processes.

The non-metals which feature in the anions of salts include the well-known and industrially important elements, sulphur, phosphorus, iodine, bromine, and the common gases oxygen, nitrogen, and chlorine. **Table 1 (F23)** provides a summary of the classification of a few of the more common elements according to the number of electrons in their outer shell. Although some of these elements, *e.g.*, aluminium, undoubtedly possess metallic properties and others, *e.g.*, nitrogen, are non-metals, the dividing lines are not always so clearly defined and most of the compounds formed by elements near the centre of **Table 1** are of the covalent type.

ACIDS AND BASES.

pH Values.

Hydrogen occupies a unique position in **Table 1** According to its electronic structure it can be classified with sodium and potassium, as having one electron in its outer shell. It therefore readily forms cations, H^+, but it can hardly be called a metal. Having lost its electron, what remains is a proton (**F10**), a single positive charge. Thus we can compare sodium chloride, $Na^+ Cl^-$, with $H^+ Cl^-$, but whereas sodium chloride exists in the ionic form in the solid and liquid states and in solution, HCl is a covalent gas in the pure state, but readily ionises in solution, because the H^+ does not exist on its own, but attaches itself to a solvent molecule. Thus when HCl is dissolved in water, it ionises and the H^+ combines with the water: $HCl + H_2O \rightarrow (H^+ H_2O) + Cl^-$. This is a typical example of what is known as an *acid-base reaction*, an acid being defined as a substance which in solution can produce one or several protons (hydrogen ions), and the base as being a substance which can accept protons from an acid. In the above reaction HCl is the acid and H_2O the base, and the reaction consists of the transfer of the proton from acid to base. Other common acids include sulphuric acid ($2H^+ + SO_4^{--}$) and nitric acid ($H^+ + NO_3^-$). When ammonia (NH_3), a covalent gas, is dissolved in water, an acid base reaction also occurs: $NH_3 + HOH \rightarrow (NH_3.H^+) + OH^-$. Here water acts as acid, since it donates a proton to the ammonia, forming NH_4^+, the ammonium ion. When a proton is removed from water, the remainder, a negatively charged ion, is called the hydroxyl ion, OH^-. It has now been established that water can act either as an acid or a base, and in pure water two molecules of water can react: $H_2O + H_2O = (H^+ H_2O) + OH^-$, so that one molecule behaves as an acid and the other as a base. This phenomenon is called self-ionisation and also occurs in other solvents.

The extent to which water ionises is very small, thus 1 litre of "pure" water contains 10^{-7} moles each of H^+ and OH^- ions. However, when a stronger acid, *i.e.*, one that can produce more hydrogen ions than water, is added, the concentration of hydrogen ions increases and that of OH^- ions decreases correspondingly, so that the product of the amounts of H^+ and OH^- ions will always be constant and equal to 10^{-14} (see law of chemical equilibrium). It is important to be able to compare the strengths of acid solutions and this is done by reference to the concentration of hydrogen ions. The numerical measure is obtained by taking minus the logarithm of the hydrogen ion concentration and this number is called the *pH value* of the solution. Thus in pure water, the hydrogen ion concentration is 10^{-7} moles per litre and the *pH* value is therefore 7.

Vinegar, which is a dilute solution of acetic acid in water, has a hydrogen ion concentration of about 10^{-4} moles per litre; its *pH* is 4. Thus, solutions with a *pH* value below 7 are acidic (they contain an excess of hydrogen ions) and those with a *pH* value greater than 7 are basic (they contain an excess of OH^- ions). Many chemical and most biological reactions are extremely sensitive to small changes in the *pH* and steps must frequently be taken to adjust the *pH* to an optimum value for a given reaction. This is achieved by means of substances known as buffers, which have the capacity of mopping up or producing hydrogen ions and to maintain a constant *pH*. An example of this buffering action is the prevention of stomach acidity by the use of bicarbonates.

THE HYDROGEN BOND AND WATER.

Where hydrogen is covalently bonded to a small, fairly strongly electronegative atom, *i.e.*, one which requires 1, 2, or 3 electrons to fill its outer shell, the one electron which can be supplied by hydrogen is not shared equally by the two atoms but is pulled closer to the electronegative atom. The most common examples of this phenomenon are liquid water and ice. Here the electronegative atom is oxygen, as shown in **Fig 3.** The dots represent the outer shell electrons of oxygen and the crosses the electrons contributed by hydrogen. The oxygen atom 1 exerts a strong pull on the lone electron supplied by the hydrogen, so that at the position of the oxygen atom 2 it appears as though the hydrogen is in fact an ion (H^+), devoid of electrons, and since a pair of electrons of oxygen atom 2 are already pointing in the direction of this hydrogen atom, a weak bond will be formed. Thus the " hydrogen bond " consists of one hydrogen atom between two oxygen atoms. The actual strength of such a bond is only about 10 per cent of that of an ordinary covalent bond, and not very much energy is required to disrupt it. In terms of most chemical reactions the hydrogen bond is therefore not of great significance, but it is vital in reactions which occur with small changes in energy, *i.e.*, biochemical reactions, where the making and breaking of hydrogen bonds is frequently of supreme importance. It must also be

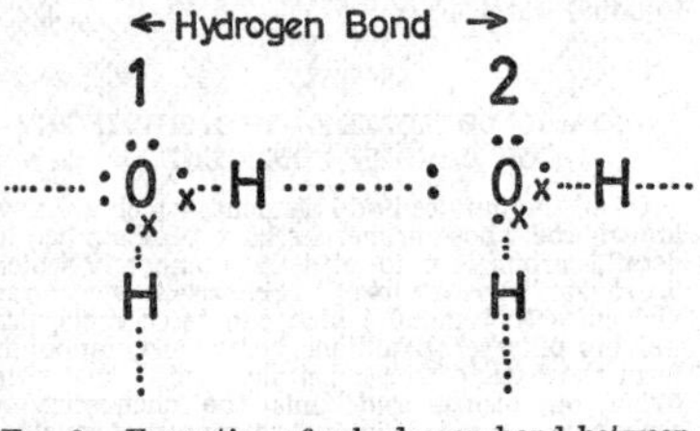

FIG. 3. Formation of a hydrogen bond between neighbouring water molecules.

borne in mind that all biological reactions take place in an aqueous medium which is highly hydrogen-bonded and it is well known that water is the essential substrate for all life processes, although it is not always appreciated that water is also the most anomalous of chemical compounds. It is one of very few substances that are denser in the liquid than in the solid state (ice floats on water) and it is unique in that upon heating the liquid from its melting point to 4°C, a further contraction takes place. From our discussion on intermolecular forces it is apparent that a chemical compound made up of small molecules, being not very easily polarised, should exist in the gas state at ordinary temperature, and this is the case for other substances whose molecules have approximately the same dimensions as those of

TABLE 1.

ELECTRONS IN OUTER SHELL (VALENCE ELECTRONS)

1	2	3	4	5	6	7	8
Hydrogen							
	Magnesium	Aluminium	Carbon	Nitrogen	Oxygen		Neon
Sodium	Calcium		Silicon	Phosphorus	Sulphur	Chlorine	Argon
Potassium						Bromine	
Silver	Radium					Iodine	

Metals Positive ions ——— Covalent ———→ Non-metals Negative ions or covalent

TABLE 2.

Class of Compound	Elements	Example	Origin or Use
Hydrocarbon	C,H	Octane Benzene	Nat. oil deposit, fuel Coal tar, solvent, and raw material
Alcohols	C,H,O	Ethyl alcohol	Formed by fermentation of sugar
Amides	C,H,O,N	Acetamide	Constituents of synthetic polymers, *e.g.*, nylon
Lipids	C,H,O	Olive oil	Found in plant seeds, used as food energy
Carbohydrates	C,H,O	Sugar, starch, cellulose	Occur in Nature—sources of energy and plant structural materials
Amino acids	C,H,N,O,(S)	Glycine, alanine	Building blocks of proteins
Steroids	C,H,O	Cholesterol	Hormone substances
Terpenes	C,H,O	Geraniol	Occur in Nature—perfumes

water, *viz.*, CO_2 (carbon dioxide), NH_3, and HCl. The abnormal physical properties of water are due to the extensive hydrogen bonding which exists in its liquid and solid forms. Indeed, ice is the most perfectly hydrogen-bonded structure, and liquid water appears to retain some of this regular crystalline order, the main difference being that such crystalline regions are short-lived, forming and melting many million times every second. Nevertheless a snapshot of short enough exposure would no doubt reveal ice-like regions in liquid water.

ORGANIC CHEMISTRY—THE CHEMISTRY OF CARBON COMPOUNDS.

Of all the hundred-odd elements which are now known and whose properties have been studied in detail, carbon is unique in the manner in which it can combine with itself to give rise to very large molecules (polymers) which can have molecular weights of several millions. Carbon compounds form the basis of the substances which make up living organisms, and thus the chemistry of carbon compounds is known as organic chemistry. Reference to **Table 1 (F23)** shows that carbon is capable of forming 4 covalent bonds, and the simplest organic compound is methane, CH_4 (the main constituent of North Sea gas). The hydrogen atoms are capable of being replaced by other atoms or groups of atoms, including carbon. Thus by replacing one of the C—H bonds by a C—C bond, $CH_3.CH_3$ (or C_2H_6) can be obtained. This process can continue and result in long chains of carbon atoms and the compounds so obtained form a series whose general formula is C_nH_{2n+2}, where n is any whole number. The compound C_8H_{18} is known as octane and forms the basis of petrol. The larger members of the series are the paraffin waxes. Starting again from methane and replacing one hydrogen atom by oxygen + hydrogen so that the carbon is covalently bonded to the oxygen, methyl alcohol, CH_3OH is obtained. Once again this is the first member of a series, the alcohols, whose second member, C_2H_5OH (ethyl alcohol), forms the basis of all alcoholic drinks.

In addition to ordinary 2-electron covalent bonds carbon also forms bonds involving 4 and 6 shared electrons. These bonds are much less stable than the ordinary covalent bonds so that compounds possessing them are extremely reactive. Carbon atom chains can also form side branches or closed rings, usually containing 5 or 6 carbon atoms. Furthermore, the important group of aromatic compounds are based on benzene, C_6H_6, in which the 6 carbon atoms form a planar ring and each has one hydrogen atom bonded to it. The remaining electrons form a mobile pool, so that the whole molecule is easily polarised and can be made to react with many other substances. It follows that a large variety of compounds can be obtained using only the elements carbon, hydrogen, and oxygen. If the elements nitrogen, phosphorus, sulphur are included, as well as chlorine, bromine, and iodine, the number of possible compounds becomes even larger. Table 2 provides some examples of classes of organic compounds and their occurrence in nature or their industrial application.

To achieve the growth of molecules by the elongation of the carbon chains is not usually feasible technically, although in nature this is a common process, brought about by enzymes (**F25(1)**). However, some molecules, especially those with four or six electron bonds, can react with one another to form polymers. In addition many molecules can be made to react (condense) to form more complex molecules with the elimination of a simple molecule, such as water or ammonia. Examples of the latter type of polymer are the proteins which are composed of amino-acid units (**Table 2**), the polysaccharides (carbohydrates), such as starch and cellulose, made up of condensed sugar molecules (**Table 2**), and synthetic condensation polymers of acids and alcohols known as polyesters, *e.g.*, Terylene. Additional polymers also figure largely in chemical technology, examples being polyvinyl chloride (PVC), polyolefines (*e.g.*, polythene) and polystyrene.

CHEMICAL REACTIONS.

Laws Governing Chemical Reactions.

Large amounts of energy are locked up within molecules and some of this energy is used up in chemical reaction. Like other forms of energy (*e.g.*, electrical and mechanical) it is subject to certain laws, such as the law of conservation of energy which states that energy cannot be created or destroyed, but can be converted from one form to another. Thus, part of the chemical energy during the reaction may be converted into heat, and this is frequently the case (**F17**).

Another very important law deals with the extent to which a chemical reaction will proceed. The reaction of nitrogen with hydrogen, which combine to give ammonia, forms the basis of the fixation of atmospheric nitrogen in the manufacture of fertilisers. The two gases combine in the molecular ratio of 1: 3, two molecules of ammonia being produced, *i.e.*, $N_2 + 3H_2 = 2NH_3$. However, ammonia also decomposes to form nitrogen and hydrogen, and at a certain stage the rates of the two opposing reactions will be equal and the mixture is then said to be at equilibrium. The position of the equilibrium, *i.e.*, the amount of ammonia formed, can be influenced by changes in temperature, pressure, or the amounts of the reacting substances, and the law of chemical equilibrium states that, if any factor governing an equilibrium is altered, then the equilibrium will shift in an attempt to counter the imposed alteration. Thus, in the ammonia synthesis, if ammonia is removed then more nitrogen and hydrogen will react in trying to re-establish the equilibrium. Furthermore, the reaction between hydrogen and nitrogen proceeds with the evolution of heat, so, if the temperature of the gas mixture is raised (*i.e.*, heat is added) then the equilibrium will readjust itself in an attempt to nullify the imposed change, and accordingly some ammonia will decompose into hydrogen and nitrogen, because this process *absorbs* heat.

The laws governing the influence of temperature, pressure, and chemical composition on reactions are termed chemical thermodynamics and the effects described can be calculated in quantitative terms. Some of the problems of chemical engineering are concerned with maximising yields of chemical reactions, while at the same time reconciling the necessary conditions with the economics of the process, *e.g.*, cost of plant, materials, and fuel.

One other important consideration is the speed with which chemical reactions proceed, and the time taken to reach equilibrium (chemical kinetics). This cannot be predicted by the laws of chemical thermodynamics. According to thermodynamic calculations, gaseous hydrogen and oxygen will react to form liquid water, but this reaction is so slow that even in a million years not very much water would be formed.

Catalysts.

Molecules react as a result of collisions, during which the energy due to the collision must be channelled into the chemical bond which is to be broken or to be made. Although at ordinary pressure and temperature molecules collide many million times every second, if all these collisions were to result in chemical reaction, then all reactions would occur with explosive violence. In fact, only a very small number of collisions are of a high enough energy for reaction to take place. This energy, termed the energy of activation, is therefore an important factor controlling the rate of a chemical reaction. The combination of hydrogen and oxygen normally has a large energy of activation and the two gases do not react to form water, although thermodynamics predicts that the reaction is feasible. Reaction rates can be increased, *i.e.*, the activation energy lowered, if certain solids are added, on which one or several of the reacting species are adsorbed. The bond formed between the added solid (*e.g.*, platinum) and the reacting gas is strong enough to weaken other bonds in the molecules, so that, on collision with another molecule, reaction takes place more readily. The solid which itself does not participate in the chemical reaction, is called a *catalyst.* Its function is to promote chemical reactions between substances which, because of the high activation energy, would not react in its absence. Catalysts find applications not only in many industrial processes but are also extensively used by living organisms, where they are called *enzymes*. Current theories hold that the reacting molecule fits into a hole or groove, like a key into a lock, on the enzyme protein where it is held while the reaction takes place; an example of an enzyme catalysed reaction is the breakdown of starch by the body. This consists of several steps, each of which is controlled by its own specific enzyme. These biological catalysts are much more efficient than those used in synthetic reactions, both in their specificity and in the lowering of the energy of activation (*i.e.*, the increase in the reaction rate). Sometimes a foreign molecule which bears a similarity to the molecule whose reaction is to be catalysed, will combine with a catalyst. If this foreign molecule is very strongly held by the catalyst then the latter can no longer perform its function and is said to be poisoned. This is also true for enzymes: *e.g.*, carbon monoxide and cyanides act as poisons by combining with certain important enzymes and thus inhibit the biochemical reactions on which the functioning of organs depends.

SOME USEFUL APPLICATIONS OF CHEMISTRY.

The application of basic chemical and physical principles to the manufacturing industries has led to the technological revolution which began at the turn of the century and is still gathering momentum. Although it is impossible to cover fully the areas in which the chemical sciences find application, a few of the more important fields are noted below:

Electrochemistry.

Electrochemistry deals with processes in which chemical energy is converted into electrical energy or *vice versa*. The most common examples are the dry battery and the lead storage battery (**L13**), although the generation of electricity by fuel cells (**L43**) is fast becoming of industrial importance. Conversely, if a current is passed through an ionic solution, a chemical reaction will take place, and this principle is employed in the electrolytic refining of metal ores and in metal plating processes.

Surface Chemistry.

Surface chemistry is based on the fact that solid and liquid surfaces have properties which are different from those of matter in the bulk state. A molecule A situated in the bulk interacts with its neighbours, but the various forces will cancel, as shown in **Fig. 4**. For a molecule B in the surface there is a net inward pull. The surface is therefore a high energy state and thermodynamics predicts that substances will try to minimise their total surface area. In a liquid this leads to the formation of spherical drops. The solid, on the other hand, will attract vapours and liquids which deposit surface films and thus reduce its surface energy. One application of adsorbed films, catalysis, has already been discussed.

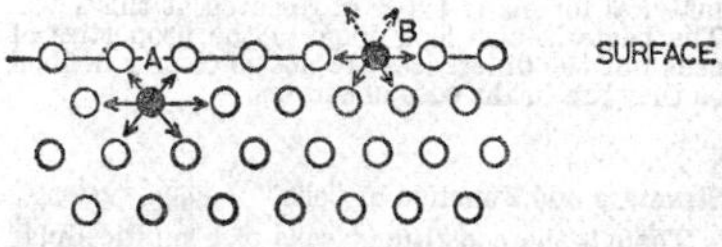

FIG. 4—Surface Forces: molecules within the solid (or liquid) are subject to balanced forces, but for molecules in the surface there is a resultant downward force.

Surface effects become significant in processes where the ratio of surface area to bulk volume is large, for instance, where matter is finely dispersed. This is the case in the technology of paints, printing inks, detergency, dairy products, air and water pollution, and solutions of polymers. The above-mentioned properties are also utilised in processes which involve the deposition of substances on surfaces, *e.g.*, textile finishing (water- and crease-proofing), metal coating, herbicides, cosmetics, and adhesives. Perhaps the most important field in which surface behaviour is one of the determining factors is biology. All living cells are separated from each other by membranes, and nutrients and other chemicals are adsorbed on, and diffuse through, these membranes, the nature and action of which are as yet very imperfectly understood (**F27(1)**).

Photochemistry.

Like other forms of energy, light, both visible and ultraviolet, can cause chemical changes to take place and, conversely, some reactions will give rise to the emission of radiation, *e.g.*, fluorescence. The ultimate source of most of the energy on each is the radiation from the sun which, by the process of photosynthesis (**F28(1)**), can be converted by green plants into the chemical energy stored in coal, oil, and carbohydrates. The mechanism of photosynthesis is one of the most baffling problems in chemical kinetics.

In photography a film of gelatin, in which are embedded small grains of silver bromide, is exposed to light, when a " latent image " is formed. This is believed to consist of submicroscopic specks of silver in some of the grains, but the mechanism of its formation is still uncertain. The latent image can be " developed " into a negative image (silver) which is then " fixed " by dissolving away the unreduced silver bromide.

Analytical Chemistry.

This is an important branch of Chemistry and deals with the identification and quantitative estimation of substances, often in complex mixtures. Where a quantitative analysis is to be achieved, the component under study has first to be separated in the pure state and then a suitable method must be found to determine its concentration in the mixture. In earlier days most analytical techniques were based on chemical reactions which were specific for the compound to be separated. Thus, sodium chloride and sodium sulphate can be separated by making use of the fact that many metal sulphates are insoluble in water, so that if a solution of, say, barium chloride is added to the mixture, barium sulphate will precipitate as solid and can be removed from the sodium chloride by filtration. If the amount of mixture initially used and the amount of precipitated barium sulphate are known, then, from the chemical formulae for barium and sodium sulphates, $BaSO_4$ and Na_2SO_4, it is easy to calculate the percentage of sodium sulphate in the original mixture.

During the last 25 years chemical analytical techniques have gradually been superseded by much more refined physical methods. Most important among these are the spectroscopic methods which can distinguish between small differences in energies associated with the vibrational motions of different chemical bonds. Some of these techniques not only measure energy differences but can detect minute amounts of energy, such as the energy liberated by a burning candle at a distance of 1 mile.

The detection, identification, and sometimes the quantitative estimation of very minor constituents of mixtures is frequently of great importance in industrial processes and products. For instance the presence of 1 g of iron in a ton of edible oil will rapidly cause the oil to turn rancid. Another example of the importance of traces of chemical compounds is provided by flavour and aroma of foodstuffs and perfumes. Frequently the characteristic, agreeable odour of a product is due to minute concentrations of one or several fairly simple organic compounds which at higher concentrations possess a quite unpleasant odour. The isolation of these compounds from natural products such as fruit or flowers and their identification provides a continuous challenge to the ingenuity of the analytical chemist.

Conclusion.

It will now be readily seen that the science of chemistry covers a large field which extends from the very simple molecules, such as H_2O, to the complex naturally occurring molecules with molecular weights of several millions. It involves very fundamental studies, ranging from the nature of the forces between atoms and the how and why of apparently simple chemical reactions, to the very applied problems encountered in the manufacture of high-strength construction materials. Among new fields which have developed rapidly during recent years petroleum chemicals rank high. This industry, which is centered on the oil companies, produces a large variety of substances, such as detergents, polymer raw materials, solvents, dyestuffs, fats and waxes, from by-products obtained during oil refining. Pharmaceutical chemistry, too, is rapidly developing and attempts are being made not only to synthesise new drugs but to gain a better understanding of the mechanism of drug action.

Probably the most significant developments during the next twenty years will occur in the field of biochemistry. The elucidation of the structure and genetic functions of nucleic acids and some proteins has provided the impetus for further investigation into the chemistry and physics of these and other biologically active molecules. Other outstanding problems which may well be solved in the not too distant future include the mechanism of membrane action, muscle contraction and nerve impulse propagation in molecular terms. Where a hundred years ago the sciences of physics, chemistry, and biology parted ways to follow their own separate paths, they are now seen to be converging and the areas of overlap are gradually increasing, as the molecular concepts of chemistry are providing a means of studying biological processes in terms of established physical laws and mechanisms. This part of the story will now be taken up in the section that follows.

IV. BIOLOGY—THE SCIENCE OF LIFE

WHAT BIOLOGY IS ABOUT.

Biology embraces the study of all living things which exist on earth at the present time and also the recognisable remains of those that are extinct. Living things or organisms range from the apparently simple micro-organisms such as viruses and bacteria to the largest animals and plants.

Living Processes.

The enormous variation and complexity of living processes make the task of understanding and defining life a very difficult one. Every living organism undergoes continual physical and chemical changes which, in spite of their diversity, are referred to as the metabolism of the organism. Metabolism involves the processing of food materials, the production of waste products, and all the intermediate stages between these whereby energy and matter are provided for the operation, maintenance, and growth of the organism. These reactions are under very exact chemical or nervous control at every stage and can be slowed down or speeded up as the need arises. Thus the organism can react to changes in the environment in which it lives, adjusting its activities in relation to the external changes. Finally, organisms can reproduce either in an identical or very slightly modified form. In this process new individuals are produced and the species continues to survive. Differences between offspring and parents can, under certain circumstances, act cumulatively over many generations and so form the basis of evolutionary change in which new species of organism are ultimately formed.

Molecular Biology.

It has been evident for many years that the most fundamental aspects of these living processes occur in basic structural units known as cells. We shall examine this level of organisation first before we attempt to look at the larger questions of the organisation of multicellular animals and plants and their interactions in groups or populations. The study of living processes at the molecular and cell level has been given a tremendous impetus in recent years by the advent of new techniques which enable microscopic and submicroscopic parts of cell to be examined. Physicists, chemists, and mathematicians have found themselves working alongside biologists in this field and several of the very notable advances have been made by physical scientists. At this level of organisation the traditional division of Biology into Botany, the study of plants, and Zoology, the study of animals, has little meaning. Even the more recent Genetics, the study of inheritance, Biophysics and Biochemistry, concerned with the physics and chemistry of organisms, and Cytology, the study of cell structure, are losing such identity as they may once have had. Molecular biology is a term frequently used in describing this rapidly expanding and fascinating field of research.

THE CELL.

Cells were first seen in 1665 by Robert Hooke when he looked at a piece of cork under his primitive microscope. It was not until 1839, however, that Schlieden and Schwann produced the cell doctrine which visualised the cell as both the structural and functional unit of living organisation. Exceptions may be found to the cell doctrine. For example, some protozoa, algae, and fungi show very complex internal organisation but are not divided into cells; they are usually called acellular organisms. The viruses also constitute a difficulty since in many ways they are intermediate between living and dead matter. They are absolutely dependent on cells of other organisms for their continued existence. Outside living cells they are inert molecules which may take a crystalline form. Inside a host cell, however, they become disease-producing parasites which multiply and show many of the other properties of living organisms. They are minute and lack the complex organisation usually associated with cells. Notwithstanding their somewhat ambiguous position, the viruses are often treated as though they were single cells or parts of cells and their extreme simplicity has made them ideal material for many types of research at this level. The bacteria also lack some of the properties of cells but the differences are not so clearly defined as they are in the case of viruses.

Structure and Function of Cells.

Though the constituent cells of a multicellular organism are usually specialised to perform particular functions, they have a great many features in common. The cell is often said to be made up of a substance called protoplasm, a term for the fundamental material of life which dates from the 19th cent. Protoplasm has two main constituents, the cytoplasm and the nucleus, and is bounded on the outside by a cell or plasma membrane. Plant cells generally have an additional wall composed primarily of cellulose and used for support. The nucleus is the controlling centre of the cell and has rather limited metabolic capabilities. The cytoplasm contains various subunits which operate to produce energy and new cell structure during the normal metabolism of the cell.

Cells take up the raw materials for metabolism

through the cell membrane from extracellular fluid which surrounds them. The nutrients include carbohydrates, fats, proteins, minerals, vitamins, and water. Fats and carbohydrates are important principally as sources of energy, though both types of compound are found in permanent cell structure. Proteins are complex substances of high molecular weight which contain nitrogen in addition to the carbon, hydrogen, and oxygen found in the other compounds. They are of fundamental importance in the structure and function of the cell and are built up of a number of simple nitrogen-containing organic molecules called amino acids. There are twenty amino acids occurring commonly in nature so that the number of possible combinations in large protein molecules is quite clearly enormous. A group of proteins whose significance is well established are the enzymes which are the catalysts of chemical reactions in living cells. Each enzyme will control and speed up a specific reaction even though it is present in very small amounts and is usually unchanged at the end of the process. A large number of inorganic mineral salts are essential for cells to function normally. Some, such as sodium, potassium, and calcium salts, are needed in considerable quantity; others are required only in trace amounts and these include iron, copper, and manganese. The trace elements are usually important constituents of enzyme systems. Vitamins are also necessary in very small amounts and it seems reasonable to conclude that their function is also a catalytic one in parts of some enzyme systems.

I. CYTOPLASM.

For a long time cytoplasm was thought to be a homogeneous and structureless substrate in which enzymes occurred as part of a general colloidal system. With the refinement of techniques such as electron microscopy and ultracentrifugation, more and more identifiable components have been found within the cytoplasm. It now seems certain that the material other than these recognisable particles is not a structureless matrix but a highly organised and variable complex at the molecular level.

Identification of Components: recent techniques.

Ultracentrifuge.

When soft tissues such as liver are ground up in a homogeniser, which usually takes the form of a plunger fitting fairly tightly into a glass tube, the cells are broken up but the smaller particles escape destruction. The particles remain in a highly active biochemical state if the salt concentration of the liquid into which they are released by homogenisation is more or less the same as that within the cell from which they came. Early failures to isolate cell fractions were almost all attributable to osmotic difficulties in which differences of salt concentration led to the movement of water into or out of the particles and to their subsequent destruction. The homogenate can be treated in a centrifuge in which high speed rotation subjects the particles to forces many thousands times greater than gravity. As a result the heaviest particles, such as the nuclei, are deposited first on the bottom of the centrifuge tube. The liquid is then transferred to another tube and the process repeated at a higher speed which brings down slightly lighter particles called mitochondria. The next collection of particles which can be obtained is called the microsomal fraction. By careful use of this technique, biochemists can produce a variety of cell constituents which can be studied in the absence of all the other reacting systems of the cell.

Radioactive Isotopes.

In many of the studies of cell chemistry which have been made on whole cells, on cell fractions, or on isolated enzyme systems, progress has been due in a large part to the availability of isotopes. With the aid of compounds prepared in the laboratory and labelled with the radioactive isotopes of elements such as carbon, hydrogen, nitrogen, oxygen, sulphur, and phosphorus, biochemists can now follow the metabolic fate of these substances in living organisms. The presence of a radioactive "labelled" element in any of the products of metabolism can be determined by means of Geiger and scintillation counters. The studies involving radioactive isotopes have shown more clearly than any others that living material is never static but is in a state of dynamic equilibrium. Substances are constantly broken down and replaced by other substances so that an organism may appear to be more or less unchanging but its components are always turning over.

Light Microscopy.

Many of the particles which can be isolated and studied have been identified within the living cell by means of the light microscope. Especially useful in this respect have been the phase contrast and interference modifications which make structures of different refractive index visible and do not depend on differences in light absorption as does the ordinary instrument.

Electron Microscope.

In light microscopy true images of particles smaller than the wavelength of light cannot be formed. Great difficulty is experienced in resolving particles much smaller than 0·5 microns (0·0005 millimetre) in size. The electron microscope, which uses a beam of electrons instead of light, is capable of much greater resolution because electrons behave as rays of extremely short wavelengths. Details as fine as 20 Ångstroms (0·002 microns) have been resolved and a tremendous amount of structure has been revealed by this instrument. However, many of the objects which are well known from electron microscope studies have not been isolated nor have functions been ascribed to them. Conversely, much of the biochemistry of cells cannot be linked to known structures. One of the great limitations of the electron microscope is that it can only be used to examine very thin slices of dead material.

X-ray Diffraction.

A method which can reveal a great deal of information about the arrangement of constituent parts in very complex biological molecules is that of X-ray diffraction. In this method X-rays are reflected from regularities in the molecular structure so as to form a pattern characteristic of the structure. Studies of X-ray diffraction patterns can be made on living material so that the internal shape of biological molecules can be worked out and the changes, if any, followed during phases of activity. In many ways X-ray diffraction has been useful in filling the gaps between biochemical studies of molecular behaviour and the essentially static view of cell structure obtained from the electron microscope.

Constituents of Cytoplasm.

The following are some of the particulate and membranous constituents of cytoplasm which have been identified and analysed with varying degrees of success by these and many other techniques:

1. Mitochondria and Oxidation.

Mitochondria vary in shape from cylindrical rods to spheres and in size from 0·2 to 3·0 microns. When seen in the living cell they are in constant motion. The whole structure is enclosed within a thin double membrane, the inner layer of which is thrown into folds extending across the central cavity of the mitochondrion and dividing it into small chambers. The function of mitochondria is to provide energy for the reactions of the rest of the cell. Almost the whole machinery for the oxidation of foodstuffs is to be found in the mitochondria and, as might be expected, is related in some way to the complex structure. Slight damage to the mitochondrion will render it unable to carry out a complete cycle of oxidative processes. Destruction of parts of the double membrane system prevents the production of energy-rich phosphate bonds in adenosine triphosphate (ATP) in which energy is stored and transported about the cell.

The Krebs Cycle.

The oxidative reactions which produce the energy are quite unlike those in which hydrocarbons are burnt in the laboratory. They proceed through a large number of controlled steps during which the energy is slowly evolved. The basic fuel substances, carbohydrates, fats, and proteins, are broken down outside the mitochondria to four major intermediate products which are pyruvic acid, oxalacetic acid, acetic acid and ketoglutaric acid. These acids diffuse into the mitochondria and are oxidised in a cyclical system of reactions called the Krebs or citric acid cycle which ultimately leads to the production of carbon dioxide and water. The actual oxidation of the various compounds participating in the cycle is brought about by a series of enzymes described as an electron transport chain. Oxidation in these cases is essentially a removal of electrons from the substrate, invariably accompanied by an equal number of hydrogen nuclei. The electrons, sometimes with and sometimes without the hydrogen nuclei, are passed from one compound to another until eventually they combine with oxygen to form water. One of the best known electron transport systems is that involving iron-containing substances called cytochromes.

An example of a typical stage in the Krebs cycle is the conversion of succinic acid to fumaric acid under the control of the enzyme succinic dehydrogenase. Both acids are compounds containing four carbon atoms but the latter has two electrons and two hydrogen nuclei fewer than the former which is therefore said to be oxidised during the conversion. The electrons are accepted by the first member of a chain of cytochromes which is thus reduced and the hydrogen is set free as hydrogen ions. The electrons are passed down the chain of cytochromes which are reduced in turn and re-oxidise the earlier members of the chain. In the final stage the reduced cytochrome is oxidised by oxygen which accepts the electrons and combines with the hydrogen ions to form water. These steps produce energy, but this does not all appear as heat because some is used to drive a reaction which consumes energy. The first law of thermodynamics states that such a coupling is necessary if a high energy compound is to be produced. The energy consuming reaction is the conversion of adenosine diphosphate (ADP) to adenosine triphosphate (ATP) with its energy-rich phosphate bond. The whole process is known as oxidative phosphorylation. The mitochondria produce far more energy than they require and the ATP passes into the cytoplasm for use in the rest of the cell.

2. Chloroplasts and Photosynthesis.

Chloroplasts are particles found in cells in the green parts of plants, in fact they contain the green pigment which is called chlorophyll. They are involved in the extremely important process known as photosynthesis in which energy absorbed from light is used to synthesise carbohydrates from carbon dioxide and water, oxygen being formed as a by-product.

Chloroplasts are disc-shaped or flat ellipsoids from 2 to 20 microns across, possessing a complex structure which in many ways is reminiscent of that found in mitochondria. A typical double membrane surrounds the structure and the inside is made up very largely of a stack of discs consisting of paired membranes connected at their ends to form closed systems. This seems to be a further development of the type of lamellated structure seen dividing the central cavity of a mitochondrion. The chlorophylls and other pigments, such as the orange yellow carotenoids, seem to be arranged in layers a single molecule thick in the chloroplast discs so that they are maximally exposed to light.

Photosynthesis.

In photosynthesis there are two somewhat independent sets of reactions, one needing light and the other going on in the dark. The primary process is the absorption of light quanta by the chlorophyll which causes some of the electrons of its molecule to pass from one orbital to another and thus enter an excited state. It is thought that chlorophyll then loses electrons which pass either to a recently discovered protein called ferrodoxin or to another oxidising agent, plastoquinone. The electrons from plastoquinone are transferred via a complex series of steps involving a cytochrome chain back to the chlorophyll. During these sequences oxygen is liberated from water molecules and energy-rich phosphate bonds are produced. The production of ATP in this reaction, which can only take place in the light, is called photosynthetic phosphorylation and, in this respect, makes plants independent of stored carbohydrate as their primary energy source.

The reactions so far described have not involved carbon dioxide and though it is possible to make the system operate solely in this way it is not usual for it to do so. Normally the electrons from ferrodoxin are passed to another electron accepting system together with hydrogen ions from water. At the same time, as recent isotope studies have revealed, carbon dioxide is combined with a 5-carbon sugar and the resulting compound immediately splits into two molecules of a 3-carbon, phosphoglyceric acid. The reduced electron system which has oxidised ferrodoxin now comes into operation and, together with energy from ATP, is used to synthesise sugar and starch from the 3-carbon compounds. The reactions in which carbon dioxide is taken up or "fixed" and then reduced during the formation of sugar, can go on in the dark unlike those of photosynthetic phosphorylation described earlier.

The importance of this process whereby plants can make use of the energy in sunlight to fix carbon dioxide and produce carbohydrates is quite clear. The whole animal population of the world, including man, is dependent on plants for food since even the meat-eating carnivores prey upon herbivores. Although scientists continue to make efforts to produce adequate food materials from simple compounds, there is still no better machinery known for doing this than the plant cell. Man is dependent on photosynthesis not only for his supplies of food but also for much of

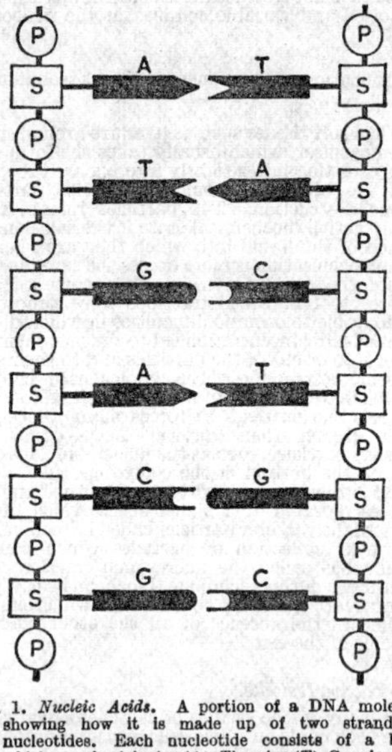

FIG. 1. *Nucleic Acids.* A portion of a DNA molecule showing how it is made up of two strands of nucleotides. Each nucleotide consists of a base, which may be Adenine (A), Thymine (T), Guanine (G), or Cytosine (C), united to the Pentose Sugar, Desoxyribose (S), in turn joined to Phosphoric Acid (P). The nucleotides are linked through the phosphoric acid groups. The two strands are held together by hydrogen bonds between bases, adenine linking only with thymine, and guanine only with cytosine.

his fuel, since much of the combustible material removed from the earth is of plant origin. In this respect atomic energy may eventually prove to be an adequate alternative.

3. Endoplasmic reticulum, Ribosomes, and Protein Synthesis.

A network of elaborate and oriented double membranes existing within parts of the cytoplasm can be seen in the electron microscope. In the space between the pairs of double membranes small granules are visible, either free in the space or attached to a membrane. The whole system is called the endoplasmic reticulum or ergastoplasm. When the cell is homogenised and centrifuged the endoplasmic reticulum appears as the microsomal fraction. Biochemical analysis after separation of the membranous from the granular components reveals that the former is composed largely of phospholipids and cholesterol, which are compounds closely related to fats, and the latter of ribonucleic acid (RNA).

Nucleic Acids.

The term nucleic acid covers a class of substances, usually of great complexity, built up from smaller units called nucleotides. Each nucleotide consists of a base, united to a sugar, in turn united to phosphoric acid. Nucleotides are joined together in a linear fashion by means of the phosphoric acid residues to form a chain from which the bases project at right angles (Fig. 1). Two types of sugar are found in naturally occurring nucleic acids and these are the ribose of RNA and the desoxyribose of desoxyribonucleic acids (DNA). We shall return to the latter when the nucleus is considered. Four nitrogen-containing bases occur in nucleic acids and in RNA—adenine, cytosine, guanine, and uracil. In DNA the uracil is replaced by thymine.

Protein Synthesis.

There is good evidence that RNA is manufactured exclusively within the nucleus and subsequently moves out into the cytoplasm. Some of it, called ribosomal RNA, unites with protein to form the granules, or ribosomes, of the endoplasmic reticulum. Another form, called messenger RNA, also migrates from the nucleus to associate with ribosomes but does not become incorporated into their permanent structure. It is also well established that the ribosomes are closely linked with protein synthesis in the cell because radioactive amino acids, when fed to an animal, are always found first in the ribosomes before any other cell structure. The specification for a particular protein is not carried on the ribosome which is merely the factory for making these complex molecules. It is thought that messenger RNA carries instructions from the nucleus which specify exactly the protein to be synthesised at a ribosome. This is done by means of a code in which a "triplet" of three nucleotide bases codes one amino acid (Fig. 2). Thus on a long molecule of RNA, three adjacent uracil bases would specify an amino acid called phenylalanine. If these were followed on the RNA molecule by one uracil and two guanines then the amino acid tryptophan would be specified and this would be

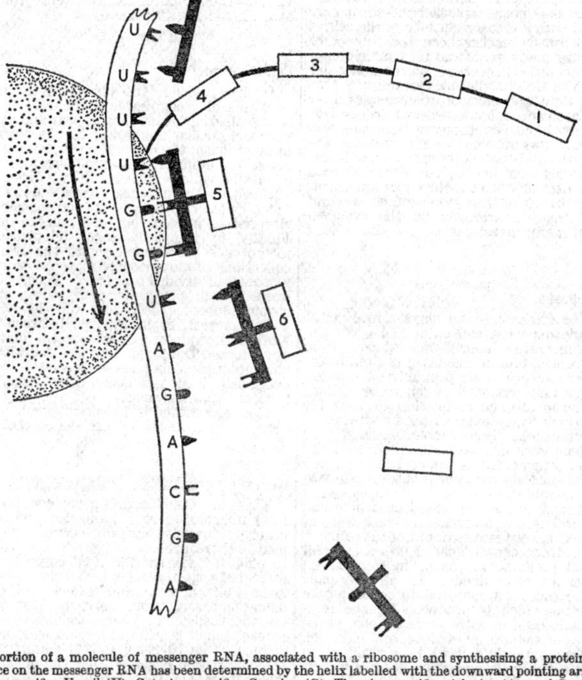

FIG. 2. A portion of a molecule of messenger RNA, associated with a ribosome and synthesising a protein. The base sequence on the messenger RNA has been determined by the helix labelled with the downward pointing arrow in Fig. 3. Adenine specifies Uracil (U), Cytosine specifies Guanine (G), Thymine specifies Adenine (A), and Guanine specifies Cytosine (C). The ribosome is moving down the messenger RNA strand "reading" the triplet code. Amino acid 4, which is phenylalanine specified by UUU, has just been joined to three other amino acids and its carrier RNA released to the cytoplasm. Amino acid 5, tryptophan specified by UGG, is attached to its carrier RNA and in position ready to be joined to the protein chain by the ribosome. Amino acid 6, methionine specified by UAG is attached to its carrier RNA but has not been brought into position on the messenger RNA strand. Other amino acids and carrier RNA molecules exist free in the cytoplasm and have not yet associated.

joined to the phenylalanine. In this way complex protein molecules can be built up according to instructions emanating from the nucleus for each of the 20 different amino acids. It is far from clear how the amino acids in the cytoplasm are brought into position on the RNA "template" and how they are activated so as to combine and form protein. It is thought that they are first attached, by appropriate enzymes, to small molecules of so-called carrier RNA in the cytoplasm before associating on the template of messenger RNA. The association is then accomplished by a ribosome which moves along the messenger RNA chain, as it were "reading" the code, and taking appropriate carrier RNA-amino acid complexes from the surrounding medium. There are still many gaps in our knowledge of the exact sequence of events.

This system is responsible for building and maintaining much of the organisation of the cytoplasm. All the enzymes, for example catalysing every reaction within the cell will be specified and built up on the appropriate RNA template. The understanding of protein synthesis is of fundamental importance to the whole of biology and has particular significance in studies on cancer where cell growth becomes abnormal.

4. The Golgi Apparatus.

The characteristic features of the Golgi apparatus are numbers of large vacuoles or spaces, bordered by closely packed layers of double membranes. The latter look very much like the membranes of the endoplasmic reticulum but do not have the ribosome particles along their edge. They are therefore known as "smooth" membranes in contrast to the "rough" membranes of endoplasmic reticulum. The function of the Golgi apparatus is not established though it may be associated with secretory activity of the cell.

The Golgi apparatus has been the subject of controversy for many years and illustrates one of the major difficulties in working at the molecular cell level. The Golgi structure can only be seen through the light and electron microscopes after the cell has been through a number of preparative stages. Many biologists thought that the preparation itself was responsible for creating the Golgi apparatus and that nothing like the objects seen would really exist in the living cell. Though there is now little doubt that the Golgi apparatus is a real constituent of the cytoplasm, the general problem of creating artefacts by the involved treatment in many investigations remains a very real one.

5. Cell Membrane.

Though the cell membrane plays a most vital part in regulating what can enter and leave the cell, it remains rather poorly understood. It is thought to consist of a double layer of lipid molecules with a layer of protein probably outside the lipid. Fairly large molecules seem to be able to penetrate the membrane in relation to their fat solubility, which would support the hypothesis of its lipid framework. Small molecules and ions appear to penetrate in relation to their size, the smaller ones getting through more readily than the larger. This suggests that pores of a certain size exist in the membrane.

The cell membrane has mechanisms which can move ions and other substances against concentration differences either into or out of the cell. A fine microelectrode can be pushed into a cell and the electrical potential of the inside determined with respect to the outside. In all the cells studied so far there is a potential difference across the membrane which is produced by the non-uniform distribution on either side of ions, particularly those of sodium, potassium, and chloride. Though these potentials have been studied in animal and plant cells generally, they are best known from the work on nerve cells where sudden changes in the membrane potential are the basis of nerve impulses. A great deal is now known about the mechanism whereby the potential change, and thus the nerve impulse, is propagated from one end of a nerve to the other. The basic process which produces the nerve impulse in any region of the nerve fibre has been shown to be a sudden increase in permeability of the membrane to sodium ions in that region. A problem of much interest is how such activity can be passed from one nerve to the next, that is to say how a change of potential in one cell membrane can be made to affect an adjacent cell membrane. Such a process is fundamental to the large collections of nerve cells which form the nervous systems of animals. Transmission takes place at a special region called a synapse and when an impulse reaches this region it causes the release of a small amount of chemical transmitter substance which diffuse to the membrane of the adjacent cell. There it combines with the membrane in such a way as to change its permeability to ions and so produce a nerve impulse in the second cell. A number of transmitter substances have now been identified and many of them are related chemically to tranquillisers and other drugs affecting the nervous system.

II. NUCLEUS.

The main regions of the nucleus are the surrounding nuclear membrane, a mass of material known as chromatin, and a small sphere called the nucleolus. The nuclear membrane is a double structure very much like the membranes of the cell surface and endoplasmic reticulum. Suggestions have been made that these membranes are continuous at some regions within the cell. The status of chromatin was in doubt for many years. Light microscope studies reveal very little structure in the nucleus until the time when the cell is preparing for, and undergoing, division or mitosis. At this time a number of discrete double strands, the chromosomes, are revealed by virtue of their chromatin content—the material stains heavily with basic dyes.

Cell Division.

During division the chromosomes behave in regular and recognisable sequence. In the first stage called prophase they appear and at the same time the nuclear membrane breaks down. Next, in metaphase, the chromosomes become arranged across the equator of a spindle-shaped collection of fibrils which appears in the area formerly outlined by the nucleus. Then follows anaphase in which the two threads of each chromosome, the chromatids, move to opposite poles of the spindle. Finally in the last stage, telophase, nuclear membranes are formed round the two separate collections of chromosome material and the cytoplasm itself divides into two. Thus two cells are formed each containing the same number of chromosomes as the parent and the cells enter a period of rest, or interphase, between divisions. During interphase the chromatin material disappears and the possibility was considered of the chromosomes being assembled as a prelude to every cell division and then being dispersed in the nuclear sap afterwards.

This suggestion is in direct conflict with the view that chromosomes are the carriers of genes.

Genes.

These are the elements which contain all hereditary information and the medium whereby hereditary features are transmitted from one cell to the next, either in the same organism or from parents to offspring via the fertilised egg. Experiments indicated that the same genes always occupy the same position on chromosomes and this really demands a structural continuity through the life of the cell. The chromosomes undoubtedly persist, but it is still not certain why or how they change so as to become visible during division. One suggestion has been that the nucleic acids of which they are very largely made up condense during the period of prophase. In the resting nucleus the chromosomes may be much more swollen and occupy much of the nucleus.

The problem that has attracted the most attention and is possibly the most fundamental that biology has to offer is that of the nature of the genes. The important material of the genes is known to be desoxyribosenucleic acid (DNA), made up of nucleotides as is RNA, though in this case the bases are adenine, cytosine, guanine, and thymine. The DNA molecule is large and complex. Two long chains of nucleotides are known to coil round in a double helix with the pairs of bases on each helix directed towards one another and linked by means of hydrogen bonds (Fig. 3).

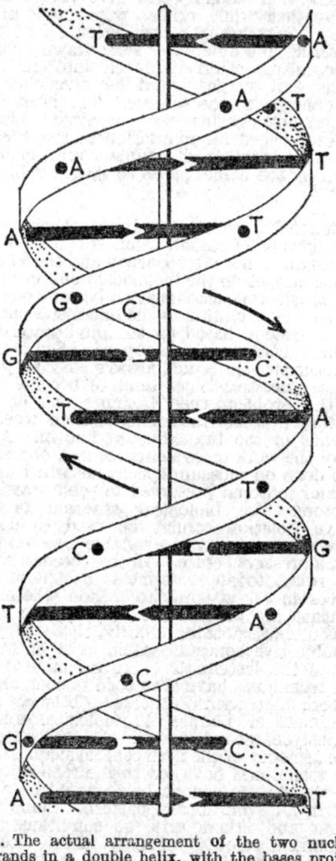

FIG. 3. The actual arrangement of the two nucleotide strands in a double helix, with the bases projecting and linking the two helices as shown.

Furthermore, if adenine is the base on one chain, thymine must be its partner on the other and similarly guanine can link only with cytosine. Because of this pairing off of bases there is sufficient information in a single chain of nucleotides to resynthesise the double helix once more. Thus if we examine a section of a single strand of the helix and find bases in the order adenine, thymine, guanine, adenine, cytosine, we can predict that in similar positions on the other strand we shall find thymine, adenine, cytosine, thymine, guanine. The capacity of one half of a DNA molecule to specify the othe half exactly, enables the system to be self-replicating in a way that is essential in a hereditary transmitter and fits in well with what is known of chromosome behaviour during cell division.

Transmission of Genetic Information.

Accepting that DNA is the material of the gene it remains now to examine the nature of the information which it passes from cell to cell and organism to organism. Long before the structure and significance of the DNA molecule was known, geneticists were finding that alterations in a gene, known as a mutation, usually affected a particular chemical reaction and this in turn caused the changes seen in the organism as a whole. The effect was due to the failure to synthesise a necessary enzyme and so the hypothesis "one gene = one enzyme" gathered currency. This view has now been extended to include proteins other than enzymes and it is now certain that specific genes control the synthesis of specific proteins. The DNA of the genes transmits the instructions about protein synthesis to the ribosomes via messenger RNA. In the nucleus, messenger RNA is made with specific base sequences in its molecule by using DNA as the template; thus a group of three adjacent adenine bases in DNA would produce a group of three adjacent urocil bases in the synthesised RNA and this would lead to the specification of phenylalanine at the ribosome as we have seen. Only one of the two strands in the DNA double helix participates in the production of RNA.

Within the nucleus, the nucleolus is believed to play an important part in the synthesis of RNA since its turnover of this material is very rapid. It has been suggested that the nucleolus supplements the RNA produced by chromosomes and acts as the channel through which this material is released to the cytoplasm. There is now some good evidence which points to the nucleolus as the source of ribosomal RNA since cells which lose the nucleolus have no ribosomes.

The processes involved in nuclear control and the transmission of information from cell to cell is summarised in the aphorism "DNA makes RNA and RNA makes protein." The system of carrying that information in the base sequences of DNA molecules has become known as the "genetic code." A remarkable landmark in the study of DNA occurred when, towards the end of 1967, Kornberg and his colleagues managed to synthesise a virus DNA in a test tube. The synthesised molecules proved to be capable of infecting bacteria in the same way that the naturally occurring virus would. The DNA was synthesised using an extracted virus DNA molecule as template and attaching nucleotides by means of appropriate enzymes. The newly made molecules were then separated from the template. It can hardly be claimed that this is the creation of life in a test tube since the template was extracted from a living virus. The experiment suggests many possibilities in experimental modification of the genetic constitution of an organism with all the far reaching ethical consequences.

MULTICELLULAR ORGANISATION.

It is axiomatic, if evolutionary theory is accepted, that in the course of very long periods of time there has been a general change in multicellular organisation from the simple aggregation of cells with little individual differentiation, to the highly specialised and differentiated cells and tissues seen in complex animals and plants. It is fascinating to speculate on the environmental variations and internal mechanisms which together produced this result. The problem is so vast, however, that a complete analysis is impossible and even a statement of the sequence of changes is in many cases highly controversial.

Another aspect of becoming multicellular, where the problems offer more hope of analysis, is that the complex organisation must be built up in the lifetime of each animal or plant from the single-celled stage of the fertilised egg. We have already seen how cells can divide repeatedly, handing on self-replicating chromosomes so that each cell is apparently identical. If this were really so then division of the fertilised egg would result in an unorganised mass of cells showing no differentiation. The essential problems in development are: (1) how is the smooth succession of shape changes produced during cell division so that an appropriate and recognisable end product is reached?; (2) how do the cells differentiate during this temporal sequence so that those which form part of the eye, say, are different from those of liver and blood?

Method of Development.

There are some important differences in the method of development in animals and plants. In animals there tends to be a relatively short period during which the basic structure is produced and after which growth, repair, and replacement may cause adjustment rather than major change. In higher plants, on the other hand, the apical regions of both roots and shoots remain in a permanently embryonic state and add material, which then differentiates, in a continuous process throughout the life of the plant. In spite of these differences—and in any case there are many exceptions—the two main problems in development are essentially similar in both animals and plants.

A great deal of work has been done on animal development since this takes place in a fairly stereotyped way during a short period of time. The fertilised egg of an animal divides in such a way as to form a hollow ball of cells, the blastula, which folds in on itself to produce a two-layered sac, the gastrula. A third layer, the mesoderm, is now added between the two layers, known as ectoderm on the outside, and endoderm on the inside. At this stage much of the animal's basic structure is established. Many aspects of this orderly sequence can be explained in terms of specific adhesive properties of cells, so that a cell will stick to others of the same type but not to unrelated types. Other mechanical properties such as elasticity, particularly in surface layers, are important in maintaining shape and producing appropriate changes during processes when one layer is folded in on another. Why cells should have the different physical properties necessary to produce an integrated whole embryo is not known, but certainly it cannot be thought that every cell has an absolutely fixed constitution and therefore a predetermined role in development. Large parts of developing embryos can be removed in early stages and their places taken by remaining cells so that intact organisms are still produced. One is led to conclude that the surroundings of a cell have a great deal of influence on the way it reacts and that there is a great deal of adaptability in the developing system, especially in its early stages.

Formation of Specialised Tissues.

These points lead us on to the second major question concerning the differences which appear progressively in cells during development so that specialised tissues are ultimately formed. This is essentially a problem in the regulation of gene activity since we know that each cell division produces daughter cells which are genetically identical. It seems likely therefore that instructions are carried on the chromosomes to cope with all requirements of the organism, but that in specialised cells only a small fraction of this full potential is realised. For a long time embryologists have known that egg cytoplasm shows regional differences which make identical nuclei behave differently, and it is thought that regional cytoplasm can in some way control gene activity. Techniques for the transplantation of nuclei in developing frog embryos have been perfected and it has been possible to put a nucleus from an intestinal cell of a tadpole into an enucleate egg. The egg will go on to develop normally even though its nucleus came from a fully specialised cell derived from endoderm. The embryo will form blood and muscle from the mesodermal layer and all the other components of an organism, under the influence of a nucleus which normally would have produced none of these things. One can conclude that all the genes are present, even in the nuclei of specialised cells, but that they have to be placed in a suitable cytoplasmic environment in order to be activated. Similar nuclear transplantation experiments indicate that genes can be " turned off " as well as " turned on " by an appropriate cytoplasmic environment, even though the nuclei come from cells which are so specialised as to stop dividing. The components of cytoplasm which control gene activity are still quite unknown.

A study of cell differentiation and the development of multicellular organisation leads us to the view that, important though the nucleus and its genes are in controlling cell activity, an integrated organism is the result of complex interactions between its constituent cells and between the cytoplasm of those cells and their nuclei.

THE CLASSIFICATION OF ORGANISMS.

It was clear to the biologists of the 17th cent. that animals and plants could be fitted into different groups or species. John Ray, a leading biologist of the day, defined a species as a group of individuals capable of interbreeding within the group. This criterion, with its corollary that a species is reproductively isolated from organisms outside the group, has survived more or less unchanged to the present day. The early workers also saw that some species were very similar to one another while others were obviously dissimilar. Systems of classification based on the similarities and differences were drawn up so that all organisms could be fitted into an orderly scheme and species could be given names in accordance with the scheme. The most famous collector and classifier was the Swede, Linnaeus, who established his reputation in the 1730s. A very large number of animals and plants are known by the names given to them by Linnaeus.

Systematics, as the study of species and of higher groups of classification is called, acquired a new significance after Darwin and the Theory of Evolution. From the biological point of view the most satisfactory classification became one which reflected the evolution of the organisms classified. Such a system, based on the phylogeny or evolutionary history of a group, is called a natural classification. It is not always easy to produce because ancestral types tend to become extinct and the problem then becomes one of reconstructing a whole branching system when only the ends of the branches are known. A great deal of the work on systematics has, of necessity, to be done on museum specimens which may be fossils or material preserved in some way by the collectors. The biological criterion of reproductive isolation cannot be used to define a species when the only available representatives are in a preserved state. In this case the scientist must resort to an assessment of structural differences in an attempt to decide whether two organisms are of different or the same species. It has often been said, unfairly, that such species are subjective concepts which exist only in the mind of the systematist. In recent years computer techniques have been used to compare large numbers of structural differences between groups of animals or plants. Physiological and biochemical characteristics are also becoming part of the armoury of the 20th cent. systematist. All these techniques have led to the realisation that even the species cannot be regarded as a static point in an evolutionary pattern. Some species die out and others arise as conditions in the environment slowly change. This essentially dynamic view of a continually shifting equilibrium between animals, plants and their environment has given rise to what Huxley has aptly called " The New Systematics " in his book of that title.

When the systematist shifts his attention to the higher levels of classification the problems are just as great as at the species level. Different species having features in common can be grouped together into genera, genera into families, families into orders, orders into classes, and classes into phyla. The dividing lines between different groups at all levels is always difficult and in the final analysis somewhat arbitrary since at these levels we do not have any biological criterion such as exists for the species. The evolutionary status of the larger groups is also poorly defined. Many are now recognised to be polyphyletic, which is to say that there are several main evolutionary lines running right through the group.

THE ANIMAL KINGDOM.

The animal kingdom is divided into about 24 large groups or phyla though the number varies between different classifications. Ten of the more important phyla are listed below.

1. Protozoa.—Microscopic, unicellular forms of great variety. Some may have more than one nucleus and others form colonies. Many are able to swim by waving hair like flagella or cilia

Others move by putting out extensions of the body or pseudopodia into which the rest of the body then flows. Protozoa are found in the sea, in fresh water and in the soil. Some are parasitic and cause important diseases in animals and man such as sleeping sickness and malaria.

2. Porifera.—Sponges. Very primitive multicellular animals whose cells display considerable independence of one another. Largely marine. The body which may become branched and plant-like is supported by a framework of spicules and fibres. The bath sponge is the fibrous skeleton of certain species.

3. Coelenterates.—Hydra, jellyfish, sea anemones, corals. Simple animals which have a body only two cells thick surrounding a gut cavity with a single opening to the outside. Largely marine. Many are colonial. Coral reefs are formed from the calcareous skeletons of these animals.

4. Platyhelminths.—Flatworms, which are free living in water, and liver flukes and tapeworms, which are parasitic. A third, solid block of cells, the mesoderm, has been developed between the two layers of cells seen in the coelenterates. A simple gut may be developed and the reproductive system is complex especially in the parasitic forms.

5. Nematodes.—Roundworms. The body is smooth and pointed at each end. Some of the most numerous and widespread of all animals. Free living in all environments and parasitic in practically all groups of plants and animals. At the same level of complexity as the Platyhelminths.

6. Annelids.—Segmented worms such as earthworms, marine worms and leeches. A system of spaces, the body cavity, is developed in the mesoderm so that movements of the main body of the animal and movements of the gut become more or less independent. Digestive, excretory, circulatory, nervous and reproductive systems are all well developed.

7. Arthropods.—A very large, diverse and important group of animals which includes crustaceans such as crabs, shrimps and water fleas; myriapods, such as centipedes and millepedes; insects; and arachnids, such as spiders and scorpions. The arthropods show many of the developments seen in annelids and in addition they possess a jointed, hard exoskeleton. Paired appendages grow out from the segments of the body and form antennae, mouth parts, walking legs, etc. The muscles within the skeleton are able to exert a fine control over the movement of the appendage. In order to grow these animals have to shed the exoskeleton periodically.

8. Molluscs.—Mussels, clams, oysters, squids, octopods and snails. Complex body form but somewhat different from annelid–arthropod type. Unsegmented body protected by shell which is variously developed in different types. It forms two valves in mussels and oysters, a spiral structure in snails, is reduced and internal in squids and completely lost in octopods.

9. Echinoderms.—Starfish, brittle stars, sea cucumbers, sea urchins, and sea lilies. All marine and all radially symmetrical, usually with five radii. Completely unlike the other advanced, major groups. Circulatory, excretory and nervous systems differently developed. Locomotion and feeding by means of hundreds of tube feet projecting from under surface.

10. Chordates.—Sea squirts, Amphioxus, fish, amphibia, reptiles, birds and mammals. Segmented animals which at some stage in their life have gill slits leading from pharynx to the outside and a supporting notochord from which, in all chordates except sea squirts and Amphioxus, is developed a vertebral column or backbone. Those animals with a backbone are commonly referred to as vertebrates, *all* those without as invertebrates. These are obviously names of convenience having no phylogenetic significance since they lump together totally unrelated phyla in one case and align these with a part of a single phylum in the other. The vertebrates have been investigated more completely than any other animals because of their direct structural and functional relationship with man himself. There are five well defined classes which are listed below. The first vertebrates were the fish and from them came the amphibia. The amphibia gave rise to the reptiles and both birds and mammals evolved from different reptilian stock.

(*a*) *Fish*

Cold blooded, aquatic animals breathing by means of gills. Sharks, rays and dogfish belong to a group known as the elasmobranchs characterised by a skeleton made of cartilage. Bony fish, or teleosts, include almost all the fresh water fish and the common marine fish such as cod, mackerel, plaice, herring, etc.

(*b*) *Amphibia*

Cold blooded, more or less terrestrial animals which have to return to water to breed. Five fingered limbs are developed in place of the fins of fish. The egg hatches into a tadpole larva which is aquatic and breathes by gills. At metamorphosis the larva changes into the terrestrial adult which possesses lungs. Some amphibia such as the axolotl may become sexually mature as a larva and so never metamorphose into the adult. The class includes newts, salamanders, frogs and toads.

(*c*) *Reptiles*

Cold blooded and terrestrial. These animals do not return to water to breed because they have an egg with a relatively impermeable shell containing the food and water requirements of the developing embryo. There is no larval stage. Present day reptiles such as lizards, snakes and crocodiles are all that remains of a tremendous radiation of dinosaur-like creatures which occurred in the Mesozoic (F44).

(*d*) *Birds*

Warm blooded and adapted for aerial life. The characteristic feathers act both to insulate the body against heat loss and to provide the airfoil surfaces necessary for flight. The birds are an astonishingly uniform group and show less diversity of structure than much lower classification categories (*e.g.*, the teleosts) in other classes. The relationships of the 19,000 or more species of bird are difficult to establish because of this uniformity. It is clear that the flightless forms such as the ostrich are primitive and that the penguins are also in a separate category but the typical modern birds are classified in a large number of rather arbitrary orders. About half of all the known species are placed in one enormous order called the Passeriformes or perching birds.

(*e*) *Mammals*

Warm blooded animals which have been successful in a tremendous variety of habitats. Mammals are insulated from the environment by the characteristically hairy and waterproofed skin. They are, with two exceptions, viviparous which means that their young are born alive and in typical mammals at an advanced stage of development. In the marsupials of Australia the young are born at an early stage and transferred to a pouch where they develop further. The two exceptions referred to are primitive monotreme mammals known as the duck-billed platypus and spiny ant-eater and these animals lay eggs. The young of mammals are suckled by means of the milk producing mammary glands. The mammals include aquatic whales and dolphins, hoofed ungulates, flesh eating carnivores, rodents and insectivores, the aerial bats, and the tree climbing primates to which man himself belongs.

THE PHYSIOLOGY OF ANIMALS.

Some basic features of cell organisation have already been dealt with, and in unicellular animals all life processes, such as respiration, movement, growth and reproduction, proceed in the single cell. However in multicellular animals cells are of various types, constituting distinct tissues and organs which perform special functions in the body. Although each cell has its own complex metabolism there must be co-ordination between cells forming special tissues and between the tissues which form the whole organism in order for the body to function efficiently. The study of these functional interrelationships at the tissue and organism level of organisation is the province of the physiologist.

1. Movement, Fibrils and Skeletons.

(*a*) **Muscles.**—The prime movers in almost all animal movement are large protein molecules in the form of microscopic fibrillar threads. In some way not yet fully understood these fibrils can convert the chemical energy stored in the high energy phosphate bonds of ATP into mechanical energy. In the long, thin cells forming the muscles of animals, it has been discovered that there are two sets of fibrils, one formed of a protein called myosin, the other of actin, arranged in a regular, interdigitating fashion. When the muscle contracts the fibrils slide into one another so that, although the fibrils themselves do not change in length, the muscle as a whole develops tension and shortens. This, the Sliding Filament Theory of Muscle Contraction, was formulated in 1953 by A. F. Huxley, H. E. Huxley and J. Hanson. Fine bridges extend from the myosin fibrils to attach on to the actin and it is here that the conversion of chemical to mechanical energy goes on.

(*b*) **Skeletons.**—In order for muscles to work effectively it is necessary for them to operate in some sort of skeletal system. Contraction but not relaxation is an active process; muscles must be arranged in antagonistic pairs so that one muscle can extend the other. A skeleton also provides a system of levers so that the muscles can do work against the environment in an efficient manner. A simple type of skeleton found in fairly primitive animals is the hydrostatic system of coelenterates and worms. Here the animal can be thought of as a fluid filled bag or tube which can change shape but whose volume remains constant. By contraction of circular muscles the tube will become long and thin and conversely contraction of longitudinal muscles makes the tube short and fat. Examination of an earthworm will demonstrate how alternating waves of activity of this type passing from head to tail can move the animal over the ground. The earthworm shows an advance over the simplest systems because the hydrostatic tube is broken up into small units by the segmentation of the body. This makes local responses possible. The next advance to be seen is the development in animals such as arthropods and vertebrates of a firm skeleton to which muscles are directly attached. The skeleton can then be used to support the body and to engage the environment. It seems to matter little whether an endoskeleton (vertebrates) or exoskeleton (arthropods) is developed since in both cases a tremendous radiation of fins for swimming, legs for walking and wings for flying can be seen. However in other respects these two types of skeleton show significant differences. The exoskeleton for example offers more protection than the endoskeleton while apparently setting an upper size limit. All the really big animals have endoskeletons.

(*c*) **Cilia.**—Fibrillar systems are also seen in the fine hair-like cilia which project from the surface of some cells. Cilia are important in a number of ways. They are the organelles of movement in many Protozoa, they are used to produce water currents past the bodies of some aquatic animals, and they are of great importance in moving fluid within the body of almost all animals. They beat in a regular fashion, the effective stroke being accomplished with the cilium held straight out from the surface and the recovery stroke with the cilium flexed at the base.

Cilia possess the same structure no matter where they come from. In transverse section eleven fibrils can be seen which run the whole length of the organelle. Two of the fibrils are single and situated centrally while the other nine are double fibrils arranged in a circle around the periphery of the cilium. Work is still going on in this field, but it has been suggested that the peripheral fibrils are contractile and cause the cilium to bend. The function of the central fibrils is unknown.

2. Nutrition and the Alimentary Canal.

All animals must take in and digest food materials. As well as water they require complex organic substances, proteins, fats and carbohydrates, together with small amounts of salts and vitamins. These materials are obtained by eating the dead bodies of plants and other animals. They are taken into the alimentary canal and there broken down or digested by enzymes into simpler, soluble amino acids, sugars and fatty acids. These substances are absorbed and distributed to various parts of the body where they are used in cell metabolism (**F26, 27**) or stored for future use.

(a) The Size of Food—Microphagy and Macrophagy.

Many animals, called macrophagous feeders, take in relatively large masses of food. Some such as frogs and snakes swallow their food whole, but many break it up first. Arthropods have modified appendages arranged round the mouth for cutting, some molluscs have a rasp-like radula with which to scrape off particles, and many mammals break up their food with jaws and teeth. The teeth are usually well adapted to the type of food. Carnivores have large, sharp canines, premolars and molars with which to tear the flesh of the prey, fish eating seals have small peg-like teeth to grip the fish and herbivorous ungulates have flat grinding teeth with which they break up hard plant material.

In contrast, microphagous feeders collect small particles of food material from the environment by continuous filtration. In bivalve molluscs and many marine worms water currents are produced by beating cilia. Food is trapped within the confined space through which the water flows by means of a plentiful supply of sticky mucus in the filtering region. Some crustacea use fine hairs to sieve off food material, often from water currents created by the swimming movements. The most startling of filter feeders is the whalebone whale. As the whale swims forward a stream of water flows in at the front of the mouth and out at the sides via sheets of whalebone which filter off the organisms on which the animal feeds. Though macrophagy seems to favour the attainment of larger size there are exceptions! Another type of particulate feeding is seen in those animals which eat deposits of detritus as do many worms. Finally some animals take in only soluble food materials. These fluid feeders include internal parasites like the tapeworm which absorb substances over the surface of the body, and insects such as the aphid with sucking mouth parts.

(b) Reception and Storage.

The food now passes into the alimentary canal which may be fairly simple, straight tube but more usually becomes long and coiled. The gut tube may be divided into several functional components though the divisions must not be regarded as absolute. The first section is usually involved in the selection, by taste, smell and texture, and the reception of food. A lubricating mucus, together with some digestive enzymes, may be added at this stage from glands such as salivary glands. A large crop for food storage occurs in animals as diverse as insects and birds but in mammals this region remains as a simple tube called the oesophagus.

(c) Mixing, Grinding and Early Digestion.

Waves of contraction in the muscles of the gut move the food onwards. This peristaltic action delivers the food to a region known variously in different animals as the stomach, gizzard or gastric mill. Here the further disintegration and mixing with enzymes is accomplished in many forms simply by contraction of the muscle of the stomach wall. Stones may assist the action in the gizzard of birds for example, and more bizarre modifications are seen in some crustaceans and molluscs. In the former there is a complicated gastric mill with grinding surfaces, teeth and a filter, and in the latter a long rod, called the crystalline style, is rotated by ciliary action against a hard pad on the opposite wall of the stomach. In the ruminating mammals such as sheep and cattle the stomach is divided into four chambers. The function of the first two of these is to mix food with a bacterial culture which exists in this region and to regurgitate the cud for further grinding. The bacteria break down plant cell walls and so benefit the host which cannot deal unaided with the main component known as cellulose. The final two chambers of the ruminant stomach are more typical in function.

A variety of digestive enzymes are released into the stomach region. Carbohydrates, fats and proteins are all broken down to some extent. The main enzyme in the stomach of vertebrate animals is a proteinase which works under acid conditions.

(d) Final Digestion and Absorption.

The finely divided food now passes on to the intestine where digestion continues, using enzymes liberated in the preceding region, or under the action of new enzymes released from intestinal glands. In the vertebrates the pancreas secretes a number of enzymes acting on all types of food material, one of the most important being the protein-breaking trypsin. The pancreatic secretion is liberated into the anterior end of the intestine known as the duodenum and operates in an alkaline medium.

Soluble products of the process of digestion are absorbed through the wall of the intestine into the blood stream. Blood vessels carry the food material to the liver where it is put to use in the animal's metabolism or stored as liver glycogen. The surface for absorption is increased by tremendous folding of the intestine interior, seen as finger-like villi in higher vertebrates or as the so called spiral valve in some fish.

(e) Processing of Waste Material.

The undigested remains of the food now pass through the most posterior regions of the alimentary canal known simply as the hindgut in many forms or as the colon and rectum in others. A major function of this region, particularly in terrestrial animals, is the removal of water so as to conserve this vital material. In the rectum the faeces are formed and stored before being eliminated from the body.

3. Respiration. Gills, Lungs and Tracheae.

The oxidations which consume oxygen and produce carbon dioxide go on at the cellular level as explained earlier (F20). All living cells respire and remain alive only if supplied with oxygen. In a multicellular body, however, many cells are remote from the oxygen of the environment and the need arises for an efficient respiratory system by which oxygen can be taken up and carbon dioxide released. In addition a circulatory system is necessary to transport the oxygen to and from the respiring cells.

(a) Simple Gas Exchange Systems.

Animals such as protozoa which because of their size have a high surface area to volume ratio do not need special structures for gas exchange. Diffusion over the whole body surface ensures an adequate supply of oxygen. Much larger animals such as earthworms also find it possible to rely on diffusion alone, partly because their consumption of oxygen is fairly low, and partly because their bodies are permeable all over. For various reasons most animals restrict the permeability of the outer layers of the body and under these conditions special respiratory areas have to be developed.

(b) Gas Exchange in Water.

Aquatic animals, except those such as whales breathing at the surface, have to obtain their oxygen from the supplies which are dissolved in the water. This presents several problems because water is a dense medium, there is not a lot of oxygen in solution, and its diffusion rate is low. For these reasons there is a surprising functional uniformity in gill systems and they are very different from lungs. Gills are fine, finger-like processes with a good blood supply which are held out in a water stream. The water current is brought very close to the gill filaments so that the length of diffusion pathway for oxygen is minimal. There is a "counter current" flow of water and blood so that the water containing most oxygen comes into contact with the blood just leaving the gill. This ensures that most of the oxygen can be transferred from water to blood through the thin gill cells. The efficiency of "counter current" systems is well known to the engineer but they were invented by aquatic animals long before they were by man. These features can be seen in the gills of molluscs, crustacea and fish. The pumping devices which maintain the water currents also operate economically. Flow is maintained in crustacea by appendages modified to form beating paddles, in many molluscs by ciliary movement, and in fish by the operation of a double pump in mouth and opercular cavities. In almost all cases there is a continuous current over the gills, the water coming in one way and going out another. Thus the animal avoids reversing the flow with the consequent waste of energy in accelerating and decelerating a large mass of water. Fish, for example, take water in at the mouth and force it out through the gill slits (sharks) or operculum (teleosts).

(c) Gas Exchange in Air.

Air breathing animals do not encounter these problems since the medium is less dense, contains a great deal (20%) of oxygen and diffusion rates are high. Lungs are therefore in the form of sacs whose walls are well supplied with blood. The area of the walls may be increased by folding so that the lung becomes spongy and full of minute air spaces called alveoli where the gas exchanges goes on. Only the main airways receive fresh air as the lung expands; oxygen is renewed in the alveoli by diffusion. Ventilation of the lung is accomplished by a tidal flow of air in and out of the same tubular opening known as the trachea. The actual ventilating mechanism varies in different animals. In the amphibia for example air is forced into the lungs when the floor of the mouth is raised with the mouth and nostrils shut. The lungs are emptied by elastic recoil and by lowering the floor of the mouth. Higher vertebrates use a costal pump which changes the volume of chest and lungs by movements of the ribs. This change in volume is further assisted in mammals by the diaphragm, a sheet of muscle which lies beneath the lungs and separates thorax and abdomen. In many animals sound producing organs are associated with the lungs and trachea. The larynx is a vocal organ in frogs, some lizards, and most notably mammals. In birds voice production takes place in the syrinx situated further down at the base of the trachea.

A completely different gas exchanging system is seen in insects. Branching tubes, known as tracheae, run throughout the body and carry oxygen directly to the cells without the intervention of a blood system. The tracheae communicate with the outside world via a series of holes called spiracles. Although the main tubes may be actively ventilated, diffusion in the system accounts for a large part of the movement of oxygen between the outside world and cells.

4. Circulation.

In simple, small animals there is no blood system and dissolved oxygen, nutrients and other materials move about the body solely by diffusion, assisted to a certain extent by streaming movements of protoplasm within the cells. In larger animals a transport system is necessary to convey materials about the body and in many, but not all, it is in the form of a blood system. Blood systems are of two types, closed and open.

(a) Open Systems.

In an open circulatory system blood is pumped from the heart into a few major arteries but these very quickly give way to large tissue spaces or sinuses so that the tissues and organs of the body are directly bathed in blood. Blood flows slowly from the sinuses back to the heart. Both molluscs and arthropods possess an open system. The heart in most arthropods is a long, thin tube in the dorsal part of the body, pumping blood towards the head. Auxiliary muscles may be attached to the heart to pull it out and refill it after the pumping cycle. Mollusc hearts on the other hand are of the chambered type, with thin walled auricles receiving blood from the gills and pumping it to a more muscular ventricle. The ventricle in turn contracts to pump blood to the body. In squids and octopods two auxiliary hearts are seen, receiving blood at low pressure from the body and pumping it through the gills and thence to the main heart.

(b) Closed Systems.

In a closed system blood is pumped round the body in a branching network of arteries, and comes into contact with tissues and cells via very thin walled vessels called capillaries. Substances diffuse into and out of the blood through capillary walls. From capillaries, blood enters the veins and so returns to the heart. Blood flow in the tubes of a closed system is much more brisk and blood pressures tend to be higher than in an open system. In annelids the closed system is fairly simple with a vessel above the gut in which blood moves forward connecting to one below in which blood moves backwards. The blood is pumped by peristaltic contraction of the vessels and this system must be regarded as the precursor of a localised pump. Simple hearts are in fact seen in some annelids.

In vertebrates a well defined heart is always present, situated ventrally at the level of the forelimbs. In fish there is a single auricle and ventricle and the latter pumps blood directly to the gills. From the gills the blood is collected into a dorsal aorta which then branches to serve the rest of the body. Associated with the development of lungs and loss of gills in the tetrapods, we see a progressive modification of this simple pattern. The most posterior gill vessel is taken over as the lung or pulmonary artery and slowly a completely separate circuit evolves. This involves the division of the single heart into right and left sides, the former pumping blood to the lungs and the latter to the body. In the birds and mammals where the division is complete the system can be seen to be functionally satisfactory. Blood flows along the following route: left auricle to left ventricle, to body, to right auricle, to right ventricle, to lungs, to left auricle, and so on. Thus blood charged with oxygen in the lungs returns to the heart before being pumped to the body. In the lower tetrapods, division of the heart is incomplete and considerable interest centres on the function of these apparently imperfect systems. Amphibian hearts have two auricles but only a single ventricle. In spite of this, evidence is accumulating to show that blood from the lungs and body is not mixed as it passes through the ventricle. A further complication in amphibia is due to the moist skin also being used for gas exchange. Some oxygen is thus contained in blood returning from the body. Reptiles show a further advance in that the ventricle is almost completely divided into two. The system appears still to be functionally inadequate because one of the major arteries to the body leaves from the deoxygenated side along with lung vessels.

(c) Function of the Blood.

Most of the materials transported by the blood such as nutrients, waste materials and hormones are carried in solution in the plasma. The respiratory gases, oxygen and carbon dioxide, are present in greater quantity than would be possible if they were in simple solution. Carbon dioxide is carried in the form of bicarbonate and oxygen combines with blood pigment. The best known blood pigment is haemoglobin which is found in a variety of animals and gives the red colour to blood. When oxygen is present in high concentration, as it is in the lungs, combination occurs to give oxyhaemoglobin. If the concentration of oxygen is low, as it is in the tissues, dissociation occurs and oxygen is given off leaving reduced haemoglobin. Carbon monoxide will combine more readily than oxygen with haemoglobin so that in carbon monoxide poisoning the blood cannot transport oxygen. The haemoglobin of vertebrates is contained in high concentration in red blood corpuscles. The amount of haemoglobin and, hence, oxygen carried is greater than if the pigment is not in corpuscles. In mammals the oxygen carrying capacity of blood is thirty times that of a similar quantity of water. Other blood pigments are the blue haemocyanin found in crustacea and molluscs, and the violet haemerythrin found in some worms. Also present in the blood are various types of white corpuscle which are part of the defence mechanism of the body and ingest invading bacteria. Special blood proteins such as fibrinogen, causing clot formation, and antibodies effective against foreign substances occur in the plasma.

5. Excretion, Ionic Regulation and Kidney Tubules.

As the chemical reactions included under the term metabolism proceed, so numerous waste products accumulate. The most important of these are compounds containing nitrogen, such as ammonia, urea and uric acid, arising from the use of protein as an energy source. In terrestrial animals they are removed from the blood by the kidney. The basic unit of a kidney is the tubule; in worms these tubules are not concentrated into a solid kidney but occur, a pair in every segment, right down the body. The kidney tubule begins with an end sac, corpuscle or funnel which is closely associated with the body cavity or the blood system. Fluid is filtered from the body cavity or blood into the corpuscle whence it passes to the tubule proper. During passage down the tubule, useful materials are reabsorbed through the tubule cells into the blood whereas unwanted materials remain and pass to the outside world.

Although it is usual to think of kidney function being primarily one of nitrogenous excretion, it is quite common to find that in aquatic animals the kidneys are hardly used for this purpose. In these animals the tubules are primarily concerned in regulating the salt and water levels in the body, nitrogenous wastes being eliminated by diffusion through any permeable surface. In fresh water for example all animals have osmotic problems since the body fluids have a much greater osmotic pressure than the environment. Water tends to enter the body and salts tend to leave. Fresh water animals produce large quantities of very dilute urine, filtering off a lot of blood plasma into the tubules but reabsorbing all wanted materials including the invaluable salts. Fresh water crustacea, molluscs and fish all possess tubules of different morphology which show very similar functional properties.

Different environmental conditions impose different demands on the osmotic and ionic regulating machinery. In very dry conditions, such as in deserts, it is obviously of advantage to reabsorb as much water from the tubule as possible. All animals do this but it is interesting that only birds and mammals have discovered the secret of so concentrating the urine that its salt concentration is higher than that in the blood. This is done by means of a hairpin-like loop in the tubule called the Loop of Henle, another example of a counter current device.

6. Co-ordinating Systems.

Overall co-ordination of the animal's body, so that it functions as a whole and reacts appropriately to environmental changes, is largely the province of two systems, one chemical or hormonal, the other nervous. In one respect these are systems for homeostasis, that is for preserving the *status quo*, in spite of considerable environmental fluctuation. Paradoxically they can also initiate change as, for example, one can see in the daily repertoire of complicated behaviour patterns produced by almost any animal.

(a) Nervous Systems.

(i) *Sensory Information.*

Before appropriate reactions can be produced to any stimulus it is necessary to measure its intensity, position, duration and, most important, character. This is done by sense organs which are usually specialised to receive stimuli of a single modality or character. Thus photoreceptors detect light, mechanoreceptors detect mechanical disturbance and chemoreceptors detect specific chemicals. In all cases the sense organs produce a message about the stimulus in the form of nerve impulses (see **F30**—Cell Membrane) which travel up the nerve from the sense organ to the rest of the nervous system. Change of stimulus intensity is usually signalled as a change in frequency of nerve impulses. The position of the sense organ which is active indicates the position of the stimulus within or without the body. The duration of the repeated discharge of nerve impulses indicates the duration of the stimulus.

(ii) *Simple Networks.*

The simplest type of nervous system is the network of interconnected nerve cells (neurones) found in the coelenterates. Branching processes of the nerve cells communicate with neighbouring processes at special regions called synapses (**F30**). Quite complicated behaviour is possible even with this relatively simple system. If a sea anemone is prodded violently it will close up equally violently, showing that activity has spread throughout the network. If it is tickled gently it will respond with local contractions around the site of stimulation. The movements of feeding and locomotion are very delicately performed at appropriate times.

(iii) *Central Nervous Systems.*

In the majority of animals all the nerve cells tend to become collected into a solid mass of tissue referred to as a central nervous system (C.N.S.). Within the mass the nerve cells are interconnected via synapses in the same way as in a nerve net. The connexions with sense organs and muscles are made via long processes called axons. Numbers of axons are usually bound together with connective tissue to form a nerve trunk. In annelids and arthropods the C.N.S. is seen as a ventral cord lying beneath the gut with a swelling or ganglion in each segment of the body. In molluscs, the ganglia are usually more closely grouped around the oesophagus, with the possible provision of a pair of ganglia further back in the viscera. Vertebrates possess a dorsal nerve cord which is uniform in diameter and not ganglionated, though nerves emerge from it in a segmental fashion. The segmental nerves arise in two separate bundles or roots. The dorsal root is made up entirely of sensory nerves conveying information to the C.N.S. The ventral root consists of motor nerves which convey nerve impulses to the muscles of limbs and alimentary canal together with other effector organs such as glands.

(iv) *Reflexes.*

A reflex, in which stimulation of a sense organ or sensory nerve results in the almost immediate contraction of a muscle, is the simplest type of C.N.S. activity. Reflexes have been studied in all animals but the best known ones can be seen in frogs, cats, dogs, and sometimes humans. The very simplest is the stretch reflex, in which a stretched muscle is made to contract by activity coming into the C.N.S. from stretch receptors in the muscle. The activity is relayed directly to the motor neurones of the muscle concerned, making them active and thus causing the muscle to contract. This reflex is monosynaptic, *i.e.* there is only the single synaptic connexion between sensory nerve and motor neurone. The knee jerk in humans is a stretch reflex, the stretch being caused by hitting the muscle tendon as it passes over the knee. Much of the recent work on reflexes has been done on this simple system, notably by Eccles. The flexor reflex, which is seen as the sudden withdrawal of a limb from any painful stimulus, is more complicated. Although the stimuli may vary, the withdrawal response is always accomplished by contraction of flexor muscles which bring the limb in towards the body. The reflex is polysynaptic, *i.e.* several intermediate neurones connect the sensory nerves through to the motor neurones. More complicated still is the scratch reflex in which an animal is made to scratch its flank in response to an irritation or tickling in that region. This reflex demonstrates some of the more involved properties of the C.N.S. For example a dog will continue to scratch for a time after the tickling has stopped, so that the C.N.S. must continue to be active in the absence of sensory stimulation. This has been called after-discharge.

(v) *The Brain.*

The C.N.S. functions in a more complicated way than is suggested by study of the reflexes and most of these higher activities are co-ordinated by the brain. A greater condensation of neurones is seen at the front end of the C.N.S. of all animals because of the larger numbers of sense organs in that region. Brains, which become the dominant part of the C.N.S., can be seen in arthropods, molluscs and vertebrates. The close association with sense organs is illustrated by the vertebrate brain which is divided into three regions: (*a*) forebrain (nose), (*b*) midbrain (eye) and (*c*) hindbrain (ear and taste). However, the brain is much more than a relay station for these stimulus modalities and it receives information from other parts of the body via the spinal cord. All this information is correlated and activity patterns initiated and transmitted to appropriate regions. In lower vertebrates, the roof of the midbrain (the optic tectum) is the important correlation centre and its effectiveness has been well established in studies on instinct and learning in fish. Another region of the brain of importance in all vertebrates is a dorsal upgrowth of the hindbrain called the cerebellum. This is a motor co-ordinating centre which ensures that all activities are performed in a smooth and well balanced way by the muscles and limbs of the body. In reptiles, the forebrain begins to take over the correlation role and in mammals this development reaches its peak in the cerebral cortex. In man the cortex overshadows the rest of the brain and contains some 1000,000,000 neurones. It is easy to see the magnitude of the problem of understanding a system of this complexity. The bee's brain with far, far fewer cells can initiate complicated behaviour such as the hive dances. The possibilities offered by the human cortex seem vastly greater, though they are often realised in ways which give cause for concern. At the moment it would be quite impossible to build a computer with the properties of the human brain. To do this in the future would depend on major advances in computer technology and even greater advances in the knowledge of central nervous systems.

(b) Hormonal Regulation.

Many aspects of an animal's metabolism are regulated, not by the nervous system, but by specific chemical signals known as hormones which are circulated in the blood stream. Growth, carbohydrate metabolism, salt balance, activity of ovaries and testes and their associated structures, and colour change are all regulated in some way by hormones. The substances are secreted by endocrine glands or ductless glands as they are often called. The important endocrine glands in vertebrates are the thyroid, parathyroid, adrenal, pancreas, the sex glands, and the pituitary.

In the past the endocrine and nervous systems were regarded as exerting an independent control in slightly different functional areas of the body. It is clear now that the integration of the two systems is much greater than was formerly envisaged and in vertebrates is accomplished through the pituitary gland. Secretions of this gland regulate almost all other endocrine glands and the secretions of the pituitary are either produced in the C.N.S. with which it is directly connected or are controlled by C.N.S. secretions. An astonishing, parallel development of other neurosecretory systems, such as those of the pituitary, has been found in a variety of animals and in all types the neurosecretory organ complex is the dominant endocrine gland of the body. In crustacea the so-called X organ complex found within the eyestalk, and in insects neurosecretory cells connecting to the corpora cardiaca glands, occupy the functional position of the vertebrate pituitary. They all regulate growth, metabolism and reproductive physiology, either directly or through the mediation of other endocrine glands.

7. Animal Behaviour.

In discussing the nervous system we have already dealt with simple mechanisms such as the reflex. Very much more complicated are the instinctive and learned patterns of behaviour which are studied by animal psychologists and ethologists such as Lorenz and Tinbergen.

(a) Instinct.

Instinct is inborn behaviour which does not have to be learnt and is usually performed in a stereotyped way. For example a gull will retrieve an egg taken out of its nest by shovelling it back with the underside of its beak. The gull will never replace an egg in its nest in any other way, for example by using a wing or leg, and once it has begun a retrieval it will usually continue the movements back to the nest even though the egg is taken away. An instinctive behaviour pattern is triggered off by a particular stimulus or "releaser" which may be a very small part of the total environment. A male stickleback will attack a very crude model with a red belly but will not attack an exact model without it. The red underside appears to be a much more important stimulas than general shape. A particular instinctive pattern cannot always be elicited and the reaction of an animal very largely depends on when the behaviour was last produced. The longer the time that elapses, the easier it is to trigger off the instinctive pattern until eventually it may appear in the absence of an appropriate set of environmental circumstances.

(b) Learning.

Learning is that behaviour acquired during the organism's lifetime as a result of experience. Evidence of learning has been seen in many animals from worms upwards though, as might be expected, the more complicated types of learning are found only in those animals with elaborate nervous systems. A simple type of learning is seen when an animal, upon repeated exposure to a stimulus, gradually decreases the normal response which is usually one of flight, until eventually the response may disappear completely. This process is called habituation. More complex are the conditioned reflexes, which were first discovered by Pavlov. In these an animal can in some way connect a conditioned stimulus such as a bell, with an unconditioned stimulus such as meat, so that eventually it salivates when the bell is rung. Trial and error learning of the type needed to be successful in running a maze is more complicated still. In this there is a retrospective element because the reward at the end of the maze comes after all the responses. Many animals can run mazes but the white rat has been extensively used in experiments of this nature and there is a huge literature on this one animal. A final category of learning can be called insight learning; in this an animal shows evidence of resolving a new problem without trial and error. This type of learning involves the perception of relations between different parts of the environment and though there may be examples in arthropods and molluscs the clearest evidence of it is seen in the behaviour of birds and mammals.

8. Reproduction.

A single animal may live for a short or long time, but eventually it dies, and the continuance of the species is dependent upon reproduction. Some protozoa, such as *Amoeba*, reproduce asexually by the simple division of the cell to produce two new individuals. Asexual reproduction also occurs in some coelenterates, such as jelly-fish, in which there is an alternation of sexual and asexual generations. However, the vast majority of animals only reproduce sexually. This involves the fusion of two cells, the gametes, produced by adult individuals, and each zygote thus formed develops into an individual of the next generation. The gametes are of two kinds, the large, spherical, immobile ova produced by the female gonad or ovary and the much smaller motile sperms produced by the male gonad or testis. The motility of the sperms helps them to reach the passive ovum, which contains food reserves to support the early development of the embryo.

Worms.—The flat worms, particularly parasitic forms, have complicated life cycles, and many are hermaphrodite, *i.e.*, each individual has both male and female organs. Cross-fertilisation usually occurs, the sperms from one worm being introduced into the female duct of another. The round worms are unisexual, and internal fertilisation also occurs. Of the annelids the polychaete worms are unisexual, but the ova and sperms are shed into the sea, where fertilisation takes place. However, *Lumbricus* and the leeches are hermaphrodite, cross-fertilisation takes place and the eggs are laid in cocoons.

Arthropods.—Many crustacea are unisexual, though the sedentary barnacles are hermaphrodite. Internal fertilisation may occur, but in the crabs and crayfish pairing takes place and the sperms are deposited on the tail of the female. When the eggs are shed they become fertilised and remain attached to the abdominal appendages. Most crustacea have motile larval stages into which the eggs first develop. In *Daphnia*, the water-flea, parthenogenesis sometimes occurs, *i.e.*, the eggs develop without being fertilised. The sexes are separate in the arachnida and there are usually no larval stages except in the primitive king-crabs. The insects are also unisexual, and the fertilised eggs are laid after copulation. In some, *e.g.*, dragon-flies, an immature nymph similar to the adult is formed, but in flies, beetles, moths, and many others the egg hatches into a larval form. This then develops into a pupa, from which the final adult or imago is produced. In the social ant's nest the workers are sterile females with large heads, reduced eyes, and no wings. The males and queens are winged, and insemination of the latter occurs during the "nuptial" flight.

Molluscs and Echinoderms.—Most lamellibranchs are unisexual, although some species of scallops and oysters are hermaphrodite. There are motile larval forms, and in the swan mussel, *Anodonta*, the larvae develop in the mantle cavity of the parent and when liberated become attached to the gills or fins of fish, where they remain parasitic for some time. Some gasteropods are unisexual, but the slugs and snails are hermaphrodite. In the latter cross-fertilisation occurs, the two approaching snails being stimulated to copulate by firing small sharp darts of calcium carbonate into each other. The echinoderms are unisexual, and fertilisation takes place in the sea. The egg first develops into a ciliated larval form.

Vertebrates.—The sexes are always separate in the vertebrates. In some cartilaginous fish, *e.g.*, dogfish, internal fertilisation occurs and the eggs are laid in protective sacs. In contrast, the bony fish shed ova and sperms into the water, where fertilisation takes place. Although pairing may take place in the amphibia, fertilisation occurs in water, and there is usually an aquatic larval stage. The reptiles, birds, and mammals are independent of water for fertilisation, as copulation takes place and the sperms from the male are introduced directly into the female. Most reptiles and all birds lay eggs with hard shells. Development of the embryo in marsupial mammals begins in the female uterus, but is continued in a ventral pouch which surrounds the teat of the mammary gland. In the two living species of monotreme mammals the eggs are incubated in a similar pouch. Finally, in the eutherian mammals the embryo develops in the female uterus and is born at an advanced stage.

Diversity of Sexual Reproduction.— This brief survey will give some idea of the diversity of sexual reproduction in animals. External fertilisation is very much a matter of chance, and large numbers of gametes are produced which offset the great losses of gametes and embryos that this method involves. Internal fertilisation is more certain, and is also independent of external water—an important factor in land animals. In vertebrates particularly there is increase in the care of the young by the parents, involving the development of characters of behaviour as well as those of structure. Some fish lay their eggs in holes or nests which are protected by the male. Similarly, a few frogs build nests, while others carry the eggs about. The eggs of birds require a constant high temperature for their development, and they are usually incubated by the parents. After hatching the young are fed and guarded by the parents until they can leave the nest and fend for themselves. In the eutherian mammals the embryos are attached to the uterus wall by the placenta, *via* which food materials pass from the mother. The period of gestation is long, and after birth the young are supplied with milk from the mother until they are weaned and can feed themselves. Another feature in mammals is the period of "childhood" during which they play and learn and are protected and fed by their parents. The internal fertilisation, internal development, and care and protection of the young after birth which is so conspicuous in the higher vertebrates results in the reduction of losses during the vulnerable embryonic and young stages, and in consequence relatively few progeny are produced by a pair of individuals.

THE PLANT KINGDOM.

There are various ways in which the main classes of the plant kingdom can be grouped, but a simple, up-to-date arrangement is given in the chart. Vascular plants are often known as the *Tracheophyta* because they all possess woody conducting elements. These are absent in non-vascular plants, and the bacteria, fungi, and algæ are often called *Thallophyta*, *i.e.*, they have a relatively simple plant body or thallus. Many of the bryophytes also possess a thallus, but in some there is a stem bearing leaves, although a true vascular system is absent. Many thallophytes are aquatic, whereas the tracheophytes are mostly land plants in which the development of woody tissues can be related to the attainment of the land habit as the plant kingdom evolved. However, the chart should not be taken as indicating the evolutionary relationships of the various groups. It is more a convenient arrangement which reflects the relative complexity of the plant body.

1. Bacteria.—This is a vast group of minute organisms of very simple structure. They are spherical or rod shaped and may exist as separate cells, some species being motile, or as long chains or irregular masses. Their minute size makes the elucidation of their structure very difficult. There is a wall of complex composition, and cytoplasm which contains glycogen and fat. Electron-microscope studies have revealed the presence of structures which appear to consist of nuclear material. Multiplication is by simple division, which may take place very rapidly. For example, *Bacillus subtilis* can divide every 20 minutes, so that in 8 hours a single cell may give rise to 16 millions. Recent research indicates that a sexual process may also occur. Bacteria can survive unfavourable conditions by producing a resistant spore within the cell. They do not possess chlorophyll, though a few are pigmented. Most obtain their food already formed, and are thus either saprophytes or parasites. The saprophytic bacteria occupy a vital position in the living world. They are responsible for most of the decay of dead organic matter, and it has been truly said that without them the surface of the earth would soon become completely covered with the dead bodies of animals and plants. Bacteria also play a vital part in the circulation of nitrogen in nature. By breaking down organic material, ammonia is released and ammonium carbonate is formed in the soil. This is oxidised by other bacteria to form nitrates, which can be absorbed by plants again. Yet other bacteria can "fix" atmospheric nitrogen, and one species, *Rhizobium leguminosum*, occurs in the root nodules of the pea plant. Such plants are often grown on poor soils and ploughed in, thus improving the fertility of the soil. The parasitic bacteria are also of great importance, as they are responsible for many diseases of plants, animals, and man. (*See* **P7(1)**.)

2. Fungi.—This is a large group of plants, none of which contain chlorophyll. Hence, like the bacteria, they are either parasites on other living plants and animals or saprophytes which live on dead organic matter. Some are unicellular aquatic plants, but many have a body called a mycelium composed of many branched threads or hyphæ. In the higher fungi (*e.g.*, toadstools, bracket fungi, and puff-balls) complex reproductive structures are formed. All fungi produce spores. In the aquatic species these may be motile, but the majority form minute, airborne spores. The spore output is often very great, and a single mushroom may produce 1,800 million spores. Some fungi are serious diseases of crop plants, such as potato blight and wheat rust.

3. Algæ.—These are essentially aquatic plants which contain chlorophyll. They range from microscopic forms to the large seaweeds. The green algæ (*Chlorophyceæ*) live mostly in fresh water and may be unicellular, motile or non-motile, or filamentous, though a few found in tropical seas are more complex. The brown algæ (*Phæophyceæ*) are mostly seaweeds which possess a brown pigment, fucoxanthin, which masks the green chlorophyll. They include the bladder-wracks (*Fucus*) and kelps (*Laminaria*) of our coasts and the seaweeds which form dense floating masses over hundreds of square miles of the Sargasso Sea. Other groups are the red algæ (*Rhodophyceæ*), mostly seaweeds of delicate form, the unicellular motile diatoms (*Bacillariophyceæ*), and the blue-green algæ (*Cyanophyceæ*). All algæ possess unicellular reproductive organs. Various types of life cycle occur, the most complex being found in the red algæ.

4. Bryophyta.—These are the liverworts (*Hepaticæ*) and the mosses (*Musci*). They are all small plants characterised by a sharply defined life-cycle. This consists of an alternation of generations, the "plant" being a gametophyte bearing sex organs. The latter are multicellular, the female archegonium containing a single stationary ovum and the male antheridium producing many motile sperms. The latter are released and swim in water to the archegonium, where fertilisation takes place. After this a sporophyte is formed

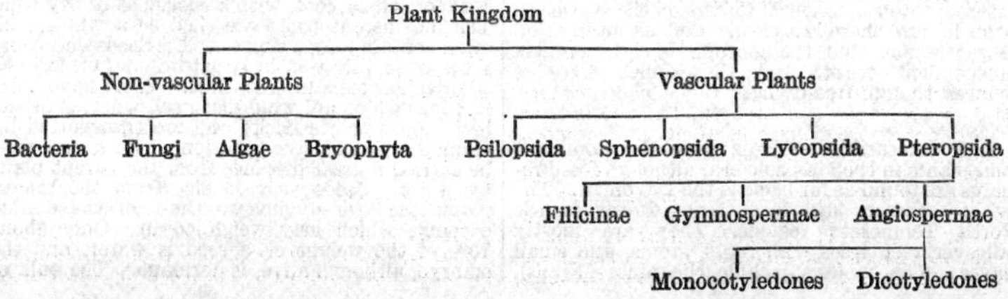

which is always dependent on the gametophyte and never becomes free living. The sporophyte usually consists of an absorbing foot buried in the tissue of the gametophyte and a stalk or seta bearing at the top a single sporangium. In many mosses this is a complex structure with hygroscopic teeth which move apart only when dry, thus releasing the minute spores only when conditions are suitable for their dissemination in the air. The bryophytes are of little economic importance, and may be looked upon as an evolutionary sideline. However, they occupy suitable " niches " in many plant communities, and species of the bog-moss *Sphagnum* cover large areas where rainfall is high.

5. Psilopsida.—This is a small group of primitive, vascular, spore-bearing plants. Its only living representatives are two rare genera of the Southern Hemisphere. However, a number of fossil forms are known from the Devonian period. The best known are those found in the chert at Rhynie in Scotland. The plants are excellently preserved, and their internal structure can be easily seen. They were probably marsh plants with prostrate and erect leafless stems, although *Asteroxylon* had simple leaves.

6. Sphenopsida.—The only living members of this group are about twenty-five species of horsetails (*Equisetum*). In the Carboniferous period many tree forms existed (*e.g.*, *Calamites*), the remains of which are very common in coal deposits.

7. Lycopsida.—In the Carboniferous period the tree clubmosses were also prominent members of the forests (*e.g.*, *Lepidodendron*). They often reached 100 ft. in height, were branched or unbranched, and had large simple leaves. They also had extensive root systems. The only living members belong to a few genera of small herbaceous clubmosses, such as *Lycopodium* and *Selaginella*. Like the true mosses, they have an alternation of generations, but the elaborate plant with stem, leaves, and roots is the sporophyte, and the gametophyte is very small. In *Lycopodium* only one kind of spore is produced, and the resultant gametophyte is bisexual. *Selaginella* produces numerous small microspores which give rise to the very reduced male gametophytes and motile sperms and the few large megaspores which produce the female gametophytes. The latter are formed within the megaspore wall, which splits to allow the sperms to reach the small archegonia.

8. Filicinæ.—These are the true ferns, which in some classifications are put with the horsetails and clubmosses in the Pteridophyta or vascular cryptogams (*i.e.*, vascular plants without seeds). The ferns have a long fossil history, and remains very similar to the living Royal ferns (*Osmunda*) are known from the Carboniferous. The ferns are widespread and particularly abundant in tropical forests. The majority are herbaceous perennial plants, but a few are aquatic, and there are some tree ferns, which may reach 20 ft. in height. Most ferns possess a stem bearing roots and large leaves or fronds. The plant is the sporophyte and produces numerous spores in sporangia borne on the fronds. Each spore gives rise to a minute green free-living gametophyte known as the prothallus, which bears the archegonia and antheridia. After fertilisation a young sporophyte develops, which at first draws nourishment from the prothallus. Thus, as in the *Bryophyta*, external water is essential for the motile sperms to swim in, and there is a clearly defined alternation of generations, but the sporophyte is a complex independent plant, and the gametophyte is reduced though free-living.

9. Gymnospermæ.—These were the dominant land plants in the Mesozoic era, although fossil remains are found as far back as the Devonian. The living members still form large forests in the North Temperate regions. They are mostly tall evergreen trees with roots, stems, and small leaves. The conifers include the pines (*Pinus*), larches (*Larix*), and yews (*Taxus*). The cycads are a relic group of tropical plants with thick, unbranched trunks and large fern-like leaves. The maiden-hair tree of Japan (*Ginkgo biloba*) has also had a long geological history. Another interesting Gymnosperm is *Metasequoia*, a genus well known to palæobotanists. In 1948 a few living specimens were found in a remote area of China. Seeds were collected and plants are now being grown in botanical gardens all over the world. The Gymnosperms are characterised by the production of " naked " seeds, which are usually borne on cones. The male pollen grains, which are equivalent to the microspores of *Selaginella*, are carried by wind to the ovule of the female cone. The pollen germinates and the pollen tube carries the male gametes to the reduced archegonia borne on the female prothallus, which, unlike those of the ferns, is retained within the ovule on the parent plant. After fertilisation an embryo is formed, the prothallus becomes the food store or endosperm, and the outer part of the ovule becomes the seed coat. The cycads and *Ginkgo* retain a primitive feature in that the male gametes are motile and they swim to the archegonia from the pollen tube.

10. Angiospermæ.—The apparent sudden rise of the Angiosperms in the Cretaceous period is still the " abominable mystery " it was to Darwin. Various suggestions have been put forward, but nothing definite is known about the origin of the group. The Angiosperms or flowering plants are now the dominant group over most of the land surface of the earth, and at least 250,000 species are known. Apart from the natural vegetation, the majority of our crop and garden plants are Angiosperms. They occur in every type of habitat and range in form from gigantic trees to minute plants, such as the duck-weeds. Some are climbers, others succulents, and a number have reverted to the aquatic habit. Although most possess chlorophyll, a few are partial (*e.g.*, Mistletoe) or complete parasites (*e.g.*, Dodder).

Flower, Fruit and Seeds.—The diagnostic feature of the group is the production of seeds, which are completely enclosed within the female part of the flower, the ovary. Basically a flower is a short reproductive shoot which bears several whorls of lateral organs. At the base are several, often green, protective sepals forming the calyx, and above this are the often brightly coloured petals of the corolla. Within this are the stamens of the androecium or male part of the flower. Centrally is the female gynœcium of one or more carpels containing the ovules. The parts of the flower may be free, as in the buttercup, or fused together. In many species the petals are fused (sympetalous), the stamens are borne on the corolla (epipetalous), and the carpels are fused to form a compound gynœcium (syncarpous). The stamens possess anthers, which produce pollen grains. These are shed and carried by insects or wind to the receptive stigmas of the carpels. Each produces a tube which grows down the style to the ovary and enters an ovule. The ovule is a complex structure containing an ovum and a primary endosperm nucleus. Two male nuclei are discharged from the pollen tube, one fuses with the ovum and the other fuses with the primary endosperm nucleus. After this " double fertilisation " an embryo is formed which is embedded in the nutritive endosperm and the outer tissues of the ovule form the seed coat or testa. The ovary of the carpel develops into the fruit containing the seeds. Fruits are of various kinds, being either dehiscent and opening when mature to release the seeds or indehiscent, with a succulent or dry wall. The indehiscent fruits are shed as a whole, and often contain only a single seed. Seeds and fruits show great variation in structure, and often have adaptations assisting dispersal. Some have hairs or wings which aid wind dispersal, whereas others have hooks or are sticky and are transported by animals. Some have flotation devices and may be carried a great distance from the parent plant by water. Seeds vary in size from the microscopic seeds of orchids to those of the double coconut, which may weigh 40 lb. Only about 10% of the weight of a seed is water, and the embryo, although alive, is dormant. The bulk of a seed consists of stored food material, commonly fats or starch and proteins, which may be contained in the endosperm surrounding the embryo, although in some species the endosperm is absorbed during seed development and the food is stored in the one or two swollen seed leaves or cotyledons of the embryo.

Classification of Flowering Plants.—John Ray (1627–1705) was the first botanist to recognise the two great divisions of the Angiosperms—the dicotyledons with two seed leaves and the monocotyledons with only one. This primary division of the flowering plants has stood the test of time and is still recognised. Other differences are also found between the two groups. The dicotyledons usually have net-veined leaves and the floral parts are in fours or fives, whereas the monocotyledons usually have leaves with parallel veins and the floral parts are in threes.

THE PHYSIOLOGY OF PLANTS.

Some of the fundamental differences between animals and plants can be ascribed to the ways in which the two groups of living organisms satisfy their requirements for food material. In a simple way at least, an animal can be thought of as a mobile gastro-intestinal tract which is highly specialised to search out and receive food in convenient, concentrated packets. In typical land plants, however, a quite different organisation exists because the organic nutrition is based on the process of photosynthesis in which carbon dioxide from the air is combined with water from the soil to form simple carbohydrates. An expanded foliage system is necessary to absorb carbon dioxide and to expose the photosynthetic pigment, chlorophyll, to sunlight. Similarly, an expanded root system is needed to absorb the other ingredients of nutrition, water and mineral salts, from the soil.

The work of the plant physiologist is devoted to understanding the functional relationships between these two expanded systems of root and shoot. The production of carbohydrates by photosynthesis has already been discussed (F28). Absorption and transport of water and mineral salts from root to leaf and transport of the synthesised organic compounds from leaves to other parts of the plant continue to be challenging problems. In addition, the physiologist is concerned with the progressive elaboration of root and shoot as the plant grows. Plants show much less specialisation of their cells into discrete tissues and organs than do animals and they also retain special areas, at root and shoot tips for example, where new cells are added to the structure throughout the life of the plant. In some cases whole plants can be regenerated from very few cells taken almost anywhere from a growing plant body. The orderly regulation of growth and differentiation is thus a basic property of much plant tissue.

1. Movement of Solutes and Water.

The movement of water and inorganic solutes in a plant is primarily upwards from the roots where they are absorbed, to the leaves or growing regions where evaporation of water or the use of both water and salts occurs. Water and inorganic ions permeate freely through the cell walls and air spaces of the more peripheral cells of the roots. Equilibrium is established between the insides of cells in this region and the water and salts outside, water tending to enter by osmosis and the salts by diffusion or active transport. Increase in cell volume which would be caused by continual influx of materials is, of course, restricted by the inextensible cell wall. In the centre of the root is a region packed with the specialised conducting tissues called xylem and phloem. These form continuous channels through the root and into the shoot and clearly serve for the conduction of water and substances in solution. In the root this central region is separated from the more peripheral tissue by a single layer of cells, the endodermis. The endodermal layer can actively pump water and salts from the outer regions through into the longitudinal conducting strands of, in this case, the xylem. Evidence for this pumping activity can be seen in the exudation of liquid from the base of a plant stem cut close to ground level. In some cases pressures of 8 to 10 atmospheres have been generated in roots as a result of the pumping action of the endodermal cells.

Water is also moved up a plant by forces generated in the leaves. Constant evaporation from the walls of leaf cells, both on the surface and within the substance of the leaf, causes loss of water from the plant. The process is called transpiration and, within limits, the plant can control transpiration rate by regulating the ease with which water-saturated air passes to the exterior through perforations in the leaf surface called stomata. The diameter of these apertures can be regulated by movements of guard cells surrounding the stomatal openings. Loss of water from the leaf cells is made good by withdrawing more water from the xylem elements within the leaves and stem of the plant. Cohesive forces between water molecules prevent the continuous water columns within the xylem from breaking. The net result is that water is drawn up the stem as transpiration occurs in the leaves. Considerable suction pressures have been measured by suitable manometer systems attached to the cut stems of actively transpiring plants. In addition materials such as dyes or radioactive isotopes have been followed as they move up the conducting xylem vessels at rates which can usually be related to the rate of transpiration.

2. Movement of Organic Substances.

The organic substances, whose site of manufacture is primarily in the leaves, have to be distributed to the rest of the plant body. It is thought that a second conducting tissue, the phloem, is mainly responsible for the distribution of these materials in solution. Phloem is found as a layer of tissue to the outside of the xylem vessels in a plant stem. It consists of conducting cells which are rather different from those of the xylem, which serve, as we have seen, mainly in the transport of water and salts. Whereas xylem tissues are composed of dead cells whose cell walls form effective longitudinal conducting channels, phloem is made up mainly of living cells. Elements called sieve tubes are the most important conducting cells in phloem and, during the initial stages of differentiation, a sieve tube has a full complement of cytoplasm and cell organelles. Later differentiation sees the protoplasmic structures break down, but even in mature sieve tubes protoplasmic strands join through the perforated ends of adjacent cells and may extend longitudinally through the conducting elements.

Ringing experiments in which a complete ring of phloem is cut from the outside of a plant, provide evidence of the tissue's function in longitudinal conduction of carbohydrates. Sugars accumulate above such a ring but not below it. Samples of fluid taken from sieve tubes have also revealed high concentrations of carbohydrates in the sap. The method used to obtain such samples is very ingenious. Several aphids (insects such as green fly) are known which parasitise the phloem translocation channels of plants. The aphid is allowed to insert its stylet tip into the phloem vessels and is then anaesthetised and cut off the inserted stylet. Sap exudes from the stylet stump and can be collected and analysed.

Although the phloem is definitely implicated in transport of organic food materials in solution, the mechanism of this transport is still the subject of controversy. One theory suggests a mass flow of material such as occurs in the xylem; in this case the driving force is generated because of a concentration difference between the region of production of a carbohydrate and the regions of use. The sieve tubes with their interconnections blocked by protoplasmic strands are obviously not ideally adapted to mass flow of liquid. Moreover there are several observations which suggest that materials move simultaneously in both directions and that different substances can move at different rates. An alternative theory proposes that phloem transport is due to cytoplasmic streaming. Strands of protoplasm may move from cell to cell through the sieve plate connections, carrying metabolic products with them. A transport system such as this would require energy and it is known that translocation is frequently associated with high levels of metabolic activity in the phloem tissue. However, direct observations of cytoplasmic streaming in phloem vessels have not been made.

3. Growth.

Growth is usually, but not always, thought of as involving increase of size as measured by length, volume, or weight. In these terms any unit in a plant, whether root, shoot or fruit would follow a sigmoid growth curve with growth starting slowly, then speeding up, before finally slowing down at maturity leading on to death. Growth may also be considered as an increase in the number of cells, an increase in substances such as water, protein or DNA in the growing system, or an increase in complexity of organisation.

The organisation of growth, no matter how it is measured, presents a number of interesting problems. In the first divisions of a fertilised egg, all cells divide. Very soon this property becomes localised, polarity is established, and the young embryo develops a shoot tip and a root tip. These have then become discrete regions of cell division. The cells behind them cease active division, enlarge by developing large vacuoles and form mature plant tissue. A circular strand of dividing tissue, called the cambium, is left in the stem between differentiated xylem and phloem. The cambium is responsible for growth in girth. The acquisition of polarity has far-reaching consequences, for the behaviour of a shoot tip is very different from that of a root. The shoot tip, for example, gives rise to leaf cells with photosynthesising chloroplasts and it grows upwards away from gravity and towards light. The root tip gives rise to cells which absorb salt and water, and it grows towards gravity and away from light.

Quite a lot is known about the mechanisms which regulate growth by cell enlargement in the regions behind the actively dividing tips. Cell enlargement is achieved by the secretion of water and solutes to form a substantial vacuole within the cell, thus causing an overall increase of volume and expansion of the cell wall. The degree of enlargement is affected by external stimuli such as light and gravity, producing the differential growth patterns seen when plants orientate to these stimuli. Substances, called plant hormones or auxins, are now known to be produced at the growing apex and to move back causing vacuole formation in the actively elongating region. The distribution of auxin is affected by light or gravity so that the plant will turn towards or away from the stimulus. Indoleacetic acid is the active growth substance occurring naturally in many plants. Several man-made substances are also effective and are widely used as weedkillers. Evidence is also accumulating to show that a group of substances exists in plants to control cell division, just as auxins regulate cell enlargement.

ECOLOGY—THE STUDY OF LIVING ORGANISMS IN THEIR ENVIRONMENT.

So far we have examined biological organisation at the level of the cell through to the whole, multicellular organism. The important branch of biology which deals with the relationship between living organisms and their environment must now be considered. Living organisms and the physical environment in which they exist form what is termed an ecosystem. Obviously it would be possible to regard the whole world as a giant ecosystem, though for purposes of study it would be extremely unrewarding and impractical to adopt such an extreme attitude. A pond, a rocky or sandy shore, a forest, and a peat bog are examples of ecosystems on a somewhat smaller scale, possessing different properties and containing populations of animals and plants that are different both in number of individuals and in species represented. The ecologist seeks to understand why a particular species is present in certain numbers in an ecosystem in terms of that species' interaction with all other living organisms (biotic factors) and with the physical (abiotic) factors of the ecosystem.

1. Abiotic Factors.

All living organisms will show ranges of tolerance for abiotic factors such as temperature, humidity, salinity, oxygen levels, amount of light, etc. Clearly, if any factor in the environment moves outside the range of tolerance of a species, it becomes limiting for that particular species which is then excluded from the environment. Within the range of tolerance there will be an optimum value for each abiotic factor at which a species will survive best.

There is not a firm line separating suitable and unsuitable environments, but rather a steady shift from optimum values into conditions in which an organism finds it more and more difficult to survive. The interaction of different abiotic factors in an environment produces a complex situation which will make the environment suitable for one species but will exclude another species having slightly different abiotic optima from the first, even though the conditions are not outside the tolerance ranges of either species. Thus trout and carp show considerable overlap in the ranges of temperature, oxygenation of the water, and speed of water current in which they can survive and it is possible for both species to live in the same pool or tank. In the wild, however, they tend to form part of different ecosystems because trout have a lower temperature optimum, need more oxygen, and are more active than carp. Trout are found in rapidly-flowing, cool, unpolluted chalk streams whereas carp live best in shallow lakes which are somewhat warmer and rather stagnant.

One of the most important abiotic factors in an environment is the nature of the substrate upon or within which an organism moves and settles.

(*a*) **The Terrestrial Environment.**—Soil is the commonest substrate for terrestrial organisms. Particle sizes, ranging from the coarsest gravel soils, through sands and silts to the finely textured clays, have extensive effects on the flora and fauna of any area. Coarsely textured soils are obviously penetrated most easily both by roots and by soil animals. Soils of this type also allow the rapid movement of water and soil gases, but they have the serious disadvantage of poor water retention. The level at which water saturation occurs is known as the water table and is an important abiotic factor. The terrestrial environment tends on the whole to dehydrate organisms and there is always a marked dependence on water supplies.

Soil characteristics also vary with depth. A vertical section through any soil is referred to as its profile and has considerable bearing on the ecosystems in which the soil is involved. The layers, or horizons, of a soil profile vary enormously from one soil to another. Below a surface layer of organic debris one can, in general terms, distinguish a layer of soil from which substances have been leached (A horizon), soil containing the leached-out substances from the layer above (B horizon), the weathered parent material (C horizon), and finally the parent rock or some other stratum beneath the soil (D horizon).

Humus, which is formed from animal and plant remains and is located in the lower parts of the A profile, is of great importance in providing food for soil organisms and chemical elements such as nitrogen, phosphorus, and calcium for plant growth. It is also important in maintaining good soil structure and, though inorganic fertilisers can supply chemical elements, they have little or no effect on structure. Soil requires careful cultivation, and structure is easily disturbed by such things as heavy farm machinery. The smearing of soils by spinning tractor wheels as wet land is ploughed, or the winter harvesting of crops such as sugar beet in adverse conditions, eventually leads to the creation of impermeable layers with the disastrous exclusion of oxygen and oxygen-consuming organisms.

(*b*) **The Aquatic Environments.**—Marine and freshwater environments together cover more than 75 per cent of the earth's surface and, since they can be occupied throughout their entire depth, offer a much greater volume of living space than does the land. There is only a slight difference between the density of water and of living tissues, so that the bodies of aquatic organisms are very largely supported by the environment and do not need strong woody stems or powerfully muscled limbs to hold them up. Water has a high specific heat, which means that large amounts of heat are needed to raise its temperature. The result is that aquatic environments tend to show much smaller fluctuations in temperature than the terrestrial ones. In general, the larger the volume of water the smaller are the fluctuations in temperature, and so the fauna and flora of the oceans will not show wide temperature tolerance, whereas that of small pools will, but in neither case will the tolerance be so great as that shown by many terrestrial forms. Oxygen and carbon dioxide concentrations are very different in water and in air and this has led in animals to the development of gill systems for gas exchange rather than the lungs, or lung-type structures, of terrestrial forms. Gas concentrations are also variable from one aquatic environment to another, making them suitable for the support of different fauna and flora.

An important difference between the sea and freshwater is seen when their salt concentrations are determined. This is usually done experimentally by measuring the temperature at which the medium freezes, because a well-established relationship exists between the salt concentration in a solution and the extent to which the freezing point is lowered below that of the solvent (in this case distilled water) alone. Thus, freshwater freezes at 0 °C or just below whereas sea water, with its high salt content, freezes at −1·9 °C, and a mixture of half fresh and half sea water freezes at −0·95 °C. Organisms living in fresh or in sea water face quite dissimilar problems in osmotic and ionic regulation. Life evolved originally in the sea and the salt concentration in the blood of marine molluscs, crustaceans, and echinoderms, for example, produces precisely the same freezing point depression as does sea water itself. Marine organisms have, on several occasions in the course of their evolution, moved into freshwater. Representatives of the worms, crustaceans, molluscs, and vertebrates have all independently invaded this very dilute habitat. What is more, all these animals show approximately the same types of modification to cope with the change. Their outer layers, in the main, become impermeable and the salt concentration of their blood is reduced considerably (to a freezing point of −1·0 °C in fish and to a spectacularly low level in the freshwater mussel, depressing the freezing point to a mere −0·2 °C). The kidneys become enlarged and produce a large volume of dilute urine. By these means freshwater animals can cut down loss of their salts to the dilute medium and can also remove the large volume of water that enters their bodies by osmosis. It is interesting that all terrestrial vertebrates, including the mammals, have retained a salt concentration in their blood of about half the seawater level and this is partly attributable to their freshwater ancestry. The transition between seawater and freshwater was achieved via brackish water estuaries and the organisms which live under brackish water conditions today are of great interest in showing how tolerance of substantial fluctuations in salinity can be achieved. The ultimate development of salinity tolerance is seen in such animals as the salmon and eel which move from fresh to salt water and back again during their life cycle.

2. Biotic Factors.

(*a*) **Associations between Organisms.**—No organism can be considered to be independent of any other organism in an ecosystem but in some cases close associations of various types can be developed between different species or different members of the same species.

Commensalism is an association which benefits one member but has little effect on the other. Small organisms can live within the protective covering offered by a larger individual, as, for example, commensal crabs living within the shell of some species of oyster.

Symbiosis is a somewhat closer association in which both members benefit, as do certain species of green algae and the coelenterates in whose body tissues they live. The algae are protected and the coelenterates benefit from the food produced by the photosynthetic plant. Some symbiotic organisms are unable to survive outside the association. The lichens which are associations of algae and fungi, are examples of this type of symbiosis, as are some of the food-processing **micro-organisms** together with the animals in whose intestinal tracts they live.

Social animals. In some cases animals of the same species form social groups in which co-operative effort and division of labour makes them more successful in exploiting a particular environment. Social development is most obvious among certain insects such as termites, ants, wasps, and bees, and among the vertebrates. Social organisation in these groups may lead to the development of different behaviour patterns and ultimately, as in ants and bees, for example, to the evolution of a variety of structural modifications so that different castes are recognisable.

Parasitism. Not all associations are of mutual benefit and when one organism becomes sufficiently specialised so that it can live successfully on materials extracted from another, the latter is always adversely affected. Parasites, by causing disease in, and sometimes the death of, the host, can influence population growth and size. Important groups are bacteria, protozoa, fungi, nematodes (roundworms), and platyhelminths (tapeworms and liver flukes). Viruses are also important disease-producing agents which are incapable of an independent existence outside the cells of the host and utilise the host cell's metabolic pathways directly to synthesise new virus material.

Many parasites (and other pests which may disturb the comfort and health of man) can now be controlled to some extent, and, for a variety of reasons, such control procedures have extensive effects on the ecosystems involved. The regulation of some bacterial parasites by means of antibiotics, and control of the insect vectors of organisms such as the malaria parasite by means of insecticides, have both been important factors in the increase in human population. Though the beneficial effects of pest control of all types are clear, the process is not without its difficulties and dangers. Indiscriminate use of many chemical agents has led to the development of resistant strains. In any group of organisms, some will naturally be more resistant to a pesticide or antibiotic than others and these will be the survivors of any treatment that is less than totally effective. They will form the breeding stock for subsequent generations and so progressively more and more resistant types will evolve. Thus, there are now many strains of bacteria resistant to penicillin and other antibiotics. Even more alarming is the recent discovery that this resistance can be transferred in an infective way between bacteria of different species. Another complication associated with chemical control is that the agent concerned frequently affects a wide spectrum of organisms, including those that are in no sense injurious to man or his crops. Thus DDT kills bees and other pollinating insects unless its application to a crop is very precisely timed. In addition, the accumulation of quantities of chlorinated hydrocarbons such as DDT in the environment is known to have an injurious effect on organisms other than insects. Because these chemicals are broken down very slowly they now form a serious problem in environmental pollution.

Predation. A less direct association than that between parasite and host is the one which exists between predators and the prey which they capture and kill. However, interactions in both parasitism and predation have features in common, particularly those affecting population numbers. If the abundance of prey increases, the effort and time required for a capture is reduced so that the rate of predation must also go up. Eventually, however, predators do not respond to further increases in prey; because they are satiated, or for some other behavioural reason, a maximum predation rate is reached in a population of a certain size. Increased prey density also tends to result in larger numbers of predators, produced either by aggregation from outside areas or by increased reproduction rate. The density of predators then begins to have its limiting affect on the rate of predation. The total response may lead to stability in numbers but more often periodic oscillations in the number of both predators and prey are seen.

(*b*) **The Food Factor.**—Plants are the ultimate source of organic food for all animals. The most important food plants are those capable of photosynthesis (**F28**) in which organic material is synthesised from carbon dioxide and water, using radiant energy from the sun to drive the reaction.

Food Chains. Plants are eaten by herbivores which in turn are eaten by carnivores. It is possible to see many such sequences, called food chains, in all ecosystems. For example, in the open sea, green algae are the important photosynthetic organisms; these are eaten by a small crustacean, *Calanus*, which in turn forms a large part of the diet of the herring. Feeding relationships are usually of much greater complexity than is suggested by a simple food chain. Thus, Calanus represents about 20 per cent of the herring's diet but it is also eaten by many other marine animals as well. For example, it forms about 70 per cent of the total diet of larval sand eels. The larval eels are eaten in turn by the herring and may form 40 per cent of its diet. Because an animal's diet is usually quite varied and one species of animal or plant may be part of the food of a wide range of different animals, interactions are set up which are referred to as food webs. The more knowledge there is about a particular food web, the more complex it becomes. However, for general comparative purposes it is possible to disregard the detail of species and to group together all organisms with similar food habits. When this is done a relationship known as pyramid of numbers often appears in which organisms at the base of a food chain (the primary producers) are extremely abundant, while those at the apex (the final consumers) are relatively few in number.

Productivity. The validity of using numbers of individuals in such an analysis is often open to question, especially when ecosystems are to be compared. For example, a comparison between numbers of herring and numbers of whales as final consumers in two pyramidal systems is not very informative. This difficulty is partially overcome by using estimates of the total weight (biomass) of organisms at each level rather than their number. Even this has disadvantages because determinations of biomass give a measure of the amount of material present at any one time (the standing crop) but give no indication of the amount of material being produced or the rate of its production (the productivity). In some parts of the sea, for example, the biomass of small animals forming the zooplankton is greater than that of the plant life or phytoplankton on which it depends for food. This seems to contravene the pyramid concept. However, the rate of production of new material by the phytoplankton is very much greater than by the zooplankton so that, if taken over a year, the total amount of plant material produced would far exceed the total production of animal material. Productivity is a concept of great practical and theoretical importance. It may be determined in terms of the actual organic material produced in an area over a set period of time or, more usefully, in terms of the amounts of energy transferred and stored at each food level, again over a set period of time.

Under natural conditions only 1 to 5 per cent of the light falling on a plant is converted by its photosynthetic system into chemical energy contained in the material of its tissues. Similarly herbivores which consume plants will pass on to their predators only some 10 per cent of the energy contained in the plant material they eat. These low values for photosynthetic efficiency and ecological efficiency respectively are due to the fact that most of the energy appears as heat during the metabolic reactions needed to sustain life and only a small amount is incorporated into new tissue. It is easy to see that the form of a pyramid of numbers can be explained in terms of low ecological efficiency, as can the observation that a food chain rarely has more than five links. The loss of energy at each stage must mean that each succeeding stage becomes smaller and smaller in number and that the number of stages is severely limited.

Human Population and Food. The present very large increase in human population and the predicted rise from 3,300 million in 1968 to 6,000 million in the year 2000 has led to a pressing need for the controlled exploitation of food resources in the world. Consideration of the processes of energy transfer suggests that man should be mainly herbivorous. They also suggest that present agricultural crops, with the possible exception of sugar cane do not achieve as high a primary productivity as that encountered in some natural ecosystems. Crops rarely achieve complete plant cover of the land throughout the growing season so as to trap the maximum amount of sunlight. It would be necessary to mix crops to do this effectively and there would then be complicated harvesting problems.

If man remains an omnivore, as he almost certainly will, then his domestic food animals will continue to be herbivorous as they are at present, though whether they will be the same herbivores is less easy to predict. Beef cattle raised on grassland convert only 4 per cent of the energy in the plants of their environment into similar chemical energy in their tissues. At the present time intensive farming practices are being empoyed to improve conversion, usually by harvesting plant material, processing it, and bringing it to the animals which are housed in special buildings. This cuts down on the wastage of plant food because it can be grown under better conditions and less of it is consumed by animals other than the cattle. Careful breeding and the limitation of the period over which livestock is raised to that of maximum growth efficiency have also contributed to conversions of some 35 per cent, achieved in the case of broiler chickens and calves. The moral problems raised by these methods and the circumstances which make them necessary give rise to widespread concern.

Fish are also an important part of man's diet and again an understanding of the ecology of food fish is important in running efficient fisheries. Many populations have been overfished so that returns have gone down in spite of intensified fishing effort. The fisheries scientist is concerned to discover the limit at which the maximum number of fish can be taken without depleting the population year by year. Research is also going on into possible methods of enclosing and farming areas of the sea or estuaries.

Population Dynamics.

Factors such as those outlined above interact to determine the size and character of any population of living organism. Study of the numbers of organisms in a population, together with their change and regulation, forms a branch of the subject of considerable practical importance known as population dynamics.

Numbers of animals and plants tend to increase up to the capacity of the environment, at which stage some essential resource will exert a limiting effect. The rate of increase will be determined by the balance between reproduction rate and mortality. As Malthus appreciated, adults of any organism tend to replace themselves by a greater number of progeny and, in the absence of losses by mortality and other factors, there is a vast potential for increase in all populations. If an organism doubles its number in a year, there will be a 1,000-fold increase in 10 years, and a 10 million-fold increase in 20 years. Increase of this type soon leads to shortages and overcrowding so that mortality goes up, the net rate of increase diminishes, and finally an equilibrium is reached with no further increase in number. The change from low to high numbers with the passage of time follows an S-shaped curve, starting slowly, becoming faster and faster, and then slowing down to equilibrium.

When a population reaches equilibrium, the numbers are kept at a steady level by factors such as competition for food, refuge, or space. These factors are said to be density-dependent because greater numbers in the population intensify the competition and increase mortality, lower numbers decrease competition and favour survival. Abundance is therefore regulated by density-dependent processes arising from interactions, first, between individuals making up the population, and secondly, between the population under consideration and other populations whose members may be competitors, predators, or food. The level of abundance at which this regulation occurs may vary greatly and will be determined, at least in part, by general environmental factors such as temperature, rainfall, amount of sunlight, the nature of the vegetation, and so on.

Human population is increasing rapidly at the present time, mainly because of the fall in death-rate. Food production is also increasing, but in some areas of the world supply and requirement are so evenly matched that drought or war are inevitably followed by a famine. Though the human population has not yet reached the stage of equilibrium, it is clear that ultimately it must be subject to forces of regulation similar to those that control populations of other organisms. Birth-rate cannot exceed death-rate indefinitely in any living organism. By limiting the size of families it is possible for man to achieve a population equilibrium at levels lower than those at which regulative factors such as famine or aggression must begin to operate. Rational control of birth-rate seems to offer the best chance of averting a global population disaster.

THE GEOLOGICAL RECORD.

The various stages in the history of the earth can be read by the geologists in the strata or layers of rock laid down since the planet began to solidify, and it is in these rocks, too, that the record of life upon earth may be traced.

No Life Rocks.—The earliest rocks in the record are known as the Azoic (no life) rocks, because they show no trace of living things, and these layers are of such thickness that they occupy more than half of the whole record. That is to say, for more than half of the earth's history nothing living existed upon any part of the globe. For millions of years the surface of our planet was nothing but bare rock without soil or sand, swept by hot winds exceeding in violence the wildest tornadoes of today, and drenched by torrential downpours of tropical rain, which, as we have seen elsewhere, gradually tore away the surface to form sandy sediments at the bottom of the seas. In such ancient rocks pushed above the surface by later upheavals we can still trace the marks of primeval oceans as they rippled upon the barren shores or of raindrops which left their imprint perhaps 1,500 million years ago.

Primitive Sea-life.—As we move upwards through the strata, however, traces of life begin to appear and steadily increase as we come to the more recent levels. The earliest signs appear in what is known as the Early Paleozoic Age (or by some writers as the Proterozoic Age), when we find the fossilised remains of small shellfish, seaweeds, and trilobites—the latter were creatures somewhat like the plant-lice of modern times. All these primitive animals and plants lived in the shallow tidal waters of ancient seas; for as yet life had not invaded either the dry land or the deep oceans. It is, of course, clear that these creatures of Early Paleozoic times were not the first living things: they were merely the first creatures capable of leaving fossilised remains, and without doubt must have had more primitive ancestors—amœbic-like forms, jellyfish, bacteria, and so on whose bodies were too soft to leave any traces in the record of the rocks.

The Age of Fishes.—Towards the end of the Early Paleozoic Era, in what we now know as the Silurian period, there arose a new form of life: the first backboned animals, primitive fishes somewhat similar to the sharks of today; and in the division of the Upper Paleozoic Era known as the Devonian, they had come to multiply so greatly that this is frequently described as the Age of Fishes.

First Land Animals and Plants.—It is about this time, too, that we begin to find traces of animal and plant life upon the dry land. Both animals and plants had acute problems to solve before it became possible for them to live out of water; for both animals and plants had hitherto been supported by the surrounding water and respired by removing oxygen dissolved in the water. In land animals this problem was solved by a long series of adaptations from gills to lungs. Plants were able to invade the land because of the evolution of an impermeable outer cuticle which prevented water loss and also the development of woody tissues which provided support and a water-conducting system for the whole plant body.

Amphibia and Spore-bearing Trees.—The first type of vertebrates (backboned animals) to live upon dry land was the group of amphibia in the Carboniferous Age, which is today represented by the newts, frogs, toads, and salamanders. In

THE GEOLOGICAL TIME SCALE

ERAS	PERIODS	AGE (millions of years)	LIFE
CAENOZOIC	Pleistocene	1	Man
	Pliocene		Birds, Mammals and modern plants; Molluscs
	Miocene	25	
	Oligocene		
	Eocene	70	
MESOZOIC	Cretaceous	135	Dinosaurs, Cycads; Earliest Birds; Ammonites and Sea-urchins
	Jurassic	180	
	Triassic	225	
PALAEOZOIC	Permian	270	First mammals; Early reptiles
	Carboniferous	350	Amphibians, tree-ferns, first insects
	Devonian	400	Fishes, first land plants
	Silurian	440	Mainly invertebrate animals; no life on land. Trilobites and graptolites
	Ordovician	500	
	Cambrian	600	
PRE-CAMBRIAN (also PROTEROZOIC, ARCHAEOZOIC)		2,000	Life emerges
		4,600	Age of Earth

all these forms the eggs give rise to a tadpole stage with gills which lives for some time entirely in water. Later the gills give place to a primitive form of lung which enables the animal to live upon land. Even so, amphibia are restricted more or less to swampy or marshy land, and without a damp environment they would dry up and shrivel to death. The most abundant forms of plant life in the Carboniferous period were the tree-like horsetails, clubmosses, and ferns, the fossilised tissues of which are found in the coal measures and are burned as household coal. But these plants also, as in the case of the amphibia, could exist only amongst the swamps and marshes, and life, although it had freed itself from the necessity of existence in the waters of the earth, still had to return to the water in order to reproduce itself. The highlands and the deeper waters of the planet were still empty of living things. Although the Carboniferous period had been a period of warmth and abundance, the Paleozoic Era came to an end with a long cycle of dry and bitterly cold ages. Such long-term climatic changes were due, it is now supposed, to such factors as changes in the earth's orbit, the shifting of its axis of rotation, changes in the shape of the land masses, and so on. Long before the Ice Ages of more recent times, there are records in the rocks of alternating periods of warmth and cold as far back as the Azoic and Early Paleozoic Eras. This long cold spell at the close of the Paleozoic era came to an end about 220 million years ago, and was succeeded by a long era of widely spread warm conditions—the Mesozoic Era, the so-called Age of Reptiles.

The Mesozoic Era.—The reptiles first appeared in the Permian, but it was during the Mesozoic era that they became the dominant group of animals. The giant reptiles included the stegosaurus, the gigantosaurus, the diplodocus, and many other kinds which were far larger than any land animals living today. Some, for example the diplodocus, were 100 ft. long, although they were vegetarian in habit and were preyed upon by other almost equally huge flesh-eating reptiles. Some species, such as the plesiosaurs and icthyosaurs, became secondarily aquatic, while the pterodactyl possessed wings with which it could glide and perhaps fly short distances. However, they all differed from the amphibia in that they had hard, dry skins, their lungs were more efficient, fertilisation was internal due to the development of copulatory organs, and they laid eggs with hard, protective shells.

It was also during the Mesozoic era that the warm-blooded birds arose. The birds, like the reptiles, lay eggs with hard shells, and they have several internal features found in the reptiles. The fossil bird Archæopteryx, three specimens of which have been found in Germany, lived in the Jurassic period. Although it was obviously a bird, it retained many reptilian features. Earliest mammals are recognised in rocks of the late Palaeozoic but in the Mesozoic considerable evolution of the group took place. The fossil Trituberculata which are also found in the Jurassic, are believed to be related to forms from which both the marsupial and placental mammals arose. Although insects were present as far back as the Carboniferous, it was in the Mesozoic that many of the groups we know today first appeared.

Great changes also took place in the plant cover of the land during this era. The spore-bearing giant horsetails and tree clubmosses declined and were replaced by gymnosperms—trees bearing naked seeds. One large group of these, the cycadeoids, has become extinct, but the conifers and a few of the once abundant cycads still remain. The flowering plants or angiosperms also made their appearance, and towards the end of the Cretaceous their evolution was extremely rapid. In fact, many of the fossil leaves found in rocks of Cretaceous age are indistinguishable from those of some present-day flowering plants.

A New Era.—But, perhaps 150 million years later, all this seemingly everlasting warmth and sunshine, the lush tropical life, the giant reptiles who had ruled the world, were wiped out by a new period of bitter cold which only the hardy species could survive. A new Era known as the Caenozoic was beginning, ushered in by a period of upheaval and volcanic activity, following which the map of the world came to resemble more closely the picture we know today. The cold period may have lasted several million years, and the main species to survive it were those which had come into existence towards the end of the Mesozoic Era, the seed-bearing flowering plants, the birds, and the mammals. The once all-powerful reptiles from this time onwards are represented only by the comparatively few and relatively small reptilian species of today: the snakes, lizards, crocodiles, and alligators. It was at this time, too, that, long after the creation of the mountains of Scotland and Norway (the so-called Caledonian revolution), or even of the Appalachian mountains (the Appalachian revolution), there arose the great masses of the Alps, the Himalayas, the Rocky Mountains, and the Andes. These are the mountain chains of the most recent, the Caenozoic revolution. Initially, as we have seen, the climate of the Caenozoic Era was cold, but the weather grew generally warmer until a new period of abundance was reached, only to be followed at the end of the Pliocene by a period of glacial ages generally known as the First, Second, Third, and Fourth Ice Ages.

THE EVOLUTION OF ORGANISMS.

(*see also* Special Topic, F58)

Introduction.—It is commonly thought that the great 19th cent. naturalist Charles Darwin was the first person to suggest that life had continually evolved. However, the idea that species of living organisms could change over long periods of time was considered by some Greek writers and, much later, by the Frenchmen Buffon and Lamarck at the end of the 18th cent. Further, the work of the 18th cent. geologists such as James Hutton and William Smith provided a basis without which Darwin's contribution would have been impossible. Hutton showed that the earth's surface had undergone prolonged upheavals and volcanic eruptions with consequent changes in sea level. This implied that the earth was much older than had previously been supposed. Smith developed a method of dating the geological strata by means of the fossils found in them and demonstrated that widely different types of animals and plants existed at different periods of the earth's history. As described in the previous section a general picture is presented of the evolution of organisms from the simple to the complex and from the aquatic to the terrestrial environment. These discoveries were in conflict with the Biblical account in the book of Genesis and, although various attempts were made to explain them away or discredit them, it became abundantly clear that through millions of years life has been continually changing, with new species constantly arising and many dying out. Before considering Darwin's major contribution to the theory of evolution it will be appropriate to outline briefly the various lines of evidence which indicate that, in fact, evolution has taken place.

The Evidence for Evolution.

1. *The Geological Record.*—It has already been pointed out that successively younger rocks contain fossil remains of different and relatively more complex organisms. The spore-bearing plants preceded the gymnosperms and the angiosperms arose much later. Similarly in the vertebrate series the fish appeared before the amphibia which were followed by the reptiles and later by the air breathing, warm-blooded birds and mammals. On a more restricted level the rocks provide even greater support for the occurrence of evolution. For example, the evolution of the horse has been worked out in great detail from the small Eohippus which was about a foot high and had four digits on the forefeet and three on the hind feet to the large one-toed animal living today. However, such complete series are rare and the geological record is very incomplete. There are a number of gaps, particularly between the major groups of organisms. No satisfactory fossil evidence is known of the ancestors of the angiosperms (F40) and although some may be discovered it could be that they did not grow in conditions which favoured

their preservation as fossils. On the other hand, Archæopteryx provides an indisputable link between the reptiles and the birds.

Another important point should also be made about the geological record. Although we talk about the age of fishes, the age of reptiles and so on it must be emphasised that these are the periods during which particular groups were abundant or even dominant. Each group probably originated many millions of years before it became widespread. Further, some groups, such as the giant reptiles and the seed-ferns, died out completely whereas others, the fishes and true ferns for example, are still common today. However, even in the latter groups there is evidence that they have continued to evolve so that many fishes and ferns that exist today are very different from those of the Devonian and Carboniferous periods (F45). On the other hand, the geological record also shows that some species, for example the Maiden-hair tree, have remained unaltered for many millions of years.

2. *Geographical Distribution.*—Nearly all the marsupials or pouched mammals are found in the Australian continent which was cut off from the mainland about 60 million years ago. All the fossil evidence indicates that at that time the eutherian or placental mammals did not yet exist. The marsupials are the only naturally occurring mammals in Australia (F33(2)) but since the isolation of the continent the group has given rise to a large number of species very similar in appearance to those which evolved elsewhere in the world among the eutherian mammals. There are marsupials which look like wolves, dogs, cats and squirrels; yet they have no close biological relationships to these animals. Further, some marsupials such as the kangaroos have evolved which are unlike any other creatures in the rest of the world. Quite clearly the isolation of Australia so long ago has resulted in the evolution of these distinct types. A similar small-scale effect of isolation was studied by Darwin in the Galapagos islands where each has its own distinct flora and fauna which differ also from those of the S. American mainland.

3. *Anatomy.*—The comparative study of the development and mature structure of the mammalian body provides much evidence that all the species have evolved from a single ancestral stock. Although the arm of an ape, the leg of a dog, the flipper of a whale and the wing of a bat appear very different externally they are all built on the same skeletal plan. It would be difficult to explain such similarities unless they had all evolved from a common type. There is also evidence that the early development of an animal recapitulates its biological history to a certain extent. For example, the gill slits found in fish are formed during the early stages in the development of a mammal although later they disappear. Finally, apparently useless vestigial structures sometimes occur which would be inexplicable unless regarded in the light of an evolutionary history. In man a small appendix and vestiges of a third eyelid occur but these are functionless although in other animals such structures are well developed and functional, *e.g.*, the appendix in the rabbit.

4. *Human Selection.*—During his brief history on earth modern man has continually selected and bred animals and plants for his own use. We have only to look at the various breeds of dogs which have been developed from a single wild type to see that under certain circumstances great structural divergence can occur in a species even in a relatively short time.

The Darwinian Theory of Evolution.—Darwin amassed a great deal of information such as that outlined above which convinced him that evolution of life had taken place over millions of years. His was the first real attempt to collect all the evidence scientifically and no other satisfactory alternative explanation of all the facts he presented has been proposed. Perhaps even more important was his attempt to explain *how* evolution had actually occurred. He published his theory after many years of work in his book *The Origin of Species by Means of Natural Selection* in 1859. Some of his ideas have since been modified owing to our increased knowledge of genetics but they are so important that it is worth while recounting the main points of his theory.

1. *The Struggle for Existence.*—It is clear that in nature there is a severe struggle for existence in all animals and plants. Over a period of time the number of individuals of a species in a given community does not vary greatly. This implies that the number of progeny which survive to become mature breeding individuals more or less replaces the number of mature ones that die. Generally speaking the reproductive output of a species is much greater than this. For example, a single large foxglove plant may produce half a million seeds each one of which is potentially capable of giving rise to a new individual. Obviously nearly all the progeny die before reaching maturity and the chance of any single one surviving is very remote.

2. *Variation.*—The individuals of any generation of human beings obviously differ from one another and such differences are found in other organisms. No two animals of the same species (except perhaps for identical twins) are exactly alike and when a large number of individuals are examined it is clear that they vary considerably in structure, colour, activity and so on. Darwin also pointed out that generally these variations were passed on from one generation to the next, for example, the children of tall parents tend to grow tall.

3. *Survival of the Fittest.*—If there is an intense struggle for existence in their natural environment among individuals of a species having different characteristics, those which are best "fitted" to a given set of conditions are most likely to survive to maturity. These will reproduce and the features which enabled them to survive will be passed on to their offspring. This process is liable to continue and a species will become better adapted to its environment.

4. *Natural Selection.*—Over a long period of time the environment of a given species is never stable but will change in various ways. As it does so the characters which best fit the individuals to the changed environment will be selected (not consciously of course) and the species will change. The environment may change only in part of the range of the species and thus lead to divergence and the production of a new species alongside the old one.

Darwin and Lamarck.—Darwin pictured evolution as a slow continuous process with natural selection operating on the small inheritable variations found between the individuals of a species which are undergoing intense competition. This neglects the important effect of the environment on the growth and structure of the individual. It is obvious that external conditions will affect the development of an organism, for example the effect of various soil conditions on the growth of a plant or the amount of food material available to an animal. Lamarck maintained that the characters acquired by an individual owing to the effect of its environment could be passed on to its offspring. Undoubtedly characters are acquired by the individual during its growth but in spite of many attempts to prove otherwise no experiments have been done which prove conclusively that these are inherited by the offspring. Thus Lamarck's theory that evolution has occurred by the inheritance of acquired characters is not generally acceptable today.

Mutation Theory.—The data accumulated by Darwin showed that the variations between individuals of a species are small and graded into one another. If a particular character in a group of individuals is measured it is found that it varies symmetrically about a mean or average, with most values clustered about the mean and with few extreme ones. Darwin himself was worried about this fact because, although selection over a long period of time might shift the position of the mean, he did not see how it could bring about the discontinuity necessary for the establishment of a distinct new species. De Vries in his *Mutation Theory* published in 1901 put forward the view that evolution depends, not on the accumulation of continuous minute variations, but primarily upon large discontinuous variations or mutations. The importance of such spontaneous "sports" was considered by Darwin but he rejected the idea because when they appear they are usually "monstrous". Such individuals are less "fitted" to their environment and therefore they will not survive to reproduce and give rise to a new species. That mutations are important factors in evolution is undoubtedly true but modern work has shown that the whole problem is far more complex than either Darwin or De Vries supposed.

Mendelism.—It is remarkable that in spite of carrying out many careful experiments on inheritance in plants Darwin did not discover the simple laws which are the basis of modern genetics. Mendel investigated inheritance in the garden pea and published his results in 1865, *i.e.*, at the time that Darwin's work was being widely discussed. However, Mendel's important discoveries were not generally known until 1900. When he crossed a pure breeding tall plant with a pure breeding dwarf plant all the progeny were tall. When these plants were self-pollinated the next generation consisted of approximately one quarter dwarf plants and three quarters tall. From this and similar experiments Mendel deduced that the "factors" passed from parents to offspring were paired, only one of the pair came from each parent and that one could be dominant over the other. When he dealt with two pairs of characters, *e.g.*, tall or dwarf plants and round or wrinkled seeds, he found that they segregated and recombined independently and in predictable ratios.

The importance of Mendel's work in relation to evolution is that it showed that there was no blending of the characters in the offspring.

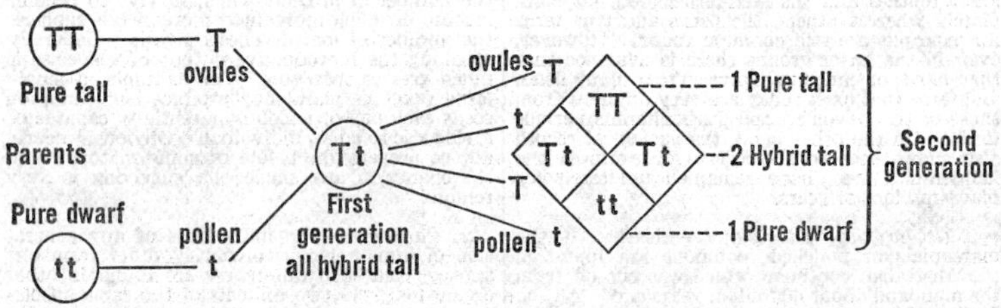

Mutations can be hidden as recessive characters in a population and are not diluted or lost. Although they may not be of importance when they first appear they may be so if the selection pressure changes and they become of survival value. Thus specific characters may change or diverge and evolution will take place. His investigations also showed that recombination of factors could give rise to plants with new characteristics. By crossing a pure bred tall plant having round seeds with a dwarf plant having wrinkled seeds he produced in the second generation some tall plants with wrinkled seeds and dwarf plants with round seeds. When a large number of characters are involved it is obvious that considerable variation and recombination occurs upon which natural selection can work.

Mendel was fortunate in his choice of experimental material with its easily recognisable contrasting characters. It is now known that his "factors" are the genes carried by the chromosomes in the nucleus of the cell. At the present time the biochemical basis of heredity is being vigorously investigated. *See* F31.

V. MAN AND HIS ENVIRONMENT

THE CHALLENGE TO MANKIND.

I. INTRODUCTION.

We are now more than ever aware that we live in a world where events in one place affect people thousands of miles away. A dramatic example of this inter-relationship was the oil crisis that followed the Arab–Israel war of October 1973. The oil producers of the world, led by the Arab states, welded their organisation OPEC into an effective cartel which raised the price of oil to consumers fivefold by the end of 1974. This sudden action rocked the economies of countries one after another and increased the threat of world recession. In a country like India, dependent on importing oil, the extra drain on foreign exchange curbed her other imports, notably fertilisers. Another example can be drawn from the turn of the century. Successful synthesis of indigo by Professor Adolf Bayer of Munich in 1880 created havoc within a generation in the Indian villages depending on the cultivation of the natural indigo plant. Export of indigo from India fell from 187,000 tons in 1895–6 to the pitiful level of 11,000 tons in 1913–14 as synthetic production developed into a thriving industry in Europe: success in one part of the world meant economic devastation in another. Today we have reached the stage where we must take account of both the wider repercussions of new developments and also the consequences in using up irreplaceable resources.

In this part of the Science Section we shall be looking at key aspects of the environment in which we live—quality of life, population food, energy, pollution. We shall see them as inter-acting parts of a system which includes all living things, the air, water and soil, accessible parts of the earth's crust and the exchange of radiation with the rest of the universe, the most important being the receipt of vast amounts of energy from the sun. Whether we can meet the challenge of living in equilibrium with that environment depends entirely upon ourselves. Those of us living in the "developed" (or "industrialised" or "advanced") countries have a great responsibility in finding lasting solutions to the problems since we have

* greater wealth
* more technology
* better educated populations

than many of those in the less-developed (or "underdeveloped" or "poor") countries whose poverty limits the extent to which they can help themselves.

The reader may like to refer to **Section G** (Part III) for a review of the economic problems of the less-developed countries.

An informal international group of scientists and economists known, because of their first meeting place, as the Club of Rome, have made a series of studies since 1968 of the effects of unrestrained economic and population growth. Their first report, "The Limits of Growth" by Professor Dennis Meadows of the Massachusetts Institute of Technology, warned of mass starvation and of mineral resources becoming exhausted if present trends continued. Other researchers criticised aspects of his methods and of his choice of relationships for the equations used in the computer exercises on which those conclusions were based. Further work published under the title "Mankind at the turning point" by M. Mesarovic and E. Pestel (1974) continued to rely on computer analyses of the future interplay between population, resources and the environment. But this is based on dividing the world into ten interacting regions, then examining results of a number of hypotheses (or "scenarios") in each case considered in terms of attempts to resolve problems by conflict or by co-operation. Scenarios based on conflict assume that individual nations or regions try to act on their own; those based on co-operation show regions of the earth banding together in a concerted attack on problems regardless of political, social and other differences. The work confirms analytically that it is essential for nations to overcome their animosities, work closely together, make short-term sacrifices for long-term gains and share access to resources.

II. QUALITY OF LIFE.

Some people would say that one of the main objectives of human activity is to achieve a better standard of living or a more congenial environment and not only for ourselves but for others less well off. The concept "quality of life" is difficult to define as it depends upon the criteria used as to what is desirable for human welfare. There is no correlation between level of income and level of cultural development (we have only to think of Ancient China and modern Kuwait). One writer suggests "we have to find ways of creating and maintaining a civilisation and at the same time to keep people fully employed earning their living producing the right kinds of goods in conditions that foster human attitudes." However, the results of some changes in our way of life can be objectively measured, and it is on these that we shall later dwell.

Ultimately, however, all attempts to define the quality of life must include "recognition of the inherent dignity and of the equal and inalienable rights of all members of the human family" set out in the Universal Declaration of Human Rights adopted in 1948 by the United Nations. This states that all human beings are born free and equal in dignity and rights, naming among these the right to life, liberty and security of person, freedom from slavery, from torture or degrading treatment, from arbitrary arrest, from arbitrary interference; it also names freedom of movement, of thought, conscience, religion, opinion, the right to take part in government and of equal access to public service; in the economic and social spheres it covers the right to social security, to work, to rest and leisure, to a standard of living adequate for health and well-being, including food, clothing and medical care and to education. The list of rights concludes with an article referring to everyone's duties to the community for free and full development of his personality subject to such limitations as are determined by law solely for the purpose of securing due recognition and respect for the rights and freedoms of others and of meeting the just requirements of morality, public order and the general welfare in a democratic society.

Policies directed at ensuring that man lives in equilibrium with his environment must be kept consistent with these humane and reasonable requirements. For example, it would not be acceptable to argue that the need to conserve resources demanded that consumption levels should be kept low in the countries that are at present poor; nor would it be consistent with the view that all human beings are equal to suggest that population should be more severely controlled in the poorer developing countries than in the richer developed ones. These are not "abstract" issues. They arose very forcefully at the World Food Conference and the World Population Conference, both held in 1974.

Broadly, the aspects of the quality of life that are felt to be most relevant in the developing countries are those dealing with such basics as food, health services, shelter, employment, education, which are generally seen as linked with industrialisation and technological development. The industrialised countries tend to interpret the issues in terms of preventing pollution of air, water and land, reducing noise, reclaiming land that has become an eyesore, cleaning up the residues of the industrial past, renewing the older towns and building the newer ones in aesthetically pleasing styles, minimising damage to the surroundings in new municipal, social and industrial building or activity. Social reformers add that these concerns should include providing for those with disadvantages—the poor, the sick, the physically and mentally handicapped, and above all, the child in need of care. *See also* G12.

Several of the industrialised countries now have projects in progress to improve the *quality of working life*, particularly for workers engaged in operations likely to induce stress. What types of operations would these be? They are production or clerical jobs involving forced uniform pacing, especially when the pace is rapid; repetitiveness and very short time cycles leading to monotony, triviality and meaninglessness in work; large impersonal structures of organisation and also objectives which seem distant and unreal. To combat these undesirable features, Dr. N. A. B. Wilson in 1973 in a report published by the UK Government ("On the quality of working life") recommended re-arrangements to induce the worker to be less passively subordinate, more versatile, more self-directed and to link this with making all desirable work behaviour obviously rewarding. Generally, the efforts at job enrichment start by giving the worker more variety, making him part of a group with shared responsibility and some degree of autonomy. Measures of the results, in addition to replies to questionnaires, will be the effects on absenteeism, quality of products, proportion of rejects, rate of turnover of staff, labour disputes and other indices.

Another aspect receiving attention in many countries is protecting the health of workers at work. The EEC have proposals for a planned programme of social reform of employment conditions which, they specify, must include the interests of immigrant workers in Europe. In the UK under the Health and Safety at Work Act 1974 the conditions of virtually all employed persons in the country now come under one unified control, a new Health and Safety Commission is established, and a series of Codes of Practice to supplement regulations and give practical guidance are being introduced.

Habitat: 1976 UN Conference on Human Settlements.

In June 1976 the UN held a conference on human settlements under the title of Habitat. It resulted in a declaration and two groups of recommendations. Its Vancouver Declaration reflected a major commitment on the part of Governments and the international community to improve the quality of life for all peoples. Recommendations for specific action to put this into effect were grouped into those for national action and others demanding international co-operation.

Major attention was given to the right of all people to a pure supply of water—an apparently simple provision that is nevertheless denied to a large proportion of the world's population. It was agreed to hold a UN conference in 1977 devoted wholly to this single, important issue.

Committee on the World Disarmament Conference.

A further factor affecting the quality of life is the continuing build-up of armaments and the anxieties produced notably by the growing stocks of nuclear arms and of "improved" methods for delivering them on to enemies. This has been systematically documented in a series of reports by the Swedish-government-sponsored Stockholm International Peace Research Institute (SIPRI).

The UN Committee on the World Disarmament Conference has had a series of meetings to prepare the objectives of the conference. The period from 1970 has already been declared by the UN as the Disarmament Decade; the General Assembly during 1975 examined a number of relevant reports including a comprehensive study of nuclear-weapon-free zones.

Distribution and Forecast Increase of World Population

Year		North America	Latin America	Africa	Europe and USSR	Asia and Australasia	Total
1970		226/6·3	280/7·8	346/9·6	704/19·5	2,051/56·8	3,607
1980	A	250/5·6	378/8·5	457/10·3	760/17·1	2,596/58·5	4,441
	B	249/5·7	372/8·5	453/10·3	757/17·2	2,558/58·3	4,389
	C	248/5·7	367/8·4	451/10·4	754/17·4	2,521/58·1	4,341
1990	A	280/5·0	517/9·2	619/11·0	815/14·6	3,377/60·2	5,608
	B	275/5·1	491/9·2	597/11·1	809/15·1	3,196/59·5	5,368
	C	271/5·3	465/9·0	578/11·2	801/15·5	3,039/59·0	5,154
2000	A	308/4·3	710/9·9	861/11·9	870/12·1	4,447/61·8	7,196
	B	297/4·5	635/9·7	783/12·0	854/13·1	3,968/60·7	6,536
	C	288/4·8	567/9·5	677/11·4	843/14·1	3,583/60·1	5,958

Above: first figure indicates population in millions; second figure represents proportion per cent. Assumptions: A, constant fertility; B, "medium" fertility decline; C, "fast" fertility decline.

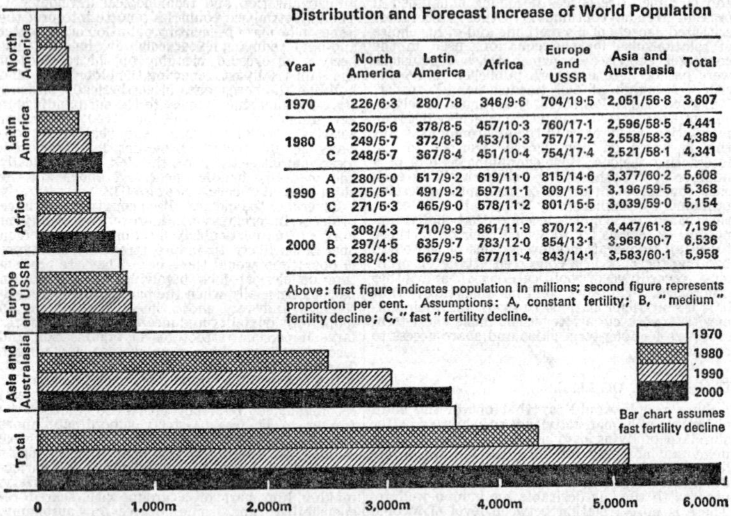

All three of these projections, first published by the World Bank (Finance and Development, vol. 10. no. 4), assume declining mortality rates. The concept of fertility is based on the number of births during a woman's reproductive period, at current rates.

"Constant" fertility assumes that rates will remain at their present levels until 2000. "Fast" decline assumes that rates will fall by between 1 and 3 per cent annually until replacement level is reached, and could amount to a halving of the rate in 30 to 40 years.

III. POPULATION.

In recent years there has been a growing realisation that the rapid increase in population is exerting pressures on existing resources, aggravating many social problems, especially attempts to combat poverty in developing countries. Significant of these worldwide anxieties was the holding of the first world intergovernmental conference on population in August 1974 under the auspices of the United Nations. It nevertheless proved to be a controversial subject since many countries placed more emphasis on industrial and technological development as the solution to their problems of rapidly rising population than on campaigns for population control. The final Plan of Action adopted was based on striving to reconcile these two policy approaches.

1. Background.

The basic worrying demographic trend is that world population is growing by 2% a year: if this rate is sustained it will result in the doubling of world population every 35 years. Within this overall figure regional rates vary and national rates range from a negative rate to well over 3%. Generally, the rapid increase reflects decline in death rate while birth rate either does not decline or does so much more slowly. Nevertheless in the developing countries death rate remains high. In Africa average expectation of life is estimated by the UN to be less than 40 years and one baby in four dies before its first birthday. As the Plan reveals, many couples are unable to exercise the right to have the number of children they desire. Poor economic conditions, social norms, inadequate knowledge of effective methods of family regulation, unavailability of contraceptive devices result in a situation where couples have more children than they desire or feel they can properly care for. High birth rate means that in developing countries 41% of the population is under the age of 15. Though population of the rural areas continues to grow, that of town areas is increasing so fast that for the first time in history the majority of the world's people will be living in urban areas by the end of the century. Very often this movement takes place in an uncontrolled fashion accompanied by overcrowding, unemployment, slums and deterioration of the environment.

Change in fertility rate takes some decades before it has any effect on the growth rate of the population. Thus the demographers calculate that even if the developing countries now had on average only a little over 2 children per family—the replacement level—their population would still grow until the latter half of the next century; this effect is sometimes called "demographic inertia". The Plan urged countries wishing to affect their population growth to anticipate future demographic trends and take appropriate decisions on plans for economic and social development well in advance.

2. Principles and Objectives.

Formulating and implementing population policies was declared to be the sovereign right of each nation. A statement of principles opened by setting the aim of development to be the improvement of the levels of living and the quality of life of the people. Development was seen as playing a crucial role in affecting population trends so that population policies were elements of development policies. As we noted above, the conference decided that these should be consistent with human rights, individual freedom, justice and the survival of national, regional and minority groups; furthermore "respect for human life is basic to all human societies". Other principles adopted included:

* couples have the basic human right to decide freely and responsibly the number and spacing of their children
* the family is the basic unit of society
* women have the right to complete integration in the development process
* consideration must be given to natural resources, the environment, food supply, minimising waste

* because of growing interdependence of nations, international strategies must enable the under-privileged to attain an early improvement in living conditions.

3. Recommendations for Action.

Countries which consider their growth rate hampers their goals of promoting human welfare were invited to consider adopting population policies. It will be noted that this is far from a rousing call for campaigns to restrict population growth. The wording deliberately adopted throughout was neutral so that it could be interpreted to cover those said to desire population growth as well as those wishing to restrict it. The UN's "low variant projections"—reflecting assumptions about successful progress in development and implementing population policies—are based on the world rate of population growth declining from 2% to about 1·7% by 1985. These projections presume decline in the birth rate of the developing countries as a whole from the present level of 38 per thousand to 30 per thousand in 1985; that in the developed countries is projected as remaining at 15 per thousand. Achievement of these levels was recognised as requiring substantial national effort in both socio-economic and population policies, supported on request by adequate international assistance.

Countries "which consider their birth rate detrimental to their national purposes" were invited to consider setting goals. Among recommendations adopted were:

* efforts to reduce mortality levels
* encouraging family planning
* ensuring full participation of women in the educational and general life of their countries on an equal basis with men
* as part of promoting knowledge recommending a population census in each country between 1975 and 1985
* inviting all countries to co-operate in a World Fertility Survey.

In addition to recommending actions in areas directly concerned with possible control of population size there was strong emphasis on the indirect factors which are thought to have reduced birth rates dramatically in the richer countries, notably promoting the status of women.

4. Recommendations for Implementation.

The Plan recommended continuous monitoring of population trends and policies by the UN, biennially beginning in 1977 and more comprehensively every 5 years after 1979. All this should be closely co-ordinated with the Strategy for the Second United Nations Development Decade.

In relation to world resources the conference expressed concern over disproportionate consumption in some countries which were asked to reduce such consumption and to refrain from any action that would adversely affect the ability of developing countries to promote their own development. Countries were urged to participate fully in the food conference (discussed later), giving priority to food and fertiliser production and consideration as to how shortages could best be overcome by national effort, regional and international co-operation.

The UN General Assembly has continued to monitor progress, receiving reports from the committees responsible. UN has supported a range of relevant researches and training courses in family-planning administration though all on a scale that appears to some observers to be small in relation to global trends and needs. The latest major review is entitled "Concise Report on the World Population Situation in 1970–1975 and Its Long Range Implications" (UN E/5624).

As part of its aid programme, the UK in 1975/6 has contributed £1·8 million to the UN Fund for Population Activities and £1·2 million to the International Planned Parenthood Federation.

5. "Social and political change may prove to be the key, the only key, to solving the population problem."

This quotation comes from Robert Cassen, Fellow of the Institute of Development Studies (University of Sussex). According to this analysis health, education, employment and reduced birth and death rates are all intimately connected. In the short run family planning is the only thing that has much effect, since other policy measures are slow to operate, difficult to pursue. Dr. Cassen's conclusion in advance of the conference was much the same as the compromise decisions reached. If the rich countries "are concerned about population growth in the Third World, we should be working much harder to create an international order more favourable to the elimination of poverty." In a nutshell, where we pursue trade and other policies that perpetuate poverty, we help to perpetuate high birth rates.

6. Britain is One of the Most Crowded Countries.

Though these discussions tend to centre on the problems of poor countries remote from our shores, Britain is very directly involved in population problems. For England and Wales the number of persons per square kilometre in 1971 was 323 compared with 93 for Europe as a whole, 10 for North America and 11 for Africa, and it is forecast to go on growing. However, Bernard Benjamin, Professor of Actuarial Science at the City University, has analysed the effects of allowing the British population of 56 million to fall steadily until it reaches 35 million in helping reduce the strain on world resources, while easing our own crowding and the scramble for land and housing. His conclusion is that this is likely to be achieved without any real economic difficulty. It should be added that there is already a marked fall in births. Live births in England and Wales were 867,000 in the year ending June 1965 compared with an estimated 594,000 in 1976 (when deaths, by the way, numbered 600,000). The balance of migration is outward and we lost some 85,000 emigrants in 1974, resulting in an overall decline in population. However, there have been previous periods in the country's history when trends have been markedly changed and there is some evidence that births may in fact be about to rise. The Office of Population Censuses and Surveys expects a fall in the total population of England and Wales of nearly 100,000 over the years 1975 to 1980; but from 1980 onwards they estimate that population will grow steadily to a total of nearly 53 million in 2014, about 3·5 million above the 1975 level. For the UK as a whole the corresponding rise is from 56 million in 1975, through a small fall to a total of over 59 million. The situation is thus one of uncertainty. Meanwhile an organisation has been set up in Britain called Population Countdown, supporting voluntary family planning programmes throughout the world and any projects that work towards stabilising world population by means which also promote human welfare, personal freedom and the quality of life. They quote analyses showing that Britain has now lost the special world privileges it once had, so that the British people are now once again exposed to the penalties normally incurred when population outstrips resources. And the officially sponsored, though advisory, Report of the Population Panel (Cmnd. 5258, 1973) advocated a stationary population for Britain.

IV. FOOD.

Projecting the present growth rates for population, food production and demand, the UN estimates that the vast majority of the developing countries will have a deficiency of 85 million tons each year by 1985. Urgent action was therefore proposed to the 1974 World Food Conference to prevent these developments and find a way of avoiding millions of people in the Third World dying of starvation during the next few years.

1. Demand.

Demand for food is calculated to grow at 2·5% per annum; 2·0% represents population increases as quoted above and 0·5% increased purchasing power. But these overall figures are composed of a growth rate of only 1·6% in the developed countries and 3·7% in developing ones. Despite this expected growth there would still be some 34 countries by 1985 with a total of 700 million people where the intake of food energy per head on the average would fall short of basic nutritional requirements. For cereals (providing the bulk of human food) the projections are for demand to grow from 1,200 million tonnes in 1970 to 1,700 million tonnes in 1985; 300 million of the increase would be needed in poorer countries.

2. Supply.

Here the basis for projections was felt to be less sure but growth rates were estimated at 2·4% for the developed, 2·6% for the developing countries and up to 3·5% for Eastern Europe and the USSR. These figures suggest approximate balance between supply and demand. But this would ignore fluctuations due to bad years. World stocks are now so low that bad harvests would have catastrophic effects. Furthermore, when a bad harvest occurs in a country with some financial resources they go out and buy, thus aggravating the supply position for others with similar crop failures but fewer other resources.

3. Malnutrition

The human cost of the inadequate food supplies at present is assessed by the UN as resulting in malnutrition for some 400 million people. In the report to the conference this condition was described as "the daily physical privation of fellow human beings, adversely affecting health and physical growth and seriously reducing the capacity of children to learn and adults to work." Overall no fewer than 61 countries were reckoned to have a deficit in food supplies in 1970. In the Far East, Near East and Africa this was considered to mean that up to a quarter of the population suffered from under-nutrition.

Furthermore the Food and Agriculture Organisation of the United Nations (FAO) has sponsored a Protein–Calorie Advisory Group to ensure that in food planning adequate attention is paid also to nutritional balance. They draw attention to the value of including in the diet such sources of protein as fish from the sea or from aquaculture, and recommend attention being given to exploiting Antarctic krill (little-known shrimp-like animals). They also reinforce the advice of the voluntary aid organisations such as War on Want and Oxfam that mothers in developing countries should be encouraged to continue breast feeding babies rather than weaning them on to infant foods too early and this was endorsed by a resolution of the 27th World Health Assembly. PAG has also drawn attention to the value of coconut flour, notably in the Philippines, as a food resource with many desirable characteristics for blending into foods to raise protein intake. To assess both current situations and the value of nutrition programmes, the Group has proposed a group of indicators to be used concurrently. They are mortality at individual ages 1, 2, 3 and 4; proportion of low birth weights; height at school entry age; age at menarche.

4. 1974 World Conference Conclusions.

Results of the 1974 World Food Conference disappointed many observers, though the mere fact that it was held at all indicated the level of world concern. Its President assessed its work as having only sketched the beginnings of a world food policy. And Mr. Sayed Marei, its Secretary-General, was disappointed that wealthier countries had not offered sufficient help to countries already suffering from famine. Though the issues concerned people starving to death, there were political disputes among the assembled nations on the aid issue. The USA has in the past made large quantities of food available as aid. At this conference they stated that they would also expect a number of the newly-rich oil exporting countries to be willing to help finance the necessary food aid programme. These were to ensure forward planning of food aid, including at least ten million tons of grains as food aid every year and supplementary arrangements for other foods such as oils, oilseeds and dairy products.

Four principal recommendations to emerge from the proceedings were:

1. establishing a World Food Council to co-ordinate the activities of various international agencies;

2. creating an international fund for agricultural development to channel investment toward improving agriculture in the developing world;

3. agreeing on a co-ordinated system of cereal reserves as a world food security system; these reserves would be nationally held but supported by a service of worldwide information and detection of food shortage;

4. providing, on a three-year forward planning basis, both commodities and finance for food aid to a minimum level of ten million tons of grains a year and other foods, as stated above.

The final declaration included a pledge that "within a decade no child will go to bed hungry, that no family will fear for its next day's bread" and a statement that "every man, woman and child has the right to be free from hunger and malnutrition". These are, of course, historic declarations of intent but it is difficult to see how the limited decisions taken will in practice enable the world's wealthier nations to fulfil them. In terms of immediate need, Mr. Marei quoted that the most seriously affected countries needed some eight million tons within the half year following the conference and no specific offers were made to meet this need. On a longer term basis, local and international efforts need to reverse the trends discernible over the last few years.

5. World Situation 1977.

Though the situation continued to give rise to concern, there was a marked increase in activities of the World Food Programme and by May 1976 over $600 million of contributions had been pledged to it and increased quantities of food grains placed at its disposal. The US Agriculture Department expected a record world harvest of 1·3 (US) billion tonnes of grain and rice in 1976, leaving some 25 million tonnes over after satisfying demands.

Thus the immediate food situation was improved. Yet the Executive Director of the World Food Council commented "The basic world food situation remains insecure." Long-run food production trends in the developing countries were still inadequate to meet their rising needs and large numbers still suffered from malnutrition. He therefore continued to press for further support for the World Food Programme and for aid that would not discourage food production in recipient countries nor disturb the stability of their markets.

Under the present UK Government, a "central objective" of aid policy has become promotion of development in country areas where the overwhelming majority of the poor of the Third World live, and thus to aid in increasing world food production. This is not an imposed view; it has been adopted as a consensus decision at the Commonwealth Ministerial Meeting on Food Production and Rural Development in 1975. Even after some degree of cutting, the UK gross aid programme for 1975–6 (all aspects, not only food) was £471 million.

However, the extensive use of grain—suitable for human consumption—for feeding animals has rightly been severely criticised. The World Development Movement accuses Britain and other rich meat-eating countries of supporting famine by buying grain to feed the animals. In more restrained terms similar criticism has been voiced by Dr. H. C. Pereira, F.R.S., Chief Scientist, Ministry of Agriculture.

If we were willing to obtain more protein from grain and reduce our consumption of meat we could contribute to world food supplies—and reduce our import bill.

6. Fertilisers and Pesticides.

Prices of fertilisers were generally four times as much in 1974 as in 1971, a major influence being the big rise in oil prices. In addition critical shortages of fertilisers and pesticides, and of quality seeds were reported by the UN as impeding efforts to increase food production in the poorer parts of the world. Even taking into account heavy investment in fertiliser manufacturing plants, world production of nitrogenous and phosphate fertilisers in 1980–81 was estimated to be likely to fall short by 19 million nutrient tons of the projected needs of almost 97 million. The FAO in mid-1974 set up an International Fertiliser Supply Scheme seeking to mobilise financial and technical assistance for buying fertilisers and for making them in developing countries. However, little has been reported of its success. FAO also call for better organised use of plant, animal and human wastes, estimating that these sources in developing countries could supply up to eight times more nutrient than the total they now consume of inorganic fertilisers.

Pests are reckoned to consume about a third of the crops of the developing countries and FAO have urged reserve stocks of pesticide and equipment for applying them, as well as the organisation of training courses and of industries to manufacture pesticides.

Output could be expanded by *quality seeds.* FAO recommends expanding their international Seed Industry Development Programme and also establishing stocks of these in various areas of the world; improved seeds are seen as a relatively cheap and simple input that can lead to higher yields and to plants with greater disease resistance. Some successes in this area have been achieved but on a limited scale.

7. Credit Facilities.

Credit facilities may seem remote from this subject but they are of crucial importance to poor farmers. Without them the farmers cannot take advantage of the new technological package of better seeds, fertilisers and pesticides. FAO assess, for example, that in south Asia the average small farmer spends $6 per hectare a year when he should be spending between $20 and $80 according to crop. To purchase the means of increasing his output the farmer needs credit. Governments of developing countries should therefore expand credit and ensure that it reaches the smaller farmer.

8. Aquaculture.

Noted briefly above, this is the production of freshwater and marine organisms by the equivalent of farming methods. The UN Protein-Calorie Advisory Group (PAG) estimates that it now contributes annually about 6 million tons of food in the world valued at $2,500 million. It could be greatly expanded and could contribute particularly to the nutrition of landlocked countries. Eel, shrimp and some oysters have long been cultivated for the luxury market but common carp, Chinese and Indian carp, milkfish and mussels have been reared for local human consumption. PAG gives the figures in the table as conservative estimates, stressing the

WORLD PRODUCTION BY AQUACULTURE
(excluding sport, bait and ornamental fish and pearls.)

Species	Annual production, thousands of tons
Finfish	3,680
Shrimps and prawns	14
Oysters	711
Mussels	180
Clams	56
Other molluscs	20
Seaweeds	373
Total	5,034

Source: PAG Bulletin, Vol. IV, No. 2

economic as well as nutritional importance in the Philippines, Korea, Indonesia. To expand this valuable source of food they recommend more research, better data on fish eggs, larvae and juveniles, genetic improvement, disease control, predator and competitor control, training in the expertise, issuing instruction material and training teachers, the so-called extension workers who give technical advice and assistance—the whole being run as an international programme.

9. The Intermediate Technology (IT).

Appropriate Technology (as some prefer to call the concept) is beginning on a small scale to contribute to improving farming in poorer countries. This is based on the view that it is impracticable and even damaging to transfer technology (tools, equipment, organisation) directly from industrialised countries to developing ones. Consequently, they argue, modern knowledge should be applied *not* to developing inferior technology but to assisting in developing technologies appropriate to the developing countries themselves with the co-operation of those living there. In farming, applying IT offers wide opportunities for diversifying and upgrading rural life, especially if new and improved farming equipment can be locally manufactured and serviced. For example, field projects in Zambia and Nigeria have resulted in innovations, including planting machines for maize and other crops, weeders, improved animal-drawn equipment; in India they have introduced an improved version of a thresher first designed in Iran; in Chad, improved pit silos for safely preserving crops to keep as cattle feed. In all cases, the design is at a suitable price level for the country concerned, developed by their own countrymen and at a level of complexity suited to local skills.

This approach was endorsed in the UN World Economic Survey 1974 and by Dr. Kurt Waldheim, Secretary-General of the UN, in his report to the UN Seventh Special Session 1975; in this he urged a New International Economic Order to aid in spreading the benefits of technological progress to all countries equitably. For the less-developed countries, the greatest impact is likely to be in rural areas.

This is of the greatest significance since the UN Industrial Development Organisation (UNIDO) is actively promoting industrialisation of developing countries.

V. ENERGY.

Until recently interest in energy sources on a practical industrial scale centred on coal, oil and gas. These of course remain the main sources in projections in terms of decades ahead but it is significant that a Survey of Energy Resources prepared for the World Energy Conference 1974 opened with a wider theme. All energy in its various forms of use is traceable to four sources which are, it pointed out:

1. solar radiation
2. subterranean heat from radioactive decay
3. inertial forces from gravitational and rotational phenomena
4. nuclear reactions releasing energy from fission or fusion of atomic nuclei.

Mankind has had a long period of dependence on the irreplaceable stores of energy derived from past solar radiation. Now there is active interest and research into the possibilities of utilising power derived from all of the above sources, which are effectively inexhaustible. A further significant feature was the theme of the conference itself "The economic and environmental challenges of future requirements". The grouping of its subject matter was equally indicative of present anxieties, for sections were devoted to relating energy to population, to environmental constraints and to recovery of resources as well as the more traditional subjects of energy conversion, transport and utilisation. This reflects the growing concern by the

WORLD ENERGY CONSUMPTION AND POPULATION, BY MAJOR REGIONS, 1950 1960, 1970

Region	1950		1960		1970	
	Population (million)	Consumption per capita (million Btu)	Population (million)	Consumption per capita (million Btu)	Population (million	Consumption per capita (million Btu)
North America	166·1	221·9	198·7	245·1	226·2	329·3
Canada	13·7	197·6	17·9	217·0	21·4	328·9
United States	152·3	224·3	180·7	248·0	204·8	329·3
Western Europe	302·4	57·8	326·5	79·8	356·4	134·3
Oceania	12·2	73·0	15·4	90·8	19·2	127·7
Latin America	161·9	14·8	212·4	23·3	282·0	32·4
Asia (excl. Communist)	805·4	4·7	970·6	8·5	1,231·3	16·9
Japan	82·9	21·0	93·2	39·4	103·4	108·9
Other Asia	722·5	2·9	877·4	5·2	1,127·9	8·5
Africa	217·0	6·0	276·0	7·8	349·5	10·5
USSR and Comm. Eastern Europe	269·8	47·6	312·9	83·0	348·4	128·5
USSR	180·0	46·8	214·4	83·5	242·8	131·8
Eastern Europe	89·7	49·2	98·5	82·0	105·6	120·9
Communist Asia	569·8	2·2	677·5	9·7	795·6	14·2
WORLD	2,504·5	30·7	2,989·9	41·5	3,608·6	59·4

Source: J. Darmstadter. Royal Society conference " Energy in the 1980s ", pub. 1974.

general public at the profligate use of many natural resources, particularly in the industrially advanced parts of the world. Other features of concern have been the heavy and growing dependence of the developed countries on oil, a large part of which comes from a politically unstable region. The oil crisis of 1973–4 led all consumer countries to take urgent measures to speed the search for other sources of energy and to seek economies in use.

The growth in world production and the marked differences in usage in different parts of the world are shown in the table.

1. Energy Consumption: the growing problem.

Global energy needs have not only been growing but accelerating (up to the time of the exceptional events of 1973/4). In the inter-war years the figures rose by about 1½% a year, in the 'fifties by nearly 5% a year, and in the 'sixties by 5½% a year. In recent years (until 1974) demand for oil alone has grown at 7% a year. But coal production has remained constant, the decline in production in Western Europe (including the UK) being counterbalanced by increased output in the USA, USSR and Eastern Europe. The world market for energy is dominated by the USA where energy consumption per head per year is the highest in the world, roughly double that of any other developed country. Meanwhile two-thirds of the world's inhabitants living in the developing countries use so little per head that they consume only about one-tenth of global supplies.

Nuclear energy, hailed as the great hope early in the 'fifties has not as yet lived up to its early promise. Though reactors have so far operated at high levels of safety, their use has led to extensive debate internationally about possible future risks, including the liability to exploitation militarily by terrorist groups. The UK was the first country to generate electricity from nuclear stations on an industrial scale (1956) (*see* **Section L**). Of other possible sources only hydroelectricity makes any appreciable contribution. A barrage scheme (*see* **Tidal Power, Section L**) is already in operation on the River Rance in France and is the subject of research in England (the Severn estuary is particularly appropriate because its range from high to low tide is very large). Such a scheme could make an important contribution to electricity generation and storage but the cost would be high. Solar energy and geothermal energy are in use only to a very limited extent.

An immediate result of the oil price rise was a decline in global oil consumption in two successive years—1974 and 1975—reversing the consistent well-established long-term trend. On a world scale, total energy consumption was estimated by BP in its statistical review as having risen by less than 1% in 1975 compared with the preceding year. This was composed of a large proportionate rise (a small absolute one) in contribution by nuclear power and rises in solid fuels and water power.

UK ENERGY CONSUMPTION IN MILLION TONS COAL EQUIVALENT

	1973	1974	1975
oil	161	150	134
coal	131	116	118
gas	44	52	54
nuclear	10	12	11
hydroelectric	2	2	2
Total	348	332	319

In the UK, a separate Department of Energy was set up in January 1974 to concentrate on " energy problems arising from developments in the supply and price of oil ". Energy and conservation problems were also examined by the National Economic Development Office (NEDO) and by the so-called Think-Tank—the Central Policy Review Staff—in published reports. As the table shows, energy consumption fell but analysis of the causes was complicated by the poor levels of economic activity which reduces the demand for energy. Policy measures taken include establishing greater public control in respect of offshore oil and gas development, supporting a 10-year investment programme in the coal industry to provide 42 million tons of new coal-producing capacity by 1985 with a target for that year by the NCB of 150 million tons (including opencast) thus ending the rundown of the industry, undertaking a 4,000 MW programme based on the Steam Generating Heavy Water Reactor (SGHWR), and a programme of energy conservation. For the longer term, work is proceeding on the Fast Breeder Reactor (FBR). From 1980 onwards North Sea oil (100–140 million tons p.a.) should meet our oil needs. Meanwhile the Social Science Research Council is promoting work on energy economics to ensure that this aspect is adequately taken into account and that the problem is not treated purely as one of technology.

2. The Future.

For Britain, an important discussion document was published by the Advisory Council on Research and Development for Fuel and Power (ACORD) as Energy Paper No. 11 (London, HMSO, 1976). This accepted the widely-held view that the UK would be self-sufficient in energy throughout the 1980s due to large supplies of oil, coal and gas, with a supplement from nuclear reactors. Yet it warned that it would be a "grave mistake" to lapse into complacency. The breathing space should be used to improve the efficiency of energy use and to establish technologies upon which this country's future is likely to depend. After examining several possible lines of future development of policy, it concludes that we need

* more attention to coal utilisation and conversion
* high priority to technologies connected with North Sea oil and gas expanded nuclear technology
* wider R & D on "alternative sources" (solar, wind, wave and tidal power, waste materials, geothermal and—longer-term—nuclear fusion)
* new technology for gas and liquid fuel from coal
* improving efficiency in converting primary fuel to electricity
* major effort on energy-saving with economic equipment

An ingenious idea quoted by the Programmes Analysis Unit is calcining limestone to give CO_2, reacting this with hydrogen obtained in nuclear reactors by decomposing water, and thus yielding methanol fuel. Alternatively, the hydrogen might be used directly as the fuel. There are many critics of growing dependence on nuclear reactors since these create plutonium—a poisonous material and one that can be used to make devastatingly destructive bombs; thus distributing reactors disseminates potential nuclear explosive material. The Secretary of State for Energy, Tony Benn, has stated that he welcomes extensive public debate on the human/political/economic/technological issues involved.

3. Other Research Areas.

In the new situation of vastly increased energy cost, work on "alternative sources" has been greatly stimulated. Throughout the industrialised countries there are small groups working on projects applying particularly wind and solar power. In addition, in several countries there are now major officially funded projects in these and similar types of area—now removed from characterisation as "cranky" and accepted into the fold or formal scientific/technological development. In 1976, Dr. W. Marshall FRS, Chief Scientist at the UK Department of Energy, reported on the assessments of the Energy Technology Support Unit; the table shows the possible contributions to UK energy supplies in the year 2000.

These are regarded largely as research projects during the next few years; it is reckoned to take decades before new technology in energy can make a worthwhile contribution. The programme on solar energy also involves the Department of the Environment who have responsibility for housing; it will also incorporate material from a detailed review by the UK section of the International Solar Energy Society. There are, however, informed critics of the view that greater energy supplies will continue to be needed to support economic growth; broadly these place emphasis on more conservation and recovery of discharged heat at present wasted notably in generating electricity. They also suggest that we may be approaching saturation of the market for energy in some areas. Studies along these lines are in progress in the Energy Research Group at the Open University.

4. Energy and Environment in the Less-developed Countries.

At its meeting in 1975 the Governing Councils of UNEP requested its Director to give high priority to establishing in typical rural areas in Asia, Africa and Latin America demonstration centres for harnessing locally available renewable sources of energy. Their grounds were recognition that small amounts of energy for cooking, desalination of water, lighting, could alleviate some of the conditions of abject poverty. Sources suggested were solar, wind, hydro-, biogas from organic wastes, planting quicker-growing trees. The aim was "to enhance the quality of life".

VI. ECONOMIC GROWTH.

1. Is Growth Desirable?

Until recently the value of economic growth was little questioned. It was assumed that increases in national output were desirable and would improve standards of living. Until the last decade or so, the availability of resources received relatively little attention. But in recent years these concepts of the value of economic growth have come under attack generally on the grounds that world resources will be quickly depleted, that a large part of the increased volume of products are worthless baubles and there should be more emphasis on re-distribution to give a more socially just society between and within countries. In the Introduction we quoted the main conclusions of the weighty, though unofficial, Club of Rome on the risks of exhausting resources and of major economic catastrophes unless all countries co-operate in the use of world resources.

A so-called "Blueprint for Survival", published in 1972 by Ecosystems Ltd., emphasised the extreme gravity of the situation. For it contended that if current trends are allowed to persist the breakdown of society and the irreversible disruption of the life-support systems on this planet, possibly by the end of the century, certainly within the lifetime of our children, are inevitable. The principal defect of the industrial way of life with its ethos of expansion, according to this critique, is that it is not sustainable. It will end *either* in a succession of famines, epidemics, social crises and wars *or* under human control in a succession of humane and measured changes. Policy advocated was to move towards a stable society based on:

1. minimum disruption of ecological processes;
2. maximum conservation of materials and energy;
3. a population in which recruitment equals loss;
4. a social system in which the individual can enjoy, rather than feel restricted by, the first three conditions.

Thoughtful reaction has been that these criticisms draw attention to real major problems, that the dire consequences are over-stated but that the pressures are valuable in speeding up corrective trends already emerging in response to world difficulties as noted earlier.

However, there have been strong hostile reactions from the poorer countries, illustrated by the comments of Dr. Abdel-Rahman, Executive Director of UN Industrial Development Organisa-

Source	Form of use	Annual mtce *	Growth beyond 2000
Solar			
i. Solar heating .	heat	5	large
ii. Fuel from plants . .	fluid fuel	3	uncertain
Geothermal . . .	heat	4	modest
Wind	electrical	6	small
Tides	electrical	3–10	small
Waves	electrical	15	very large

* mtce = million tons coal equivalent

tion. Examining the possibility of reducing consumption in the developing countries, he understandably commented "if it goes on the average any lower it will mean starvation, famine and actual death for hundreds of millions today and in the next 25 years". It would also increase tension between advanced countries with decreasing population and developing countries with increasing population at relatively lower standards of living. He therefore urged for developing countries accelerated and effective industrialisation. This in essence formed the subject of the UN Special Session 1975 mentioned above.

The UN is strongly committed to promoting technical co-operation for the developing countries and the UN Development Programme reported that in 1975 these activities exceeded a value of $1 (US) billion. They ranged from a small irrigation project in Mali to a 133 acre industrial park in El Salvador with 52 factory sites. This programme plans "new dimensions" of expansion of efforts in response to varied needs of countries in diverse stages of development.

From within the economically advanced countries comes the reply to queries on exhausting resources that there will be compensating adjustments. Increasing scarcity will raise prices, speed the search for new sources, justify working leaner and more remote sources, increase the pressure for re-cycling and speed the search for substitutes; all these reactions invalidate the assumptions on which estimates are based for the period in which existing resources are being exhausted. On the proposal for aiming at zero economic growth the counter-arguments—for example by Fremont Felix in *World Markets of Tomorrow*—are that this zero economic growth would actually hinder social progress, deny minority groups the chance to improve their positions, deny all under-privileged groups the opportunity to better their lots, deny to all countries the resources for more schools, universities and hospitals and to continue the fight against pollution and other environmental ills. Furthermore, he contends that the historical trends after the earliest stages of industrialisation are for the rate of growth to decline and for the consumption of electrical energy per unit of growth also to decline; growth is *not* in fact exponential, but diminishing. Dr. Wilfred Beckerman (in his book *In Defence of Economic Growth*) carries this counter-attack further. The developed countries with higher rates of growth (W. Germany, Denmark, Norway, Sweden) provide much more generous social insurance programmes—16% of the National Product than those with lower ones such as UK and USA which allot only 9% to these purposes. What is more, these types of expenditure tend to rise at 2½ times the growth rate of per capita National Product. Ironically he asks whether a starving man, say in Calcutta, in an unpleasant environment, would prefer an improved environment or a square meal. In the light of the situation described above (**IV**) this is a valid question. On mineral resources, Beckerman argues that priority must be given to current human welfare; there is no "correct" rate of usage, since things are for people; we might even be using resources too slowly. Concerning our duties to posterity, it can be added that since each successive generation has been richer than its predecessors and has successfully found ways of meeting its increased needs of goods and energy, this concern may well be misplaced.

Nevertheless the views of the critics of growth have led to many re-appraisals. Typical of the newer mood was the comment by Denis Healey, Chancellor of the Exchequer, in his 1974 autumn Budget speech favouring improvement in the standard of living but adding "the senseless accumulation of material goods of exactly the same type as the Western world had been producing since the war can no longer be regarded as the only guarantee of human happiness or the only measure of economic success."

In fact, during 1974 and 1975 the industrialised countries did suffer reductions in economic wealth due to both the recession and the greatly increased oil prices. But it is generally expected that economic growth will shortly be resumed.

2. War on Waste: re-cycling.

Throughout the developed world there is growing interest in the re-use of materials, largely because of anxieties about resources in relation to economic growth, but also on more limited normal grounds of economy. And of course within companies and trades, industrial scrap is already extensively salvaged and re-used. Extensions of the principle have led to difficulties in some cases and it is useful to examine the proposals made in the UK to overcome these.

Introduced by Anthony Crosland, Secretary of State for the Environment, as a policy designed to aid growth, the Government in 1974 launched a campaign with a Green Paper entitled "War on Waste". This discussed specifically problems in recovering ferrous metals, non-ferrous metals, paper, glass, plastics, rubber and other materials. The Government set up a Waste Management Advisory Council, and a special group to promote collecting waste paper for re-cycling. They planned to extend research and to study financial incentives, disincentives, grants, awards and regulations. Appeals were issued to local authorities, commercial firms, voluntary organisations and industry to increase efforts. A major difficulty—the Green Paper picked it out as a "critical factor"—is the instability of markets for recovered materials. The Government declared that it would consult the relevant industries so as to provide a firmer basis for the long-term development of the reclamation industry associated with more stable conditions, longer term contracts and less movement in prices. For bulk wastes that might be of industrial interest they also set up a waste exchange market dealing (in confidence) with offers or requests in this field without disclosing company details at the enquiry stage. It might be assumed that the normal working of industry would ensure that efforts were made to extract values from wastes or to sell it. But the Warren Spring Laboratory reports that its investigations showed that industry often did not know what it was throwing away. This laboratory in fact operates a Waste Recovery Service to aid industry in assessing the possibilities.

Overall the scale of the problem can be seen from the fact that in 1973 Britain produced 20 million tonnes of household and trade refuse, with an approximately equal quantity produced by industry, far larger quantities of mining and quarry waste, plus further agricultural waste. Much of this, it is now considered, could be put to use, producing economic wealth without any drain on resources, often improving the environment, often also reducing dependence on imports.

An officially commended scheme is operated by the charity Oxfam with a national collection of rag waste from their Oxfam shops and a central sorting depot run in co-operation with the local authority at Kirklees. They are also running an intensive segregated waste collection in the nearby area which is reported to have had a very good response.

The first published study of the WMAC has put forward to the government a set of recommendations to encourage waste paper collection by local authorities to overcome their reluctance based on the "critical factor" noted above which has led

NON-FERROUS METALS. RATE OF USE AND RECOVERY 1973

	Aluminium	Copper	Lead	Zinc	Platinum
UK consumption . . .	668,000 tonnes	699,000 tonnes	364,000 tonnes	391,000 tonnes	18·7 tonnes (600,000 troy oz)
Approximate scrap recovery as a proportion of consumption . .	26%	37%	62%	21%	58%

to losses in some cases and therefore local criticism.

VII. POLLUTION.

Responding to worldwide anxieties about this subject the UN held a conference at Stockholm in 1972 on the human environment. Though dealing with many other aspects, it gave major attention to pollution risks. Since then the UN Environment Programme (UNEP) has established an earthwatch system of global monitoring and information services to provide early warning of environmental risks and providing governments with access to the latest scientific knowledge to deal with them. It gave high priority to monitoring radionuclides resulting from nuclear tests. It also adopted a number of decisions concerned with the preservation of the marine environment. (For completeness it should also be mentioned that it launched a major attack on the advance of deserts, with programmes to restore productivity of arid areas to prevent a future Sahel-type tragedy.)

In November 1973 the EEC similarly adopted an Environmental Action Programme. Items on which they have promoted action include reducing the amount of lead in petrol, of sulphur in diesel oil, and preparing for decisions on air pollution by sulphur compounds and dusts by starting a programme of exchanging information on them as the basis for a survey. However at this stage sulphur trioxide and suspended particles in air are the only pollutants under systematic and intense surveillance in every EEC state. Using the British Food Research Association as their agents, EEC are also investigating N-nitroso compounds in the environment; they will check the levels of nitrites, nitrates and amine precursors in root crops, grains, fruits, water supplies and elsewhere, including any relevant pesticide residues.

Within the UK considerable progress has been made because of public awareness and official pressures, though there can never be justification for complacency. The booklet "Clean Air Today" (issued by the Department of the Environment) presents photos—for example of Widnes at the end of the 19th cent. and today—and diagrams to illustrate how remarkably the air has improved over the last couple of decades. Domestic smoke emissions estimated at about 1·3 million tons p.a. in 1953 were reckoned at below 0·5 million by 1972 as a result of the Clean Air Act 1956 (a pioneering step by the UK) and changing social habits, notably the switch from crude coal burning in inadequate appliances to refined fuels, smokeless solid fuels and greatly improved appliances if the user chose to stay with coal. Sulphur dioxide *emissions* have slightly increased with time but strangely enough the amount in the air has fallen. From power stations it is discharged from very tall chimneys and the Scandinavian countries contend that the oxides of sulphur are being carried over the North Sea to them. This is disputed by the UK authorities and the problem is under study. Other theories include the suggestion that they are brought down sorbed on to particles. The Warren Spring Laboratory operates the National Survey of Smoke and Sulphur Dioxide and conducts research on, for example, pollutants in rain and other pollution topics. Other bodies involved in work on pollution are the Meteorological Office, the Ministry of Agriculture, Fisheries and Food, the National Environmental Research Council and the Atomic Energy Research Establishment.

Increasing concern about pollution from motor vehicles has resulted in a detailed survey by Warren Spring Laboratory of roadside levels of vehicle pollutants in five cities. The great spur to all this work in Britain was the London "smog" of 1952 when the death rate was doubled for that period. Some have compared the pressure for clean air just after this catastrophe to that for clean water supply and adequate sewerage of the 19th cent.

An important self-inflicted source of lethal pollution is smoking. A series of medical-statistical reports have pinpointed smoking as the largest single cause of both bronchitis and lung cancer (*see* **Section P**). This is evidently more severe a factor than air pollution, in general, today, since the Report on Air Pollution of the Royal College of Physicians in 1970 found evidence of association between *air* pollution and lung cancer to be *in*conclusive. It is reported that under present conditions—in sharp contrast to those in the more polluted ones of twenty years ago—there is very little correspondence between periods of heavier air pollution and mortality and sickness rates.

Radioactivity in the air and in milk is constantly monitored and, after rising to a peak, has steadily fallen since the signing of the agreements on banning atmospheric tests of nuclear weapons. When France and China carried out their nuclear tests, the effects were noted worldwide in surges of increased radioactivity.

A series of reports on river pollution has demonstrated a welcome improvement in river water quality. For example, the Report of 1972 showed that the numbers of discharges to rivers complying with the standards of the authorities rose from 63% to 67% for sewage effluents and from 43%to 47% for industrial effluents. Sewage flows are receiving better treatment, whilst discharges of sewage to estuaries are also being controlled.

Pesticides used for non-agricultural purposes have been more closely supervised since 1974, in the same way as those used in agriculture; food storage and related areas are already covered by the Pesticides Safety Precautions Scheme. And —reverting to international aspects—the FAO maintain a running control on hazards to health arising from contamination of foods with pesticide residues. In the UK the British Ecological Society seeks, among other objectives, to promote control of crop pests by biological means so avoiding environmental hazards from pesticides. The need for research into pollution of the stratosphere and its effects on the ozone layer (which protects our health and our crops from potentially harmful ultra-violet radiation) is now recognised.

Though this is very much a recent story of increasing awareness and of great advances in combating pollution, *eternal vigilance* remains the watchword. The large expansion in generation of electricity by nuclear power carries grave risks of greater quantities of radiation contaminating the biosphere. So does the conduct of two major powers (China and France) in carrying out nuclear explosions in the atmosphere. And the growing risks of 20 million tonnes of manufactured organic chemicals entering the environment annually (largely due to the development of the petrochemical industries) have received the attention of the Royal Society. The Health and Safety at Work Act 1974 also places some responsibility on industry for dealing with pollution problems arising from their activities. Research Associations are correspondingly beginning to introduce environmental services to aid industry in adjusting their processes to prevent possible ill-effects; and this ties in of course with pressures for re-cycling, for economising in world resources and for ending the casual throwaway attitude.

Disclosures of irresponsible casual dumping of toxic materials in dumps that were both unsightly and suspected to drain to water-courses led to the passing of the Deposit of Poisonous Waste Act 1972, which gave local authorities greatly increased powers to control this potentially lethal danger. Controls were further extended under the Control of Pollution Act 1974. There are now specialist companies willing to take such offensive and poisonous wastes and treat them before depositing them in protected areas. And the Warren Spring Laboratory advises companies, placing heavy emphasis on the possibilities of recovering values from waste. New features in recent years have been attention to controlling smells and controlling noise. Both have been the subject of special researches and surveys, then of government circulars urging action by local authorities. Further reflecting the mood of the times is the fact that in all new projects considered, even those arising from the crisis in energy supplies, a high priority is given to avoiding pollution or even despoiling the environment. Thus these considerations have been urged in respect of bringing in the oil from below the continental shelf around Britain (contaminating the sea, damaging Scottish coastal areas of outstanding natural beauty) in a way that would not have been a feature of the discussions in earlier periods.

VIII. APPRAISAL.

Final decisions on the relative weight to be given to environmental issues are heavily influenced by value judgments. There are no correct, fixed or final answers. For starving people, the urgent necessity is food, and beyond that the facilities and means for making a living by their own efforts, with self-respect. But once man emerges beyond the stage of meeting his most basic needs, it becomes possible to make choices of how to live, what proportion of resources to give to keeping the air and water pure, land and coastlines attractive and inviolate, factories landscaped. Yet much of this is dependent on the mood of public opinion. In making the necessary decisions, the public needs to have information and knowledge of the technical possibilities for each case, the consequences of adopting particular options and also the consequences of drift without a strategic policy. In many of the topics discussed in this section, life and death are at stake. This is obvious for food, but no less so for preventing smog or the death from hyperthermia of old people unable to afford enough fuel. These are the most dramatic aspects of examining how we can learn to live in the modern world. But at a less critical level, action or inaction in respect of the environment affects our enjoyment of life, as, for example, in determining whether we look out on to a squalid tip or, after restoration, on to an attractive landscape; whether resources are used to pile up personal baubles or better social amenities: whether we are content to over-feed (particularly on meat which wastes grain) and risk later world upheavals or alter our mode of life to aid some re-allocation of food to those in need: whether part of our population should continue to spend their working days in almost mindless tedium or be stimulated to take an active interest in what they do.

Apart from calling a halt to the ceaseless accumulation of un-needed further personal possessions by those with spare, disposable income, such options mean contributing to (relatively small) changes in personal behaviour. If salvage from municipal refuse is widely introduced, we may be called upon to give support by sorting our domestic refuse, keeping some things like paper and metals separate. And fuel and space economies may turn us towards more use of public transport and less use of our precious personal cars. In attempting to provide a background, this section has striven to put forward a fair selection of the facts and issues guided throughout by the major considerations that we in the UK share the surface of the planet with the whole community of mankind and that we must accept the statement of the UNEP Governing Council in April 1975 . . that the issues of population, resources environment and development are inter-related problems . . . that environmental management implies sustainable development of all countries aimed at meeting basic human needs without transgressing the outer limits set to man's endeavours by the biosphere.

VI. SPECIAL TOPIC

MAN'S EARLY ANCESTORS

In the early Tertiary the earth's climate was generally warmer than it is today and extensive tropical forests covered much of North America and Europe as well as Africa and Asia. It is from geological deposits in these northern latitudes that the earliest fossil remains clearly attributable to the Primate order of mammals have been found. Three Families are represented in the Palaeocene period: the Carpolestidae, the Phenacolemuridae and the Plesiadipidae; the first two exclusively North American but the third known also from Europe. Most of the remains are of teeth and pieces of jaw but other parts of the skull and even bones from the rest of the skeleton have been preserved of some species. All the forms show many primitive characteristics as is to be expected in such early forms; more surprisingly they show little similarity in their special characteristics with later families, but they are judged to be Primate on the basis of the morphology of their molar teeth. By the next geological period, the Eocene, however, fossils are to be found which are fairly certainly the ancestors of present-day Primates. The Families known from the Eocene are the Adapidae, from which the Lemurs were probably descended, the Tarsiidae, containing the ancestor of the present-day *Tarsius*, the Anaptomorphidae which seem to have become extinct at the end of the Eocene and the Omomyidae, representatives of which seem to have given rise to the higher primates or Anthropoidea. The Palaeocene and Eocene primates along with the extant lemurs, lorises and tarsiers are referred to taxonomically as "prosimians". Little is known of their evolution after the Eocene until the Pleistocene, partly because of poor conditions for fossilisation where they lived, but partly also because they experienced a marked reduction in numbers following competition with evolving rodents and their own anthropoid descendants. Today the lemurs are confined to the island of Madagascar where they escaped this competition; the lorises have a restricted distribution in tropical Africa and Asia and are nocturnal in habit and the tarsier is confined to some of the islands in the East Indies.

The first definite anthropoids are known from the Oligocene period, mainly from deposits of a former swamp in the Fayum of Egypt. Among the fossils here have been identified the first Old World Monkeys (Cercopithecoidea) in *Parapithecus* and *Apidium*; the first gibbons (Hylobatidae) in *Aelopithecus*; and the earliest ancestor of the Great Apes (Pongidae) in *Aegyptopithecus*. It has also been suggested that a form known only from a few teeth and a lower jaw *Propliopithecus* might represent the origin of the lineage giving rise to man, but this is now thought to be unlikely. Some Oligocene fossils are also known from South America and appear to be the beginnings of the New World Monkeys (Ceboidea) which are probably descended from New World prosimians and have evolved quite separately from Old World anthropoids.

From the Miocene, which follows the Oligocene, remains of a number of different apes have been found in East Africa, India (the Siwalik hills) and parts of Europe. Most are collectively referred to as the *Dryopithecinae* and still retain many monkey-like characteristics. Their skeleton indicates that they ran and jumped through the branches of trees, as most monkeys tend to do, but intermittently they probably moved by swinging from their arms; a mode of locomotion termed semi-brachiation. Present-day apes, the Orang, the Chimpanzee and the Gorilla are almost certainly descended from the Dryopithecinae. The group, however, is also seen as containing the ancestors of the human or hominid lineage. With regard to the early divergence of this lineage a fossil, known as *Ramapithecus* and found in both India and East Africa (where it was first called *Kenyapithecus*) assumes particular importance. It is known only from teeth and jaws, but in contrast with apes these show a rounded shape to the dental arcade, small canine teeth and spatulate shaped incisors; all of which are hominid characters. It is surmised that *Ramapithecus* lived on seeds and had probably given up an arboreal life for a terrestrial one, and what is more, in becoming terrestrial had adopted an erect bipedal mode of locomotion. The fossil is dated to about 14 million years ago. Mention should also be made here of another fossil anthropoid known best from Pliocene deposits in Italy: *Oreopithecus*. This, in a well-preserved skeleton, shows many features of bipedalism, but other characteristics, particularly of the teeth indicate that it is not closely related to man but is rather an aberrant ape.

Major features of Primate and Human evolution.

The distinctive characteristics of Primates arise from the fact that all species in the group either themselves live in trees or have had ancestors which were tree-living. They, therefore, show, though to varying degrees, a number of arboreal adaptations. 1. Special development of the limbs. The arboreal environment is characterised by being not only three-dimensional but also irregular and precarious. Animals in it therefore require special mechanisms for hanging on to branches and moving through trees. Primates have adapted to these needs by evolving thumbs and big toes which are opposable to the other digits so as to form grasping organs. Associated with this is the tendency to replace claws with nails and the development of friction pads on the palmar surface of hands and feet. A considerable flexibility and wide range of movement is evolved in the fore limb and primates have the ability to sit back on their haunches and explore the irregularity in their environment with their hands, thus emancipating the fore limb from a solely locomotor function. The grasping hand can also be used for collecting food and transferring it to the mouth. 2. Development of Special Senses. Unlike terrestrial environments the world of the trees is not a world of smells and the sense of olfaction tends to be poor in Primates. Concomittently there is a reduction in the snout, also made possible by the development of the hand. On the other hand, vision becomes an increasingly important sense and the eyes of Primates tend not only to be large but also to move from a lateral position on the skull on to the front of the face. Eventually there is overlapping in visual fields and the evolution of stereoscopy. In higher Primates colour vision arises. Tactile sense is also increased and balance and fine movement are improved. These changes in the senses are reflected in brain structure and size and Primates tend characteristically to have large brains for their body size. 3. Reduction in offspring number. The arboreal environment because of its precarious nature puts a premium on parental care and if there are many offspring to be cared for dissipation of parental effort may lead to none surviving. The arboreal environment is thus one of the few where animals who reduce their litter size can have a higher reproductive fitness than those with large litters. Primates typically give birth to only one or two offspring at any one time. This also means that there is little or no competition between offspring and therefore no premium for rapid development. Primates tend to be characterised by slow maturation and a long dependence on parents.

Clearly many of the features we see in man are an extension of his Primate heritage. But man, of course, has his own very distinctive characteristics. Anatomically these are to be seen particularly in his adaptations to a terrestrial bipedal existence, his much reduced face and jaws and his greatly enlarged brain. In evolution it would seem that it was the acquisition of the bipedalism which was critical. Why man's ancestors abandoned an arboreal habit is obscure, though there must have been a particular terrestrial ecological niche available, perhaps grain eating. Why in becoming terrestrial these same ancestors became bipedal is also unknown. Other Primates, such as the baboons and their relatives on re-colonising the ground continued to be quadrupedal. Perhaps the fact that the dryopithecine apes were semi-brachiators and therefore in many ways preadapted to an erect posture was significant. But whatever the explanation bipedalism, superimposed upon a Primate heritage, offered important evolutionary opportunities. This is not because bipedalism itself is a particularly effective means of locomotion but rather that it completes a Primate tendency of emancipating the forelimbs from locomotor function. They could therefore be used for many other purposes. One of the most important of these was tool use and subsequently tool-making. When early hominids colonised the terrestrial habitat they had few inbuilt defence mechanisms and the ability to use stones sticks and bones to ward off carnivores and other predators must have been of considerable survival value, as has been shown by observation of present-day chimpanzees when they are on the ground. The ability was enhanced and extended as it became possible to fashion these natural objects into shapes for particular purposes, and throughout the later stages of hominid evolution there is evidence of increasing refinement of the use of stone and flints in the making of tools. Initially of use in defence, the tools became of value in offence, and there is evidence quite early in hominid evolution of a lineage changing from the traditional herbivorous diet of Primates to a carnivorous one, indicating the adoption of a hunting mode of life. Tool making must have been one of the practices which favoured the development of language, and, since it came to require fine manipulative skill, hand and brain evolved together; particularly those parts of the brain concerned with precise motor control and tactile sensation. Man is sometimes defined as the tool making animal and although other creatures use tools and some fashion them at least occasionally, only man makes tools of a consistent and repeated pattern. Another consequence of freeing of the forelimbs through bipedalism was that carrying became so much easier. Thus food and other materials could be carried over considerable distances and this facilitated the establishment of a home base. Perhaps even more importantly the human infant could be carried in its mother's arms and held close to her body, allowing a much closer and intimate relationship between mother and child than is possible in other animals. The human infant is born in a very immature state; in part because of the limitations to the size of the birth canal imposed by the demands of bipedalism. It is therefore long dependent on maternal care. This raises problems in a hunting economy where nursing mothers become dependent upon males for the catching and providing of food. It has been argued that the evolution of the particular form of reproductive cycle found in man, in which the female is receptive to the male throughout most of her menstrual cycle should be seen as a means of ensuring that a hunting male will provide for his female and offspring. Certainly the type of behaviour found in many monkeys in which a female in heat abandons her offspring to consort with dominant males would not be compatible with survival of the human baby.

In recent years a great deal of attention has been devoted by physical anthropologists to studying the behaviour and ecology of many different Primates, especially Old World Monkeys and Apes. One of the aims of this has been to try and understand the origins of human sociality. Except in the most general of terms little can be said definitively about this, mainly, of course, because the non-human Primates have themselves evolved since the time they shared common ancestry with man. And even among quite closely related forms an immense diversity of social structures exist. But these new ethological studies have added a fascinating dimension to physical anthropology and allow a much more functional interpretation of Primate variety than was possible before.

THE HOMINID LINEAGE

Australopithecinae.

This group of creatures are presumed to be descended from a form like *Ramapithecus* and lived during Pliocene and Lower Pleistocene periods. They are well known from many finds made by R. Dart, R. Brown and J. T. Robinson in South Africa and more recently from East Africa, where L. S. B. Leakey and his family have been the main discoverers. For a number of years controversy raged as to whether they were apes or hominids: the brain size is small, in most cases well within the ape range, and they have heavy projecting jaws and large teeth. However they also show a number of human characteristics; their canine teeth were not projecting dagger like structures; their jaw movement was a rotatory grinding one not just directly up and down as in apes and most importantly, as evidenced from their post-cranial skeleton, they were terrestrial bipeds. In East Africa at least, there is also evidence that they made stone tools.

The taxonomy of the Australopithecines has been a source of great confusion. In South Africa the fossils were recovered from various former caves in Botswana and the Transvaal and those from a particular cave were given a distinct scientific name: *Australopithecus africanus* from Taung, *Australopithecus prometheus* from Makapansgat, *Pleisianthropus transvaalensis* from Sterkfontein, *Paranthropus robustus* from Kromdrai and *Paranthropus crassidens* from Swartkrans. Today it is generally agreed that only two forms are represented and that they are probably distinct only at the species level. They are known as *Australopithecus robustus* representing the forms previously known as *Paranthropus* and *Australopithecus africanus* the rest. The former, as its scientific name suggests, was a heavy rugged creature and, on the evidence of its extremely large premolar and molar teeth, was probably herbivorous. *A. africanus* was a much more gracile creature and, it is surmised, may well have been an active hunter.

A major problem in discussing the evolutionary significance of the South African australopithecines has been the difficulty in establishing accurately their age, since they were found in limestone breccias which cannot be geologically dated with present techniques. The situation is much better in East Africa where the fossils are found in or nearby igneous rocks which can be dated, particularly by the potassium/argon method. This indicates that australopithecine forms existed as long as 5 million years ago and occupied the region till at least 1·5 million years. The major sites from which specimens have been recovered are Olduvai Gorge in Tanzania, East of Lake Rudolph in Kenya and Omo and Afar in Ethiopia. Again there is evidence of two distinct forms as in South Africa; one robust, such as the well-represented "Nutcracker man" *Zinjanthropus boisei* (now known as *A. boisei* or *A. robustus boisei*) from Bed I at Olduvai Gorge; and the other gracile and comparable to *A. africanus*. At Olduvai Gorge, where it occurs in Bed I and the lower part of Bed II with dates ranging from 1·90 million—1·6 million the gracile form is more advanced than in South Africa with a larger braincase and more human teeth and has been termed *H. habilis*. It was almost certainly the maker of the Olduvan pebble culture and its advance on the South African form is probably because it was later in time. However, an anomaly which has not yet been explained is the discovery at East Rudolph of a form known as ER 1470 which appears more advanced, particularly in its large cranial capacity, than any other australopithecine and yet has a date of around 2·5–2 million years.

Homo erectus.

Although evolution along a lineage is a process of slow and gradual change, it is necessary taxonomially to divide the continuum into stages. When the fossil record is incomplete the gaps in it are used for separating the stages, but as these gaps are filled by further discovery the divisions become increasingly arbitrary. Bearing this difficulty in mind we can refer the stage of human evolution after the australopithecines (probably from a form like *A. africanus*) to *Homo erectus*. Most of the finds of this species are dated to the upper part of the Lower Pleistocene and to the Middle Pleistocene period. *H. erectus* is characterised by very thick skull bones, the development of heavy bony ridges, particularly above the eye region, and neither chin nor forehead. However the brain is much larger than in australopithecines and with a cranial capacity of 1,000 ccs or more, *H. erectus* is intermediate between australopithecines and *H. sapiens*. Further the post-cranial skeleton is essentially indistinguishable from modern man and *H. erectus* was fully bipedal and made complex stone tools.

The first finds of *H. erectus* were made in middle Pleistocene river terrace deposits in Java at the end of the last century by E. Dubois. They were named *Pithecanthropus erectus*. Subsequently further fossils of the same form were recovered in the region, and some remains showing particularly primitive features were recovered from Lower Pleistocene strata. Most of the latter were originally named *P. robustus* but a particularly massive jaw fragment termed *Meganthropus palaeojavanicus* shows australopithecine features.

In 1927 and 1929 the first remains of Pekin Man (long known as *Sinanthropus pekinensis*) were found in Chou kou Tien cave near Pekin. These remains tend to show some advances on the Javanese fossils such as larger cranial capacities but otherwise are very similar. Although the first finds of *H. erectus* were in Asia it is now known that the species had a wide distribution in the Old World and remains now attributed to it have been recovered in Europe, at Heidelberg, Germany; Vertesszöllös, Hungary and Petrolona, Greece, and in Africa at Ternifine, Algeria; Sidi Abderrahman, Morocco (both initially called *Athanthropus mauritanicus*) and Olduvai Gorge, Tanzania. Some very recent discoveries in East Africa also indicate that *H. erectus* may have evolved much earlier than was formerly thought and been present 1·75 million years ago. It may thus be contemporaneous with late australopithecines.

Prior to the Middle Pleistocene all the varieties of primates, including hominids, had been confined to the tropical parts of the world. Now with cultural advances including knowledge of fire, man was able to leave the tropical areas and to utilise the space and resources of the more northerly parts of the Old World. Both at Choukoutien and Vertesszöllös there is clear evidence of the use of fire.

ELEMENTS

Element (Symbol)	Atomic Number	Atomic Weight	Valency
actinium(Ac)*	89	227	
aluminium (Al)	13	26·9815	3
americium (Am)*	95	243	3, 4, 5, 6
antimony (Sb)	51	121·75	3, 5
argon (A)	18	39·948	0
arsenic (As)	33	74·9216	3, 5
astatine (At)*	85	210	1, 3, 5, 7
barium (Ba)	56	137·34	2
berkelium (Bk)*	97	247	3, 4
beryllium (Be)	4	9·0122	2
bismuth (Bi)	83	208·980	3, 5
boron (B)	5	10·811	3
bromine (Br)	35	79·904	1, 3, 5, 7
cadmium (Cd)	48	112·40	2
calcium (Ca)	20	40·08	2
californium (Cf)*	98	251	
carbon (C)	6	12·0111	2, 4
cerium (Ce)	58	140·12	3, 4
caesium (Cs)	55	132·905	1
chlorine (Cl)	17	35·453	1, 3, 5, 7
chromium (Cr)	24	51·996	2, 3, 6
cobalt (Co)	27	58·9332	2, 3
copper (Cu)	29	63·546	1, 2
curium (Cm)*	96	247	3
dysprosium (Dy)	66	162·50	3
einsteinium (Es)*	99	254	
erbium (Er)	68	167·26	3
europium (Eu)	63	151·96	2, 3
fermium (Fm)*	100	253	
fluorine (F)	9	18·9984	1
francium(Fr)*	87	223	1
gadolinium (Gd)	64	157·25	3
gallium (Ga)	31	69·72	2, 3
germanium (Ge)	32	72·59	4
gold (Au)	79	196·967	1, 3
hafnium (Hf)	72	178·49	4
helium (He)	2	4·0026	0
holmium (Ho)	67	164·930	3
hydrogen (H)	1	1·00797	1
indium (In)	49	114·82	3
iodine (I)	53	126·904	1, 3, 5, 7
iridium (Ir)	77	192·2	3, 4
iron (Fe)	26	55·847	2, 3
krypton (Kr)	36	83·8	0
lanthanum (La)	57	138·91	3
lawrencium(Lw)*	103	257	
lead (Pb)	82	207·19	2, 4
lithium (Li)	3	6·941	1
lutetium (Lu)	71	174·97	3
magnesium (Mg)	12	24·305	2
manganese (Mn)	25	54·9380	2,3,4,6,7
mendeleevium (Mv)*	101	256	
mercury (Hg)	80	200·59	1, 2

Element (Symbol)	Atomic Number	Atomic Weight	Valency
molybdenum (Mo)	42	95·94	3, 4, 6
neodymium (Nd)	60	144·24	3
neon (Ne)	10	20·17	0
neptunium (Np)*	93	237	4, 5, 6
nickel (Ni)	28	58·71	2, 3
niobium (Nb)	41	92·906	3, 5
nitrogen (N)	7	14·0067	3, 5
nobelium (No)*	102	254	
osmium (Os)	76	190·2	2, 3, 4, 8
oxygen (O)	8	15·9994	2
palladium (Pd)	46	106·4	2, 4, 6
phosphorus (P)	15	30·9738	3, 5
platinum (Pt)	78	195·09	2, 4
plutonium (Pu)*	94	244	3, 4, 5, 6
polonium (Po)*	84	210	
potassium (K)	19	39·102	1
praseodymium (Pr)	59	140·907	3
promethium (Pm)*	61	145	3
protactinium (Pa)*	91	231	
radium (Ra)*	88	226	2
radon (Rn)*	86	222	0
rhenium (Re)	75	186·2	
rhodium (Rh)	45	102·905	3
rubidium (Rb)	37	85·47	1
ruthenium (Ru)	44	101·07	3, 4, 6, 8
samarium (Sm)	62	150·35	2, 3
scandium (Sc)	21	44·956	3
selenium (Se)	34	78·96	2, 4, 6
silicon (Si)	14	28·086	4
silver (Ag)	47	107·870	1
sodium (Na)	11	22·9898	1
strontium (Sr)	38	87·62	2
sulphur (S)	16	32·064	2, 4, 6
tantalum (Ta)	73	180·947	5
technetium (Tc)*	43	99	6, 7
tellurium (Te)	52	127·60	2, 4, 6
terbium (Tb)	65	158·925	3
thalium (Tl)	81	204·37	1, 3
thorium (Th)	90	232·038	4
thulium (Tm)	69	168·934	3
tin (Sn)	50	118·69	2, 4
titanium (Ti)	22	47·90	3, 4
tungsten (*see* wolfram)			
uranium (U)	92	238·03	4, 6
vanadium (V)	23	50·942	3, 5
wolfram (W)	74	183·85	6
xenon (Xe)	54	131·30	0
ytterbium (Yb)	70	173·04	2, 3
yttrium (Y)	39	88·905	3
zinc (Zn)	30	65·37	2
zirconium (Zr)	40	91·22	4

* In the cases of these elements, which are very rare or not found in nature, but have been artificially prepared, atomic weight in the chemical sense is meaningless; the integral mass of the most stable isotope known is given.

Note: In 1961 the isotope of Carbon-12 replaced Oxygen as a standard, the weight of its atom being taken as 12. This change of standard has meant a slight adjustment in atomic weights from the old chemical scale.

The new elements with an atomic number higher than that of uranium 238 (element 92) are termed Transuranics.

GAS LAWS

The Perfect or Ideal Gas Law: $pV = nRT$
where n is the number of moles in volume V at pressure p and absolute temperature T, and R is a universal constant.

Van der Waals' equation: $\left(p + \frac{a}{V^2}\right)(V - b) = nRT$
where a and b are constants, different for each gas.

PERIODIC TABLE OF THE ELEMENTS

GROUP →	1A	2A	3B	4B	5B	6B	7B	8			1B	2B	3A	4A	5A	6A	7A	0
Period ↓	Alkali metals	Alkaline earth metals	← Transition metals →								Noble metals							Inert gases
1	1 **H** **1·00797**																	2 **He** **4·0026**
2	3 Li 6·941	4 Be 9·0122											5 **B** **10·811**	6 **C** **12·0111**	7 **N** **14·0067**	8 **O** **15·9994**	9 **F** **18·9984**	10 **Ne** **20·17**
3	11 Na 22·9898	12 Mg 24·305											13 Al 26·9815	*14* *Si* *28·086*	15 **P** **30·9738**	16 **S** **32·064**	17 **Cl** **35·453**	18 **Ar** **39·948**
4	19 K 39·103	20 Ca 40·08	21 Sc 44·956	22 Ti 47·90	23 V 50·942	24 Cr 51·996	25 Mn 54·938	26 Fe 55·847	27 Co 58·933	28 Ni 58·71	29 Cu 63·546	30 Zn 65·37	31 Ga 69·72	*32* *Ge* *72·59*	*33* *As* *74·922*	*34* *Se* *78.96*	35 **Br** **79·904**	36 **Kr** **83·80**
5	37 Rb 85·47	38 Sr 87·62	39 Y 88·905	40 Zr 91·22	41 Nb 92·906	42 Mo 95·94	43 Tc 99	44 Ru 101·07	45 Rh 102·905	46 Pd 106·4	47 Ag 107·870	48 Cd 112·40	49 In 114·82	50 Sn 118·69	*51* *Sb* *121·75*	*52* *Te* *127·60*	53 **I** **126·904**	54 **Xe** **131·30**
6	55 Cs 132·905	56 Ba 137·34	57 La* 138·91	72 Hf 178·49	73 Ta 180·947	74 W 183·85	75 Re 186·2	76 Os 190·2	77 Ir 192·2	78 Pt 195·09	79 Au 196·967	80 Hg 200·59	81 Tl 204·37	82 Pb 207·19	83 Bi 208·980	84 Po 210	85 **At** **210**	86 **Rn** **222**
7	87 Fr 223	88 Ra 226	89 Ac† 227															

* Lanthanides (*see* L72)

58 Ce 140·12	59 Pr 140·907	60 Nd 144·24	61 Pm 145	62 Sm 150·35	63 Eu 151·96	64 Gd 157·25	65 Tb 158·925	66 Dy 162·50	67 Ho 164·930	68 Er 167·26	69 Tm 168·934	70 Yb 173·04	71 Lu 174·97

† Actinides (*see* L3)

90 Th 232·038	91 Pa 231	92 U 238·03	93 Np 237	94 Pu 244	95 Am 243	96 Cm 247	97 Bk 247	98 Cf 251	99 Es 254	100 Fm 253	101 Md 256	102 No 254	103 Lw 257

Roman type—metals
Italic type—semiconductors
Bold type—non-metals

These designations refer to the normal materials, usually at room temperature. Processes like heating or compressing can turn metals into insulators and vice versa.

BACKGROUND TO ECONOMIC EVENTS

The aim of this section is to help the ordinary reader to follow economic events as they happen, and to understand the controversies that accompany them.

TABLE OF CONTENTS

BACKGROUND TO ECONOMIC EVENTS

This section is divided into four parts. Part I gives a brief description of the most important problems of economic policy. Part II is concerned with a more detailed survey of the British economy and the way in which it operates. In the course of this survey, the specialised terms used by economists are explained, and the attempt is made to present an intelligible summary of the information, facts, and figures relevant to an understanding of economic events. There are five main sub-sections: International Trade and Payments; Employment, Production, and Industry; Incomes, Wages, and Prices; Money, Banking, and Finance; and Economic Aspects of the Public Services. Part III outlines the main economic problems faced by the underdeveloped countries, and the economic policies of Britain and other developed countries towards the underdeveloped world. Some suggestions for further reading are given at the end of Parts II and III. Part IV is written as shortly before publication as possible, and contains a survey of recent developments in the British economy.

I. CENTRAL PROBLEMS OF ECONOMIC POLICY

Unemployment.

Between the wars, unemployment was Britain's most urgent economic problem. Quite the worst slump was that of the early 1930s: in 1932, nearly 3 million workers were without a job. But in no year between 1919 and 1939 were there fewer than a million workers unemployed. Economists make a distinction between *structural* unemployment and *cyclical* unemployment. Structural unemployment appears when the structure of industry gets out of line with the pattern of demand for industrial products. In Britain, unemployment was particularly severe and persistent in areas which were dependent on the coal, textile, and shipbuilding industries, and some sections of the engineering industry. Cyclical unemployment appears when there is a general decline in the level of demand for goods and services, which leads to a decline in the employment of workers producing those goods and services. In the slump years unemployment was so high because of a combination of structural and cyclical unemployment; in the best years, unemployment was largely structural.

Unemployment means waste. Men willing to work, who could produce valuable goods and services, are idle; the economy produces fewer goods and services than it is capable of producing. Unemployment also means hardship and low standards of living for those out of work, and for their families. The avoidance of mass unemployment has been accepted as a primary objective of economic policy by all political parties. It is only with the advent in the 1970s of new and greater problems of inflation and the balance of payments that this commitment has faltered. Cyclical unemployment can be tackled through measures to increase total spending by consumers, by investors, and by the Government. The problem which has daunted Governments in recent years is that such expansionary policies may not be possible without fuelling inflation and worsening the deficit in the balance of payments.

There have been ups and downs in unemployment in the post-war years, but these have been very slight until recently, compared to those before the war. In most post-war years, less than 2 per cent of the working population was unemployed—a sharp contrast with the 11 per cent for 1937 and the 22 per cent for 1932. But there are still areas of the country where structural unemployment is serious. In Northern Ireland, for example, despite the efforts which have been made to attract new industries, unemployment ranged between 6 and 10 per cent in the last decade.

Inflation.

A characteristic of the British economy in post-war years has been a persistent rise in prices and money incomes. For example, between 1960 and 1970, retail prices went up by about 52 per cent or—expressed as an annual rate—by 4·3 per cent per annum, export prices rose by 40 per cent (or 3·4 per cent per annum), and weekly wage rates by about 67 per cent (5·3 per cent per annum). However, these rates of increase were somewhat slower than the corresponding rates in the immediately post-war decade, or the annual inflation of 14 per cent between 1970 and 1976. Inflation can be harmful in various ways. Firstly, it is associated with an arbitrary redistribution of purchasing power. Prices rise for everyone, but some members of the community are better placed than others to secure increases in their money incomes which offset, or more than offset the rise in the price of the goods and services they buy. The feeling that particular groups are falling behind, in that their money incomes have not risen as fast as those of other groups is a source of much unrest and discontent. Secondly, and crucially for the British economy, an inflation of prices makes it more difficult to achieve a satisfactory balance of payments. As prices of our exports rise, it becomes harder to sell them in foreign markets; and as imports become cheap in comparison with goods produced at home there is a tendency to buy more of them.

Two main explanations have been advanced to account for the inflation which has occurred. The first stresses the role of an excess of demand or spending power in the economy—of too much money chasing too few goods, and so leading to a rise in prices. The inflationary problem is seen as the obverse of the cyclical unemployment problem: the latter involves a deficiency of spending, and the former an excess. Those who consider an excess of demand (*demand-pull*) to be an important factor in the inflationary situation favour policies designed to reduce purchasing power: for example, the reduction of spendable income by levying higher taxes, or the reduction of spending financed through borrowing by making credit more expensive or more difficult to get. The second stresses the role of an excessive increase in incomes: it is argued that prices have risen mainly because costs have increased faster than productivity (*cost-push*). Those who take this view favour measures to restrain or control increases in wages, profits, rents, and other forms of income. Neither explanation excludes the other. Many would agree that both demand-pull and cost-push factors have contributed—with different strengths at different times—to the inflationary spiral in prices and incomes, and that measures both to control demand and to restrain or control incomes may be necessary.

But it is easier to specify in general terms the measures needed to combat inflation than it is to apply policies which are successful in practice. In particular, policy measures to restrain or control wage increases are difficult to reconcile with widely-accepted procedures of collective bargaining.

The Balance of Payments.

Britain is heavily dependent on imports. This country must import food: it cannot produce enough food within its borders to feed its population. Many of the raw materials necessary for its industry have to be purchased from abroad. Furthermore, some manufactured goods produced in other countries will be purchased because they are cheaper or more attractive than similar goods produced at home. All these goods, and our imports of services, have to be paid for in foreign currency. Foreign currency is earned by exporting goods and services to other countries. It is not, however, considered sufficient to earn enough foreign currency from our exports to pay for our imports. The objective is to earn considerably more than that, so that we have a surplus of foreign currency available to pay off external debts, to build up our external assets by investing abroad, to enable us to lend and give aid to underdeveloped countries, and to increase our foreign exchange resources.

Since the war, our balance of payments position has been precarious. Exports have increased considerably, but so have imports; and the margin of safety has been so narrow that unfavourable turns of events have led to crises in the balance of payments. In several years, our earnings from the export of goods and services have not even been sufficient to cover our payments for imports, and in almost none has the surplus been as large as is considered necessary. With the balance of payments delicately poised even in favourable years, and with corrective action necessary in crisis years, economic policies have been much influenced by our foreign trade problems. It is easy to say that most of the problems would disappear, or would become less urgent, if we could achieve a major expansion of our exports. But most export markets are highly competitive, and we cannot expect to sell more unless the price, quality, and terms of delivery of our goods and services are at least as attractive as those of our rivals in export markets.

Economic Growth.

Taking a longer view, the most important objective of internal economic policy must be to raise the standard of living. The standard of living can increase only if more goods and services are produced per head of population. In a fully-employed economy, the main source of increased output is a higher productivity—output per person—of the working population.

British living standards have until recently been rising: the output of goods and services per head of population increased by about 21 per cent between 1960 and 1970; *i.e.* by 2 per cent per annum on average. Nevertheless, many economists are of the opinion that the rate of growth of output and productivity can be, and should be, increased. In particular, they point out that our rate of growth compares unfavourably with that achieved by some other countries. The potentialities for higher productivity are enormous. In many United States industries, output per person employed is twice or more than yet attained in Britain. Higher productivity will require more and better capital equipment, and better planning and organisation in the use of labour and machinery.

Less Developed Countries.

Britain and the other developed countries of the world have important responsibilities towards the less developed countries. The poorest two-thirds of the world's population account for only a sixth of total world income and output, while two-thirds of world income accrue to the richest sixth of world population, a category which includes Britain. The poorest two-thirds suffer from poverty, hunger, malnutrition, debilitating diseases, and widespread illiteracy. To make matters worse, most of the poor countries are experiencing a rapid growth of population. Output has to rise as fast as population just to prevent standards of living from falling, and an increase in standards of living requires an even faster growth of output.

Few of these countries can hope to solve the increasing problems they face without active and generous help from developed countries. This help must take many forms. Financial aid in the form of grants or loans in order to place resources at the disposal of less developed countries which they would otherwise not be able to obtain; technical aid to assist in the solution of the many technical problems which have to be solved; trading policies which do not hinder underdeveloped countries from getting the imports they need or from selling their exports—these are all activities in which Britain should play her part. In particular, Britain must contribute to the development of the underdeveloped countries of the Commonwealth. *See* **Part III.**

The Inter-relationship of Economic Problems.

Each of the problems briefly described above is extremely complex. The difficulties of achieving successful solutions are further aggravated by the fact that the problems are inter-related in such a way that measures which are helpful for one problem can make others more difficult to solve. For example, a reduction of purchasing power might be considered helpful in the control of inflation, and might ease balance of payments problems by reducing—or slowing down the increase of—imports. But it could also lead to an increase in unemployment, and to a slowing down in the rate of growth of the economy. Or again, a reduction in aid to underdeveloped countries could make it easier to balance our external accounts, but such action could hardly be reconciled with our responsibilities towards underdeveloped countries. In the next section, particular aspects of the British economy are considered in some detail; the final section discusses the main features of the development of the economy since 1960.

The Worsening Economic Climate.

In the mid-1970s, after 30 years of rapid growth and unprecedented prosperity for the major Western economies, the prospects for continued growth became much less favourable. This resulted partly from the acceleration of inflation in many countries, bringing with it insecurity and militancy in industrial relations. However, the main cause was the remarkable increase in the price of oil, a fuel on which the Western economies had become heavily dependent. This produced a strong burst of inflation; and, because much of the oil revenue accruing to producers could not be spent, gave rise to an unprecedented balance of payments problem and a very severe world recession. There was a danger that, through a lack of international co-ordination and of business confidence and through misplaced attempts by countries to cure their immediate economic problems by means of deflation, mass unemployment on the scale of the 1930s would again appear. In the changing situation both the problems of economic policy and the inter-relationships between them became more difficult.

II. SURVEY OF THE BRITISH ECONOMY

1. INTERNATIONAL TRADE AND PAYMENTS

International Trade.

(i) Imports and Exports.

In 1970 the United Kingdom bought from abroad goods to the value of £9,037 million, or about £160 per head. Food was a large item in this bill, accounting for 23 per cent of the total. Fuel, largely oil, cost about 10 per cent, basic materials for industry, 15 per cent, and manufactured goods (a category that includes a large number of semi-manufactured goods bought for further processing) 51 per cent. This last category of imports has increased sharply in recent years. In 1954 it represented only 20 per cent in an import bill of only £3,359 million. All this can be seen in the table.

There are three main determinants of the level of British imports. One is the competitiveness of British with foreign producers. Britain imports those commodities which—at the ruling exchange rate between the pound and foreign currencies—can be bought more cheaply from foreign than from home producers. Secondly, the level of imports depends on the extent to which free trade is prevented by tariffs on imported goods or by other devices. Thirdly, as total incomes in the economy expand, there is a general increase in the demand for goods and services, including imports. Therefore imports can be expected to vary directly with the total

UNITED KINGDOM IMPORTS AND EXPORTS

Imports of goods (c.i.f.)	£ million.		Percentage of total.	
	1954.	1970.	1954.	1970.
Food, drink, and tobacco	1,314	2,047	39	23
Basic materials	1,015	1,362	30	15
Fuels and lubricants	329	945	10	10
Semi-manufactures	513	2,500	15	28
Finished manufactures	174	2,072	5	23
TOTAL *	3,359	9,037	100	100
Exports of goods (f.o.b.)				
Food, drink, and tobacco	154	514	6	6
Basic materials	101	273	4	3
Fuels and lubricants	151	207	6	3
Metals	338	959	13	12
Engineering products	1,007	3,510	38	44
Textiles	324	396	12	5
Other manufactured goods	490	1,941	18	24
TOTAL *	2,650	8,061	100	100

* The column figures do not add up to the totals because the former exclude postal packages.

of incomes in the economy, known as the *national income*.

One would expect that the liberalisation of trade since the early 1950s, together with a decline in the competitiveness of British producers, would have produced an expansion of imports relative to national income. In fact imports as a proportion of national income were the same—23 per cent—in 1970 as in 1954. One reason why the proportion of imports did not rise was the sluggish demand for *primary products* such as food and raw materials. The British spend little of their additional income on imported food, and the development of synthetic substitutes and new products has slowed down the growth in demand for raw materials. Moreover, since the demand for primary products of this sort has been sluggish on a world scale, while supply has increased, their price has fallen in relative terms, and this too has reduced the total cost of British imports.

Since the exports of one country must be the imports of another, the same factors in reverse, foreign competitiveness, access to foreign markets, and the level of foreign incomes determine the level of British exports. In 1970 these amounted to £8,061 million, of which no less than 85 per cent were manufactures, mainly engineering products. In 1954 it was true to say that Britain gained from trade by exporting manufactures, in which she had a *comparative advantage*, in return for food and raw materials, which she was not suited to produce. This is still partly true; but increasingly—with the growth of trade and specialisation among the major economies—Britain gains from trade by exporting those manufactures in which her producers specialise and importing other manufactures. Among the main manufacturing exports are cars and commercial vehicles, tractors, aircraft and aircraft engines, finished steel, various forms of machinery, woollen fabrics, man-made fibres, and books; among the main manufactured imports are wood products, aluminium, newsprint, cars, and aircraft.

(ii) The Terms of Trade.

Between 1954 and 1970 the value of British exports and imports approximately tripled. These changes can be separated into two components, price and volume. Imports rose in price by only 27 per cent, whereas export prices rose by 58 per cent. The ratio of the average price of exports to that of imports is known as the *terms of trade*; and a rise in the price of exports relative to imports indicates an improvement in the terms of trade. Thus, when we note in the table that the terms of trade improved by 20 per cent between 1954 and 1970, we mean that, in 1970, 20 per cent less exports by volume would have been needed to buy the same amount of imports as in 1954. This improvement in the terms of trade reflects the fact that the prices of many primary products—food and raw materials such as wool, cocoa, rubber, or oil—fell or stagnated in world markets over the period (*see* G30).

VISIBLE TRADE: VOLUME AND PRICES

	1961 = 100.		Percentage increase 1954–70.
	1954.	1970.	
Value			
Imports	76	204	168
Exports	72	219	204
Volume			
Imports	74	156	111
Exports	80	155	94
Price			
Imports	103	131	27
Exports	89	141	58
Terms of trade	116	93	−20

(iii) The Volume of Trade.

Superficially it would appear that any improvement in the terms of trade raises the value of British exports relative to imports. However, this is not always true: faster inflation in this country, leading to a more rapid increase in export prices, would harm rather than help the balance of payments. If the prices of our export goods rise faster than the prices of our competitors in overseas markets, it will become progressively more difficult to sell our exports. Conversely, an inflation in Britain will make it progressively more attractive to buy goods produced abroad. Partly because of the slower growth of import prices than of export prices, the volume of imports increased more rapidly than the volume of exports over the period 1954–70. The trade balance may well be helped by a fall in the price of imported primary products; but the balance of trade in manufactures will be worsened by an improvement in their terms of trade.

In the post-war period there was a considerable fall in Britain's share of world exports; from 20·0 per cent of exports of manufactures in 1954 to 16·4 in 1961 to 12·3 in 1967, the year of sterling devaluation, to 10·8 in 1970. The fall was persistent: in no year did Britain's share increase. Her competitors in export markets—and particularly Germany, Italy, and Japan—were more successful in expanding their exports. Had the prices of British exports risen less rapidly over the period, Britain's share of world exports would have been higher in 1970.

The Balance of Payments.

The *balance of payments* is an account of the total transactions of one country with the rest of the world. To illustrate the balance of payments and its components, the British accounts for two years are presented in the table; accounts for a bad year, 1964, and for a good year, 1970. A detailed examination of recent movements in the British balance of payments is made in Part IV (*see* G35–8).

BALANCE OF PAYMENTS OF THE UNITED KINGDOM, 1964 AND 1970
(£ millions)

	1964.	1970.
Exports (f.o.b.)	4,521	7,907
Imports (f.o.b.)	5,021	7,919
Visible balance	−500	−12
Invisible balance	+145	+747
of which: private services	+184	+675
Government military transfers	−268	−285
other Government services and transfers	−164	−200
interest, profits, and dividends	+393	+557
Current balance	−355	+735
Official long-term capital	−116	−204
Net private investment	−256	+51
of which: overseas investment in U.K.	+143	+838
U.K. investment overseas	−399	−787
Other capital flows	+71	+858
Balancing item	−39	−20
Total currency flow	−695	+1,420
Net borrowing from IMF*	+357	−134
Net borrowing from other monetary authorities*	+216	−1,161
Change in reserves*	+122	−125
Total official financing*	+695	−1,420

* A plus sign denotes a rise in liabilities or a fall in assets, and a minus sign a fall in liabilities or a rise in assets.

(i) The Balance of Visible Trade.

The *balance of (visible) trade* is the difference between exports and imports of goods. It is said to be in *surplus* if exports exceed imports and in *deficit* if imports exceed exports. In estimating the balance of trade it is important that imports and exports be valued on the same basis. The normal method in the trade returns is to measure imports *c.i.f.* (cost, insurance, and freight) and exports *f.o.b* (free on board). In other words import prices are shown to include the costs of transporting them to Britain, and exports are valued at the prices when loaded in British ports. Our table shows both imports and exports *f.o.b.*

Britain's visible balance is normally in deficit. The trade balance in 1970 was the best achieved since 1958. On the other hand, the year 1964 was exceptional in the large size of its deficit.

(ii) The Balance of Invisible Trade.

The chronic deficit in the balance of visible trade has in normal years been offset by a surplus in the *balance of invisible trade*. This relates to international transactions in services as opposed to goods. It comprises four main groups of transactions. The first covers receipts from non-residents *less* payments to non-residents for services such as shipping, civil aviation, tourism, insurance, and financial services. The second covers receipts from foreign governments in respect of military bases in the country *less* payments by this country in respect of military bases abroad. The third covers receipts of gifts and grants made to this country, *less* gifts and grants made by this country. The fourth includes all receipts of interest, dividends, and profits earned on overseas investment *less* interest, dividends, and profits paid out on foreign investment in this country.

(iii) The Balance on Current Account.

The surplus on invisibles usually exceeds the deficit on visibles, so that Britain earns a surplus in the *balance on current account*, comprising both visible and invisible trade. The year 1964 was exceptional in this respect.

In 1970 just over a quarter of British visible trade was with the countries of the *Overseas Sterling Area*—comprising the independent Commonwealth countries other than Canada, the remaining colonial territories, and a few countries such as South Africa, the Republic of Ireland, and some Arab oil-producing states. Until 1972 these were known as *the scheduled territories*. Since then only Ireland and Gibraltar were so defined, the change being important for U.K. exchange control regulations. Almost 40 per cent of our visible trade was with Western Europe—20 per cent with the EEC and 15 per cent with the EFTA countries (*see* **G42**)—and rather less than 20 per cent with North America. The current balance of payments surplus found in normal years is generally made up of a large surplus with sterling area countries partially offset by a deficit with the non-sterling areas.

(iv) Capital Flow.

It is not sufficient simply to avoid deficits on current account. It has been the Government's objective to earn a surplus in order to finance investment abroad, to repay foreign debts previously incurred, and to build up reserves of gold and foreign exchange which can help to tide us over periods of deficit in the future. In fact a surplus of the magnitude aimed at by the Government was only rarely achieved.

The capital account of the balance of payments contains net official long-term capital movements (*e.g.*, inter-government loans to less developed countries), net private investment abroad (being the difference between investment abroad by United Kingdom residents and investment by foreigners in the United Kingdom). Both these items are normally in deficit and tend to be long-term movements. Usually they involve a deficit with the sterling area and only minor imbalance with the rest of the world.

There are also large, short-term capital flows, sometimes referred to as *monetary movements*. These include trade credits, changes in sterling reserves held by foreign governments, and Eurodollar transactions. Such funds can be highly volatile, moving out of a currency if there is a risk of its devaluation and into it if there is a chance of revaluation upwards or if other currencies are suspect. Therefore, monetary movements often accentuate a surplus or deficit in the other items of the balance of payments; as happened in 1970.

(v) Total Currency Flow.

The bookkeeping identity of international payments and receipts may be illustrated by reference to the year 1964. In that year the United Kingdom had a deficit on current and capital account of no less than £656 million. In other words, there was a net demand to transfer funds from sterling into other currencies. Since the monetary authorities would not permit the market price of sterling to fall, this excess demand had to be met from official sources. The deficit could be financed by an increase in liabilities, *i.e.*, by government borrowing from abroad, or by a reduction in assets, *e.g.*, a depletion of the official gold and foreign exchange reserves. Total net official financing recorded was in fact £695 million, so that there must have been an unrecorded capital outflow equal to £39 million, known as the *balancing item*. The *total currency flow*, equal to the *total official financing*, was therefore £695 million.

(vi) Foreign Exchange Reserves.

The gold and convertible currency reserves are used to finance payments abroad which cannot be financed in any other way: they are a last line of defence in international trade. The reserves held in London belong to the sterling area as a whole, and not just to this country. Members of the sterling area are willing to pay into these central reserves some or all of their net earnings of gold and convertible currencies in exchange for sterling balances. They do this on the understanding that they can, should they wish to do so, call upon the central reserves by exchanging sterling balances for gold and convertible currencies.

The central reserves of gold and foreign currencies amounted to £1,180 million at the end of 1970; a level which, though higher than in many previous post-war years, was still low. There are bound to be imbalances in international trade and payments, and the function of these reserves is to tide over temporary imbalances by increasing reserves in favourable periods and running down reserves in unfavourable periods. If reserves are not sufficient to withstand temporary pressures, measures to protect the reserves will have to be taken—*e.g.*, raising Bank Rate and tightening up monetary policies generally—and these measures may create unemployment and recession, and restrict the growth of the economy.

Correcting a Deficit.

If an imbalance in the total currency flow persists, the deficit cannot be met indefinitely from official financing. At some stage the Government must take action to remove the deficit. What action can it take? There are a number of alternatives available, each with its advantages and disadvantages, and economic opinion is by no means unanimous on the choice of policy. Let us consider each of these alternatives in turn.

(i) Variation of the Exchange Rate.

The *exchange rate* is the ruling official rate of exchange of pounds for gold and other currencies. It determines the value of British goods in relation to foreign goods. If the pound is devalued in terms of gold and other currencies, British exports (which are paid for in pounds) become cheaper to foreigners and British imports (paid for by purchasing foreign currency) become more expensive to holders of pounds. In this way *devaluation* can improve the British balance of payments position by encouraging exports and discouraging imports.

But there are certain disadvantages attached to devaluation. The prospect of devaluation results in a speculative outflow of capital funds: and one devaluation may be taken as a sign that there will be further devaluation in the future. Secondly, until 1968 it was true that the sterling area countries—many of them underdeveloped—would suffer a capital loss, because they hold their reserves largely in the form of sterling rather than gold (*see* G9). Thirdly, the rise in the price of imports of raw materials and consumption goods results in higher costs and prices and then in wage demands to maintain the British standard of living. It is possible that inflation will in this way neutralise the beneficial effects of devaluation.

The pound was devalued in 1949, when an official exchange rate of £1 = \$2·8 was established, and again in 1967, to a rate of £1 = \$2·4. During 1971, when, as a result of the dollar crisis, exchange rates were allowed to fluctuate, the rate varied between £1 = \$2·4 and £1 = \$2·5. After the devaluation of the dollar in December 1971, the rate with gold remained unchanged, but the exchange rate with dollars became £1 = \$2·6. After June 1972 the value of sterling in relation to other currencies was allowed to *float*. It fluctuated, but the tendency was to float downwards: in January 1977 the pound equalled \$1·71 (*see* G37).

(ii) Exchange Controls and Convertibility.

A currency is fully *convertible* if it can be freely exchanged for any other currency, or for gold, at the ruling official rates of exchange. Exchange controls impose restrictions on convertibility by limiting the powers of holders of a currency to exchange their holdings for other currencies or gold at the official rate of exchange. In the post-war period there was a world-wide shortage of dollars: if sterling had been convertible, there would have been a rush to obtain dollars, with the consequence that the dollar reserves of the sterling area would soon have been exhausted. In fact, a premature attempt to establish sterling convertibility in 1947 led to such a drain on reserves that strict exchange controls had to be re-imposed.

Exchange controls on residents can be enforced by requiring that earnings of foreign currencies (*e.g.*, the proceeds from the sale of exports) be handed over to the exchange control authority—the Bank of England acts as the Government's agent—in exchange for sterling; and by permitting the exchange of sterling for foreign currencies (*e.g.*, to enable the purchase of imports) only for transactions approved by the exchange control authority. There was a move towards convertibility of sterling during the 1950s, and the sterling held by non-residents was made fully convertible in 1958. Residents, however, continued to be subject to exchange controls.

By restricting convertibility the Government can make it more difficult for funds to move into or out of sterling. In this way the Government can impede capital movements, *e.g.*, British private investment abroad, or it can restrict current spending abroad, *e.g.*, on foreign holidays.

(iii) Import Controls and Tariffs.

Import controls impose limitations on the quantity or value of goods which are permitted to enter a country: tariffs are duties levied on imported goods so that the price of those goods to consumers in a country is higher than the price received by the foreigners supplying the goods. In the early post-war years, Britain maintained strict import controls over a wide range of goods. These were gradually dismantled, until in 1959 the last remaining import controls on goods were abandoned, except on habit-forming drugs and some agricultural products and textiles from the Far East—to give a measure of protection to British producers.

All countries impose tariffs. Some tariffs are primarily intended to raise revenue for the Government, and others are primarily intended to protect home industries by raising the price of competing goods from abroad. The rights of countries to raise tariffs, or to operate tariffs in a discriminatory way (*i.e.*, to offer lower tariffs on goods from some sources than on similar goods from other sources), are closely circumscribed by the rules of the *General Agreement on Tariffs and Trade* (GATT). The object of the GATT is to work towards free trade, especially through a reduction in tariffs. In the post-war period GATT held several major conferences, at which bargaining to reduce tariffs was attended by modest success. The most significant moves towards free trade in this period were on a regional basis.

The disadvantage of introducing import controls or tariffs to correct a deficit in the balance of payments is that the benefits of free trade are lost. Moreover, there is always the possibility of retaliation by Britain's trading partners. Nevertheless, import controls or tariffs may well be preferable to another measure which has been used to correct a deficit, deflation.

(iv) Deflation.

Throughout the post-war period the U.K. balance of payments was far from secure. As a result, domestic economic policies were much influenced by balance of payments considerations. Devaluation was turned to only as a last resort. The movement in the 1950s and 1960s was towards greater freedom of trade. By ruling out devaluation and trade restrictions, the authorities had to fall back on *deflation* of the economy to correct periodic deficits. In other words, the Government took measures to discourage demand and so cut back incomes and employment. By reducing demand in general, the authorities secured a fall in demand for imports. However, it was necessary to cut back national income by many times the ensuing fall in imports. Deflation is a painful method of correcting a deficit. Not only does it have a direct effect on the level of incomes and employment, but it is also liable to slow down the rate of growth of the economy. This can happen because deflation can weaken the incentive to expand productive capacity by investing in new plant, machinery, and other capital goods.

The problem which faced British policy-makers attempting to raise the rate of economic growth was this: as total demand for goods and services expands, it is difficult to prevent growth in the demand for imports and diversion of exports to the home market, particularly when home industries reach the limit of their productive capacity.

Yet if consequent balance of payments difficulties are met by restrictions on total demand, it is difficult to maintain the investment necessary for growth in the productive capacity of the economy. The main need during the 1970s was the same as that during the 1950s: to achieve an expansion of exports relative to imports so as to secure economic growth without running into balance of payments difficulties.

The international monetary system is partly to blame for the British decisions to resort to periodic deflation of the economy. The use of sterling as a reserve currency has subjected the balance of payments to violent swings in short-term capital flows. Moreover, if there is a world-wide shortage of *international liquidity, i.e.*, gold and foreign exchange reserves, this means that countries have an incentive to maintain a surplus in their balance of payments and so increase their reserves. In this situation surplus countries do not help to correct an imbalance in foreign transactions: the burden of correcting the imbalance is placed on the deficit country. If the Government of the deficit country feels itself unable to devalue its currency or to impose trade restrictions, it has to deflate the economy. The international monetary system has contained a "deflationary bias," which the International Monetary Fund (*see below* and **G39**) has at most only ameliorated.

The International Monetary System.

(i) International Liquidity.

Imbalance in payments between countries is financed by transfers of gold or foreign exchange (*see* **G8**). These reserves of gold and foreign exchange are known as *international liquidity*. Their basic characteristic is general acceptability: they can perform their function only if they retain the confidence of those engaged in international transactions. Unless it is ultimately convertible into goods and services, gold has merely an industrial and ornamental value. But since most central banks are prepared to buy and sell gold at a fixed price in terms of their local currency, confidence in gold is maintained.

Two *international reserve currencies* have emerged to supplement gold: the pound and the dollar. The pound has performed this function since World War I, but the dollar has become the main reserve currency since World War II. Surplus countries are prepared to hold short-term debt in pounds or dollars—so earning a rate of interest—confident that their future trading deficits can be financed by payment of these currencies or by their conversion into gold. These holdings are known as the *dollar* and *sterling balances*. Like gold, they can perform their function as international reserves only if there is confidence that they can be converted into other currencies and hence into goods and services at current exchange rates. There is one other form of international liquidity—drawing rights on the IMF (*see* **G10**). Near the end of 1976 gold accounted for 17 per cent of total international liquidity, foreign exchange reserves for 71 per cent, the IMF for 8 per cent, and the newly created Special Drawing Rights (*see* **G40**) for 4 per cent.

In recent years two developments have undermined the present international monetary system. First, the growth of international trade has outstripped the growth of reserves with which to finance imbalances in this trade. Between 1952 and 1972 world trade, measured in dollars, rose by 375 per cent, whereas international liquidity, measured in dollars, rose by only 175 per cent. Gold reserves have been a declining proportion of international liquidity, partly because gold production has been hampered by the fixed price in the face of rising costs of gold production, and also because an increasing proportion of newly-mined gold has found its way into private speculative hoards and not into official stocks. The other main source of new international liquidity was an increase in dollar balances. By the late 1960s dollar balances actually exceeded the United States gold reserves.

The second problem to have emerged is the weakness in the balance of payments of the reserve currency countries. Both Britain and the United States have had persistent deficits in recent years. As a result there have been periodic fears that the dollar or the pound would be devalued in terms of gold and other currencies; and this has resulted in speculation against the dollar and the pound (*see* **G35**). The inadequacy of international liquidity and the weakness of the reserve currencies produce a dangerous "deflationary bias" in the world economy.

(ii) The Sterling Balances.

Governments and individuals may hold balances in sterling (*e.g.*, Treasury bills, Government stocks and bank accounts) for many reasons. Sterling area countries reckon to keep a high proportion of their international trade reserves in the form of sterling balances. It is convenient to hold sterling to finance trading transactions because sterling is widely acceptable in settlement of trading debts. Sterling balances will also be held to the extent that they are considered a profitable and safe way of holding liquid assets. It may be profitable to hold sterling if the rate of interest paid on balances in London is higher than that paid in other financial centres. And it may be considered safe to hold sterling if the chances of sterling devaluation (which would automatically reduce the value of the balances in terms of any currency which did not devalue) are thought to be remote.

An increase in the sterling balances enables Britain to finance an adverse balance of payments without reducing the gold and foreign exchange reserves. Conversely, a reduction in sterling balances can impose a drain on reserves even if there is no adverse balance.

At the end of 1970 liquid sterling balances held by non-residents (excluding the International Monetary Fund) amounted to £2,800 million; far in excess of Britain's reserves of gold and convertible currencies, equal to £1,180 million. Nearly threequarters of this amount was held by the rest of the sterling area. However, it is unlikely that Britain would be able to finance a persistent deficit in her balance of payments through a progressive increase in the sterling balances. In the long run the sterling balances will probably be reduced, *e.g.*, many underdeveloped countries of the sterling area will want to run down their sterling balances in order to help finance the imports required for their development programmes, and all sterling area countries have faced the risk of capital loss through sterling devaluation. Additionally, their financial links with the U.K. have been weakened by the latter's entry into the EEC.

Sterling holdings outside the sterling area, and particularly the unofficial (*i.e.*, private) holdings, are highly volatile, in that they may be withdrawn very rapidly if for any reason it is thought less profitable or less safe to hold sterling than some other currency or gold. Since confidence in sterling is weakest (*i.e.*, fear that it will be devalued is greatest) when the balance of payments is in deficit, sterling balances tend to move perversely, so accentuating movement in the reserves. Such was the case, for instance, in the sterling crisis of 1964.

It is ironical that Britain's position as an international currency country makes it more and not less difficult to rely on a running down of reserves to meet a temporary deficit in the balance of payments. However, under the Basle agreement of 1968 the major central banks granted the United Kingdom new credit facilities of up to £800 million for 10 years with which to finance sales of sterling as the sterling balances were run down. Also the British Government guaranteed the value, in terms of U.S. dollars, of most of the official sterling reserves held by sterling area countries, in return for their holding at least a certain proportion of their reserves in sterling. These arrangements helped to protect sterling against the dangers of being a reserve currency (*see also* **G38**).

(iii) The International Monetary Fund.

The *International Monetary Fund* (IMF) was set up after the war with the objective of working towards free trade at stable exchange rates. Under the original agreement setting up the Fund, members agreed to make their currencies convertible into other currencies and gold at fixed rates of exchange, and agreed not to impose exchange or import controls without the permission of the Fund. Any alteration in the rates of exchange by more than 10 per cent also requires the permission of the Fund. For many years after the war, the imbalances in world trade—and particularly the acute shortage of dollars—were such that many countries had to invoke the clauses in the agreement which permitted them to impose restrictions during a "transitional" period. During the 1950s the progressive relaxation of exchange and import controls by this country was paralleled in some other countries, and most of the currencies important in world trade and payments were declared convertible.

The function of the Fund is to make foreign exchange resources available to members who run into balance of payments difficulties. Each member country makes a deposit (called its quota) partly in gold and partly in its own currencies, with the Fund. The size of the deposit is fixed in relation to the country's share in world trade. In return, it is granted certain automatic drawing rights, which entitle it to borrow foreign currencies from the Fund. Furthermore, the Fund has power to make larger loans, and to grant stand-by credits to be drawn on if required. Before the Fund will make such loans and credits available, it has to be satisfied that the borrowing country is taking appropriate action to correct the balance of payments disequilibrium.

In 1964 and 1965, when there was a severe deficit in total currency flow and heavy speculation against sterling, the British Government borrowed from the IMF £369 million in 1964 and £499 million in 1965. In this way the country could ride out crises of confidence in sterling without a severe loss of reserves.

For an account of recent international monetary crises and attempts at reform, involving the IMF, see Part IV, G39–42.

(iv) The Eurodollar Market.

The Eurodollar market is a market for bank deposits which are denominated in foreign currencies. It derives its name from the fact that most of the banks which accept these foreign currency deposits are in Europe (including Britain) and most of the deposits are denominated in U.S. dollars. The Eurodollar market has grown at remarkable speed. A phenomenon of the 1960s, the market involved deposits of $9 billion in 1964 and $37 billion in 1969. The reason for that growth was the profitability of Eurodollar transactions. Banks found that, particularly if only large units of money were handled, they could profitably borrow funds in country A and lend in country B, while paying interest rates higher than those paid in country A and charging rates lower than those charged in country B. Its growth was helped by the continuous deficit in the United States balance of payments, since this meant that banks and institutions received dollars which they were willing to hold and lend. London is very important in the Eurodollar market: London banks accounted for no less than 57 per cent of the total external liabilities in U.S. dollars reported by European banks in 1968.

The Eurodollar market—involving great mobility of short-term funds—creates problems for the regulation of economic activity. The market affects the rates of interest and the availability of credit in different countries, and money movements can thwart both restrictive and expansionist monetary policies (*see* G24).

2. EMPLOYMENT, PRODUCTION, AND INDUSTRY

Population.

In June 1973 the population of the United Kingdom was estimated to be 55·9 million—49·2 m. in England and Wales, 5·2 m. in Scotland, and 1·5 m. in Northern Ireland. The total was rising slowly, at a rate of about 0.3 per cent per annum. The *crude birth rate* (the number of live births per 100 people) was about 1·5 in the early 1970s, and the *crude death rate* about 1·2; giving a *rate of natural increase* of 0·3 per cent. Net migration was slightly negative over the previous decade as a whole.

The official estimate of the population of the United Kingdom in the year 2001 is 59·4 million. But prediction of future trends is difficult. For instance, it depends on immigration and emigration policies, the effect of improving medical services on the average length of life, trends in the age at which people marry, advances in techniques of birth control, and attitudes towards desirable family size. The average age of women on first marriage fell between 1951 and 1973 from 24·6 to 22·7 years. The expectation of life at birth was 66·2 years in 1951 and 68·9 years in 1973 in the case of males; being 71·2 years in 1951 and 75·3 years in 1973 in the case of females.

It is sometimes said that Britain is an overpopulated island. However, the apparent increase in overcrowding may be more the result of increasing prosperity, *e.g.*, the impact of the motor car on our environment, than of increasing population.

The Population of Working Age.

Of the total population only some are of *working age, i.e.*, between the minimum school leaving age of 16 (15 before 1973) and retiring age—65 years for men and 60 for women. Of course, not all those of working age do work and not all those above working age have retired; nevertheless, the ratio between population not of working age and the total is a useful statistic, as it does provide a rough guide to the numbers who have to be supported out of the national income but who do not contribute to it. This ratio was 41 per cent in 1973; 24 per cent being below working age and 17 per cent above. It is likely to rise over time as people live longer and particularly if the age of retirement is reduced.

The Labour Force.

Not all persons of working age actually work, although the vast majority do; but only a part are gainfully employed, *i.e.*, work for wages, salaries, or profits. It is only those *gainfully employed* who are counted in the *labour force* (or working population), *e.g.*, housewives and mothers are excluded unless they do some work for cash. In 1973, when the total population of the United Kingdom was 55·9 million, of whom

DISTRIBUTION OF WORKING POPULATION, UNITED KINGDOM, JUNE 1973
(Thousands)

Primary Industries:	
Agriculture, forestry, and fishing	434
Mining and quarrying	363
TOTAL	797
Production Industries:	
Construction	1,380
Gas, electricity, and water	344
Transport and communication	1,524
Manufacturing	7,828
of which:	
food, drink, and tobacco	754
chemicals and allied industries	427
metal manufacture	518
engineering	1,935
shipbuilding	187
vehicles	797
textiles	594
clothing and footwear	440
paper, printing, and publishing	574
other manufacturing	1,602
TOTAL	11,076
Services:	
Distributive trades	2,744
Financial, business, professional and scientific services	4,308
Catering, hotels, etc.	794
Miscellaneous services	1,359
National government service	614
Local government service	969
TOTAL	10,788
GRAND TOTAL	22,661

33·3 million were of working age, the total labour force (including the unemployed who are seeking employment) was only 25·6 million. Of the 16.0 million women of working age only about 9 million were gainfully employed. So for every person who was gainfully employed there was just over one other person to be supported. One feature of the post-war years was an increase in the proportion of adults going out to work. Whereas in 1955, 66 per cent of the working-age population was gainfully employed, in 1973 the figure was 77 per cent.

Most of the labour force work for wages and salaries as employees. Of the total for the United Kingdom in June 1973 of 25·6 million, 2·0 m. were employers or self-employed, 0.36 m. were in the Forces, 22·6 m. were employees and 0·57 m. were registered as unemployed.

The table shows the industries in which people work. Some 3·5 per cent of the total work in the *primary sector* (agriculture and mining) and 49 per cent in the *production industries*, 35 per cent being in manufacturing (the main production industry). As an economy develops there is a tendency for employment in the primary sector to decline at the expense of the production industries. At high levels of income a large proportion of income is spent on services, and employment in services expands as a proportion of the total. Thus, in 1955 services accounted for only 36 per cent of total employment; whereas by 1973 the proportion had risen to 48 per cent.

Employment and Unemployment.

In 1970 an average of 582,000 persons—2·5 per cent of the labour force—were unemployed in Great Britain. In most post-war years the average was lower than 1·5 per cent. Even in January 1959, the worst month of the 1950s, the rate rose only to 2·8 per cent, and in February 1963—an exceptional month owing to weather—to 3·9 per cent. These contrast with an average figure in 1937, the best year of the 1930s, of 11 per cent, and with a figure of 22 per cent at the bottom of the slump in 1932. The low unemployment of the post-war years was not maintained in the late 1960s. Unemployment grew and in 1971 averaged 3·4 per cent. In January 1972 unemployment had reached the remarkable level of 928,600 unemployed—not less than 4·1 per cent of the labour force.

UNEMPLOYMENT AND VACANCIES
(Great Britain, thousands)

	Unemployment. (Annual average)	Vacancies. (End of period)	Unemployment as percentage of total employees
1932*	2,829	n.a.	*22·1*
1937*	1,482	n.a.	*10·9*
1958	410	163	*1·9*
1960	346	294	*1·5*
1962	432	157	*1·9*
1964	372	311	*1·6*
1966	331	234	*1·4*
1968	549	267	*2·4*
1970	582	211	*2·5*
1972	844	225	*3·8*
1973	600	168	*2·6*

* Figures relate only to population insured against unemployment.

Until the late 1960s 1–1·5 per cent unemployment was somewhere near the practicable minimum; for some unemployment is more or less inevitable. Some seasonal rise in unemployment in the winter must be expected, *e.g.*, in seaside towns, and for this reason unemployment in January is half a per cent or so higher than in June. Moreover, some unemployment is bound to be involved in job-changing and as the demands of industries change. "Full employment" means that there should be about as many jobs vacant as there are workers looking for jobs. A large excess of vacancies is evidence of inflationary pressure in the labour market, for it means that the employers needing workers to meet the demands for their products will have to compete with each other by bidding up wages. Most commentators feel that the practicable minimum level of unemployment has increased since the late 1960s One explanation of this is that as the fixed costs (like National Insurance contributions) of employing workers have gone up, so employers have been more careful to economise on labour.

To some extent unemployment figures are misleading, as not all unemployed workers are eligible for unemployment benefit under the National Insurance Scheme. Most married women who go out to work normally opt not to pay the full National Insurance contributions, so that, when they become unemployed, they just drop out of the "working population." Unemployment figures definitely understate the seriousness of recessions, as they do not count all the persons who would like to have, but cannot find, jobs.

Regional Unemployment.

A peculiarly dreadful feature of the inter-war years was the emergence of the depressed areas—the regions of the country where a third of the men had not had a job for a year or more. Such extreme regional unemployment has not recurred in the post-war period: only in Northern Ireland was unemployment very high. Between 1954 and 1970 unemployment there ranged between 6 and 10 per cent. Nevertheless, regional inequalities exist.

PERCENTAGE OF WORKERS UNEMPLOYED, BY REGIONS

	Annual average 1965	November 1971
North	2·5	6·4
Yorkshire and Humberside	1·1	4·5
East Midlands	0·9	3·3
East Anglia	1·3	3·3
South East	0·8	2·2
South West	1·5	4·0
Wales	2·5	5·2
West Midlands	0·7	5·5
North West	1·6	4·7
Scotland	2·9	6·6
Great Britain	*1·4*	*3·8*
Northern Ireland	6·1	8·4

In November 1971 the proportion of all workers unemployed in Great Britain was 3·8. But the table shows a lower proportion was unemployed in the South East, East Anglia, and East Midlands, and that there was a much higher proportion unemployed in the north and west of England, in Wales, Scotland, and Northern Ireland. Moreover, the labour shortage of 1965 was not shared equally; unemployment remained at 2·5 per cent or above in the North, Wales, Scotland, and Northern Ireland. In this situation checks have to be placed on the economy before full employment is reached, because in the booming areas vacancies far exceed unemployment.

DECREASE IN EMPLOYMENT IN SELECTED INDUSTRIES, 1950–1970

	Thousands.	Per cent.
Textiles	373	34
Mining and quarrying	446	48
Shipbuilding	118	37
Agriculture, forestry, and fishing	457	55

One of the main reasons for the regional pattern of unemployment is that certain industries and services, in which big changes have been taking place, tend to be grouped in specific regions. Most of our early industrial centres had to be established close to coal, iron ore, and adequate water supplies. But employment in many long-established industries has recently been declining. The scale of this contraction can be seen from the table. On the other hand new and growing industries, and their related offices, have been concentrated in Greater London, the South East, and the Midlands. The growth of services, too, has centred on the areas where industry is booming and population is increasing. In the absence of government intervention, the process would tend to become cumulative, and regional inequalities would grow rather than diminish.

National Income.

Gross domestic income (GDY) is the sum total of incomes received for the services of labour, land, or capital in a country. Gross domestic product (GDP) is the money value of all the goods and services produced in the country. So as to avoid double-counting, only the *value added* at each stage of production is included: firms' purchases of goods and services from other firms are excluded. The revenue from selling the GDP is either paid out to the hired factors of production—labour, land, and capital—or retained in the form of profits. Therefore, provided it is calculated net of taxes on goods produced, GDP must equal GDY. To estimate gross national income (GNY) from GDY it is necessary to add the net income—such as profits and interest—received from abroad. If an allowance is made for wear and tear of the nation's capital equipment, *i.e.*, for *capital consumption*, we arrive at net national income, better known as the *national income*.

In 1970 the national income of the United Kingdom was £39,375 million, implying a national income per head of £710. In 1955 the corresponding figures had been £15,523 million and £305 per head. However, only part of the increase in value was due to an increase in the quantity of goods and services produced; some of the increase simply reflected a rise in prices. It is important to calculate changes in the volume of output—known as *real output*—as well as changes in its value. Real output is calculated by the statistical device of constructing an index number. This is done by calculating the volume of goods and services provided in each year and then valuing these goods and services at the prices found in one particular year. Thus between 1955 and 1970 the money value of national income rose by 153 per cent, whereas real income increased by only 46 per cent, and the difference represented a rise in prices.

The Quality of Life.

In real terms national income per head rose by 31 per cent between 1955 and 1970, or by 1·2 per cent per annum. National income per head is the most useful indicator of the standard of living. However, this measure is necessarily a crude one. For instance, it cannot take into account new and better products, *e.g.*, television, man-made fibres, faster flight, long-playing records, or the lowly plastic bucket; nor does it indicate changes in the distribution of income between rich and poor; nor in the length of working week.

Data of national income per head may also conceal important changes in the "quality of life", *e.g.*, in our physical environment. This is affected by such things as traffic congestion, noise, water- and air-pollution. Between 1960 and 1970 the number of cars on British roads more than doubled, from 5·5 million to 11·5 million; the number of road goods vehicles with unladen weight exceeding 8 tons growing five-fold over the same decade. Movement of civil aircraft over Britain doubled during the 1960s, and aircraft tended to become noisier. On the other hand, air in London has become cleaner: in the period 1949–54 there were on average 1·29 hours of winter sunshine per day, whereas in the period 1964–69 the average was 1·66 hours.

Industrial Production.

It is fairly easy to measure output in the main manufacturing industries, and in many of the other industries producing goods. It is much more difficult to do so for the service industries: the output of a doctor or a teacher is not easily measured. So each month the Central Statistical Office calculates the *index of industrial production* covering the main production industries. Industrial production is thus an early indicator of economic trends (*see* **G43**), but it is prone to fluctuate more than do the other components of GDP.

Manufacturing industry accounts for more than three-quarters of industrial production. Within manufacturing the following industries have expanded most rapidly—chemicals, which include drugs, plastics, cosmetics and detergents, coal and petroleum products, including oil refining, and instrument and electrical engineering. The slowest growing manufacturing industries are textiles, clothing, leather and shipbuilding, which are losing their markets to cheaper competitors. Those industries in which demand has stagnated tend to be the industries in which output per employee, *i.e.* productivity, has stagnated.

International Comparisons.

In recent years Britain's GDP has grown less rapidly than that of almost any other major Western country. The British economy is also characterised by a relatively slow growth of output per head, *i.e.*, productivity. Britain has fallen behind many of the European countries in terms of income per head. Some comparisons with other countries are made in the table. However, these may be misleading because incomes are converted into pounds at official exchange rates, and these need not reflect relative costs of living.

Many explanations of Britain's poor performance have been suggested, and there is by no means agreement on this matter among economists. It has been argued that the U.K.—like the U.S.A.—has a highly advanced economy in which there is a relatively high demand for services: and that it is difficult to raise productivity in the large services sector. Another argument is that Britain has been hampered by its slowly growing labour force, which has restricted growth not only in output but also in output per man. The reason given is that an expanding labour force needs to be equipped with additional plant and machinery

AN INTERNATIONAL GROWTH LEAGUE TABLE

	Percentage change per annum, 1958–60 to 1970–72				
	Output.	Employment.	Output per head.	Fixed investment as percentage of GDP, 1960s.	Income per head, 1972 £ p.a.
Japan	10·6	1·3	9·3	32	1,042
France	5·5	0·4	5·1	24	1,449
W. Germany	4·7	0·2	4·5	26	1,605
Italy	4·5	−0·6	5·1	21	845
U.S.A.	4·4	1·8	2·6	17	2,126
U.K.	3·1	0·2	2·9	18	1,066

so that its capital equipment tends to be newer on average than that used by a static labour force, and thus more up-to-date and efficient.

Some commentators have put the blame on the inefficiency of our business management; some on our educational system, biased towards the humanities; some on the social milieu which looks down on money-making as a career; some on over-manning and other restrictive practices of trade unions. A good deal of attention has also been paid to the proportion of output which different countries devote to *investment*, *i.e.*, expenditure on commodities—such as plant and machinery—for use in future production. These investment ratios are shown in the table. With the exception of the U.S.A., all countries have investment ratios considerably higher than in the U.K., with correspondingly higher growth rates of output and productivity. Since investment in dwellings contributes very little to growth, it may be appropriate to exclude this investment: however, similar results are obtained. This leads to the hypothesis that Britain's growth rate could be raised if a higher proportion of output were devoted to investment, particularly in plant and machinery. There is probably some truth in many of these explanations, and it is unlikely that any one remedy will be sufficient to raise the British growth rate.

Investment.

In 1970 gross investment in capital assets amounted to £9,380 million in the United Kingdom. This was about 21 per cent of the GNP. The net addition to the nation's stock of capital assets was just over half of total investment, and just under half the total was needed to offset the wastage of assets already in use, *i.e.*, to make good the *capital consumption*.

There are four main kinds of investment: plant and machinery, vehicles, dwellings, and other construction. In 1970 the four categories accounted for 38 10, 18, and 34 per cent respectively. Investment may also be analysed by the purpose for which it is used. Social services such as education and health (7 per cent) take a surprisingly small proportion of total investment. Distribution and other service industries (15 per cent) and public corporations (18 per cent) take a large proportion: investment in electricity alone accounts for over 5 per cent of the total. It is clear that some sectors of the economy are more capital-intensive than others. Manufacturing investment accounts for 23 per cent of the total. This is small in relation to the contribution of manufacturing to ouput. However, many of the fast-growing manufacturing industries—*e.g.*, chemicals, electronics, steel—use much machinery and equipment per unit of output produced. These capital-intensive plants cannot pay unless they are worked at near full capacity. With the growing capitalisation of industry it is increasingly necessary to introduce shift work.

Increasing Investment.

The proportion of total output invested—the *investment ratio*—is lower in Britain than in other countries with faster growth rates of output and productivity; and there is reason to believe that a higher proportion would improve the growth rate to some extent (*see* **G12**). But in a fully employed economy it is not possible to increase investment expenditures without curtailing other forms of expenditure, notably private and public consumption. This curtailment would have to be brought about by increasing taxation or encouraging people to save or by pruning public services. Yet the very act of restricting private consumption may induce private firms to *reduce* their investment expenditures.

In 1970, 56 per cent of total investment in the United Kingdom was carried out in the private sector, 26 per cent by public authorities and 18 per cent by the public corporations. The Government has more control over investment in the public sector than in the private sector. Governments do possess various policy measures by which to influence private investment (*see* **G21–5, 43–9**) but private investment is volatile and highly dependent on businessmen's expectations, especially their expectations about the future growth of their markets. It is no easy matter to raise the British investment ratio.

If a higher investment ratio could be achieved, a faster rate of economic growth—and therefore higher consumption in the future—would involve a sacrifice in current consumption. A choice must be made between the loss in current consumption and the ensuing gain in future consumption. Of course not all consumption expenditure is equally important to the standard of living: some would argue that if British defence expenditure was pruned to permit more investment, there would be no loss to set against the future gain.

The Finance of Investment.

Any business is allowed to charge as a cost the depreciation of its assets. Normal depreciation allowances are based on the original cost of the asset and on its expected useful life. In a time of price inflation depreciation allowances will not provide sufficient finance to permit the replacement of assets at higher prices, and there are many supporters of depreciation allowances being based on replacement costs. Many firms do set aside extra funds specifically to cover these extra replacement costs.

Governments have, however, adopted certain fiscal devices to encourage replacement and net investment. Soon after the war initial allowances were introduced. Under this system firms were permitted to charge against profits in the first year of its life 20, or at times 40, per cent of the cost of any new equipment, and the system amounted to a loan of the tax saved in the first year, repaid over the life of the asset. In 1954 initial allowances for machinery were replaced by a system of investment allowances, under which a firm could charge against profits 20 per cent of the cost of any new machine, with the difference that all ordinary depreciation allowances were still chargeable. So the investment allowance was a grant, not a loan, of the saved tax. In 1966, initial and investment allowances on new plant and machinery in three sectors—manufacturing, mining, and shipping—were replaced by cash grants. Other plant and machinery and industrial building received higher initial allowances. In 1970 the Conservative Government reintroduced initial allowances in place of investment grants but in 1972 tried to encourage investment by granting free depreciation (*see* **G49**).

Depreciation allowances and government allowances and grants for investment are sufficient to cover more than half of investment (excluding dwellings) by the private sector, and to cover a minor part of public (non-housing) investment. The residue of investment, and housebuilding, has to be provided from other sources of funds. Companies rely mainly on retained profits, which are often larger, taking companies as a whole, than their net investment. Other sources of company finance are borrowing in financial markets and the issue of company shares (*see* **G23**). Much public investment must be financed by the Treasury (*see* **G22**).

Automation.

Accompanying the accumulation of capital is a tendency towards automation in production. With automation, much of the manual semi-skilled work should come to an end. So far the impact of automation has been small. The main use has been in the office, where computers can carry out far more efficiently much of the routine calculating, recording, and checking operations previously done by clerks. But it will continue to spread, and must do so if the growth in incomes is to continue. This revolution will take many decades to effect. It raises no spectre of widespread redundancy; but it does mean that over the years more and more emphasis will need to be laid on the training of workers for skilled work, and indeed on raising the general level of education.

Monopoly and Competition.

A trend to increasing size and increasing capitalisation has been going on now for many decades, and in the process it has changed the face of British industry. In the early 19th century the typical firm was the owner-managed textile mill. Then in the 1860s and 1870s came the discovery of cheap methods of making steel, with the consequential immense growth in the engineering industries. Most of the chemical industry is still newer, and there are a number of entirely 20th cent. industries such as aircraft and electronics.

In the capital-intensive industries the big firm predominates. In some it has become almost a monopoly; in others the pattern is of a few firms, all large. In 1970 the top British companies —each with sales exceeding £1,000 million— included oil firms (British Petroleum and Shell), tobacco firms (British American Tobacco and Imperial Tobacco), chemical firms (Imperial Chemical Industries and Unilever) and one in the motor industry (British Leyland Motor Corporation). There is evidence that the extent of *concentration* of British industry—according to measures such as the proportion of the output of an industry produced by the largest three firms—has increased steadily since 1945.

Competition goes on, but it has changed its form. In the old days competition was largely by price. Now it is largely by advertising and by variations in the quality and other features of the product—detergents and motor cars being good examples. In many industries groups of firms producing similar products entered into agreements which had the effect of restricting competition, for example through schemes for price-fixing.

Regulation of Monopoly and Competition.

(i) Restrictive Practices Court.

The Restrictive Trade Practices Acts of 1956 and 1968 outlawed many of the main forms of restrictive agreements to prevent competition. Collective price fixing was declared to be illegal unless the industry could show that the practice brought substantial benefit to the public. Collective price-fixing was the system under which a central association for the industry lays down minimum prices at which members may sell. Usually such a system was backed by arrangements for collective boycotts, under which members of the association would refuse to sell goods to wholesalers or retailers who broke the rules. Collective boycotts were also found in industries without collective price-fixing, one common purpose being to make sure that retailers did not sell a manufacturer's products below his recommended price. This form of collective resale price maintenance was also outlawed by the Acts.

Under the Acts any restrictive agreements of several specified kinds had to be registered with the Registrar of Restrictive Practices. He then had to decide whether there was a *prima facie* case for the discontinuation of the agreement, and, if he thought there was, the case was referred to a Restrictive Practices Court, containing both judicial and lay members. For an agreement to be upheld, the agreeing parties had to prove to the Court that the agreement conferred some substantial benefit on the public which outweighed any injury it did to the public.

(iii) Resale Prices Act.

The Act of 1956 permitted individual manufacturers to enforce *resale price maintenance* (r.p.m.) for their own products. Few suppliers would want the publicity of enforcing r.p.m. through the courts, but individual suppliers could still put some commercial pressure on price-cutters, *e.g.*, by offering less favourable terms or by refusing them supplies. The Resale Prices Act of 1964 prohibited all methods of enforcing minimum resale prices. However, goods which had been registered in due time with the Registrar of restrictive trading agreements or had been approved by the Restrictive Practices Court, were exempted, temporarily in the former case and permanently in the latter. For r.p.m. to be approved by the Court, it must be shown that some ensuing benefit to customers (*e.g.*, of increased quality or more retail outlets) outweighs any detriment. It is also lawful to withhold supplies to retailers selling goods at a loss to attract customers.

As a result of the Act r.p.m. has ceased to be a common practice, and has largely been replaced by "recommended" retail prices, which are in effect maximum prices. This practice has been investigated by the Monopolies Commission, which found that it was not always against the public interest.

(iii) The Monopolies Commission.

The Restrictive Practices Acts left untouched the industries in which one firm is dominant: these remained the responsibility of the Monopolies Commission. This is an independent administrative tribunal, established in 1948 with powers to investigate and decide whether a monopoly (defined in terms of market share) is contrary to the "public interest." The Commission reports on industries referred to it by the Department of Trade and Industry (formerly the Board of Trade) and makes recommendations.

The Monopolies and Mergers Act of 1965 strengthened control over monopolies and mergers. With regard to monopolies, the Government wished to provide itself with legal powers of enforcement: previously monopolies had been expected to comply voluntarily with the findings of the Monopolies Commission. The Act also permitted the Government to refer a merger or a proposed merger to the Monopolies Commission in cases where the merger would lead to monopoly (defined as control of at least one third of the market) or would increase the power of an existing monopoly, or where the value of the assets taken over exceeded £5 million.

In interpreting the public interest, the Monopolies Commission has criticised monopolies for various practices, *e.g.*, if they attempt to deter entry to the industry, or earn abnormally high profit rates, or show weakness in research and innovation.

(iv) The Industrial Reorganisation Corporation.

Mergers may lead to monopoly and to the abuse of monopoly power. But it would be wrong to presume that mergers are always bad: mergers— by facilitating research and other economies of large-scale production—may increase industrial efficiency. For this reason the *Industrial Reorganisation Corporation* (IRC) was set up in 1966 under Government auspices. Its functions were to promote industrial reorganistion in the interests of industrial efficiency, *e.g.*, by enabling industries to achieve economies of scale or by reorganising inefficiently managed firms. It assisted firms in agreed regroupings and could intervene to encourage a particular takeover which, in its estimation, was in the public interest. However its objective in making loans was to "prod" and not to "prop" inefficient firms. It supported mergers in electronics, trawling, nuclear power, mechanical engineering, and other industries. In 1970 the Conservative Government decided to wind up the IRC. However, some of the proposed functions of the National Enterprise Board, set up in 1975, were similar to those performed by the IRC (*see* **G48**).

(v) Restrictive Labour Practices.

Restrictive labour practices—which result in the "over-manning" of plant or the "under-employment" of men—are common in British industry. These stem from such causes as the fear of redundancy and unemployment, anxiety to preserve a craft skill threatened by technical progress, the desire to work at overtime rates, and sometimes just inertia. Governments have made attempts to eliminate this underemployment. In its incomes policy the Labour Government specifically made *productivity agreements*— agreements to change working practices in return for higher pay—an exception to the norm laid down for wage increases (*see* **G51**). One of the objectives of the Conservative Government taking office in 1970, in condoning and maintaining the recession in the economy, was to achieve a "shakeout" of underemployed labour. The permanent elimination of restrictive labour practices requires more enlightened management, more union co-operation, and more Government measures to promote the mobility of labour between occupations.

(vi) The Fair Trading Act.

The 1973 Fair Trading Act placed the previously dispersed responsibilities for overseeing competition policies in the hands of a civil servant—the Director General of Fair Trading. The Monopolies Acts of 1948 and 1965 were repealed and replaced by rather more comprehensive rules. Monopoly was now defined as control of one quarter of the market instead of one-third. For the first time local monopolies were made subject to control. The Director General of Fair Trading—as well as the Department of Trade and Industry—was enabled to refer monopoly situations to the Monopolies Commission; though it was still only the Department which could make references on mergers. Additionally the Director General took over the functions of the Registrar of Restrictive Practices. The Act also gave him responsibilities for general consumer protection, and set up a new body to assist in that aim—the Consumer Protection Advisory Committee In 1975 the Restrictive Trades Practices Act was extended to service industries.

Nationalised Industries.

Nationalised industry accounts for over 10 per cent of British production. Local authorities also run some services, *e.g.*, bus transport and water provision. In many cases—*e.g.*, the railways, gas, electricity, and postal services—these industries are natural monopolies, in which the provision of competing services would obviously be wasteful. They were thus obvious candidates for public ownership. With the exception of steel—nationalised 1951–3 and renationalised in 1967—nationalisation was for a long time not extended into manufacturing industry. The post-1974 Labour Government nationalised the shipbuilding and aerospace industry, and established the British National Oil Corporation and the National Enterprise Board (*see* **G48**), with powers to take holdings in private industry.

The nationalised industries are required normally to cover their costs, and to earn a target rate of return on their investment. However, it is government policy that subsidies can be made for some services which are justified on social grounds, *e.g.*, grants are made to British Rail to continue unremunerative rail services. Cross-subsidisation of non-commercial services by commercial services within a nationalised industry is discouraged, and costing according to the *marginal cost* of a service is encouraged. To give an example of marginal costing: once all the gas production equipment and gas pipes have been installed the cost incurred in supplying additional gas is low; thus consumers are charged a low price per unit of gas consumed and, to avoid a financial loss, the Gas Boards make a standing charge to cover overheads.

The nationalised industries are voracious users of capital, as they are nearly all highly-capitalised industries (*see* **G13**). Until 1956 they raised new capital, when they wanted it, by borrowing on the Stock Exchange; this fixed interest stock being guaranteed by the Treasury. Since then the nationalised industries have drawn directly on the Exchequer for most of their capital. In 1971–75, for example, £5,700 million was raised from the government, and £1,600 million from other (mainly overseas) sources. This system has been criticised. The advocates of equity issue have pointed to the strain it puts on the Exchequer and the possibility of nationalised industries cutting investment when surpluses fall or become deficits because of the ensuing difficulties in meeting interest obligations. It is also said that nationalised industries have suffered from their dependence on the Exchequer. In times of balance of payments crises the nationalised industries have been forced by the Government to cut back their planned expansion, sometimes at serious cost of disorganisation. But any alternative system of financing would also be open to criticism.

3. INCOMES, WAGES, AND PRICES

Personal Income.

National income is a measure of the total income accruing to the residents in a country in return for services rendered (*see* **G12**). It therefore consists of the sum of wages, salaries, profits, and rents. But not all this income accrues to persons, *e.g.*, companies do not distribute all their profits to shareholders and some nationalised industries earn profits. This is part of national income but not of *personal income*. On the other hand some personal incomes are not payments for services rendered. Such incomes are called *transfer incomes* to emphasise that their payment does not add to the national income, but only transfers income from one recipient to another. Included in this category are retirement pensions, family allowances, and student grants. In the United Kingdom in 1971 income accruing to companies and public corporations and not distributed exceeded £6,000 million, but the central and local governments made transfer payments of nearly £5,000 million to the personal sector; so that personal income (£47,800 million) was only slightly less than gross national income (£49,300 million).

Personal Disposable Income.

Not all personal income is available for spending. In 1971 the State took 14 per cent of personal income in *direct taxation*, *i.e.*, income tax and surtax; and 6 per cent went as National Insurance contributions, which being compulsory are in effect a form of tax. The remaining 80 per cent of personal income—called *personal disposable income*—was available for spending. However, not all disposable income need be spent on consumer goods and services: income can instead be saved. There are many possible motives for saving, *e.g.*, to meet future contingencies, for a future purchase such as a house or car, for retirement, or for the income to be derived from saving. Saving as a fraction of personal disposable income was fairly steady at between 7 and 9 per cent, but from 1972 increased appreciably.

Types of Personal Income.

Compare the sources of personal income in Britain in 1938 and in 1971. We see in the table that the share of income from employment increased considerably, especially that of wages and salaries. The share of salaries grew relative to that of wages, not because average salaries rose faster than average wages but because the number of salaried workers expanded rapidly. With the development of the Welfare State there was an increase in the percentage of incomes derived from public grants—pensions, social security payments, student grants, etc.

SOURCES OF PERSONAL INCOME, 1938 AND 1971
(As percentage of total)

	1938	1971
Income from employment	*59·5*	*70·1*
of which:		
wages and salaries	55·5	62·1
Forces' pay	1·5	1·6
employers' contributions*	2·5	6·4
Income from self-employment	*12·5*	*9·2*
of which:		
professional persons	2·0	1·5
farmers	1·5	1·8
others	9·0	5·9
Income from property	*22·5*	*10·6*
Grants from public authorities	*5·5*	*10·1*

* To National Insurance and other superannuation schemes.

The types of income which fell as a percentage of the total are incomes of self-employed persons—a diminishing group—and incomes from property. During the war and for several years afterwards property incomes changed little—the effects of rent control, excess profits tax, and low interest rates were such that these incomes did not rise, while other incomes increased sharply. Subsequently there was a rise, as rent control on some property was lifted and as interest rates increased. In the latter part of the 1960s there was a growing

BRITISH INCOMES BY SIZE, 1972/73

Range of incomes before tax.	As percentage of total.			Rate of tax as percentage.
	Number of incomes.	Incomes before tax.	Incomes after tax.	
–£999	18·2	7·4	8·4	5·4
£1000–1499	22·5	14·3	15·3	10·9
£1500–1999	22·2	19·8	20·6	13·4
£2000–2999	25·9	31·9	32·4	15·2
£3000–4999	8·9	16·6	15·9	20·0
£5000–9999	1·8	6·2	5·2	30·2
£10,000–19,999	0·4	2·7	1·8	44·9
£20,000–	0·06	1·0	0·4	65·5
Total . . .	20·319m	£39,764m	£33,192m	16·5

recession in the economy. There was also an acceleration in the rate of wage increases but often prices could not be raised correspondingly because of the need to keep British products competitive with those of other countries. These developments contributed to a squeezing of the share of profits in national income. We see that the share of property incomes (profits, interest, and rents) in 1971 was less than half of what it had been in 1938. Over this third of a century there was a fundamental redistribution of income away from property-owners towards employees.

Inequality of Income.

In the tax-year 1972/73 nearly one-fifth of income-receivers had incomes under £1,000 and over two-fifths under £1,500. The richest 37 per cent received 58 per cent of total income, the richest 11 per cent received 26 per cent, and the top 2 per cent received nearly 10 per cent of the total. Thus Britain is far from being an egalitarian society. Income is still unevenly distributed, but not so unevenly as before the war, when the top 1 per cent received 16 per cent of total income.

Taxes on income are of course highly progressive, rising sharply as income increases. Those with no incomes pay no income tax, and in so far as they are pensioners, no compulsory contributions either. We see from the table that the proportion of income paid in direct taxes is about 5 per cent on incomes under £1,000 per annum, is 15 per cent in the income range £2,000–2,999, and is 45 per cent on incomes over £10,000.

This tax burden somewhat changes the distribution of incomes. After tax the top 11 per cent received 23 per cent of income and the top 2 per cent 7·4 per cent. But the redistributive effect of taxation must not be overstressed: the levelling of incomes before tax has been of greater importance in making Britain rather more egalitarian than has been taxation policy.

WEALTH OF INDIVIDUALS IN BRITAIN, 1972

Range of net wealth. (£000)	As percentage of total.	
	Number of cases.	Value of wealth (£m).
0·9	21·0	1·7
1–2·9	25·2	5·8
3–4·9	13·8	6·6
5–9·9	21·6	19·3
10–14·9	8·8	13·4
15–19·9	3·0	6·4
20–24·9	1·8	5·3
25–49·9	3·1	13·7
50–99·9	1·2	9·9
100–199·9	0·4	6·5
200–	0·2	11·4
Total	17·017m	£138,400m

Income and Spending Power.

In various ways figures for incomes alone underestimate the degree of inequality in British society. First, incomes are incomes as defined for income tax purposes. Any allowed expenses are excluded; and for the self-employed and the higher ranks of management the expense allowance now adds substantially to spending power. Second, if one buys an asset which then rises in value one gains extra spending power. Such capital gains can be very important to the wealthy in periods of boom in ordinary share prices, land prices and house prices—as experienced in Britain in the 1950s and 1960s. Yet only in 1965 did capital gains become taxable and even then the rate of tax on capital gains was low in relation to the rate on additional income (*see* G55).

Inequality of Wealth.

Spending power depends not only on income and capital gains but also on the sheer amount of capital owned. Data on the ownership of capital in Britain have to be estimated indirectly from information arising in connection with the payment of death duties, and therefore cannot be relied upon. However, it appears from the table that individuals owning more than £10,000—less than a fifth of all individuals—owned two thirds of total wealth in 1972, while the richest 5 per cent owned over 41 per cent of the total. And this in spite of a growing tendency for the rich to pass on their capital before death to avoid death duties (so distorting the statistics). The vast majority own very little, and Britain is still far from being a property-owning democracy. There is a natural tendency for the inequality of wealth to grow because the higher income groups tend to save a higher proportion of their income, and so to accumulate capital more readily. The Government by imposing estate duties has had to neutralise this tendency. There is some evidence that in the last decade the inequality of wealth has been reduced. Between 1962 and 1973 the share of the wealthiest 1 per cent fell from 27 to 22 per cent of total wealth, and that of the wealthiest 25 per cent from 79 to 73 per cent.

Wages and Salaries.

In 1971 no less than 62 per cent of personal income was paid in the form of wages and salaries. The distinction between the two is very much a matter of convention; many salary-earners now earn less than wage-earners, and a more important division is between those salary-earners who are paid monthly and the rest. Even though weekly-paid staff do not now earn more than wage-earners, they may still in effect be better off; for they generally work shorter hours, are more likely to be covered by private superannuation schemes, and usually work in better conditions. The table shows the earnings of manual and non-manual workers.

GROSS WEEKLY EARNINGS, GREAT BRITAIN

(Median earnings, adults, 1976)

	Manual	Non-Manual
Men . . .	£62·1	£73·9
Women . . .	£38·4	£44·2

Earnings by Occupation.

Different occupations command different pay, as the table shows. The figures are of *median* earnings, *i.e.*, the earnings of the middle worker within each occupation when workers are arranged in descending order of pay. The structure of pay reflects in part the amount of responsibility which the different jobs entail. The differentials reflect also the ease of entry into various occupations. This in turn depends on the degree of specialised knowledge, skill or talent required, and in a few cases it depends on the extent to which artificial barriers to entry have created scarcity. The structure of pay is also influenced, of course, by the degree of organisation and bargaining strength of workers in different occupations.

MEDIAN GROSS WEEKLY EARNINGS OF FULL-TIME ADULT MALE EMPLOYEES, BY SELECTED OCCUPATION, APRIL 1976.

	£ per week
Medical practitioner	123·3
University teacher	120·4
Architect	100·8
General manager	93·9
Engineer, civil or structural	87·7
Primary teacher	86·3
Works or production manager	83·8
Accountant	81·9
Furnaceman	76·3
Coal miner, face-trained	75·1
Policeman (below sergeant)	74·8
Docker, stevedore	74·4
Electrician, maintenance	71·6
Railway engine driver	69·7
Compositor	67·5
Bus conductor	65·3
Plumber, pipe fitter	62·7
Postman, mail sorter	61·5
Bricklayer	60·4
Telephonist	59·3
Dustman	56·4
Junior clerk	54·8
Hospital porter	54·2
Unskilled building worker	53·6
Butcher, meat cutter	46·0
Shop assistant	45·1
General farm worker	43·6
Total workers	65·8
of which: *Manual*	62·1
Non-manual	73·9

Within the manual occupations the difference between skilled, semi-skilled and unskilled pay is now small. There has been a narrowing over the years. This was most marked during the war, in the years immediately after the war and since 1970 when skilled workers were granted the same flat rate advances as unskilled.

Occupational differentials have been a major source of industrial strife in some industries. In engineering, for instance, there has been continued conflict between unions with membership largely among the skilled and those with membership largely among the less skilled, over what forms demands for wage increases should take. On the railways there has been similar strife. Because of the importance placed on occupational differentials in collective bargaining there exist powerful rigidities in the structure of earnings in Britain.

Earnings by Industry.

Even within the manual occupations there are significant differences in earnings among industries. These are associated with the bargaining strength of different groups of workers, with the prosperity of the industry, and with the average skill levels required in production. Coal mining is the highest paying industry. Manufacturing industries also pay relatively well. Public administration (including local government road-men and the like) is a low-wage sector.

Earnings by Sex.

The table also shows very significant earnings differences within each industry between men and women. There are two possible reasons why women are paid less than men. One is that they are crowded into lower-paying occupations. This may be because their attachment to the labour force is weak, and therefore neither they nor their employers have much incentive to invest in training. The second reason is that they may have lower pay than men within the same occupation. The Equal Pay Act (1970) obliged a firm to pay men and women, who are doing the same job, the same wage by the end of 1975. In 1970 women in manual occupations had average earnings which were only half those of men, but by 1976 this figure had risen to over 60 per cent. This change is explained by the impact of the Act and by flat rate general increases agreed under incomes policies

Overtime and Short-time.

The earnings of any individual worker depend on many factors, and are usually well above the basic wage rate payable for a *standard working-week*. They include overtime earnings; and overtime working is common for men. In most weeks about 2 million operatives in manufacturing—about a third of the total—will be working overtime to the extent of 8 to 9 hours. Even in 1971—a year of high unemployment—the average amount of overtime worked by full-time male manual employees over all industries was 6 hours per employee (including those who worked none); with the average standard working-week being 40 hours, the average hours actually worked were therefore 46. The average working week has fallen very little since before the war, although the standard week has been significantly reduced. In most industries it was cut from 48 to 44 hours soon after the war, a 42-hour week was introduced between 1960 and 1962, and there was a movement towards a 40-hour standard working-week in the late 1960s.

AVERAGE WEEKLY EARNINGS OF MANUAL WORKERS IN CERTAIN INDUSTRIES (£p)
(April 1976)

	Men	Women
Paper, printing and publishing	70·5	42·8
Chemicals	68·2	40·5
Mechanical engineering	66·9	43·7
Food, drink and tobacco	66·8	40·9
Textiles	60·9	38·0
*All manufacturing**	67·4	40·3
Transport and communication	70·8	51·8
Distributive trades	53·9	33·8
*All industries**	65·1	39·4

* Including industries not listed.

Short-time, the working of less than the standard week, has not been common since the war. It has been important in particular industries at particular times; but even at the end of 1971—with a national rate of unemployment of over 4 per cent—it was far smaller than overtime. Then 100,000 operatives in manufacturing were on an average short-time of 12 hours a week—a total 1·2 million hours lost as against 12·8 million hours of overtime in the same week.

Earnings and Rates.

Overtime is not, however, the main reason why earnings exceed minimum wage-rates; for most workers earn very much more than the minimum in the standard working-week. One reason is payment by results, the system of payment under which the worker's wage depends partly on output. The commonest form is still the piecework system, under which pieceworkers are paid a fixed low rate per hour for each hour worked plus a fixed piecework price for each operation performed; but increasingly employers tend to prefer, as a more effective incentive, some scheme under which the bonus payment is related to the output of a larger group or to that of a whole factory. With payment by results systems—these cover about 40 per cent of the workers in manufacturing industry—earnings rise as productivity rises, and, as usually such workers also participate in advances in wage-rates negotiated between employers and unions, the gap between earnings and wage-rates tends to widen for them. So workers not paid by results press for similar advances for themselves, and in times of booming trade get them under a wide variety of names and forms—merit payments, lieu rates, compensation bonuses, etc.

Between 1955 and 1974 wage-rates rose by 254 per cent and earnings by 344 per cent. The advance in rates was more than the rise in prices, which was 152 per cent, but for much of the period anyone who actually earned the minimum rate throughout was not much better off. Earnings, on the other hand, rose considerably more than prices, so that a major source of the extra real income of the working class is to be found in the widening gap between earnings and rates.

Wage Negotiation.

In Britain there were *c.* 12 million trade union members in 488 unions in 1975. Most of these unions are very small, almost 326 having less than 2,500 members, but 25 have a membership of over 100,000. The main job of unions is collective bargaining with employers, and in most industries most employers also belong to associations which bargain collectively on their behalf. Some big firms, however, prefer to remain outside the associations, and strike their own bargain with the unions. Before the war many firms tried to encourage the formation of Company Unions, *i.e.*, of unions confined to employees of a single firm; but this is now uncommon. In some lowly paid trades—catering, baking, dressmaking, agriculture and others—minimum wages are fixed by Wages Boards or Councils set up by the Department of Employment: and representatives of the workers and employers, and indepedent members, meet together to reach agreement on the settlement to be recommended to the Minister. But over most of industry the aim of collective bargaining is to reach voluntary agreement, and the Department of Employment intervenes only when no agreement is reached. In 1974 the Labour Government set up the *Advisory Conciliation and Arbitration Service*, to provide independent mediation and arbitration services.

The usual pattern of negotiation is like this. First, the union puts in a claim for an all-round increase, usually much larger than it expects to get. Then after a time the employers reply, often offering a much smaller increase, and sometimes none at all. They then argue round a table until either they reach agreement or they definitely fail to reach agreement. If the latter happens the next step varies considerably from industry to industry. Many industries have their own "conciliation" machinery, in which outsiders try to help the two sides to reach agreement. Some, though not many, also have their own "arbitration" machinery, in which outsiders can recommend a solution of the dispute, which is sometimes binding and sometimes not. It depends on what the two sides have agreed on in advance. Many industries have no machinery of their own and until 1974 depended on the general facilities the Minister responsible could offer. Since then they have relied on the services of the A.C.A.S. Just as neither unions nor employers were obliged to call in the Minister, so now they are under no obligation to call in the A.C.A.S.; the unions may opt to put pressure on the employers immediately either by strike action, or by banning overtime or piecework, or by other action.

Thus the British Government traditionally has little power to control wages directly or to impose agreements. The recent attempts to introduce compulsion in wage-determination are described in **Part IV.**

Important Negotiations.

A few negotiations are particularly important in determining how wages rise in a year; for the pattern of later settlements tends roughly to follow those of earlier settlements. Probably the most important of all are those between the Confederation of Engineering and Shipbuilding Unions—an organisation representing 3 million workers—and the Engineering Employers' Federation, as this single negotiation directly affects the wages of $3\frac{1}{2}$ million workers, and indirectly many more. On several occasions since the war negotiations between these two have broken down, and only finally been settled after a Court of Enquiry had recommended a compromise wage-advance. The Confederation is a special negotiating body comprising all the unions who have members working in the engineering and shipbuilding industries These include many small, skilled workers' unions, such as the Patternmakers' Union, but they also include, besides the 1-million-strong Amalgamated Engineering Union, the two large general unions, the Transport and General Workers' Union, with about $1\frac{3}{4}$ million members, and the General and Municipal Workers' Union, with not far short of a million. These last two represent the semi-skilled and unskilled workers, and conflict between them and the skilled unions concerning differentials is common.

Strikes.

The strike is the unions' weapon of last resort. Most unions maintain strike funds in order to support their members when they call them out on strike; but these funds are small, and strike pay is usually very much below normal wages. So unions cannot afford to call strikes irresponsibly, and major official strikes are uncommon. In most years there will be one or two, but not more, and the total number of working-days lost is usually negligible—less than one day per head. Even in the industry affected the lost working-days are usually made up in the following weeks by overtime. Nevertheless, the big strikes are important; for the success or failure of one big strike can affect the results of all the other collective bargaining under way at the time.

Most strikes are neither large nor official nor about wages. An official strike is one called by a union, usually by decision of the national executive, and is usually the result of collective bargaining about wages. But unofficial strikes called by local leaders are often about other matters. Few of the big unofficial strikes which have plagued the docks since the war were about wages; rather they reflected job insecurity and the poor state of labour relations in that industry. Much the same may be said about the continual strikes in shipbuilding, many of them caused by demarcation disputes concerning which jobs should be done by which type of skilled worker. Other strike-prone industries are mining and vehicles. In most industries there are very few strikes, and even in shipbuilding, with the worst record of disputes, losses average little more than one day a year. But strikes are often a symptom of industrial trouble—frequently occurring in industries with stagnant productivity and declining employment. They are sometimes really a form of industrial protest, and employers have to bear their share of the blame.

From the mid 1950s the number of strikes in Britain tended to increase, except in coal mining. In 1969 and 1970 there was a huge jump in both the number of stoppages and working days lost. After that industrial disputes fell to a more normal level. But is Britain particularly strike prone compared with other countries? Making allowances for the size of their labour forces, Sweden and West Germany have fewer strikes and lose fewer working days than Britain. The United States has less strikes, but the ones they have are very large, and thus they lose more working days than the U.K. The strike records of Australia and France are most comparable with the U.K.'s.

In its Industrial Relations Act of 1971 the Conservative Government laid down new laws for the regulation of industrial relations and for the curbing of strikes. However, the Act was repealed by the incoming Labour Government in 1974.

Prices and Real Incomes.

The aim of a trade union is to get for its members a higher stardard of living, and its success depends on the extent to which wage advances exceed the rise in the cost-of-living. Prices rose very rapidly (by over 30 per cent) between 1949 and 1953, and earnings only just kept ahead in this period. But since then *real earnings* (*i.e.*, the command which money earnings have over goods and services) rose steadily until 1974. Between 1974 and 1976 there was some interruption to this trend (*see* **Part IV**).

Price Changes.

In the calculation of real wages it is usual to make use of the *index of retail prices*, commonly called the cost-of-living index. The index is calculated monthly by the Department of Employment, and it naturally has an influence on the course of wage negotiations. Indeed, up to 1958 it was probably the dominant influence and sometimes automatic adjustment for cost-of-living was written into wage agreements.

The table shows how consumers allocate their expenditure among different commodities in Britain, and how the prices of these commodities have moved over time. Almost 30 per cent of expenditure in 1970 was on food; and housing, fuel, and light between them accounted for 18 per cent. Drink and tobacco represented 11 per cent; and expenditure on transport and vehicles no less than 12 per cent. Comparing the allocation of expenditure in 1952 and in 1970, we see in particular the growing importance of housing and the declining importance of food in household budgets.

Price changes have not been the same for all types of goods. For instance between 1956 and 1970, when the total index rose by 65 per cent, housing went up by 122 per cent and fuel and light by 90 per cent; but the prices of food, clothing and especially durable household goods rose less than the average. It is partly the fall in the *relative* price of food and partly the fact that as people grow richer they choose to spend less of their income on food which accounts for the declining share of food in total expenditure.

The general retail price index is calculated by weighting each of the commodity price indexes by the proportionate importance of that commodity in total expenditure in a particular year, and then summing all the indexes, *i.e.*, the general index is a *weighted average* of its constituent indexes. A different pattern of expenditure would mean a different set of weights, and hence a different cost-of-living index. For instance, the poor—and particularly pensioners—spend a higher proportion on the basic necessities: food, fuel and light, and housing. It is possible that the cost-of-living rose more for the poor than for the rich over these years.

The cost-of-living index has not risen evenly in Britain. There were spurts of rapid inflation in the periods 1950–52 and 1954–56, followed by a decade of relatively little inflation (averaging 2·9 per cent per annum). After 1967, however, the rate of inflation accelerated, rising progressively from 2·5 per cent per annum between 1966 and and 1967 to 7·1 per cent between 1971 and 1972.

The Causes of Inflation.

(i) **Import Prices.**

Prices charged in the shops are determined by a great many factors, over many of which the Government has little or no control. First among these is the price of imports. Prices of imported food and raw materials are determined in the world markets, in which Britain is only one of many purchasers. In the raw material markets the U.S.A. is usually the dominant purchaser, and prices depend greatly on the level of economic activity there. In the food markets British purchases are more important, since the U.S.A. grows most of its own food, and is a large exporter of some foods. Prices in raw material markets are continually changing, and can fluctuate wildly. For instance, the average price of copper rose 70% between 1972 and 1973, and almost halved in six months during 1974. The free market price of sugar quadrupled in the period

WAGES AND PRICES
(1955=100)

	Weekly wage rates.	Weekly earnings.	Index of retail prices.	Real wage rates.	Real earnings.
1950	73	68	77	96	91
1955	100	100	100	100	100
1960	124	130	114	109	114
1965	151	175	136	112	129
1970	202	250	170	119	147
1976	549	614	365	150	168

INDEX OF RETAIL PRICES
(January 1956 = 100)

	1952 Weight*.	1970 Weight*.	Monthly average index.					
			1950	1955	1960	1965	1970	1975
Food	399	298	98	98	107	124	155	320
Drink	78	66	}94	100	98	127	156	343
Tobacco	90	64		98	112	146	169	251
Housing	72	119	83	98	132	169	222	396
Fuel and light	66	61	65	92	117	150	190	362
Durable household goods	62	60	80	94	98	107	129	213
Clothing and footwear	98	86	83	98	104	114	132	223
Transport and vehicles	—	126	—	—	118	135	167	319
Services	91	55	73	97	115	147	200	374
Other goods	44	65	77	96	120	140	183	324
All items	*1000*	*1000*	*74*	*97*	*111*	*132*	*165*	*304*

**I.e.*, proportionate importance of items in total expenditure in 1952 and in 1970.

from October 1973 to October 1974. The big increases in commodity prices occurred during the Korean war and in the well-synchronised world boom of 1972 and 1973 (*see* G37–8). The sharp increases in the prices of primary commodites contributed to British inflation at these times, but for most of the post-war period the rise in import prices has been less rapid than the domestic inflation. Imports cannot be primarily blamed for the continuing inflation, nor for the acceleration of inflation after 1967 (*see* G49–50). The source has to be looked for in the tendency of wages, salaries, profits, and other incomes to rise faster than real output; and this they have done in almost every year since the war.

(ii) Demand-Pull Inflation.

An alternative explanation of inflation is that it arises not so much from increased costs as from demand pressures increasing prices and profits. If there is an increase in aggregate demand for goods and services in the economy, how does the economy respond? If it is operating at less than full employment, producers are able to expand their production to meet the additional demand. But if full employment has already been achieved, it is the price level and not production which rises. Given an excess demand for goods and services, there is competitive bidding for the limited supplies and producers are able to sell at higher prices. A more sophisticated version of this argument recognises that full employment cannot be precisely defined: rather, there are degrees of less or more unemployment. Bottlenecks appear in different firms and industries at different stages; so that any increase in demand is met by an increase in both prices and production. But the lower the rate of unemployment, the more does the response take the form of price increases.

A variant of the demand-pull theory is the so-called *quantity theory of money*, in which inflation is seen as a response to an increase in the supply of money: there is too much money chasing too few goods. The theory dates back at least to David Hume, but it was generally discredited as a result of the writings of Maynard Keynes in the 1930s (*see* G21). However, it was recently revived by Milton Friedman and has received some measure of acceptance among economists in the United States (*see* G25).

The evidence for the demand-pull theory of inflation in Britain is very slight. No doubt there are times at which demand contributes to inflation in the economy as a whole or in particular sectors. Thus, for instance, the great shortages during and immediately after the war would no doubt have generated rapid demand inflation had it not been for rationing and price controls; and the spurt of inflation between 1954 and 1956 was associated with a very high pressure of demand. On the other hand, inflation has occurred even in periods of relatively high unemployment. Moreover, the method by which most firms price their products is on the basis of their costs; so that most prices are not directly sensitive to the pressure of demand. A more plausible mechanism by which demand might influence prices indirectly is through its effect on wages.

(iii) Wages and Inflation.

When a trade union negotiates a wage advance for all or most employees in an industry, firms will immediately consider whether they should increase their prices to cover their increased wage-costs. As it is common practice for firms to fix the selling prices of their products by first calculating the direct cost of labour and of materials, and then adding on a percentage to cover overhead costs and profits, they will tend to want to raise their prices not only to cover the cost of the wage advance, but also to cover their percentage addition. Moreover, in deciding whether or not their customers will stand for such increases, firms will be influenced by the knowledge that their competitors have to pay the increased wages too, and will probably therefore be raising their prices. So industry-wide wage advances—and changes in costs of materials—are particularly likely to be passed on to the consumer; and, as wage-earners are also consumers, to generate further demands for wage advances to cover the increased prices. Profits per unit also go up under this tendency to set prices on a *cost-plus* basis; but it is the wage advance which tends to set the spiral off, by providing the opportunity for price increases.

Once this spiral gets going, it is very hard to stop it. In general, the requirement is that wage earnings should not rise faster than productivity (output per man). But as in some industries productivity is very slow to rise, and as it would be unfair and impracticable to exclude their workers from participating in any general rise in the standard of living, this requirement means that in industries with a rapid growth of productivity wage advances should be kept well below the rate of rise of productivity. For two reasons this is rather difficult. First, rising productivity often raises the wages of some workers in these industries automatically, because they are paid by results or through some incentive scheme. The rise of wages from this source takes the form of a tendency on the part of earnings in these industries to rise faster than wage-rates; but that does not mean that all employees benefit, or that the unions in these industries will not press for the same rate of increase in wage-rates as is achieved in the slowly-growing industries. Second, employers in the rapidly-growing industries have far less reason to resist demands for wage increases than those in slowly-growing industries. Indeed, they are quite likely to bid up wages in order to get the labour they need, rather than to try to hold down wages.

There are therefore major problems in preventing a faster rise in wages than in productivity, with its consequence of rising prices. And once a wage-price spiral has started, the problems become more acute because unions and employers become accustomed to substantial annual advances in money wages. A main source of continuing price inflation has been the tendency of money wages to continue to advance at a rate that was appropriate when the cost-of-living was going up sharply, but ceased to be appropriate in later years.

(iv) The Phillips Curve.

Even if wage behaviour is primarily responsible for inflation, the pressure of demand may still be important. If unemployment is low and unfilled vacancies high, there is competitive bidding among employers to obtain or retain their workers. Moreover, with the economy booming the bargaining strength of trade unions increases: employers are more willing to concede wage demands. These possibilities have led economists to postulate—and indeed to measure—the so-called *Phillips Curve* relationship: the lower the level of unemployment, the faster the rate of increase in wages. Such a relationship has been found to exist in the British economy over some periods. But events after 1967 reveal the danger of postulating "general laws" in economics: inflation accelerated despite high and growing unemployment (*see* G50). Clearly, changes in the cost-of-living, expectations for the future, Government policies and the degree of militancy of trade unionists can all have a significant influence on wage behaviour; and the level of demand may at times be relatively unimportant.

The Effects of Inflation.

British Governments have been concerned about inflation mainly because of its effects on British competitiveness, and hence on the balance of payments. If our costs rise relative to competitors' costs, British exporters find it more difficult to compete in foreign markets if they raise their prices; and if they keep prices down in order to compete, this implies their having to accept lower profit margins on exports than on sales in the home market, and so discourages exporting.

But inflation can have other harmful consequences. It often produces a redistribution of income, with the strong gaining at the expense of the weak, *i.e.*, the poorly organised workers and the pensioners. In inflationary conditions income gains can appear to result not so much from work or sacrifice as from ingenuity and speculation and the exercise of economic and political power. Inflation can breed uncertainty, insecurity and industrial unrest. For instance, during the rapid inflation of 1970 the number of strikes was up by 60 per cent on the annual average for 1960–66, and the number of working days lost was up by 250 per cent. This was partly a cause but also partly an effect of the inflation.

Government Policy against Inflation.

There are several possible methods of attack on the inflationary spiral of wages and prices. Their usefulness will depend on the causes of the inflation.

One policy appropriate to most inflations, and also helpful to other objectives of economic policy, is to achieve a faster rate of productivity growth. The faster the growth of average productivity the faster can average incomes rise without an increase in average prices. Only if faster growth in productivity raised the growth of money wages proportionately would the inflation not be reduced. Comprehensive and detailed government control of wages except as an emergency policy must probably be ruled out for political and institutional reasons, and so must comprehensive and detailed control of prices. Experience suggests that such detailed policy, except as a temporary general "freeze", would be very difficult to operate and, if successful, would involve a major loss of flexibility in the economy. At the other extreme, general exhortations to unions to exercise restraint on wages, and to manufacturers to exercise restraint on prices, have probably had little effect.

The Government can attempt to regulate inflation by controlling purchasing power through its monetary and fiscal policies, the nature of which will be examined below. There is a danger that curbing demand also curbs the growth of output and productivity in the economy; so conflicting with other objectives of economic policy. Moreover, there is no certainty that inflation is sensitive to the rate of unemployment over the politically acceptable range of unemployment; and experience in Britain after 1967 suggests that it is not.

There is no easy solution—difficulties and disadvantages are attached to every measure for controlling inflation. In Part IV we shall discuss the solutions which have been attempted since 1960 (*see* **G51-4**).

4. MONEY, BANKING, AND FINANCE.

Money.

In Britain money consists of bank-notes, coinage, and banks' debt. Bank-notes—mainly in denominations of £10, £5, and £1—are issued by the Bank of England, which has been publicly owned since 1946, and which acts in effect as an agent of the Government. We shall see below (G22) how commercial banks can also create money.

The total size of the bank-note issue is not a good guide to the amount of purchasing power in the economy. The Bank of England has stated that it was now its policy to issue bank-notes in accordance with the convenience of the public, and not to use this means of controlling the amount of purchasing power. As a result, the various checks on the size of the note issue—in particular the Parliamentary control over the fiduciary issue, *i.e.*, the permitted maximum level of the note issue—have become functionless and may be ignored. An increase in the value of the note issue is now only a symptom and not a cause of inflation.

Determination of Income and Employment.

What matters is the amount of purchasing power available to the public. Most private expenditure is financed out of income—after paying taxes—and most government expenditure out of taxes; but most investment, public and private, and a growing amount of purchases of durable goods by consumers, is not financed out of income, but out of borrowing of one kind or another. And the primary purpose of monetary policy must be to keep the total of this kind of expenditure out of credit in line with the amount of savings private individuals and profit-making companies are prepared to make out of their incomes.

A more accurate distinction is between expenditure, the amount of which is related to current income, and expenditure which is not related to income. The community tends to spend a fairly constant proportion of its disposable income on non-durable consumer goods and to save the residual proportion (*see* **G15**); whereas investment decisions and expenditure on consumer durables are generally unrelated to income. The amount of saving being undertaken therefore depends on the community's *propensity to save* and on the level of community income; the higher total income, the higher is total saving. Thus there must always be some level of income at which saving would equal the amount of expenditure not related to income.

Total demand for goods and services in the economy is the sum of consumption and investment expenditures. The value of whatever is produced accrues to the factors of production—wage-earners, profit-recipients, rentiers—as income; *i.e.* national product necessarily equals national income (*see* **G12**). Income is either consumed or saved. To recap: total demand equals consumption plus investment expenditures, and total output equals consumption plus saving. Therefore if investment expenditure exceeds the amount which the community wishes to save out of its current level of income, it means that the total demand for goods and services exceeds total current output. If output cannot be increased because men and machines are already fully-employed, prices and wages and also imports are forced up in response to the demand. If, on the other hand, investment expenditure falls short of saving out of full-employment income, production and employment are reduced below the full-employment level.

There is no automatic mechanism in our economic system which ensures full-employment of resources, and it is the task of Government to balance saving and investment at the right level of employment. This important fact was first established by the great economist J. M. (later Lord) Keynes. Prior to the Great Depression, economists believed that any divergence from full-employment was a temporary phenomenon, which would right itself. However, in the 1930s Keynes produced a new explanation of how income and employment are determined; and so brought about what has come to be known as the *Keynesian Revolution* in economics.

Government Control of Income and Employment.

The Government can control the level of income and employment in various ways. First, in many fields the Government has only very restricted powers to influence behaviour. It cannot compel persons or companies to save; it can only offer them inducements to do so in the form of higher interest rates or of tax concessions on receipts from interest; and their effectiveness is limited. Nor in general has it very much direct power over expenditure out of credit. It can control the conditions under which hire-purchase agreements are made—and this does, temporarily at any rate, make a great deal of difference to the amount of goods bought on hire-purchase. It can to a certain extent influence private companies in their investment policies by granting and withdrawing incentives to investment (*see* **G13**); but it is doubtful quite how much influence these changes have. And it can, if it chooses, exercise direct control over building, by allowing building only on licence. This power, however, is not now used in order to control the level of investment, but only in order to encourage it in depressed areas and discourage it elsewhere The only authorities over whose investment the Government does have real control are the nationalised industries; and there are obvious disadvantages in any system whereby investment in public utilities is determined, not by the need for such investment, but by the need to balance saving and investment.

The two main means remaining are fiscal and monetary control. If the Government thinks there is going to be a shortage of private saving it raises more in taxation or reduces its current expenditure and so increases the Budget surplus (*see* **G28**). The second form of control is more complex; in principle, the aims are twofold. One is to keep the amount of credit-creation down (or up) to the required extent; the second is to ensure that the Government gets the share of saving it needs to cover its investment programmes. The complexity arises from the interrelations between these two tasks.

The Government as Borrower.

The Government is a heavy borrower from the rest of the economy. In 1970 total outstanding public borrowing—by government, nationalised industries, and local authorities—stood at over £43,000 million, equivalent to 1·1 times the annual national income. Most of this immense National Debt was built up during the war, when government expenditure far exceeded taxation; but the total continues to advance year by year, owing to the heavy capital requirements of the nationalised industries.

The Government borrows in six main ways. First, the issue of bank-notes is in effect a form of government borrowing. Second, it borrows from foreign governments. Third, it borrows from companies through tax reserve certificates, which are a means by which companies let the Government have the taxes they would have to pay on profits as the latter are earned, rather than when the taxes legally become due. Fourth, it borrows direct from private individuals through the various forms of national savings. In all forms of national savings the Government pays interest—or in the case of premium bonds prizes in *lieu* of interest to the winners of the monthly draw—to the holders, who have the right either on demand or at short notice to the repayment of their loans.

Gilt-edged Securities and Treasury Bills.

The fifth and sixth methods of borrowing are through the market. The main method is through the Stock Exchange by the issue of fixed-interest securities, called *gilt-edged securities*. In 1970 the net amount owing to the public on all such securities was nearly £22,000 million—a half of total public debt. Most gilt-edged securities are promises to repay at a specified date in the future the amount originally borrowed; and in the meantime to pay a fixed amount of interest each half-year. Some gilt-edged securities are irredeemable, and consist therefore simply of a promise to pay the interest in perpetuity.

Most gilt-edged securities are held by institutions: the banks, discount houses, and other major financial institutions of the country, and foreign governments (whose holdings represent their sterling balances, *see* G9); only a small part of the total being held by private individuals. Gilt-edged securities, unlike national savings, are not liquid assets. Until they become due for replacement they can only be sold on the Stock Exchange for what they will fetch, and variations in their market value are quite considerable. Dealings in second-hand securities can have important effects on the economy. Variation in the market price of securities implies an inverse variation in the effective rate of interest which they earn. This in turn can influence the general level of interest rates, hence the amount of investment which it is profitable to carry out, and hence the general level of economic activity.

The sixth form of borrowing is by means of *Treasury Bills*, of which £1,400 million were outstanding in 1970. A Treasury Bill is an extremely short-term loan to the Government—usually for three months. Each week the Treasury offers for sale some £300 million of these, and a number of specialised institutions bid for them. The difference between their bids and the value of the bills on repayment is called discount, and is a substitute for interest. These bills play a crucial role in the monetary system.

Government Borrowing and Liquidity.

Monetary policy consists largely in varying the way in which the Government borrows to finance its expenditure. This is because the form of borrowing affects the amount of *liquidity* in the economy. All financial institutions have some policy regarding liquidity. In general they try to maintain sufficient reserves either of cash or of assets which can be immediately converted into cash to meet any foreseeable sudden increase in their commitments. But they do not hold all their assets in liquid form. The chance that all their creditors simultaneously demand their money back can be ruled out, and therefore most of them act on the principle that they should maintain cash or other liquid assets to cover some percentage of their total outstanding commitments. Whereas currency and Treasury Bills are regarded as liquid assets, government securities and most other forms of government borrowing are illiquid.

If therefore the Government borrows more by issuing currency or Treasury Bills and less by other means, this action increases the amount of liquid assets about and therefore the total lending which financial institutions think it safe to make. And, conversely, if the Government borrows less by issuing currency or Treasury Bills and more by other means, this tends to decrease the total amount of loans which financial institutions are prepared to make. However, government control over the way in which it borrows is circumscribed. The public can be persuaded to hold more government securities only if the rate of interest earned on securities is increased. In the 1950s the British Government was unable to prevent a rapid accumulation of short-term debt, even though it allowed the rate of interest earned by irredeemable government securities to rise from less than 4 per cent in 1950 to over 5 per cent in 1960.

LONDON CLEARING BANKS, 1974
(£ million)

Liabilities.		Assets.		Percentage of deposits.
Capital and reserves	2,428	Cash	974	3·6
Deposits	24,715	Other liquid assets	3,704	13·5
Other	228	Special deposits	615	2·3
		Investments	1,689	6·2
		Advances	17,433	63·7
		Other	2,956	10·8
Total	27,371	Total	27,371	

The Commercial Banks.

In the centre of the financial world stand the commercial banks. In England these are known as the London clearing banks. In this country, unlike the United States, the banking system is highly concentrated; there being four main banks with branches in every town. The commercial banks are important because their debts are used by the public as money. Anyone who has a bank current account can sign cheques or withdraw cash on demand up to the limit of his account. Because they can be used as a means of payment just as readily as bank-notes, bank deposits are money.

Commercial banks earn a profit by borrowing funds and then lending part of these funds at higher rates of interest. Because it is unlikely that all deposits will be withdrawn at once the banks hold only a small proportion of their deposits in the form of cash. Until September 1971 the Bank or England required them to hold 8 per cent; and we see in the table that the average cash ratio in 1974 was 3·6 per cent. Before September 1971 they also held by convention liquid assets (cash plus Treasury bills and money at call and short notice) equal to at least 28 per cent of their deposits; the ratio being 17·1 per cent in 1974. These liquid assets are easily transferable into cash. Their remaining assets are more remunerative; the majority being advances made to the public and earning a rate of interest higher than the rate at which the banks can borrow from the public or from the Bank of England. In 1974 cash held by the commercial banks amounted to £974 million, whereas the public had deposits with the banks totalling £24,715 million. Thus the banking system can create money: it does so by accepting bank deposits far in excess of the cash held to meet demands for these deposits.

In September 1971 the Bank of England introduced new arrangements for the control of credit in the United Kingdom. The clearing banks were required to observe a minimum reserve ratio of 12·5 per cent between their *eligible reserve assets* and their *eligible liabilities*. The eligible reserve assets comprise balances with the Bank of England, Treasury Bills, company tax certificates, money at call, and a few short-dated bills, *i.e.*, the banks' holdings of cash were excluded; and eligible liabilities are sterling deposits.

The Control of Commercial Banks.

The first step in any credit squeeze is to put pressure on the commercial banks by reducing their liquidity; so causing them to restrict their advances to would-be investors. This can be done in various ways. One is by means of *open market operations* in which the Bank deliberately sells more government stock than it otherwise would. The purchasers pay by cheque, and thus create a debt from the commercial banks to the Bank of England. Such debts have to be settled in cash, and so pressure is put on the banks' liquidity. Another method is through the Bank's *minimum lending rate*, *i.e.*, the rate at which the Bank is prepared to lend to the clearing banks. Until October 1972 this was known as *Bank Rate*. If this rate is raised the rate of discount on Treasury Bills is pushed up. A high rate of discount on these makes them appear attractive investments to those who do not normally buy them, and the commercial banks find it difficult to get as many of them as they would like. So again there is pressure on the banks' liquidity.

Since 1958, the monetary authorities have had the power to call upon the banks to make *special deposits* in cash with the Bank of England. Unlike other deposits of the banks with the Bank of England, special deposits cannot be treated as forming part of the liquid assets of commercial banks. This is in effect another way of putting pressure on the liquidity position of banks: the necessity of making such deposits could force them to sell securities or reduce advances. Special deposits amounted to 2·5 per cent of the banks' total deposits in 1970. In December 1973 a new non-interest bearing special deposits scheme was announced, to supplement the existing scheme. The Bank of England was to declare a maximum rate of growth of interest-bearing deposits over a specified period of time. If the banks allowed a higher rate of growth than this, they would have to supply progressively increasing special deposits to the Bank of England.

Faced by pressure on their liquidity, the banks have to take steps to restore their liquidity either by selling securities or by calling in advances. Neither method brings in much cash directly; for since the banks will be paid by cheque rather than in cash, they have to go on until the depletion of deposits caused by the paying of these cheques cuts down the total of deposits to the level where liquid assets once again meet the minimum reserve ratio required. To this there is one major exception: if the Bank of England buys the securities the banks sell—and the need to ensure an orderly market may force it to do so—then selling securities brings more cash into the banks, and thus enables them to replenish their liquidity.

This exception became important in the 1960s, when the monetary authorities appeared to give greater priority to the management of the National Debt than to the regulation of the commercial banks' liquidity. An alternative technique of monetary control was therefore increasingly used in the 1960s, *viz.*, the imposition of quantitative controls on bank lending by means of directives. These controls were often of a selective nature, *e.g.*, giving preference to exporters and investors.

The arrangements introduced in 1971 involved a return to earlier methods of credit control. Quantitative lending directions were abolished and less emphasis was to be placed on the regulation of interest rates. Instead, greater emphasis would be placed on the control of credit and the money supply, by means of the new minimum reserve ratio and calls for special deposits.

Bank Advances and Other Credit.

Bank advances are the simplest form of credit: the customer is simply given the right to sign cheques beyond his credit account and interest is charged on the overdraft. Alternatively, he is granted a personal loan, with more specific rules for repayment. Most bank advances are made to business. It is a common practice in business to finance working capital—stock and work-in-progress—out of bank advances, and to depend on more permanent forms of borrowing for the purchase of fixed capital. But there are no fixed rules: business gets its finance wherever it can.

Apart from clearing banks there are many other banks and financial institutions from which to borrow. For this reason a squeeze on bank advances alone is unlikely to be an effective way of restricting credit. Large firms, in particular, are in a good position to tap other sources of credit if necessary. The two forms of expenditure which have been most affected by credit squeezes are business stocks and housebuilding. Housebuilding depends on the availability of building society loans, and these depend on the amount of money which the public deposits with the building societies. When other interest rates rise building society deposits become less attractive.

When there is a squeeze on bank advances and borrowers have to resort to other sources of credit, the cost of borrowing is usually more expensive. But this need not be a deterrent to borrowing, as interest payments normally form only a small part of business costs. Most business capital expenditure is not sensitive to the rate of interest. Expenditure on stocks and on housebuilding are the two sorts of expenditure likely to be influenced by interest charges. But housebuilding is made less sensitive by the fact that when the rate of interest rises, it is the repayment period for the mortgage, and not the annual interest charge, which is usually increased.

It was the Government's intention in introducing the 1971 arrangements that there should be both greater control over credit and greater competition among the different financial institutions. The eligible reserve assets ratio was therefore imposed not only on the clearing banks but on all banks; and also on other finance houses with eligible liabilities exceeding £5 million, for whom the minimum ratio would be 10 per cent. The scheme for the calling of special deposits was also extended to these other financial institutions.

The Stock Exchange.

The banks through their advances are the main providers of short-term credit; but most long-term credit is provided through the Stock Exchange. In 1970 the total market value of all securities traded on the Stock Exchange was £120,000 million, of which £100,000 million represented stocks or shares in public companies. There are three main types. *Debenture Stock* is simply a fixed-interest loan. *Preference Stock* is a fixed-interest loan, with provisions for waiving the interest if the company fails to earn profits. Preference shareholders cannot get a company declared bankrupt if it does not pay them a dividend; but Debenture holders can. The third type—and much the most important—is *Ordinary Shares*. Nominally the owner of an Ordinary Share is a part-owner of the company concerned, with most of the rights of ownership. He has no right to any particular dividend or interest payment but only the right to participate in net profits if there are any. In addition to stocks or shares in public companies, British Government gilt-edged securities worth £17,000 million were quoted on the Stock Exchange.

The Return on Financial Assets.

Each type of holding has obvious advantages. The fixed-interest security brings in a guaranteed income; the Ordinary Shareholder has no such guarantee, though in practice during much of the post-war period the risk of a decline in dividend was small. Inflation, provided that it is not accompanied by recession in the economy and a weakening of business confidence, encourages investors to hold Ordinary Shares instead of fixed-interest securities. This is because product prices —and hence dividends—can rise, but interest payments fixed in terms of money lose their value. If inflation is expected to erode the value of the loan repayment the amount of lending dries up unless lenders are compensated by higher interest payments. For this reason there is likely to be a general increase in interest rates on new loans in times of inflation, and a corresponding decrease in the value of existing securities. The growth of the economy tends, even without inflation, to raise the value of Ordinary Shares by increasing the value of companies. So for private investors the Ordinary Share was a much better bet in the 1950s and early 1960s; and because Ordinary Shares were so popular, the yield on such shares—the ratio of dividends to market value fell below the yield obtainable on Government securities (*see* table).

PERCENTAGE YIELD ON FINANCIAL ASSETS

	Bank Rate. (range during year)	Treasury bill rate.	Irredeemable government bond rate.	Ordinary Share rate.
1950	2	0·5	3·5	5·3
1955	3–4·5	3·6	4·2	5·4
1960	4–6	4·9	5·4	4·6
1965	6–7	5·6	6·4	5·7
1970	7–8	6·9	9·2	4·8
1976	9–15*	11·2	14·3	6·2

* These figures relate to Bank of England Minimum Lending Rate, and are therefore not strictly comparable with earlier entries in this column.

Most Ordinary Shares are held by private individuals, some indirectly through Unit Trusts; but increasingly in recent years holdings by insurance companies and pension funds have become more important, because of the growth of private superannuation schemes. Insurance companies and pension funds cannot afford to take risks, so the main bulk of their funds is still invested in fixed-interest securities; but they have shown a growing tendency to increase the proportion of their funds invested in Ordinary Shares. This switch, by lowering the demand for gilt-edged securities relative to Ordinary Shares, contributed to the downward pressure on the prices of gilt-edged securities.

The more rapid rate of inflation in the late 1960s and early 1970s reduced the attractiveness of gilt-edged and paper assets of fixed value, and increased the attractiveness of assets likely to appreciate in value. However, the accompanying recession in the economy, giving rise to pessimistic profit expectations, acted to discourage shareholding. Land and housing were much in demand as a good hedge against inflation, and consequently their price rose rapidly (*see* G26).

Monetary Policy.

Monetary policy in Britain in the post-war period has been subject to waves of fashion: it has undergone periods of popularity and of disfavour.

(i) Cheap Money Policy.

The post-war Labour Government pursued a *cheap money policy*. There was no major use of monetary policy as an economic regulator: Bank Rate, for instance, was kept at 2 per cent throughout, and the rate on Treasury Bills was only ½ per cent. Instead the Government relied on controls and on fiscal measures to keep inflation in check. For this neglect of monetary controls there was, in fact, a very good case: the pent-up demand for goods was so strong, and the funds available to companies and individuals so large, that monetary restrictions would not have made very much difference.

(ii) Revival of Monetary Policy

The Conservative Government reintroduced active monetary policy in 1951. Bank Rate was raised—reaching a peak of 7 per cent in 1957—and manipulated in an attempt to control demand. In addition to influencing the cost of credit by manipulating interest rates, the Government influenced the availability of certain sorts of credit through the credit-squeeze. At times it made it more difficult for the banks to extend their lending by operating on the banks' liquidity position, and it also issued more or less strongly-worded "requests" that banks should restrict the growth of, or secure a reduction in, their advances.

A form of monetary control which was particularly important after 1950 was the control of hire-purchase. By raising or lowering the proportion of the price which has to be paid as a down-payment, and by shortening or lengthening the time over which repayments can be made, the Government was able greatly to influence the volume of hire-purchase transactions, and therefore the use of this particular form of credit. These controls, of course, only affect the rather narrow class of goods—cars, furniture, washing machines, television sets, etc.—for which a substantial proportion of sales are on hire-purchase terms. In consequence, the output of those industries concerned with the manufacture of these goods fluctuated widely.

(iii) The Radcliffe Report.

In 1959 the Report of the Radcliffe Committee on the working of the monetary system was published. It is complicated, because the monetary system is complicated; but it is written in terms which can be understood by the layman. Running through the Report is a scepticism concerning the likely general effectiveness of monetary policy, both as an anti-deflationary and as an anti-inflationary weapon of control. In the former case, it is clearly difficult to encourage spending by making credit more easily available, if business prospects are so poor that no investment looks profitable. On the use of monetary policy to counter inflation in the 1950s, the Committee felt that, because only some of the channels of finance had been obstructed, monetary restrictions had little effect on the pressure of total demand but did create financial inefficiency. The more conventional instruments (*e.g.*, Bank Rate) failed to keep the economy in balance; and when high pressure of demand, through its effect on inflation or the balance of payments, drove the Government to take quick action, it concentrated on hire-purchase restrictions and on public sector investment cuts. There was no smooth adjustment of the economy to monetary policy; rather there were vicious and harmful effects on the sectors singled out in this way. However, Radcliffe recognised that monetary measures do influence confidence in sterling.

(iv) The New Monetarism.

From 1964 onwards Britain has, with only brief respite, been hampered by severe balance-of-payments difficulties. Interest rate policy was used in times of sterling crises to stem speculative outflows of capital. A rise in interest rates increases the attractiveness of holding sterling balances, and stern monetary measures may be

THE COST OF PUBLIC SERVICES
(£ million)

Expenditure.	1960.	1972.	Percentage increase 1960–72.	Percentage of total 1972.
Defence	1,612	3,106	93	11·3
External relations	172	387	125	1·4
Roads, transport and communication	739	1,985	169	7·2
Industry and trade	562	2,190	290	8·0
Research	99	247	149	0·9
Agriculture, forestry and fishing	324	454	40	1·7
Housing	490	1,448	196	5·3
Environmental services	332	1,368	312	5·0
Libraries, museums and arts	30	137	357	0·5
Police and prisons	150	586	291	2·1
Education	917	3,559	288	13·0
National health service	861	2,645	207	9·7
Social Security benefits	1,488	5,119	244	18·7
School meals, milk and welfare foods	85	170	200	0·6
Local welfare services and child care	58	407	602	1·5
Debt interest	1,165	2,438	109	8·9
Other expenditure	316	1,161	267	4·2
Total expenditure	9,400	27,407	192	100·0

taken as indicative of the Government's determination to solve its problems without recourse to devaluation. Bank Rate reached a new peak of 8 per cent late in 1967. In the 1960s the monetary authorities did not attempt to regulate the money supply. Rather, they were concerned to control and to stabilise the structure of interest rates in order to protect sterling and to manage the financing of the National Debt. It was apparently thought that a stable interest rate—and therefore price—of government securities would boost the demand for these securities and so reduce the cost of servicing the National Debt.

After 1968 the monetary authorities became increasingly concerned with control of the money supply. Partly this reflected the influence of Britain's creditor, the International Monetary Fund (*see* G9); and partly the emergence of a school of "Monetarist" economists. The new monetarism, of which Professor Milton Friedman of Chicago is the leading exponent, attributes great powers to the money supply in influencing the level of activity and the rate of inflation in the economy (*see* G20). These claims have been vigorously disputed: many economists regard them as far too simple an explanation of the working of the economy. Moreover, the empirical support for the theory is ambiguous, *e.g.*, the mere fact that the money supply and the price level rise together does not necessarily mean that it is the growth of the money supply which causes the inflation, rather than that the inflation induces the banking system and the monetary authorities to expand the money supply. Nor do all monetarists claim that monetary policy is the best short-run regulator of the economy. Friedman acknowledges that the size and timing of the effects of monetary policy are unpredictable, and himself advocates a slow but steady growth of the money supply.

Through its 1971 reforms the British Government intended in future to concentrate more on the money supply and the availability of credit, and less on stabilising interest rates in the pursuit of its debt policy.

5. ECONOMIC ASPECTS OF THE PUBLIC SERVICES

The Cost of Public Services.

In 1972 total public expenditure was £27,407 million, about £490 per head. Of this total the central government spent about two-thirds, the local authorities about a quarter, and the public corporations' investment programme was responsible for the remaining one-twelfth. Total public expenditure almost tripled between 1960 and 1972; and rose as a proportion of the national income from 45 to 55 per cent.

The Government collects in revenue considerably more than it spends itself, but transfers funds to the local authorities, to the National Insurance Fund, and to the nationalised industries. The expenditure of the public sector as a whole generally exceeds its revenue, and the difference is met by net borrowing.

A breakdown of public expenditure is shown in the table. Not all categories of expenditure expanded at the same rate: expenditure on industry and trade (mainly the investment of public corporations and capital grants to the private sector), environmental services (water, sewerage, public health, parks, etc.), police and prisons, social security benefits, education, libraries, museums and arts, and local welfare services and child care increased faster than the total; and expenditure on defence, external relations, the agricultural subsidy, roads, transport and communication, research, and debt interest fell behind the total. Nevertheless, defence expenditure accounted for over 11 per cent of the total (*i.e.* 6·3 per cent of national income) in 1972.

Council Housing.

Expenditure on council housing amounted to 5·3 per cent of public expenditure in 1972. Housing expenditure consists of two quite different items. There is the capital cost of building new council houses. This is financed out of borrowing by local authorities, both from the Government and from the market. There is also a recurrent cost, in the form of subsidies on council housing. This represents the difference between the cost of housing, including the cost of borrowing, and rents received on council housing. In 1970 costs exceeded the rents of £1,005 million by £323 million, so that the average council house tenant was paying 75p in the £ of the cost of accommodation.

Up to 1957 the Government contracted to pay a flat subsidy per year on every council house built. From 1957, government subsidies were no longer paid on ordinary new council houses, but in 1961 were reintroduced, in a form intended to encourage councils to charge higher rents on their existing houses. The Labour Government substantially increased the subsidy in 1967; it being calculated as the difference between interest payable on new housing at current interest rates and at 4 per cent.

The 1972 Housing Finance Act made major changes to the system of council housing finance. Councils were in future to charge "fair rents"—the likely market rent for a dwelling if supply and demand for rented accommodation were in balance in the area concerned. The Government was also prepared to finance a rent rebate scheme whereby people in need, both council tenants and private tenants, could claim a rebate according to a formula based on family size and income. A slum clearance subsidy was also to be paid to councils and—to encourage housebuilding—a "rising costs" subsidy whereby the additional costs resulting from council house building were to be subsidised. The system of "fair rents" was ended by the Housing Rents and Subsidies Act of 1975.

Under the new Act most Government help would go to new building, the acquisition of land and housing and improving the stock of council housing. Additionally the 1975 Community Land Bill was designed after a period of about five years to give local authorities the power to acquire all land for development at prices based on its value in current use as distinct from its value for development.

The Housing Market.

Government housing policy must be seen in terms of the housing market as a whole. In 1972 there were some 19·7 million dwellings in the United Kingdom, 51 per cent being owner-occupied, 31 per cent being council houses, and the remaining 18 per cent privately rented. The importance of owner-occupation has grown and that of private renting has declined: 12 years previously they had accounted for 42 per cent and 32 per cent of the total respectively.

This switch is largely the result of Government policy. Rent controls have meant that there is little incentive to build houses for renting, nor even to maintain existing rented houses: in 1971 over half the dwellings which had been declared "unfit" in England and Wales were privately rented. On the other hand, Government has given considerable tax advantages to owner-occupiers. Owner-occupied houses are exempt from the capital gains tax introduced in 1964 (*see* **G54**), and owner-occupiers can obtain tax relief on mortgage-interest payments. Since the abolition of the Schedule A tax in 1961—whereby owner-occupiers paid tax on the rental income imputed to their houses—this tax relief on interest payments must be justified as an inducement to home-ownership; but it is also a considerable subsidy to owner-occupiers, who tend to be the relatively well-off. In the tax-year 1973/74 the British Government gave tax-relief of £500 million to house-mortgagees; averaging £95 for each of the 5½ million owner-occupiers benefiting. This total was slightly more than the whole of the public subsidy on council housing in the same year.

The year 1953 was a peak for public sector housebuilding in the United Kingdom when 262,000 council dwellings were completed. There was a trough in 1961 (122,000), a peak in 1967 (211,000) and a subsequent fall to 113,000 in 1973. On the other hand, the number of private dwellings completed rose steadily from 65,000 in 1953 to a peak of 226,000 in 1968. This was also the peak year for the total number of dwellings completed (426,000); the total falling to 304,000 in 1973. Over the 15 years 1955–70 the rate of inflation in the price of modern existing houses averaged 5 per cent per annum: somewhat faster than the rise in the cost of living. After 1970 there was a great surge in house prices: between December 1970 and December 1972 the average rise was no less than 30 per cent per annum. There are various reasons for this remarkable inflation. Partly it reflected the acceleration of general inflation (*see* **G50**); in such times it is sensible to hold one's wealth in the form of assets which will appreciate in value. It also reflected the decline in housebuilding after 1968, and a slowing-down in the rate at which building land became available. The precise timing of the inflation resulted from the sudden and large increase in the availability of building society mortgages. And as the inflation grew, so optimistic expectations helped to raise house prices still further. By 1974 the rate of increase had slowed down considerably, and the average price of existing houses for that year as a whole was less than 10 per cent higher than in 1973.

Education.

Educational expenditure rose by no less than 288 per cent between 1960 and 1972, and accounted for 13 per cent of public expenditure in 1972. Between 1961 and 1972 enrolment in all schools in the United Kingdom increased by 18 per cent. In addition, expenditure rose because the more expensive types of education—secondary schools and universities—expanded more rapidly. University enrolment more than doubled, reaching 242,000 in 1971/72. In that year there were also about the same number of people enrolled for advanced courses at polytechnics and other institutions of further education. More children stayed on at school after reaching the school-leaving age of 15. For instance, the number of children aged 15 and over at school in England and Wales rose from 14 per cent of the age-group 15–19 in 1960 to 24 per cent in 1970. This percentage increased again with the raising of the school-leaving age to 16 in 1973.

In December 1972 the Conservative Government published a White Paper setting out plans for the expansion of education over the next decade. More emphasis was to be placed on nursery schooling for the 3- and 4-year-olds: within 10 years it would be available to all children whose parents want them to attend. There would be a school building programme to replace the bad old school buildings. Teacher training would be expanded to reduce pupil-teacher ratios further. In 1970 there were on average 27 pupils per teacher in primary schools and 18 in secondary schools in England and Wales; but these averages covered a wide dispersion. Higher education would be expanded less rapidly than in the previous decade, and the emphasis would be placed on polytechnics and other non-university colleges.

It is increasingly recognised that education can be an economic investment for the future just as much as capital formation in, say, machinery or roads. There is a "private return" on "investment in education", which takes the form of higher earnings over the lifetime of the person educated; and there is a "social return" on public resources devoted to education, being the greater contribution to the national product which trained and educated people can make.

Social Security.

There are two forms of social security: *National Insurance* and *supplementary benefits.*

(i) National Insurance.

Under this scheme employees receive rights to unemployment benefit, sickness benefit, retirement pensions, widows' benefits, injury and disablement benefits, etc. For instance, in 1974 294 thousand persons received unemployment benefit, 1·0 million received sickness benefit, there were 8·0 million retirement pensioners and 528 thousand receiving widows' benefits. Weekly rates are laid down for each benefit, *e.g.* in late 1976 a weekly rate of £12·90 was paid to a single person receiving unemployment benefit or sickness benefit. The basic rate was increased according to the number of dependants: £8·00 for one adult, so much for the first child, etc. In 1966 an earnings-related supplement was introduced for benefits paid to persons between 18 and 65 (men) or 60 (women): the supplement in 1976 being one-third of average weekly earnings between £11 and £30 and 15 per cent of any earnings lying between £30 and £69, and a maximum total benefit, including increases for dependants, of 85 per cent of earnings.

By far the most important benefit is the retirement pension, paid as of right to contributors on retirement. Individuals may increase their rate of pension by staying on at work after the minimum retiring age of 65 for men and 60 for women. In November 1976 the Chancellor raised retirement pensions to £15·30 per week single persons and to £24·50 for a married couple. *See also* **G56**.

(ii) The Financing of National Insurance.

The main source of finance for National Insurance payments is the National Insurance and Industrial Injury Funds; accounting for some £4,200 million in 1974. These funds are built up largely from the compulsory weekly National Insurance contributions which most of the adult population have to pay. In April 1975 there was a fundamental change in the system of contributions (*see* **G56**). The scheme prior to that date is described in what follows. For employees, both employer and employee pay a contribution. The self-employed also pay contributions of smaller size than the sum of the employer's and employee's contribution, but they are not entitled to unemployment benefit and one or two other benefits.

Most non-employed persons, other than married women and the retired, have to pay still lower contributions and are entitled to even fewer benefits. Weekly contributions include a contribution to the cost of the National Health Service. Both ordinary and contracted-out workers pay a graduated contribution on their earnings between £15 and £105 per week to meet the cost of the earnings-related supplements introduced in 1966.

The National Insurance Scheme is an odd mixture of insurance and tax. The levels of contributions, when the scheme started in 1948, were fixed on the actuarial principle that contributions by or on behalf of an individual plus a specified State contribution should on average suffice to pay for the benefits to which he was entitled. But the scheme did not allow for inflation and a rising standard of living, and a succession of increases granted in the rate of pensions has put an end to this actuarial probity. Instead the principle became established that the rate of contributions in each year, together with a minor transfer from the Government, should equal the total benefits paid out in that year.

(iii) Reform of Pensions.

A scheme for graduated pensions was introduced for employees in 1961. Under the scheme there were two kinds of employees—*ordinary* and *contracted-out*. In the case of contracted-out workers, their employer (on whom the decision whether to contract out rested) had to institute a private superannuation scheme that gave at least as favourable terms as the new State scheme, including the provision that rights under the scheme should be transferable up to the limits of the State scheme. Transferability was the guarantee that the individual did not lose his pension rights when he changed his job. For ordinary workers the contribution depended on earnings. Until April 1975, those earning less than £9 a week paid a flat-rate contribution, which was lower than that paid by contracted-out workers. Those earning more than £9 paid in addition a percentage of the amount by which earnings exceeded £9 up to a limit of £62 and in return received the right to an increased pension on retirement.

In 1969 the Labour Government made proposals in a White Paper to replace the National Insurance Scheme by a new scheme of superannuation and social insurance, in which both contributions and benefits would be related to the earnings of the individual. It argued that the existing scheme failed to provide security in old age. The new earnings-related contributions would be mostly higher than contributions under the existing scheme, especially among higher earners; and in return higher pensions and other benefits would be paid.

An important feature of the proposed scheme was that benefits were to take into account both changes in prices and in general living standards. Thus, for instance, a contributor who received earnings equal to the national average throughout his working life would receive a pension calculated on the national average earnings at the time he reached pension age, not on the money he received over his working like. Some two-thirds of employed men were contracted out, *i.e.*, in occupational pension schemes, in 1970. The Government intended that these schemes should continue to exist together with the State scheme, and it proposed to allow for partial contracting out of the State scheme.

These plans lapsed with the change of Government in 1970. The Conservative Government announced its proposals for reform in a White Paper published in 1971. It considered that the costs of earnings-related benefits would be too great; instead it favoured earnings-related contributions for basically flat-rate pensions. In addition it wished to encourage contracting out, so that almost all employees would also be members of a private occupational pension scheme, in which pensions would be related to past contributions. The Government recognised that it would have to ensure that occupational pension rights were transferable between jobs. Like the previous Government, it envisaged a legal guarantee that State pensions would be revised every two years. It also envisaged that the share which the State provides from taxation for National Insurance—about 18 per cent of contributions in 1970—would be maintained. For important changes in 1975 in both the provision for pensions and the system of National Insurance contributions, *see* G56.

(iv) Poverty in Britain.

Despite the existence of National Insurance there are many people in Britain whose income falls below that which the Government regards as adequate. These people are supported from Government revenues by means of *supplementary benefits*, before 1966 known as *National Assistance*. It is a fault of the National Insurance Scheme that so many have required this assistance. In 1974 there were no less than 2·7 million recipients of supplementary benefits, of whom two-thirds —1·8 million—were persons over pension age. Another 260 thousand were sick and disabled 300 thousand unemployed and 245 thousand women with dependent children. Including dependants, no less than 4·3 million people benefited. Just over a quarter of those on National Insurance retirement pensions also received supplementary benefits.

Supplementary benefits ensure that a certain minimum weekly income is maintained: in late 1976, in the case of a single pensioner £15·70, a pensioner couple £24·85, and an unemployed man with wife and children aged 4 and 7, £30·57. In addition an allowance for housing expenditure is paid. The operation of social security is illustrated in the following example, utilising the data and regulations in force in 1975. Take a worker earning the average weekly gross earnings for adult male workers in November 1975. Assume that this individual has a wife and two children aged 4 and 8 years. While he is working his gross income is reduced by National Insurance contributions and income tax, and supplemented by family allowance; his net income being £46·32. If he becomes unemployed or sick, he receives National Insurance benefit, including an earnings-related supplement, and family allowance; his net income being £33·35. But after 6 months the earnings-related supplement lapses: he receives only £25·01 in National Insurance benefits, and is eligible for supplementary benefits to raise his income to £30·57 plus an allowance for housing expenditure. A major fault with the supplementary benefits scheme was that they could not be paid to those in employment whose earnings were below the benefit level, and if such persons became unemployed they could claim benefits only up to their normal earnings level. The *Family Income Supplement* was introduced in 1971 to alleviate hardship amongst low earners, but it has been estimated that only half of those eligible have claimed F.I.S.

Public Revenue.

We see from the table (G28) that, of the sources of revenue, personal income tax, National Insurance contributions and taxes on capital were the most buoyant over the decade. No less than 46 per cent of the total public revenue in 1970 came from taxes on income; more than half of this being personal income tax. Taxation of profits amounted to only 6 per cent of total public revenue. Taxes on expenditure accounted for 38 per cent of the total. It is interesting to note the growing importance of *direct taxation* (taxes on income) relative to *indirect taxation* (taxes on expenditure on goods and services) over the decade.

Two commodities in particular were heavily taxed: alcoholic drink and tobacco. Together they accounted for almost 10 per cent of public revenue. These commodities are singled out partly for social reasons and partly because—in economists' jargon—the demand for them is *inelastic*; *i.e.*, the public reduces its consumption of drink and tobacco only slightly in response to a rise in their price. Indirect taxation—taking the form of excise duties and purchase taxes—was spread unevenly over the different sorts of expenditure. In 1970 taxation increased the price of cigarettes by 203 per cent; drink by 69 per cent; consumer durables such as cars by 26 per cent; the running of cars (*e.g.*, petrol) by 93 per cent; clothing by 10 per cent; and food hardly

SOURCES OF PUBLIC REVENUE

Revenue.	1960. £m	1970. £m	Percentage increase 1960–70.	Percentage of total revenue 1970.
Taxes on income	*3,626*	*10,064*	*178*	*46·0*
of which paid by:				
personal sector	1,991	5,850	194	26·7
companies	612	1,283	110	5·9
national insurance contributions	913	2,654	191	12·1
Taxes on capital	*236*	*673*	*185*	*3·1*
of which:				
death duties	236	378	60	1·7
capital gains tax	—	264	—	1·2
Taxes on expenditure	*3,391*	*8,433*	*149*	*38·5*
of which levied on:				
alcohol	400	919	130	4·2
tobacco	818	1,150	41	5·3
rates	771	1,824	137	8·3
Surplus of public corporations	*534*	*1,447*	*171*	*6·6*
Other revenues	*901*	*1,281*	*42*	*5·8*
Total revenue	8,688	21,898	152	100·0
Net borrowing	710	−18		
Total expenditure	9,398	21,880		

at all. For goods and services in general, tax raised prices by 23 per cent on average. The introduction of Value Added Tax in 1973 tended to even out the incidence of indirect taxes on different goods and services (*see* G56).

The Budget.

Each year in April the Chancellor of the Exchequer announces his Budget for the coming fiscal year. The most important and most difficult task in drawing up the Budget is to decide on the size of deficit to aim for. The deficit is the excess of public expenditure over public revenue; and it has to be financed by borrowing from the private sector. A large deficit is reflationary: sometimes that may be required to get the economy out of recession. A small deficit—and even more, a surplus—is deflationary, and is a means of holding a demand-pull inflation in check (*see* (G20). In 1970 there was a small surplus, and thus the net borrowing requirement was negative (£−18m). Since then the borrowing requirement has become increasingly large, and in 1974 was no less than £6,371 million.

The calculation of the precise deficit or surplus needed is a chancy business; for the level that is required depends on the amount of saving and on the amount of spending out of credit that people intend to do—and this is not easily predictable. It also depends on the change in the foreign balance. Nor can the Chancellor be sure his figures are right: estimating next year's revenue, and even next year's expenditure, by the Government is difficult enough, but he needs to estimate also the likely trends of private income and expenditure, without really reliable information as to what they were in the past year.

Nevertheless, fiscal policy—running large deficits when economic activity is low, and small ones when it seems to be excessively high—is the most important action through which the economy can be kept on an even keel. Monetary policy may help; but the Budget decision of the Chancellor on changes in taxation and public expenditure is the key one.

6. SOURCES OF STATISTICS, AND SOME SUGGESTIONS FOR FURTHER READING

The non-specialist will find that most of the statistics he needs are given in the *Annual Abstract of Statistics*, published every year by Her Majesty's Stationery Office. This comprehensive document includes figures on population, social conditions, education, labour, production, trade and balance of payments, national income and expenditure, wages and prices, and many other topics. For more up-to-date information, reference should be made to the *Monthly Digest of Statistics* which has a similar coverage and gives month-by-month figures. A selection of the more important series, presented in a manner which can more easily be understood by the layman, is given in another Stationery Office publication, *Economic Trends*, also issued monthly.

Fuller information on labour problems is given in the *Department of Employment Gazette*, on trade in *Trade and Industry*, and on financial matters in the *Bank of England Quarterly Bulletin*. These three periodicals include discussions on the statistics presented. An important new Government annual publication in 1970 was *Social Trends*, containing articles and detailed statistics on social and economic conditions in Britain.

For an analysis of developments in the economy see the official *Economic Report*, published just before the Budget by the Treasury, and the *Economic Review*, a private publication issued by the National Institute for Economic and Social Research. To explain economic events and policy the Treasury publishes a monthly *Economic Progress Report*, available free of charge to the public. The periodic *British Economic Survey* (Oxford University Press) contains up-to-date articles on aspects of the economy.

For a comprehensive and systematic introduction to the British economy the reader is referred to A. R. Prest and D. J. Coppock, *The U.K. Economy: a Survey of Applied Economics* (Weidenfeld and Nicolson). An excellent, North American survey of the British economy is found in the Brookings Institution Report, *Britain's Economic, Prospects*, edited by Richard E. Caves (George Allen and Unwin). Easier to read is S. Brittan *Steering the Economy* (Penguin).

An entertaining account of economic ideas and their application is found in Michael Stewart, *Keynes and After* (Penguin Books). Other Pelicans include Joan Robinson, *Economic Philosophy*, and J. Pen, *Modern Economics*. A thorough explanation of international monetary affairs is given in Fred Hirsch. *Money International* (Allen Lane). E. J. Mishan in *Growth: The Price We Pay* (Staples Press) produces an interesting criticism of economists' and politicians' "obsession" with economic growth and affluence. A. B. Atkinson examines inequality in Britain in *The Economics of Inequality* (Oxford).

Readers with an appetite for economic theory may wish to try the introductory books *Economic Theory* by G. B. Richardson (Hutchinson University Library) and *Introduction to Positive Economics* by R. G. Lipsey (Weidenfeld and Nicolson).

III. THE LESS DEVELOPED ECONOMIES

Income Levels.

Two-thirds of the world's population live in dire poverty—a poverty which can scarcely be imagined by those accustomed to the standards of living attained in the relatively few developed countries of the world. The orders of world inequality may be seen from the table comparing annual income per capita by region, converted into pounds sterling at official exchange rates. These figures are only very approximate because exchange rates are misleading indicators of purchasing power and because the averages conceal considerable income inequalities within some regions and countries. Nevertheless, it is clear that poverty is widespread in the world. The alleviation of this poverty is widely recognised as the most important economic—and indeed political—task of the second half of the twentieth century.

NATIONAL INCOME PER CAPITA BY REGION, 1970

	(£ p.a.)
North America	1,788
Oceania	894
Europe	873
Latin America	217
Middle East	155
Africa	79
Asia (excl. Japan)	46

What is a Less Developed Country?

There are no less than 140 countries comprising the so-called "Third World," known variously as "less developed" or "developing" or "underdeveloped" or "poor" countries. There is a great diversity among them, and yet they have a number of features in common. Foremost among these is their poverty, but even poverty is not universal: some of the oil-producing countries such as Saudi Arabia, Kuwait and Libya have achieved very high levels of income per capita while retaining many of the other characteristics of less developed countries.

Most of the developing countries are primarily agricultural economies, with the bulk of the population engaged in *subsistence agriculture*. For many millions of peasant farmers the primary objective is to produce enough food for their family to subsist. India is a classic example, with no less than 70 per cent of its 574 million people dependent on agriculture for a living. Most less developed countries have only a small industrial sector as yet: it is rare for the output of the manufacturing sector to exceed 10 per cent of the gross domestic product. The main exceptions to this rule are the successful exporters of labour-intensive manufacturing goods, such as Hong Kong, Singapore and Puerto Rico. Many of the less developed countries lack the necessary ingredients for successful industrialisation—capital, skills and entrepreneurship.

The developing countries vary enormously in size—from the teeming masses of India and China to scores of countries with less than a million people, including Bahrain, Botswana, Fiji, Gabon, Mauritius and many West Indian islands. The development problems and possibilities facing large and small countries are very different. The small size of most developing economies forces them to concentrate on the production of one or two primary products for world markets. Their high degree of specialisation and heavy dependence on exports and imports makes these economies dangerously vulnerable to the vagaries of world trade and the world economy.

Enough has been said to show that, apart from their poverty, the less developed countries have other economic characteristics and problems in common. However, it is dangerous to generalise because there are also important differences. In particular, they vary in their degree of development and in their potential for development. A semi-industrialised, urbanised country such as Argentina has little in common with an utterly backward country such as Chad, and the economic prospects for an oil-rich country such as Iran are far brighter than for a country with few natural resources such as Tanzania.

Population Growth.

Many underdeveloped countries are experiencing an unprecedented population explosion: annual rates of increase of between 2 and 3 per cent—which double population in as little as 35 and 24 years respectively—are common. This is a phenomenon of the last three decades. Death rates have fallen sharply in response to improved health services and modern methods of control, *e.g.*, the eradication of malaria through DDT spraying. On the other hand, birth rates have been kept up by such factors as tradition, social prestige, religion, the need for security in old age and a lack of facilities for family planning.

POPULATION SIZE, GROWTH AND DENSITY BY REGION

	Population 1973 (m).	Growth rate 1965–72 (% p.a.).	Density 1973 (per sq. kilo).
North America	236	1·2	11
Europe	472	0·8	96
U.S.S.R.	250	1·0	11
Oceania	20	2·1	2
Africa	374	2·7	12
Latin America	309	2·9	15
China	814	1·7	85
India	574	2·1	175
Other Asia	816	2·5	55
World Total	3,860	2·0	28

The table indicates that over half the world's population lives in Asia, and that the developed regions account for under a third of the total. Apart from Australasia (into which immigration is high) the developed countries show slower rates of population growth than Africa, Latin America and Asia. The figures of population density may easily be misleading, since they take no account of the nature of the area, *e.g.*, deserts are included. But it is clear that Asia is more densely populated than Africa or Latin America.

The Population Problem.

In many developing countries there is population pressure on the land, and many people want more land for farming. Population density is a hindrance in agricultural economies, but not necessarily in industrial economies: because it is industrialised and has accumulated much capital Europe can support at a high standard of living a population more concentrated even than that of Asia.

As a result of rapid population growth the pressure of population on the land has increased. The consequences have been far more serious in countries such as Bangladesh (with a population density of 497 people per square kilometre in 1973) or India (175 per sq. km) than in Zambia (6 per sq. km) or Brazil (12 per sq. km). In those countries with abundant land the expanding population can spread into unused areas; but as land becomes increasingly scarce, less and less productive land must be brought into cultivation and soil erosion and loss of fertility become major problems. A substantial increase in output is required to prevent a fall in per capita income as population grows, and an even greater increase is required if living standards are to be improved. Between 1963 and 1973 food production in the developing countries as a group increased by 28 per cent, but per capita food production fell by 2 per cent.

Even in those countries with plenty of land a rapid increase in population can have harmful effects. For instance, it diverts scarce investment resources away from directly productive investments such as factories and irrigation projects so as to meet the needs of the expanding population for more schools, hospitals, housing, cities and other public services.

Problems of Agriculture.

There are many millions of peasant farmers throughout the Third World eking out a subsistence from the soil. The margin between what can be produced and what is required to support life is narrow: the failure of crops because of drought, floods or pests can lead to famine unless food is quickly supplied from outside the area affected. For instance, relief action by the international community was too slow to prevent the drought which struck the Sahel area of Africa in 1973 and 1974 from claiming some 100,000 lives, endangering future income by destroying seeds and livestock, and breaking up rural communities.

Agricultural production may be held back by a shortage of land, or by the use of primitive tools and methods of cultivation (which may in turn be due to a lack of farming knowledge and skills or to a lack of funds for investment in land improvement or equipment), or by an unjust system of land tenure which deprives the farmer of incentive to raise his production. Perhaps all these problems must be tackled simultaneously.

The Green Revolution.

A technology is being introduced which can increase the yields from foodgrains by 50 per cent or more in tropical areas. This new technology is commonly thought to have caused a *green revolution*. It consists of new high-yielding seeds, largely for wheat and rice. Not only are the yields per acre higher but also shorter cropping cycles permit multiple cropping. The new technology economises on land and, being labour-intensive, provides more farm employment.

However, we cannot assume that it is going to solve the problem of foodgrain shortage in the underdeveloped countries. As yet, the new seeds are less resistant to drought, floods and disease. To be effective, they require substantial inputs of fertiliser and of water: in many areas expensive irrigation will be essential to their success. Moreover, the fact that fertiliser and water are complementary inputs has meant that the green revolution has caught on—and been encouraged by governments—among the larger, more prosperous farmers in the better-watered, more prosperous regions. This is true of, *e.g.*, Mexico, Pakistan and the Philippines. Unless governments ensure that the benefits of the green revolution are widely spread, the effect might even be to harm small peasant farmers by increasing the competition from large farmers.

Land Reform.

There are many forms of land tenure in less developed countries. In black Africa communal or tribal ownership of land is common, with members of the community or tribe receiving rights to use the land individually. In parts of Asia and Latin America, there is private ownership of land, which—particularly where the land is densely populated—has often led to great inequality of land ownership. In some cases land tenure is characterised by absentee landlords and share-cropping tenants. The development of large estates produces a class of landless labourers.

The need for land reform varies according to the circumstances. In most cases the main argument is for greater social justice. In some cases it may be possible also to expand production by redistributing land more evenly or by giving land to share-cropping tenants and so improving their incentives. On the other hand, large farmers may have access to technology, skills and capital which small farmers lack: there is a danger that greater equity will be achieved only at the expense of efficiency. Hence the need to ensure that land reform is accompanied by a package of measures, *e.g.*, education, training and advice, and credit for fertiliser, tools and land improvements. Few governments have succeeded in implementing serious land reform programmes. The main reason is that the system of land tenure in a country often reflects the balance of political power: land reform invariably faces political opposition from entrenched interests. By the same token, a successful land reform may alter the balance of political power so as to facilitate broad-based development.

A Case-study of Land Reform.

Egypt provides a case-study of relatively successful land reform. It began in 1952 after the overthrow of a régime which relied heavily on the support of big landlords. It was necessary because of the gross inequality of land ownership and the acute shortage of arable land in Egypt. In 1952 more than 2 million families, making up two-thirds of land proprietors, held no more than an acre each and only 13 per cent of the land in total; whereas 12,000 families, each with more than 50 acres, owned a third of agricultural land. A ceiling was imposed on the size of family holding and gradually brought down, and the requisitioned land redistributed to landless families and small farmers. Yet progress was slow: only 14 per cent of agricultural land had been redistributed by 1971 and only the richest and the poorest were affected. An important element in the success of the reforms was the formation of state-supervised co-operatives which organised cultivation, channelled credit and marketed produce. Agricultural yields rose significantly, particularly after 1960.

A grave problem facing the poor in agriculture which land reform cannot solve is population growth, currently estimated in Egypt to be 2·2 per cent per annum. Between the census years 1947 and 1966, the rural population increased from 12·6 million to 17·7 million people.

Exports of Primary Products.

Almost all underdeveloped countries export primary products (foodstuffs, industrial raw materials or minerals) and import manufactured goods, especially the capital goods (plant, machinery and vehicles) required for development. This international division of labour has recently operated to the disadvantage of the underdeveloped countries. The world demand for their primary products has increased only very slowly. This is because people spend just a small part of their additional income on food (*e.g.*, tea, coffee, cocoa), because synthetic substitutes have been developed for many raw materials (*e.g.*, rubber, cotton, jute), because developed countries protect their own agriculture (*e.g.*, sugar) and because demand in the developed countries has moved towards commodities with low raw material content (*e.g.*, from heavy industries to services).

In consequence, the general trend has been for the prices of primary products to fall in relation to those of manufactured goods. This was an important cause of the improvement in Britain's terms of trade (*see* G6). The reverse of the coin was a deterioration in the terms of trade of many underdeveloped countries, *i.e.*, they could now buy fewer imports for a given quantity of exports. Primary commodities exported by developing countries actually decreased in price on average by 12 per cent over the period 1957–62, and increased by only 2 per cent between 1962 and 1970. Most poor countries benefited from the soaring prices of various commodities in world markets during 1972 and 1973. These were years of world economic boom, food shortages and speculative purchasing of primary commodities. However, the non-oil-producing developing countries suffered as a result of the oil price rise after October 1973. The world recession of 1974 and 1975 depressed primary commodity prices, and inflation in developed countries increased the price of manufactured imports (*see* G41). Unsatisfactory prices of primary commodities (other than oil) have contributed to the shortage of foreign exchange which restricts investment expenditure in many less developed countries.

The prices of various primary products tend to fluctuate violently from one year to another. Many underdeveloped economies depend heavily on the exports of one or two commodities. For instance, coffee is the most important product in

Brazil, cotton in Egypt, copper in Zambia, sugar in Cuba, cocoa in Ghana and rice in Burma. Fluctuations in the world price of its main export cause instability in the export revenues of a country, and this in turn can produce fluctuations in income throughout its domestic economy.

Problems of Industrialisation.

In those underdeveloped countries where there is population pressure on the land, alternative employment has to be created in industry or services. Even in countries with a surplus of land, if there is heavy dependence on one or two primary products, industrialisation provides a means of diversifying the economy.

But industrialisation is not an easy course. Because the margin between agricultural production and food consumption is narrow, the surplus from the agricultural sector exchangeable for the products of other sectors—*e.g.* industry and services—is small; *i.e.*, the demand for the goods and services produced by other sectors is low. A second constraint on industrialisation is imposed by competition from abroad; new industries in an underdeveloped country have to compete with established industries in developed countries, which have the advantage of experience, a trained labour force and markets big enough for them to reap all the potential economies of large-scale production.

Industrialisation Strategies.

One means of overcoming the small size of market is to export manufactures to the developed countries. Developing countries with cheap labour are likely to have a comparative advantage in the manufacture of relatively labour-intensive commodities. A number of less developed countries have had remarkable success in following this strategy, *e.g.*, Hong Kong, Taiwan, South Korea, Mexico and Puerto Rico. Among their successful activities are textiles, clothing and labour-intensive components of electronic equipment. However, the markets for such products are limited—so that not all developing countries can succeed—and the developed countries often impose protective tariffs. Another form of manufacturing is the processing of primary products before exporting them. Here developing countries sometimes face the problem that tariffs are higher on the processed than on the unprocessed products.

A means of overcoming competition from the industries of the developed countries is by nurturing an infant industrial sector behind tariff walls—which is how the United States and Germany developed their industries in the face of British competition in the nineteenth century. A number of developing countries have adopted this strategy. However, it has its drawbacks. Sometimes the "infants" never grow up, and vested interests press for continued protection. Import-substituted industrialisation often means that raw materials or semi-processed goods are imported for local processing. There is a danger that fluctuations in export proceeds will periodically curtail imports of necessary intermediate goods. The under-utilisation of capital in the manufacturing sector because of foreign exchange shortages has frequently occurred in countries such as India, Sri Lanka and Ghana.

Unemployment and Underemployment.

Unemployment and underemployment occur on a very considerable scale in both the rural and the urban areas of developing countries. Consider first the rural case. Because farm work is normally shared, underemployment—disguised unemployment—is more common than open unemployment. People work for only a part of the day or year. Where land is scarce, underemployment is chronic: people would like to work more if only they had more land. Unless the yield from the land can be raised, growth in population causes greater underemployment and reduces income per head on the land. Where land is abundant, underemployment is a seasonal phenomenon. People are fully employed in the busy season—harvesting and planting—but underemployed at other times of the year.

In the towns open unemployment is common with people queueing for *modern sector* jobs at the labour exchanges and at the factory gates. Rates of urban open unemployment in excess of 10 per cent are frequently recorded, *e.g.*, in Ghana, Colombia, Puerto Rico, Trinidad, Sri Lanka and the Philippines. Few developing countries can afford unemployment benefits, so that job-seekers remain openly unemployed only until their savings are used up or support by their relations is withdrawn. Then they have to scrape out a subsistence in the urban *traditional sector* while waiting and hoping for something better. Underemployment is rife in the easily entered traditional sector activities such as petty trading, hawking, beer brewing, fetching and carrying. A shoeshiner may be on the streets for ten hours a day but have only a couple of customers. The more people enter these activities, the further average income per worker is depressed. In many less developed countries this self-employment in the traditional sector accounts for the majority of urban workers.

Migration to the Cities.

Urbanisation is proceeding at an unprecedented pace in much of the Third World. Rural people are being drawn to the cities at a rate well in excess of the capacity of the cities to absorb them productively. The reason for this migration might be economic or social. The economic explanation runs in terms of an income differential between the urban and the rural areas. Relatively unskilled wages in the modern sector of the economy—often governed by minimum wage legislation or trade union bargaining—can be well above the incomes to be derived from peasant agriculture. People go to the towns in search of modern sector wage jobs, although they may actually end up underemployed in the low-income traditional sector. Rural–urban migration may be a social phenomenon: rural people are attracted by the facilities and "bright lights" of the cities. The recent expansion of education in many countries may also play a part, since a high proportion of the migrants are school leavers.

Whatever the reasons the consequences are socially harmful and politically explosive. Shanty towns and slums proliferate in the cities and their outskirts; poverty, disease and crime flourish.

Employment Creation.

As recognition has grown that unemployment, in its open and disguised forms, is both high and rising in many of the developing countries, so the objective of creating productive employment has received higher priority. For various reasons the growth of modern sector employment has been tardy and has lagged behind the growth of output. One reason is that the modern sector normally uses capital equipment and technology which is imported from the developed countries. This means that, even in countries with cheap and abundant labour, the most profitable techniques of production are often highly capital-intensive, so that the amount of scarce investment funds required to equip a worker is high. Hence the case for developing an *intermediate technology* which is both profitable and suited to the needs of the underdeveloped countries.

There is some danger that the establishment of capital-intensive factories may actually harm existing labour-intensive production. For instance, sandals can be made by small cobblers using local leather (or old car tyres) or by a large plant using imported plastic materials: a new factory employing a few machine operators might displace many more traditional craftsmen who have no alternative employment opportunities.

Governments, by encouraging or discouraging particular forms and areas of investment, have the power to influence the growth of employment. In the rural areas the encouragement and organisation of labour-intensive developmental or community projects can assist in harnessing the one abundant resource which almost all developing countries possess: unskilled labour.

Educated Manpower.

Many underdeveloped countries are faced with the dual problem of unskilled labour surpluses and scarcities of skilled and educated manpower. The problem is particularly acute in some of the recently independent countries of Africa. To give an extreme example: at the time of its independence in 1964, Zambia had only 100 Zambian university graduates and 1,200 secondary school graduates in a population of 3·5 million. In such countries the great shortage of educated and skilled people enables them to earn high incomes—with the result that there is a very unequal distribution of income. And even in countries where surpluses have developed, the existence of an international market for professional people such as doctors and engineers helps to keep up their earnings: these countries suffer from a "brain drain" to the developed world.

Because teachers are educated people, education in underdeveloped countries can be very expensive. In Uganda in the 1960s only 45 per cent of the children in the relevant age-group were at primary school and only 2 per cent were at secondary school. Yet the salary bill paid to their teachers exceeded 2 per cent of the gross domestic product. In such circumstances it is difficult to meet the demands for universal primary education; especially if the sort of primary education provided does not enable children to become better farmers.

Economic development is not just a matter of capital accumulation: it requires also an increase in educated manpower. Not only more knowledge but also new habits and attitudes—*e.g.*, attitudes towards risk-taking, hard work and thrift. Education—of the right sort and with suitable content—is generally acknowledged to be important for development, although the benefits of education cannot be quantified at all satisfactorily.

Economic Aid.

The gap between living standards in the underdeveloped areas of the world and in the areas already developed has tended to widen in recent years. In the 1950s real income per capita rose in the developed countries by 2·7 per cent per annum on average, and in the less developed countries by 2·3 per cent per annum. It was through a growing world recognition of the situation that the 1960s were designated "The United Nations Development Decade." But between 1960 and 1970 these rates of growth widened to 3·8 and 3·0 per cent per annum respectively. World inequalities continued to increase: hence the "Second United Nations Development Decade" in the 1970s.

The main industrial countries—organised as a 17-member *Development Assistance Committee* (DAC)—have provided economic aid to the developing countries. The total net flow of economic assistance from the DAC countries was $40 billion (about £18 billion) in 1975. Roughly $23·3 billion of this was net private investment and $13·6 billion official aid from governments. A third of the net *official development assistance* (ODA) was contributed by the United States: the other principal donors were France, West Germany, Japan, Canada and Britain in that order.

The DAC nations have accepted three aid targets. One is that the net flow of private and official resources combined should exceed 1 per cent of each country's gross national product. In 1973 only 5 of the 17 countries had achieved this percentage. The second target is that net ODA should exceed 0·7 per cent of GNP: not one country managed this in 1973. The third target, more generally achieved, concerns the "grant element"—the extent to which ODA contains an element of grant as opposed to commercial loans.

Although the money value of ODA increased between 1963 and 1973, in real terms it remained roughly constant. As a proportion of the combined GNP of the DAC countries, it fell from 0·51 per cent to 0·30 per cent over the decade. By their own standards the countries of the First World were failing to assist the Third World on an adequate scale. Yet, since the oil crisis of October 1973, the situation has worsened. Many of the developing countries are in greater need of assistance, and in the developed countries the unprecedented balance of payments deficits and the fall in real incomes has made the provision of aid both economically and politically more difficult.

Forms of Aid.

Aid to the developing countries takes many forms, it serves many purposes and it is given for many reasons. Underdeveloped countries need aid to provide finance for development projects; to provide foreign exchange with which imports for development purposes can be bought; and to provide the trained manpower and technical knowledge they lack. The motives of the donor are not always humanitarian. "Aid" can take a military form; it can be used to prop up an incompetent or unjust government, or to buy support in the cold war. Nor is aid always beneficial to the recipient country. It may be wasted on ill-conceived or prestige projects, or cause the government simply to relax its own efforts. Sometimes schools or hospitals are built with aid but there is a lack of local revenues with which to staff and run these institutions. Concern over donor's motives and instances of waste has led some people to react against aid-giving. However, the correct remedy is not to cut off aid but rather to prevent its misuse.

Donor governments may finance specific projects, or they may contribute to the general pool of funds available for expenditure by the governments of underdeveloped countries. But financial aid is not always enough. Most underdeveloped countries need technical assistance in planning their development, to ensure that development possibilities are exploited and that scarce resources are used to best advantage. Hence the many schemes for providing experts by individual countries and by the technical agencies of the United Nations, such as the Food and Agriculture Organisation (FAO), the World Health Organisation (WHO), the International Labour Organisation (ILO), the United Nations Educational, Scientific and Cultural Organisation (UNESCO), the Technical Assistance Board (UNTAB) and so on. Hence also the schemes for educating and training people from the developing countries.

Foreign Private Investment.

One possible form of aid is private investment by firms from developed countries. These investments—setting up branch factories, for example—are concentrated in those projects which appear profitable to the investor. However, it is a characteristic of underdevelopment that there are few openings for profitable investment. Most of the U.K. private investment overseas, for example, has been concentrated in relatively highly developed countries of the sterling area. Private investment cannot be relied upon to provide an adequate flow of resources.

Indeed, it has been questioned whether private investment constitutes aid to less developed countries at all. Its opponents argue that the benefits are often small or even negative: foreign-owned firms repatriate high profits and avoid tax by means of royalty payments to the parent company or unrealistic pricing of their transactions with the parent company; and these firms deter local enterprise. Supporters of foreign investment point to the high political risks which necessitate high profits in order to attract investors to developing countries, and question whether resources are available for any alternative path to development. A form of compromise which has become common in the Third World is a partnership arrangement between multinational companies and the host country's government.

British Aid.

The table shows how British assistance to developing countries has grown over the years, and how it has measured up to the international aid targets now accepted by the British Government. The first target is that the total net financial flow to developing countries should exceed 1 per cent of GNP. The large but fluctuating flows of private capital meant that this target was achieved in 1974 and in some previous years. The second target is for a net official development assistance (ODA) in excess of 0·7 per cent of GNP. We see that British ODA as a percentage

FINANCIAL FLOWS FROM BRITAIN TO DEVELOPING COUNTRIES 1965–1975

	Net total flows, official and private.		Net official development assistance.		
	£m.	% of GNP.	£m.	% of GNP.	£m. (1970 prices).
1964	328	0·98	176	0·53	201
1967	287	0·72	173	0·44	203
1970	520	1·02	186	0·36	186
1972	584	0·92	243	0·39	201
1973	601	0.83	246	0·34	182
1974	980	1·20	309	0·38	195
1975	1012	0·98	393	0·38	201

of GNP was only slightly more than half of the officially accepted target in 1974, and was lower than it had been ten years previously. The table also shows that ODA has grown in value; in 1975 it equalled £7·00 per head of British population. However, if we allow for inflation by expressing official aid in real terms, we see that the volume of aid has stagnated.

Government aid may be divided into multilateral aid and bilateral aid. Multilateral aid is given through the medium of the international development institutions; bilateral aid is given directly to the developing countries. Multilateral aid constituted over a quarter of total British aid in 1975. Nearly half of British bilateral disbursements in 1975 took the form of grants, and just over half were loans. Most of the loans were fairly "soft", with maturity averaging 25 years and the rate of interest averaging 2 per cent. About half of expenditure on aid is formally tied to the purchase of British goods and services. Other aid is not tied formally, and may be used directly to finance local expenditure; but when it is used to finance imports directly, it has to be spent on British goods if these are available on competitive terms. Multilateral aid is untied. The tying of aid tends to raise the costs to developing countries; but it also enables countries with precarious foreign balances—such as the United Kingdom—to be more generous.

Aid takes the form not only of financial but also of technical assistance. Government expenditure on technical assistance amounted to a third of net bilateral disbursements in 1975. At the end of 1975 British technical assistance personnel overseas totalled 8,400 (excluding volunteers recruited by voluntary societies); over 1,000 administrators, 4,000 teachers, 800 agricultural advisers, 600 doctors and medical workers, and 1,800 involved in the economy.

All British official aid is channelled and coordinated by the Ministry of Overseas Development. In addition there are various private associations concerned with promoting development, such as Oxfam, War on Want and the World Development Movement.

The World Bank.

The International Bank for Reconstruction and Development (IBRD) known as the *International Bank* or as the *World Bank*, is an agency of the United Nations established in 1945. It has the primary function of making funds available to assist developing countries. Member nations agreed to subscribe quotas—fixed in much the same way as the quotas for the IMF—to the Bank. In fact, only a small proportion of the quotas has been called up by the Bank; the major part of the Fund's resources are borrowed—on the security of the remainder of the quotas—in financial centres.

Usually, loans are made to finance specific projects of investment in underdeveloped countries; and the Bank will normally make a loan only if it is satisfied that the investment will yield a revenue sufficient to enable the payment of interest on the loan, and the repayment of the sum lent. In 1974 the Bank made loans to the value of over £700 million. Thus a sizeable amount of lending is channelled through the Bank, but it is clear that some projects of great value to underdeveloped countries cannot be financed in this way, because they would not yield returns quickly or large enough to meet the Bank's requirements for interest and repayment. Accordingly a new institution, the *International Development Association*, was set up in 1960 with the power to make loans at low rates of interest and with more generous repayment conditions. The IDA contributes towards the development of education and agriculture (£400 million in 1974).

UNCTAD.

In 1964 the United Nations Conference on Trade and Development (UNCTAD) was held. For the first time the poorer nations of the world—77 were represented—came together to act as a pressure group on trading matters. The Conference made the following recommendations. Developing countries should be given free access to world markets for their manufactures and semi-manufactures by the elimination of quotas and tariffs. International *commodity agreements* should be made for each major primary commodity in world trade, to stabilise commodity prices. Compensation schemes—whereby countries are compensated for the declining prices of their primary products—were recommended for consideration. The Conference also resolved that the developed countries should aim to provide at least 1 per cent of their national income as aid for the underdeveloped countries.

Nothing concrete resulted from the 1964 Session: no significant trade measures in favour of the developing countries were taken, and the international transfer of financial resources diminished in relation to the income of the developed countries. A second Session of the Conference was held in 1968. Again, no action resulted from the Session; but the developed countries did accept more firmly the principle of discrimination in favour of developing countries in trade and shipping, and the 1 per cent target for aid. Progress was subsequently made in introducing tariff preferences on poor countries' exports of some manufactures to rich countries.

UNCTAD III, held in Chile in 1972, appeared to be more a political tournament than a constructive Conference. Perhaps the most promising outcome was the greater likelihood of a future *Link* between SDRs and international aid; *i.e.*, the issue of the new international paper currency to less developed countries—so easing the problems both of international liquidity and of development (*see* G40).

The Impact of the Oil Price Rise.

In October 1973, during the Arab–Israeli war, the members of the Organisation of Petroleum Exporting Countries (OPEC) cut supplies of oil and increased their prices drastically. The price of oil subsequently rose fourfold above its initial level. By acting as a cartel to control supplies the OPEC countries were able to maintain the higher prices without surpluses accumulating and a competitive price war breaking out. The impact on all countries was great (*see* G41); on a number of less developed countries it was disastrous.

Some idea of the magnitude of the problem can be given by expressing the *additional* oil bill in 1974 as a percentage of the total import bill and of the GNP in 1973 of various countries. For Uruguay the figures were 39 and 4·9 per cent respectively, for Thailand 26 and 5·4 for South

Korea 20 and 9·0, and for Turkey 19 and 3·3 per cent. The bout of inflation in the industrial countries resulting from the oil crisis meant that the developing countries also had to pay more for their other imports. They were further hit by the world recession generated by the oil crisis, because the resultant fall in world demand produced a slump in the prices of primary commodities. Between June 1974 and June 1975 the primary commodity exports (other than oil) of developing countries fell in price by nearly 40 per cent, and their imports of manufactures rose in price by 40 per cent. The developing countries had to cut back on the volume of their imports, to the detriment of development programmes. However, they were partly cushioned by the emergency loans provided through the *oil facility* scheme introduced by the IMF.

Of course, a number of less developed countries benefited from the oil price increases. These included the five rich oil countries (Saudi Arabia, Kuwait, Qatar, Abu Dhabi and Libya), whose levels of income per capita now exceed those in the industrial countries. Their use of the new revenues is limited by the ability of their economies to absorb them: for that reason they continue to need technical assistance. How they use their unabsorbed oil revenues can greatly affect the economies of both developed and developing countries. Other, less wealthy, oil-producing countries—including Iran, Iraq, Venezuela, Indonesia and Nigeria—have much larger populations and more absorptive capacity. They now have an opportunity to transform their economies with the oil revenues.

Reappraisal of Development and Aid Policies.

By the mid-1970s it was generally recognised that there was a case for a drastic reappraisal of development policies and of aid priorities. One of the important considerations was the new situation created by the increased price of oil. Many developing countries would require substantially more aid to offset its various adverse effects. The success of OPEC in raising the oil price aroused the hopes and expectations of developing countries producing other primary commodities that they too could improve their terms of trade with the developed world. A "New International Economic Order" was envisaged by the General Assembly of the United Nations, in which the formation of producers' associations and new commodity agreements could play a part. These were the main issues debated, but with little agreement being reached, in the fourth session of UNCTAD held in May 1976.

Other factors calling for a reappraisal of policies included a growing recognition of the precarious food situation in many developing countries, and an increased awareness of large and growing income inequalities both within and among the developing countries.

The Food Crisis.

In the last couple of decades food production in the developing countries has done no more than keep pace with the growth of population. F.A.O. projections of demand and supply over the decade 1975–85 indicate no increase in food production per capita in the developing countries. Many developing countries have become net food importers, and this trend is likely to continue. In the period 1970–72 food imports represented no less than 14 per cent of the total imports of the less developed countries.

The years 1972–74 were ones of poor harvests in various parts of the developed and developing world. Famines occurred in the Sahel area of Africa, in Bangladesh and in parts of India. In response to vast imports of grain by the Soviet Union and many other countries, world grain stocks were reduced to very low levels and the price of grain rocketed. At the same time an acute shortage of fertiliser emerged, and its price also soared. These circumstances led to the calling of a World Food Conference in 1974 (*see also* **F61**).

The Conference foresaw the possibility of inadequate food supplies and famines in the developing countries in future years. It called for a building up of world food stocks and increased emergency *food aid*—aid provided in the form of foodstuffs. However, the long-run solution was seen to come from a fundamental attack on the problems of agricultural development. In response, most of the DAC donor countries decided to increase very substantially their aid to agriculture in the recipient countries.

Concern for food shortages leads inexorably to the population issue. Although the urgency of the problem of rapidly expanding population is not appreciated in some developing countries, growing attention is being paid to the economic benefits of population planning, *e.g.*, with the calling of the World Population Conference in 1973. Aid for family planning increased tenfold between 1965 and 1973; but in 1973 it still represented only 2·3 per cent of total aid.

Inequality Within Countries.

The growth performance of the less developed countries taken together—growth of GNP per capita of 2·3 per cent per annum in the 1950s and 3·0 per cent per annum in the 1960s—is good by the standards of the past, although worse than the corresponding performance of the developed countries. However, in many less developed countries these growth rates have been achieved without any apparent improvement in the lot of the masses.

The majority of the people are engaged in agriculture in the rural areas, whereas much of the development has taken place in industry and services in the urban areas. A minority of people have benefited—industrialists, bureaucrats, educated and skilled workers, organised labour in the modern sector of the economy—but the poor living in the urban slums, often in open or disguised unemployment, and the enormous numbers in the rural areas have been little affected by development. In many countries the fruits of development have not been widely spread. It is a growing criticism that development policies have been biased towards industry and towards the cities, and that rural people in agriculture have been neglected. This outcome may be a reflection of the uneven distribution of political power within a developing country.

Increasingly, the growth of GNP per capita as a goal of development has been questioned, both within the less developed countries and among national and international aid agencies. Both recipient and donor governments have recently shown a greater concern for poverty, employment creation and social equity. Many donors have modified their aid policies to try to reach the poor. Of course, this redirection coincides to a considerable extent with the increased concern for agricultural development.

Inequality Among Countries.

Not all less developed countries have fared equally well in recent years. In particular, there appears to be a tendency for disparities among less developed countries to widen. Dividing such countries into the 46 with GNP per capita of less than £85 ($200) and the 96 with GNP per capita above £85 in 1972, we find that no less than half of the poorer group failed to raise average income per capita by more than 1 per cent per annum between 1960 and 1972, whereas only a tenth of the less poor group failed to do so. The countries which have performed well tend to be semi-industrialised and able to respond to opportunities for exporting manufactures to the developed countries, or to be well endowed with mineral or oil resources. Recent growth success stories include Brazil, Colombia, South Korea, Taiwan, Mexico and Turkey. Some of these are on the way to becoming self-reliant economically.

The poorest countries—25 of which have been designated the *least developed countries*—are experiencing the greatest difficulty in escaping from the vicious circle of poverty. A growing recognition of their problem has led the DAC countries to reallocate aid in favour of the least developed countries, and to offer aid on more concessionary terms to these countries.

Revision of British Aid Policies.

The revision of DAC aid policies mentioned above also occurred in the British aid programme. In 1974 the British Government began to direct more of its aid towards the poorest developing countries, and all future ODA to countries with a GNP per capita of less than $200 (£85) per annum was to take the form of outright grants. A Disaster Unit was established to respond to emergencies. Aid for family planning was stepped up. Increasing weight would be placed on rural development and the expansion of agricultural production, in particular on helping the poor in rural areas, *e.g.*, small farmers and landless labourers.

Some Suggestions for Further Reading.

For an introduction to the subject the reader is referred to Jagdish Bhagwati, *The Economics of Underdeveloped Countries* (World University Library). A recent book concerned with international disparities, and addressed to the general reader, is *Development in a Divided World*, edited by Seers and Joy (Pelican). An interesting account of life in rural India is found in Kusum Nair, *Blossoms in the Dust* (Duckworth). On Asia the reader may wish to dip into the three volumes of Gunnar Myrdal entitled *Asian Drama: An Enquiry into the Poverty of Nations* (Alan Lane, The Penguin Press). A helpful introduction to African problems is found in Andrew M. Kamarck, *The Economics of African Development* (Praeger). On South America there is Celso Furtado, *Economic Development of Latin America* (Cambridge University Press). Introductory books on particular topics include G. K. Helleiner, *International Trade and Economic Development* and Peter Dorner, *Land Reform and Economic Development* (both Penguins).

The Overseas Development Institute has published a number of pamphlets on aid topics, including *World Development Handbook*, *British Development Policies* and *Volunteers in Development*. The Ministry of Overseas Development has compiled a handbook of *British Aid Statistics* (H.M.S.O.). A recent publication of the World Bank, *The Assault on World Poverty* (Johns Hopkins), examines the causes of poverty, especially in the rural areas, and the remedies. The Organisation for Economic Co-operation and Development, comprising all the major non-communist developed countries, publishes an Annual Review of aid and development entitled *Development Co-operation* (O.E.C.D.).

An interesting quarterly publication of the I.M.F. and the World Bank, *Finance and Development*, is available free of charge: applications should be sent to *Finance and Development*, I.M.F. Building, Washington, D.C. 20431. U.S.A.

IV. RECENT DEVELOPMENTS IN THE BRITISH ECONOMY

1. INTERNATIONAL DEVELOPMENTS

The Balance of Payments.

The balance of payments problem has dominated events in the British economy in recent years. It is therefore important to analyse the balance of payments in some detail; to understand why the balance of payments has been a problem; and to see its effects on economic policy. The balance of payments and its components are explained in detail on **G6–8**. The balance of payments in each year since 1961 is shown in the table on **G36**.

The 1964 Crisis.

We begin our story as we end it: with the British balance of payments heavily in deficit and under severe pressure. The late 1950s and early 1960s saw a decline in British competitiveness. The British share in world exports of manufactures fell steadily, and there was a rapid increase in imports of manufactured goods. The record current account deficit of 1964 was made worse by the sharp pre-election boom which depleted stocks and diverted demand to imports as domestic bottlenecks were reached. After the General Election of October 1964 the new Labour Government took immediate remedial action. This included a *temporary import surcharge* on all imports of manufactures and semi-manufactures, and a system of *export rebates*, representing the indirect taxes paid in Britain by British exporters.

The deficit on capital account was no less than that on current account. The United Kingdom was not an attractive investment proposition. A crisis arose in the second half of the year, when an outflow of short-term capital—a " flight of hot money "—took place in the expectation that a devaluation would be necessary to cure the worsening imbalance. Once this feeling developed, the process became cumulative: the greater the outflow, the more likely it seemed that Britain would be forced to devalue. A great deal of sterling was offered for sale by speculators holding pounds—the " Gnomes of Zurich "—and by British and foreign importers and exporters. In order to prevent the price of sterling from falling below the official minimum limit to the exchange rate of £1 = $2.78 (*i.e.*, to " support sterling ") the Bank of England was itself forced to buy pounds. To do this the Bank had to draw on the country's reserves of gold and foreign exchange. The vast drain on the reserves could not be allowed to continue, and in late November, Bank Rate was raised by 2 per cent to 7 per cent. The aim of this measure was to lure back short-term capital funds with the high rate of interest, and also to convince speculators that the pound would not be devalued. Speculators were not convinced, however, and the crisis continued. Two days later it was announced that an enormous loan totalling over £1 billion (*i.e.* £1,000 million) would be made available to Britain from all the leading Western central banks. This news was sufficient to slow down the speculative outflow, and by the close of 1964 the selling had come to an end.

Events Leading to Devaluation.

The current account improved gradually in 1965 and again in 1966. Nevertheless, there was still a substantial deficit in total currency flow, which had somehow to be financed. Confidence in the pound remained weak and was further upset by the seamen's strike in May and June. Yet another flight of short-term capital occurred, and this led the Government in panic to introduce a policy of deflation, in a package-deal known as the " July measures " (*see* **G44**). To improve the balance of payments directly, the personal travel allowance outside the Sterling Area was reduced to £50 per annum. The fall in demand resulting from the deflationary policy, together with a wage-freeze introduced at the same time (*see* **G52**), helped to improve the trade balance, but of course at a cost of more unemployment and slower growth.

The trade gap widened to a record level in 1967. No single factor can be held responsible, but the following contributed: a continued decline in competitiveness, the removal of the temporary import surcharge, the building up of imported stocks which had been depleted, and the exceptionally slow growth of world production in 1967 (which meant that demand in the countries importing British goods was fairly stagnant). With the trade returns deteriorating, sterling came under unremitting speculative pressure, reaching a climax in November.

Devaluation of the Pound, 1967.

The Government recognised that action would have to be taken to improve the balance of payments, and to obtain further foreign loans to protect the depleted reserves. The alternatives were: deflation, import controls, tariffs and devaluation. Simple deflation to reduce imports was ruled out politically as the economy was now already in recession. Import controls and tariffs would meet with resistance from Britain's competitors and the GATT, and tariffs had been tried in 1964 without

BALANCE OF PAYMENTS

	1964	1965	1966	1967	1968
Exports (f.o.b.)	4,521	4,848	5,204	5,139	6,282
Imports (f.o.b.)	5,019	5,071	5,268	5,693	6,949
Visible balance	−498	−223	−64	−554	−667
Invisible balance	+145	+196	+167	+256	+395
Current balance	−353	−27	+103	−298	−272
Official long-term capital	−116	−85	−81	−59	+17
Net private investment	−256	−130	−39	−96	−160
Other capital flows	+71	−111	−503	−445	−863
Balancing item	−41	—	−72	+227	−132
Total currency flow	−695	−353	−591	−671	−1,410
Net borrowing from IMF*	+357	+489	+15	−339	+506
Other net borrowing*	+216	+110	+294	+691	+790
Transfer from portfolio to reserves*	—	—	+316	+204	—
Change in reserves*	+122	−246	−34	+115	+114
*Total official financing**	+695	+353	+591	+671	+1,410

* A plus sign denotes a rise in liabilities or a fall in assets, and a minus sign a fall in liabilities or a are included as changes in the official reserves.

success. The Government decided to devalue the pound.

The case for devaluation is a mixed one (*see* G8). It makes imports more expensive in relation to home-produced goods, and so demand for manufactured goods shifts away from imports; but in the case of food and raw materials, Britain must continue to import these essentials at the higher price because there are no domestic substitutes. It is possible, therefore, that devaluation will actually raise the import bill. However, export receipts should be increased by a greater amount: Britain exports its products in a highly competitive market, so that the reduced price of British goods in terms of foreign currencies should lead to a considerable increase in the amount of exports.

This improvement in the trade balance depends on Britain being able to retain at least part of the price advantage gained by devaluation. However, since devaluation raises the price of imported goods, it raises the cost of living both directly and indirectly, *e.g.*, imported raw materials rise in price, so increasing production costs, which are passed on as higher prices. The trade unions react to this cut in the standard of living by demanding wage increases. In this way a spiralling inflation can occur which entirely neutralises the gain from devaluation. Devaluation makes an incomes policy both more difficult and more important (*see* G51–4).

In November 1967, the pound was devalued by 14·3 per cent, from $2.8 to $2.4 to the £. Devaluation was anticipated by speculators, and on the day before, there was a run on the pound said to be greater than any previously experienced. The devaluation was unfortunately delayed by the need to achieve international co-operation so as to prevent a flurry of competitive devaluations. It was also agreed among central bankers that Britain should be given credits of up to $3 billion, including $1·4 billion standby credit from the IMF (*see* G9 and 10). This credit protected the reserves against speculation; but it would have to be paid back out of balance of payments surpluses over the next few years.

Devaluation increases the demand for domestically produced goods and services: imports are replaced by local substitutes and foreign demand for British goods increases. This switch in demand requires also a switch in scarce resources—labour and capital—into the exporting and import substituting industries, if the new demand is to be met. To release resources for these industries it is necessary to reduce the demand for resources elsewhere in the economy. Accordingly, the devaluation was accompanied by a series of deflationary measures (*see* G44).

Improvement after Devaluation.

In his Letter of Intent to the IMF immediately after devaluation, the Chancellor stated the Government's aim to improve the balance of payments by at least £500 million a year. However, progress after devaluation was initially disappointing: the current account deficit for 1968 was only slightly less than that for 1967. Moreover, this improvement came in the invisible account: the trade gap actually widened.

The balance of payments was transformed in 1969, improving strongly throughout the year. British exports were helped by the rapid increase in world trade. The volume of imports hardly rose, partly because of the *import deposit scheme*, introduced in November 1968, by which importers were required to deposit with H.M. Customs for a period of six months money equal to half (later reduced) of the value of certain imports.

The improvement in the balance of payments enabled the Government in 1970 to abolish the restrictions on travel expenditure and the import deposit scheme. The balance of payments continued to improve, and in 1971, for the first time in many years, the British share of world exports of manufactures rose. On the other hand, the growth of imports was constrained by the stagnation of the economy. Most unusually for Britain, the visible trade balance showed a large surplus in 1971.

The surplus on current account was no less than £500 million in 1969, £700 m. in 1970 and £1,000 m. in 1971. This improvement occurred both in visibles and invisibles. Between 1968 and 1971 the trade balance improved by over £900 m. and the invisible balance by nearly £400 m.; its most improved components being private services (*e.g.*, financial, insurance and travel services) and net income from abroad. The total currency flow was transformed from an enormous deficit in 1968 (when the authorities were forced to borrow £1·3 billion) to surpluses of £740 m. in 1969, £1·42 b. in 1970 and no less than £3·35 b. in 1971, some of which represented short-term capital flight from the dollar.

Was the improvement in the balance of payments after 1968 an indication that the policy of devaluation had eventually succeeded? The efficacy of devaluation can only be judged after a few years, and then with difficulty since we need to know what would have happened in the absence of devaluation. Economists have not produced a unanimous answer. The National Institute for Economic Research has suggested that the current account surplus of £600 million in 1970 might have been over £400 m. smaller (£300 m. less on invisible trade) had it not been for devaluation. Undoubtedly the balance of payments was aided by the depressed state of the economy.

Britain's Debt Repayments.

At the end of 1968 the British Government had short- and medium-term debts outstanding to central banks and the IMF of no less than £3·4

1964–76 (£ MILLION)

1969	1970	1971	1972	1973	1974	1975	1976
7,075	7,907	8,810	9,141	11,772	15,899	18,768	25,294
7,231	7,932	8,530	9,843	14,106	21,119	21,972	28,886
−156	−25	+280	−702	−2,334	−5,220	−3,204	−3,592
+616	+758	+804	+856	+1,598	+1,873	+1,531	+2,169
+460	+733	+1,084	+154	−736	−3,347	−1,673	−1,423
−99	−204	−273	−255	−254	−276	−288	−156
−6	+49	+216	−631	−260	+1,066	+355	+219
−60	+728	+1,874	+172	+416	+749	+121	−2,001
+392	−19	+245	−705	+45	+136	+6	−267
+687	+1,287	+3,146	−1,265	−789	−1,672	−1,479	−3,628
−30	−134	−554	−415	—	—	—	+1,018
−613	−1,161	−1,181	+864	+999	+1,751	+810	+1,757
—	—	—	—	—	—	—	—
−44	−125	−1,536	+692	−210	−79	+669	+853
−687	−1,420	−3,271	+1,141	+789	+1,672	+1,479	+3,628

rise in assets. From July 1972 transactions with IMF affecting the U.K. reserve position in the Fund

billion. This represented about 10 per cent of the national income in 1968 and compared with gold and foreign exchange reserves of only £1·0 billion. The continued improvement in the balance of payments after 1968 and the first allocation of Special Drawing Rights (*see* G40) enabled the Chancellor to announce in his April 1970 budget that the outstanding debts were down to £1·65b. while the reserves stood at £1·13 b. The vast balance of payments surplus of 1971 eliminated almost all of these debts, and indeed the Bank of England lent to foreign monetary authorities under the "swap agreement" among central banks. The British reserves rose to the record level of over £2·7 b. early in 1972. By the end of 1972 the official short- and medium-term indebtedness was nil.

Renewed Balance of Payments Problems.

The competitive position of the United Kingdom was weakened after 1971 by an inflation more rapid than in other countries (*see* G50) and by the dollar devaluation of 1971 (*see* G40). These developments contributed to the sharp deterioration in the balance of payments which occurred in 1972. There were sharp increases in demand for such consumer goods as cars and colour television sets—no doubt set off by the abolition of hire-purchase restrictions in 1971 (*see* G44)—and the inability of domestic producers to expand their production correspondingly both constrained exports and accelerated imports. The import bill was also up on account of a rapid increase in the world prices of a number of primary products, especially of such foodstuffs as beef, wheat, sugar and coffee. The trade balance deteriorated from a surplus in 1971 to a record deficit in 1972; and the current account was just in balance. A large private capital net outflow occurred, so that there was a deficit of over £1·1 billion in the total currency flow.

Floating of the Pound.

The deterioration in the balance of payments contributed to a large outflow of short-term funds in mid-1972, which culminated in a sterling crisis and a floating of the pound in June. This was the first time that sterling had been allowed to float since a period in the 1930s, and it represented a contravention of the increasingly criticised IMF system (*see* G40). The pound floated downwards after June, from about \$2.60 = £1 to an average value of roughly \$2.40 during 1973, and to a low of below \$2.30 in early 1974. It fluctuated between \$2.30 and \$2.40 until June 1975 when the rate dropped to \$2.20. The downward slide continued, and in March 1976 the pound fell below \$2.00 for the first time and continued to slide. Sterling depreciated even further in relation to such currencies as the mark, the franc and the yen, as the dollar was itself devalued in 1971 and 1973 (*see* G40).

The falling value of the pound was of no immediate assistance to the balance of payments: experience suggests that the improvement occurs only after a lag of a year or two. In the meantime the devaluation pushed up the domestic price of imports of raw materials and foodstuffs, so raising both the costs of production and the cost of living. The downward floating of the pound made a counter-inflation policy both more difficult and more important (*see* G51–4).

Inflation in Commodity Markets.

The current account of the balance of payments deteriorated sharply in 1973, to reach the unprecedented deficit of £1·12 billion. Exports did reasonably well, rising by 25 per cent in terms of value and by 11 per cent in terms of volume. However, the import bill soared, increasing by no less than 41 per cent. Import volume increased by 14 per cent, reflecting the rapid upsurge of the economy during 1972, and the emergence of shortages and a need for stockbuilding during 1973. More important was the higher price of imports: up by an average of 26 per cent between 1972 and 1973. This period witnessed a remarkable inflation in the prices of various primary products in world markets. To give some examples, between the first quarter of 1972 and the last quarter of 1973 average price increases in major world markets were as follows: cocoa 173 per cent, copper 115 per cent, cotton 127 per cent, rubber 123 per cent, wool 138 per cent and zinc 308 per cent.

This unprecedented jump in primary commodity prices stemmed from the sharp and well-synchronised expansion of the major industrial economies during 1972 and 1973, and it was assisted by some speculative buying as a hedge against inflation. Commodity prices generally reached their peak in the second quarter of 1974. Food prices continued to rise after this, while the prices of other commodities, especially fibres and metals, fell as the world economy moved into recession.

The Oil Crisis.

An event of great importance to Britain and to other industrial countries was the decision of the Arab oil-producing states, taken in October 1973, to restrict oil supplies and to raise oil prices. The restriction of supplies was initiated as a short-run political weapon in the Arab–Israeli conflict; but it revealed a potential for obtaining higher prices which had not previously been exploited by the Organisation of Petroleum Exporting Countries (OPEC). In the past the world demand for oil has grown very rapidly—by about 8 per cent per annum between 1960 and 1973—but it has been successfully met by expansion of pro duction. A slower growth of oil supply in relation to demand produces scarcity and a rocketing of price. Alternative sources of energy cannot be developed—and thus the demand for oil cannot be curtailed or even its growth retarded—for many years: little can be done about the prices charged by OPEC until the 1980s. However, maintenance of high prices depends on the ability of the OPEC group to restrict oil supplies to the market despite the incentive of each individual country to take advantage of the high prices by expanding its sales.

It seemed initially that the oil restrictions would produce physical shortages in the economy which would harm production and require rationing and direct controls. By February it appeared that demand would be met, but only at a much higher price. Between September 1973 and January 1974 the oil-producing governments raised their "take" on a barrel of crude oil from $1.75 to $7.00, and the import price was increased from $3.45 to $8.70 a barrel, *i.e.*, an increase of 150 per cent. Comparing 1974 with 1973 the price of oil imported into Britain almost trebled.

Oil and the Balance of Payments.

Largely because of higher import prices Britain's current balance deteriorated sharply in 1974. The value of imports rose by about 50 per cent. This was all accounted for by price increases, and not only oil prices: imported basic materials rose in price by 47 per cent, semi-manufactures by 42 per cent, and food by 28 per cent. Meanwhile the price of exports increased by 30 per cent but, because of world inflation, this involved little loss of competitiveness. In 1974 Britain recorded her worst ever current account deficit: no less than £3·65 billion. It represented a worsening of over £2·5 billion; in fact the additional oil bill amounted to £2·8 billion The deficit was of an order of magnitude—no less than 5 per cent of GDP—which made the deficits of previous crisis years appear puny.

In the wake of the oil crisis the world economy moved into severe recession (*see* **G41**). To this the British economy was no exception: real GDP stagnated in 1974 and fell in 1975. The domestic recession reduced the demand for imports, which fell in volume by 8 per cent in 1975. With rapid inflation at home and abroad, both exports and imports again rose sharply in price. The world recession made it difficult for OPEC to raise oil prices further (although an increase of 10 per cent was announced late in 1975); and the depressed state of world demand caused the prices of primary commodities actually to fall. Britain therefore benefited from a 6 per cent improvement in the terms of trade. Moreover, British exports suffered less than the exports of most other countries, falling in volume by only 3 per cent in 1975; and the British share of world exports of manufactures rose slightly, against the long-run trend. The net result of these changes was that the current account deficit of the balance of payments was halved, to £1·7 billion, in 1975.

In 1976 the world economy began to emerge from its severe recession, and output of the OECD countries grew by 5 per cent on average. This helped the British balance of payments; despite this, the current account deficit, at £1·5 billion, did little more than mark time. Exports rose by 30 per cent in value and by 8 per cent in volume; they were assisted by the depreciation of sterling and by the domestic price controls which encouraged producers to switch to foreign markets. The import bill rose by 35 per cent and import volume by 9 per cent. There was a particularly large increase in imports of cars: British producers appeared unable to expand production to meet the demand. Although the current account was no worse in 1976, the deficit in total currency flow rose to no less than £3·6 billion. To understand the reason we must examine the way in which the oil deficits have been financed and movements of the exchange rate.

Financing the Deficit.

In 1974 the oil exporting countries financed the largest part of the current account deficit by adding £2·2 billion to their sterling balances. There was also an unusual net inflow of private investment and considerable public sector borrowing in the Eurodollar market. The reduced deficit of 1975 actually posed a greater problem of financing, because the oil producers were less willing to accumulate balances in sterling. Britain's foreign exchange reserves fell by £500 million, the Government borrowed another £500 million in the Eurodollar market and announced that it would borrow £1 billion from the IMF in 1976.

Interest rates were kept high in London during 1975 to attract short-term capital and to discourage its withdrawal. However, during 1975 the rate of inflation in Britain was some 15 per cent above the average for the OECD countries: it became increasingly clear that sterling would have to be depreciated further. In March and April 1976 speculative outflows of funds forced the authorities to intervene strongly in the foreign exchange market by selling foreign exchange, and even then the pound depreciated substantially to a new low level. The British economy had again become precariously dependent on creditors and speculators.

In March the value of the pound fell below $2.00: in the space of two months it depreciated by 9 per cent. The pound slipped further with large withdrawals of officially held sterling balances, until it was checked in June by the announced agreement of a $5·3 billion standby credit facility made available to the Bank of England by the "Group of Ten" countries; this would be available for six months. With the trade returns worsening, sterling came under pressure again in September and October. The exchange rate slid to a low point of $1.57 in October, and the Bank of England's minimum lending rate (*see* **G23**) was raised to the unprecedented level of 15 per cent. Drawings on the credit facility exceeded $1 billion, and these had to be repaid in December. Accordingly, the Government applied to the IMF to draw on the United Kingdom's credit tranche of $3·9 billion. The successful conclusion of these negotiations in January 1977, and the borrowing of more than $1 billion from the IMF, helped to restore confidence. However, the terms of the agreement involved some loss of control over domestic affairs: in his Letter of Intent to the IMF, the Chancellor agreed to restrictions on the rate of domestic credit expansion (dce) and on the public sector borrowing requirement (psbr) (*see* **G47**).

Over the year 1976 the pound depreciated by some 15 per cent against other currencies. However, with the British rate of inflation running at 16 per cent and well above that in the other major countries, the ensuing gain in competitiveness was small.

The Sterling Balances.

The official sterling holdings (*see* **G9**) have been very volatile in recent years. They rose sharply after the oil crisis, as oil funds were invested in Britain; early in 1975 they amounted to £4·9 billion. In 1976, however, much of the oil money was withdrawn during the bouts of speculation against the pound, and the sterling balances fell by some £1·1 billion over the year to reach £2·6 billion in December. It had become increasingly necessary to reduce the vulnerability of the British economy to fluctuations of this sort.

The IMF agreement of January 1977 was followed by the successful negotiation of a "safety net" for the officially held sterling balances. The new facility, for an amount of $3 billion, was to operate with the support of various major central banks. Under the scheme, the British Government offers official holders of sterling the opportunity to convert all or part of their holdings into medium-term foreign currency bonds. But in addition, the UK is able to draw on the credit facility in respect of any other net reductions in the official sterling holdings.

North Sea Oil.

In 1974 the "oil deficit" in the balance of payments was £3·4 billion, in 1975 £3·1 billion, and in 1976 £3·0 billion. This is to be contrasted with a current account deficit (including oil) in these years of £3·4 billion, £1·5 billion, and £1·4 billion, respectively. The future course of the British balance of payments depends crucially on the rate of expansion of British oil production. The official forecast was that the net effect of North Sea oil production on the current account would rise steadily from a negligible sum (£90 million) in 1976 to some £5·4 billion (3 per cent of the GNP) in 1980, when Britain would be self-sufficient in oil. Of course, such a forecast involves many imponderables, including the price of oil itself. This depends on the ability of the OPEC cartel to survive and on the growth of world demand (influenced by the pace of economic recovery) in relation to supply (influenced by the development of new fields such as the North Sea and Alaska).

The Prospects for Restoring Balance.

World economic recovery should increase the demand for British exports, although it could also worsen the British terms of trade by raising the prices of primary commodities. It is the growth of exports, together with the terms of trade, which puts a ceiling on the growth of imports if the current account deficit is to be eliminated. Since the expansion of the economy raises the demand for imports, the foreign exchange constraint in imports in turn limits the extent to which production and employment can be permitted to increase. The balance of payments will therefore act as the crucial constraint on the growth of the economy in the years up to 1980.

Economic forecasters charting the likely course of the economy up to 1980 have drawn pessimistic conclusions, despite the expected gains from North Sea oil. If resources are to be released for correcting the balance of payments and for investment, there will have to be very severe restriction on the growth of real wages, private consumption and public expenditure. Unless this restriction is accepted by the community, the rate of unemployment in Britain might actually have to rise above the 5·5 per cent level reached at the end of 1976. If a 2·5 per cent unemployment rate is to be restored by 1980, very substantial improvement in the balance of payments will be necessary. For this to be achieved, inflation will have to be curbed drastically, and either further depreciation of the exchange rate or the imposition of import controls seems all too likely.

Should Imports be Controlled?

Pressure was brought to bear on the British Government to ease the balance of payments and unemployment problems by imposing import duties or quotas. The Government acceded to these pressures in a selective and minor way. For instance, in 1975 new quota levels on cotton yarn and man-made fibre imports from certain countries, and a licensing system for imports of television tubes and colour television sets, were introduced. However, in his budget of April 1976, the Chancellor rejected general and semi-permanent controls on manufactured goods: they would infringe treaty obligations to the GATT and the EEC, and he feared that they would lead to retaliation and the danger of an international trade war.

The economics profession, as on so many issues, is by no means in agreement on the relative merits of devaluation and import controls for remedying Britain's balance of payments deficit. The protagonists of import controls point to their scope for selectivity, *e.g.*, permitting concentration on manufactures and excluding raw materials and food, to the possibility of using price controls to avoid subsequent price increases in the sheltered industries, and to the avoidance of financial crises which would result from the prospect of devaluation. The devaluationists, on the other hand, argue that import controls are more likely to provoke retaliation by other countries, that controls breed inefficiency in production, that selective controls need to be very substantial to have the same impact as devaluation, and may have to be progressively intensified.

Foreign Investment.

One of the more successful items in the UK balance of payments has been net interest, profit, and dividends from private sources. In 1975 the net figure was a £1·49 billion surplus, to be compared with £0·57 billion a decade before. Much of this is made up of the overseas earnings of British companies.

Should the British Government discourage or encourage private investment abroad? An economic study has suggested that for every £100 of British investment abroad, British exports immediately increase by about £11, *i.e.*, there is an initial drain on the balance of payments of £89. The average rate of profit on capital overseas is thereafter about £8 per annum, or only £5 if capital appreciation is allowed for. The short-term balance of payments loss must therefore be weighed against the long-term gain. The importance of the short-term considerations depends on the state of the balance of payments, *e.g.*, if more investment overseas causes the Government to take deflationary measures the national cost is great.

The Rise of Multinational Companies.

The remarkable expansion since 1960 of international investment, both by foreign companies in the United Kingdom and by British companies abroad, reflects the growing importance of *multinational companies* in the world economy. Some 165 multinationals account for 80 per cent of British private investment abroad. The multinationals tend to dominate the world markets for technologically advanced products. They account for no less than 60 per cent of trade in manufactures in the developed world. Their financial and market power, their global investment strategies, and their ability to avoid national taxation pose a challenge to the economic sovereignty of national governments.

Reform of the International Economic System.

The international monetary system and international liquidity are explained on **G9–10**. The main problem facing the international economic system during the 1960s was an increasing shortage of international liquidity in the face of expanding world trade. This gave a deflationary twist to the world economy and threatened the continuation of free trade. In the 1970s the focus moved to the problems of world inflation and to the international imbalance caused by the increased price of oil, and the resultant threat to economic growth. We trace the issues and events as they unfolded.

Methods of Increasing International Liquidity.

There were three main alternatives: greater flexibility in exchange rates, a rise in the price of gold in terms of all currencies, and the creation of an international paper money.

The advocates of greater flexibility in exchange rates (*see* **G8**) argued that greater flexibility would reduce the need for international liquidity: the size and duration of deficits in the balance of payments would be smaller and therefore the reserves required to tide over deficits would be smaller. The critics of greater flexibility pointed to the possibility of instability in the exchange markets resulting from speculation and to the danger of a cumulative spiral of devaluation and inflation occurring in some countries.

A rise in the gold price would increase international liquidity; first, by increasing the money value of existing and future gold reserves, and second, by encouraging gold production. However, there are certain disadvantages. It helps those countries most which need help least—those with large gold reserves; it represents a victory for the gold speculators and so acts as a stimulus to further hoarding and speculation in the future; it helps in particular the gold-producing countries Russia and South Africa; and finally, it represents a sheer waste of economic resources: gold has little value except as a means of international payment.

The domestic currency of the United Kingdom is not backed by gold: on a one pound note the Governor of the Bank of England promises to pay the bearer on demand the sum of one pound—another pound note! Yet, within Britain, there is complete confidence in the currency, because it is generally acceptable and so convertible into goods and services. Just as gold no longer backs the domestic currency, there is no need for gold in settlement of international payments. All we need is a generally acceptable international currency, *i.e.*, one in which all countries have confidence.

Such a currency could be created by an international authority constituted for this purpose; and it could be made available to deficit countries, which could then pay their creditors in the new currency. In this way the current shortage of international liquidity coud be made good, and indeed gold—Keynes' "barbarous relic"—could be supplanted. There are various difficulties in such a scheme. It involves some loss of national autonomy and the vesting of considerable power in the international authority issuing the paper currency. Decisions have to be made as to which countries should receive the new currency, and in what quantities. And there is a fear that it will enable reckless governments to pursue inflationary policies without the discipline imposed by shortage of reserves, and that their inflation will be infectious. Many variations on this basic scheme have been devised in an attempt to surmount these—largely political—objections.

Special Drawing Rights.

The main function of the IMF has been to provide deficit countries with loans, to be repaid over a certain period (*see* G9–10). The amount of these credit facilities has been increased over time, but the level has remained low in relation to needs, and the IMF facility has therefore been supplemented in various ways. In order to increase the resources available to neutralise the movements of short-term funds which so disrupted the balance of payments at that time, the IMF initiated a scheme for a "Lenders' Club" in 1961. According to the scheme, the main trading countries—the *Group of Ten*—undertook (subject to some control by lending countries over the use of the funds) to make available loans totalling over £2 billion to the IMF for relending to countries of the Group suffering an outflow of short-term funds.

In 1967 the members of the IMF agreed in principle to a scheme according *special drawing rights* (SDRs) to member countries, and in 1970 the scheme came into operation. SDRs are distributed annually to all members in proportion to their quotas with the IMF. They initially had a fixed value in terms of gold, and are generally accepted as a means of payment. Thus a deficit country can use its SDRs to buy the currency of the countries with which it has a deficit, and the surplus countries, in accumulating SDRs, earn a rate of interest on them. This is a movement towards an international paper currency, since the SDRs, unlike IMF loans, do not have to be repaid: they are a permanent addition to international reserves. Allocations were made in 1970, 1971, and 1972; none has been made since then. The scheme was launched on a scale which is small in relation to the size of the problem: the value of SDRs amounted to $10 billion, or 4 per cent of total world reserves, in early 1977. However, it is expected that the SDR will eventually become the principal reserve asset of the international monetary system. The IMF, in its statistics, now values all reserves, including gold and dollars, in terms of SDRs.

The Gold Crisis.

The United States ran a large and persistent payments deficit in the 1950s and 1960s. This was initially financed through the willingness of foreigners to run up dollar balances. However, distrust of the dollar grew, and between 1960 and 1967 U.S. gold reserves were run down, from $19·5 billion to $12·1 b. After the devaluation of sterling in November 1967, the interest of speculators transferred from the pound to the dollar. Since many speculators expected the devaluation of the dollar in terms of gold to be followed by a corresponding devaluation of other currencies there was a growing demand for gold.

After 1961 the central banks of the major trading nations operated a *gold pool* in the London market, whereby they agreed to exchange gold for currencies at existing official exchange rates. But with the growing speculation against the dollar, the system could not be continued without endangering the U.S. gold reserves. The central bankers gathered for a crisis meeting in Washington in March 1968, and decided to terminate the gold pool. They introduced two markets for gold, with private transactions taking place in the free market at a price determined by supply and demand, and transactions among central banks taking place in the official market at the official gold price. The United States was now prepared to convert dollars into gold only for central banks, *i.e.*, to finance a deficit only on its current plus long-term capital account. In this way speculation against the dollar could be controlled; but the problem of the U.S. deficit on current and long-term capital account was still to be solved. The free market price of gold initially rose in response to speculative demand, but, after a currency re-alignment in 1969, tension in the foreign-exchange markets was relaxed and the price fell back to $35 per fine ounce.

The Dollar Crisis.

In 1970 the deficit in the United States balance of payments rose to a record level. This was financed by creditor countries increasing their dollar balances. They had little choice: a large-scale conversion of dollar balances would force the United States to renounce its obligation to supply gold to central banks at $35 per ounce. It became increasingly clear that if the United States failed to reduce its deficit, *e.g.*, by restricting capital outflows or military expenditures abroad, the creditor countries would either have to go on financing American deficits by accumulating dollars or allow their currencies to appreciate in terms of the dollar.

In May 1971, in response to speculative capital movements mainly from the United States to West Germany, the deutschmark was allowed to float upwards, *i.e.*, the authorities allowed its price to rise above the official ceiling. But massive speculation against the dollar continued and in August the United States Government imposed a surcharge on imports and suspended the convertibility of dollars into gold. Currencies of the major trading countries were then allowed to float upwards against the dollar by varying amounts.

Adjustment of Exchange Rates.

The Smithsonian Agreement of December 1971 set the seal in the biggest realignment of exchange rates for nearly a quarter of a century. After negotiations among the Group of Ten it was agreed that the United States would withdraw its surcharge and devalue the dollar against gold if other countries would revalue upwards or at least not devalue. In terms of gold Japan revalued by 8 per cent, West Germany by 5 per cent, 44 countries including the United Kingdom and France did not alter their exchange rates, and 44 countries, all underdeveloped, followed the United States in devaluing by 8 per cent. It was also agreed that there should be a period of greater flexibility in exchange rates, with countries being allowed to alter their exchange rates by 2¼ per cent from the par value in each direction.

The year 1972 saw a rise in the free market price of gold to almost $70 per fine ounce—well above the new official rate of $38. This development reflected the doubts of speculators that the new exchange rates would be permanent. The pound came under speculative pressure in June; and this, combined with a deteriorating balance of payments and the imminence of accession to the EEC, led the British Government to float the pound downwards (*see* G37). Various countries—including Britain, West Germany, Italy and Japan—took measures to try to control speculative capital flows. Partly to prevent speculative capital outflows, interest rates were raised competitively by various governments during the year.

Despite the devaluation of the dollar in December 1971 the U.S. balance of payments on current account actually deteriorated in 1972. Speculation against the dollar broke out early in 1973: the West German central bank was believed to have taken in no less than $6 billion in ten days despite its capital controls. The chief foreign exchange markets were closed, and in February the dollar was devalued by 10 per cent and the Japanese yen—the strongest currency—was allowed to float upwards. In March the EEC countries agreed that their currencies would float jointly against the dollar, but with the currencies of Britain, Ireland and Italy—then in balance of payments difficulties—temporarily floating independently. In early 1974 France left the joint EEC float. Though individual governments intervened to stop their currencies changing value too rapidly or too far, it would be true to say that the international monetary system had entered a new era of flexible exchange rates.

Oil and the International Balance of Payments.

In 1973 the oil-producing countries exported oil worth $27 billion, and their surplus on current account was $13 billion. Their surplus for 1974 was estimated at $56 billion. This surplus involved a corresponding deficit for the oil-importing countries as a group. Such a transformation in the international balance of payments was unprecedented in its scale and speed. It involved a massive transfer of purchasing power from consumers to producers of oil. Since only a small part of the additional oil revenue was spent, this had a severe deflationary effect on the world economy. This effect was not remedied, and it was even compounded by the restrictive monetary and fiscal policies introduced by many of the major countries to stem their oil-induced inflation and balance of payments deficits.

The oil-producing countries have to invest their surplus funds abroad, so that there is a corresponding surplus on the capital account of the oil importing group of countries. However, it is unlikely that the current account deficit of each individual country will be offset by a corresponding capital inflow. There is a danger that these funds will be highly mobile between recipient countries, thus introducing considerable instability in the currency flows of the western oil consumers. There is also a danger that each country will take undesirable and self-defeating measures, *e.g.*, deflation and import controls, to improve its own current account.

The Response to Oil Deficits.

Faced with these problems, the major industrial countries agreed in 1974 that capital transfers among themselves should be used to overcome individual imbalances. Despite this, many governments took restrictive measures to combat both domestic inflation and their balance of payments deficits. In 1974 and 1975 the industrial countries experienced the worst economic recession of the post-war period. For instance, the level of industrial production in the OECD group of countries was 10 per cent lower at the end of 1975 than it had been at the end of 1973. At the end of 1975, unemployment rates were 8 per cent in the United States, 7 per cent in Canada, 5 per cent in Britain, and 4 per cent in France and West Germany.

The economic recession meant that the price of primary products fell—on average by 13 per cent between 1974 and 1975—and the price of oil could not be raised much further. As a result, the terms of trade of the developed countries improved in 1975. The recession also brought a sharp fall in their imports—by 8 per cent in volume terms in 1975—while the OPEC countries increased their imports very rapidly. The net effect was that the OECD countries returned to near balance on current account in 1975. In November the leaders of the six major non-communist countries held a summit meeting in France and agreed to various forms of economic co-ordination and co-operation, *e.g.*, rejecting protectionist, retaliatory *beggar-my-neighbour* trade policies.

Financing the Oil Deficits.

The OPEC group ran a surplus on current account of $56 billion in 1974 and $32 b. in 1975. The United Kingdom attracted $21 b. of these funds in 1974 but only $4 b. in 1975, the United States received $11 b. and $6 b., other countries $21 b. and $17 b., and international organisations $3·5 b. and $4 b. respectively. This last mainly represents the oil producers' financing of the IMF's *oil facility*: a loan fund intended to help countries cope with their oil deficits. By the end of 1975 drawings on the oil facility exceeded $5 billion.

In 1975 the OECD group formally established a *recycling* fund which would be used to help member countries in balance of payments difficulties: since most of the oil surpluses are invested within the OECD group, inter-governmental transfers of funds are possible. In January 1976 the IMF agreed to give all its member countries a temporary increase in borrowing rights of 45 per cent. These various methods of financing oil deficits provide a temporary accommodation but they do not obviate the need for a long-run correction of the new imbalance in world trade and payments.

The Prospects for World Recovery.

In 1976 the world economy began gradually to recover from the recession, and the output of the OECD countries as a whole increased by 5 per cent over the year. Unemployment remained high, but was lowest in those countries (*e.g.*, West Germany) which were able to "export" their unemployment by repatriating migrant workers. The effect of renewed expansion was to reopen the current account deficit of the OECD, to increase the OPEC trade surplus, and to reduce a little the large deficit of the less developed countries as their terms of trade improved. Between the third quarter of 1975 and the fourth quarter of 1976 the price of primary commodities (other than oil) rose on average by 28 per cent.

The deficit countries' strategy of borrowing in 1974, 1975, and 1976 was increasingly seen to be based on a false assumption. They had assumed that their oil deficits were not a normal imbalance requiring domestic adjustment policies, and were relying on a reflation of the world economy to permit repayment of their debts. Unfortunately, the large surplus of the oil producers is likely to be exacerbated by world expansion, implying a corresponding deficit in the rest of the world which will somehow have to be accommodated. It is this problem of a greater trade deficit, together with the fear that expansion will fuel inflation, which is likely to restrain the growth of the major economies up to 1980.

SDRs and Gold.

By the end of 1976 total international reserves were valued at 213 billion SDRs or $246 billion. Of this gold accounted for $41 b., foreign exchange for $175 b., IMF drawing rights for $14 b., and SDRs for $10 b. Originally the SDR had been set equal to the par value of the U.S. dollar, but when the dollar was devalued the SDR maintained its value in terms of gold (SDR1 = 0·889 grammes of fine gold = $1.206). With the general floating of exchange rates after March 1973, the volatility of the SDR in terms of currencies conflicted with the aim of developing it as the principal reserve asset of a reformed international monetary system, and its adoption as the unit of account for all IMF transactions. The IMF therefore introduced, as from July 1974, a new system of valuation based on the value of a group of 17 major currencies in specified proportions. In March 1977 the dollar was worth 0·86 SDRs.

The rapid inflation and great uncertainty in the world economy contributed to the speculative demand for gold; this raised its price many times over in the free market. In December 1974 the London gold price exceeded $180 per fine ounce. However, the IMF in 1975 decided that the official price of gold should be abolished, and that it would auction 25 million oz (equivalent to a year's production) over a period of 4 years. The profits from the sale of the gold would go as aid to less developed countries. The effect of this decision was to depress the free market price of gold, which fell to under $130 in April 1976. It was agreed that central banks should be allowed to buy and sell gold among themselves and on the open market at free market prices, as opposed to the old official price, provided that there is no net accrual of gold by the countries concerned.

Experience of Exchange-rate Flexibility.

It is not clear from recent experience that greater exchange-rate flexibility can produce equilibrium in international payments. It seems that the balance of payments takes a long time—

perhaps two or three years—to adjust to a depreciation of the exchange rate. In the meantime there might be wage increases to compensate for the increase in the cost of living brought about by the depreciation, which in turn tend to neutralise the depreciation. For instance, between the date of the Smithsonian agreement in 1971 and February 1977 the pound had depreciated against other currencies by 43 per cent, the dollar by 5 per cent, the yen had appreciated by 7 per cent and the deutschmark by 30 per cent. Yet, because of their different rates of inflation, the signs were that the British current balance and the competitiveness of British goods were no stronger relative to the German than they had been in December 1971. One of the worrying features of the flexible exchange-rate system is that it not only permits but also generates a far wider spread of inflation rates among the major countries.

Prospects for Further Reform.

The system of correcting international imbalances operating in the post-war period under the articles of the International Monetary Fund became increasingly unsatisfactory in the 1960s. The attempts to maintain stable exchange rates in the face of rapid change in the competitiveness of different countries, increasingly inadequate international liquidity and more massive speculative capital movements produced a series of foreign exchange crises and deflationary internal policies.

The movements in the 1970s towards greater control of "hot money" flows, greater flexibility of exchange rates, and increased international liquidity would help to correct international imbalances. But there were various reasons for believing that they would not provide a permanent solution. Reasons have been given above for questioning whether exchange-rate flexibility can cope with the international imbalances of the 1970s. Moreover, the amount of short-term funds and the scope for speculation with them is greater than ever. The surpluses of the OPEC countries —with their *increase* in funds totalling over $100 billion in the three years 1974–76—present a considerable problem. International companies, with structures that span exchange control barriers, have accumulated vast sums which they move about in search of security and profit. These developments, together with the growth of the Eurodollar market (*see* G10), makes control of short-term capital flows very difficult and gives rise to the possibility of exaggerated and destabilising movements in international exchange rates.

International liquidity grew very rapidly during the early 1970s, mainly because the United States deficit was financed by other countries accumulating dollars. But the fact that official dollar holdings were not in general convertible meant that the apparent increase in liquidity was to a large extent illusory.

The severe imbalance in international payments resulting from the oil crisis made it all the more important that there be international monetary reform to help in the correction of such imbalances without sacrificing full employment, trade and economic growth.

The European Economic Community.

The *European Economic Community* (EEC), otherwise known as the Common Market, was set up by the Treaty of Rome, ratified in 1958. It consisted of six full members—Belgium, France, Holland, Italy, Luxembourg, and Western Germany. Britain had participated in the negotiations which led up to its formation, and had argued in favour of a looser "free trade area" without a common external tariff, and excluding trade in agricultural products. No compromise acceptable to the Six was found, and Britain joined with six other European countries—Austria, Denmark, Norway, Portugal, Sweden, and Switzerland—in forming the *European Free Trade Area* (EFTA).

Economic Arrangements of the EEC.

The EEC forms a common market with no tariffs or trade controls within it and a Common External Tariff (CET). There is a Common Agricultural Policy (CAP), which is maintained by a system of variable import levies setting *threshold prices* on imports of agricultural products from outside the Community, and by means of *intervention prices* at which agricultural products of the Community are purchased. The intervention price is slightly higher than the threshold price of a product. The EEC has a large Budget required mainly for supporting the CAP, *i.e.*, for subsidising Common Market farmers. There is free movement of both capital and labour within the Community, and a certain degree of fiscal harmonisation.

Prospects for Economic Union.

In 1970 the Commission of the European Economic Community published the Werner Plan, a report on the establishment of economic and monetary union of the EEC. The plan aimed at transferring within a decade the principal economic decisions from the national to the Community level, and at establishing within the Community complete freedom of movement of goods, services, persons and capital, with fixed and constant rates of exchange between national currencies or, preferably, a common currency. A centre of decision for economic policy would be established and made responsible to a European parliament.

These proposals have far-reaching economic and political implications, since they involve a considerable reduction of national sovereignty. For instance, the loss of power to correct balance of payments deficits by means of trade controls or variation in the exchange rate implies either that the deficit country's currency should be generally acceptable to its creditors (so that the country within the Community—like a region within a country—simply cannot have a balance of payments problem), or the country must resort to deflation. And even if there is a common currency, it is very likely that resources will concentrate in some regions of the Community to the neglect of other regions, possibly those far from the main centres of production and consumption. Complete mobility of resources is likely to produce a regional problem within the Community just as it can produce a regional problem within a country. But the Community may not, to the same extent as a country, possess the political power and determination required to remedy the problem. It is not surprising, therefore, that the Werner Plan has been pursued in only limited respects and that its eventual implementation is not certain: economic union cannot precede political union.

The Terms of British Entry.

After the resignation in 1969 of General de Gaulle, who had vetoed British membership of the EEC, the path was clear for British entry. In 1971 entry terms were negotiated and published in a White Paper.

Tariffs and trade between Britain and the Community were to be eliminated and the CET imposed on imports from other countries; the changes would be made gradually over five years. Britain also agreed to introduce the CAP in the first year of membership and gradually to raise both threshold and intervention prices over five years. In the meantime, to ensure that prices to producers were equated, levies and compensation payments would be made on agricultural trade between Britain and the rest of the Community. It was agreed that Britain should eventually contribute to the Community Budget according to its share of the total GNP of the Community. Thus Britain would build up its contribution over five years from 9 per cent to about 20 per cent of the total. Britain also had to follow all the EEC countries in introducing a *value added tax* (*see* **G55**). The high British customs duties on oil, alcoholic beverages, and tobacco could be retained and yet avoid contravention of the Treaty of Rome by becoming internal taxes.

Accession to the Community 1973.

The United Kingdom acceded as a full member of the EEC on 1 January 1973. Two of Britain's EFTA partners—Ireland and Denmark—joined on the same date, so forming an expanded Community of nine countries. The economic ties with the Sterling Area were weakened and those with the Community strengthened. For instance in 1972 the Government relaxed restrictions on direct investment by British firms in the EEC and introduced controls on capital transactions with the Overseas Sterling Area. In 1972 trade with the original six members of the EEC accounted for about 23 per cent of total British trade, trade with the EFTA partners about 13 per cent, and with the Commonwealth 19 per cent. After accession, trade with the EEC expanded sharply and the proportion of trade with the former EFTA countries and the Commonwealth fell. Excluding trade with the oil-exporting countries, British trade with the original EEC countries rose from 25 per cent of the total in 1972 to 30 per cent in 1974.

It was on the issue of monetary union that the first major economic problem for Britain arose after entry. In conformity with the Werner Plan (above), the Community agreed in March 1973 to fix the exchange rates between member currencies and to float them together against the dollar (*see* G40). Britain and Italy—then in balance of payments difficulties—insisted that they be permitted temporarily to float independently. There is a danger that the right to vary exchange rates be withdrawn from member countries without there being uniformity in other policies. If there is to be a monetary union, there should also be conformity in industrial relations and incomes policies! For if inflation is more rapid in Britain than in her partner countries, and if Britain is prevented from adjusting the exchange rate or imposing import restrictions against her partners to correct the ensuing balance of payments deficit, the Government might see no alternative but to deflate the economy: stagnation could ensue.

In fact, the "snake in the tunnel"—*i.e.*, Community currencies being permitted to fluctuate against each other only within limited bands—has not proved a success. Countries other than Britain, including France, have dropped out.

Labour Government Policy.

The Labour Party in opposition had criticised the terms of British entry to the EEC negotiated by the Conservative Government. When it came to power in 1974 the Labour Government was determined to renegotiate terms. The Government wanted major changes in the CAP and in the method of financing the Community Budget, and other safeguards of British and Commonwealth interests. Some concessions were negotiated, *e.g.*, in the contributions to the Community Budget and on New Zealand butter. Moreover, the Lomé Convention of March 1975 effectively safeguarded the interests of most poor Commonwealth countries. It was left to the British electorate to vote in a referendum in June 1975 on the renegotiated terms. There was an overwhelming vote in favour of the United Kingdom remaining a member of the EEC: 67 per cent voted "yes" and 33 per cent "no."

The Green Pound.

It is in the British interest that the CAP—with its heavy support of Common Market farmers—be reformed. Community funds are available to protect farmers by buying excess food and building up stocks of food if the free market price falls below the intervention price. As a result "food mountains" have developed, surviving even the drought of 1976, *e.g.*, in the autumn of that year the stockpile of milk products amounted to 1·3 million tonnes.

Nevertheless, the British contribution to the EEC Budget has been much smaller than expected. The *net* contribution (payments *less* benefits) was £104 million in 1973, £31 million in 1974, and there was a net gain of £54 million in 1975. Britain gained from "monetary compensation amounts," *i.e.*, refunds associated with the difference between the values of the pound in the foreign exchange markets and the *green pound*. The green pound is the agreed exchange rate between the pound and the other Community currencies which is used in calculating contributions to the Budget. As the market value of the pound has floated below the agreed green pound rate, so the United Kingdom has had the difference refunded.

2. INTERNAL DEVELOPMENTS

Economic Fluctuations and Government Policies.

We begin with an account of fluctuations in economic activity and of Government attempts to control them.

Government Budgetary Policies.

There is probably no country in the world which has made fuller use than Britain of budgetary policy as a means of stabilising the economy. Since 1941, almost all adjustments to the total level of taxation have been made with the object of reducing the excess in total demand or of repairing a deficit. British Governments have accepted Keynesian principles—first laid down by Lord Keynes—for managing the economy by adjusting the level of taxation and private saving in relation to public expenditure and private investment. This does not mean to say that British policies have always been successful. Apart from the difficulty of deciding when demand is excessive or deficient, there are the difficulties that data are available only with a serious time-lag, and may be inaccurate; that economic events cannot be predicted with any certainty; and that the quantitative effects of Government measures are not easy to estimate.

Economic Fluctuations.

That Governments were unable to eliminate fluctuations in the economy is made clear in the table below. Indeed, some commentators have argued that Governments, misjudging movements in the economy, have tended to do "too much too late" and so have actually accentuated the "stop-go". The table shows that the period 1961–62 was one of recession. 1963–65 upswing and boom, 1966–67 stagnation, 1968 slight reflation, 1969–71 recession and growing unemployment, 1972–73 sharp upswing, and 1974–76 recession. Industrial production was more unstable than GDP and investment more unstable still.

An Electoral Cycle 1958–65?

The sharp pre-election boom of 1958–60 was accompanied by a worsening balance of payments.

ECONOMIC FLUCTUATIONS IN THE BRITISH ECONOMY 1962–76

	Percentage change over previous year in:			
	GDP*	Industrial Production*	Investment*	Number Unemployed†
1962	1·3	0·9	0·2	33·9
1963	3·7	3·0	1·3	18·8
1964	5·9	8·5	16·8	−27·0
1965	2·8	3·0	4·8	−14·1
1966	1·9	1·7	2·5	4·5
1967	2·1	1·2	8·4	54·9
1968	4·0	6·0	4·6	5·0
1969	2·1	2·7	0·4	−1·4
1970	1·9	0·2	2·6	6·3
1971	1·7	0·5	2·4	28·9
1972	2·6	2·2	2·0	10·2
1973	5·8	7·4	4·1	−28·5
1974	−0·2	−3·5	−1·7	−1·8
1975	−2·0	−4·8	−1·2	54·8
1976	0·9	0·1	−4·4	33·2

* At constant prices.
† Average number unemployed during the year.

After the General Election of 1959 economic policy became increasingly deflationary. For instance, in July 1961 the Chancellor introduced a collection of restrictive measures, primarily intended to ease the critical foreign balance, but not without effect on the domestic economy. Bank rate was raised, a 10 per cent surcharge on indirect taxation—the *regulator*—was imposed, the increase in Government spending was cut, and the banks were required to increase their special deposits at the Bank of England.

The recession continued during 1961 and 1962, and in early 1963 there was substantial underutilisation of capacity in many branches of industry. Consequently the economy could respond to the expansionary April budget: national output rose by 6 per cent over the year. By 1964 the economy was beginning to show signs of strain, and there was a rapid deterioration in the balance of trade. However, the 1964 budget was again reflationary, and both industrial production and consumption expenditure responded. By the end of 1964 there were reports of growing labour shortage and the balance of payments was heavily in deficit (*see* **G35**). Nothing was done about it, however, until after the General Election of October. The incoming Government attempted to tackle the balance of payments directly, without recourse to deflation. Its first budget was not deflationary, and full employment was maintained up to and beyond the General Election of 1965.

On the basis of British experience in the decade prior to 1966, it is apparent that either General Elections were timed to coincide with booms or that booms were timed to coincide with elections, or a little of both! The evidence points to the existence of an electoral trade cycle, in which booms were determined by politics and recessions by the balance of payments.

Stagnation 1966–71.

Balance of payments difficulties eventually produced a deflation of the economy. In mid-1966, during yet another run on the pound, the Government panicked. In its "July measures" the Government raised indirect taxation 10 per cent and introduced a variety of deflationary measures. As a result, the economy went into recession in the second half of 1966. Employers now began to lay off workers, and unemployment rose from 1·3 per cent of the labour force in early 1966 to average 2·3 per cent in 1967.

Despite growing unemployment the Chancellor produced a "no-change" April Budget in 1967. The balance of payments prevented him from taking reflationary measures. The balance of payments deteriorated, and, since further deflation was politically unacceptable, the Government devalued the pound. Devaluation was itself strongly reflationary—increasing demand for exports and for import-substitute goods—and had to be accompanied by measures to release resources for these industries. Taxes were raised and monetary restrictions imposed. Further cuts in government spending were announced in December, and again in January, when future defence spending was considerably reduced because of the decision to withdraw forces from East of Suez, and the planned rise in the school-leaving age from 15 to 16 was put off until 1972.

The 1968 budget was highly deflationary. The Chancellor increased taxation to yield an additional £920 million per annum. Most of this came from indirect taxation, with purchase tax and taxes on spirits, wines, tobacco, vehicles, and petrol all raised. Partly to gain support for the incomes policy, the Chancellor raised family allowances and placed a heavy "special levy" for one year on unearned income above £3,000 per annum. In deflating the economy the Chancellor was attempting to reduce private consumer demand so as to free resources for the export market and for replacing imports. His strategy was to produce an overall balance of payments surplus of the order of £500 million before resuming growth, and in this way to break the vicious circle of "stop-go."

In February 1969 Bank Rate was raised, partly to help reduced bank lending and partly to retain short-term funds in London: owing to the shortage of international liquidity (*see* **G39**) central banks competed for short-term capital by raising their discount rates. The April budget was somewhat restrictive; additional taxation was raised mainly by increasing corporation tax to 45 per cent. The budget continued the strategy of improving the balance of payments at the expense of consumption. In June the Chancellor published a Letter of Intent to the IMF stating his intention to limit the annual increase in *domestic credit expansion* to £400 million. Domestic credit expansion is defined as the increase in the money supply adjusted for changes resulting from external transactions. In fact domestic credit expansion turned out to be negative in the financial year 1969/70: credit was extremely tight except for the manufacturing sector. The growth of the economy in 1969 was slight, output being about 2 per cent up on 1968. Investment and consumption stagnated, and the main impetus for expansion came from exports.

In 1970, with the balance of payments improved and an election not far ahead, the Chancellor reduced taxation. Even then, because expenditure was to be restrained and income tax receipts rise with the inflation, he expected a Government budget surplus of £620 million. It could not be claimed that this was an electioneering budget: output was planned to rise by 3·5 per cent in the next year. But the period of severe restraint on private consumption was over.

In October the new Conservative Government announced cuts in both public expenditure and taxation. There was to be a 2·5p cut in the standard rate of income tax and a cut in corporation tax. Prescription charges and dental charges were increased, the subsidy on welfare milk was ended, the price of school meals was raised, and the system of import levies on farm produce was extended. These changes involved a redistribution of income away from the poor. However, a *family income supplement* (FIS) was introduced to provide a cash benefit for poor families with children (*see* **G27**). Although real output grew by only very little in 1970, the Chancellor did not take any measures which would have an immediate reflationary effect.

With business profits and liquidity down and business confidence weak, private investment was low and the economy continued to stagnate. The 1971 budget, therefore, was somewhat reflationary with tax reductions of £550 million in the financial year 1971–72. The Chancellor claimed as his objective an increase in output of about 3 per cent per annum. The main measures were a further cut in corporation tax to 40 per cent, an increase in the tax allowances for children, a reduction in surtax particularly for very high income earners, and a general increase in national insurance benefits and contributions. The economy did not appear to respond to the budget measures, and further but minor reflationary action was taken during the year.

1971 was also a year of important monetary changes. The Bank of England abolished the ceiling for lending by banks and repaid outstanding special deposits. Associated with the large inflow of short-term funds from abroad, the money supply expanded rapidly and Bank Rate fell from 7 per cent to 5 per cent. Many interest rates were thus below the rate of price inflation, so that the effective rate of interest incurred on borrowing could actually be negative! In September the Bank of England introduced new techniques of monetary control which are outlined on **G23**. Also the Government removed all restrictions on hire-purchase, credit sale and rental agreements.

Reflation 1972–73.

By January 1972 the economy showed little sign of reflation and total unemployment in the United Kingdom approached one million. How was the Government's inaction to be explained? Part of the explanation may be that the Chancellor underestimated the degree of recession in 1971 and the delay before his reflationary measures would take effect: when demand increases stocks are first run down before production is expanded, and employment tends to lag behind movements in production. There is the possibility that the economy was not as depressed as the unemployment figures would suggest. Given higher unemployment benefits, workers were choosing to remain unemployed in search of the right job longer than in the past. At the same time, it was argued, SET (*see* **G55**) was causing employers to lay off workers who in previous recessions might have been retained on short-time or to do non-routine maintenance. It is also likely that the Government was purposely timid in its reflationary policy in order to stem the rapid inflation of prices. Nevertheless, the conclusion cannot be avoided that the Government had acted too little and too late.

1972.

The March budget was highly reflationary: in aiming for an annual growth rate of 5 per cent the Chancellor reduced taxation in 1972/3 by an estimated £1·4 billion. The main tax reduction (£960 m.) took the form of increased personal allowances (deducted from income before assessment of income tax). Old age pensions and other National Insurance benefits were to be raised in the autumn, but National Insurance contributions on earnings between £18 and £48 a week were put up to finance this. Rates of purchase tax of 30 and 45 per cent were reduced to 25 per cent in anticipation of its abolition and replacement by a *value added tax* (*see* **G55**). To encourage private investment the Chancellor introduced free depreciation—*i.e.* an allowance of 100 per cent of investment expenditure against income liable to tax in the year of the investment—for all investment in plant and machinery, and an initial allowance of 40 per cent for expenditure on industrial buildings (*see* **G13**).

The reflationary budget had an effect primarily on consumption. Between 1971 and 1972 private consumption grew in real terms by 6 per cent. Real expenditure on consumer durables—encouraged by the ready availability of credit and the abolition of restrictions on hire-purchase—increased by no less than 17 per cent. The money supply grew rapidly until mid-1972, and this kept interest rates down. Despite the low interest rates and the Budget incentives, gross investment did not pick up significantly. The danger of a "consumption led", rather than "export led", reflation of the sort initiated in 1972 is that it may impair the balance of payments. Indeed, a remarkable expansion of imports of consumer goods and in particular consumer durables did take place in 1972 (*see* **G37**).

1973.

Although unemployment was falling sharply and production growing rapidly, in early 1973 there was still plenty of plant capacity and labour in reserve: unemployment stood at over 700,000. Measures were urgently needed to improve the deteriorating balance of payments, but there was no case for restraining the economy, since idle resources were available to produce additional exports and import substitutes. The Chancellor in his March Budget stated his objective to be sustained economic growth, maintained at an annual rate of 5 per cent over the following year. To this end he presented a fairly neutral budget.

The money supply had expanded very rapidly until mid-1972, and the Chancellor proposed to continue the monetary restraint imposed in the second half of that year. Probably this had as much to do with the need to raise interest rates so as to prevent a capital movement out of sterling as with domestic policy. The public sector borrowing requirement was expected to be no less than £4 4 billion in the financial year 1973/4. To meet this, it seemed that the Government would have to accept rapid increases either in the money supply or in interest rates. In the event, both occurred.

The most immediate economic problem facing the Government in 1973 was the rapid inflation of costs and prices. It could be said, therefore, that the most important test of the budget would be its success or failure in gaining public support for the Government's pay and prices policy (*see* **G52**). Here the Chancellor could have done more: he was not willing to increase family allowances, nor to subsidise the foods which had risen sharply in price, nor to withdraw the £300 million a year tax concession for surtax payers and those receiving investment income which he had announced in his 1972 Budget to take effect in 1973.

Growth in the economy slowed down during 1973, coming almost to a halt by the end of the year. Although unemployment did not drop below 500,000, unfilled vacancies rose to the record level of 360,000 in the fourth quarter. Production was increasingly held back by supply bottlenecks, owing to shortages of labour in certain places and with certain skills, and of materials and components. The startling rise in the price of oil and of other imports acted to deflate the economy, *i.e.*, these higher prices meant lower real incomes and therefore a fall in the demand for other goods and services. But the oil shortage also curtailed production. To prevent the growth of excess demand in the economy, the Chancellor introduced a December budget. His most important measure was to cut public spending, particularly on capital projects, beginning in 1974 and amounting to £1·2 b. in the financial year 1974–75. Severe hire-purchase and other credit controls were also re-established.

Slumpflation 1974–77.

The period 1974–77 was one of "Slumpflation": a remarkable combination of the most rapid inflation and the most severe recession of the post-war period.

1974.

1974 saw a simultaneous failure to meet all four main policy objectives—of adequate economic growth, full employment, a stable balance of payments and stable prices. The volume of consumer spending fell for the first time in 20 years, GDP rose year-on-year by only a small amount, and by January 1975 over 700,000 people were unemployed, 140,000 more than at the beginning of the previous year. Despite this, the balance of payments deficit on current account was the largest ever recorded (*see* **G38**), and retail prices in January 1975 were over 19 per cent higher than in January 1974 (*see* **G50**). Production in the first quarter fell by 5 per cent, affected as it was by the three-day working week, imposed by the Government in response to the overtime ban and subsequent strike in the coal mining industry (*see* **G53**). Shortage of coal was now the problem: indeed, the restrictions on exports of oil to Britain had been relaxed. With the fall in production there was a running down of stocks, a diversion of exports to the home market and a sharp increase in imports. The trade deficit increased to unprecedented levels; nearly £1·3 billion in the first three months. The miners' strike was settled and full-time working was restored by the incoming Labour Government in March.

Because the oil-producing countries could absorb only a small part of their increased balance of payments surpluses, and because any feasible reduction by western countries of their oil consumption could make only a relatively minor impact on the surpluses, the British Government felt that industrial countries should agree to collectively run current account deficits and finance them by borrowing from the oil producers (*see* **G38**). This was the alternative to taking strongly deflationary measures which could only exacerbate the recession.

Three weeks after taking office the new Chancellor presented his first budget. Overall, the budget was only mildly deflationary in its intended effort on demand. Taxation was to be raised by about £1·5 billion. The standard rate of income tax was raised by 3p to 33p in the pound and the income at which higher rates were to be paid was lowered; but personal tax allowances and child allowances were increased. Corporation tax was raised to 52 per cent, and employers were to pay a higher flat rate contribution to finance the higher National Insurance benefits announced in the budget (*see* **G26**). The Chancellor announced various measures to reduce tax avoidance. Tax relief of interest payments would apply only to the interest on a mortgage of up to £25,000 in respect of an owner-occupier's main house. The main forms of additional planned expenditure were higher retirement pensions, £500 million additional subsidies on basic foodstuffs, and provision for an expanded local authority housing programme. The Chancellor announced very large increases in the prices of coal, electricity, steel, postage and rail fares, in order to reduce the growing need for State subsidisation of these nationalised industries. As it turned out, this express intention to run down the level of subsidies (except on food) did not materialise; some price increases were delayed until 1975.

The second budget of the year, in July, was mildly expansionary. Value added tax was reduced from 10 per cent to 8 per cent; the Regional Employment Premium (*see* **G49**) was doubled; dividend controls (*see* **G53**) were eased. The main aim of yet another supplementary budget in November was to bring relief to companies which were suffering heavy taxation on "paper profits." These had resulted from inflation driving up the value of their stocks of goods and materials, which meant an increase in their declared profits. It was argued that at least part of this was an unreal increase, because the cost of replacing these stocks had gone up *pari passu*. The budget also eased some of the provisions of the Price Code (*see* **G53**), increased VAT on petrol to 25 per cent, made minor income tax concessions, and announced an increase in pensions and related benefits and in family allowances.

Though GDP recovered from its first quarter level, the recovery was very weak, and over the year as a whole it was virtually stagnant. This reflected mainly the weakness of private sector demand, since public expenditure rose through the year. Consumers' expenditure was down slightly. The demand for cars fell sharply, reflecting the higher cost of petrol. Factors affecting the more general sluggishness of consumption were the stricter hire-purchase controls introduced late in 1973 and the negligible rise in personal disposable income through 1974. The biggest slump in demand was in private investment. Though investment in manufacturing rose by nearly 10 per cent, housing investment shot down by nearly 25 per cent. Investment in the construction, distribution and other service industries also fell. Stockbuilding was lower than in 1973.

1975.

The picture in early 1975 was, therefore, a gloomy one. Weak or even falling output and final sales in the fourth quarter of 1974 was reflected in the unemployment figures. By February 1975 736,700 (or 3·2 per cent of the workforce) were unemployed. Despite this significant weakening in the pressure of demand, inflation showed little sign of slowing down.

One of the most alarming features of the situation was the massive increase in the public sector financial deficit. In the financial year 1974–75 it had risen to £5·5 billion, and was forecast to reach £8·9 billion in 1975–76. This latter figure would represent more than 10 per cent of the value of our total national output. This huge deficit was partly due to inflation affecting both the income and expenditure sides of the account, and thus magnifying the existing deficit. But it also represented a real increase in public expenditure. Such a deficit might be financed either by increasing the money supply or by selling government securities. Whichever way it was to be financed, the government obviously did not want to encourage the high rate of inflation. Additionally if there were large sales of government securities, interest payments would constitute a large claim on the resources of the country.

In the budget of April 1975 the Chancellor announced that he planned to cut back the public deficit to 8 per cent of national output in 1975–76 and to 6 per cent in 1976–77. To do this he increased taxation in 1975, and aimed to reinforce this by cutting back public spending in the following year, to the tune of £900 million. Defence spending was to be cut as were food and housing subsidies. Subsidies on nationalised industry prices were to be reduced in 1975, and probably phased out altogether in 1976. Income tax rates were raised by 2p in the pound, so bringing the standard rate up to 35p. This was partly offset by increasing the amount of income which could be earned before tax was levied. Though the standard rate of VAT remained at 8 per cent, it was raised to 25 per cent on most domestic electrical appliances, radios, television sets, hi-fi equipment, cameras, furs, jewellery, and on other "luxury" goods. Excise duties were raised substantially. The company sector, already in difficulties, did not suffer as much as the personal sector. Corporation Tax was unchanged, and no surcharge on advance payment was levied. There was to be some slight further relief from the Price Code provisions. More money was made available for retraining workers, and a temporary employment subsidy was planned to encourage the deferment of redundancies. Some capital gains tax relief was announced for farmers and small businessmen. A new scheme of family allowances was proposed for the future, which, amongst other things, would give an allowance for the first child.

This was one of the harshest of recent budgets. Yet it would be hard to call it excessively restrictive. It still meant the biggest peacetime deficit in government accounts on record, and was intended to cut the flow of spending in the economy by only about £330 million by the end of 1975. The hope was that it would create enough spare capacity to enable the U.K. to take advantage of the expected upswing of world trade in 1976.

Though there was some recovery of world trade towards the end of the year, it was less strong than had been expected. The volume of U.K. exports fell between 1974 and 1975. The major components of domestic demand also declined. Although real personal disposable income was slightly higher, consumers' expenditure on durable goods declined and saving increased. Thus the ratio of saving to real personal disposable income rose to 14 per cent, compared with 13 per cent in 1974, which was itself a very high figure. One explanation for this is that people were trying to restore the real value of their assets which had been eroded by inflation. Another is that people felt exceptionally uncertain in the face of rising unemployment. Uncertainty about the future together with very low profit margins and a severe liquidity shortage explained negative stockbuilding (*i.e.*, a running down of stocks) by industrialists and also the fall in manufacturing investment. Investment as a whole remained more or less stable because of an increase in private housebuilding and investment in mining and quarrying. The current spending of public authorities expanded in volume terms—and, because of inflation, very rapidly in value terms—but not sufficiently to offset the fall in private demand. Despite the rapid inflation, the money supply grew by only 8 per cent over the year. As a result of the contraction in real demand, GDP fell by 1·7 per cent and industrial production by 5 per cent.

1976.

Although there was some evidence of recovery, the economy was still in deep recession in early 1976. Unemployment, which reacts with a lag to changes in production, was still rising and in February 1976 exceeded 1·2 million. In that month the Chancellor announced a £215 million package designed to create or save 70,000 jobs. Money was put into industrial investment and construction, and into the temporary employment subsidy and a job creation scheme. Inflation, though it eased off, was still uncomfortably high compared to that suffered by our major competitors. Between December 1975 and February 1976 retail prices rose at an annual rate of over 12 per cent. The problem faced by the government was to prevent any recovery leading to higher inflation and to further balance of payments difficulties.

The Budget of April 1976 was broadly neutral in its intent. The Chancellor's intention was to give a mild stimulus to the economy by encouraging the demand for consumer durables, while at the same time keeping a tight hold on inflationary pressure. The higher VAT rate (which applied to consumer durables and luxury goods) of 25 per cent was halved to 12½ per cent, but the duty on beer, spirits, wine, cigarettes, cigars and petrol was increased. Pensions were to be increased from November (*see* **G26**), and Family Income Supplement (*see* **G27**) was to be raised from July. The temporary employment subsidy was increased from £10 to £20, and the scheme was extended by 4½ months until the end of December 1976. An extra £40 million was made available for various industrial schemes receiving government aid. The profit level at which smaller companies qualify for the preferential rate of corporation tax was raised (*see* **G55**) and tax relief for stock appreciation was continued. In the field of personal taxation age allowances were increased by £60 for single people and by £130 for married couples. The child allowance was raised by £60.

There were two novel aspects to the Budget. The first was an offer of tax cuts, through increased personal allowances (*see* **G55**), conditional upon obtaining trade union agreement to a new round of incomes policy (*see* **G54**). The second major innovation was in the control of public expenditure. In the tax year 1975–76 both government revenue and, even more so, spending increased by more than had been anticipated in the 1975 Budget. The result was that the public sector's borrowing requirement was £10,770 million, representing $11\frac{1}{2}$ per cent of GNP; this was 16 per cent above the predicted level. The unanticipated increase was partly a result of the recession being more severe than was thought likely and consequently higher social security payments and the like; but probably more important was inflation magnifying the difference between revenue and expenditure. The borrowing requirement for 1976/7 was forecast at £11,960 million, which it was expected would be a smaller proportion of GNP than the 1975/6 deficit. When Supply Estimates were presented with the Budget, they were calculated on the basis of price levels prevailing at the time. As inflation proceeded, therefore, Supplementary Estimates were needed, and of course the greater the inflation the greater this unplanned expenditure. The introduction of strict advance *cash limits* was therefore announced. Three quarters of central government expenditure, other than social security benefits, was to be subject to these. There would also be stricter control of grants to local government and of the spending of nationalised industries.

During the course of the year, inflation moderated (*see* G50) and there was a slight rise in output, which was 1·6 per cent higher in the last quarter of 1976 than in the last quarter of 1975. The fastest rising component of demand was exports, whose volume increased by $8\frac{1}{2}$ per cent. Consumers' expenditure rose by $\frac{1}{2}$ per cent, despite a fall of $1\frac{1}{2}$ per cent in real personal disposable income. This meant a fall in the personal savings ratio, from 14 per cent in 1975 to 12 per cent in 1976—still a high level compared to the 1960s. Spending increased most on durable goods, especially cars and motor-cycles, and was financed by borrowing. There was a rise in net credit extended for the first time in two years. Most other items of consumer spending were stagnant. Investment fell by 4 per cent, there being particularly large falls in manufacturing industry and private services. There was, however, some recovery in the second half of the year. There was also some fall in stocks held, especially in manufacturing, which implied that employers were far from sanguine about the immediate prospects for economic recovery. Despite the moderate increase in demand, there were still large margins of unused capacity, and unemployment rose by 150,000 to 1·42 million in February 1977: an unprecedentedly high level for the post-war period. This rise was, however, less than a third as large as the increase in unemployment in 1975.

Later in the year, the Chancellor took further measures. In July he announced £1 billion cuts in previous public spending estimates for 1977/78, whilst a further £1 billion was pruned off the estimates for that year in a December mini-budget. This budget also announced 10 per cent increases in alcohol and tobacco duties from 1 January 1977, and the sale of some of the government stake in British Petroleum. This latter decision was confirmed in the March 1977 Budget, with the Government still holding 51 per cent of the shares.

Many commentators argued that during the year fiscal policy, as it had been known, ceased to exist. It was no longer primarily seen as the instrument with which to manage domestic demand fluctuations. Rather the concern was with controlling the public sector borrowing requirement, with reducing cost inflation and the balance of payments deficit, and at the end of the year with satisfying our IMF creditors by imposing limits on both the public sector borrowing requirement (p.s.b.r.) and domestic credit expansion (d.c.e.). Certainly the Government achieved some measure of success in reducing p.s.b.r. From a figure of £10·5 billion in 1975, which represented over 11 per cent of GNP, in 1976 it was brought down to £10·3 billion or less than 10 per cent of GNP. Cash limits on public spending were undoubtedly in large part responsible for this success. Early in 1977 it was announced that they would be extended to some items of expenditure not previously covered, such as new housing investment and slum clearance. Monetary policy was not so successfully controlled, and for a period in the summer of 1976 the money supply was expanding at a rate of almost 30 per cent per annum. Over the year as a whole, however, it rose by about 10 per cent. The restriction in the latter part of the year, in the face of a huge p.s.b.r., pushed up interest rates: in October the Bank of England's minimum lending rate rose to a record 15 per cent.

1977

In early 1977, then, the economy was still in recession. Output growth was sluggish, and unemployment had not started to fall. The rate of inflation, though lower than it had been a year earlier, was still uncomfortably high in comparison with our major competitors. The Government was committed to strict limits on the public sector borrowing requirement and on domestic credit expansion, as a result of the IMF loan and subsequent " safety net " arrangements.

In the March 1977 Budget the Chancellor announced that he hoped to cut p.s.b.r. to £7·5 billion for the 1977/78 financial year. There were to be tax cuts of £1·29 billion, to be achieved by raising tax thresholds and increasing personal allowances (*see* G55). He also promised to reduce the standard rate of income tax from 35p in the pound to 33p, if satisfactory agreement could be reached with the trade unions on a new stage of incomes policy from August. This would take another £960 million off the tax bill. V.A.T. remained unchanged, but the duties on such items as cigarettes and the vehicle excise tax were increased. Corporation tax was not altered, though extra relief was given to small companies, whilst the scheme for relief on stock appreciation (see G49) was continued. The temporary employment subsidy, which had been due to expire, was extended for the whole 1977/78 tax year. The Government calculated that the scheme had so far saved 200,000 jobs. They regarded such direct policies against unemployment as effective and safer than general reflation, which might have alarming inflationary consequences. The Government's strategy hinged on obtaining a new round of pay restraint from the summer. If this could be obtained there was the prospect of at least very small increases in output and in real personal disposable income over the year.

Criticism of Monetary Policy.

Many commentators felt that the impact of Competition and Credit Control (*see* G23) and the associated supplementary deposits scheme had been minimal. Indeed, the latter was suspended in February 1975, though it was reintroduced in November 1976. They felt that the basic problem was the unwillingness of the authorities to curtail the rate of growth of bank deposits, that the cash was always provided to allow this growth. Critics also pointed out that the Government had retained control over short-term interest rates, and that in 1973–74 it had broken one of its new rules. It had intervened to raise the minimum lending rate without reference to the Treasury Bill rate in order to prevent a drain of capital abroad. The rest of the market followed this increase, with the exception of the clearing banks, who kept their interest rates down. Other financial institutions could therefore borrow funds from the banks and lend them at a much higher rate to property speculators. When the property boom collapsed with many debts unpaid the result was general financial panic. The Government had to intervene to support the banks, and in August 1976 introduced measures into Parliament designed to control the non-bank deposit-taking institutions.

Prospects for Economic Growth.

There has not only been dissatisfaction with the uneven way in which the economy has grown. There has also been increasing dissatisfaction with the rate of growth achieved in the economy since the war. The economies of most other industrial countries have expanded at a much faster rate (*see* G12). To try to improve our growth performance, the Labour Government introduced the National Plan in 1965. By setting a target annual rate of growth until 1970, it aimed to bolster firms' expectations and hence their investment and to co-ordinate their decisions. Unanticipated balance of payments difficulties meant that the Plan was short-lived, but some of the institutions associated with the Plan survived. The National Economic Development Council had been established in 1962 to stimulate a more systematic study of the problems involved in securing a faster rate of growth. Twenty-one Economic Development Committees for different industries were set up under its umbrella.

(i) The National Enterprise Board.

In 1974 The Labour Government published a White Paper entitled *The Regeneration of British Industry*, setting out ideas which found their legislative expression in *The Industry Act* of 1975. Underlying this Act was the feeling that private enterprise, on its own, had not done enough to stimulate a high rate of growth. The Act aimed to remedy this by setting up *The National Enterprise Board*. Its proposed functions were to assist the establishment, development or maintenance of any industrial enterprise or industry, to extend public ownership into profitable areas of manufacturing, to promote industrial democracy in undertakings controlled by it, and to hold and manage the securities of any other property in public ownership. The Board was not, without the consent of the Minister for Industry, to acquire shares if this would give the Board control of more than 30 per cent of the voting rights of the company, or to invest more than £10 million in the shares of any one company. The Board's borrowings were to be limited to £700 million, which could be increased to £1,000 million by order. These sums are very modest in relation to the market value of the share capital of major British firms. Funds for aid which the Minister directed the Board to give were to be additional to the above figures. Both the Minister and the Treasury were to ensure that the Board earned an "adequate" return on capital employed. The Act also contained provisions for the compulsory disclosure of information by firms both to the Minister and to trade unions. It also introduced the idea of voluntary *planning agreements*, which private companies might enter into with the Government. In return such companies would be assured of regional development grants at the rates prevailing at the time the agreement was made. Critics argued both that the Act was doctrinaire socialism and that it was not proved that such state intervention would have more favourable effects than the workings of free private enterprise. As presently financed, it is clear that the National Enterprise Board cannot proceed much further with the extension of public ownership, since it has available only £225 million per annum until 1980. Guidelines issued in early 1976 further restricted its ability to act without reference to the Secretary of State for Industry. He must be consulted in all cases involving share purchases of more than £½ million if shareholders object.

(ii) An Approach to Industrial Strategy.

In 1975 a White Paper, entitled *An Approach to Industrial Strategy*, set out the Government's general views on planning for growth. It envisaged a systematic and continuing study of the past performance of thirty or so sectors of manufacturing, assessing the implications for medium-term growth assumptions. It further suggested consultations about these studies between government and industry at the national, industry, and company level. At present it is too early to judge whether anything will come of this.

Even before the NEB was effectively operational, state acquisitions in the private sector had proceeded apace. Normally the government had provided financial help to ailing companies on condition of taking a shareholding, under the provisions of the Conservatives' 1972 Industry Act. By early 1976 the companies which were wholly or partly state-owned included Ferranti, Alfred Herbert, British Leyland, Rolls Royce, Dunford and Elliot, Triang and Harland and Wolff.

(iii) British Oil Production.

The discovery of oil in British waters has implications for Britain's long-term growth prospects. The oil crisis of 1973 and the subsequent rocketing of the price of oil drove the economy into recession and engendered concern about Britain's medium-term growth rate. Whilst these early fears may have been somewhat exaggerated, so also might expectations of a bonanza in the late 1970s from oil production in British waters. Though by early 1976 extraction of British oil had fallen behind schedule, it was still expected that by 1980 production would be enough for the U.K. to be almost self-sufficient. But there were a number of doubts about the costs of exploitation and about the extent to which the Government would have already mortgaged future returns by heavy borrowing abroad. By 1975 new investment in exploration had slowed down dramatically. This was a result largely of the general financial climate and of cost escalation. It was therefore uncertain how long after 1980 the U.K. would continue to be self-sufficient. Unless new oil-fields were discovered, it was estimated that production would decline from a peak of 2·3 million barrels per day in 1981 to only 0·8 million in 1990.

Meanwhile the Government was trying to ensure that the state got a substantial share of the returns from offshore oil extraction. A major concern was the large degree of foreign ownership of the oil companies involved in the operations. In February 1975, therefore, a Bill was introduced into Parliament, which proposed a *petroleum revenue tax* of 45 per cent and royalties of 12½ per cent. Corporation tax was to be deducted from the residue at the standard rate. It was envisaged that this would allow the oil companies a 20 per cent return on capital. Concern had been expressed that such a tax system would discourage exploitation of the "marginal fields", that is the smaller oil-fields which might not justify the huge initial expenditure needed to make them productive. Several safeguards were, therefore, proposed. No petroleum revenue tax would be levied until a field had earned back 175 per cent of its capital outlay. Fields returning less than 30 per cent on investment after paying p.r.t. would have the tax refunded. There was also to be discretionary provision to return all or part of the 12½ per cent royalties. The Government reiterated its intention to press for 51 per cent state participation in the oil-fields. It was later made clear that the licensing for new operations, due in the spring or early summer of 1976, would involve a 51 per cent stake for the British National Oil Corporation. Prior to this, participation agreements were concluded with some of the smaller oil companies like Gulf and Conoco.

(iv) Pressures on the Industrial Sector.

Between 1961 and 1974 employment outside industry increased by over one-third relative to employment in industry; *i.e.* employment grew much faster in private services and in public services and utilities. This larger non-industrial sector imposed extra demands on industrial production. Capital goods for investment in services had to be provided from the output of the industrial sector, whilst more industrial production was needed for consumers employed in the services and elsewhere. Thus less was left over for investments in industry itself and for industrial exports. This meant an inadequate growth of industrial capacity. Thus when the Government attempted to stimulate the economy, bottlenecks quickly developed and imports of consumer goods increased rapidly. The result was balance of payments difficulties, which were only partially alleviated by increasing exports of services like insurance, and therefore the government took deflationary action. This vicious circle could only be broken by an upsurge in industrial investment, which was prevented by declining profitability.

Some commentators have argued that the problem was a direct result of the growth in public sector employment. This had to be paid for either by workers or private employers, and trade unions made sure that it was the employers; if, for example, income tax was raised, this was passed on in successful wage demands. The result was declining profitability. This analysis is at best speculative. It is not, for example, at all evident that public sector employment has grown nearly as rapidly as implied. In certain activities such as local government there was a very rapid growth, but overall the ratio of public sector to total employment increased only modestly—from 23·9 per cent in 1961 to 27·2 per cent in 1974. Similarly over the same period public sector spending increased only from 21·5 per cent to 26·8 per cent of gross domestic product. On the other side it was argued that such figures understate the true change: the spending figures are in constant prices; in current money terms the change was more striking because of the *relative price effect*, *i.e.*, items like teachers' and civil servants' salaries rising faster than the general price level. The figures also exclude transfers from people who produce to those who do not, such as pensioners. Finally, it was argued that the claim of the public sector on output which could be sold increased by almost 50 per cent between 1961 and 1974, thus reducing the resources available for industrial investment. If such arguments are borne out by further investigations, a conflict between industrial growth and the humanitarian aims of society—such as the provision of health services and of education—may arise. But before that argument begins, research will be needed into how productively the extra resources apparently claimed by the public sector have been used.

Regional Planning.

Much publicity has been given since the early 1960s to the varying degrees of prosperity and levels of unemployment in the United Kingdom (*see* **G11–12**). Government measures are necessary to reduce disparities and probably even to prevent them from growing.

There are essentially two ways of tackling the problem of regional imbalances: taking jobs to the people or bringing people to the jobs. In so far as the latter alternative is chosen, the Government should encourage the mobility of labour, *e.g.*, through retraining schemes or a rehousing subsidy. However, the migration of population may damage community life in the denuded areas, and cause congestion, housing shortages, and overcrowding in the booming regions. The Government can create employment opportunities in the relatively depressed regions in various ways. It can try to induce expanding industries to set up new plants in these regions by offering tax incentives; it can authorise additional expenditure on public works —*e.g.*, by accelerating road-building programmes —to provide additional employment; it can place orders for the goods it needs—*e.g.* defence contracts—where work is required. It can also use physical controls on expansion in the better-off areas; since 1947 factory building over a particular size, which has been changed from time to time, has required the granting of an *Industrial Development Certificate.*

(i) Labour's Policy.

On taking office in October 1964, the Labour Government made regional planning the responsibility of its Department of Economic Affairs. Britain was divided into eight regions, with the intention of producing a plan for each region. The Government also established two kinds of planning body: regional economic planning Councils and Boards to advise on and co-ordinate the planning of each region.

Labour Government policy to cure regional unemployment took the following forms. Various measures to defer public construction programmes excluded the *Development Areas.* Fiscal incentives to locate industry in the depressed regions were given, *e.g.*, the cash grants provided in 1966 for new plants and machinery in manufacturing were at twice the national rate in the Development Areas. By contrast, office building in the main conurbations, London and Birmingham, was strictly limited. To encourage the mobility of labour, the Government introduced redundancy compensation and achieved some expansion in both public and private training facilities. In 1967 regional differentials in the selective employment tax were introduced (*see* **G56**). Under this scheme manufacturers in Development Areas were paid £1·50 per week for each full-time adult male employee and lower amounts in respect of other workers; so giving the Development Areas a wage cost advantage in manufacturing of 5–10 per cent.

In 1965/6 special assistance to industry in the Development Areas was only £29 million. The estimate for the financial year 1970/1 was £309 million; taking the form mainly of the Regional Employment Premium and investment grants.

(ii) Conservative Policy.

In 1970 the incentive to invest in the Development Areas was affected by the Conservative Government's replacement of cash grants by a system of initial allowances against tax. Whereas cash grants had been 40 per cent of investment in plant and machinery in Development Areas and 20 per cent in other areas, there was now to be free depreciation in Development Areas and 60 per cent initial allowances in other areas.

Early in 1972, with the national unemployment rate no less than 4·0 per cent, unemployment rates in Northern Ireland, Scotland, Wales and Northern England had reached appalling levels. At the time of the Budget the Government produced a White Paper on regional development. In the Budget the Chancellor had introduced free depreciation throughout the country on all investment in plant and machinery (*see* **G45**): the previous preferential treatment of investment in Development Areas was therefore ended. Instead *regional development grants*, in the form of cash payments towards investment in plant, machinery and buildings, were introduced. These were to be made by *regional industrial development boards*, at rates equal to 22 per cent of investment expenditure in Special Development Areas and 20 per cent in Development Areas and Intermediate Areas. The Government also proposed in four years to triple expenditure on retraining facilities, and to pay a worker who had undergone retraining a rehousing grant of £600 if he moved house to take a new job; and also £400 to any worker in an assisted area who moved house to take a new job. It should be remembered, however, that strong measures were necessary merely to replace the Labour Government's system of cash grants, and the Regional Employment Premium which was to be phased out beginning in 1974. The incoming Labour Government, however, announced that the Regional Employment Premium would be retained but it was finally replaced by more selective measures in 1977 (*see* **G46–7**).

Slumps normally affect the poorest regions most. This was not so in the recession of 1974–1975. Between mid-1974 and mid-1975 unemployment rose by 47 per cent in the development regions, as against 81 per cent in the unassisted areas. It is doubtful whether this was due to government regional policy. It is more likely to be attributable to the following factors. North Sea oil created jobs in Scotland and the North East. Nationalised industries, which tend to be concentrated in the poor areas, cut back their labour force by relatively little. The slump in the demand for consumer durables and cars badly affected production and therefore employment in one of the better-off areas—the West Midlands.

Though regional problems remain, recent studies have shown that IDCs, financial incentives, and REP have to a limited extent mitigated them.

Inflation.

(i) Wages and Prices.

Retail prices continued to edge upwards in the 1960s (*see* **G19–20**). In 1975 they were 150 per cent higher than in 1963. Very little of this increase can be attributed to an increase in import prices. To explain the inflation we must look at the behaviour of labour costs. Between 1963 and 1975 the nationally negotiated weekly wage rates rose by 232 per cent, and weekly earnings—including overtime payments and payments negotiated on the factory floor—by 249 per cent. Since the increase in productivity during this period was slow, income from employment per unit of output (indicating labour costs per unit of output) rose by about 150 per cent. These increased costs were passed on to the public in the form of increased prices, so that real earnings rose by only 40 per cent. The table shows annual average prices, earnings, real earnings, and also real disposable incomes (*i.e.*, the purchasing power of total personal incomes after income tax), all as indexes with 1963 = 100.

AVERAGE RETAIL PRICES, WEEKLY EARNINGS, REAL WEEKLY EARNINGS AND REAL DISPOSABLE INCOMES
1963 = 100

	Retail prices	Weekly earnings	Real weekly earnings	Real disposable incomes
1964	103·3	107·1	103·7	103·9
1965	108·2	115·1	106·4	106·3
1966	112·5	122·5	108·9	108·6
1967	115 3	126·2	109·5	110·0
1968	120·7	136·8	113·3	112·0
1969	127·2	147·5	115·9	112·8
1970	135·3	164·4	121·5	116·8
1971	148·1	182·8	123·4	119·9
1972	158·6	205·7	129·7	128·7
1973	173·2	234·1	135·2	136·7
1974	201·0	275·2	136·9	138·1
1975	249·5	349·1	139·8	139·2
1976	290·9	399·0	137·2	137·1

(ii) The Growing Inflation.

A disturbing feature of the table is the growth in the rate of inflation in Britain after 1967. Between 1968 and 1970 retail prices rose by an average of 5·9 per cent per year, between 1970 and 1971 by 9·5 per cent, between 1971 and 1972 by 7·1 per cent, between 1972 and 1973 by 9·2 per cent, between 1973 and 1974 by 16 per cent and between 1974 and 1975 by 24·1 per cent. The increase in average weekly earnings also accelerated.

Why has there been this acceleration in the rate of inflation? In 1968 and 1969, it resulted partly from the increase in import prices consequent upon the devaluation of the pound in November 1967 (*see* **G35**), partly from the increase in indirect taxes introduced after devaluation in order to free resources for exports (*see* **G44**), and partly from the spurt in money wages when the Government's incomes policy weakened (*see* **G52**). But in 1970 the blame could be placed squarely on the " wage explosion ". Normally money wages rise more rapidly the greater the pressure of demand in the labour market (*see* **G20**). But with unemployment high in 1970, pressure of demand for labour could not be the explanation. Rather, the wage explosion appeared to reflect a general increase in militancy by trade unionists angered by the near-stagnation of real earnings and real disposable incomes after 1967 and possibly influenced by events in other countries (*see* below). Once begun it was maintained by the growth of expectations that prices would continue to rise rapidly.

In 1970 there was a sharp increase in real earnings (by 5 per cent), implying a decline in the share of profits. This share (gross trading profits as a proportion of domestic income) is normally low during a recession, but the share in 1970 dropped to 10 per cent compared with 14 per cent in the recession of 1962. The share rose in 1971 when the increase in labour costs had a delayed effect on prices: retail prices were up by no less than 9 per cent on 1970. There was a danger that this in turn might set off further wage demands and so maintain, or even accelerate, a vicious spiral of inflation. Indeed, that is what happened in 1972. Both wage and price increases accelerated, and the Government was forced to intervene in November by introducing a pay and price standstill (*see* **G52**). The inflation of 1972 was caused mainly by increased wage payments, although the effective devaluation of the pound in June and the rising world prices of food and raw materials also contributed, both directly to prices and indirectly through their effects on wage demands. The rising price of imports—particularly of food which accounted for half of the 10 per cent increase in the cost of living between end-1972 and end-1973—was mainly responsible for the inflation during 1973, but labour costs also rose markedly. There was a temporary slowdown in the rate of inflation following the July 1974 budget, but apart from this it accelerated fairly steadily through 1974 as a whole. Whilst import prices had been the fastest growing item of costs for the two years up to the middle of 1974, by then domestic wage and salary costs had taken over this role. Average earnings increased by no less than 25 per cent between the fourth quarters of 1973 and 1974. Since productivity growth was very slow, this meant a 23 per cent rise in labour costs. Government policy had some effect in dampening down the rate of inflation, both through the operation of the Price Code (*see* **G53**) and through increased subsidies.

(iii) The Attack on Inflation.

1975 saw an even higher rate of inflation than 1974. Average weekly earnings rose by nearly 27 per cent. Productivity fell and prices rose by about 25 per cent. Import prices made a smaller contribution to inflation than in the previous two years. They were 13 per cent higher than in 1974, much of this being the result of an 8 per cent fall in the value of sterling. Real earnings rose by 2·1 per cent, implying a further drop in the share of profits in domestic income to less than 6 per cent, after a larger fall from 9·7 per cent in 1973 to 6·6 per cent in 1974. But through 1975 inflation moderated. Average earnings started to slow down in the second quarter, and wholesale and retail prices followed with a lag. By the third quarter they were all increasing at about 15 per cent. The slowdown of average earnings started before the imposition of the £6 limit (*see* **G54**), and it has been suggested that this was caused by growing unemployment. Such an effect was, however, small compared with the direct impact of the £6 rule.

Domestic inflation moderated still further in 1976, retail prices being 16 per cent higher than in 1975. The main contributor to this was the deceleration in the rate of increase in labour costs. Average weekly earnings were 14 per cent higher than in 1975. Real earnings were therefore 2 per cent lower than in the previous year, implying some recovery in the share of profits in domestic income. By far the largest influence on the deceleration of wage inflation was the voluntary incomes policy, first the £6 limit and from August its successor, which aimed at a 4½ per cent increase in basic wage rates (*see* **G54**). In the last few months of the year price inflation showed a small increase. Whereas in July the retail price index was only 13 per cent higher than a year earlier, by December this figure was 15 per cent. This upturn is explained by the sharp fall in the value of the pound during the year putting up the cost of raw materials and fuel purchased by British industry. Over the year as a whole the largest price increases were in food, fuel, and light, and the smallest were in durable household goods, tobacco, and services.

(iv) International Inflation.

The acceleration of inflation in Britain coincided with similar trends in other countries, including the United States, Japan, W. Germany, France, and Italy, as the table shows. It is also apparent that inflation has generally been more rapid in the United Kingdom than in the other countries since 1968.

Was this the result of a series of coincidences; did the inflations have a common cause; or were they " contagious "? Both France and Italy had major strikes and subsequent " wage explosions "; Britain's inflation too was " cost-push " not " demand pull " in character (*see* **G4**); Japan and W. Germany experienced strong demand pressures; and in the United States the price increases could be explained as a lagged reaction to the demand pressure of 1966–69. Nevertheless, it is likely that inflation was to some extent transmitted from one country to another—particularly from the United States and particularly to small, trading countries—through its effects on the prices of imports and exports, and possibly through its effects on workers' expectations. In all countries, whatever the initial impetus to the inflation, expectations came to play an important rôle in sustaining it.

Policies against inflation were also similar. Heartened by the apparent success of the statutory wages and prices policies introduced in the United States in August 1971, a growing number of European countries, including the United Kingdom, introduced or tightened direct controls on pay and prices. But these policies did not prevent inflation from accelerating. The sharp increase in inflation experienced by all the major economies in 1973 reflected the rising prices of primary products in world markets. World inflation accelerated further during 1974 as the increased oil price had its full effect on costs and prices in the industrial countries. The high price of oil meant a transfer of purchasing power from its consumers to its producers, and therefore a fall in effective demand in industrialised countries. Many foreign countries exacerbated the consequent recession by much more restrictive fiscal and monetary policies than those employed by the British Government. The result was a fall in their inflation rates in the first half of 1975; and, though there was a renewed rise in the second half of the year, the rise of consumer prices in 1975 as a whole was somewhat lower than in 1974. Britain is the only one of the countries listed in the table whose inflation rate increased in 1975. In all major trading countries the inflation rate fell in 1976, and Britain remains near the top of the inflation league table. Only Italy, of the countries listed in the table, had a higher rise in consumer prices.

Incomes Policy.

Britain's competitive position in world trade has deteriorated in relation to that of her main rivals the United States, West Germany, and France; this is one major reason for her recurrent balance of payments difficulties. The British share in total world exports of manufactures fell from 17·7 per cent to 12·3 per cent between 1959 and 1967; and further, to 8·8 per cent, between 1967 and 1975. There are essentially two methods of remedying this situation. We must secure either a relative fall in the external value of the pound, or a relative rise in its internal value. In other words, either there must be a devaluation of the pound in terms of other currencies, or we must have a policy to limit the increase in the British price-level. Up to 1967 the Government concentrated on the latter alternative; and attempts were made to introduce some form of *incomes policy*. In 1967, and from 1972 it allowed the pound to depreciate or float downwards; but incomes policy was still necessary if the devaluation was to be successful, and if harshly restrictive monetary and fiscal policies were to be avoided.

Other harmful effects of inflation, giving rise to the need for some form of incomes policy, are discussed on G20–1.

(i) The Pay Pause.

In July 1961 the Chancellor of the Exchequer called for a "pause" in wages, salaries, and dividend payments. Exhortations for restraint have been a familiar feature of ministerial statements for many years, but on this occasion the Government soon made it clear that it intended to use such power as it has to influence the amount and timing of wage and salary awards. It had the power to decide when the pay awards recommended by the Wages Councils—which fix minimum wages for 3½ million workers—should be implemented. The Government's power is strongest over workers which it directly or indirectly employs, *e.g.*, civil servants, teachers, and Post Office workers. Their pay awards were cut back. The Government also had a limited influence on awards made in nationalised industries.

The "pay pause" came to an end in April 1962. It was envisaged as a temporary policy, and its effects are difficult to assess. It certainly postponed some wage awards which would otherwise have been made in that period, and it may have contributed to a stiffening of resistance to wage claims. But because the pause affected some groups of people more severely than others, this form of incomes policy was seen to be discriminatory.

(ii) The National Incomes Commission.

In February 1962 the Government issued a White Paper which outlined its incomes policy for the period after the pause. It stated that "the objective must be to keep the rate of increase in incomes within the long-term rate of growth of national production." The Government stressed that most of the arguments which had in the past been advanced in justification of wages and salary claims—*e.g.*, increases in the cost of living, trends in productivity or profits in particular industries, and comparisons with levels or trends in other employments—should be given less weight; and that "general economic considerations"—*i.e.*, the increases which the economy can afford given the prospective rate of increase in national production—should be given more weight.

Late in 1962 the Government set up the *National Incomes Commission* (NIC). However, the powers of this body were limited. It had, for example, no power to cancel or modify a wage agreement on which it reported. NIC produced only 4 reports, and was wound up after the change in Government.

(iii) The National Board for Prices and Incomes.

In October 1964 the Labour Government's new Department of Economic Affairs was made responsible for achieving an incomes policy. The lessons of the past had been learned; the Government recognised that a successful incomes policy would require the support of both sides of industry. Its first objective was to achieve a "Joint Statement of Intent on Productivity, Prices and Incomes"; this was signed in December 1964. In this document the T.U.C. and the employers' organisations undertook to co-operate with the Government in producing an effective machinery for the implementing of an incomes policy.

It was Government policy that growth in earnings per employee should equal the planned growth in national output per employee of 3–3½ per cent per annum. Thus, in those industries (*e.g.*, engineering) in which productivity growth exceeded this "norm", earnings should rise less rapidly than productivity, and in those industries (*e.g.*, railways) in which productivity growth fell short of the norm, earnings could rise more rapidly than productivity. Moreover, prices would be expected to fall in industries such as engineering, and permitted to rise in industries such as railways. Growth in earnings per employee should exceed the norm only in exceptional cases; *i.e.*, as a reward for increasing productivity by eliminating restrictive working practices; if necessary to transfer labour from one industry to another; if earnings were too low to maintain a reasonable standard of living; or if a group of workers had fallen seriously out of line with earnings for similar work.

To make specific recommendations on the basis of this policy, the Government set up a *National Board for Prices and Incomes*. The Prices Review Division of the Board could investigate the price of any goods in the economy, and the Incomes Review Division had power to investigate all

RISE IN CONSUMER PRICES

	1959–1971*	1971–1972	1972–1973	1973–1974	1974–1975	1975–1976
U.S.	2·8	3·3	6·2	11·0	9·1	5·7
Japan	5·6	4·9	11·7	23·2	11·7	9·3
France	4·1	5·9	7·3	13·7	11·7	9·7
W. Germany	2·8	5·5	6·9	7·0	6·0	4·5
Italy	3·8	5·6	10·4	19·4	17·2	16·5
U.K.	4·3	6·8	8·3	16·0	24·1	15·8

* Annual average.

claims and settlements relating to wages, salaries, and other incomes. In less than 5 years of operation the Board had produced over 150 reports on prices and earnings.

There was no statutory authority to enforce the recommendations of the Board: reliance was placed on voluntary methods and the power of persuasion and public opinion. However, in late 1965 the Government introduced a compulsory "Early Warning" system, where by it was notified in advance of any intended increase in incomes or in certain prices. As a result, the Government and the Board had time to consider increases before they were put into effect.

(iv) The Prices and Incomes Standstill.

A voluntary incomes policy is very difficult to implement, since it depends on co-operation among Government, workers, and employers; moreover, co-operation among representatives at the top may be undermined by "wage-drift" at the factory level. Thus the annual average of weekly wage-rates rose by no less than 5 percentage points between 1965 and 1966. In fact all of this increase took place in the period before July 1966. Clearly the voluntary incomes policy was meeting with little success.

Therefore, as part of the July measures taken to deal with the balance of payments problem, the Government introduced a "prices and incomes standstill." Increases in prices and incomes were as far as possible avoided altogether until the end of 1966. The only exceptions in the case of incomes were pay increases resulting directly from increases in output (*e.g.*, piece-work or overtime earnings) and from genuine promotion or regular increments on a predetermined scale. Increases already negotiated but not yet implemented were deferred for 6 months. The first half of 1967 was a period of "severe restraint." Any price increases were carefully examined, and the norm for income increases was zero. Any increase in earnings had to be justified by one of the four conditions for exception, referred to above. To enforce its "freeze" the Government took the unprecedented step of asking Parliament for reserve powers (including penalties for offenders), which were to be used only if the need should arise. For the most part, there was a voluntary observation of the standstill; but from October 1966 the Government found it necessary to exercise its power of compulsion in a few cases, *e.g.*, laundry and dry cleaning charges, and a wage agreement in the electrical engineering industry. The power of compulsion lapsed in August 1967.

There then followed a year in which there was to be a "nil norm" except where increases in incomes could be justified by one of the four criteria listed above. The Government could no longer legally enforce its policy, but it did retain the power to delay price and pay increases, through reference to the Board, by up to 7 months. Whereas the Government succeeded in slowing down the rise in wages and prices during the year in which it took compulsory powers, in the second half of 1967 weekly wage rates rose at an annual rate of 6 per cent. The advantage gained from the previous restraint was reduced but not entirely lost.

(v) Incomes Policy after Devaluation.

Incomes policy was made both more difficult and more important by the devaluation of the pound: more difficult in that devaluation involved a cut in the standard of living, and more important in that the trading benefit from devaluation should not be neutralised by inflation.

In April 1968 the Government published a White Paper outlining its policy for the period until the end of 1969. Wage increases had still to be justified by the four criteria, and there was a "ceiling" to increases in income of 3½ per cent per annum except for "productivity agreements" and low-paid workers. Price increases were permitted only as a result of unavoidable increases in cost per unit of output, and price reductions were required when costs fell. Dividend increases were also subject to the ceiling of 3½ per cent per annum, and home rent increases restricted. The Government intended to rely on the voluntary co-operation of unions and employers over pay; but it decided to lengthen its delaying powers for pay and price increases up to 12 months, and take powers to enforce price reductions recommended by the Board.

Between November 1967 and November 1968 the retail price index rose by 5·2 per cent, mainly due to the effect of devaluation on import prices. In the face of this rise in the cost of living the incomes policy met with firm resistance. In practice the nominal ceiling of 3½ per cent per annum rapidly became the normal increase. In the first year after devaluation basic wage rates rose by 6·0 per cent and average earnings by 7·5 per cent. Workers were able to protect themselves against the inflation and to increase slightly their real incomes.

During 1969 the process of wage and price inflation accelerated. In December the Government published a White Paper on its incomes policy for the period after 1969. It laid down a norm for wage increases of 2·5 to 4·5 per cent per annum: increases should exceed the upper limit only in exceptional circumstances, *e.g.*, in productivity agreements, in cases where an inappropriate pay structure is rationalised, *e.g.* by means of job evaluation, in the case of low-paid workers, and in the achievement of equal pay for women. Comparisons with other workers should not be used, except in the case of public servants (*e.g.*, teachers and nurses) whose productivity cannot be measured and whose pay tends to fall behind that of the private sector. The limit on the increase in company dividends of 3·5 per cent per annum was ended and the Government powers to delay the implementation of proposed wage and price increases were reduced. However, the incomes policy laid down in the White Paper was tempered by the imminence of a General Election and the recent cost of living increases; and it did not prevent a "wage explosion" occurring in 1970.

(vi) Conservative Policy.

On taking office in June 1970 the Conservative Government eschewed its predecessor's approach to incomes policy and disbanded the National Board for Prices and Incomes. To curb the inflation it maintained the economy in recession and squeezed company liquidity, hoping in this way to weaken wage pressures and strengthen the resistances of employers. In addition it attempted to resist demands for wage increases in the public sector, at the cost of prolonging strikes, *e.g.*, in electricity supply, postal services and coal mining. In the former two cases it met with some success; in the case of the coal miners' strike early in 1972 the Government was unable to enforce its policy. In any case this form of incomes policy—like the "pay pause" of 1961—was both partial and discriminatory. The Government also intervened to curb price rises in the nationalised industries, *e.g.*, postal charges and steel prices. The main initiative on prices came from the Confederation of British Industry (CBI): in July 1971, it asked its members to avoid price increases over the next twelve months or to limit them to 5 per cent or less in unavoidable increases. Over 170 leading British companies agreed to comply.

The Government measures were by no means a sure remedy for the inflation spiral. Moreover, even its apparent strategy of deterring wage demands by maintaining high unemployment was dropped in the reflationary budget of 1972 (*see* **G45**). The Government appeared to be placing its faith in its Act for the Reform of Industrial Relations to solve the problem of wage inflation in the long run.

(vii) The Pay and Price Standstill.

In 1972 wage demands became more difficult to contain because of the increase in the cost-of-living resulting from the effective devaluation of the pound in June and the rise in world food prices during the year. There was a marked increase in the number and seriousness of strikes (*see* **G18**). This was fairly widespread, although the national miners' strike accounted for 10·8 million of the 23·9 million working days lost in 1972. Nevertheless, on average only very slightly more than one working day was lost per employee during the year. The principal cause of the rise in disputes was a sharp rise in disagreements over pay claims: this increase being both cause and effect of the rapid inflation. In the six months between the first and third quarters of 1972 average weekly earnings rose by no less than 7 per cent. It was inevitable that the Government should intervene. The expectation of an impending freeze now encouraged further wage and price increases, especially after the CBI's period of voluntary restraint had elapsed.

The Government first tried to achieve a tripartite voluntary agreement with the CBI and the TUC to combat inflation. After this attempt had failed, on 6 November the Conservative Government reversed its previous policy on inflation and introduced a Statutory Prices and Pay Standstill. In effect there was a standstill on all prices of goods and services other than imports and fresh foods, a standstill on rents, on dividends, and on all negotiated wages and salaries including those previously negotiated but not yet in operation. The freeze was to last for 90 days, and possibly for a further 60 days. Offenders were liable to be fined.

(viii) The Price Commission and the Pay Board.

In early 1973 the Government formulated its policy for after the standstill in a series of documents, culminating in a Price and Pay Code. Two new agencies—a *Price Commission* and a *Pay Board*—were established to regulate prices, pay, dividends, and rent in accordance with the Price and Pay Code.

In Stage Two of the policy—lasting from the end of the pay standstill on 31 March until the autumn—the following criteria on pay were to apply. The total annual pay increase for any group of employees should not exceed £1 a week plus 4 per cent of the current pay bill excluding overtime. There was flexibility for negotiation of increases within a group: emphasis was to be on the lower paid and the maximum allowable increase was £250 a year. Exceptions to the limit were made for, *e.g.*, movement towards equal pay between the sexes, reduction in standard hours worked to not less than 40 hours a week, increased annual holidays up to a three week maximum, personal increments and promotion, and some improved pension benefits. The Pay Board had to be notified of all settlements involving less than 1,000 employees but settlements involving more than 1,000 employees required its prior approval. It became an offence to strike or threaten to strike to force an employer to contravene an order of the Pay Board.

Prices in Stage Two could be increased only to take account of *allowable* cost increases, and were to reflect only the percentage increases in these costs per unit of output since 1 October 1972. Moreover to allow for productivity growth, firms were permitted to pass on as price increases only a fraction of the increase in the wage costs allowed by the Code. Prices were also limited by the requirement that net profit margins should not exceed the average percentage level of the best two of the last five years. Exceptions were made for companies which could show that without higher profits their investment would be held back. Large firms had to give prior notice of price increases to the Price Commission, medium firms had to report regularly on prices, and small firms had to keep price records. Imports, fresh foods, auctioned goods, secondhand goods and interest charges were among the exemptions from the price controls. Dividends could not be raised by more than 5 per cent over the previous year. The standstill on business rents was extended into Stage Two.

One of the problems facing the price policy was the continued sharp rise in world food prices after the standstill was declared. This made public acceptance of the Government policy more difficult to achieve.

(ix) Stage Three.

Stage Three of the counter-inflation policy was announced in October 1973. Price controls were similar to those under Stage Two. Wage increases negotiated for any group of workers would be statutorily limited to an average of either £2·25 a week per head, or if preferred, 7 per cent per head, with a limit of £350 a year on the amount to be received by any one individual. However, further increases were permitted beyond these limits, to deal with certain specific matters: changes in pay structures, better use of manpower, efficiency schemes, "unsocial" hours, and progress towards equal pay for women. A novel aspect of the pay policy was the *threshold agreement* to safeguard against increases in the cost of living. It was possible for wage negotiators to bargain for a pay increase of up to 40p a week, payable if the retail price index reached 7 per cent above its level at the beginning of Stage Three, with up to another 40p a week for each percentage point it rose thereafter until the end of Stage Three in November 1974. Other countries, Canada for example, have recently experimented with various forms of *indexation* similar to threshold agreements. In Britain many people claimed that these agreements were responsible for a large part of the wage and price inflation of 1974. Indeed in a purely statistical sense this was correct. The threshold was triggered eleven times, which meant an extra £4.40 per week for anyone under the scheme. It was estimated that 10 million workers were covered by such arrangements by October 1974. The idea behind thresholds was that unions, when negotiating wage increases, might have unduly pessimistic expectations about inflation. By introducing automatic compensation, such expectations would be taken out of the bargaining situation. Without this compensation, it might be argued, many groups would have refused to settle under Stage Three terms, and their pay increases would have been just as large or even larger than the ones which they actually obtained.

(x) The Miners' Strike.

An increasing number of settlements were made under the Stage Three conditions; the number of workers covered rising to over 6 million by the end of February 1974. The National Union of Mineworkers, however, feeling strongly that their relative pay had fallen and recognising their new bargaining powers resulting from the oil crisis, refused to settle under Stage Three. A national overtime ban was begun in November which in January 1974 became a national strike. In November the Government declared a State of Emergency and in January introduced a three-day week for industry in order to conserve coal and electricity (which depended on coal). It was unwilling to waive the Stage Three legislation in the miners' case, despite a declaration by the Trade Union Congress that its member unions would not invoke a settlement of the miners' dispute in support of their own claims. By using the maximum flexibility permitted in the legislation, *e.g.*, on payment for unsocial hours, the National Coal Board had been able to offer an average increase of some 17 per cent within the Stage Three rules. The Government referred the NUM claim to the Pay Board, for the Board to determine whether the miners constituted a special case which justified a further increase in their relative pay. The Government then called a General Election. The Pay Board reported just after the election, and recommended that an additional increase be paid, on the grounds that the long-run contraction of the industry would in future be reversed and that higher relative pay would be necessary to recruit and retain sufficient mineworkers. The incoming Labour Government settled with the miners on terms very similar to those recommended by the Pay Board.

(xi) The Social Contract.

The Labour Party came to power pledged to deal firmly with prices but to abandon statutory wage controls. It took early action on house rents and food prices, by means of controls and subsidies. The Pay Board was abolished and the policy of compulsory wage restraint thus finally ended in July 1974. The Price Code and the Price Commission were, however, retained.

During the February 1974 general election campaign an agreement between the TUC and the Labour Party was announced. This became known as the *social contract*, and formed the backbone of the Labour Government's attempts to stem wage inflation. The hope was that, in return for the repeal of the 1972 Industrial Relations Act, the TUC would be able to persuade its members to cooperate in a programme of voluntary wage restraint. In this way it was hoped to avoid the strains caused by formal incomes policies, which have always appeared to trade unionists to leave them without any role to play. Under a voluntary system they could still do their job—that is bargain about wage rates. The terms of the contract were that there should be a twelve-month interval between wage settlements; and that negotiated increases should be confined either to compensating for price increases since the last settlement, or for anticipated future price increases before the next settlement. An attempt by the TUC's general secretary to tighten up the interpretation of the contract, so that nothing was generally allowed apart from compensation for past increases, was unsuccessful.

(xii) Voluntary Restraint.

By early 1975 it was evident that this policy had failed. Some wage settlements were of the order of 30 per cent. In July 1975 the Government announced that there would be a limit of £6 per week on pay increases, £6 representing 10% of average earnings. There were to be no exceptions to this, and those earning more than £8,500 a year were to get nothing at all. The Government had the prior agreement of the TUC to such a policy, and the TUC agreed to try to persuade its members to comply. The policy was voluntary to the extent that there were no legal sanctions against individual unions, but in another sense there were very powerful sanctions. These operated through the Price Code. No firms could pass on in price rises any part of a pay settlement above the limit; this applied not only to the excess but to the whole of the increase. Apart from avoiding the threat of penalties on trade unionists, this form of sanctions has the advantage of covering all payments made at the plant level; many previous incomes policies had been relatively successful at monitoring national negotiations, but had failed to keep a check on extra payments made below this level.

The £6 limit was due to lapse in July 1976, and the April 1976 Budget gave the first indications of a possible successor. The Chancellor announced that he would make cuts in the effective amount of tax paid by private individuals, if he could secure trade union agreement to a second year of pay restraint. Other countries, like Norway, have linked fiscal policy and incomes policy in this way. Its attraction was that it would allow an increase in take-home pay with the employers bearing less than half the cost. Therefore prices would rise by less and our competitive position deteriorate by less than if the whole increase had been achieved by putting up money wages. There were, however, those who felt that the integrity of Parliament was threatened by making taxation decisions conditional on trade union agreement. Be that as it may, agreement was reached with the TUC. From August 1976 more severe limits on pay operated than under the £6 limit. For those earning less than £50 a week, wage increases were limited to £2·50; for those earning between £50 and £80 the limit was 5 per cent, whilst those earning more than £80 could get no more than a £4 per week increase. Average earnings in August were about £75 per week, and the implied overall limit was about 4½ per cent.

There is no doubt that the pay policy was successful in holding down earnings. During the £6 policy earnings rose by 14 per cent. An all-round increase of £6 would have meant a 10 per cent rise. Another 2 per cent can be explained by the implementation of agreements made before August 1975, by moves towards equal pay, and by increased overtime earnings. This leaves only 2 per cent unaccounted for. Some of this "slippage" was no doubt evasion of the limits. There was no reason to think that there had been any greater slippage by March 1977 from the new 4½ per cent limit. That there was so little slippage was possibly due as much to the sanctions imposed by the Price Code and to the recession in the economy as to the voluntary co-operation of the trade unions. There are three possible disadvantages to this sort of incomes policy. The first is that price control is not as rigorous on small companies as on large ones. The second may become more important the longer this form of policy is applied; it may be that a company will be faced with the choice of taking a total strike from a workforce bent on securing an increase over the limit or paying what the unions want. Both courses may be very expensive for the firms, but the latter more so than the former. Finally, the policy could put the Government in direct conflict with unions in the nationalised industries.

The 4½ per cent policy was due to lapse at the end of July 1977, and in the March 1977 Budget the Chancellor offered the prospect of tax cuts, if trade union agreement to a new stage could be achieved. Though major trade union leaders were talking much more loudly than a year earlier about "a return to free collective bargaining," most of them were agreed that it should be an "orderly" return. This implied some support for a continuing incomes policy, at least in the short-run. There were, however, severe obstacles to be overcome before agreement could be reached. Many felt that any new policy would have to allow some restoration of pay differentials, particularly skill differentials, which had been severely squeezed during recent years. Such a restoration of differentials might be necessary for two reasons. First, unless this happened, the more highly skilled or the more highly paid might refuse to co-operate. Second, pay differences are necessary to reflect differing contributions to the economy and to allow the labour market to operate efficiently. One possible tactic which was suggested was to impose a limit for a bargaining group; how the cash amount to which they were entitled was distributed would be up to members of the group. The danger was that any increased flexibility would increase the likelihood of restraint being circumvented. In the meanwhile strike activity, which had been very low during 1975 and 1976, increased in the early months of 1977. This to a large degree reflected frustration with nearly two years of income restraint.

Tax Reforms.

(i) Capital Gains Tax.

A tax on short-term gains was introduced in 1962, but a more comprehensive innovation was the *capital gains tax* of 1965. This tax is levied on the gain realised on an asset between its purchase and sale, provided this does not exceed the gain between 6 April 1965 and sale. It applies to all assets, with limited exceptions: the most important being owner-occupied houses, and annual disposals of goods and chattels realised for less than £1,000. Gains realised by companies over any period are taxed at corporation tax rates, though from 1973 they were effectively taxed at only 30%, since a fraction of the gain was left out of account. Gains by individuals on assets held for more than a year are taxed at a flat rate of 30 per cent. Gains realised within a period of one year were treated as ordinary income and taxed accordingly. However, in his 1971 Budget the Chancellor made these gains also subject to the 30 per cent flat rate. He also exempted individuals' capital gains where the assets sold during the year were valued at less than £500, and taxed individuals at their personal income tax rate on only half their gains up to £5,000. The 1972 Budget effectively eliminated double taxation on unit trust capital gains. In the April 1975 budget the Chancellor gave some relief to farms by limiting the valuation (for tax purposes) of transferred land to twenty times its agricultural rental value. He also gave relief to small businessmen by allowing tax due on certain assets to be paid in instalments over eight years, no interest being charged on the tax due on the first £250,000.

There are many administrative difficulties in implementing such a tax. Nevertheless, it is an important attempt to remedy the inequality in the taxation of earned and unearned incomes (*see* G16).

(ii) Corporation Tax.

In 1965 the Labour Government also introduced a *corporation tax*, to replace the existing company income tax and profits tax. This tax, at a rate of 40 per cent, was imposed on distributed as well as undistributed profits, so as to encourage the retention of profits for the financing of business expansion. The tax rate was subsequently raised to 42·5 per cent and then to 45 per cent.

In 1970 the incoming Conservative Government reduced the rate of tax to 42·5 per cent and in 1971 to 40 per cent. It was also announced that the Government intended to remove the discrimination in favour of retained and against distributed profits, by decreasing the rate on distributed profits so that the burden of corporation tax and income tax together would be equal to the corporation tax alone on retained profits. This would have the effects of reducing profit retentions, which would discourage investment, and of easing share issue, which would encourage investment. The new corporation tax was introduced in 1973, and there was preferential treatment for small companies with profits of less than £25,000 a year. This figure was subsequently raised, and stood at £50,000 after the March 1977 budget. In the March 1974 budget the Chancellor set corporation tax for 1973–74 at a rate of 52 per cent, which was left unchanged by subsequent budgets in 1975, 1976 and 1977.

(iii) Selective Employment Tax

The *selective employment tax* (SET) was introduced in the 1966 budget and became partly an instrument of regional policy in 1967. It was abolished when VAT was introduced in 1973. All firms were required to pay SET on each employee, but it was refunded in full to employers in non-taxable industries, such as agriculture and the nationalised industries. Until November 1967 it was refunded with a premium to all manufacturing concerns. From then until 1970 the premium was paid only to manufacturers in the development areas. Its aim was to switch labour from the services and construction into manufacturing, which, it was thought, made a greater contribution to exports and growth.

(iv) Value Added Tax.

In his 1971 Budget the Chancellor of the Exchequer announced that SET and purchase tax would be replaced by a *value added tax* (VAT) in April 1973. A value added tax was seen to have certain advantages: it could be applied evenly to almost all goods and services unlike purchase tax which was imposed on only a limited range of goods; without infringing international rules exports could be exempted from the tax and so encouraged; and it would be in line with practice in the Common Market countries.

The tax is levied as a certain percentage of *value added* at each stage of production (*see* **G12**). Here is a simple example on the assumption of a uniform 10 per cent rate. A producer imports raw materials valued at £100 and pays a tax of £10. He makes an intermediate product and sells it to a manufacturer for £200. The producer's value added is £100, so he pays another £10. The manufacturer makes a final product and sells it to a retailer for £500. His value added—accruing either as wages to his workers or as profits—is therefore £300, and he pays tax of £30. The retailer sells the product to domestic consumers for £700, his value added being £200 and his tax liability £20. The sum total of tax paid is £70, *i.e.*, 10 per cent of the final product price, but it is collected at each stage of production.

VAT was initially set at 10 per cent, but the rate was subject to regulation upwards and downwards. In the interests of simplicity there was only one, uniform rate, but there were exceptions. Some activities were exempt from the tax: *e.g.*, insurance, postal services, education and health services, and small firms with turnover of less than £5,000 per annum. These do not pay tax on their sales but cannot reclaim tax on their purchases. Still more favoured were zero-rated activities which could get complete relief from the tax both on sales and on purchases. They included all food for humans, newspapers, periodicals, books, housebuilding, rents, rates, fares, domestic fuel and light, children's clothing and footwear, and of course exports. Because cars are a major source of revenue from purchase tax, there was, in addition to VAT, a separate tax on new and imported cars of 10 per cent. By introducing exceptions—*e.g.*, no tax on food and housing—the Chancellor went some way to meet the charge that the replacement of purchase tax by VAT would widen the gap in living standards between rich and poor.

In July 1974 the rate was reduced to 8 per cent, but in November the rate on petrol was increased to 25 per cent. In the April 1975 budget this higher rate of 25 per cent was extended to a range of so-called "luxury" goods (*see* **G46**). The thinking behind this move was that higher taxation would bear most heavily on the expenditure of the well-off, who could afford to buy such goods. The 25 per cent rate was reduced to 12½ per cent in the April 1976 budget.

(v) Income Tax and Surtax.

In the 1971 budget the Conservative Government proposed to replace the existing income tax and surtax with a single graduated personal tax in 1973, with the following principal features. The existing pattern of personal allowances would be retained, there would be a basic rate covering a broad band of income and corresponding to the standard rate less earned income relief, there would be higher rates above the basic rate applicable to the higher incomes, and the distinction between earned and unearned income would be made by way of a surcharge on investment income above a certain level of such income. The purpose of the proposals was to simplify tax assessment and collection to avoid misunderstanding as to the true marginal rates of tax, and to encourage saving.

In the 1972 budget the Chancellor, giving further details of the 1973 innovation, announced that on the first £5,000 of annual taxable income, the personal tax would be charged at the basic rate of 30 per cent. On the slice of income between £5,000 and £6,000 it would be 40 per cent, and it would reach a maximum of 75 per cent on the slice of income in excess of £20,000. There would be a surcharge of 15 per cent on investment income only above £2,000. These changes implied a much simpler system, but one in which the rate of tax increased less rapidly with income than before, *i.e.*, it was a less *progressive* tax.

In the March 1974 budget the Chancellor in the incoming Labour Government took measures to make income tax more progressive. The standard rate was raised to 33 per cent but personal and child allowances were increased. Additions to the standard rate begin at a taxable income of £4,500 per annum and the surcharge on investment income at £1,000 (£1,500 for the over 65s). The maximum rate of tax was raised to 83 per cent (98 per cent for investment income). In April 1975 all rates, except for the highest one, were raised by 2 per cent, so that the standard rate became 35 per cent. Personal allowances were raised, but inflation meant that the real value of these was actually lower than the ones prevailing a year earlier. The April 1976 budget increased allowances by £60 for single persons and £135 for married men, making them £735 and £1,085 respectively, and the income thresholds, at which people started to pay higher rates of tax, by £500; this concession applied only to tax rates up to and including 60 per cent. In the March 1977 budget these tax thresholds were raised still further. The basic tax rate now applied to the first £6,000 of taxable income. The highest rate of 83 per cent applied to taxable income of over £21,000. Personal allowances were also raised. The single person's allowance went up by £70 to £805, and the married man's allowance by £140 to £1,225. The Chancellor also promised a reduction in the standard rate of income from 35 to 33 per cent, if a satisfactory agreement on a new phase of incomes policy could be reached with the trade unions (*see* **N31–32**).

As inflation occurs, so income recipients move into higher tax brackets. Thus the proportion of personal income taken in income tax rises unless there is compensatory upward adjustment of tax allowances and tax brackets by the Chancellor. Although in recent years there have been many such adjustments, they have not been sufficient to compensate the average wage earner. This is the main reason why an increasing proportion of the labour force has become liable for income tax over the last decade. Consider the case of a married couple with two young children, with no income except the husband's earnings from employment and family allowances. In the tax-year 1966–7, if the husband received the median earnings of full-time adult men manual employees (£1,059 per annum), 7 per cent of his income would be taxed; to escape income tax, his earnings would have to be less than 70 per cent of the median. In 1975/6 20 per cent of the median income of £3,107 per annum would be taxed; and to escape income tax, his earnings would have to be less than 45 per cent of the median. This tendency for inflation to increase the burden of taxation is known as *fiscal drag*, because the reduced personal spending has a deflationary effect on the economy.

(vi) Capital Transfer Tax.

Transfers of private wealth from one generation to another used to be taxed through estate duty, but it was possible to avoid this by making gifts seven years before death. In his March 1974 Budget the Chancellor announced that he would introduce a *gifts tax*, retrospective to March 1974, to close this loophole. The tax, which was renamed the *Capital Transfer Tax*, was finally approved by Parliament in March 1975, and replaced estate duty. It applies to all gifts made since March 1974, and is payable by the donor. Gifts between husband and wife are exempt. Until the total value of gifts made by an individual reaches £15,000 the rate of tax is zero. To give a simple example, suppose that in one year a person makes gifts worth £14,000. The first £2,000 (before April 1976 £1,000) per year is exempt. The remaining £12,000 bears a zero rate of tax, but is carried forward to be added to the chargeable value of gifts made in subsequent years. In the next year this person gives away £6,000. Again the first £2,000 is exempt. £3,000 of the remaining £4,000 carries zero tax. The limit of £15,000 has then been reached, so that the individual has to pay 10 per cent tax on the remaining £1,000. At the end of two years, therefore, this individual's chargeable gifts stand at £16,000. The value of any subsequent gifts will be added to this figure to determine the new total chargeable value; and the rate at which the new gifts are taxed will depend on this value. The higher it is the higher will be the rate of tax. In the 1976 Budget partial reliefs were announced for small businesses, owned by a single person or in partnership. This new tax, then, covers transmissions of personal wealth. At some future date, the Labour Government plans to introduce a *Wealth Tax*, which will tax individuals according to the value of their wealth. A House of Commons Select Committee reported on this in December 1975, but the report provided no real foundation for legislation, since there was substantial disagreement both on the rate of tax and on the level of wealth at which taxation should begin.

Means-tested Social Services.

In 1972 there existed at least 45 different types of benefits or services which were provided on test of means, some of them administered by Central Government and some by Local Authorities. They included supplementary benefits, free school meals, rent and rate rebates, legal aid, free welfare milk and foods, higher education awards, dental and optical charges, and family income supplements (*see* G26–27). The selective system has grown in recent years, in three ways: an increase in the number of such benefits and in the number of families qualifying, and a restriction of benefits which were formerly universal.

Means-tested schemes have been criticised on four main grounds: it is argued that they are expensive to operate; that they reduce the incentive to work or to earn more (there are cases in which additional income is entirely neutralised by loss of selective benefits); that they are considerably under-utilised through ignorance or pride (probably only two-thirds of those eligible for supplementary benefits, only half of those eligible for free welfare milk and food, and only a third of those eligible for rate rebates actually receive them); and that they are socially divisive. Under the present income tax system, people in poverty pay no tax. A possible alternative might be a tax credit scheme under which they would not only pay nothing but they would actually receive a "negative income tax" from the Government. Such a system might be capable of reducing the need for the various means-tested benefits currently provided to alleviate poverty and of avoiding the defects to which the critics have pointed; but much would depend on the precise details of the system.

A New Pensions Scheme.

There are nearly eight million pensioners in Britain. 25 per cent of these are kept out of poverty only by receiving a supplementary pension. It is estimated that another 10 per cent are entitled to a supplementary pension, but do not draw it. Many of the remainder find their living standards considerably reduced from when they were working. This is because the existing state retirement pension is inadequate. There are some occupational pension schemes which offer a better income, but these are rather restricted in their coverage, being available to many more non-manual than manual workers. Like personal savings, many of them also tend to have only limited safeguards against inflation. In an era of rapidly rising prices, the pensioner is at a particular disadvantage. Widows form the poorest group among them, with about 60 per cent of them needing to draw a supplementary pension.

From the summer of 1974 until April 1975 the full pension entitlement was £10 for a single person and £16 for a married couple. In April 1975 the rates were raised to £11·60 and £18·50. In November of the same year they were put up to £13·30 and £21·10, and there was a further increase in November 1976, taking the rates to £15·30 and £24·50. So in little more than two years basic pensions increased by more than 50 per cent.

It was clear that the Government had become aware of the need for a frequent adjustment of rates. The real need, however, was for fundamental reform. Successive governments have tried to develop new pensions schemes (*see* G27) and the latest of them went before Parliament in February 1975. The idea is for a two-tier pension. The bottom tier is a common flat-rate for everyone. The top tier will be earnings related—that is, it will be a fixed proportion of the pensioner's previous earnings. Because of the flat-rate element, a low earner will be able to expect a pension which is a higher percentage of his working income than that obtained by a higher earner. Contributions to the scheme will be earnings related. The pensions will be fully protected against inflation, and women will enter the scheme on the same footing as men. There was an obvious emphasis on the need to protect women from poverty in retirement, after the death of the husband. There will be a maximum pension entitlement and a maximum contribution. For this reason among others, the Government plans to encourage new and improved occupational schemes, to exist alongside the state scheme. It is hoped that the scheme will come to full maturity in twenty years, this long delay reflecting the formidable difficulties in financing the plan. In the meantime fully earnings-related contributions started in 1975. These replaced flat-rate National Insurance payments and graduated pension contributions.

THE CONTEMPORARY THEATRE

Since the 1950s our stage has seen far-reaching changes. Influential foreign plays long neglected have been produced here for the first time and contemporary writers, both indigenous and foreign, have experimented with new techniques and been concerned with urgent social problems. This section is concerned with the revival in the theatre, the differing types of drama, and with premières of the most outstanding plays of the last 25 years.

TABLE OF CONTENTS

THE CONTEMPORARY THEATRE

This section concerns the English theatre since 1950 and since a shared experience between actors and playgoers has long been vital to the full enjoyment of drama it is limited to plays acted live to a live audience. There are four sections:

I. INTRODUCTION

Although recently some of our most popular plays have been Ayckbourn's clever social comedies in the style of the " well-made play " between the wars, yet the work of many eminent dramatists has been very different in theme and technique. The theme of Hampton's *Savages* and Fugard's *Sizwe Bansi* was social injustice in other continents and Shaffer's *Equus* explored the anquish of the disturbed personality. The visual image of Beckett's *Not I* and *That Time* was a dimly lit mouth and young writers like Brenton and Hare constantly use surprising images as they question our social structure.

Such plays are more fully appreciated in the context of the many innovations in drama dating from the mid-1950s and this section is concerned with the more significant plays of this period.

The Function of Dramatic Art.

It is not the function of art to make a statement but to induce an imaginative response, and the spectator receives not an answer to a question but an experience.

Drama, like the other arts, gives expression to that subtle and elusive life of feeling that defies logical definition. By feeling is to be understood the whole experience of what it feels like to be alive—physical sensations, emotions, and even what it feels like to think.

This flux of sensibility cannot be netted down in logical discourse, but can find expression in what Clive Bell, when discussing the visual arts, called " significant form. "

The contemporary philosopher, Susanne Langer, in her book, *Feeling and Form*, has developed Clive Bell's concept, arguing that all artistic form is an indirect expression of feeling. The artist, be he painter, poet, or dramatist, creates an image, a form that gives shape to his feeling, and it is for the sensitive recipient to interpret its significance.

The especial province of drama, as was pointed out by Aristotle, is to create an image, an illusion of action, that action " which springs from the past but is directed towards the future and is always great with things to come." Both tragedy and comedy depict such action and the conflict which it normally entails.

The Therapeutic Effect of Drama.

One of the achievements of serious drama is to create an image that will objectify and help to resolve deep human conflicts.

Most people have at some time or another come away from a fine play feeling in some inexplicable way exhilarated and released, and it has long been recognised that drama can have a beneficial, even a therapeutic effect.

It is easy to understand the exhilarating effect of comedy but extremely difficult to comprehend that of tragedy. In the 4th cent. B.C. Aristotle claimed that tragedy accomplishes a beneficial purgation of pity and terror (*see* The Aristotelian Play) and Helen Gardner in *Religion and Literature*, 1971, again examines the paradox as to why a dramatisation of catastrophe should give us some kind of release and satisfaction. Discussing such influential theories as those of Hegel, Bradley, Schopenhauer, Nietzsche, Unamuno and Niebuhr, she elucidates the tragic conflict as opposition between such contraries as man and fate, man's incompatible ideals and inner conflicts, reason and emotion. She concludes that the power of tragedy lies in reconcilement of harshly discordant contraries—the passionate protest at inevitable suffering and its agonised acceptance—which realised together have power to console.

Helen Gardner's book is especially relevant today for she denies tragic stature to the modern serious play. Studying two of those rare periods productive of tragedy, she points out that social and religious conditions in 5th cent. Athens had a parallel in Elizabethan London. In both cultures a consciousness of guilt and sin and the need for propitiation and salvation involved a conviction that human action was profoundly significant, helping to create a climate propitious to tragedy which Helen Gardner following Aristotle defines as " the imitation of a complete action. "

Today's climate she considers adverse. The contemporary metaphysical despair and sense of meaninglessness together with post-Freudian emphasis on " sickness " rather than wrong-doing have helped to erode a sense of responsibility for actions, so that today's serious play is either eventless, pathetic rather than tragic, or as in the " theatre of cruelty " (*q.v.*). preoccupied with violent event for event's sake, while the unrelieved despair inevitably lacks that conflict of protest and acceptance, which exhilarates and consoles.

Another distinguished woman critic, Muriel Bradbrook, has put forward a most interesting psychological explanation of the effect of serious drama on the audience. She suggests that in watching a mature play we are encouraged to sympathise with many different characters at one and the same time, and it may be that the imaginative effort entailed has a corresponding movement in the unconscious mind. There, at the most primitive level, is an " internal society ", the petrified infantile images of father, mother and siblings, to which we are linked by inflexible attitudes. It may be that the sympathetic response to the playwright's images of these figures helps us to relax our rigid attitudes towards them so that the internal pattern of relationships shifts, and we experience a sense of release and a new access of energy.

It is noteworthy also that drama can be fully appreciated only in a public performance, a social event demanding the co-operation and understanding between author, players and audience. Because it can flourish only in a community, normally a city, it has been called the metropolitan art.

The Constituents of Drama.

Drama is a complex art in that it uses two very different kinds of ingredient or material, one speech, the literary constituent, the other the gesture movement, and confrontation of actors on an actual stage. Speech is man's most precise, subtle, and mature means of expression. Gesture and confrontation, which he shares to some degree with animals, is more primitive and some of the power of drama is its fusion of civilised speech and primitive gesture into one organic whole.

It is just possible to conduct brief scenes using only one of these media. The chorus in Shakespeare's *Henry V* is virtually confined to speech and there is in Galsworthy's *Justice*, revived in 1968, a moving wordless scene, showing a criminal in solitary confinement that is reputed to have led to amendment of the penal code.

Perhaps the more primitive gesture has the greater emotional force, but words made permanent in the literary script have constituted the commanding form of drama. Even the wordless mime is given permanence by the script.

The Ritual Element.

While speech and the confrontation of actors are essential to full drama, there is an element that has sometimes been neglected and that is ritual, perhaps the most primitive and evocative of all. The early tragedy of Greece was probably organically connected with the religious ritual of Dionysus and the matrix was song and dance. Similarly in England the origins of drama are to be found in church liturgy and ritual and civic occasion, both of which used procession, pageantry, costume, and symbolic insignia to great effect and also clowning which served as comic relief.

There have naturally been few dramatists able to combine literary ability, a sense of stage situation and skill in the use of ritual. The enduring power of Shakespeare is due to his manifold genius in that he could deploy inimitable poetry, swift action, and such ritual enrichments as royal processions, crowning and dethroning, duelling and wrestling, masque, pageantry, song and dance.

The Background of Modern Drama.

The happy fusion of excellence which is to be found in Shakespeare's plays is extremely rare, for it demands not only a versatile genius but also a receptive audience and a suitable building. By the Restoration the delicate balance was already disturbed and by the middle decades of the 19th cent. popular taste had all but banished literature from the stage. The disorderly audiences of the time demanded only spectacular and sensational theatrical and musical effects, and in the vast monopoly theatres of Drury Lane and Covent Garden they could hardly have heard, let alone appreciated, good dialogue. The managers discouraged men of genius, so that poets like Browning, who had no practical knowledge of the theatre, produced wordy " closet dramas " which were virtually unactable, while the popular theatrical melodramas like *Maria Marten* or *Murder in the Red Barn*, are today unreadable.

With the gradual establishment of smaller theatres, catering for a sober middle-class audience, men of talent again began to write for the stage. It was the turn of literature to take command, and more popular and traditional techniques such as music and clowning were now banished to the music-hall and pantomime.

T. W. Robertson, Henry Arthur Jones and Pinero all furthered the trend towards realism but it was the genius of Ibsen that set a high standard of excellence for the literary and realistic play of middle-class life. He expressed profound insight into personal and social problems in finely constructed plays, the overtones of poetic universality being conveyed in symbolism that was usually verbal.

Able writers, like Granville Barker and Galsworthy, although they lacked the poetic power of Ibsen, firmly established in England a similar type of literary play, realistic, well-constructed, serious-minded, concerned with the middle class and almost exclusively verbal.

Some of the few exceptions to this type of play are to be found in Shaw. Like Shakespeare, he was not only a literary genius. He was also well acquainted with stage-production and although much too wordy in old age, in his best comedies he combined some of the wittiest dialogue in English drama along with the delightful shocks and surprises of total theatre. Androcles' engaging Lion belongs to the same family as Titania's Ass.

But Shaw in his prime was unique, and between the wars the verbal, realistic play was perpetuated by such writers as Maugham and Coward. Not over-concerned with psychological or social issues, they used it to portray the leisured classes.

By the 'forties the conventional West End play had come to imitate not life but photography. Confined to the proscenium arch and realistic to the last trivial detail, it presented a prosaic picture of middle- and upper-class life, with stereotyped situation, demanding only stock responses and lacking interest in ideas, poetic intensity, and genuine wit. With the star cast and the long commercial run, theatre-going had become not an artistic experience but a social occasion.

Apart from the novel comedies of such writers as Rattigan and the verse plays of T. S. Eliot and Fry, it was the revivals of the classics, English and European, that were bringing genuine drama to the stage. Shakespeare could be enjoyed not only at Stratford and the Old Vic, but in the West End. It was largely due to Gielgud that Shakespeare was now a box-office draw.

Gielgud's fine histrionic sense, and his highly sensitive and poetic interpretation had earned him that rare distinction of being the Hamlet of his generation. As actor and producer, working with other fine artists, such as Edith Evans, Peggy Ashcroft, Olivier, Guinness and Scofield, Gielgud later confirmed his success. Enthralling interpretations of plays by Shakespeare, Webster, and the like, demonstrated that the classics could have a wide popular appeal.

Such achievements reminded audience and aspiring playwright that there are many other dramatic styles than fashionable realism and so may even have helped to further the dramatic revival that began in the 'fifties.

The Modern Revival.

Although artistic work overflows the tidy schemes of chronology, it is helpful to distinguish two main phases of contemporary drama, beginning with plays produced during the first sudden outburst of creativity.

The decade beginning 1955.

Many new playwrights first became known during an exciting decade. There were British premières of plays by continental writers such as Brecht, Ionesco, Genet, Dürrenmatt, Frisch, Vian, Hochbuth and Weiss and by the American Albee. British dramatists who soon established their reputation included Beckett, Osborne, Behan, Pinter, N. F. Simpson, Mortimer, Wesker, Arden, Shaffer, Saunders and Bolt. Most of these, fortunately, still continue to write.

It is never easy to identify causes of artistic renewal but one reason was that young men like Wesker injected new vigour into jaded realism by using it to express the stresses of the working people they knew. Hence the settings in shabby basements and attics (*see* Neo-realism). It was in such a setting in Osborne's *Look Back in Anger* (*q.v.*) that there suddenly exploded that blast of confused and impotent anger which expressed the frustration of many of his contemporaries.

More far-reaching was the general awareness among avant-garde playwrights that verbalism was not enough, and their readiness to experiment with the resources of " total theatre ". Here the way had been shown by scholarly research into the history of the theatre which gave dramatists confidence to revive valid techniques such as song, music and clowning that the early 20th cent. had banished to the music-hall.

The most vital stimulus was the challenge of genius. Brecht's Epic Theatre (*q.v.*) offered a more free and fluid form than that of the " well-made play " (*q.v.*) and his novel uses of traditional theatrical devices (such as song, masks, extravagant costume and settings, direct address to the audience) were quickly adapted by dramatists like Arden, Bolt and Osborne.

Meanwhile Ionesco, whole-hearted devotee of the Theatre of the Absurd (*q.v.*), introduced monsters like the rhinoceros and exploited stage properties like empty chairs to satirise man's frightened and empty existence. He was soon followed by Saunders and by Simpson, whose weighing-machines symbolised the dominance of imagination by machinery. Devices recently restricted to pantomime were reviving.

A pervasive and growing influence was that of Artaud's demand for a Theatre of Cruelty (*q.v.*). This is both the most novel and the most atavistic type of theatre, for it attempts to re-create in modern terms that primitive, even barbaric ritual from which drama evolved. It was clearly exemplified in 1964 in a play by Weiss (*q.v.*) and in England is still best known in translations.

Developments since 1965.

One of the most interesting aspects of theatre was a fresh topical approach to Shakespeare.

Some critics and producers have traced in his plays the bleak disenchantment of post-war Europe, owing much to the Polish critic, Jan Kott, whose book *Shakespeare, our Contemporary*, was published here in 1964.

Kott, who lived through the Nazi tyranny and the Stalinist occupation of Poland, urges that the power-politics of twentieth century Europe have their counterpart in the Wars of the Roses and the Tudor disturbances. He finds in Shakespeare's Histories and Tragedies, what he terms the " Grand Mechanism " of history, the blood-stained struggle for power and claims that Shakespeare " condemns war by showing up the Feudal butchery. "

The series, " The Wars of the Roses ", which was produced for the B.B.C. during 1965–6 by Peter Hall and John Barton with the R.S.C., vividly demonstrated the crime-ridden lust for power and the Feudal butchery. Meanwhile at Stratford and the Aldwych, the production of *Henry V* showed the king, grimy and battle-scarred, leading a tattered army, plagued by corrupt camp-followers. Played on a bare, gaunt stage, grey, metallic and cavernous, it was strikingly similar in tone and significance to Brecht's *Mother Courage*, running concurrently at the Old Vic.

Shakespearean comedy was also approached afresh. In Clifford Williams' enchanting production for the National Theatre in 1967 of *As You Like It*, with an all-male cast, the women's parts were not taken as in Shakespeare's time by boys with unbroken voices but by young men. Williams was aware of the unorthodox theories expressed in Kott's *The Bitter Arcadia*. Kott observing the almost identical appearance of modern youths and girls was reminded of those Shakespearean comedies where the girl appears disguised as a youth. He argues that their theme is that of the sonnets—" the impossibility of choice between the youth and the woman, the fragile boundary between friendship and love . . . the universality of desire which cannot be contained or limited to one sex."

The sober fact remains that Shakespeare is not our contemporary. Historical accuracy of presentation is comparatively recent and the text can even be illuminated by anachronism as in Brook's production of *A Midsummer Night's Dream* with techniques borrowed from Persia. The plays can even be abbreviated as in most productions of *Hamlet*.

But violations such as Nahum Tate's notorious happy ending to *King Lear* now appear ridiculous. Helen Gardner castigates as " outrageous arrogance " attempts to present Shakespeare as " our contemporary, " an existentialist confounding " the tragic " with " the meaningless ", and sacrificing poetry to spectacle and violence.

Recent perspectives.

Meanwhile there have since 1965 been diverse influences from abroad through plays by Soyinka, Duras, Jarry, Fugard, Feiffer, Lowell, Triana and Chayavsky. A new generation of British dramatists has become prominent including Mercer, Bond, McGrath, Storey, Terson, Nichols, Wood, Hampton and Stoppard. Some have experimented in fresh dramatic genres and techniques but generally speaking the most novel contribution of native authors and producers has been a new candour in the presentation of social problems.

Joe Orton, whose best play had been produced in 1964, popularised a peculiar brand of " black comedy " (*q.v.*).

A more serious innovation was the " theatre of fact ". *The Investigation* of Peter Weiss set an example for plays which constitute a kind of " documentary " of the stage, the dramatist endeavouring to present objectively a selection of the actual events of contemporary history. But however detached, selection involves bias.

One of the most sober of such factual plays, Kipphardt's on Oppenheimer, followed Weiss in presenting a judicial enquiry. Later examples were Hare's *Fanshen*, 1975, and Brook's production of *The Ik*, 1976.

The R.S.C. also carried out an experiment in a new genre, that of " Director's Theatre ", and the involvement of the audience was certainly the purpose of *US*, directed by Peter Brook as a direct assault on our apathy concerning the war in Vietnam.

A refreshing candour in the approach to social problems has been evident in plays involving biting criticism of the military mentality and recourse to war, notably McGrath's *Bofors Gun*, Vian's *The Generals' Tea Party*, and Charles Wood's *Dingo* and " *H* ".

Meanwhile the pressing international problem of relations between black and white has been illuminated in plays by Fugard and Lowell.

Illness both physical and mental is now frankly presented. Peter Nichols in 1967 used remarkable theatrical skill in revealing the effects on the parents of the incurable illness of a spastic shild. His ironic *The National Health* (1969) was set in a grim hospital ward.

It is no longer unusual to see a play depicting the distressed mind. Storey's touching work *Home* (1970) is set in the grounds of a mental hospital. Both he and Mercer have been concerned with the malaise of a generation educated beyond the parents.

There has steadily developed a sympathetic attitude towards sexual deviation. In 1965 *A Patriot for Me*, Osborne's uncompromising record of a homosexual, could be performed only privately. But in 1968 Christopher Hampton's *Total Eclipse* was devoted to a candid exploration of the historic relationship between Verlaine and Rimbaud.

The abolition in September 1968 of the Lord Chamberlain's powers of theatre censorship removed official taboos on the dramatist's freedom of expression, which are now conditioned by the public's response. There has been an increasing vogue for four-letter words and sexual reference. The revue *Oh! Calcutta!* (1970), sponsored by Tynan, included a representation of sexual intercourse and total nudity. The taboo on stage nakedness was broken. Although nudity has proved commercially successful the plays in which it is employed have been unremarkable.

Four-letter words are now a commonplace. Chaucer used them precisely and effectively and after Victorian repression they needed a good airing. In realistic plays such as Whitehead's they give a valid impression of actual speech. Pinter is very conscious of the explosive force of an erotic taboo word suddenly erupting to the surface and for that very reason uses it rarely. Lesser playwrights have used such words freely so as to shock, when they show diminishing returns, and degenerate into a modish gutter slang and like false money depreciate the vocabulary.

In the avant garde Living Theatre coherent narrative sequence is discarded in favour of a series of "happenings"—disparate theatrical images, involving movement, mime, inarticulate cries, rhythmic sound and music. These are frequently violent, sometimes in a talented company surprising and beautiful, but often unintelligible. Living Theatre is often imbued with the spirit of Artaud's "Theatre of Cruelty". Sometimes "audience participation" is invited, actors and spectators mingling with each other both on stage and in the auditorium.

Recently much experimental work has made its appearance on the Fringe. An increasing number of enterprising companies—such as McGrath's 7.84—have presented plays in shabby makeshift quarters such as basements, disused rooms and pubs. Some were founded some time ago, such as the Unity, N.W.1, 1937, or the Traverse Theatre, Edinburgh, 1963. Recently there have been successful pub theatres like the King's Head, Islington, and the Bush, W.12. A fortunate few have good modern buildings such as the Cockpit, 1970, the Soho Poly, and the Half Moon of 1972, all in London.

The late '60s and early '70s have seen a rise in the importance of provincial theatres, with many new ones being opened in towns such as Exeter, Colchester and Worcester. More established provincial theatres, particularly the Nottingham Playhouse, have combined programmes of neglected classics with premières of important new plays.

Criteria of Judgment.

How can the value of novel and experimental plays be estimated? The ultimate test of time is obviously impossible and some of the critical principles by which traditional drama has been interpreted are no longer relevant.

The first canon of criticism is that every art form determines the criteria by which it is judged, and the good dramatic critic does not approach any play with a pontifical set of rules but endeavours to keep an open mind.

Since artistic form is an expression of human feeling, the first encounter with a work of art should be in a mood of extreme receptivity, so that one may be aware of the feeling implicit in the work, however novel or even bizarre the expression may be. The initial reaction to drama should be intuitive.

The nature and quality of the implicit feeling can then be considered. Is it an original and genuine response to experience, or perfunctory and stereotyped, is it intense or diffuse, profound or shallow, subtle or commonplace, reasoned or irrational?

Drama is an especially complicated art, in that part of its material being words, it may also involve discussion of ideas. This discussion, however, should not be mistaken for a statement of the author's convictions. In a good play it is an expression of his characters' *feeling* about ideas.

Another enquiry concerns the appropriateness and beauty of the form in which the feeling is conveyed. Many consider that Beckett's *Waiting for Godot*, while lacking the tragic greatness of *King Lear*, conveys its implicit mood, and that each play is an image of man, disillusioned, adrift, assailed by despair in an alien universe. This recognised, the critic's task is to explore the form of the two plays. Apart from the fact that they both use a most improbable fable, they could hardly be more different. Yet in either case the form of the play has artistic significance and appropriateness and repays analysis, and here again the critic needs to be flexible.

The most searching question to be asked of a play is whether it is life-enhancing, whether it gives delight or deepens understanding.

Most difficult to estimate are those plays like *Lear* or *Godot*, which express a mood of despair. But if man's honesty and endurance are ultimately affirmed, the play is not negative in import. Lear begs forgiveness and the tramps still wait. Similarly a biting satire may be positive if it helps to clear away old wood. A facile optimism may be a betrayal.

Ideally the best way to know a play is first to see it on the stage, when its theatrical qualities can be enjoyed, and later to read it at leisure, when its literary value can be appreciated.

II. EMINENT THEATRICAL GROUPS

We are greatly indebted to a few enterprising and devoted groups—chiefly repertory companies and theatre clubs—which help to keep drama alive.

Foremost are the Royal Shakespeare Company and the National Theatre, which have earned an international reputation by their superb productions of both classics and new plays. Some groups, such as the English Stage Company and the Traverse Theatre, Edinburgh, have been particularly concerned with new dramatists.

Many repertory theatres do exciting work and there is a comprehensive list in the *Stage Year Book.*

The Royal Shakespeare Company.

When Peter Hall was appointed managing director in January 1960 he decided to supplement the annual season of Shakespeare at Stratford-on-Avon by a continuous repertory of classical and contemporary plays at the Aldwych, and in 1962 to hold a special experimental season at the Arts Theatre. Under the directors, Peter Hall, Peter Brook and Paul Scofield, a brilliant team of over 100 actors was gathered together and the imaginative direction and artistic perfection of the ensemble playing became world famous.

Each year at the Aldwych arresting Shakespearean productions from Stratford alternate with other classics and stimulating modern work. There have been new experimental plays by native writers, such as Beckett, Mercer, Pinter, Saunders and Whiting. Stimulating foreign playwrights have included Albee, Arrabal, Brecht, Chayavsky, Duras, Dürrenmatt, Feiffer, Gorky, Günter Grass, Hochhuth, Triana and Weiss. Their work is discussed in Part IV.

The annual World Theatre Season, organised by Peter Daubney, has given a unique opportunity for seeing ensembles from other countries with apparatus for simultaneous translation.

The National Theatre.

Sixty years after Granville Barker and William Archer had formulated plans for a National

Theatre, the inaugural production of *Hamlet* took place on 22 October 1963 at its temporary home, the Old Vic.

Laurence Olivier already appointed director, the nucleus of a distinguished company was formed and soon established its high reputation for exquisite ensemble playing, guest artists also appearing on occasion.

The intention was to build up a large repertoire of classical and modern plays from all countries and the wide and varied list included works by Euripides, Shakespeare, Ben Jonson, Webster, Congreve, Farquhar, Molière, Feydeau, Pinero, O'Neill, Strindberg, Shaw, O'Casey and Brecht. Contemporary dramatists represented were often Arden, Arrabal, Griffiths, Miller, Nichols, Peter Shaffer, Stoppard and Wood.

The imaginative quality of production and acting was enthusiastically acclaimed by packed houses and the scenery was often breathtaking.

In April 1973 Peter Hall became co-director with Olivier and in the autumn assumed full responsibility.

In March 1976 the new National Theatre on the South Bank at last opened. It has three auditoria. The Lyttleton, with its proscenium arch familiar in England during the last 300 years, opened first, later The Olivier, with the type of stage used in Greek and Elizabethan times, but the smaller Cottesloe was not ready in 1976.

The English Stage Company.

Formed to promote contemporary drama, the company acquired in 1956 a long lease of the Royal Court with George Devine (d. 1965) as director and Tony Richardson as assistant. Declaring themselves a Writers' Theatre, they were extraordinarily successful in sponsoring new playwrights, such as Arden, Bond, Osborne, N. F. Simpson, Storey and E. A. Whitehead. The première of *Dingo* by the promising Charles Wood, was seen here, as were new plays by established authors like Beckett and Wesker. New plays appeared by stimulating foreign writers, including Ionesco, Genet, Sartre and Arthur Miller.

An interesting departure was to present for the first time seminal plays from the past, including the first Brecht staged in London and work by Jarry and Wedekind. In 1968 D. H. Lawrence's plays were at last produced.

In 1973 the Court was particularly successful with premières by Brenton and Hampton, and from '73 to '74 with 3 plays by Fugard, acted by his South African black collaborators.

These writers are all discussed in Part IV.

The Mermaid Theatre.

It was largely due to the efforts of Bernard Miles that in 1959 the City of London's first new theatre since Shakespeare's time was opened at Blackfriars. Commerce, industry and the general public had generously given money, the City Corporation had granted the site at a peppercorn rent and the surviving walls of a blitzed warehouse had been used as the shell for a delightful little theatre of 499 seats with an open stage, based on that of Shakespeare's day.

The Mermaid is now part of the City's artistic life with foyer exhibitions, films, concerts, and lectures. The enterprising "Molecule Club" for children uses ingenious theatrical means to demonstrate basic scientific principles.

The Mermaid has a fine varied record of productions, including British premières of works by Brecht, Camus, and O'Casey. There have been revivals of Shakespeare, Ford, Dekker, Beaumont and Fletcher and Shaw, and of foreign plays by Ibsen, Pirandello, Henry James Lessing and Euripides. Lowell's *Benito Cereno* (*q.v.*) and James Joyce's *Exiles* (*q.v.*) both had their premières here.

The National Youth Theatre.

Originating in Alleyn's School and the enterprise of Michael Croft, the N.Y.T. fosters in young people an appreciation of theatre, whether as audience or performers. Since 1959 it has performed annually in the West End and abroad. In 1971 Camden Council generously offered the N.Y.T. fine permanent headquarters—the new Shaw Theatre.

Terson (*q.v.*) has written for the N.Y.T. plays specially commissioned, admirably suited to the company and enthusiastically received. Several young amateur actors have become professional, including Derek Jacobi and John Stride.

Theatre Workshop and Joan Littlewood.

Between 1953 and 1961 Joan Littlewood as director of Theatre Workshop at Stratford East introduced several new playwrights, including Behan. Spontaneity, pseudo-Brechtian techniques and social commitment rather than careful construction were the hall-marks of her work, her masterpiece being *Oh What a Lovely War* (M). This paradoxically used a period piece brilliantly to satirise the tragic futility of the first world war.

In 1967 Littlewood directed *MacBird* and *Mrs. Wilson's Diary*. *MacBird* (P), by Barbara Garson, is an American parody on *Macbeth* in doggerel blank verse, attacking the American "Establishment", under Lyndon Johnson. Unfortunately Joan Littlewood made such alterations to the text that the satirical parallel with Shakespeare was blurred. *Mrs. Wilson's Diary* (M), in form a jolly prewar musical, was described by its authors, Ingrams and Wells, as "an affectionate lampoon" on the Wilson administration.

In 1970 Joan Littlewood returned to Stratford East, where she has produced Hill's *Forward Up Your End* and Wells' *The Projector*, set in Walpole's age but suggesting parallels with the collapse of flats at Ronan Point.

III. GLOSSARY OF DRAMATIC TERMS

Absurd Drama.

The Theatre of the Absurd, originating in Paris, was introduced here through the plays of Beckett and translations of Ionesco and Vian. It has had considerable impact on Pinter, N. F. Simpson, Saunders and Stoppard, while absurdist plays by the Americaan Albee and the Swiss Frisch have also been produced here.

The concept of the Absurd was first formulated by Camus to indicate the discrepancy between human reason and aspiration and an indifferent and hostile universe. But like Sartre he expressed his convictions through the traditional dramatic form.

Not every playwright of the Absurd is an existentialist and many are more concerned with an irrational human society than with the universe. What they have in common is a technique. All have discarded traditional realism and express absurdity through images that are themselves absurd, including bizarre situations and objects, both sad and comic, such as aged parents consigned to dustbins.

There is in the Absurd an element of Surrealism and Dr. Bradbrook has suggested that a better term might be Theatre of Dream, for it is the unconscious dream mind that juxtaposes objects and incidents that in the waking state have no connection, such as a rhinoceros in a provincial street. Pinter seems to have an intuitive awareness of the hinterland of dream, while Simpson makes a conscious manipulation of Surrealism.

Frisch has ably demonstrated that the Absurd can be an effective vehicle for satire and absurdist writers like Ioneso and Simpson have satirised the modern corruption of language by salesmen and politicians, using conversations of vapid emptiness to demonstrate its breakdown and relying more on ludicrous objects and situations, thus extending the range of total theatre.

The Aristotelian Play.

Brecht and Ionesco have disparagingly referred somewhat inaccurately, to "Aristotelianism". Strictly speaking, this means the concept of tragedy which Aristotle first analysed in his *Poetics*, basing it primarily on the poetic tragedies of Sophocles, especially the *Oedipus Rex* (P), *c.* 425 B.C. The Aristotelian concept, revived since the Renaissance, has obviously been much modified, but certain basic principles can still be discerned.

Aristotle claims that poetry in general aims at that rational pleasure which is part of the good life. He defines tragedy as the imitation of an action. By imitation he does not mean the description of an actual happening but of one that is possible. Hence the poetic licence whereby the dramatist may adapt historical material to his own theme.

Aristotle stresses that the action should be complete in itself and have inner coherence. Tragedy must have an intelligible beginning, a middle necessitated by the beginning and which itself necessitates the end. "The story . . . must represent one action, a complete whole, with its several incidents so closely connected that the transposal or withdrawal of any one will disjoint and dislocate the whole."

The action should be of some magnitude, with "incidents arousing pity and fear wherewith to accomplish the purgation of such emotions." Here is Aristotle's celebrated doctrine of purgation or "catharsis" which has been variously interpreted, some considering that something like a ceremonial purification is intended, with an ethical end in view, others that bodily or psychological relief from tension is meant.

Aristotle emphasised the paramount importance of action or plot, the characters being revealed in and through the action. The kind of plot recommended is one where the hero is an eminent man, neither inordinately good nor bad, whose misfortune is brought upon him by some error of judgment.

Here is the germ of the splendid Renaissance tragedy concerned with the fall of princes and also of the modern finely constructed play, such as Ibsen's *Ghosts*. Such a play has classical symmetry, the beginning, middle and end, becoming in modern parlance the exposition, development and climax or dénouement. It has its own organic unity and inevitability. But although many writers, such as Sartre, still work within the classical disciplines many have discarded the traditional form.

Brecht and his followers have repudiated the whole pattern in favour of a sequence of self-contained episodes strung along a narrative thread, where ironic detachment supersedes the emotional involvement and catharsis of Greek tragedy.

In this day of the common man few are concerned with the fall of princes, and it is interesting to examine some of the more striking modern plays and to ask how far they stand up to the Aristotelian canon. Should a new concept of tragedy be evolved, that of potentiality unrealised, not a fall from greatness but a failure to rise?

Black Comedy.

Orton (*q.v*) popularised a genre in which human suffering is presented as comic. The basic technique is the shock of violent juxtapositions both in language and incident. Death, mental illness, murder, sexual perversion, suddenly excite laughter because they are conveyed in deadpan jests and genteel terms, or are promptly succeeded by the bathos of farce. Like circus clowning, the style has some value, especially in satire, but it easily stifles compassion.

The Brechtian or Epic Play.

Many British dramatists have felt the pervasive influence of the Bavarian Brecht (*q.v.*), who developed a new kind of Epic or narrative play of debate, with a loose sequence of episodic scenes linked by commentary or songs. Discarding realism, Brecht attempted not to arouse the onlooker's emotions but to stimulate him to think about social issues and to take left-wing action. In the event his ambiguous central situation appealed to deeper levels of experience.

There have been several instances of the ambiguous protagonist, but English playwrights have tended to adopt not the political intentions but the style of the Epic genre. Esslin has said that Shaffer in *The Royal Hunt of the Sun* has joined "Bolt, Arden and John Whiting of *The Devils* in the select group of British dramatists who have genuinely benefited from the conception of epic . . . techniques in drama."

Theatre of Cruelty.

In 1938 Antonin Artaud published *The Theatre and its Double*, a collection of essays and letters, which forms the theoretic basis of the Theatre of Cruelty, his central purpose being a ritual of cruelty to exorcise fantasies.

Professor Brustein has described how Artaud hated industrial civilisation, believing, like Freud and D. H. Lawrence, that it stifled instinctual life. He claimed that the theatre, as the heart of a common culture, should enact a primitive ritual of cruelty, a sacrificial frenzy and exaltation. In this way it would bring to the surface and exorcise the spectator's latent anarchy, violence, and eroticism, serving as an "outlet for repressions".

Artaud's theories have yet to be proved. Anthropology has shown that a sacrificial blood ritual was long practised by primitive tribes without diminishing man's urge to cruelty, as is poetically conveyed in Edith Sitwell's *Gold Coast Customs* (*see* **M, Part III**). A modern dramatic enactment can certainly make us aware of repressed violent impulses but does it clear them away?

As to technique, Artaud envisaged a total theatre appealing to total man, primarily visual, where the all-important director would deploy "music, dance, plastic art, pantomime, mimicry, gesticulation, intonation, architecture, scenery and lighting" to induce a state of trance. Attacking the inadequacy of a pallid conceptual language, Artaud demanded that dramatic language should have an emotional and incantatory effect.

Genet fulfils Artaud's demands and in England the specific Theatre of Cruelty has been best represented by his plays, the *Marat Sade* of Weiss, Triana's *The Criminals* and *The Architect and the Emperor of Assyria* of Arrabal. But the methods of production advocated by Artaud have had a wide and pervasive influence on the movement towards total theatre.

Expressionism.

The genre flourished in Germany after the first world war, where its chief exponents were Kaiser and Toller, and in Czechoslovakia in the plays of Capek. O'Neill and O'Casey have also occasionally experimented with Expressionism.

Reacting from Realism with its insistence on individual psychology and the detailed representation of actual life, Kaiser, Toller and Capek deliberately rejected the particular in favour of the typical. Living at a time of social upheaval they were preoccupied with the class struggle and with man's fear of the encroaching machine.

Their subject was social flux and clash and they sought to project on to the stage the aspirations and fears of large social groups or of the generality of mankind.

Their characters are types, sometimes even symbolic figures such as the Nameless one representing the mob in Toller's *Man and the Masses*. Their décor is stylised with occasional use of film, the dialogue staccato and the brief scenes are characterised by mass movement and swift action.

Allardyce Nicoll carefully distinguishes between the aims and the methods of Expressionism. He considers that although some impressionistic plays of Strindberg and later subjective writers sometimes employ similar techniques they cannot justly be considered as expressionist because their aim is to reveal subjective feelings.

Naturalism.

Naturalism in drama may be regarded as a special case of Realism, and it is not easy, nor perhaps always desirable, to make a sharp distinction between the two.

Naturalistic drama attempts to record as faithfully as possible the actual experiences of life, however banal, and to present life, undistorted by the playwright's theories or too much concern for artistic form. The virtues of Naturalism are fidelity and spontaneity. Its danger is that it may keep so close to life as to lose artistic form and tension, becoming the stage version of the tape recorder. *See* **Slice-of-Life Play.**

Zola in the 1870s propounded the principles of Naturalism. Distrusting both the play of ideas and the well-constructed play as tending to impose on life a falsifying pattern, he urged that drama should record as objectively as possible the actual course of man's life, especially the way it is conditioned by environment.

Strindberg's *Miss Julie*, 1888, is an essay in Naturalism but the genre is found in its most accomplished form in the Russian theatre, especially in Stanislavsky's production at the Moscow Art Theatre of the plays of Chekhov and in 1902 of Gorky's *The Lower Depths*.

Neo-Realism.

There is nothing new in dramatic Realism (*q.v.*) as such. What is novel is the realistic presentation of the shabby lodgings and streets of the underprivileged. Gorky in *The Lower Depths* was perhaps the first dramatist to reveal the wretched condition of the destitute and this play influenced O'Neill's *The Iceman Cometh*. Their production in London, with a starkly realistic background, had some effect on those modern plays where the kitchen-sink and dustbin were as much in vogue as was formerly the fashionable drawing-room.

Any worthwhile play has significance far beyond its milieu and modern neo-realistic plays vary greatly in theme and purpose. Several playwrights like Wesker have themselves been workers and their plays are an authentic interpretation of their own culture, once inaccessible to the middle-class audience. The fact that their work is occasionally loose in structure may be attributable to the influence of Naturalism (*q.v.*) or to the author's unacademic background. The advent of this fresh and vigorous drama from a group that has seldom been articulate is most valuable.

Realism.

Writers of realistic drama, such as Galsworthy, attempt to create a stage illusion of actual life, usually through the medium of the well-constructed play. It is not always easy to distinguish between Realism and Naturalism—its extreme form—but one salient difference is that the latter tends to discard organised plot as imposing a false pattern on the flux of life.

The Satirical Play.

Recent years have seen heartening revivals of plays by Shaw, triggered off by Stage Sixty's production of *Widowers' Houses*, with its topical relevance to Rachmanism. There followed a long succession of Shaw revivals.

Shaw has found few successors, for genuine satire is a most demanding art. Subjective hostility and negative criticism are not enough. The motive power in Ibsen and Shaw was rational indignation, a most difficult fusion of strong emotion and objective reasoning, and their satire was constructive in that it implied and indicated positive values. It was also characterised by a precise aim at a specific target. Vague and wholesale denunciation diffuse a disagreeable tone which has a boomerang effect for it becomes associated not with the targets but with the playwright himself.

The graces of satire are detachment, irony and wit and it flourishes apparently in a stable society such as that of the 18th cent. which produced Swift and Voltaire. The European upheavals of the last half century have been unpropitious for satire and it is significant that the best plays in this genre, those of Frisch and Dürrenmatt, have come from neutral Switzerland.

The " Slice of Life " Play.

Here is an extreme kind of Naturalism, where the author has been so anxious to preserve fidelity to the natural spontaneity of living, that he has all but discarded form, as having a cramping and distorting effect.

Verse Drama.

During the 20th cent. several attempts have been made to revive drama in verse—the normal vehicle for the Renaissance playwright. Although the verse plays of Shakespeare and his contemporaries, kept alive in excellent revivals, still rise like the Himalayas above the contemporary scene, the dramatist today who tries to use verse has not the benefit of an unbroken tradition. T. S. Eliot and Christopher Fry succeeded in getting their verse plays on the stage but at the moment the most successful poetic drama achieves its effect through poetic prose and the theatrical poetry of its situation and stage imagery. Beckett, Arden and Pinter have captured this poetry.

The finest verse play seen on the English stage for many years is Robert Lowell's *Benito Cereno*.

The Well-made Play.

The term " well-made play " was frequently used in a derogatory sense. Eric Bentley has pointed out that the " well-made play " is a form of classical tragedy, degenerate in that although the plot is ingeniously contrived, with arresting situation, intrigue and suspense, the play is mechanical and devoid of feeling.

IV. INDIVIDUAL DRAMATISTS

This part, alphabetical in arrangement, includes representative plays of dramatists whose work, whether English or in translation, has had its British première since 1950. Unless otherwise stated the quotation of date and actor refers to the British première.

Some less expensive editions are referred to thus: F: Faber and Faber. M: Methuen. P: Penguin. Inexpensive acting editions can usually be obtained from French's Theatre Bookshop, 26 Southampton Street, W.C.2.

Arthur Adamov (b. 1908).

Adamov first wrote plays such as *Professor Taranne* (P), which translate his own personal neuroses into images of the absurd, until with the propagandist *Paolo Paoli* he adopted a Brechtian technique. His *Spring 1871*, an epic panorama of the Paris Commune, had its world première in London in 1962.

Edward Albee (b. 1928).

The American Albee is a brilliant satirist, master of a hostile dialogue of barbed intellectual wit, and an adept in utilising diverse styles. He was adopted by wealthy foster parents and his major plays express the claustrophobia, the emptiness that may lurk behind the deceptively secure façade of wealth.

His early plays include the absurdist *Zoo Story* (P) and *The American Dream* (P), and the realistic *The Death of Bessie Smith.*

Who's Afraid of Virginia Woolf? 1964. P.

A brilliant and scarifying satire on sterility in an American campus uses a ritual movement. George and Martha, named after the Washingtons, are an unsuccessful and childless middle-aged couple. They cherish a fantasy "son", whom George, to spite Martha, symbolically "murders" during a drunken night party, when they attack each other and their guests (a young couple also childless) with ferocious mental cruelty.

A Delicate Balance. 1969. P.

An icy surface glasses over treacherous depths in the well-to-do home of Tobias (Hordern) and Agnes (Peggy Ashcroft) and the play begins and ends with her virtual monologue—phrased with the elegance of a Henry James—on how it will be if she goes mad.

Agnes holds the "delicate balance" of polite manners, while tolerant Tobias is now ineffectual and her alcoholic sister Claire persists in her sarcastic utterance of unwelcome truths. The most galling, obliquely hinted at, is that Tobias is more drawn to Claire than to Agnes.

Their son long since dead, and Tobias having then withdrawn from Agnes, their sole offspring is the neurotic Julia, who now returns home at the breakdown of her fourth marriage.

Suddenly their "oldest friends", Harry and Edna, arrive seeking asylum from some inexplicable terror of "nothing". Bewildered, but courteous, the hosts accept their guests, but after Julia has threatened to shoot the "intruders", Agnes forces Tobias to realise that they bring "the plague".

Tobias, unable to discard his last ideal of friendship, begs them to stay, while telling them this truth, but they depart, realising that they demand a sacrifice they themselves could not make.

Here is a microcosm of a society where love and friendship have died, humanism crumbles, and little but polite diplomacy survives, often a vehicle for fear and hostility. In tone it is a bitter inversion of the Apocryphal *Tobit*, with its touching pictures of religious faith, family love and neighbourliness, and the "entertaining of Angels unaware".

The literary provenance in subject and style is Eliot's *Family Reunion*, where another Harry, fleeing the furies, comes to a Wishwood, also dominated by a woman whose husband had loved her sister, like Claire also a visionary. But in Eliot the visionary is healer not destroyer and Harry departs to "follow the bright angels."

With literary subtlety Albee exposes the "panic and emptiness" in a society losing its confidence and sense of values.

Tiny Alice. 1970.

A "metaphysical melodrama", of great emotional tension, possibly personal, is at surface level, like Dürrenmatt's *The Visit* (*q.v.*), a satire on materialism, with the victim sold to Mammon. It has another facet, the schema being primitive magic, the sexual initiation and ritual sacrifice of the victim. Here Albee draws on techniques of the Theatre of Cruelty (*q.v.*). There are also echoes of T. S. Eliot's *The Cocktail Party* (*q.v.*) and of Lewis Carroll's *Alice.*

A brilliant first scene initiates a bargain between two astute and unsavoury men, literally "of the same school", who detest each other—the Cardinal, corrupt representative of the Church, and the Lawyer, emissary of Miss Alice, embodiment of Croesus. She is to confer immense wealth on the Church on condition that the lay brother Julian shall collect it.

With Julian, the gentle and compassionate protagonist, a deeper theme is developed, the distinction between actuality and symbol. His ideals being service, obedience and possible martyrdom, Julian has fought against accepting illusion and a false god, the puppet made in man's image, instead of God the Creator.

But in Miss Alice's echoing castle he is confronted and confused by an extraordinary image, a huge model, an exact replica of the castle, and within it a tiny model of the model Sometimes events within castle and model synchronise.

The play's sinister dimension now becomes clearer, as Miss Alice, her brutal lover, the lawyer, and the butler, a former lover, plan, with the acquiescence of the cardinal, to entrap Julian. Their purpose is consummated as Miss Alice by witchery and her appeal "Help me", seduces Julian, when she utters the cry "Alice." (On the satirical plane this may signify that only by orgasm can the millionairess realise her identity).

Later, after Julian's marriage to Alice by the reluctant cardinal, the four participants in the plot circle round Julian drinking to "the ceremony" and "Alice." Julian is now told that Miss Alice is an illusion, a surrogate for the real Alice who is within the model. Refusing to accept this, he is callously shot by the lawyer and left to die alone, slumped against the model.

The disparate elements in this exciting and disturbing play are not perfectly fused. Although Miss Alice experiences conflict between her "awesome" rôle and genuine tenderness for Julian, the characters are, with the exception of the complex Julian, two-dimensional. He, in his shy integrity, is touchingly portrayed. But his problem of faith although clinically scrutinised is not penetrated. This is especially apparent in his ambiguous and over-long dying soliloquy.

The work is meticulously plotted and worded, motifs, gestures, and phrases poetically recurring with ironic and suggestive shifts of meaning.

All Over. 1971.

In the handsome room of a dying celebrity there "gather" his Wife aged seventy-one, his Mistress, a fading voluptuous beauty for whom he had twenty years ago deserted the Wife, his Best Friend with whom the Wife had had a brief affair on her husband's desertion, and his Son and Daughter. The characters are not named.

The Wife's question, "Is he dead yet?" opens the play and her chilly clinical detachment is reflected in the older generation's dispassionate reminiscences. The Wife's haughty aloofness is a defence against desperate emotion, but she does not disguise her contempt for her ineffectual Son and unstable Daughter. The only event and climax of Act 1 is the unhappy Daughter's revengeful attempt to let the waiting Pressmen into the room.

Only at the final intimation of death does the Wife's control crumble, as with slow self-discovery she says, "I don't love *anyone.* (Pause) Any more . . . I LOVE MY HUSBAND!! . . ." She finally breaks into incontrollable sobbing, crying, "Because I'm unhappy."

This is a hint that the Wife may have realised the significance for herself of her former vindictive taunt to her daughter, "Do you love anyone?" She may realise that the plight of her despised children may not be unconnected with the parents for twice she had said, "We made them."

But characterisation in depth is not the mainspring here, for Albee has attempted to endistance and universalise the situation. There are many references to ritual and echoes of T. S. Eliot's *The Family Reunion.* But in *All Over* the power of communal emotion which inspires the ritual of death is lacking. There is little love and no religious awe, and ritual has dwindled to convention.

This is a static play, like the fifteenth-century *Everyman*, a paradigm of the human predicament but enacted now in a "sad and shabby time".

Jean Anouilh (b. 1910).

Anouilh is a playwright of remarkable theatrical versatility and skill. Following Giraudoux, he has frequently employed classical themes, as in *Eurydice* (M), and *Antigone*, 1949 (M), with Olivier and Vivien Leigh. More recently he has treated historical figures, Saint Joan in *The Lark* (M), and Becket in the play of that name (M). The play within a play is a favourite expedient of his and he used it again in *The Fighting Cock* (M), produced at Chichester, 1966.

Anouilh's outlook is deeply pessimistic. A recurring theme is that purity is incompatible with experience of life and many of his protagonists say, "No." His plays fall into two categories—the fatalistic *pièces noires* and the romantic fantasies *pièces roses*. Anouilh's amoral attitude has been reflected in many West End successes.

Aleksei Arbuzov (b. 1908).

The Russian producer and playwright Arbuzov has been writing since 1930.

The Promise. 1966.

In the Chekhovian tradition *The Promise* is a moving and positive work free from both illusion and despair. During the siege of Leningrad two boys and a girl contrive to survive in a bombed house, and here in brief episodic scenes their hardship, gaiety, and the slow awakening of love are shown with a delicate and touching naturalism.

Four years later Lika must choose between the two men and although she loves the engineer Marat she chooses the dependent, poetic Leonidik. The decision brings fulfilment to no one and finally Leonidik courageously summons back Marat and leaves him and Lika together.

Produced in 1976 were *Evening Light* and *Once Upon a Time*—humane and scrupulously non-political plays.

John Arden (b. 1930).

Arden is a vigorous and gifted playwright, who has experimented with a variety of subjects and methods, sometimes too original and complex to find quick acceptance.

He has the rare gift of the poet and his diction is often richly suggestive and evocative. He has said in interview that plays should use speech in the way that a poet uses individual images and that the playwright "should *form* language rather than just report it", so that even colloquial speech is given a tension and dramatic rhythm.

With the exception of *The Island of the Mighty* Arden's major work has been produced before 1967 and since some more recent plays have differed in approach and key it is appropriate first to discuss his earlier work.

His characters have been full-blooded and rich in human contradictions, and he has sympathetically brought to life even such bogeys as Herod and King John. He has chosen to dwell on some ambiguous personality, where generosity conflicts with violence, and to consider the problems of directing man's unruly vitality.

His favourite theme has been the dispute between instinctual energy and good government and he has pleaded the case cogently for both sides, giving no facile judgment or direct "message" unless it be "the recognition of the fallibility of man". Thus although, like Brecht, he is deeply concerned with social and political issues, he remained politically "uncommitted." He has above all been the dramatist of the dilemma.

There has been a fruitful cross-fertilisation of Arden's interest in current events and his literary studies; and his historical plays, like Brecht's *Mother Courage*, have combined a fine sense of period and a sharp relevance to some current issue.

His plays have been poetic in structure, depending in part on the recurrent image and metaphor and, like Arthur Miller in *The Crucible*, he has skilfully devised for each an appropriate dialect of time and place. At the same time he has a keen sense of theatre, and has successfully adapted techniques from Miracle plays, Elizabethan drama, music-hall, puppet stage, and Brechtian epic play.

Apart from *The Island of the Mighty*, most of Arden's recent plays have been more theatrical in effect. They lack his poetic intensity both in style and structure, despite a more lavish use of verse and song. They are still much concerned with social problems but there is not the same many-angled approach and personalities are often deliberately presented in caricature.

Live Like Pigs. 1958. P.

Seventeen realistic scenes full of comic and frightening incident reveal how fatal conflicts develop between households at different social levels in a new housing estate. Street ballads in Brechtian style preface some scenes.

The Happy Haven. 1960. P.

Here, in a good-tempered satirical fable, enlivened by a dash of magic, Arden touches on problems of longevity.

Doctor Copperthwaite, the superintendent of the Happy Haven, an old people's home, is, like a mediaeval alchemist, bent on producing an Elixir of Life and Youth, intending to use his five unsuspecting patients as guinea-pigs. But outwitted by them he is himself transformed into a small boy.

The theme is childishness. The egocentric demands of the very old are seen as amusing childish foibles, while Doctor Copperthwaite brings childishness on himself.

In form the play is an extended puppet show. The characters wear masks, the set is formalised.

Serjeant Musgrave's Dance. 1959. M.

For a fine play, which explores the ethical dilemma of war, Arden drew on two sources—contemporary events in Cyprus and a journal written by a deeply devout N.C.O. during the Crimean War. He has fused his material into vivid incidents, which he projects against the background of a fictitious colonial war of the 1880s.

In a frost-bound colliery town there arrive three private soldiers, led by the dominating Serjeant Musgrave. They claim to have come recruiting but are in fact deserters from a colonial war.

In spite of his rigid sense of military duty, Musgrave had been horrified by the terrible five-fold reprisals taken by the British for the assassination of a comrade, Billy Hicks. Believing himself to be God's agent, he has now come to Billy's town, obsessed by one purpose, to expose war's horrors.

Exhibiting Billy's skeleton in the market-place, he at first wins sympathy in his denunciation of atrocities. Then bewildered by his own confused "logic", he demands twenty-five deaths in return for the five taken by the British and turns the Gatling on the astonished crowd.

Suddenly, with the thaw, the Dragoons arrive and Musgrave finds himself awaiting execution, stunned that no one has learned the lesson he yearned to teach.

Fierce incident and macabre surprise are used for a play of ideas which enunciates no facile answer. It is typical of Arden's fair and non-doctrinaire approach that the dilemma of the religious man in face of war should be embodied in the fanatical and confused Musgrave. This has sometimes misled the audience, but the spirit of compassion implicit throughout the play is clearly revealed in the gentle, pacific Private Attercliffe, also to be executed with Musgrave. The women's parts are also significant expecially that of Mrs. Hitchcock, the owner of the inn, who visits Musgrave in prison and shows him how he had erred in trying to use war itself to end war. In his darkest despair she gives him hope, and he accepts wine from her.

The complex play weaves together many tensions; harsh discord between colliery owner and strikers; contention between the three privates, each of whom is strongly individualised; the discrepancy between a woman's love and the careless soldier's life; Musgrave's own bitter inner struggle.

The dialogue has a wonderful period character and the soldiers' ballads and lyrical songs occur with complete naturalness.

The Workhouse Donkey. 1963. M.

Styled by Arden as a "vulgar melodrama", this ample Brechtian play shows jockeying for power in a northern town between the Tory Alderman Sweetman, a wealthy brewer, and Alderman Butterthwaite (Frank Finlay), the Labour ex-mayor. Both attempt to manipulate the police and to enlist the support of the electorate, represented by the shifty turncoat Doctor Blomax, until all these four elements of the community are deeply corrupted.

Butterthwaite, called "the workhouse donkey" because born in the workhouse, is the dominating Rabelaisian character. A Dionysiac figure, he is drunken, lecherous and amoral, yet devotedly loyal and generous. Finally in an attempt to help the treacherous Blomax he robs the Borough safe and brings disaster on himself and the town.

The personality of the late Mr. Joseph D'Arcy of Dublin inspired much of the play.

Armstrong's Last Goodnight. 1964. M.

The old "Ballad of Johnie Armstrang", *c.* 1603, forms the framework of a play concerning the dilemmas of government. Armstrong of Gilnockie, the Scots Border laird, freebooter and rebel, is invited to a meeting by the young Scottish King James V and then treacherously hanged. Arden has introduced into this stark story the historical character of the king's herald, Sir David Lindsay, poet and politician, and shows him at first striving by devious diplomatic expedients to persuade Armstrong (Albert Finney) to loyalty, before he finally advises force. The play is diversified by minor characters and incidents which overcomplicate the impressive ballad line.

The introduction of Lindsay was suggested to Arden by his reading of Conor Cruise O'Brien's book *To Katanga and back*, for he was struck by "a basic similarity of moral" between 20th-cent. Africa and 16th-cent. Scotland, the rôle of O'Brien being similar to that which he invents for Lindsay.

Arden makes free use of Elizabethan pageantry and of Brechtian ballad-singing and the setting is the mediaeval convention of "simultaneous mansions", Gilnockie, the Border, and the Court all being formally represented on the stage at one and the same time.

Arden "constructed" a dialect to suggest place and period, but it is difficult to follow.

Left-handed Liberty. 1965. M.

Commissioned by the Corporation of the City of London to write a play to commemorate the 750th anniversary of Magna Carta, Arden presents the historical facts with very little transposition and addition.

He approaches his theme of liberty from an unusual angle, showing the aftermath of Runnymede in the apparent failure of the Charter, and demonstrating that the agreement had to take place in people's minds before it could become effective.

Arden does not present a clash of black and white. John is a rounded character, a slippery villain, but shrewd and energetic and gifted with the Plantagenet charm, while some of the barons are coarse and unscrupulous fighters.

The use of stylised scene emblems gives mediaeval colour to the simple staging and Arden has again invented a suitable dialect.

The Royal Pardon. 1967. M.

A play for young teenagers, was written in collaboration with Arden's Irish wife Margaretta D'Arcy.

Squire Jonathan. 1968.

In a grim Gothic tower, centuries ago, threadbare old Jonathan, descended from kings, gloats over his treasure chest, suspicious of the Dark Men outside and desiring the White Woman. A foolish, clumsy blonde, she appears wearing a chastity belt and eventually refusing his jewels, goes to the Dark Men. The play, was interpreted as an image of Britain's current situation, Jonathan dressed as Wilson and the White Woman like a Britannia or Boadicea.

The Hero Rises Up. 1968. M.

Written with his wife, this burlesque of melodrama is a sardonic enquiry into the motivation and deeds of Nelson, and the very differing reactions he occasioned. The authors use the racy style of period ephemera, such as street ballads, broadsheets and caricature and "stage spectacles of sensational splendour" like "tuppence-coloured prints".

The Ballygombeen Bequest. 1972.

Arden and his wife assert exploitation in Galway. An absentee English landlord so takes advantage of the tourist trade inflating the price of land that he evicts the ignorant local smallholder.

Although Arden disclaims the rôle of activist, this play of protest, conveyed in pantomime style, has been called his first "agit prop" work.

The Island of the Mighty. 1972. M.

A play written as a television trilogy for the B.B.C. went unproduced and Arden collaborated with his wife in the long work produced by the R.S.C.

The Celtic Arthurian legends and the *Golden Bough* form a misty background to Arden's convincing picture of what were probably the harsh realities of life in the chaotic Dark Age that succeeded Rome's withdrawal from Britain.

The Romano-British Arthur, now nearing seventy, is a limping hero who has striven for thirty years to maintain order during the break-up of a civilisation. Nominally Christian and boasting Imperial descent he cherishes the Roman ideals of "justice, restraint of power and protection of the weak". He relies on his highly disciplined but ageing armoured cavalry, the loyalty of the handsome young Medraut, his nephew, and the diplomacy of Merlin.

Merlin, a subtle and complex personality, shares Arthur's ideal of unity but is increasingly distressed by war's cruelties. A radical young pagan poet, Aneurin, is concerned with the oppression of obscure individuals and the poets act as commentators offering differing insights.

Britain is ravaged by persistent English raids and torn internally by rival chieftains, blood feuds and vengeful bandits, while the indigenous matriarchal fertility religions, suppressed by the Romans, linger secretly in distorted forms.

Again Arden skilfully presents the interplay of social forces through arresting individuals such as the turbulent roving brothers Balin and Balan, dispossessed by the English, and the pathetic young bondwoman, passed like a chattel from man to man.

The commanding theme is land hunger. Arthur realises that Britain's chief peril is the remorseless English attacks, but unable to persuade the British to unite all he can do is to fight to preserve *some* patch of fertile ground. But he is gradually worn down by British disunity, the growing ambition of Medraut and his own inner conflicts.

Arthur's final undoing is the resurgence of the matriarchal pagan cults. This is early foreshadowed in the frightening annual fertility rituals of a desperately poor tribe of pagan Picts, the Wild Cats, who assume weird cat masks. The captured Balan becoming consort to the princess has to fight his lame predecessor and is himself ritually lamed. But the avaricious old queen, finding his brother Balin shipwrecked, orders that this ritual be re-enacted prematurely. The doomed brothers fight and kill each other and the fertility magic is also lost.

Arthur is similarly destroyed. For reasons of political expediency he marries the mischievous young Gwenhwyvar. Taught by the crone Morgan, Arthur's sister, that she represents the ancient cult, Gwenhwyvar sets her sign on Medraut, who is wildly acclaimed by the people. But due ceremony has been neglected and as Medraut announces that he will claim Imperial rule Morgan despairingly tears to shreds her symbolic green fertility robe.

Meanwhile Arthur has gradually revealed that he also has been involved in the ancient superstition and that Medraut is in fact his son by ritual incest, instigated by Morgan. In a final catastrophic battle Medraut and Arthur destroy each other and the way is wide open for the English invasion. As Merlin had forseen, five hundred years of history were " swept away to nowhere in a pagan bog of blood and mud " and Merlin loses his reason.

The play is alive with a host of convincing characters, complex inter-relationships, violent unruly emotion and exciting incident. The dialogue is clearly individualised and with some few exceptions has both a period flavour and yet immediate freshness. The style varies between prose and verse with some passages of poetic intensity and power, especially in the weird and erotic sequences, and it conjures up a landscape of Roman ruins, wildwood and desolate shore. Interspersed are ballads, some almost doggerel, others like genuine early ballads, are richly suggestive, especially the final refrain.

Some incidents seem superfluous and it is confusing that in a confessedly anti-imperialist play Arthur should be the centre of the action.

The play has been called untidy, but " tidiness " would be inappropriate in this image of civilisation in breakdown. Arden has so orchestrated his themes that there is a poetic resonance in its design.

It is regrettable that the play could not be shown as planned, as a trilogy, when the complexities of its rich and intricate tapestry could be gradually assimilated and its relevance to our own divided and hungry world fully realised.

Fernando Arrabal (b. 1932).

Born in Spanish Morocco, Arrabal was early involved in cruelty. He was four years old when the Spanish Civil War broke out and his father was condemned to thirty years' imprisonment. When he was nine Arrabal was told that his father had escaped. He never heard of him again. The father, whom he had deeply loved, had been completely abandoned by his mother and this harrowing experience is given dramatic expression in *The Two Executioners*, P. He retains vivid memories of the Civil War, the mass executions and the cries of tortured prisoners and says that in schooling and religion he was " brought up on sado-masochism ". When of age he broke free from his extraordinary mother and in 1955 he moved finally to France.

Arrabal's work is in the tradition of Spanish surrealism, and even before reading Ionesco and Beckett he wrote plays considered as absurdist. " His main preoccupation," says Esslin, " is with the absurdity of ethical and moral rules. He looks at the world with the incomprehension of a child that simply cannot understand the logic of conventional morality." His work, which is " a highly disturbing mixture of innocence and cruelty ", has been much influenced by Artaud's Theatre of Cruelty and from 1962 he developed his ritualistic theatre as a Panic Ceremony, so called after the god Pan.

Arrabal has also experimented with abstract drama. The *Orchestration Théâtrale* of 1959 attempted to create a dramatic spectacle devoid of human content and consisting solely in the manipulation of three-dimensional shapes—some mechanical and others moved by dancers—to the accompaniment of coloured diagrams.

Arrabal's work is increasingly characterised by surrealist fantasy and the grotesque. Disclaiming imagination, he has said, " What I do is to copy my memories or my dreams . . . almost exactly, without changing a word."

The Architect and the Emperor of Assyria. 1971.

After terrifying intensity of noise the lordly Emperor descends from the skies calmly announcing to a cowering man whom he later dubs his architect that he is the sole survivor.

The situation recalls *The Tempest*, the Emperor, like Prospero, an embodiment of civilisation, the Architect an amalgam of Caliban and Ariel, a primitive, at first ignorant even of language, yet retaining magical powers over nature.

These two, the sole inhabitants of a desert island, play out an unending repetition of sado-masochistic fantasies, springing from infantile traumas. All but naked they circle each other in balletic movement and mime, instantaneously exchanging such rôles as master, persecutor, judge, lover and mother.

In Act I the Emperor is usually dominant, though sometimes sobbing for comfort in the arms of his " mummy ". In Act II he is judged by the Architect for murdering his own mother whom he gave to his dog to eat. He demands the same punishment and is killed and eaten by the Architect, who in his cannibalism sucks in the Emperor's civilisation but loses his former magical power.

Again come darkness and deafening noise, but this time the Architect descends, taking over the Emperor's rôle.

As in Triana's more disciplined *The Criminals*, the dramatic movement is cyclical, the remorseless, self-destroying recurrence of obession, especially guilt-ridden hate and dependence on the mother. The play has some root in anthropology and recalls Artaud's theories, exposing man's most grisly unconscious motivation and deploying a most extensive range of theatrical devices. Garcia, the producer, used brilliant lighting and baroque music.

Tense and exciting, the work can yet have a shattering effect on the audience, which is implicity called on to play the exhausting rôle of untrained and helpless psychiatrist. The basic subject is that of Aeschylus' *The Eumenides*—matricide pursued by guilt. But the Greek tragedy exhilarates and achieves an Aristotelian catharsis.

And They Handcuffed the Flowers. 1973.

The title is derived from words of Lorca who in 1936 was executed by fascists. The play was stimulated by requests that the playwright would bear witness to what he had seen during his few weeks of political imprisonment in 1967 but its chief source of inspiration is his anguished childhood.

Apart from a few casual references and brief readings by a little girl sitting on a stool, few factual details about prison life emerge for Arrabal is preoccupied with the terrible distortion of the psyche caused by long years of incarceration. His three principal characters are the three inmates of a prison cell now degraded by their inhuman conditions. Their pathological urges are enacted in sado-masochistic fantasies, religious and sexual, in which the prison chaplain, hated because evasion of mass is punished by solitary confinement, is ritually castrated, the mass is parodied, there is a pornographic Christ and harsh grotesque whores invade the scene.

In contrast to the extravagant surrealist fantasies, the simplicity of some direct questions is all the more effective. "Who invented the prison? Animals don't have them."

It is interesting to compare more restrained plays written by ex-prisoners, such as Genet's *Deathwatch* and Behan's *The Quare Fellow.*

Alan Ayckbourn (b. 1939).

Ayckbourn is a successful writer of social comedy with a sharp eye for the trivial distinctions and snobberies within the middle class. He is adept in contriving ingenious incident and witty rejoinder. His craftsmanlike plays include *Relatively Speaking*, 1967, *How the Other Half Loves*, 1970, and *Time and Time Again*, 1972.

Absurd Person Singular. 1973.

A farcical comedy shows three couples participating in three successive Christmas Eve parties.

In the first, Sidney, a pushing property developer, tries vainly to force party games on his more sophisticated guests. But at the third party he is so secure in his new wealth that he easily imposes on his hosts the humiliating games they had once scorned.

In a symmetrical and eventful play Ayckbourn reveals character development and implies criticism of a social order easily reversed by the thrusting plutocrat.

The Norman Conquests. 1974.

The Norman Conquests is a *tour de force*, a trilogy of 3 farcical comedies: *Table Manners, Living Together* and *Round and Round the Garden.* The action is not consecutive but simultaneous and interlocking, the off-stage events of one play providing the material of the others. Each is limited to either dining-room, living-room or garden of the same home and spanning a family weekend they expose the relationships between only six people. Success within these stringent limits demonstrates Ayckbourn's assured theatrical expertise.

The home is that of a demanding invalid mother who does not appear. Here the spinster daughter, Annie, entertains her capable sister, Ruth, married to the philandering Norman, her brother Reg, with his bossy, prudish wife, Sarah, and her own suitor the hilariously slow-witted Tom.

Norman has persuaded Annie to go away with him for a weekend but is foiled by Sarah. Piqued he sets himself to persuade Sarah herself to an illicit assignation. Then he misinterprets his wife's attempts to bring him to his senses as passion for himself and is finally rejected by all three women.

The plays exemplify Ayckbourn's clever observation of human folly, acute but not unkindly, and his deft farcical timing. Each play claims to be self-subsistent, but enjoyment of one is enhanced by what is made explicit by its fore-runners.

Absent Friends. 1975.

Colin, whose fiancée had been lost at sea, is entertained to tea by Paul (whose wife Colin had once courted) along with other friends of bachelor days. Much empty jocularity is a smoke-screen for hurt feelings.

Confusions. 1976.

Five short plays, presented by a cast of five, again ingeniously reveal the pain engendered by middle-class snobbery.

Samuel Beckett (b. 1906). *See also* Section M.

Beckett, an Anglo-Irishman, who has made his home in France, is both novelist and the most distinguished of the English dramatists of the Absurd. His world is drastically limited, peopled chiefly by old men awaiting their death, and conceived with the suggestiveness of the true poet.

His work is poetic in its verbal imagery, sometimes as searching and macabre as that of Webster, and his dramatic prose has an underlying rhythm often more flexible and effective than that of Eliot's verse. In structure his plays have a poetic symbolism, like that of James Joyce, Beckett's close friend, and their striking visual imagery has a kind of theatrical poetry, as for instance the two tramps at the foot of a bare tree in *Waiting for Godot.* It is remarkable that so literary a playwright should also have succeeded with the wordless mime play.

Beckett's chief weakness as a dramatist is that the action and visual imagery are frequently too static, as in the motionless dustbins in *End Game*, much less effective theatrically than Ionesco's movable chairs.

Waiting for Godot. 1955. F.

This tantalising and compelling tragi-comedy, Beckett's masterpiece, originally written in French and produced in Paris in 1953, was later translated and performed in more than twenty countries.

Character and incident are pared to the bone and only a skeleton situation remains. At evening, on a desolate road, bare but for a single tree, two wretched tramps, Vladimir and Estragon, nicknamed Didi and Gogo, wait for a mysterious Mr. Godot. As they while away the time with desultory talk and clowning, a tragi-farcical diversion is provided by the entry of Pozzo and Lucky, bullying master and wretched slave, and a boy later brings a message that Mr. Godot cannot come but will arrive the next evening. After discussing whether or not they shall hang themselves from the tree, the tramps decide to go away for the night, but remain on the spot.

Act II presents "Next day, same place," the only difference being that the tree has sprouted a few leaves, and the basic pattern of Act I is repeated.

Although by the skilful use of music-hall techniques Beckett presents his tramps in the guise of amusing clowns, they are at the same time pathetically human as they waver between suicide and irrational hope. A fretful affection has kept them together over fifty years, and their dispositions are complementary, possibly even representing different aspects of the one personality.

Pozzo and Lucky, another pair of contrasting characters, are portrayed more farcically. The loud, confident Pozzo drives Lucky in as if he were a beast of burden. Lucky carries in his mouth the whip with which he is beaten and humbly obeys every insolent command. He dances for Pozzo and even thinks for him. In their second appearance Pozzo is blind and Lucky dumb.

They may be considered personifications respectively of master and slave, worldly materialism and higher values, the physical and the intellectual, body and soul, or the two aspects of a sado-masochistic relationship.

The play as a whole is a most complex dramatic symbol expressing man's anxiety and suffering as to his origin and destination.

The uncertainty is symbolised by the characters' confusion as to even the physical actualities of time and place, but the dominating symbol is the tramps' doubt as to Godot's identity and purpose.

To equate Godot with God is inadequate, yet the play has Christian references. A tree is frequently used as an emblem of the Cross. Beckett, questioned about his theme, quoted Saint Augustine, . . . "Do not despair; one of the thieves was saved. Do not presume; one of the thieves was damned."

Beckett neither affirms nor denies Saint Augustine's statement but inverts it into a question, more distressing than direct denial. Can we any longer accept the existence of divine grace and judgment? It is a question such as this that gives to the play its symbolic shape of doubt, and which is cogently expressed in the theatrical image of two outcasts at the foot of a tree, a tree of life which puts forth leaves, a tree of death which they contemplate using as a gallows.

Yet the significance of the play is even deeper than an exploration of religious doubt, its appeal wider and more contemporary. The anguished uncertainty of the 20th cent. is whether life has any meaning whatsoever.

Some have considered it to be written from the point of view of existentialism: continuing vainly to hope for a supernatural revelation, the tramps lack the courage to come to terms with the nothingness of our existence and the need to choose and create our own destiny.

A Jungian psychologist, Eva Metman, has made a similar interpretation, remarking, "Godot's function seems to be to keep his dependents unconscious."

"Habit is a great deadener," says Vladimir. If Beckett's play enables the audience to escape the drug of habit and to face this image of anguish and so find some relief, then it may have the therapeutic value of that inner knowledge advocated by Freud and Jung.

It is not a play for those who cannot bear to suffer. When performed in San Francisco Gaol, the first play there for forty-four years, it held its audience of fourteen hundred convicts spellbound. They realised that each must find his own personal message. All knew that it spoke to those who must suffer and wait.

Endgame. 1958. F.

Also re-created from the French, this play again depicts a static situation. In a single, claustrophobic room, the selfish, materialistic Hamm, who keeps his senile and legless parents in dustbins, is now paralysed and blind and dependent on his servant Clov, who longs to leave him. But if Clov should leave, both would die, for Hamm owns the only store of food in a devastated and dead world. Finally Clov sees outside what may be a small boy, "a potential procreator," and he prepares for departure but remains immobile.

The play like poetry can be interpreted in several ways. Since Hamm and Clov are mutually dependent, it probably represents tension between complementary aspects of personality, Hamm sensation and emotion, and Clov intellect. As Clov has vision and sees the boy, the situation suggests the struggle of the mystic endeavouring to escape from a deadening materialism to a vital awakening of the spirit. It may also depict a period of traumatic depression when the whole external world seems dead and unreal. The play's overall impression is that of the dissolution of the personality in death, both personal and global.

Endgame lacks the wry humour of *Godot.*

Krapp's Last Tape. 1958. F.

In the briefest sketch, Krapp, a solitary, decrepit, unsuccessful old man listens to his own autobiographical tape-recording of thirty years ago, but the moment of miraculous insight it commemorates is now so meaningless to him that he switches off that section of the recording and broods on a description of his love-making.

Beckett employs a most effective stage device to pose contemporary queries as to the limitations of verbal communication and the continuity of personal identity.

Happy Days. 1962. F.

Winnie, buried to her waist in a mound of earth, assiduously tries to fill in the time between the waking bell and the bell for sleep with the routine of nail filing, with rummaging in her capacious bag, with memories of her first kiss and of her husband's proposal and with a flood of talk adjuring cheerfulness, "ah yes . . . great mercies". In rare moments with bent head and breaking voice she says, "What *is* one to do? All day long. Day after day", but soon, lifts her head with a smile—"The old style!"

She shows tender concern for her husband, Willie, whose bald head topped by a boater is just visible behind the mound. ". . . just to know you are within hearing and conceivably on the semi-alert, is—er—paradise enow," she says, overjoyed at his rare and monosyllabic replies. To his answer, "It", she cries, "Oh you are going to talk to me today. This is going to be a happy day!"

In a brief second act Winnie is buried to her neck. Willie "dressed to kill" in a morning coat crawls from behind the mound and collapses while trying to reach her. She is shocked that he may have gone out of his "poor old wits". Just audibly he says, "Win", and the happy expression grows on her face.

It is possible to conjecture several interpretations, the most obvious being that of the woman becoming paralysed by illness and unable any longer to make contact with or help the husband who appears to have psychological difficulties. Poor Willie had always been in "dire need of a hand". In her bag is the revolver he had asked her to take from him. Now he can barely communicate, hardly crawl and has to reverse into a hole which shelters him, an image suggesting Beckett's recurring theme of a desire to regress to childhood and the womb.

The theme is suffering but the surface of the play is rich comedy.

Play. 1964. F.

Beckett's own directions best describe the striking imagery of a brief one-act play. "Three identical grey urns . . . From each a head protrudes, the neck held fast in the urn's mouth . . . They face undeviatingly front throughout the play. Faces so lost as to age and aspect as to seem almost part of the urns."

The heads are those of a man between two women, apparently his wife and mistress. With impassive faces and normally toneless voices each utters a monologue. At first there builds up a vivid and amusing picture of a man who had passionately loved two women who were possessive and bitterly jealous. When the man suddenly disappears from an impossible situation the voices become dim and lower, for all three are left isolated living in a limbo of obsessive memory and sadness, touched by pity.

The imprisoning urns effectively symbolise their self-absorbed condition.

Not I. 1973. F.

In a play of only fifteen minutes Beckett pares every thing down to bare essentials. On a dark stage there is a dimly lit mouth appearing totally disconnected from the rest of the body and downstage a faintly visible Auditor, intent on Mouth, cloaked, silent and all but immobile.

Mouth (Billie Whitelaw) pours forth a flood of disjointed phrases, voicing the anguish of a woman nearing seventy to whom she persistently refers as "She". Some few facts emerge. Born prematurely and deserted by the mother she had been an unloved waif with "no love of any kind" and "practically speechless . . . all her days".

One early April morning "wandering in a field" she had suddenly experienced some extraordinary shock, finding herself barely sentient and aware only of darkness with a beam of light "ferreting around" and a "dull roar in the skull".

Later, came thoughts that she was being punished, that she was "not suffering" at any rate "so far" and then the sudden realisation that "words were coming" and that "a voice she did not recognise . . . at first" must be her own, followed by the sensation of her mouth actually moving, "mouth on fire" but "no idea what she's saying" and with "the brain . . . raving away on its own . . . trying to make sense of it . . . or make it stop".

The frenzied monologue is four times punctuated by a vehement disclaimer that Mouth is speaking of herself, when, as if in answer to questions she cries, "what? . . . who? . . . no! . . . she!" while the silent Auditor raises and drops his or her arms in a gesture of hopeless compassion. The play expresses complete despair save that the closing words suggest a desperate courage as Mouth gasps, "not knowing . . . what to try" but "no matter . . . keep on . . . hit on it in the end" while her repetition of religious phrases is no longer accompanied by harsh laughter but may express acceptance, "God is love . . . tender mercies . . . new every morning".

The monologue has some basis in commonplace fact and it might be interpreted as occasioned by a stroke or as expressing the agony of an autistic or schizophrenic personality. But the play has a much wider and deeper reference, for it is a poignant dramatic image of the lonely anguish of man enmeshed in the dark enigma of human suffering and desperately seeking meaning.

Footfalls and *That Time.* 1976.

Footfalls. Mrs. Winter was in her forties when May (Billie Whitelaw) was born. When the mother was bedridden May nursed her devotedly. Now locked in her past May paces rhythmically up and down, the dim light concentrated on her feet although her dead mother's voice implores her, "Will you never have done revolving it all?" Such are the few theatrical images. *That Time.* Dimly lighted an old man's face is immobile, while three unseen voices disjointedly represent his past.

Brendan Behan (1923–64).

Behan, a Dubliner, had only two plays produced in his life. *The Quare Fellow*, 1956 (M), is set in a prison the day before the hanging of a brutal fratricide and is incidentally an effective plea for the abolition of capital punishment. *The Hostage*, 1958 (M), is set in a Dublin brothel where a captured young Cockney soldier expects death during Irish political strife. Both were given shape by Joan Littlewood. *Richard's Cork Leg*, 1972 (M), lacks her sense of tension. The personnel of Behan's plays are generally wildly eccentric and their world randy and bizarre, relying on a vivid impressionistic style and lively ribald speech—an innovation in the '50s.

Alan Bennett.

Bennet was one of the participants in the witty, satirical revue, *Beyond the Fringe*, and in the television programmes that followed.

Forty Years On. 1968. F.

The retiring Head Master (Gielgud) of Albion House, a minor public school, is entertained by a cavalcade of 20th-cent. British history, devised by his Radical successor and enacted by the boys.

The rather loose organisation of the play gives opportunity for entertaining, satirical skits on the public school and on the middle class, where Bennett can exercise his special talent for parody.

Esslin has pointed out that the format is similar to that of the *Marat Sade* of Weiss.

Getting On. 1971. F.

In his cluttered Highgate home George Oliver, Labour M.P. in his forties, surveys with dismay the onset of age and the prospect of a mediocre future, where the hand has been dealt.

His youthful enthusiasm for the Welfare State now disregarded, George voices Bennett's free-wheeling satire on current trends in a picturesque idiom, biting, witty, comic, sometimes merely facetious.

Although concerned, he is too busy talking to be fully aware of the lonely predicament of his wife, teenage son, and friend, his Tory pair. Social satire constitutes not only the surface but the driving force of a comedy which, like Nichols' *Forget-me-not Lane* (*q.v.*) is very funny but sad.

Habeas Corpus. 1973. F.

Mrs. Swabb, sturdy daily help, presents her employers as caricatures in the style of seaside postcards.

Most are preoccupied with their bodily idiosyncracies. The ageing Dr. Wickstead still desires his female patients, his wife contemplates her menopause with consternation, his son Dennis is hypochondriac, his spinster sister Constance is wretched because she is flat-chested. Of their guests, Sir Percy Shorter feels furious that his name matches his short stature and lovely Felicity has just become pregnant from a chance encounter.

The action is a whirl of accidents, assignations, intrigue and mistaken identities, ending in an improbable double marriage. Felicity gladly marries Dennis for, unknown to himself, he has only three months to live, and Constance glamorous in her falsie bra has found an ardent suitor.

Bennett ingeniously uses the classical ingredients of farce, transforming them by his wryly caustic wit. The far-fetched comparison and outrageous statement delivered in a flat prim tone are now his hallmark.

Robert Bolt (b. 1924).

Bolt has recently said, "I do like plays in which the people have ideas as well as predicaments" and he is one of the few dramatists who have scored West End successes with the play of ideas. He holds the balance of discussion so fairly that only in the outcome is it clear that he himself is committed. His earlier work, represented by *The Flowering Cherry* (1957), with Ralph Richardson, was in the realistic convention, but later he experimented with other dramatic techniques, owing something to Brecht and to the Theatre of Cruelty and of the Absurd.

The Tiger and the Horse. 1960.

This play takes its title from Blake's "The Tygers of wrath are wiser than the horses of instruction." It is concerned with the inadequacy of detachment, the philosophy held by Jack Dean, (Michael Redgrave), the Master of an Oxbridge college, the well-balanced man who represents Blake's "horse", while his wife, Gwen, the "tiger", passionately concerned for the world's suffering, shows signs of neurosis. The action revolves round her wish to sign a petition for unconditional nuclear disarmament and Dean eventually, to save her from mental breakdown, bravely identifies himself with her, thereby deserting his philosophy and his career.

In its outcome the play stresses the value of social idealism. It is typical of Bolt's dialectic that this value should be upheld by the disturbed Gwen.

A Man for All Seasons. 1960. P.

Here Bolt attempts to give his characters heroic dimensions by striking back into history.

Believing that our need today is a sense of personal individuality he chooses as his hero of "selfhood" Sir Thomas More. Bolt consciously uses the dramatist's privilege to adapt history to his own purpose, for the theory of conscience accepted by More was not subjective and existentialist but identical with that of Thomas Aquinas. Hence some inconsistency in his portrayal.

More was described by one of his contemporaries as "a man for all seasons" and Bolt presents More (Scofield) as not only flexibly adjusted to Renaissance society but also preserving an inner core of unassailable integrity. Suspected of a critical attitude to Henry VIII's divorce, he used his skill in "the thickets of the law", yet resolutely refused to swear the oath to the Act of Succession that would have released him from the Tower and the block, because for him perjury meant the loss of the soul, the self. His constancy is thrown into relief by the growing corruption of Richard Rich, whose final perjury sends More to his death.

Bolt's More challenges comparison with Brecht's Galileo. He also is a man of supreme intelligence, whose inner certitude of truth is persecuted by an absolute power. He also skilfully avoids open clash until he must eventually make a final choice between astute temporising and commitment of his life to his belief. The difference is that More opts unequivocally for constancy.

Bolt uses what he calls a "bastardised version" of Brecht's style. Episodic scenes are strung along a strong thread of intellectual argument. There is also a commentator in the form of the Common Man, who with the aid of property box takes a swift succession of minor parts, changes of rôle which throw into relief the steadfast individuality of More.

Bolt, like Brecht, believing that beauty of language is a means of "alienation", matches fine passages from More himself with his own appropriate use of wit and imagery, using images of land to suggest society and its laws and those of water and sea the superhuman context.

The film version has been highly praised.

Gentle Jack. 1963.

Bolt contrasts inhibited society with natural spontaneity and its potential violence. But he was unable like Euripides in *The Bacchae* to rely on a familar myth and his allegory proved too cerebral.

Vivat! Vivat Regina! 1970.

The play has two " heroines "—Elizabeth I and Mary Queen of Scots. In the same predicament, the conflict between royal statecraft and woman's desire for husband, child, and heir, they are in temperament sharply contrasted. Mary is shown as sophisticated, sensuous, passionate and self-willed, ruthlessly conniving at plots to murder her rival. Elizabeth, listening to Cecil and Walsingham, foregoes her love for Leicester in the interest of the realm.

Since the period spanned is virtually that of Mary's return from France until her execution (with a hint of England's coming victory over the Armada) she is the main dramatic focus although Elizabeth's astute dialogues with her advisers are more interesting.

Bolt does not attempt the subtle complexity of *A Man For All Seasons* but he cleverly employs emblematic properties, such as thrones, pulpits, desks and heraldic blazons so that with selective lighting the action shifts unhindered through space and time.

Edward Bond (b. 1935).

Bond had a most unfortunate start in life. The son of a labourer in North London, twice evacuated to the country, he says that his whole relationship with his family " was one of total suspicion ", and that his education at a London secondary modern school " consisted of one evening ", when he was taken to see Wolfit in *Macbeth.* He left at fifteen to take up casual employment, and generalising from an apparently meagre experience asserted " There's really no difference between our State prisons and our State schools " since they both are " training alienated slaves who will fit into our society. "

He appears to have read widely, not always with the ability to discriminate, even in drama.

Bond shares the appalled dismay of most sensitive people at contemporary violence and war, the drab monotony of industrialisation and the stifling of individuality but he is not yet in full control of his material. Early interviews with him endorsed the impression that much of his work is motivated by the compelling need to exorcise his own emotional difficulties. Hence the strange, emotive power of his images, often as violent and gruesome as nightmare. But there is an uneasy alliance between his bold intuitive imagery and his conviction that his work serves as a timely warning of genocide. The tenuous moral fable fabricated to rationalise the episodic violence is seldom very convincing. Lucid reasoning is not his forte.

At one time Bond attempted to rationalise his intense hostility to all authority by a naïve Romantic anarchy, asserting, " Society . . . makes men animals." In *Lear* there are signs that he now recognises individual responsibility.

Opinions are divided. Some critics, like Esslin, rate Bond highly and he is appreciated on the Continent. Many playgoers remain doubtful.

Saved. 1965. M.

As a result of casual intercourse with the promiscuous Pam, Len gets involved with her morose South London family, with Fred, the putative father of her baby, and with Fred's lewd gang, which murders the baby on the stage.

Since the play is largely in delinquents' argot, and is limited to a photographic study of inarticulate people, it is in itself somewhat inarticulate.

Early Morning. 1968.

Esslin interprets this play as infantile fantasy. The archetypal authoritarian figures of mother, father, nurse, and grown-ups appear as Queen Victoria and the Consort at deadly enmity, Florence Nightingale, on whom Victoria has a Lesbian crush, and Gladstone and Dizzy waging civil war. The princes, Siamese twins, suggest sibling rivalry, and the final scene is a nightmare eternity of mutual cannibalism, whose psychoanalytic significance is oral eroticism and sadism. Esslin judges the play absurdist, innocuous as satire, but with an underlying substance " of great seriousness and poetic power. "

Wardle says Bond is writing like a wrathful " omnipotent baby " presenting a " solipsistic muddle, " meriting case-book study rather than dramatic criticism.

Narrow Road to the Deep North. 1968. M.

The setting, visually very beautiful, is 17th-cent. Japan, where the War Lord, Shogo, is eventually overthrown by the Commodore, a " bragging mindless savage, " representing Western civilisation, with the tambourine-banging Georgina, a somewhat outdated image of missionary zeal supporting imperialism.

Shogo maintains order by sheer atrocity, Georgina by inculcating also a puritan sense of sin, the " message " being that government is *per se* evil and our only hope the naked man, who finally rises from the river (recalling the Romantic myth of the " noble savage ").

Bond's dubious dogma overlays the most moving aspect of the play, its latent plea for individualism.

Black Mass. 1970.

For the Sharpeville commemoration Bond wrote a bitter satire, showing a priest corrupted by the power of politician and police.

Lear. 1971. M.

Bond employs two devices. He drastically alters the basic situation and story line of Shakespeare's *King Lear*, whittling it down to a political fable, and he presents a symbolic object, a huge wall, representing man's possessiveness, fear and aggression.

The furious Lear visits the wall which he is erecting against two hostile dukes, whereupon one of the workers is promptly executed, and his two daughters, Bodice and Fontanelle, provocatively announce their marriage to the dukes. They soon make away with their husbands, seizing power and defeating Lear, who is left wretched and vagrant. Cordelia, a priest's daughter, who had been urging her husband to erect a fence (evidently a microcosm of the wall), is now in ruthless command of victorious guerrilla forces. She has the sisters killed and Lear blinded by a " scientific device. " He lives on, accompanied by the ghost of Cordelia's husband, who experiences a second death. Finally, Lear, feebly attempting to dismantle the wall which Cordelia now feverishly maintains, is shot dead.

The horror of gruesome maimings and killings indicates that Bond is beginning to recognise that evil is inherent in man but still argues that contemporary life is bearable to no one " unless he'd been made morally insane " by our education and the pressure to conform.

To convey his message Bond eventually resorts to crude verbalism, as when Lear says, " We have only one thing to keep us sane; pity, and the man without pity is mad." But this is moral preaching not drama.

In *King Lear* Shakespeare did not have to resort to preaching, for his play is permeated by loyalty and compassion which reach their apotheosis in the tender reconciliation of Lear and Cordelia. *King Lear.* IV. 7.

Bond however says, " The Cordelia figure was very unsatisfactory in Shakespeare . . . He can't deal with her. My view is that she is a moralised person and moralised people are not good people."

As criticism this is poppycock.

The Sea. 1973. M.

Bond enters new territory in a play which although bizarre has a realistic setting, an East

Coast village in 1907, dominated by the imperious Mrs. Rafi (Coral Browne), a wealthy widow. It begins with the drowning of Colin, the fiancé of her niece Rose, and his death is the pivot of the play.

The village draper Hatch, who faces bankruptcy through Mrs. Rafi's capricious cancelling of orders, is becoming paranoic and suffers hallucinations. He had been on the beach the night Colin drowned and repelled his friend Willy who yet survived. When Mrs. Rafi again cancels a commission he threatens her. Eventually as she conducts Colin's strange cliff-top funeral he attacks her and is taken away mad.

The play described as a comedy has a long and irrelevant farcical scene. There is also satiric comedy at the funeral which changes to the macabre as Colin's ashes are spilled and pelted at Hatch.

The spirit of comedy is more evident in a new sympathy for the individual. The grief of the bereaved Rose and Willy and their growing love are tenderly depicted and their decision to marry and leave the village sounds a new note of hope.

The theme of *The Sea* is the crippling of human nature by a social élite but the indications in *Lear* that evil is not solely attributable to society is here explicitly expressed by one who acts as commentator: "People are cruel and boring and obsessed."

Bingo. 1973. M.

In *Bingo* or "scenes of money and death" Bond again limits himself to a precise locality and period, Stratford-on-Avon in the early seventeenth century, and his portrayal of Shakespeare the man finds support in an interpretation of an extant document and in literary tradition.

Bond seizes on the oft-discussed anomaly between the humane spirit of reconciliation that animates *The Winter's Tale* and the shrewd business acumen of the owner of New Place, and his Shakespeare is a deeply divided and withdrawn man, sensitive and concerned for the suffering of the poor yet trapped by his own desire for gain. He allows the ruthless William Coombe, predecessor of the modern property-developer, to secure his agreement to the enclosure of common land regardless of the impoverishment of the common people seen in the homeless woman who strays into his garden, is flogged for vagrancy and later hanged.

Shakespeare's wealth brings him nothing but increasing disillusion and despair. His daughter Judith, grown bitter, is harshly obsessed with what he may bequeath her. Ben Johnson comes to Stratford to borrow money and persuade him to return to the theatre but fails on both counts and Shakespeare stumbles home from their drinking bout, carrying the fatal potion Jonson has just handed him. Locking the bedroom against his furious wife he slips the famous will under the door and dies wretchedly on the floor.

In a letter to *The Times* Bond stated that "the contradictions in Shakespeare are those in our own society" and his more disciplined focus certainly gives the play a sharper relevance.

The Fool. 1975.

Although Bond makes free use of "poetic licence" in distorting and inventing characters, his play is broadly based on the life of the Northamptonshire poet, John Clare (1793–1864), labourer and herdsmen.

Bond early contrasts him with a fellow peasant, "Darkie", who scorns Lord Milton's patronage. Clare is absorbed in poetry and although engaged to Patty has a brief affair with Mary, Milton's servant. Meanwhile enclosures are impoverishing the villagers and the rebellious "Darkie" is eventually hanged.

Act II shows Clare in London, patronised by the litterati; but his poems prove too radical in politics, too frank about love. Clare is quickly dropped. A London patron brings back quantities of unsold books and Milton has him permanently assigned to an asylum.

Clare's thwarted genius gives Bond a moving human story and his political "message" is the more effective for the discipline.

Bertold Brecht (1898–1956).

Perhaps the most original and vigorous dramatist and producer of the century the Bavarian Brecht, was remarkable in his command of both literary and theatrical genius.

His practice and theory underwent constant modification. Early plays, like *Baal*, written to provide entertainment, reveal a satiric and anarchic attitude, and in 1928 the ironic *The Threepenny Opera* (P), made him famous. From 1930 onward his work became explicitly communistic, marked by the rejection of the individual in favour of a social ideal. But although Brecht always remained "committed" to Marxist ideology, most of his later plays, written after his withdrawal from Nazi Germany, are less didactic than humanist in spirit and it is by these mature works that he is best known in Britain.

After 1949 Brecht consolidated the famous Berliner Ensemble in East Berlin, where he developed his influential techniques of production.

The most permanent feature of Brecht's mature drama are the Epic form and the *Verfremdung*, or "alienation" effect, both developed in reaction to the traditional dramatic form, which he dubbed "Aristotelian". He considered that the closely constructed Aristotelian play, which encourages the audience's emotional participation in the action, syphons off the spectator's emotion, leaving him a passive and acquiescent member of society.

According to Brecht, the drama should be not ritual but debate. The spectator should be a detached observer, calmly investigating the view of the world that confronts him, rationally considering arguments and stimulated to decisive social action. It is taken for granted that he will find the solution to problems in communism.

Brecht therefore developed his "Epic", or narrative play, loosely constructed with a sequence of individual scenes, functioning as independent dramatic illustrations or quotations to the narrative.

He uses a variety of techniques to establish the narrative tone, such as an actual story-teller on the stage, explanatory verses relayed before the scenes, and banner headlines which foretell the events to be portrayed. Although by throwing the action thus into the past tense, he discards the lure of suspense, his dramatic intelligence, vigour, and inventiveness excite lively interest and curiosity.

To break down the traditional identification of the spectator with the action, Brecht developed his celebrated "alienation" effect, devising techniques to keep him at a critical distance. This implies using an image that suddenly makes the familiar appear strange and novel to the onlooker, so that he is shocked into recognising its significance.

His productions were thus avowedly non-realistic and theatrical, sometimes appearing like an inspired charade. He used not only direct narration but direct address to the audience, formalised settings and properties, masks and stylised make-up, sometimes grotesque in character. His text, "scarcely more than prompter's copy," was freely adapted during rehearsal, so that an acquaintance with the pattern of Brecht's mime and gesture is often necessary to the full understanding of his plays.

Few find in Brecht's mature work the plea for communism that he intended, and many of his protagonists, designed as exponents of capitalist villainy, appeal strongly to the sympathy. The compelling and fascinating central ambiguity can be ascribed, as Esslin has pointed out, to the tension between Brecht's conscious reason and the unconscious emotional experience on which every creative writer must intuitively draw. This profound tension is the major source of Brecht's power.

Brecht's influence has been pervasive, especially through the plays written between 1937 and 1945, the first to be produced here. He has left his mark on Arden, Bolt, Whiting and Joan Littlewood and his plays, major and minor, are still being revived. Above all his iconoclastic attitude and his fertile experiment have been invaluable in encouraging a new and empirical approach to drama.

Esslin's book *Brecht: a Choice of Evils*, 1959, is authoritative.

Baal. Written 1918.

The amoral vagabond poet, Baal (O'Toole), driven by instinct and emotion, expresses the subjective experience of the youthful Brecht.

Man is Man. Written 1924–25.

An amusing comedy marks the turning point between the anarchic hedonism of plays like *Baal* and didactic Marxism. Three raffish soldiers, losing a fourth, persuade a pacific, gentle companion to take his identity. Through their manipulation he becomes a fierce, aggressive soldier. The theme of brain-washing is apparent.

Galileo. Written 1938–9. M.

Brecht intended Galileo's recantation as an image of the scientist's allowing the State to assume authority over science. It has also been interpreted as Galileo's cunning expedient, allowing him to continue research.

Mother Courage. Written 1939. M.

In his panorama of war's futility, Brecht designed Mother Courage—a camp follower in the Thirty Years' War—as an epitome of the haggling profiteer. But his intuitive understanding of this dynamic, maternal figure, bereaved eventually of all three children, has endowed her with an ambiguous fascination.

The Good Person of Szechwan. Written 1938–40. M. P.

Shen Te (Peggy Ashcroft), the benevolent prostitute, has to disguise herself as Shui Ta, the harsh task-master, in order to survive in an unjust commercial society.

Puntila. Written 1940–1.

The drunken generosity of the mean landowner, Puntila, designed by Brecht to highlight his harshness when sober, has however given him an attractive inconsistency. The chauffeur who rejects Puntila's daughter, is a Schweikian character.

The Resistable Rise of Arturo Ui. Written 1941.

The late British première, 1967, of a minor play vividly illuminates Brecht's principles and method. The Chicago thug, Ui, and his cronies burlesque Hitler and his entourage and the horror of Nazism is offset by the brilliant clowning by Rossiter of Ui's abject cowardice and monstrous arrogance. The play successfully parodies Shakespeare's verse, especially in *Richard III*, but the picture of Chicago gangsters as vegetable dealers is unconvincing.

The Caucasian Chalk Circle. Written 1944–5. M. P.

The prologue to this delightful fairy-tale constitutes an overt plea for communism rare in Brecht's later work. The rascally judge Adzak, who takes bribes from the rich and gives judgment in favour of the poor, is one of Brecht's typical contradictory characters.

Howard Brenton (b. 1942).

Brenton is one of the foremost writers of the Fringe, his early plays *Revenge*, *Fruit* and *Christie in Love* being cleverly tailored for the small touring company, but his full-length *Magnificence*, 1973, was commissioned for the Royal Court.

Brenton is a modest writer. " One of my blazing faults ", he says, " is that I understand the ' agit ' bit but I have difficulty with the ' prop '." Like many of his generation he is stirred by a sense of impotent rage. His originality is his struggle to clarify his ideals for a just society and the struggle mirrored in his plays is more telling than overt propaganda.

Fruit. 1970.

An osteopath exploits his privileged knowledge of the failings of eminent men who are his patients, including a Socialist leader who drinks and a homosexual prime minister. Brenton's sweeping condemnation of the corruption engendered by power involves all but a Leninist working man.

Lay By. 1971.

Brenton and Hare (*q.v.*) combining with five others to write a play found their starting point in a laconic newspaper report about the legal aspects of a case of fellatio.

The play takes as subject sex perversion, pornography and drug addiction.

The girl Lesley, a pornographic photographer's model, and a drug addict, is given a lift by Jack. In the back of his van in a lay-by he commits fellatio with her and assaults her, in the presence of his mistress. Jack and his mistress, now pregnant, are convicted and imprisoned. Later all three are brought together again, dead, in a hospital mortuary.

A final surrealist incident is introduced as satire on society's callous indifference to the individual but the imagery, although gruesome in the extreme, is in its implications not sufficiently clear, and many consider that the sensational portrayal of perversion is in itself degrading.

Brassneck. 1973. M.

The collaborators Brenton and Hare have said of their disturbing work " We wrote the play line by line together. The work is indivisible."

" Brassneck " is a Midlands' word meaning " impudence ", and has " a criminal inference ". The play, which is a sweeping indictment of corruption, financial and political presents a panoramic view of civic life in a Midland town between 1945 and 1973, traced through the dubious activities of three generations of one family, the Bagleys. Their progress is cleverly synchronised with the decline of post-war England by means of topical background photographs, music and song.

The parvenu Bagley, making contact with a shady solicitor and a venal Tory house agent, forces his way to civic power by means of unscrupulous property speculation and membership of the Masonic Lodge, of which he becomes Master, the Conservative Club and the golf club. Members of these establishments moved by self interest, reluctantly admit as members the newly elected Edmunds, Labour M. P., and the Marxist representative who becomes Mayor and the Bagleys' servile agent. All seeking personal gain they work in collusion.

In the second generation Roderick, a dubious architect, continues to extend the affluent Bagley empire by means of the calculated gift and prearranged tender, until he is suddenly bankrupt, his bribery disclosed and his accomplices involved. Edmunds, now Leader of the Opposition, has to retreat to the Lords.

Finally in the third generation, Sidney, Etonian spiv and owner of a strip-tease night club and brothel, gathers together the family and cronies and launches a combine in Chinese heroin. As they drink to " the last days of capitalism " the play ends.

This successful and devasting satire has constant variety of incident, bravura and pace.

Magnificence. 1973. M.

In an interesting and original political play three high-spirited young men and two women decide to attract attention to the plight of the homeless by squatting in an empty house. Their leader is Jed. There follows a struggle with a bailiff who evicts them and accidentally kicks a girl, causing a miscarriage, thus enraging Jed and sparking off a wish for revenge.

Act One is followed by Jed's remarkable speech describing how after nine months in prison he emerges as a Marxist Leninist.

He decides that the assassination of " Alice ", a Tory minister, shall be his " magnificent " protest against the establishment. But the gelignite fails to go off. Alice cunningly tries to undermine Jed's confidence with hospitable drinks and a parade of humanism. Then the gelignite explodes accidentally and kills them both.

His fellow squatter Cliff speaks Jed's epitaph. What horrifies Cliff is not the violence but the tragic waste of effort that could have been diverted to constructive political action.

Magnificence, like Brenton's earlier film script *Skin Flicker* explores " the question of individual terrorism ". He has said that his emotional sympathy is with Jed's urge to " distrupt the spectacle " and expose the " obscene parade " of the privileged establishment. But it is Cliff's insight that he endorses.

The Churchill Play. 1974.

The play is set in 1984 at the Churchill camp for internees. The spokesman is tough Sergt. Baxter who after fighting the Irish in Ulster had fought the English at home. When a new liberal doctor suggests that the internees act a play for visiting M.P.s they grasp this outlet for their bitterness and also the chance of a break-out. The subject is Churchill. The theme is that like the human body so can the state contract fatal ills and the Churchill cult encouraged neglect of our democratic freedom.

The play poses unanswered questions and theatrically follows Weiss's *Marat Sade* and Hochhuth's *Soldiers.*

Weapons of Happiness. 1976.

In 1952 Josef Frank was executed after the Slansky trial in Czechoslovakia, but Brenton imagines him alive and working in a London factory where the workers unsuccessfully stage a sit-in on learning that the business is to be closed and they dismissed.

Frank is through a woman unwillingly drawn into the protest, and when the workers escape down a sewer " dies " of a heart attack while for a moment Stalin's tanks are seen entering Prague. Finally the factory hands consider taking over a disused farm.

Brenton brilliantly contrasts the experienced communist of 1952, his reluctant phantom and the English workers, placing them in the European context.

Peter Brook (b. 1925). Director.

US (or ambiguously *U.S.*). 1966.

US is a collaboration between director, actors, designers, musicians, and writers in an attempt to confront the Vietnam war and to involve the audience.

Brook admits anti-American bias.

The First Act is a violent theatrical assault on apathy. Brook re-employs techniques from Weiss's *Marat-Sade* and alternates utmost stillness, as in the initial mime of a Buddhist self-immolation, with loud music and noise. In the hideous uproar and confusion of a bombing raid at the climax a giant war-effigy from the proscenium crashes across the stage. Shattering assault is succeeded in Act Two by a penetration in depth, its centre being a dialogue between a white man about to burn himself alive and a girl whose cold, detached criticism gradually gives way to a bitter indictment of English parochial indifference. In an ambiguous poetic finale an actor silently releases butterflies, one of which he burns.

This daring and controversial use of theatre directly to involve the emotion of the audience in confrontation with contemporary political tragedy marked a new departure.

The Ik. 1976.

Peter Brook (whose last major experiment had been *Orghast*, where the actors communicated ceremony by gesture and non-verbal sound) produced *The Ik* as a dramatisation from Colin Turnbull's anthropological study, *The Mountain People*, scripted by Denis Cannen and Colin Higgins who use Turnbull as the Investigator. The appalling story is of a group of hunters between Kenya and Uganda whose grounds have become a nature reserve, consigning them to an almost barren area.

Vividly shown is the shocking degradation where food is the sole concern. Children aged 3 are discarded and the old (aged 30) turned out to die. Even the priest is deserted by his son. Save for a private reverence for the mountain the tribe is devoid of spiritual sense and ritual. An effective contrast is the unusual migration of one tribe to be closer to the Sudan, where food is less scarce, the people hospitable and ritual survives.

Brook stresses the danger of any society, including our own, where communal ritual declines.

Albert Camus (1913–60).

The French existentialist philosopher and novelist, Camus, first enunciated the concept of the Absurd as whatever is incompatible with man's desire for reason, justice, happiness and purpose. Like Sartre, Camus expressed his views through the traditional dramatic form, and the plays most familiar here were those written before he had moved on to a more humanistic philosphy. They include *Caligula* (P), *Cross Purposes* (P) and *The Price of Justice.*

Paddy Chayvesky (b. 1923).

The Latent Heterosexual. 1968.

This American play begins as a hilarious caricature of homosexuality and drug addiction as embodied in the outrageous poet, Morley. His novel has just earned him $72,000 and his accountant advises him to evade taxation by a token marriage and by turning himself into a Corporation.

The marriage, to an expensive prostitute, is a sensational success, but soon the Corporation usurps Morley's personal identity. Almost paralysed, he makes a frantic effort to liberate himself and can find his only resource in suicide.

The remorseless and impressive final scenes change the tone of the play and constitute a serious satire on the atrophy of the human personality by Big Business.

Marguerite Duras (b. 1914).

The French novelist and script-writer of the film *Hiroshima Mon Amour*, has a sensitive flair for dialogue and for exploring the ebb and flow of feeling. Her naturalistic plays move subtly towards their climax, often the agony of parting, as in the one-act *La Musica*, 1966 (P).

Days in the Trees. 1966.

The theme of the play, virtually a trio, is the love–hate relationship between mother (Peggy Ashcroft) and son. She had indulged her own emotions by conniving at his playing truant for " whole days in the trees, " so that he is now incapable of love for anyone else. Finally, the ageing woman admits to herself his callous egoism and misery, as now a gambler and pimp he lives contemptuously with the devoted girl for whom he procures.

The Lovers of Viorne. 1971.

Marguerite Duras returns to the subject of an earlier play, *The Viaduct*—an actual murder committed in provincial France in the 1940s when a married woman killed her husband and disposed of the corpse by dropping dismembered portions from a viaduct on to passing trains.

Apart from changing the identity of the victim to a deaf-mute cousin, housekeeper to the couple, Duras keeps closely to the facts and concentrates on penetrating the motive.

This demanding play is almost exclusively verbal and spare in design. After a loudspeaker announcement of the discovered crime an impersonal " Interrogator " probes the husband about the twenty-year barren marriage and in Act II he questions the wife herself, Claire Lannes (Peggy Ashcroft), apathetic yet deeply suffering.

He elicits complementary pictures of their meaningless existence, devoid of emotion or thought, the husband finding a cold response to his early love, the wife obsessed by thoughts of the former lover who had destroyed her religious faith, exasperated by the stifling house and revolted by her cousin's cooking.

Duras has spoken of " their totally asphyxiated life " saying, " the silence between them has to be destroyed. "

It is significant that the victim is the deaf and dumb cousin.

Suzanna Andler. 1971.

For many years Suzanna (Eileen Atkins) has brought her children to the same rented house for the summer but now she contemplates change.

In the off-season an agent shows her over a larger empty villa, again in St. Tropez. She worries about the expense but gradually deep levels of anxiety are disclosed. Married for seventeen years Suzanna had long accepted the infidelities of the wealthy husband who still cares for her, but recently she has agreed to a brief affaire with Michel, a rough and struggling journalist, which involves her in new emotional conflicts. Confused as if in a dream she struggles with that paralysis of will that often accompanies suffering, as she strives to come to terms with her tenderness for her husband and the need she and her aggressive lover now feel for each other although they have little else in common.

This sensitive play reveals with faithful naturalism the loneliness and anguish of indecision. As literature and vocally it is exquisite. Theatrically it is less successful for apart from brief meetings with the agent and a confidante and a long telephone conversation with her husband, Suzanna's indecisive encounter with Michel provides the only external action. A radio production with Vivien Merchant as Suzanna indicated that radio is the play's ideal medium.

Friedrich Dürrenmatt (b. 1921)

The German-Swiss Dürrenmatt acknowledges the Greek dramatists, Shakespeare, and Swift as major influences. He describes his work as " theatre of paradox ", revealing " precisely the paradoxical effects of strict logic. " He is an unsparing critic of contemporary society, whose dangerous tendencies he exposes in striking and bizarre fictions, reminiscent of the later Shaw.

The Marriage of Mr. Mississippi. 1959.

An extravaganza poses the opposition between two principles carried to their logical and farcical extreme. One is a passion for the law of Moses, interpreted as retributive justice. The other is pure Marxism. The two characters embodying these principles, together with a Quixotic lover, are manipulated and destroyed by an unscrupulous politician.

The Visit.

An old multi-millionairess revisits her birthplace and offers the inhabitants £1,000,000 to murder her former lover, who had denied her paternity order. Gradually persuading themselves that they are acting justly they comply.

Dürrenmatt cleverly maintains suspense in his withering satire on love of money, hypocrisy and the sycophancy of press and radio.

The Physicists. 1963.

Dürrenmatt has said that this arresting play is not so much about the hydrogen bomb as about society itself and the impossibility of escaping the consequences of one's thinking.

The central character, attempting to suppress scientific discoveries that may lead to the hydrogen bomb, retires to a private asylum pretending to be in contact with King Solomon. There he is first in danger of two spies, pretending to the delusion that they are Einstein and Newton, and eventually of the mad proprietress whose use of his discoveries will lead to the destruction of the human race.

The Meteor. 1966.

Another play of paradox has as hero a man who wishes to die but cannot.

Schwitter (Patrick Magee), famous dramatist and Nobel prizewinner, already proclaimed dead in hospital, returns to the garret of his youth to die. In vain. As the old egoist swaggers, drinks, makes love, one by one those who touch his orbit meet their death.

The symbolism is unclear. Is Schwitter the egoistic kind of artist who feeds on the lives of others? The most effective incident—his dialogue with an ancient tart—cynically suggests that his art also has been prostitution, for he too has supplied artificial emotion to meet public demand.

The chief weakness of the play is that the surprise wears thin. An original idea adequate to a one-act play has been inflated too far.

T. S. Eliot (1888–1965). *See also* **Section M.**

In his attempt to revive poetic drama the distinguished poet, T. S. Eliot, was moved by deeply religious and social aims, modestly regarding his work as experimental, " that of the first generation only. " The verse he evolved was of a flowing poetic rhythm, " close to contemporary speech " and based on natural stress. Normally he used a line with three stresses and varying length.

In his two plays of the 'thirties Eliot had adopted the ritualistic themes and patterns of Greek drama and had achieved a certain tragic intensity. But the *Cocktail Party* inaugurated a new style, the theme still being Christian redemption and the plot deriving from Greek drama, but the idiom, that of the fashionable comedy of manners. In spite of subtle organisation the liaison has been an uneasy one.

It is curious that the creator of Prufrock should seem unable fully to animate his dramatis personae. This is partly because their inspiration is literary, partly because they are used to illustrate Anglican doctrine and to convey a message. Nor do they belong to the impeccable background against which they are so carefully placed.

The wealth and subtlety of reference of these plays and the beauty of the language make them a delight to the reader, but they are less compelling on the stage.

The Cocktail Party. 1949. F.

This play, revived in 1968, has its literary origin in Euripides' tragi-comedy *Alcestis*, the demi-god Hercules being replaced by Reilly, the psychiatrist, whose intervention breaks the back of the play, for it is not easy to sympathise with people who let their actions be so directed.

The Confidential Clerk. 1953.

Described as " high farce ", this play derives from another tragi-comedy of Euripides, the *Ion*, whose theme of parents seeking their lost children reappears in Terence, Plautus and Shakespeare.

The Elder Statesman. 1955.

Eliot here returns to a tragedy, the *Oedipus at Colonus* of Sophocles, but the youthful peccadilloes of Lord Claverton appear pallid compared with the patricide and incest of Sophocles' protagonist.

Jules Feiffer.

Feiffer, the New York strip-cartoonist of international fame, now writes plays.

Little Murders. 1967. P.

The blustering Newquist family of New York embody what Feiffer has called the " national paranoia " in face of " random violence ", and when the daughter, Patsy, introduces her fiancé, Alfred, who is so strong that he never retaliates, they are incredulous. But Patsy is killed by some stray bullet, Alfred adopts the Newquist ethos, and the family is happily united sniping down harmless passers by.

The main theme is clear. "Man hates war but is fascinated by it. . . . Peace is a Sissy." The play began as a novel, which may account for the plethora of other stimulating ideas which are never fully integrated, and also for some highly entertaining satirical vignettes not entirely relevant.

God Bless. 1968.

This Shavian satire scintillates with dramatic and verbal paradox, epigram and ironic understatement, and improves on reading.

It is timed in "the immediate future," with America waging war in three continents, and is set in the library of the Liberal Brackman (Dotrice), America's "oldest elder statesman."

On his 110th birthday he is cynically dictating the record of his shilly-shallying career, used by Feiffer as an image of the American Liberal compromise as a betrayal of principle, a "sellout". His narrative is punctuated by teletype and television presentations of mounting insurrection off-stage. Then two heavily armed agitators, for Peace and Civil Rights, formerly Brackman's Harvard students, enter, soon to be followed by the President himself.

As forty-six cities go up in flames, the President reveals that the agitators have actually been financed by him as a tactic to shake up Congress! But the "tactic has gotten out of hand" and while Civil War breaks out the four men settle down to effect yet another compromise. The revolutionaries insist on bombing ten cities, but the President is to decide which ten!

The play operates as an urgent warning.

Max Frisch (b. 1911).

Frisch, a German-Swiss who has been influenced by Shaw and Brecht, dramatises current issues in ingenious, apt and witty parables that have a lucid economy of outline.

The Fire-Raisers. 1961. M.

A delightful Absurdist satire on bourgeois self-delusion and ineptitude shows Biedermann (Alfred Marks) persuading himself that he can cajole the incendiaries about to set fire to his house by inviting them to a good dinner. The situation is analogous to that of Benes of Czechoslovakia who included communists in his government, and to that of the Germans who connived at Hitler.

Andorra. 1964. M.

An incisive and moving satire on the vicious pervasiveness of antisemitism shows the Andorrans' betrayal of the lad Andri, reputedly a Jewish foundling, to the invading totalitarian state. Andri is in fact a Gentile and his assumption of Jewish traits is an example of identity imposed from without by society.

Christopher Fry (b. 1907).

Fry, widely acclaimed in the 'forties for bringing verse back to the stage, has written comedies and religious plays, the latter culminating in *A Sleep of Prisoners*, 1951, commissioned for enactment in churches during the Festival of Britain.

Fry devises ingenious situations, often in terms of poetic fable, informed by implicit affirmation and hope, lightly and gaily conveyed. His special talent is the creation of a dramatic atmosphere, unique to each play. But like *Love's Labours Lost* they tend to be too static and are carried by the dynamic and magic of verse. His delightful early verse was sometimes too lavish and discursive and with *Curtmantle* he began to use a plainer style with brief, telling images.

His mature work completes the quartet of the Seasons that had begun with the Spring comedy, *The Lady's Not for Burning*, 1948, O.U.P., and *Venus Observed*, 1950, O.U.P., an unusual and felicitous comedy of Autumn.

The Dark is Light Enough. 1954.

In a play of Winter an eccentric and saint-like old Countess (Edith Evans) gives asylum to men of both sides in the Hungarian rising of 1948. The theme of non-intervention is presented with an elegance that saves it from didacticism.

Curtmantle. 1962.

A vigorous play has as tragic protagonist Henry II, shown as an imperious autocrat, brilliant, generous and headstrong. Redeeming England from anarchy by his firm foundation of Common Law, he yet makes the tragic error of promoting as Archbishop his tried friend, Becket, who then proves intransigent and inconsistent and triumphs by his martyrdom.

With remarkable skill Fry incorporates the truly tragic hero and emotional power of the Aristotelian play (*q.v.*) in a work modern in structure. The main themes interpenetrate: the progressive discovery of Henry's contradictory personality in his relations with Becket, his people, and the wife and sons who deserted him, and the "interplay of different laws." The drama moves swiftly through the years 1158–89, the events successfully telescoped as in William Marshall's memory.

Some prose is appropriately used and the poetry is disciplined and vivid.

A Yard of Sun. 1970.

It is July 1946 in Siena, time of the first post-war Palio, that tense horse-race, which is also a "galvanic liturgy of life." In war's aftermath two neighbouring families strive towards renewal.

In one there are still brothers' conflicts to be resolved. Angelino's eldest son, the rebellious Roberto, ex-Partisan, now a devoted doctor, is scathingly scornful of easy-going Luigi, failed politician and Blackshirt, and also of the long-missing Edmondo, who suddenly turns up. A war-profiteer, Edmondo is smugly eager to use his financial expertise to contrive the families' fortunes.

Unwillingly Roberto is stirred by Edmondo's dazzling wife, embodiment of the passionate excitement of the Palio. But her husband's machinations go comically awry and they soon depart.

Roberto now realises that he loves the simple Grazia, daughter of the neighbour Giosetta, whose putative husband has just returned from a concentration camp, and now believes in his duty to return to his legal invalid wife. There is a hint of union between Giosetta and Angelino.

Although the scheme of this quiet, humorous comedy is somewhat too neat and flat it is true to its theme of resurgence. The fruits of Autumn may come. The poetic imagery well expresses the differing personalities and the volatile Italian temperament.

Athol Fugard (b. 1932).

Fugard, an Afrikaner, has now emerged as one of the most remarkable playwrights writing in English.

He left the University of Cape Town before completing his degree in Philosophy and spent two years as a seaman in the Far East, subsequently working in Europe. Economic circumstances obliged him to direct and act in his own plays and he had his own theatre group in Port Elizabeth, but he has now given up acting and hopes soon to devote himself entirely to writing.

As a liberal Fugard is in a most difficult situation. His roots and source of inspiration are in his Afrikaans kinship and his over-riding drive is to reveal to South Africans the "social circumstances that do terrible things to people," *apartheid* being one of these circumstances. He depicts them with unsparing realism and while constantly facing the risk of police interference and taboo he has tried "to be as courageous as possible . . . in indicting a social system", his aim being "to get plays performed not banned". Although the social implications of his plays seem inescapable, they do reach the stage in South Africa, for they are not committed to political criticism. Indeed they rise above it and perhaps it is the tensions that inhibit emotional self-indulgence that give to his work its characteristic fusion of passionate caring and disciplined objectivity.

A dominant theme is the human courage that survives appalling odds, a courage especially evident in women such as Milly, Lena and Hester. He is especially skilful in his handling of confrontation between two people who are closely involved emotionally, some complete plays being limited to a cast of two. The playwright Fugard most admires is Samuel Beckett.

In about 1963 seven men from New Brighton, the black ghetto in Port Elizabeth, asked his help in starting an amateur drama group, which became the precursor of several other groups of black actors, who, because of *apartheid* can play to black audiences only. The Serpent Players presented works of Brecht, Genet, Strindberg, Sophocles and Euripides and became the seed-bed of a remarkable partnership in creative writing between Fugard and the black South Africans John Kani and Winston Ntshona. Their *Sizwe Bansi* and *The Island* when brought to England in 1973–4 were enthusiastically received.

The Blood Knot. 1966. P.

Of two brothers belonging to the mixed race of "Cape Coloureds", one "tries for white." The dialogue between them, both comic and naïve, and fraught with intense love and hate, is a microcosm of the terrible strains imposed by racial segregation.

People Are Living There. 1970. O.U.P.

In a shabby Johannesburg kitchen, the slatternly landlady, Milly, just deserted by her lover, frenziedly tries to whip up a party for her fiftieth birthday. The only guests are her lodgers, a "retarded poor white," and a student immersed in Sartre's anguish.

They get down to the grim "rock bottom" of mutual self-knowledge, of society's indifference to poverty, of the loss of joy in the aging process, measured by the frail chiming of a shaky clock. Only Milly's outburst of laughter at the ridiculous spectacle of the whole animal world saves their precarious companionship.

This compassionate play recalls Sartre's *In Camera* but has a more valid conclusion than Sartre's dictum, "hell is other people."

Boesman and Lena. 1971.

Uprooted from their shanty town near Port Elizabeth, the aging coloured couple, Boesman and Lena, can find no other refuge than a succession of rubbish dumps.

"We're whiteman's rubbish," exclaims Boesman. "He can't get rid of his rubbish. He throws it away, we pick it up. Wear it. Sleep in it. Eat it. We're made of it now. His rubbish is people."

When they encounter an old and dying Kaffir, Boesman adopts the bullying tone of the *baas*, but Lena tries to befriend him only to find that he speaks an obscure dialect and they cannot communicate.

In spite of inhuman conditions, Lena, like Milly in *People are Living There*, somehow preserves some courage and resilience.

In an authentic film version Fugard himself takes the part of Boesman.

Hello and Goodbye. 1973.

The scene is the slum home of the Smits, poor whites in Port Elizabeth.

Hester, now on the streets, returns unexpectedly to search for and claim from her brother Johnny her share of the compensation paid to their father, who having lost a leg in an industrial accident was also crippled by resentment and self-pity. Tough and forceful she obliges her neurotic brother to fetch from the father's bedroom all the cardboard boxes which when searched disclose nothing but the ugly and worthless cast-offs from their squalid past. These like the furniture in Miller's *The Price* focus the emotional strain between the two; Johnny having given up personal ambition to act as nurse has identified himself with the invalid father, Hester with the mother, the patient bread-winner.

Eventually Hester is shocked to find the bedroom empty for Johnny had deliberately hidden from her the fact that the father had died. Suddenly moved, she asks Johnny to come away with her. But he, a victim of agoraphobia symbolically takes his father's crutches and adopts his defeated pose.

As in *The Blood Knot* Fugard skilfully used a taut dualogue to reveal the pain of conflict between siblings but this later play lacks the wider resonance of the social suffering endemic in *apartheid.*

Sizwe Bansi is Dead. 1973.

Sizwe is a triumph of collaboration, both dramatic and racial, between Fugard and two members of the black Serpent Players, John Kani and Winston Ntshona, who are also the only actors. The piece is rooted in the personal experience of these two men, given shape by the literary talent of Fugard, and it creates a wonderful illusion of spontaneous dramatic interchange, story-telling and mime. Kani and Ntshona, who appear professionally for the first time, give a dazzling performance. They play the three characters while incidental figures are brilliantly conjured up by lightning impersonations. The action is continuous, the simple set being quickly adaptable to change of locale.

Initially it is the one room "Photographic Studio" of Styles (Kani). In a richly humorous monologue he recalls the day when the anxious bosses at the Ford plant, where he once worked for six years, ordered frenzied and long overdue cleaning and safety precautions in hasty preparation for an unexpected visit by Ford himself. They had called on Styles to translate their exhortations to the workers and their injunctions to "Smile", and he re-enacts with relish his highly individual interpretation and mimics their fawning reaction to Ford's three-minute entry.

Now proudly independent in his studio Styles confides his desire to take photographs that will confirm the black man's dream of self-respect and give him a symbol of permanent identity.

Robert timidly enters for a photograph to send his wife. Styles gives him confidence posing him with a cigarette in one hand and a fancy pipe in the other, and as the flashbulb goes for a second snapshot there is a blackout and a flashback to Robert's past, when Kani now takes on the part of Buntu.

Robert's real name in Sizwe Bansi. A bewildered countryman, he has walked from his famished village to Port Elizabeth in search of work and has been picked up in a police raid, but is too simple to realise that his Passbook is now stamped with an order to return home. Buntu befriends him and eventually gets across the harsh complications of the Pass Laws. Then Buntu stumbles over the corpse of one Robert Zwelima, and urges the reluctant Sizwe for the sake of his starving family to adopt Robert's Passbook with its work permit. He rehearses Sizwe in his new role by improvising possibly risky encounters and drilling into his mind the new identity number. "Burn that into your head, my friend . . . It's more important than your name." Buntu wishes him luck as long as he "stay out of trouble." "Impossible, Buntu. Our skin is trouble."

But Sizwe agrees to try and the play closes as again in the "Studio" he jauntily responds to Styles' encouragement, "Now smile Robert . . . Smile . . . Smile . . ."

An enthralling play brings home the massive hypocrisy and ruthlessness of a regime that would mutilate and reduce manhood to an identity number and a set of finger prints. Yet the work is devoid of self-pity and has none of that stridency which sometimes mars the British play of protest. In their warmth and generosity, their creativity and sense of humour, the black people find the rueful courage to survive and beyond courage evince even a rare "gaiety transfiguring all that dread."

The Island. 1973.

Like *Sizwe Bansi* the play was devised by Fugard and the two actors Kani and Ntshona.

The setting is a prison recalling the notorious Robben Island to which some members of the Serpent Players had been relegated. The two prisoners are locked by their isolation into a symbiotic relationship which they describe as a "marriage", hating each other as they toil digging and carting sand, comforting each other huddled in their cell. When John learns that his ten years' sentence has been reduced and he will be free in three months, Winston at first joyfully hugs him but then is overcome by jealousy.

But John urges Winston to go forward with the rehearsal for a prison concert of their version of *Antigone*, and notwithstanding Winston's pathetic drag, their performance gives a universal significance to their incarceration.

Statements After an Arrest Under the Immorality Act. 1974.

In 1957 the Queen gave royal assent to an Act prohibiting any sexual relationship between white and coloured or black people living in South Africa (even those legally married). The Act's effects are the theme of a brief ninety-minute play, which opens with a scene of lyrical tenderness between a coloured schoolmaster (Ben Kingsley) and his white mistress (Yvonne Bryceland). Gradually it appears that the man is suffering the common torment of one pulled between love for his mistress and responsibility for his wife and family, who he fears will discover his unfaithfulness. The lovers' private joy and anguish are rudely interrupted. Starkly illuminated by the flashbulbs of police cameras they seek panic-stricken to cover their nakedness with shabby blankets, but are given no opportunity to dress before being interrogated by the dispassionate police officer (Wilson Dunster).

Jean Genet (b. 1910).

The French Genet, abandoned as a child, has lived as social outcast and criminal and, while politically "uncommitted", has mirrored his bitter repudiation of society in plays of frightening impact.

His dramatis personae have been the rejected, murderers (*Deathwatch* (F)), despised servants (*The Maids* (F)), prostitutes (*The Balcony* (F)), Negroes (*The Blacks* (F)), and Algerian peasants (*The Screens*). These have realised their fantasies of sex, power, violence, and revenge only by compulsive ritual acts, so that sequences of arresting ceremonial, sometimes Absurdist, replace character study and coherent plot.

In his destructive scorn of contemporary society, his recourse to rituals of violence, and his incantatory language, Genet satisfies the requirements of Artaud's Theatre of Cruelty.

The Maids. 1956. F.

Two sisters, maids to a fine lady, continually take it in turn to enact the rôle of mistress and maid so that each can vent her envy and rancour on the mistress. When their plot to murder the mistress misfires, one of them herself drinks the poisoned cup of tea.

Their compulsive charade, designed originally for a cast of young men, mirrors the obsessive and self-destroying conflict of envious love and hate in the mind of the outsider.

Triana's *The Criminals* has a similar theme and technique.

The Balcony. 1957. F.

This censored play had its world première at the Arts Theatre Club. It opens in a brothel, where the frequenters enact their fantasies of power by dressing up as bishop, judge, or general, until after an abortive revolution they are called upon by the Court to impersonate these authorities in actuality. Eventually the defeated revolutionary leader visits the brothel to enact the part of Chief of Police, who is then satisfied that his image also has been established in popular regard. The film gives a softened version of the play.

The Screens. 1973.

A rather sprawling play to be acted against movable screens with a cast of ninety-seven and lasting five hours was with Genet's permission presented in three hours with a cast of nine, the adaptor being Howard Brenton (*q.v.*).

Written in 1961 it differs from Genet's previous plays in representing his views on a specific issue, the French-Algerian conflict of 1954–62 and attacks colonialism as represented by decadent exploiters and cruel, sexually perverted soldiers. But the revolution of the wretched Algerian peasants is focused on yet another of Genet's rejected outcasts, the treacherous criminal Said, driven by his mother "to go to extremes" and so impoverished that he can marry only the ugliest girl.

There is an uneasy juxtaposition of political incidents with obsessive fantasies of sex and power, and the play is less concentrated and effective than earlier work.

Maxim Gorky (1868–1936).

Enemies. 1971. M.

Although the delayed British première of *The Lower Depths* influenced Neo-Realism (*q.v.*) Gorky's later plays, concerned with the Russian class struggle, are unfortunately little known here. The première of *Enemies*, written the year after the 1905 uprising, was therefore doubly welcome, as, in Bryden's words, it is "the missing link between Chekhov and the Russian Revolution."

Workers in the Bardins' factory, next to their peaceful country estate, are demanding the dismissal of a harsh foreman, and Bardin, a gentle liberal, reluctantly agrees that his reactionary partner Skrobotov, shall enforce a lock-out. In the ensuing dispute the latter is shot and carried back dead. The excellent first act is followed by the identification and trial of the murderer.

While Gorky's sympathies are with the oppressed, he is not doctrinaire and depicts with Chekhovian detail the complicated personal and political tensions among the leisured gentry and their consternation that liberal concessions carry no weight with the embittered workers, now "enemies".

Trevor Griffiths.

The Party. 1974.

In the expensive flat of an impotent young husband a heterogeneous group of left-wingers meet during the French uprising of students and workers of May 1968. They indulge in interesting political monologue and there is little action.

Comedians. 1975.

Emphasing the need for humanity in today's permissive and often cruel atmosphere, the famous ex-comedian Eddie Waters tries to train a few students as stand-up comics for the brief interludes tolerated in working men's clubs—the shabby setting of the play. An agent's scout is to spot talent, but the attempts of all save one miscarry. Especially hurtful to Waters is the failure of his favourite pupil Gethin, who has violently accused a dummy pair in evening dress, piercing the woman so that "blood" flows. The play ends as Waters and Gethin discuss Gethin's methods and intentions, and the relation of comedy to cruelty.

Günter Grass (b. 1927).

Grass, a notable German novelist and author of some early absurdist plays, has recently written propaganda for the Social Democratic Party of Federal Germany.

The Plebians Rehearse the Uprising. 1968.

Produced here first by amateurs in 1968, and then by the R.S.C. in 1970, *The Plebians* is set in a theatre in East Berlin. The date, 17 June 1953, is that of the spontaneous yet formidable rising of the workers in East Germany against the Ulbricht régime.

The play imagines a situation in which the Boss, clearly a counterpart of Brecht the dramatist-producer, is rehearsing his Germanised version of *Coriolanus*, whose protagonist is the aristocrat, who, spurning the rebellious plebians, all but betrays his country.

Into the Boss's theatre intrude rebellious workers, asking him to write a manifesto which will give coherence to their inarticulate demands. But the dramatist who has indefatigably urged intelligent revolution, scorns their amateur incompetence. Despite the advice of his wife, he temporises.

Finally, moved by the enthusiasm of a girl, herself inspired by Katrin in Brecht's *Mother Courage* (*q.v.*), the Boss resolves to support the uprising. But already the Russian tanks are moving in. Bitterly he realises that he has himself played the part of Coriolanus.

The play reflects not only Grass's disquiet about Brecht's rôle in a satellite dictatorship. It concerns the predicament of the modern artist—that of Grass himself—as to whether art or political commitment should take precedence. A significant minor incident in the play is that the response of the University to the workers' cry, "Intellectuals, Solidarity", is merely to bar their windows. Grass clearly indicates that the lack of effective support of artists and intellectuals to the revolution they advocate results in a tragic cleavage in the nation—hence the sub-title, *A German Tragedy*.

Christopher Hampton (b. 1946).

When Did You Last See My Mother? 1960. **F.**

Hampton frankly explores homosexuality.

Total Eclipse. 1968. **F.**

The story of Verlaine's passionate infatuation for the younger poet Rimbaud (prototype of Brecht's Baal) is dispassionately and convincingly presented, almost like a chronicle, the open ing and closing scenes being particularly skilful.

The Philanthropist. 1970. **F.**

An ingenious comedy, ironic parallel of Molière's *The Misanthropist* (M), is "set in the near future" in the room of a bachelor don, Philip, the "philanthropist."

In an arresting *coup de théâtre* an aspiring dramatist, trying to convince Philip and his friend Donald of the likelihood of his protagonist's suicide, unfortunately blows out his own brains.

Shortly afterwards a dinner party for six occasions some brilliantly precise and apt repartee. As in Molière, the characters are boldly contrasted. Philip, a literal-minded philology don, disclaims critical judgment, but is fascinated by words in isolation, his lonely pastime devising anagrams. He is terrified of hurting people, but his mumbling evasions give more offence than Don's trenchant criticisms.

The evening culminates in comic fiasco. Philip, too imperceptive to realise that his fiancée, Celia, wants to stay, lets her be "taken home" by an unscrupulous acquaintance, and out of pique she sleeps with him. Meanwhile Philip is too timid to refuse the nymphomaniac, Araminta, who stays the night "under conditions too appalling to relate."

Next day, Celia, having discovered Araminta at breakfast, returns again to break off her engagement with one too weak to control her. Philip, crestfallen, decides to approach Liz, only to find that she has spent the night with Don!

Harking back to Scene 1, Philip transposes "Imagine the theatre as real" into "I hate thee, sterile anagram." Then, taking a cigarette and a small pistol, he goes to join Don and Liz. Is this ambiguous finale a token suicide, Philip having previously given up smoking for fear of cancer, or does the anagram indicate a new fruitful involvement in life?

A theme shared with Molière is the foibles of the age, in Molière courtly hypocrisy, in Hampton growing indifference to violence. Hampton's characters are of the same metal as their prototypes but the coin is reversed. The idealistic misanthropist, Alceste, rebukes flatterers, even his beloved, the coquettish Célimène, finally deciding to withdraw from society. The gentle Philip, diffidently condones even the "frivolous" Celia. The play is too derivative to be entirely self-subsistent but Hampton skilfully incorporates a penetration of Philip's complex nature into his meticulously structured comedy.

Savages. 1973. **F.**

A play informed by an icy indignation is grounded in topical political events and in Hampton's personal experience. After reading how the Indians of the upper Amazon were being progressively exterminated so that their land might be developed by speculators, Hampton visited Brazil to investigate. He set his play in the Brazil of 1970–1, when during a brief revolutionary movement foreign diplomats of four different countries were kidnapped.

Hampton invents a fifth, West (Scofield), a British diplomat, collector and translator of Indian myths. West is seized by urban guerrillas revolting against a brutal fascist military dictatorship in cahoots with American speculators. A series of scenes between West and his captor Carlos form the framework of the play.

Handcuffed to a bed the sceptical liberal diplomat is confronted by an enthusiastic and friendly Marxist and their sophisticated and ironic dialogue reveals their growing personal sympathy and opposed ideology—Carlos's dedication to action and West's stance as humane observer. The kidnapping is in fact the diplomat's first close contact with Brazil, for hitherto he has thought only in a "distanced" way, typical, considers Hampton, of the English people.

To Carlos obsessed by the massive squalor of a country where wealth is owned by three per cent of the people, the plight of the Indians is a "marginal problem" but West is aware of their systematic extermination by violent murder and by such gifts as poisoned food. Interspersed with discussion are film-style flashbacks demonstrating the Indians' predicament, one depicting the infamous hunting party of 1963, whose simple expedient was the mass murder of the villagers and firing of their homes. Scattered scenes of West's translations and the enactment of myths lack cumulative impact.

The climax of the play is Carlos's reluctant shooting of West followed by a scene of the ruthless bombing raid exterminating a whole tribe during their ritual fertility ceremony.

The ambiguous title, indicating that the savages are the "civilised" exploiters, is underlined by contrasting public concern at West's assassination with indifference to mass genocide.

Treats. 1976.

Ann's lover Dave, a loutish, promiscuous journalist, is in Cyprus when the conventional Patrick supplants him in her flat but is eventually rejected in favour of Dave. The play had a mixed reception.

David Hare (b. 1947).

Hare is one of our younger experimental writers and has on occasion collaborated with Brenton (*q.v.*).

Slag. 1970.

Hare claims that his play set out "to show what was good about women" but admits that it ends up "as rather a vicious slur on them."

Slag relies on parody of girls' schools, women's lib. and political jargon.

What Happened to Blake. 1970.

A pantomime-style dramatisation of William Blake's career distorts the quality of his life.

The Great Exhibition. 1972.

Like *Slag* the play deals with self-isolated members of the middle class.

Hammett, once a reasonably energetic Labour M.P., can now find no motive for action but simply stays in his flat brooding on his life's futility. His disillusioned wife entertains a disaffected boyfriend and together they smoke pot. When she leaves Hammett, in a desperate resort to action he exposes himself on Wimbledon Common but without effect save on his wife's best friend. Hare combines a picture of existentialist despair with some farcical comedy and random satire.

Knuckle. 1974.

A fast-moving play is in the style of a Mickey Spillane private-eye thriller. Curly is a tough gun-runner from Peru, yet he returns to his home town Guildford to unravel the mysterious death of his sister, who had disappeared from there and been seen in Surbiton and Eastbourne before her deserted clothes had been discovered in a lonely spot. He is unable to learn anything even from their father, a suave, wealthy merchant-banker, or the dead girl's lover, but at last he accidentally realises the truth through his relationship with Jenny, a hostess in Guildford's night club.

Hare has daringly used parody to satirise the forces of ruthless materialism and corruption that have distorted life's values not in distant Peru but Surrey.

Fanshen. 1975.

Fanshen means "to turn over" and Hare, writes a convincing resumé of William Hinton's 700-page documentary of how between 1945 and 1949 the people of Long Bow in Shensi turned over to Chinese communism.

Using nine people as a microcosm of the village, with occasional advisers from the Party, Hare shows the peasants' mounting revenge against the extortionate landlord and more gradually an honest evaluation of their own possessions.

Teeth n' Smiles. 1975.

Hare emphasises the social gulf between a rock group playing for a Cambridge May ball and the privileged members of college.

Rolf Hochhuth (b. 1931).

Hochhuth, like his predecessor Schiller, is specially interested in the historical play, using poetic licence to organise and adapt factual material to his own dramatic purpose.

The Representative. 1963. M. P.

Using some dramatis personae who represent historical personages, this play in verse exposes the failure of Pope Pius XII, Christ's "representative", to protest against the massacre of the Jews. Film sequences of the horrors of Auschwitz are used with harrowing effect.

Soldiers. 1968.

Hochhuth's inordinately long play had its genesis in his horror and protest at the bombing of non-combatants. It is set symbolically at Coventry Cathedral but contains a realistic play-within-the-play, the only part produced in 1968 and here discussed.

This is timed for the crucial months, May to July, 1943, and historical persons are assigned fictional parts. Hochhuth embodies his theme by presenting Cherwell as the "eminence grise" who advocates to Churchill (John Colicos), the commanding protagonist, a policy of ruthless saturation bombing. The theme is counterpointed by the suggestion that success in modern warfare demands not only barbarity but treachery. This is given personal urgency in Churchill's confrontation with his ally, the Polish General Sikorski, whose intransigent hostility to Russia was proving a threat to our precarious alliance with Stalin.

Hochhuth's sensational insinuation that Churchill connived at Sikorski's death is a striking and poignant dramatic image and is defended by some critics on the grounds that a play is an agreed fiction. Hochhuth himself, however, claims to have seen secret evidence and has by some been sharply criticised for traducing Churchill when he cannot produce this.

In the final Act, Bishop Bell is presented in a fictional impassioned protest to Churchill against civilian atrocities, but the arguments assigned to him do not unfortunately proceed to their logical conclusion that modern warfare is *per se* an atrocity and here the moral pressure of the play is dissipated.

Hochhuth boldly handles his dominant theme while organising the intricate political detail in a gripping and enthralling way. The presentation of historical characters is remarkably convincing and Churchill emerges as an idiosyncratic, massive and tragic hero, fully aware of his moral dilemmas and ironically prescient of his rôle as the servant of history in winning a war that destroyed the balance of Europe.

Eugene Ionesco (b. 1912).

Ionesco, one of the leading Parisian playwrights of the Absurd, differs from Camus and Sartre in that he expresses his conviction of life's absurdity, not rationally, but through images that are in themselves absurd.

In 1948, while learning English from a primer, Ionesco stumbled on his vocation, his shocked reaction to the platitudes he was memorising being dramatised in *The Bald Prima Donna*. Here he singled out aspects of contemporary life which remain as the chief targets of his ridicule.

One is the empty, myopic existence of the petit bourgeois, his lack of passion and thought, the yielding to conventional pressures, the urge to conform. Another is the desiccation of language which, stereotyped and inadequate, has become "nothing but clichés, empty formulas and slogans."

Ionesco's sense of life's absurdity has deep roots, for he is keenly aware of the anguish of the modern world, of the flight from reason, both tragic and absurd in its potentialities. He believes that by dramatising his own inner hurt he can best reveal a universal experience. In *The Shepherd's Chameleon* he has plainly stated that for him "the theatre is the projection on to the stage of the dark world within," the world of dream, anguish, dark desires, inner contradictions and obsessions.

It follows naturally that he is little preoccupied with specific social problems. Regarding the human condition as wider and deeper than the social condition, he dislikes any kind of political message or conformism and deliberately repudiates the "committed" and didactic play.

Iconoclastic in both his principles and technique, Ionesco—as he indicated in *Victims of Duty*—has challenged most dramatic assumptions, including realism, the concept of the "Aristotelian play", consistent characterisation, motivation, plot and the distinction between tragedy and comedy.

Discarding so much, Ionesco has evolved a new technique of shock tactic, using most ingenious theatrical devices to express his convictions. He attempts "to go right down to the very basis of the grotesque, the realm of caricature . . . to push everything to paroxysm, to the point where the sources of the tragic lie. To create a theatre of violence—violently comic, violently tragic."

In his plays as in those of Pinter, the traditional dividing lines between tragedy and comedy melt away, for his amusing images are at the same time poignant, expressing as they do human disappointment and folly, so that his hilarious comedy may have a tragic import.

A charactistic technique is the use of proliferating material objects, which externalise the anxieties of his characters—an accumulation of chairs or eggs, for instance, or an expanding corpse. He hopes thus "to make the stage settings speak: to translate action into visual terms; to project visible images of fear, regret, remorse, alienation."

The discarding of proved theatrical techniques is risky. Shock tactics are successful only as long as they surprise by their novelty. It is a measure of Ionesco's talent that he continues to invent the novel and arresting.

In two of his most recent plays, *Rhinoceros* and *Exit the King*, the nihilism for which Ionesco has been criticised has been relieved by the assertion of the human value of fortitude.

Ionesco's plays were introduced into England in the 'fifties and they have had a marked and specific impact on English drama, especially on Simpson and Saunders. Although Pinter has a philosophy and style all his own, his early work is based on similar presuppositions.

The Bald Prima Donna. Written 1948.

Characters from an English language manual come to life and pour out their clichés in a "parody of a play", which Ionesco first considered to be a "tragedy of language", but which proved theatrically very funny. The first dialogue between husband and wife is now a classic.

Thus Ionesco, almost by accident, wrote the first of many satirical exposures of the sterile language of those who live a merely mechanical existence.

The Lesson. Written 1950. P.

A nervous old professor coaches an eager young girl. Elaborately "proving" the impossibility of communicating by words, he arbitrarily decides what various words shall mean, until he rapidly gains assurance and eventually rapes and murders his pupil, the fortieth that day.

Ionesco illustrates the prostitution of language as a means to power, the sexual element in power, and the sadism lurking in the teacher-pupil relationship and indeed in all authority.

Jack. Written 1950.

Urged by his conventional family to settle down to married life, the Bohemian son, Jack, resists Roberte, the proposed bride, because having only two noses she is not ugly enough. He eventually succumbs to Roberte II with three noses. Ionesco parodies submission to bourgeois conformity.

The Chairs. Written 1951. P.

An ancient concierge and his wife prepare for a crowd of guests who are to hear his final message to posterity. As the totally invisible guests arrive the couple fetch more and more chairs for them, until with the entry of the professional orator who is to pronounce the message, they jump into the sea. But the orator is deaf and dumb and his writing on the blackboard is a meaningless jumble.

The empty chairs constitute a most effective theatrical image for man's failure to communicate, and the dumb orator makes the record of a lifetime seem utterly futile. It may also suggest how meaningless can be the words of author and actor. Ionesco says, "The theme of the play is nothingness made concrete."

Victims of Duty. Written 1952.

By transforming a detective into a psychoanalyst, Ionesco argues that there is little difference between the psychological drama and the mere detective play.

Amédée. Written 1953. P.

A corpse in the flat of a married couple, constantly growing at a frightening rate, is a gruesome and appropriate image of their dead love.

Rhinoceros. Written 1958. P.

More and more rhinoceroses appear in a small provincial town. They are the inhabitants who, one after the other, want to be turned into these thick-skinned, aggressive animals. Finally only Bérenger (Olivier) resists the urge to conform.

The terrifying lure of conformity is here skilfully and movingly illustrated.

Exit the King. Written 1963.

In an agnostic counterpart of the 15th cent. *Everyman*, Ionesco shows King Bérenger (Alec Guinness), in his disintegrating palace, reluctantly submitting to the process of dying, his final resource being fortitude alone. This dramatic elegy, inspired by the final scenes of Richard II, is designed with bold simplicity, presenting man's mortal dissolution with unflinching honesty and a tenderness new in Ionesco.

Alfred Jarry (1873–1907).

Ubu Roi. 1966. M.

In 1896, Jarry initiator of the "Pataphysics" movement, scandalised Paris with his startling *Ubu Roi*, precursor of Absurd drama.

The characters appear as grotesque puppets, shocking and comic. The shameless, greedy Ubu caricatures both Macbeth and bourgeois vulgarity and in his brutal conquest of Poland becomes a monstrous prototype of ruthless cruelty

James Joyce (1882–1941). *See also* **Section M.**

Exiles. P.

Joyce's only play, rejected by both Yeats and Shaw, was wonderfully justified under Pinter's direction in 1970.

Its theme is the agony of mind and spirit engendered by a courageous attempt to live beyond the confines of law, convention and habit. Richard Rowan returns to Dublin, a famous writer, after nine years' voluntary exile. He brings Bertha, his wife by common-law, who had devotedly left Ireland with him, and their little son, Archie.

Rowan again meets Beatrice, who has always loved him and with whom he has for years corresponded voluminously about his work. From complex motives, partly to assure himself that Bertha's union with him is still absolutely free of conventional ties, he encourages her growing intimacy with his old friend and disciple, Robert. But Bertha, who in her simplicity is envious of Beatrice's education and subtlety of mind, feels rejected and confused, Robert that he is acting in an underhand way, and Richard that he must be ever wounded by doubt as to their fidelity.

Only parental feeling for Archie and Bertha's profound tenderness for Richard save them. For Bertha, with "something wiser than wisdom in her heart," has an intuitive insight beyond Richard's probing manipulating intelligence. Since Richard is to some degree a self-portrait, objective self-criticism is remarkable.

This taut and close-knit play in "three cat and mouse acts," where the past "is present here now," recalls Ibsen.

Heiner Kipphardt.

In the Matter of J. Robert Oppenheimer. 1966. M.

The play, already performed in 23 capitals, concerns Oppenheimer, "father of the A bomb." The source is documentary, the 3,000 pages of proceedings before the Personnel Security Board of the US Atomic Energy Commission in 1954.

A hearing taking over a month with 40 witnesses has been condensed and shaped so that evidence is represented by only 6 witnesses. Kipphardt's aim was to follow Hegel in stripping away the adventitious circumstances so that the essential situation clearly emerges. He has made a few additions and all deviations from the literal documents are based on historical data.

The play therefore has an extraordinary authenticity and grip while the central dilemmas are lucidly presented. As *The New Scientist* pointed out, it is for the audience to answer the searching questions raised. Was Oppenheimer, with his communist connections, a security risk? Can a scientist work with state authorities and keep his integrity? Is he responsible for the use made of his discoveries?

D. H. Lawrence (1885–1930). *See also* **Section M.**

In 1968 at the Royal Court Peter Gill staged three Lawrence plays in a special season acclaimed by the critics. They were *A Collier's Friday Night* (P), *The Daughter in Law* (P) and *The Widowing of Mrs. Holroyd* (P).

They depict Lawrence's Nottinghamshire mining community and share the themes already familiar through the contemporary *Sons and Lovers*, moving foward with a leisurely naturalism, undisturbed by any forced plot.

Robert Lowell (b. 1917). *See also* **Section M.**

The first dramatic work of the distinguished American poet, Robert Lowell, is *The Old Glory*, a trilogy of plays in free verse based on stories of Hawthorne and Melville. Their unifying motif is the flag.

Benito Cereno. 1967.

The third and best play of Lowell's trilogy is based on a short story by Melville.

About 1800, while off Trinidad, Delano, Captain of an American trader, observes that a Spanish trader, the *San Domingo*, is in great difficulties and generously goes to her aid.

Captained ostensibly by Benito Cereno, the *San Domingo* is in fact in the hands of her cargo of revolted slaves who have spared his life only that he may navigate them back to Africa. The effete and exhausted Cereno lives at the knife point at the hands of Babu, their wily leader.

Delano fails to realise this, for Cereno dare not speak plainly, and the American is too opaque and self-assured to interpret hints. Only when Babu openly defies him is he enlightened, but too late. The only safe course now left is open violence and instantly his seamen massacre all the Negroes.

In a final ominous incident the last survivor, Babu, cries out " The future is with us " before Delano empties his pistol into the Negro's body, crying, " This is your future."

This truly poetic play in lucid verse is rich in themes and suggestive power and austere in design, while mimes, rituals and masques are used with ironic significance. The Director, Jonathan Miller, envisaged it as a kind of inverted *Tempest*, the Spanish ship a black magic island and Cereno a drugged Prospero held captive by Babu, and he produced it in the formal and stylised manner of opera.

The play was also remarkable in its relevance to America's dilemma, domestic and foreign, including her ambiguous attitude to the contemporary Negro. Miller points out that Lowell here shows " the penalties of uniformed generosity ".

Prometheus Bound. 1971.

Lowell has adapted the first and only surviving play of Aeschylus's trilogy, where Prometheus, whose name means " forethought " and who had stolen fire from heaven for the benefit of mankind, is manacled to a crag at the command of a vengeful and violent Zeus.

Jonathan Miller's stylised production emphasised the tragic significance for today of an archetypal myth—the situation of one who refuses to compromise with arbitrary dictatorship and is consigned to solitary imprisonment and torture.

John McGrath (b. 1935).

Of Irish extraction, McGrath, who had wide experience in the army before reading English at Oxford, has now had several plays published.

His early realistic plays were critical of some aspects of society and recently McGrath has become a thoroughly committed writer, identifying himself with the 7.84 Theatre Company, one of the leading so-called " fringe " groups. This radical socialist company, which presents plays in the small theatre, factory and pub, is so named because 7% of the people in the country own 84% of the wealth. McGrath and his company are convinced that the under-privileged are also exploited culturally by mass media which erode their sense of values. In plays following *Plugged In* he aimed to give his audience of workers self-confidence, while providing lively entertainment.

Events while Guarding the Bofors Gun. 1966. M.

In situation, McGrath's masculine and disciplined play is a realistic counterpart of Giles Cooper's radio fantasy *Mathry Beacon.*

The futility of military routine is exposed with steely irony as, on a freezing night in Germany, during the Cold War, seven men guard the obsolete Bofors gun. The frustrating situation also engenders personal conflict. The uncontrollable desperado O'Rourke defies Lance Bombardier Evans. An insecure boy of 18, Evans is so obsessed by the hope that promotion may provide him a way of escape to England that he connives at insubordination. Finally O'Rourke's reckless suicide destroys them both.

Bakke's Night of Fame. 1968.

A play, faithfully based on the novel, *A Danish Gambit*, by William Butler, takes as subject the prisoner's last night in the condemned cell of an American prison.

Bakke, condemned for an apparently motiveless murder, enjoys being as provocative as possible, discomforting the well-meaning guard by first requesting then contemptuously rejecting the traditional routine of food and consolation. He entangles the priest with his contention that society is exercising not justice but revenge, his only constant demand being that he shall meet his " buddy ", the executioner.

This granted, Bakke so needles and infuriates the executioner that the man is betrayed into a violent outburst, gloating over his imminent task. Bakke, gleeful and triumphant, has proved his point about revenge.

McGrath shows great expertise in manoeuvre and sudden surprise, but he has not achieved the tension and progression of the *Bofors Gun.* The significant encounter with the executioner comes too late.

Plugged In. 1972.

The theme of three original one-act plays is the massive indifference of monopoly capitalism to individual human need. Free from didacticism they work indirectly, played in a cartoon-like setting of giant contemporary objects such as a Daz packet, symbolic of mass production, an Ionesco-like absurdity which in the first two plays is reflected in the dramatic situation. Both of these derive power from the association of the latent violence inherent in capitalism with loveless sexuality, repression and licence.

In *Plugged In*, the best of the trio, Kay, wife of a managing director, wearily sits on a street bench and obsessively recites disconnected newspaper reports of violence and disaster. She is joined by Derek, a sympathetic young working man who, preferring country walks, refuses to work more than one week in three.

He cannot stem her recital until his account of how in anger he had beaten his mistress excites Kay's own erotic masochistic feelings. Of her newspapers she cries, " I feel plugged in to history . . . taken over, crushed, by many many men . . . I need pain. It stops me suffering "; of her husband she says, " At night he drinks cocoa."

In this, the most powerful of the three plays, Kay is presented with psychological insight. Not only is her personality swamped by the mass media but she is sexually frustrated and repressed. In some ways she is a contemporary Lady Chatterley, now urban and demented.

Fish in the Sea. 1975.

The subject, like the sit-in at Fisher Bendix, is the occupation by the workers of a factory that would otherwise be dismantled. The play, set fictionally in Liverpool, shows the varied repercussions in the complex left-wing family of the Maconochies and the daughters' suitors. Only the last part of the play culminates in the sit-in. Songs abound.

David Mercer (b. 1928).

Since 1961 Mercer has written television plays and also the film-script *Morgan or a Suitable Case for Treatment.* His first stage play, *Ride a Cock Horse*, was produced in 1965. He is concerned with the psychological predicament of today's able, educated young man of artisan origin (a reflection of his own situation as son of a Yorkshire engine-driver). He usually depicts him as estranged from his parents, disorientated and childless.

Originally drawn to Marxism, Mercer has recently said that whatever the society he is examining, "whether the Vatican or the Kremlin," he is most concerned with the individual "who's catching the muck that's flying off the ideological fan," but he has not yet successfully dramatised this concern on the stage.

Belcher's Luck. 1966.

The rickety English class structure is the framework of a complex play.

On his ramshackle country estate, contemptuously served by his former batman, Belcher, Sir Gerald is becoming senile, Helen, his icy, avaricious niece, persuades Belcher to goad her uncle to his death so that they may together inherit the property. She then scornfully dismisses Belcher in favour of Victor, his bastard son.

Victor, expensively educated by Sir Gerald, is mentally unstable and impotent, but this familiar Mercer figure is now on the periphery. The conflict between the chaste and physically timid Sir Gerald and the coarse and drunken Belcher has become the compelling focus.

After Haggerty. 1970. M.

Bernard Link, dejected after two unsuccessful marriages, suddenly finds his new flat invaded by the vociferous American Claire, deserted wife of the former tenant Haggerty. She brings her baby. Idiosyncratic "decorators" from "Rely-On" add to the comic confusion.

Meanwhile rather stereotyped flashbacks in the form of monologue reveal emotional stalemate: Bernard, international drama critic, addresses his parochial engine-driver father (invisible to the audience); and the adoring heiress, Claire, talks to the indifferent and anarchical Haggerty (also unseen).

Bernard's weary embarrassment is intensified by the unheralded arrival of his father, prejudiced and censorious, yet pathetic.

The play ends with two acts of cruelty. An empty coffin arrives from Haggerty indicating his demise, and Bernard, exasperated by his father's mental atrophy, symbolically hangs the funeral wreath round his neck.

A latent topic is disillusion with communism and violent protest, but Mercer's favourite theme, the alienation of artisan father and educated son, finds no resolution. The dialogue is vigorous and inventive, especially in invective.

Flint. 1970. M.

The play presents the improbable situation of a kindly septuagenarian Kensington vicar, Flint (Michael Hordern), agnostic since ordination, whose sexual obsessions and irregularities have long been the scandal of the diocese.

While conducting his latest affair in the vestry with the teen-age Dixie, a Liverpool Irish "scrubber" from Holloway gaol, already pregnant by another, Flint inadvertently sets the vestry on fire. Meanwhile his wife, hysterically crippled since her honeymoon, sets fire to the church. She is then murdered by her sister, formerly Flint's mistress, who promptly goes mad. Flint and Dixie escape abroad on his motor-bike and side-car. While she is in labour by the roadside, he helplessly crashes into an ammunition lorry and is killed.

Mercer has claimed that Flint's "humanity is more valuable and more deserving of our love and compassion than the institution to which he belongs." But to contrast the hero, presented as endearing, with some stagy clerics is unconvincing demonstration. Recent revivals of Shaw make *Flint* look paltry as a "play of ideas", especially as the individuals who "catch the muck" are the vicar's hapless women!

There is melodrama in plenty and some lively farcical comedy, but wordy meditations, virtually monologues, clog the action.

Duck Song. 1974. M.

Maurice, 71, wealthy, inept, is an artist passé, terrified of death. He reluctantly supports his brother Herbert, 61, formerly an expert cracksman, Herbert's daughter Jane, "an angry psychiatrist", and her unemployed lover. On this ménage there intrude first a burglar, Herbert's latest accomplice, then Herbert's ex-wife from America, now thrice married. She introduces her young lover Lee, alias Swift Arrow, a Red Indian, their only luggage being a buffalo head on a pole like a totem. The act ends in a blinding flash of light.

The second act shows the same scene but devoid of furniture and Lee, now in Red Indian dress, meditates on the Indians' virtual extinction (as indicated by the buffalo head) and foresees a similar fate for the white imperialists. There is a series of desultory conversation and monologues as each expresses his regrets, disillusion, sense of futility and uncertainty. In this limbo death is apparently impossible, for three people are deliberately murdered without any effect, and the play ends amid signs of final cataclysm as all mournfully cluster around the totem unable even to sing their "swan song".

Themes include art, imperialism, sex and love, confusion and disintegration, but characters and situation are unconvincing and the fable obscure.

Arthur Miller (b. 1915).

Arthur Miller, an admirer of Ibsen, shares his strong sense of moral purpose and of the individual's responsibility to the community. This is balanced by a sympathetic understanding of the insecurity of the individual in modern society.

Miller's characters, deeply felt and realised, are fallible men who suffer through their own errors of character or judgment in social conditions which are incomprehensible, indifferent, or even hostile to them.

A recurrent pattern is that of paternal responsibility within a patriarchal family unit, and the father's distress as he sees his errors hurting wife and sons. But the sense of responsibility flows outwards to society as a whole, of which the family is but the growing point. Significantly—apart from the benign mother-figures—Miller's most balanced characters are lawyers.

His plays are well constructed, the dialogue economic and telling, and he has progressed from the realism of *All My Sons*, published 1947, to much freer experimental techniques, while the prose style has become more fluid and eloquent.

Death of a Salesman. Published 1949. P.

A compassionate and finely-balanced play exposes the impingement of hire-purchase commercialism on the ageing salesman, Willy Loman, a weak, foolish, and deeply affectionate man, and also reveals his overwhelming sense of guilt towards wife and sons. The play is worked out on two planes, the inexorable present and Willy's past which obsessively enacts itself within his mind. The film version with Frederic March, is excellent.

The Crucible. Published 1953. P.

In 1949 Marion Starkey's *The Devil in Massachusetts* dealt with a witch-hunt in Salem in 1692, and pointed out its relevance to our own age, also rent by "ideological intensities." In 1952 the activities of McCarthy gave it a special urgency.

In this powerful play Miller uses this historical incident to depict not an indifferent society but one in which positive evil is unleashed. The evils he explores are the persecution of a minority and the interference of the Establishment in the individual conscience.

Characteristically Miller focuses attention on the plain man, John Proctor, and he invents his former adultery with Abigail, so that the play is not a partisan manifesto but a study of the complex contradictions of actual life. The self-righteous fanaticism of the persecutors and Proctor's own growth in self-knowledge and courage are faithfully and poignantly portrayed.

A View From the Bridge. 1956. P.

Eddie Carbone, a Brooklyn docker, is so gripped by jealous possessiveness of his wife's niece, that he eventually betrays her two kinsmen, illegal immigrants, to the Authorities.

In a play of repressed sexual passion, with hints of incest and homosexuality, Miller shows mastery of a kind of situation new to him and the heightening tension is realised in taut and disciplined sequences.

A lawyer, Alfieri, acts as a Greek chorus but is powerless to intervene, for Eddie infringes something more primitive than the legal code and it is by the primitive vendetta that he is eventually killed.

Incident at Vichy. 1966. P.

Miller here turns to the responsibility of society for the individual in a play which exposes the latent racial hostility which even the best men may unconsciously harbour.

The example he takes is antisemitism, the place and time Vichy in 1942, the scene a bleak anteroom within sound of a railway, where sealed trucks are deporting Jews to the furnaces of Auschwitz. Here a group of men and a boy, Jewish suspects, await investigation. There is an atmosphere of chill horror and suspense as each tries to summon up his own pitiful defence against the premonition of the ghastly journey he must embark on, once he is summoned behind the closed door.

Eventually only two men remain, the two most aware and articulate, Doctor Leduc, a Jewish analyst (Anthony Quayle) and Von Berg (Alec Guinness), the only Gentile of the group, a cultured and humane Viennese Prince, who is horrified by the vulgarity and barbarism of the Nazis.

In their final dialogue Doctor Leduc convinces the Prince of his unconscious antisemitism and the Prince gives his safe-conduct to the doctor.

A subsidiary theme of the play is the way society imposes extrinsically an identity on the individual, in this instance, as in Frisch's *Andorra*, the rôle of victim on the Jewish people. Through Leduc, Miller also criticises the Jews' acceptance of their rôle.

This disturbing play makes the greatest demands on the emotions, intelligence and humanity of the audience, who like the Prince to some degree undergo psycho-analysis. But the play is also characterised by a fine restraint. As in Aeschylus' *Agamemnon* the violence takes place behind closed doors, with the significant difference that in Miller's play the chorus and victims are identical.

The Price. 1969.

Two brothers confront each other in an attic crowded with the heavy furniture of their dead father, a financier ruined in the Depression. Its imminent sale is the occasion of their first encounter in sixteen years.

Victor Franz, who had given up a scientific career to support his father, is now a policeman at retiring age but too immobilised by his past to begin a new career in spite of the hysterical pressure of his wife. Walter, a surgeon, in his slick pursuit of success has had a prolonged breakdown and a broken marriage. The "price", ostensibly that of the furniture, is the price each has paid for his decision in life and its inexorable results.

The brothers ruthlessly dissect and probe back to the motivation of their choice. Walter is forced to admit calculated callousness but drives Victor to realise that his sense of social responsibility was also flawed, for he had sentimentally sacrificed his potentiality to a disingenuous father too cowardly to work again.

But no reconciliation ensues, Victor angrily refusing the dubious job which Walter offers as a salve to conscience.

Miller describes his play as stripped to the skeletal structure of two lives, the home the dead husk from which they had developed. But the characters are complex and through the Ibsen-like situation runs a thread of delightful and significant comedy. Solomon, a ancient Jew, survivor of wildly differing professions and four marriages, is the furniture appraisor and embodies the resilience lacking in the Franzes. When he falls, he bounces. He shrewdly decides to buy all the furniture at a fair price and at curtain fall sits gleefully in the chair of the beaten father, chuckling exuberantly at his decision to begin life afresh.

The play is realistic, but the muted significance of various remnants of bric-a-brac is symbolic in effect. Organised with meticulous artistry, it is lucid and profound, and rich in the wisdom of experience distilled. Acted without a break it holds the audience absorbed.

John Mortimer (b. 1923).

Mortimer, a barrister, first won success with his short plays, such as *The Dock Brief*, 1957, and *Lunch Hour*, 1960 (M). Here his talents are seen at their best, especially his gift for seizing on an unusual encounter between "the lonely, the neglected, the unsuccessful", whom he envisages in realistic settings of shabby gentility, and he is particularly sympathetic to those who allow their fantasy to swamp actuality.

But the moment of insight that gives pathos to his short plays is not enough to illuminate those of full length, like *What Shall We Tell Caroline?* and *The Wrong Side of the Park*, which lack substance. *Two Stars for Comfort*, 1960 (M), is also unsatisfactory. *The Judge*, 1967, (M), and *A Voyage Round thy Father*, 1970 (M), were more successful.

Peter Nichols.

Nichols has long been interested in music-hall and revue and he expertly deploys their techniques of direct address to the audience. He successfully uses one of the dramatis personae as an ironical commentator able to step easily in and out of the action.

He has a remarkable talent for conveying with comedy and compassion the sharp pain that can underlie the absurdities of personal relationships and he is intelligently concerned with specific social problems.

A Day in the Death of Joe Egg. 1967. F.

Nichols has shown remarkable sensitivity and skill in developing his theme—the especial difficulties of monogamy when the only child, a ten-year-old girl, is hopelessly spastic. He uses comic techniques of revue as the parents re-enact their frustrating encounters with doctors and clergy. But below the jesting facade grows the realisation that the wife's compulsive maternity blinds her to her husband's needs and that his endurance is crumbling.

Nichols has a spastic child and says "It's a play about marriage. . . . Not autobiographical."

The National Health. 1969. F.

In a bleak men's ward in a decaying hospital the staff are reasonably competent but faceless. Interpolated are brief TV scenes of *Nurse Norton's Affair*, a burlesque of the rosy view of the medical profession as seen on popular TV.

The vignettes of the consultant, the chaplain, and the visitor, have the pungency of revue. The male nurse acts as compère to the whole, and also as devil's advocate who maliciously destroys the beginning of a positive relationship between a neurotic but protective schoolmaster and the alcoholic he is helping.

The play has the sharp comedy associated not with impartial enquiry but with astringent criticism. It has been seen as an image of Britain's own condition.

Forget-me-not Lane. 1971. F.

With easy expertise Nichols presents psychological strain in terms of hilarious domestic and social comedy. He spans the generations deftly conveying the manners of each and presenting a recurring pattern of the marriage strained to breaking-point and the children caught in "the genetic trap" enacting in middle age the parental traits they most disliked.

As he moves in and out of the action Frank, now in his forties, is able to re-live crucial experiences and ruefully and sardonically to interpret them. His adolescent self (taken by a young actor) is seen in war-time Britain, the only child in a divided home, siding with his easy-going mother against the father, Charles, absurdly unsuccessful in all he attempts, whether as petty commercial traveller, martinet or entertainer. Frank's mind is on girls, but he is too repressed to respond to the frank overture of Ursula (later his wife) and takes refuge with pin-ups and fantasy.

Later Frank, sexually frustrated, faces the breakdown of his own marriage and to his dismay finds himself echoing his father's mannerisms. Too late he understands the pathetic Charles, also the son of incompatible parents, his awkward affection for his wife constantly rebuffed.

Chez Nous. 1974. F.

Nichols here uses realistic comedy of character to satirise the malaise underlying an affluent and permissive group.

Dick, 40, is a paediatrician who has written a book advocating sexual freedom at puberty. By changing the title to *The Nubile Baby* and issuing it in a dust jacket depicting a schoolgirl wearing only a satchel, his publishers have promoted this into a best-seller. To avoid tax he and his homely wife, Liz, have bought and modernised the old farm in France they previously rented.

The scene is an ancient barn modishly furnished with farming relics where they welcome their "oldest friends", Phil, provincial and immature, and Di, his languid, actressy wife, but the strains in their relationships soon show. While the others had enjoyed a promiscuous youth, Dick had chastely waited for Di who had instead married Phil while she was pregnant by another man. She was then sterilised and Phil left pining for a son.

Nichols adroitly places three successive shocks, the first that the hosts have acquired a fourth child, Sammy, now in his pram. Then the talkative Liz blurts out that he is in fact the son to her eldest daughter Jane, now aged 14. Last, an old French peasant informs Dick that he recognises Phil as Jane's lover, having seen them lying together naked the previous summer.

The act closes to general consternation with Dick indignant and cheated, Phil struggling between shame and pride in his paternity, while Di angrily bolts her door against him.

Long pent-up recriminations ensue. Phil's longing to adopt his son is opposed by Di's disdain and Liz's maternity, while Dick urges Di to join him in a romantic elopement. Their wrangles are punctured by the arrival of two American journalists whose questioning neatly incapsulates the disparity between Dick's precepts and his apparently conventional domesticity.

But "the family is like the car. Out of date but we go on using it" and after each couple has spent a conjugal night neither Di nor Dick can finally cut adrift and in a muddled compromise they agree that Sammy should somehow be shared between them.

Dick echoes Nichols' Frank, sadly gnawed by vain regrets, but he is now presented with a greater detachment.

Eugene O'Neill (1888–1953).

Although O'Neill's work belongs to the first half of the century, three of his later works had their delayed première here in the 'fifties, two of them making a great impression.

The Iceman Cometh. Published 1947.

In a naturalistic play, whose prototype is Gorky's *The Lower Depths*, down-and-outs await the arrival of the dionysiac Hickey. But Hickey has just murdered his wife and his abortive attempt to rouse them from "pipe dreams" to reality leaves them sunk even more deeply than before in drink and self-deceit. The pessimistic theme is that of Ibsen's *The Wild Duck* and the situation that of Beckett's *Waiting for Godot*.

Long Day's Journey Into Night. Published 1955.

An avowed autobiographical play depicts O'Neill's family on the day when his mother (Gwen Ffrancgon Davies) relapses into drug addiction and Eugene learns that he must leave the doomed circle for a sanatorium. As it was there that he chose his vocation, this constitutes the one note of hope in a deeply mournful reverie. The Freudian love-hate relationships are unfolded with tender understanding.

Joe Orton (1933–67).

Orton was a successful commercial exponent of black comedy who also won praise from serious critics especially for his dialogue.

His range is narrow and he is preoccupied with crime, perverted sexuality, and violence portrayed without inhibition as hilariously comic, sometimes with satiric effect. The macabre plots occasion a flow of deadpan repartee, normally smutty, sometimes merely facetious, often very apt and funny indeed, always a parody of the genteel. Nearly all Orton's characters speak alike and are as undifferentiated in their lingo as in their lack of morality.

The satire is in the form of caricature or parody and apart from its implications it is almost impossible to discover in Orton any expression of human value or aspiration. It is not always easy to discriminate between the unsavoury matter of his plays and the expertise and aplomb with which it is manipulated, and some feel that he defaces the image of life.

Entertaining Mr. Sloane. 1964. P.

The handsome young wastrel, Sloane, already a murderer, finds a cosy refuge with Kath. A slattern of forty, she smothers him with motherliness and, sexually insatiable, she seduces him from the first night. Her brother, Ed, a homosexual, soon employs Sloan as his "chauffeur". When Sloane tries to escape their possessiveness, his brutal murder of their father puts him into their power and they agree quite literally to share him, each having him for six months at a time.

The play scores by a skilfully handled plot, an ironic "poetic justice" and the sly and genteel euphemisms of the salacious dialogue, and it won the London Critics Variety Award as the best play of 1964.

Loot. 1966. M. P.

Helped by his accomplice a young criminal secretes the loot from a burglary in his mother's coffin. This is the key situation in a macabre and complicated farce, which is also an exuberant caricature of funeral ritual, of a police which is represented as hamhanded and venal, and of cheap detective fiction. The characters are cardboard puppets manipulated by the plot and the play is notable for the fact that vice is completely triumphant.

Crimes of Passion. 1967. M.

A double bill consists of *The Ruffian on the Stair*, 1966, Orton's first play, and *The Erpingham Camp*, 1967. Frequent and fussy scene changes betray their origin in radio and television respectively.

The Ruffian on the Stair. 1967. M.

The occupants of the room are Mike, a criminal living with an ex-prostitute, Joyce. The intruder is a boy ostensibly seeking revenge for his brother with whom he had lived in homosexual incest, and whom Mike had murdered. He is in fact seeking his own death and provokes Mike to murder him by pretending that he has seduced Joyce.

The Erpingham Camp. 1967. M.

A satire on holiday camps shows an uprising of the merrymakers who eventually kill Erpingham. The ebullient parody has some highly comic incidents. Orton's sketch lacks complexity and Erpingham meets his fate because he is stupid and dictatorial.

What the Butler Saw. 1969. M.

A farce in a psychiatric clinic is typically Orton in its discrepancy between decorous speech and indecent behaviour. In the original production pace and invention seemed to flag but a revival by the Royal Court in 1975 revealed the play's inherent potential.

John Osborne (b. 1929).

Osborne is endowed with considerable theatrical talent and a torrential rhetoric, most effective in impetuous monologue and in hostile denunciation.

These gifts were at once apparent in *Look Back in Anger*, 1956, where the protagonist, Jimmy Porter, makes a strident attack on the assumptions and values of the middle class. The play was perfectly timed and its success immediate, for Jimmy voiced the pent-up frustrations of the radicals of his generation, baffled by the complacence of an establishment which had muddled through two wars and left them without any sense of security or direction. Moreover, the frisson of surprise at sight of Jimmy's shabby provincial attic delighted playgoers jaded by the convention of stage drawing-room.

Osborne had broken new ground and for some years went on to experiment, attempting in 1957 and 1961 Brechtian techniques. But his two plays of 1968 are conventional in both structure and plushy, affluent settings, while the heady tirade of invective has dwindled, as the characters spew out a bitter personal malaise in disconnected complaint.

Osborne is most successful in the portrayal of his dominating and eloquent protagonists, like Archie Rice, Bill Maitland and Laurie. Even when disorganised by self-pity they convince us as we watch them driven on by sado-masochistic urges to destroy both themselves and their circle. A succession of famous actors have brought them unforgettably to life. But the other dramatis personae, serving as "feed", are often presented perfunctorily, distinguishable only by a few mannerisms and in the assertions of their fellows.

This kind of characterisation is damaging to structure. Dramatic confrontation is spasmodic so that the play becomes slack. Time has disclosed Osborne's tenuous grip on structure generally. His expositions are sometimes maladroit or even misleading, the development desultory and the climax superimposed.

The mood of Osborne's protagonists, rejection of the present and sentimental nostalgia for the era of Britain's imperial and colonial power, has now invaded the minor characters, so the play tends to be uniformly negative and sometimes downright dreary. Such an idiom cannot be defended as satire, which is positive in its implications.

Look Back in Anger. 1956. F.

Jimmy Porter, product of "white-tile" university, has married Alison a colonel's daughter and their misalliance triggers off his furious diatribe against her and her family. When she returns to her parents because pregnant, her friend Helena promptly becomes Jimmy's mistress, until Alison, having lost her baby returns and is reduced to grovelling to Jimmy before they can resume their unstable relationship.

The play, with its fusion of sexual and social tension, made an immediate impact on Osborne's contemporaries. It cleverly synthesises a strident denunciation of Alison and of the privileged classes, so that Jimmy's marriage is like a token rape and plunder of the establishment, the excitement given a sensational fillip by his liaison with Helena.

Jimmy's torrential rhetoric is inebriating and the surprises well judged, but the surrounding characters are too compliant to be convincing. This dramatic defect and the author's ambivalent attitude to Jimmy himself, give a false authority to an immature and wantonly destructive protagonist.

The Entertainer. 1957. F.

Osborne here attempts to use the Brechtian device of "endistancing", employing a framework of music-hall scenes, where Archie Rice (Olivier), a seedy comedian, tries to hold the stage with tawdry patter and songs in a dubious show with nudes called "Rock'n Roll New'd Look." These are intended to "endistance" realistic scenes of Archie's shabby home. But the "endistancing" device serves little purpose for the overall mood of unquestioned disillusion "whooped up" by drink and patter is in both planes unrelieved. Querulous complaint that England has lost the glory and glamour of Edwardian days is crystallised on the realistic plane by the report of the death of Archie's son at Suez and in the music-hall by the presentation of a nude Britannia, wearing only her helmet.

Luther. 1961. F.

Luther is a less subjective work, although Osborne again takes for his hero a rebel, the son of an unsympathetic mother, and emphasises the emotional and not the intellectual sources of Luther's protests.

The play is imitative of Brecht's *Galileo* both in its loose "epic" structure and also in the attempt to present the protagonist in an equivocal light. The first two acts give a sympathetic and leisurely portrayal of Luther's early conflicts of conscience and vigorous attack on superstition while in the third act he is hurriedly presented as having treacherously let down the peasants who had been encouraged to rise against the Emperor. But the political reasons for Luther's dilemma are not even hinted at and we are invited not to think, as in *Galileo*, but to condemn while ignorant of relevant facts. Structurally this sudden *volte face* is most damaging to the play.

The most effective scenes, such as Tetzel's selling of indulgences and Martin's sermon at Wittenberg are splendid rhetoric, without a word of dialogue and directed straight at the audience.

Skilful period production and the acting of Albert Finney as Luther made the play theatrically effective.

Two Plays for England. 1962.

Two slight pays make a double bill. *The Blood of the Bambergs*, a send-up of royal weddings, and *Under Plain Cover*, an attack on press sensationalism, rely on parody and mimicry.

Inadmissible Evidence. 1964. F.

The play provides the sensational spectacle of a middle-aged solicitor, Bill Maitland (Nicol Williamson), obsessed with sex, and disintegrating under the influence of drink and drugs.

The play opens with a dream sequence as Maitland is tried in the court of his own mind. What follows is his rancid outpouring of self-pity, as during forty-eight hours, he is progressively deserted by staff, clients and mistress. Maitland's flagellation of himself and his fate is unrelieved.

A Patriot for Me. 1965.

The protagonist of a play, produced privately, is Redl, a distinguished army officer of the Austro-Hungarian Empire, who through his homosexuality is blackmailed into becoming a spy for Tsarist Russia.

Osborne is here objective and ironic. He uses a series of brief scenes with significant juxtaposition of characters and swift dialogue. The first act, showing Redl's gradual discovery of his nature is discriminating and adroit and the drag ball which opens Act Two is an astonishing *tour de force*.

Act Three shows a decline of tension as Redl, now a spy, himself declines, his fibre coarsened through a sequence of sordid infidelities by male lovers and prostitutes. His final unmasking and suicide is almost a foregone conclusion.

A Bond Honoured. 1966.

Osborne, in a free translation of *La Fianza Satisfecha*, is said to have distorted Lope de Vega's play.

Time Present. 1968. F.

The protagonist, Pamela, is a neurotic actress. Emotionally strangled by the familiar "Electra complex", an exaggerated devotion to her father, a once famous actor, now dying off-stage, she is unable to establish any satisfactory human relationship, in spite of love affairs and the friendship of the devoted Constance, a successful Labour M.P., in whose flat she is living.

Pamela's role is static and verbal; reiteration of her shallow scheme of values (a preference for style over vulgarity), sentimental reminiscences of her father and a relentless spate of contemptuous and indiscriminate derision. Phrased in modish argot some gibes have a bitter wit, pleasing to the prejudices of the illiberal.

Pamela's alienation, which should arouse compassion, becomes tiresome because of the play's apparent assumption that her outpourings have objective value.

The Hotel in Amsterdam. 1968. F.

United by fear and dislike of their employer, a film magnate, cryptically referred to as K.L., three couples retreat to a luxury hotel in Amsterdam as a hide-out from his encroachments.

They pass the weekend in denouncing K.L., drinking, and exchanging desultory jokes and complaints about homosexuals, mothers and "the working class", until the unwelcome arrival of a relative and the news that K.L. has killed himself disturb the tenuous camaraderie.

Such a structure is perfunctory. Only the garrulous and petulant Laurie (Scofield) is individualised and the characters reveal and discover little of value about themselves or each other.

A revealing sidelight is that Laurie fancies himself as an authority on "the creative process", boasting, "What I do, I get out of the air." Is this Osborne's method?

West of Suez. 1971. F.

In a sub-tropical island, formerly British, an expatriate couple entertain her family; three sisters, two with husbands, and her father, Wyatt (Ralph Richardson), once a distinguished writer.

The relatives and a host of supernumeraries drift in and out, usually preceded by a dissection of their deficiencies, but Wyatt firmly holds the centre. Now a television sage, he is a consummate poseur, effusively professing that consideration for others which he conspicuously lacks and pathetically anxious for adulation.

He and his coterie are privileged but bored and uneasy, "perched between one civilisation and the next", and nostalgically recalling army officer life in India.

The play is without incident until a sudden melodramatic finale. First a hippie American student makes a violent verbal onslaught and almost immediately armed islanders enter and gun Wyatt down.

Osborne obviously follows Chekhov in depicting a decaying and powerless society but fails to catch Chekhov's humane portrayal of the complex and subtle relationships within a closely knit group.

Later plays, *A Sense of Detachment*, 1972 (F), *The End of Me Old Cigar*, 1975, and *Watch it Come Down*, 1976, did not enhance Osborne's reputation.

Alexander Ostrovsky (1823–86).

The eminent Russian playwright is unfortunately little known in this country.

The Storm. 1966.

Written in 1859, Ostrovsky's fine realistic play portrays a social group unfamiliar to us, the petty tradesmen of an isolated township, who are avaricious, ignorant and bigoted.

The widow, Kabanovna, is a warped and ruthless matriarch, who saps the vitality of her weak son and cruelly tyrannises over his hapless wife, Katerina. The lonely, susceptible girl yields to the love of a young stranger from Moscow. Then sheltering in a church during a violent storm, she is overcome by superstitious dread and remorse. She confesses and later kills herself.

Harold Pinter (b. 1930).

The versatile Pinter, one of our foremost playwrights, began as an actor and also directs plays and films.

He exerts an almost hypnotic effect over his audience with his uncanny sense of tension and the telling pause. Whether his novel situations find resolution in final surprise or disturb with teasing uncertainty, they have a satisfying elegance of design.

His art developed quickly and two main phases can now be distinguished. The plays culminating in *The Caretaker*, 1960, were concerned with the underprivileged and showed a growing sense of compassion. His later plays were much concerned with sexual dominance and jealousy, the background usually sophisticated, the attitude detached.

Whatever the subject, the plays have a poetic resonance, due in part to Pinter's intuitive understanding of man's subconscious life, especially his memories and fears. The basis is actuality. As a Jewish boy growing up in East London he had personal experience of hostility and aggression, intensified by his knowledge of Europe's suffering Jewry.

His recurring image is of a room that is invaded and he has said, "I don't think it is all that surrealistic and curious because surely this thing of people arriving at the door has been happening in Europe in the last twenty years. Not only the last twenty years, the last two to three hundred."

But his basic situation is so striking, that, like poetry, it can be interpreted on more than one level. Those periods of private anxiety, when the distraught individual holds on precariously to some tiny foothold, also image the predicament of the whole human race, where existence is threatened by ungovernable forces. Like Kafka, whom he admires, Pinter expresses vividly the feeling of some inscrutable menace from some vague hinterland invading humdrum human life.

Some of the disturbing fascination Pinter exerts is due to the state of uncertainty he creates but the questions posed have become increasingly significant. He deliberately rejects the Ibsenite rôle of the omniscient, for people's memories are inconsistent and it is particularly difficult to be precise about people's inner lives and motives, especially if they are inarticulate.

Pinter has affinities with dramatists of the absurd and is closest in feeling to Beckett. He shares with Ionesco an awareness that tragedy can co-exist with comedy, saying "Even tragedy is funny."

Pinter is a stylist in dialogue, especially in Cockney and the shabby genteel, in clichés and non-sequiturs. He records talk rather than conversation, what Martin Buber calls "monologue disguised as as dialogue". His characters' monologues are spiced with boasting as each strives for ascendancy.

The theme of power over others is indeed the keynote of much of his best work.

Esslin's study "*The Peopled Wound*" (M. 1970), is scholarly and illuminating.

Pinter's early one-acters include *The Room*, 1957 (M), which includes some insignificant factual contradictions and ends in melodrama, and *The Dumb Waiter*, 1960 (M and P), which shows Ben and Gus, hired assassins, harrassed by an Ionesco-like dumb-waiter, while awaiting their victim in a basement. It is then revealed that Ben is deputed to kill Gus.

The Birthday Party. 1958. M.

In Pinter's first full-length play, the room is in a shabby boarding-house kept by the motherly Meg. Here Stanley, who claims to have been a concert pianist, has taken refuge, until he is suddenly unnerved by the arrival of a sinister pair, the specious Goldberg and the brutal McCann. They subject Stanley to a fantastic catechism, a parody of brain-washing, and during his phoney and ludicrous birthday party he is blindfolded and his glasses broken—symbolic of destruction of vision. Next morning the pair lead Stanley away, conventionally dressed, incapable of speech, his personality disintegrated.

The menace here is economically sustained, and the fact that the identity of the three main characters is never revealed adds to the terror. Some see Stanley as the political refugee; some, since he was a pianist, as the artist made to conform. But by its deliberate lack of definiteness, the play has a wide reference to all who seek refuge from a hostile world.

The Caretaker. 1960. M.

The play is set in a junk-filled room, where the kindly Aston lives in his brother's derelict house. He brings home an old tramp, Davies, who grudgingly agrees to stay as "caretaker" and then tries to encroach further by playing off one brother against the other, until finally rejected by both.

In a naturalistic background Pinter has created two unforgettable characters, presented in psychological depth with reference to their past, and has depicted their failure to come to terms with compassion and restraint.

Davies is one who bites the hand that feeds him. His very identity is suspect for he passes under an assumed name, having "left his papers" years ago "at Sidcup." But he never retrieves them. Aston haltingly tells Davies how he once had periods of unique lucidity, now destroyed by a terrifying shock-treatment in mental hospital, but Davies' only reaction is later to threaten him. It is remarkable that when Aston finally rejects Davies' last encroachment the plight of the tramp should seem as pitiful as Aston's own, Pinter having wisely rejected his first intention to end the play with the violent death of Davies.

This mature play shows a man actually opening the door to his fears and mastering them. Aston in his long speech faces the wrong done to him by "people". His unique vision destroyed, his only creative outlet has been tinkering with his junk, but as he tries to break out of his isolation by befriending another crippled human being, he unhappily meets a man so twisted by his own suffering and resentment that he cannot respond. Some find in Aston a moving image of the mystic and artist in man whose creative insight is destroyed by an imperceptive and mechanical society.

There followed four short plays, *A Slight Ache* and *A Night Out*, 1961 (M), and then two with a chic setting, *The Collection*, 1962 (M), and *The Lover*, 1961 (M).

The Homecoming. 1965. M.

Teddy, a Doctor of Philosophy in an American University, brings his wife, Ruth, on a surprise visit to his former home in North London, where Max, his widowed father, still lives with his two younger sons, Lenny and Joey. It is gradually revealed that Ruth before her marriage had been a "model" and the family decide to keep her as their common mistress, while the brutal Lenny, a pimp, arranges that she shall earn her keep as a prostitute.

Because this is presented with clinical detachment, the audience is induced to suspend emotion. Only at the last moment is this cool acceptance shattered when Max, aged 70, crawls sobbing to Ruth asking to be kissed and the audience is shocked into feeling the degradation.

On the surface the play is a disillusioned glance at life. It may also be interpreted as a fantasy of sexual gratification, which in a dream state escapes the taboo of ethical and humane feeling. The use of some accepted sex symbols and the slow and trance-like acting, especially that of Ruth, is dream-like and the final shock is analogous to waking up and realising what the dream has implied.

It is possible also to see in Teddy an acquiescent Hamlet. He returns home from a foreign university to find marital infidelity, for it is disclosed that his mother had been unfaithful with an uncle figure and Hamlet's scornful words to Ophelia suggest that Ruth may represent her.

Landscape and Silence. 1969. M.

Beckett's influence is apparent in two short plays, where inconclusive words and action are pared to the bone and whose theme is personal isolation. Both recall *Krapp's Last Tape* in their repetitive memories of past love.

Landscape, originally broadcast, is set in the kitchen of a country house, where the middle-aged caretaker appears to be telling his wife (Peggy Ashcroft) of the day's commonplace events and recalls an infidelity. She, absorbed in dreaming of a former tender encounter on the sea-shore, ignores him.

Silence is even more spare and brief. Ellen sits between two men. Both have loved her in vain, although she has all but forgotten them. They are almost immobile, their only speech interlacing, fragmentary memories of love. These are redolent of the country, mostly at nightfall. The men are faintly characterised and setting is discarded in favour of "three areas". *Silence* recalls Beckett's *Play*. Pinter was later to develop further the theme of nostalgic memory.

The Tea Party and *The Basement.* 1970. M.

Two plays originally seen on television were perfectly suited to the medium since both make swift transitions from objective happenings to subjective fantasies. They were however translated as faithfully as possible to the stage. Both involve the theme of encroachment.

The Basement, written first, is like a chic version of *The Caretaker*. A fastidious bachelor, Law, welcomes to his flat an old friend, Stott, who brings his girl friend. Both promptly take possession, even of the host's bed. Law alternates between friendly chat and suppressed fantasies, such as romantic seduction of the girl and violent duelling with Stott. The play suddenly concludes with rôles reversed, Law being the visitor demanding admittance.

The Tea Party centres on Disson, a middle-aged plumbing tycoon. Just before his marriage to a young woman socially his superior, he engages a new secretary, Wendy, with whom he is soon infatuated. But his patronising wife comes to the office as his secretary, and he suspects an incestuous liaison between her and her parasite brother.

Since wife, secretary and even he as husband have each a curious distorted double, Disson's vision, not surprisingly, becomes confused. A single table-tennis ball appears to him as two and he can only touch Wendy when blindfolded. His hysterical blindness culminates, at an office tea party, in complete loss of sight. Poor Disson had from the outset been blind to his social position and his sexual needs.

The play has echoes of *The Birthday Party*, but now all on a fashionable level.

Old Times. 1971. M.

Deeley and his wife Kate await the first visit of Anna, her friend in London twenty years before. As Deeley jestingly questions the laconic Kate he is startled to learn that the two girls "lived together", and the waiting Anna then comes forward from the symbolic half-light.

In an exchange of conflicting memories Deeley and Anna begin to strive for possession of Kate, even in retrospect.

In the second act Deeley alone with Anna insists that he recognises her as the girl he had picked up at a pub. Anna's riposte is that she was then wearing Kate's underwear so that his memory of the two girls becomes more confused.

His jealousy of Anna, inflamed by her talk of her expensive home, flares out in anger at her mention of the word "passion". But Kate remains withdrawn until a strange final speech.

She had, she says, seen Anna lying dead in their room with earth on her face and her place taken by a man. She had tried to plaster his face with earth but he had resisted. Is this Kate's rejection of both rivals? Anna turns to go. Deeley sobs silently. Then brightly lit all three are seen as in their opening conversation, as though locked together by their past.

In this taut, suggestive and ambiguous play Pinter has admirably fused the themes of nostalgia and sexual dominance.

No Man's Land. 1975.

Hirst (Ralph Richardson), a wealthy alcoholic in his sixties, once a man of letters, brings home a shabby contemporary, Spooner (John Gielgud), a self-styled poet he has met in a fashionable pub on Hampstead Heath. Spooner's first attempt to insinuate himself permanently into this luxurious home is maladroit. Mistaking one of Hirst's remarks as an admission of impotence, he scornfully offers himself as friend. Hirst, dead drunk, says, "No man's land . . . does not move . . . or change . . . or grow old . . . remains . . . forever . . . icy", falls twice and crawls from the room.

Alone, Spooner is startled by the arrival of two tough men-servants, Briggs, fortyish, who recognises Spooner as a pub potman, Foster, younger, and Spooner realises he must struggle with them also for ascendancy. When Hirst returns he professes not to know Spooner and is plied with drink by Briggs. Even here Spooner seizes a chance to ingratiate himself, claiming that he and Hirst are both fathers. The men-servants threaten him violently and Briggs leading Hirst off, Foster plunges the room into darkness.

Next day Hirst comes forward to Spooner saying "Charles. How nice of you to drop in", and charming him as one of his Oxford set. Hirst boasts how he seduced Spooner's wife and after a ludicrous rigmarole of names of friends, still preserved in Hirst's photograph albums, Spooner accuses him of "insane and corrosive absolutism". They quarrel, the men-servants return and Spooner makes his supreme effort. He could bring to life the nostalgia embalmed in "the albums". He could act as chef and secretary to Hirst, who would be chief guest at poetry readings he is organising. The bodyguard stand dumbfounded. There is silence. Hirst's ambiguous reply is "Let us change the subject. For the last time. What have I said?" By sleight of words Briggs and Foster trap Hirst. "So that nothing else will happen forever", says Foster.

Spooner replies with Hirst's own words telling him he is in no man's land. "I'll drink to that," replies Hirst and there is a slow fade.

The confrontation between Hirst and Spooner is arresting and Gielgud was hailed as "actor of the year". The difference between Briggs and Foster is carelessly indicated and the play less well integrated than *Old Times*.

Terence Rattigan (b. 1911).

Rattigan, with his flair for light comedy, is an expert in the well-made play. His later, more serious work, includes *The Deep Blue Sea*, 1952, and *Ross*, 1960, about T. E. Lawrence.

A Bequest to the Nation. 1970.

A somewhat ornate historical play spans Nelson's final days in England. Like *Ross*, it sympathetically probes intimate problems of a national hero, its theme the conflict between Nelson's infatuation for Emma and his duty, to which finally she generously yields. Rattigan cleverly uses Nelson's schoolboy nephew to emphasise duty, to act as dramatic link with Lady Nelson and as the "juvenile sensibility", whereby Emma's tipsy decline is sharply focused.

In Praise of Love. 1973.

In a double bill a thirty-minute curtain-raiser proved unsuccessful while many critics considered the second play one of Rattigan's best.

Before Dawn. An unfortunate inversion of Puccini's *Tosca* represents the police chief successfully seducing the heroine while her lover faces execution. It is further marred by some clumsy puns.

After Lydia. Lydia is married to the successful literary critic, the gruff Sebastian. Lydia keeps from him the fact that she is dying of leukaemia, unaware that he already knows. Husband and wife each trying to save the other pain is suffering in consequence. Eventually Lydia is able to face death secure in the realisation of her husband's love.

David Rudkin.

David Rudkin who has also written for radio and television won a drama award for the most promising playwright of 1962. But it was not until 1973 that any other reckonable stage play appeared. He has wide and unusual interests, uses words evocatively, and has the power of creating an uncanny sense of suspense and the macabre. His plays are deeply felt but sometimes overloaded in implication and theme.

Afore Night Come. 1962. P.

Revived by the R.S.C. in 1974, the play shows a Midland pear orchard, where a gang of superstitious pickers prepare to re-enact a gruesome fertility murder. Chance witnesses are threatened with the asylum from which the pathetic Johnny has been allowed out for only a few hours to act as carter.

During a tense afternoon the gang ominously focus their hostility on a filthy old tramp who they believe brings misfortune and blight. Increasingly agitated Johnny incoherently tries to persuade Larry, a casual student worker, to escape with him but is repulsed. Then "afore night come" the gang plunge their knives into the tramp's body, score it with the cross and then behead and bury it, their grisly ritual once more accomplished.

In a coda Larry gives the shivering Johnny his fountain-pen, transforming Johnny's shame to a radiant confidence.

Cries from Casement as his bones are brought to Dublin. 1973.

A radio play, somewhat disappointing when staged, concerns Sir Roger Casement, the F.O. diplomat secretly in league in 1916 with the Sinn Fein and executed as a traitor. When his bones are taken to Dublin for ceremonial reburial, he emerges from his coffin to describe and re-enact his life. Rudkin, connecting Casement's espousal of rebellion with his homosexual experiences in Black Africa, sees him as a outsider. The play ends with a plea for Irish unity.

Ashes. 1974.

The title is symbolic. In their desperate efforts to have a child Colin and Anne undergo a humiliating sequence of medical tests and advice, and the strain and domestic confusion of a "pregnancy at risk". When Anne eventually reaches the maternity ward there is a mishap, she suffers hysterectomy and her uterus is consigned to ashes. Even the couple's application to adopt is refused.

In the closing sequences there is a sudden change of subject, having little structural connection with the rest but expanding its theme.

Colin, just returned from Belfast, tells Anne of the death of his Protestant uncle dismembered by a bomb in "an atrocious anagram of people". Unable to share the violent obsessions of his cousin, who says "We shall fight till Ulster is in ashes", he feels rejected by his own kinsfolk and connects this with his own childlessness. "So there's another self for the rubbish heap—my self as 'tribal son'. Yet: if we do not change, tomorrow has no place for us."

One theme is inheritance, but at a deeper level it is man's survival. This passionate play, in part autobiographical, is presented with unflinching clinical realism made viable by a clever manipulation of screens. A sardonic accompaniment of sound and music underline its indignant irony.

The Sons of Light. 1976.

An inordinately long play, springing from a deep personal struggle, was thrice rejected both by the R.S.C. and the National, before a short version of over 3 hours was produced at Newcastle University.

The scene is a blighted island where from a monstrous ikon Nebewohl forces his slave gang to work in an underworld of agony and death. Finally the evangelical son of a new pastor urges the gang to destroy the false ikon, the island is torn by a tremendous geological upheaval and its inhabitants freed.

Jean-Paul Sartre (b. 1905).

The plays of the French philosopher Sartre (*see* **J18**) can be fully appreciated only in the light of his atheistic existentialist convictions. As a communist Sartre vindicates violence and his protests against the absurdity of existence, especially that of the bourgeoisie, are expressed not as Ionesco's in images themselves absurd but through the medium of the well-made play.

Influential British premières seen since 1950 include *Lucifer and the Lord* (P), *Nekrassov* (P) and *Altona* (P).

James Saunders (b. 1925).

In Saunders' very early work, as *Alas Poor Fred* and *Ends and Echoes*, 1960, the influence of Ionesco is apparent. But his most promising work was in the '60s. In *Next Time I'll Sing to You*, 1963, on the hermit of Canfield who died in 1942, Saunders uses the style of Pirandello's *Six Characters* to explore the theme of solitude. In *A Scent of Flowers*, 1964, the protagonist is a young girl who, because of a moral conflict, has just committed suicide. It shows her touching encounters with friends and relatives from whom she had vainly sought help. *The Borage Pigeon Affair*, produced in 1969 by amateurs, was seen as an image of Enoch Powell's protests at immigration. But in 1975 it was produced by professionals with stress on the lively and amusing conflict between a Labour Councillor who keeps pigeons in his attic to the indignation of the Borage Medical Officer of Health, a Conservative Councillor, a situation further distorted by the media.

Anthony Shaffer (b. 1926).

The playwright, once a barrister, is twin brother of Peter Shaffer (*q.v.*). In *Sleuth*, 1970, a famous writer of stories about a wealthy amateur detective plans to outwit his wife's lover, and inviting him to their country house he there emulates his own fictional hero.

Shaffer combines an ingenious detective thriller all suspense and surprise with a witty parody of the genre he presents. *The Murderer*, 1975, proved less successful.

Peter Shaffer (b. 1926).

Shaffer is an assured and ingenious dramatist whose first success was with the realistic well-made play and who has since 1964 moved on to freer modes of composition.

His plays operate successfully on two levels: they offer insight into the subtleties of personal relationships, especially into the difficulties of adjustment between people of different cultural background, and they also involve discussion of ideas.

Shaffer's early realistic plays include the skilful *Five Finger Exercise*, 1958 (P), and *The Private Ear and The Public Eye*, 1962, two spare triangular plays both demonstrating the influence of artistic taste on the relationship between the sexes.

The Royal Hunt of the Sun. 1964.

A sweeping "epic" drama of Pizarro's fantastic conquest of Peru skilfully uses, as narrator, "old Martin", who watches his own boyhood as page to Pizarro. Shaffer deploys "total theatre" in dazzling ceremonial, processions and masks, in ritual dancing, mime and strange, metallic music.

There is rich thematic material in the clash of "two immense and joyless powers," in the conflict of Christianity and Sun worship. Personal tragedy develops in the mutual attraction felt by the grizzled Pizarro (Colin Blakeley) and the young Inca, Atahualpa (Robert Stephens). Captor and prisoner, they painfully seek for the god in each other and the Inca accepts death both as a sacrifice to friendship and the final test of his faith.

Black Comedy. 1965.

A highly successful brief comedy frankly uses an effective device of Chinese theatre. During a party the lights fail and the stage, although supposed to be in darkness, is still fully illuminated, so that the ludicrous behaviour of the dramatis personae is visible only to the audience.

The Battle of Shrivings. 1970.

In a return to realistic drama, Shaffer shows the conflict between the eminent philosopher, Sir Gideon, a humanist and pacifist who believes in human perfectibility and his friend and guest, Mark, a famous and amoral poet. A painful weekend together results in a deliberate contest of wills, in which both win but both are broken. This attempt to dramatise the discrepancy between man's ideals and his personal relationships proved too wordy and contrived.

Equus. 1973.

In attempting to penetrate the motive of a shocking crime of which he had been told, Shaffer has created a compelling work of art.

Dysart (Alec McCowen), overworked child psychiatrist in a provincial hospital, accepts as patient Alan Strang, a part-time stable boy who has inexplicably blinded six horses. Shaffer's vivid imagination has been brilliantly interpreted in John Dexter's inventive production.

An open stage with a palisaded square within a circle and selective lighting are so skilfully deployed that they instantly indicate such diverse locations as the stable, the psychiatrist's consulting room, Alan's hospital cubicle, the Strangs' home, a beach, and often two locations at the same time, so that Dysart's interviews with Alan and others melt into enactment of the deeds he is uncovering.

Alan's well-meaning parents are incompatible, his mother religious, his father a self-educated atheist. The boy's first memorable experience had been on a beach when a stranger took him onto his horse, until his ecstatic ride was roughly interrupted by his parents. His fascination with horses was fostered by his mother's constant re-reading of a favourite story and also of splendid Biblical passages such as that from Job. Thus Alan's erotic and religious emotions become fused. A harrowing picture in his bedroom of Christ on the way to Calvary was torn down by his outraged father and replaced by one of a horse gazing directly at the onlooker, and Alan came to worship this image of Equus the chained god, devising his own ritual of obeisance and self-flagellation.

He had no chance to ride until he found a week-end job as a stable boy. There he would fondle his favourite horse, Nugget, like a lover and one night in every three weeks would gallop naked and bareback in a lonely field, in secret ecstasy.

One night the stable girl excited Alan by taking him to a blue film, where to his dismay he saw his respectable father. She then attempted to seduce Alan in the stable, but unsuccessfully, for he was agonised by his treachery to Equus. Driving the girl away he vainly implored forgiveness from Nugget's implacable stare and in desperation stabbed out the eyes of all six horses in the stable.

Since the audience watch Dysart's meetings with Alan's parents and his gradual winning of the boy's confidence and at one and the same time the actual events which he elicits, the play is a gripping detective story and fascinating psychiatric study.

But the extraordinary relationship between doctor and patient gives it a special depth. For Alan has the psychotic's instinct for sensing Dysart's own problems and throughout presents an urgent challenge. For Dysart's own life is devoid of sexual or religious passion, his marriage sterile, his only contact with the intuitive life he values his prim annual holidays in Greece. In his own terrible nightmare he sees himself as a masked priest sacrificing children and tearing out their entrails. He has lost faith in his vocation and says that in bringing Alan back to the drab normal he is destroying his capacity for reverence and rapture.

Some critics have assumed that Dysart's estimate of his own worth is that of Shaffer and that the playwright is decrying psychiatry itself. This is a misreading, for the wise and humane woman J.P., who first brings Alan to Dysart feels only gratitude for pain banished and Shaffer, acknowledging his debt to the advice and expert comment of a distinguished child psychiatrist says, " I have also come to perceive that psychiatrists are an immensely varied breed . . . Dysart is simply one doctor in one hospital."

N. F. Simpson (b. 1919).

N. F. Simpson's plays of the Absurd are in the peculiarly English vein of Lewis Carroll and Edward Lear, a world of surrealist fantasy, nonsequitur and nonsense. It is almost a contradiction in terms to organise such material coherently and to do so in a full-length play is a *tour de force* which Simpson brought off in his *One Way Pendulum.* His best work ridicules the mechanical and conventional existence, the attenuation of feeling, of the little suburban home, his usual milieu.

The Resounding Tinkle. 1957. P. F.

A most unusual play, which pokes fun at suburban life, discards plot, progress and characterisation, and the uniform dialogue is one continuous flow of clever verbal paradoxes and non-sequiturs. The apologetic " author " appears at intervals and in the final act there is a parody discussion of the play by a panel of " critics "—devices used by Ionesco in *The Shepherd's Chameleon.* Simpson's verbal agility is exhilarating, but some find the play over-cerebral.

One Way Pendulum. A Farce in a New Dimension. 1959. F.

Here Simpson has devised a framework built of whimsy and yet firm enough to carry its own logic and to be dramatically satisfying. The characters are drawn simply, but consistently, each with his own " humour " in the manner of Ben Jonson and the dialogue is a close parody of banal family interchange.

The play concerns a suburban family, the Groomkirbys, whose son, Kirby, is teaching a collection of weighing-machines to sing the Hallelujah Chorus. His ineffectual father is combining his two favourite hobbies of law and " do it yourself" carpentry, by building an enormous model of the Old Bailey in the living-room, where the phlegmatic mother pays a charwoman to eat up the " left-overs ".

Finally a trial takes place in the Old Bailey and Kirby is convicted of murdering forty-three people in order that he may wear black, the weighing-machines being part of a complicated device to cause a holocaust of death.

The main theme of the play is the tyranny of things, which is exemplified by the absurd Ionesco-like objects. These are treated with the respect due to human beings while human beings are treated as things, and father and son are so obsessed by things that they cannot get into touch with one another.

The tyranny of mechanical routine and social custom is also indicated. Kirby will only eat when a cash-register rings and will only wear black when it is sanctioned by funeral convention.

The anxiety and guilt which result from a starved and mechanical existence are finally symbolised in the nightmare parody of a trial scene in the final act.

Although the stage objects are novel and intriguing and can be assigned a clear meaning they lack the suggestive power of Ionesco's chairs or rhinoceroses. Contrived rather than intuitive, they illustrate more than they illuminate the human condition. But the play is an original and successful experiment and the implied comment on the unconscious assumptions and compulsive habits of the Groomkirbys has a wide reference.

The Cresta Run. 1965.

A play about counter-espionage proved disappointing, partly because its mockery is directed at a schoolboy dream rather than at a general malaise, partly because it lacks the bold structural outline of *One Way Pendulum.* Even the absurd objects—keys, codes, disguises—are trivial compared with the " Old Bailey ". Simpson has also lost some of the claustrophobic compulsion of his earlier plays by his constant switching of the action from the home of the suburban couple to the Ministry and back again.

It is unfortunate that a promising latent theme —the compulsion felt by the Security man to divulge his secret information—is swamped by trivia, while the best jest is only a casual aside—the suggestion that in England Intelligence should logically be in the hands of private enterprise!

Was He Anyone? 1972. F.

On a cargo-boat, " several sizes too small for him ", Whitebrace, a bookie's runner, absent-mindedly runs into the sea. He treads water for over a year, while his plight is elaborately discussed by bureaucratic and charitable organisations and is depicted on the media.

So that he may improve himself culturally while waiting he is given a baby-grand on which he learns to play. The World's National Help-You-Out Week professes concern, the P.M. hopes to gain popularity with photographs of himself shaking hands with the wife and cruise ships stop to watch her husband's struggles. Eventually a private citizen thinks to throw a life-belt, but it causes concussion and death.

Appropriately the actress playing Mrs. Whitebrace is the only one of the cast not to change rôles during the play. The other six, as in a cabaret, quickly impersonate a number of figures devious, foolish or pompous.

A lively surrealistic comedy satirises popular voyeurism and the procrastination of official and charitable organisations in helping " the drowning man ".

Wole Soyinka (b. 1934). *See also* **Section M.**

Soyinka, a Nigerian and an English graduate, is an admirer of Brecht, Arden and Dürrenmatt.

The Road. 1965.

The Road, set in a drivers' haven in Nigeria, successfully produced with a large cast of coloured actors, later won a Dakar award.

The Lion and the Jewel. 1966. O.U.P.

In a lively comedy, presented by the Ijinle Company of African actors, the jewel is Sidi, the belle of a Yoruba village. Elated at being photographed for a glossy magazine, she rejects both the native schoolmaster and the old chieftain, the Lion, until cunningly seduced by him she exultantly joins his harem.

Native culture, with vivid ritual dance and music, is presented as more alluring and virile than European, which is mocked both in amusing mimes and in the shabby, ineffective schoolmaster infatuated with Western gadgets.

Tom Stoppard (d. 1937).

Stoppard is a shrewd observer and the most versatile, ingenious and witty of all our playwrights.

Rosencrantz and Guildenstern are Dead. 1966. F.

Stoppard's diverting play is a gloss on *Hamlet* and he dovetails snatches of Shakespeare's tragedy with his own action or rather inaction, for his archetype is Beckett's *Waiting for Godot*.

He humorously chooses as protagonists the two nonentities, Rosencrantz and Guildenstern. Summoned inexplicably to Elsinore, they hang about, always on the fringe of great events they do not understand, passing the time, like Shakespearean jesters, in witty word play and fruitless speculation as to their situation and destiny.

Their predicament is a suggestive image of the bewilderment of the ordinary man faced with world events beyond his grasp and, at a deeper level, with the existential problem of man's very being on this earth, and the imminence of death.

The rehearsal of the Players creates a further film of unreality and illusion.

The play is too long, the second act not sufficiently contrasted, but it is remarkable that so derivative a play should be so delightfully fresh and original.

Enter a Free Man. 1968. F.

Reilly is a self-styled "inventor" of disastrous Heath Robinson gadgets to the discomfort of the unfortunate wife and daughter who support him. The situation, though funny and pathetic, is not adequate to a full-length play.

The Real Inspector Hound. 1968. F.

A crisp burlesque of an absurd whodunnit with a neglected corpse stage centre, uses the device of the play-within-a-play, for interest is focused on two critics, each nursing his obsession, Birdfoot susceptible and fickle, Moon jealous of Higgs, his superior.

At the ringing of the stage telephone zany absurdity takes over. First Birdfoot goes on stage to soothe his jealous wife; then Moon thinking the corpse is Higgs! Finally both are shot. Beneath the play's glittering surface is shrewd observation.

After Magritte. 1970. F.

Stoppard has himself interpreted his one-act surrealistic comedy. Fascinated by the paintings of Magritte, with their quirky juxtaposition of objects painted in the finished style of a nineteenth-century academician, Stoppard has tried to emulate the painter in theatrical terms. Within the orthodox framework of the well-made play he has presented unrelated incidents, even using some of Magritte's favourite images, such as the tuba, apple and woman with her head covered, as well as one of his own favourites, the detective. He has felt compelled to invent a logical causation for the bizarre sequence. The result is a playlet that is visually and verbally most ingenious, but much too static—an amusing trifle that resembles a clever five-finger exercise.

Jumpers. 1972. F.

In a hilarious virtuoso piece Stoppard displays the farcical inventiveness of a Marx brothers' film, with proliferation of zany incident and slapstick, all sizzling with verbal wit. He juggles with wildly incongruous incidents and yet sustains a serious theme, that of "credibility", for Stoppard is extremely sceptical of claims to certainty of knowledge or belief. He ridicules political dogmatism and the pretensions of psychiatry and in two-fold guise he parodies the contortions of academic philosophy as physical and mental acrobatics.

The scene is the flat of George Moore, a dishevelled Professor of Moral Philosophy, and the action, set on a revolving stage, shifts swiftly from one room to another. George has married the lovely Dorothy, or Dotty, a musical comedy star now retired with a nervous breakdown, for since a landing on "that Juney old moon", she can no longer sing her romantic moon songs with any conviction.

In her sumptuous bedroom Dotty is accustomed to receive the suave and immaculate Vice-Chancellor, Archie, her lover and, most opportunely, her psychiatrist also, while in his study George worries away at moral abstractions like a tousled dog with a bone.

At a victory party thrown by Dotty celebrating a Radical–Liberal *coup d'état*, Archie compères a performance by his "jumpers", gymnast philosophers—logical positivists, linguistic analysts and the like, for Archie professes strict rationalism in both philosophy and politics. They form a human pyramid but at its base McFee, Professor of Logic, is unaccountably shot dead. The pyramid collapses and Dotty is left alone with the body, which is later seen hanging from a door in her bedroom.

This symbolic collapse of philosophic coherence is paralleled by George's verbal fumblings on the credibility of God and of moral absolutes as, oblivious of the murder, he dictates his refutation of McFee's contribution to the annual symposium on "Man—good, bad or indifferent?" George retains some confidence in man's ability to discern moral value by intuition and since "to sustain the attention of rival schools of academics by argument alone is tantamount to constructing a Gothic arch out of junket", he intends to demonstrate his points with Zeno's bow and arrow and a specially trained pet hare and tortoise. Inadvertently he shoots the hare, Thumper, (*cf.* jumper) and in his dismay crushes the tortoise underfoot.

Dotty, suspected of McFee's murder, is questioned by Inspector Bones, an ardent fan of hers, who arrives with a bouquet since he can hardly arrest her "by Interflora". But the all-accomplished Archie, whose jumpers have deftly disposed of the body in a plastic bag, is also Dotty's lawyer and even the coroner and easily manipulates Bones.

A further dimension is given to the play by political events, for Archie's party, the Rad–Libs are rationalising the Church, like the railways, and have appointed as Archbishop their spokesman for Agriculture, an agnostic. "It's like the Chairman of the Coal Board believing in oil", concedes Dotty.

The progress of the lunar landing, seen on a huge television screen, provides an even more remote perspective. The two amoral astronauts, Captain Scott and Captain Oates, have fought each other for survival. For Dorothy this makes earth's morality parochial while conversely, McFee had been reminded of the self-sacrifice of the Antarctic Captain Oates and had had ruefully to admit that if irrational altruism is indeed a possibility then his logical arguments were "up a gum tree".

The contrast between the successful Archie, a cocksure and cynical opportunist, and the ineffectual George, oddly engaging our sympathy in his desperate search for truth, effectively dramatises an underlying concern with genuine values. These like the identity of the murderer, remain unverified.

In using such stock situations as cuckolded husband and detection of murder as vehicle for erudite parody, Stoppard has brought off a *tour de force* both theatrical and literary.

Travesties. 1974.

Staying in Zürich in 1917 are 3 men destined to influence our culture, the Rumanian poet Tristan Tzara (a founder of Dadaism which affected Surrealism), Lenin and James Joyce, while at the British Consulate is youthful Henry Carr, who had accepted Joyce's invitation to participate in a production of *The Importance of Being Earnest.* So much is factual but round this nub Stoppard spins complex webs of fantasy, these being the reminiscences of Carr, both as an old man remembering and as a youthful participant, and these recollections form the framework of the play.

Stoppard invents a friendship between Carr and Tzara resembling that between Wilde's Algy and Jack, and the names of the girls are Gwendolen (Carr's sister) and Cecily. Fitting settings for their wit and persiflage are the private drawing rooms of Tzara and Joyce. Another setting is

Zürich library where Tzara works at one table, concocting his random verses, Joyce at another dictating part of *Ulysses* to Gwendolen, and Lenin at a third with his secretary Cecily. Here the girls accidentally swap their author's folders, and Lenin and his wife, planning the historic secret return to revolted Russia, are unsuccessfully spied on by Carr.

Again a play of Stoppard's displays his fertile invention and verbal wit, and his interest in Surrealism and the absurd, this time linked with a serious subject. Its full appreciation demands considerable erudition.

Dirty Linen and New-Found-Land. 1967.

In a *jeu d'esprit* satire and farce fuse as members of a Parliamentary Select Committee on Promiscuity in High Places eventually have to investigate their own liaisons with their own secretary, Miss Gotobed, who has been " going through the ranks like a lawnmower in knickers ". Sandwiched into the play is *New-Found-Land*, an investigation into Ed Berman's application for naturalisation.

David Storey (b. 1933). *See also* **Section M.**

Storey, also a novelist, is the son of a Yorkshire miner and helped to support himself at the Slade by playing professional Rugby for Leeds. He wrote the film-script for his own novel, *This Sporting Life*, and Lindsay Anderson, while directing it encouraged him to revise his discarded play, *Arnold Middleton*.

Anderson has directed Storey's four subsequent plays and the imaginative rapport between producer and playwright has led to their being interpreted with singular insight and restraint.

One theme in Storey's work, as in Mercer's, is the stress felt by the educated offspring of working folk. Many plays involve reference to mental trouble or instability and he is much interested in the theories of R. D. Laing.

The plays are grounded in every-day life, frequently in Storey's own experience. Yet they have become increasingly poetic in approach, in that their significance is consciously ambiguous, and " escapes and refuses definitions. " Storey deliberately leaves " all the options open. " He also says that, if on reading something through, he " knows completely what it is all about, then it is dead, " but if it mystifies him then it has " taken on an independent life of its own. "

Storey is refreshingly versatile in subject and approach and each new work shows a growing mastery and maturity. A genuine and unassuming artist, he is now one of our best playwrights.

The Restoration of Arnold Middleton. 1967. **P.**

Arnold, a young schoolmaster (as Storey once was) is a jesting eccentric, his latest acquisition an outsize suit of armour introduced during the play's revision. But Arnold's clowning disguises the fact that he is going mad.

The theme is reminiscent of Mercer's *Morgan*, with the gorilla suit, but the exuberant comedy tends to blur the issue and the interpretation of the hero's instability and lightning recovery is inadequate.

In Celebration. 1969. **P.**

Three sons return home to celebrate the fortieth wedding anniversary of their parents, doting collier husband and complacent matriarch, who considers herself his social superior.

With first-hand realism Storey conveys the disorientation and embarrassed filial feeling of sons educated beyond their origins. The eldest brother, the iconoclastic Andrew, is hell-bent on tearing down the family facade and tries to force on stolid Colin and sensitive Steven his theory that their ambitious mother had distorted their lives into a false respectability to appease her own sense of guilt. When six months pregnant, she had felt obliged to marry the collier father and after the firstborn had died at the age of seven, she had tried to commit suicide.

After an extravagant dinner at the local hotel Andrew lashes the bewildered father with his scorn and only the concerted efforts of Colin and Steven can help to reassure the old man and get Andrew away next morning before he can confront the mother.

The psychological motivation is not fully credible but this compassionate and close-knit play, with the past haunting the present, recalls Ibsen, especially since Andrew is an ignoble counterpart of Gregers Werle in *The Wild Duck*.

The Contractor. 1969. **P.**

Five men leisurely assemble and later dismantle a huge tent for the wedding of the contractor's daughter, while members of the family drift in and out. The workers' banter and taunts and the family casual talk hint at hidden hurts, but the focus of the play is the actual work on the tent—as in Ionesco a " thing "—presented here with no absurdity or phantasy but with almost the faithfulness of documentary, for Storey can draw on his own experience of the job.

The image is however metaphorical and because the play cannot " be confined to any one definition, " Storey finds it one of his most satisfying works. He sometimes sees it as " somehow related to the decline and falling away of capitalist society " or " as a metaphor for artistic creation. " Yet " it still continues to make sense—and complete sense—as the story of these men who put up this tent and that's that. "

Home. 1970. **P.**

Sitting at a garden table, on the only two chairs available, two aging gentlemen, Jack (Ralph Richardson) and Harry (Gielgud), gently and diffidently make conversation. Jack, slightly more dapper, and prone to pointless family anecdote, usually takes the initiative in their exchange of dated clichés and banalities. The broken phrases refer to wives now separated, ambitions unfulfilled, the clouds, but real communication can only be unspoken and there is sad irony in Jack's, " So rare these days nowadays to meet someone to whom one can actually talk."

When these leave, their places are taken by two rough, " Cor blimey " women, full of prurient innuendo and scandal, and when the gentlemen return and courteously escort " the ladies " to " corn beef hash ", it has gradually become apparent that this is a mental " home ". Act II begins with the entry of a leucotomised young man who aimlessly shifts the furniture about.

The play, heart-breaking in its naturalistic fidelity to human inadequacy, is handicapped by some monotony of incident and dialogue. But, like Beckett's *Godot*, also a strange quintet, it works through poetic suggestion. The ironic title and the furniture, inadequate for 2000 people, are significant as is the apparently irrelevant juxtaposition of phrases, which are in themselves ambiguous metaphors. (" This little island." " Shan't see its like." " Oh, no." " The sun has set." " Couple of hours.")

But the decline of hope and vitality (perhaps that of England herself) is most potently expressed by the unadorned shape of the play, the decline of the day from morning to evening, the sky overcast, the rain that of the old men's silent tears.

The Changing Room. 1971. **P.**

Storey can rely on his own memories of Rugby League football when he paints the bare, chilly, changing room. Opened up by the caretaker, a muttering old pensioner, it is gradually taken over by the players, clearly individualised and arriving in ascending order of their social status, to be treated by the masseur, advised by the trainer, briefly encouraged by the Chairman, until changed into their kit they stand as a team, silent for a moment before trotting down the tunnel to the icy pitch and the roar from the stands.

The second act includes the brief half-time when the battered players, committed by their common hazard and purpose are now welded into a corporate body. In the third, exultant after victory, they joke and bath in easy comradeship until with his everyday clothes each man assumes his separate identity and only the caretaker is left.

Storey here develops and refines the deceptively easy naturalism and the novel pattern of *The Contractor*, but peripheral and rather conventional interest such as that of the Contractor's family, which intrudes on the work scene, is now pared away and Storey wholly commits himself to the re-creation of men thrown together by the exigencies of their job yet temporarily finding themselves a community.

To create out of such simple materials and means a shapely and invigorating work of art is a remarkable achievement.

Cromwell. 1973. Cape.

In a play which took shape in 1968–9, a time of conflict in Vietnam and Ireland, Storey abandons naturalism for a kind of dramatic fable, where brief, swiftly-moving scenes, occasionally using some verse, depict "people wandering through woods and a war". Although Cromwell is never mentioned the setting suggests the Ireland of his time.

Amid the refugees, rigid partisans and turncoats of a confused guerrilla war, the protagonist Proctor emerges as a man of principle, constantly searching for the right course of action. Two amiable Irish layabouts, shameless opportunists, serve as a foil to Proctor and their comic lackadaisical backchat acts as cynical running commentary on his devotion to ideals. He is fighting on behalf of dispossessed Catholics but disillusioned by the futility of inconclusive reprisals he withdraws from war, marries Joan and finds deep satisfaction in restoring her ravaged farm. Then, because he gives shelter to some wounded anarchist Levellers the farm is devastated a second time by the Protestants and their child killed.

After bitter heart searching, Proctor finally eschews all political and social ideology and in a final scene a boatman ferries him and Joan across a river. Storey says that the scene indicates "just the transference from one kind of life to another", although it may be interpreted both literally and also symbolically as purification and absolution.

Storey's theme is the irrelevance of theoretical and political standpoints and he has said that "it has become immaterial which side you choose to be on". Yet the value of integrity is stressed as paramount and the boatman significantly refuses to carry the layabouts, who "hang like leeches", for "hands which always receive can offer nought".

An interesting play of ideas suffers from structural imbalance, for there is an extremely long and leisurely first act while Proctor's deepest conflicts are hurried into brief and rather obscure final scenes. There are literary echoes from Dante and Bunyan but Storey says Shakespeare is his only model.

The Farm. 1973.

The play reverts to the realistic style of *In Celebration.* It is dominated by the rough Yorkshire farmer, Slattery, who after a dangerous stroke still drinks inordinately.

After a lifetime of toil he is angered and bewildered by the sterility of his offspring. Three daughters still live at home. Two are teachers in their thirties, Wendy early separated from her husband and Jenny restlessly seeking one, while Brenda, aged twenty-three, a fierce and naïve subvertionist, is still supported by her father. Slattery is passionately scornful of the son Arthur, a poet manqué, idolised by his mother. Now twenty-one, he has left home and drifts impecuniously from job to job.

One night Wendy finds that Arthur has returned unexpectedly. He is shaking with apprehension and next morning tells his father he is about to marry Alison, a divorced woman of forty-two. Slattery, incredulous and furious, lashes him with invective yet agrees to receive Alison that evening. But Arthur's courage fails and he arrives late and alone. Slattery's paroxysm of rage is such that he almost collapses and during the night the despondent Arthur leaves as unobtrusively as he had come.

Next morning a brief final scene shows Slattery genially welcoming to the breakfast table Brenda's diffident suitor, who has at last found courage to come openly to the house.

The play is looser in texture than *In Celebration* and the portrayal of the sisters rather flat and repetitive. But the frustration of their unfulfilled lives is peripheral, although probably stemming from the mutually destructive relationship between father, mother and son. Slattery gradually betrays his misery that his wife has withheld from him the love she has lavished on Arthur and in his final outburst he even accuses his son of trying to supplant him by deliberately contriving an emotional shock that will cause his death. Storey's compassionate presentation of this Oedipal situation is powerful and moving'

Life Class. 1973.

In a play related to his novel *A Temporary Life* Storey portrays a mixed group of students in a shabby Yorkshire art college drawing a nude woman from the life.

Their teacher Allott, the educated son of working folk, and unhappily married, is a failed artist, deeply alienated. His attitude to his students is ironic and remote.

Their personalities and attitudes to their task differ widely and Allott's provocative questions on the woman as artist, the place of art in modern society and its relation to illusion and reality are unanswered. He remains aloof even when two of his randiest students apparently rape the model, but the act like art itself is also a simulation. Summarily dismissed by his conventional and rigid Principal, Allott is still nonchalantly unperturbed.

Critics differ in their estimates. Some consider that this third play in his once novel genre (the naturalistic portrayal of a group at work) is becoming conventional. Others see deeper implications.

Peter Terson (b. 1932).

Terson is a prolific writer, with a talent for fertile, fluent dialogue, which immediately establishes personalities and relationships. His most successful work has been done in active co-operation with two directors, Cheeseman and Croft.

In 1963, while working as a games master in the Vale of Evesham, Terson first contacted Cheeseman, director at Stoke-on-Trent, and through his encouragement wrote several plays located in the Vale. A recurrent theme of these is the mysterious power of nature as opposed to urban sophistication, and as in Rudkind's *Afore Night Come* (*q.v.*), a sinister theme often runs through them.

The Evesham plays include *A Night to Make the Angels Weep*, 1963, *The Mighty Reservoy*, 1964 (P), *I'm in Charge of These Ruins*, 1966, *All Honour Mr. Todd*, 1966, and *Mooney and His Caravans*, 1967 (P).

Recently Cheeseman has produced plays which break new ground and whose first drafts had been written at an earlier date. Most notable are *The Samaritan*, 1971 (begun 1968) and *But Fred Freud is Dead*, 1972 (written 1964). Both plays involve a sympathetic and wittily accurate picture of a man who feels emotionally insecure and inferior and who finds over-compensation in a false bravura.

Cheeseman rightly considers Terson's greatest gift is "his capacity to write in a way that is both very funny and profoundly serious at the same time."

Terson became known nationally through his remarkable collaboration with Michael Croft, director of the N.Y.T.

He writes about youngsters with affectionate zest and exuberant humour, vividly aware of the lack of opportunity offered them by society.

Terson's plays tailored for the N.Y.T. include:—*Zigger Zagger*, 1967 (P), which depicts the Dionysiac frenzy of a young football crowd; *The Apprentices*, 1968 (P); *Fuzz*, 1969; *Spring-Heeled Jack*, 1970; *Good Lads at Heart*, 1971, one of Terson's most successful plays, showing conflict between modern and authoritarian methods in an approved school; *Geordie's March*, 1972, where apprentices encounter every kind of unexpected setback when marching to London from Sunderland to protest at a fatal accident to one of their fellows.

Jose Triana (b. 1931).

Triana, born in Cuba, has written several plays.

The Criminals. 1967.

The first Cuban play staged here depicts three adults, a brother and his two sisters, acting out fantasies of childhood, hatred of thwarting parents, which culminate in a frenzied ritual of their murder at the end of Act One. The trial of the children in Act Two gradually develops into an enactment of the parents' mutual detestation. As the curtain falls the ritual begins afresh.

This intense play, in the genre of "Theatre of Cruelty" (*q.v.*), has less wealth of imagery than Weiss's *Marat-Sade* but a greater universality of reference than Genet's world. It may have been influenced by the work of Arrabal.

Triana shows great psychological insight; children's play is often a dramatic projection of their inner conflicts and at all ages the sterile process of fantasy gives only temporary relief and must be exhaustingly repeated. The most significant moment of the play is when the word "love" is timidly offered as an alternative only to be rejected.

An apt parallel to Triana's vision was the contemporary Reith lecture (26 Nov. 1967), when Dr. Leach, the social anthropologist, criticised our unthinking acceptance of the inward turning family life, where "The parents fight: the children rebel." "The strain is greater than most of us can bear," and the source of our social discontents.

Triana's play shows it as a potent source of man's aggression. Some critics have seen in it implications of Castro's resistance to the dominance of America.

Boris Vian (1920–59).

The French Vian was influenced by the Absurdist approach of Ionesco.

The Empire Builders. 1962. M.

Man's futile flight from death is imaged in a family trying to escape from a terrifying noise by moving up to a higher and higher floor and meaner quarters. Eventually the father alone reaches the attic, where he dies.

The General's Tea Party. 1966. P.

Written in 1951, Vian's biting, absurdist satire on the military mentality represents his general behaving like a small boy, afraid of Mama, and asking his playfellows—other generals—to tea. After deciding that war would be a nice idea, they then select the target—prophetically Algeria.

Frank Wedekind (1864–1918).

The plays of the German Wedekind, a passionate amoralist, are preoccupied with the mysterious power of sex and in their intensity they sporadically break through the bounds of realism into fantasy and symbolism—techniques later to be deployed in Expressionism (*q.v.*).

Spring's Awakening. 1863.

Published in 1891, the play which concerns the lyrical rapture and the agony of puberty, is a fervid indictment of a disastrous and repressive "morality", of secretive or hypocritical parents and grotesquely tyrannical schoolmasters.

Finally in a scene of nightmare fantasy, the ruined adolescent, Melchior, searching for the grave of his sweetheart, dead through an abortion, is encountered by the ghost of his suicide friend and is himself only restrained from the same fate by the symbolic Man in the Mask.

Lulu. 1970.

Lulu is the title given by Peter Barnes to his adaptation of two plays, *Earth Spirit*, 1895, and its sequel *Pandora's Box*, 1903. Barnes keeps to the substance if not the spirit of the original.

Wedekind's protagonist, Lulu, the incarnation of the instinctual life, symbolises sexual passion in its beauty, rapture and terror. In her narcissism and uninhibited passion she destroys all who become hopelessly infatuated with her.

In Barnes's Act I, corresponding to *Earth Spirit*, Lulu causes the death of her first husband by shock, the suicide of the second and shoots the third, Schön.

In Act II, the sequel, she gradually degenerates to amateur prostitute, still adored by two ruined devotees, a lesbian countess and Schön's son. To him she has been successively foster-sister, stepmother and mistress, the incarnation of a Freudian dream. These two also die and she is herself assassinated by a pervert casual client.

Barnes's adaptation neglects the mystery and pathos of the original. Only the countess and Schön's son are a little more than two-dimensional. Fantasy is abruptly succeeded by grotesque bathos as in black comedy (*q.v.*).

The Marquis of Keith. 1974.

The protagonist of Wedekind's favourite play is an imposter and adventurer. The familiar theme is the conflict of sexuality and pleasure, with ethics.

Peter Weiss (b. 1916).

The German-speaking Weiss has adopted Swedish nationality and Marxist doctrine.

The "Marat Sade." 1964.

The full title of this verse play, one of the most impressive exemplifications of Artaud's Theatre of Cruelty, is *The Persecution and Assassination of Jean-Paul Marat as Performed by the Inmates of the Asylum of Charenton under the Direction of the Marquis de Sade!* As the title indicates this complex work operates on receding planes of cruelty, thus exciting in the audience that vivid experience of violence which is the aim of Artaud.

Artaud's demand for primitive ritual which shall exorcise repressed fantasy is met by Corday's threefold visit and murder of Marat and also by the lunatics' frenzied miming of the ceremony of the guillotine—a background motif to the whole play. The use of pantomime and gesticulation on the open stage satisfy Artaud's demands for spectacle, for "poetry in space."

Peter Brook pointed out that these elements are not inconsistent with a Brechtian "alienation"—achieved by the device of a play within a play, the protesting comments of the director of the asylum, the intellectual debates between Sade and Marat and the ribald songs of a grotesque quartet of zanies. The effect is an inextricable blend of the comic and the violent.

The Investigation. 1965.

A documentary of the Frankfurt War Crime Trials, edited by Weiss, had a multiple première in East and West Germany and at the Aldwych. Described by Weiss as an "Oratorio in 11 Cantos", after Dante's *Inferno*, it indicts the millions, including the German monopoly capitalists, who tacitly supported the Nazi atrocities.

At the first impact the grisly facts leave an overwhelming impression of horror. It is remarkable that the author's restraint and dignity in presenting them and the formal austerity of his design have in retrospect the effect of catharsis.

The Song of the Lusitanian Bogey. 1969.

A passionate indictment of Portuguese colonial exploitation and oppression of Angola recalls in some of its techniques Peter Brook's *US*. It was splendidly acted by the New York Negro Ensemble.

Arnold Wesker (b. 1932)

Wesker's work is best understood in the light of his Jewish background and his didactic socialism. He is no naïve optimist but has always represented the tension between idealism and practicality and is most trenchant in his criticism of characters like Ronnie who reveal this dichotomy.

His sense of dramatic structure is erratic but he sometimes evinces an exhilarating sense of stage movement. His chief weakness is diction and he succeeds best in plays like *Roots*, *Chips* and *Golden City* where the use of an unaccustomed idiom necessitates disciplined study. The reportage of the voluble converse of some Jewish people is all too easy for him and in some plays action is drowned in a garrulous flood.

After 1962 he devoted much energy to the founding of Centre 42 to bring good art to the masses, and their own apathy has been his greatest disappointment especially as he is member of a race which highly values education and culture.

Wesker first worked as a chef in Norwich, London and Paris, but soon achieved fame through the "kitchen sink" naturalism of his trilogy of plays.

The first, **Chicken Soup with Barley**, 1958 (P), shows a Jewish socialist family, the Kahns, on 4 October 1936, helping to prevent Mosley's march through the East End. It concludes in 1957 with the disillusion of the vacillating son Ronnie at the Russian invasion of Hungary. The theme of the play is "caring", not only politically but in the home, for the stalwart mother must cope with the inertia of Ronnie and of her shiftless husband.

In *Roots*, 1959 (P), Beatie, who is engaged to Ronnie, revisits her Norfolk family (the coarse roots of her origin), ignorant, prejudiced and inarticulate. Although she fails to understand him Beatie constantly parrots Ronnie's teaching about the power of words, or "bridges" to communicate ideas. Then on the day he is to arrive she receives a letter saying their marriage would not work. Beatie, galvanised by shock and ecstatic with self-realisation, discovers that she is at last speaking thoughts of her own. This play, the best of the trilogy, is well-constructed, the characters convincing and the concept of "roots" and "bridges" develop organically from the situation.

I'm Talking about Jerusalem. **1960. P.**

Kahn's daughter and her husband Dave go to Norfolk to put into practice the ideas of William Morris, but find they cannot compete with factory products and in 1960 return to London, Dave's self-respect contrasting with the bitter cynicism of a friend. But he is not sufficiently commanding to save a play weak in structure.

The Kitchen. **1959. P.**

In a two-acter, Wesker draws on his experience as a chef to give a vivid impression of a day in the kitchen of Marango's restaurant. The play is notable for its skilful contrasts in pace and movement. The quiet morning quickens to a frenzy of anxiety at lunch-time, and the doldrums of the afternoon are succeeded by the sudden outburst of a German who goes beserk.

The swirling vortex is a microcrosm of the world, where men with their casual contacts find themselves in a situation beyond their grasp. The play ends with the dramatic irony of Marango's failure to perceive that work and food alone cannot satisfy man's desires.

Chips with Everything. **1962. P.**

In *R.U.R.* the Expressionist playwright Capek used robots as dramatis personae. In *Chips with Everything* Wesker illustrates the process whereby military discipline can reduce both men and officers to robot-like uniformity.

A squad of nine R.A.F. conscripts are subjected to a battery of bullying abuse from the corporal and pychological manipulation by the officers, until, their personal identity submerged, they learn to move as one mechanical unit and pass out to the blaring of a military band playing 'God Save the Queen".

Wesker employs a new stylised, streamlined technique which appropriately shares some of the techniques of expressionism. Type characters are used and the identity of the recruits, with two exceptions, indicated very lightly. The dialogue is usually staccato while brief, symbolic scenes such as square bashing, bayonet practice and the comic mime of stealing coke succeed one another rapidly, an instance of Wesker's command of stage movement.

As to the two recruits presented in more detail: the plight of the gentle Smiler broken and suffering gives pathos to the play without disturbing its tone, but the somewhat unconvincing predicament of Thompson is treated with too much detail to be in key. The son of a general, he is at first resistant to authority and seems to be trying to assume leadership of the squad, but accused by them of "slumming" and assailed by the officers' blandishments he finds the habits of those who can "eat chips with everything" too distasteful for him and he suddenly capitulates and assumes officer's uniform.

The overall effect is tense and powerful for the audience facing the same direction as the recruits cannot avoid feeling the obliterating effect of the military machine.

The Four Seasons. **1965. P.**

Wesker deliberately ignoring "any recognisable social context" indicates his milieu of old house and garden only symbolically. He limits his characters to a man and woman whose previous marriages had floundered and they live together from winter to the following autumn. The play relies on lyrical interchange followed by alienation but even the final quarrel is too unmotivated to convince. Wesker forgetting that drama is the imitation of an action is attempting the impossible.

Their Very Own and Golden City. **1966. P.**

The driving force of a vigorous play may be Wesker's own frustrated struggle to realise a communal artistic ideal in Centre 42, intended to make good art accessible to the people.

The opening dream-like scene in Durham Cathedral in 1926 shows Andrew Cobham and fellow apprentices with Jessie his future wife, when Andy is so exhilarated by the soaring splendour that he is inspired to his life work as architect. This seminal experience is flashed forward and developed in the early part of the play as if nurturing his vision of the twelve Golden Cities he is inspired to design where the centre shall not be the town hall but museums, art galleries and theatres.

When he is already married an aristocratic girl, Kate, befriends him and holds him determinedly to his purpose. Future householders enthusiastically finance the buildings of one city but Andy is so frustrated by ten years of fruitless waiting for the T.U.C. that he yields to Kate's persuasion and compromises his principles by accepting support from a Tory minister and a capitalist industrialist.

Similarly Andy's private life is jeopardised, for Kate scorns Jessie from whom he is gradually estranged. Eventually knighted and a member of the Establishment, he is seen a cantakerous old man playing bridge with his three influential friends while Jessie sews. A final scene is a sad ironic flash-back to the Cathedral, where the youngsters discover themselves locked in until one door is discovered open, symbolic perhaps of Wesker's fears and hopes.

He ably portrays the dilemma of the socialist artist caught between an obscurantist labour movement and the privileged Establishment which fosters cultural values. He uses with assurance techniques worked out in *Chips* integrating a panorama of social trends with type characters, but here those at the heart of the play are realised in depth.

In spite of some mawkish phrases in the Cathedral and some over-long political speeches the dialogue is usually sharp and incisive.

The Friends. 1970.

Her brother, lover and friends surround Esther's deathbed. Of Jewish working-class origin, they have become affluent and cultured but have lost direction. The situation is static and the dialogue often embarrassingly introverted and self-conscious.

The Old Ones. 1972.

A kaleidoscopic play with seven contrasting settings, demanding a revolving stage, shows an ageing Jewish family and their friends.

At the centre is a triangular pattern of contrasts. The seventy-year-old tailor, Manny, and his younger brother, Boomy, living in Manny's house, constantly challenge each other with learned quotations. Although he is suffering an agonising depression Manny's citations are optimistic, while Boomy is a "catastrophe-monger". Meanwhile their cheerful sister Sarah, in her council flat, prepares for "Succoth", the Jewish harvest festival.

"Defiant old age," is reflected in Manny's much-tried wife and in two old women, picturesque eccentrics. All are Jewish and described as "pellets of steel" by their Cockney friend Jack, who assumes the rôle of moral leper, complete with bell—an effective contrast to the rest.

In the final scene all gather at Sarah's and with her daughter and nephew try to enact the half-forgotten Succoth ritual of "merriment and rejoicing". Here Manny regains confidence and joy. This climax is an instance of Wesker's individual use of stage movement.

This picturesque play is more extroverted and successful than *The Friends*, but the stage is cluttered with minor characters all parroting their sentiments, and there is little dramatic confrontation.

E. A. Whitehead.

Whitehead, who later won a scholarship to Cambridge, was brought up as a poor Catholic in Liverpool and set his two first plays there, asserting its bigotry and his conviction that a new pattern of mating and breeding should now be found. The plays are stark and sincere but narrow in scope and the limited verbal idiom becomes monotonous.

The Foursome. 1971. F.

Two youths take two girls they have successfully picked up the previous evening to a sandy hollow of the beach but they are sexually frustrated and infuriated by the girls' sham reluctance. The dialogue of the men's bawdy taunts and the girls' prurient and prudish repartee is seldom relieved.

Alpha Beta. 1972. F.

A vigorous two-character play spanning nine years shows a working-class married couple in their thirties suffering the inexorable collapse of their marriage. Frank (Albert Finney) feeling trapped by convention and children, Nora grimly refusing divorce, they fight physically, until both are worn down. Finally Frank, now 38, can envisage freedom in two years time under the new Act. Nora sardonically asks, "Free for what?"

Old Flames. 1975.

Edward entertained by Sally on her houseboat is disturbed to find three other guests, his wife now deserted, his former wife and his mother. Edward disappears and the women all frankly discuss their hostile relationships to the other sex. Only at the end of the play does the audience see pieces of flesh brought in from the kitchen. Marriage had already been stigmatised in *Alpha Beta* as "ritual slaughter" and this extraordinary surrealistic ending to a naturalistic play suggests a nightmare misogyny which Whitehead feels can only adequately be conveyed by an image of cannibalism.

John Whiting (1915–63)

John Whiting was an original playwright preoccupied with the theme of self-destruction. He was slow to find his own style but his last two subtle plays are still influential, despite his early death.

A Penny for a Song, 1951, written at a time of personal happiness, is an agreeable whimsy depicting two wealthy eccentric brothers preparing to repel Napoleon with such gadgets as a home-made fire engine. *Saints Day*, an earlier play not performed until 1951, shows an angry octogenerian, once a famous revolutionary poet, but the play becomes swamped by extraneous action and melodrama.

Marching Song. 1954. P.

In a play much concerned with the existentialist stress on the inescapability of choice, Whiting returns to the theme of self-destruction.

The setting is generalised—a wealthy house "above a capital city in Europe." Rupert Forster, formerly a general, who seven years previously had inexplicably lost a decisive battle, here meets his dilemma. He must either face a trial, which might cause political unrest, or commit suicide. The choices are represented by two people.

In Act II Forster encounters Dido, a young woman who revives his sense of humanity and will to live. She represents the female side of personality, the Jungian anima; and her name recalls the Dido of the *Aeneid*, who by her love deflected Aeneas from the path of military duty.

In Act III he has a very different meeting with Captain Bruno, the embodiment of military ambition. To him Forster at last confesses the cause of his fatal defeat. He had been so overcome with compassion for children whom he had destroyed while they were impeding his tanks that he had been unable to follow up his advance. Bruno stigmatises the delay as military error and guilt and Forster commits suicide rather than face disgrace and imprisonment.

This is a strongly constructed play, its dominating theme worked out with single-minded austerity. Forster's reversion to his original decision to commit suicide gives it a circular movement. It is concerned to clarify judgment and in the contrast between military code and humane ethic is stimulating and relevant.

The Devils. 1962. P.

Suggested to Whiting by Peter Brook, this intricate and distinguished play is based on Aldous Huxley's *The Devils of Loudun*, which treats of an actual case of suspected diabolism in France between 1623 and 1634.

Whiting employs two focal points. One is Grandier (Richard Johnson), again a man who invites his own destruction, a worldly and sensual priest who is yet gifted with a rare religious insight and compassion. The other is a hunchback prioress (Dorothy Tutin). Although she has not met Grandier, she becomes obsessed by fantasies of his amorous adventures and her resulting hysteria, which spreads throughout the convent, is suspected as diabolical possession, instigated by Grandier. Richelieu, for political reasons, uses this as a pretext to get rid of him. Grandier, in spite of excruciating torture and degradation, the prelude to his being burnt alive, struggles to retain his faith.

In its subject and theme *The Devils* is strikingly similar to Miller's *The Crucible*.

There are significant differences. Whiting's intricate play is not realistic but Brechtian in style, with a series of brief episodes and a commentary by a sewerman, whose ironic and sceptical remarks counterpoint Grandier's eloquence. Its final note is one of harsh pessimism, as the sewerman tells the prioress that Grandier's bones are being prized by the crowd as superstitious "charms".

The final act presents an almost unbearable spectacle of a barbarous ritual of physical torture as the maimed and twitching Grandier is paraded in public procession through the streets.

Tennessee Williams (b. 1914).

Since 1950 the works of the American playwright seen here, have included, *The Rose Tatoo*, 1951 (P), *Cat on a Hot Tin Roof* 1955 (P) and *Suddenly Last Summer* 1958 (P), with its crescendo of violence. Williams' plays often breathe the atmosphere of the deep south and he is preoccupied with the inner emotions of his vulnerable people, a prey to guilt, aggression and despair, and caught in a web of relationships which they only break at great cost. Especially poignant are Williams' picture of life's pathetic failures.

The Two Character Play. 1967.

Believing them to be mad, a touring company desert their fellow actors Felice and Clare. This brother and sister then hysterically enact Felice's work, *The Two Character Play*, that may perhaps mirror their own unhappy relationship.

Small Craft Warnings. 1973.

In Monk's foggy bar on the Pacific his customers are misfits and failures, such as a disqualified doctor, Violet, a destitute nymphomaniac, the sensual Bill supported by Leona (Elaine Stritch) in her trailer. But when Leona discovers Violet trying to seduce Bill her fury is lacerating. The play is less powerful than usual, for the kindly Monk devises facile solutions. He warns the doctor and wryly befriends Violet. Only Leona firmly rejecting Bill sets out once more on the vagrant course.

The original title was *Confessional*, each character revealing his hurts in soliloquy.

Charles Wood (b. 1932).

Descended from actors and once a regular soldier, Wood has made stage and army the province of his plays. He skilfully devises for each an appropriate dialogue.

The triple bill *Cockade*, 1963, was concerned with the army and *Fill the Stage with Happy Hours*, 1966 (P), set in a tatty provincial theatre was, says Wood, " about theatrical failure " and serves as a contrast to *Veterans*.

Dingo. 1967. P.

Wood employs Expressionism to present a phantasmagoria of the last War, beginning in the desert and grinding through Stalag to the unconditional surrender of Germany. It is an assault on the emotions and sensations in a passionate attempt to bring home war's physical horror and spiritual attrition, Wood exposing latent jingoism and political expedience and the futile heroism they exact.

The scurrilous words matter less than certain persistent images: the ranker, Dingo, epitome of bitter disillusion; Tanky, rendered simple-minded because he was powerless to release his mate, screaming to death in a flaming tank; an ENSA comedian who serves to parody Churchillian rhetoric, and breezy morale-boosting of High Command; a young subaltern, dressed as a blonde in a bikini for a concert party designed to cover an escape from Stalag, and now, with Tanky, lolling dead from the barbed wire.

The play is sprawling but powerful, attacking the idea that Britain's rôle was disinterested. It was fought, says Dingo, "for all the usual reasons."

" H ". 1969. M.

Wood's subject is the heroic march of the elderly General Havelock, or " H ", during the Mutiny. His column vastly outnumbered and decimated by disease, he yet relieved Cawnpore and won twelve desperate battles before relieving Lucknow where he died of dysentery.

A chivalrous Christian and a disciplined commander, Havelock yet ordered some of the terrible reprisals then current, hanging mutinous sepoys or shooting them alive from the mouths of cannon. His equivocal behaviour helps to focus Wood's own conflicting impulses, his fascination with military discipline and his horror at war's bestiality, so that the play is more unified than *Dingo*.

The core of the play is irony, centred in the action of the protagonist. But the irony proliferates, as in the contrast between the stylised Victorian language and the brutal deed, and unconnected episodes sometimes distract and confuse.

The fact that Havelock's aide-de-camp is his own son suggests the tender perspective of home. Resolute in courage and obedience, the son differs from his father in opinion and faith and his eventual confession of Christianity at Havelock's death gives pathos to the scene.

The Brechtian epic style is well suited to the simple episodic structure. Brechtian devices are also used:—direct address to the audience, map titles and symbolic emblems, such as the simple blood-stained floor and awning, conveying the Indian atrocities at Cawnpore, and the deliberate theatricality of short scenes projected within a little replica of the popular travelling stage.

Although Havelock on the surface resembles the Brechtian ambiguous protagonist, he does not attain the commanding stature of a Galileo or a Mother Courage.

Veterans. 1972. M.

Wood has imagined his own play *H* being filmed in Turkey near the Hellespont and the filming of his screenplay, *The Charge of the Light Brigade*, has given him an authentic background.

The play is set in or near the small Greek amphitheatre of Prieria and the veterans are two famous actors, Sir Geoffrey Kendle (John Gielgud) as Havelock, and d'Orsay (John Mills), as Outram. Sir Geoffrey spends nearly all day waiting, tired and frustrated. His conversation with his jealous friend d'Orsay and the younger star, Bryan, " a curled young man ", is that of the green room but uncovers some of their problems. The tenuous action consists in their transient contact with each other, and with the exuberant young director. d'Orsay is early sent off the set for indecent exposure, Bryan walks off in dudgeon and Sir Geoffrey, as he says " fell off " the rickety rostrum on which he had been directed to climb, only to find that producers and camera crew had all unaccountably vanished.

What emerges is a delightful dramatic portrait of Sir Geoffrey, generally believed to represent Gielgud himself. Idioms of speech and personal idiosyncracies are painted in affectionate detail—the unflinching honesty about others at odds with innate courtesy and concern, the *faux pas* hastily withdrawn, above all the integrity and self-effacing modesty of the true artist.

The play especially appeals to theatrical cognoscenti but it has another dimension. It is, says Wood, " about the failure of theatrical success " and it comically exposes the absurdities of costly film epics. The setting in the Greek theatre is effective visual irony and the final impression is of the futility of a mammoth enterprise that leaves the ancient site littered with indestructible plastic cups tossed everywhere among the Hittite débris.

Jingo. 1975.

The play, set in the last days of Singapore, centres round the promiscuous Gwendoline and her relations with her ex-husband and lover and with her present husband, an impotent and masochistic brigadier, reiterating his fatuous denigration of the Japs. As satire it is sadly out of date.

IDEAS & BELIEFS

This section explains many of the ideas and beliefs that have dominated men's minds during the centuries. The arrangement is alphabetical and the subjects fall broadly into four groups: religious, philosophical, political, and offbeat cults and ideas.

IDEAS AND BELIEFS

THIS section explains many of the ideas and beliefs which people have held at different periods in history. Beliefs may be true or false, meaningful or totally meaningless, regardless of the degree of conviction with which they are held. Since man has been moved to action so often by his beliefs they are worth serious study. The section throws a vivid light on human history.

Man has always felt a deep need for emotional security, a sense of "belonging." This need has found expression in the framing of innumerable religious systems, nearly all of which have been concerned with man's relation to a divine ruling power. In the past people have been accustomed to think of their own religion as true and of all others as false. Latterly we have come to realise that in man's religious strivings there is common ground, for our need in the world today is a morality whereby human beings may live together in harmony.

There is also to be found in man an irresistible curiosity which demands an explanation of the world in which he finds himself. This urge to make the world intelligible takes him into the realm of science where the unknown is the constant challenge. Science is a creative process, always in the making, since the scientist's conjectures are constantly being submitted to severe critical tests. Basic scientific ideas are discussed in Section **F**.

A

Activists, those in a political movement who insist on taking active steps towards their objectives rather than merely putting forward a programme. Lately activism has become an increasingly common facet of political life. This is probably because the undeniably rapid social changes which are taking place across the world at the moment are not generally being followed by appropriate shifts in political structures and ideals.

Acupuncture, a quasi-medical system originating in China and based on the supposedly therapeutic effects of implanting fine gold needles in the spinal cord and other specific parts of the body. The site of needle implantation is decided according to traditional texts. The apparent lack of any logical relationship between the implantation sites and any known physiological or anatomical systems within the body has caused acupuncture to be held in low regard by Western medicine. Indeed it is certainly true that acupuncture and other similar practices tend to flourish in parts of the world where orthodox medicine has made little progress or where doctors and trained staff are scarce.

Recent years however have seen a curious and unexpected revival of interest in acupuncture in Europe and America, prompted in large part by the considerable press publicity which has surrounded a number of major surgical operations performed without anaesthesia upon human patients and which have been witnessed by sceptical Western specialists. Considerable controversy still surrounds acupuncture and is likely to continue for many years—possibly because it is hard to envisage a theory to explain its effects which is consistent with orthodox medicine. No doubt the immensely powerful effects of suggestion and hypnosis need to be taken into account. Some recent discoveries on the psychology and physiology of pain which show that severe wound pain may be alleviated by electrical stimulation of the nerve endings in the site of the wound may also have some relevance. It is tempting to take the line that acupuncture is based on some "forgotten" or "hidden" medical system and to assume that it is only because Western scientists are blinkered and hide-bound that it is not being incorporated in a big way into European and American hospitals. But there are always two sides to an argument; whereas the first reports from Western specialists visiting China were filled with grudging acceptance and genuine puzzlement, more recent visitors have brought back a subtly different story. One of the world's leading experts on pain, for example, who has himself witnessed acupuncture-based surgery, reports four significant findings: (1) contrary to earlier reports, patients *are* sedated, sometimes heavily so, before surgery; (2) those patients who do go for surgery using acupuncture are only chosen after a fairly rigorous selection procedure to see whether they have complete faith in the method; (3) acupuncture does not appear to work with children; and (4) its use appears to be on the decline in the major hospitals in China. Despite this rather sceptical analysis, it is clear that the full story about acupuncture, its nature and its practical value has not yet been told.

Adlerian Psychology. In 1911 the Viennese psychoanalyst Alfred Adler (1870–1937) together with his colleague Carl Gustav Jung broke with their friend Sigmund Freud over disputes concerning the latter's theoretic approach to psychoanalysis. Jung and Adler were themselves shortly also to part company, each to set up and develop his own "school" of psychoanalysis. Adler's system of psychotherapy is based on the idea, not of sex as a driving force as in the case of Freud, but on the concept of "compensation" or a drive for power in an attempt to overcome the "inferiority complex" which he held to be universal in human beings. The child naturally feels inferior to adults, but bullying, making him feel insignificant or guilty or contemptible, even spoiling, which makes him feel important within the family but relatively unimportant outside, increases this feeling. Or the child may have physical defects: he may be small or underweight, have to wear glasses, become lame, be constantly ill, or stupid at school. In these ways he develops a sense of inferiority which for the rest of his life he develops a technique to overcome.

This may be done in several ways: he may try to become capable in the very respects in which he feels incompetent—hence many great orators have originally had speech defects; many painters poor eyesight; many musicians have been partially deaf; like Nietzsche, the weakling, he may write about the superman, or like Sandow, the strong man, be born with poor health.

On the other hand he may overdo his attempt and overcompensate. Hence we have the bully who is really a coward, the small man who is self-assertive to an objectionable degree (Hitler, Napoleon, Stalin, and Mussolini were all small men) or the foreigner who like three of these men wanted to be the hero of their adopted country—Hitler the Austrian, Napoleon the Italian, Stalin the Georgian.

But what about the man who can do none of these things, who continues to fail to compensate? He, says Adler, becomes a neurotic because neurosis is an excuse which means "I could have done so-and-so but . . ." It is the unconscious flight into illness—the desire to be ill. Adler's treatment involves disclosing these subterfuges we play on ourselves so that we can deal with the real situation in a more realistic way. Adlerian psychoanalysis still attracts supporters, but its golden days were when the founder was at the head of the movement in the U.S.A., when his views were considered to provide a more "acceptable" theory of the mind than the enormously controversial theories of Freud with their strong sexual orientation.

Adventists, a group of American religious sects, the most familiar being the Seventh-Day Adventist Church, which observes Saturday as the true Sabbath. With more than a million members throughout the world, it shares with other Adventists a belief in the imminent second coming of Christ (a doctrine fairly widespread in the U.S.A. during the early decades of the 19th cent. when the end of the world was predicted by William Miller for 1843, then for 1844). Modern Adventists content themselves with the conviction that the "signs" of the Advent are multiplying, the "blessed event" which will solve the world's ills. Believers will be saved, but the sects differ as to whether the unjust will be tortured in hell, annihilated, or merely remain asleep eternally.

Agnosticism. *See* **God and Man.**

Albigenses, also known as **Cathari.** French heretical sect (named after the town of Albi in Provence) who appeared in the 11th cent. to challenge the Catholic Church on the way true Christians should lead their lives. They followed a life of extreme asceticism in contrast to the local clergy and their faith was adopted by the mass of the population, especially in Toulouse. Condemned as heretics by Pope Innocent III, the sect was exterminated in the savage Albigensian Crusade (1208–29), initially led by Simon de Montfort. (In his thoroughness, de Montfort also succeeded in destroying the high culture of the Troubadors.)

Alchemy, ancient art associated with magic and astrology in which modern chemistry has its roots. The earliest mention of alchemy comes from ancient Egypt but its later practitioners attributed its origins to such varied sources as the fallen angels of the Bible, to Moses and Aaron, but most commonly to Hermes Trismegistus, often identified with the Egyptian god Thoth, whose knowledge of the divine art was handed down only to the sons of kings (cf. the phrase "hermetically sealed"). Its main object was the transmutation of metals. Egyptian speculation concerning this reached its height during the 6th cent. in the Alexandrian school. Brought to Western Europe by the Moslems, one of its most famous Arab exponents was Jabir (*c.* 760–*c.* 815), known to the Latins as Geber, who had a laboratory at Kufa on the Tigris. One school of early Greek philosophy held that there was ultimately only one elemental matter of which everything was composed. Such men as Albertus Magnus (1206–80) and Roger Bacon (1214–94) assumed that, by removing impurities, this *materia prima* could be obtained. Although Bacon's ideas were in many ways ahead of his time, he firmly believed in the philosopher's stone, which could turn base metals into gold, and in an elixir of life which would give eternal youth. Modern science has, of course, shown in its researches into radioactivity the possibility of transmutation of certain elements, but this phenomenon has little bearing on either the methods of the alchemist or the mysteries with which he surrounded them. In line with the current considerable revival of interest in the occult, alchemy appears to be staging a comeback, at least as a literary if not an experimental topic.

Anabaptists. *See* **Baptists.**

Analytical Psychology, the name given by Carl Gustav Jung (1875–1961) of Zürich to his system of psychology which, like Adler's (*see* **Adlerian psychology**), took its origin from Freud's psychoanalysis from which both diverged in 1911. Briefly, Jung differed from Freud: (1) in believing that the latter had laid too much emphasis on the sexual drive as the basic one in man and replacing it with the concept of *libido* or life energy of which sex forms a part; (2) in his theory of types: men are either extrovert or introvert (*i.e.* their interest is turned primarily outwards to the world or inwards to the self), and they apprehend experience in four main ways, one or other of which is predominant in any given individual—sensing, feeling, thinking, or intuiting; (3) in his belief that the individual's unconscious mind contains not only repressed material which, as Freud maintained, was too unpleasant to be allowed into awareness, but also faculties which had not been allowed to develop—*e.g.*, the emotional side of the too rational man, the feminine side of the too masculine one; (4) in the importance he attaches to the existence of a collective unconscious at a still deeper level which contains traces of ancient ways of thought which mankind has inherited over the centuries. These are the *archetypes* and include vague primitive notions of magic, spirits and witches, birth and death, gods, virgin mothers, resurrection, etc. In the treatment of neuroses Jung believed in the importance of (*a*) the present situation which the patient refuses to face; (*b*) the bringing together of conscious and unconscious and integrating them.

In the 1940s and 50s interest in Jung's ideas waned, at least in academic circles, as the emphasis among experimental psychologists shifted closer and closer to the "hard" scientific line. This was also true in the field of psychoanalysis where the Jungian as opposed to the Freudian point of view became progressively less popular. At the present time this trend is beginning to reverse, and while Jung's offbeat views on astrology, telepathy, etc., are still unfashionable, a reappraisal of the significance of his views on the nature of the unconscious is taking place and many psychologists feel that his contribution to our understanding of the nature of human mental processes has been greatly underated. *See also* **Psychoanalysis.**

Anarchism, a political philosophy which holds, in the words of the American anarchist Josiah Warren (1798–1874), an early follower of Robert Owen, that "every man should be his own government, his own law, his own church." The idea that governmental interference or even the mere existence of authority is inherently bad is as old as Zeno, the Greek Stoic philosopher, who believed that compulsion perverts the normal nature of man. William Godwin's *Enquiry Concerning Political Justice* (1793) was the first systematic exposition of the doctrine. Godwin (father-in-law of Shelley) claimed that man is by nature sociable, co-operative, rational, and good when given the choice to act freely; that under such conditions men will form voluntary groups to work in complete social harmony. Such groups or communities would be based on equality of income, no state control, no property; this state of affairs would be brought about by rational discussion and persuasion rather than by revolution.

The French economist Proudhon (1809–65) was the first to bring anarchism to the status of a mass movement. In his book *What is Property?* he stated bluntly that "property is theft" and "governments are the scourge of God." He urged the formation of co-operative credit banks where money could be had without interest and goods could be exchanged at cost value at a rate representing the hours of work needed to produce each commodity. Like Godwin, he disapproved of violence but, unlike Marx, disapproved of trades unions as representing organised groups.

In communistic anarchism these ideas were combined with a revolutionary philosophy, primarily by the Russians Michael Bakunin (1814–76) and Peter Kropotkin (1842–1921) who favoured training workers in the technique of "direct action" to overthrow the state by all possible means, including political assassination. In 1868 anarchists joined the First International which broke up a few years later after a bitter struggle between Bakuninists and Marxists. Subsequently small anarchist groups murdered such political figures as Tsar Alexander II of Russia, King Humbert of Italy, Presidents Carnot of France and MacKinley of America, and the Empress Elizabeth of Austria.

Anarchism and communism differ in three main ways: (1) anarchism forms no political party, rejects all relationship with established authority, and regards democratic reform as a setback; (2) communism is against capitalism, anarchism against the state as such; (3) both have the final goal of a classless society, but anarchism rejects the idea of an intermediate period of socialist state control accepted by communism. Philosophical anarchists, such as the American writer Henry David Thoreau (1817–62), were primarily individualists who believed in a return to nature, the non-payment of taxes, and passive resistance to state control; in these respects Thoreau strongly influenced

Gandhi as did the Christian anarchist Tolstoy.

Anarchism has traditionally been criticised as being impractical—*e.g.*, in a non-authoritarian society, who is going to look after the sewers or clean the streets?—and there is a good deal of force to this argument. In fact anarchistic ideas became progressively less fashionable in the first half of this century. A curious and probably significant revival of interest has taken place in the past decade, however, probably because of a growing sense of disillusion, particularly on the part of young people, with the progress of orthodox political systems. *See also* **Syndicalism.**

Anglicanism, adherence to the doctrine and discipline of the Anglican, as the genuine representative of the Catholic Church. *See* **Church of England.**

Anglo-Catholicism. To Queen Elizabeth I the Church of England was that of the "middle way" in which human reason and commonsense took their place beside Scripture and Church authority. The extent to which these various factors are stressed creates the distinctions between "high" and "low" church. Anglo-Catholics tend to reject the term "Protestant" and stress the term "Catholic" and, although few accept the infallibility of the Pope, some Anglo-Catholic churches have introduced much or all of the Roman ritual and teach Roman dogmas. *See* **Catholicism, Tractarianism.**

Animism. To early man and in primitive societies the distinction between animate and inanimate objects was not always obvious—it is not enough to say that living things move and non-living things do not, for leaves blow about in the wind and streams flow down a hillside. In the religions of early societies, therefore, we find a tendency to believe that life exists in all objects from rocks and pools to seas and mountains. This belief is technically known as *animatism*, which differs from *animism*, a somewhat more sophisticated view which holds that natural objects have no life in themselves but may be the abode of dead people, spirits, or gods who occasionally give them the appearance of life. The classic example of this, of course, is the assumption that an erupting volcano is an expression of anger on the part of the god who resides in it. Such beliefs may seem absurd today, but it is worth realising that we are not entirely free of them ourselves when we ascribe "personalities" of a limited kind to motor cars, boats, dolls, or models which incur our pleasure or anger depending upon how well they "behave."

Anthropomorphism, the attribution of human form, thoughts or motives to non-human entities or life forms from gods to animals. At one end this can be summed up in the once widespread image of God as a "white-bearded old gentleman sitting on a cloud." At the other end is the very common tendency to invest domestic animals and pets with man-like wishes and personalities. At both extremes the belief could be seriously misleading. Firstly, it could be very unwise to assume that God, if he exists, necessarily thinks as humans do and has human interests at heart. Secondly, we shall learn very little about animal behaviour if we look upon them as mere extensions of our own personality, and we do them less than justice if we see them simply as human beings of diminutive intelligence.

Anthroposophy, a school of religious and philosophical thought based on the work of the German educationist and mystic Rudolf Steiner (1861–1925). Steiner was originally an adherent of Madame Blavatsky's theosophical movement (*see* **Theosophy**) but in 1913 broke away to form his own splinter group, the Anthroposophical Society, following ideological disputes over the alleged "divinity" of the Indian boy Krishnamurti. Steiner was much influenced by the German poet and scientist, Goethe, and believed that an appreciation and love for art was one of the keys to spiritual development. One of the first tasks of his new movement was the construction of a vast temple of arts and sciences, known as the Goetheanum, to act as the headquarters of the society. This structure, which was of striking and revolutionary architectural style, was unfortunately burnt down in 1922 to be replaced by an even more imaginative one which today is one of the most interesting buildings of its kind in the world. Anthroposophy, which ceased to expand greatly following its founder's death, is nevertheless well-established in various parts of the world with specialised, and often very well equipped, schools and clinics which propagate the educational and therapeutic theories of the movement. These, which include the allegedly beneficial powers of music, coloured lights, etc., have made little impact on modern educational ideas, but the schools have acquired a reputation for success in the training of mentally handicapped children, though one suspects that these successes are due to the patience and tolerance exercised in these establishments rather than to the curative value of colour or music "therapy" itself. Despite its apparent eccentricities, anthroposophy has made its mark on art and architecture, the outstanding modern painter Kandinsky, for example, being particularly influenced by Steiner's ideas and teachings.

Anticlericalism, resentment of priestly powers and privileges, traceable in England to Wyclif's insistence in the 14th cent. on the right of all men to have access to the Scriptures. The translation of the Bible into the common tongue was a great landmark in the history of the Bible and the English language. Wyclif's principles were condemned by the Roman Church of his time but were readily accepted during the Reformation. Tudor anticlericalism arose from motives ranging from a greedy desire to plunder the riches of the Church to a genuine dislike of the powers of the priesthood whose spiritual courts still had the right to decide on points of doctrine or morals in an age when the layman felt he was well able to decide for himself. In innumerable ways the Church was permitted to extort money from the laity. It is generally agreed, says Trevelyan, that the final submission of church to state in England was motivated quite as much by anticlericalism as by Protestantism. The rise of the Reformed churches in England satisfied the people generally and anticlericalism never became the fixed principle of permanent parties as happened in France and Italy from the time of Voltaire onwards.

Antisemitism, a term first applied about the middle of the last century to those who were anti-Jewish in their outlook. Although this attitude was prevalent for religious reasons throughout the Middle Ages, modern antisemitism differed (*a*) in being largely motivated by economic or political conditions, and (*b*) in being doctrinaire with a pseudo-scientific rationale presented by such men as Gobineau (1816–82) and Houston Stewart Chamberlain (1855–1927), and later by the Nazi and Fascist "philosophers." Beginning in Russia and Hungary with the pogroms of 1882 it gradually spread south and westwards where, in France, the Dreyfus case provided an unsavoury example in 1894. Thousands of Jews from Eastern Europe fled to Britain and America during this period; for in these countries antisemitism has rarely been more than a personal eccentricity. During the last war the murder of six million Jews by the Nazis and their accomplices led to a further exodus to various parts of the world and finally to the creation of the state of Israel.

The individual Jew-hater makes unconscious use of the psychological processes of projection and displacement: his greed or sexual guilt is projected on to the Jew (or Negro or Catholic) because he cannot bear to accept them as his own emotions, and his sense of failure in life is blamed on his chosen scapegoat rather than on his own inadequacy.

But there are social causes too and politicians in some lands are well versed in the technique of blaming unsatisfactory conditions (which they themselves may have in part produced) upon minority groups and persuading others to do the same. Historically, the Jew is ideally suited for this role of scapegoat: (1) in the Middle Ages when usury was forbidden to Christians but not to Jews, the latter often became moneylenders incurring the opprobrium generally associated with this trade (*e.g.*, to the simple-minded Russian peasant the Jew often represented, not only the "Christ-killer," but also the moneylender or small shopkeeper to whom he owed money); (2) many trades being closed to Jews, it was natural that they concentrated in others, thus arousing suspicions of "influence" (*i.e.* Jews are felt to occupy a place in certain trades and professions which far exceeds their numerical proportion to the population as a whole); (3) even with the ending of ghetto life, Jews often occupy *en masse* some parts of cities rather than others and this may lead to resentment on the part of the original inhabitants who begin to feel themselves dispossessed; (4) Jews tend to form a closed society and incur the suspicions attached to all closed societies within which social contacts are largely limited to members; marriage outside the group is forbidden or strongly disapproved of, and the preservation, among the orthodox, of cultural and religious barriers tends to isolate them from their fellow citizens. Discrimination, hateful as it is, does not come from one side only and it is such barriers as these that help to maintain an old and cruel folly. *See* **Racism, Zionism, Judaism.**

Antivivisection, opposition to scientific experimentation upon live animals based, according to its supporters, both on the moral grounds of the suffering imposed, and on the less secure claim that many doctors and scientists of repute have rejected the value of information gained in this way. It is true that the protagonists of the movement during its early days in the mid-19th cent. included a number of eminent physicians and surgeons, but few today—whatever their moral scruples—would deny the value of the results obtained. Without animal experiments we would be unable to test out new drugs for safety before using them on human beings. There are in Britain two or three large national anti-vivisection societies and several smaller ones. Much of their work is co-ordinated through the British Council of Anti-Vivisection Societies. Animal experimentation is controlled by Act of Parliament which makes obligatory the possession of licences by experimenters, inspection of laboratories by the Home Office, and the issue of annual returns of experiments. Many people would like the number of experiments on animals reduced and the law changed to prohibit any experiment in which there is any risk of inflicting suffering. A recent opinion survey showed that while the public approves of medical experiment it strongly disapproves of animals being used for the testing of cosmetics and other chemicals which have nothing to do with medical research. Reform of the Cruelty to Animals Act 1876 has been called for in view of the enormous increase in the number and variety of live animal experiments.

Apartheid, an Afrikaans word meaning "apartness," referred to by South African Government spokesmen as "separate development" or "self-development." To others it means the system of total racial discrimination between black and white South Africans—the permanent inhabitants of the country—as enforced by the Nationalist Party since it came to power in 1948. Some degree of racial segregation has existed in South Africa since the earliest days of colonialism in the mid-17th cent. and the policy was continued by the United Party under Smuts and Hertzog from 1934 onwards though it was never a political issue. This changed when the Nationalist Party gained power and oppressive measures against the non-White segment of the population have grown steadily under Malan, Strydom, Verwoerd, and Vorster. *Apartheid* involves the beliefs in racial purity and *baaskap*, or white supremacy. It means keeping vast African populations in a condition of helotry. Thousands of families are broken up by the pass laws. The official policy of the South African Government is to create separate self-governing black states in which the Africans would be guided to self-government and, it is claimed, eventually to independence. The first so-called bantu reserve was set up in the Transkei in 1962. But Africans with 70 per cent of the population would have only about 13 per cent of the land, and the poorest land at that; cities and mineral areas would remain the reserve of the whites. Total *apartheid* or complete separation of the black and white races in South Africa remains unlikely to be realised since mining, the main industry of the country, is based on low-paid African labour.

The sports boycott, the conflict between the churches and the government, and the economic need to make more use of African labour, could bring an impetus for change. The increasing economic power of some of the black African states – Nigeria, for example, is rich in oil resources – and the elimination of "Europeanism" from the Arab cultures of the North, has led to a steady erosion of the power-base of the white dominant countries such as South Africa and Rhodesia. Inevitably, apartheid has shown signs of weakening in response to these external pressures, and in early 1976 the South African government, for example, began to soften its objections to genuinely multi-racial sport. As the political situation in the African continent gets progressively more fluid in the latter half of the 70s, it seems likely that the days of total doctrinaire apartheid are numbered. *See also* **Africa, Section C, Part II.**

Aquarius, one of the twelve "signs of the Zodiac." This has recently achieved special significance in the mythology of our time because of the pronouncements of astrologers that the world is shifting out of the 2000-years-old cycle of the Age of Pisces, the fish, into that of Aquarius the water-carrier. The exact date of the transition is a matter of astrological controversy, but the consensus is that it began in 1960 and will be completed sometime in the 24th century. The Aquarian Age is predicted to be one of peace and harmony, replacing the era of strife which, ironically, has marked the dominance of the Christian symbol of the fish. Such speculations are totally without scientific backing and are mentioned here only to draw attention to the grip which astrological and other mythical concepts still have on human thinking. One of the first spaceships to carry man to the moon, for example, was named Aquarius by its crew. *See also* **Astrology.**

Arianism, formed the subject of the first great controversy within the Christian Church over the doctrine of Arius of Alexandria (d. 336) who denied the divinity of Christ. The doctrine, although at first influential, was condemned at the Council of Nicaea (325), called by the Emperor Constantine, at which Arius was opposed by Athanasius, also of Alexandria, who maintained the now orthodox view that the Son is of one substance with the Father. Arius was banished and the heresy had died out by the end of the 4th cent., but disbelief in the divinity of Christ has formed part of the doctrine of many minor sects since, notably in Unitarianism (*q.v.*).

Assassins, a sect of Moslem Shi'ites, founded by the Persian Hasan i Sabbah (*c.* 1090), which for more than two centuries established a rule of terror all over Persia and Syria. The coming of the Mongols in 1256 destroyed them in Persia and the Syrian branch suffered a similar fate at the hands of the then Mamluk sultan of Egypt, *c.* 1270. It was a secret order, ruled over by a grand master, under whom the members were strictly organised into classes, according to the degree of initiation into the secrets of the order. The devotees, belonging to one of the lower groups, carried out the actual assassinations under strict laws of obedience, and total ignorance of the objects and ritual of the society. It is believed that the latter were given ecstatic visions under the influence of hashish, whence the term *hashshashin*, which became corrupted to "assassin."

Associationism. In psychology, the Associationist school of the 19th cent. accepted the association of ideas as the fundamental principle in mental life. It was represented in Britain by the two Mills and Herbert Spencer, in Germany by J. F. Herbart (1776–1841). To these, mental activity was nothing but the association of "ideas" conceived of as units of both thought and feeling—the emotion of anger or the perception of a chair were both "ideas"—and apart from them the self did not exist. Personality was simply a series of these units coming and going, adding to or cancelling each other out, in accordance with rigid and mechanistic scientific laws.

Astrology was once the best available theory for explaining the course of human life and bears much the same historical relationship to astronomy as alchemy does to chemistry. Originally it was divided into the two branches of Natural Astrology which dealt with the movements of the heavenly bodies and their calculations, and Judicial Astrology which studied the alleged influence of the stars and the planets on human life and fate. It was the former that developed into modern astronomy; the latter was, and remains, a primitive myth.

Astrology owes most to the early Babylonians (or Chaldeans) who, being largely nomadic in an environment which permitted an unobstructed view of the sky, readily accepted the idea that divine energy is manifested in the movements of the sun and planets. Gradually this concept became enlarged and the relative positions of the planets both in relation to each other and to the fixed stars became important together with the idea of omens—that, if a particular event occurred whilst the planets were in a particular position, the recurrence of that position heralded a recurrence of the same sort of event. Soon the planets became associated with almost every aspect of human life. They were bound up with the emotions, with parts of the body, so that astrology played quite a large part in medicine up to late mediaeval times. Not only was the position of the planet to be considered but also the particular sign of the zodiac (or house of heaven) it was occupying, and it was believed possible to foretell the destiny of an individual by calculating which star was in the ascendant (*i.e.* the sign of the zodiac nearest the eastern horizon and the star which arose at that precise moment) at the time of his birth. Astrology was popular among the Egyptians, the Romans (whose authorities found the Chaldean astrologers a nuisance and expelled them from time to time), and during the Middle Ages when astrologers were often highly respected.

Despite the apparent absurdity of astrological beliefs—for example, how could the pattern of light from stars billions of miles away possibly influence the temperament of single individuals on earth—a substantial number of intelligent and well-educated people take its study in all seriousness. The most interesting "convert" was the psychologist and philosopher, Carl Jung, who conducted a complex experiment in which he compared the "birth signs" of happily married and divorced couples and claimed to find that those most favourably matched in astrological terms were also those more likely to have permanent wedded bliss. Jung's findings were subsequently shown to have been based on a simple statistical fallacy, which did not prevent the brilliant but eccentric psychologist from offering them up as evidence in support of his own theory of "synchronicity" (**J51**), an involved and vaguely metaphysical notion which suggests that events in the universe may be significantly related in a "non-causal" fashion. To add fuel to the controversy however, the French mathematician, Michel Gauquelin, has recently offered up fresh data which apparently supports the general astrological view. In a carefully controlled study he noticed statistically significant correspondences between certain astrological signs and the professions of a large number of Frenchmen whose birth time and date were accurately recorded. Gauquelin claims to have repeated his study on a second large sample of his fellow countrymen, though he has been unable to use English people as the exact times of birth are not recorded on their birth certificates! This apparent shot in the arm for astrology is still a matter of great scientific controversy, though Gauquelin's work has been given support from the distinguished British psychologist, H. J. Eysenck, who has pronounced his statistical data to be incontrovertible. Both scientists, however, carefully refrian from discussing the implications of these curious findings, and the controversy will no doubt increase rather than decrease in the near future.

Atheism. *See* **God and Man.**

Atlantis, a mythical continent supposed to have lain somewhere between Europe and America and a centre of advanced civilisation before it was inundated by some great natural catastrophe in pre-Christian times. There is little, if any, serious historical or archaeological evidence for its existence, but the legend of the Golden Land destroyed when the waters of the Atlantic closed over it has remarkable staying power and is believed by large numbers of people. Plato wrote convincingly about the wonders of Atlantis in his dialogues *Timaeus* and *Critias*, while other writers gave suggested that the biblical story of the Flood is based on fragmentary accounts of the Atlantean deluge. The lost continent is also of occult significance, largely as the result of the writings of W. Scott-Elliott whose book, *The Story of Atlantis* (recently re-published by the Theosophical Society), alleged that by clairvoyance he had been able to contact the spirits of Atlanteans who had been destroyed because of their addiction to black magic. There even exists in Britain today a minor but ardent religious group, "The Atlanteans," who hold that Atlantis still exists today, but on a different metaphysical plane, and that it is possible to communicate with it via individuals with supposedly mediumistic powers (*see* **Spiritualism**). Members of the Atlanteans meet regularly to hear "trance addresses" by one of the high priests of Atlantis, Helio-Arconaphus. Such beliefs are essentially harmless and merely reflect the great variety of religious attitudes which human beings enjoy.

Atomism. In philosophy, the atomists were a group of early Greek thinkers, the most important of whom were Leucippus (fl. *c.* 440 B.C.) and his younger contemporary Democritus (*c.* 460–370 B.C.). Prior to these men, although it had been agreed that matter must be composed of tiny ultimate particles and that change must be due to the manner in which these mingled or separated from each other, it was supposed that there existed different types of particle for each material—*e.g.* for flesh, wood, hair, bone. The atomists taught that atoms were all made of a single substance and differed only in the connections (pictured as hooks, grooves, points, etc.) which enabled them to join each other in characteristic ways. Theirs was the first move towards modern atomic theory and a predecessor of the modern concept of chemical linkages.

Authoritarianism, a dictatorial form of government as contrasted with a democratic one based on popular sovereignty. Its alleged advantages are the avoidance of the delays and inefficiency said to be characteristic of the latter.

Automatism, the production of material, written or spoken in "automatic" fashion—*i.e.*, apparently not under the conscious or volitional control of the individual. This psychologically perplexing phenomenon has occurred from time to time throughout the history of literature and art, and while it has occasionally produced work of great merit (much of William Blake's poetry, Coleridge's "Kubla Khan," etc.) the bulk of it is indifferent and often simply rubbish. Spiritualists claim that the work is produced under the direct guidance of the spirit world, and their argument has recently attracted considerable attention through the compositions of the pianist Rosemary Brown who, with little or no academic background in musical theory, has produced a number of "original" piano pieces allegedly composed by Beethoven, Mozart, etc., from the astral plane. While few music critics doubt Mrs. Brown's honesty and integrity, most consider her work to be clever pastiche and barely comparable in quality to the masterworks of the dead composers. Nevertheless automatism wants some explaining, and most psychologists today defer judgement, taking the view that it serves to remind us of the fund of material which lies in the unconscious mind, and which is prone to pop up from time to time without warning. Rather similar is the case of Matthew Manning, a young English student who produces clever and artistically intriguing drawings and sketches, allegedly guided by the hands of famous dead artists.

B

Baconian Method, the use of the inductive (as opposed to the deductive or Aristotelian) method of reasoning as proposed by Francis Bacon in the 17th cent. and J. S. Mill in the 19th cent. Deduction argues from supposedly certain first principles (such as the existence of God or Descartes's "I think, therefore I am") what the nature of the universe and its laws *must* be, whereas the only means of obtaining true knowledge of the universe, in Bacon's view, was by the amassing of facts and observations so that when enough were obtained the certain truth would be known in the same way that a child's numbered dots in a playbook joined together by a pencilled line create a picture. However, this is not the way science progresses in practice (*see* **F3(1)**). Bacon underrated the importance of hypothesis and theory and overrated the reliability of the senses. In discussing the scientific tradition, Sir Karl Popper in his book, *Conjectures and Refutations*, says: "The most important function of observation and reasoning, and even of intuition and imagination, is to help us in the critical examination of those bold conjectures which are the means by which we probe into the unknown." Two of the greatest men who clearly saw that there was no such thing as an inductive procedure were Galileo and Einstein.

Bahá'í Faith, a faith which teaches the unity of all religions and the unity of mankind. It arose in Iran from the teachings of the Bab (Mirza Ali Mohammed, 1820–50) and the Bahá'u'lláh (Mirza Husain Ali, 1817–92), thought to be manifestations of God, who in his essence is unknowable. Emphasis is laid on service to others. It has communities in many states and is surprisingly strong in England with a substantial following among university students. Its aims—universal peace, love, fellowship, etc.—are so laudable that it is hard to disagree with anything in the movement. On the other hand it is equally hard to see what it can offer, apart from more good intentions, over and above the teaching of more orthodox religious systems. The movement is now guided and administered by an elected order, "The Universal House of Justice".

Baptists, a Christian denomination whose distinctive doctrines are that members can only be received by baptism "upon the confession of their faith and sins" and that "baptism in no wise appertaineth to infants." Baptism is therefore by total immersion of adults. Modern Baptists base their doctrines upon the teaching of the Apostles and some hold that the Albigenses (*q.v.*) maintained the true belief through what they regarded as the corruption of the Roman Church in mediaeval times. On the other hand any connection with the Anabaptist movement during the Reformation is rejected and the beginning of the modern Church is traced to John Smyth, a minister of the Church of England who in Amsterdam came under the influence of the Arminians (*q.v.*) and Mennonites. Smyth died in 1612 when the first Baptist church in England was built at Newgate. This, the "General" Baptist Church, rejected Calvinistic beliefs and held the Arminian doctrine of redemption open to all, but some years later a split occurred with the formation of the "Particular" Baptist Church which was Calvinist in doctrine. In 1891 the two bodies were united in the Baptist Union and today the sect is spread throughout the world notably in the U.S.A.

The Anabaptist movements of Germany, Switzerland, and Holland also practised adult baptism in addition to a primitive communism and demanded social reforms. Persecuted by both Catholics and Protestants, their leader, Thomas Münzer, and many others were burned at the stake (1525). However, this sect was noted for its violence under a religious guise, and its taking over of the state of Münster in 1533 was characterised by wild licentiousness, since, as Antinomians, they believed that the "elect" could do no wrong. A revival begun by Menno Simons (d. 1561), a Dutch religious reformer, led to the formation of the Mennonite sect which, whilst rejecting infant baptism, gave up the objectionable features of the Anabaptists. This reformed sect still exists as small agricultural groups in the original strongholds of the movement and in the United States.

Beat Generation, a term first used by the American writer Jack Kerouac (d. 1969), author of *The Town and the City* and *On The Road*, to define various groups spread across the face of the country, but notably New York and San Francisco, who, belonging to the post-war generation, represented a complex of attitudes. Briefly, these were: rejection of the values of the past and lack of conviction in the possibility of a future for humanity—hence an acceptance of nothing but the immediate present in terms of experience and sensations; rebellion against organised authority, not out of any political conviction (as in the case of anarchism), but rather from lack of any interest or desire to control events, nature, or people; contempt for the "Square"—the orthodox individual who, stuck firmly in his rut, "plays it safe" and remains confident of the rightness and decency of his moral values. *See* **Beat Poets, Section M.**

The Beat generation of the 1940s and 50s gave way to the Love generation or Flower people, with their flowers, beads, and cowbells. Their social philosophy was the same—living in the present, unconventionally, seeking personal freedom, believing drugs to be essential, claiming to be acting against the rat race, dissociating themselves from politics, taking a superficial interest in the religions of the East, borrowing much of their language, music, and ideas on dress from the American "hippy"; yet believing in the creation of a new and gentler society based on different forms and values.

Both the Beat and Love generations were forerunners in America of an increasing and certainly welcome social awareness on the part of American students. This led in turn to the "campus revolutions" which were disruptive in their early stages but were also influential as part of the wave of public protest against the American involvement in Vietnam.

Behaviourism, a school of psychology founded in 1914 by J. B. Watson (1878–1958), an animal psychologist at Johns Hopkins University, Baltimore. Its main tenet was that the method of introspection and the study of mental states were unscientific and should be replaced by the study of behaviour. When animals or human beings were exposed to specific stimuli and their responses objectively recorded, or when the development of a child, as seen in its changing behaviour, was noted, these alone were methods which were truly scientific. Watson contributed an important idea to psychology and did a great deal towards ridding it of the largely philosophical speculations of the past. But he also went to absurd extremes, as in his view that thought is nothing but subvocal speech, consisting of almost imperceptible movements of the tongue, throat, and larynx (*i.e.*, when we think, we are really talking to ourselves), and his further opinion that heredity is, except in grossly abnormal cases, of no importance. He claimed that by "conditioning," the ordinary individual could be made into any desired type, regardless of his or her inheritance.

The work of Ivan Pavlov had begun about 1901, but was unknown in America until about ten years later, and it was through another Russian, Vladimir Bekhterev, that the concept of "conditioning" was introduced into the country. Bekhterev's book *Objective Psychology*, describing his new science of "reflexology," was translated in 1913 and played a great part in the development of Behaviourist ideas. The conditioned reflex became central to Watson's theory of learning and habit formation (*e.g.*, he showed that a year-old child, at first unafraid of white rats, became afraid of them when they came to be associated with a loud noise behind the head). Finally all behaviour, including abnormal behaviour, came to be explained in terms of conditioned responses; these were built up by association on the infant's three innate emotions of fear, rage, and love, of which the original stimuli were, for the first, loud noises and the fear of falling; for the second, interference with freedom of movement; and for the third, patting and stroking.

Because of its considerable theoretical simplicity and its implicit suggestion that human behaviour could be easily described (and even modified or controlled), Pavlovian psychology appeared very attractive to the Communist regime in Russia, and before long it became the "official" dogma in universities and research laboratories. Whereas in America and Western Europe its severe limitations became gradually apparent, in Russia these were ignored or disguised for ideological reasons with the inevitable outcome that Soviet psychology failed to evolve and, at one stage, seemed to be no more than a pallid offshoot of physiology. The recent liberalisation which has been taking place throughout Soviet society has led to a considerable broadening of scientific horizons and Pavlovian ideas are no longer looked upon with such unquestioning reverence. In non-Communist countries simple Watsonian behaviourism has evolved into more sophisticated studies of animal learning, largely pioneered by the Harvard psychologist, Skinner. These techniques, which have shown that animals, from monkeys to rats, may be taught to solve a remarkable range of physical problems such as pressing complex sequences of buttons or levers to escape from a cage) have themselves turned out to be rather disappointing in terms of advancing our general understanding of the workings of the human and animal brain. There is a growing feeling among psychologists that the real keys to the understanding of mankind will only be found through the study of man himself, and not of his simpler animal cousins. *See also* **Gestalt psychology** and **Q18–20.**

Benthamism. *See* **Utilitarianism.**

Black Power. The division of the world's population into races is now generally agreed by scientists to have arisen as the result of climatic and environmental pressures—the darker, more highly pigmented peoples tending to be better equipped to withstand higher solar output than the fairer, more northerly based types. For various reasons, again largely climatic and environmental, the first great advances in civilisation came from the temporary ascendancy over the black or near-black. Until quite recently—not much more than a century ago—the technological gulf between white and black was so vast that the negroid races were often held in slavery by the Europeans and while such a thought might be repugnant to most today, attitudes to coloured people still reflect a notion of inherent white "superiority" which it is easy to deny intellectually but difficult to shake-off emotionally. In the U.S.A., the most advanced and at the same time the most tormented multi-racial society in the world, the role of the substantial negroid population has changed dramatically in the last hundred years, shifting from that of slave to friendly servant, and then to near, or theoretical, equal. With this shift has come a corresponding change in the black community's view of itself, from relief at being no longer slaves, to gratitude at being allowed to do the menial jobs in the American society. More recently, with advances in educational opportunity and increasing political liberalisation, the attitude of the Negro in the U.S.A. has shifted yet again—from subservience to intellectual and physical equality, and even, perhaps, to inherent superiority. This new stand, rare at first, but spreading rapidly across America and other parts of the world throughout the 1960s, has crystallised in the concept and ideology of "Black Power," a movement of growing significance and importance in modern society. It is hard to trace the moment at which this formally emerged but one of its first expressions was the use by Negroes of the phrase "Black is beautiful," an apparent wakening of the belief that their colour, physique, features, hair, etc., were in no way aesthetically inferior to those of Europeans. Suddenly, in Negro communities it became no longer fashionable to artificially straighten hair, to bleach the skin or even to copy white American clothing, social habits, speech, and mannerisms. Alongside this highly important psychological jump—a rejection of the white man's social patterns—came an increasing rejection of his political machinery as well, a belief that the black races should have political autonomy and power of their own and not as part of an integrationist evolution of Caucasian societies.

The Black Power movement at this moment has no formal political representation in the United States, largely because it spurns the normal democratic approach of offering up candidates for election, but its strength and growing potency is well understood by enlightened American politicians who take careful account of its views on current or proposed "racialist" legislation. Its present strategy is a declared one of attaining black supremacy and autonomy rapidly by violence and revolution if necessary, and it has supporters in all sections of the Negro population—and among many of the younger whites as well. In the late 60s when the Black Power movement was in its most aggressive phase of expansion, there were real fears that open conflict, almost of civil war dimensions, might break out in American cities, but increasing liberalisation and better opportunities for social advancement and education for Negroes has slightly dulled its sense of purpose. The early 70s in fact have seen a dramatic change in the state of the Negro, with blacks penetrating middle-class and professional strata of society – medicine, law, politics, business, science, etc.—at a rate which would have seemed incredible 20 years ago. Urban ghettoes, however, still exist and provide numerous flashpoints for black-white conflict—the city of Boston is a particularly good example—but most observers (black and white) now view the future with more optimism than pessimism. However, the fact that America is fast becoming the best integrated country in the world is at least partly due to the conflicts and injustices which launched Black Power into being.

Bolshevism, an alternative name for **Communism** (*q.v.*), usually used in the West in a derogatory sense. When the Russian Social Democratic Party at a conference held in London in 1903 split over the issue of radicalism or moderation, it was the radical faction headed by Lenin (who subsequently led the 1917 Revolution and became first Head of State of the Soviet Union) which polled the majority of votes. The Russian for majority is *bolshinstvo* and for minority *menshinstvo*; hence the radicals became known as Bolsheviki and the moderates as Mensheviki, anglicised as Bolsheviks and Mensheviks. *See* **Communism, Marxism.**

British Israelites, a religious group who hold the race-theory that the English-speaking peoples (of the White Race) are the lineal descendants of the "lost Ten Tribes" of Israel (deported by Sargon of Assyria on the fall of Samaria in 721 B.C.). They believe the Anglo-Saxons to be God's "Chosen People" in the literal sense of the term as it is used in the Old Testament, by whom the world will be brought in readiness for the Millennium. The official organisation is the British–Israel World Federation of which the official journal is the *National Message*. Some British Israelites have the notion that the future can be foretold by the measurements of the Great Pyramid.

Buchmanism. *See* **Moral Re-Armament.**

Buddhism, one of the great Oriental religions. It arose against the background of Hinduism in north India in the 6th cent. B.C., its founder (real or legendary) being the Hindu prince Siddhartha Gautama, known as the Buddha or "Enlightened One." Distressed by the problem of human suffering from which even death allowed no escape—since Buddha accepted the Hindu doctrine of a cycle of lives—he left his palace and his beloved wife and child to become a religious mendicant and ascetic, studying without success for six years the beliefs of Brahmin hermits and self-torturing recluses. After this fruitless search he sat down under a tree (the Bo-tree) and finally came to understand the cause and cure of suffering. The result of his meditations are enshrined in the "four noble truths" which are: (1) that existence is unhappiness; (2) that unhappiness is caused by selfish desire or craving; (3) that desire can be destroyed; (4) that it can be destroyed by following the "noble eightfold path" whose steps are: right views; right desires; right speech, plain and truthful; right conduct, including abstinence not only from immorality but also from taking life, whether human or animal; right livelihood, harming no one; right effort, always pressing on; right awareness of the past, the present, and the future; and lastly, right contemplation or meditation. The more man acquires merit by following these rules in his chain of lives, the sooner is *Nirvana* attained; he loses his individuality, not by annihilation, but "as the dewdrop slips into the shining sea," by merging with the universal life.

Buddhism teaches the way of liberation through ethics and discipline. A universal God plays no part in this religion, and in many Buddhist nations no word exists for the concept which was neither affirmed nor denied by Buddha himself but simply ignored. Nor did Buddha claim to be other than a man, although much superstition entered the religion at a later date; prayers were made to Buddha, ritual developed, sacred relics preserved under stupas, and the belief in a succession of Buddhas introduced; the sacred writings (*Tipitaka*) are divided into three parts: for the layman, the monks, the philosophers. They were produced by devotees at three councils—the first held immediately after the death of Buddha at the age of 80, the last at the order of King Asoka in 244 B.C. The founder himself wrote nothing.

Buddhism spread to Sri Lanka, Nepal, Tibet, Mongolia, Indo-China, Burma, Siam, China, and Japan, although on the whole losing influence in India. In Tibet, Buddhism developed into Lamaism (*q.v.*). In Sri Lanka and Burma it persisted in its pure form (the Hinayana), while in China and Japan it developed into the Mahayana with its bodhisattvas and avatars.

Bushido, the traditional code of honour of the Samurai or Japanese military caste corresponding to the European concept of knighthood and chivalry with which it took its separate origin in the 12th cent. Even today it is a potent influence among the upper classes, being based on the principles of simplicity, honesty, courage, and justice which together form a man's idea of personal honour.

C

Cabala, originally a collection of Jewish doctrines about the nature of the Universe, supposedly handed down by Moses to the Rabbis, which evolved into a kind of mystical interpretation of the Old Testament. Students of the history of religious belief have found its origins to be in fact extremely obscure, and some aspects appear to have been lifted from ancient Egyptian sources. Skilled Cabalists hold that the system contains a key to biblical interpretation based on the numerical values of the words and letters of the scriptures which reveal hidden depths of meaning behind the allegorical Old Testament stories.

Calvinism, the branch of Protestantism founded basically (although preceded by Zwingli and others) by Jean Chauvin (1509–64), who was born in Noyon in Picardy. John Calvin, as he is usually called, from the Latin form of his name, Calvinius, provided in his *Institutions of the Christian Religion* the first logical definition and justification of Protestantism, thus becoming the intellectual leader of the Reformation as the older Martin Luther was its emotional instigator. The distinctive doctrine of Calvinism is its dogma of predestination which states that God has unalterably destined some souls to salvation to whom "efficacious grace and the gift of perseverance" is granted and others to eternal damnation. Calvinism, as defined in the Westminster Confession, is established in the Reformed or Presbyterian churches of France, Holland, Scotland, etc., as contrasted with the Lutheran churches, and its harsh but logical beliefs inspired the French Huguenots, the Dutch in their fight against Spanish Catholic domination, and the English Puritans. The rule set up under Calvin's influence in Geneva was marred by the burning at the stake of the anatomist Servetus for the heresy of "pantheism," or, as we should say, Unitarianism.

Perhaps its greatest single influence outside the Church was the result of Calvinist belief that to labour industriously was one of God's commands. This changed the mediaeval notions of the blessedness of poverty and the wickedness of usury, proclaimed that men should shun luxury and be thrifty, yet implied that financial success was a mark of God's favour. In this way it was related to the rise of capitalism either as cause or effect. Max Weber, the German sociologist, believed that Calvinism was a powerful incentive to, or even cause of, the rise of capitalism (*q.v.*); Marx, Sombart, and in England, Tawney, have asserted the reverse view—that Calvinism was a result of developing capitalism, being its ideological justification.

Capitalism is an economic system under which the means of production and distribution are owned by a relatively small section of society which runs them at its own discretion for private profit. There exists, on the other hand, a propertyless class of those who exist by the sale of their labour power. Capitalism arose towards the end of the 18th cent. in England where the early factory owners working with small-scale units naturally approved of free enterprise and free trade. But free enterprise has no necessary connection with capitalism; by the beginning of this century monopolies were developing and state protection against foreign competition was demanded. Capitalism is opposed by those who believe in socialism (*q.v.*), first, for the moral reasons that it leads to economic inequality and the exploitation of labour and the consuming public, and that public welfare rather than private profit should motivate the economic system; secondly, for the practical reason that capitalism leads to recurrent economic crises. The recent world economic crisis has led to great hopes on the part of Marxists and Communists that capitalism is now involved in its final death throes. It is worth commenting, however, that the European war of the 1940s, the great depression of the 30s, the first world war and the Russian Revolution were also, in their turn, confidently held up by Communists as heralding capitalism's imminent collapse.

Cartomancy, the art of telling fortunes or predicting the future by playing cards or by the Tarot pack. The elegant Tarot cards number 78 in all and are probably mediaeval in origin. They are rich in symbolism and include trump cards depicting the devil, the pope, death, the moon, the wheel of fortune, etc., and are an interesting part of our cultural mythology. There is no evidence whatsoever that they can be used in any objective way to divine the future, and professional fortune tellers and clairvoyants who use them almost certainly rely on a little native, basic psychology to achieve their results.

Catholicism. For those who are not Roman Catholics the term "Catholic" has two separate meanings. The more general refers to the whole body of Christians throughout the world, the more specific refers to a particular view of Christianity. In this latter sense the Church of England, the Orthodox Eastern Churches, and others consider themselves "Catholic" meaning that (*a*) they belong to Christ's Church as organised on an accepted basis of faith and order; (*b*) they insist on the necessity of "liturgical" worship through established forms (*e.g.*, baptism, holy communion); (*c*) they emphasise the continuity of Christian tradition by the use of ancient creeds (*e.g.*, the Apostles' Creed, the Nicene Creed) and regard the ministry as a succession (Apostolic succession) deriving from early practice. In this sense there is thought to be no necessary contradiction between Catholicism and Protestantism regarded as a renewal of the Church in the 16th cent. by an appeal to the Scriptures as interpreted by the early Fathers of the Church. This definition obviously excludes Quakers, Christian Scientists, and many Nonconformist sects.

The Roman Catholic Church is the religious organisation of all those who acknowledge the bishop of Rome as head of the Christian

Church, recognizing him as the lawful successor of St. Peter, who was the apostle appointed by Christ to be the head of the Church. Whereas in the Protestant Churches prayer and preaching play a central part (each individual soul seeking direct communication with God), in Roman Catholic worship the central service is the Mass, or Holy Eucharist, the seven sacraments (baptism, confirmation, eucharist, penance, extreme unction, orders, and marriage) being administered by a special priesthood. Church discipline and organisation are strong and authoritarian. *See* **Papal Infallibility.**

Characterology, the attempt made over many centuries to classify people into personality types on the basis of physical or psychological characteristics. The first attempt was made by Hippocrates in the 5th cent. B.C. who classified temperaments into the *sanguine* (or optimistic), the *melancholic*, the *choleric* (or aggressive), and the *phlegmatic* (or placid); these were supposed to result from the predominance of the following " humours " in the body: red blood, black bile, yellow bile, or phlegm respectively. Theophrastus, a pupil of Aristotle, described, with examples, thirty extreme types of personality (*e.g.* the talkative, the boorish, the miserly, etc.); these were basically literary and imaginative but about the same time " physiognomy " arose which attempted to interpret character from the face. Physiognomy became of importance again during the Renaissance and there are still those today who believe in it in spite of the fact that, broadly speaking, there is no connection whatever between facial features and personality (*i.e.* although it may be possible to tell from the features that a man is an idiot or some extreme abnormal type and some idea of character may be obtained from an individual's characteristic facial expressions, it is not possible to tell (as Johann Lavater, the best-known physiognomist of the late 18th cent. believed) from the shape of the nose, height of the brow, or dominance of the lower jaw, whether anyone is weak, intellectual, or determined). The contention of the 19th cent. Italian criminologist Cesare Lombroso that criminals show typical facial characteristics—prominent cheekbones and jaw, slanting eyes, receding brow, large ears of a particular shape—was disproved by Karl Pearson early this century when he found that 3,000 criminals showed no significant differences of features, carefully measured, from a similar number of students at Oxford and Cambridge.

It has, however, been noted that people in general tend to be intellectual or emotional, inward- or outward-looking, and this observation is reflected in the classifications of the Scottish psychologist, Alexander Bain (d. 1903), into intellectual, artistic, and practical; Nietzsche's Apollonian and Dionysian types; William James's " tender " and " tough-minded "; and C. G. Jung's introvert and extrovert. Careful experiments have shown that these are not clear-cut and that most individuals fall in between the extremes.

Some connection has been found between temperament and body-build. The German psychiatrist Ernst Kretschmer (b. 1888) showed that manic-depressive patients and normal people who are extroverted and tend to alternate in mood (as do manic-depressives to an exaggerated degree) were usually short and stout or thick-set in build; schizophrenics and normal people, who both show shyness, serious or introverted reactions, were usually tall and slender. The former of " pyknic " body-build are " cyclothyme " in temperament, the latter with " schizothyme " temperament are of two bodily types—the tall and thin or " asthenic " and the muscularly well-proportioned or " athletic." The American Sheldon has confirmed these observations on the whole and gone into further details. According to him the basic body types are: (1) *endomorphic* (rounded build), corresponding to Kretschmer's pyknic, normally associated with the *viscerotonic* temperament (relaxed, sociable); (2) *mesomorphic* (squarish, athletic build), normally associated with the *somatotonic* temperament (energetic, assertive); and (3) *ectomorphic* (linear build) normally associated with the *cerebrotonic* temperament (anxious, submissive, restless). Glandular and metabolic factors have considerable effect on human personality and also, to some extent, on physique. It is not too surprising, therefore, to find an association between body build (or " somatotype " as Sheldon termed it) and general mood. However, Sheldon's original clear-cut and oversimplified categories of body-type are no longer looked upon as reliable indicators of personality.

Chartism, a socialistic movement in England (1837–55) which attempted to better the conditions of the working classes. Named after " The People's Charter " of Francis Place (1838), its programme demanded: (1) universal manhood suffrage; (2) vote by ballot; (3) equal electoral districts; (4) annual parliaments; (5) payment of members; (6) abolition of their property qualifications. Chartism was supported by the Christian socialists (*q.v.*), J. F. D. Maurice (1805–72), and Charles Kingsley (1819–75) with certain qualifications. The movement, the first mass organisation of the industrial working class, had considerable influence on the evolution of socialist ideas in England. It is worth noting that its demands—with the exception of the unworkable " annual parliament "—have largely been met today, though at the time they were thought by many to be both outrageous and impossible.

Chauvinism, a term applied to any excessive devotion to a cause, particularly a patriotic or military one. The word is derived from Nicholas Chauvin whose excessive devotion to Napoleon made him a laughing-stock.

Chirognomy, the attempt to read character from the lines in the hand (as contrasted with chiromancy or palmistry, in which an attempt is made to tell the future in the same way) is an ancient practice which, like astrology (*q.v.*) has no discernible scientific basis but a very considerable popular following. As with astrology, where it is hard to see what kind of link could exist between the constellations and human behaviour, so it is equally hard to see how the configuration of lines on the hand could be paralleled by psychological attributes. This argument might be thought of as irrelevant if palmistry, etc. actually had predictive power, but the plain fact is that when put to a scientific test, practitioners of these arts turn out to show no abilities beyond those with which a normally perceptive individual is equipped.

Chiropractice, the art of manipulation of the joints, in particular the spine, as a means of curing diseases, is a slightly fashionable quasi-medical practice. Few qualified doctors employ its questionable principles though, as with its near-neighbour osteopathy, it seems on occasions to be a useful complement to medical treatment. Much controversy surrounds the status of practitioners of fringe medicine of this kind. In America osteopathy (bone manipulation), which seems to be beneficial in many cases for the condition known as prolapsed or " slipped" disc, is becoming gradually merged into orthodox medical practice.

Christadelphians, a religious denomination formed in the U.S.A. about 1848 at the time of the American Civil War by John Thomas, an Englishman from London. They claim to represent the simple apostolic faith of the 1st cent., and, in common with many other sects, hold that they alone interpret the Scriptures truly. They believe that Christ will return soon to set up the Kingdom of God with Jerusalem as its capital. In social life Christadelphians keep to themselves and hold aloof from organisational activities, though they do take an interest in political events if only from the point of view of their belief in biblical prophecy.

Christianity, the religion founded by Jesus Christ whose teaching is found in the New Testament's four Gospels. Simple as His creed may seem it soon became complicated by the various ways in which Christians interpreted it, and the differences within the early Church are reflected in the numerous Councils held to define truth from heresy. The Eastern Church of the Byzantine Empire from the 5th cent. onwards had differed in various ways from the See of Rome and by 1054 the breach became permanent. The 16th cent. Reformation was the other great break in the unity of the Church and once Protestantism had given in effect the right to each man to interpret the Scriptures in his own way, the tendency to fragmentation increased so that, by 1650, there were no fewer than 180 sects, mostly dogmatic and intolerant towards each other. Today there are many more, some of which are mentioned in this section under the appropriate headings. Nevertheless there are signs today that the trend of disunity is being reversed. The modern ecumenical movement, which has its roots in the great missionary movement of the 19th cent., aims to bring about a reunion of Christendom by uniting Christians throughout the world on the simple basis of the acceptance of Jesus Christ as God and Saviour, *i.e.*, on the basis of Christian fellowship. The movement finds expression in the World Council of Churches (*q.v.*). The Christian life is expressed in the words of Christ: "Thou shalt love the Lord thy God with all thy heart and thy neighbour as thyself." For many it is the humanitarian side of Christianity that has meaning today: to accept responsibility for others, as well as for oneself. *See* chart, below.

Christian Science, a religious denomination founded by Mary Baker Eddy (1821–1910), an American lady who sought to organise a church which would reinstate primitive Christianity and its lost element of healing. The sacred books of the movement are the Bible and *Science and Health with Key to the Scriptures* (1891), a revision of *Science and Health*, first published by Mrs. Eddy in 1875. Its main tenets (quoting from an official Christian Science source) are "that nothing is real save God and His spiritual creation, including man in His image and likeness; that man's essential nature is spiritual and wholly good; that matter, evil, disease and sickness are unreal—illusions existing only through ignorance of God. Therefore Christian Scientists renounce for themselves medicine, surgery and drugs and rely on healing through prayer."

The name of the movement seems misleading since it has nothing to do with any of the natural sciences of which Mrs. Eddy had no first-hand knowledge. In using the word, Mrs. Eddy meant that the teaching and acts of Jesus were rooted in unchanging divine law. Mrs. Eddy was at first interested in Spiritualism and afterwards, having been a patient of a faith-healer named Quimby, claimed to have been divinely healed.

There is a good deal of controversy about the efficacy of the Christian Science methods. In principle believers argue that if one has total, unquestioned faith in the healing power of Christ, then all sickness will be revealed as illusion and vanish. The trouble of course is that total faith is almost impossible to achieve, and hence even Christian Scientists inevitably fall ill and die. This makes the Church's argument irrefutable, but there is some evidence that the argument is convincing fewer individuals than it once did. On the other hand the growth of interest in "divine healing" within the more orthodox churches has led to a softening of barriers between Mrs. Eddy's splinter group and the hard-core Christian religions. Christian Science may well fade away after handing over to orthodoxy its single key concept.

Christian Socialism, a movement launched in 1848, a year of revolutions throughout the continent, by a group in England designed to commit the Church to a programme of social reform. The leaders, notably J. F. D. Maurice, Charles Kingsley (both Anglican clergymen), and John Ludlow were deeply moved by the wretched conditions of the British working class and the two priests had, indeed, given active support to the Chartist movement (*q.v.*). However, all insisted that socialism in its existing forms ignored the spiritual needs of mankind and must be tempered with Christianity. Tracts were written to expose the sweated industries, the consequences of unrestrained competition, and the evils following the enclosure system; but, more concretely, Christian socialism fostered co-operative workshops and distributive societies based on those of the Rochdale pioneers, organised a working-man's college and set up elementary classes for education. It also supported the trade-union movement's right to organise and bargain for its members.

The traditions of Christian socialism have

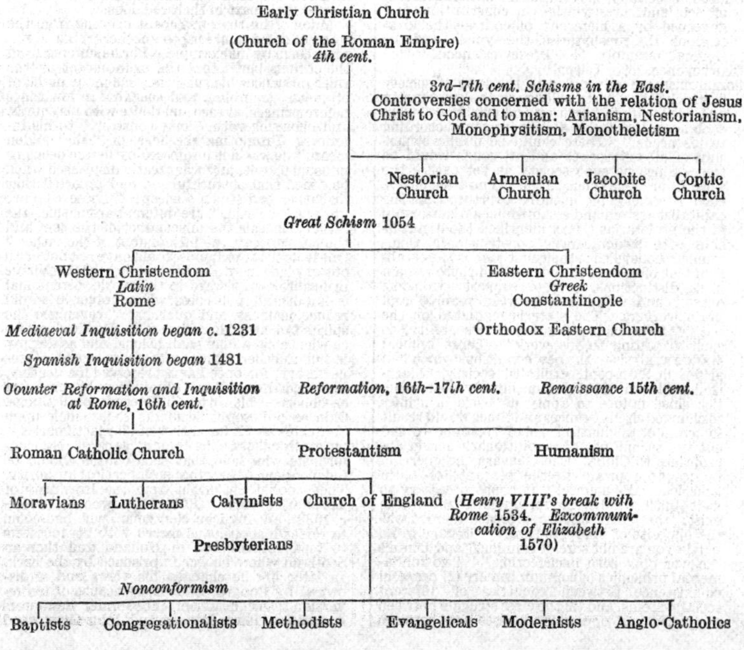

been carried on by the Fabian Society, by adherents of Guild Socialism, and by individuals who reject Marx's teaching of revolutionary change, and seek to bring it about by the methods of action through political parties, education, and encouragement of the unions. They believe that Christ's teachings can only be fully realised in a new society since Christianity implies social responsibility, and material factors are admitted to have an important bearing on the ability to lead a truly religious life. *See also* **Fabian Society, Guild Socialism.**

Church of England. There is some evidence of possible continuity with the Christianity of Roman Britain, but in the main the Church derives from the fusion of the ancient Celtic church with the missionary church of St. Augustine, who founded the See of Canterbury in A.D. 597. To archbishop Theodore in 673 is ascribed its organisation in dioceses with settled boundaries, and in parishes. St. Augustine's church was in communion with Rome from the first, but the Church of England was not brought within papal jurisdiction until after the Norman conquest, and was at no time under the complete domination of Rome. It remains the Catholic Church of England without break of continuity, but during the Reformation the royal supremacy was accepted and that of the pope repudiated. It is the Established Church (*i.e.*, the official church of the realm), crowns the sovereign, and its archbishops and bishops in the House of Lords can act as a kind of "conscience of the state" at every stage of legislation. The policy of religious toleration has been accepted since the 16th cent. The Church is organised in two ecclesiastical provinces (Canterbury and York) and 43 dioceses. Its form of worship is embodied in the Book of Common Prayer.

The Anglican Communion comprises the churches in all parts of the world which are in communion with the Church of England. All the bishops of the Anglican Communion meet every ten years in the Lambeth Conference (first held in 1867), over which the Archbishop of Canterbury by custom presides as *primus inter pares*. The theme of the 1968 Conference was "The Renewal of the Church," and for the first time observers and laymen were admitted.

Church of Scotland, the established national church of Scotland, presbyterian in constitution, and governed by a hierarchy of courts—the kirk-sessions, the presbyteries, the synods, and the General Assembly. *See* **Presbyterianism.**

Clairvoyance. *See* **Telepathy.**

Communism, ideally refers to the type of society in which all property belongs to the community and social life is based on the principle "from each according to his ability, to each according to his needs." There would be public ownership of all enterprises and all goods would be free. Since no such society as yet exists, the word in practice refers to the attempt to achieve such a society by initially overthrowing the capitalist system and establishing a dictatorship of the proletariat (Marx identified the dictatorship with a democratic constitution). Communists believe that their first task is the establishment of socialism under which there remain class distinctions, private property to some extent, and differences between manual and brain workers. The state is regulated on the basis "from each according to his ability, to each according to his work." Lenin applied Marx's analysis to the new conditions which had arisen in 20th-cent. capitalist society. Marxism–Leninism develops continously with practice since failure to apply its basic principles to changed circumstances and times would result in errors of dogmatism. Mao Tse-tung worked out the techniques of revolutionary action appropriate to China; Che Guevara the guerrilla tactics appropriate to the peasants of Latin America. His counsel "It is not necessary to wait until conditions for making revolution exist; the insurrection can create them," was the opposite of Mao Tse-tung's "Engage in no battle you are not sure of winning," and Lenin's "Never play with insurrection." Two fundamental principles of communism are (1) peaceful co-existence between countries of different social systems, and (2) the class struggle between oppressed and oppressing classes and between oppressed and oppressor nations. China, for example, holds that it is a mistake to lay one-sided stress on peaceful transition toward socialism otherwise the revolutionary will of the proletariat becomes passive and unprepared politically and organisationally for the tasks ahead.

In Russia the civil war developed *after* the revolution; in China the communists fought their civil war *before* they seized power: the Yugoslav partisans won their own guerrilla war during their stand against the fascist powers—differences which had important political consequences. Russia suffered three decades of isolationism and totalitarian suppression ("an isolated and besieged fortress") before the death of Stalin. Then came a marked, if zigzagging shift towards "liberalisation." Mao Tse-tung held to the orthodox Leninist view about capitalism and communism, regarded détente as a dangerous illusion and compromise and "revisionism" as a fatal error. The ideological dispute which has developed since 1960 between these two great communist powers has been likened to the East–West schism in the Christian church. Today, communist parties in some countries, *e.g.*, Italy, are taking the democratic road to socialism and believe that a communist government should be installed by the ballot box and not by force. *See also* **Maoism, Marxism, Trotskyism, and Section C, Part II.**

Confucianism. Confucius (Latinised form of K'ung-Fu-tzu) was born in 551 B.C. in the feudal state of Lu in modern Shantung province. He was thus a contemporary of Buddha, although nobody could have been more dissimilar. Where Buddha was metaphysical in his thought, Confucius was practical; Buddha was original, Confucius had hardly an original idea in his head; Buddha wanted to convert individuals to an other-worldly philosophy, Confucius wanted to reform the feudal governments of his time, believing that in this way their subjects would be made happier. Other religions have, in their time, been revolutionary; Confucius was a conservative who wanted to bring back a golden age from the past. The only respect in which Confucius agreed with the Buddha was that neither was particularly interested in the supernatural, and God or gods played little part in their religions.

Much of his time was spent in going from the court of one feudal lord to another trying to impress them by his example. For he suffered from the curious belief that the example set by the ruler influences his subjects. He made much of etiquette, trembling and speaking in low tones before princes, at ease and polite with his equals, and behaving with "lofty courtesy" to his inferiors. Promoting the idea of "the golden mean," he was not impressed by heroic deeds or unusual people, and was greatly displeased when he heard that a truthful son had reported that his father had stolen a sheep: "Those who are upright," he said, "are different from this; the father conceals the misconduct of the son, and the son conceals the misconduct of the father." One feels that Confucius would have felt not at all out of place in an English public school. Virtue brings its own reward in this world, ceremonial is important, politeness when universal would reduce jealousy and quarrels; "reverence the spirits but keep them far off." Destiny decides to what class a man shall belong, and as destiny is but another name for Nature prayer is unnecessary, for once having received his destiny, a man can demand and obtain from Nature what he chooses—his own will determines all things. Chinese philosophy students today look upon Confucius as "a forefather of all reactionaries."

Congregationalists, the oldest sect of Nonconformists who hold that each church should be independent of external ecclesiastical authority. They took their origin from the Brownists of Elizabeth's days. Robert Browne (*c.* 1550–*c.* 1633), an Anglican clergyman, who had come to reject bishops, was forced with his followers to seek refuge, first in Holland and then in Scotland where he was imprisoned by the Kirk. In later life he changed his views and is disowned by Congregationalists because of his reversion to Anglicanism. His former views were spread by Henry Barrow and John Greenwood who, under an Act passed in 1592 "for the punishment of persons obstinately refusing to come to church" (and largely designed for the suppression of this sect), were hanged at Tyburn. They had preached (*a*) that the only head of the church is Jesus Christ; (*b*) that, contrary to Elizabethan doctrine, the church had no relationship to the state; (*c*) that the only statute-book was the Bible whereas the Articles of Religion and the Common Prayer were mere Acts of Parliament; (*d*) that each congregation of believers was independent and had the power of choosing its own ministers. The body fled once more to Holland and were among the Pilgrims who set sail in the *Mayflower* for America in 1620 whilst those who remained were joined by Puritans fleeing from Charles I. They became free once more to live in England under the Commonwealth only to be repressed again under Charles II. Finally full liberty of worship was granted under William III. In 1833 the Congregational Union of England and Wales was formed which has no legislative power. It has issued a Declaration of Faith by which no minster is bound; he is responsible to his own church and to nobody else. The sect is widespread both in Britain and the U.S.A. where it is held in special honour because of its connection with the Pilgrim Fathers. In 1972 the Congregational Church in England and Wales and the Presbyterian Church of England decided to unite to form the United Reformed Church. The majority of members who did not join comprise the Congregational Federation.

Conservatism. The term "Conservative" came into general use after 1834 in place of the older name of "Tory." The modern Conservative Party has its origins in the period of "Tory Democracy" introduced by Disraeli between 1874 and 1880. Originally the party of church, aristocracy and landed gentry, Conservatism has been increasingly supported since the turn of the century by large business interests. Under Baldwin, Conservative-dominated administrations held office for much of the inter-war period. The 1945 Labour victory caused the Conservative Party to undertake a basic review of its philosophy. From 1951 to 1964, Conservatives held office continuously, reaching a peak in Harold Macmillan's 1959 election victory. Though defeated by Labour in 1964 and 1966, the party regained power in 1970 under Edward Heath. The subsequent troubled administration, plagued with problems on the industrial front, ended with the February 1974 election. The subsequent defeat in October 1974, followed by the battle for the Conservative leadership, again caused the party to seek to review its philosophy as it had developed in recent years. Most particularly, sections of the party were disturbed over the party's approach to economic problems and its increasingly narrow electoral base.

On the continent, Conservatism has generally adopted a more right-wing stance, being identified with the established order and fearing most forms of social change. *See also* **Section C, Part I.**

Coptic Church, the sect of Egyptian Christians who, holding "Monophysite" opinions (*i.e.*, refusing to grant the two natures, God and Man, of Christ), were declared heretical by the Council of Chalcedon in 451. They practise circumcision and have dietary laws. Their language is a direct descendant of ancient Egyptian. Like the Armenians, they are regarded as an heretical branch of Eastern Christianity. Their religious head is the patriarch of Alexandria.

Cynics, a school of philosophy founded in the time of Alexander the Great by Diogenes. Choosing to live like a dog by rejecting all conventions of religion, manners, or decency, and allegedly living in a tub, Diogenes unwittingly brought on his school the title "Cynic," meaning not "cynical," as the word is understood today, but "canine." His teacher, Antisthenes, who had been a disciple of Socrates, decided, after the latter's death, that all philosophy was useless quibbling and man's sole aim should be simple goodness. He believed in a return to nature, despised luxury, wanted no government, no private property, and associated with working men and slaves. Far from being cynics in the modern sense, Diogenes and Antisthenes were virtuous anarchists rather like old Tolstoy (except that in the practice of their beliefs they were more consistent).

D

Deism. *See* **God and Man.**

Demonism, Demons, and the Devil. Demons are ethereal beings of various degrees of significance and power which are believed to be implicated in men's good, but especially evil, fortune. They are common to most cultures. From the anthropological point of view the demon arose as a widespread concept in the following ways: (1) as a psychological projection into the outer world of man's own good or evil emotions and thoughts; (2) as a survival of primitive animism (*q.v.*), thus spirits are believed to haunt places, trees, stones, and other natural objects; (3) when by warlike invasion the gods of the vanquished become the devils of the conquerors (as when the Jews occupied Canaan); (4) as a primitive belief that spirits of the dead continue after death to hover near their former habitation, and not always entirely welcome to the living; (5) the conception of a supreme source of evil (the Devil or Satan) which took shape among the Jews during their sojourn in Babylon under the influence of Zoroastrianism (*q.v.*), a religion in which the struggle between the two spirits, Good and Evil, reached its height in the imagination of the ancient world. The Satan of the Old Testament was first regarded as one of God's servants (in the Book of Job he goes up and down the earth to see whether God's commands are obeyed), but when the Jews returned from their captivity he had become identified with Ahriman, the spirit of evil, who was in continual conflict with Ahura Mazda, the spirit of good. As Dr. Margaret Murray has pointed out, the primitive mind ascribed both good and evil to one power alone; the division into God and the Devil, priest and witch, belongs to a higher stage of civilisation. The worship of evil itself, or of its personification in Satan, is a curious practice which seems to have developed hand-in-hand with Christianity and to have received steady support from a small but measurable minority. Many of the ceremonies involved in Satanism or in the so-called Black Mass appear to have been no more than opportunities for sexual excesses of one kind or another—such indulgences being traditionally barred to devout Christians. The alleged power of sex as a form of magic was propagated by the talented but rather mad poet, Aleister Crowley (1875–1947), who scandalised pre-war Europe with his very well-publicised dabblings into Satanism. The self-styled "wickedest man in the world," Crowley was a pathetic rather than shocking figure and died a drug addict. He can hardly be said to have significantly advanced the cause of Demonology, though it has to be admitted that he tried very hard. *See also* **Witchcraft, Magic.**

Determinism and Free-will. The question of whether man is, or is not, free to mould his own destiny is one which has exercised the minds of philosophers since Greek mythology conceived of the Fates as weaving a web of destiny from which no man can free himself. Socrates emphasised that man could through knowledge influence his destiny whilst ignorance made him the plaything of fate; Plato went further in pointing out that man can, and does, defeat the purposes of the universe and its divine Creator. It is our duty to live a good life, but we can live a foolish and wicked one if we choose. Aristotle wrote "Virtue is a disposition or habit involving deliberate purpose or choice." If this were not so morality would be a sham.

The Problem for Theology. The last of the great philosophers of antiquity and one of the great influences in moulding Catholic theology was Plotinus (*c.* 204–270). Soul, he taught, is free, but once enmeshed in the body loses its freedom in the life of sense. Nevertheless, man is free to turn away from sensuality and towards God who is perfect freedom; for even when incarnated in matter the soul does not entirely lose the ability to rescue itself. This conception was carried over into the beliefs of the Early Christian Apologists because it appeared to be in line with the teaching of Jesus that He had come to save man from sin. Sin implies guilt, and guilt implies the freedom to act otherwise; furthermore an all-good God cannot be responsible for the sin in the world which must be man's responsibility and this again implies freedom. Pelagius (*c.* 355–*c.* 425), a Welsh priest, not only believed in freewill but, questioning the doctrine of original sin, said that when men act righteously it is through their own moral effort, and God rewards them for their virtues in heaven. This belief became fairly widespread and was declared a heresy by the Church, being attacked notably by St. Augustine (354–430), a contemporary of Pelagius, who believed in predestination—that, since the sin of Adam, God had chosen who in all future history would be saved and who damned. This represents one tradition in Christianity: the determinism which leads to **Calvinism** (*q.v.*). St. Thomas Aquinas (1227–74), the greatest figure of scholasticism and one of the principal saints in the Roman Catholic Church, compromised between the two positions in the sense that, believing man to be free, he yet held that Adam's sin was transmitted to all mankind and only divine grace can bring salvation. But even when God wishes to bestow this salvation, the human will must cooperate. God foresees that some will not accept the offer of grace and predestines them to eternal punishment.

The Problem for Philosophy. With the Renaissance, thinkers began to free themselves from the domination of the Church and to study the world objectively and freely without preconceptions. But the more man turned to science, the more he discovered that the world was ruled by apparently inexorable laws and, since the scientist must believe that every event has a cause, he was led back to determinism. Man as part of the universe was subject to law too and all that existed was a vast machine. Francis Bacon (1561–1626) separated the fields of religion and science but left man subject completely to the will of God. Thomas Hobbes (1588–1679) was a rigid determinist and materialist although, having had trouble with the church in France whence, as a royalist, he had fled, he took care to announce that the Christian God is the Prime Mover.

Modern philosophy begins with René Descartes (1596–1650), a Frenchman who tried to reconcile the mechanical scientific universe of his time with the spiritual need for freedom He did this by separating completely mind and body; the former, he said, is free, the latter completely determined. But, by admitting that the will can produce states of body, he was left with the problem of how this could happen—a problem which the so-called Occasionists solved to their own satisfaction by stating that the will is free and God so arranges the universe that what a person wills happens. Baruch Spinoza (1632–77), a Dutch Jew whose independence of thought had led to his excommunication from the Amsterdam Synagogue in 1656, was a complete determinist. He asserted that God and Nature are one, everything that happens is a manifestation of God's inscrutable nature, and it is logically impossible that things could be other than they are. Thus both Hobbes and Spinoza were determinists for entirely opposed reasons. The former as a materialist, the latter because he believed in the absolute perfection and universality of God. Yet the great religious mystic and mathematician Blaise Pascal (1623–62) held that, no matter what reason and cold logic may indicate, we *know* from direct religious experience that we are free. John Calvin (1509–64) and Martin Luther (1483–1546) were both determinists. *See* **Calvinism, Lutheranism.**

To the more practical British philosophers, John Locke (1632–1704) and David Hume (1711–76), free-will was related to personality. Locke believed that God had implanted in each individual certain desires and these determine the will; the desires are already there, but we use our will to satisfy them. Hume argued that a man's behaviour is the necessary result of his character and if he had a different character he would act otherwise. Accordingly, when a man's actions arise from his own nature and desires he is free. He is not free when external events compel him to act otherwise (*e.g.*, if he strikes another because his own nature is such he is free as he is not if he is compelled to do so against his desire). Leibnitz (1646–1716), although as a German metaphysical philosopher holding very different general views, said much the same thing—that choice is simply selecting the desire that is strongest. But most of the 18th cent. from Voltaire onwards, with the great exceptions of Rousseau and the later German philosophers Kant, Fichte, Schopenhauer, and Hegel, who were initially influenced by him, accepted determinism. Rousseau (1712–78) began to stem the tide by his declaration that man is a free soul striving to remain free and only prevented from being so by society and the cold science which stifles his feeling heart. Once again the will became important as Kant (1724–1804) asserted that belief in freedom is a moral necessity although it cannot be proved by reason; the moral nature of man shows that there is a "transcendental" world beyond the senses where freedom applies. Fichte and Schelling found freedom in the Absolute ego or God of whom each individual was part and thus also free. Hegel (1770–1831) saw the whole universe as evolving towards self-awareness and freedom in man although this could only be fully realised in a society that makes for freedom. Even God himself only attains full consciousness and self-realisation through the minds of such individuals as are free. This is the goal of the dialectical process. (*See* **Dialectical Materialism.**)

The Scientist's View. For the scientist the law of cause and effect is a useful hypothesis since, by and large, it is necessary for him to assume that all events are caused. Nevertheless the modern tendency is to think in terms of statistical probability rather than relentless mechanistic causality, and, although the free-will problem does not concern the scientist as such, it is clear that freedom and determinism (assuming the terms to have any meaning at all) are not necessarily opposed. In sociology, for example, we *know* that certain actions will produce certain results upon the behaviour of people in general, *e.g.*, that raising the bank rate will discourage business expansion. But this does not mean that Mr. Brown who decides in the circumstances not to add a new wing to his factory is not using his free-will. Even in the case of atoms, as Dr. Bronowski has pointed out, the observed results of allowing gas under pressure in a cylinder to rush out occur because most of the atoms are "obeying" the scientific "law" relating to such situations. But this does not mean that some atoms are not busy rushing across the stream or even against it—they are, but the general tendency is outwards and that is what we note. Lastly, the modern philosophical school of Logical Analysis would probably ask, not whether Free-will or Determinism is the true belief, but whether the question has any meaning. For what scientific experiment could we set up to prove one or the other true? The reader will note that some of the philosophers mentioned above are using the words to mean quite different concepts.

Dialectical Materialism, the combination of Hegel's dialectic method with a materialist philosophy produced by Karl Marx (1818–83) and his friend Friedrich Engels (1820–95). It is the philosophical basis of **Marxism** (*q.v.*) and **Communism** (*q.v.*). "Dialectic" to the ancient Greek philosophers meant a kind of dialogue or conversation, as used particularly by Socrates, in which philosophical disputes were resolved by a series of successive contradictions: a thesis is put forward and the opposing side holds its contradiction or antithesis until in the course of argument a synthesis is reached in which the conflicting ideas are resolved.

From Thesis through Antithesis to Synthesis. Hegel in the 19th cent. put forward the view that this process applies to the course of nature and history as they strive towards the perfect state. But to him, as to the Greeks, the conflict was in the field of ideas. The "universal reason" behind events works through the ideas held by a particular society until they are challenged by those of another which supersedes them and in turn, usually by war, becomes the agent of universal reason until the arrival of a new challenger. Hegel therefore regarded war as an instrument of progress and his Prussian compatriots found no difficulty in identifying their own state as the new agent of progress by universal conquest. Feuerbach, Lassalle, and other early socialists were impressed by some of Hegel's ideas: *e.g.*, that societies evolved (with the assumption that finally their own ideal society would be achieved) and that truth, morals, and concepts were relative so that a type of society that was "good" at one time was not necessarily so at another. But Marx and Engels in effect turned Hegel upside-down, accepted his dialectic but rejected his belief that ideas were the motive force. On the contrary, they said, ideas are determined by social and economic change as a result of materialistic forces. (*See* **Calvinism**, where it is pointed out that the Marxist view is not that Calvin changed men's economic ideas but rather that a developing capitalism unconsciously changed his.) The historical materialism of Marxism purports to show that the inexorable dialectic determines that feudalism is displaced by capitalism and capitalism by creating a proletariat (its antithesis) inevitably leads to socialism and a classless society. The state, as a tool of the dominant class, withers away. Dialectical materialism is applied in all spheres. As a philosophy there is little to be said for it save that it has shown us the close dependence of man's thoughts upon current material and social conditions. But as a battle-cry or a rationalisation of Marxism it wields immense power over the minds of men. *See* **Marxism.**

Dianetics. *See* **Scientology.**

Diggers, one of the many sects which flourished under the Commonwealth (others were the Muggletonians, the Levellers, the Millenarians, and the Fifth Monarchy Men), so-called because they attempted to dig (*i.e.* cultivate) untilled land. Gerrard Winstanley, a profoundly religious man, and leader of the Diggers, believed in the economic and social equality of man and castigated the clergy for upholding the class structure of society. In his book *The True Leveller's Standard Advanced* (1649) he wrote: "Every day poor people are forced to work for fourpence a day, though corn is dear. And yet the tithing priest stops their mouth and tells them that 'inward satisfaction of mind' was meant by the declaration 'the poor shall inherit the earth'. I tell you, the Scripture is to be really and materially fulfilled. You jeer at the name 'Leveller'; I tell you Jesus Christ is the Head Leveller."

Doukhobors, a religious sect of Russian origin, founded by a Prussian sergeant at Kharkov in the middle of the 18th cent., and now mainly settled in Canada. Like many other sects they belong to that type of Christianity which seeks direct communication with God and such bodies tend to have certain traits in common, such as belief in the "inner light," opposition to war and authority in general, and often ecstasies which show themselves in physical ways such as shaking, speaking in strange tongues (glossolalia), and other forms of what to the unbeliever seem mass hysteria. Liturgy, ritual, or ceremony is non-existent. The Doukhobors were persecuted in Tsarist Russia, but in 1898 Tolstoy used his influence to have them removed to Canada where the government granted them uninhabited land in what is now Saskatchewan and seven or eight thousand settled down in peace which they enjoyed for many years. Recently, however, their practices have caused difficulties once more; for even the most tolerant government which is prepared to accept pacifism, total dependence on communally-owned agriculture, refusal to engage in commerce, non-payment of taxes, rejection of the marriage ceremony and separation "when love ceases," finds it difficult to tolerate, as civilisation advances ever closer to Doukhobor communities, their proneness to "put off these troublesome disguises which we wear"—*i.e.*, to walk about naked in the communities of their more orthodox neighbours. What the future of the Doukhobors in their various sects (for even they have their differences) will be it is impossible to say, but it is difficult to believe that these simple people can long resist the pressure of modern civilisation.

Dowsing. *See* **Radiesthesia.**

Druidism, the religion of Celtic Britain and Gaul of which Druids were the priesthood. They were finally wiped out by the Roman general Suetonius Paulinus about A.D. 58 in their last stronghold, the island of Anglesey. There are two sources of our present beliefs in Druidism: (1) the brief and factual records of the Romans, notably Pliny and Julius Caesar, which tell us that they worshipped in sacred oak groves and presumably practised a religion doing reverence to the powers of nature which must have had its roots in early stone age times and had many cruel rites, *e.g.*, human sacrifice; (2) the beliefs put forward by William Stukeley, an amateur antiquarian who from 1718 did valuable work by his studies of the stone circles at Stonehenge and Avebury. However, influenced by the Romantic movement, he later put forward the most extravagant theories which unfortunately are those popularly accepted by those without archaeological knowledge today. Stonehenge and Avebury were depicted as the temples of the "white-haired Druid bard sublime" and an attempt was made to tie up Druidism with early Christianity, above all with the concept of the Trinity. In fact, these circles have no connection with the Druids. They may have made ceremonial use of them but recent evidence suggests that the megalithic stones at Stonehenge belong to a Bronze Age culture (2100–1600 B.C.). Nor have Druidism and Christianity any relationship. Almost nothing is known of the religion. Yet such were its romantic associations that, even today, one hears of "Druidic" ceremonies practised at the appropriate time of year on Primrose Hill in the heart of London (though whether seriously or with tongue in cheek one does not know). In Wales the name Druid survives as the title for the semi-religious leaders of the annual festivals of Celtic poetry, drama, and music known as Eisteddfods. Lingering, but now tenuous, druidic connections are to be found in all Celtic parts including Cornwall and Brittany, where Eisteddfods are also held.

Dualism, any philosophical or theological theory which implies that the universe has a double nature, notably Plato's distinction between appearance and reality, soul and body, ideas and material objects, reason and the evidence of the senses, which infers that behind the world as we perceive it there lies an "ideal" world which is more "real" than that of mere appearance. In religions such as Zoroastrianism or the Gnostic and Manichaeism heresies, it was believed that the universe was ruled by good and evil "principles"—in effect that there was a good God and a bad one. In psychology, dualism refers to the philosophical theories which believe mind and body to be separate entities. The opposite of dualism is monism which asserts the essential unity of the substance of the universe.

An essential problem in the dualistic view lies in the question as to how and where the two separate and distinct properties of the universe interact. Where, for example, does the "mind" actually mesh with the physical mechanics of the brain and body—where does the ghost sit in his machine? Descartes decided that mind and body must interact somewhere and he selected the pineal gland (an apparently functionless part of the brain) as the spot. But this did nothing to explain how two *totally different* aspects of nature can possibly influence each other, and today most philosophers and psychologists reject dualistic views of life and personality as posing more problems than they solve. *See also* **Psychology, Occam's Razor.**

E

Ecomovement. In the early 1970s widespread publicity was for the first time given to the urgent warnings of ecologists that the current exponential increase in (a) world population, (b) depletion of natural resources, and (c) pollution of the environment could not continue without global catastrophe. The most significant single event in the evolution of what is now being known as the "ecomovement" was probably the publication of the Club of Rome's paper on *The Limits to Growth.* From this sprang a movement, unfortunately initially drawn only from the middle class and better educated, which aimed to reduce environmental pollution, the extravagances of advertising and needless waste of natural resources. Its first campaigns were directed against such obvious targets as disposable glass bottles and unnecessary packaging and wrapping in shops and supermarkets. The ecomovement also protests against industrial firms which pollute rivers and seas, against aircraft noise and waste in general. Its early campaigns were greeted with some derision but have achieved dramatic point with the world energy and economic crisis which developed towards the end of 1973. *See* **Economic Growth, Section F, Part V.**

Ecumenism, a world movement which springs from the Christian belief that all men are brothers and that the Christian Church should be re-structured to give reality to the belief. Christ's church exists not to serve its own members, but for the service of the whole world. Some see the answer in a united church of a federal type (unity in diversity), others in an organic structure with one set of rules. The period since the convening of the Second Vatican Council by Pope John has been one of fervent discussion among Christian theologians with the aim of promoting Christian unity. *See* World Council of Churches.

Education. Education was no great problem to primitive man, but as societies became more complex people began to ask themselves such questions as: *What* should young people be taught? *How* should they be taught? Should the aim of their education be to bring out their individual qualities or rather to make them good servants of the state?

The first teachers were priests who knew most about the traditions, customs, and lore of their societies and thus the first schools were in religious meeting places. This was notably true of the Jews who learned from the rabbis in the synagogue.

The Greeks. We begin, as always, with the Greeks whose city-states, based on slavery, educated men (not women) for the sort of life described in Plato's *Dialogues*—the leisured life of gentlemen arguing the problems of the universe at their banquets or in the market-place. This made it necessary to learn debate and oratory (or rhetoric) especially for those who proposed to take up politics. The Sophist philosophy taught the need to build up convincing arguments in a persuasive manner, to learn the rules of logic and master the laws and customs of the Athenians, and to know the literature of the past so that illustrations might be drawn from it. These strolling philosophers who taught for a fee were individualists showing the student how to advance himself at all costs within his community.

Socrates had a more ethical approach, believing that education was good in itself, made a man happier and a better citizen, and emphasised his position as a member of a group. His method of teaching, the dialectic or "Socratic" method, involved argument and discussion rather than overwhelming others by rhetoric and is briefly mentioned under **Dialectical Materialism** (*q.v.*). Today this method is increasingly used in adult education where a lecture is followed by a period of discussion in which both lecturer and audience participate; for psychologists have shown that people accept ideas more readily when conviction arises through their own arguments than when they are passively thrust down their throats.

Socrates' pupil Plato produced in his book *The Republic* one of the first comprehensive systems of education and vocational selection. Believing that essentially men have very different and unequal abilities he considered that in an idealistic or utopian society they should be put into social classes corresponding to these differences, and suggested the following method: (1) For the first 18 years of a boy's life he should be taught gymnastics and sports, playing and singing music, reading and writing, a knowledge of literature, and if he passed this course sent on to the next stage; those who failed were to become tradesmen and merchants. (2) From 18–20 those successful in the first course were to be given two years of cadet training, the ones thought incapable of further education being placed in the military class as soldiers. (3) The remainder, who were to become the leaders of society, proceeded with advanced studies in philosophy, mathematics, science, and art. Such education was to be a state concern, state supported and controlled, selecting men and training them for service in the state according to their abilities.

Plato's pupil Aristotle even suggested that the state should determine shortly after birth which children should be allowed to live and destroy the physically or mentally handicapped; that marriage should be state-controlled to ensure desirable offspring. However, in their time the leisured and individualistic Sophists held the field and few accepted the educational views of Plato or his pupil.

Rome. The Romans were not philosophers and most of their culture came from Greece. Administration was their chief aptitude and Quintilian (A.D. *c.* 35–*c.* 95) based his higher education on the earlier classical tuition in public speaking, but he is important for emphasising the training of character and for his humanistic approach to the method of teaching that caused his *Institutio oratoria* to be influential for centuries later—indeed one might almost say up to the time of the great Dr. Arnold of Rugby. Education, he believed, should begin early but one must "take care that the child not old enough to love his studies does not come to hate them" by premature forcing; studies must be made pleasant and interesting and students encouraged by praise rather than discouraged when they sometimes fail; play is to be approved of as a sign of a lively disposition and because gloomy, depressed children are not likely to be good students; corporal punishment should never be used because "it is an insult as you will realise if you imagine it yourself." The world became interested not in *what* he taught but *how* he taught it; he was the pioneer of humanistic education and character-training from Vittorino da Feltre (1378–1446) of Mantua, through Milton and Pope who commended his works, to the modern educationists who have studied their pupils as well as their books.

The Middle Ages: The Religious View. With the development of Christianity education once more became a religious problem. The earliest converts had to be taught Christian doctrine and were given instruction in "catechumenal" schools before admission to the group, but as the religion came increasingly into contact with other religions or heresies a more serious training was necessary, and from these newer "catechetical" schools, where the method used was the catechism (*i.e.*, question and answer as known to all Presbyterian children today), the Apologists arose among whom were Clement of Alexandria and the great Origen. From this time education became an instrument of the church and in 529 the Emperor Justinian ordered all pagan schools to be closed.

As typical of the best in mediaeval education whilst the lamp of civilisation burned low during the Dark Ages, after the fall of Roman power, and survived only in the monasteries, we may mention St. Benedict (*c.* 480–*c.* 547) of Monte Cassino. There, in southern Italy, a rule was established which became a part of monastic life in general. Monastic schools were originally intended for the training of would-be monks, but later others were admitted who simply wanted some education; thus two types of school developed, one for the *interni* and the other for *externi* or external pupils. Originally studies were merely reading in order to study the Bible, writing to copy the sacred books, and sufficient calculation to be able to work out the advent of holy days or festivals. But by the end of the 6th cent. the "seven liberal arts" (grammar rhetoric, dialectic, arithmetic, geometry, music, and astronomy) were added.

The Renaissance. The close of the Middle Ages saw the development of two types of secular school. One came with the rise of the new merchant class and the skilled trader whose "guilds" or early trade unions established schools to train young men for their trades but ultimately gave rise to burgher or town schools; the other was the court school founded and supported by the wealthy rulers of the Italian cities—Vittorino da Feltre (mentioned above) presided over the most famous at Mantua.

These Renaissance developments are paralleled in northern Europe by the Protestant reformers who, having with Martin Luther held that everyone should know how to read his Bible in order to interpret it in his own way, were logically committed to popular education, compulsory and universal. In theory this was intended for biblical study, but writing, arithmetic, and other elementary subjects were taught and Luther said that, even if heaven and hell did not exist, education was important. Universal education is a Protestant conception.

Views of Philosophers. From this period onwards people were free to put forward any ideas about education, foolish or otherwise, and to create their own types of school. Of English philosophers who theorised about, but did not practise, education we may mention the rationalist Francis Bacon (1561–1626) who saw learning as the dissipation of all prejudices and the collection of concrete facts; the materialist and totalitarian Hobbes (1588–1679) who, as a royalist, believed that the right to determine the kind of education fit for his subjects is one of the absolute rights of the sovereign power or ruler; the gentlemanly Locke (1632–1704) whose ideal was a sound mind in a sound body to be attained by hard physical exercise, wide experience of the world, and enough knowledge to meet the requirements of the pupil's environment. The end result would be one able to get on with his fellows, pious but wise in the ways of the world, independent and able to look after himself, informed but reticent about his knowledge. Classics and religious study were not to be carried to excess, since Locke held that these subjects had been overrated in the past. Locke's pupil was the well-to-do, civilised young man of the 17th cent. who knew how to behave in society.

Jean-Jacques Rousseau (1712–78), a forerunner of the Romantic movement (*q.v.*), which despised society and its institutions, put emotion at a higher level than reason. His book *Emile* describes the education of a boy which is natural and spontaneous. Society, he holds, warps the growing mind and therefore the child should be protected from its influences until his development in accordance with his own nature is so complete that he cannot be harmed by it. During the first 4 years the body should be developed by physical training; from 5 to 12 the child would live in a state of nature such that he could develop his powers of observation and his senses; from 13 books would be used and intellectual training introduced, although only in line with the child's own interests, and he would be given instruction only as he came to ask for it. Moral training and contact with his fellows to learn the principles of sympathy, kindness, and helpfulness to mankind would be given between 15 and 20. Girls, however, should be educated to serve men in a spirit of modesty and restraint. His own five children he deposited in a foundling hospital.

Summary. Broadly speaking, then, there have been four main attitudes to education: (1) religious, with a view to a life beyond death; (2) state-controlled education, with a view to uniform subservience to authority; (3) "gentlemanly" education, with a view to social graces and easy congress in company; (4) the "child-centred" education, which attempts to follow the pupil's inner nature. It is unnecessary to mention the ordinary method of attempting to instil facts without any considerable degree of co-operation between pupil and teacher in order that the former may, with or without interest, follow some occupation in adult life; for this the philosophers did not consider. Today there remain the two fundamental principles: education for the advantage of the state and its ideology or education for individual development and freedom.

Four educationists of the modern period who have influenced us in the direction of freedom were Johann Pestalozzi of Switzerland (1746–1827) who, by trying to understand children, taught the "natural, progressive, and harmonious development of all the powers and capacities of the human being"; Friedrich Froebel (1782–1852) of Germany, the founder of the Kindergarten who, like Pestalozzi, was influenced by Rousseau but realised the need to combine complete personal development with social adjustment; Maria Montessori (1869–1952) whose free methods have revolutionised infant teaching; John Dewey (1859–1952) who held that the best interests of the group are served when the individual develops his own particular talents and nature.

Eleatics, the philosophers of Elea in ancient Greece who, at the time when Heraclitus (*c.* 535–475 B.C.) was teaching that change is all that exists and nothing is permanent, were asserting that change is an illusion. Of the three leaders of this school, Xenophanes asserted that the universe was a solid immovable mass forever the same; Parmenides explained away change as an inconceivable process, its appearance being due to the fact that what we see is unreal; and Zeno (the best-known today) illustrated the same thesis with his famous argument of the arrow which, at any given moment of its flight, must be where it is since it cannot be where it is not. But if it is where it is, it cannot move; this is based, of course, on the delusion that motion is discontinuous. The Eleatics were contemporaries of Socrates.

Empiricism. While not a single school of philosophy, empiricism is an approach to knowledge which holds that if a man wants to know what the universe is like the only correct way to do so is to go and look for himself, to collect facts which come to him through his senses. It is, in essence, the method of science as contrasted with rationalism (*q.v.*) which in philosophy implies that thinking or reasoning without necessarily referring to external observations can arrive at truth. Empiricism is typically an English attitude, for among the greatest empirical philosophers were John Locke, George Berkeley, and David Hume. *See* **Rationalism.**

picureanism. The two great schools of the Hellenistic period (*i.e.* the late Greek period beginning with the empire of Alexander the Great) were the Stoics and Epicureans, the former founded by Zeno of Citium (*not* to be confused with Zeno the Eleatic) (*q.v.*), the latter by Epicurus, born in Samos in 342 B.C. Both schools settled in Athens, where Epicurus taught that "pleasure is the beginning and end of a happy life." However, he was no sensualist and emphasised the importance of moderation in all things because excesses would lead to pain instead of pleasure and the best of all pleasures were mental ones. Pleasures could be active or passive but the former contain an element of pain since they are the process of satisfying desires not yet satiated. The latter involving the absence of desire are the more pleasant. In fact, Epicurus in his personal life was more stoical than many Stoics and wrote "when I live on bread and water I spit on luxurious pleasures." He disapproved of sexual enjoyment and thought friendship one of the highest of all joys. A materialist who accepted the atomic theory of Democritus, he was not a determinist, and if he did not disbelieve in the gods he regarded religion and the fear of death as the two primary sources of unhappiness.

Epiphenomenalism. *See* **Mind and Body.**

Erastianism, the theory that the state has the right to decide the religion of its members, wrongly attributed to Erastus of Switzerland (1524–83) who was believed to have held this doctrine. The term has usually been made use of in a derogatory sense—*e.g.*, by the Scottish churches which held that the "call" of the congregation was the only way to elect ministers at a time when, about the turn of the 17th and 18th cent., they felt that Episcopalianism was being foisted on them. "Episcopalianism" (*i.e.* Anglicanism) with its state church, ecclesiastical hierarchy, and system of livings presented by patrons was to them "Erastian" in addition to its other "unscriptural practices."

Essenes, a Jewish sect which, during the oppressive rule of Herod (d. 4 B.C.), set up monastic communities in the region of the Dead Sea. They refused to be bound by the scriptural interpretations of the Pharisees and adhered rigorously to the letter of Holy Writ, although with additions of their own which cause them by orthodox Jews today to be regarded as a break-away from Judaism. Among their practices and beliefs were purification through baptism, renunciation of sexual pleasures, scrupulous cleanliness, strict observance of the Mosaic law, communal possession, asceticism. Akin in spirit, although not necessarily identical with them, were the writers of Apocalyptic literature preaching that the evils of the present would shortly be terminated by a new supernatural order heralded by a Messiah who would reign over a restored Israel. The casting out of demons and spiritual healing formed part of these general beliefs which were in the air at that time. The sect has an importance far beyond its size or what has been known about it in the past since the discovery from 1947 onwards of the Dead Sea Scrolls (*see* **Section L**) of the Qumran community occupying a monastery in the same area as the Essenes and holding the same type of belief. These scrolls with their references to a "Teacher of Righteousness" preceding the Messiah have obvious relevance to the sources of early Christianity and have given rise to speculations as to whether Jesus might have been influenced by views which, like His own, were unacceptable to orthodox Jews but in line with those of the Dead Sea communities. At the very least they seem to show that early Christianity was not a sudden development but a gradual one which had its predecessors.

Ethical Church, a movement typical of 19th cent. rationalism which attempted to combine atheism (or at any rate the absence of any belief in a God which was inconsistent with reason or based on revelation) with the inculcation of moral principles. Prayers were not used and ordinarily the service consisted in the singing of edifying compositions interspersed with readings from poems or prose of a similar nature by great writers holding appropriate views. It terminated in a talk on an ethical or scientific theme. There is an Ethical Church in London and the South Place Institution where Moncure Conway preached from 1864 to 1897 still exists.

Ethnocentrism, the exaggerated tendency to think the characteristics of one's own group or race superior to those of any others.

Eugenics, a 19th-cent. movement largely instigated by the British scientist and mathematician, Sir Francis Galton. Galton argued that many of the most satisfactory attributes of mankind—intelligence, physical strength, resistance to disease, etc.—were genetically determined and thus handed down in the normal process of inheritance. From this he reasoned that selective mating of physical "superior" individuals, and its converse, the controlled limitation on the breeding of criminals or the insane, would lead inevitably to a progressive improvement in the overall standards of the human race. In their simplest form these proposals are incontestable, though they do of course introduce marked restrictions on the choice of the individual for marriage and procreation. Worse yet is the way in which the argument can be misapplied or elaborated—as it was in Nazi Germany—to include the sterilisation of alcoholics, confirmed criminals and even epileptics. Nevertheless there remains the feeling that there are some aspects of eugenics which intuitively at any rate make good sense and of course the widespread application of birth control is itself an enactment of eugenic principles.

Evangelicanism, the belief of those Protestant sects which hold that the essence of the Gospel consists in the doctrine of salvation by faith in the atoning death of Christ and not by good works or the sacraments; that worship should be "free" rather than liturgical through established forms; that ritual is unacceptable and superstitious. Evangelicals are Low Churchmen.

Evangelism, the preaching of the Gospel, emphasising the necessity for a new birth or conversion. The evangelistic fervour of John Wesley and George Whitefield (*see* Methodism) aroused the great missionary spirit of the late 18th and 19th cent. George Fox, founder of the Society of Friends (*q.v.*), was also an evangelist. Evangelists can be Low, High, or Middle Churchmen.

Existentialism, a highly subjective philosophy which many people connect with such names as Jean-Paul Sartre (b. 1905) or Albert Camus (1913–60) and assume to be a post-war movement associated with disillusion and a sordid view of life. However, existentialism stems from Sören Kierkegaard (1813–55), the Danish "religious writer"—his own description of himself—in such works as *Either/Or*, *Fear and Trembling*, and *Concluding Unscientific Postscript*. Between the two wars translations of Kierkegaard into German influenced Martin Heidegger's great work *Being and Time* and the other great existentialist Karl Jaspers; it has strongly influenced modern Protestant theology notably in Karl Barth, Reinhold Niebuhr, and Paul Tillich and beyond that field the French philosopher Gabriel Marcel, the Spanish writer Unamuno in his well-known *The Tragic Sense of Life*, and Martin Buber of Israel in his *I and Thou*. We have it on Heidegger's authority that "Sartre is no philosopher" even if it is to his works that modern existentialists often turn.

Existentialism is extremely difficult for the non-metaphysically-minded to understand; it deals, not with the nature of the universe or what are ordinarily thought of as philosophical problems but describes an attitude to life or God held by the individual. Briefly, its main essentials are: (1) it distinguishes between *essence*, *i.e.*, that aspect of an entity which can be observed and known—and its *existence*—the fact of its having a place in a changing and dangerous world which is what really matters; (2) existence being basic, each self-aware individual can grasp his own existence on reflection in his own immediate experience of himself and his situation as a free being in the world; what he finds is not merely a knowing self but a self that fears, hopes, believes, wills, and is aware of its need to find a purpose, plan, and destiny in life; (3) but we cannot grasp our existence by thought alone; thus the fact "all men must die" relates to the essence of man but it is necessary to be involved, to draw the conclusion as a person that "I too must die" and experience its impact on our own individual existence; (4) because of the preceding, it is necessary to abandon our attitude of objectivity and theoretical detachment when faced by the problems relating to the ultimate purpose of our own life and the basis of our own conduct; life remains closed to those who take no part in it because it can have no significance; (5) it follows that the existentialist cannot be rationalist in his outlook for this is merely an escape into thought from the serious problems of existence; none of the important aspects of life—failure, evil, sin, folly—nor (in the view of Kierkegaard) even the existence of God or the truth of Christianity—can be proved by reason. "God does not exist; He is eternal," was how he expressed it; (6) life is short and limited in space and time, therefore it is foolish to discuss in a leisurely fashion matters of life or death as if there were all eternity to argue them in. It is necessary to make a leap into the unknown, *e.g.*, accepting Christ (in the case of the Christian existentialist) by faith in the sense of giving and risking the self utterly. This means complete commitment, not a dependence on arguments as to whether certain historical events did, or did not, happen.

To summarise: existentialism of whatever type seems to the outsider to be an attitude to life concerning itself with the individual's ultimate problems (mine, not yours); to be anti-rationalist and anti-idealist (in the sense of being, as it seems to the believer, practical)—in effect it seems to say "life is too short to fool about with argument, you must dive in and become committed" to something. Sartre who calls himself an "atheist existentialist" is apparently committed to the belief that "hell is other people," but for most critics the main argument against existentialist philosophy is that it often rests on a highly specialised personal experience and, as such, is incommunicable.

Existential psychology, a new if rather diffuse movement in modern psychology with no specific founder but with a number of figures who have, perhaps against their will, acquired leader status. One of the key figures is the British psychiatrist, R. D. Laing, whose radical views on psychotherapy are counted as being heretical by the vast majority of his medical colleagues. Laing holds that many so-called neurotic and psychotic conditions are essentially not "abnormal" and merely represent extreme strategies by which an individual may adjust to environmental and personal stress. Instead of attempting to suppress or eliminate the psychosis in the traditional manner, one should lead the patient through it thus allowing the individual's "unconscious plan" for his own adjustment to be fulfilled.

Exorcism, the removal or ejection of an evil spirit by a ritual or prayer. It is easy to forget that the concept of insanity as representing a disorder of the brain, analogous to physical sickness of the body, is fairly recent in origin. Barely two centuries ago it was considered to be appropriate treatment to put lunatics into chains and beat them daily in the hope that the malevolent beings inhabiting them might be persuaded to depart. Tragically, many of the symptoms of severe forms of mental disorder induce such an apparent change in the personality of the individual as to suggest that an alien individual has indeed taken over their body, and this belief is still common in many parts of the world. Most religious systems have developed some ritual or set of rituals for expelling these demons, and while, not surprisingly, the practice of exorcism by the clergy has declined dramatically in the past century, it is still brought into play now and again in such circumstances as alleged hauntings, poltergeist phenomena, etc. From a scientific point of view exorcism must be counted as a superstitious rite, but its suggestive power in cases of hysteria, and perhaps even more serious mental illnesses, cannot be completely ruled out. General interest in the topic has been stimulated in part by the resurgence of the practice of Black Magic and witchcraft, largely in the form of experimental dabbling by young people, who no doubt become disillusioned when it fails to live up to its promise. Testimony to the pulling-power of this remnant of our superstitious past is the fact that a sensational and terrifying novel, *The Exorcist*, which its author claimed was based on fact, topped the best-seller lists in 1972, and the even more horrific movie-version became one of the most successful (in box office terms) films of all time. The Church of England, incidentally, takes anything but a dismissive line on the matter, and in fact employs a number of ordained priests as "licensed exorcists". These services are apparently much in demand.

Extra-sensory Perception. *See* **Section Q, VI.**

F

Fabian Society. In 1848 (the year of *The Communist Manifesto* by Marx and Engels) Europe was in revolt. In most countries the workers and intellectuals started bloody revolutions against the feudal ruling classes which were no less violently suppressed; hence on the continent socialism took on a Marxist tinge which to some extent it still retains. But at the same time England was undergoing a slow but nonviolent transition in her political and industrial life which led the workers in general to look forward to progress through evolution. Marxism never became an important movement in England even though it took its origin here. There were many reasons for this: the agitation of the Chartists (*q.v.*); the writings of Mill, Ruskin, and Carlyle; the reforms of Robert Owen; the religious movement led by the Wesleys; the Co-operative societies; the Christian socialists. Furthermore legislation stimulated by these bodies had led to an extension of the franchise to include a considerable number of wage-earners, remedial measures to correct some of the worst abuses of the factory system, recognition of the trade unions, etc.

This was the background against which the Fabian Society was founded in 1884 with the conviction that social change could be brought about by gradual parliamentary means. (The name is derived from Quintus Fabius Maximus, the Roman general nicknamed "Cunctator," the delayer, who achieved his successes in defending Rome against Hannibal by refusing to give direct battle.) It was a movement of brilliant intellectuals, chief among whom were Sidney and Beatrice Webb, H. G. Wells, G. B. Shaw, Graham Wallas, Sidney Olivier, and Edward Pease. The Society itself was basically a research institution which furnished the intellectual information for social reform and supported all contributing to the gradual attainment by parliamentary means of socialism.

The Webbs's analysis of society emphasised that individualist enterprise in capitalism was a hang-over from early days and was bound to defeat itself since socialism is the inevitable accompaniment of modern industrialism; the necessary result of popular government is control of their economic system by the people themselves. Utopian schemes had been doomed to failure because they were based on the fallacy that society is static and that islands of utopias could be formed in the midst of an unchanging and antagonistic environment. On the contrary, it was pointed out, society develops: "The new becomes old, often before it is consciously regarded as new." Social reorganisation cannot usefully be hastened by violent means but only through methods consonant with this natural historical progression—gradual, peaceful, and democratic. The Fabians were convinced that men are rational enough to accept in their common interest developments which can be demonstrated as necessary; thus public opinion will come to see that socialisation of the land and industries is essential in the same way that they came to accept the already-existing acts in respect of housing, insurance, medical care, and conditions of work.

The Society collaborated first in the formation of the Independent Labour Party and then with the more moderate Labour Party and the trade unions and Co-operative movement. But in general it disapproved of independent trade union action since change should come from the government and take political form. The class-war of Marx was rejected and so too was the idea of the exclusive role of the working class—reform must come from the enlightened co-operation of all classes—not from their opposition.

Faith Healing, the belief and practice of curing physical and mental ills by faith in some supernatural power, either allegedly latent in the individual (as with Christian Science) or drawn in some way from God. It is a characteristic of faith healing that it is supposed to be publicly demonstrable—*i.e.*, a "healer" will hold public meetings and invite sick people to come up to be cured on the platform. In the emotionally charged atmosphere which the healer generates, it is not unusual for people to show immediate and striking improvement in their illness, but the almost invariable rule is for relapses to occur within days or hours after the event. When remission is more permanent, the illness is generally hysterical in origin and will often return to the individual in some other form. Spiritualists claim that the healing in such cases is done not by "faith" but by direct intervention of the spirits of doctors, etc., who have died and passed on to another world. Perhaps the world's most famous faith healer in recent years was Harry Edwards (d. 1976), who had literally millions of letters from all parts of the world asking for the healing attention of his spirit guides. Many doctors, while remaining immensely sceptical about the origins and extent of this kind of therapy, are inclined to admit that it might have benefits when the sickness is mildly hysterical in origin. The real danger, of course, comes when patients seek unorthodox therapy before consulting their doctors in the first place.

Falangists. The Fascist Party of Spain founded in 1933 by José Antonio Primo de Rivera, son of the man who was dictator of the country from 1923 to 1930; he was shot by the Republicans. In 1937 the falangists who had shown unwelcome signs of social radicalism were merged with the other right-wing political groups to form the *Falange Española Tradicionalista y de las Juntas de Ofensive Nacional Sindicalistas* which replaced the Cortes (*i.e.* the Government) between 1939 and 1942 when the Cortes was reinstituted. The Falange is the only political party allowed in Spain. *See* **Fascism.**

Fascism. From the end of mediaeval times with the opening up of the world, the liberation of the mind and the release of business enterprise, a new spirit arose in Europe exemplified in such movements as the Renaissance, the Reformation, the struggle for democracy, the rise of capitalism, and the Industrial Revolution. With these movements there developed a certain tradition which, in spite of hindrances and disagreements or failures, was universally held both by right- and left-wing parties however strongly they might fail to agree on the best means of attaining what was felt to be a universal ideal. The hard core of this tradition involved: belief in reason and the possibility of human progress; the essential sanctity and dignity of human life; tolerance of widely different religious and political views; reliance on popular government and the responsibility of the rulers to the ruled; freedom of thought and criticism; the necessity of universal education; impartial justice and the rule of law; the desirability of universal peace. Fascism was the negation of every aspect of this tradition and took pride in being so. Emotion took the place of reason, the "immutable, beneficial, and fruitful inequality of classes" and the right of a self-constituted élite to rule them replaced universal suffrage because absolute authority "quick, sure, unanimous" led to action rather than talk. Contrary opinions are not allowed and justice is in the service of the state; war is desirable to advance the power of the state; and racial inequality made a dogma. Those who belong to the "wrong" religion, political party, or race are outside the law.

The attacks on liberalism and exaltation of the state derive largely from Hegel and his German followers; the mystical irrationalism from such 19th cent. philosophers as Schopenhauer, Nietzsche, and Bergson; from Sorel (*see* **Syndicalism**) came the idea of the "myth," and an image which would have the power to arouse the emotions of the masses and from Sorel also the rationale of violence and justification of force. But these philosophical justifications of fascism do not explain why it arose at all and why it arose where it did—in Italy, Germany, and Spain. These countries had one thing in common—disillusionment. Germany had lost the 1914–18 war, Italy had been on the winning side but was resentful about her small gains, Spain had sunk to the level of a third-rate power, and people were becoming increasingly restive under the reactionary powers of the Catholic Church, the landed aristocracy, and the army. In Marxist theory, fascism is the last fling of the ruling class and the bourgeoisie in their attempt to hold down the workers.

Italian Fascism. The corporate state set up by Benito Mussolini in Italy claimed to be neither capitalist nor socialist, and after its inception in 1922 the Fascist Party became the only recognised one. Its members wore black shirts, were organised in military formations, used the Roman greeting of the outstretched arm, and adopted as their slogan "Mussolini is always right." Membership of the Party was not allowed to exceed a number thought to be suited to the optimum size of a governing class and new candidates were drawn, after strict examinations, from the youth organisations. The Blackshirts, a fascist militia, existed separately from the army and were ruled by Fascist Headquarters.

At the head of government was Mussolini, "Il Duce" himself, a cabinet of fourteen ministers selected by him and approved by the King to supervise the various functions of government, and the Grand Council or directorate of the Fascist Party, all the members of which were chosen by the Duce. Parliament, which was not allowed to initiate legislation but only to approve decrees from above, consisted of a Senate with life-membership and a Chamber of Fasci and Corporations composed of nominated members of the Party, the National Council of Corporations, and selected representatives of the employers' and employees' confederations. Private enterprise was encouraged and protected but rigidly controlled; strikes were forbidden, but a Charter of Labour enforced the collaboration of workers and employers whose disputes were settled in labour courts presided over by the Party. All decisions relating to industry were government-controlled (*e.g.*, wages, prices, conditions of employment and dismissal, the expansion or limitation of production), and some industries such as mining, shipping, and armaments were largely state-owned.

Italian fascism served as a model in other countries, notably for the German National Socialist Party, in Spain and Japan, and most European nations between the wars had their small Fascist parties, the British version led by Sir Oswald Mosley being known as the British Union which relied on "strong-arm tactics", marches and violence. The Public Order Act of 1936 was passed to deal with it. Although fascism in all countries has certain recognisable characteristics, it would be wrong to think of it as an international movement taking fixed forms and with a clearly thought-out rationale as in the case of communism. While there have been minor revivals of interest in Fascism in Italy—presumably as a counter-move against the considerable inroads being made by the Communist party in that country—Fascism's final remaining bastion in Europe—Spain—began to crumble with the death of its dictator, General Franco, in 1975.

See **Falange, Nazism.**

Fatalism. *See* **Determinism.**

Feedback Cult is the name given to a curious fad which began in America in 1970 and which is interesting because it incorporates complicated scientific equipment and experimental psychological methods into its practice. The basis of the cult is as follows: for nearly fifty years it has been known that the brain is the source of varied electrical signals of very low power which can be detected by attaching electrodes to the scalp and amplifying the pulses emitted. Much scientific controversy has surrounded these pulses, and their interpretation by skilled clinicians can lead to the detection of hidden cerebral disorders such as tumours, epileptic foci, etc. The presence of one particular rhythm the so-called alpha wave, which beats at 14 cycles per second—is believed to be dependent upon whether or not the individual is "attending" to something, particularly in the visual field. It is this alpha rhythm, or rather its control, that is the basis of the feedback cult.

Within the past decade it has been discovered that when some people are connected to an electroencephalograph (the device which records brain rhythms) and are shown the recorded tracings of their own brain waves as they actually occur, they find it possible to modify and control the nature of the waves—the alpha in particular. This, a scientific curiosity rather than a major discovery, soon caught the attention of followers of yoga and other systems seeking enhanced relaxation, "mental discipline," etc. The argument was advanced that for centuries man had been seeking to exercise control over his own mental activities, without however having much opportunity to assess his success—or lack of it. The use of the EEG with the individual's brain waves "fed back" to him for inspection would remedy this. The result has been a sudden surge of lay interest in electroencephalography and a boom in the sale of small, portable EEG machines. Followers of the cult, who may sit for hours inspecting the output from their own brains and attempting to modify it at will, claim that the activity promotes mental "relaxation" and a greater and deeper understanding of their own personal problems. Psychologists are extremely dubious about the reality of this as mental therapy, and the feedback cult will probably die away as soon as some new and equally attractive scientific toy is developed.

Fetichism, originally a practice of the natives of West Africa and elsewhere of attributing magical properties to an object which was used as an amulet, for putting spells on others, or regarded as possessing dangerous powers. In psychology the term refers to a sexual perversion in which objects such as shoes, brassières, hair, etc., arouse sexual excitement.

Feudalism. The feudal system took its origins from Saxon times and broadly speaking lasted until the end of the 13th cent. It was a military and political organisation based on land tenure, for, of course, society throughout this period was based almost entirely on agriculture. The activities of men divided them into three classes or estates. The First Estate was the clergy, responsible for man's spiritual needs; the Second was the nobility, including kings and emperor as well as the lesser nobles; the Third was composed of all those who had to do with the economic and mainly agricultural life of Europe. The praying men, the fighting men and administrators, and the toilers were all held to be dependent on each other in a web of mutual responsibilities.

The theory of feudalism, although it by no means always worked out in practice, was as follows: the earth was God's and therefore no man owned land in the modern sense of the word. God had given the pope spiritual charge of men, and secular power over them to the emperor from whom kings held their kingdoms, and in turn the dukes and counts received the land over which they held sway from the king. Members of the Second Estate held their lands on the condition of fulfilling certain obligations to their overlord and to the people living under them, so when a noble received a fief or piece of land he became the vassal of the man who bestowed it. To him he owed military service for a specified period of the year, attendance at court, and giving his lord counsel. He undertook to ransom his lord when he fell into enemy hands and to contribute to his daughter's dowry and at the knighting of his son. In return the lord offered his vassal protection and justice, received the vassal's sons into his household and educated them for knighthood.

The system was complicated by the fact that large fiefs might be subdivided and abbots often governed church lands held in fief from nobles. The serf or toiling man dwelt on the land of a feudal noble or churchman where he rendered service by tilling the soil or carrying out his craft for his manorial lord in return for protection, justice, and the security of his life and land. He was given a share in the common lands or pastures from which he provided for his own needs. In the modern sense he was not free (although at a later stage he could buy his freedom) since he was attached to the soil and could not leave without the lord's permission. On the other hand he could neither be deprived of his land nor lose his livelihood. Feudal tenures were abolished in England by statute in 1660, although they had for long been inoperative. In Japan a feudal system existed up to 1871, in Russia until 1917, and many relics of it still linger on (*e.g.* the *mezzadria* system of land tenure in parts of Italy).

Flying Saucers. In June 1947 an American private pilot, Kenneth Arnold, saw a series of wingless objects flying through the air at a speed which he estimated at thousands of miles an hour. He later told the press that the objects "flew as a saucer would if you skipped it across the water," and the phrase "flying saucers" was erroneously born. What Arnold actually saw has never been satisfactorily explained—it was probably a flight of jet fighters reflecting the sun's rays in a way that made them appear as discs—but since that date literally hundreds of thousands of people all over the world have reported the sighting of strange objects in the sky, coming in a bewildering range of shapes and sizes. Initially the American Air Force launched an official enquiry—Project Bluebook—to attempt to solve the mystery of these "unidentified flying objects" or "U.F.O.s," which finally folded in 1969 after concluding that the bulk of the sightings were probably misinterpretations of natural phenomena and that there was no evidence for the commonly held view that earth was being visited by spacecraft from some other planetary system. A rather similar conclusion was arrived at by the famous University of Colorado project—the Condon Committee—which published its findings in 1968. Despite this clear-cut official attitude, belief in the existence of flying saucers and their origin as alien space vehicles is exceedingly widespread and is held very strongly by people in all walks of life. In 1959 this striking social phenomenon attracted the attention of the psychologist, C. G. Jung. He noticed that the press were inclined to report statements that saucers existed when made by prominent people and not publish contrary statements made by equally prominent people. He concluded that flying saucers were in some way welcome phenomena and in his brilliant little book, *Flying Saucers—a modern myth* he hypothesised that the U.F.O.s were the modern equivalent of "signs in the skies." It was Jung's contention that the saucers were looked upon as the harbingers of advanced alien civilisations who had come to save the world from its descent into nuclear catastrophe—archangels in modern dress in fact.

Whatever the validity of this imaginative view of U.F.O.s, it is undeniably true that they exercise a great fascination for millions of people, some of whom invest them with definite religious significance. The best example of the open incorporation of flying saucers into a religious belief system is to be found in the Aetherius Society, an international organisation with headquarters in Los Angeles but founded by a former London clerk, George King. Mr. King, who claims to be the mediumistic link between earth and the largely benevolent beings from outer space, regularly relays messages—notably from a Venusian known as Aetherius—to enthusiastic congregations at religious meetings. The sect, which is entirely sincere and dedicated in its beliefs, also makes pilgrimages to the tops of various mountains which have been "spiritually charged" with the aid of the spacebeings in their flying saucers.

Odd though such ideas may seem to most people, they can be readily understood within the context of the very marked decline in orthodox religious belief which we have seen in the past two decades. To an increasing number of people, many of whom feel a desperate need for spiritual guidance and enlightenment, the concepts of the traditionally Western religions seem somehow unsatisfactory. Many therefore turn to cults and splinter groups which use ideas and terminology which to them seem more at home in the twentieth century than those that sprung to life thousands of years ago. To members of the Aetherius Society, for example, the idea that Jesus Christ lives on Venus and rides around in a flying saucer is neither blasphemous nor ludicrous. As long as empty churches testify to the growing, if perhaps only temporary loss of contact between orthodox religions and the man-in-the-street, then one can expect such offbeat ideas as the cults surrounding flying saucers, and the science-fiction-like cult of Scientology (*q.v.*) to expand and flourish.

Fourierism. *See* **Utopianism.**

Freemasonry, a widespread, influential secret organisation of English origin. Although it can be traced back to the Middle Ages when itinerant working masons in England and Scotland were organised in lodges with secret signs for the recognition of fellow-members, modern freemasonry first arose in England in the early decades of the 18th cent. The first Grand Lodge was founded in London in 1716 and Freemasons' Hall was opened in 1776. With its clubs for discussion and social enjoyment (women were excluded) it met a need and became a well-known feature of English life. The movement quickly spread abroad to places which had direct trade links with England. The graded lodge structure, the social prestige conferred by membership, the symbolism, ritual and ceremony, and the emphasis on mutual help have had a lasting appeal. Interest in the occult had more appeal on the continent than in England. Until a decade or so ago, membership conferred definite business and social advantages, particularly in small communities where the leading middle-class figures were generally members. Recently this advantage has markedly declined and freemason lodges nowadays tend to be little more than worthy charitable organisations. Fear of secret societies has given freemasonry many opponents; it was condemned by the Roman Catholic Church, banned by Fascist dictators, and denounced by the Comintern. The fact that the movement's influence on religious and economic matters is slowly waning may be evidenced by the recent rumours that the Roman Catholic Church was expecting to lift its ban on Freemasonry.

Freudian theory. *See* Psychoanalysis.

Friends, The Society of. *See* Quakers.

Fundamentalism is a term covering a number of religious movements which adhere with the utmost rigidity to orthodox tenets; for example the Old Testament statement that the earth was created by God in six days and six nights would be held to be factual rather than allegorical or symbolic. There is a strong minority undercurrent of support for various Fundamental religions, including such sects as Jehovah's Witnesses, the Seventh Day Adventists, etc. Although the holding of rigid beliefs in the literal truth of the Bible might seem to be frequently contrary to modern scientific findings, the fundamentalists at least do not have the problems of compromise and interpretation to face, and among many simple-minded and poorly educated people this is no doubt a great attraction.

G

Game Theory, an approach to understanding human and animal behaviour which takes the view that psychological insight is best gained by studying the decisions which all living things make constantly and which govern the course of their lives. It proposes that life is basically a strategic game following complex rules which can probably only be understood by a study of the "decision units" as and when they occur. Because one is dealing with highly variable animals controlled by highly complex brains, and not with simple clockwork or electro-mechanical systems, the study of the rules which operate in the game of life is enormously complicated and thus game theory has quickly taken off into advanced mathematics. Game theory, incidentally, can be used to apply to individual action or to the behaviour of groups. Little of any predictive value has been put forward by the protagonists of this approach, but the use of computers to tackle the complex mathematics involved may well lead to some interesting advances.

Gestalt Psychology. In the latter half of the 19th cent. it became evident to psychologists that in principle there was no good reason why "mental" events should not be just as measurable and manageable as "physical" ones. Intensive studies of learning, memory, perception, and so on were therefore undertaken and the beginnings of an empirical science of psychology were underway. In the early part of the 20th cent. the experiments of Pavlov (*see* Behaviourism) and his co-workers suggested that the behaviour of an animal, or even men, might ultimately be reduced to a descriptive account of the activities of nervous reflex loops—the so-called conditioned reflexes. With the publication of Watson's important book on Behaviourism in 1914 it looked as though the transfer of psychological studies from the field of philosophy to that of science could now take place. Actually the over-simplified picture of cerebral and mental pictures which Behaviourism offered was rather comparable to the billiard ball view of the universe so fashionable in Victorian science. Just as Behaviourism implied that there was a fundamental building block (the conditioned reflex) from which all mental events could be constructed, so Victorian physics assumed that the entire universe could be described in terms of a vast collection of atoms pushing each other around like billiard balls. The development of nuclear physics was to shatter the latter dream and at the same time a challenge to the naive "reflex psychology" came from the Gestalt experimental school.

The founders of this school were Max Wertheimer, Kurt Koffka and Wolfgang Köhler three young psychologists who in 1912 were conducting experiments—notably in vision—which seemed to expose the inadequacies of the behaviourist position. The Pavlov–Watson view, as we have said, implied that complex sensory events were no more than a numerical sum of individual nervous impulses. Wertheimer's group proposed that certain facts of perceptual experiences (ruled out of court as subjective and therefore unreliable by Watson) implied that *the whole (Gestalt) was something more than simply the sum of its parts.* For example, the presentation of a number of photographs, each slightly different, in rapid series gives rise to cinematographic motion. In basic terms, the eye has received a number of discrete, "still" photographs, and yet "motion" is perceived. What, they asked, was the sensory input corresponding to this motion? Some processes within the brain clearly *added* something to the total input as defined in behaviourist terms. An obvious alternative—in a different sense modality—is that of the arrangement of musical notes. A cluster of notes played one way might be called a tune; played backwards they may form another tune, or may be meaningless. Yet in all cases the constituent parts are the same, and yet their relationship to one another is evidently vital. Once again the whole is something more than the simple sum of the parts.

The implications of all this appeared to be that the brain was equipped with the capacity to organise sensory input in certain well-defined ways, and that far from being misleading and scientifically unjustifiable, human subjective studies of visual experience might reveal the very principles of organisation which the brain employs. Take a field of dots, more or less randomly distributed; inspection of the field will soon reveal certain patterns or clusters standing out—the constellations in the night sky are a good illustration. There are many other examples, and Wertheimer and his colleagues in a famous series of experiments made some effort to catalogue them and reduce them to a finite number of "Laws of Perceptual Organisation" which are still much quoted today. *See* Q19, Q21.

Ghosts, belief in ghosts is one of the most common features of supernatural and mystical philosophy. At its roots it is based on the assumption that Man is essentially an individual created of two separate and distinct substances, mind and body. Most religious systems hold to this dualistic view (*see* Dualism), arguing that whereas the body is transient and destructible, the mind or spirit is permanent and survives the death of its physical host. The discarnate spirit is normally assumed to progress to some other realm ("Heaven," "Nirvana," "The Spirit World," etc.) whereupon it loses contact with the mortal world. Occasionally, however, for one reason or another, the spirits may not progress and may become trapped and unable to escape the material world. Traditionally this is supposed to occur when the death of the individual is precipitated by some great tragedy—murder, suicide, etc.—when the site of the tragedy is supposed to be haunted by the earthbound spirit. Although the library of the Society for Psychical Research is crammed with supposedly authentic accounts of hauntings of this kind, scientific interest in ghosts has been waning rapidly in recent years. At one time, in particular in the latter part of the 19th cent., with the upsurge of scientific interest in Spiritualism (*q.v.*), there were even attempts to call up ghosts in the laboratory. These led to spectacular opportunities for fraud on the part of Spiritualist mediums and the like, but in the long run added little to the cause of science. As we have said, belief in ghosts is largely dependent upon a parallel belief that the mind or soul of man is something essentially separate from the body. With the decline in belief of this notion (it is now almost totally dismissed by most scientists and philosophers) has come an inevitable decline in belief in ghosts.

Gnosticism. Among the many heresies of early Christianity, especially during its first two centuries, was a group which came under the heading of Gnosticism. This was a system or set of systems which attempted to combine Christian beliefs with others derived from Oriental and Greek sources, especially those which were of a mystical and metaphysical nature, such as the doctrines of Plato and Pythagoras. There were many Gnostic sects, the most celebrated being the Alexandrian school of Valentius (fl. *c.* 136–*c.* 160). "Gnosis" was understood not as meaning "knowledge" or "understanding" as we understand these words, but "revelation." As in other mystical religions, the ultimate object was individual salvation; sacraments took the most varied forms. Many who professed themselves Christians accepted Gnostic doctrines and even orthodox Christianity contains some elements of Gnostic mysticism. It was left to the bishops and theologians to decide at what point Gnosticism ceased to be orthodox and a difficult task this proved to be. Two of the greatest, Clement of Alexandria and his pupil Origen, unwittingly slipped into heresy when they tried to show that such men as Socrates and Plato, who were in quest of truth, were Christian in intention, and by their lives and works had prepared the way for Christ. Thus they contradicted Church doctrine which specifically said *Extra ecclesiam nulla salus*—outside the Church there is no salvation.

God and Man. The idea of gods came before the idea of God and even earlier in the evolution of religious thought there existed belief in spirits (*see* **Animism**). It was only as a result of a long period of development that the notion of a universal "God" arose, a development particularly well documented in the Old Testament. Here we are concerned only with the views of philosophers, the views of specific religious bodies being given under the appropriate headings. First, however, some definitions.

Atheism is the positive disbelief in the existence of a God. **Agnosticism** (a term coined by T. H. Huxley, the 19th cent. biologist and contemporary of Darwin) signifies that one cannot know whether God exists or not. **Deism** is the acceptance of the existence of God, not through revelation, but as a hypothesis required by reason. **Theism** also accepts the existence of God, but, unlike Deism, does not reject the evidence of revelation (*e.g.*, in the Bible or in the lives of the saints). **Pantheism** is the identification of God with all that exists (*i.e.*, with the whole universe). **Monotheism** is the belief in one God, **Polytheism** the belief in many (*see also* **Dualism**).

Early Greek Views. Among the early Greek philosophers, Thales (*c.* 624–565 B.C.) of Miletus, in Asia Minor, Anaximander (611–547 B.C.), his pupil, and Anaximenes (b. *c.* 570 B.C.), another Miletan, were men of scientific curiosity and their speculations about the origin of the universe were untouched by religious thought. They founded the scientific tradition of critical discussion. Heraclitus of Ephesus (*c.* 540–475 B.C.), was concerned with the problem of change. How does a thing change and yet remain itself? For him all things are flames—processes. "Everything is in flux, and nothing is at rest." Empedocles of Agrigentum in Sicily (*c.* 500–*c.* 430 B.C.) introduced the idea of opposition and affinity. All matter is composed of the so-called four elements—*earth, water, air*, and *fire*—which are in opposition or alliance with each other. All these were materialist philosophers who sought to explain the working of the universe without recourse to the gods.

Socrates, Plato, and Aristotle. Socrates (470–399 B.C.) was primarily concerned with ethical matters and conduct rather than the nature of the universe. For him goodness and virtue come from knowledge. He obeyed an "inner voice" and suffered death rather than give up his philosophy. He believed in the persistence of life after death and was essentially a monotheist. Plato (427–347 B.C.) was chiefly concerned with the nature of reality and thought in terms of absolute truths which were unchanging, logical, and mathematical. (*See* **Mind and Matter**.) Aristotle (384–322 B.C.) took his view of matter not from Democritus (atomic view) but from Empedocles (doctrine of four elements), a view which came to fit in well with orthodox mediaeval theology. Matter is conceived of as potentially alive and striving to attain its particular form, being moved by divine spirit or mind (*nous*). (An acorn, for example, is matter which contains the form "oak-tree" towards which it strives.) Thus there is a whole series from the simplest level of matter to the perfect living individual. But there must be a supreme source of all movement upon which the whole of Nature depends, a Being that Aristotle describes as the "Unmoved Mover," the ultimate cause of all becoming in the universe. This Being is pure intelligence, a philosopher's God, not a personal one. Unlike Plato, Aristotle did not believe in survival after death, holding that the divine, that is the immortal element in man, is mind.

Among the later Greek thinkers the Epicureans were polytheists whose gods, however, were denied supernatural powers. The Stoics built up a materialist theory of the universe, based on the Aristotelian model. To them God was an all-pervading force, related to the world as the soul is related to the body, but they conceived of it as material. They developed the mystical side of Plato's idealism and were much attracted by the astrology coming from Babylonia. They were pantheists. The Sceptics were agnostics.

From Pagan to Christian Thought. Philo, "the Jew of Alexandria," who was about 20 years older than Jesus, tried to show that the Jewish scriptures were in line with the best in Greek thought. He introduced the *Logos* as a bridge between the two systems. Philo's God is remote from the world, above and beyond all thought and being, and as His perfection does not permit direct contact with matter the divine *Logos* acts as intermediary between God and man. Plotinus (204–70), a Roman, and the founder of Neoplatonism, was the last of the great pagan philosophers. Like Philo, he believed that God had created the world indirectly through emanations—beings coming from Him but not of Him. The world needs God but God does not need the world. Creation is a fall from God, especially the human soul when enmeshed in the body and the world of the senses, yet (*see* **Determinism**) man has the ability to free himself from sense domination and turn towards God. Neoplatonism was the final stage of Greek thought drawing its inspiration from the mystical side of Plato's idealism and its ethics from Stoicism.

Christianity: The Fathers and the Schoolmen. It was mainly through St. Augustine (354–430), Bishop of Hippo in North Africa, that certain of the doctrines of Neoplatonism found their way into Christianity. Augustine also emphasised the concept of God as all good, all wise, all knowing, transcendent, the Creator of the universe out of nothing. But, he added, since God knows everything, everything is determined by Him forever. This is the doctrine of predestination and its subsequent history is discussed under **Determinism**.

In the early centuries of Christianity, as we have seen, some found it difficult to reconcile God's perfection with His creation of the universe and introduced the concept of the *Logos* which many identified with Christ. Further, it came to be held that a power of divine origin permeated the universe, namely the Holy Spirit or Holy Ghost. Some theory had to be worked out to explain the relationships of these three entities whence arose the conception of the Trinity. God is One; but He is also Three: Father, Son (the *Logos* or Christ), and Holy Ghost.

This doctrine was argued by the Apologists and the Modalists. The former maintained that the *Logos* and the Holy Spirit were emanations from God and that Jesus was the *Logos* in the form of a man. The Modalists held that all three Persons of the Trinity were God in three forms or modes: the *Logos* is God creating, the Holy Spirit God reasoning, and God is God being. This led to a long discussion as to whether the *Logos* was an emanation from God or God in another form; was the *Logos* of like *nature* with God or of the same *substance*? This was resolved at the Council of Nicaea (325) when Athanasius formulated the orthodox doctrine against Arius (*q.v.*): that the one Godhead is a Trinity of the same substance, three Persons of the same nature—Father, Son, and Holy Ghost.

St. Thomas Aquinas (1227–74), influenced greatly by Aristotle's doctrines, set the pattern for all subsequent Catholic belief even to the present time. He produced rational arguments for God's existence: *e.g.*, Aristotle's argument that, since movement exists, there must be a prime mover, the Unmoved Mover or God; further, we can see that things in the universe are related in a scale from the less to the more complex, from the less to the more perfect, and this leads us to suppose that at the peak there must be a Being with absolute perfection. God is the first and final cause of the universe, absolutely perfect, the Creator of everything out of nothing. He reveals Himself in his Creation and rules the universe through His perfect will. How Aquinas dealt with the problem of predestination is told under **Determinism**.

Break with Mediaeval Thought. Renaissance thinkers, free to think for themselves, doubted the validity of the arguments of the Schoolmen but most were unwilling to give up the idea of God (nor would it have been safe to do so). Mystics (*see* **Mysticism**) or near-mystics such as Nicholas of Cusa (*c.* 1401–64) and Jacob Boehme (1575–1624) taught that God was not to be found by reason but was a fact of the immediate intuition of the mystical experience. Giordano Bruno held that God was immanent in the infinite universe. He is the unity of all opposites, a unity without opposites, which the human mind cannot grasp. Bruno was burned at the stake in 1600 at the instigation of the Inquisition (a body which, so we are told, never caused pain to anyone since it was the civil power, not the Inquisition, that carried out the unpleasant sentences) for his heresy.

Francis Bacon, who died in 1626, separated, as was the tendency of that time, science from religion. The latter he divided into the two categories of natural and revealed theology. The former, through the study of nature, may give convincing proof of the existence of a God but nothing more. Of revealed theology he said: " we must quit the small vessel of human reason . . . as we are obliged to obey the divine law, though our will murmurs against it, so we are obliged to believe in the word of God, though our reason is shocked at it." Hobbes (d. 1679) was a complete materialist and one feels that obeisance to the notion was politic rather than from conviction. However, he does mention God as starting the universe; in motion infers that God is corporeal but denies that His nature can be known.

From Descartes Onwards. Descartes (1596–1650) separated mind and body as different entities but believed that the existence of God could be deduced by the fact that the idea of him existed in the mind. Whatever God puts into man, including his ideas, must be real. God is self-caused, omniscient, omnipotent, eternal, all goodness and truth. But Descartes neglected to explain how mind separate from body can influence body, or God separate from the world can influence matter.

Spinoza (1632–77) declared that all existence is embraced in one substance—God, the all-in-all. He was a pantheist and as such was rejected by his Jewish brethren. But Spinoza's God has neither personality nor consciousness, intelligence nor purpose, although all things follow in strict law from His nature. All the thought of everyone in the world, make up God's thoughts.

Bishop Berkeley (1685–1753) took the view that things exist only when they are perceived, and this naturally implies that a tree, for example, ceases to exist when nobody is looking at it. This problem was solved to his own satisfaction by assuming that God, seeing everything, prevented objects from disappearing when we were not present. The world is a creation of God but it is a spiritual or mental world, not a material one.

Hume (1711–76), who was a sceptic, held that human reason cannot demonstrate the existence of God and all past arguments to show that it could were fallacious. Yet we must believe in God since the basis of all hope, morality, and society is based upon the belief. Kant (1724–1804) held a theory similar to that of Hume. We cannot know by reason that God exists, nor can we prove on the basis of argument anything about God. But we can form an idea of the whole of the universe, the one Absolute Whole, and personify it. We need the idea of God on which to base our moral life, although this idea of God is transcendent, *i.e.*, goes beyond experience.

William James (1842–1910), the American philosopher (*see* **Pragmatism**), held much the same view: God cannot be proved to exist, but we have a will to believe which must be satisfied, and the idea works in practice. Hegel (1770–1831) thought of God as a developing process, beginning with " the Absolute " or First Cause and finding its highest expression in man's mind, or reason. It is in man that God most clearly becomes aware of Himself. Finally Comte (1798–1857), the positivist, held that religion belongs to a more primitive state of society and, like many modern philosophers, turned the problem over to believers as being none of the business of science.

Golden Dawn, Order of, a strange but intellectually influential secret society founded in 1887 by three former Rosicrucians (*q.v.*). The Society, which was but one of the large number of occult organisations which flourished in the latter half of the 19th cent., was particularly interesting because it attracted so many scholarly eccentrics to its ranks. These included the poet W. B. Yeats, the actress Florence Farr, the writers Arthur Machen and Algernon Blackwood and the poetess Dion Fortune. A member with a less savoury reputation was the notorious Aleister Crowley who was ultimately expelled from the order for practising Black Magic. Essentially the movement, like others of its kind, professed to offer important secrets of occult knowledge, and taught its followers the basic principles of White, as opposed to Black Magic. Mainly harmless in their aims and activities, societies such as this served largely as pastimes for individuals of intellectual and academic standing who found the concepts and rituals of the Established Church too dull for their inquisitive minds. Most members of the Order of the Golden Dawn either became disillusioned when the white magic, which they had so arduously studied, failed to provide any genuine supernatural results and gave up in disgust, or broke away to form their own rival groups. Though these often had equally glamorous names and rituals, they tended to be no more successful and themselves vanished into the mists of obscurity. Today so-called White Magic has become fashionable with many young people, no doubt as the result of the almost total collapse of the authority of orthodox religion, but it is noticeable that such interest is generally to be found among the less well-educated and intelligent. White Magic had its intellectual heyday in the 19th cent. and it is unlikely ever to attract such sustained academic interest again.

Good and Evil.

Early Philosophers' Views. The early Greek philosophers were chiefly concerned with the laws of the universe, consequently it was common belief that knowledge of these laws, and living according to them, constituted the supreme good. Heraclitus, for example, who taught that all things carried with them their opposites, held that good and evil were like two notes in a harmony, necessary to each other. " It is the opposite which is good for us." Democritus, like Epicurus (*q.v.*), held that the main goal of life is happiness, but happiness in moderation. The good man is not merely the one who *does* good but who always *wants* to do so: "You can tell the good man not by his deeds alone but by his desires." Such goodness brings happiness, the ultimate goal. On the other hand, many of the wandering Sophist teachers taught that good was merely social convention, that there are no absolute principles of right and wrong, that each man should live according to his desires and make his own moral code. To Socrates knowledge was the highest good because doing wrong is the result of ignorance: "no man is voluntarily bad." Plato and Aristotle, differing in many other respects, drew attention to the fact that man is composed of three parts: his desires and appetites, his will, and his reason. A man whose reason rules his will and appetites is not only a good but a happy man; for happiness is not an aim in itself but a by-product of the good life. Aristotle, however, emphasised the goal of self-realisation, and thought that if the goal of life is (as Plato had said) a rational attitude towards the feelings and desires, it needs to be further defined. Aristotle defined it as the "Golden Mean"—the good man is one who does not go to extremes but balances one extreme against another. Thus courage is a mean between cowardice and foolhardiness. The later philosophers Philo and Plotinus held that evil was in the very nature of the body and its senses. Goodness could only be achieved by giving up the life of the senses and, freed from the domination of the body, turning to God, the source of goodness.

Christian Views. St. Augustine taught that everything in the universe is good. Even those things which appear evil are good in that they fit with the harmony of the universe like shadows in a painting. Man should turn his back on the pleasures of the world and turn to the love of God. Peter Abelard (1079–1142) made the more sophisticated distinction when he suggested that the wrongness of an act lies not in the act itself, but in the intention of the doer: "God considers not what is done but in what spirit it is done; and the merit or praise of the agent lies not in the deed but in the intention." If we do what we believe to be right, we may err, but we do not sin. The only sinful man is he who deliberately sets out to do what he knows to be wrong. St. Thomas Aquinas agreed with Aristotle in that he believed the highest good to be realisation of self as God has ordained, and he also agreed with Abelard that intention is important. Even a good act is not good unless the doer intended it to have good consequences. Intention will not make a bad act good, but it is the only thing that will make a good act genuinely good.

In general, Christianity has had difficulties in solving the problem of the existence of evil; for even when one accepts that the evil men do is somehow tied up with the body, it is still difficult to answer the question: how could an all-good God create evil? This is answered in one of two ways: (*a*) that Adam was given free-will and chose to sin (an answer which still does not explain how sin could exist anywhere in the universe of a God who created everything); (*b*) by denying the reality of evil as some Christians have chosen to do (*e.g.*, Christian Science *q.v.*). The Eastern religions, on the other hand (*see* **Zoroastrianism**), solved the problem in a more realistic way by a dualism which denied that their gods were the creators of the whole universe and allowed the existence of at least two gods, one good and one evil. In Christianity there is, of course, a Devil, but it is not explained whence his evil nature came.

Later Philosophic Views. Hobbes equated good with pleasure, evil with pain. They are relative to the individual man in the sense that "one man's meat is another man's poison." Descartes believed that the power to distinguish between good and evil given by God to man is not complete, so that man does evil through ignorance. We act with insufficient knowledge and on inadequate evidence. Locke, believing that at birth the mind is a blank slate, held that men get their opinions of right and wrong from their parents. By and large, happiness is good and pain is evil. But men do not always agree over what is pleasurable and what not. Hence laws exist and these fall into three categories: (1) the divine law; (2) civil laws; (3) matters of opinion or reputation which are enforced by the fact that men do not like to incur the disapproval of their friends. We learn by experience that evil brings pain and good acts bring pleasure, and, basically, one is good because not to be so would bring discomfort.

Kant (*see* **God and Man**) found moral beliefs to be inherent in man whether or not they can be proved by reason. There is a categorical imperative which makes us realise the validity of two universal laws: (1) "always act in such a way that the maxim determining your conduct might well become a universal law; act so that you can will that everybody shall follow the principle of your action; (2) "always act so as to treat humanity, whether in thine own person or in that of another, in every case as an end and never as a means."

Schopenhauer (1788–1860) was influenced by Buddhism and saw the will as a blind impelling striving, and desire as the cause of all suffering. The remedy is to regard sympathy and pity as the basis of all morality and to deny one's individual will. This is made easier if we realise that everyone is part of the Universal Will and therefore the one against whom we are struggling is part of the same whole as ourselves.

John Stuart Mill and Jeremy Bentham were both representatives of the Utilitarian school, believing that good is the greatest good (happiness) of the greatest number (*see* **Utilitarianism**). Lastly, there is the view held mostly by political thinkers that good is what is good for the state or society in general (*see* **State and Man**).

Graphology, the study of the analysis of human handwriting. There are two approaches to this topic and it is important to separate them clearly. The first involves the attempt on the part of an expert to decide from looking at a signature (*a*) to whom it belongs, and (*b*) whether or not it is forgery. This art is a legitimate, though tricky area of study, and graphologists have been called in as expert witnesses in courts of law. The second approach involves attempts to detect such tenuous variables as character from a study of an individual's handwriting, and the facts here are altogether less clear. Psychologists find it difficult enough to assess character or personality in a face-to-face interview and even when they are equipped with a range of special tests. The general opinion here would seem to be that some slight information might be revealed by a careful study of handwriting, but that the overall effect would be too unreliable for this kind of graphology to be of practical value.

Greater World Spiritualists. Spiritualism, as an organised religion, holds the view that the human personality survives death, and that it is possible to communicate with the spirits of those who have died in the physical sense. Relatively little importance is attached to the divinity of Jesus Christ, which is of course the cornerstone of the Christian faith. Some Spiritualists, however, hold a kind of halfway house position, believing both that Jesus was the son of God, and also that communication with the spirit world is not only possible but also a "lost aspect" of Christian teachings. The most significant group holding this view are the Greater World Christian Spiritualists Association, founded in 1931. Their teachings are based on trance addresses received through the mediumship of Winifred Moyes. Despite the fact that her control in the spirit world was named "Zodiac," Christian Spiritualists claim that their philosophy is closer to the original teachings of Jesus than that of the orthodox Church today.

Guild Socialism, a British form of syndicalism (*q.v.*) created in 1906 by an architect, A. J. Penty, who was soon joined by A. R. Orage, S. G. Hobson, and G. D. H. Cole. The background to the movement was the situation that, although at that time the Labour Party had 29 members in the House of Commons, a period of severe economic crisis had shown the government unwilling and the Labourites unable to do anything about it; the workers were resorting again to direct action to secure their demands and the democratic and constitutional methods to which the Fabians had partly persuaded them seemed to have failed. The guild socialists advocated a restoration of the mediaeval guild system as was being recommended by the French syndicalists whose programme involved a return to direct economic action, a functional industrial structure, return of craftsmanship, and distrust of the state. Guild socialists believed that value was created by society as a whole rather than by individuals singly, and that capitalist economists had recommended the acquisition of wealth without emphasising the social responsibilities which wealth should bring. The trade unions were to be organised to take over and run their own industries after nationalisation. Thus guild socialists were not only against capitalism but also against state socialism in which the state took over the control of industry. Political authority was held to be uncongenial to human freedom and therefore nothing was to be gained by the substitution of state bureaucracy for capitalist control. The National Guilds League, formed in 1915, advocated the abolition of the wages system, self-government in industry, control by a system of national guilds acting in conjunction with other functional democratic organisations in the community. This body was dissolved in 1925, but the theories of guild socialism have undoubtedly influenced British socialism.

Gurdjieff, Russian–Greek mystic who set up an occult commune near Paris in the 1930s, to which were attracted a host of the intellectual and literary avant garde of the time. His teachings, which are immensely obscure, are presented in allegorical form in a lengthy philosophical novel, *All and Everything*, which has the peculiar sub-title "Beelzebub's Tales to his Grandson." Opinions as to the merits of Gurdjieff's ideas are strikingly varied, some commentators hold that he was one of the century's leading philosophers, others that he was a brazen confidence trickster with a vivid personality and the gift of making trivial observations sound pregnant with meaning. The truth probably lies somewhere in between the two extremes and, despite the fact that a number of highly intelligent individuals still espouse his cause two decades after his death, most people continue to find his books largely unreadable and his philosophy muddled and pretentious.

H

Heresy, originally meant a sect or school of thought holding views different from others (*e.g.*, Pharisees and Sadducees within Judaism). Later it came to mean beliefs contrary to orthodox teaching (*e.g.*, Arianism, Apollinarianism, Nestorianism).

Hinduism, the religion and social institutions of the great majority of the people of India. Hinduism has no fixed scriptural canon but its doctrines are to be found in certain ancient works, notably the *Veda*, the *Brahmanas*, the *Upanishads*, and the *Bhagavad-gita*. The dark-skinned Dravidians invaded India between about 3250 and 2750 B.C. and established a civilisation in the Indus valley. They were polytheists who worshipped a number of nature-gods; some elements of their beliefs persisted into Hinduism. They were subdued by a light-skinned Nordic people who invaded from Asia Minor and Iran about 1500 B.C. The language of these Aryan people was Vedic, parent of Sanskrit in which their religious literature (the Vedas) came to be written after many centuries of oral transmission.

The *Veda* or Sacred Lore has come down to us in the form of mantras or hymns of which there are four great collections, the best-known being the *Rig-Veda*. These Vedic Aryans worshipped nature-deities, their favourites being Indra (rain), Agni (fire), and Surya (the sun). Their religion contained no idolatry but became contaminated by the more primitive beliefs of the conquered Dravidians. Sacrifice and ritual became predominant in a ceremonial religion.

As a reaction a more philosophic form arose (*c.* 500 B.C.) with its scriptures in the *Upanishads*. At its highest level, known as Brahmanism, belief is in a subtle and sophisticated form of monotheism (Brahman is an impersonal, all-embracing spirit), but there is a tolerant acceptance of more primitive beliefs. Thus Vishnu (a conservative principle) and Siva (a destructive principle) grew out of Vedic conceptions. The two great doctrines of Hinduism are *karma* and transmigration. The universal desire to be reunited with the absolute (*atman* or Brahman) can be satisfied by following the path of knowledge. Life is a cycle of lives (*samsara*) in which man's destiny is determined by his deeds (*karma*) from which he may seek release (*moksa*) through ascetic practices or the discipline of Yoga (*q.v.*). Failure to achieve release means reincarnation—migration to a higher or lower form of life after death—until the ultimate goal of absorption in the absolute is reached.

In the great Sanskrit epic poems *Ramayana* and *Mahabharata* the deity takes three forms, represented by the divine personalities of Brahma, Vishnu, and Siva. There are also lower gods, demi-gods, supernatural beings, and members of the trinity may even become incarnate, as Vishnu became identified with Krishna, one of the heroes of the *Mahabharata* and the well-known *Bhagavad-gita*.

The ritual and legalistic side of Brahmanism is the caste system based on the elaborate codes of the *Law of Manu*, according to which God created distinct orders of men as He created distinct species of animals and plants. Men are born to be Brahmans, soldiers, agriculturists, or servants, but since a Brahman may marry a woman from any of these castes, an endless number of sub-castes arises.

Hinduism has always shown great tolerance for varieties of belief and practice. Ideas pleasant and unpleasant have been assimilated: fetichism, demon-cults, animal-worship, sexual-cults (such as the rites of *Kali* in Calcutta). Today, as would be expected in a country which is in the throes of vast social change, Hinduism itself is changing. Under the impact of modern conditions new ideas are destroying old beliefs and customs. *See also* Jainism, Sikhism.

Holy Rollers. Contrary to general belief there is no single individual religious group calling themselves Holy Rollers; rather this is a generic term referring to a number of minor revivalist groups whose members work themselves into an ecstatic frenzy in the course of religious worship. Swooning and fainting are probably the most popular methods of expressing this kind of religious ecstasy, but "speaking with tongues" (*i.e.*, babbling nonsense), snake handling (many believers die from snake venom as a consequence) and uncontrolled dancing are also featured. Athletic religious worship of this kind is of course of great interest to psychologists. Anthropologists are equally interested, for they see in such behaviour patterns vivid reminders—if such are needed—that mankind has a history that predates our present culture by millions and not just by thousands of years.

Homoeopathy, a branch of fringe medicine whose motto *Similia Similibus Curantur* (like cures like) sums up its controversial approach to therapy. In essence the homoeopathists claim that a disease can be treated by administering quite minute doses of a substance which produce symptoms (in the healthy person) similar to those induced by the disease itself. The founder and populariser of this unusual approach to medicine was the German Samuel Hahnemann who was born in 1775, a friend of the physician Mesmer who propagated hypnotherapy. Hahnemann lived to see his ideas spread across the civilised world and despite the grave theoretical difficulties implicit in the question of how the very minute dosages actually achieve any result at all, it remained a respectable approach of medicine until the latter half of the last century. Even today a number of qualified doctors still employ homoeopathic ideas within the framework of the national health service, and the late King George V was treated by the eminent homoeopathist, Sir John Weir, but it seems nevertheless to be in slow but steady decline. This is probably due not to any revealed deficiences in homoeopathy itself, but rather to the extraordinary advances which have been made in orthodox medicine in the last few decades.

Humanism, the term applied to (1) a system of education based on the Greek and Latin classics; and (2) the vigorous attitudes that accompanied the end of the Middle Ages and were represented at different periods by the Renaissance, the Reformation, the Industrial Revolution, and the struggle for democracy. These include: release from ecclesiastical authority, the liberation of the intellect, faith in progress, the belief that man himself can improve his own conditions without supernatural help and, indeed, has a duty to do so. "Man is the measure of all things" is the keynote of humanism. The humanist has faith in man's intellectual and spiritual resources not only to bring knowledge and understanding of the world but to solve the moral problems of how to use that knowledge. That man should show respect to man irrespective of class, race or creed is fundamental to the humanist attitude to life. Among the fundamental moral principles he would count those of freedom, justice, tolerance and happiness.

Today the idea that people can live an honest, meaningful life without following a formal religious creed of some kind does not seem particularly shocking. It is an interesting gauge of the rapid change in social attitudes to religion that when, less than twenty years ago, the psychologist Margaret Knight tentatively advanced this thesis in a short B.B.C. talk, public opinion seemed to be outraged and both Mrs. Knight and the B.B.C. were openly attacked by the popular press for immoral and seditious teachings.

Hussites, the followers of John Hus, the most famous pupil of John Wyclif. He was the rector of Prague University and, although it is now by no means certain that his beliefs were heretical, he was condemned to death for heresy and burnt at the stake in 1415 at Constance whence he had come with a safe conduct issued by the Emperor Sigismund of Hungary. The latter based his action on the doctrine that no faith need be kept with heretics, but it is obvious that the main objection to Hus was his contempt for authority of any kind. After their leader's death, the Hussites became a formidable body in Bohemia and Moravia. They took up arms on behalf of their faith, their religion being strongly imbued with political feeling (hostility to Germanism and to the supremacy of the Roman Church). Their religious struggles for reform led to the Hussite Wars during which the movement splintered into several groups.

I

I Ching, the Chinese "Book of Changes" which is supposed to provide a practical demonstration of the truths of ancient Chinese philosophy. The method consists of casting forty-nine sticks into two random heaps, or more simply, of tossing three coins to see if there is a preponderance of heads or tails. The coins are cast six times whereupon the head-tail sequence achieved is referred to a coded series of phrases in the book, which are supposed to relate in some way to the question held in the mind when the sticks or coins are being cast. The phrases are without exception vague, and platitudinous remarks such as "Evil people do not further the perseverance of the superior man," etc., abound. Consequently it is not difficult to read into such amorphous stuff a suitable "interpretation" or answer to one's unspoken question. The I Ching might well be looked upon as an entertaining parlour game, but it is currently a great fad in Europe and America and is taken with great seriousness by an astonishing number of people.

Idealism, in a philosophical sense, the belief that there is no matter in the universe, that all that exists is mind or spirit. *See* **Mind and Matter** and **Realism**.

Illuminati, a secret society founded in 1776 by Adam Weishaupt, a Bavarian professor of canon law at Ingolstadt, in an attempt to combat superstition and ignorance by founding an association for rational enlightenment and the regeneration of the world. "He tried to give the social ideals of the Enlightenment realisation by conspiratorial means" (J. M. Roberts, *The Mythology of the Secret Societies*, 1972). Under conditions of secrecy it sought to penetrate and control the masonic lodges for subversive purposes. Among its members were Goethe and Schiller. The Order spread to Austria, Italy and Hungary but was condemned by the Roman Catholic Church and dissolved in 1785 by the Bavarian government.

Immortality. The belief in a life after death has been widely held since the earliest times. It has certainly not been universal, nor has it always taken a form which everyone would find satisfying. In the early stages of human history or prehistory everything contained a spirit (*see* **Animism**) and it is obvious from the objects left in early graves that the dead were expected to exist in some form after death. The experience of dreams, too, seemed to suggest to the unsophisticated that there was a part of man which could leave his body and wander elsewhere during sleep. In order to save space, it will be helpful to classify the various types of belief which have existed in philosophical thought regarding this problem: (1) There is the idea that, although *something* survives bodily death, it is not necessarily eternal. Thus most primitive peoples were prepared to believe that man's spirit haunted the place around his grave and that food and drink should be set out for it, but that this spirit did not go on forever and gradually faded away. (2) The ancient Greeks and Hebrews believed for the most part that the souls of the dead went to a place of shades there to pine for the world of men. Their whining ghosts spent eternity in a dark, uninviting region in misery and remorse. (3) Other people, and there were many more of these, believed in the transmigration of souls with the former life of the individual determining whether his next life would be at a higher or lower level. Sometimes this process seems to have been thought of as simply going on and on, by others (*e.g.*, in Hinduism and Buddhism) as terminating in either non-sentience or union with God but in any case in annihilation of the self as self. Believers in this theory were the Greek philosophers Pythagoras, Empedocles, Plato (who believed that soul comes from God and strives to return to God, according to his own rather confused notions of the deity. If it fails to free itself completely from the body it will sink lower and lower from one body to another.) Plotinus held similar views to Plato, and many other religious sects in addition to those mentioned have believed in transmigration. (4) The belief of Plato and Aristotle that if souls continue to exist after death there is no reason why they should not have existed before birth (this in part is covered by (3)), but some have pointed out that eternity does not mean "from now on," but the whole of time before and after "now"—nobody, however, so far as one knows, held that *individual* souls so exist. (5) The theory that the soul does not exist at all and therefore immortality is meaningless: this was held by Anaximenes in early Greek times; by Leucippus, Democritus, and the other Greek atomists; by the Epicureans from the Greek Epicurus to the Roman Lucretius; by the British Hobbes and Hume; by Comte of France; and William James and John Dewey of America. (6) The thesis, held notably by Locke and Kant, that although we cannot prove the reality of soul and immortality by pure reason, belief in them should be held for moral ends. (For the orthodox Christian view *see* **God and Man, Determinism and Free-will.**) From this summary we can see that many philosophies and religions (with the important exceptions of Islam and Christianity) without denying a future life do deny the permanence of the individual soul in anything resembling its earthly form (*see* **Spiritualism, Psychic research**).

Imperialism, the practice by a country, which has become a nation and embarked upon commercial and industrial expansion, of acquiring and administering territories, inhabited by peoples usually at a lower stage of development, as colonies or dependencies. Thus the "typical" imperialist powers of the 19th cent. and earlier were Britain, Belgium, Holland, Spain, and Portugal, whilst Germany, Italy, and Japan, which either did not have unity during this period or adequate industrial expansion, tried to make good their lacks in this direction by war in the 20th cent. The term "imperialism" is not easy to define today (although often enough used as a term of abuse). There is economic imperialism exerted, not through armies, but through economic penetration. There is what may be described as ideological imperialism, *e.g.*, the anti-communist crusade that led America (in the name of freedom) into acts of appalling inhumanity in Vietnam; the dogmatism that led the Soviet Union into the invasion of Czechoslovakia. The Afrikaners in South Africa pass laws to permit the exploitation of the black and coloured peoples in their midst. Imperialism is a dangerous word and, before using it, we would do well to remember the retort of a British statesman who, when lecturing in America prior to Indian independence, was asked by an elderly matron "What are you going to do about the Indians?" "Which Indians, madam —ours or yours?"

Irrationalism. An attitude that puts emotion and passion before reason, and which can be exploited for dubious ends.

Islam, the religion of which Mohammed (570–632) was the prophet, the word signifying submission to the will of God. It is one of the most widespread of religions. Its adherents are called Moslems or Muslims. Islam came later than the other great monotheistic religions (Judaism and Christianity) and may be regarded in some respects as a heresy. Mohammed accepted the inspiration of the Old Testament and claimed to be a successor to Moses, and although he did not recognise Jesus as God, he did recognise Him as a prophet.

The sacred book of Islam is the Koran, the most influential book in the world next to the Bible. According to Islamic belief the words were revealed to the prophet by God through the angel Gabriel at intervals over a period of 20 years, first at his native Mecca, and then at Medina. The book is divided into 114 *suras* or chapters: all but one begin with the words: "In the name of Allah, the Merciful, the Compassionate." It is written in classical Arabic, and Moslems memorise much or all of it. The Koran superseded the Gospel as Mohammed superseded Christ. Its ethical teachings are high.

The great advantage of Mohammedism is that, like orthodox Judaism, it is a literal-minded religion lived in everyday life. No Moslem is in any doubt as to exactly how he should carry on in the events of his day. He has five duties: (1) Once in his life he must say with absolute conviction: "There is no God but Allah, and Mohammed is His Prophet." (2) Prayer preceded by ablution must be five times daily—on rising, at noon, in mid-afternoon, after sunset, and before retiring. The face of the worshipper is turned in the direction of Mecca. (3) The giving of alms generously, including provisions for the poor. (4) The keeping of the fast of Ramadan, the holy month, during which believers in good health may neither eat nor drink nor indulge in worldly pleasures between sunrise and sunset. (5) Once in his life a Moslem, if he can, must make the pilgrimage to Mecca. In addition, drinking, gambling, and the eating of pork are forbidden and circumcision is practised. Polygamy is permitted, although decreasing; sexual relations outside marriage are disapproved of; marriage is only with the wife's consent; and divorce may be initiated by either husband or wife. A great advantage in the spread of Islam has been its lack of race prejudice.

Mohammed's main achievements were the destruction of idolatry, the welding of warring tribes into one community, the progress of a conquest which led after his death to the great and cultured empire which spread throughout the Middle East into north Africa, north India, and ultimately to Spain. That it did not spread all over Europe was due to the Muslim defeat by Charles Martel at Tours in 732 A.D.

J

Jainism. The Jains are a small Indian sect, largely in commerce and finance, numbering about 2 million. Their movement founded by Vardhamana, called Mahavira (the great hero), in the 6th cent. B.C. arose rather earlier than Buddhism in revolt against the ritualism and impersonality of Hinduism (*q.v.*). It rejects the authority of the early Hindu Vedas and does away with many of the Hindu deities whose place is largely taken by Jainism's twenty-four immortal saints; it despises caste distinctions and modifies the two great Hindu doctrines of *karma* and transmigration. Jain philosophy is based on *ahimsa*, the sacredness of all life, regarding even plants as the brethren of mankind, and refusing to kill even the smallest insect.

Jehovah's Witnesses, a religious body who consider themselves to be the present-day representatives of a religious movement which has existed since Abel "offered unto God a more excellent sacrifice than Cain, by which he obtained witness that he was righteous." Abel was the first "witness," and amongst others were Enoch, Noah, Abraham, Moses, Jeremiah, and John the Baptist. Pre-eminent among witnesses, of course, was Jesus Christ who is described in the Book of Revelation as "the faithful and true witness." Thus they see themselves as "the Lord's organisation," in the long line of those who through the ages have preserved on earth the true and pure worship of God or, as the Witnesses prefer to call Him, "Jehovah-God."

So far as other people are aware, the movement was founded by Charles Taze Russell (Pastor Russell) of Allegany, Pittsburgh, Pennsylvania, U.S.A. in 1881 under the name, adopted in 1896, of the Watch Tower Bible and Tract Society, which has continued as the controlling organisation of Jehovah's Witnesses. Its magazine, *The Watch Tower Announcing Jehovah's Kingdom*, first published in 1879, and other publications are distributed by the zealous members who carry out the house-to-house canvassing. The movement has a strong leadership.

Their teaching centres upon the early establishment of God's new world on earth, preceded by the second coming of Christ. Witnesses believe this has already happened, and that Armageddon "will come as soon as the Witness is completed." The millennial period will give sinners a second chance of salvation and "millions now living will never die" (the title of one of their pamphlets).

The dead will progressively be raised to the new earth until all the vacant places left after Armageddon are filled. There is, however, some doubt about the "goatish souls" who have made themselves unpleasant to the Witnesses, those who have accepted (or permitted to be accepted) a blood-transfusion contrary to the Scriptures, and others who have committed grave sins.

Every belief held by the movement, it is claimed, can be upheld, chapter and verse, by reference to the Scriptures. Witnesses regard the doctrine of the Trinity as devised by Satan. In both wars Witnesses have been in trouble for their refusal to take part in war and it is only fair to add that six thousand suffered for the same reason in German concentration camps.

Jensenism, name given to the minority group of psychologists and educationalists who, in general, support the view of the American professor, Arthur Jensen. The latter's studies of individual variation in learning and of the genetic factor in mental ability has led him to argue that heredity is more crucial in determining intellectual ability than environment. By implication this has put him and his colleagues at the centre of a divisive "race and intelligence" controversy which has acquired some political overtones. In 1973 Professor H. J. Eysenck was physically assaulted by students at a university lecture because he was reputed to be supporting the Jensenist position.

Jesus People, naïve and exhibitionist revival of interest in the teaching and personality of Jesus Christ which has recently featured as part of the American "Hippy" scene. The Jesus people or Jesus Freaks, as they are sometimes called, are generally white but not necessarily of an orthodox Christian background. The cult, like so many others of its kind seems to have developed in California and its adherents adopt the regimental attire (colourful costumes, long hair, beards, etc.) of the modern American Hippy, who is himself a descendant of the Beatnik (*see* **Beat Generation**). Apart from the fact that the long hair and beards are vaguely reminiscent of the Victorian pictorial representation of Jesus, the followers of the present-day cult would seem to have little genuinely in common with the ethos of Christianity, and the movement and its ideals appear to be superficial and probably transitory. A recent highly successful rock musical, "Jesus Christ, Superstar," blatantly cashes in on the Jesus Freak vogue.

Judaism, the religion of the Jews, the oldest of the great monotheist religions, parent of Christianity and Islam, the development of which is presented in the Old Testament. The creed of Judaism is based on the concept of a transcendent and omnipotent One True God, the revelation of His will in the *Torah*, and the special relation between God and His "Chosen People." The idea of Incarnation is rejected, Jesus is not recognised as the Messiah. The *Torah* is the Hebrew name for the Law of Moses (the Pentateuch) which, Judaism holds, was divinely revealed to Moses on Mount Sinai soon after the exodus of the Israelites from Egypt (1230 B.C.). Many critics deny the Mosaic authorship of the first five books of the Bible and believe them to be a compilation from four main sources known as J (Jahvist), E (Elohist), D (Deuteronomist) and P (Priestly Code), distinguished from each other by the name used for God, language, style, and internal evidence. From the historical point of view an important influence on Judaism may have been the monotheism of Akhenaten, the "heretic" Pharaoh (note, for example, the striking resemblance between Psalm 104 and Akhenaten's "Hymn to the Sun").

The Talmud is a book containing the civil and canonical laws of the Jews and includes the Mishna, a compilation from oral tradition written in Hebrew, and the Gemara, a collection of comments and criticisms by the Jewish rabbis, written in Aramaic. There are in fact two Talmuds: the one made in Palestine (the Jerusalem Talmud), finished at the beginning of the 5th cent., and the other made in Babylon, completed at the end of the 6th cent.

Judaism at the beginning of the Christian era had a number of sects: (1) the Pharisees (whose views include the first clear statement of the resurrection of the just to eternal life and the future punishment of the wicked) who held to the *Torah* and the universality of God; (2) the Sadducees, the upper class of priests and wealthy landowners, to whom God was essentially a national God and who placed the interests of the state before the *Torah*; they rejected ideas of resurrection and eternal life; (3) the Essenes (*q.v.*) who were regarded as a puritanical break-away movement by both parties. The views of the Pharisees prevailed.

Jewish writing continued through the years and some books were added to the *Torah*, among them the Three Major Prophets and certain books of the Twelve Minor Prophets. There were also the Apocalyptic writers who were unorthodox in their preaching of a divinely planned catastrophic end to the world with a "new Heaven and a new earth," preceded by a divine Messiah, and a future life—all of which beliefs influenced early Christianity. Judah Halevi of Toledo (*c.* 1085–*c.* 1140) and Moses Maimonides of Cordova (1135–1204) were the great Jewish philosophers.

Modern movements in Judaism stem from the Enlightenment, notably with Moses Mendelssohn in the 18th cent. who accepted, as was the tendency of the period, only that which could be proved by reason. He translated the Pentateuch into German thus encouraging German Jews to give up Yiddish and Hebrew for the language of the land and thereby preparing them for their vast contribution to Western civilisation. One of his disciples, David Friedländer (d. 1834) instituted "reform" Judaism. He wanted to eliminate anything that would hamper the relationships of Jews with their neighbours or tend to call in doubt their loyalty to their adopted state. A similar movement in America (1885) called for the rejection of dietary laws, the inauguration of Sunday services, and the repudiation of Jewish nationalism. Between "reform" and orthodoxy there arose the conservative movement which, in England, includes prayers in English in the service, does not segregate men and women in the synagogue, and translates the Law in a more liberal way. (The fact is that it would be almost impossible for a strictly orthodox Jew to live in a modern industrialised community at all.)

Judaism is essentially a social and family religion which, more than almost any other, concerns itself with the observances of every aspect of daily life. As in Islam (*q.v.*) details are laid down in the most minute way for the behaviour of the orthodox.

The home is the main Jewish institution and Jews, like Catholics, cannot surrender their religion. Circumcision takes place eight days after birth, and a boy becomes a man for religious purposes at his Bar Mitzvah at the age of thirteen. Women are spared most of this because their place in the home is considered sufficiently sacred. Among festivals are Passover, recalling the Exodus; Rosh Hashanah (the Jewish New Year), the anniversary of the Creation and the beginning of ten days of penitence ending with Yom Kippur (the Day of Atonement), a day of fasting spent in the synagogue; Purim, celebrating the deliverance of the Jews from Haman; and Chanukah, celebrating their victory against the Syrians under their leader Judas Maccabeus. A new and semi-religious festival is the Yom Haatzmaut, the anniversary of the birth of the new Jewish state of Israel.

K

Kabbala. *See* **Cabala.**

Ku Klux Klan. After the American Civil War (1861–65) southern conservatives and ex-Confederate leaders began to fear (as they had every reason to do) both Negro and poor White rule. Taxes were rising owing to radical legislation and the tax-burdened and disenfranchised planters finally took to illegal means to achieve their ends by trying to effect an alliance with the poor White and small farmer through appealing to his anti-Negro prejudice.

Hence the Ku Klux Klan was formed in 1866 as a secret society by a small group of Confederate veterans in Tennessee with the intention of frightening Negroes by dressing in ghostly white robes in the guise of the spirits of dead soldiers. But the movement spread like wild-fire throughout the South encouraged by small farmers and planters alike. General Nathan Bedford Forrest was appointed "Grand Wizard" of the Klan "empire" and in every community armed Klansmen riding at night horsewhipped "uppity" Negroes, beat Union soldiers, and threatened carpet-bag politicians (*i.e.*, fortune-hunters from the North). Soon several similar organisations arose, many of which did not stop at torture, burning property, and murder. In fact, although claiming to be a "holy crusade" the Klan was a vicious and contemptible organisation in which former Southern leaders trying to regain control deliberately set poor and middle-class Whites against the Negroes by appeal to race-prejudice. Congress struck back with laws and intervention of Federal troops, and after a large number of convictions in South Carolina much of the violence stopped even if the feelings continued.

After the 1914–18 war the movement, dormant since 1900, revived as a sadistic anti-Negro, anti-Jewish, anti-Catholic society, spreading to the north as well as the south. By 1926, with its white-gowned hooligans and fiery crosses, the Klan began to subside once more. While it revived again in the mid-60s, the Klan has suffered a sensational loss of support in recent years as the notion of the essential inferiority of black people has wilted among the new generations of America.

Kuomintang, a Chinese Nationalist party founded in 1891 by Sun Yat Sen. It took part in the first Chinese revolution of 1911 and led the second the following year, dominating south China by 1930 and, under Chiang Kai-shek, who succeeded Sun Yat Sen on his death in 1925, conducted China's defence against Japanese invasion from 1937–45. Sun Yat Sen had attempted to found a democratic republic based on Western parliamentary democracy and in his famous *Testament* laid down the principles upon which the constitution of China should be based. In 1946, Sun Fo, the son of Sun Yat Sen, deplored the party's departure from the principles of social democracy and the welfare of the people in which his father had believed. Beginning as a movement largely inspired by Russia, the Kuomintang under Chiang Kai-shek degenerated into a reactionary and corrupt military oligarchy which, collapsing in 1949, was replaced by the Communist party, leaving Chiang and his followers to rule Formosa with American aid.

L

Lamaism, the religion of Tibet. Its beliefs and worship derive from the Mahayana form of Buddhism which was introduced into Tibet in 749 A.D. The emphasis laid by its founder on the necessity for self-discipline and conversion through meditation and the study of philosophy deteriorated into formal monasticism and ritualism. The Dalai Lama, as the reincarnated Buddha, was both king and high priest, a sort of pope and emperor rolled into one. Under him was a hierarchy of officials in which the lowest order was that of the monks who became as numerous as one man in every six or seven of the population. The main work carried out by this vast church-state was the collection of taxes to maintain the monasteries and other religious offices. Second in power to the Dalai Lama was the Panchen or Tashi Lama believed to be a reincarnation of Amitabha, another Buddha. The last Dalai Lama fled to India in 1959 when the Chinese entered his country. For a brief period following his departure, the Panchen Lama surprised the Western world by publicly welcoming the Communist invasion, but he later renounced the regime and the suppression of Lamaism in Tibet continued unchecked.

Levellers, an English military-politico-religious party prominent in the Parliamentary Army about 1647 which stood for the rights of the people *See* Diggers.

Liberalism. The Liberal Party is the successor to the Whigs (a nickname derived from *Whiggamore*, used in the 17th cent. for Scottish dissenters) of the 18th and 19th cent. Under Gladstone's two great ministries (1868–74; and 1880–85), and again under Campbell-Bannerman and Asquith (1906–1914) much reforming legislation was enacted. The Asquith–Lloyd George split of 1916, and the advent of Labour as a major party after 1918, have caused the Liberals to be relegated as a smaller, third party. In the decade after 1945, there were times when the Liberal Party nearly disappeared altogether. But under Grimond's leadership, a revival followed the Orpington by-election triumph of March 1962. Another revival in 1972–3, with Jeremy Thorpe as leader, culminated in a Liberal vote of over 6 million in February 1974. But in October 1974, the party lost both seats and votes.

Liberal philosophy is moderately radical and progressive in terms of social reform. But the party strongly disapproves of state control or any form of monopoly, private or public. The main proposals favoured by the party are co-ownership in industry, proportional representation, greater protection of individual liberties, and separate Parliaments for Wales and Scotland. Many younger members of the party hold views to the Left or official party policy. The phenomenon of "community politics" has owed much to these younger, radical Liberals.

Logical Positivism, a school of philosophy founded in Vienna in the 1920s by a group known as "the Vienna circle": their work was based on that of Ernst Mach, but dates in essentials as far back as Hume. Of the leaders of the group, Schlick was murdered by a student, Wittgenstein came to Britain, and Carnap went to America following the entry of the Nazis. Briefly the philosophy differs from all others in that, while most people have believed that a statement might be (*a*) true, or (*b*) false, logical positivists consider there to be a third category; a statement may be meaningless. There are only two types of statement which can be said to have meaning: (1) those which are tautological, *i.e.*, those in which the statement is merely a definition of the subject, such as "a triangle is a three-sided plane figure" ("triangle" and "three-sided plane figure" are the same thing); and (2) those which can be tested by sense experience. This definition of meaningfulness excludes a great deal of what has previously been thought to be the field of philosophy; in particular it excludes the possibility of metaphysics. Thus the question as to whether there is a God or whether free-will exists is strictly meaningless, for it is neither a tautological statement nor can it be tested by sense-experience.

Lollards, a body of religious reformers and followers of Wyclif who were reviled and persecuted in the reign of Richard II. The name "Lollard" comes from a Flemish meaning "mutterer"—a term of contempt used to describe the sect. After his accession Henry IV renewed persecution of the group, even condemning one of his own personal friends, the Lollard leader Sir John Oldcastle, to be burnt at the stake.

Luddites, a group of peasants and working men who deliberately destroyed spinning and farm machinery in England in the early part of the 19th cent., fearing that such devices would destroy their livelihood. Their name was taken from the eccentric Ned Lud who had done the same in a less organised way two or three decades earlier. The Luddites' worst fears were of course not realised, for far from putting human beings out of work the industrial revolution created jobs for a vastly increased population. Luddism, dormant for over a century, is beginning to appear again, if in muted form. Public anxiety about the rapid growth in computer technology is manifesting itself in the form of such groups as the Society for the Abolition of Data Processing Machines, which while not of course dedicated to the physical destruction of computers, urge for social and even governmental checks on the development of such things as "data banks." These are vast computer memory stores listing comprehensive records concerning all the people living in a city or country and able to cross-reference them in a way that has never previously been possible. The arguments for and against such data banks and other developments in computer technology are beyond the scope of this section, but the rise of this 20th cent. Luddism is of considerable historical and social significance.

Lutheranism. The Reformation had a long history before it became, under Luther and Calvin, an accepted fact. The mediaeval Church had held (as the Catholic Church holds today) that the sacraments were the indispensable means of salvation. Since these were exclusively administered by the clergy, any movement which attacked clerical abuses was forced by sheer necessity to deny the Church's exclusive control of the means of salvation, before it could become free from dependence on a corrupt priesthood. Hence the Albigenses and the Waldenses (*qq.v.*), the followers of John Hus and Wyclif (*see* **Anticlericalism**), were bound to deny the authority of the Church and emphasise that of the Bible. Luther began his movement primarily in order to reform the Church from its gross abuses and the famous ninety-five theses nailed to the door of the Church at Wittenberg in 1517 were not primarily theological but moral complaints dealing with the actual behaviour of the clergy rather than Church beliefs. But unlike the earlier reformers, Luther had arrived at the right moment in history when economic individualism and the force of nationalism were bound, sooner or later, to cause the authorities in Germany to line up on his side. Thus he began with the support of the peasants who were genuinely shocked at the abuse of indulgences and other matters, but ended up by being supported by the noblemen who wanted to destroy the power of the pope over the German states and looked forward to confiscating the lands and property of the Church. When the peasants wanted the reform of actual economic abuses relating to the feudal system, Luther took the side of the nobles against them. The contemporary movement in Switzerland led by Ulrich Zwingli had no such secular support, and Zwingli was killed in 1531.

Martin Luther (1483–1546) was the son of a miner in Eisleben in Saxony, entered the order of Austin Friars in 1505, and later taught at the newly founded university of Wittenberg. After the publication of the theses the real issue so far as the Church was concerned was whether he was willing or not to submit to the authority of his superiors; Luther refused to compromise with his conscience in the famous words: "Here I stand; I can do no other." In a further statement Luther recommended the formation of a German national church, the abolition of indulgences and other means whereby Rome obtained money from Germany, and an end to the celibacy of the clergy. For this he was naturally excommunicated. His teaching was based on the German translation of the Bible, but he was by no means a fundamentalist: *e.g.*, he denied that the Book of Hebrews was written by Paul, would have nothing to do with the Apocrypha, and regarded the letter of James as "an epistle of straw." The Scriptures were open to all and could be interpreted by private judgment enlightened by the Spirit of God. Like Calvin, Luther was a predestinarian and determinist, but he was also a conservative and soon became alarmed about the position taken by many extremists once the Reformation was under way. He had really wanted the Church to reform itself, but when he alienated Rome he had perforce to rely more and more on the secular powers which finally resulted in the state-church form which became pronounced in Prussia and later elsewhere. Whereas Calvin wished the Church to be at least the equal of the State and in some respects its superior, Luther's rebellion resulted in the reverse, a state-controlled episcopalianism. *See* **Calvinism, Presbyterianism.**

Lycanthropy, the belief that men may, by the exercise of magical powers or because of some inherited affliction, occasionally transform into wolves. The so-called werewolf is an important feature of mid-European folklore and much the same can be said of the were-tigers and were-bears of Africa and the Far East. There is, needless to say, no such thing as a genuine werewolf known to biology, but it is not hard to see how legends of their existence could arise. There are a number of mental illnesses in which men may deliberately or unconsciously mimic the actions of animals and there are a number of endocrinological disorders which may cause gross changes in the features of the individuals, including the excessive growth of hair. In times when the physiological bases of such afflictions were not properly understood, sufferers from such complaints could easily be persuaded, either by themselves or others, that they were in fact wolfmen. Once the mythology of lycanthropy is established in a society, then of course it will be used by unscrupulous individuals for their own ends—for example revenge killings by people dressed as animals—thus helping to perpetuate the legend.

M

McLuhanism. According to Marshall McLuhan, a Canadian, and former professor of English at Toronto University, the *way* people communicate is more important than *what* they communicate: hence his famous slogan, "the medium is the message." There have been two great landmarks in human understanding since we learnt to speak and write: the invention of the printed book and the present electronic revolution. The printed word took us step by step along the linear, logical path to understanding; television comes at us from all directions at once. "Electronic circuitry has overthrown the regime of 'time' and 'space' . . . Its message is Total Change." Thus the spectacle of the Chicago police force clubbing people outside the Democratic Convention in August 1968 was described by Alistair Cook, in a despatch to *The Guardian*, as "a terrifying demonstration of McLuhanism: the millions frozen with terror in front of their television screens." In his essay, "On Reading Marshall McLuhan," Dr. George Steiner (one of the first critics in England to understand him) writes: "Marshall McLuhan posits that Western civilisation has entered, or is about to enter an era of electromagnetic technology. This technology will radically alter the milieu of human perception, the reality co-ordinates within which we apprehend and order sense data. Experience will not present itself serially, in atomized or linear patterns of casual sequence, but in 'fields' of simultaneous interaction." McLuhan's importance lies in alerting us to the present clash between two great technologies, the literate and the electromagnetic, and in his vision, beyond the present chaos, of a world drawn tighter together in a "global village" where identity will merge in collectivity and we shall all be able to cooperate for the common good instead of being split up into warring nations.

Magic, a form of belief originating in very early days and based on the primitive's inability to distinguish between similarity and identity. The simplest example would perhaps be the fertility rites in which it is believed that a ceremony involving sexual relations between men and women will bring about fertility in the harvest. Or the idea that sticking pins in an image of an individual will bring about harm or even death to the real person. Magic is regarded by some as a form of early science in that man in his efforts to control Nature had recourse to magical practices when the only methods he knew had failed to bring the desired results. It filled a gap. By others magic is regarded as an elementary stage in the evolution of religion. It can be said to have served a purpose there too. Yet magic differs from religion, however closely at times it may come to be related with it, in this important respect: religion depends upon a power *outside and beyond* human beings, whereas magic depends upon nothing but the casting of a spell or the performance of a ceremony—the result follows automatically.

The idea that "like produces like" is at the roots of imitative magic, and it is interesting to note that in some languages (*e.g.*, Hebrew and Arabic) there is no word for "resembles" or "similar to." Hence one says "All thy garments are myrrh" instead of "are *like* myrrh." It follows that an event can be compelled by imitating it. One engages in swinging, not for pleasure, but to produce a wind as the swing does; ball games are played to get rainy weather because the black ball represents dark rain-clouds; other ball games, in which one attempts to catch the ball in a cup or hit it with a stick, represent the sexual act (as some gentlemen at Lords may be distressed to hear) and bring about fertility; in medicine up till a few centuries ago herbs were chosen to cure a disease because in some respects their leaves or other parts looked like the part of the body affected (*e.g.*, the common wildflower still known as "eyebright" was used in bathing the eyes because the flower looks like a tiny eye). *See* **Witchcraft, Demonism.**

Malthusianism, the theory about population growth put forward by the Rev. Thomas Malthus (1766–1834) in *An Essay on Population* (1798). His three main propositions were: (1) "Population is necessarily limited by means of subsistence." (2) "Population invariably increases where means of subsistence increase, unless prevented by some very powerful and obvious checks." (3) "These checks, and the checks which repress the superior power of population, and keep its effects on a level with the means of subsistence, are all resolvable into moral restraint, vice and misery." In other words, no matter how great the food supply may become, human reproductive power will always adjust itself so that food will always be scarce in relation to population; the only means to deal with this is by "moral restraint" (*i.e.*, chastity or not marrying), "vice" (*i.e.*, birth-control methods), or misery (*i.e.*, starvation). More specifically, Malthus claimed that while food increases by arithmetical progression, population increases by geometrical progression. It is true that these gloomy predictions did not take place in Malthus's time largely owing to the opening up of new areas of land outside Europe, the development of new techniques in agriculture, the growth of international trade to poorer areas, the increased knowledge of birth-control, and developments in medical science which reduced the misery he had predicted. Furthermore, we now know that as a society becomes industrialised its birth-rate tends to fall. Nevertheless there are very few scientists who are not perturbed by the growth in the world's population which has increased from about 465 million in 1650 to 3,890 million today.

Manichaeism, an Asiatic religion which developed from Zoroastrianism (*q.v.*) and shows the influence of Buddhism (*q.v.*) and Gnosticism (*q.v.*), being founded by Mani, a Persian, who was born in Babylonia, *c.* 216 A.D. Mani presented himself to Shapur I as the founder of a new religion which was to be to Babylonia what Buddhism was to India or Christianity to the West. His aspiration was to convert the East and he himself made no attempt to interfere directly with Christianity although he represented himself as the Paraclete (the Holy Ghost or "Comforter") and, like Jesus, had twelve disciples. His success in Persia aroused the fury of the Zoroastrian priests who objected to his reforming zeal towards their religion and in 276 Mani was taken prisoner and crucified.

Of Mani's complicated system little can be said here, save that it is based on the struggle of two eternal conflicting principles, God and matter, or light and darkness. Although its founder had no intention of interfering with the West, after his death his followers soon spread the religion from Persia and Mesopotamia to India and China. (Manichaeism flourished in China until the 11th cent.) It reached as far as Spain and Gaul and influenced many of the bishops in Alexandria and in Carthage where for a time St. Augustine accepted Manichaeism. Soon the toleration accorded it under Constantine ended and it was treated as a heresy and violently suppressed. Yet it later influenced many heresies, and even had some influence on orthodox Catholicism which had a genius for picking up elements in other religions which had been shown to appeal to worshippers provided they did not conflict unduly with fundamental beliefs.

Maoism is the branch of communism that reigns in China. It has been shaped by one of the most remarkable statesmen of modern times, Mao Tse-tung (1893–1976), who set the pattern of revolution for poor peasant societies and restored pride and confidence to his fellow countrymen after years of turmoil and brutality. Although Marxist theory guided the Chinese communists in their struggle for liberation from the old bourgeois and feudal China, it was interpreted in a manner peculiar to China and developed to fit into the Chinese way of life and the "thoughts" of Chairman Mao. As early as 1926 Mao had pointed out that the Chinese proletariat had in the peasanty its staunchest and most numerous ally. "A rural revolution", he said, "is a revolution by which the peasantry overthrows the authority of the feudal landlord class." The struggles of 1925–49 (the Long March of the Red Army, the Anti-Japanese War, the Civil War against Chiang Kai-shek) were the foundations on which present-day China has been built. Maoism is against authoritarianism and for self-reliance; against bureaucracy and for revolutionary momentum: against rivalry between individuals and for common effort. One of the great achievements has been the removal of poverty, ignorance and disease from China. Mao taught that struggle is necessary for the revolution to endure. "Running water does not go stale and door-hinges do not become worm-eaten", Mao reminded his comrades. "We must", he said, "make every comrade understand that the highest criterion for judging the words and deeds of the communists is whether they conform with the best interests and win the support of the broadest masses of the people". It remains to be seen what effect the death of Mao Tse-tung will have on Chinese communism and whether political direction will be towards the modernisation of China and away from "continuous revolution". *See also* **China, Section C, Part II.**

Marxism. The sociological theories founded by Karl Marx and Friedrich Engels on which modern communist thought is based. Marx and Engels lived in a period of unrestrained capitalism when exploitation and misery were the lot of the industrial working classes, and it was their humanitarianism and concern for social justice which inspired their work. They co-operated in 1848 in writing the *Communist Manifesto*, and in his great work, *Das Kapital* (1867), Marx worked out a new theory of society. He showed that all social systems are economically motivated and change as a result of technical and economic changes in methods of production. The driving force of social change Marx found to be in the struggle which the oppressed classes wage to secure a better future. Thus in his celebrated theory of historical materialism he interpreted history in terms of economics and explained the evolution of society in terms of class struggle. (*See* **Dialectical Materialism.**) "In the social production of their means of existence," he wrote, "men enter into definite and unavoidable relations which are independent of their will. These productive relationships correspond to the particular stage in the development of their material productive forces." Marx's theory of historical materialism implies that history is propelled by class struggle with communism and the classless society as the final stage when man will have emancipated himself from the productive process. Marx was the first to put socialism on a rational and scientific basis, and he foretold that socialism would inevitably replace capitalism. His prophecy, however, came to realisation not in the advanced countries as he had envisaged but in backward Russia and China. *See also* **Communism.**

Mesmerism, a rapidly vanishing name to denote the practice of hypnosis, which owes its popularity, though not its discovery, to the Austrian physician, Anton Mesmer (1733–1815). Mesmer's contribution was the realisation that a large number of what we would today call psychosomatic or hysterical conditions could be cured (or at least temporarily alleviated) by one or another form of suggestion. Mesmer himself relied on the idea of what he called "animal magnetism," a supposedly potent therapeutic force emanating from the living body which could be controlled by the trained individual. Mesmer used wands and impressive gadgetry to dispense the marvellous force and he effected a remarkable number of cures of complaints, hitherto looked upon as incurable or totally mysterious in origin—the most typical of these being hysterical blindness, paralysis or deafness, nervous skin conditions, and so on. Hypnosis, which is a valid if very poorly understood psychological phenomenon even today, would probably have been developed much further had not efficient general anaesthetics such as ether, nitrous oxide, etc., been discovered, thus greatly diminishing its role as a pain reliever in surgery. Mesmer, who was three parts charlatan, never really troubled to think deeply about the cause of his undoubted successes. The first man to treat hysteria as a formal class of illness and who made a scientific attempt to treat it with hypnosis was Ambrose Liébeault (1823–1904). He and his colleague Hippolyte Bernheim (1840–1919) believed: (*a*) that hysteria was produced by suggestion, and particularly by autosuggestion on the part of the patient, and (*b*) that suggestion was a normal trait found in varying degrees in everyone. These conclusions are true, but as Freud showed later are far from being the whole truth.

Messianism. Most varieties of religious belief rely on the assumption that the deity is a supernatural being either permeating the universe or dwelling in some other sphere, and normally inaccessible to man. Where divine intervention is necessary, the deity is traditionally believed to nominate a human being—in the case of Christianity, for example, Jesus is believed to be the actual son of God. Messianic cults introduce a novel variant on the traditional theme. In these a human being is held to be God himself. He may either nominate himself for this role, relying on his own personality or native talent to acquire the necessary following, or for one reason or another large numbers of people may alight on one individual and declare him the Messiah. While it might seem that beliefs of this kind would be confined to earlier epochs in man's recorded history, this is in fact not the case. In the past century, and even within recent decades, a number of individuals have been held by groups to be actually divine. Among these were the Dutchman Lourens van Voorthuizen, a former fisherman who declared himself to be God in 1950 and got large numbers to accept his claim; the Anglican priest Henry James Prince, who did much the same thing in 1850; and of course the famous Negro George Baker, who convinced hundreds of thousands of other Negroes that he was "Father Divine." To simple people the idea that God is to be found on earth and that one may even be personally introduced to him, is an obviously attractive one. The trouble is that all self-styled Gods to this present date have sooner or later seriously disappointed their supporters by performing that most human of acts—dying.

Metapsychology. Not to be confused with parapsychology (*q.v.*). The branch or off-shoot of psychology which goes beyond empirical and experimental studies to consider such philosophical matters as the nature of mind the reality of free will and the mind/body problem. It was originally used by Freud as a blanket descriptive term denoting all mental processes, but this usage is now obsolete.

Methodism, the religious movement founded by John Wesley in 1738, at a time when the Anglican Church was in one of its periodic phases of spiritual torpor, with the simple aim of spreading "scriptural holiness" throughout the land. Up to that time Wesley had been a High Churchman but on a visit to Georgia in the United States he was much impressed by the group known as Moravians (*q.v.*), and on his return to this country was introduced by his brother Charles, who had already become an adherent, to Peter Böhler, a Moravian minister in England. Passing through a period of spiritual commotion following the meeting, he first saw the light at a small service in Aldersgate in May 1738 "where one was reading Luther's preface to the Epistle to the Romans" and from this time forth all Wesley's energies were devoted to the single object of saving souls. He did this for fifty years and at the end of his life confessed that he had wasted fifteen minutes in that time by reading a worthless book. Even when he was over eighty he still rose at 4 a.m. and toiled all day long.

Soon Whitefield, a follower with Calvinist views, was preaching throughout the country and Charles Wesley was composing his well-known hymns; John's abilities at this time were taken up in organising the movement described as "People called Methodists." They were to be arranged in "societies" which were united into "circuits" under a minister, the circuits into "districts" and all knit together into a single body under a conference of ministers which has met annually since 1744. Local lay preachers were also employed and to maintain interest the ministers were moved from circuit to circuit each year. These chapel services were not originally meant to conflict with the Church of England of which Wesley still considered himself a member. They were purely supplementary, and it used to be the custom (before the Methodists began to count themselves as Nonconformists) for Methodists to attend Church in the morning and Chapel in the evening.

The class-meeting was the unit of the organisation where members met regularly under a chosen leader to tell their "experiences" upon which they were often subjected to severe cross-examination. At the end of every quarter, provided their attendances were regular, they received a ticket of membership which entitled them to come to monthly sacramental services. If attendance was inadequate the name was removed from the list, without appearance on which nobody was deemed a member. The price of the ticket was "a penny a week and a shilling a quarter" but Wesley was not interested in receiving money from anyone who was not utterly devoted to the cause.

John Wesley introduced four other innovations, some of which were regarded by Churchmen who had previously been willing to commend his efforts in bringing religion to the poorer classes as dangerous: (1) He started the Sunday-school scheme and afterwards enthusiastically supported that of John Raikes, often regarded as the founder of the idea; this was of immense importance in the days before the Education Acts. (2) He reintroduced the Agapae or "love feasts" of the early Church which were fellowship meetings deepening the sense of brotherhood of the society. (3) He began to copy the open-air meetings of the eloquent Whitefield and soon unwittingly produced the most extraordinary results, finding that his sermons led to groans, tears, fainting-fits, and all sorts of emotional expression. Even his open-air lay speakers produced like results and these came to be associated with Methodism and gave significance to the proud Anglican claim that *their* services would be "without enthusiasm." (4) After some hesitation he ventured to consecrate Dr. Thomas Coke, who was being sent as a missionary to America, as a bishop of his church. In addition to Wesley's religious work he was a great educator of the common man. Thus he introduced the cheap book and the church magazine, publishing books of any sort which he thought would edify and not harm even when the views expressed were different from his own—*e.g.*, Thomas à Kempis's *Imitation of Christ* and works of history, biography, science, and medicine in some cases written by himself. In this way the movement with its cheap books and reading rooms had an influence far beyond its actual membership. Both the Anglican Church and the Evangelical movement of Wilberforce and others profited from Wesley's work. Some social historians, rightly or wrongly, have claimed that it was Wesley's influence among the working classes that spared England the revolutionary activity which characterised most other European countries during the first quarter of the 19th cent.

Methodism, especially after Wesley's death in 1791, began, like other movements, to develop schisms. There were the long-standing differences which the Baptist movement (*q.v.*) had shown too between Arminian and Calvinist sections—*i.e.*, between those who did and those who did not accept the doctrine of predestination. In the case of the Methodists, this led to a complete break in 1811. Then there were differences associated with the status of the laity, or the relationship of the movement with the Anglican Church. The "Methodist New Connection" of 1797 differed only in giving the laity equal representation with the ministers but the more important break of the Primitive Methodists in 1810 gave still more power to the laity and reintroduced the "camp-meeting" type of service. In 1815 the Bryanites or "Bible Christians" were formed, and a further schism which was even brought before the law courts was ostensibly over the foundation of a theological college. The real reason, of course, was that the ministers were becoming more Tory, whilst the laity were becoming more Radical. Finally in 1932, at a conference in the Albert Hall in London, the Wesleyan Methodists, the Primitive Methodists, and the United Methodists became one Church, the Methodist Church.

Mind and Matter.

Early Greek Views: Idealism and Dualism. Primitive peoples could see that there is a distinction between those things which move and do things by themselves and others, such as stones, which do not. Following the early state of **Animism** (*q.v.*), in which spirits were believed to have their abode in everything, they began to differentiate between matter or substance and a force which seems to move it and shape it into objects and things. Thus to the Greek Parmenides (fl. *c.* 475 B.C.), who was a philosopher of pure reason, thought or mind was the creator of what we observe and in some way not quite clear to himself it seemed that mind was the cause of everything. This is perhaps the first expression of the movement known as Idealism which says, in effect, that the whole universe is mental—a creation either of our own minds or the mind of God. But from Anaxagorus (488–428 B.C.) we have the clearer statement that mind or *nous* causes all movement but is distinct from the substance it moves. He does not, however, think in terms of individual minds but rather of a kind of generalised mind throughout the universe which can be used as an explanation of anything which cannot be explained otherwise. This is the position known as **Dualism** (*q.v.*) which holds that both mind and matter exist and interact but are separate entities.

Most people in practice are dualists since, rightly or wrongly, mind and body are thought of as two different things; it is the "commonsense" (although not necessarily the true) point of view. Plato in a much more complex way was also a dualist although he held that the world of matter we observe is in some sense not the genuine world. The real world is the world of ideas and the tree we see is not real but simply matter upon which mind or soul has imprinted the idea of a tree. Everything that exists has its corresponding form in the world of ideas and imprints its pattern upon matter. Mind has always existed and, having become entangled with matter, is constantly seeking to free itself and return to God.

Plato's pupil Aristotle had a much more scientific outlook and held that, although it was mind which gave matter its form, mind is not *outside* matter, as Plato had thought, but *inside* it as its formative principle. Therefore there could be no mind without matter and no matter without mind; for even the lowest forms of matter have some degree of mind which increases in quantity and quality as we move up the scale to more complex things.

So far, nobody had explained how two such different substances as matter and mind could influence each other in any way, and this remains, in spite of attempts to be mentioned later, a basic problem in philosophy.

Two later ideas, one of them rather foolish and the other simply refusing to answer the question, are typified by the Stoics and some members of the Sceptic school. The first is that only matter exists and what we call mind is merely matter of a finer texture, a view which as an explanation is unlikely to satisfy anyone; the other, that of some Sceptics, is that we can know nothing except the fleeting images or thoughts that flicker through our consciousness. Of either mind or matter we know nothing.

Renaissance Attitude. Christian doctrines have already been dealt with (*see* **God and Man, Determinism and Free-will**), and the past and future of the soul is dealt with under **Immortality.** Nor need we mention the Renaissance philosophers who were really much more concerned about how to use mind than about its nature. When they did consider the subject they usually dealt with it, as did Francis Bacon, by separating the sphere of science from that of religion and giving the orthodox view of the latter because there were still good reasons for not wishing to annoy the Church.

17th-cent. Views: Hobbes, Descartes, Guelincx, Spinoza, Locke, Berkeley. Thomas Hobbes in the 17th cent. was really one of the first to attempt a modern explanation of mind and matter even if his attempt was crude. As a materialist he held that all that exists is matter and hence our thoughts, ideas, images, and actions are really a form of motion taking place within the brain and nerves. This is the materialist theory which states that mind does not exist.

Thus there are three basic theories of the nature of mind and body: idealism, dualism, and materialism, and we may accept any one of the three. But, if we accept dualism, we shall have to explain precisely the relationship between body and mind. In some of his later writings Hobbes seems to suggest that mental processes are the effects of motion rather than motion itself; *i.e.*, they exist, but only as a result of physical processes just as a flame does on a candle. This theory of the relationship is known as *epiphenomenalism.*

Descartes, the great French contemporary of Hobbes, was a dualist who believed that mind and matter both exist and are entirely different entities; therefore he had to ask himself how, for example, the desire to walk leads to the physical motion of walking. His unsatisfactory answer was that, although animals are pure automatons, man is different in that he has a soul which resides in the pineal gland (a tiny structure in the brain which today we know to be a relic of evolution with no present function whatever). In this gland the mind comes in contact with the "vital spirits" of the body and thus there is interaction between the two. This theory is known as *interactionism,* and since we do not accept its basis in the function of the pineal gland, we are simply left with the notion of interaction but without the explanation of how it takes place.

One of Descartes's successors, Arnold Guelincx, produced the even more improbable theory of *psychophysical parallelism,* sometimes known as the theory of the "two clocks." Imagine you have two clocks, each keeping perfect time, then supposing you saw one and heard the other, every time one points to the hour the other will strike, giving the impression that the first event causes the second, although in fact they are quite unrelated. So it is with the body and mind in Guelincx's view, each is "wound up" by God in the beginning in such a way as to keep time with the other so that when I have the desire to walk purely unrelated physical events in my legs cause them to move at the same time. A variety of this theory is *occasionism,* which says that whenever something happens in the physical world, God affects us so that we *think* we are being affected by the happening.

The trouble about all these theories is (*a*) that they really explain nothing, and (*b*) that they give us a very peculiar view of God as a celestial showman treating us as puppets when it would surely have been easier to create a world in which mind and matter simply interacted by their very nature. Spinoza, too, believed in a sort of psychophysical parallelism in that he did not think that mind and body interacted. But since in his theory everything is God, mind and matter are simply two sides of the same penny.

John Locke, another contemporary, thought of the mind as a blank slate upon which the world writes in the form of sensations, for we have no innate or inborn ideas and mind and matter do interact although he does not tell us how. All we know are sensations—*i.e.*, sense impressions. Bishop Berkeley carried this idea to its logical conclusion: if we know nothing but sensations, we have no reason to suppose that matter exists at all. He was, therefore, an idealist.

18th cent. Views: Hume, Kant. David Hume went further still and pointed out that, if all we know are sensations, we cannot prove the existence of matter but we cannot prove the existence of mind either. All we can ever know is that ideas, impressions, thoughts, follow each other. We do not even experience a self or personality because every time we look into our "minds" all we really experience are thoughts and impressions. Hume was quick to point out that this was not the same as saying that the self did not exist; it only proved that we cannot know that it does.

Kant made it clear that, although there is a world outside ourselves, we can never know what it is really like. The mind receives impressions and forms them into patterns which conform not to the thing-in-itself but to the nature of mind. Space and time, for example, are not realities but only the form into which our mind fits its sensations. In other words our mind shapes impressions which are no more like the thing-in-itself than the map of a battlefield with pins showing the position of various army groups at any given moment is like the battlefield. This, of course, is true. From physics and physiology we know that the sounds we hear are "really" waves in the air, the sights we see "really" electromagnetic waves. What guarantee do we have that the source is "really" like the impression received in our brain? Kant was the leader of the great German Idealist movement of the 18th cent. which in effect said: "why bother about matter when all we can ever know is mental?"

19th and 20th cent. Views. The Englishman Bradley, and the Frenchman Henri Bergson in the 19th and early 20th cent. both held in one form or another the belief that mind in some way creates matter and were, therefore, idealists, whereas Comte, the positivist (*q.v.*), and the Americans William James and John Dewey, held that mind is a form of behaviour. Certain acts (*e.g.*, reflexes) are "mindless" because they are deliberate; others which are intended may be described for the sake of convenience as "minded" (*i.e.*, purposeful). But like the majority of modern psychologists—insofar as they take any interest in the subject—they regarded mind as a process going on in the living body. Is there any reason, many now ask why we should think of mind as being any different in nature from digestion? Both are processes going on in the body, the one in the brain the other in the stomach and intestines. Why should we regard them as "things"? *See also* J43–4 and Section Q.

Mithraism, a sun-religion which originated in Persia with the worship of the mythical Mithra, the god of light and of truth. It was for two centuries one of early Christianity's most formidable rivals, particularly in the West since the more philosophical Hellenic Christianity of the East had little to fear from it. (Arnold Toynbee has described Mithraism as "a pre-Zoroastrian Iranian paganism—in a Hellenic dress"; Manichaeism as "Zoroastrianism—in a Christian dress".) Mithraism was a mystery-faith with secret rites known only to devotees. It appealed to the soldiers of the Roman Army which explains its spread to the farthest limits of the Roman empire and its decline as the Romans retreated. The religion resembled Zoroastrianism (*q.v.*) in that it laid stress on the constant struggle between good and evil and there are a number of parallels with Christianity, *e.g.*, a miraculous birth, death, and a glorious resurrection, a belief in heaven and hell and the immortality of the soul, a last judgment. Both religions held Sunday as the holy day of the week, celebrated 25 December (date of the pagan winter solstice festival) as the birthday of the founder; both celebrated Easter, and in their ceremonies made use of bell, holy water, and the candle. Mithraism reached its height about 275 A.D. and afterwards declined both for the reason given above and, perhaps, because it excluded women, was emotional rather than philosophical, and had no general organisation to direct its course. Yet even today, from the Euphrates to the Tyne, traces of the religion remain and antiquarians are familiar with the image of the sun-god and the inscription *Deo Soli Mithrae, Invicto, Seculari* (dedicated to the sun-god of Mithra, the unconquered). Mithraism enjoyed a brief revival of popular interest in the mid-1950s when workers excavating the foundations of the skyscraper, Bucklersbury House in the City of London, found the well-preserved remains of a Roman Mithraic temple. A campaign to save the temple as a national monument resulted in its now being on open display on a site in front of the skyscraper.

Mohammedanism. See Islam.

Monasticism. When in the 4th cent. A.D. Constantine in effect united state and church there were naturally many who hastened to become Christians for the worldly benefits they expected it to bring in view of the new situation. But there were others who, in their efforts to escape from worldly involvement, went into the deserts of North Africa and Syria to live as hermits and so in these regions there grew up large communities of monks whose lives of renunciation made a considerable impression on the Christian world. They were men of all types but the two main groups were those who preferred to live alone and those who preferred a community life. Among the first must be included St. Anthony, the earliest of the hermits, who was born in Egypt *c.* 250 and who lived alone in a hut near his home for fifteen years, and then in the desert for a further twenty. As his fame spread Anthony came forth to teach and advocate a life of extreme austerity, until by the end of his life the Thebaid (the desert around Thebes) was full of hermits following his example. (Not unnaturally, he was constantly assailed by lustful visions which he thoughtfully attributed to Satan.) In the Syrian desert St. Simeon Stylites and others were stimulated to even greater austerities and Simeon himself spent many years on the top of a pillar in a space so small that it was only possible to sit or stand. With some of these men it is obvious that ascetic discipline had become perverted into an unpleasant form of exhibitionism.

The first monastery was founded by Pachomius of Egypt *c.* 315 and here the monks had a common life with communal meals, worship, and work mainly of an agricultural type. In the Eastern part of the Empire St. Basil (*c.* 360) tried to check the growth of the extreme and spectacular practices of the hermits by organising monasteries in which the ascetic disciplines of fasting, meditation, and prayer, would be balanced by useful and healthy activities. His monasteries had orphanages and schools for boys—not only those who were intended for a monkish life. But the Eastern Church in general continued to favour the hermit life and ascetic extremes. Originally a spontaneous movement, the monastic life was introduced to the West by St. Athanasius in 339 who obtained its recognition from the Church of Rome and St. Augustine introduced it into North Africa beyond Egypt. The movement was promoted also by St. Jerome, St. Martin of Tours, who introduced it into France, and St. Patrick into Ireland. The monastery of Iona was founded by St. Columba in 566. But it must be remembered that the Celtic Church had a life of its own which owed more to the Egyptian tradition than to Rome. Unlike the more elaborate monasteries of the continent those of the early Celtic Church were often little more than a cluster of stone bee-hive huts, an oratory, and a stone cross. It had its own religious ceremonies and its own art (notably its beautifully carved crosses and the illuminated manuscripts such as the Lindisfarne Gospel (*c.* 700) and the Irish Book of Kells dating from about the same time). The Scottish St. Ninian played a major part in introducing Egyptian texts and art to Britain where, mixed with Byzantine influences and the art of the Vikings, it produced a typical culture of its own. Strangely enough, it was the relatively primitive Celts who played almost as large a part in preserving civilisation in Europe during the Dark Ages as did the Italians since. It was St. Columbanus (*c.* 540–615) who founded the great monasteries of Annegray, Luxeuil, and Fontaine in the Vosges country, St. Gall in Switzerland, and Bobbio in the Apennines. So, too, it was the Anglo-Saxon Alcuin (*c.* 735–804) who was called from York by Charlemagne to set up a system of education throughout his empire; the most famous of the monastic schools he founded was at Tours. Among those influenced by him was the philosopher John Scotus Erigena.

Meanwhile from the south, as the disintegrating Roman empire became increasingly corrupt, St. Benedict of Nursia (*c.* 480–*c.* 543) fled the pleasures of Rome to lead a hermit's life near Subiaco. Here he founded some small monasteries, but *c.* 520 made a new settlement, the great monastery of Monte Cassino in southern Italy, where he established a "Rule" for the government of monks. This included both study and work and emphasised that education was necessary for the continuance of Christianity. As his influence spread his Rule was adopted by other monasteries, and schools became part of monastic life. It is not possible to describe the many different orders of monks and nuns formed since, nor the mendicant orders of friars (*e.g.*, Franciscans, Dominicans, Carmelites, Augustinians). In many ways even those outside the Roman Catholic Church owe much to the monastic movement. Monasticism, of course, is not peculiar to Christianity and forms a major aspect of Buddhism, especially in the form of Lamaism in Tibet (*q.v.*)

Montanism, a Phrygian form of primitive Puritanism with many peculiar tenets into which the early Christian theologian Tertullian (*c.* 150–*c.* 230) was driven by his extremist views that the Christian should keep himself aloof from the world and hold no social intercourse whatever with pagans. The sect had immediate expectation of Christ's second coming and indulged in prophetic utterance which they held to be inspired by the Holy Ghost but which their enemies put down to prompting by the Devil. In seeking persecution and martyrdom they antagonised the Church and were suppressed.

Moral Re-Armament, a campaign launched in 1938 by an American evangelist of Lutheran background, Frank N. D. Buchman (1878–1961), founder of the Oxford Group Movement, and at first associated with the First Century Church Fellowship, a fundamentalist Protestant revivalist movement. On a visit to England in 1920 Buchman preached "world-changing through life-changing" to undergraduates at Oxford, hence the name Oxford Group. This revivalist movement was based on Buchman's conviction that world civilisation was breaking down and a change had to be effected in the minds of men.

Two of the Group's most typical practices were group confession of sins openly and the "quiet time" set aside during the day to receive messages from the Almighty as to behaviour and current problems. In the eyes of non-Groupers the confession (often of trivial sins) appeared to be exhibitionist and there was felt to be a certain snobbery about the movement which made it strongly conscious of the social status of its converts.

The Oxford Group gave way to Moral Re-Armament, the third phase of Buchmanism. M.R.A. men and women lay stress on the four moral absolutes of honesty, purity, love, and unselfishness. They believe they have the ideas to set the pattern for the changing world and, indeed, claim to have aided in solving many international disputes—political, industrial, and racial. Theologians complained of the Groups that their movement lacked doctrine and intellectual content; M.R.A. is no different in this respect.

The peak of public interest in M.R.A. was probably reached in the 1950s. Like so many movements of its kind it relied heavily for its motive force on the dynamism of its founder and leader. With the death of Dr. Buchman and the unexpected demise at an early age of his most promising protégé and successor-designate, the journalist Peter Howard, the movement began to lose its public impact.

Moravian Church, a revival of the Church of the "Bohemian Brethren" which originated (1457) among some of the followers of John Hus. It developed a kind of Quakerism that rejected the use of force, refused to take oaths, and had no hierarchy. It appears to have been sympathetic towards Calvinism but made unsuccessful approaches to Luther. As a Protestant sect it was ruthlessly persecuted by Ferdinand II and barely managed to survive. However, in the 18th cent. the body was re-established by Count Zinzendorf who offered it a place of safety in Saxony where a town called Herrnhut (God's protection) was built and this became the centre from which Moravian doctrine was spread by missionaries all over the world. Their chief belief (which had a fundamental influence on John Wesley—*see* **Methodism**) was that faith is a direct illumination from God which assures us beyond all possibility of doubt that we are saved, and that no goodness of behaviour, piety, or orthodoxy is of any use without this "sufficient, sovereign, saving grace."

Mormons, or Latter-day Saints, one of the very numerous American religious sects; founded in 1830 by Joseph Smith, the son of a Vermont farmer, who, as a youth, had been influenced by a local religious revival though confused by the conflicting beliefs of the various denominations. He said that while praying for guidance he had been confronted by two heavenly messengers who forbade him to join any existing church but prepare to become the prophet of a new one. Soon, in a series of visions, he was told of a revelation written on golden plates concealed in a nearby hillside. These he unearthed in 1827 and with the help of "Urim and Thummim" translated the "reformed Egyptian" characters into English. Described as the *Book of Mormon*, this was published in 1830 and at the same time a little church of those few who accepted his testimony was founded in Fayette, N.Y. In addition the first of Joseph Smith's "miracles"—the casting out of a devil—was performed. The *Book of Mormon* purports to be a record of early American history and religion, the American Indians being identified as the ten Lost Tribes of Israel, whose fate has never failed to attract the attention of those who prefer myth to fact (cf. British Israelites). Jesus Christ is alleged to have appeared in America after His ascension. Yet Smith's eloquence was able to influence quite educated people, including Sidney Rigdon with whom he went into business for a time. *Doctrine and Covenants* is the title of another book dealing with the revelations Smith claimed to have received. Soon the sect was in trouble with the community both because its members insisted on describing themselves as the Chosen People and others as Gentiles and because they took part in politics, voting as Smith ordered them to. Smith was constantly in trouble with the police. Therefore they were turned out from one city after another until they found themselves a dwelling-place at Nauvoo, Illinois, on the Mississippi.

That would probably have been the end of the story had not Smith been murdered in 1844 and thereby made to appear a martyr, and had there not appeared Brigham Young, a quite extraordinary leader, who stamped out warring factions and drove out the recalcitrant. While persecutions continued Brigham Young announced that it had been revealed that he must lead the faithful to Salt Lake, then outside the area of the United States. There followed the famous trek of more than a thousand miles across desert country in which he led the way, reaching his journey's end in the forbidding valley of the Great Salt Lake on 24 July 1847. By 1851 30,000 Mormons had reached the Promised Land. Here they held their own in a hostile environment and under the practical genius of their leader carried through a vast irrigation scheme and built Salt Lake City which still serves as the headquarters of their sect. In 1850 their pioneer settlement was made Utah Territory, and in 1896 incorporated in the Union. The church was strictly ruled by its leader who also looked after affairs of state for thirty years until his death in 1877.

Polygamy, although opposed by some Mormons, and only sanctioned by Brigham Young when Salt Lake City had been built, is the best-known of Mormon doctrines. It brought the sect into much disrepute and was renounced in 1890. Mormons are millenarians, believing that some time Christ will appear and rule for a thousand years.

There are two orders of priests or leaders: the Melchizedeks, or higher order, include the apostles or ruling elders, and the high priest; the Aaronic priesthood, or lower order, attends to the temporal affairs of the church as the Melchizedeks attend to the spiritual. Members abstain from alcohol, tobacco, coffee, and tea. The church lays stress on the importance of revelation through visions, on education to meet the social, spiritual, and cultural needs of its members, and on community welfare. Members of the Church of Jesus Christ of Latter-day Saints now number over three million in congregations throughout the world.

The Reorganised Church of Jesus Christ of Latter-day Saints with its headquarters at Independence, Missouri, has been separate and distinct since 1852.

Muggletonians, one of the many sects which arose during the Commonwealth but, unlike most of the others (**Levellers** (*q.v.*), **Diggers** (*q.v.*, Fifth-Monarchy Men, and the Millenarians) which tended to have a strongly political aspect, this was purely religious. Founded by two journeymen tailors, Lodowick Muggleton and John Reeve, who interpreted the Book of Revelation in their own peculiar way, it was decided that Reeve represented Moses, and Muggleton, Aaron. They also believed that the Father, not the Son, had died on the cross (an ancient heresy) but added the strange statement that He left Elijah in control during His period on earth. Rejecting the doctrine of the Trinity, they also asserted that God has a human body. Nevertheless, for a time, they had a large number of followers.

Mysticism, a religious attitude which concerns itself with direct relationship with God, "reality" as contrasted with appearance, or the "ultimate" in one form or another. All the higher religions have had their mystics who have not always been regarded without suspicion by their more orthodox members, and, as Bertrand Russell points out, there has been a remarkable unity of opinion among mystics which almost transcends their religious differences. Thus, characteristic of the mystical experience in general, have been the following features: (1) a belief in insight as opposed to analytical knowledge which is accompanied in the actual experience by the sense of a mystery unveiled, a hidden wisdom become certain beyond the possibility of doubt; this is often preceded by a period of utter hopelessness and isolation described as "the dark night of the soul"; (2) a belief in unity and a refusal to admit opposition or division anywhere; this sometimes appears in the form of what seem to be contradictory statements: "the way up and the way down is one and the same" (Heraclitus). There is no distinction between subject and object, the act of perception and the thing perceived; (3) a denial of the reality of time, since if all is one the distinction of past and future must be illusory; (4) a denial of the reality of evil (which does not maintain, *e.g.*, that cruelty is good but that it does not exist in the world of reality as opposed to the world of phantoms from which we are liberated by the insight of the vision). Among the great mystics have been Meister Eckhart and Jakob Boehme, the German religious mystics of the 13th and 16th cent. respectively, Acharya Sankara of India, and St. Theresa and St. John of the Cross of Spain. Mystical movements within the great religions have been: the Zen (*q.v.*) movement within Buddhism; Taoism in China; the Cabalists and Hasidim in Judaism; the Sufis within Islam; some of the Quakers within Christianity.

Mystery Religions. *See* **Orphism.**

N

Natural Law, the specifically Roman Catholic doctrine that there is a natural moral law, irrespective of time and place, which man can know through his own reason. Originally a product of early rational philosophy, the Christian form of the doctrine is basically due to St. Thomas Aquinas who defined natural law in relation to eternal law, holding that the eternal law is God's reason which governs the relations of all things in the universe to each other. The natural law is that part of the eternal law which relates to man's behaviour. Catholic natural law assumes that the human reason is capable of deriving ultimate rules for right behaviour since there are in man and his institutions certain stable structures produced by God's reason which man's reason can know to be correct and true. Thus, the basis of marriage, property, the state, and the contents of justice are held to be available to man's natural reason. The rules of positive morality and civil law are held to be valid only insofar as they conform to the natural law, which man is not only capable of knowing but also of obeying.

Protestant theologians criticise this notion. Thus Karl Barth and many others hold that sinful and fallen man cannot have any direct knowledge of God or His reason or will without the aid of revelation. Another theologian Niebuhr points out that the principles of the doctrines are too inflexible and that although they are the product of a particular time and circumstance, they are regarded as if they were absolute and eternal. In fact, as most social scientists would also agree, there is no law which can be regarded as "natural" for all men at all times. Nor does it seem sensible to suppose that all or even many men possess either the reason to discern natural law or the ability to obey it; whether or not we accept man's free-will (and all Protestant sects do not), we know as a fact of science that people are not always fully responsible for their actions and some not at all.

Nazism, the term commonly used for the political and social ideology of the German National Socialist Party inspired and led by Hitler. The term *Nazi* was an abbreviation of National Socialist. Those in the Federal Republic today sympathetic to National Socialist aims are known as neo-Nazis. *See* **Fascism.**

Neoplatonism. *See* **Determinism and Free-will** and **God and Man.**

Nihilism, the name commonly given to the earliest Russian form of revolutionary anarchism. It originated in the early years of Tsar Alexander II (1818–81), the liberator of the serfs, who, during his attempts to bring about a constitutional monarchy, was killed by a bomb. The term "nihilist," however, was first used in 1862 by Turgenev in his novel *Fathers and Children*. *See* **Anarchism.**

Nominalism. Early mediaeval thinkers were divided into two schools, those who regarded "universals" or abstract concepts as mere names without any corresponding realities (Nominalists), and those who held the opposite doctrine (**Realism**) that general concepts have an existence independent of individual things. The relation between universals and particulars was a subject of philosophical dispute all through the Middle Ages.

The first person to hold the nominalist doctrine was probably Roscelin or Roscellinus in the late 11th cent., but very little is known of him and none of his works remains except for a single letter to Peter Abelard who was his pupil. Roscelin was born in France, accused twice of heresy but recanted and fled to England where he attacked the views of Anselm, according to whom Roscelin used the phrase that universals were a *flatus voci* or breath of the voice. The most important nominalist was the Englishman William of Occam in the 13th cent. who, once and for all, separated the two schools by saying in effect that science is about things (the nominalist view), whereas logic, philosophy, and religion are about terms or concepts (the Platonic tradition). Both are justified, but we must distinguish between them. The proposition "man is a species" is not a proposition of logic or philosophy but a scientific statement since we cannot say whether it is true or false without knowing about man. If we fail to realise that words are conventional signs and that it is important to decide whether or not they have a meaning and refer to something, then we shall fall into logical fallacies of the type: "Man is a species, Socrates is a man, therefore Socrates is a species." This, in effect, is the beginning of the modern philosophy of logical analysis which, to oversimplify, tells us that a statement is not just true or untrue, it may also be meaningless. Therefore, in all the philosophical problems we have discussed elsewhere, there is the third possibility that the problem we are discussing has no meaning because the words refer to nothing and we must ask ourselves before going any further "what do we mean by God," has the word "free-will" any definite meaning?

Nonconformism, the attitude of all those Christian bodies which do not conform to the doctrines of the Church of England. Up to the passing of the Act of Uniformity in 1662 they were called "puritans" or "dissenters" and were often persecuted. The oldest bodies of nonconformists are the Baptists, Independents, and (in England) the Presbyterians; the Methodists, although dating from 1738, did not consider themselves nonconformists until some time later. The Presbyterians are, of course, the official Church of Scotland where it is the Anglicans (known as "Episcopalians") who are the nonconformists, although not generally described as such.

O

Objectivism, a semi-political philosophy expounded by the American novelist, Ayn Rand, and interesting in as much as it was first propagated through two of her own best-selling novels. The thesis of Objectivism is the inherent suitability of the competitive capitalist system for the well-being and advancement of the human race. The seeds of man's destruction, Miss Rand believes, are to be found in the creeping menace of socialism, which by its tendency to encourage the individual to rely on the state rather than himself, undermines the dynamic power of human hard work and self-interest. In her first, and perhaps most significant novel, *The Fountainhead*, she tells the story of an unconventional and highly self-motivated architect, Howard Roark, who achieves world fame and success by a combination of hard work, talent, and refusal to compromise. Her second major novel, *Atlas Shrugged*, which is over 1100 pages long, pictures a world in which the "objectivists" (the hard-working, self-motivated, highly talented individuals in the human race) decide to pull out from society and set up a secret nation of their own. Left to its own devices, the world of socialist slackers and loafers slides into grey destruction. Objectivism seems to have arisen as a kind of counterblast to the growing tendency within some sections of the United States to decry capitalism as impersonal profiteering, and followers sport as their insignia a small badge depicting the dollar sign—the emblem incidentally of the secret states in *Atlas Shrugged*. The movement, which relies heavily on the talent and personality of its founder, has made little headway into formal American politics, but Miss Rand's books, which have sold literally by the millions, obviously touch a chord in many readers' minds.

Occam's Razor, the philosophical maxim by which William of Occam, the 14th cent. Franciscan has become best-known. This states in the form which is most familiar: "Entities are not to be multiplied without necessity" and as such does not appear in his works. He did, however, say something much to the same effect: "It is vain to do with more what can be done with fewer." In other words, if everything in some science can be interpreted without assuming this or that hypothetical entity, there is no ground for assuming it. This is Bertrand Russell's version, and he adds: "I have myself found this a most fruitful principle in logical analysis."

Occultism. *See* **Magic, Alchemy, Astrology,** and **Theosophy.**

Orangemen, members of an Irish society formed in Ulster in 1795 to uphold Protestantism. Their name is taken from King William III, Prince of Orange, who defeated James II at the Battle of the Boyne (1690), hence the enormous banners depicting "King Billy on the Boyne" carried in procession on 12 July each year. The Unionist Party of Northern Ireland (the ruling political party from 1921 to 1972) is largely maintained by the Orange Order. The Order has branches in many English-speaking countries but flourishes chiefly in Ulster.

Orgonomy, a pseudo-psychological theory advanced by the German psychiatrist Wilhelm Reich (1897–1957), a pupil of Freud, who was expelled from Germany for attacking the Nazis and who started life afresh in the U.S.A. like so many of his colleagues. Moving quickly away from orthodox psychoanalytic theories, Reich became increasingly obsessed with the view that all living things were permeated with a unique force or energy which he termed "orgone" and which he believed could be photographed and measured with a geiger counter. The key to the successful flow of orgone throughout the body was sexual intercourse and the resulting orgasm (hence "orgone"). Reich achieved a substantial following for his increasingly bizarre views and when he was sentenced to two-years' imprisonment in 1956 for alleged medical malpractice a "civil rights" controversy developed which has not died down to this date. His unfortunate and rather tragic death in prison has fanned the emotional issues and granted him the important role of martyr to his cause. There is presently a strong revival of interest in Reich and orgonomy, partly in tune with the general occult revival. A recent witty, but not totally unsympathetic film about his work "W R—Mysteries of the Organism" has drawn the attention of a large new audience to his teachings.

Orphism. The Greeks in general thought very little of their gods, regarding them as similar to human beings with human failings and virtues although on a larger scale. But there was another aspect of Greek religion which was passionate, ecstatic, and secret, dealing with the worship of various figures among whom were Bacchus or Dionysus, Orpheus, and Demeter and Persephone of the Eleusinian Mysteries. Dionysus (or Bacchus) was originally a god from Thrace where the people were primitive farmers naturally interested in fertility cults. Dionysus was the god of fertility who only later came to be associated with wine and the divine madness it produces. He assumed the form of a man or a bull and his worship by the time it arrived in Greece became associated with women (as was the case in most of the Mystery Religions) who spent nights on the hills dancing and possibly drinking wine in order to stimulate ecstasy; an unpleasant aspect of the cult was the tearing to pieces of wild animals whose flesh was eaten raw. Although the cult was disapproved of by the orthodox and, needless to say, by husbands, it existed for a long time.

This primitive and savage religion in time was modified by that attributed to Orpheus whose cult was more spiritualised, ascetic, and substituted mental for physical intoxication. Orpheus may have been a real person or a legendary hero and he, too, is supposed to have come from Thrace, but his name indicates that he, or the movement associated with him, came from Crete and originally from Egypt, which seems to have been the source of many of its doctrines. Crete, it must be remembered, was the island through which Egypt influenced Greece in other respects. Orpheus is said to have been a reformer who was torn to pieces by the Maenad worshippers of Dionysus. The Orphics believed in the transmigration of souls and that the soul after death might obtain either eternal bliss or temporary or permanent torment according to its way of life upon earth. They held ceremonies of purification and the more orthodox abstained from animal food except on special occasions when it was eaten ritually Man is partly earthly, partly heavenly, and a good life increases the heavenly part so that, in the end, he may become one with Bacchus and be called a "Bacchus"

The religion had an elaborate theology. As the Bacchic rites were reformed by Orpheus, so the Orphic rites were reformed by Pythagoras (*c.* 582–*c.* 507 B.C.) who introduced the mystical element into Greek philosophy which reached its heights in Plato. Other elements entered Greek life from Orphism. One of these was feminism which was notably lacking in Greek civilisation outside the Mystery Religions. The other was the drama which arose from the rites of Dionysus. The mysteries of Eleusis formed the most sacred part of the Athenian state religion, and it is clear that they had to do with fertility rites also, for they were in honour of Demeter and Persephone and all the myths speak of them as being associated with the supply of corn to the country. Without being provocative, it is accepted by most anthropologists and many theologians that Christianity, just as it accepted elements of Gnosticism and Mithraism, accepted elements from the Mystery Religions as they in turn must have done from earlier cults. The miraculous birth, the death and resurrection, the sacramental feast of bread and wine, symbolising the eating of the flesh and drinking of the blood of the god, all these are common elements in early religions and not just in one. None of this means that what we are told about Jesus is not true, but it surely does mean: (*a*) that Christianity was not a sudden development; (*b*) that the early Church absorbed many of the elements of other religions; (*c*) that perhaps Jesus Himself made use of certain symbols which He knew had a timeless significance for man and invested them with new meaning.

Orthodox Eastern Church. There are two groups of Eastern churches: (1) those forming the Orthodox Church dealt with here which include the ancient Byzantine patriarchates of Constantinople, Alexandria, Antioch, and Jerusalem, and the national churches of Russia, Greece, Yugoslavia, Bulgaria, Rumania, etc. (although Orthodox communities exist all over the world and are no longer confined to geographical areas); (2) the churches which rejected Byzantine orthodoxy during various controversies from the 5th to the 7th cent., notably the Coptic church (*q.v.*) and the Armenian church. Although all Orthodox churches share the same doctrine and traditions they are arranged as national independent bodies each with its own hierarchy. They do not recognise the pope, and the primacy of the patriarch of Constantinople is largely an honorary one. Although claiming to be the One Holy, Catholic, and Apostolic Church its alleged infallibility rests on universal agreement rather than on any one individual, and agreement over the faith comes from the Scriptures interpreted in the light of the Tradition. The latter includes dogmas relating to the Trinity, Christology, Mariology, and Holy Icons; the testimony of the Fathers (St. Athanasius, St. Basil, St. John Chrysostom, St. Cyril of Alexandria, etc.); the canons or rules as formulated by the Councils and the Fathers. The Orthodox Church did not take part in the great Western controversies about the Bible, nor, of course, in the Reformation. Attempts have recently been made to improve relations between Rome and Constantinople: the two Churches agreed in 1965 to retract the excommunications cast on each other in A.D. 1054, which formalised the Great Schism.

Ouspensky, a contemporary of Gurdjieff (*q.v.*), Peter Ouspensky was another obscure mystic of Eastern European origin who believed he had an occult philosophical message to bring to the West. This he embodied in a series of lengthy books which are both humourless and self-indulgent.

Oxford Group. *See* **Moral Re-Armament.**

Oxford Movement. *See* **Tractarianism.**

P

Pantheism. *See* **God and Man.**

Papal Infallibility. The basis of papal infallibility is (*a*) that every question of morals and faith is not dealt with in the Bible so it is necessary that there should be a sure court of appeal in case of doubt, and this was provided by Christ when he established the Church as His Teaching Authority upon earth; (*b*) ultimately this idea of the teaching function of the Church shapes the idea of papal infallibility which asserts that the pope, when speaking officially on matters of faith or morals, is protected by God against the possibility of error. The doctrine was proclaimed in July 1870.

Infallibility is a strictly limited gift which does not mean that the pope has extraordinary intelligence, that God helps him to find the answer to every conceivable question, or that Catholics have to accept the pope's views on politics. He can make mistakes or fall into sin, his scientific or historical opinions may be quite wrong, he may write books that are full of errors. Only in two limited spheres is he infallible and in these only when he speaks officially as the supreme teacher and lawgiver of the Church, defining a doctrine that must be accepted by all its members. When, after studying a problem of faith or morals as carefully as possible, and with all available help from expert consultants, he emerges with the Church's answer—on these occasions it is not strictly an answer, it is *the* answer.

Historically speaking, the Roman Catholic Church of the early 19th cent. was at its lowest ebb of power. Pope Pius IX, in fear of Italian nationalism, revealed his reactionary attitude by the feverish declaration of new dogmas, the canonisation of new saints, the denunciation of all modern ideals in the Syllabus of Errors, and the unqualified defence of his temporal power against the threat of Garibaldi. It is not too much to say that everything regarded as important by freedom-loving and democratic people was opposed by the papacy at that time. In 1870, after a long and sordid struggle, the Vatican Council, convened by Pius IX, pronounced the definition of his infallibility. Döllinger, a German priest and famous historian of the Church, was excommunicated because, like many others, he refused to accept the new dogma. It is difficult not to doubt that there was some connection between the pronouncement of the pope's infallibility and his simultaneous loss of temporal power.

After the humanism of the Second Vatican Council (1962–5) the Pope's encyclical *Humanae Vitae* (1968), condemning birth control, came as a great disappointment to the many people (including theologians, priests, and laymen) who had expected there would be a change in the Church's teaching. The Church's moral guidance on this controversial issue, however, does not involve the doctrine of infallibility. (The Roman Catholic Church teaches that papal pronouncements are infallible only when they are specifically defined as such.) That there is unlikely to be any immediate softening of the Church's line on infallibility was made clear in July 1973 when the Vatican's Sacred Congregation for the Doctrine of the Faith published a document strongly reaffirming papal infallibility. The document also reminded Catholics of their obligation to accept the Catholic Church's unique claims to authenticity.

Parapsychology, the name given to the study of psychical research (*q.v.*) as an academic discipline, and chosen to denote the topic's supposed status as a branch of psychology. The impetus behind parapsychology came from the psychologist William MacDougall who persuaded Duke University in North Carolina, U.S.A., to found a department of parapsychology under J. B. Rhine. Throughout the 1930s and 40s the work of Rhine and his colleagues, who claimed to have produced scientific evidence for the existence of E.S.P., attracted world-wide attention. Increasing reservations about the interpretation of Rhine's results and an apparent lack of any readily repeatable experiments, however, gradually eroded scientific confidence in the topic. The academic status of parapsychology is at the present time exceedingly uncertain. Rhine retired from university life in 1965 and the world-famous parapsychology laboratory at Duke University was closed. On the other hand the American Association for the Advancement of Science recently admitted the Parapsychology Association (the leading organisation for professional parapsychologists) as an affiliated member society. An American government body, the National Institute of Mental Health, has also officially supported some medical research into alleged telepathic dreams, the first "official" grant support of this kind. In Britain a recent poll of readers in the weekly journal, *New Scientist*, revealed a very high interest in the subject matter of parapsychology, though no British university actively supports research into the topic. Stories of intensive parapsychological research in Soviet Russia are however without foundation and are not supported by Western parapsychologists who have visited Russia. *See also* **Extra-sensory Perception, Q31-3.**

Parsees. *See* Zoroastrianism

Pavlovian theory. *See* Behaviourism.

Pentecostalism, a religious movement within the Protestant churches, holding the belief that an essential feature of true Christianity is a vigorous and profound spiritual or mystical experience which occurs after, and seemingly reinforces the initial conversion. The origins of modern Pentecostalism appear to lie in the occasion on 1 January 1901 when a member of a Bible College in Topeka, Kansas, one Agnes N. Ozman, spontaneously began to speak in an apparently unknown language at one of the College's religious meetings. This "speaking in tongues" was assumed to be evidence of her conversion and "spirit baptism", and became a feature of most Pentecostal meetings in due course. The movement spread rapidly across America, particularly in rural communities, and also was a strong feature of Welsh religious life in the early part of the century. Pentecostal services are enthusiastic and rousing, with a strong emphasis on music and participation on the part of the congregation. Pentecostalism is evangelistic in nature and seems to be gaining in strength at the present time, at the expense of more orthodox and staid versions of Christianity. The fiery character Aimee Semple McPherson was one of its most prominent evangelists.

Phrenology, a psychological "school" founded in 1800 by two Germans, Franz Josef Gall and Johann Gaspar Spurzheim. Gall was an anatomist who believed there to be some correspondence between mental faculties and the shape of the head. He tested these ideas in prisons and mental hospitals and began to lecture on his findings, arousing a great deal of interest throughout both Europe and America, where his doctrines were widely accepted. Phrenology became fashionable, and people would go to "have their bumps read" as later men and women of fashion have gone to be psychoanalysed. Roughly speaking, Gall divided the mind into thirty-seven faculties such as destructiveness, suavity, self-esteem, conscientiousness, and so on, and claimed that each of these was located in a definite area of the brain. He further claimed that the areas in the brain corresponded to "bumps" on the skull which could be read by the expert, thus giving a complete account of the character of the subject. In fact, (*a*) no such faculties are located in the brain anywhere for this is simply not the way the brain works; (*b*) the faculties described by Gall are not pure traits which cannot be further analysed and are based on a long outdated psychology; (*c*) the shape of the brain bears no specific relationship to the shape of the skull. Phrenology is a pseudo-science; there is no truth in it whatever. But, even so, like astrology, it still has its practitioners.

Physiocrats. A French school of economic thought during the 18th cent., known at the time as *Les Economistes* but in later years named physiocrats by Du Pont de Nemours, a member of the School. Other members were Quesnay, Mirabeau, and the great financier Turgot. The physiocrats held the view, common to the 18th cent., and deriving ultimately from Rousseau, of the goodness and bounty of nature and the goodness of man "as he came from the bosom of nature." The aim of governments, therefore, should be to conform to nature; and so long as men do not interfere with each other's liberty and do not combine among themselves, governments should leave them free to find their own salvation. Criminals, madmen, and monopolists should be eliminated. Otherwise the duty of government is *laissez-faire, laissez passer*. From this follows the doctrine of free trade between nations on grounds of both justice and economy; for the greater the competition, the more will each one strive to economise the cost of his labour to the general advantage. Adam Smith, although not sharing their confidence in human nature, learned much from the physiocrats, eliminated their errors, and greatly developed their teaching.

Physiognomy. *See* **Characterology.**

Pietism, a movement in the Lutheran Church at the end of the 17th cent.—the reaction, after the sufferings of the thirty years' war, of a pious and humiliated people against learning, pomp and ceremony, and stressing the importance of man's personal relationship with God. The writings of Johann Georg Hamann (1730–88) who came from a Pietist family of Königsberg influenced Kierkegaard. The Pietist movement was the root of the great Romantic movement of the 18th cent.

Plymouth Brethren, a religious sect founded by John Nelson Darby, a minister of the Protestant Church of Ireland, and Edward Cronin, a former Roman Catholic, in 1827. Both were dissatisfied with the lack of spirituality in their own and other churches and joined together in small meetings in Dublin every Sunday for "the breaking of bread." Soon the movement began to spread through Darby's travels and writings and he finally settled in Plymouth, giving the popular name to the "Brethren." Beginning as a movement open to all who felt the need to "keep the unity of the Spirit," it soon exercised the right to exclude all who had unorthodox views and split up into smaller groups. Among these the main ones were the "Exclusives," the Kellyites, the Newtonites, and "Bethesda" whose main differences were over problems of church government or prophetical powers. Some of these are further split among themselves. Readers of *Father and Son* by Sir Edmund Gosse, which describes life with his father, the eminent naturalist Philip Gosse, who belonged to the Brethren, will recall how this basically kind, honest, and learned man was led through their teachings to acts of unkindness (*e.g.*, in refusing to allow his son and other members of his household to celebrate Christmas and throwing out the small tokens they had secretly bought), and intellectual dishonesty (*e.g.*, in refusing for religious reasons alone to accept Darwinism when all his evidence pointed towards it).

Today, the majority of Brethren belong to the "Open Brethren" assemblies and, unlike the "Exclusives," hold that the Lord's Supper (a commemorative act of "breaking the bread" observed once a week) is for all Christians who care to join them. Baptism is required and Brethren believe in the personal premillenial second coming of Christ.

Poltergeist, allegedly a noisy type of spirit which specialises in throwing things about, making loud thumpings and bangings, and occasionally bringing in "apports," *i.e.*, objects from elsewhere. Most so-called poltergeist activities are plain frauds, but the others are almost invariably associated with the presence in the house of someone (often, but not always a child) who is suffering from severe mental conflicts usually of a sexual nature. The inference is that those activities which are not simply fraudulent are either due to some unknown influence exuded by such mentally abnormal people, or that they are actually carried out by ordinary physical means by such people when in a state of hysterical dissociation—*i.e.*, unconsciously. The second hypothesis is much the more probable. *See* **Psychic Research.**

Polytheism. *See* **God and Man.**

Positivism, also known as the **Religion of Humanity**, was founded by Auguste Comte (1798–1857), a famous mathematician and philosopher born in Montpellier France. His views up to the end of the century attracted many and it would have been impossible throughout that time to read a book on philosophy or sociology that did not mention them, but today his significance is purely of historical interest. In his *Cours de Philosophie Positive* (1830) he put forward the thesis that mankind had seen three great stages in human thought: (1) the theological, during which man seeks for supernatural causes to explain nature and invents gods and devils; (2) the metaphysical, through which he thinks in terms of philosophical and metaphysical abstractions; (3) the last positive or scientific stage when he will proceed by experiment and objective observation to reach in time "positive truth."

Broadly speaking, there is little to complain of in this analysis; for there does seem to have been some sort of general direction along these lines. However, Comte was not satisfied with having reached this point and felt that his system demanded a religion and, of course, one that was "scientific." This religion was to be the worship of Humanity in place of the personal Deity of earlier times, and for it he supplied not only a Positive Catechism but a treatise on Sociology in which he declared himself the High Priest of the cult. Since, as it stood, the religion was likely to appear somewhat abstract to many. Comte drew up a list of historical characters whom he regarded as worthy of the same sort of adoration as Catholics accord to their saints. The new Church attracted few members, even among those who had a high regard for Comte's scientific work, and its only significant adherents were a small group of Oxford scholars and some in his own country. Frederic Harrison was the best-known English adherent and throughout his life continued to preach Comtist doctrines in London to diminishing audiences.

Pragmatism, a typically American school of philosophy which comes under the heading of what Bertrand Russell describes as a "practical" as opposed to a "theoretical" philosophy. Whereas the latter, to which most of the great philosophical systems belong, seeks disinterested knowledge for its own sake, the former (*a*) regards action as the supreme good, (*b*) considers happiness an effect and knowledge a mere instrument of successful activity.

The originator of pragmatism is usually considered to have been the psychologist William James (1842–1910) although he himself attributed its basic principles to his life-long friend, the American philosopher, Charles Sanders Peirce (1839–1914). The other famous pragmatist is John Dewey, best-known in Europe for his works on education (for although American text-books on philosophy express opinions to the contrary, few educated people in Europe have taken the slightest interest in pragmatism and generally regard it as an eccentricity peculiar to Americans). James in his book *The Will to Believe* (1896) points out that we are often compelled to take a decision where no adequate theoretical grounds for a decision exist; for even to do nothing is to decide. Thus in religion we have a right to adopt a believing attitude although not intellectually fully convinced. We should believe truth and shun error, but the failing of the sceptical philosopher is that he adheres only to the latter rule and thus fails to believe various truths which a less cautious man will accept. If believing truth and avoiding error are equally important, then it is a good idea when we are presented with an alternative to believe one of the possibilities at will, since we then have an even chance of being right, whereas we have none if we suspend judgment. The function of philosophy, according to James, is to find out what difference it makes to the individual if a particular philosophy or world-system is true: "An idea is 'true' so long as to believe it is profitable to our lives," and, he adds, "the true is only the expedient in our way of thinking . . . in the long run and on the whole of course." Thus "if the hypothesis of God works satisfactorily in the widest sense of the word, it is true." Bertrand Russell's reply to this assertion is: "I have always found that the hypothesis of Santa Claus 'works satisfactorily in the widest sense of the word'; therefore 'Santa Claus exists' is true, although Santa Claus does not exist." Russell adds that James's concept of truth simply omits as unimportant the question whether God really *is* in His heaven; if He is a useful hypothesis that is enough. "God the Architect of the Cosmos is forgotten; all that is remembered is belief in God, and its effects upon the creatures inhabiting our petty planet. No wonder the Pope condemned the pragmatic defence of religion."

Predestination. *See* Calvinism.

Presbyterianism, a system of ecclesiastical government of the Protestant churches which look back to John Calvin as their Reformation leader. The ministry consists of presbyters who are all of equal rank. Its doctrinal standards are contained in the *Westminster Confession of Faith* (1647) which is, in general, accepted by English, Scottish, and American Presbyterians as the most thorough and logical statement in existence of the Calvinist creed. The Church of Scotland is the leading Presbyterian church in the British Isles.

The Reformation in Scotland was preceded by the same sort of awareness of the moral corruption of the Roman Church as had happened elsewhere, but for various political and emotional reasons, which need not be discussed here, the majority of the Scottish people (unlike the English who had been satisfied with the mere exchange of Crown for Pope) were determined on a fundamental change of doctrine, discipline, and worship, rather than a reform of manners. The church preachers had learned their Protestantism not from Luther but from Calvin and their leader John Knox had worked in Geneva with Calvin himself and was resolved to introduce the system into Scotland. In 1557 the "Lords of the Congregation" signed the Common Band (*i.e.*, a bond or covenant) to maintain "the blessed Word of God and his congregation" against their enemies, and demanded the right to worship as they had chosen. However, the real date of the Scottish Reformation is August 1560 when Mary of Guise (the regent for Mary Queen of Scots who was not yet of age) died and the Estates met to settle their affairs without foreign pressure; the *Scots Confession* was drawn up and signed by Knox and adopted by the Estates.

The ideas on which the Reformed Kirk was based are found in the *Scots Confession*, the *Book of Discipline*, and the *Book of Common Order*, the so-called Knox's liturgy. Knox's liturgy, the same as that used in Geneva but translated into English, was used until Laud's attempt to force an Anglican liturgy on the Kirk led to an abandonment of both in favour of "free prayers."

The Presbyterian tradition includes uncompromising stress upon the Word of God contained in the Scriptures of the Old and New Testaments as the supreme rule of faith and life, and upon the value of a highly trained ministry, which has given the Church of Scotland a high reputation for scholarship and has in turn influenced the standard of education in Scotland. The unity of the Church is guaranteed by providing for democratic representation in a hierarchy of courts (unlike the Anglican Church, which is a hierarchy of persons). The local kirk-session consists of the minister and popularly elected elders (laymen). Ministers, elected by their flocks, are ordained by presbyters (ministers already ordained). Above the kirk-session is the court of the presbytery which has jurisdiction over a specified area; above that the court of synod which rules over many presbyteries; and finally the General Assembly which is the Supreme Court of the Church with both judicial and legislative powers, and over which the Moderator of the General Assembly presides. The function of the elders is to help the minister in the work and government of the kirk. The episcopacy set up by James VI and I, and maintained by Charles I was brought to an end by the Glasgow Assembly (1638), but General Assemblies were abolished by Oliver Cromwell and at the Restoration Charles II re-established episcopacy. The Covenanters who resisted were hunted down, imprisoned, transported, or executed over a period of nearly thirty years before William of Orange came to the throne and Presbyterianism was re-established (1690). Today Presbyterians no less than other Christian communities are looking at Christianity as a common world religion in the sense that the principles which unite them are greater than those which divide them. A small but significant step in the direction of international Christian unity was made in 1972 when the Presbyterian and Congregationalist Churches in England were merged to form the United Reformed Church. *See* Church of Scotland, Calvinism.

Protestant, the name first applied to those who favoured the cause of Martin Luther and who protested against the intolerant decisions of the Catholic majority at the second Diet of Speyer (1529), revoking earlier decisions of the first Diet of Speyer tolerating the Reformers in certain cases (1526). In general the name "Protestant" is applied to those Churches which severed connection with Rome at the time of the Reformation. The essence of Protestantism is the acceptance by the individual Christian of his direct responsibility to God rather than to the Church. *See* Lutheranism, Presbyterianism, Calvinism.

Psychedelism. For all his recorded history man

has relied upon drugs of one kind or another to make his life more tolerable. These have generally been central nervous system depressants—*i.e.*, alcohol, hashish, etc.—and their use in most societies has been brought under careful government control. Most societies have also at some stage experimented with the use of certain drugs of another class—the hallucinogens. These, far from having the mentally tranquillising characteristics of small doses of alcohol, provoke striking changes in mental alertness, frequently coupled with visionary or hallucinatory experiences. The confusion and disorientation which accompany such states has led to social disapproval of their use in Western countries. and the favoured "legal" drug for centuries has been alcohol. In the 1950s the novelist Aldous Huxley in his essay *The Doors of Perception* wrote of his experiences with the drug mescalin, a derivative of the South American peyotl and a powerful hallucinogen. Huxley put forward the hypothesis that mescalin had given him not only an entirely original psychological experience but had also significantly "heightened" his perceptual ability—a development of the greatest possible interest to artists, writers, and poets. Huxley's book had considerable impact, stimulating other creative individuals into similar experiments, not always with such euphoric results. In England the author Richard Ward reported some frightening moments under the drug LSD in his *A Drug-taker's Notebook* and Huxley amplified the unpredictable nature of the drug-experience in *Heaven and Hell*, published in 1956. Although such experiments were technically illegal, public interest had been considerably aroused and in the 1960s, when it became easy to synthesise the most effective of the hallucinogens, LSD, its use began to be common among certain sections of society. In 1964 a sensational scandal rocked the great American university of Harvard when senior members of the teaching staff, including the psychologist Timothy Leary, were dismissed for using LSD and encouraging students in its use. Unrepentant, Dr. Leary set up a community near New York from whence the cult of psychedelism was propagated.

Psychedelism—which is not really an organised system of belief, but rather an attitude of mind—preaches that through the controlled use of drugs, particularly of the hallucinogenic variety, an individual may be made aware for the first time of the rich fields of experience which lie latent in the unconscious mind. The exploration of these territories will have both a liberating and an enriching effect, the outcome being to "turn on" the individual to the total reality of mind. So convinced do many of the proponents of psychedelia become of the significance of the experience of the so-called LSD "trip," that they are inclined to urge non-trippers to experiment with the drug. Herein, of course, lies one obvious danger, for the drug LSD is potentially a toxic substance which needs to be administered in minute doses if it is not to cause madness or even death. There is also much uncertainty about the possible long-term effects of "tripping," many psychologists and scientists believing that it leads to a progressive disorientation and destruction of the personality, a disintegration of which the individual drug-taker is seldom aware. If there is a credit side to psychedelism it may lie in the clear, if limited, evolution in popular music, art, and design and to a lesser extent, literature which has been inspired by these excursions. The wave of interest in LSD and similar drugs is beginning to slacken off, possibly because of an increasing awareness of the possible grievous side-effects and of the largely illusory nature of the "insights" which the "trip" is supposed to provide. The controversial Dr. Leary, the movement's most literate and influential figure, has himself disavowed many of his original statements, and today warns young people against the indiscriminate use of drugs as an aid to insight or self-awareness.

Psychic Research is a general term for the various approaches to the scientific investigation of the paranormal, in particular supposed extra-sensery powers of the mind, but also manifestations such as ghosts, poltergeists, spiritualistic phenomena, etc. In recent years the word parapsychology has also come into use, particularly for the investigation of ESP in a laboratory setting, but it is really part of psychic research as the subject's fascinating history reveals.

For all recorded history, and no doubt very much earlier, man has been puzzled at his apparent ability to perceive features of the universe without the use of the normal senses—mind-to-mind contact, dreams about the future which come true, etc. He has also been intrigued by the notion that in addition to the natural world of people and things, there exists in parallel, a *supernatural* world of ghosts, spirits and other similar strange manifestations. Belief in such oddities has been tremendously widespread and still forms one of the major casual conversational topics raised when people see each other socially today. Of course, until the 19th cent. or thereabouts such phenomena, while bizarre, unpredictable and possibly frightening, were not at odds with man's view of himself and his world as revealed through basic religious beliefs. Man was supposed to be in essence a supernatural being with eternal life, and the world was seen as the happy hunting ground of dynamic evil forces which could intervene directly in the lives of humans. The rise of material science in the 19th cent. however began to shake the orthodox religious framework, and as a result in due course scientists began to question the basis of all supernatural powers and manifestations, putting forward the reasonable argument: "if such things *are* real then they should be demonstrable in scientific terms—just as all other aspects of the universe are."

Once having advanced this argument, the next step was to carry it to its conclusion and set about the systematic investigation of the phenomena to see whether they *did* conform in any way to the immensely successful framework of 19th cent. science, and from this step psychic research was born. In fact one can date its origins rather precisely—to 1882 when a group of scholars formed the Society for Psychical Research in London—an organisation which still exists today. The first experiments in this slightly eccentric field of science were haphazard and tended to be confined to spiritualistic phenomena such as table tapping, mediumistic messages, ectoplasmic manifestations, etc., which were having a great wave of popularity among the general public at the time. In fact what one might term as the first phase of psychic research—it has gone through three phases in its history—was really heavily tied up with Spiritualism. Before ridiculing it for this, it is only fair to point lut that many of the most eminent figures of the time—the great physicists Sir Oliver Lodge and Sir William Crookes, Alfred Russell Wallace, co-discoverer with Darwin of the theory of evolution by natural selection, the brilliant author and creator of Sherlock Holmes, Sir Arthur Conan Doyle, and many others—became convinced Spiritualists as the result of their early experiments. Nevertheless, despite the ardent support of such intellectual giants, medium after medium was in due course detected in fraud—sometimes of the most blatant kind—and the majority of scientists gradually became more critical and less likely to be taken in by even the subtlest of trickery. As a result, interest slowly shifted from the séance room to a different realm, and as it did so the first phase of psychic research drew to a close.

The second phase was, broadly speaking, the era of the ghost hunter. With the idea of spirits materialising in laboratories seeming intrinsically less and less credible, scientists began to study what struck them at the time to be basically more "plausible" matters—haunted houses, poltergeist phenomena and so on. For some reason the idea of a house dominated by a psychic presence as the result of some tragic history seemed (at the turn of the century) *somehow* scientifically and philosophically more acceptable than did the old spiritualist notions about direct communication with the spirit world. The key figure in the "ghost hunting" era was Mr. Harry Price, an amateur magician who became the scourge of fraudulent mediums, but who staked his name and credibility on the authenticity of the alleged poltergeist phenomena at Borley Rectory in Suffolk, which became world famous through his book "The Most Haunted House in England." The ancient rectory's catalogue of ghosts and marvels allegedly witnessed by numerous "reliable witnesses" seemed irrefutable. Unfortunately investigations by the Society for Psychical Research some years after Price's death now make it seem certain that Price was responsible for faking some of the Borley phenomena himself, and with these disclosures scientifically "respectable" ghost hunting took a nasty tumble. Thus, with an increasingly critical attitude developing among scientists, haunted houses and poltergeists gradually began to shift out of favour to usher in the third phase of psychic research.

The date of the commencement of this phase can be identified as 1927 when the Parapsychology Laboratory at Duke University in North Carolina was formed by Dr. J. B. Rhine. Here the emphasis was on laboratory studies along the traditional lines of experimental psychology; spirit forms and poltergeists were ignored in favour of the routine testing of literally thousands of people for telepathy, precognition (the ability to see into the future), etc., almost always involving card tests which could be rigidly controlled and the results statistically analysed. By the 1940s Rhine was claiming irrefutable evidence of telepathy achieved by these means, but once again critical forces began to gather and it was pointed out that results obtained in Rhine's laboratory rarely seemed to be replicable in other scientists' laboratories in different parts of the world. In fact the failure of ESP experiments of this kind to be easily repeatable has turned out to be crucial and has led to a growing scepticism on the part of uncommitted scientists who now question whether psychic research and parapsychology have really advanced our understanding of the world of the paranormal in any way. At the present time the topic is in a highly controversial phase; Rhine's university parapsychology laboratory has closed with his retirement, allegations of cheating and faking experimental results have been made against some parapsychologists (and apparently substantiated) and the topic is racked with controversy both internal and external. On the other hand public as opposed to scientific interest in the topic remains exceedingly high, though interest in the more sensational and bizarre phenomena, such as the alleged fork bending abilities of the Israeli Uri Geller, seems to be growing at the expense of the routine, admittedly dull, but at least scientifically controllable, card guessing experiments by Rhine.

To sum up the topic one could say that in a curious way, while the third phase of psychic research is now drawing to a close, the evidence suggests that a fourth phase is appearing, and that this may well feature a return to the study of the more sensational and dramatic phenomena characteristic of Uri Geller, and in its way so reminiscent of the Victorian séance room. If this is so, a century after its foundation the wheel will have turned full circle and psychic research will be back where it started, without in the opinion of most scientists, having solved any of the basic questions which it had set out to answer. *See* **Poltergeist, Telepathy, Spiritualism.**

Psychoanalysis, an approach to the study of human personality involving the rigorous probing, with the assistance of a specially trained practitioner, of an individual's personal problems, motives, goals and attitudes to life in general. Often, and quite understandably, confused with psychology (of which it is merely a part), psychoanalysis has an interesting historical background and has attracted the interest of philosophers, scientists and medical experts since it emerged as a radical and controversial form of mental therapy at the turn of the century. The traditionally accepted founder is the great Austrian Sigmund Freud, but he never failed to acknowledge the impetus that had been given to his own ideas by his talented friend, the physiologist Joseph Breuer, who for most of his working life had been interested in the curious phenomena associated with hypnosis. Breuer had successfully cured the hysterical paralysis of a young woman patient and had noticed that under hypnosis the girl seemed to be recalling emotional experiences, hitherto forgotten, which bore some relationship to the symptoms of her illness. Developing this with other patients Breuer then found that the mere recalling and discussing of the emotional events under hypnosis seemed to produce a dramatic alleviation of the symptoms—a phenomenon which came to be known as *catharsis*. Breuer also noticed another curious side-effect, that his women patients fell embarrassingly and violently in love with him, and he gradually dropped the practice of "mental catharsis," possibly feeling that it was a bit too dangerous to handle. This left the field clear for Freud, whose brilliant mind began to search beyond the therapeutic aspects of the topic to see what light might be thrown on the nature of human personality and psychological mechanisms in general. The most important question concerned the "forgotten" emotional material which turned up, apparently out of the blue, during the hypnotic session. Freud rightly saw that this posed problems for the current theories of memory, for how could something once forgotten (a) continue to have an effect on the individual without his being aware of it, and (b) ultimately be brought back to conscious memory again. It must be remembered that at this time memory was considered to be a fairly simple process—information was stored in the brain and was gradually eroded or destroyed with the passage of time and the decay of brain cells. Once lost, it was believed, memories were gone for ever, or at best only partially and inaccurately reproducible. Furthermore, human beings were supposed to be rational (if frequently wilful) creatures who never did anything without thinking about it (if only briefly) beforehand and without being well aware of their reasons for so doing. It was within this framework that Freud had his great insight, one which many people believe to be one of the most important ideas given to mankind. This was simply the realisation that the human mind was not a simple entity controlling the brain and body more or less at will, but a complex system made up of a number of integrated parts with at least two major subdivisions—the conscious and the unconscious. The former concerned itself with the normal round of human behaviour, including the larger part of rational thought, conversation, etc., and large areas of memory. The latter was principally devoted to the automatic control of bodily functions, such as respiration, cardiac activity, various types of emotional behaviour not subject to much conscious modification and a large storehouse of relevant "memories" again not normally accessible to the conscious mind. Occasionally, Freud proposed, an exceedingly unpleasant emotional or otherwise painful event might be so troublesome if held in the conscious mind's store, that it would get shoved down into the unconscious or "repressed" where it would cease to trouble the individual in his normal life. The advantages of this mechanism are obvious, but they also brought with them hazards. With certain kinds of memory, particularly those involving psychological rather than physical pain—as for example a severe sexual conflict or marital problem—repression might be used as a device to save the individual from facing his problem in the "real" world, where he might be able ultimately to solve it, by merely hiding it away in the unconscious and thus pretending it did not exist. Unfortunately, Freud believed, conflicts of this kind were not snuffed out when consigned to the basements of the mind, but rather tended to smoulder on, affecting the individual in various ways which he could not understand. Repressed marital conflicts might give rise to impotence, for example, or even to homosexual behaviour. Guilt at improper social actions similarly repressed might provoke nervous tics, local paralysis, etc. etc. Following this line of reasoning, Freud argued that if the unwisely repressed material could be dredged up and the individual forced to face the crisis instead of denying it, then dramatic alleviations of symptoms and full recovery should follow.

To the great psychologist and his growing band of followers the stage seemed to be set for a dramatic breakthrough not only in mental therapy but also in a general understanding of the nature of human personality. To his pleasure—for various reasons he was never too happy about hypnosis—Freud discovered that with due patience, skill and guidance an individual could be led to resurrect the material repressed in his unconscious mind in the normal, as opposed to the hypnotic, state. This technique, involving long sessions consisting of intimate discussions between patient and therapist became known as psychoanalysis, and it has steadily evolved from its experimental beginnings in the medical schools and universities of Vienna to being a major system of psychotherapy with a world-wide following and important theoretical connotations. Psychoanalysis, as practised today, consists of a number of meetings between doctor and patient in which the latter is slowly taught to approach and enter the territory of his subconscious mind, and examine the strange and "forgotten" material within. A successful analysis, it is claimed, gives the individual greater insight into his own personality and a fuller understanding of the potent unconscious forces which are at work within him and in part dictating his goals.

Freud's initial ideas were of course tentative, and meant to be so. He was however a didactic and forceful personality himself, unwilling to compromise on many points which became controversial as the technique and practice of psychoanalysis developed. The outcome was that some of his early followers, notably the equally brilliant Carl Jung and Alfred Adler, broke away to found their own "schools" or versions of psychoanalysis, with varying degrees of success. Today, psychoanalysis is coming under increasingly critical scrutiny, and its claims are being treated with a good deal of reservation. Notable antagonists include the English psychologist Professor H. J. Eysenck who points out that there is little if any solid experimental data indicating that psychoanalysis is a valid method of treating or curing mental illness. Analysts respond by saying that their system is closer to an art than a craft and not amenable to routine scientific experiment. The controversy will no doubt continue for some time to come, but whatever its validity as therapy, the basic ideas behind psychoanalysis—notably the reality and power of the unconscious mind—are beyond question and have given human beings definite and major insights into the greatest enigma of all—the workings of the human mind. *See also* **Section Q.**

Psychokinesis (alternatively **Telekinesis**), the supposed faculty of the human mind to influence objects at a distance by "thought" or the act of will. Scientific evidence for the existence of PK (as it is abbreviated) is very slender indeed and people claiming to have witnessed it have probably been the victims of simple trickery or a skilful illusion. Almost 20,000,000 people watched an alleged demonstration of PK on British television in 1973 when a young Israeli, Uri Geller, purported to bend cutlery by mental power. Despite their spectacular appearance, such demonstrations have no scientific validity and little can be inferred about the powers of Mr. Geller and other similar claimants unless they have demonstrated their abilities to professional magicians, in order that simple sleight of hand can be ruled out.

Psychometry, the supposed talent or faculty of divining something about the history and previous owners of an object by holding it in the hand. A common feature of modern Spiritualistic practice, and to a certain extent synonymous with clairvoyance, psychometry is based on an ancient magical assumption that objects somehow take on traces or "memories" of their surroundings which are detectable by specially sensitive individuals. Controlled scientific tests on people claiming to have this power have however proved totally negative. *See also* **Psychic Research.**

Pyramidology, a curious belief that the dimensions of the Great Pyramid at Giza, if studied carefully, reveal principles of fundamental historical and religious significance. The perpetrator of this was a Victorian publisher, John Taylor, who discovered that if you divide the height of the pyramid into twice the side of its base you get a number very similar to *pi*—a number of considerable mathematical importance. Later discoveries in the same vein include the finding that the base of the pyramid (when divided by the width of a single casing stone) equals exactly 365—number of days in the year. Many books have been written on the interpretation of the dimensions of the pyramid, none of which has any scientific or archaeological validity. Pyramidology is simply a classic example of the well-known fact that hunting through even a random array of numbers will turn up sequences which appear to be "significant"—always provided that one carefully selects the numbers one wants and turns a blind eye to those that one doesn't! A peculiar variant of pyramidology has recently arisen through the publication of a claim that razor blades kept beneath a cardboard model of a pyramid never lose their cutting edge! Scientific tests have shown that this is not so, but the belief persists—implicit testimony to the mystical power of certain common emblems and symbols.

Pyrrhonism, a sceptical philosophy which doubts everything.

Q

Quakers, a religious body founded in England in the 17th cent. by George Fox (1624–91). The essence of their faith is that every individual who believes has the power of direct communication with God who will guide him into the ways of truth. This power comes from the "inner light" of his own heart, the light of Christ. Quakers meet for worship avoiding all ritual, without ordained ministers or prepared sermons; there is complete silence until someone is moved by the Holy Spirit to utter his message.

In the early days Quakers gave vent to violent outbursts and disturbed church services. Friends had the habit of preaching at anyone who happened to be nearby, their denunciation of "steeple-houses" and references to the "inner light," their addressing everyone as "thee" and "thou," their refusal to go beyond "yea" and "nay" in making an assertion and refusing to go further in taking an oath, must have played some part in bringing about the savage persecutions they were forced to endure. Many emigrated to Pennsylvania, founded by William Penn in 1682, and missionaries were sent to many parts of the world. The former violence gave way to gentleness. Friends not only refused to take part in war but even refused to resist personal violence. They took the lead in abolishing slavery, worked for prison reform and better education. As we know them today Quakers are quiet, sincere, undemonstrative people, given to a somewhat serious turn of mind. The former peculiarities of custom and dress have been dropped and interpretation of the Scriptures is more liberal. Although Quakers refuse to take part in warfare, they are always ready to help the victims of war, by organising relief, helping refugees in distress, or sending their ambulance units into the heat of battle.

Quietism, a doctrine of extreme asceticism and contemplative devotion, embodied in the works of Michael Molinos, a 17th cent. Spanish priest, and condemned by Rome. It taught that the chief duty of man is to be occupied in the continual contemplation of God, so as to become totally independent of outward circumstances and the influence of the senses. Quietists taught that when this stage of perfection is reached the soul has no further need for prayer and other external devotional practices. Similar doctrines have been taught in the Moslem and Hindu religions. *See* **Yoga.**

R

Racism, the doctrine that one race is inherently superior or inferior to others, one of the bases of racial prejudice. It has no connection whatever with the study of race as a concept, nor with the investigation of racial differences, which is a science practised by the physical anthropologist (who studies physical differences), or the social anthropologist (who studies cultural differences). Racism is simply a vulgar superstition believed in by the ignorant or mentally unbalanced, and it may be categorically stated as a scientific fact that racial superiority is a myth believed in by no scientist of repute. *See also* **Race, Section L.**

Radiesthesia, the detection, either by some "psychic" faculty or with special equipment, of radiations alleged to be given off by all living things and natural substances such as water, oil, metal, etc. The word radiesthesia is in fact a fancy modern name for the ancient practice of "dowsing," whereby an individual is supposed to be able to detect the presence of hidden underground water by following the movements of a hazel twig held in his hands. Dowsers, or water diviners, as they are sometimes called, claim also to be able to detect the presence of minerals and, hard though it may seem to believe, have actually been hired by major oil companies to prospect for desert wells—though without any notable successes. The theory of dowsing is that all things give off a unique radiation signal which the trained individual (via his twig, pendulum, or whatever) can "tune in" to, a theory which, while not backed up by any data known to orthodox sciences, is at least not too fantastically far-fetched. It is when radiesthesists claim to be able to detect the presence of oil, water, or precious metals by holding their pendulum *over a map* of the territory and declare that it is not necessary for them to visit the area in person to find the required spot that the topic moves from the remotely possible to the absurdly improbable. Some practitioners of this art state that they are able to perform even more marvellous feats such as determining the sex of chickens while still in the egg, or diagnosing illness by studying the movements of a pendulum held over a blood sample from the sick individual. Such claims when put to simple scientific test have almost invariably turned out as fiascos. Yet belief in dowsing, water-divining, and the like is still very widespread.

There is an important link between radiesthesia and the pseudo-science of *radionics*, which holds that the twig or pendulum can be superseded by complicated equipment built vaguely according to electronic principles. A typical radionic device consists of a box covered with knobs, dials, etc., by which the practitioner "tunes in" to the "vibration" given off by an object, such as a blood spot, a piece of hair, or even a signature. By the proper interpretation of the readings from the equipment the illness, or even the mental state, of the individual whose blood, hair, or signature is being tested, may be ascertained. The originator of radionics seems to have been a Dr. Albert Abrams who engaged in medical practice using radionic devices in America in the 1920s and 30s. The principal exponent in this country was the late George de la Warr who manufactured radionic boxes for diagnosis and treatment of illnesses, and even a "camera" which he believed to be capable of photographing thought. In a sensational court case in 1960 a woman who had purchased one of the diagnostic devices sued de la Warr for fraud. After a long trial the case was dismissed, the Judge commenting that while he had no good evidence that the device worked as claimed, he felt that de la Warr sincerely believed in its validity and thus was not guilty of fraud or misrepresentation. Some practitioners hold this as in some way justifying or accrediting the science of radionics but most observers feel that the case was more a triumph for British justice and the right of the individual to promote his beliefs whatever they may be—provided they are sincerely held and do no obvious social harm.

Ranters, a derisive term for the Primitive Methodists (*see* **Methodism**).

Rationalism is defined as "the treating of reason as the ultimate authority in religion and the rejection of doctrines not consonant with reason." In practice, rationalism has a double significance: (1) the doctrine as defined above, and (2) a 19th cent. movement which was given to what was then known as "free-thought," "secularism," or agnosticism—*i.e.*, it was in the positive sense anti-religious and was represented by various bodies such as the Secular Society, the National Secular Society, and the Rationalist Press Association (founded in 1899).

In the first sense, which implies a particular philosophical attitude to the universe and life, rationalism is not easy to pin down although, at first sight, it would appear that nothing could be simpler. Does it mean the use of pure reason and logic or does it mean, on the other hand, the use of what is generally called the "scientific method" based on a critical attitude to existing beliefs? If we are thinking in terms of the use of pure reason and logic then the Roman Catholic Church throughout most of its history has maintained, not that the whole truth about religion can be discovered by reason, but as St. Thomas Aquinas held, the basis of religion—*e.g.* the existence of God—can be rationally demonstrated. Nobody could have made more use of logic than the schoolmen of the Middle Ages, yet not many people today would accept their conclusions, nor would many non-Catholics accept St. Thomas's proofs of the existence of God even when they themselves are religious. The arguments of a First Cause or Prime Mover or the argument from Design on the whole leave us unmoved, partly because they do not lead us to the idea of a *personal God*, partly because we rightly distrust logic and pure reason divorced from facts and know that, if we begin from the wrong assumptions or premises, we can arrive at some very strange answers. If the existence of a Deity can be proved by reason, then one can also by the use of reason come to the conclusions, or rather paradoxes, such as the following: God is by definition all good, all knowing, all powerful—yet evil exists (because if it does not exist then it cannot be wrong to say "there is no God"). But if evil exists, then it must do so either because of God (in which case He is not all good) or in spite of God (in which case He is not all powerful).

Arguments of this sort do not appeal to the modern mind for two historical reasons: (1) many of us have been brought up in the Protestant tradition which—at least in one of its aspects—insists that we must believe in God by faith rather than by logic and in its extreme form insists on God as revealed by the "inner light"; (2) our increasing trust in the scientific method of observation, experiment and argument. Thus, no matter what Aristotle or St. Thomas may say about a Prime Mover or a First Cause, we remain unconvinced since at least one scientific theory suggests that the universe did not have a beginning and if scientific investigation proved this to be so, then we should be entirely indifferent to what formal logic had to say.

The secularist and rationalist movements of the 19th cent. were anti-religious—and quite rightly so—because at that time there were serious disabilities imposed even in Britain by the Established Church on atheism or agnosticism and freedom of thought. They are of little significance now because very little is left, largely thanks to their efforts, of these disabilities.

Finally, although most people are likely to accept the scientific method as the main means of discovering truth, there are other factors which equally make us doubt the value of "pure" logic and reason unaided by observation. The first of these is the influence of Freud which shows that much of our reasoning is mere rationalising—*e.g.*, we are more likely to become atheists because we hated our father than because we can prove that there is no God. The second is the influence of a movement in philosophy which, in the form of logical positivism or logical analysis, makes us doubt whether metaphysical systems have any meaning at all. Today, instead of asking ourselves whether Plato was right or wrong, we are much more likely to ask whether he did anything but make for the most part meaningless noises. Religion is in a sense much safer today than it ever was in the 19th cent. when it made foolish statements over matters of science that could be *proved* wrong; now we tend to see it as an emotional attitude to the universe or God (a "feeling of being at home in the universe," as William James put it) which can no more be proved or disproved than being in love.

Realism is a word which has so many meanings, and such contradictory ones, in various spheres, that it is difficult to define. We shall limit ourselves to its significance in philosophy. In philosophy, "realism" has two different meanings, diametrically opposed. (1) The most usual meaning is the one we should least expect from the everyday sense of the word—*i.e.*, it refers to all those philosophies from Plato onwards which maintained that the world of appearance is illusory and that ideas, forms, or universals are the only true realities, belonging to the world beyond matter and appearance—the world of God or mind. In early mediaeval times St. Thomas Aquinas was the chief exponent of this doctrine which was held by the scholastics as opposed to the Nominalists (*q.v.*). (2) In its modern everyday meaning "realism" is the belief that the universe is real and not a creation of mind, that there is a reality that causes the appearance, the "thing-in-itself" as Kant described it. Material things may not really be what they appear to be (*e.g.* a noise is not the "bang" we experience but a series of shock-waves passing through the atmosphere), yet, for all that, we can be sure that matter exists and it is very possible (some might add) that mind does not.

Reformation, the great religious movement of the 16th cent., which resulted in the establishment of Protestantism. John Wyclif (d. 1384), John Hus (d. 1415) and others had sounded the warning note, and when later on Luther took up the cause in Germany, and Zwingli in Switzerland, adherents soon became numerous. The wholesale vending of indulgences by the papal agents had incensed the people, and when Luther denounced these things he spoke to willing ears. After much controversy, the reformers boldly propounded the principles of the new doctrine, and the struggle for religious supremacy grew bitter. They claimed justification (salvation) by faith, and the use as well as the authority of the Scriptures, rejecting the doctrine of transubstantiation, the adoration of the Virgin and Saints, and the headship of the Pope. Luther was excommunicated. But the Reformation principles spread and ultimately a great part of Germany, as well as Switzerland, the Low Countries, Scandinavia, England, and Scotland were won over to the new faith. In England Henry VIII readily espoused the cause of the Reformation, his own personal quarrel with the Pope acting as an incentive. Under Mary there was a brief and sanguinary reaction, but Elizabeth gave completeness to the work which her father had initiated. *See* **Lutheranism, Calvinism, Presbyterianism, Baptists, Methodism.**

Renaissance is defined in the *Oxford English Dictionary* as: "The revival of art and letters, under the influence of classical models, which began in Italy in the 14th century." It is a term which must be used with care for the following reasons: (1) Although it was first used in the form *rinascita* (re-birth) by Vasari in 1550 and people living at that time certainly were aware that something new was happening, the word had no wide currency until used by the Swiss historian Jacob Burchardt in his classic *The Civilization of the Renaissance in Italy* (1860). (2) The term as used today refers not only to art in its widest sense but to a total change in man's outlook on life which extended into philosophical, scientific, economic, and technical fields. (3) Spreading from Italy there were renaissance movements in France, Spain, Germany, and northern Europe, all widely different with varying delays in time. As the historian Edith Sichel says: "Out of the Italian Renaissance there issued a new-born art; out of the Northern Renaissance there came forth a new-born religion. There came forth also a great school of poetry, and a drama the greatest that the world had seen since the days of Greece. The religion was the offspring of Germany and the poetry that of England."

The real cause of the Renaissance was not the fall of Constantinople, the invention of printing, the discovery of America, though these were phases in the process; it was, quite simply, money. The rise of a new merchant class gave rise to individualist attitudes in economic affairs which prepared the way for individualism and humanism. The new wealthy class in time became patrons of the arts whereas previously the Church had been the sole patron and controller. Thus the artist became more free to express himself, more respected, and being more well-to-do could afford to ignore the Church and even, in time, the views of his patrons.

It is true that art continued to serve to a considerable extent the purposes of faith, but it was judged from the standpoint of art. Mediaeval art was meant to elevate and teach man; Renaissance art to delight his senses and enrich his life. From this free and questing spirit acquired from economic individualism came the rise of modern science and technology; here Italy learned much from the Arab scholars who had translated and commented upon the philosophical, medical, and mathematical texts of antiquity, while denying themselves any interest in Greek art and literature. Arabic-Latin versions of Aristotle were in use well into the 16th cent. The Byzantine culture, though it had preserved the Greek tradition and gave supremacy to Plato, had made no move forward. But the Greek scholars who fled to Italy after the fall of Constantinople brought with them an immense cargo of classical manuscripts. The recovery of these Greek masterpieces, their translation into the vernaculars, and the invention of printing, made possible a completer understanding of the Greek spirit. It was the bringing together of the two heritages, Greek science, and Greek literature, that gave birth to a new vision. But it was not only Aristotle and Plato who were being studied but Ovid, Catullus, Horace, Pliny and Lucretius. What interested Renaissance man was the humanism of the Latin writers, their attitude to science, their scepticism.

The period *c.* 1400–1500 is known as the **Early Renaissance.** During this time such painters as Masaccio, Uccello, Piero della Francesca, Botticelli, and Giovanni Bellini were laying the foundations of drawing and painting for all subsequent periods including our own. They concerned themselves with such problems as anatomy, composition, perspective, and representation of space, creating in effect a grammar or textbook of visual expression. The term **High Renaissance** is reserved for a very brief period when a pure, balanced, classical harmony was achieved and artists were in complete control of the techniques learned earlier. The High Renaissance lasted only from *c.* 1500 to 1527 (the date of the sack of Rome), yet that interval included the earlier works of Michelangelo, most of Leonardo's, and all the Roman works of Raphael.

Ritualism, a tendency which, during the 19th cent., developed in the High Church section of the Church of England to make use of those vestments, candles, incense, etc. which are usually regarded as features of the Church of Rome. Since some opposition was aroused, a Ritual Commission was appointed in 1904 to take evidence and try to find some common basis on which High and Low Church could agree with respect to ceremonial. The report of 1906 in effect recommended the giving of greater powers to bishops to suppress objectionable practices. Although they are often associated together, it is worth while pointing out that there was no special connection between the Oxford Movement or Tractarians (*q.v.*) and Ritualism because Pusey disliked ritual and even Newman, who eventually went over to Rome, held extremely simple services at his church of St. Mary's.

Roman Catholic Church, the Christian organisation which acknowledges the Pope as the lawful successor of St. Peter, the apostle appointed by Christ to be the head of His Church. The reforming impulse at the Second Vatican Council (1962–5), summoned by Pope John, set in train movements towards religious unity and the reform and modernisation of the Church. Pope Paul made changes in the government and liturgy of the Church but refused to allow birth control, the marriage of priests and a greater role for women in the Roman Catholic Church. In fact the apparent trend towards increasing liberalism within the body of the Church has been reversed with a highly conservative papal pronouncement on sexual conduct which produced sharp controversy in the early part of 1976. The 1970s, incidentally, have shown a sharp decline in the number of worshippers at Roman Catholic Churches in Europe and America—a development of considerable significance in the light of the Roman Church's traditional solid support from its rank and file. *See also* **Cardinals, Section L.**

Romantic Movement or **Romanticism** is the name given not so much to an individual way of thinking but to the gradual but radical transformation of basic human values that occurred in the Western world round about the latter part of the 18th cent. It was a great breakthrough in European consciousness and arose through the writings of certain men living during the half-century or more following, say, 1760. It arose then because both time and place were propitious for the birth of these new ideas. There was a revolution in basic values—in art, morals, politics, religion, etc. The new view was of a world transcending the old one, infinitely larger and more varied.

To understand the Romantic movement it is necessary first to take note of the climate of thought preceding the great change; then to account for its beginning in Germany where it did (*see* **Pietism**) during the latter part of the 18th cent., and finally to appraise the writings of those men whose ideas fermented the new awakening. Briefly, the shift was away from French classicism and from belief in the all-pervasive power of human reason (the Enlightenment) towards the unfettered freedom that the new consciousness was able to engender. What mattered was to live a passionate and vigorous life, to dedicate oneself to an ideal, no matter what the cost (*e.g.*, Byron).

The ideas of the Enlightenment (*e.g.*, Fontenelle, Voltaire, Montesquieu) had been attacked by the Germans Hamann and Herder and by the ideas of the English philosopher Hume, but Kant, Schiller, and Fichte, Goethe's novel *Wilhelm Meister*, and the French Revolution all had profound effects on the aesthetic, moral, social, and political thought of the time. Friedrich Schlegel (1772–1829) said: "There is in man a terrible unsatisfied desire to soar into infinity; a feverish longing to break through the narrow bonds of individuality." Romanticism undermined the notion that in matters of value there are objective criteria which operate between men. Henceforth there was to be a resurgence of the human spirit, deep and profound, that is still going on.

Rosicrucians, an ancient mystical society founded in the 16th cent. by Christian Rosenkreuz which attempted to forge a theoretical link between the great Egyptian religions and the Church of Rome, drawing rituals and philosophy from both camps. The Society did not long survive the death of its founder (he managed to reach the age of 106 incidentally) but has been revived in succeeding centuries by a series of rivalling factions. Perhaps the most famous of these is the Rosicrucian Order (A.M.O.R.C.) which has become well-known in the Western world as a result of its heavy advertising in the popular press. Founded by the American H. Spencer Lewis, this offers a simple and good-natured doctrine preaching the Brotherhood of Man, the reincarnation of the soul and the immense latent potential of the human mind. As with many American-based organisations of this kind, the boundary between business and religion is hard to define. The A.M.O.R.C. Rosicrucian order, for example, proudly advertises that it is not a religion, and it is probably best summed up as a modern secret society which serves an important function in the lives of many people of mystical inclinations.

S

Salvation Army. The religious movement which in 1878 became known by this name arose from the Christian Mission meetings which the Rev. William Booth and his devoted wife had held in the East End of London for the previous thirteen years. Its primary aim was, and still is, to preach the gospel of Jesus Christ to men and women untouched by ordinary religious efforts. The founder devoted his life to the salvation of the submerged classes whose conditions at that time were unspeakably dreadful. Originally his aim had been to convert people and then send them on to the churches, but he soon found that few religious bodies would accept these "low-class" men and women. So it was that social work became part of their effort. Practical help like the provision of soup-kitchens, accompanied spiritual ministration. Soon, in the interests of more effective "warfare" against social evils, a military form of organisation, with uniforms, brass bands, and religious songs, was introduced. Its magazine *The War Cry* gave as its aim "to carry the Blood of Christ and the Fire of the Holy Ghost into every part of the world."

General Booth saw with blinding clarity that conversion must be accompanied by an improvement of external conditions. Various books had earlier described the terrible conditions of the slums, but in 1890 he produced a monumental survey entitled *In Darkest England and the Way Out*. From that time forward the Army was accepted and its facilities made use of by the authorities. Today the Army's spiritual and social activities have spread to countries all over the world; every one, no matter what class, colour, or creed he belongs to is a "brother for whom Christ died."

Sandemanians or **Glassites**, an obscure religious sect whose sole claim to fame is that one of its members was the great Michael Faraday, founder of the science of electromagnetism, who never failed to attend its Sunday services.

Sceptics. From Thales of Miletus (*c.* 624–565 B.C.) to the Stoics in the 4th cent. B.C. philosophers had been trying to explain the nature of the universe; each one produced a different theory and each could, apparently, prove that he was right. This diversity of views convinced the Sceptic school founded by Pyrrho (*c.* 360–270 B.C.) that man is unable to know the real nature of the world or how it came into being. In place of a futile search for what must be for ever unknowable, the Sceptics recommended that men should be practical, follow custom, and accept the evidence of their senses.

Schoolmen. From the time of Augustine to the middle of the 9th cent. philosophy, like science, was dead or merely a repetition of what had gone before. But about that time there arose a new interest in the subject, although (since by then Western Europe was entirely under the authority of the Catholic Church) the main form it took was an attempt to justify Church teaching in the light of Greek philosophy. Those who made this attempt to reconcile Christian beliefs with the best in Plato and Aristotle were known as "schoolmen" and the philosophies which they developed were known as "scholasticism." Among the most famous schoolmen must be counted John Scotus Erigena (*c.* 800–*c.* 877), born in Ireland and probably the earliest; St. Anselm, archbishop of Canterbury (1033–1109); the great Peter Abelard whose school was in Paris (1079–1142); Bernard of Chartres, his contemporary; and the best-known of all, St. Thomas Aquinas of Naples (1225–74), who was given the name of the "Angelic Doctor."

The philosophies of these men are discussed under various headings (God and Man, Determinism and Free-will), but being severely limited by the Church their doctrines differed from each other much less than those of later philosophical schools. However, one of the great arguments was between the orthodox Realists (*q.v.*) and the Nominalists (*q.v.*) and a second was between the Thomists (or followers of St. Thomas Aquinas) and the Scotists (followers of John Duns Scotus—not to be confused with John Scotus Erigena). The two latter schools were known as the Ancients, whilst the followers of William of Occam, the Nominalist, were known as the Terminalists. All became reconciled in 1482 in face of the threat from humanism of which the great exponent was Erasmus of Rotterdam (1466-1536) who hated scholasticism.

Scientology, an unusual quasi-philosophical system started by the American science-fiction writer L. Ron Hubbard, which claims to be able to effect dramatic improvement in the mental and physical well-being of its adherents. Originally developed in the United States as "Dianetics, the modern science of mental health," it was hailed in Hubbard's first book to be "a milestone for Man comparable to his discovery of fire and superior to his inventions of the wheel and the arch." Such extravagant statements exemplify the literature of the movement, which in the late 1950s began to expand in England when its founder came to live in East Grinstead. Followers of Dianetics and Scientology advance within the cult through a series of levels or grades, most reached by undertaking courses of training and tuition, payment for which may amount to hundreds and, in total, even thousands of pounds. These courses consist largely of specialised and complex mental exercises based on Hubbard's own variation of psychology and known as "processing" and "auditing." One of the principal goals of a Scientologist is the attainment of the state known as "Clear" (roughly speaking, one "cleared" of certain mental and physical handicaps) when it is believed he (she) will be a literally superior being, equipped with a higher intelligence and a greater command over the pattern of his (her) own life.

The Scientologists' claims that their movement is a genuine religion have generally been met with resistance from establishment bodies. In recent years the situation seems to have changed however, and acceptance of their claim is now much more widespread. Religious services moulded on the movement's philosophy are held, and the organisation is becoming involved in social work, notably the drug rehabilitation scheme known as Narconon.

Shakers, members of a revivalist group, styled by themselves "The United Society of Believers in Christ's Second Appearing," who seceded from Quakerism in 1747 though adhering to many of the Quaker tenets. The community was joined in 1758 by Ann Lee, a young convert from Manchester, who had "revelations" that she was the female Christ; "Mother Ann" was accepted as their leader. Under the influence of her prophetic visions she set out with nine followers for "Immanuel's land" in America and the community settled near Albany, capital of New York state. They were known as the "Shakers" in ridicule because they were given to involuntary movements in moments of religious ecstasy.

Central to their faith was the belief in the dual role of God through the male and female Christ: the male principle came to earth in Jesus; the female principle, in "Mother Ann." The sexes were equal and women preached as often as men at their meetings which sometimes included sacred dances—nevertheless the two sexes, even in dancing, kept apart. Their communistic way of living brought them economic prosperity, the Shakers becoming known as good agriculturists and craftsmen, noted for their furniture and textiles. After 1860, however, the movement began to decline and few, if any, are active today.

Shamans, the medicine men found in all primitive societies who used their magical arts to work cures, and protect the group from evil influences. The *shaman* was a man apart and wore special garments to show his authority. Shamanism with its magical practices, incantations, trances, exhausting dances, and self-torture is practised even today by tribes that have survived in a primitive state of culture.

Shiites or Shia, a heretical Moslem sect in Persia, opposed by the orthodox Sunnites. The dispute, which came almost immediately after the death of the Prophet and led to bitter feuding, had little to do with matters of doctrine as such, but with the succession. After Mohammed's death, there were three possible claimants: Ali, the husband of his daughter Fatima, and two others, one of whom gave up his claim in favour of the other, Omar. The orthodox selected Omar, who was shortly assassinated, and the same happened to his successor as Ali was passed over again. The Shiites are those who maintain that Ali was the true vicar of the Prophet, and that the three orthodox predecessors were usurpers.

Shintoism, literally means "teaching of the Gods" and is the specifically Japanese splinter version of Buddhism with a strong bias towards ancestor worship and the divine powers of natural forces. Unusual in that it had no recognised founder nor written dogma, Shintoism permeated Japanese life in a most vigorous way until the defeat of the country at the hands of the Allied Powers in 1945. In the 1500 years of its existence the Shinto religion produced tens of thousands of unique and beautiful shrines throughout Japan. Vast numbers of these were destroyed by bombing in the war, but a tolerant decision by the American airforce spared the Shinto capital, Kyoto, from air-attack. Shintoism was disestablished by the American occupying forces in 1945 and the Emperor Hirohito "abdicated" his divine powers. Current dissatisfaction among many Japanese with the worldly extravagance of their heavily industrialised society has led to a recent revival of interest in their ancient and selfless religion.

Sikhism. The Sikh community of the Punjab, which has played a significant part in the history of modern India, came into being during a period of religious revival in India in the 15th and 16th cent. It was originally founded as a religious sect by Guru (teacher) Nanak (1469–1538) who emphasised the fundamental truth of all religions, and whose mission was to put an end to religious conflict. He condemned the formalism both of Hinduism and Islam, preaching the gospel of universal toleration, and the unity of the Godhead, whether He be called Allah, Vishnu, or God. His ideas were welcomed by the great Mogul Emperor Akbar (1542–1605). Thus a succession of Gurus were able to live in peace after Nanak's death; they established the great Sikh centre at Amritsar, compiled the sacred writings known as the *Adi Granth*, and improved their organisation as a sect. But the peace did not last long, for an emperor arose who was a fanatical Moslem, in face of whom the last Guru, Govind Singh (1666–1708), whose father was put to death for refusal to embrace Islam, had to make himself a warrior and instil into the Sikhs a more aggressive spirit. A number of ceremonies were instituted by Govind Singh; admission to the fraternity was by special rite; caste distinctions were abolished; hair was worn long; the word singh, meaning lion, was added to the original name. They were able to organise themselves into 12 *misls* or confederacies but divisions appeared with the disappearance of a common enemy and it was not until the rise of Ranjit Singh (1780–1839) that a single powerful Sikh kingdom was established, its influence only being checked by the English, with whom a treaty of friendship was made. After the death of Ranjit Singh two Anglo-Sikh wars followed, in 1845–46, and 1848–49, which resulted in British annexation of the Punjab and the end of Sikh independence. In the two world wars the Sikhs proved among the most loyal of Britain's Indian subjects. The partitioning of the continent of India in 1947 into two states, one predominantly Hindu and the other predominantly Moslem, presented a considerable problem in the Punjab, which was divided in such a way as to leave 2 million Sikhs in Pakistan, and a considerable number of Moslems in the Indian Punjab. Although numbering less than 2 per cent. of the population (*c.* 8 million) the Sikhs are a continuing factor in Indian political life. In 1966 the Punjab was divided on a linguistic basis—Punjabi-speaking Punjab and Hindi-speaking Hariana

Socialism, is a form of society in which men and women are not divided into opposing economic classes but live together under conditions of approximate social and economic equality, using in common the means that lie to their hands of promoting social welfare. The brotherhood of man inspires the aims of socialism in foreign, colonial, social, and economic policies alike. The word "socialism" first came into general use in England about 1834 in connection with Robert Owen's "village of co-operation" at New Lanark. About the middle of the 19th cent., Charles Kingsley and others established a form of Christian socialism, and William Morris, John Burns, and others founded a Socialist League in 1886. With the development of trade unions the socialist movement took a more practical trend. Fabianism (*q.v.*) associated in its early days with the names of Beatrice and Sidney Webb and George Bernard Shaw, aims at the gradual reorganisation of society by creating intelligent public opinion by education and legislation. The British Labour Party believes in peaceful and constitutional change to socialism by democratic methods based upon popular consent. The Labour Government of 1945–51 initiated a major period of social reform and public ownership. Though beset by economic difficulties, the 1964–70 Labour Government continued a policy of radical reform. The minority Labour Government (of February–October 1974) and the subsequent administration have continued this process, particularly in the area of state intervention in industry, although not all sections of the party are united on the extent of public ownership and state intervention. *See also* **Section C, Part I.**

Southcottians, followers of Joanna Southcott, who died in 1814 shortly after announcing that (although over 50) she was about to give birth to a divine human being named Siloh. Miss Southcott certainly produced all the symptoms of pregnancy, and was even examined by the Royal physician who pronounced her unquestionably "with child." Although she even went "into labour," no child, divine or otherwise, appeared and she seems to have died of something rather close to a broken heart. Her interesting symptoms would today be classed as "hysterical pregnancy"—a not uncommon condition which may mimic real pregnancy in a remarkable way. Joanna's followers remained loyal to her memory, however, and a tiny sect still survives to this day. Shortly before her death, incidentally, she handed to followers a number of locked and sealed boxes which she indicated contained, among other things, the secret of the universe. These were only to be opened 100 years after her death and then in the presence of 12 bishops. In 1927 one of these boxes unexpectedly turned up and it was ceremoniously opened at the Caxton Hall before a public audience. The organisers had to make do with only one bishop as most of the country's senior clerics pronounced themselves to be too busy to attend. Perhaps it was just as well for Miss Southcott's marvellous box was found to contain only a few rare coins, a horse pistol, a woman's embroidered nightcap, and a slightly improper novel, *The Surprises of Love.* One of the most endearing qualities of Joanna Southcott must have been her sense of humour.

Spiritualism is a religion which requires to be distinguished from **psychical research** (*q.v.*) which is a scientific attempt carried on both by believers and non-believers to investigate psychic phenomena including those not necessarily connected with "spirits"—*e.g.*, telepathy or clairvoyance and precognition. As a religion (although for that matter the whole of history is filled with attempts to get in touch with the "spirit world") Spiritualism begins with the American Andrew Jackson Davis who in 1847 published *Nature's Divine Revelations*, a book which is still widely read. In this Davis states that on the death of the physical body, the human spirit remains alive and moves on to one or another of a considerable range of worlds or "spheres" where it commences yet another stage of existence. Since the spirit has not died, but exists with full (and possibly even expanded) consciousness, there should be no reason, Davis argues, why it should not make its presence known to the beings it has temporarily left behind on earth. In 1847, the year of the publication of Davis's book, two young girls, Margaret and Kate Fox, living in a farmhouse at Hydesville, New York, began apparently to act as unwitting mediums for attempts at such between-worlds communication. The girls were the focus for strange rappings and bangs which it was alleged defied normal explanation and which spelt out, in the form of a simple alphabetical code, messages from the spirits of "the dead." The Fox sisters were later to confess that they had produced the raps by trickery, but by that time the fashion had spread across the world and before long "mediums" in all lands were issuing spirit communications (often in much more spectacular form). In the late 19th cent. Spiritualism went into a phase of great expansion and for various reasons attracted the attention of many scientists. Among these were Sir William Crookes, Sir Oliver Lodge, Professor Charles Richet, Alfred Russell Wallace, to say nothing of the brilliant and shrewd creator of Sherlock Holmes, Sir Arthur Conan Doyle. Today many people find it astonishing that people of such brilliance should find the phenomena of the seance room of more than passing interest, but the commitment of the Victorian scientists is understandable if we realise that Spiritualists, after all, claim to do no more than demonstrate as fact what all Christians are called on to believe—that the human personality survives bodily death. Furthermore, at the time of the late 19th cent. peak of Spiritualism, much less was known about human psychology and about the great limitations of sensory perception in typical seance conditions, when lights are dimmed or extinguished and an emotionally charged atmosphere generated. Today the most striking phenomena of the seance room—the alleged materialisation of spirit people and the production of such half-spiritual, half-physical substances as ectoplasm—are rarely if ever produced at Spiritualist meetings. Some say that the most probable explanation for this is that too many fraudulent mediums have been caught out and publicly exposed for the profession to be worth the risks. The movement today, which still has a large and often articulate following, now concentrates on the less controversial areas of "mental mediumship," clairvoyance and the like, or on the very widespread practice of "spirit healing." Where people are not deliberately deluded by bogus mediums acting for monetary reward (a practice which largely died out with the "death" of ectoplasm) Spiritualism probably has an important role to play in the life of many people whose happiness has been removed by the death of a much loved relative or spouse. It certainly does not deserve the violent attacks that are often made on it by orthodox clergy who allege that Spiritualists are communicating not with the souls of the departed but with the devil or his emissaries. To many people today belief in the devil would be looked upon as somewhat odder than belief in the survival of the individual spirit after death.

State and Man. Most of the early civilisations such as those of Egypt and Babylonia were theocratic, that is to say, they were arranged in a hierarchy with, at the peak, a king who was also an incarnation of the god. Needless to say, in such circumstances there was no room for philosophising about the nature of the state and the relationship which ought to exist between state and citizens. As usual, we have to turn to ancient Greece for the beginnings of thought about this problem. We do so as briefly as possible since in general it is only the later philosophers whose work has much contemporary interest and, in any case, most people today realise that the political philosophy of a particular time is bound to reflect the actual conditions prevailing then and as such is of mainly theoretical interest today.

The Greek Approach. The early pre-Socratic philosophers Democritus and the Pythagorean school for example, held that the individual should subordinate himself to the whole; they had no doubt that the citizen's first duty was to the state. The Greeks until the time of Plato were not really thinking in terms of individual rights, nor had they given much thought to what form the state should take—they simply accepted it. The first great attempt to describe the ideal state is to be found in Plato's *The Republic* which is referred to elsewhere (*see* **Education**). His pupil Aristotle did not try to form a utopia but made many comments on the nature of government. Thus, while agreeing that the state was more important than any individual person, he distinguished between good and bad states, and pointed out that to the extent that the state does not enable its citizens to lead virtuous and useful lives it is evil. A good constitution must recognise the inequalities between human beings and confer on them rights according to their abilities: among these inequalities are those of personal ability, property, birth, and status, as freeman or slave. The best forms of rule were monarchy, aristocracy, and democracy; the worst forms—tyranny, oligarchy (or rule of a powerful few), and ochlocracy (or mob-rule). The later Greek thinkers of Hellenistic times held two opposed points of view. The Epicureans (*q.v.*) taught that all social life is based upon self-interest and we become members of a group for our own convenience; therefore there are no absolute rights and laws—what is good is what members decide at that time to be good, and when they change their minds the law must change too. Injustice is not an evil in any god-given sense; we behave justly simply because if injustice became the general rule, we ourselves should suffer. The Stoics (*q.v.*), on the other hand, held that the state must dominate the individual completely and everyone must carry out, first and foremost, his social duties and be willing to sacrifice everything for it; but the state of the Stoics was no narrowly national one, but one that strove to become a universal brotherhood.

The Christian Approach. The orthodox Christian view is expressed in St. Augustine's book *The City of God*. Here it is held that the church, as the worldly incarnation of the City of God, is to be supreme over the state, and the head of the church is to be supreme over secular rulers. In addition it must be recognised that, whilst the secular ruler can make mistakes, the church does not, since it is the representative of God's kingdom on earth.

The Secular State. During the Renaissance (*q.v.*) people began to think for themselves and the results of their cogitations were not always pleasant; for it was during this time that many rulers, petty and otherwise, were seeking absolute authority. Two notable thinkers at this stage were Niccolo Machiavelli (1469–1527) in Italy and Thomas Hobbes (1588–1679) in England, where, of course, the Renaissance arrived later in history. Both supported absolute monarchy against the former domination of the church. The name of Machiavelli has become a by-word for any behaviour that is cunning and unscrupulous, but he was not really as bad as he is usually painted. It is, indeed, true that in his book *The Prince* he showed in the greatest detail the methods by which a ruler could gain absolute control and destroy civic freedom, but this despotism was intended as merely a necessary intermediate stage towards his real idea which was a free, united Italian nation wholly independent of the church. Hobbes was a materialist whose thesis was that man is naturally a ferocious animal whose basic impulse is war and pillage and the destruction of whatever stands in his way to gain his desires. But if he allowed himself to behave in this way his life would be "nasty, brutish, and short" so he creates a society in which he voluntarily gives up many of his rights and hands them over to a powerful ruler in his own interest. But having done this he must obey; even when the ruler is unjust, as he has no right to complain because anything is better than a return to his natural state. The religion of the king must be the religion of the people and the only things no ruler has the right to do is to cause a man to commit suicide or murder or to make him confess to a crime.

Views of Locke: Live and Let Live. John Locke (1632–1704) disagreed with these views. Man is naturally peaceful and co-operative and therefore social life comes readily to him. He sets up an authority in order to preserve the group and that is why laws are made; but the function of the state is strictly limited to maintaining the public good and beyond this men are to be left free. Therefore absolute power and the doctrine of the Divine Right of Kings were wrong because power ultimately rests with the people who have the right to make and break governments. It is also wrong that those who make the laws should be able to execute them. This is the important British doctrine of the separation of powers between the legislature and the executive which, in Britain and America, is regarded as one of the bases of democracy. *See* **Section C, Part I.**

Rousseau's Social Doctrine. The only other views we need consider here are those of Jean-Jacques Rousseau (1712–78) and Herbert Spencer (1820–1903), since the views of the two important intervening figures, Hegel and Karl Marx, are dealt with elsewhere (*see* Dialectical Materialism) and after Spencer we come to a stage where political philosophy begins to merge with sociology and the social sciences. Rousseau is a puzzling figure. On the one hand he has been hailed as the prophet of freedom and on the other as the father of modern totalitarianism. His book *Social Contract* (1762) begins with the words: "Man is born free, and everywhere he is in chains." He says that he is in favour, not merely of democracy, but of direct democracy in which everyone has to give his assent to all measures as in the Greek city-states and in Geneva, of which city he was a citizen. (This method is still in force in respect of some measures in the Swiss cantons.) Natural society is based on a "social contract" or mutual agreement and Rousseau speaks of a "return to nature" which would ensure the sovereignty of the people at all times. Thus far, he seems to agree with Locke but soon we find that he is more akin to Hobbes, since (as we are learning in our own day) nothing is more tyrannical than the absolute rule of all the people. (Public opinion is more Hitlerian than Hitler.) As it turns out, then, the "social contract" consists in "the total alienation of each associate, together with all his rights, to the whole community" and "each of us puts his person and all his power in common under the supreme direction of the general will." Rousseau admired direct democracy in the small city-state, but if his doctrine is applied to large states, then the "general will" becomes absolute. It is in this sense that he is regarded as the forerunner of totalitarianism. Herbert Spencer is quoted only as an example of the inappropriate application of a biological theory to social issues. Influenced by Darwin's thesis of natural selection, he saw in society a struggle in which the fittest survived and the less fit perished. Each individual had the right to preserve himself, but in the case of human beings this depended upon group life in which, to some extent, each individual is limited by the rights of others. But this should not go too far, and he condemned the socialism of J. S. Mill which (*a*) would give over-much protection to the unfit, and (*b*) would give the state powers which it has no right to since the best government is the least government. In accordance with Darwinism free competition was essential.

Stoics, the followers of Zeno, a Greek philosopher in the 4th cent. B.C., who received their name from the fact that they were taught in the Stoa Poikile or Painted Porch of Athens. They believed that since the world is the creation of divine wisdom and is governed by divine law, it is man's duty to accept his fate. Zeno conceived virtue to be the highest good and condemned the passions. (*See* **God and Man, State and Man, Determinism and Free-will** for a more detailed account of their beliefs.)

Subud, a cultish movement surrounding the Javanese mystic Pak Subuh which established its headquarters in England in 1958 and made newspaper headlines because of alleged "miracle" cures of both psychological and physical ills. The basis of Subud (which is a contraction of three Sanskrit words, Susila Budhi Dharma, meaning "the right living of the soul") is a single spiritual exercise, the *latihan*, in which the individual comes into contact with, or is overwhelmed by a metaphysical force of some kind which is supposed to produce great mental and physical changes. During the latihan people may make strange movements, some violent, and utter unusual cries or chants. Now better known in America than in Britain, Subud did not live up to the expectations of its early followers, many of whom were people of considerable intelligence and professional standing. It is of particular interest because it represents a unique incursion of a rather obscure Eastern cult into Western life, and suggests again that there is growing dissatisfaction in many quarters with orthodox religion and its contribution to the philosophy of the modern world.

Sunnites, the orthodox sect of Islam as contrasted with the Shiites or Shia (*q.v.*).

Swedenborgianism. The Church of the New Jerusalem, based on the writings of Emanuel Swedenborg (1688–1772), was founded by his followers eleven years after his death. The New Church is regarded by its members not as a sect but as a new dispensation bearing the same relationship to Christianity as Christianity does to Judaism.

Synchronicity, an attempt by the psychologist, Carl Gustav Jung, to explain the apparently significant relationship between certain events in the physical universe which seem to have no obvious "causal" link. This rather involved concept is easily understood if one realises that almost all scientific and philosophical beliefs are based on the notion that the continuous process of change which is taking place in ourselves and in the universe around us is dependent upon a principle known as causality. We can express this another way by saying that an object moves because it has been pushed or pulled by another. We see because light strikes the retina and signals pass up the nervous system to the brain. A stone falls to the ground because the earth's gravity is pulling it towards its centre etc., etc. For all practical purposes every event can be looked upon as being "caused" by some other prior event and this is obviously one of the most important principles of the operation of the universe. Jung, however, felt that there is a sufficiently large body of evidence to suggest that events may be linked in a significant (*i.e.*, non-chance) way without there being any true causal relationship between them. The classic example he held to be the supposed predictive power of astrology by which there appears to be a relationship between the stellar configurations and the personality and life-pattern of individuals on earth. Jung was scientist enough to realise that there could be no causal connection between the aspect of the stars and the lives of people billions of miles from them, yet felt the evidence for astrology was strong enough to demand an alternative non-causal explanation. The trouble with synchronicity, which has not made much impact on the world of physics or of psychology, is that it is not really an explanation at all but merely a convenient word to describe some puzzling correspondences. The real question, of course, is whether there really are events occurring which are significantly but not *causally* linked, and most scientists today would hold that there were probably not. Still it was typical of the bold and imaginative mind of Jung to tackle head-on one of the principal mysteries of existence and come up with a hypothesis to attempt to meet it.

Syndicalism, a form of socialist doctrine which aims at the ownership and control of all industries by the workers, contrasted with the more conventional type of socialism which advocates ownership and control by the state. Since syndicalists have preferred to improve the conditions of the workers by direct action, *e.g.* strikes and working to rule, rather than through the usual parliamentary procedures, they have been closely related to anarchists (*q.v.*) and are sometimes described as anarcho-syndicalists. Under syndicalism there would be no state; for the state would be replaced by a federation of units based on functional economic organisation rather than on geographical representation. The movement had bodies in the United Kingdom, where guild socialism (*q.v.*) was strongly influenced by its doctrines, in France, Germany, Italy, Spain, Argentina, and Mexico, but these gradually declined after the first world war losing many members to the communists. Fascism (*q.v.*) was also strongly influenced by the revolutionary syndicalism of Georges Sorel in making use of his concept of the "myth of the general strike" as an emotional image or ideal goal to spur on the workers: with Mussolini the "myth" became that of the state. Mussolini was also influenced by Sorel's doctrine of violence and the justification of force. Syndicalism had a certain influence in the Labour Party in its early days, but was crushed by men like Ernest Bevin who began to fear that by involving the workers in direct responsibility for their industries, it would put them at a disadvantage when bargaining for wages.

T

Taoism, a religion which, although in a degenerate state, is still one of the great Eastern creeds. Its alleged founder, Lao-tze, is said to have been born in Honan about 604 B.C.; he is also said to be the author of the bible of Taoism, the *Tao-te-ching*, or in English *The Way of Life*, and to have disapproved of Confucius. This, if true, would hardly be surprising; for Taoism is eminently a mystical religion recommending doing nothing and resisting nothing, whereas Confucianism (*q.v.*) is eminently a practical code of living and its founder insisted on intervening in everything to do with social life. But the truth as revealed by modern scholarship is rather different. We are told that the poems of the *Tao-te-ching* are anonymous and probably originated among recluses in lonely valleys long before the time of Confucius; they were collected and given form at some time late in the 3rd cent. B.C. and their authorship attributed to Lao-tze. It is entirely possible that no such person ever existed (unlike Confucius, who certainly did), but if there were such a man he appears to have used a pseudonym since "Lao" is not a surname but an adjective meaning "old" and it was customary to attribute important works to old men on account of their supposed wisdom. Lao-tze simply means "the old philosopher," and although the *Tao-te-ching* is one of the most remarkable and instructive books ever written it is as anonymous as the Border Ballads.

It is apparent that the religion learned both from the ancient Chinese mystics and from Brahmanism: *Tao*, the Way, is impalpable, invisible, and incapable of being expressed in words. But it can be attained by virtue, by compassion, humility, and non-violence. Out of weakness comes true strength whereas violence is not only wrong but defeats its own ends. There is no personal God and such gods as men imagine are mere emanations of *Tao* which gives life to all things. *Tao* is Being. Works are worthless and internal renunciation is far better than anything that follows from the use of force because passive resistance convinces the other from within that he is in error, whereas violence only compels the external appearance of conviction whilst inwardly the individual is as before. "It is wealth to be content; it is wilful to force one's way on others."

Later Lao-tze became a divinity and indeed one of a Trinity each worshipped in the form of idols (which the founder had hated). Soon there was worship of the forces of nature: the stars, the tides, the sun and moon, and a thousand other deities among whom Confucius was one. The purest mysticism and wisdom had been utterly corrupted by contact with the world.

Telepathy and Clairvoyance. Telepathy is the alleged communication between one mind and another other than through the ordinary sense channels. Clairvoyance is the supposed faculty of "seeing" objects or events which, by reason of space and time or other causes, are not discernible through the ordinary sense of vision. Such claims have been made from time immemorial but it was not until this century that the phenomena were investigated scientifically. The first studies were undertaken by the Society for Psychical Research, which was founded in 1882 with Professor Henry Sidgwick as its first president. Since then it has carried out a scholarly programme of research without—in accordance with its constitution—coming to any corporate conclusions. In America the centre of this research was the Parapsychology Laboratory at Duke University (*see* **Parapsychology**) where at one time it was claimed clear scientific evidence for extra-sensory perception (ESP) had been obtained. These claims have been treated with great reservation by the majority of scientists but despite the belief that the study of ESP was going into eclipse, there remains a small but measurable residue of interest in scientific research in this area. It would be odd if some scientists were not interested in ESP because of the enormous weight of anecdotal evidence which has built up over centuries to support it. The weakness of the scientific as opposed to the casual evidence is however exemplified by the failure of ESP researchers to produce a reliable "repeatable" experiment. *See* **Section Q, VI.**

Theism. *See* **God and Man.**

Theosophy (Sanskrit *Brahma Vidya* = divine wisdom), a system of thought that draws on the mystical teachings of those who assert the spiritual nature of the universe, and the divine nature of man. It insists that man is capable of intuitive insight into the nature of God. The way to wisdom, or self-knowledge, is through the practice of **Yoga** (*q.v.*). Theosophy has close connections with Indian thought through Vedic, Buddhist, and Brahmanist literature. The modern Theosophical Society was founded by Mme H. P. Blavatsky and others in 1875, and popularised by Mrs. Annie Besant.

Tractarianism, a Catholic revival movement, also known as the **Oxford Movement** (not to be confused with the so-called Oxford Group), which had its beginnings at Oxford in 1833. The leaders included the Oxford high churchmen E. B. Pusey, J. Keble and J. H. Newman. Through the *Tracts for the Times* (1833–41), a series of pamphlets which were sent to every parsonage in England, they sought to expose the dangers which they considered to be threatening the church from secular authority. The immediate cause of the movement was the Reform Act (1832) which meant that the state was no longer in the safe keeping of Tories and Churchmen but that power was falling into the hands of Liberals and Dissenters. They advocated a higher degree of ceremonial in worship nearer the Roman communion. In *Tract 90* (the last) Newman showed how the Thirty-nine Articles themselves, which were regarded as the bulwark of Protestantism, could be made to square with Roman doctrine. It was obvious which direction the movement was taking and the romanizing tendency was widely resented. In 1845 Newman went over to Rome. Pusey and Keble persisted in their efforts to secure recognition of Catholic liturgy and doctrine in the Anglican Church. Catholicism of the Anglican type (*i.e.*, Catholic in ritual, ceremony, and everything save submission to the Pope) is termed Anglo-Catholicism (*q.v.*).

Transcendental Meditation, popularised in the West by the Maharishi Mahesh Yogi, who achieved sensational worldwide publicity by his "conversion" of the Beatles a few years ago. This is a simple meditational system which it is claimed is an aid to relaxation and the reduction of psychological and physical stress. It is reported that the technique can be taught in under five minutes provided that someone trained by the Maharishi is the teacher. The pupil or would-be meditator is given a mantra—a meaningless word which acts as a focal point for the imagination—and told to concentrate on the word while sitting in a comfortable position. Extraordinary claims are made on behalf of the system. As with most cults, religious and occult systems, there is an initial psychological benefit to anyone who becomes deeply involved. Nevertheless, apart from this simple "participation-effect," there is some evidence that the body's autonomic functions (heart rate, respiratory cycle, brain waves, etc.) can be modified by certain individuals including yogis. Whether it is ultimately beneficial to be able to modify these autonomic functions or not is another matter. The latest evidence from laboratory studies in fact shows that subjects in the most relaxed phase of TM are in fact in a (quite normal) stage of light sleep. *See also* **Feedback Cult.**

Transmigration of Souls. *See* **Immortality, Buddhism, Hinduism.**

Transubstantiation, the conversion in the Eucharist of the bread and wine into the body and blood of Christ—a doctrine of the Roman Catholic Church.

Trotskyism, a form of communism supporting the views of Leon Trotsky, the assumed name of Lev Bronstein (1879–1940) who, in 1924, was ousted from power by Stalin and later exiled and assassinated in Mexico. Trotsky held that excessive Russian nationalism was incompatible with genuine international communism and that Stalin was concentrating on the economic development of the Soviet Union to an extent which could only lead to a bureaucratic state with a purely nationalist outlook. After the Hungarian uprising in 1956, which was ruthlessly suppressed by the Soviet Armed Forces, a wave of resignations from Western Communist parties took place, many of the dissident elements taking to Trotskyism in its place.

U

Ufology, cultish interest in the study of strange and unexplained aerial phenomena (unidentified flying objects, hence UFOs). *See* **Flying Saucers.**

Underground, the name given to an increasingly well-organised group, mainly composed of young people, university students, etc., which propagates anti-establishment and often highly controversial views. Its history, and to some extent its aims, are obscure, but it is a force of increasing power in Western society and its evolution is worth watching with care. The 1960s were years of great metamorphosis in Europe and America with rapid changes taking place in our attitudes to war and peace, to sex and morals, to marriage and family, to church and state. For large sections of the population these changes have been too rapid and too radical by far, but for others they have been too slow. In particular, the liberalisation of the law on the so-called "soft drugs," notably marijuana, is advocated by a vocal and increasing minority of young people. The expression of their views has been finding outlet in magazines and newspapers, privately published and printed, which reach a wide circulation despite the disinclination of many newsagents to stock them. These publications, while frequently containing material of an obscene and, to many people, highly offensive nature, also contain articles, features, and poems by writers of repute, many of whom contribute regularly to more orthodox publications and yet are sympathetic to the "underground cause." The word underground here, incidentally, refers back to the "underground press" that published revolutionary material at great risk in Nazi occupied territories during the last war. With the exception of the risqué magazine *Private Eye*, which is largely concerned with acid political satire, the first of the genuine underground newsheets was the *International Times* (IT) which was followed in due course by *Oz* and *Rolling Stone.* All three papers were strongly anarchistic in flavour, uneven in literary merit, openly in favour of legalising marijuana ("pot"), and generally quite scandalous to the middle-class and middle-aged. This is not the place to argue the pros and cons of the underground arguments, nor to decide whether our "permissive society" has gone too far or not yet far enough. The important message that the appearance of the whole underground movement implies is that young people, because of greater financial independence, wider opportunities for travel, better education, and easier access to communication channels, such as printing presses, radio transmitters, etc., are beginning to make their admittedly controversial views more widely publicised. Furthermore, this is a trend which will inevitably develop rather than diminish and in the absence of authoritarian repression, these forces will have an increasing impact on our lives. By 1973 however signs of the decline in the power of the underground seemed to be appearing. One of its leading publications *Oz* had folded and its "drop-out" arguments seemed to be appealing less and less to students and young people. The most likely reason for this is that the movement in its decade of vigorous life was successful in inducing a number of reforms ranging from the propagation of a more liberal attitude to what may be printed, spoken about or shown on stage and screen, and an acceptance by school and university authorities that students should have a greater voice in academic affairs. These reforms, whether welcome or not to the middle-aged and the middle class, have nevertheless reached fruition in the "permissive" society which in turn appears to have taken much of the steam out of the underground itself. *See also* Weathermen.

Unitarianism has no special doctrines, although clearly, as the name indicates, belief is in the single personality of God, *i.e.*, anti-trinitarian. This general statement, however, can be interpreted with varying degrees of subtlety. Thus unitarian belief may range from a sort of Arianism which accepts that, although Christ was not of divine nature, divine powers had been delegated to him by the Father, to the simple belief that Christ was a man like anyone else, and his goodness was of the same nature as that of many other great and good men. Indeed, today, many Unitarians deny belief in a personal God and interpret their religion in purely moral terms, putting their faith in the value of love and the brotherhood of man. The Toleration Act (1689) excluded Unitarians but from 1813 they were legally tolerated in England. Nevertheless attempts were made to turn them out of their chapels on the ground that the preachers did not hold the views of the original founders of the endowments. But this ended with the Dissenting Chapels Act of 1845. In America no such difficulties existed, and in the Boston of the 19th cent. many of the great literary figures were openly unitarian both in belief and name: *e.g.*, Emerson, Longfellow, Lowell, and Oliver Wendell Holmes.

Utilitarianism, a school of moral philosophy of which the main proponents were J. S. Mill (1806–73) and Jeremy Bentham (1748–1832). Bentham based his ethical theory upon the utilitarian principle that the greatest happiness of the greatest number is the criterion of morality. What is good is pleasure or happiness; what is bad is pain. If we act on this basis of self-interest (pursuing what we believe to be our own happiness), then what we do will automatically be for the general good. The serious failing of this thesis is (1) that it makes no distinction between the quality of one pleasure and another, and (2) that Bentham failed to see that the law might not be framed and administered by men as benevolent as himself. J. S. Mill accepted Bentham's position in general but seeing its failings emphasised (1) that self-interest was an inadequate basis for utilitarianism and suggested that we should take as the real criterion of good the social consequences of the act; (2) that some pleasures rank higher than others and held that those of the intellect are superior to those of the senses. Not only is the social factor emphasised, but emphasis is also placed on the nature of the act.

Utopias. The name "utopia" is taken from a Greek word meaning "nowhere" and was first used in 1516 by Sir Thomas More (1478–1535) as the title of his book referring to a mythical island in the south Pacific where he sited his ideal society. Since then it has been used of any ideal or fanciful society, and here a few will be mentioned. (The reader may recall that Samuel Butler's 19th cent. novel, describing an imaginary society in New Zealand where criminals were treated and the sick punished, was entitled *Erewhon* which is the word "nowhere" in reverse.) It should be noted that not all utopias were entirely fanciful—*e.g.*, Robert Owen's and François Fourier's beliefs, although found to be impractical, were, in fact, tried out.

Sir Thomas More. More wrote at a time when the rise of the wool-growing trade had resulted in farming land being turned over to pasture and there was a great wave of unemployment and a rise in crime among the dispossessed. More began to think in terms of the mediaeval ideal of small co-operative communities in which class interests and personal gain played a decreasing part, a society which would have the welfare of the people at heart both from the physical and intellectual points of view. His utopia was one in which there was no private property, because the desire for acquisition and private possessions lay at the root of human misery. There was, therefore, only common ownership of land and resources. Each class of worker was equipped to carry out its proper function in the economic scheme and each was fairly rewarded for its share in production so that there was neither wealth nor poverty to inspire conflict. Nobody was allowed to be idle, until the time came for him to retire when he became free to enjoy whatever cultural pleasures he wished, but, since the system was devoid of the waste associated with competition, the working day would be only six hours. There was to be compulsory schooling and free medical care for everybody, full religious toleration, complete equality of the sexes, and a modern system of dealing with crime which was free from vindictiveness and cruelty. Government was to be simple and direct by democratically-elected officials whose powers would be strictly limited and the public expenditure kept under close scrutiny. It will be seen that More was far in advance of his age, and to most democratically-minded people in advance of an earlier utopia, Plato's *Republic*, which is described under the heading of Education.

James Harrington. James Harrington published his book *The Commonwealth of Oceana* in 1656 and offered it to Oliver Cromwell for his consideration but without tangible results. Better than any other man of his time Harrington understood the nature of the economic revolution which was then taking place, and, like More, saw the private ownership of land as the main cause of conflict. He put forward the theory that the control of property, particularly in the shape of land, determines the character of the political structure of the state; if property were universally distributed among the people the sentiment for its protection would naturally result in a republican form of government. The Commonwealth of Oceana was a society "of laws and not of men"—*i.e.*, it was to be legally based and structured so as to be independent of the good or ill-will of any individuals controlling it. Thus there must be a written constitution, a two-house legislature, frequent elections with a secret ballot, and separation of powers between legislature and executive—all today familiar features of parliamentary democracy, but unique in his time.

Saint-Simon. The utopias of the late 18th and 19th cent. come, of course, into the period of the industrial revolution and of laissez-faire capitalism. Individual enterprise and complete freedom of competition formed the outlook of the ruling class. Naturally the utopias of this period tended to have a strongly socialist tinge since such theories are obviously produced by those who are not satisfied with existing conditions. Saint-Simon's *New Christianity* (1825) is one such, and by many, Claude Henri, Comte de Saint-Simon (1760–1825) is regarded as the founder of French socialism. His book urged a dedication of society to the principle of human brotherhood and a community which would be led by men of science motivated by wholly spiritual aims. Production property was to be nationalised (or "socialised" as he describes the process) and employed to serve the public good rather than private gain; the worker was to produce according to his capacity and to be rewarded on the basis of individual merit; the principle of inheritance was to be abolished since it denied the principle of reward for accomplishment on which the society was to be founded. Saint-Simon's proposals were not directed towards the poorer classes alone, but to the conscience and intellect of all. He was deeply impressed with the productive power of the new machines and his scheme was, first and foremost, intended as a method of directing that power to the betterment of humanity as a whole.

Fourier. François Marie Charles Fourier (1772–1837), although by conviction a philosophical anarchist who held that human beings are naturally good if allowed to follow their natural desires, was the originator of what, on the face of it, one would suppose to be the most regimented of the utopias. It consisted of a system of " phalanxes " or co-operative communities each composed of a group of workers and technicians assured of a minimum income and sharing the surplus on an equitable basis. Agriculture was to be the chief occupation of each phalanx and industrial employment planned and so carefully assigned that work would become pleasant and creative rather than burdensome. One of his ideas was that necessary work should receive the highest pay, useful work the next, and pleasant work the least pay. The land was to be scientifically cultivated and natural resources carefully conserved. Most of the members' property was to be privately owned, but the ownership of each phalanx was to be widely diffused among members by the sale of shares. Such " parasitic and unproductive " occupations as stockbroker, soldier, economist, middle-man and philosopher would be eliminated and the education of children carried out along vocational lines to train them for their future employment.

The strange thing was that Fourier's suggestions appealed to many both in Europe and the U.S.A. and such men (admittedly no economic or technical experts) as Emerson, Thoreau, James Russell Lowell, and Nathaniel Hawthorne strongly supported them. An American Fourier colony known as Brook Farm was established and carried on for eight years when it was dissolved after a serious fire had destroyed most of its property.

Robert Owen. Robert Owen (1771–1858), a wealthy textile manufacturer and philanthropist, established communities founded on a kind of utopian socialism in Lanarkshire, Hampshire, and in America. Of his New Lanark community an American observer wrote: " There is not, I apprehend, to be found in any part of the world, a manufacturing community in which so much order, good government, tranquillity, and rational happiness prevail." The workers in Lanark were given better housing and education for their children, and it was administered as a co-operative self-supporting community in Scotland. Later in life Owen returned to sponsoring legislation that would remove some of the worst evils of industrial life in those days: reduction of the working day to twelve hours, prohibition of labour for children under the age of ten, public schools for elementary education, and so on. But he lived to see few of his reforms adopted. He also promoted the creation of co-operative societies, the formation of trades unions, labour banks and exchanges, the workers' educational movement, and even an Anglo-American federation. There can be no doubt that, if he saw little result himself, he left the imprint of his convictions to benefit future communities who may not even know his name.

V

Vitalism, the philosophical doctrine that the behaviour of the living organism is, at least in part, due to a vital principle which cannot possibly be explained wholly in terms of physics and chemistry. This belief was at one time held strongly by the late Professor C. E. M. Joad and is implicit in Henri Bergson's (1859–1941) theory of creative evolution. It was maintained by Bergson that evolution, like the work of an artist, is creative and therefore unpredictable; that a vague need exists beforehand within the animal or plant before the means of satisfying the need develops. Thus we might assume that sightless animals developed the need to become aware of objects before they were in physical contact with them and that this ultimately led to the origin of organs of sight. Earlier this century a form of vitalism described as " emergent evolution " was put forward. This theory maintains that when two or more simple entities come together there may arise a new property which none of them previously possessed. Today biologists would say that it is the *arrangement* of atoms that counts, different arrangements exhibiting different properties, and that biological organisation is an essentially dynamic affair, involving the lapse of time.

W

Wahabis, members of an Arabian sect of Islam which originated in the teaching of Muhammad Ibn 'Abd-al-Wahab, born at the end of the 17th cent. He was deeply resentful of the Turkish rule which, in addition to its tyranny, had brought about innovations in the religion which Muhammad regarded as a perversion of its original form. He proceeded to reform Islam to its primitive conditions and impressed his beliefs on Mohammed Ibn Saud, a sheikh who spread them with the aid of his sword. Under the successors of Ibn Saud the power of the Wahabis spread over much of Arabia where it is dominant today in Saudi Arabia. Its particular characteristic is that it refuses to accept symbolic or mystical interpretations of the words of the Prophet and accepts quite literally the teaching of Islam. It is, in fact, a sort of Moslem fundamentalism. Although crushed by the Turks in 1811–15, the movement remains an important element in Mohammedanism.

Waldenses, a movement also known as " The Poor Men of Lyons," founded by Peter Waldo of that city about the same time, and in the same part of southern France, as the Albigenses (*q.v.*) with whom, however, they had nothing in common. Their main belief was a return to Apostolic simplicity, based on reading the Bible in their own language; their doctrines were somewhat similar to those of the Mennonites and the Quakers. However, they did not wish to separate themselves from the Church and were originally protected by several popes until the Lateran Council of 1215 excluded them mainly for the crime of preaching without ecclesiastical permission. From this time they were subjected to persecution, yet maintained some contact with the Church until the Reformation when they chose to take the side of the Protestants. Situated mainly on the sides of the Alps, half in Piedmont and half in France, they were persecuted or not according to the contemporary political convenience of the Dukes of Savoy, and the major attempt to destroy them called forth Oliver Cromwell's intervention and the famous sonnet of Milton. In spite of torture, murder, deportation, and even the kidnapping of their children, to have them brought up in the Roman Catholic faith, the sect survived, and still exists, having been granted full equality of rights with his Roman Catholic subjects by Charles Edward of Piedmont in 1848.

Weathermen, the rather incongruous name for the most radical and volatile of the many groups making up the so-called "underground" in the United States of America. Unlike most of the loosely-structured organisations involved in the growing anti-establishment front, the Weathermen appear to have direct rather than anarchistic political goals, taking a stand far to the left of traditional politics. Their avowed aim is the total overthrow of the current American political structure, with specific and carefully planned acts of violence as the tools of their trade and the civil police force as one of their prime targets. This has led to a series of bomb explosions, often cunningly planned, and brutal murders of police patrolmen which have deeply shocked the average American citizen. A particularly sinister and ominous feature, to most people's eyes, is the fact that the Weathermen appear to be largely drawn from the highly intelligent and well-educated strata, many of them with well-to-do and/or academic backgrounds. Members of this group make no secret of their contempt for the intellect and political attitudes of the American middle-class, and claim to demonstrate the impotence of Society by their ability to commit flagrant acts of violence with such ease and the equal ease with which they subsequently escape detection and arrest. The elusive nature of the organisation and its uncertain background have led to a number of fantastic speculations about its true origins. One of the oddest of these is the notion, widely held in America, that the Weathermen are in reality financed and backed by the country's extreme *right*—as a means of discrediting in the public eye the slow but steady move towards socialism that seems to be developing there. The Weathermen appear to have ceased activity in the early 1970s, but bomb outrages in early 1975 were once more perpetrated in their name.

Witchcraft. There are various interpretations and definitions of witchcraft from that of Pennethorne Hughes who states that "witchcraft, as it emerges into European history and literature, represents the old paleolithic fertility cult, plus the magical idea, plus various parodies of contemporary religions" to that of the fanatical Father Montague Summers who says that Spiritualism and witchcraft are the same thing. A leading authority on witchcraft, however, the late Dr. Margaret Murray, distinguishes between Operative Witchcraft (which is really Magic (*q.v.*)) and Ritual Witchcraft which, she says, "embraces the religious beliefs and ritual of the people known in late mediaeval times as 'witches.'" That there were such people we know from history and we know, too, that many of them—the great majority of them women—were tortured or executed or both. Many innocent people perished, especially after the promulgation of the bull *Summis desiderantes* by Pope Innocent VIII in 1484. Himself "a man of scandalous life", according to a Catholic historian, he wrote to "his dear sons," the German professors of theology, Johann Sprenger and Heinrich Kraemer, "witches are hindering men from performing the sexual act and women from conceiving . . ." and delegated them as Inquisitors "of these heretical pravities." In 1494 they codified in the *Malleus Maleficarum* (Hammer of Witches) the ecclesiastical rules for detecting acts of witchcraft. Dr. Murray points out that there have ordinarily been two theories about witchcraft: (1) that there were such beings as witches, that they possessed supernatural powers and that the evidence given at their trials was substantially correct; (2) that the witches were simply poor silly creatures who either deluded themselves into believing that they had certain powers or, more frequently, were tortured into admitting things that they did not do. She herself accepts a third theory: that there were such beings as witches, that they really did what they admitted to doing, but that they did not possess supernatural powers. They were in fact believers in the old religion of pre-Christian times and the Church took centuries to root them out. That there existed "covens" of witches who carried out peculiar rites Dr. Murray has no doubt whatever. The first to show that witchcraft was a superstition and that the majority of so-called witches were people suffering from mental illness was the physician Johann Weyer of Cleves (1515–88). His views were denounced by the Catholic Church. Few people realise how deeply the notion of witchcraft is implanted in our minds and how seriously its power is still taken. For example, the Witchcraft Act was not repealed in this country until the 1950s. Furthermore, as recently as 1944, when the allied armies were invading Europe, the Spiritualist medium Mrs. Helen Duncan was charged with witchcraft and actually sent to prison—a prosecution which brought forth caustic comments from the then prime minister, Winston Churchill. *See also* Demonism.

Women's Liberation Movement, the name given to a loosely organised collection of women drawn from all ages and walks of life which appears to be emerging as a latter-day "super-suffragette" movement. Unlike the original suffragette movement, however, which advocated "Votes for Women," the 1970s' version seems to have less definite aims. The principal argument hinges on the fact that with the development of highly efficient methods of contraception (the "pill") women need no longer be "slaves" to their family commitments and the traditional dominant and decision-making role of the male in our society must go. At the same time there should be no more wage or job discrimination against women. The movement has been going from strength to strength in America and is acquiring definite power in local and state politics. In Europe it has made somewhat less dramatic inroads. To many spectators, the movement's bible is the witty if polemical book *The Female Eunuch* by the Australian author Germaine Greer. An equally amusing, if perhaps somewhat less serious counterblast *The Manipulated Man* by the German woman doctor. Esther Vilar, traitorously takes an anti-feminist line. A small victory for the feminist cause has been the slow advance of the abbreviation "Ms" as an acceptable alternative for Mrs or Miss. 1975 saw the passage, in the United Kingdom, of the "Equal Opportunities Act"—a development which would have delighted the suffragettes of half a centrury ago.

World Congress of Faiths, an inter-religious movement which aims to break down barriers between faiths. The first step was taken by the world's parliament of religions held in Chicago in 1893; similar gatherings were held subsequently at intervals in Europe; but the actual organisation was formed in 1936 by Sir Francis Younghusband; and now an annual conference is held and educational activity carried on.

World Council of Churches, a union of Christian Churches from all over the world (including the Churches of the Protestant, Anglican, and Orthodox traditions, but excluding the Roman Catholic Church), engaged in extending Christian mission and unity throughout the world. All Churches which "accept our Lord Jesus Christ as God and Saviour" are eligible. This modern ecumenical movement stems from the great World Missionary Conference held at Edinburgh in 1910. The World Council was founded in 1948 and meets for consultation from time to time In the light of the 1975 assembly in Nairobi, the Churches plan to monitor the suppression of human rights throughout the world.

Y

Yoga, a Hindu discipline which teaches a technique for freeing the mind from attachment to the senses, so that once freed the soul may become fused with the universal spirit (*atman* or Brahman), which is its natural goal. This is the sole function of the psychological and physical exercises which the Yogi undertakes, although few ever reach the final stage of *Samadhi* or union with Brahman which is said to take place in eight levels of attainment. These are: (1) *Yama*, which involves the extinction of desire and egotism and their replacement by charity and unselfishness; (2) *Niyama*, during which certain rules of conduct must be adopted, such as cleanliness, the pursuit of devotional studies, and the carrying out of rituals of purification; (3) *Asana*, or the attainment of correct posture and the reduction to a minimum of all bodily movement (the usual posture of the concentrating Yogi is the "lotus position" familiar from pictures); (4) *Pranayama*, the right control of the life-force or breath in which there are two stages at which the practitioner hopes to arrive, the first being complete absorption in the act of breathing which empties the mind of any other thought, the second being the ability almost to cease to breathe which allegedly enables him to achieve marvellous feats of endurance; (5) *Pratyahara* or abstraction which means the mind's complete withdrawal from the world of sense; (6) *Dharana* in which an attempt is made to think of one thing only which finally becomes a repetition of the sacred syllable OM; (7) *dhyana*, meditation, which finally leads to (8) *Samadhi* the trance state which is a sign of the complete unity of soul with reality.

Yoga is very old, and when the sage Patanjali (*c.* 300 B.C.) composed the book containing these instructions, the *Yoga Sutras*, he was probably collecting from many ancient traditions. Some of the claims made by Yogis seem, to the Western mind, frankly incredible; but in the West and especially in recent years Yoga methods have been used at the lower levels in order to gain improved self-control, better posture, and improved health. Whether it achieves these ends is another matter, but the genuine Yogi regards this as a perversion of the nature and purpose of the discipline.

Z

Zen Buddhism, a Buddhist sect which is believed to have arisen in 6th cent. China but has flourished chiefly in Japan; for some reason it has of recent years begun to attract attention in the West thanks to the voluminous writings of Dr. D. T. Suzuki and the less numerous but doubtless much-read books of Mr. Christmas Humphreys. But the fact that these writings exist does not explain their being read, nor why of all possible Eastern sects this particular one should be chosen in our times. What is Zen's attraction and why should anyone take the trouble to read about something (the word "something" is used for reasons that will become evident) that is not a religion, has no doctrine, knows no God and no after-life, no good and no evil, and possesses no scriptures but has to be taught by parables which seem to be purposely meaningless? One of the heroes of Zen is the fierce-looking Indian monk Boddhidharma (fl. *c.* 516–534) who brought Buddhism to China, of whom it is recounted that when the Emperor asked him how much merit he had acquired by supporting the new creed, the monk shouted at him: "None whatever!" The Emperor then wished to know what was the sacred doctrine of the creed and again the monk shouted: "It is empty—there is nothing sacred!" Dr. Suzuki, having affirmed that there is no God in Zen, goes on to state that this does not mean that Zen denies the existence of God because "neither denial nor affirmation concerns Zen." The most concrete statement he is prepared to make is that the basic idea of Zen is to come in touch with the inner workings of our being, and to do this in the most direct way possible without resorting to anything external or superadded. Therefore anything that has the semblance of an external authority is rejected by Zen. Absolute faith is placed in a man's own inner being. Apparently the intention is that, so far from indulging in inward meditations or such practices as the Yogi uses, the student must learn to act spontaneously, without thinking, and without self-consciousness or hesitation. This is the main purpose of the *koan* the logically insoluble riddle which the pupil must try to solve. One such is the question put by master to pupil: "A girl is walking down the street, is she the younger or the older sister?" The correct answer, it seems, is to say nothing but put on a mincing gait, to *become* the girl, thus showing that what matters is the experience of being and not its verbal description. Another *koan*: "What is the Buddha?" "Three pounds of flax" is attributed to T'ung-shan in the 9th cent. and a later authority's comment is that "none can excel it as regards its irrationality which cuts off all passages to speculation." Zen, in effect, teaches the uselessness of trying to use words to discuss the Absolute.

Zen came to Japan in the 13th cent., more than five centuries after Confucianism or the orthodox forms of Buddhism, and immediately gained acceptance whilst becoming typically Japanese in the process. One of the reasons why it appealed must have been that its spontaneity and insistence on action without thought, its emphasis on the uselessness of mere words, and such categories as logical opposites, had an inevitable attraction for a people given to seriousness, formality, and logic to a degree which was almost stifling. Zen must have been to the Japanese what nonsense rhymes and nonsense books, like those of Edward Lear and Lewis Carroll, were to the English intellectuals. Lear's limericks, like some of the *koans*, end up with a line which, just at the time when one expects a point to be made, has no particular point at all, and *Alice in Wonderland* is the perfect example of a world, not without logic, but with a crazy logic of its own which has no relationship to that of everyday life. Therefore Zen began to impregnate every aspect of life in Japan, and one of the results of its emphasis on spontaneous action rather than reason was its acceptance by the Samurai, the ferocious warrior class, in such activities as swordsmanship, archery, Japanese wrestling, and later Judo and the Kamikaze dive-bombers. But much of Japanese art, especially landscape gardening and flower-arrangement, was influenced similarly, and Zen is even used in Japanese psychiatry. The very strict life of the Zen monks is based largely on doing things, learning through experience; the periods of meditation in the Zendo hall are punctuated by sharp slaps on the face administered by the abbot to those who are unsatisfactory pupils. Dr. Suzuki denies that Zen is nihilistic, but it is probably its appearance of nihilism and its appeal to the irrational and spontaneous which attracts the Western world at a time when to many the world seems without meaning and life over-regimented. However, it has influenced such various aspects of Western life as philosophy (Heidegger), psychiatry (Erich Fromm and Hubert Benoit), writing (Aldous Huxley), and painting (Die Zen Gruppe in Germany).

Zionism, a belief in the need to establish an autonomous Jewish home in Palestine which, in its modern form, began with Theodor Herzl (1860–1904), a Hungarian journalist working in Vienna. Although Herzl was a more or less assimilated Jew, he was forced by the Dreyfus case and the pogroms in Eastern Europe to conclude that there was no real safety for the Jewish people until they had a state of their own. The Jews, of course, had always in a religious sense thought of Palestine as a spiritual homeland and prayed "next year in Jerusalem," but the religious had thought of this in a philosophical way as affirming old loyalties, not as recommending the formation of an actual state. Therefore Herzl was opposed both by many of the religious Jews and, at the other extreme, by those who felt themselves to be assimilated and in many cases without religious faith. Even after the Balfour Declaration of 1917, there was not a considerable flow of Jews to Palestine, which at that time was a predominantly Arab state. But the persecutions of Hitler changed all this and, after bitter struggles, the Jewish state was proclaimed in 1948. Today Zionism is supported by the vast majority of the Jewish communities everywhere (although strongly disapproved of in the Soviet Union as "Western imperialism") and Zionism is now an active international force concerned with protecting the welfare and extending the influence of Israel.

Zoroastrianism, at one time one of the great world religions, competing in the 2nd cent. A.D. on almost equal terms from its Persian home with Hellenism and the Roman Imperial Government. Under the Achaemenidae (*c.* 550–330 B.C.) Zoroastrianism was the state religion of Persia. Alexander's conquest in 331 B.C. brought disruption but the religion flourished again under the Sassanian dynasty (A.D. *c.* 226–640). With the advance of the Mohammedan Arabs in the 7th cent. Zoroastrianism finally gave way to Islam. A number of devotees fled to India there to become the Parsees. In Persia itself a few scattered societies remain.

The name Zoroaster is the Greek rendering of Zarathustra, the prophet who came to purify the ancient religion of Persia. It is thought that he lived at the beginning of the 6th cent. B.C. He never claimed for himself divine powers but was given them by his followers. The basis of Zoroastrianism is the age-long war between good and evil, Ahura Mazda heading the good spirits and Ahriman the evil ones. Morality is very important since by doing right the worshipper is supporting Ahura Mazda against Ahriman, and the evil-doers will be punished in the last days when Ahura Mazda wins his inevitable victory.

The sacred book of this religion is the *Avesta*. If Zoroastrianism has little authority today, it had a very considerable influence in the past. Its doctrines penetrated into Judaism (*q.v.*) and, through Gnosticism, Christianity. The worship of Mithra by the Romans was an impure version of Zoroastrianism. Manichaeism (*q.v.*) was a Zoroastrian heresy and the Albigensianism of mediaeval times was the last relic of a belief which had impressed itself deeply in the minds of men.

GAZETTEER OF THE WORLD

An index and guide to the maps with up-to-date descriptive matter, together with a list of the sovereign members of the Commonwealth and British dependent territories, information on the reorganisation of local government in the United Kingdom and on some aspects of the social structure of the world economy.

GAZETTEER OF THE WORLD

This edition of the gazetteer is the result of a major revision which has attempted to provide an index and guide to the maps. Gazetteer and maps (also newly revised) should be used in conjunction, although it is impractical for reasons of clarity to include every place mentioned in the gazetteer within the map section.

Measurement of Geographical Phenomena.

(1) Physical Features.

In using the gazetteer the reader should note that it is impossible to make absolutely correct measurements of geographical phenomena. For example, measurement of height of land above sea-level depends, in the first instance, upon the definition of the elusive concept of sea-level itself. This is constantly changing and so an arbitrary value of *mean sea-level* is normally used, but the value adopted varies from country to country. As a result, height above sea-level has inbuilt inconsistencies and inaccuracies. Similarly, the length of a river will depend upon the scale of the survey from which measurements are made. Large-scale maps and aerial photographs can show in great detail the sinuous course of rivers, whereas a map on a smaller scale must reduce the amount of information shown and thereby the apparent length. We hope to include in a later edition the results of a yet unpublished work by a commission of the United Nations which is attempting to define in precise terms the area of the world's seas and oceans.

The gazetteer now records the heights of mountains, lengths of rivers, and land and sea areas in metric units. English equivalents will be found on **K183** and p. 1 of the **Atlas**.

(2) Definition of Urban Area.

An even more difficult problem of measurement relates to the definition of the urban area of a town or city. It is possible to define the extent of urban areas in three major ways, by using (1) the administrative area, (2) the physically built-up area, and (3) the socio-geographic, metropolitan area. This latter concept is in many ways the most meaningful for it relates to the notion that a city exerts a strong influence over the population resident beyond its administrative or built-up boundary. For example, the city may provide employment opportunities or shopping and entertainment facilities for a population resident some distance away from it. In order to define "city" in these terms some means of measuring the degree of connection between it and its surrounding hinterland (the city-region) must be found and, needless to say, there is considerable disagreement among workers in this field as to what are the most suitable criteria to use. Different criteria produce different definitions and even the most recent measurements are obsolete within a short space of time. However, the real significance of this less tangible concept of "city" may be illustrated by the fact that recent proposals for the reform of local government in England rest in part upon the concept of the city-region.

The population figures given in the gazetteer normally relate to the city's administrative area. In the case of some large cities two figures are given—(1) for the administrative city, and (2) for the more extensive metropolitan area which surrounds and includes the administrative city.

Place Names.

Where there have been recent changes in place names, the old name is given in brackets and a cross reference directs the reader to the new name. *See also* **K183**.

Reorganisation of Local Government in the United Kingdom.

The gazetteer has been modified to incorporate the new system of local government in the United Kingdom. Details of the changes will be found on **K186**.

Editor's Note to Readers.

As a result of the indeterminate and dynamic nature of geographical phenomena inconsistencies and inaccuracies are bound to occur in a gazetteer of this size. The editor welcomes comments and criticisms of the entries based upon local knowledge and will try to make the fullest possible use of information received from readers.

ABBREVIATIONS USED IN THE GAZETTEER

Geographical Names

Ala. = Alabama
Ark. = Arkansas
ASSR = Autonomous Soviet Socialist Republic
Atl. Oc. = Atlantic Ocean
B.C. = British Columbia
Brit. = British
Cal. = California
Col. = Colorado
Conn. = Connecticut
ČSSR = Czechoslovak Socialist Republic
Del. Delaware
Eng. = England
Fla. = Florida
Fr. = French
Ga. = Georgia
Ill. = Illinois
Ind. = Indiana
Kan. = Kansas
Ky. = Kentucky
La. = Louisiana
Land = prov. (W. Germany)
Mass. = Massachusetts
Md. = Maryland
Me. = Maine
Mich. = Michigan
Minn. = Minnesota
Miss. = Mississippi
Mo. = Missouri
Mont. = Montana
N.B. = New Brunswick
N.C. = North Carolina
N.D. = North Dakota
Neth. = Netherlands
N.H. = New Hampshire
N.J. = New Jersey
N.M. = New Mexico
N.S.W. = New South Wales
N.T. = Northern Territory (Australia)
N.Y. = New York
N.Z. = New Zealand
Oblast = aut. prov. (USSR)
O.F.S. = Orange Free State
Okla. = Oklahoma
Okrug = aut. dist. (RSFSR)
Ore. = Oregon
Pac. Oc. = Pacific Ocean
Penns. = Pennsylvania
R.I. = Rhode Island
R.o.I. = Republic of Ireland
RSFSR = Russian Soviet Federal Socialist Republic
S.C. = South Carolina
Scot. = Scotland
S.D. = South Dakota
SSR = Soviet Socialist Republic
Tenn. = Tennessee
USA = United States of America
USSR = Union of Soviet Socialist Republics
Va. = Virginia
Vt. = Vermont
Wash. = Washington
W.I. = West Indies
Wis. = Wisconsin
Wyo. = Wyoming

Other Abbreviations

a. = area
admin. = administrative
agr. = agriculture
alt. = altitude
anc. = ancient
arch. = archaeological
a.s.l. = above sea-level
ass. = associated
aut. rep. = autonomous republic
bdy. = boundary
bldg. = building
bor. = borough
bdr. = border
C. = cape
c. = city; circa = about
can. = canton
cap. = capital
cas. = castle
cath. = cathedral
ch. = chief
cm = centimetres
co. = county
C.B. = county borough
col. = colony
colly. = colliery
comm. = commercial
conurb. = conurbation
cst. = coast
ctr. = centre
cty. = country
dep. = department
dist. = district
div. = division
E. = east or easterly
elec. = electrical
engin. = engineering
esp. = especially
est. = estimate
exp. = exports
F. = firth
fed. = federal
fish. pt. = fishing port
fortfd. = fortified
G. = Gulf
gen. = general
G.N.P. = gross national product
gr. = great, group
ha = hectares
gtr. = greater
hgst. = highest
I. = island
impt. = important
inc. = including
indep. = independent
inds. = industries
industl. = industrial
Is. = Islands
km = kilometres
km^2 = square kilometres
L. = lake
l. = length
lge. = large
l. gov. dist. = local government district
lgst. = largest
lt. = light
m = metres
machin. = machinery
met. a. = metropolitan area
met. co. = metropolitan county
mftg. = manufacturing
mkg. = making
mkt. = market
mm = millimetres
mnfs. = manufactures
mng. = mining
mtn. = mountain
mun. = municipality
N. = north or northerly
nat. = national
non-met. co. = non-metropolitan county
nr. = near
p. = population
par. = parish
penin. = peninsula
pref. = prefecture
prin. = principal
prod. = products
prot. = protectorate
prov. = province
pt. = port
R. = river
rep. = republic
residtl. = residential
rly. = railway
S. = south or southerly
shipbldg. = shipbuilding
sm. = small
spt. = seaport
st. = state
sta. = station
sub. = suburb
t. = town
Tan-Zam = Tanzania-Zambia rly.
terr. = territory
tr. = trade
trib. = tributary
Turk-Sib = Turkestan-Siberia rly.
univ. = university
U.D. = urban district
v. = village
W. = west or westerly
wat. pl. = watering place
wks. = works
wkshps. = workshops

A

Aachen (Aix-la-Chapelle), t., N. Rhine-Westphalia, W. Germany; anc. spa t. in coal-field dist.; industl., route ctr.; contains tomb of Charlemagne; p. (est. 1969) 176,800.

Aalen, t., Baden-Württemberg, **W. Germany**; on R. Kocher; iron, textiles, lens mkg.; p. (est. 1969) 34,773.

Aalst (Alost), t., E. Flanders, **Belgium**, 24 km N.W. Brussels; industl., comm. ctr. at rly. junc.; agr. tr.; p. (1968) 45,881.

Aarau, t., cap. of Aargau can., **Switzerland**; precision tools and instruments, shoes, textiles; hydroelectric power; p. (1969) 17,800.

Aare, R., **Switzerland**, flows through Brienz and Thun Ls., thence into Rhine; Aare gorges above Meiringen; lgst R. wholly in Switzerland, 290 km long.

Aargau, can., N. Switzerland; occupies lower Aare R. valley; agr. in valleys, wooded uplands; cap. Aarau; a. 1,404 km²; p. (1969) 422,000.

Aba, t., Nigeria; N.E. of Pt. Harcourt; mkt., palm oil processing; p. (1971) 158,330.

Abaco, Gt., I., Bahamas, **W.I.**; sheltered harbours, yachting; exp. crayfish; p. (est. 1969) 6,500.

Abādān, c., **Iran**; spt., major oil terminal and refining ctr. on A.I. in Persian G.; p. (est. 1971) 300,000.

Abakan, t., **RSFSR**, on R. A.; recent rly.; saw-milling, food inds.; p. (1970) 90,000.

Abashiri, t., N. cst. Hokkaido, **Japan**; impt. fishing base; p. (1970) 43,904.

Abaza, t., **USSR**; E. Siberia; iron ore.

Abbeville, t., N. **France**; on R. Somme; connected with Paris and Belgium by canals; sugar-milling, carpets, biscuits, beer; p. (1968) 25,702.

Abbots-Langley, v., Herts., **Eng.**; birthplace of Nicholas Breakspeare (Pope Adrian IV).

Åbenrå, spt., S.E. Jutland, **Denmark**; at head of A. fjord and admin. ctr. of S. Jutland prov.; vehicles, clothing, food processing; p. (1970) 20,264.

Abeokuta, t., **Nigeria**; cap. Ogun st.; N. of Lagos; palm oil, textiles; p. (est. 1971) 226,361.

Aberaeron, t., Dyfed, S. Wales; p. (1971) 1,324.

Abercarn, t., Gwent, **Wales**; tinplate, knitting pins; former colliery t.; p. (1971) 18,468.

Aberdare, t., Mid Glamorgan, **Wales**; on R. Cynon; wire cables; former coalmng.; p. (1971) 37,760.

Aberdare Range, mtns., Nat. Park, **Kenya**; rise to 4,000 m; form a section of E. rim of Gr. Rift Valley; equable climate attractive to white settlers; camphor forests, fruit and pastoral agr. at higher alts.

Aberdeen, royal burgh, l. gov. dist., Grampian Reg., **Scot.**; between mouths of Rs. Dee and Don; impt. fishing pt. under competition from claims of rapidly growing N. Sea oil ind.; "granite-city"—much granite used in central bldgs.; univ., cath.; p. (1971) 182,071.

Aberdeen, t., S.D., **USA**; ctr. for wheat and live-stock region; rly. wks., farm machin.; p. (1970) 26,476.

Aberdeenshire, former co., E. Scot. *See* **Grampian Region.**

Aberdovey, t., Gwynedd, **Wales**, on estuary of R. Dovey; resort.

Aberfeldy, burgh, Perth and Kinross, **Scot.**; in Strath Tay, 6 km below Loch Tay; mkt.; salmon and trout fishing resort; p. (1971) 1,537.

Abergavenny, t., Gwent, **Wales**; on R. Usk; light engin., concrete prods.; cattle mkt.; cas.; p. (1971) 9,388.

Abergele, t., Clwyd, **Wales**; p. (1971) 12,257.

Aberlour, Charlestown of, burgh, Moray, **Scot.**; on R. Spey, 19 km S. of Elgin; p. (1971) 763.

Abernethy, burgh, Perth and Kinross, **Scot.**; on R. Tay, once the cap. of the Pictish Kings; p. (1971) 698.

Abersoch, t., Gwynedd, **Wales**; yachting resort.

Abertillery, t., Gwent, **Wales**; collieries, tinplate; p. (1971) 21,140.

Aberystwyth, t., Dyfed, **Wales**; on Cardigan Bay at mouth of R. Ystwyth, resort; cas., univ. college; Nat. Library of Wales; p. (1971) 10,680.

Abidjan, c., cap. of **Ivory Coast**; pt.; exp. palm oil, cocoa, copra, hardwood, rubber; oil refining at Vridi nearby; p. (est. 1964) 282,000 (met. a.).

Abilene, t., Texas, **USA**; univ.; agr. processing oil refining; p. (1970) 88,433 (c.), 112,168 (met. a.).

Abilene, t., on Smoky Hill R. Kansas, **USA**; childhood home of Eisenhower; p. (1970) 6,661.

Abingdon, Oxon., **Eng.**; mkt. t. on R. Thames; cars, leather gds.; mediaeval and Georgian bldgs.; p. (1971) 18,596.

Abingdon, t., Va., **USA**; timber inds., agr. processing and tr., tobacco; tourist ctr.; p. (1970) 4,376.

Abinger Hammer, v., Surrey, **Eng.**; former centre of Weald iron industry.

Abkhazskaya, aut. rep., Georgian SSR, **USSR**; borders Black Sea; sub-tropical crops, tourism; cap. Sukhumi; a. 8,599 km²; p. (1970) 487,000.

Abo. *See* **Turku.**

Abomey, anc. cap., **Dahomey**, former slave mkt.; cotton; p. (est. 1970) 34,000.

Abovyan, t., Armeniyan SSR, **USSR**; 16 km from Yerevan; new model t. founded 1963; planned p. 50,000.

Aboyne and Glentanner, par., Kincardine and Deeside, **Scot.**; on R. Dee nr. Ballater; Highland games; resort.

Abraham, Plains of, nr. Quebec, **Canada**; Wolfe's victory over French under Montcalm, 1759.

Abram, t., Gtr. Manchester, **Eng.**; engin.; p. (1971) 6,472.

Abrantes, t., **Portugal**, on Tagus R.; French won battle here in Napoleonic Wars, 1807.

Abruzzo Molise, region, central **Italy**; high limestone plateaux, narrow cstl. plain bordering Adriatic; poor agr., livestock; methane; forms part of Mezzogiorno; a. 15,229 km²; p. (1969) 1,202,071.

Abu Dhabi, I., emirate, lgst. of **United Arab Emirates**; S.E. Arabian pen.; rich oil reserves; a. 207,200 km²; p. (est. 1968) 46,375.

Abu Qir, v. on A. Bay, **Egypt**; site of anc. Canopus; Battle of the Nile fought in the Bay 1798; p. 7,086.

Abu Simbel, Nile Valley, **Egypt**; anc. temples carved out of solid sandstone, one to Rameses II and the other to his Queen; saved from waters of Lake Nasser.

Abydos, anc. t. of Phrygia, **Asia Minor**, in present Turkey; resisted Philip of Macedon; famed for story of Leander and Hero.

Abydus, ruined c., Upper **Egypt**; celebrated for its temple of Osiris.

Acajutla, spt., **El Salvador**; exp. coffee; cement, oil refining, fertilisers; p. (1960) 15,475.

Acapulco de Juárez, spt., Pac. cst., **Mexico**; major modern resort in bay surrounded by steep mtns.; exp. agr. prods.; p. (1970) 174,378.

Accra, c., cap. of **Ghana**; spt.; univ.; airpt.; consumer gds.; p. (1970) 564,194 (c.), 738,498 (met. a. inc. Tema).

Accrington, t., Lancs., **Eng.**; 32 km N. of Manchester; former cotton ctr.; textile machin., more diversified new inds.; p. (1971) 36,838.

Achill I., Mayo, **R.o.I.**; mtnous.; agr., fishing, tourism at Dugort and Keal; a. 148 km²; p. (1966) 3,598.

Acireale, spt., Sicily, **Italy**; cath.; sulphur springs, p. (est. 1968) 47,581.

Aconcagua, mtn., Andes, **Argentina**; highest peak of Western Hemisphere, alt. 6,956 m.

Aconquija, Nevada de, mtn. range, in E. Andes, N. **Argentina**; rises steeply from Chaco lowland to 5,500 m.

Acre. *See* **'Akko.**

Acre, st. E. **Brazil**; isolated within Amazon basin; cap. Rio Branco; a. 153,170 km²; p. (est. 1968) 204,081.

Acton. *See* **Ealing.**

Adamawa Highlands, Nigeria; rise to over 5,490 m; stock rearing.

Adam's Bridge, chain of sandbanks, 35 km long, in Palk Strait, between India and Sri Lanka; construction of rail causeway mooted.

Adana, t., **Turkey**; on Seijhan R.; agr. processing and tr.; cas.; cap. of A. prov.; 4th. t. of Turkey; p. (1965) 289,918 (t.), 347,093 (met. a.).

Adapazari, t., **Turkey**; rly. junction; agr. and tr. ctr., silk, linen; high-grade concentrate from low-grade iron ore deposits in Camdagi a.; p. (1970) 152,171.

Adda, R., N. **Italy**; flows through L. Como to R. Po.; agr. in wide valley above L. Como; 240 km long.

Addis Ababa, c., cap. of **Ethiopia**; at 2,440 m in central highlands; terminus of Djibouti rly., ctr. of coffee tr., light inds.; admin. ctr.; univ., palaces; p. (1971) 881,400.

Adelaide, c., spt., cap. of **South Australia**; on R. Torrens, which flows into G. of St. Vincent; transcontinental rly. connections; univ.; cars, steel tubes, electrical appliances, chemicals, sugar and oil refining; p. (1972) 16,331 (c.), 842,611 (met. a.).

Adélie Land (Terre Adélie), Antarctica; French terr. and dependency of Réunion.

Adelsberg, t., **Yugoslavia**. *See* **Postojna**.

Aden, spt., cap. of **Democratic Rep. of Yemen**; former Brit. col.; bay behind headlands of Aden t. and Little Aden, excellent anchorage; p. (est. 1970) 250,000 (met. a.).

Aden, G. of W. **Arabian Sea**; one of most impt. shipping lanes in world; pts. of Aden, Berbera, Djibouti; length 880 km, width 480 km at mouth.

Adige, R., N. **Italy**; upper course forms impt. routeway through Alps between Italy and N.; flows via Verona to Adriatic; 360 km long.

Adirondack, mtns., **USA**; hgst. peak Mt. Marcy (1,630 m), average height 1,200 m; scenically attractive, ski resorts, sanatoria, iron ore deposits.

Adlington, t., Lancs., **Eng.**; nr. Chorley; former cotton spinning t.; p. (1971) 4,991.

Admiralty Is., 27 km of sm. coral Is., one lge. I., S.W. **Pac. Oc.**; N. of New Guinea; forms part of Bismarck Archipelago; Australian mandate; anc. civilisation; pearl fishing, coconuts; ch. t. Lorengau.; a. 2,072 km^2; p. (1966) 20,202.

Adour, R., S.W. **France**; rises in Pyrenees, enters Bay of Biscay below Bayonne; 331 km long.

Adria, mkt. t., Rovigo, **Italy**; formerly on cst., now 22 km inland, old Etruscan c.; p. (est. 1968) 22,703.

Adrianople. *See* **Edirne**.

Adriatic Sea, branch of the Mediterranean, between Italy and Balkan Peninsula; forms G. of Venice on the N.; chief trading pts., Venice, Trieste, and Ancona on the N., Brindisi and Dürres on the S.; a. 134,680 km^2, 720 km long.

Adriatic Highway, Yugoslavia; cst. road (in need of repair) across Dinaric Alps motivated by tourist boom.

Adullam or **Aidelma**, Judean c. of Canaanite origin, S.W. Jerusalem, **Israel**, where David hid in cave from Saul.

Adwick le Street, t., South Yorks, **Eng.**; coal; home of George Washington's family; p. (1971) 18,000.

Adygeyskaya (Adygei), aut. region, **RSFSR**; in foothills of Caucasus; mainly agr. and lumbering; cap. Maykop; a. 7,599 km^2; p. (1970) 386,000.

Adzharskaya, aut. rep., Georgian SSR, **USSR**; borders Turkey; mtnous.; sub-tropical crops; cap. Batumi; a. 2,849 km^2; p. (1970) 310,000.

Aegades, gr. of rocky Is. off W. cst. of Sicily, **Italy**; ch. t. Favignana on I. of that name.

Aegean Is., between Greece and Turkey; called the Grecian Archipelago, inc. Crete, Cyclades, Sporades, and Dodecanese; a. 3,901 km^2.

Aegean Sea, branch of the Mediterranean; studded with Is., between Greece and Turkey; connected through the Dardanelles with Sea of Marmara and thence through the Bosporus Strait with the Black Sea; rich cultural history; coral, sponge fishing; recent oil finds; length 640 km, width 320 km.

Afars and Issas, French Territory of the, N.E. **Africa**; formerly French Somaliland (renamed 1967); indep. planned for 1977; extends inland from straits of Bab-el-Mandeb; plain, mainly below 180 m; hot, dry climate; shark and mother of pearl fisheries; little cultivable land; cap. Djibouti; a. 23,051 km^2; p. (1967) 126,000.

Affric, Glen, Inverness, **Scot.**; 48 km S.W. of Inverness; hydroelectric power.

Afghanistan, rep. (1973), former kingdom, **Asia**; lies N. and W. of Pakistan; cap. Kabul; comm. ctrs. Kabul, Kandahar; mtnous.; ch. Rs., Kabul and Helm; intense summer heat, severe winter cold, scanty rainfall; races, Afghans, aboriginal hill-tribes; languages, official Persian, spoken Pushtu; religion, Islam; cereals, fruit, sheep, horses, camels; inds. carpets, woollens, silks; coal-mng. at Dara-i-Suf; natural gas at Shibarghan; rich copper, lead, iron ore resources undeveloped; no rly. a. 647,500 km^2; p. (est. 1969) 16,516,000.

Africa, second lgst. continent contains 22 per cent of world's land a. but only 8 per cent of p.; diverse physical and cultural conditions; plateaux interrupted in N. and S. by steeply folded, sharply eroded mtn. ranges and by mtn. massifs of Sahara and E. Africa; climate and vegetation vary from hot desert to equatorial rain forest and from Mediterranean woodland to tropical savannah; sparse but ethnically varied p., concentrated mainly along N.W. Mediterranean cst., Nile valley, cst. of W. Africa and N.E. of L. Victoria; little urbanisation; economic development hindered by colonial legacy and neo-colonial international companies, poorly developed transport network, poor soils, inadequate rainfall and low economic value of natural vegetation; schemes like Volta R. multipurpose development and the Cabora Bassa dam designed to alleviate this natural poverty; continent contains 40 per cent of world hydroelectric potential and is storehouse of non-energy producing minerals, but many are exported in unprocessed form; agr. predominant economic activity, except in industl. enclaves of Egypt, Rhodesia and S. Africa; 60 per cent land devoted to subsistence crops; 46 ctys. had achieved independence by 1977 compared with 4 in 1945; a. *c.* 30,259,000 km^2; p. (est. 1974), 391,000,000.

Agadir, spt., S. cst. **Morocco**; wrecked by earthquake, 1960; new t. built S. of former c. in a. of greater geological stability; p. (est. 1970) 34,000.

Agana, cap. of **Guam**; reconstructed after second world war; p. (1970) 2,131 (exc. armed forces).

Agen t., cap. of Lot-et-Garonne, **France**; mkt. t.; aqueduct and bridge over Garonne R.; fruit tr. and processing; p. (1968) 37,470.

Agincourt, v., Pas-de-Calais, **France**; famed for battle in 1415 between English, led by Henry V and French under d'Albert; p. (1968) 220.

Agra, c., Uttar Pradesh, **India**; on Jumna R., 184 km S.S.E. of Delhi; formerly cap. of Mogul Empire; famous Taj Mahal mausoleum; univ.; footwear; p. (1971) 591,197 (c.), 634,622 (met. a.).

Agrigento, t., S. Sicily, **Italy**; spt., exp. sulphur, salt. Formerly Girgenti, founded Akragas, c. 580 B.C., famous for its temples; birthplace of Empedocles; p. (1969) 52,283.

Aguadilla, spt., **Puerto Rico**; exp. coffee and sugar; p. (1970) 21,087.

Aguascalientes, st., **Mexico**; on central plateau at 1,800 m; agr.; mineral springs; cap. A.; a. 6,472 km^2; p. (1969) 316,000.

Aguascalientes, t., cap. of A. st. **Mexico**; alt. over 1,800 m; 416 km N.W. of Mexico City; wide range of local inds.; hot springs; p. (1970) 181,277.

Agulhas, C., rocky projection, 160 km E. of C. of Good Hope, most southerly point of **Africa**.

Ahlen, t., N. Rhine-Westphalia, **W. Germany**; on R. Werse; coalmng., metal and engin. wks.; p. (est. 1969) 45,175.

Ahmadabad, temporary cap. of Gujarat, **India**; Jain temple, mosques; univ.; impt. textile ctr.; oilfield at Nawagam nearby; p. (1971) 1,585,544 (c.), 1,741,522 (met. a.).

Ahmadnagar, c., Maharashtra, **India**; admin. ctr.; old Bahmani cap.; lge. tr. in cotton and silk gds.; p. (1971) 118,236 (c.), 148,405 (met. a.).

Ahvāz (Ahwāz), c., cap. of Khuzestan prov., **Iran**; airpt.; oil, aluminium, steel pipes; p. (est. 1971) 270,100.

Aigues-Mortes, t., Gard dep., **France**; on Rhône delta; canal ctr., once spt., now 5 km from Mediterranean; salt-works; much of mediaeval t. preserved; tourism; p. (1968) 4,197.

Aiguille d'Arves, mtn., Dauphiné Alps, S.E. **France**; 3 rock needles; hgst. alt. 3,511 m.

Aiguille du Midi, mtn., Mt. Blanc massif, S.E. **France**; rock needle, funicular rly.; alt. 3,845 m.

Aiguille Verte, mtn., Mt. Blanc massif, S.E. **France**, rock needle overlooking Chamonix; alt. 4,130 m.

Ailefroid, mtn., Dauphiné Alps, S.E. **France**; double summit; alt. 3,962 m.

Ailsa Craig, rocky I., Kyle and Carrick, **Scot.**; alt. 340 m; gannetry.

Ain, dep., **France**; in Jura; mainly agr., famous for pigs and poultry; a. 5,822 km²; p. (1968) 339,262.
Ain, R., **France**; trib. of R. Rhône, flows S.S.W. from Jura; hydroelectric power; 194 km long.
Airdrie, burgh, Strathclyde Reg., **Scot.**; 19 km E. of Glasgow; iron inds., brick and concrete wks., steel tubes, pharmaceutics; p. (1971) 37,740.
Aire, R., West Yorks., **Eng.**; trib. of Ouse; length 112 km.
Aireborough, t., West Yorks., **Eng.**; woollens; p. (1971) 29,477.
Aisne, dep., **France**; borders Ardennes; forested; mainly agr., sugar beet; sm. textile ts.; cap. Laon; a. 7,423 km²; p. (1968) 526,346.
Aisne, R., N.E. **France**; navigation improved by regularisation; 240 km long.
Aitolia and Akarnania, **Greece**; mtnous. prov. on N. side G. of Patras; arable cultivation on cstl. plain; cap. Missolonghi; a. 5,390 km²; p. (1971) 228,719.
Aix-en-Provence, t., Bouches-du-Rhône, **France**; 29 km N. of Marseilles; old cap. of Provence; thermal springs; cultural and comm. ctr., agr., inds.; p. (1968) 93,671.
Aix-la-Chapelle. *See* **Aachen**.
Aix-les-Bains, health resort, Savoy, **France**; p. (1968) 20,718.
Aizuwakamatsu, t. N. Honshu, **Japan**; lacquer ware, candles; p. (est. 1971) 105,000.
Ajaccio, spt., cap. Corse du Sud, Corsica, **France**; tiber, flour, olive oil, tobacco; tourism; birthplace of Napoleon; p. (1968) 42,300.
Ajman, emirate, one of **United Arab Emirates**; p. (est. 1968) 4,000.
Ajmer, t., Rajasthan, **India**; salt extraction, vegetable oils; p. (1971) 262,851 (c.), 264,291 (met. a.).
Akhaia, prov., **Greece**; impt. currant producing a.; livestock; inc. pt. of Patras; a. 3,134 km²; p. (1971) 238,594.
Akhisar, t., **Turkey**; anc. Thyatira; in fertile agr. basin; p. (1965) 47,422.
Akita, pref., **Japan**; a. 11,663 km²; contains Japan's lgst. oilfield and copper mine; mtns. and fertile lowlands; p. (1970) 1,241,376.
Akita, c., **Japan**; cap. Akita pref.; old cas. t., pt; oil refining ctr., fertilisers, wood pulp; p. (est. 1971) 245,000.
'Akko (Acre), c., spt., **Israel**; famous for sieges during Crusades; withstood Napoleon for 61 days in 1799; pt. functions now assumed by Haifa; p. (est. 1970) 33,900.
Akmolinsk. *See* Tselinograd.
Akola, t., Maharashtra, **India**; cotton; p. (1971) 168,438.
Akosombo, pt., **Ghana**; pt. and new t. S. of L. Volta; textile factory being built; planned p. 50,000.
Akranes, t., **Iceland**; N. of Reykjavik; lge. cement wks.
Akron, c., Ohio, **USA**; lge. rubber mftg. ctr.; maize mills, woollens, machin., chemicals; univ.; p. (1970) 273,266 (c.), 673,485 (met. a.).
Aktyubinsk, t., N.W. Kazakh SSR, **USSR**; at S. end of Ural mtns.; ferro-alloys, engin., lignite, elec. power, chemicals, copper; p. (1970) 150,000.
Akureyri, t., N. **Iceland**; herring fishery, textiles, food processing; 2nd. t. of Iceland; p. (1970) 10,755.
Akyab, *See* **Sittwe**.
Alabama, st., **USA**; cap. Montgomery, ch. pt. Mobile; " cotton st.", cattle-rearing; fertilisers, chemicals, mng.; a. 133,667 km²; p. (1970) 3,373,006.
Alagôas, st., N.E. Brazil; hot, dry cattle rearing a., poor st. with low literacy rate; cap. Maceió; a. 28,648 km²; p. (1968) 1,400,248.
Alameda, spt. Cal., **USA**; on I. in San Francisco Bay; impt. naval and air base; pt. inds.; p. (1970) 70,968.
Aland Is. (Ahvenanmaa), group belonging to **Finland** at entrance of G. of Bothnia; a. 1,481 km²; p. (1968) 21,500.
Alaska, Arctic st., **USA**; separated from other sts.; bought from Russia (1868); mtnous.; furs, timber, salmon; major oil discoveries on N. slope present difficult ecological problems for exploitation; route of pipeline from Prudhoe Bay to Valdez now approved; a. 1,518,776 km²; p. (1970) 294,607.
Alaska G. of, S. cst. A., **USA**.; semi-circular G. with precipitous csts.; oil in Cook Inlet and Controller B.; a. 5,000 km².
Alaska Highway, from Dawson Creek, B.C., Canada, to Fairbanks, Alaska, **USA**; 2,443 km long; built for second world war programme; main supply base and H.Q., Edmonton, Alberta.
Alaska Range, mtn. massif, S.A., **USA**; extends in arc of 640 km; separates S. cst. and N. tundra; S.E. flowing glaciers; many peaks over 3,000 m; Mt. McKinley, 6,182 m.
Alatau, mtns., bdy. of Kazakhstan, **USSR**; and Sinkiang, **China**; group of 5 ranges, outliers of Tien-Shan; alt. up to 4,600 m; highest peak Khan Tengri, 6,954 m.
Alava, Basque prov., N. **Spain**; ch. t. Vitoria; viticulture; a. 3,043 km²; p. (1970) 204,323.
Albacete, prov., S.E. **Spain**; stock-raising; a. 14,864 km². p. (1970) 335,026.
Albacete, t., cap. of A. prov., **Spain**; agr. mkt., fruit, saffron; p. (1967) 83,495.
Alba-Iulia, t., **Romania**; on R. Mures, formerly Carisburgh; union of Transylvania with Romania proclaimed here 1918; p. (1966) 22,225.
Albania, rep., **S.E. Europe**; lying along Adriatic, adjacent to Yugoslavia and Greece; politically aligned with China; recent industl. development with Russian and Chinese aid; food ch. ind.; petroleum reserves and refining, hydroelectric power, coal, chrome ore, copper, iron ore; fastest growing p. in Europe; cap. Tirana; a. 27,529 km²; p. (1973) 2,322,600.
Albano, crater L., **Italy**; tourist attraction 24 km S.E. of Rome; steep sides; a. 8 km².
Albany, mkt. t., Ga., **USA**; on Flint R.; agr. ctr.; cotton, food; p. (1970) 72,623.
Albany, c., cap. of N.Y. st., **USA**; R. pt. on Hudson R.; admin. and industl. ctr.; p. (1970) 113,857 (c.), 710,602 (met. a.).
Albany, t., **W. Australia**; pt. on King George Sound; fruit ch. exp.; founded (1826) as penal col.; p. (1972) 13,055.
Albert, L. *See* **Mobutu Seso, L.**
Alberta, prov., W. **Canada**; part of prairies; Rockies in W.; wheat, livestock, feed crops; coal less impt. with development of rich oil and gas resources; chemicals, timber; cap. Edmonton; a. 661,188 km²; p. (1971) 1,627,874.
Albertville. *See* **Kalemi**.
Albi, t., cap. of Tarn dep., **France**; cath., industl. and comm. ctr.; p. (1968) 46,613.
Ålborg, c., cap. of N. Jutland prov., **Denmark**; spt. on S. side of Lim fjord; shipbldg., cement, textiles; airpt. 11 km to N.W.; p. (est. 1970) 154,737.
Albula Alps, mtn. range, Rhaetian Alps, E. **Switzerland**; summits intersected by low passes; inc. several impt. Dolomitic peaks.
Albuquerque, t., N.M., **USA**; on Rio Grande; alt. 1,525 m, univ.; food prod., engin.; resort; p. (1970) 242,411 (c.), 313,829 (met. a.).
Albury, t., N.S.W., **Australia**; on Murray R.; wool sales; clothing; p. (1966) 32,029.
Alcalá de Henares, t., **Spain**; nr. Madrid; univ.; birthplace of Cervantes; p. (1970) 59,783.
Alcamo, t., Sicily, **Italy**; nr. ruins of anc. Segesra; p. (est. 1968) 42,758.
Alcatraz, I., Cal., **USA**; San Francisco Bay; former prison.
Alcoy, t., **Spain**; textiles, paper; p. (1970) 61,371.
Aldabra Is., **Seychelles Rep.**; 400 km N.W. of Malagasy Rep.; leased (1971–1985) to Royal Society for wildlife research (unique animal and plant species).
Aldan, R., E. Siberia, **USSR**; flows from Stanovoy Range to Lena R. via Tommot gold-mng. dist.; coal in lower course; 2,682 km long.
Aldeburgh, spt., Suffolk, **Eng.**; 48 km from Ipswich; famous for annual music festival; p. (1971) 2,793.
Alderley Edge, t., Cheshire, **Eng.**; residtl.; viewpoint N. over Cheshire plain; p. (1971) 4,458.
Aldermaston, Berkshire, **Eng.**; atomic weapons research ctr.
Alderney, I., Channel Is., **Eng.**; horticulture, tourism; a. 794 ha; p. (est. 1973) 1,700.
Aldershot, t., Hants., **Eng.**; bricks; lge. military camp; p. (1971) 33,311.
Aldridge, t., West Midlands, **Eng.**; plastics packing cases; expanded t.; p. with Brownhills (1971) 88,475.

Alençon, t., cap. of Orne dep., **France**; textiles; p. (1968) 31,656.
Aleppo, c., Syria; 2nd. c. of Syria; in limestone hills; univ.; mkt. and textile ctr.; p. (1970) 639,000.
Alès, t., Gard dep., France; sm. coalfield; chemicals; p. (1968) 42,818.
Alessandria, t., N. Italy; rly. ctr. on Tanaro R.; engin.; p. (est. 1968) 99,023.
Ålesund, spt. on Giske I. W. **Norway**, fishing, fish processing; airpt. on separate I. to N.; p. (1968) 38,544.
Aletsch, glacier, Switzerland; in Bernese Alps; lgst. in Europe; length 24 km.
Aletschhorn, mtn., Bernese Alps, **Switzerland**; alt. 4,198 m.
Aleution Is.; Bering Sea, Alaska, **USA**; chain of over 150 Is. formed from partially submerged peaks of volcanic A. mtn. range; on earthquake belt; U.S. air base.
Alexander Archipelago, S.E. Alaska, **USA**; dense I. system; fjord scenery; well populated; furs, lumbering, fishing; a. 33,670 km².
Alexandria, ch. pt., **Egypt**; founded by Alexander the Great, 332 B.C.; floating dock; exp. cotton, wheat, rice, gum; second lgst. c. in Africa; p. (est. 1974) 2,146,000.
Alexandria, t., La., **USA**; rice, foundries; p. (1970) 41,557.
Alexandria, c., spt., Va., **USA**; on Chesapeake Bay; indusl. t.; p. (1970) 110,938.
Alford, t., Lincs., **Eng.**; mkt.; brewing, food processing; p. (1971) 2,278.
Alfreton, t., Derbys., **Eng.**; mkt. t.; formerly coal-mng.; hosiery, knitwear; p. (1971) 21,670.
Algarve, prov., anc. kingdom, **Portugal**; in extreme S. of cty.; tourism, fishing, fruit; p. (est. 1970) 316,200.
Algeciras, spt., **Spain**; W. of Gibraltar on A. Bay; nearby Campo de Gibraltar scheme for social and economic development to break down Gibraltar's economic isolation; p. (1967) 73,292.
Algeria, indep. st. (1962), **N. Africa**; formerly under French rule; 13 deps.; fertile valleys, rugged mtns.; barren plateaux; Mediterranean climate; Berbers, Kabyles, Arabs, Tuaregs; cap. Algiers; wine, fruit, olive oil, tobacco; oil, natural gas and iron ore in Sahara; developing tourism; land reform in progress; a. 2,373,994 km²; p. (est. 1969) 13,349,000.
Algiers (renamed **El Dzejair**, 1972), pt., cap. c. of Algeria; old t. surmounted by 16th cent. Casbah (fortress); univ.; exp. wine, citrus fruit, iron ore; oil refining at Maison Carrée; airpt. at Maison Blanche, 16 km E. of c.; p. (1966) 903,530 (c.), 943,142 (met. a.).
Alhambra, Cal., **USA**; sub. Los Angeles; fruit mkt.; mftg.; p. (1970) 62,125.
Alicante, spt., cap of A. prov., **Spain**; wine, fruits; oil refinery; p. (est. 1969) 137,500.
Alice Springs, t., N.T., Australia; ch. t. of desert a.; major cattle raising ctr.; p. (1972) 11,118.
Aligarh, t., **Uttar Pradesh, India**; 128 km S.E. of Delhi; univ.; p. (1971) 252,314.
Alkmaar, t., **Netherlands**; impt. cheese mkt. on N. Holland canal; p. (1967) 48,561.
Allahabad, t. Uttar Pradesh, **India**; at confluence of Jumna and Ganges Rs.; univ.; Hindu pilgrimage ctr.; p. (1971) 490.622 (c.), 513,036 (met. a.).
Allegheny Mtns., **USA**; part of Appalachian system, inc. several parallel ranges; water-shed between Atlantic and Mississippi R. drainage; forested, tourism; average alt. 1,500 m.
Allegheny R., Penns., N.Y., **USA**, rises in A. mtns., flows to Ohio R.; Pittsburg met. a. on lower reaches where R. entrenched 120 m below plateau making urban development difficult; used for coal and oil transport; 520 km long.
Allen, Bot of, R.o.I.; peat bogs, peat cutting, cultivation; a. 958 km².
Allenstein. *See* **Olsztyn.**
Allentown, t., Penns., **USA**; coal, textiles, cement; p. (1970) 210,301 (c.), 538,388 (met. a.).
Alleppey, spt., Kerala, S. **India**; on sand spit; coconut prods.; p. (1971) 160,166.
Alliance, t., Ohio, **USA**; iron, steel, engin.; p. (1970) 26,547.
Allier, dep., France; N. of Massif Central; coal- and iron-mng.; mineral springs, wine, wheat; a. 4,786 km²; p. (1968) 386,553.
Alloa, sm. burgh, Clackmannan, **Scot.**; on N. bank of R. Forth; bricks, tiles, glass, distilling; p. (1971) 14,100.
Alma-Ata, c., cap. of Kazakh SSR, **USSR**; in foothills of Tien-Shan mtns.; univ.; comm. agr., and ind. ctr.; food processing, machin., printing; p. (1970) 730,000.
Almada, t., **Portugal**; on R. Tagus estuary opposite Lisbon; Salazar bridge (opened 1966) links it with Lisbon; p. (1970) 43,537.
Almadén, t., Ciudad Real, Spain; anc. Sisapon; mercury mines nearby; p. (1970) 10,774.
Almelo, t., Overijssel, **Neth.**; 40 km S.E. of Zwolle; cotton textile mnfs.; p. (1968) 58,155.
Almeria, spt., on G. of A., S.E. Spain; cath.; exp. grapes, oranges; p. (1967) 99,653.
Alnwick, t., Northumberland, **Eng.**; cas.; mkt. t.; p. (1971) 7,113.
Alor Star, t., cap. of Kedah, **W. Malaysia**; on main W. cst. road and rly.; p. 32,424.
Alost. *See* **Aalst.**
Alpes-de-Haute-Provence (**Basses-Alpes**), dep., S.E. France; mtnous., infertile a. bordering Italy; olives, wines; cap. Digne; a. 6,988 km²; p. (1968) 104,813.
Alpes-Maritimes, dep., S.E. **France**; ceded by Italy in 1860; ch. t. Nice; olives, wines, fruit; a. 3,737 km²; p. (1968) 722,070.
Alphen, t., S. Holland, **Neth.**; on Old Rhine, 16 km S.E. of Leiden; mkt. for dairy produce; p. (1967) 30,980.
Alps, hgst. mtns. in **Europe**; 960 km long, inc. 1,200 glaciers; separates S. and central Europe, forming a climatic divide; major tourist a., winter sports; hydroelec. power; main peaks Mont Blanc (4,814 m), Mont Rosa (4,641 m), Matterhorn (4,509 m).
Als, I., S. Denmark; in the Little Belt, a. 337 km²; linked to Jutland by bridge; p. (1965) 48,676.
Alsace-Lorraine, region, E. France; bordered to E. by W. Germany and Rhine R; incorporated into Germany at time of unification (1871), returned to France by Treaty of Versailles (1919); impt. iron-ore and iron and steel inds. in Lorraine; regional aid for economic development; well wooded.
Alsager, t., Cheshire, **Eng.**; nr. Crewe; mkt. t.; p. (1971) 10,202.
Alsdorf, t., N. Rhine-Westphalia, **W. Germany**; 16 km N. of Aachen; tar-distillation plant; p. (est. 1969) 31,420.
Alston, t., Cumbria, **Eng.**; in upper reaches of south Tyne in N. Pennines; limestone quarrying; p. with Garrigill (1971) 1,909.
Altai Mtns., Mongolia, **USSR**; border China; steppes and glaciers; silver and mercury; multi-purpose R. project at Kamenna-Obi; ctr. of USSR atomic ind. at Ust Kamenogorsk; stock-rearing; average alt. 3,000 m, hghst. alt. 4,656 m at Tabun Bogdo.
Altamira, caves, N. Spain; prehistoric shelters, paintings of animals (Magdalenian).
Altamura, t., Apulia, **Italy**; at foot of Apennines; wines, wool; cath.; p. (est. 1968) 45,988.
Altdorf, t., cap. of Uri can., Switzerland; rubber gds., wood workings; statue of William Tell and Tell Theatre; p. (1970) 8,647.
Altenahr, t., N. Rhine-Westphalia, **W. Germany**; site of anc. cas. of Counts von der Marck; metals, wine; p. (est. 1969) 31,391.
Altenburg, t., Leipzig, E. Germany; lignite mng., engin., metallurgy, mnfs. playing cards, textiles; p. (est. 1970) 46,737.
Alton, t., Hants., **Eng.**; breweries, lt. engin.; p. (1971) 12,686.
Alton, t., Ill., **USA**; on Mississippi R.; oil refining; p. (1970) 39,700.
Altona, R. pt. of Hamburg, **W. Germany**; on the Elbe; chemical and fishing inds.; trawler pt.
Altoona, c., Penns., **USA**; rly. t.; p. (1970) 62,385 (c.), 134,142 (met. a.).
Altrincham, mkt. t., Gtr. Manchester, **Eng.**; engin.; residtl.; p. (1971) 40,752.
Alva, burgh, Clackmannan, Scot.; at S. foot of Ochil Hills, 5 km N. of Alloa; woollens, printing fruit and fish canning; p. (1971) 4,180.
Alwar, c., Rajasthan, **India**; in hilly agr. region; former cap. of A. princely st.; fort, palace; p. (1971) 100,378.
Amagasaki, c., **Japan**; nr. Osaka; chemicals polyethylene; iron and steel; oil refining; p. (est. 1971) 543,000.
Amalfi, spt., **Italy**; on G. of Salerno; tourist resort; fisheries; p. (est. 1968) 7,162.

Amapá, fed. terr., N. Brazil; on equator; tropical rain forest, sparse p.; a. 137,423 km²; p. (est. 1968) 109,076.
Amārah, Al, pt., **Iraq**; on left bank of R. Tigris 400 km below Baghdad; Arab t. and agr. mkt. at R. crossing; p. (1965) 104,000 (met. a.).
Amārapura, t., **Burma**; on R. Irrawaddy 10 m. S.W. of Mandalay; former cap.; craft inds.
Amarillo, t., Texas, **USA**; oil refining, creameries, meat packing; p. (1970) 123,973 (c.), 140,876 (met. a.).
Amasya, t., **Turkey**; on Yesil-Cekerek R.; tr. ctr.; p. (1965) 33,539.
Amazon, gr. R., **S. America**; drains lgst. a. and carries more water than any other R. in world; main Andean headstreams Ucayali and Marañón from Peru unite to flow across Brazil to Atl. Oc., receiving waters of many Rs., inc. the Madeira; lgst. rain forest in world; ocean steamers penetrate to Iquitos, Peru, c. 3,680 km from mouth; a. drained c. 6 million km² of sparsely populated cty., mostly in Brazil; length 6,712 km, longest R. in world; basin inc. 40% of S. America; ocean pt. Belém.
Amazonas, lgst. st. of **Brazil**; isolated; tropical rain forest; tree prods.; cap. Manáus; a. 1,595,823 km²; p. (est. 1968) 921,390, (mainly Indian).
Amazonas, fed. terr., **Venezuela**; cap. Puerto Ayacucho on Orinoco R., isolated, tropical rain forest; a. 181,300 km²; p. (est. 1970) 12,831.
Amazonia, Peru, Columbia, Brazil; a. covered by Amazon R. and its tribs. and the surrounding lowland; thickly forested; underdeveloped.
Ambala, c., Haryana, **India**; cotton, flour; p. (1971) 102,493 (c.), 200,576 (met. a.).
Ambato, c., **Ecuador**; S. of Quito, on slope of Mt. Chimborazo; alt. 2,702 m; textiles, canned fruits, leather gds.; p. (1966) 89,541.
Amberg, t., Bavaria, **W. Germany**; mediaeval walled t. on R. Vils; specialist steels, textiles; p. (est. 1969) 42,300.
Ambès, t., Gironde, **France**; nr. Bordeaux; oil refining.
Ambleside, tourist ctr., Cumbria, **Eng.**; N. of L. Windermere.
Amboise, t., Indre-et-Loire dep., **France**; 24 km E. of Tours; famous cas. and prison; p. (1968) 8,899.
Ambon, I., Moluccas, **Indonesia**; spices, coconuts; a. 818 km²; p. 73,000.
America, the lands of the Western hemisphere, comprising the continents of North and South America, separated by narrow Isthmus of Panama; most N. point over 14,400 km from C. Horn, the extreme S. point; p. (est. 1967) 479,000,000. *See also* **North, South,** and **Central America.**
Amersfoort, c., Utrecht, **Neth.**; walled c. on R. Eem; rapid growth of light inds.; p. (1968) 76,285.
Amersham, t., Bucks., **Eng.**; radiochemical ctr.; lt. inds., 17th cent. mkt. hall; p. (1971) 68,413 (dist.).
Ames, t., Iowa, **USA**; Iowa State Univ. of. Science and Technology and many fed. and st. institutes; p. (1970) 39,505.
Amesbury, t., Wilts. **Eng.**; nr. Stonehenge; p. (1971) 27,611 (dist.).
Amiens, c., cap. of Somme dep; major textile ctr. of **France**, on R. Somme; cath.; p. (1968) 117,888 (c.), 136,713 (met. a.).
Amirante Is., British group **Indian Ocean**; S.W. of Seychelles.
Amlwch, t., Gwynedd, **Wales**; N. cst. of Anglesey; resort; pt.; oil terminal; p. (1971) 3,681.
Amman, c., cap. of **Jordan**; N.E of Dead Sea; site of biblical Raboth Ammon; textiles, cement, tobacco; airpt.; univ.; p. (est. 1971) 520,700.
Ammanford, t., Dyfed, **Wales**; anthracite, brick mkg.; p. (1971) 5,795.
Amoy (Xiamen), c., Fukien, **China**; rail link to Yingtang, Kiansi; tea, fruit, bricks; univ.; former treaty-pt.; p. (est. 1970) 400,000.
Ampthill, Beds., **Eng.**; mkt. t.; p. (1971) 5,575.
Amravati, c., Maharashtra, **India**; cotton ctr., univ.; p. (1971) 193,800.
Amritsar, c., Punjab, N.W. **India**; Golden Temple sacred to Sikhs; trade ctr. for shawls and carpets; soaps, paints, engin.; p. (1971) 407,628 (c.), 458,029 (met. a.).
Amroha, t., Uttar Pradesh, **India**; pilgrimage ctr.; p. (1961) 68,965.
Amsterdam, spt., cap. of **Netherlands**; at junction of R. Amstel and the IJ; built on 96 Is. joined by 300 bridges, harbour at terminus of N. Sea canal can hold 1,000 ships; two univs., Royal Palace, Bourse; extensive tr.; exp. dairy prod., sugar, tobacco; shipbldg., diamond polishing, aeronautical, marine, elec. machin., oil refining; p. (1968) 857,635 (c.), 1,047,588 (met. a.).
Amu-Dar'ya (Oxus), R., marks boundary between **USSR** and **Afghanistan**; flows from Pamir mtns. to Aral Sea; Kara- and Kzyl-Kum deserts on either bank; rich in fish; irrigation in lower course; 1,395 km long.
Amur (Hei-Lung Chiang), major R. of **E. Asia**; flows from Mongolia between N.E. China and E. Siberia into Pac. Oc. opposite Sakhalin I.; with tribs. Argun and Ussuri forms lgst. R. frontier in world; crossed by Trans-Siberian rly. at Khabarovsk; 2,827 km long.
Anaconda, t. Mont, **USA**; one of lgst. copper mines in world; p. (1970) 9,771.
Anaheim, t., Cal., **USA**; tourism; Disneyland; p. (1970) 441,327 (c.), 1,409,335 (met a.).
Ahahuac, pleateau, **Mexico**; average alt. 2,000 m; surrounded by higher cty. inc. volcano Popocatapetl (5,456 m); contains Mexico City, heartland of Aztec Mexico; a. c. 3,900 km².
Anambas Is., Indonesia; 240 km W. of W. Malaysia; little development; p. c. 12,000.
Anatolia (Asia Minor), penin. approx. coextensive with **Turkey** bounded by Black Sea (N.), Mediterranean (S.), Aegean (W.)
Anching, c., Anhwei prov., **China**; R. pt. on Yangtse; tr. in agr. prods.; p. (est. 1970) 160,000.
Anchorage, t., Alaska, **USA**; timber, salmon fishing and canning; earthquake 28 Mar. 1964; spt.; airpt.; p. (1970) 48,081.
Ancona, spt., central **Italy**; on the Adriatic Sea; founded by Dorians, 1500 B.C.; sugar refineries, shipbldg.; p. (1969) 109,422.
Andalucia, region, covering southern **Spain**; Córdoba, Seville, Jaén and Granada, celebrated ctrs. in Moorish times; irrigation for wines, olives, fruits.
Andaman and Nicobar Is., Bay of Bengal; constituted a union terr., **India**, 1956; hilly remnants of drowned mtn. chain; primitive pygmy tribes; a. 8,327 km²; p. (1967) 80,000.
Anderlecht, t., residtl. and industl. sub. of Brussels, **Belgium**; p. (est. 1969) 104,157.
Andermatt, v., Uri, **Switzerland**; at foot of Mt. St. Gotthard; tourist ctr., winter health resort; p. (1970) 1,589.
Anderson, t., Ind., **USA**; car components; p. (1970) 49,061 (c.), 125,819 (met. a.).
Andes, gr. volcanic mtn. system, **S. America**; extends over 6,400 km from N.–S.; physical and climatic divide rising to over 6,000 m; densely populated; high tropical plateaux; rich in minerals; hgst. peak, Aconcagua (6,965 m).
Andhra Pradesh, st. S.E. **India**; cap. Hyderabad; inc. valleys of lower Godavari and Krishna Rs.; sugar, rice; a. 275,278 km²; p. (1971) 43,394,951.
Andizhan, c. Uzbek SSR, **USSR**; once residence of Khans of Khokan; industl. ctr.; in irrigation a.; cotton, silk; oil fields; p. (1970) 188,000.
Andorra, sm. mtn. st., **E. Pyrenees**; under joint suzerainty of French President and Bishop of Urgel (Spain); virtually indep.; livestock, wines, tobacco; tourism having fundamental social and economic consequences; alt. 900–3,000 m; a. 495 km²; p. (est. 1967) 15,000.
Andover, mkt. t., Hants., **Eng.**; prehistoric earthwks.; expanded t.; p. (1971) 25,538.
Andria, t., S. **Italy**; Roman remains, cath., palaces; p. (est. 1968) 76,482.
Andros, lgst. I., **Bahamas**; sponges, sisal, hemp; p. (est. 1969) 75,000.
Andújar, t., **Spain**; on Guadalquivir R.; mineral springs, pottery, soap, textiles, uranium plant; p. (1970) 31,464.
Angara, R., Siberia, **USSR**; trib. of Yenisey; navigable almost its entire length., rises nr. and flows through L. Baykal; length 2,080 km; hydro-electric power.
Angarsk, t., E. Siberia, **USSR**; on R. Angaar 32 km N.W. Irkutsk; engin. saw milling; p. (1970) 204,000.
Angel Falls (Salto del Angel), waterfall, **Venezuela**; nr. Ciudad Bolivar; 980 m drop.

Angerman, R., N. **Sweden** rises nr. Norwegian border, falls to G. of Bothnia; timber transport; 448 km long.

Angers, t., cap. of Maine-et-Loire dep., **France**; on R. Maine; mkt. t. for local produce, fruit, vegetables, Anjou wines, Cointreau; textiles; cath., cas.; p. (1968) 128,533 (t.), 163,191 (met. a.).

Angkor, c., Cambodia; jungle-covered ruins of c. from Khmer civilisation; discovered 1860.

Anglesey, I., former co., N.W. Wales. *See* Gwynedd.

Angola, People's Rep. of (Port. W. Africa), W. Africa; interior forms part of central African plateaux, bounded by transitional escarpments in W. which face on to narrow coastal plain; rainfall diminishes from N.–S. with consequent crop zoning; coffee, cotton, oil palm in N., corn, peanuts, sisal in drier interior, cattle in S., semi-desert in S.E.; economy dependent upon primary inds., especially agr.; coffee major exp., produced on foreign (mainly Portuguese) owned plantations; newly discovered oilfields; diamonds in remote N.E. Luanda dist.; iron ore mng. impt. at Cassinga; little mftg.; hydroelectric scheme on Cuarza R.; pts. on natural harbours impt. transhipment points for land-locked central African ctys.; indep. 1975, followed by civil war between rival guerrilla groups; cap. Luanda; a. 1,246,375 km²; p. (est. 1970) 5,466,600.

Angoulême, mftg. t., Charente, **France**; on R. Charente; cognac, paper; cath.; suffered during Huguenot wars; p. (1968) 50,883.

Angra do Heroismo, t., cap. admin. dist. **Azores**; pt. on Terceira I.; p. (est. 1970) 105,800 (dist.).

Angren, t., Uzbek SSR, **USSR**; E. of Tashkent; lgst. ctr. of lignite mng. in central Asia; p. (est. 1968) 94,000.

Anguilla I., Leeward Is., W.I.; dry climate, thin limestone soil; exp. cotton, salt; a. 91 km²; reverted to Brit. Crown after secession from St. Kitts–Nevis ass. st. 1967; plans for autonomy; p. (est. 1967) 5,800.

Angus, l. gov. dist., former co., **Scot.**; part of Tayside Reg.; a. 1,937 km²; p. (1971) 84,660.

Anhwei, prov., E. central China; in delta region of Yangtse R.; a. 140,686 km²; cap. Hofei; soya-beans, rice, tea, coal and iron; p. (est. 1968) 35,000,000.

Aniakchak, volcano, S.W. Alaska, **USA**; rich variety of flora and fauna on crater floor. alt.; 1,384 m.

Anjou, former prov. of **France**; mainly S. of lower R. Loire; ch. t. Angers.

Ankara, c., cap. of **Turkey** since 1923; alt. 1,037 m; univ., cultural and admin. ctr.; p. (est. 1970) 1,162,000 (met. a.).

Anklesvar, t., Gujarat, **India**; natural gas, oil; gas pipelines to Ultaran and Barodi; p. (1961) 20,287.

'Annaba, spt., Algeria; on fertile plain; phosphates, iron and steel wks.; p. (1966) 152,006 (c.) 168,790 (met. a.).

Annaberg–Bucholz, t., Karl-Marx-Stadt, **E. Germany**; in Erz Mtns.; cobalt, tin, uranium mng.; p. (est. 1970) 27,892.

Annam, region, **Vietnam**; formerly within French Union; divided by 17th parallel bdy. (1957); a 147,560 km²; ch. t. Hué.

Annamese Cordillera, cstl. mtn. range, **Laos, Vietnam**; N.–S. watershed between Mekong and S. China Sea, rising to 2,000 m in Ngoc Linh; forested; inhabited by hill tribes.

Annan, royal burgh, Annandale and Eskdale, **Scot.**; on R. Annan, 3 km from its mouth in Solway F.; Chapelcross reactor sta.; p. (1971) 6,051.

Annapolis, c., cap. of Maryland, **USA**; naval academy; p. (1970) 29,592.

Annapolis Valley, Nova Scotia, **Canada**; famous fruit growing a., especially for apples.

Annapurna, massif, **Nepal**; part of Himalayas; many glaciers in W. and N.W.; alt. 8,080 m.

Ann Arbor, c., Mich., **USA**; on the Huron; Univ. of Michigan.; motor lorries, farm implements, scientific instruments; p. (1970) 98,414 (c.), 230,128 (met. a.).

Annecy, t., France; dep. of Haute-Savoie; at lower end of beautiful L. Annecy; textiles, paper, watches; resort; p. (1968) 56,689.

Ansbach, t., Bavaria, **W. Germany**; machin., metallurgy, furniture indus.; rly. ctr.; p. (est. 1968) 30,768.

An-shan, c., Liaoning, N. **China**; at foot of Changpai Shan, 96 km S.W. of Mukden; lgst. iron and steel complex in China (fully automated steel plant), elec. and locomotive ind.; p. (1957) 805,000.

Antakya (Antioch), anc. c. S. **Turkey**; on R. Orontes; cap. of Hatay prov., major Roman cap. and early ctr. of Christian culture; p. (1965) 57,584.

Antalya, c., S.W. **Turkey**; spt. with shallow harbour from which Paul and Barnabas sailed to Antakya; tourism; p. (1965) 71,632.

Antarctica, plateau continent within A. circle; snow-covered, extensive ice sheets and glaciers; volcanoes and Is.; alt. 2,000–3,000 m; owned by U.K., Australia, N.Z., France, Norway but a. S. of 60° S reserved for peaceful international scientific research; a. 16 million km².

Antarctic Ocean, parts of Pac., Atl. and Indian Oceans, S. of 60°S.; cold and dangerous; no mammalian life other than whales.

Antibes, t., Alpes-Martimes, N. of Cap d. A., S.E. **France**; spt. on Fr. Riviera; exp. oranges; flowers for perfume mnfs.; resort; Roman remains; p. (1968) 48,013.

Anticosti, barren I. in G. of St. Lawrence, Quebec, **Canada**; well wooded game reserve, lumbering; 224 km by 45 km.

Antigua, anc. c. **Guatemala**; 32 km W. of Guatemala c.; former cap., destroyed by earthquake 1773; comm. ctr. in coffee dist.; notable colonial ruins; tourism; p. (1964) 21,984.

Antigua, Leeward gr., **W.I.**; aut. st. in ass. with Gt. Britain; semi-arid limestone; 75 per cent p. in N.E.; sugar, cotton, tourism; cap. St. Johns; a. (inc. Barbuda and Redonda) 440 km²; p. (1970) 65,000.

Antilles, Greater and Lesser, archipelago enclosing Caribbean Sea and G. of Mexico, **W.I.**; complex political structure, tropical climate and crops; a. c. 259,000 km².

Antioquia, mtnous. dep. **Colombia**; colonial mng.; agr. now more impt.; one of major p. clusters in Colombia inc. dep. cap. Medellin; a 65,791 km²; p. (est. 1968) 2,828,000.

Antisana, volcano, central **Ecuador**; alt. 5,708 m.

Antofagasta, spt., Chile; cap., comm. and industl. ctr. of A. prov; exps. copper from Chuquicamata; situated in desert, water supply 240 km by adqueduct from Andes; p. (1970) 137,968.

Antony, t., Hauts-de-Seine, **France**; brick wks., toys; sub. of Paris; p. (1968) 56,878.

Antrim, former co.; l. gov. dist., **N. Ireland**; fertile lowland a., arable agr.; borders L. Neagh in S.W. and A. mtns. in N.E.; p. of former co. (est. 1971) 352,549.

Antrim, mkt. t., **N. Ireland**; on Lough Neagh; linen, nylon; p. (1966) 5,468.

An-tung c., Liaoning, **China**; pt. on R. Yalu, 24 km from mouth; Chinese frontier sta. on main rly. from China into N. Korea; mkt. for agr. prod.; lumbering; p. (est. 1968) 450,000.

Antwerp, low-lying prov., N. **Belgium**; grain, flax; a. 2,859 km²; p. (1968) 1,518,464.

Antwerp, spt., Belgium; on Scheldt R., 88 km from sea; major transit pt. for EEC, competes with Rotterdam; oil pt., refineries; diamonds; Gothic cath.; of artistic and historic interest; p. (est. 1969) 230,184 (c.), 673,040 (met. a.).

Anuradhapura, anc. cap., **Sri Lanka**; ctr. of Buddhism; comm. ctr of irrigated rice-growing a. in dry zone; p. (est. 1968) 30,000.

An-yang, c., Honan prov., **China**; coal, cotton ind.; former cap. of Shang dynasty; p. (est. 1970) 225,000.

Anzhero-Sudzhensk, t., S.W. Siberia, **USSR**; nr. Tomsk; coalmng., mng. equipment, pharmaceutics; p. (1970) 106,000.

Anzio, t., Italy; Roman resort and fishing pt., 53 km S. of Rome; p. (est. 1968) 22,108.

Aomori, spt., N. Honshu, **Japan**; on A. Bay; cstl., tr. of timber, fish with Hokkaido; S. outlet of Seikan Tunnel between Honshu and Hokkaido; cap. of apple-growing A. prov.; p. (est. 1971) 250,000.

Aosta, t., cap. of Val d'Aosta, N. **Italy**; in valley of Dora Baltea at node of trans-Alpine routes; iron inds.; Mont Blanc road tunnel links to Chamonix, Switzerland, opened 1964; cath.; p. (1969) 35,577.

Apapa, spt., sub. of Lagos, **Nigeria**; on mainland opposite I. on which Lagos is situated; modern pt. terminus of W. Nigerian rly. system; exp. agr. prods.; imports industl. prods.

Apeldoorn, c., Gelderland, **Netherlands**; holiday resort; royal summer palace of Het Loo; p. (est. 1969) 122,287.

Apennines, mtn. "backbone" of **Italy**; rich in minerals inc. Carrara marble; cultivation on lower slopes; earthquakes, in S.; barrier to E.–W. communications; hgst. alt. 2,916 m, (Grand Sasso d'Italia); length N.–S. 1,280 km; width 120 km.

Apia, spt., N. Upolu, cap. of **W. Samoa**; exp. agr. prods.; p. (est. 1971) 30,593 (met. a.).

Apolda, t., Erfurt, **E. Germany**; ball-casting and museum; p. (est. 1970) 29,087.

Appalachian Mtns., parallel ranges between Atl. Oc. and Mississippi basin, stretching for 2,560 km from Me. to Ala., **USA**; afforestation, hydro-elec. power, coal in N., iron ore in S.; region of human poverty; average alt. 900 m; Mt., Mitchell 2,039 m.

Appenzell, can., N.E. **Switzerland**; divided into the half-cans. Appenzell Inner-Rhoden, a. 174 km², cap. Appenzell; p. (1970) 13,124; and Appenzell Ausser-Rhoden; textiles, agr.; a. 243 km², cap. Herisau; p. (1970) 49,023.

Appenzell, picturesque t., cap. of A. can., **Switzerland**; on R. Sitter; lace, embroidery; p. (1970) 5,217.

Appian Way, anc. highway; runs from Rome to Campania and S. **Italy**.

Appleby, t., Cumbria, **Eng.**; mkt. t. on R. Eden; cas.; p. (1971) 1,946.

Appleton, c., Wis., **USA**; industl. c. in rich dairy dist.; p. (1970) 57,143.

Apsheron, peninsula, E. Azerbaydzhan SSR, **USSR**; on W. side of the Caspian; petroleum wells (nr. Baku) and mud volcanoes.

Apulia, region, S.E. **Italy**; hilly, cstl., pastoral plain; grain, fruits, livestock; wine, olive oil; a. 19,347 km²; p. (1969) 3,628,909.

Aqaba, t., **Jordan's** only spt. at head of G. of A., 88 km from Israeli Elat; exp. phosphates, imports petroleum; p. (est. 1964) 10,000.

Aqaba G., Red Sea, between Sinai Peninsula and Saudi Arabia; impt. Biblical waterway; few natural harbours, Dahab, Elat, Aqaba main pts; Elat ctr. of mng. a., and airpt.; length 160 km, width 24 km.

Aquila (L'Aquila), t., cap. of Abruzzi prov., **Italy**; on R. terrace of R. Aterno; mkt. and sm. inds. ass. with local farming; holiday resort; cath.; p. (1969) 58,845.

Aquitaine, Basin of, geographical region, S.W. **France**; to W. and S.W. of Central Massif, to N. of Pyrenees, bordered on W. by Atl. Oc.; warm, wet, oceanic climate; rich agr. lowland; inc. Landes, reclaimed sandy area; ch. ts. Bordeaux, Toulouse.

Arabia, peninsula, **S.W. Asia**; mainly desert plateau, lying between Red Sea and Persian Gulf; inc. Saudi Arabia, South Yemen, North Yemen, Oman, United Arab Emirates, Kuwait, Bahrain, Qatar; coffee, dates, gums, horses, camels; E. Arabia rich in oil reserves; a. 2,590,000 km²; p. 8,000,000.

Arabian Desert, E. **Egypt**; between R. Nile and Red Sea; alt. approx. 350–2,000 m; a. 207,200 km².

Arabian Mtns., ridge along W. and S.W. csts. of Arabia; volcanic, hgst. peaks in Yemen Arab Rep.; average alt. 1,500 m, rising to over 3,500 km.

Arabian Sea, N.W. part of Indian Oc., tr. in Arab dhows; width 2,880 km.

Aracaju, spt., cap. of Sergipe st., **Brazil**; sugar, soap, textiles, tanneries; p. (1970) 179,512.

Arad, new t. (1962) **Israel**; in Negev desert, nr. Beersheba; inds. to be based on gasfields at Zohar and Kanaim; chemicals.

Arad, t., **Romania**; industl., route ctr. on R. Mures; p. (est. 1969) 135,181.

Arafura Sea, N. of Australia, S.W. of Papua–New Guinea, and E. of Timor.

Aragua, sm. upland cstl. st., **Venezuela**; lies in densely populated industl., agr., urban and political region of cty.; tropical climate; good road network; cap. Maracay in fertile Aragua valley; a. 7,014 km²; p. (est. 1970) 429,344.

Araguaia R., **Brazil**; trib. of Tocatins R.; splits into 2 parts in middle course to form Banaral I.; rapids; length 1,800 km.

Arak, t. **Iran**; mkt. and agr. processing ctr. for surrounding region on Trans-Iranian rly.; carpets; p. (1966) 72,087.

Aral Sea (**Aral'skoye More**), inland sea with no outlet, **USSR**; fed by Amu-Dar'ya and Syr Dar'ya Rs.; sparse p. on shore but attempts to develop agr.; a. 63,805 km².

Aran Is.; Galway, **R.o.I.**; inc. anc. religious ctr. and I. of Inishmore; fishing; agr.; a. 47 km²; p. (1966) 1,612.

Arandelovac, t., **Yugoslavia**; industl. a. based on local sources of refractory clays; tourist resort.

Aranjuez, t., **Spain**; 18th cent. planned t. on R. Tagus; mkt. gardens; strawberries, asparagus; p. (1970) 29,548.

Ararat, volcanic mtn., **Turkey**; supposed resting-place of Noah's Ark.; 5,168 m.

Ararat, t., Victoria, **Australia**; on W. Highway; ctr. of fertile lava agr. a.; forestry; p. (1972) 8,317.

Aras (**Araxes**) **R.**, flows from Bingöl Dağlari mtns. (**Turkey**) to Caspian Sea forming long sections of **USSR–Iran** frontier; valley in rich fruit growing a.; home of anc. civilisation; length 880 km.

Araucania, terr., **Chile**; concentration of A. Indians, especially in Rio Tolten valley.

Arbroath, royal burgh, Angus cst., **Scot.**; engin., textiles, fishing; pt.; holiday resort; p. (1971) 22,586.

Arcachon, t., Gironde, S.W. **France**; on S. side of Bassin d'Arcachon, Bay of Biscay; fish. pt., oysters; resort; p. (1968) 15,755.

Arcadia, region of anc. **Greece** in Peloponnesus; tradition of pastoral agr. in dry a.; ch. c. was Megalopolis.

Arctic Ocean, almost landlocked sea extending from N. Pole to Atl. Oc.; flora and fauna of scientific interest; a. 14,089,600 km².

Ardabil, anc. c. in fertile agr. a., Azerbaijan, **Iran**; tr. and route ctr.; carpets; p. (1966) 83,546.

Årdal, t., **Norway**; on Sogne fiord; site of aluminium wks.

Ardèche, dep. S. **France**; Cevennes Mtns.; olives, wine, silk, minerals; cap. Privas; a. 55,530 km²; p. (1968), 256,927.

Ardennes, hilly wooded region, **Belgium**, **N. France**, **Luxembourg**, rising to over 600 m; infertile; heavy fighting in both world wars.

Ardennes, dep., N.E. **France**; farming, woollens, iron; cap. Mézières; a. 5,250 km²; p. (1968) 309,380.

Ardglass, sm. t., Down, **N. Ireland**; one of N.I.'s impt. fishing pts.

Ardnacrusha, Clare, **R.o.I.**; power sta. on R. Shannon, 5 km N. of Limerick.

Ardnamurchan, most westerly point of mainland of Scot., Lochaber.

Ardrishaig, sm. spt., Argyll and Bute, **Scot.**; on Loch Gilp, at entrance to Crinan canal.

Ardrossan, burgh, Cunninghame, S.W. **Scot.**; resort and spt. on Firth of Clyde; oil storage, ship-bldg., road bitumen, engin.; p. (1971) 10,562.

Ards, l. gov. dist., **N. Ireland**; formerly part of Down; N. of Strangford L.; main t. Newtownards.

Arecibo, spt., N. cst. **Puerto Rico**; sited in rich agr. a.; local hydro-elec. power; p. (1970) 72,283.

Arendal, spt. **Norway**; on Skagerrak; wood pulp, aluminium, shipping; p. (est. 1970) 11,831.

Arequipa, c., **Peru**; cap. of A. prov. and former Inca c.; impt. wool mkt.; alpaca wool inds.; growth point for prov. industl. development; copper mng. nearby; earthquakes frequent; p. (est. 1970) 194,700.

Arezzo, c., cap. of Arezzo prov., Tuscany, **Italy**; hill site in basin within Apennines at junc. of valley routes; in mediaeval times ctr. of learning and the arts; birthplace of Petrarch and Vasari; Gothic cath.; mkt. for silk, wine, olives; p. (est. 1969) 85,954.

Argenteuil, t., Val-d'Oise, **France**; N.W. sub. of Paris; industl., mkt. gardens; p. (1968) 90,929.

Argentina, fed. rep., **S. America**; 2nd. in a., 3rd. in p. of S. American sts.; p. predominantly of European origin and highly urbanised; varied relief and climate, inc. Andes, tropical N., Chaco, Pampas, Patagonia in S.; agr. less impt. internally than other S. American sts., yet provides most of exp., inc. meat, wool, wheat, maize, cotton; petroleum, natural gas; cap. Buenos Aires; a. 2,797,109 km², p. (est. 1970) 23,360,000.

Argonne, hill ridge, S.E. Paris basin, **France**; composed of greensand; wooded; fighting in 2nd world war; alt. 300 m; a. approx. 650 km².

Argos, c. of anc. Greece; N.E. Peloponnesus; leading c. in 7th cent. B.C. under King Pheidon.

Argostolion, cap. of Cephalonia I., **Greece**; shipbldg.; earthquake 1953; p. (1971) 7,521.

Argyll, former co., N.W. **Scot.**; now divided between Highland and Strathclyde Regs.

Argyll and Bute, l. gov. dist., Strathclyde Reg., **Scot.**; rural a. N.W. of Glasgow conurb.; a. 6,754 km²; p. (1971) 63,265.

Århus, c., **Denmark**; prin. spt. on E. cst. Jutland; admin. ctr. of A. prov.; Gothic cath.; univ.; comm. and industl. ctr.; pt. processing inds., oil refining; p. (est. 1969) 111,266 (c.), 193,573 (met. a.).

Arica, spt., N. **Chile**, free zone; exp. tin, copper, sulphur mainly from Bolivia; rly. to La Paz and oil pipeline connects to Sica-Sica in Bolivia; p. (est. 1966) 63,160.

Ariège, dep., S. **France**; Pyrenees in S., fertile lowland in N.; livestock, fruit, iron, copper; cap. Foix; a. 4,900 km²; p. (1968) 138,478.

Arizona, st., **USA**; home of Apache Indians; much desert, rainfall increasing to E.; many lge. irrigation schemes for cotton, grain, fruit, vegetables; inc. Col. Plateau and Grand Canyon to N.; copper, lead mng. and refining; prin. ts. Phoenix (cap.), Tucson; a. 295,024 km²; p. (1970) 1,752,122.

Arkansas, st., **USA**; highland in N.W., inc. Ozark, Ouachita mtns.; lowland in S.E. where Arkansas R. and Mississippi alluvium; humid climate; cotton cultivation; bauxite, coal, petroleum; cap. Little Rock; a. 137,534 km²; p. (1970) 1,886,210.

Arkansas, R., **USA**; rises in Rockies, trib. of Mississippi; completion (1971) of 704 km waterway (17 dams and locks), opening Okla. and Ark. to sea; flows through impt. agr. as.; several major cs. on banks; length 2,334 km.

Arkhangel'sk, c., major spt., **USSR**; on E. side Dvina estuary, White Sea; lge. harbour kept open in winter by ice breakers; fishery headquarters; exp. and inds. from local softwood resources; engin.; hydro-elec. power; p. (1970) 343,000.

Arklow, U.D. spt., Wicklow, **R.o.I.**; fisheries, pottery; fertiliser plant under construction; resort; p. (1966) 6,056.

Arlberg, Alpine pass, 1,803 m; main western entry to **Austria**; rly. tunnel 10 km long.

Arles, t., Provence, S. **France**; on Rhône delta; anc. Roman t.; historic bldgs and monuments; Van Gogh and Gauguin painted here; p. (1968) 46,136.

Arlington, t., Mass., **USA**; residtl. sub. of Boston; agr. ctr.; p. (1970) 53,524.

Arlington, t., Texas, **USA**; aircraft, missiles; rapid expansion; p. (1970) 89,723.

Arlington, t., Va., **USA**; Arlington National Cemetery contains tombs of the Unknown Soldier and President Kennedy.

Arlon, t., cap. of Luxembourg prov., **Belgium**; p. (est. 1970) 14,343.

Armadale, burgh, West Lothian, **Scot.**; 16 km S.W. Linlithgow; extractive inds.; p. (1971) 7,152.

Armagh, former co.; l. gov. dist., **N. Ireland**; lowland in N. rising to over 450 m adjoins R.o.I. border; mainly rural; p. of former co. (est. 1971) 133,196.

Armagh, t., A., **N. Ireland**; caths.; linen, whiskey; p. (est. 1971) 12,297.

Armavir, c., Krasnodar Terr., **RSFSR**, on Kuban R.; rly. junc.; engin.; food processing; p. (1970) 146,000.

Armenia, constituent rep., **USSR**; former a. divided between Turkey, Russia, Iran; rich mineral deposits, mineral inds.; sub-tropical agr.; hydro-elec. stas. under constr.; cap. Yerevan; a. 30,821 km²; p. (1970) 2,493,000.

Armenia, t., **Colombia**; coffee; p. (est. 1972) 172,300 (t.), 189,100 (met. a.).

Armentières, mftg. t., Nord, **France**; base of British operations against Lille in first world war; textiles; p. (1968) 28,469.

Armidale, t., N.S.W., **Australia**; univ.; caths.; ctr. of wool industry; p. (1966) 14,990.

Arnhem, c., cap. of Gelderland prov., **Neth.**; on R. Neder-Rhine; lge. tin smelter; lt. inds. using rubber and rayon; p. (est. 1969) 133,391 (c.), 268,987 (met. a.).

Arnhem Land, N. part of N.T., **Australia**; an aboriginal reserve.

Arno, R., central **Italy**; flows past Florence and Pisa into Mediterranean; Val d'Arno is the fruitful valley of the R.; length 120 km.

Arnold, t., Notts., **Eng.**; almost continuous with Nottingham; hosiery, brick mkg.; p. (1971) 33,254.

Arnstadt, t., Erfurt, **E. Germany**; on R. Gera, 16 km S. of Erfurt; artificial silk, leather gds., engin.; p. (est. 1970) 28,762.

Aroostook, dist., New England, **USA**; produces 12 per cent of USA potatoes.

Arran, I., Cunninghame, **Scot.**; in Firth of Clyde; contains many summer resorts; a. 427 km²; p. (1971) 3,576.

Arras, t., cap. of Pas-de-Calais dep., **France**; historic cap. of Artois; renowned for tapestry; agr. mkt.; brewing, textiles, metal inds.; almost destroyed in first world war; p. (1968) 53,573.

Árta, t., cap. of Árta prov., Epirus. **Greece**; agr. tr. ctr.; Ambracia was its name in anc. Greece; p. (1970) 20,333.

Artemovsk, t., Ukrainian SSR, **USSR**; industl. ctr. in Donets Basin; salt, coal, iron, mercury; p. (est. 1969) 81,000.

Arthur's Seat, famous hill, Edinburgh, **Scot.**; 251 m.

Artois, former prov. of N. **France**; now mainly with dep. of Pas-de-Calais.

Aru Is., gr., **Indonesia**; S.W. of W. Irian; fertile; sago, rice, sugar, coconuts, tobacco; a. 8,402 km²; p. 18,139.

Aruba, I., Leeward Is., **Neth. Antilles**; oil refining, shipping; guano; a. 176 km²; p. (1968) 59,020.

Arunachal Pradesh, new union terr. (1972), N.E. Assam, **India**; formerly N.E. Frontier Agency; in Himalayas bordering Tibet and Burma; tribal p.; cap. Itanagar; a. 81,424 km²; p. (est. 1971) 440,000.

Arundel, t., West Sussex, **Eng.**; mkt. t. on Arun R.; Arundel Castle, seat of Duke of Norfolk; p. (1971) 2,382.

Arusha, t., **Tanzania**; S.W. of Mt. Meru; mkt. for coffee; H.Q. of E. African Common Market; airpt. at 1,388 m (W. of t.); p. (1967) 32,452.

Aruwimi, R., **Zaïre**; trib. of R. Zaïre; route of Stanley's famous forest march in 1887; 992 km long.

Arvida, t., S. Quebec, **Canada**; aluminium plant; nearby Saguenay power development; p. (1971) 18,433.

Arvika, t., N. of L. Vänern, **Sweden**; agr. machin. and implements, pianos, organs; p. (est. 1970) 15,998.

Asahigawa, c., Hokkaido, **Japan**; on Ishikari R.; industl., comm. and rly. ctr. for gr. agr. region; p. (est. 1971) 305,000.

Asansol, t., W. Bengal, **India**; in Damodar valley; rly. junc.; coal mng., iron, steel; p. (1971) 155,968 (c.), 241,792 (met. a.).

Ascension I., part of Brit. col. **St. Helena**, 1,216 km to S.E.; volcanic; ch. settlement Georgetown; nesting place of sooty tern; Brit. earth satellite sta. (1966); airstrip known as Miracle Mile; some arable and pastoral agr.; a. 88 km²; p. (1967) 1,486.

Aschaffenburg, t., Bavaria, **W. Germany**; pt. on R. Main; cas.; synthetic fibres, scientific-based inds.; p. (est. 1969) 55,772.

Aschersleben, t., Halle, **E. Germany**; potash and lignite mng., chemicals, textiles, engin., horticulture; p. (est. 1970) 37,196.

Ascoli Piceno, cath. c., central **Italy**; cap. of A.P. prov.; lies in wooded hills; agr. inds.; (1969) 55,247.

Ascot, v., Berks., **Eng.**; famous racecourse at Ascot Heath.

Ashanti, admin. region, central **Ghana**; formerly powerful native st.; timber, cocoa, goldmines; cap. Kumasi; a. 24,390 km²; p. (1970) 1,477,397.

Ashbourne, t., Derbys., **Eng.**; nr. Dovedale; mkt. t.; quarrying, milk processing; p. (1971) 5,575.

Ashburton, t., Devon, **Eng.**; old mkt. t., S. gateway to Dartmoor; anc. stannary t.; p. (1971) 3,495.

Ashburton, t. S. Island, **N.Z.**; ctr. of gr. wheat growing dist.; p. (1971) 13,299.

Ashby-de-la-Zouch, t., Leics., **Eng.**; local coal-mng. hosiery; ruined cas. in which Mary Queen of Scots was imprisoned; p. (1971) 8,291.
Ashby Woulds, t., Leics., **Eng.**; clay mng., pottery; p. (1971) 2,994.
Ashdod, pt., Israel; new modern deepwater pt. on Med. cst., 32 km S. of **Jaffa.**
Ashdown Forest, East Sussex, **Eng.**; heath and woodland; site of former iron industry.
Asheville, c., N.C., **USA**; economic and cultural ctr. of mtnous. region; winter resort; glass; p. (1970) 55,444 (c.), 135,424 (met. a.).
Ashford, t., Kent, **Eng.**; mkt. t., rly. ctr.; agr. implements, beer, bricks; expanded t.; p. (1971) 35,560.
Ashikaga, c., Honshu, **Japan**; cultural ctr.; old silk-weaving ctr.; anc. school with library of Chinese classics; p. (est. 1971) 159,000.
Ashington, t., Northumberland, **Eng.**; coal mng.; p. (1971) 25,645.
Ashkhabad, c., cap. of Turkmen SSR, **USSR**; in foothills of Kopet-Dag mtns.; textiles, clothing, food processing; univ.; p. (1970) 253,000.
Ashland, t., Ky., **USA**; on R. Ohio; iron, steel, lumber, leather; p. (1970) 29,245.
Ashtabula, t., Ohio, **USA**; pt. on L. Erie handling iron ore, coal; many diversified inds.; p. (1970) 24,313.
Ashton-in-Makerfield, t., Gtr. Manchester, **Eng.**; nr. Wigan; former coal-mng.; p. (1971) 26,271.
Ashton-under-Lyne, t., Gtr. Manchester, **Eng.**; textiles, lt. engin. rubber, tobacco; p. (1971) 48,865.
Asia, largest continent, extends over nearly one-third of the land surface of the earth; chief mtn. ranges, Himalayas, Kunlun, Tien Shan, Altai, Tibetan plateau; ch. Rs., Ob, Yangtze, Yenisey, Lena, Amur, Hwang-ho, Mekong; deserts, Arabia, Thar, Takla Makan, Gobi; some very fertile valleys and plains; climate very varied, extreme in N., monsoonal in S. and E.; gold, coal, oil, iron, manganese, antimony, tin; principal countries in Asia: Turkey in Asia, Israel, Jordan, Iran, Iraq, Afghanistan, India, Pakistan, Sri Lanka, Burma, China, Vietnam, Indonesia, Thailand, Malaysia, Korea Japan, Bangladesh, Cambodia, Laos, Philippines, Korea, Syria, Lebanon, Taiwan, and Soviet Asia; industrialisation greatest in Japan, China, India, and Soviet Asia; a. c. 43,250,000 km^2; p. (1972) 2,154,000,000 (57 per cent of world total).
Asia Minor. *See* **Anatolia.**
Asir, dist., S.W. **Saudi Arabia**; desert cstl. plain with parallel A. mtns.
Askja, volcanic crater, L. and lava plain, E. Iceland; surrounded by Dyngju-fjöll Hills; alt. 1,450 m.
Asmara, c., Ethiopia; alt. 2,226 m; on rly.; textiles, matches, soap, brewing; p. (est. 1971) 240,700.
Asnières, t., sub. N.W. Paris, Hauts-de-Seine, **France**; dyes, perfumery; machin.; regattas; p. (1968) 80,530.
Aspra Spitia, t. central **Greece**; new industl. t. close to Andikira Bay; aluminium wks.
Aspull, t., Gtr. Manchester, **Eng.**; nr. Wigan; former coal mng.; p. (1971) 7,510.
Assab, pt. on Red Sea, **Ethiopia**; oil refinery; p. (est. 1970) 14,900.
Assam, st., India; on Brahmaputra R.; valley enclosed by mtns.; forested; extensive tea plantations; rice, cotton, coal; oil development at Rudrasagar; former cap. Shillong; since 1956 4 new sts. carved out – Nagaland (1963), Meghalaya, Manipur, Tripura (1972), and union terrs. of Arunachal Pradesh and Mizoram (1972); a. (1972) 121,973 km^2; p. (1972) 14,857,314.
Assen, t., prov. cap. Drenthe, **Neth.**; route ctr.; food processing; p. (1968) 39,940.
Assiniboine, R., Manitoba, **Canada**; joins Red R. at Winnipeg; 720 km long.
Assissi, t., Umbria, central **Italy**; 24 km S.E. of Perugia; birthplace of St. Francis; cath. and old cas.; p. (est. 1968) 24,755.
Assyria, gr. anc. empire, northern plain Mesopotamia (Iraq), cap. Neneveh; drained by R. Tigris; now mainly pastoral farming a.
Astara, pt., Azerbaydzhan, **USSR**; on Caspian Sea, at frontier with Iran; natural gas pipeline.
Asti, t., Italy; route, industl., comm. ctr.; cath.; sparkling wines; p. (1969) 75,032.
Astin Tagh, (Aerchin Shan), mtn range, S., Sinkiang, **China**; N. branch of Kunlun mtn. system which separates Tibet from Turkestan; rises to 5,000 m.
Astrakhan', c., **RSFSR**; major air and sea pt. on delta of R. Volga, 80 km from Caspian Sea; handles petroleum, timber; lge. fishing fleet; caviar; food and pt. processing inds.; astrakhan fur; cap. A. oblast; univ.; p. (1970) 411,000.
Asturias, region and former kingdom, N.W. **Spain**; S. of Bay of Biscay; now Oviedo prov.; isolated from rest of Spain by Cantabrian mtns.; coalmng.
Asunción, c., cap. of **Paraguay**; at confluence of Rs. Paraguay and Pilcomayo; 25 per cent of p. of Paraguay in and around A.; admin., industl., comm. ctr.; cath.; p. (1968) 411,500 (met. a.).
Aswan, t., Upper **Egypt**; on Nile at first cataract; anc. name Syene. Aswan dam built 1902, 5 km S. of t., to control Nile flood; lge. cement plant; univ. proposed; p. (est. 1970) 201,500.
Aswan High Dam (107 m high) opened 1971, on R. Nile, Egypt, 6 km S. of old Aswan dam, has harnessed R. to bring electricity and irrigation to hundreds of vs. and prevent Nile's flood from being lost into Mediterranean. *See also* **Nile.**
Asyût, major c. of Upper **Egypt**; nr. A. dam on Nile R.; anc. Lycopolis; noted pottery, wood, ivory carving; caravan tr. ctr.; cap. of A. prov.; p. (est. 1970) 175,700.
Atacama Desert, N. **Chile**; arid coastal tract rich in nitrates; one of world's driest deserts.
Ataléia, t., Minas Gerais, **Brazil**; W. of Sierra des Aimorés; p. (est. 1967) 118,112.
Atami, t., Honshu, **Japan**; on Sagami Bay; seaside hot-spring resort; p. (1970) 51,281.
Atbara, t., **Sudan**; at confluence of Atbara R. with Nile; heavy inds.; international airpt.; p. (est 1969) 53,110.
Atbara R., or **Black Nile, Ethiopia and Sudan**; trib. of Nile; provides irrigation water for Sudan; length 1,264 km.
Athelney, hill, formerly encircled by marsh nr. Taunton, Somerset, **Eng.**; between the Rs. Tone and Parret; King Alfred's hiding-place.
Athens (Athinai), c., cap of **Greece**; on plain of Attica; admin., economic and cultural ctr.; varied mnfs., notably textiles; anc. c. of Greek art and learning; Acropolis and many splendid temples; univ.; airpt; p. (1971) 862,133 (c.), 2,530,207 (met. a.).
Athens, t., Ga., **USA**; univ.; cotton gds., lumber; p. (1970) 44,342.
Athens, t., Ohio, **USA**; univ.; coal, lt. inds.; p. (1970) 24,168.
Atherstone, t., Warwicks., **Eng.**; N. of Coventry; mkt. t., coalmng., footwear, granite quarrying; p. (1971) 38,611.
Atherton, t., Grt. Manchester, **Eng.**; 21 km N.W. Manchester; lt. engin.; former coal-mng.; p. (1971) 21,758.
Athlone, U.D., Westmeath, **R.o.I.**; on R. Shannon; radio sta.; textiles; p. (1966) 9,616.
Atholl, dist., N. Perth and Kinross, **Scot.**; extensive deer forests and grouse moors; a. 1,166 km^2.
Athos, peninsula, Khalkidhiki, N.E. **Greece**; Mt. Athos (2,034 m) at S. tip, known as Holy Mountain, home of monastic community; ch. t. Karves.
Athy, U.D., Kildare, **R.o.I.**; on Grand Canal; agr. machin.; p. (1968) 4,055.
Atitlán L., S.W. Guatemala; volcanic; famed for beauty; dense p. on shore; maize, fishing; a. 137 km^2.
Atlanta, c., st. cap. Ga., **USA**; univ.; cotton, paper, farm implements, printing, clothing; p. (1970) 487,553 (c.), 1,373,629 (met. a.).
Atlantic City, c., N.J., **USA**; summer resort, convention c.; p. (1970) 45,386 (c.), 170,492 (met. a.).
Atlantic Ocean, 2nd lgst ocean; a. est. 82,440,000 km^2; connected to Pac. Oc. by Panama Canal; central ridge of volcanic activity runs S. from Iceland to Antarctic, some peaks emerging as Is. mainly in N. (*e.g.*, Azores, Ascension, Tristan da Cunha); S. mainly a barren waste of water; chief deeps: Milwaukee Deep (9,225 m) nr. Bahamas and Nares Deep (8,531 m) nr. Puerto Rico.
Atlas, mtn. range, N.W. **Africa**; extends 2,400 km through Morocco, Algeria, to Tunisia; formed

of several chains; mineralised, roads across passes; long been home of Berber tribes; average height 2,500–3,000 m; hgst. peak Jebel Toubkal, 4,141 m.

Atlixco Valley, t., **Mexico**; 16 km S.W. of Puebla; fertile volcanic soils; wheat, fruit, vegetables.

Attica, (Attiki), dep., **Greece**; agr., serving cap. Athens; a. 3,761 km^2; p. (1971) 201,460.

Attleboro, c., Mass., **USA**; founded (1669) by immigrants from English Attleborough (Norfolk); jewellery, silverware; p. (1970) 32,907.

Attock, t., **Pakistan**; on Indus R. between Peshawar and Islamabad; oil wells, oil refining; impt. crossing of R. Indus.

Aubagne, t., Bouches-du-Rhône, **France**; bricks, tiles, corks, meat processing; p. (1968) 27,938.

Aube, dep., N.E. **France**; arid, infertile chalk in ctr. and N.W.; wooded and fertile S.E.; drained by Seine and A. Rs.; cap. Troyes; a. 6,024 km^2; p. (1968) 270,325.

Aubervilliers, t., Seine-St. Denis, **France**; sub. of Paris; industl.; p. (1968) 73,808.

Auburn, t., N.Y., **USA**; shoes, woollens, farm implements; st. prison; p. (1970) 34,599.

Aubusson, t., Creuse dep., **France**; sited on Creuse R.; fine tapestries and carpets; p. (1968) 6,761.

Auch, t., cap. of Gers dep., **France**; agr. mkt., tr. in Armagnac brandy; agr. processing; p. (1968) 23,718.

Auchterarder, burgh, Perth and Kinross, **Scot.**; 24 km S.W. of Perth; health resort on S. slopes of vale of Strathearn; woollen inds.; p. (1971) 2,446.

Auchtermuchty, burgh, North East Fife, **Scot.**; at S. foot of Ochil Hills, 40 km N.E. of Alloa; distilling; p. (1971) 1,475.

Auckland, spt., c., N.I., **N.Z.**; lgst. c. in N.Z.; seat of government 1845–64; univ.; extensive tr. and shipping; univ.; sawmills, sugar refinery, shipbldg., glass; steelwks. projected 40 km S. of A., in Waikato iron sand a.; p. (1971) 151,567 (c.), (est. 1970) 603,500 (met. a.).

Auckland Is., uninhabited gr. of **S. Pac. Oc.**; 320 km off N.Z.; discovered by British (1806); fur seals; a. 606 km^2.

Aude, dep., S. **France**; mtnous.; fertile N., salt from S. cstl. lagoons; drained by A. R. to Mediterranean; cap. Carcassonne; a. 6,340 km^2 p. (1968) 278,323.

Audenshaw, t., Gtr. Manchester, **Eng.**; metals, leather, pharmaceutics; p. (1971) 11,887.

Aue, t., Karl-Marx-Stadt, **E. Germany**; 32 km S.E. of Zwickau; uranium mng., metallurgy, textiles; p. (est. 1970) 30,930.

Aughrim, v., Galway, **R.o.I.**; battle (1691) between William III and James II.

Augsburg, c., Bavaria, **W. Germany**; at confluence of Rs. Lech and Wertach; cath.; theological institute; major industl. ctr., textiles, engin.; route ctr.; p. (est. 1969) 213,000.

Augusta, t., Sicily, **Italy**; on E. cst. peninsula; gd. harbour used as naval base; fishing; lubricants; p. (est. 1968) 31,602.

Augusta, c., Ga., **USA**; pt.; on Savannah R. and boundary with S.C.; cotton, cotton-seed oil, chemicals, foundries; p. (1970) 58,483 (c.), 249,842 (met. a.).

Aulnay-sous-Bois, t., Seine-St. Denis, **France**; residtl. sub. of Paris; p. (1968) 61,758.

Aurangabad, t., admin. ctr., Maharashtra, **India**; textiles, grain tr.; p. (1971) 150,483 (t.), 165,253 (met. a.).

Aurès, mtn. massif, **Algeria**; Berber stronghold.

Aurignac, v., Haute-Garonne, S. **France**; at foot of Pyrenees; caves, paleolithic remains.

Aurillac, t., cap., mkt. t. for dep. of Cantal, **France**; cheeses, umbrellas, leather goods; p. (1968) 31,143.

Aurora, t., Ill., **USA**; rly. wks., foundries, office equipment; p. (1970) 74,182.

Aussig. *See* **Usti Nad Labem**.

Austin, st. cap., Texas, **USA**; educational and artistic ctr., st. univ.; food processing; international airpt.; p. (1970) 246,904 (c.), 289,597 (met. a.).

Australasia, div. of **Oceania**; inc. Australia, Tasmania, N.Z., New Guinea and neighbouring archipelagos.

Australia, Commonwealth of, lgst. I., smallest continent in world; forms part of **Australasia**; Cook took possession for Britain 1770; Commonwealth proclaimed 1901; fed. of N.S.W., Victoria, Queensland, S.A., W. Australia, Tasmania; inc. also Cap. Terr. (Canberra) and N.T.; p. and inds. concentrated around cst. and in st. caps.; agr. economy (sheep, wheat, dairying) giving way to mineral inds. esp. in W.A. where lge. and diverse deposits abound; offshore petroleum deposits; N. cst. tropical, interior dry, S.E. cst. more moderate, Mediterranean climate in S.W.; mtns. in E. form Gr. Dividing Range separating E. cst. from interior, where plains drained by Murray-Darling and L. Eyre R. systems (used for hydroelec. power and irrigation); cap. Canberra; a. 7,686,884 km^2; p. (1972) 12,728,461.

Australian Alps, form S. part of Gr. Dividing Range, between E. cst. and interior, **Australia**; extend for 320 km S.W. from Australian Cap. Terr. to Goulburn R. in Victoria; plateau with average height of 300–600 m; tablelands extend to 1,500 m; dense vegetation cover; popular tourist and naturalist a.

Australian Antarctic Terr., part of **Antarctica**; between 45° E. and 160° E. and S. of 60° S. excluding Adélie Land; research stas. of Mawson, Davis and Wilkes.

Australian Bight, Gr.; gr. cstl. indentation S. of Nullarbor Plain, **Australia**.

Australian Capital Territory, fed. terr. surrounding Canberra, seat of Fed. Govt. of **Australia**; predominantly pastoral; highest point Mt. Bimberi, 1,912 m; a. 2,432 km^2; p. (1972) 143,843.

Austria, rep., **Europe**; after long and glamorous history under the Hapsburgs (**L53**), instability between A. and Hungary a cause of first world war; forcibly incorporated in German Reich, 1938, liberated 1945, recovered indep. 1955; almost entirely within Alps; drained mainly by Danube; continental climate; magnificent scenery generates a major tourist ind. but much food must be imported; forests and timber inds.; mineralised, iron-ore of Styria; hydroelec.; inds. located in ts.; cap. Vienna; a. 83,898 km^2; p. (est. 1969) 7,371,000, mainly Roman Catholic.

Austria, Lower, st., **Austria**; impt. agr. a.; cap. Vienna; a. (excluding Vienna) 18,384 km^2; p. (excluding Vienna) (est. 1968) 1,365,090.

Auvergne, old French prov. forming the present deps. of Puy-de-Dôme, Cantal and a small part of Haute-Loire; part of Massif Central; volcanic scenery; ch. t. Clermont-Ferrand.

Auvergne Mtns., mtns., central **France**; in N.W. of Central Massif; highest peak Puy de Sancy in Mt. Dore, 1,887 m; volcanic landscape.

Auxerre, t., cap. of Yonne dep., **France**; comm. and industl. ctr.; wine; tr.; Gothic cath.; p. (1968) 38,066.

Ava, c., **Burma**; on the Irrawaddy R.; former cap.; many pagodas, now ruins; bridge over R.

Avebury, v., Wilts., **Eng.**; mediaeval v. outside Neolithic circle and avenues, nr. Silbury Hill; lgst. prehistoric structure in England.

Aveiro, t., **Portugal**; on Vouga estuary, connected to sea by canal; fish. pt., salt from lagoons; p. (1963) 16,011.

Avellaneda, industl. sub. of Buenos Aires, **Argentina**; hides, wool; p. (1960) 329,626.

Avellino, t., cap. of A. prov., **Italy**; on motorway from Naples to W.; monastery; sulphur mng. and refining; hats; p. (est, 1968) 49,455.

Aversa, t. **Italy**; in fertile plain of Campania; agr. and route ctr.; p. (est. 1968) 47,018.

Avesta, t., Kopparberg, **Sweden**; on Dal R.; iron, aluminium and charcoal wks.; p. (est. 1970) 28,545.

Aveyron, dep., **France**; on S.W. rim of Central Massif, inc. Causses limestones; extensive forests; grain, dairying, sheep; coal; cap. Rodez; a. 8,767 km^2; p. (1968) 281,568.

Aviemore, t., Badenoch and Strathspey, **Scot.**; on R. Spey, 19 km S.W. of Grantown; rly. junction; winter sports.

Avignon, t., cap. of Vaucluse, dep., **France**; anc. Roman t. at crossing of R. Rhône; Provençal tourist ctr.; diversified inds. inc. wine tr.; p. (1968) 86,096 (t.), 139,134 (met. a.).

Avila, t., cap. of A. prov., **Spain**; in Old Castile; univ., cath.; mediaeval architecture; birthplace of St. Teresa; p. (1970) 30,938.

Avon, non-met. co., S. **Eng.**; based on Lower

Avon valley and Severnside; major ctrs. of p. at Bristol and Bath; pt. at Avonmouth; cstl. resort at Weston-super-Mare; bordered by Mendips in S.; a. 1,336 km²; p. (1971) 902,000.

Avon, R., Avon/Wiltshire, **Eng.**; flows from Cotswolds to enter Bristol Channel at Avonmouth; spectacular limestone gorge between Bristol and the sea; length 128 km.

Avon, R., Warwicks, **Eng.**; flows past Stratford-on-A., to reach Severn R. at Tewkesbury; fertile agr. valley; string of ts. along course; length 152 km.

Avon, R., Wilts./Hants./Dorset, **Eng.**; flows past Salisbury into English Channel at Christchurch; length 112 km.

Avonmouth, outport of Bristol, at mouth of R. Avon, **Eng.**; docks; seed crushing, petrol refinery, non-ferrous metal and chemical plants.

Avranches, t., Manche, **France**; Normandy mkt. t.; cider and dairy produce; p. (1968) 11,102.

Awe, Loch, Argyll and Bute, **Scot.**; 13 km W. of Inveraray, bordered by Ben Cruachan; a. 41 km², length 40 km; salmon and trout fishing; hydroelec. sta. at Cruachan.

Axholme, Isle of, flat lowland a., N.W. Lincs., **Eng.**; W. of Trent R.; drained by Vermuyden in 17th cent.; p. (1971) 14,882 (dist.).

Axminster, t., Devon, **Eng.**; brushes; flour and sawmills; carpet and press tool mftg.; p. (1971) 15,301 (dist.).

Ayacucho, t., **Peru**; cap. of A. dep.; founded by Pizarro in 1539; lies in equable, fertile valley; agr. processing, local mng.; p. (est. 1969) 27,900.

Aydin, t., **Turkey**; anc. Tralles; rly. and agr. tr. ctr. for surrounding a.; p. (1965) 43,289.

Aylesbury, co. t., Bucks., **Eng.**; mkt. t., dairy processing, printing; expanded t.; p. (1971) 41,288.

Aylesford, mkt. t., Kent, **Eng.**; N.W. Maidstone; cement, paper mills; antiquities in vicinity.

Aylsham, t., Norfolk, **Eng.**; on R. Bure; p. with St. Faith's (1971) 60,168 (dist.).

Ayr, royal burgh, Kyle and Carrick, **Scot.**; pt. on F. of Clyde, 48 km S.W. of Glasgow; Burns born nearby; racecourse; carpets, engin., footwear; p. (1971) 47,896.

Ayrshire, former co., **Scot.**; now part of Strathclyde Region.

Aysgarth, v. North Yorks., **Eng.**; on R. Ure in Wensleydale; famous waterfalls.

Ayutthaya, t., **Thailand**; former cap., on Menam Chao Phraya R. delta; ruins; tourism; p. (est. 1969) 40,352.

Azarbaijan, E. and W., provs., **N. Iran**; border USSR (Azerbaydzhan SSR) and Turkey; cap. (E.A.) Tabriz; p. (1967) 2,598,022; cap. (W.A.) Rezayeh; p. (1967) 1,087,702.

Azerbaydzhan, Transcaucasia, constituent rep. **USSR**; Caucasus and Lesser Caucasus separated by hot dry irrigated steppe; impt. oil ind.; 86,661 km²; p. (1970) 5,111,000.

Azores, Portuguese gr. of physically and climatically attractive Is. in mid-Atlantic about 1,440 km W. of Lisbon; separatist moves; volcanic; fruit, wine; ch. spts: Ponta Delgada, Horta (a major whaling ctr.), Angra do Heroismo; U.S. air bases on Terceira I.; a. 2,569 km²; p. (est. 1970) 336,100.

Azov Sea (Azouskoye More), **USSR**; joins Black Sea by Kerch strait; receives Don R.; fisheries; a. 36,000 km².

Azpeitia, t., **N. Spain**; mineral springs; local quarrying; timber inds., agr. processing; p. (1970) 10,797.

Azraq Desert Nat. Park, Jordan; first Jordanian nat. park around oasis of Azraq, 96 km E. of Amman; a. 3,900 km².

B

Baalbek, c., **Lebanon**, S.W. Asia; old Heliopolis; ruins; tourism.

Bab-al-Mandab, strait connecting Red Sea and Indian Oc.; dangerous but impt. shipping lane; length 32 km. width 27 km.

Babol, t., **Iran**, Mazandaran prov.; airport; p. (1966) 49,973.

Babylon, anc. cap. of Babylonian Empire, in Euphrates valley about 96 km S. of Baghdad, **Iraq**.

Bačau, t., **E. Romania**; on R. Bistrita; oil, sawmilling, textiles; p. (1968) 79,079.

Bacolod City, t., Negros, **Philippines**; sm. pt.; exp. sugar; p. (1968) 156,900.

Bacton, v., Norfolk, **Eng.**; terminal for S. gasfields in N. Sea.

Bacup, t., S.E. Lancs., **Eng.**; 32 km N. of Manchester; textiles, felts, footwear; p. (1971) 15,102.

Badagri, t., W. of Lagos, **Nigeria**; on the Bight of Benin: formerly a gr. slave pt.; coir sacks.

Badajoz, lgst. prov., **Spain**; gr. reclamation scheme in progress; a. 21,624 km²; p. (1970) 687,599.

Badajoz, c., cap. of B. prov., **W. Spain**, in Estremadura; anc. fortress c.; transit tr.; p. (est. 1969) 112,836.

Badalona, t., sub. of Barcelona; **Spain**; p. (est. 1967) 139,223.

Baden, t., **Switzerland**; health resort, mineral springs; p. (1969) 15,700.

Baden-Baden, t., Baden-Württemberg. **W. Germany**; fashionable spa; p. (est. 1969) 39,074.

Baden-bei-Wien, wat. pl., **Austria**; 22 km S.W. of Vienna; p. (1961) 22,484.

Baden-Württemberg, *Land*, **S. W. Germany**; created 1952; bounded by Rhine in W., drained by Neckar and Donau R. systems; mtnous., inc. Black Forest and Swabian Jura; received much immigrant ind. from E. Europe, so encouraging prosperous and diversified industl. structure; several impt. industl. regions centred on Mannheim, Karlsruhe, and cap. Stuttgart; a. 35,750 km²; p. (1969) 8,910,000.

Bad Lands, S.D., **USA**; stretches of infertile badly eroded soil.

Badrinath, mtn. and t., **Uttar Pradesh, India**; pilgrim shrine of Vishnu.

Badulla, t., **Sri Lanka**; tea; anc. t.; rly. terminus; ctr. of tea estates; p. (est. 1968) 30,000.

Badwater, salt pool, Cal., **USA**; 85 m below sea-level, lowest point in N. America.

Baeza, t., **S. Spain**; anc. Moorish c.; olives, wine; p. (1970) 14,834.

Baffin B., between **Greenland and Canada**; joined to Atl. Oc. by Davis Strait, to Arctic Oc. by Nares Strait; open 4 months per year; B. I., in W., ctr. of Arctic research and communications; length 1,120 km, width 100–650 km.

Bagé, t, **S. Brazil**; ctr. of cattle tr.; p. (est. 1968) 90,593.

Baghdad, c., cap. of **Iraq**; anc. c. on R. Tigris; terminus Baghdad rly.; airport; univ.; textiles, gum, bricks, tiles, metal inds.; p. (1967) 1,169,655.

Baghdad, prov. or liwa, **Iraq**; between Iran and Syrian Desert; inc. some of the most fertile lands in the Tigris and Euphrates valleys; p. (est. 1967) 2,270,639.

Baghlan, t., **Afghanistan**; new industl. t. in ctr. of sugar producing a.; alt. 518 m; p. (est. 1971) 105,944.

Bagnoli, t., **Italy**; sub. of Naples; spt.; iron and steel wks.

Bagnolet, t., Seine-St. Denis, **France**; sub. of Paris; famous for " plaster of Paris " from local gypsum; textiles; p. (1968) 34,039.

Bagshot, t., Surrey, **Eng.**; heath of same name; historically old postal town, 42 km S.W. of London; residtl.; p. (1971) 21,021 (dist.).

Baguio, Luzon, N.W. of Manila, summer cap. of **Philippines**, alt. 1,500 m; gold mines; p. (est. 1969) 71,400.

Bahamas, indep. st. (1973) within Brit. Commonwealth, **W.I.**, more than 700 coral atolls; subtropical climate; infertile but valuable tourist tr.; exp. crayfish; cap. Nassau; a. 11,406 km²; p. (1970) 168,812.

Bahawalpur, t., **Pakistan**; former cap. of B. princely st.; impt. bridging point over Sutlej R.; p. (est. 1969) 147,000.

Bahia, st., **Brazil**, cap. Salvador; cattle, cacao, sugar, coffee, tobacco; oil, extensive mineral deposits; a. 560,139 km²; p. (est. 1968) 6,914,658.

Bahia Blanca, spt., **Argentina**; industl. ctr., oil refining; prin. shipping point of S.; exp. oil, grain, wool, hides; p. (1970) 175,000 (met. a.).

Bahrain Is., indep. st. (1971) in Persian G.; low sandy Is., springs allow cultivation of dates; oil wells, oil and aluminium refining; trading ctr.; cap. Manamah; airpt. at Muharraq; a. 570 km²; p. (est. 1974) 220,000.

Baia, historic v., Campania, **Italy**; beautifully situated on Bay of Naples; celebrated Roman pleasure resort.
Baia-Mare, t., N.W. **Romania**; on Somesul R., in region mining copper, lead, zinc, gold, silver; mtn. resort; p. (1968) 68,077.
Baikal L. *See* Baykal L.
Baildon, t., West Yorks., **Eng.**; nr. Bradford; moorland resort; p. (1971) 14,690.
Baja, t., **Hungary**; impt. bridging point of R. Danube in Gr. Plain; p. (1966) 33,800.
Baja California. *See* Lower California.
Bakar, pt., **Yugoslavia**; S. of Rijeka; new pt. and oil harbour.
Bakersfield, t., Cal., **USA**; ctr. of oil prod. and refining; aircraft assembly; p. (1970) 67,955 (c.), 325,090 (met. a.).
Bakewell, t., Derbys., **Eng.**; tourist ctr. Peak District; agr., mng.; p. (1971) 4,240.
Bakhchisaray, t., Crimea, Ukrainian SSR, **USSR**; old cap. of Tartar Khans; copper, leather; p. 16,000.
Bakhuis Gebergte mtns., W. **Surinam**; major aluminium complex based on local power and bauxite.
Bakony Wald, mtns., **Hungary**; forested; vineyards; bauxite, manganese.
Baku, cap. of Azerbaydzhan SSR, **USSR**; pt. on Caspian Sea; univ.; oil-wells; oil pipeline connects with Batumi; shipbldg.; p. (1970) 847,000 (c.), 1,261,000 (met. a.).
Bala, t., Gwynedd **N. Wales**; nr. Denbigh, lt. engin.; resort; p. (1971) 1,580.
Bala, L., Gwynedd, **N. Wales**; drained by the Dee.
Balaklava, pt., S. Crimea, **USSR**; scene of the charge of the Light Brigade (1854); p. 2,000.
Balashov, t., Saratov area, **RSFSR**; on Khoper R.; engin., aircraft plant; p. (est. 1969) 76,000.
Balaton, L., lgst. in **Hungary**; a. 596 km²; long history of settlement in a.; shores forested; vineyards; tourism.
Balboa, t., **Panama Canal Zone**; pt. on Pac.; p. (1970) 2,568.
Balbriggan, spt., Dublin, **R.o.I.**; hosiery; p. (1966) 3,249.
Baldock, t., Herts., **Eng.**; on N. edge of Chiltern Hills and Gr. N. Road; hosiery, malting, lt. engin.; p. (1971) 6,270.
Baldwin, t., N.Y., **USA**; on S. Long I.; fisheries; p. (1970) 34,525.
Balearic Is., in Mediterranean Sea, **Spain**; inc. Majorca, Minorca, Ibiza, Formentera; limestone scenery and mild climate encourage tourism which has swamped Moorish influence; agr.; ch. t. Palma; a. 5,014 km²; p. (1970) 558,287.
Bali, I. off Java, **Indonesia**, in Lesser Sundas; equable climate, fertile soil, luxurious vegetation; p. mainly engaged in agr.; noted native dancers; a. (inc. Lombok) 10,196 km²; p. (est. 1970) 2,247,000.
Balikesir, t., **Turkey**; rly. junc.; ctr. of fertile agr. region; p. (1965) 69,256.
Balikpapan, t., Kalimantan, **Indonesia**; new oil refinery; p. (1971) 137,340.
Baliuag, t., Luzon, **Philippines**; rice, bamboo hats, mkt.; p. (est. 1969) 51,400.
Balkan Mtns., **Bulgaria**; fine alpine meadows, forested; tourism based on Sofia; average alt. 900–1,200 m, hgst. point Botev Peak, 2,377 m.
Balkan Peninsula, the easternmost of the three gr. southern peninsulas of Europe, between the Adriatic and Ionian seas on the W., and the Black Sea, Sea of Marmara and the Aegean Sea on the E., with an area of, roughly, 500,000 km²; includes Turkey, Yugoslavia, Bulgaria, Albania, Greece; ch. mtns.: Rodopi, Pindhus, Balkan; ch. Rs.: Danube, Maritsa, Vardar; ch. Ls.: Scutari, Okhrida.
Balkh. *See* Wazirabad.
Balkhash, t., Kazakh SSR, **USSR**; on N. shore of L.B.; smelting, esp. local copper; vermiculite deposits nearby, salt; p. (est. 1969) 77,000.
Balkhash, L., Kazakh SSR, **USSR**; receives Ili R., but has no outlet; salt water; fishing, salt-panning; a. 17,301 km².
Ballachulish, v., Argyll and Bute, **Scot.**; on S. shore of Loch Leven, N.E. of Oban; tourism; ferry across Loch Linnhe, new road bridge.
Ballarat, t., Victoria, **Australia**; 117 km N.W. of Melbourne, former gold-field dist.; mkt ctr.; engin., timber, bricks, and tiles; caths.; p. (1972) 58,434.
Ballater, burgh, Kincardine and Deeside, **Scot.**; on R. Dee, 59 km S.W. of Aberdeen; tourist resort, mineral wells; nr. the royal Highland residence of Balmoral; p. (1971) 982.
Ballina, U.D., spt., Mayo, **R.o.I.**; agr. machin. salmon fishing; p. (1966) 6,187.
Ballina, t., N.S.W., **Australia**; at mouth of Richmond R.; resort, fishing; p. (1972) 6,133.
Ballinasloe, U.D., Galway and Roscommon, **R.o.I.**; agr. ctr.; cattle mkt.; terminus of Grand Canal; p. (1966) 5,826.
Ballinrobe, R.D., Mayo, **R.o.I.**; E. of Lough Mask; trout fishing; p. (1961) 13,492.
Ballybunion, resort, Kerry, **R.o.I.**; at mouth of R. Shannon; p. (1966) 1,160.
Ballycastle, spt., mkt. t., Moyle, **N. Ireland**; abbey and cas. ruins; seaside resort; p. (1966) 2,949.
Ballyclare, t., Newtownabbey, **N. Ireland**; paper, linen, dyeing, asbestos-cement prod.; p. (1966) 4,583.
Ballymena, mkt. t., l. gov. dist., **N. Ireland**; on R. Braid; linen and dyeing; p. (est. 1971) 16,487.
Ballymoney, mkt. t., l. gov. dist., **N. Ireland**; 64 km N.W. of Belfast; linen; p. (1966) 3,520.
Ballynahinch, t., Down, **N. Ireland**; 19 km from Downpatrick.
Ballyshannon, spt., Donegal, **R.o.I.**; at mouth of R. Erne; salmon fishery; resort; hydro-electric power plant; p. (1966) 2,233.
Balmoral Cas., Kincardine and Deeside, **Scot.**; royal residence, on R. Dee, 13 km W. of Ballater.
Balsas, R., and lowland, **Mexico**; R. flows E. to Pacific through rich agr. valley of Morelos; length 800 km.
Baltic Sea, an arm of Atl. Oc., opens into N. Sea by narrow channels between Denmark and Sweden; joined to Arctic by White Sea Canal; low. dune-backed cst.; shallowness, tendency to freeze reduce its importance for shipping; a. 414,000 km².
Baltic White Canal. *See* **Volga Baltic Waterway.**
Baltimore, industl. c., spt., Md. **USA**; fine harbour nr. head of Chesapeake B.; pt. processing and diversified inds.; steel wks. at Sparrow's Point; educational, cultural ctr., seat of Johns Hopkins univ.; many fine public bldgs. despite disastrous fire of 1904; p. (1970) 895,222 (c.), 2,045,200 (met. a.).
Baltoro Glacier, Karakoram Mtns., **Pakistan**; drains into tribs. of Indus; alt. 3,532 m.
Baluchistan, prov. (revived 1970), **Pakistan**; S. of Afghanistan; largely desert and rugged barren mtns.; cap. Quetta; cereals, potatoes, fruits, dates; new oil and natural gas discoveries; a. 137,011 km²; p. (1972) 2,409,000.
Bamako, cap. c. of **Mali**; impressive site at foot of escarpment on R. Niger; admin. and agr. tr. ctr.; R. pt.; univ.; p. (est. 1970) 196,800.
Bamberg, c., Bavaria, **W. Germany**; cath.; textiles, elec., leather and engin. inds.; impt. R. pt.; p. (est. 1969) 69,303.
Bamburgh, t., Northumberland, **Eng.**; former cap. of Bernicia and Northumbria; cas.; birthplace of Grace Darling.
Banaba I. *See* **Ocean I.**
Banagher, v., Offaly, **R.o.I.**; impt. crossing of R. Shannon.
Banam, t., **Cambodia**; on Mekong R.; boat-bldg., rice milling; p. 28,000.
Banat, terr., Vojvodina, **Yugoslavaia**; major source of petroleum, natural gas, vineyards, but economically backward.
Banbridge, t., l. gov. dist., **N. Ireland**; on Bann R.; linen; p. (1966) 6,551.
Banbury, mkt. t., Oxford, **Eng.**; 128 km from London; aluminium ind., furniture, printing, ladies wear; expanded t.; p. (1971) 29,216.
Banchory, burgh, Kincardine and Deeside, **Scot.**; on R. Dee, 27 km S.W. of Aberdeen; p. (1971) 2,355.
Banda Is., volcanic gr. in Moluccas, in Banda Sea, **Indonesia**; nutmegs and mace; a. 103 km².
Bandama, R., **Ivory Coast**; major power and irrigation scheme at Kossou Dam; length c. 320 km.
Bandar. *See* **Masulipatnam.**
Bandar 'Abbās, spt., S. **Iran**; airport; oil exploration; new deepwater harbour; p. (1967) 163,133.

Bandar-e-Būshehūr (Bushire), spt., S.W. **Iran**; on Persian G., Iran's major pt.; petro-chem. complex project; p. (est. 1971) 40,000.
Bandar-e-Pahlavi, spt., N. **Iran**; on Caspian Sea; p. (1967) 59,737.
Bandar-e-Shāh, spt., N. **Iran**; on Caspian Sea, on rly. from Tehran; p. (1966) 13,081.
Bandar-e-Shāhpūr, spt., **Iran**, on Persian G., terminus of rly. from Tehran; petrochemical plant; p. (1966) 6,013.
Bandjarmasin, c., cap. of Kalimantan, **Indonesia**; pt. on Martapura R., nr. confluence with Barito R.; tr. ctr.; oil, timber, rubber, printing plant; p. (1971) 281,673.
Bandon, t., Cork, **R.o.I.**; on B.R.; agr. processing; p. (1966) 2,294.
Bandung, c., W. Java, **Indonesia**; industl. and tourist ctr.; technical institute; radio sta. at nearby Malabar; p. (est. 1971) 1,114,000 (met. a.).
Banff Nat. Park, Canada; first Canadian Nat. Park; in Rocky Mtns.; variegated scenery, many tourist facilities; a. 6,695 km².
Banff, royal burgh, Banff and Buchan, **Scot.**; on Moray Firth at mouth of R. Deveron; fisheries; tourism; p. (1971) 3,723.
Banffshire, former co., **Scot.**; lge. part now forms Banff and Buchan l. gov. dist., Grampian Reg.; a. of dist. 1,525 km²; p. of dist. (1971) 73,880.
Bangalore, c., Karnataka, **India**; well-planned c., former Brit. military sta. and admin. H.Q.; route ctr.; textiles, engin.; p. (1971) 1,540,741 (c.), 1,653,779 (met. a.).
Bangka (Banka), I., between Sumatra and Kalimantan, **Indonesia**; tin; a. 11,942 km²; p. 280,000.
Bangkok (Krung Thep), cap. c., **Thailand**; pt. on Menam Chao Phraya R., 32 km from sea; built originally round canals; major industl. ctr.; royal palace, univ.; p. (1970) 2,132,000.
Bangladesh (East Pakistan), indep. sov. st., S. Asia; within Commonwealth (1972); occupies former Indian prov. of E. Bengal and E. part of Ganges delta; dense rural p. engaged in intensive farming of rice and jute; susceptible to flooding and cyclones, cstl. embankment project; open warfare between India and Pakistan (Dec. 1971) resulted in creation of indep. st.; cap. Dacca; a. 142,776 km²; p. (1975) 76,200,000 (+40 per cent since 1961).
Bangor, t., North Down, **N. Ireland**; spt. on S. shore of Belfast Lough, 16 km N.E. of Belfast; lt. inds.; carpets, hosiery; seaside resort; p. (est. 1971) 35,178.
Bangor, t., S. Me., **USA**; pt. of entry on Penobscot R.; timber inds., shoes; p. (1970) 33,168.
Bangor, t. Gwynedd, **Wales**; pt. on S. shore of Menai Strait; cath., univ. college; lt. engin.; tourist ctr.; p. (1971) 14,526.
Bangui, c., cap. of **Central African Rep.**; pt. on R. Ubangi; airpt.; p. (est. 1971) 187,000 (met. a.).
Bangweulu, L., **Zambia**; 240 km long, 128 km wide, contains 3 islands. Dr. Livingstone died at Illala on S. shore of this L., in 1873.
Baniyas, spt., **Syria**; terminus of oil pipeline from Kirkuk, opened 1952.
Banja Luka, t., N. Bosnia, **Yugoslavia**; caths., mosques; recent industl. development; cellulose; rly. junc.; p. (1971) 89,866.
Banjul (Bathurst), t., cap. of **Gambia**; pt. at mouth of Gambia R., exp. groundnuts; airport; p. (1967) 31,800.
Banks I., Canada, Arctic Oc.; separated by McClure Strait from Melville I.
Banks Is., gr. of sm. Is. in S. Pacific; N.E. of New Hebrides.
Banks Peninsula, on E. cst. of S.I., **N.Z.**
Banks Strait, separating Furneaux Is. from Tasmania, **Australia**.
Bankura, t., W. Bengal, **India**; on Hooghly R.; shellac, silk; p. (1961) 62,833.
Bann, Upper and Lower R., **N. Ireland**; rises in Mtns. of Mourne, and flows through Lough Neagh to Atlantic nr. Coleraine; length 144 km.
Bannockburn, moor, nr. Stirling, **Scot.**; Bruce's victory over Edward II on June 23–24, 1314, established Scotland's independence.
Banovici, basin, **Yugoslavia**; in Bosnia; brown coal.
Banská Bystrica, region, Slovakia, **ČSSR**; copper and silver mng., metal wks.; a. 9,230 km²; p. (est. 1968) 38,865 (commune).
Banstead, Surrey, **Eng.**; dormitory t.; p. (1971) 44,986.
Bantam, t. and dist., W. Java, **Indonesia**; suffered severely from fever and volcanic eruption; former pt. and sultanate; cattle rearing.
Bantry, t., Cork, **R.o.I.**; tweed; p. (1966) 2,341.
Bantry Bay, Cork, **R.o.I.**; Atlantic inlet; natural harbour utilised mainly by oil-storage depot.
Bar, spt., Dalmatian cst., **Yugoslavia**; terminal of new Belgrade-Bar rly.; p. 5,500.
Baracaldo, pt., N.E. **Spain**; rapidly growing industl. t. on Bilbāo estuary; p. (est. 1967) 110,516.
Baracoa, spt., **Cuba**; exp. bananas, coconuts; p. (est. 1967) 105,090.
Baranovichi, c., Belorussiya, **USSR**; admin. ctr. of agr. dist.; impt. rly. ctr.; p. (1970) 102,000.
Barataria Bay, S.E. Louisiana, **USA**; 56 km S. of New Orleans; ctr. of shrimp ind., petroleum extraction; picturesque stilt vs.; a. 466 km².
Barauni, t., N. Central Bihar, **India**; oil refining; oil pipelines to Gauhati, and Kanpur and from Haldia; p. (1961) 40,321.
Barbados, I., indep. sovereign st., within Brit. Commonwealth, **W.I.**; fertile soils; economy based on intensive agr. supporting dense p.; sugar, molasses, rum; fishing; tourism; cap. and spt. Bridgetown; a. 429 km²; p. (1969) 250,686.
Barbary Coast, gen. name applied to Mediterranean cst. of N. Africa between Strait of Gibraltar and C. Bon.
Barberton, t., Ohio, **USA**; S.W. of Akron; tyre mftg.; p. (1970) 33,052.
Barberton, t., Transvaal, **S. Africa**; developed from 19th cent. gold rush; ctr. of rich agr. dist.; p. (est. 1967) 13,200.
Barbican, dist., City of London, **Eng.**; inc. major housing scheme to attract p. back into c.; cultural amenities.
Barbizon, v., nr. forest of Fontainebleau, **France**; haunt of painters, especially those ass. with the Barbizon school.
Barbuda and Redonda, Is., Leeward Is., **W.I.**; dependencies of Antigua; sea-island cotton; a. 163 km²; p. (1960) 1,145.
Barcellona, t., N.E. cst., Sicily, **Italy**; mkt. t.; p. (est. 1968) 34,526.
Barcelona, c., cap. of B. prov., major spt. of **Spain**; industl. and comm. ctr., "Manchester of Spain", textiles and varied inds.; exp. agr. prod. inc. cork; cath., univ.; p. (est. 1969) 1,827,838.
Barcelona, t., N. **Venezuela**; cap. of Anzoátegui st.; agr. tr.; brewing; p. (est. 1970) 54,916.
Barcoo Creek. *See* **Cooper's Creek**.
Bardsey, I., Irish Sea; off cst. of Wales, nr. N. point of Cardigan Bay; lighthouse.
Bareilly, c., Uttar Pradesh, **India**; mkt., sugar tr. and processing, cotton mills, bamboo furniture; p. (1971) 296,248 (c.), 326,106 (met. a.).
Barents Sea, part of Arctic Oc., E. of Spitzbergen to N. Cape; impt. cod fisheries; oil potential.
Bari, c., cap. of B. prov., Apulia, **Italy**; spt. on Adriatic handling agr. prods.; agr. processing inds., oil refinery; p. (1969) 352,425.
Barinas, t., cap. of B. st., **Venezuela**; cattle oil in surrounding Llanos; p. (est. 1970) 50,576.
Barisal, t., **Bangladesh**; nr. Tetulia at mouth of Ganges; river pt.; gr. damage and loss of life from cyclone 1965; p. (est. 1969) 79,300.
Barito R, Borneo, **Indonesia**; a. of swampland in lower valley; proposals to develop valley for rice cultivation; length *c.* 440 km.
Barking, outer bor., E. London, **Eng**; on Rs. Roding and Thames; diversified inds. inc. huge R.side Ford motor wks.; high proportion of council housing; p. (1971) 160,499.
Barlad, t., Moldavia, **Romania**; soap, textiles; p. (1966) 41,060.
Bar-le-Duc, t, cap. of Meuse dep., **France**; in picturesque Ornain valley; many fine old houses; varied inds.; p. (1968) 20,384.
Barletta, t., spt., **Italy**; diversified pt. processing inds.; wine tr.; p. (est. 1968) 75,097.
Barmouth, t., Gwynedd, **Wales**; pt. on Cardigan Bay; chemicals; resort; p. (1971) 2,103.
Barnard Castle, Durham, **Eng.**; mkt. t., resort; woollens, penicillin; cas.; p. (1971) 5,228.
Barnaul, t., W. Siberia, **RSFSR**; route ctr. in cotton-growing dist. nr. industl. Kuznetsk Basin; varied inds.; p. (1970) 439,000.
Barnet, former U.D., Herts., **Eng.**; now outer bor., Greater London; comprising Finchley,

Hendon, Barnet, East Barnet and Friern Barnet; p. (1971) 303,578.
Barnoldswick, t., Lancs., **Eng.**; cotton weaving; p. (1971) 9,937.
Barnsley, t., South Yorks., **Eng.**; machin., plastics; carpets; coal-mng. ctr.; p. (1971) 75,330.
Barnstaple, Devon, **Eng.**; mkt. t., pt. on R. Taw; seaside resort; p. (1971) 17,342.
Baroda, t., Gujarat, **India**; univ.; palaces, Hindu temples; natural gas pipeline from Ankleshwar; oil refining nearby at Jawaharnagar; p. (1971) 467,422.
Barquisimeto, t., **Venezuela**; well built c.; comm. ctr. for fertile agr. a.; p. (est. 1970) 281,600.
Barra Is., Outer Hebrides, **Scot.**; a. 901 km²; lighthouse on Barra Head; p. (1971) 1,088.
Barrancabermeja, R. pt., **Colombia**; oilfield, oil refining, paper mkg., petrochemicals; p. (est. 1972) 94,000 (t.), 106,000 (met. a.).
Barranquilla, t., **Colombia**; major spt. nr. mouth of Magdalena R.; impt. industl. ctr.; international airpt.; p. (est. 1972) 682,300 (t.), 693,900 (met. a.).
Barreiro, t., Setúbal, **Portugal**; on S. bank of Tagus estuary; agr. processing; p. (1970) 35,622.
Barrhead, burgh, Renfrew, **Scot.**; 11 km S.W. of Glasgow; p. (1971) 18,289.
Barrowford, t., Lancs., **Eng.**; p. (1971) 5,130.
Barrow, R., **R.o.I.**; rises in Slieve Bloom mtns.; flows to Waterford; navigable; linked to Dublin by canal from Athy; 192 km long.
Barrow-in-Furness, spt., Cumbria, **Eng.**; iron and steel ind. once based on local haematite ores; shipbldg., submarines; p. (1971) 63,998.
Barrow Point, most N. headland in Alaska, **USA**.
Barry, pt., South Glamorgan, **Wales**; rapid growth in 19th cent. as outport of Cardiff; modern light inds., replacing coal and tinplate inds.; p. (1971) 41,578.
Barth, spt., Rostock, **E. Germany**; shipyard engin., furniture, sugar; p. (1963) 12,406.
Bartlesville, t. Okla., **USA**; oil refining, metal inds.; p. (1970) 29,683.
Barton-on-Humber, mkt. t., Humberside, **Eng.**; anc. Eng. pt.; S. site of new Humber Bridge; p. (1971) 7,496.
Basel, c., cap. of B. can., 2nd. t. of **Switzerland**; cath., univ.; burial place of Erasmus; comm., industl. rly. ctr. at head of barge navigation on R. Rhine; p. (est. 1969) 213,200 (c.), 364,800 (met. a.).
Basel, can., **Switzerland**; divided into 2 half cantons; (1) B.—Stadt; in immediate vicinity of B.c.; cap. B.; a. 36 km²; p. (1969) 238,000; (2) B.—Land; on N. Jura slopes; watchmaking; cap. Liestal; a. 427 km²; p. (1969) 200,500.
Basford, t., Notts. **Eng.**; outskirts of Nottingham; hosiery; p. (1971) 70,763. (dist.).
Bashkir (Bashirskaya) ASSR, occupies Belaya R. basin in S.W. Urals, **RSFSR**; impt. mng. and metal inds., inc. major oilfield; arable agr.; cap. Ufa; a. 143,486 km²; p. (1970) 3,819,000.
Basildon, t., Essex, **Eng.**; in lower Thames valley; new t. 1949; light inds.; p. (est. 1974) 84,900.
Basilicata, region, S. **Italy**; mtnous. in W., drains to G. of Taranto; arable agr.; a. 9,984 km²; p. (1969) 626,041.
Basingstoke, N. Hants., **Eng.**; 80 km W. of London; expanded t.; engin., light inds.; p. (1971) 52,502, (1951) 17,012.
Basle. *See* Basel.
Basotho ba Borwa (S. Sotho) Bantu Terr. Authority, O.F.S., **S. Africa**; cap. Witzieshoek; a. 52,000 hectares; p. (est. 1969) 144,000.
Basque Provs., N. **Spain**; comprise 3 provs.: Alava, Guipuzcoa and Vizcaya where Basque language spoken; recent claims that French dep. of Pyrénées-Atlantiques should be inc. within an indep. Basque prov.; lgst. c. Bilbão. p. (1970) 1,878,636.
Basra, t., **Iraq**; cap. of B. prov.; R. pt., 64 km from mouth of Tigris R., on main rly. from Baghdad; exp. agr. prods.; p. (1965) 310,950.
Bas-Rhin, dep., E. **France**; N. part of Alsace; extends to Rhine rift valley, inc. Vosges Mtns.; impt. agr. dist.; many industl. ts.; cap. Strasbourg; a. 4,791 km²; p. (1968) 827,367.
Bass Rock, lighthouse in Firth of Forth, opposite Tantallon Cas., E. Lothian, **Scot.**; gannetry.
Bass Strait, Australia; between Victoria and Tasmania; length 320 km; width 224 km.
Bassano del Grappa; cap. of Vicenza prov., on R. Brenta, **Italy**; light and craft inds,; cath.; p. (est. 1968) 34,763.
Bassein, t., **Burma**; on mouth of Irrawaddy R., univ.; airfield; rice tr. and milling; p. (est. 1969) 175,000 (met. a.).
Bassenthwaite, L., L. Dist., Cumbria, **Eng.**; most N. of lge. Ls.; drained to Solway Firth by R. Derwent; length 6 km, width 1 6 km.
Basses-Alpes. *See* Alpes-de-Haute-Provence.
Basses-Pyrénées. *See* Pyrénées-Atlantique.
Basse-Terre, I., cap. of Guadeloupe, **Fr. W.I.**; pt.; p. (est. 1969) 16,000.
Basseterre, t., St. Kitts I., **W.I.**; cap. St. Kitts-Nevis-Anguilla ass. st.; pt.; sugar refining; p. (est. 1970) 14,133.
Bastia, c. spt., cap. Haute Corse, N.E. Corsica, **France**; lgst. t. of Corsica; agr. exp. and inds.; tourism; p. (1968) 50,100.
Basutoland. *See* Lesotho.
Bata, t., ch. spt., **Equatorial Guinea**; cap. of Rio Muni prov.; airpt.; p. (1960) 27,024.
Bataan, peninsula and prov., W. Luzon, **Philippines**; mtnous.; inc. t. of Balanga; timber inds., oil refining.
Batangas, prov. and spt., S.W. Luzon, **Philippines**; oil refining; agr. tr.; p. (est. 1966) 102,100 (t.).
Batavia. *See* Djakarta.
Bath, c., Avon **Eng.**; Roman baths. hot springs medicinal waters; fine Regency architecture; univ.; elec. engin., metal inds.; p. (1971) 84,545.
Bathgate, burgh, W. Lothian, **Scot.**; coal mng. automobile ind.; p. (1971) 14,224.
Bathurst, t., N.S.W. **Australia**; ctr. of mng. pastorial agr. and fruit dist. on Macquarie R.; light inds., tourism; p. (1972) 17,169.
Bathurst, I., off cst. of N.T., **Australia**; separated from Melville I. by Apsley Str.; aboriginal reserve; cypress pine milling.
Bathurst, t., N.B., **Canada**; pt. on Nipisiguit Bay; paper mill; salmon fishing; local mng.; p. (1971) 16,404.
Bathurst. *See* Banjul.
Bātinah, Al, fertile coastal plain, **Oman**, Arabia; produces early-ripening dates famous for flavour.
Batley, t. West Yorks., **Eng.**; heavy woollens shoddy; p. (1971) 42,004.
Baton Rouge, st. cap., La., **USA**; on Mississippi; major tr. ctr.; univ.; oil refining, chemical plants; p. (1970) 161,783 (c.), 276,763 (met. a.).
Battambang, t., **Cambodia**; 288 km N.W. of Phnom-Penh; cotton mill; p. (1962) 38,846.
Battersea, dist., London, **Eng.**; S. of R. Thames; famous park; lge. power sta.; part of Wandsworth.
Batticaloa, t., cap. of E. Prov., **Sri Lanka**; on E. cst.; comm. ctr.; p. (est. 1968) 24,000.
Battle, t., East Sussex, **Eng.**; battle of Hastings fought here 1066; abbey; p. (1971) 33,563 (dist.).
Battle Creek, t., Mich., **USA**; on Kalamazoo R.; engin., local cereal prod.; p. (1970) 39,931.
Batu Arang, t., **Malaya**; ctr. of only worked coalfield in Malaya; 45 km from Kuala Lumpur.
Batumi, t., spt. on E. shore of Black Sea; Georgian SSR, **USSR**; oil, engin., citrus fruits, tea; oil pipeline connects with Baku; resort; airpt; p. (1970) 101,000.
Bauchi, t., **Nigeria**; cap. Bauchi st.; ctr. of Jos plateau; tin-mng. ctr.
Bauld, C., northernmost part of Newfoundland, **Canada**.
Bauru, t., São Paulo st., **Brazil**; comm. ctr.; food inds.; p. (1970) 120,178.
Bautzen, t., Dresden, **E. Germany**; on R. Spree; textiles, engin., iron inds.; cath.; p. (est. 1970) 43,670.
Bavaria (Bayern), *Land*, **W. Germany**; mtnous., bounded in S. by Alps, inc. Böhmerwald, Fichtelgebirge, Franconian Forest; main Rs. Danube and Main; fertile agr. valleys; forestry and agr.; economic life concentrated in ts., esp. cap. Munich, now a focus of p. immigration; rural beauty attracts tourist tr.; celebrated beer; a. 70,220 km²; p. (1967) 10,280,400.
Bavarian Alps, mtn. range, **W. Germany**, along Austrian border; Zugspitze (2,969 m) highest mtn. in W. Germany.
Bavarian Forest. *See* Böhmerwald.
Bawdwin, t., **Burma**; in Shan plateau; impt. mng. ctr.; wolfram, lead, zinc, silver, rubies.

Bayamón, t., **Puerto Rico**; in fertile valley; oil refining; p. (1970) 147,552 (t.), 156,192 (met. a.).
Baybay, t., Leyte, **Philippines**; impt. comm. pt.; p. (est. 1969) 70,200.
Bay City, t., Mich., **USA**; comm. pt. nr. head of Saginaw B.; fishing; pt. processing inds.; automobile parts; p. (1970) 49,075 (c.), 116,628 (met. a.).
Bayeux, t., Calvados, **France**; mkt. t.; cath., museum, Bayeux tapestry; p. (1968) 12,871.
Baykal, L. (Ozero Baykal), Siberia, **RSFSR**; sixth largest fresh-water L. in world; basin forms deepest depression in world (1,616 m); many pts. around shores but frozen Nov.–May; skirted by Trans-Siberian rly.; sturgeon, salmon; tourism; a. 35,483 km².
Bay of Biscay. *See* Biscay, Bay of.
Bayonne, spt., Pyrénées-Atlantique, S.W. **France**; cath.; noted for invention of bayonet; Basque Museum; p. (1968) 42,743 (t.); 110,163 (met. a.).
Bayonne, t., N.J., **USA**; 10 km from New York; chemicals, oil refining; dry docks; p. (1970) 72,743.
Bayreuth, t., Bavaria, **W. Germany**; home of Wagner; famous for musical festivals in national theatre; textiles, porcelain, engin.; p. (est. 1969) 65,530.
Bayswater, dist., London, **Eng.**; residtl. dist., now part of Westminster.
Baytown, pt., S.E. Texas, **USA**; industl. t., oil refining and exp.; p. (1970) 43,980.
Beachy Head, chalk headland, S.W. of Eastbourne, East Sussex, **Eng.**; 175 m high.
Beaconsfield, t., Bucks., **Eng.**; residtl.; home of Edmund Burke; p. (1971) 11,861.
Beardmore Glacier, Antarctica; one of world's lgst. valley glaciers; over 176 km in length.
Bear I. (Björnöya I.), **Norway**; in Arctic Oc. 208 km S. of Spitzbergen; cod fisheries.
Bearsden, burgh, l. gov. dist. with Milngavie, **Scot.**; residtl.; p. (1971) 25,013.
Beas (Bias), R., Punjab, **India**; trib. of Sutlej R.; one of the "five rivers"; part of irrigation scheme.
Beattock, pass, S. Uplands, **Scot.**; gives access from valley of R. Clyde to R. Annan; used by main W. cst. rly. route from Carlisle to Glasgow and Edinburgh; alt. 309 m.
Beauce, region, central **France**; flat limestone plateau; arid, few surface streams; thin layer of loam (limon) permits agr.; impt. wheat growing a. ("the granary of France"); p. mainly grouped in vs.
Beaufort Sea, off N. Alaska, **USA**; part of Arctic Oc.
Beaujolais, France; in upper Rhône valley, N.E. Massif Central; wine-growing dist.
Beaulieu, v., Hants, **Eng.**; on Beaulieu R.; Cistercian abbey; car museum.
Beauly, t., Inverness, **Scot.**; on B. R.; ruined priory.
Beaumaris, t., Anglesey, Gwynedd, **N. Wales**; pt. on Menai Strait; lt. engin.; resort; p. (1971) 2,096.
Beaumont, t.; 2nd. pt. of Texas, **USA**; ctr. of petrochemical inds.; p. (1970) 115,716 (c.), 306,016 (met. a.).
Beaune, t., Cote d'Or, **France**; mediaeval walled t.; ctr. of wine tr.; p. (1968) 17,377.
Beauvais, agr. mkt. t., cap. of Oise dep., N. **France**; cath.; Gobelin tapestry removed to Paris; p. (1968) 49,347.
Bebington, Merseyside, **Eng.**; part of pt. of Liverpool; soap, chemicals, engin.; p. (1971) 61,488.
Becancourt, t., Quebec, **Canada**; on S. bank of St. Lawrence; integrated steel mill projected.
Beccles, Suffolk, **Eng.**; mkt. t. on R. Waveney S. of Broads; resort, agr. inds.; p. (1971) 8,015.
Béchar (Colom-Béchar), t., N.W. **Algeria**; airpt.; coal; p. (1966) 42,090.
Bechuanaland. *See* Botswana.
Beckum, t., N. Rhine-Westphalia, **W. Germany**. cement, chalk, engin. wks.; p. (est. 1969) 22,189.
Bedale, mkt. t., North Yorks., **Eng.**; at N. end of Vale of York; tent mkg.; p. (1971) 8,544 (dist.).
Beddington and Wallington. *See* Sutton.
Bedford, co. t., Beds., **Eng.**; on R. Ouse, 80 km N. of London; gen. engin., inc. marine and elec., bricks, ironfounding aero research; p. (1971) 73,064.
Bedfordshire, non-met. co., **Eng.**; co. t. Bedford; crossed by Chilterns; agr., mkt. gardening, brickmkg., cement, vehicles, engin.; a. 1,232 km²; p. (1971) 463,493.
Bedford Level, once over 162,000 ha of peat marsh in S. Fenland, **Eng.**; first successful draining initiated by Earl of Bedford 1634.
Bedlington, t., Northumberland, **Eng.**; nr. Blyth; coal mng.; electronics; p. (1971) 28,167.
Bedloe's I., or **Liberty I.**, N.Y., harbour, **USA**; on which the statue of Liberty stands.
Bedwas and Machen, t., Mid Glamorgan, **Wales**; gas, coal and coke by-prods.; new anthracite mine; p. (1971) 12,548.
Bedwellty, t., Gwent, **Wales**; elec. gds., car upholstery; p. (1971) 25,326.
Bedworth, t., Warwicks., **Eng.**; nr. Coventry; coal mng., limestone quarrying, engin., textiles; p. (1971) 40,535.
Bedzin, t., S. **Poland**; coalmng. t. in Upper Silesia; p. (1970) 42,800.
Beerenberg, mtn., Jan Mayen I., **Norway, Arctic** Oc.; one of lgst. volcanic cones in world; glaciated; alt. 2,546 m.
Beersheba, t., **Israel**; ctr. for development of the Negev; p. (1968) 69,500.
Beeston and Stapleford, Notts., **Eng.**; sub. of Nottingham; engin., drugs, telephones; p. (1971) 63,498.
Bègles, t., Gironde, **France**; mftg.; p. (1968) 27,330.
Begovat, t., E. Uzbek SSR, **USSR**; on Syr Dar'ya R.; iron and steel wks.; hydroelectric power; p. (1967) 59,000.
Beira, spt., **Moçambique**; airpt.; rly. runs inland to Salisbury (Rhodesia) and Blantyre (Malawi); exp. sugar, maize, cotton; oil pipeline to Umtali; p. (1960) 64,600.
Beirut, c., cap. of **Lebanon**; pt. on Mediterranean; anc. Phoenician c., now busy shipping and mercantile ctr.; silk, wool, fruits; 4 univs.; p. (1964) 700,000.
Beisan (Bet She'an), t., **Israel**; in Jordan valley, *c.* 90 m below sea level; archaeological finds date from 1500 B.C.; rebuilt since 1948 by Israelis; p. (est. 1970) 11,900.
Bejaia (Bougie), spt., **Algeria**; impt. tr. ctr.; exp. wood, hides; oil pipeline connection to Hassi-Messoud; p. (1967) 63,000.
Belaya Tserkov, t., N. Ukrainian SSR, **USSR**; agr. and comm. ctr.; p. (1970) 109,000.
Békéscsaba, t., **Hungary**; milling; rly. junc.; poultry processing plant; p. (1968) 53,000
Belém, spt., cap. of Pará st., **Brazil**; comm. ctr., ch. pt. of Amazon basin (rubber, Brazil nuts, cacao, timber); univ.; p. (1970) 565,097.
Belfast, l. gov. dist., cap. of **N. Ireland**; pt. on Belfast Lough; Britain's lgst. single shipyard; linen mnf., rope, tobacco, distilling, aircraft, fertilisers, computers; oil refinery on E. side of harbour; univ.; Stormont Castle; p. (est. 1976) 385,000.
Belfort, t., cap. of Belfort dep., E. **France**, in Alsace; fortress t. between Jura and Vosges; heavy inds., rly. wks., cotton ind.; elec. engin.; p. (1968) 55,833.
Belfort (Territoire de), dep., **France**; ch. t. Belfort; a. 608 km²; p. (1968) 118,450.
Belgaum, t., Karnataka, **India**; cotton; alt. 760 m; Jain temples; p. (1971) 192,427 (t.), 213,872 (met a.).
Belgium, kingdom, **W. Europe**, comprises 9 admin. provs.; low-lying except in Ardennes in S.E.; very high density of p., intensive agr. and highly industl.; severe social and economic problems have resulted from decline of Sambre-Meuse coalfield and associated heavy engin. inds., similar difficulties in textile inds. in N.W.; industl. expansion on Kempenland coalfield in N.E. and around Brussels, Antwerp, and Ghent; heavily dependent upon foreign tr. for economic survival; member of EEC; major spt. of Antwerp competing with Rotterdam for hinterland of N. EEC; 2 language groups: Flemish (Dutch dialect) in N., French dialect in S. (Walloon a.); univs. at Brussels, Ghent, Liège, Louvain; cap. Brussels; a. 30,445 km²; p. (1970) 9,650,944.
Belgorod, t., **RSFSR**; N.W. of Kharkov, on N. Donets R.; rly. junc. in agr. region; p. (1970) 151,000.
Belgrade (Beograd), c., cap. of **Yugoslavia**; inland pt. on Danube at mouth of Sava R.; industl., admin. and cultural ctr.; univ.; airport; p. (est. 1969) 772,000.

Belitung or **Billiton, I.**, between Sumatra and Kalimantan, **Indonesia**; tin; a. 4,832 km²; p. 102,375.

Belize (British Honduras), self-gov. Brit. col., **Central America**; proposed indep. postponed as result of internal disorder; heavy rainfall, hurricanes; tropical forests; poor agr., underdeveloped; fishing, pine, mahogany; new cap. Belmopen; a. 22,962 km²; p. (est. 1969) 120,000.

Belize, c., former cap. of **Belize**; mahogany, dyewoods, bananas; almost devastated by hurricane 31 Oct. 1961; cap. moved to Belmopan 80 km further inland; spt.; p. (1966) 38,482.

Bellary, c., Karnataka, **India**; fort; cotton processing and tr.; p. (1971) 125,183.

Bell Bay, pt., Tasmania, **Australia**; on bank of Tamar R.; modern pt. and site of aluminium refinery.

Bell, I., Newfoundland E. Canada; in Conception Bay, 32 km N.W. of St. Johns; impt. Wabana iron-ore deposits outcrop on N.W. cst., smelted on Pictou coalfield, Nova Scotia; a. 31 km².

Belle Isle Strait, Canada; between Newfoundland and Labrador on N. shipping route to Canada from Europe.

Belleville, pt., L. Ontario, **Canada**; agr. processing; white marble nearby cement; light inds.; p. (1971) 34,498.

Belleville, t., Ill., **USA**; industl. ctr., domestic prod., coal; air force training school; p. (1970) 41,699.

Belleville, t., N.J., **USA**; machin., chemicals; p. (1970) 37,629.

Bellingham, t., spt., Wash., **USA**; agr. distribution ctr.; timber inds.; salmon canning; p. (1971) 34,498.

Bellingshausen Sea, borders Antarctica; part of S. Pac.; ice floes obstruct passage.

Bellinzona, t., **Switzerland**; on R. Ticino; 22 km N. of Lugano; three castles built on hills dominating t.; rly. engin.; tourism; p. (1969) 16,500.

Bell Rock, (Inchcape I.), rock and lighthouse 19 km S.E. of Arbroath, **Scot.**

Belluno, t., cap. of B. prov., Venezia, **N. Italy**; route ctr. at S. foot of Dolomites; cath.; engin.; p. (1969) 34,129.

Belmopan, new cap., **Belize**; at geographic ctr. of cty.; replaces Belize.

Belo Horizonte, c., cap. of Minas Gerais st. **Brazil**; impt. inland c.; ctr. rich agr. and mng. region; steel mills, food inds., textiles, diamond cutting; oil pipeline from Guanabara; univ.; p. (1970) 1,106,722.

Beloretsk, t., Bashkir ASSR, **RSFSR**; in Ural Mtns. on Belaya R.; iron, metal inds.; p. (est. 1969) 66,000.

Belorussiyan SSR, constituent rep., **USSR**; lowlying; timber; agr. on drained marshes; peat; 209,790 km²; p. (1970) 9,003,000.

Belovo, t., W. Siberia, **RSFSR**; in Kuznetsk basin; coal mng., zinc. engin.; p. (1970) 108,000.

Belper, mkt. t., Derbys., **Eng.**; hosiery, textiles, oil wks., iron foundries; p. (1971) 16,665.

Belsen, v., 24 km N.W. of Celle, **W. Germany**; notorious second world war concentration camp.

Belterra, t., dist., Pará st., N.E. **Brazil**; nr. confluence of Tapajós and Amazon Rs; site of Fordlandia scheme.

Beltsy, t., Moldavian SSR, **USSR**; on trib. of Dniester R.; agr. ctr., food processing; p. (1970) 102,000.

Belvoir, Vale of, Lincs., **Eng.**; clay vale; cattle, sheep; Stilton cheese; recent discovery of valuable coal deposits.

Bembridge, v., E. cst., I. of Wight, **Eng.**; resort, yachting.

Benalla, t., dist., Victoria, **Australia**; pastoral and agr.; p. (1972) 8,235 (t.).

Benares. *See* Varanasi.

Benbecula I., Outer Hebrides, Western Isles, **Scot.**; between Is. of N. and S. Uist; airpt. in N.; fishing; a. 93 km²; p. 900.

Bendigo, c., Victoria, **Australia**; former goldmng. dist., gold rush 1851; food processing and tr.; varied inds.; p. (1972) 45,860.

Benevento, c., Campania, **Italy**; cap. of B. prov. which contains many Roman remains; cath.; agr. processing; p. (1969) 60,082.

Benfleet, t. Essex **Eng.**; residtl.; p. (1971) 47,924.

Bengal, Bay of, part of **Indian Oc.** washing E. shores of India and W. shores of Burma; receives waters of Rs. Krishna, Ganges, Brahmaputra, Irrawaddy.

Benghazi, joint cap. (with Tripoli) of **Libya**; spt. and airpt. on G. of Sirte; univ.; former Greek Hesperides; p. (est. 1970) 170,000.

Benguela, t., **Angola**, S.W. Africa; rly. runs inland to Zaïre and Zambia; seaport now lost much tr. to Lobito; p. (est. 1969) 35,162.

Benha, t., **Egypt**; impt. mkt. t., rail and road ctr. in heart of cultivated a. of Nile delta 48 km N. of Cairo; airpt.; p. (est. 1970) 72,500.

Benin City, t. **Nigeria**; cap. of Benin st.; former notorious slave ctr.; p. (1971) 121,699.

Benin, People's Rep. of (Dahomey), W. Africa; indep. from France 1960; name changed 1975; limited transport system, agr. mainstay of comm. economy; exp. groundnuts, palm-kernels, palm oil via major pt. of Cotonou; some industl. development; brewing, chemicals, tobacco; equatorial climate, much tropical rain forest; cap. Porto Novo; a. 115,640 km²; p. (est. 1969) 2,640,000.

Beni Suef, t., **Egypt**; on Nile, 96 km S. of Cairo; ctr. of fertile agr. a.; carpets, cotton; p. (est. 1970) 99,400.

Ben Lawers, mtn., Perth and Kinross, **Scot.**; by Loch Tay; arctic and alpine flora; alt. 1,215 m.

Ben Macdhui, mtn., Kincardine and Deeside, **Scot.**; Cairngorm gr.; second highest peak in Brit. Is.; alt. 1,310 m.

Ben Nevis, mtn., Lochaber, **Scot.**; volcanic; hgst. peak in Brit. Isles alt. 1,344 m.

Benoni, t., Transvaal, **S. Africa**; gold mng. ctr.; engin.; p. (1970) 162,794.

Benrath, t., **W. Germany**; on Rhine R. nr. Düsseldorf; R. pt. and industl. t.; chemicals, machin.

Bensberg, t., N. Rhine-Westphalia, **W. Germany**; 16 km from Cologne; leather gds.; mainly residtl.; foundries; cas.; p. (est. 1969) 40,516.

Bensheim, t., Hesse, **W. Germany**; ctr. of fruit and wine dist. on E. edge Rhine valley; textiles, paper, metallurgy; p. (est. 1969) 26,975.

Bentley with Arksey, t., South Yorks., **Eng.**; p. (1971) 22,888.

Benton Harbor, t., Mich., **USA**; midway along E. cst. L. Michigan; p. (1970) 16,481.

Benue R., **Nigeria-Cameroon**; rises in Adamawa mtns.; forms ch. trib. of Niger R.; R. pts. and agr. tr.; length 1,392 km.

Ben Vorlich, mtn., Perth and Kinross, **Scot.**; alt. 983 m.

Benwell, t., Tyne and Wear, **Eng.**; sub. of Newcastle.

Ben Wyvis, mtn., Ross and Cromarty, **Scot.**; nr. Dingwall; alt. 1,046 m.

Ben-y-Gloe, mtn., Glen Tilt, Perth and Kinross, **Scot.**; alt. 1,120 m.

Beograd. *See* Belgrade.

Beppu, c., Kyushu, **Japan**; hot spring resort; p. (est. 1971) 124,000.

Berbera, pt., **Somalia**, on G. of Aden; exp. livestock from pastoral hinterland; new deep-sea pt. completed 1969; airport; p. (est. 1963) 12,219.

Berchtesgaden, v., **W. Germany**; mtn. resort 24 km S. of Salzburg; Hitler's mtn. retreat; tourism; potash.

Berck-Plage, resort, Pas-de-Calais, **France**, on Eng. Channel; p. (1968) 13,690.

Berdichev, t., Ukrainian SSR, **USSR**; ctr. of sugar a.; engin., lt. inds.; p. (est. 1969) 61,000.

Berdyansk, c., Ukrainian SSR, **USSR**; pt. on Sea of Azov; agr. ctr.; machin.; health resort; p. (1970) 100,000.

Bere Regis, mkt. t., Dorset, **Eng.**; Saxon royal residence.

Berezina, R., **USSR**; trib. of Dnieper; forms part of Baltic-Black Sea waterway; 608 km long.

Berezniki, t., E. European **RSFSR**; pt. on Kolva R., W. Urals; salt, chemicals, paper; p. (1970) 145,000.

Bergama, t., **Turkey**; anc. Pergamos, ruins; morocco leather inds.; agr. tr.; p. (1965) 24,113.

Bergamo, c., Lombardy, **Italy**; 54 km N.E. Milan; cath. and academy; silk industry; p. (1969) 125,310.

Bergen, spt., W. cst. **Norway**; univ.; most impt. comm. pt. in kingdom; shipping, fishing; mftg. inds.; birthplace of Grieg; p. (est. 1969) 115,964.

Bergen op Zoom, t., N. Brabant, **Neth.**; sugar refining, engin.; p. (1968) 38,489.

Bergerac, t., Dordogne, S.W. **France**; impt. bridge over Dordogne R.; mkt. for wines and luxury foods; anc. Huguenot stronghold; p. (1968) 28,015.
Bergisches Land, terr., N. Rhine-Westphalia, **W. Germany**; specialised iron and steel prod.; chemicals, machin.; inc. ts. of Solingen, Remscheid, Velbert, Wuppertal.
Bergisch-Gladbach, t. N. Rhine-Westphalia, **W. Germany**; 11 km E. of Cologne, paper, metallurgy, textiles; p. (est. 1969) 49,704.
Berhampur, t., Orissa, **India**; admin. and educational ctr.; p. (1971) 117,662.
Bergstrasse, region, Baden-Württemberg, **W. Germany**; fruit-growing.
Bering Current (**Okhotsk Current**, or **Oyashio**), ocean current, N. **Pac. Oc.**; flows through Bering Strait from Arctic, along E. cst. of Kamchatka and Japanese Is. Hokkaido, Honshu; relatively cold; moderate summer temperatures along csts. causes fogs.
Bering Sea, part of N. Pac. **Oc.** between Aleutian Is. and B. Strait; fishing; a. 2,274,020 km².
Bering Strait, narrow sea which separates Asia from N. America, and connects Bering Sea with Arctic Oc.; 58 km wide at narrowest part.
Berkeley, v., Gloucs., **Eng.**; nr. R. Severn, 24 km N. of Bristol; civil nuclear power-sta.
Berkeley, c., Cal., **USA**; univ.; chemicals; now inc. in San Francisco; p. (1970) 116,716.
Berkhamsted, Herts., **Eng.**; mkt. t.; chemicals; cas. ruins, 17th cent. school; birthplace of William Cowper the poet; p. (1971) 15,439.
Berkshire, non-met. co., **Eng.**; chalk downland inc. Inkpen Beacon, White Horse Hills; drained by Thames and tribs.; residtl.; electronics, biscuits; dairying; Windsor Gr. Park; Ascot racecourse; a. 1,256 km²; p. (1971) 620,000.
Berlin, c., former cap. of **Germany**, Europe; on Spree R.; divided into 4 occupied zones 1945; Soviet (now E. Berlin), British, American, French (now W. Berlin); W. Berlin forms enclave within E. Germany; focal point of escape attempts from E. to W. led to construction of "Berlin Wall"; W. Berlin major industl. ctr. aided by American and W. German capital; educational, cultural and tourist ctr.; relaxation of cold war adding to metropolitan character of c. as meeting place between E. and W.; wartime reconstruction has lagged in E. Berlin; p. (est. 1970) 2,134,256 (W. Berlin); 1,200,000 (E. Berlin).
Bermondsey. *See* **Southwark**.
Bermuda, Brit. gr. coral Is. (360 in no. of which 20 are inhabited) N. Atlantic; about 1,120 km E. of S.C.; Hamilton, on Long I. is the ch. t.; Brit. and US air and naval stas.; favourite winter resort for Americans; inds. attracted by tax incentives; no surface water; total a. 54 km²; p. (est. 1969) 52,000.
Bern, c., cap. of B. can. and fed. cap. **Switzerland**; on Aare R.; cath., univ.; textiles, musical instruments chocolate; H.Q. of Postal Union; bear pit; p. (1969) 166,800 (c.), 258,000 (met. a.).
Bern, can., **Switzerland**; fertile valleys, dairying; watches; hydroelectric power; plans for separate can. in Jura reg.; a. 6,881 km²; p. (1969) 1,005,000.
Bernard, Great St., one of the Alps in the S. of the Valais, **Switzerland**; highest point 3,390 m; height of mtn. pass between Italy (Aosta) and Switzerland (Martigny), 2,477 m; famous hospice for travellers in monastery on mtn.; road tunnel completed 1962.
Bernard, Little St., one of Graian Alps, Savoy, S. of Mt. Blanc, **France**; pass traversed by Hannibal 218 B.C.
Bernburg, t., Halle, **E. Germany**; cas.; chemicals, salt mng.; p. (est. 1970) 45,322.
Bernese Oberland (**Berner Alpen**), alpine region, **Switzerland**; 35 peaks over 3,000 m inc. Finsteraarhorn and Jungfrau; tourist a. inc. resorts of Interlaken and Grindelwald.
Bernina Alps, **Switzerland**; alt. 4,050 m.
Berri, t., S. **Australia**; ctr. of irrigated fruit growing a. on R. Murray; wines; p. (1966) 2,224.
Berri, oilfield, **Saudi Arabia**; 72 km N.W. of Ras Tannura; the field extends offshore.
Berwick, l. gov. dist., former co., Borders Reg., **S.E. Scot.**; a. of sheep rearing and woollen inds. in S. Uplands; a. 875 km²; p. (1971) 17,200.
Berwick-upon-Tweed, Northumberland, **Eng.**; spt. on mouth of Tweed; border t.; fishing, lt. engin., tweeds, knitwear; cas. ruins; p. (1971) 11,644.
Berwyn, t., Ill., **USA**; sub. of Chicago; p. (1970) 52,502.
Besançon, t., cap. of Doubs dep., **France**; cath., observatory, univ.; farm implements, textiles; watch- and clock-making; birthplace of Victor Hugo; p. (1968) 113,220 (t.), 116,197 (met. a.).
Besche, t., Saarland, **W. Germany**; oil refining.
Beskids, W. and E., (**Beskidy Zachodnie**), mtn. range, **Poland**, **ČSSR**, E. **Europe**; northern range of Carpathian mtn. system, seldom exceeds alt. 1,200 m, many passes; forested; tourism; length 352 km.
Bessarabia, terr., ceded to **USSR** by Romania 1940, and now part of Moldavian SSR; agr. region.
Bessemer, t., Ala., **USA**; iron and steel; p. (1970) 33,428.
Bethany (**El Azarieh**), v., on Mt. of Olives 6 km W. of Jerusalem, **Jordan**.
Bethel, anc. c., the modern **Beitin**, **Jordan**; 16 km N. Jerusalem.
Bethesday, t., Gwynedd, **Wales**; slate, lt. engin. p. (1971) 4,167.
Bethlehem, t., **Jordan**; 9 km S.W. Jerusalem; birthplace of Christ; p. (est. 1967) 16,313.
Bethlehem, t., Penns., **USA**; 80 km N. of Philadelphia; iron-wks.; univ.; p. (1970) 72,686.
Bethnal Green, dist., London, **Eng.**; in E. End of London; furniture, clothing; now in Tower Hamlets.
Béthune, t., Pas-de-Calais, **France**; rail and canal ctr. for coalfield; mkt. t.; p. (1968) 28,379 144,678 (met. a.).
Betteshanger, v., Kent, **Eng.**; on N. flank of N. Downs, 6 km W. of Deal; coal mng.
Bettws-y-Coed, t., Gwynedd, **Wales**; waterfalls; tourism; p. (1971) 726.
Beuel, t., N. Rhine-Westphalia, **W. Germany**; on E. bank R. Rhine opposite Bonn; chemicals, furniture; p. (est. 1969) 38,668.
Beuthan. *See* **Bytom**.
Beverley, mkt. t., Humberside, **Eng.**; famous minster (13th cent.); agr. processing; p. (1971) 17,124.
Beverly, c., Mass., **USA**; footwear, machin.; p. (1970) 38,348.
Beverly Hills, t., Cal., **USA**; sub. of Los Angeles; home of many film celebrities; p. (1970) 33,416.
Beverwijk, t., nr. Haarlem, N. Holland, **Neth.**; agr. prods.; p. (1968) 42,008.
Bewdley, Hereford and Worcs. **Eng.**; mkt. t. on R. Severn; residtl.; p. (1971) 7,212.
Bexhill-on-Sea, t. East Sussex **Eng.**; resort; p. (1971) 32,849.
Bexley, former bor., W. Kent; now outer bor., Greater London, **Eng.**; inc. Chislehurst and Sidcup (N. of the A.20) Crayford and Erith; p. (1971) 216,172.
Béziers, t., Hérault, **France**; ctr. of wine, brandy tr. and inds.; chemicals; p. (1968) 82,271.
Bezwada. *See* **Vijayawada**.
Bhadravati, t., Karnataka, **India**; steel; p. (1971) 61,155 (t.), 101,358 (met. a.).
Bhagalpur, t., Bihar, **India**; agr. tr. ctr. on R. Ganges; p. (1971) 172,202.
Bhamo, t., Upper **Burma**; on Irrawaddy; inland limit of steam boats; mkt. ctr.; ruby mines; p. 10,000.
Bhandara, cap. of Bhandara dist., Maharashtra, **India**; 48 km E. of Nagpur; cotton cloth, brass mftg.; p. (1961) 27,710.
Bhatpara, t., W. Bengal, **India**; on R. Hooghly; industl. t.; jute, engin.; p. (1971) 204,750.
Bhaunager, t., Gujarat, **India**; pt. on G. of Cambay; exp. cotton, oilseeds; p. (1971) 225,358.
Bhilai, t., Madhya Pradesh, **India**; steel plant; rails and rly. sleepers; p. (1961) of industl. t. 86,116; of Durg 47,114.
Bhim-Gora, sacred pool, place of Hindu pilgrimage, Uttar Pradesh, **India**.
Bhopal, c., cap. of Madhya Pradesh, **India**; impt. tr. ctr.; varied inds.; prehistoric cave paintings nearby; p. (1971) 298,022 (c.), 384,859 (met. a.).
Bhutan, kingdom, indep. mtn. st., E. Himalayas; heavy monsoon rain, rich tropical vegetation., valuable forests; N.–S. ridges and valleys result in semi-closed communities; first motor link with India opened 1962; cap. Thimbu:

a. c. 46,620 km²; alt. 7,558 m (Kula Kangri); p. scattered and nomadic (est. 1969) 770,000.
Bhubaneswar, t., cap. of Orissa, **India**; 29 km from Cuttack; admin. ctr.; Hindu temples, pilgrimage ctr.; p. (1971) 105,491.
Biafra, Bight of. *See* **Bonny, Bight of.**
Bialystok, t., **Poland**; cap. of B. prov., nr. Grodno; major, diversified industl. ctr.; rly. ctr.; p. (1970) 158,500.
Biarritz, t., Pyrénées-Atlantique dep., **France**; on Bay of Biscay; seaside resort; p. (1968) 26,985.
Biberach, t., Baden-Württemberg, **W. Germany**; on R. Kinzig; spa; wood, metal and engin. inds.; p. (est. 1969) 25,456.
Bicester, Oxford, **Eng.**; anc. mkt. t., N.E. of Oxford; p. (1971) 12,340.
Biddulph, t., Staffs., **Eng.**; coal mng., machin., textiles, furniture; residtl.; p. (1971) 17,372.
Bideford, N. Devon, **Eng.**; pt. on estuary R. Torridge; mkt., boat-bldg.; resort; p. (1971) 11,766.
Biel (Bienne), t., Berne, **Switzerland**; nr. Lake B.; watches; impt. industl. ctr.; p. (1969) 67,800.
Bielawa, t., Wroclaw prov., S.W. **Poland**; textiles; p. (1970) 31,000.
Bielefeld, t., Rhine-Westphalia, **W. Germany**; ch. ctr. of linen industry; machin., bicycles; p. (est. 1969) 168,700.
Biella, t., Vercelli, **Italy**; textiles; p. (1961) (est. 1968) 53,839.
Bielsko-Biala, t., Katowice prov. **Poland**; woollens, linen, metal, chemicals; p. (est. 1969) 102,700.
Bien-hoa, t., nr. Ho Chi-minh City, **S. Vietnam**; sugar refining; cotton mills.
Bies-Bosch, reclaimed fenland area between N. Brabant and S.W. **Neth.**; sugar refining, dairying; a. 142 km².
Biggar, sm. burgh, Lanark, **Scot.**; 213 m in Southern Uplands; p. (1971) 1,637.
Biggin Hill, Greater London, **Eng**; nr. Orpington; famous airfield of Battle of Britain.
Biggleswade, t., Beds. **Eng.**; in valley of R. Ivel, 14 km S.E. of Bedford; ctr. of fruit-growing and mkt. gardening dist.; hydraulic machin. tools, hosiery, caravans; p. (1971) 9,598.
Big Horn Mtns., Wyo. and Mont., **USA**; Rockies; favourite film location; attractive agr. valleys; highest alt., 3,600 m.
Bihać, t., **Yugoslavia**; on R. Una; recent industl. development; timber processing.
Bihar, st., N.W. **India**; in Ganges basin; hilly; bulk of p. in agr. N.; irrigation; minerals in S.E.: coal, iron, mica; steelwks. at Jamshedpur, oil refining at Barauni; cap. Patna, admin. ctr. Ranchi; a. 173,882 km²; p. (1971) 56,387,296.
Bihar, t., Bihar, **India**; within middle Ganges valley nr. Patna; p. (1971) 100,046.
Biisk, c., Siberia, **USSR**; ctr. of rich agr. a.; meat packing, textiles; p. (1970) 186,000.
Bijagós, Achipelago dos (Bissagos Is.); off W. cst. **Guinea-Bissau**; c. 14 Is.; coconuts, rice; ch. t. Bolama on Bolama I.; a. 1,554 km².
Bijapur, t., Karnataka, **India**; cotton tr. and inds.; ruins; former cap. of B. kingdom; p. (1971) 103,931.
Bikaner, t., Rajasthan, **India**; in Thar desert; on former caravan route; wool tr., bldg. stone, handicrafts; p. (1971) 188,518 (t.), 208,894 (met. a.).
Bikini, atoll, **Pac. Oc.**; scene of atomic-bomb tests (1946).
Bilaspur, t., Madhya Pradesh, **India**; silks, cottons; p. (1971) 98,410 (t.), 130,740 (met. a.).
Bilbao, spt., N. **Spain**; cap. Basque prov. of Viscaya; formerly famous for rapier making; iron ore, smelting; pipeline from Ayoluengo oilfield; p. (est. 1969) 369,559.
Billinge and Winstanley, t., Lancs., **Eng.**; former coal-mng. a.; p. (1971) 11,379.
Billingham, t. Cleveland, **Eng.**; on N. of Tees estuary; major petro-chemical plant.
Billings, t., Mont., **USA**; agr. tr. ctr. in irrigated a.; sulphur plant; p. (1970) 61,581.
Billingsgate, London, **Eng.**; old river-gate and wharf, now ch. fish mkt. of England.
Bilma (Kawar), oasis t., **Niger**; on caravan route from Tripoli to Agadés and L. Chad; salt tr., dates; p. c. 1,000.
Billiton I. *See* **Belitung.**
Biloxi, t., Miss., **USA**; fishing, tourist ctr.; US Coast Guard air base; p. (1970) 47,814 (c.), 131,268 (met. a.).
Bilston, t., West Midlands, **Eng.**; part of Wolverhampton; iron and steel.
Bingen, t., Rhineland Palatinate, **W. Germany**; at S. entrance to Rhine gorge; wine; beautiful scenery; tourism; p. (est. 1967) 20,700.
Bingerville, spt., **Ivory Coast, W. Africa**; rubber processing.
Bingham Canyon, t., N. Utah, **USA**; silver, gold, lead; major open pit copper mine; p. (1970) 31.
Binghampton, N.Y., **USA**; on Susquehanna R.; boot factories, aircraft components, cameras; p. (1970) 63,229 (c.), 297,959 (met. a.).
Bingley, West Yorks., **Eng.**; mkt. t. on R. Aire, 26 km N.W. of Leeds; textiles, engin., agr.; p. (1971) 26.540.
Bintan I., lgst. island of Riouw archipelago, **Indonesia**; bauxite, tin.
Bintenne, dist., **Sri Lanka**; remote a., sparse p.; lge. Gal Oya reservoir; tea and rubber estates.
Biratnagar, t., S.E. **Nepal**, in the Tarai; jute, sugar, cotton milling, stainless steel; p. (1971) 44,938.
Birbhum, dist., W. Bengal, **India**; cap. Suri; healthy climate; rice, sugar; mnfs. silk, cotton; a. 4,550 km²; p. (1961) 1,446,158
Birkenhead, Merseyside, **Eng.**; spt. on R. Mersey, opposite Liverpool; handles industl. goods; heavy and pt. processing inds.; ship-bldg.; p. (1971) 137,738.
Birmingham, c., West Midlands, **Eng.**; industl. cap. Midlands, second lgst. c. Gt. Britain; metal inds.; motor vehicles, components and accessories; major growth due to Industl. Revolution; univ., cath.; p. (1971) 1,031,366.
Birmingham, t., cap. of Ala., **USA**; coal, iron, limestone, steel, aircraft, chemicals, textiles; p. (1970) 297,364 (c.), 729,984 (met. a.).
Birnam, v., Perth and Kinross, **Scot.**; location of Birnam Wood in *Macbeth*; former royal forest.
Birobidzhan, or Jewish aut. oblast, **RSFSR**; in Khabarovsk terr.; agr., timber and mng. inds.; a. 35,988 km²; cap. Birobidzhan City; p. (1968) 174,000 (inc. 15,000 Jews).
Birr, U.D. Offaly, **R.o.I.**; mkt. t. on Brosna R.; observatory; p. (1966) 3,266.
Bir Tlacsin, Libya; 192 km S.W. Tripoli; oilfields.
Bisbee, t., Arizona, **USA**; very rich copper deposits, gold, silver, lead; p. (1970) 8,328.
Biscarosse, Landes dep., **France**; 72 km S.W. Bordeaux; rocket and missile testing range projected; p. (1968) 7,781.
Biscay, Bay of, stormy a. of Atl. Oc., W. of France and N. of Spain, from Ushant to C. Ortegal; the Roman Sinus Aquitanicus; heavy seas.
Bisceglie, t., Apulia, **Italy**; spt. on E. cst. 35 km N.W. of Bari; tr. in wine and olives; light inds.; cath.; p. (est. 1968) 44,317.
Bischofswerda, t., Dresden, **E. Germany**; quarrying, glass and iron inds.; rly. ctr.; p. (1963) 11,285.
Bishop Auckland, t., Durham, **Eng.**; palace of Bishop of Durham; iron, lt. engin.; former coal mng.; p. (1971) 33,292.
Bishopbriggs, sm. burgh, Strathkelvin, **Scot.**; p. (1971) 21,684.
Bishop Rock, isolated rock, lighthouse, Scilly Is., **Eng.**; 58 km S.W. of Land's End, Cornwall; recognised internationally as E. end of trans-Atlantic ocean crossing.
Bishop's Stortford, Herts., **Eng.**; mkt. t. on Stort R.; light inds.; Hatfield forest nearby; Norman cas.; p. (1971) 22,054.
Biskra, t., **Algeria**; admin. ctr., winter resort; oasis nearby; date mkt.; p. (1966) 59,052.
Bisley, v., Surrey, **Eng.**; ranges of Nat. Rifle Ass. on B. common.
Bismarck, t., st. cap. N.D., **USA**; on Missouri R.; agr. mkt. ctr.; p. (1969) 33,700.
Bismarck Archipelago, volcanic gr., S.W. Pac. Oc., off New Guinea, admin. by **Australia**; p. (est. 1962) 174,115.
Bisotūn, t., **Iran**; in ruins; monuments to Darius I (the Great).
Bissagos Is. *See* **Bijagós, Achipelago dos.**
Bissau, t., cap. of **Guinea-Bissau**; former ctr. of slave tr.; airpt.; p. (1970) 62,101.
Bitola, t., Macedonia, **Yugoslavia**; varied mnfs., recent industl. development; mosques; p. (1971) 65,851.

Bitonto, t., Apulia, on E. cst. 11 km N.W. of Bari; Italy; olive oil, wine; cath.; p. (est. 1968) 41,749.
Bitterfeld, t., Halle, **E. Germany**; lignite mng., engin., chemicals; p. (est. 1970) 28,964.
Bitter Lakes, Isthmus of Suez, **Egypt**, utilised by Suez Canal.
Biwa-ko, lgst. lake in **Japan**, S. Honshu; 101 m a.s.l.; canal to Kyoto provides hydroelectric power; superb scenery, historical associations; tourism; a. 675 km^2.
Biysk or **Bisk**, c., Altai terr., **RSFSR**; pt. on Biya R.; terminus of branch of Turk-Sib. rly.; p. (est. 1967) 181,000.
Bizerte, c., N. **Tunisia**; pt. and naval sta. on Med.; the anc. Hippo Zaritus; fishing, oil refining, steelwks., tyres; p. (1966) 95,023.
Björnborg. *See* **Pori.**
Black Belt, coastlands of Miss. and Ala., **USA**, where black soil prairie land is good for cotton.
Blackburn, t., Lancs., **Eng.**; once major cotton weaving ctr.; engin., lt. inds.; p. (1971) 101,672
Black Country, Midlands **Eng.**; formerly impt. iron-working and coal-mng. dist. mainly in S. West Midlands; now a. of lt. engin.; about 130 km^2 in extent.
Blackdown Hills, Devon and Somerset, **Eng.**; sandstone hills rising over 305 m.
Black Forest. *See* **Schwarzwald.**
Blackheath, open common, S.E. London **Eng.**; mustering place of Wat Tyler's (1381) and Jack Cade's (1450) revolutionary peasants; now forms main attraction of expensive residtl. a.; a. 108 ha.
Black Hills, mtns., between S.D. and Wyo., **USA**; highest, Horney Peak, 2,208 m; form part of Nat. Park.
Black Isle, peninsula, between Cromarty and Beauly Firths, Ross and Cromarty, **Scot.**; agr., fisheries, quarrying; a. 621 km^2.
Black Mtns., Powys and Dyfed, S. **Wales**; rise to 802 m in Brecknock Van, sandstone plateau; moorland; valleys used for reservoirs; Nat. Park.
Black Mtns., Powys, S. **Wales**; rise to 811 m in Waun Fach.
Blackpool, t., Lancs., **Eng.**; on cst. of Fylde dist.; one of major Brit. resorts; p. (1971) 151,311.
Black Prairie, region, Texas, **USA**; extends 560 km S.W. from Ouachita Mtns. to Austin; contains very fertile Black Waxy and Grande Prairie sub-regions devoted almost entirely to cotton growing; ch. ts., Dallas, Fort Worth, Austin; a. 77,700 km^2.
Blackrod, t., Gtr. Manchester, **Eng.**; nr. Chorley; former cotton weaving; p. (1971) 4,801.
Black Sea, bordered by 4 sts., **USSR** (N. and E.), **Turkey** (S.), **Bulgaria**, **Romania** (W.); receives waters of Danube, Dniester, Dnieper, Don, Bug; stagnant and lifeless below 146 m; fisheries in N. and W.; oil exploration by Turkey; a. 424,760 km^2 (exc. Sea of Azov).
Blacksod Bay, cst. of Mayo, **R.o.I.**
Black Volta, R., rises in **Upper Volta**, flows E. and S. into L Volta, **Ghana**; length *c.* 1,200 km.
Blackwater R., **N. Ireland**; rising in Dungannon, it forms border with R.o.I.; enters L. Neagh; 80 km long.
Blackwater R., **R.o.I.**; flows from Knockanefune to enter Atl. Oc. at pt. and resort of Youghal; chain of sm. ts. along course; 144 km long.
Blaenavon, t., Gwent, **Wales**; former coal mng.; p. (1971) 7,182.
Blagoveshchensk, t., E. Siberia, **RSFSR**, on Chinese bdr. and R. Amur; wat. pl.; engin., sawmilling, flour milling; on Trans-Siberian rly.; p. (1970) 128,000.
Blair Atholl, v., Perth and Kinross, **Scot.**; tourist resort; cas.; seat of Duke of Atholl.
Blairgowrie and Rattray, burgh, Perth and Kinross, **Scot.**; at foot of Scot. Highlands; mkt. t. in Strathmore fruit growing dist.; p. (1971) 5,553.
Blakeney, v., N. Norfolk, **Eng.**; nr. sand spit; yachting; wild fowl.
Blanc, Mt. *See* **Mont Blanc.**
Blandford or **Blandford Forum**, Dorset, **Eng.**; on R. Stour; pastoral mkt. t. since 13th cent.; p. (1971) 3,643.
Blantyre, c., **Malawi**; in Shire Highlands; linked by rail to Beira (Moçambique); comm. ctr.; timber processing; p. (1966) 109,795 (met. a.).
Blantyre, v., East Kilbride, **Scot.**; Lower B. birthplace of David Livingstone.
Blarney, v., 6 km N.W. Cork, **R.o.I.**; cas. and Blarney stone; p. (1966) 932.
Blasket Is., Kerry, **R.o.I.**; rocky Is.; uninhabited since 1953.
Blaydon, t., Tyne and Wear, **Eng.**; former coal mng.; p. (1971) 32,018.
Bled, glacial L., Slovenia, **Yugoslavia**; tourism.
Blenheim, t., S.I., **N.Z.**; fruit; p. (1971) 14,760.
Blenheim, v., **W. Germany**; scene of battle (1704) when English and Austrians under Marlborough defeated the French and Bavarians; Blenheim Palace, Woodstock, Oxon, **Eng.**, named in honour of this victory.
Blessington, L., Wicklow, **R.o.I.**; glacial L., now serves as reservoir for Dublin.
Bletchley, Bucks., **Eng.**; expanded t.; p. (1971) 30,608.
Blida, t., **Algeria**; agr. tr., citrus fruits; p. (1967) 87,000.
Bloemfontein, t., cap. O.F.S., **S. Africa**; on plateau, alt. 1,393 m; route and tr. ctr.; univ.; p. (1970) 180,179 (met. a.).
Blois, t., cap. of Loire-et-Cher dep., **France**; historic t. on Loire R.; Renaissance château; wines; p. (1968) 44,762.
Bloomfield, t., N.J., **USA**; pharmaceuticals, metal and elec. gds.; sub. N.J. c.; p. (est. 1969) 53,000.
Bloomington, t., Ill., **USA**; comm. ctr. and industl. t. in rich agr. and coalmng. a.; univ.; p. (1970) 39,398 (c.), 103,308 (met. a.).
Bloomington, t., Ind., **USA**; electronic equipment, furniture, structural glass; univ.; p. (est. 1969) 48,000.
Bloomsbury, dist., London, **Eng.**; fashionable dist. with many squares; famous for B. gr. of authors in first quarter of 20th cent.; inc. Brit. Museum, Univ. of London.
Bludenz, t., W. **Austria**; cotton, watches; p. (est. 1965) 11,400.
Bluefields, t., **Nicaragua**; spt. on E. cst.; exp. bananas, timber; p. (1967) 17,706.
Blue Grass, dist., Ky., **USA**; area where blue grass abundant; horse breeding.
Blue Mountains, t., N.S.W., **Australia**; tourist ctr.; new t. (1947); p. (est. 1968) 32,110.
Blue Mtns., **Jamaica**; famous for coffee; dense forest; tourism; average alt. 900–1,200 m, rising to 2,294 m in Blue Mtn. peak.
Blue Nile (Bahr-el-Azraq), R., rises in tablelands of Ethiopia, joins the White Nile at Khartoum; its seasonal flooding provides the bulk of water for irrigation in Sudan and Egypt.
Blue Ridge Mtns., S. Penn., Ga., **USA**; inc. Shenandoah valley; superb scenery, resorts; average alt. 600–1,200 m, rising to 1,737 m in Grandfather Mtn.
Bluff, S.I., **N.Z.**; 29 km from Invercargill; spt. for Southland prov.; major aluminium ctr.; p. (1971) 3,246.
Blumenau, mkt. t., Santa Catarina st., **Brazil**; butter, sugar; p. (est. 1968) 84,139.
Blyth., spt., Northumberland, **Eng.**; on coalfield; shipbldg.; p. (1971) 34,617.
Bo, t., **Sierra Leone**; gold; admin. H.Q.; p. (1963) of dist. 209,000.
Boa Vista, t., R. pt., cap. Roraima st., **Brazil**; p. (est. 1967) 34,659.
Bobbio, t., Emilia-Romagna, **Italy**, in northern Apennines; ctr. European cultural life, 9th-12th cent.; St. Columban founded monastery, 612.
Bobo Dioulassa, t., **Upper Volta**; agr. tr., gold mng.; p. (1967) 68,000.
Bobigny, N.E. sub. of Paris, cap. of Seine-St. Denis dep., **France**; varied inds.; p. (1968) 39,453.
Bobruysk, t., Belorussiyan SSR, **USSR**; pt. on R. Berezina; engin., sawmilling, paper, cellulose, grain; p. (1970) 138,000.
Boca Costa, south-facing volcanic escarpment, **Guatemala**; ch. coffee belt.
Bocholt, t., N. Rhine-Westphalia, **W. Germany**; machin., textiles, elec. gds.; p. (est. 1967) 47,200.
Bochum, t., N. Rhine-Westphalia, **W. Germany**; heart of Ruhr iron and steel ind.; known since 9th cent.; new (1962) Univ. of Ruhr; p. (1968) 346,805.
Boden, t., **Sweden**; on Luleå R.; military and comm. ctr.; p (est. 1970) 24,727.
Bodensee (**L. Constance**), S.W. West Germany and

Switzerland; 72 km long, 14 km wide.; R. Rhine flows through; fruit and horticulture on warmer slopes of L.

Bodmin, co. t., Cornwall, **Eng.**; on S.W. flank of Bodmin moor; china clay, lt. engin.; p. (1971) 9,204.

Bodmin Moor, upland, N.E. Cornwall, **Eng.**; lower slopes cultivated, higher slopes used for sheep pastures; average alt. 300 m, highest point, Brown Willy, alt, 419 m; major ctr. of china clay quarrying.

Bodö, t., **Norway**; nr. Lofoten Is.; spt., fish processing; N. rly. terminus; p. (est. 1967) 14,000.

Boeotia, region of anc. **Greece**; scene of many battles; Thebes was the ch. c.; home of Hesiod and Pindar.

Bogdo Ula, massif, Sinkiang, **China**; forms N. perimeter of Turfan depression; 240 km wide, average alt. 4,000 m, rising to 5,479 m in Turpanat Targh.

Bognor Regis, t., West Sussex, **Eng.**; residtl.; seaside resort; p. (1971) 34,389.

Bogor, t., Java, **Indonesia**; rubber factory, textiles, footwear; p. (1971) 195,882.

Bogota, cap. and lgst. c. of **Colombia**; in E. Cordilleras, 2,745 m a.s.l.; univ., nat. observatory, colonial architecture; political, social and financial ctr. of rep.; p. (est. 1972) 2,680,100 (c.), 2,818,300 (met. a.).

Bohemia, historic region, former kingdom, W. **ČSSR**; plateau drained by R. Elbe; borders W. Germany; agr. dist.; minerals inc. lignite, graphite; textiles, sugar, pottery.

Böhmerwald (Bohemian Forest), forested range of mtns. between ČSSR and Bavaria, **W. Germany**; 240 km long; alt. 1,479 m at Aber; region of poor soils; sm. farms; some mng. and quarrying.

Bohol I., **Philippines**; maize, coconuts, rice; a. 3,864 km²; p. (1970) 674,806.

Boise, t., cap. of Idaho, **USA**; financial ctr.; timber mills; hot springs; p. (1970) 73,330 (c.), 109,398 (met. a.).

Bois-Colombes, sub. of Paris, Hauts-de-Seine dep., **France**; p. (1968) 28,934.

Boksburg, t., Transvaal, **S. Africa**; industl., former coal-mng.; t. p. (1970) 104,745.

Bolama, spt., Bijagós Is., **Guinea-Bissau**; p. c. 4,000.

Bolan Pass, Baluchistan, **Pakistan**; pass from Pakistan to Afghanistan; summit 1,800 m.

Bolbec, t., Seine-Maritime, **France**; 19 km E. of Le Havre; textiles; elec. engin.; p. (1968) 13,053.

Boldon, t., Tyne and Wear, **Eng.**; coal mng.; p. (1971) 23,904.

Boleslawiec (Bunzlau), t., Lower Silesia, **Poland**; German before 1945; on the Bóbr R., pottery; p. (1970) 30,500.

Boliden, t., N. **Sweden**; impt. deposits of copper and arsenic.

Bolivia, inland rep., S. **America**; land-locked, 9 deps.; cap. nominally Sucre, actual admin. H.Q. La Paz; politically unstable; much US investment but discouraged by nationalism from late 1960s; p. dispersed over wide a.; relief makes transport difficult; forests; savannahs; agr. in backward conditions; rubber, quinine, cattle, hides; ch. exp. tin; petroleum; language Spanish; a. 1,331,661 km²; p. (est. 1969) 4,804,000.

Bollington, t., Cheshire, **Eng.**; nr. Macclesfield; textile finishing; p. (1971) 6,610.

Bologna, c., N. **Italy**; cap. of B. prov. on N. flank of Apennines; impt. route ctr. commanding road (over Futa Pass) and rly. (through Apennine Tunnel) across Apennines to Florence; mnfs. sugar, macaroni; nuclear research ctr.; long-standing cultural and educational ctr.; p. (1969) 490,675.

Bologoye, **RSFSR**; depot and impt. junc. on Leningrad and Moscow rly.; p. 10,000.

Bolsa Island, Cal., **USA**; nuclear power and desalination project in progress.

Bolsena, L., Latium region, **Italy**; occupies lge. extinct volcanic crater in S. of Tuscan Hills 96 km N.W. of Rome; a. (approx.) 129 km².

Bolshoya Volga, t., **RSFSR**; 128 km N. of Moscow, at junc. of Volga and Moscow Volga Canal; Soviet Institute of Nuclear Studies.

Bolsover, t., Derbys., **Eng.**; limestone, coal, textiles; cas.; Hardwick Hall 6 km to S.; p. (1971) 10,956.

Bolt Head, headland, Devon, **Eng.**; alt. 131 m.

Bolton, t., Gtr. Manchester, **Eng.**; cotton, textiles, engin.; p. (1971) 153,977.

Bolton, Abbey, North Yorks., **Eng.**; ruined Augustinian Priory.

Bolus Head, C., Kerry, **R.o.I.**

Bolzano, t., Trentino Alto Adige, **Italy**; on R. Isarco at S. approach to Brenner Pass; resort; p. (1969) 104,699.

Boma, t., **Zaïre**; pt. on estuary of R. Zaïre; exp. timber, cocoa, palm prods., bananas; p. (est. 1967) 79,230.

Bombay, spt., cap. of Maharashtra st., **India**; harbour, docks, rly. ctr.; univ.; greatest cotton ctr. in republic; pt. handles nearly half of India's foreign tr.; oil refinery; film industry; univ., fine public bldgs.; p. (1971) 5,970,575.

Bonaire I., **Neth. Antilles**; a. 287 km²; p. (1968) 7,537.

Bondy, N.E. sub. of Paris, Seine-St. Denis dep., **France**; brewing, chemicals; p. (1968) 51,692.

Bône. *See* Annaba.

Bo'ness, burgh, W. Lothian, **Scot.**; spt. on Firth of Forth, 6 km E. of Grangemouth; foundries, timber yards; p. (1971) 12,853.

Bonifacio, spt., Corse du Sud, Corsica, **France**; opposite Sardinia, on Strait of Bonifacio; p. (1968) 2,433.

Bonin Is., Pac. Oc., **Japan**; 15 Is., volcanic; 960 km S. of Tokyo; a. 103 km²; p. (1965) 203.

Bonn, c., fed. cap. of **W. Germany**; at confluence of Rs. Sieg and Rhine; univ.; seat of W. German parliament; birthplace of Beethoven; founded in Roman times; varied inds. inc. printing, publishing; p. (est. 1967) 138,000 (c.); (est. 1969) 300,400 (met. a.).

Bonnet a l'Eveque, mtn., **Haiti**; sheer sides, flat top; site of La Ferrière fortress, alt. 900 m.

Bonneville Dam, Ore., Wash., **USA**; across R. Columbia 64 km above Portland (Ore.), provides irrigation to valleys in Columbia-Snake Plateau; locks permit navigation and provide hydroelectric power.

Bonneville Salt Flats, Utah, **USA**; remains of anc. lake; world automobile speed test, 1937–47.

Bonny, t., S. **Nigeria**; at mouth of R. Bonny, Niger delta; oil terminal.

Bonny, Bight of (Bight of Biafra until 1975), **W. Africa**; bay lying E. of the G. of Guinea between the Niger and C. Lopez.

Bonnyrigg and Lasswade, burgh, Midlothian, **Scot.**, 11 km S.E. of Edinburgh, p. (1971) 7,102.

Boothia, peninsula on Arctic cst., Franklin dist., **Canada**; separated from Baffin I., by G. of B.

Bootle, t. Merseyside, **Eng.**; on E. side of entrance to Mersey estuary; shares line of docks with Liverpool; dockside inds. inc. tanning, ship-repairing; tin plant; p. (1971) 74,208.

Bor, t., Serbia, **Yugoslavia**; copper mng. and processing; p. (est. 1965) 20,000.

Borås, t., S. **Sweden**; on R. Viske, nr. Göteborg; ctr. of textile and clothing inds.; p. (1968) 70,144.

Bordeaux, spt., cap. of Gironde, **France**; nr. mouth of R. Garonne; cath., univ.; exp. wines, liqueurs, sugar, potatoes, pit props; oil refining nearby; p. (1968) 266,662 (c.), 555,152 (met. a.).

Borders Region, l. gov. reg., **Scot.**; occupies E. half of Southern Uplands; hilly cty. drained by R. Tweed and tribs.; rural a. interspersed by mkt. and mill ts., a. 4,670 km², p. (1971) 98,840.

Bordighera, t., **Italy**; Riviera winter resort; p. (est. 1968) 12,172.

Boreham Wood, t., Herts., **Eng.**; lt. engin., computers, film studios.

Borinage, dist. around Mons, **Belgium**; impt. but declining coalfield.

Borislav, t., Ukrainian SSR, **USSR**; formerly Polish (1919–39); oilfield, natural gas; richest ozocerite deposits in Europe; oil pipeline links to Drogobych and Dashava; p. (est. 1967) 32,000.

Borisoglebsk, t., **RSFSR**; food processing; p. (est. 1969) 65,000.

Borisov, t., Belorussiyan SSR, **USSR**; defeat of Napoleon, 1812; chemicals, sawmills, hardware; p. (est. 1967) 74,000.

Borkum, I., **W. Germany**; off Ems R. estuary; a. 36 km²; p. (est. 1967) 5,774.

Borlänge, t., **Sweden**; iron, paper, engin. and chemical wks.; p. (1968) 29,060.

Borneo, lgst. I. in Malay archipelago and 3rd lgst. in world; high mtn. range extends from ctr. to N. rising to 4,180 m; low-lying swamp in S.; politically divided into Kalimantan (Indonesian B.), Sabah and Sarawak (E. Malaysia) and Brunei; jungle-covered and underdeveloped; scattered tribes inc. Dyaks; few nodes of development around oilfields (Sarawak and Brunei), as. of forest exploitation (Sabah); new settlement in Barito valley (Kalimantan); a. 738,150 km²; p. (est. 1970) 6,800,000.

Bornholm, I. in Baltic Sea, **Denmark**; mostly granite with poor soils; cattle rearing; kaolin; tourism and fishing impt.; cap. Rønne; a. 543 km²; p. (1971) 47,241.

Bornu, region, **Nigeria**; S.W. of L. Chad; former Moslem st.; a. 132,090 km²; p. (est.) 5,000,000.

Borobudur, Java, Indonesia; gr. Buddhist temple; ruins now restored.

Borrowdale, valley, Cumbria, **Eng**; tourist resort; former graphite mines.

Boscastle, spt., Cornwall, **Eng.**; resort; pilchard fishing; sm. harbour built for slate exp.

Bosnia and Hercegovina, rep., Yugoslavia; mtnous., forested, watered by R. Sava and tribs.; one-fourth cultivated; tobacco, cereals, fruit; cattle, sheep, pigs; mineral deposits in Bosnia; cap. Sarajevo; a. 51,199 km²; p. (1971) 3,742,842.

Bosporus or Strait of Constantinople (Karadeniz Boğazi), between Black Sea and Sea of Marmara; suspension bridge, first to link Europe and S.W. Asia, opened 1973.

Bossier City, t., La., **USA**; oil refineries, rly. wks., chemical and processing plants; p. (1970) 41,592.

Boston, t., Lincs., **Eng.**; sm. pt. on Witham R., 6 km from Wash; agr. mkt., fruit and vegetable canning; p. (1971) 25,995.

Boston, c., st. cap. Mass., **USA**; fine harbour and leading pt. at head of Boston Bay; cultural, comm. and financial ctr., impt. mkt. for fish and wool; 3 univs.; leading c. in 19th cent.; varied inds. inc. leather, rubber, textiles, shoes and elec. gds.; p. (1970) 628,215 (c.), 2,730,228 (met. a.).

Bosworth or **Market Bosworth,** t., Leics., **Eng.**; battle between Richard III and Henry VII, 1485; p. (1971) 32,219 (dist.).

Botany Bay, N.S.W., Australia; inlet of Tasman Sea on E. cst., 16 km S. of Sydney; resort; first settled by Brit. in 1787; old penal colony; deep-water pt. planned.

Botaşani, t., N. Moldavia, **Romania**; in rich pastoral a.; flour milling, tanning; p. (1968) 35,707.

Bothnia, G. of, N. of Baltic; between Finland and Sweden, breadth about 160 km; shallow sea, many Is.

Botswana, Rep. of, indep. sov. st. within Brit. Commonwealth (1966) S.W. **Africa**; stretches from Orange R. to Zambesi R., and merges W. into Kalahari desert; Bamangwato ch. tribe; cap. Gaborone; cattle-rearing; lge. potential copper and nickel ores; a. 574,980 km²; p. (est. 1969) 629,000

Bottrop, t., N. Rhine-Westphalia, **W. Germany**; once a sm. t., now ctr. of Ruhr coal basin; p. (est. 1969) 108,200.

Bouches-du-Rhône, dep., S. **France**; covers Rhône delta and inc. the Camargue and Crau; lagoon cst.; mainly agr. but inc. industl. complex ass. with cap. of Marseilles; a. 5,270 km²; p. (1968) 1,470,271.

Bougainville, I. seceded from **New Guinea** to form Rep. of N. Solomons; major reserve of copper in Panguna valley; new mng. ts. of Anewa Bay and Panguna; forested; a. 10,619 km²; p. (1966) 72,490.

Bougie. *See* Bejaia.

Boulder, t., **W. Australia**; included in Kalgoorlie mun.; p. (1966) 19,892 (joint p.).

Boulder, t., Col. **USA**; gold- and silver-mng. dist.; univ.; resort; p. (1970) 66,870.

Boulder City, t., Nevada, **USA**; nr. Gr. Boulder Dam, gr. engin. project; model t., ctr. for Nat. Park services; p. (1970) 5,223.

Boulogne-Billancourt, S.W. sub. of Paris, **France**; motor car, aircraft inds.; p. (1968) 109,008.

Boulogne-sur-Mer, t., Pas-de-Calais dep., **France**; on English Channel; comm. and fish. pt.; Channel ferry; pt. inds.; p. (1968) 50,138.

Bounty I., N.Z., S. Pac. Oc.; uninhabited.

Bourg-en-Bresse, t., cap. of Ain dep., **France**; route ctr., varied inds.; p. (1968) 40,407.

Bourges, t., cap. of Cher dep., **France**; cath., univ.; industl. and transit ctr.; p. (1968) 73,998.

Bourget, L., Savoie, France; tourist a.

Bourne, t., Lincs., **Eng.**; agr. machin.; p. (1971) 6,461.

Bournemouth, t., Dorset, **Eng.**; on S. cst., E. of Poole Harbour; seaside resort; conference ctr.; p. (1971) 153,425.

Bournville, garden sub. founded by George Cadbury (1897), 6 km S.W. of Birmingham **Eng.**; chocolate and cocoa wks.

Bourton-on-the-Water, v., Gloucs., **Eng.**; tourist ctr.

Bouvet I., uninhabited island in S. Atlantic belonging to **Norway**; a. about 56 km².

Bovey Tracey, v., Devon, Eng.; ball clay excavating.

Bow or Stratford-le-Bow, Tower Hamlets, E. London, **Eng.**; 5 km from St. Paul's.

Bow, R., Alberta, N.W. Canada; head of Saskatchewan R., flows through Banff Nat. Park; irrigation; 504 km long.

Bowdon, t., Gtr. Manchester, **Eng.**; p. (1971) 4,825.

Bowen, spt. N. Queensland, **Australia**; meat wks.; coke plant; p. (1966) 5,134.

Bow Fell, mtn., Cumbria, **Eng.**; at head of Borrowdale, 6 km N.W. of Wast Water, alt. 903 m.

Bowland, Forest of, W. offshoot of Pennines Lancs., **Eng.**; between Rs. Lune and Ribble; designated a. of outstanding natural beauty; reservoirs.

Bowling, v., Dunbarton, **Scot.**; on N. bank of R. Clyde, 16 km N.W. of Glasgow; lge. oil refinery.

Bowling Green, t., Ky., **USA**; tr. ctr. for agr. a. producing tobacco, livestock, limestone and dairy prods.; univ.; p. (1970) 36,253.

Bowness, v., Cumbria, **Eng.**; W. end of Hadrian's Wall.

Bowness, t., Cumbria, **Eng.**; on L. Windermere; tourist ctr.

Box Hill, nr. Dorking, Surrey, **Eng.**; E. of R. Mole gap through N. Downs; chalk; wooded, fine views; alt. 233 m.

Boyle, mkt. t., Roscommon, **R.o.I.**; on R. Boyle; dairying; p. (1966) 1,789.

Boyne, R., **R.o.I.**; flows to Irish Sea; Battle of the Boyne (1690) fought at Oldbridge, 5 km W. of Drogheda; salmon fishing; 128 km long.

Boyoma Falls (Stanley Falls), on Upper Zaïre R., **Zaïre**; nr. equator; originally named after the explorer.

Bozrah, c. of anc. Edom, probably modern Buseira (Jordan), S.E. of Dead Sea.

Brabant, prov., **Belgium**; S. section of former Duchy; fertile and wooded; many breweries; mnfs. linen, cloth, paper, lace; cap. Brussels; a. 3,281 km²; p. (1968) 2,148,513.

Brabant, North, prov., **Neth.**; S. of Gelderland; N. half of former Duchy; cattle rearing; grain, hops, beetroot; cap. 's-Hertogenbosch; a. 4,972 km²; p. (1968) 1,725,292.

Brač, I., Adriatic Sea, **Yugoslavia**; lgst. of Dalmatian Is.; tourism, fishing; a. 393 km².

Brackley, t., Northants., **Eng.**; flour milling, brewing; former prosperous wool tr.; Magdalen College School (1447); p. (1971) 4,615.

Bracknell, t., Berks., **Eng.**; on Thames Valley terrace, 16 km S. of Windsor; new t. designated 1949 to meet overspill needs from London; extends N. and W. of old v. of Bracknell; Meteorological Office H.Q.; engin., sealing compounds, plastics; p. (est. 1974) 41,300.

Brackwede, t. N. Rhine-Westphalia, **W. Germany**; iron and machin.; p. (1969) 26,448.

Bradford, c., West Yorks., **Eng.**; 14 km W. of Leeds; comm. ctr. of wool-textile inds.; impt. for worsted; engin. and chem. inds.; univ.; p. (1971) 293,756.

Bradford-on-Avon, t., Wilts., **Eng.**; on E. flank of Cotswolds from which bldg. stone derived; former ctr. of wool ind.; p. (1971) 8,001.

Bradwell, v., Essex, **Eng.**; at mouth of R. Blackwater; civil nuclear power-sta.; p. (1961) 1,116.

Braemar, dist. in Grampians, Kincardine and Deeside, **Scot.**; containing Balmoral estate.

Braeriach, mtn., **Scot.**; borders Badenoch and Strathspey, alt. 1,296 m.

Braga, t., cap. of B. dist. N.W. **Portugal**; agr. tr. ctr.; hats, cutlery; religious ctr.; cath.; p. (1970) 101,877.
Bragança, t., cap. of B. dist., N.E. **Portugal**; agr. tr.; p. (1970) 33,928.
Brahmaputra, one of longer Rs. in **Asia**; flows for much of its length through Himalayas and Assam; called **Tsangpo** in Tibet; fertile agr. valley subject to flooding and silting; 2,880 km long.
Braich-y-Pwll, headland, Gwynedd, **Wales**.
Brăila, t., **Romania**; R. pt. on Danube, nr. Galati; grain tr., boatbldg., reed processing; p. (est. 1969) 149,686.
Braintree, t., Mass., **USA**; elec. machin., rubber gds., glassware; p. (1970) 35,050.
Braintree and Bocking, ts., former U.D., Essex, **Eng.**; on Blackwater; rayon mftg., metal windows, engin.; p. (1971) 24,839.
Brakpan, t., Transvaal, **S. Africa**; gold mng.; p. (1970) 113,115.
Brampton, t., Ontario, **Canada**; noted for its greenhouses; p. (1971) 41,238.
Brandenburg, t., **E. Germany**; on R. Havel; former cap. of prov. of B.; cath.; tractors, textiles, machin.; p. (est. 1970) 93,660.
Brandenburg. *See* **Neubrandenburg**.
Brandon, t. Manitoba, **Canada**; on Assiniboine R., W. of Winnipeg; comm. ctr. wheat a.; agr. equipment, oil refining; p. (1971) 30,832.
Brandon, t. Suffolk, **Eng.**; ctr. of Breckland; expanded t.
Brandon and Byshottles, ts., former U.D., Durham, **Eng.**; former coal-mng. a.; p. (1971) 16,849.
Brandywine Creek, R., Penns., **USA**; Americans defeated by British 1777; length 32 km.
Branford, t, Conn., **USA**; lt. mnfs., fishing, oysters; resort; p. (1970) 20,444.
Brantford, t., Ontario, **Canada**; on Grand R., S.W. of Hamilton; leading mnf. t.; farm implements, cycles, bus and truck parts; p. (1971) 62,853.
Brasilia, cap. of **Brazil**, Goiás st., 960 km N.W. of Rio de Janeiro; ch. of many cities designed to open up interior of rep.; modern architecture; inaugurated 1960; designed for p. 500,000; p. (1970) 272,002.
Braşov, t., **Romania**; at foot of Transylvanian Alps; aircraft, engin., lge. German and Hungarian p.; p. (est. 1969) 179,316 (c.); (1966) 263,158 (met. a.).
Bratislava, c. cap. of Slovakia, **ČSSR**; pt. on Danube 48 km below Vienna; univ.; industl. and comm. ctr.; textiles, chemicals engin., oil refining; linked to Mozyr', USSR, by "friendship oil pipeline"; p. (est. 1968) 283,234.
Bratsk, c., central Irkutsk oblast, **RSFSR**; on Angara R., ship repair yards, lumber, iron-ore, wood processing chemicals; lge. hydroelectric sta.; p. (1970) 155,000.
Brava, spt., **Somalia**; leather, shoes; p. (est. 1965) 7,665.
Bray, U.D., Wicklow **R.o.I.**; on Irish Sea cst.; popular resort; p. (1966) 12,657.
Brazil, United States of, rep., **S. America**; a. 8,512,035 km²; 5th lgst cty. in world, exceeded in size only by USSR, China, Canada and USA; covers variety of land and climate; in S., gr. Brazilian plateau, in N., Amazon R. basin (thickly forested); leading industl. nation of Latin America; agr.; coffee, cotton, sugar, cocoa, rubber, fruits, hardwoods; cattle-raising; manganese, iron, gold, diamonds; admin. through 22 sts., 4 terrs., and Fed. Dist.; cap. Brasilia; lgst. industl. ctr. São Paulo; p. mainly White, Negro, Indian, Mestizo; Portuguese official language; p. concentrated in coastal belt, leaving vast a. of interior relatively underdeveloped; p. (1975) 107,145,168.
Brazos, R., Texas, **USA**; flows through agr. and industl. Young Co. via Waco to industl. Brazosport; length 1,520 km.
Brazzaville, c., cap. of **Congo Rep.**; connected by rly. with the Atlantic at Pointe-Noire; R. pt. under construction; airport; p. (1966) 156,000.
Brechin, royal burgh, Angus, **Scot.**; on S. Esk; cath.; linen, paper, whisky; p. (1971) 6,578.
Breckland, dist., S.W. Norfolk, N.W. Suffolk, **Eng.**; chalk overlain by glacial sands; heathland and coniferous plantations; ch. ts. Brandon, Lakenheath; a. 518 km².
Brecknock (Breconshire), former co., **Wales**; now mostly inc. in Powys; sm. parts in Mid-Glamorgan and Gwent.
Brecon (Brecknock), t., Powys, **Wales**; on R. Usk; agr. ctr.; p. (1971) 6,283.
Brecon Beacons, mtns., **S. Wales**; 8 km S. of Brecon; highest peak 888 m; sandstone moorland; Nat. Park.
Breda, c. N. Brabant prov. **Neth.**; mnf. ctr.; machin., foundries, canneries, refineries; historic t., 13th cent. cath.; p. (est. 1969) 120,582 (c.) 146,173 (met. a.).
Bredbury and Romiley, ts., Gtr. Manchester, **Eng.**; paper, engin., dyeing, textiles; p. (1971) 28,472.
Bregenz, t., cap. of Vorarlberg, **Austria**; on Bodensee; hydroelectric power; textiles, lt. inds.; resort nr. Bregenz Forest; p. (est. 1968) 23,600.
Breidha Fjord, lge. inlet, W. cst. **Iceland**.
Breman, *Land*, **W. Germany**; a. 404 km²; cap. Bremen; p. (1967) 751,800.
Bremen, c., cap. of *Land* B., **W. Germany**; old t. on right bank of Weser R., 64 km from N. Sea; new t., founded 17th cent., on left bank; leading pt., industl. and comm. ctr.; but hinterland divided by post-war division of Germany; former member of Hanseatic League; p. (est. 1969) 606,100.
Bremerhaven, c., Bremen, **W. Germany**; outport of Bremen at mouth of R. Weser; docks; impt. passenger and fish. pt.; shipbldg.; united with Wesermünde 1941; p. (est. 1969) 149,300.
Bremerton, t., Wash., **USA**; on Puget Sound; naval dockyard; elec. equipment, machin.; p. (1970) 35,307.
Brendon Hills, Somerset, **Eng.**; extension of Exmoor, rising to over 400 m.
Brenner Pass, lowest Alpine pass from Bolzano (Italy) to Innsbruck (**Austria**); used by road and rail; frequent meeting place of Mussolini and Hitler (1940–2).
Brent, outer bor., Greater London, **Eng.**; inc. Wembley and Willesden; p. (1971) 278,541.
Brenta, R., N. **Italy**; rises in picturesque Alpine valley; forestry, silk, tourism; flows to Adriatic Sea; navigable in lower course; length 180 km.
Brentford and Chiswick. *See* **Hounslow**.
Brentwood, t., Essex, **Eng.**; residentl.; p. (1971) 57,976.
Brescia, c., cap. B. prov., Lombardy, N. **Italy**; industl. ctr.; iron, steel, engin., textiles; many historic bldgs.; p. (1969) 206,379.
Breslau. *See* **Wroclaw**.
Bressay I., Shetland Is., **Scot.**; p. (1971) 251.
Brest, naval pt., Finistère dep., N.W. **France**; base of French Atlantic fleet; used by Germans as fortfd. submarine base 1940–4; exp. agr. prods.; impt. industl. ctr.; p. (1968) 159,857 (c.), 169,279 (met. a.).
Brest (Brest-Litovsk), c., Belorussiyan SSR, **USSR**; nr. Polish border; route ctr. and agr. mkt.; timber, food-processing, textiles. Captured by Germans in 1915. Treaty of Brest-Litovsk signed with Soviet Russia 1918; p. (1970) 122,000.
Bretton Woods, resort, N.H., **USA**; site of US monetary and financial conference, 1944, leading to establishment of the International Monetary Fund and the World Bank.
Briançon, t., Hautes-Alpes, **France**; in upper Durance R. valley; winter sports; p. (1968) 10,497.
Bridgend, t., Mid-Glamorgan, **S. Wales**; industl. trading estate; iron, stone, paper; coal mng.; p. (1971) 14,531.
Bridge of Allen, burgh, Stirling, **Scot.**; 3 km N. of Stirling; p. (1971) 4,314.
Bridgeport, c., Conn., **USA**; on Long Island Sound; impt. industl. c., firearms, hardware, elec. equipment, metal products, plastics; p. (1970) 155,359 (c.), 385,746 (met. a.).
Bridgeton, t., N.J., **USA**; founded by Quakers; glasswks., fruit; p. (1970) 20,435.
Bridgetown, t., spt., cap. **Barbados**; deepwater harbour opened 1961; comm. ctr.; exp. sugar, molasses, rum; tourism; p. (1970) 8,789.
Bridgewater Canal, Worsley–Manchester–Runcorn, Gtr. Manchester and Cheshire **Eng.**; crosses ship canal by means of Barton swing bridge; 61 km long.
Bridgnorth, t., Salop, **Eng.**; cas.; carpets, radio equipment; p. (1971) 31,961 (dist.).
Bridgwater, t., Somerset, **Eng.**; on R. Parrett, 16 km from Bristol Channel; bricks and tiles,

engin., wire rope, fibre fabrics, cellophane; p. (1971) 26,598.

Bridlington, t., Humberside, Eng.; on Bridlington Bay, S. of Flamborough Head; fishing; seaside resort; p. (1971) 26,729.

Bridport, Dorset, Eng.; mkt. t.; rope, line and twine, engin., concrete prods.; seaside resort; p. (1971) 6,362.

Brie, region, Marne and Seine-et-Marne deps., France; low, level plateau of limestones and clays, S.E. of Paris; loam (limon) cover and plentiful water supply encourage agr.; grains, sugar-beet, fruit, dairy cattle; famous cheese; densely populated.

Brienz, t., Switzerland; resort on L. Brienz; wood carving; p. (1970) 2,796.

Brierfield, t., Lancs., Eng.; p. (1971) 7,572.

Brierley Hill, t., West Midlands, Eng.; on W. edge of Black Cty.; cut glass, castable metal gds., firebricks, roofing and tiling, iron and steel.

Brigg, mkt. t., Humberside, Eng.; ctr. of agr. dist. between Lincoln Heights and Wolds; sugar-beet, jam, seed crushing, canning; p. (1971) 4,793.

Brighouse, t., West Yorks., Eng.; on R. Calder, 5 km S.E. of Halifax; textiles and engin.; p. (1971) 34,111.

Brightlingsea, t., Essex, Eng.; on R. Colne; oysters, boatbldg., yachting; p. (1971) 6,515.

Brighton, t., East Sussex, Eng.; 80 km S. of London on S. cst.; seaside resort and residtl. t.; Royal Pavilion (1817), univ.; lt. inds.; birthplace of Aubrey Beardsley; p. (1971) 166,081.

Brindisi, c., Apulia, S. Italy; spt. on Adriatic cst., sea and air connections to Middle E.; cath.; cas.; wine, olive oil, silk, petrochemicals; oil refining; p. (1969) 81,576.

Brisbane, t., cap. of Queensland, Australia; spt. 800 km N. of Sydney; fine streets and parks, univ., pt. exp. agr. prods.; pt. processing and agr. based inds., oil refining: p. (1972) 699,371 (c.), 866,207 (met. a.).

Bristol, c. Avon, Eng.; pt. on R. Avon 14 km from Bristol Channel; outport at Avonmouth; cath., univ.; docks; aircraft engin., tobacco, paint, printing and lt. inds.; p. (1971) 425,203.

Bristol, t., Conn., USA; foundries, ball bearings, clocks, bells; p. (1970) 55,487.

Bristol Channel, arm of Atl. Oc. between S. cst. of Wales and Somerset and Devon, Eng.; noted tidal bores.

British Antarctic Territory, Brit. col., created 1962; consists of all land and Is. S. of lat. 60° S. and between 20° and 80° W. longitude; comprising Graham Land peninsula, S. Shetlands, S. Orkneys and smaller Is., excluding S. Georgia and S. Sandwich Is.; a. 1,222,500 km².

British Columbia, W. prov. separated from rest of Canada by Rockies, borders Pac. Oc.; little lowland; parallel N.W.–S.E. ranges of Rockies crossed by Rs. Fraser, Columbia, Kootenay and Peace; vast coniferous forest and hydroelec. resources; salmon fishing on cst.; mng.; p. concentrated in S.W. around Vancouver; a. 948,600 km²; p. (1971) 2,184,621.

British East Africa, formerly comprised Kenya, Tanganyika, Uganda, together with the Is. of Zanzibar and Pemba. *See* under their respective headings.

British Guiana. *See* Guyana.

British Honduras *See* **Belize**.

British Indian Ocean Terr., Brit. col., created 1965; consists of the Chagos Archipelago (of which Diego Garcia [Anglo-American naval communications ctr.] is lgst. I.) 1,920 km N.E. of Mauritius, and formerly Is. of Aldabra, Farquhar, and Desroches in the W. Indian Oc. now part of Seychelles Rep.; p. (est. 1971) 560.

British Is., archipelago, N.W. **Europe**; comprising 2 lge. Is.; Great Britain, Ireland; and 5,000 sm. Is.; a. 315,029 km².

British Solomon Is. *See* **Solomon Is.**

British West Africa, formerly comprised Gambia, Sierra Leone, Gold Coast (Ghana), Nigeria, and parts of Togoland and Cameroons. *See* under their separate headings.

Briton Ferry, t., West Glamorgan, S. Wales; pt. at mouth of R. Neath; steel wks., engin., shipbreaking.

Brittany, region, N.W. France; penin. between Eng. Channel and Bay of Biscay; contrast between productive cst. lands (fishing, early vegetables, tourism) and barren moorland interior; economically depressed; oil refinery projected at St. Livy; p. (est. 1968) 2,468,000.

Brive-la-Gaillarde, t., Corrèze dep., France; regional mkt. in fertile basin on edge of Central Massif; p. (1968) 49,325.

Brixham, S. Devon, Eng.; incorporated in Torbay; fishing; resort.

Brixton, dist., S.W. London, Eng.; prison.

Brno (Brünn), c., ČSSR; cap. of Moldavia; finely situated at confluence of Svratka and Svitava Rs., 109 km N. of Vienna; industl. and communications ctr. with mnfs. of machin., precision tools, textiles; annual tr. fair; p. (est. 1968) 335,935.

Broach, t., Gujarat, India; lowest bridging of R. Narbada; textiles.

Broad Haven, t., new t. planned on St. Brides Bay, Wales.

Broadstairs, Kent, Eng.; seaside resort; 5 km N.E. of Ramsgate; p. (1971) 19,996.

Broads, The, Norfolk, Eng.; series of Ls. formed by mediaeval turf cutting in lower alluvial reaches of Rs. Bure, Waveney, and Yare; yachting, fishing, tourism; plans to create a Nat. Park to help relieve pollution.

Brockton, c., Mass., USA; S. of Boston; lge shoe and leather ind., machin.; annual tr. fair; p. (1970) 87,444 (c.), 186,839 (met. a.).

Brockville, t., Ontaria, Canada; R. pt. on St. Lawrence R. below Thousand Is.; telephone equipment, wire cables, elec. tools; p. (1971) 19,707.

Broken Hill, t., N.S.W., **Australia**; major mng. industl. t., silver, lead, zinc; p. (1972) 29,743.

Bromberg. *See* **Bydgoszcz.**

Bromley, outer bor. of London, Eng.; inc. Beckenham, Orpington, Penge, and part of Sidcup; p. (1971) 304,357.

Bromsgrove, Hereford and Worcs., Eng.; mkt. t., 21 km S.W. Birmingham; wrought ironwk., lt. engin.; p. (1971) 40,668.

Bromyard, Hereford and Worcs., Eng.; sm. mkt. t.; p. (1971) 8,568.

Bronx, The, one of the five bors. of New York City, **USA**; connected by bridges to bor. of Manhattan; residtl. with parks, zoological and botanical gardens, colleges and professional schools; p. (1970) 1,472,216.

Brookline, sub. of Boston, Mass., **USA**; residtl.; p. (1970) 58,689.

Brooklyn, bor., N.Y. City, **USA**; linked with Manhattan bor. by Brooklyn, Manhattan, and Williamsburgh suspension bridges across East R.; and with Staten I. by Verrazano-Narrows bridge (longest in world); mainly residtl. with numerous mftg. and comm. interests; p. (1970) 2,601,852.

Brooks Range, mtns., N. Alaska, **USA**; forms N. section of Rocky Mtns.; Eskimo p.; Arctic climate, flora and fauna; alt. 2,000 m rising to 2,818 m (Mt. Michelson).

Broom, loch on N.W. cst. of Ross and Cromarty, Scot.

Brora, t., Sutherland, Scot.; on E. cst., 19 km N.E. of Dornoch Firth; ctr. of sm. coalfield; Harris Tweed ind.; tourism.

Brownhills, t., West Midlands, Eng.; former mng. t.; expanded t.

Brownsville, t., Texas, **USA**; pt. on Rio Grande nr. Mexican border; livestock, sugar-cane, fruit processing, chemicals; p. (1970) 51,080 (c.), 137,506 (met. a.).

Broxbourne, t., Herts., Eng.; on gravel terrace to W. of R. Lea; ctr. of very intensively cultivated dist.; lt. inds.; "dormitory" t. linked with London.

Bruay-en-Artois, t., Pas-de-Calais, **France**; coal mng.; p. (1968) 28,628 (t.), 126,520 (met. a.).

Bruchsal, t., Baden-Württemberg, W. Germany; tobacco, paper, machin.; p. (est. 1969) 26,506.

Brugge (Bruges), c., cap. of W. Flanders prov., N. Belgium; mediaeval t. connected by canal to its outer pt. Zeebrugge; univ.; impt. mkt. for grain, cattle, horses; engin., ship-repairing, elec. gds., glass mkg., textiles, lace; p. (est. 1967) 51,900 (c.), 113,828 (met a.).

Brühl, t., N. Rhine-Westphalia, W. Germany; 13 km S. of Cologne; cas.; lignite; p. (est. 1969) 41,475.

Brunei, intern. self-gov. Brit. prot. st., N.W.

Borneo; enclave of Sarawak (Malaysia); Seria oilfields (output now declining); underdeveloped elsewhere; rubber, natural gas, sago, pepper, timber; cap. Bandar Seri Begawan; a. 5,765 km²; p. (est. 1972) 200,000.

Brünn. *See* Brno.

Brunsbüttelkoog, pt. at mouth of R. Elbe opposite Cuxhaven, W. Germany.

Brunswick (Braunschweig), c., Lower Saxony, W. Germany; on R. Oker; formerly cap. of st. of Brunswick, now a comm. and industl. ctr.; mnfs. inc. canning, tinplate, optics, pianos, lorries; p. (est. 1969) 225,600.

Brussels (Bruxelles), cap. of Belgium and of prov. of Brabant; impt. comm., industl. and cultural ctr.; varied mnfs., inc. pharmaceuticals, electronic equipment, machine tools; lge. oil refinery at Feluy; noted for carpets and lace; occupied by the Germans 1914–18, 1940–4; univ.; mediaeval and Renaissance monuments; H.Q. of EEC; p. (est. 1969) 164,013 (c.), 1,073,111 (met. a.).

Bryan, t., Texas, **USA**; mkt. ctr., agr. college; p. (1970) 33,719.

Bryansk, c., cap. of B. oblast, **RSFSR**, on Desna R.; rly. junc.; a fortress until 19th cent.; sawmilling, engin., textiles, chemicals, steel; oil pipeline from Kuybyshev; p. inc. Bezhitsa (1970) 318,000.

Brynmawr, t., Gwent, Wales; former coal-mng. a.; industl. estate; rubber prods.; p. (1971) 5,930.

Brzeg (Brieg), t. Silesia, **Poland**; on R. Oder; German until 1945; textiles, leather, chemicals; p. (1968) 29,900.

Bucaramanga, c., N. central **Colombia**, 900 m a.s.l. in E. highlands of Andes; ctr. of coffee-growing dist.; cigar and cigarette mkg.; p. (est. 1972) 324,400 (c.), 347,400 (met. a.).

Buchan Ness, C., nr. Peterhead, E. Scot.

Bucharest (Bucureşti), cap. and lgst c. of **Romania**; "Little Paris," on the Dambovita, trib. of Danube; cath., univ.; textiles, chemicals, pharmaceuticals, oil refining, engin.; 20 per cent industl. ouput of rep.; p. (est. 1969) 1,457,802.

Buckfastleigh, t., S. Devon. **Eng.**; wool, quarrying; nearby Benedictine abbey on site of mediaeval Cistercian abbey; p. (1971) 2,657.

Buckhaven and Methil, burgh, Kircaldy, **Scot.**; on N. Side of Firth of Forth, 13 km N.E. of Kirkcaldy; coal; p. (1971) 18,396.

Buckie, burgh, Moray, **Scot.**; boat- and yacht-bldg.; fisheries; p. (1971) 7,919.

Buckingham, Bucks., **Eng.**; mkt. t. on R. Ouse, 24 km N.W. of Aylesbury; p. (1971) 5,075.

Buckinghamshire, non-met. co., **Eng.**; crossed by Chilterns and Vale of Aylesbury; rural and wooded, emphasis is on dairy farming; co. t. Aylesbury; mnfs. chiefly in High Wycombe; decline in traditional handicrafts (lace-mkg. and furniture parts); a. 1,882 km²; p. (1971) 476,00.

Buckley, t., Clwyd. **Wales**; sm. castings; p. (1971) 11,866.

Budapest, cap. and lgst. c. of **Hungary**; stands on both banks of Danube (Buda on right, Pest on left); attractive townscape; univ.; varied mnfs., inc. steel, textiles, chemicals, engin., motorbuses, oil refining; employs 40 per cent industl. workers of Hungary; p. (est. 1969) 1,934,000 (c.); (est. 1967) 2,335,000 (met. a.).

Budaun, t., Uttar Pradesh, **India**; agr. processing; ruins; p. (1961) 58,770.

Bude. *See* Stratton and Bude.

Budel, t., N. Brabant, S. **Neth.**; 19 km S. of Eindhoven; major zinc smelter project.

Budge-Budge, t., W. Bengal, **India**; on lower Hooghly R.; hemp, rice; p. (1961) 39,824.

Budleigh Salterton, E. Devon, **Eng.**; resort; birthplace of Walter Raleigh nearby; p. (1971) 4,139.

Buena Park, t., Cal., **USA**; agr. processing, mkt.; oilfields; p. (1970) 63,646.

Buenaventura, spt., Colombia; lumber yards, tanning, fish canning; p. (est. 1972) 102,300 (t.), 133,600 (met. a.).

Buenos Aires, c., cap. of **Argentina**; ch. spt. at head of Rio de la Plata, on E. edge of Pampa; connected to Uruguay, Paraguay, and Brazil by gr. R. system; industl. and tr. ctr. for outlying regions; p. (1970) 2,972,453 (c.). 8,352,900 (met. a.).

Buffalo, c., N.Y. **USA**; pt. on L. Erie; focus of communications on Gr. Ls. has encouraged many heavy inds.; diversified lt. inds.; univ.; p. (1970) 457,808 (c.), 1,334,485 (met. a.).

Bug R., Ukrainian SSR, **USSR**; known as S. or Ukrainian B.; flows from Volyno–Podolsh upland to Black Sea; navigable in lower course; 853 km long.

Bug, R., the western Bug rises in the Ukraine, **USSR**, not far from the southern Bug and flows N. to join the Vistula below Warsaw; forms bdy. between Poland and Ukrainian SSR; 774 km long.

Bugul'ma, t., Tatar ASSR, **RSFSR**; oil ctr.; p. (est. 1967) 74,000.

Buganda, prov., Uganda, E. Africa; located W. of L. Victoria largely at alt. between 1,300 and 1,800 m; intensive cultivation, cotton (ch. comm. crop), plantains, millets; cap. Kampala.

Builth Wells, t., Powys, Wales; on upper course of R. Wye; medicinal springs; p. (1971) 1,481.

Buitenzorg. *See* Bogor.

Bujumbura, t., cap. of Burundi; pt. on L. Tanganyika; varied inds.; airpt.; p. (est. 1970) 78,810 (met. a.).

Bukavu, t., Zaire; cement, quinine processing; p. (est. 1972) 156,078 (met. a.).

Bukhara (Bokhara), t., Uzbek SSR, **USSR**; in Amu-Dar'ya valley at W. foot of Tien Shan; agr. mkt. at W. terminus of anc. caravan route from China; modern route ctr.; local natural gas, textiles; p. (1970) 112,000.

Bukittinggi, t., Sumatra, **Indonesia**; in Padang Highlands at 1,068 m; p. 53,700.

Bukoba, t., **Tanzania**; pt. midway along W. shore of L. Victoria; exp. coffee, rice, plantains and other foodstuffs to L. pts. in Kenya and Uganda.

Bukovina, Northern; terr., formerly belonging to Romania, ceded to **USSR** in 1940; now part of Ukrainian SSR; a. 5,542 km²; ch. t. Chernovitsy; Carpathian Mtns., forested; farming, cereals; cattle.

Bulawayo, t., **Rhodesia**; impt. rly. ctr.; iron and steel, brewing, agr. mnfs.; airpt.; p. (est. 1972) 295,000 (met. a.).

Bulgaria, **People's Rep.** of, **S.E. Europe**; in E. Balkans, bounded by Black Sea in E., and by Danube R. in N. which separates it from Romania; Rodopi range in S.W.; Maritsa R. basin forms central lowland a.; sharp climatic contrasts between winter and summer; fertile lowland areas organised into lge.-scale cooperative farms producing grain; impt. exp. tr. in agr. prods., inc. fruit, vegetables, tobacco; rapidly increasing industl. output; mineral and oil resources; popular tourist a. on Black Sea cst.; cap. Sofia; a. 110,911 km²; p. (est. 1974) 8,706,000.

Bunbury, t., **W. Australia**; spt. on cst. 179 km S. of Fremantle; comm. ctr. of lge. pastoral, fruit-growing and timber dist.; new bauxite refinery to serve Hotham R. deposits; p. (1972) 17,762.

Buncrana, U.D., mkt. t., Donegal, **R.o.I.**; salmon fishing; seaside resort; p. (1966) 3,120.

Bundaberg, t., Queensland, **Australia**; on Burnett R.; sugar factories, timber, butter, iron; p. (1972) 26,570.

Bundoran, v., Donegal, **R.o.I.**; fish. pt. and resort; p. (1966) 1,421.

Bungay, Suffolk, **Eng.**; mkt. t. on R. Waveney; printing, malting, leather gds.; p. (1971) 3,961.

Bungosuido Channel, Japan; E. entrance into Inland Sea.

Bunzlau. *See* **Boleslawiec.**

Buraimi, oases lying between **Oman** and **United** Arab Emirates; rich in oil.

Buraydah (Buraida), t. Nejd., **Saudi Arabia**; oasis; tr. ctr.; p. (est.) 70,000.

Burbank, c., Cal.. **USA**; airpt.; aeroplanes, film studios; p. (1970) 88,871.

Burdwan, t., W. Bengal, India; agr. processing and tr. ctr. in Damodar valley close to Raniganj coalfield; p. (1971) 143,318.

Bure, R., Norfolk, **Eng.**; lower course forms part of Norfolk Broads; joins Yare at Yarmouth; 93 km.

Burg, t., Magdeburg, **E. Germany**; on Ihle Canal; p. (est. 1970) 29,994.

Burgas, c., **Bulgaria**; spt. and comm. ctr. on Black Sea; ch. exp. pt. for rep.; pt. for oil tankers under construction; p. (1968) 122,212.

Burgenland, prov., **Austria**; bordered on E. by Hungary; low-lying in N., agr.; hilly in S.; cap. Eisenstadt; a. 3,962 km²; p. (1968) 267,300.
Burgess Hill, t., West Sussex, **Eng.**; bricks, tiles; p. (1971) 19,309.
Burghausen, t., **W. Germany**; chemicals, oil refining; pipeline to Munich.
Burghead, burgh. Moray, **Scot.**; fish pt., resort; p. (1971) 1,282.
Burgos, c., **N. Spain**; cap. of B. prov.; anc. cap. of Castile and cap. of Franco's regime 1936–9; cath; home of the Cid; tourism, varied inds.; p. (1967) 100,413.
Burgos, prov., Old Castile, **Spain**; cap. B.; a. 14,050 km²; p. (1970) 358,075.
Burgstädt, t., Karl-Marx-Stadt, **E. Germany**; textiles, machin.; p. (1963) 17,167.
Burgundy, former kingdom and prov., **N.E. France**; composed largely of upper valley of R. Saône; famous vineyards; strategic position on route leading between plateau of Vosges and Jura Mtns., from Rhône valley to Rhine valley.
Burhanpur, t., Madhya Pradesh, **India**; anc. walled Mogul c.; textiles, brocades; p. (1971) 105,246.
Burlington, t., S. Ontario, **Canada**; on L. Ontario, sub., N.E. of Hamilton; in fruit-growing a.; industl.; tourism; p. (1971) 86,125.
Burlington, t., Iowa. **USA**; on bluffs of Mississippi R.; machin., furniture; p. (1970) 32,360.
Burlington, t., Vt., **USA**; on L. Champlain; pt. of entry and ch. industl. and comm. t. in st.; numerous mnfs.; p. (est. 1969) 38,500.
Burma, Union of, rep., **S.E. Asia**; Irrawaddy R. basin, developed by British in 19th cent., forms major cluster of p., routeways and source of rice of which B. is one of few exporters; surrounding mtns. relatively underdeveloped, although they are a source of teak and hardwood exps.; almost self-sufficient in petroleum from deposits in N.; monsoon climate; ch. ts., Mandalay, cap. Rangoon; a. 676,580 km²; p. (est. 1972) 28,874,000.
Burnham Beeches, Berks./Bucks., **Eng.**; part of anc. forest acquired 1879 for public use; 243 ha.
Burnham-on-Crouch, t., Essex. **Eng.**; pt., yachting, boat-bldg.; p. (1971) 4,546.
Burnham-on-Sea, t., Somerset, **Eng.**; on Bridgwater Bay; resort; p. (1971) 12,281.
Burnie, spt., Tasmania, **Australia**; mnfs., paper pulp, chemicals; oil terminal; p. (1972) 20,088.
Burnley, t., Lancs., **Eng.**; textiles, engin., car accessories; p. (1971) 76,483.
Burntisland, royal burgh, Kirkcaldy, **Scot.**; on F. of Forth; shipbldg., aluminium inds.; p. (1971) 5,699.
Burray, one of the Orkney Is., **Scot.**; p. (est. 1969) 595.
Burrinjuck, t., N.S.W., **Australia**; on Murrumbidgee R., N. of Canberra; site of impt. dam providing irrigation in Riverina dist.
Burry Port, t., Dyfed, **Wales**; p. (1971) 5,880.
Bursa, c., **N.W. Turkey**; noted for its textiles; cap. of anc. Bithynia (3rd cent B.C.) and later of Ottoman empire; mosques; p. (1965) 211,644 (c.), 307,753 (met. a.).
Burslem. *See* Stoke-on-Trent.
Burton-on-Trent, t., Staffs., **Eng.**; brewing, malting, rubber gds.; p. (1971) 50,175.
Burujird, t., **Iran**; textiles and mkt. ctr. at alt. 1,678 m; p. (1966) 71,486.
Burundi, rep., **E. central Africa**; high plateau on N.E. shore of L. Tanganyika; tropical climate, irregular rainfall; economy based on agr., inc. subsistence crops of manioc, sweet potatoes, and cash crops of cotton, coffee; coffee major exp.; sm. mftg. inds. developing but no rlys.; home of ruling Tutsi and rebel Hutu; cap. Bujumbura; a. 27,834 km²; p. (est. 1970) 3,340,000.
Bury, t., Gtr. Manchester, **Eng.**; on R. Irwell to S. of Rossendale Fells; cotton, textiles; birthplace of Robert Peel; p. (1971) 67,776.
Buryat (Buryatskaya), aut. rep., **RSFSR**; borders L. Baykal; mtnous., forested; lge. mineral deposits; cap. Ulan Ude; a. 350,945 km²; p. (1970) 812,000.
Bury St. Edmunds, Suffolk, **Eng.**; old mkt t., on R. Lark, abbey ruins; farm implements, sugar beet processing; expanded t.; p. (1971) 25,629.
Bushey, t., Herts. **Eng.**; residtl.; p. (1971) 23,729.
Bushir. *See* Bandar-e-Būshehr.
Busto Arsizio, t., Varese prov., **N. Italy**; 30 km. N.W. of Milan; cotton milling ctr., iron, steel, rayon, textile machin.; p. (est. 1968) 75,565.
Bute, Kyles of, strait, 10 km between isles of Bute and Argyll, Scot.
Buteshire, former co., now part of Strathclyde Region, **Scot.**
Butte, t., Mont., **USA**; mng. t. (copper, zinc, silver, manganese, gold, lead, arsenic); also a farming ctr.; p. (est. 1969) 26,000.
Buttermere, L., Cumberland, Eng.
Butt of Lewis, promontory with lighthouse; Lewis, Hebrides, Scot.
Buxton t., Derbys., **Eng.**; spa nr. High Peak dist.; lime-quarrying nearby; p. (1971) 20,316.
Buzau, t., **Romania**; rly. ctr.; cath.; wheat, timber, petroleum; p. (1968) 59,114.
Bydgoszcz, prov., **Poland**; cap. B.; drained by Rs. Vistula, Brda, and Notec; formerly called Pomorze; salt and lime deposits aid chemical inds.; a. 20,800 km²; p. (1970) 1,912,000.
Bydgoszcz (Bromberg), c., N. central **Poland**; on R. Brda; R. pt., rly. ctr.; elec. equipment, machine tools, timber mnfs.; p. (est. 1969) 275,200.
Byelorussian SSR. *See* **Belorussiyan SSR.**
Byron C., most E. point of **Australia**, Pacific cst. of N.S.W.
Bytom, c., **S.W. Poland**; formerly in Prussian prov. of Upper Silesia; ctr. of Katowice mng. a.; p. (est. 1969) 186,700.

C

Cabinda, enclave, **Angola**; separated by Zaïre R. estuary from Angola; tropical climate encourages thick forest cover; tropical crops; offshore oil production; uranium; attempts at secession; a. 7,236 km²; p. (1960) 58,547.
Cabot Strait, entrance of G. of St. Lawrence between C. Breton I. and Newfoundland, **Canada**.
Cáceres, c., and cap. of C. prov., **W. Spain**; in Estremadura, above Tagus valley; mkt. t. lies below the old t. topping the hill; p. (est. 1969) 56,274.
Cachar, dist., Assam, **India**; tea-growing ctr.; a. 6,961 km²; p. (1961) 1,378,476.
Cachoeira, t., Bahia, **Brazil**; historic c.; p. (1968) 32,432.
Cachoeira do Sul, t., Rio Grande do Sul, **Brazil**; p. (est. 1968) 98,927.
Cadarache, t., **S. France**; nr. Aix-en-Provence; nuclear research centre.
Cader Idris, mtn., Gwynedd, **Wales**; alt. 893 m.
Cádiz, maritime prov., **S.W. Spain**; cap. Cádiz; a. 7,321 km²; p. (1967) 818,847.
Cádiz, c., cap. of C. prov., **S.W. Spain**; in Andalusia; pt. on Bay of C.; fortress t., naval base; exp. sherry, cork, fruit, olive oil, tunny fish; univ., cath.; one of the most anc. ts. in Europe, built by Phoenicians, *c.* 1100 B.C.; p. (est. 1969) 134,315.
Caen, c., cap. of Calvados dep., **France**; church and abbey, tomb of William the Conqueror; univ.; iron ore mng. and processing; severely damaged in second world war; p. (1968) 110,262 (c.), 152,332 (met. a.).
Caerleon, t., Gwent, **Wales**; on R. Usk, 5 km N.E. of Newport; Roman remains; agr. machin., tools, bricks; p. (1971) 6,235.
Caernarvon, t., Gwynedd, **N. Wales**; pt. on S. shore of Menai strait; cas. where first Prince of Wales (Edward II) was christened; bricks, plastics; p. (1971) 9,253.
Caernarvonshire, former co., **N. Wales**. *See* **Gwynedd.**
Caerphilly, t., Mid-Glamorgan, **S. Wales**; cas.; lt. inds.; former coal-mng. a.; p. (1971) 40,689.
Caesar Mazaca, anc. c., Asia Minor; residence of the Cappadocian Kings; the modern Kayeri, **Turkey**.
Caesarea Palestinae, old c., **Israel**, 32 km S. Mt. Carmel; cap. of Herod the Great.
Caeté, t., Minas Gerais st., **Brazil**; lge. iron and steel wks.; p. (est. 1968) 36,411.

Cagliare, cap. and ch. pt. of Sardinia, **Italy**; univ., cath.; p. (1969) 223,002.
Caha, mtns., on bdy. of Cork and Kerry, **R.o.I.**; cas.; highest point 686 m.
Cahir, t., Tipperary, **R.o.I.**; on R. Suir; anc. cas. and abbey; salmon fishing; p. (1966) 1,740.
Cahors, t., cap. of Lot dep., **France**; comm. ctr.; many historic bldgs., inc. cath., palace; distilleries, shoe factory; p. (1968) 20,903.
Cairngorm, mtns., Moray, Badenoch and Strathspey, **Scot.**; rise to 1,310 m (Ben Mac Dhui); form part of Highlands; nat. nature reserve of arctic flora and fauna; winter sports.
Cairns, spt., Queensland, **Australia**; on Trinity Bay; bulk sugar pt.; tourist ctr.; p. (1972) 32,570.
Cairntoul, mtn., Kincardine and Deeside, **Scot.**; alt. 1,294 m.
Cairo (El Qâhira), c., cap. of **Egypt**; on E. bank of Nile, at head of delta; lgst. c. in rep.; mnfs. cotton, paper, silk; univ.; mosques, palace, fortress of Babylon in old c.; p. (est. 1974) 5,384,000
Cairo, Ill., **USA**; at confluence of Mississippi and Ohio; busy traffic ctr.; p. (1970) 6,277.
Caistor, t., Lincs., **Eng.**; site of Roman camp in Lincs. Wolds; p. (1971) 14,575 (dist.).
Caithness, l. gov. dist., former co., **Scot.**; most N. part of mainland; flat, with much moorland; herring fishery; poor agr.; quarrying; ch. ts. Wick, Thurso; a. 3,152 km²; p. (1971) 29,755.
Cajamarca, t., cap. of C. dep., **Peru**; in mtn. valley, 2,745 m; impt. in Inca times; p. (est. 1969) 27,600.
Calabar, spt., S.E. **Nigeria**; cap. Cross River st.; exp. palm oil, kernels, rubber, ivory, cement; p. (est. 1969) 88,621.
Calabria, region, extreme S.W. **Italy**; mtnous. pen.; highest point Mt. Pollino 2,234 m; ch. R. Crati; agr., fruit, sheep, goats; socially and economically underdeveloped; cap. Catanzaro; p. (1969) 2,057,182.
Calais, spt., Pas-de-Calais, N.E. **France**; cross-channel ferry pt. opposite to and 33·6 km distant from Dover; p. (1968) 74,908.
Calama, oasis, Antofagasta prov., N. **Chile**; in Atacama desert at foot of Andean Cordillera; water from R. Loa supplies Antofagasta and used for irrigation locally.
Calatafimi, t., Sicily, **Italy**; Garibaldi defeated Neapolitans, May 1860; p. (est. 1968) 9,627.
Calbayog, t., Samar, **Philippines**; hemp tr., fisheries; p. (est. 1968) 103,100.
Calbe, t., Magdeburg, **E. Germany**; on R. Saale; iron smelting, lignite mng., machin., chemicals; p. (est. 1970) 16,296.
Calcutta, c., cap. of W. Bengal st., **India**; pt. on Hooghly R., lgst. c. in rep. and one of most densely populated areas of world; vast tr. from Ganges plain; univ.; jute-mills, textiles, chems., engin.; exp. jute, cotton, sugar-cane, rice, tea, coal; "black hole" (1756); p. (1971) 3,148,746 (c.), 7,031,382 (met. a. covering 1,036 km²).
Calder, R., West Yorks., **Eng.**, trib of Aire R.
Calder Hall, Cumbria, **Eng.**; first full-scale nuclear power sta. in world (1956) owned and operated by AEA, produces electricity for nat. grid.
Caldy I., off Dyfed cst., **Wales**; lighthouse; Trappist monastery.
Caledonian Canal, from Moray Firth to Loch Linnhe, **Scot.**, connecting North Sea with Atl. Oc.; 100 km long; opened 1822.
Calf of Man, sm. I., S.W. I. of Man, **Eng.**; a. 250 ha.
Calgary, ch. t., Alberta, **Canada**; ctr. of ranching cty.; lumber mills, tanneries, oil refining, flour milling; p. (1971) 400,514.
Cali, c., cap. of Valle del Cauca dep., W. **Colombia**; 1,068 m on Cauca R.; comm. and transport ctr. for rich agr. a.; p. (est. 1972) 1,003,900 (c.), 1,022,200 (met. a.).
Calicut (Kozhikade), t., Kerala, **India**; first pt. reached by Vasco da Gama (1498); gave its name to calico cloth; exp. coffee, spices; p. (1971) 333,979.
California, st., W. **USA**; mtnous., forested, fertile valleys; subject to earthquakes from San Andreas fault; rich in minerals, oil, natural gas, gold, silver, copper; fruits; film ind.; attractive climate and scenery; cap. Sacramento; ch. pt. San Francisco, lgst. c. Los Angeles; most populous st. in USA; a. 411,014 km²; p. (1970) 19,696,840.
California Current, E. **Pac. Oc.**; flows N. to S. along cst. of Ore., and Cal., USA; relatively cold water; reduces summer temp. and causes fog in cst. a. especially nr. San Francisco.
California, G. of, arm of Pac. Oc., N.W. **Mexico**; 1,120 km long; same rift as Imperial and Coachella valleys in S.E. Cal.
Callan, R.D., Kilkenny, **R.o.I.**; mkt. t. on Kings R.; p. (1961) 5,963.
Callander, burgh, Stirling, **Scot.**; mkt. t. on R. Teith, 24 km N.W. of Stirling; "the gate of the Highlands," tourism; p. (1971) 1,768.
Callao, c., W. **Peru**; pt. of Lima; sheltered harbour; sacked by Drake in 16th cent.; p. (est. 1970) 335,400.
Calne, Wilts., **Eng.**; mkt. t. on Marden R.; lge. bacon factory; p. (1971) 9,685.
Caltagirone, t., Catania, Sicily, **Italy**; cath.; majolica ware; p. (est. 1968) 43,455.
Caltanissetta, t., cap. of C. prov., Sicily, **Italy**; cath.; agr., sulphur ctr.; p. (1969) 64,048.
Calumet, v., Mich., **USA**; on Keweenaw peninsula, L. Superior; copper mine; p. (1970) 1,007.
Calvados, dep., N.E. **France**; low-lying cty. and damp climate aid dairying; butter and cheese prods.; apple orchards produce Calvados brandy; cap. Caen; a. 5,690 km²; p. (1968) 519,695.
Cam (Granta), R., Cambridge, **Eng.**; trib. of R. Ouse; flows through the "backs" at Cambridge; 64 km long.
Camagüey, c., **Cuba**; comm. ctr. in rich agr. region; cattle, sugar-cane; p. (est. 1967) 178,600.
Camargue, delta dist., Bouches-du-Rhône, **France**; at mouth of R. Rhône; famous col. of flamingoes; gypsies; bull-rearing; a. 777 km².
Camberley, t., Surrey, **Eng.**; Royal Military Staff College.
Cambodia, Democratic (Khmer Rep.), S.E. **Asia**, between Thailand and S. Vietnam; former associate st. of Fr. Union; cap. Phnom-Penh on Mekong R.; mainly agr., rice, rubber, maize, pepper, kapok, livestock; Gr. L., or Tonle Sap, impt. for fisheries, car assembly, cigarette-mkg., textiles, plywood, paper, tyres, cement; oil refinery nr. Sihanoukville; new constitution established after civil war 1970–5; a. 181,300 km²; p. (est. 1969) 7,000,000.
Cambourne, t., Cornwall, **Eng.**; 18 km S.W. Truro; old tin-and copper-mines; engin., radio-television assembly; textiles, chemicals; p. (1971) 42,029 (inc. Redruth).
Cambrai, t., Nord dep., **France**; on R. Scheldt; textiles (gave its name to cambric), agr. processing; suffered in both world wars; p. (1968) 39,922.
Cambrian Mtns., **Wales**; collective name for mtns. of N. and Central Wales inc. Snowdonia and Cader Idris.
Cambridge, univ. c., co. t., Cambridgeshire, **Eng.**; on Cam R.; famous univ. with residtl. colleges; leading ctr. of research-based inds.; p. (1971) 98,519.
Cambridgeshire, non-met. co., **Eng.**; low-lying, sloping from E. Anglian Heights in S.E. to Fens in N.; crossed by Rs. flowing to Wash; rich soils aid intensive agr. and mkt. gardening; inc. former cos. of Huntingdon, Peterborough and Isle of Ely; ch. t. Cambridge; a. 3,408 km²; p. (1971) 505,000.
Cambridge, c., Mass., **USA**; 5 km from Boston; seat of Harvard Univ. and MIT; mftg.; impt. research ctr.; now inc. in Boston met. a.
Cambuslang, par., Strathclyde Reg., **Scot.**; dye-works, hosiery, engin., plate mill; on Clyde R.
Camden, inner bor., N. London, **Eng.**; inc. Hampstead, Holborn, and St. Pancras; p. (1971) 200,784.
Camden, c., N.J., **USA**; pt. of entry on Delaware R., opposite Philadelphia; comm., mftg. and residtl.; iron foundries, chemicals, shipbldg.; p. (1970) 102,551; inc. in Philadelphia met. a.
Camden Town, industl. and residtl. dist., London, **Eng.**; N.E. of Regent's Park.
Camerino, t., central **Italy**; in Appennines; univ., cath.; the anc. Camerium; p. (est. 1968) 9,180.
Cameroon, United Rep. of, unitary st. (1972) W. **Africa**; on G. of Guinea; fed. cap. Yaoundé; timber, cocoa, palm kernels, palm oil, groundnuts, bananas, coffee; a. 475,500 km²; p. (est. 1969) 5,680,000.
Cameroon Mtn., volcano, massif, **Cameroon**; cstl.

mtn., hgst. in W. Africa; last eruption 1922; alt. 4,072 m.

Campagna di Roma, Latium, **Italy;** malarial coastal plain around Rome; now reclaimed and used for pasture.

Campania, region, S. **Italy;** comprising provs. Avellino, Benevento, Caserta, Naples, Salerno; admin. and comm. ctr. Naples; high p. density; fertile; intensive agr.; p. (1969) 5,159,038.

Campbelltown, t., N.S.W., **Australia;** dairy and poultry ctr.; proposed as satellite t. for Sydney; p. (1966) 22,812.

Campbeltown, royal burgh, spt., Kintyre, Argyll and Bute, **Scot.;** distilling, fishing; planned ctr. for construction of off-shore oil platforms; p. (1971) 5,960.

Campeche, spt., S.E. **Mexico;** on G. of Campeche; gives its name to prov. (a. 56,099 km²; p. (1969) 239,000); clothing; exp. timber, sisal hemp; p. (est. 1969) 44,000.

Campina Grande, t., Paraiba, **Brazil;** agr.; textiles, veg. oils; p. (1970) 163,206.

Campinas, t., **Brazil;** 88 km N. of São Paulo; coffee; machin.; rubber gds.; p. (1970) 328,629.

Campine or Kempenland, region in Limburg and Antwerp provs., **Belgium;** concealed coalfield in heathland a.

Campobasso, t., cap. of C. prov., S. **Italy;** agr. ctr.; famed for cutlery; 15th cent. cas.; p. (est. 1967) 33,800.

Campo Belo, t., Minas Gerais st., **Brazil;** impt. cattle ctr. nr. L. formed by Furnas Dam on Rio Grande; p. (est. 1968) 30,810.

Campo Duran, terr., **Argentina;** oil-field and refining.

Campos, c., Rio de Janeiro st., **Brazil;** ctr. for rich agr. region; sugar-refining; p. (1970) 153,310.

Campos do Jordão, t., **Brazil;** alt. 1,699 m; health resort, known as the Switzerland of Brazil; p. (est. 1968) 19,676.

Campsie Fells, range of hills, **Stirling, Scot.;** highest point, 578 m.

Campulung, t., **Romania,** in Walachia, at foot of Transylvanian Alps; summer resort; p. (est. 1970) 26,675.

Canada, indep. st., within Commonwealth; occupies N. part of **N. America;** enclave of Alaska (USA) in N.W.; second lgst. cty. in world, consisting of 10 provs., 2 terrs.; coastal mtns. and Rockies in W., interior plains in ctr., Hudson Bay lowlands in N., plateau a. of Quebec and Newfoundland in E.; many Is. off Arctic cst.; continental climate, severe in interior but moderated on csts.; less than 8 per cent of total land a. classified as cultivated land but agr. prods. (especially wheat) very valuable exp.; enormous forest resources but many economically inaccessible; fur trapping in N., impt. fishing inds. in both Pac. and Atl. csts.; considerable mineral resources; lgst. world producer of asbestos, silver, nickel, zinc.; major oil and gas resources in Alberta; one of most urbanised ctys. in world; p. concentrated along E.–W. axis in S. parts of W. provs. and along Gr. Ls. and St. Lawrence lowland; economy highly integrated with USA; 80 per cent of mftg. inds. based on US investment and 70 per cent of external tr. with USA; major cultural differences between English and French communities; both nat. languages official (30 per cent p. speak French); cap. Ottawa; a. 9,976,185 km²; p. (est. 1972) 21,815,978.

Canada Dam, Bihar, **India;** on R. Mayurakshi, 256 km from Calcutta.

Canadian Coast Range, mtns., B.C., W. **Canada;** penetrated by deep inlets (fjords) with very little cst. plain; crossed only by R. Skeena in N., R. Fraser in S.

Canadian R., S.W. **USA;** trib. of Arkansas R., not navigable but impt. for irrigation; 1,440 km long.

Canadian Shield (Laurentian Shield), Canada; vast region of hard anc. rock surrounding Hudson Bay, deeply eroded by ice, and lake covered; mng. and forestry.

Canal du Centre, canal, **France;** links Rhône-Saône valley at Chalon-sur-Saône with R. Loire at Digoin; serves Le Creusot coalfield; length 96 km.

Canal Zone, Panama; strip of land leased to USA since 1903 for Panama Canal; a. 1,678 km² (714 km² water); p. (1970) 44,650.

Canaries Current, ocean current, flows S. along N.W. coast of Africa from El Dar-el-Beida to C. Verde; relatively cold and has very marked cooling effect on Saharan coastlands.

Canary Is., or Canaries, **N. Atl. Oc.;** gr. of 7 volcanic Is. belong to Spain, 96 km off cst. Africa; inc. Tenerife (the lgst. I.), Gran Canaria, La Palma, Gomera, Hierro, Fuerteventura, Lanzarote; dry sunny climate and impressive volcanic landscape encourage tourism; intensive, irrigated agr. for bananas, tomatoes, oranges and vegetables; cap. Las Palmas, the "Fortunate Isles" of many myths and legends; a. 7,272 km²; p. (1970) 1,170,224.

Canberra, Australian Capital Territory, **Australia;** in Gr. Dividing Range (highest point Mt. Bimberi, 1,912 m) 317 km S.W. of Sydney; planned (1911) as seat of govt. of Commonwealth; univ.; a. 2,356 km²; p. (1972) 158,594 (met. a.).

Candia. *See* **Iráklion.**

Canea. *See* **Khaniá.**

Canna, sm. I., Hebrides, **Scot.;** basaltic pillars.

Cannanore, t., Kerala, **India;** exp. timber, coconuts; p. (1961) 48,960.

Cannes, spt., dep. Alpes-Maritimes, **France;** 32 km S.W. Nice; famous resort; perfumes; airpt.; annual spring international film festival; p. (1968) 67,152 (t.), 213,397 (met. a.).

Cannock and Hednesford, ts., former U.D., Staffs., **Eng.;** on S.W. flank of Cannock Chase, expanded t.; engin., bricks, tiles, tools, elec. gds., car parts; p. (1971) 55,813.

Canopus, c. of anc. **Egypt;** 19 km E. of Alexandria; here bdy. between Asia and Africa was drawn; Aboukir nr. ruins of temple of Serapis.

Cantabrians (Sierra de Cantabria), mtns., N. **Spain;** stretch from Pyrenees to C. Finisterre; form barrier between sea and central plateau; thick vegetation on lower slopes; coal, iron, hydro-elec. power; hgst. peak Peña Vieja (2,673 m).

Cantal, dep., S.E. **France;** volcanic a., part of Massif Central; hgst. peak Plomb du Cantal (1,859 m); difficult agr., sparse p.; cap. Aurillac; a. 5,778 km²; p. (1968) 169,330.

Canterbury, c., Kent, **Eng.;** at foot of N. Downs on R. Stour; univ.; cath. founded A.D. 597 by St. Augustine; shrine of Thomas Becket; for centuries a place of pilgrimage; p. (1971) 33,157.

Canterbury, prov., S.I., **N.Z.;** cap. Christchurch; a. 36,104 km²; p. (1971) 398,318.

Canterbury Plains, rich grazing and wheat-growing dist. S.I., **N.Z.;** ch. t. Christchurch; ch. pt. Lyttelton.

Can-tho, t., S. **Vietnam;** on Mekong R. delta, tr. ctr.; rice, fish; p. (est. 1967) 61,000.

Canton. *See* **Kuangchow.**

Canton R. *See* **Chu-kiang.**

Canton, c., Ohio, **USA;** iron and steel, pulleys, hydraulic presses; p. (1970) 108,872 (c.), 368,876 (met. a.).

Canvey I., Essex, **Eng.;** fronting the Thames; expanded t.; resort; radio components, bookbinding, iron and wire wk., oil storage; oil refinery projected; liquid gas terminal; p. (1971) 26,462.

Cap de la Madeleine, t., S. Quebec, **Canada;** varied mnfs.; p. (1966) 29,433.

Cape Breton I., Nova Scotia, **Canada;** coalmng., steelwks; farming, timber, fishing; ch. t., Sydney; discovered in 1497 by John Cabot; a. 9,324 km²; p. (1966) 166,943.

Cape Canaveral, E. Fla., **USA;** formerly Cape Kennedy; barrier I. separating Banana R. lagoon from Atl. Oc.; military base for testing missiles.

Cape Coast, t., **Ghana;** pt. of G. of Guinea, 96 km S.W. of Accra; cap. of Gold Coast until 1876; exp. cacao; cas.; p. (1970) 51,764.

Cape Cod, low sandy penin., Mass. Bay, **USA;** resort; fishing, boat bldg.; encloses C. C. Bay where Pilgrim Fathers first arrived in America 1620.

Cape Giradeau, t., Mo., **USA;** on Mississippi R.; footwear, clothing; p. (1970) 31,282.

Cape Kennedy. *See* **Cape Canaveral.**

Cape of Good Hope, S. **Africa;** famous headland, S. of Cape Town; 305 m high.

Cape Province, prov., Rep. of **S. Africa;** formerly Cape of Good Hope Colony; southernmost tip of Africa; cap. Cape Town; mostly plateau; inc. Transkeian terrs. in E.; sheep raising; wheat, citrus fruits, grapes, tobacco; fisheries; diamond and copper mng. in Namaqualand;

automobile assembly, textiles, food canning; a. 721,224 km²; p. (1970) 4,235,376.
Capernaüm, in time of Christ impt. place in Palestine, on N. shore of L. Galilee; the modern Tell Hum (Israel).
Cape Town, c., cap. of Cape Province, and legislative cap. of **Rep. of S. Africa**; spt. on Table Bay, 48 km N. of C. of Good Hope; communication by rail direct with Rhodesia, Transvaal, O.F.S., and Natal; docks; cath.; univ.; exp. wool, gold, diamonds; oil refinery under construction at Milnerton 10 km N.E., p. (1970) 1,096,257 (met. a.).
Cape Verde Is., archipelago off **W. cst. Africa**; former Portuguese col.; 15 volcanic Is. and islets, divided into two grs.; windward and leeward; a. 4,040 km²; cap. Praia; agr. sugar, fruit-growing; São Vicente fuelling sta. for navigation to S. America; indep. achieved 1975; irrigation and reafforestation projects; p. (est. 1969) 250,000.
Cap-Haitien, t., **N. Haiti**; spt., on N. cst.; exp. coffee, cacao, sugar; p. (1971) 44,123.
Capraia, I., 26 km E. of Corsica, belonging to **Italy**; volcanic; part of Genoa prov.
Caprera, I. off N.E. cst. Sardinia, **Italy**; Garibaldi buried here.
Caprese Michelangeo, v., Tuscany, **Italy**; birthplace of Michelangelo; p. (est. 1968) 2,220.
Capri, I. and tourist resort in Bay of Naples, **Italy**; famous Blue Grotto; celebrated in times of Augustus and Tiberius; wines; a. 10 km².
Capua, t., Campania, S. **Italy**; on Volturno R.; founded by Etruscans, impt. ctr. under Roman rule, sacked by Gaiseric; modern t. 5 km N. of site of anc. Capua; cath., Roman bridge; p. (est. 1968) 19,176.
Caracas, c., cap. of **Venezuela**; in mtn. valley 921 m a.s.l.; 13 km inland from its pt. La Guaira; modern c.; contains 20 per cent of p. of rep.; cath., univs.; oil, textile mills, sugar refining; p. (est. 1970) 2,175,400 (met. a.).
Carbon County, N. Utah, **USA**; contains immense reserves of gd. coking coal suitable for blast furnaces; not yet developed.
Carbonia, t., Sardinia, **Italy**; built 1937–8 nr. lignite and barytes a.; p. (est. 1968) 32,661.
Carcassonne, c., cap of Aude dep., S. **France**; historic citadel guarding impt. routeway from Aquitaine to Rhône valley; old c. divided from new by Aude R.; tourism; p. (1968) 46,329.
Cardamom Hills, Kerala, S. **India**; highland formed where W. and E. Ghats meet; rise to over 2,400 m; hgst. land of Indian penin.; rainfall less seasonal than most of India; " China " tea plantations on middle slopes.
Cárdenas, t., **W. Cuba**; pt. on Cárdenas Bay; processes and exp. sugar; p. (est. 1967) 67,400.
Cardiff, c., South Glamorgan, cap. of **Wales**; at mouth of R. Taff on Bristol Channel, one of world's gr. coal-shipping pts.; univ., cath., cas.; docks inc. Penarth and Barry; iron and steel wks., flour mills; p. (1971) 278,221.
Cardigan, t., Dyfed, **S. Wales**; at mouth of Teifi R.; former pt., now mkt. ctr.; p. (1971) 3,800.
Cardiganshire, former co., **Wales**. *See* **Dyfed.**
Caribbean Sea, part of **Atl. Oc.**, between W.I. and Central and S. America; warm sea, entirely within tropics; a. 19,425 km².
Cariboo Range, mtns., B.C., W. **Canada**; mass of anc. crystalline rocks inside the gr. bend of R. Fraser; widespread occurrence of lode and alluvial gold; mainly above 1,500 m; hgst. point Mt. Sir Wilfred Laurier (3,584 m).
Carinthia (Karnten), prov., **Austria**; cap. Klagenfurt; contains hgst. mtn. in Austria, Grossglockner, alt. 3,801 m; many Ls.; p. (1968) 522,600.
Carlisle, c., Cumbria, **Eng.**; on Eden R.; pt. and route ctr.; Norman cas.; cath.; textiles, plasterboard, flour, bacon, biscuits, metal boxes; p. (1971) 71,497.
Carlow, co., S.E. Leinster, **R.o.I.**; arable agr. and livestock; co. t. Carlow; a. 896 km²; p. (1966) 33,479.
Carlow, co. t., Carlow co., **R.o.I.**; cath.; mkt., agr. processing; p. (1966) 7,791.
Carlsbad, t., N.M., **USA**; tourist resort; impt. potash deposits; p. (1970) 21,297.
Carlsbad Caverns National Park, N.M., **USA**; in foothills of Guadalupe mtns.; limestone caves; 18,600 ha.
Carlton, t., Notts., **Eng.**; 3 km N.E. Nottingham; hosiery; p. (1971) 45,211.
Carluke, mkt. t., Lanark, **Scot.**; 198 m above Clyde valley; preserve factory.
Carmarthen, t., Dyfed, **Wales**; on Towy R.; impt. agr. ctr.; cas. ruins; p. (1971) 13,072.
Carmarthen Bay, Dyfed, **Wales**; 29 km across.
Carmarthenshire, former co., **Wales**. *See* **Dyfed.**
Carmel, Mount. *See* **Mount Carmel.**
Carmiel, t., N. **Israel**; new t. built between Acre and Safad, in the Galilean hills; planned for p. 50,000.
Carmona, t., **Spain**; Roman walls and necropolis; p. (1970) 24,378.
Carnac, sm. t., Brittany, N.W. **France**; famous for its megalithic monuments.
Carnarvon, t., **W. Australia**; on R. Gascoyne; NASA tracking sta.; p. (1966) 2,957.
Carnatic. *See* **Coromandel.**
Carnoustie, burgh, Angus, **Scot.**; on N. Sea; 10 km S.W. of Arbroath; resort; p. (1971) 6,232.
Caroline Is., archipelago in **W. Pac. Oc.**; 549 in no., lying between the Philippines and the Marshall gr., former Japanese mandate now part of US Pac. Trust Terr.; ch. exp. copra; a. 1,193 km²; p. (est. 1967) 66,900.
Caroni, R., **Venezuela**, hydroelec. complex at confluence Orinoco R.; steelwks.
Carpathian Mtns., range, **E. Europe**; arc of mtns. extending from ČSSR into Ukrainian SSR and Romania; major European range; 1,288 km long; contain oil fields.
Carpentaria, G. of, **N. Australia**; between C. Arnhem and C. York.
Carpentras, t., Vaucluse, **France**; on R. Auzon; antiquities; sweetmeats; p. (1968) 22,130.
Carpi, t., central **Italy**; 16 km N. of Modena; cath.; food processing; p. (est. 1968) 52,186.
Carrantuohill, mtn., Kerry, **R.o.I.**; 1,041 m, loftiest in Magillicuddy's Reeks and in all Ireland.
Carrara, t., Massa-e-Carrara, central **Italy**; famed for white marble used by Michelangelo; p. (1966) 66,592.
Carrickfergus, t., l. gov. dist., **N. Ireland**; pt. on N. shore of Belfast Lough; textiles, nylon fibres, tobacco inds.; p. (est. 1971) 15,162.
Carrickmacross, mkt. t., U.D., Monaghan, **R.o.I.**; p. (1966) 2,094.
Carrick-on-Shannon, co. t., R. D., Leitrim, **R.o.I.**; on flat land in Upper Shannon valley; p. of t. (1966) 1,636.
Carrick-on-Suir, mkt. t., U.D., Tipperary, **R.o.I.**; leather prods.; N.W. of Waterford; p. (1966) 4,830.
Carron, v., Falkirk, **Scot.**; nr. Falkirk; site of first ironwks. in E. Lowlands of Scot.
Carron, Loch, inlet, W. cst., Ross and Cromarty, **Scot.**; followed by rly. from Dingwall to Kyle of Lochalsh.
Carse of Gowrie, Perth and Kinross, **Scot.**; fertile coastal dist. between Perth and Dundee, S. of Sidlaw Hills; soft fruits, especially raspberries.
Carshalton. *See* **Sutton.**
Carson City, cap. Nevada, **USA**; smallest st. cap. at 1,427 m; tourist ctr.; p. (1970) 15,468.
Carstenz Mtns., W. Irian, **Indonesia**; major copper and base metal deposits and mng.; slurry pipeline to pts. on Tipoeka R.
Cartagena, spt., cap. dep. Bolivar, **Columbia**; shares with Barranquilla tr. from Magdalena R. valley; platinum, coffee, chemicals, textiles, fertilisers; oil refinery; p. (est. 1972) 315,200 (t.), 347,600 (met. a.).
Cartagena, c., Murcia prov., S.E. **Spain**; on Mediterranean; spt. and naval base; cath.; shipbldg., metalwkg.; p. (est. 1967) 144,316.
Cartago, t., **Colombia**; in Cauca valley, ctr. of rich agr. a.; coffee, tobacco, cattle; ft. 64,830.
Cartago, c., **Costa Rica**; former cap.; 1,504 m at foot of volcanic Mt. Irazu; coffee, fruits; subject to earthquakes; p. (est. 1967) 20,200.
Cartago Basin, Meseta Central, **Costa Rica**; alt. 5,000 ft.; a. of early Spanish settlement.
Carter Fell, mtn., a summit of the Cheviot hills, on the **Eng./Scot.** border, 554 m.
Carthage, anc. c., **N. Africa**; on Bay of Tunis; destroyed by Romans 146 B.C.; site is sub. of Tunis.
Casablanca. *See* **El Dar-el-Beida.**
Casale Monferrato, t., Piedmont, **Italy**; on R. Po; cath.; cement; p. (est. 1968) 43,896.

Casas Grandes, t., N.W. Chihuahua st., **Mexico**; Aztec ruins; p. (1970) 11,207.

Cascade Range, USA and Canada; extends N. and S. through B.C., Wash., and Ore. between Rocky Mtns. and Pac. cst.; timber resources, hydroelec. power; hgst. peak Mt. Rainier, 4,395 m.

Cascade Tunnel, longest rly. tunnel in N. America, Wash., **USA**; carries trunk rly. from Spokane to Seattle through Cascade Mtns.; length 12·5 km.

Caserta, t., **Italy**; on N.E. edge of plain of Campania; impt. route ctr. and agr. mkt.; cath.; palace; p. (1969) 60,196.

Cashel, mkt. t., U.D. Tipperary, **R.o.I.**; anc. seat of kings of Munster; ruins of cath. on Rock of Cashel; p. (1966) 2,682.

Casiquiare, R., and canal, **Venezuela**; joins Orinoco to the Rio Negro, a trib. of the Amazon.

Casper, t., Wyo., **USA**; petroleum; airpt.; p. (1970) 39,361.

Caspian Sea, salt lake, **USSR** and **Iran**, between Europe and Asia; lgst. inland sea in world; a. 422,170 km² but shrinking; 28 m below sea level; maximum depth 975 m; fed by R. Volga; agr. and dense p. on S. shore; pts.: Astrakhan, at mouth of Volga, Baku (oil ctr.).

Casquets, dangerous rocks, 11 km W. of Alderney, Channel Is. **Eng.**; lighthouse.

Cassino, t., Frosinone, **Italy**; in Apennines, on Rapido R.; t. and nearby monastery destroyed 1944, now rebuilt.

Castel Gandolfo, t., central **Italy**; in Alban Hills; papal summer residence; p. (est. 1968) 8,044.

Castellammare del Golfo, spt., N.W. Sicily, **Italy**; wat. pl., tuna fishing; p. (est. 1968) 15,498.

Castellammare di Stabia, t., Campania, **Italy**; on Bay of Naples, at foot of Vesuvius; historic arsenal and dockyards; mineral springs; cath.; resort; p. (est. 1968) 70,287.

Castellón de la Plana, prov., **Spain**; on Mediterranean, part of anc. Valencia, mainly mtns., a. 6,679 km²; cap. Castellón; p. (est. 1970) 385,823.

Castellón de la Plana, t., **Spain**; on plain inland from Mediterranean cst.; varied agr. inds.; oil refining; p. (1967) 81,187.

Castelnaudary, t., Aude dep., **France**; in strategic gap between Central Massif and Pyrenees; captured by Black Prince 1355; mkt. for cereals; pottery; p. (1968) 10,844.

Castelo Branco, t., **Portugal**, prov. cap. Beira Baixa; agr. mkt. t.; p. (1970) 21,730.

Castelvetrano, agr. t., W. Sicily, **Italy**; wine-mkg.; p. (est. 1968) 31,123.

Castile, region in the high plateaux of central **Spain**; former kingdom; divided into Old Castile in N. (Avila, Burgos, Logroño, Santander, Segovia, Soria) and New Castile in S. (Ciudad Real, Cuenca, Guadalajara, Madrid, Toledo). Its dialect became the standard language of Spain.

Castlebar, U.D., cap. Mayo, **R.o.I.**; mkt. t.; pursuit of Brit. by Fr. who captured t. 1798 known as "Castlebar races"; p. (1966) 5,630.

Castleblayney, U.D., Monaghan, **R.o.I.**; nr. Dundalk; mkt. t.; shoes; p. (1961) 2,125.

Castle Cary, mkt. t., Somerset, **Eng.**; N.E. of Yeovil; dairy prods.; cas. ruins.

Castlecary, v., Central Reg., **Scot.**; sta. on Roman wall; silica, fire clay deposits.

Castle Donington, t., Leics., **Eng.**; airpt; power sta.; p. (1971) 11,851. (dist.).

Castle Douglas, burgh, Stewartry, **Scot.**; nr. R. Dee; nearby cas.; stock mkt.; p. (1971) 3,331.

Castleford, t., West Yorks., **Eng.**; 16 km S.E. of Leeds at confluence of Rs. Aire and Calder; coal mng., chemical, glass, and clothing mnfs, flour milling, brick mkg.; p. (1967) 38,210.

Castlemaine, t., Victoria, **Australia**; at foot of Gr. Dividing Range, 40 km S. of Bendigo; dairying, sheep; engin.; wool; p. (1972) 7,547.

Castlereagh, l. gov. dist., **N. Ireland**; inc. S.E. outskirts of Belfast.

Castleton, v., Derbys., **Eng.**; on Hope R.; tourist ctr. for the Peak District; nearby fluorspar mines.

Castletown, t., Isle of Man, **Eng.**; former cap.; pt., cas. tower.

Castres, t., Tarn, **France**; on R. Agout; former Huguenot stronghold; cath.; textiles, soap, earthenware; p. (1968) 42,920.

Castries, t., cap. St. Lucia, Windward Is. **W.I.**; fine harbour; p. (1964) 5,100.

Castrop-Rauxel or **Kastrop Rauxel**, t., N. Rhine-Westphalia, **W. Germany**; part of Ruhr conurb.; industl.; coal, cement, tar prod., tiles, brandy; p. (est. 1969) 83,892.

Catalonia, region, N.E. **Spain**; ch. industl. a.; comprises 4 provs.; Barcelona, Gerona, Lérida, Tarragona; cap. Barcelona; hilly, drained by Ebro R.; cereals, olive oil, wines; textiles, cars; hydroelec. power stas.; nuclear power sta. projected; a. 32,185 km²; p. (1970) 5,122,567.

Catamarca, t., cap. of Catamarca prov., N.W. **Argentina**; in Andean foothills 128 km S. of San Miguel de Tucumán; ctr. of irrigated oasis producing vines, apricots, cherries, cotton; thermal springs; p. (1960) 42,291.

Catanduanes, I., off S. Luzon, **Philippines**; hilly, fertile; rice, corn, cotton, hemp, coconuts; a. 1,429 km²; p. (1970) 162,679.

Catania, c., Sicily, **Italy**; cap. of C. prov.; pt. on E. cst. at foot of Mt. Etna; rebuilt several times after earthquakes and volcanic eruption; cath., univ., cas.; p. (1969) 412,721.

Catanzaro, t., S. **Italy**; univ.; service ctr., regional cap. of Calabria; p. (1969) 82,243.

Catastrophe, C., S. extremity of Eyre Peninsula, **S. Australia**.

Catawba, R., S. and N.C., **USA**; rises in Blue Ridge Range, flows to Santee R.; extensively dammed; 480 km long.

Caterham and Warlingham, ts., former U.D. Surrey, **Eng.**; on N. Downs; residtl.; p. (1971) 35,781.

Cathay, anc. name for China and E. Tartary.

Catoche, C., N.E. point of Yucatan, **Mexico**.

Catskill Mtns., N.Y., **USA**; gr. in Appalachians, W. of Hudson R.; well wooded; resort for p. of N.Y. c.; alt. c. 900 m.

Cauca, dep., **Colombia**; cap. Popayán; a. 30,191 km²; p. (est. 1968) 664,003.

Cauca, R., **Colombia**; trib. of Magdalena; 960 km long.

Caucasia, region between Black Sea and Caspian, **USSR**; divided by Caucasus Mtns. into N. or Cis-Caucasia and S. or Trans-Caucasia.

Caucasus (Bol'shoy Kavkaz), mtns., separate RSFSR from Georgian SSR and Azerbaydzhan SSR, **USSR**; run from Black Sea to Caspian Sea; divided into 3 ranges; hgst. summits Mt. Elbruz (5,631 m) and Kasbek (5,047 m); many lofty passes and glaciers; total l. c. 1,520 km.

Caucun, I., off Yucatan penin., **Mexico**; developing tourist ctr.; airpt.

Causses, Les, limestone plateau, Aveyron, Tarn deps., S. **France**; on S.W. flank of Central Massif; caverns, gorges of Rs. Lot and Tarn; sheep provide milk for Roquefort cheese; alt. 900–1,800 m.

Cauvery, R., S. **India**; rises in W. Ghats, flows into Bay of Bengal through Karnataka and Tamil Nadu; length 640 km; lge. irrigation and hydroelec. power project.

Caux, region of Normandy, **France**; fertile loess-covered chalk plateau adjacent to English Channel; arable agr.

Cava de' Tirreni, t., Salerno, **Italy**; summer resort; textiles; p. (est. 1968) 46,657.

Cavaillon, t., Vaucluse, **France**; cath.; ctr. of mkt. gardening dist.; p. (1968) 18,544.

Cavan, inland co., **R.o.I.**; agr. a. with many Ls.; depopulation; borders Ulster; a. 1,932 km²; p. (1966) 53,815.

Cavan, U.D., co. t., Cavan, **R.o.I.**; 115 km S.W. Belfast; mkt.; cath.; p. (1966) 4,165.

Cavite, spt., Luzon, **Philippines**; walled t.; oil refining nearby; p. (est. 1970) 77,100.

Cavour Canal, irrigation canal, Piedmont and Lombardy regions, N. **Italy**; links R. Po nr. Chivassa with R. Ticino 16 km N.E. of Novara; provides water for 101,000 ha of rice-fields and meadow-land; length 128 km.

Cawnpore. *See* Kanpur.

Caxias, t., Maranhão, **Brazil**; on Itapicuru R.; p. (1968) 124,403.

Caxias do Sul, t., Rio Grande do Sul, **Brazil**; wines; p. (1970) 107,487.

Cayambe, volcanic mtn., Andes, **Ecuador**; alt. 5,958 m.

Cayenne, c., cap. of **French Guiana**, at mouth of Cayenne R.; exp. gold; gave its name to Cayenne pepper; p. (1967) 24,518.

Cayman Is., **W.I.**; consists of Grand Cayman, cap. Georgetown; Little Cayman; and Cayman

Brac.; turtle and shark fishing; a. 259 km²; p. (1970) 10,652.

Ceará, st., N. **Brazil**; stretches from Brazilian Plateau to Atl. cst.; poor cattle rearing a. with many droughts; cap. Fortaleza; a. 148,078 km²; p. (est. 1968) 3,838,329.

Cebu, one of Visayan Is., **Philippines**; mtnous.; forested; coal, oil, gold; coconuts, maize; a. 4,408 km²; p. (1970) 1,632,642 (prov.).

Cebu, one of Visayan Is., Philippines; mtnous.; forested; coal, oil, gold; coconuts, maize; a. 1,702 sq. m.; p. (1970) 1,632,642 (prov.).

Cebu, t., Cebu I., **Philippines**; tr. ctr. of Visayan Is.; pt. for abaca and copra; p. (1968) 332,100.

Cedar Falls, t., N. Iowa, **USA**; on Cedar R.; p. (1970) 29,597.

Cedar Mountain, hill, Va., **USA**; here Stonewall Jackson defeated Banks in Civil War (second battle of Bull Run, 1862).

Cedar Rapids, c., Iowa **USA**; distribution and rly. ctr. for agr. a.; p. (1970) 109,111 (c.), 160,832 (met. a.).

Cegléd, t., **Hungary**; on edge of Central Plain in fruit growing a.; vehicle repair shops; p. (1966) 37,200.

Celaya, mkt. t., Guanajuato, **Mexico**; rly. junc.; ctr. of rich farming a.; many inds.; sweetmeats; p. (1970) 143,703.

Celebes. *See* **Sulawesi.**

Celje, t., **Yugoslavia**; industl., agr. ctr., zinc refining, fertilisers; close to Austrian border; p. (est. 1965) 30,000.

Celle, t., Lower Saxony, **W. Germany**; on R. Aller; cas. was residence of dukes of Brunswick-Lüneburg until 1705; oil refining, machin., textiles; p. (est. 1967) 56,500.

Celtic Sea, a. bounded by S. Ireland, Wales, Cornwall and Brittany: rich natural gas deposits 48 km S.W. of Kinsale.

Central African Republic, indep. st. within Fr. Community, **Equatorial Africa**; formerly Fr. colony of Ubangi-Shari; landlocked upland plateau covered by savannah grassland; cotton, diamonds; cap. Bangui; a. 616,420 km²; p. (est. 1969) 1,518,000.

Central America, stretch of land between Mexico and S. America, from the Isthmus of Tehuantepec to that of Panama; includes Guatemala, Honduras, Nicaragua, Salvador, Costa Rica, Panama, Belize; tropical climate; forests, savannahs; p. (est. 1970) 16,630,000.

Central Asia, usually applied to regions between 30° and 40° N. lat. and 55° and 85° E. long.; Soviet C.A. is the land between China and Afghanistan and the Caspian, consisting of Kazakh SSR, Tadzhik SSR, Turkmen SSR, Uzbek SSR, and Kirghiz SSR.

Central Massif. *See* Massif Central.

Central Region, l. gov. reg., **Scot.**; stretches from Grampian mtns. to Central Lowlands, inc. Forth valley; main ts. Falkirk and Stirling; a. 2,631 km²; p. (1971) 262,600.

Central Valley, Cal., **USA**; valleys of Rs. San Joaquin and Sacramento; main agr. a. of Cal.; vast scheme for irrigation, hydroelec. power, flood control and protection of wildlife.

Cephalonia (Kefallinia), lgst. of Ionian Is., **Greece**; mtnous. with fertile valleys; impt. harbours of Argostólion and Lexourion; currant production; a. 751 km².

Ceram. *See* Seram.

Cérignola, t., Apulia, **Italy**; agr. ctr.; Spanish victory over French in Italian wars 1503; p. (est. 1967) 42,200.

Cerigo (Kithira) I., **Greece**; sm. I. between Crete and Peloponnesus.

Cernauti. *See* Chernovtsy.

Cerro de Pasco, t., Pasco dep., **Peru**; mng. ctr. at 4,403 m; univ.; copper, gold, lead, zinc; p. (1961) 19,354.

Cerro Rico, mtn., **Bolivia**; in Andes, W. of Potosi; alt. 4,782 m; rich silver, tin, tungsten ores.

Cesena, t., Emillia-Romagna, **Italy**; flourished in Renaissance times; cath., Malatesta library; agr. mkt. t.; p. (est. 1967) 53,300.

České Budějovice (Budweis), t., **ČSSR**; on R. Vitava, 128 km S. of Prague, major industl. ctr.; pencils, porcelain, brewing, anthracite; p. (1967) 72,000.

Cesky Těšín, t., **ČSSR**; on Olše R., trib. of Oder; part of former t. of Teschen on Czech side of frontier with Poland; coal mng.

Cessnock-Bellbird, t., N.S.W., **Australia**; coal-mng. declining since 1968; clothing wks.; p. (1972) 16,141.

Cetina R., Dalmatia, **Yugoslavia**; hydroelec. power.

Ceuta, spt., **Spanish N. Africa**, naval base; opposite to and 26 km from Gibraltar; cath.; the anc. Abyia, one of the Pillars of Hercules; p. (est. 1970) 88,468.

Cevennes, mtns., S. **France**; separating basins of Rhône, Loire, and Tarn; highest point Mt. Mézenc, alt. 1,767 m.

Ceylon. *See* Sri Lanka.

Chaco, prov., N. **Argentina**; farming and prairie land; cap. Resistencia; a. 99,632 km²; p. (1970) 566,613.

Chad, indep. st. within Fr. Community, **Equatorial Africa**; cap. Ndjamene; desert and dry savannah; cotton, livestock; a. 1,282,050 km²; p. (est. 1969) 3,510,000.

Chad, L., lge. sheet of water bordering **Nigeria, Niger, Chad** and **Cameroon**; a. 129,500 km² when in flood; varies in extent with season, and is drying up; shallow, many Is., lies between the wooded region of the Sudan and the steppes leading to the Sahara desert; joint project for devel. by neighbouring ctys.

Chadderton, t., Gtr. Manchester, **Eng.**; engin., chemicals, textiles; p. (1971) 32,406.

Chagos Is., 5 coral Is., **Indian Oc.**; admin. by Seychelles since 1965; fine harbour in Diego Garcia (Anglo-American naval communications ctr.).

Chainat, t., **Thailand**; on Menam Chao Phraya; major barrage for hydroelec. power and flood control.

Chalcis, t., **Greece**; resort for Athens; joined to mainland by swing bridge; p. (1971) 36,381.

Chalfont St. Giles, v., Bucks, **Eng.**; in London commuter belt; home of Milton.

Châlons-sur-Marne, t, cap. of Marne dep., N.E. **France**; comm. and industl; cath., churches; p. (1968) 54,025.

Châlon-sur-Saône, t., Saône-et-Loire dep., E. **France**; R. pt., comm. ctr. for Burgundy; historic t.; p. (1968) 52,746.

Chambal, R., trib. of R. Jumna, rising in Vindhya hills, Madhya Pradesh, **India**; major power, irrigation and industl. scheme; agr. in lower valley causing soil erosion, major soil conservation projection; 880 km long.

Chambéry, t., cap. of Savoie dep., S.E. **France**; leather gds.; tourism; p. (1968) 53,813.

Chambord, v., Loir-et-Cher dep., **France**; on R. Cosson, trib. of Loire; Renaissance château; p. (1968) 267.

Chamonix, t., Haute-Savoie, **France**; at foot of Mont Blanc, in valley of R. Arve; winter sports ctr.; road tunnel links to Aosta; p. (1968) 8,403.

Champagne, region and former prov., **France**; covers deps. of Aube, Marne, Haute-Marne, Ardennes, and parts of Yonne, Aisne, Seine-et-Marne, and Meuse; famous for its champagne wine; wheat, sheep; impt. tr. fairs in Middle Ages., main ctr. Reims. *See* **Champagne Humide and Champagne Pouilleuse.**

Champagne Humide, region, **France**; clay vale, runs 160 km N.E. from Auxerre to Bar-le-Duc; drained by Seine, Aube, Marne, Aisne, and many tribs.; heavily wooded, marshy; where cleared and drained, grain cultivation.

Champagne Pouilleuse, region, **France**; barren chalk plateau, extends 128 km N.E. from Sens to Reims; drained by Aisne, Vesle, Seine, Aube, Marne; dusty chalk downland pastures; sheep; vine growing on S.-facing valley sides and S.E.-facing escarpment of Falaise de l'Île de France favours production of Champagne wines; ch. producing ctrs.: Châlons-sur-Marne, Reims, Epernay.

Champaign, t., Ill., **USA**; close to Urbana; univ.; foundries; food processing; p. (1970) 55,976 (c.), 162,107 (met. a.).

Champigny-sur-Marne, t., Val-de-Marne dep., **France**; E. sub. of Paris; varied inds.; p. (1968) 70,564.

Champlain Canal, N.Y., **USA**; follows gap between Adirondack Mtns. and Green Mtns. occupied by Hudson R.; links Albany with L. Champlain and allows through barge traffic between New York and St. Lawrence valley.

Champlain, L., **USA**; N. frontier of N.Y. st.;

discharges by Richelieu R. into St. Lawrence; flanked by trunk route from New York to Montreal; forms link between Hudson R. and St. Lawrence waterway; a. 1,126 km².
Chañaral, spt., N. Atacama, **Chile**; lies in gold and copper-mng. a.; p. (1960) 21,098.
Chanda, t., Nagpur, Maharashtra, **India**; anc. temples; p. (1961) 51,484.
Chandausi, t., Uttar Pradesh, **India**; cotton, hemp; rly. ctr.; p. (1961) 48,557.
Chandernagore, t., W. Bengal, **India**; on Hooghly R., N. of Calcutta; founded by French 1686; p. (1961) 67,105.
Chandigarh, union terr. (1966) and cap. of both Punjab and Haryana sts., **India**; new c. designed by Le Corbusier to replace former cap. Lahore, now in Pakistan; on plateau at foot of Himalayas, S.W. of Simla; univ.; a. of terr. 114 km², p. of c. (1971) 218,743.
Changchow (Changzhou), c., Kiangsu, **China**; in valley of Yangtze R., on Grand Canal 112 km S.E. of Nanking; mkt. for intensively cultivated dist.; silk; p. (1953) 297,000.
Changchun, c., Kirin, **China**; rly. ctr.; univ.; China's biggest motor vehicle plant, machine tools; p. (est. 1970) 1,500,000.
Changnacheri, t., Kerala, S. **India**; tea, cotton-spinning, silk; p. (1961) 42,376.
Changpai Shan, mtns.; form bdy. between **China** and N. **Korea**; drained by Rs. Yalu and Tumen; hgst. point Pai-t'ou-shan, 2,442 m.
Changsha, c., cap. of Hunan prov., **China**; pt. on Hsiang R.; univ.; tea, rice, antimony; p. (est. 1970) 850,000.
Changshu, c., Kiangsu, **China**; in valley of Yangtze R., 104 km S.W. of Shanghai; mkt. for local agr. prod.; p. (est. 1970) 150,000.
Channel Is., gr. of self-governing Is. belonging to the Brit. Crown off N.W. cst. France, of which the lgst. are Jersey, Guernsey, Alderney, and Sark; part of the old duchy of Normandy; vegetables, flowers, fruit, granite; two famous breeds of dairy cattle; tourist resort; impt. banking and insurance ctr. encouraged by low taxes; retirement ctr.; a. 194 km²; p. (est. 1973) 125,000.
Chantilly, t., Oise, **France**; famous race-course; formerly famous for lace and porcelain; p. (1968) 10,501.
Chaochow (Chaozhou), c., Kwangtung, S. **China**; on Han R., 32 km N. of Swatow; ctr. of cultivated plain; rice, sugar, tea; linked to Swatow by rly.; p. (1953) 101,300.
Chao Phraya. *See* **Menam Chao Phraya**.
Chapala, L., **Mexico**; chiefly in Jalisco st.; attractive site and climate encourage tourism; pastoral agr. on shores; a. 1,080 km².
Chapayevsk, t., Kuybyshev region, **RSFSR**; in Volga valley; chemicals, agr. machin.; p. (est. 1969) 87,000.
Chapelcross, nr. Annan, Annandale and Eskdale, **Scot.**; AEA nuclear power sta., producing electricity for nat. grid.
Chapel-en-le-Frith, mkt. t., Derbys., **Eng.**; brake-linings; p. (1971) 18,689 (dist.).
Chapra, t., Bihar, **India**; on Ganges R.; ctr. of former saltpetre and indigo tr.; p. (1961) 75,580.
Chard, mkt. t., Somerset, **Eng.**; lace, engin., shirt and cotton mftg.; p. (1971) 7,905.
Chardzhou, t., Turkmen SSR, **USSR**; inland pt. on Amu-Dar'ya R.; shipyards, textiles, chemicals; major oil refinery project; p. (1967) 85,000.
Charente, dep., S.W. **France**; cap. Angoulême; ctr. of distilling tr., cognac; a. 5,970 km²; p. (1968) 331,016.
Charente, R., S.W. **France**; rises W. of Limoges and flows into Bay of Biscay below Rochefort; valley slopes beyond Angoulême produce celebrated grapes from which brandy is made at Cognac and Jarnac.
Charente-Maritime, dep., S.W. **France**; cap. La Rochelle; borders Bay of Biscay; wine, wheat; oysters, pilchards; a. 7,229 km²; p. (1968) 483,622.
Charleroi, t., Hainaut, **Belgium**; on R. Sambre; coal mng.; glass; p. (est. 1967) 24,500 (c.); (est. 1969) 217,349 (met. a.).
Charleston, c., spt., S.C., **USA**; industl. and comm. ctr. on Atl. cst. founded 1670; scene of onset of Civil War; p. (1970) 64,591 (c.), 285,916 (met. a.).
Charleston, t., cap. W. Va., **USA**; on Kanawha R.; in bituminous coal dist.; chemicals, glass, tools, oil, natural gas, lumber, coal processing; p. (1970) 69,531 (c.), 224,054 (met. a.).
Charleville, t., Queensland, **Australia**; on Warrego R., 640 km W. of Brisbane; pastoral dist.; p. (1966) 4,799.
Charleville-Mézières, twin t., Ardennes dep., N.E. **France**; on Meuse R.; iron, bricks, nails, hardware; p. (1968) 55,543.
Charlotte, c., N.C., **USA**; key rly. junc.; machin., chemicals, textiles; p. (1970) 239,056 (c.), 405,976 (met. a.).
Charlotte Amalie, t., cap. of Virgin Is. of **USA**; on St. Thomas I.; excellent natural harbour; former coaling sta.; p. (1970) 12,372.
Charlottenburg, sub. of Berlin, **Germany**; (in W. Berlin); on R. Spree.
Charlottesville, t., Va., **USA**; on Rivanna R.; in apple-growing region; univ.; Monticello nearby, home of Jefferson; textiles; p. (1970) 38,880.
Charlottetown, t., ch. pt. Prince Edward I., **Canada**; named after Queen Charlotte, consort of George III; univ.; p. (1971) 18,631.
Charlton Kings, t., Gloucs., **Eng.**; at foot of Cotswolds nr. Cheltenham; p. (1971) 10,088.
Charnwood Forest, upland dist., Leics., **Eng.**; to W. of Soar valley, 19 km N.W. of Leicester; composed of anc. rocks; stone-crushing; largely forests; used for recreation by industl. ts. of E. Midlands; alt. 180–275 m.
Charters Towers, t., N. Queensland, **Australia**; pastoral ctr.; former gold-mng. a.; p. (1972) 7,529.
Chartres, t., cap. of Eure-et-Loir dep., **France**; mkt. for cereals from Beauce region; famous Gothic cath.; p. (1968) 36,881.
Châteauroux, t., cap. of Indre dep., **France**; 96 km S.E. of Tours, on R. Indre; agr. ctr., food processing; woollens, pottery; p. (1968) 51,201.
Chateau Thierry, t., Aisne, **France**; on R. Marne; mkt. t.; cas.; precision instruments; p. (1968) 11,629.
Châtellerault, t., Vienne, **France**; 64 km S. of Tours on R. Vienne; cutlery, metallurgical and aeronautical engin. Descartes lived here; p. (1968) 35,337.
Chatham, t., Kent, **Eng.**; on estuary of R. Medway; lt. inds.; naval dockyard established by Henry VIII; p. (1971) 56,921.
Chatham, t., spt., N.B., **Canada**; lumbering, fish exporting; p. (1971) 7,812.
Chatham, c., Ont., **Canada**; on extinct L. plain on R. Thames; agr. prods.; p. (1971) 34,601.
Chatham Is., N.Z. dependency, S. Pac. Oc.; volcanic Is.; sheep rearing and fishing; a. 963 km²; lgst. I. Wharekauri; p. (est. 1968) 500.
Chatsworth, par., Derbys., **Eng.**; on R. Derwent; seat of the dukes of Devonshire.
Chattanooga, c., Tenn., **USA**; on Tennessee R.; univ.; rly. ctr.; cottons; iron, steel, chemicals, paper, metals; p. (1970) 113,033 (c.), 293,034 (met.a.).
Chatteris, Cambridge, **Eng.**; mkt. t.; p. (1971) 5,566.
Chaudière Falls, on Ottawa R., above Ottawa, **Canada**; hydroelec. sta.
Chauk, t., **Burma**; on R. Irrawaddy; ctr. of oilfield; oil refining; fertilisers.
Chaumont, t., cap. of Haute-Marne dep., **France**; on R. Marne; gloves, leather; p. (1968) 27,569.
Chautauqua, L., N.Y., st., **USA**; summer resort; vineyards.
Chaux-de-Fonds, La, t., can. Neuchâtel, **Switzerland**; ctr. of watchmkg. ind.; p. (1969) 43,200.
Cheadle, t., Staffs., **Eng.**; metal mnfs.; former coal-mng. a.; p. (1971) 4,070 (dist.).
Cheadle and Gatley, ts., Gtr. Manchester, **Eng.**; textile finishing and bleaching, engin.; residtl.; p. (1971) 60,648.
Cheb, t., **ČSSR**; nr. Bavarian frontier; industl. ctr.; motor cycles, machin., textiles; p. (1967) 25,633.
Cheboksary, c., cap. of Chuvash ASSR, **RSFSR**; R. pt. on Volga; agr. ctr.; hydroelec. plant; p. (1970) 216,000.
Checheno-Ingush ASSR, USSR; oilfield, petrochemicals; p. (1970) 1,065,000.
Cheddar, v., Somerset, **Eng.**; famous limestone caves in Mendips; cheese, strawberries.
Chefoo (Yentai), c., N. Shantung prov., **China**; pt. on G. of Pohai; former treaty pt.; noted for its pongee silk ("shantung"); p. (est. 1970) 180,000.

Cheju (Quelpart), **I.**, off **S. Korea**, E. China Sea; extinct volcano Mt. Halla, 1,968 m.
Chekiang (Zhijiang), coastal prov., S.E. **China**; cap. Hangchow; impt. rice-growing a.; major natural gas field; a. 102,269 km²; p. (est. 1968) 31,000,000.
Che-ling Pass, on bdy. between Kwangtung and Hunan, S. **China**; historic route across Nanling mtns., now followed by Wuhan to Kuangchow trunk rly.; alt. 300 m.
Chelm, t., E. **Poland**; nr. Lublin; cath.; flour-milling; p. (1968) 37,100.
Chelmer, R., Essex, **Eng.**; joins R. Blackwater at Maldon.
Chelmsford, co. t., Essex, **Eng.**; 48 km N.E. London; cath.; agr. mkt.; radio, elec. engin., brewing; p. (1971) 58,125.
Chelsea, dist., London, **Eng.**; fashionable residtl. dist. *See* **Kensington**.
Chelsea, t., Mass., **USA**; industl. sub. on Boston harbour; p. (1970) 30,625.
Cheltenham, t., Gloucs. **Eng.**; spa; educational ctr.; precision instruments; birthplace of Gustav Holst; p. (1971) 69,734.
Chelyabinsk, t., **RSFSR**; major industl. ctr. on Miass R., Siberian lowlands; steel wks.; metallurgy, machin.; on natural gas pipeline from Gazli gasfield; p. (1970) 874,000.
Chelyuskin, Cape, most N. point in Asia, in Krasnoyarsk Terr., **RSFSR**; named after Russian navigator who discovered it in 1742.
Chemnitz. *See* **Karl-Marx-Stadt**.
Chemulpo. *See* **Inchon**.
Chenab, R., W. Punjab, **Pakistan**; one of "five rivers" of Punjab; rises in Himalayas, flows S.W. into R. Sutlej; dams at Marala and Khanki provide water for Upper and Lower Chenab Irrigation Canal Systems; approx. 1,440 km long.
Chengchow (Zhengzhou), c., cap. Honan prov., **China**; 24 km S. of Hwang-ho (Yellow R.), where it emerges on to N. China Plain; impt. route ctr. and rly. junc. where Peking to Wuhan rly. crosses Sian to Tunghai rly.; p. (est. 1970) 1,500,000.
Chengtu (Chengdu), c., cap. of Szechwan prov., **China**; ctr. of tobacco and cotton-growing a.; oil refinery; chemicals, textiles, machin.; p. (est. 1970) 2,000,000.
Chepstow, mkt. t., Gwent, **Wales**; on R. Wye, 3 km above confluence with R. Severn; Severn Bridge links to Aust (Avon); ruined cas.; lt. engin., brush mkg., asphalt, limestone; p. (1971), 16,096.
Chequers, official residence of Brit. prime ministers, 3 km S. of Wendover, Bucks., **Eng.**; gift of Lord Lee of Fareham.
Cher, dep., **France**; cap. Bourges; crossed by Cher R.; chiefly pastoral agr.; a. 7,301 km²; p. (1968) 304,601.
Cher, R., central **France**; rises in Central Massif, joins Loire below Tours; length 320 km.
Cherbourg, spt., Manche, **France**; N. cst. of Contentin peninsula; opposite to and 128 km dist. from Portsmouth; naval arsenal, shipbldg.; metals, ropes, fishing; p. (1968) 40,333.
Cheremkhovo, t., **RSFSR**; N.W. of Irkutsk; coal, engin., chemicals; on Trans-Siberian rly.; p. (est. 1969) 104,000.
Cherepovets, c., **RSFSR**; on Rybinskoye reservoir of R. Volga; steel, engin., sawmills, shipbldg.; p. (1970) 189,000.
Cheribon. *See* **Tjirebon**.
Cherkassy, t., Ukrainian SSR, **USSR**; nr. Kiev, on reservoir formed by Dnieper R.; sugar, engin., sawmilling; p. (1970) 159,000.
Cherkessk, t., **RSFSR**; rly. terminus, industl. ctr.; p. (1970) 76,000.
Chernigov, t., Ukrainian SSR, **USSR**; on Desna R.; caths.; univ.; flour, textiles, chemicals; p. (1970) 159,000.
Chernogorsk, t., **RSFSR**; 16 km N.W. of Abakan; ctr. of Minusinsk coal-mng. basin; p. (est. 1967) 63,000.
Chernovtsy, t., Ukrainian SSR, **USSR**; univ.; Greek cath.; wheat, dairy produce, textiles, engin., chemicals; p. (1970) 187,000.
Chernyakhovsk (Insterberg), t., Lithuanian SSR, **USSR**; chemicals, textiles; p. (est. 1967) 29,000.
Cherrapunji, t., Assam, **India**; in Khasi Hills; reputed wettest place in world, average annual rainfall 12,700 mm.
Chertsey, t., Surrey, **Eng.**; on S. bank of R. Thames, 6 km below Staines; residtl.; aircraft components, cement; p. (1971) 44,886.
Cherwell, R., trib. of Thames, nr. Oxford, **Eng.**; length 48 km.
Chesapeake Bay, inlet on Atl. cst., **USA**; extending 320 km from mouth of Susquehanna R. to C. Charles; shellfish ind.; bridge-tunnel (opened 1964) spans entrance to Bay.
Chesham, t., Bucks., **Eng.**; in heart of Chiltern Hills; printing, textiles, lt. engin.; residtl.; p. (1971) 20,416.
Cheshire, non-met. co., N.W. **Eng.**; lowland a. drained by Rs. Dee and Mersey, bounded by Pennines in E.; dairying and mkt. gardening; chemical ind. based on salt deposits around Northwich; heavy inds. in and around Warrington; much of co. residtl. for Liverpool and Manchester; cap. Chester; a. 2,323 km²; p. (1971) 865,000.
Cheshire, t., Conn., **USA**; agr.; formerly copper, and barytes mined; p. (est. 1967) 42,900.
Cheshunt, t., Herts., **Eng.**; in Lea valley, 11 km S. of Hertford; bricks, mkt. gardening, horticulture; p. (1971) 44,947.
Chesil Bank, Dorset, **Eng.**; shingle ridge enclosing the Fleet lagoon running from I. of Portland to Bridport.
Chester, c., Cheshire, **Eng.**; at head of estuary of R. Dee; cath., anc. walls and old timbered houses; Roman c. of Deva site of legionary barracks; engin., metal gds.; p. (1971) 62,696.
Chester, t., Penns., **USA**; on Delaware R., S.W. Philadelphia; called Uppland by Swedish settlers 1643, renamed by William Penn; pt. of entry; shipbldg.; p. (est. 1969) 61,000.
Chesterfield, mkt. t., colly. dist., Derbys., **Eng.**; on Rother R.; 13 km S. of Sheffield; variety of heavy inds.; 14th-cent. church with crooked spire; p. (1971) 70,153.
Chesterfield Inlet, arm of Hudson Bay, **Canada**; 400 km by 40 km.
Chester-le-Street, t., Durham, **Eng.**; clothing confectionery, sand wkg.; p. (1971) 20,531.
Cheviot Hills, range between Scot. and **Eng.**; hgst. summit, the Cheviot, 816 m.
Cheyenne, t., cap. of Wyo., **USA**; cattle-ranching dist.; rly. ctr.; p. (1970) 40,914.
Cheyenne, R., S.D., **USA**; trib. of Missouri; irrigation; length 800 km.
Chiana, Val di, valley, central **Italy**; separates Tuscan hills from central Apennines; occupied by upper course of R. Arno, middle course of R. Tiber; followed by main route from Florence to Rome.
Chiang Mai, c., cap of C. prov., and 3rd c. of **Thailand**; rly. terminus on Ping R.; tr. ctr.; teak; p. (1970) 89,272.
Chiapa, R., flows N. from **Guatemala** through **Mexico** to G. of Campeche; impt. routeway in lower course; length 320 km.
Chiapas, Pac. st., **Mexico**; mtnous., forested; bananas, tobacco, sugar and cocoa; cattle; oil reserves; close associations with Guatemala; cap. Tuxtla-Gutierrez; a. 74,408 km²; p. (1970) 1,578,180.
Chiasso, frontier t.; S. **Switzerland**; rly. sta. on Italian border; p. (1970) 8,868.
Chiatura, t., Georgian SSR **USSR**; impt. manganese deposits; p. (est. 1967) 27,000.
Chiba, c., cap. of C. pref. **Japan**; part of Keihin conurb. on Tokyo B.; tr. ctr., giant shipyard, oil refining, aluminium, chemicals, iron and steel; airpt.; p. (est. 1971) 512,000.
Chicago, c., Ill., **USA**; on S. shore of L. Michigan; second lgst. US c.; economic heart of Mid-West; comm. ctr. called "The Loop"; immense tr. by rail and Gr. Ls.; univs.; grain mills, meat packing plants, iron and steel wks., major iron-ore mkt., electronic equipment, furniture; lgst. airpt. in world; p. (1970) 3,322,855 (c.), 6,892,509 (met. a.).
Chichester, t., West Sussex, **Eng.**; on S. cst. plain, 18 km W. of Arundel; cath.; yachting basin; p. (1971) 20,547.
Chickamauga Creek, **USA**; branch of Tennessee R. above Chattanooga, forming part of Tenn. Valley Authority scheme; Civil War battles; site of Nat. Park.
Chickerell, E. Dorset, **Eng.**; 5 km N.W. of Weymouth; site of nuclear power sta. on shores of East Fleet R.
Chiclayo, c., Lambayeque dep., **Peru**; mkt. ctr. for irrigated desert a. between Andes and

Pac. Oc. producing mainly rice and sugar; p. (est. 1970) 140,800.
Chicopee, t., Mass., **USA**; on Connecticut R. nr. Springfield; hardware, carpets, cars; p. (1970) 66,676.
Chicoutimi, t., Quebec, **Canada**; pt. on Chicoutimi R.; lumber, pulp, paper; hydroelectric power; p. (1971) 32,890.
Chiemsee, L., lge. lake nr. Munich, **W. Germany**; c. 460 m a.s.l.
Chieti, t., cap. of C. prov., S. **Italy**; cath.; anc. Teate Marrucinorum; Europe's lgst. glass plant, using methane from Abruzzi field; p. (1969) 53,324.
Chignecto Bay, inlet of Bay of Fundy, **Canada**; bordered by C. isthmus.
Chigrik, t., Uzbek SSR, **USSR**; new t. (1963) 34 km S. of Tashkent.
Chigwell, t., Essex, **Eng.**; on borders of Epping Forest; Hainault Estate now incorporated in Redbridge, Greater London; residtl.; p. (1971) 53,620.
Chihli, Gulf of. *See* **Pohai.**
Chihauhua, lgst. st. in **Mexico**; dry climate impedes agr.; mng., cotton, cattle, Chihuahua dogs; a. 247,024 km²; p. (1969) 1,826,000.
Chihuahua, c., cap. Chihuahua st., **Mexico**; univ., cath.; ctr. silver-mng. ind.; p. (1970) 257,027.
Chikchi, peninsula, **RSFSR**; world's first Arctic nuclear power sta. being built.
Chikugo, t., N. Kyushu, **Japan**; lgst. coalmines in country.
Chilaw, t., **Sri Lanka**; ctr. of coconut plantations.
Chile, rep., **S. America**; extends between Andes and Pac. for 4,160 km to C. Horn, E. to W. 400 km; Atacama desert; Spanish language; Roman Catholic; similar climate to that of Argentina but lacks space for extensive agr., dairying, sheep, wool; ch. exp. nitrates, copper, iron ore, coal, iodine, petroleum, paper; cap. Santiago; ch. pt. Valparaíso; earthquake 1960, hgst. recorded magnitude; a. 738,494 km²; p. (est. 1969) 9,566,000.
Chillán, t., cap. of Nuble prov., **Chile**; destroyed 1939 by one of world's worst recorded earthquakes; since rebuilt; agr. and comm. ctr.; p. (est. 1966) 77,654.
Chiloé, I. and S. prov., **Chile**; cap, San Carlos, earthquakes 1939 and 1960; ch. pt. Ancud destroyed 1960; heavy rainfall, tropical forest; a. 23,460 km²; p. (1970) 110,728.
Chilpancingo de los Bravos, t., cap. of Guerrero st., **Mexico**; ctr. of pre-Aztec culture; univ.; p. (1970) 56,904.
Chiltern Hills, chalk escarpment, Oxon., Bucks., Beds., and Herts., **Eng.**; cut by no. of impt. gaps used by main communications; sheep and barley; hgst. point 276 m nr. Wendover.
Chimborazo, mtn., **Ecuador**, 6,286 m; Andes; extinct volcano, first explored by von Humboldt (1802), first scaled by Whymper (1880).
Chimbote, spt., **Peru**; steel, iron-ore, coal; tinned fish fish-meal; p. (est. 1970) 102,800.
Chimkent, t., Kazakh SSR, **USSR**; in W. foothills of Tien Shan; nearby oasis fed by Arys R.; major industl. ctr.; lead smelting; p. (1970) 247,000.
China, People's Republic of, Asia; second lgst. cty. of world; anc. conservative civilisation overthrown by long civil war and establishment of communist régime (1949); lge. p. crowded on cultivable valleys of Hwang-ho (Yellow R.), Yangtze and Si-kiang in E.; rest of cty. either mtnous. (plateau of Tibet) or desert (Sinkiang); rapid economic growth following onset of communist régime; agr. organised on commune basis, becomes increasingly intensive in S. where climate is less extreme; vast mineral resources, many undeveloped; recent industl. growth; heavy inds. at Wuhan, Paotow and in N.E. (Manchuria); poor communications except in E.; cap. Peking; a. 11,137,000 km²; p. (est. 1974) 827,850,000, lgst. p. of any cty.
China Sea, part of W. Pacific between Korea and Philippines; divided by the narrow Formosa Strait into two areas; E. China Sea, inc. Yellow Sea, and S. China Sea.
Chinandega, mkt. t., cap. of C. dep., **Nicaragua**; sugar-refining; p. (1967) 36,885.
Chinchow (Jinzhou), c., Liaoning prov., **China**; cement, glass, bricks, tiles, paper and wood pulp, oil; p. (est. 1970) 750,000.
Chindwin, R., **Burma**; ch. trib. of Irrawaddy; rises in Patkai Hills, navigable in rainy season; dense p. in power reaches; 800 km long.
Chinghai (Tsinghai), prov., W. **China**; between Sinkiang and Tibet, inc. C. plateau; local coal and iron-ore but exploitation hindered by isolation; two new iron and steel plants; a. 721,004 km²; p. (est. 1970) 2,000,000.
Chingola, t., **Zambia**; copper mng.; metal prod., printing; p. (est. 1972) 181,500 (met. a.).
Chinkiang (Zhenjiang), c., Kiangsu, **China**; former treaty pt., Yangtse R., 77 km below Nanking; tr. ctr.; p. (est. 1970) 250,000.
Chinon, t. Indre-et-Loire, central **France**; on R. Vienne, industl.; ruined cas., once a royal residency; nuclear power sta.; p. (1968) 8,035.
Chinqui, volcano, **Panama**; 3,480 m.
Chinwangtao (Qinhuangdao), c., spt., former treaty pt., Hopeh, N. **China**; on Yellow Sea cst. 240 km N.E. of Tientsin; only gd. natural harbour on N. China cst.; exp. coal from Kailan mines; p. (1953) 186,800.
Chioggia, spt., cath. t., N. **Italy**; on I. in G. of Venice; fishing; p. (est. 1968) 48,347.
Chios (Khios) I., in Aegean Sea, **Greece**; mainly agr.; wines, fruits and figs; supposed birthplace of Homer; p. (1971) 53,942.
Chippenham, Wilts., **Eng.**; mkt. t. on R. Avon; rly. signal and brake equipment, bacon curing, tanning; p. (1971) 18,662.
Chipping Campden, v. Gloucs., **Eng.**; in Cotswold Hills; formerly impt. for woollens; tourism.
Chipping Norton, mkt. t., Oxford, **Eng.**; nr. Banbury; formerly impt. for woollens; p. (1971) 4,763.
Chipping Sodbury, mkt. t., Avon, **Eng.**; 13 km N.E. of Bristol; p. (1971) 67,040 (dist.).
Chirchik, c., Uzbek SSR, **USSR**; 32 km N.E. Tashkent; engin., chemicals; hydroelec. power stas.; p. (1970) 108,000.
Chiricahua Mtns., Arizona, **USA**; form part of Coronado Nat. Forest; long inhabited by Apache Indians; spectacular volcanic scenery; alt. 2,987 m.
Chirk, t., Clwyd, **Wales**; on R. Cleriog, S. of Wrexham; slate, former coal-mng. a.; cas.
Chislehurst. *See* **Bromley.**
Chistyakovo. *See* **Torez.**
Chita, c., rly. ctr., Siberia, **RSFSR**; on upper R.Ingoda, 640 km E. of L. Baykal; coal, engin., chemicals, sawmilling; p. (1970) 242,000.
Chittagong, c., **Bangladesh**; main pt. on Karnafuli R., nr. Bay of Bengal; exp. jute. tea; oil refining; steel mill; hydroelec. power; p. (1974) 416,733.
Chittaranjan, t., Bihar, **India**; new t. on Barakhar R., in steel ctr. of Damodar valley; rly. locomotive wks.; p. (1961) 28,957.
Chkalov. *See* **Orenburg.**
Choisy-le-Roi, t., Val-de-Marne dep., **France**; industl. sub. of Paris on R. Seine; p. (1968) 41,711.
Cholet, t., Maine-et-Loire, **France**; textile ctr. on R. Seine; p. (1968) 41,711.
Cholon (Cho Lon), t., S. **Vietnam**; 16 km S.W. of Ho Chi-minh City; ctr. of rice tr.; p. inc. Ho Chi-minh City (1968) 1,682,000.
Cholula, anc. c. of Puebla prov., **Mexico**; Aztec temple, pyramid of Cholula, and other remains.
Chomo Lhari, mtn., Tibet, **China** and **Bhutan**; sacred to Buddhists; part of Himalayas; alt. 7,319 m.
Chomutov, t., N. **ČSSR**; industl. ctr. of lignite mng. a.; coal, steel, glass; p. (1967) 38,000.
Chooz, t., Ardennes, **France**; pressurised water reactor; nuclear power sta. linked with Belgian grid.
Cho Oyu, mtn., between Nepal and Tibet, **China**; sixth hgst. in world; alt. 8,225 m.
Chorley, t., N. Lancs., **Eng.**; on W. flank of Rossendale Fells, 11 km S.E. of Preston; cotton, engin.; expansion as new t. with Leyland (20,200 ha); p. (1971) 31,609.
Chorleywood, t., Herts., **Eng.**; nr. Watford; p. (1971) 8,427.
Chorrilos Pass, Argentina; in E. cordillera of Andes at alt. 4,470 m; used by rly. from San Miguel de Tucumán to Antofagasta.
Chorzów (Królewska Huta), t. Upper Silesia, **Poland**; coal, iron and steel, chemicals, engin.; p. (est. 1969) 151,300.
Chota Nagpur, plateau, Madhya Pradesh, **India**; produces lac; impt. mng. ctr.; bauxite, mica.
Chou Kou Tien, site nr. Peking, **China**; dis-

covery of fossil bones of Peking man (*Sinanthropus pekinensis*).
Christchurch, t., Dorset, **Eng.**; on S. cst. 8 km E. of Bournemouth; holiday resort, aircraft, lt. inds.; p. (1971) 31,373.
Christchurch, c., Canterbury dist., S.I., **N.Z.**; comm. ctr. for lamb, wool, and grain; cath., univ.; airpt; p. (1971) 165,198 (c.); (est. 1970) 260,200 (met. a.).
Christianshåb, Danish settlement on Disko Bay, W. Greenland; meteorological sta.
Christmas I., in Indian Oc., Australian terr. since 1958; a. 161 km², healthy climate, phosphate deposits; p. (1966) 3,381.
Christmas I., lge. coral atoll in Pac. Oc., one of Line Is.; discovered by Cook 1777; a. 135 km²; nuclear test site, 1957–64.
Chu, R. Kazakh SSR, **USSR**; rises in Tien Shan flows N.W. for 800 km into inland drainage basin; Chumysh Dam provides hydroelectricity and water for intensive cultivation under irrigation of cotton, sugarbeet, citrus fruits.
Chuanchow (Quanzhou), c., Fukien prov.; **China**; former pt. now silted up; p. (est. 1970) 130,000.
Chubut, R., **Argentina**; drains from Andes into Atl. Oc.; continual irrigation reducing soil fertility of valley; 640 km long.
Chuchow (Zhuzhou), c., Hunan prov., **China**; on Siang R.; rly. p. (est. 1970) 350,000.
Chudleigh, mkt. t., Devon, **Eng.**; on R. Teign; stone quarrying.
Chu-kiang (Canton R. or Pearl R.), Kwangtung, S. **China**; one of most impt. waterways of China; 176 km long, from Kuangchow to Hong Kong; fertile delta known as "land of fish, rice, and fruit"; around Kuangchow network of elec. drainage and irrigation stas., built since 1959; R. estuary now silting.
Chukotskiy, peninsula, **USSR**; extreme N.E.; rich gold deposit; hunting.
Chukyo, industl. area, Honshu, **Japan**; centred on Nagoya; textiles, ceramics, chemicals.
Chula Vista, t., Cal., **USA**; agr., aircraft; p. (1970) 67,901.
Chungking (Zhongqing), c., S.E. Szechwan prov., **China**; on Yangtze R.; comm. ctr. W. China; ctr. of rich agr. dist. of Red Basin of Szechwan; coal, iron and steel, heavy machin., lorries, vans, chemical fertilisers; former treaty pt.; p. (est. 1970) 3,500,000.
Chuquibamba Mtns., (alt. *c.* 6,400 m), **Peru.**
Chuquicamata, t., N. **Chile**; 3,050 m in Andes; lgst copper mine in world; p. (est. 1966) 28,786.
Chur (Coire), t., cap. Graubünden, **Switzerland**; in valley of upper Rhine; historic bldgs.; fruit, wine, tourist ctr.; p. (1969) 30,900.
Church, sub. of Accrington, Lancs., **Eng.**; engin.; p. (1971) 5,310.
Churchill, R., formerly Hamilton R., flows into Hamilton inlet, cst. of Labrador, **Canada**; magnificent waterfall, Churchill Falls with lge. hydroelec. scheme.
Church Stretton, mkt. t., Salop, **Eng.**; tourism.
Chusan, I., and archipelago off E. cst. **China**; ch. ctr. Tinghai on Chusan I.; rich off-shore fishing grounds.
Chusovoy, t., **RSFSR**; in Urals; iron and steel; p. (est. 1969) 62,000.
Chuvash ASSR, aut. rep., **RSFSR**; in middle Volga valley; arable agr., lumbering, food processing; a. 18,407 km²; p. (1970) 1,224,000.
Chysauster, Cornwall, **Eng.**; prehistoric v.
Cibao, lowland a., **Dominican Rep.**, Central America; extends along N. side of Cordillera de Cibao for 180 km; 16–56 km wide; early a. of Spanish settlement; E. part called Vega Real; richest agr. a. of Hispaniola; cacao, tobacco, maize; dense p.; ch. t. Santiago.
Cicero, t., Ill., **USA**; adjoins Chicago; electrical appliances, hardware; p. (1970) 67,058.
Ciechanów, t., **Poland**; 78 km N.W. of Warsaw; agr. inds.; p. (1970) 23,200.
Cienaga, spt., N. **Colombia**; exp. cotton, bananas, cacao; p. (est. 1972) 69,100 (t.), 168,100 (met. a.).
Cienfuegos, t., **Cuba**; sugar, tobacco; picturesque; nuclear power sta. proposed, built with Soviet assistance; p. (est. 1967) 91,800.
Cieszyn, t., Katowice prov., **Poland**; part of former Teschen on Polish side of frontier with **ČSSR**; p. (1970) 25,200.
Cîmpina, t., **Romania**, in Walachia; petroleum ctr.; oil pipeline links to Ploieşti and Constanta on Black Sea.
Cincinnati, c., Ohio, **USA**; route and comm. ctr. on terraces of Ohio R.; food processing and many varied inds.; univs.; p. (1970) 448,492 (c.), 1,373,225, (met. a.).
Cinderford, t., Gloucs., **Eng.**; former ctr. of coal-mng. a. of Forest of Dean; new lt. industl. estate.
Cinque Ports, confederation of anc. Eng. pts. on cst. of Kent and Sussex; original 5: Sandwich, Dover, Hythe, Romney, Hastings; Winchelsea, and Rye added later. *See* L23.
Cirencester, t., Gloucs., **Eng.**; the Roman Corineum; former woollen t.; p. (1971) 13,022.
Ciskei, Bantu Terr. Authority, **S. Africa**; established 1961 between Fish and Kei Rs. on S.E. cst.; self-gov. (1972); cap. Zwelitsha; p. (1970) 527,159.
Citta di Castello, walled t., **Italy**; in upper Tiber valley; impt. in Roman times; Renaissance cath., palaces; p. (est. 1968) 36,274.
Citta Vecchia (Mdina), c., central **Malta**; former cap.; Roman remains; cath.
Ciudad Bolivar, c., Bolivar st., **Venezuela**; pt. on Orinoco R.; formerly called Angostura; coffee, cattle; ctr. of new industl. development on lower Orinoco; p. (est. 1970) 109,600.
Ciudad Juarez, c., **Mexico**; comm. ctr. on USA border; agr. processing; tourism; p. (1970) 407,370.
Ciudad Madero, t., **Mexico**; styrene and detergent plants, oil refining; p. (1970) 89,994.
Ciudad Obregón, t., Sonora, **Mexico**: on Yaqui R.; ctr. of irrigated agr. a.; p. (1970) 114,407.
Ciudad Real, c., cap. of Ciudad Real prov., **Spain**; mkt. t. founded 1255; textiles; p. (1970) 41,708.
Ciudad Real, prov., central **Spain**; mostly at 600 m; covering la Mancha dist.; agr.; cap. C.R.; a. 19,741 km²; p. (1970) 507,650.
Ciudad Rodrigo, old fortress t., Salamanca prov., **Spain**; strategic position nr. Portuguese bdy.; in Peninsular War fell to Fr. (1810) and captured by Wellington (1812); p. (1970) 13,320.
Civitavecchia, t.. Latium, **Italy**; pt. for Rome on Tyrrhenian cst., 48 km N. of mouth of R. Tiber; p. (est. 1968) 42,570.
Clackmannan, former co., l. gov. dist., Central Reg., **Scot.**; a. 161 km²; p. (1971) 46,340.
Clacton-on-Sea, t., Essex, **Eng.**; on E. cst. 19 km S.E. of Colchester; seaside resort; lt. inds.; residtl.; p. (1971) 37,942.
Clairvaux, v., Aube, **France**; famous Cistercian abbey.
Clamart, t., Hauts-de-Seine, **France**; sub. of S.W. Paris; p. (1968) 55,299.
Clare, co., Munster, **R.o.I.**; cstl. co. bounded in S. and E. by R. Shannon; mainly agr. and tourism; inc. cliffs of Moher; Shannon airpt. and tax-free industl. development scheme; co. t. Ennis; a. 3,351 km²; p. (1966) 73,539.
Clare I., Clew Bay, Mayo, **R.o.I.**
Clarence, R., N.S.W., **Australia**; length 384 km.
Clarence Strait, between Melville I. and Darwin, N.T., **Australia**.
Clarksburg, t., W. Va., **USA**; industl. ctr. for coal-mng. a., oil and natural gas fields; machin., glass, pottery; p. (1970) 24,684.
Clarksdale, t., Miss., **USA**; processing ctr. for rich farming a.; p. (1970) 21,105.
Clarksville, t., Tenn., **USA**; on Cumberland R.; tobacco mkt.; p. (1970) 31,719.
Clausthal-Zellerfeld, t., Lower Saxony, **W. Germany** in Harz mtns.; tourism.
Clay Cross, t., Derbyshire, **Eng.**; former ctr. coal-mng. (first developed by George Stephenson 1838) iron, engin.; p. (1971) 10,153.
Clayton-le-Moors, t., Lancs., **Eng.**; nr. Blackburn; textile machin., cotton and blanket weaving, bristles, soap; p. (1971) 6,760.
Clear C., southernmost point of Ireland, Clear I., **R.o.I.**; off S.W. cst. of Cork.
Cleare, c., Alaska, **USA**; site of ballistic missile early warning sta.
Clearwater, t., Fla., **USA**; citrus fruit, flowers, fish; resort; p. (1970) 52,074.
Cleator Moor, t. Cumbria, **Eng.**; former colly. t.
Cleckheaton, t., West Yorks., **Eng.**; nr. Bradford; woollens, blankets, asbestos.
Clee Hills, Salop, **Eng.**; between Rs. Severn and Teme; alt. 550 m.
Cleethorpes, t., Humberside, **Eng.**; 5 km S. of Grimsby; resort; p. (1971) 35,785.
Clent Hills, Hereford and Worcs., **Eng.**; about

16 km S.W. of Birmingham, overlooking valley of R. Stour; recreation; maximum alt. 316 m.

Clerkenwell, industl. dist., London, Eng.; immediately N. of the City; noted for watchmkg.

Clermont-Ferrand, c., cap. Puy-de-Dôme dep. central France; in Auvergne; rubber tyres, chemicals, food inds.; Gothic cath., Romanesque church; p. (1968) 148,896 (c.), 204,699 (met. a.).

Clevedon, t., Avon **Eng.**; at mouth of R. Severn; seaside resort; quarrying, bricks, footwear; p. (1971) 14,285.

Cleveland, c., Ohio, **USA**; impt. Gr. Ls. pt. handling iron ore and coal which support a major iron and steel ind.; oil refining, food processing, many varied inds.; univ.; p. (1971) 738,956 (c.), 2,064,194 (met. a.).

Cleveland, non-met. co., N.E. **Eng.**; heavy industl. region centred around ts. of Tees estuary; chems., iron and steel mftg.; inc. part of N. York Moors to S.; a. 583 km^2.; p. (1971) 567,000.

Cleveland Hills, North Yorks./Cleveland, **Eng.**; part of N. York Moors; once mined for iron ore, impt. potash deposit.

Clichy, t., Hauts-de-Seine, **France**; N.W. sub. of Paris; oil refining, aircraft, automobile components; p. (1968) 52,704.

Clifton, sub., Bristol, Avon, **Eng.**; on R. Avon; mineral springs; famous suspension bridge.

Clifton, t., N.J., **USA**; industl. t., nr. Passaic; p. (1970) 82,437.

Clinton, t., Iowa, **USA**; on Mississippi R.; iron and steel, machin.; p. (1970) 34,719.

Clitheroe, t., Lancs. **Eng.**; in Ribble valley; mkt. t. for rural a.; limestone quarrying nearby; p. (1971) 13,191.

Clonakilty, t., Cork, **R.o.I.**; nr. Bandon; sm. harbour; agr. prods.; p. (1966) 2,341.

Cloncurry, t., Queensland, **Australia**; in pastoral and copper-producing dist.; p. (1966) 2,174.

Clones, mkt. t. on Ulster border, Monaghan, **R.o.I.**; rly. ctr.; p. (1961) 2,107.

Clonmacnoise, v., Offaly, **R.o.I.**; ecclesiastical ruins.

Clonmel, t., Tipperary, **R.o.I.**; on R. Suir; agr. ctr.; fairs; cider, footwear; p. (1966) 11,026.

Clovelly, v., Devon, **Eng.**; seaside resort.

Clowne, t., Derbys., **Eng.**; coal mng.; p. (1971) 18,869 (dist.).

Cluj, c., Romania; in Transylvania on Somesul R.; univs., historic bldgs.; industl. ctr.; p. (est. 1969) 197,902 (c.), (1966) 222,491 (met. a.).

Clutha R., longest R. of S.I., **N.Z.,** hydroelec. power; 320 km long.

Clwyd, co., N. Wales; inc. most of Denbigh and Flintshire; mtnous. to S.; N. cstal. resorts inc. Colwyn Bay, Prestatyn and Rhyl; sm. coalfield; lgst. t. Wrexham; a. 2,424 km^2; p. (1971) 358,159.

Clwyd, R., Clwyd, N. Wales; flows into Irish Sea at Rhyl; length 48 km.

Clydach, t., West Glamorgan, Wales; on R. Tawe, 8 km N.E. Swansea; steel wks., nickel refineries.

Clyde, R., Strathclyde Reg., S.W. Scot ; flows through industl. belt into Firth of C.; Glasgow, Greenock, Clydebank main pts.; hydroelec. stas.; twin-road tunnel under R. in Glasgow (Whiteinch–Linthouse) completed 1963; 170 km long.

Clydebank, t., l. gov. dist., Strathclyde Reg., **Scot.**; on Clyde adjoining Glasgow; shipbldg., sewing machin., tyres, biscuits; p. (1971) 48,300.

Clyde, Firth of, stretches from Dumbarton to Ailsa Craig, **Scot.**; Bute, Arran, Gr. and Little Cumbrae ch. Is.; 102 km long.

Coachella Valley, arid region, S.E. Cal., **USA**; part of G. of Cal.; dates and citrus fruits under irrigation from Imperial Valley irrigation system.

Coahuila, st., **Mexico**; 3rd st. of Mexico; lies S. of Texas, bordering Rio Grande valley; main coal deposits; mnfs. impt.; irrigated agr.: cap. Saltillo; a. 142,611 km^2; p. (1969) 1,225,000.

Coalbrookdale, v., Salop., **Eng.**; old coal- and iron-mines; home of iron master Abraham Darby. *See* **Bridges, Section L.**

Coalville, t. Leics., **Eng.**; nr. Ashby-de-la-Zouch; coal mng., engin., elastic webbing; p. (1971) 28,334.

Coast Range, mtns., **USA**; along Pac. cst.; wooded ranges causing rain shadow to E. valleys; alt. up to 600 m.

Coatbridge, burgh, Strathclyde Reg., **Scot.**, 16 km E. of Glasgow; coal, iron and steel, prefabricated houses, tubes engin.; p. (1971) 52,344.

Coats I., S. of Southampton I., Hudson Bay, Canada.

Coatzacoalcos (Puerto Mexico), spt., **Mexico**; on G. of Campeche; oil refinery; chemicals, fertilisers; p. (est. 1970) 108,818 (met. a.).

Cobalt, t., Ont., **Canada**; silver, cobalt, arsenic, nickel; p. (1971) 2,191.

Cobán, t., Guatemala, mkt. t.; coffee and Peruvian bark tr.; p. (1964) 38,426.

Cóbh (Queenstown), U.D., Cork, **R.o.I.**; spt. on Great I. in Cork Harbour; lge. docks; H.Q. of Royal Cork Yacht Club; seaside resort; p. (1966) 5,608.

Coburg, t., Bavaria, **W. Germany**; old cas.; wickerwork, furniture, metal, machines, toy inds.; p. (est. 1969) 41,456.

Cochabamba, dep., Bolivia; E. of Andes; lgst. p. concentration of Bolivia in C. basin; a. 65,496 km^2; p. (est. 1969) 780,500.

Cochabamba, c., cap. of C. dep., **Bolivia**; second lgst. c. in rep.; alt. 2,559 m; univ., cath.; oil refining, shoes, rubber tyres, fruit-canning, modern milk plant; hydroelectric power; p. (1969) 157,000.

Cochin, spt., Kerala, **India**; on Malabar cst.; exp. coconut oil, tea; oil refining; silting pt.; p. (1971) 439,066.

Cochin China, region, formerly part of Indo-China; now roughly coincides with S. Vietnam; comprises the Mekong delta. *See* **Vietnam.**

Cockenzie and Port Seaton, small burgh, E. Lothian, Scot.; two fishing pts. on F. of Forth; p. (1971) 3,580.

Cockermouth, t., Cumbria, **Eng.**; slate, shoe mftg., plywood, concrete prods.; birthplace of Wordsworth; p. (1971) 6,356.

Cockpit Country, upland a., W. **Jamaica**; classic karst landscape forming rugged upland; some cultivation in hollows; a. 500 km^2; alt. 300–800 m.

Coco, R., Honduras and Nicaragua; flows to Caribbean Sea through economically impt. valley; agr., forestry, mng.; potential as routeway; 480 km long.

Cocos or Keeling Is., 27 coral atolls, **Indian Oc.**; since 1955 terr. of Australia; ch. prod. coconuts; strategic position S.E. of Sri Lanka, 848 km W. of Christmas I., N.E. of Mauritius; radio and cable sta.; civil aviation marine base; German cruiser *Emden* destroyed by Australian cruiser *Sydney* on N. Keeling I. in 1914; a. 13 km^2; p. (est. 1970) 611.

Coesfeld, t., N. Rhine–Westphalia, **W. Germany**; textiles, machin.; p. (est. 1969) 21,924.

Cognac, t., Charente, **France**; cognac, bottles; p. (1968) 22,515.

Coiba I., off S. cst. of Panama.

Coimbatore, t., Tamil Nadu, **India**; commands Palghat Gap; varied inds. benefit from local hydroelec. power; p. (1971) 356,368 (c.) 736,203 (met. a.).

Coimbra, t., **Portugal**; cath., oldest univ. in Portugal; wine-growing; earthenware mnfs.; p. (1970) 108,046.

Colac, t., Victoria, **Australia**; nr. Melbourne; farming and dairying dist.; engin., and brickmkg.; p. (1972) 10,418.

Colchester, t., Essex, **Eng.**; pre-Roman t. of Camulodunum on R. Colne; univ.; lt. inds., engin., oyster fisheries; pt.; p. (1971) 76,145.

Cold Fell, mtn., Northumberland, **Eng.**; 622 m.

Cold Harbour, v., Va., **USA**; battles between Grant and Lee 1864.

Coldstream, t., Berwick, **Scot.**; on Eng. border; agr. machin., knitwear; p. (1971) 1,278.

Coleraine, t., l. gov. dist., **N. Ireland**; pt. on R. Bann, 6 km from sea; univ.; linen, acrilan mftg., distilling; p. (est. 1971) 14,871.

Coleshill, t., West Midlands, **Eng.**; lurgi gasification plant; new colly. 1965.

Colima, mkt. t., **Mexico**; on Colima R. in fertile valley; univ.; agr. processing; p. (est. 1969) 44,000.

Colima, st., **Mexico**; on Pac. cst.; cap. Colima; pt. Manzanillo; cotton, sugar, rice, coffee; a. 5,203 km^2; p. (1969) 238,000.

Colima, volcano (48 km N.E. of c.), **Mexico,** alt. 3,869 m.

Coll, I. off cst. of Mull, Argyll and Bute, **Scot.**; agr., lobster fishing.
Collie, t., **W. Australia**; sub-bituminous coal; p. (1972) 5,832.
Collingwood, t., Ont., **Canada**; on Georgian Bay, L. Huron; shipbldg., steel; p. (1971) 9,719.
Colmar, t., cap. Haut-Rhin dep., **France**; ctr. of Alsace textile ind.; attractive mediaeval t.; mkt. for vineyards; p. (1968) 62,341.
Colne, t., E. Lancs., **Eng.**; cotton mnfs., felts; p. (1971) 18,873.
Colne, R., Essex, **Eng.**; oysters.
Colne, R., Eng.; trib. of R. Thames rising in Chilterns.
Colne Valley, t., West Yorks., **Eng.**; woollens; p. (1971) 21,188.
Cologne (Köln), c., N. Rhine-Westphalia, **W. Germany**; on Rhine at N. end of Rhine gorge; cath., univ.; impt. R. pt., route and comm. ctr.; eau-de-Cologne, electro-technical ind., machin., metallurgy, paper, chemicals, cars, oil refining, textiles; p. (est. 1969) 860,800.
Colombes, t., Hauts-de-Seine dep., **France**; mftg. sub. of Paris on R. Seine; p. (1968) 80,616.
Colombia, rep., N.W. **S. America**; cap. Bogotá; Andes contain most of p.; the savannahs (llanos) to S.E. are almost uninhabited; industl. employment growing; birth and death rates high in mainly tropical climate and many diseases endemic; agr. impt.; coffee petroleum, bananas; a. 1,139,592 km²; p. (est. 1969) 20,463,000.
Colombo, c., cap. of **Sri Lanka**; on W. cst.; univ.; impt. pt. (artificial) built by British; exp. tea, rubber, coconuts; p. (est. 1968) 558,500.
Colón, t., **Panama**; at Atl. end of Panama Canal; free tr. zone; comm. and industl. ctr.; oil refining nearby; p. (1970) 95,308.
Colonsay, I., Inner Hebrides, Argyll and Bute, **Scot.**; 13 km long; ecclesiastical antiquities; p. (inc. Jura 1971) 349.
Colorado, st., **USA**; hgst. st. in USA; in the Rockies extending up to 4,401 m (Mt. Elbert), no land below 1,000 m; drained by headwaters of Rs. Arkansas and Colorado; major stock-rearing a.; many valuable minerals esp. uranium, radium and molybdenum; cap. Denver; a. 270,000 km²; p. (1970) 2,195,887.
Colorado, plateau, Arizona, Utah, Col., N.M., **USA**; arid upland with spectacular scenery, inc. Grand Canyon; alt. 1,500–3,300 m.
Colorado, R., Argentina; flows from Andes to Atl. Oc.; limited irrigation in pastoral valley; length 848 km.
Colorado, major R. of W. **USA**; drains 8% of USA; formed by confluence of Green and Grand Rs.; spectacular canyons inc. Grand Canyon; hydroelec. power from many dams inc. Hoover Dam; irrigation supplies intensive horticultural a. in S. section and consequent rapid decrease in volume to a sm. stream in lower course; length 2,320 km.
Colorado, R., rises N.W. Texas, **USA**; and flows to G. of Mexico; irrigation and power; length 1,552 km.
Colorado Desert, Cal., **USA**; inc. Imperial Valley, a fertile irrigated a.
Colorado Springs. t. Col., **USA**; 102 km S. Denver; resort; p. (1970) 124,856 (c.), 228,572 (met. a.).
Colton, t., S.E. Cal., **USA**; fruit- and vegetable-canning; mkt. gardening; p. (1970) 20,016.
Columbia, t., Mo., **USA**; W. of St. Louis; st. univ.; flour, lumber; p. (1970) 58,804.
Columbia, t., st. cap. S.C., **USA**; in ctr. of rich farming a.; textiles, clothing; burned down in Civil War 1865; p. (1970) 111,706 (c.), 315,716 (met. a.).
Columbia, District of (D.C.); area on east bank of Potomac R., coterminus with c. of Washington, cap. of **USA**; a. 179 km²; p. (1970) 764,000 (c.); (1968) 2,750,700 (met. a.).
Columbia, R., major R. of western **N. America**; rises in Rocky Mtns., B.C., flows through Washington, **USA**; power sources, inc. Grand Coulee Dam, Bonneville Dam; deepwater harbour at mouth; length 2,240 km.
Columbus, c., Ga., **USA**; at head of navigation on Chattahoochee R.; industl. and shipping ctr.; textile mills, food-processing; cotton-ginning machin.; p. (1970) 152,123 (c.), 234,288 (met. a.).
Columbus, t., Ind., **USA**; engin.; leather gds.; p. (1970) 26,457.
Columbus, t., Miss. **USA**; agr. prods.; p. (1970) 25,795.
Columbus, c., st. cap. Ohio, **USA**; rly. ctr.; st. univ.; machin., paper, aircraft machin., chemicals; p. (1970) 533,418 (c.), 904,725 (met. a.).
Colwyn Bay, t., Clwyd, **N. Wales**; on cst. 10 km E. of Llandudno; furniture; seaside resort; p. (1971) 25,535.
Comayagüela, c., former cap. of **Honduras**; twin c. of Tegucigalpa from which it is separated by Choluteca R.; both cs. administered together as Central Dist.
Combe Martin, v., Devon, **Eng.**; 8 km E. of Ilfracombe; seaside resort.
Comber, t., Ards, **N. Ireland**; linen; p. (1966) 3,925.
Como, c., N. **Italy**; at foot of Alps, on L. Como; oranges, olives; textiles; cath.; tourism; p. (1969) 94,379.
Como, L., N. **Italy**; beautiful mtn. scenery, tourism, villas; a. 145 km².
Comodoro Rivadavia, spt., Chubut prov., **Argentina**; on San Jorge G., 880 km S.W. of Bahia Blanca; military zone; univ.; ch. source of oil in Argentine; oil refining; p. (1960) 40,000.
Comorin, C., most S. point of **India**.
Comoro Is., arch., **Indian Oc.**; in Moçambique channel, midway between Africa and Malagasy Rep.; cap. Moroni; total a. 2,170 km²; turtle fishing; vanilla, copra, sisal, timber, perfume plants; indep. from France declared 1975 but rejected by Mayotte Is; p. (est. 1907) 280,000.
Compiègne, t., Oise, **France**; sugar mills, rope; Armistice signed between Allies and Germany 1918; Fr. surrendered to Hitler 1940; resort; p. (1968) 32,653.
Compton, t., Cal., **USA**; residtl. for Los Angeles; heavy engin., glass, oil refining; p. (1970) 78,611.
Conakry, c., cap. of **Rep. of Guinea**; impt. pt. on offshore islet; exp. iron ore and alumina; experimental fruit gardens; p. (1967) 197,267 (met. a.).
Concarneau, pt., Finistère, **France**; 19 km S.E. Quimper; fisheries; p. (1968) 18,150.
Concepción, c., prov. cap., **Chile**; shipping ctr. through its pt. Talcahuano; univ.; comm. and cultural t.; severe earthquakes 1939 and 1960; nr. to coalfield; p. (est. 1970) 196,317.
Concepción, prov., **Chile**; cap. C.; Lota-Coronel coalfield lgst. in Chile; a. 5,701 km²; p. (1970) 638,118.
Concepción, t. cap. of C. prov., **Paraguay**; main comm. ctr. for Chaco, pt. on R. Paraguay; p. (est. 1968) 17,200.
Conchos, R., Chihuahua prov., **Mexico**; flows N.E. from Madre Occidental to Rio Grande; cotton under irrigation in upper valley; hydroelec. power; length 560 km.
Concord, t., Cal., **USA**; residtl. and comm. ctr. in San Francisco met. a.; rapid p. growth; p. (1970) 85,164.
Concord, t., Mass., **USA**; literary ctr.; textiles; p. (1970) 16,148.
Concord, t., st. cap., N.H., **USA**; on Merrimack R.; granite, machin., textiles; p. (1970) 30,022.
Concordia, t., **Argentina**; pt. on Uruguay R.; exp. agr. prod.; p. (1960) 56,000.
Condamine, R., Queensland, **Australia**; trib. of R. Darling; used for irrigation.
Coney I., t., N.Y., **USA**; on Long I., 8 km long, comprises Manhattan Beach, Brighton Beach, W. Brighton, and W. End; seaside resort.
Congleton, t., E. Cheshire, **Eng.**; on S.W. margin of Pennines; clothing, textiles; once impt. for silk; p. (1971) 20,324.
Congo, People's Rep. of the, indep. st. within Fr. Community, **Equatorial Africa**; cap. Brazzaville; agr. and forestry; hardwoods; a. 341,880 km²; p. (est. 1969) 880,000.
Congolese Republic. *See* Zaïre.
Congo R. *See* Zaïre R.
Conisborough, t., South Yorks., **Eng.**; limestone, bricks, tiles; p. (1971) 16,800.
Coniston, t., Ont., **Canada**; on rly. 13 km E. of Sudbury; nickel smelting; t. built by and for nickel-mng. company.
Coniston Water, L., Cumbria, **Eng.**; focus of tourism in L. Dist.; 8·8 km long.
Conjeeveram. *See* Kanchipuram.
Connacht, prov., **R.o.I.**; inc. Galway, Mayo Sligo, Leitrim, Roscommon; mtnous. in W.;

farming, fishing; a. 17,775 km²; p. (1966) 401,518.
Connah's Quay, t., Clwyd, Wales; p. (1971) 12,296.
Connaught Tunnel (Can. Pac. Rly.), B.C., Canada; longest in N. America (8 km) 1,500 m under mt. Sir Donald (Selkirk Mtns.).
Connecticut, R., New Eng.; USA; middle course forms fine agr. land; investment in navigation. irrigation and flood control; 566 km long.
Connecticut, st., New England, USA; one of original 13 sts.; humid climate; arable agr.; diversified inds.; many natural harbours on cst.; cap. Hartford; lgst. c. New Haven; a. 12,973 km²; p. (1970) 2,987,950.
Connemara, mtns., dist., R.o.I.; Co. Galway; many lakes and bogs; tourist resort.
Conowingo Dam, Md. USA; on lower Susquehanna R.; hydroelec. power sta. supplies power to inds. in Philadelphia.
Consett, t., Durham, Eng.; on edge of Pennines, 16 km S.W. Newcastle; iron, steel, coal mng.; p. (1971) 35,391.
Constance (Konstanz), c., Baden-Württemberg, W. Germany; on Bodensee; cath.; textiles, machin., chemicals, elec. inds.; route ctr.; tourism; p. (est. 1969) 60,821.
Constance, L. *See* Bodensee.
Constanța, ch. spt. S.E. Romania; on Black Sea; oil pipeline to Ploiești and Cimpina; exp. petroleum, wheat; cement, chemicals, machin.; p. (est. 1969) 170,026 (c.); (1966) 202,024 (met. a.).
Constantine, c., N.E. Algeria; stands 650 m high on gorge of Rhumel R.; planned textile and engin. wks.; p. (1966) 243,558.
Constantinople. *See* Istanbul.
Conwy (Conway), Gwynedd, spt., N. Wales; mediaeval walled t.; at mouth of R. Conway; sm. seaside resort; cas.; quarrying, lt. engin.; p. (1971) 12,158.
Cook, mtn., alt. 3,764 m; hgst. point in S. Alps. N.Z.; 3 peaks.
Cookham, t., Berks., Eng.; on R. Thames nr. Maidenhead; tourism; p. (1971) 19,372 (dist.).
Cook Inlet, S. cst. Alaska, USA; oil pipeline connects oilfields of Granite Point with marine terminal at Drift R.
Cook Is., Brit. gr. (Rarotonga, lgst.) in S. Pac., annexed to N.Z., 1901; internal self-govt. 1965; bananas, oranges, copra; a. 241 km²; p. (1966) 19,247.
Cookstown, mkt. t., l. gov. dist., N. Ireland; cement wks.; p. (1966) 5,542.
Cook Strait, channel between N. and S. Is. of N.Z.; 24–29 km wide; undersea cable completed 1965.
Cooma, t., N.S.W., Australia; mkt. t. and pastoral ctr.; tourism; H.Q. of Snowy Mts. Authority; p. (1966) 9,101.
Coonoor, t., Tamil Nadu, India; in Nilgiri Hills; sanatorium *c.* 1,800 m a.s.l.; p. (1961) 30,690.
Coopers Creek (Barcoo), intermittent R., central Australia; rises in Warrego Range, Gr. Dividing Range, flows S.W. into marshes of L. Eyre; provides water for livestock in semi-arid region; 1,408 km long.
Copenhagen (København), ch. spt., cap. of Denmark; on E. cst. of Sjaelland I.; royal palace, univ., library; naval sta.; steel, metal, textiles, clothing, breweries; airpt.; p. (est. 1969) 643,262 (c.), 1,381,312 (met. a.).
Copiapó, t., cap. of Atacama prov., Chile; copper and iron-mng. ctr.; p. (est. 1966) 36,767.
Coquet, R., Northumberland, Eng.; rises in the Cheviots and flows into North Sea.
Coquimbo, spt., Chile; exp. iron, copper, and manganese ores; p. (est. 1966) 39,610.
Coral Sea, Pac. Oc., extends from the New Hebrides to Australia.
Coral Sea Islands Territory, Fed. terr., Australia; scattered Is., E. of Gr. Barrier Reef, off Queensland cst.; possibility of oil exploration.
Corbeil-Essonnes, t., Essonne, France; on R. Seine, 19 km S.E. of Paris; flour mills, printing, paper; p. (1968) 32,192.
Corbridge, t., Northumberland, Eng.; on R. Tyne, nr. Hexham; 17th cent. bridge; Roman t. nearby.
Corby, t., Northants., Eng.; 11 km N. of Kettering; new t.; steel wks., shoes, clothing, lamps; p. (est. 1974) 53,750.
Córdoba, c., central Argentina; univ.; cultural and comm. ctr.; exp. wheat, cattle, lumber; health resort; local hydroelec. power from La Vina; p. (1970) 789,663 (met. a.).
Córdoba, t., Veracruz, Mexico; mkt. t. in coffee-growing a.; p. (1970) 92,870.
Córdova, prov., Andalusia, Spain; cap. Córdova; olives, vines, livestock; a. 13,724 km²; p. (1970) 724,116
Córdova, c., Andalusia, Spain; cap. of C. prov., on Guadalquivir R.; cath. originally built as a mosque in 8th cent.; tourist ctr.; p. (est. 1969) 229,407.
Corfu (Kérkira), most N. of Ionian Is., Greece; traversed by mtns. but largely lowland producing olive-oil, figs, wine, oranges; a. 637 km²; p. (1971) 92,261 (prov.).
Corinth (Kórinthos), t., cap. Corinthia prov. Greece; at end of Isthmus of C.; occupies site 5 km from anc. classic c. destroyed by earthquake 1858; raisins, wine; p. (1961) 15,892.
Corinth Canal, ship canal, S. Greece; traverses Isthmus of Corinth, links G. of Corinth and Ionian Sea with Saronic G. and Aegean Sea; opened 1893; length 5·6 km, depth 8 m.
Corinth, Isthmus of, connects the Peloponnesus with the mainland of Greece; cut across by canal.
Corinto, ch. spt., N.W. Nicaragua; handles 50 per cent of cty's tr.; exp. hides, sugar, coffee; p. (est. 1970) 12,985.
Cork, co., R.o.I.; lgst. and most S.; mtns.; dairying, brewing, agr., fisheries; cap. Cork; a. 7,485 km²; p. (1966) 339,525.
Cork, spt., C.B., Cork, R.o.I.; at mouth of R. Lee; cath., univ.; woollens, butter, cattle, brewing, cars, rubber; p. (1966) 122,146 (c.), 125,283 (met. a.).
Corner Brook, c., W. Newfoundland, Canada; gd. harbour; iron foundries, cement, gypsum; one of world's lgst. newsprint mills; p. (1971) 25,929.
Cornwall, t., Ont., Canada; on St. Lawrence R.; H.Q. of Seaway Authority; textiles, pulp. paper, flour; p. (1971) 46,429.
Cornwall, non-met. co., S.W. Eng.; penin. bordering Atl. Oc. and Eng. Channel; granite moorlands supply kaolin and tin; mild maritime climate encourages tourism, dairying, and mkt. gardening; many small fishing vs.; co. t. Bodmin; a. 3,515 km²; p. inc. Isles of Scilly (1971) 379,892.
Coro, c., Falcón, Venezuela; on Paraguaná penin.; agr. processing; nearby oil refineries; p. (est. 1970) 55,955.
Corocoro, t., La Paz dep., Bolivia; at alt. *c.* 4,000 m in central Andes, 80 km S. of La Paz; impt. copper-mng. ctr.
Coromandel Coast (Carnatic region), cst. of Tamil Nadu, India; where earliest European settlements established; extensive a. of flat land built up by R. Cauvery.
Coronation Gulf, arm of Beaufort Sea; extreme point N. Canadian mainland; discovered by Franklin.
Coronel, spt., Chile; coal mng., pt. inds.; p. (est. 1966) 43,324.
Coronel Oviedo, t., Paraguay; comm. ctr.; p. (est. 1970) 59,307.
Corpus Christi, c. Texas, USA; cotton, oil refining, chemicals; resort; p. (1970) 201,581 (c.), 278,443 (met. a.).
Corréze, dep., S. central France; part of Massif Central, mostly over 600 m; sparse p. based on livestock agr. and forestry; cap. Tulle; a. 5,884 km²; p. (1968) 237,858.
Corrib, Lough, Galway and Mayo, R.o.I.; drained by Corrib R. into Galway Bay; impt. brown trout fishery; a. 176 km².
Corrientes, t., Argentina; agr. tr. ctr. on Paraná R.; univ.; cattle, sugar, rice, cotton; river navigation reduces isolation; p. (1970) 131,392 (met. a.).
Corryvreckan, strait and whirlpool between Jura and Scarba Is., Inner Hebrides, Scot.; whirlpool caused by tidal movement over variable sea bed.
Corsica (Corse), I. France; in Mediterranean Sea; violent history in 16th and 17th cent.; high granite peaks (Monte Cinto), mtn. torrents, fertile plains; inland and sea fishing; rapid growth of tourism with little benefit to indigeneous Corsicans; split into 2 deps. to help overcome autonomist agitation (1975); Haute

Corse, cap. Bastia, Corse du Sud, cap. Ajaccio; a. 8,721 km²; p. (1968) 269,831.
Corsicana, t., Texas, USA; site of first oil drilling in USA; p. (1970) 19,972.
Cortona, t., Tuscany, Italy; nr. Perugia; Roman remains, cath.; p. (est. 1968) 23,564.
Corumbá, pt., Mato Grosso, Brazil; on R. Paraguay; exp. agr. products; mkt. t.; p. (est. 1968) 89,199.
Corunna. *See* La Coruña.
Corvallis, t., Ore., USA; in fertile farming valley; lumbering; univ.; p. (1970) 35,056.
Coryton, t., Essex, Eng.; on Thames, oil refining; oil pipeline to Stanlow refinery.
Cos (Kos) I., Dodecanese, Greece; in Aegean Sea, second lgst. of gr.; gave name to Cos lettuce; birthplace of Hippocrates.
Cosenza, prov., Calabria, Italy; a. 6,646 km²; p. (1969) 716,916.
Cosenza, c., S. Italy; ctr. for figs, oranges, olive oil, wine; cath., cas.; p. (1969) 96,515.
Costa Brava, region, Catalonia, Spain; tourism.
Costa del Sol, region, Málaga cst., Spain; tourism.
Costa Rica, rep. Central America; over half p. in equable Meseta Central; forests, volcanic mtns.; agr. 40 per cent G.N.P.; coffee, bananas, cacao; high literacy and living standards; a. 50,909 km²; p. (est. 1969) 1,695,000.
Côte d'Argent, France; cstl. resort a. at S. end of Bay of Biscay.
Côte d'Azur, France; Mediterranean littoral E. of Rhône R.; inc. resorts of Nice, Cannes, Monte Carlo, and St. Tropez.
Côte d'Or, dep., E. France; heart of anc. Burgundy, traversed by R. Saône; cap. Dijon; wines, livestock, iron and steel; a 8,783 km²; p. (1968) 431,192.
Cotentin, peninsula, N. France; 80 km long; Cherbourg, at its extremity, 128 km from Portsmouth.
Côtes-du-Nord, dep., N. Brittany, France; rugged cst. and Is. and mild climate encourage tourism; mkt. gardens along cst.; many fishing ts.; cap. St. Brieuc; a. 7,218 km²; p. (1968) 506,102.
Cotonou, pt., Benin Rep.; new artificial pt.; fishing; lt. inds.; p. (est. 1970) 208,000.
Cotopaxi, volcano, (alt. 5,982 m) in the Andes of Ecuador, nr. Quito; loftiest active volcano in the world; recent eruptions have caused great damage to Ecuador.
Cotswold Hills, W. Eng.; limestone escarpment; Gloucs., Oxon.; once famous for woollens; source of Thames and tribs.; highest point Cleeve Cloud, 309 m; tourism.
Cottbus or Kottbus, E. Germany; on R. Spree; rly. ctr.; textile and metal mnfs.; p. (est. 1970) 82,897.
Cottian Alps, mtn. range on border of France and Italy crossed by Hannibal; craggy; max. alt. 2,844 m (Monte Viso).
Coulsdon and Purley. *See* Croydon.
Council Bluffs, t., Iowa, USA; on Missouri R. nr. Omaha; rly. ctr.; farm implements, paper, machin.; p. (1970) 60,348.
Courbevoie, north-western industl. sub. of Paris, France; p. (1968) 58,283.
Courantyne, R., Guyana; rises in Serra Acari; passes through bauxite mng. region to Atl. Oc.; navigation in lower course; 720 km long.
Courtrai. *See* Kortrijk.
Cove and Kilcreggan, burgh, Dumbarton, Scot.; at junc. of Loch Long and R. Clyde; p. (1971) 1,343.
Coventry, c., West Midlands, Eng.; 29 km E.S.E. of Birmingham; ctr. of cycle, motor-cycle, motor-car ind.; aircraft, tools; chemicals; projectiles, textiles; cath.; univ.; p. (1971) 334,839.
Covilhã, t., Portugal; cloth factories; p. (1970) 60,768.
Covington, t., Ky., USA; on R. Ohio, opp. Cincinnati; machin., leather, furniture; p. (1970) 52,535.
Cowbridge, t., South Glamorgan, S. Wales; nr. Cardiff; p. (1971) 1,221.
Cowdenbeath, burgh, Dunfermline, Scot.; 8 km N.E. of Dunfermline; coal; p. (1971) 10,464.
Cowes, resort and pt., I. of Wight, Eng.; on estuary of R. Medina; regattas and yacht bldg.; hovercraft; p. (1971) 18,895.
Cowley, sub., Oxford, Oxon., Eng.; 5 km S.E. of Oxford; mnfs. motor vehicles.
Cowra, t., N.S.W., Australia; famous wheat dist. and site of state experimental farm; sm. mftg. ctr.; p. (1966) 7,082.
Cozumel I., E. of Yucatan peninsula, Mexico.
Cracow. *See* Kraków.
Cradle, Mt., mtn., Tasmania, Australia; alt. 1,546 m; Nat. Park.
Cradock, t., Cape Prov., S. Africa; wool tr.; p. (est. 1967) 21,300.
Craigavon, c., l. gov. dist. N. Ireland; new "city in a garden" under construction, 16 km long, merging Portadown and Lurgan, linked by motorway, to provide major base for ind.; p. (est. 1971) 12,594.
Crail, royal burgh, North East Fife, Scot.; cstl. resort; p. (1971) 1,075.
Craiova, c., S. Romania, in Wallachia; tr. ctr.; agr. processing textiles, engin., chemicals; p. (est. 1969) 171,676.
Cramlington, t., Northumberland, Eng.; 13 km N. of Newcastle; new t., proposed p. 60,000.
Cranborne Chase, Wilts., Eng.; chalk upland of over 275 m; extension of Salisbury Plain.
Cranbrook, mkt. t., Kent, Eng.; hops and grain; former weaving t.; p. (1971) 16,022 (dist.).
Cranston, t., R.I., USA; machin., chemicals, textiles; p. (1970) 74,287.
Crater L., Ore., USA; in Nat. Park, is a body of water 600 m deep and 10 m across, set in a crater of an extinct volcano, *c.* 2,400 m high; varied flora and fauna on shore.
Craters of the Moon, dist., Idaho, USA; Nat. Monument of volcanic craters and cones; a. 192 km².
Crato, t., Ceara st., Brazil; ctr. of irrigated area producing cotton, sugar, rice; p. (1960) 27,649.
Crau, La, region, Bouches-du-Rhône dep., S.E. France; dry, pebbly area E. of Rhône delta; winter pasture for sheep.
Craven, dist., central Pennines, Eng.; relatively low limestone plateau, alt. mainly below 240 m; drained by R. Ribble to S.W., R. Aire to S.E.; sheep rearing in valleys, cattle for fattening, root and fodder crops.
Crawley, t., West Sussex, Eng.; on N.W. flank of Weald, 14 km S. of Reigate; new t. (1947); engin., pharmaceuticals, metal, leather, wooden gds.; p. (est. 1974) 71,000.
Crayford. *See* Bexley.
Creag Meagaidh, mtn., Lochaber, Scot.; alt. 1,128 m.
Crediton, mkt. t., Devon, Eng.; p. (1971) 5,144.
Cree, R, Wigtown, Scot.; flows into Wigtown Bay.
Crema, industl. and agr. t., N. Italy; S.E. of Milan; cath.; p. (est. 1968) 32,070.
Cremona, t., cap. of C. prov., Lombardy, N. Italy; famed as a ctr. of learning and later for mnf. of violins and violas; birthplace of Stradivari; cath.; pt. on new Milan-Adriatic Waterway; p. (1969) 81,061.
Crete (Kriti), I., E. Mediterranean, lgst. I. of Greece; cradle of Minoan civilisation between 1600 and 1400 B.C.; mild climate; sm. a. of cultivable land; few minerals; part of Greece since Balkan Wars (1913); cap. Khaniá; birthplace of El Greco; a. 8,379 km²; p. (1971) 456,208. (admin. reg.).
Creus, C., juts out into Mediterranean Sea, Spain; nr. Fr. border.
Creuse, dep., in Massif Central, France; soil infertile, harsh climate, limited agr.; a. 5,605 km² p. (1968) 156,876.
Crewe, t., Cheshire, Eng.; 32 km. S.E. of Chester; lge. rly. wks.; impt. rly. junc.; aircraft and refrigerator wks., clothing, engin., motor vehicles; expanded t.; p. (1971) 51,302.
Crewkerne, mkt. t., Somerset, Eng.; 13 km S.W. of Yeovil; leather gds.; grammar school (1499); p. (1971) 4,819.
Criccieth, t., Gwynedd, N. Wales; on N. shore of Cardigan Bay; seaside resort; p. (1971) 1,509.
Cricklade, t., N. Wilts., Eng.; on R. Thames, 13 km N.W. of Swindon; fortified township in Saxon times; p. (1971) 22,368 (dist.).
Crieff, t., Perth and Kinross, Scot.; on R. Earn; egg hatchery, preserve wks.; summer resort; p. (1971) 5,467.
Crimea (Krym) Peninsula, juts into Black Sea, Ukrainian SSR, USSR; wheat, tobacco, fruit; campaign 1854–55 between Russia and Allied Forces of Turkey, Britain, France, and Sardinia was chiefly fought out here (Alma, Balaclava, and Sevastopol); tourism.

Crimmitschau, t., Karl-Marx-Stadt, **E. Germany**; nr. Zwickau; impt. textile ctr.; p. (est. 1970) 29,932.
Crinan Canal, across peninsula of Argyll and Bute, S.W. Scot.; connects Loch Gilp with Atl. Oc.; 14 km long.
Cristóbal, dist., **Panama Canal Zone**; adjoins Colon at N. entrance to Canal; p. (1970) 11,600.
Croaghpatrick, mtns., May, **R.o.I.**; 766 m.
Croatia, constituent rep., **Yugoslavia**; stretches from Istria on Adriatic cst. to Dinaric Alps; crossed by Drava and Sava Rs.; traditional agr. being replaced by new inds.; impt. aluminium wks. based on local bauxite; chemicals, shipbldg.; new oilfields supply 70 per cent of Yugoslavia's needs; cap. Zagreb; a. 56,524 km²; p. (1971) 4,422,564.
Crocodile R. *See* **Limpopo**.
Cromarty, burgh, Ross and Cromarty, **Scot.**; N.E. cst. of Black Isle; p. (1971) 484.
Cromer, t., Norfolk, **Eng.**; on N. cst. of E. Anglia; seaside resort; p. (1971) 5,336.
Cromford, v., Derbys., **Eng.**; Richard Arkwright's first waterpowered mill (1771); cotton.
Crompton, t., Gtr. Manchester, **Eng.**; 3 km S. of Rochdale; cotton, engin., elec. lamps; p. (1971) 17,027.
Crook and Willington, ts., former U.D., Durham, **Eng.**; varied inds. to replace coal mng.; p. (1971) 21,485.
Crosby, t., Merseyside, **Eng.**; on Liverpool Bay, 5 km N. of Bootle, Seaforth container pt.; residtl.; seaside resort; p. (1971) 57,405.
Cross, R., S.E. **Nigeria**; rises in Cameroon Highlands, flows W. and S. into G. of Guinea at Calabar; useful inland waterway; 640 km long.
Cross Fell, mtn., Cumbria, **Eng.**; on E. border of co.; alt. 894 m; highest point of the Pennines.
Crotone, t., S. **Italy**; pt. on E. cst. Calabria; electro-chemicals and metallurgical inds.; on site of anc. Crotona founded as Greek col.; home of Pythagoras; p. (1966) 41,300.
Crowland, t., Lincs., **Eng.**; mkt. t. in the Fens, on R. Welland; 8th-cent. abbey ruins.
Crows Nest Pass, B.C., Alberta, **Canada**; southernmost pass across Canadian Rocky Mtns.; used by rly. from Medicine Hat to Syokane (USA); summit 1,360 m.
Croydon, residtl. t., **Eng.**; now outer bor. Greater London; inc. Coulsdon and Purley; lt. inds.; major office ctr.; p. (1971) 331,851.
Crummock Water, L. Dist., Cumbria, **Eng.**; ribbon L.
Csepel, sub., Budapest, **Hungary**; iron and steel, oil refining, leather, paper; p. incorporated with Budapest 1950.
Csongrád, mkt. t., agr. dist., **Hungary**; at junc. of Rs. Tisza and Körös; p. (1970) 20,331.
Cuba, I., indep. rep., **W.I.**; cap. Havana; lies within tropics; highly fertile although half land a. is mtnous.; exp. sugar, nickel, tobacco, rum, citrus fruits; revolution (1959) reoriented economic and political connections away from USA towards USSR; 70 per cent of cultivated land in state farms or cooperatives; recent attempts to diversify economy but sugar still mainstay; a. 114,494 km²; p. (1970) 8,553,395.
Cuckfield, mkt. t., West Sussex, **Eng.**; p. (1971) 25,883.
Cuckmere, R., Sussex, **Eng.**; passes through S. Downs in beautiful gap; length 37 km.
Cúcuta, t., cap. of Norte de Santander, **Colombia**; close to Venezuelan border; nr. oilfield; destroyed by earthquake, 1875; new planned t.; p. (est. 1972) 219,400 (t.), 248,900 (met. a.).
Cuddalore, spt., Tamil Nadu, **India**; nr. Pondicherry; exp. oilseeds, cottons; p. (1971) 101,335.
Cuddapah, t., Andhra Pradesh, **India**; cotton, cloth factories, millet, rice; p. (1961) 49,027.
Cudworth, South Yorks., **Eng.**; p. (1971) 8,838.
Cuenca, t., cap. of Azuay prov., 3rd. c. of **Ecuador**; in fertile agr. basin of Andes; sugar, tyres, flour mills, Panama hats; p. (1970) 77,300.
Cuenca, agr. and mng. prov., central **Spain**; furniture, leather, paper; a. 17,063 km²; p. (1970) 247,158.
Cuenca, t., cap. of C. prov., **Spain**; on gorge above R. Júcar; mkt. t.; famed in mediaeval times for silver and cloth mnfs.; p. (1966) 28,173.
Cuernavaca, t., cap. of Morelos st., central **Mexico**; anc. Indian t. captured by Cortes; tourist resort; univ.; p. (1970) 134,117.
Cuiabá, t. cap. of Mato Grosso st., **Brazil**; ctr. pastoral a.; gold and diamonds produced; galena deposit nearby; p. (est. 1968) 87,316.
Cuillin Hills, mtns., I. of Skye, **Scot.**; attaining 992 m in Sgurr Alasdair.
Culiacán, c., of Sinaloa, N.W. **Mexico**; anc. c.; Pacific pt. Altata; p. (1970) 167,956.
Culloden Moor, 10 km E. of Inverness, **Scot.**; defeat of Prince Charles Edward Stuart's highlanders by duke of Cumberland's forces (1746).
Culross, royal burgh, Dunfermline, **Scot.**; belong. to Nat. Trust; abbey; p. (1971) 523.
Culver City, t., Cal., **USA**; sub. of Los Angeles; lge. motion-picture plant; electronic equipment, machin., chemicals, tools; p. (1970) 34,526.
Cumaná, c., N.E. **Venezuela**; pt. on Caribbean; European settlement since 1510; exp. coffee, cacao; sardine canning; airpt.; p. (est. 1970) 100,500.
Cumaná, G., N. cst., **Venezuela**.
Cumberland, former co., **Eng.**; now part of Cumbria non-met. co.
Cumberland, industl. t., Md., **USA**; on Potomac R.; iron and steel, tyres, glassware; p. (1970) 29,724.
Cumberland Gap, Ky., **USA**; ch. break in high E. wall of Cumberland plateau; gives access from upper Tennessee valley to Cumberland and Ohio valleys; impt. routeway in colonisation of Ky.
Cumberland Is., off cst. of Queensland, **Australia**.
Cumberland Plateau, mtn. region, Ky., Tenn., Ala., **USA**; forms S.W. zone of Appalachian mtn. system terminating abruptly towards Tennessee valley to E., Cumberland valley to W.; drained W. by tribs. of Cumberland and Ohio Rs; composed of horizontal sandstones overlying coal; thinly populated by backward farming communities except where mng. ts. occur in valleys cut down to coal; mainly between 360–900 m.
Cumberland R., Tenn. and Ky., **USA**; trib. of Ohio R., rises in C. plateau; upper course forested; crosses coalmng. a. and fertile agr. valley; part of Tenn. Valley Authority scheme; hydroelec. power; 1,104 km long.
Cumbernauld, new t. (1955), l. gov. dist., Strathclyde Reg., **Scot.**; to house 50,000 overspill from Glasgow; adding machines; p. (est. 1974) 38,500.
Cumbrae, Gt and Little, Is., in F. of Clyde, off cst. of Cunninghame, **Scot.**
Cumbria, non-met. co., N.W. **Eng.**; centred on L. Dist. where rugged glaciated scenery encourages tourism, sheep-farming, forestry and water storage; Cumberland coalfield on W. cst. where declining heavy inds. being replaced by new lt. inds.; major ts. Carlisle and Barrow; a. 6,809 km²; p. (1971) 476,000.
Cumbrian Mtns., L. Dist., Cumbria, **Eng.**
Cumnock, burgh, Cumnock and Doone Valley, **Scot.**; p. (1971) 5,714.
Cundinamarca, dep., **Colombia**; contains many Andean Ls. and the fed. cap Bogotá; a. 23,585 km²; p. (est. 1968) 1,165,095.
Cunene. *See* **Kunene R.**
Cuneo, prov., **Italy**; a. 7,433 km²; p. (1969) 541,251.
Cuneo, t., cap. of C. prov., Piedmont, **Italy**; mkt. for prod. of surrounding a.; withstood many sieges under the rule of house of Savoy; p. (1969) 53,233.
Cupar, royal burgh, North East Fife, **Scot.**; on R. Eden, W. of St. Andrews; linen; sugar beet; p. (1971) 6,603.
Curaçao, I. (**Neth. Antilles**), off N. cst. Venezuela; major ctr. for refining and trans-shipping Venezuelan oil; picturesque Dutch architecture in cap. Willemstad; a. 544 km²; p. (1968) 139,211.
Curepipe, t., central **Mauritius**; health resort; p. (est. 1968) 50,000.
Curicó, t., **Chile**; agr. and comm. ctr.; earthquake 1928; p. (est. 1966) 39,392.
Curitiba, c., cap. of Paraná st., **Brazil**; univ.; industl. and comm. ctr. at c. 900 m; coffee, maté, chemicals, pharmaceutical and forest prods., foodstuffs; p. (1970) 483,038.
Curragh, plain, Kildare, **R.o.I.**; turf; racecourse.
Curtis I., Queensland, **Australia**; low volcanic I.; wooded; cattle.
Curzola. *See* **Korčula**.

Cuttack, t., Orissa st., **India**; on Mahanadi R.; long famous for gold and silver filigree work; p. (1971) 194,068 (t.), 205,759 (met. a.).
Cuxhaven, spt., Lower Saxony, **W. Germany**; outport of Hamburg at the mouth of R. Elbe; fine harbour, docks, fishing; p. (est. 1969) 45,383.
Cuyahoga Falls, t., Ohio, **USA**; industl. and residtl.; p. (1970) 49,678.
Cuzco, dep., **Peru**; inc. Central Cordilleras, reaching *c.* 5,800 m; tropical climate; agr. varies with alt.; minerals; cap. C.; a. 144,304 km²; p. (est. 1969) 742,100.
Cuzco, t., cap. of C. dep., S. **Peru**; in Andes at alt. 3,418 m in valley of Urubamba R.; once cap. of Incas; sacked by Francisco Pizarro 1533; cath., ruins of Inca fortress; tr. ctr. for agr. prod.; cottons, woollens; p. (est. 1970) 108,900.
Cwmamman, t., Dyfed, **Wales**; on R. Loughor; p. (1971) 3,955.
Cwmbran, t., Gwent, **Wales**; in valley of Avon-Lwyd, 8 km N. of Newport; new t. (1949); motor accessories, wire, elec. gds., bricks, tiles, pipes; p. (est. 1974) 43,500.
Cwm Dyli, Gwynedd, **Wales**; hydroelec. sta.
Cyclades (Kirkádhes), gr. of about 220 Is., **Greece**; rugged and barren csts. conceal sheltered agr. valleys; ch. t. and pt. Hermoupolis; a. 2,650 km²; p. (1971) 86,084.
Cyprus, Rep. of, I., indep. federated state, E. Mediterranean, 64 km S. of Turkey; civil war between Greek and Turkish Cypriots 1974; varied cst., limestone hills in N., forested mtns. in S., central plains of Messaoris in which cap. Nicosia is situated; agr. employs 30 per cent of p.; many irrigation schemes also aid soil and water conservation; land reform programmes to reduce fragmentation of holdings; copper in Troodos mtns. but asbestos of increasing importance; lt. inds. and tourism helping to restructure economy but agr. provides over 50 per cent of exp., inc. wine, citrus fruit, vegetables exported via main pt. of Famagusta; a. 9,251 km²; p. (est. 1969) 630,000.
Cyrenaica, prov. **Libya**; impt. region in anc. times; Greek col. 7th cent. B.C., Roman prov. 1st cent. B.C., captured by Arabs A.D. 642, part of Ottoman Empire 16th cent.; animal grazing, dates, oil-wells; a. 854,700 km²; p. (est. 1963) 350,024.
Czechoslovak Socialist Republic (ČSSR), fed. two-rep. st. (Czech Socialist Rep. and Slovak Socialist Rep.); **Central Europe**; ch. ts. Prague (cap.) Brno, Bratislava, Ostrava, Plzeň; Rs. Danube, Elbe, Vltava, Oder of gr. economic importance for landlocked cty.; inds. highly developed; high standard of living; coal, non-ferrous metals, little petroleum; hydro-elec. power; a. 127,897 km²; p. (est. 1969) 14,418,000.
Czeladz, t., S.W. **Poland**; coal; p. (1970) 31,800.
Czernowitz. *See* **Chernovtsy**.
Czestochowa, c., Katowice prov., S. **Poland**; on Warta R.; rly. and industl. ctr.; iron and steel, textiles; celebrated religious ctr.; monastery; p. (est. 1969) 186,200.

D

Dacca, c., cap. of **Bangladesh**; on Buriganga R., old channel of Ganges; jute, muslin, paper mnfs.; medical radioisotope ctr., univ.; p. (1974) 1,310,976.
Dabrowa Gornicza, t., Katowice, **Poland**; coal, zinc, iron ore; p. (1970) 61,700.
Dachau, t., Bavaria, **W. Germany**; paper, elec. gds., brewing; concentration camp during last war; p. (est. 1969) 32,713.
Dachstein, mtn., Salzkammergut, **Austria**; alt. 2,998 m.
Dadra and Nagar Haveli, union terr., **India**; admin. ctr. Silvassa; a. 490 km²; p. (1962) 57,963.
Dagenham, dist., former M.B., **Eng.**; now forms part of Greater London bor. of Barking; on N. bank of R. Thames; motor cars, iron, drugs, chemicals; residtl.
Dagestan, Caucasian aut rep., **RSFSR**; mtnous.; cap. Makhachkala; cotton, orchards and vineyards; machin., engin. oil; a. 50,246 km²; p. (1970) 1,429,000.
Dagupan, t., Pangasiman, Luzon, **Philippines**; on Lingayen Bay; comm. ctr.; p. (est. 1970) 89,000.
Daharki Mari, t., **Pakistan**; 560 km N.E. of Karachi; fertiliser plant.
Dahlak Archipelago, **Ethiopia**; in Red Sea; only 2 Is. inhabited; noted for pearl fishing.
Dahomey. *See* **Benin, People's Rep. of.**
Daimiel, mkt. t., Ciudad Real, **Spain**; cheeses, oil, wine; p. (1970) 17,710.
Dakar, spt., cap. of **Senegal, W. Africa**; S.E. of C. Verde behind Gorée I. on Atl. cst.; exp. groundnuts and groundnut prods.; some industl. development; international airport; univ. and medical ctr.; p. (est. 1969) 581,000 (met. a.).
Dakhla, oasis, Libyan Desert, **Egypt**; 272 km S.W. of Asyût; dates, olives; stage on caravan route from Cyrenaica to Upper Egypt; site of New Valley Project for irrigation.
Dalälven, R., S. central **Sweden**; length 520 km, used for timber transport.
Da Lat (Dalat), t., **Vietnam**; 224 km N.E. Ho Chi-minh City; in Annamite hills; nuclear reactor (1963); airport.
Dalbeattie, burgh, Stewartry, **Scot.**; granite, dairy prod., gloves; p. (1971) 3,412.
Dalby, t., Queensland, **Australia**; p. likely to increase with development of Moonie oilfield; dairying, timber; p. (1972) 8,890.
Dalgety, t., on Fife cst., **Scot.**; new t. proposed p. 10,000.
Dalkeith, burgh, Midlothian, **Scot.**; 10 km S.E. of Edinburgh; route ctr.; mkt. t.; p. (1971) 9,532.
Dalkey, t., Dublin, **R.o.I.**; on E. cst.; 6 km N. of Wicklow border; seaside resort; residtl.; p. 5,526.
Dallas, c., Texas, **USA**; in cotton- and grain-growing a.; machin., aircraft, petroleum prod.; univ.; scene of assassination of President Kennedy (1963); p. (1970) 836,121 (c.), 1,539 472 (met a.).
Dalmatia, region of **Yugoslavia** and prov. of Croatia, N.E. Adriatic cst.; high Karst plateaux; olive oil, wine; tourism; contains many resorts; a. 12,732 km²; p. 622,000.
Daltonganj, t., Bihar, **India**; on R. Koël; coal, cement; p. (1961) 25,270.
Dalton-in-Furness, t., Cumbria, **Eng.**; limestone quarrying, textiles; abbey ruins; p. (1971) 11,217.
Daman (Damão), spt., **India**; 160 km N. Bombay; fishing, ship-bldg., cotton; former Portuguese settlement; p. (1960) 22,388.
Damanhûr, t., **Egypt**; on W. margin of Nile delta, 40 km S.E. of Alexandria; mkt. for local agr. produce; p. (est. 1970) 161,400.
Damaraland, region, **South-West Africa**; high plateau; admin. by Rep. of S. Africa; pt., Walvis Bay; cattle rearing.
Damascus (Arabic Esh-Sham), cap. c., **Syria**; 91 km S.E. of its pt. Beirut; claims to be oldest continuously inhabited c. in world; metal-wk., glass, cement; univ.; p. (1970) 835,000.
Dambovitta (Dîmbovița), R., **Romania**; rises in Mt. Omul (Transylvanian Alps), flows S. through Bucharest to R. Danube, via impt. oilfields; 320 km long.
Damietta (Dumyât), t., Lower **Egypt**; on main distributary of R. Nile delta; cotton; p. (est. 1970) 98,000.
Dammam, spt. on Persian G. **Saudi Arabia**; oil pt.; planned industl. growth.
Damodar R., Bihar, **India**; flows through India's major coalfields; valley forms ch. industl. a. of India; multipurpose scheme for hydro-electric power, irrigation and flood control.
Dampier, spt., **W. Australia**; on Indian Oc.; new pt. (1965) for shipping iron ore from Mt. Tom Price and Mt. Wittenoom; pelletising plant.
Dampier Archipelago, gr. of sm. Is., off N.W. **Australia, in Indian Oc.**
Dampier Strait, Bismarck Archipelago, channel between W. New Britain and Umboi I.
Dampier Strait, channel between West Irian and Waigeo I.

Danakil Land (Dankalia) coastal desert a., mainly in **Ethiopia**, but partly in **Afars and Issas**; includes D. depression; potash; sm. pt. and road projected.
Da-nang (Tourane), c., **S. Vietnam**; ch. pt. of Annam on S. China Sea; exp. agr. prod.; p. (1968) 334,229.
Danao, t., Cebu, **Philippines**; rice and sugar dist.; p. (est. 1970) 45,500.
Danapur, t., Bihar, **India**; on Ganges R., nr. Patna; p. (1961) 70,766.
Dandenong, t., Victoria, **Australia**; 30 km E. of Melbourne; growing industl. ctr.; p. (est. 1968) 28,700.
Dannemora, t., **Sweden**; 40 km N.E. of Uppsala; iron ore worked since 1579; p. (est. 1970) 4,147.
Danube (Donau), R., second longest R. in Europe; rises in Black Forest, Germany, and flows E. into Black Sea; forms comm. highway; linked by canals with Main, Rhine and Oder; Vienna, Budapest, Belgrade, and other lge. cs. on its banks; 2,706 km long.
Danube-Tisa Canal, N. **Yugoslavia**; irrigation, flood control, navigable; 261 km long.
Danville, t., Ill., **USA**; coal; mftg tr.; p. (1970) 42,570.
Danville t., Va., **USA**; cotton, tobacco; p. (1970) 46,391.
Danzig. *See* Gdańsk.
Dap Cau, t., **Vietnam**; bamboo pulp and paper factories.
Darbhanga, t., Bihar, **India**; rice, oil-seeds, grain, sugar tr.; univ.; p. (1971) 132,059.
Dardanelles, strait between European and Asian Turkey, connecting Aegean Sea with Sea of Marmara; (the anc. Hellespont), 64 km long.
Daresbury, v., Cheshire, **Eng.**; birthplace of C. L. Dodgson (Lewis Carroll).
Dar-es-Salaam, spt., cap. of **Tanzania**; univ.; textile mill projected; oil refining; pipeline to Ndola, Zambia; naval base and Tanzam rly. built with Chinese aid; p. (1970) 343,911.
Darfield, t., South Yorks., **Eng.**; p. (1971) 7,739.
Darien, region, **Panama**; tortoiseshell, pearls, gold, but agr. is basis of economy; cap. La Palma; a. 15,540 km²; p. (1968) 24,100.
Darien, Gulf of, inlet of Caribbean Sea; separates Colombia and Panama.
Darjeeling, hill t., W. Bengal, **India**; tea, quinine; Himalayan resort; p. (1961) 40,651.
Darkhan, new t., **Mongolia**, on R. Hara; industl.
Darlaston, t., West Midlands, **Eng.**; nuts, bolts, fabricated steel mnfs., drop forgings, car components.
Darling Downs, plateau, S.E. Queensland, **Australia**; grazing region; ch. t. Toowoomba.
Darling R., N.S.W., **Australia**; longest trib. of the Murray, forming part of the Murray-Darling Rs. scheme for irrigation and flood control; 2,723 km long.
Darlington, t., Durham, **Eng.**; bridge bldg., woollen yarn mnf., engin., rly. wagons, steel wks.; p. (1971) 85,889.
Darmstadt, c., Hesse, **W. Germany**; cas.; comm. ctr.; metallurgical prods., paper, machin., radio, chemicals, plastics; technical univ.; p. (est. 1969) 140,200.
Dart, R., Devon, **Eng.**; rises in Dartmoor, flows S. into English Channel at Dartmouth; picturesque estuary; 74 km long.
Dartford, t., Kent, **Eng.**; nr. S. cst. of Thames estuary; Dartford–Purfleet road tunnel (1963); engin., chemicals, quarrying, paper; mkt.; p. (1971) 45,670.
Dartmoor, high granite plateau, S.W. Devon, **Eng.**; rough moorland; sheep, cattle, and wild ponies; granite tors; Nat. Park; tourism; granite quarries, reservoirs; prison at Princetown; a. 583 km²; hgst. point High Willays, 622 m.
Dartmouth, spt., S. Devon, **Eng.**; on W. of estuary of R. Dart; Royal Naval College; pottery; yachting, holiday resort; p. (1971) 5,696.
Dartmouth, industl. spt., sub. of Halifax, Nova Scotia, **Canada**; oil refining, shipbldg.; p. (1971) 64,002.
Darton, t., South Yorks., **Eng.**; nr. Barnsley; coal mng.; p. (1971) 15,145.
Darvel, burgh, Strathclyde Reg., **Scot.**; on R. Irvine, 13 km E. Kilmarnock; p. (1971) 3,209.
Darwen, t., N.E. Lancs., **Eng.**; on flank of Rossendale Fells, 5 km S. of Blackburn; tile and glaze bricks, paint, wallpaper, plastics; p. (1971) 28,880.
Darwin, c., spt., N.T., **Australia**; international airpt. serves Frances Creek iron ore mines; mineral deposits; tourism; devastated by cyclone 1974; to be rebuilt; p. (1972) 35,281.
Daryal Gorge, Caucasus, Georgian SSR, **USSR**; deep gorge (1,800 m) cut by Terek R.; identified as the classical Caspian or Iberian Gates from which distances were reckoned; forms part of Georgian military road.
Dashava, settlement on Lvov oblast, W. Ukraine, **USSR**; ctr. of rich natural gas field and starting point of gas pipeline to Kiev and Moscow, built after second world war.
Datia, t. Madhya-Pradesh, **India**; stone-walled, palaces; p. (1961) 29,430.
Datteln, t., N. Rhine-Westphalia, **W. Germany**; coal, leather, iron; p. (est. 1969) 34,659.
Daugavpils, t., Latvian SSR, **USSR**; on Dvina R.; textiles, engin., rly. repair wks., food prods.; p. (1970) 101,000.
Dauphiné Alps, mtn. range, S.E. **France**; 24 peaks over 3,050 m.
Daura, t., nr. Baghdad, **Iraq**; oil refining.
Davangere, t., Karnataka, S. **India**; on 600 m plateau in Indian Penin.; p. (1971) 121,110.
Davao, t., Mindanao, **Philippines**; pt. for sugar; p. (est. 1968) 337,000 (met. a.).
Davenport, t., Iowa, **USA**; on Mississippi R. where it is spanned by bridges to Rock Island, Molise and East Molise; rly., comm. and industl. ctr.; p. (1970) 97,614 (c.), 358,917 (met. a.).
Daventry, t., Northampton, **Eng.**; 14 km S.E. of Rugby; boot-mkg., lt. engin.; wireless-transmission sta.; expanded t.; p. (1971) 11,813.
David, t., cap. of Chiriqui prov., **Panama**; timber, coffee, cacao, sugar; p. (1970) 58,827.
Davis Strait, channel between Greenland and Baffin I., N.W. Terr., **Canada**; connects Atl. Oc. with Baffin Bay; navigable.
Davos-Platz and Dörfli, ts., Grisons, **Switzerland**; Alpine winter resorts; alt. 1,478 m; p. (1970) 10,238.
Dawley, t., Salop, **Eng.**; on S.E. flank of the Wrekin; ironwks., pipe, cement, roadstone, asphalt and brick wks., engin.; new t. (1963); p. (1971) 25,935.
Dawlish, t., S. Devon, **Eng.**; on S. cst. between estuaries of Rs. Exe and Teign; seaside resort; flower tr.; p. (1971) 9,505.
Dawson, t., Yukon Terr., **Canada**; on Yukon R., nr. Klondike goldfields; asbestos mng. projected 1968; p. (1966) 881.
Dax, t., Landes, S.W. **France**; on Adour R.; hot sulphur spring; horse mart; p. (1968) 19,348.
Dayton, c., Ohio, **USA**; on Great Miami R.; univ.; aircraft, elec. machin., rubber gds.; p. (1970) 239,591 (c.), 842,157 (met. a.).
Daytona Beach, t., Fla., **USA**; resort; shipping, ctr.; motor speed trials; p. (1970) 45,327.
De Aar, t., rly. junc., Cape Prov., **S. Africa**; 500 m. from Cape Town; rlys. from N.W. (Luderitz, Walvis Bay) and S.E. (Pt. Elizabeth, E. London) join Cape Town to Johannesburg trunk rly.; p. (est. 1967) 16,600.
Dead Sea, salt-water L. between **Israel and Jordan**; surface 392 m below level of Mediterranean; a. 881 km², length 76 km, greatest width 15 km, greatest depth 399 m; receives waters of Jordan; high mineral content, very saline.
Deal, anc. pt., E. Kent, **Eng.**; on S.E. cst., 11 km N.E. Dover; opposite Goodwin Sands; seaside resort; lifeboat service; p. (1971) 25,415.
Dean, Forest of, Gloucs., **Eng.**; between Wye and Severn Rs.; former Royal Forest; Forestry Commission plantations; former coal-mng. a.; tourism; new lt. industl. estates.
Dearborn, t., Mich., **USA**; birthplace of Henry Ford; p. (1970) 104,199.
Dearne, t., South Yorks., **Eng.**; p. (1971) 25,029.
Death Valley, depression, Cal., **USA**; N. of Mojave Desert, 240 km N.E. of Los Angeles; completely arid; floor covered with saline deposits; tourist attraction; depth of valley floor 84 m below sea-level.
Deauville, seaside resort, Calvados dep., N. **France**; on Eng. Channel; racecourse, casino; p. (1968) 5,370.
Debra Markos, t., cap. of Gojam prov., **Ethiopia**, vegetable oil extraction; p. (est. 1970) 27,170.

Debrecen, t., **Hungary**; 183 km E. of Budapest; univ.; ctr. of pastoral dist.; fairs; pharmaceutics, medical instruments, furniture; ctr. of Calvinism; p. (est. 1969) 154,000.

Decatur, t. Ala., **USA**; steel, textiles; industl. development after establishment of Tenn. Valley Authority; p. (1970) 38,044.

Decatur, t., Ill., **USA**; on Sangamon R.; industl.; rly. engin., food processing; univ.; p. (1970) 89,468 (c.), 123,926 (met. a.).

Decazeville, t., Aveyron, S. **France**; ctr. of sm. coalfield (no longer worked), metallurgy; p. (1968) 10,532.

Deccan, The, upland of S. **India**, bounded by the Narbada and Kistna Rs.; coincides with Maharashtra st.; area of very fertile lava soils; impt. cotton-growing region.

Děčin, R. pt., **ČSSR**; industl. ctr.; cas.; p. (1967) 42,000.

Dedza, t., **Malawi**, new t.; p. (1966) 2,261.

Dee, R., N. **Wales** and Cheshire, **Eng.**; 144 km long; lge. silted estuary, use for water storage planned.

Dee, R., Louth, **R.o.I.**; flows to Dundalk Bay; 32 km long.

Dee, R., Kincardine and Deeside, **Scot.**; picturesque, tourism; 139 km long.

Dehiwala-Mt Lavina, t., **Sri Lanka**; on cst. S. of Colombo; p. (est. 1968) 122,500.

Dehra Dun, t.. Uttar Pradesh, **India**; scientific research ctr.; sawmills; p. (1971) 166,073 (t.), 203,464 (met. a.).

Deir-ez-Zor, t., **Syria**; on Euphrates R.; on motor route between Damascus and Baghdad; p. (1962) 59,757.

Dej, t.. **Romania**; on Somesul R., distillery; p. (est. 1970) 30,869.

Delabole, v., Cornwall, **Eng.**; on N.W. flank of Bodmin Moor; slate quarries.

Delagoa Bay, natural harbour, **Moçambique**; ch. pt. Lourenço Marques.

Delaware, st., **USA**; low-lying a. of Atl. cst. plain; agr., lumber; fertilisers, minerals, leather, chemicals, machin.; cap. Dover; ch. pt. Wilmington; a. 6,138 km^2; p. (1970) 542,979.

Delaware Bay, inlet, Atl. cst., **USA**; drowned estuary of R. Delaware, extends 128 km inland from C. May into heart of highly industl. a. of Philadelphia.

Delaware R., flows between N.Y. st., **USA** along the Penns. border, through N.J. to Delaware Bay; 504 km long.

Delft, c., pt., S. Holland, **Neth.**; on Schie R. (canalised), nr. Rotterdam; technical univ.; ceramics (delft-ware), tool mftg., precision instruments; 13th cent. Old church and 15th cent. New church; p. (1968) 80,545.

Delhi, c., cap. of **India**; on watershed between Rs. Indus and Ganges; made up of Old Delhi with walls, palace, and fort, and New Delhi with admin. ctr.; univ.; p. (1971) 3,287,883 (c.), 3,647,023 (met. a.).

Delhi, union terr., **India**; hot and arid region between Indus valley and alluvial plain of Ganges; irrigation to support agr ; New Delhi and Old Delhi ch. ctrs.; a. 1,497 km^2; p. (1971) 4,044,338.

Delitzsch, t., Leipzig, **E. Germany**; 26 km E. of Halle; sugar, chemicals; p. (est. 1970) 24,270.

Delmarva, peninsula, Del., **USA**; between Chesapeake Bay and Del. Bay; horticulture, poultry, forestry, fishing.

Delmenhorst, t., Lower Saxony, **W. Germany**; nr. Bremen; jute, woollens, linoleum, foodstuffs; p. (est. 1969) 63,068.

Delphi, anc. Phocis, central **Greece**, N. of G. of Corinth; famous for Delphic oracle on Mt. Parnassus.

Del Rio, t., Texas, **USA**; pt. of entry on Rio Grande; mkt. for agr. a.; grapes; exp. wool; border t., bridge to Mexico; p. (1970) 21,330.

Demavend, dormant volcano; **Iran**; hgst. peak in Elburz range, *c.* 5,673 m.

Demerara, co., **Guyana**; between Essequibo and Demerara Rs.; exp. sugar, molasses, rum.

Demerara, R., **Guyana**; drains N. to Atl. Oc.; bauxite transport.

Demirtas, t., **Turkey**; nr. Bursa; car wks.

Denain, t., Nord dep., **N. France**; industl. ctr.; coal, steel; p. (1968) 27,988 (t.), 126,740 (met. a.).

Denbigh, former co., N. **Wales**; now mostly in Clwyd; sm. part in Gwynedd.

Denbigh, t., Clwyd, **Wales**; in Vale of Clwyd, 16 km S. of Rhyl; cas.; tourism; dairy prods.; birthplace of Stanley the explorer; p. (1971) 8,100.

Denby Dale, t., West Yorks., **Eng.**; 13 km W. of Barnsley; woollen textiles; earthenware pipes; p. (1971) 11,093.

Den Haag. *See* **Hague, The.**

Den Helder. *See* **Helder.**

Denholme, t., West Yorks., **Eng.**; nr. Bradford; dairying, textiles; p. (1971) 2,587.

Denizli, t., **Turkey**; 75 km S.E. of Izmir; gardens —"the Damascus of Anatolia"; nr. site of Laodicea; p. (1965) 61,820.

Denmark, kingdom, N.W. **Europe**; part of Scandinavia; consists of Jutland peninsula, Is. of Sjaelland, Fyn, Falster, Lolland, and Bornholm, and 400 smaller Is., between N. Sea and Baltic; emphasis on dairy agr., producing butter, eggs, and bacon; increasing industrialisation; industl. prods. now account for 62 per cent of exp.; cap. Copenhagen; a. 42,932 km^2; p. (est. 1970) 4,921,156.

Denny and Dunipace, burgh, Falkirk, **Scot.**; 10 km W. of Falkirk; steel castings, precast concrete, p. (1971) 9,841.

Dent du Midi, mtn. gr., Vaud can., S.W. **Switzerland**; rises to 10,694 ft. in Haut Cime.

Denton, t., Gtr. Manchester **Eng.**; nr. Manchester; felt-hat mkg.; p. (1971) 38,107.

Denton, mkt. t., Texas, **USA**; univs.; food processing p. (1970) 39,874.

D'Entrecasteaux Is., volcanic gr. off S.E. New Guinea, Pac. Oc., part of **Papua-New Guinea.**

Denver, c., cap. of Col., **USA**; on E. slope of Rockies, on South Platte R.; univs.; oil, electronic equipment, mng. machin., livestock, canning; tourism; p. (1970) 512,691 (c.); 1,223,142 (met. a.).

Deogarh, t., Bihar, **India**; temples, place of pilgrimage; p. (1961) 30,813.

Deptford. *See* **Lewisham.**

Dera Ghazi Khan, t., **Pakistan**; on W. bank of Indus R.; silk, brass, ivory gds.; mosques; p. (1961) 47,105.

Dera Ismail Khan, t., **Pakistan**; on Indus R.; admin. ctr., caravan ctr.; p. (1961) 46,100.

Derbent, c., S.E. Dagestan, **RSFSR**; on Caspian Sea; textiles, fish inds., glass; oil and natural gas nearby; anc. c. founded by Persians; p. (est. 1967) 59,000.

Derby, t., Derbys., **Eng.**; on R. Derwent; general engin., aero-engines, man-made fibres; p. (1971) 219,348.

Derbyshire, non-met. co., **Eng.**; much of a. occupied by Pennines and Peak Dist. Nat. Park.; coalfield and industl. a. in E.; forms part of Manchester met. a. in N.W.; co. t. Derby; a. 2,631 km^2; p. (1971) 886,000.

Derg, Lough, in basin of R. Shannon, **R.o.I.**; separating Galway and Clare from Tipperary.

Derg, L., Donegal, **R.o.I**, with cave on I. visited by R.C. pilgrims and known as "St. Patrick's Purgatory".

Derwent, lgst R., Tasmania, **Australia**; flows to Storm Bay; used for hydroelectric power; length 48 km.

Derwent, R., Derbys., **Eng.**; trib. of R. Trent; length 96 km.

Derwent, R., North Yorks./Humberside, **Eng.**; trib. of R. Ouse; length 91 km.

Derwentwater, L., Cumbria, **Eng.**; nr. Keswick; 5 km long.

Desaguadero, R., **Bolivia**; outlet of L. Titicaca; used for irrigation; 320 km long.

Desborough, t., Northants., **Eng.**; boot and shoe mnfs., iron mng.; p. (1971) 5,294.

Désirade, I., **Fr. W.I.**; nr. Guadeloupe; a. 26 km^2; p. 1,581.

Des Moines, c., cap. of Iowa st., **USA**; in heart of corn belt; transport and industl. ctr.; univ.; p. (1970) 198,427 (c.), 281,478 (met. a.).

Des Moines, R., Iowa, **USA**; trib. of Mississippi rising in Minn.; 880 km long.

Desna, R., main trib. of Dnieper R., **USSR**; navigable below Bryansk; 1,184 km long.

Des Plaines, t., Ill., **USA**; sub. of Chicago on Des Plaines; R. p. (1970) 57,239.

Dessau, t., Halle, **E. Germany**; at confluence of Mulde and Elbe Rs.; cas.; machin., rly. carriages, paper, sugar, chemicals; route ctr.; p. (est. 1970) 98,261.

Detmold, t., N. Rhine-Westphalia, **W. Germany**; cas.; paints, wood inds.; p. (est. 1969) 28,347.

Detroit, ch. c., pt., Mich., **USA**; busy comm. and industl. ctr.; univ.; gr. grain mart; and ctr. of the "Ford" motor-car wks., aeroplanes, military tanks, synthetic diamonds, pharmaceutics, tools, chemicals, steel; lgst exporting t. on Great Lakes; 850 murders per year; p. (1970) 1,492,914 (c.), 4,163,517 (met. a.).

Detroit, R., channel between L. St. Clair and L. Erie (40 km) separates st. of Mich., USA, from Ontario, **Canada**; carries more shipping than any other inland waterway in the world.

Deurne, t., **Belgium**; nr. Antwerp, airport; p. (1968) 77,159.

Deux Sèvres, dep., Poitou-Charentes, **France**; mainly agr.; vineyards; cap. Niort; a. 6,053 km²; p. (1968) 326,462.

Deventer, t., Overijssel, **Neth.**; on IJssel R.; industl. ctr., machin., textile and carpet inds.; Hanse t. in Middle Ages; p. (1968) 62,777.

Devil's Island (I. du Diable), I., Atl. Oc. off **Fr. Guiana**; former penal settlement where Dreyfus was confined in 1894.

Devils Tower, N.E. Wyo., **USA**; tower rock of volcanic origin with fluted columns of igneous rock; alt. 264 m.

Devizes, Wilts. **Eng.**; mkt. t., on Kennet and Avon canal at foot of Marlborough Downs; bricks, tiles, bacon-curing; p. (1971) 10,170.

Devonport, spt., Tasmania, **Australia**; 131 km from Launceston; agr. dist.; canning, foundry inds.; p. (1972) 18,150.

Devonport, fortfd. spt., S. Devon, **Eng.**; naval sta. to become nuclear submarine base; road bridge to Saltash across Tamar; p. included with Plymouth.

Devonport, bor., Auckland, **N.Z.**; naval base and dockyard; sub. of Auckland; p. (1971) 10,925.

Devon, non-met. co., S.W. **Eng.**; between English and Bristol Channels; attractive cstl. scenery, Nat. Parks of Dartmoor and Exmoor encourage tourism; mixed farming; modern lt. inds.; major ctrs. of p. at Plymouth, Torbay, Exeter; a. 6,713 km²; p. (1971) 896,000.

Dewsbury, t., West Yorks., **Eng.**; on R. Calder, 13 km from Leeds; heavy woollens, shoddy, coalmng.; dyewks.; p. (1971) 51,310.

Dez Dam, over Dez R., Khurzistan prov., **Iran**; opened 1963.

Dezfūl, t., **Iran**; mkt. ctr.; oil fields nearby; p. (1966) 105,381.

Dhahran, spt., **Saudi-Arabia**; main oil pt. of S.A.; airpt.; College of Petroleum and Minerals; p. 12,001.

Dhanbad, t., Bihar, **India**; lead, zinc, tools, radio assembly, fertilisers; p. (1971) 79,838 (t.), 434,031 (met. a.).

Dhanushkodi, t., Tamil Nadu, **India**; on I. in Palk Strait; ferry pt. for passenger traffic from India to Sri Lanka.

Dhar, t., Madhya Pradesh, **India**; cultural and tr. ctr.; p. (1961) 28,325.

Dharmsala, hill sta., Himachal Pradesh, **India**; 160 km N.E. of Amritsar; sanatorium; *c.* 1,800 m; imposing mtn. scenery; p. (1961) 10,255.

Dharwar, t., Karnataka, **India**; 112 km E. of Goa; univ.; cotton mnf.; p. (1961) 77,163.

Dhaulagiri, mtn. peak, 8,172 m, **Nepal**, 4 summits in Himalayas.

Dhekélia, **Cyprus**; Brit. sovereign a. within Rep.; p. (1960) 3,602.

Dhufar, fertile prov., **Oman**, Arabia; sugar-cane, cattle; ch. t. Salālah; ch. pt. Mirbat.

Dhulia, t., Khandesh dist., Maharashtra, **India**; cotton ind.; rly. ctr.; p. (1971) 137,129.

Diamante, R., Mendoza prov., **Argentina**; rises in Andes, flows E. to R. Salado; irrigates oasis of San Rafael; 320 km long.

Diamantina, t., Minas Gerais, **Brazil**; ctr. of former diamond mng. dist.; p. (est. 1968) 34,267.

Dibrugarh, t., Assam, **India**; terminus of rail communications along Brahmaputra from Calcutta; coal, tea; p. (1961) 58,480.

Didcot, sm. t., Oxon., **Eng.**; 16 km S. of Oxford; ordnance depots.

Diego Garcia, I., Brit. Indian Oc. Terr.; Anglo-American naval communications ctr.; c. 1,000 islanders evacuated to Mauritius 1966–71; major US military staging base projected 1975.

Diego Suarez, t., extreme N. of **Malagasy Rep.**; oxygen plant; Fr. naval base; p. (1965) 38,484.

Dieppe, pt., Seine-Maritime, **France**; 56 km N. of Rouen; fisheries, shipbldg., machin.; cross-Channel ferry; p. (1968) 30,404.

Differdange, t., S.W. **Luxembourg**; iron ore; cattle; p. (est. 1970) 17,963.

Digboi, N.E. Assam, **India**; oil fields and refinery; p. (1961) 35,028.

Digne, t., cap. of Alpes-de-Haute-Provence, **France**; nr. Aix; cath.; p. (1968) 14,661.

Dijon, c., cap. Cote-d'Or, E. **France**; the Roman Divonense castrum; route ctr.; Seine-Saône watershed; wine tr.; industl. ctr.; univ., cath.; casino; p. (1968) 145,357 (c.), 183,989 (met. a.).

Dili, t., cap. of E. Timor, **Indonesia**; major spt.; exp. cotton, copra, coffee; p. (1970) 29,312.

Dillingen, t., Bavaria, **W. Germany**; on R. Danube, heavy inds.; p. (est. 1967) 11,600.

Dimitrovgrad, t., **Bulgaria**; founded 1947; fertilisers, chemicals, superphosphate plant, iron, thermo-electric sta.; p. (est. 1968) 44,302.

Dimitrovo. *See* Pernik.

Dinajpur, t., **Bangladesh**; comm. ctr.; univ.; p. (1961) 37,711.

Dinan, t., Brittany, **France**; mediaeval t. above Rance R.; hosiery, brewing; holiday resort; p. (1968) 9,901.

Dinant, t., Namur, **Belgium**; on R. Meuse; mkt. t., tourist resort; exported copperware (*dinanderie*) in Middle Ages; cath., citadel (1040); p. (1968) 9,901.

Dinard, t., Brittany, **France**; resort, especially for English; p. (1968) 9,162.

Dinaric Alps, mtn. range, **Yugoslavia**, **Albania** and **Italy** (Trieste); extend 640 km along Adriatic; hgst. peak Durmitor, 2,515 m.

Dindigul, t., Tamil Nadu, **India**; 40 km S. of Tiruchirapalli; cigars, tobacco; p. (1971) 128,429.

Dingle B., Kerry, **R.o.I.**; long inlet of sea on Atl. cst.

Dingle, t., D. peninsula, Kerry, **R.o.I.**; agr. mkt.; creamery, fishing.

Dingwall, royal burgh, Ross and Cromarty, **Scot.**; at head of Cromarty F.; rly. junc.; cattle mkt., admin. ctr.; distilling, handloom weaving; p. (1971) 4,232.

Dinslaken, t., N. Rhine-Westphalia, **W. Germany**, N. of Duisburg; coal, steel, iron, footwear, timber; oil pipeline from Wesseling under construction; p. (est. 1969) 53,991.

Diomede Is., two barren granitic islets in Bering Strait between Alaska and Siberia; accepted bdy. between Soviet and US terr.

Diredawa, t., **Ethiopia**; 40 km N. of Harar; rly. wks.; mkt and comm. ctr.; p. (est. 1970) 60,925.

Dirk Hartog I., off Shark Bay, **W. Australia**.

Disko I., off W. cst. of **Greenland** in Baffin Bay; contains harbour of Godhavn, cap. N. Greenland; rendezvous for whalers; shrimp beds; a. 8,288 km².

Dismal Swamp, morass, S. Va. and N.C., **USA**; contains L. Drummond and extends 50–65 km S. from nr. Norfolk.

Diss, Norfolk, **Eng.**; mkt t. on R. Waveney, 45 km S.W. of Norwich; agr. implements; p. (1971) 4,477.

Distaghil, major peak, Gr. Karakoram, N. Kashmir, **Pakistan**; two summits connected by a ridge, max. alt. 7,890 m.

Distrito Federal, federal dist., **Brazil**; inc. cap. c. of Brasilia; a. 5,815 km²; p. (1967) 142,000.

Ditchling Beacon, 10 km N. of Brighton, East Sussex, **Eng.**; hgst point of South Downs, 248 m.

Diu, spt., I., off S. cst. of Bombay, **India**; oil nearby at Kayakov; p. (1960) 14,271.

Diwānīyah, Ad, t., **Iraq**; cap. D. prov.; on Baghdad–Basra rly.; p. (1965) 181,000 (met. a.).

Diyarbakir, c., cap. of D. prov., central **Turkey**; on Tigris R.; comm. and mnf. ctr.; flour and rice mills; the anc. Amida, old walls, gates, citadel; p. (1965) 102,653 (c.), 163,691 (met. a.).

Djajapura (Sukarnapura), t., cap. of West Irian, **Indonesia**; on Humboldt B., an inlet of Pac. Oc.

Djakarta (Batavia), c., cap. of **Indonesia**, N.W. Java; comm. ctr.; textiles; exps. rubber, tea; printing; airport; p. (1971) 4,576,009.

Djambi, dist., and t., Sumatra, **Indonesia**; on E.

cst. plain 160 km N.W. of Palembang; univ.; field; a. (dist.) 44,924 km²; p. (1971) 158,559 (t.).

Djerba, t. and I., **Tunisia,** at S. entrance to G. of Gabès, joined to mainland by causeway; olives, dates, textiles, pottery; a. 510 km²; p. (1966) 62,445.

Djibouti, c., cap. of **Afars and Issas**; rly. terminus; main pt. and transit ctr.; p. (est. 1970) 62,000 (met. a.).

Dneprodzerzhinsk, t., Ukrainian SSR, **USSR**; W. of Dnepropetrovsk on Dnieper R.; iron and steel, engin., chemicals; hydroelec. sta. nearby; p. (1970) 227,000 (c.), 239,000 (met. a.).

Dneproges (abbrev. Dnieper hydroelectric sta.), Ukrainian SSR, **USSR**; nr. Zaporoz'ye, on Dnieper; lgst dam and power sta. in Europe; destroyed by Germans, rebuilt 1944–9.

Dnepropetrovsk, c., Ukrainian SSR, **USSR**; on R. Dnieper; univ.; impt. rly. and industl. ctr., using iron ore (from Krivoy Rog), coal (Donbas), manganese (Nikopol) and electric power from Dnieper dam; heavy machin., chemicals; p. (1970) 863,000 (c.), 918,000 (met. a.).

Dneprorudnyy, t., Ukrainian SSR, **USSR**; new t. on S. shore of Kakhvota reservoir; p. (1964) 6,000.

Dneprostroy. *See* **Zaporoz'ye.**

Dnieper (Dnepr), gr. R. of Ukrainian SSR, **USSR**; 3rd longest R. of Europe; rises in Valdai hills, flows into Black Sea, 2,240 km long; connected by canals to Baltic; tribs. inc. Berezina, Pripet, Desna, Orel, Samara; since erection of Dneproges dam navigable for almost entire length.

Dniester (Dnestr), R., Ukraine SSR, **USSR**; rises in Carpathians and flows into the Black Sea; 1,403 km long.

Döbeln, t., Leipzig, **E. Germany**; machin., metallurgy, wood, cigar and sugar inds.; p. (est. 1970) 27,754.

Dobrich. *See* **Tolbukhin.**

Dobruja, historic region, S.E. **Europe**; along Black Sea cst., S.E. Romania, and N.E. Bulgaria; mainly agr.; ch. pt. Constanta.

Dobšiná, t., **ČSSR**; cave containing ice-field of 0·8 ha; asbestos, iron ore; p. 5,300.

Dodecanese (S. Sporades), gr. of some 20 Greek Is. (originally 12) in S. Ægean Sea; most impt. are Rhodes, Cos, and Leros; Italian 1912–46; p. (1971) 120,258.

Dodoma, proposed new cap. of **Tanzania**; at geographical ctr. of T. in rural a.; transfer planned for 1983.

Dodworth, t. South Yorks., **Eng.**; nr. Barnsley; coal; p. (1971) 4,551.

Dogger Bank, sandbank in N. Sea, between England and Denmark; depth varies from 6 to 37 m; valuable fishing ground; action between British fleet under Beatty and German fleet under Hipper; *Blücher* sunk Jan. 1915.

Dogs, I. of, riverside dist., formed by bend in the R. Thames off Greenwich, London, **Eng.**; Millwall and India docks, shipbldg. yards.

Doha, t., cap. of **Qatar**; spt. on E. of Qatar peninsula, Persian Gulf; internat. airpt., deep sea pt.; contains 80 per cent of p.; p. (est. 1970) 80,000.

Dokai Bay, inlet, N. Kyushu, **Japan**; landlocked bay on S. side of Shimonoseki straits; flanked by highly industl. zone inc. Yawata, Wakamatsu, Tobata cs.; requires constant dredging; length 6 km, width 0·8–2·4 km.

Dôle, t., Jura, **E. France**; on R. Doubs, nr. Dijon; industl. ctr.; anc. cap. of Franche-Comté, ceded to France in 1678; birthplace of Pasteur; p. (1968) 28,774.

Dolgarrog, sm. t., Gwynedd, **Wales**; site of hydroelectric sta.

Dolgellau, t., Gwynedd, **N. Wales**; agr., quarrying, timber; p. (1971) 2,564.

Dollar, burgh, Clackmannan, **Scot.**; at foot of Ochil hills; p. (1971) 2,280.

Dollar Law, mtn., nr. Peebles, **Scot.**; alt. 817 m.

Dolomites, gr. of limestone mtns., S. Tyrolese Alps, N.E. **Italy**; tourist dist.; peaks assume fantastic forms; principal peak Marmolada 3,355 m.

Dominica, **W.I.**, most N. of Windward Is.; 25 per cent under cultivation; volcanic soils highly suitable for bananas; N.–S. mtn. range has spectacular volcanic scenery; cap. Roseau; Ass. St. within Brit. Commonwealth (1967); a. 751 km²; p. (1968) 70,177.

Dominican Rep., rep., **W.I.**, shares I. of Hispaniola with Haiti; comprises Nat. Dist. (inc. cap. Santo Domingo) and 25 admin. provs.; mtnous. with sub-tropical climate; in path of tropical cyclones; comm. economy mainly agr.; transport system geared to exp. of sugar; govt. investment in agr. and mng.; oil refining at Nigua; exp. bauxite; tourism growing; official language Spanish; a. 48,430 km²; p. (est. 1974) 4,900,000.

Domodossola, frontier t., Piedmont, **N. Italy**; nr. Alpine tourist resort in Toce valley, nr. Simplon.

Don, R. South Yorks., **Eng.**; trib. of R. Ouse, 112 km long.

Don, R., Gordon, **Scot.**; flows into N. Sea nr. Aberdeen; salmon; 131 km long.

Don, major R. of southern **RSFSR**; falls into Sea of Azov below Rostov, its ch. pt.; navigable to Voronezh; ch. trib., Donets; access to Volga by Don-Volga canal; fisheries; 1,955 km long.

Donaghadee, t., Ards, **N. Ireland**; nearest point to Scot.; spt. and seaside resort; p. (1966) 3,649.

Donauwörth, t., W. Bavaria, **W. Germany**; bridge t. on N. bank of Danube at Wörnitz confluence; p. (est. 1968) 11,130.

Donawitz, t., Styria prov., **Austria**; lignite, iron and steel; p. circa 18,000.

Donbas, industl. region, Ukrainian SSR, **USSR**; in valleys of Rs. Donets and lower Dnieper; about 23,300 km²; produces 60 per cent of Russia's coal; adjoins Krivoy Rog ironfields; many lge. industl. ts.

Doncaster, t. South Yorks., **Eng.**; on Don R. 27 km N.E. of Sheffield; coal mines, tractors nylon mftg.; racecourse; p. (1971) 82,505.

Donegal, spt., Co. Donegal, **R.o.I.**; on W. cst. on Donegal Bay; homespun tweeds, carpets; p. (1966) 1,507.

Donegal (Tirconnail), co., N.W. **R.o.I.**; fishing poor agr.; cloth, hydroelectric power; co. t. Lifford; a. 4,830 km²; p. (1966) 108,486.

Donets, R., rises in uplands of central **RSFSR**, N.E. of Belgorod, flows S.E. to join R. Don; crosses Donets coalfield; length 1,040 km. *See* **Donbas.**

Donetsk (Stalino), t., Ukrainian SSR, **USSR**; industl. ctr. of Donets coal basin; iron, steel, engin., chemicals; p. (1970) 879,000 (c.), 890,000 (met. a.).

Donges, t., Loire Atlantique, **France**; nr. St. Nazaire; oil refinery; synthetic textiles, plastics.; p. (1968) 6,458.

Dongola (Dunqulah), t., **Sudan**; on left bank of Nile above Third Cataract; Old D. was 120 km to S.; p. (est. 1965) 4,970.

Donner Pass, E. Cal., **USA**; highway pass through Sierra Nevada at 2,176 m.

Donzère-Mondragon, Vaucluse, **France**; site of Rhône barrage supplying hydroelectric power.

Doon, R., Kyle and Carrick, **Scot.**; flows from Loch Doon to F. of Clyde; 42 km long.

Dora Baltea, R., **N. Italy**; rises in Mt. Blanc, flows E. and S. through Val d'Aosta to R. Po at Chivasso; impt. routeway from N. Italy to Switzerland (through Gr. St. Bernard Pass) and France (through Little St. Bernard Pass); 152 km long.

Dora Riparia, R., **Italy**; trib. of R. Po, flowing from Cottian Alps past Turin; 96 km long.

Dorchester, co. t., Dorset, **Eng.**; mkt. t. on R. Frome; lime, agr., engin.; Roman remains; nearby prehistoric Maiden Castle; linked with the name of Thomas Hardy; p. (1971) 13,737.

Dordogne, dep., S.W. **France**; cap. Périgueux; crossed by Dordogne R.; fertile valleys; p. (1968) 374,073.

Dordogne, R., S.W. **France**; rises in Central Massif, joins Garonne to form Gironde; vineyards; upper reaches used for hydroelectric power.

Dordrecht, c., nr. Rotterdam, **Neth.**, on R. Merwede; timber, shipbldg., seaplanes; p. (1968) 88,461.

Dorking, t., Surrey, **Eng.**; on R. Mole to S. of gap through N. Downs; mkt., residtl; lt. inds.; p. (1971) 22,354.

Dormagen, t., N. Rhine–Westphalia, **W. Germany**; petrochemicals, artificial fibres.

Dornbirn, t., Vorarlberg, **Austria**; textiles; p. (est. 1966) 32,200.

Dornoch, burgh, Sutherland, **Scot.**; N. of Dornoch F.; resort; p. (1971) 838.

Dorset, non-met. co., S. **Eng.**; borders Eng. Channel along attractive cliffed cst. formed by E.–W. limestone ridges; Portland stone quarried; many tourist resorts inc. Bournemouth; mkt. ts. serve agr. interior; a. 2,655 km²; p. (1971) 553,000.

Dorset Heights, hills, extend E. to W. across central Dorset, Eng.; chalk; pastoral farming, sheep; some cultivation where soil is deep enough; rise to 250–275 m.

Dorsten, t., N. Rhine–Westphalia, **W. Germany**; on R. Lippe; coal, iron, elec., chemical inds.; p. (1969) 39,354.

Dortmund, c., N. Rhine–Westphalia, **W. Germany**; on Dortmund–Ems Canal; industl. ctr. and pt. of Ruhr; coal, iron, steel, machin.; p. (est. 1969) 647,000.

Dortmund–Ems Canal, N. Rhine–Westphalia, **W. Germany**; links Dortmund on Ruhr coalfield with R. Ems 8 km above Lingen; coal, iron-ore traffic; 144 km long.

Douai, t., Nord, **France**; nr. Lille on Scarpe R.; coal, iron and engin. wks.; bell founding, arsenal; p. (1968) 49,187 (t.), 205,432 (met. a.).

Douala, spt., **Cameroon**; rly. to Yaoundé; exp. hardwoods; p. (1970) 250,00 (met. a.).

Douarnenez, spt., Finistère, N.W. **France**; on D. Bay; sardine fisheries; p. (1968) 20,184.

Doubs, dep., E. **France**; traversed by Jura range and R. Doubs; mainly agr.; watchmkg., motor vehicles; cap. Besançon; a. 5,315 km²; p. (1968) 426,363.

Douglas, t., cap. of I. of Man; 120 km W. of Liverpool, **Eng.**; spt.; seaside resort; p. (1966) 19,517.

Douglas Point, on shore of L. Huron, Ont., **Canada**; nuclear power sta.

Dounreay, Caithness, **Scot.**; fast-breeder nuclear reactors.

Douro, R., **Portugal** and **Spain**; enters Atl. Oc. below Oporto; known as Duero R. in Spain; l. 776 km; famous port wine a.

Dove, R., Derbys. and Staffs., **Eng.**; trib. of Trent; flows through beautiful dales; 77 km long.

Dovedale, valley, Derbys., **Eng.**; steeply sloping limestone ravine of R. Dove; tourism.

Dover, packet pt., Kent, **Eng.**; one of old Cinque pts.; nearest spt. to France the Strait of D. being only 34 km wide; ch. pt. for passenger and mail traffic with Continent; cas.; p. (1971) 34,322.

Dovey, R., **Wales**; flows from Cambrian Mtns. and enters Cardigan Bay by a wide estuary.

Dowlais, dist., Merthyr Tydfil, Mid Glamorgan, **S. Wales**; coal mng., iron founding, engin.

Down, former co.; l. gov. dist., **N. Ireland**; borders Strangford Lough and Dundrum Bay; agr. and fisheries; p. of former co. (est. 1971) 310,617.

Downham Market, t., Norfolk, **Eng.**; on R. Ouse; flour-milling malting, sheet-metal wks.; p. (1971) 3,608.

Downpatrick, t., Down, **N. Ireland**; on R. Quoile; linen; p. (1966) 4,291.

Downs, natural harbour of refuge for shipping between Kent cst. and Goodwin Sands in the English Channel.

Downs. *See* **North Downs, South Downs.**

Drachenfels, mtn. peak on the Rhine, **W. Germany**; the steepest of the Siebengebirge range, nr. Königswinter; alt. 325 m; ascended by lt. rly.; famous cave of legendary dragon.

Draguignan, t., S.E. **France**; cap. of Var. dep. until 1974; mkt. t., service ctr.; p. (1968) 18,376.

Drakensberg, mtn. chain between Natal and Orange Free State, **S. Africa**, and **Lesotho**; extending 800 km from Gt. Fish R. to Olifants R.; hgst. peak Mont-aux-Sources 3,283 m; rly. crosses range by Van Reenen Pass.

Drama, pref. Macedonia, **Greece**; cap. Drama; a. 3,504 km²; p. (1971) 91,015.

Drammen, spt., **Norway**; nr. Oslo, on the Drammen R.; shipyard; exp. timber, wood-pulp, paper; p. (1968) 47,827.

Drancy, t., Seine-St. Denis, **France**; N.E. sub. of Paris; p. (1968) 69,528.

Drava (Drau), R., trib. of Danube, **Austria** and **Yugoslavia**; flows from the Tyrol across Carinthia and Styria, joining Danube nr. Osijek; length 720 km; used for hydroelec. power.

Drenthe, prov., **Neth.**; on German frontier; cap. Assen; a. 2,663 km²; p. (1968) 354,124.

Dresden, c., **E. Germany**; R. pt. on Elbe, 80 km E. of Leipzig; impt. route ctr.; engin., chemicals, optical and photographic apparatus, porcelain, glass, brewing; fine art collections; scientific research; oil pipeline from Schwedt under construction; p. (est. 1969) 500.726 (c.). 635,000 (met. a.).

Driffield, t., Humberside, **Eng.**; on Yorks. Wolds 21 km N. of Beverley; oil-cake wks.; p. (1971) 7,899.

Drin, R., N. **Albania**; rises in Yugoslavia and flows through deep gorges into Adriatic; hydroelec. power; 288 km long.

Drina, R., trib. of Sava R., **Yugoslavia**; ch. source of hydroelec. power in rep.; 480 km long.

Dröbak, spt., S.E. **Norway**; winter pt. for Oslo; summer resort.

Drogheda, spt., Louth, **R.o.I.**; considerable tr. in agr. produce, salmon, etc.; stormed by Cromwell in 1649; p. (1966) 17,823.

Drogobych, t., Ukranian SSR, **USSR**; 64 km S.W. of Lvov; ctr. of lge. oilfields, refineries; mftg.; p. (est. 1968) 56,000.

Droitwich, t., Hereford and Worcs., **Eng.**; brine baths, salt wks., wireless-transmission sta.; lt. inds.; expanded t.; p. (1971) 12,766.

Drôme, dep., S.E. **France**; traversed by Alps and watered by Rs. Rhône, Drôme, and Isère; cap. Valence; agr., forestry, sericulture, textile ind.; a. 6,560 km²; p. (1968) 342,891.

Dromore, mkt. t., Banbridge, **N. Ireland**; on Lagan R.; linen; p. (1966) 2,081.

Dronfield, t., Derbys, **Eng.**; between Chesterfield and Sheffield; edged tools, engin. and agr. implements; p. (1971) 17,826.

Droylsden, t., Gtr. Manchester, **Eng.**; sub. of Manchester; chemicals; textiles; p. (1971) 24,134.

Drumochter Pass, Grampian Mtns., **Scot.**; carries main Perth to Inverness rly. from Glen Garry into valley of R. Spey; highest alt. reached by any main rly. in Gt. Britain, 453 m.

Dschang, t., **Cameroon**; quinine processing; bauxite mng.

Dubai (Dubayy), emirate, one of **United Arab Emirates, Arabian Gulf**; recently developed as free pt. (modelled on Singapore), major comm. ctr. of a.; offshore oil with vast underwater storage tanks; international airpt.; deepwater pt. (Port Rashid) under construction; p. (est. 1970) 70,000.

Dubbo, t., N.S.W., **Australia**; on Macquarie R., timber, wool, flour, meat wks.; p. (1966) 15,568.

Dublin. co., **R.o.I.**; co. t. Dublin; a. (inc. c. of Dublin) 922 km²; p. (1966) 795,047.

Dublin (Irish *Baile Atha Cliath*), C.B., cap. of **R.o.I.**; co. t. Co. Dublin; at mouth of R. Liffey; ctr. of govt., commerce, ind., and culture; cath., univ., Abbey Theatre; brewing, distilling, food processing; Swift was buried here; p. (1966) 568,271 (c.), 650,153 (met. a.).

Dubrovnik (Ital. Ragusa), t., **Yugoslavia**; impt. pt. on Adriatic; retains much of its mediaeval architecture; tourism; airport; p. (est. 1965) 26,000.

Dubuque, t., Iowa, **USA**; pt. on Mississippi R.; varied inds. inc. meat-packing; p. (1970) 62,309.

Dudinka, Arctic spt. on R. Yenisey, **RSFSR**; nickel.

Dudley, t., West Midlands, **Eng.**; cas.; engin.; cables, chains; p. (1971) 185,535

Duisburg, c., N. Rhine–Westphalia, **W. Germany**; R. pt. on E. bank of Rhine at confluence with R. Ruhr. 16 km N. of Düsseldorf; iron and steel inds., machin., textiles, chemicals, pt. inds., route and R. tr. ctr.; p. (est. 1969) 460,500.

Dukeries, dist., Sherwood Forest, Notts., **Eng.**; so called from ducal mansions in dist.; tourism.

Dukinfield, t., Gtr. Manchester, **Eng.**; 10 km S.E. of Manchester; textiles, engin., rope and twine; p. (1971) 17,294.

Dukla Pass, anc. and easy route across Carpathians, linking **Poland, Hungary** and **Slovakia**, 497 m a.s.l.

Duluth, pt., Minn., **USA**; at W. end of L. Superior; gr. tr. in grain, timber and iron ore; natural gas pipeline into the Mesabi Iron Range; p. (1970) 99,761 (c.), 261,963 (met. a.).

Dulwich, residtl. sub. in bor. of Southwark, Greater London, **Eng.**; village character with lge. park and public school.

Dumbarton, royal burgh, l. gov. dist., Strathclyde Reg., **Scot.**; on N. bank of R. Clyde, 19 km below Glasgow; shipbldg., valve and tube-mkg., iron and brassware; p. (1971) 25,640.

Dum-Dum, t., W. Bengal, **India**; ammunition; impt. airpt.; p. (est. 1970) 195,693.

Dumfries, royal burgh, Nithsdale, **Scot.**; on R. Nith, 16 km from Solway F.; p. (1971) 29,382.

Dumfries and Galloway Region, l. gov. reg., **Scot.**; occupies W. half of Southern Uplands; drained by S. flowing rivers to Solway F.; sparse rural p.; a. 6,369 km²; p. (1971) 143,295.

Dumfriesshire, former co., **Scot.**; now part of Dumfries and Galloway Reg.

Dunaujváros, t., **Hungary**; new t. built from v. of Dunapentele; iron and steel wks.; paper inds., engin.; p. (1966) 43,400.

Dunbar, royal burgh, E. Lothian, **Scot.**; sm. fishing pt.; Cromwell's victory 1650; p. (1971) 4,611.

Dunbartonshire, former co., **Scot.**; now part of Strathclyde Reg.

Dunblane, mkt. burgh, Stirling, **Scot.**; on Allan Water, 8 km from Stirling; Gothic cath. now used as par. church; p. (1971) 4,497.

Dundalk, U.D., cap. of Co. Louth, **R.o.I.**; harbour, rly. ctr.; engin., footwear, tobacco, brewing; p. (1966) 19,834.

Dundee, c., spt., royal burgh, l. gov. dist., Tayside Reg., **Scot.**; on F. of Tay, 80 km N. Edinburgh; jute mnf., shipbldg., engin., computers, refrigerators, clocks, watches, preserves, linoleum; univ.; p. (1971) 182,204.

Dunedin, c., Otago, S.I., **N.Z.**; univ.; wool and dairy produce; named after the old name of Edinburgh; p. (1971) 82,289 (c.); (est. 1970) 110,100 (met. a.).

Dunfermline, royal burgh, l. gov. dist., Fife Reg., **Scot.**; 22 km E. of Alloa; linen, rubber gds., synthetic fibre; birthplace of Charles I and Andrew Carnegie; p. (1971) 49,897.

Dungannon, mkt. t., l. gov. dist., **N. Ireland**; linen, bricks; p. (1966) 7,335.

Dungarvan, U.D., Co. Waterford, **R.o.I.**; spt., mkt. t.; leather processing; p. (1966) 5,376.

Dungeness, headland of shingle, Kent, **Eng.**; 16 km S.E. of Rye; civil nuclear power stas.; linked by power cable to France 1961; gravel wking., fishing.

Dunkeld, t., Perth and Kinross, **Scot.**; on R. Tay at entrance to Strathmore; cath.; tourist resort.

Dunkirk, spt., Nord dep., **France**; strong fort; gd. harbour and tr.; fisheries, shipbldg., oil refining; steel mill; scene of evacuation of B.E.F. 1940; p. (1968) 28,082 (t.), 143,425 (met. a.).

Dun Laoghaire (Kingstown), C.B., Dublin, **R o.I.**; spt., mail packet sta., fishing; ferry to Eng.; p. (1966) 55,885.

Dunmanway, t., Cork, **R.o.I.**; on R. Brandon; tweeds, blankets.

Dunmow, Great, mkt. t., Essex, **Eng.**; on R. Chelmer; 16 km N.W. of Chelmsford; p. (1971) 23,600 (dist.).

Dunmow, Little, v., 3 km E. of Great Dunmow; Essex, **Eng.**; historic Dunmow Flitch (side of bacon).

Dunoon, burgh, Argyll and Bute, **Scot.**; on N. side of F. of Clyde, anc. cas.; holiday resort; p. (1971) 9,718.

Duns, burgh, Berwick, **Scot.**; agr. and allied inds.; mkt. t.; cas.; p. (1971) 1,768.

Dunsinane, hill, Sidlaws, **Scot.**; nr. Perth; alt. 309 m; referred to by Shakespeare in *Macbeth*.

Dunstable, t., Beds., **Eng.**; on N. edge of Chiltern Hills, 6 km W. of Luton; motor vehicles, engin., cement, rubber, and plastic gds.; p. (1971) 31,790.

Duque de Caxias, t., **Brazil**; oil refining; pipeline to Volta Redonda; p. (1970) 256,582.

Durance, R., S.E. **France**; trib. of Rhône: rapid current, 347 km long; provides irrigation and hydroelec. power.

Durango, c., cap. of D. st., **Mexico**; cath.; silver, gold, copper, iron-ore; p. (1970) 150,541.

Durango, st., N.W. **Mexico**; mng., agr., cotton, wheat; a. 109,484 km²; p. (1969) 959,000.

Durant, t., S. Okla., **USA**; cotton gins and compresses, cottonseed oil; p. (1970) 11,118.

Durban, c., **S. Africa**; on Durban Bay; ch. comm. c. of Natal; exp. coal, manganese, wool, hides; oil and sugar refining, chemicals, textiles, engin.; oil pipeline to Johannesburg; univ.; main pt. and seaside resort; p. (1970) 721,265 (met. a.).

Düren, t., N. Rhine-Westphalia, **W. Germany**; on R. Rur 37 km S.W. of Cologne; rly. ctr.; iron and steel wks., vehicles; p. (est. 1969) 54,745.

Durgapur, t., W. Bengal, **India**; site of barrage on Damodar R.; p. (1971) 206,638.

Durham, c., co. t., Durham, N.E. **Eng.**; sited within a meander of R. Wear; cath., cas., univ.; carpets, organ mftg., confectionery; p. (1971) 24,744.

Durham, non-met. co., N.E. **Eng.**; between Rs. Tyne and Tees; stretches from attractive Pennine moorland in W. to coalfield and industl. a. with many sm. ts. in E.; borders the N. Sea; a. 2,437 km²; p. (1971) 608,000.

Durham, t., N.C., **USA**; tobacco factories, textiles; univ.; p. (1970) 93,935 (t.), 188,786 (met. a.).

Durrës (Durazzo), ch. spt., **Albania**; on Adriatic; pt. for Tirana; tobacco ind., plastics; tourism; p. (1967) 53,000.

Dursley, t., Gloucs., **Eng.**; 21 km S.W. of Gloucester; engin., agr. machin.; 18th cent. mkt. house; p. (1971) 21,149 (dist.).

Dushanbe, c., cap. of Tadzhik SSR, **USSR**; univ., industl. and agr. ctr.; rly. junc.; engin., textiles, meat-packing, cement; earlier called Stalinabad; p. (1970) 374,000.

Düsseldorf, c., cap. of N. Rhine-Westphalia, **W. Germany**; on R. Rhine, 32 km N. of Cologne; admin. and cultural ctr., art and medical academies; iron, steel, machin., soap, cars, paper, chemical inds.; impt. trans-shipment pt.; p. (est. 1969) 683,000.

Dust Bowl, region, **USA**; name applied to great plains on E. flank of Rocky Mtns.; subject to severe soil erosion by wind, particularly in drought years (1933, 1936) due to destruction of natural vegetation by over-grazing or by excessive ploughing.

Dutch Guiana. *See* **Surinam.**

Dutch Harbour, t., Unalaska I., Aleutian gr., N. Pac. Oc.; strategic American naval base.

Dvina or Northern Dvina, R., **RSFSR**; flows to White Sea at Arkhangelsk, formed by the junction of Rs. Sukhona and Vychegda at Kotlas; connected by canal with Neva and Volga; used for timber transport; 744 km long.

Dvina or Western Dvina, R., Latvian SSR, RSFSR, **USSR**; rises in Valdai Hills nr. sources of Volga and Dnieper, flows through Latvia to G. of Riga; connected by canal to Berezina and Dnieper; *c.* 1,016 km long.

Dyfed, co., S.W. **Wales**; inc. former cos. of Cardiganshire, Carmarthenshire and Pembroke; upland a. crossed by valleys of Teifi and Towy Rs.; stock rearing and fattening; tourism impt. around cst.; industl. in S.E.; a. 5,765 km²; p. (1971) 314,452.

Dzaudzhikau. *See* **Ordzhonikidze.**

Dzerzhinsk, c., **RSFSR**; R. pt. on Oka; chemicals (fertilisers, explosives); p. (1970) 221,000 (c.), 273,000 (met. a.).

Dzhalil, t., **RSFSR**; new t. 48 km N.E. of Almetyevsk to serve new oilfield there.

Dzhambul, c., Kazakh SSR, **USSR**; on Talas R. and on Turk-Sib rly.; chemicals, food-processing; p. (1970) 188,000.

Dzhezkazgan, t., Kazakh SSR, **USSR**; 560 km W. of L. Balkhash; copper-mines; manganese ore nearby; p. (est. 1967) 58,000.

Dzierzoniow (Reichenbach), t., Wroclaw, S.W. **Poland**; mnf. ctr.; textiles, machin., elec. equipment; formerly in Germany; p. (1970) 32,900.

Dzungaria, inland basin, Sinkiang prov., N.W. **China**; lies between Tien-Shan highlands of Soviet-Chinese frontier and Altai mtns.; former historic kingdom of Zungaria.

E

Ealing, outer bor., Greater London, **Eng.**; comprising former bors. of Acton, Ealing, and Southall; p. (1971) 299,450.

Earl's Court, residtl. a., London, **Eng.**; Bor. of Kensington and Chelsea, contains E.C. exhibition hall.
Earn R., Perth, and Kinross, **Scot.**; issues from Loch Earn (10 km long) and flows into Tay R.; 74 km long.
Easington, Durham, **Eng.**; colly. v.; now part of Peterlee new t.; p. (1971) 85,410 (dist.).
Easington, v., Humberside **Eng.**; nr. Hull; natural gas terminal.
East Anglia, comprises Norfolk and Suffolk, **Eng.**; former Anglo-Saxon kingdom; one of Britain's most productive agr. regions.
East Anglian Heights, hills, extend S.W. to N.E. across N.E. Hertfordshire, N. Essex, and S.W. Suffolk, **Eng.**; chalk overlain by glacial clays and sands; smooth, rolling surface; region of lge. farms and lge. fields, mixed farms mainly grain; rarely exceed 180 m.
East Bergholt, v., Suffolk, **Eng.**; birthplace of Constable.
Eastbourne, t., East Sussex **Eng.**; on S. cst. to E. of Beachy Head; seaside resort; p. (1971) 70,495.
East Cape, extreme N.E. point of Asia; on Chukchi peninsula, **RSFSR**; Russian name Cape Dezhneva.
East Cape, extreme E. point of **N.Z.**, named by Cook on his first voyage in 1769.
East Chicago, t., Ind., **USA**; L. Michigan; iron and steel wks., oil refining; p. (1970) 46,982.
East Cleveland, t., Ohio, **USA**; residtl.; p. (1970) 34,600.
East Dereham, t., Norfolk, **Eng.**; 22 km W. of Norwich; agr. implements; p. (1971) 9,391.
Easter Island, S. Pac. Oc., 3,760 km W. of Chile; various theories to explain origin of gigantic statues; p. *c.* 850.
Eastern Province, **Zambia**; groundnuts, maize, tobacco; prov. ctr. Fort Jameson; a. 57,887 km²; p. (1964) 507,000.
East Grinstead, t. West Sussex, **Eng.**; in ctr. of Weald, 14 km W. of Tunbridge Wells; agr. mkt.; famous hospital for plastic surgery; p. (1971) 18,569.
East Ham. *See* **Newham**.
East Hartford, t., Conn., **USA**; industl.; p. (1970) 57,583.
East Indies, name commonly applied to Is. between S.E. Asia and N. Australia, variously known as Malay archipelago, Malaysia, Indonesia.
East Kilbride, t., l. gov. dist., Strathclyde Reg., **Scot.**; 11 km S.S.E. of Glasgow; new t. 1947; lge. agr. machin., aero engines, engin., elec. gds. seawater distillation plant; knitwear, clothing; p. (est. 1974) 71,500.
East Lansing, t., Mich., **USA**; residtl.; univ.; p. (1970) 47,540.
Eastleigh, t., Hants., **Eng.**; rly. engin., many new inds.; p. (1971) 45,320
East London, spt. C. Prov., **S. Africa**; at mouth of Buffalo R.; holiday resort; trading ctr.; inds. inc. car assembly, textiles, engin.; titanium deposits nearby; p. (1970) 123,294 (met. a.).
East Lothian (Haddington), former co., l. gov. dist., **Scot.**; part of Lothian Reg.
East Main R., Quebec, **Canada**; flows into James Bay; 432 km long.
Easton, t., Penns., **USA**; on Delaware R.; rly. ctr., coal, steel, machin., furniture; p. (1970) 30,256.
East Orange, t., N.J., **USA**; residtl. sub. of New York; p. (1970) 75,471.
East Pakistan. *See* **Bangladesh**.
East Point, t., Ga., **USA**; textiles, fertilisers; p. (1970) 39,315.
East Providence, t., Rhode I., **USA**; textiles, machin.; p. (1970) 48,207.
East Retford, t., Notts., **Eng.**; on R. Idle, 10 km E. of Worksop; rubber, wire ropes, engin.; p. (1971) 18,402.
East Riding, Yorkshire. *See* **Yorkshire**.
East River, tidal strait about 26 km long and from 180–1,200 m wide; separates the bors. of Manhattan and Bronx from the bors. of Queens and Brooklyn, N.Y., **USA**.
East St. Louis, t., R. pt., Ill., **USA**; on Mississippi R.; lge stockyards, meat-packing, aluminium, chemicals; p. (1970) 69,996.
East Sussex, non-met. co., S.E. **Eng.**; mainly rural, urban growth on cst. where resorts, retirement and dormitory ts. for London, inc. Brighton, Hastings and Eastbourne; crossed by S. Downs in S. terminating at Beachy Head, Ashdown Forest in N.; a. 1,795 km²; p. (1971) 650,000.
East Timor, prov., **Indonesia**; Port. terr. until 1975; mtnous; underdeveloped; cap. Dili; a. 14,693 km²; p. (est. 1968) 559,563.
Eastwood, t., Notts., **Eng.**; birthplace of D. H. Lawrence; coal; p. (1971) 10,864.
Eau Claire, t., Wis., **USA**; on Chippewa R.; agr. mkt.; univ. food processing, varied mnfs.; p. (1970) 44,619.
Ebal, Mt., **Israel**; opposite Gerizim; alt. 911 m.
Ebbw Vale, t., Gwent, **Wales**; 27 km N.W. of Newport; coal, iron, tinplate, bricks, pipes, precast concrete; some steel wks. to close; p. (1971) 26,049.
Eberswalde, t., Frankfurt, **E. Germany**; N.E. of Berlin; iron, wood, and cardboard wks., chemicals; p. (est. 1970) 46,090.
Ebro, ch. R. of N.E. **Spain**; flows to Mediterranean from Cantabrian Mtns.; feeds hydroelectric plants, irrigation, esp. around Zaragoza; 928 km long.
Eccles, Gtr. Manchester, **Eng.**; 6 km W. of Manchester; chemicals, oil refining, engin.; p. (1971) 38,413.
Echo L., Tasmania, **Australia**; used to store water for hydroelectric power.
Echuca, t., Victoria, **Australia**; on R. Murray; rly. ctr.; irrigation wks.; dairy prods., timber; p. (1972) 7,510.
Écija, t., Seville, **Spain**; olive oil, wine, pottery; the Roman Astigi; p. (1970) 36,506.
Eckernförde, spt., Schleswig-Holstein, **W. Germany**; on Baltic, N. W. of Kiel; p. (est. 1969) 21,925.
Ecrins, mtn. peak, S.E. **France**; hgst. point of massif du Pelvoux and Dauphiné Alps; alt. 4,106 m.
Ecuador, rep., **S. America**; on equatorial Pac. cst., bounded by Colombia to N. and Peru to W. and S.; inc. Galapagos Is. in Pac. Oc.; lowland to E. and W. of central Andes; climate temperate in Andes and hot and humid in lowlands; comm. economy mainly agr. with impt. exp. of bananas; petroleum increasingly impt.; pipeline across Andes to pt. of Esmeraldas; communications difficult but vital for economic development; major pts. Guayaquil and Manta; official language Spanish; cap. Quito; a. inc. Galápagos Is. 454,752 km²; p. (est. 1969) 5,973,300.
Edam, t., N. Holland, **Neth.**; on cst. IJsselmeer; cheese, tool mftg.; p. (1967) 16,558.
Eday, I., Orkney Is., **Scot.**; the Ocelli of Ptolemy. p. (1971) 179.
Eddystone, rock with lighthouse, Eng. Channel; S.W. of Plymouth.
Ede, t., Gelderland, **Neth.**; livestock; pianos; p. (1968) 68,772.
Edea, t., pt., **Cameroon**; aluminium smelting based on nearby hydroelectric power plant.
Eden, Vale of, fertile belt in Cumbria, **Eng.**; between barren hills of Pennines and L. Dist.; occupied by R. Eden; mkt. ts. Appleby and Penrith.
Eder R., **W. Germany**; joins Fulda R. S. of Kassel; Eder dam lgst. in Germany.
Edessa (Edhessa), t., N.E. **Greece**; agr. tr. ctr.; the anc. Ægae, burial place of Macedonian kings; p. (1971) 16,521.
Edgehill, ridge, 24 km S. of Warwick, **Eng.**; scene of first battle of civil war, 1642.
Edgewater, t., N.J., **USA**; sub., connected by ferry with New York; sugar refining; p. (1970) 4,987
Edgware, N. sub. of London, **Eng.**; inc. in outer London bor. of Barnet.
Edinburgh, c., cap. of Scot., l. gov. dist., Lothian Reg.; royal burgh on F. of Forth; univ., cas.; palace (Holyrood); printing, publishing, brewing, electronics equipment, rubber gds.; Edinburgh Festival in August; Leith, with docks is joined to E.; p. (1971) 453,584.
Edirne, t., **Turkey**; in Thrace, on R. Maritsa; comm. ctr. with tr. in wine, tobacco, silk, perfume; the anc. Adrianople, named after the emperor Hadrian, later cap. of Ottoman sultans 1366–1453; p. (1965) 46,264.
Edmonton, c., cap. of Alberta, **Canada**; fast-growing c. (119 km²) on both sides of N. Saskatchewan R.; high-level bridge links

Strathcona; major military ctr.; univ.; international air ctr.; oilfields and farming; oil and chemical inds.; p. (1971) 490,811 (met. a.).

Edremit, t., Balikesir, N.W. **Turkey**; cereals, opium; silverwk.; p. (1965) 25,003.

Edward, L. *See* **Idi Amin Dada.**

Eger, t., N.E. **Hungary**; mkt. t. in wine producing region; mediaeval fortress t.; p. (1968) 44,000.

Egersund pt., S. cst. **Norway**; fishing; mentioned in Norwegian sagas; p. (est. 1970) 10,197.

Egham, t., Surrey, **Eng.**; on R. Thames, nr. Staines; contains field of Runnymede; residtl.; p. (1971) 30,510.

Egmont, mtn., N.I., **N.Z.**; extinct volcano; alt. 2,501 m.

Egremont, mkt. t., Cumbria, **Eng.**; 16 km S. of Whitehaven; limestone; former iron ore mng.

Egypt, Arab Republic of, indep. st., N.E. corner Africa; member of Federation of Arab Reps.; 96 per cent a. is desert except Nile valley and delta where 95 per cent of p. live; agr. depends on annual rise of Nile waters and irrigation; cereals, sugar-cane, vegetables, fruit; cotton main cash crop; phosphates; oilfield in Israeli-occupied Sinai and recent finds offshore in G. of Suez and in Western Desert; cap. Cairo; ch. spts. Alexandria, Port Said, Suez; Aswan High Dam has produced problems: (1) silting up of reservoir (L. Nasser) behind dam; (2) reduction in fertilising silt deposits in lower Nile valley; (3) erosion of Nile delta itself; (4) reduction of fish p. in E. Med.; a. 999,740 km²; p. (1976) 38,000,000 (75 per cent illiterate).

Eider, R., **W. Germany**; separates Holstein from Schleswig; flows into N. Sea; 125 m. long.

Eifel, plateau of volcanic rocks, **W. Germany**; lies N. of R. Moselle, forming W. edge of Rhine gorge between Koblenz and Bonn; formerly cultivated, now largely woodland and moorland; farming in valleys; rises to just over 600 m.

Eiger, mtn., one of the hgst. peaks of the Bernese Oberland, **Switzerland**; famous for steep N. wall; alt. 3,978 m.

Eigg, I., Inner Hebrides, **Scot.**; 24 km S.W. of Mallaig; basaltic rocks on cst.; rises to 393 m.

Eilat, new spt., Negev, **Israel**; on G. of Aqaba; copper at Timna; oil pipeline from Ashdod (1970).

Eildon Hills, Roxburgh, **Scot.**; S. of Melrose; hgst. point 422 m.

Eindhoven, c., N. Brabant, **Neth.**; electronic equipment, motor vehicles, tobacco and textile inds.; technical univ.; p. (est. 1969) 187,930, 331,397 (met. a.).

Eire. *See* **Ireland, Republic of.**

Eisenach, t., Erfurt, **E. Germany**; on R. Hörsel, at foot of Thuringian forest; ctr. of Werra potash field; cars, machin., textiles; birthplace of J. S. Bach; p. (est. 1969) 50,777.

Eisenerz Alps, mtn. range, **Austria**; most N. range of Alps, overlooking Danube valley between Linz and Vienna; impt. iron-ore deposits; alt. from 1,800–2,700 m.

Eisenhüttenstadt, t., Frankfurt, **E. Germany**; iron smelting; terminus of Oder-Spree canal; p. (est. 1970) 45,194.

Eisleben, t., Halle, **E. Germany**; machin., copper- and silver-mng. ctr.; birthplace of Luther; p. (est. 1970) 30,386.

Ekibastuz, t., Kazakh SSR, **USSR**; 120 km S.W. of Pavlodar; ctr. of rapidly developing mng. a. coal, gold, metals; coal-fed generating plant projected to supply power to European Russia; p. (est. 1967) 40,000.

El Aaiun, pt., **Western Sahara**; main pt. for exp. of phosphates.

El Alamein, v., **Egypt**; in Libyan Desert 96 km S.W. of Alexandria, scene of Allied victory, second world war; oilfield nearby; terminal nr. Sidi Abd el-Rahman.

Elan, R. Powys, **Wales**; rises on S.E. sides of Plynlimon, flows into R. Wye; lower valley contains series of 4 lge reservoirs, capacity 45,460 million litres; ch. source of water for Birmingham.

Elâzig, t., **E. Turkey**; dam and hydroelec. project at Keban, 48 km to N.W. at confluence of E. and W. branches of Euphrates; p. (1965) 78,899.

Elba, I., off Tuscan cst., **Italy**; iron ore, wine, marble, salt; ch. t. Porto Ferrajo; Napoleon's first exile here; a. 363 km²; p. (1960) 26,000.

Elbe (Labe), R., in **ČSSR** and **Germany**; rises in Riesengebirge and flows into N. Sea at Cuxhaven; navigable for 840 km of total l. of 1,160 km; connected with Rhine and Weser Rs. by Mittelland canal; forms part of border between E. and W. Germany.

Elbert, mtn., Col., **USA**; hgst. peak of Rocky Mtns. in USA, 4,401 m.

Elblag or **Elbing**, spt., Gdansk, **N. Poland**; shipbldg., machin., vehicles; p. (1970) 89,800.

Elbruz Mt., Caucasus, Georgian SSR, **USSR**; hgst. in Europe (5,636 m), over-topping Mont Blanc by 822 m; twin volcanic peaks.

Elburz, mtn. range, **N. Iran**; bordering on Caspian Sea; hgst. peak, Demavend, 5,642 m.

Elche, t., Alicante, **Spain**; palm groves; oil, soap, footwear; p. (est. 1967) 101,028.

El Dar-el-Beida (Casablanca), c., **Morocco**; pt. on Atl. Oc.; artificial harbour; fish canning, textiles; exp. phosphate; p. (1971) 1,371,330 (c.), 1,561,280 (met. a.).

Eldorado, radium mine, N.W. Terr., **Canada**; on E. shore of Gr. Bear Lake nr. Arctic Circle; produces 40 per cent of world's radium, sent to Pt. Hope, Ontario, for refining.

El Dzejair. *See* **Algiers.**

Electrona, Tasmania, **Australia**; carbide wks. based on local limestone and hydroelec. power.

Elektrenai, t., Lithuanian SSR, **USSR**; new township nr. Vievis, at site of thermal power sta.

Elektrostal, t., **RSFSR**; 56 km E. of Moscow; steel. engin.; p. (1970) 123,000.

Elephanta I., Bombay Harbour, **India**; Brahmanic caves with monolithic carvings.

Elephant Butte Dam, N.M., **USA**; on Rio Grande; built to control flood water; lake, a. 155 km² supplies irrigation water to 2,020 km² in N.M. and Texas, water also supplied to Mexico.

El Ferrol del Caudillo, spt., **Spain**; on N.W. cst.; fortfd., fishing; p. (1967) 84,866.

Elgin, royal burgh, Moray, **Scot.**; pt. Lossiemouth; woollens, whisky; ruins anc. cath.; p. (1971) 16,407.

Elgin, t., Ill., **USA**; watches, electrical equipment; p. (1970) 55,691.

Elgon Mt., extinct volcano, bdy. of **Kenya** and **Uganda**; 4,300 m; cave dwellings on slopes.

El Hasa, dist., **Saudi Arabia**; on Persian Gulf, ch. t. Hofuf.

Elie and Earlsferry, burgh, North East Fife, **Scot.**; summer resort; p. (1971) 895.

Elisabethville. *See* **Lubumbashi.**

Elizabeth, t., S. **Australia**; planned t. built in 1954; residtl.; chemical wks.; p. (1971) 33,389.

Elizabeth, c., N.J., **USA**; univ.; sewing machines, iron, oil refining, automobiles, aircraft components; now inc. in Newark; p. (1970) 112,654.

Elk I., Nat. Park, **Canada**; animal reserve, tourism.

El Khârga, oasis, Libyan desert, **Egypt**, 136 km S.W. of Asyût; site of New Valley Project for irrigation.

Elkhart, t., Ind., **USA**; E. of Chicago; paper, machin.; elec. equipment, musical instruments; p. (1970) 43,152.

Elk Mtns., W. Col., **USA**; highest point Castle Peak, 4,305 m.

Elland, t., West Yorks., **Eng.**; on R. Calder, 5 km S.E. of Halifax; textiles; p. (1971) 17,817.

Ellesmere, agr. dist., S.I., **N.Z.**; on Canterbury Plain nr. Christchurch.

Ellesmere, mkt. t., N. Salop, **Eng.**; nearby lake; tourism.

Ellesmere I., extreme N. of Arctic **Canada**; barren, uninhabited; a. 106,200 km².

Ellesmere Port, t., N.W. Cheshire, **Eng.**; on Manchester Ship Canal and 14 km S.S.E. of Liverpool; metal mftg., paper, engin., oil refineries; cars; expanded t.; p. (1971) 61,556.

Elliot Lake, t., N. Ont., **Canada**; ctr. of uranium mines.

Ellice Is. *See* **Tuvalu I.**

Ellis I., N.Y. harbour, **USA**; served as ch. immigration ctr., 1892–1943.

Ellon, burgh, Gordon, **Scot.**; on R. Ythan; p. (1971) 8,505.

Elmira, t., N.Y., **USA**; rly. gds., farm implements; burial place of Mark Twain; p. (1970) 39,945.

El Misti, mtn., **S. Peru**; dormant volcano with snow cap; alt. 5,846 m.

Elmshorn, t., **W. Germany**; N.W. of Hamburg; shipbldg.; p. (est. 1969) 40,896.
El Paso, c., Texas, **USA**; on E. bank Rio Grande opposite Ciudad Juárez (Mexico); natural gas distribution, oil refining, metallurgy; tourism; p. (1968) 276,687 (c.), 351,400 (met. a.).
El Salvador. *See* **Salvador**.
El Segundo, t., Cal., **USA**; lge oil refinery; assembly of aircraft components.
El Sharana, t., N.T., **Australia**; mng. base for uranium; uranium processing.
Elsinore (**Helsingör**), t., spt., **Denmark**; shipbldg.; setting of Shakespeare's *Hamlet*; p. (1970) 3,530.
Elstow, v., Beds., **Eng.**; birthplace of Bunyan.
Elstree, t., Herts., **Eng.**; 6 km W. of Barnet; residtl.; films, lt. engin., silk hosiery; p. (1971) 33,516 (dist.).
El Teniente, Andean t., central **Chile**; copper mng. and smelting; p. 11,761.
Eltham, residtl. sub. in London Bor. of Greenwich, **Eng.**
Eluru, t., Andhra Pradesh, **India**; cotton, carpets, hosiery, oil; p. (1971) 127,023.
Elvas, mkt. t., **Portugal**; on Guadiana R.; plums, olives, jams; cath.; once strongly fortfd.; p. (1970) 24,510.
Ely, t., Cambridge, **Eng.**; on S. fringe of Fens; mkt., cath.; agr. ctr.; p. (1971) 9,969.
Ely, I. of. *See* **Cambridgeshire**.
Elyria, t., Ohio, **USA**; mftg.; p. (1970) 53,427.
Emba, R., Kazakh SSR, **USSR**; rises in Urals, flows S.W. to Caspian Sea; crosses productive Ural–Emba oilfield; 608 km long.
Emden, t., Lower Saxony, **W. Germany**; impt. N. Sea pt. nr. mouth of R. Ems and on Dortmund–Ems and Ems–Jade canals; exp. coal and iron from Ruhr; shipyards, fisheries; p. (est. 1967) 47,300.
Emene, t., **Nigeria**; nr. Enugu; steel plant; cement.
Emilia-Romagna, region, N. **Italy**; S. of Po R.; divided into 8 provs.; fertile agr. a.; a 22,124 km²; p. (1969) 3,834,468.
Emmen, t., Drenthe, **Neth.**; 48 km S.E. of Groningen; elec. machin., ball bearings, tinplate, iron wks.; p. (1968) 76,599.
Emmental, dist., **Switzerland**; dairy produce, especially cheese.
Empoli, t., Tuscany, **Italy**; on R. Arno; textile mnfs., glass; p. (est. 1968) 42,768.
Ems, R., N. **W. Germany**; rises in Teutoburger Wald, flows N. to N. Sea at Emden; 333 km long.
Emscher, R., **W. Germany**; rises in Sauerland, flows W. through heart of Ruhr coalfield to enter R. Rhine at Hamborn; canalised for most of its course; highly polluted; 88 km long.
Encarnación, pt., cap. of Itapuá dep., S.E. **Paraguay**; on Paraná R.; exp. timber, maté, tobacco, cotton, hides; p. (est. 1970) 47,333.
Enderby Land, Australian terr., S. of C. of Good Hope, **Antarctica**.
Enfield, former M.B., Middlesex, **Eng.**; now outer bor. Greater London; comprising Edmonton, Enfield, and Southgate; p. (1971) 266,788.
Enfield, t., Conn., **USA**; mftg.; p. (1970) 46,189.
Engadine, **Switzerland**; upper valley of Inn R.; health resort; ch. t. St. Moritz; Swiss Nat. Park.
Enggano, I., Sumatra, **Indonesia**; sparse primitive p.; hunting, fishing, shifting cultivation.
Engelberg, t., Unterwalden, **Switzerland**; tourism.
Engels, c., **RSFSR**; on Volga; R. pt., mftg. and food-processing ctr.; engin., petroleum refining, textiles; p. (1970) 130,000 (c.), 151,000 (met. a.).
England, southern and lgst political div. of U.K.; bounded by Wales on W., by Scot. on N. and separated from continent of Europe by English Channel and North Sea; highly industl., circa 80 per cent of p. live in urban areas; major trading nation through main pts. London, Liverpool, Southampton; increasing contrast between prosperous S. and depressed N. and W.; very varied geology and topography produce contrasts in landscape, matched by climatic variability; increasingly attractive as tourist area although urban and agr. pressures on rural countryside cause concern in such a densely populated cty.; excellent road and rail network improved by construction of motorways and rly. electrification between London and Glasgow (Scot.); rich and varied cultural heritage and historic bldgs.; developing welfare st.; cap London; a. 130,368 km²; p. (1971) 45,870,062.
Englewood, t., Col., **USA**; sub. of Denver; glasshouses; p. (1970) 33,695.
Englewood, t., N.J., **USA**; elevators, leather gds.; p. (1970) 24,985.
English Channel (**La Manche**), narrow sea separating England from France; extends from Strait of Dover to Land's End in Cornwall; length 480 km, greatest width 248 km.
Enham-Alamein, Hants., **Eng.**; rehabilitation ctr. for disabled ex-service men; 4 km N. of Andover; lt. inds.
Enid, t., Okla., **USA**; univ.; ironwks., farm implements; wheat mkt.; p. (1970) 44,986.
Enkhuizen, t., R. pt., **Neth.**; on IJsselmeer; p. (1967) 11,231.
Enna (**Castrogiovanni**), t., Sicily, **Italy**; sulphur-mines; famous for its connection with the Proserpine legend; p. (1969) 28,767.
Ennepetal, t., N. Rhine-Westphalia, **W. Germany**; t. created 1949 with merging of Milspe and Voerde; iron, machin.; p. (est. 1969) 36,922.
Ennerdale Water, L., Cumbria, **Eng.**
Ennis, mkt. t., U.D., Clare, **R.o.I.**; p. (1966) 5,831.
Enniscorthy, mkt. t., U.D., Wexford, **R.o.I.**; cath.; p. (1966) 5,762.
Enniskillen, t., Fermanagh, **N. Ireland**; brewing, nylon mftg., meat processing; p. (1966) 7,154.
Enns, R., **Austria**; S. trib of Danube; 179 km.
Enschede, c., Overijssel, **Neth.**; textile ctr.; technical univ.; p. (est. 1969) 138,064 (c.), 228,228 (met. a.).
Ensenada, t., **Mexico**; spt., exp. cotton; fishing and fish processing; p. (1970) 113,320.
Entebbe, t., **Uganda**; on L. Victoria; univ.; cotton ginning; airport; p. (1969) 10,900.
Entre Rios, prov., **Argentina**; between Paraná and Uruguay Rs.; wheat, linseed, livestock; cap. Paraná; a. 76,216 km²; p. (1970) 811,691.
Enugu, cap. of E. prov., **Nigeria**; coal; cloth mill; p. (est. 1971) 167,339.
Epernay, t., on S. bank of Marne, **France**; champagne ctr.; p. (1968) 27,767.
Ephesus, anc. Ionian c., in what is now **Turkey**, S. of Izmir; sacked by Goths A.D. 262; excavations.
Epinal, t., cap. of Vosges dep., **France**; on Moselle R.; textiles, printing, liqueur; p. (1968) 39,991.
Epirus, dist., N.W. **Greece**; a. 9,552 km²; p. (1971) 314,558.
Epping Forest, Essex, **Eng.**; forest a. N.E. of London free to public (opened by Queen Victoria 1882); formerly part of royal hunting forest.
Epsom and Ewell, ts., former M.B., Surrey, **Eng.**; 29 km S.W. of London; residtl., racecourse; p. (1971) 72,054.
Epworth, v., Humberside, **Eng.**; birthplace of John Wesley.
Equatorial Guinea, unitary state, W. **Africa**; former Spanish col.; indep. 1968; comprises 2 provs.; Rio Muni (mainland and Is of Corisco, Elobey Grande, Elobey Chico) and Marcias Nguema (Is. of Marcias Nguema and Pagalu); narrow coastal plain and dissected upland plateau (600 m); economy almost entirely based on agr. and timber; exploration for oil; cap. Malabo on Marcias Nguema I.; a. 45,392 km²; p. (est. 1968) 250,000.
Erbil, t., **Iraq**; comm. ctr.; rly. terminus; p. (1965) 134,000 (met. a.).
Erebus, mtn., active volcano, Victoria Land, **Antarctica**; alt. 4,027 m.
Erfurt, admin. dist., **E. Germany**; a. 7,322 km²; p. (1968) 1,256,034.
Erfurt, c., **E. Germany**; on Gera R.; cath., ctr. of mkt. gardening and seed-growing dist., textiles, machin., foodstuffs, footwear, radios, heavy engin.; p. (est. 1969) 193,997.
Ericht, loch, **Scot.**; in central Grampians; 25 km long; hydroelec. scheme.
Erie, c., N.W. Penns., **USA**; pt. on L. Erie; coal, iron, grain, petroleum; machin., domestic appliances; p. (1970) 125,941 (c.), 257,860 (met. a.).

Erie Canal. *See* **New York State Barge Canal.**
Erie, one of Great Lakes (the shallowest), N. America, separating Canada from USA; 386 km long, 48–91 km wide; polluted waters; petroleum resources.
Erith, former M.B., Kent, **Eng.**; on Thames estuary; plastics, paints, varnishes, timber, concrete; now inc. in London bor. of Bexley.
Eritrea, prov., **Ethiopia**; tobacco, cereals, pearl fishing; demands for autonomy; cap. Asmara, a. 118,503 km²; p. (est. 1970) 1,836,800.
Erivan. *See* **Yerevan.**
Erlangen, t., Bavaria, **W. Germany**; univ.; textiles, elec. and precision engin., gloves; p. (est. 1969) 84,619.
Ermelo, t., **Neth.**; ctr. of agr. dist.; p. (1968) 35,434.
Ernakulam, t., Kerala, **India**; cotton, coffee, hides; p. (est. 1970) 213,811 (c.), 493,460 (met. a.).
Erne R., N. Ireland/ R.o.I.; links Ls. in Cavan and Fermanagh; 115 km long.
Erode, t., S. Tamil Nadu, **India**; on R. Cauvery; p. (1971) 105,111 (t.), 169,613 (met. a.).
Erzgebirge (**Ore Mtns.**), mtn. range along border of ČSSR and Germany, reaching highest peak in Mt. Klinovec (1,240 m) in ČSSR; uranium; tourism.
Erzurum, t., **Turkey**; agr. ctr. on fertile plateau *c.* 1,890 m a.s.l.; formerly of gr. strategic importance; univ.; p. (1965) 105,317 (t.), 174,155 (met. a.).
Esbjerg, spt., **Denmark**; W. cst. of Jutland; export harbour on N. Sea cst.; exp. agr. prod.; fishing; airport; p. (est. 1970) 76,056.
Esch-sur-Alzette, t., **Luxembourg**; mng. ctr.; steel; p. (1968) 27,466.
Eschwege, t., Hesse, **W. Germany**; cas.; machin., textiles, leather, cigars, chemicals; p. (est. 1969) 22,227.
Eschweiler, t., N. Rhine-Westphalia, **W. Germany**; N.W. of Aachen; lignite mng., steel, iron, metallurgy, leather, textiles; p. (est. 1969) 39,756.
Esdraelon, plain, **Israel**; between Carmel and Gilboa Mtns.
Esfahān (**Isfahan,** anc. **Aspadana**), c., central **Iran**; prov. cap.; historic, picturesque c. noted for carpets and metal ware; tourism, airpt.; new steel mill; p. (est. 1971) 546,200.
Esher, t., Surrey, **Eng.**; on R. Mole, residtl.; Sandown Park racecourse; p. (1971) 64,186.
Eshowe, health resort, Natal, **S. Africa**; 64 km from Tugela R.; p. (est. 1967) 4,800.
Esk R., Annandale and Eskdale, **Scot.**; Cumbria, **Eng.**; attractive agr. valley; flows into Solway F. from confluence of Black and White Esk Rs.; 37 km long.
Eskilstuna, t., **Sweden**; on R. of same name; iron, steel, machin., machin. tools; p. (1968) 173,900.
Eskişehir, t., **Turkey**; W. of Ankara, anc. Dorylaeum; rly. ctr.; meerschaum; p. (1965) 173,882 (t.), 243,033 (met. a.).
Esmeraldas, prov., **Ecuador**; cap. E. on R. of same name; cacao, tobacco; a. 14,152 km²; p. (est. 1970) 177,600.
Esmeraldas, pt., **Ecuador**; bananas, timber, tobacco, cacao, rubber; gold mines nearby; p. (1970) 59,000.
Esneh. *See* **Isna.**
Espirito Santo, st., **Brazil**; sugar, cotton, coffee, fruits, lumber, thorium; cap. Vitória; a. 40,883 km²; p. (est. 1968) 1,921,353.
Espiritu Santo, I., New Hebrides; volcanic I., lgst. of gr.; depopulation.
Essaouira (**Mogador**), spt., **Morocco**; cereals, almonds, gum-arabic, crude oil; p. (1960) 26,392.
Essen, c., N. Rhine-Westphalia, **W. Germany**; gr. industl. c., ctr. of Ruhr conurbation; coal, steel (Krupp), electric power, engin.; canal links with Dortmund-Ems and Mittelland canals and with Rhine; minster severely damaged in second world war; p. (est. 1969) 705,700 (c.); (est. 1967) 5,150,000 (met. a.).
Essequibo R.; flows N. from Brazilian border draining half Guyana; lower course navigable, rapids; timber in upper valley; 960 km long.
Essex, non-met. co., **Eng.**; bounded on S. by Thames, on E. by N. Sea; co. t. Chelmsford; on London clay and chalk; agr.; wheat, barley, sugar-beet; mkt. gardens; S.W. of co. forms part of Greater London with mftg. subs.; oil refineries at Shell Haven; civil nuclear power sta. at Bradwell; univ. at Colchester; a. 2,637 km²; p. (1971) 1,354,000.
Esslingen, t., Baden-Württemberg, **W. Germany**; on R. Neckar; mach. and rly. shops; textiles, chemicals, leather gds.; Liebfrauen church (1440); p. (est. 1969) 85,350.
Essonne, dep., **France**; S. of Paris; cap. Ivry; a. 1,810 km²; p. (1968) 674,157.
Esteli, cap. Esteli, **Nicaragua**; on Inter-American Highway; p. (1963) 26,764.
Eston, t., Cleveland, **Eng.**; 5 km E. of Middlesbrough; shipbldg. and repairing.
Estonia (**Estoniya**), constituent rep., **USSR**; borders on Baltic, G. of Finland, G. of Riga; lowland with many Ls.; farming and dairying, fishing; oil deposits; hydroelec. power; mainly Lutheran; univ.; cap. Tallinn; a. 45,610 km²; p. (1970) 1,357,000.
Estoril, wat. pl. and thermal spa, **Portugal**; N. side of Tagus estuary; holiday resort.
Estremadura, maritime prov., **Portugal**; agr., tourism; cap. Lisbon; a. 5,348 km²; p. 1,600,000.
Estremadura, region, S.W. **Spain**; on the border of Portugal; largely plateau, alt. 450–900 m.; heathy moorland; sheep; less arid conditions than in remainder of central Spain allow olives, vines, cereals; irrigation in valleys of Tagus, Guadiana; govt. project to develop a. in progress.
Esztergom, t., **Hungary**; R. pt. on Danube; iron foundries, machine tools; mineral springs; cath.; p. (est 1966) 26,000.
Etang de Berre, lagoon, Bouches-du-Rhône, S.E. **France**; E. of Rhône delta; traversed by Rhône-Marseille canal; salt pans; oil refineries in a.; approx. a. 260 km².
Étaples, t., Pas-de-Calais, **France**; seaside resort; p. (1968) 9,108.
Etawah, t., Uttar Pradesh, **India**; textiles; p. (1961) 69,681.
Ethiopia (**Abyssinia**), indep. st. N.E. **Africa**; temperate climate as a result of high plateau terrain; coffee most impt. comm. crop, but poor communications inhibit economic development; low per capita income and rapid growth of p.; ch. pt. Assab; English widely spoken; univs. at Addis Ababa and Asmara; cap. Addis Ababa; monarchy abolished 1975; a. 1,221,900 km²; p. (est. 1967) 23,667,400.
Ethiopian Highlands, mtns., **Ethiopia**; rise over 4,500 m; source of headwaters of tribs. of R. Nile.
Etna, volcano, N.E. Sicily, **Italy**; most recent eruption 1971; alt. 3,276 m.
Eton, t., Berks., **Eng.**; on N. bank of R. Thames opposite Windsor; public school, founded by Henry VI; p. (1971) 3,954.
Etruria, anc. dist., **Italy**; now forms Tuscany; home of the Etruscans and part of the Roman empire by 400 B.C.
Etruria, t., Staffs., **Eng.**; part of Stoke-on-Trent; seat of Josiah Wedgwood's potteries (1769).
Euboea (**Evvoia**), lgst. of Greek Is. Aegean Sea; mtnous. (Mt. Delphi 1,746 m); vines and olives in lowlands, sheep and goats in highlands; a. 3,864 km²; p. (1971) 165,822.
Euclid, t., Ohio, **USA**; electrical and agr. machin.; p. (1970) 71,552.
Eucumbene Dam and L., N.S.W., **Australia**; major storage of Snowy Mtns. hydroelectric scheme; holds eight times as much water as Sydney harbour.
Eugene, c., Ore., **USA**; univ.; mkt. ctr. for rich agr. and lumbering region; fruit-canning, saw-milling; headquarters of Willamette National Forest; p. (1970) 77 284 (c.), 212,644 (met. a.).
Euphrates, lgst. R. in S.W. Asia; rises in Armenian uplands and joined by the Tigris enters Persian G. as the Shatt-al Arab; anc. ctr. of civilisation; modern irrigation, navigation, high dam opened 1973; 2,848 km long.
Eure, dep., Normandy, **France**; agr., fruit, livestock, textiles; cap. Evreux; a. 6,037 km²; p. (1968) 383,385.
Eure-et-Loire, dep., N. **France**; mainly agr.; cap. Chartres; a. 5.934 km²; p. (1968) 302,207.
Europe, continent; W. peninsula of Eurasian land mass; no well-defined bdy. with Asia but line normally accepted runs along Ural Mtns. to Caspian Sea and Caucasus to Black Sea, Sea of Marmara and Dardanelles; after

Australia, Europe is smallest continent in a., but contains 20 per cent of world's p. and even more of world's economic activity; climate varies from Arctic to Mediterranean and from temperate maritime to severe continental; major physical features inc. Alps, Pyrenees in S., Baltic Shield in N.; major political div. between E. and W. Europe along Iron Curtain; W. Europe also divided into economic grs. EEC and EFTA; major concentration of p. and economic activity within Golden Triangle (q.v.), total a. c. 10,360,000 km^2; p. (est. 1974) 470,000,000 (excl. USSR).

Europort, name of the post-war expansion of the port of Rotterdam, **Neth.**; capable of handling 100,000 tonne oil-tankers; oil refining; European oil supply ctr.; joined to Rotterdam by the New Waterway.

Evanston, t., Ill., **USA**., on L. Michigan, sub. of Chicago; univ.; p. (1970) 79,808.

Evansville, c., Ind., **USA**; on Ohio R.; shipping and comm. ctr. for agr. region; coal mng.; p. (1970) 137,997 (c.), 230,708 (met. a.).

Eveneki National Area, Siberia, **RSFSR**; forest and tundra covered; home of Eveneki people; cap. Tura; a. 740,740 km^2; p. (1970) 13,000.

Everest, Mt. (Chomolungma = Goddess Mother of the Earth), Himlaya, on frontier of **Nepal** and Tibet, **China**, alt. 8,854 m; hgst. mtn. in the world; Hillary and Tenzing first to reach summit in 1953; within Nepal Nat. Park.

Everett, mftg. t., Mass., **USA**; nr. Boston; iron and steel; p. (1970) 42,485.

Everett, t., Wash., **USA**; on Puget Sound; harbour; comm. ctr.; timber; tourism; p. (1970) 53,622.

Everglades, Fla., **USA**; subtropical a., extensive marshes; home of Seminole Indians; lge. scale drainage since 1905; early vegetables.

Evesham, mkt. t., Hereford and Worcs. **Eng.**; on R. Avon, in Vale of Evesham, 24 km S.E. of Worcester; fruit ctr.; tourism; p. (1971) 13,847.

Évora, t., cap. of Upper Alentejo prov. S. **Portugal**; mkt. for agr. prod.; cath.; p. (1970) 47,806.

Évreux, t., cap. of Eure dep., **France**; mkt. ctr.; p. (1968) 45,441.

Evros, prov., **Greece**; borders Bulgaria and Turkey; a. 4,191 km^2; p. (1971) 141,002.

Exe, R., Somerset and Devon, **Eng.**; rises on Exmoor, flows S. via Exeter to English Channel at Exmouth; 86 km long.

Exeter, cath. c., co. t., Devon, **Eng.**; former Roman Isca; E. of Dartmoor on R. Exe; mkt. t.; univ.; aircraft components; airport; p. (1971) 95,598.

Exmoor, Somerset and Devon, **Eng.**; sandstone, moorland, deep wooded valleys; Nat. Park.

Exmouth, t., Devon, **Eng.**; on estuary of R. Exe; holiday resort; p. (1971) 25,815.

Exploits, R., Newfoundland, **Canada**; length 240 km; used for hydroelectric power.

Eye, mkt. t., Suffolk, **Eng.**; 29 km N. of Ipswich; anc. church; p. (1971) 1,659.

Eyemouth, burgh, Berwick, **Scot.**; on E. cst. 14 km N. of Berwick; fishing; p. (1971) 2,530.

Eyre Lake, shallow salt L., S. **Australia**; 12 m below sea-level and practically dry; a. 9,065 km^2.

Eyre Peninsula, S. **Australia**; between Gr. Australian Bight and Spencer G.; iron-ore deposits; a. 51,800 km^2.

F

Fabriano, t., Marches, **Italy**; in Apennines; cath.; paper mills; p. (est. 1968) 27,252.

Faenza, t., Ravenna, **Italy**; at foot of Apennines; majolica, textiles; p. (est. 1968) 54,065.

Fagersta, t., Västmanland, **Sweden**; iron, steel smelting; p. (est. 1970) 17,054.

Failsworth, t., Gtr. Manchester, **Eng.**; N.E. of Manchester; textiles, elec. gds.; p. (1971) 23,233.

Fairbanks, t., Alaska, **USA**; univ.; sawmilling; mng.; p. (1970) 22,640.

Fairfield, t., Conn., **USA**; chemicals, automobile parts; univ.; p. (1970) 56,487.

Fair I., midway between Shetland and Orkney, **Scot.**; bird sanctuary; famous for brightly patterned, hand-knitted articles.

Fairmont, t., W. Va., **USA**; glass, machin., coal by-products; p. (1970) 26,093.

Faiyum (El Faiyûm), t. and region, N. **Egypt**; oasis nr. L. Karun (anc. L. Moeris), fertilised by Nile water and silt; cereals, sugar-cane, fruits, cotton; archaeological finds; p. of t. (est. 1970) 150,900.

Faizabad, t., Uttar Pradesh, **India**; rly. junc.; sugar refining; p. (1971) 102,835.

Falaise, t., Calvados, **France**; birthplace of William the Conqueror; p. (1968) 7,599.

Falaise de l'Ile de France, low S.E.-facing escarpment, 80 km S.E. and E. of Paris, **France**; overlooks Champagne Pouilleuse; ch. vine-growing dist. for champagne-wine ind. of Reims, Epernay.

Falcón, st. **Venezuela**; bordering Caribbean Sea; cap. Coro; p. (est. 1970) 408,051.

Falconara Marittima, t., **Italy**; nr. Ancona; spt.; oil refining, shipbldg.

Falkirk burgh, l. gov. dist., Central Reg., **Scot.**; 16 km S.E. of Stirling; foundries, bricks, chemical, aluminium wks., concrete, timber yards, battles 1298 and 1746; p. (1971) 37,579.

Falkland, burgh, North East Fife, **Scot.**; 5 km S. of Auchtermuchty; mkt.; p. (1971) 896.

Falkland Is., Brit. Crown col., S. Atl., comprises E. and W. Falkland and adjacent Is.; sheep rearing (for wool); cap. Port Stanley on E. Falkland I.; claimed by Argentina; a. 12,173 km^2; p. (1969) 2,098.

Falkland Is. Dependencies, S. Atl.; inc. Is of S. Georgia and S. Sandwich; a. 4,092 km^2; p. (of S. Georgia) 11 males; now form part of Brit. Antarctic Terr.

Fall River, c., Mass., **USA**; on Mt. Hope Bay; pt. of entry; clothing, rubber gds., food prods., paper; p. (1970) 95,679 (c.), 148,430 (met. a.).

Falmouth, t., Cornwall, **Eng.**; on W. side of estuary of R. Fal. 16 km S. of Truro; sheltered harbourage; offshore oil supply base; seaside resort; fisheries, ship repairing, mng., quarrying, lt. engin.; cas.; pt.; p. (1971) 17,883.

False Bay, inlet on E. side of C. of Good Hope peninsula, **S. Africa**.

Falster, I. Baltic, **Denmark**; cap. Nyköbing; p. (1965) 45,906.

Falun, t., Kopparberg, **Sweden**; paper; copper mines now exhausted; p. (est. 1970) 34,550.

Famagusta, t., spt., **Cyprus**; on E. cst.; resort; anc. crusade pt.; p. (est. 1970) 42,500.

Famatina, t., La Rioja prov., **Argentina**; in foothills of Andes, 576 km N.W. of Córdoba; copper-mines.

Fano, t., **Italy**; sm. pt on Adriatic cst., N. of Ancona; seaside resort; p. (est. 1968) 45,879.

Fareham, t., Hants., **Eng.**; at N.W. corner of Portsmouth Harbour; p. (1971) 60,296.

Farewell (Kap Farvel), C., southernmost tip of Greenland.

Farewell, C., most N. point S.I., **N.Z.**

Fargo, t., N.D., **USA**; rly. ctr. and R. pt.; grain, farm machin.; p. (1970) 52,697 (t.), 118,555 (met. a.).

Faringdon, mkt. t., Oxon., **Eng**; on N. edge of Vale of White Horse; Faringdon Folly.

Farnborough, t., Hants., **Eng.**; 5 km N. of Aldershot military camp; Royal Aircraft Establishment; p. (1971) 41,233.

Farne Is. gr. of islets off Northumberland cst., **Eng.**; bird sanctuary; National Trust.

Farnham, t., Surrey, **Eng**; at N. foot of N. Downs, 16 km W. of Guildford; mkt.; p. (1971) 31,175.

Farnworth, t., Gtr. Manchester, **Eng.**; nr. Bolton, textiles, engin., paper; p. (1971) 26,841.

Faro, spt., cap. of Algarve prov., **Portugal**; cork, figs, oranges; p. (1970) 30,269.

Faroe Is., 320 km N.W. of the Shetlands, **Scot.**; cap. Thörshavn (Strömö I.); Danish possession but not member of EEC; impt. fisheries; a. 1,399 km^2; p. (1966) 37,122.

Farrukhabad, t., Uttar Pradesh, **India**; on Ganges R.; gold, lace, brass wk.; p. (1971) 102,768.

Fars, prov., S. **Iran**; agr.; cap. Shirāz; p. (1967) 1,499,472.

Fastnet, lighthouse in Atl. Oc., 7·2 km S.W.C. Clear, Irish cst.

Fatima, v., W. **Portugal**, nr. Leiria; R.C. pilgrimage.

Fatshan (Foshan), c., Kwangtung, **China**; S.W. of Kuangchow; iron and steel, textiles; p. (1953) 123,000.
Faversham, pt., N.E. Kent, **Eng.**; at head of F. creek; mkt.; fruit, hops, bricks, brushes, engin.; p. (1971) 13,807.
Fawley, t., Hants., **Eng.**; on W. shore Southampton Water; lge. oil refinery with pipeline to Staines and Heathrow Airpt; synthetic rubber.
Fayal I., one of the **Azores**; fruit and wine; cap. Horta.
Fayetteville, t., N.C., **USA**; agr. processing; p. (1970) 51,606 (t.), 206,446 (met. a.).
Feather, R., N. Cal., **USA**; R. project for water supply, irrigation, and hydroelectric power.
Featherstone, t., West Yorks., **Eng.**; p. (1971) 15,242.
Fécamp, sm. spt. on cst. of Normandy, **France**; fishing, tourism, 12th cent. abbey; p. (1968) 21,745.
Fedchenko, glacier, lgst in **USSR**; in Pamir-Altai mtns. of central Asia; 80 km long.
Federal German Republic. *See* **Germany, Fed. Rep. of.**
Feira de Santana, t., Bahia, **Brazil**; cattle, tobacco, beans, manioc; p. (1970) 127,105.
Feldberg, highest peak in Black Forest, **W. Germany**; alt. 1,495 m.
Feldkirch, t., Vorarlberg, **Austria**; on Swiss frontier; p. (1961) 17,343.
Felixstowe, pt., Suffolk, **Eng.**; dock development with container facilities; seaside resort; p. (1971) 18,888.
Felling, Tyne and Wear, **Eng.**; Tyneside mftg. dist.; p. (1971) 38,595.
Feltham. *See* **Hounslow.**
Fens, The, low-lying dist. around the Wash, **Eng.**; artificial drainage begun in 17th cent.; impt. agr. dist.; root crops, wheat, fruit, bulbs; a. 3,367 km².
Feodosiya, t., Ukrainian SSR, **USSR**; in Crimea; major Black Sea pt., tobacco, hosiery; exp. wheat; resort and sanatoria; p. (est. 1968) 59,000.
Ferghana, region, Uzbek SSR, **USSR**; deep basin at W. end of Tien Shan Mtns.; drained W. by R. Syr Dar'ya; semi-arid but extensive irrigation system allows intensive cultivation of cotton, citrus fruits, silk, rice; ch. ts., Kokand, Namangan.
Ferghana, c., Uzbek SSR, **USSR**; hydroelectric power, petroleum refining, textiles; deposits of ozocerite nearby; p. (1970) 111,000.
Fermanagh, former co.; l. gov. dist., **N. Ireland**; bisected by R. Erne and lakes; stock raising, dairying; p. of former co. (est. 1971) 49,960.
Fermoy, t., Cork, **R.o.I.**; on R. Blackwater; cath.; woollens; p. (1966) 3,207.
Fernando de Noronha, I., fed. terr., N.E. cst. Brazil; penal settlement and met. sta.; cap. Vila dos Remédios; a. 26 km²; p. (est. 1968) 2,400.
Fernando Po. *See* **Marcias Nguema.**
Ferozepore, t., Punjab st. N.W. **India**; rly. t.; admin. ctr.; p. (1961) 97,932.
Ferrara, c., N. **Italy**; nr. head of Po delta; cath., univ., palaces; mkt. for fertile plain; silk, hemp, wine; oil refinery nearby; petrochemicals; birthplace of Savonarola; p. (1969) 156,207.
Ferro (Hierro), most S. of the Canary Is., a. 275 km²; cap. Valverde; chosen by Ptolemy (A.D. 56) for his prime meridian and used by French scientists in 17th cent.; reckoned as exactly W. 20° of Paris.
Ferryhill, v., Durham, **Eng.**; 8 km S. of Durham, in gap through limestone ridge which separates Wear valley from Tees valley; commands main N. to S. route along lowland E. of Pennines.
Fertile Crescent, an arc of fertile land from the Mediterranean Sea, N. of the Arabian Desert, to Persian G.; home of some very early civilisations and migrations.
Fez (Fès), c., **Morocco**; lies inland 160 km E. of Rabat; one of the sacred cities of Islam; univ. attached to mosque (one of lgst. in Africa); comm. ctr.; p. (1971) 321,460 (c.), 379,790 (met. a.).
Fezzan, prov., S.W. **Libya**; desert plateau with numerous wells and inhabited oases; p. (1964) 78,326.
Ffestiniog (Festiniog), t. Gwynedd, **N. Wales**; at head of Vale of Ffestiniog, 14 km E. of Portmadoc; contains Ffestiniog and Blaenau Ffestiniog; slate quarries; pumped-storage hydroelec. sta. (1963); cement; p. (1971) 5,751.
Fianarantsoa, t., **Malagasy Rep.**; rice mills, meat preserves; p. (est. 1968) 45,790.
Fichtelgebirge, mtn. range, N.E. Bavaria, **W. Germany**; extending into ČSSR, rising to 1,051 m in Schneeberg; forested slopes.
Fiesole, t., Tuscany, **Italy**; on summit of wooded hill overlooking Florence and the Arno; residtl.; 11th cent. cath.; p. (est. 1968) 13,401.
Fife, l. gov. reg., former co., **E. Scot.**; occupies a. between Tay and Forth estuaries; industl. dist. based originally on coalfields; a. 1,305 km²; p. (1971) 327,690.
Fiji, S.W. Pac. Oc., former Brit. col., gained independence in 1970; comprises over 800 Is.; tropical climate; agr. basis of economy, especially sugar and coconut prods.; gold an impt. exp.; forestry and tourism developing; forms ctr. of communications in S.W. Pac. Oc.; international airport at Nadi, ch. pt. and cap. Suva; a. 18,272 km²; cosmopolitan p. (1970) 513,000.
Filey, t., North Yorks., **Eng.**; 8 km S.E. of Scarborough; seaside resort; p. (1971) 5,337.
Filton, Bristol, Avon, **Eng.**; aircraft wks.
Finchley. *See* **Barnet.**
Findhorn, v., Moray, **Scot.**; resort; 12th cent. abbey; fishing.
Findlay, t., Ohio, **USA**; on Blanchard R.; agr. machin., tyres, beet sugar refining; p. (1970) 35,800.
Findochty, sm. burgh, Moray, **Scot.**; p. (1971) 1,203.
Fingal's Cave, Staffa I., Inner Hebrides, **W. Scot.**; basaltic columns.
Finger Lakes, gr. of narrow glacial Ls., N.Y., **USA**; picturesque resorts and state parks.
Finistère (Lat. *finis terrae* = land's end), dep. N.W. **France**, in Brittany; cap. Quimper; fishing, tourism; a. 7,071 km²; p. (1968) 768,929.
Finland, rep., N. **Europe**; part of Scandinavia; low-lying plateau severely eroded by ice to form 60,000 Ls.; economy based on timber (forests cover 72 per cent of a.); world's leading exporter of pulp and paper; increasing importance of metal and engin. inds.; cap. Helsinki; a. 360,318 km²; p. concentrated in S.; p. (1970) 4,707,000.
Finland, G. of, E. arm of Baltic Sea, between Finland and USSR.
Finnart, Dumbarton, **Scot.**; crude oil terminal situated in Loch Long, N.W. Glasgow; pipeline to Grangemouth.
Finnmark, most N. co., **Norway**; inhabited by Lapps; whale fisheries; lge. copper deposits discovered nr. Reppan fjord; a. 48,125 km²; p. (est. 1972) 77,060.
Finsbury. *See* **Islington.**
Finsteraarhorn, highest peak in Bernese Oberland, **Switzerland**; 4,277 m.
Finucane I., pt. W. **Australia**; deepwater pt. to ship iron ore and new t. projected.
Firenze. *See* **Florence.**
Firozabad, t., Uttar Pradesh, **India**; glassware; agr. tr.; p. (1961) 98,611.
Fishguard and Goodwick, spt., Dyfed, **Wales**; on S. of Cardigan Bay; steamer connection to Cork and Rosslare (Ireland); p. (1971) 4,933.
Fitchburg, t., Mass., **USA**; paper, machin., textiles; p. (1970) 43,343.
Fitzroy, R., W. **Australia**; flows into King Sound; dry in winter; irrigation; 560 km long.
Fiume. *See* **Rijeka.**
Flamborough Head, promontory of Yorks. cst. **Eng.**; steep chalk cliffs; lighthouse; anc. Brit. earthwork (Danes' dyke).
Flanders, region between R. Scheldt and cst. crossed by Franco-Belgian frontier; Dunkirk, Lille ctrs. of French F.; Belgian F. (p. (1970) 5,416,583) divided into 2 provs., E. and W.; caps. Bruges and Ghent.
Fleet, t., Hants., **Eng.**; 6 km N.W. of Aldershot; p. (1971) 21,362.
Fleetwood, spt., Lancs., **Eng.**; at mouth of Wyre, Morecambe Bay; deep-sea fish. pt.; fish processing; lge chemical plant nearby; p. (1971) 28,584.
Flensburg, spt., Schleswig-Holstein, **W. Germany**;

on Baltic, close to Danish border; shipbldg., machin., chemicals, rum distilleries, fishing; p. (est. 1969) 95,488.
Flevosted, t., **Neth.**; admin. ctr. of new S.E. Polder.
Flinders I., Australia; lgst I. in the Furneaux gr., Bass Strait; a. 2,077 km²; p. 900.
Flinders Range, chain of mtns., S. **Australia**; extending 400 km N.E. from head of Spencer G., reaching 1,190 m in St. Mary's Peak; named after Matthew Flinders; uranium ore at Mt. Painter.
Flint, t., Clwyd, **Wales**; viscose textile yarn, cas. ruins; p. (1971) 14,660.
Flint, t., Mich., **USA**; motorcars, aircraft engines; p. (1970) 193,571 (t.), 493,402 (met. a.).
Flintshire, former co., N. Wales; now part of Clwyd.
Flodden, v., Northumberland, **Eng.**; on R. Till; battle between James IV of Scot. and the English under the Earl of Surrey, 1513.
Flora, t., **Norway**; new t. 136 km N. of Bergen; p. (1965) 7,700.
Florence (Firenze), c., Tuscany, **Italy**; on R. Arno; univ.; leather-work; famous for art treasures, cath. and churches; ruled by Medici 1421–1737; birthplace of Dante and Machiavelli; severely affected by heavy floods Nov. 1966; plans for new EEC univ.; p. (1966) 459,058.
Florence, t., N.W. Ala., **USA**; on Tennessee R., nr. Wilson dam; textile, steel plants; p. (1970) 34,031.
Flores, I., most northwesterly of Azores gr.; Portuguese; cap. Santa Cruz; French to set up ballistic missiles tracking sta.; a. 142 km; p. (1960) 6,617.
Flores, I., **Indonesia**; mtnous.; volcanic, densely forested; a. 22,973 km²; p. (1961) 803,000.
Flores Sea, between Sulawesi and Flores, **Indonesia**.
Florianópolis, spt., cap. of Santa Catarina st., **Brazil**; comm. ctr., fishing; p. (1970) 115,665.
Florida, st., **USA**; between Atl. Oc. and G. of Mexico; low-lying, swampy, inc. Everglades; sea resorts on Atl. cst.; citrus fruit and subtropical agr.; agr. processing; cap Tallahassee; a. 151,670 km²; p. (1970) 6,671,162.
Florida Keys, archipelago, **USA**; extends in an arc from S.E. cst. Florida W.S.W. to Key West in G. of Mexico; fishing resorts.
Florida Strait, between Florida and Bahama Is.; course of Gulf Stream from G. of Mexico.
Florina. *See* **Phlorina**.
Florissant (St. Ferdinand), t., Mo., **USA**; sub. of St. Louis on Missouri R.; p. (1970) 65,908.
Flushing. *See* **Vlissingen**.
Fly, lgst. R. of **Papua New Guinea**; flows S.E. from Victor Emmanuel Range to G. of Papua; 1,280 km long.
Fochabers, v., Moray, **Scot.**; nr. mouth of Spey; tourist resort; food canning; p. (1971) 4,230.
Focsani, t. **Romania**; at foot of Transylvanian Alps; wine and grain ctr.; p. (est. 1970) 39,629.
Foggia, cath. c., S. **Italy**; rly. ctr. and mkt. ctr. for plain of Apulia; site of cas. of Frederick II; p. (1969) 139,981.
Foix, t., cap. of Ariège dep., S. **France**; historic t.; p. (1968) 9,331.
Foligno, t., central **Italy**; in Apennines, on Topino R.; cath., textiles, paper; p. (est. 1968) 50,237.
Folkestone, t., Kent **Eng.**; seaside resort; pt. for Folkestone–Boulogne route to France 46 km; p. (1971) 43,760.
Fond du Lac, t., Winnebago L., Wis., **USA**; cath.; machine tools, domestic appliances; resort; p. (1970) 35,515.
Fonseca, Gulf of, Honduras; lgst indentation along Pac. cst. of Central America; sm. pt. of Amapala, US naval base, and new deepwater pt.
Fontainebleau, t., Seine-et-Marne, **France**; on R. Seine, 56 km S.E. Paris; in former royal forest (a. 17,200 ha); magnificent palace; p. (1968) 19,803.
Fontenoy, v., **Belgium**; nr. Tournai; scene of battle (1745) when the French under Marshal Saxe defeated the English and their allies; p. (est. 1969) 655.
Foochow (Fu-chou), c., cap. of Fukien prov., **China**; at mouth of Min R.; major comm. and industl. ctr.; became impt. with tea exp.; former treaty pt.; p. (est. 1970) 900,000.
Fordlandia. *See* **Belterra**.
Foreland, N. and S., two headlands on E. cst. Kent, **Eng.**; between which are the Goodwin Sands and Pegwell Bay; lighthouses; sea battle between de Ruyter and Monk (1666).
Forest Hills, residtl. a., central Queen's bor., N.Y., **USA**; national and international matches played at West Side Tennis Club.
Forest of Dean. *See* **Dean, Forest of**.
Forfar, royal burgh, Angus, **Scot.**; jute, linen; p. (1971) 10,499.
Forli, c., Emilia-Romagna, central **Italy**; route ctr. in Apennine foothills; felt, textiles, footwear; p. (1969) 104,175.
Formby, t., Merseyside, **Eng.**; on W. cst., 10 km S.W. of Southport; residtl.; p. (1971) 23,501.
Formosa, prov., N. **Argentina**; bordering on Paraguay; timber; cap. Formosa; a. 72,067 km²; p. (1970) 234,075.
Formosa. *See* **Taiwan**.
Forres, royal burgh, Moray, **Scot.**; on Findhorn R. nr. Moray F.; agr., forestry, engin., distilleries; cas.; p. (1971) 4,718.
Forst, t., Cottbus, **E. Germany**; on R. Neisse; E. section of t. Polish since 1945; textiles; p. (est. 1970) 29,284
Fortaleza, c., cap. of Ceará st., **Brazil**; exp. sugar cotton, hides, carnauba wax; p. (1970) 520,175.
Fort Collins, t., Col., **USA**; ctr. of rich farming a.; grain, sugarbeet, livestock; univ.; p. (1970) 43,337.
Fort Dauphin, pt., **Malagasy Rep.**; mica production; exp. sisal; sacks, twine.
Fort de France, cap. of **Martinique**, Fr. W.I.; landlocked harbour; exp. sugar, rum; comm. ctr.; Fr. naval base; p. (1967) 99,051.
Fort Dodge, t., Iowa, **USA**; on Des Moines R., in rich agr. a.; grain, gypsum, coal; p. (1970) 31,263.
Fort George, R., W. Quebec, **Canada**; rises in Labrador and flows into Hudson Bay; 880 km long.
Fort Gouraud, t., **Mauritania**; modern iron-ore mines.
Forth, R., **Scot.**; formed by two headstreams rising to N. of Ben Lomond which meet nr. Aberfoyle; takes meandering course to Alloa, whence it expands into Firth of Forth (q.v.); 165 km long.
Forth, Firth of, lge. inlet, E. cst. of **Scot.**; submerged estuary of R. Forth; navigable by lge. vessels for 64 km inland to Grangemouth; other pts., Leith, Rosyth (naval), Bo'ness; l. (to Alloa) 80 km; the Forth rly. bridge (1890) spans the F. at Queensferry; the road bridge (1964) is the longest suspension bridge in Europe.
Forth and Clyde Canal, Scot.; links F. of Forth at Grangemouth and F. of Clyde at Glasgow; 61 km long.
Fort Johnston, t., S. **Malawi**, on L. Malombe; new t., 1966; tobacco; airpt.
Fort Knox, Ky., **USA**; nation's gold bullion depository; military air-base.
Fort Lamy. *See* **Ndjamene**.
Fort Lauderdale, c., Fla., **USA**; on Atl. cst. N. of Miami; lge. marina; citrus fruits, mkt. garden prod.; holiday resort; p. (1970) 139,122 (c.), 612,003 (met a., inc. military personnel and families).
Fort Myers, t., Fla., **USA**; on G. of Mexico; resort; Eddison experimented here; p. (1970) 27,351.
Fortrose, t., royal burgh, Ross and Cromarty, **Scot.**; on S. cst. of Black Isle, on Moray F.; p. (1971) 1,081.
Fort Smith, c., Ark., **USA**; on Arkansas R.; mkt. ctr. for agr. a.; varied mnfs., inc. furniture, glass; coal and zinc mined nearby; p. (1970) 61,549 (c.), 156,750 (met. a.).
Fort Victoria, t., **Rhodesia**, agr. and mng. ctr., cattle, historic ruins in Zimbabwe Nat. Park; p. (est. 1970) 13,000.
Fort Wayne, c., Ind., **USA**; at confluence of 2 headstreams of Maumee R.; rly. repair shops; elec. machin. and domestic appliances, originally a Fr. fort; p. (1970) 175,082 (c.), 277,721 (met. a.).
Fort William. *See* **Thunder Bay**.
Fort William, burgh, Lochaber, **Scot.**; nr. head of Loch Linnhe, at base of Ben Nevis; aluminium factory; pulp- and paper-mill at Corpach; p. (1971) 4,214.
Fort Worth, c., Texas **USA**; rly. and comm. ctr, on Trinity R.; livestock and grain mkt.; oil

refining, meat packing, oilfield equipment; p. (1970) 388,123 (c.), 757,105 (met. a.).

Fort Yukon, trading sta. on Yukon R., N.E. Alaska, **USA**.

Fos-sur-Mer, t., Bouches-du-Rhône, S. **France**; nr. Marseilles; new deepwater pt. and oil refinery; bauxite terminal; iron and steel plant.

Fotheringhay, v., Northampton, **Eng.**; on R. Nene; Mary Queen of Scots beheaded (1587) in F. Castle.

Fougères, t., Ille-et-Vilaine, **France**; cas.; footwear, clothing; p. (1968) 26,854.

Foulness I., S. Essex, **Eng.**; at mouth of R. Crouch; owned by Min. of Defence; site of projected third London airport of Maplin, now abandoned; projected container and oil pt.

Fountains Abbey, ruined 12th cent. Cistercian abbey North Yorks., **Eng.**; nr. Ripon.

Fowey, sm. spt., Cornwall, **Eng.**; nr. mouth of R. Fowey; exp. kaolin; resort; fishing; p. with St. Austell (1971) 32,252.

Foxe Basin and Channel, to N. of Hudson Bay, between Baffin I. and Southampton I., **Canada**.

Foyers, Falls of, Inverness, **Scot.**; E. of Loch Ness, nr. Fort Augustus; aluminium wks., the first hydroelectric plant erected in Britain (1896).

Foyle, Lough, inlet, **N. Ireland**; between Donegal (R.o.I.) and Londonderry; outlet of R. F.; Londonderry t. at head of inlet.

Foynes Is., **R.o.I.**; oil terminal on N. side, E. of Battery Point.

Foz do Iguacú, t., Paraná, **Brazil**; highway (coffee road) from Paranaguá

Framingham, t., Mass., **USA**; 32 km W. of Boston; lt. inds.; p. (1970) 64,048.

Framlingham, mkt. t., Suffolk, **Eng.**; N.E. of Ipswich; cas. remains.

Francavilla Fontana, t., Apulia, **Italy**; rly. junc.; agr. tr.; p. (est. 1968) 31,241.

France, rep., W. **Europe**; bounded by 3 seas: Eng. Channel, Atl. Oc., Mediterranean; variety of climate and relief; leading agr. cty. of Europe; 75 per cent under cultivation; exps. grain, fruit, vegetables, wine; industl. expansion since second world war; lgst. inds. inc. iron and steel, motor vehicles, aircraft, engin., textiles, chemicals; tourism impt.; EEC member; cap. Paris; 96 deps.; excessive social, economic, and political concentration around Paris promotes description of France as "Paris and the French Desert"; recent attempts to break this down using framework of 21 economic planning regions; a. 550,634 km^2; p. (1975) 52,655,802.

Franceville, t., Gabon, **Equatorial Africa**; on R. Ogooué; linked to Libreville as part of the Trans-Gabon rly. project; manganese mines opened 1962; founded by De Brazza.

Francistown, t., **Botswana**, S. Africa; airpt.; butter, coppermng; p. (est. 1969) 11,000.

Frankenthal, t., Rhineland-Palatinate **W. Germany**; in industl. dist. of Mannheim-Ludwigshafen; engin., machin.; p. (est. 1969) 39,920.

Frankfurt-on-Main, c., Hesse, **W. Germany**; focal point in Rhine-Main urban region; rly. ctr., transit pt.; machin., cars, chemicals, elec. engin., publishing; airport; cath., univ.; birthplace of Goethe; p. (est. 1969) 661,880 (c.); (est. 1967) 1,520,000 (met. a.).

Frankfurt-on-Oder, c., Brandenburg, **E. Germany**; agr. ctr., R. pt., rail junc.; machin., chemicals; E. part of t. (Slubice) Polish since 1945; p. (est. 1967) 60,200.

Frankischer (Franconian) Jura, plateau with steep N.-facing edge, S.E. of **W. Germany**; runs 128 km S.W. from Fichtelgebirge; drained by Regnitz and Altmühl Rs.

Franklin, t., Tasmania, **Australia**; 32 km from Hobart; principal fruit-growing dist. in I.

Franklin, dist., N.W. Terr., **Canada**; comprising the Is. of Arctic Canada from Banks I. to Baffin I., including Boothia Peninsula and Melville Peninsula; sparsely populated; furs; a. 1,434,943 km^2.

Františkovy Lázne (Franzensbad), famous spa, W. Bohemia, **ČSSR**; 445 m a.s.l., between the the Erzgebirge and the Fichtelgebirge.

Franz Josef Land (Zemlya Frantsalosifa), **RSFSR**; archipelago in Arctic Oc. N. of Novaya Zemlya; a. 20,720 km^2; mainly ice-covered.

Frascati, t., **Italy**; 19 km S.E. of Rome; summer resort; famous villas and arch. remains; nuclear research ctr.; p. (est. 1968) 18,023.

Fraser I., Queensland, **Australia**; low sandy I., 128 km long; timber reserve.

Fraser, R., B.C., **Canada**, rises at *c.* 1,800 m on W. slopes Rocky Mtns.; famous salmon fisheries: routeway; Vancouver nr. delta; 1,360 km long.

Fraserburgh, spt., burgh, Banff and Buchan **Scot.**; one of the main E. cst. herring pts.; p. (1971) 10,606.

Frauenfeld, t., cap. of Thurgau can., **Switzerland**; 11th cent. cas.; textiles; p. (1970) 17,576.

Fray Bentos, t., cap. of Rio Negro dep., **Uruguay**; pt. on R. Uruguay 80 km from mouth; meat-processing; p. (1963) 14,000.

Fredericia, t., pt., E. Jutland, **Denmark**; major rly. junc.; textiles, silver and electroplated gds., fertilisers: oil refinery; p. (est. 1970) 43,513.

Fredericton, c., cap. of N.B., **Canada**; on St. John R.; univ., cath.; timber, shoes, plastics; p. (1971) 23,612.

Frederiksberg, sub. of Copenhagen, **Denmark**, with indep. municipal status; p. (est. 1969) 103,621.

Frederikshaab, sm. spt. on W. cst. of **Greenland**; fish processing.

Frederikshavn, fish. pt., N. Jutland, **Denmark**, on Kattegat; p. (est. 1970) 32,826.

Frederikstad, t., **Norway**; at mouth of Glomma R.; ctr. of pulp and paper-producing ind.; electrotechnical inds., shipbldg., fish canning; p. (1968) 30,089.

Frederiksvaerk, t., Sjaelland, **Denmark**; impt. iron and steel wks.

Freetown, c., cap. of **Sierra Leone**; pt. on Atl. Oc.; one of lgst. natural harbours in world; humid, oppressive climate; exp. diamonds, palm oil; engin., food processing, oil refining; fishing; p. (est. 1970) 178,600.

Freiberg, t., **E. Germany**; S.W. of Dresden, at foot of Erzgebirge; mng. academy (silver discovered 12th cent).; metallurgy, textiles, glass, porcelain; p. (est. 1967) 49,100.

Freiburg im Breisgau, c., Baden-Württemberg, **W. Germany**; in Black Forest; cath., univ.; cultural ctr.; tourism; p. (est. 1969) 163,500.

Freising, t., Bavaria, **W. Germany**; N.E. of Munich; cath.; agr. machin., textiles, chemicals; p. (est. 1969) 29,788.

Freital, t., **E. Germany**; S.W. Dresden; glass, uranium ore processing; coalmines nearby; p. (est. 1970) 42,159.

Fréjus, t., Var dep., S.W. **France**; cath., Roman ruins; resort on Fr. Riviera; p. (1968) 25,736.

Fréjus, Col de, Alpine pass, **France** and **Italy**, 2,083 m, under which runs the Mont Cenis tunnel (13·6 km).

Fremantle, spt., W. **Australia**; at mouth of Swan R., 19 km S.W. from Perth, principal pt. of commerce in W. Australia and first Australian pt. of call for mail steamers; oil refining; wheat, wool; p. (1966) 32,134.

French Equatorial Africa, formerly included Gabon, Congo (Brazzaville), Ubangi-Shari and Chad, sts. which are now independent.

French Guiana, Fr. overseas dep., on N. cst. of **S. America**, between Surinam to W. and Brazil to S. and E.; tropical climate; little developed and thinly populated; ch. ctr. of p. and spt. at cap. of Cayenne; economy based on agr., especially sugar and forestry; some gold and bauxite mng.; a. 90,650 km^2; p. (est. 1969) 48,000.

French Polynesia, Fr. overseas terr., in S. Pac. **Oc.**, comprising several archipelagos: Society Is., Marquesas Is., Tubuai Is., Tuamotu Is., and Gambier Is; cap. Papeete; a. 4,002 km^2; p. (est. 1970) 109,000.

French Somaliland. *See* Afars and Issas.

French S. and Antarctic Terrs., Fr. overseas terr., comprising several grs. of Is. and Antarctic terr. of Adélie Land; a. 409,220 km^2; p. 132 (mainly scientists).

French West Africa, comprised former Fr. cols. of Dahomey (Benin), Ivory Coast, Mauritania, Niger, Fr. Guinea, Upper Volta, Senegal, Fr. Soudan (Mali).

Freshwater, sm. t., I. of White, **Eng.**; at W. end of I., 13 km W. of Newport; resort.

Fresnillo de Gonzalez Echeverria, t., Zacatecas, **Mexico**; alt. 2,227 m; mkt. t., silver mng.; p. (1970) 101,316.

Fresno, c., Cal., **USA**; ctr. of vast irrigated fruit-growing dist.; p. (1970) 162,326 (c.), 407,048 (met. a.).

Fribourg (Freiburg), c., cap. of F. can. **Switzerland**; between Berne and Lausanne; viaduct and bridges; cath., univ.; p. (1969) 40,500.

Fribourg (Freiburg), can., **Switzerland**; mainly dairy farming; cereals, sugarbeet, cheese; a. 1,671 km²; p. (1969) 174,000.

Friedrichshafen, t., **W. Germany**; on Bodensee; machin., boat bldg., motors; resort; p. (est. 1967) 40,300.

Friendly Is. *See* **Tonga.**

Friern Barnet. *See* **Barnet.**

Friesland, prov., **N. Neth.**; cap. Leeuwarden; dairying, horses, cattle; natural gas on Ameland I.; a. 3,432 km²; p. (1968) 511,330.

Frimley and Camberley, ts., former U.D., Surrey, **Eng.**; 5 km N. of Farnborough; lt. engin., plastics; military training ctr.; p. (1971) 44,784.

Frinton and Walton, Essex, **Eng.**; on E. cst., 8 km N.E. of Clacton; seaside resort; p. (1971) 20 ,431.

Frisches Haff, shallow freshwater lagoon, Baltic cst. of Poland; 85 km long, 6–18 km broad.

Frisian Is., chain of Is. stretching from Den Helder to Jutland, along csts. of Neth., Germany, and Denmark; ch. Is. are Texel, Vlieland, Terschelling, Ameland (West F. Is), Nordeney, Borkum (East F. Is.), Sylt, Föhr, Rømø (North F. Is.).

Friuli-Venezia Giulia, aut. reg. (created 1963), N.E. **Italy**; comprising 3 provs. Udine, Gorozia, Trieste; p. (1969) 1,228,927.

Frobisher Bay, inlet in S. Baffin I., **N. Canada**, extending 320 km between Cumberland Sound and Hudson Strait.

Frodingham, t., Humberside, **Eng.**; on W. flank of limestone ridge, Lincoln Edge; impt. iron-ore open-cast mines; mnfs. iron and steel; p. with Scunthorpe (1971) 70,800.

Frome, mkt. t. Somerset, **Eng.**; on R. Frome, 18 km S. of Bath; p. (1971) 13,384.

Frome, R., Dorset, **Eng.**; flows from N. Dorset Downs into Poole Harbour.

Frontignan, t., Hérault, **S. France**; oil refining; pipeline under sea from Sète; produces muscat; p. (1968) 11,141.

Frunze, c., cap. of Kirghiz SSR, **USSR**; univ.; engin., textiles, meat-packing; p. (1970) 431,000.

Fuerteventura, I., **Canary** gr.; a. 1,717 km²; p. (1970) 18,192.

Fujayrah, emirate, one of **United Arab Emirates**, Persian G.; p. (est. 1968) 10,000.

Fujisawa, t., Honshu, **Japan**; bearings machin.; p. (est. 1971) 240,000.

Fujiyama, extinct volcano, **Japan**; 96 km S.W. of Tokyo; pilgrim resort; hgst. peak of Japan; alt. 3,780 m.

Fukien (Fujian), prov., **China**; cap. Foochow (Fuzhou); intensive agr., rice and sugar-cane; shellfish raised along cst.; a. 123,103 km²; p. (est. 1968) 17,000,000.

Fukui, c., cap. of F. pref., central Honshu, **Japan**; synthetic fibres, paper; old silk-weaving ctr.; p. (est. 1971) 216,000.

Fukuoka, c., N. Kyushu, **Japan**; pt. on Hakata Bay; univ. ctr., old cas. t.; textiles, dolls, shipbldg.; p. (est. 1971) 878,000.

Fukushima, c., N. Honshu, **Japan**; ceramics, foods, steel; publishing; p. (est. 1971) 232,000.

Fukuyama, c., S. Hokkaido, **Japan**; p. (est. 1971) 265,000.

Fulda, t., Hesse, **W. Germany**; nr. Kassel; on R. Fulda; palace, abbey; textiles, metallurgy, rubber; route ctr.; p. (est. 1967) 44,400.

Fulham. *See* **Hammersmith.**

Fulwood, t., Lancs., **Eng.**; 3 km N.E. of Preston; p. (1971) 21,741.

Funchal, cap. of **Madeira Is.**, pt., winter resort; cath.; p. (1970) 105,791.

Fundy, Bay of, inlet between Nova Scotia and New Brunswick, **Canada**; lge. tidal range of 21 m.

Furka Pass, Switzerland; between Valais and Uri cans.; 2,433 m.

Furneaux Is., S.E. **Australia**; in Bass Strait, belonging to Tasmania; lgst is Flinders I.; p. (1966) 1,220.

Furness, dist., Cumbria, **Eng.**; between Morecambe Bay and the Irish Sea.

Fürstenwalde, t., Frankfurt, **E. Germany**; on R. Spree; metallurgy, leather, tyres; p. (est. 1970) 30,830.

Fürth, t., Bavaria, **W. Germany**; nr. Nürnberg; toy and glass inds.; p. (est. 1967) 94,800.

Fusan. *See* **Pusan.**

Fuse, t., Honshu, **Japan**; machin., textiles, chemicals; now part of Higashiosaka; p. (1966) 253,000.

Fushimi, c., Honshu, **Japan**; sub. of Kyoto.

Fushun, c., Liaoning, **N. China**; at foot of Changpai Shan, 35 km N.E. of Shenyang; major industl. ctr.; possesses world's thickest bituminous coal seam (127 m) worked by deep and opencast mines; oil refinery based on local oil shales; steelwks. chemicals; p. (est. 1970) 1,700 000.

Fusin (Fuxin), c., Liaoning, **N. China**; ctr. of lge. coalfield; p. (1953) 188,600.

Fuskiki, spt., Honshu, **Japan**; serves Toyama c. with metals, coal.

Futa, La, pass, Tusco-Emilian Apennines, **N. Italy**; used by main road from Bologna to Florence; alt. 903 m.

Futa Jalon (Fouta Djalon), upland dist., mostly in **Guinea, W. Africa**, with outliers in **Liberia** and **Sierra Leone**.

Futseling, t., Anhwei, **China**; site of lge. dam on Hwai Ho, built 1954.

Fylde, W. Lancs., **Eng.**; low plain behind coastal sand dunes; pig- and poultry-rearing dist.; ch. t. Blackpool; p. (1971) 20,251 (dist.).

Fylingdales, ballistic missile early warning sta. on N. Yorks. moors, Eng.

Fyn, I., **Denmark**; in Baltic Sea; a. 3,419 km²; cap. Odense; dairying, sugarbeet; p. (1971) 433,765.

Fyne, loch on Argyll and Bute cst., **W. Scot.**; an arm of F. of Clyde; offshore oil platform construction; 64 km long.

Fyzabad, t., Uttar Pradesh, **India**; mkt. t.; sugar refineries; p. (1961) 88,296.

G

Gabès, spt., **Tunisia**; on G. of Gabès, 320 km S. of Tunis: dates, henna, wool; p. (1966) 76,356.

Gabon, rep., **W. Africa**; Cameroon to N., Zaïre to S. and E.; tropical climate, hot, humid; much tropical rain forest; forestry main ind. but mng. increasingly impt.; petroleum exp. creating increasing prosperity; manganese at Moanda (S.), iron-ore at Mekambo (N.E.); communications geared mainly to mng. areas; major pts. Libreville (cap.), Port Gentil; Trans-Gabon rly. project to promote exploitation of timber; intense forest cover makes internal air services very impt.; airport at Libreville; a. 266,770 km²; p. (est. 1970) 475,000.

Gaborone (Gaberones), cap. **Botswana**; formerly sm. v.; chosen as cap. for new rep., bldg. began 1964; p. (est. 1970) 15,000.

Gadag-Betgeri, t., Karnataka, **India**; cotton and silk weaving; p. (1961) 76,614.

Gaeta, t., naval pt., **Italy**; on promontory on shore of G. of Gaeta; the anc. Caietae Portus; cath.; p. (est. 1968) 22,799.

Gafsa, t., **Tunisia**; phosphate mng. ctr.; p. (1966) 32,408.

Gaillard Cut, excavated channel, **Panama Canal** Zone; carries Panama Canal through Culebra Mtn. from L. Gatun to Pac. Oc.; 11 km long.

Gainesville, t., Fla., **USA**; univ.; mkt. gardening; electronics, wood prod.; p. (est. 1969) 67,000.

Gainsborough, t., Lincs., **Eng.**; on R. Trent; agr. implements, milling, packing and wrapping machin.; some R. traffic; mkt.; George Eliot's St. Ogg's in *Mill on the Floss*; p. (1971) 17,420.

Gairdner, salt L., **S. Australia**; a. 4,766 km².

Gairloch, sea loch and v., W. Ross and Cromarty, **Scot.**; resort, fishing; p. (1971) 1,783.

Galapagos, volcanic Is., Pac. Oc.; 960 km W. of **Ecuador** (to whom they belong) on equator; flora and fauna peculiar to each I.; visited by Darwin 1835; now a wildlife sanctuary; a. 7,428 km²; p. (1967) 3,100.

Galashiels, burgh, Ettrick and Lauderdale, **Scot.**; on Gala Water, 3 km above confluence with R. Tweed; tweeds, woollens; p. (1971) 12,609.

Galati or **Galatz**, c., E. **Romania**; major inland pt. on lower Danube; cath.; p. (est. 1969) 172,687.

Galesburg, t., Ill., **USA**; engin., coal mng.; p. (1970) 36,290.

Galicia, historic region, S.E. **Poland** and W. Ukraine, **USSR**.

Galicia, region, N.W. **Spain**; comprising provs. La Coruña, Lugo, Orense, and Pontevedra.

Galilee, northern div. of Palestine in Roman times, containing the ts. Cana, Capernaum, Tiberias, Nazareth; the ch. scene of Christ's ministry.

Galilee, Sea of (**Lake Tiberias**), also known as L. Gennesaret; Biblical associations; 207 m below level of Med.; Israel plans to draw water from L. to irrigate Negev; a. 166 km².

Gallarate, t., **Italy**; nr. Milan; textiles; p. (est. 1968) 41,208.

Galle, c., pt. on S.W. cst. of **Sri Lanka**; exp. tea, rubber, coconut oil; suffered from competition with Colombo after construction of modern harbour there; p. (est. 1968) 73,000.

Gallego, R., N.E. **Spain**; rises in Pyrenees, flows S. to R. Ebro at Zaragoza; provides irrigation around Zaragoza; valley used by main rly. across Pyrenees from Pau (France) to Zaragoza; 176 km long.

Gallipoli. *See* **Gelibolu**.

Gällivare, dist., N. **Sweden**, in Norrbotton prov.; rich iron-ore deposits; p. (1968) 26,625.

Galloway, anc. dist. S.W. **Scot.**; inc. l. gov. dists. of Stewartry and Wigtown; dairying.

Galloway, Mull of, the extremity of the Rinns of G., the most southern pt. of Scot.

Galston, burgh, Kilmarnock and Loudoun, **Scot.**; on R. Irvine, nr. Kilmarnock; p. (1971) 4,239.

Galt., t., Ont., **Canada**; textiles, shoes; p. (1971) 38,134.

Galveston, c., spt., Texas, **USA**; on I. in Bay at entrance to G. of Mexico; gr. cotton and sulphur pt. with lge. exp. of agr. prod.; mills, foundries, food-processing, chemicals; univ., resort; p. (1970) 60,714 (c.), 165,669 (met. a.).

Galway, co., Galway Bay, Connacht, **R.o.I.**; fishery, cattle, marble quarrying; a. 6,351 km²; p. (1966) 148,190.

Galway, co. t., Galway, **R.o.I.**; univ.; spt., fishing; sawmills, textiles, printing; p. (1966) 24,495.

Gambia, The, rep. (1970), **W. Africa**, on Atl. Oc.; comprises St. Mary's I. (on which is Banjul, the cap.) and narrow mainland enclave (average width 32 km) extending 320 km inland astride R. Gambia, hot all year, summer rain, but savannah inland; agr. is basis of economy, esp. groundnuts; economic aid from Taiwan; communications developed around Banjul (spt. and airpt.); a. 10,368 km²; p. (est. 1968) 360,000.

Gambia, R., **Senegal** and **Gambia**, rises in Futa Jalon Plateau, flows N. and W. into Atl. Oc. at Banjul; forms main means of communication through Gambia, 1,120 km long.

Gambier Is., Fr Polynesia, **S. Pac. Oc.**, 4 coral Is.; a. 31 km².

Gandhinagar, new cap. of Gujarat, **India**; on Sabarmati R., 21 km N. of Ahmadabad; under construction; planned initial p. 75,000 rising to 200,000.

Ganges (**Ganga**), sacred R. of **India**; rises in Himalayas and flows to Bay of Bengal via alluvial cones at foot of Himalayas and by several delta mouths, on one of which stands Calcutta; navigable for lge. ships from Allahabad; delta alone larger than Eng. and Wales; flood plain and delta very fertile and densely populated; 2,400 km long.

Gangtok, t., cap. of **Sikkim**, E. Himalayas; agr. tr. ctr.; carpets; p. (est. 1968) 9,000.

Gap, t., Hautes Alpes, S.E. **France**; textiles; p. (1968) 23,994.

Gard, dep., S. **France**; in Languedoc, on Mediterranean; cap. Nîmes; vines, olives, sericulture; a. 5,879 km²; p. (1968) 478,544.

Garda, L., between Lombardy and Venezia, **Italy**; variety of scenery, winter resort; a. 370 km²; greatest depth, 346 m.

Garden Grove, residtl. c., sub. S.E. Los Angeles, Cal., **USA**; p. (1970) 121,504.

Gardéz, t., **Afghanistan**; alt. 2,287 m; ctr. of comm. and transport; p. (est. 1969) 39,142.

Garforth, t., West Yorks., **Eng.**; coalmng., lt. inds.; p. (1971) 25,296.

Garigliano, R. and dist., S. central **Italy**; where Liri R. joins Gari R. below Cassino; nuclear power plant.

Garmisch-Partenkirchen, t., Bavaria, **W. Germany**; winter sports; p. (est. 1969) 27,267.

Garo Hills, mtnous. dist., Assam, **India**; a. 8,078 km²; dense forests; p. (1961) 307,228.

Garonne, R., S.W. **France**; rises at foot of Mt. Maladetta (Pyrenees), flows via Toulouse and agr. valley, and enters Gironde estuary 32 km below Bordeaux; 720 km long.

Garrigue, region, Languedoc, S. **France**; low limestone hills, run N.E. to S.W., W. of Rhône delta; semi-arid; scanty vegetation; winter pasture for sheep; olives; Montpellier, Nîmes located on S. flank.

Garston, spt., southern end Bootle and Liverpool docks; Merseyside, **Eng.**

Garut, t., W. Java, **Indonesia**, mtn. resort, lge. spinning mill; p. 24,219.

Gary, c., Ind., **USA**; on S. shore of L. Michigan; leading producer of steel, tinplate, cement; p. (1970) 174,132 (c.), 628,969 (met. a.).

Gascony, anc. prov., S.W. **France**; now comprises deps. along Atl. cst. and Pyrenees; Landes, Gers, Hautes-Pyrenees, and parts of Lot-et-Garonne, Tarn-et-Garonne, Haute Garonne, Gironde, and Ariège. Battleground in Hundred Years War.

Gastein (**Bad Gastein**), t., Salzburg, **Austria**; mineral springs; resort; p. 5,700.

Gastonia, t., N.C., **USA**; impt. textile ctr.; p. (1970) 47,142.

Gateshead, t., Tyne and Wear, **Eng.**; on R. Tyne opposite Newcastle; engin., food-processing, pumps, paper; pt.; p. (1971) 94,457.

Gatineau, R., **Canada**; trib. of Ottawa R., which it joins nr. Ottawa; length 480 km; hydroelec. power; forested valley.

Gatwick, West Sussex, **Eng.**; 40 km S. London; first airport in world where trunk road, main rly. line and air facilities combined in one unit.

Gauhati, t., temporary cap., Assam, **India**; univ.; silk, cotton, lace, oil refinery; pipeline from Barauni; p. (1971) 123,783 (t.), 200,377 (met. a.).

Gaul (Lat. *Gallia*), embraced the lands inhabited by Celtic peoples in Roman times, covering what is now modern France (Gaul proper), Belgium, N. Italy, and parts of Germany, Neth., and Switzerland. South of the Alps was known as Cisalpine Gaul, north of the Alps as Transalpine Gaul.

Gauri-Sankar, mtn. in Himalayas, **Nepal** and **Tibet, China**; 56 km W. of Mt. Everest; alt. 7,149 m.

Gävle, spt., **Sweden**; timber, textiles, steel, porcelain; p. (1968) 60,990.

Gävleborg, co., **Sweden**; ch. t., Gävle; a. 18,544 km²; p. (est. 1970) 293,377.

Gaya, t., Bihar, **India**; Buddhist pilgrim ctr.; cottons, silks; p. (1971) 179,884.

Gaza, t., N.E. **Egypt**; ch. t. of Gaza Strip (q.v.); anciently the t. where Samson brought down the temple.

Gazankulu (**Machangana**), Bantu Terr. Authority (1969), **S. Africa**; home of Shangana and Tsonga p.; cap. Giyana; p. (est. 1969) 392,000.

Gaza Strip, coastal a. under Egyptian admin. since 1949; occupied by Israeli troops, Nov. 1956–March 1957, and since June 1967.

Gaziantep, t., **Turkey**; S.W. of Malatya; mkt. t.; p. (1965) 160,152 (t.), 235,472 (met. a.).

Gazli, Uzbek SSR, **USSR**; 96 km N.W. of Bukhara; natural gas field; pipeline to Chelyabinsk opened 1963; destroyed by earthquake (1976).

Gdańsk (**Danzig**), c., spt., N. **Poland**; Baltic pt.; on branch of Vistula; annexed to Germany 1939, restored to Poland 1945; shipbldg., machin., chemicals, metals; Gdańsk, Gdynia and Sopot admin. as single c. (Trójmiasto = tricity); p. (1970) 364,000.

Gdynia, spt., Gdańsk, N. **Poland**; competes with spt. of Gdańsk for Polish hinterland; impt. comm., rly. and industl. ctr.; part of the Trójmiasto; p. (1970) 190,000.

Geelong, c., spt., Victoria, **Australia**; on Corio Bay; exp. flour, wool, meat; oil refining, agr. machin., cars, carpets; p. (1972) 17,775 (c.), 121,966 (met. a.).

Gela, t., S. Sicily, **Italy**; in cotton-growing a.; petrochemicals; p. (est. 1968) 65,289.

Gelderland, prov., **Neth.**; E. and S. of Utrecht prov., a. 5,022 km²; cap. Arnhem; cereals, tobacco; cattle rearing; p. (1968) 1,456,544.

Gelibolu (Gallipoli), pt. and penin. on the Dardanelles, **Turkey**; scene of unsuccessful landing by British and Anzac troops 1915; 176 km. long.

Gelligaer, t., Mid Glamorgan, **Wales**; 6 km. N.E. of Pontypridd; coal mng.; p. (1971) 33,670.

Gelsenkirchen, t., N. Rhine–Westphalia, **W. Germany**; in Ruhr conurb. on Rhine–Herne canal; collys., ironwks., glass, chemicals, oil refining; p. (est. 1969) 351,000.

Geneva, c., cap. of G. can., **Switzerland**; at exit of Rhône from L. Geneva; cath., univ.; former H.Q. of League of Nations; H.Q. of ILO, WHO, and Red Cross; watchmkg., jewellery, elec. gds., optical instruments; tourist resort; birthplace of Rousseau; p. (est. 1969) 169,500 (c.), 307,500 (met. a.).

Geneva (**L. Léman**), L., S.W. corner of **Switzerland**; forms a gr. crescent of water, source of poetic inspiration; 371 m a.s.l.; a. 578 km².

Génissiat, **France**; site of gr. barrage and hydro-elec. power sta. on Rhône below Geneva; completed 1950.

Genk, t., Limburg, **Belgium**; stainless steel wks., petrochemicals; p. (1968) 56,031.

Gennevilliers, t., Hauts-de-Seine **France**; N.W. sub. of Paris; R. pt.; p. (1968) 46,074.

Genoa (**Genova**), c., ch. pt. **Italy**; cath., univ., palaces; handles one-third of Italy's foreign tr.; pt. and airpt. expansion, shipyards, steelwks., engin., textiles, tanning; p. (est. 1970) 842,114 (met. a.).

George L., N.Y., **USA**; Adirondack mtns.; picturesque resort.

Georgetown, cap., **Cayman Is.**; pt.; p. (1970) 3,975.

Georgetown (**Demerara**), c., cap. of **Guyana**; on Demerara R.; exp. sugar, cocoa, coffee, timber, gold, diamonds, bauxite; airpt. nearby; botanical gardens; p. (1970) 99,989.

Georgetown. *See* **Penang**.

Georgia, st., S.E. **USA**; one of 13 original sts., on Atl. cst.; rising to Appalachians; impt. arable agr.; cotton and lumber inds.; major source of kaolin; ch. ts., Atlanta (cap.), Savannah; a. 152,489 km²; p. (1970) 4,492,038.

Georgia (**Gruziya**), constituent rep., **USSR**; rich agr., fruit, tobacco, grain; mng. inc. manganese, gold, oil; several hydroelectric power plants; coastal and mtn. resorts; active Jewish community; cap. Tbilisi; a. 69,671 km²; p. (1970) 4,688,000.

Georgian Bay, arm of L. Huron, S. Ont., **Canada**; separated from L. by Manitoulin I. and Saugeen peninsula; *c.* 160 km long, *c.* 80 km wide; L. pts., Owen Sound, Midland, Parry Sound; Georgian Bay Is., Nat. Park.

Gera, c., cap. of G. admin. dist., **E. Germany**; on White Elster R.; woollens, printing; lignite mined nearby; p. (est. 1969) 111,188.

Geraldton, spt., **W. Australia**; N. outlet for wheat belt; also exps. wool and manganese; early tomatoes; super phosphate; p. (1972) 15,330.

Germany, Democratic Rep. of, and **E. Berlin** (**E. Germany**), rep., **Central Europe**; partition from W. Germany complete by 1948; part of N. European Plain; 7th industl. nation of world; lignite field supplies 70 per cent of energy; main inds., optics, electronics and precision machin., chemicals, heavy engin.; member of Comecon; 15 admin. dists. (Bezirke); cap. E. Berlin; a. 108,267 km²; p. (1969) 17,074,504.

Germany, Fed. Rep. of (**W. Germany**), **W. Europe**; partition complete by 1948; N. half part of N. European Plain; rises in S. to Bavarian Alps; 2nd lgst. trading nation of world; mainly industl. with core in Ruhr conurb.; motor vehicles, chemicals, precision engin.; member of EEC; tourism; 10 admin. dists. (Länder) and W. Berlin; cap. Bonn; a. (inc. W. Berlin) 248,459 km²; p. (1975) 61,645,000.

Germiston, t., Transvaal, **S. Africa**; nr. Johannesburg; gold-mng.; rly. wkshps., engin., machin., chemicals; gas pipeline from Sasolburg, p. (1970) 281,494 (met. a.).

Gerona, c., cap. of G. prov., **Spain**; cath.; textiles, chemicals; p. (1970) 50,338.

Gerrards Cross, t., S.E. Bucks., **Eng.**; 14 km E. of High Wycombe; residtl.

Gers, dep., S.W. **France**; cap. Auch; grain, vines, brandy; a. 6,291 km²; p. (1968) 181,577.

Gersoppa Falls, Sharavati R., Karnataka, **India**; hgst. cascade 253 m; hydroelec. power.

Gezira, dist., **Sudan**, N.E. Africa; between Blue and White Niles; *c.* 12,173 km² capable of irrigation provided by Blue Nile at Sennar Dam; lge-scale growing of high-quality cotton; total a. *c.* 20,200 km².

Ghadames (**Ghudamis**), oasis, Sahara Desert, **Libya**; at point where Tunis, Algeria, Libya converge 480 km S.W. of Tripoli.

Ghaghara (**Gogra**), sacred R., **India**; trib. of Ganges, rises in Tibet, flows through Uttar Pradesh; lge. catchment a. but poorly developed floodplain; 960 km long.

Ghana, rep., **W. Africa**; indep. st., member of Brit. Commonwealth; tropical monsoon climate, but rainfall decreases inland; S. Ghana more developed than N.; agr. basis of comm. economy and cocoa (of which Ghana is world's lgst producer) major exp.; Volta R. scheme produces power from main dam at Akosombo and an aluminium smelter plant began production in 1967; oil refining and production; communications network based on Accra and Takoradi on cst., and inland ctr. of Kumasi; development of road network vital for expansion of comm. agr.; 3 univs.; pts. at Takoradi and Tema closely linked with internal economic growth; cap. Accra; a. 238,539 km²; p. (1970) 8,545,561.

Ghardaia, t., **Algeria**; N. of Sahara; ch. t. of Mzab valley; p. (1966) 30,167.

Ghats, mtn. ranges which border the Deccan plateau in S. **India**. The **Eastern Ghats** are broken by many Rs. and rise only to 1,362 m in Northern Circars. The **Western Ghats** form an almost unbroken range, reaching 2,672 m in Dodabetta in Nilgiri hills; rainfall extremely heavy; forests; hydroelectric power.

Ghaziabad, t., Uttar Pradesh, **India**; on R. Jumna opposite Delhi; p. (1971) 118,836.

Ghazipur, t., Uttar Pradesh, N. **India**; on Ganges, E. of Varanasi; p. (1961) 37,147.

Ghaznī, mtn. t., E. **Afghanistan**; once cap. of empire of Mahmud, *c.* A.D. 1000; now mkt. t.; p. (est. 1969) 43,423.

Ghent, c., cap. of E. Flanders prov., **Belgium**; pt. at confluence of Rs. Scheldt and Lys; cath., univ.; textiles, steel, plastics, chemicals; oil refinery; p. (est. 1969) 151,614 (c.), 228,100 (met. a.).

Ghor, El, depression, **Jordan** and **Israel** between Sea of Galilee and Dead Sea 3–24 km wide; agr. resettlement scheme.

Giant's Causeway, basaltic columns on promontory of N. cst. of Moyle, **N. Ireland**.

Gibraltar, City of, Brit. terr. at W. entrance to Mediterranean; rocky I., 426 m, joined to Spain by sandy isthmus; few natural resources; economy depends on tourism, Admiralty dockyard, services to shipping, and entrepot tr.; Spanish govt. lays claim to terr.; a. 6·5 km²; p. (1971) 28,964.

Gibraltar, Strait of, connects Mediterranean with Atl., 13·6 km wide; of strategic importance.

Gidgelpha-Moomba, dist., S. **Australia**; lge. natural gas field; pipeline to Adelaide.

Giessen, t., Hesse, **W. Germany**; on R. Lahn; univ.; tobacco, engin., textiles; p. (est. 1969) 74,380.

Gifu, t., Central Honshu, **Japan**; cas.; fans, lanterns, textiles; tourism for cormorant fishing; p. (est. 1971) 393,000.

Gigha., I, Argyll and Bute, **Scot.**; off W. cst. of Kintyre; 10 km by 3 km.

Gijón, spt., Oviedo, **Spain**; on Bay of Biscay; gd. harbour; tobacco, petroleum, coal, earthenware; steel wks. nearby; p. (1967) 144,987.

Gila, R., N.M. and Arizona, **USA**; trib. of R. Colorado; used for irrigation in Imperial valley; 1,040 km long.

Gilan, prov., N.W. **Iran**; on Caspian Sea, bounded by USSR; sub-tropical climate; agr., inc. cotton and rice; cap Rasht; p. (1967) 754,650.

Gilbert Is., Brit. col. terr., internal self-gov. delayed by Ocean I. dispute; central **Pac. Oc.**; chain of coral Is. across equator; economy based on phosphate mng. and copra; cap. Tarawa; Ellice Is. separated 1976 and renamed Tuvalu Is.; a. 956 km²; p. (1968) 53,517.

Gilgit, dist., Kashmir, **India**; mtnous., exceeding 6,000 m on N. and W.; with Ladakh links India with Tibet; p. 77,000.

Gillingham, t., Kent. **Eng.**; 3 km E. of Chatham; Chatham; on R. Medway; naval and military establishments; cement, lt. inds.; p. (1971) 86,714.
Gippsland, dist., S.E. Victoria, **Australia**; mtnous; intensive dairying, pig-rearing, mkt. gardening; a. 36,001 km².
Girardot, t., **Colombia**; R. pt. and airport on upper course of Magdalena R.; linked by rly. to Bogotá; coffee, hides, ceramics; p. (est. 1968) 82,310.
Girgenti. *See* **Agrigento**.
Gironde, dep., S.W. **France**; vineyards, grain, fruit, wines; cap. Bordeaux; a. 10,723 km²; p. (1968) 1,009,390.
Gironde, estuary, S.W. **France**; formed by junc. of Rs. Garonne and Dordogne; navigable to Pauillac and Bordeaux.
Girvan, burgh, Kyle and Carrick, **Scot.**; on F. of Clyde, 29 km S.W. of Ayr; summer resort; p. (1971) 7,410.
Gisborne, t., spt., N.I. **N.Z.**; on Poverty Bay, 96 km N.E. of Napier; freezing-wks.; fishing; p. (1971) 25,709.
Giuba, R. *See* **Juba R.**
Giurgiu, t., **Romania**; pt. on Danube; opposite Ruse, Bulgaria; linked by oil pipelines with Ploiesti; p. (1966) 32,300.
Givors, t., Rhône dep., **France**; on Rhône R. 16 km S. of Lyons; mnfs.; oil refining near by at Feyzin; p. (1968) 19,048.
Giza, El, t. **Egypt**; on Nile, sub. of Cairo; nr. pyramids of Khufu (Cheops), Khafra (Chephren), and the Sphinx; film ind.; p. (est. 1970) 711,900.
Gjövik, t., S. **Norway**; on L. Mjösa; furniture, footwear, lt. inds.; p. (est. 1970) 25,164.
Glace Bay, t., Cape Breton I., Nova Scotia; **Canada**; coal; fishing harbour; p. (1971) 22,276.
Glacier National Park, B.C., **Canada**; mtn. scenery, resorts; a. 1,349 km².
Glacier National Park, Mon., **USA**; Rocky mtns., picturesque; a. 4,040 km².
Gladbeck, t., N. Rhine-Westphalia, **W. Germany**; N. of Essen; coalmng; p. (est. 1967) 82,500.
Gladstone, t., Queensland, **Australia**; alumina refining, oil, chemicals; p. (1972) 15,365.
Glamis, v., Angus, **Scot.**; G. cas. childhood home of Queen Elizabeth the Queen Mother, and featured in Shakespeare's *Macbeth*.
Glamorgan, former co., S. **Wales**; now divided into 3 cos., **South, West** and **Mid-Glamorgan**.
Glamorgan, Vale of. *See* **Gwent, Plain of**.
Glarus, can., **Switzerland**; E. of Schwyz; a. 684 km²; sheep, cheese, cottons; p. (1969) 42,500.
Glarus, t., cap. of can G. **Switzerland**; on R. Linth, nr. Wessen; p. (1970) 6,189.
Glasgow, c., burgh, l. gov. dist., Strathclyde Reg., **Scot.**; on R. Clyde; leading spt. and 3rd lgst. c. in Gt. Britain; major problems of urban renewal; ctr. of industl. belt; shipbldg., iron and steel, heavy and lt. engin., electronics equipment, printing; univ., cath.; p. (1971) 897,483.
Glas Maol, mtn., Angus, Kincardine and Deeside, **Scot.**; part of the Braes of Angus; 1,068 m.
Glatz. *See* **Klodzko**.
Glauchau, t., Karl-Marx-Stadt, **E. Germany**; on R. Mulde; woollens, calicoes, dyes, machin.; p. (est. 1970) 32,127.
Gleiwitz. *See* **Gliwice**.
Glen Affric, Inverness, **Scot.**; drained E. to Moray F.; hydroelectric scheme.
Glencoe, Lochaber, **Scot.**; S.E. of Ballachulish; scene of massacre of MacDonalds 1692.
Glendale, c., Cal., **USA**; science-based inds.; p. (1970) 132,752, now inc. in Los Angeles met. a.
Glendalough, Wicklow, **R.o.I.**; scenic valley with Ls. and monastic ruins; round tower; tourism.
Glenelg, t., S. **Australia**; on St. Vincent G.; sub. of Adelaide; first free settlement in Australia; p. (1966) 14,800
Glen Garry, Perth and Kinross, **Scot.**; used by Perth to Inverness rly. on S. approach to Drumochter Pass.
Glen More, Scottish valley traversed by Caledonian canal, from Fort William to Inverness.
Glenrothes, t., Kirkaldy, **Scot.**; new t. (1948); coal, transistors, mng. machin., photoprecision ind.; p. (est. 1974) 32,500 .
Glen Roy, Lochaber, **Scot.**; 24 km N.E. of Fort William; remarkable terraces, remains of series of glacial lakes.
Glen Spean, Lochaber, **Scot.**; used by Glasgow to Fort William rly.
Glittertind, mtn., Opland co., S. **Norway**; highest peak in Scandinavia; alt. 2,483 m.
Gliwice (Gleiwitz), c. S.W. **Poland** (since 1945); coal mng. and steel ctr. of Katowice region; machin., chemicals; p. (1970) 171,000.
Glomma (Glommen), R., S. **Norway**; lgst. R. in Scandinavia; flows to Skaggerak; timber inds.; hydroelec. power; 400 km long.
Glossop, t., Derbys., **Eng.**; at foot of Pennines; paper, food-canning, textile finishing; mkt.; p. (1971) 24,174.
Gloucester, cath. c., **Eng.**; on R. Severn; the Roman Glevum; cath., on site of Benedictine abbey; aircraft mftg. and repair; engin., nylon; p. (1971) 90,134.
Gloucester, t., Mass., **USA**; pt. at head of G. Harbour; resort fish-processing; p. (1970) 27,941.
Gloucestershire, non-met. co., W. **Eng.**; situated around lower Severn basin, Cotswolds, Forest of Dean; sheep, dairy and fruit farming; major ctrs. of p. at Gloucester and Cheltenham; a. 2,639 km²; p. (1971) 463,000.
Glyncorrwg, t., West Glamorgan, **Wales**; 6 km N. of Maesteg; coal-mng. dist.; p. (1971) 8,642.
Glynde, v., Sussex, **Eng.**; nearby Tudor manor and opera house of Glyndebourne.
Gmünd. *See* **Schwäbish-Gmünd**.
Gniezno (Gnesen), c., **W. Poland**; E. of Poznan; first cap. of Poland (11th cent.); cath.; p. (1970) 50,600.
Goa, Daman and Diu, terr., **India**; former Portuguese enclaves; iron pyrites, manganese, coconuts, fish, spices, cashew nuts, salt, copra; a. 3,693 km²; p. (1971) 857,791.
Goat Fell, mtn., I. of Arran, Cunninghame, **Scot.**; alt. 874 m.
Gobi, steppes and stony or sandy desert, **China** and **Mongolia**; divided into two principal divs.; Shamo in Central Mongolia, and the basins of the Tarim, E. Turkestan; l. about 2,400 km (E. to W.), breadth 800–1,120 km; average elevation 1,200 m; crossed by Kalgan–Ulan Bator highway.
Godalming, t., Surrey, **Eng.**; 6 km S.W. of Guildford; first public supply of elec. 1881; Charterhouse School; p. (1971) 18,634.
Godavari, sacred R., **India**; rises in W. Ghats, flows E. across Deccan through gap in E. Ghats to Bay of Bengal; forms lge. delta; used for irrigation and hydroelec. power; *c.* 1,440 km long.
Godesberg, Bad, t., N. Rhine-Westphalia, **W. Germany**; nr. Bonn; spa; meeting place of Chamberlain and Hitler 1938; p. (est. 1969) 73,512.
Godhavn, Danish settlement, Disco I., W. of Greenland; arctic research sta.; fish processing.
Godstone, v., Surrey, **Eng.**; nr. Reigate; p. (1971) 43,706 (dist.).
Godthåb t., admin. ctr., **Greenland**; first Danish col. 1721; sm. pt.; fish processing; p. (est. 1968) 6,104.
Godwin Austen, Mt. or **K2**, peak (8,616 m) in Karakoram between Tibet and Sinkiang, China, after Everest highest in world; summit reached by Prof. Desio 1954; also named Chobrum.
Gogmagog Hills, Cambs., **Eng.**; low chalk upland, S. of Breckland; traces of Roman entrenchment.
Gogra. *See* **Ghaghara R.**
Goiana, t., Pernambuco st. **Brazil**; p. (est. 1968) 47,631.
Goiânia, t., cap. of Goiás st., **Brazil**; comm. and industl. ctr.; p. (1970) 362,152.
Goiás, st., central **Brazil**; mtnous., forested; stock-raising, tobacco; gold, diamonds; cap. Goiânia, on Vermelho R.; a. 642,061 km²; p. (est. 1968) 2,745,711.
Gökçeada I. (Imbroz I.), off W. Turkey, in Ægean Sea at entrance to Dardanelles; a. 280 km²; p. (est. 1970) 1,856.
Golborne, t., Lancs., **Eng.**; man-made fibres; p. (1971) 28,178.
Golconda, fort and ruined c., nr. Hyderabad, S. **India**; famous for its legendary diamond troves.
Gold Coast, c., Queensland and N.S.W., **Australia**; tourist ctr.; p. (1972) 74,121.
Golden Gate, strait, between San Francisco Bay

and Pac. Oc., Cal., **USA**; spanned by Golden Gate Bridge, opened 1937.

Golden Horn, peninsula on the Bosporus, forming the harbour of Istanbul, **Turkey.**

Golden Triangle, a. of Britain and Europe roughly bounded by Birmingham, Frankfurt, and Paris: economic core a. of W. **Europe.**

Golden Vale, dist., Limerick, Tipperary, **R.o.I.**; drained W. to Shannon and E. to Suir; rich farming a., beef and dairy cattle, pigs.

Gold River, t., B.C., **Canada**; on W cst. of Vancouver I. at junc. of Heber and Gold Rs.; new t. 1967.

Golspie, co. t., Sutherland, **Scot.**; p. (1971) 3,186 (inc. Rogart and Lairg).

Gomal Pass, a pass in Sulaiman ranges, **Pakistan,** leading from Indus valley to Afghanistan.

Gomel', c., S.E. Belorussiyan SSR, **USSR**; on R. Sozh, trib. of Dnieper; R. pt., agr. ctr.; engin., chemicals, clothing inds.; p. (1970) 272,000.

Gomera, I., Canaries; 21 km S.W. Tenerife; cap. San Sebastian; p. (1970) 19,389.

Gondar, t., N.W. **Ethiopia**; N. of L. Tana; airport; p. (est. 1970) 35,331.

Goodwin Sands, dangerous sandbanks off E. cst. of Kent, **Eng.**; shielding the Down roadstead.

Goodwood, v., West Sussex, **Eng.**; racecourse and motor racing; home of Dukes of Richmond.

Goole, t., Humberside, **Eng.**; second pt. to Hull on Humber; shipbldg., flour milling, fertilisers, alum and dextrine mftg.; p. (1971) 18,066.

Goonhilly Downs, Cornwall, **Eng.**; satellite communications sta. of Post Office.

Goose Bay, t., Labrador, **Canada**; on Churchill R., international airpt.

Göppingen, t., Baden-Württemberg, **W. Germany**; between Ulm and Stuttgart; machin., iron, wood, chemicals; p. (est. 1969) 47,119.

Gorakhpur, t., Uttar Pradesh, **India**; on Rapti R., N. of Varanasi; grain, timber; fertilisers; univ.; p. (1971) 230,911.

Gore Peninsula, N.T., **Australia**; N.E. extremity of Arnhem Land; bauxite deposits and new t.; alumina plant.

Gorgān, c., **Iran**, Mazandaran prov.; nr. Caspian Sea; p. (1967) 300,878 (met. a.).

Gori, t., central Georgian SSR, **USSR**; at confluence of Bolshoy, Liakhvi, and Kura Rs.; birthplace of Stalin; p. (1968) 33,100.

Gorinchem, t., S. Holland, **Neth.**; on R. Waal; p. (1967) 24,786.

Goring Gap, Berks./Oxon., **Eng.**; where R. Thames cuts through Chilterns and Berkshire Downs.

Gorizia (Görz), c., cap. of Gorizia prov., N.E. **Italy**; on Yugoslav border; cas.; agr. mkt., fruit, wine; cotton mills, textile machin.; p. (1969) 43,655.

Gorki or **Gorky** (formerly Nizhni-Novgorod), c., **RSFSR**; cap. of forested G. region, on Rs. Oka and Volga; univ., churches, 13th cent. kremlin; gr. industl. ctr. with heavy engin., steel, textiles, chemicals, oil refining, cars, glass, timber inds.; birthplace of Maxim Gorky; p. (1970) 1,170,000.

Görlitz, t., **E. Germany**; on W. Neisse on Polish border; lignite mines; textile mills; religious mystic Jacob Boehme lived here; p. (1968) 88,824.

Gorlovka, t., Ukrainian SSR, **USSR**; in Donets Basin; coal, chemicals, engin.; oil pipeline connects with Grozny oilfields; p. (1970) 335,000; (1970) 362,000 (met. a.).

Gorno-Altai, aut. region, S.E. Altai terr., **RSFSR**; in Altai mtns. on Mongolian border; cap. Gorno-Altaisk; forested, pastoral agr., mng. (gold, manganese, mercury); a. 92,567 km; p. (1970) 168,000.

Gorno-Altaisk, t., **RSFSR**; cap. of Gorno-Altai aut. region; nr. Chuya highway to Mongolia; food-processing of agr. prod. from region; p. (1970) 34,000.

Gorno Badakhshan, aut. region, S.E. Tadzhik SSR, **USSR**; in Pamirs, bordered by China and Afghanistan; mng. (gold, mica, salt, limestone); livestock; cap. Khorog; a. 63,688 km^2; p. (1970) 98,000.

Gornyy Snezhnogorsk, t., **RSFSR**; new t. in Siberian Arctic on R. Hantaiki, 56 km W.N.W. Komsomolsk; tin-mng.

Gorseinon, v., West Glamorgan, **S. Wales**; nr. Loughour estuary, 6 km N.W. of Swansea; steel-wks., zinc refineries.

Gorzów Wielkopolski (Landesberg an der Warthe), c., **W. Poland** (since 1945); industl. ctr.; lignite mines; p. (1970) 74,300.

Gosainthan (Sisha Pangma), mtn. massif, **Nepal–Tibet (China)** border; part of Himalayas; rises to 8,091 m.

Gosford-Woy Woy, t., N.S.W., **Australia**; 80 km N. of Sydney; resort and commuter t.; food processing, bldg. materials; p. (1972) 38,093.

Gosforth, t., sub. to Newcastle upon Tyne, Tyne and Wear, **Eng.**; coal; p. (1971) 26,826.

Goslar, t., Lower Saxony, **W. Germany**; mng. ctr. at foot of Harz mtns.; lt. inds., tourism; p. (est. 1967) 40,900.

Gosport, t., Hants., **Eng.**; naval depot W. of Portsmouth to which it is linked by ferry; marine engin.; p. (1971) 75,974.

Göta, R. **Sweden**; flows from L. Vänern to the Kattegat; also canal connecting L. Vänern with the Baltic; the G. Canal provides a popular tourist trip from Stockholm to Göteborg.

Götaland, southernmost of 3 old provs. of **Sweden**; a. 101,010 km^2; name used only in weather forecasts.

Göteborg or **Gothenburg,** c., cap. of Göteborg and Bohus, S.W. **Sweden**; at mouth of R. Göta on Kattegat; second c. in Sweden for commerce and ind.; univ.; shipbldg., oil refining; deepwater tanker terminal; p. (1970) 446,875 (c.), (est. 1969) 661,308 (met. a.).

Göteborg and Bohus, co., **Sweden**; on cst. of Kattegat; a. 5,152 km^2; p. (est. 1970) 699,395.

Gotha, t., Erfurt, **E. Germany**; iron, machin., engin., musical instruments, textiles, porcelain, printing, cartography; p. (est. 1967) 57,400.

Gotham, v., Notts., **Eng.**; gypsum mng. and plaster wks.

Gotland, I. in the Baltic, **Sweden**; many historic bldgs.; cap. Visby; tourism; a. 3,173 km^2; p. (1968) 53,939.

Göttingen, t., Lower Saxony, **W. Germany**; univ.; scientific instruments, pharmaceutics, film studios; p. (est. 1969) 114,000.

Gottwaldov (Zlin), t., **ČSSR**; 64 km E. of Brno; footwear, leather and domestic woodware inds.; home of Bata footwear; p. (1967) 64,000.

Gouda, t., S. Holland, **Neth.**; on R. IJssel, 18 km from Rotterdam; cheese, candles, ceramics, pipes; p. (1968) 46,262.

Gough I., Atl. Oc. dependency of St. Helena; breeding ground of the great shearwater; guano.

Goulburn, t., N.S.W., **Australia**; commands route across Gr. Dividing Range; in agr. dist. W. of Sydney; cath.; wool, shoes; p. (1972) 21,568.

Goulburn Is., N.T., **Australia**; 2 sm. Is. off N. cst. of Arnhem Land; Methodist Mission sta.

Goulburn R., Victoria, **Australia**; irrigation.

Gourock, burgh, Inverclyde, **Scot.**; on F. of Clyde, 3 km W. of Greenock; ferry to Dunoon; resort; p. (1971) 10,922.

Gower, peninsula, W. Glamorgan, **Wales**; tourism.

Gowrie, Carse of, fertile tract N. side F. of Tay, **Scot.**; includes Dundee, Kinnoul, Perth.

Gozo, I. in Mediterranean, belonging to **Malta**; the anc. Gaulos; surrounded by perpendicular cliffs; a. 67 km^2; p. (1961) 27,506.

Graaff-Reinet, t., Cape Prov., **S. Africa**; fruit-growing, wool; p. (est. 1967) 17,700.

Grado-Aquileia, t., Friuli-Venezia Giulia, N.E. **Italy**; pleasure resort and former Roman spt.; rich in early Christian mosaics and antiquities; Grado joined to mainland by bridge; p. (est. 1968) 10,065.

Graengesberg, dist., Kopparberg co., **Sweden**; on S. fringe of Scandinavian mtns.; iron ore deposits.

Grafton, t., N.S.W., **Australia**; on Clarence R.; dairy prod., timber; p. (1972) 16,354.

Graham Land, Falkland Is. Dependencies, **Antarctica**; mtnous., icebound; discovered 1832.

Grahamstown, t., C. Prov., **S. Africa**; univ.; cath ; p. (1970) 41,086.

Graian Alps, mtns. between Savoie, **France** and Piedmont, **Italy**; hgst. point Gran Paradiso, 4,063 m.

Grain Coast, name formerly applied to cst. of Liberia, W. Africa; "grain" refers to pepper, spices, etc.

Grammichele, t., E. Sicily, **Italy**; 37 km S.W. of Catania; planned settlement after 1968 earthquake.

Grampian Region, l. gov. reg., N.E. **Scot.**; inc. former cos. of Aberdeenshire, Banff, Kincardine and Moray; highland a.; rapid devel. of cst. with N. Sea oil discoveries; a. 8,702 km²; p. (1971) 436,995.

Grampians, mtns. of **Scot.**; forming natural bdy. between Highlands and Lowlands; inc. Ben Nevis, the hgst. peak (1,344 m), the Cairngorms and Schiehallion.

Granada, t., W. **Nicaragua**; on L. Nicaragua; in rich agr. region; distilling, soap, furniture; p. (1967) 40,200.

Granada, c., cap. of G. prov., S. **Spain**; in Andalusia, at foot of Sierra Nevada; formerly cap. of Moorish kingdom of G.; univ, cath., famous 14th cent. Alhambra; tourism; p. (est. 1969) 158,477.

Granada, prov., S. **Spain**; traversed by Sierra Nevada; wheat, olives, textiles, liqueurs, paper; a. 12,530 km²; p. (1970) 773,375.

Granby, t., Quebec, **Canada**; on Yamaska R.; sawmills, leather, textiles, rubber, plastics; p. (1966) 34,349.

Gran Chaco, extensive lowland plain, **Argentina, Paraguay**, and **Bolivia**, between Andes and Paraguay–Paraná Rs.; hot, wet, swampy region with forests containing quebracho trees, a source of tannin; potential for petroleum.

Grand Banks, submarine plateau, extending S.E. from Newfoundland, **Canada**; a. 1,295,000 km²; impt. cod fisheries.

Grand Bassam, t. spt., **Ivory Coast**; exp. bananas, palm-kernels; mnf. prefabricated houses; p. (est. 1963) 22,994.

Grand Canal, canal, N. **China**; *c.* 1,600 km long from Tientsin to Hangchow; built between A.D. 605–18 and 1282–92; rebuilt for navigation and flood control.

Grand Canal, main water thoroughfare through Venice, **Italy**.

Grand Canary, I., Canaries; cap. Las Palmas; tomatoes, bananas, potatoes; tourism; extinct volcanoes; p. (1970) 519,606.

Grand Cayman I., **W.I.**; a. 220 km²; coconuts; cap. Georgetown; p. (1966) 7,323.

Grand Combin, mtn. **Switzerland**; part of Pennine Alps nr. Italian border; alt. 4,320 m.

Grand Coulee Dam, Wash., **USA**; on Columbia R., 176 km below Spokane; one of lgst. concrete dams in world (1,924,000 kW); reservoir (Franklin D. Roosevelt Lake) recreational a.; supplies irrigation water to 4,900 km² between Rs. Columbia and Snake.

Grande Chartreuse, limestone massif, Isère, **France**; brandy from monastery of La Grande Chartreuse.

Grand Falls, t., Newfoundland, **Canada**; newsprint; falls provide hydroelectric power; p. (1966) 7,451.

Grand Island, t., Nebraska, **USA**; cattle and grain t.; p. (est. 1969) 30,000.

Grand' Mère, t., Quebec, **Canada**; pulp and paper mills; p. (1971) 17,144.

Grand Prairie. *See* Black Prairie.

Grand Rapids, c., Mich., **USA**; on Grand R.; furniture mkg., car and aircraft parts, chemicals, paper; p. (1970) 195,892 (c.), 535,702 (met. a.).

Grand R., Mich., **USA**; enters L. Mich. at Grand Haven, navigable to Grand Rapids; hydroelec. power; 400 km long.

Grand Turk, I., cap. of **Turks and Caicos Is.**; p. (1970) 2,300.

Grange, t., Cumbria, **Eng.**; on N. cst. of Morecambe Bay; summer resort; p. (1971) 3,627.

Grangemouth, burgh, Falkirk, **Scot.**; on F. of Forth; shipbldg. and repair, marine engin., oil refining, projected oil tanker terminal; petroleum prods., chemicals, pharmaceutics; electronics and elec. ind.; oil pipeline to Finnart; p. (1971) 24,569.

Granite City, Ill., **USA**; iron and steel, tinplate, rly. engin., chemicals; p. (1970) 40,440.

Gran Sasso d'Italia, rugged limestone highlands, Abruzzi e Molise, central **Italy**, in highest part of Apennines, rising to 2,923 m in Monte Corno; Mussolini was rescued from here by German paratroopers 1943; Aquila at foot of Gran Sasso winter sports ctr.

Grantham, t., Lincs., **Eng.**; on Witham R.; tanning, agr. machin., engin., brewing, malting, basket mkg.; expanded t.; p. (1971) 27,913.

Grantown-on-Spey, burgh, Moray, **Scot.**; on R. Spey; resort; p. (1971) 1,600.

Granville, spt., Manche dep., **France**; on Golfe de St. Malo; fisheries, food-processing; p. (1968) 12,715.

Grasmere, v., Cumbria, **Eng.**; at head of Grasmere L.; home of Wordsworth.

Grasse, t., Alpes-Maritimes dep., S.E. **France**, in Provence in hills above Cannes; perfumes; birthplace of Fragonard; p. (1968) 32,096.

Graubünden. *See* **Grisons**.

Graudenz. *See* **Grudziadz**.

's-Gravenhage. *See* **Hague**.

Graves, Pointe de, N. point of Médoc peninsula, **France**; in famous wine dist.

Gravesend, spt., Kent, **Eng.**; S. bank R. Thames facing Tilbury; pilot sta. for Port of London; paper, cement; oil refinery projected; p. (1971) 54,044.

Graz, c., cap. of Styria, **Austria**; on R. Mur at foothills of Alps; second lgst. c.; univ., cath.; machin., iron and steel, rly. wks.; p. (est. 1969) 253,800.

Great Altai, range of mtns., lying mainly in **Outer Mongolia** but also in Western Siberia, **USSR**; rising to 4,200 m.

Great Atlas (Haut Atlas), mtns., N.W. **Africa**; alt. *c.* 2,000 m; part of the Atlas mtns.

Great Australian Basin, artesian basin, **Australia**; underlies plains of Queensland, N.S.W., S. Australia; water supply used on sheep-farms, cattle-ranches, in a. from Normanton in N. to Renmark in S., Oodnadatta in W. to Roma in E.; a. 1,476,300 km².

Great Australian Bight, wide inlet of Indian Oc., S. cst. of Australia.

Great Barrier Reef, coral reef barrier off N.E. cst. of **Australia**; 1,600 km long, 120–160 km from cst.; currently being eaten away by the starfish, *Acanthaster planci*.

Great Basin, high plateau region between the Wasatch and Sierra Nevada mtns., **USA**; inc. most of Nevada, parts of Utah, Cal., Idaho, Ore., Wyo.; inland drainage ctr. Great Salt Lake; a. 543,900 km²; much desert; sparse p.

Great Bear Lake, lge L., N.W. Terr., **Canada**; *c.* 280 km long; a. 36,260 km²; outlet through Great Bear R. to Mackenzie R.

Great Belt (Store Bælt), strait, **Denmark**; separates Fyn I. from Sjaelland I.; sinuous shape makes navigation difficult; rly. ferry at narrowest point (18 km) between Nyborg and Korsør; 64 km long; proposed bridge.

Great Britain. *See* England, Scotland, Wales, British Isles.

Great Dividing Range, mtn. system, E. **Australia**; extends, under different local names, from Queensland to Victoria and separates E. cst. plains from interior; reaches max. alt. in Mt. Koskiusko (2,230 m), in Australian Alps, on bdy. between Victoria and N.S.W.

Greater Manchester, met. co., N.W. **Eng.**; lge. urban a. centred on major comm. ctr. of M., with former cotton spinning ts. to N., inc. Bolton, Bury and Rochdale; dormitory ts. to S.; former concentration on textile mftg. now reduced and inds. diversified; major industl. estate at Trafford Park; p. (1971) 2,727,000.

Great Falls, c., Mont., **USA**; on Missouri R.; lgst c. in st.; mkt. for irrigated farming a.; ctr. of hydroelectric power, called the "electric city"; copper- and oil-refining, flour mills; p. (est. 1969) 61,000.

Great Fisher Bank, submarine sandbank in N. Sea; 320 km E. of Aberdeen, 160 km S.W. of Stavanger; valuable fishing-ground; depth of water, from 45–75 m.

Great Gable, mtn., Cumbria, **Eng.**; alt. 899 m.

Great Harwood, t., Lancs., **Eng.**; 8 km N.E. of Blackburn; textiles, aero-engin.; p. (1971) 11,000.

Great Lake, Tasmania, **Australia**; lgst. freshwater L. in Australia.

Great Lakes, N. **America**; 5 freshwater Ls.; Superior, Michigan, Huron, Erie, Ontario; glacial genesis; frozen 4 to 5 months in winter; traffic in cereals, iron, coal, etc.; major ctr. of heavy inds.; resorts; serious pollution; a. 248,640 km².

Great Plains, lowland a. of central N. **America**; extending E. from Rocky mtns. and S. from Mackenzie to S. Texas; stock rearing, grain, oilfields.

Great Rift Valley, geological fault system extending from S.W. Asia to E. Africa, 4,800 km in l.; inc. L. Tiberias (Sea of Galilee), Jordan valley, Dead Sea, G. of Aqaba, Red Sea, and chain of Ls., notably L. Rudolf and L. Malawi; a branch runs through Ls. Tanganyika, Mobutu and Idi Amin Dada.

Great St. Bernard. *See* St. Bernard Pass, Gt.

Great Salt Lake, shallow salty L., N. Utah, **USA**; in Great Basin plateau of N. America; remnant of L. Bonneville; alt. 1,286 m; varies in size and depth; receives Bear, Jordan and Beaver Rs.; many Is., no outlet.

Great Slave Lake, N.W. Terr., **Canada**; a. 28,490 km^2; 496 km long; drained by Mackenzie R.; navigable.

Great Smoky Mtns., Tenn., **USA**; with Blue Ridge mtns. form E. zone of Appalachian mtn. system; hgst peak Clingmans Dome 2,026 m; largely preserved as Nat Park.

Great Torrington, t., Devon, **Eng**.; on R. Torridge; mkt., processing of agr. prod.; p. (1971) 3,536.

Great Wall of China, wall built in N. China along S. edge of Mongolian plateau to keep out invading Mongols; length 2,400 km; begun in Ch'in dynasty by Shih Huang Ti, *c.* 220 B.C.; present form dates from Ming dynasty (1368–1644).

Great Whale R. (R. de la Baleine), Quebec, **Canada**; rises in L. Bienville, flows to Hudson Bay; difficult transport; 400 km long.

Great Yarmouth. *See* Yarmouth.

Greece, rep., S.E. **Europe**; mtnous. peninsula, between Mediterranean and Ægean Sea, inc. many sm. Is. to S., lgst. Crete; inds. increasingly impt. but agr. prods. still ch. exp. (tobacco, olive oil, cotton, citrus fruit, wine); only 25 per cent a. cultivable; economy also helped by lge. merchant fleet and tourism; deposed king in exile; executive power held by military junta 1967–74; cap. Athens; a. 132,561 km^2; p. (1971) 8,736,367.

Greenland, I., between Arctic Oc. and Baffin Bay; lofty ice-capped plateau; peopled by coastal settlements of Eskimos; fisheries; whale oil, seal skins; lge. uranium deposits, potential for petroleum; some coal, lead, zinc; US base at Thule; part of Danish kingdom; cap Godthåb; a. 2,175,600 km^2 of which 1,833,720 km^2 are under a permanent ice-cap; p. (1966) 39,600.

Greenland Sea, Arctic Oc., between Greenland and Spitzbergen; ice-covered.

Green Mtns., Vt., **USA**; part of Appalachians reaching 1,340 m (Mt. Mansfield); Nat. Forest, tourism.

Greenock, spt., burgh, Inverclyde, **Scot.**; on S. shore of F. of Clyde, 40 km W. of Glasgow; container facilities; shipbldg., sugar refining, woollens, chemicals, aluminium casting, tinplate inds.; birthplace of James Watt; p. (1971) 69,502.

Green River, Wyo., Utah, **USA**; rises in Wind R. Range (major watershed in Rockies); flows via spectacular scenery to Colorado R.; impt. routeway; 1,168 km long.

Greensboro', c., N.C., **USA**; cotton, tobacco, chemicals; regional financial ctr.; educational institutes; p. (1970) 140,672 (c.), 598,905 (met. a.).

Greenville, t., Miss., **USA**; on Mississippi R.; deep-water harbour; tr. ctr. for cotton, agr. prod.; chemicals, metal gds.; p. (est. 1969) 44,000.

Greenville, t., S.C., **USA**; univ.; industl. and comm. ctr.; textile mills, farm prod. processing; p. (1970) 61,242 (c.), 294,220 (met. a.).

Greenwich, inner bor., London, **Eng.**; inc. most of former bor. of Woolwich on S. bank of R. Thames; famous for its hospital, observatory (now moved to Herstmonceux) and R.N. College; longitudes conventionally calculated from Greenwich meridian; p. (1971) 216,441.

Greenwich Village, lower Manhattan, N.Y. city, **USA**; bohemian quarter.

Greifswald, spt., Rostock, **E. Germany**; on Baltic inlet; shipbldg., textiles, wood inds.; p. (est. 1967) 45,800.

Greiz, t., Gera, **E. Germany**; paper, textiles, chemicals; p. (est. 1970) 39,058.

Grenada, W.I., most S. of Windward Is.; inc. archipelago of Grenadines; known as the "spice islands" as major exp. is nutmeg; cloves and vanilla also grown; sugar and sugar prods.; cotton-ginning; cap. St. George's; former Brit. col., achieved indep. 1974; a. 344 km^2; p. (1970) 104,000.

Grenadines, dependency of Grenada I., W.I.; gr. of over 100 sm. Is., between Grenada and St. Vincent. Windward Is.; sea-island cotton.

Grenoble, c., cap. of Isère dep., S.E. **France**; on Isère R.. at foot of Alps; univ.; thriving cultural and scientific ctr.; impt. hydroelectric ctr.; science-based inds., joint Franco-German nuclear research reactor; gloves, paper, cement, liqueurs; p. (1968) 161,616 (c.), 332,423 (met. a.).

Gretna Green, v., Annandale and Eskdale, **Scot.**; on Eng. border; famous as place of runaway marriages 1754–1856.

Greymouth, spt., S.I., **N.Z.**; on W. cst. at mouth of Grey R.; ch. t. prov. of Westland; coal; p (1971) 7,739.

Grey Range, mtns., S.W. Queensland, **Australia**; forms divide between streams draining E. to R. Darling and those draining W. to L. Eyre.

Grimaldi, caves, N.W. **Italy**; remains of prehistoric man, late Paleolithic, found there.

Grimsby, spt., Humberside, **Eng.**; on S. bank o R. Humber; major distant waters fish. pt.; food-processing; chemical ind. at nearby Immingham; p. (1971) 95,685.

Grindelwald, v., Bernese Oberland, **Switzerland**; tourist ctr.; p. (1970) 3,511.

Gris-Nez, C., N.E. **France**; nearest point on Fr. cst. to Dover.

Grisons (Graubünden), can., E. **Switzerland**; region of glaciers and magnificent peaks; ch. resorts Davos, Arosa, St. Moritz; Swiss Nat. Park; lgst can.; sparse p.; ctr. Romansch language; a. 7,112 km^2; p. (1969) 153,000.

Grodno, c., W. Belorussiyan SSR, **USSR**; pt. on Neman R.; a Polish t. until 1939; machine parts, cloth; historic bldgs.; p. (1970) 132,000.

Groningen, c., cap. of G. prov., **Neth.**; univ.; impt. trading ctr.; p. (est. 1969) 168,256 (c.), 200,532 (met. a.).

Groningen, prov., N.E. **Neth.**; agr. and dairying; major natural gas deposits at Slochteren; a. 2,157 km^2; p. (1968) 511,753.

Groote Eylandt, I., G. of Carpentaria; off cst. of N.T., **Australia**; manganese ore-mng.

Grosseto, t., cap. of G. prov., Tuscany, **Italy**; cath.; agr. mkt.; severely affected by floods 1966; p. (1969) 61,534.

Gross Glockner, mtn. (3,801 m) and pass (2,370 m), **Austria**, part of Hohe Tauern range; hgst. peak in Austria.

Groznyy, t., N. Caucasia, **RSFSR**; on R. Terek; naphtha wells, refinery, engin.; starting point of oil pipelines to Makhachkala, Tuapse and Gorlovka; p. (1970) 341,000.

Grudziadz (Graudenz), t., on R. Vistula, Bydgoszcz, **Poland**; mftg.; p. (1970) 75,500.

Grünberg. *See* **Zielona Góra.**

Gruyères, dist., can. Fribourg, **Switzerland**; cattle; cheese.

Guadalajara, c., cap. of Jalisco st., W. **Mexico**; *c.* 1,500 m high; impt. industl. and comm. ctr.; textiles, agr. processing, traditional pottery and glassware; cath.; gas pipeline from Salamanca; health resort; p. (1970) 1,196,218.

Guadalajara, c., cap. of G. prov., **Spain**; on Henares R., N. of Madrid; palace of Mendoza family; battle of Spanish Civil War, March 1937, fought nearby; p. (1970) 31,917.

Guadalaviar, R.. E. **Spain**; flows into Mediterranean, below Valencia; 208 km long.

Guadalcanal, volcanic I., **Pac. Oc.**; lgst. of Solomon Is.; jungle and mtns.; exp. copra; ch. t. Honiara.

Guadalquivir, R. S. **Spain**; flows through Andalusia via Seville to Atl.; *c.* 560 km long; hydroelec. plants; agr.

Guadalupe Hidalgo, place of pilgrimage, N.W. Mexico City, **Mexico**; basilica and shrine; treaty ending Mexican–U.S. war signed here 1848.

Guadarrama, Sierra de, mtn. range, central **Spain**; rugged, forest covered; affects Madrid's climate; reaches 2,431 m.

Guadeloupe, overseas dep. France, **W.I.**; comprises most S. of Leeward gr., Basse-Terre, Grande-Terre, Marie-Galante and other Is.; economy based on sugar exports to France; rapidly rising p. aggravates process of econ. development; attempts to develop tourism and food-processing inds.; ch. comm. ctr. and pt. Pointe à Pitre (Grande Terre); cap. Basse-Terre; a. 1,748 km²; p. (1967) 312,724.

Guadiana, R., forms part of Spanish and Portuguese frontier; flows into G. of Cádiz; Estremadura valley reclamation scheme in progress; 816 km long.

Guadiana del Caudillo, new t., nr. Badajoz, **Spain**.

Guam, I., U.S. air and naval base in **W. Pac.**; developing tourist ind.; free-port and tax incentives aid investment; ch. t. Agaña; a. 541 km²; p. (1968) 58,598.

Guanabara, st., S.E. **Brazil**; cap. Rio de Janeiro; formerly the Fed. Dist., before Brasilia became the cap.; a. 1,357 km²; p. (est. 1968) 4,207,322.

Guanajuato, st., central **Mexico**; average elevation 1,800 m; mng. (silver, gold, tin, copper, iron, lead, opals); a. 30,572 km²; p. (1969) 2,326,000.

Guanajuato, cap. of G. st., **Mexico**; 1,990 m high in gorge; resort; p. (1970) 65,258.

Guantánamo, c., S.E. **Cuba**; sugar, coffee, bananas, cacao; pt. at Caimanera on G. Bay; p. (est. 1967) 135,100.

Guaporé, R., **Brazil**; rises in Mato Grosso st., forms Brazil–Bolivia bdy. before joining the Mamoré; length 1,440 km.

Guatemala, rep., **Central America**; straddles Central American isthmus; interior mtnous. with temperate climate; coastal lowlands hot and humid; economy based on agr., coffee accounting for half exp.; timber exploitation, food processing; two oil refineries; trades mainly with USA. ch. pts. Puerto Barrios, San José. Santo Tomas de Castilla; 4 univs.; cap. Guatemala City; a. 108,889 km²; p. (est. 1975) 6,090,000.

Guatemala City, c., cap. of G. rep.; cath., univ.; fruit and vegetable mkts.; coffee tr., mftg.; remains of Mayan civilisation; partially destroyed by earthquake (1976); p. (est. 1970) 730,991.

Guayama, t., **Puerto Rico**; ctr. of agr. region; sugar-milling and food-processing; p. (1970) 36,159.

Guayaquil, ch. pt., **Ecuador**; cap. of Guayas prov. on Guayas R., nr. Bay of G.; recent new pt. nearby and improvement to transport in hinterland; univ., cath.; sawmills, foundries, machin., brewing, oil refinery; p. (est. 1972) 860,600.

Gubin (Polish **Guben**), border t., **E. Germany/Poland**, on R. Neisse; comm. ctr.; textiles, machin., leather, synthetic fibre.

Gudbrandsdal, valley, S. **Norway**; leads S.E. from Dovrefjell towards Oslo; drained by R. Logan; used by main road Oslo to Trondheim; provides relatively lge. a. of cultivable land; hay, oats, barley, dairy cattle; 368 km long.

Guelph, t., Ont., **Canada**; on Speed R.; univ.; mkt. ctr. in rich farming a.; cloth, elec. equipment; p. (1971) 58,364.

Guernsey, I., Channel Is., between cst. of France and Eng., tomatoes, grapes (under glass), flowers, cattle, tourist resort, t. and ch. spt. St. Peter Port; banking; a. 6,335 ha; p. (est. 1973) 52,000.

Guerrero, st., S. **Mexico**; on Pac. cst.; mtnous.; cereals, cotton, coffee, tobacco; cap. Chilpancingo; ch. pt. Acapulco; a. 64,452 km; p. (1969) 1,620 000.

Guiana Highlands, platueau, **S. America**; extend c. 1,440 km from E. to W. across S. parts of Venezuela, Guyana, Surinam, Fr. Guiana; steep sides, rounded tops c. 900 m but rise to 2,852 m in Mt. Roraima; chiefly composed of crystalline rocks rich in minerals.

Guienne, former prov., **France**, partly coincides with the Aquitaine basin (q.v.); controlled by England 1154–1451.

Guildford, co. t., Surrey, **Eng.**; 48 km S.W. London; on gap cut by R. Wey through N. Downs, cath., univ.; vehicles, agr. implements, lt. inds.; residtl., cas.; p. (1971) 56,887.

Guinea, rep., **W. Africa**; climate hot and humid on cst. but temperate in higher interior; 95 per cent p. engaged in agr., but bauxite dominates exp. from deposits at Boké; hydroelectric dam and aluminium smelter at Konkouré; all foreigners barred from business in G. (1968); poorly developed transport system; major spt. at cap. Conakry; socialist economic policies have been adopted since independence from France (1958); a. 245,861 km²; p. (est. 1970) 4,000,000.

Guinea, gen. name for W. African coastlands from Senegal to Angola.

Guinea-Bissau, formerly Portuguese Guinea, **W. Africa**; indep. 1974; poor econ. infrastructure; no manf. inds.; depends on agr. of rice, groundnuts and stock raising; cst. edged by mangroves; offshore oil potential; a. 36,125 km² p. (est. 1969) 550,000.

Guinea, Spanish. *See* Equatorial Guinea.

Guinea Current, ocean current, flows W. to E. along Guinea cst., diverted away from cst. in Bight of Benin by C. Three Points.

Guinea, Gulf of, arm of Atl. Oc. formed by gr. bend of cst. of W. Africa between Ivory Coast and Gabon; Bight of Benin and Bight of Bonny are inner bays.

Guisborough, t., Cleveland, **Eng.**; at foot of Cleveland hills; former ctr. of iron-mng.; 12 cent. abbey ruins; p. (1971) 13,852.

Gujarat, st. **India**; formerly part of Bombay st.; cap. temporarily Ahmedabad; new cap. Gandhinager, 21 km N. of A. under construction; oil development in Cambay area; fertiliser plant projected; a. 187,115 km²; p. (1971) 26,661,000.

Gujranwala, c., **Pakistan**; N. of Lahore; power plant, engin.; p. (1969) 289,000.

Gujrat, t., Rawalpindi, **Pakistan**; agr. ctr., handicraft inds.; p. (est. 1969) 73,000.

Gulbarga, t., Karnataka, **India**; cotton, flour, paint; (1971) 145,588.

Gulfport, t., Miss., **USA**; pt. of entry; exp. wood, cottonseed; mnfs., textiles, fertilisers; resort; p. (est. 1969) 47,000.

Gulf Stream, warm current of the Atl. Oc., issuing from G. of Mexico by Fla. Strait. *See* L50.

Guntur, c., Andhra Pradesh, **India**; on E. cst. N. of Madras; cotton mkt.; p. (1971) 269,991.

Gur'yev, c., Kazakh SSR, **USSR**; pt. on R. Ural at entrance to Caspian Sea; oil refining; pipeline to Orsk; p. (1970) 113,000.

Gus-Khrustalnyy, t., **RSFSR**; 64 km S. of Vladimir; impt. ctr. of glass ind.; p. (est. 1969) 65,000.

Güstrow, t., Schwerin, **E. Germany**; S. of Rostock; cas., cath.; mkt. t.; p. (est. 1970) 37,213.

Gütersloh, t., N. Rhine–Westphalia, **W. Germany**; nr. Bielefeld; silk and cotton inds.; famous for its Pumpernickel (Westphalian rye bread); machin., furniture, publishing, metallurgy; p. (est. 1967) 55,200.

Guyana, rep., N. cst. **S. America**; former Brit. col.; largely covered by dense jungle. p. concentrated on narrow coastal belt; economy based on agr., especially sugar and rice; forestry inds. limited by lack of transport; impt. bauxite deposits; high birth-rate creates social and economic problems, especially on overpopulated coastal belt; airport at Timehri; univ. at Turkeyen; cap. Georgetown; a. 214,970 km²; p. (est. 1970) 721,098.

Gwalior, t., Madhya Pradesh, **India**; adjoins Lashkar (q.v.); dominated by rock of Gwalior with Jain sculptures; p. (1971) 384,722 (t.), 406,140 (met. a.).

Gwelo, t., **Rhodesia**; ctr. of farming dist.; shoes, glass, containers; p. (1967) 39,500.

Gwent, co., S.E. **Wales**; inc. most of Monmouth and sm. part of Brecon; upland in N. where coalfield and former mng. ts., lowland a. bordering Severn estuary to S. where lge. industl. ts. inc. Newport; a. 1,375 km² (1971) 439 903.

Gwent, Plain of (Vale of Glamorgan), lowland dist., South and Mid Glamorgan, S. **Wales**; lies S. of moorland of S. Wales coalfield, extends E. into Monmouth; fertile soils; mixed farming except in industl. areas of Cardiff, Barry.

Gwynedd, co., N.W. **Wales**; comprises former cos. of Anglesey, Caernarvon, most of Merioneth and a sm. part of Denbigh; mtnous. a. except cst. and Anglesey; inc. Snowdonia Nat. Park; sparse p. inland where hill farming; cstl. resorts inc. Llandudno; a. 3,867 km²; p. (1971) 219,895.

Gympie, t., Queensland, **Australia**; on Mary R., 106 m. from Brisbane; former goldfield; now dairying and pastoral dist., tropical fruits, especially pineapples; p. (1972) 11,131.

Györ, t., **Hungary**; at confluence of Rs. Rába and Danube; cath.; textile ctr., rolling stock, chemicals, machine tools; p. (1968) 80,000.

H

Haarlem, c., cap. of N. Holland prov., **Neth.**; nr. N. Sea cst.; tulip-growing, textiles, printing; 15th cent. church; p. (est. 1969) 172,588 (c.), 239,089 (met. a.).
Hachinohe, c., Honshu, **Japan**; cas.; fishing, fish-processing, metal-refining; p. (est. 1971) 217,000.
Hackney, inner bor., N.E. London, **Eng.**; incorporates former bors. of Shoreditch and Stoke Newington; furniture, clothing, p. (1971) 216,659.
Haddington, burgh, E. Lothian, **Scot.**; on R. Tyne, 26 km E. of Edinburgh; woollen mnf.; grain mkt., corn mills, lt. engin., hosiery; p. (1971) 6,501.
Haderslev, t., Denmark; tobacco, clothing, knitted gds.; p. (est. 1970) 29,647.
Hadhramaut, dist., S. Yemen; ch. pt. and c. Al Mukallā; fertile coastal valley; frankincense, aloes, tobacco, shawls, carpets; p. (1961) 240,000.
Hadleigh, t., Suffolk **Eng.**; mkt.; flour-milling; p. (1971) 5,101.
Hadrian's Wall, part of frontier barrier, **N. Eng.**; stretching across Tyne–Solway isthmus, 118 km long. *See* **Roman Walls, Section L.**
Hafnarfjördur, t., S. of Reykjavik, **Iceland**; p. (1970) 9,696.
Hagen, t., N. Rhine-Westphalia, **W. Germany**; N.E. of Wuppertal; iron, steel, chemicals, textiles, paper; p. (est. 1969) 201,500.
Hagerstown, t., Md., **USA**; machin., furniture, chemicals, aircraft; p. (1970) 35,862.
Hagersville, t., Ont., **Canada**; main producer of gypsum in Canada.
Hagfors, t., Värmland, **Sweden**; site of lge. iron and steel wks. since 1878.
Hague, The or 's-Gravenhage or Den Haag, c., S. Holland, **Neth.**; seat of government; permanent court of international justice; admin. ctr.; urban inds., machin. and metal wares; engin., printing; p. (est. 1969) 557,114 (c.), 723,753 (met. a.).
Haifa, c., ch. spt., **Israel**; on Bay of Acre at foot of Mt. Carmel; terminus of Iraq oil pipeline; oil refining and heavy inds.; p. (1972) 217,400 (c.), 447,800 (met. a.).
Hail, t., and oasis, Nejd, Saudi Arabia; p. 30,000.
Hailsham, mkt. t., East Sussex, **Eng.**; 8 km N. of Eastbourne; mats, rope, and twine; p. (1971) 35,502 (dist.).
Hainan, I., S. cst. of **China**; densely wooded; camphor, mahogany, rosewood, sugar; new rubber plantations; ch. t. Hoihow; a. 36,193 km².
Hainaut, prov., **Belgium**, adjoining N.E. border of France; industl. and agr.; coal- and iron-mines; a. 3,719 km²; p. (1968) 1,336,677.
Haiphong, c., ch. pt. **Vietnam**; on Red R. delta; comm. and trading ctr.; cotton, thread, soap, glass, enamel ware, fish-canning; former naval base of Fr. Indo-China; p. (1963) 369,000.
Haiti, rep., **W.I.**, W. third of I. of Hispaniola; tropical climate modified by alt.; agr. basis of economy; coffee accounts for 45 per cent exp.; irrigation scheme in Artibonite valley; unexploited mineral resources, some bauxite mng. and exp.; sm.-scale inds.; well-developed road network and international shipping services; cap. Port-au-Prince; a. 27,713 km²; p. (est. 1975) 5,400,000 (predominantly Negro).
Hakodate, c., S. Hokkaido, **Japan**; Seikan tunnel to Honshu (Aomori) under construction; fishing pt.; fish food processing; p. (est. 1971) 239,000.
Halberstadt, t., Magdeburg, **E. Germany**; cath.; metallurgy, rubber inds., engin., sugar refining; rly. junc.; p. (est. 1970) 46,774.
Halden, t., S.E. Norway; wood-pulp, paper, footwear, cotton spinning; nuclear research reactor; p. (est. 1970) 26,271.
Haldia, pt., W. Bengal, **India**; nr. mouth of R. Hooghly; satellite pt. for Calcutta to handle coal, ore, grain; oil pipeline to Barauni; refinery.
Hale, t., Gtr. Manchester, **Eng.**; residtl.; p. (1971) 7,030.
Halesowen, t., S.W. of Birmingham, West Midlands, **Eng.**; weldless tubes, elec. gds., stainless steel forgings, engin.; p. (1971) 53,933.
Halesworth, t., Suffolk, **Eng**; on R. Blyth, 14 km S.W. of Beccles; p. (1971) 3,250.
Halifax, spt., cap. of Nova Scotia, **Canada**; univ.; naval sta. and dockyard, open in winter; machin., iron foundries, footwear, oil refining, food-processing; p. (1971) 86,290 (c.), 129,309 (met. a.).
Halifax, t., West Yorks., **Eng.**; on E. flanks of Pennines; carpets, textiles, machine tools; p. (1971) 91,171.
Halle, c., cap. of H. admin. dist., **E. Germany**; on R. Saale; univ.; lignite and potash mined nearby; engin., chemicals, food-processing; p. (est. 1969) 261,190.
Hallein, t., Salzburg, **Austria**; on Austro-German frontier, 21 km S. of Salzburg; salt-mines; p. (1961) 13,329.
Hallstatt, v., Upper **Austria**; in the Salzkammergut; early Iron Age culture type site.
Halmahera, I., **Indonesia**; mtnous., active volcanoes, tropical forests; spices, pearl fisheries, sago, rice; a. 17,218 km².
Halmstad, spt. Kattegat, **Sweden**; iron and steel wks., machin. engin., cycles, textiles, leather, jute, wood-pulp; p. (1968) 46,548.
Hälsingborg, spt., Malmöhus, **Sweden**; industl. ctr.; train ferry to Elsinore, **Denmark**; p. (1968) 80,648.
Halstead, t., Essex, **Eng.**; on R. Colne, 19 km N.W. of Colchester; rayon weaving; p. (1971) 7,621.
Haltemprice, t., Humberside, **Eng.**; p. (1971) 52,239.
Haltwhistle, mkt. t., Northumberland, **Eng.**; on R. South Tyne; former coal-mng. dist.; p. (1971) 6,531 (dist.).
Hama, c., N. Syria, on R. Orontes; the anc. Hamath, ctr. of Hittite culture; food tr., rural inds.; p. (1970) 137,000.
Hamadān, t., W. **Iran**; alt. *c.* 1,800 m; the anc. Ecbatana, cap. of Media; carpets, pottery; airport.; tomb of Avicenna; p. (est. 1971) 139,600.
Hamamatsu, c., S. Honshu, **Japan**; on cst. plain 96 km S.E. of Nagoya; ctr. of impt. cotton-mftg. region; textiles, dyeing, musical instruments, motor cycles; p. (est. 1971) 447,000.
Hamar, t., **Norway**; on L. Mjösa; ctr. of rich agr. dist.; tr. and mftg. inds.; p. (est. 1970) 15,189.
Hamble, Hants, **Eng.**; popular yachting ctr.
Hamburg, c., *Land* H., **W. Germany**; astride R. Elbe, nr. N. Sea; 2nd. lgst. German c. and ch. pt.; pt. to be extended by reclaiming Is. of Neuwerk and Scharhörn; diversified tr. inc. liner traffic, barge traffic down Elbe, entrepôt goods; major pt. processing inds., airpt., univ.; cultural and musical ctr.; heavily bombed in second world war; p. (est. 1969) 1,818,600.
Hämeenlinna (Tavastehus), c., cap. of Häme co., S.W. **Finland**; L. pt.; tourist ctr.; birthplace of Sibelius; p. (est. 1966) 36,400.
Hameln (Hamelin), t., Lower Saxony, **W. Germany**; pt. on R. Weser; iron, textiles; scene of legend of the Pied Piper; p. (est. 1967) 47,200.
Hamhung, c., **N. Korea**; industl. and comm. ctr., oil refinery, petrochemicals; coal nearby; p. (est. 1962) 125,000.
Hamilton, t., W. Victoria, **Australia**; mkt. ctr. for dairying and grazing a.; p. (1972) 9,662.
Hamilton, spt., cap. of **Bermuda**; tourism, comm. and service ctr.; p. (est. 1968) 3,000.
Hamilton, c., and L. pt., S.E. Ont., **Canada**; at W. end of L. Ont.; univ.; varied metallurgical mnfs., fruit ctr.; p. (1971) 307,473 (c.), 495,864 (met. a.).
Hamilton, t., N.I., **N.Z.**; pt. on Waikato R.; univ.; p. (1971) 74,762.
Hamilton, burgh, l. gov. dist., Strathclyde Reg., **Scot.**; in Clyde valley, 16 km S.E. of Glasgow; admin. ctr.; elec. gds., carpet mftg., cottons, woollens, knitwear; Rudolf Hess landed on Duke of Hamilton's estate 1941; p. (1971) 46,349.
Hamilton, t., Ohio, **USA**; on Great Miami R.; industl. ctr.; mnfs. metal prods., paper, machin.; p. (1970) 64,058 (t.), 218,201 (met. a.).
Hamilton, R. *See* **Churchill R.**
Hamm, t., N. Rhine-Westphalia, **W. Germany**; on R. Lippe, in Ruhr conurb.; rly. marshalling yards, iron and steel foundries; p. (est. 1967) 72,000 (c.), 159,000 (met. a.).
Hamme, t., E. Flanders, **Belgium**; rope, textiles; p. (est. 1969) 17,493.
Hammerfest, spt., **Norway**; world's most N. t., on Kvalöya I.; fishing; p. (est. 1967) 6,800.
Hammersmith, Thames-side inner bor., London,

Eng.; inc. former bor. of Fulham; industl., residtl.; elec. and car accessories, synthetic rubber; p. (1971) 184,935.

Hammond, c., N.W. Ind., **USA**; on Grand Calumet R., nr. Chicago; originally slaughtering and meat-pkg. ctr., now ch. mnfs., petroleum and steel prods., soap; p. (1970) 107,108.

Hampshire, non-met. co., S. **Eng.**; inc. Hampshire basin of chalk covered in clay and sand; inc. infertile heath and New Forest; leading pts Southampton, Portsmouth; lt. inds.; tourism, seaside resorts; impt. planned p. growth in S. H.; co. t. Winchester; a. 3,771 km²; p. (1971) 1,370,000.

Hampstead, former v., now inc. in Greater London, **Eng.**; hilltop v. with nearby heathland. *See* **Camden.**

Hampton, Thames-side t., inc. in Richmond upon Thames, outer London bor., **Eng.**; Hampton Court Palace in the par.; Hampton Wick is a mile E. of H. Court.

Hampton, t., S.E. Va., **USA**; oldest English community in U.S.; fishing, oyster and crab packing; p. (1970) 118,584.

Han, R., Hupeh, **China**; rises in S.W. Shensi prov., flows E. between Tsingling mtns. and Tapa range of N. Szechwan into Yangtze R. at Wuhan; ch. trib. of Yangtze; *c.* 1,280 km long.

Han, R., S. **China**; forms rich agr. delta nr. Swatow; *c.* 400 km long.

Hanau, t., Hesse, **W. Germany**; on Rs. Main and Kinzig; jewellery ctr., rubber and non-ferrous metals inds.; birthplace of Jakob and Wilhelm Grimm, Paul Hindemith; p. (est. 1967) 52,600.

Hanchung, c., S.W. Shensi prov., **China**; on Han R.; nr. Szechwan border; agr. and tr. ctr.; former Nancheng; p. (est. 1970) 120,000.

Hangchow (Hang-chou), c., cap. of Chekiang prov., E. **China**; picturesque setting at head of H. Bay; former treaty pt., now silted up; silk-weaving, chemicals, jute cloth; tourism; p. (est. 1970) 1,100,000.

Hanko (Hango), t., on S. point, **Finland**; spt.; iron-wks.; p. (1966) 9,414.

Hankow, c., Hupeh, China; at junc. of Han and Yangtze Rs., 960 km from mouth of Yangtze but accessible to ocean-going ships; ch. comm. and mnf. ctr. of central China; former treaty pt., now part of Wuhan conurb.; machin., chemicals, cigarettes, silk. *See* **Wuhan.**

Hanley. *See* **Stoke-on-Trent.**

Hannibal, t., Mo., **USA**; on Mississippi R.; shoes, cement, metal gds.; boyhood home of Mark Twain; p. (1970) 18,698.

Hanoi, c., cap. of **Vietnam**; on Red R.; old Annamese fort, now modern comm. ctr.; univ.; cotton, silks, tobacco, pottery; superphosphate and magnesium phosphate nearby; bricks, concrete, rubber; p. (est. 1965) 850,000.

Hanover (Hannover), c., cap. of Lower Saxony, **W. Germany**; route ctr.; iron, textiles, machin., paper, biscuits, cigarettes, cars, rubber-processing, chemicals; p. (est. 1969) 519,700.

Hanyang, c., Hupeh, **China**; on Yangtze R.; linked by bridge with Hanchow and Wuchang; one of earliest iron-wks. in Asia; now inc. in conurb. of Wuhan. *See* **Wuhan.**

Haparanda, spt., **N. Sweden**; salmon fishing; exp. timber, and prod. of the Lapps; p. (est. 1970) 8,963.

Hapur, t., W. Uttar Pradesh, **India**; tr. in sugar, timber, cotton, brassware; p. (1961) 55,248.

Harar, t., cap. of Harar prov., **Ethiopia**; walled t., alt. *c.* 1,800 m; anc. c. of Islamic learning; mkt.; p. (est. 1970) 45,033.

Harbin (Haerhpin), c., cap. of Heilungkiang prov., **China**; pt. on Sungari R.; tr. and comm. ctr. of N.E. China; exp. soyabeans; food-processing, machin., paper-mills, oil refining, hydro-turbines, textiles; former treaty pt.; p. (est. 1970) 2,750,000.

Harburg-Wilhelmsburg, industl. pt. of Hamburg, **W. Germany**; oil refining.

Hardanger Fjord, W. cst. **Norway**; 120 km long; magnificent scenery; tourism.

Hardt Mtns., **W. Germany**; northward continuation of Vosges on W. of Rhine rift valley; formerly forested, now largely cleared for pasture; hgst. points reach just over 600 m.

Hardwar, t., Uttar Pradesh, **India**; on R. Ganges; gr. annual fair and pilgrimage; nearby dam; p. (1961) 58,513.

Hargeisa, t., **Somalia**; comm. ctr. of livestock-raising region; airport; p. (1963) 40,255.

Hariana. *See* **Haryana.**

Haringey, outer bor., Greater London, **Eng.**; comprising former bors. of Hornsey, Tottenham, and Wood Green; p. (1971) 236,956.

Hari-Rud, R., N. **Afghanistan** and **Iran**; the anc. "Arius"; length 1,040 km; (*Rud* = river).

Harlech, t., Gwynedd, **Wales**; on Cardigan Bay 16 km N. of Barmouth; farming; cas.; seaside resort.

Harlem, upper Manhattan, N.Y. city, **USA**; residtl. and business section of c. with lge. Negro p.; depressed economic a. with much poverty.

Harlem, R., N.Y., **USA**; separates Manhattan I. from bor. of Bronx; with Spuyten Duyvi Creek forms waterway 13 km long from East R. to Hudson R.

Harlingen, spt., Friesland, **Neth.**; margarine, mixed farming, fish; natural gas; p. (est. 1970) 12,522.

Harlingen, spt., S. Texas, **USA**; ctr. of productive agr. a.; food-processing; p. (est. 1969) 37,000.

Harlow, t., Essex, **Eng.**; in valley of R. Stort, 35 km N.E. of London; new t. (1947); spreads S.W. from nucleus of old mkt. t. of H.; engin., glass, furniture mkg. metallurgy; p. (est. 1974) 82,250.

Härnösand, t., **Sweden**; on G. Bothnia; engin. sawmills, pulp, graphite prod.; p. (est. 1970) 27,023.

Harpenden, t., Herts., **Eng.**; in Chiltern Hills, 8 km N. of St. Albans; Rothamsted agr. experimental sta.; residtl.; p. (1971) 24,161.

Harringay. *See* **Haringey.**

Harris, S. part of Lewis I., Outer Hebrides, **Scot.**; and several sm. Is.; p. (1971) 2,879.

Harrisburg, c., cap. of Penns., **USA**; on Susquehanna R.; iron and steel ind.; machin., cigarettes, cotton gds.; p. (1970) 65,828 (c.) 405,387 (met. a.).

Harrogate, t., North Yorks., **Eng.**; in valley of R. Nidd, 22 km N. of Leeds; spa; favoured a. for retirement; p. (1971) 62,290.

Harrow, outer bor., Greater London, **Eng.**; public school; camera mftg.; p. (1971) 202,718.

Harsprånget, t., Norrbotten, **Sweden**; lge. hydro-electric plant.

Harstad, ch. t., Lofoten Is., N.W. **Norway**; herring ind., woollen gds.; p. (1960) 4,028.

Hartebeestpoort, Dam, Transvaal, **S. Africa**; on R. Crocodile (Limpopo), 40 km W. of Pretoria; supplies water for cultivation, under irrigation, of cotton, maize, tobacco.

Hartford, c., cap. of Conn., **USA**; comm. and insurance ctr.; univ.; sm. arms, typewriters, elec. machin., aircraft engin., ceramics, plastics; Mark Twain lived here; p. (1970) 155,868 (c.), 657,104 (met. a.).

Hartland Point, Barnstaple Bay, N. Devon, **Eng.**

Hartlepool, spt., Cleveland, **Eng.**; on E. cst., 5 km N. of Tees estuary; shipbldg., lt. inds., timber. iron and steel inds., pipe making; gd. sands for holiday-makers to the S.; p. (1971) 96,898.

Harvey, t., N.E. Ill., **USA**; nr. Chicago; rolling stock, diesel engines, heavy machin.; p. (1970) 34,636.

Harwell, v. Oxon., **Eng.**; 19 km S. of Oxford; AEA nuclear power research establishment.

Harwich, spt., Essex, **Eng.**; on S. cst. of estuary of R. Stour; packet sta. for Belgium, Neth., Denmark; docks, container facilities, naval base; p. (1971) 14,892.

Haryana, st., **India**; formed 1966 from Hindi-speaking areas of Punjab; cap. Chandigarh (also of Punjab st. until its own cap. is built); a. 45,584 km²; p. (1971) 9,971,164.

Harz Mtns., range, **E.** and **W. Germany**; between the Weser and the Elbe; highest peak the Brocken; ch. t. Goslar (W. Germany); forested slopes; rich in minerals; tourism.

Haslemere, t., Surrey, **Eng.**; nr. Hindhead; mkt., residtl.; lt. inds., p. (1971) 13,252.

Haslingden, t., Lancs., **Eng.**; on Rossendale Fells, 5 km S. of Accrington; heavy industl. textiles, waste-spinning; textile-finishing; p. (1971) 14,953.

Hasselt, t., prov. Limburg, **Belgium**; mkt t.; gin distilleries; p. (1968) 38,886.

Hassi Messaoued, t., **Algeria**; lge. oilfield; pipeline to Bejaia.

Hassi R'Mel, t., **Algeria**; lge. natural gasfield.
Hastings, t., East Sussex, **Eng.**; on S. cst., midway between Beachy Head and Dungeness; seaside resort; one of the Cinque Ports; cas.; p. (1971) 72,169.
Hastings, t., N.I., **N.Z.**; on Hawke's Bay, nr. Napier; fruit-canning; p. (1971) 29,736.
Hatay (Sanjak of Alexandretta), dist., S. **Turkey**, comprising Antioch (now Antakya) and its pt. Alexandretta (now Iskenderun), ceded to Turkey by France 1939; p. (1960) 441,209.
Hatfield, t., Herts., **Eng.**; 30 km N. of London; new t. (1948) which grew around old t. of Bishops Hatfield; lt. engin., aircraft; p. (est. 1974) 26,000.
Hathras, t., Aligarh dist., Uttar Pradesh, **India**; sugar, cotton, carved work; p. (1961) 64,045.
Hatteras, Cape, promontory on I. and cays off N.C., **USA**; stormy region, marked by lighthouse.
Hattiesburg, t., Miss., **USA**; sawmilling, clothing, fertilisers; p. (est. 1969) 40,500.
Haugesund, spt., S. **Norway**; on S.W. cst., 35 m. N. of Stavanger; ch. ctr. of herring fishery; canning inds.; p. (1968) 27,294.
Hauraki Gulf, arm of Pac. Oc.; E. cst. N.I., **N.Z.**; forming entrance to harbour of Auckland.
Haute Garonne, dep., S. **France**; in Languedoc; cap. Toulouse; a. 6,366 km²; p. (1968) 690,712.
Haute-Loire, dep., **France**; mainly in Massif Central; cap. Le Puy; cattle, fruit, vineyards; a. 4,999 km²; p. (1968) 208,337.
Haute-Marne, dep., **France**; mainly in Champagne; metallurgical inds.; a. 6,268 km²; p. (1968) 214,336.
Hautes-Alpes, dep., **France**; mtnous.; on Italian border; sheep; cap. Gap; a. 5,641 km²; p. (1968) 91,790.
Haute-Saône, dep., **France**; inc. part of Vosges mtns.; mainly agr.; cap. Vesoul; a. 5,372 km²; p. (1968) 14,776.
Haute-Savoie, dep., **France**; borders on Italy and Switzerland; reaches highest alt. in Mont Blanc; cap. Annecy; winter sports; a. 4,595 km.; p. (1968) 378,550.
Haute-Pyrénées, dep., S. **France**; rises in S. to steep peaks of Pyrenees, forming bdy. with Spain; Basques live on both sides of border; cap. Tarbes; Lourdes place of pilgrimage; a. 4,533 km²; p. (1968) 225,730.
Haute-Vienne, dep., **France**; entirely in Massif Central; cap. Limoges; cattle-raising; a. 5,488 km²; p. (1968) 341,589.
Haut-Rhin, dep., E. **France**; in lower Alsace; cap. Colmar; ch. industl. t. Mulhouse; a. 3,507 km²; p. (1968) 585,018.
Hauts-de-Seine, new dep., **France**; W. of Paris; cap. Nanterre; a. 176 km²; p. (1968) 1,461,619.
Havana (La Habana), c., cap. of **Cuba**; ch. pt. of W.I., with lge. harbour; cigars, tobacco, sugar, rum, coffee, woollens, straw hats, iron-ore; oil refining on outskirts of c.; p. (est. 1967) 1,008,500 (c.), 1,557,200 (met. a.).
Havant and Waterloo, ts., former U.D., **Eng.**; at foot of Portsdown Hill, 10 km N.E. of Portsmouth; p. (1971) 108,999.
Havel, R., **E. Germany**; rises in Neubrandenburg L. region; flows to Elbe R.; partially canalised nr. Berlin; 354 km long.
Haverfordwest, t., Dyfed, **Wales**; 10 km N.E. of Milford Haven; agr. mkt.; Norman cas.; p. (1971) 9,101.
Haverhill, t., Suffolk **Eng.**; expanded t.; textiles, clothing; p. (1971) 12 430.
Haverhill, t., Mass., **USA**; industl.; shipping containers; p. (est. 1969) 42,000.
Havering, outer bor., E. London, **Eng.**; inc. Hornchurch and Romford; p. (1971) 246,778.
Hawaii, I., N. central Pac. Oc.; lgst. of Hawaiian gr.; three gr. volcanic mtns., Mauna Kea (4,208 m), Mauna Loa (4,172 m), Hualalai (last erupted, 1801); ch. pt. Hilo (devastated by tidal wave, 1946); lava deserts, bamboo forests; sugar-cane, cattle, coffee; tourism; deep-sea fishing; p. (1970) 61,332.
Hawaiian Is. (Sandwich Is.), st., Pac. Oc., admitted 1959 as 50th st. of **USA**; chain of coral and volcanic Is.; cap. Honolulu on S.E. cst. of Oahu I.; tourism; ctr. of international shipping routes; sugar, pineapples; a. 16,638 km²; p. (1970) 748,575.
Hawarden, t., Clwyd, N. **Wales**; steel plant; home of Gladstone; p. (1971) 42,467 (dist.).
Hawes Water, L., Cumbria, **Eng.**; 4 km long.
Hawick, burgh, Roxburgh, **Scot.**; on R. Teviot, 28 km S.W. of Kelso; hosiery, tweed, and woollens; p. (1971) 16,286.
Hawke's Bay, prov. dist., N.I., **N.Z.**; on E. cst.; cap. Napier; a. 11,033 km²; p. (1971) 133,814.
Hawkesbury, R., N.S.W., **Australia**; 528 km long.
Haworth, t., West Yorks., **Eng.**; nr. Keighley; home of the Brontës.
Hawthorne, t., S.W. Cal., **USA**; residtl.; in gas- and oil-producing a.; aircraft and electronics; p. (1970) 53,304.
Hay, t., N.S.W., **Australia**; situated on R. Murrumbidgee; collecting ctr. for fruit and wheat; p. (1966) 2,957.
Hay, t., Powys, **Wales**; on R. Wye; cas.; mkt.; p. (1971) 1,230.
Hay, R., Alberta, **Canada**; flows into G. Slave Lake; 560 km long.
Haydock, t., Merseyside, **Eng.**; coal mng.; inc. H. Park racecourse; p. (1971) 14,180.
Hayes and Harlington. *See* **Hillingdon**.
Hayling Island, resort, Hants, **Eng.**; E. of Portsmouth.
Hayward, t., Cal., **USA**; fruit-canning, poultry; p. (1970) 93,058.
Hayward's Heath, residtl. a., West Sussex, **Eng.**
Hazel Grove and Bramhall, sub. of Stockport Gtr. Manchester, **Eng.**; p. (1971) 39,534.
Hazleton, t., Penns., **USA**; anthracite region; textiles, iron and steel mnfs.; p. (est. 1969) 29,000.
Headingley, sub., Leeds, West Yorks., **Eng.** mainly residtl.; county cricket ground.
Heanor, t., Derbys., **Eng.**; 11 km N.E. of Derby; hoisery, pottery, prefabricated timber bldgs. mftg.; p. (1971) 24 352.
Heard, I., S. **Indian Oc.**; 448 km S.E. of Kerguelen I.; Australian possession; volcanic.
Heathrow, site of London airport, **Eng.**; 24 km W. of central London, S. of M4 motorway; residtl. a.
Hebburn, t., Tyne and Wear, **Eng.**; on R. Tyne 6 km below Gateshead; shipbldg., engin.; p. (1971) 23,597.
Hebden Royd, t., West Yorks., **Eng.**; cotton factories, dyewks., heavy engin., woollens and worsteds; p. (1971) 8,648.
Hebrides or Western Is., Scot.; grouped as Outer and Inner Hebrides; ch. t. Stornoway, Lewis; a. 7,382 km².
Hebron, t., **Jordan**; 26 km. S.W. of Jerusalem; p. (1967) 43,000.
Heckmondwike, t., West Yorks., **Eng.**; wool textiles; p. (1971) 9,361.
Hedon, t., Humberside, **Eng.**; former spt.; p. (1971) 2,600.
Heerenveen, t., Friesland prov., N. **Neth.**; bicycles; p. (1968) 30.282.
Heerlen, t., Limburg, **Neth.**; 22 km E. of Maastricht; coal mng.; p. (1968) 76,515.
Heide, t., Schleswig-Holstein, **W. Germany**; ctr. of Ditmarschen oilfields; p. (est. 1969) 23,352.
Heidelberg, c., Baden-Württemberg, **W. Germany**; on R. Neckar, nr. Mannheim; celebrated univ., cas.; tobacco, wood, leather, rly. carriages; nylon plant projected; p. (est. 1969) 122,000.
Heidenheim, t. Baden-Württemberg, **W. Germany**; N.E. of Ulm; textiles, machin., metallurgy, furniture; p. (est. 1969) 50,007.
Heilbronn, t., R. pt. Baden-Württemberg, **W. Germany**; engin., vehicles, foodstuffs; p. (est. 1969) 98,481.
Heilungkiang (Heilungjiang), prov., N.E. **China**; separated from USSR by Amur and Ussuri Rs.; mtnous.; crossed by Sungari R. in central plain; maize, soya beans, millets; opencast coalmines; gold; cap. Harbin; a. 466,200 km²; p. (est. 1967) 21,000,000.
Hejaz, region, **Saudi Arabia**; mainly desert; very poor communications; ch. t. Mecca; a. 388,500 km²; p. (est. 1963) 2,000,000, mainly Bedouin.
Hekla, volcano, **Iceland**; erupted in 1970; alt. 1,554 m.
Helder (Den Helder), t., N. Holland, **Neth.**; on strait between peninsula and I. of Texel; naval base; on cst. 80 km N. of Amsterdam; p. (1968) 58,356.
Helena, st. cap., Mont., **USA**; grew up as gold- and silver-mng. t.; bricks, pottery; resort; p. (1970) 22,730.
Helensburgh, t., Dumbarton, W. **Scot.**; on the Clyde; resort; p. (1971) 11,296.

Helford, R., Cornwall, **Eng.**; oysters, tourism.
Helicon, mtn. gr., **Greece**; abode of classical muses.
Heligoland (Helgoländ), sm. I., N. Sea; off mouth of Elbe; ceded by Britain to Germany 1890 in return for Zanzibar.
Hellendoorn, t., Overijssel, **Neth.**; textiles; p. (1968) 28,766.
Hellespont. *See* **Dardanelles.**
Helmand or **Helmund, R., Afghanistan**; flows *c.* 1,360 km from mtns. of Kabul to Hamun-i-Helmand swamp on Iranian border; cultivation in valley; major irrigation project.
Helmond, t. N. Brabant, **Neth.**; on Zuid-Willemsvaart (canal); textiles; p. (1968) 56,976.
Helmsley, mkt. t., North Yorks., **Eng.**; cas.; p. (1971) 4,828 (dist.).
Helmstedt, t., Lower Saxony, **W. Germany**; E. of Brunswick; on E. German border; textiles, machin.; p. (est. 1969) 27,267.
Helsingör. *See* Elsinore.
Helsinki or **Helsingfors**, c., cap. of **Finland**; spt. on G. of Finland; harbour ice-bound Jan. to Apr., channel opened by ice-breakers; cultural ctr., univ.; timber, textiles, carpets; exp. mainly timber prods.; p. (1968) 529,091 (c.), 700,856 (met. a.).
Helston, mkt. t., Cornwall, **Eng.**; on R. Cober, 13 km W. of Falmouth; tourist ctr.; famous for festival of floral dance (8 May); fishing, soup-canning; p. (1971) inc. Porthleven, 9,827.
Helvellyn, mtn., L. Dist., Cumbria, **Eng.**; severely eroded by ice; alt. 951 m; sharp ridge of Striding Edge.
Helwan, t., **Egypt**; 24 km S. of Cairo; sulphur springs; iron and steel complex, fertilisers, cement; car assembly; p. 51,000.
Hemel Hempstead, t., Herts., **Eng.**; new t. (1947), on S. slopes of Chilterns; scientific glass, elec. engin., cars; p. (est. 1974) 73,000
Hempstead, t., Long I., N.Y., **USA**; textiles, radios; p. (est. 1969) 39,500.
Hemsworth, t., West Yorks., **Eng.**; 10 km S.E. of Wakefield; p. (1971) 14,856.
Hendon. *See* Barnet.
Hengelo, t., Overijssel, **Neth.**; industl. ctr.; cattle mkt.; metals, textiles; p. (1968) 68,348.
Hengyang (Hengchow), c., Hunan, **China**; on Siang R. in foothills to S. of Yangtze plain; on main Kuangchow–Peking rly.; lead and zinc mines nearby; p. (est. 1970) 240,000.
Henin-Liétard, t., Pas-de-Calais, **France**; on coalfield; p. (1968) 25,067.
Henley-in-Arden, v., Warwicks., **Eng.**; many old buildings; residtl.
Henley-on-Thames, t., Oxford, **Eng.**; 8 km N.E. of Reading; mkt. gardening, brewing; annual regatta; p. (1971) 11,402.
Hensbarrow, upland a., Cornwall, **Eng.**; granite; kaolin-mng. dist., kaolin exp. by sea from Fowey; rises to over 300 m; a. 70 km^2.
Henzada, t., **Burma**, on Irrawaddy delta; in tobacco- and rice-growing dist.; p. (est. 1962) 896,836.
Herakleion. *See* **Iráklion.**
Herāt, c., cap. of H. prov., N.W. **Afghanistan**; on Hari Rud R.; of historic and strategic importance, has been called "the key of India"; crude petroleum and chrome-ore nearby; tr. ctr.; textiles; p. (est. 1971) 103,915.
Hérault, dep., S.W. **France**; in Languedoc; agr.; cap. Montpellier; govt.-sponsored tourist developments along shores of Mediterranean; a. 6,221 km^2; p. (1968) 596,392.
Herculaneum, anc. c., S. **Italy**; 6 km E. of Naples; buried along with Pompeii by eruption from Vesuvius A.D. 79; rediscovered 1709; site of modern Resina and Portici.
Hereford and Worcestershire, non-met. co., **Eng.**; crossed by Wye and Severn valleys, separated by Malvern Hills; mainly agr., beef, dairy and fruit farming; major ts. Hereford and Worcester; a. 3,906 km^2; p. (1971) 562,000.
Hereford c., Hereford and Worcs., **Eng.**; on R. Wye; cath.; mkt.; tiles, engin., timber, cider and preserves; furniture, brassware; p. (1971) 46,503.
Herford, t., N. Rhine-Westphalia, **W. Germany**; on R. Werra; cotton, flax, furniture, cigars, confectionery, metallurgy; p. (est. 1967) 54,900.
Herisau, t., cap of Appenzell Ausser-Rhoden half-can., N.E. **Switzerland**; muslin, embroideries; p. (1970) 14,597.
Herm, sm. I. of **Channel Is.**, English Channel; 6 km N.W. Sark and N.E. of Guernsey; remarkable shell-beach; a. 130 ha; p. (1971) 96.
Hermon, Mount (Jebel esh Sheikh), mtn., in Anti-Lebanon range, on **Syria–Lebanon** bdy., nr. Israel; alt. 2,862 m.
Hermosillo, c., cap. of Sonora st., N.W. **Mexico**; on San Miguel R.; oranges; agr. and mng. ctr.; p. (1970) 176,596.
Hermoupolis or **Hermopolis**, t., Syros I., **Greece**; cap. of Cyclades; Ægean pt. and comm. ctr.; p. (1971) 13,460.
Herne, t., N. Rhine–Westphalia, **W. Germany**; pt. on Rhine–Herne canal; industl. t. of Ruhr conurb.; p. (est. 1969) 101,500.
Herne Bay, t., Kent. **Eng.**; on cst., 19 km W. of Margate; p. (1971) 25,117.
Herning, t., Jutland, **Denmark**; knitting ind.; p. (est. 1970) 32,512.
Heröya, S. **Norway**; nuclear power plant; chemicals, fertilisers.
Herstal, t., **Belgium**; nr. Liège; armaments, aero-engines; p. (1968) 29,894.
Herstmonceux, v., nr. Hastings, Sussex, **Eng.**; cas.; site of Royal Greenwich Observatory.
Hertford, non-met. co., **Eng.**; borders Greater London on S.; co. t., Hertford, ch. ctr. St. Albans; drained by Rs. Thames and Lea; intensive agr., lt. inds.; new ts. Welwyn, Stevenage, Hatfield, Hemel Hempstead; a. 1,637 km^2; p. (1971) 922,188.
Hertford, co. t., Herts., **Eng.**; on R. Lea, 32 km N. of London; pharmaceutics, flour milling, rolling stock, diesels, brewing; p. (1971) 20,379.
's-Hertogenbosch, t., **Neth.**; on Rs. Dommel and Aa; cap. of N. Brabant prov.; cath.; cattle mkt.; industl. development; p. (1968) 80,425.
Hesse, *Land*, **W. Germany**; part of former Prussian prov. Hesse-Nassau; mainly upland; inds. at Frankfurt, Kassel, Darmstadt; wine produced along Rhine valley; cap. Wiesbaden; tourism; a. 21,103 km^2; p. (1968) 5,333,000.
Heston and Isleworth. *See* **Hounslow.**
Hetch Hetchy Dam, Cal., **USA**; on R. Toulumne upstream from San Joaquin R.; ch. source of irrigation for middle San Joaquin valley; supplies water and generating power to San Francisco.
Hetton, t., Tyne and Wear, **Eng.**; 8 km N.E. of Durham; coal-mng. dist.; p. (1971) 16,871.
Hexham, mkt. t., Northumberland, **Eng.**; on R. Tyne, 32 km W. of Newcastle; priory; p. (1971) 9,799.
Heysham. *See* **Morecambe and Heysham.**
Heywood, t., Gtr. Manchester **Eng.**; 5 km E. of Bury; chemicals, engin.; p. (1971) 30,418.
Hialeah, t., Fla., **USA**; sub. of Miami; race-course; p. (1970) 102,297.
Hidalgo, st., central **Mexico**; mtnous. with fertile valleys in S. and W.; cap. Pachuca; mng. (silver, gold, copper. lead, iron, sulphur); maguey (type of lily), tobacco. cotton, coffee; a. 20,868 km^2; p. (1969) 1,282,000.
Hierro. *See* Ferro.
Higashiosaka, c., **Japan**; E. of Osaka; formed from amalgamation of Fuse, Kawachi, Hiraoka and many sm. ts.; p. (est. 1971) 485,000.
Higham Ferrers, mkt. t., Northants, **Eng.**; 5 km E. of Wellingborough; footwear and leather dressing; p. (1971) 4,700.
Highbury, residtl. dist., N. London, **Eng.**; in bor. of Islington; Arsenal football ground.
Highgate, residtl. dist., N. London, **Eng.**; hilltop v. in bor. of Camden.
Highland Park, t., Mich., **USA**; sub. of Detroit; grew up with expansion of motor-car ind.; p. (1970) 32,263.
Highland Region, l. gov. reg., **N. Scot.**; rugged mtns. inland; p. concentrated around cst.; off-shore oil development; stock raising, forestry, tourism; a. 25,128 km^2; p. (1971) 172,720.
High Point, t., N.C., **USA**; furniture ctr., hosiery; p. (est. 1969) 64,000.
High Willhays, hgst. summit, Dartmoor, Devon, **Eng.**; 621 m.
High Wycombe, t., Bucks., **Eng.**; 13 km N. of Maidenhead; furniture, paper-mkg., egg processing; in London commuter belt; p. (1971) 59,298.
Hildesheim, t., Lower Saxony, **W. Germany**; at foot of Harz mtns.; cath.; machin., farm implements, textiles, ceramics; p. (est. 1967) 97,000.

Hillah, Al, mkt. t., **Iraq**; on R. Euphrates; nr. anc. Babylon; food tr. rugs, leather; p. (1965) 84,717 (t.), 110,795 (met. a.).

Hilleröd, t., **Denmark**; admin. ctr. of Frederiksborg prov.; agr. implements; p. (est. 1970) 23,500.

Hillingdon, outer bor., Greater London, **Eng.**; comprising former U.D.s of Hayes and Harlington, Ruislip and Northwood Yiewsley, W. Drayton, and former M.B. of Uxbridge; p. (1971) 234,718.

Hilo, t., Hawaii; pt. of entry and main tr. and shipping ctr. of I.; tourism; Mauna Loa volcano nearby; p. (1970) 26,353.

Hilversum, t., **Neth.**; nr. Utrecht; radio broadcasting ctr.; noteworthy modern architecture; p. (est. 1969) 100,098.

Himachal Pradesh, st., N.W. **India**; bounded by Tibet on E.; forested mtns., cultivated valleys; cap. Simla; a. 56,019 km^2; p. (1971) 3,424,332.

Himalayas, vast chain of mtns. along N. border of India, between the Indus and Brahamaputra Rs., and lying in Pakistan, India, Nepal, Sikkim, Bhutan, and China; made up of several parallel ranges inc. the Siwaliks, the Hindu Kush, and the Karakorams; crossed by passes, mainly in W.; 2,560 km long; hgst. peak Mt. Everest, 8,854 m.

Himeji, c., S. Honshu, **Japan**; mkt. ctr. on shore of Inland Sea, 48 km W. of Kobe; iron and steel ind., heavy engin.; oil refining; p. (est. 1971) 414,000.

Hinckley, mkt. t., Leics., **Eng.**; hosiery, cardboard boxes, dye-wks., engin.; nr. Watling Street; p. (1971) 47,982.

Hinkley Point, Somerset, **Eng.**; civil nuclear power-sta.; second sta. now being built.

Hindenburg. *See* **Zabrze.**

Hindhead, hilly common, Surrey, nr. Haslemere, **Eng.**

Hindiya Barrage, dam, **Iraq**; across R. Euphrates, 48 km above Al Hillah; provides flood control and irrigation in a. between Shatt al Hillah and R. Euphrates.

Hindley, t., Gtr. Manchester, **Eng.**; 3 km S.E. of Wigan; paint, knitwear, rubber, asbestos; p. (1971) 24,307.

Hindu Kush, mtn. range, mainly in N.E. **Afghanistan**; hgst peak Tirich Mir (7,755 m) in Chitral dist., **Pakistan**; Salang tunnel (opened 1964) with 2-lane motor highway cuts H.K. at height of 3,300 m, runs 240 m below mtn. top, 3·2 km.

Hindustan, former name of part of N. **India** between Himalayas and Vindhya ranges.

Hirfanli Dam, project on R. Kizilirmak, 144 km S.E. Ankara, **Turkey**, 1961.

Hirosaki, c., Honshu, **Japan**; mkt., lacquer-ware; cas.; p. (est. 1971) 160,000.

Hiroshima, c., S.W. Honshu, **Japan**; on delta of Ota R.; first c. to be destroyed by atomic bomb (6 Aug. 1945); since rebuilt; motor vehicles, shipbldg.; p. (est. 1971) 567,000.

Hirschberg. *See* **Jelenia Góra.**

Hispaniola, second lgst I. of **W.I.**; lies between Cuba and Puerto Rico; divided between Haiti (Fr.-speaking) and Dominican Rep. (Spanish-speaking); complex relief, climate, and vegetation, but strong cultural differences make international bdy. a sharp divide; a. 76,498 km^2.

Hitchin, t., Herts., **Eng.**; in gap through Chiltern Hills, 56 km N. of London; lt. engin., tanning, chemicals, distilling; mkt.; p. (1971) 26,680.

Hjälmaren Lake, central **Sweden**; drained into L. Malaren by Esk R.; linked by canal to Arboga; a. 474 km^2.

Hjörring, t., Jutland, N. **Denmark**; biscuit and clothing wks.; p. (est. 1970) 15,699.

Hobart, cap. and ch. pt. of Tasmania, **Australia**; on R. Derwent; univ.; fruit exp.; zinc; cadmium, superphosphates, textiles; p. (1972) 52,425 (c.), 153,024 (met. a.).

Hoboken, t., Antwerp, **Belgium**; shipbldg.; refractory metals; p. (1968) 32,184.

Hoboken, t., N.J., **USA**; on Hudson R. above Jersey City, opp N.Y. to which it is linked by subway and ferry; pt. for ocean commerce; industl. ctr.; p. (est. 1969) 45,000.

Ho Chi-minh City (Saigon), c., spt., **Vietnam**; former cap. of S. Vietnam; on Saigon R. to E. of Mekong Delta; tree-lined boulevards; cath., univ., modern airport; comm. ctr.; exp. rice, rubber; food processing; p. (est. 1968) 1,682,000.

Höchst, t., Hesse, **W. Germany**; industl. sub. of Frankfurt-on-Main; site of German chemical ind.

Hochstetter, mtn., S.I., **N.Z.**; in Southern Alps; alt. 3,416 m.

Hoddesdon, t., Herts., **Eng.**; in Lea valley, 6 km S. of Ware; nursery tr., tomatoes, etc.; p. (1971) 26,071.

Hodeida (Al Hudaydah), t., **Yemen Arab Rep.**, on Red Sea; pt. and naval base; exp. dates, hides, coffee; p. (est. 1970) 90,000.

Hódmezövásárhely, t., S.E. **Hungary**; wheat, fruit, tobacco, cattle; natural gas pipeline from Szeged; p. (1966) 52,800.

Hof, t. Bavaria, **W. Germany**; on R. Saale; textiles, iron, machin., porcelain, glass, brewing; p. (est. 1967) 55,000.

Hofei or Hefei, c., cap. of Anhwei prov., **China**; rice-growing a.; cotton and silk, iron and steel; p. (est. 1970) 400,000.

Hoffman mtn. peak of the Sierra Nevada, Cal., **USA**; alt. 2,473m.

Hofuf (Al Hufuf), t., El Hasa, **Saudi Arabia**; dates wheat, fruit; textiles, brass- and copper-ware; oil-fields nearby; p. (est. 1967) 85,000.

Hog's Back, Surrey, **Eng.**; steep chalk ridge; alt. 154 m.

Hohenlimburg, t., N. Rhine-Westphalia, **W. Germany**; nr. Dortmund; cas.; textiles, iron, steel; p. (est. 1969) 26,176.

Hohenstein-Ernstal, t., Karl-Marx-Stadt, **E. Germany**; textiles, metal gds.; p. (est. 1970) 16,800.

Hohe Tauern, Alpine range, Tyrol, **Austria**; rugged crystalline rocks; highest point Gross Glockner, 3,801 m; traversed by rly. tunnel 8 km long.

Hoihow (Hai-k'ou), c., ch. pt. of Hainan I. Kwangtung prov., **China**; p. (est. 1970) 500,000.

Hokkaido, lge I., **Japan**, N. of Honshu; colder than other Is.; less dense p.; temperate agr.; skiing; a. 88,775 km^2; p. of pref. (1970) 5,184,287.

Holbaek, t., Sjaelland, **Denmark**; W. of Copenhagen; engin. and motor wks.; p. (est. 1970) 17,892.

Holbeach, mkt. t. S. Lincs., **Eng.**; in Fens, 11 km E. of Spalding; brewing; ctr. of bulb-growing dist.

Holborn. *See* **Camden.**

Holderness, peninsula, Humberside, **Eng.**; between R. Humber and N. Sea; agr.; p. (1971) 24,256 (dist.).

Holguin, t., N.E. **Cuba**; comm. ctr.; sugar, tobacco, coffee, cattle; exps. handled by pt. Gibara; p. (est. 1967) 350,250.

Holland. *See* **Netherlands.**

Holland, N., prov., **Neth.**; inc. W. Frisian Is.; dairying; a. 2,629 km^2; p. (1968) 2,215,876.

Holland, Parts of. *See* **Lincolnshire.**

Holland, S., prov., **Neth.**; crossed by R. Rhine; mkt. gardening; a. 2,927 km^2; p. (1968) 2,922,450.

Hollandia, former name of cap. W. Irian, **Indonesia**; renamed Kota Baru by Indonesia, then Sukarnapura, now Djajapura.

Holloman, t., N.M., **USA**; atomic and space research ctr.; site of 1st. man-made atomic explosion.

Holloway, N. dist., Islington bor., London, **Eng.**; women's prison.

Hollywood, t., Fla., **USA**; seaside resort on Atl. cst.; cement, furniture; p. (1970) 104,018; part of Fort Lauderdale met. a.

Hollywood, sub. of Los Angeles, Cal., **USA**; ctr. of film industry.

Holmesdale, Vale of, Kent, E. Surrey, **Eng.**; extends along foot of N. Downs escarpment; drained by Rs. Mole, Darent, Medway, Len, Stour; heavy clay soils; ch. ts., Dorking, Reigate, Sevenoaks, Maidstone, Ashford, which have grown up in gaps through hills to N. and S. of Vale; length 96 km, average width 2 km.

Holmfirth, t., West Yorks., **Eng.**; 8 km S. of Huddersfield, textiles, engin.; p. (1971) 19,319.

Holt, mkt. t., N. Norfolk, **Eng.**; 8 km S.W. of Sheringham; 16th-cent. school.

Holt, t., Clwyd, **Wales**; on R. Dee, 11 km S. of Chester; cas. ruins.

Holyhead, spt., Anglesey, Gwynedd, **Wales**; on Holyhead I.; mail packet sta. for Ireland;

lt. engin., woodwkg., clocks; site for aluminium smelter; pt. traffic reduced as result of damage to Menai Bridge; p. (1971) 10,608.
Holy I. (**Lindisfarne**), off cst. of Northumberland, **Eng.**
Holy I., Scot., in F. of Clyde, nr. I. of Arran; submarine base.
Holy I., off cst. of Anglesey, Gwynedd, **Wales.**
Holyoke, t., Mass., **USA**; on Connecticut R., above Springfield; paper, machin.; p. (est. 1969) 52,000.
Holywell, mkt. t., Clwyd, N. Wales; woollen, rayon and paper inds.; p. (1971) 8,536.
Holywood, spt., North Down, **N. Ireland**; on S. shore of Belfast Lough; seaside resort; p. (1966) 7,795.
Homburg (**Bad Homburg**), c., Hesse, **W. Germany**; famous spa; p. (est. 1969) 40,485.
Home Counties, term applied to the geographical counties adjoining London, *i.e.*, Middlesex, Surrey, Essex, and Kent; sometimes Hertfordshire, Buckinghamshire, and Berkshire are included, and occasionally Sussex; (Middlesex and parts of Essex, Surrey, Kent, and Hertfordshire incorporated in Greater London 1965).
Homs, t., W. **Syria**; on R. Orontes; anc. Emesa; silk, textiles, cement; oil refinery; pipeline from Kirkūk oil fields; p. (1970) 216,000.
Honan (**Henan**), prov., N.E. **China**; traversed by Hwang-ho; cap. Chengchow; densely p. in fertile E.; mainly agr.; wheat, kaolin, cotton, anthracite; a. 167,172 km²; p. (est. 1968) 50,000,000.
Honda, old Spanish t., **Colombia**; on Magdelena R., at rapids; former comm. ctr.; p. (est. 1968) 22,315.
Honduras, rep., straddles Central American isthmus with longest cst. on Caribbean; comprises 18 deps. inc. offshore Bay Is.; coastal lowlands hot and humid, more temperate in interior highlands which rise to over 2,000 m; agr. basis of economy, especially American-owned banana plantations; bananas almost half exp.; some mng.; rlys. oriented to banana-producing areas to facilitate exp.; nationalised forests; land reform; cap. Tegucigalpa; 5 airports.; a. 111,958 km²; p. (est. 1969) 2,500,000.
Honduras, British. *See* **Belize.**
Hong Kong, Brit. Crown Col., S.E. cst. **China**, comprises Hong Kong I., Kowloon peninsula and New Territories (on lease from China until 1997); tunnel (1972) links H.K. with Kowloon; deepwater harbour of Victoria has lost much tr. from China; industl. development rapid since second world war yet few natural resources; dense p. aggravated by immigration from China; a. 1,031 km²; p. (1971) 3,950,802.
Honiara, t., cap. of **Solomon Is.**; on Guadalcanal I.; p. (1970) 11,191.
Honiton, t., E. Devon, **Eng.**; on R. Otter, 26 km E. of Exeter; mkt.; trout-fishing; once produced lace; p. (1971) 5,058.
Honolulu, c., cap. of **Hawaii**; on Oahu I.; social and comm. ctr. and ch. pt. of archipelago; gd. harbour; univ.; airport; fruit-canning, sugar-processing; tourism; p. (1970) 319,784 (c.), 613,114 (met. a.).
Honshu, lgst. I. of **Japan**; contains most of p. along E. cst. in 320 km industl. belt; new Seikan tunnel links I. to Hokkaido; a. 230,300 km²; p. (1970) 82,569,581.
Hoogeveen, t., Drenthe, **Neth.**; fruit- and vegetable-canning; p. (1968) 35,375.
Hooghly, R., arm of Ganges R., **India**; flows into Bay of Bengal; used in jute-milling and navigable as far as Calcutta; 256 km long.
Hooghly Chinsura, t., W. Bengal, **India**; on Hooghly R.; rice-milling; p. (1971) 105,241 (part of Calcutta met. a.).
Hook of Holland (**Hoek van Holland**), spt., **Neth.**; packet sta. with steamer connections to Harwich, Eng.
Hoorn, old fishing t., N. Holland, **Neth.**; on IJsselmeer, 32 km N. of Amsterdam; cheese and cattle mkts.; birthplace of Tasman, discoverer of Tasmania and N.Z., founder of Batavia; p. (1967) 17,072.
Hoover Dam, **USA**; on Colorado R.; used for irrigation (parts of Cal., Arizona, and Mexico), flood control and hydroelectric power; Lake Mead, 184 km long, 2–13 km wide, one of world's lgst man-made Ls.
Hopeh (**Hebei**), prov., N.E. **China**; part of N. China plain; bounded on N. by Great Wall; cap. Tientsin; wheat, kaoliang, cotton; coal mng.; a. 194,250 km²; p. (est. 1968) 47,000,000.
Hor, unlocated biblical mtn. between Dead Sea and G. of Aqaba, the place of Aaron's death.
Horbury, t., West Yorks., **Eng.**; nr. Wakefield; p. (1971) 8,914.
Horeb. *See* **Sinai.**
Horn, C., S. **Chile**, most S. point of S. America; severe gales.
Horncastle, mkt. t., Lincs., **Eng.**; at confluence of Rs. Bain and Waring at foot of Lincoln Wolds; mkt.; vegetable-processing; p. (1971) 4,096.
Hornchurch. *See* **Havering.**
Hornsea, t., Humberside, **Eng.**; on E. cst., N.E. of Hull; seaside resort; lge. freshwater L.; p. (1971) 7,021.
Hornsey. *See* **Haringey.**
Horsens, t., **Denmark**, E. Jutland; on inlet of Kattegat; industl. and comm ctr.; p. (est. 1970) 35,621.
Horsforth, t., West Yorks., **Eng.**; in Aire valley N.W. of Leeds; cloth, tanning, lt. engin.; p. (1971) 19,336.
Horsham, t., Victoria, **Australia**; on R. Wimmera; pastoral, dairying and agr. dist.; agr. machin.; p. (1972) 11,046.
Horsham, t., West Sussex, **Eng.**; on R. Arun at W. end of forested dist. of the High Weald; agr., timber, engin., chemicals; Horsham stone once quarried here; Shelley's birthplace; p. (1971) 26,378.
Horta, t., cap. of H. dist., **Azores**; on Fayal I.; excellent harbour and base for transatlantic flights; p. (1960) 7,109 (t.), 49,735 (dist.).
Horten, spt., **Norway**; nr. Oslo; naval base; ship-bldg., mftg. inds.; p. (est. 1970) 14,050.
Horton, R., N.W. Terr., **Canada**; flows into Beaufort Sea, Arctic Oc.; reindeer reserve along cst.
Horwich, t., Gtr. Manchester, **Eng.**; on W. edge of Rossendale Fells, N.W. of Bolton; rly. t.; engin.; p. (1971) 16,433.
Hospitalet, t., **Spain**; sub. of Barcelona, in Llobregat valley; p. (1967) 206,512.
Hot Springs, c., Ark., **USA**; in Ouachita mtns. S.W. of Little Rock; Nat. Park since 1832; health resort; p. (est. 1969) 38,000.
Houghton-le-Spring, t., Tyne and Wear, **Eng.**; S.W. of Sunderland; former colly. t.; coal-mng. dist.; p. (1971) 32,666.
Hounslow, outer bor., Greater London, **Eng.**; inc. former bors. of Brentford and Chiswick, Heston and Isleworth, Feltham and Hounslow; rubber goods; p. (1971) 206,182.
Housatonic, R., W. Mass., Conn., **USA**; falls attracted early Puritan settlement and industrialisation; dairy farming; 240 km long.
Houston, c., spt., S. Texas, **USA**; on Galveston Bay; gr. pt., lgst. c. of S.; univ.; oil refineries, oilfield machin., steel, chemicals, paper, processing, milling and assembling plants; NASA's manned space flight ctr. and lunar science institute; p. (1970) 1,213,064 (c.), 1,958,491 (met. a.).
Houston Ship Canal, Texas, **USA**; links Houston to head of shallow Galveston Bay and continues through bay to deep water; provides site for heavy inds.; opened 1915; total length 72 km.
Hove, t., East Sussex, **Eng.**; on S. cst., continuous with Brighton; residtl.; holiday resort; p. (1971) 72,659.
Howrah, c., W. Bengal, **India**; on W. bank of Hooghly R., in met. a. of Calcutta; p. (1971) 737,877.
Hoy, I., Orkneys, **Scot.**; lofty cliffs along W. cst.; separated from Mainland I. by Sound of Hoy; Old Man of Hoy rock 137 m high; p. (1971) 531 (inc. Walls).
Hoylake, t., Merseyside, **Eng.**; on N. cst. of Wirral peninsula; residtl.; golf course; p. (1971) 32,196.
Hradec Králové, t., **ČSSR**; at confluence of Elbe (Labe) and Orlice Rs.; industl. ctr.; mnfs. machin., precision instruments; 14th-cent. cath. and town hall; p. (1967) 64,000.
Huancayo, t., cap. of Junin dep., **Peru**; in high valley of Andes, *c.* 3,300 m; textiles; p. (est. 1969) 91,200.
Huarás or **Huaráz**, cap. of Ancash dep., **Peru**; on Santa R., *c.* 3,000 m; mainly agr., some mng.; avalanche 1941 killed 6,000 inhabitants; p. (1961) 11,628 (predominantly Indian).

Huascarán, extinct volcano, Peruvian Andes, nr. Huarás, 6,773 m high; avalanche 1970 killed 20,000 people.

Hubli, c., Karnataka, India; E. of Goa; textiles, rly. engin.; p. (1971) 377,166.

Hucknall, t., Nottingham, Eng.; hosiery, coal; p. (1971) 26,394.

Huddersfield, t., West Yorks., Eng.; on edge of Pennines, 16 km S. of Bradford; wool, textiles, chemicals, engin.; p. (1971) 130,964.

Hudson, R., N.Y., USA; flows from Adirondacks to N.Y. harbour; with valley of Mohawk R. makes gr. highway of tr. between Great Ls. and N.Y.; scenic beauty; hydroelec. power; 560 km long.

Hudson Bay, gr. inland sea, Canada; communicates by Hudson Strait with Davis Srait (Atl. Oc.); ice-free mid-July to Oct.; salmon, cod; a. 1,398,600 km².

Hué, c., Vietnam; on Hué R., 16 km from S. China Sea; pt. and tr. ctr.; former cap. of Annam; royal palace; p. (est. 1968) 156,537.

Huelva, coastal prov., S.W. Spain; copper mng., vine- and olive-growing, stock-raising, fisheries, brandy distilling; a. 10,117 km²; p. (1970) 397,683.

Huelva, c., cap. of Huelva prov., Spain; pt. on G. of Cadiz; oil refining, chemicals, food processing; exp. of minerals from nearby Rio Tinto; p. (1967) 90,740.

Huesca, c., cap. of H. prov., N.E. Spain; at foot of Pyrenees on R. Isuela; cath.; agr. ctr.; wine and timber tr. with France; p. (1970) 33,185.

Huhehot, c., Inner Mongolia, China; diesel engines; new woollen mill; p. (est. 1970) 700,000.

Hula L. *See* Waters of Merom.

Hull, t., S.W. Quebec, Canada; within met. a. of Ottawa; sawmills, paper; p. (1971) 62,842 (c.), 137,759 (met. a.).

Hull or Kingston-upon-Hull, c., Humberside, Eng.; major spt. of U.K.; at influx of R. Hull in estuary of Humber; lge. docks; premier distant waters fishing pt.; inds. inc. oil-extracting, flour milling, sawmilling, chemicals, engin.; p. (1971) 285,472.

Humber, estuary of Rs. Ouse and Trent, Eng.; fine waterway; 2–13 km wide, 61 km long.

Humberside, non-met. co., Eng.; inc. most of E. Riding of Yorks., and Humber estuary where growth of pt. processing and chem. inds. and impt. pts. of Hull and Grimsby; iron and steel at Scunthorpe; cstl. resort of Bridlington in N.E.; a. 3,512 km²; p. (1971) 838,000.

Humboldt, R., N. Nevada, USA; rises in Ruby Mtns., flows for 480 km before disappearing by evaporation and percolation; impt. 19th cent. routeway.

Humboldt Bay, inlet, Cal., USA; nuclear experimental breeder reactor.

Humboldt Current. *See* Peru Current.

Hume Lake, reservoir, N.S.W., Australia; formed by dam where R. Murray leaves Gr. Dividing Range; supplies water for irrigation in upper Riverina dist.; approx. capacity 113 million m³.

Hugh Town, cap. of the Scilly Isles, Eng.; on St. Mary's I.

Hunan, prov., central China; S. of the Yangtze; hilly in S. and W.; rice, wheat, beans; rich mineral resources, inc. mercury, tin, tungsten; cap. Changsha; Mao Tse-tung came from Hunan peasant stock; a. 205,589 km²; p. (est. 1968) 38,000,000.

Hunedoara, t., H. dist., Romania; iron and steel; p. (1966) 68,300.

Hungary, rep., E. Europe; bounded by USSR, ČSSR, Romania, Yugoslavia, and Austria; lies in basin of middle Danube (Duna), with plain in E. and Carpathian mtns. in W.; mainly agr.; exp. meat, fruit, vegetables to W. Europe; inds. increasingly impt. and now account for over 50 per cent of income; plans to make H. leading exporter of buses in Europe; 19 cos., cap. Budapest; a. 93,012 km²; p. (1970) 10,314,152.

Hungnam, spt., N. Korea; on Sea of Japan; on rly. to Seoul.

Hunsrück (= dog's back), forested highlands, Rhineland–Palatinate, W. Germany; between Mosel and Nahe Rs.; vineyards on S. slopes; hgst. point 816 m.

Hunstanton, t., Norfolk, Eng.; S.E. shore of Wash; seaside resort; p. (1971) 3,901.

Hunter, R., N.S.W., Australia; rises in Liverpool range of Gr. Dividing Range, flows S. and E. into Tasman Sea at Newcastle; *c.* 400 km long.

Hunterston, Cunninghame, Scot.; civil nuclear power sta.; integrated iron and steel wks., engin. of oil platforms and oil terminal planned.

Huntingdon, t., Cambs., Eng.; on R. Ouse; expanded t.; canning, engin., processed rubber, confectionery; birthplace of Cromwell and home of the poet Cowper; p. inc. Godmanchester (1971) 16,540.

Huntingdon and Peterborough, former co., Eng.; now part of Cambridgeshire non-met. co.

Huntington, c., W. Va., USA; on Ohio R.; R. pt. comm. ctr.; rly. wks., steel; p. (1970) 72,970 (c.), 247,059 (met. a.).

Huntly, burgh, Gordon, Scot.; at confluence of Rs. Bogie and Deveron; agr. mkt.; angling resort; p. (1971) 3,645.

Huntsville, c., Ala., USA; textiles; rocket research ctr.; p. (1970) 136,102 (c.), 224,217 (met. a.).

Hupeh (Hubei), prov., central China; N. of the Yangtze; many Ls. and Rs.; rice, wheat, cotton; iron ores; Hankow, Hanyang, Wuchang form tri-city of Wuhan, the major industl. region of central China; cap. Wuchang; a. 186,363 km²; p. (est. 1968) 32,000,000.

Huron, L., between Canada and USA; one of the Gr. Ls. of the St. Lawrence basin; a. 59,596 km²; 330 km long.

Husum, spt., Schleswig-Holstein, W. Germany; on N. Sea cst.; cattle mkt.; p. (est. 1969) 25,069.

Hutchinson, t., Kan., USA; salt-mng., meat-packing, flour milling, oil refining; p. (est. 1969) 40,000.

Hutt, Upper and Lower, t., N.I., N.Z.; meat-freezing, vehicle assembly textiles; p. (est. 1970) 59,400 (c.), 122,000 (met. a.).

Huyton with Roby, Merseyside, Eng.; sub. of Liverpool; p. (1971) 66,629.

Hwai-ho (Huai-ho), R., N. China; rises in Hwaiyang Shan, flows E. between N. China plain and lower Yangtze; subject to disastrous floods and changes of course; since 1950 flood control and irrigation canal to sea; *c.* 1,224 km long.

Hwainan (Huainan), c., Anhwei prov., central China; ctr. of China's ch. coalmng. region; p. (est. 1970) 350,000.

Hwang-hai (Yellow Sea), arm of Pac. Oc. between Korea and China; branches into Gs. of Pohai and Liaotung; shallow sea rapidly infilling; named after yellow silt coming from the Hwang-ho; length 960 km, greatest width 640 km.

Hwang-ho (Yellow R.), China; rises in Kunlun range, S. Chinghai prov.; flows c. 4,800 km into G. of Pohai; cuts through Shensi in a deep gorge; filled with yellow silt (loess) from this a.; floods frequently and changes course (once entered sea S. of Shantung); in lower part forms fertile plain; now part of multipurpose scheme for hydroelectric power, irrigation and flood control; lgst. dam in China opened at Liuchia in 1975; 4,640 km long.

Hwangshih (Huangshi), c., Hupeh prov., China; main iron and steel ctr. of central China, built since 1950; p. (est. 1970) 200,000.

Hyde, t., Gtr. Manchester, Eng.; on R. Tame, 8 km S.E. of Manchester; paints, chemicals, food-processing, tobacco, rubber; p. (1971) 37,075.

Hyderabad, ch. c., Andhra Pradesh, India; on R. Musi; walled t. and impt. comm. ctr.; univ.; p. (1971) 1,607,396 (c.), 1,796,339 (met. a.).

Hyderabad, c., Pakistan; 5 km W. of Indus; 144 km N.E. of Karachi; old cap of Sind; univ.; noted for silk, gold and silver embroidery; now varied mnfs.; dam at nearby Kotri; p. (1969) 698,000.

Hythe, t., Kent, Eng.; on S. cst., 5 km W. of Folkestone; one of the Cinque pts.; military canal passing through t., used for boating; p. (1971) 11,949.

I

Iasi (Jassy), c., Romania; former cap. of Moldavia; in fertile agr. region; univ., cath.; cultural ctr.; textiles, plastics, chems.; p. (est. 1969) 179,405.

Ibadan, c., cap. Oyo st.; S.W. Nigeria; univ.; ctr.

of rich agr. a., between the savannah and forest regions; p. mainly Yoruba; crafts, small inds.; p. (est. 1971) 758,332.

Ibagué, c., cap. of Tolima dep., **Colombia**; transport ctr.; cotton, tobacco, sugar, leather gds.; p. (est. 1972) 194,800 (c.), 218,600 (met. a.).

Ibarra, t., **Ecuador**; alt. 2,226 m at foot of Imbabura volcano; on Pan-American highway; p. (est. 1970) 37,100.

Iberian Peninsula, S.W. peninsula of **Europe**; containing sts. of Spain and Portugal; lge. a. of high tableland; interior isolation and regionalism; historical and contemporary importance for minerals; a. 593,250 km²; p. (1968) 41,500,000.

Iceland, rep., **N. Atl. Oc.**; volcanic I. with ice-covered plateaux; glacier fields cover 13,000 km²; only 1 per cent of a. cultivated; cold climate; hot house cultivation using thermal springs; economy dependent on fishing and fish-processing inds.; high standard of living; tourism increasingly impt.; 7 admin. dists.; cap. Reykjavik; a. 102,846 km²; p. (1969) 203,442.

Ichang (I-ch'ang), c., S.W. Hupeh, **China**; on R. Yangtze; site of famous gorges; terminus for lge. vessels from Shanghai.

Ichinomiya, c., S.E. Honshu, **Japan**; anc. Shinto shrine; textiles, pottery; p. (est. 1971) 223,000.

Ichow. *See* **Lin-i.**

Icknield Way, prehistoric route running from near Avebury, Wilts., along the Berkshire Downs, Chilterns and East Anglian Heights into Norfolk, crossing the Thames at Streatley.

Idaho, st., **USA**; one of the Rocky Mtn. sts.; rich in minerals; agr. mainly in irrigated Snake R. valley; cap. Boise; a. 216,413 km²; p. (1970) 698,275.

Idaho Falls, c., Idaho, **USA**; on Snake R.; food-processing, lumbering; silver, lead, and gold mines nearby; nuclear experimental breeder reactor; p. (est. 1969) 36,500.

Ida Mountains, range, N.W. **Turkey**; volcanic, hot springs; max. alt. Mount Gargarus, 1,768 m.

Idi Amin Dada (L. Edward), on frontier of **Uganda** and **Zaïre**, one of the sources of R. Nile; occupies Gr. Rift Valley; alt. *c.* 900 m, 70 km long, breadth 51 km; salt, fishing, wildlife.

Idle, t., West Yorks., **Eng.**; in Aire valley, 5 km N. of Bradford; woollens.

Ife, t., **Nigeria**; ctr. of the cacao tr.; univ.; p. (est. 1971) 157,178.

Ifni, enclave, S. **Morocco**; ceded by Spain to Morocco (1969); cap. Sidi Ifni; a. 1,500 km²; p. (1964) 51,517.

Igarka, sm. t., Siberia, **RSFSR**; on R. Yenisey, 640 km from its mouth; graphite plant, nickel-mines, lumber mills; p. 15,200.

Iglesias, t., Sardinia, **Italy**; N.W. of Cagliari; mng. for lead, pyrites, zinc; p. (est. 1968) 28,316.

Iguaçu, R., trib. of Paraná; mostly in Brazil; famous falls where Argentina, Brazil, and Paraguay meet, excelling Niagara, height 64 m; hydroelec. power potential.

IJmuiden, c., N. Holland, **Neth.**; on cst. at mouth of N. Sea canal; fishing; gasification plant, major iron and steel plant; p. (1968) 67,864 (c.), 135,334 (met. a.).

IJsselmeer (Lake IJssel), freshwater reservoir, **Neth.**, formerly Zuider Zee; separated from N. Sea by Wieringen–Friesland Barrage; active land reclamation in progress; Wieringermeer drained 1930, N.E. Polder 1942, E. Flevoland 1957, S. Flevoland 1968, Markerwaard still to be drained; when reclamation complete by end of cent. a. of Neth. will have been increased by some 6 per cent.; ch. c. on inlet (IJ) Amsterdam.

Ilchester, t., Somerset, **Eng.**; on R. Yeo; N.W. of Yeovil; birthplace of Roger Bacon.

Iles d'Hyères, I. gr., **France**; in Mediterranean off Toulon; tourism.

Ilesha, t., **Nigeria**; tr. ctr., cotton weaving; p. (est. 1971) 200,434.

Ilford. *See* **Redbridge.**

Ilfracombe, t., N. Devon, **Eng.**; sm. pt. on cst. of Bristol Channel; seaside resort; p. (1971) 9,846.

Ilhéus, spt., Bahia, **Brazil**; exp. cacao, timber; losing tr. to lge. pts.; p. (est. 1968) 100,687.

Ili, R., **Central Asia**; rises in Tienshan, China, and flows into L. Balkhash in Soviet terr.; new t. of I. at site of hydroelec. sta.; *c.* 1,200 km long.

Iligan, t., Mindanao, **Philippines**; integrated steel mill; cement; p. (est. 1969) 66,100.

Ilkeston, t., Derbys., **Eng.**; W. of Nottingham; iron, engin., locknit fabrics, needles, plastics; p. (1971) 34,123.

Ilkley, t., spa, West Yorks., **Eng.**; on R. Wharfe, N.W. of Leeds; local mkt.; p. (1971) 21,828.

Illawara, dist., N.S.W., **Australia**; forming belt of land between S. tableland and cst.; very fertile; dairy farming; coal seams; ch. ts., Kiama, Wollongong, Bulli, Gerringong.

Ille-et-Vilaine, dep., N.W. **France**; on English Channel; a. 6,990 km²; agr.; cap. Rennes; p. (1968) 652,722.

Illimani, one of the high peaks of the Cordillera Real, Andes, **Bolivia**, 6,461 m, E. of La Paz.

Illinois, st., **USA**; in Middle West; named after its principal R., a lge. trib. of Mississippi; many Rs.; cap. Springfield, metropolis Chicago; rich agr.; fuel and mineral resources; major coal-mng. st.; inds. inc. meat-processing, farm implements; a. 146,076 km²; p. (1970) 10,973,986.

Illinois, R., Ill., **USA**; glacial valley; long history of settlement; impt. routeway; 437 km long.

Illyria, region, mainly in **Yugoslavia**, stretching along Adriatic Sea from Trieste in N. to **Albania** in S. and inland as far as Rs. Danube and Morava.

Ilmen, L., **RSFSR**, nr. Novgorod; drained by Volkhov R. into L. Ladoga; a. 932 km²; fisheries.

Ilminster, t., Somerset, **Eng.**; 16 km S.E. of Taunton; cutstone, concrete, collars, radio valves; p. (1971) 3,375.

Iloilo, c., cap. of I. prov., Panay, **Philippines**; ctr. of rly. network; impt. pt. exp. sugar, rice, copra, hemp; p. (est. 1968) 201,000.

Ilorin, t., N. **Nigeria**; on Lagos–Kano rly.; agr. and caravan ctr.; govt. sugar-growing scheme at Bacita; p. (est. 1971) 252,076.

Imabari, t., spt., N.W. Shikoku, **Japan**; on shore of Inland Sea; mnfs. cotton textiles, paper, canned fruits; p. (est. 1971) 111,000.

Imatra, t., Kymi, **Finland**; hydroelec. power sta. supplies S. Finland; electro-metallurgy; p. (1968) 35,694.

Imbroz. *See* **Gökçeada I.**

Immingham, pt., Humberside, **Eng.**; on the Humber, N.W. of Grimsby; lge. docks; new deep-sea oil and coal terminals; chemicals engin., refinery nearby at Killingholme.

Imola, t., **Italy**; S.E. of Bologna; cath.; glass, pottery; p. (est. 1968) 55,580.

Imperia, t., **Italy**; on G. of Genoa; sm. pt., olive-growing ctr.; resort; p. (1969) 38,831.

Imperial Valley, S. Cal., **USA**; extends 48 km S.E. from Salton Sea to Mexican bdy.; mainly below sea-level; hot, arid climate; irrigation from Colorado R. chiefly by All-American Canal nr. Yuma; total irrigated a. 405,000 ha; principal crops, fruit, dates, tomatoes, cotton, and dairy prod.

Imphal, cap. of Manipur, **India**; in rice-growing basin in hills of Assam nr. Burma bdy.; p. (1971) 100,366.

Inari L., extensive L., Lappi, **Finland**; outlet into Barents Sea; hydroelec. power; a. 1,774 km².

Ince-in-Makerfield, t., Gtr. Manchester, **Eng.**; nr. Wigan; engin.; p. (1971) 15,925.

Inchon, c., **S. Korea**; on Yellow Sea; pt. for Seoul; exp. soyabeans, rice; textile ctr., steel mill, glass, diesel engines; p. (1966) 525,072.

Independence, c., Mo., **USA**; E. of Kansas; oil refining; agr. machin.; p. (est. 1969) 112,000.

India, rep., indep. st. (since 1947), S. **Asia**; second cty. of world by p.; 22 sts. and 9 union terrs.; peninsula bounded by Himalayas in N. extends in wide plateau to Indian Oc. in S.; most of p. concentrated in Indo-Gangetic Plain; unpredictable monsoon climate; heavy dependence on agr.; 70 per cent of p. farmers; few cash crops except cotton (the Deccan), tea (Himalayas), and jute (W. Bengal); 854 languages and dialects impede economic development; strong caste system; high illiteracy rate (70 per cent); little industl. development except in Damodar region; cap. New Delhi; main pts. Bombay, Calcutta; a. 3,268,580 km²; p. (1976) 605,000,000 (+25 per cent since 1961).

Indiana, st., **USA**; in Middle West, bounded by Mich., Ohio, Ill. and sep. from Ky. by Ohio R.; agr.; coal, limestone, petroleum; steel, metal prods., machin., food prod.; cap. Indianapolis; a. 93,994 km²; p. (1970) 5,143,422.

Indianapolis, c., cap. of Ind., USA; on White R.; univ.; rly. ctr.; meat-packing, jet engines, aircraft parts, chemicals, pharmaceutics; p. (1970) 742,613 (c.), 1,099,628 (met. a.).

Indian Ocean extends from S. of Asia and E. of Africa to the C. of Good Hope and C. Leeuwin in Australia, separated from the Pacific by the Malay Archipelago and Australia; a. 75,990,600 km².

Indigirka R., Yakut ASSR, **RSFSR**; flows into Arctic Oc.; hydroelec. power; 1,760 km long.

Indo-China, S.E. Asia; federation in Fr. Union until end of hostilities July 1954; consisted of the three sts. of Vietnam, Cambodia, and Laos.

Indo-Gangetic Plain, India, Bangladesh and **Pakistan**; name applied to flat land created by the Indus and Ganges basins; densely populated a.

Indonesia, rep., **S.E. Asia**; former Neth. E. Indies; made up of many sm. Is. straddling equator for over 4,800 km; many Is. in W. volcanic and E. coral; lgst. Is. inc. Java, Sumatra, Kalimantan (S. Borneo), Sulawesi, and Irian (W. New Guinea); mostly underdeveloped except Java; rapidly developing oil industry; 64 per cent p. on Java, planned decentralisation to other Is.; cap. Djakarta; a. 1,907,566 km²; p. (1974) 124,600,000; (+21 per cent since 1961).

Indore, c., Madhya Pradesh, India; nr. valley of Narbada R.; comm. ctr.; cotton-mills; p. (1971) 543,381 (c.), 560,936 (met. a.).

Indre, dep., central France; agr. and industl.; cap. Châteauroux; a. 6,905 km²; p. (1968) 247,178.

Indre-et-Loire, dep., central France; drained by Indre and Loire Rs.; vineyards, orchards; cap. Tours; a. 6,156 km²; p. (1968) 437,870.

Indus, R., Pakistan, rises in Tibet, flows through Kashmir, Punjab, Sind, to Arabian Sea; 5 tribs. Jhelum, Chenab, Ravi, Beas, Sutlej, form one of world's major R. systems, now used extensively to irrigate the Punjab and the Sind; impt. cotton, wheat, and sugar dist.; hydroelec. power; supported Indus valley civilisation 3,000–1,500 B.C.; 2,880 km long.

Ingleborough, mtn., near Settle, North Yorks., Eng.; underground caves, stalactites; made of limestone and millstone grit; alt. 724 m.

Inglewood, t., S. Cal., USA; sub. of Los Angeles; chinchilla farms; furniture, lt. engin., aircraft parts; p. (est. 1969) 85,000.

Ingolstadt, t., Bavaria, **W. Germany**; on Danube, nr. Munich; cas.; machin., cars, tobacco, oil refining; pipeline from Genoa; transalpine oil pipeline from Trieste, through N.E. Italy and Austria to I.; p. (est. 1967) 69,000.

Inhambane, spt., **Moçambique**; sugar, copra, oilseeds, bricks, soap, tiles; p. (1970) 745,911.

Inishboffin, I., Galway, **R.o.I.**, sm. I. off Connemara; farming, fishing.

Inishmore, lgst. of Aran gr., Galway, **R.o.I.**; fishing.

Inkpen Beacon, hill, Berks., Eng.; highest point reached by chalk hills in Eng.; alt. 297 m.

Inland Sea, Japan; between Honshu on N. and Shikoku and Kyushu on S.; sheltered sea with many Is.; ch. spts. Osaka, Amagaski, Kōbe, Okayama, Hiroshima, Kure; Nat. Park; a. c. 9,500 km².

Inn, R., traversing **Switzerland**, the Tyrol, **Austria** and **Bavaria**; enters R. Danube at Passau; hydroelec. plants; 512 km long.

Innerleithen, burgh, Tweeddale, **Scot.**, on R. Tweed, 8 km S.E. of Peebles; woollen cloth and knitwear; mineral springs; p. (1971) 2,218.

Inner Mongolia, Chinese aut. region, N.E. **China**; stretches along S. border of Mongolian People's Rep.; vast steppelands, sparse p.; st. farms for animal husbandry; peat beds; milk-processing; cap Huhehot; a. 1,177,518 km²; p. (est. 1967) 13,000,000.

Innisfail, t., Queensland, **Australia**; ch. sugar-producing ctr. of Australia; p. (1972) 7,475.

Innsbruck, c., cap. of the Tyrol, **W. Austria**; on R. Inn; commands N. approach to Brenner Pass; univ.; tourism; fortfd. 12th cent.; p. (est. 1969) 112,824.

Inowroclaw, t., N. **Poland**; nr. Bydgoszcz; rock-salt, iron pyrites; agr. prod.; p. (1970) 54,800.

Insterburg. *See* **Chernyakhovsk.**

Inter-American Highway, section of Pan-American Highway system, from Mexico to Panama.

Interlaken, t., Bernese Oberland, Berne, **Switzerland**; on R. Aare between Ls. Thun and Brienz; tourist resort; p. (1970) 4,735.

Intracoastal Waterway, **USA**; toll-free waterway along Atl. and Gulf of Mexico csts.; completed 1949 using bays, rivers and canals; 4,960 km long.

Inuvik, t., Arctic, **Canada**; above the permafrost.

Inveraray, burgh, Argyll and Bute, **Scot.**; nr. head of Loch Fyne; herring fishing; p. (1971) 438.

Inverbervie, burgh, Kincardine and Deeside, **Scot.**; on E. cst., 13 km S. of Stonehaven; linen, rayon inds.; p. (1971) 850.

Invercargill, t., S.I., **N.Z.**; on S.E. cst.; sawmills, freezing wks.; aluminium smelter; served by Bluff Harbour; p. (1971) 47,092.

Inverell, t., N.S.W., **Australia**; 613 km N. of Sydney; wheat and lamb cty.; tin; p. (1966) 8,411.

Invergordon, burgh, spt., Ross and Cromarty, **Scot.**; on N. side of Cromarty F., 19 km N.E. of Dingwall; former naval pt.; whisky distillery; lge. chemical ind. and aluminium smelter projected; p. (1971) 2,350.

Inverkeithing, royal burgh, Dunfermline, **Scot.**; on F. of Forth, nr. Dunfermline; shipbreaking, papermkg., quarrying; p. (1971) 5,861.

Inverkip, par., v., Inverclyde, **Scot.**; 10 km S.W. of Greenock; par. contains Gourock; resort; car ferry.

Inverness, royal burgh, Inverness, N.E. **Scot.**; on Moray F.; distilling, lt. engin., tweeds; sm. pt. for coal, timber; tourism; p. (1971) 34,839.

Inverness-shire, former co., l. gov. dist., N.E. **Scot.**; part of Highland Reg.; a. 11,269 km²; p. (1971) 49,285.

Inverurie, royal burgh, Gordon, **Scot.**; on R. Don, 22 km N.W. of Aberdeen; rly. ctr., mkt. t.; tourism; p. (1971) 5,437.

Inyokern, t., E. Cal., **USA**; naval ordnance research sta.

Ioánnina (Janina), t., Epirus, **Greece**; nr. Albanian frontier; agr. tr.; embroidery; univ.; p. (1971) 39,814.

Iona, I., off cst. of Mull, Argyll, **Scot.**; early Scottish Christian ctr.; restored abbey; St. Columba's burial place; anc. burial place of Scottish kings.

Ionian Is., gr. in Mediterranean, belonging to Greece; comprising Corfu, Paxos, Levkas, Cephalonia, Zakinthos, Ithake; severe earthquake 1953; total a. 1,948 km²; p. (1971) 183,633.

Ionian Sea, Mediterranean; between Greece on E.; Italy and Sicily on W.

Iowa, st., **USA**; in Middle West; prairie cty.; watered by Mississippi and Missouri; rich farm land; maize, oats, and other grains; hogs, pigs; processing of farm prod.; flood control, reforestation; diverse inds.; cap. Des Moines; a. 145,791 km²; p. (1970) 2,789,893.

Iowa City, c., S.E. Iowa, USA; former st. cap. (1839–56); univ.; p. (est. 1969) 47,000.

Ipin (Yibin), c., Szechwan prov., **China**; at junc. of Yangtze and Min Rs.; p. (est. 1970) 275,000.

Ipoh, c., cap. of Perak st., N.W. **Malaya**; tin-mng. ctr.; Chinese rock temples; p. (1970) 247,689.

Ipswich, t., S.E. Queensland, **Australia**; nr. Brisbane; coalmng. ctr.; woollens; p. (1966) 53,396.

Ipswich, co. t., Suffolk, **Eng.**; pt. on estuary of R. Orwell; diesel engines, gen. engin.; p. (1971) 122,814.

Iquique, t., N. **Chile**; pt. on Pac. Oc.; exp. nitrates and iodine from Atacama desert; fish-canning; p. (1966) 48,000.

Iquitos, t., N.E. **Peru**; on Amazon, 3,680 km from mouth; comm. ctr.; exp. timber, cotton; sawmills, oil refining; p. (est. 1969) 74,000.

Iráklion (Candia or Herakleion), t., Crete, **Greece**; impt. spt. on G. of I., arm of Aegean Sea; at foot of terraced hill slopes; wine, olive oil, fruit, fishing; tourism; p. (1971) 77,783.

Iran, kingdom, **S.W. Asia**; interior plateau at

c. 900 m, ringed by mtn. ranges of up to c. 5,500 m; much of a. is desert; settled agr. limited to Caspian plain; heavy dependence on oil; oilfields centred on Abādān; high quality carpets exported, esp. to USA; cap. Tehran; a. 1,626,520 km²; p. (est. 1969) 28,386,000.

Irapuato, c., central **Mexico**; agr. tr. and processing; iron-founding; p. (1970) 116,651.

Iraq, rep., S.W. **Asia**; the anc. Mesopotamia; dominated by 2 Rs., Tigris and Euphrates; much of a. desert and semi-desert but irrigation in S. and centre enables settled agr. for barley, wheat, dates, and tobacco; only outlet to sea at N.W. end of Persian G.; oil principal source of wealth; main oilfield at Kirkūk; main oil pt. at Basra; pipelines to Lebanon and Syria; new inds. based on oil; 14 provs.; cap. Baghdad; a. 435,120 km²; p. (est. 1970) 9,465,800.

Irazú, active volcano, 3,437 m high, central **Costa Rica**.

Irbid, t., **Jordan**; comm. and agr. tr. ctr.; p. (est. 1971) 115,000.

Ireland, I., W. of Gt. Britain, separated by Irish Sea; divided politically into R.o.I. (Eire) and N. Ireland (Ulster, part of U.K.); ch. physical features, L. Neagh in N.E., Ls. of Killarney in S.W.; Rs. Shannon, Boyne, Blackwater; mtns. of Mourne, Wicklow, and Kerry; mild moist climate; called "emerald isle" because of grasslands; pastoral agr., especially dairying; tourism; a. 83,937 km²; p. (1966) 3,088,759.

Ireland, Republic of, ind. st., W. **Europe**; comprises 26 of 32 cos. making up I. of Ireland; remaining 6 cos. belong to U.K.; ring of highlands surround central lowland basin, much of which is peat-covered; economy based on agr., especially dairying; exps. butter, cheese, bacon; new govt.-encouraged inds.; mineral resources; tourism; cap. Dublin; a. 68,894 km²; p. (1971) 2,978,248.

Irish Sea, **Brit. Is.**; between Gt. Britain and Ireland, connecting N. and S. with Atl. Oc.; 320 km long; 80–224 km wide; greatest depth 840 m; a. 18,130 km².

Irkutsk, c., cap. of I. oblast, **RSFSR**; on Angara R. in E. Siberia; on Trans-Siberian rly., 64 km W. of L. Baykal; univ.; engin., sawmilling, petroleum refining, chemicals, hydroelec. power sta.; p. (1970) 451,000.

Irlam, t., Gtr. Manchester, **Eng.**; engin., tar, soap, glycerine, margarine; steel wks. to close; overspill p.; p. (1971) 20,571.

Ironbridge, t., Salop, **Eng.**; scene of Darby's iron ind.; derives name from first cast-iron bridge (1779) which here crosses Severn; now inc. in Dawley new t.

Iron Country, Utah, **USA**; vast reserves of iron ore; undeveloped due to inaccessibility.

Iron Gate (Portile de Fier), **Romania**; famous rapids in R. Danube; Romanian–Yugoslavian hydroelectric and navigation project, 1964–71.

Irrawaddy, R., **Burma**; flows S. to Bay of Bengal; navigable for lge. steamers 1,440 km; irrigation wks.; major Asian rice bowl; 2,000 km long.

Irthlingborough, t., Northants., **Eng.**; p. (1971) 5,145.

Irtysh, R., W. Siberia, **USSR**; ch. trib. of R. Ob'; crossed by Turk-Sib rly. at Semipalatinsk and by Trans-Siberian rly. at Omsk; hydroelectric power stas.; 2,960 km long.

Irvine, royal burgh, Cunninghame, **Scot.**; nr. mouth of R. Irvine; new t. (1966); cas.; hosiery, lt. engin., bottle wks., chemicals; p. (est. 1974) 50,100.

Irvington, t., N.J., **USA**; industl. sub. of Newark; machin.; p. (est. 1969) 62,000.

Irwell, R. Gtr. Manchester **Eng.**; flows through Manchester to the Mersey via Manchester Ship Canal: 48 km long.

Isar, R., **Austria** and **W. Germany**; rises in Austrian Tyrol, flows N.E. to Danube; hydroelectric power stas. below Munich; 261 km long.

Isarco, R., N. **Italy**; rises nr. Brenner Pass, flows S. into R. Adige at Bolzano; 80 km long.

Isa Town, new t., **Bahrain**; 6 km from Al Manāmah; proposed p. 35,000.

Ischl or **Bad Ischl**, famous Alpine spa, **Austria**, in Salzkammergut.

Isdud, anc. c. of the Philistines. *See* **Ashdod**.

Ise (Ujiyamada), t., Honshu, **Japan**; sacred c. of Shintoism; p. (1970) 103,576.

Ise Bay, inlet, S. Honshu, **Japan**; flanked by ch. textile mftg. a. of cty. with 5 million people centred on Nagoya; 64 km long, 24–32 km wide.

Iselle, t., N.W. **Italy**; S. terminal Simplon tunnel.

Iseo, L., N. **Italy**; E. of Bergamo; 124 km².

Isère, dep., S.E. **France**; drained by Rs. Isère and Rhône; cap. Grenoble; mtnous.; cereals; wine, butter, cheese; iron, coal, lead, silver, copper; gloves, silks; a. 8,231 km²; p. (1968) 768,450.

Isère, R., S.E. **France**; rises in Graian Alps, flows W. into R. Rhône nr. Valence; used to generate hydroelec. power; used, with trib. R. Arc, by main rly. from France to N. Italy through Mt. Cenis (Fréjus) tunnel.

Iserlohn, t., N. Rhine-Westphalia, **W. Germany**; S.E. of Dortmund; metal gds.; p. (est. 1967) 57,400.

Isfahan. *See* **Eşfahān**.

Ishikari, t., Hokkaido, **Japan**; on cst. of Otaru Bay, 16 km N. of Sapporo; ctr. of second lgst. coalfield in Japan; sm. petroleum production.

Ishimbay, c., Bashkir ASSR, **RSFSR**; on R. Belaya; ctr. of Ishimbay oilfields; pipelines to Ufa, Orsk, and Shkaparo; p. (est. 1967) 53,000.

Isiro (Paulis), t., N.E. **Zaire**; admin. offices; cotton ginneries; rly. repair shops.

Isis, R., headstream of R. Thames, **Eng.**; so named around and above Oxford.

Iskenderun (Alexandretta), spt., S. **Turkey**; recent modernisation for new Iran/Turkey rly.; new steel wks.; p. (1965) 69,259.

Islamabad, new cap. of **Pakistan**, to N. of Rawalpindi below Himalayas; nuclear power sta.; p. (1972) 235,000.

Islay, I. Inner Hebrides, Argyll and Bute. **Scot.**; a. 609 km²; farming, dairying, distilleries; p. (1971) 3,827.

Isle of Grain, Kent, **Eng.**; flat promontory at confluence of Thames and Medway, once separated from mainland by a tidal estuary; lge oil refinery; pipelines to Walton-on-Thames and Heathrow Airport.

Isle of Man, Irish Sea; 43 km from Eng. (Cumbria) and N. Ireland (Down); high plateau N.E. to S.W.; ch. t. Douglas; old cap. Castletown; admin. according to own laws; tourism; a. 572 km²; p. (1971) 49,743.

Isleworth. *See* **Hounslow**.

Islington, inner bor., London, **Eng.**; N. of City; incorporates Finsbury; univ.; residtl.; clocks, precision engin.; p. (1971) 199,129.

Ismailia (Ismâ'ilîya), t., **Egypt**; at mid-point of Suez Canal on L. Timsah; rail connections with Cairo, Suez, Port Said; declined during canal closure; p. (est. 1970) 167,500.

Isna (Esneh), t., Upper **Egypt**; on Nile; agr. ctr.; cottons, pottery; p. (1966) 27,400.

Ispra, t., Varese, **Italy**; nr. L. Maggiore; nuclear research ctr.

Israel, rep., S.W. **Asia**; occupies narrow corridor between Jordan valley and Mediterranean Sea; extends S. into the Negev desert (half a. of rep.); Mediterranean climate enables cultivation of early fruits and vegetables, especially citrus fruits; most highly industrialised cty. of S.W. Asia, especially for textiles and clothing; petroleum of increasing impt.; tourism; Jewish rep. since 1948; until then part of the mandate Palestine; surrounded by hostile Arab sts.; difficulties of increasing Jewish immigration; cap. Jerusalem; a. 20,850 km²; nat. a. in dispute, particularly since Arab-Israeli wars of 1967 and 1973; p. (1970) 2,995,000 (75 per cent Jewish).

Issyk Kul, mtn. L., Kirghiz SSR, **USSR**; in Tien-Shan mtns., alt. 1,568 m; a. 6,216 km²; ice-free in winter.

Issy-les-Moulineaux, sub. S.W. Paris, Hauts-de-Seine, **France**; engin.; p. (1968) 51,666.

Istanbul (Constantinople), ch. spt., former cap., **Turkey**; on Golden Horn peninsula on European cst. at entry of Bosporus into Sea of Marmara; divided into old "Stamboul" on S. side, and dists. of Galata and Beyoglu (Pera) on N.; the anc. Byzantium; magnificent mosque of Sta. Sophia; univ.; industl. and comm. ctr.; tourism; p. (1970) 2,312,751.

Istria, peninsula, N. Adriatic, **Yugoslavia**; ch. c. Pula; agr., olives, vines, oranges, maize; p. Yugoslav and Italian; a. c. 5,200 km².

Itabira, t., Minas Gerais st., **Brazil**; on Brazilian

Plateau, 96 km N.E. of Belo Horizonte; lgst. deposits of iron ore in Brazil; p. (est. 1968) 42,836.

Itabuna, t., Bahia, E. **Brazil**; cocoa, livestock; p. (est. 1968) 87,561.

Itajaí, spt., Santa Catarina, S. **Brazil**; exp. lumber, cement, agr. prods.; p. (est. 1968) 59,423.

Italy, rep., S. **Europe**; peninsula extending into Mediterranean; inc. 2 main Is. of Sicily and Sardinia; bounded by Alps to N.; central spine of Apennines; Mediterranean climate; contrast between industrialised N. and less developed agr. S. (Mezzogiorno); agr. impt., especially in Po basin; tourism attracted by Roman and Renaissance architecture and by climate; inds. based on hydroelectric power in N., inc. elec. engin., motor vehicles and textiles, centred at Milan and Turin; 19 admin. regions; cap. Rome; a. 301,049 km²; p. (1976) 56,024,000.

Ithaca, t., N.Y., **USA**; on Cayuga L.; seat of Cornell Univ.; elec. clocks; machin.; p. (est. 1969) 29,500.

Ithake, one of the Ionian Is., **Greece**; a. 96 km²; ch. t. Ithake; severe earthquake, 1953.

Itzehoe, t., Schleswig-Holstein, W. **Germany**; founded by Charlemagne; wood, cement, machin.; p. (est. 1969) 35,874.

Ivano-Frankovsk (**Stanislav**), c., Ukrainian SSR, **USSR**; in Carpathian foothills; industl. ctr.; oilfields nearby; oil refineries, engin.; p. (1970) 105,000.

Ivanovo, t., **RSFSR**; N.E. of Moscow; textiles, iron and chemical wks.; peat-fed power stas.; p. (1970) 419,000.

Iviza, I., Balearic gr. in the W. **Mediterranean**; Spanish; cath.; tourism.

Ivory Coast, rep., on G. of Guinea, **W. Africa**; formerly a Fr. overseas terr.; hot, humid climate; coastal lagoons, interior plateau (300–1,200 m); economy based on subsistence agr. although an impt. coffee and timber producer; underdeveloped mineral resources; poorly developed rail network but extensive road system; new pt. at San Pedro; Pt. Bouet outport of cap. Abidjan; a. 322,481 km²; p. (est. 1969) 4,200,000.

Iwaki, t., Honshu, **Japan**; ctr. of apple producing dist.; p. (est. 1971) 331,000.

Iwakuni, t., Honshu, **Japan**; on Inland Sea; p. (est. 1971) 108,000.

Iwo, t., **Nigeria**; nr. Ibadan; tr. ctr.; p. (est. 1971) 191,684.

Izhevsk, c., cap. of Udmurt ASSR, **RSFSR**; steel ctr., engin.; p. (1970) 422,000.

Izmail, c., Ukrainian SSR, **USSR**; in Bessarabia, on Danube delta, nr. Romanian border; naval base of Soviet Danube flotilla; former Turkish fortress; p. (est. 1967) 63,000.

Izmir (**Smyrna**), c., **Turkey**; at head of G. of I., Anatolia; exp. figs, raisins, tobacco, carpets, rugs; anc. and historic c.; ch. comm. ctr. of the Levant; univ.; p. (1970) 753,443.

Izmit, c., **Turkey**; E. end of Sea of Marmara; cereals, tobacco, oil refinery and polythene plant under construction; p. (1965) 90,061.

J

Jabalpur (**Jubbulpore**), c., Madhya Pradesh, **India**; rly. ctr.; ordnance wks.; p. (1971) 426,224 (c.), 534,845 (met. a.).

Jablonec nad Nisou, t., **ČSSR**; on R. Neisse; glassware ctr., inc. glass jewellery and imitation stones; p. (est. 1968) 33,722.

Jáchymov, t., **ČSSR**; spa; uranium mines, pitchblende, lead, silver, nickel, cobalt.

Jackson, t., Mich., **USA**; on Grand R.; locomotives, motorcar accessories, electronic equipment, metal gds.; p. (1970) 45,733 (c.), 142,422 (met. a.).

Jackson, t., cap. of Miss., **USA**; comm. and industl. ctr.; birthplace of Harry S. Truman; p. (1970) 150,332 (c.), 252,713 (met. a.).

Jacksonville, c., Fla., **USA**; pt. on St. John's R.; impt. ctr. on Atl. cst.; chemicals, shipbldg. and repair, printing, lumber, cigar mftg.; tourism; p. (1970) 513,439.

Jacobabad, t., Sind, **Pakistan**; driest and hottest place in Indian sub-continent; p. (1961) 35,200.

Jacuí, R., S. **Brazil**; rises in S. edge of Brazilian Plateau, enters Atl. Oc., through lagoon, Lagoa dos Patos; 560 km long.

Jadotville, t., **Zaïre**; copper mng. and refining; p. (est. 1966) 102,187.

Jaduguda, Bihar, **India**; uranium plant.

Jaén, t., cap. of prov. of Jaén, S. **Spain**; in foothills of Andalusian mtns.; cath.; olive oil, wine, chemicals; p. (1967) 71,508.

Jaffna, spt., N. **Sri Lanka**; on J. peninsula; second t. of rep.; p. (est. 1968) 101,700.

Jaipur, c., cap. of Rajasthan, **India**; univ.; fine fabrics, jewellery; tourism; old cap. Amber is 8 km away; p. (1971) 615,258 (c.), 636,768 (met. a.).

Jajce, t., **Yugoslavia**; in Bosnia, at junc. of Rs. Vrbas and Pliva (hydroelectric power); Fed. People's Rep. of Yugoslavia declared here by Tito (1943).

Jakarta. *See* **Djakarta**.

Jalalabad, c., E. **Afghanistan**; on Kābul R., nr. Khyber Pass; univ.; agr. tr. ctr.; p. (est. 1969) 48,919.

Jalapa, c., cap. of Veracruz st., **Mexico**; *c.* 1,370 m; a.s.l.; luxuriant vegetation; agr. ctr.; tourism; p. (1970) 122,377.

Jalgaon, t., Maharashtra, **India**; in Tapti R. valley nr. Bhusawal; p. (1971) 106,711.

Jalisco, st., **Mexico**; on Pac. Oc.; traversed by Sierra Madre; well timbered, agr.; minerals; tourism; a. 80,876 km²; p. (1969) 3,344,000.

Jalón, R., **Spain**; rises in Iberian Mtns., flows N.E. into R. Ebro nr. Zaragoza; valley forms main rly., road route from Madrid to Ebro valley.

Jalpaiguri, t., W. Bengal, **India**; frontier t.; rly. ctr.; p. (1961) 48,738.

Jamaica, rep., **W.I.**; member of Brit. Commonwealth; mtnous.; Blue Mtn. range runs E. to W. and rises to 2,258 m; tropical climate modified by alt.; economy based on agr. and mng.; major exp. crops sugar and bananas; major world producer of bauxite and alumina; tourist ind. expanding; member of Caribbean Free Trade Association; 25 per cent unemployment; major pts. Kingston, Montego Bay, Pt. Antonio; international airpt.; univ. at cap. Kingston; a. 11,424 km²; p. (est. 1975) 2,100,000, of which 45% are in Kingston.

James, R. Va., **USA**; hydroelec. power in upper reaches, wide estuary in lower course; outlet to Chesapeake Bay; 544 km long.

James Bay, S. arm of Hudson Bay, **Canada**; *c.* 480 km long, 224 km wide.

Jameshedpur, c. Bihar, **India**; W. of Calcutta; major industl. ctr. of rep.; Tata iron and steel wks.; engin.; p. (1971) 199,709 (c.), 227,640 (met. a.).

Jamestown, spt., cap. of **St. Helena I.**; flax; p. (1966) 1,475.

Jamestown, t., dist., Va., **USA**; nr. mouth of James R., where first English permanent settlement was founded 1607.

Jammu, t., J. and Kashmir, **India**; winter cap. of st.; univ., fort, palace; p. (est. 1970) 135,522.

Jammu and Kashmir, st., N.W. **India**; traversed by ranges of Himalayas; in Jhelum valley is celebrated vale of Kashmir, producing abundant crops of wheat and rice; cap. Srinagar; Muzaffarabad ch. c. of a. occupied by Pakistan (Azad Kashmir); total a. 222,823 km²; p. (1971) 4,615,176.

Jamnagar, t., Gujarat, **India**; on G. of Kutch; p. (1971) 199,709 (t.), 227,640 (met. a.).

Janina. *See* **Ioánnina**.

Jan Mayen I., volcanic I. between Spitzbergen and Iceland, Arctic Oc.; annexed by **Norway** 1929; meteorological sta.; a. 373 km²; p. (1967) 36.

Japan, monarchy, E. **Asia**; 4 main Is., Honshu (lgst.), Hokkaido, Shikoku, Kyushu; mtnous.; 18 active volcanoes; subject to earthquakes; only 17 per cent of land cultivable; intensive and mechanised agr.; rice, fruits, vegetables; few animals; inds. highly developed and based on imports of raw material and export of finished prods.; rapid industrialisation since second world war; inds. inc. shipbldg., motor vehicles, textiles, steel, chemicals, cheap consumer gds.; cap. Tokyo; a. 370,370 km²; p. (1975) 111,933,818 (inc. Okinawa and Ryuku Is.).

Japan Current. *See* **Kuroshio**.

Japan, Sea of, portion of **Pac. Oc.** between Korea, USSR, and Japan.
Japurá, R., Colombia, Brazil; rises as Caquetá in Colombian Andes, flows S.E. through Brazil to Amazon; 2,080 km long.
Jaroslaw, t., Rzeszow prov., S.E. **Poland;** on R. San; food-processing; founded 11th cent.; impt. tr. ctr. 16th cent.; p. (1970) 29,100.
Jarrow, t., Tyne and Wear, **Eng.;** on S. bank of Tyne, 11 km below Gateshead; grew up as shipbldg. ctr.; hit by depression of 1930s; new enterprises introduced; steel and tube wks., oil storage; die-castings, knitting-wool-mkg. at Bede trading estate; the Venerable Bede lived and died here; p. (1971) 28,779.
Jasper National Park, Alberta, **Canada;** Rocky mtns.; tourism.
Jaunpur, t., Uttar Pradesh, **India;** mkt. t.; ctr. of Moslem learning and architecture in 15th cent.; p. (1961) 61,851.
Java, I., **Indonesia;** most developed of Indonesian Is.; traversed E. to W. by forested volcanic mtns.; fertile volcanic soils aid intensive rice cultivation; over-populated; contains 70 per cent of cty.'s p. yet only 8 per cent of land a.; exps. inc. coffee, rubber, sugar, copra, teak; noted for silver craft and batik work (anc. craft of fabric decoration); a. 130,510 km^2; p. (est. 1970) 78,660,000.
Javari, R., forms bdy. between **Peru** and **Brazil;** trib. of R. Amazon.
Java Sea, part of the **Pac. Oc.** between N. cst. Java, Borneo, and Sumatra.
Jebba, t., **Nigeria;** on R. Niger; dam proposed for 1982.
Jebel Aulia, v., **Sudan;** S. of Khartoum; dam across White Nile R.
Jebel, Arabic term for mtn., mtn. range, or highland.
Jebel-Hauran, high tableland of **Syria,** alt. *c.* 1,800 m.
Jedburgh, royal burgh, Roxburgh, **Scot.;** on Jed Water, S.W. of Kelso; tweeds, woollens, rayon; abbey ruins; ctr. of Border warfare in Middle Ages; p. (1971) 3,874.
Jeddah. *See* **Jiddah.**
Jefferson City, st. cap. Mo., **USA;** on Missouri R.; univ.; comm. and processing ctr. of agr. a.; shoes, tiles, farm implements; p. (est. 1969) 29,500.
Jelenia Góra (Hirschberg), t., S.W. **Poland** (since 1945), formerly in Lower Silesia; mftg.; spa; p. (1970) 55,700.
Jelgava (Mitau), t., Latvian SSR, **USSR;** on Lielupe R.; textiles, foodstuffs, refractory materials; p. (est. 1967) 49,000.
Jemappes, t., **Belgium;** 5 km W. of Mons; industl.; Fr. victory over Austria 1792; battle of Mons 1914; p. (est. 1969) 12,548.
Jena, c., **E. Germany;** on R. Saale, 72 km S.W. of Leipzig; univ., observatory; optical glassware, precision instruments; leading cultural ctr. late 18th and early 19th cent.; defeat of Prussians by Fr. 1806; p. (est. 1967) 83,900.
Jensen, t., Utah, **USA;** oil refinery; on R. Green.
Jerez de la Frontera, t., **Spain;** in Andalusia, 22 km N.E. of Cádiz; in fertile agr. a.; sherry; p. (est. 1967) 147,633.
Jericho, v., Jordan Valley, **Jordan;** est. through recent excavations as one of oldest towns in the world (6000 B.C.); p. (1961) 10,284.
Jersey, I., lgst of **Channel Is.,** 21 km W. of **Fr.** cst.; potatoes, tomatoes, cauliflowers, flowers, fruit. cattle; tourist resort; banking; ch. t. St. Helier; a. 117 km^2; p. (est. 1973) 72,000.
Jersey City, c., N.J., **USA;** E. of Newark, on Hudson R.; comm. and industl. ctr.; diverse inds.; rly. ctr.; p. (1970) 253,467 (c.), 597,091 (met. a.).
Jerusalem, c., **Israel** and **Jordan;** 811 m a.s.l.; between Dead Sea and Mediterranean; the "Holy City" of the Jews and the sacred c. of the Christians and Moslems; divided between Israel and Jordan; Israeli sector cap. of Israel; Old City annexed by Israel June 1967; modern mftg.; p. (1972) 304,500 inc. E. Jerusalem.
Jervis Bay, inlet of Pac. Oc., N.S.W., **Australia;** acquired by Fed. Govt. as site for establishment of pt. for Canberra 1909; a. 73 km^2.
Jesenice, t., **Yugoslavia;** integrated iron and steel wks.; terminal of Brotherhood and Unity Highway.
Jesselton. *See* **Kota Kinabalu.**
Jhang Maghiana, t., **Pakistan;** textiles; mkt.; on R. Chenab; p. (1969) 118,000.
Jhansi, c., Uttar Pradesh, **India;** rly. ctr., mkt.; formerly of strategic importance; p. (1971) 173,292 (c.), 198,135 (met. a.).
Jharia, t., Bihar, **India;** ctr. of most impt. coalfield in India; p. (1961) 33,683.
Jhelum, R., W. Punjab, **Pakistan;** most W. of the five Rs. of the Punjab; forms Vale of Kashmir in upper course; Mangla Dam under Indus Waters Treaty, completed 1967.
Jhelum, t., **Pakistan;** on Jhelum R.; p. (1961) 52,585.
Jiddah or Jeddah, c., Hejaz, **Saudi Arabia;** on Red Sea, pt. of Mecca; pilgrims; steel mill projected; new King Faisal Port nearby; univ. (with Mecca); p. (est. 1965) 194,000.
Jihlava, t., Moravia, **ČSSR;** on Jihlava R.; 519 m a.s.l.; timber, grain, textiles; Prague Compactata signed here 1436; p. (1967) 38,000.
Jimma, t., **Ethiopia;** ch. prod. Jimma coffee; connected by road with Addis Ababa; Agricultural Technical School.
Jinja, t., **Uganda;** on N. shore of L. Victoria where Nile drains from L. over Ripon Falls; (now inundated by Owen Falls dam 2·4 km upstream); cotton mnfs., copper smelting, flour and maize milling; rly. to Kampala; p. (1961) 29,741.
João Pessoa, t., cap. of Paraíba st., **Brazil;** through its pt. Cabedelo expts. cotton, sugar, minerals; p. (1970) 197,398.
Joban, dist., N.E. Honshu, **Japan;** third lgst. coalfield in Japan; ch. t. Fukushima.
Joda, Orissa, **India;** ferromanganese plant.
Jodhpur, t., Rajasthan, **India;** ctr. of Thar desert; old fortress t.; p. (1971) 317,612.
Jogjakarta, c., Java, **Indonesia;** univ., cultural ctr.; handicrafts; citadel with palace; p. (1971) 342,367.
Johannesburg, c., Transvaal, **S. Africa;** univ.; gold-mng. ctr. of Witwatersrand; diamond cutting, engin., textiles, chemicals; oil pipeline from Durban; p. (1970) 1,432,643 (met. a.).
John o'Groat's House, place nr. Duncansby Head, Caithness, **Scot.**
Johnstone, burgh, Renfrew, **Scot.;** on R. Black Cart, nr. Paisley; machine tools, textiles, iron and brass foundry; p. (1971) 22,617.
Johnstown, industl. t., Penns., **USA;** on Conemaugh R.; coal-mng. and steel ctr.; machin.; p. (1970) 42,065 (t.), 260,692 (met. a.).
Johore, st., **Malaysia;** at S. end of Malaya; forested; cap. Johor Baharo; rubber, rice, copra, pineapples; tin, iron, bauxite; a. 18,985 km^2; p. (1967) 1,297,962.
Joina Falls, Mali; dam projected for hydro-electric power and irrigation under auspices of Organisation of Riparian States of R. Senegal (Guinea, Mali, Mauritania, Senegal).
Joinville, t., Santa Catarina, **Brazil;** exp. timber, maté tea; textiles, machin., car parts, plastics; p. (est. 1968) 88,647.
Joliet, c., Ill., **USA;** on Des Plaines R., S.W. of Chicago; R. pt.; coal and limestone nearby; rly. engin., oil refining; p (est. 1969) 77,000.
Joliette, t., Quebec, **Canada;** textile mills, paper, tobacco-processing; p. (1970) 78,887.
Jönköping, t., cap. of J. co., **Sweden;** safety-matches, textiles, footwear; p. (1968) 53,815.
Jonquière, t., S. Quebec, **Canada;** paper and pulp mills; p. (1971) 28,080.
Joplin, t., Mo., **USA;** in dairy and livestock region; lead and zinc mng.; mnfs. metal and leather gds.; p. (est. 1969) 38,500.
Jordan, kingdom, S.W. Asia; bounded by Israel, Syria, Saudi Arabia, and Iraq; consists of high plateau (600 m), Jordan valley, and hill cty. to W. of R. Jordan; only 25 per cent of a. sufficiently humid for agr., much is migratory herding of animals and subsistence agr.; sm. mineral wealth; only outlet to sea Aqaba, pt. on G. of Aqaba; only one single-track rly.; cap. Amman; W. Bank of R. Jordan occupied by Israeli forces since June 1967; plan mooted (1972) to unify J. and W. Bank to form United Arab Kingdom; a. 101,140 km^2; p. (est. 1969) 2,250,000 (80 per cent Moslem and 70 per cent under 24).
Jordan, R., **Israel** and **Jordan;** flows S. from Anti-Lebanon along sinuous course, mostly below sea-level to Dead Sea; its rapidity and variant

depth render it unnavigable, and no t. of any importance has ever been built on its banks; Jesus was baptised in its waters; contemporary strife over use for irrigation; 368 km long.
Jos, t., central **Nigeria**; on Bauchi Plateau, 96 km S.W. of Bauchi; impt. tin mines; p. (est. 1969) 104,838.
Jostedalsbre, icefield, W. **Norway**, lgst. icefield of European mainland; a. 881 km²; rises to 2,043 m.
Jotunheimen, mtn. region, central **Norway**; hgst. in Scandinavia; Galdhopiggen 2,470 m, Glitter tind 2,482 m.
Juan Fernández, two rocky volcanic Is., S. Pac. Oc., belonging to Chile; a. 98 km²; the buccaneer Alexander Selkirk marooned here 1704–9 gave idea for Defoe's *Robinson Crusoe*.
Juan les Pins, resort, Alpes-Maritimes dep., S.E. France.
Juba (Giuba), R., **Somalia**; narrow fertile valley, impt. agr. a.; 872 km long.
Jubbulpore. *See* **Jabalpur**.
Júcar, R., E. **Spain**; rises in Montes Universales, and flows to Mediterranean; irrigation and hydroelec. power; 400 km long.
Judaea, div of Palestine in the Roman period.
Juggernaut. *See* **Puri**.
Jugoslavia. *See* **Yugoslavia**.
Juiz de Fora, t., Minas Gerais, **Brazil**; textile ctr.; p. (1970) 218,832.
Julfa (Jolfa), c., N. **Iran**; on frontier with USSR, customs and transit ctr. on overland route from Europe.
Julian Alps, mtn. range, **Yugoslavia** and **Italy**; hgst. peak 2,865 m.
Julianehåb, t., S.W. **Greenland**; N.W. of C. Farewell; tr. ctr., fish. pt.
Jülich, t., N. Rhine–Westphalia, **W. Germany**; nuclear reactor.
Jullundur, c., Punjab, **India**; rly. ctr.; st. cap. until Chandigarh was built; p. (1971) 296,106.
Jumna, R., N. **India**; ch. trib. of R. Ganges; rises in the Himalayas and flows past Delhi and Agra to Allahabad; 1,376 km long.
Junagadh, t., Gujarat, **India**; agr. tr. and food-processing; industl. ctr.; formerly cap. of principality of J.; p. (1961) 74,298.
Jundiai, t., São Paulo st., **Brazil**; industl. ctr.; nr. São Paulo; p. (1970) 145,785.
Juneau, c., cap. of Alaska, **USA**; at foot of Chilkoot mtns.; lumbering; fisheries; gold settlement (1881); p. (1970) 13,556.
Jungfrau, peak, Bernese Oberland, **Switzerland**; height 4,161 m; electric rly. from Kleine Scheidegg to Jungfraujoch.
Junin, t., **Argentina**; agr. tr., rly. engin., pottery, furniture; p. (1960) 53,489.
Jura, dep., E. **France**; named from mtn. range on Franco-Swiss border; agr. and pastoral; cap. Lons-le-Saunier; a. 5,053 km²; p. (1968) 233,547.
Jura, I., Argyll and Bute, **Scot.**; off W. cst.; a. 378 km²; p. (1971) 349 inc. Colonsay.
Jura, mtn. range, **Switzerland** and **France**; folded parallel ranges separated by deep R. valleys; hgst. peak Crêt de la Neige, 1,724 m; 240 km long, breadth 48–64 km.
Juruá R., lge. trib. of Amazon; rises in E. **Peru** and flows through Acre and Amazonas sts., **Brazil**; over 3,200 km long.
Jutland (Jylland), peninsula, **Denmark**; intensive agr. and poultry farming; sandy heath in W.; more fertile clay in E. used for dairying; a. 29,554 km²; p. (1971) 2,193,070.
Jyväskylä, t., central **Finland**; pt. on L. Päijänne; pulp, paper, plywood; univ.; p. (1968) 55,328.

K

K2. *See* **Godwin-Austen, Mt.**
Kabardin-Balkar ASSR, aut. rep., Transcaucasia, **RSFSR**; cap. Nalchik; livestock, lumber, wheat, fruit; non-ferrous metals; hydro-metallurgy plant; a. 12,432 km²; p. (1970) 589,000.
Kabelega Falls (Murchison Falls), on Victoria Nile, **Uganda**; falls between L. Kioga and L. Mobutu Seso.
Kabinda. *See* **Cabinda**.
Kābul, c., cap. of **Afghanistan**; on Kābul R. S. of Hindu Kush; 2,104 m a.s.l.; excellent climate; univ.; comm. and cultural ctr.; textiles, leather, timber inds.; p. (est. 1971) 318,094 (c.), 498,821 (met. a.).
Kābul, R., flows from Hindu Kush through gorges in Khyber Pass to Indus; site of dam for hydroelec. power and irrigation; length c. 480 km.
Kabwe (Broken Hill), Zambia; comm. and mng. ctr.; lead, zinc, cadmium, silver; p. (est. 1966) 44,600.
Kachin State, semi-aut. st., **Burma**; comprising former Myitkyina and Bhamo dists.; home of Kachins; a. 89,042 km².
Kadiyevka, t., Ukrainian SSR, **USSR**; coal, iron and steel, synthetic rubber; p. (1970) 137,000.
Kaduna, t., N. **Nigeria**; cap of Kaduna st.; rly. junc.; aluminium wks.; spinning and weaving; p. (est. 1971) 181,201.
Kaffa, region, **Ethiopia**; mtnous., forested; natural habitat of coffee plant.
Kagoshima, c., at S. end of Kyushu I., **Japan**; pt. on K. Bay; univs., cas.; porcelain, silk and cotton clothing, food-processing, publishing; rocket launching site nearby at Uchinoura; p. (est. 1971) 412,000.
Kahoolawe, I., **Hawaiian Is.**; a. 117 km²; uninhabited.
Kaieteur Falls, waterfall, **Guyana**; where R. Potaro leaves Guiana Highlands; among world's hgst falls (226 m).
K'ai-feng, c., Honan, **China**; nr. S. bank of Hwang-ho; one of the most anc. cities in China; cottons, chemicals; p. (est. 1970) 330,000.
Kai Islands, Is., **Indonesia**; between New Guinea and Timor; timber; a. 1,761 km²; p. 51,000.
Kaikoura, t., S.I., **N.Z.**; on E. cst., 128 km N.E. of Christchurch; in this region are the Kaikoura ranges, in which the hgst. peaks are Tapuaenuku (2,887 m) and Alarm (2,867 m); p. (1971) 1,607.
Kailas (Kang-ti-ssu Shan), range and peak, S.W. Tibet, **China**; unclimbed sacred mtn.; source of Indus, Ganges, Sutlej and Tsangpo (headstream of Brahmaputra).
Kainji Dam, Nigeria; power sta. transmission system and river transportation on R. Niger.
K'ai-ping, t., Hopeh, N. **China**; second lgst. coal-mng. a. (Kailan mines) in China; coal exported through Chinwangtao.
Kairouan, holy c. of Moslems, **Tunisia**; 128 km S.S.E. of Tunis; founded A.D. 670; mosque; p. (1966) 82,299.
Kaiserslautern, c., Rhineland–Palatinate, **W. Germany**; nr. Mannheim; iron, textiles, machin., tobacco, wood; p. (est. 1969) 84,900 (c.), 107,000 (met. a.).
Kaiser Wilhelm's Land, Australian dependency, **Antarctica**.
Kakamega, t., **Kenya**; E. Africa; 48 km N. of Kisumu; ctr. of gold-mng. dist.
Kakinada, t., spt., Andhra Pradesh, **India**; cotton, oilseeds; p. (1971) 164,200.
Kalahari Desert, region of semi-desert, southern **Africa**; between Orange and Zambesi Rs.; mainly in **Botswana**; alt. 1,128 m; a. 51,800 km²; inhabited chiefly by Bushmen.
Kalamata, t., Peloponnesus, **Greece**; nr. Sparta; figs, currants, flour-milling, cigarette mftg.; p. (1971) 39,346.
Kalamazoo, c., Mich., **USA**; industl. and comm. ctr. in farming a.; paper, pharmaceuticals; fish hatchery nearby; p. (1970) 84,444 (c.), 199,287 (met. a.).
Kalemie (Albertville), t., **Zaïre**; on L. Tanganyika; rail-steamer transfer point; p. (est. 1967) 86,687.
Kalewa, t., **Burma**; at confluence of Irrawaddy and Chindwin Rs.; coal deposits.
Kalgan (Chang-chia-k'ou), c., Hopeh, **China**; nr. Great Wall, 160 km N.W. of Peking; on main route to Mongolia; tea, wool, hides; p. (est. 1970) 1,000,000.
Kalgoorlie, t., **W. Australia**; on transcontinental rly. route 560 km E. of Perth; semi-desert conditions; nickel, gold-mng. a.; p. (1972) 20,784 (inc. Boulder).
Kalimantan (Indonesian Borneo); straddles equator; sparse p.; poor soils; lge. areas of swamp; plans for reclamation; coal, oil, diamonds, gold in sm. quantities; rice, pepper, copra; a 539,461 km²; p. est. (1970) 626,000.
Kalinin (Tver), c., **RSFSR**; on upper Volga; diversified inds.; 17th cent. cath. and cas.; p. (1970) 345,000.

Kaliningrad (Königsberg), c., RSFSR; former cap. of E. Prussia; on R. Pregel, linked by canal to outer pt. Pillau; univ., cath.; shipbldg., machin., wood-pulp, chemicals, exp. agr. prods.; Kant lived here all his life; p. (1970) 297,000.

Kalisz, t., Poznan, **Poland**; on R. Prosna; industl. ctr., textiles; oldest Polish t., mentioned in 2nd cent. A.D. by Ptolemy; p. (1970) 81,200.

Kalmar, t., spt., S. **Sweden**; on I. in Kalmar Sound; cath., cas.; matches, food inds., shipbldg.; p. (1968) 37,965.

Kalmuk (Kalmytskaya) ASSR, aut. rep., **RSFSR**; on Caspian Sea; harsh and infertile steppe; pastoral agr.; cap. Elista; a. 75,887 km^2; p. (1970) 268,000.

Kalna, v., on Mt. Stara Planina, **Yugoslavia**; uranium mine and plant; nuclear power sta.

Kaluga, c., **RSFSR**; pt. on Oka R.; chemicals, engin., hydroelec. power plant; p. (1970) 211,000.

Kalyan, spt., Maharashtra, **India**; nr. Bombay; bricks, tiles; p. (1971) 168,462.

Kalymnos, I., Dodecanese, **Greece**; mtnous.; a. 106 km^2; p. 13,600

Kama, R., **RSFSR**; ch. trib. of Volga which it joins below Kazan; rises in foothills of Urals; lge. hydroelectric sta. at Perm; navigable; 2,016 km long.

Kamaishi, t., spt., N.E. Honshu, **Japan**; serves Kamaishi–Sennin iron-ore field, lgst. worked deposits and reserves in Japan; impt. iron and steel ind.; p. (1970) 72,923.

Kamakura, t., Honshu, **Japan**; on shore of Sagami Bay; tourism; p. (est. 1971) 147,000.

Kamaran I., Red Sea; **Democratic Rep. of Yemen**; formerly under Brit. occupation, 1915–67; a. 57 km^2.; p. 2,200

Kamchatka, peninsula, E. Siberia, **USSR**; volcanic ranges; geothermal power sta.; mineral wealth, fisheries on cst., climate cold, wet and foggy; contains part of Koryak nat. okrug; cap. Petropavlovsk.

Kamenets-Podolskiy, t., Ukrainian SSR, **USSR**; on Smotrich R.; lt. inds.; mediaeval fortress t.; p. (est. 1967) 52,000.

Kamensk-Shakhtinskiy, c., **RSFSR**; on Donets R.; coal-mng. ctr., engin., food processing, artificial fibres; p. (est. 1967) 71,000.

Kamensk-Uralsk, c., **RSFSR**; aluminium, iron, steel, engin.; p. (1970) 169,000.

Kamet, Himalayan peak, on border of **India** and **Tibet, China**, 7,761 m; highest mtn. climbed (Smythe, 1931) until 1953 (Everest).

Kamloops, t., B.C., **Canada**; on Thompson R.; formerly Fort Thompson; on transcontinental rlys.; supply ctr. for mng. and grazing dist.; fruit and livestock mkts.; p. (1971) 25,599.

Kampala, c., cap. of **Uganda**; univ., ch. comm. ctr.; lt. inds., coffee-processing; p. (1969) 331,889.

Kampen, t., Overijssel, **Neth**; on R. IJssel; cigar-mkg.; p. (1968) 29,041.

Kampot, t., **Cambodia**., spt. on G. of Siam; ctr. of pepper ind.; p. (1962) 12,949.

Kamyshin, t., **RSFSR**; pt. on Volga; textiles, mkt. gardening, grain; p. (est. 1967) 77,000.

Kan, R., S. **China**; rises in Nanling Shan, flows N. into L. Poyang; valley provides route for main road from Kiangsi prov. to Kwangtung prov. over Meiling Pass; *c.* 880 km long.

Kananga (Luluabourg), c., cap. of Kasai Occidental prov., **Zaïre**; on Lulua R.; comm. and communications ctr. in cotton-growing a.; p. (est. 1972) 506,033 (met. a.).

Kanawha, R., W. Va., **USA**; rises in Allegheny mtns., flows into R. Ohio; runs through ch. mng. a. of W. Va. coalfield nr. Charleston.

Kanazawa, c., Honshu, **Japan**; in Kaga plain, on Sea of Japan; machin., silk and cotton textiles; landscape gardens, *No* theatre; p. (est. 1971) 366,000.

Kanchenjunga, mtn., on Nepal–Sikkim bdy., N.E. **India**; third hgst. mtn. in world, 8,585 m.

Kanchipuram (Conjeeveram) t., Tamil Nadu, S. **India**; on plain S.W. of Madras; pilgrimage ctr.; textiles; p. (1971) 110,657 (t.), 119,693 (met. a.).

Kandahar, c., former cap. of **Afghanistan**; alt. 1,037 m; 592 km from Herāt; linked by road to Kushka (Turkmen SSR) via Herat; fruit preserving and canning; textiles; p. (est. 1971) 133,799.

Kandy, c., **Sri Lanka**; in mtns. in ctr.of **I.**; 120 km from Colombo; univ. at sub. of Peradeniya; resort in hot season; tea, cocoa; p. (est. 1968) 78,000.

Kangaroo, I., S. **Australia**; eucalyptus; gypsum; summer resorts; p. (1966) 3,380.

Kano, c., N. **Nigeria**; emporium for whole of Sudan region; impt. airport and rly. terminus; groundnut ctr.; p. (est. 1971) 357,098.

Kanpur (Cawnpore), c., Uttar Pradesh, N. **India**; on R. Ganges; impt. mftg. ctr.; textiles, chemicals, leather goods, foodstuffs; p. (1971) 1,154,388 (c.), 1,275,242 (met. a.).

Kansas, st., **USA**; called the "sunflower state"; prairie; farming, maize, wheat; cattle, dairying, pigs; coal, petroleum, natural gas, lead, meat packing, flour milling, aircraft, chemicals, machin.; cap. Topeka; a. 213,095 km^2; p. (1970) 2,222,173.

Kansas, R., Kan., **USA**; trib. of Missouri R., confluence at Kansas City; vegetable growing in valley; periodic flooding; 272 km long.

Kansas City, Mo., **USA**; at confluence of Kansas and Missouri Rs.; univ.; gr. livestock mart, car and aircraft assembly, steel prods., meat-packing, food processing; p. (1970) 495,405; adjoins **Kansas City, Kansas**; p. (est. 1969) 172,000; 1,240,575 (joint met. a.).

Kansu (Gansu), prov., N.W. **China**; borders Inner Mongolia; cap. Lanchow; pastoral agr., wheat, cotton, tobacco; coal reserves; rich iron-ore deposits; a. 391,507 km^2; p. (est. 1968) 13,000,000

Kant, t., Kirghiz SSR, **USSR**; 19 km E. of Frunze; to be expanded to industl. c.; proposed p. 100,000.

Kanye, t., **Botswana**, S. Africa; lgst. t. in rep.; p. (est. 1969) 34,045.

Kaohsiung, spt., **Taiwan**; on S.W. cst.; industl. ctr., road and rly. terminus; oil refining, aluminium wks.; p. (est. 1970) 828,191.

Kaolack, inland pt., **Senegal**; 112 km up Saloum R.; groundnut ctr., p. (est. 1969) 95,000.

Kaposvár, t., S.W. **Hungary**; on Kapos R.; comm. ctr.; textiles, foodstuffs; p. (1968) 50,000.

Kara-Bogaz-Gol, lge shallow bay, Turkmen SSR, **USSR**; an arm of Caspian Sea; rapid evaporation allows huge quantities of salt from Caspian to be deposited along its shores (world's lgst. source of Glauber's salt); a. 18,130 km^2.

Karabuk, t., **Turkey**; N. of Ankara; steel wks.; p. (1965) 47,660.

Karacheyevo-Cherkesskaya, aut. region, **RSFSR**; in Greater Caucasus; cap. Cherkessk; livestock, grain; coal, lead, zinc; a. 14,095 km^2; p. (1970) 345,000.

Karachi, c., **Pakistan**; on Arabian Sea, nr. Indus delta; former cap. of Pakistan; univ.; spt., air ctr.; oil refining, industl. gases, steel mill, natural gas from Sui; nuclear power sta.; p. (1972) 3,469,000.

Karaganda, c., Kazakh SSR, **USSR**; on impt. coalfield developed since 1926; supplies industl. ctrs. of Urals; iron and steel wks., power sta.; p. (1970) 522,000.

Kara-Kalpak ASSR, aut. rep., N.W. Uzbek SSR, **USSR**; inc. Ust-Urt plateau, Kyzyl-Kum desert; irrigated agr.; cap. Nukus; a. 165,553 km^2; p. (1970) 702,000.

Karakorum Range, part of Himalayas between Kashmir and China; many lofty peaks, inc. Mt. Godwin-Austen; Karakorum highway, linking Pakistan with Sinkiang prov. of China, opened 1971.

Kara-Kum, sand desert, Turkmen SSR, **USSR**; E. of S.E. shore of Caspian Sea; a. 349,650 km^2; canal 1,440 km long across desert recently built.

Karamai (K'o-la-ma-i), t., Sinkiang, **China**; ctr. of lge. oilfield; pipeline to Fushantzu refinery.

Kara Sea, Arctic Oc.; E. of Novaya Zemlya; navigation to and from Siberian pts. July–Sept.

Karbala, c., **Iraq**; N.W. of Al Hillah; ctr. of pilgrimage; sacred c. of Moslem Shiite sect; p. (1965) 247,000 (met. a.).

Karelian ASSR, aut. rep., **RSFSR**; between Kola peninsula and Finland; lake-covered, coniferous forests; cap. Petrozavodsk; rich in timber, minerals, precious metals; granite and mica quarried; paper and pulp milling; a. 179,408 km^2; p. (1970) 714,000.

Karelian Isthmus, **RSFSR**; strategic route

between Finland and USSR impt. for defence of Leningrad.

Kariba Dam, in Kariba gorge of Zambezi R., on Rhodesia–Zambia border; operated jointly by the two govts.; one of lgst. dams in world with vast artificial lake supplying hydroelectric power to Rhodesia, Malawi, and the copperbelt of Zambia; involved resettlement of Batonka peoples; completed 1960; since Rhodesian U.D.I., construction has begun on a second generating sta. on the Zambian side.

Karikal, former Fr. settlement on E. cst. of **India**; p. (1961) 22,252.

Karkonosze. *See* **Riesengebirge.**

Karl-Marx-Stadt (Chemnitz), c., Karl-Marx-Stadt dist., **E. Germany**; leading industl. ctr.; cotton, woollens, machin., cars, furniture, chemicals, engin.; nr. lignite mines; p. (est. 1969) 297,133.

Karlovac, t., Croatia, **Yugoslavia**; S.W. of Zagreb; chemicals, textiles, food processing; p. (est. 1965) 38,000.

Karlový Vary (Carlsbad), t., Bohemia, **ČSSR**; on R. Ohře; hot mineral springs; health resort; porcelain; p. (1967) 46,000.

Karlskoga, t., **Sweden**; E. of L. Vänern; seat of Bofors armament wks.; iron and steel, explosives, chemicals; p. (1968) 38,203.

Karlskrona, spt., S. **Sweden**; on Baltic Sea; main naval sta.; lighting fixtures, china; p. (1968) 37,249.

Karlsruhe, c., Baden–Württemberg, **W. Germany**; road and rly. ctr.; outport on Rhine; chemicals, engin., elec., tobacco inds., oil refining; nuclear reactor; oil pipeline to Lavera, nr. Marseilles; p. (est. 1969) 256,200.

Karlstad, t., **Sweden**; on N. shore L. Vänern; ironwks., engin., machin.; p. (1968) 53,208.

Karnak, t., **Egypt**; on Nile, E. of Luxor; site of the anc. Thebes; ruined temples; p. *c.* 11,000.

Karnal, t., Haryana, **India**; clothing inds.; p. (1961) 72,109.

Karnataka (Mysore), st., S.W. **India**; borders Arabian Oc.; inc. W. Ghats where high rainfall and hydroelec. power; rainfall decreases to E.; cap. Bangalore; a. 192,203 km²; p. (1971) 29,263,334.

Karpathos, I., Dodecanese, **Greece**; Aegean Sea; between Rhodes and Crete; p. 8,747.

Karroo, W. Cape Prov., **S. Africa**; high plateau, scrub-covered; irrigated by Verwoerd dam on Orange R.

Kars, t., N.E. **Turkey**; in Armenia, alt. *c.* 1,800 m, in strategic position nr. Soviet border; p. (1965) 41,200.

Karst, dist., **Yugoslavia**; in Dinaric Alps; gives name to limestone landforms which are well developed here.

Karun, R., S.W. **Iran**; mainly mtn. torrent; difficult access, sparse p.; 752 km long.

Karvina, t., **ČSSR**; on Polish border; ctr. of Ostrava-Karvina coalfield; p. (1967) 73,000.

Kasai, R., Angola and **Zaïre**, Central Africa; rises in Bihé Plateau (Angola) and flows over 1,920 km into R. Zaïre 192 km above Kinshasa; alluvial diamond mng. at Chicopa.

Kasai, former prov., **Zaïre**; agr.; impt. source of industl. diamonds; attempted secession 1960; now divided into E. Kasai (cap. Mbuji-Mayi), and W. Kasai (cap. Luluabourg).

Kāshān, c., central **Iran**; in agr. oasis; carpets, velvet; p. (1967) 58,500 (c.), 153,980 (dist.).

Kashgar (K'a-shih), c., W. Sinkiang prov., **China**; on anc. imperial silk route through central Asia; growth rapid with irrigation; visited by Marco Polo 1275; p. (est. 1970) 175,000.

Kashmir. *See* **Jammu and Kashmir.**

Kassala, t., N.E. **Sudan**; ctr. of cotton-growing dist.; p. (est. 1966) 68,100.

Kassel, c., Hesse, **W. Germany**; on R. Fulda; cas.; machin., vehicles, science-based inds.; route ctr.; p. (est. 1969) 213,100.

Kastamonu, t., N. **Turkey**; cap. of K. prov.; ctr. of dist. rich in minerals; textiles, copper gds.; p. (1965) 23,485.

Katanga. *See* **Shaba.**

Kathiawar, peninsula, Gujarat, **India**; between G. of Kutch and G. of Cambay; ch. pt. Bhaunagar; very dry a.

Katmai, Mount, S. Alaska, **USA**; active volcano with crater L.; alt. 2,135 m.

Katmandu (Kathmandu), cap. of **Nepal**; on Vishnumati R., 120 km from Indian frontier; highway to Kodari; hydroelec. sta.; brick and tile wks.; many palaces and temples; p. (1971) 153,405.

Katoomba, t., N.S.W., **Australia**; holiday resort; alt. 1,006 m; p. (1972) 11,573 inc. Wentworth Falls.

Katowice, prov., S. **Poland**; in Upper Silesia; cap. K.; mng. and industl. a. drained by Warta R.; a. 9,516 km²; p. (1970) 3,691,000.

Katowice, c., S. **Poland**; cap. of K. prov.; impt. iron-mng. and industl. ctr.; heavy machin., chemicals; p. (1970) 303,000 (c.) (est. 1966) 2,010,000 (met. a.).

Katrine, Loch, S.W. Stirling, **Scot.**; beautiful woodland and moorland scenery; source of Glasgow water supply; scene of Scott's *Lady of the Lake*; 13 km long, *c.* 1·6 km wide.

Katsina, t., **Nigeria**; nr. Niger border; agr. tr. ctr., groundnuts, cotton; rural craft inds.; Hausa cultural ctr.; p. (est. 1971) 109,424.

Kattegat, arm of N. Sea linked with Baltic; separates **Denmark** (Jutland) from **Sweden**; 64–112 km wide.

Katwijk, t., S. Holland, **Neth.**; on N. Sea 24 km from the Hague; resort; synthetic resins; p. (1968) 34,730.

Kaufbeuren, t., Bavaria, **W. Germany**; on R. Wertach; textile mnfs.; p. (est. 1969) 39,542.

Kaunas (Kovno), c., Lithuanian SSR, **USSR**; on R. Nemen; R. pt. and comm. ctr.; univ.; 11th cent. c.; metal gds., chemicals, textiles, hydroelec. power; Jewish p. (circa 30 per cent) exterminated during German occupation 1941–4; p. (1970) 309,000.

Kavalla, c., E. Macedonia, **Greece**; on Bay of Kavalla; processes and exp. tobacco; the anc. Neapolis; nearby peat deposits; p. (1971) 46,679.

Kawagoe, c., Honshu, **Japan**; in Kanto plain; silk textiles; p. (est. 1971) 179,000.

Kawasaki, S. sub. Tokyo, Honshu, **Japan**; pt. for import of industl. raw materials; heavy inds.; p. (est. 1971) 963,000.

Kawthoolei State, st., **Burma**; former Karen st., extended to inc. areas in Tenasserim and Irrawaddy; a. 30,383 km².

Kayah State, semi-aut. st., **Burma**; on Thai border; forested plateau; tungsten mines; teak; a. 11,730 km².

Kayseri, c., **Turkey**; S.E. of Ankara; textiles, carpets, food tr.; anc. Hittite c.; p. (1965) 126,653 (c.); 222,699 (met. a.).

Kazakh SSR (Kazakhstan), constituent rep., **USSR**; in central Asia; cap. Alma-Ata; steppe with stock-raising; lge. desert areas being made fertile by irrigation; grain in N.; coal at Karaganda; asbestos at Dzhetygara; minerals inc. metaborite (richest boron mineral); oil; atomic power sta. to W. of Caspian Sea; cosmodrome at Leninsk, E. of Aral Sea; a. 2,778,544 km²; p. (1970) 12,850,000.

Kazan', c., **RSFSR**; cap. of Tatar ASSR; pt. on Volga; impt. tr. ctr. for E. USSR, Turkestan Bokhara and Iran; cath., univ. (where Tolstoy and Lenin were educated); engin., chemicals, synthetic rubber, textiles, paper, oil refining; natural gas pipeline to Minnibayevo; p. (1970) 869,000.

Kazanluk, t., central **Bulgaria**; in region famous for attar of roses; p. (est. 1968) 48,816.

Kazan-retto or Volcanic Is., gr. of Is., W. Pac. Oc. S. of Tokyo; sugar plantations, sulphur; returned to Japan by USA 1968.

Kazbek, extinct volcano, N. Georgian SSR, **USSR**; second hgst. peak of Caucasus; alt. 5,045 m.

Kāzerūn, t., S.W. **Iran**; ctr. of agr. dist. where fruit, tobacco, opium, cotton grown; p. (1966) 39,758.

Kazvin or Qazvin, c., N.W. **Iran**; transit tr.; carpets, textiles; p. (1966) 88,106.

Kearsley, t., Gtr. Manchester, **Eng.**; chemicals, paper; p. (1971) 11,243.

Keban Dam, S.E. **Turkey**; at confluence of the E. and W. branches of Euphrates.

Kecskemet, c., central **Hungary**; fruit-canning and wine-distilling from locally grown prods.; 4th cent. c.; p. (1966) 74,400.

Kedah, st., **Malaysia**; on Strait of Malacca, N.W. Malaya; rice, rubber, coconuts, tungsten; cap. cap. Alor Star; a. 9,479 km²; p. (1967) 925,105.

Kediri, t., E. Java, **Indonesia**; food processing; p. (1971) 178,865.

Keeling Is. *See* **Cocos Is.**

Keelung (Chi-lung), c., N. **Taiwan**; on E. China

Atlas of the World

Contents

Symbols

- Principal Railways
- Motorways
- Principal Roads
- International Boundaries
- Internal Boundaries
- 4125 Heights in Metres
- Principal Airports

Height of Land

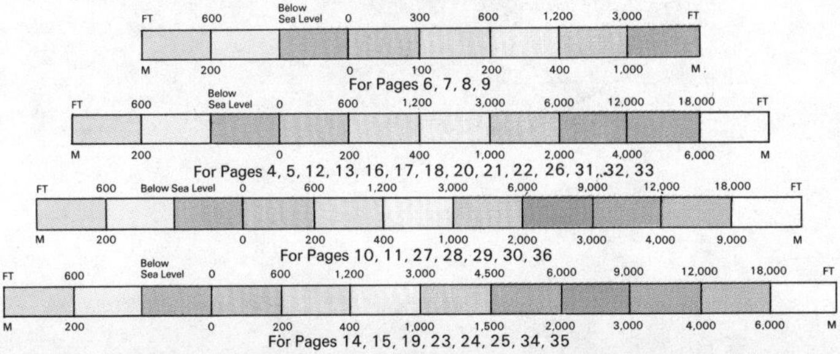

WORLD : Political

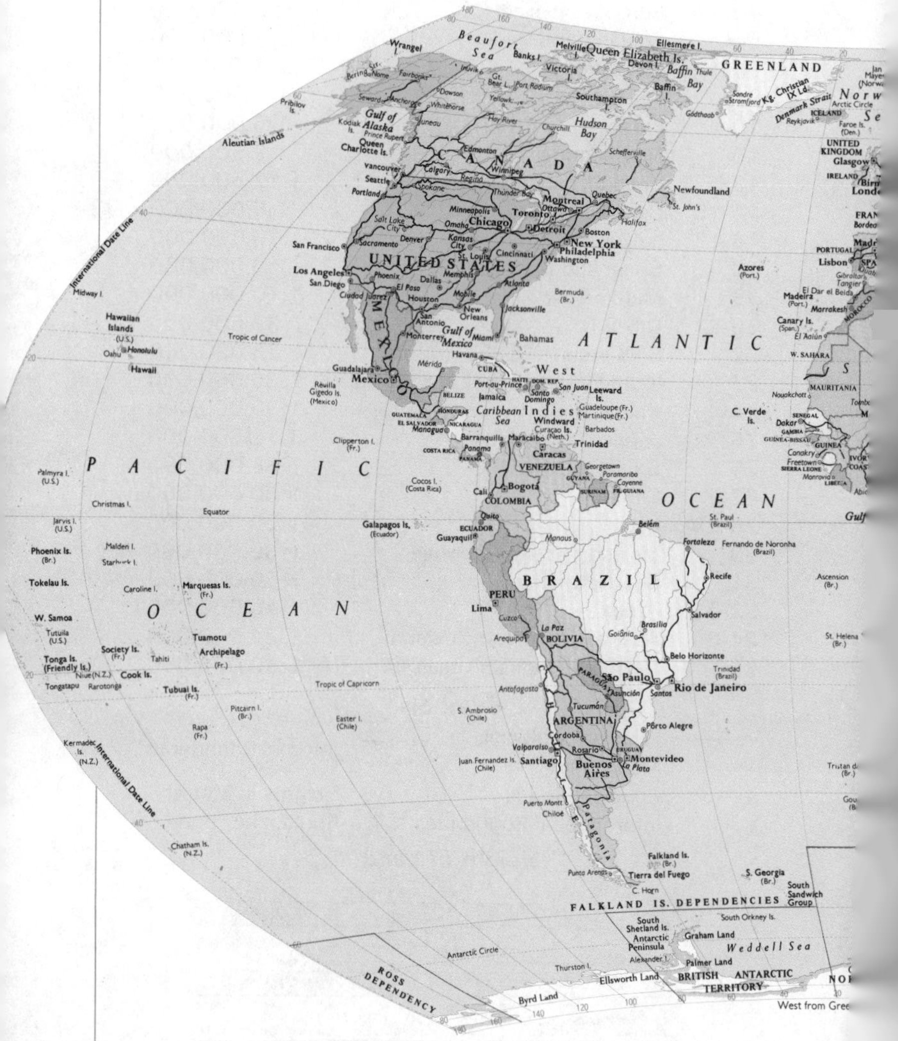

Scale 1:135,000,000

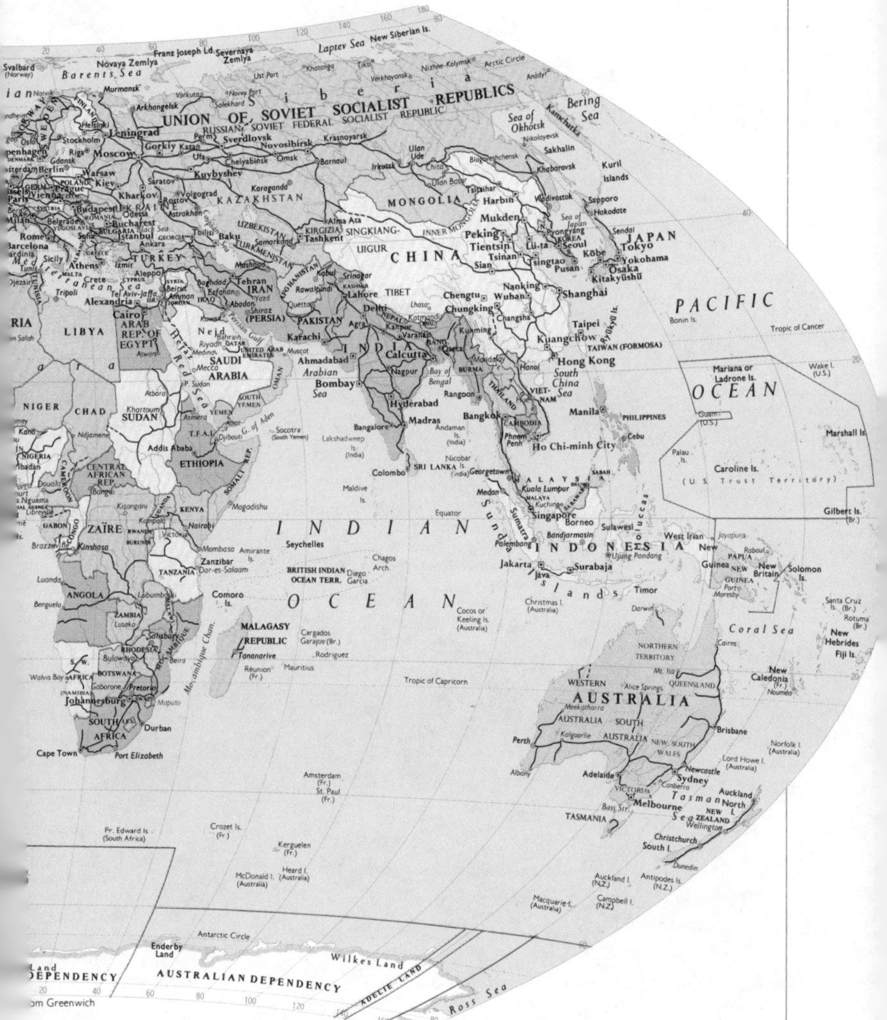

30
25
20
15
10
5
0
5
10
15
Tromsø
Reykjavik
Husavik
Akureyri
ICELAND
Arctic Circle
Narvik
60
A T L A N T I C   O C E A N
Faroe Is.
(Dan.)
Kristiansund
Trondheim
Östersund
Indals
N O R W A Y
S W E D E N
Shetland
Is.
Sogne Fd.
Sundsvall
Bergen
Lillehammer
55
Hardanger Fd.
Oslo
Gävle
Orkney
Is.
Hebrides
UNITED
KINGDOM
Drammen
Stavanger
Uppsala
Inverness
Aberdeen
Vanern
Örebro
Eskilstuna
Glasgow
Dundee
SCOTLAND
Skagerrak
Göteborg
Londonderry
Edinburgh
Vattern
Jönköping
N.I.
NORTH
SEA
Aalborg
Kattegat
REP
OF IRELAND
Belfast
I. of
Man
Carlisle
Newcastle
DENMARK
Kalmar
Galway
Aarhus
Limerick
Dublin
Manchester
Leeds
York
COPENHAGEN
Karlskrona
Liverpool
Hull
Esbjerg
Malmö
Cork
Sheffield
50
Flensburg
BALTIC
C. Clear
WALES
Birmingham
Kiel
Gdynia
Gdańsk
Swansea
ENGLAND
Norwich
Amsterdam
Groningen
Hamburg
Rostock
Cardiff
The Hague
NETHERLANDS
Bremen
Elbe
Szczecin
Bydgoszcz
Bristol
Rotterdam
Plymouth
Southampton
LONDON
Hanover
East
BERLIN
Poznań
Portsmouth
Dover
Ostend
Weser
Magdeburg
Scilly Is.
English Channel
Calais
Antwerp
GERMANY
Oder
Łódź
Cherbourg
Le Havre
BELGIUM
BRUSSELS
Dortmund
Essen
POLAND
Lille
Bonn
Cologne
Halle
Leipzig
Ushant
Rouen
West
Karl-Marx-Stadt
Dresden
Wrocław
Brest
Caen
Seine
Wiesbaden
Frankfurt
Rennes
Reims
LUX.
Mainz
PARIS
Meuse
Würzburg
PRAGUE
Katowice
45
Le Mans
Metz
Rhine
Nuremberg
Plzen
CZECHOSLOVAKIA
Loire
Strasbourg
Ostrava
Orléans
Stuttgart
Brno
Nantes
BAY OF BISCAY
Tours
FRANCE
Danube
Munich
VIENNA
Dijon
Mulhouse
Freiburg
Linz
Bratislava
Basel
Salzburg
Limoges
Clermont
Ferrand
Zürich
AUSTRIA
Bern
La Coruña
Saône
SWITZERLAND
BUDAPEST
C.
Finisterre
Oviedo
Santander
San Sebastian
Bordeaux
Perigueux
Geneva
Innsbruck
Graz
HUNGARY
Bilbao
Bayonne
St. Etienne
Lyons
Trento
Vigo
Grenoble
Milan
Brescia
Trieste
Ljubljana
Pécs
Garonne
Oporto
Turin
Zagreb
Toulouse
Rhône
Rijeka
Douro
Venice
Genoa
Montpellier
Avignon
Valladolid
Duero
Ebro
Bologna
Coimbra
Monaco
Nice
La Spezia
Ravenna
40
Perpignan
Sète
Andorra
San Marino
Florence
YUGOSLAVIA
PORTUGAL
Marseilles
Toulon
Leghorn
Ancona
Belgrade
SPAIN
Zaragoza
Tagus
Split
Sarajevo
MADRID
LISBON
Toledo
Corsica
Barcelona
ADRIATIC SEA
Guadiana
Ajaccio
Dubrovnik
Badajoz
ITALY
Tiber
ROME
Valencia
Lagos
Balearic Is.
Sassari
Minorca
Sevilla
Córdoba
Palma
Bari
Guadalquivir
Sardinia
Naples
Majorca
Cádiz
Murcia
Str. of
Málaga
Taranto
Brindisi
Gibraltar
Granada
Alicante
Tyrrhenian Sea
Gibraltar (Br.)
Almeria
Cartagena
Cagliari
MEDITERRANEAN SEA
Tangier
35
Ceuta (Sp.)
Ionian
Palermo
Messina
El Djezair
Ouahran
Reggio
Rabat
Melilla (Sp.)
Skikda
Annaba
Bizerta
Sicily
Fès
Blida
Tunis
Catania
Meknes
MOROCCO
Tlemcen
Constantine
ALGERIA
TUNISIA
Pantelleria
(Ital.)
Sousse
MALTA
5
West from Greenwich
0
East from Greenwich
5
10
15

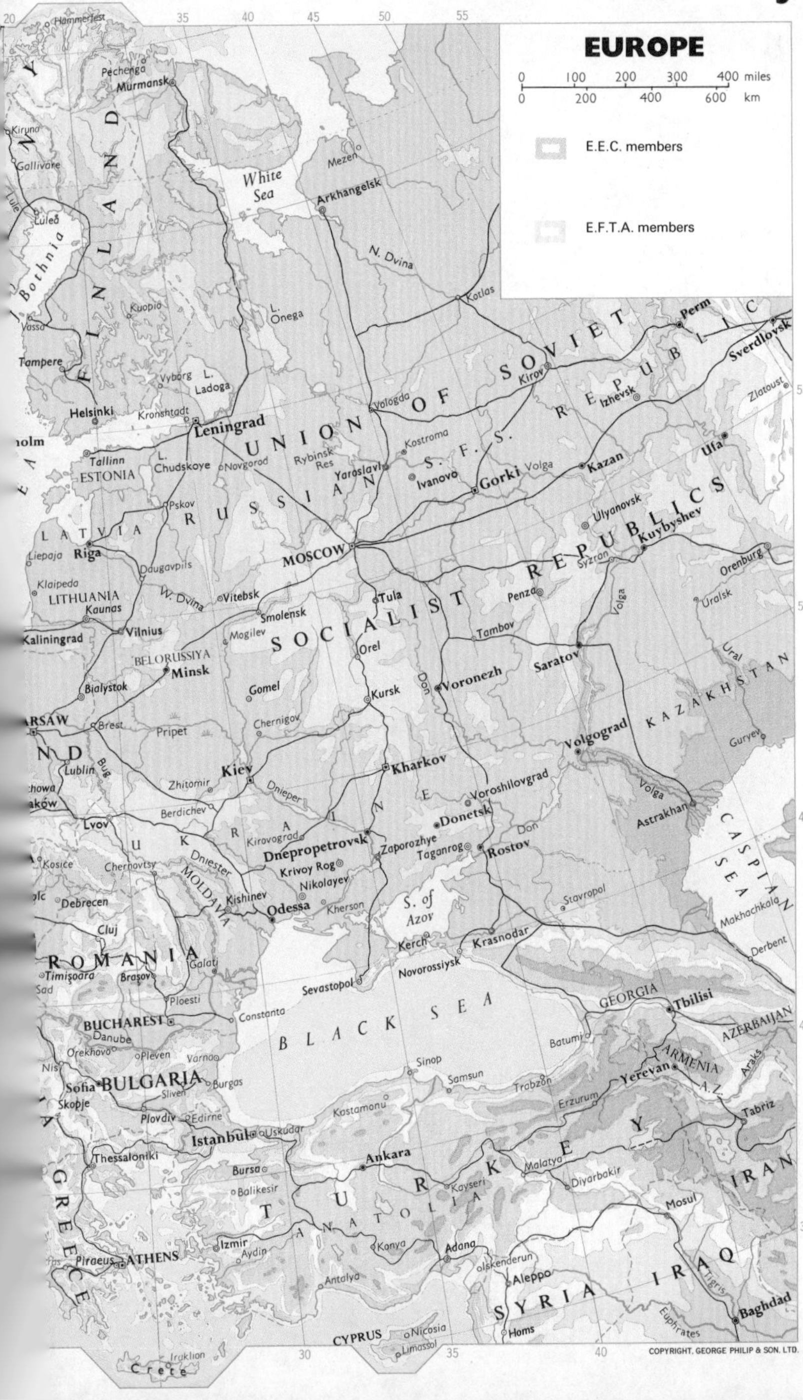
EUROPE
0 100 200 300 400 miles
0 200 400 600 km
E.E.C. members
E.F.T.A. members
White Sea
Arkhangelsk
Mezen
N. Dvina
Kotlas
Murmansk
Pechenga
Hammerfest
Kiruna
Gallivare
Lulea
Vassa
Tampere
Helsinki
Kuopio
FINLAND
Bothnia
L. Onega
L. Ladoga
Vyborg
Kronshtadt
Leningrad
Tallinn
ESTONIA
L. Chudskoye
Novgorod
Pskov
LATVIA
Riga
Liepaja
Daugavpils
Klaipeda
LITHUANIA
Kaunas
Vilnius
Kaliningrad
W. Dvina
Vitebsk
Smolensk
Mogilev
BELORUSSIYA
Minsk
Bialystok
Brest
Pripet
Gomel
Chernigov
Kiev
Zhitomir
Berdichev
Lublin
Bug
Lvov
Dnieper
UNION OF SOVIET SOCIALIST REPUBLICS
RUSSIAN S.F.S. REPUBLIC
MOSCOW
Vologda
Kostroma
Rybinsk Res
Yaroslavl
Ivanovo
Gorki
Volga
Kirov
Perm
Sverdlovsk
Izhevsk
Zlatoust
Kazan
Ufa
Ulyanovsk
Kuybyshev
Syzran
Orenburg
Uralsk
Ural
Penza
Tula
Orel
Kursk
Tambov
Voronezh
Don
Saratov
KAZAKHSTAN
Volgograd
Guryev
Astrakhan
CASPIAN SEA
Kharkov
UKRAINE
Voroshilovgrad
Donetsk
Dnepropetrovsk
Kirovograd
Zaporozhye
Taganrog
Rostov
Krivoy Rog
Nikolayev
Kherson
Odessa
Dniester
Chernovtsy
MOLDAVIA
Kishinev
Kosice
Debrecen
Cluj
ROMANIA
Timişoara
Braşov
Galati
Ploesti
Constanta
BUCHAREST
Danube
S. of Azov
Kerch
Krasnodar
Novorossiysk
Stavropol
Makhachkala
Derbent
Sevastopol
BLACK SEA
GEORGIA
Tbilisi
AZERBAIJAN
ARMENIA
Yerevan
Batumi
Araks
A.Z.
Tabriz
Orekhovo
Pleven
Varna
Nis
Sofia
BULGARIA
Sliven
Burgas
Skopje
Plovdiv
Edirne
Istanbul
Uskudar
Sinop
Samsun
Trabzon
Erzurum
Kostamonu
Thessaloniki
Ankara
Bursa
Balikesir
TURKEY
ANATOLIA
Malatya
Kayseri
Diyarbakir
Mosul
IRAN
Izmir
Aydin
Konya
Adana
Iskenderun
Aleppo
Antalya
GREECE
Piraeus
ATHENS
SYRIA
IRAQ
Tigris
Euphrates
Baghdad
Homs
CYPRUS
Nicosia
Limassol
Iraklion
Crete
20 35 40 45 50 55
30 35 40
55 50 45 40 35

ENGLAND AND WALES
0 20 40 60 miles
0 20 40 60 80 100 km
NORTH SEA
IRISH SEA
North Channel
Firth of Clyde
Firth of Lorn
Solway Firth
Dogger Bank
SCOTLAND
NORTHERN IRELAND
IRELAND
ULSTER
ISLE OF MAN
STRATHCLYDE
TAYSIDE
FIFE
CENTRAL
LOTHIAN
BORDERS
DUMFRIES AND GALLOWAY
NORTHUMBERLAND
TYNE AND WEAR
DURHAM
CLEVELAND
CUMBRIA
NORTH YORKSHIRE
HUMBERSIDE
LANCASHIRE
MERSEYSIDE
GREATER MANCHESTER
CHESHIRE
Southern Uplands
Galloway
Cheviot Hills
Pennine Range
Cumbrian Mts.
N. York Moors
Lincoln Wolds
Mourne Mts.
Edinburgh
Glasgow
Dundee
Perth
Stirling
Newcastle
Sunderland
Carlisle
Berwick-upon-Tweed
Middlesbrough
Teesside
Darlington
Scarborough
York
Leeds
Bradford
Hull
Blackpool
Preston
Lancaster
Liverpool
Manchester
Sheffield
Belfast
Dublin (Baile Atha Cliath)
Dundalk
Douglas
Lincoln
Skegness

6 4 West from Greenwich 2 0 East from Greenwich

West from Greenwich

IRELAND
0 20 40 60 miles
0 20 40 60 80 100 km
8
6
56
54
52
10
ATLANTIC
OCEAN
Tiree
Staffa
Mull
B. More 996
Iona
Oban
Firth of Lorn
STRATHCLYDE
L. Awe
SCOTLAND
Colonsay
Lochgilphead
Jura
Sound of Jura
L. Fyne
Rudh a' Mhail
Islay
Bowmore
Gigha
Kintyre
Arran
Campbeltown
Rathlin I.
Fair Hd.
Mull of Kintyre
North Channel
Malin Hd.
Giant's Causeway
Ballycastle
Portrush
Lough Swilly
Sheep Haven
Tory I.
Horn Hd.
Inishowen Pen.
Moville
Buncrana
L. Foyle
Bloody Foreland
Coleraine
Ballymoney
Trostan 554
Errigal 752
Derryveagh Mts.
Aran I.
Londonderry
Letterkenny
DONEGAL
Gweebarra B.
Sperrin Mts.
Sawel 683
Bann
Ballymena
Larne
Main
Antrim
Loughros More B.
Glenties
Finn
676
Lifford
Strabane
Bluestack
Carrickfergus
Rossan Pt.
Rathlin O'Birne I.
Killybegs
Donegal
Derg
Lough Neagh
Antrim
Belfast L.
Bangor
NORTHERN IRELAND
Newtownards
Belfast
ULSTER
Omagh
Donegal Bay
Ballyshannon
Dungannon
Lagan
Strangford L.
Ards Pen.
Lisburn
Erne
L. Erne
Portadown
Lurgan
(Craigavon)
Broad Haven
Killala Bay
Erris Hd.
Sligo B.
Sligo
Blackwater
Enniskillen
Armagh
Banbridge
Downpatrick
Ardglass
Mullet Peninsula
LEITRIM
Finn
MONAGHAN
Monaghan
Slieve Donard 852
Newcastle
Mourne Mts.
Dundrum Bay
Ballina
Ox Mts.
SLIGO
L. Allen
Upper L. Erne
Newry
Sl. Gullion
Blacksod Bay
L. Conn
Nephin 806
Warrenpoint
Castleblayney
Carlingford L.
Achill Head
MAYO
Leitrim
CAVAN
Cootehill
Achill I.
Castlebar
Boyle
Carrick-on-Shannon
Dundalk
Dundalk Bay
LOUTH
Louth
Clare I.
Clew Bay
ROSCOMMON
L. Gowna
Ardee
Westport
Claremorris
Blackwater
Croagh Patrick 765
CONNACHT
Longford
L. Sheelin
Ceanannus Mor (Kells)
Killary Harbour
Mweelrea 819
Inishbofin
LONGFORD
An Uaimh (Navan)
Drogheda
L. Mask
Roscommon
L. Ree
Inny
MEATH
Balbriggan
Twelve Pins
Tuam
Connemara
L. Corrib
Mullingar
WESTMEATH
Boyne
DUBLIN
Slyne Hd.
GALWAY
REPUBLIC OF IRELAND
Athlone
Maynooth
Howth Hd.
Galway
Athenry
Ballinasloe
Clara
Tullamore
Dublin (Baile Atha Cliath)
Dun Laoghaire
Kilkieran B.
Brosna
OFFALY
Allen
Celbridge
Galway Bay
Loughrea
Shannon
Bog of
Naas
Kippure 754
Bray
Inishmore
Slieve Aughty
KILDARE
Kildare
Aran Is.
Gort
Birr
Sl. Bloom
Mountmellick
Port Laoighise
Poulaphouca Res.
LEINSTER
WICKLOW
Wicklow
L. Derg
LAOIS
Athy
Barrow
Wicklow Mts.
Liscannor Bay
Mal Bay
Roscrea
Lugnaquilla 923
CLARE
Ennis
Nenagh
Carlow
Mizen Hd.
Slaney
Arklow
Kilkee
Keeper 694
Thurles
Nore
CARLOW
Muine Bheag
Kilrush
Gorey
Loop Hd.
Limerick
TIPPERARY
Kilkenny
Mt. Leinster 796
Foynes
KILKENNY
Shannon
Rathkeale
Cahore Pt.
Listowel
LIMERICK
Golden Vale
Tipperary
Sl. Naman 722
Enniscorthy
WEXFORD
St. George's Channel
Feale
Galtymore 920
Brandon Bay
Tralee Bay
Rath Luirc (Charleville)
Galty Mts.
Caher
Carrick-on-Suir
Penit
Brandon Hill 953
Tralee
MUNSTER
Clonmel
New Ross
Wexford Harbour
Wexford
Rosslare
Suir
Greenore Pt.
Great Blasket I.
Dingle
Sl. Mish
Mitchelstown
Comeragh Mts.
Waterford
Tuscar Rock
Knockmealdown Mts.
Tramore
Carnsore Pt.
KERRY
Laune
Mallow
Blackwater
WATERFORD
Hook Hd.
Dingle Bay
Killarney
Fermoy
Waterford Harbour
Saltee Is.
Macgillycuddy's Reeks
Boggeragh Mts.
Dungarvan
Dungarvan Bay
Valentia Harbour
Carrantuohill 1040
Lakes of Killarney
CORK
Youghal
Cahirciveen
Cork
Valentia I.
Macroom
Midleton
Youghal Harbour
Kenmare
Lee
Cobh
Ballinskelligs B.
Kenmare River
Caha Mts.
Bandon
Cork Harbour
Castletown Berehaven
Bantry
Clonakilty
Crow Head
Bantry Bay
Clonakilty Bay
Old Head of Kinsale
Dunmanus Bay
Baltimore
Galley Hd.
Mizen Hd.
Clear I.
Fastnet Rock
C. Clear
West from Greenwich

FRANCE
0 20 40 60 80 100 miles
0 40 80 120 160 km
ENGLAND
LONDON
Swansea
Newport
Cardiff
Bristol
Bath
Swindon
Southend
Margate
Dover
Folkestone
Hastings
Calais
C. Gris Nez
Str. of Dover
Boulogne
Montreuil
Somme
Taunton
Southampton
Brighton
Newhaven
Chichester
Portsmouth
Ryde
Bournemouth
Weymouth
Portland
Exeter
Exmouth
Torquay
Dartmouth
Tamar
Plymouth
Eddystone
St. Ives
Truro
Falmouth
Land's End
Penzance
ENGLISH CHANNEL
C. de la Hague
Alderney
Guernsey
St. Peter Port
Sark
Channel Is. (Br.)
Jersey
St. Helier
Cherbourg
Pte. de Barfleur
Valognes
Cotentin
Le Tréport
Dieppe
St. Valery
Fécamp
Caux
Yvetot
Bolbec
Le Havre
Rouen
S.Me.
Trouville
Honfleur
Elbeuf
Lisieux
Bessin
Bayeux
St. Lo
Caen
M.
C.
E.
Bocage
NORMANDY
Falaise
Évreux
Mantes
Versailles
Granville
Mt. St. Michel
Vire
Avranches
Or.
Perche
Dreux
Ushant
Brest
Pte de St. Mathieu
Morlaix
Guingamp
Mts. Bd'Arree
St. Brieuc
St. Malo
Dinard
Dinan
F.
C.N.
BRITTANY
Mts. Noire
Pte. du Raz
Quimper
Pte. de Penmarch
Quimperlé
Lorient
Mo.
Vannes
Carnac
Quiberon
Belle I.
Rennes
I.V.
Vilaine
Fougères
Alençon
Mayenne
MAINE
Laval
May.
Châteaubriant
Le Mans
S.
Sarthe
E.L.
Chartres
Beauce
Orléans
Loir
Blois
L.C.
Angers
M.L.
ANJOU
Tours
Amboise
Loire
TOURAINE
I.L.
Loches
Saumur
Chinon
L.A.
Nantes
St. Nazaire
Loire
Cholet
Ile de Noirmoutier
Vendée
Bocage
Ile de Yeu
La Roche
Ve.
POITOU
D.S.
Châtellerault
Châteauroux
Creuse
Les Sables d'Olonne
Fontenay
Gâtine
Poitiers
Vi.
Vienne
Niort
BAY OF BISCAY
Ile de Ré
La Rochelle
AUNIS
Ile d' Oléron
Rochefort
Saintes
ANGOUMOIS
SAINTONGE
Ch.M.
H.V.
Limoges
Royan
Le Verdon
Gironde
Cognac
Angoulême
Ch.
Uzerche
Médoc
Pauillac
Périgueux
D.
Perigord
Bordeaux
Gi.
Libourne
Dordogne
Sarlat
Bergerac
Garonne
Arcachon
GUYENNE
Landes
L.G.
Cahors
Agen
T.G.
L.
Mont-de-Marsan
GASCONY
Armagnac
Auch
Ge.
Toulouse
Adour
Gulf of Gascony
Gijón
S. Vicente de la Barquera
Llanes
Oviedo
Torrelavega
Santander
Santona
Guecho
Picos de Europa 2648
Guernica
Sestao
Bilbao
Biarritz
Fuenterrabia
Bayonne
Orthez
P.A.
San Sebastián
BEARN
Pau
Tarbes
G.H.
Sa. de. Alba
Reinosa
Durango
Tolosa
Lourdes
Bigorre
H.P.
Ebro
Vitoria
Roncesvalles
Pic du Midi 2887
León
Pancorbo P.
Miranda
Pamplona
Canfranc P. 1631
Mt. Perdu 3355
Pyrenees
Astorga
Saldaña
Pisuerga
SPAIN
Burgos
Logroño
Tafalla
Rioja
Jaca
Sahagún
Arlanzon
Andorra
50
48
46
44
6
4
2
0
West from Greenwich
East from Greenwich

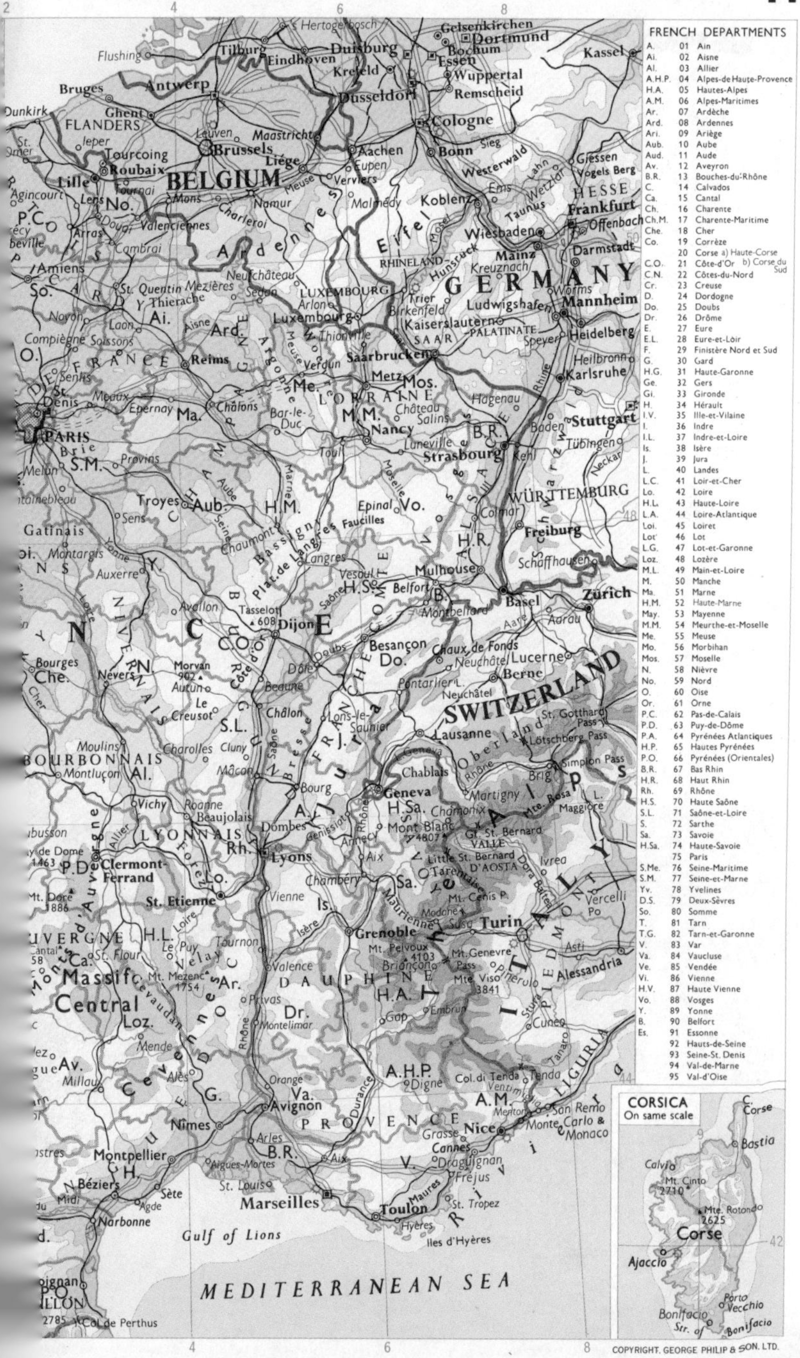

FRENCH DEPARTMENTS

A.	01	Ain
Ai.	02	Aisne
Al.	03	Allier
A.H.P.	04	Alpes-de Haute-Provence
H.A.	05	Hautes-Alpes
A.M.	06	Alpes-Maritimes
Ar.	07	Ardèche
Ard.	08	Ardennes
Ari.	09	Ariège
Aub.	10	Aube
Aud.	11	Aude
Av.	12	Aveyron
B.R.	13	Bouches-du-Rhône
C.	14	Calvados
Ca.	15	Cantal
Ch.	16	Charente
Ch.M.	17	Charente-Maritime
Che.	18	Cher
Co.	19	Corrèze
	20	Corse a) Haute-Corse b) Corse du Sud
C.O.	21	Côte-d'Or
C.N.	22	Côtes-du-Nord
Cr.	23	Creuse
D.	24	Dordogne
Do.	25	Doubs
Dr.	26	Drôme
E.	27	Eure
E.L.	28	Eure-et-Loir
F.	29	Finistère Nord et Sud
G.	30	Gard
H.G.	31	Haute-Garonne
Ge.	32	Gers
Gi.	33	Gironde
H.	34	Hérault
I.V.	35	Ille-et-Vilaine
I.	36	Indre
I.L.	37	Indre-et-Loire
Is.	38	Isère
J.	39	Jura
L.	40	Landes
L.C.	41	Loir-et-Cher
Lo.	42	Loire
H.L.	43	Haute-Loire
L.A.	44	Loire-Atlantique
Loi.	45	Loiret
Lot	46	Lot
L.G.	47	Lot-et-Garonne
Loz.	48	Lozère
M.L.	49	Main-et-Loire
M.	50	Manche
Ma.	51	Marne
H.M.	52	Haute-Marne
May.	53	Mayenne
M.M.	54	Meurthe-et-Moselle
Me.	55	Meuse
Mo.	56	Morbihan
Mos.	57	Moselle
N.	58	Nièvre
No.	59	Nord
O.	60	Oise
Or.	61	Orne
P.C.	62	Pas-de-Calais
P.D.	63	Puy-de-Dôme
P.A.	64	Pyrénées Atlantiques
H.P.	65	Hautes Pyrénées
P.O.	66	Pyrénées (Orientales)
B.R.	67	Bas Rhin
H.R.	68	Haut Rhin
Rh.	69	Rhône
H.S.	70	Haute Saône
S.L.	71	Saône-et-Loire
S.	72	Sarthe
Sa.	73	Savoie
H.Sa.	74	Haute-Savoie
	75	Paris
S.Me.	76	Seine-Maritime
S.M.	77	Seine-et-Marne
Yv.	78	Yvelines
D.S.	79	Deux-Sèvres
So.	80	Somme
T.	81	Tarn
T.G.	82	Tarn-et-Garonne
V.	83	Var
Va.	84	Vaucluse
Ve.	85	Vendée
Vi.	86	Vienne
H.V.	87	Haute Vienne
Vo.	88	Vosges
Y.	89	Yonne
B.	90	Belfort
Es.	91	Essonne
	92	Hauts-de-Seine
	93	Seine-St. Denis
	94	Val-de-Marne
	95	Val-d'Oise

NETHERLANDS
0 10 20 30 40 50 miles
0 20 40 60 80 km
NORTH SEA
WEST FRISIAN IS
Norderney
Juist
Borkum
Rotummeroog
Schiermonnikoog
Ameland
Terschelling
Vlieland
Texel
Den Burg
Norddeich
Norden
Ems
Uithuizen
Zoutkamp
Delfzijl
Holwerd
Dokkum
West Terschelling
Waddenzee
Leeuwarden
Franeker
Harlingen
Bolsward
Sneek
FRIESLAND
Bergum
Zuidhorn
Groningen
Slochteren
Drachten
Hoogezand
Veendam
Winschoten
Onstwedde
Heerenveen
Stadskanaal
Wolvega
Assen
Borger
Beilen
Ter Apel
Emmen
DRENTHE
Den Oever
Workum
Den Helder
Hippolytushoef
Stavoren
Lemmer
Schagen
Medemblik
IJsselmeer
Noordoost-Polder
Steenwijk
Hoogeveen
Emmeloord
Coevorden
Enkhuizen
Bergen
Alkmaar
Hoorn
Urk
Vollenhove
Meppel
Hardenberg
Emlichheim
Ommen
Purmerend
Edam
Kampen
Zwolle
Vechte
Mariënberg
Beverwijk
IJmuiden
Velsen
Zaandam
Lelystad
Marken
Elburg
Hellendoorn
Nordhorn
Haarlem
AMSTERDAM
Nunspeet
Heerde
IJssel
Wierden
Almelo
Zandvoort
Harderwijk
Ermelo
Epe
Nijverdal
OVERIJSSEL
Oldenzaal
Heemstede
Hillegom
Bussum
Putten
107
Deventer
Rijssen
Hengelo
Noordwijk
Lisse
Aalsmeer
Nijkerk
Hilversum
Baarn
Apeldoorn
Goor
Katwijk-aan-Zee
Wassenaar
Leiden
Soest
Amersfoort
Enschede
Gronau
Scheveningen
Oude Rijn
UTRECHT
Barneveld
Zutphen
Lochem
THE HAGUE
Voorburg
Utrecht
Zeist
Ede
GELDERLAND
Ahaus
Hoek van Holland
Delft
Rijswijk
Gouda
Veenendaal
Rheden
Ruurlo
Dieren
Doetinchem
Berkel
EUROPOORT
Lek
Arnhem
Winterswijk
Stadtlohn
Maassluis
Vlaardingen
ROTTERDAM
Wageningen
Renkum
Aalten
Hellevoetsluis
Schiedam
Tiel
Waal
Gendringen
Bocholt
Oudorp
Sliedrecht
Geldermalsen
Nijmegen
Emmerich
Goeree
Borken
Brouwershaven
Dordrecht
Gorinchem
Kleve
Schouwen
Overflakkee
ZUID
NETHERLANDS
Oss
Gennep
Rhein
Rhine
Zierikzee
's-Hertogenbosch
Goch
Noord Beveland
Vught
Veghel
Xanten
Wesel
Dorsten
Domburg
Oosterhout
Niers
Walcheren
Bergen-op-Zoom
Breda
Boxtel
Venraij
Gelsenkirchen
Middelburg
Goes
Roosendaal
Tilburg
Geldern
Bottrop
Oosterschelde
Baarle Nassau
Helmond
Oberhausen
Flushing
Essen
Eindhoven
Deurne
Maas
DUISBURG
Westerschelde
Geldrop
Venlo
Ruhr
Breskens
Valkenswaard
Tegelen
Krefeld
Sluis
Terneuzen
Brasschaat
Turnhout
DÜSSELDORF
Maldegem
Hulst
ANTWERPEN
Weert
Viersen
Neuss
Eekloo
Merksem
Mol
Overpelt
Mönchen-gladbach
Zelzate
St. Niklaas
Antwerp
Roermond
Gladbach
Rheydt
Solingen
FLANDRE
Deurne
Scheldt
Lier
Lokeren
Hoboken
Herentals
Maaseik
Ghent
Boom
Nethe (Nete)
Leopoldsburg
W. GERMANY
Leie
Mechelen
Diest
Beringen
95
Sittard
Brunssum
Leverkusen
Wetteren
Dendermonde
Geilenkirchen
Bergheim
Deinze
Aalst
Asse
Vilvoorde
Aarschot
Demer
Genk
Geleen
ORIENTALE
Hasselt
Jülich
COLOGNE
Heerlen
Eschweiler
Brühl
Oudenaarde
Ninove
BRUSSELS
Leuven
Tienen
Maastricht
Kerkrade
Düren
157
Geraardsbergen
St. Truiden
Tongeren
Stolberg
Erft
Ronse
Enghien
BRABANT
Landen
Visé
Aachen
Bonn
Lessines
Halle
Waterloo
Wavre
Jemeppe
Herstal
Zülpich
Raeren
Euskirchen
Tournai
BELGIUM
Ath
Liège
Eupen
Mechernich
Rheinbach
Soignies
St. Georges
Verviers
Münstereifel
Ahrweiler
Leuze
HAINAUT
Nivelles
Gembloux
Seraing
Meuse
Spa
Hohe Venn
694
Schleiden
Mons
Namur
Huy
Malmedy
Condé
La Louvière
Jumet
Andenne
Comblain
Ahr
Binche
Sambre
Ohey
746
Charleroi
Stavelot
Valenciennes
Thuin
Florennes
Ciney
Havelange
St. Vith
Ernstberg
le Quesnoy
Aulnoye
Maubeuge
313
Dinant
Ourthe
652
697
Gerolstein
700
Solesmes
Hautmont
Philippeville
Marche
Bovigny
Prüm
4
5
6
7
54
53
52
51
East from Greenwich
COPYRIGHT. GEORGE PHILIP & SON

SCANDINAVIA
0 100 200 miles
0 100 200 300
ICELAND
On same scale as general map
West from 20 Greenwich
East from Greenwich
Arctic Circle
Horn
Ísafjörður
Húnaflói
Akureyri
Jökulsá
Breiðafjörður
Neskaupstaður
Hvítá
Faxaflói
Akranes
Reykjavík
Keflavík
Þjórsá
Vatnajökull
Öraefajökull 2119
Vestmannaeyjar
North Cape
Nordkinn
Hammerfest
Söröya
Vardö
Vadsö
Tana
Senja
Tromsö
Vesterålen
Inari
L. Inari
Lofoten
Narvik
L. Torne
Torne
Porttipahta Res.
Lokka Res.
Lapland
West Fjord
2123 Kebnekaise
Kiruna
Kemi
Storlulea
Kelloselkä
Bodö
Sulitjelma 1913
Gällivare
ATLANTIC OCEAN
Lule
Rovaniemi
Hornavan
Tornio
Kemi
Mosjöen
Boden
Haparanda
Vega
Storavan
Luleå
Piteå
Oulu
Storuman
Skellefte
Vikna
Skellefteå
Raahe
Folda Fjord
Vilhelmina
Oulu
L. Oulu
Kajaani
Norrland
Trondheim Fjord
Steinkjer
Levanger
Ume
Vännäs
Umeå
Iisalmi
Gulf of Bothnia
Kristiansund
Trondheim
Örnsköldsvik
Östersund
Kuopio
Molde
Storsjön
Angerman
Vaasa
Ålesund
Dovre Fjell
Snöhetta 2286
Bräcke
Ånge
Indals
Härnösand
FINLAND
Stadlandet
Ljusnan
Sundsvall
Jyväskylä
Florø
Galdhöpiggen 2469
Jotun Fjell
Glåma
Hudiksvall
Höyanger
Lillehammer
Easter Dal
Tampere
Sogne Fjord
Söderhamn
Pori
Hamar
Moras
Wester Dal
Uusikaupunki
Hämeenlinna
Lahti
Bergen
Mjösa L.
Gävle
Kotka
Hardanger Fjord
Klar
Falun
Ahvenanmaa Is.
Turku
Helsinki
Dal
Dannemora
Oslo
Svealand
Hanko
Porkkala
Gulf of Finland
Haugesund
Drammen
Sala
Uppsala
Tallinn
Västerås
L. Mälar
Skien
Karlstad
Fredrikstad
Hjälmaren
Hiiumaa
Larvik
Oslo Fjord
Halden
Örebro
Eskilstuna
Stockholm
ESTONIA
Stavanger
L. Vaner
Pärnu
Egersund
Arendal
Canal
Norrköping
Saaremaa
Kristiansand
Trollhättan
L. Vätter
Linköping
Volga
Lindesnes
Mandal
Gulf of Riga
Skagen
Västervik
Visby
Skagerrak
Göteborg
Jönköping
Gotland
Borås
Götaland
Ventspils
LATVIA
Aalborg
Varberg
Oskarshamn
Riga
Kattegat
Lim Fjord
Halmstad
Kalmar
Öland
Liepaja
Jelgava
Dvina
Randers
Jutland
The Sound
Aarhus
U.S.S.R.
DENMARK
Hälsingborg
Karlskrona
Esbjerg
Copenhagen
Lund
Klaipeda
BALTIC SEA
LITHUANIA
Odense
Great Belt
Fyn
Sjælland
Malmö
Sovetsk
Kaunas
Neman
Bornholm
Flensburg
Kaliningrad
Vilnius
Gdynia
Heligoland
Gedser
Sassnitz
Gdańsk
Kiel Canal
Kiel
Stralsund
Rügen
Rostock
Lübeck
Altona
Hamburg
POLAND
Groningen
GERMANY
NETH.
WEST
Bremen
EAST
Szczecin
NORWAY
SWEDEN

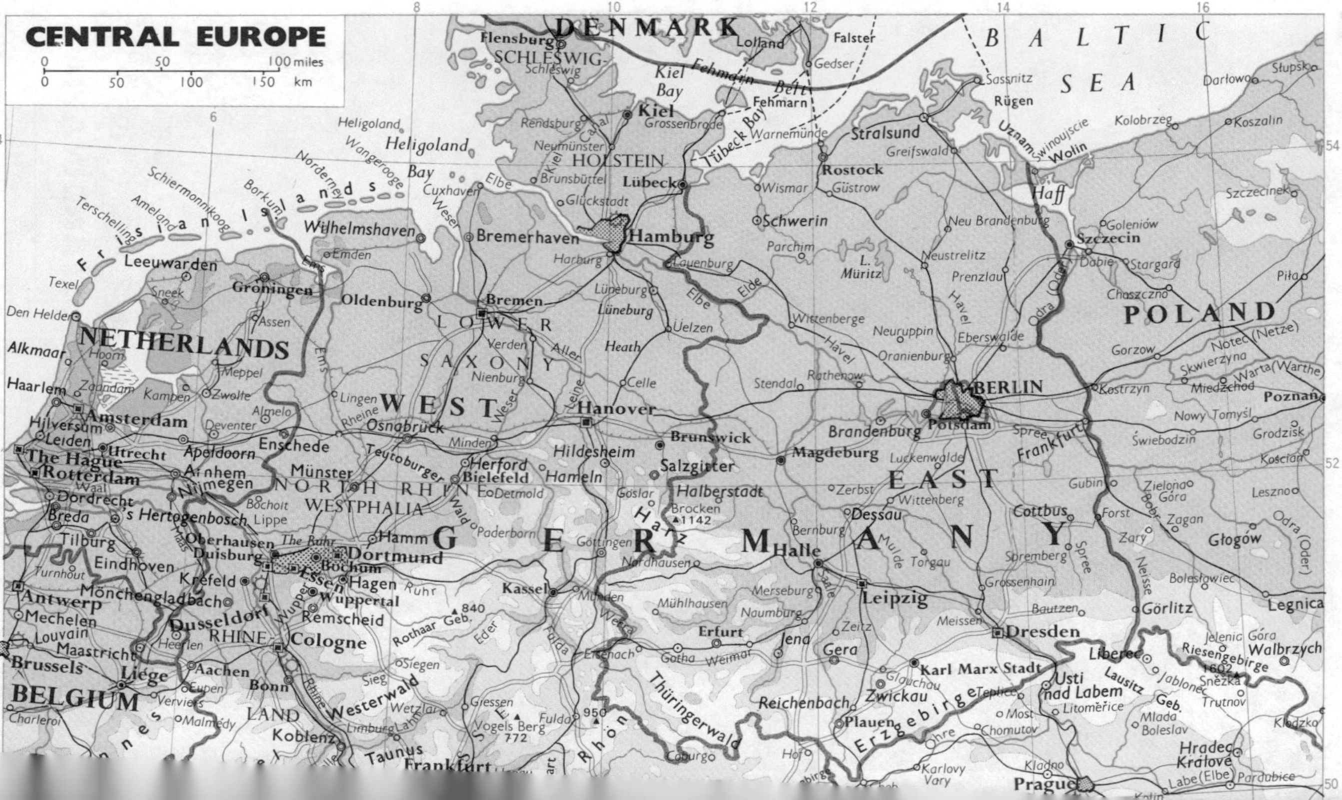
CENTRAL EUROPE
0 50 100 miles
0 50 100 150 km
DENMARK
BALTIC SEA
POLAND
NETHERLANDS
BELGIUM
WEST GERMANY
EAST GERMANY
LOWER SAXONY
NORTH RHINE WESTPHALIA
SCHLESWIG-HOLSTEIN
Frisian Islands
Flensburg
Schleswig
Lolland
Falster
Gedser
Kiel Bay
Fehmarn Belt
Fehmarn
Lübeck Bay
Kiel
Grossenbrode
Rendsburg
Neumünster
Kiel Canal
Brunsbüttel
Glückstadt
Lübeck
Warnemünde
Rostock
Stralsund
Greifswald
Sassnitz
Rügen
Uznam
Swinoujscie
Wolin
Haff
Kolobrzeg
Koszalin
Darłowo
Słupsk
Szczecinek
Goleniów
Szczecin
Dąbie
Stargard
Chaszczno
Piła
Heligoland
Heligoland Bay
Wangerooge
Norderney
Borkum
Schiermonnikoog
Ameland
Terschelling
Texel
Cuxhaven
Elbe
Weser
Wilhelmshaven
Bremerhaven
Hamburg
Harburg
Lauenburg
Wismar
Güstrow
Schwerin
Parchim
L. Müritz
Neu Brandenburg
Neustrelitz
Prenzlau
Oder
Odra
Leeuwarden
Emden
Ems
Groningen
Sneek
Assen
Oldenburg
Bremen
Lüneburg
Lüneburg Heath
Elde
Uelzen
Wittenberge
Havel
Neuruppin
Eberswalde
Oranienburg
Gorzow
Notec (Netze)
Skwierzyna
Warta (Warthe)
Międzychód
Poznań
Den Helder
Alkmaar
Hoorn
Meppel
Zwolle
Kampen
Zaandam
Haarlem
Amsterdam
Hilversum
Leiden
Utrecht
The Hague
Rotterdam
Waal
Dordrecht
Breda
's Hertogenbosch
Tilburg
Eindhoven
Turnhout
Antwerp
Mechelen
Louvain
Maastricht
Brussels
Liège
Charleroi
Verviers
Malmédy
Eupen
Heerlen
Aachen
Mönchengladbach
Krefeld
Duisburg
Oberhausen
Essen
Bochum
Dortmund
The Ruhr
Hagen
Ruhr
Wuppertal
Wupper
Remscheid
Dusseldorf
Cologne
Bonn
RHINE LAND
Rhine
Koblenz
Lahn
Limburg
Wetzlar
Westerwald
Taunus
Frankfurt
Sieg
Siegen
Rothaar Geb.
840
Eder
Deventer
Almelo
Apeldoorn
Arnhem
Nijmegen
Enschede
Bocholt
Lippe
Münster
Lingen
Rheine
Osnabrück
Teutoburger Wald
Minden
Herford
Bielefeld
Detmold
Paderborn
Hamm
Verden
Nienburg
Aller
Celle
Leine
Hanover
Hildesheim
Hameln
Brunswick
Salzgitter
Goslar
Halberstadt
Brocken
1142
Harz
Göttingen
Nordhausen
Kassel
Münden
Werra
Fulda
Mühlhausen
Eisenach
Gotha
Weimar
Erfurt
Jena
Gera
Zeitz
Naumburg
Merseburg
Saale
Halle
Leipzig
Bernburg
Dessau
Mulde
Zerbst
Wittenberg
Torgau
Magdeburg
Stendal
Rathenow
Brandenburg
Potsdam
BERLIN
Luckenwalde
Spree
Frankfurt
Kostrzyn
Nowy Tomyśl
Grodzisk
Świebodzin
Kościan
Gubin
Zielona Góra
Bóbr
Zagan
Żary
Forst
Cottbus
Spremberg
Leszno
Głogów
Odra (Oder)
Bolesławiec
Legnica
Neisse
Görlitz
Bautzen
Grossenhain
Meissen
Dresden
Karl Marx Stadt
Glauchau
Zwickau
Reichenbach
Plauen
Erzgebirge
Teplice
Usti nad Labem
Litoměřice
Most
Chomutov
Ohre
Karlovy Vary
Kladno
Prague
Liberec
Jablonec
Lausitz Geb.
Jelenia Góra
Riesengebirge
1602
Sněžka
Trutnov
Wałbrzych
Kłodzko
Mlada Boleslav
Hradec Kralove
Labe (Elbe)
Pardubice
Thüringerwald
Coburg
Hof
Rhön
950
Gressen
Vogels Berg
772
8
10
12
14
16
6
54
52
50

CZECHOSLOVAKIA
BOHEMIA
LOWER AUSTRIA
UPPER AUSTRIA
AUSTRIA
BURGENLAND
STYRIA
CARINTHIA
SALZBURG
TYROL
VORARLBERG
LIECHTENSTEIN
BAVARIA
BADEN-WÜRTTEMBERG
SAAR
LORRAINE
FRANCE
FRANCHE COMTÉ
SWITZERLAND
ITALY
LOMBARDY
VENETO
TRENTINO-ALTO ADIGE
FRIULI-VENEZIA GIULIA
PIEDMONT
V. D'AOSTA
Böhmerwald
Schwarzwald
Swabian Jura
Bernese Oberland
Carnic Alps
Karawanken
Karst
Dolomites
Plateau de Langres
Vienna
Munich
Zürich
Milan
Turin
Venice
Trieste
Zagreb
Ljubljana
Graz
Linz
Salzburg
Innsbruck
Klagenfurt
Nürnberg
Regensburg
Augsburg
Ingolstadt
Stuttgart
Mannheim
Heidelberg
Karlsruhe
Strasbourg
Freiburg
Mulhouse
Basel
Berne
Lucerne
Lausanne
Geneva
Besançon
Dijon
Nancy
Metz
Saarbrücken
Grenoble
Villeurbanne
Verona
Padua
Vicenza
Brescia
Bergamo
Bolzano
Trento
Udine
Rijeka
Maribor
Gulf of Venice
Istria
East from Greenwich

ITALY AND S.E. EUROPE
0 50 100 150 200 miles
0 100 200 300 km
10
15
45
40
35
East from Greenwich
GERMANY
CZECHOSL
Nuremberg
Plzeň
Ostrava
Jablunka P.
Jihlava
Brno
Slavkov
Regensburg
Isar
Danube
Vltava
Váh
Ulm
Augsburg
Munich
Inn
Linz
Vienna
Bratislava
Salzburg
AUSTRIA
Schutt I.
Graz
Bruck
Raab
HU
Klagenfurt
Mur
Drava
L. Balaton
Pécs
Belfort
Basel
L. of Constance
Zürich
Besançon
Dijon
Jura
Berne
SWITZERLAND
Innsbruck
Brenner P. 1371
TYROL
ALPS
Lausanne
L. Geneva
St. Gotthard P.
Ortler 3899
Geneva
Simplon P.
Mâcon
Chalon
Saône
FRANCE
Lyons
Mt. Blanc 4807
Bergamo
Como
Milan
Brescia
L. Garda
Trento
Piave
Udine
Gorizia
Ljubljana
Zagreb
Isère
Grenoble
Mt. Cenis P. 2083
Turin
Novara
Po
Adda
Oglio
Verona
Vicenza
Padua
Venice
Trieste
Isonzo
Rijeka
Istria
Rhône
Durance
Alessandria
Pavia
Parma
Reggio
Ferrara
G. of Venice
Pula
YUGOSLAVIA
Brod
Una
Banja Luka
Genoa
Modena
Bologna
Ravenna
BOSNIA
Avignon
Monaco
Riviera
La Spezia
Forli
Cannes
Nice
Menton
Gulf of Genoa
Rimini
Marseilles
Toulon
Pisa
Florence
San Marino
Zadar
Dinaric Alps
Bosna
Leghorn
Arno
Arezzo
Ancona
Sibenik
Dalmatia
Ligurian Sea
C. Corse
Siena
Split
Mostar
Elba
Perugia
APENNINES
Vis
Bastia
2710 Mte. Cinto
Corsica
Ajaccio
Sabine Mts.
Gran Sasso 2914
Lastovo
Dubrovnik
ADRIATIC SEA
Civitavecchia
ROME
Tiber
Str. of Bonifacio
Caprera
Mt. Gargano
Foggia
Barletta
Gaeta
Volturno
Sassari
Olbia
Tirso
Naples
Vesuvius 1277
Ofanto
Bari
Capri
Salerno
Brindisi
Sardinia
Mt. del Gennargentu 1834
3719
Taranto
G. of Taranto
Mannu
Cagliari
Tyrrhenian Sea
Cosenza
La Sila 1929
Stromboli
Lipari Is.
Catanzaro
MEDITERRANEAN
Palermo
Messina
Trapani
Egadi Is.
Marsala
Sicily
Mt. Etna 3340
Catania
Reggio
C. Spartivento
Str. of Messina
Skikda
Annaba
Bizerta
Agrigento
Caltanissetta
Siracusa
C. Bon
Tunis
Constantine
Pantelleria (It.)
C. Passero
G. of Hammamet
Sousse
Kairouan
Gozo
Valletta
MALTA
ALGERIA
Tébessa
TUNISIA
Lampedusa (It.)
4135
Sfax
Kerkennah
Tozeur
Chott Djerid
Gabès
Djerba

20
25
30
Przemysl
Lvov
Vinnitsa
Cieszyn
Galicia
Carpathians
U. S. S. R.
UKRAINE
Tatra
2655
OVAKIA
Kamenets-Podolskiy
Uman
Mogilev-Podolski
Kirovograd
Pervomaysk
Krivoy Rog
Kolomyia
Prut
RUTHENIA
Košice
Dnestr (Dniester)
MOLDAVIA
Balta
Voznesensk
Banská Štiavnica
Chernovtsy
Tisza
Beltsy
Bug
Nikolayev
Miskolc
Tokaj
Botoşani
Somes
Pietrosul 2305
Iaşi
Siret
Debrecen
Kishinev
Tiraspol
Kherson
Budapest
HUNGARY
Oradea
Pietrosul 2102
Bessarabia
Bendery
Odessa
Kecskemét
Körös
Cluj
Belgorod Dnestrovski
G. of Karkinitsk
Szeged
Hódmezővásárhely
ROMANIA
Arad
Galaţi
Izmail
C. Tarkhankut
Subotica
Mureş
Sibiu
Negoiu 2535
Braşov
45
Sombor
Timişoara
Transylvanian Alps
Brăila
Sulina
Novi Sad
Petrovaradin
Ploieşti
Dobrogea
Sava
Belgrade
Iron Gate
Turnu-Severin
Piteşti
Constanţa
Smederevo
Orşova
Bucharest
Craiova
Silistra
Drina
Kragujevac
Danube
Ruse
Tolbukhin
BLACK SEA
SERBIA
Morava
Vidin
Pleven
Iskŭr
Sarajevo
Niš
Balkan Mts.
Tŭrnovo
Varna
Novi Pazar
Shipka P.
Durmitor 2522
Sliven
Burgas
MONTENEGRO
YUGOSLAVIA
Sofia
BULGARIA
Cetinje
Musala 2925
Maritsa
Zonguldak
Shkodër
Plovdiv
Edirne
Ereğli
Šar Pl. 2764
Skopje
Rhodope
İstanbul
Bosporus
Tiranë
Vardar
Strumica
Xanthi
Üsküdar
İzmit
Bolu
Durrës
Bitolj
Serrai
Komotini
Tekirdağ
Sea of Marmara
İznik Gölü
Elbasan
ALBANIA
Kavalla
Alexandroupolis
Enez
Bilecik
Sakarya
Aliakmon
Thessaloniki
Gelibolu
Bursa
40
Vlorë
Áthos 2033
Gökçeada
Bandırma
Eskişehir
Olympus 2917
Çanakkale
Sivrihisar
Str. of Otranto
Pindus
Lemnos
Dardanelles
Balıkesir
Kütahya
GREECE
Trikkala
Afyon Karahisar
Corfu
Larissa
Aegean Sea
Ayvalık
TURKEY
Ioannina
Vólos
N. Sporades
Lésvos
Belvadin
Ionian Is.
Eğridir Gölü
Euboea
Manisa
Turgutlu
Eğridir
Levkás
Návpaktos
Chios
İzmir
Alaşehir
Menderes
Isparta
Cephalonia
Thebes
G. of Corinth
Athens
Andros
Samos
Aydın
Burdur
Patras
Corinth
Piraeus
Ikaría
Denizli
Taurus Mts.
Zákinthos
Olympia
Nauplia
Hermoupolis
Syros
Cyclades
Muğla
Antalya
Peloponnesus
Náxos
Dodecanese
Elmalı
3086
Kalamata
Sparta
Pílos
Milo
Ios
Rhodes
Kastellorizon
5121
Thira
Rhodes
4486
C. Matapan
Cerigo
Scarpanto
Andikithira
Khaniá
Mt. Ídhi 2456
Iráklion
35
Crete
AEGEAN SEA
20
25

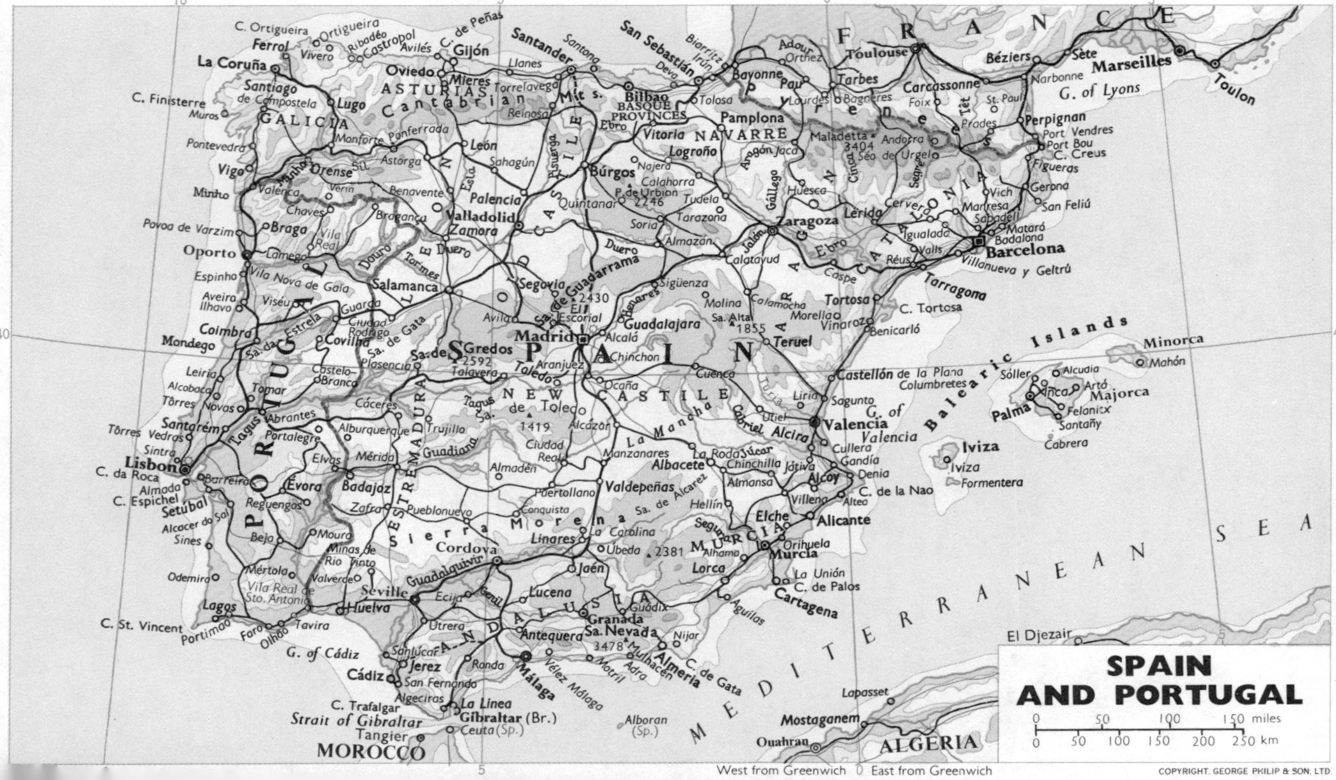
SPAIN
AND PORTUGAL
0 50 100 150 miles
0 50 100 150 200 250 km
COPYRIGHT. GEORGE PHILIP & SON. LTD.
West from Greenwich 0 East from Greenwich
F R A N C E
S P A I N
P O R T U G A L
M E D I T E R R A N E A N S E A
MOROCCO
ALGERIA
Balearic Islands
NEW CASTILE
OLD CASTILE
ARAGON
CATALONIA
NAVARRE
BASQUE PROVINCES
GALICIA
ASTURIAS
LEON
ESTREMADURA
ANDALUSIA
MURCIA
Cantabrian Mts.
Pyrenees
Sierra Morena
Sa. de Guadarrama
Sa. de Gredos
Sa. Nevada
G. of Lyons
G. of Valencia
G. of Cádiz
Strait of Gibraltar
La Coruña
Ferrol
Santiago de Compostela
Lugo
Oviedo
Gijón
Santander
Bilbao
San Sebastián
Vitoria
Pamplona
Logroño
Búrgos
León
Palencia
Valladolid
Zamora
Salamanca
Segovia
Madrid
Toledo
Guadalajara
Zaragoza
Lérida
Barcelona
Tarragona
Tortosa
Teruel
Cuenca
Castellón de la Plana
Valencia
Alicante
Murcia
Cartagena
Albacete
Valdepeñas
Ciudad Real
Badajoz
Cáceres
Mérida
Córdova
Jaén
Granada
Almería
Málaga
Seville
Huelva
Cádiz
Jerez
Gibraltar (Br.)
La Linea
Ceuta (Sp.)
Tangier
Oporto
Braga
Coimbra
Lisbon
Setúbal
Évora
Lagos
C. St. Vincent
C. Finisterre
C. Ortigueira
C. da Roca
C. Espichel
C. Trafalgar
C. de Gata
C. de Palos
C. de la Nao
C. Tortosa
C. Creus
Majorca
Minorca
Iviza
Formentera
Cabrera
Palma
Mahón
Toulouse
Tarbes
Carcassonne
Béziers
Perpignan
Marseilles
Toulon
Sète
Bayonne
Pau
Andorra
Maladetta 3404
Mostaganem
Ouahran
Lapasset
El Djezair
Tagus
Douro
Duero
Ebro
Minho
Guadiana
Guadalquivir
Júcar
Turia
Segura
Genil
Tormes
Alboran (Sp.)

MIDDLE EAST

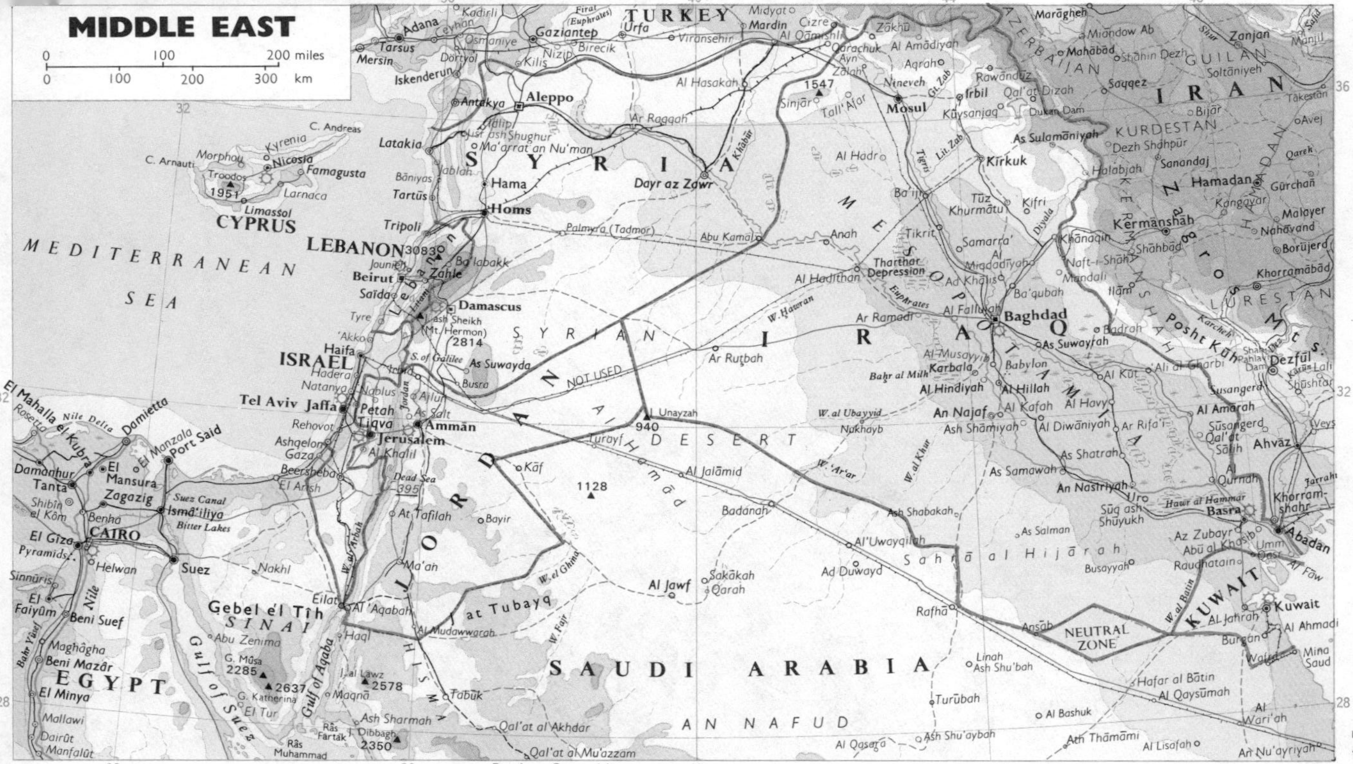
0 100 200 miles
0 100 200 300 km
TURKEY
SYRIA
IRAQ
IRAN
JORDAN
LEBANON
ISRAEL
CYPRUS
EGYPT
SAUDI ARABIA
KUWAIT
NEUTRAL ZONE
MEDITERRANEAN SEA
SYRIAN DESERT
NOT USED
MESOPOTAMIA
SINAI
AN NAFUD
Sahrā al Hijārah
Al Hamād
Zagros Mts.
KURDESTAN
LURESTAN
AZERBAIJAN
GUILAN
HAMADAN
KERMANSHAH
Posht Kūh
Gulf of Suez
Gulf of Aqaba
Gebel el Tîh
HISMA
Adana
Tarsus
Mersin
Iskenderun
Antakya
Aleppo
Gaziantep
Urfa
Mardin
Latakia
Hama
Homs
Tartūs
Tripoli
Beirut
Zahle
Damascus
Saïda
Tyre
Haifa
Tel Aviv Jaffa
Jerusalem
Ammān
Petah Tiqva
Dayr az Zawr
Palmyra (Tadmor)
Abu Kamal
Mosul
Kirkuk
Baghdad
Karbala
An Najaf
Basra
Abadan
Ahvāz
Dezfūl
Kermanshah
Hamadan
Kuwait
Cairo
Port Said
Suez
Alexandria
Damietta
Tanta
Zagazig
El Giza
Beni Suef
El Minya
Nicosia
Famagusta
Limassol
Kyrenia
Larnaca
Ar Rutbah
Al Jawf
Tabūk
Rafhā
Hafar al Bātin
'Aqabah
Eilat
Ma'an
1951
3083
2814
1547
940
1128
2578
2637
2285
2350
36
40
44
48
32
28
East from Greenwich

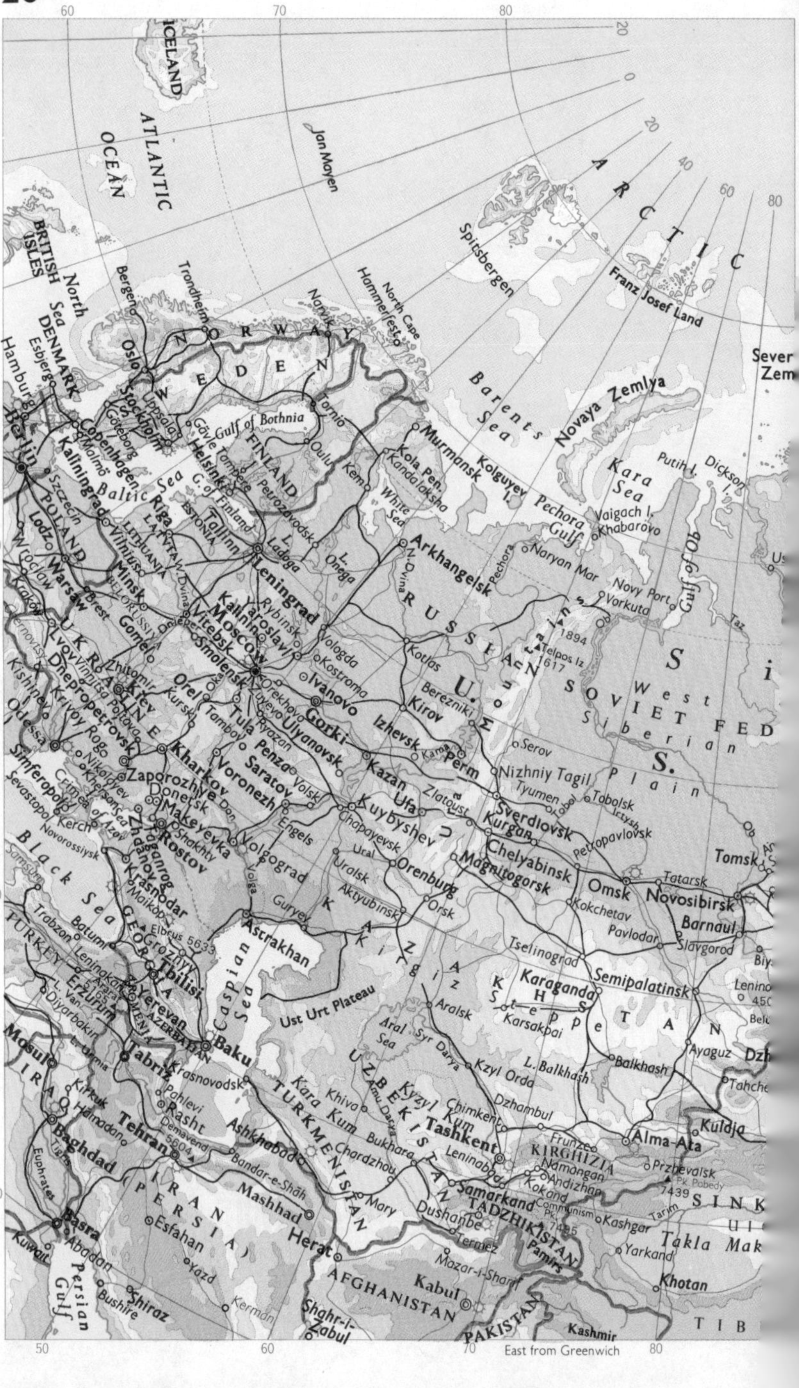
ICELAND
ATLANTIC
OCEAN
Jan Mayen
A R C T I C
Spitsbergen
Franz Josef Land
Sever
Zem
BRITISH ISLES
North Sea
DENMARK
Bergen
Trondheim
Narvik
Hammerfest
North Cape
N O R W A Y
S W E D E N
Oslo
Esbjerg
Hamburg
Stockholm
Uppsala
Göteborg
Copenhagen
Malmö
Berlin
Kaliningrad
Gulf of Bothnia
Gävle
Tornio
Oulu
Kem
Tampere
FINLAND
Helsinki
G. of Finland
Baltic Sea
Szczecin
POLAND
Lodz
Wroclaw
Krakow
Warsaw
Riga
LATVIA
ESTONIA
Tallinn
LITHUANIA
Vilnius
Minsk
BELORUSSIA
Brest
Gomel
Murmansk
Kola Pen.
Kandalaksha
White Sea
Barents Sea
Novaya Zemlya
Kolguyev I.
Pechora Gulf
Kara Sea
Vaigach I.
Khabarovo
Putih I.
Dickson I.
Gulf of Ob
Arkhangelsk
N. Dvina
Pechora
Naryan Mar
Novy Port
Vorkuta
Petrozavodsk
L. Ladoga
L. Onega
Leningrad
Rybinsk
Yaroslavl
Kalinin
Moscow
Vitebsk
Smolensk
Dnieper
Vologda
Kostroma
Ivanovo
Kotlas
R U S S I A N
S O V I E T
F E D
U. S. S. R.
West Siberian Plain
Telpos Iz 1617
1894
Taz
Ob
UKRAINE
Lvov
Chernovtsy
Vinnitsa
Zhitomir
Kiev
Kishinev
Odessa
Dnepropetrovsk
Krivoy Rog
Poltava
Kursk
Orel
Oka
Tula
Tambov
Ryazan
Orekhovo Zuyevo
Gorki
Kirov
Bereznik
Izhevsk
Kama
Perm
Serov
Nizhniy Tagil
Ulyanovsk
Penza
Kazan
Ufa
Zlatoust
Tyumen
Tobol
Tobolsk
Irtysh
Sverdlovsk
Kurgan
Petropavlovsk
Nikolayev
Kherson
Crimea
Simferopol
Sevastopol
Zaporozhye
Kharkov
Voronezh
Saratov
Volsk
Donetsk
Makeyevka
Don
Kerch
Sea of Azov
Zhdanov
Taganrog
Rostov
Shakhty
Novorossiysk
Kuybyshev
Chapayevsk
Engels
Volgograd
Volga
Ural
Uralsk
Orenburg
Chelyabinsk
Magnitogorsk
Omsk
Tatarsk
Novosibirsk
Tomsk
Barnaul
Biy
Black Sea
Samsun
Trabzon
TURKEY
Krasnodar
Maikop
GEORGIA
Batumi
Elbrus 5633
Grozny
Tbilisi
Leninakan
Ararat 5165
Erzurum
L. Van
Diyarbakir
Yerevan
ARMENIA
AZERBAIJAN
Baku
Astrakhan
Guryev
Caspian Sea
Aktyubinsk
Orsk
Kokchetav
Pavlodar
Slavgorod
Tselinograd
Karaganda
Semipalatinsk
K A Z A K H S T A N
Kirgiz Steppe
Karsakpai
Ust Urt Plateau
Aralsk
Aral Sea
Syr Darya
L. Balkhash
Balkhash
Ayaguz
Dzh
Tahche
Lenino
450
Belu
Mosul
IRAQ
L. Urmia
Tabriz
Kirkuk
Hamadan
Krasnovodsk
Pahlevi
Rasht
Tehran
Demavend 5604
Baghdad
Euphrates
Tigris
Kara Kum
Khiva
Amu Darya
UZBEKISTAN
Kyzyl Kum
Kzyl Orda
Chimkent
Dzhambul
Tashkent
TURKMENISTAN
Ashkhabad
Bukhara
Chardzhou
Bandar-e-Shah
Mashhad
Mary
Samarkand
Leninabad
Frunze
KIRGHIZIA
Alma-Ata
Kuldja
Namangan
Andizhan
Kokand
Przhevalsk
Pk. Pobedy 7439
Dushanbe
TADZHIKISTAN
Communism Pk. 7495
Kashgar
Tarim
SINK
Takla Mak
IRAN (PERSIA)
Basra
Kuwait
Abadan
Esfahan
Yazd
Persian Gulf
Bushire
Shiraz
Kerman
Herat
AFGHANISTAN
Termez
Mazar-i-Sharif
Pamirs
Yarkand
Khotan
Kabul
Shghr-i-Zabul
PAKISTAN
Kashmir
TIB
50
60
70
80
40
30
20
0
East from Greenwich

U.S.S.R.
0 200 400 600 800 miles
0 200 400 600 800 1000 1200 km
80
70
60
50
40
30
100
110
180
160
140
120
100
ALASKA
Bering Strait
St. Lawrence I. (U.S.A.)
Bering Sea
Wrangel I.
Chukot Sea
Chukot Range
Gulf of Anadyr
Anadyr
OCEAN
Komsomolets I.
October Revolution I.
Bolshevik I.
New Siberian Is.
De Long Is.
East Siberian Sea
Beruang I.
Amabarchik
Lyakhov Is.
Nizhne Kolymsk
Sredne Kolymsk
Kolyma
Kolyma Ra.
Gizhiga
Shelekhov Gulf
Kamchatka
Komandorskiye Is.
Ust Kamchatsk
4750 Klyuchevsk Vol.
Petropavlovsk-Kamchatskiy
Laptev Sea
Tiksi
Byrrang Mts.
Taimyr Pen.
L. Taimyr
Nordvik
Khatanga
Kotuy R.
Buluno
Yana
Verkhoyansk
Verkhoyansk Range
Magadan
Okhotsk
Sea of Okhotsk
Zhigansk
Lena
Aldan
Central Siberian Plateau
Vilyuisk
Yakutsk
Dzhugdzhur Ra.
Shantar Is.
Okha
Sakhalin
Aleksandrovsk
Kuril Is.
Lower Tunguska
Noginsk
Olekminsk
Aldan
Nikolayevsk
Sovetskaya Gavan
Yuzhno-Sakhalinsk
Korsakov
Stony Tunguska
Kirensk
Bodaibo
Stanovoi Ra.
Skovorodino
Komsomolsk
Birobidzhan
Sikhote Alin Range
Gulf of Tartary
Angara
Bratsk
Yablonovy Ra.
Amur
Belogorsk
Blagoveshchensk
Khabarovsk
Sapporo
Otaru
Hakodate
JAPAN
Achinsk
Krasnoyarsk
Taishet
Kansk
Nizhneudinsk
L. Baikal
Chita
Sretensk
Nerchinsk
Kuznetskiy
Tulun
Cheremkhovo
Angarsk
Ulan-Ude
Olovyannaya
Hailar
Sungari
Vladivostok
Minusinsk
Munku-Sardyk 3491
Irkutsk
Petrovsk
Khilok
Harbin
Ussuriysk
Yenisei
Kyakhta
Selenga
Sea of Japan
Dzhibkhalantu
Ulan Bator
Changchun
MONGOLIA
Mukden
Yingkow
Antung
N. Wonsan
Seoul
S. KOREA
Pusan
Hiroshima
Gobi or Shamo
INNER MONGOLIA
Pyongyang
Inchon
Kunsan
Lü-ta
Peking
Tatung
Tientsin
Mokpo
Masan
Nagasaki
JAPAN
Hami
Paotow
Tsingtao
Sinhailien
CHINESE REPUBLIC
GREAT WALL
Hwang
Tsinan
Lanchow
Sian
Chengchow

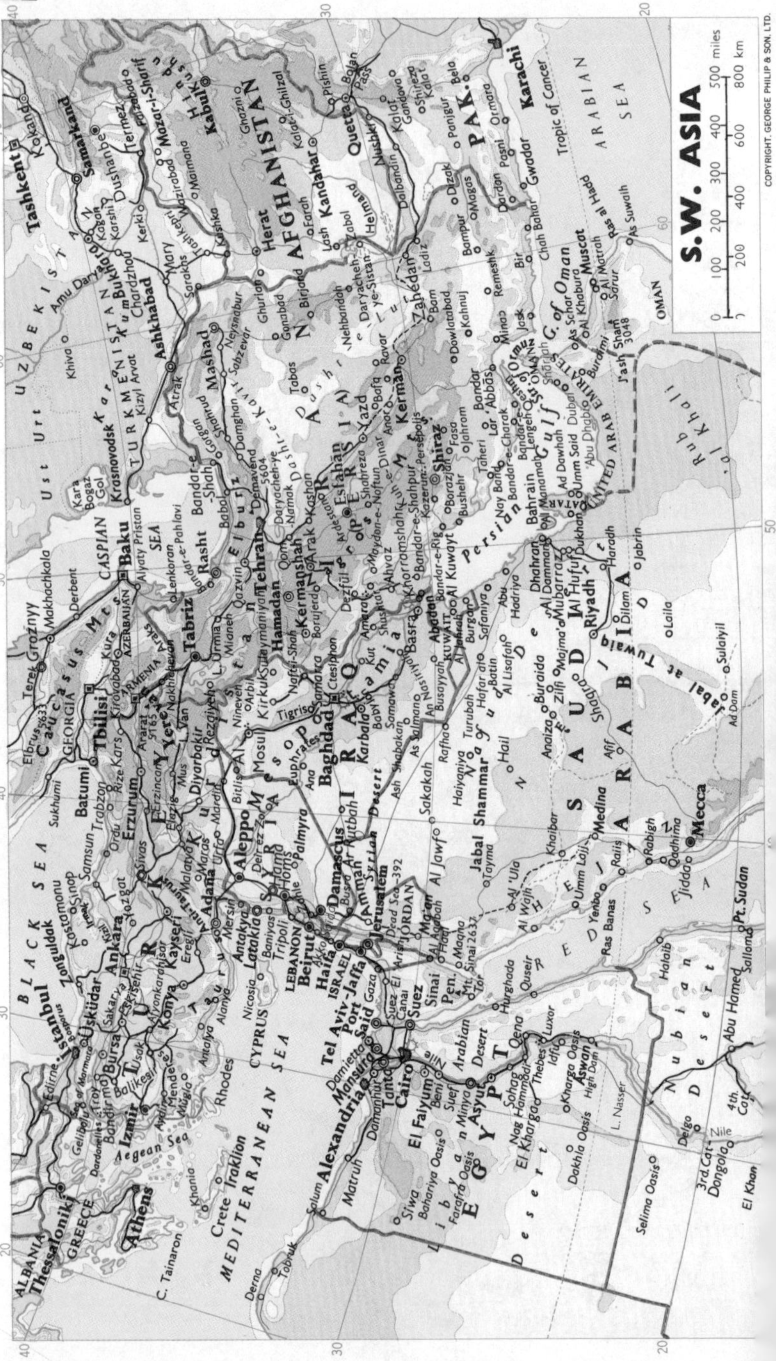
S.W. ASIA
COPYRIGHT, GEORGE PHILIP & SON, LTD.
0 100 200 300 400 500 miles
0 200 400 600 800 km
Tropic of Cancer
BLACK SEA
CASPIAN SEA
MEDITERRANEAN SEA
Aegean Sea
RED SEA
ARABIAN SEA
Persian Gulf
G. of Oman
Caucasus Mts.
Elburz
Ust Urt
Kara Kum
Dasht-e-Kavir
Dasht-e-Lut
Rub al Khali
Jabal at Tuwaiq
Jabal Shammar
Syrian Desert
Libyan Desert
Arabian Desert
Nubian Desert
Mesopotamia
Hindu Kush
TURKEY
GREECE
ALBANIA
CYPRUS
SYRIA
LEBANON
ISRAEL
JORDAN
IRAQ
IRAN
PERSIA
KUWAIT
QATAR
BAHRAIN
UNITED ARAB EMIRATES
OMAN
SAUDI ARABIA
AFGHANISTAN
PAK.
EGYPT
GEORGIA
ARMENIA
AZERBAIJAN
TURKMENISTAN
UZBEKISTAN
Istanbul
Ankara
Izmir
Athens
Thessaloniki
Baku
Tbilisi
Tehran
Baghdad
Damascus
Beirut
Jerusalem
Amman
Cairo
Alexandria
Port Said
Suez
Mecca
Medina
Riyadh
Kuwait
Tabriz
Esfahan
Shiraz
Mashad
Herat
Kandahar
Kabul
Quetta
Karachi
Muscat
Tashkent
Samarkand
Ashkhabad
Aleppo
Mosul
Basra
Tel Aviv-Jaffa
Haifa
Aswan
Nile
Euphrates
Tigris
Demavend 5604
Elbrus 5633
Ararat 5165
L. Van
L. Urmia
L. Nasser

INDIA, PAKISTAN, SRI LANKA & BURMA

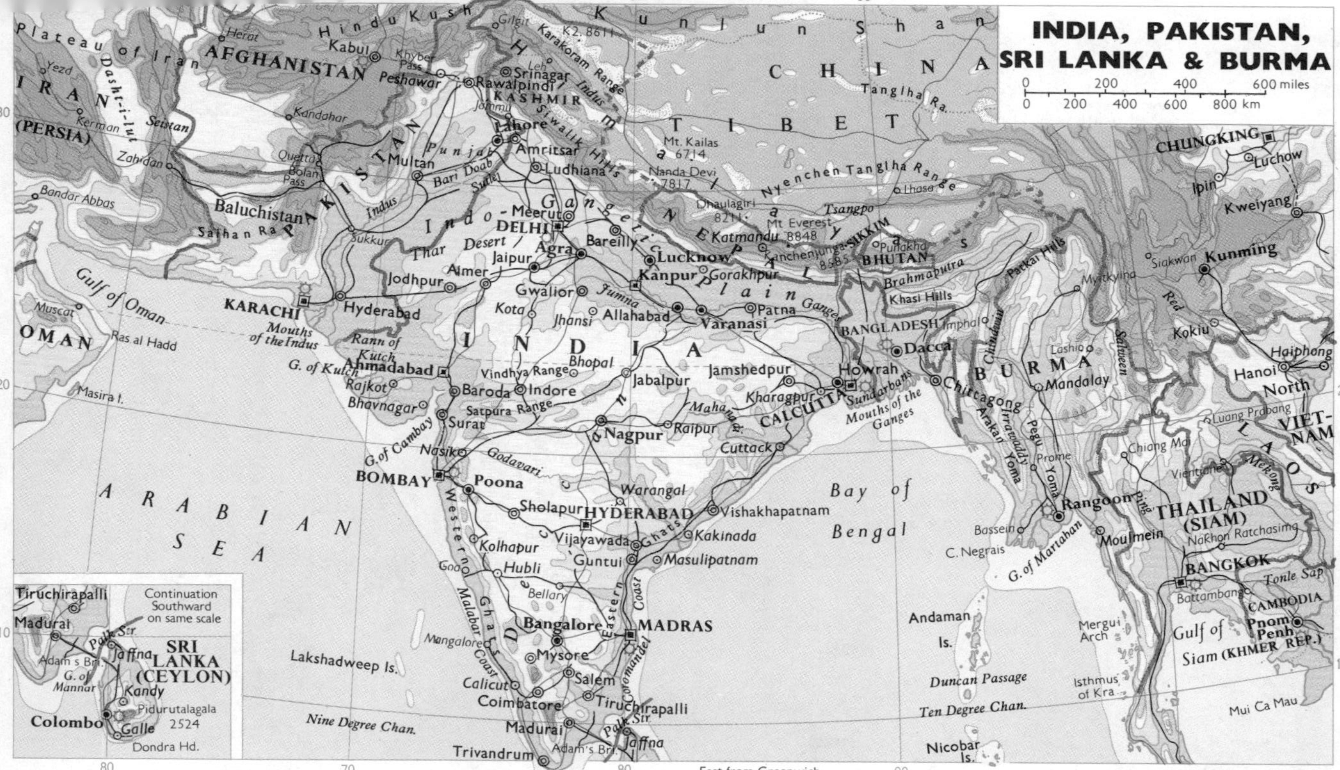

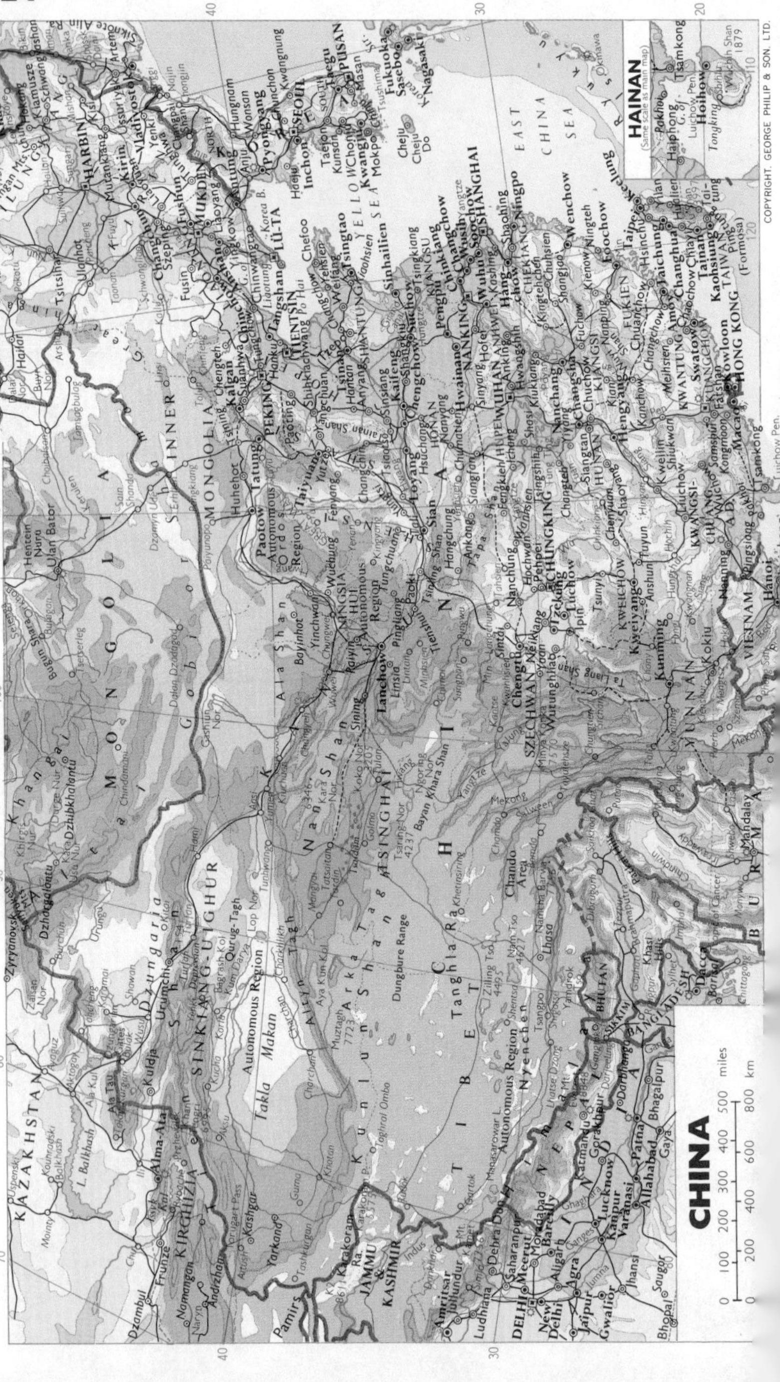

CHINA
0 100 200 300 400 500 miles
0 200 400 600 800 km
HAINAN
(Same scale as main map)
COPYRIGHT. GEORGE PHILIP & SON. LTD.

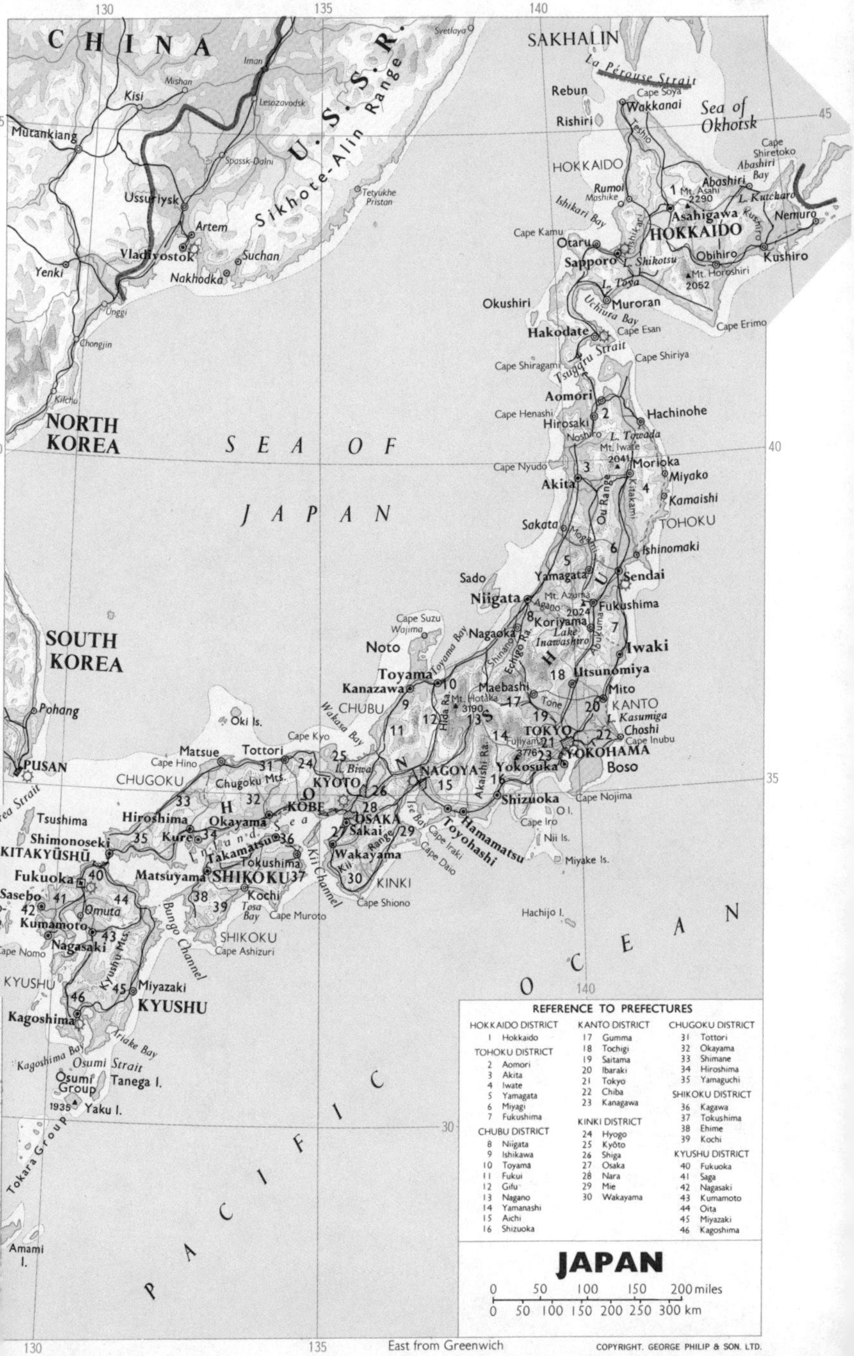
CHINA
U.S.S.R.
Sikhote-Alin Range
SAKHALIN
La Pérouse Strait
Cape Soya
Wakkanai
Rebun
Rishiri
Sea of Okhotsk
Cape Shiretoko
Abashiri Bay
Abashiri
Mt. Asahi 2290
L. Kutcharo
Asahigawa
HOKKAIDO
Nemuro
Obihiro
Kushiro
Mt. Horoshiri 2052
Sapporo
Otaru
L. Shikotsu
L. Toya
Muroran
Uchiura Bay
Cape Erimo
Hakodate
Cape Esan
Tsugaru Strait
Cape Shiriya
Cape Shiragami
Okushiri
Ishikari Bay
Rumoi
Mashike
Cape Kamui
Teshio
Aomori
Hachinohe
Hirosaki
Cape Henashi
L. Towada
Noshiro
Mt. Iwate 2041
Morioka
Miyako
Kamaishi
Cape Nyudo
Akita
Ou Range
Kitakami
TOHOKU
Sakata
Mogami
Ishinomaki
Yamagata
Sendai
Sado
Niigata
Mt. Azuma 2024
Agano
Fukushima
Koriyama
Lake Inawashiro
Abukuma
Nagaoka
Iwaki
Cape Suzu
Wajima
Noto
Toyama Bay
Toyama
Kanazawa
Shinano
Echigo Ra.
Utsunomiya
Maebashi
Mito
Tone
KANTO
L. Kasumiga
Choshi
Cape Inubu
Mt. Hotaka 3190
Hida Ra.
Akaishi Ra.
CHUBU
Wakasa Bay
TOKYO
Fujiyama 3776
YOKOHAMA
Yokosuka
Boso
Cape Nojima
O I.
Cape Iro
Nii Is.
Miyake Is.
Hachijo I.
Shizuoka
Hamamatsu
Toyohashi
NAGOYA
Ise Bay
Cape Irako
Cape Daio
L. Biwa
KYOTO
KOBE
OSAKA
Sakai
Wakayama
Kii Range
Kii Channel
KINKI
Cape Shiono
Cape Kyo
Oki Is.
Tottori
Matsue
Cape Hino
CHUGOKU
Chugoku Mts.
Okayama
Hiroshima
Kure
Inland Sea
Takamatsu
Tokushima
Matsuyama
SHIKOKU
Kochi
Tosa Bay
Cape Muroto
Cape Ashizuri
Bungo Channel
Shimonoseki
KITAKYŪSHŪ
Fukuoka
Sasebo
Omuta
Kumamoto
Nagasaki
Cape Nomo
Kyushu Mts.
Miyazaki
KYUSHU
Kagoshima
Kagoshima Bay
Ariake Bay
Osumi Strait
Osumi Group
Tanega I.
1935
Yaku I.
Tokara Group
Amami I.
Tsushima
Korea Strait
PUSAN
Pohang
SOUTH KOREA
NORTH KOREA
Kilchu
Chongjin
Unggi
Yenki
Vladivostok
Nakhodka
Suchan
Artem
Ussuriysk
Mutankiang
Kisi
Mishan
Iman
Lesozavodsk
Spassk-Dalni
Tetyukhe Pristan
Svetlaya
SEA OF JAPAN
PACIFIC OCEAN
REFERENCE TO PREFECTURES
HOKKAIDO DISTRICT
1 Hokkaido
TOHOKU DISTRICT
2 Aomori
3 Akita
4 Iwate
5 Yamagata
6 Miyagi
7 Fukushima
CHUBU DISTRICT
8 Niigata
9 Ishikawa
10 Toyama
11 Fukui
12 Gifu
13 Nagano
14 Yamanashi
15 Aichi
16 Shizuoka
KANTO DISTRICT
17 Gumma
18 Tochigi
19 Saitama
20 Ibaraki
21 Tokyo
22 Chiba
23 Kanagawa
KINKI DISTRICT
24 Hyogo
25 Kyōto
26 Shiga
27 Osaka
28 Nara
29 Mie
30 Wakayama
CHUGOKU DISTRICT
31 Tottori
32 Okayama
33 Shimane
34 Hiroshima
35 Yamaguchi
SHIKOKU DISTRICT
36 Kagawa
37 Tokushima
38 Ehime
39 Kochi
KYUSHU DISTRICT
40 Fukuoka
41 Saga
42 Nagasaki
43 Kumamoto
44 Oita
45 Miyazaki
46 Kagoshima
JAPAN
0 50 100 150 200 miles
0 50 100 150 200 250 300 km
East from Greenwich

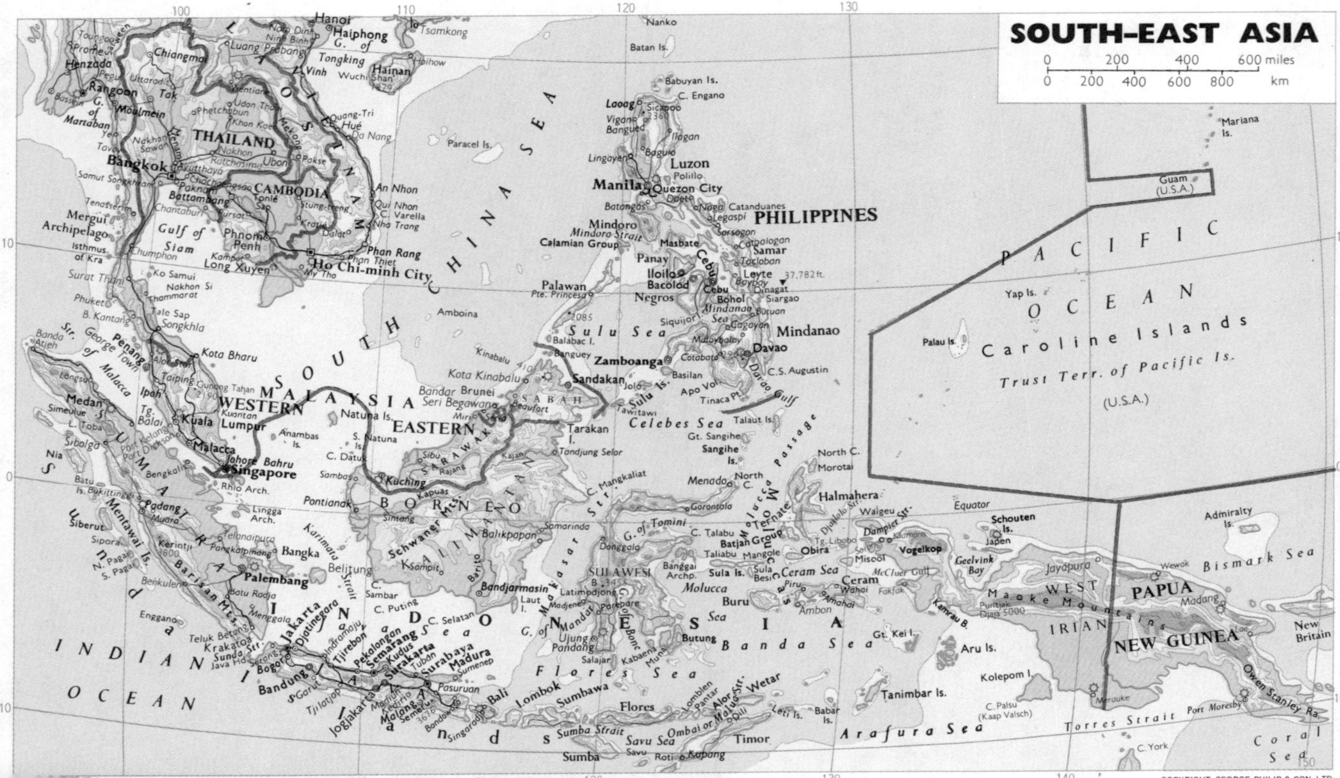
SOUTH-EAST ASIA
0 200 400 600 miles
0 200 400 600 800 km
SOUTH CHINA SEA
PACIFIC OCEAN
Caroline Islands
Trust Terr. of Pacific Is.
(U.S.A.)
Guam
(U.S.A.)
Mariana Is.
PHILIPPINES
Luzon
Manila
Quezon City
Mindanao
Davao
Zamboanga
Sulu Sea
Celebes Sea
THAILAND
Bangkok
CAMBODIA
Phnom Penh
Ho Chi-minh City
Hanoi
Haiphong
Hainan
Gulf of Siam
MALAYSIA
WESTERN
EASTERN
Kuala Lumpur
Singapore
SABAH
SARAWAK
BORNEO
KALIMANTAN
SULAWESI
INDONESIA
Jakarta
Bandung
Semarang
Surabaya
Palembang
Medan
Banda Sea
Flores Sea
Java Sea
Molucca Sea
Ceram Sea
Arafura Sea
Timor
Halmahera
Equator
Bismark Sea
Admiralty Is.
WEST IRIAN
PAPUA
NEW GUINEA
Maoke Mountains
Owen Stanley Ra.
Port Moresby
Torres Strait
Coral Sea
INDIAN OCEAN
East from Greenwich

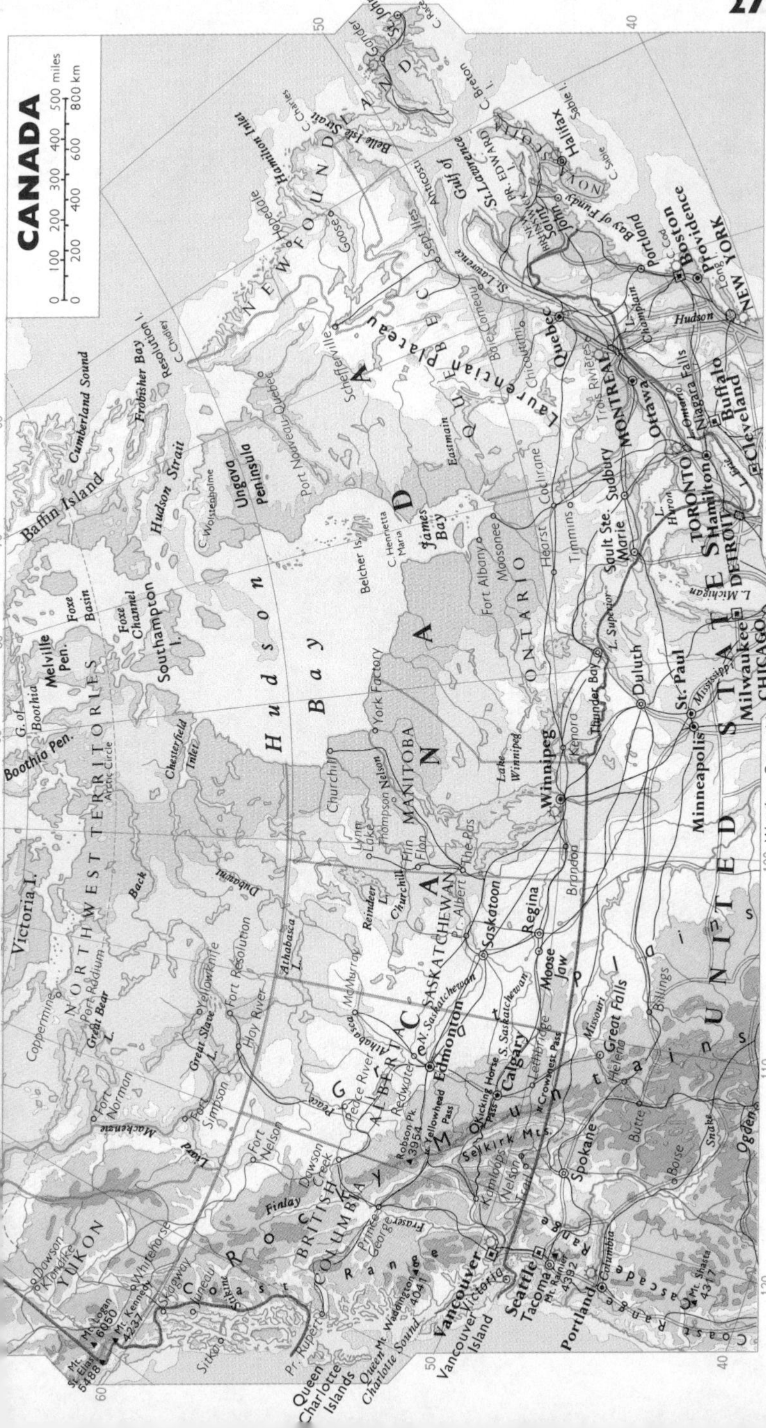
CANADA
0 100 200 300 400 500 miles
0 200 400 600 800 km
Baffin Island
Cumberland Sound
Frobisher Bay
Resolution I.
C. Chidley
Hudson Strait
Ungava Peninsula
C. Wolstenholme
Port Nouveau-Quebec
Schefferville
Laurentian Plateau
Hopedale
Hamilton Inlet
Goose
NEWFOUNDLAND
Belle Isle Strait
C. Charles
St. John's
C. Race
Gander
Sept Iles
Anticosti
Gulf of St. Lawrence
PR. EDWARD I.
NEW BRUNSWICK
NOVA SCOTIA
Halifax
Sable I.
C. Sable
C. Breton
Saint John
Bay of Fundy
QUEBEC
Quebec
Baie Comeau
Chicoutimi
Trois Rivières
MONTREAL
Ottawa
L. Champlain
Portland
C. Cod
Boston
Providence
Long I.
NEW YORK
Hudson
L. Ontario
Niagara Falls
Buffalo
Cleveland
L. Erie
TORONTO
Hamilton
DETROIT
L. Huron
Sudbury
Cochrane
Eastmain
James Bay
C. Henrietta Maria
Belcher Is.
Moosonee
Fort Albany
Hearst
Timmins
Sault Ste. Marie
L. Michigan
L. Superior
ONTARIO
Thunder Bay
Duluth
St. Paul
Minneapolis
Mississippi
Milwaukee
CHICAGO
UNITED STATES
Hudson Bay
Victoria I.
Melville Pen.
Foxe Basin
Foxe Channel
Southampton I.
G. of Boothia
Boothia Pen.
NORTHWEST TERRITORIES
Arctic Circle
Chesterfield Inlet
Back
Dubawnt
Churchill
York Factory
Nelson
MANITOBA
Lynn Lake
Thompson
Flin Flon
The Pas
Lake Winnipeg
Winnipeg
Kenora
Brandon
Reindeer L.
SASKATCHEWAN
Pr. Albert
Saskatoon
Regina
Moose Jaw
N. Saskatchewan
S. Saskatchewan
Missouri
Great Falls
Billings
Athabasca L.
Athabasca
McMurray
Fort Resolution
Hay River
Great Slave L.
Yellowknife
Port Radium
Great Bear L.
Coppermine
Fort Norman
Mackenzie
Fort Simpson
Liard
Fort Nelson
Peace
Peace River
ALBERTA
Edmonton
Redwater
Calgary
Lethbridge
Crowsnest Pass
Kicking Horse Pass
Yellowhead Pass
Robson Pk. 3954
ROCKY MOUNTAINS
Selkirk Mts.
Helena
Butte
Spokane
Boise
Snake
Ogden
Nelson
Trail
Kamloops
Dawson Creek
Finlay
BRITISH COLUMBIA
Prince George
Fraser
Coast Range
Mt. Waddington 4041
Vancouver
Victoria
Vancouver Island
Seattle
Tacoma
Mt. Rainier 4392
Columbia
Portland
Cascade Range
Mt. Shasta 4317
Queen Charlotte Sound
Queen Charlotte Islands
Pr. Rupert
Sitka
Juneau
Stikine
Skagway
Whitehorse
YUKON
Dawson
Klondike
Mt. Logan 6050
Mt. Kennedy 4237
Mt. St. Elias 5488
West from Greenwich
40
50
60
70
80
90
100
110
120

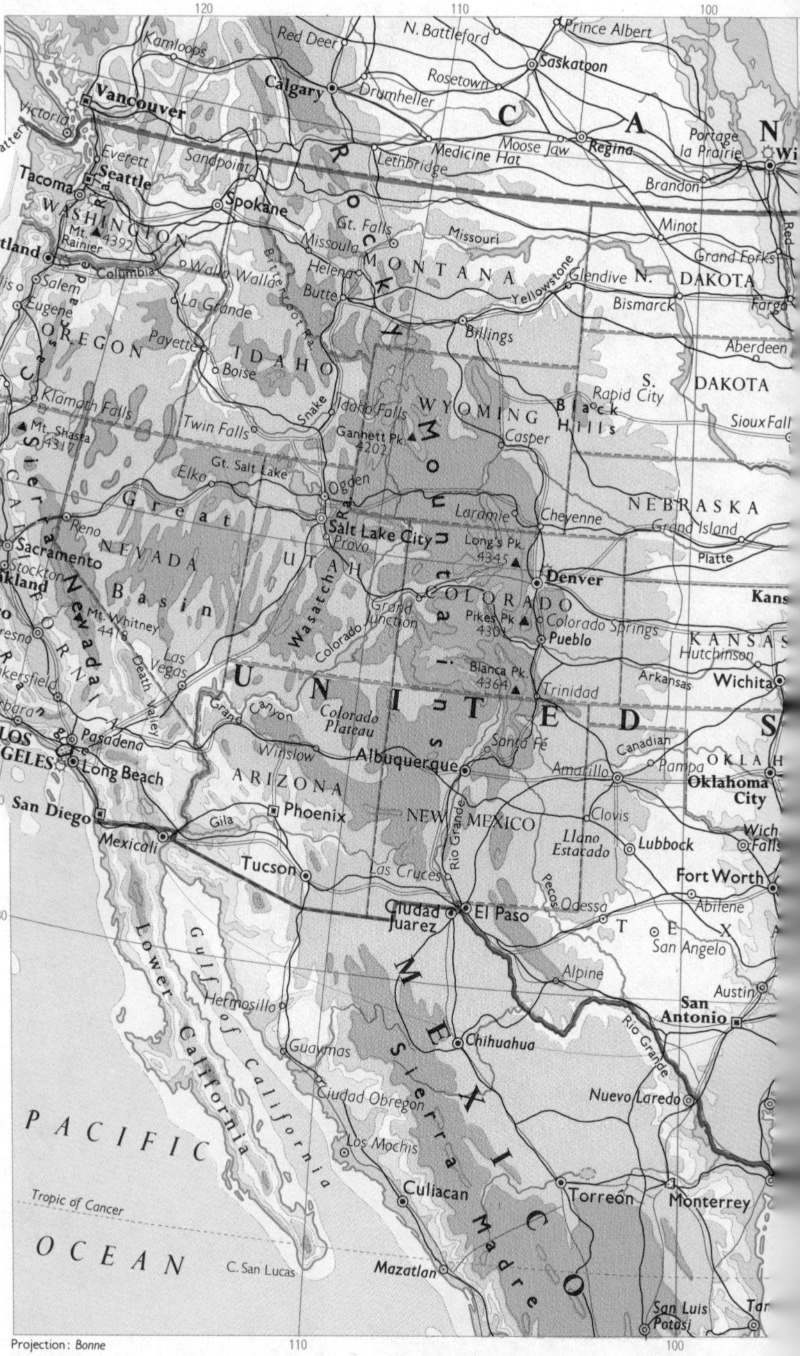
120
110
100
50
Kamloops
Red Deer
N. Battleford
Prince Albert
Saskatoon
Calgary
Drumheller
Rosetown
Vancouver
Victoria
C. Flattery
C A N
Moose Jaw
Regina
Portage la Prairie
Medicine Hat
Lethbridge
Sandpoint
Everett
Seattle
Tacoma
Spokane
WASHINGTON
Mt. Rainier 4392
Brandon
Minot
Gt. Falls
Missouri
Missoula
Portland
Columbia
Walla Walla
Helena
MONTANA
Glendive
N. DAKOTA
Grand Forks
Corvallis
Salem
Eugene
Butte
Yellowstone
Bismarck
Fargo
La Grande
Billings
OREGON
Payette
IDAHO
Boise
Aberdeen
Medford
S. DAKOTA
Rapid City
Klamath Falls
Idaho Falls
WYOMING
Black Hills
Mt. Shasta 4317
Twin Falls
Snake
Gannett Pk. 4202
Casper
Sioux Falls
Gt. Salt Lake
Elko
Ogden
Great
Reno
Salt Lake City
Laramie
Cheyenne
NEBRASKA
Grand Island
Sacramento
NEVADA
Provo
UTAH
Long's Pk. 4345
Platte
Oakland
Stockton
San Francisco
Basin
Wasatch Ra.
Grand Junction
COLORADO
Denver
Mt. Whitney 4418
Colorado
Pikes Pk. 4301
Colorado Springs
Pueblo
KANSAS
Fresno
Death Valley
Las Vegas
Hutchinson
Bakersfield
Blanca Pk. 4364
Trinidad
Arkansas
Wichita
Santa Barbara
UNITED STATES
Grand Canyon
Colorado Plateau
LOS ANGELES
Pasadena
Long Beach
Winslow
Albuquerque
Santa Fe
Canadian
Pampa
Amarillo
OKLAHOMA
Oklahoma City
ARIZONA
San Diego
Phoenix
NEW MEXICO
Clovis
Gila
Mexicali
Rio Grande
Llano Estacado
Lubbock
Wichita Falls
Tucson
Las Cruces
Fort Worth
Pecos
Abilene
Ciudad Juarez
El Paso
Odessa
30
TEXAS
San Angelo
Alpine
Austin
Hermosillo
San Antonio
Gulf of California
Lower California
MEXICO
Chihuahua
Guaymas
Sierra Madre
Ciudad Obregon
Nuevo Laredo
PACIFIC
Los Mochis
Tropic of Cancer
Culiacan
Torreon
Monterrey
OCEAN
C. San Lucas
Mazatlan
San Luis Potosi
Projection: Bonne
110
100

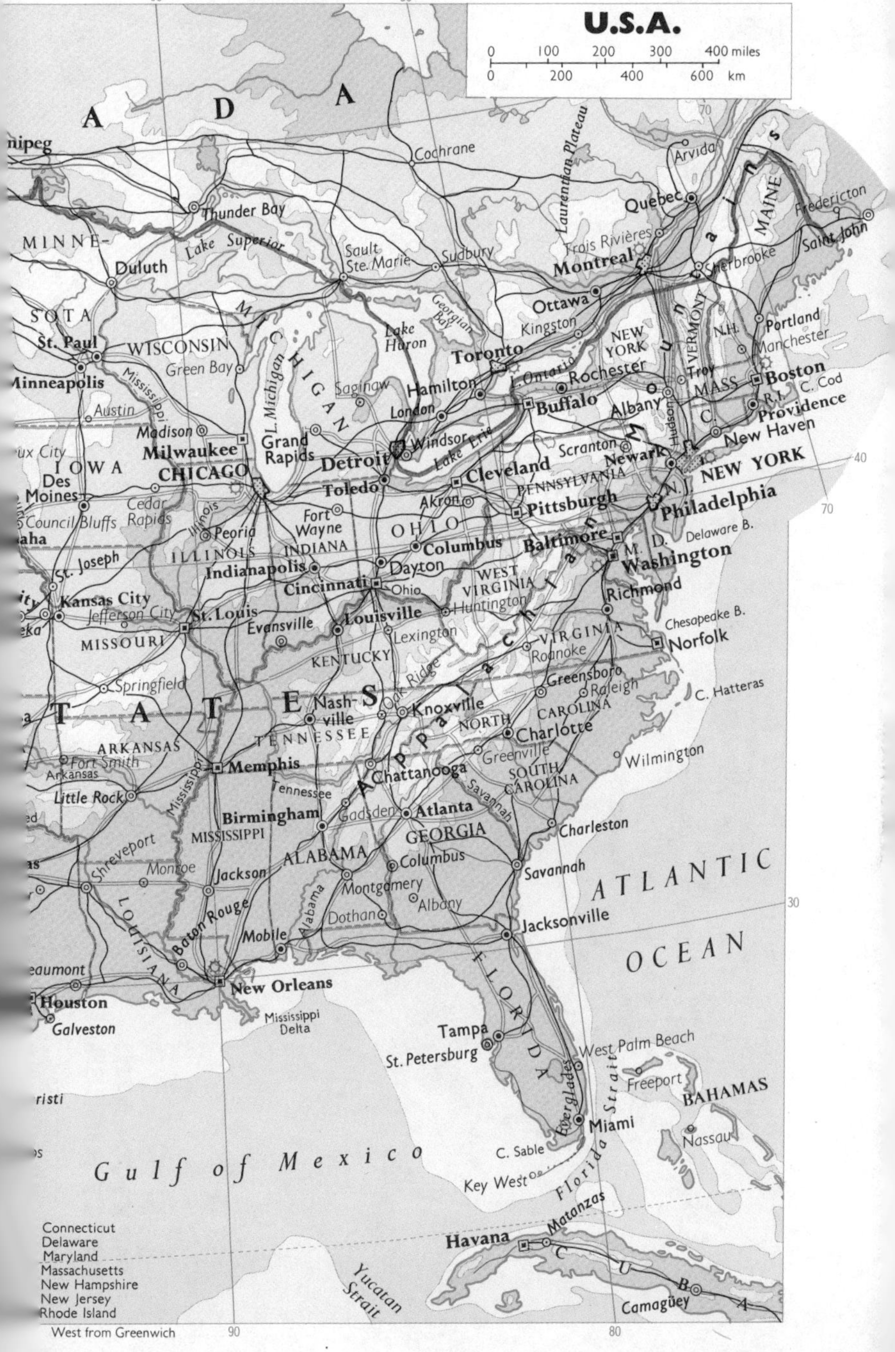

West from Greenwich

MEXICO AND THE CARIBBEAN
0 100 200 300 400 500 miles
0 200 400 600 800 km
UNITED STATES
MEXICO
ATLANTIC OCEAN
PACIFIC OCEAN
Gulf of Mexico
Caribbean Sea
Greater Antilles
Tropic of Cancer
West from Greenwich
Mexicali
Lower California
Gulf of California
Nogales
Hermosillo
Guaymas
Ciudad Juarez
El Paso
Chihuahua
Western Sierra Madre
Mexican Plateau
Eastern Sierra Madre
Torreón
Durango
Mazatlan
C. San Lucas
Aguascalientes
Guadalajara
C. Corrientes
Revilla Gigedo Is. (Mexico)
Leon
San Luis Potosi
Saltillo
Monterrey
Nuevo Laredo
Piedras Negras
Rio Grande
Matamoros
Tampico
MEXICO CITY
Balsas
Popocatepetl 5452
Citlaltepetl 5700
Puebla
Veracruz
Oaxaca
Acapulco
Salina Cruz
G. of Tehuantepec
Coatzacoalcos
Villahermosa
Tuxtla Gutierrez
Gulf of Campeche
Merida
Yucatan
C. Catoche
Yucatan Strait
BELIZE
Belmopan
Gulf of Honduras
GUATEMALA
Guatemala
San Salvador
EL SALVADOR
HONDURAS
Tegucigalpa
C. Gracias á Dios
Chinandega
Managua
NICARAGUA
L. Nicaragua
COSTA RICA
San José
Colon
Panama
PANAMA
G. of Panama
Fort Worth
Dallas
Austin
San Antonio
Houston
Baton Rouge
Jackson
Birmingham
Mobile
New Orleans
Corpus Christi
Atlanta
Columbus
Montgomery
Charleston
Savannah
Jacksonville
Florida
Tampa
Miami
C. Sable
Florida Strait
BAHAMAS
Turks & Caicos Is. (Br.)
Havana
Cuba
Sta. Clara
Camagüey
Holguin
Santiago de Cuba
JAMAICA
Kingston
Hispaniola
HAITI
Port au Prince
DOMINICAN REP.
Santiago
Santo Domingo
PUERTO RICO
San Juan
Virgin Is.
Anguilla (Br.)
St. Kitts
Nevis
Antigua
Guadeloupe (Fr.)
Dominica
Martinique (Fr.)
St. Lucia
St. Vincent
Barbados
Grenada
Tobago
Port of Spain
TRINIDAD & TOBAGO
Curaçao (Neth.)
G. of Venezuela
Maracaibo
L. Maracaibo
CARACAS
Barquisimeto
Orinoco
Ciudad Bolivar
Caroni
Caura
Apure
VENEZUELA
Sa. Pacaraima
Cord. de Merida
Sa. Nevada de S. Marta
5800
Barranquilla
Cartagena
G. of Darien
Magdalena
Cauca
Cucuta
Bucaramanga
Medellin
Meta
COLOMBIA
30
20
10
110
100
90
80
70

SOUTH AMERICA
0 200 400 600 800 miles
0 200 400 800 1200 km
Sierra Maestra
Hispaniola
Santiago de Cuba
Jamaica
Kingston
HAITI
DOM. REP.
Port au Prince
S. Juan
PUERTO RICO (U.S.)
Leeward Is.
CARIBBEAN SEA
Windward Is.
Barbados
G. of Venezuela
Curaçao (Neth.)
NICARAGUA
CANAL ZONE (U.S.)
COSTA RICA
PANAMA
Panama
Gulf of Panama
Barranquilla
Maracaibo
Cabimas
La Guaira
Port of Spain
Trinidad
Puerto de la Cruz
Maturín
Santo Tomé
G. of Darien
Cartagena
Bucaramanga
Sa. de Merida
Barquisimeto
Caracas
Orinoco
Ciudad Bolivar
Llanos
Magdalena
VENEZUELA
Kaieteur Falls
GUYANA
Demerara
Georgetown
SURINAM
Paramaribo
FR. GUIANA
Cayenne
Medellín
Manizales
Pereira
Bogotá
Roraima 2810
Sa. Pacaraima
Courantyne
Suriname
Tumucumaque
Sa. de Tumucumaque
Cali
COLOMBIA
Popayán
Orinoco
Casiquiare
Pasto
Macapá
Amazon
Marajo I.
Pará
Equator
ECUADOR
Quito
Chimborazo 6267
Cotopaxi 5897
Guayaquil
Cuenca
Loja
Putumayo
Japurá
Solimões
Negro
Manaus
Amazon
Santarém
Belém
São Luis
Tocantins
C. Pariña
Piura
Marañon
Iquitos
Benjamin Constant
Selvas
Tapajós
Xingu
Teresina
Fortaleza
Imperatriz
Parnaíba
Natal
C. de São Roque
Chiclayo
Trujillo
Ucayali
Pucallpa
Purus
Madeira
S. Antonio Falls
Roosevelt
Araguaya
Picos
João Pessoa
Recife
C. Branco
Paulistana
São Francisco
Andes
PERU
Rio Branco
Guaporé
BRAZIL
Barreiras
Salvador
Alagoinhas
Maceió
Aracaju
Callão
Lima
Huancayo
Pisco
Cuzco
Plateau of Mato Grosso
Ilhéus
Lomas
Juliaca
Titicaca
Illampú 6550
BOLIVIA
Cuyaba
Brasília
Goiânia
Montes Claros
Vitória de Conquista
Pirapora
Arequipa
La Paz
Mollendo
Tacna
Cochabamba
Oruro
Santa Cruz
Sucre
Potosí
Arica
Bolivian Plateau
Corumbá
Gran Chaco
Paraguay
Brazilian Highlands
Uberaba
Belo Horizonte
Caravelas
Iquique
Uyuni
Tarija
Paraná
Ribeirão Preto
Sa. da Mantiqueira
Vitória
Campos
Tropic of Capricorn
Antofagasta
Atacama Desert
Pilcomayo
PARAGUAY
Campinas
Niteroi
São Paulo
Santos
Rio de Janeiro
C. Frio
Taltal
Salta
Ojos del Salado 6863
Asunción
Curitiba
Iguaçu Falls
Tucumán
Corrientes
Sa. do Mar
Blumenau
PACIFIC
Santiago del Estero
Entre Rios
Uruguay
Santa Maria
La Serena
ARGENTINA
Uruguaiana
Pôrto Alegre
Aconcagua 6960
Córdoba
Santa Fé
Paraná
Bagé
Lagoa dos Patos
Pelotas
Rio Grande do Sul
Mendoza
Juan Fernández (Chile)
Viña del Mar
Valparaíso
Rosario
URUGUAY
Rocha
Santiago
Mercedes
Pampas
Buenos Aires
Montevideo
ATLANTIC
Rio de la Plata
La Plata
OCEAN
Talca
Azul
Concepción
Santa Rosa
Mar del Plata
Pta. Mogotes
Colorado
Neuquen
Temuco
Bahia Blanca
Negro
Valdivia
Osorno
Viedma
G. of San Matias
Puerto Montt
Chiloé
Chubut
Rawson
OCEAN
Chonos Arch.
Comodoro Rivadavia
G. of San Jorge
Patagonia
Rio Gallegos
Falkland Is. (Br.)
Punta Arenas
Stanley
Magellan's Str.
Tierra del Fuego
Staten I.
South Georgia (Br.)
C. Froward
C. Horn
Drake Passage
West from Greenwich
80
70
60
50
40
90
20
10
0
30

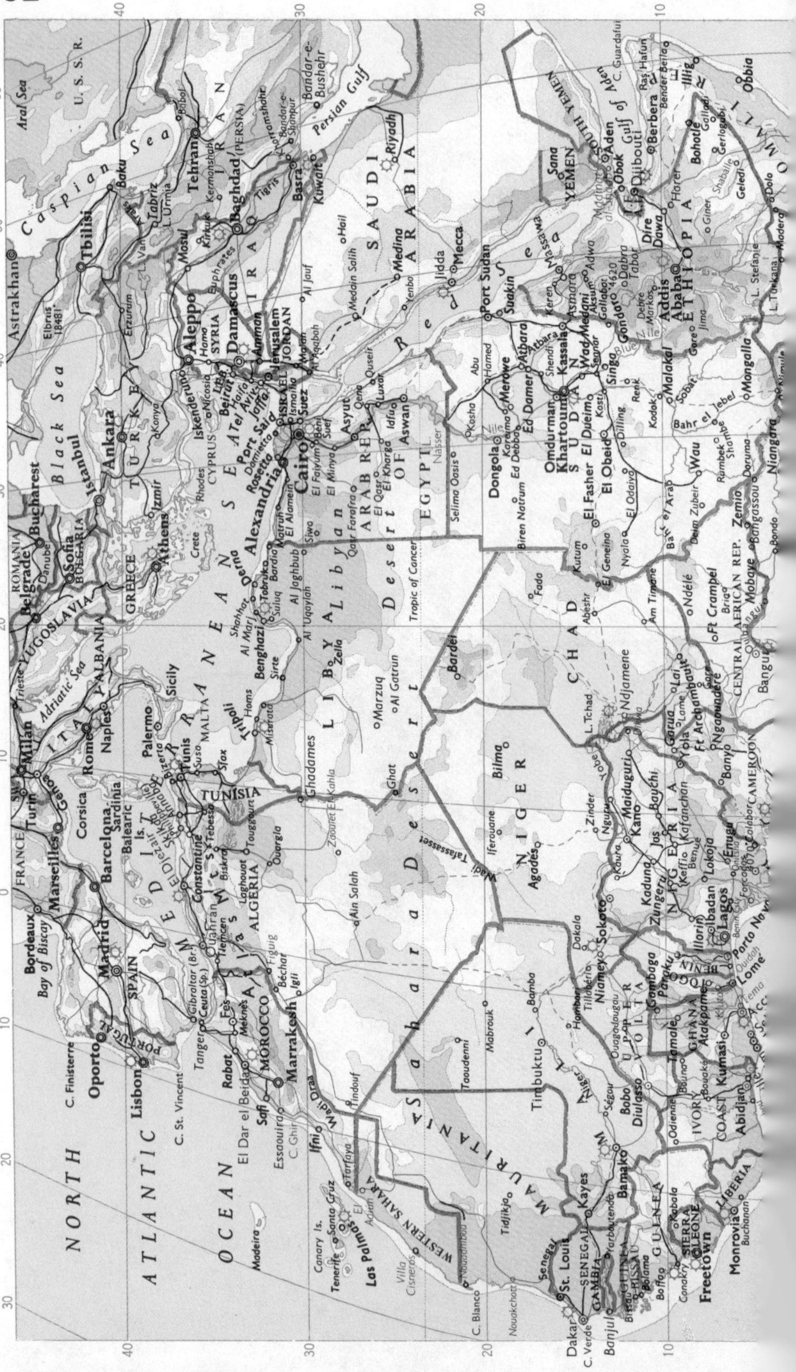
NORTH ATLANTIC OCEAN
Mediterranean Sea
Black Sea
Caspian Sea
Aral Sea
Red Sea
Persian Gulf
Gulf of Aden
Bay of Biscay
Adriatic Sea
Sahara Desert
Libyan Desert
Tropic of Cancer
Atlas Mts.
U. S. S. R.
PORTUGAL
SPAIN
FRANCE
ITALY
YUGOSLAVIA
ALBANIA
GREECE
BULGARIA
ROMANIA
TURKEY
CYPRUS
SYRIA
LEBANON
ISRAEL
JORDAN
IRAQ
IRAN (PERSIA)
SAUDI ARABIA
YEMEN
SOUTH YEMEN
MOROCCO
ALGERIA
TUNISIA
LIBYA
EGYPT
ARAB REP. OF EGYPT
SUDAN
ETHIOPIA
SOMALI
CHAD
NIGER
MALI
MAURITANIA
WESTERN SAHARA
SENEGAL
GAMBIA
GUINEA
GUINEA BISSAU
SIERRA LEONE
LIBERIA
IVORY COAST
UPPER VOLTA
GHANA
NIGERIA
CAMEROON
CENTRAL AFRICAN REP.
Lisbon
Madrid
Barcelona
Marseilles
Bordeaux
Rome
Milan
Naples
Tunis
Tripoli
Algiers
Rabat
Marrakesh
Casablanca
Cairo
Alexandria
Port Said
Suez
Aswan
Khartoum
Omdurman
Addis Ababa
Athens
Istanbul
Ankara
Sofia
Belgrade
Bucharest
Tbilisi
Baku
Tehran
Baghdad
Damascus
Beirut
Jerusalem
Amman
Aleppo
Mecca
Medina
Riyadh
Kuwait
Basra
Jidda
Port Sudan
Aden
Djibouti
Berbera
Dakar
St. Louis
Banjul
Bamako
Timbuktu
Niamey
Kano
Lagos
Ibadan
Accra
Kumasi
Abidjan
Monrovia
Freetown
Las Palmas
Canary Is.
Madeira
Sicily
Sardinia
Corsica
Crete
Malta
L. Tchad
L. Nasser
Nile
Niger

AFRICA
0 200 400 600 800 miles
0 200 400 600 800 1000 1200 km
West from Greenwich 0 East from Greenwich 10
SOUTH ATLANTIC
OCEAN
INDIAN
OCEAN
Ascension I.
St. Helena
São Tomé
Tropic of Capricorn
Mocambique Channel
GABON
CONGO
ZAÏRE
ANGOLA
ZAMBIA
MALAWI
TANZANIA
KENYA
UGANDA
RWANDA
BURUNDI
RHODESIA
BOTSWANA
SOUTH WEST AFRICA
(NAMIBIA)
MOÇAMBIQUE
MALAGASY REP.
SOUTH AFRICA
TRANSVAAL
ORANGE FREE STATE
NATAL
LESOTHO
SWAZILAND
CAPE PROVINCE
TRANSKEI
Kalahari
Mogadishu
Brava
Kismayu
Mombasa
Malindi
Lamu
Nairobi
Kampala
Entebbe
Kisangani
Mbandaka
Brazzaville
Pointe Noire
Kinshasa
Matadi
Boma
Cabinda
Banana
Luanda
Ambriz
Malange
Lobito
Benguela
Huambo
Sá da Bandeira
Mossâmedes
Kananga
Kasongo
Kindu
Kalemie
Tabora
Dodoma
Tanga
Zanzibar
Dar-es-Salaam
Kilwa
Lindi
Mtwara
Livingstonia
Lusaka
Livingstone
Salisbury
Bulawayo
Gwelo
Umtali
Blantyre
Beira
Sofala
Quelimane
Chinde
Moçambique
Inhambane
Maputo
Pretoria
Johannesburg
Germiston
Mafeking
Pietersburg
Kimberley
Bloemfontein
Ladysmith
Pietermaritzburg
Durban
East London
Port Elizabeth
Grahamstown
Cape Town
Paarl
Mossel Bay
C. of Good Hope
Windhoek
Swakopmund
Walvis Bay
Lüderitz
Keetmanshoop
Port Nolloth
Tananarive
Tamatave
Majunga
Fianarantsoa
Farafangana
Tulear
Fort Dauphin
Morondava
Comoro Is
Aldabra
C. Amber
Kenya 5199
Kilimanjaro 5895

AUSTRALIA
0 100 200 300 400 500 miles
0 200 400 600 800 km
East from Greenwich
INDONESIA
Ujung Pandang
Muna
Baubau
Bonthain
Salajar
Flores Sea
Lombok
Sumbawa
Mojo
Mataram
3728
Flores
Ruteng
Ende
Maumere
Sumba Str.
Sumba
Waingapu
Sawu Sea
Alor
Ombai Str.
Dili
Timor
Kefannanu
Wetar
Leti Is
South East Is.
Tanimbar Is.
Aru Is.
Durga Str.
Frederik Hendrik I.
Arafura Sea
Timor Sea
Melville I.
Bathurst I.
Van Diemen Gulf
Castlereagh B.
Junction B.
Elcho I.
Darwin
Gove
C. Arnhem
P. Bradshaw
Gul
Blue Mud B.
Groote Eylandt
Limmen Bight
Carpe
Rum Jungle
Pine Creek
Anson B.
Katherine
Daly
Roper
Cambridge G.
Queens Chan.
Admiralty G.
Brunswick Bay
Gulf Basin
Wyndham
Birdum
Daly Waters
Collier Bay
King Sd.
Kimberley
Durack Range
Newcastle Waters
Wave Hill
Derby
Hall's Creek
Barkly Tableland
Broome
Roebuck B.
Gordon Downs
L. Sylvester
Tennant Creek
NORTHERN TERRITORY
Lagrange
Desert Basin
Gregory Salt Sea
Port Hedland
Point Samson
Goldsworthy
De Grey
Dampier
Roebourne
Barrow I.
Yule
Shaw
Marble Bar
Throssell Ra
L. Dora
L. Mackay
Barrow Creek
Sandover Cr.
Tropic of Capricorn
Alice Springs
Hay
Exmouth G.
Onslow
Hamersley Ra.
Mt. Enid
Tom Price
Mt. Bruce
1227
Opthalmia Ra
Ethel Creek
L. Disappointment
Gibson Desert
Learmonth
Mt. Whaleback
WESTERN AUSTRALIA
AUSTRALIA
North West Basin
Carnarvon
Mt. Augustus
1105
L. Buchanan
Musgrave Ranges
1549
Mt. Woodroffe
Charlotte Waters
L. Carnegie
Wiluna
Oodnadatta
Meekatharra
Yeo L.
Great Victoria Desert
L. Maurice
L. Austin
Sandstone
Mt. Magnet
Laverton
L. Rason
Leonora
Malcolm
SOUTH AUSTRA
L. Torrens
Woomera
Ajana
Yalgoo
Maralinga
Ooldea
L. Harris
Geraldton
L. Monger
L. Moore
Kalgoorlie
Premier Downs
Eucla Basin
Deakin
Bonnie Rock
Coolgardie
Loongana
Nullarbor Plain
Eucla
Head of Bight
L. Gairdner
Gawler Ranges
Coastal Plain Basin
Northam
Southern Cross
L. Dundas
Eyre
Penong
Whyalla
Perth
Fremantle
Narrogin
The Johnston Lakes
Great Australian Bight
Collie
Wagin
Pingrup
Esperance
Rocky Pt.
Port Lincoln
Spencer Gulf
Bunbury
Esperance B.
Albany
Kangaroo I.
Pt. D'Entrecasteaux
5
10
15
20
25
30
35
40
115
120
125
130
135

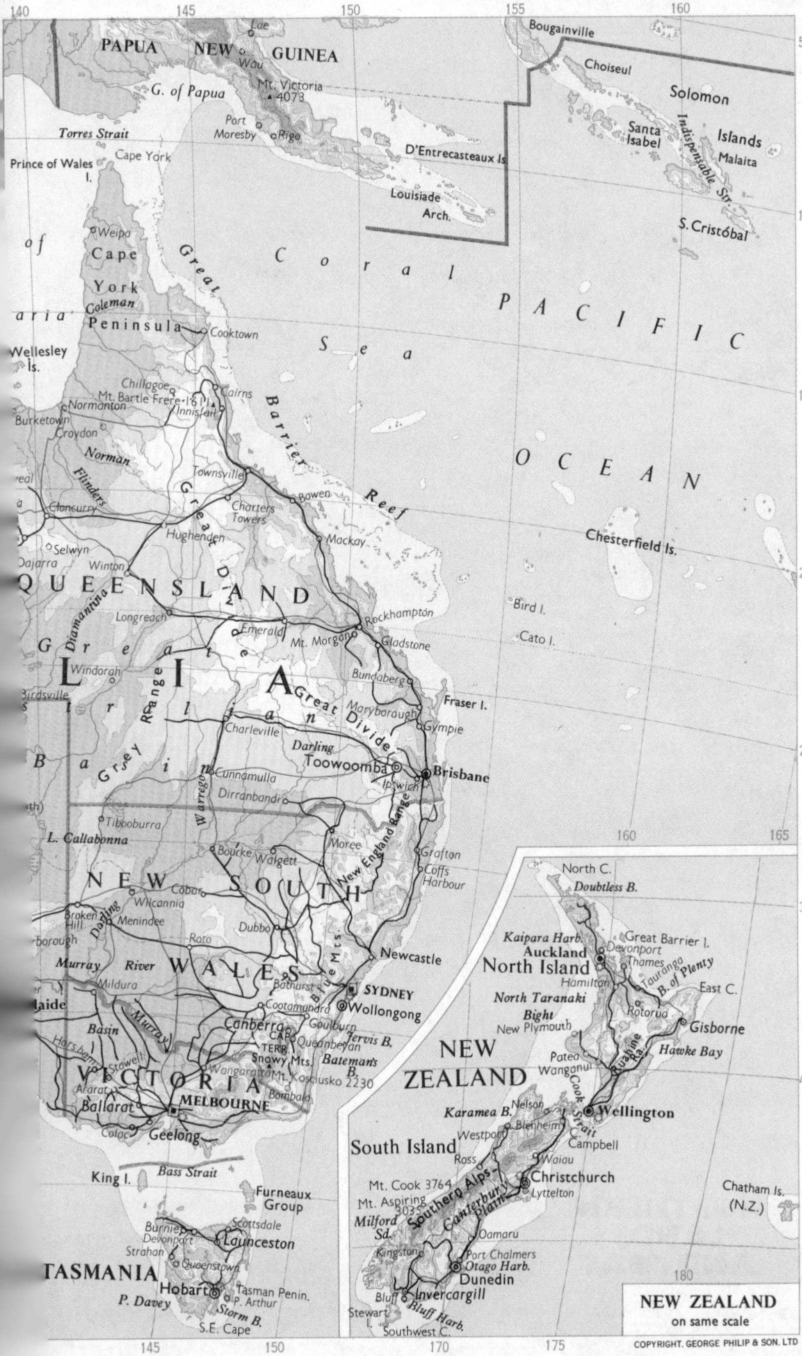
140
145
150
155
160
165
170
175
180
PAPUA NEW GUINEA
Lae
Wau
Mt. Victoria 4073
G. of Papua
Port Moresby
Rigo
Torres Strait
Cape York
Prince of Wales I.
D'Entrecasteaux Is.
Louisiade Arch.
Bougainville
Choiseul
Solomon Islands
Santa Isabel
Indispensable Str.
Malaita
S. Cristóbal
Weipa
Cape York Peninsula
Coleman
Wellesley Is.
Great Barrier Reef
Coral Sea
PACIFIC OCEAN
Cooktown
Chillagoe
Mt. Bartle Frere 1611
Cairns
Innisfail
Normanton
Burketown
Croydon
Norman
Flinders
Townsville
Cloncurry
Charters Towers
Bowen
Hughenden
Mackay
Selwyn
Winton
Chesterfield Is.
QUEENSLAND
Diamantina
Longreach
Emerald
Mt. Morgan
Rockhampton
Gladstone
Bird I.
Cato I.
Great Dividing Range
Windorah
Birdsville
Bundaberg
Maryborough
Fraser I.
Gympie
Charleville
Grey Range
Darling
Toowoomba
Brisbane
Ipswich
Cunnamulla
Warrego
Dirranbandi
Tibooburra
L. Callabonna
Moree
New England Range
Bourke
Walgett
Grafton
Coffs Harbour
NEW SOUTH WALES
Cobar
Wilcannia
Broken Hill
Menindee
Dubbo
Roto
Newcastle
Murray
River
Mildura
Blue Mts.
Bathurst
SYDNEY
Wollongong
Cootamundra
Goulburn
Canberra
CAP. TERR.
Queanbeyan
Jervis B.
Basin
Horsham
Stawell
Snowy Mts.
Mt. Kosciusko 2230
Bateman's B.
VICTORIA
Wangaratta
Ararat
Ballarat
MELBOURNE
Bombala
Colac
Geelong
Bass Strait
King I.
Furneaux Group
Burnie
Devonport
Scottsdale
Launceston
Strahan
Queenstown
TASMANIA
Hobart
Tasman Penin.
P. Arthur
P. Davey
Storm B.
S.E. Cape
North C.
Doubtless B.
Kaipara Harb.
Great Barrier I.
Auckland
Devonport
Thames
North Island
Tauranga
B. of Plenty
Hamilton
East C.
North Taranaki Bight
Rotorua
New Plymouth
Gisborne
Hawke Bay
Ruahine Ra.
NEW ZEALAND
Patea
Wanganui
Cook Strait
Wellington
Karamea B.
Nelson
Blenheim
Westport
South Island
Campbell
Ross
Waiau
Mt. Cook 3764
Christchurch
Southern Alps
Mt. Aspiring 3035
Canterbury Plain
Lyttelton
Milford Sd.
Oamaru
Kingston
Port Chalmers
Otago Harb.
Dunedin
Bluff
Invercargill
Bluff Harb.
Stewart I.
Southwest C.
Chatham Is. (N.Z.)
NEW ZEALAND
on same scale

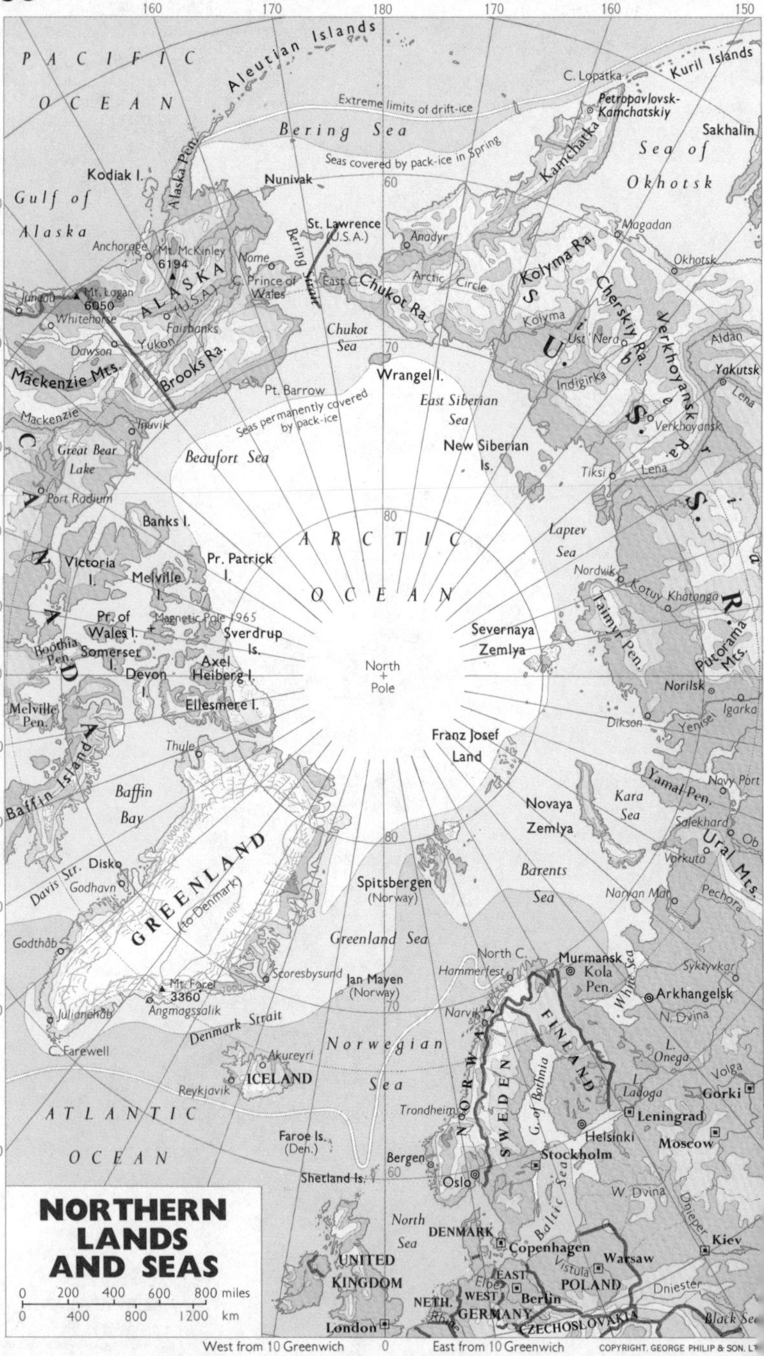
NORTHERN LANDS AND SEAS
0 200 400 600 800 miles
0 400 800 1200 km
PACIFIC OCEAN
Aleutian Islands
Extreme limits of drift-ice
Bering Sea
Seas covered by pack-ice in Spring
C. Lopatka
Kuril Islands
Petropavlovsk-Kamchatskiy
Sakhalin
Sea of Okhotsk
Kamchatka
Kodiak I.
Alaska Pen.
Nunivak
Gulf of Alaska
St. Lawrence (U.S.A.)
Bering Strait
Anadyr
Magadan
Okhotsk
Anchorage
Mt. McKinley 6194
ALASKA (U.S.A.)
Nome
C. Prince of Wales
East C.
Chukot Ra.
Arctic Circle
Kolyma Ra.
Cherskiy Ra.
Verkhoyansk Ra.
Juneau
Mt. Logan 6050
Whitehorse
Fairbanks
Yukon
Dawson
Brooks Ra.
Mackenzie Mts.
Chukot Sea
Kolyma
Ust' Nera
Aldan
Yakutsk
Lena
Indigirka
Wrangel I.
Pt. Barrow
Seas permanently covered by pack-ice
East Siberian Sea
Verkhoyansk
Mackenzie
Inuvik
CANADA
Great Bear Lake
Port Radium
Beaufort Sea
New Siberian Is.
Tiksi
U.S.S.R.
Banks I.
ARCTIC OCEAN
Laptev Sea
Victoria I.
Melville I.
Pr. Patrick I.
Nordvik
Kotuy
Khatanga
Taimyr Pen.
Putorama Mts.
Pr. of Wales I.
Magnetic Pole 1965
Sverdrup Is.
Severnaya Zemlya
Boothia Pen.
Somerset I.
Axel Heiberg I.
Devon I.
North Pole
Norilsk
Igarka
Melville Pen.
Ellesmere I.
Dikson
Yenisei
Thule
Franz Josef Land
Baffin Island
Baffin Bay
Yamal Pen.
Novy Port
Novaya Zemlya
Kara Sea
Salekhard
Ob
Ural Mts.
Vorkuta
Disko
Davis Str.
Godhavn
GREENLAND (to Denmark)
Barents Sea
Spitsbergen (Norway)
Naryan Mar
Pechora
Godthåb
Greenland Sea
North C.
Hammerfest
Murmansk
Kola Pen.
Syktyvkar
Scoresbysund
Jan Mayen (Norway)
White Sea
Arkhangelsk
Mt. Forel 3360
Angmagssalik
Julianehåb
Denmark Strait
Narvik
N. Dvina
C. Farewell
Norwegian Sea
NORWAY
SWEDEN
FINLAND
G. of Bothnia
L. Onega
Volga
Akureyri
ICELAND
Reykjavik
L. Ladoga
Gorki
Trondheim
Leningrad
Helsinki
ATLANTIC OCEAN
Faroe Is. (Den.)
Moscow
Bergen
Stockholm
Shetland Is.
Oslo
W. Dvina
North Sea
Dnieper
Baltic Sea
DENMARK
Copenhagen
Kiev
UNITED KINGDOM
Vistula
Warsaw
EAST
Elbe
POLAND
Dniester
NETH.
WEST GERMANY
Berlin
Rhine
CZECHOSLOVAKIA
London
Black Sea
West from 10 Greenwich
East from 10 Greenwich

Sea; naval base and ch. pt.; exp. agr. prods.; chemicals; gold, sulphur, copper mined nearby; p. (est. 1970) 324,040.

Keewatin, dist., N.W. Terr., **Canada**; barren grounds; fur-trapping; a. 590,934 km²; p. 2,400.

Keighley, t., West Yorks., **Eng.**; in Aire valley, 24 km N.W. of Leeds; engin., woollen and worsteds; p. (1971) 55,263.

Keihin, vast conurb. of Tokyo, Yokohama and Kawasaki, **Japan**; p. (1971) 14,650,000.

Keith, burgh, Moray, **Scot.**; mkt. t. in agr. dist.; p. (1971) 4,177.

Kelantan, st., **Malaysia**; one of most fertile areas on E. cst. Malaya; cap Kota Bharu; rice, coconuts, rubber; a. 14,815 km²; p. (1967) 677,205.

Kells or Ceannanus Mor, mkt. t., Co. Meath, **R.o.I.**; notable for monastic remains and illuminated Book of Kells, now in library of Trinity College, Dublin; p. (1966) 2,274.

Kelso, burgh, Roxburgh, **Scot.**; at confluence of Rs. Teviot and Tweed; p. (1971) 4,852.

Kemerovo, c., **RSFSR**; S.E. of Tomsk; coalmng. ctr.; chemicals, textiles, plastics; p. (1970) 385,000 (c.), 417,000 (met. a.).

Kemi, t., N.E. **Finland**; spt. on G. of Bothnia; sawmills; p. (1968) 30,259.

Kemi, R., N.E. **Finland**; used for hydroelectric power and timber transport; 480 km long.

Kempston, t., Beds., **Eng.**; on R. Ouse, 5 km S.W. of Bedford; p. (1971) 12,790.

Kempten, t., Bavaria, **W. Germany**; nr. Bodensee; mkt. for dairying ind.; Benedictine abbey; p. (est. 1969) 44,057.

Kendal, Cumbria, **Eng.**; mkt. ctr., footwear, woollens, paper; tourism; p. (1971) 21,572.

Kene. *See* **Qena**.

Kenilworth, t., Warwicks., **Eng.**; 6 km S.W. of Coventry; mkt.; lt. engin., agr. repair wk.; ruined cas.; p. (1971) 20,121.

Kenitra. *See* **Mina Hassan Tani**.

Kennet, R., Wilts. and Berks., **Eng.**; trib. of R. Thames; followed by main rly. London to W. of Eng.; 70 km long.

Kennington, dist., in London bor. of Lambeth, **Eng.**; inc. the Oval cricket ground, home of Surrey C.C.

Kenosha, t., Wis., **USA**; on W. shore of L. Mich.; cars, furniture; p. (1970) 78,063 (c.), 116,734 (met. a.).

Kensington and Chelsea, Royal Borough of, inner bor., W. London, **Eng.**; mainly residtl.; contains Kensington Palace and Gardens; p. (1971) 184,392.

Kent, non-met. co., **Eng.**; intensive agr., mkt. gardening, orchards, hops; "Garden of England"; crossed by N. Downs and Weald; industl. zone bordering Thames and Medway estuaries; tourist resorts and cross-channel ferry pts. on cst.; London commuter hinterland; co. t. Maidstone; a. 3,730 km²; p. (1971) 1,396,030.

Kentucky, E. central st., **USA**; in W. foothills of Appalachians and crossed by tribs. of Mississippi; "Bluegrass" st.; mainly agr.; some coal; cap. Frankfort; lgst. c. Louisville, at falls of Ohio R.; hydroelec. power; tourism; a. 104,623 km²; p. (1970) 3,160,555.

Kentucky, R., Ky., **USA**; flows from Cumberland plateau to Ohio R.; length 400 km.

Kenya, rep., E. **Africa**; member of Brit. Commonwealth; comprises 7 provs.; straddles equator but climate modified by alt; marked contrast between sparsely populated and arid N. and well-developed S. where S.W. upland climate has attracted the European p.; economy based on prod. and processing of arable and pastoral prods., inc. dairy prod.; relatively well developed cooperative African farming; ch. spt. Mombasa, airports at Nairobi and Mombasa; famous for big game; extensive a. of agr. land owned by white p. source of social friction; univ.; cap. Nairobi; a. 582,646 km²; p. (1969) 10,890,000.

Kenya, Mt., volcano, **Kenya**; just S. of equator; snow-covered; alt. 5,197 m; 2nd hgst. peak in Africa; Nat. Park.

Kephallenia. *See* **Cephalonia**.

Kerala, st., **India**; cap. Trivandrum; plantations producing rubber, tea, pepper; higher proportion of literacy than in any other st.,; a. 38,855 km².; p. (1961) 16,903,715.

Kerch, c., Ukrainian SSR, **USSR**; in Crimea, commanding K. strait connecting Black Sea and Azov Sea; spt. and industl. ctr.; metallurgical plant, iron and steel mills, shipbldg., fisheries; iron-ore, vanadium, natural gas nearby; p. (1970) 128,000.

Kerguelen, archipelago, S. **Indian Oc.**; part of Fr. Antarctic terr.; whaling, fishing; famous for K. cabbage (*Pringlea antiscorbutica*) discovered by Cook.

Kerkrade, t., Limburg prov., **Neth.**; coal mng.; anc. abbey; p. (1968) 50,206.

Kérkira. *See* **Corfu**.

Kermadec Is., volcanic gr. **Pac. Oc.**; 960 km N.E. of N.Z.; a. 34 km²; met. sta. on Sunday I. (lgst of gr.); annexed to N.Z. 1887; p. (1961) 10.

Kerman, region, S.E. **Iran**; mtnous., much desert land; agr.; carpet-weaving; coal and iron-ore mng. being developed; recent copper find; irrigation scheme projected; p. (1967) 243,770.

Kermān, c., S.E. **Iran**; prov. cap.; carpet-weaving ctr.; textile mftg.; airpt.; mediaeval mosques; p. (est. 1971) 100,000.

Kermānshāh, t., N.W. **Iran**; cap. of Kermānshāhān prov.; agr., comm. and route ctr.; airpt.; oil refinery; p. (est. 1971) 229,800.

Kern, R., E. Cal., **USA**; one of most impt. power-generating Rs. in st.

Kerry, coastal co., Munster, **R.o.I.**; deeply indented cst.; cap. Tralee; tourism; a. 4,703 km²; p. (1966) 112,642.

Kerulen, R., N.E. **Mongolia** and **China**; flows parallel to edge of Gobi Desert; a. designated for economic development; 1,256 km long.

Kesteven. *See* **Lincolnshire**.

Keswick, Cumbria, **Eng.**; on Greta R.; at N. end of L. Derwentwater; tourist ctr.; mkt.; pencils; p. (1971) 5,169.

Kettering, mkt. t., Northants, **Eng.**; nr. Wellingborough; footwear; iron mng.; p. (1971) 42,628.

Kew, dist., London bor. of Richmond-upon-Thames, **Eng.**; contains Kew botanical gardens.

Keweenaw, peninsula, L. Superior, **USA**; former impt. copper deposits.

Keynsham, t., Avon, **Eng.**; expanded t.; p. (1971) 19,007.

Key West, c., Fla., **USA**; on I. c. 240 km from mainland; naval sta., coastguard base; cigar-mftg.; nearest US pt. to Panama canal; tourism; p. (est. 1969) 39,500.

Khabarovsk, c., **RSFSR**; cap. of K. terr., E. Siberia, on Amur R.; cath.; oil refining, aircraft engin., wood and paper inds.; pipeline links with oilfields in N. Sakhalin; transport ctr. of Far East; p. (1970) 437,000.

Khairpur, t., **Pakistan**; nr. Sukkur barrage; textiles; p. (1961) 34,144.

Khakass Autonomous Oblast, admin. div. of Krasnoyarsk region, **RSFSR**; pastoral agr., timber and mng. inds.; a. 61,784 km²; p. (1970) 446,000.

Khandwa, t., Madhya Pradesh, **India**; S. of Indore; cotton, oil-pressing; p. (1961) 63,505.

Khaniá, or Canea, c., cap. of Crete, **Greece**; in sheltered bay on W. cst.; historic sites; p. (1971) 40,452.

Khanka, L., China–**USSR** border; dairy farming, fishing; branch of Trans-Siberian rly. to W. shore; a. 4,403 km².

Khanty-Mansi, admin. div., **RSFSR**; in W. Siberian lowland; sparse p.; cap. Khanty-Mansiisk (at confluence of Ob' and Irtysh Rs.); natural gas; a. 556,850 km²; p. (1970) 272,000.

Kharagpur, c., W. Bengal, **India**; industl., scientific research ctr.; rly. junc.; p. (1971) 161,911.

Khārk, I., Persian Gulf, **Iran**; oil terminal for super-tankers, 48 km from mainland.

Khar'kov, c., Ukrainian SSR, **USSR**; impt. industl. ctr. in Donets coal region; cap. of K. region; univ., cath.; rly. ctr.; extensively rebuilt after second world war; p. (1970) 1,223,000.

Khartoum, c., cap. of the **Sudan**; at confluence of Blue and White Niles; univ.; famous siege under Gordon 1884–5; p. (est. 1971) 261,840.

Khashm el Girba, t., **Sudan**; new t. on Atbara R., between Khartoum and Ethiopian border; for p. of Wadi Halfa inundated by Aswan L.; sugar refinery.

Khasi Hills, Meghalaya, N.E. **India**; form abrupt S. edge to middle Brahmaputra valley; very heavy monsoon rains on S.-facing slopes; lower slopes forested; middle slopes impt. tea-growing region; rise to over 1,800 m.

Khaskovo, t., **Bulgaria**; woollens, carpets, tobacco; p. (est. 1968) 63,840.

Kherson, c., Ukrainian SSR, **USSR**; 24 km up R. Dnieper from Black Sea; sea and R. pt., rly. junc.; grain, oil refining, engin., textiles, shipbldg; founded by Catherine the Great as fortress t.; p. (1970) 261,000.

Khingan, Gr. and **Little**, mtn. ranges, Inner Mongolia and Heilungkiang prov., N.E. **China**; rich timber resources; rise to over 1,800 m.

Khios or **Chios, I., Greece**; in Aegean Sea; wines, figs, fruits; marble; cap. Khios; supposed birthplace of Homer; p. (1972) 53,942.

Khiva, former vassal st. of Russia; now part of Uzbek SSR and Turkmen SSR, **USSR**.

Khiva, c., N.W. Uzbek SSR, **USSR**; in oasis nr. Kara-Kum desert; cottons, carpets; anc. c.; p. (est. 1967) 22,000.

Khmel'nitskiy (Proskurov), c., Ukrainian SSR, **USSR**; on R. Bug; machin. tools, textiles, food inds.; p. (1970) 113,000.

Khmer Republic. *See* **Cambodia, Democratic.**

Khor Abdulla, Iraq; in Persian G. nr. Basra; deepwater oil-loading island terminal (1963).

Khorāsan or **Khurasan**, prov., N.E. **Iran**; bounded by USSR and Afghanistan; sparsely p.; agr.; wool; turquoises; cap. Mashhad; p. (1967) 2,494,283.

Khorramshahr, spt., S.W. **Iran**, leading pt. on Persian G.; increased in importance in second world war when harbour facilities expanded; handles major part of foreign trade; main exp. dates; linked by pipeline to oilfields and by road and rail to Ahvāz and Tehran; p. (1967) 150,322 (met. a.).

Khotan (Ho-t'ien), c., S.W. Sinkiang prov., **China**; in fertile K. oasis at base of Kunlun mtns.; silk, carpets, jade-ware; on anc. Silk Road; early ctr. of Buddhism; visited by Marco Polo 1274; p. 50,000.

Khovu-Aksy, t., Tuva ASSR, **RSFSR**; on R. Elegest, 80 km S.W. of Kyzyl; new t. 1956; cobalt deposit being developed.

Khulna, c., **Bangladesh**; in low-lying a. in W. Ganges delta; p. (1974) 436,000.

Khuzestan, prov., W. **Iran**; frontier Iraq; leading petroleum ctr.; lge. dams; cap. Ahvāz; p. (1967) 1,614,576.

Khyber Pass, pass in Hindu Kush mtns., between **Pakistan** and **Afghanistan**; followed by route from Peshawar to Kabul; historically most famous route into India, used by many invaders, inc. Alexander the Great.

Kiamusze (Chia-mu-ssu), c., Heilungkiang prov., **China**; ch. pt. on lower Sungari R.; p. (est. 1970) 275,000.

Kianga-Moura, dist., Queensland, **Australia**; lge coalfield; coking coal exp. to Japan via Gladstone.

Kiangsi (Jiangxi), prov., S.E. **China**; in basin of navigable Kan R., which drains through Poyang L. to Yangtze R.; ch. cs. Shanghai, Chingkiang, Wusih, Nanchang (cap.); rice, wheat, tea, cotton; tungsten, coking coal, kaolin; a. 172,494 km²; p. (est. 1968) 22,000,000.

Kiangsu (Jiangsu), coastal prov., **China**; on Yellow Sea; low-lying a. N. of Yangtze delta; rich agr., densely p.; cotton, sericulture, tea, sugar, fish (many Ls.); cap. Nanking; a. 109,000 km²; p. (est. 1968) 47,000,000.

Kicking Horse Pass, mtn. pass (1,628 m), over Rocky Mtns., B.C., **Canada**; used by Canadian Pac. rly.

Kidderminster, t., Hereford and Worcs., **Eng.**; on R. Stour 6 km above its confluence with R. Severn; carpets, engin., sugar-beet refining, textile machin., elec. vehicles, drop forgings; p. (1971) 47,255.

Kidsgrove, t., "Potteries," Staff., **Eng.**; 5 km N.W. of Stoke-on-Trent; chemicals, metal wks., rayon, silk and nylon spinning, precast concrete, ceramics; p. (1971) 22,036.

Kidwelly, Dyfed, **Wales**; mkt. t.; sm. harbour; cas.; p. (1971) 3,076.

Kiel, spt., cap. of Schleswig-Holstein, **W. Germany**; univ.; Baltic naval pt.; shipbldg. and allied inds., elec. gds., textiles, fishing; p. (est. 1969) 269,200.

Kiel Canal (North Sea-Baltic Canal or **Kaiser-Wilhelm-Kanal), W. Germany**; connects Elbe estuary on North Sea with Baltic; 98 km long; opened 1895, reconstructed 1914; internationalised 1919 by Treaty of Versailles, but repudiated by Hitler 1936.

Kielce, c., central **Poland**; cap. of K. prov.; in Swietokrzyskie mtns.; cath., route ctr.; agr. machin., chemicals; minerals qurraied in prov.; founded 12th cent.; p. (1970) 126,000.

Kiev (Kiyev), c., cap. of Ukrainian SSR, **USSR**; on R. Dnieper; leading cultural, industl. and comm. ctr.; cath., univ.; machin., textiles; in a. of rich mineral deposits; natural gas pipeline runs from Dashava; historic c., once cap. of Muscovite empire; p. (1976) 1,974,000.

Kigali, cap. of **Rwanda**; comm. ctr.; airport; p. (est. 1970) 60,000 (met. a.).

Kigoma, t., W. **Tanzania**; pt. on E. shore of L. Tanganyika; W. terminus of Central rly. to Dar-es-Salaam; p. (est. 1967) 21,639.

Kii, peninsula, **Japan**; highland area and inlet of same name, S. Honshu.

Kikinda, t., Vojvodina, **Yugoslavia**; agr. tr.; rly. junc.; p. (est. 1965) 33,000.

Kilauea, crater, 1,112 m high, on S.E. slope of Mauna Loa, **Hawaii**, one of lgst. active craters in world; over 3 km in diameter.

Kildare, inland co., Leinster, **R.o.I.**; dairying cereals; a. 1,694 km²; p. (1966) 66,486.

Kildare, mkt. t., cap. of Kildare, **R.o.I.**; cath.; close by is the famous racecourse, the Curragh of Kildare; p. (1966) 2,731.

Kilimanjaro, volcanic mtn., N. **Tanzania**; hgst. peak in Africa, 5,895 m; international airpt. at 894 m on Sanya Plain; Nat. Park.

Kilindini, spt., **Kenya**; adjoins Mombasa; the finest harbour on E. cst. of Africa.

Kilkenny, inland co., Leinster, **R.o.I.**; cap. Kilkenny; pastoral farming, black marble; a. 2,062 km²; p. (1966) 60,472.

Kilkenny, t., cap. of Kilkenny, **R.o.I.**; on R. Nore; local mkt., caths., cas.; p. (1966) 10,057.

Kilkieran Bay, inlet, Galway, **R.o.I.**

Killala Bay, Mayo and Sligo, **R.o I.**, wide bay fed by R. Hoy.

Killaloe, v., Co. Clare, **R.o.I.**; crossing point for R. Shannon; cath.; p. 500.

Killarney, t., U.D., Kerry, **R.o.I.**; local mkt.; tourist ctr. for the Ls. of K.; p. (1966) 6,870.

Killarney, Lakes of, Kerry, **R.o.I.**; Lower, Middle, and Upper, celebrated for their beauty; tourist resorts; Muckross on Middle L. site of anc. abbey.

Killiecrankie, Pass of, Scot.; on R. Garry; at S. approach to Drumochter Pass; used by main rly. Perth to Inverness; scene of battle 1691.

Killingworth, t., Tyne and Wear, **Eng.**; 6 km N.E. of Newcastle; new t.; proposed p. 20,000.

Kilmarnock, burgh, l. gov. dist., Strathclyde Reg., **Scot.**; on R. Irvine, 17 km N.E. of Ayr.; carpet factories, textiles; rly. ctr.; p. (1971) 48,787.

Kilo-Moto, goldfield, **Zaïre**; in N.E. of st., 80 km W. of L. Mobutu Seso; linked by motor road to R. Zaïre (Kisangani) and L. Mobutu Seso (Kasenyi).

Kilrenny and Anstruther, t., North East Fife, **Scot.**; at entrance to F. of Forth; fishing, hosiery, oilskin mnfs.; p. (1971) 3,037.

Kilrush, sm. spt., U.D., Co. Clare, **R.o.I.**; on R. Shannon; p. (1966) 2,734.

Kilsyth, burgh, Stirling, **Scot.**; at S. foot of Campsie Fells, 16 km W. of Falkirk; p. (1971) 10,165.

Kilwinning, burgh, Cunninghame, **Scot.**; 8 km E. of Ardrossan; to be incorporated in new t. Irvine; p. (1971) 8,290.

Kimberley, former goldfield dist., W. **Australia**; big deposits of bauxite discovered 1965.

Kimberley, t., B.C., **Canada**; on R. Kootenay; site of Sullivan mine, silver, lead, zinc; ores smelted at Trail; p. (1971) 7,441.

Kimberley, t., C. Prov., **S. Africa**; diamond-mng. dist.; asbestos, manganese, iron, cement, engin.; founded 1871; p. (1971) 103,789.

Kinabalu, Mount, Sabah, **Malaysia**; in Crocker mtns.; hgst. peak in Borneo, alt. 4,104 m.

Kincardine, former co., **Scot.**; with Deeside forms l. gov. dist. in Grampian Reg.; a. 2,546 km²; p. (1971) 33,260.

Kinder Scout, mtn., N. Derbys., **Eng.**; hgst. point of the Peak dist.; alt. 637 m.

Kindia, t., **Guinea**; rich bauxite deposits.

Kineshma, c., **RSFSR**; on Volga, N.W. of Gorki; pt. for Ivanovo industl. a.; textiles; dates from early 15th cent.; p. (est. 1967) 94,000.

King George's Sound, W. Australia; nr. Albany; fine harbour and bay.
Kinghorn, t., Kircaldy, Scot.; on F. of Forth, 5 km S. of Kirkcaldy; p. (1971) 2,146.
Kingsbridge, t., S. Devon, Eng.; at head of Kingsbridge estuary, 16 km S.W. of Dartmouth; mkt.; p. (1971) 3,535.
Kingsclere and Whitchurch, N. Hants., Eng.; on R. Test, 16 km N.W. of Basingstoke; mkt.; p. (1971) 27,928 (dist.).
King's Lynn, spt., Norfolk, Eng.; at mouth of Gr. Ouse; docks; fishing base; agr. machin., canning, chemical fertilisers, shoes; expanded t.; p. (1971) 30,120.
Kingston, t., Ont., Canada; E. end of L. Ontario; univ., military college; heavy inds.; p. (1971) 61,870.
Kingston, spt., cap. of Jamaica; ch. comm. ctr. for J.; landlocked harbour; agr.-processing; univ.; p. (1970) 117,400 (c.), (1967) 376,520 (met. a.).
Kingston-upon-Hull. *See* **Hull.**
Kingston-upon-Thames, former M.B., Surrey, Eng.; now The Royal Borough of Kingston-upon-Thames, outer bor. of Greater London; inc. bors. of Malden and Coombe and Surbiton; residtl. with Richmond Park, Hampton Court, Bushey Park nearby; aircraft parts; p. (1971) 140,210.
Kingstown. *See* **Dun Laoghaire.**
Kingstown, spt., cap. of St. Vincent, W.I.; cath., botanic gardens; p. (1966) 20,688.
Kingswood, t., Avon, Eng.; nr. Bristol; elec. vehicles, motor cycles, boots, brushes, tools; school founded by John Wesley; p. (1971) 30,269.
Kington, mkt. t., Hereford and Worcs., Eng.; 19 km W. of Leominster; p. (1971) 1,916.
Kingussie, burgh, Badenoch and Strathspey, Scot.; between Cairngorm mtns. and Monadhliath mtns., on R. Spey; summer resort; p. (1971) 1,104.
Kinki, dist., S.W. Honshu, Japan; agr., industl. and comm. complex centred on Osaka, Kyoto, and Kōbe.
Kinlochleven, v., Lochaber, Scot.; at head of Loch Leven; hydroelec. power sta.; aluminium smelting.
Kinnairds Head, promontory, nr. Fraserburgh, on N.E. cst., Scot.
Kinross, burgh, Perth and Kinross, Scot.; on Loch Leven, 26 km N.E. of Alloa; textiles; resort; p. (1971) 2,418.
Kinross-shire, former co., Scot.; now part of Perth and Kinross l. gov. dist., Grampian Reg.
Kinsale, U.D., Cork, R.o.I.; sm. fish pt. on K. harbour; tourism; p. (1971) 1,628.
Kinshasa (Leopoldville), c., cap. of Zaïre; above the cataracts on R. Zaïre; univ.; textiles, shoes; founded by Stanley 1887; p. (est. 1972) 1,623,760 (met. a.).
Kinta Valley, S.E. Perak, W. Malaysia; tin mng., rubber plantations.
Kintyre, peninsula, Argyll and Bute, Scot.; terminates in Mull of Kintyre; 67 km long, 16 km wide.
Kioga (Kyoga), L., Uganda; on R. Nile midway between L. Victoria and L. Mobuto Seso; very shallow, fringed with marsh; land reclamation.
Kiölen or Kjölen, mtn. range, Norway and Sweden; hgst. point Mt. Sulitjelma, 1,876 m.
Kirghiz SSR (Khirghizia), constituent rep., USSR; S.W. of Siberia; mtnous. cty., in Tienshan and Pamir systems; livestock breeding; mineral resources; food processing; cap. Frunze; a. 196,581 km²; p. (1970) 2,933,000.
Kirin (Jilin), prov., N.E. China; N. of Korea and Liaotung peninsula; crossed by Sungari R.; in fertile Manchurian plain; impt. industl. a.; soyabeans, grain, lumber, coal, gold, lead; gd. rly services; cap. Changchun; a. 186,998 km²; p. (est. 1968) 17,000,000.
Kirin (Jilin), c., Kirin, N.E. China; former prov. cap.; on Sungari R. at outlet of Sungari reservoir; impt. position on rly. from Changchun to coastal pts.; chemical fertilisers, steel, oil refinery; p. (est. 1970) 1,200,000.
Kirkburton, t., West Yorks., Eng.; S.E. of Huddersfield; woollens; p. (1971) 19,520.
Kirkby, t., Merseyside, Eng.; p. (1971) 59,759.
Kirkby in Ashfield, t., Notts., Eng.; 16 km N.W. of Nottingham; coal mng.; p. (1971) 23,638.
Kirkby Moorside, t., North Yorks., Eng.; nr. Vale of Pickering; mkt.-place; sailplanes, gliders; p. (1971) 4,175 (dist.).
Kirkcaldy, royal burgh, l. gov. dist., Fife Reg., Scot.; spt. on N. side of F. of Forth; submarine coal mng.; linoleum, potteries, engin.; birthplace of Adam Smith; p. (1971) 50,360.
Kirkcudbright, royal burgh, Stewartry, Scot.; on R. Dee at influx into K. Bay, S.W. of Dumfries; agr. ctr., hosiery; cas., abbey; p. (1971) 2,502.
Kircudbrightshire, former co., Scot.; now part of Stewartry l. gov. dist., Dumfries and Galloway Reg.
Kirkenes, t., Finnmark prov., N.E. Norway; on S. arm of Varanger fjord, nr. Soviet border; pt. for iron-mng. dist.
Kirkham, t., Lancs., Eng.; textiles; p. (1971) 6,422.
Kirkintilloch, burgh, Strathkelvin, Scot.; on Forth and Clyde canal; engin.; p. (1971) 25,206.
Kirkstone Pass, mtn. pass, Cumbria, Eng.; used by main road between Ullswater and Windermere Ls.
Kirkūk, t., Iraq; mart for Arab horses; oilfield with pipelines to Tripoli, Haifa and Banias; p. (1965) 175,303 (t.), 183,981 (met. a.).
Kirkwall, royal burgh, Mainland I., Orkneys, Scot.; cath.; p. (1971) 4,617.
Kirov, c., RSFSR; pt. on Vyatka R.; rly. junc.; engin., saw milling, chemicals, leather inds.; cath.; p. (1970) 332,000.
Kirovabad, c., W. Azerbaydzhan SSR, USSR; on Gandzha R.; industl. ctr.; textiles, agr. implements, wine; copper and manganese mines; aluminium plant; p. (1970) 190,000.
Kirovograd, c., Ukrainian SSR, USSR; on Ingul R.; cap. of K. oblast; agr. ctr.; engin.; p. (1970) 189,000.
Kirovsk, c., RSFSR; on Kola peninsula; apatite and nephelite mng.; chemicals; p. (est. 1967) 50,000.
Kirriemuir, burgh, Angus, Scot.; on N. margin of Strathmore, 8 km W. of Forfar; jute-weaving; birthplace of J. M. Barrie; p. (1971) 4,138.
Kirtland, t., N.M., USA; atomic and space research sta.
Kiruna, t., N. Sweden; inside Arctic Circle, N.W. of Luleå; linked by rly. to Narvik (Norway); impt. deposits of iron ore; p. (1968) 28,968.
Kiryu, c., Honshu, Japan; major textile ctr.; p. (est. 1971) 135,000.
Kisangani (Stanleyville), t., Zaïre; on R. Zaïre nr. Boyoma Falls; airpt.; univ.; p. (est. 1972) 261,496 (met. a.).
Kiselevsk, c., S.W. Siberia, RSFSR; coal-mng. ctr. in Kuznetsk basin; p. (1970) 126,000.
Kishinev, c., cap. of Moldavian SSR, USSR; on Byk R., trib. of Dniester; cath., univ.; industl., comm. ctr. in rich farming a.; tourism; p. (1970) 357,000.
Kislovodsk, c., RSFSR; in N. Caucasus; famous spa; p. (est. 1967) 84,000.
Kismayu, pt., Somalia; new deep-water harbour; airpt.
Kistna R. *See* **Krishna R.**
Kisumu, spt., cap. of Nyanza prov., Kenya; at head of Kavirondo G. on L. Victoria; handles bulk of cotton from Buganda and coffee from N. Tanzania for transhipment E. by rail; p. (1969) 30,700.
Kitakyūshū, c., N. Kyushu, Japan; one of Japan's lgst. muns. on merging (1963) of ts. Moji, Kokura, Tobata, Yawata, and Wakamatsu; sixth c. to enjoy special aut. rights; p. (est. 1971) 1,307,000.
Kitami, c., Hokkaido, Japan; mkt.; food-processing; p. (1970) 82,727.
Kitchener, c., Ont., Canada; agr. machin., tyres, hardware, agr. processing; p. (1971) 109,954 (c.) 224,390 (met. a.).
Kithira. *See* **Cerigo.**
Kitimat, t., B.C., Canada; lge. aluminium smelter powered by hydroelectricity from diversion of R. Fraser trib. through the Rockies.
Kitwe, t., Zambia; contiguous to mng. township of Nkana, ctr. of copperbelt; p. (est. 1972) 290,100 (met. a.).
Kiukiang (Chiu-chiang), c., N. Kiangsi prov., China; pt. on Yangtze R., at foot of forested mtn. of Lu-shan; entrepôt tr.; former treaty pt.; p. (est. 1970) 120,000.
Kivu, L., on border of Zaïre and Rwanda; in highlands of Gr. Rift Valley, 1,473 m high, 96 km long.
Kizel, c., RSFSR; on Kizel R., on W. slopes of

Urals; coal-mng. ctr.; mng. equipment; p. (est. 1967) 55,000.

Kizil, lgst R. of Turkey; rises in Kisil Dagh, flows to Black Sea via Sivas; 1,120 km long.

Kladno, t., **ČSSR**; 16 km N.W. of Prague; coal-mng. ctr.; iron and steel wks., machin.; p. (1967) 55,000.

Klagenfurt, t., cap. of Carinthia, Austria; winter sports ctr.; varied mnfs.; p. (est. 1969) 73,156.

Klaipeda (Memel), c., Lithuanian SSR, **USSR**; ice-free spt. on Baltic Sea; exp. timber, textiles, chemicals, paper; p. (1970) 140,000.

Klamath, mtns., N. Cal., S.W. Ore., **USA**; beautiful ranges containing Nat. Park and Indian reserve; hgst. alt. Mt. Eddy, 2,757 m.

Klamono, t., W. Irian, Indonesia; ctr. of oilfield; pipeline to Sorong harbour.

Klatovy, t., S.W. Bohemia, **ČSSR**; mkt.; rose-growing a.; textiles; p. (est. 1968) 16,493.

Klerksdorp, t., S. Transvaal, S. Africa; gold, diamonds; p. (1970) 75,686.

Klodzko (Glatz), t., S.W. **Poland**; formerly in Prussian Silesia; rly. junc.; on R. Neisse; comm. and mftg.; p. (1970) 26,100.

Klondike, R., Yukon, **Canada**; sm. trib. of Yukon in gold-mng. region; gold rush 1896; 160 km long.

Klyuchevskaya Sopka, one of 18 active volcanoes, **RSFSR**; in N.E. Siberia, on Kamchatka peninsula; alt. 4,748 m.

Knaresborough, t., North Yorks., **Eng.**; 5 km N.E. of Harrogate; mkt.; cas. ruins; p. (1971) 11,863.

Knighton, t., Powys, **Wales**; on R. Teme; mkt.; p. (1971) 2,010.

Knockmealdown Mtns., Waterford and Tipperary, **R.o.I.**; highest point 796 m; tourism.

Knob Lake. *See* **Schefferville.**

Knossos, ruined c., cap. of anc. Crete, **Greece**; S.E. of **Iráklion**; ctr. of Cretan bronze age culture, 1800 B.C.; archaeological source of knowledge about the Minoans.

Knottingley, t., West Yorks., **Eng.**; on R. Aire, 19 km S.E. of Leeds; engin., glass, tar distilling, chemicals; coal mng; p. (1971) 16,360.

Knoxville, c., Tenn., **USA**; univ.; livestock and tobacco mkt.; textiles, marble, plastics, chemicals, aluminium; p. (1970) 169,766 (c.), 391,974 (met. a.).

Knutsford, t., N.E. Cheshire, **Eng.**; mkt.; home of Mrs. Gaskell, author of *Cranford*; p. (1971) 13,765.

Kōbe, c., spt., Honshu, **Japan**; at E. end of Inland Sea; 5th c. of Japan; developed as pt. for Osaka and Kinki plain; iron and steel, shipbldg., rubber; p. (est. 1971) 1,307,000.

Koblenz (Coblenz), t., Rhineland-Palatinate, **W. Germany**; at confluence of Rs. Rhine and Moselle; fine buildings; wine, paper, machin., leather, ceramics; p. (est. 1969) 105,700.

Kōchi, plain and c., Shikoku, **Japan**; early vegetables, double rice cropping; p. (est. 1971) 246,000.

Kodiak I., lgst. of Is. of Alaska, **USA**; 144 km long; forested mtns.; fur-trading, salmon-fishing, canning; earthquake 1964; p. (1970) 3,798.

Kōfu, basin and c., Honshu, **Japan**; rice, vineyards, orchards, silk, wine; p. (est. 1971) 189,000.

Kohat, t., **Pakistan**; on trib. of Indus; military t.; cement wks.; p. (1961) 49,800.

Koh-I-Baba Mtns., Afghanistan, spur of the Hindu Kush; highest point 5,380 m.

Kokand, c., Uzbek SSR, **USSR**; in the Ferghana Valley; mftg. ctr., textiles, chemicals, engin.; p. (1970) 133,000.

Kokiu (Gejiu), t., Yunnan prov., **China**; leading tin-mng. ctr. of China; p. (1953) 159,700.

Kokkola (Gamla Karleby), t. **Finland**; on cst. of G. of Bothnia; sulphur plant; p. (est. 1970) 20,748.

Kokomo, c., Ind., **USA**; on Wild Cat R.; ctr. of agr. region; car components; p. (est. 1969) 48,000.

Koko-Nor, salt L., Chinghai prov., **China**; at over 3,000 m in Tibetan highlands; a. 5,957 km²; no outlet.

Kokura. *See* **Kitakyūshū.**

Kola Peninsula, peninsula, **RSFSR**; extension of Lapland; rich mineral deposits; hydro-electric plants.

Kolar, c., Karnataka, **India**; the ctr. of the Indian gold-mng. ind.; textiles; p. (1967) 167,610.

Kolarovgrad (Shumen), c., cap. of K. prov., N.E. **Bulgaria**; agr. tr., leather, cloth, metal gds.; Moslem architecture; p. (est. 1968) 68,124.

Kolding, c., at head of Kolding fjord, Jutland, **Denmark**; spt. and fishing base; lt. inds.; p. (est. 1970) 39,609.

Kolhapur, c., Maharashtra, S.W. **India**; cap. of former princely st. of K.; bauxite; anc. Buddhist ctr.; p. (1971) 259,050 (c.), 267,513 (met. a.).

Kolobrzeg (Kolberg), t., N.W. **Poland**; spt. on Baltic cst.; comm. and fishing harbour; resort and spa; p. (1970) 25,400.

Kolomna, c., **RSFSR**; on Moskva R., nr. confluence with Oka R.; industl. ctr.; engin., locomotives, machin., synthetic rubber; p. (1970) 136,000.

Kolomyya, c., Ukrainian SSR, **USSR**; on Pruth R.; in Carpathian foothills; agr. tr., metal gds., oil refining, textiles; p. (est. 1967) 39,000.

Kolwezi, c., S. Shaba, **Zaïre**; comm. ctr. for mng. dist. (cobalt and copper); p. (est. 1968) 70,558.

Kolyma, R., N.E. Siberia, **RSFSR**; flows into Arctic Oc., via Kolyma goldfields; navigable in summer; basin largely covered with tundra, sparsely p.; 2,560 km long.

Komárno, c., **ČSSR**; on left bank, of Danube, opposite Hungarian Komárom, on right bank; R. pt., shipbldg., oil refining.

Komi ASSR, aut. rep., **RSFSR**; wooded lowland, pastoral agr.; coal from Pechora basin, oil at Ukhta and Troitsko-Pechorsk; mng. now ch. economic activity; cap. Syktyvkar, lumber ctr.; a. 415,799 km²; p. (1970) 965,000.

Komló, t., **Hungary**; new mng. t.; coking coal; p. (1965) 27,800.

Kompong Som. *See* **Sihanoukville.**

Kommunarsk (Voroshilovsk), t., Ukrainian SSR, **USSR**; 40 km S.W. of Lugansk; ctr. of iron, steel and coking inds.; p. (1970) 123,000.

Komsomolsk, c., **RSFSR**; built by volunteer youth labour, after 1932; heavy industl. development; oil refining; pipeline connects with oilfield in N. Sakhalin; p. (1970) 218,000.

Komi-Permyak, admin. div., **RSFSR**; forestry, cellulose, paper; cap. Kudymbar; a. 31,080 km²; p. (1970) 212,000.

Konstantinovka, industl. t., Ukrainian SSR, **USSR**; in heart of Donbas industl. region, 61 km N. of Donetsk; heavy engin., iron and steel, zinc smelting, fertilisers; p. (1970) 106,000.

Konya, c., **Turkey**; cap. of K. prov.; agr. tr. ctr.; mnfs. textiles, carpets, leather gds.; the anc. Iconium, fortress of the Hittite empire; p. (1965) 157,934 (c.), 242,414 (met. a.).

Koolan I., W. **Australia**; rugged I. with iron-ore deposits worked since 1960.

Koolyanobbing, mng. t., W. **Australia**; high-grade haematite and limonite ores; linked to rly. between Kwinana and Kalgoorlie 1968.

Kootenay or **Kootenai**, R., flows from B.C., **Canada**; through Montana and Idaho, **USA**, into K. L., draining it by narrow channel into Columbia R.; beautiful scenery; resort at Radium Hotsprings; upper reaches inc. K. Nat. Park; 720 km long.

Kopeysk, t., **RSFSR**; in Urals; lignite mng., agr. and mng. machin.; p. (1970) 156,000.

Korat Plateau, E. **Thailand**; headwaters of Mekong tribs.; cattle-rearing; tr. ctr. Korat.

Korcë (Koritsa), t., S.E. **Albania**; in infertile basin at 854 m nr. Greek border; mkt.; cultural ctr.; p. (1967) 46,000.

Korcula (Curzola), I., **Yugoslavia**; sm. I. in Adriatic Sea; ch. pt. K.; a. 277 km²; p. (1961) 10,223.

Korea, Democratic People's Republic of, (N. Korea); occupies N. part of Korean peninsula (N. of 38th parallel), E. Asia; bounded on N. by China and USSR; continental climate; cold dry winters, hot humid summers; predominantly mtnous. with many uninhabited offshore Is.; all inds. nationalised and collective agr.; agr. employs half working p.; development emphasis on mng. resources of coal, iron-ore and on growth of heavy inds.; most industl. resources located in N. Korea; transport network under reconstruction after devastation of Korean war; some R. transport, international airport at cap. of Pyongyang; proposed union with S. Korea; a. 121,248 km²; p. (est. 1969) 13,300,000.

Korea, Rep. of (S. Korea), occupies S. part of Korean peninsula (S. of 38th parallel); climate and topography resemble N. Korea's; massive US aid revitalised economy after Korean war; 50 per cent work-force engaged in agr.; industl. growth hampered by lack of resources, but iron and steel ind. at Pusan; fishing is both source of subsistence and exp.; irrigation and power project (1971–81) for 4 Rs.—Hangang, Naktangang, Kum-Gang, and Yongsan-Gang; proposed union with N. Korea; cap. Seoul; a. 99,591 km²; p. (est. 1974) 33,959,000.
Korea Bay, Yellow Sea; between N. Korea and North-East China (Manchuria).
Koriyama, Honshu, **Japan**; textiles, chemicals; p. (est. 1971) 251,000.
Korsör, spt., Sjaelland I., **Denmark**; fine harbour; glass wks.; p. (est. 1970) 13,674.
Kortrijk (Courtrai), t., W. Flanders prov., N.W. **Belgium**; textiles; 13th cent. Notre Dame church; battle of the Spurs 1302; p. (1968) 45,170.
Koryak, admin. div., N.E. Siberia, **RSFSR**; sparse p.; a. 393,680 km²; p. (1970) 31,000.
Kos, I. *See* **Cos, I.**
Kosciusko, Mount, N.S.W., in Australian Alps; highest peak in **Australia**; 2,230 m.
Kosi R., India; flows from Himalayas to Ganges; site of barrage for hydroelectric power and irrigation.
Košice, c., S.E. Slovakia, **ČSSR**; lies in fertile basin; major industl. ctr.; heavy inds., iron and steel plant; agr.-processing; univ., Gothic cath.; mediaeval fortress t.; p. (est. 1968) 119,757.
Kosovo-Metohija, aut. region, S.W. Serbia, **Yugoslavia**; mtnous., fertile valleys; stock raising, forestry; ch. t. Priština; a. 10,352 km²; p. (1971) 1,244,755.
Kostroma, c., cap. of K. oblast, **RSFSR**; at confluence of Volga and Kostroma; in flax growing a.; textiles, engin.; cath.; p. (1970) 223,000.
Koszalin (Köslin), c., cap. of K. prov., N.W. **Poland**; nr. Baltic cst.; paper mills, textiles, building materials; p. (1970) 64,400.
Kota, t., Rajasthan, **India**; on R. Chambal; textiles; p. (1971) 212,991.
Kota Kinabalu (Jesselton), t., cap of Sabah, **Malaysia**; on W. cst.; main rubber pt.; rly. terminal; p. (1970) 41,830.
Köthen, t., Halle, **E. Germany**; in former st. of Saxony-Anhalt; lignite mines, sugar-refining, machin., chemicals; p. (est. 1970) 36,587.
Kotka, spt., S.E. **Finland**; on G. of Finland, at mouth of Kymi R.; major exp. pt. for timber, paper, pulp; p. (1968) 33,553.
Kotor, spt., S. Montenegro, **Yugoslavia**; on Bay of K., inlet of Adriatic; cath.; tourism.
Kotri, t., **Pakistan**; on R. Indus, opposite Hyderabad; barrage N. of the t., to help irrigate Sind; p. (1961) 52,685.
Kottbus. *See* **Cottbus.**
Koulikoro, t., **Mali**, W. Africa; on upper course of R. Niger; mkt. for groundnuts, gum-arabic, sisal; linked by R. to Timbuktu and Gao; rly. terminus, 1,216 km from Dakar.
Kovrov, c., **RSFSR**; on Gorki rly. line and R. Klyazma; impt. agr. exp. ctr.; engin., textiles; p. (1970) 123,000.
Kowloon, peninsula, S.E. **China**; on mainland opposite Hong Kong I.; pt. installations; major industl. and tr. ctr.; held by Britain on lease expiring 1998; p. (1961) 726,976.
Kozáni, dep., Macedonia, **Greece**; cap. K.; mainly agr.; a. 6,143 km²; p. (1971) 135,619.
Kozhikode. *See* **Calicut.**
Kra Isthmus, neck of land between B. of Bengal and G. of Thailand, linking Malay peninsula with continent of Asia.
Kragujevac, t., central Serbia, **Yugoslavia**; on both banks of Lepenica R. (trib. of Morava R.); cath.; arsenal and garrison; route ctr., developing agr. and industl. ctr.; p. (est. 1965) 59,000.
Krakatoa (Rakata), volcanic I., Sunda strait, **Indonesia**; between Java and Sumatra; greater part blown up by violent eruption 1883.
Kraków (Cracow), c., cap. of K. prov., S. **Poland**; pt. on Vistula; cultural ctr., univ. (Copernicus matriculated here); many historic monuments; inc. c. of Nowa Huta, lgst iron and steel ctr. of rep.; machin., chemicals, farm implements; p. (1970) 583,000.
Kramatorsk, c., Ukrainian SSR, **USSR**; in Donets basin; heavy engin., metallurgy; p. (1970) 151,000.
Kramfors, t., **Sweden**; on G. of Bothnia; paper-mill and sulphite pulp wks.
Krasnodar Territory, region, **RSFSR**; extends from Sea of Azov and Black Sea to N.W. end of Caucasus; contains Kuban steppe and Maikop oilfields; fertile black soil; main pt. Tuapse; many health resorts.
Krasnodar, c., cap. of K. region, **RSFSR**; R. pt. Kuban R.; ctr. of industl. and agr. region; p. (1970) 465,000.
Krasnoturinsk, t., **RSFSR**; in Urals, 9 km N.W. of Serov; aluminium, coal; p. (est. 1969) 61,000.
Krasnovodsk, c., Turkmen SSR, **USSR**; pt. on Caspian Sea; oil-refining ctr.; handles agr. and oil prods.; p. (est. 1967) 48,000.
Krasnoyarsk Territory, extensive region, **RSFSR**; extends across Siberia to Arctic Oc.; traversed by Yenisey and tribs.; minerals, grain from Minusinska basin and timber from coniferous forests; cap. K.; a. of labour camps in Stalin era.
Krasnoyarsk, c., cap. of K. terr., E. Siberia, **RSFSR**; on Trans-Siberian rly. at crossing of Yenesey R.; hydroelectric sta.; industl. ctr.; local copper and iron-ore deposits; ctr. for grain and timber; p. (1970) 684,000.
Krefeld, t., N. Rhine-Westphalia, **W. Germany**; chemicals, steel, machin., textiles, soap; former ctr. of silk inds.; p. (est. 1969) 226,800.
Kremenchug, c., Ukrainian SSR, **USSR**; on R. Dnieper; timber, engin., textiles; hydroelectric sta.; oil refining; p. (1970) 148,000.
Krems, mkt. t., **Austria**; on R. Danube; fruit processing; founded in 10th cent. as imperial fortress; p. (1961) 21,046.
Kreuznach Bad, t., Rhineland Palatinate, **W. Germany**; on R. Nahe; metallurgy, leather optical and chemical inds.; viticulture, mineral baths; p. (est. 1969) 44,139.
Krishna (Kistna), R., S. **India**; rises in W. Ghats, flows E. across Deccan plateau into Bay of Bengal; lower valley and delta under intensive rice cultivation; densely populated; 1,360 km long.
Kristiansand, spt., S. **Norway**; on Skagerrak; shipbldg., ships timber, paper, pulp, fish; electro-metallurgy; p. (1968) 53,736.
Kristianstad, c., cap. of K. prov., **Sweden**; on Helge R.; its pt. Ahus is on Baltic; food-processing, clothing, machin.; founded 1614 as fortress; p. (1968) 42,456.
Kristiansund, spt., W. cst. **Norway**; built on 3 Is.; trawler fleet base; exp. dried fish; heavily damaged in second world war; since rebuilt; p. (1969) 18,588.
Kristinehamn, L. pt. on L. Vänern, central **Sweden**; p. (est. 1970) 22,018.
Krivoy Rog., c., Ukrainian SSR, **USSR**; on R. Ingulets; ctr. of ch. iron-mng. a. of USSR; p. (1970) 573,000.
Krk, I., N. Adriatic Sea, **Yugoslavia**; S. of Rijeke; agr.; tourism; ch. t., K.; p. 14,500.
Krkonose. *See* **Riesengebirge.**
Kronshlot (Kronstadt), spt., on I. of Kotlin, **RSFSR**; at head of G. of Finland, nr. Leningrad; Baltic pt. and naval base; scene of naval mutiny which precipitated the Russian revolution; founded by Peter the Great 1710; p. 50,000.
Kroonstad, t., O.F.S., **S. Africa**; on R. Vals; rly. junc.; agr. mkt.; engin., milling; p. (1970) 50,898.
Kropotkin, c., E. Krasnodar Terr., **RSFSR**; food-processing, engin.; p. (est. 1967) 62,000.
Kruger Nat. Park, N.E. Transvaal, **S. Africa**; game reserve; a. 20,720 km².
Krugersdorp, t., Transvaal, **S. Africa**; gold mng., uranium, manganese; p. (1970) 91,202.
Kuala Lumpur, c., fed. terr., **W. Malaysia**; cap. of Fed. of Malaysia and of Selangor st.; univ.; ctr. of rubber and tin dist.; outport Port Kelang; p. (1968) 592,785.
Kuangchow (Kuang-chou), formerly Canton, c., cap. of Kwantung prov., S. **China**; industl. and educational ctr.; mnfs. inc. silk, paper, cement; univ.; former treaty pt. and major spt. of S. China but site on Chu-kiang delta results in silting and expensive harbour wks., hence Chinese interest in Hong Kong; ctr. of revolu-

tionary movement from days of Sun Yat-Sen; p. (est. 1970) 2,300,000.

Kuantan, main t. on E. cst. W. **Malaysia**; linked to Kuala Lumpur; tin mng; p. (1970) 43,391.

Kuching, c., cap. of Sarawak, **Malaysia**; pt. on Sarawak R.; gold discovered nearby at Bau; p. (1967) 70,000.

Kucovë (Qyteti Stalin), **Albania**; nr. Berat; oil prod. and refining; pipeline connects to Vlore.

Kufra, oasis, **Libya**; dates, barley; on caravan route.

Kuldja (I-ning), c., W. Sinkiang prov., **China**; on highway to Turkestan and on Ili R.; coalfield; recent industl. development inc. iron and steel; p. (est. 1970) 160,000.

Kumamoto, c., W. Kyushu, **Japan**; 3rd c. of K.; cas., univs.; food inds.; business ctr.; p. (est. 1971) 447,000.

Kumasi, c., cap. of Ashanti region, **Ghana**; univ., aerodrome; road and rly. junc.; ctr. of cocoa-producing a.; bauxite nearby; jute bags; p. (1970) 260, 286 (c.), 345,117 (met. a.).

Kumba Konam, t., Tamil Nadu, **India**; on Cauvery delta; silks, cotton; sacred Hindu c.; p. (1971) 113,130.

Kunene (Cunene), R., **Angola**; scheme to channel water from Angola to S.W. Africa; 1,200 km long.

Kungur, t., **RSFSR**; S.E. of Perm; oil ind. equipment; p. (est. 1967) 70,000.

Kun Lun (Kwen Lun), mtn. ranges, Tibet, **China**; extend 2,900 km E. from Pamirs along N. edge of high plateau of Tibet; drained N. into inland drainage basin of Lop Nor; alt. frequently exceeds 5,400 m; rising to 7,729 m.

Kunming, c., cap. of Yunnan prov., S.W. **China**; univ.; comm. and cultural ctr., noted for its scenic beauty; iron and steel, milling and boring machin., textiles, chemicals; p. (est. 1970) 1,700,000.

Kunsan, spt., S.W. **S. Korea**; on Yellow Sea, on estuary of R. Kum; p. (1966) 102,800.

Kununurra Dam, Ord R., W. **Australia**; opened 1963; to irrigate 81,000 ha of semi-arid land for cotton, rice, and cattle.

Kuopio, t., **Finland**; on L. Kalki; timber inds.; tourism; p. (1968) 55,067.

Kura, R., rises in **Turkey**, chief R. of Transcaucasia, **USSR**, flows into Caspian Sea; agr., fishing, hydroelec. power; 1,504 km long.

Kurdistan (Country of the Kurds), includes parts of E. Turkey, Soviet Armenia, N.E. Iraq, and N.W. Iran; attempts at autonomy.

Kure, c., S.W. Honshu, **Japan**; spt. and naval base; engin.; shipbldg.; p. (est. 1971) 239,000.

Kurgan, c., **RSFSR**; on Tobol R.; impt. junc. on Trans-Siberian rly.; tr. in cattle and foodstuffs; agr. engin.; p. (1970) 244,000.

Kuria Muria Is., 5 barren Is. in Arabian Sea off cst. of Oman; admin. by U.K. until 1967.

Kurile Is., chain of volcanic Is., N. Pac., **RSFSR**; extend from Kamchatka to Hokkaido; mainly mtnous.; sulphur, hunting, fishing; Japan claims sovereignty over 4 Is.; a. 15,592 km²; p. 18,000.

Kurisches Haff (Kuršiu Martos), shallow lagoon, Baltic cst. of Lithuanian SSR, **USSR**; receives water of R. Niemen; narrow entrance to Baltic Sea at N. end of lagoon commanded by pt. of Klaipeda (Memel); length 92 km, maximum width 32 km.

Kurische Nehrung, sandspit, Baltic Sea; almost cuts off Kurisches Haff from Baltic Sea; 88 km long.

Kurnool, t., Andhra Pradesh, **India**; agr. comm. ctr.; p. (1971) 136,710.

Kuroshio (Japan Current), ocean current, flows N.E. along Pac. cst. of Kyushu, Shikoku and S. Honshu, relatively warm water, exerts slight warming influence on this cst. in winter.

Kursk, c., cap. of K. oblast, **RSFSR**; on Tuskor R.; rly. junc.; in fertile fruit-growing a.; engin., textiles, synthetic rubber; p. (1970) 284,000.

Kurume, t., W. Kyushu, **Japan**; on Chikugo plain; comm. ctr.; p. (est. 1969) 190,000.

Kushiro, spt., S.E. Hokkaido, **Japan**; exp. lumber; local coal; fishing; p. (est. 1971) 201,000.

Kustanay, c., Kazakh SSR, **USSR**; on Tobol R.; agr.-processing, lt. inds.; p. (1970) 123,000.

Kütahya, t., cap. of K. prov., central **Turkey**; agr. mkt. ctr.; ceramics; p. (1965) 49,227.

Kutaisi, c., Georgian SSR, **USSR**; on R. Rion (hydroelectric plant); chemicals, textiles, mng. equipment; big coal deposits being mined; mkt. gardening a.; p. (1970) 161,000.

Kut-al-Amara, t., cap. of K. prov., **Iraq**; on R. Tigris; agr. tr. ctr.; p. (1965) 104,000 (met. a.).

Kutch, peninsula, Gujarat st., N.W. **India**; bounded on N. by Pakistan; largely barren except for fertile strip along Arabian Sea; p. (1961) 696,440.

Kutch, Rann of, desert region covered with salt, but flooded during monsoons; nine-tenths belongs to **India**; one-tenth to **Pakistan**.

Kutchan, t., S.W. Hokkaido, **Japan**; ctr. of lge. iron-ore field; ore smelted at Muroran.

Kutno, t., Lodz, **Poland**; route ctr.; sm. textile ind.; p. (1970) 30,300.

Kuwait, indep. Arab st., **S.W. Asia**; under Brit. protection until 1971; lies at head of Persian G.; mainly desert with a few oases; imports most of food requirements; possesses 17 per cent of the proved world reserves of oil; heavily dependent on oil and natural gas exports; industl. complex of petrochemical inds. at Shuaiba projected, 48 km S. of Kuwait (cap)., which contains nearly half of p.; one of hgst. incomes per capita in world, but most of p. remains poor; a. 24,235 km²; p. (1974) 862,200.

Kuwait, c., cap. of Kuwait; pt. with natural harbour on Persian G.; univ.; p. (1970) 80,008.

Kuybyshev, c., cap. of K. oblast, **RSFSR**; on R. Volga; major R. pt., rly. junc. on Moscow–Siberian line, airport; hydroelectric power sta.; comm. ctr. with varied mnfs., inc. cars, aircraft, textiles, synthetic rubber; oil refining; grain and livestock exp.; p. (1970) 1,047,000.

Kuzbas (Kuznetsk Basin), industl. region, Siberia, **USSR**; lies S. of Trans-Siberian rly. in upper valleys of Rs. Ob and Tom; second lgst. coal output in USSR, iron and steel mftg., heavy metallurgical ind.; ch. ts., Novosibirsk, Novokuznetsk, Kemerovo, Leninsk-Kuznetsky.

Kvalöy. *See* Hammerfest.

Kwangsi Chuang (Guang Zhuang), aut. region, **S. China**; borders on Vietnam; cap. Nanning; drained by Si-kiang and tribs.; rice most impt. crop; timber from sub-tropical forests; home of the Chuang people (over 7 million); a. 221,321 km²; p. (est. 1968) 24,000,000.

Kwantung (Guangdong), prov., S. **China**; on S. China Sea; cap. Kuangchow; occupied by delta of Si-kiang and its confluents; Hong Kong in estuary; tropical monsoon climate; densely p. on R. plains and valley slopes; intensive farming of rice, sugar, fruits; a. 221,308 km²; p. (est. 1968) 40,000,000.

Kwanto Plain, S.E. Honshu, **Japan**; lgst. a. of continuous lowland in Japan, extends 128 km inland from Tokyo; plain devoted to intensive rice cultivation; higher, drier terraces under mulberry, vegetables, tea, tobacco; very dense rural p.; lge. number of urban ctrs., inc. Tokyo, Yokohama; a. 13,000 km²; p. (1960) 27,000,000.

Kwazulu, Bantu Terr. Authority (1970), **E. S. Africa**; runs 480 km from Moçambique to Cape Prov. but in 29 separate as. interspersed by white as.; cap. Nongoma in N. highland; p. (1971) 2,100,00.

Kweichow (Guizhou), inland prov., S.W. **China**; upland a. with p. concentrated in valley urban areas; cap. Kweiyang; cereals; tung oil; forestry; coal, mercury; a. 176,480 km²; p. (est. 1968) 17,000,000.

Kweilin (Guilin), c., Kwangsi prov., **China**; on Kwei R.; univ.; textiles, sugar refining, timber; noted for its beautiful setting; p. (est. 1970) 235,000.

Kweiyang (Guiynag), c., Kweichow prov., **China**; univ.; comm. and industl.; coal; iron and steel, textiles, chemicals; p. (est. 1970) 1,500,000.

Kwidzyn (Marienwerder), c., Gdansk, N. **Poland** (since 1945); cath., cas.; industl. ctr. nr. Vistula R.; p. (1970) 23,100.

Kwinana, new t., W. **Australia**; oil refinery and steel plant, alumina reduction, blast furnace; integrated steelwks. by 1978; p. (1972) 10,096.

Kyle of Lochalsh, v., Skye and Lochalsh, **Scot.**; at entrance to Loch Alsh, facing S. end of I. of Skye; terminus of rly. across Highlands from Dingwall; ch. pt. for steamers to N.W. cst., I. of Skye, Outer Hebrides.

Kymi, R., **Finland**; rises in L. Päijänne, flows to

G. of Finland; many Ls., timber transport, hydroelec. power; 144 km long.
Kyoto, c., Honshu, **Japan**; cultural and religious ctr., without lge.-scale inds.; former cap. 794–1868; univ.; shrines, old Imperial palace; p. (est. 1971) 1,424,000.
Kyushu, most S. of 4 major Is. of Japan; mtnous.; coal mng. in Chikugo basin; heavy inds.; agr. on coastal lowlands; joined to Honshu by bridge and rly.; a. 42,007 km²; p. (1960) 12,903,515.
Kyustendil, t., **Bulgaria**; in foothills of Osogovo mtns.; lge. lead and zinc deposits; combined plant for mng. and ore dressing projected.
Kzyl Orda, R. and t., Kazakh SSR, **USSR**; lge. dam to irrigate rice plantations.

L

Laaland I. *See* Lolland I.
Labrador, mainland a. of prov. Newfoundland, **Canada**; separated from I. by Strait of Belle I.; barren, severe climate; impt. cod fisheries; rich iron ore reserves nr. Quebec bdy.; Churchill R. power project; cap. Battle Harbour; a. 292,219 km²; p. (1966) 21,157.
Labrador City, t., Newfoundland, **Canada**; new t. built 1965, nr. Wabush L. to house workers of iron-ore mines.
Labuan, I., Sabah, **Malaysia**; rubber, rice, coconuts; cap. Victoria; a. 81 km²; former free pt.; p. (1960) 14,904.
Laccadive, coral Is., Arabian Sea; about 320 km off Malabar cst. joined with Minicoy and Amindivi Is. to form union terr., **India**; renamed Lakshadweep Is. (1974); coir, coconuts; cap. Kavaratti; a. 28 km²; p. of terr. (1971) 31,798.
La Ceiba, spt., **Honduras**; on Caribbean cst.; exp. bananas; p. (1966) 31,951.
Lachine, c., Quebec, **Canada**; on Montreal I. where St. Lawrence R. leaves St. Louis L.; iron and steel, wire, rope; Lachine canal by-passes rapids; summer resort; p. (1966) 43,155.
Lachlan, R., N.S.W., **Australia**; trib. of R. Murrumbidgee; irrigation; 1,472 km long.
La Coruña, spt., cap. of La Coruña prov., N.W. **Spain**; fishing; import tr.; p. (est. 1969) 224,055.
Ladakh, dist., of the Upper Indus, **India**, bordering Tibet; ch. t. Leh; isolated and remote; alt. 3,600 m; p. (1961) 88,651.
Ladoga (Ladozhskoye), L., Leningrad, **USSR**; a. 18,389 km²; (lgst. in Europe); drained to G. of Finland by R. Neva; fishing; link in new deep-water canal between White and Baltic Seas.
Ladybank, burgh, North East Fife, **Scot.**; 8 km S.W of Cupar; p. (1971) 1,176.
Ladysmith, t. Natal, **S. Africa**; cotton mills; besieged by Boers 1899–1900; p. (1968) 32,750.
Lae, t., **Papua New Guinea**; pt. on Huon Gulf serving goldmng. dist;. outlet for Morobe plywood; air ctr.
Lagan (Laggan), R., **N. Ireland**; flows into Belfast Lough; canal link to Lough Neagh; 16 km long.
Lagôa dos Patos, L., **Brazil**; drained by Rio Grande do Sul; 224 km long.
Lagôa Mirim, L., on bdy. between **Brazil** and **Uruguay**; drains N.; 176 km long.
Lagos, spt., cap. of **Nigeria**; unhealthy and congested; cap. to be moved to Abuja by 1986; on G. of Guinea; gd. natural harbour; exp. cocoa, groundnuts, palm oil and kernels, timber, hides and skins, cotton, rubber, crude oil; mnfs. textiles, confectionery, chemicals, car assembly; univ.; p. (est. 1971) 900,979 (c.), 1,476,837 (met. a.).
La Grande Chartreuse, limestone region between Chambéry and Grenoble, **France**; famous monastery and liqueur.
La Grande Rivière, N. Quebec, **Canada**; major hydroelec. scheme; mineral and timber inds.
Laguna, dist., Durango st. **Mexico**; former L. bed irrigated by Rs. Nazas and Aguanaval; ch. cotton-growing region in Mexico; ch. t., Torréon; a. 259,000 km².
Lahore, ch. c., **Pakistan**; univ., cath., temples, mosques; textiles, pottery, carpets, industl. gases; atomic research ctr.; second c. of Pakistan; p. (1972) 2,148,000.
Lahti, t., S. **Finland**; wood, plywood, brewing textiles; p. (1968) 85,409.
Lake Champlain, N.Y., **USA**; forms lowland a. for main routes between Montreal and N.Y.
Lake Charles, c., La., **USA**; spt. at mouth of Calcasieu R.; connected to G. of Mexico by channel; exp. oil, chemicals, rice, cotton; p. (1970) 76,522 (c.), 142,288 (met. a.).
Lake District, almost circular mtnous. a.. Cumbria, **Eng.**; 17 major and many smaller Ls. formed by glacial erosion and deposition; increasing tourist pressure on Nat. Park as motorways improve accessibility.
Lakeland, c., Fla., **USA**; citrus fruit ctr.; holiday resort; p. (est. 1969) 43,000.
Lake of the Woods, L., Ont., S.E. of Winnipeg, on bdy. between **Canada** and **USA**; in pine forest; tourism.
Lakeview, t., Ont., **Canada**; thermal elec. power plant projected; to be lgst. in world.
Lakshadweep, union terr., **India**; made up of Laccadive, Minicoy and Amindivi Is.
La Linea, t., **Spain**; on isthmus connecting Gibraltar with mainland; vegetables, fruit; p. (1970) 52,127.
La Mancha, plain, Cuidad-Real prov., S. **Spain**; in shallow depression on central plateau, alt. between 450–900 m, drained by headstreams of R. Guadiana; semi-arid climate with hot summers, cold winters; widespread salt deposits; Merino sheep, esparto grass; Spain's lgst. grape-growing region.
Lambarene, t., **Gabon**; site of Schweitzer's hospital on Ogooué R.
Lambayeque, prov., N.W. **Peru**; ctr. of irrigated dists.; sugar, cotton, tobacco; cap. Chiclayo, ch. pt. Pimental; a. 11,948 km²; p. (est. 1969) 468,800.
Lambeth, inner bor., London, **Eng.**; L. palace, residence of Archibishop of Canterbury; p. (1971) 302,616.
Lammermuir Hills, E. Lothian, **Scot.**; highest peak Lammer Law, 529 m.
Lampang, t., **Thailand**; modern sugar plant; p. (est. 1969) 39,400.
Lampedusa, lgst of Pelagi Is., between Malta and Tunisian cst., belonging to **Italy**; barren limestone; a. 21 km²; p. (est. 1968) 4,620.
Lampeter, t., Dyfed, **S. Wales**; on R. Teifi; mkt.; univ. college of Wales; p. (1971) 2,189.
Lanark, former co., central **Scot.**; now forms several sm. l. gov. dists. within Strathclyde Reg.
Lanark, royal burgh, Lanark, **Scot.**; in Clyde valley 35 km S.E. of Glasgow; hosiery; ctr. of mkt. gardening a.; nr. New Lanark model t. built by Robert Owen; p. (1971) 8,700.
Lancashire, non-met. co., N.W. **Eng.**; major growth of p. in 19th cent. based on prod. of cotton and coal; main industl. ctrs. now outside co. in Merseyside and Gtr. Manchester met. cos.; Pennines in E.; extensive lowland in W.; admin. ctr. Preston, co. t. Lancaster; a. 2,738 km²; p. (1971) 1,341,000.
Lancaster, c., co. t., Lancs., **Eng.**; 10 km up R. Lune; mediaeval cas., univ.; linoleum, vinyl, clothing; p. (1971) 49,525.
Lancaster, c., Penns., **USA**; agr. ctr., tobacco mkt.; stockyards; mnfs. linoleum, watches; birthplace of Robert Fulton; p. (1970) 57,693 (c.), 319,531 (met. a.).
Lanchow (Lanzhou), c., cap. of Kansu prov., **China**; on Hwang-ho; tr. ctr.; oil refining, gaseous diffusion plant, woollen mills, coal mng. nearby; p. (est. 1970) 1,500,000.
Lancing, v., West Sussex, **Eng.**; on S. cst., 3 km E. of Worthing; seaside resort; lt. inds.; public school.
Landau, t., Rhineland-Palatinate, **W. Germany**; on R. Queich; cigar mftg., wine, iron ind.; here the carriages called Landaus were first made; p. (est. 1969) 32,094.
Landes, dep., S.W. **France**; on Atl. cst.; agr., vineyards, resin; cap. Mont-de-Marsan; a. 9,334 km²; p. (1968) 277,381.
Landes, Les, region, Aquitaine, S.W. **France**; fringes Bay of Biscay from Pointe de Grave to Biarritz; coastal sand dunes and lagoons backed by low, flat plain of alternate sandy tracts and marsh; reclaimed by drainage and afforestation, now over half a. covered by pine forests; turpentine, timber; oilfield.
Land's End, extreme S.W. point of **Eng.** on Cornish cst.
Landshut, t., Bavaria, **W. Germany**; on R. Isar; cas.; elec. inds., glass, metallurgy, textiles, coal; rly. junc.; p. (est. 1969) 51,182.
Landskrona, spt., **Sweden**; on the Sound; ship-

ping and tr. ctr.; agr.-processing; on nearby I. of Ven Tycho Brahe built his observatory; p. (1968) 32,125.

Langdale Pikes, L. Dist., **Eng**; 2 peaks Harrison Stickle (733 m), Pike-o'-Stickel (709 m); popular rambling and climbing a.; 5 km W. of Grasmere.

Langebergen, mtns., Cape Prov., **S. Africa**; 240 km E. to W. parallel to S. cst. of Africa; form barrier to access from cst. plain to Little Karroo, broken across by valley of R. Gouritz; max. alt, exceeds 1,370 m.

Langholm, mkt. burgh, Annandale and Eskdale, **Scot.**; on R. Esk; 29 km N. of Carlisle; textiles; p. (1971) 2,344.

Langnau, t., **Switzerland**; ch. t. of the Emmental; cheese, cloth mills, pottery.

Langreo, t., **N. Spain**; in Asturias, 19 km S.E. of Oviedo; coal and iron mines; p. (1970) 58,864.

Langres, t., Haute-Marne, **France**; cath., mediaeval fortifications; famous for its cutlery; birthplace of Diderot; p. (1968) 10,846.

Languedoc, region, former prov., S. **France**; inc. deps. Gard, Aude, Hérault, Lozère, Ardèche, Tarn, and parts of Haute Garonne, Tarn-et-Garonne, and Haute Loire; major govt. sponsored investment in tourist inds., along Mediterranean cst.; mono-cultural vine prod., irrigation scheme to aid agr. diversification.

Lannemezan, region, Aquitaine, S.W. **France**; belt 80 km wide stretches over 160 km along foot of Pyrenees W. of Toulouse; consists of immense deltas of glacial gravel deeply cut by tribs. of Rs. Garonne and Adour; valleys liable to severe floods in summer, intervening plateau dry, bare; scantily populated.

Lanpung, dist., Sumatra, **Indonesia**; a. of early colonial settlement; rice surplus.

Lansing, c., cap. of Mich., **USA**; on Grand R. at confluence with Cedar R.; automobiles, chemicals; p. (1970) 129,021 (c.), 373,474 (met. a.).

Lanzarote, I., **Canary Is.**; volcanic mtns.; developing tourist ind.; cochineal; cap. Arrecife; p. (1970) 41,912.

Laoag, t., N. Luzon I., **Philippines**; agr.-processing; p. (1970) 69,300.

Laoighis or **Leix** Co., Leinster, **R.o.I.**; mtns. and bog; inland pasture and tillage; cap. Port Laoighise (Maryborough); a. 1,720 km²; p. (1966) 44,622.

Laon, t., cap. of Aisne dep., **France**; on rocky height above plain; historic fortress t.; cath.; p. (1968) 28,613.

Laos, People's Dem. Rep. of, S.E. Asia; kingdom until 1975; bordered by China, Vietnam, Cambodia, Thailand and Burma; formerly part of Fr. Indo-China; under-developed and isolated cty; economic ctr. is Mekong valley, scene of recent Mekong R. Development Project; elsewhere thickly forested mtns.; 90 per cent of p. engaged in subsistence agr. for dry rice; lge. food imports necessary; main exp., hardwoods; no rlys.; royal cap. Luang Prabang admin. cap. Vientiane; a. 231,339 km²; p. (est. 1970) 2,962,000.

La Paz, dep., **Bolivia**; traversed by Andes; de facto cap. La Paz, legal cap. Sucre; cocoa, coffee, rubber, tin-mng. at Catari; a. 105,377 km²; p. (est. 1969) 1,509,100.

La Paz, c., **Bolivia**; seat of govt.; comm. ctr.; copper, alpaca wool, cinchona, textiles; p. (1969) 525,000.

Lapland, terr., **N. Europe**, in Norway, Sweden, Finland, and USSR, extending from Norwegian cst. to White Sea; mainly mtn. and moorland, with many lakes; Lapps are nomadic pastoralists with reindeer herds; iron-ore at Kiruna and Gällivare; a. 336,700 km²; p. (est. 1968) 36,500.

La Plata, c., spt., **Argentina**; cap. of Buenos Aires prov., univ.; mftg. ctr.; iron and steel, oil refining, refrigerated meat prods.; p. (1970) 506,287 (met. a.).

La Plata, Rio de. *See* **Plata, Rio de la**.

Laptev Sea (Nordenskjöld Sea), inlet of Arctic Oc.; between Severnaya Zemlya and New Siberian Is., **RSFSR**.

Larache, spt., **Morocco**; on Atl. cst. 64 km S. of Tangier; exp. cork, wool; p. (1960) 30,769.

Laramie, t., Wyo., **USA**; univ.; industl. ctr. for cattle and timber region; rly. engin.; p. (1970) 23,143.

Laredo, t., Texas, **USA**; frontier t. on Rio Grande; smuggling; ctr. of Chicanos; p. (est. 1969) 73,000 (c.), 195,000 (met. a.).

Largo, v., North East Fife, **Scot.**; fishing, holiday resort; birthplace of Alexander Selkirk.

Largs, burgh, Cunninghame, **Scot.**; on F. of Clyde opposite Is. of Bute and Cumbrae; seaside resort, fishing; battle 1263; p. (1971) 9,771.

Larissa, dep., Thessaly, **Greece**; inc. infertile basin of R. Pinios; cap. Larissa; ch. pt. Volos; p. (1971) 232,157.

Larkhall, t., Strathclyde Reg., **Scot.**; industl. estate; foundry, hosiery, silk dye wks.

Larnaca, spt., **Cyprus**; the anc. Citium; grain, cotton, fruit; oil refinery; growing tourist ctr.; p. (est. 1970) 21,400.

Larne, spt., l. gov. dist., **N. Ireland**; at entrance to Larne Lough; cross channel service to Stranraer; tourism; p. (est. 1971) 18,242.

La Rochelle, spt., cap. of Charente-Maritime dep., **France**; on Atl. cst.; its deepwater pt. is La Pallice; cath.; fishing pt.; chemicals, food-processing; tourism; p. (1968) 75,497.

Larut Hills, W. Malaysia; rise to over 1,500 m; lge. tin-field.

Larvik, spt., **Norway**; S.W. of Oslo; seaside resort; engin., pulp, stone; former whaling pt.; p. (est. 1970) 10,376.

Las Cruces, t., N.M., **USA**; on Rio Grande R.; irrigated agr.; univ.; p. (1970) 37,857.

La Serena, c., cap. of Coquimbo prov., **Chile**; 14 km inland from its pt. Coquimbo; cath.; resort; p. (est. 1966) 48,647.

Lashio, t., **Burma**; on R. Salween; rly. terminus; Burma road links with China; ctr. of silver-lead mines; p. 4,638.

Lashkar, c., Madhya Pradesh, central **India**; modern industl. t., adjoining Gwalior.

La Skhirra, pt., on G. of Gabès, **Tunisia**; oil; pipeline to Edjelé.

Las Palmas, prov., Canary Is., **Spain**; inc. Gran Canaria, Lanzarote, Fuerteventura and smaller Is.; intensive irrigated agr. of bananas, tomatoes, potatoes; tourism encouraged by climate and volcanic landscape; a. 4,053 km²; p. (1970) 579,710.

Las Palmas, c., N.E. Gran Canaria, ch. pt. of **Canary Is.**; exp. agr. prods.; cath.; p. (1968) 218,072.

La Spezia, spt., Liguria, N.W. **Italy**; on Bay of Spezia; ch. Italian naval sta., arsenal and docks; maritime inds., elec. machin., olive oil, oil refining; p. (1969) 128,652.

Lassen Peak, Nat. Park, Cascade Range, **Cal.**; only active volcano in **USA**.

Lasswade. *See* Bonnyrigg and Lasswade.

Las Vegas, c., Nevada, **USA**; noted for its gambling casinos; ranching and mng. a.; p. (1970) 124,161 (c.), 270,045 (met. a.).

Latacunga, t., **Ecuador**; at *c.* 2,740 m in Andean basin, not far from Cotopaxi volcano; anc. Inca t.; tr. ctr.; p. (est. 1970) 17,300.

Latakia, spt., **Syria**; exp. tobacco, olive oil, sponges; p. (1970) 126,000.

Latina (Littoria), c., cap. of Latina prov., in Latium, central **Italy**; in ctr. of reclaimed a. of Pontine marshes; mkt ctr., on which planned road system converges; built since 1932; nuclear power sta. nearby; p. (est. 1967) 45,600 (c.), 65,600 (dist.).

Latin America, the Spanish-, Portuguese- and Fr.-speaking countries of N. America, S. America, Central America, and the W.I., inc. the reps. of Argentina, Bolivia, Brazil, Chile, Colombia, Costa Rica, Cuba, Dominican Republic, Ecuador, Salvador, Guatemala, Haiti, Honduras, Mexico, Nicaragua, Panama, Paraguay, Peru, Uruguay, and Venezuela; sometimes Puerto Rico, Fr. W.I., and other Is. of the W.I. are included, and occasionally Belize, Guyana, Fr. Guiana, and Surinam.

Latium (Laszio), region, central **Italy**; between Apennines and Tyrrhenian Sea, comprising provs. of Rome, Frosinone, Latina, Rieti, Viterbo; a. 17,182 km²; p. (1969) 4,635,528.

Latvia, constituent rep., **USSR**; borders on Baltic Sea; dairying, stock-raising, forestry; cap. Riga; spts. Ventspils, Liepaya; a. 66,278 km²; p. (1970) 2,365,000.

Launceston, t., **Tasmania, Australia**; wool, textiles, cars; p. (1792) 62,181.

Launceston, t., Cornwall, **Eng.**; agr. mkt.; quarrying, lt. engin.; p. (1971) 4,725.

Laurencekirk, burgh, Kincardine and Deeside, Scot.; agr. ctr. in the Howe of Mearns; p. (est. 1976) 1,500.
Laurion or **Laurium**, pt. on Attic peninsula, Greece; lead, manganese, zinc, and silver mines; silver mined 5th cent. B.C.
Lausanne, c., cap. of Vaud can., **Switzerland**; nr. L. Geneva; cath., univ.; impt. rly. junc.; seat of Swiss high courts of justice; tourism; p. (est. 1969) 13,8300 (c.), 214,900 (met. a.).
Lauterbrunnen, Alpine valley, Bern can., Switzerland; famous for its waterfalls, the highest of which is Staubbach 299 m; tourist and winter sports ctr.
Laval, t., cap. of Mayenne dep., **France**; Mayenne R. divides old and modern parts; cotton, paper, machin., marble; cas., church; p. (1968) 49,052.
Lavenham, t., Suffolk, **Eng.**; a ctr. of the wool tr. in 15th cent., still preserves its mediaeval character.
Lavera, pt., nr. Marseilles, S.E. France commencement of 752 km oil pipeline to Karlsruhe, W. Germany; oil refining.
Lawrence, t., Mass., **USA**; on Merrimac R., N.W. of Boston; textiles, paper, footwear, engin.; p. (1970) 66,216 (c.), 229,325 (met. a.).
Lawton, t., Okla., **USA**; mnfs. cottonseed oil; p. (1970) 69,069 (c.), 104,504 (met. a.).
Laxey, v., I. of Man, **Eng.**; flour milling, woollen mills, meerschaum pipes.
Lea or **Lee**, R., **Eng.**; rises in Chiltern Hills nr. Luton, flows S. and E. into R. Thames through industl. zone of N.E. London; valley to become a regional park; mkt. gardening a.; 74 km long.
Leamington (Royal Leamington Spa), t., Warwicks., **Eng.**; on R. Leam, trib. of Avon, 3 km N.E. of Warwick; fashionable spa; engin. inds.; p. (1971) 44,989.
Leatherhead, t., Surrey, **Eng.**; on R. Mole to N. of gap through N. Downs; residtl.; p. (1971) 40,112.
Lebanon, mtn. range, **Lebanon**, extending to cst. of Syria; snow-capped most of year; highest peak Timarum, 3,214 m; famous in anc. times for cedar forests.
Lebanon, rep., S.W. Asia; at E. end of Mediterranean Sea; bordered by Syria to N. and Israel to S.; narrow coastal strip backed by mtnous. interior; free mkt. a., with economy based on transit tr.; most of p. involved in tourism, finance and commerce; oil refining based on imports; cap. Beirut; strife-torn by civil war 1975–6; a. 8,806 km²; p. (est. 1972) 2,960,000.
Le Bourget, t., N.E. of Paris, **France**; airpt.; p. (1968) 9,797.
Lebórk (Lauenburg), t., Gdansk, **Poland** (since 1945); in agr. dist.; timber and food inds.; p. (1970) 25,000.
Lebowa Territory, Bantu Terr., **S. Africa**; home of N. Sotho and Ndebele peoples; self-gov. Oct. 1972; cap. Seshego; p. (1970) 1,087,095.
Lecce, c., Apulia, S. **Italy**; agr. and route ctr. with ceramic and glass inds.; anc. Greek col.; baroque churches and palaces; p. (1969) 81,769.
Lecco, t., **Italy**; in Lombardy, on L. Como; iron and copper wks., agr.-processing, cheese; one of first ts. in Europe to be run by elec.; p. (est. 1967) 51,500.
Lech, R., rises in Austria and flows past Augsburg in Bavaria, **W. Germany**, to join Danube; 283 km long.
Le Creusot, t., Saône-et-Loire, **France**; ctr. of one of sm. coalfields bordering the Massif Central; steel, engin.; p. (1968) 34,109.
Ledbury, t., Hereford and Worcs., **Eng.**; at W. foot of Malvern hills; fruit preserving, tanning; 17th cent. mkt. hall; birthplace of John Masefield; p. (1971) 11,184 (dist.).
Leeds, c., West Yorks., **Eng.**; on R. Aire; at E. margin of Pennines; univ.; lge. clothing ind., varied engin. mnfs., paper and printing; with Bradford forms conurb. of W. Yorks.; p. (1971) 494,971.
Leek, mkt. t., Staffs., **Eng.**; 18 km N.E. of Stoke-on-Trent; silk mnfs., butter; expanded t.; p. (1971) 19,368.
Lee-on-Solent, t., Hants., **Eng.**; on Southampton Water.
Lees, t., Gtr. Manchester, **Eng.**; textiles; p. (1971) 4,367.
Leeton, t., N.S.W., **Australia**; new t., ctr. of fruit and rice farming as part of Murrumbidgee irrigation a.; p. (1966) 5,814.
Leeuwarden, c., cap. of Friesland prov., **Neth.**; noted cattle mkt.; rly. junc.; p. (1968) 87,414.
Leeuwin, C., S.W. point of **Australia**; notorious storms.
Leeward Is., **W.I.**, northern gr. of Lesser Antilles archipelago; so-called because winds in this a. generally blow from E.; inc. Virgin Is. of US; Fr. I. of Guadloupe, Dutch Is. of St. Eustatius and Saba, and Brit. Leeward Is. (Montserrat, Virgin Is., and former cols. of Antigua, St. Kitt-Nevis, Anguilla).
Legaspi, t., cap. of Albay prov., **Philippines**; spt. in S.E. Luzon; linked by rly. with Manila; p. (est. 1970) 84,700.
Leghorn. *See* Livorno.
Legionowa, t., Poland; new t. (1951) on outskirts of Warsaw; nr. artificial L. in R. Bug valley; p. (1970) 20,800.
Legnano, t., Lombardy, **Italy**; N.W. of Milan; textiles, machin.; p. (est. 1967) 45,900.
Legnica (Liegnitz), c., Wroclaw, S.W. **Poland** (since 1945); on Katzbach R., in rich agr. region; p. (1970) 75,800.
Leh, cap. of Ladakh, Kashmir, **India**; isolated t. in Himalayas on caravan route to Tibet; p. (1961) 3,700.
Le Havre, spt., Seine-Maritime dep., N. **France**; at mouth of Seine on English Channel; shipbldg., engin., chemicals, ropes, cottons, oil refining; pipeline to Grandpuits; p. (1968) 200,940 (c.), 247,374 (met. a.).
Leicester, c., co. t., Leics., **Eng.**; on R. Soar; univ.; footwear, hosiery, knitwear, textile machin.; Roman remains; p. (1971) 283,549.
Leicestershire, non-met. co., **Eng.**; mainly rural, low-lying Midland co., but inc. Charnwood Forest; mixed agr., sm. coalfield; hosiery and footwear inds.; now inc. Rutland; ch. t. Leicester; a. 2,554 km²; p. (1971) 799,000.
Leiden or **Leyden**, c., S. Holland prov., **Neth.**; on Oude Rijn; famous univ.; printing, textiles, medical equipment; gr. weaving ctr. in Middle Ages; revolt against Spanish rule 1573–4; birthplace of Rembrandt; p. (est. 1969) 101,878 (c.), 161,341 (met. a.).
Leigh, t., Gtr. Manchester, **Eng.**; 8 km S.E. of Wigan; mkt.; coal mng.; textiles; p. (1971) 46,117.
Leigh-on-Sea, t., Essex, **Eng.**; on N. cst. of Thames estuary, 3 km W. of Southend; holiday resort, fishing.
Leighton Buzzard, t., Beds., **Eng.**; at N.E. end of Vale of Aylesbury; tiles, engin., sand quarrying; p. (1971) 20,326 (inc. Linslade).
Leinster, S.E. prov., **R.o.I.**; bulk of recent Irish p. increase; a. 19,736 km²; p. (1966) 1,412,465.
Leipzig, c., **E. Germany**; comm., industl., and cultural ctr. at junc. of Rs. Pleisse, Elster, and Parthe; famous univ.; inds. inc. publishing, steel, textiles, chemicals, machin., cars; tr. fairs; Bach was organist at Thomaskirche; birthplace of Leibnitz and Wagner; p. (est. 1969) 587,761.
Leiston-cum-Sizewell, t., Suffolk, **Eng.**; on cst., 6 km E. of Saxmundham; agr. implements; nuclear power sta.; p. (1971) 4,864.
Leith, t., Edinburgh City, **Scot.**; shipbldg., timber, whisky; outport for Edinburgh.
Leith Hill, Surrey, **Eng.**; nr. Dorking; alt. 294 m; Lower Greensand crest.
Leitmeritz. *See* Litoměřice.
Leitrim, co., Connacht, **R.o.I.**; agr.; cap. Carrick-on-Shannon; a. 1,588 km²; p. (1966) 30,532.
Leix. *See* Laoighis.
Leixões, the modern harbour of Oporto, **Portugal**; oil refinery.
Lek, R., **Neth.**; one of the branches of the Neder Rijn; from Wijk-bij-Duurstede to Krimpen nr. Rotterdam; 64 km long.
Le Locle, t., Neuchâtel, **Switzerland**; ctr. of watch-mkg. ind.; p. (1969) 15,200.
Léman L. *See* **Geneva, L.**
Le Mans, t., cap. of Sarthe dep., N.W. **France**; cath.; linen, ironmongery, chemicals, motor cars, aeroplanes; motor-racing; p. (1968) 147,651.
Lemnos, Greek I., Aegean Sea, **Greece**; 64 km S.W. of Dardanelles; ch. t. Kastro (the anc. Myrina); tobacco, wine; a. 466 km²; part of Lesvos dep.

Lena, one of gr. Siberian Rs., **RSFSR**; rises in Oc.; navigable; 4,480 km long.
Leninabad, c., Tadzhik SSR, **USSR**; on Syr Dar'ya R., S. of Tashkent; silks, cottons, fruit-preserving; hydroelectric power sta.; p. (1970) 103,000.
Leninakan, c., Armenian SSR, **RSFSR**; nr. Turkish border; textiles, engin., rug-mkg.; p. (1970) 164,000.
Lenin Dam (Dnieper Dam). *See* **Zaporozh'ye.**
Leningrad, c., cap. of Leningrad oblast, **RSFSR**; at mouth of Neva R.; cultural ctr. with many fine bldgs., inc. winter palace, Hermitage museum, cath., admiralty bldg.; former cap. of Russia; major pt. and industl. ctr.; exp. timber, furs, and raw materials; ice-bound December–March; founded (1703) by Peter the Great as St. Petersburg; p. (1970) 3,513,000 (c); 4,311,000 (met. a.).
Leninogorsk, c., Kazakh SSR, **USSR**; in Altai mtns.; lead zinc, and silver mines; metallurgical plants; p. (est. 1967) 70,000.
Lenin Peak (Mt. Kaufmann), Trans-Altai Range, Kirghiz-Tadzhik SSR border, 2nd. hgst. mtn. of **USSR**; adjoining glacier; alt. 7,132 m.
Leninsk-Kuznetski, t., **RSFSR**; in W. Siberia on Inya R.; coalfield in Kuznetsk basin; heavy engin., power sta.; p. (1970) 128,000.
Lenkoran, c., pt., Azerbaydzhan SSR, **USSR**; on Caspian Sea, nr. Iranian border; rice, citrus fruits, tea, fisheries, food-processing; p. (est. 1967) 31,000.
Lennoxtown, t., Stirling, **Scot.**; alum. wks.
Lens, t., Pas-de-Calais dep., **N. France**; industl. ctr. in coal a.; p. (1968) 41,874 (c.), 325,696 (met. a.).
Leoben, t., Styria, **Austria**; lignite mng. ctr.; p. (1961) 36,257.
Leominster, mkt. t., Hereford and Worcs., **Eng.**; 19 km N. of Hereford; once famed for woollen inc.; p. (1971) 7,071.
León, c., central **Mexico**; at *c.* 1,700 m; comm., agr. and mng. ctr. (gold, copper, silver, lead, tin); textiles, leather; p. (1970) 364,990.
León, c., cap. of León dep., N.W. **Nicaragua**; cath., univ.; ctr. for agr. and industl. prods.; footwear, textiles; p. (est. 1970) 90,897.
León, cap. of L. prov., N.W. **Spain**; gothic cath.; craft inds.; p. (1967) 92,814.
Léopoldville. *See* **Kinshasa.**
Lepontine Alps, major gr., **Switzerland–Italy**; alt. over 3,300 m.
Le Puy, t., cap. of Haute Loire dep., **France**; lace, liqueurs; cath. sited on old volcanic plug; tourism; p. (1968) 29,549.
Lérida, t., cap. of L. prov., **Spain**; on R. Segre; 2 caths.; textiles, leather, glass; p. (1967) 75,467.
Lerwick, t., Shetland Is., **Scot.**: on Mainland; fishing; p. (1971) 6,127.
Lesbos. *See* **Lesvos.**
Les Causses. *See* **Causses, Les.**
Leskovac, t., Serbia, **Yugoslavia**; on Morava R.; in economically backward a.; textiles, soap, furniture, tobacco-processing; p. (est. 1965) 40,000.
Les Landes. *See* **Landes, Les.**
Leslie, burgh, Kirkcaldy, **Scot.**; 11 km N. of Kirkcaldy; paper, bleaching; p. (1971) 3,342.
Lesotho (Basutoland), kingdom, southern **Africa**; surrounded by Rep. of S. Africa; at head of Orange R. and enclosed by Drakensberg mtns.; economy mainly agr., especially pastoral farming; exp. livestock, wool, mohair, diamonds; 50 per cent revenue from U.K. grants; inds. underdeveloped; poor communications; cap. Maseru; a. 30,344 km²; p. (est. 1969) 930,000.
Lesser Antilles. *See* **Antilles.**
Lesvos (Lesbos, Mytilene), I., off Turkey, Aegean Sea, belonging to **Greece**; highest point 939 m; agr., antimony, marbles; cap. Mytilene; a. 1,601 km²; p. (1971) 114,504 (dep.).
Leszno, t., Poznan, **W. Poland**; engin., distilling, tobacco; p. (1970) 33,900.
Letchworth (Garden City), t., Herts., **Eng.**; at foot of Chiltern Hills, 3 km N.E. of Hitchin; first garden c., founded by Sir Ebenezer Howard 1903; engin., office equipment; expanded t.; p. (1971) 30,884.
Lethbridge, c., Alberta, **Canada**; in foothills of Rockies; ctr. of lge coal-mng. dist. and of irrigated wheat-growing a.; p. (1971) 40,706.
Le Touquet-Paris Plage, fashionable resort, W. cst. **France**, S. of Canche estuary.
Letterkenny, t., Co. Donegal, **R.o.I.**; on Lough Swilly; tourist ctr.; p. (1966) 4,513.
Leuna, t., Halle, **E. Germany**; 5 km S. of Merseburg; synthetic chemical ind.; oil pipeline from Schwedt; p. (1963) 12,702.
Levant, French and Italian name for E. cst. of Mediterranean.
Leven, burgh, Kirkcaldy, **Scot.**; on N. side of F. of Forth; resort; p. (1971) 9,472.
Leven, L., Perth and Kinross, **Scot.**; ass. with escape of Mary Queen of Scots from Castle I., 1568.
Leverkusen, t., N. Rhine–Westphalia, **W. Germany**; on R. Rhine, N. of Cologne; iron, machin., textiles, chemicals; p. (est. 1969) 110,800.
Levkás or **Santa Maura**, one of Ionian Is., off W. **Greece**; wine, olive oil, currants.
Lewes, co. t., East Sussex, **Eng.**; on R. Ouse at N. entrance to gap through S. Downs; mkt., agr. ctr.; p. (1971) 14,015.
Lewis, I., Outer Hebrides, **Scot.**; fishing, tweeds; ch. t. Stornoway; a. 1,994 km²; p. (1971) 15,174.
Lewisham, inner bor., London, **Eng.**; inc. Deptford; residtl.; industl.; p. (1971) 264,800.
Lewiston, t., Maine, **USA**; power for textile mill supplied by waterfall since early 19th cent.; p. (est. 1969) 40,500.
Lexington, c., Ky., **USA**; in heart of Blue Grass region; univ.; ch. tobacco mkt. and horse-breeding ctr. of USA; p. (1970) 107,944 (c.), 172,927 (met. a.).
Lexington, t., Mass., **USA**; nr. Boston; residtl.; first battle in war of independence 19 Apr. 1775; p. (est. 1969) 34,000.
Leyburn, t., North Yorks., **Eng.**; in lower Wensleydale; mkt.; p. (1971) 5,896 (dist.).
Leyden. *See* **Leiden.**
Leyland, t., Lancs., **Eng.**; 8 km S. of Preston; motor vehicles, rubber; p. (1971) 23,391.
Leyte, one of Visayan Is., central **Philippines**; maize, abaca, rice; Japanese fleet defeated by US in battle of Leyte Gulf 1944; a. 7,213 km²; p. (1970) 1,340,015.
Leyton. *See* **Waltham Forest.**
Lhasa (Lasa), c., cap. of Tibet, **China**; "forbidden" c.; Buddhist ctr., temple, monasteries, shrines; caravan tr. in carpets, silk, lace, gold, tea; pharmaceutical factory, turbine pumps, fertilisers; p. (est. 1970) 175,000.
Lhotse, mtn., Tibet, **China–Nepal**; 4th hgst. mtn. in world; alt. 8,506 m.
Liao-ho, R., Liaoning, N.E. **China**; flows into G. of Liaotung, Yellow Sea; navigable for last 640 km of course; *c.* 1,600 km long.
Liaoning, prov., N.E. **China**; inc. lower course and delta of Liao-ho; part of N.E. China (formerly called Manchuria); maize, millets, soyabeans; lge. mineral reserves of coal and iron ore; cap. Shenyang; a. 150,220 km²; p. (est. 1968) 28,000,000.
Liaotung, peninsula, N.E. **China**; nr. G. of same name.
Liaoyang, c., E. Liaoning prov., N.E. **China**; in fertile valley of Liao-ho; cotton-growing; textile mills; p. (est. 1970) 250,000.
Liao-yuang, c., S.W. Kirin, **China**; lge. coal-mng. ctr.; p. (1953) 120,100.
Liberec, t., **ČSSR**; on R. Neisse; univ.; textiles, chemicals, tr. ctr.; p. (1967) 71,000.
Liberia, rep., W. **Africa**; tropical climate; 90 per cent of p. involved in agr.; few cash crops, inc. rubber and cocoa; rich iron deposits provide main exp.; world's lgst. merchant fleet as result of "flag of convenience"; cap. and ch. pt. Monrovia; a. 99,068 km²; p. (est. 1969) 1,134,000.
Libourne, t., Gironde, **France**; on R. Dordogne, 35 km N.E. of Bordeaux; wine tr.; p. (1968) 22,123.
Libreville, c., cap. of **Gabon**; pt. on G. of Guinea; exp. tropical hardwoods, rubber, cacao; Trans-Gabon rly. project to link L. to Booué to promote timber exploitation; p. (1965) 31,000 (c.); (1967) 57,000 (met. a.).
Libya, rep., N. **Africa**; on Mediterranean cst.; desert conditions prevail; radical attitude towards oil cos., as oil accounts for 99 per cent of exp. earnings and forms basis of new-found wealth; petro-chemical inds.; over half working p. are foreigners; most of p. engaged in subsistence agr.; joint caps. Tripoli (site of govern-

ment deps.), Benghazi; union with Egypt proposed 1973; a. 1,759,537 km²; p. (est. 1969) 1,875,000.

Libyan Desert, part of the Sahara, **Africa**.

Licata, t., Sicily, **Italy**; spt.; sulphur-processing; p. (est. 1968) 40,422.

Lichfield, c., Staffs. **Eng.**; cath.; agr. and lt. inds.; expanded t.; birthplace of Dr. Samuel Johnson; p. (1971) 22,672.

Lickey Hills, gr. of hills, Hereford and Worcs., **Eng.**; 6 km S.W. of Birmingham; reveal anc. rocks underlying younger sediments; rise to 292 m, largely wooded.

Liechtenstein, principality, between Austria and Switzerland; official language German; economy based on sm.-scale inds. and tourism in picturesque Alpine scenery aided by mild climate; wine; cap. Vaduz; a. 161 km²; p. (1969) 21,758; 20 per cent p. in Vaduz.

Liège (Luik), industl. c., E. **Belgium**; on R. Meuse nr. confluence of Ourthe; cath., univ.; conurb. inc. Herstal, Bressoux, Ougrée, Angleur, Grivegnée; metallurgy, armaments, vehicles, chemicals, textiles, glassware, tyres; p. (est. 1969) 148,599 (c.), 445,347 (met. a.).

Liepaja (Libau), c., Latvian SSR, **USSR**; ice-free pt. on Baltic Sea, second to Riga; shipyards, steel-wks., paper mills, chemicals; exp. timber, grain; p. (1969) 88,000.

Liestal, t., cap. of the half-can. Baselland, **Switzerland**; p. (1970) 12,500.

Liffey, R., **R.o.I.**; rises in Wicklow Mtns. and enters Irish Sea at Dublin; water supply for Dublin; inds. along estuary, 80 km long.

Liguria, region, N.W. **Italy**; inc. provs. of Genoa and Porto Maurizio; a. 5,411 km²; p. (1969) 1,873,039.

Ligurian Sea, Mediterranean; N. of Corsica.

Lille, c., cap. of Nord dep., N. **France**; on R. Deûle; mftg., comm. and cultural ctr.; former cap. of Fr. Flanders (1668); textiles (the term lisle is derived from an earlier spelling of the city's name), metallurgy, engin.; univ., art museums; p. (1968) 194,948 (c.), 881,439 (met. a.).

Lilongwe, c., main ctr. of Central Region, **Malawi**; replaced Zomba as cap. 1975; p. (1966) 19,176.

Lima, c., cap. of **Peru**; 13 km from its pt. Callao; dominates comm., industl. and social life of cty.; cath., univ., imposing architecture; seaside subs. Miraflores, Barranco, Chorillos; shanty ts. on outskirts; p. (est. 1970) 2,541,300 (met. a.).

Lima, t., Ohio, **USA**; on Ottawa R.; rly. wks., oil, car bodies, refrigerators; p. (1970) 53,373 (c.), 170,687 (met. a.).

Limassol, t., S. **Cyprus**; spt. on Akrotiri Bay; new artificial harbour; ctr. of admin. dist.; wine, agr.-processing; exp. foodstuffs; tourism; p. (est. 1970) 51,500.

Limavady, t., l. gov. dist., **N. Ireland**; mkt.; linen; p. (1966) 4,811.

Limbach, t., Karl-Marx-Stadt, **E. Germany**; hosiery, textiles, machines; p. (est. 1970) 25,460.

Limbe. *See* **Blantyre-Limbe**.

Limburg, prov., N.E. **Belgium**; bordering Neth.; mainly agr.; coal-mng. in Campine region; cap. Hasselt; a. 2,409 km²; p. (1968) 638,593.

Limburg, prov., S.E. **Neth.**; bordering on Belgium and W. Germany; drained by R. Maas; former coalmng.; new inds. to relieve unemployment; a. 2,191 km²; p. (1968) 985,738.

Limburg-on-Lahn, t., Hesse, **W. Germany**; on R. Lahn; machin., glass, paper; rly. junc.; cath.; p. (est. 1969) 14,708.

Limeira, t., São Paulo, **Brazil**; ctr. of orange cultivation; hats, matches; p. (est. 1970) 71,690.

Limerick, co., Munster, **R.o.I.**; agr., livestock, fishing; a. 3,385 km²; p. (1966) 137,276.

Limerick, C.B., cap. of Limerick, **R.o.I.**; spt. at head of Shannon estuary; bacon, tanning, shipbldg.; p. (1966) 55,885.

Limmat, R., **Switzerland**; trib. of R. Aare; flows through c. of Zürich; 128 km long.

Lim Fjord, shallow strait, Jutland, **Denmark**; connects N. Sea with Kattegat; contains I. of Mors.

Limoges, c., cap. of Haute-Vienne dep., **France**; to N.W. of Central Massif; anc. t., celebrated in middle ages for goldsmith's work, later for enamel ware and porcelain; cath.; p. (1968) 132,935.

Limón, spt., **Costa Rica**; on Caribbean; coffee, bananas; oil refining nearby; p. (est. 1968) 22,555.

Limousin, region and former prov., central **France**; to W. of Auvergne; now divided into deps. Haute-Vienne, Corrèze, Dordogne; plateau, average alt. 300 m, composed of old crystalline rocks; exposed damp climate; infertile, some pastoral agr.; kaolin; ch. t. Limoges.

Limpopo or **Crocodile R.**, **S. Africa**, **Moçambique**, and **Rhodesia**; lower R forms a fertile valley 1,600 km long.

Linares, prov., central **Chile**; thermal springs in Andes; cereals and vineyards in valleys; cap. Linares; a. 9,816 km²; p. (1970) 189,010.

Linares, t., Jaén prov., **Spain**; silver-lead mines; metallurgical inds.; p. (1967) 61,593.

Lincoln, c., C.B., co. t., Lincs., **Eng.**; on R. Witham in gap through Lincoln Edge; impt. Roman t.; cath., cas.; heavy engin., iron foundries, bricks, lime, seed milling, malting; p. (1971) 74,207.

Lincoln, c., cap. of Nebraska, **USA**; univ.; educational ctr.; grain and cattle mkt.; flour mills, agr. machin., cars, chemicals, rubber gds.; p. (1970) 148,092.

Lincoln Edge, limestone ridge, Lincs. and Humberside, **Eng.**; runs N. from Ancaster through Lincoln to Humber; narrow ridge with steep scarp slope to W., broken by R. Witham at Lincoln; iron-ore deposits worked in N. nr. Scunthorpe; sheep, barley; rarely exceeds 90 m alt.

Lincolnshire, non-met. co., **Eng.**; between Humberside non-met. co. and the Wash; fertile soil on low-lying fenland; intensive agr., arable crops, bulbs, market gardening; food-processing; formerly divided into 3 admin. parts: Holland, Kesteven, and Lindsey; a. 5,884 km²; p. (1971) 503,000.

Lincoln Wolds, low plateau, Lincs. and Humberside, **Eng.**; runs N. 72 km from Wash to Humber; chalk covered with glacial deposits; mixed farming, grains, roots, sheep; lge. farm units; scantily populated; rise to approx. 135 m.

Lindau, t., Baden-Württemberg, **W. Germany**; on I. in Bodensee; tourist resort; p. (est. 1967) 25,900.

Lindisfarne or **Holy I.**, off cst. of Northumberland, **Eng.**; connected to mainland by stretch of sand at low tide; abbey founded 635 A.D. as first establishment of Celtic Christianity in Eng.

Lindsey. *See* **Lincolnshire**.

Line Is., Pac. Oc., coral gr. admin. by U.K., except Palmyra, Kingman and Jarvis, which belong to USA; coconuts; airfields, meteorological stas.

Lin-i (formerly **Ichow**), t., Shantung, **China**; at foot of Shantung Highlands.

Linköping, t., S.E. **Sweden**; aero-engin., pianos, furniture; cath.; p. (1968) 78,032.

Linlithgow, burgh, W. Lothian, **Scot.**; distilling, brewing, paper, shoes; birthplace of Mary Queen of Scots; p. (1971) 5,684.

Linnhe, Loch, Lochaber, Argyll and Bute, **Scot.**; 21 m. long; entrance to Caledonian canal.

Linslade. *See* **Leighton Buzzard**.

Linz, c., cap. of Upper **Austria**; pt. on Danube; comm. and industl. ctr. with iron and steel wks.; cath.; p. (est. 1969) 205,808.

Lipa, t., Luzon, **Philippines**; sugar, tobacco, cocoa, maize; processing; p. (est. 1970) 96,500.

Lipari Is. or **Aeolian Is.**, volcanic gr. between Sicily and toe of **Italy**; inc. Stromboli (927 m), Lipari, Vulcano, Salina; olives, grapes, currants, pumice.

Lipetsk, c., **RSFSR**; on Voronezh R.; ctr. of iron-ore mng. a.; engin., steel, ferro-alloys; health resort; p. (1970) 290,000.

Lippe, R., **W. Germany**; trib. of Rhine; paralleled by L. canal; forms N. bdy. of Ruhr industl. dist.; 176 km long.

Lippstadt, t., N. Rhine-Westphalia, **W. Germany**; on R. Lippe; metallurgy, textiles, rly. ctr.; p. (est. 1967) 40,400.

Liri, R., central **Italy**; rises in Alban Hills, flows S.E. to Cassino and then S.W. to G. of Gaeta; valley followed by main road from Rome to Naples; length 168 km.

Lisbon (**Lisboa**), c., cap of **Portugal**; on **R. Tagus**, 14 km from mouth; spt. with fine natural harbour; cas., cath., univ.; admin., comm., and industl. ctr.; expanding inds., airpt.; attracts p. from rural areas; p. (est. 1969) 830,600.

Lisburn, t., l. gov. dist., **N. Ireland**; on R. Lagan, 10 km S.W. of Belfast; tyre valves; p. (est. 1971) 27,405.

Lisieux, t., Calvados dep., **N. France**; historic t., severely damaged in second world war; cath.; Camembert cheese; p. (1968) 25,223.

Liskeard, mkt. t., Cornwall, **Eng.**; on R. Looe at S. edge of Bodmin Moor; p. (1971) 5,255.

Lismore, t., N.S.W., **Australia**; pt. on Richmond R.; dairying, sugar refining, maize, potatoes, textiles, engin.; p. (1972) 20,901.

Lismore, mkt. t., R.D., Waterford, **R.o.I.**; on Blackwater R.; dairy prod.; cas.; p. (1966) 894 (t.).

Listowel, U.D., Kerry, **R.o.I.**; on R. Feale; cas. ruins; p. (1966) 2,822.

Litherland, t., Merseyside, **Eng.**; N. sub. of Liverpool; tanning, rubber-processing, tar-distilling, tin-smelting; p. (1971) 23,670.

Lithuania (Litva SSR), constituent rep., **USSR**; borders Baltic Sea; agr. development on reclaimed marshland; dairy farming, stock-raising, fishing, timber inds., food-processing, ship bldg., textiles, machin.; cap. Vilna; a. 65,201 km^2; p. (1970) 3,129,000.

Litoměřice, t., **ČSSR**; in Bohemia on R. Elbe (Labe); cath.; brewing, agr. ctr.; p. (est. 1968) 18,894.

Little Belt (Lille Bælt), strait, **Denmark**; separates Fyn I. from Jutland; too shallow for lge. ships; road/rly., motorway bridges cross narrow N. section nr. Frederidicia; 48 km long.

Little Bighorn R., Wyo, Mont., **USA**; Custer's last battle on ridge overlooking R. (1876); 144 km long.

Littleborough, t., Gtr. Manchester, **Eng.**; textiles and textile finishing; p. (1971) 11,987.

Littlehampton, t., West Sussex, **Eng.**; on S. cst. at mouth of R. Arun; holiday resort, sm. spt.; p. (1971) 18,621.

Little Lever, t., Gtr. Manchester, **Eng.**; 5 km S.E. of Bolton; residtl. and industl.; p. (1971) 9,124.

Little Rock, c., cap. of Ark., **USA**; N.E. of Hot Springs, on Ark. R. opposite N. Little Rock; comm. and mnf. ctr. in rich cotton and dairy farming a.; bauxite nearby; p. (1970) 128,880 (c.), 315,375 (met. a.).

Littoria. *See* **Latina.**

Liuchow, c., Kwangsi prov., **S. China**; on trib. of Si-kiang; route ctr. and R. pt.; p. (1958) 190,000.

Liverpool, c., spt., Merseyside, **Eng.**; second pt. in Gr. Britain, on N. bank at entrance to Mersey estuary; deep-sea container berths at Seaforth; shipping and ship-repairing; elec. mnfs. and engin., flour milling, sugar refining, seed and rubber processing, cars; cath., univ.; second Mersey tunnel opened 1971; p. (1971) 606,834 (c.), 1,368,630 (met. a.).

Liverpool, t., N.S.W., **Australia**; within met. a. of Sydney; mkt. and processing ctr. for dairy prod.; elec. gds., woollens; p. (1966) 60,552.

Livingston, new t. (1962), W. Lothian, **Scot.**; p. (est. 1974) 22,470.

Livingstone, t., **Zambia**; on Zambesi R. where rly. bridges R.; stands at *c.* 900 m; former cap.; sawmilling ctr.; p. (est. 1967) 41,000.

Livorno (Leghorn), spt., cap. of L. prov., **Italy**; on Ligurian Sea; shipbldg., machin., chemicals, iron and steel wks., oil refining; exp. wine, olive oil, textiles, marble; p. (1969) 173,839.

Lizard, The, C., Cornwall, **Eng.**; S. point of Eng.

Ljubljana, c., cap. of Slovenia, **N.W. Yugoslavia**; on trib. of Sava R.; industl. ctr., local coal, hydroelectric power; route ctr.; airport; univ., mediaeval fortress; ctr. of Slovene nat. movement in 19th cent.; p. (est. 1969) 172,000.

Llanberis, pass, Gwynedd, **N. Wales**; between Snowdon and Clyder Fawr; road carries heavy tourist traffic; summit 356 m; nearby tourist resort of Llanberis.

Llandaff, t., South Glamorgan, **S. Wales**; part of Cardiff; cath.

Llandarcy, v., West Glamorgan, **S. Wales**; on cst. Swansea Bay, Bristol Channel; lge oil refinery; pipeline to Angle Bay, Pembroke.

Llandeilo, mkt. t., Dyfed, **Wales**; in vale of Towy, E. of Carmarthen; cas.; p. (1971) 1,794.

Llandovery, t., Dyfed, **Wales**; on R. Bran, nr. confluence with Towy; mkt. ctr. for rural a.; p. (1971) 1,999.

Llandrindod Wells, t., Powys, **Wales**; medicinal waters; p. (1971) 3,379.

Llandudno, t., Gwynedd, **Wales**; between Gr. Ormes and Little Ormes headlands; resort; p. (1971) 19,009.

Llanelli, Dyfed, **Wales**; pt. on Burry inlet, 18 km. N.W. of Swansea; industl. and comm. ctr.; coal mng., steel, and tinplate wks., mng. machin.; cas.; p. (1971) 26,320.

Llanfairfechan, t., Gwynedd, **Wales**; at foot of Penmaenmawr mtn.; seaside resort; granite quarrying; p. (1971) 3,430.

Llanfyllin, t., Powys, **Wales**; anc. mkt. t.; p. (1971) 1,117.

Llangefni, t., Anglesey, Gwynedd, **Wales**; in ctr. of the I.; mkt. and agr. t.; p. (1971) 3,949.

Llangollen, t., Clwyd, **Wales**; on R. Dee; vale of L., tourist ctr.; annual Eisteddfod; p. (1971) 3,108.

Llanidloes, t., Powys, **Wales**; on R. Severn; surrounded by hills; anc. mkt. house; p. (1971) 2,333.

Llanos, lowland region, **Venezuela** and **Colombia**, **S. America**; drained by R. Orinoco and tribs.; high temperatures throughout year, but rain chiefly in summer; ch. vegetation, coarse grass which withers during dry season (Dec. to May); little developed, some cattle-rearing.

Llanos de Urgel, upland region, Lérida, **N.E. Spain**; semi-arid; formerly steppe-land, now irrigated by R. Segre; vine, olive, maize, tobacco.

Llanrwst, mkt. t., Gwynedd, **Wales**; on R. Conway; tourist ctr.; p. (1971) 2,736.

Llanstephan, v., Dyfed, **Wales**; at mouth of R. Towy; ruins of Norman cas.

Llantrisant, new t., Mid Glamorgan, **S. Wales**; iron-ore quarrying; Royal Mint; p. (1971) 37,087 (dist.).

Llanwrtyd Wells, t., Powys, **Wales**; once a spa; resort; p. (1971) 488.

Lleyn, peninsula, Gwynedd, **N. Wales**; from Snowdonia to Bardsey I.; crystalline rocks form hills in E., otherwise low, undulating; pastoral farming, sheep, cattle; sm. seaside resorts; ch. t. Pwllheli; a. 466 km^2; p. (1971) 15,200 (dist.).

Llwchwr, t., West Glamorgan, **S. Wales**; p. (1971) 26,845.

Llwchwr or **Loughor**, R., **S. Wales**; in lower course forms bdy. between Dyfed and West Glamorgan, empties into Burry inlet.

Loanhead, burgh, Midlothian, **Scot.**; 8 km S.E. of Edinburgh; coal, engin.; p. (1971) 5,963.

Lobito, spt., **Angola**; on Atl. Oc.; 29 km N. of Benguela; fine natural deepwater harbour; rly. terminus; varied exps.; oil-refinery under construction; p. (est. 1969) 97,758.

Locarno, t., **Switzerland**; on L. Maggiore; tourist ctr.; L. treaty 1925; figs, olives, pomegranates; p. (1969) 13,400.

Lochaber, mtnous. l. gov. dist., Highland Reg., **Scot.**; bounded by Loch Linnhe and Loch Leven; inc. Ben Nevis; hydroelec. power; a. 4,465 km^2; p. (1971) 18,920.

Lochalsh. *See* **Kyle of Lochalsh.**

Lochgelly, burgh, Dunfermline l. gov. dist., **Scot.**; nr. Dunfermline; p. (1971), 7,980.

Lochgilphead, co. t., Argyll and Bute, **Scot.**; at head of Loch Gilp, 3 km N. of Ardrishaig; tourist ctr.; p. (1971) 1,184.

Lochmaben, burgh, Annandale and Eskdale, **Scot.**; in Annandale, 11 km N.E. of Dumfries; p. (1971) 1,261.

Lockerbie, burgh, Annandale and Eskdale, **Scot.**; in Annandale, 16 km E. of Dumfries; sheep mkt.; p. (1971) 3,624.

Lockport, t., N.Y., **USA**; on N.Y. st. barge canal, 38 km N.E. of Buffalo; power from Niagara falls supplies paper, metal, and other inds.; p. (1970) 25,399.

Lodi, t., **Italy**; on R. Adda, S.E. of Milan; cheese, majolica ware; cath.; scene of Napoleon's victory over Austrians 1796; p. (est. 1968) 42,757.

Lodore Falls, waterfalls, Cumbria, **Eng.**; in Watendlath beck at foot of Derwentwater.

Łódź, c., cap. of L. prov., **central Poland**; second c. of rep. and ctr. of textile ind.; machin., elec. equipment, chemicals, metals; univ.; cultural ctr.; problems of water-supply; p. (1970) 761,800.

Lofoten Is., storm-swept chain of Is. off N.W. cst.

Norway within Arctic Oc., stretching 240 km; cod and herring fisheries among richest in world.

Loftus, t., Cleveland, **Eng.**; on N.E. flank of Cleveland Hills; p. (1971) 7,706.

Logan, Mount, S.E. Yukon, Canada, E. of Alaska; alt. 6,054 m; highest mtn. in Canada and second highest in N. America.

Logroño, t., N. **Spain**; on Ebro R.; in wine growing a.; industl. and agr. ctr.; p. (1967) 75,157.

Loire, R., **France**; longest in cty., flows from Cevennes mtns. to Atl. Oc. at St. Nazaire; vineyards and many castles in attractive valley; 1,000 km long.

Loire, dep., E. central **France**; in part of the former provs. of Beaujolais and Lyonnais; agr., coal mng., cattle raising; cap. St. Etienne; a. 4,799 km²; p. (1968) 722,383.

Loire-Atlantique, dep., W. **France**; mainly agr., salt-marsh on cst.; inds. at cap. Nantes; a. 6,980 km²; p. (1968) 861,452.

Loiret, dep., N. central **France**; agr., vineyards, distilling, mftg.; cap. Orléans; a. 6,812 km²; p. (1968) 430,629.

Loir-et-Cher, dep., central **France**; contains fertile a. of Beauce; cap. Blois; a. 6,421 km²; p. (1968) 267,896.

Lokeren, industl. t., **Belgium**; between Ghent and Antwerp; textiles, chemicals, tobacco; p. (1968) 26,569.

Lokoja, t., **Nigeria**; at confluence of Rs. Niger and Benue; R. pt.; iron-ore nearby.

Lolland or **Laaland**, Danish I. in Baltic Sea; a. 1,241 km²; agr., forests; ch. ts. Maribo, Nakshov; p. (1965) 81,760.

Lomami, R., central **Zaïre**; trib. of Zaïre R., rich coal-bearing strata at confluence; 1,812 km long.

Lombardy, Plain of, N. **Italy**; extensive lowland flanked by Alps, Apennines, Adriatic Sea; built up by alluvium from R. Po, its tribs. and R. Adige; intensively cultivated rice, maize, flax, clover, lucerne, wheat, apples, dairy cattle; densely populated; many industl. ts., Milan, Novara, Pavia, etc.; length 400 km, width 80–192 km.

Lombok, one of the lesser Sunda Is., **Indonesia**; mtnous. volcanic terrain; Wallace's Line passes between Lombok and Bali; ch. t. Mataram; p. 1,300,000.

Lomé, spt., cap. of **Togo**, W. Africa; on G. of Guinea; deepwater pt.; exp. cacao, cotton, palm prods.; phosphates; p. (1970) 192,745.

Lomond, Loch, Stirling, lgst. loch in **Scot.**; studded with Is., surrounded by hills with Ben Lomond on E. side; a. 70 km².

Lomża, t., Bialystok, **Poland**; on Narew R., metal inds., foodstuffs; p. (1970) 25,500.

London, cap. of UK, **Eng.**; at head of Thames estuary; seat of govt., world ctr. of finance and communication; cultural and artistic ctr.; comprises the City, 12 inner and 20 outer bors.; Port of London one of lgst pts. in world; dockyard system expanding downstream to Tilbury; currently losing p. and inds. to outer met. a.; univs. (London, Brunel, City), caths., many historic bldgs., theatres, museums, galleries, libraries, and parks; p. (1971) 4,234 (City of London), 7,379,014 (met. a.).

London, t., Ont., **Canada**; on R. Thames, 104 km W. of Hamilton; industl. ctr.; univ.; p. (1971) 221,430 (c.), 284,469 (met. a.).

Londonderry, former co.; l. gov. dist., **N. Ireland**; borders R.o.I. and L. Foyle; Sperrin Mtns. in S.; inds. concentrated in L.c.; p. of former co., (est. 1971) 130,296.

Londonderry (or **Derry**), c., l. gov. dist. **N. Ireland**; on left bank of R. Foyle, 6 km upstream from Lough Foyle; shirt mftg.; textiles; acetylene from naphtha; training ctr. for ind.; p. (est. 1971) 51,850.

Londrina, c., Paraná, **Brazil**; industl. and agr. ctr., coffee, maize, cotton, livestock; p. (1970) 156,670.

Long Beach, c., Cal., **USA**; Pac. cst. resort and industl. suburb of Los Angeles met. a.; p. (1970) 346,975.

Longbenton, t., Tyne and Wear, **Eng.**; 5 km N.E. of Newcastle; former coal mng.; expanded t.; p. (1971) 48,970.

Long Eaton, t., Derbys., **Eng.**; on R. Trent, 8 km S. W. of Nottingham; rly. wks., lace mftg., elec. cables, flexible tubing, hosiery; p. (1971) 33,694.

Longford, co., Leinster, **R.o.I.**; peat bogs; dairy farming; co. t. Longford; a. 1,090 km²; p. (1966) 28,943.

Longford, co. t., Longford, **R.o.I.**; cas., cath.; mkt. t.; p. (1966) 3,454.

Long Forties Bank, submarine sandbank, N. Sea; 128 km E. of Aberdeen; valuable fishing-grounds; depth of water, from 45–75 m.

Long I., part of N.Y., **USA**; separated from mainland by East R.; contains Queens and Brooklyn bors. of N.Y. City; mkt. gardening, fisheries, oysters, holiday resorts; a. 4,356 km².

Longreach, t., Queensland, **Australia**; in ctr. of Gr. Australian (artesian) basin; collecting ctr. for cattle and wool; p. (1966) 3,864.

Longridge, t., Lancs., **Eng.**; 10 km N.E. of Preston; nails; p. (1971) 6,507.

Longview, t., Texas, **USA**; oil, chemicals, plastics; p. (est. 1969) 48,000.

Longwy, t., Meurthe-et-Moselle dep., N.E. **France**; on Belgian–Luxembourg frontier; upper part fortfd.; lower part industl. with iron and steel ind.; p. (1968) 21,087.

Lons-le-Saunier, cap. of Jura dep., E. **France**; saline springs; agr. ctr.; p. (1968) 18,769.

Looe, t., Cornwall, **Eng.**; on Looe estuary; holiday resort; p. (1971) 4,051.

Lopburi, t., **Thailand**; ctr. of haematite iron deposits; former cap.

Lop Nor, marsh, Sinkiang, W. **China**; in Tarim Basin at foot of Altyn Tagh; ctr. of inland drainage, receives water from R. Tarim; atomic testing grounds.

Lorain, t., Ohio, **USA**; on L. Erie; shipbldg., steelwks., fisheries; p. (1970) 76,733 (c.), 255,612 (met. a.).

Lorca, t., Murcia, **Spain**; agr. prod., woollens, chemicals; bishop's palace; p. (1967) 61,445.

Lord Howe I., forested volcanic I., S. Pac. Oc., 698 km N.E. of Sydney; palm seed ind.; admin. by N.S.W.

Lorient, spt., Morbihan dep., N.W. **France**; on Atl.; naval shipyard, fishing harbour; p. (1968) 68,960.

Lorraine, region and former prov., N.E. **France**; inc. deps. Moselle, Meurthe-et-Moselle, Meuse, and Vosges; ch. t. Nancy; rich iron-ore deposits; impt. but declining industl. a.; mkt. gardening, vineyards; with Alsace long disputed between Germany and France.

Los Alamos, t., N.M., **USA**; site of research for first atomic bomb; p. (1970) 11,310.

Los Angeles, c., S. Cal., **USA**; booming modern c. ("the city of angels"), busiest pt. in Cal.; fine harbour; one of world's lgst. urban areas; miles of freeway (2,400 km. planned by 1980); many prosperous inds., inc. aircraft, missiles, chemicals, machin., electronic equipment, food-processing, oil refining; film ctr.; p. (1970) 2,781,829 (c.), 6,974,103 (met. a.).

Lossiemouth, burgh, Moray, **Scot.**; on Moray F., 8 km N. of Elgin; fishing; p. (1971) 5,849.

Lot, dep., S.W. **France**; livestock, wine, cereals, coal, iron; a. 5,227 km²; cap. Cahors; p. (1968) 151,198.

Lot, R., S. **France**; trib. of Garonne R.; 435 km long.

Lota, pt., **Chile**; coal-mng. ctr.; ceramics, copper smelting; p. (est. 1966) 57,773.

Lot-et-Garonne, dep., S.W. **France**; agr. (cereals, vines, fruit); cap. Agen; a. 5,385 km²; p. (1968) 290,592.

Lothian Region, l. gov. reg., central **Scot.**; borders F. of Forth, and inc. a. around Edinburgh; mainly industl.; a. 1,753 km²; p. (1971) 741,275.

Lötschental, picturesque valley, Valais, **Switzerland**; ch. v. Kippel.

Loughborough, t., Leics., **Eng.**; on R. Soar 16 km N. of Leicester; engin., elec. gds., chemicals, textiles; univ.; former hosiery t.; bell foundry; p. (1971) 45,863.

Loughrea, mkt. t., Galway, **R.o.I.**; cotton mill; p. (1966) 3,001.

Louisiana, southern st., **USA**; leading producer of rice, sugarcane, sweet potatoes, also cotton, maize, tobacco, oil, natural gas, lumber; cap. Baton Rouge; New Orleans major pt.; a. 125,675 km²; p. (1970) 3,564,310.

Louisville, c., Ky., **USA**; on Ohio R.; univ.; lgst. tobacco mkt. in world; chemicals, paints, cars, machin., elec. gds., synthetic rubber; p. (1970) 356,982 (c.), 819,057 (met. a.).

Lourdes, t., **France**; on R. Pau; Catholic pilgrim ctr.; slate, marble; p. (1968) 18,310.
Lourenço Marques. *See* **Maputo.**
Louth, t., Lincs., **Eng.**; on E. edge of Lincoln Wolds; abbey ruins; cattle mkt., farm implements, rope mkg., lime, malting, canning; p. (1971) 11,746.
Louth, maritime co., Leinster, **R.o.I.**; mtns., bog and barren land; salmon fishing; cap. Dundalk; a. 818 km^2; p. (1966) 69,162.
Louvain (Leuven), c., Brabant prov., **Belgium**; on R. Dyle; univ. (Erasmus taught here); brewing ctr., bell foundries; p. (1968) 32,224.
Low Archipelago. *See* **Tuamotu Is.**
Low Countries, name applied to Belgium and the Neth.
Lowell, c., Mass., **USA**; at junc. of Merrimac and Concord Rs.; 48 km N. of Boston; textiles, machin., chemicals, carpets; birthplace of Whistler; p. (1970) 92,929 (c.), 101,048 (met. a.).
Lower California (Baja California), peninsula, N.W. **Mexico**; separating G. of Cal. and Pac. Oc.; isolated, arid; divided into 2 sts., Baja California (cap. Tijuana), and Baja California, Territorio Sur (cap. La Paz); a. 143,963 km^2; p. (1969) 1,150,000.
Lower Saxony (Nieder Sachsen), *Land*, **W. Germany**; inc. Lüneburg heath and Harz mtns.; cap. Hanover; a. 47,205 km^2; p. (1968) 7,039,000.
Lowestoft, fish. pt., Suffolk, **Eng.**; on E. Anglian cst. 14 km S. of Gr. Yarmouth; holiday resort, nr. Broads; food and fish processing plants; base for N. Sea gas; p. (1971) 51,182.
Lowther Hills, mtns., between Strathclyde and Dumfries and Galloway Regs., **Scot.**; hgst. point 733 m.
Loyalty Is., S. **Pac. Oc.**; included in Fr. administration of New Caledonia; copra; lgst. Is., Maré, Lifou, Uvéa; a. *c.* 2,100 km^2.
Loyang, c., Honan prov., **China**; industl.; ball bearing and mng. machin.; lge. car and tractor plant, oil refinery, textiles; p. (est. 1970) 750,000.
Lozère, dep., S.E. **France**; traversed by Cevennes mtns.; cap. Mende; a. 5,170 km^2; p. (1968) 77,258.
Lualaba, R., **Zaïre**, central **Africa**; rises nr. Lubumbashi in Shaba prov., flows N. circa 800 km to Kikondja, where joined by R. Lufira to form R. Zaïre; name also applied to main stream of R. Zaïre as far downstream as Ponthierville.
Luanda, c., cap. of **Angola**; pt. on Atl. Oc.; exp. coffee, cotton, palm prod.; industl. ctr.; foodstuffs, tobacco, clothing, plastics; oil refining; hydroelectric power; p. (est. 1971) 346,763.
Luang Prabang, c., N.W. **Laos**; at confluence of Mekong and Kahn Rs.; rubber, rice, teak; former royal cap.; p. (est. 1970) 25,000.
Lubbock, c., N.W. Texas, **USA**; on Double Mountain fork of Brazos R.; ctr. of cotton-growing a.; p. (1970) 146,379 (c.), 175,757 (met. a.).
Lübeck, c., pt. of Schleswig-Holstein, **W. Germany**; on Baltic Sea at mouth of Trave R.; cath.; shipbldg., machin., chemicals, textiles, iron, foodstuffs; birthplace of Thomas Mann; p. (est. 1969) 242,900.
Lublin, c., cap. of L. prov., E. **Poland**; motor vehicle and elec. engin.; agr. tr. and processing; cultural ctr., univ.; cas.; p. (1970) 235,900.
Lubumbashi (Elisabethville), t., Shaba, **Zaïre**; copper-mng. ctr.; p. (est. 1972) 357,369 (met. a.).
Luce Bay, Wigtown, **Scot.**; enclosed by Mull of Galloway.
Lucca, c., cap. of L. prov., Tuscany, **Italy**; cath., churches, palaces; noted for olive oil, pasta, wine; silk, cotton, jute, tobacco inds.; p. (1969) 91,708.
Lucena, t., Córdoba, **Spain**; olive oil, ceramics, gilt metals, wine; p. (1970) 27,920.
Lucenec, t., **ČSSR**; on Hungarian border; magnesite, textiles, sawmilling; p. (est. 1968) 20,156.
Lucerne (Luzern), can., **Switzerland**; agr., pastoral, vineyards; oil refinery projected at Schötz/Ettiswil; cap. Lucerne; a. 1,492 km^2; p. (est. 1969) 284,000.
Lucerne (Luzern), c., cap. of L. can., **Switzerland**; at N.W. end of L. Lucerne; aluminium gds., sewing machin.; tourist ctr.; p. (1969) 73,000 (c.), 148,500 (met. a.).
Lucerne, L., **Switzerland**; also known as L. of the Four Cantons; length 37 km; a. 70 km^2.
Luchon or Bagnères-de-Luchon, resort in Fr. Pyrenees, Haute-Garonne dep., S. **France**; warm sulphur springs; winter sports ctr.
Luchow (Luzhou), c., Szechwan prov., **China**; coal, iron, kaolin; synthetic ammonia plant; p. (est. 1970) 225,000.
Luckenwalde, t., **E. Germany**; on R. Nuthe; textiles, footwear, machin., wood and metals, chemicals; p. (est. 1970) 28 984.
Lucknow, c., cap. of Uttar Pradesh st., N. **India**; on R. Gumti (trib. of Ganges); educational and cultural ctr. with textile inds.; rly. ctr.; scene of 1857 mutiny; p. (1971) 749,239 (c.), 813,982 (met. a.).
Lüdenscheid, t., N. Rhine-Westphalia, **W. Germany**; metal mnfs., domestic hardware; supplied structures for first Zeppelins; p. (est. 1967) 57,500.
Lüderitz, t., **South-West Africa**; rly. pt. on desert cst.; diamonds, fishing; p. (1960) 3,604.
Ludhiana, t., Punjab st., N.W. **India**; S. of Sutlej R.; industl. ctr.; hosiery, knitwear; p. (1971) 397,850 (t.), 401,176 (met. a.).
Ludlow, t., Salop, **Eng.**; agr. mkt.; agr. engin. cas.; p. (1971) 23,481 (dist.).
Ludwigsburg, t., Baden-Württemberg, **W. Germany**; N. of Stuttgart; cas ; textiles, foodstuffs, machin., toys; p. (est. 1969) 78,812.
Ludwigshafen, t., Rhine-Palatinate, **W. Germany**; on R. Rhine, opposite Mannheim; chemicals, marine diesel engines, metallurgy, glass; R. pt. and rly. junc.; oil pipeline from Rotterdam under construction; p. (est. 1969) 174,000.
Lugano, t., Ticino can., **Switzerland**; on L. Lugano; tourist resort; p. (est. 1968) 22,500.
Lugano, L., lies at S. foot of Alps between Switzerland and **Italy**; attractive scenery, tourism; a. 49 km^2.
Lugansk (Voroshilovgrad), industl. t., Ukrainian SSR, **USSR**; S. of R. Donets in Donbas region; impt. rly. engin. factories; textiles; p. (1970) 382,000.
Lugnaquilia, mtn., loftiest summit in Wicklow, **R.o.I.**, 927 m.
Lugo, c., cap. of L. prov., N.W. **Spain**; in Galicia, on Miño R.; in fertile agr. a.; cath.; p. (1967) 67,918.
Lukuga, intermittent outlet of L. Tanganyika, **Zaïre**, linking with R. Zaïre.
Luleå, spt., N. **Sweden**, cap. of Norrbotten co.; on Lule R. at head of G. of Bothnia; iron ore; smelting plant, engin.; p. (1968) 36,296.
Luluabourg. *See* **Kananga.**
Lulworth Cove, sm. inlet, Dorset, **Eng.**; formed by sea breaching limestone cliffs and eroding clay behind; tourism.
Lund, t., S. **Sweden**; 16 km N.E. of Malmö; 11th cent. Romanesque cath.; univ.; publishing ctr.; p. (1968) 50,669.
Lundy I., Bristol Channel, N. Devon, **Eng.**; 19 km N.W. of Hartland Point; wildlife sanctuary; about 5 km long and 1 km wide.
Lune, R., Cumbria, **Eng.**; flows 72 km to Irish Sea; attractive valley.
Lüneburg, t., Lower Saxony, **W. Germany**; on Ilmenau R., S.E. of Hamburg; rly. junc., R. pt.; iron wks., chemicals; dates from 8th cent.; p. (est. 1967) 60,300.
Lüneburg Heath, Lower Saxony, **W. Germany**; lies to S. of Lüneburg; glacial outwash plain of sands and gravels; heather, scrub; some agr. but infertile acid soils.
Lünen, t., N. Rhine-Westphalia, **W. Germany**; in Ruhr conurb.; coal, metallurgy, glass, wood; R. pt. and rly. ctr.; p. (est. 1967) 71,000.
Lunéville, t., Meurthe-et-Moselle dep., N.E. **France**; in Lorraine, on R. Meurthe; 18th cent château; p. (1968) 25,367.
Lungi, t., **Sierra Leone**, W. **Africa**; nr. Freetown; only civil airport in st.
Lupata Gorge, **Moçambique**, E. **Africa**; narrow pass occupied by R. Zambesi.
Lurgan, t., Craigavon, **N. Ireland**; textiles, tobacco mftg.; merging with Portadown to form new c. of Craigavon; p. (est. 1971) 24,055.

Lusaka, c., cap. of **Zambia**; comm. and admin. ctr.; at junc. of routes to Tanzania and Malawi; motor assembly, footwear, metal prods., clothing; p. (est. 1972) 347,900 (met. a.).

Luta, special mun., S. Liaoning prov., **China**; comprising Port Arthur Naval Base District and the pts. of Port Arthur and Talien (Dairen); chemicals, machin., shipbldg., textiles; p. (est. 1970) 4,000,000.

Luton, t., Beds., **Eng.**; in Chiltern Hills nr. source of R. Lea; motor vehicles, engin., hat mkg., aircraft, gear instruments, chemicals; expanded t.; p. (1971) 161,178.

Lutong, main oil pt. of Sarawak, **E. Malaysia**; oil refining.

Lutsk, c., Ukrainian SSR, **USSR**; pt. on Styr R.; one of oldest ts. in Volhynia; coal mng., machin.; architectural monuments; p. (1968) 94,000.

Luxembourg, prov., S.E. **Belgium**; on Fr. border; wooded and hilly; a. 2,784 km²; cap. Arlon; p. (1968) 219,368.

Luxembourg, grand duchy, **W. Europe**; lies between Belgium, W. Germany, and France; divided into 12 admin. cans.; official language French though German frequently used; well wooded, most of a. over 300 m; economic prosperity based upon iron and steel inds. and lge. deposits of iron-ore; agr. and cattle raising impt.; sm. size of home market makes L. keen protagonist of European economic unity and cap. of L. contains many European organisations; tourist ind. based upon scenery and cas. ts.; a. 2,587 km²; p. (est. 1969) 338,500.

Luxembourg, c., cap. of grand duchy of **Luxembourg**; historic t., perched above valleys of Alzette and Petrusse Rs.; cath.; seat of European Court of Justice; p. (est. 1969) 77,463.

Luxor, v., Upper **Egypt**; on E. bank of Nile; site of Thebes; tomb of Tutankhamun; p. (est. 1970) 84,600.

Luzon, I., lgst and most N. of **Philippines**; mtn. ranges; fertile Cagayan valley; rice, sugar cane, cotton, coffee, hemp, tobacco; mineral deposits; cap. Manila; a. 104,688 km²; p. (1970) 16,669,724.

L'vov, c., Ukrainian SSR, **USSR**; founded 13th cent.; univ., caths.; major industl. ctr.; petroleum refining; natural gas nearby; p. (1970) 553,000.

Lyalpur, t., W. Punjab, **Pakistan**; univ.; cotton, chemicals, fertilisers; p. (est. 1969) 854,000.

Lydd, Kent, **Eng.**; anc. t. on Romney marsh, at edge of Dungeness shingle; name given to explosive lyddite mnf. here; airport; p. (1971) 4,301.

Lydda, c., **Israel**, S.E. of Tel-Aviv; major airport; mentioned in the Bible, and reputed birthplace of St. George; p. (est. 1967) 26,100.

Lydney, t., Gloucs., **Eng.**; in Forest of Dean; spt. on Severn estuary; timber imports; new lt. inds.; p. (1971) 14,447 (dist.).

Lyme Regis, spt., Dorset, **Eng.**; on bdy. between Devon and Dorset; holiday resort; p. (1971) 3,394.

Lymington, t., Hants., **Eng.**; on the Solent; ferry to I. of Wight; abbey; p. (1971) 35,644.

Lymm, t., Cheshire, **Eng.**; 8 km W. of Altrincham; mainly residtl.; p. (1971) 10,458.

Lynchburg, c., Va., **USA**; on James R. in foothills of Appalachians; tobacco ctr.; p. (1970) 53,134 (c.), 121,832 (met. a.).

Lyndhurst, v., Hants, **Eng.**; recognised as cap. of New Forest; tourism.

Lynemouth, nr. Blyth, Northumberland, **Eng.**; aluminium smelter.

Lynn, industl. c., Mass., **USA**; on Mass. Bay; footwear, elec. appliances; Mary Baker Eddy lived here; p. (est. 1969) 90,500.

Lynton, t., N. Devon, **Eng.**; 27 km W. of Minehead on Bristol Channel; tourist ctr. for Exmoor; sm. harbour of Lynmouth 130 m below; devastating flood of R. Lyn 1952; p. (1971) 1,981.

Lyons, c., cap. of Rhône dep., **France**; at confluence of Rs. Saône and Rhône; silk, rayon, chemicals, engin., heavy lorries; oil refinery nearby; univ.; world ctr. for cancer research; p. (1968) 527,800 (c.), 1,074,823 (met. a.).

Lytham St. Annes, t., N. Lancs., **Eng.**; on N. cst. of Ribble estuary, 6 km S. of Blackpool holiday ctr.; p. (1971) 40,089.

Lyttleton, spt., S.I., **N.Z.**, on N. cst. of Banks peninsula; ch. pt. of Canterbury plain; p. (1971) 3,277.

M

Ma'an, t., S. **Jordan**, terminus of rly. through Amman to Beirut; Hijaz rail line to Medina; p. (1961) 6,899.

Maas, R., Dutch name for the R. Meuse after it has entered the Neth.

Maastricht, t., cap. of Limburg prov., **Neth.**; on R. Maas; pottery, glass, textiles, brewing; p. (1968) 94,986.

Mablethorpe and Sutton, t., Lincs., **Eng.**; holiday resort; p. (1971) 6,156.

Macao, Portuguese col., S.E. China; increased indep. since 1975; gambling, tourism, recreation for Hong Kong; new deep water port.; oldest European col. in Far East (1557); a. 16 km²; p. (est. 1968) 250,000.

Macapá, c., cap. of Amapá st., **Brazil**; at mouth of R. Amazon; rubber, cattle tr.; p. (est. 1968) 74,464.

MacArthur (**Ormoc**), t., W. Leyte, **Philippines**; pt. and agr. ctr., exp. hemp, rice; p. (est. 1970) 85,900.

Macclesfield, t., Cheshire, **Eng.**; at foot of Pennines, 16 km S. of Stockport; on R. Bollin; mkt., textiles, clothing, paper prods., engin.; expanded t.; p. (1971) 44,240.

Macdonald Is., terr. of Australia, **Antarctica**.

Macdonnell Range, mtns., N.T., **Australia**; highest part of desert tableland, centrally situated within the continent; some gold and mica mines, but development hampered by aridity and isolation; highest alt. 1,367 m.

Macduff, spt., burgh, Banff and Buchan, **Scot.**; 3 km E. of Banff; fishing; p. (1971) 3,709.

Macedonia, region of Baltic peninsula, covering parts of Greece, Yugoslavia, and Bulgaria.

Macedonia, dist., **Greece**; mtnous.; cereals, tobacco; chromium; cap. and pt. Salonika; a. 33,945 km²; p. (1971) 1,883,156.

Macedonia, constituent rep., **Yugoslavia**; agr., chromium; cap. Skopje; a. 27,436 km²; p. (1971) 1,647,104.

Maceió, spt., cap. of Alagôas st., **Brazil**; cotton, sugar, tobacco, soap, sawmills, distilleries; p. (1970) 242,867.

Macerata, t., cap. of M. prov., **Italy**; cath., univ.; terracotta, glass, chemicals; p. (1969) 42,909.

Macgillicuddy's Reeks, mtns., Kerry, **R.o.I.**; highest peak, Carrantuohill, 1,041 m.

Machala, t., Tibet, China; hgst. coalmine in world.

Machynlleth, t., Powys, **Wales**; on R. Dovey; clothing; tourism; p. (1971) 1,766.

Macintyre, R., N.S.W., **Australia**; forms border between Queensland and N.S.W.; trib. of R. Darling; 560 km long.

Mackay, spt., Queensland, **Australia**; on R. Pioneer; sugar, dairying, banana ctr.; p. (1966) 24,566.

Mackenzie, R., N.W. Terr., **Canada**; lgst in N. America; rises in Rocky mtns. as Athabaska, flows into Athabaska L., leaves as Slave R., thence into Gr. Slave L., below which it is known as Mackenzie R., across arctic plains to Beaufort Sea; 4,000 km long.

Mackenzie Mtns., N.W. Terr., Canada; range of Rockies, still much unexplored; game preserve; max. alt. 2,760 m.

Mâcon, t., cap. of Saône-et-Loire dep., **France**; on R. Saône; Burgundy wines; p. (1968) 35,264.

Macon, c., Ga., **USA**; on Ocmulgee R.; industl. and shipping ctr. for agr. a., cotton, livestock; cotton mftg.; p. (1970) 118,764 (c.), 201,108 (met. a.).

Macquarie, I., Australian I., S. Pac.; 1,440 km S.E. of Tasmania; 34 km long, 3 km wide; meteorological and research base.

Macquarie, R., N.S.W., **Australia**; trib. of R. Darling; 960 km long.

Macroom, t., Cork, **R.o.I.**; on R. Sullane; agr. fishing; p. (1966) 2,224.

Madagascar. *See* **Malagasy Republic**.

Madang, t. and dist., **Papua New Guinea**; entrepôt pt. on N. cst.; international airpt.; p. of dist. (1966) 150,306.

Madeira, R., **Brazil**; trib. of Amazon; with Mamoré R., *c.* 3,200 km long.

Madeira Is., volcanic archipelago, Atl. Oc., part of met. Portugal; separatist moves; wine, sugar, fruits; tourism; cap. Funchal on Madeira I., lgst. of gr.; a. 790 km²; p. (est. 1970) 268,700.

Madhya Pradesh, st., **India**; absorbed sts. Bhopal, Vindhya Pradesh, Madhya Bharat, 1956; rice, jute, pulses, oilseeds, cotton; forests; manganese, coal, marble, limestone; cotton textile mftg.; cap. Bhopal; a. 443,452 km²; p. (1971) 41,449,729.

Madinat ash Sha'b (Al Ittihad), cap. of Democratic Rep. of Yemen; N.W. of Aden.

Madison, c., cap. of Wis., **USA**; educational and admin. ctr.; univ.; mnfs. agr. tools, footwear; p. (1970) 170,073 (c.), 287,501 (met. a.).

Madiun, t., Java, **Indonesia**; agr. and comm. ctr.; engin.; p. (1971) 136,147.

Madras, c., cap. of Tamil Nadu st., **India**; spt. on Bay of Bengal, on Coromandel cst.; cath., univ.; comm. and mftg. ctr.; textile mills, tanneries, potteries, chemical plants; oil refinery projected; p. (1971) 2,469,449 (c.), 3,169,930 (met. a.).

Madras. *See* **Tamil Nadu**.

Madre de Dios, R., **Bolivia**; trib. of R. Madeira; rises in Peru; 960 km long.

Madrid, c., cap. of **Spain**; and of M. prov., on Manzanares R.; stands at 665 m (highest cap. in Europe) in vast open plain; although remote with relatively few inds. is ctr. of Spanish admin. and communications; univ., cath., Prado gallery; printing, publishing; p. (1968) 2,850,631.

Madura, I., **Indonesia**; off N.E. Java; dry climate, limestone soils; arable and pastoral agr.; salt; a. 4,584 km²; p. *c.* 2,000,000.

Madurai, t., Tamil Nadu, **India**; univ.; impt. textile ctr.; p. (1971) 549,114 (t.), 711,501 (met. a.).

Maebashi, c., central Honshu, **Japan**; N.W. Kanto plain; silk textile ctr.; p. (est. 1971) 237,000.

Maelstrom, tidewater whirlpool, in Lofoten Is., **Norway**.

Maentwrog, v., Gwynedd, **N. Wales**; in Vale of Ffestiniog, 3 km E. of Ffestiniog; ch. hydro-electric power sta. in N. Wales.

Maesteg, t., Mid Glamorgan, **Wales**; dormitory t. for steel wks. at Pt. Talbot; coal mng., cosmetics; p. (1971) 20,970.

Mafeking, t., N.E. Cape Prov., **S. Africa**; famous siege at outbreak of Boer War 1899–1900; p. (est. 1967) 6,200.

Magadan, spt., **RSFSR**; on N. side of Sea of Okhotsk; marine engin.; fishing; p. (1970) 92,000.

Magadi, L., **Kenya**; in Gr. Rift valley; carbonate of soda extracted.

Magdalena, R., **Colombia**; forms basis of inland navigation system, opening up interior; 1,600 km long.

Magdeburg, c., Magdeburg, **E. Germany**; on R. Elbe; cath.; beet-sugar ctr., sugar-refineries; chemicals, steel, mng. machin., heavy engin.; route ctr. and lge. inland pt.; p. (est. 1969) 269,031.

Magelang, t., Java, **Indonesia**; tr. ctr.; tannery; p. (1971) 110,308.

Magellan, strait, between Tierra del Fuego and Chile, separates Atl. and Pac. Ocs.

Maggiore, L., **N. Italy–Switzerland**; a. 212 km²; contains Borromean Is.; tourist resort.

Magherafelt, l. gov. dist., centred on t. of M., **N. Ireland**; agr. a. bordering L. Neagh.

Maghreb, collective name given to Arabic-speaking countries bordering Mediterranean in **N. Africa**, inc. Algeria, Morocco and Tunisia.

Magnet Mtn., S. Urals, **RSFSR**; very rich deposit of magnetite iron ore; smelted at Magnitogorsk, and in Kuzbas region.

Magnitogorsk, c., **RSFSR**; in S. Urals, on R. Ural; sited on magnetite deposits; metallurgical ctr.; oil pipeline from Shkapovo in Bashkiria; p. (1970) 364,000.

Mahalla El Kubra, t., Lower **Egypt**; cotton textile ctr.; p. (1966) 225,700.

Mahanadi, R., **India**; flows from Orissa to Bay of Bengal; forms extensive delta; sugar and rice growing; 832 km long.

Maharashtra, st., W. **India**; on Arabian Sea; ch. ts. Bombay (cap.), Poona, Nagpur; fertile lava soils; impt. cotton-growing dist. of Deccan; a. 307,477 km²; p. (1971) 50,295,081.

Mahé, former Fr. prov., S. **India**; united with India 1954; cap. Mahé.

Mahon, spt., cap. of Minorca, **Balearic Is., Spain**.

Maidenhead, t., Berks., **Eng.**; on R. Thames, 14 km above Windsor; residtl.; p. (1971) 45,306.

Maidens, The, gr. of dangerous rocks off Larne cst. **N. Ireland**.

Maidstone, co.t., Kent, **Eng.**; on R. Medway; regional ctr.; brewing, paper, agr. tools, confectionery, timber inds.; p. (1971) 70,918.

Maiduguri, t., **Nigeria**; cap. Bornu st.; on rly. from Bornu; mkt.; p. (est. 1971) 169,180.

Maikop, c., cap. of Adygei aut. oblast, Krasnodar terr., **RSFSR**; oilfields nearby; oil-refineries, woodwkg., food-processing; p. (1970) 111,600.

Main, R., **W. Germany**; joins Rhine opposite Mainz; linked with Danube via Ludwig canal; 486 km long.

Main Range, central mtns. of **W. Malaysia**; rise to over 2,100 m.

Maine, st., New England, **USA**; mtnous., with much forest; potatoes, paper pulp, metals, woollens, shoes, processed foods; cap. Augusta; ch. spt. Portland; a. 86,027 km²; p. (1970) 977,260.

Maine-et-Loire, dep., **France**; agr., vineyards; cap. Angers; a. 7,280 km²; p. (1968) 584,709.

Mainland. (1) I., lgst of Shetlands, **Scot.** (2) I., lgst of Orkneys, *see* **Pomona**.

Mainz, c., cap. of Rhineland-Palatinate, **W. Germany**; at confluence of Rs. Rhine and Main; R. pt.; cath., univ., cas.; cement, engin., optical glass, food-processing; p. (est. 1969) 174,100.

Maisons-Alfort, t., **France**; S.E. sub. of Paris; p. (1968) 53,761.

Maitland, t., N.S.W., **Australia**; on R. Hunter, nr. Newcastle; agr., pastoral ctr., coal mng., textiles; p. (1972) 24,530.

Majes, R., S. **Peru**; valley a. site of projected irrigation scheme; 240 km long.

Majorca (Mallorca), lgst. of Balearic Is., **Spain**; major tourist ctr.; ch. t. and pt. Palma; a. 3,639 km²; p. (1970) 460,030.

Majunga, t., **Malagasy Rep.**; second t. and pt.; meat conserves, sacks, cement; p. (est. 1970) 53,993.

Makalu, mtn., **Nepal** and Tibet, **China**; fifth hgst. mtn. in world; part of Himalayas; alt. 8,486 m.

Makasar. *See* **Ujung Pandang**.

Makasar, strait, **Indonesia**; separates Kalimantan from Sulawesi; 384 km wide.

Makeyevka, c., Ukrainian SSR, **USSR**; in Donets basin; metallurgical and coal-mng. ctr.; p. (1970) 393,000 (c.), 511,000 (met. a.).

Makhachkala, c., cap. of Dagestan ASSR, **RSFSR**; pt. on Caspian Sea; comm. and industl. ctr.; oil refineries linked by pipeline to Grozny fields; p. (1970) 186,000.

Makó, t., **Hungary**; on Maros R., nr. Romanian bdy.; comm. and agr. ctr.; p. (1966) 29,600.

Makran, dist., **Pakistan** and **Iran**; coastal dist.; lowland route between India and Middle E.

Makurdi, t., **Nigeria**, W. Africa; on R. Benue; mkt. for palm prod., groundnuts; rly. bridge across R. Benue.

Makwar, v., **Sudan**, N.E. Africa; on Blue Nile; site of Sennar Dam.

Malabar Coast, **India**; name applied to W. cst. of India from Goa to southern tip of peninsula at C. Comorin; sand dunes backed by lagoons; coastlands intensively cultivated, rice, spices, rubber, coconuts; ch. pt. Cochin.

Malabo (Santa Isabel), cap. of **Equatorial Guinea**; on Marcias Nguema I.; ch. pt. for I., exp. cacao; comm. and financial ctr.; p. (est. 1965) 37,152.

Malacca, st., S.W. **W. Malaysia**; originally part of Brit. Straits Settlements (*q.v.*); cap. M.; a. 1,658 km²; p. (1970) 403,722.

Malacca, strait, separates Sumatra, **Indonesia**, from **W. Malaysia**; 38 km wide at narrowest point; international routeway but attempts by Malaysia and Indonesia to claim it as territorial water.

Maladetta, with Pic d'Anéto, highest point in Pyrenees, **Spain**; alt. 3,408 m.

Malaga, c., cap. of Malaga prov., **Spain**; in Andalusia on Bay of M.; impt. spt.; olive oil, wine, fruit; oil pipeline from Puertollano refinery; winter resort; cath., citadel; birthplace of Picasso; p. (1968) 319,235.

Malagasy Republic (Madagascar), I. off Moçambique; former Fr. col.; distinctive evolution of flora and fauna; p. engaged in agr.; rice staple food, coffee ch. exp.; inds. based on agr.-processing; many minerals; exp. graphite, and petroleum from new refinery at ch. pt. of Tamatave; cap. Tananarive; a. 590,002 km²; p. (est. 1969) 6,600,000.

Malakoff, t. S.W. sub. of Paris, Hauts-de-Seine, France; residtl. and industl.; p. (1968) 36,297.

Malang, t., Java, **Indonesia**; ctr. of fertile agr. basin; p. (1971) 422,428.

Mälar, L., S.E. **Sweden**; connected with Baltic by Södertelge canal; 1,260 Is.; length 128 km; a. 1,235 km².

Malatya, c., cap. of M. prov., central **Turkey**; at foot of Taurus mtns.; ctr. of rich agr. a.; fruit, opium; p. (1965) 104,428 (c.), 174,472 (met. a.).

Malawi, rep., Central **Africa**; L. Malawi to S. and E.; tropical climate modified by alt.; few natural resources; economy based on agr.; lge. prod. of tung oil; exp. tobacco and tea; new cap. at Lilongwe (old cap. Zomba): a. 117,614 km²; p. (est. 1970) 4,530,000.

Malawi, L., central **Africa**; southward extension of the Gr. Rift valley; *c.* 450 m a.s.l.; 560 km by 64 km; drains by R. Shire into R. Zambesi.

Malaya. *See* **Malaysia, West.**

Malay Archipelago, lge. gr. of Is. extending 7,680 km from Nicobar Is. in Bay of Bengal to Solomon Is. in Pac.; inc. Sumatra, Java, Kalimantan, Sulawesi, Philippines, New Guinea, Bismarck archipelago.

Malaysia, East, part of **Fed. of Malaysia**; inc. Sarawak and Sabah (formerly Brit. N. Borneo); less developed than W. Malaysia; p. concentrated on cst.; hill tribes engaged in hunting in interior; oil major exp., exploration off cst.; separated from W. Malaysia by S. China Sea; a. 200,971 km²; p. (1698) 1,582,000.

Malaysia, Federation of, indep. federation (1963), S.E. **Asia**; member of Brit. Commonwealth; inc. W. Malaysia (Malaya) and E. Malaysia (Borneo sts. of Sarawak and Sabah); cap. Kuala Lumpur; a. 334,110 km²; p. (1968) 10,455,000.

Malaysia, West (Malaya), part of **Federation of Malaysia**; consists of wide peninsula, S. of Thailand; most developed in W.; world's leading producer of natural rubber, grown in plantations; oil palm and pineapples also grown; world's leading exporter of tin; nearly half p. Chinese; a. 131,588 km²; p. (1968) 8,899,000.

Malbork (Marienburg), t., Gdansk, **Poland**; R. pt. on Nogat R.; cas.; p. (1970) 30,900.

Malden, t., Mass., **USA**; mftg. sub. of Boston; rubber gds., hosiery furniture; p. (est. 1969) 54,000.

Malden and Coombe. *See* **Kingston-upon-Thames.**

Maldive Is., indep. rep. (1968), **Indian Oc.**; chain of coral atolls *c.* 640 km S.W. of Sri Lanka; 1,067 Is., 193 inhabited; economy based on fishing (bonito and tuna); dried fish main exp.; coconuts, copra, coconut oil, coir, cowrie shells,; cap. Malé; Britain to withdraw R.A.F. sta. on Gan I. in Addu Atoll; a. 298 km²; p. (1970) 114,469.

Maldon, t., Essex, **Eng.**; sm. pt. at head of Blackwater estuary; agr. machin., steel window-frames, flour-milling; p. (1971) 13,840.

Malegaon, t., Maharashtra, **India**; in Satmala Hills N.E. of Bombay; p. (1971) 191,847.

Malham Cove, North Yorks., **Eng.**; in Craven dist. of N. Pennines, 16 km N.W. of Skipton; semi-circular amphitheatre limestone cliffs from base of which emerges R. Aire.

Mali, Rep. of, W. **Africa**; landlocked st.; former Fr. col. of Soudan; dry semi-desert climate in S.; extends into Sahara desert in N.; few natural resources; nomadic pastoralist p. in N.; only 20 per cent of a. cultivable; livestock basis of inds. (hides, wool, etc.) and exps.; cap. Bamako; a. 1,204,350 km²; p. (1969) 4,929,000.

Malin Head, Donegal, **R.o.I.**; most N. point.

Malines (Mechelen), t., **Belgium**; on R. Dyle; cath.; rly. ctr., textiles, furniture; once famous for lace; p. (1969) 65,730.

Malling, t., Kent, **Eng.**; 5 km W. of Maidstone; fruit, chemicals; p. (1971) 54,251 (dist.).

Mallow, mkt. t., Cork, **R.o.I.**; on R. Blackwater; agr., fishing, flour mills, tanneries, condensed milk, dehydrated foods; p. (1966) 5,539.

Malmesbury, t., Wilts., **Eng.**; anc. hilltop t. in Cotswolds; mkt.; abbey; elec. engin.; birthplace of Thomas Hobbes; p. (1971) 2,526.

Malmesbury, t., Victoria, **Australia**; on R. Campaspe, 32 km S.E. of Bendigo; dam across R.

Malmö, c., spt., S. **Sweden**; on the Sound opposite Copenhagen; third lgst c. in cty.; naval and comm. pt.; shipbldg., textiles, machin.; founded in 12th cent.; proposed terminus of tunnel to Denmark; p. (1970) 258,311 (c.) (est. 1969) 435,634 (met. a.).

Malta, indep. st. within Br. C. (1964), rep. (1974); I. in Mediterranean, 93 km S. of Sicily; strategic location; British naval and military base; agr. ch. occupation with ship-repairing at dry-docks of Valletta; sm.-scale inds. growing; tourism exploits Mediterranean climate; major airport at Luqa; awarded George Cross for bravery in second world war; cap. Valletta; a. 316 km²; p. (est. 1971) 322,070 (inc. Gozo and Comino).

Maltby, t., South Yorks., **Eng.**; p. (1971) 14,050.

Malton, mkt. t., North Yorks., **Eng.**; on R. Derwent, in S.W. of Vale of Pickering; brewing, p. (1971) 3,980.

Malvern, t., Hereford and Worcs., **Eng.**; at E. foot of Malvern hills; spa; annual dramatic festival; Elgar lived here; p. (1971) 29,004.

Malvern Hills, narrow ridge forming bdy. between Worcs. and Hereford, Eng.; rises very abruptly from Severn valley to over 300 m between Malvern and Bromsberrow; moorland, woodland on lower slopes; length 13 km, width under 2 km, maximum alt., 425 m.

Mammoth Cave, Ky., **USA**; to S. of Green R. in hilly forested parkland; spectacular limestone formations (stalactites, stalagmites), lakes and rivers (e.g., Echo R., 110 m below surface) in avenues aggregating 240 km long; included in Nat. Park.

Mamoré, R., N. **Bolivia** and **Brazil**; rises in Andes; 1,920 km long.

Mam Soul, mtn., Kyle of Lochalsh and Inverness **Scot.**; alt. 1,178 m.

Manacle Rocks, dangerous reef off cst. of Cornwall, **Eng.**; 12 km S. of Falmouth.

Manacor, t., Majorca, **Spain**; artificial pearls, wine; stalactite caves of Drach and Hams; p. (1970) 23,278.

Managua, c., cap. of **Nicaragua**; on S. Shore of L. Managua; industl. and comm. ctr.; oil refining agr. processing, textiles, steel; univ.; 48 km from pt. Puerto Somoza; violent earthquake Dec. 1972; p. (1971) 398,514.

Managua, L., **Nicaragua**; second lgst. L. in Central America.

Manãmah, Al, cap. and ch. pt. Bahrain, **Persian G.**; free pt., comm. ctr.; declining pearl-fishing ind.; linked by causeway to internat. airpt.; p. (1971) 89,728.

Manáus (Manaos), c., cap. of Amazonas st., N.W., **Brazil**; on Rio Negro nr. confluence with Amazon; impt. R. pt., airpt.; oil refinery; former rubber ctr.; in free zone (10,360 km²) recently set up to encourage development in Amazonas; p. (1970) 284,118.

Manche, dep., N.W. **France**; on English Channel; agr. and dairying; cap. Saint Lô; ch. pt. Cherbourg; a. 6,410 km²; p. (1968) 451,939.

Manchester, c., major pt., Gtr. Manchester, **Eng.**; on R. Irwell; terminus of Manchester Ship Canal; ctr. of cotton and man-made fibre textile inds.; heavy, lt., and elec. engin., machine tools, petro-chemicals, dyestuffs, pharmaceutical gds.; univ.; comm., cultural, and recreational cap. of N.W. Eng.; p. (1971) 541,408 (c.); (1968) 2,451,660 (met. a.).

Manchester, t., Conn., **USA**; textiles (silk); p. (est. 1969) 47,000.

Manchester, c., N.H., **USA**; at Amoskeag falls, on the Merrimac R.; textiles, footwear, machin.; p. (1970) 87,342 (c.), 107,675 (met. a.).

Manchester Ship Canal, ship canal, Cheshire/ Merseyside/Gtr. Manchester, **Eng.**; joins Manchester to Mersey estuary at Eastham; can be used by ocean steamers; 57 km long.

Manchuria. *See* **North-East China.**

Mandalay, c., **Burma**; on R. Irrawaddy, 640 km N. of Rangoon; former cap.; lost importance with rise of Irrawaddy delta; many temples, palaces; p. (1969) 360,000.

Manfredonia, mkt. t., Foggia, **Italy**; fish. pt.; cath.; p. (est. 1968) 44,998.

Mangalore, spt., Karnataka, **India**; exp. coffee, coconuts, rice spices, fertilisers; p. (1971) 165,174 (c.), 215,122 (met. a.).
Mangere, N.I., N.Z.; 21 km S. of Auckland; international airport (opened 1965).
Mangla Dam, Pakistan; world's lgst. earth-filled dam, on Jhelum R., part of Indus Basin irrigation scheme.
Manhattan, I., N.Y., **USA**; at mouth of Hudson R.; a. 57 km^2; forms major part of bor. of Manhattan of N.Y. City.
Manila, c., S.W. Luzon, **Philippines**; leading c. and ch. pt. of Is.; entrepôt tr.; modern skyscrapers; univ., cath.; major airpt.; p. (1969) 1,550,000 (c.), 2,989,300 (met. a.).
Manipur, new st. (1972), E. India; borders Burma; former princely st.; cap. Imphal; a. 22,274 km^2; p. (est. 1972) 1,070,000.
Manisa, c., cap. of M. prov., W. **Turkey**; agr. ctr.; mineral deposits nearby; p. (1965) 69,394.
Manitoba, prov., Canada; wheat, rich mineral deposits, fisheries; diverse inds.; cap. Winnipeg; a. 650,090 km^2; p. (1966) 936,066.
Manitowoc, c., Wis., **USA**; on L Mich.; shipbldg., aluminium wks., flour mills; p. (est. 1969) 33,500.
Manizales, c., cap. of Caldas, **Colombia**; at 2,155 m in the Central Cordillera; in rich coffee a.; route ctr.; p. (est. 1972) 286,100 (c.), 306,500 (met. a.).
Mannar, G., with Palk Strait separates **India** from **Sri Lanka**.
Mannheim, c., Baden-Württemberg, **W. Germany**; major R. pt. at confluence of Rs. Neckar and Rhine, opposite Ludwigshafen; heavy and lt. inds., notably precision instruments, machin., vehicles; p. (est. 1969) 328,000.
Manono, t., **Zaire**; ctr. for tin-mng.; foundries.
Manresa, industl. t., N.E. **Spain**; in Catalonia; textiles; associated with Ignatius of Loyola; place of pilgrimage; p. (est. 1965) 57,200.
Mansfield, t., Notts., **Eng.**; on E. flank of Pennines, 19 km N. of Nottingham; coal mng., sand-quarrying, textiles, footwear, metal boxes, machin.; p. (1971) 57,598
Mansfield, t., Ohio, **USA**; machin. farm tools, paper, rubber gds.; p. (1970) 54,154 (t.), 129,162 (met. a.).
Mansfield Woodhouse, t., Notts., **Eng.**; 3 km N. of Mansfield; stone quarries; Roman remains; p. (1971) 24,787.
Mansûra, c., Lower **Egypt**; pt. on Nile; cotton mftg.; univ. proposed; p. (est. 1970) 212,300.
Mantua, c., cap. of M. prov., N. **Italy**; on R. Mincio; comm. and agr. ctr.; old fortfd. c.; p. (1969) 66,577.
Manukau, new t., N.I., **N.Z.**; in subs. of Auckland; p. (1971) 104,096.
Manukau Harbour, N.I., **N.Z.**; lge. shallow inlet on W. cst. of Auckland peninsula; provides additional harbour facilities for spt. of Auckland; recreational sailing; fishing.
Manych, R., **RSFSR**; trib. of R. Don; 480 km long; canal being built through R. to Caspian to provide through connection with Black Sea.
Manzala (Menzala), lagoon, Mediterranean cst., **Egypt**; extends E. from Damietta mouth of Nile to Pt. Said; fringed by salt marsh; a. 2,072 km^2.
Manzanillo, spt., S.E. **Cuba**; exp. sugar, rice, tobacco; p. (1966) 87,000.
Manzanillo, c., Colima, W. **Mexico**; ch. pt. on Pac. Oc.; exp. coffee, timber, minerals; p. (est. 1969) 29,347.
Maputo (Lourenço Marques), spt., cap. of **Moçambique**; at head of Delagoa Bay; rly. terminus; oil refining, deposits of bentonite worked nearby; ore terminal for 1976; p. (est. 1967) 90,000 (c), 250,000 (met. a.).
Maracaibo, spt., cap. of Zulia st., **Venezuela**; deepwater harbour; on W. of narrow entrance to L. Maracaibo; univ.; oilfields and refineries; exp. coffee, cocoa, hardwoods; p. (est. 1970) 690,400.
Maracaibo, G., and L., Zulia st., **Venezuela**; brackish lake, 192 km long, 96 km wide; oilwells on fringes and drilled into lake floor.
Maracay, c., N. **Venezuela**; on L. Valencia, 112 km from Carácas; agr. and industl. ctr.; p. (est. 1970) 192,900.
Maragheh, t., **Iran**; on N. end of L. Urmia; comm. and fruit ctr.; p. (1966) 54,106.
Marajó, I., at mouth of the Rs. Amazon and Pará **Brazil**; a. 38,850 km^2.
Maralinga, S. **Australia**; 320 km N.E. Eucla; joint U.K.-Australian atomic testing ground, first weapon exploded here 27 Sept. 1956.
Maranhão, st., N.E. **Brazil**; rice, cotton sugar, tobacco, coffee, cattle, gold, copper; oil in the Barrierinhas a.; cap. São Luiz; a. 334,812 km^2; p. (est. 1968) 3,497,890.
Marañon, R. *See* Amazon, R.
Maras, t., S. central **Turkey**; tr. in Kurdish carpets; p. (1965) 63,315.
Marathon, v. and plain, **Greece**; 32 km N.E. of Athens; here the Athenians defeated the Persians 490 B.C.
Marazion, mkt. t., Cornwall, **Eng.**; on Mount's Bay, nr. St. Michael's Mount; pilchard fisheries.
Marble Bar, t., W. **Australia**. 136 km inland by rail from Pt. Hedland; ctr. of Pilbara goldfields.
Marburg on Lahn, t., Hesse, W **Germany**; univ., cas.; noted for optical instruments; p. (est. 1967) 49,900.
March, mkt. t., Cambs., **Eng.**; on R. Nene, in Fens; rly. junc.; farm tools; p. (1971) 14,268.
Marches, The, region, central **Italy**; extending from eastern slopes of Apennines to Adriatic cst.; embracing provs. of Macerata, Ascoli-Piceno, Acona, and Pesaro e Urbino; maize, wine, tobacco, silk, paper; a. 9,697 km^2; p. (1969) 1,363,685.
Marchfeld, plain, Lower **Austria**, between Rs. Danube and Morava which here forms bdy. between Austria and ČSSR.
Marcias Nguema (Fernando Po), I., **Equatorial Guinea**; in Bight of Bonny; mtnous.; coffee, cocoa, bananas, timber; p. (1968) 61,000.
Mar del Plata, c., **Argentina**; on C. Corrientes; Atl. cst. resort; p. (1970) 299,700 (met. a.).
Maree, L., Ross and Cromarty, **Scot.**; 21 km long, c. 3 km wide; rocky shores; studded with wooded islets.
Maremma, coastal region along Tyrrhenean Sea, S. Tuscany, **Italy**; once malarial, now drained with wide fertile areas.
Mareotis or **Birket-el-Mariut**, L., Lower **Egypt**; separated from Mediterranean by ridge of sand on which stands Alexandria; 80 km long, 32 km wide.
Margam, t., in Pt. Talbot, West Glamorgan, S. **Wales**; on cst. of Swansea Bay; lge. new steel-wks., lgst. steel-rolling mill in Europe.
Margarita, I., in Caribbean off N. **Venezuela**; tourism; formerly pearl-fishing ctr.; cap. Asunción; a. 1,166 km^2; p. (1961) 87,500.
Margate, t., Kent, **Eng.**; W. of N. Foreland, in the Isle of Thanet; seaside resort; p. (1971) 50,145.
Margelan, t., E. Uzbek SSR, **USSR**; in Ferghana Valley; noted for silk ind.; p. (est. 1967) 89,000.
Mari, aut. rep., **RSFSR**; timber, paper inds.; p. (1970) 685,000.
Mariana Is. (**Marianas**), chain of Is., W. Pac.; US. Trust Terr.; most impt. are Guam, Saipan, and Tinian; US Commonwealth status planned for N. Mariana Is.; a. 479 km^2; p. (1968) 10,986.
Maribor, t., Slovenia, **Yugoslavia**; on Drava R., nr. Austrian border; metallurgical inds.; ctr. of agr. a.; p. (1971) 97,167.
Marilia, t., São Paulo st., **Brazil**; coffee, cotton, oil peanuts; p. (est. 1968) 107,305.
Mariinsk Canal. *See* Volga Baltic Waterway.
Marion, c., Ind., **USA**; mkt. ctr. within corn belt; varied inds.; p. (est. 1969) 38,500.
Marion, t., Ohio, **USA**; agr. ctr., with varied agr. mnfs.; p. (est. 1969) 37,500.
Maritime Provinces, include Canadian provs. of Nova Scotia, New Brunswick, Prince Edward I.
Maritsa, R., **Bulgaria** and **Greece**; used for irrigation and hydroelectric power; 416 km long.
Market Drayton, t., Salop, **Eng.**; on R. Tern, 21 km S.W. of Newcastle-under-Lyme; agr. implements, nylon mftg.; p. (1971) 17,154 (dist.).
Market Harborough, t., Leics., **Eng.**; on R. Welland, 13 km N.W. of Kettering; elec. engin., foodstuffs, corsetry; p. (1971) 14,527.
Market Rasen, t., Lincs., **Eng.**; agr. ctr.; racecourse; p. (1971) 2,430.
Markinch, burgh, Kirkcaldy, **Scot**; 13 km N. of Kirkcaldy; paper mftg., whisky blending and bottling; p. (1971) 2,225.

Marl, t., N. Rhine-Westphalia, **W. Germany**; in Ruhr; coal mng.; chemicals; p. (est. 1967) 76,100.
Marlborough, t., Wilts., **Eng.**; on R. Kennet in heart of Marlborough Downs; public school; p. (1971) 6,031.
Marlborough, prov. dist., S.I., **N.Z.**; pastoral; a. 10,930 km²; cap. Blenheim; p. (1971) 31,533.
Marlborough Downs, hills, Wilts., **Eng.**; chalk; highest point, Milk Hill, 298 m.
Marlow, t., Bucks., **Eng.**; on R. Thames; mkt., tourist ctr.; home of Shelley; p. (1971) 11,706.
Marmara, Sea of, separates Europe from Asia; connected with Black Sea through the Bosporus, with Aegean Sea through Dardanelles; shores belong to Turkey.
Marne, dep., N.E. **France**; in Champagne; ctr. of champagne ind.; cap. Châlons-sur-Marne; a. 8,205 km²; p. (1968) 485,388.
Marne, R., central **France**; rises in Plateau de Langres, flows across Champagne Humide, Champagne Pouilleuse, and Beauce, joins R. Seine just above Paris; with Marne-Rhine and Marne-Saône canals forms impt. inland waterway linking Seine with Rhine and Rhône valleys; *c.* 520 km. long.
Marple, t., Gtr. Manchester, **Eng.**; 5 km E. of Stockport; engin., residtl.; p. (1971) 23,217.
Marquesas Is., volcanic gr. in central **Pac. Oc.**, part of Fr. Polynesia; lgst. Nukuhiva and Hivaoa; mtnous., fertile; exp. copra, vanilla, tobacco, cotton; a. 1,274 km²; p. (1967) 5,147.
Marrakesh, c., **Morocco**; tourist ctr.; leather gds., carpets; p. (1971) 330,400 (c.), 390,480 (met. a.).
Marsa el-Brega, new pt., G. of Sirte, **Libya**; oil pipeline from Zelten; gas liquefaction plant opened 1970; airport.
Marsala, pt., Sicily, **Italy**; on site of anc. Carthaginian settlement; wine ctr.; p. (est. 1967) 42,400.
Marseilles, c., spt., cap. of Bouche-du-Rhône dep., S. **France**; on Provence cst.; passenger and gds. traffic; pt. inds., marine engin., oil refining; oil pipeline to Karlsruhe; industl. expansion at G. of Fos; cath., univ., palace; founded as Massilia by Phocaean Greeks of Asia Minor 600 B.C.; p. (1968) 889,029 (c.), 964,412 (met. a.).
Marshall Is., gr. of coral Is., central **Pac. Oc.**; comprising 34 atolls; exp. copra, sugar, coffee; admin. ctr. Jaluit I.; US Pac. Trust Terr.; a. 181 km²; nuclear bomb tests; p. (1968) 18,998.
Martha's Vineyard, I., S.E. Mass., **USA**; state forest; summer resort; ch. ts., Vineyard Haven, Oak Bluffs, Edgartown; summer resort.
Martigny, t., Valais, **Switzerland**; linked by road tunnel to Aosta, Italy; p. 6,572.
Martina Franca, t., S. **Italy**; in Apulia; wine, olive oil; summer resort; p. (est. 1968) 38,771.
Martinique, I., Fr. overseas dep., Windward Is., **W.I.**; dominated by volcanic peak Mt. Pelée which erupted 1902 destroying t. of St. Pierre; hurricanes, earthquakes; economy based on sugar-cane and fruit prod.; much emigration to France; cap. Fort de France; a. 1,088 km²; p. (1970) 345,000.
Martos, t., Jaén prov., Andalusia, **Spain**; castled hilltop t.; wines, sulphur springs; mftg. p. (1970) 21,493.
Mary (Merv), c., Turkmen SSR, **USSR**; in oasis in Kara-Kum desert; anc. c. founded 3rd cent. B.C.; textile ctr.; p. (1969) 61,000.
Maryborough, t., Queensland, **Australia**; pt. on Mary R.; exp. fruit, sugar, timber, coal; shipyards, steelwks.; p. (1972) 19,962.
Maryborough. *See* **Port Laoighise, Ireland.**
Mary Kathleen, t., Queensland, **Australia**; new t., nr. uranium field in Cloncurry a.
Maryland, one of original 13 sts. of **USA**; on shores of Chesapeake Bay; humid continental climate; arable agr. and mkt. gardening; seafishing; cap. Annapolis; lgst. c. Baltimore; a. 27,394 km²; p. (1970) 3,874,642.
Maryport, t., Cumbria, **Eng.**; former pt.; modern lt. inds. in industl. estate to S. of t.; p. (1971) 11,615.
Masaya, t., W. **Nicaragua**; comm ctr. in rich agr. a ; p. (est. 1970) 49,691.
Masbate, I., **Philippines**; gold mng.; a. 3,269 km²; p. (1970) 492,868.
Mascarene Is., collective name of Mauritius, Rodriguez and Réunion, in Indian Oc.
Maseru, t., cap. **Lesotho**; nr. border with S. Africa on Caledon R.; p. (1972) 17,000.
Masham, t., North Yorks., **Eng.**; on R. Ure; 14 km N.W. of Ripon; mkt.; p. (1971) 1,473 (dist.).
Mashhad, c., N.E. **Iran**; cap. of Khorassan prov.; p. (est. 1971) 530,500.
Mashonaland, dist., **Rhodesia**; a. inhabited by the Mashona tribe; ch. t. Salisbury.
Masjid-i-Sulamain, t., **Iran**; impt. oilfield and refinery.
Mask, L., Mayo and Galway, **R.o.I.**; 19 km long, 3–6 km wide.
Mason City, t., Iowa, **USA**; on Sheel Rock R.; tr. ctr. of lge. agr. a.; p. (est. 1969) 30,711.
Mason-Dixon Line. *See* **Section L.**
Massachusetts, st., New England, **USA**; on Atl. cst.; humid continental climate; hilly interior severed by N.–S. Connecticut valley; major fishing ind.; replacement of traditional textile inds. by modern science-based inds., especially around M. Institute of Technology; impt. arable gr. a.; cap. Boston; a. 21,386 km²; p. (1970) 5,630,224.
Massa di Carrara. *See* **Carrara.**
Massawa, spt., **Ethiopia**, on Red Sea; fine harbour; fishing; fish meal; p. (est. 1970) 18,490.
Massif Central, upland a., **France**; variable geology and scenery inc. volcanic Auvergne and limestone Causses; much rural depopulation, pastoral agr.; industl. ts. inc. St. Etienne based on sm. coalfields in N.E.; other ts. inc. Limoges and Clermont-Ferrand.
Masterton, t., N.I., **N.Z.**; meat-packing; dairy prods., woollen mills; p. (1971) 18,556.
Masulipatam (Bandar), spt., Andhra Pradesh, **India** on Coromandel cst.; cotton mftg., rice; p. (1971) 129,905.
Matabeleland, dist., **Rhodesia**; a. inhabited by Matabele tribe; ch. t. Bulawayo.
Matadi, spt., **Zaïre**; on R. Zaïre; main pt.; exp. forest prod.; proposed Inga power project nearby; p. (est. 1972) 125,585 (met. a.).
Matagalpa, t., **Nicaragua**; ctr. of agr. a., food processing; second lgst. t. of Nicaragua; p. (est. 1967) 20,718.
Matamoros, irrigated region, **Mexico**; around t. of M. on Rio Grande delta; Mexico's leading producer of cotton.
Matamoros, t., **Mexico**; on Rio Grande; livestock tr. ctr.; p. (1970) 137,990.
Matanzas, spt., cap. of M. prov., **Cuba**; exp. sugar, cigars; rayon plant; p. (est. 1967) 84,100.
Matarani, new spt., S. **Peru**; oil refinery.
Mataró, spt., **Spain**; nr. Barcelona; fisheries, textiles, chemicals, paper; p. (1970) 73,129.
Matera, t., cap. of M. prov., S. **Italy**; stands on limestone ridge cleft by canyon; agr. ctr.; cave dwellings; 13th cent. cath. and cas.; p. (1969) 44,635.
Mathura (Muttra), t., Uttar Pradesh, **India**; sacred t. on R. Jumna; Hindu pilgrimage ctr.; textiles; p. (1971) 132,028 (t.), 140,150 (met. a.).
Matlock, t., Derbys., **Eng.**; on R. Derwent; 24 km N. of Derby; tourist ctr., limestone quarrying, lt. inds.; p. (1971) 19,575.
Mato Grosso, st., **Brazil**; cap. Cuiabá; a. 1,232,081 km²; p. (est. 1968) 1,363,980.
Mato Grosso, plateau, Mato Grosso st., **Brazil**; average alt. 900 m, acts as divide between Amazon and Paraná-Paraguay R. systems; reserves of gold, diamonds, manganese but largely undeveloped; lge. areas of tropical rain forest.
Matozinhso, t., **Portugal**; fish. pt. at mouth of Leca R.; seaside resort; p. (1960) 37,694.
Matrah, t., **Oman**; ch. comm. ctr.; agr. tr.; site of Port Qaboos, new deep water pt.; p. 14,119.
Matsue, c., S.W. Honshu, **Japan**; on L. Shinji; old cas.; p. (est. 1971) 118,000.
Matsumoto, c., central Honshu, **Japan**; machin., food-processing, paper; once impt. for silk; remains of 16th cent. cas.; p. (est. 1971) 165,000.
Matsuyama, c., **Japan**; pt. based inds. of oil refining and petrochemicals; univ.; feudal cas.; p. (est. 1971) 339,000.
Matterhorn (Fr. **Mt. Cervin**, It. **Monte Cervino**); alt. 4,477 m; Pennine Alps, **Switzerland**.
Mauchline, mkt. t., Strathclyde Reg., **Scot.**; associated with Robert Burns.
Mauna Kea, volcano, **Hawaii**; alt. 4,208 m; now dormant.

Mauna Loa, volcano, **Hawaii**; alt. 4,172 m; one of world's lgst. volcanoes.
Mauritania, Islamic Rep. of, **W. Africa**; desert in N., S. more fertile; Senegal R. forms main artery of transport; mainly pastoral agr. (nomadic); deposits of iron ore (Fort Gouraud) and copper (Bakel Akjoujt); fishing being developed; new pt. development at Nouadhibou; cap. Nouakchott; a. 1,085,210 km²; p. (est. 1969) 1,120,000.
Mauritius, I., indep. st. within Brit. Commonwealth; **Indian Oc.**; volcanic I., 800 km E. of Malagasy Rep.; subtropical climate, prone to cyclones; racially mixed; dependent on sugar for 95 per cent of exps.; dense p. and unemployment cause social tension; former residents of Chagos Arch. resettled on 2 of Agalega Is.; cap. Port Louis; a. (inc. Rodrigues and Agalega) 2,038 km²; p. (1969) 798,684.
Mawson, Australian national research base, **Antarctica**.
Mayagüez, c., spt., **Puerto Rico**; ctr. of fertile region producing sugar, coffee, tobacco; cultural and educational ctr.; p. (1970) 69,485.
Maybole, burgh, Kyle and Carrick, **Scot.**; 13 km S. of Ayr; footwear, agr. implements; cas.; p. (1971) 4,523.
Mayenne, dep., N.W. **France**; pastoral and agr.; cap. Laval; a. 5,146 km²; p. (1968) 252,762.
Mayfair, dist., City of Westminster, London, **Eng.**; fashionable residtl. and comm. a., to E. of Hyde Park; clubs and hotels.
Maynooth, mkt. t., Kildare, **R.o.I.**; college for Roman Catholic clergy; cas.; p. (1966) 1,254.
Mayo, maritime co., Connacht, **R.o.I.**; broken cst., much barren mtn. land, many lge. lakes; agr., fishery; co. t. Castlebar, a. 5,506 km²; p. (1966) 115,588.
Mayotte, ch. I., Fr. terr., Comoro Archipelago, Mocambique Channel; rejected indep. to remain Fr. dep. (1975); sugar-cane, vanilla, cacao; a. 363 km²; p. (est. 1970) 48,000.
Mazandaran, prov., N.E. **Iran**; Caspian Sea, borders USSR; subtropical climate; agr.; cap. Sari; p. (1967) 1,843,388.
Mazar-i-Sharif, c., **Afghanistan**; chemical fertilisers from natural gas; textiles, bricks, flourmilling; noted mosque; p. (est. 1969) 43,197.
Mazatenango, t., S.W. **Guatemala**; agr. comm. ctr.; p. (est. 1971) 23,932.
Mazatlán, c., N.W. **Mexico**; major spt. on Pac. cst.; comm. and industl. ctr.; exp. metals, hides, fish prods., woods; oil refinery; fishing, tourism.; p. (1970) 119,553.
Mazzara, t., Sicily, **Italy**; cath., ruined cas.; agr. prod.; p. (est. 1968) 16,563.
M'babane, cap. of **Swaziland**; stands at *c.* 1,160 m; admin. ctr.; tin mng.; p. (1966) 13,803.
M'Bao, Senegal, W. Africa; oil refinery.
McMurdo Sound, ice-locked channel, **Antarctica**; base for many expeditions.
Mead, L., Cal., **USA**; on R. Colorado behind Boulder (Hoover) Dam; world's lgst. reservoir; stores water for irrigation in Imperial Valley and Yuma dist.; tourist attraction; 184 km long.
Meath, maritime co., Leinster, **R.o.I.**; pastoral; co. t., Trim; a. 2,347 km²; p. (1966) 67,279.
Meaux, t., Seine-et-Marne dep., **France**; on R. Marne; cath.; comm. and industl. ctr.; p. (1968) 31,420.
Mecca, holy c. of Islam, cap. of **Saudi Arabia**; birthplace of Mohammed; pilgrimage ctr.; Gr. Mosque enclosing the Kaaba; univ. (with Jidda); p. (est. 1965) 185,000.
Mechelen. *See* **Malines**.
Mecklenburg, region, **E. Germany**; former *Land*, Soviet Zone of admin.; part of N. European plain, bordering Baltic Sea; abolished as admin. unit 1952; Schwerin was the cap.; a. 22,947 km².
Medan, c., cap. of N. Sumatra prov., **Indonesia**; ctr. for rubber, tobacco, tea; printing; univ.; pt. is Belawan; p. (1971) 635,562.
Médéa, t., 80 km S. of El Djezair, **Algeria**; projected industl. complex; p. (1966) 53,951.
Medellin, c., cap. of Antiquia prov., **Colombia**; at 1,533 m in Central Cordillera; second c. of rep.; univ.; cultural ctr.; coffee; textiles, steel, sugar refining, glass; coal, gold, silver mined nearby; hydroelec. power; p. (est. 1972) 1,091,600 (c.), 1,207,800 (met. a.).
Medicine Hat, t., Alberta, **Canada**; on S. Saskatchewan R.; rly. junc.; coal, natural gas, flour mills; p. (1971) 26,058.
Medina, c., Hejaz, **Saudi Arabia**; 352 km N. of Mecca; tomb of Mohammed; place of Moslem pilgrimage; univ.; harbour at Yanbu' on Red Sea; p. (est. 1965) 100,000.
Mediterranean, gr. inland sea, almost tideless, dividing Europe from Africa; communicating with Atl. by Strait of Gibraltar and Black Sea by Dardanelles, Sea of Marmara and Bosporus, E. part touches Asia in the Levant; total length W. to E. 3,520 km; greatest width of sea proper *c.* 1,120 km; water a. 2,331,000 km²; greatest depth 4,482 m; ch. Is.; Corsica, Sardinia, Sicily, Crete, Cyprus, and the Balearic, Lipari, Maltese, Ionian grs., also Greek arch.
Mednogorksk, t., S. Ural mtns; copper mines; lgst. in **USSR**; copper-refining.
Médoc, region, Gironde, **France**; extending for about 77 km along Garonne R.; noted for wines.
Medway, R., Kent, **Eng.**; flows N.E. past Tonbridge, Maidstone and Rochester (where it becomes estuarial) to mouth of Thames; 112 km long; Medway Bridge (part of London–Dover motorway) completed 1962.
Meekatharra, t., W. **Australia**; Flying Doctor and School of the Air ctr.
Meerut, c., Uttar Pradesh, **India**; scene of outbreak of Indian mutiny 1857; p. (1971) 270,993 (c.), 367,754 (met. a.).
Meghalaya ("Home of the Clouds"), new st. (1972), **India**; former Khasi-Jaintra Hills and Garo Hills dists. of Assam; cap. Shillong; a. 22,549 km²; p. (est. 1972) 1,000,000.
Meiling Pass, on bdy. between Kwangtung, Kiangsi, **S. China**; provides historic routeway across Nanling mtns., followed by old imperial highway from Nanking to Kuangchow; alt. c. 300 m.
Meiningen, t., **E. Germany**; on R. Werra; cas.; machin., chemicals, timber inds.; drama ctr. in second half 19th cent.; p. (est. 1970) 25,357.
Meiringen, t., **Switzerland**; nr. to Aar gorge; resort; wood carving, hand weaving; p. 3,285.
Meissen, t., Dresden, **E. Germany**; on R. Elbe; cath.; famous porcelain popularly known as Dresden china; p. (est. 1970) 45,571.
Meknès, t., **Morocco**; one of the caps. of M.; agr. ctr., olives; p. (1971) 244,520 (t.), 362,840 (met. a.).
Mekong, R., S.E. **Asia**; rises in Tibet, flows through China, Laos, Cambodia, and S. Vietnam, entering China Sea in extensive swampy delta; used for sm. boats but many rapids; longest R. in Asia; 4,000 km long; new R. project for flood control, irrigation and hydroelectric power.
Melanesia, archipelago, S.W. **Pac. Oc.**; inc. Admiralty, Solomon, Santa Cruz, New Hebrides, Loyalty, New Caledonian, and Fiji Is.; New Guinea is sometimes included; ethnic region; arable subsistence agr.
Melbourne, spt., cap. of Victoria, **Australia**; at mouth of Yarra R. in Hobson's Bay at N. end of Port Philip Bay; comm. ctr. of lge region; international airpt.; mnfs. inc. textiles, machin.; botanical gardens; univ., caths.; p. (1972) 74,877 (c.), 2,497,993 (met. a.).
Melilla, spt. and enclave in **Morocco**, on Mediterranean cst., belonging to Spain; exp. iron ore; p. (1969) 77,239.
Melitopol, c., Ukrainian SSR, **USSR**; on Molochnoy R.; ctr. of rich fruit-growing a.; heavy machin., food-processing; p. (1970) 137,000.
Melksham, t., Wilts., **Eng.**; on R. Avon, 8 km N.E. of Bradford-on-Avon; rubber wks., engin., flour mills, creameries, rope and matting; p. (1971) 9,803.
Melrose, burgh, Ettrick and Lauderdale, **Scot.**; on R. Tweed; 6 km E. of Galashiels; ruined abbey; p. (1971) 2,185.
Meltham, t., West Yorks., **Eng.**; 6 km S.W. of Huddersfield; woollen textiles; p. (1971) 17,181.
Melton Mowbray, t., Leics., **Eng.**; on Lincoln Heights, 24 km N.E. of Leicester; mkt., hunting dist.; famous pork pies; footwear, pet foods, Stilton cheese; p. (1971) 19,932.
Melun, t., cap. of Seine-et-Marne dep., **N. France**; on R. Seine; agr. tools and prod.; Romanesque church; p. (1968) 34,518.
Melville I., off N. cst., Arnhem Land, **Australia**; Aboriginal settlement; a. 4,350 km².

Melville I., N.W. Terr., Arctic **Canada**; natural gas; a. 41,958 km².

Memaliaj, t., **Albania**; new mng. t. on banks of R. Vjosa.

Memel. *See* **Klaipeda.**

Memmingen, t., Bavaria, W. **Germany**; rly. junc.; machin., textiles; p. (est. 1969) 35,142.

Memphis, anc. c., **Egypt**; on R. Nile; 19 km S. of Cairo; nearby are Sakkara ruins.

Memphis, c., Tenn., **USA**; on R. Mississippi; rly. ctr., pt. of entry, lgst c. in st., mkt. ctr. for cotton and hardwoods; cottonseed oil, textiles, farm machin.; natural gas and hydroelectric power; univ.; Martin Luther King assassinated here (1968); p. (1970) 620,873 (c.), 770,160 (met. a.).

Menado, t., Sulawesi, **Indonesia**; second t. of I.; pt. for transit tr.; p. (1971) 169,684.

Menai Bridge, t., Anglesey, Gwynedd, **Wales**; p. (1971) 2,608.

Menai Strait, separates Isle of Anglesey from mainland, **Wales**; crossed by Telford's suspension bridge (1825) and Britannia rly. bridge (1850).

Menam Chao Phraya, R., **Thailand**; main R. of cty.; dense p. in valley; lge. multi-purpose scheme for hydroelectric power and irrigation; 1,120 km long.

Mendip Hills, Avon/Somerset, **Eng.**; limestone range containing many karst features inc. Cheddar gorge and Wookey Hole; a. of outstanding natural beauty; quarrying; motorway; hgst. point, 325 m.

Mendoza, prov., W. **Argentina**, on Chilean border; Andean peaks Aconcagua and Tupungato; oilfields; alfalfa, vines, olives, fruit, peppermint; cap. M.; a. 148,783 km²; p. (1970) 973,075.

Mendoza, c., cap. of M. prov., W. **Argentina**; stands at c. 730 m in oasis known as "garden of the Andes"; starting point of Transandine rly.; univ.; wine, fruit; petroleum, agr. processing; p. (1970) 470,896 (met. a.).

Mendoza, R., **Argentina**; enters L. Guanacache; used for hydroelectric power; 320 km long.

Menin (Meenen), t., **Belgium**; on R. Lys on Fr. border; mediaeval cloth ctr.; tobacco tr., textiles, rubber gds., soap; scene of fierce fighting in first world war; p. (est. 1969) 22,195.

Mentawei Is., S.W. Sumatra, **Indonesia**; hilly and forested; primitive p.; fishing, shifting cultivation.

Menteith, Lake of, Stirling, **Scot.**; contains 3 Is.; 2·4 km by 1·6 km.

Menton, t., Alpes-Maritimes dep., S. **France**; Riviera resort; p. (1968) 25,271.

Meppel, t., Drenthe, **Neth.**, 21 km N. of Zwolle; shipbldg.; p. (1967) 19,192.

Merauke, t., W. Irian, **Indonesia**; pt. on S. cst.; ctr. of livestock raising region.

Mercedes, t., S.W. **Uruguay**; livestock ctr., E. of its pt. Fray Bentos; p. (1963) 34,000.

Mergui, archipelago, Tenasserim cst., S. **Burma**; teak, rice, pearl fishing.

Mérida, c., cap. of Yucatan st., S.E. **Mexico**; sisal-hemp; Spanish colonial architecture; tourism; Mayan ruins; p. (1970) 212,097.

Mérida, c., Badajoz prov., S.W. **Spain**; on Guadiana R.; comm. ctr. of Estremadura; impt. Roman remains; p. (1970) 40,059.

Mérida, t., cap. of M. st., **Venezuela**; in Andes; univ., cath.; tourist ctr.; world's highest cable rly. to Espejo peak (4,690 m); p. (est. 1970) 75,634.

Meriden, t., Conn., **USA**; hardware mftg.; p. (est. 1969) 58,000.

Meridian, t., Miss., **USA**; mkt. ctr. in cotton, livestock, lumber a.; rly. and route ctr.; textiles, clothing; p. (est. 1969) 53,000.

Merioneth, former co., **Wales**. *See* **Gwynedd.**

Merksem, industl. t., Antwerp, **Belgium**; p. (1968) 39,659.

Merrick, mtn., Wigtown, **Scot.**; hgst. peak in S. Uplands of Scot.; alt. 843 m.

Mersea, I., at mouth of R. Colne, Essex, **Eng.**; oysters; holiday resort; 8 km long, 3 km wide.

Merseburg, c., Halle, E. **Germany**; on R. Saale; ctr. of gr. lignite field; paper mills, chemical wks.; historic c.; p. (est. 1970) 55,986.

Merse of Berwick, region, S.E. **Scot.**; lower valleys of Rs. Tweed and Teviot; glacial clays; arable agr. for barley, wheat; dairy cattle; ch. t. Berwick-on-Tweed; a. 570 km².

Mersey, R., Cheshire/Gtr. Manchester/Merseyside, **Eng.**; enters Irish Sea by fine estuary at Liverpool; 109 km long.

Merseyside, met. co., N.W. **Eng.**; a. around lower Mersey estuary inc. N. Wirral penin., pts. of Liverpool, Birkenhead and Bootle; many chem. and pt. processing inds.; p. (1971) 1,659,000.

Mersin, c., S. **Turkey**; spt. on Mediterranean cst.; oil refinery; dates from c. 3,600 B.C.; p. (1965) 87,267.

Merthyr Tydfil, t. Mid Glamorgan S. **Wales**; in narrow valley of R. Taff, 35 km N.W. of Cardiff; coal-mng. ctr.; hosiery, aircraft, bricks, elec. domestic gds.; p. (1971) 55,215.

Merton, outer bor., Greater London, **Eng.**; inc. former bors. of Mitcham, Wimbledon, and Merton and Morden; p. (1971) 176,524.

Meru, mtn., **Tanzania**, E. Africa; extinct volcano overlooking E. arm of Gt. Rift valley; coffee plantations at alt. 1,500–1,800 m, some rubber below 1,200 m; alt. summit 4,560 m.

Merv. *See* **Mary.**

Mesa, t., Arizona, **USA**; in Salt River Valley, founded by Mormons 1878; agr. ctr., helicopter mftg.; p. (est. 1969) 55,000.

Mesa Central, plateau, **Mexico**; part of Mexican plateau, major a. of comm. agr. (maize, wheat, agave); contains cap. Mexico City; dense p. and industl. comm. ctrs.

Mesa del Norte, plateau, **Mexico**; northern part of Mexican plateau.

Mesabi Range, hills, N.E. Minn., **USA**; vast iron ore deposits, now running out.

Mesa Verde National Park, S.W. Col., **USA**; Indian cliff dwellings.

Mesopotamia, anc. region, S.W. **Asia**; between Tigris and Euphrates Rs.; a. of early civilisation.

Messenia, anc. region, Peloponnesus, **Greece**; corresponding to present Messinia, densely p. agr. dep., cap. Kalamata; a. 3,406 km²; p. (1971) 172,850.

Messina, c., spt., Sicily, **Italy**; opposite Reggio; univ.; exp. fruit, wine, oil; p. (1969) 272,312.

Messina, strait, between Sicily and Italian mainland; length 35 km, minimum width 5 km.

Mesta, R., **Bulgaria, Greece**; rises in Rodopi mtns., flows S.E. into Aegean Sea 24 km E. of Kavalla; valley famous for tobacco; known in Greece as Nestos; c. 280 km long.

Mestre, t., **Italy**; on lagoon at landward end of causeway linking Venice to mainland.

Meta, R., **Colombia** and **Venezuela**; navigable for 640 km; trib. of R. Orinoco; 1,200 km long.

Metz, c., cap. of Moselle dep., N.E. **France**; on R. Moselle 40 km N. of Nancy; cultural and comm. ctr. of Lorraine; impt. iron mines; wines, preserved fruits; mediaeval bldgs.; birthplace of Verlaine; p. (1968) 107,537.

Meudon, t., Hauts-de-Seine, **France**; S.W. sub. of Paris; observatory; glass, linen, ammunition; p. (1968) 51,481.

Meurthe, R., N.E. **France**; rises in Vosges and joins Moselle N. of Nancy.

Meurthe-et-Moselle, dep., N.E. **France**; borders on Belgium and Luxembourg; cap. Nancy; a. 5,276 km²; p. (1968) 705,413.

Meuse, dep., N.E. **France**; borders on Belgium; cap. Bar-le-Duc; a. 6,237 km²; p. (1968) 209,513.

Meuse (Maas), R., **France**; rises in Haute-Marne, flows past Verdun into **Belgium** past Namur, and Liège into the **Neth.** and joins the Waal, left arm of the Rhine; impt. routeway; 912 km long.

Mexborough, t., South Yorks., **Eng.**; on R. Don, 16 km above Doncaster; potteries; p. (1971) 15,946.

Mexicali, c., Baja Cal., **Mexico**; border resort; p. (1970) 263,498.

Mexican Plateau, central plateau, **Mexico**, between the branches of the Sierra Madre; highest point over 2,400 m; impt. landform and a. of human settlement.

Mexico, fed. rep., **Central America**; inc. 31 sts., and fed. dist. of Mexico City; mtnous.; Sierra Madre covers most of rep.; variety of climate according to alt.; W. mostly desert; agr. requires irrigation; major world exporter of cotton, sisal, sulphur, silver; oil impt.; 14 oil refineries, new petrochemical complex at Cosoleacaque; rapid industl. expansion for

consumer gds.; decentralisation of inds. from Mexico City; tourism for Americans; cap. Mexico City; a. 1,972,360 km²; p. (1970) 48,377,363.
Mexico, st., Mexico; encircles fed. dist. of Mexico City; cap. Toluca; a. 21,412 km²; p. (1969) 2,803,000.
Mexico City, c., cap. of **Mexico**; lgst. c. in Latin America; on plain at 2,275 m; many noteworthy bldgs., cath., univ.; admin., comm. and industl. ctr.; nuclear reactor nearby; p. (1970) 6,874,165 (c.), 8,589,630 (met. a.).
Mexico, Gulf of, lge. inlet of Atl. Oc. (1,600 km E. to W. by 1,280 km N. to S.) lying S. of USA and E. of Mexico; communicates by Florida strait with Atl. and by Yucatan strait with Caribbean Sea; submarine oil drilling.
Mexico, Valley of, Meseta Central, **Mexico**; major industl. zone; over 60 per cent by value of Mexican mnfs. produced; wide range of inds.; major ctr. Mexico City; attempts to decentralise p. and economic activity throughout Mexico; once ctr. of Aztec p.
Meyrin, t., **Switzerland**; H.Q. of CERN, nr. Geneva.
Mezhdurechensk, t., **RSFSR**; W. Siberia, on R. Tom'; new coal-mng. ctr.; p. (est. 1969) 81,000.
Mézières. *See* **Charleville-Mézières**.
Mezötur, t., **Hungary**; mkt., flour, pottery; p. (1966) 22,200.
Mezzogiorno, lge underdeveloped region, southern **Italy**; comprising Abruzzo and Molise, Campania, Basilicata, Apulia, Calabria and the Is. of Sicily and Sardinia; major govt. attempts to develop a.; agr. reforms and industl. growth, oil refining, iron and steel, petrochemicals; contains 40 per cent of p. of Italy, much emigration; p. (est. 1969) 19,000,000.
Miami, c., Fla., **USA**; on Biscayne Bay, at mouth of Miami R.; famous resort and recreational ctr.; varied inds.; international airport; M. beach across Biscayne Bay; p. (1970) 331,553 (c.), 1,259,176 (met. a.).
Miass, c., **RSFSR**; in Urals, 90 km S.W of Chelyabinsk; gold-mng. ctr.; cars; p. (1970) 132,000.
Michigan, st., **USA**; in valley of Gr. Ls.; industl.; cars, iron and steel gds., petroleum, minerals; some agr.; cap. Lansing; a. 150,779 km²; p. (1970) 8,776,873.
Michigan City, t., Ind., **USA**; on L. Mich.; rly. wks., furniture, hosiery; p. (est. 1969) 39,500.
Michigan Lake, 3rd lgst of Gr. Ls. and the only one wholly in **USA**; in basin of St. Lawrence R., enclosed by two peninsulas of the st. of Mich. and by Wis., Ill., and Ind.; a. 61,901 km²; discharges by Straits of Mackinac to L. Huron.
Michipicoten, R., Ont., **Canada**; flows 200 km to L. Superior; iron ore deposits in valley.
Michoacan, st., **Mexico**; on Pac. Oc.; mtnous., rich in minerals; cap. Morelia; a. 60,088 km²; p. (1969) 2,452,000.
Michurinsk, t., **RSFSR**; N.W. of Tambov; engin., textiles, food inds.; agr. exp. ctr.; p. (est. 1967) 91,000.
Micronesia, Is., S. Pac.; inc. the Carolines, Marshalls, Marianas, and Gilbert Is.; most are coral atolls.
Middleburg, t., cap. of Zeeland prov., **Neth.**; on Walcheren I. nr. Flushing; margarine, timber, optical instruments; cloth ctr. in mediaeval times; p. (1968) 28,416.
Middlesbrough, t., Cleveland, **Eng.**; expanded t.; pt. on S. side of Tees estuary; impt. iron and steel ind., heavy engin., chemicals.
Middlesex, former co., S.E. **Eng.**; N. of R. Thames; largely absorbed in Greater London 1964; a. 601 km².
Middleton, mkt. t., Durham, **Eng.**; on R. Tees; civil airport projected; nearby waterfall.
Middleton, t., Gtr. Manchester, **Eng.**; in valley of R. Irk; textiles, engin. chemicals, foam rubber; p. (1971) 53,419.
Middleton, t., Ohio, **USA**; on Miami R. and canal; steel, paper; p. (est. 1969) 46,500.
Middlewich, t., Cheshire, **Eng.**; on Rs. Dane, Wheelock and Croco, 8 km N. of Crewe; salt, chemicals, clothing; p. (1971) 7,783.
Mid Glamorgan, co., S. **Wales**; upland in N. dissected by deep R. valleys containing former coal-mng. settlements; lowland to S. borders Bristol Channel; a. 1,018 km²; p. (1971) 530,639.
Midhurst, t., West Sussex, **Eng.**; on R. Rother; famous polo grounds; birthplace of Richard Cobden; p. (1971) 18,983 (dist.).
Midland, t., Texas, **USA**; oilfield ctr., cotton ginning, natural gas; p. (est. 1969) 61,500.
Midlands, region, **Eng.**; comprises non-met. cos. of Staffs., Derbys., Notts., Leics., Warwicks., Northants., and met. co. of West Midlands; impt. a. for lt. engin.
Midlothian, former co., l. gov. dist., Lothian Reg., **Scot.**; adjoins Edinburgh; a. 357 km²; p. (1971) 80,235.
Midnapore, t., W. Bengal, **India**; mkt. for agr. prods.; p. (1961) 59,532.
Midway Island, I., **Pac. Oc.**; calling-place on air-routes between San Francisco and Asia, midway between Asia and USA (to which it belongs).
Mieres, t., Oviedo prov., N. **Spain**; in Asturias; coal-mng. ctr., iron and steel inds.; p. (1967) 68,458.
Mihama, Fukui, **Japan**; nuclear reactor under construction 1968.
Mihoro, Gifu, **Japan**; power plant under construction.
Mikkeli, c., cap. of M prov., **Finland**; L. pt. in Saimaa L. region; p. (est. 1970) 25,188.
Milan, c., cap. of M. prov., N. **Italy**; route ctr. in Lombard plain; second lgst. c. in rep.; ctr. of commerce and ind.; textiles, chemicals, printing, publishing, machin., cars, aircraft, porcelain; cath., univ.; p. (1969) 1,701,612 (met. a.).
Mildenhall, t., Suffolk, **Eng.**; on R. Lark; 13th cent. church; R.A.F. sta. nearby; expanded t.; p. (1971) 26,613 (dist.).
Mildura, t., Victoria, **Australia**; on R. Murray; irrigation ctr.; fruit-canning, food-processing; p. (1972) 13,190.
Milford Haven, spt., Dyfed, **Wales**; magnificent deepwater harbour recently developed; major tanker terminal (250,000 tonnes); 2 refineries; pipeline from Angle Bay to Llandarcy (nr. Swansea); major white fish pt.; trawlers built and repaired; net mkg.; p. (1971) 13,745.
Milford Sound, inlet, at S. of S.I., **N.Z.**, tourist resort; noted for scenery and rare birds.
Millau, t., Aveyron, **France**; on R. Tarn; glove mnfs.; p. (1968) 22,595.
Millom, t., Cumbria, **Eng.**; on N.W. cst. of Duddon estuary; ironwks. (closed 1968 after 100 years); hosiery; declining p.; p. (1971) 14,070 (dist.).
Millport, burgh, Cunninghame, **Scot.**; on Gr. Cumbrae I., in F. of Clyde; resort; cath.; quarries; p. (1971) 1,254.
Milngavie, burgh, Bearsden and M., Strathclyde Reg., **Scot.**; 8 km N.W. of Glasgow; textiles; p. (1971) 10,741.
Milnrow, t., Gtr. Manchester, **Eng.**; sub. of Rochdale; cotton and waste spinning engin., brick mkg., paper and tube mftg.; p. (1971) 10,329.
Milo or Melos, I., Cyclades, **Greece**; cap. Plaka, nr. site of anc. c.; famous statue of Venus of Milo (now in Louvre) found here in 1820.
Milton Keynes, v., Bucks., **Eng.**; a. 9,000 ha; site and name of new c. for London overspill to comprise Bletchley, Wolverton and Stoney Stratford; Open University at Bletchley; p. (est. 1974) 64,000.
Milwaukee, c., Wis., **USA**; lgst. c. and ch. pt. of st.; on L. Mich.; 112 km N. of Chicago; univ.; major mftg. ctr. with numerous inds., notably machin. and transport equipment, meat-canning, beer; p. (1970) 709,537 (c.), 1,393,260 (met. a.).
Min, R., Fukien, S. **China**; descends steeply on S.E. course to enter S. China Sea nr. Foochow, length 480 km, navigable.
Min, R., Szechwan, N.W. **China**; flows S., diverted at Kwanhsien into irrigation channels, joining Yangtze at Ipin; length 800 km, navigable.
Mina Hassan Tani (Kenitra), spt., **Morocco**; exp. grain; p. (1971) 135,960 (c.), 302, 390 (met. a.).
Minas Gerais, st., **Brazil**; vast iron ore reserves; gold, diamonds, manganese, uranium, aluminium; cotton, coffee; hydroelec. power sta.; cap. Belo Horizonte; plans for development of heavy inds.; a. 585,472 km²; p. (est. 1968) 11,776,817.

Minas Novas, t., Minas Gerais, **Brazil**; p. (est. 1968) 24,003.
Mina Sulman, free transit pt., **Bahrain**; deepwater pt., dry dock for OPEC super-tankers, entrepôt tr.
Minatitlán, t., E. **Mexico**; petroleum refineries; petrochemicals; p. 18,539.
Minch, The, channel between the mainland of **Scot.** and the N. portion of Outer Hebrides, 38–64 km wide; very rapid current.
Minch, The Little, channel between I. of Skye, Scot., and the middle portion of Outer Hebrides, 22–32 km wide.
Minchinhampton, t., Gloucs., **Eng.**; in Cotswolds, 6 km S.E. of Stroud.
Mindanao, second lgst. I. of **Philippines**; forested mtns., volcano Mt. Apo; exp. pineapples, hemp, coconuts, coffee; iron, gold, copper mined; plywoods and veneer, paper, pulp; ch. ts. Zamboanga, Davao; a. of govt. sponsored immigration; lge. Muslim p. seeking indep. for I.; greatest depth Mindanao Deep, off Philippines, 11,524 m; a. 94,628 km²; p. (1970) 7,292,691.
Minden, c., N. Rhine-Westphalia, **W. Germany**; on R. Weser at crossing of Mittelland canal; pt., rly. junc.; cath. (12th–14th cent.) destroyed in second world war; p. (est. 1967) 51,100.
Mindoro, I., **Philippines**, S. of Luzon; mtnous., thickly forested; rice, coconuts grown on cst., a. 9,376 km²; p. (1970) 473,940.
Minehead, t., Somerset, **Eng.**; at N. foot of Exmoor, on Bristol Channel cst.; mkt., holiday resort; p. (1971) 8,063.
Minho, R., separates Portugal from Spain in N.W.; length 272 km.
Minicoy Is., Arabian Sea; joined with Laccadive and Amindivi Is. to form union terr. of **India**.
Minneapolis, c., Minn., **USA**; on Mississippi R., at falls of St. Anthony; lgst. c. of st., pt. of entry, rly. terminus; wheat mkt., comm. and industl. ctr.; wide range of inds.; univ.; p. (1970) 431,977 (c.), 1 805,081 (met. a.).
Minnesota, st., **USA**; W. of L. Superior; studded with Ls., many Rs.; iron ore; maize, wheat, livestock, dairying; cap. St. Paul; a. 217,736 km²; p. (1970) 3,767,975.
Minorca (Menorca), I. off **Spain**; 2nd lgst. of Balearic Is.; Mediterranean agr.; developing tourism; cap. Mahón; a. 733 km²; p. (1970) 50,217.
Minsk, c., cap. of Belorussiyan SSR, **USSR**; lge. rly. junc.; cultural and industl. ctr.; univ.; engin., computers; rebuilt since second world war; p. (1970) 907,000 (c.), 916,000 (met. a.).
Minya, c., central **Egypt**; on Nile; cotton tr. ctr.; p. (est. 1970) 122,100.
Minya Konka, mtn., S.W. Szechwan prov., **China**; in Himalayas; highest peak in China; 7,570 m.
Mirfield, t., West Yorks., **Eng.**; on R. Calder, 5 km S.W. of Dewsbury; woollens; p. (1971) 16,871.
Miri, t., Sarawak, **E. Malaysia**; impt. oil ctr.; p. (1960) 13,350.
Mirzapur, t., Uttar Pradesh, **India**; on R. Ganges; carpets, brassware; p. (1971) 105,939.
Miskolc, c., N.E. **Hungary**; impt. industl. ctr.; iron ore, lignite nearby; varied inds., inc. textiles, porcelain, engin., bricks, refrigeration plants; p. (est. 1969) 172,000.
Mississippi, st., S. **USA**; in lower M. valley; bounded on S. by G. of Mexico; cotton, sweet potatoes, pecan nuts, rice, sugar-cane, sorghum-cane, fruit, livestock raising; petroleum, natural gas; cotton textiles, chemicals, fish-processing; cap. Jackson; a. 123,584 km²; p. (1970) 2,158,872.
Mississippi, principal R. of **USA**; rises in N. Minn. nr. L. Itasca; drains c. 3,170,000 km²; enters G. of Mexico in lge. delta nr. New Orleans; navigable, flood control problems; length 3,760 km (Mississippi–Missouri–Red Rock 6,176 km).
Missolonghi, t., **Greece**, pt. on inlet of G. of Patras; fish, tobacco; Byron died here 1824; p. (1971) 12,368.
Missoula, t., Mont., **USA**; on Klark R.; univ.; rly. wks., agr., fruit, oil refinery; tourism; p. (1970) 29,497.
Missouri, st., central **USA**; dominated by Mississippi and Missouri Rs.; predominantly agr.; livestock, maize; coal, iron; transport equipment; cap. Jefferson City; ch. t. St. Louis; a. 180,456 km²; p. (1970) 4,636,247.
Missouri, longest R. of **USA**; 3,942 km; trib of Mississippi R.; main headstream Jackson R.; flood, power and irrigation schemes.
Missouri Coteau, hill ridge, **N. America**; runs N.W. to S.E. across prairies of Saskatchewan (Canada), N. and S. Dakota (USA); rises abruptly from 480–600 m.
Mistassini, L., Quebec, **Canada**; 160 km long.
Misurata, t., Tripolitania, **Libya**; on cst. of Mediterranean, 176 km E. of Tripoli; mkt. for local agr. produce; p. (1964) 37,000.
Mitau. *See* **Jelgava**.
Mitchelstown, t., Cork, **R.o.I.**; nr. Fermoy; dairy prods.; p. (1966) 2,617.
Mitidja, plain, **Algeria**; N. Africa; borders Mediterranean; intensive cultivation of vine; ch. ts. Algiers, Blida.
Mito, c., Honshu, **Japan**; cas., comm. ctr.; famous for lime trees; p. (est. 1971) 179,000.
Mittelland Canal, inland waterway system, **W. Germany**; system of canals and canalised Rs.; links Dortmund–Ems canal nr. Rheine through Minden, Hanover, Magdeburg, Berlin to R. Oder at Frankfurt-on-Oder; makes use of natural E.–W. troughs across the N. German plain.
Mittweida, t., Karl-Marx-Stadt, **E. Germany**; metallurgy, textiles; p. (est. 1970) 19,600.
Miyazaki, c., Kyushu, **Japan**; famous shrine; ctr. of sandy plain with lagoons; p. (est. 1971) 207,000.
Mizoram ("Land of Highlanders"), new union terr. (1972), Assam, N.E. **India**; former Mizo Hills dist. of Assam; 80 per cent p. Christian; 44 per cent literate, higher proportion than any other a. except Kerala; cap. Aizawl a. 21,238 km²; p. (est. 1971) 400,000.
Mjosa, lgst. L., **Norway**; 88 km long.
Mladá Boleslav (Jungbunzlau), t., Bohemia, **ČSSR**; vehicles, agr. machin., textiles; once ctr. of Bohemian Brethren (followers of John Hus); p. (est. 1968) 28,790.
Moanda, spt. at mouth of Zaïre R., **Zaïre**; oil refinery, aluminium smelter.
Mobutu Seso, L., (L. Albert), **Zaïre, Uganda**; on floor of Gt. Rift Valley; crocodile farming; tourism; main pt. Kasenyi; 160 km long, 32 km wide; alt., 640 m; a. 5,346 km².
Mobile, c., spt., Ala. **USA**; on R. M.; shipbldg. pt. inds.; exp. cotton; p. (1970) 129,009 (c.). 231,105 (met. a.).
Moçambique, former Portuguese prov., indep. st. (1975), **E. Africa**; wide cstl. plain rising inland to 2,100 m; crossed by Zambesi R.; few exp. inc. cashew nuts, cotton, sugar, tea; deposits of coal and bauxite; Beira and Maputo (cap.) serve as import pts. for transit tr.; 40% GNP from tourism and transport; Cabora Bassa dam project in Tete dist.; border with Rhodesia closed March 1976; a. 771,820 km²; p. (est. 1969) 7,376,000.
Moçambique Channel, strait, **Indian Oc.**; separates Malagasy Rep. from mainland of Africa; 1,600 km long, 400–960 km wide.
Moçambique Current, ocean current, flows N. to S. along E. cst. of Moçambique and Natal, E. Africa; relatively warm water.
Moçâmedes, pt., **Angola**, W. Africa; ore pier; linked by rail to Cassinga mines; fishing; p. 8,000.
Mocha or Al-Mukha, t., **N. Yemen**; S.W. Arabia; on Red Sea; formerly noted for exp. of coffee; p. 5,000.
Modane, t., S.E. Savoie, **France**; commands routes via Mont Cenis Pass and tunnel; electro-metallurgy; p. (1968) 5,767.
Modena, t., cap. of M. prov., **Italy**; cath., univ.; textiles, leather, engin.; p. (1968) 167,310.
Modesto, t., Cal., **USA**; fruit (especially peaches), vegetable-processing; p. (est. 1969) 52,000.
Modica, t., S.E. Sicily, **Italy**; agr. ctr.; limestone grottoes, cave dwellings; Cava d'Ispica; p. (est. 1968) 44,574.
Moffat, burgh, Annandale and Eskdale, **Scot.**; 24 km N.W. of Lockerbie; resort; p. (1971) 2,031.
Moffat Tunnel, Col., **USA**; carries trunk rly. from Chicago to San Francisco under Rocky mtns. between Denver and Salt Lake City; 10 km long; alt. 2,774m.

Mogadishu, c., cap. of Rep. of Somalia; on Indian Oc.; modernised deep-sea pt., airpt.; p. (est. 1972) 230,000.
Mogador. *See* Essaouira.
Mogi das Cruzes, t., São Paulo, Brazil; agr.; bauxite mng.; p. (est. 1968) 111,554.
Mogilev, c., Belorussiyan SSR, USSR; on R. Dnieper; industl.; rly. and route junc.; p. (1970) 202,000.
Mohács, t., S. Hungary; on Danube; impt. R. pt.; strategic site; battle 1526; p. (est. 1967) 15,900.
Mohammedia, t., Morocco, N. Africa; oil refining; p. (1960) 35,010.
Mohawk, R., N.Y., USA; trib. of Hudson R.; followed by impt. road, rly. and canal routes across Appalachian mtns.; 280 km long.
Mojave or **Mohave**, S. Cal., USA; desert region of mtns. and valleys; a. 38,850 km².
Moji, spt., Kyushu, Japan; exp. coal, cement, timber; linked by bridge to Honshu. *See* Kitakyushu.
Mokpo, spt., W. cst. S. Korea; ctr. of food-processing and cotton-ginning; p. (1966) 162,322.
Mol, t., N.E. Belgium; nuclear energy research ctr.; p. (est. 1969) 28,440.
Mold, t., Clwyd, N. Wales; on R. Alyn; chemicals roadstone; p. (1971), 8,239.
Moldau. *See* Vltava.
Moldavian SSR, constituent rep., USSR; fertile fruit growing a. especially for vines; inds. based on fruit; cap. Kishinev; a. 34,188 km²; p. (1970) 3,372,000.
Mole, R., Surrey, Eng.; rises in central Weald, flows N. into R. Thames nr. Molesey; cuts impt. gap through N. Downs between Dorking and Leatherhead; 80 km long.
Molenbeek-Saint-Jean, t., Belgium; nr. Brussels; lge mftg. ctr.; p. (est. 1967) 67,500.
Molesey, E. and W., t., Surrey, Eng.; at junc. of Rs. Mole and Thames; residtl.
Molfetta, spt., Apulia, Italy; olive oil, macaroni, wine; caths.; p. (est. 1967) 65,100.
Moline, t., Ill., USA; on Mississippi R.; agr. implements, ironwks., flour; p. (est. 1969) 49,000.
Mollendo, t., S.W. Peru; pt. on Pac. Oc.; former outlet for Arequipa; replaced by Matarani; wool textiles, fishing; p. (1961) 18,000.
Mölndal, t., S.W. Sweden; paper, textiles; margarine; p. (1968) 31,125.
Moluccas or **Spice Is.**, prov. Indonesia; gr. of Is. between Sulawesi and W. Irian; mtnous., fertile; spices, sago, timber, pearls, rice, copra, ch. t. Ternate; attempts at secession by S. Moluccans; a. 496,454 km²; p. (est. 1970) 995,000.
Mombasa, spt., Kenya; ch. harbour, Killindini; rly. terminus; oil refinery; exp. tropical produce (ivory, hides, rubber, etc.); p. (est. 1970) 255,400.
Mon, I., off cst. of Sjaelland, Denmark; a. 233 km².; cap. Stege; p. (1965) 12,318.
Monaco, principality, on Mediterranean cst. between France and Italy, W. Europe; economy based on tourism; benefits from climate and amenities, inc. famous casino; tax laws attract p. and shortage of land causes M. to build out into sea; much revenue derived from transactional laws, sales of tobacco and postage stamps; cap. Monte Carlo; a. 146 ha; p. (1968) 23,035.
Monadhliath Mtns., Badenoch and Strathspey, Scot.; between Spey R. and Loch Ness; hgst. peak Carn Mairg 1,216 m.
Monadnock Mt., peak, 965 m high, N.H., USA; name used as term for the geomorphological feature of an isolated hill which has successfully resisted erosion.
Monaghan, co., R.o.I.; mainly pastoral and agr.; a. 1,295 km²; p. (1966) 45,726.
Monaghan, co. t., Monaghan, R.o.I.; on the Ulster canal; cath.; p. (1966) 4,019.
Mona Passage, strait, Caribbean Sea; separates Hispaniola from Puerto Rico.
Monastir. *See* Bitola.
Mönch, peak, Bernese Alps, Switzerland; 4,101 m.
Monchegorsk, t., RSFSR; on L. Imandra; copper and nickel smelting; p. (est. 1969) 53,000.
Mönchengladbach, t., N. Rhine-Westphalia, W. Germany; 26 km W. of Düsseldorf; rly. ctr., textiles; p. (est. 1969) 152,200.
Monchique, t., Algarve, Portugal; spa; wine, oil, chestnuts; p. 10,000.
Moncton, t., N.B., Canada; rly. ctr., textiles; oil nearby; p. (1971) 47,781.
Mondego, R., Portugal; 208 km long.
Monfalcone, t., N.E. Italy; on Adriatic; modern industl. t.; shipbldg., oil refining; p. (1968) 27,907.
Monferrato, low hills, Piedmont, N. Italy; S. and S.E. of Turin between valleys of Po and Tanaro; celebrated vineyards, produce Asti Spumante wines; alt. never exceeds 460 m.
Monghyr, t., Bihar, India; on R. Ganges; mkt. ctr.; p. (1971) 102,474.
Mongla, pt., Bangladesh; on Pussur R.; shipping pt. under construction.
Mongolia, vast elevated plateau in heart of Asia between China and USSR. *See* Mongolian People's Rep. and Inner Mongolia.
Mongolia, Inner. *See* Inner Mongolia.
Mongolia, People's Rep. of (Outer Mongolia), central Asia; extensive plateau at 1,200 m bordering Gobi desert in S.; dry continental climate with extremely cold winters; pastoral agr. collectively organised for horses, sheep, camels, oxen, and goats; extensive state farms for cereals; 60 per cent of tr. with USSR; cap. Ulan Bator; a. 1,564,360 km²; p. (1970) 1,227,000.
Monmouth, t., Gwent, Wales; at confluence of Rs. Wye and Monnow; mkt. ctr.; timber, crushed limestone, wrought ironwk.; p. (1971) 6,545.
Monmouthshire, former co., S. Wales; mostly inc. in Gwent; parts in South and Mid Glamorgan.
Monongahela, R., W. Va., USA; joins Allegheny R. at Pittsburgh to form Ohio R.; impt. waterway.
Monopoli, spt., Apulia, Italy; oil, wine, fruit, flour tr.; p. (est. 1968) 39,746.
Monroe, t., La., USA; cotton ctr., natural gas, paper, printing ink; p. (1970) 54,647 (c.), 111,527 (met. a.).
Monrovia, c., cap. of Liberia, W. Africa; pt. on Atl. at mouth of St. Paul R.; exp. rubber, palm oil; ship registration; p. (est. 1970) 96,226.
Mons, c., cap. of Hainaut prov., W. Belgium, nr. Fr. border; cath.; inds linked with Borinage coal-mng. dist.; varied mnfs.; scene of many battles; NATO (SHAPE) H.Q. nearby at Casteau; p. (1968) 27,680.
Montana, st., N.W. USA; in Rocky mtns. region; cap. Helena; lgst c. Great Falls; copper, silver, gold, zinc, lead, manganese; coal, petroleum, natural gas; pastoral agr.; Glacier Nat. Park, tourism; a. 377,456 km²; p. (1970) 682,133.
Montauban, t., Tarn-et-Garonne dep., France; on R. Tarn; cath.; agr. prod., wines; p. (1968) 48,555.
Montbéliard, t., Doubs dep., France; S. of Belfort; textiles, watches, typewriters, vehicles; p. (1968) 23,908 (t.), 114,670 (met. a.).
Mont Blanc, mtn., Alps; on confines of Italy and France; alt. 4,814 m; longest road tunnel in world (opened to traffic 1965) linking Courmayeur (Italy) and Chamonix (France), length 12 km.
Montceau-les-Mines, t., Saône-et-Loire dep., France; coal, textiles, metal-working; p. (1968) 27,421.
Mont Cenis Pass, W. Alps; on bdy. between France and Italy; approached from W. by Isère–Arc valleys, from E. by Dora Riparia; alt. 2,097 m.
Mont Cenis Tunnel, W. Alps; on bdy. between France and Italy; carries main rly. from Lyons to Turin under Col de Fréjus; approached from W. by Isère–Arc valleys, from E. by Dora Riparia; opened 1871; 12 km long.
Montclair, t., N.J., USA; residtl. sub. of N.Y.; paper gds. mnfs.; p. (1970) 44,043.
Mont-de-Marsan, t., Landes dep., France; mkt. ctr.; p. (1968) 24,458.
Mont-Dore, spa, Puy-de-Dôme dep., France; 48 km S.W. of Clermont-Ferrand; Puy de Sancy (1,887 m) hgst. peak of Mont-Dore mtn. gr.; p. (1968) 2,419.
Monte Bello Is., gr. off N.W. cst., Australia; about 136 km N. of pt. of Onslow; first Brit. atomic weapon exploded here 3 Oct. 1952.

Monte Carlo, t., **Monaco**; tourist resort, casino; p. (1961) 9,516.

Monte Corno, mtn., **Italy**; in Central Apennines; alt. 2,923 m.

Monte Cristo, Italian I., 42 km S. of Elba, in Tyrrhenian Sea; famed by novel by Dumas.

Monte Gargano, peninsula, S. **Italy**; projects into Adriatic Sea nr. plain of Foggia; formed by limestone plateau, alt. over 900 m; pasture on upper slopes, woodland on lower slopes; a. 1,030 km^2.

Montego Bay, spt., **Jamaica**; main ctr. for tourism; p. (est. 1970) 42,800.

Montélimar, t., Drôme dep., **France**; bricks, tiles, nougat; hydroelectric barrage on R. Rhône; p. (1968) 27,483.

Montenegro, constituent rep., S.W. **Yugoslavia**; agr., pastoral; cap. Titograd; a. 13,812 km^2; p. (1971) 530,361.

Monterey, t., Cal., **USA**; S. of San Francisco, resort of artists and writers; sardine ind., fruit and vegetable canneries; p. (est. 1969) 26,500.

Monteria, c., cap. of Cordoba prov., **Colombia**; tobacco, cacao, cotton, sugar; p. (est. 1972) 121,200 (c.), 167,600 (met. a.).

Monte Rosa, hgst. peak, 4,637 m, Pennine Alps, on border of **Italy** and **Switzerland**.

Monte Rotondo, hgst. mtn., Corsica, **France**; 2,767 m.

Monterrey, t., cap. of Nuevo León prov., **Mexico**; third lgst. c.; cath.; textiles, brewing, ironwks., minerals; thermoelec. plant; sheet metal; p. (1970) 858,107 (c.), 1,213,479 (met. a.).

Monte Sant'Angelo, hilltop t., **Italy**; on Gargano promontory; notable ctr. of pilgrimage; p. (est. 1968) 20,092.

Montevideo, c., cap. of **Uruguay**; major pt. on Rio de la Plata; dominates life of rep. as financial, comm. and industl. ctr.; fisheries, oil-refining, food-processing, tourism; cath., univ.; p. (est. 1967) 1,280,000.

Montgomery, t., Powys, central **Wales**; in upper Severn valley, 13 km N.E. of Newtown; agr. mkt.; cas.; p. (1971) 968.

Montgomery, t., W. Punjab, **Pakistan**; livestock; leather, cotton; p. (1961) 25,100.

Montgomery, c., cap. of Ala., **USA**; at head of Alabama R.; cotton, livestock, timber, dairying, fertilisers; hydroelec. power; p. (1970) 129,375 (c.), 194,522 (met. a.).

Montgomeryshire, former co., Central **Wales**. *See* **Powys**.

Montluçon, t., Allier dep., **France**; on R. Cher; terminus of Berry canal, linking Commentry coalfields with Loire; iron foundries, glass-making; cas.; p. (1968) 59,983.

Montmartre, dist., N. Paris, **France**; on Butte de M. (101 m), commands superb view S. over Paris; picturesque square, frequented by artists; basilica of Sacré Coeur.

Montparnasse, dist., Paris, **France**; on left bank of Seine R.; haunt of artists and writers.

Montpellier, t., cap. of Hérault dep., **France**; 8 km N. of Mediterranean cst. on coastal low-land route to S.W. France; comm. and cultural ctr.; univ.; wines, fruit tr.; silk, chemicals; many anc. bldgs. inc. cath.; p. (1968) 161,910 (c.), 171,467 (met. a.).

Montreal, c., spt., Quebec, **Canada**; at confluence of Ottawa and St. Lawrence Rs.; caths., univs.; major industl., comm. and financial ctr.; extensive harbour installations, lge. grain exp.; diverse mnfs.; lgst c. and spt. in Canada; p. mainly French-speaking; p. (1971) 1,197,753 (c.); 2,720,413 (met. a.).

Montreuil-sous-Bois, E. sub. Paris, **France**; hot-house flowers and fruit for Paris mkt.; peach growing; mnfs.; p. (1968) 95,859.

Montreux, t., **Switzerland**; on L. Geneva; tourist ctr.; Chillon cas.; p. (1969) 19,900.

Montrose, spt., burgh, Angus, **Scot.**; on E. cst. at mouth of S. Esk R.; chemicals, rope wks., vegetable-canning, boat-bldg., fishing; supply base for N. Sea oil; p. (1971) 9,959.

Mont-Saint-Michel, rocky granite I., in English Channel, off Normandy cst., **France**; tourist ctr. with Benedictine abbey; connected to mainland by causeway; surrounding marshland reclaimed for agr.; alt. 79 m.

Montserrat, volcanic I., Leeward Is., **W.I.**,; chiefly agr.; exp. sea-island cotton, limes, sugar-cane and tomatoes; cap. Plymouth; a. 101 km^2; p. (1968) 14,500.

Montserrat, mtn., Catalonia, **Spain**; Benedictine monastery, alt. 1,236 m.

Monument Valley, Utah and Arizona, **USA**; home of Navajo Indians.

Monza, c., Lombardy, N. **Italy**; 14 km from Milan; cath.; textiles, leather, hats; former royal residence; motor-racing circuit; p. (1968) 103,460.

Moonie, t., Queensland, **Australia**; 320 km W. of Brisbane; oilfields; pipeline to Lytton, at mouth of Brisbane R.

Moose Jaw, c., Saskatchewan, **Canada**; rly. junc.; agr. ctr.; agr. implements, oil refining. p. (1966) 33,417.

Moradabad, c., Uttar Pradesh, N. **India**; rly. junc.; cotton mills, brassware; mosque; p. (1971) 258,590 (c.), 272,652 (met. a.).

Morava, R., **ČSSR** and **Austria**; trib. of R. Danube; navigable in lower course; 339 km long.

Morava, R., **Yugoslavia**; formed from W. Morava and S. Morava, flows N. into Danube 80 km below Belgrade to Istanbul; 560 km long.

Moravia, region, **ČSSR**; part of Bohemian plateau, drained by Morava R.; inc. fertile agr. a.; mineral resources and industl. ts.

Moray, former co., l. gov. dist., Grampian Reg., **Scot.**; borders M. Firth; arable agr. benefiting from glacial soils; a. 2,230 km^2; p. (1971) 76,595.

Moray Firth, arm of N. Sea; on Scottish E. cst., between Highland and Grampian Regs.; plans for lge.-scale industl. expansion.

Morbihan, dep., N.W. **France**; on Bay of Biscay; agr., fishing; cap. Vannes; a. 7,094 km^2; p. (1968) 540,474.

Mordovian ASSR, RSFSR; forested steppe between Rs. Oka and Volga; pastoral agr., lumbering; food processing; a. 25,493 km^2; p. (1970) 1,030,000.

Morea. *See* **Peloponnesus**.

Morecambe and Heysham, t., N. Lancs., **Eng.**; on S. shore of M. Bay; M. holiday resort; H., pt. for N. Ireland and oil refinery; nuclear power sta. being built on cst. S. of M.; p. (1971) 41,863.

Morecambe Bay, between Lancs. and Cumbria, **Eng.**; isolates Furness dist. of Lancs.; many proposed barrages across Bay, now project increasingly probable as water shortage in N.W. Eng. grows.

Morelia, c., cap. of Michoacán st., W. **Mexico**; on rocky hill, 1,891 m in fertile valley; cath.; textiles, pottery; p. (1970) 161,040.

Morelos, inland st., **Mexico**; mtns., forested; arable agr.; cap. Cuernavaca; a. 4,962 km^2; p. (1969) 597,000.

Morez, t., Jura dep., **France**; precision instruments, optical equipment; winter sports.

Morgan, t., R. pt., S. **Australia**; on R. Murray, handles transhipment of Murray and Darling R. traffic to rail for despatch to Adelaide.

Morgantown, c. W. Va., **USA**; univ.; coal, oil, gas fields; chemicals, heavy ind.; p. (1970) 29,341.

Morioka, c., N. Honshu, **Japan**; textiles, ironwks.; p. (est. 1971) 202,000.

Morlaix, spt., Finistère, **France**; tobacco, paper, brewing, agr.; p. (1968) 21,516.

Morley, t., West Yorks., **Eng.**; 5 km S.W. of Leeds; woollens, stone quarrying; p. (1971) 44,340.

Morocco, kingdom, N.W. **Africa**; csts. on Atl. Oc. and Mediterranean Sea; rises to Atlas mtns. inland; leading world producer of phosphates; other minerals inc. iron-ore, lead and manganese; agr. main occupation, wheat, barley, maize and livestock; fishing and tourism well developed; cap. Rabat; a. 466,200 km^2; p. (1969) 15,030,000.

Morogoro, t., **Tanzania**, E. Africa; on E. edge of Central African plateau, alt. *c.* 900 m, 176 km by rail W. of Dar-es-Salaam; ctr. of sisal- and cotton-growing a.

Moron, t., **Venezuela**; on cst. nr. Puerto Cabello; industl.; natural gas, oil refining.

Morón de la Frontera, t., S.W. **Spain**; agr. tr. ctr.; ruined Moorish cas.; p. (1970) 29,488.

Morpeth, t., Northumberland, **Eng.**; finely situated in valley of Wansbeck; coal mng., iron-founding; mkt.; Norman cas. remains; p. (1971) 14,055.

Morriston, v., West Glamorgan, S. **Wales**; on R. Tawe, 3 km N.E. of Swansea; zinc. inds.

Morro Velho, gold mng. dist., Minas Gerais, **Brazil**; in Serra do Espinhaco; ch. t. Nova Lima.

Mors, I., N. Jutland, **Denmark**; in Lim fjord; a. 357 km²; p. (1965) 25,739.

Morwell, t., Victoria, **Australia**; industl.; coal mng.; p. (1972) 16,827.

Moscow, c., cap. of **USSR**, and of **RSFSR**; leading cultural, political, comm., industl. and route ctr. of USSR; on Moskva R.; served by several airpts., R. and canal pts.; contains Kremlin in c. ctr. with Red Square; caths., univs., palaces, many famous theatres and art galleries; p. (1970) 6,942,000 (c.); (1976) 7,632,000 (met. a.).

Moscow Sea (Ucha Reservoir), artificial L., **RSFSR**; created behind dam on R. Volga at Ivankovo; supplies water to Moscow, maintains level on Moscow–Volga canal, and supplies water to 8 hydroelec. power-stas.; a. 329 km².

Moscow–Volga Canal, RSFSR; links R. Volga at Ivankovo with Khimki sub. of Moscow; forms part of Leningrad–Moscow inland waterway; opened 1937; 128 km long.

Moselle, dep., N.E. **France**; iron-ore, coal mng.; metal inds.; cap. Metz; a. 6,224 km²; p. (1968) 971,314.

Moselle, R., **France** and **Germany**; trib. of R. Rhine; canalised between Thionville and Koblenz (269 km); lower valley forms famous wine dist.; 525 km long.

Moshi, t., N. **Tanzania**; on southern slope of Mt. Kilimanjaro; ctr. of coffee-growing dist.; airpt. at 854 m (S.W. of t.).

Mosi-oa-Toenja. *See* **Victoria Falls**. The local name means "Smoke of the Thunders."

Mosjoen, t., N. **Norway**; recent aluminium wks.

Moskva, R., central **RSFSR**; trib. of R. Oka; Moscow stands on its banks; linked with upper Volga by Moscow–Volga canal (128 km long); 400 km long.

Mosonmagyaróvár, t., **Hungary**; aluminium wks.; agr. machin.; p. (1966) 24,100.

Mosquito Cst., lowland, E. cst. **Nicaragua**; 400 km N.–S., 192 km E.–W.; lumbering, bananas; ch. t. Bluefields; sparse p.

Moss, spt., **Norway**; pulp, paper, machin., textile inds.; p. (est. 1970) 24,580.

Mossamedes. *See* **Moçâmedes**.

Mossel Bay, pt. and seaside resort, Cape Prov., **S. Africa**; between Cape Town and Port Elizabeth; p. (est. 1967) 15,600.

Mossley, t., Gtr. Manchester, **Eng.**; 5 km E. of Oldham; mkt. t., textiles; p. (1971) 10,055.

Most, t., **ČSSR**; lignite, chemicals; Druzhba crude oil pipeline extended to chemical wks.; p. (1967) 56,000.

Mostaganem, t., **Algeria**; spt. on Mediterranean cst., E. of Oran; exp. wine and fruits; gas pipeline from Hassi Messoud; p. (1967) 64,000.

Mostar, t., Herzegovina, **Yugoslavia**; on R. Naretva; bauxite, lignite; developing inds., wine, food-processing, aluminium plant; p. (est. 1965) 56,000.

Mosul, t., N. **Iraq**; on R. Tigris; in region producing cereals, citrus fruit, cattle; impt. oilfields nearby; metal work; impt. during crusades; p. (1965) 264,146.

Motala, t., on L. Vättern, **Sweden**; radio sta.; engin., woollen gds.; p. (1968) 27,887.

Motherwell and Wishaw, burgh, l. gov. dist., Strathclyde Reg., **Scot.**; in Clyde valley, 24 km S.E. of Glasgow; iron, steel, machin., engin., textiles; p. (1971) 73,658.

Moulins, c., cap. of Allier dep., **France**; on Allier R.; leather gds., clothing; cath., ruined château, art treasures; p. (1968) 27,408.

Moulmein, spt., **Burma**, on R. Salween; exp. teak, rice; p. (1966) 156,968.

Mountain Ash, t., Mid Glamorgan, **Wales**; in narrow valley 5 km S.E. of Aberdare; coal-mng. a.; p. (1971) 27,806.

Mount Adams, mtn., S. Wash. **USA**; beautiful volcanic scenery in Cascade Range; pine forests; alt. 3,803 m.

Mount Albert, bor., Auckland, **N.Z.**; p. (1972) 26,150.

Mount Alberta, mtn., W. Alberta, **Canada**; in Canadian Rockies and Jasper Nat. Park; alt. 3,622 m.

Mount Assiniboine, mtn., Alberta, B.C., **Canada**; "Matterhorn" of Canadian Rockies; alt. 3,620 m.

Mount Carmel, mtn., N.W. **Israel**; rises to 554 m and extends 19 km as penin. into Mediterranean Sea, forming S. limit to Bay of Acre; ass. with prophets Elijah and Elisha.

Mount Eden, bor., Auckland, **N.Z.**; p. (1972) 20,061.

Mount Goldsworthy, t., **W. Australia**; new t. being developed in iron ore mng. a.

Mount Isa, t., W. Queensland, **Australia**; in Selwyn Range 128 km W. of Cloncurry; copper mng.; p. (1972) 25,240.

Mount Lofty Range, mtn. range, **S. Australia**; forms barrier to routes leaving Adelaide; lower slopes support vineyards and outer suburbs of Adelaide; rises to over 900 m.

Mount Lyell, Tasmania, **Australia**; impt. copper mines, and refinery.

Mount McKinley, Alaska, **USA**; in Alaska Range and Nat. Park; highest point in N. America, c. 6,191 m.

Mountmellick, t., R.D., Laoighis, **R.o.I.**; p. (1961) 22,596 (R.D.).

Mount Newman, W. Australia; new t. built 1967 to exploit nearby iron ore.

Mount of Olives, Jordan; ridge (817 m), E. of Jerusalem; Garden of Gethsemane on lower slopes.

Mount Roskill, bor., Auckland, **N.Z.**; p. (1971) 33,842.

Mount's Bay, inlet, S. cst., Cornwall, **Eng.**; 32 km wide; fishery grounds.

Mount Tom Price, t., **W. Australia**; new t., being developed in iron ore mng. a.

Mount Vernon, c., N.Y., **USA**; on Bronx R.; sub. of N.Y.; residtl.; takes name from George Washington's house on Potomac, Va., 24 km S. of Washington D.C.; varied inds., notably electronic equipment; p. (1970) 72,778.

Mount Wellington, bor., Auckland, **N.Z.**; p. (1971) 20,178.

Mourenx, t., S.W. Aquitaine, **France**; nr. Lacq; new t. in oil dist.; p. (1966) 8,660.

Mourne Mtns., Newry and Mourne, **N. Ireland**; hgst. peak, 853 m.

Mouscron, t., **Belgium**; textile ctr. nr. Fr. border; p. (1968) 37,746.

Moyle, l. gov. dist., **N. Ireland**; borders N.E. cst.; inc. Rathlin I., Giants Causeway; main t. Ballycastle.

Mozambique. *See* **Moçambique**.

Mühlhausen, t., Erfurt, **E. Germany**; on R. Unstrut; textiles, machin., tobacco; p. (est. 1970) 45,385.

Mukden. *See* **Shenyang**.

Mulhaćen, mtn., Sierra Nevada range, **Spain**; 3,483 m (hgst. peak Europe, outside Alps).

Mülheim-an-der-Ruhr, t., N. Rhine–Westphalia, **W. Germany**; on R. Ruhr; cas.; coal mng., iron, steel, tobacco, engin., elec., oil refining; airpt.; p. (est. 1969) 190,400.

Mulhouse, t., Haut-Rhin dep., **France**; impt. textile ctr.; potash deposits to N. supply chemical inds.; p. (1968) 116,336 (c.), 199,037 (met. a.).

Mull, I., Argyll and Bute, **Scot.**; included in Hebrides; a. 925 km²; pastoral farming, fishing, tourism; ch. t. Tobermory; p. (1971) 1,569.

Mullet, The, peninsula, W. cst. Mayo, **R.o.I.**

Mullingar, co. t., Westmeath, **R.o.I.**; on Brosna R.; mkt., agr. ctr.; cath.; p. (1966) 6,453.

Mull of Galloway, S. point of Wigtown, **Scot.**

Multan, t., W. Punjab, **Pakistan**; on R. Chenab; carpets, silks, pottery; steel, thermal sta.; gas pipeline to Lyallpur; p. (est. 1969) 597,000.

Muncie, t., Ind. **USA**; on White R.; iron, steel, glass and paper; p. (1970) 68,066 (c.), 127,861 (met. a.).

Munich or München, c., cap. Bavaria, **W. Germany**; on R. Isar; cultural ctr. with univ., cath., many old bldgs.; inds. varied, notably scientific instruments, brewing, elec. engin., chemicals; film studios; p. (est. 1969) 1,302,600.

Münster, c., N. Rhine–Westphalia, **W. Germany**; pt. on Dortmund–Ems canal; heavy machin., with varied mnfs.; cath., univ. and mediæval bldgs. damaged or destroyed in second world war; p. (est. 1969) 203,300.

Munster, prov., S.W. **R.o.I.**; includes cos. Waterford, Kerry, Cork, Limerick, Clare, Tipperary; a. 24,540 km²; p. (1966) 969,902.

Muonio, R., part of bdy. between **Finland** and **Sweden**; flows into G. of Bothnia.

Murano, t., Venice, **Italy**; famous since Middle Ages for glass ind.

Murchison Falls. *See* **Kabelega Falls.**

Murchison, R., W. Australia; length 1,280 km; near-by gold-field.

Murcia, prov. and former Moorish kingdom, S.E. **Spain**, on Mediterranean ("Almonds and Raisins Coast"); irrigated agr., cereals and fruit; cap. Murcia; a. 8,467 km²; p. (1970) 832,313.

Murcia, c., cap. of Murcia prov., S.E. **Spain**; on R. Segura; cath., univ.; textiles and food inds.; p. (1968) 274,560.

Murgab or **Murghab, R., Agfhanistan**; flows 400 km to desert swamps.

Murmansk, spt., **RSFSR**; on Kola peninsula; ice-free throughout year; engin., elec. power; fishing, shipbldg.; submarine base; marine power sta. utilising tidal energy projected; p. (1970) 309,000.

Murom, t., **RSFSR**; pt. on Oka R.; anc. t.; textiles, engin.; p. (est. 1967) 96,000.

Muroran, spt., Hokkaido, **Japan**; on W. cst.; impt. iron and steel ctr.; p. (est. 1971) 170,000.

Murray, R., separates N.S.W. and Victoria, **Australia**; major irrigation schemes; hydro-electric power; 2,560 km long; length Murray-Darling system 3,696 km.

Murrumbidgee, R., N.S.W., **Australia**; trib. of R. Murray; used extensively for irrigation; 2,160 km long.

Musa Jebel, mtn., **Egypt**; 2,249 m; identified with the biblical Sinai.

Muscat, t., cap. of **Oman**, Arabia; on S. cst. of G. of Oman; gd. harbour; dates, mother-of-pearl; terminal of oil pipeline; p. (est. 1969) 9,973.

Muscat and Oman. *See* **Oman.**

Musgrave Range, mtns., on bdy. between S. Australia and N.T., **Australia**; isolated highland in ctr. of continent; arid; rise to over 900 m.

Muskingum, R., Ohio, **USA**; trib. of Ohio R.; canalised for navigation; 384 km long.

Musselburgh, burgh, East Lothian, **Scot.**; on F. of Forth at mouth of R. Esk; wire, cables, nets, twine; paper mkg.; golf course; p. (1971) 16,790.

Mutankiang (Mudanjiang), c., Heilungkiang prov., **China**; pulp, paper, machin., flour milling; site of dam on R. Mutang; oil shale found locally; p. (est. 1970) 400,000.

Muttra. *See* **Mathura.**

Muzaffarnagar, t., Uttar Pradesh, **India**; N.E. of Delhi; p. (1971) 114,783.

Muzaffarpur, t., Bihar, **India**; in middle Ganges valley N. of Patna; p. (1971) 126,379.

Mwanza, t., N. **Tanzania**; pt. on L. Victoria; rly. term.; gold and diamonds mined; p. (1967) 34,186.

Mweelrea, mtn., Mayo, **R.o.I.**; 820 m.

Mweru, L., between **Zaïre** and **Zambia**; a. 6,993 km² at *c.* 900 m.

Mycenae, anc. c., N.E. Peloponnesus, **Greece**; excavations by Schliemann.

Myingyan, t., **Burma**; on R. Irrawaddy, S.W. of Mandalay; cotton spinning mill, zinc smelting, chemicals, fertilisers.

Myitkyina, t., **Burma**; on R. Irrawaddy; terminus of caravan route to China.

Mymensingh, t., **Bangladesh**; rice, jute; p. (1961) 53,200.

Mynyddisiwyn, t., Gwent, **Wales**; in narrow valley of W. Ebbw R., 11 km N.W. of Newport; elec. gds., kerb- and flagstones; p. (1971) 15,369.

Mystowice, t., Katowice, **Poland**; ctr. of coal-mng. dist.; technical porcelain; p. (1970) 44,700.

Mysore. *See* **Karnataka.**

Mysore, t., Karnataka, **India**; univ.; new inds. based on hydroelec. power; p. (1971) 355,685.

Mytilene, pt. on Aegean Sea, **Greece**; ch. c. of I. of Lesvos (sometimes called Mytilene).

N

Naantali, t., S.W. **Finland**; pt. for Turku, on Baltic Sea; oil-refining, chemicals; founded 15th cent.; p. (est.) 2,778.

Naas, co. t. Co. Kildare, **R.o.I.**; former cap. of Leinster prov.; p. (1966) 4,528.

Nabeul, t., **Tunisia**, N. Africa; winter resort; p. (1966) 34,134.

Nablus, t., **Jordan**, N. of Jerusalem; nr. site of anc. Schechem and Jacob's Well; p. (1967) 44,223.

Nadiad, t., Gujarat, **India**; S. of Ahmadabad; p. (1971) 108,269.

Nagaland, st., **India** (1963); incorporates Naga Hills and Tuengsang; tribal a., formerly parts of Assam; cap. Kohima; a. 16,488 km²; p. (1971) 515,561.

Nagano, c., central Honshu, **Japan**; on R. Sinanogawa, 160 km S.W. of Niigata; cultural ctr.; publishing, machin., food-processing; textiles; p. (est. 1971) 290,000.

Nagaoka, t., N.W. Honshu, **Japan**; lge. oil production ctr.; p. (est. 1971) 163,000.

Nagapattinam, t., Tamil Nadu, **India**; spt. at mouth of R. Vettar; exp. cotton, tobacco, groundnuts; rly. terminus; p. (1961) 59,063.

Nagasaki, c., spt., Kyushu, **Japan**; on narrow peninsula; second c. destroyed by atomic bomb in second world war; impt. shipbldg. ctr. and associated engin.; p. (est. 1971) 427,000.

Nagercoil, t., Tamil Nadu, **India**; extreme S. of Indian peninsula; coconut-processing; p. (1971) 141,288.

Nagh Hamadi (Nag' Hammâdi), t., Upper **Egypt**; on R. Nile 256 km above Asyût; site of barrage (opened 1930) to regulate Nile flood and ensure irrigation of Girga prov.; barrage carries Cairo–Shellal rly. across Nile.

Nagorno-Karabakh, aut. oblast, S.W. Azerbaydzhan SSR, **USSR**; on E. of Lesser Caucasus; forested mtns.; cap. Stepanakert; a. 4,403 km²; p. (1970) 149,000.

Nagoya, third c. of **Japan**; on Ise Bay, central Honshu; major pt. and industl. ctr.; univ.; textile mills, ceramic ctr., oil-refining; 16th cent. fortress t.; p. (est. 1971) 2,052,000.

Nagpur, c., Maharashtra st., **India**; univ.; admin. ctr.; textiles; Hindu temples; p. (1971) 866,076 (c.), 930,459 (met. a.).

Nagy Banya. *See* **Baia-Mare.**

Nagykanizsa, t., S.W. **Hungary**; industl. ctr.; heavy equipment, glasswks., beer; p. (1966) 37,800.

Nagykőrös, mkt. t., S.W. **Hungary**; in fruit-growing region; wine, food-processing; p. (1966) 25,400.

Naha, spt., cap. of Okinawa I., **Ryuku Is.**; (under 1971 treaty U.S. returns Is. to **Japan**); p. (est. 1971) 281,000.

Nailsworth, t., Gloucs., **Eng.**; in Cotswold Hills 6 km S. of Stroud; p. (1971) 3,974.

Nain, t., **Iran**; noted for very fine carpets; p. (1967) 40,289.

Nairn, former co., l. gov. dist., Highland Reg. **Scot.**; on Moray F., agr. a.; a. 420 km²; p. (1971) 9,665.

Nairn, royal burgh, Nairn, N.E. **Scot.**; fishing ctr.; cas.; p. (1971) 8,037.

Nairobi, c., cap. of **Kenya**; stands at *c.* 1,500 m on edge of Kenya highlands; modern c., 528 km from Mombasa; univ.; tourist ctr.; lt. inds.; wildlife game reserve; p. (est. 1970) 535,200. (met. a.).

Naivasha, L., **Kenya**; on floor of Gt. African Rift Valey; alt. 1,800 m.

Najaf or **Nejef**, c., **Iraq**; in Euphrates valley; Shiite Moslem pilgrimage ctr.; p. (1965) 134,027.

Nakhichevan, c., Azerbaydzhan SSR, **USSR**; food and wine inds.; ctr. of Nakhichevan aut. region; p. (1970) 33,000.

Nakhichevan ASSR, aut. rep., Azerbaydzhan SSR, **USSR**; borders Iran and Turkey; cotton, tobacco, rice, wheat in irrigated lowlands; salt and mineral deposits; a. 5,439 km².

Nakhodka, t., **RSFSR**; outpt. for Vladivostok on Sea of Japan; new t. 1950; p. (1970) 105,000.

Nakhon Pathom, t., **Thailand**; in central plain, S.W. of Bangkok; mkt. t.; p. (est. 1964) 31,746.

Nakhon Ratchasima, t., **Thailand**; on Mun R., in Korat plateau; rly. junc.; copper deposits nearby; p. (est. 1965) 54,310.

Nakhon si Thammarat, t., **Thailand**; in S. of Isthmus of Kra, on G. of Siam; anc. t.; mkt.; p. (est. 1964) 29,237.

Nakshov, spt., Lolland I., **Denmark**; sugar-refining; p. (est. 1970) 15,994.

Nakuru, t., **Kenya** rift valley (1,837 m), E. Africa; protected bird sanctuary (flamingoes) on L. Nakuru; wool-processing, fertilisers; p. (1969) 47,800.

Nalchik, c., cap. of Kabardino-Balkar ASSR, **RSFSR**; in foothills of N. Caucasus; food-processing; tourist resort; p. (1970) 146,000.
Namangan, c., Uzbek SSR, **USSR**; on Syr Dar'ya R., in Ferghana Valley; textiles, leather; p. (1970) 175,000.
Namaqualand, region, S.W. cst. of **Africa**; divided by Orange R. into Gr. N. in S.W. Africa, and Little N. in Cape Prov., Rep. of S. Africa; semi-arid; a. 259,000 km²; copper, diamonds.
Nam Dinh, t., **N. Vietnam**, nr. mouth of Red R.; cotton spinning, silk-weaving, glass; mkt.; p. 25,000.
Namhoi. *See* **Fatshan.**
Namib Desert, desert a. along coastal strip of S.W. Africa for 1,200 km; very dry a., and almost unused.
Namibia. *See* **South West Africa.**
Namsos, spt., central **Norway**; on Folda fjord; lumber, fish canning; textiles; copper; p. (est. 1970) 11,223.
Nam Tso, L., Tibet, **China**; lge. L. in ctr. of plateau of Tibet at 4,630 m.
Namur, c., cap. of N. prov., **Belgium**; at confluence of Meuse and Sambre Rs.; agr. processing, cutlery, glass; p. (1968) 32,418.
Nanaimo, t., B.C., **Canada**; pt. on Vancouver I.; timber and allied inds.; fisheries; boating and yachting; tourism; p. (1971) 14,762.
Nanchang, c., Kiangsi, **China**; on Kan R.; major transportation and industl. ctr.; textiles, machin., chemicals, paper; tractor wks.; dates from Sung dynasty (12th cent.); p. (est. 1970) 900,000.
Nancheng. *See* **Hanchung.**
Nancy, c., Meurthe-et-Moselle dep., **France**; industl. and admin. ctr.; univ., cath.; chemical ind. (based on local salt); anc. cap. of duchy of Lorraine; p. (1968) 123,428 (c.), 257,829 (met. a.).
Nanda Devi, mtn., Uttar Pradesh, **India**; in Himalayas, 7,822 m; first scaled, 1936.
Nanded, t., Maharashtra, **India**; on R. Godovari; tr. ctr.; p. (1971) 126,538.
Nanga Parbat, mtn., N.W. Kashmir, **India**, in W. Himalayas; alt. 8,131 m.
Nanking (Nanjing), c., Kiangsu, **China**; on Yangtze; cap. of China during Kuomintang régime 1928–49; famous seat of learning; tombs of founders of Ming dynasty; lge. motor vehicle plant, precision instruments, insecticides, cotton cloth, oil-refining; road-rail bridge over lowest reaches of Yangtze opened 1969; p. (est. 1970) 2,000,000.
Nanling, mtns., S. **China**; form divide between Rs. flowing N. to Yangtze R. and S. to Si R.; crossed by historic Cheling and Meiling Passes; alt. mainly below 1,800 m.
Nanning, c., cap. of Kwangsi prov. **China**; on Yu R.; ch. mkt. on S. frontier; rice transplanter factor; p. (est. 1970) 375,000.
Nan Shan, mtns., central **China**; branch range of Kunlun; rise to over 3,600 m.
Nanterre, N.W. sub. of Paris, **France**; cap. of Hauts-de-Seine dep.; aluminium mftg.; p. (1968) 90,632.
Nantes, spt., cap. of Loire-Atlantique dep., W. **France**; on R. Loire; ocean pt. St. Nazaire; impt. industl. and shipping ctr.; univ., cath., cas.; p. (1968) 259,208 (c.), 393,731 (met. a.).
Nantucket, I., Mass., **USA**; official W. end of trans-Atlantic sea-crossing; summer resort; fishing; p. (1970) 3,774.
Nantung (Nantong), c., Kiangsu, **China**; on N. bank of Yangtze R. estuary; cotton; p. (est. 1970) 300,000.
Nantwich, mkt. t., Cheshire, **Eng.**; on R. Weaver, 5 km S.W. of Crewe; brine baths; clothing, food prods.; p. (1971) 11,666.
Nantyglo and Blaina, t., Gwent, **Wales**; in narrow valley 3 km N. of Abertillery; footwear, rubber prods.; p. (1971) 10,609.
Napier, c., N.I., **N.Z.**; pt. and ch. c. of Hawke's Bay prov. dist.; exp. frozen meat; timber processing, fishing; p. (1971) 40,181.
Napo, R., rises in Ecuador, flows S.E. into Peru where it joins the Amazon; 880 km long.
Naples (Napoli), c., Campania, S. **Italy**; spt. on Bay of N., at foot of Vesuvius, opposite anc. Pompeii; exp. food prods.; impt. industl. ctr.; shipbldg., oil refining, food-processing; cultural and artistic ctr.; univ., cath.; tourism; p. (1969) 1,276,824.
Nara, c., S. Honshu, **Japan**; anc. religious ctr. and place of pilgrimage; colossal image of Buddha (16·3 m high); cap. of Japan 710–84; tourism; p. (est. 1971) 214,000.
Nara Basin, Honshu, **Japan**; agr. dist. serving the Kinki plain; intensive rice and vegetable cultivation.
Narayanganj, c., **Bangladesh**; S. of Dacca in middle Ganges delta; p. (est. 1972) 425,000.
Narberth, mkt. t., Dyfed, **Wales**; nr. head of Milford Haven; p. (1971) 936.
Narbonne, t., Aude dep., S. **France**; in Languedoc; nr. Mediterranean cst.; in wine-growing a.; impt. in Roman times; cath., palace (now town hall); p. (1968) 40,035.
Narew, R., **Poland** and **USSR**; flows to R. Vistula nr. Warsaw, *c.* 432 km long; ch. trib. W. Bug.
Narmada, R., central **India**; flows W. through Madhya Pradesh and Gujarat to G. of Cambay; 1,280 km long.
Narrabri, t., N.S.W., **Australia**; 480 km N. of Sydney; observatory with stellar interferometer (1964); p. (1966) 5,953.
Narrandera, t., N.S.W., **Australia**; on R. Murrumbidgee; collecting ctr. for wool, mutton, wheat, fruits produced in irrigated a.; p. (1966) 4,897.
Narrogin, t., W. **Australia**; major ctr. of wheat belt; p. (1966) 4,864.
Narva, t., N.E. Estonia, **USSR**; textiles, machin., sawmills; hydroelectric power; founded by Danes 1223; p. (est. 1967) 49,000.
Narvik, pt., N.W. **Norway**; sheltered by Lofoten Is.; ice-free; linked by rly. to iron-ore fields in N. Sweden; scene of fierce sea-battles between British and Germans 1940; p. (1969) 13,422.
Naseby, v., Northants., **Eng.**; battle where parliamentarians under Fairfax and Cromwell beat royalists under Charles I and Prince Rupert 1645.
Nashville, c., st. cap. Tenn., **USA**; pt. on Cumberland R.; rly. ctr.; impt. shipping, industl. and educational ctr.; food and tobacco prods., cellophane, rayon; univs. and colleges; p. (1970) 444,489 (c.), 535,932 (met. a.).
Nasik, t., Maharashtra, **India**; on R. Godavari; Hindu pilgrimage ctr.; metal work; p. (1971) 176,091 (t.), 271,681 (met. a.).
Nassau, spt., cap. Bahamas, **W.I.**; exp. forest, sea and agr. prods.; resort; p. (1970) 3,233 (t.), 101,503 (met. a.).
Nassau, I., Cook Is., **S. Pac. Oc.**; N.Z. terr.; uninhabited.
Nasser City, t., **Egypt**; rural development at Kom Ombo, N. of Aswan, for resettlement of 50,000 Nubians before formation of Lake Nasser behind the High Dam.
Natal, spt., cap. of Rio Grande do Norte st., **Brazil**; above mouth of Potengi R.; exp. sugar, cotton, salt, carnauba wax, hides; new textile mills; airport on main routes from Africa to S. America; p. (1970) 250,787.
Natal, prov., **S. Africa**; subtropical coastal climate; sugar-cane, tea, cereals; coal; oil at Dannhauser; cap. Pietermaritzburg; a. 91,385 km²; p. (1970) 2,138,907.
Natanya or **Nathania**, t., **Israel**; resort on Mediterranean cst.; food-processing; p. (1968) 57,900.
Natuna Is., **Indonesia**; I. gr. in S. China Sea, N.W. of Borneo; little developed; a. 2,113 km²; p. 27,000.
Naucratis, anc. c., **Egypt**; between Cairo and Alexandria; excavated by Flinders Petrie and Gardiner.
Naumburg, t., Halle, **E. Germany**; on R. Saale; cath.; textiles, leather, toys, chemicals; p. (est. 1967) 38,300.
Nauplia (Gr. Nauplion), pt. and comm. ctr., on E. cst. Peloponnesus, **Greece**; the anc. Argos; first cap. of indep. Greece 1830–4, when it was superseded by Athens.
Nauru, I., indep. rep. (1968), central **Pac. Oc.**; formerly admin. by Australia; coral I., heavily dependent on phosphate-mng.; deposits nearly exhausted and plans to ship out new soil by UN; a. 21 km²; p. (1970) 6,664.
Navan (An Uamh), U.D., Meath, **R.o.I.**; carpets; lead and zinc ores; p. (1971) 4,607.
Navarre, prov., N. **Spain**; bounded by Pyrenees; thickly wooded; cap. Pamplona; sugar-beet, cereals, cattle, hardwoods, vineyards; former kingdom; p. Basque; p. (1970) 832,313.

Naver, R., Sutherland, **Scot.**; flows N. to Pentland Firth; valley once densely p., cleared early 19th cent. to make room for sheep.
Naxos, I., **Greece**; in Aegean Sea, lgst of the Cyclades; famous for wine and fruit; a. 425 km^2; p. 19,000.
Nazareth, t., **Israel**; 34 km S.E. Acre; home of Jesus Christ; p. (est. 1970) 34,000.
Naze, The, C., S. point of Norway.
Nazilli, t., S.W. **Turkey**; on R. Menderes; agr., especially olives; p. (1965) 41,121.
Ndjamene (Fort Lamy), c., cap. of **Chad Rep.**; at confluence of Shari and Logone Rs.; isolated but ctr. of caravan tr.; airpt.; p. (est. 1972) 179,000. (met. a.).
Ndola, t., **Zambia**; nr. bdy. with Zaïre, 176 km by rail N. of Kabwe; ctr. of rich copper-mng. a., less impt. lead- and zinc-mng.; minerals despatched by rail E. to Beira and W. to Lobito Bay; oil refining nearby; international airpt. being built; p. (est. 1972) 201,300 (met. a.).
Neagh, Lough, L., **N. Ireland**; lgst. freshwater L. in Brit. Is.; a. 396 km^2; drained by R. Bann.
Neath, t., West Glamorgan, **Wales**; 10 km up R. Neath from Swansea Bay; coal, aluminium inds., oil refining; cas., abbey; p. (1971) 28,568.
Nebraska, st., **USA**; mainly prairie; cap. Lincoln; farming, meat-packing, wheat, maize, hay, potatoes, sugar-beet, apples, wool, livestock, petroleum, cement; a. 200,147 km^2; p. (1970) 1,468,101.
Neckar, R., **W. Germany**; rises between Swabian Jura and Black Forest; flows through Baden-Württemberg to Rhine at Mannheim; 384 km long.
Needles, chalk stacks in English Channel, off W. cst. of I. of Wight, **Eng.**
Neftyne Kamni, t., **USSR**; built on piles over Caspian Sea for Russian oil workers.
Negev, desert, region, S. **Israel**; new a. of irrigated agr.; oil and natural gas; p. (1962) c. 33,000.
Negombo, t., S.W. **Sri Lanka**; at mouth of Negombo lagoon; ctr. of coconut belt; metalware, ceramics; p. (est. 1968) 53,000.
Negril Beach, Jamaica; 40 km W. of Montego Bay; new resort to further Jamaica's tourist tr.
Negri Sembilan, st., **W. Malaysia**; on Strait of Malacca; tin and rubber; cap. Seremban; a. 6,682 km^2; p. (1970) 479,312.
Negro Rio, R., **Argentina**; flows into G. of St. Mathias, Atl. Oc.; used for irrigation, partly navigable.
Negro Rio, R., **Brazil**; one of ch. tribs. of R. Amazon; rises in Colombia, joins Amazon nr. Manaus; *c.* 1,520 km long.
Negro, Rio., Uruguay; flows from Brazil border to Uruguay R.; major multi-purpose project at Rincon del Bonete; 800 km long.
Negros, I., **Philippines**; S. of Mindanao; impt. sugar producing I.; copper deposits; a. 12,704 km^2; p. (1970) 2,307,493.
Neheim-Hüsten, t., N. Rhine-Westphalia, **W. Germany**; at confluence of Rs. Möhne and Ruhr; lamps, metals, chemicals; p. (est. 1969) 36,787.
Neikiang (Neijiang), c., Szechwan prov., **China**; on To R.; agr. ctr.; p. (est. 1970) 240,000.
Neisse or Nisa, two tribs. of R. Oder, (1) Western or Glatzer Neisse, frontier between Poland and E. Germany, 224 km long; (2) Eastern or Lausitzer Neisse, E. Silesia, Poland, 192 km long.
Neiva, t., **Colombia**; at head of navigation of R. Magdalena; tr. in cattle and coffee; panama hats; p. (est. 1972) 117,900 (t.), 124,700 (met. a.).
Nejd, dist., central Arabia; with Hejaz, forms kingdom of Saudi Arabia; mainly desert; impt. oil wells, horses, camels, dates, various fruits; cap. Riyadh; a. 1,087,800 km^2; p. (est.) 4,000,000.
Nellore, t., Andhra Pradesh, **India**; admin. ctr.; p. (1971) 133,590.
Nelson, R., **Canada**; drains L. Winnipeg to Hudson Bay; length (with its gr. trib. the Saskatchewan) 2,320 km.
Nelson, t., Lancs., **Eng.**; on N. flank of Rossendale 5 km N.E. of Burnley; cotton, iron and brick wks., lt. engin., paper; p. (1971) 31,225.
Nelson, t., S.I., **N.Z.**; pt. nr. head of Tasman Bay; fishing, fruit-packing, timber; coalfield; cath.; p. (1971) 29,270.
Neman (Pol. Niemen, Ger. Memel), R., Luaithnian SSR and Belorussiyan SSR, **USSR**; rises S.W. of Minsk and flows *c.* 920 km into Kurisches Haff (Courland Lagoon), Baltic Sea, forming sm. delta.
Nene, R., Northants., **Eng.**; rises nr. Naseby and flows 144 km to the Wash.
Nepal, indep. kingdom, S.E. **Asia**; on S. slopes of Himalayas and inc. Mt. Everest; isolated from India by malarial forested zone of Terai; N. mostly tropical forest and jungle; home of Gurkhas; poor transport; only 1,600 km of road; agr. in fertile valleys, rice, wheat, maize; cap. Katmandu; a. 141,414 km^2; p. (est. 1969) 10,845,000..
Nerbudda. *See* **Narmada.**
Ness, Loch. L., Inverness, **Scot.**; occupies N.E. end of Glenmore; forms link in Caledonian Canal; very deep; 36·4 km long.
Neston, t., Cheshire, **Eng.**; on N. side of Dee estuary; residtl.; p. (1971) 16,848.
Nestos, R. *See* **Mesta.**
Netherlands, kingdom, N.W. **Europe**; bounded by N. Sea, Belgium and W. Germany; comprises 11 provs.; since second world war has taken advantage of location at mouth of Rhine, opposite Thames estuary, to develop lge.-scale coastal inds., inc. iron and steel at IJmuiden, oil refining, petrochemicals at major European pt. complex of Rotterdam–Europort; similarly major industl. growth in conurbation of Randstad Holland in steering economy far away from formerly predominant agr. basis; agr. still impt. and major sea-flood control schemes around IJsselmeer and Rhine estuary are creating valuable land for intensive agr. in a densely populated cty.; recent discoveries of natural gas in Groningen have also turned cty. into major supplier of energy for European mkts.; practises advanced policy of social welfare; cap. Amsterdam; seat of govt. at The Hague; a. 36,175 km^2; p. (est. 1970) 12,957,621.
Netherlands Antilles (Curaçao), 2 gr. of Is. in Caribbean Sea, part of Lesser Antilles; main gr. off Venezuela inc. Curaçao, Bonaire and Aruba; 2nd gr. inc. volcanic Is. of St. Eustatius, Saba, and St. Maarten (S. part only); agr. of sm. importance as a result of low rainfall; benefits from Venezuelan oil ind.; oil refineries in Curaçao and Aruba; petrochemical inds.; indep. planned for 1980; cap. Willemstad; a. 1,020 km^2; p. (1969) 216,355.
Netze. *See* **Notec.**
Neubrandenburg, c., cap. of N. admin. dist., **E. Germany**; fibreglass, machin., chemicals; p. (est. 1970) 45,685.
Neuchâtel, can., **Switzerland**; in Jura mtns.; forested with some pastures; cattle, cheese, wine; watches, cutlery, cottons, hosiery; asphalt from Val de Travers; a. 800 km^2; p. (1969) 167,000.
Neuchâtel cap. of Neuchâtel can., **Switzerland**; on N. slope of Lake Neuchâtel; cas.; univ.; watches, jewellery, condensed milk; p. (1969) 36,800.
Neuchâtel, L., **Switzerland**; at S.E. foot of Jura mtns.; drains N.E. to R. Aare; vineyards on S. facing slopes; remains of lake dwellings, anc. Celtic site of La Tène culture.
Neuilly-sur-Seine, sub., W. of Paris, Hauts-de-Seine, **France**; fine bridge and cas.; engin.; p. (1968) 71,215.
Neumünster, t., Schleswig-Holstein, **W. Germany**; rly. ctr.; leather, paper and textile inds.; p. (est. 1969) 73,175.
Neunkirchen, t., Saarland, **W. Germany**; iron and steel mnfs.; coal mng.; p. (est. 1969) 44,633.
Neuquén, t., cap. of N. prov., **Argentina**; at confluence of Rs. Limay and Neuquén, in ctr. of fruit-farming dist.; p. (1960) 17,500.
Neusalz. *See* **Nowa Sól.**
Neusandetz. *See* **Nowy Sacz.**
Neuss, c., N. Rhine-Westphalia, **W. Germany**; rly. junc., canal pt.; nr. Rhine, opposite Düsseldorf; metal gds., food-processing; p. (est. 1969) 116,500.
Neustadt, t., Rhineland-Palatinate, **W. Germany**; on R. Haardt; agr. machinery; impt. wine tr.; p. (est. 1969) 50,882.
Neustadt. *See* **Wiener-Neustadt.**
Neutitschein. *See* **Nový Jičin.**
Neva, R., **RSFSR,** on which Leningrad stands;

drains L. Ladoga to G. of Finland; navigable but liable to flooding; 74 km long.

Nevada, st., **USA**; in Rocky mtns., continental climate; mng. basis of economy gold, silver, copper, tungsten, gypsum, iron, lead; livestock agr., timber; tourism; ts. inc. Las Vegas and cap. Carson City; a. 286,299 km²; p. (1970) 481,893, grew rapidly during 1960s.

Nevers, c., cap. of Nièvre dep., **France**; on R. Loire; anc. iron and steel ind.; porcelain and faience; cath., historic bldgs.; p. (1968) 45,068.

Neves, t., Rio de Janeiro st., S.E. **Brazil**; sugar, coffee; p. (1960) 85,741.

Nevis, I., Leeward Is., **W.I.**; cotton, sugar; ch. t. Charlestown; desire for indep. from **St. Kitts**; a. 130 km²; p. (1966) 15,072.

New Albany, c., Ind., **USA**; on R. Ohio; domestic glassware, furniture, leather, iron and steel, car bodies; p. (est. 1969) 38,000.

New Amsterdam, spt., **Guyana**; on Berbice R.; processes agr. prods. from surrounding lowland; p. (1970) 18,199.

New Amsterdam, t., Manhattan I., **USA**; taken by English from Dutch, 1664, and renamed New York.

Newark, mkt. t., Notts., **Eng.**; on R. Trent 27 km N.E. of Nottingham; ball bearings, brewing and malting; cas.; p. (1971) 24,631.

Newark, c., N.J., **USA**; meat-packing, printing, elec. gds., paints, chemicals, cars, aircraft, leather; route ctr.; p. (1970) 378,222 (c.), 1,847,542 (met. a.).

New Bedford, c., spt., Mass., **USA**; on estuary of R. Acushnet; whale-fishery ctr.; mnfs. cottons, cordage, glass, shoes; resort; p. (1970) 101,262 (c.), 151,934 (met. a.).

Newbiggin-by-the-Sea, t., Northumberland, **Eng.**; sm. seaside resort; coal mng.; p. (1971) 10,661.

New Brighton, t., Merseyside, **Eng.**; at entrance to Mersey estuary; residtl. dist. of Wallasey resort.

New Brighton, t., S.I., seaside resort, nr. Christchurch, **N.Z.**; p. (1961) 10,219.

New Britain, lgst. I., Bismarck Archipelago, **Papua-New Guinea**; volcanic mtns.; exp. copra, cacao; a. (with adjacent Is.) 37,814 km²; p. (1966) 154,091.

New Britain, t., Conn., **USA**; iron and brass mnfs.; p. (1970) 82,685 (c.), 143,965 (met. a.).

New Brunswick, maritime prov., **Canada**; forest-clad mtns.; impt. timber inds.; fishing and fish-processing; many minerals; road and rail link with Prince Edward I.; cap. Fredericton; a. 72,481 km²; p. (1971) 634,557.

New Brunswick, t., N.J., **USA**; on Raritan R.; chemicals, motor lorries, motor parts, leather hosiery and hardware; univ.; p. (est. 1969) 41,000.

Newburgh, burgh, North East Fife, **Scot.**; on S. side of F. of Tay, 13 km E. of Perth; fish. pt.; linoleum; p. (1971) 2,062.

Newburn, t., Tyne and Wear, **Eng.**; on R. Tyne, 5 km W. of Newcastle; pure graphite for nuclear reactors; p. (1971) 39,379.

Newbury, t., Berks., **Eng.**; on R. Kennet, 27 km S.W. of Reading; engin., furniture, paper, cardboard boxmaking; mkt.; racecourse; p. (1971) 23,696.

New Caledonia, overseas terr. of **France**; volcanic I. in S. Pac. Oc.; nickel and chrome deposits; nickel processing; cap. Nouméa; a. 22,139 km²; p. (1970) 100,579.

Newcastle, c., N.S.W., **Australia**; spt. at mouth of R. Hunter, exp. agr. prod.; second c. of st.; leading industl. ctr., iron and steel, engin., shipbldg., chemicals; p. (1972) 145,718 (c.), 351,010 (met. a.).

Newcastle, spt., on Dundrum Bay; Down, **N. Ireland**; resort; p. (1966) 4,336.

New Castle, t., Penns., **USA**; tinplate, glass steel wire, iron, coal, limestone; p. (1970) 38,559.

Newcastle Emlyn, t., Dyfed, **Wales**; on R. Teifi; p. (1971) 654.

Newcastle-under-Lyme, t., Staffs., **Eng.**; 3 km W. of Stoke-on-Trent, on Lyme Brook; coal mng.; brick and tile mnfs.; p. (1971) 76,970.

Newcastle upon Tyne, c., Tyne and Wear, **Eng.**; spt. on N. bank of Tyne R., 16 km from N. Sea; shipbldg., heavy engin., iron and steel, chemicals; connected by bridges across Tyne to Gateshead; univ., cath., many fine public bldgs., partially preserved in redevelopment of c. ctr.; airport; p. (1971) 222,153.

New Delhi. *See* **Delhi.**

New England, N.S.W., **Australia**; dist. of N. Tablelands; pastoral cty. for sheep and beef; ch. ts. Armidale, Glen Innes, and Tenterfield.

New England, the six N.E. Atl. sts. of **USA**; Me., N.H., Vt., Mass., R.I., Conn.; humid-continental climate, infertile soils, poor agr. conditions; fishing; recent industl. metamorphosis as traditional inds. are replaced by modern science-based, high-value inds.; tourism; ch. t. Boston.

Newent, mkt. t. Gloucs., **Eng.**; 13 km S. of Ledbury; p. (1971) 9,376 (dist.).

New Forest, forest and heathland, Hants., **Eng.**; relic of Royal Forest; now partly owned by Forestry Commission; pasture, ponies, tourism; ch. t. Lyndhurst.

New Forest, Hants., **Eng.**; tourism; residtl.; rapid growth of p. since 1951; p. (1971) 70,673 (dist.).

Newfoundland, I., with Labrador, prov., of **Canada**; E. of the G. of St. Lawrence; in E. low; in W. rugged mtns., many Ls.; coniferous forest; fishing, cod, salmon, halibut, lobster, seal; lumber, wood-pulp, paper; iron ore, lead, zinc, copper, asbestos; hydroelec. power; climate is severe; cap. St. John's; a. prov. 404,519 km² (I. 112,300 km², Labrador 292,219 km²); p. (1971) 522,105.

New Galloway, burgh, Stewartry, **Scot.**; on R. Dee.; nearby Clatteringshaws hydroelec. sta.; p. (1971) 338.

New Guinea, I., S.W. **Pac. Oc.**; N. of Australia; equatorial climate; dense forest; central mtn. chain; lge. a. of lowland in S.; divided politically between W. Irian in W. (Indonesia) and Papua New Guinea in E.; economically underdeveloped; a. 831,390 km². *See* **Papua New Guinea, West Irian.**

Newham, outer bor. Greater London, **Eng.**; W. of R. Lea; contains Royal group of London docks; p. and industl. decentralization from a.; p. (1971) 235,700.

New Hampshire, st., New England, **USA**; borders on Canada; forested mtns.; agr., fruit-growing; paper and forest prods.; textiles, shoes; granite; cap. Concord; ch. spt. Portsmouth; ch. mftg. ctr. Manchester; a. 24,097 km²; p. (1970) 722,753.

Newhaven t., East Sussex, **Eng.**; on S. cst. at mouth of R. Ouse, 14 km E. of Brighton; passenger pt. for Dieppe; boat-bldg. and lt. inds; p. (1971) 9,977.

New Haven, c., pt., Conn., **USA**; on inlet of Long I. Sound; Yale Univ.; firearms, clocks, hardware, radiators, rubber gds.; p. (1970) 133,543 (c.), 348,424 (met. a.).

New Hebrides, Anglo-French condominion, S. **Pac. Oc.**; between New Caledonia and Fiji Is.; strong separatist moves in Santo I.; mostly subsistence agr.; few cash crops; ch. crop coconuts; no worked minerals; thickly forested; cap. Vila; a. 14,763 km²; p. (1971) 86,084.

New Holland, v., rly. terminus, ferry pt. for crossing to Hull, Humberside, **Eng.**

New Ireland, volcanic I., **Papua-New Guinea**, in Bismarck archipelago; mtnous.; ch. pt. Kavieng; exp. copra; a. (with adjacent Is.) 9,842 km²; p. (1966) 50,129.

New Jersey, st., **USA**; on Atl. cst. plain, adjacent to N.Y. c.; intensive agr., mkt. gardening; heavily industrialised; oil refining, glass sand, zinc, iron ore, clay, chemicals, motor vehicles; cap. Trenton; ch. cs. Newark, Jersey City; a. 20,295 km²; p. (1970) 7,091,995.

Newmarket, t., Suffolk, **Eng.**; at foot of E. Anglian Heights; the "racing capital of England"; p. (1971) 12,934.

New Mexico, st., **USA**; N. of Mexico, S. of Col. st.; traversed by Rocky mtns.; dry climate; agr. dependent upon irrigation; dry farming, arable crops, livestock; uranium, potash salts, pumice, beryllium, copper, petroleum; ch. ts., Albuquerque and cap. Santa Fé; a. 315,115 km²; p. (1970) 998,257.

New Milford, t., Milford Haven, Dyfed, **Wales.**

New Mills, industl. t., Derbys., **Eng.**; at W. foot of Pennines; textile printing, bleaching and dyeing; rayon, paper; confectionery; p. (1971) 9,165.

Newmilns and Greenholm, burgh, Kilmarnock and

Loudoun, Scot.; on R. Irvine, 19 km E. of Kilmarnock; mulsin and lace curtain mnf.; p. (1971) 3,406.

New Mirpir, t., Pakistan; new t. 3 km. from old Mirpur submerged by Mangla L. 1967; planned p. 40,000.

New Orleans, c., spt., La., **USA**; on delta of Mississippi R.; the gr. cotton mart of America, busy comm., mftg. and cultural ctr., home of jazz; sugar refining, oil refining; p. (1970) 585,787 (c.); 1,034,316 (met. a.).

New Plymouth, t., spt., N.I., **N.Z.**; on W. cst. at N. foot of Mt. Egmont; sm. oil deposits; ctr. of dairy-farming dist.; p. (1971) 34,165.

Newport-on-Tay, burgh, North East Fife, **Scot.**; on S. side of F. of Tay, opposite Dundee; p. (1971) 3,719.

Newport, cap. of I. of Wight, **Eng.**; on R. Medina, in gap through central chalk ridge; mkt.; brewing, joinery, bait mnfs.; prison; p. (1971) 22,286.

Newport, mkt. t., Salop, **Eng.**; 13 km N.E. of Wellington; p. (1971) 6,919.

Newport, spt., **Vietnam**; on N. outskirts of Ho Chi-minh City; lge. pt. inaugurated 1967.

Newport, t., R.I., **USA**; on Narragansett Bay; fashionable seaside resort; precision instruments; p. (1970) 34,562.

Newport, t., Gwent, **Wales**; on R. Usk, 8 km from its mouth; timber terminal and deep-water berth; engin., iron and steel, aluminium, paperboard, confectionery, chemicals, plastics; p. (1971) 112,048.

Newport News, c., spt., Va., **USA**; on N. shore of estuary of James R. on Hampton Roads; lge harbour; shipbldg.; outlet for Virginian tobacco and Appalachian coal; p. (1970) 137,348 (c.), 289,341 (met. a.).

Newport Pagnell, mkt. t., Bucks., **Eng.**; on R. Ouse; mnfs. Aston Martin cars; p. (1971) 6,337.

Newquay, t., Cornwall, **Eng.**; on N. Cornish cst.; seaside resort; p. (1971) 14,963.

New Quay, t., Dyfed, **Wales**; on cst. of Cardigan Bay; fishing; resort; p. (1971) 747.

New Radnor, t., Powys, **Wales**; on slope of Radnor Forest, 10 km S.W. of Presteign; p. (1971) 1,478 (dist.).

New River, artificial aqueduct, Herts. to Islington, London, **Eng.**; part of London's water-supply system; 58 km long.

New Rochelle, t., N.Y., **USA**; on Long I. Sound; residtl.; p. (1970) 75,385.

New Romney, t. Kent, **Eng.**; nr. S. cst. to E. of Dungeness; in rich agr. dist. of Romney Marsh; Cinque pt.; old harbour silted up by shingle, now a mile from sea; p. (1971) 3,414.

New Ross, mkt. t. U.D., Wexford, **R.o.I.**; brewing and malting; p. (1966) 4,568.

Newry, t., Newry and Mourne, **N. Ireland**; pt. at head of Carlingford Lough; machin., rope, brewing, granite; p. (est. 1971) 11,393.

Newry and Mourne, l. gov. dist., **N. Ireland**; surrounds t. of N., borders R.o.I., Irish Sea; inc. Mtns. of Mourne.

New South Wales, st., S.E. **Australia**; much mineral wealth in tablelands and mtns.; climate equable and well suited to both arable and pastoral agr.; leading agr. st. in Australia; major irrigation schemes in drier E. plains of Murray, Murrumbidgee, and Lachlan Rs.; coal mng. and heavy inds. at Newcastle, Port Kembla, Wollongong; hydroelectric power from Snowy mtns. scheme; lge concentration of p. in cap. c. of Sydney; a. 801,431 km² (excluding of Cap. Terr. of Canberra); p. (1972) 4,589,556.

Newton, t., Mass., **USA**; on R. Charles; in met. a. of Boston; lt. inds. p. (1970) 91,263.

Newtownabbey, t., l. gov. dist., **N. Ireland**; sub. of Belfast, textiles, lt. inds.; p. (est. 1971) 57,908.

Newton Abbot, mkt. t., Devon, **Eng.**; at head of Teign estuary; rly. junc.; pottery, lt. engin.; agr. processing; p. (1971) 19,367.

Newton Aycliffe, t., Durham, **Eng.**; 10 km N.W. of Darlington; new t. (1947); engin., textiles, plastics, paints; p. (1971) 20,190.

Newton-le-Willows, t., Merseyside, **Eng.**; engin., printing, sugar-refining; p. (1971) 22,380.

Newton-Stewart, burgh, Wigtown, **Scot.**; on R. Cree, 8 km N. of Wigtown; mkt.; wool, creameries and agr. inds.; p. (1971) 1,883.

Newtown and Llanllwchaiarn, mkt. t., Powys, **Wales**; on R. Severn 13 km S.W. of Montgomery; precision instruments, machine tools; plan for expansion as growth-pole for central Wales; p. (1971) 6,122.

Newtownards, spt., mkt., Ards, **N. Ireland**; 11 km E. of Belfast; textile and engin. inds.; p. (est. 1971) 15,387.

New Waterway. *See* **Nieuwe Waterweg.**

New Westminster, t., B.C., **Canada**; spt. on estuary of R. Fraser; exp. timber; agr. ctr., food-processing and canning; fishing; oil refining; forms part of Vancouver met a.; p. (1971) 42,083.

New York, st., N.E. **USA**; one of 13 original sts., borders Canada on N., faces Atl. Oc. on S.; Adirondack mtns. in N., with lowland in E. alongside L. Ontario; Hudson valley impt. routeway; humid-continental climate; second lgst st. in p. size and despite p. movement to W., remains major a. of urbanisation (megalopolis) with comm. and industl. activity; ch. ts. inc. Buffalo, Rochester, Syracuse; st. cap. Albany, metropolis New York city; dairy farming and intensive agr. serve urban mkts.; a. 128,402 km²; p. (1970) 17,979,712.

New York, c., spt., N.Y., **USA**; on N.Y. Bay at mouth of Hudson R.; lgst. c. in USA and one of 3 lgst. in world; comprises 5 bors., Manhattan, Bronx, Queens, Brooklyn, Richmond; originally founded by Dutch settlers as New Amsterdam on Manhattan I.; gr. comm. ctr. and cultural cap.; univ.; fine parks, bridges, skyscrapers, and deepwater harbour; varied inds., inc. clothing, food-processing, printing and publishing, shipbldg.; despite p. and industl. decentralisation concentration of socially needy in c. causing financial difficulties to c. govt.; 2 intern. airports; p. (1971) 7,895,000 (c.); (1970) 11,572,000 (met. a.).

New York State Barge Canal (Erie Canal), N.Y. st., **USA**; links Tonawanda on Niagara R. with Hudson R. via the Mohawk gap through Appalachian mtns.; provides through water route from N.Y. to Gr. Ls.; opened as Erie Canal 1825, improved 1918; length 542 km (with branches 840 km), depth 4 m.

New Zealand, indep. sov. st. within Brit. Commonwealth, **S. Pac. Oc.**; 1,920 km E. of Sydney, Australia; consists of two major Is., N.I. and S.I., separated by Cook Strait, and several smaller Is., inc. Stewart I. to S.; mtnous., glaciated, volcanic; landscapes with superb scenery; dependent upon pastoral prods., taking advantage of equable climate and excellent grass growing conditions, but mainly reliant on Brit. mkts.; economic diversification; expansion of lt. inds., inc. car assembly, pulp and paper, textiles; hydroelec. potential being developed; oil and natural gas recently discovered; advanced social services; cap. Wellington; ch. pt. Auckland; a. 268,676 km²; p. (1971) 2,860,475 (inc. 223,300 Maoris); N.I., 2,050,208, S.I., 810,267.

Neyland, t., Dyfed, **Wales**; on Milford Haven; rly. terminus and sm. pt.; p. (1971) 2,633.

Ngami, L., Botswana, S.W. **Africa**; swamp, the remnant of a much larger L.

Ngauruhoe, mtn., N.I., **N.Z.**; an active volcano; 2,292 m.

Niagara, R., forms part of boundary between Canada and **USA**; flows from L. Erie to L. Ontario; rapids and famous falls utilised by gr. hydroelec. power sta.; 56 km long.

Niagara Falls, waterfall, Niagara R., on bdy. of **USA** and **Canada**; in two sections, American (51 m high) and Canadian (48 m high), separated by Goat I.; major tourist attraction and hydroelec. power sta.

Niagara Falls, t., Ontario, **Canada**; opposite the falls; hydroelectric power sta.; timber and agr. inds., tourism; p. (1971) 65,271.

Niagara Falls, c., N.Y., **USA**; extends along summit of cliff for 5 km; paper, flour, aluminium, chemicals, hydroelectric power stas.; univ.; p. (est. 1969) 90,000; inc. in Buffalo met. a.

Niamey, t., cap. of Rep. of Niger, W. **Africa**; one of the termini (the other is Zinder) of the trans-Sahara motor routes; agr. tr. ctr.; p. (est. 1968) 79,991.

Nicaragua, rep., **Central America**; lies across isthmus with Pac. Oc. to W., Caribbean Sea to E.; sparsely populated; central mtn.

range, marshy E. cst.; tropical rain forest and climate; limited a. of fertile soils but 70 per cent. p. farmers; main exps. coffee, cotton; industl. growth based on US investment, gold and silver mng.; politically unstable; cap. Managua; a. 148,006 km²; p. (1969) 1,841,759.

Nicaragua, Lake, S.W. **Nicaragua**; lgst. L. in Central America; 24 km from Pac. Oc., but discharges into Caribbean via San Juan R.; fisheries; 160 km N.W. to S.E., 67 km S.W. to N.E.

Nicaraguan Depression, lowland, **Nicaragua**; contains Ls. Maragua and Nicaragua.

Nice, c., spt., cap. of Alpes Maritimes dep., **France**; on Mediterranean cst., at foot of Alps; pleasant climate and surroundings; adjoins anc. t. of Cimiez; ceded to France 1860 by Sardinia; resort; fruit and flower exp., perfume mftg.; attracting science-based inds.; major airport; p. (1968) 322,442 (c.), 392,635 (met. a.).

Nicobar Is. *See* **Andaman and Nicobar Is.**

Nicosia, c., cap. of **Cyprus**; agr. tr. ctr.; textiles, cigarettes, leather, pottery mnfs.; remains of Venetian fortifications; mosques; new airpt.; cap. of admin. dist. of N.; tourism; p. (est. 1969) 114,000.

Nidd, R., trib. of R. Ouse, North Yorks., **Eng.**; 80 km long.

Nieder Sachsen. *See* **Lower Saxony.**

Niemen R. *See* **Neman.**

Nieuwe Waterweg, ship canal, S. Holland, **Neth.**; connects R. Lek 11 km below Rotterdam with N. Sea cst. at Hook of Holland.

Nieuwveld Range, mtns., Cape Prov., **S. Africa**; part of S. terminal escarpment of African tableland; overlooks Gr. Karroo to its S.; forms impenetrable barrier to routes; mainly over 1,500 m, max. alt. 1,914 m.

Nièvre, dep., central **France**; traversed by Morvan mtns., forests, arable agr.; cap. Nevers; a. 6,887 km²; p. (1968) 247,702.

Nigel, t., Transvaal, **S. Africa**; gold mng.; industl.; p. (est. 1967) 38,400.

Niger, landlocked rep., **W. Africa**; 90 per cent p. dependent upon agr.; livestock (cattle, sheep, goats), cotton; exp. of groundnuts main source of wealth; rainfall diminishes to N. giving way to Sahara Desert; discovery and exploitation of uranium (1967); fishing in L. Chad; game hunting; close economic ties with France; cap. Niamey; a. 1,253,560 km²; p. (est. 1970) 4,016,000.

Niger, R., **W. Africa**; rises nr. sea in outer mtn. zone of W. Africa as R. Tembi, sweeps round by Timbuktu to delta in G. of Guinea, on circuitous course of 4,160 km, receiving its gr. trib., the R. Benue, about 400 km from the mouth; navigable for 1,600 km; Kainji (Nigeria) hydroelec. plant and dam opened 1969.

Nigeria, fed. rep., **W. Africa**; within Brit. Commonwealth; federation of 19 sts.; climate, wet, tropical in S., increasingly dry to N.; main economic development in S.; exp. agr. prods., especially cocoa; recent rapid increase in oil exp. based upon coastal deposits and European demand; cap. Lagos, lgst. c. Ibadan; cap. to be built at Abuja by 1986; a. 923,773 km²; p. (1973) 79,760,000.

Niigata, c., Honshu, **Japan**; pt. on W. cst. exp. locally produced petroleum; chemical inds.; p. (est. 1971) 390,000.

Niihama, c., N. Shikoku, **Japan**; on cst. of Inland Sea, 32 km S.E. of Imabari; refines copper obtained from Besshi mines 19 km to the S.; petrochemicals; p. (est. 1971) 130,000.

Nijmegen, c., E. **Neth.**; on R. Waal, nr. German bdr., 18 km S. of Arnhem; Hanse t. in Middle Ages; historic bldgs., univ.; p. (est. 1969) 101,878 (c.), 201,280 (met. a.).

Nijni-Novgorod. *See* **Gorki.**

Nikko, t., Honshu, **Japan**; famous temples and shrines; tourist resort; p. (1966) 32,031.

Nikolayev, c., cap. of N. oblast, Ukrainian SSR, **USSR**; major spt. at head of Dnieper–Bug estuary on Black Sea; shipbldg. ctr.; exp. minerals, grains; founded 1784 as fortress; p. (1970) 331,000.

Nikolayevsk, lge R. pt., Khabarovsk terr., **RSFSR**; on R. Amur; shipyards; fishing, canning, lumbering, oil refining; p. (est. 1967) 32,000.

Nikopol, c., Ukrainian SSR, **USSR**; on R. Dnieper; manganese mng. ctr.; steel, machin.; p. (1970) 125,000.

Nikšić, t., Montenegro, **Yugoslavia**; N. of Cetinje; bauxite mng., growing industl. ctr.; p. (est. 1965) 27,000.

Nile, longest R. in Africa (*see* **White Nile** (Bahr-el-Abiad) and **Blue Nile** (Bahr-el-Azrek)); flows through a longer stretch of basin (over 3,920 km in a direct line) than any other R., and along all its windings measures 6,632 km; on Upper Nile navigation is hindered by sudd (floating vegetation); R. rises April, overflows Sept.; formerly cultivation entirely dependent on annual floods, but now assisted by dams, at Asyût, Aswan, Sennar, for regulating flow and navigation; Aswan High Dam completed 1970, but complex problems of delta erosion and dam-lake silting. *See also* **Egypt.**

Nilgiri Hills, Tamil Nadu, S. **India**; tea-growing dist.; resort a.

Nîmes, c., cap. of Gard dep., S. **France**; in Cevennes; Roman antiquities, notably Maison Carrée; silk, cotton, carpets, wines; tourism; p. (1968) 123,292 (c.), 124,854 (met. a.).

Nineveh, celebrated anc. c., **Iraq**, stood on E. bank of upper R. Tigris, opposite modern Mosul.

Ningpo (Ningbo), c., spt., Chekiang, **China**; 160 km from Shanghai; leading fish. pt., comm. and mnf. ctr.; exp. agr. and fish prods.; p. (est. 1970) 350,000.

Ningsia Hui, aut. region, N.W. **China**; bounded on N. by Inner Mongolia; dry a. but modern irrigation projects allow growth of spring wheat and rice; coal reserves, salt; cap .Yinchwan; a. 66,408 km²; p. (est. 1968) 2,000,000.

Niobrara, R., **USA**; trib. of Missouri R.; flows from Wyoming to Nebraska; 960 km long.

Niort, c., cap. of Deux-Sèvres dep., W. **France**; noted for mkt. gardens and leather gds. (gloves); birthplace of Mme de Maintenon; p. (1968) 50,079.

Nipigon, Lake, in Thunder Bay dist., Ont., **Canada**; 106 km long, 74 km wide; studded with Is.; discharges by Nipigon R. to L. Superior.

Nipissing, Lake, S. Ont., **Canada**; 855 km²; drained by French R. to Georgian Bay.

Niš, t., **Yugoslavia**; on R. Nishava; route ctr.; rly. engin., developing mftg.; univ.; p. (1971) 127,178.

Nišava, R., **Yugoslavia**; flows N.W. into R. Morava nr. Niš; valley used by trunk rly. from Belgrade to Istanbul; length over 160 km.

Nishapur, mkt. t., N.E. **Iran**, S.W. of Mashhad; in fertile a.; cotton, fruits; famous turquoise mines nearby; birthplace of Omar Khayyám; impt. archaeological finds dating 9th and 10th cent.; p. (1966) 33,482.

Nishinomiya, c., S. Honshu, **Japan**; produces famous liquor called saké; machin., chemicals; p. (est. 1971) 378,000.

Niterói, t., cap. of Rio de Janeiro st., **Brazil**; shipbldg.; residtl. sub. of Rio de Janeiro c. to which it is linked by bridge; p. (1970) 291,970.

Nith, R., S.W. **Scot.**; flows to Solway F., S. of Dumfries; followed by main rly. from Carlisle to Kilmarnock and Glasgow; 114 km long.

Niue or **Savage I.,** Pac. Oc.; one of Cook Is., formerly part of N.Z., self government 1974; ch. pt. Alofi; copra, plaited basketware, sweet potatoes; a. 259 km²; p. (1970) 5,302.

Nivernais, former prov. of **France**, now forming Nièvre prov. and part of Cher.

Nizamabad, t., Andhra Pradesh, **India**; road and rly. ctr. N. of Hyderabad; p. (1971) 115,640.

Nizhneudinsk, t., W. Irkutsk, **RSFSR**; new mftg. t.; p. (est. 1967) 38,000.

Nizhni Novgorod. *See* **Gorki.**

Nizhniy Tagil, t., **RSFSR**; in Ural mtns.; metallurgical ctr. using ore from Mt. Visokaya; rly. cars, iron, and steel plants, chemicals; p. (1970) 378,000.

No, Lake, Bahr-el-Ghazal prov., **Sudan**; N.E. Africa; vast swamp a., 906 km S.W. of Khartoum; flow of water blocked by papyrus reed and floating weed (sudd).

Nobeoka, t., Kyushu, **Japan**; on E. cst.; p. (est. 1971) 133,000.

Nobi Plain, S. Honshu, **Japan**; at head of Ise Bay; composed of: (1) low, badly drained pottery mftg. a. in Japan; inc. cs. Nagoya, alluvial plain on W. under intensive rice cultivation, (2) higher, drier, terraces on E. under mulberry, vegetables, pine-woods; very dense urban and rural p.; ch. textile and pottery mftg. a. in Japan; inc. cs. Nagoya, Gifu, Yokkaichi; a. 1,865 km²; p. (1960) 5,400,000.

Nocera Inferiore, t., Italy; nr. Naples; vegetable-canning, textile mnfs.; p. (est. 1968) 49,167.

Nogales, twin ts., Sonora, **Mexico** and Arizona, **USA**; mng. and agr. ctr.; total p. (1970) 61,811.

Nogent-sur-Marne, S.E. sub. of Paris, Val de Marne dep., **France**; dep.; p. (est. 1965) 4,910.

Noginsk, t., **RSFSR**; nr. Moscow; textiles, metals; natural gas pipeline from Central Asia projected; p. (1970) 104,000.

Nola, c., **Italy**; at foot of Vesuvius, 19 km N.E. of Naples; ctr. of fertile arable agr. a. in Campania plain; anc. c., home of Giordano Bruno; p. (est. 1968) 27,009.

Nome, c., W. Alaska, **USA**; on Seward peninsula; gold rush (1900); now admin. and route ctr.; airport; tourism; p. (1970) 2,488.

Noord Brabant, prov., Neth.; cap. 's-Hertogenbosch; a. 4,973 km²; p. (est. 1967) 1,700,866.

Noord Holland, prov., Neth.; a. 2,722 km²; cap. Haarlem; natural gas in Schermer Polder nr. Alkmaar; p. (1967) 2,200,062.

Noordoostpolder, Overijssel, **Neth.**; land reclaimed from Zuider Zee, 1942; now used for intensive agr.; a. 479 km²; p. (1967) 31,016.

Noordwijk, resort, W. cst., Neth.; p. (1967) 20,563.

Nord, dep., **N. France**; borders on Belgium and N. Sea; flourishing agr., mng. iron and coal, textile and chemical mnfs.; cap. Lille; a. 5,773 km²; p. (1968) 2,417,899.

Nordenham, pt. on Lower Weser R., Lower Saxony, W. Germany; lead and zinc smelting; fishing; p. (est. 1969) 16,271.

Norderney, one of the E. Frisian Is., **W. Germany**; low-lying sand-dunes; resort and fish. pt. at Nordseebad.

Nordhorn, t., Lower Saxony, W. Germany; nr. Neth. frontier; textiles; p. (est. 1969) 42,706.

Nordkyn, Cape, northernmost pt. of European mainland, Finnmark prov., **N. Norway, E.** of North Cape.

Nordland, co., **N. Norway**; fjord cst.; p. on cst. lowlands; fishing, livestock; iron-ore, electro-chemical and metallurgical inds. based on local hydroelec. power; spt. Narvik; a. 38,146 km²; p. (est. 1972) 241,142.

Nördlingen, t., Bavaria, **W. Germany**; historic walled t.; p. (est. 1967) 14,200.

Nore, The, sandbank, lightship, Thames estuary, Eng.

Norfolk, non-met. co., E. Eng.; low-lying, fens in W.; low sandy cst. suffers from erosion; intensive arable agr. on lge farms; wheat, barley, root crops; inds. based on agr. processing and provision of agr. requisites; tourism intensively developed on Norfolk Broads; cap. Norwich; a. 5,354 km²; p. (1971) 624,000.

Norfolk, c., Va., USA; naval base on Hampton Roads; fine deepwater harbour; exp. coal, industl. prods.; shipbldg., car assembly, food-processing, timber inds., fertilisers; p. (1970) 268,331 (c.), 633,142 (met. a.).

Norfolk I. remote dependency of Australia; **Pac. Oc.**; 1,528 km N.E. of Sydney; fertile agr., inc. citrus fruit; discovered by Cook 1774; penal settlement 1788-1853; tourism; a. 34 km²; p. (1970) 1,240.

Norilsk, t., Krasnoyarsk terr., **RSFSR**; in N. Siberia; northernmost t. in Russia; mng. of coal, uranium, nickel, copper; natural gas pipeline from W. Siberia; p. (1970) 136,000.

Normandy, historic prov. of **France**; on English Channel; now divided into deps. Manche, Calvados, Eure, Seine-Maritime and part of Orne; Rouen was cap.; Channel Is. were part of the old duchy; conquered England 1066; allied invasion of Europe 1944.

Normanton, t., West Yorks., **Eng.**; 5 km N.E. of Wakefield; coal mng.,; rly. wks.; p. (1971) 17,656.

Norman Wells, t., N.W. Terr., **Canada**; at confluence of R. Mackenzie and Gr. Bear R., 112 km W. of Gr. Bear L.; ctr. of rich oil-field.

Norrbotten, prov., N. Sweden; rich iron deposits at Kiruna; ore exp. via ice-free Narvik on Norwegian cst.; many Ls. and Rs., highest peak in Sweden, Kebnekaise; cap. Pitea; a. 105,553 km²; p. (est. 1970) 256,750.

Norris Dam, Tenn., **USA**; across R. Clinch at confluence with R. Tennessee, N.W. of Knoxville; lgst. dam Tenn. Valley Authority (TVA); built for flood control and hydroelectric power.

Norristown, bor., Penns., **USA**; textiles, metal gds.; p. (1970) 38,169.

Norrköping, c., S.E. **Sweden**; nr. inlet of Baltic Sea; industl. and shipping ctr.; textiles, margarine, paper, agr. machin.; ocean-going shipping through Lindö canal; p. (1968) 93,345.

Northallerton, mkt. t., North Yorks., admin. ctr., **Eng.**; in broad gap between Cleveland hills and Pennines; in dairy farming and agr. dist.; p. (1971) 10,508.

Northam, t., Devon, **Eng.**; nr. Bideford; inc. Westward Ho!; p. (1971) 8,082.

North America, northern continent of W. hemisphere; comprises Greenland (on N. American continental shelf), Canada, USA, Mexico; high W. Cordilleras, inc. Rocky mtns., run N. to S. from Alaska to Mexico; lower range of Appalachian mtns. in E. with vast interior basin, inc. Gr. Ls., Saskatchewan, St. Lawrence, and Miss.-Mo. R. systems; gr. variation in climate and vegetation from subtropical in S. and Mediterranean in W. to Arctic in N. and continental in interior: enormous endowment of natural resources provide basis for vast economies of USA and Canada, but contemporary public concern for natural environment of continent; formerly inhabited by Indians, now mainly occupied by a white p. with lge. European minorities, and an African-based, black p.; p. (est. 1974) 338,000,000 (inc. Hawaii).

Northampton, t., Northampton, **Eng.**; on R. Nene; footwear, engin. leather gds.; expanded t.; p. (est. 1974) 145,400.

Northamptonshire, non-met. co., **Eng.**; E. Midlands; chiefly agr.; iron mng. and mftg.; footwear, engin., leather; co. t. Northampton; a. 2,367 km²; p. (1971) 468,000.

North Atlantic Drift, drift of surface waters of Atl. Oc. N.E. from Gulf Stream towards Europe; relatively warm; supplies prevailing S.W. winds with warmth and moisture to modify climate of Brit. Is. and countries on N.W. margin of European Continent.

North Bay, t., Ont., **Canada**; on L. Nipissing; air base; tourism, route ctr.; p. (1971) 49,063.

North Berwick, royal burgh, E. Lothian, Scot.; on S. of F. of Forth, 32 km E. of Edinburgh; seaside resort; golf course; fishing pt.; p. (1971) 4,392.

North Beveland, I., **Neth.**; in Scheldt estuary; arable agr.; a. 91 km².

North Carolina, st., S.E. **USA**; bounded on E. by Atl. Oc.; one of 13 original sts.; sandy, indented cst., rising in W. to Appalachian mtns.; humid subtropical climate, modified by alt.; agr. impt., maize, cotton, tobacco; mica; textiles; ch. pt. Wilmington; cap. Raleigh; a. 136,524 km²; p. (1970) 4,961,832.

North Channel, Brit. Is.; gives access from Atl. Oc. to Irish Sea between S.W. Scotland (Galloway) and N.E. Ireland (Larne); length 96 km; narrowest width 24 km.

North China Plain, China; alluvial lowland of Hwang-ho basin; notorious floods but R. now controlled; wheat and millets; very dense p.

North Crimean Canal, USSR; links R. Dnieper with Black Sea and Sea of Azov, crossing steppes of S. Ukraine and Crimea, terminating at Kerch; first section (123 km long) opened 1963; when completed will be 352 km long, 200 km of which will be navigable.

North Dakota, st., N.W. **USA**; rolling prairie, rising from E.-W.; drained by Missouri R., controlled by multi-purpose Garrison Reservoir; arable agr., mainly grains, but eroded "Badlands" in S.; coal mng., petroleum; a. 183,022 km²; p. (1970) 610,648.

North Down, l. gov. dist., **N. Ireland**; borders Belfast Lough; main ts. Bangor, Holywood.

North Downs, Surrey/Kent, **Eng.**; chalk escarpment running E. to W. across S.E. Eng., flanking the Weald to N.; form "white cliffs of Dover"; followed in part by Pilgrim's Way; Box Hill 233 m.

North-East China, formerly known as Manchuria, comprises nine provs.—Liaoning, Kirin, Heilungkiang, Liaopeh, Nunkiang, Hsingan, Sunkiang, Hokiang, and Antung; mtnous., N.W. and E.; drained to N. by Sungari and S. by Liao

Rs.; forested; soya-beans, wheat, coal, iron; impt. a. for iron and steel; occupied by Japanese in second world war; p. (est. 1968) 66,000,000.

North-East Frontier Agency. *See* **Arunachal Pradesh.**

North East Passage, along N. cst. Europe and Asia between Atl. and Pac. *See* **Section L.**

Northern Ireland, part of **U.K.**; occupies N.E. a. of Ireland, consisting of 26 l. gov. dists.; mild, temperate climate, exploited by dairy farming using excellent grass; arable agr. inc. barley, potatoes; traditional inds. inc. linen, shipbldg., food-processing, tobacco; modern inds. encouraged by extensive government aid inc. artificial fibres, carpets, elec. and aero-engin.; heavily dependent upon Brit. mkt.; serious social disturbance since 1969, based upon long-standing religious differences between Roman Catholic and Protestant as a result of discrimination against minority; Stormont Parliament replaced by Assembly (suspended 29 May 1974 and direct rule resumed); returns 12 members to Westminster; a. 14,121 km^2; p. (1971) 1,525,187. *See also* **Section C, Part I.**

Northern Territory, st., N. **Australia**; variable rainfall decreasing inland from N. to S.; land rises generally N. to S. and reaches over 1,800 m in Macdonnell ranges; lge. semi-nomadic Aboriginal p.; livestock agr. dependent upon rail, road access to mkts.; mng.; ch. ts. Darwin on N. cst., Alice Springs; a. 1,356,176 km^2; p. (1972) 85,519.

Northfleet, t., Kent, **Eng.**; on S. bank of R. Thames, adjoining Gravesend; cement, paper, rubber, tyres, cables; p. (1971) 26,679.

North Foreland, E. Kent cst., **Eng.**; chalk headland.

North Island, I., N.Z.; one of the two major Is. of N.Z.; separated from S.I. by Cook Strait; volcanic mtns.; Waikato R. drains L. Taupo; cap. Wellington, spt. Auckland; oil deposits on E. and W. csts.; a. 114,688 km^2; p. (1971) 2,050,208.

Northleach, t., Gloucs., **Eng.**; in Cotswolds; once impt. woollen tr.; p. (1971) 7,092. (dist.).

North Little Rock, t., Ark., **USA**; agr. processing, engin.; p. (1970) 60,040.

North Ossetian ASSR, RSFSR; on N. slope of Gr. Caucasus; cap. Ordzhonikidze; agr. in valleys; lead, silver, zinc, and oil deposits with metallurgical and food-processing inds.; a. 8,029 km^2; p. (1970) 553,000.

North Platte, t., Nebraska, **USA**; on N. Platte R.; in irrigated region of the Gr. Plains; grain, livestock, processed meat; p. (1970) 19,447.

North Platte, R., USA; rises N. Col., flows 1,088 km through Wyo., across W. Nebraska to join S. Platte at c. of North Platte; extensive power and irrigation developments.

North Rhine-Westphalia, *Land,* **W. Germany**; highly industrialized, coal mng., iron and steel, textiles; a. 34,066 km^2; p. (1967) 16,842,600.

North River (Pei-kiang), Kwangtung, S. **China**; rises in Nanling mtns., flows S. into Si-kiang delta; 480 km long.

North Sea, arm of the Atl., E. of Gr. Brit., W. of Norway, Sweden, and N. Germany, and N. of Holland, Belgium, and France; length 960 km, width 640 km; gd. fisheries; major natural gas, coal and oil deposits.

North Sea Canal, ship canal, N. Holland, **Neth.**; connects Amsterdam to N. Sea at Ijmuiden; depth 14 m, length 26 km.

North Shields, t., Tyne and Wear, **Eng.**; Tyne pt.; major new fishing pt. planned; marine engines, chain cables, anchors, rope; mkt.

North Solomons, Rep. of, formed 1975 when Bougainville I. seceded from Papua New Guinea.

North Tonawanda, t., N.Y., **USA**; on Niagara R.; timber tr., paper mnfs.; p. (1970) 36,012.

Northumberland, non-met. co., N. **Eng.**; on border of Scot. along Cheviots and R. Tweed; drained by Tyne, Blyth, Coquet Rs.; pastoral agr., especially sheep; coal mng., with former impt. exp. to London and S.E. Eng.; industl. a. now inc. in Tyne and Wear met. co.; isolation and wild landscape increasingly attractive as a tourist resort; a. 5,032 km^2; p. (1971) 280,000.

Northumberland Straits, separates Prince Edward I. from Nova Scotia and New Brunswick; 14 km combined road and rail tunnel, bridge and causeway to link provs. projected.

Northumbria, Anglo-Saxon kingdom stretching from the Humber to the Forth; conquered by the Danes 9th cent.

North Walsham, mkt. t., Norfolk, **Eng.**; 22 km N. of Norwich; former wool-weaving ctr.; p. (1971) 6,357.

North-West Passage, between Atl. and Pac. along Arctic cst. of **Canada**; potentially of gr. importance as a W. outlet for Alaskan oil. *See* **L.**

Northwest Territories, N.W. region and terr. of **Canada**; N. of 60° Lat. N., between Yukon (W.) and Hudson Bay (E.); comprises 3 dists., Franklin, Mackenzie, Keewatin; varied physical geography, inc. vast areas of lowland with with some of highest peaks in E.N. America; tree-line marks physical bdy. between N. and S.; drained in W. by Mackenzie R.; major inds. gold and silver mng. around cap. Yellowknife; of Norwich; former wool-weaving ctr.; p. petroleum, fur-trapping fisheries; a. 3,379,711 km^2; p. (1971) 34,807, (two-thirds Eskimos and Indians).

Northwich, t., Cheshire, **Eng.**; on R. Weaver; impt. chemical inds. based originally upon local salt deposits, now much subsidence in a. due to salt extraction; p. (1971) 18,109.

North York Moors, limestone plateau, North Yorks./Cleveland, **Eng.**; lies S. of estuary of R. Tees; heather moorland; some pastoral farming on lower slopes; alt. varies from 300–450 m; formerly impt. iron-ore quarrying along N. edge in Cleveland dist.; now potential for potash mng. threatening N.Y.M. Nat. Park.

North Yorkshire, non-met. co., N. **Eng.**; inc. much of former N. Riding; stretches from Pennines (W.) to Vale of York (centre), N. York Moors and Yorks. Wolds (E.); crossed by R. Ouse and tribs.; mainly rural, mixed agr.; major ctrs. of p. at York, cstal. resort of Scarborough and spa of Harrogate; a. 8,316 km^2; p. (1971) 629,000.

Norton-Radstock, t., Avon, **Eng.**; footwear, sm. coalfield; p. (1971) 15,232.

Norwalk, t., Cal., **USA**; oil refining; p. (est. 1969) 96,000.

Norwalk, t., Conn., **USA**; gd. harbour on Long I. Sound; lt. inds., clothing; formerly impt. oyster ind. diminished by industl. pollution; p. (1970) 78,577 (t.), 118,968 (met. a.).

Norway, kingdom, W. Scandinavia, N. **Europe**; long fjord cst. stretches from Arctic to N. Sea; mtnous.; cool damp climate, influenced by prevailing W. winds; excellent conditions for hydroelectric power and electro-inds.; sm. p. makes N. heavily dependent upon foreign tr., especially exp. of aluminium, wood-pulp, paper, fish; now possesses lge. deposits of petroleum in N. Sea; arable agr. limited to fjord lowlands and a. around cap. Oslo; pastoral transhumance in mtnous. interior; a. 322,600 km^2; p. (1969) 3,866,468.

Norwich, c.. co. t., Norfolk, **Eng.**; on R. Wensum just above confluence with R. Yare; univ.; cath., cas.; cult. and agr. ctr.; food mnfs., footwear, printing; decentralization of office employment from London; p. (1971) 121,688.

Norwich, t., Conn., **USA**; sm. pt. on Thames R.; machin., textiles; p. (1970) 41,739.

Nossi-Bé, lgst. of sm. Is., off W. cst. **Malagasy**; sugar, perfumery oils; ch. t. Hellville, resort and ctr. of cst. tr.; a. 337 km^2; p. *c.* 26,000.

Notec (Netze), R., **Poland**; trib. R. Warta; partially navigable; 224 km long.

Noto, t., S.E. Sicily, **Italy**; cath.; amid vineyards and orchards; p. (est. 1968) 25,916.

Notodden, t., S. **Norway**; nr. Tinnfoss falls which provide hydroelectric power; iron smelting, nitrates; p. (est. 1970) 13,422.

Nottingham, c., co. t., Nottinghamshire, **Eng.**; at bridging pt. over Trent R.; lace, hosiery, tobacco, pharmaceutical and cycle inds., all based upon local capital; univ., cas., lge. mkt. square in c. ctr.; p. (1971) 299,758.

Nottinghamshire, non-met. co., Midlands, **Eng.**; contains part of productive E. Midlands coalfield serving many power stas. along Trent R.; urban growth concentrated mainly on coalfield; ch. and co. t. Nottingham; engin., hosiery; wheat, barley, cattle, roses; brilliantly characterised in writings of D. H. Lawrence; a. 2,165 km^2; p. (1971) 973,000.

Nouadhibar, new pt., Mauritania, W. **Africa**; mineral exp., international airport.

Nouakchott, t., cap. of Mauritania, W. **Africa**;

comm. ctr. on caravan route; tr. in agr. prods.; p. (est. 1972) 55,000 (met. a.).

Nouméa (Port de France), t., cap. of **Fr. New Caledonia**; ch. pt. of Is.; exp. nickel, chrome; p. (est. 1969) 41,853.

Nouvelle Amsterdam, I., **Indian Oc.**; part of Fr. Southern and Antarctic Terrs.; volcanic; ctr. of meteorological research; a. 65 km².

Nova Friburgo, t., Rio de Janeiro, **Brazil**; health resort; p. (1968) 93,364.

Nova Iguaçú, t., Rio de Janeiro, **Brazil**; steel, tyres, chemicals; p. (1970) 331,457.

Nova Lima, t., Minas Gerais st., **Brazil**; in Serra do Espinhaço, 16 km S. of Belo Horizonte; adjacent to impt. gold-mines of Morro Velho; p. (est. 1968) 32,336.

Nova Lisboa (**Huambo**), central **Angola**, **Africa**; E. of Benguela; rly. repair shops; agr. comm. ctr.; p. (est. 1969) 49,823.

Novara, c., cap. of N. prov., **N. Italy**; agr. and mnf. ctr., textiles, chemicals, cheese; Romanesque church; p. (1969) 99,647.

Nova Scotia, maritime prov., **Canada**; mainly fertile uplands and rich valleys with agr. aided by temperate maritime climate; fruit, livestock, dairying; forested uplands along cst. nr. Bay of Fundy give rise to impt. timber inds. with many pts. along indented cst.; fishing and fish-processing; local coal supplies iron and steel ind.; cap. Halifax; a. 54,556 km².; p. (1971) 788,960.

Novaya Kakhovka, c., Ukrainian SSR, **USSR**; built (1951) on K. Sea nr. hydroelec. power sta. on Dnieper R.; tourism.

Novaya Zemlya, archipelago, Arctic Oc., **USSR**; 2 main Is.; lofty and rugged, severe climate; nuclear testing a.; a. 90,650 km².

Novgorod, c., **RSFSR**; on Volkhov R. nr. exit from L. Ilmen; food and timber inds., engin.; in mediaeval times gr. comm. and cultural ctr., cap. of an indep. rep.; architectural monuments; damaged by Germans in second world war; p. (1970) 128,000.

Novi Sad, c., **Yugoslavia**; R. pt. on Danube R., formerly royal free c.; almost destroyed by Austrians 1849; tr. in fruit, wine, vegetables, corn; p. (est. 1969) 162,000.

Novokuybyshevsk, t., **RSFSR**; S.W. of Kuybyshev; lge. oil processing plant; p. (1970) 104,000.

Novo Kuznetsk (**Stalinsk**), c., **RSFSR**; grew up as iron and steel ctr. of Kuznetsk Basin; engin., chemicals, aluminium, ferro-alloys; p. (1970) 499,000 (c.); (1969) 514,000 (met. a.).

Novomoskovsk (**Stalinogorsk**), c., **RSFSR**; on R. Don; lignite, fertilisers, p. (1970) 134,000.

Novorossiisk, spt., **RSFSR**; on N.E. cst. of Black Sea; engin., textiles; lgst. cement producer in USSR; exp. industl. prods.; p. (1970) 133,000 (c.); (1969) 146,000 (met. a.).

Novoshakhtinsk, c., **RSFSR**; on Rostov–Kharkov highway; coal mng., chemicals; p. (1970) 102,999 (c.); (1969) 122,000 (met. a.).

Novosibirsk, c., **RSFSR**; on Ob R. and Trans-Siberian rly.; lgst. industl. ctr. of Siberia, nr. Kuznetz Basin; hydroelec. power; varied inds., uranium nearby; univ.; p. (1970) 1,161,000.

Novo Troitsk, t., **RSFSR**; in Urals, 18 km S.W. of Orsk; cement, special steels; p. (est. 1967)82,000.

Novovoronezh, **USSR**; on R. Don, S. of Voronezh; nuclear power sta.

Nový Jičín (**Neutitschein**), t., Moravia, **ČSSR**; farm machin., and engin.; p. (est. 1968) 19,000.

Nowa Huta, t., **Poland**; 10 km S.E. Kraców on Vistula R.; newly developed Lenin metallurgical combine and modern residtl. a. within c. of Kraców; p. (1969) 112,000.

Nowa Sól (**Neusalz**), t., Lower Silesia, **Poland**; pt. on R. Oder; metal-working, food and timber inds.; p. (1970) 33,300.

Nowgong, t., Assam, **India**; agr. and comm. ctr.; rice, tea; p. (1961) 38,600.

Nowra-Bomaderry, t., N.S.W., **Australia**; on E. cst. at mouth of Shoalhaven R.; collecting ctr. for coastal agr. prod.; powdered milk, paper mill; p. (1972) 12,866.

Nowy Sącz, t., Kraków prov., **S. Poland**; on Dunajec R.; lignite nearby; rly. engin., mftg.; ctr. of a. renowned for beauty and tourist attractions; p. (1968) 39,300.

Nubia, anc. region, N.E. **Africa**, extending on both sides of Nile from first cataract at Aswan to Khartoum, Sudan; largely desert, some irrigation alongside Nile.

Nuble, prov., **Chile**; borders on Argentina; comprehensive attempt to develop agr.; most industl. development and agr. mkt. at cap. Chillán; a. 14,204 km²; p. (1970) 314,738.

Nueva Esparta, st., **Venezuela**; consists of over 70 Is.; impt. fisheries; cap. La Asunción; a. 1,150 km²; p. (est. 1970) 112,611.

Neuva San Salvador, t., **El Salvador**; agr. comm. ctr. in coffee-growing and livestock region; p. (est. 1970) 38,063.

Nuevo Laredo, c., N.E. **Mexico**; entry point for American tourists driving to Mexico; tr. ctr. in pastoral and arable agr. a.; p. (1970) 148,867.

Nuevo Léon, st., N.E. **Mexico**; arable agr. needs irrigation in arid climate; impt. iron and steel inds.; cap. Monterrey; a. 65,097 km²; p. (est. 1969) 1,678,000.

Nukualofa, cap. of Polynesian kingdom of **Tonga**; p. (1966) 15,545.

Nukus, c., cap. of Karakalpak ASSR, Uzbek SSR, **USSR**; on Amu Dar'ya R. in Khorezm oasis; clothing inds.; p. (1970) 74,000.

Nullarbor Plain, **S. Australia**; low, level, limestone plateau fringing Gr. Australian Bight; arid; treeless, salt-bush scrub; crossed by Trans-continental rly. between Naretha (W. Australia) and Ooldea; rly. is dead straight, dead level for 477 km.

Numazu, t., Honshu, **Japan**; nr. Tokyo; ctr. of industl. dist. with varied mnfs. inc. machin.; p. (est. 1971) 196,000.

Nuneaton, t., Warwicks., **Eng.**; on Anker R.; coal mng., textiles, lt. inds.; mkt.; birthplace of George Eliot; p. (1971) 66,979.

Nunivak, I., Alaska, **USA**; lge. reindeer herds.

Nunkiang, former prov., N.E. **China**; crossed by Nonni R., trib. of Sungari; now part of Heilungkiang prov.

Nürnberg (**Nuremberg**), c., Bavaria, **W. Germany**; historic c. of architectural beauty; industl. ctr. with elec. mnfs., machin., heavy vehicles, precision instruments, chemicals, toys, pencils and crayons; rly. junc.; inland pt. on Rhine–Danube waterway; p. (1969) 477,783.

Nusa Tenggara, Is., **Indonesia**; part of Lesser Sunda Is.; p. (est. 1970) 4,752,000.

Nuwara Eliya, hill t., (*c.* 1,800 m), **Sri Lanka**; health resort; p. (est. 1968) 16,000.

Nyasa, L., *See* Malawi L.

Nyasaland. *See* **Malawi**.

Nyíregyháza, t., N.E. **Hungary**; ctr. of reclaimed agr. a.; mkt. for tobacco, wine, fruits; domestic ware; p. (1968) 63,000.

Nyborg, pt., **Denmark**; on Fyn I.; terminal of train-ferry across Gr. Belt; shipyards; textile ind.; p. (est. 1970) 11,698.

Nyköbing, spt., Falster I., **Denmark**; varied inds.; admin ctr. of Storstrøms prov.; p. (est. 1970) 17,364.

Nyköping, spt., **Sweden**; at head of inlet on Baltic cst.; comm. and industl. ctr.; p. (1968) 31,226.

Nystad. *See* **Uusikaupunki**.

O

Oadby, t., Leics., **Eng.**; 5 km S.E. of Leicester; footwear; p. (1971) 19,530.

Oahu, I., **Hawaiian Is.**, **Pac. Oc.**; sugar, pineapples; tourist tr.; cap. Honolulu; a. 1,564 km²; p. (1970) 630,528.

Oakengates, t., Shrops., **Eng.**; 24 km N.W. of Wolverhampton; iron and steel, precast concrete, engin.; now part of new t. of Telford; p. (1971) 16,684.

Oakham, t., Leics., **Eng.**; mkt.; hosiery, footwear; p. (1971) 6,411.

Oakland, c., Cal., **USA**; on San Francisco Bay; residtl. sub.; cars, shipbldg., fruit canning, elec. machin., clothing, tanneries, chemicals; p. (1970) 367,548 (c.); (1968) 2,999,200 (met. a.).

Oak Park Village, t., Ill., **USA**; now included in Chicago; birthplace of Ernest Hemingway; p. (1970) 62,511.

Oak Ridge, t., Tenn., **USA**; Atomic Energy Commission's major research ctr.

Oamaru, bor., spt., S.I., **N.Z.**; wool, frozen meat; exp. agr. prods.; p. (1971) 13,090.

Oaxaca, st., Pac. cst., **S. Mexico**; mtnous.,

subsistence agr. in fertile valleys; comm. prod. of coffee, cotton, tobacco; stock-raising; mng. in mtns.; cap. Oaxaca; a. 94,201 km^2; p. (1969) 2,170,000.

Oaxaca, c., cap. of O. st., S. **Mexico**; stands at c. 1,500 m; coffee; gold and silver mines; handicraft mkt.; table linen weaving, wool zarapes; tourist ctr.; p. (1970) 116,826.

Ob', R., W. Siberia, **RSFSR**; one of the world's lgst. Rs., flows from Altai mtns. to G. of Ob'; crossed by Turk-Sib. rly. at Barnaul and by Trans-Siberian rly. at Novosibirsk; ch. trib. Irtysh; hydroelec. power; navigable; oilfields in middle section; outlet of Ob basin Novy-Port (Gdansk); 4,160 km long.

Oban, spt., burgh, Argyll and Bute, **Scot.**; on F. of Lorne; resort; ctr. for local shipping; woollens, tartans; p. (1971) 6,897.

Obed, Alberta, **Canada**; 240 km W. of Edmonton; major natural gas a.

Obeid, El, t., Kordofan, **Sudan**; economically dependent upon rly. link to Khartoum; agr. tr. ctr.; p. (est. 1969) 66,270.

Oberammergau, v., Upper Bavaria, **W. Germany**; scene of decennial Passion Play; winter sports; p. 4,700.

Oberhausen, t., N. Rhine-Westphalia, **W. Germany**; industl. ctr. of Ruhr conurb.; rly. junc., canal pt.; p. (est. 1969) 249,900.

Obidos, t., R. pt., **Brazil**; 800 km up R. Amazon; cacao, cotton; p. (est. 1968) 25,021.

Obihiro, t., Hokkaido, **Japan**; mkt; sugar-beet refining, flax, dairy prods.; p. (est. 1971) 136,000.

Obuasi, t., **Ghana**, E. Africa; ctr. of gold mng.; p. (1970) 31,018.

Obwalden, demi-canton, **Switzerland**; a. 492 km^2; p. (1970) 24,509.

Ocaña, t., Magdalena st., **Colombia**; coffee, hides; isolated by difficult transport conditions; p. (est. 1968) 43, 481.

Ocean City, t., N.J., **USA**; seaside resort founded by the Methodists; p. (1970) 10,575.

Ocean I. (Banaba), **Gilbert Is.**, Pac. Oc.; high grade phosphate (guano) worked by Brit., need for compensation and restoration of land subject of legal action 1971-76; many Banabans evacuated to Rabi I. (Fiji) 1945; p. (1968) 2,192.

Oceania, name given to the Is. of the Pacific; comprising Australasia, Polynesia, Melanesia, Micronesia.

Ochil Hills, volcanic hill-range, **Scot.**; stretching 40 km N.E. to S.W. from F. of Tay to nr. Stirling; loftiest Ben Cleugh 721 m; beautiful glens and valleys.

Odawara, t., **Japan**; pt. with rail connections to Tokyo, 48 km to N.E.; p. (est. 1971) 166,000.

Odda, t., S. **Norway**; on Haugesund; electrochemical and metallurgical inds.; p. (1961) 7,383.

Odemis, t., Asiatic **Turkey**; N.E. of Aydin; tobacco, cereals, silk, cotton, flax, olives, raisins, figs; minerals; p. (1965) 30,621.

Odense, spt., **Denmark**; admin. ctr. of Fyn prov.; varied inds.; exp. dairy prod.; birthplace of Hans Andersen; p. (est. 1969) 103,850 (c.), 138,697 (met. a.).

Odenwald, forested hills, Hesse and Baden-Württemberg, **W. Germany**; highest point Katzenbuckel 626 m.

Oder (Pol. Odra), R., central **Europe**; flows from Moravia to Baltic through Silesia and Pomerania, forming from junc. with Neisse R. frontier between Poland and E. Germany; ch. trib. Warta R.; impt. comm. waterway below Wroclaw; 896 km long.

Odessa, t., Texas, **USA**; impt. oil ctr., chemicals, foundry prod., livestock tr.; p. (1970) 78,380.

Odessa, spt., Ukrainian SSR, **USSR**; on Black Sea; cultural, industl. ctr.; cath., univ.; gr. grain exp.; engin., oil refining, chemicals; ice-bound for a few weeks in winter; p. (1970) 892,000.

Offaly, co., Leinster, **R.o.I.**; much marshy land (inc. Bog of Allen), barren uplands (inc. Slieve Bloom); pastoral agr., wheat; p. mainly rural; sm.-scale domestic prods. and agr.-processing inds. in ts.; co. t. Tullamore; a. 1,999 km^2; p. (1966) 51,707.

Offa's Dyke, earthwork constructed by Offa, king of Mercia (757-96) as bdy. between the English and the Welsh; still forms part of border between the two countries; long-distance footpath along the Welsh marches, 269 km.

Offenbach, t., Hesse, **W. Germany**; on R. Main; cas., leather museum; machin., chemicals, leather gds., metals; p. (est. 1969) 117,500.

Offenburg, t., Baden-Württemberg, **W. Germany**; on R. Kinzig; textiles, glass, rly. junc.; cas.; p. (est. 1969) 32,408.

Ogaden, arid region, S.W. **Ethiopia**; on border of Rep. of Somalia.

Ogaki, t., Honshu, **Japan**; route ctr. in lowland embayment, 40 km N.W. of Nagoya; p. (est. 1971) 137,000.

Ogbomosho, t., S.W. **Nigeria**; ctr. of agr. dist.; cotton weaving; p. (est. 1971) 386,650.

Ogden, c., Utah, **USA**; stands at 1,324 m, nr. Gr. Salt L.; rly. ctr.; beet-sugar, meat-packing, flour-milling, clothing, cement; p. (1970) 68,480 (c.), 124,035 (met. a.).

Ogdensburg, c., pt., N.Y., **USA**; on St. Lawrence R., opposite Prescott; impt. R. pt.; p. (1970) 14,554.

Ogmore and Garw, t., Mid Glamorgan, **Wales**; in narrow valley, 10 km N. of Bridgend; industl.; cas.; p. (1971) 19,415.

Ogooué R., **Gabon**, **Congo**; site of Schweitzer's hospital at Lambaréné; 800 km long.

Ohau, Lake, S.I., **N.Z.**; in Mt. Cook dist.; fed by glaciers; 19 km by 35 km; hydroelectric power potential.

Ohio, R., trib. of Mississippi R., **USA**; formed in Penns., by junc. of Monongahela and Allegheny Rs. at Pittsburgh, thence navigable for 1,560 km to Cairo in Ky.; an impt. comm. waterway for industl. raw materials; flood protection schemes.

Ohio, st., N. **USA**; gr. agr. and industl. region; maize, wheat, cattle; major deposits of coal form basis of heavy inds., especially in major ts. of Cleveland, Cincinnati, Toledo, Akron, Dayton, Youngstown; petroleum; timber inds.; cap. Columbus; a. 106,508 km^2; p. (1970) 10,542,000.

Ohre (Eger), R., Bohemia, **ČSSR**; rises in Fichtelgebirge, flows N.E. into Labe (Elbe) and through Karlovy Vary; 224 km long.

Ohrid or Ochrida, L., forms part of bdy. between **Albania** and **Yugoslavia**; alt. c. 850 m; deepest L. in Balkans; scenic tourist a.; monasteries on shores.

Ohrid or Ochrida, t., Macedonia, **Yugoslavia**; on N.E. shore of L.; airport and tourist ctr.; p. (est. 1965) 19,000.

Oich, Loch, L., Gr. Glen, Inverness, **Scot.**; forms part of Caledonian Canal.

Oise, dep., N. **France**; traversed by R. Oise; fertile, forested; cap. Beauvais; a. 5,884 km^2; p. (1968) 540,988.

Oise, R., trib. of R. Seine, **France**; canalised, navigable to Chauny; 298 km long.

Oita, c., spt., N.E. Kyushu, **Japan**; on Beppu Bay; wire, carbon, iron, and steel; oil refinery; p. (est. 1971) 274,000.

Ojos del Salado, mtn., N.W. **Argentina**; alt. 6,884 m.

Oka, R., Kursk, **RSFSR**; rises S. of Orel, flows past Kaluga, Serpukhov, Kolomna, Ryazan, Murom, to become trib. of Volga at Gorki; navigable, carrying grain and timber; 1,520 km long.

Oka, R., Irkutsk, Siberia, **USSR**; joins Angara R. below Bratsk; 800 km long.

Okanagan, R., and L., B.C., **Canada**; fruit-growing dist., especially apples.

Okayama, c., Honshu, **Japan**; textiles; lt. inds.; p. (est. 1971) 472,000.

Okazaki, t., Honshu, **Japan**; nr. G. of Ovari; industl. ctr.; textiles, chemicals, machin.; p. (est. 1971) 213,000.

Okeechobee, Lake, S. Fla., **USA**; drains to Atl. Oc. via Everglades; tourist attraction especially for fishing; also comm. fisheries.

Okefenokee, swamp, Ga./Fla., **USA**; forms O. Nat. Wildlife Refuge.

Okehampton, mkt. t., Devon, **Eng.**; on N. flank of Dartmoor; granite quarries; p. (1971) 3,908.

Okha, spt., E. cst. Sakhalin I., **RSFSR**; exp. petroleum; lge. refinery; p. 50,000.

Okhotsk, Sea of, N.E. Asia; 1,600 km by 800 km; enclosed by the Siberian mainland, Kamchatka, the Kurils and Sakhalin I.

Oki Is., off cst. of Honshu, **Japan**; a. 350 km^2.

Okinawa, I., **Japan**, under U.S. control until 1972; lgst. and most impt. of Ryuku Is.;

US air bases at Kadena and cap. Naha; a. 1,500 km²; p. (1965) 758,777.
Oklahoma, st., **USA**; prairie, plains and mtns.; continental climate; cereals, cotton, stock-raising; petroleum, gas, zinc, coal, gypsum, lead; ch. ind. petroleum refining; cap. Oklahoma City; a. 181,090 km²; p. (1970) 2,498,378.
Oklahoma City, c., cap. of Okla. st., **USA**; univ.; livestock mkt.; tr. and processing ctr.; oil and by-prods., field machin., flour mills, meat-packing; p. (1970) 362,981 (c.), 623,592 (met. a.).
Okovango, R.; rises in **Angola**, flows to Ngami depression, **Botswana**, where it forms swampy delta; 1,600 km long.
Oktyabrsky, t., Bashkir ASSR, **USSR**; on R. Ik; in new oil-mng. dist., the "New Baku"; p. (est. 1967) 79,000.
Öland, I., Baltic Sea; off E. cst. **Sweden**; connected by Europe's longest bridge to mainland; agr., limestone quarries; ch. t. Borgholm; seaside resorts; a. 1,380 km²; p. (est. 1969) 26,750.
Oldbury, t., West Midlands, **Eng.**; N.W. of Birmingham; chemicals, bricks, glass.
Oldbury-on-Severn, Avon, **Eng.**; nuclear power sta.
Old Castile, historical div., **Spain**; now divided into Santander, Soria, Segovia, Logrono, Avila, Valladolid, Palencia, and Burgos provs.
Oldenburg, c., Lower Saxony, **W. Germany**; on R. Hunte nr. Hunte–Ems canal; rly. junc.; mkt. for horses and cattle; lt. inds.; natural gas nr. to cst.; p. (est. 1969) 131,200.
Old Fletton, Cambs., **Eng.**; on R. Nene opposite Peterborough; bricks, gen. and elec. engin., beet sugar, fruit and vegetable canning; p. (1971) 13,660.
Oldham, c., Gtr. Manchester, **Eng.**; on R. Medlock, 6 km N.E. of Manchester; man-made fibre and cotton textiles, machin.; recent industl. diversification inc. electro- and aero-engin., leather, paints; p. (1971) 105,705.
Oldmeldrum, burgh, Gordon, **Scot.**; 6 km N.E. of Inverurie; p. (1971) 1,085.
Olenek, R., **RSFSR**; N. Siberia; flows W. of Lena R. into Laptev Sea, Arctic Oc.; abounds in fish; 2,160 km long, 960 km navigable
Oléron, Ile d', I., Charente-Maritime dep., **France**; lies off estuary of Charente, Bay of Biscay; oysters, early vegetables; a. 176 km².
Olifant, R., Transvaal, **S. Africa**; trib. of Limpopo; irrigation scheme for intensive agr. in valley.
Olinda, c., Pernambuco st., **Brazil**; seaside resort; phosphates; p. (1970) 187,553.
Oliva, t., Valencia, **Spain**; nr. Alicante; wine dist., ducal palace; p. (1970) 16,772.
Olivos, sub., Buenos Aires, **Argentina**.
Olmütz. *See* **Olomouc**.
Olney, t., Bucks., **Eng.**; mkt., dairy produce; annual Shrove Tuesday pancake race.
Oloibiri, S. **Nigeria**; oilfields; pipeline to Pt. Harcourt, 128 km W.
Olomouc (Olmütz), **ČSSR**; industl. ctr., steel wks., elec. equipment, textiles, food prod.; cath., univ.; formerly one of ch. fortresses of Austria; p. (1967) 78,000.
Oloron-Sainte-Marie, t., Pyrénées-Atlantique, **France**; in Pyrenean foothills; caths.; p. (1968) 13,028.
Olsztyn (Allenstein), t., N.W. **Poland**; cap. of Olsztyn prov.; on R. Alle, 160 km N. of Warsaw; cas.; machin., wood inds.; p. (1970) 94,100.
Olten, t., N. **Switzerland**; rly. junc., on R. Aare; p. (1970) 21,209.
Olympia, anc. c., Peloponnesus, S. **Greece**; at confluence of Alphaeus and Cladeus Rs.; site of gr. temple of Zeus and scene of Olympic games; modern v. of O. nearby; museum.
Olympia, cap. of Washington st., **USA**; spt. on Puget Sound; exp. timber; machin., agr.-processing inds.; p. (1970) 18,273.
Olympus, Mt., highest mtn. in **Greece**; on border of Thessaly and Macedonia, nr. Aegean cst.; alt. 2,975 m; regarded by anc. Greeks as home of the Olympian gods.
Omagh, t., l. gov. dist., **N. Ireland**; on R.; Strule agr. mkt.; tourist ctr.; p. (est. 1971) 11,953.
Omaha, c., Nebraska, **USA**; on Missouri R.; one of lgst. livestock and meat-packing ctrs. in US, gold and silver smelting and refining, steel fabrication, industl. alcohol prod.; univ.; p. (1970) 327,789 (c.), 538,718 (met. a.).
Oman (Muscat and Oman until 1970) sultanate, S.W. Asia; fertile coastal plain, interior desert plateau; irrigated agr., especially impt. for dates; recent oil discoveries (1964); oil now main exp.; a. 212,380 km²; p. (est. 1970) 750,000.
Oman, G. of, Arabian Sea; connected through strait of Ormug to Persian G.; length 480 km, width 208 km.
Omaruru, t., **S.W. Africa**; creamery; aerodrome; p. (1960) 2,689.
Omdurman, c., central **Sudan**, on Nile, opposite Khartoum; site of Mahdi's tomb; here Kitchener defeated the dervishes 1898; native mkts.; p. (est. 1971) 258,532.
Ometepe, I., L. Nicaragua, **Nicaragua**; volcanic; alt. 1,753 m.
Omsk, c., W. Siberia, **RSFSR**; at confluence of Irtysh and Om Rs.; major R. pt. on Trans-Siberian rly.; in agr. region; engin., chemicals, textiles, oil refining, food processing; cath.; founded as fortress 1716; p. (1970) 821,000 (c.); (1969) 832,000.
Omuta, t., W. Kyushu, **Japan**; on Amakusa Sea; local coal at Miike giving rise to chemical inds.; pt. exp. coal; p. (est. 1971) 197,062.
Onega, Lake, **RSFSR**; between L. Ladoga and White Sea; second lgst. L. in Europe (L. Ladoga is lgst.); a. 9,751 km²; ch. c. Petrozavodsk; Onega canal forms part of Volga–Baltic waterway.
Onega, R., **RSFSR**; flows to G. of Onega; 640 km long.
Onehunga, spt., bor., N.I., **N.Z.**; nr. Auckland; p. (1971) 15,597.
One Tree Hill, bor., Auckland, **N.Z.**; p. (1971) 12,963.
Onitsha, t., **Nigeria**; on R. Niger; agr. tr. ctr.; p. (est. 1969) 189,067.
Onstwedde, t., Groningen, **Neth.**; mnfs.; p. (1967) 27,666.
Ontario, prov., **Canada**; bounded on N. by Hudson Bay, on S. by Gr. Ls.; extreme continental climate in N., milder in S. peninsula; extensive coniferous forest in N.; temperate agr. in S.; leading mineral producer, nickel, uranium, copper, gold; well-developed inds. using plentiful hydroelectric power; agr.-processing, machin., engin.; cap. Toronto; contains fed. cap. of Ottawa a. 1,068,587 km² p. (1971) 7,703,106 concentrated in S.E.
Ontario, L., **N. America**; smallest of the Gr. Ls. of the St. Lawrence basin, separating the Canadian prov. of Ont. from N.Y., USA; navigable, carries industl. raw materials; polluted waters; a. 19,425 km²; depth 226 m.
Ontario, t., Cal., **USA**; aircraft components; fruit comm. ctr.; p. (1970) 64,118.
Onteniente, t., Valencia, **Spain**; on R. Clariano; woollen gds., paper mills; p. (1970) 23,685.
Oosterhout, t., N. Brabant, **Neth.**; nr. Breda; footwear, tobacco; p. (1968) 29,625.
Ootacamund, t., Tamil Nadu, **India**; in Nilgiri hills, *c.* 2,100 m; summer H.Q. of st. govt.; sanatorium; p. (1961) 50,140.
Opatija (It. Abbazia), t., **Yugoslavia**; tourist resort, known as the Nice of the Adriatic; p. (1961) 7,974.
Opava (Troppau), t., N. Moravia, **ČSSR**; nr. Polish border; industl. ctr. in agr. a.; p. (1967) 46,000.
Opladen, t., N. Rhine–Westphalia, **W. Germany**; on R. Wupper; metals, textiles, chemicals; p. (est. 1967) 44,700.
Opland or Oppland, co., central **Norway**; mtnous. N. inc. alpine region of Jotunheimen; forestry prods.; a. 24,885 km²; p. (est. 1972) 174,174.
Opole (Oppeln), c., S. **Poland**; on R. Oder; R. pt., rly. junc.; cement, metals, furniture; 3 univ. schools; cap. Prussian prov. of Upper Silesia 1919–45; p. (1970) 86,500.
Oporto, c., spt., **Portugal**; second c. of rep., built high above Douro R.; ctr. of port wine tr.; cath., univ., historic bldgs.; sardine fisheries, cotton and wool textiles, sugar refining, distilling, oil refining; outer harbour at Leixões; p. (est. 1969) 325,400.
Oradea (Hung. Nagy Varad), t., W. **Romania**, on

Crisul Repede R., nr. Hungarian border; p.; ctr.; baroque architecture; lge. Hungarian rly p. (est. 1969) 135,400.

Öraefa Jokull, hgst. mtn., **Iceland;** alt. 1,955 m.

Orange, historic t., Vaucluse, **France;** title founded by Charlemagne passed to William the Silent of the house of Nassau; Roman amphitheatre; tourism; p. (1968) 25,630.

Orange, R., Cape Prov., **S. Africa;** flows from Lesotho to Atl.; part forms S. bdy. between Cape Prov. and Orange Free State; Verwoerd dam (1972) for power, irrigation, flood control; 2,080 km long.

Orange Free State, prov., **Rep. of S. Africa;** plateau land, Drakensberg to N.E., Rs. Orange, Vaal and Caledon; sheep, cattle, horses, wheat, maize, fruit, tobacco, coal, diamonds; cap. Bloemfontein; a. 128,586 km²; p. (1970) 1,651,610.

Oranienburg, t., Potsdam, **E. Germany;** on R. Havel; industl.; chemicals, metals, machin.; p. (est. 1970) 20,442.

Ord of Caithness, hill, headland, nr. Helmsdale, **Scot.;** alt. 366 m.

Ordos, desert region, Inner Mongolia, **China;** lies S. of Yellow R.; mean alt. 1,000 m; dry cropping, especially millets; pastoral farming.

Ordu, spt., **Turkey;** on Black Sea; exp. manganese; p. (1965) 27,307.

Ordzhonikidze, c., cap. of N. Ossetian ASSR, **RSFSR;** on R. Terek at foot of Caucasus, ind. ctr., metallurgical inds.; natural gas pipeline to Tbilisi; hydroelec. power sta.; p. (1970) 236,000.

Örebro, c., cap. of Örebro prov., **Sweden;** on R. Svartå at entrance to Hjälmar L.; anc. t., cas.; footwear, biscuits; p. (1968) 87,430.

Oregon, st., N.W. **USA;** borders Pac. Oc.; ch. physical features, Coast ranges, Cascade mtn. region, Blue mtns., Columbia R. and tribs., Willamette valley; rainy cst., drier interior (agr. with irrigation); cereals, sugar-beet, fruit, cattle; gold, silver, copper, coal, uranium; fisheries, canning, meat-packing, timber, milling; cap. Salem; a. 250,948 km²; p. (1970) 2,056,171.

Orekhovo-Zuyevo, t., **RSFSR;** E. of Moscow, on R. Klyazma; textile inds.; p. (1970) 120,000.

Orel, c., **RSFSR;** on R. Oka; univ.; rly. junc.; engin., textile mills, food prods.; birthplace of Turgenev; p. (1970) 232,000.

Orenburg (Chkalov), c., cap. of Orenburg oblast, **RSFSR;** on Ural R.; rly. junc.; food processing, agr. machin.; oil and natural gas in region; p. (est. 1967) 326,000.

Orense, t., cap. of Orense prov., **Spain;** on R. Minho; flour, leather, iron; p. (1967) 71,768.

Ore Sound, strait, between Sjaelland, Denmark, and S. Sweden; protected by agreement of adjacent countries; freezes occasionally.

Orford Ness, coastal sandspit, Suffolk, **Eng.;** cas. keep at Orford.

Oriente, prov., **Cuba;** contains mtns. of Sierra Maestra; sugar cane grown in lowlands; manganese mng.; a. 36,592 km²; p. (est. 1970) 2,998,972.

Oriente, terr., **Peru/Ecuador;** for long in dispute between the two ctys., partially settled by treaty (1942); lies E. of Andes, between Putumayo and Marañon Rs.; mainly dense forest, reputedly rich in minerals.

Orihuela, t., Alicante, **Spain;** on R. Segura; leather, textiles, wine; univ., cath.; p. (1970) 44,938.

Orinoco, R., **Venezuela;** rises in Parima mtns., flows to Atl., connected to Rio Negro and Amazon; impt. industl. development on lower O., based on hydroelec. power and iron ore; experimental scheme to reclaim delta for agr.; 2,368 km long.

Orissa, st., **India;** agr. with few ts.; Hirakud dam across Mahanadi R.; Paradeep being developed as pt.; rice; cap. Bhuvaneshwar; a. 155,825 km²; p. (1971) 21,934,827.

Orizaba, t., Veracruz, **Mexico;** textiles, paper mills, breweries; resort; p. (est. 1970) 92,728.

Orizaba, mtn., Veracruz, **Mexico;** volcanic; called Citlatepetl in Aztec times; alt. 5,704 m.

Orkney, l. gov. reg., **Scot.;** gr. of 68 Is. in N. Sea, inc. Pomona, Sanday, Westray; 29 inhabited; antiquarian remains, stone circles; farming, fishing; North Sea oil finds; cap. Kirkwall; total a. *c.* 932 km²; p. (1971) 17,077.

Orlando, c., Fla., **USA;** winter resort; inds. based on citrus fruit and mkt. garden prods.; p. (1970) 97,565 (c.), 426,750 (met. a.).

Orléannais, region and former prov., **France;** inc. deps. of Loire-et-Cher, Loiret, and parts of Eure-et-Loire and Yonne.

Orléans, c., cap. of Loiret dep., **France;** on R. Loire; cath., univ.; regional tr. ctr.; wine, textiles, chemicals, farm implements; statue of Joan of Arc; p. (1968) 95,828 (c.), 167,515 (met. a.).

Orleans, I., Quebec, **Canada;** in St. Lawrence R., nr. Quebec; resort; a. 181 km².

Ormoc. *See* **MacArthur.**

Ormskirk, t., Lancs., **Eng.;** 22 km N.E. of Liverpool; in mkt. gardening a.; lt. engin., clothing; p. (1971) 27,618.

Orne, dep., N. **France;** agr., dairying, stock-keeping, fruit-growing, Camembert cheese; cap. Alençon; a. 6,143 km²; p. (1968) 288,524.

Orontes, R., rises in Lebanon, flows through **Syria** past Hama into **Turkey** past Antioch to Mediterranean; unnavigable but used for irrigation; part of valley followed by rly.; irrigated areas intensively cultivated; c. 400 km long.

Oroya, t., **Peru;** impt. mng. and refining ctr.; p. (est. 1969) 31,700.

Orpington. *See* **Bromley.**

Orrell, t., Gtr. Manchester, **Eng.;** W. of Wigan; p. (1971) 12,069.

Orsha, c., Belorussiyan SSR, **USSR;** impt. industl. and transport ctr. on R. Dnieper; textiles, metal wks., food-processing; once a frontier fortress; p. (1970) 101,000.

Orsk, c., Bashkir ASSR, **RSFSR;** in Ural mtns. on Ural R.; inds. based on surrounding mng. a.; oil pipeline terminus; oil refining; hydro-electric power sta. nearby; p. (1970) 225,000.

Orta, L., **Italy;** W. of Lago Maggiore; a. 18 km².

Orthez, t., Pyrénées-Atlantique, **France;** scene of Wellington's victory over Soult (1814); Bayonne hams; p. (1968) 10,640.

Oruro, t., **Bolivia;** cap. of O. prov. at alt. 3,709 m; once impt. ctr. for silver mng.; now other minerals impt.; p. (1967) 91,911.

Oruwala, t., **Sri Lanka;** steel rolling mill.

Orvieto, t., Umbria, **Italy;** on R. Paglia; cath., Etruscan antiquities; wines, olive oil, cereals; pottery; p. (est. 1968) 24,246.

Osaka, c., Honshu, **Japan;** ctr. of Kinki plain; built on delta in shallow O. Bay; comm. ctr.; banking, heavy industry, metals, machin., clothing; p. (est. 1971) 2,939,000.

Osasco, t., São Paulo st., **Brazil;** industl. ctr.; p. (1970) 283,203.

Osh, t., S.W. Kirghiz SSR, **USSR;** textiles, food-processing; one of oldest ts. in central Asia; p. (1970) 120,000.

Oshawa, t., Ont., **Canada;** pt. on L. Ont.; motor vehicles; p. (1971) 91,113.

Oshima, I., Tokyo Bay, **Japan;** lgst and most N. of Izu-shichito gr.; site of volcanic Mt. Mihara (755 m).

Oshkosh, t., Wis., **USA;** on Fox R.; meat packing, flour, motors; p. (est. 1969) 52,500.

Oshogbo, t., **Nigeria;** comm. and educational ctr.; serves agr. dist.; cotton-ginning; p. (est. 1971) 252,583.

Osijek, t., Croatia, **Yugoslavia;** on Drava R.; growing industl. ctr. for textiles and leather; p. (1971) 93,912.

Osinniki, t., **RSFSR;** W. Siberia; new ctr. of coal mng.; thermal power sta.; p. (est. 1969) 67,000.

Osipenko. *See* **Berdyansk.**

Oslo (Christiania), c., cap. of **Norway;** at head of Oslo Fjord; ch. spt., comm., industl., and cultural ctr.; ice-free harbour; cath., univ.; exp. timber, fish, matches; wood pulp, paper; occupied by Germans 1940–5; p. (est. 1969) 487,846 (c.); (1967) 685,000. (met. a.).

Osnabrück, c., Lower Saxony, **W. Germany;** on R. Hase; stands on a branch of the Mittelland canal; inland pt. and industl. ctr.; iron and steel mills; mach., textile and paper mnfs.; p. (est. 1969) 140,400.

Osorno, t., **Chile;** agr. ctr.; in beautiful forested cty.; Germanic influence; food-processing; tourism; p. (est. 1966) 69,220.

Ossett, t., West Yorks., **Eng.;** 5 km W. of Wakefield; woollens, shoddy-processing, engin.; p. (1971) 17,181.

Ostend, spt., **Belgium**; passenger route between Britain and continent of Europe; popular resort; casino, fisheries, shipbldg., textiles, tobacco; p. (1968) 57,765.

Östergötland, co., **Sweden**; on Baltic cst.; rises to uplands of Småland in S. where p. declining; lowland a. crossed by Göta canal; cap. Linköping; a. 11,050 km²; p. (est. 1970) 375,947.

Östersund, t., Jämtland, **Sweden**; on Storsjön L.; p. (1968) 26,620.

Östfold, co., S.E. **Norway**; hilly a. crossed by R. Glomma; dairy prods. for Oslo; a. 4,178 km²; p. (est. 1972) 224,041.

Ostia, anc. c., **Italy**; once pt. of Rome, at mouth of R. Tiber, founded 4th cent. B.C.; layout revealed by excavations; modern v. of O. nearby on plain reclaimed from salt marsh.

Ostrava, c., **ČSSR**; at junc. of Oder and Ostravice Rs.; industl. ctr. of Ostrava–Karvinna coal-mng. region; iron and steel, machin., chemicals, oil refining; p. (est. 1968) 273,280.

Ostrow Wielkopolski, t., Poznan, **Poland**; agr. machin., clothing; p. (1970) 49,500.

Ostrowiec Swietokrzyski (Ostrovets), t., Kielce, **Poland**; on R. Kamienna; ceramic and metallurgical inds.; p. (1970) 50,000.

Oswaldtwistle, t., Lancs., **Eng.**; at N. foot of Rossendale Fells; chemicals, textiles; p. (1971) 14,015.

Oswego, t., N.Y., **USA**; pt. on L. Ontario; mnfs. hosiery, matches, textiles, boiler engines, paper; p. (1970) 23,844.

Oswestry, t., Salop, **Eng.**; at foot of Welsh mtns., cas.; engin.; p. (1971) 30,320 (dist.).

Oświecim (Ger. **Auschwitz**), t., Kraków, **Poland**; at confluence of Rs. Iola and Vistula; lge. chemical wks.; German concentration camp (1940–44); p. (1970) 39,600.

Otago, prov., S.I., **N.Z.**; forested mtns.; gold; farming, sheep, fruit; lge. deposit of jade found at head of L. Wakatipu; coalfields; cap. Dunedin; a. 65,320 km²; p. (1971) 182,825.

Otago Harbour, Otago dist., S.I., **N.Z.**; Dunedin and Port Chalmers are ports on this harbour.

Otanmäki, **Finland**; rich deposit of magnetite-ilmenite ore.

Otaru, spt., Hokkaido, **Japan**; herring fisheries; coal mng., lumbering; p. (est. 1971) 192,000.

Otley, t., West Yorks., **Eng.**; on R. Wharfe; printing, machin., wool, paper mkg., leather, furnishings; birthplace of Thomas Chippendale; p. (1971) 13,254.

Otranto, t., S. **Italy**; on Strait O.; once a flourishing c., fine mosaic pavement, cath., cas.; submarine cable sta.; bauxite exp., fishing; p. (est. 1968) 4,530.

Otsu, t., Honshu, **Japan**; on L. Biwa; p. (est. 1971) 176,000.

Ottawa, c., cap. of **Canada**, Ont., on R. Ottawa; univ., caths., parliament bldgs.; hydroelec. power, lumbering, sawmills, paper, flour, leather, matches, machin., ironware; p. (1971) 298,087 (c.), 447,736 (met. a.).

Ottawa, R., **Canada**; trib. of St. Lawrence, forming bdy. between Ont. and Quebec; timber transport, hydroelec. power; 1,000 km long.

Ottery St. Mary, mkt. t., Devon, **Eng.**; 16 km E. of Exeter; birthplace of Coleridge; p. (1971) 5,824.

Ottumwa, t., Iowa, **USA**; on Des Moines R.; in coalfield and agr. dist.; iron and steel, meat-packing; p. (1970) 29,610.

Ötzal, valley, **Austria**; longest side valley of R. Inn; tourist dist.

Ouachita or **Washita**, R., Ark., **USA**; trib. of Red R.; 880 km long.

Ouachita National Forest, Ark., Okla., **USA**; part of forested O. highlands.

Ouagadougou, cap. of **Upper Volta**; tr. and comm. ctr.; p. (1967) 79,500.

Ouahran (Oran), spt., N. **Algeria**; founded by Moors 10th cent.; occupied by French 1831–1962; handles wines, wool, cereals, meat, skins; fine roadstead at Mers-el-Kebir; former French naval and military sta.; p. (1967) 324,000 (c.), (1966) 328,257 (met. a.).

Oudenaarde (Audenarde), t., **Belgium**, on R. Scheldt; textile ctr.; scene of Marlborough's victory over French 1708; p. (1968) 22,035.

Ouenza, c., **Algeria**; 75 per cent of Algerian iron-ore produced in dist.

Oujda, t., N.E. **Morocco**; comm. ctr.; phosphate, lead and zinc-mng. dist.; p. (1971) 155,800 (t.) 317,420 (met. a.).

Oulton Broad, L., Suffolk, **Eng.**; nr. Lowestoft. *See* **Broads**.

Oulu, spt., cap. of Oulu prov., N.W. **Finland**; on G. of Bothnia at mouth of R. Oulu; univ.; p. (1968) 83,190.

Oundle, mkt. t., Northants., **Eng.**; on R. Nene; public school; p. (1971) 3,741.

Ouro Prêto, old colonial t., **Brazil**; former cap. of Minas Gerais st.; grew as gold mng. ctr.; since p. has declined; now other minerals; school of mines; p. (est. 1968) 38,372.

Ouse or **Great Ouse**, R., **Eng.**; rises in S. Northamptonshire and flows N.E. via the Fens to the Wash; 250 km long.

Ouse, R., East Sussex, **Eng.**; flows to English Channel at Newhaven; 48 km long.

Ouse, R., North Yorks./Humberside, **Eng.**; formed by Rs. Swale and Ure, flows to Humber estuary; 208 km long.

Ovalle, t., Coquimbo prov., **Chile**; ctr. of fruit and pastoral dist.; p. (est. 1966) 29,377.

Overijssel, prov., **Neth.**; dairying, fishing; ch. ind. textiles; a. 3,364 km²; p. (1967) 887,261.

Oviedo, coastal. prov., N. **Spain**; agr., fruit, sardine, and other fisheries; cap. O.; a. 10,888 km²; p. (1970) 1,045,635.

Oviedo, c., cap. of O. prov., **Spain**; on R. Nalón; cath., univ.; industl. and comm. ctr. for agr. and mng dists. of Asturia; textiles, leather, matches and many other mnfs.; p. (1968) 144,697.

Owends, pt., **Liberia**; deepwater pt. built to serve iron-ore mines at Belinga.

Owen Falls, **Uganda**; dam inaugurated 1954; converts L. Victoria into reservoir for irrigation of Egypt and Sudan; also to supply Uganda with hydroelectric power.

Owensboro', t., Ky., **USA**; petroleum; ctr. for stock raising and tobacco growing a.; p. (1970) 50,329.

Owens, L., S. Cal., **USA**; on E. flank of Sierra Nevada, 32 km S.E. of Mt. Whitney; water taken by 360 km-long aqueduct to Los Angeles; a. 311 km².

Owen Sound, t., L. pt., Ont., **Canada**; on S.W. cst. of Georgian Bay, L. Huron; E. terminus of lgst. wheat-carrying L. steamers; linked by rly. to Toronto (200 km) and Montreal; p. (1971) 18,281.

Oxelösund, spt., E. **Sweden**; on Baltic cst., S. of Stockholm; steelwks., glass; p. (1961) 10,007.

Oxford, c., Oxon., **Eng.**; between R. Thames and R. Cherwell; 13th cent. univ. and residtl. colleges; printing, cars, elec. engin.; p. (1971) 108,564.

Oxfordshire, non-met. co., **Eng.**; formed by Chilterns and Cotswolds, drained by R. Thames and tribs.; mainly agr. with lge. arable farms; ch. t. Oxford; a, 2,611 km²; citrus fruits, sugar

Oxnard, t., Cal., **USA**; citrus fruits, sugar beet, oil refining; p. (1970) 70,128 (t.), 374,410 (met. a.).

Oxus R. *See* **Amu Dar'ya**.

Oyashio. *See* **Bering Current**.

Oyo, t., **Nigeria**; cotton weaving; mkt.; p. (est. 1971) 135,785.

Ozark Mtns., Okla. and Ark., **USA**; lead, zinc; ch. t. Joplin; forested.

Ozd, t., **Hungary**; iron and steel; p. (1966) 39,900.

P

Paarl, t., Cape Prov., **S. Africa**; summer resort extending along Gt. Berg R.; wines, fruit, tobacco; flour, saw and textile mills; p. (1970) 48,597.

Pabianice, t., **Poland**; nr. Lodz; textiles, farming implements, paper; cas.; p. (1969) 62,000.

Pabna, t., and dist., Bengal, **Bangladesh**; dist. is a fertile alluvial plain; t. serves as trading, industl. and admin. ctr. for a.; hosiery, carpets; p. (1961) 40,792 (t.).

Pacasmayo, spt., **Peru**; exp. rice, sugar, cotton, cacao, hides, copper, lead, zinc, silver; p. (1961) 6,000.

Pachitea, R., **Peru**; rises in Andes, flows N. to

R. Ucayali; sm. German immigrant colonies in upper valley; 512 km long.

Pachmarhi, Madhya Pradesh, **India**; summer cap., tourist ctr.; p. (1961) 6,142.

Pachuca, cap., Hidalgo st., **Mexico**; silver mnfs. and mng.; woollen and leather gds.; p. (1970) 84,543.

Pacific Islands, Trust Terr. of, external terr. of USA held under U.N. trusteeship; consists of Mariana Is. (except Guam), Caroline and Marshall Is., W. Pac. Oc.; inc. 2,141 Is., grouped into 6 admin. dists.; cap. (provisional) Saipan, **Mariana Is.**; total land a. *c.* 1,800 km^2; p. (1970) 102,250.

Pacific Ocean, a. 176,120,000 km^2; lgst. ocean in the world; extends from W. cst of America to E. cst. of Asia and Australia and the S. Ocean in the S.; enters Arctic Oc. via Bering Strait; greatest length N. to S. 1,280 km; breadth, 16,000 km; mean depth 3,830 m, 11,524 m in the Mindanao trench; many coral and volcanic Is. in S.W.

Padang, spt., W. cst. Sumatra, **Indonesia**; exp. agr. prods., coffee, copra, rubber and coal; cement mnfs.; univ.; p. (1971) 196,339.

Paddington. *See* Westminster, City of.

Paderborn, c., N. Rhine-Westphalia, **W. Germany**; cath. and other historic bldgs. severely damaged in second world war; foodstuffs, textiles, metals; p. (est. 1969) 64,576.

Padiham, t., Lancs., **Eng.**; at N. foot of Rossendale Fells, textiles, engin., gas appliances; p. (1971) 10,192.

Padstow, mkt. t., Cornwall, **Eng.**; on W. side of Camel estuary in which silting has caused pt. of P. to decline; lt. inds.; seaside resort; p. (1971) 17,799 (inc. Wadebridge dist.).

Padua (Padova), c., cap. of P. prov., N.E. **Italy**; cath., arcades, anc. bridges; univ. founded 1222 (Galileo taught here); flourished as artistic ctr.; birthplace of Livy; machin., chemicals, cloth, distilling; agr. ctr.; p. (1969) 226,244.

Paducah, c., Ky., **USA**; pt. on Ohio R.; saw-mills, tobacco, railway wks.; atomic energy plant; p. (1970) 31,267.

Paestum, anc. c., S. **Italy**; S.E. of Salerno; founded by the Greeks 600 B.C.; ruins of temples, Roman forum and amphitheatre.

Pagan, ruined c., central **Burma**; on Irrawaddy R.; founded circa 849, sacked 1299; in ctr. of a. covered with pagodas, place of Burmese pilgrimage; lacquer work.

Pago Pago, spt., cap. of American **Samoa**, S. Pac.; on Tutuila I., magnificent harbour; US naval and radio sta.; airport; p. (1970) 2,491.

Pahang, st., **Malaysia**, central Malaya; isolated from rest of Malaya, less economically developed; largely covered with forest; some rubber production, gold, tin mng.; cap. Kuala Lipis; a. 34,395 km^2; p. (1967) 425,552.

Pahlevi. *See* Bandar-e-Pahlevi.

Paignton, t., S. Devon, **Eng.**; incorporated in Torbay; resort.

Painted Desert, Arizona, **USA**; a. of bare multicoloured shale and sandstones; arid; a. c. 19,400 km^2.

Paisley, burgh, Renfrew, **Scot.**; 8 km W. of Glasgow; anc. abbey; shipbldg., chemicals, engin., preserves, car bodies, cotton thread; p. (1971) 95,357.

Paita, pt., **Peru**; exp. cotton, wool, flax, panama hats; lge. whaling sta. to S.; p. 37,000.

Pakistan, Islamic Rep. of, forms part of Indian subcontinent, **S. Asia**; formerly split into two separate units, E. Pakistan (cap. Dacca) and W. Pakistan (cap. Lahore), 1,600 km apart; politically separate since 1972; W. part now forms Pakistan, E. part indep. st. of Bangladesh; dry semi-desert, irrigated by Indus R. and tribs.; cash crops, sugar, wheat, cotton; natural gas fields; new cap. Islamabad; main spt. Karachi; a. 803,944 km^2; p. (1972) 64,890,000 (+51 per cent. in 12 years).

Paknampoh, t., **Thailand**; on R. Menam, at upper limit of steam navigation; terminus of private rly.; fish breeding in L. created from swamp.

Pakokku, t., **Upper Burma**; pt. on Irrawaddy R.; shipping ctr. for a. producing sugar, tobacco, peanuts, teak, petroleum; Yenangyaung oilfields nearby; p. (est. 1962) 156,960.

Paktia, prov., **Afghanistan**; mtnous., forested; difficult to govern, inhabited by sm. and indep. tribes, but sparse p.; livestock basis of agr.; timber exp.; a. *c.* 12,950 km^2; p. (est. 1970) 732,779.

Palau Is., archipelago, **Pac. Oc.**; volcanic and coral Is.; exp. agr. prods., dried fish; p. (1968) 11,904.

Palawan I., **Philippines**; elongated I., rising to 1,731 m; coffee, resin, timber; sparse p.; a. 11,784 km^2; p. (1970) 232,322.

Palembang, cap. of S. Sumatra prov., **Indonesia**; R. pt. on Musi R., 80 km from sea; terminus of S. Sumatran rly. systems; exp. coffee and petroleum prods. from nearby oilfields; inds. based on agr. processing and oil refining; p. (1971) 582,961.

Palencia, t., cap. of P. prov., N.W. **Spain**; industl. ctr.; rly. engin.; cath.; p. (1970) 58,370.

Palermo, spt., Sicily, **Italy**; cath., univ.; ship-repairing; processes agr. prod. from surrounding fertile Conca d'Oro; p. (1969) 659,177.

Palestine or **The Holy Land**, historic region, bounded by Syria and Lebanon on the N., Jordan on the E., the Egyptian prov. of Sinai on the S., and the Mediterranean on the W.; a. when under Brit. mandate 2,701 km^2; p. (est. 1948) 782,000. *See* **Israel**.

Palghat, t., Kerala, **India**; commands Palghat gap through W. Ghats; p. (1961) 77,620.

Palitana, t., Gujarat, **India**; t. of Jain temples inhabited by priests and their servants; p. (1961) 24,581.

Palk Strait, **India**; separates India from Sri Lanka.

Palma de Mallorca, spt., Mallorca I. **Spain**; cath., palaces, varied inds.; agr. exp.; well-known tourist resort; p. (est. 1969) 177,089.

Palm Beach, t., Fla., **USA**; Atl. coastal resort; permanent p. (1970) 9,086.

Palmerston North, pt. and t. N.I. **N.Z.**; rly. junc. at ctr. of Manawatu R. lowlands; sheep and dairy prod.; univ.; p. (1971) 51,859.

Palmira, t., W. **Colombia**; agr. ctr. in Cauca valley; p. (est. 1972) 154,200 (t.), 193,500 (met. a.).

Palm Springs, Cal., **USA**; resort; p. (1970) 20,936.

Palmyra, anc. c. in Syrian desert, 192 km N.E. of Damascus; Bible name Tadmor = city of palms; extensive ruins.

Palmyra Is. *See* **Line Is.**

Palo Alto, t., sub. development 48 km S.E. San Francisco, **USA**; attractive wooded site of variable relief; on shore of San Francisco Bay peninsula; Stanford Univ.; science-based inds.; p. (1970) 56,181.

Palomar, Mount, peak, 1,868 m high, S. Cal. **USA**; observatory with 5,080 mm reflecting telescope.

Palos de la Frontera t., Huelva, S.W. **Spain**; on Rio Tinto; starting point for Columbus in 1492; pt. now silted up; p. 1,900.

Palua, pt., **Venezuela**; pt. of shipment for iron mines at El Pao; nearby Caroni hydroelec. plant built to serve steel wks. and aluminium plant.

Pamir Mtns., high mtn. plateau ("roof of the world"), Tadzik SSR, Central Asia; Mt. Communism (7,500 m) climbed by Russo-British team 1962; name derives from high mtn. valleys known as "Pamirs."

Pampas, **Argentina**; vast plains stretching from the Rio Negro on the S. to the Gran Chaco in the N., and E. from the Andes to the Atl.; woodless, level country; rich pastures in E., supporting countless numbers of sheep and cattle, a major influence upon the Argentinian economy, source of livestock exps.; W. mostly barren.

Pamplona, t., Norte de Santander, **Colombia**; agr., comm. and tr. ctr.; inds. based on agr. processing; p. (est. 1968) 33,707.

Pamplona, c, cap. of Navarre, N. **Spain**; at foot of Pyrenees, anc. Basque c.; cath., fortress, univ.; industl. ctr. with varied mnfs.; p. (est. 1968) 122,005.

Panama, rep., **Central America**; narrow strip of terr. at S. end of isthmus separating N. and S. America; mtnous. and tropical, thickly forested; split by Canal Zone from which rep. earns 25 per cent of revenue; shipping registration impt.; subsistence agr.; exp. bananas, rice, maize; sea fisheries; rich copper deposits found 1975; poor communications; cap. Panama City; a. 74,009 km^2; p. (est. 1974) 1,650,000.

Panama Canal Zone, Panama; strip of land 82 km long 16 km wide on either side of Canal, leased to USA for military base; a. 1,675 km^2; p. (est. 1970) 51,400.
Panama, c. spt., cap. of **Panama**; free pt. at S. entrance to Canal; cath.; oil refining, steel rolling mill, cement plant, lt. inds.; contains 25 per cent p. Panama rep.; p. (est. 1974) 410,000.
Panama City, t., Fla., **USA**; pulp and paper mill; resort; p. (est. 1970) 418,013.
Pan American Highway, international road project, not yet fully complete, from Alaska to Chile, down W. csts. of continents; section between USA and Mexico is called Central American Inter-American Highway.
Panay, I., **Philippines**; between Negros I. and Mindoro I.; coconuts, maize grown in E., fertile lowland; ch. t. Iloilo; a. 11,515 km^2; p. (1970) 2,116,545.
Pančevo, t., N.E. Serbia, **Yugoslavia**; agr. ctr. for grain growing a., flour-milling; developing industl. ctr., fertilizers, oil refining; p. (est. 1965) 52,000.
Pangalanes Canal (Canal Des Pangalanes), **Malagasy Rep.**; follows E. cst. from Farafangana to Tamatave, through series of lagoons; 480 km long.
Panipat, t., Punjab, N.W. **India**; on Jumna R.; on route from Afghanistan to central India; scene of battles; p. (1961) 67,026.
Panjim, cap. of Goa, **India**; pt.; old cap. (Velha Goa) in ruins; p. (1961) 32,000.
Panjsher Valley, Afghanistan; silver and mica mines.
Pannonian Basin, major structural depression, N. and E. **Yugoslavia**.
Pantelleria, volcanic I., Mediterranean, **Italy**; midway between W. Sicily and Tunisia; figs, raisins, vines, capers, cereals; fishing; a. 150 km^2; ch. t. P.; p. 10,000.
Pantin, N.E. sub., Paris, Seine-St. Denis, **France**; glasswks., sugar refining, tobacco factories, chemicals, leather, tallow; p. (1968) 47,607.
Paoki (Baoji), c., Shensi prov., **China**; ctr. of arable agr. a.; cotton weaving; nearby gorge on Hwang-ho used for multi-purpose dams; p. (est. 1970) 275,000.
Paoting (Baoding), c., Hopeh prov., **China**; on the Yungting R.; p. (est. 1970) 350,000.
Paotow (Baotou), c., Inner Mongolia, **China**; on left bank of Hwang-ho, on road and rly. routes to E. China; airfield; terminus of caravan routes through Gobi desert and Tarim basin to Turkestan; tr. in non-perishable livestock prods., cereals; modern steel ind.; p. (est. 1970) 800,000.
Papakura, bor., N.I., **N.Z.**; p. (1971) 17,208.
Papoloa, R., **Mexico**; agr. and industl. development; Papaloan project for flood control and electricity generation.
Papal States, Italy; areas ruled by the Pope until 1870; comprised Latium, Umbria, the Marches, and Emilia-Romagna.
Papatoetoe, t., N.I., **N.Z.**; p. (1971) 21,804.
Papeete, t., pt., **Tahiti I.**, Pac. Oc.; cap. Tahiti and of Fr. Settlements in Oceania; exp. copra, vanilla, phosphates and mother-of-pearl; p. (est. 1970) 28,000.
Paphos, admin. dist., W. cst. **Cyprus**; anc. c.; Old P. dates from 3000 B.C., New P. impt. spt.; rich deposits of copper and iron pyrites, sulphur in Vretsia a.; p. (est. 1970) 11,800 (t.).
Papua New Guinea, E. New Guinea, **S.E. Asia**; indep. st. (1974); mtnous., thickly forested; under-developed; copra, rubber and timber prods.; cap. Pt. Moresby; a. 461,693 km^2; p. (1970) 2,522,890.
Pará, st., **Brazil**; densely forested; rubber, fruits, cacao, Brazil nuts; cap. Belem; a. 1,228,061 km^2; p. (est. 1968) 1,959,756.
Paracel Is., S. China Sea; claimed by China, Taiwan and Vietnam.
Paraguay, landlocked rep., **S. America**; undulating cty.; swamps, forest; hot summers, warm winters, high but seasonal rainfall; sm. densely populated areas, lge. areas with no p.; most economically developed in E.; in and around cap. Asunción 25 per cent p.; economy based on agr., cereals, livestock, fruit, cotton, oil-seeds, but food imported; aid from USA for rural development; few fuel resources (a few oilfields in the Chaco Boreal) and low energy consumption; hydroelectric plants on Paraná Paraguay Rs. and at Guaira Falls; some agr., based inds.; a. 406,630 km^2; p. (est. 1970) 2,386,000.
Paraguay, R., **S. America**; rises in plateau of Mato Grosso, flows S. and joins R. Paraná nr. Corrientes; forms bdy. between Brazil and Bolivia, Brazil and Paraguay; impt. navigable waterway to Cáceres (Brazil); 1,920 km long.
Paraíba, st., N.E. **Brazil**; livestock, cotton, sugar cane; tin, scheelite; cap. João Pessoa; a. 56,462 km^2; p. (est. 1968) 2,252,636.
Paraíba do Sul, R., S. **Brazil**; rises in São Paulo st., and flows between Rio de Janeiro and Minas Gerais to Atl. N.E. of Rio de Janeiro; forms routeway between São Paulo and Rio de Janeiro; 1,040 km long.
Paramaribo, spt., cap. of **Surinam**; on Surinam R.; exp. bauxite, timber, rubber, rice, fruit; t. built on grid pattern with canals and tree-lined streets; p. (1964) 110,867 (c.), 182,100 (met. a.).
Paraná, c., cap. of Entre Ríos prov., N.E. **Argentina**; pt. on Paraná R. for grain, cattle, sheep; road tunnel to Santa Fé; p. (1970) 127,836 (met. a.).
Paraná, R., S.W. **Brazil**; formed by junc. of Rs. Rio Grande and Paranaíba; flows W. between Paraguay and Argentina; flows into Rio de la Plata; navigable to Brazil frontier nr. Iguaçu Falls; forms part of international inland waterway system; hydroelec. power, Itaipú to be lgst. sta. in world; 3,280 km long.
Paraná, st., S. **Brazil**; between Paraná R. and Atl. Oc.; extensively forested; maté, timber, coffee; cap. Curitiba; a. 201,287 km^2; p. (est. 1968) 7,216,582.
Paranaguá, spt., Paraná st., **Brazil**; ch. pt. for Paraná; in lagoon harbour; modern highway links with Asunción (Paraguay); p. (est. 1968) 65,178.
Paradubice, t., **ČSSR**; univ., cath.; rly. junc., industl. ctr.; distilling, oil refining; p. (1967) 66,000.
Paricutín, Mt., Michoacán, **Mexico**; volcano formed between 1943 and 1952, 2,501 m high; of great interest to scientists.
Paris, c., cap. of **France**; dominates rep. politically, economically, and socially, partly as result of extreme centralisation of political power in cap.; on R. Seine, 176 km from mouth, in ctr. of Paris Basin; forms major ctr. of communications; planning of Haussmann gives spacious appearance, 12 boulevards radiate from Arc de Triomphe; many historic bldgs., especially on and around Île de la Cité, an I. on R. Seine, site of cath. of Nôtre Dame; major cultural and tourist ctr.; univs.; comprises 20 admin. arrondissements; major ctr. of inds. with concentration of modern science-based inds. hindering planned attempts at decentralisation; p. (1968) 2,590,771 (c.), 8,196,746 (met. a.), representing 16 per cent of Fr. p.
Paris Basin, concentric limestone escarpments form saucer-shaped depression with Paris at ctr.; impt. agr. dist., wheat, dairy prod. and wines.
Parkersburg, t., W. Va., **USA**; on Ohio R.; iron- and steel-wks., oil and natural gas, coal, glassware, rayon, porcelain; p. (est. 1969) 47,000.
Parkes, t., N.S.W., **Australia**; mkt.; rly. junc.; radio telescope; p. (1966) 8,431.
Parma, c., cap. of P. prov., **Italy**; between Apennines and Po R.; tr. ctr., rly. junc.; food-processing, wine, Parmesan cheese, precision instruments, agr. machin.; Roman remains, many historic bldgs., univ., cath.; p. (1969) 172,341.
Parma, t., Ohio, **USA**; motor vehicle parts; residtl.; p. (1970) 100,216.
Parnaíba, spt., Piauí, **Brazil**; agr. comm. ctr., cotton, cattle; exp. agr. prods.; p. (est. 1968) 69,961.
Parnaíba, R., rises in **Brazil**; flows into N. Atl. Oc., forms bdy. between Maranhão and Piauí; 1,200 km long.
Parnassos, mtn. ridge, **Greece**; 133 km N.W. of Athens, nr. the anc. Delphi, the modern Liakhura; hgst. peak Licoreia 2,461 m.
Parnu or Pyarnu, spt., S.W. Estonian SSR, **USSR**; on G. of Riga; exp. timber, flax; health resort; p. (est. 1967) 42,000.

Páros, I., Grecian Archipelago; W. of Naxos; source of Parian marble; cap. P.; a. 163 km²; p. (1961) 7,800.

Parramatta, c., N.S.W., **Australia**; pt. nr. head of Parramatta R. (spanned by lgst. concrete bridge in world) in met. a. of Sydney; chemical and engin. inds.; p. (1966) 107,006.

Parrett, R., Somerset, **Eng.**; flows to Bristol Channel, nr. Bridgewater; 56 km long.

Pasadena, c., Cal., **USA**; N. of Los Angeles; in fruit-growing region, base of San Gabriel mtns.; 5,080 mm telescope on Mt. Palomar; famous for its carnival; p. (1970) 112,981; inc. in met. a. of Los Angeles.

Pasco, t., Wash., **USA**; on Snake R.; atomic energy plant; p. (1970) 13,920.

Pasco. *See* **Cerro de Pasco.**

Pas-de-Calais, dep., N. **France**; impt. heavy industl. a. based upon local extensive coal deposits; heavy inds. inc. iron and steel, but many ts. in decline as importance of coal diminishes; prosperous agr. based on arable farming; N. cst. faces English Channel and inc. pts. of Calais and Boulogne; severe devastation in both world wars; cap. Arras; a. 6,750 km²; p. (1968) 1,397,159.

Passage West, U.D., Cork, **R.o.I.**; declining pt., fishing; p. (1961) 2,000.

Passaic, c., N.J., **USA**; rubber gds., springs, steel cabinets, tin cans; p. (1970) 55,124.

Passau, c., **W. Germany**, at confluence of Rs. Danube, Inn and Ilz, nr. Austrian frontier; trans-shipment base, inds. inc. leather, porcelain, tobacco and brewing; cath., picturesque tourist ctr.; p. (est. 1969) 31,158.

Passchendaele, t., **Belgium**; strategic point in first world war; battle 31 July–6 Nov. 1917; p. (est. 1969) 3,112.

Passero I., Mediterranean Sea; off S.E. cst. of Sicily, **Italy**.

Passy, residtl. part of W. Paris, **France**; between Bois de Boulogne and right bank of Seine; residence of Balzac.

Pasto, t., cap. of Narino dep., **Colombia**; on flank of Pasto volcano; univ.; agr. comm. ctr.; gold nearby; p. (est. 1972) 111,100 (t.), 137,200 (met. a.).

Patagonia, extensive region, E. of Andes, **Argentina/Chile**; elevated plateau, arid, sterile; prin. Rs. Colorado, Rio Negro, and Chubut; impt. source of oil at Commodoro Rivadavia; lge tracts of grazing for livestock; much of p. Welsh descendants.

Patan, Gujarat, **India**; impt. ctr. of Buddhism; gold and silver gds.; p. (1961) 50,264.

Patani or Pattani, pt., S. **Thailand**; on E. cst. of Malay peninsula; spices, rubber, coconuts; tin mng.; former Malay sultanate; p. of t. (est. 1964) 19,902.

Paterno, t., Sicily, **Italy**; N.W. of Catania; cath., cas.; mineral springs, wines; p. (est. 1968) 42,277.

Paterson, c., N.J., **USA**; on Passaic R. whose falls provide hydroelectric power for gr. silk mnf. ind.; now inds. diversified; in addition to textiles and textile machin., aeroplane engines, metallurgical inds., electronic equipment; p. (1970) 142,819 (c.), 1,369,374 (met. a.).

Patiala, t., Punjab, **India**; metal gds., flour; univ.; p. (1971) 148,686 (t.), 151,041 (met. a.).

Patino Mines. *See* **Uncia.**

Pátmos, I., one of the Dodecanese, **Greece**; in Aegean Sea; a. 34 km²; p. (est.) 3,000. (According to Rev. 1. 9. the exiled St. John wrote the Revelation here.)

Patna, c., cap. of Bihar, **India**; univ.; rly. junc.; agr. tr., rice, oilseeds, cotton; handicraft inds.; p. (1971) 473,001 (c.), 491,217 (met. a.).

Patras (Pátrai), spt., cap. of Akhaia, **Greece**; citadel and cas., exp. currants, raisins, figs, olive oil; inds. based on agr. processing; p. (1971) 111,238.

Pau, c., cap. of Pyrénées-Atlantique dep., **France**; on Gave-de-Pau; impt. mkt. and regional ctr.; summer and winter resort; linen, chocolate, hams, wine; natural gas nearby; p. (1968) 74,005 (c.), 110,377 (met. a.).

Pauillac, t., Gironde dep., **France**; pt. on Gironde estuary; ships wines, timber; oil refinery, natural gas; p. (1968) 5,691.

Paulo Affonso, falls, São Francisco R., **Brazil**; 79 m; Tres Marías dam and power sta. opened 1960; in Nat. Park.

Pavia, c., prov. cap., N. **Italy**; on R. Ticino; route ctr. and agr. mkt. in Po valley; olives, wine, Parmesan cheese; oil refining at Spineto; walled c.; battle 1525; birthplace of Lanfranc; p. (1969) 85,680.

Pavlodar, pt., Kazakh SSR, **USSR**; on R. Irtysh; chemicals, sulphates, agr. machin., locomotives, aluminium, oil processing; food prod.; p. (1970) 187,000.

Pawtucket, c., R.I., **USA**; on Pawtucket R. at head of navigation; first water-power cotton spinning factory in USA 1790; textiles remain most impt. ind.; p. (est. 1969) 76,000.

Paysandú, dep., W. **Uruguay**; rich pastoral a.; ranching, cattle, sheep; arable agr., cereals, mkt. gardening around c. of P.; a. 13,406 km²; p. (est. 1969) 90,800.

Paysandú, cap. of P. dep., W. **Uruguay**; pt. on Uruguay R. with meat-packing, soap and footwear inds.; p. (1964) 60,000.

Pazardzhik, t., **Bulgaria**; on main rly. line to Istanbul; industl., hemp spinning and weaving; p. (est. 1968) 59,532.

Paz de Rio, t., Boyacá, **Colombia**; iron and steel wks.; iron ore, coal, limestone nearby; hydro-elec. sta. projected.

Peace, R., **Canada**; one of ch. headstreams of Mackenzie R.; rises in Rocky mtns., and flows generally N. to Gr. Slave R. nr. L. Athabaska; a. of very mild climate in lower course, fertile agr. valley; 1,680 km long.

Peak Dist., Pennine hill dist., mid-**Eng.**; extends from Chesterfield to Buxton, and Ashbourne to Glossop; composed of limestone with typical karst features; within P.D. Nat. Park, tourist and recreation a. for cities to E. (Sheffield) and W. (Manchester); limestone quarrying for cement; Kinder Scout 634 m.

Pearl Harbor, landlocked harbour, Oahu I. Hawaiian Is., one of finest natural harbours in E. Pac.; US naval base; attacked by Japanese without warning 7 Dec. 1941.

Pearl Is., archipelago, G. of Panama; sea fishing, pearls.

Pearl R. *See* **Chu-kiang.**

Pechenga (Petsamo), spt., **RSFSR**; on inlet of Barents Sea; formerly Finnish, ceded to USSR Sept. 1944; ice-free throughout year,; exp. nickel, timber, cobalt.

Pechora, dist., **RSFSR**; E. of Urals; one of 4 main coalfields of USSR; coking coal; ch. ts., Vorkuta and Inta.

Pechora, R., **RSFSR**; rises in Urals and flows N. into Arctic Oc.; 1,120 km navigable between June and Sept. for transport of timber from its basin; fishing; 1,792 km long.

Pecos, R., N.M. and Texas, **USA**; trib. of Rio Grande; water control schemes provide irrigation for lge. a.; 1,482 km long.

Pécs, c., S.W. **Hungary**; on Yugoslav border; one of oldest and most pleasantly situated ts. of Hungary; cath., univ., airport; in coal-mng. a.; coke, chemicals, majolica, leather gds. engin., brewing; p. (est. 1969) 144,000.

Peebles, royal burgh, Tweeddale, **Scot.**; on upper course of R. Tweed; woollen cloth, knitwear; mkt., tourist ctr.; p. (1971) 5,884.

Peeblesshire, former co., S. **Scot.**; now part of Borders Reg.

Peel, t., I. of Man, **Eng.**; resort, fishing pt. midway along W. cst.; cas., cath.; p. (1971) 3,081.

Peel Fell, mtn., Northumberland, **Eng.**; 599 m.

Pegu, c., Pegu prov., S. **Burma**; R. pt., rly. junc.; many temples, notably Shwe May Daw Pagoda; once cap. of Burmese kingdom; came under Brit. rule 1852; p. 48,000.

Pegu Yoma, mtns., **Burma**; between valleys of Rs. Irrawadi and Sittang; thickly forested with teak which is comm. exploited and forms impt. exp.

Peine, t., Lower Saxony, **W. Germany**; N.W. of Brunswick; iron, furniture, textiles; p. (est. 1969) 30,899.

Peipus, Lake, Estonian SSR, **RSFSR**; drained by Narva R. into G. of Finland; Pskov lies to S.; scene of Alexander Nevsky's victory over the Germans 1242; a. 3,626 km².

Pekalongan, t., N. cst. Java, **Indonesia**; exp. sugar, rubber; p. (1961) 102,380.

Peking (Beijing), c. and mun., cap. of **China**; cultural ctr. and c. of gr. architectural beauty; for hundreds of years seat of Chinese emperors

(Mongol, Ming, Manchu regimes); surrounded by 35 km of towering walls, broken by 16 gates; univ.; many sm. factories; textiles, synthetic fibres, machin., precision instruments, printing, publishing; route ctr., rly. junc., airpt.; a. 8,770 km²; p. (est. 1971) 7,570,000.

Pelagi, gr. of Italian Is., inc. Lampedusa and Linosa, between Malta and Tunisian cst.

Pelagonia, terr., S. **Yugoslavia**; fertile agr. R. basin.

Pelée, mtn., **Martinique**; active volcano, devastated town of St. Pierre 1902, loss of over 30,000 lives, later eruption caused further 2,000 deaths; alt. 1,342 m.

Pella, dep of Macedonia, **Greece**; mtnous.; cotton, wheat, tobacco; cap. Edessa; a. 2,802 km²; p. (1971) 126,201.

Peloponnesus (Peloponnisos), peninsula, S. **Greece**; separated from mainland by G. of Corinth, but joined in N.E. by Isthmus of Corinth; mtnous.; livestock agr., drought-resistant sheep and goats; ch. ts., Kalamata, Tripolis; a. 21,642 km²; p. (1971) 985,620.

Pelotas, t., Rio Grande do Sul, **Brazil**; pt. on lagoon S.S.W. Pôrto Alegre; meat-packing and industl. ctr.; p. (1970) 150,278.

Pemba, I., part of **Tanzania**; cloves, copra, coconuts; exp. mangrove bark for tannin; a. 984 km²; p. (1967) 164,243.

Pembroke, mkt. t., Dyfed, **Wales**; on S. side of Milford Haven; sm. pt.; dock facilities; cas., ruins of Monkton priory; p. (1971) 14,092.

Pembroke Dock, Dyfed, **Wales**; site of government dockyard (1814) with consequent growth of a new t.

Pembrokeshire, former co., Wales. *See* **Dyfed**.

Penang, I., st. **W. Malaysia**; cap. Georgetown, pt. for N. Malaya handling rubber and tin; paper mill; the first Brit. Straits Settlement (*q.v.*); a. 1,036 km²; p. (1967) 752,059.

Penarth, t., South Glamorgan, **Wales**; sm. pt. on Severn estuary, 3 km S. of Cardiff; ship-repairing, seaside resort; p. (1971) 23,965.

Penge. *See* **Bromley**.

Pengpu (Bengbu), c., Anhwei, **China**; on Kwo-Ho, 168 km N.E. of Nanking; on Tientsin–Nanking rly.; p. (est. 1958) 330,000.

Penicuik, burgh, Midlothian, **Scot.**; on R. Esk; paper; p. (1971) 10,066.

Penistone, t., South Yorks., **Eng.**; on R. Don; steel; mkt.; p. (1971) 8,182.

Penki (Benqi), c., Liaoning prov., **China**; metallurgical ctr.; p. (est. 1970) 750,000.

Penmaenmawr, t., Gwynedd, **Wales**; 6 km. S.W. of Conway; resort; p. (1971) 3,998.

Pennine Alps, **Switzerland**; div. of Alpine system; ch. peaks; Mont Blanc (4,814 m), Monte Rosa (4,637 m), Matterhorn (4,477 m); winter sports.

Pennine Range, mtn. range, "backbone of England," extends 224 km southwards from Cheviot hills to Derbyshire; limestone, millstone grit; moorland sheep, dairying in valleys, quarrying, tourism; inc. Peak Dist. Nat. Park and Pennine Way long distance route; water supply, forestry; Cross Fell, 895 m.

Pennsylvania, st., **USA**; originally proprietary colony of Penn family, later one of the 13 original sts. in the Union; traversed N.E. to S.W. by Appalachians; ch. Rs.: Delaware, Susquehanna, Allegheny, and Monongahela; major industl. st.; iron and steel, coal (bituminous and anthracite), natural gas, petroleum; maize, wheat, oats, rye; textiles, machin., motor cars, tobacco; cap. Harrisburg; ch. ts.: Pittsburgh, Philadelphia; a. 117,412 km²; p. (1970) 11,663,301.

Penrhyn, dist., Gwynedd, **Wales**; nr. Bethesda; slate quarries.

Penrith, t., N.S.W., **Australia**; in Sydney met. a.; ctr. for mkt. gardening; p. (1966) 35,970.

Penrith, mkt. t., Cumbria, **Eng.**; at N. foot of Shap Fell, 29 km S.E. of Carlisle; agr. mkt.; tourist ctr., p. (1971) 11,292.

Penryn, t. Cornwall, **Eng.**; on R. Fal estuary; sm. pt., boat repairs; once ctr. of granite quarrying; p. (1971) 5,082.

Pensacola, t., Fla., **USA**; on N. shore of P. Bay; originally a Spanish settlement, retaining much Spanish influence in squares, bldgs., street names; fishing, sea food inds.; univ. naval air training school; p. (1970) 65,422 (t.) 237,995 (met. a.).

Penshurst, Wealden vil., S.W. of Tonbridge, Kent, **Eng.**; Penshurst Place home of the Sydney family.

Penticton, B.C., **Canada**; comm. fruit ctr.; p. (1971) 17,702.

Pentonville, dist., London, **Eng.**; prison; birthplace of John Stuart Mill.

Pentland Firth, strait, between Orkney Is. and Caithness, **Scot.**, connecting N. Sea and Atl. Oc.; dangerous tidal currents.

Pentland Hills, range, **Scot.**; extend from Lanark to Edinburgh; Scald Law, 878 m.

Pen-y-Ghent, peak, Pennines, North Yorks., **Eng.**; alt. 680 m.

Penza, c. cap. of P. oblast, **RSFSR**; on Sura R.; rly. junc.; agr. ctr., especially for grain tr. to Moscow; food-processing and wide range of mnfs.; oil pipeline from Mozyr'; p. (1970) 374,000.

Penzance, t. Cornwall, **Eng.**; on Mount's Bay; tourist ctr.; ferry to Scilly Isles; engin.; birthplace of Sir Humphry Davy; p. (1971) 19,352.

Peoria, t., Ill., **USA**; machin., domestic gds.; grain tr.; univ.; p. (1970) 125,736 (c.), 339,719 (met. a.).

Perak, st., **W. Malaysia**; ch. tin-dredging a., in basin of Perak R.; rubber; cap. Taiping; a. 20,668 km²; p. (1967) 1,636,605.

Pereira, t., Caldas, **Colombia**; cath.; comm. ctr. for coffee; p. (est. 1972) 212,200 (t.), 249,500 (met. a.).

Perekop, Isthmus of, connects Crimea with Ukraine, **USSR**.

Pergamino, t., Buenos Aires, **Argentina**; road and rail focus in maize-growing dist.

Périgord, dist., S.W. **France**; limestone plateau crossed by Dordogne R.; famous for truffles.

Périgueux, t., cap. Dordogne, **France**; on R. Isle; cath.; famous for pâté de foie gras; engin., china; p. (1968) 40,091.

Perim, I. in strait of Bab-el-Mandeb at S. entrance to Red Sea; part of **Democratic Rep. of Yemen**; former coaling sta.; a. 13 km²; p. 1,700.

Perlis, st., **W. Malaysia**; agr. dist. for rice and coconuts; tin; a. 803 km²; p. (1967) 117,606.

Perm, oblast, **RSFSR**; major mng., timber, and paper dist.; produces oil (Krasnokamsk), coal (Kizel), hydroelectricity, and potash (Solikamsh); cap. Perm.

Perm (Molotov), c., cap. of P. oblast, **RSFSR**; on Kama R.; machin., chemicals, oil refineries; univ.; p. (est. 1968) 811,000.

Pernambuco, st., N.E. **Brazil**; mtnous. interior, cst. fertile; cap. Recife; sugar, cotton, manioc, tobacco, fruits; a. 98,322 km²; p. (est. 1968) 4,728,830.

Pernik (Dimitrovo), c., **Bulgaria**; iron and steel inds.; p. (est. 1968) 79,335.

Pernis, t., opposite Rotterdam, **Neth.**; lge. oil refinery; pipeline to Wesserling (nr. Cologne). *See also* **Terneuzen**.

Perovo, t., **RSFSR**; nr. Moscow; engin., chemicals; agr. research institute; p. inc. in Moscow.

Perpignan, c., cap. of Pyrénées-Orientales dep., **France**; nr. Spanish border and Mediterranean; on Paris–Barcelona rly.; mkt. and comm. ctr. for wines and fruits; cath.; tourism; p. (1968) 102,191 (c.), 106,927 (met. a.).

Persepolis, anc. c., **Iran**; former cap. of Persian empire, now in ruins; tourism.

Pershore, t. Hereford and Worcs., **Eng.**; on R. Avon; ctr. of fruit-growing a.; p. (1971) 20,430 (dist.).

Persia. *See* **Iran**.

Persian Gulf, inlet from Indian Oc. through G. of Oman and Strait of Ormuz, between Iran and Arabia; oilfields in surrounding land and now in G. itself; ch. pts. Bandar-e-Bushehr, Abadan, Kuwait, Dubai; Bahrein, lgst. I.

Perth, c., cap. of **W. Australia**; serves lge. agr. hinterland; many inds. based upon agr. prods.; univ.; outport at Fremantle; terminus of Trans-Australian rly., airport; well planned c.; p. (1972) 97,242 (c.), 701,392 (met. a.).

Perth, c., royal burgh, Perth and Kinross, **Scot.**; on R. Tay; rly. junc.; cap. of Scot. until assassination of James I, 1437; dyeing, textiles, whisky distilling; cath., historical associations; p. (1971) 43,030.

Perthshire, former co., **Scot.**; now part of Perth and Kinross l. gov. dist., Tayside Reg.

Peru, Andean rep., **S. America**; consists of 3 N.W.–S.E. regions: Costa (cst.), Sierra (Andes, rising to over 6,100 m), and Selva (interior *montaña* and R. basins); 40 per cent p. in Costa, 60 per cent in Sierra, yet Selva covers 70 per cent total a.; ch. Rs. Ucayali, Marañon; L. Titicaca shared with Bolivia; El Misti volcano in S.; cap. Lima on Pac. cst. with 20 per cent p.; agr. diversified and being extended by irrigation schemes; fishing main single ind.; mng. impt. in Andes; major world producer of silver, phosphates potash, copper, petroleum; a. 1,249,048 km²; p. (1972) 14,100,000 (of whom 3,600,000 live in Lima-Callao met. a.).

Peru Current (Humboldt), ocean current, S. Pac. Oc.; flows N. along cst. of N. Chile and Peru; causes clouds and fog.

Perugia, spt., Umbria, **Italy**; on R. Tiber; univ., observatory; woollens, silks, lace; foodstuffs, furniture, pottery, chemicals, agr. machin.; p. (1969) 126,887.

Pervouralsk, t., **RSFSR**; in Urals; metallurgical ctr.; p. (1970) 117,000.

Pesaro, c., central **Italy**; on Adriatic cst.; agr. ctr., seaside resort; birthplace of Rossini; p. (1969) 81,689.

Pescadores Is., archipelago, between Taiwan and mainland **China**; fishing, fish-processing; a. 132 km²; p. 86,000.

Pescara, c., cap. of P. prov., S. **Italy**; on estuary of R. Aterno; fish. pt., olive oil, soap, pasta, pottery; resort; birthplace of D'Annunzio; p. (1969) 116,723.

Peshawar, c., cap. of North-West Frontier Prov., **Pakistan**; 18 km E. of Khyber pass, commanding route to Afghanistan; military sta.; univ.; handicrafts, textiles, furniture; p. (est. 1969) 296,000.

Petah Tikva, oldest modern Jewish settlement in **Israel** (1878); ctr. for oranges; mnfs. inc. textiles; p. (1968) 73,500.

Petaling Jaya, t., **W. Malaysia**; industl. estate nr. Kuala Lumpur; tyres, aluminium rolling mill.

Peter I., uninhabited I., **Antarctic Oc.**, belonging to Norway, a. *c.* 243 km².

Peterborough, t., Ont., **Canada**; flour-milling, elec. machin., trailers, agr. equipment, plastics, textiles, paper; p. (1971) 57,498.

Peterborough, c., Cambs., **Eng.**; on R. Nene on margin of Fens; cath.; rly ctr.; ctr. of brick ind. (Oxford clay around Fletton); diesel engines, agr. machin. gen. engin.; major planned expansion as new t.; p. (est. 1974) 98,000 (53,471 in 1951).

Peterborough, Soke of. *See* **Cambridgeshire.**

Peterhead, spt., burgh, Banff and Buchan, **Scot.**; on E. cst., 43 km N.E. of Aberdeen; herring fisheries, fish-processing, granite quarrying; supply base for N. Sea oil; p. (1971) 14,160.

Peterlee, new t. (1948), Durham, **Eng.**; coal-mng. dist.; textiles, science-based inds.; p. (est. 1971) 26,500.

Petersfield, t., Hants., **Eng.**; on R. Rother, 19 km N.W. of Chichester; mkt.; p. (1971) 8,958.

Petra, anc. c., **Jordan**; temples, rock tombs and Roman ruins; called Sela in Bible (2 Kings 14. 7); rediscovered by Burckhardt 1812.

Petropavlovsk, t., Kazakh SSR, **USSR**; on Ishim R.; rly. junc.; flour, leather, meat canneries, furs, engin.; p. (1970) 173,000.

Petropavlovsk-Kamchatsky, t., **RSFSR**; spt. on Pac. cst.; shipyard, timber mills, engin.; fishing and whaling fleet; p. (1970) 154,000 (c.); (1969) 157,000 (met. a.).

Petrópolis, t., Rio de Janeiro, **Brazil**; health resort, *c.* 700 m a.s.l.; cath.; p. (1970) 116,080.

Petsamo. *See* **Pechenga.**

Petten, t., **Neth.**; 48 km N.W. of Amsterdam, on cst.; atomic research ctr.

Petworth, mkt. t., West Sussex, **Eng.**; in Rother valley, 19 km N.E. of Chichester; associated with Turner; p. (1971) 11,070 (dist.).

Pevensey Levels, marshy a., East Sussex, **Eng.**; lie behind coastal sand-bars between Eastbourne and Bexhill, extend 8 km inland to Hailsham; now largely drained, cattle pastures; a. 62 km².

Pforzheim, t., Baden-Württemberg, **W. Germany**; S.E. of Karlsruhe; gold, silver, metal wks., jewellery; p. (est. 1969) 90,022.

Phan Thiet, spt., **Vietnam**; exp. dried and salt fish; p. 5,000.

Phetburi, t. and prov., **Thailand**; on Isthmus of Kra crossed by Phetburi R.; p. (1960) 24,654 (t.), 237,835 (prov.).

Philadelphia, c., pt., Penns., **USA**; on Delaware R.; comm., industl. and cultural ctr.; univ., R.C. cath., masonic temple, mint, academy of fine arts; shipbldg., locomotives, machin., surgical instruments, carpets, woollens, cottons, worsteds; sugar, and petroleum refining; ctr. of War of Independence 1790–1809; founded as Quaker col. by William Penn 1682; p. (1970) 1,927,863 (c.), 4,777,414 (met. a.).

Philae, I. in Nile R., **Egypt**; flooded by waters of Aswan Dam; contains anc. ruined temples which have been removed to a safer site.

Philippeville. *See* Skikda.

Philippines, Rep. of, S.E. Asia; island chain in Pac. Oc., stretching over 1,760 km; ch. Is. Luzon, Mindanao, Negros, Cebu, Mindoro, and Palawar; lie in track of cyclones; tropical climate; mtnous., agr. aided by intricate terracing system; most Is. underdeveloped except Luzon where p. concentrated; subsistence agr. rice and maize; cash crops sugar, coconuts, hemp, tobacco; close connections with USA; cap. Quezon City (admin. functions at Manila); a. 299,681 km²; p. (1970) 37,008,419.

Philippopolis. *See* **Plovdiv.**

Phlorina (Florina), t., Macedonia, **Greece**; in basin at 900 m, 16 km from Yugoslav border; agr. ctr.; p. (1971) 11,180.

Phnom-Penh, c., cap. of **Cambodia**, **S.E. Asia**; pt. on Mekong R.; handles ships up to 2,500 tonnes; linked to Sihanoukville by modern highway; multi-purpose dam to W.; univ., royal palace; airport; p. (1971) 1,500,000.

Phoenix, c., Arizona, **USA**; on Salt R., ctr. of Salt River Valley irrigated region; electronics research, steel, aircraft, clothing; p. (1970) 580,275 (c.), 963,132 (met. a.).

Phoenix Group, Is., **Pac. Oc.**; part of Gilbert I. col.; a. 41 km²; US have some rights over Canton and Enderbury; Canton used as international airport.; p. (1963) 1,014.

Phuket I., **Thailand**, off Kra Isthmus; main alluvial tin-working region of Thailand; ch. t. Phuket where a tin-smelting plant is to be established; a. 534 km².

Piacenza, c., cap. of P. prov., **Italy**; in Emilia-Romagna, on R. Po; agr. and comm. ctr.; cath., palaces, arsenal; cars, chemicals, cement; p. (1969) 104,092.

Piatra-Neamt, t., Moldavia, **Romania**; timber, pharmaceuticals, soap; oil refineries; p. (1968) 48,103.

Piauí, st., **Brazil**; semi-arid, underdeveloped dist.; thorn scrub; livestock rearing; cap. Teresina; a. 249,319 km²; p. (est. 1968) 1,432,634.

Piave, R., N.E. **Italy**; flows to Adriatic, 200 km long.

Picardy, former prov., **France**; included the Somme dep. and parts of Pas-de-Calais, Aisne and Oise; old battle sites, Agincourt and Crécy; rich agr. a.; textiles.

Pichincha, prov., **Ecuador**; p. concentrated in Andes; many natural resources inc. lime, gypsum, silver; tropical hardwoods; cattle raising; cap. Quito; a. 16,105 km²; p. (est. 1970) 843,000.

Pickering, mkt. t., North Yorks. **Eng.**; on N. margin of Vale of Pickering; church with murals; cas.; gas terminal, p. (1971) 4,544.

Pickering, Vale of, North Yorks., **Eng.**, wide, flat-floored vale, once occupied by glacial lake; bounded to N. by N. York Moors, to S. by York Wolds; drained W. by R. Derwent, alluvial soils, marshy in ctr.; crop farming along margins, cattle grazing in damper meadows in ctr.; ch. ts. Pickering, Malton, Helmsley.

Picos de Europa, mtn. massif, N. **Spain**; hgst. massif in Cantabrian mtns., rising to 2,650 m; partially inc. in Nat. Park.

Picton, t., S.I., **N.Z.**; freezing wks.; tourist and fishing ctr.; pt.; p. (1971) 2,825.

Pictou, t., Nova Scotia, **Canada**; on Northumberland Strait; founded by Scottish settlers.

Pidurutalagala, mtn., **Sri Lanka**; alt. 2,530 m; hgst. peak in rep.

Piedmont, region, N. **Italy**; rice, wheat, vines, fruits; cottons, woollens; a. 25,416 km²; p. (1969) 4,380,508.

Pietermaritzburg, c., cap. of Natal, **S. Africa**;

named after Piet Retief and Gerhardus Maritz, two Boer leaders; lt. inds.; tanning; iron-ore mng. in a.; part of univ. of Natal; 2 caths.; p. (1970) 158,921 (met. a.).

Pietersburg, t., Transvaal, **S. Africa**; gold, asbestos, tin; comm. ctr. for cereals, tobacco, cotton, citrus fruits; p. (1968) 36,274.

Pila (Schneidemühl), t., N.W. **Poland** (since 1945); formerly in Prussian prov. of Pomerania; tr. ctr., lignite mines nearby; p. (1970) 43,800.

Pilar, t., **Paraguay**; impt. R. pt.; sawmills; textiles; p. (est. 1970) 15,324.

Pilbara, dist., W. **Australia**; extensive iron mng.; processing and exp. to serve Japanese mkt.; rapid growth of p.

Pilcomayo, R., northernmost R. of **Argentina**; rises in Bolivian Andes, flows across the Gran Chaco, to enter Paraguay, joining the Paraguay R. nr. Asunción; hydroelec. power; 1,120 km long.

Pilibhit, t., Uttar Pradesh, N. **India**; admin. ctr.; sugar-refining; p. (1961) 57,527.

Pilsen. *See* **Plzeň.**

Pinar del Rio, c., prov. cap., **Cuba**; tobacco; p. (est. 1967) 67,600.

Pinawa, t., Manitoba, **Canada**; 88 km N.E. of Winnipeg; nuclear research; p. (1965) 8,000.

Pindus, mtn. chain, between Thessaly and Albania, **Greece**; hgst. peak 2,455 m.

Pinghsiang, t., Hunan, **China**; supplies coking coal to Wuhan.

Pinneberg, t., Schleswig-Holstein, **W. Germany**; N.W. of Hamburg; rose cultivation, metals, leather; p. (est. 1969) 36,101.

Pinsk, c., Belorussiyan SSR, **USSR**; in Pripet Marshes, pt. on Pina R.; paper, wood-working inds., matches; Jewish residents exterminated during German occupation second world war; p. (est. 1967) 57,000.

Piombino, t., **Italy**; mainland pt. for island of Elba; steel wks.; p. (est. 1968) 39,618.

Piotrkow Trybunalski, t., **Poland**; cas.; timber and glass inds.; new textile combine; p. (1970) 59,700.

Piqua, t., Ohio, **USA**; N. of Dayton; ironwks., woollens; nuclear reactor; p. (1970) 20,741.

Piracicaba, t., São Paulo, **Brazil**; ctr. of agr. dist.; sugar-refining, brandy, flour; p. (est. 1968) 137,184.

Piraeus, c., **Greece**; pt. of Athens and prin. pt. of Greece; major industl. and comm. ctr.; p. (1971) 186,223.

Pirmasens, t., Rhineland-Palatinate, **W. Germany**; S.W. of Mannheim; footwear, leather gds.; p. (est. 1969) 56,420.

Pirna, t., Dresden, **E. Germany**; on R. Elbe; textiles, paper, glass; p. (1969) 41,076.

Pirot, t., **Yugoslavia**; nr. Bulgarian border; in economic developmenta.; p. (est. 1965) 21,000.

Pisa, c., **Italy**; at head of Arno delta, 19 km N.E. of Livorno; famous leaning tower, cath., univ.; textiles, chemicals, engin.; airport; tourism; p. (1969) 103,011.

Pisco, spt., **Peru**; famous for P. brandy; p. (est. 1969) 26,700.

Pistoia, t., Tuscany, **Italy**; on Arno plain, N.W. of Florence; iron and steel gds., macaroni; p. (1969) 91,729.

Pit, R., Cal., **USA**; rises in Goose L.; cuts spectacular gorges in the Cascades; used for hydroelectric power.

Pitcairn I., E. **Pac. Oc.**, Brit. col.; inc. atolls of Ducie and Oeno and I. of Henderson; sweet potatoes, bananas, oranges, coconuts; a. 5 km²; p. mostly descendants of mutineers of the *Bounty*; p. (1970) 80.

Pitch Lake, Trinidad, **W.I.**; S. of I., 16 km S.W. of San Fernando; natural deposit of asphalt; tourism; a. 86 ha.

Pitea, spt., N. **Sweden**; on G. of Bothnia; saw-mills; p. (est. 1970) 32,365.

Pitesti, t., **Romania**; on Arges R.; petroleum, fruit, grain; lge. automobile plant; oil refinery under construction; p. (1968) 65,782.

Pitlochry, burgh, Perth and Kinross, **Scot.**; on R. Tummel, 6 km S. of Pass of Killiecrankie; summer resort; distilleries, hydros; p. (1971) 2,599.

Pittenweem, burgh, North East Fife, **Scot.**; at entrance to F. of Forth; fisheries; p. (1971) 1,518.

Pittsburgh, c., Penns., **USA**; univ.; R.C. cath.; pt. on Ohio R.; ctr. of richest American coal-field; natural gas, petroleum, iron and steel, machin., metal gds., meat-packing, glass, aluminium, chemicals, p. (1970) 512,789 (c.) 2,383,753 (met. a.).

Pittsfield, c., Mass., **USA**; textiles, paper, plastics, elec. machin.; resort; p. (1966) 144,800 (met. a.).

Piura, t., N. **Peru**; on Piura R.; oldest Spanish t. in Peru; cotton mkt. and processing, p. (est. 1970) 111,400.

Pladju, t., S. Sumatra, **Indonesia**; oil refining; linked by pipeline with Tempino and Bejubang.

Plata, Rio de la (Plate R.), estuary between **Argentina** and **Uruguay**; receives waters of Rs. Paraná and Uruguay; cst. provides sites for lge. spts., Buenos Aires, La Plata, Montevideo.

Platte, R., Nebraska, **USA**; formed by union of N. Platte and S. Platte Rs.; total length 2,240 km; irrigation, hydroelec. power.

Plauen, t., Karl-Marx-Stadt, **E. Germany**; textiles, machin., cable, leather, paper, radios; rly. junc.; p. (est. 1970) 81,907.

Plenty, Bay of, N.I., **N.Z.**; on E. cst.; 208 km wide.

Plettenberg, t., N. Rhine-Westphalia, **W. Germany**; on R. Lenne; iron wks.; p. (est. 1969) 30,172.

Pleven, mkt. t., **Bulgaria**; many mosques; famous siege 1877; textiles, wines; p. (est. 1968) 89,814.

Plitvička Jezera, lakes, **Yugoslavia**; beautiful scenery; tourism; fishing.

Ploče, new spt., **Yugoslavia**; on Dalmatian cst.; industl. and rly. ctr.

Plock, t., **Poland**; on R. Vistula, nr. Warsaw; agr.; oil refinery and petrochemical plant; food processing; agr. machin.; p. (1970) 71,700.

Ploieşti, t., Prahova dist., **Romania**; petroleum, engin.; p. (est. 1969) 160,011; (1966) 191,663 (met. a.).

Plovdiv (Philippopolis), c., **Bulgaria**; on R. Maritsa; univ., Greek cath.; second c. of rep.; agr. processing, clothing, metals, engin.; p. (est. 1969) 242,050.

Plymouth, c., spt., S. Devon, **Eng.**; on Plymouth Sound; comprises the "three towns" of Plymouth, Devonport, and Stonehouse; R.C. cath., guildhall, museum; shipbldg.; seaside resort; fishing and fish-canning, lt. inds.; p. (1971) 239,314.

Plymouth, ch. t., Monserrat I., **W.I.**; p. (1970) 3,500.

Plymouth, spt., Mass., **USA**; on Plymouth Bay, S.E. of Boston; here Pilgrim Fathers landed 1620 from *Mayflower* to form first English col.; Pilgrim Hall, Pilgrim Rock; textiles, cordage, machin.; tourism; p. (est. 1969) 11,500.

Plynlimmon, mtn., Powys and Dyfed, **Wales**; alt. 753 m; source of R. Severn.

Plzeň (Pilsen), c., W. Bohemia, **ČSSR**; ctr. of coal-mng. region; famous for beer and Lenin (former Skoda) armament wks.; p. (est. 1968) 145,299.

Po, R., **Italy**; flows from Monte Viso, through Piedmont and Lombardy to the Adriatic; valley forms a major component of N. Italian lowland; natural gas deposits in valley; liable to flooding; 648 km long.

Pocklington, mkt. t., Humberside, **Eng.**; at foot of York Wolds, 19 km E. of York; ctr. of agr. dist.; 16th cent. grammar school; p. (1971) 15,732 (dist.).

Podolsk, t., **RSFSR**; on main rly. from Moscow to S.; engin., tin-smelting, food-processing; p. (1970) 169,000.

Pohai (Chihli), G. of, N. **China**; together with G. of Liaotung forms shallow expanse of water almost cut off from Yellow Sea by Liaotung and Shantung peninsulas; receives water and silt of Hwang-Ho; a. approx. 38,900 km².

Point-à-Pierre, **Trinidad**; oil refinery; natural gas pipeline from Forest Reserve field.

Pointe-à-Pitre, ch. t. and pt. Guadeloupe, **Fr. W.I.**; on Grande Terre I.; exp. agr. prods., bananas, sugar; p. (est. 1969) 39,000.

Pointe-des-Galets or **Le Port**, ch. pt. **La Réunion** (Fr.), Indian Oc.

Pointe-Noire, spt., **Congo Rep.**; airport, rly. to Brazzaville; agr. exp.; potash deposits nearby; p. (1970) 135,000.

Point Fortin, r. **Trinidad**; oilfield and refinery.

Poitiers, c., cap. of Vienne dep., **France**; many attractive bldgs., cath.; agr. tr.; mnfs. chemicals, hosiery; Black Prince defeated Fr. 1356; p. (1968) 74,852.

Poland, People's Republic, E. Europe; history dominated by constantly changing sovereignty between E. and W. powers; mainly lowland; continental climate; economy retarded by history of political fluctuation but growth of inds. and urbanisation are both proceeding rapidly; major ctr. of mng. and heavy inds. in conurb. of Upper Silesia, agr. land remains largely in private ownership, but govt. attempts to rationalise farm structure, major pts. at Gdynia, Gdansk, and Szczecin, international airport at cap. Warsaw, 17 historic provs. to be replaced by 49 large dists., a. 311,700 km²; p. (1976) 34,180,000.

Polotsk, c., Belorussiyan SSR, **USSR**; cath.; gasoline prod., oil refining; pipeline to Latvian pt. of Ventspils; food processing; p. (est. 1967) 61,000.

Polotskiy, t. Belorussiyan SSR, **USSR**; 13 km W. of Polotsk; new oil workers' t. 1963.

Poltava, c., Ukrainian SSR, **USSR**; industl. and food-processing ctr. in rich agr. dist.; countryside described in Gogol's work; textiles, synthetic diamond plant; battle 1709 between Swedish and Russian armies; p. (1970) 220,000.

Polynesia, ethnic region, **Oceania**; I. grs. in Pac. Oc. within 30° N. and S. of equator; between longitude 135° E. and W.

Pomerania, former prov., N. Germany; in post-war redivision part E. of R. Oder to **Poland**; part W. of R. Oder incorporated in Mecklenburg, **E. Germany**; farming, shipbldg., fishing.

Pomona or **Mainland**, lgst of the Orkney Is., **Scot.**; Kirkwall (cap.) and Stromness on I.; p. (est. 1969) 6,674.

Pomorze. *See* **Bydgoszcz**.

Pompeii, ruined c., **Italy**; stood 21 km S.E. of Naples, at foot of Vesuvius; destroyed A.D. 79 by volcanic eruption, site re-discovered 1748; many interesting excavations; also modern c. nearby; fine church with famous collection of silver and gold plate.

Ponape, volcanic I., Caroline Is., W. Pac. Oc.; copra, ivory, nuts, starch, bauxite; a. 334 km².

Ponce, c., **Puerto Rico**; recently improved harbour on S. cst.; well connected with other ts. in rep.; ctr. of fertile, irrigated sugar-cane a.; industl. ctr.; p. (1970) 128,233 (c.), 158,981 (met. a.).

Pondicherry, spt., Tamil Nadu st., **India**; on Coromandel cst.; cap. of P. terr.; tr. ctr. for local prod.; p. (1971) 90,637.

Ponta Delgada, ch. t., spt., San Miguel I., **Azores**; attractive scenery, mild climate attract tourists; p. (1970) 69,930.

Ponta Grossa, t., Paraná, **Brazil**; rly. junc.; comm. ctr.; maté, rice, timber, tobacco, bananas, cattle, jerked beef; p. (est. 1968) 152,581.

Pontardawe, t., West Glamorgan, **S. Wales**; on R. Tawe, N.E. of Swansea; zinc smelting and refining; p. (1971) 29,431 (dist.).

Pontchartrain, Lake, shallow L., lower Mississippi flood plain, **USA**; connected by canal to New Orleans 10 km to S., and by deltaic channels to G. of Mexico.

Pontefract, mkt. t., West Yorks., **Eng.**; 11 km E. of Wakefield; coal, furniture, confectionery, mkt. gardening; cas. ruins; p. (1971) 31,335.

Pontevedra, prov., Spain; on deeply indented Atl. cst.; transatlantic pt. Vigo; scenery and fiesta attractions for tourists; agr., livestock, timber, fisheries; cap. P.; a. 4,390 km²; p. (1967) 63,315.

Pontevedra, c., cap. of P. prov., N.W. Spain; fish. pt., handicrafts, agr. tr.; p. (1967) 63,315.

Pontiac, t., Mich., **USA**; on Clinton R.; fishing and shooting, motor cars, rubber gds., machin., varnish; p. (1970) 85,279.

Pontianak, t., cap. of Kalimantan, **Indonesia**; exp. rubber, copra; rubber processing; p. (1971) 217,555.

Pontine Is., off W. cst. of **Italy**; in Tyrrhenian Sea; a. 11·6 km²; p. 6,000.

Pontine Marshes, region, Latium, **S. Italy**; coastal zone S.E. of Rome extending from Velletri to Terracina; formerly highly malarial fens, largely drained and colonised 1930–35; 3,200 new farms, 4 new ts.; ch. t. Littoria; a. 647 km².

Pontresina, t., Grisons, **Switzerland**; E. of St. Moritz; tourist resort; p. (1960) 1,067.

Pontypool, t., Gwent, **Wales**; coal, steel, glass, bricks, tin galvanising, nylon at Manhilad; p. (1971) 37,014.

Pontypridd, t., Mid Glamorgan, **Wales**; on R. Taff, 19 km N.W. of Cardiff; coal, iron-founding; p. (1971) 34,465.

Pool Malebo (Stanley Pool), **Congo** and **Zaïre**; lake formed by expansion of R. Zaïre; length 40 km.; width 26 km.

Poole, t., Dorset, **Eng.**; spt. on Poole Harbour, 6 km W. of Bournemouth; imports clay for local pottery inds.; tourism, yachting, marine engin., chemicals; p. (1971) 106,697.

Poona, c., Maharashtra, **India**; in W. Ghats; temperate, pleasant climate; cultural, educational (univ.) and political ctr.; military base; agr. tr. ctr.; mnfs. cotton gds., paper; p. (1971) 856,105 (c.), 1,135,900 (met. a.).

Poopó, salt L., Oruro dep., **Bolivia**; fed from L. Titicaca by R. Desaguadero, which flows over saline beds; no outlet; *c*. 3,600 m a.s.l.; a. 2,600 km².

Popayan, c., S.W. **Columbia**; 1,677 m above Cauca R.; cath., univ.; food processing, coffee, flour; mng. nearby; p. (est. 1972) 82,100 (c.), 103,900 (met. a.).

Poplar. *See* **Tower Hamlets**.

Popocatepetl, volcano, nr. Puebla, **Mexico**; alt. 5,456 m; dormant since 1702.

Porbander, spt., Gujarat, **India**; exp. silk, cotton; imports coal, dates, timber, machin., petroleum; birthplace of Mahatma Gandhi; p. (1971) 96,881.

Pori (Björneborg), spt., S. **Finland**; at mouth of R. Kokemäen; copper refinery, rolling mills, match, paper and pulp wks.; p. (1968). 70,957

Porirua, t., Wellington, N.I., **N.Z.**; p. (1971) 30,345.

Porjus, t., Norrbotten, N. **Sweden**; on R. Luleå, hydroelectric plant supplies power to iron-ore mng. dists. of Gällivare and Kiruna, also to Narvik rly.

Porsgrunn, spt., **Norway**; timber, shipping, engin., porcelain, explosives; p. (1968) 31,765.

Port Adelaide, pt., S. **Australia**; serves Adelaide; exp. agr. prods. from hinterland; iron smelting, chemicals, cement; p. (1966) 39,747.

Portadown, t., Craigavon, **N. Ireland**; on R. Bann, 40 km S.W. of Belfast; linen, food processing; merged with Lurgan to form new c. of Craigavon; p. (est. 1971) 21,906.

Portaferry, spt., Ards, **N. Ireland**; shipping fisheries; p. (1966) 1,426.

Portage la Prairie, t., Manitoba, **Canada**; sm. pt. on Assiniboine R.; grain and potato tr.; p. (1966) 13,012.

Port Alberni, spt., Vancouver I., B.C., **Canada**; exp. timber; fisheries; timber inds.; p. (1971) 19,749.

Port Alfred, pt., **Canada**; upper St. Lawrence R.; imports bauxite for smelting at Arvida.

Port Amelia, spt., **Moçambique**; sisal, coconuts, cotton, maize, groundnuts; p. (1960) 55,902.

Portarlington, mkt. t., Offaly, **R.o.I.**; farming; first place to have elec. power-sta. using local peat fuel; p. (1966) 2,804.

Port Arthur. *See* **Thunder Bay**.

Port Arthur (China). *See* **Luta**.

Port Arthur, t., Texas, **USA**; pt. on L. Sabine; exp. petroleum, chemicals., grain; p. (1970) 57,371.

Port Arzew, pt., **Algeria**; world's first plant to liquefy natural gas (1964); oil pipeline from Haoud el Hamra; oil refinery.

Port Assab, t., **Ethiopia**; oil refining.

Port Augusta, t., spt., S. **Australia**; at head of Spencer G.; fine harbour; salt field; exp. wheat, fruit; p. (1972) 12,095.

Port-au-Prince, c., cap. of **Haiti**; spt. on bay in G. of La Gonave; cultural and political ctr.; univ., cath.; iron mkt.; food processing and exp.; oil refinery; p. (est. 1975) 393,000.

Port Blair, spt., cap. of Andaman and Nicobar Is.; p. (est.) 16,000.

Port Chalmers, t., bor., S.I., **N.Z.**; docks, shipyards; p. (1971) 3,010.
Port Colborne, t., Ont., Canada; pt. on L. Erie; iron smelting; nickel and copper refining; power from Niagara falls; p. (1971) 21,388.
Port Elizabeth, spt., Cape Prov., **S. Africa**; on Algoa Bay; bilingual univ.; exp. skins, wool, ostrich feathers, mohair; foundries, soap, chemicals, car assembly, food preservation, sawmills; p. (1970) 468,577 (met. a.).
Port Erin, v., I. of Man, **Eng.**; on S.E. cst.; seaside resort, fisheries.
Port Essington, N. point. of Coburg peninsula, N.T., **Australia**; pearl culture experiments.
Port Etienne, pt., **Mauritania**; fish. pt.; exp. iron ore.
Port Francqui, t., **Zaïre**; present terminus of Zaïre rly. on Kasai R.; p. (est. 1970) 48,190.
Port Fuad, t., **Egypt**; N. entrance to Suez Canal.
Port Gentil, spt., **Gabon**, Eq. Africa; exp. palm-oil, mahogany, ebony; sawmills, fishing, oil refining; p. (est. 1970) 48,190.
Port Glasgow, burgh, spt., Inverclyde, **Scot.**; on S. bank of R. Clyde, 27 km below Glasgow; shipbldg. and repairing, textiles, rope, canvas mftg.; p. (1971) 22,398.
Port Harcourt, spt., **Nigeria**; 48 km from sea on E. branch of Niger delta; terminus of E. Nigerian rly. system; tin, palm oil, groundnuts; bitumen plant, tyres; oil refining; p. (est. 1971) 217,043.
Porthcawl, t., Mid Glamorgan, **Wales**; on cst. 16 km S.E. of Pt. Talbot; resort; p. (1971) 14,065.
Port Hedland, sm. spt., **W. Australia**; new t. being built 8 km inland to absorb impact of Mt. Newman iron ore project; twin ts. to be linked by industl. belt; exp. iron ore to Japan; p. (1972) 7,172.
Porthmadog (Portmadoc), t., Gwynedd, **Wales**; pt. on Tremadoc Bay; terminus of Ffestiniog lt. rly.; p. (1971) 3,665.
Port Hope, t., Ont., **Canada**; midway along N. shore of L. Ont., fruit, dairying, radium refining; p. (1971) 8,747.
Port Huron, t., Mich., **USA**; on L. Huron; summer resort, dry docks, grain elevators; motor-car parts; p. (1970) 35,749.
Portici, spt., Campania, **S. Italy**; on Bay of Naples; dockland sub. of Naples; p. (est. 1968) 67,888.
Potile de Fier. *See* **Iron Gate.**
Portishead, pt., Avon, **Eng.**; on Severn estuary 5 km S.W. of Avonmouth; shipping; p. (1971) 9,015.
Port Jackson, N.S.W., **Australia**; deep natural harbour used by Sydney and crossed by Sydney bridge.
Port Kelang (Port Swettenham), major spt. of **Malaysia**; 48 km W. of Kuala Lumpur; exp. primary prods. inc. tin, rubber fruit; imports mnfs.; p. 11,300.
Port Kembla, spt., N.S.W., **Australia**; S. of Wollongong; iron and steel wks., fertilisers.
Portknockie, burgh, Grampian Reg., **Scot.**; on N. Buchan cst., 8 km E. of Buckie; sm. fish. pt.; p. (1971) 1,191.
Portland, t., Dorset **Eng.**; 6 km S. of Weymouth on sheltered N.E. side of I. of Portland; lge. artificial harbour; naval base, prison; p. (1971) 12,306.
Portland, t., spt., Me., **USA**; comm. cap. of Me.; lge fisheries; paper, pulp, lumber, processed food, clothing; p. (1970) 64,304 (t.), 139,959 (met. a.).
Portland, c., Ore., **USA**; gr. wheat and wool tr.; flour milling, shipbldg., fishing and canning, aluminium, lumber; p. (1970) 375,161 (c.), 992,593 (met. a.).
Portland Canal, fjord, N.W. cst. of America, forming bdy. between Alaska and B.C.
Portland, I. of, Dorset, **Eng.**; limestone mass, linked to mainland by shingle spit, Chesil Bank, terminates S. in Portland Bill; naval base, Borstal institution; limestone quarrying; masonry wks.
Portlaoighise, mkt. t., Laoighis, **R.o.I.**; flour, malting; p. (1966) 3,435.
Port Lincoln, spt., **S. Australia**; exp. wheat, frozen meat, wool; fertilisers; p. (1972) 9,158.
Port Louis, c., cap. of **Mauritius**; pt. on Indian Oc.; exp. sugar; p. (1971) 141,100.
Port Lyautey (Kenitra). *See* Mina Hassan Tani.
Port Macquarie, t., N.S.W., **Australia**; on Hastings R.; resort; p. (1972) 9,362.
Port Moresby, t., cap. of **Papua New Guinea**, 2,880 km from Sydney; spt., airpt.; univ.; p. (est. 1971) 76,500.
Port Nelson, spt., Manitoba, **Canada**; on cst. of Hudson Bay at mouth of R. Nelson; linked by rly. to trans-continental systems via The Pas; exp. wheat, minerals; closed by ice for 7 months each year.
Port Nolloth, spt., Cape Prov., **S. Africa**; serves copper- and diamond-mng. dists.; declining crayfish pt.
Pôrto Alegre, c., cap. of Rio Grande do Sul st., **Brazil**; exp. lard, preserved meats, rice, timber, tobacco; textiles, chemicals, furniture, brewing, metallurgy; oil refinery under construction; pipeline connects with Rio Grande; 2 univs.; p. (1970) 869,795.
Portobello, resort, Midlothian, **Scot.**; on F. of Forth, 5 km E. of Edinburgh; bricks, pottery, paper.
Port of Spain, c., cap. of **Trinidad**; attractive c. with squares; 2 caths., mosque; spt. exp. cocoa, sugar, asphalt, oil; natural gas pipeline from Penal; food processing; p. (1970) 11,032 (c.), 67,867 (met. a.).
Porto Marghera, spt., Venezia, **N. Italy**; the modern pt. of Venice, reached by ship canal dredged through shallow lagoon; oil refineries; chemicals, metal refining.
Porto Novo, t., cap. of **Benin Rep.**; on coastal lagoon; spt.; fishing; many old colonial bldgs.; p. (est. 1970) 87,000.
Pôrto Velho, c., cap. of Rondônia st., **Brazil**; in a. producing maize, rice, rubber, tin; p. (est. 1968) 83,178.
Portoviejo, t., **Ecuador**; mkt. and comm. ctr. for agr. dist.; p. (1966) 96,651.
Port Phillip, lge. inlet, Victoria, **Australia**; land-locked bay, Melbourne on N., Geelong on W.
Port Pirie, t., spt., **S. Australia**; smelting ores, gold refining; exp. wheat, minerals; p. (1972) 15,506.
Port Radium, t., N.W. Terr., **Canada**; on Gr. Bear L.; pitchblende deposits; p. 300.
Portree, spt., v., I. of Skye, **Scot.**; landlocked harbour on P. Bay, Sound of Raasay; fishing; tweed mill.
Portrush, spt., Coleraine, **N. Ireland**; 8 km N. of Coleraine; tourism; p. (1966) 4,357.
Port Said, spt., **Egypt**; at N. end of Suez Canal; free tr. a.; impt. fuelling sta.; entrepôt tr.; p. (est. 1970) 313,000.
Port St. Mary, v., I. of Man, **Eng.**; on S.E. cst.; resort; fisheries, boat-bldg.
Portsdown Hill, chalk ridge, Hants, **Eng.**; extends E. to W. behind Portsmouth from Havant to Fareham.
Portsea I., fortfd. I., between Portsmouth and Langston harbours, Hants, Eng.
Portslade-by-Sea, t. East Sussex, **Eng.**; W. of Hove; p. (1971) 18,150.
Portsmouth, c., naval pt., Hants, **Eng.**; opposite I. of Wight; naval establishment; Portsmouth is the garrison t.; Portsea has the naval dockyards, Landport is residtl., and Southsea is a popular resort within the bor. a.; across the harbour is Gosport; shipbldg.; gen. mnfs.; birthplace of Charles Dickens; p. (1971) 196,973.
Portsmouth, t., N.H., **USA**; summer resort, naval dockyard, cotton; the 1905 Peace Treaty between Japan and Russia was negotiated here; p. (1970) 25,717.
Portsmouth, t., Ohio, **USA**; iron and steel gds., aircraft, boots, shoes, bricks; p. (1970) 27,633.
Portsmouth, spt., Va., **USA**; naval dockyard; farm produce, cotton, rly. wks.; p. (1970) 109,827 (c.), inc. in Norfolk met. a.
Portsoy, burgh, Banff and Buchan, **Scot.**; spt. 8 km W. of Banff; fisheries and meal milling; p. (1971) 1,667.
Port Stanvac, **S. Australia**; 24 km S. of Adelaide; oil refining.
Port Sudan, spt., **Sudan**; 48 km N. of Suakin; linked by rail to Atbara and Khartoum; oil refining; p. (est. 1971) 110,091.
Port Sunlight, Merseyside, **Eng.**; garden v. founded 1888 by Lord Leverhulme for the employees of the Port Sunlight factories.
Port Swettenham. *See* **Port Kelang.**

Port Talbot, t., West Glamorgan, **S. Wales**; on E. side of Swansea Bay; impt. iron and steel ind., copper, coal; new deep-water harbour serves as ore terminal; p. (1971) 50,658.
Port Taufiq, spt., **Egypt**; S. end of the Suez canal; p. 1,000.
Portugal, rep., Iberia, W. Europe; mild temperate climate on cst., drier and hotter in interior; economy based on an inefficient agr. sector, located in wide fertile valleys, and associated processing inds.; major exp. of cork, but few industl. raw materials; textiles; post-war growth of tourist inds.; cap. and airport Lisbon; a. 91,945 km²; p. (1968) 8,978,800.
Portuguesa, st., **Venezuela**; inc. llanos plains; most rapid increase in p.; livestock raising; cap. Guanare; a. 15,200 km²; p. (est. 1970) 284,523.
Portuguese Guinea. *See* **Guinea-Bissau**.
Portuguese Timor. *See* **East Timor**.
Porvoo, spt., S. **Finland**; on G. of Finland; exp. ctr. for forest prods.; forest inds., breweries, publishing; p. (1966) 13,687.
Porz, t., N. Rhine–Westphalia, **W. Germany**; on R. Rhine, S.E. of Cologne; glass, metals, paper; p. (est. 1967) 71,800.
Posadas, c., cap. of Misiones prov., N.E. **Argentina**; on upper Paraná R.; on border of Paraguay; yerba-maté, tobacco, cereals; connection for Iguaça falls; p. (1960) 70,691.
Posen. *See* **Poznań**.
Pössneck, t., Gera, **E. Germany**; S.E. of Weimar; porcelain, textiles, leather; p. (est. 1970) 19,074.
Postillon Is., Lesser Sunda Is., **Indonesia**; coconuts.
Postojna (Adelsberg,) t., **Yugoslavia**; 32 km N.E. of Trieste; extensive grotto and stalactite cavern.
Potchefstroom, t., Transvaal, **S. Africa**; on Mooi R.; univ.; agr.; malt, timber, engin.; p. (1970) 68,207.
Potenza, t., cap. of P. prov., **Italy**; on hill 220 m above Basento R.; agr. and industl. ctr.; p. (1969) 52,907.
Poti, spt., Georgian SSR, **USSR**; exp. manganese; fish processing, timber-milling, engin.; p. (est. 1967) 46,000.
Potomac, R., **USA**; divides Va. from Md.; flows past Wash. to Chesapeake Bay; 464 km long.
Potosi, dep., **Bolivia**; famous for silver- and tin-mines; zinc ore; cap. Potosi; a. 116,630 km²; p. (est. 1969) 850,400.
Potosi, c., **Bolivia**; on slope of Cerro Gordo de Potosi, 4,072 m a.s.l.; tin, silver, copper, lead mng.; p. (1967) 73,923.
Potsdam, c. cap. of admin. dist., **E. Germany**; on R. Havel, 29 km S.E. of Berlin; beautiful parks and gardens, many palaces; scene of conference between Allies on bdy. questions, 1945; motor and locomotive wks., engin.; precision instruments; p. (est. 1969) 110,949.
Potteries, The, dist., N. Staffs., **Eng.**; ctr. of earthenware ind., comprising ts. Burslem, Hanley, Fenton, Tunstall, Stoke and Longton.
Potters Bar, t., Herts., **Eng.**; residtl.; in London commuter belt; p. (1971) 24,583.
Poulton-le-Fylde, t., Lancs., **Eng.**; ctr. of mkt. gardening, poultry rearing dist.; p. (1971) 16,401.
Powys, co., central **Wales**; mtnous. a. made up of former cos. of Radnorshire, Montgomery and most of Brecon and bordering Eng.; forestry, stockraising and water catchment for Eng.; crossed by Rs. Wye and Severn; sparse p.; a. 5,076 km²; p. (1971) 98,765.
Powys, Vale of, Powys, **Wales**; drained by R. Severn; cattle-rearing; ch. t. Welshpool.
Poyang Hu, lge L., Kiangsi, **China**; on S. margin of Yangtze R. plain; surrounded by flat, intensively cultivated land, rice, sugar, mulberry; size varies greatly with season, max. a. (in late summer) 4,662 km².
Poznań, prov., W. **Poland**; drained by Warta and Notec Rs.; mainly agr.; stock-raising; mnfs. inc. locomotives; a. 26,705 km²; p. (1970) 2,190,000.
Poznań, c., cap. of P. prov., **Poland**; on Warta R.; route ctr., industl. and educational ctr.; cath. univ.; engin., iron-founding, chemicals; anc. c., once cap. of Poland; p. (1970) 469,000.
Pozzuoli, t., **Italy**; 3 km W. of Naples; anc. Puteoli; mineral baths, ordnance wks.; Roman ruins; p. (est. 1968) 61,912.
Prague (Praha), c., cap. of **ČSSR**; picturesque, anc. c. on R. Vltava; comm. and cultural ctr.; univ. (founded 1348); outstanding architecture; extensive mnfs.; machin., sugar, leather, milling, chemicals; p. (est. 1968) 1,102,060.
Prahova, R., Walachia, **Romania**; rises in Transylvanian Alps, flows S. into R. Ialomita; c. 176 km long.
Prato, t., **Italy**; 13 km N.W. of Florence; cath., mediaeval cas. and fortifications; cottons, woollens, machin.; p. (est. 1969) 138,717.
Predeal Pass, **Romania**; carries main road and rly. across Transylvanian Alps from Bucharest to Brasov; alt. over 1,200 m.
Preesall, t., Lancs., **Eng.**; N. of Blackpool; p. (1971) 4,066.
Pregel, R., **Poland**; flows to Frisches Haff, nr. Kaliningrad; 200 km long.
Prek Innot, **Khmer Rep.**; power and irrigation development project on lower Mekong R.
Prerov, t., **ČSSR**; S.E. of Olomouc; hardware, textiles; p. (1967) 36,000.
Prescot, mftg. t., Merseyside, **Eng.**; 6 km. S.W. of St. Helens; mkt., elec. cable ind.; p. (1971) 12,590.
Prešov, mkt. t., **ČSSR**; linen mnfs.; p. (1967) 40,000.
Prestatyn, t., Clwyd, **Wales**; on N. cst., 5 km E. of Rhyl; seaside resort; p. (1971) 14,428.
Presteign, mkt. t., Powys, **Wales**; on R. Lugg, 16 km. N.W. of Leominster; p. (1971) 1,214.
Preston, t., Lancs., **Eng.**; pt. on R. Ribble; textiles, engin., aircraft wks.; p. (1971) 97,365.
Prestonpans, burgh, E. Lothian, S.E. **Scot.**; on F. of Forth, 14 km E. of Edinburgh; scene of Jacobite victory 1745; p. (1971) 3,132.
Prestwich, t., Gtr. Manchester, **Eng.**; in valley of R. Irwell, 5 km N.W. of Manchester; cotton bleaching and dyeing, soap, furnishings; p. (1971) 32,838.
Prestwick, burgh, Kyle and Carrick, **Scot.**; on F. of Clyde, 5 km N. of Ayr; golfing ctr. and transatlantic airpt.; resort; p. (1971) 13,437.
Pretoria, c., Transvaal, admin. cap. of Rep. of **S. Africa**; univ., tr. ctr.; inds. inc. engin., chemicals, iron, and steel; p. (1970) 516,703 (met. a.).
Preveza, ch. pt. and t. of P. dep. of Epirus, N.W. **Greece**; guards G. of Arta; p. (1971) 12,816.
Pribilof Is., off S.W. Alaska, **USA**; seal fur; a. 168 km²; p. (est.) 550.
Pribram, t., Bohemia, **ČSSR**; impt. lead and silver mines, zinc, barium and antimony; p. (est. 1968) 29,689.
Prijedor, t., Bosnia and Hercegovina, **Yugoslavia**; on E. flank of Dinaric Alps, 104 km S.E. of Zagreb; rly. junc.; iron-ore mines.
Prilep, t., Macedonia, **Yugoslavia**; mkt., refractory materials, tobacco processing; p. (est. 1965) 44,000.
Primorskiy Kray, terr., **RSFSR**; S.E. Siberia, on Sea of Japan; coal, iron ore, and various metals in vicinity; fisheries; millet and rice; slow economic development results from isolation; wants economic links with China; ch. cs.. Vladivostok (cap.), Ussuriysk; a. 168,350 km²; p. (1970) 1,722,000.
Prince Albert, t., Saskatchewan, **Canada**; lumbering, furs; p. (1966) 26,269.
Prince Edward I., prov., **Canada**; sm. I. in G. of St. Lawrence; physically poorly endowed; rocky, with thin soils; pastoral agr., fur-farming, fishing; cap. Charlottetown; a. 5,657 km²; p. (1971) 111,641.
Prince George, t., B.C., **Canada**; oil refining; lumbering, mng., fur tr.; p. (1971) 32,755.
Prince Rupert, t., B.C., **Canada**; Pac. pt. of Canadian National rly.; service ctr., fishing and fish-processing; p. (1971) 15,355.
Princeton, bor., N.J., **USA**; seat of Princeton Univ.; p. (1970) 12,311.
Princetown, v., Devon, **Eng.**; in ctr. of Dartmoor; prison.
Principe. *See* **São Tomé**.
Pripet Marshes, Belorussiyan SSR, **USSR**; forested swampy region crossed by Pripet R. and its streams; greater part reclaimed; coal and petroleum; a. 46,620 km².
Pripet (Pripyat), R., Belorussiyan SSR, **USSR**; trib. of R. Dnieper; 560 km long.
Pristina, c., cap. of Kossovo aut. region, S.W.

Serbia, **Yugoslavia**; on Sitnic R.; admin. ctr.; many mosques; p. (1971) 69,524.

Prokopyevsk, t., S.W. Siberia, **RSFSR**; in Novosibirsk dist.; one of the main coalfields of Kuznetsk Basin; mng. machin., metallurgy; p. (1970) 275,000.

Prome, c., **Burma**; pt. on R. Irrawaddy; connected by rail and road to Rangoon; tr. in rice, cotton, tobacco; one of oldest cs. in Burma, founded 8th cent.; p. (est. 1962) 496,960.

Proskurov. *See* Khmel'nitskiy.

Prostejov, t., N. Moravia, **ČSSR**; rly. junc.; agr. machin., textiles; historic bldgs.; p. (1967) 36,000.

Provence, region and former prov., S.E. **France**; along Mediterranean; now embraces deps. of Var, Bouches-du-Rhône, Vaucluse and parts of Alpes-de-Haute-Provence and Alpes-Maritimes; tourism; fastest growing p. of France; mkt. gardening; intensive investment along cst.

Providence, c., R.I. **USA**; at head of Narragansett Bay; univ.; jewellery, textiles, silverware, rubber gds., machin., oil, coal; p. (1970) 176,920 (c.), 900,569 (met. a.).

Provo, t., Utah, **USA**; at base of Wasatch mtns., nr. shore of Utah L.; univ.; flour, bricks, blast furnaces; p. (1970) 53,491 (t.), 137,675 (met.a.).

Prudhoe, Northumberland, **Eng.**; former coal-mng. t.; chemicals, paper; p. (1971) 11,015.

Prudhoe Bay, N.E. Alaska, **USA**; ctr. of recent extensive oil finds; arctic conditions make extraction and transport of oil difficult and ecologically dangerous but despite opposition from environmentalist groups 1,262 km pipeline to ice-free pt. of Valdez approved (1973).

Prussia, former kingdom (1701–1806); former st. (1806–1945), **Germany**; consisted of 13 provs., cap. Berlin; formally abolished 1947; E. Prussia partitioned between USSR and Poland.

Pruszkow, t., **Poland**; nr. Warsaw; elec. plant; engin.; p. (1970) 43,000.

Prut, R., flows between **Romania** and **USSR**; from the Carpathian mtns. to the Danube R.; 576 km long.

Przemysl, c., S.E. **Poland**; on San R. (trib. of Vistula) nr. bdy. between Poland and Ukrainian SSR; anc. fortress t.; sewing machin.; p. (1970) 53,200.

Pskov, c., **RSFSR**; on R. Velikaya, nr. entry to L. Peipus; rly. junc.; flax tr.; historic bldgs.; scene of abdication of Nicholas II, March 1917; p. (1970) 127,000.

Pudsey, t., West Yorks., **Eng.**; between Leeds and Bradford; woollens; p. (1971) 38,127.

Peubia de Zaragoza, c., cap. of P. st., **Mexico**; one of oldest and most impt. cs. of rep.; fine cath., theatre, univ.; cotton mills, onyx quarries, glazed tiles; p. (1970) 401,603.

Puebla, st., **Mexico**; on interior plateau at 2,400 m; fertile valleys for coffee and sugar; mng. impt.; dense p.; a. 33,991 km²; p. (1969) 2,803,000.

Pueblo, c., Col., **USA**; on R. Arkansas, in foothills of Rockies; iron and steel ctr.; coal and various metals nearby; p. (1970) 96,746 (c.) 117,212 (met. a.).

Puente Genil, t., Córdoba, **Spain**; olive oil, quince pulp; p. (1970) 26,442.

Puerto Barrios, pt., **Guatemala**; rly. terminus; oil refining; p. (est. 1971) 29,425.

Puerto Cabello, spt., N. **Venezuela**; on Caribbean nr. Valencia; excellent harbour; linked by rail and highway to Carácas; asbestos, vegetable oils, soap, candles, meat-packing; p. (est. 1970) 70,598.

Puerto Cortés, spt., N.W. **Honduras**; on Caribbean; exp. bananas, hardwoods; p. (1961) 17,412.

Puerto de Santa Maria, spt., S.W. **Spain**; on Bay of Cadiz; exp. mainly sherry; p. (1970) 42,111.

Puerto la Cruz, t., **Venezuela**; 16 km from Barcelona; oil refining; p. (est. 1970) 82,059.

Puerto Limón. *See* Limón.

Puerto Montt, spt., **Chile**; in sheep-farming dist.; S. terminus of rlys.; devastated by earthquake 1960; p. (est. 1966) 49,473.

Puerto Ordaz. *See* Santo Tomé de la Guayana.

Puerto Rico, I., terr. of **USA**, **W.I.**; since 1952 free commonwealth ass. with USA; democratic economic growth aided recently by falling birth-rate; mtnous., eroded soils, alt. modifies tropical climate; exp. mnfs., but agr. impt. internally; 80 per cent land under cultivation, sugar, tobacco, coffee; tourism; cap. San Juan; a. 8,866 km²; p. (1970) 2,712,033.

Puerto Saurez, R. pt., **Bolivia**; on R. Paraguay; collecting ctr. for rubber, coffee, Brazil nuts.

Puerto Varas, t., **Chile**; tourist ctr. in Chilean "Switzerland"; p. (1961) 26,615.

Puget Sound, Wash., **USA**; inlet of Pac. Oc.

Puket. *See* Phuket.

Pula, spt., Croatia, **Yugoslavia**; on Adriatic; industl. ctr. with shipyards, docks, and various inds.; ch. naval base of Hapsburg empire; tourism; Roman remains; p. (est. 1965) 45,000.

Puna, cold, bleak, and barren plateau of Andes in **Peru** and **Bolivia**, 3,600–5,500 m.

Punjab, region N.W. Indus plains, Indian subcontinent; extensive irrigation from the "five rivers"—Jhelum, Chenab, Ravi, Bias, Sutlej; now divided politically between **India** and **Pakistan**; impt. cotton, wheat, and sugar dist.; coal deposits.

Punjab (East), former st., **India**; partitioned on linguistic basis 1966; Punjab-speaking Punjab st. (a. 50,375 km²; p. (1971) 13,472,972 inc. 55 per cent Sikh); and Hindi-speaking Haryana st. (a. 44,056 km²; p. (1971) 9,971,165); joint cap. Chandigarh.

Punjab (West), prov., **Pakistan**; old prov. revived 1970; p. (1972) 37,374,000.

Punta Arenas, c., cap. of Magallanes prov., S. **Chile**; most S. c. in world; mutton, wool; coal nearby; natural gas pipeline from Kimiri-Aike; p. (est. 1966) 67,514.

Puntarenas, spt., **Costa Rica**, on G. of Nicoya; fishing; fish-processing; resort; p. (1970) 31,162.

Purbeck, I. of, sm. peninsula, Dorset cst., **Eng.**; anc. v. of Corfe Castle in ctr.; limestone ("Purbeck marble") quarries; site of Britain's lgst. onshore oilfield; once a royal deer forest.

Puri, dist., Orissa, **India**; cap. P. famous for its temple and festival of the god Vishnu and his monster car, Juggernaut; p. (1961) 1,865,439.

Purley. *See* Croydon.

Purus, R., **Peru** and **Brazil**; rises in Andes, flows to Amazon R. through underdeveloped a.; 3,360 km long.

Pusan, main pt. of **S. Korea**; on Korean Strait at head of Naktong R. basin; textiles; steel mill at Pohang nearby; p. (1966) 1,425,703.

Pushkin, c., **RSFSR**; nr. Leningrad; summer palaces of Tsars; Pushkin museum; Pulkovo observatory nearby; p. (est. 1966) 66,000.

Puteaux, sub. Paris, **France**; woollens, dyes, engin., printing; p. (1968) 38,014.

Putney, sub. of London, **Eng.**; residtl.; Thames-side dist.

Putrid Sea. *See* Sivash.

Putumayo, R., trib. of R. Amazon; rises in **Colombia**, forming bdy. with **Ecuador** and **Peru**; here, in wild-rubber region, Roger Casement exposed cruel exploitation of native labour; 1,600 km long.

Puy-de-Dôme, extinct volcano, Massif Central, **France**; hgst peak of Auvergne mtns., 1,466 m.

Puy-de-Dôme, dep., **France**; in Auvergne; cap. Clermont-Ferrand, indsutl. ctr. Thiers; a. 8,003 km², p. (1968) 547,743.

Puymorens Tunnel, Pyrenees, on bdy. between **France** and **Spain**; carries main rly. between Toulouse and Barcelona.

Pwllheli, t., Gwynedd, **N. Wales**; sm. pt. on S. cst. Lleyn peninsula; seaside resort; inshore fishing, boat-bldg., p. (1971) 3,832.

Pyatigorsk, c., N. Caucasus, **RSFSR**; ctr. of Caucasian mineral water springs; Lermontov shot here in duel 1841; p. (est. 1969) 84,000.

Pylos, pt., S.W. Peleponnesus, **Greece**; shipbldg. and repair yard, heavy metal wks. projected; sea-battles 1827 (Navarino), 425 B.C.

Pyongyang, c., cap. of **N. Korea**; stands high above Taedong R.; major industl. ctr. with coal and iron ore deposits nearby; univ.; many historic relics; p. (est. 1966) 1,364,000.

Pyrenees, range of mtns., S.W. **Europe**; dividing **France** from **Iberian Peninsula**; 432 km long; hgst peak Pic d'Anéto (Maladetta) 3,408 m.

Pyrénées-Atlantique, dep., S.W. **France**; mainly agr., sheep and cattle raising; ch. ts. Pau (cap.), Bayonne, Biarritz; a. 7,713 km²; p. (1968) 508,734.

Pyrénées-Orientales, dep., S. **France**; on Mediterranean; wine, fruit, olives; cap. Perpignan; a. 4,141 km²; p. (1968) 281,976.

Pyrgos, t., Elis, S.W. Greece; has suffered from earthquakes; p. (1971) 20,380.

Q

Qarun (Karun). *See* **Birket el Qarun.**

Qatar, emirate, indep. st. (1971), **Arabia**; peninsula on Persian G.; economy based on oil; inland production declining, but increasing offshore drilling; political stability less certain after withdrawal of Brit. military protection (1971); cap. Doha; a. 10,360 km²; p. (1971) 130,000.

Qattara Depression, N. **Egypt**; 134 m below sea level, salt marsh produced by seepage and evaporation of artesian water; marshes; few inhabitants.

Qena or **Kene,** t., central **Egypt**; on R. Nile; water jars and bottles; agr. tr., cereals, dates; p. (est. 1970) 77,600.

Qisil-Qum, desert region, **Central Asia**; covering dried-up a. of extended Pleistocene Aral Sea.

Qizan, spt., **Saudi Arabia**; cereals, pearl-fishing, salt.

Qom (Qum), c., **Iran**; pilgrimage ctr., shrine of Fatima; rly. junction; p. (1967) 179,434 (met. a.).

Qornet es Sauda, mtn., Lebanon range, Levant, **Lebanon**; max. alt. 3,050 m.

Quantock Hills, Somerset, **Eng.**; S. of Bridgewater Bay; hgst. pt. 385 m; a Nat. Park.

Queanbeyan, t., N.S.W. **Australia**; 13 km from Canberra; pastoral, dairying dist.; mkt. and service ctr.; p. (1972) 15,368.

Quebec, c., cap. of Q. prov., **Canada**; spt. with fine harbour on St. Lawrence R. at mouth of St. Charles; cultural cap. of French Canada; inds. based on local raw materials of timber, agr. prods.; oil refining at St. Romauld; historic c. with many fine bldgs., univ., tourism; p. (1971) 182,418 (c.), 476,232 (met. a.).

Quebec, prov., **Canada**; mainly within Canadian Shield; continental climate; forests and timber inds.; agr. in S.; hydroelectric power and abundant minerals; p. mainly French-speaking; ch. cs., Quebec (cap.), Montreal; strong separatist movements; a. 1,540,687 km²; p. (1971) 6,027,764.

Quebec-Labrador Trough, Canada; geological formation extending through central Quebec prov. to Ungava Bay, Hudson Strait; immense reserves of iron-ore (locally "red-gold").

Quedlinburg, t., Halle, **E. Germany**; at foot of Harz mtns.; cas. cath.; aniline dyes, metals, engin., horticultural mkt. t.; p. (est. 1970) 30,829.

Queenborough, sm. pt., on R. Swale, I. of Sheppey, Kent, **Eng.**

Queen Charlotte's Is., archipelago, N. of Vancouver I., off cst. B.C., **Canada**; halibut fishing, lumbering; p. (1966) 2,222.

Queen Charlotte Sound, strait, separating Vancouver I. from B.C. mainland, a continuation of Johnstone Strait.

Queen Elizabeth Is., Canada; I. gr. in Canadian Arctic; most N. land of N. America; a. 349,443 km²; p. (1961) 310.

Queen Mary Land, Norwegian sector of **Antarctica**; ice crystal mtns., 3,050 m high for 160 km along cst.

Queens, bor., N.Y. City, **USA**; residtl. dist.; lgst bor. of N.Y. c.; p. (1970) 1,973,708.

Queensbury and Shelf, t., West Yorks., **Eng.**; textiles; p. (1971) 10,603.

Queensferry, royal burgh, Edinburgh City, **Scot.**; at S. end of Forth road and rail bridges; p. (1971) 5,127.

Queensland, st., N.E. **Australia**; rises from E. cst. plain to Gr. Dividing Range; sub-tropical climate; p. concentrated on E. cst. where sugar-cane, pineapples, bananas, cotton; inland grassland support cattle and sheep; mng. impt for copper, lead, zinc; oil discovered at Moonie; Gr. Barrier Reef along cst.; cap. Brisbane; a. 1,736,595 km²; p. (1972) 1,823,362.

Queenstown. *See* **Cobh.**

Queenstown, t., Tasmania, **Australia**; mng. ctr. for copper, silver, gold; p. (1966) 4,292.

Queenstown, t., Cape Prov., **S. Africa**; in agr. region producing wool and wheat; p. (1968) 42,997.

Quelimane, pt., **Moçambique**; at head of estuary; rly. terminus; exp. copra, sisal, tea; notorious in 18th and 19th cent. as slave mkt.; p. c. 10,000.

Quelpart. *See* **Cheju.**

Quemoy, gr. of Is. off Chinese mainland nr. Amoy, held by Nationalist forces; p. (est.) 50,000 (plus garrison of 40,000).

Querétaro, t., cap. of Q. st., **Mexico**; site of pre-Aztec settlement at 1,881 m; cath., many colonial bldgs.; old cotton ind.; p. (1970) 140,379.

Querétaro, st., **Mexico**; in Central Plateau; arid with fertile valleys; variety of crops; mng. impt.; famous for opals; cap. Q.; a. 11,479 km²; p. (1969) 112,993.

Quetta, t., cap. of Baluchistan, **Pakistan**; at 5,000 ft., commands routes to Bolan Pass; ctr. of irrigated agr. a.; military ctr.; coal mng. nearby; damaged by severe earthquake (1935); p. (est. 1969) 130,000.

Quezaltenango, t., S.W. **Guatemala**; second c. of rep.; at 2,333 m at foot of Santa Maria volcano; univ.; comm. ctr. for rich agr. region; textiles, handicrafts; p. (est. 1971) 54,475.

Quezon City, cap. **Philippines**; new sub. 16 km N.E. of Manila; cap. since 1948; univ.; p. (est. 1968) 545,500.

Quibdó, t., **Colombia**; in forested a. on R. Atrato; platinum, gold mng.; p. (est. 1968) 46,871.

Quillon, t., Kerala, **India**; on Malabar cst., ctr. of coconut tr. and processing; p. (1971) 124,208.

Quilmes, t., Buenos Aires, **Argentina**; on Rio de la Plata estuary; English public school; resort; oil refining, textiles, chemicals, glass; p. (1960) 318,144.

Quimper, ch. t., Finistère, **France**; tourist ctr. for S. Brittany; Breton pottery; Gothic cath.; p. (1968) 57,678.

Quincy, t., Ill., **USA**; at bridging point of R. Mississippi; agr. machin., clothing, footwear, food inds.; p. (1970) 45,288.

Quincy, t., Mass., **USA**; in Mass. B., 13 km S.E. of Boston; shipbldg. ctr.; p. (1970) 87,966.

Quindio, pass, **Colombia**; provides impt. route-way through Cordillera Central; 11,099 ft.

Qui Nhon, t., **S. Vietnam**; on E. cst.; tr. in coconut prods.; fishing; p. (est. 1968) 116,821.

Quintana Roo, st., S.E. **Mexico**; on Caribbean; low-lying swamp, underdeveloped; cap. Chetumal; a. 50,344 km²; p. (1969) 80,000.

Quito, c., cap. of **Ecuador**; in Andes at 2,852 m, 24 km S. of equator; anc. Inca c., cath., univ., slower growth than coastal ts.; impt. textile ctr.; p. (est. 1972) 564,900.

Quorndon or **Quorn,** sm. t., Leics., **Eng.**; on R. Soar, 5 km S. of Loughborough; ctr. of fox-hunting dist.

R

Raake, t., N. **Finland**; spt.; iron wks.

Raasay, I., E. of Skye, Skye and Lochalsh, **Scot.**; 21 km long, 5·6 km wide.

Rab I., at head of Adriatic, **Yugoslavia**; tourism; a. 192 km²; p. (1961) 8,369.

Rabat, c., cap. of **Morocco**; spt. at mouth of Bu Regreg R. on Atl. cst.; cath., univ.; textiles, carpets, rugs; p. (1971) 435,510 (c.), 534,270 (met. a.).

Rabaul, spt., New Britain, **Papua New Guinea**; ch. pt., exp. copra; damaged by volcanic eruption (1937) former cap. of New Guinea; p. (1966) 10,589.

Racibórz (Ratibor), t., Upper Silesia, **Poland** (since 1945); on R. Oder; textiles, metals, wood engin.; p. (1970) 40,400.

Racine, c., Wis., **USA**; sm. pt. on L. Mich., 16 km S. of Milwaukee; agr. machin., tractors, car parts; p. (1970) 94,720 (c.), 171,218 (met. a.).

Radcliffe, t., Gtr. Manchester, **Eng.**; N.W. of Manchester; paper, rubber, paint, engin.; p. (1971) 29,320.

Radebeul, t. Dresden, **E. Germany**; on R. Elbe; satellite of Dresden; p. (est. 1970) 39,626.

Radium Hill, v. S. Australia; ctr. for radium mng. 1920–30 and uranium later; mines now closed.
Radnorshire, former co., Central Wales. *See* Powys.
Radom, t., Kielce, Poland; in Radomska Plain; route ctr.; metal and chemical inds.; lge. tobacco factory; p. (1970) 158,700.
Radomosko, t., Poland; on edge of Lodz Upland; metallurgical wks., food inds.; bentwood chairs for exp.; p. (1970) 31,200.
Radstock (Norton Radstock), t., Somerset, Eng.; 16 km S.E. of Bristol; former coal-mng. a.; p. (1971) 15,232.
Radzionkow, t., Katowice, Poland; new t. (1951); p. (1970) 27,800.
Ragaz, Bad, spa, St. Gall can., Switzerland; at mouth of Tamina R.; hot springs from nearby v. of Pfäfers; p. (1960) 2,699.
Ragusa. *See* Dubrovnik.
Ragusa, t., Sicily, Italy; oil and asphalt production; p. (1969) 60,413.
Rahway, t., N.J., USA; on R. Rahway; residtl. for N.Y. business men; p. (1970) 29,114.
Raichur, t., Karnataka, India; comm. ctr.; agr. processing; p. (1961) 63,329.
Rainer, mtn., Wash., USA; 4,432 m; forms Nat. Park.
Rainford, t., Merseyside, Eng.; nr. St. Helens; former coal-mng. a.; p. (1971) 8,381.
Rainy, L., on border of Canada and Minn., USA; drained by Rainy R. to L. of the Woods.
Raipur, t., Madhya Pradesh, India; ctr. of fertile rice growing a.; p. (1971) 174, 518 (t.), 205,986 (met. a.).
Rajahmundry, t., Andhra Pradesh, India; on delta of Godivari R.; agr. tr.; p. (1971) 165,912 (t.), 188,805 (met. a.).
Rajasthan, st., India; dry a. inc. Thar desert; sparse p. where primitive irrigation; agr., millets, pulses, cotton; impt. gypsum deposits; cap. Jaipur; a. 342,274 km²; p. (1971) 25,742,142.
Rajkot, t., Gujarat, India; p. (1971) 300,612.
Rajshahi, t., Rajshahi dist., Bangladesh; on R. Ganges; univ.; silk inds.; p. (est. 1969) 76,000.
Raki-Ura I. *See* Stewart I.
Raleigh, c., cap. of N.C., USA; educational ctr. univ.; printing, cotton tr. and processing; p. (1970) 117,676 (c.), 225,634 (met. a.).
Ralik, W. chain of Is., Marshall gr., Pac. Oc.; lgst atoll Kwajalein; parallel with Ratak chain.
Ramat Gan, t., Israel; in plain of Sharon; univ.; lt. inds.; p. (1972) 120,100.
Rambouillet, t., Yvelines, France; nr. Versailles; anc. château; p. (1968) 14,499.
Rameswaram, t., S. India; on Rameswaram I., Palk Strait; contains Dravidian temple, Hindu holy place of pilgrimage; p. (1961) 6,801.
Ramla, t., Israel; S. of Lydda; former cap. of Palestine; ass. with crusaders; p. (est. 1970) 30,800.
Rampur, t., Uttar Pradesh, India; N.W. of Bareilly; agr. tr.; sugar refining; chemicals; cap. of former princely st. of R.; p. (1971) 161,417.
Ramree I., Burma; in Bay of Bengal, off Arakan cst.; 80 km long.
Ramsbottom, t., Lancs., Eng.; on R. Irwell, 6 km N. of Bury; engin., paper, textiles; p. (1971) 15,872.
Ramsey, mkt. t., Cambs., Eng; on edge of Fens, 11 km N. of St. Ives; engin.; abbey ruins; p. (1971) 5,646.
Ramsey, t., spt., I. of Man, Eng.; on N.E. cst.; holiday resort; p. (1971) 5,048.
Ramsgate, t., Kent, Eng.; on S. cst. of I. of Thanet; seaside resort; p. (1971) 39,482.
Rancagua, t., Colchagua prov., Chile; ctr. of fertile valley in Andean foothills; tractors, agr. processing; p. (est. 1966) 63,116.
Rance, R., Brittany, France; world's first major tidal hydroelectric power sta. (opened 1966).
Ranchi, t., Bihar, India; hot season seat of govt. in Chota Nagpur plateau; univ.; heavy engin.; p. (1971) 175,943 (c.), 255,551 (met. a.).
Rand. *See* Witwatersrand.
Randers, pt., Denmark; on Randers Fjord, inlet of Kattegat; machin., foundries; exp. dairy prod.; mediaeval monastery; p. (est. 1970) 41,253.
Randfontein, t., Transvaal, S. Africa; gold-mng. ctr.; uranium plant; p. (1968) 46,370.
Randstad, conur b., Neth.; Dutch "urban ring," inc. Rotterdam, the Hague, Leiden, Amsterdam. and Utrecht, contained within radius of 16 km; a. of rapid industrialisation.
Rangitaiki R., N.I., N.Z.; flows into Bay of Plenty; 192 km long.
Rangoon, c., cap. of Burma; on E. arm of Irrawaddy delta; 2 caths., many mosques, temples and pagodas; replaced Mandalay as cap. with the increasing importance of delta under the Brit. as ctr. of rice tr. and exp.; oil refining; teak collecting ctr.; p. (1970) 1,821,752.
Rangpur, t., Bangladesh; on R. Ghaghat; jute; p. (1961) 40,600.
Raniganj, t., W. Bengal, India; coalfield in Damodar basin; engin.; p. (1961) 30,113.
Rannoch, Loch, Perth and Kinross, Scot.; 14 km long, 1·6 km wide; drained to R. Tay.
Rapallo, t., Liguria, N.W. Italy; on G. of Genoa 35 km E. of Genoa; most celebrated resort on Italian Riviera di Levante; p. (est. 1968) 25,311.
Rapanui. *See* Easter I.
Rapid City, t., S.D., USA; second t. of st.; comm. ctr. for agr. and mng. a.; p. (est. 1969) 43,000.
Rarotonga, volcanic I., Pac. Oc.; cap. of Cook Is.; fruit canning; ch. t. and pt. Avarua; p. (est. 1968) 10,853.
Ra's al Khaymah. *See* United Arab Emirates.
Rasht (Resht), c., Iran; cap of Gilan prov., in a. producing rice, cotton, silk; carpets; nearby Pahlevi serves as pt.; p. (est. 1971) 164,400.
Ras Lanug, oil terminal, on G. of Sidra, Libya; pipeline from Hofra oilfield.
Ras Tannura, spt., Nejd, Saudi Arabia; lge. oil refinery; oil exp.
Ratak, E., chain of Is., Marshall gr., Pac. Oc.; ch. I. Majuro; parallel with Ralik chain.
Rathenow, t., Potsdam, E. Germany; on R. Havel; optical and precision instruments; p. (est. 1970) 29,823.
Rathlin, I., off Fair Head, Moyle, N. Ireland; 8 km by 1·6 km.
Ratibor. *See* Racibórz.
Ratingen, t., N. Rhine-Westphalia, W. Germany; N.E. of Düsseldorf; textiles, machin., glass; famous for Blue L.; p. (est. 1969) 42,256.
Ratisbon. *See* Regensburg.
Ratlam, t., Madhya Pradesh, India; rly. junc. in Malwa Plateau; p. (1971) 106,666.
Ratnapura, t., Sri Lanka; former ctr. of gem mng.; p. (est. 1968) 24,000.
Rauma, spt., S.W. Finland; on Baltic Sea; p. (1966) 23,952.
Raunds, t., Northants., Eng.; 8 km N.E. of Wellingborough; p. (1971) 5,945.
Raurkela, t., Orissa, India; steel, tinplate, iron, fertilisers; p. (1961) 90,287.
Ravenglass, t. Cumbria, Eng.; nr. mouth of R. Esk; old pt.; Roman remains.
Ravenna, c., cap. of Ravenna prov., Emilia-Romagna, Italy; on reclaimed plain nr. Po delta; connected to Adriatic by canal; ctr. of fertile agr. dist., agr. processing; new inds. aided by discovery of methane N. of c.; oil refineries, chemicals, fertilisers; cath., mausoleum, famous mosaics; p. (1969) 131,279.
Ravenna, prov., Emilia-Romagna, Italy; N. Italian plain rising to Apennines; fertile agr. a.; cap. R.; a. 1,852 km²; p. (1969) 352,146).
Ravensburg, t., Baden-Württemberg, W. Germany; nr. Konstanz; engin., textiles; p. (est. 1969) 31,908.
Ravenscraig, t., nr. Motherwell, Strathclyde Reg., Scot.; hot strip steelmill; cold reduction mill at Gartcosh 13 km away.
Ravi, R., Punjab, India; trib. of Chenab; used for irrigation; 720 km long.
Rawalpindi, c., Pakistan; seat of govt. until completion of Islamabad; admin., comm. and rly ctr.; foundries, oil refining, industl. gases; p. (est. 1969) 455,000.
Rawmarsh, t., South Yorks., Eng.; 3 km N.E. of Rotherham; engin.; p. (1971) 19,884.
Rawtenstall, t., Lancs., Eng.; on R. Irwell in ctr. of Rossendale Fells; felts; footwear, textiles; p. (1971) 21,404.
Rayleigh, t., Essex, Eng.; 8 km N.W. of Southend; lt. inds.; dormitory for London; p. (1971) 26,265.
Ré, Ile de, I., W. cst. of Charente-Maritime dep. France; off La Rochelle; citadel (built 1681) at St. Martin de Ré is now a prison.

Reading, t., Berks., **Eng.**; at confluence of Rs. Thames and Kennet; univ.; biscuits, engin., electronics, mkt. gardening, tin-box mftg. printing; p. (1971) 132,023.
Reading, c., Penns., **USA**; on Schuylkill R.; steelwks. using local coal, optical gds.; p. (1970) 86,470 (c.), 294,104 (met. a.).
Recife, spt., cap. of Pernambuco st., N.E. **Brazil**; fine natural harbour; univ.; processing and exp. of sugar from surrounding a.; "Venice of Brazil" because of I. and peninsula site; lge. petrochemical wks. nearby; p. (1970) 1,046,454.
Recklinghausen, t., N. Rhine–Westphalia, **W. Germany**; nr. Dortmund; collieries, iron, machin., textiles, chemicals; p. (est. 1969) 125,700.
Recôncavo, dist., Bahia st., N.E. **Brazil**; surrounds bay at mouth of R. Paraguassu; intensive cultivation of sugar-cane, cotton, tobacco, rice, by Negro farmers; oil production; ch. ts. São Salvador, Cachoeira.
Redbridge, outer bor., E. London, **Eng.**; incorporates Ilford, Wanstead and Woodford, Chigwell (Hainault Estate), Dagenham (N. Chadwell Heath ward); mainly residtl.; p. (1971) 238,614.
Redcar, t., Cleveland, **Eng.**; lge. iron and steel wks.
Redcliff, t., **Rhodesia**; iron-mng.; iron and steel wks.; fertilisers.
Red Deer, t., Alberta, **Canada**; on Red Deer R.; mkt. t. in farming a.; lge. natural gas processing plant nearby; p. (1971) 27,428.
Redditch, t., Hereford and Worcs., **Eng.**; 19 km S. of Birmingham; needles, fishing tackle, cycles, springs, aluminium alloys; new t. (1964); p. (est. 1974) 49,730.
Redlands, t., Cal., **USA**; univ.; citrus fruit packing and canning; p. (1970) 36,355.
Redonda, I., Leeward gr., **Caribbean Sea**; between Montserrat and Nevis; uninhabited.
Redondo Beach, t., Cal., **USA**; residtl.; tourism; p. (1970) 57,425.
Red R. (**China and Vietnam**). *See* **Song-koi.**
Red R., **USA**; southernmost of lge. tribs. of Mississippi R.; derives name and colour from red clay in upper course; dammed for flood control and hydroelec. power; 2,560 km long.
Red R. of the North, **USA**; rises in Minn., flows N. into Canada to empty into L. Winnipeg; 1,040 km long.
Redruth, t., Cornwall, **Eng.**; once major ctr. of tin mng.; most mines now closed, although recent revival of some; p. (1971) 42,029 (inc. Camborne).
Red Sea, arm of sea separating Arabia from Africa; connects with Indian Oc. by Straits of Bab-el-Mandeb; extension of Great African Rift Valley which further N. encloses the Dead Sea; 2,240 km long.
Redwood City, t., W. Cal., **USA**; timber tr.; electronics; p. (1970) 55,686.
Ree, Lough, L., **R.o.I.**; between Roscommon, Longford and Westmeath, an extension of R. Shannon; 27 km long.
Regensburg (**Ratisbon**), c., R. pt., Bavaria, **W. Germany**; N.E. of Munich on R. Danube; timber processing, chemicals; p. (est. 1969) 126,600.
Reggio di Calabria, spt., Calabria, **Italy**; on Strait of Messina; cath.; fishing, ferry to Sicily; mkt. for citrus fruit; tourism; agr. processing; rebuilt after 1908 earthquake; p. (1969) 166,022.
Reggio nell' Emilia, c., cap. of prov. of same name, in Emilia-Romagna, N. **Italy**; at foot of Apennines; Renaissance church of the Madonna della Ghiara; locomotives, aircraft, agr. engin.; birthplace of Ariosto; p. (1969) 127,269.
Regina, t., cap. of Saskatchewan, **Canada**; ctr. of wheat growing dist. of Prairies; connected by pipeline to Alberta oilfields; oil refining, chemicals, agr. machin.; p. (est. 1969) 140,000.
Rehovoth, **Israel**; t., in citrus fruit dist.; Weizmann Institute of Science; p. (est. 1970) 36,600.
Reichenbach, t., Karl-Marx-Stadt, **E. Germany**; at foot of Erzgebirge; textile ctr.; p. (est. 1970) 28,818.
Reichenberg. *See* **Liberec.**
Reigate, t., Surrey, **Eng.**; at foot of N. Downs, 8 km E. of Dorking; inc. Redhill; dormitory for London; p. (1971) 56,088.
Reims, c., Marne dep., N.E. **France**; on R. Vesle; famous Gothic cath.; univ.; champagne ctr., textiles; p. (1968) 152,967 (c.); 167,830 (met. a.).
Reindeer L., Saskatchewan, Manitoba, **Canada**; Indian settlement on shore; a. 6,475 km^2.
Rejang R., **Sarawak**; navigable for 72 km by ocean boats; main R. of Sarawak.
Rembang, pt., N. cst. Java, **Indonesia**; in dry limestone R. plateau; p. (est. 1960) 75,000.
Remscheid, t., N. Rhine–Westphalia, **W. Germany**; nr. Düsseldorf; iron and steel ctr.; machin. tools; p. (est. 1969) 136,400.
Renaix. *See* **Ronse.**
Rendsburg, t., Schleswig-Holstein, **W. Germany**; on Kiel Canal; shipbldg., elec. gds.; p. (est. 1969) 35,464.
Renfrew, royal burgh, Renfrew, **Scot.**; nr. R. Clyde, 8 km W. of Glasgow; p. (1971) 18,595.
Renfrewshire, former co., central **Scot.**; now reduced in size and forms l. gov. dist. within Strathclyde Reg.; a. of l. gov. dist. 308 km^2; p. (1971) 203,995.
Renkum, t., Gelderland. **Neth.**; 13 km W. of Arnhem; paper mnfs.; p. (1968) 32,815.
Rennes, c., cap. of Ille-et-Vilaine dep., **France**; only major inland t. of Brittany, in fertile agr. basin; univ., comm. ctr.; cars, engin.; p. (1968) 180,943 (c.), 192,782 (met. a.).
Reno, lgst. t. of Nevada, **USA**; univ.; st. agr. college; famous for easy divorce procedure and gambling; p. (1970) 72,121 (t.), 119,965 (met. a.).
Repton, t., Derbyshire, **Eng.**; famous public school in priory; former Saxon cap. of Mercia; p. (1971) 32,667 (dist.).
Resende, t., Rio de Janeiro st., **Brazil**; chemicals, rly. junc.; univ.; p. (est. 1968) 64,950.
Resht. *See* **Rasht.**
Resina, t., S. **Italy**; on Bay of Naples at W. foot of Vesuvius; nr. site of anc. Herculaneum; resort; p. (est. 1968) 51,124.
Resistencia, t., cap. of Chaco terr., **Argentina**; served by R. pt. of Barranqueras on R. Paraná; tr. in cattle, timber, cotton; agr. processing; p. (1970) 142,736 (met. a.).
Resita, t., Banat region, **Romania**; developing steel inds. based on local iron ore; heavy engin.; p. (1968) 58,679.
Retalhuleu, t., cap. of R. dep., **Guatemala**; comm. ctr. for coffee, sugar; p. (est. 1964) 36,919.
Réunion (**Ile de Bourbon**), I., overseas terr. of France; in **Indian Oc.**, between Mauritius and Malagasy Rep.; volcanic I.; impt. sugar producer; cap. St. Denis; a. 2,512 km^2; p. (1969) 430,000.
Reus, t., Tarragona, prov., **Spain**; textiles; agr. tr.; p. (1970) 59,095.
Reuss, R., **Switzerland**; flows N. from the St. Gotthard Pass through L. Lucerne, joining Aare R. nr. Brugg; 157 km long.
Reutlingen, t., Baden–Württemberg, **W. Germany**; S. of Stuttgart; textiles, metals, machin., leather; p. (est. 1969) 77,034.
Reval. *See* **Tallin.**
Revelstoke, t., B.C., **Canada**; rly. junc.; in timber producing a.; ctr. for R. Nat. Park; p. (1966) 4,791.
Revere, t., Mass., **USA**; sub. of Boston; resort; p. (1970) 43,159.
Revillagigedo Islands, archipelago, Pac. Oc., off S.W. **Mexico**; ch. Is., Socorro, San Benedicto (volcano suddenly arose on I. 1952).
Reykjavik, c., cap. of **Iceland**; on S.W. cst.; impt. fish. pt.; fish exp. and processing; water piped from geysers; airport; univ.; 2 caths.; p. (est. 1969) 81,288 (c.).
Rezayeh, c., **Iran**; cap. of W. Azerbaijan prov.; comm. ctr. of agr. region; p. (1966) 110,749.
Rheidol, R., Dyfed, **Wales**; flows from Plynlimmon in deeply incised valley (Devil's Bridge) to Aberystwyth; hydroelec. power; 38 km long.
Rheine, t., N. Rhine–Westphalia, **W. Germany**; on R. Ems; textiles, machin.; p. (est. 1969) 51,028.
Rheingau, dist., **W. Germany**; famous wine a. on right bank of Rhine from Biebrich to Assmanshausen.
Rheinhausen, t., Rhine–Westphalia, **W. Germany**; on left bank of Rhine opposite Duisburg; coal mng., iron, textiles; p. (est. 1969) 71,740.
Rheydt, t., N. Rhine–Westphalia, **W. Germany**;

twin c. of adjacent Mönchengladbach; textiles, machin.; p. (est. 1969) 100,300.

Rhin (Bas), dep., N.E. France; cap. Strasbourg; a. 4,786 km²; p. (1968) 827,367.

Rhine, R., rises in Switzerland, can. Grisons, passes through L. Constance, skirts Baden, traverses Hesse, Rhineland, and the Neth., flowing to N. Sea by two arms, Oude Rijn and the Waal (the latter discharging finally by the Maas); famous for its beauty, especially between Bonn and Bingen; ch. falls at Schaffhausen; once a natural barrier between E. and W. Europe, spanned by 30 rly. bridges; linked to Rhône by 1985 and only 105 km incomplete of Rhine-Danube canal; very polluted; 1,280 km long.

Rhine-Hern, canal, **W. Germany**; impt. Ruhr waterway, part of Mitelland Canal; 38 km long.

Rhineland Palatinate (Rheinland-Pfalz), *Land*, **W. Germany**; borders France, Luxembourg and Belgium; drained by Rhine and Moselle, inc. Hunsrück and Eiger mtns.; arable agr. in Rhine valley; vineyards; cap. Mainz; a. 19,852 km; p. (1970) 3,684,000.

Rhode Island, st., New England, **USA**; washed by Atl. Oc., surrounded by Mass. and Conn.; divided by Narragansett Bay, with many Is. lgst. being that from which the st. takes its name; smallest and most densely populated st.; famous for poultry; major ind. textiles; cap. Providence; a. 3,144 km²; p. (1970) 922,461.

Rhodes (Rhodos), I., Dodecanese Is.; off S.W. cst., Anatolia, belonging to **Greece**; cap. R.; p. c. 60,000

Rhodes, cap. of I. of Rhodes, **Greece**; on N.E. cst.; picturesque; p. (1971) 32,019.

Rhodesia (Southern Rhodesia), **Central Africa**; former Brit. col.; illegal rep. since 1969; landlocked st.; much of land high veld above 900 m, covered in savannah; agr., maize, cattle and tobacco (main exp.); mng. also impt.; Wankie coal mine lgst. in world; also asbestos, chrome and copper; power from Kariba dam encourages lt. inds.; cap. Salisbury; a. 389,329 km²; p. (est. 1970) 5,310,000 (5,050,000 Africans).

Rhodope Mtns. *See* Rodopi Mtns.

Rhondda, t., Mid Glamorgan, **Wales**; in narrow R. valley; coal-mng. ctr.; lt. inds. introduced since 1930s depression; picturesque a. in upper R. valley; p. (1971) 88,924.

Rhône, dep., S.E. **France**; drained by R. Rhône, and its trib. R. Saône, which unite at Lyons; agr. grain, potatoes, wine; vine-growing, many mnfs., silks, textiles; cap. Lyons; a. 2,859 km²; p. (1968) 1,325,611.

Rhône, R., **Switzerland** and **France**; rises in Rhône glacier of St. Gotthard mtn. gr., and flows through L. of Geneva and E. France to G. of Lyons in Mediterranean; power stas. at Sion and Geneva; canals, dams, locks and power stas. form part of Fr. Rhône Valley project (1937–72); linked to Rhine by 1985; 811 km long.

Rhône-Saône Corridor, routeway, **France**; impt. transport artery using Rhône, Saône R. valleys as a means for linking Paris, Lorraine and Rhine rift valley with Mediterranean cst.; rlys., roads, with major pt. of Marseilles serving the S. terminus.

Rhyl, t., Clwyd, **N. Wales**; at entrance Vale of Clwyd; resort developed from sm. fishing v.; serves Lancs. conurbs.; p. (1971) 21,715.

Rhymney, t., Mid Glamorgan, **Wales**; on R. Rhymney, 6 km E. of Merthyr Tydfil; former colly. and iron founding ctr.; engin.; p. (1971) 8,051.

Ribble, R., North Yorks., Lancs., **Eng.**; rises in Pennines, flows W. to Irish Sea nr. pt. of Preston; 120 km long.

Ribe, mkt. t., Jutland, **S. Denmark**; admin. ctr. of R. prov.; impt. mediaeval c.; Romanesque cath.; many fine bldgs.; p. (est. 1970) 8,224.

Ribeirão Prêto, t., São Paulo st., **Brazil**; mkt. in rich agr. a., coffee, cotton, sugar; p. (1970) 190,897.

Riberalta, R. pt., Colonia terr., **Bolivia**; on R. Beni above rapids; collecting ctr. for wild rubber; p. c. 7,000.

Richard's Bay, Natal, **S. Africa**; new pt. to supplement congested Durban; on natural harbour; silting problem but designed for bulk carriers; plans to attract ass. industl. development.

Richborough, pt., Kent, **Eng.**; at mouth of R. Stour; Caesar's ch. pt., Roman remains; pt. has been privately redeveloped; chemicals, antibiotics.

Richmond, t., North Yorks., **Eng.**; at E. foot of Pennines on R. Swale; mkt. t., agr. tr.; 14th cent. grammar school; Norman cas.; p. (1971) 7,245.

Richmond, c., Cal., **USA**; deepwater pt.; oil refining; car assembly, chemicals, electronics; p. (1970) 79,043.

Richmond, c., cap. of Va., **USA**; on falls on R. James; pt. at head of navigation; financial, and tr. ctr.; tobacco inds., and mkt.; chemicals, iron and steel; p. (1970) 248,074 (c.), 515,586 (met. a.).

Richmond-upon-Thames, outer bor., Greater London, **Eng.**; inc. Barnes, Richmond and Twickenham; industl. and residtl.; beautiful park and riverside scenery; p. (1971) 173,592. *See also* Kew.

Rickmansworth, t., Herts., **Eng.**; residtl. sub. of London; p. (1971) 29,510.

Rideau Canal, Ont., **Canada**; from Ottawa R. at Ottawa to Kingston on L. Ontario; 211 km long.

Riesa, t., Dresden, **E. Germany**; R. pt. on Elbe R. nr. Meissen; steel, rubber; p. (est. 1970) 49,746.

Riesengebirge, mtn. range, between Silesia (Poland) and Bohemia (ČSSR); highest peak Schneekoppe (Czech Sněžka, Polish Sniezka), 1,604 m.

Rieti, Latium, **Italy**; an anc. Sabine c. with mediaeval townscape, in fertile Apennine basin; route ctr. and cap. of R. prov.; chemicals, sugar refinery, textiles; p. (1969) 39,108.

Riff or **Rif**, mtns., **Morocco**, N.W. Africa; extend along N. African cst. for 320 km from Straits of Gibraltar; inaccessible and economically unattractive, terr. of semi-nomadic tribes; rise to over 2,100 m in many places.

Riga, cap. of Latvian SSR, **USSR**; Baltic pt.; exp. wheat, flax, hemp, dairy produce; industl. ctr., diesel rly. engin., furniture; univ.; local bathing beaches; p. (1970) 733,000.

Rigi, mtn., nr. L. Lucerne, **Switzerland**; famous view-point, reached by a rack and pinion rly.; 1,801 m.

Rijeka-Susak, c., Croatia, **Yugoslavia**; formerly Fiume, ceded to Yugoslavia by Italy after second world war; rival pt. to Trieste on Adriatic Sea; oil refining, shipbldg., tobacco, chemicals; hydroelectric power; p. (est. 1971) 133,000.

Rimac, R., Lima dep., **Peru**; rises in W. cordillera of Andes and flows W. to Pac. Oc.; provides water for irrigation and for c. of Lima; 120 km long.

Rimini, c., Emilia-Romagna, **Italy**; on Adriatic cst. at junc. of Via Emilia and Via Flamina; mkt. for fertile agr. a.; sm. inds.; bathing resort; p. (est. 1969) 115,573.

Ringerike, t., Buskerud, **Norway**; new t. 40 km N.W. of Oslo and inc. former t. of Hönefoss; p. (est. 1970) 28,828.

Riobamba, t., Chimborazo, **Ecuador**; on R. St. Juan; woollens, cotton gds., cement, ceramics; Inca palace ruins; p. (1966) 61,393.

Rio Branco, R., flows *c.* 560 km from Guiana Highlands through **Brazil** to join Rio Negro.

Rio Branco, t., cap. of Acre st., **Brazil**; p. (est. 1968) 70,730.

Rio Cuarto, t., Cordoba prov., **Argentina**; agr. ctr.; p. (1960) 70,000.

Rio de Janeiro, c., spt., S.E. **Brazil**; cap. of Guanabara st., on G. Bay, Atl. Oc.; former fed. cap.; beautiful natural harbour, many fine bldgs., Sugar Loaf mtn., Copacabana beach; flourishing tr. and inds.; mnfs. inc. textiles, foodstuffs, pharmaceutics, china, sheet glass; oil refining; p. (1970) 4,252,009.

Rio de Janeiro, st., S.E. **Brazil**; on Atl. Oc.; consists of cst. plain, central Sero do Mar escarpment, fertile Paraíba R. basin in W.; coffee, sugar, fruit; ctr. of heavy ind.; cement, textiles, sugar refineries at Campos, steel wks. at Volta Redonda; cap. Niterói; a. 42,735 km²; p. (est. 1968) 4,505,938.

Rio de la Plata. *See* Plata, Rio de la.

Rio Gallegos, cap. of Santa Cruz prov., **Argentina**; sm. agr. pt. at mouth of Gallegos R.; refrigeration wks.; p. c. 15,000.

Rio Grande, headstream of R. Paraná., **Brazil;** Furnas dam, Estreito dam for hydroelec. power; 1,040 km long.

Rio Grande, R., flows from st. of Col. through N.M. to G. of Mexico; forms bdy. between Texas, **USA** and **Mexico;** Elephant Butte, Caballo, and Falcon multi-purpose dams; known also as Rio Grande do Norte and Rio Bravo; c. 3,016 km long.

Rio Grande do Norte, st., N.E. **Brazil;** cst. plain rising to S. plateau; climate semi-arid; cotton, sugar, salt, scheelite; cap. Natal; a. 53,038 km²; p. (est. 1968) 1,291,195.

Rio Grande do Sul, st., S. **Brazil;** grassy plains, rolling plateaux; cool climate; stock-raising, meat-processing, wheat, wine, wool; lge coal deposits at São Jeronimo; cap. Pôrto Alegre; a. 267,684 km²; p. (est. 1968) 6,560,504.

Rioja, region, N. **Spain;** upper Ebro valley; famous for wines and orange groves; ch. ctr. Logroño.

Riom, t., Puy-de-Dôme dep., **France;** former cap. of Auvergne; old bldgs. built of lava; p. (1968) 15,467.

Río Muni, terr., **Equatorial Guinea;** former Spanish terr., on cst. between Cameroon and Gabon, inc. offshore Is. of Corisco, Elobey Grande, Elobey Chico; with **Marcias Nguema** forms Equatorial Guinea; equatorial forest; exp. tree prods. of cacao, coffee, hardwoods; ch. t. Bata; a. 26,003 km²; p. (1968) 183,000.

Rion, R., Georgian SSR, **USSR;** flows from Caucasus to Black Sea; lower half navigable; hydroelec. sta. at Kutaisi. (In Greek mythology the R. Phasis of the Argonauts.)

Rio Negro, prov., **Argentina;** in N. Patagonia; irrigated agr. in R. valley, fruits, grain crops; elsewhere stock-raising; cap. Viedma; a. 201,010 km²; p. (1970) 193,848.

Rio Negro, dep., **Uruguay;** livestock fattening from N. Uruguay; grain crops; ch. t. and cap. Fray Bentos; a. 8,466 km²; p. (est. 1969) 48,700.

Rio Tinto, t., **Spain;** at W. end of Sierra Morena 64 km N.E. of Huelva; major world ctr. of copper production.

Riouw-Lingga Archipelago, I. gr., **Indonesia;** S. of Malaya; Bintan lgst. I. where bauxite mng.; pepper and rubber cultivation; a. 5,905 km²; p. (1961) 278,966.

Ripley, mkt. t., Derbys., **Eng.;** 11 km N.E. of Derby; coal, iron, heavy engin., bricks, agr. implements; p. (1971) 17,825.

Ripon, c. North Yorks., **Eng.;** on R. Ure; cath.; old mkt. square; old custom of wakeman; tourism; p. (1971) 10,987.

Ripponden, t., West Yorks., **Eng.;** nr. Halifax; p. (1971) 4,782.

Risca, t., Gwent, **Wales;** on R. Ebbw; former coal-mng. dist.; limestone quarrying; bricks, plastics; p. (1971) 15,799.

Risdon, t., Tasmania, **Australia;** oldest settlement in Tasmania, opposite Hobart; electrometallurgy.

Rishton, t., Lancs., **Eng.;** at N. foot of Rossendale Fells, 6 km N.E. of Blackburn; p. (1971) 6,010.

Rive-de-Gier, t., Loire dep., **France;** on R. Gier, nr. Lyons; coal mng., iron and steel, glass; p. (1968) 16,855.

Rivera, dep., **Uruguay;** on Brazilian border; noted for cattle and sheep ranches; cap. R.; a. 9,824 km²; p. (est. 1969) 80,700.

Rivera, t., cap. of R. dep., **Uruguay;** on Brazilian frontier opposite Santa Ana; agr. mkt.; p. (1964) 40,000.

Riverina, pastoral cty., N.S.W., **Australia;** between Lachlan-Murrumbidgee and Murray Rs.; sheep, agr. with irrigation; gold, coal; ch. ts., Wagga Wagga, Albury; a. 68,894 km².

River Rouge, t., Mich., **USA;** ctr. of Ford car mnf.; many heavy inds.; rapidly growing t. p. (1970) 15,947.

Riverside, t., Cal., **USA;** ctr. for citrus fruit packing and tr.; resort; p. (1971) 139,217.

Riviera, the belt of cst. between the Alps and the Mediterranean from Spezia to Hyères, **France** and **Italy;** picturesque scenery, sheltered, mild climate; fashionable health resorts.

Riyadh, t., cap. of **Saudi Arabia;** 368 km inland from Persian G.; palace; univ.; route and tr. ctr., linked by rail with pt. of Zahran; p. (est. 1965) 225,000.

Rizaiyeh (Urmia), c., cap. of Azerbaijan prov., **Iran;** nr. L. Urmia; comm. ctr.; birthplace of Zoroaster; p. (1966) 110,749.

Rizal, prov., central Luzon, **Philippines;** rapidly growing prov. in fertile Central Plain; new inds. developing; cap. Pasig; a. 2,049 km²; p. (1970) 2,781,081.

Rize, t., **Turkey;** nr. Trabzon, on Black Sea; ctr. of Turkish tea inds.; p. (1965) 27,069.

Road Town, spt., Tortola; cap. of the **Brit. Virgin Is.;** tr. in fish, poultry; p. (1960) 900.

Roanne, t., Loire dep., **France;** on R. Loire; château ruins; textiles; p. (1968) 54,748.

Roanoke, R., Va., and N.C., **USA;** flows into Albemarle Sound; hydroelec. power; 656 km long.

Roanoke, c., S.W. Va., **USA;** between Blue Ridge and Allegheny mtns.; rly. junc.; engin. p. (1970) 90,955 (c.), 179,352 (met. a.).

Roanoke I., off cst. N.C., **USA;** attempted settlement of colony by Raleigh.

Roaring Creek, Belize, Central America; site of new cap. 80 km inland, at junc. of W. highway with Hummingbird highway.

Robben I., at entrance of Table Bay, Cape Prov., **S. Africa;** penal settlement and former leper colony.

Robin Hood's Bay, v., North Yorks., **Eng.;** picturesque site in inlet; tourism, fishing.

Robson, Mt., Canada; on B.C. and Alberta border; alt. 3,956 m; in Nat. Park.

Rocha, dep., **Uruguay;** borders Atl. Oc.; a. of cattle and sheep rearing; cap. R.; a. 11,085 km²; p. (est. 1969) 57,800.

Rochdale, t., Gtr. Manchester, **Eng.;** at S. foot of Rossendale Fells, on R. Roch; textiles, engin. asbestos; co-operative movement started here 1844; p. (1971) 91,344.

Rochefort, t., Charente-Maritime dep., **France;** fishing pt.; former impt. naval base; p. (1968) 34,780.

Rochelle, La, t., cap. of Charente-Maritime dep., **France;** on Bay of Biscay; fishing pt.; shipbldg.; pt. tr. declining; p. (1968) 75,498.

Rochester, c., Kent, **Eng.;** on R. Medway, adjoining Chatham; cath., cas.; aeronautical, elec. and mechanical engin., paint, varnish, cement; p. (1971) 55,460.

Rochester, t., Minn., **USA;** famous for Mayo clinic, and Mayo medical research ctr.; p. (1970) 53,776.

Rochester, c., N.Y., **USA;** on Genesee R.; univ.; cameras, films, optical instruments, thermometers, electronic equipment; hydroelec. power; p. (1970) 293,695 (c.), 875,636 (met. a.).

Roche-sur-Yon, La, t., cap. of Vendée dep., **France;** on R. Yon; built by Napoleon I; p. (1968) 38,249.

Rock, R., Wis., Ill., **USA;** formerly home of native Indians; focus of white settlement since 1830; 456 km long.

Rockall, sm. I., **Atl. Oc.;** lies 320 km W. of Outer Hebrides; forms hgst. part of submarine bank which forms gd. fishing-ground; uninhabited; annexed by Britain 1955; formally incorporated into Inverness-shire (1972) to ensure control of suspected oil and natural gas deposits; rock samples aged 1,000 million years place it with some Canadian rocks.

Rockall Deep, submarine trench, **N. Atl. Oc.;** between N.W. Ireland and Rockall I.; suspected oil and natural gas reserves.

Rockford, c., Ill., **USA;** serves agr. dist.; agr. machin., machin. tools; p. (1970) 144,707 (c.), 269,829 (met. a.).

Rockhampton, t., pt., Queensland, **Australia;** on R. Fitzroy; comm. cap. of central Queensland; meat-preserving; fruit-canning; cotton-ginning; rly. wks.; p. (1972) 48,188.

Rock Island, c., Ill., **USA;** on R. Mississippi; former site of US arsenal; agr. machin., timber and agr. processing; p. (est. 1969) 52,000.

Rocky Mount, t., N.C., **USA;** ctr. of tobacco tr. and processing; p. (1970) 34,284.

Rocky Mtns., vast mtn. chain, **N. America;** extend from Alaska, through Canada, USA to Mexico; made up of several parallel ranges separated by intermontane basins and plateaux; barrier to spread of settlers to W. cst. in 19th cent.; climatic barrier; extensive snow and glacier fields in N.; dry, desert landscapes in S.; many Nat. Parks; sparse p.; hydroelectric

power; hgst. peak Mt. Logan (6,054 m); length 5,120 km.
Rodez, t., cap. of Aveyron dep., France; on R. Aveyron; cath.; woollens; p. (1968) 23,328.
Rodopi (Rhodope) Mtns., range S. **Bulgaria**; rise to 3,100 m.
Rodosto. *See* **Tekirdag.**
Rodriguez, I., Brit. dependency of **Mauritius**, Indian Oc.; 560 km N.E. of Mauritius; mainly agr. and fishing; cap. Port Mathurin; a. 109 km²; p. (est. 1968) 20,000.
Roermond, t., Limburg prov., **Neth.**; on R. Maas; minster; textiles; p. (1968) 37,011.
Roeselare. t., W. Flanders **Belgium**; on R. Lys, nr. Kortrijk, textile ctr.; p. (1968) 40,091.
Rogerstone, t., Gwent, **Wales**; on R. Ebbw; lge. aluminium wks.
Rohtak, t., Haryana, **India**; N.W. of Delhi; p. (1971) 124,755.
Roissy-en-France; 26 km N.E. of Paris, **France**; site of new Charles de Gaulle airpt.
Roman, t., **Romania**; on R. Moldava; cath.; agr. processing; p. (est. 1970) 43,188.
Romania (Rumania), Socialist Rep. of, S.E. **Europe**; bounded by USSR, Hungary, Yugoslavia, Bulgaria, and Black Sea; Carpathian mtn. arc., Transylvanian Alps, wide Walachian plain, Moldavian plateau; drained by Danube and its tribs.; climate predominately continental with cold winters and hot summers; since second world war transformation of economy from agr. to industl. basis, although agr. still impt., contributing many exps., especially timber, wine, fruit; major pt. Constanta on Black Sea; oilfields at Ploiesti; cap. Bucharest; ch. tr. partners USSR and E. Europe; Danube used for navigation; Iron Gates power and navigation system being constructed in co-operation with Yugoslavia; tourism from W. Europe and N. America encouraged; a. 237,428 km²; p. (1970) 20,040,000.
Rome (Roma), cap of **Italy**, and of Latium and Rome prov.; on R. Tiber, 24 km from sea; in Roman legend founded by Romulus 753 B.C.; once cap. of anc. Roman empire; inc. Vatican c., ctr. of Roman Catholic Church; situated on original "seven hills," and along the R.; leading cultural ctr.; St. Peter's church, Colosseum, Pantheon; univ.; admin. ctr.; tourism; created cap. of United Italy 1871; p. (est. 1970) 2,778,872.
Romford. *See* **Havering.**
Romney Marsh, coastal marsh, Kent, **Eng.**; formed by blocking of R. Rother by shingle spit of Dungeness which extends from Rye to Hythe; largely drained; pastures for special Romney Marsh breed of sheep; a. 129 km².
Romsey, t., Hants., **Eng.**; on R. Test, 14 km N.W. of Southampton; mkt. ctr.; Norman abbey; p. (1971) 10,057.
Ronaldshay, North, most N. of **Orkney Is., Scot.**; p. (1971) 134.
Ronaldshay, South, most S. of **Orkney Is. Scot.**; p. (1971) 991.
Roncesvalles, mtn. pass in Pyrenees, Navarre, **Spain**; 32 km N.E. of **Pamplona**; **defeat and** death of Roland 778.
Ronda, t., Málaga, Spain; in **Andalusia**; anc. Moorish t., divided by deep gorge crossed by bridge; p. (1970) 30,080.
Rondônia, fed. terr., Brazil; on Bolivian border; forest covered; forest prods.; nomadic Indian tribes; cap. Pôrto Velho; a. 243,071 km²; p. (est. 1968) 116,233.
Rønne, t., Denmark; cap. of Bornholm I., fish. pt.; shipyards, ceramics; p. (est. 1970) 12,440.
Ronse (Renaix), t., Belgium; nr. Ghent; textile ctr.; p. (1968) 25,255.
Roodepoort-Maraisburg, t., Transvaal, **S. Africa**; ctr. Witwatersrand goldfields; p. (1970) 114,191.
Roosendaal, t., S.W. of N. Brabant, **Neth.**, sugar-refining; p. (1968) 45,038.
Roosevelt Dam (1903–11), Arizona, **USA**; on R. Salt in canyon E. of Phoenix on edge of Col. plateau; used for irrigation and hydroelectric power; part of Salt river project.
Roquefort-sur-Soulzon, t., S.E. Aveyron, **France**; caves in limestone cliffs used for ripening cheese; p. (1968) 1,349.
Roraima, mtn., at junc. of boundaries of Brazil, **Guyana**, and **Venezuela**; 2,852 m, hgst point of Guiana Highlands.
Roraima (Rio Branco), fed. terr., **Brazil**; under-developed rain forest; cap. Boa Vista; a. 214,320 km²; p. (est. 1968) 41,344.
Rosa, Monte, Pennine Alps, Swiss-Italian border; alt. 4,637 m.
Rosario, t., Santa Fé, **Argentina**; second t. of rep.; R. pt. on Paraná R.; agr.-processing, iron and steel, lt. inds.; univ., cath.; p. (1970) 810,840 (met. a.)
Roscommon, co. t., Roscommon, **R.o.I.**; mkt.; cas., priory; p. (1966) 1,659.
Roscommon, inland co., Connaught, **R.o.I.**; extensive peat bog and Ls.; pastoral agr., cap. R.; a. 2,458 km²; p. (1966) 56,130.
Roscrea, mkt. t., Tipperary and Offaly, **R.o.I.**; on Little Brosna R.; p. (1966) 3,510.
Rosetta (Rashid), t., Lower **Egypt**; nr. Rosetta mouth of Nile; Rosetta stone found nearby gave key to Egyptian hieroglyphs; p. (1966) 36,700.
Roskilde, t., spt., Sjaelland, **Denmark**; former cap.; cath. contains tombs of kings; admin. ctr. of R. prov.; p. (est. 1970) 39,984.
Ross and Cromarty, former co., l. gov. dist. Highland Reg.; **Scot.**; extends from N. Sea to Atl. Oc.; most of a. over 300 m, lake-covered; cattle breeding, fishing, tourism; a. 4,999 km²; p. (1971) 34,805.
Rossendale Fells (or Forest), upland, S.E. Lancs./Gtr. Manchester, **Eng.**; extension of Pennines between Rs. Mersey and Ribble; millstone grit moorland used for reservoirs; alt. mainly above 360 m.
Ross Dependency, Antarctica; N.Z. sector; inlet of Ross Sea; a. 414,400 km²; p. (1961) 198.
Rosslare, spt., Wexford, **R.o.I.**; on extreme S.E. of Ireland; steamer connections to Fishguard (Wales).
Ross-on-Wye, t. Hereford and Worcs., **Eng.**; agr.-processing; mkt., tourism; p. (1971) 6,399.
Ross Sea, sea extending to 85° S. in Antarctic.
Rostock, c., cap. of R. dist., **E. Germany**; pt. nr. Baltic cst., outport of Warnemünde; shipbldg., fish-processing, chemicals; univ.; mediaeval t.; p. (est. 1969) 193,699.
Rostov, c., **RSFSR**; pt. on R. Don, nr. Azov Sea (Black Sea); one of Russia's finest and oldest cs.; ctr. of agr. dist.; grain mkt.; agr.-processing; univ.; p. (1970) 789,000.
Rosyth, t., Dunfermline, **Scot.**; naval dockyard.
Rothamsted, v., Herts. **Eng.**; in Chiltern Hills, S. of Harpenden; world-famous agr. research sta.
Rother, R., Derbys. and South Yorks., **Eng.**; flows to R. Don at Rotherham; 34 km long.
Rother, R., East Sussex and Kent, **Eng.**; rises in the Weald, flows S.E. into English Channel at Rye; 50 km long.
Rotherham, t., South Yorks., **Eng.**; on R. Don, 6 km N.E. of Sheffield; iron, steel, wire, springs, glass; p. (1971) 84,646.
Rothes, burgh, Moray, **Scot.**; on R. Spey 19 km S.E. of Elgin; p. (1971) 1,204.
Rothesay, royal burgh, Argyll and Bute,, **Scot.**; on E. cst. of I. of Bute in F. of Clyde; tourism; p. (1971) 6,595.
Rothwell, t., Northants, **Eng.**; 5 km N.W. of Kettering; footwear; p. (1971) 4,762.
Rothwell, t., West Yorks., **Eng.**; on R. Aire, 5 km S.E. of Leeds; coal-mng. ctr., engin.; p. (1971) 28,353.
Rotorua, leading spa of **N.Z.**; on volcanic plateau, Auckland, N.I.; hot springs; p. (1971) 31,230.
Rotterdam, c., spt., **Neth.**; Europe's lgst spt., on Nieuwe Maas, part of Rhine-Maas-Scheldt delta; linked to outport Europort (*q.v.*) by New Waterway; serves hinterland of Rhine valley and central Europe; processing of imports, especially oil refining and petrochemical inds.; badly damaged in second world war; p. (est. 1969) 692,915 (c.), 1,060,448 (met. a.).
Roubaix, t., Nord dep., France; nr. Lille; on Roubaix canal close to Belgian frontier; major textile ctr., especially for woollens; p. (1968) 114,547.
Rouen, c., Seine-Maritime dep., **France**; gr. R. pt., 125 km up R. Seine; oil refining, textiles, chemicals; cath.; Joan of Arc burned here; birthplace of Corneille and Flaubert; badly damaged in second world war; p. (1968) 120,471 (c.), 369,793 (met. a.).
Rourkela, t., Orissa, **India**; W. of Jamshedpur; p. (1971) 125,426 (c.), 172,502 (met. a.).
Rousay, Orkney Is., **Scot.**; p. (1971) 256.

Roussillon, former prov., **S. France**; now dep. of Pyrénées-Orientales; irrigated by many sm. streams; olives, wine, fruit; historical cap. Perpignan.
Rouyn, t., Quebec, **Canada**; at end of L. Abitibi; copper-mng. ctr.; p. (1966) 18,581.
Rovaniemi, t., **Finland**; on Kemi R.; timber and saw mills; p. (1968) 27,832.
Rovereto, t., S. Tyrol, **Italy**; on R. Adige; leather, paper, cottons; cas.; p. (est. 1968) 28,015.
Rovigo, prov., Venetia, **Italy**; part of N. Italian plain extending to Adriatic; impt. agr. dist.; cap. R.; a. 218 km²; p. (1969) 225,161.
Rovigo, t., cap. of R. prov., **Italy**; on R. Adige, cath., cas. ruins, palace; p. (1969) 48,702.
Rovno, c., cap. of R. oblast, Ukrainian SSR, **USSR**; rly. junc.; industl. ctr.; ruins of mediaeval palace; p. (1970) 116,000.
Roxburgh, former co., **S. Scot.**; sheeprearing hilly cty. with wool-based inds.; now forms l. gov. dist. in Borders Reg.; a. 1,538 km²; p. (1971) 35,865.
Royal Leamington Spa. *See* Leamington.
Royal Oak, t., Mich., **USA**; residtl.; Detroit zoological park here; p. (1970) 86,238.
Royston, mkt. t., Herts., **Eng.**; at N. foot of E. Anglian Heights, 11 km N.E. of Baldock; p. (1971) 8,272.
Royston, t., South Yorks., **Eng.**; in coal-mng. dist.; p. (1971) 8,839.
Royton, t., Gtr. Manchester, **Eng.**; 6 km N.E. of Manchester; textiles; p. (1971) 20,319.
Ruanda-Urundi. *See* Rwanda and Burundi.
Ruapehu, highest mtn., N.I., **N.Z.**; volcanic peak at S. extremity of central volcanic dist.; alt. 2,798 m.
Rubicon, R., central **Italy**; flows to Adriatic; crossed by Julius Caesar and his armies 49 B.C.; has been identified with the Fiumicino or the Uso. There is also a R. Rubicon (It. Rubico) a few m. N. of Rimini and S. of Cervia.
Rubtsovsk, t., W. Siberia, **RSFSR**; agr. engin.; p. (1970) 145,000.
Ruby Mines, dist., Mandalay, Upper **Burma**; hilly region of Shan plateau, once famous for rubies.
Ruda Slaska, t., Katowice, **Poland**; coal-mng. ctr.; iron and steel wks.; p. (1970) 142,400.
Rudnyy, t., Kazakh SSR, **USSR**; new t. 48 km S.W. of Kustanay; iron-ore mng. and dressing plant supplying Magnitogorsk; p. (est. 1969) 97,000.
Rudolf, L., N.W. **Kenya**; in Great Rift Valley; a. 9,065 km²; ctr. of semi-arid region.
Rudolph I., N. of Franz Josef Land, **Arctic Oc.**; Russian naval base; met. sta.
Rudolstadt, t., **E. Germany**; on R. Saale, in former st. of Thuringia; seat of counts of Schwarzburg-Rudolstadt (1584–1918); tourism; porcelain; p. (est. 1970) 31,539.
Rueil Malmaison, sub. of Paris, **France**; château; tomb of the empress Josephine; p. (1968) 62,933.
Rufiji, R., **Tanzania**; E. Africa; flows to Indian Oc.; 720 km long.
Rufisque, t., **Senegal**; sm. spt. nr. Dakar; growing industl. ctr. for consumer gds.; p. (est. 1967) 60,000.
Rugby, mkt. t., Warwicks, **Eng.**; on R. Avon, 18 km E. of Coventry; famous public school; elec. and gen. engin., motor and aircraft patterns; p. (1971) 59,372.
Rugeley, mkt. t., Staffs., **Eng.**; on R. Trent, 14 km S.E. of Stafford; coal, iron, tanning; expanded t.; p. (1971) 22,234.
Rügen, I., **E. Germany**; in Baltic Sea, off Stralsund; ch. t. Bergen; pt. Sassnitz, terminus of train ferry; steamer services to Trelleborg, Sweden.
Ruhr, industl. dist., **W. Germany**; lies to E. of R. Rhine, on either side of R. Ruhr; rich coalfield; impt. iron and steel, heavy engin. inds. based on local coal and iron ore from Luxembourg, Spain, Sweden; water communications to N. Sea along R. Rhine and Dortmund–Ems Canal; ch. ts. Essen, Duisburg, Düsseldorf, Dortmund, Bochum.
Ruhr, R., **W. Germany**; trib. of Rhine; flows S. of Ruhr conurb.; 232 km long.
Ruislip-Northwood. *See* Hillingdon.
Rukwa, L., **E. Africa**; between L. Tanganyika and L. Malawi in the rift valley; 48 km by 19 km, a. increasing.
Rum, I., Inner Hebrides, Lochaber, **Scot.**; nature reserve, highland ecology; a. 168 km².
Rumaila, **Iraq**; oilfield; pipeline links to the Zubair–Fao system.
Rumania. *See* Romania.
Rum Jungle, N.T., **Australia**; 112 km S.E. of Darwin; uranium mng.; silver, lead and copper deposits.
Runcorn, t., Cheshire **Eng.**; on S. side of Mersey estuary; new t. (1964); chemicals; pipeline carrying petrochemical feedstocks from Teesside; new Runcorn–Widnes bridge over Mersey and Manchester Ship Canal opened 1961 (lgst. span arch in Europe); p. of new t. (est. 1970) 48,213.
Rungis, Paris, **France**; site of major new mkt. to replace Les Halles; nr. Orly airpt.
Ruse, t., **Bulgaria**; on R. Danube, opposite Giurgiu in Romania; univ.; Roman t.; agr. processing; p. (1969) 142,894.
Rushden, t., Northants., **Eng.**; 5 km E. of Wellingborough; shoes; p. (1971) 20,156.
Rüsselsheim, t., **W. Germany**; impt. car factory; p. (est. 1969) 55,373.
Russian Soviet Federated Socialist Republic (RSFSR), constituent rep., **USSR**; lgst. rep. by a. and p.; economic development; inds. centred on Leningrad and Moscow with new inds. being developed in Urals and Kuznetz basin; extends from Baltic to Pac. Oc. (8,000 km), from Arctic to Caspian Sea (4,000 km); part of N. European plain in W. and Siberian plain in E., separated by Ural mtns.; major Rs. Volga, Don, Ob, Yenisey, Lena, Amur; gr. variety in climate and p. density; major agr. region for wheat, sugar-beet, livestock; vast mineral deposits have aided economic growth; oil around Volga valley; metallic ores from Urals and Black Sea; hydroelectric power from Volga, Yenesey, and Ob Rs.; cap. Moscow; a. 16,838,885 km²; p. (1970) 130,090,000.
Rustavi, t., Georgian SSR, **USSR**; new t. 32 km S.E. Tbilisi; iron and steel; lge. metallurgical plant; p. (est. 1969) 102,000.
Rustenburg, t., Transvaal, **S. Africa**; on N.W. edge of High Veld, 96 km W. of Pretoria; local mkt. for agr. produce; agr.-processing; p. (1970) 52,657.
Rutbah, t., **Iraq**; on oil pipeline from Iraq to Haifa; impt. ctr. on trans-desert routes.
Rutherglen, royal burgh, Strathclyde Reg., **Scot.**; on R. Clyde, S.E. of Glasgow; chemicals, tubes, paper, wire ropes, bolts; p. (1971) 24,732.
Ruthin, t., Clwyd, **Wales**; Vale of Clwyd, 13 km S.E. of Denbigh; p. (1971) 4,331.
Rutland, former Midland co., **Eng.**; sm. co. of 394 km², now part of Leics.
Ruwenzori mtn. range, on **Uganda-Zaire** border; overlooking W. arm of Gt. Rift Valley, midway between L. Mobutu Seso and L. Idi Amin Dada; hgst. peaks, Mt. Margherita (5,123 m), Mt. Alexandra (5,109 m); lower slopes covered in equatorial rain forest, coffee plantations on middle slopes above 1,500 m.
Rwanda, indep. rep., **Central Africa**; former kingdom of Ruanda, part of UN trust terr. of Ruanda-Urundi under Belgian admin. (until 1962); sm., landlocked st., S. of equator, consisting of upland plateau at 1,200 m; mainly subsistence agr.; coffee (ch. exp.), cotton, pyrethrum, cattle; tin-mng. impt.; little ind.; cap. Kigali; a. 26,338 km²; p. (est. 1969) 3,667,000.
Ryazan, c., cap. of R. oblast, **RSFSR**; on Oka R.; food inds., agr. machin., footwear, chemicals; mediaeval architecture; p. (1970) 351,000.
Rybinsk, c., major R. pt., **RSFSR**; on upper Volga; tr. and shipping ctr. since 16th cent.; site of hydroelectric power sta.; shipbldg., engin.; p. (1970) 218,000.
Rybinsk Sea (Rybinsk Reservoir), **RSFSR**; artificial L.; created behind dams on R. Volga and R. Sheksna at Rybinsk; part of scheme to regulate flow of R. Volga and to incorporate it in a vast inland waterway system; opened 1945; a. 3,885 km.
Rybnik, t., Katowice prov., S.W. **Poland**; ctr. of coal-mng. dist.; p. (1970) 43,400.
Rydal Water, L., nr. Ambleside, Cumbria, **Eng.**; adjacent v. contains Rydal Mount, home of Wordsworth.
Ryde, t., I. of Wight, **Eng.**; on N.E. cst.; yachting ctr. and seaside resort; boat and yacht bldg.;

steamer connection across Spithead to Portsmouth; p. (1971) 23,171.

Rye, t., East Sussex, Eng.; at mouth of R. Rother to W. of Dungeness; one of the Cinque pts.; Ypres cas.; tourist ctr.; p. (1971) 4,434.

Ryton, t., Tyne and Wear, Eng.; on R. Tyne, W. of Newcastle; p. (1971) 14,831.

Ryuku Is., archipelago, between Kyushu I., Japan, and Taiwan; ch. t. Naha on Okinawa I.; following second world war Is. S. of Lat. 30° N. occupied by USA; Amami and Tokara grs. returned to Japan 1953; American military installations on Okinawa withdrawn 1972; lge. Is. mtnous., volcanic; sweet potatoes, sugarcane, pineapples; 3 lge. oil refineries; a. 2,196 km²; p. (1969) 977,000.

Rzeszów, c., cap. of R. prov., S.E. Poland; at foot of Carpathian highlands; route ctr.; growing industl. t.; p. (1970) 82,200.

Rzhev, c., RSFSR; on Volga R.; rly. ctr. on main line to Moscow; agr. processing; p. (est. 1967) 59,000.

S

Saale, R., E. Germany; rises in Fichtelgebirge flows N. through Thuringia to Elbe; attractive, well wooded valley; irrigation; hydroelec. power; 360 km long.

Saalfeld, t., Gera, E. Germany; on R. Saale; famous cas., iron-mng.; machin., chocolate; p. (est. 1970) 33,405.

Saarland, *Land*, W. Germany; heavy inds. based on lge. coalfields; drained by R. Saar; cap. Saarbrücken; admin. by League of Nations 1919–35, returned to Germany after plebiscite; economic attachment to France after second world war reunited politically with W. Germany 1957; a. 2,567 km²; p. (1970) 1,127,000.

Saarbrücken, c., cap. of Saarland, W. Germany; on R. Saar, nr. Fr. border; cas.; rich coalfield; iron and steel wks., textiles, leather, paper, oil refining at Klarenthal nearby; p. (est. 1970) 130,765.

Saaremaa (Osel), I., Baltic Sea; at entrance to G. of Riga, Estonian SSR; low plateau, bleak and barren; ch. t. Kingisepp (Kuressaare); a. 2,720 km².

Saarlouis (Saarlautern), Saarland, W. Germany; on R. Saar; coal mng.; wood and metal inds.; founded by Louis XIV; birthplace of Marshal Ney; p. (est. 1967) 36,400.

Sabadell, t., Spain; N.W. of Barcelona; textiles, fertilisers, paper; p. (est. 1967) 145,979.

Sabah, E. Malaysia; attempted secession 1975; formerly N. Borneo; underdeveloped; tropical forest; forest prods., inc. rubber, the major exp.; main pt. Sandakan; cap. Kota Kinabalu; a. 76,112 km²; p. (est. 1970) 656,000.

Sabahiyah, t., Kuwait; new t. being built between Ahmadi and Fahahil.

Sabara, t., Minas Gerais, Brazil; historic c.; museum of gold; p. (est. 1968) 26,464.

Sabine, R., Texas and La., USA; flows through S. Lake (an expansion of the R. 29 km long) to G. of Mexico; 936 km long.

Sable I., off S.E. cst. Nova Scotia, Canada; sandy I., scene of many shipwrecks.

Sacramento, c., st. cap. Cal., USA; on R. Sacramento; shipping and industl. ctr.; rly. wkshps., smelting, meat and fruit packing, flour, lumber, metal prods., rocket and missiles ind.; p. (1970) 257,860 (c.), 803,149 (met. a.).

Sacramento R., Cal., USA; forms N. section of Central Valley project for irrigation, hydroelectric power and flood control; 624 km long.

Saddleback (Blencathara), mtn., Cumberland, Eng.; nr. Keswick; alt. 868 m.

Saddleworth, t., Gtr. Manchester, Eng.; in Pennines, 8 km N.E. of Oldham; woollens, paper mkg., engin.; p. (1971) 20,525.

Saffron Walden, mkt. t., Essex, Eng.; on E. Anglian heights; cas., abbey ruins; saffron crocus once cultivated here; p. (1971) 9,945.

Safi, spt., Morocco; on Atl. Oc.; linked by rail to phosphate deposits at Youssoufia; pottery, fish-processing; resort; p. (1971) 129,100 (t.) 194,030 (met. a.).

Saga, c., cap. of S. pref., Kyushu, Japan; coalmng. ctr., textiles, ceramics; p. (est. 1971) 148,000.

Saganoseki, t., N.E. Kyushu, Japan; on Bungo strait; impt. gold, copper, and silver mines; smelting.

Sagar, t., Karnataka, India; nr. Krishna R. valley; p. (1971) 118,574 (t.), 154,785 (met. a.).

Saginaw, c., Mich., USA; on R. Saginaw; former fur and lumbering region; coal; beans, sugarbeet; various mnfs.; p. (1970) 90,603 (c.), 217,787 (met. a.).

Saguenay, R., Quebec, Canada; trib. of St. Lawrence R.; outlet of L. St. John; used for hydroelec. power; tourism; length *c.* 176 km.

Sagunto, t., Spain; nr. Valencia; integrated steelwks. projected; anc. t., sieged by Hannibal; p. (1970) 47,026.

Sahara, the gr. N. African desert between the Sudan and the Barbary sts., extending from the Atl. to the Nile, inc. Tripoli and Fezzan; a. 16,835,000 km²; numerous oases with ts. and tr. ctrs.; oil pipelines to Algerian and Tunisian csts.; p. (est. 2,500,000), nomadic Arab and Berber tribes.

Saharan Arab Democratic Rep. *See* Western Sahara.

Saharan Atlas, S. range of Atlas mtns. in Algeria; ch. peaks., Jebel Aurès, 2,331 m, J. Aissa, 2,242 m J. Ksel, 2,011 m.

Saharanpur, c., Uttar Pradesh, N.W. India; woodcarving, furniture, agr.-processing inds.; p. (1971) 225,396.

Sahel, region of W. Africa, inc. Chad, Mali, Mauritania, Niger, Senegal and Upper Volta, which suffered severe famine and drought 1972–4.

Saïda (Sidon), t., Lebanon; on Mediterranean, S. of Beirut; terminus of oil pipeline from Saudi Arabia; refinery; p. (1963) 22,000.

Saigon. *See* Ho Chi-minh City.

Saimaa, L. system, Finland; a. of water which forms basin of R. Vuoksi; canal connects with G. of Finland and runs partly through Soviet terr.; a. 1,699 km².

Saingdin Falls, Burma; on Kaladan R.; site of new hydroelec. power sta.

St. Abb's Head, rocky promontory, Berwick, Scot.

St. Albans, c., Herts., Eng.; on N. margin of Vale of St. Albans, 32 km N.W. of London; faces remains of Roman Verulamium across R. Ver; lt. inds., electronics, instrument mkg.; cath.; residtl.; p. (1971) 52,057.

St. Amand, t., Cher dep., France; on R. Cher; Roman remains; new recreational park.

St. Andrews, royal burgh, North East Fife, Scot.; seaside resort; univ.; famous golf course; p. (1971) 11,630.

St. Anthony, waterfalls, on R. Mississippi; USA; predominant factor in site of Minneapolis.

St. Asaph, t., Clwyd N. Wales; on R. Clwyd; cath.; p. (1971) 11,755 (dist.).

St. Austell with Fowey, mkt. ts., Cornwall, Eng.; on S. flank of Hensbarrow; ctr. of Cornwall's china clay ind.; p. (1971) 32,252.

St. Barthelemy, Fr. I., W.I.; dependency of Guadeloupe; cash crops of sugar, bananas, cacao; cap. Gustavia; p. (1960) 2,079.

St. Bees Head, promontory, 4 km N.W. of St Bees, Cumbria, Eng.; freestone quarries, anhydrite.

St. Bernard Pass, Great, on Italian–Swiss bdy., W. Alps; carries main road from W. Switzerland to Plain of Lombardy; 2,477 m a.s.l.; road tunnel (5·6 km) constr. 1958–62 links Cantine de Proz (Valais can., Switzerland) and St. Rhémy (Italy); under tunnel will run projected 416 km pipeline from Genoa to Aigle.

St. Bernard Pass, Little, on French–Italian bdy., W. Alps; links Isere valley with Val d'Aosta; alt. 2,190 m.

St. Boniface, t., Manitoba, Canada; sub. of Winnipeg; meat-packing, petroleum prods.; p. (1971) 46,661.

St. Bride's Bay, Dyfed, Wales.

St. Brieuc, t., cap. of Côtes-du-Nord dep., N.W. France; sm. fish. pt.; iron and steel wks.; cath ; p. (1968) 54,763.

St. Catharines, c., Ont., Canada; on Welland Ship Canal; mkt. for Niagara fruit-growing region; agr. implements, textile, paper and flour mills, vehicle components; resort; p. (1971) 109,636.

St. Chamond, t., Loire, **France**; nr. St. Etienne; ribbons, rayon; rly. wks.; coal mng.; p. (1968) 37,728.

St. Clair, L., **Canada–USA**; part of link between L. Huron and L. Erie; a. 1,191 km^2.

St. Clair, R., **N. America**; flows from L. Huron through L. of St. Clair into L. Erie; forms bdy. between Mich. (USA) and Ont. (Canada); impt. link in Gr. Ls. waterway; length 136 km, depth dredged to 6 m.

St. Clair Shores, t., Mich., **USA**; residtl. sub. of Detroit; p. (1970) 88,093.

St. Cloud, W. sub. of Paris, **France**; fine park; porcelain; p. (1968) 28,560.

St. Cloud, t., Minn., **USA**; on R. Mississippi; granite quarries; st. college; p. (1970) 36,691.

St.-Cyr-l'Ecole, t., Yvelines, **France**; once famous for military school founded by Napoleon; bldgs. destroyed second world war.

St. Davids, t., **Dyfed, Wales**; 24 km S.W. of Fishguard; on site of anc. Minevia; cath., ruins of Bishop Gower's palace (1342); p. 1,595.

St. David's Head, promontory, Dyfed, Wales.

St. Denis, t., N. sub., Paris, **France**; on R. Seine; abbey, burial place of Fr. kings; chemicals., machin.; p. (1968) 100,060.

St. Denis, spt., cap. of Ile de la Réunion (Fr.), Indian Oc.; p. (1967) 85,444.

St. Dié, t., Vosges, **France**; on R. Meurthe; cath.; textile ctr., hosiery; p. (1968) 25,117.

St. Dizier, t., Haute-Marne, dep. **France**; on R. Marne; metallurgy; p. (1968) 39,034.

St. Elias, mtns., Alaska, **USA**; and Yukon, **Canada**; inc. Mt. McKinley (5,780 m); source of world's lgst. icefield outside polar regions.

Saintes, t., Charente-Maritime dep., **France**; cath.; Roman antiquities; suffered in Huguenot wars; agr. implements; earthenware; p. (1968) 26,507.

St. Etienne, t., cap. of Loire dep., **France**; nr. Lyons; in sm. coal basin on edge of Central Massif; famous for firearms; modern inds. inc. engin., dyes, chemicals, textiles, glass; p. (1968) 213,468 (t.), 331,414 (met. a.).

St. Gall (St. Gallen), t., cap. of can. St. G., **Switzerland**; founded around Benedictine monastery (7th–8th cent.); embroidered cottons; p. (1969) 80,200.

St. Gall (St. Gallen), can., **Switzerland**; borders L. Constance, rising to S.; mainly industl.; ch. ind. textiles; cap. St. G.; a. 2,012 km^2; p. (1969) 378,000.

St. George's Channel, Brit. Isles, part of Irish Sea, separating Wales from Ireland.

St. George's, t., cap. of Grenada, **W.I.**; ch. spt.; built around submerged volcanic crater forming St. G. Bay; p. (1970) 7,303.

St. Germain-en-Laye, t., Yvelines, **France**; on R. Seine; outer sub. of Paris; residtl.; popular resort; birthplace of Debussy; p. (1968) 41,190.

Saint Gotthard, mtn. gr., Alps, S. central **Switzerland**; crossed by St. G. pass (2,115 m); rly. passes through St. G. tunnel (14·8 km, max. alt. 1,155 m); road tunnel (10·4 km) under pass Göschenen to Airolo projected; motorways linking pass with Zürich, Basle, and Lugano being built.

St. Gowan's Head, promontory, Dyfed Wales.

St. Helena, I., Brit. col., **Atl. Oc.**; 1,920 km from W. cst. Africa; spt. and only t. Jamestown; Napoleon imprisoned 1815–21, and Boer captives 1900; famous for its wirebird, species of plover peculiar to I.; a. 122 km^2; p. (1967) 4,707.

St. Helens, t., Merseyside, **Eng.**; 19 km E. of Liverpool; connected by canal with R. Mersey; coal, iron, alkali; copper smelting, glass, fibreglass, plastics; p. (1971) 104,173.

St. Helier, spt., Jersey, Channel Is., **Eng.**; resort; cas.; tr. in early vegetables; p. (1971) 28,135.

St. Hyacinthe, t., spt., Quebec, **Canada**; on Yamaska R.; cath.; famous for organs; lt. inds.; p. (1966) 23,781.

St. Ives, t., Cornwall, **Eng.**; at entrance to St. Ives Bay; fishing, holiday resort; p. (1971) 9,710.

St. Ives, t., Cambs., **Eng.**; on R. Ouse, 6 km E. of Huntingdon; borders the Fens; R. Ouse crossed by 16th cent. bridge containing a chapel; p. (1971) 7,130.

St. Jean, t., Quebec, **Canada**; on Richelieu R.; timber, grain exps.; textiles, sewing machines, p. (1966) 27,784.

St. Jérôme, t., Quebec, **Canada**; tourist ctr.; pulp, paper, knitted gds.; p. (1971) 26,131.

St. John, c., spt., N.B., **Canada**; lgst. c. of N.B.; ice-free pt.; lge. dry docks; rly. terminus; impt. inds. inc. sugar- and oil-refining, paper, textiles; p. (1971) 87,910 (c.), 105,227 (met. a.).

St. John, L., Quebec, **Canada**; on Saguenay R.; tourism; a. 971 km^2.

St. John, R., Maine, N.B., **Canada, USA**; flows to B. of Fundy forming section of international boundary; 720 km long.

St. John's, t., cap. of Antigua **W.I.**; pt., airpt.; cath.; ch. comm. ctr. of I.; p. (1963) 13,000.

St. John's, c. spt., cap. of Newfoundland, **Canada**; on E. cst.; first English settlement in America early 16th cent.; gr. tr. in fish with allied inds.; univ., 2 caths.; p. (1971) 86,290 (c.), 129,304 (met. a.).

St. Johns, R., **USA**; drains swamps of central Fla., 21 km from Atl. Oc.; 560 km long.

St. John's Wood, residtl. dist., Westminster, London, **Eng.**; contains Lord's Cricket Ground.

St. Joseph, t., Mich., **USA**; pt. on L. Mich.; ctr. of fruit-growing a.; resort; p. (1970) 11,042.

St. Joseph, t., Mo., **USA**; declining pt. on R. Mississippi; agr. tr. and processing; p. (1970) 72,691.

St. Just, t., Cornwall, **Eng.**; nr. Lands End, 10 km W. of Penzance; former tin-mng. ctr.; p. (1971) 3,573.

St. Kilda, rocky I., most W. of the Hebrides, **Scot.**; 5 km long; bird sanctuary, famous for its wren, a sub-species.

St. Kitts-Nevis, Leeward gr. of Is., **W.I.**; aut. st. in association with Gt. Britain (Anguilla unilaterally seceded from union 1967); sugar, sea island cotton, molasses; a. 262 km^2; cap. Basse-Terre; p. (est. 1967) 58,000.

St. Laurent, t., Quebec, **Canada**; industl. t. on Montreal I., W. of Montreal; p. (1966) 59,479.

St. Lawrence, G. of, Canada; arm of Atl. Oc., partly enclosed by Newfoundland and Nova Scotia; impt. fisheries.

St. Lawrence I., Alaska, **USA**; in Bering Sea; 160 km long.

St. Lawrence, R., **Canada**; major outlet from Gr. Lakes; forms bdy. between USA and Canada; ch. tribs. Ottawa, Richelieu, St. Maurice, Saguenay Rs.; with St. L. Seaway forms a major waterway facing Europe; grain, timber, oil, iron-ore traffic; used for hydroelectric power; total length from source (St. Louis) 3,360 km.

St. Lawrence Seaway, N. America; joint Canada–USA project links head of the Gr. Lakes with Atl. Oc., providing channel 8 m min. depth enabling lge. ocean-going vessels to reach American continent; provides major source of hydroelectric power to industl. a.; opened 1959.

St. Lô, t., cap. of Manche dep., N.W. **France**; built on rocky hill overlooking R. Vire; cath.; p. (1968) 18,615.

St. Louis, t., Ile de la Réunion, Indian Oc.; p. (1962) 7,753.

St. Louis, t., **Senegal**, W. Africa; at mouth of R. Senegal; cath.; former cap.; comm. ctr.; impt. fish. pt.; p. (est. 1969) 75,000.

St. Louis, c., Mo., **USA**; on R. Mississippi 16 km below confluence of Rs. Mississippi and Missouri; two univs., impt. rly. and river junc.; mkt. for furs, livestock, grain, farm prod.; banking and fin. ctr.; varied mnfs.; machin., cars, aircraft, leather gds., beer, chemicals; p. (1970) 607,718 (c.), 2,331,016 (met. a.).

St. Lucia I., aut. st. in association with Gt. Britain, Windward Is., **W.I.**; volcanic, forested, fertile valleys; exp. bananas and other tropical agr. prod.; airpt.; cap. Castries; a. 616 km^2; p. (est. 1968) 108,000.

St. Malo, spt., Ille-et-Vilaine dep., N.W. **France**; on Normandy cst.; cath.; once fortfd.; shipping, fishing, and tourist inds.; p. (1968) 43,722.

St. Martin, I., Leeward Is., **W.I.**; N. part Fr. dependency of Guadeloupe, S. part belongs to Neth. Antilles; divided since 1648; ch. exp. salt; total p. (est. 1969) 11,000.

St. Marylebone. *See* **Westminster, City of.**

St. Mary's I., Scilly Is., Brit. Isles.
St. Maur-des-Fossés, residtl. garden sub. of Paris, Val-de-Marne dep., France; p. (1968) 77,569.
St. Maurice, v., Valais, Switzerland; nr. Martigny; 6th-cent. abbey; once a leading Burgundian t.; p. c. 10,000.
St. Maurice, R., Quebec, Canada; trib. of St. Lawrence R.; used for timber transport and hydroelec. power; 520 km long.
St. Mawes, v., Cornwall, Eng.; on E. cst. of estuary of R. Fal; cas.; holiday resort, fishing.
St. Michael's Mt., castled rock, Cornwall, Eng.; the anc. Ictis; alt. 70 m.
St. Monance, burgh, North East Fife, Scot.; resort; p. (1971) 1,257.
St. Moritz, resort and winter sports ctr., Switzerland; in the Upper Engadine; alt. 1,857 m; p. (1970) 5,699.
St. Nazaire, t., Loire-Atlantique dep., W. France; spt. at mouth of R. Loire, outport for Nantes; growing pt. and industl. ctr.; shipyds., iron and steel, fertilisers, aircraft, oil refining; p. (1968) 64,003 (t.); 110,897 (met. a.).
St. Neots, mkt. t., Cambs. Eng.; on R. Ouse, 16 km N.E. of Bedford; brewing, milling, papermkg.; expanded t.; p. (1971) 15,137.
St. Niklaas, mftg. t., E. Flanders, Belgium; nr. Antwerp; textile ctr., carpets; p. (1968) 48,873.
St. Omer, t., Pas-de-Calais dep., N. France; ctr. of mkt.-gardening a.; textiles, food inds.; cath., abbey ruins; p. (1968) 19,957.
St. Ouen, N. sub. of Paris, Seine-St. Denis dep., France; on R. Seine at base of Butte de Monmarte; metals, chemicals, glues, tanning; p. (1968) 48,886.
St. Pancras. *See* Camden.
St. Paul, spt., Ile de la Réunion, Indian Oc.; p. (1968) 43,129.
St. Paul, c. cap. of Minn., USA; faces Minneapolis across Mississippi; cath.; univ.; ctr. of agr. dist.; agr. mkt. and processing; car assembly, oil refining, electronics; p. (1970) 308,686 (part of Minneapolis met. a.).
St. Paul, I., Indian Oc.; bare volcanic islet rising to 493 m; part of Fr. Southern and Antarctic Terr.; uninhabited.
St. Peter Port, spt., cap. of Guernsey, Channel Is.; exp. fruit, flowers, vegetables; resort; p. (1971) 16,303.
St. Petersburg, c., Fla., USA; resort on Tampa Bay; p. (1970) 213,189 (part of Tampa met. a.).
St. Pierre, t., Martinique I., Fr. W.I.; utterly destroyed and all inhabitants save one by eruption of Mt. Pelée 1902; tourism.
St. Pierre, t., Réunion, Indian Oc.; sm. artificial harbour; p. (est. 1971) 43,808.
St. Pierre and Miquelon, Fr. dep., consisting of 8 sm. Is. off S. cst. of Newfoundland; a. of St. Pierre gr. 26 km²; a. of Miquelon gr., 215 km²; ch. t. St. Pierre, fisheries; p. of St. P. and M. (1967) 5,235.
St. Pölten, t., Lower Austria; nr. Vienna; founded round an abbey; textiles, machin.; p. (1961) 40,112.
St. Quentin, t., Aisne dep., France; on R. Somme; impt. textile ctr.; p. (1968) 66,161.
St. Raphaël, t., Var dep., S.E. France; resort on Fr. Riviera, S.W. of Cannes; marina.
St. Rémy, t., Bouches-du-Rhône dep., France; Roman antiquities.
St. Thomas, t., Ont., Canada; ctr. of agr. dist.; rly. ctr.; lt. inds.; p. (1971) 25,062.
St. Thomas, I., Atl. Oc.; main economic ctr. of USA Virgin Is.; 80 per cent of p. live in pt. of Charlotte Amalie; tourism; p. (est. 1968) 31,867.
St. Thomas I. *See* São Tomé.
St. Trond, t., Limburg, Belgium; impt. fruit mkt.; p. (est. 1969) 21,364.
St. Tropez, t., Var dep., S.E. France; on Fr. Riviera; popular, expanding tourist resort; marina; p. (1968) 6,151.
St. Vincent, C., S.W. Portugal; Spanish fleet defeated by British 1797.
St. Vincent, Gulf of, lge. inlet, S. Australia; penetrates 160 km inland, max. width 56 km; Pt. Adelaide is on E. side.
St. Vincent, I., aut. st. in association with Gt. Britain; one of Windward gr., W.I.; volcanic; exp. bananas, arrowroot from alluvial soils in S.W. which has majority of p.; subsistence agr. on hill slopes; cap. Kingstown; inc. 5 Is. in Grenadines; a. 389 km²; p. (est. 1967) 85,000.
Sakai, sub. of Osaka, Honshu, Japan; industl. ctr., engin., chemicals, textiles, electricity generation; p. (est. 1971) 622,000.
Sakhalin, I., off cst. of Siberia; with Kuriles forms Sakhalin oblast of RSFSR; herring fisheries, coal, naphtha, alluvial gold, oil, timber, natural gas; oil pipelines connect to Komsomolsk and Khabarovsk refineries; a. c. 63,610 km²; p. (1970) 616,000.
Sakashima Is. *See* Ryuku.
Sakura-jima, peninsula, S. Kyushu, Japan; former I. joined to mainland by lava flows; famed for fruit and vegetables.
Sala, t., Västmanland, Sweden; silver mine worked for over 400 years, now to limited extent; lime, bricks; p. (1961) 11,015.
Salado, R., N.W. Argentina; impt. Andean trib. of Paraná R.; 800 km long.
Salamanca, t., Guanajuato st., Mexico; oil refining; ammonia plant; natural gas pipeline to Guadalajara.
Salamanca, t., cap. of S. prov., Spain; on R. Tormes; old univ., 2 caths., many convents; p. (1970) 103,740.
Salamis, I., Greece; opposite harbour of Athens; spt. and ch. t. S.; famous naval battle 480 B.C.; p. c. 20,000.
Salar de Uyumi, windswept, dry, salt flat, S.W. Bolivia.
Salavat, t., RSFSR; in Bashkiria, 144 km S. of Ufa; ctr. of oilfield; glass factory; became t. in 1954; p. (1970) 114,000.
Sala-y-Gomez, barren, uninhabited volcanic I., Pac. Oc.; belonging to Chile, 328 km E.N.E. of Easter I.
Salazar, Mexico; nr. Mexico City; alt. 2,897 m; nuclear reactor for radioisotopes for medical, industl. and agr. purposes.
Salcombe, t., S. Devon, Eng.; mkt.; fishing; resort; p. (1971) 2,471.
Saldanha Bay, inlet on W. cst. C. of Good Hope, S. Africa; whaling, fishing; fish-canning at t. of S.B.; p. (1960) 2,195 (t.).
Sale, t., Victoria, Australia; 205 km from Melbourne; ctr. of lge. agr. and pastoral dist.; food processing, plastics, engin.; p. (1972) 10,404.
Sale, t., Gtr. Manchester, Eng.; residtl. sub. of Manchester; p. (1971) 55,623.
Sale or Salch, spt., Fez, Morocco; former pirate headquarters; fishing, fish-processing, carpets; p. (1960) 75,799.
Salekhard, t., R. pt., N.W. Siberia, RSFSR; on R. Ob; fisheries, collecting ctr. for furs; exp. timber; p. c. 22,000.
Salem, t., Tamil Nadu, India; industl. ctr., rly. junc. in picturesque valley; local iron ore, manganese mng.; mineral processing, textiles; p. (1971) 308,716 (t.), 416,440 (met. a.).
Salem, t., Mass., USA; 24 km from Boston; one of oldest New England ts.; many fine bldgs.; textiles, leather prods., machin., electronics; p. (est. 1969) 40,000.
Salem, t., st. cap. Ore., USA; on Willamette R.; univ.; fruit packing, flour milling and canning; p. (1970) 63,309 (t.), 182,569 (met. a.).
Salemi, t., Sicily, Italy; the anc. Halicyæ; famous Norman cas., terracotta vases; p. (est. 1968) 13,778.
Salerno, c., cap. of Salerno prov., in Campania, S. Italy; on G. of S.; fishing pt. and comm. ctr.; machin., textiles, food processing; univ.; Allied landing 1943; p. (1969) 150,677.
Salford, c., Gtr. Manchester, Eng.; on R. Irwell, adjoining Manchester; inc. terminal docks of Manchester Ship Canal; varied inds.; p. and industl. decentralization; p. (1971) 130,641.
Salgótarján, t., N. Hungary; coal mng., agr. machin., tools, glass; p. (1968) 35,000.
Salina, t., Kan., USA; on Smoky Hill R.; univ.; flour milling, cattle mkt., farm implements; p. (1970) 37,714.
Salinas, t., Cal., USA; comm., tr. and processing ctr. for fertile Salinas valley; birthplace of John Steinbeck; p. (1970) 58,265 (t.), 248,831 (met. a.).
Salinas, R., Cal., USA; rises in US Coast Range, flows N.W. into Bay of Monterey, Pac. Oc.; fertile valley floor irrigated to produce hard and stone fruits, mkt. garden produce (especially lettuce), alfalfa; 166 km long.

Salinas-Grandes, Las, gr. salt marsh region, **Argentina**; provs. Santiago del Estero and Cordoba; dry, no Rs.

Salisbury, t., **South Australia**; varied light inds.; p. (1971) 56,279.

Salisbury (New Sarum), cath. c., **Wilts., Eng.**; on S. edge of Salisbury Plain at confluence of Rs. Avon and Wily; Old Sarum to N. was the Roman Sorbiodunum and present site represents a move (1220) to a more sheltered and better watered a. in valley; cath. pure Early English with tallest spire in Eng. (123 m); ctr. mediaeval woollen ind.; regional ctr. with engin. and food-processing inds.; p. (1971) 35,271.

Salisbury, c., cap. of **Rhodesia**; admin. and industl. ctr. in agr. region with gold and chrome mines nearby; tr. in agr. prods., inc. tobacco; clothing, furniture, fertilisers, machin.; univ., airways ctr.; p. (est. 1972) 477,000 (met. a.).

Salisbury Plain, Wilts., Eng.; chalk upland, N. of Salisbury; Stonehenge; army training a.; a. 777 km².

Salop (Shropshire), non-met. co., **Eng.**; on Welsh border, crossed by R. Severn; fine pastoral cty. with hills and woodland, agr. and dairying; industl. activity at co. t. Shrewsbury; a. 3,489 km²; p. (1971) 336,934.

Salpau Selka, Finland; most S. gravel ridge; forested; winter sports.

Salsette I., India; connected by bridge and causeway with Bombay; popular seaside resort at Juhu; a. 624 km².

Salt R., Arizona, **USA**; rises in Colorado plateau, flows into Gila R. below Phoenix; rich, irrigated fruit growing valley in lower course; many multipurpose schemes in Salt River Valley project; length 384 km. *See also* **Roosevelt Dam.**

Salta, c., cap. of Salta prov., **Argentina**; on R. Salta; picturesque c. with colonial atmosphere, cath.; comm. ctr. for rich agr. a.; p. (1970) 176,130 (met. a.).

Saltash, mkt. t., **Cornwall, Eng.**; on W. side of Tamar estuary; lowest bridging point of Tamar by Brunel's rly. bridge (1859) and toll road bridge; p. (1971) 9,923.

Saltburn and Markse-by-the-Sea, t., **Cleveland, Eng.**; seaside resort; 16 km E. of Middlesborough; p. (1971) 19,562.

Salcoats, burgh, Cunninghame, **Scot.**; on Firth of Clyde 3 km S. of Ardrossan; sm. harbour; hosiery; mainly residtl.; p. (1971) 14,904.

Saltillo, c., cap. of Coahuila st., **Mexico**; comm., industl., and mng. ctr.; p. (1970) 161,114.

Salt Lake City, c., cap. of Utah, **USA**; nr. Gr. Salt L., H.Q. of Mormonism; temple and univ.; agr. comm. ctr. for irrigated a.; meat packing; p. (1970) 175,280 (c.), 556,896 (met. a.).

Salto, c., cap. of S. dep., **Uruguay**; on Uruguay R., nr. Concordia (Argentina); rly. and tr. ctr. for agr a.; citrus fruit, grapes, wine; p. (1963) 57,958.

Salton Sea, L., S. Cal., **USA**; 80 m below sea-level in depression which extends N.W. from head of G. of Cal.; ctr. of inland drainage; a. 699 km². *See also* **Imperial Valley.**

Salvador, spt., cap. of Bahia, **Brazil**; coffee, cocoa, tobacco, hides, castor seed, sisal; oilfield and refinery at Matanipe; p. (1970) 998,258.

Salvador, El, rep., on Pac. cst. of **Central America**; bounded by Guatemala to W. and Honduras to N. and E.; comprises 14 administrative departments; temperate volcanic uplands, hot humid coastal lowlands; comm. economy mainly agr., especially coffee, also developing comm. fisheries and iron and steel ind.; electric power from dam across Lempa R.; well-developed transport system, inc. Pan-American Highway; pt. at Acajutla and airport at Ilopango; member of Central American Common Market; cap. San Salvador; a. 21,331 km²; p. (est. 1975) 4,100,000.

Salween, R., **S.E. Asia**; rises in E. Tibet, crosses Yunnan, descending into Burma to empty in G. of Martaban; many rapids; navigable to Moulmein; hydroelec. scheme; 2,880 km long.

Salzach, R., **Austria**; trib. of R. Inn; 208 km long.

Salzburg, c., cap. of Salzburg prov., **Austria**; on R. Salzach; cath., cas.; birthplace of Mozart; tourist resort; annual music festival; p. (1968) 120,204.

Salzburg, prov., **Austria**; adjoins Bavaria and the Tyrol, on N. slope of E. Alps; pastoral agr.; timber and some mineral wealth; hydroelectric power; cap. Salzburg; a. 7,154 km²; p. (1971) 399,000.

Salzgitter, t., Lower Saxony, **W. Germany**; S.W. of Brunswick; steel, engin., wagon bldg., fertilisers; p. (est. 1969) 117,300.

Salzkammergut, lake dist., **Upper Austria**; saline baths at Aussee and Ischl; tourist region; stock-raising, forestry.

Samar, I., **Philippines**; separated from Leyte by narrow strait; mainly forested mtns.; hemp, rice in lowlands; cap. Catbalogan; typhoons; a. 13,080 km²; p. (1970) 997,336.

Samara. *See* **Kuybyshev.**

Samarkand, c., Uzbek SSR, **USSR**; one of oldest cs. in world, sited in productive oasis on Zeravshan R.; many historical associations and anc. bldgs.; agr. tr. ctr.; food processing; cotton, silk; univ.; p. (1970) 267,000.

Samarra, t., **Iraq**; on Tigris R., N. of Baghdad; holy c. of Shiite sect; p. c. 10,000.

Sambalpur, t., Orissa, **India**; on Hirakud reservoir of Mahandi R.; p. (1971) 64,675.

Sambhar, salt lake, Rajasthan, **India**; exploited on lge. scale; a. 233 km.²

Sambre, R., trib. of R. Meuse at Namur; crosses Franco-Belgian coal basin; part of N. Fr.–S. Belgian waterway system; 176 km long.

Samnan, t., N. **Iran**; in foothills of Elburz mtns.; iron, sulphur ores, petroleum.

Samoa, archipelago, **S. Pac. Oc.**; volcanic mtns., tropical climate; agr., fishing; comprises (1) American Samoa, a. 197 km²; p. (1970) 27,769; (2) Western Samoa, indep. st., cap. and ch. spt. Apia; a. 2,841 km²; p. (est. 1969) 141,000. *See* Western Samoa.

Sámos, I., Aegean Sea, off W. cst. Anatolia, belonging to **Greece**; mtnous., fine climate, fertile soils; wine, tobacco, Med. crops; ch. t. Vathy; a. 466 km²; p. (1971) 41,687 (dep.).

Samothrace, I., Aegean Sea, **Greece**; barren, mtnous.; sparse p.; goats, grain, olives, sponge fishing; a. 184 km²; p. *c.* 4,000.

Samsö, I., Kattegat, **Denmark**; a. 109 km²; p. (est. 1965) 5,852.

Samsun, spt., Trabzon, **Turkey**; on Black Sea cst.; exp. tobacco, grain, timber, wax, wool, skins, copper gds., antimony; p. (1965) 107,510.

San, R., S.E. **Poland**; trib. of R. Vistula; bdy. between Poland and Ukraine; navigable in lower course; 442 km long.

Sana'a, c., cap. of **Yemen Arab Rep**; walled c. at 2,217 m; tr. in silk, cottons, hides, grapes; handicraft inds.; Islamic cultural and educational ctr.; p. (est. 1970) 120,000.

San Andreas Fault, Cal., **USA**; shearing plate bdy. which extends from G. of Cal. to San Francisco; stress liable to cause sudden sharp earthquake as it did in 1906. *See* **F9.**

San Angelo, t., Texas, **USA**; on R. Concho; cattle, wool, mohair mkt.; dairy produce, petroleum, machine-shop prod.; p. (est. 1969) 67,000.

San Antonio, sm. coastal t., **Angola, Africa**; at mouth of R. Zaïre; serves as occasional pt. of embarkation for travellers from lower regions of Zaïre.

San Antonio, spt., **Chile**; nearest pt. for Santiago; holiday resort; agr. prods.; exp. copper; p. (est. 1966) 34,051.

San Antonio, C., most W. point of **Cuba.**

San Antonio, c., cap. of Bexar co., Texas, **USA**; in fertile San Antonio valley; serves farming and livestock a.; oil refining, food processing, meat packing; military installations in a.; warm climate attracts winter tourist tr.; Mexican atmosphere; siege of Alamo (1836); p. (1970) 650,188 (c.), 864,014 (met. a.).

San Bernardino, c., Cal., **USA**; founded and planned by Mormons (1852) rly. ctr.; citrus fruit packing and tr.; p. (1970) 106,676 (c.) 1,122,041 (met. a.).

San Bruno, t., Cal., **USA**; 16 km S. of San Francisco; site of international airpt.; printing, mainly residtl.; p. (1970) 36,254.

San Carlos, t., Luzon, **Philippines**; p. (est. 1968) 165,200.

San Cristóbal, c., cap. of Táchira st., **Venezuela**; at 830 m nr. Colombian bdy.; mng. and comm. ctr.; coffee, cacao, sugar; food-processing, cement; cath.; p. (est. 1970) 156,600.

Sancti Spiritus, t., Las Villas, **Cuba**; comm. ctr

in grazing dist.; tr. in sugar, tobacco; agr. processing; p. (est. 1967) 146,450.

Sandakan, t., Sabah, Malaysia; fine natural harbour on N.E. cst.; exp. agr. prods., timber, rubber; sawmilling, fishing; p. (1960) 28,806.

Sanday, I., Barra Is., Orkney, Scot.; flat, many shipwrecks; agr. fishing; p. (1971) 592.

Sandbach, mkt. t., Cheshire, Eng.; 8 km N.E. of Crewe; salt, chemicals, comm. vehicles; p. (1971) 13,303.

Sandefjord, t., Vestfold prov., S.E. Norway; whaling pt. nr. mouth of Oslo Fjord; shipyds., whale-processing; chemicals; p. (est. 1970) 31,723.

Sandhurst, v., Berkshire, Eng.; 16 km S.E. of Reading; Royal Military Academy, National Army Museum.

Sandia, t., N.M., **USA**; atomic research ctr.

San Diego, c., Cal., **USA**; first Spanish settlement in Cal. 1542; on Pac. cst., 16 km N. of Mexican border; fine natural harbour, naval base; fish-canning, aircraft; comm. ctr. for fruit- and vegetable growing dist,; p. (1970) 675,788 (c.), 1,357,854 (met. a.).

Sandlings, The, S.E. Suffolk, Eng.; a. of glacial sands, forming heathland; difficult agr. conditions.

Sandown-Shanklin, t., I. of Wight, Eng.; on Sandown Bay; resort; p. (1971) 15,807.

Sandringham, v., Norfolk, Eng.; Royal residence since 1861.

Sandusky, c., Ohio, **USA**; on S. cst. L. Erie; tr. in coal, fruit, foodstuffs; paper, farm implements, chemicals; summer resort of Cedar Point nearby; p. (1970) 32,674.

Sandviken, t., Gävleborg, Sweden; impt. steel inds.; p. (1968) 25,497.

Sandwich, t., Kent, Eng.; Cinque pt. at mouth of Stour R.; harbour silted up 16th cent.; mkt., lt. inds.; p. (1971) 4,467.

Sandwich Is., dependency of Falkland Is., Brit. Crown col. S. Atlantic.

Sandy, t., Beds. Eng.; 5 km N.W. of Biggleswade; mkt. gardening; p. (1971) 5,274.

Sandy Hook, peninsula, N.J., **USA**; projects into lower bay of N.Y.; government reservation.

San Felipe, cap. of Aconcagua prov., **Chile**; 72 km N. of Santiago; agr., copper and gold-mng. ctr.; p. (est. 1966) 21,979.

San Felipe, cap. of Yaracuy st., Venezuela; ctr. of agr. dist. producing coffee, sugar and other tropical prods.; p. (est. 1970) 43,402.

San Fernando, N.W. sub. of Buenos Aires, **Argentina**; spt. on Rio de la Plata; industl. ctr., footwear, furniture, fish canning.

San Fernando, cap. of Colchagua prov., **Chile**; agr. mkt. ctr.; p. (est. 1966) 25,271.

San Fernando, t., Bay of Cadiz, S. Spain; pt. has naval arsenal; salt mftg.; much of surrounding marshland now reclaimed; p. (1967) 61,330.

San Fernando, spt., Trinidad, W.I.; on W. cst. 40 km S. of Port of Spain; exp. sugar, asphalt petrol; p. (1970) 37,313.

San Fernando, t., Venezuela; ctr. cattle ranching region of upper Llanos; oil; p. (est. 1970) 44,358.

San Francisco, c., Cal., **USA**; spt. on S. F. Bay; entrance spanned by Golden Gate Bridge; attractive hilly site; cosmopolitan c. with several immigrant quarters; comm. and financial ctr. with many varied inds.; univ.; sudden earthquake (1906) destroyed much of c. (*see* F9); p. (1970) 704,209 (c.), 3,109,519 (met. a.).

Sangihe Is., Indonesia; volcanic archipelago between Kalimantan and Philippines; sago, nutmeg, copra; ch. t. and spt. Tahuna; a. 813 km²; p. *c.* 90,000.

San Gimignano, hill t., Tuscany, Italy; overlooks Val d'Elsa; 13th cent. mediaeval t., preserved as national monument; tourist ctr.; p. (est. 1968) 8,227.

San Giovanni in Fiore, t., Calabria, Italy; agr. ctr. at 1,006 m nr. confluence of Neto and Arvo Rs.; p. (est. 1968) 22,012.

Sangli, t., Maharastra, India; nr. Miraj on Karnataka border; p. (1971) 115,138 (t.), 201,597 (met. a.).

Sangre de Cristo Mtns., part of Rocky mtns. **USA**; name (Span. — Blood of Christ) derives from reddish hue seen at sunset; highest summit Blanca Peak 4,367 m.

San Isidro, t., E. Argentina; N. sub. Buenos Aires; resort.

San Joaquin, R., Cal., **USA**; forms part of Central Valley project for irrigation of farmlands of R. valley; 512 km long.

San José, prov., Costa Rica; bauxite mng. nr. San Isidro del General projected with road to Punta Uvita where sm. pt. will be built; cap. San José.

San José, c., cap. of **Costa Rica**; sited at *c.* 1,160 m in S. J. basin; cath., univ., observatory, theatre, parks; ch. industl. and comm. ctr. of rep.; oil refining, agr. processing; major route ctr., international airport; p. (1970) 436,965 (c.), 1,057,032 (met. a.).

San José, t., cap. of San José prov., **Uruguay**; impt. mkt.; flour-milling; p. (1963) 20,000.

San José, c., Cal., **USA**; in fertile Santa Clara valley; fruit and vegetable canning and processing, chemicals, paper, electronics; p. (est. 1969) 425,000 (c.); (1970) 1,064,712 (met. a.).

San Juan, prov., Argentina; at foot of Andes, gold, copper mng.; cap. S. J.; a. 89,179 km²; p. (1960) 352,000.

San Juan, c., cap. of San Juan prov., **Argentina**; comm. ctr. of agr. a., tr. in wine, fruit, cattle; p. (1970) 224,000 (met. a.).

San Juan, c., cap. of **Puerto Rico**; built in part on I.; major spt. on N.E. cst.; exp. agr. prod. to USA; agr. processing; modern inds. inc. oil refining, cement, metallurgy, pharmaceuticals; cath., univ.; p. (1970) 452,749 (c.) 820,422 (met. a.).

San Juan, R., **Central America**; divides Nicaragua and Costa Rica; plans made for its canalisation, which would give both countries a clear waterway from Caribbean to Pac.; 144 km long.

San Juan, R., Col., N.M., and Utah., **USA**; flows in goose-neck incised meanders; Navajo Dam part of Colorado River storage project, bringing irrigation to Navajo Indian reservation; 640 km long.

San Juan del Norte (Greytown), pt. on Caribbean cst. of **Nicaragua**; silting; sm. exp. of bananas, hardwoods; p. (1963) 599.

San Juan del Sur, spt., on Pac. cst., **Nicaragua**; exp. ctr. for coffee, sugar, cocoa, balsam; p. (1960) 4,223.

Sankt Ingbert, t., Saarland, **W. Germany**; N.E. of Saarbrücken; coal mng.; iron, glass, machin., textiles, leather; p. (est. 1969) 28,818.

Sankt Pölten, t., **Lower Austria**; rly. and industl. ctr.; hydroelectric power sta.; p. c. 41,000.

San Leandro, t., Cal., **USA**; food processing; Portuguese residents have annual religious festival; p. (1970) 68,698.

San Lorenzo, t., **Argentina**; 22 km N. Rosario; lge. chemical wks., oil refining.

Sanlúcar de Barrameda, pt., Cadiz prov., **Spain**; nr. mouth of R. Guadalquivir; wines and agr. prod.; mediaeval cas.; bathing resort; p. (1970) 41,072.

San Luis, c., cap. of S. L. prov., **Argentina**; ctr. of cattle, grain, wine producing dist.; rich mineral deposits in surrounding a.; hydro-electric power sta. and irrigation dam nearby; p. (1960) 38,000.

San Luis Potosí, st., **Mexico**; leading mng. st.; metal smelting, food-processing; cap. San Luis Potosí; a. 63,235 km²; p. (1969) 1,436,300.

San Luis Potosí, t., cap. of San Luis Potosí st., **Mexico**; industl. and comm. ctr.; metallurgy, textiles; cath., palace; p. (1970) 230,039.

San Marino, sm. indep. rep., Italy; in Apennines nr. Rimini; has kept its independence since 4th cent. A.D.; exp. wine, textiles, building stone; cap. San Marino; a. 62 km²; p. (1968) 18,360.

San Marino, t., cap. of San Marino rep.; on slope of Mt. Titano, 19 km. S.W. of Rimini; tourism; p. (1968) 4,150.

San Miguel, c., El Salvador, at foot of San Miguel volcano; sisal-fibre, coffee, cattle, cotton, indigo; cath.; p. (est. 1969) 107,658.

San Miguel de Allende, t., Guanajuato st., **Mexico**; picturesque hilly site; famous art institute.

San Millán de la Cogolla, Spain; oldest (6th cent.) monastic foundation in Spain; in Cárdenas valley (Logrono prov.).

San Miguel de Tucumán, c., cap. Tucumán prov., **Argentina**; on R. Sali; univ.; breweries, saw-mills, flour, sugar; p. (1970) 365,757 (met. a.).

San Nicolas, R. pt., **Argentina**; on Paraná R.; cattle, flour, agr. prod., distillery, steel plant; p. (1960) 55,000.

Sanniya Hor, shallow L., **Iraq**; linked to R. Tigris; acts as flood control reservoir.

Sanok, t., Rzeszow prov., S.E. **Poland**; picturesque site on steep banks of San R.; industl. ctr., comm. vehicles, rubber gds.; p. (1970) 21,600.

San-Pedro, spt., **Ivory Coast**; new pt. (1970) linked with development of timber production in hinterland; p. (planned for 1980) 50,000.

San Pedro, spt., a. of Los Angeles, Cal., **USA**; shipyds., oil refining, fruit canning.

San Pedro de Macoris, spt., **Dominican Rep.**; on Caribbean; exp. sugar, sugar prods.; clothing, soap; p. (1970) 70,092.

San Pedro Sula, t., **Honduras**; ctr. for banana and sugar inds; food processing; p. (est. 1970) 102,516.

Sanquhar, burgh, Nithsdale, **Scot.**; coal mng., brick mkg.; p. (1971) 1,991.

San Rafael, t., W. **Argentina**; comm. ctr. for agr. a.; food processing, meat, wine, fruit; p. c. 46,000.

San Remo, sm. pt., **Italy**; winter resort on Italian Riviera; flower mkt., olive oil, lemons, wine; 12th cent. church; p. (est. 1968) 63,735.

San Salvador (Watling's I.), Bahama Is., **W.I.**; discovered by Columbus 1492, his first sight of the New World; a. 155 km²; p. (1963) 968.

San Salvador, c., cap. of **El Salvador**; stands c. 600 m a.s.l.; ch. comm. and industl. ctr.; food processing, textile and tobacco inds.; univ., observatory; oil refining; liable to earthquakes; p. (1971) 337,171.

Sansanding, t., **Mali**, W. Africa; lge. barrage across R. Niger.

San Sebastian, c., cap. of Guipúzcoa prov., N. **Spain**; spt. on Bay of Biscay, at foot of Mt. Urgull; seaside resort; fishing, textiles, paper, glass; captured by Wellington 1813; p. (est. 1969) 155,346.

San Severo, mkt. t., S. **Italy**; hilltop site, 24 km N.W. of Foggia, Apulia; cath.; wine ctr., cream of tartar, bricks; p. (est. 1968) 52,458.

Santa Ana, c., W. **El Salvador**; second lgst. c. of rep.; coffee, sugar, cattle; Santa Ana volcano nearby; p. (est. 1969) 168,047.

Santa Ana, c., Cal., **USA**; S.E. of Los Angeles; in fruit farming a.; fruit pkg., walnuts, oranges; p. (1970) 154,640 (c.), inc. in Anaheim met. a.

Santa Barbara, c., Cal., **USA**; resort on Pac. cst., picturesque setting, mild climate; p. (1970) 69,631 (c.), 260,299 (met. a.).

Santa Barbara Is., USA; along S. cst. of Cal.; inc. Santa Catalina I., a favourite resort.

Santa Catarina, st., **Brazil**; between Atl. and Argentina; tobacco, manioc, fruit, hogs; impt. coal producer; cap. Florianópolis; a. 95,830 km²; p. (1968) 2,705,394.

Santa Clara, c., **Cuba**; attractive site at over 360 m; agr. and comm. ctr. for sugar and tobacco; decisive victory for guerrilla army of Fidel Castro 1959; p. (1970) 213,296.

Santa Clara, c., W. Cal., **USA**; citrus fruit pkg.; electronics, plastics, chemicals; univ.; p. (est. 1969) 84,000.

Santa Clara Valley, Cal., **USA**; extends S. from San Francisco Bay; intensive fruit-growing under irrigation, prunes; ch. t. San José.

Santa Cruz, c., cap. of S.C. dep., **Bolivia**; alt. 457 m; agr. mkt. for sugar, coffee, rice, cattle; oil refining; international airport; impt. reserves iron ore; univ.; p. (est. 1969), 108,720.

Santa Cruz de la Sierra, t., **Bolivia**; on R. Piray; sugar, flour; distilling; p. (1967) 96,000.

Santa Cruz de Tenerife, pt. on Tenerife I., **Canary Is.**; cap. of S.C. de T. prov., Spain; gd. harbour, oil refinery; exp. agr. prods.; developing resort in attractive a. with mild climate; p. (est. 1969) 163,763.

Santa Cruz Is., volcanic gr., S. Pac. Oc.; part of Solomon Is.; exp. copra.

Santa Fé, c., cap. of S.F. prov., **Argentina**; impt. R. pt. on I. in Salado R.; comm. ctr. for surrounding grain and livestock a.; food processing; univ., cath.; p. (1970) 244,579 (met. a.).

Santa Fé, t., N.M., **USA**; at base of Sangre de Cristo range; oldest capital in US founded by Spaniards 1610; tourist and comm. ctr.; p. (1970) 41,167.

Santa Isabel. *See* **Malabo**.

Santa Maria, t., Rio Grande do Sul, **Brazil**; rly. junc., rly. engin., agr. tr. and processing; p. (1970) 120,667.

Santa Maria de Gerona, Spain; nr. Burgos; nuclear power plant being built.

Santa Marta, spt., cap. of Magdalena dep., **Colombia**; banana pt. on deep bay at mouth of Manzanares R., serving local plantations; p. (est. 1972) 141,300 (c.), 165,500 (met. a.).

Santa Monica, c., Cal., **USA**; W. of Los Angeles; attractive site on Santa Monica Bay; aircraft, plastics, cosmetics; p. (est. 1969) 91,500.

Santander, c., cap. of Santander prov., N. **Spain**; spt. and seaside resort on Bay of Biscay; exp. iron and zinc ore, agr. prods.; heavy inds., shipbldg., oil refining, chemicals; former summer resort of Spanish court; cath.; p. (est. 1969) 133,014.

Santarém, t., Pará, **Brazil**; rubber, cacao, Brazil nuts, sugar; p. (est. 1968) 111,706.

Santarém, t., cap. of Ribatejo prov., **Portugal**; on slope of hill overlooking Tagus R.; Moorish cas.; mkt. for agr. prod.; p. (1970) 57,292.

Santa Rosa, t., cap. of La Pampa terr., **Argentina**; p. (1960) 17,000.

Santa Rosa, t., Cal., **USA**; tr. and industl. ctr. for Somona Valley fruit-growing a.; p. (1970) 50,006.

Santiago, c., cap. of **Chile** and of S. prov.; planned t. ctr. in broad valley of Mapoche R., one of lgst. and most attractive cs. in S. America; cultural, comm., political and financial ctr., focus of routes; univ.; textiles, chemicals, paper, iron and steel; rapidly growing p.; p. (1970) 2,661,920 (met. a.).

Santiago de Compostela, c., Corunna, **Spain**; on R. Sar, surrounded by hills, univ., palace, cath. (with tomb of St. James); famous place of pilgrimage; agr. tr., food processing, tourism; p. (1970) 70,893.

Santiago de Cuba, c., **Cuba**; spt. on S. cst., exp. minerals, agr. prods., sugar, tobacco; oil refining, cigars, soap; cath., univ.; p. (est. 1967) 259,000.

Santiago del Estero, c., cap. of S. del E. prov., **Argentina**; transportation ctr. of Argentine Chaco; agr. tr. ctr., cattle, food processing; p. (1970) 105,209 (met. a.).

Santiago de los Caballeros, t., **Dominican Rep.**; comm. agr. ctr. in fertile a.; food processing, coffee, rice, tobacco; cigars, cigarettes; p. (1970) 155,151.

Santis, mtn., on border cans. St. Gallen and Appenzell, **Switzerland**; alt. 2,506 m, Europe's hgst. television transmitter on summit.

Santo Domingo, c., cap. **Dominican Rep.**; spt. on S. cst., exp. agr. prod.; food processing; 3 univs.; cath.; p. (est. 1975) 705,000.

Santo Tomé de la Guayana (Puerto Ordaz) c., S.E. **Venezuela**; new industl. c. nr. confluence of Orinoco and Caroni Rs.; iron mines, steel, hydroelec. power and aluminium plants in a.; vast industl. complex projected.

Santorine. *See* **Thira**.

Santos, c., spt., São Paulo, **Brazil**; world's ch. coffee pt.; also exp. oranges, bananas, cotton, and industl. prod. from modern harbour; p. (1970) 341,317.

San Vicente, t., cap. of S.V. dep., **El Salvador**; ctr. for coffee, sugar, tobacco; mnfs. leather gds., shawls, hats; p. (est. 1968) 19,314.

São Carlos, t., São Paulo st., **Brazil**; 192 km N.W. of São Paulo; ctr. of coffee-growing a.; textiles, refrigerators, furniture; p. (est. 1968) 73,256.

São Francisco, R., **Brazil**; flows from Minas Gerais prov. to Atl.; navigable for 1,440 km of middle course; used for hydroelectric power at Paulo Afonso falls and Três Marias dam; 2,560 km long.

São Goncalo, t., Rio de Janeiro, **Brazil**; fast-growing t.; p. (1970) 161,392.

São Jeronimo, t., Rio Grande do Sul, **Brazil**; low-grade coal; p. (1970) 36,531.

São João do Meriti, t., Rio de Janeiro, **Brazil**; industl. and comm. ctr.; p. (1970) 163,934.
São José dos Campos, t., São Paulo, **Brazil**; industl. ctr.; cattle; p. (1970) 130,118.
São Leopoldo, t., Rio Grande do Sul, S. **Brazil**; 32 km N. of Porto Alegre; mkt. t.; p. (est. 1968) 53,398.
São Luis, pt., cap. of Maranhão st., **Brazil**; on São Luis I.; noted cultural ctr. in 19th cent.; p. (1970) 167,529.
São Miguel, I., **Azores**; lgst. and most productive I. of archipelago; ch. t. and spt. Ponta Delgada, exp. agr. prods., pineapples; volcanic landscape a tourist attraction; p. c. 170,000.
Saône, R., **France**; rises in Vosges and flows to R. Rhône at Lyons; navigable, canalised; 451 km long.
Saone-et-Loire, dep., **France**; mtnous.; noted vineyards; cap. Mâcon; a. 8,627 km²; p. (1968) 550,362.
São Paulo, st., **Brazil**; on Atl. cst.; major industl. a. of S. America; coffee, cotton, sugar, rice, maize; vehicles, elec. gds., chemicals, textiles, telecomm. equipment, metal-wkg. plants; cap. São Paulo; Santos lgst pt. in Brazil; a. 247,226 km²; p. (est. 1968) 16,631,060.
São Paulo, c., cap. of São Paulo st., **Brazil**; fast-growing c., comm. and industl. ctr. of rep. and leading c. of S. America; vehicles, machin., elec. gds., textiles, pharmaceutics; aluminium refinery; nearby pt. Santos ships rich agr. prod. from hinterland; 2 univs., cath.; p. (1970) 5,186,752.
São Roque, Cape of, Rio Grande do Norte, N.E. **Brazil**; most N.E. point of S. America.
São Tomé, cap. **São Tomé and Principe**; p. (1960) 714.
São Tomé and Principe, former Port. col.; **W. Africa**; volcanic Is. in G. of Guinea; cocoa, coffee; cap. São Tomé; a. 963 km²; indep. achieved as democratic rep. 1975; p. (est. 1969) 66,000.
São Vicente, c., S.E. São Paulo, **Brazil**; first Portuguese settlement in Brazil (1532), on I. off mainland; sub. of Santos; fashionable beach resort; p. (1970) 116,075.
Sapele, t., Benin st., **Nigeria**; S. of Benin; lge. lumber mill and plywood plant.
Sapporo, c., Hokkaido, **Japan**; main t. of Hokkaido; planned t.; univ.; brewing, dairy processing, sawmills; p. (est. 1971) 1,031,000.
Saqqara, v., **Egypt**; necropolis of anc. Memphis; step pyramids; p. (1966) 12,700.
Sarajevo, c., cap. of Bosnia and Herzegovina, **Yugoslavia**; major route ctr., airport; ctr. of Yugoslav Moslems; mosques, caths.; diversified mnfs., metallurgy, elec. prods., textiles, tobacco, pottery; assassination 28 June 1914 of Archduke Francis Ferdinand precipitated First World War; p. (1971) 292,000.
Saransk, c., Mordvinian ASSR, **RSFSR**; 232 km S.E. of Gorki; univ.; elec. equipment, engin., agr. processing; p. (1970) 190,000.
Sarapul, c., **RSFSR**; pt. on R. Kama; radio equipment, machin., footwear, gloves; p. (est. 1967) 91,000.
Sarasota, Fla., **USA**; exp. fruit, veg.; resort; p. (est. 1969) 40,000 (c.), 158,000 (met. a.).
Saratoga Springs, N.Y., **USA**; summer resort at foot of Adirondack mtns., mineral springs; horse-racing; casino; p. (1970) 18,845.
Saratov, c., **RSFSR**; pt. on R. Volga; regional ctr. for agr. prod. of lower Volga valley and oil from Baku; univ.; engin., ball-bearings, textiles, oil refining, sawmilling; p. (1970) 758,000.
Sarawak, st., **E. Malaysia**; mtnous. inland with sparse p.; rubber, sago, pepper grown along cst.; oil; cap. Kuching; a. 121,914 km²; p. (1967) 903,000.
Sardinia, I., aut. region, **Italy**; mtnous., dry climate; fertile Campidano plain with fruit, wines, sheep; zinc and lead mng.; tourism; fishing; major petrochemical complex at Ottana; part of former kingdom of Sardinia belonging to house of Savoy; a. 24,002 km²; p. (1969) 1,495,383.
Sargasso Sea, zone S.W. of **N. Atl. Oc.**; relatively still sea within swirl of warm ocean currents; noted for abundance of gulf-weed on its surface, rich in marine life; named by Columbus.
Sari, c., cap. of Mazandaran prov., **Iran**; p. (1967) 206,463.
Sark, I., **Channel Is.**; 10 km E. of Guernsey; picturesque scenery; tourist ctr.; farming; a. 516 ha; p. (est. 1973) 580.
Sark, R., forms extreme W. bdy. between Scot. and Eng.
Sarnia, c., and pt., Ont., **Canada**; on St. Clair R.; connected to Port Huron by rly. tunnel; oil refineries, petrochemical inds., agr. tr.; p. (1971) 56,727.
Sarno, t., Campania, **Italy**; spa at foot of mtns. on E. edge of fertile Sarno plain; agr. mkt., textile ctr.; cas.; p. (est. 1968) 31,357.
Šar-Planina, **Yugoslavia**; nr. Skopje; impt. chrome deposits; attractive site, ctr. of mtn. tourism.
Sarpsborg, t., **Norway**; on R. Glommen; lgst. pulp and paper concern in kingdom; hydro-electric power sta.; p. (est. 1970) 13,165.
Sarreguemines, t., Moselle dep., **France**; in Lorraine; potteries based on local clay; coal mng.; p. (1968) 24,284.
Sarthe, dep., N.W. **France**; undulating surface; farming, apples, livestock; coal, linen, potteries; cap. Le Mans; a. 6,247 km²; p. (1968) 461,839.
Sarthe, T., **France**; trib. of R. Loire; 265 km long.
Sasebo, spt., Kyushu, **Japan**; ctr. of coalfield; engin., shipbldg.; p. (est. 1971) 262,000.
Saskatchewan, prov., **Canada**; coniferous forests and plains; Rs. Saskatchewan and Churchill; many lge. Ls.; extreme climate; hydroelec. power; gr. wheat prov.; livestock, dairying; oil, copper, uranium, helium plants, furs, fisheries; cap. Regina; a. 651,903 km²; p. (1971) 926,242.
Saskatchewan, R., **Canada**; flows from Rocky mtns. through L. Winnipeg and thence by R. Nelson to Hudson Bay; 2,320 km long.
Saskatoon, c., Saskatchewan, **Canada**; grew rapidly after arrival of rly. (1890); comm. ctr. for grain producing a.; meat packing and tr.; varied inds., cement, oil refining; univ.; p. (est. 1969) 129,000.
Sasolburg, t., O.F.S., **S. Africa**; oil from coal production; gas pipeline to Germiston a. p. (1960) 12,557.
Sassari, t., Sardinia, **Italy**; nr. G. of Asinara; cath., univ., palaces; tobacco and macaroni wks., cheese; p. (1969) 107,308.
Sattahip, pt., **Thailand**; new pt. inaugurated 1967.
Satu-Mare, t., N.W. **Romania**; agr. machin., handicraft inds. based on local prods., food-processing; cath.; p. (est. 1970) 78,812.
Saudi Arabia, kingdom, Arabian peninsula, **S.W. Asia**; mainly desert, agr. in oases and S.W. upland region of Asir; lgst. producer of oil in Middle East; oil sales account for 85 per cent govt. revenue; steel inds. and oil refinery at Jidda, petrochemicals developing at Dammam; Moslem holy cs. Mecca and Medina; cap. Riyadh (royal), Mecca (religious); main pt. King Faisal Port.; a. 2,400,930 km²; p. (est. 1969) 7,200,000.
Sauerland, dist., N. Rhine-Westphalia, **W. Germany**; plateau, alt. from 150–450 m E. of Rhine; agriculturally poor, largely forested; crossed by R. Wupper, with which are associated industl. ts. Wuppertal (textiles), Solingen and Remscheid (cutlery and special steel); supplies hydroelectric power to Ruhr.
Sault Ste. Marie, t., Ont., **Canada**; pt. on St. Mary's R., opposite Sault Ste. Marie, Mich., to which it is connected by bridge; pulp, paper iron and steel; tourist ctr. for L. and forest region; p. (1971) 78,175.
Sault Ste. Marie, t., Mich., **USA**; pt. on St. Mary's R.; opposite Sault Ste. Marie, Ont.; calcium carbide; tourist ctr. for fishing, hunting a.; p. (1970) 15,136.
Sault Ste. Marie Canals ("Soo"), **Canada** and **USA**; twin canals on Canadian and American side of shallow channel linking L. Superior and L. Huron; traversed by all wheat and iron-ore traffic from L. Superior pts.; length (Canadian) 2 km; depth 5 m.
Saumur, t., Maine-et-Loire dep., **France**; on R. Loire, 48 km S.W. of Tours; sparkling wines, brandy; flower, vegetable mkt.; cas.; p. (1968) 23,175.
Sauternes, v., Gironde, **France**; name applied to white wines of dist.

Sava, R., Slovenia, **Yugoslavia**; joins Danube at Belgrade; used for hydroelectric power; agr. in valleys; transport axis; 928 km long.

Savage or Niue, Cook Is., **Pac. Oc.**; under N.Z.; ch. exp. native plaited ware, bananas, copra, and sweet potatoes; ch. pt. Alofi; a. 259 km²; p. (1968) 5,240.

Savaii I., lgst. of Samoan gr., **Pac. Oc.**; volcanic, mtnous., fertile; exp. bananas, copra, cocoa; a. 1,821 km²; p. c. 30,000.

Savannah, c., Ga., **USA**; spt. nr. mouth of Savannah R.; rly., fishing and comm. ctr. for Sea Is., Savannah valley and surrounding plantations; mkt. for naval stores; sugar refining, paper, oil refining, diverse mnfs.; tourist ind. stimulated by mild climate; p. (1970) 114,155 (c.), 182,959 (met. a.).

Savannah, R., **USA**; flows between Ga. and S.C. to Atl. Oc.; used for hydroelectric power; 720 km long.

Saverne, Col de, low pass, N.E. **France**; carries trunk rly. from Paris to Strasbourg and the East between Vosges and Hardt mtns.; gradual approach from W., steep descent to E. into Rhine valley.

Savoie (Savoy), dep., **France**; borders Italy in Savoy Alps; part of former duchy; dairying and vineyards; hydroelectricity forms basis of metallurgical inds.; first Fr. National Park (Vanoise Park); cap. Chambéry; a. 6,188 km²; p. (1968) 288,921.

Savona, spt., Genoa, **Italy**; cath.; iron, shipbldg., glass and tinplate wks.; exp. preserved fruits and tomatoes; imports coal, oil, iron ore; p. (1969) 78,748.

Savonlinna, t., Mikkeli, E. **Finland**; in Saimaa L. region; route ctr.; timber inds.; p. (est. 1970) 17,942.

Sawankalok, t., **Thailand**; impt. teak collecting ctr.

Sawbridgeworth, t. Herts., **Eng.**; on R. Stort, 6 km S. of Bishops Stortford; malting, fruit preserving; p. (1971) 7,083.

Saxham, t. Suffolk, **Eng.**; agr. machin.

Saxmundham, mkt. t., Suffolk, **Eng.**; 29 km N.E. of Ipswich; p. (1971) 1,700.

Saxony, region, **E. Germany**; turbulent political and territorial history, now comprises admin. dists. of Leipzig, Dresden, Karl-Marx-Stadt, Halle and Magdeburg; inc. Erzgebirge in S., Vogtland in W. and N. European plain; drained by N. flowing Rs. Elster, Pleisse, Mulde, Elbe, Neisse, Spree; kaolin deposits basis for porcelain ind. at Meissen; industrialised in 19th and 20th cent. with notable textile ind.; coal mng. nr. Zwickau; inds. concentrated around Karl-Marx-Stadt; cap. Dresden; comm. ctr. at Leipzig; a. 16,996 km².

Sayan Mtns., range of mtns.; between Rs. Yenisey and Angra, **RSFSR**; form part of Sino-Soviet border; mineral resources.

Scafell Pike, mtn., Cumbria, **Eng.**; in N. Pennines; highest in Eng.; alt. 979 m.

Scalby, t., North Yorks., **Eng.**; 5 km N.W. of Scarborough; p. (1971) 8,672.

Scalloway, Shetlands, **Scot.**; on W. cst. of Mainland; the anc. cap.; ruined cas.; fish. pt.

Scalpay, I., off E. cst. of Skye, **Scot.**

Scalpay, I., Harris, Outer Hebrides, **Scot.**

Scandinavia, name given to lge. peninsula in N.W. **Europe**; comprises kingdoms of Sweden and Norway; sometimes inc. Denmark, Finland and Iceland; rugged a. of anc. peneplained rocks; climate varies from arctic (N.) to humid maritime (S.W.); rich in timber and mineral ores, esp. iron and copper; W. cst. waters valuable fishing grounds.

Scapa Flow, strait, N. **Scot.**; between Pomona and Hoy, Orkney Is.; surrendered German fleet scuttled 1919; Brit. battleship *Royal Oak* sunk at anchor 1939.

Scarba, I., Argyll and Bute, **Scot.**; off N. end of Jura, red deer in woods and moorlands.

Scarborough, t., North Yorks., **Eng.**; on E. cst.; seaside resort; cas.; former spa; p. (1971) 44,370.

Scarpanto. *See* **Karpathos.**

Schaffhausen, most. N. can., **Switzerland**; on R. Rhine; pastoral, forested; cereals, fruit, vegetables, wine; hydroelectric power from S. falls on Rhine; cap. S.; a. 298 km²; p. (1969) 73,000.

Schaffhausen, c., cap. of S. can., **Switzerland**; on Rhine below L. Constance; falls to S.W. of c.; hydroelectricity supplies power for electrochemical ind. and aluminium wks.; p. (1969) 38,900.

Schaumburg-Lippe, former st., between provs. of Hanover and Westphalia, Germany, now part of Lower Saxony, **W. Germany**; farming, coal mng.

Schefferville, t., **Canada**; 576 km N. of St. Lawrence estuary and connected to it (at Seven Islands) by rly.; ctr. of iron-ore mines in Quebec-Labrador trough; p. (1966) 3,086.

Scheldt (Dutch Schelde, French Escaut), R., **France, Belgium, Neth.**; rises in Aisne, France, flows to N. Sea forming extensive delta with Rhine (Rijn) and Meuse (Maas) in Netherlands; navigable; 432 km long; network of canals.

Schenectady, c., N.Y., **USA**; on Mohawk R., N.W. of Albany; electrical plants, locomotive wks.; p. (est. 1969) 71,000.

Scheveningen, seaside resort, **Neth.**; 3 km N.W. of The Hague; fish. pt.

Schiedam, t., **Neth.**, on Nieuwe Maas, 4 km downstream from Rotterdam; forms part of Rotterdam–Europort; diverse pt.-based inds.; gin; p. (1968) 82,596.

Schiehallion, mtn., Perth and Kinross, **Scot.**; alt. 1,082 m.

Schio, t., Veneto, **Italy**; at foot of Alps on Leogra R.; woollens, textiles, machin.; p. (est. 1968) 32,176.

Schlei, narrow inlet of Baltic, Schleswig-Holstein, **W. Germany**; 40 km long.

Schleswig, t., Schleswig-Holstein, **W. Germany**; fish. pt. on Schlei inlet; lt. inds.; p. (est. 1969) 33,265.

Schleswig-Holstein, *Land*, **W. Germany**; occupies S. part of Jutland peninsula; a. disputed between Denmark and Prussia in 19th cent.; mainly agr.; many sm. pts.; crossed by Kiel Canal; cap. Kiel; a. 15,664 km²; p. (1968) 2,499,700.

Schneidemühl. *See* **Pila.**

Schönebeck, t., Magdeburg, **E. Germany**; pt. on R. Elbe; metals, chemicals, machin.; p. (est. 1970) 46,146.

Schoonebeek, v., Drenthe, **Neth.**; S. of Emmen; lge. oilfield; p. (1967) 7,473.

Schouten I., W. Irian, **Indonesia**; in Geelvink Bay; p. 25,487.

Schouwen-Duiveland, I., Zeeland prov., **Neth.**; cap. Zierikee; formerly 2 separate Is.

Schuylkill R., Penns., **USA**; flows into Delaware R.; navigable; length 208 km.

Schwäbish-Gmünd, t., Baden-Württemberg, **W. Germany**; at foot of Swabian Jura, E. of Stuttgart; clocks, glass, optical, precious metal and jewellery inds.; mediaeval and baroque bldgs.; p. (est. 1969) 44,134.

Schwarzwald (Black Forest), forested mtn. range, Baden-Württemberg, **W. Germany**; highest peak Feldberg 1,496 m; tourism; famous for clock and toy inds.

Schwechat, t., **Austria**; nr. Vienna; oil refining; pipeline to Trieste; p. (1961) 13,403.

Schwedt, t., Frankfurt, **E. Germany**; on R. Oder; lge. oil refinery; pipeline from Mozyr' (USSR); paper, fertilisers; p. (est. 1970) 34,134.

Schweinfurt, t., Bavaria, **W. Germany**; on R. Main, N.E. of Würzburg; metals, machin., ball bearings, dyes, brewing; p. (est. 1969) 59,402.

Schwelm, t., N. Rhine-Westphalia, **W. Germany**; E. of Wuppertal; metals machin., textiles; p. (est. 1969) 32,969.

Schwenningen, t., Baden–Württemberg, **W. Germany**; clocks, precision instruments, optical apparatus; p. (est. 1969) 34,954.

Schwerin, c., cap. of Schwerin, **E. Germany**; on Schwerin L., surrounded by smaller Ls.; comm. and industl. ctr. of agr. dist.; food processing, engin., furniture; cath., cas.; p. (est. 1970) 96,949.

Schwyz, can., **Switzerland**; mtnous. in S.; forested; dairying impt.; original member of confederation; cap. S.; a. 907 km²; p. (1969) 85,500.

Schwyz, c.,. of Schwyz can., **Switzerland**; tourist ctr. nr. Lucerne; p. (1969) 12,500.

Sciacca, sm. pt., Sicily **Italy**; nr. Agrigento; mineral springs; p. (est. 1968) 33,524.

Scilly Is., archipelago, 30 m. S.W. of Land's End, Cornwall, **Eng.**; early flowers and vegetables benefit from mild winter climate; tourism; p. (1971) 2,428.

Scioto, R., Ohio, **USA**; joins Ohio at Portsmouth; 400 km long.

Scone, par., Perth and Kinross, **Scot.**; place of residence and coronation of early Scottish kings; from here Edward I. removed Stone of Destiny to Westminster Abbey 1297; tourist ctr.; civil aerodrome.

Scoresby Sound, E. **Greenland**; lgst. fjord system in the world; length 304 km; fishing and hunting.

Scotland, Brit. Is., N. part of **Gt. Britain**; 11 Gov. Regs.; home affairs admin. by Dept. of Sec. of State for Scot.; physically divided into 3 parts: (1) the Highlands and Is., an upland a. suffering from depopulation, economically reliant on stock-rearing, tourism, hydroelec. power, whisky and fishing; intrusive impact of N. Sea oil on N.E. cst.; (2) the Central Lowlands, containing most p., based in industl. ts. on sm. coalfields, inc. lgst. c. Glasgow and cap. Edinburgh; (3) the S. Uplands, a stock-rearing a. bordering Eng.; a. 78,772 km²; p. (1971) 5,228,963.

Scranton, c., Penns., **USA**; on Lackawanna R.; anthracite ctr.; chemicals, shoes, textiles; univ.; p. (1970) 102,294 (c.), 231,433 (met. a.).

Scunthorpe, t., Humberside, **Eng.**; on Lincoln Edge, 10 km S. of Humber; iron, limestone mng. and major iron and steel ind.; p. (1971) 70880.

Scutari. *See* **Shkodër**.

Scutari (Turkey). *See* **Usküdar**.

Seaford, t., East Sussex, **Eng.**; 5 km E. of Newhaven; seaside resort; declined as a pt. with shift of Ouse R. channel to Newhaven; p. (1971) 16,196.

Seaforth Loch, Lewis, Outer Hebrides, **Scot.**; 22 km long.

Seaham, spt., Durham, **Eng.**; Seaham Harbour on E. cst. 6 km S. of Sunderland; modern colly. workings extend under sea; p. (1971) 23,410.

Sea Islands, **USA**; chain of Is. off Atl. cst. of S.C., Ga. and Fla.; formerly impt. for sea island cotton but since 1919 infested with boll weevil.

Seathwaite, v., Cumbria, **Eng.**; 11 km from Keswick, close to Styhead (436 m); exceptionally heavy annual rainfall (above 3,800 mm).

Seaton, t., S. Devon, **Eng.**; on Lyme Bay at mouth of R. Axe; seaside resort; freestone quarries; p. (1971) 4,134.

Seaton Carew, t., Cleveland, **Eng.**; site for nuclear power sta. nr. mouth of R. Tees; seaside resort.

Seaton Valley, t., Northumberland, **Eng.**; nr. Blyth; coal mng.; expanded t.; p. (1971) 32,011.

Seattle, c., Wash., **USA**; spt. between Puget Sound and L. Wash.; S.E. is Mt. Rainier, N.E. Mt. Baker; tr. with Far East and Alaska from wooded, agr. hinterland; fishing and fish exp.; lgst c. of Wash., a major industl. and comm. ctr.; aircraft (home of Boeing), shipbldg., food processing; univs., cath.; p. (1970) 524,263 (c.), 1,404,432 (met. a.).

Secunderabad, t., Andhra Pradesh, **India**; now incorporated within Hyderabad; comm. ctr., rly. junc.; p. (1961) 78,412.

Sedan, t., Ardennes dep., **France**; on R. Meuse; machin., metal ware, woollens, flour; Napoleon III surrendered to Prussians 1870; p. (1968) 24,499.

Sedbergh, mkt. t., Cumbria, **Eng.**; woollen ind., public school; p. (1971) 3,547 (dist.).

Sedgefield, t., S.E. Durham, **Eng.**; in fertile agr. a.; cattle mkt.; racecourse; p. (1971) 35,017 (dist.).

Sedgley. *See* **Wolverhampton**.

Ségou, t., R. pt., **Mali**; W. Africa; on R. Niger; ctr. of irrigation scheme; cotton, hides, cattle; once cap. of former kingdom.

Ségou Canal, **Mali**, W. Africa; leaves R. Niger 6 km below Bamako, extends 208 km N.E. to Ségou; irrigates 7,770 km² on right bank of Niger and assists navigation.

Segovia, c., cap. of S. prov., Old Castile, **Spain**; on rocky hill above Eresma R.; flour milling, tanning, pottery, handicrafts; Roman aqueduct, cath.; p. (1970) 41,880.

Segovia, R., rises in N.W. Nicaragua, flows N.E. to Caribbean; forms part of S. limit of Mosquito cst., and bdy. between **Honduras** and **Nicaragua**; 480 km long.

Segre, R., Lerida, N.E. **Spain**; rises in E. Pyrenees, flows S.W. into R. Ebro; water irrigates the a. around Lérida, the lgst. block of irrigated land in Spain; *c*. 272 km long.

Segura, R., **Spain**; flows to Mediterranean at Guardamar; 288 km long.

Seibersdorf, **Austria**; ENEA experimental food irradiation project.

Seikan Tunnel, **Japan**; links Honshu with Hokkaido under Tsugaru strait; 37 km long.

Seim, R., Ukrainian SSR, **USSR**; trib. of R. Desna; 480 km long.

Seine, R., **France**; rises in Côte d'Or dep., and flows past Paris and Rouen to English Channel at Havre; navigable, part of French waterway network; 757 km long.

Seine-et-Marne, dep., N. **France**; agr., stock-raising, dairying; impt. source of food for Paris mkts.; Brie cheese; cap. Melun; a. 5,892 km²; p. (1968) 604,340.

Seine-Maritime, dep., N. **France**; undulating and fertile; grain, dairying; heavy inds. at cap. Rouen; oil refineries; beach resorts; p. (1968) 1,113,977.

Seine-Saint Denis, dep., N.E. Paris, **France**; mkt. gardens; cap. Bobigny; p. (1968) 1,251,792.

Seistan and Baluchistan, twin prov., **Iran**; co. ts. Zabol, Zahedan (rly. terminus Pakistan rly. from Quetta through Mirjaveh, the customs post on Iranian frontier).

Sekondi-Takoradi, t., S.W. **Ghana**; spt. on G. of Guinea; developed after construction of rly. (1903) to tap mineral, agr. and forest wealth of hinterland; deepwater harbour at Takoradi constructed 1928; fisheries, saw milling; p. (1970) 91,874 (c.), 160,868 (met. a.).

Selangor, st., central Malaya, **W. Malaysia**; former sultanate; economically well developed; chemicals, rubber, tin, coal, pineapples; ch. pt., Pt. Swettenham; fisheries; new st. cap. designated at Klang to relieve congestion of Kuala Lumpur; p. (1967) 1,408,881.

Selby, mkt. t., North Yorks., **Eng.**; on R. Ouse, 13 m. S. of York; anc. abbey church; flour milling, flax, oil-cake; rich coal deposit recently found; p. (1971) 11,610.

Sele, R., S. **Italy**; rises in S. Apennines, flows W. into G. of Salerno; headwaters carried E. through gr. Apennine tunnel (11 km) to irrigate plateau of Apulia in S.E. Italy.

Selenga, Asiatic R., rises in **Mongolia**, enters **USSR** nr. Kiachta from where it is navigable to its delta in L. Baykal; *c* 1,100 km long.

Selkirk, royal burgh, Etterick and Lauderdale, **Scot.**; on Etterick Water; 6 km S. of Galashiels; mkt. t.; tartans, tweeds; p. (1971) 5,684.

Selkirk Mtns., B.C., **Canada**; run N.W. to S.E. parallel with Rocky mtns.; anc. rocks, highly mineralised; rise to over 2,700 m.

Selkirkshire, former co., S. **Scot.**; now part of Borders Reg.

Selma, t., Ala., **USA**; on Alabama R., in cotton, dairying, lumbering region; food processing, fertilisers; p. (1970) 27,379.

Selsey, t., West Sussex, **Eng.**; on Selsey Bill 11 km S. of Chichester; coastal resort; fishing.

Selsey Bill, peninsula between Bognor Regis and Portsmouth, West Sussex, **Eng.**

Selukwe, t., **Rhodesia**; alt. 1,444 m; gold mng. chrome ore, molybdenum; ranching.

Selwyn Range, mtns., Queensland, **Australia**; extend 560 km W. from Gr. Dividing Range.

Semarang, spt., Java, **Indonesia**; exp. sugar, tobacco, tapioca, kapok; shipbldg., rly. repairs, cement, sawmills, tyres, elec. equipment; univ.; p. (est. 1971) 560,000.

Semipalatinsk, t., Kazakh SSR, **USSR**; on R. Irtysh; lge. meat-packing plant; textiles, engin.; rich gold deposit found in a. 1965; p. (1970) 236,000.

Semmering Pass, low pass, **Austria**; provides route across E. Alps for rly. from Vienna to Venice; scenic resort; alt. below 915 m.

Semnan, t., Central Prov., **Iran**; comm. ctr. for tobacco growing region; p. (1966) 31,058.

Sena, t., **Moçambique**; on R. Zambesi; iron ore mng.

Sendai, t., Honshu, **Japan**; cas.; univ.; metallurgy, food processing, lacquer ware; p. (est. 1971) 560,000.

Senegal, rep., W. cst. **Africa**; flat savannah; tropical climate with long dry season; agr. main occupation, groundnuts accounting for 72 per cent exp.; groundnut and agr. processing provide industl. basis; bauxite, phosphate, titanium, zirconium mng.; oil refinery at cap.

Dakar; a. 197,109 km²; p. (est. 1969) 3,800,000.

Senegal, R., W. Africa; flows from Kong mtns. W. and N.W. to Atl. at St. Louis, above Cape Verde; lower valley forms fertile agr. land; partially navigable; plans for economic development of valley (1972); 1,600 km long.

Senftenberg, t., Cottbus, E. Germany; inds. based on local lignite deposits; glassware, tiles; p. (est. (1970) 24,301.

Senigallia, t., Italy; resort and spt. on Adriatic; fishing and agr. ctr.. food processing, agr. machin.; p. (est. 1968) 36,730.

Senlis, t., Oise dep., France; Gallo-Roman wall; tourist ctr. in forested region, 43 km N.E. of Paris; mkt. t., furniture, rubber gds.; p. (1968) 11,169.

Sennar, t., Sudan; on Blue Nile, on rly. route to Khartoum, Suakin, Pt. Sudan; dam for irrigation, flood control and hydroelectric power; p. c. 8,000.

Sens, t., Yonne dep., France; on R. Yonne; known to Romans as Agedincum; Gothic cath.; agr. tr., food processing, farm implements, boots, chemicals, cutlery; p. (1968) 24,563.

Sensuntepeque, t., E. Salvador; pottery, distilling; p. (1968) 6,006.

Senta, t., Yugoslavia; pt. on Tisa R.; agr. ctr.; food processing, agr. machin., chemicals; p. (est. 1965) 22,000.

Seoul, c., cap. of S. Korea; in Han R. valley; food processing, textiles, rly. engin.; univs., anc. walls; international airport, connected by rly. to outport of Inchon; p. (est. 1971) 5,536,000.

Sepik, R., N. New Guinea; flows E. to Bismarck Sea; drains vast mtn. a.; very fast flow; navigable by shallow craft; 800 km long.

Sept Isles (Seven Islands), pt., on St. Lawrence, Quebec, Canada; iron brought by rail from Schefferville; airline service but no highway.

Sequoia National Park, Cal., USA; sequoia trees.

Seraing, t., Liège, Belgium; on R. Meuse; coal mng.; iron and steel heavy inds.; seat of famous Cockerill ironwks. (1817) and glasswks. (1825); p. (1968) 40,850.

Seram (Ceram), I., Moluccas, Indonesia; W.-E. mtn. range rising to 3,357 m; tobacco, sago; a. 17,148 km²; p. (1961) 73,453.

Serampore, t., W. Bengal, India; former Danish settlement; cotton and silk weaving, pottery, jute- and paper-mills; p. (1971) 102,023.

Serbia, constituent rep., N.E. Yugoslavia; lgst and most impt. rep., "bread basket" of Yugoslavia; grain, fruit; mng. copper and antimony; cap. Belgrade; a. 87,879 km²; p. (1971) 8,436,574.

Seremban, t., cap. of Negri Sembilan st., W. Malaysia; on Linggi R.; linked by rly. to Pt. Dickson; comm. ctr. for rubber and tin a.; p. (1970) 79,915.

Sereth, R., rises in Carpathians, W. Ukrainian SSR, USSR, and enters Romania to join Danube above Galati; 720 km long.

Sergipe, cst. st., Brazil; sandy cst. rising to undulating plateau in interior; est. well wooded and cropped for sugar, cotton; drier interior devoted mainly to stock-raising; oil deposits; a. 21,054 km²; p. (est. 1968) 850,603.

Sergo. *See* Kadiyevka.

Seria, t., Brunei; coastal t., protected from sea by 8 km dyke; oil ctr., linked by pipeline with Lutong; p. (1971) 20,801.

Serov, t., RSFSR; in Urals; iron and steel; natural gas pipeline from Ingrim; p. (1970) 100,000.

Serowe, t., Botswana, S.W. Africa; seat of Bamanguato tribe; mkt. ctr.; p. (est. 1969) 34,186.

Serpukhov, t., R. pt., RSFSR; on R. Oka, planned canal link to Moscow; p. (1970) 124,000.

Serra da Mantiqueira, mtn. range, hgst. in Brazil.

Serra do Espinhaco, mtns., Brazil; highest peak, Itambe, 2,045 m; iron-ore deposits.

Serra do Mar, mtns., Brazil; form steep E. edge of Brazilian Plateau S. from Rio de Janeiro.

Serrai (Seres), dep., Macedonia, N. Greece; N. mtns. form frontier with Bulgaria in gorge of Struma R. valley; lower Struma R. basin fertile agr. a., producing cotton, tobacco; mkt. ctr. at cap. Serrai; a. 4,053 km²; p. (1971) 202,771.

Sertão, semi-arid hinterland, N.E. Brazil; stock-raising, but drought causes migration to Amazon basin; hydroelectric power and irrigation schemes; focus of social unrest documented in Brazilian novels.

Sesto San Giovanni, sub., Milan, Italy; machin., glass, chemicals, plastics; p. (est. 1968) 85,094.

Sète, spt., Hérault dep., France; on Med. cst.; chemicals, fisheries; exp. oysters, brandy, wine; oil pipeline under sea to Frontignan; importance originally based upon canal network, now supplanted by rlys.; tourism of growing importance; p. (1968) 41,044.

Setesdal (Saetersdal), Aust-Agder, S. Norway; remote valley retaining traditional social customs; arable pastoral agr.

Sétif, cap. of Sétif dep., N.E. Algeria; agr. ctr. for surrounding plateaux; grain, livestock; phosphates in a.; p. (1967) 98,000.

Seto, t., central Honshu, Japan; porcelain ctr. (since 13th cent.); based on local deposits of kaolin; p. (1970) 92,681.

Setouchi, dist., S.W. Honshu, Japan; rice, mandarin oranges, reeds, salt, textiles; part of Japan's industl. belt.

Setté Cama, spt., Gabon, Equatorial Africa; open roadstead, landing difficult owing to swell; exp. timber; oil nearby.

Settle, mkt. t., North Yorks., Eng.; on R. Ribble in heart of Craven dist.; tourist ctr. for limestone cty. of N. Pennines; textiles; p. (1971) 13,994 (dist.).

Settsu Plain, S. Honshu, Japan; at head of Osaka Bay at E. end of Inland Sea; intensively cultivated alluvial lowlands, ch. crops, rice, vegetables, oranges; gr. industl. belt extends along cst. through Kobe, Osaka, Kishiwada; engin., chemicals, textiles; a. 1,295 km².

Setubal, t., Estremadura, S. Portugal; impt. pt. on Sado R. estuary; exp. cork, wine, oranges; fishing, fish processing, shipyds.; p. (1970) 64,531.

Sevan (Gokcha), lge L., Armenian SSR, USSR; alt. 1,934 m; never freezes; surrounded by high barren mtns.; drained by Razdan R.; several hydroelectric power stas.

Sevastopol, spt., Ukrainian SSR, USSR; built on ruins left after famous siege 1855; Black Sea resort; rebuilt after second world war; one of most beautiful Crimean cs.; p. (1970) 229,000.

Sevenoaks, mkt. t., Kent, Eng.; in Vale of Holmesdale; residtl.; agr., lt. inds.; Knole Park; public school founded in 1432; p. (1971) 18,240.

Severn, R., Ont., Canada; flows to Hudson Bay; tr. post at mouth; 560 km long.

Severn, R., W. of Eng. and N. Wales; rises in Powys and flows to Bristol Channel; suspension bridge at estuary opened 1966; several proposals for major economic development around shores of estuary; 344 km long.

Severn Tunnel, Eng.; under estuary of R. Severn between Pilning (Avon) and Severn Tunnel Junction (Gwent); carries main rly. from London to S. Wales; longest main-line rly. tunnel in Brit. Is.; 7 km long.

Severodvinsk, t., RSFSR; on Dvina Bay, White Sea; metals, bldg. materials; p. (1970) 145,000.

Seville, c., cap. of Seville prov. and of Andalusia, Spain; spt. on Guadalquivir R., canal link with Atl. Oc.; exp. agr. prod., imports industl. raw materials; major industl., comm. and cultural ctr.; diverse mnfs.; beautiful c. with Moorish influence, prominent in narrow streets of ctr. a.; Alcázar palace; Gothic cath.; bull-fighting, tourist ctr.; p. (est. 1970) 650,000.

Sèvres, t., Hauts-de-Seine, dep., N. France; S.W. sub. of Paris on Seine R.; celebrated porcelain mnfs.; headquarters of International Bureau of Weights and Measures; p. (1968) 20,288.

Seward, t., S. Alaska, USA; rly. terminal, airfield and ice-free harbour make it an impt. supply ctr. for interior Alaska; p. (1970) 1,587.

Seychelles Is., indep. rep. (1976), Indian Oc.; consists of 86 Is. (37 granitic, 49 coralline), among most beautiful in world; lgst. I. Mahé; cap. Victoria; fishing, tourism; exp. copra, cinnamon bark; famous for species of nut; total a. 404 km²; p. (1968) 49,981.

Seyne, or **La Seyne-sur-Mer**, t., Var dep., France; nr. Toulon; shipbldg.; p. (1968) 43,783.

Sfax, spt., Tunisia; admin. ctr.; exp. phosphate, olive oil, salt, esparto grass, cereals, dates, hides; imports food, coal, textiles, soap; sponges; fishing; natural gas found in a.; surrounded by irrigated gardens and olive groves; p. (1966) 79,595 (c.), 215,836 (met. a.).

Sgurr Mor, mtn., Ross and Cromarty, Scot.; alt. 1,109 m.

Shaba (Katanga), prov., Zaïre; many varied mineral deposits inc. copper, tin, iron-ore, cobalt, radium; cap. Lubumbashi; a. 466,200 km^2; (est. 1969) 2,174,404.

Shaftesbury, mkt. t., N. Dorset, Eng.; Saxon hilltop t., abbey ruins; ctr. for agr. a.; p. (1971) 3,976.

Shahjahanpur, t., Uttar Pradesh, India; on Deoha R.; agr. mkt. t. and rly. junc.; grain, sugar tr. and processing; p. (1971) 135,604 (t.), 144,065 (met. a.).

Shakhty (Alexandrovsk Grushevski), t., RSFSR; anthracite mng. in Donets Basin; leather, textiles, metal wkg., food inds.; p. (1970) 205,000.

Shamaldy-Say, t., Kirghiz SSR, USSR; new t. on site of Uch-Kurgan hydroelectric power sta.

Shandakan Tunnel, N.Y. st., USA; carries water under Catskill mtns to augment water supply of c. of N.Y.; 29 km long.

Shanghai, c. and mun., Kiangsu, China; major spt. on left bank of Hwangpu (main waterway of Yangtze delta); despite marshy site its strategic location developed, largely by Brit. businessmen (1843); handles major share of Chinese shipping, but much dredging required; in part a modern W. style c., but distinctively Chinese in original Chinese site; inds. developed in response to location at transit point for major economic region of China in Yangtze basin; major educational ctr.; world's most populous c.; a. 5,799 km^2; p. (est. 1971) 10,820,000.

Shanhaikwan, c., N.E. Hopei, China; on double-track rly. to N.E. China; p. (est. 1957) 598,000.

Shanklin. *See* Sandown-Shanklin.

Shannon Airport, Clare, R.o.I.; N.W. of Limerick; on main transatlantic air route; ctr. of customs-free industl. estate.

Shannon, R., Ireland; separates Connaught from provs. of Leinster and Munster, flows to Atl. at Loop Head; hydroelectric power sta. at Ardnacrusha; 358 km long.

Shansi (Shanxi), prov., N. China; bounded W. and S. by Hwang-ho (Yellow R.); mainly high plateaux; fertile loess deposits, but drought conditions limit agr. potential; dry crops and livestock; coal, iron ore, petroleum; cap. Taiyuan; a. 156,420 km^2; p. (est. 1967) 18,000,000.

Shan State, div., Burma; elevated plateau through which flows Salween R.; impt. mng. dist., lead, zinc, silver at Bawdwin, smelters at Namtu; also tungsten, tin, antimony, manganese; home of Shan people; former Shan and Wa sts.; cap. Taunggyi; a. 155,801 km^2.

Shantung, coastal prov., N. China; S. of fertile plain of Hwang-ho; dense p. but agr. potential limited by dry climate; wheat, millet, maize, soyabeans, cotton, hemp, fruits; E. mtns. contain coal, iron, bauxite, kaolin; iron and steel inds. and cotton mills at main industl. ts. of Tsinan and Tsingtao; birthplace of Confucius at foot of sacred peak Tai; cap. Tsinan; a. 146,198 km^2; p. (est. 1967) 57,000,000.

Shaohing (Shaoxing), c., N. Chekiang prov., S.E. China; agr. ctr. on Hangchow Bay; rice, wheat, cotton; p. (est. 1970) 225,000.

Shaoyang, c., Hunan prov., China; coal and iron mng.; timber; p. (est. 1970) 275,000.

Shap, mkt. t., Cumbria, Eng.; nearby is Shap Fell 279 m, an impt. pass traversed by rly. and by a main road; granite quarries.

Shapinsay, Orkney Is., Scot.; p. (1971) 346.

Shari, R., central Africa; formed by several headstreams in Central African Rep., flows across Chad Rep. into L. Chad in wide delta; navigable.

Shārjah, emirate, member of the United Arab Emirates (1971), Persian Gulf; international airport at cap. Shārjah (p. 25,000); natural harbour at Khawr Fakhan; oil exploration, fishing; p. (est. 1970) 40,000.

Sharon, plain, Israel; citrus fruits, vines, poultry.

Shasi, t., S. Hupei prov., China; agr. mkt. ctr. and canalised R. pt.; tr. in cotton, grain; flour milling, textiles; p. (est. 1970) 125,000.

Shasta Dam, Cal., USA; dams water of Rs. Pit, McCloud, Sacramento for hydroelectric power; irrigation, flood control and reclamation of lower Sacramento valley.

Shatt-al-Arab, R., Iraq; formed by union of Tigris and Euphrates, flows thence to head of Persian G.; swampy delta in rich agr. a.; deepest-water line of R.'s estuary defined (1975) as new Iraq/Iran bdy.; 192 km long.

Shawinigan Falls, c., Quebec, Canada; pulp and paper, chemicals, aluminium inds., powered by hydroelectric power from falls on St. Maurice R.; p. (1966) 30,777.

Shawnee, c., Okla., USA; rly. and tr. ctr. for rich agr. a.; electronics, aircraft components; p. (1970) 25,075.

Sheaf, R., South Yorks., Eng.; rises in S.E. Pennines, flows N.E. to join R. Don at Sheffield; 18 km long.

Shebelinka, natural gas fields nr. Kharkov, Ukrainian SSR, USSR; pipelines to Kharkov-Bryansk and Dnepropetrovsk–Odessa.

Sheboygan, t., Wis., USA; on L. Michigan; ctr. for dairy farming and resort a.; cheese, leather gds., hardware; p. (1970) 48,484.

Sheerness, Kent, Eng.; on I. of Sheppey at entrance to estuary of R. Medway; former royal dockyard and garrison; deepwater comm. pt.; electronics, furniture, coach bldg.

Sheffield, c., South Yorks., Eng.; on cramped site at confluence of Rs. Sheaf and Don; univ.; heavy engin. ctr., famous for high quality steels, cutlery, tools; major post-war redevelopment of c. ctr. with ambitious and imaginative housebldg. programme by a socially conscious local council, taking advantage of hilly site has turned S. into a very attractive modern c.; p. (1971) 519,703.

Sheksna, R., RSFSR; rises in L. Beloye and flows S. to Rybinsk Reservoir; forms part of Volga–Baltic waterway; 160 km long.

Shellhaven, oil refineries, Essex, Eng.; on N. side of Thames estuary, nr. Standord-le-Hope.

Shenandoah National Park, Va., USA; extends along forested Blue Ridge mtns.; views of Shenandoah valley and Alleghenny mtns.

Shenandoah, R., Va., USA; trib. of Potomac R.; picturesque valley noted for rich apple orchards and pastures; scene of several campaigns in Civil War; 272 km long.

Shendi, t., Sudan; on R. Nile; ctr. of Jaalin tribe; p. c. 15,000.

Shensi, prov., N. China; Great Wall runs nr. N. border with Inner Mongolia; from N.–S. four main regions: (1) dry, fertile loess plateau, notorious famine region, but increasingly irrigated; (2) fertile Wei R. valley, ctr. of p. and agr.; (3) Tsinling divide; (4) agr. a. of upper Han R.; grain, livestock; coal, petroleum; developing transportation network aiding economic development; cap. Sian; a. 188,860 km^2; p. (est. 1968) 21,000,000.

Shen-yang (Mukden), c., cap. of Liaoning prov., N.E. China; on Hun R. in narrowest part of lowland with hilly country on both sides; impt. rly. junc. with main routes N. to Harbin and Trans-Siberian rly., S. to Peking, Luta and into Korea; comm. and educational ctr.; impt. textile ctr., heavy inds., cement, chemicals, machin.; agr. tr.; p. (est. 1970) 3,750,000.

Shepperton, t., Victoria, Australia; ctr. of vegetable and orchard a.; fruit canning, metal and brick wks.; p. (1972) 19,409.

Sheppey, I. of, Kent, Eng.; in Thames estuary E. of mouth of R. Medway; cereals, sheep-raising; new steel wks.; ch. t., Sheerness; a. 117 km^2.

Shepshed, t., Leics., Eng.; 5 km W. of Loughborough; hosiery; p. (1971) 8,456.

Shepton Mallet, mkt. t., Somerset Eng.; at foot of Mendip Hills, 8 km S.E. of Wells; old woollen ctr.; bacon curing, brewing; p. (1971) 5,910.

Sherborne, mkt. t., Dorset, Eng.; 6 km E. of Yeovil; famous abbey and school; Norman cas. ruins; glass fibre; p. (1971) 7,265.

Sherbrook, t., S.E. Quebec, Canada; comm. and mkt. ctr. for surrounding agr. region; inds. based on local sources of hydroelectric power from Magog R.; textiles, paper mills, machin., flour milling; deposits of asbestos nearby; p. (1966) 75,960.

Sheringham, t., Norfolk, **Eng.**; on cst. 6 km W. of Cromer; seaside resort; fishing; p. (1971) 4,666.

Sherwood Forest, anc. royal woodland, Notts., **Eng.**; now restricted to infertile Bunter Sandstone cty.; inc. several estates and parks, notably the Dukeries.

Shetland Is., Scot.; 80 km N.E. of the Orkneys; about 100 in gr., ch. I., Mainland; lge. number of rainy days, but climate mild and tourism attracted by isolation, scenery and wildlife; Fair Isle famous for knitted clothes; fishing, livestock, agr., potatoes; offshore oil exploration; oil service bases; lge. elderly p. due to attractions as a retirement a.; ch. t. Lerwick; a. 1,427 km^2; p. (est. 1971) 17,327.

Shibin el Kôm, Menûfiya, **Egypt**; rly. and mkt. ctr. in agr. a. of Nile delta; tobacco, textiles; p. (est. 1970) 75,600.

Shigatze, t., Tibet, **China**; on R. Tsangpo; tr. ctr. on main caravan routes; p. c. 20,000.

Shihkiachwang (Shijiazhuang), c., Hopeh prov., **China**; cotton milling, glass mftg.; grew rapidly with coming of rly.; p. (est. 1970) 1,500,000.

Shikarpur, t., N. Sind, **Pakistan**; tr. ctr. for grain, precious stones; engin., food processing; p. (est.1969) 62,500.

Shikoku, I., **Japan**; S. of Honshu; smallest of Japan's 4 main Is.; sparsely populated, mtnous. interior, heavily forested; arable agr. in lowlands; ch. cs., Matsuyama, Kochi, Tokushima; a. 18,772 km^2; p. (1970) 3,904,014.

Shildon, t., Durham, **Eng.**; 5 km S. of Bishop Auckland; rly. wks.; p. (1971) 14,499.

Shilka, R., E. Siberia, **RSFSR**; trib. of R. Amur; 552 km long.

Shillelagh, v., R.D., Wicklow, **R.o.I.**; oak forest, gave its name to oak or blackthorn cudgel.

Shillong, c., cap. of Assam, **India**; at alt. 1,372 m. in Khasi hills; ctr. of impt. tea-growing dist.; admin., technical education; pleasant climate attracts summer tourists; p. (1971) 87,659 (c.), 122,752 (met. a.).

Shimizu, spt., **Japan**; exp. tea, oranges; fishing; p. (est. 1971) 237,000.

Shimoda, spt., Honshu, **Japan**; between Nagoya and Yokohama; fishing; p. (1970) 30,318.

Shimoga, t., Karnataka, **India**; on Tunga R.; cotton-ginning, rice-milling; p. (1971) 102,709.

Shimonoseki, spt., Honshu I., **Japan**; at extreme S.W. of I.; tunnel and bridge links island of Kyushu; rly. ctr.; engin., chemicals based on local coal; fishing; p. (est. 1971) 264,000.

Shin, Loch, Sutherland, **Scot.**; 26 km long; drained by R. Shin to R. Oykell.

Shipka Pass, **Bulgaria**; over the Balkan mtns., 75 km N.E. of Plovdiv.

Shipley, t., West Yorks., **Eng.**; on R. Aire, 13 km N.W. of Leeds; worsted mnfs.; inc. model v. of Saltaire, built by Titus Salt (1851) to house his alpaca mill workers; p. (1971) 28,444.

Shiraz, c., cap. of Fars prov., **Iran**; beautifully sited in vine-growing dist.; textiles, rugs, metalwk., lt. elec. ind.; tourist ctr.; tombs of mediaeval poets Saadi and Hafez; known as "city of roses and nightingales"; pleasant winter climate; univ., airpt.; oil refinery projected; p. (est. 1971) 335,700.

Shire, R., flows out of L. Malawi south through **Malawi** and **Moçambique** to Zambesi; 592 km long.

Shirwa or **Chilwah**, shallow L., **Malawi**; 64 km long, 22 km wide; has 4 Is.

Shizuoka, c., cap. of S. pref., Honshu, **Japan**; pt. on Suruga Bay; impt. ctr. for tea and oranges; lacquerware, textiles; p. (est. 1971) 428,000.

Shkodër (Scutari), c., N. **Albania**; stands at foot of L. Scutari, 26 km from Adriatic; mkt. ctr., tobacco, cement, textiles; enjoyed greatest comm. prosperity after Ottoman conquest; several mosques; p. (1967) 50,000.

Shkodër (Scutari), L., on borders of Montenegro (**Yugoslavia**) and **Albania**; outlet via R. Boyana into Adriatic, 46 km long.

Shoeburyness, t., Essex, **Eng.**; on N. side of Thames estuary, 5 km E. of Southend.

Sholapur, c., Maharashtra, **India**; between Hyderabad and Poona; rly. junc., impt. textile ctr.; p. (1971) 398,361.

Shoreditch. *See* **Hackney.**

Shoreham-by-Sea, t., West Sussex, **Eng.**; at mouth of R. Adur, 6 km E. of Worthing; spt. and mkt. t.; oil jetty; boat bldg., chemicals soap, preserves; p. (1971) 18,804.

Shoshone Falls, on Snake R., Idaho, **USA**; height 61 m, used for irrigation projects.

Shott el Jerid, **Algeria** and **Tunisia**; deep depression in the desert.

Shotts, plateau, N. **Africa**; upland region with salt Ls., within Atlas mtns.

Shreveport, c., La., **USA**; industl. ctr. in cotton-growing dist.; petroleum; p. (1970) 178,061 (c.), 289,909 (met. a.).

Shrewsbury, co. t., Salop, **Eng.**; on R. Severn 19 km above Ironbridge gorge between the Wrekin and Wenlock Edge; agr. and diary equipment, machin., elec. gds.; cattle and sheep mkt.; public school; p. (1971) 56,140.

Shropshire. *See* **Salop.**

Shusha, t., Azerbaydzhan SSR, **USSR**; health resort; silk spinning, rug making; Armenian p. massacred by Tatars 1926; p. c. 6,000.

Shustar, t., **Iran**; carpets, woollens, pottery; shallow-draught boats can reach Shallili, nr. S. by R. Karun; p. (1966) 21,999.

Sialkot, t., **Pakistan**; N.E. of Lahore; sports gds., musical and surgical instruments, paper; agr. tr. and processing ctr.; p. (est. 1969) 167,000.

Siam. *See* **Thailand.**

Siam, G. of, lge. inlet, S. China Sea; sheltered with shallow water; length 616 km N.W. to S.E.

Sian (Xian), cap. of Shensi prov., **China**; impt. route and industl. ctr.; food processing and tr., flour, grain, tea, tobacco, iron and steel, textiles, chemicals; p. (est. 1957) 1,310,000.

Siangtan (Xiangtan), c., Hunan prov., **China**; on navigable Siang R.; regional tr. ctr., tea, cotton; electrical gds., machin., textiles; Mao Tse-tung born nearby; p. (est. 1970) 300,000.

Siauliai, t., Lithuanian SSR, **USSR**; 184 km N.W. of Vilna; impt. rly. junc.; food and leather inds. p. (est. 1969) 88,000.

Sibenik, t., Croatia, **Yugoslavia**; Adriatic spt.; exp. timber, bauxite; aluminium, chemical and textile inds.; p. (est. 1965) 29,000.

Siberia, terr., **USSR**; extends from Urals to Sea of Okhotsk and Bering Strait, bounded by Arctic on N. and by Mongolia and Turkestan on S.; climate mostly severe; ch. ts., Novosibirsk (cap. W. S.) and **Irkutsk** (cap. E. S.); rich in coal, iron, minerals; oil and gas in W. Siberian lowland; resources not yet fully known but Soviet economic policy is to develop S. in order to use its natural resources to the full; p. and economic activity clustered around rlys., esp. Trans-Siberian rly.; a. c. 12,950,000 km^2.

Sibiu, t., central **Romania**; picturesque site at foot of Transylvanian Alps; retains mediaeval character despite being an impt. industl. ctr.; textiles, agr. machin., chemicals, leather; lge. German minority p.; caths.; p. (est. 1969) 118,893.

Sibu, t., Sarawak, **E. Malaysia**; 128 km up R. Rejang; comm. ctr. at head of ocean navigation; airport; p. (1960) 29,630.

Sicily, lgst I., Mediterranean Sea; former kingdom and now aut. region of **Italy**; pleasant climate, mtnous.; fertile lowlands, especially plain of Catania, but agr. hampered by primitive methods, absentee landlords and need for irrigation; lge. range of Mediterranean crops; fishing; sulphur; petroleum reserves, refining and petrochemical inds.; volcanic Mt. Etna erupted in 1971; a. 25,708 km^2; p. (1969) 4,876,624.

Sidi-bel-Abbès, t., W. **Algeria**; old fortress t., became H.Q. of Fr. Foreign Legion; agr. mkt. ctr. for region producing grain, grapes, olives, livestock; cement, furniture mnfs.; p. (1967) 101,000.

Sidlaw Hills, low mtn. range, Tayside Reg., **Scot.**; max. alt. 455 m.

Sidmouth, mkt. t., Devon, **Eng.**; on S. cst., 24 km S.E. of Exeter; seaside resort; retirement ctr.; p. (1971) 12,039.

Sidon. *See* Saida.

Siebengebirge, sm. wooded range of seven hills, W. Germany; of volcanic origin rising to 457 m on right bank of Rhine; famous for Drachenfels association with the Siegfried saga.

Siedlce, t., **Poland**; 88 km E. of Warsaw; rly. junc.; agr. inds.; p. (1970) 39,000.

Siegburg, t., N. Rhine-Westphalia, **W. Germany**; on R. Sieg; Benedictine abbey; dyes, iron, ceramics; p. (est. 1969) 33,940.

Siegen, t., N. Rhine-Westphalia, **W. Germany**; on R. Sieg; 2 cas.; ironmng. and smelting, machin., leather; p. (est. 1969) 57,946.

Siemianowice Slaskie, t., **Poland**; nr. Katowice; ctr. of mng., industl. region; iron and steel, machin.; cas.; p. (1970) 67,300.

Siena, hill-town, Tuscany, **Italy**; 51 km S. of Florence; spreads over three hilltops with Piazza del Campo in between where celebrated Palio festival (horse-races) are held; 13th- and 14th-cent. arch., cath.; agr. mkt., tanning, glass, textiles, bricks; *panforte* confectionery; tourist ctr.; p. (1969) 66,084.

Sierra Leone, rep., W. cst. **Africa**; mangrove swamps on cst., high plateau, with peaks over 1,800 m in interior; climate hot, humid; economy based on agr. and mng.; palm kernels, coffee, cocoa, rice, timber, iron ore; main exp. diamonds, notorious smuggling problem; fishing along cst.; cap. Freetown; a. 72,326 km²; p. (est. 1970) 2,500,000.

Sierra Madre Occidental, mtn. range, **Mexico**; volcanic, forms W. edge of Mexican plateau; average alt. 2,100 m.

Sierra Madre Oriental, mtn. range, **Mexico**; limestone, forms E. edge of Mexican plateau; average alt. 2,400 m.

Sierra Maestra, mtn. range, Oriente prov., S.E. **Cuba**; rises abruptly from cst.; rich in minerals.

Sierra Morena, mtn. range, **Spain**; between Guadalquivir and Guadiana basins, highest point 1,677 m; rich in minerals.

Sierra Nevada, mtn. range, Granada, **Spain**; highest summit Mulhacén 3,483 m.

Sierra Nevada, mtn. chain, Cal., **USA**; highest peak Mt. Whitney 4,544 m; nat. parks.

Sierra Nevada de Mérida, mtn. range, **W. Venezuela**; extends N.E. from San Cristóbal to Barquisimeto; extension of E. range of Andes, alt. over 4,880 m; impt. coffee plantations from 900-1,800 m on slopes.

Sierra Pacaraima, mtn. range, **Brazil, Venezuela**; forms part of international bdy. and watershed between Amazon and Orinoco basins.

Sighet, frontier t., N. **Romania**; on R. Tisa, on border with USSR; extreme, continental climate; timber, agr. and livestock tr.; cotton textiles; p. (est. 1970) 33,361.

Siglufjörd, spt., N. **Iceland**; impt. herring fisheries; p. (1970) 2,161.

Sigtuna, t., Stockholm, **Sweden**; on Mälaren L.; first cap. of Sweden; educational ctr., tourist resort; p. c. 3,300.

Sihanoukville (Kompong Som), c., **Cambodia**; deepwater pt. on G. of Thailand; linked to Phnom Penh by modern highway; textile mills, tractors, oil refining; p. (1962) 6,578.

Sikang, region, S.W. **China**; mtnous., mostly above 3,600 m; E. part in Szechwan prov., W. part in Chamdo region, Tibet; deep gorges of Salween, Mekong, Yangtze, and Hwang-ho provide severe obstacles to E.-W. communications; highest summit Minya Konka 7,570 km.

Sikhote-Alin, mtn. range, S.E. Asiatic **RSFSR**; rises to 1,800 m and extends for 1,200 km parallel to Pac. cst.; hinders access to W. basins forestry, minerals.

Si-Kiang, ch. R., S. **China**; headstreams rise in Yunnan plateau, form main R. nr. Sunchow; R. then flows E., enters S. China Sea through lge. delta nr. Hon Kong; lower valley intensively cultivated, rice, sugar-cane, tea; tropical climate permits continuous cultivation of most crops through year; valley very densely populated; c. 2,000 km long.

Sikkim, st., **India**; on S. slopes of Himalayas; incorporated as 22nd st. 1975; forest covered; economically underdeveloped; scene of rivalry between India and China; cap. Gangtok; a. 7,110 km²; p. (est. 1968) 187,000.

Sila, La, massif, Calabria, S. **Italy**; granite mass occupying full width of peninsula; alt. over 1,060 m, max. 1,930 m.

Silchester, par., Hants, **Eng.**; between Basingstoke and Reading; ruins of Roman t., Calleva Atrebatum; impt. ctr. of Roman communications network.

Silesia (Polish **Śląsk**, Czech **Slezsko**, German **Schlesien**), geographical region, **Central Europe**; since 1945 divided between Poland, ČSSR and E. Germany; extends along both banks of Oder R.; bounded in S. by Sudeten mtns.; forested mtns., fertile arable agr. in lowlands; major concentration of economic activity based on coalfield of Upper Silesia (ceded to Poland 1922); complex territorial history; now forms highly urbanised industl. conurb. mainly in Poland, admin. by Katowice, Opole, Wroclaw, Wroclaw (c.), and part of Zielona Gora; ČSSR portion forms part of N. Moravia; E. Germany retains sm. part of Lower Silesia W. of Neisse R.; total a. 46,600 km².

Silistria, t., **Bulgaria**; on Danube opposite Romanian t. of Calarasi; cereals and timber tr.; mnfs. foodstuffs, ceramics, furniture; mosques; p. (est. 1968) 36,151.

Silkeborg, t., Jutland, **Denmark**; tourist resort in beautiful forest and lake region; p. (est. 1970) 26,129.

Silsden, t., West Yorks., **Eng.**; wool textiles; p. (1971) 5,588.

Silver Spring, t., Md., **USA**; sub. N. of Washington, D.C.; science-based inds. and research laboratories; p. (1970) 77,496.

Simcoe, L., S. Ont., **Canada**; several resorts; boating, fishing; 48 km by 42 km.

Simeulue, I., S.W. of Sumatra, **Indonesia**; primitive islanders; fishing and shifting cultivation.

Simferopol, t., Ukrainian SSR, **USSR**; on R. Salghir nr. Sevastopol; industl. ctr. in rich agr. a., fruit-canning, tobacco, machin.; p. (1970) 250,000.

Simla, t., Himachal Pradesh, **India**; famous hill-station c. 2,158 m high on forested ridge of Himalayas, 280 km N. of Delhi.

Simonstown, W. Cape Prov., **S. Africa**; naval sta., docks; p. (est. 1967) 8,900.

Simplon, mtn., **Switzerland**; alt. 3,567 m; the pass over the Simplon (alt. 2,011 m) from Domodossola, Italy, to Brig in the Rhône valley, Switzerland, was originally made by Napoleon I. The Simplon rly. tunnel leads from Brig on the Swiss side to Iselle in the Val di Vedro on the Italian and is the longest in the world, 19·7 km.

Simpson Desert, Australia; S.E. of Alice Springs, N.T., extends into S. Australia.

Sinai, peninsula, easternmost part of **Egypt**; between Gs. of Aqaba and Suez, at head of Red Sea; mainly desert in N., granitic ridges in S. rising to 2,592 m at Jebel Katrun; Jebel Musa or Mt. Sinai (2,244 m) is one of numerous peaks; mineral resources; coalmine at Maghâra; occupied by Israeli troops, Nov. 1956-March 1957 and since June 1967; a. 28,632 km².

Sinaia, t., S. **Romania**; health and winter sports resort in Transylvanian Alps; until 1947 summer residence of Romanian kings; palaces; p. (1966) 11,976.

Sinaloa, st., **Mexico**; on G. of Cal.; agr. and mng., rich in gold, silver, copper, iron and lead; cereals on uplands; sugar, cotton on lowlands; cap. Culiacán; a. 48,482 km²; p. (1969) 1,185,000.

Sind, prov. (revived 1970), **Pakistan**; lower Indus valley; dry climate; E. part reaches edge of Thar desert; agr. depends on irrigation; irrigated by Sukkur and Kotri systems; wheat, rice, cotton, oilseeds, sugar-cane, fruits; handicraft inds. in ts.; ch. ts., Karachi, Hyderabad, Sukkur, Shikarpur; a. 129,500 km² p. (1972) 13,965,000.

Singapore, rep., S.E. **Asia**; I. separated from Malaysian mainland by Johore Strait and linked by causeway; equatorial climate; cap. Singapore on S. cst. has fine natural harbour; major entrepôt tr. for Malaysia and S.E. Asia; world ctr. of rubber and tin mkts.; tr. in rubber, tin, petroleum, imported foodstuffs; growing industl. estates; oil refining, shipbldg.; only 20 per cent land cultivated; fruit, mkt. gardening; offshore fishing; reduction in Brit. military presence from base on N. cst. of I.; a. 580 km²; p. (1970) 2,074,507 (rep.); (est. 1969) 2,016,800 (c.).

Singhbhum, dist., Bihar, **India**; iron- and steelwks. based on local iron mng.; a. 13,445 km²; p. (1961) 2,049,911.

Sinhailien (Xinhailion), c., Kiangsu, **China**; formed by merger of Sinput, Tunghai and Lienyienkang; agr. comm. ctr., tr. in cereals, cotton; p. (1953) 207,600.

Sining (Xining), cap of Chinghal prov., **China**;

ctr. of spring wheat a.; woollen mills, iron and steel; p. (est. 1970) 250,000.

Sinkiang-Uighur (Xinjiang), aut. region, **N.W. China**; borders on USSR and Kashmir; very dry climate; remote until new roads and rlys. penetrated a.; pastoral agr., sheep, goats; new st arable farms, wheat, maize, millet; lge oil reserves; cap. Urumchi; a. 1,646,800 km²; p. (est. 1968) 8,000,000.

Sinop, cap. of S. prov., **Turkey**; sm. pt. with gd. harbour on Black Sea but poor communications with hinterland; p. (1965) 13,354.

Sintra (Cintra), t., **Portugal**; summer resort, 29 km from Lisbon; Moorish castle, royal palace; p. (1970) 20,321.

Sinuiju, c., **W. N. Korea**; spt. at mouth of Yalu R. on Yellow Sea; linked by bridge to Antung (China); industl. ctr.; chemicals, aluminium inds., using power from Supung Dam; p. (est. 1970) 125,000.

Sinyang, t., S. Honan, **China**; regional ctr. for S. Honan and N. Hupei; p. c. 75,000.

Sion, t., cap. of Valais can., **Switzerland**; on R. Rhône; built on two castled hills; cath.; horticultural mkt. ctr.; hydroelectric power stas. and coal mines nearby; p. (1969) 21,600.

Sioux City, Iowa, **USA**; on R. Missouri: meat-packing, foundries, elec. gds. cement; p. (1970) 83,626 (c.), 113,929 (met. a.).

Sioux Falls, t., S.D., **USA**; on Big Sioux R.; in rich wheat region; machin., cars, farming implements; nuclear reactor; p. (1970) 72,488.

Siret, R., **Romania, USSR**; flows E. from Carpathians to Danube; steep forested left bank, fertile terraced right bank; hydroelectric power and irrigation schemes; 448 km long.

Sisak, t., Croatia, **Yugoslavia**; developing industl. ctr. and R. pt.; iron and steel, oil refining.

Sistan and Baluchistan, twin prov., **Iran**; bounded by Afghanistan and Pakistan; cap. Zahedan; much desert land; arid, very hot; p. (1967) 456,435.

Sitapur, t., Uttar Pradesh, **India**; rly. junc.; agr. tr. ctr.; eye hospital; p. (1961) 53,884.

Sitra, I., Persian G.; forms part of st. of Bahrain, 5 km long and 1·6 km wide; oil pipeline and causeway carrying road extends out to sea for 5 km to deep-water anchorage.

Sittang, R., **Burma**; rises in Pegu Yoma, flows S. to G. of Martaban through delta; valley intensively cultivated, delta forested; irrigation project; 976 km long.

Sittard, mkt. t., Limburg, **Neth.**; tanning; p. (1968) 33,804.

Sittingbourne and Milton, mkt. t., Kent, **Eng.**; on Milton Creek, 14 km E. of Chatham; paper-mills, brick-wks.; cement; insecticides; ctr. of fruit-growing dist.; p. (1971) 30,861.

Sittwe (Akyab), spt., **Burma**; at mouth of Kaladan R.; exp. rice; pt. suffered during war; p. (est. 1962) 86,451.

Sivas, c., cap. of S. prov., **Turkey**; impt. tr. and agr. ctr. in Kizil Irmak valley; cement, rugs; copper mng. nearby; foundations of modern Turkey laid here by Atatürk 1919; p. (1965) 108,320 (c.), 169,964 (met. a.).

Sivash Sea or **Putrid Sea**, lagoon on N.E. cst. of Crimea, **USSR**; 20 per cent salt; a. 2,590 km².

Siwa, oasis, **Egypt**; in Libyan Desert, *c.* 480 km S.W. of Alexandria; dates, olives; remains of temple of Zeus Ammon (visited by Alexander the Great); 32 km long, 1·6 km wide; p. (1966) 3,600.

Sizewell, Suffolk, **Eng.**; nuclear power sta.

Sjaelland, I., **Denmark**; lgst. I., separated from Fyn I. by the Gr. Belt; fertile glacial clays but rapidly spreading ts.; ch. c. Copenhagen; a. 7,356 km²; p. (1965) 2,055,040.

Skagerrak, arm of N. Sea, giving access to the Kattegat, between Norway and Denmark, 112–144 km wide.

Skagway, sm. spt., Alaska, **USA**; at head of Lynn Canal inlet, 640 km N.W. of Prince Rupert; linked by rly. to Whitehorse on upper R. Yukon; boomed in gold rush (1898), p. 15,000, subsequently declined; p. (1970) 675.

Skåne (Scania), peninsula, extreme S. of **Sweden**; corresponds approx. to cos. Malmöhus, Kristianstad; most favoured part of Sweden in relief, soil, climate; intensive farming, wheat, barley, sugar-beet, fodder crops, dairy cattle; ch. ts. Malmö, Lund, Hälsingborg; a. 10,360 km².

Skaraborg, co., **Sweden**; between Ls. Väner and Vätter; dairy agr.; a. 8,467 km²; p. (est. 1970) 255,964.

Skara Brae, prehistoric v., Mainland, Orkneys, **Scot.**; v. excavated from under sand dunes.

Skarzysko-Kamienna, t., Kielce, **Poland**; ctr. of developing metallurgical ind.; p. (1970) 39,200.

Skaw The (Grenen), C., at extreme N. of **Denmark**.

Skeena, R., B.C., **Canada**; rises in N. Rocky mtns., flows S.W. to Pac. Oc. at Prince Rupert; lower valley used by Canadian National Rly.; 640 km long.

Skegness, t., Lincs., **Eng.**; on E. cst.; resort; lt. engin.; p. (1971) 13,557.

Skelleftea, t., N. **Sweden**; on Bothnia G.; growing since discovery of Boliden ores nearby; iron and copper ore smelting; p. (1968) 61,949; (1961) 22,000.

Skelmersdale and Holland, t., Lancs., **Eng.**; coal, bricks, drainpipes; new t. (1961); p. (est. 1970) 39,000.

Skelton and Brotton, t., Cleveland, **Eng.**; at N. foot of Cleveland hills, 16 km E. of Middlesbrough; steel flooring; p. (1971) 15,083.

Skiddaw, mtn., Cumbria, **Eng.**; E. of Bassenthwaite L.; alt. 931 m.

Skien, spt., Bratsberg, **Norway**; on R. Skien; saw-mills, timber tr.; birthplace of Ibsen; p. (1968) 44,213.

Skikda (Philippeville), t., spt., **Algeria**; exp. prods. from Saharan oases; oil pipeline to Mesdar; p. (1967) 85,000.

Skipton, t., North Yorks., **Eng.**; on R. Aire; cotton and rayon inds.; cas.; p. (1971) 12,422.

Skopje, t., cap. of Macedonia, **Yugoslavia**; anc. Scupi, one of oldest ts. in Balkans; oriental appearance; destroyed by earthquake (1963); food processing, iron and steel wks.; new oil refinery; airpt., route ctr.; p. (est. 1971) 388,000.

Skövde, t., **Sweden**; between Ls. Vänern and Vättern; garrison t., chemicals, cement; p. (1968) 28,028.

Skye, I., lgst. of Inner Hebrides, Skye and Lochalsh, **Scot.**; mtnous.; sheep-farming and fisheries; tourism; only t. Portree; a. 1,417 km²; p. (1971) 7,364.

Skyros, I., Sporades, **Greece**; in Aegean Sea; mainly agr.; a. 199 km²; p. (1961) 2,882.

Slagelse, t., Sjaelland, **Denmark**; food inds.; iron wks.; 11th cent. church; p. (est. 1970) 23,169.

Slask. *See* Silesia.

Slave Coast, name given to the Guinea cst. of **W. Africa** between the Volta and Niger deltas where slaves were shipped from 16th to 19th cent.

Slave, R., N.W. Terr., **Canada**; flows into Gr. Slave L.; length 416 km.

Slavonia, historic region, **Yugoslavia**; between Drava R. (N.) and Sava R. (S.); now part of rep. of Croatia; ch. t. Osijek.

Slavyansk, t., Ukrainian SSR, **USSR**; in Donets basin; chemicals, engin.; p. (1970) 124,000.

Sleaford, mkt. t., Lincs., **Eng.**; 19 km N.E. of Grantham; agr. and agr. implements; p. (1971) 7,975.

Sleat, Sound of, Lochaber, Skye and Lochalsh, **Scot.**; separates I. of Skye from the mainland; 11 km wide.

Slezsko. *See* Silesia.

Sliema, t., **Malta**; E. of Valletta; resort; p. (1971) 21,887.

Slieve Bloom, hill range, Offaly and Laoghis cos., **R.o.I.**; highest point 529 m.

Slieve Donard, mtn., **N. Ireland**; highest of the Mourne mtns.; alt. 835 m.

Sligo, co., Connacht, **R.o.I.**; borders Atl. Oc.; rises to Ox Mtns. over 600 m; pastoral agr., fishing; co. t. S.; a. 1,909 km²; p. (1966) 51,078.

Sligo, co. t., Sligo, **R.o.I.**; on S. Bay; pt., exp. agr. prods.; abbey ruins; cath.; p. (1966) 13,297.

Slioch, mtn., Ross and Cromarty, **Scot.**; 981 m.

Sliven, t., **Bulgaria**; in Balkan mtns.; impt. woollen mnf. ctr.; carpets; p. (est. 1968) 77,458.

Slough, t., Berks., **Eng.**; on river terrace N. of R. Thames, 37 km W. of London; many lt. inds.; p. (1971) 86,757.

Slovakia (Slovak Socialist Rep.), **ČSSR**; extends from Carpathians to Danube valley; prosperous agr.; cap. Bratislava; with Czech Socialist Rep. forms Fed. Rep. of Czechoslovakia; a. 48,956 km²; p. (est. 1970) 4,563,460.

Slovenia, constituent rep., **Yugoslavia**; mtnous., but many minerals inc. coal; highly developed region; cap. Ljubljana; a. 16,229 km²; p. (1971) 1,725,088.

Slupsk (Stolp), t., N.W. **Poland** (since 1945); formerly in Pomerania; on R. Stupia, nr. Baltic Sea; cas.; wood, metal, food processing; p. (1970) 68,300.

Småland, historic prov., S. **Sweden**; barren upland a. S. of L. Vättern; moorland, deciduous forest; contrasts greatly with remainder of S. Sweden.

Smederevo, t., Serbia, **Yugoslavia**; nr. Belgrade; pt. on R. Danube; walled t.; steel wks.; p. (1971) 27,182.

Smethwick. *See* Warley.

Smolensk, c., cap. of S. oblast, **RSFSR**; on upper Dnieper; anc. c. damaged in many wars; route ctr.; vehicles, machin., food processing; p. (1970) 211,000.

Smyrna. *See* **Izmir**.

Snaefell, highest mtn., **I. of Man**; alt. 620 m.

Snake R. or Lewis Fork, trib. of Columbia R., flows from Wyo. to Wash., **USA**; gorges; hydroelectric power; 1,680 km long.

Sneek, t., Friesland, Neth.; butter, cheese mkt.; yachting ctr.; p. (1967) 24,464.

Sneeuwbergen, mtn. range, Cape Prov., **S. Africa**.

Snöhetta, mtn., highest in Dovrefjell range, Norway; alt. 2,307 m.

Snowdon, mtn., Gwynedd, **Wales**; highest in Eng. and Wales, alt. 1,086 m; forms part of Snowdonia Nat. Park.

Snowy Mtns., N.S.W., **Australia**; part of Australian Alps; rise to over 2,000 m; S.M. scheme (1950) diverts water from headstreams in tunnels through mtns. to provide water for irrigation and hydroelectric power; completed 1972.

Snowy, R., N.S.W. and Victoria, **Australia**; rises in Mt. Kosciusko, flows S. into Bass strait 128 km W. of C. Howe; part of Snowy Mtn. scheme; 432 km long.

Soar, R., Leics., Notts., **Eng.**; rises S. of Leics., flows N.W. to join R. Trent; 69 km long.

Sobat, R., **Sudan** and **Ethiopia**; made up of several sm. Rs.; trib. of White Nile; 800 km long.

Soche. *See* **Yarkand**.

Sochi, t., **RSFSR**; on Black Sea at foot of main Caucasian range; health resort with subtropical climate and sulphur springs; developed since 1933; p. (1970) 224,000.

Society Is., Fr. Polynesia, **S. Pac. Oc.**; comprise Windward Is. (Tahiti, Moorea, Mehetia, etc.) and Leeward Is. (Huahune, Raiatea, etc.); discovered by Captain Cook; main prods. phosphate and copper; cap. Papeete; a. 1,647 km²; p. (1967) 61,519.

Socotra, I., G. of Aden, Indian Oc.; since 1967 part of **Democratic Rep. of Yemen**; under Brit. protection 1886–1967; lofty tableland; myrrh, frankincense, aloes; cap. Tamrida; a. 3,626 km²; p. (est.) 12,000.

Sodbury, t., Avon, **Eng.**; former coal-mng. ctr.; expanded t.; p. (1971) 67,040 (dist.).

Söderhamn, spt., **Sweden**; on G. of Bothnia, N. of Gavle; timber, wood-pulp; p. (est. 1970) 13,911.

Södermanland, co., **Sweden**; between Baltic cst. and L. Mälar; cattle-rearing; mng.; a. 6,822 km²; p. (est. 1970) 247,703.

Södertälje, t., **Sweden**; on S. canal linking L. Mälar with Baltic cst.; vehicles, chemicals, tobacco; p. (1968) 52,503.

Soest, c., N. Rhine–Westphalia, **W. Germany**; one of oldest ts., member of Hanseatic league; suffered heavily in second world war; soap, textile machin., engin.; p. (est. 1969) 35,731.

Soest, t., Utrecht, **Neth.**; residtl., agr. ctr.; p. (1968) 33,190.

Sofia, c., cap. of **Bulgaria**; Roman Serdica, and Triaditsa of Byzantine Greeks; nr. Yugoslav border; impt route ctr. and ch. industl. ctr. of rep.; machin., textiles, chemicals, elec. engin.; cath., univ., and many historic bldgs.; p. (est. 1969) 858,140 (c.); (1967) 923,400 (met. a.).

Sogne Fjord, Norway; longest fjord in Norway; length 176 km; tourism.

Sogn og Fjordane, co., W. **Norway**; borders Atl. Oc., indented by Sogne Fjord; lge. hydroelectric power resources; tourism; a. 18,480 km²; p. (est. 1972) 101,740.

Sohag, t., **Egypt**; on R. Nile; cotton processing; p. (1960) 62,000.

Soho, dist., London, **Eng.**; settled by Fr. Huguenots 16th cent.; high proportion of foreign residents, sometimes known as London's "Latin quarter"; night-clubs, theatres, restaurants, film-company offices.

Soissons, t., Aisne dep., **France**; anc. Augusta Suessionum; commands N.E. approaches to Paris; cath.; agr. tr.; p. (1968) 27,641.

Sokoto, t., **Nigeria**, W. Africa; founded 1809 as cap. of native st. of S., p. mainly Hausa and Fulani; tr. ctr.; p. (est. 1969) 104,160.

Solent, The, strait separating I. of Wight from Hampshire mainland, **Eng.**

Solihull, t., West Midlands, **Eng.**; 8 km S.W. of Birmingham; residtl.; motor vehicles, chemicals; p. (1971) 106,968.

Solikamsk, t., **RSFSR**; on R. Kama; chemicals from local potash; rapidly growing t.; p. (est. 1969) 89,000.

Solingen, t., N. Rhine–Westphalia, **W. Germany**; 24 km E. of Düsseldorf; cutlery ctr.; p. (est. 1969) 175,200.

Solnechnyy. *See* **Gornyy Snezhnogorsk**.

Solomon Is., **S. Pac. Oc.**; internal self-gov. (1976), indep. by 1977; archipelago of volcanic Is.; N. Is. form part of Papua New Guinea; remainder Brit.; dependent on exp. of copra, timber, fish; threatened by insect pests; a. 29,785 km²; p. (1966) 221,290 (mostly Melanesian).

Solothurn (Soleure), can., N.W. **Switzerland**, crossed by Jura mtns., and R. Aare; 97 per cent cultivated; dairying; many industl. ts.; cap. S.; a. 793 km²; p. (1969) 228,000.

Solothurn (Soleure), t., cap. of S. can., **Switzerland**; on R. Aare; anc. t.; cath.; watches, motor mnf.; p. (1969) 19,100.

Solway Firth, arm of **Irish Sea**, Dumfries and Galloway Reg., Scot., and Cumbria, Eng.; 6 km long.

Somalia (**Somali Democratic Rep.**), E. cst. **Africa**; narrow cst. plain in N., widens in S., interior plateau reaching *c*. 2,400 m; dry, hot climate; 75 per cent. p. nomadic; livestock herding; permanent agr. in irrigated R. valleys; sugar, banana plantations in Webi Shebeli and Juba Rs. in S.; potential for mineral exploitation; cap. Mogadishu; a. 637,658 km²; p. (est. 1969) 2,730,000.

Somaliland, French. *See* **Afars and Issas**.

Sombor, t., Serbia, **Yugoslavia**; cattle, grain tr.; textiles; p. (est. 1965) 32,000.

Somersby, v., Lincs., **Eng.**; birthplace of Tennyson.

Somerse, non-met. co., S.W. **Eng.**; inc. part of Exmoor, Mendips, Quantocks and Blackdown hills; to N. is drained marshland of Somerset levels; dairying; coastal resorts; co. t. Taunton; a. 3,458 km²; p. (1973) 387,000.

Somme, dep., N. **France**; borders Eng. Channel; crossed by R. Somme; low-lying agr. a.; textile inds.; cap. Amiens; a. 6,327 km²; p. (1968) 512,113.

Somme, R., **France**; flows in deps. Aisne and Somme to English Channel; scene of battles 1916; linked to Rs. Oise and Scheldt by canal; 186 km long.

Somport Tunnel, on bdy. **France–Spain**; carries main rly. from Pau to Zaragoza under Pyrenees; 8 km long.

Sönderborg, spt., S. Jutland, **Denmark**; older part of c. on Als I.; palace; textiles; p. (est. 1970) 23,069.

Sondrio, t., cap. of S. prov., **Italy**; commands the Adda valley, impt. routeway through Alps; agr. mkt.; textiles; p. (1969) 22,792.

Songkhla, t., **Thailand**; most S. t.; ctr. of rubber growing dist.; third t. of cty.; p. (est. 1964) 36,277.

Song-koi (Red R.), R., rises in Yunnan plateau, S.W. **China**, flows S.E. through N. **Vietnam**, enters G. of Tongking; Hanoi is nr. head of delta; Haiphong nr. one of R. mouths; lower valley densely populated and intensively cultivated; *c*. 1,280 km long.

Sonora, st., **Mexico**; on G. of Cal.; crossed by Sierra Madre Occidental; irrigated agr.; ch. producer of wheat, cattle; fish exp.; cap. Hermosillo; a. 182,535 km²; p. (1969) 1,249,000.

Sonoran Desert, Arizona, **USA**; alt. 900 m; enclosed basins and salt marshes.

Sonsonate, t., El Salvador; old t. with cath.; comm. ctr. of richest agr. region of rep., famed for coffee and dairy prod.; nr. Isalco volcano; p. (est. 1968) 31,435.

" Soo " Canals. *See* **Sault Ste. Marie Canals.**

Soochow (Suzhou), c., Kiangsu, **China**; nr. Shanghai; former treaty pt.; textile ctr.; p. (est. 1970) 1,300,000.

Sopot, spt., **Poland**; on Gdansk Bay; resort, spa; part of Trójmiasto; p. (1970) 47,600.

Sopron, t., N.W. **Hungary**; on R. Hunte; nr. Austrian border; textiles, chemicals; p. (1966) 44,700.

Sorau. *See* **Zary.**

Soria, t., cap. of prov. of Soria, **Spain**; on R. Duero at *c.* 900 m; agr.-processing; retains mediaeval appearance; p. (1970) 25,030.

Sorocaba, t., São Paulo st., **Brazil**; rly. wks.; textiles, cement, footwear, wines, fertilisers; p. (1970) 165,990.

Sorrento, cst. t., S. **Italy**; nr. S. extremity G. of Naples; popular resort, celebrated for its wines in anc. times; p. (est. 1968) 14,364.

Sosnowiec, t., Katowice prov., **Poland**; coal-mng. ctr., iron wks.; metal and textile inds.; cas.; p. (1970) 144,700.

Soufrière, volcano, St. Vincent, **W.I.**; alt. 1,235 m.

Sound, The, channel between Kattegat and Baltic, 5 km across at narrowest part; proposed tunnel between Denmark and Sweden.

Sousse (Susa), spt., **Tunisia**, exp. olive oil, phosphates; resort; p. (1966) 82,666.

South Africa, Republic of, lies in most S. part of Africa between Atl. and Indian Ocs.; comprises 4 provs., Cape Prov., Natal, O.F.S., Transvaal; narrow cst. plain, several interior plateaux (600–1,800 m) with upland grasslands (Veld) and fringed by escarpments; climate warm and sunny; most highly developed cty. in Africa, based on mineral resources of gold and diamonds, and more recent successful economic diversification; coal in Witbank and Vryheid dists. serves iron and steel ind. at Pretoria; growing textile, food-processing inds. at pts. Cape Town, Durban and rubber at Pt. Elizabeth; agr. dependent upon water supply; rich fruit growing a. around Cape Town, extensive grain growing and pastoral areas extended by irrigation; enforces practice of apartheid; caps. Pretoria (admin.), Cape Town (legislative), Bloemfontein (judicial); a. 1,224,254 km²; p. (1970) 21,300,000 (inc. 3,800,000 whites).

Southall. *See* **Ealing.**

South America, S. continent of Western Hemisphere; inc. all ctys. S. of Panama. *See* **Latin America.**

Southampton, c. spt., Hants., **Eng.**; at head of Southampton Water on peninsula between estuaries of Rs. Test and Itchen; univ.; extensive docks for passenger-liners; container facilities; ship repairing, oil refining, cable mkg., electronics, synthetic rubber; p. (1971) 214,826.

Southampton Water, inlet, Hants., **Eng.**; comprises drowned estuaries of Rs. Itchen and Test; gives access from Solent and Spithead to spt. of Southampton; 14 km by 1·6–2·4 km.

South Australia, st. of the Australian **Commonwealth**; the " desert state "; undulating interior forms part of central plateau of continent but inc. mtns. in S. and S.E. and L. Eyre basin 12 m below sea level; Nullarbor Plain in S.W.; sheep in S.E., intensive agr. in Murray R. valley; some interior mng. inds. but st. cap. of Adelaide contains most inds. and 60 per cent p.; a. 984,381 km²; p. (1972) 1,172,774.

South Bend, c., Ind., **USA**; on St. Joseph R.; ctr. of fruit and dairy region; motorcars, aircraft, agr. machin.; p. (1970) 125,580 (c.); (1968) 275,000 (met. a.).

Southborough, t., Kent, **Eng.**; 3 km N. of Tunbridge Wells; residtl.; p. (1971) 9,750.

South Carolina, st., **USA**; level in E., mtns. in W.; sub-tropical climate; part of cotton belt; pigs and maize also impt.; cotton textiles; cap. Columbia; a. 80,432 km²; p. (1970) 2,522,881.

South Dakota, st., **USA**; lies in Gt. Plains; crossed by R. Missouri; irrigated agr.; part of spring wheat belt, but now more diversified crops; agr. processing; cap. Pierre; a. 199,552 km²; p. (1970) 661,406 (inc. 25,000 Indians).

South Downs, chalk escarpment, East and West Sussex and Hants., **Eng.**; stretch from Chichester to Eastbourne; rise to over 240 m.

Southend-on-Sea, t., Essex, **Eng.**; on N. side of Thames estuary; varied lt. inds.; air ferry terminal; resort; dormitory for London; p. (1971) 162,326.

Southern Alps, mtns., S.I., **N.Z.**; alt. 3,000 m.

Southern Ocean, surrounds **Antarctica**; pack ice.

Southern Uplands, region, S. **Scot.**; broad belt of hilly cty., N. part bleak moorland, S. part deeply cut by glens; sheep-rearing; dairying in valleys.

South Georgia, Brit. I., S. Atl. Oc.; dependency of **Falkland Is.**; former whaling ctr.; a. 4,144 km²; p. (1967) 22.

South Glamorgan, co., S. **Wales**; mostly lowland borders Bristol Channel; inc. lge. industl. ts. and pts. of Cardiff and Barry; a. 417 km²; p. (1971) 389,916.

South I., lge. I., **N.Z.**; inc. S. Alps (highest Mt. Cook, 3,764 m), Canterbury Plains, impt. sheep-rearing dist.; cool climate; considerable hydroelectric power resources; tourism; a. 150,461 km²; p. (1971) 810,267.

South Kensington, dist., W. London, **Eng.**; contains Victoria and Albert Museum, Geological and Science Museums, British Museum of Natural History, Commonwealth Institute, Albert Hall.

Southland, prov., S.I., **N.Z.**; part of provincial dist of Otago; S. plains, an impt. mixed farming a.; tourism; coalfields; a. 28,930 km²; p. (1971) 106,084.

South Orkney Is., Antarctica; S.W. of S. Georgia; part of Brit. Antarctic Terr. (1962); meteorological sta.

South Ossetian, aut. oblast, Georgian SSR, **USSR**; in Caucasus mtns.; goat and sheep rearing dist.; a. 3,898 km²; p. (1971) 100,000.

Southport, t., Merseyside, **Eng.**; on S. side of Ribble estuary; 29 km N. of Liverpool; seaside resort; residtl.; p. (1971) 84,349.

South Sandwich Is., Antarctica; dependency of **Falkland Is.**; sm. volcanic Is.; a. 337 km².

South Shetland, archipelago, S. Atl. Oc.; 640 km S. C Horn; part of **Brit. Antarctic Terr.** (1962).

South Shields, t., Tyne and Wear, **Eng.**; on S. bank at mouth of R. Tyne; coming holiday resort; marine engin., new lt. inds.; p. (1971) 100,513.

Southwark, inner bor., London, **Eng.**; S. of R. Thames, incorporating former bors. of Bermondsey and Camberwell; cath.; site of former Globe theatre; p. (1971) 259,982.

Southwell, mkt. t., Notts., **Eng.**; lge. minster; p. (1971) 57,365 (dist.).

South West Africa (Namibia), mandated terr., under U.N. responsibility but disputedly admin by S. Africa; planned indep. for 1979; desert, scanty rainfall, part of southern African plateau; stock rearing; alluvial diamonds from Lüderitz on Orange R.; copper, lead, zinc mng. in Grootfontein dist.; ch. pt. Walvis Bay; cap. Windhoek; summer cap. Swakopmund; a. 824,296 km²; p. (1970) 746,328.

Southwick, t., West Sussex, **Eng.**; on S. cst. 6 km W. of Brighton; p. (1971) 11,850.

Southwold, spt., Suffolk, **Eng.**; on E. cst. 13 km S. of Lowestoft; fishing; resort; p. (1971) 1,992.

South Yorkshire, met. co., **Eng.**; mainly industl. a. E. of Pennines; inc. productive coalfield nr. Barnsley and Doncaster and steel producing ts. of Sheffield and Rotherham; p. (1971) 1,315,000.

Sovetsk (Tilsit), t., **RSFSR** (since 1945); on R. Niemen, formerly in E. Prussia; timber and paper inds.; famous for Treaty of Tilsit between Napoleon and Russia 1807; p. (est. 1967) 36,000.

Sowerby Bridge, t., West Yorks., **Eng.**; on R. Calder, 5 km W. of Halifax; woollens; p. (1971) 16,260.

Spa, t., Liège, **Belgium**; mineral springs, resort; gave name to " spas "; p. (est. 1969) 9,487.

Spain, indep. sov. st., Iberia, S.W. **Europe**; lge. land a. takes up 80 per cent of Iberian peninsula and helps to make climate continental;

mtnous. interior and narrow coastal strip encourages regional isolation and development of regional culture; civil war 1936–9 hindered modern economic growth; economy based on agr., but much of land is arid and although industl. raw materials in N. Spain and an oil refinery under construction at Bilbao economic development has depended largely upon the spectacular growth of tourism; monarchy revived 1975; cap. Madrid; a. 504,747 km²; p. (1975) 35,355,039.

Spalding, mkt. t., Lincs., **Eng.**; in Fens, 16 km up R. Welland from Wash; agr., bulb mkt. agr. machin., sugar-beet, fruit canning; p. (1971) 16,950.

Spandau, t., Potsdam, **E. Germany**; previously gr. military ctr.; at confluence of Rs. Havel and Spree; now part of Berlin.

Spanish Guinea. *See* Equatorial Guinea.

Spanish Sahara (Spanish West Africa), *See* Western Sahara.

Sparrows Point, t., Md., **USA**; situated on Chesapeake Bay; impt. iron and steel inds.

Sparta (Spárti), famous anc. c., **Greece**; on R. Eurotas, in Peloponnesus; passed under Roman rule 146 B.C.; modern c. dates from 1834; p. (1971) 11,981.

Spenborough, t., West Yorks., **Eng.**; textiles, plastics, wire; p. (1971) 40,693.

Spencer Gulf, lge. inlet, S. **Australia**; penetrates 384 km inland, max. width 120 km.

Spennymoor, t., Durham, **Eng.**; growing industl. t. S. of Durham; p. (1971) 19,063.

Sperrin Mtns., Strabane, **N. Ireland**; peat-covered schists; Sawell, 683 m.

Spey, R., Moray, Badenoch and Strathspey, the most rapid in Scot., flows N.E. to Moray Firth; used for hydroelec. power; 1,712 km long.

Speyer, t., Rhineland–Palatinate, **W. Germany**; tobacco, footwear, paper, sugar, brewing, oil refining; cas., cath.; famous Diet 1529 condemning Reformation gave rise to term "Protestant"; p. (est. 1969) 41,957.

Spitalfields, par., E. London, **Eng.**; formerly noted for silk weaving, introduced by Huguenots 17th cent.; name derives from spital or hospital of St. Mary, founded 12th cent.

Spithead, roadstead, between Portsmouth and I. of Wight, **Eng.**; used by ships of Royal Navy.

Spitsbergen (Svalbard), I. gr. belonging to **Norway**; within Arctic; mtnous.; sealing and whaling; coal mng.; asbestos, copper, gypsum; a. 62,921 km²; p. (1968) 2,808 (Norwegian 908, Russian 1,900).

Split (Spalato), t., **Yugoslavia**; spt. on Adriatic; second spt. of rep.; airport; food processing; p. (est. 1969) 108,000.

Spokane, c., Wash., **USA**; on R. Spokane at falls used for hydroelec. power; timber tr. impt.; flour and saw mills, elec. gds.; lge. aluminium wks.; p. (1970) 168,654 (c.), 283,077 (met. a.).

Spoleto, c., Umbria, central **Italy**; cath., many Roman remains; textiles, leather; p. (est. 1968) 37,036.

Sporades, scattered Is. belonging to **Greece** in Aegean Sea, inc. Skyros, Skiathos and Skopelos.

Spratley Is., S. China Sea; cluster of about 50 reefs and sand bars, thought to contain petroleum; ownership disputed by China, Taiwan, Philippines, and Vietnam.

Spree, R., **E. Germany**; flows W. past Berlin to the Havel at Spandau; 363 km long.

Spremberg, t., Cottbus, **E. Germany**; on R. Spree; cas., older part of t. on I.; glass, textiles; p. (est. 1970) 22,629.

Springfield, c., cap. of Ill., **USA**; in rich agr and coal mng. a.; farming and elec. machin., food processing; tomb of Abraham Lincoln who lived here; (1970) 89,816 (c.), 159,432 (met. a.).

Springfield, c., Mass., **USA**; mnfs. cars, elec. apparatus and paper; p. (1970) 162,078 (c.), 523,502 (met. a.).

Springfield, c., Mo., **USA**; agr. ctr.; flour milling, engin.; p. (1970) 118,950.

Springfield, t., Ohio, **USA**; agr. implements, motor lorries; p. (1970) 82,188 (c.), 153,197 (met. a.).

Springs, t., Transvaal, **S. Africa**; E. of Johannesburg; gold mng., engin., machin., cars, elec. gds.; uranium plant; p. (1970) 104,090 (met. a.).

Spurn Head, Humberside, **Eng.**; sand spit at mouth of Humber estuary.

Sri Lanka (Ceylon), indep. rep. (1972) within Brit. Commonwealth (1948); in **Indian Oc.**; S.E. of India; fertile plains with cash crops of coconuts and rubber (S.W.) but dry in N.; mtnous. interior ameliorates climate where tea cultivation; varied p. composition inc. Sinhalese, Tamils, Burghers (Portuguese and Dutch); dependent on exp. of primary produce; inds. growing; cap. and ch. spt. Colombo; a. 65,610 km²; p. (est. 1969) 12,240,000.

Srinagar, t., cap. of Kashmir, **India**; in vale at c. 1,600 m. on Jhelum R. in W. Himalayas; beautiful surrounding cty.; summer resorts; mnfs. silks, woollens, carpets; tourism; p. (1967) 325,000.

Sriracha, t., **Thailand**; sawmills; oil refinery; p. (1960) 10,472.

Srirangam, t., Tamil Nadu, **India**; on R. Cauvery; temple dedicated to Vishnu; pilgrimage ctr.; p. (1961) 41,949.

Stade, t., Lower Saxony, **W. Germany**; nr. Hamburg; pt. on R. Schwinge; leather, wood, textiles; p. (est. 1969) 31,658.

Staffa, I. in Inner Hebrides, W. **Scot.**; 10 km N. of Iona, off W. cst. Mull; grand basaltic caverns, inc. Fingal's Cave, 69 m long, 13 m wide, 20 m high.

Stafford, co. t., Staffs., **Eng.**; on R. Sow, 24 km N. of Wolverhampton; heavy elec. and other engin.; expanded t.; p. (1971) 54,890.

Staffordshire, non-met. co., W. Midlands, **Eng.**; plain drained by R. Trent and tribs.; N. Staffs. coalfield inc. a. of "Potteries"; S. Staffs. coalfield now inc. in W. Midlands met. co.; a. 2,717 km²; p. (1971) 963,000.

Staines, mkt. t., Surrey, **Eng.**; on R. Thames, 6 km S.E. of Windsor; linoleum, machin.; nr. birthplace of Matthew Arnold; p. (1971) 56,386.

Stainmore, pass, North Yorks./Durham, **Eng.**; crosses N. Pennines from Greta valley into upper Eden valley; used by main road but only minor rly.; alt. 418 m.

Staithes, v., North Yorks., **Eng.**; potash mng.

Stalin. *See* **Brasov.**

Stalinabad. *See* **Dushanbe.**

Stalingrad. *See* **Volgograd.**

Stalino. *See* **Varna.**

Stalino. *See* **Donetsk.**

Stalinogorsk. *See* **Novomoskovsk.**

Stalinsk. *See* **Novo Kuznetsk.**

Stalybridge, t., Gtr. Manchester, **Eng.**; on R. Tame, 8 km E. of Manchester; cotton and wool, engin., plastics, rubber gds., elec. cables; p. (1971) 22,782.

Stamboul. *See* **Istanbul.**

Stamford, mkt. t., Lincs., **Eng.**; old bldgs., one of 5 Danelaw ts.; agr. inds., elec. gds., plastics; p. (1971) 14,485.

Stamford, c., Conn., **USA**; on shore of Long I. Sound; chemicals, engin.; p. (1970) 107,907 (c.), 204,888 (met. a.).

Standerton, t., Transvaal, **S. Africa**; on R. Vaal; agr. mkt.; p. (est. 1967) 22,500.

Standish-with-Langtree, t., Gtr. Manchester, **Eng.**; 6 km N.W. of Wigan; former colly. dist.; p. (1971) 11,159.

Stanislav. *See* **Ivano-Frankovsk.**

Stanley, t., Durham, **Eng.**; former colly. dist.; p. (1971) 41,940.

Stanley, t. West Yorks., **Eng.**; p. (1971) 20,776.

Stanley, spt., cap. of **Falkland Is.**; former whaling pt., contains over half p. of Falklands; p. (est. 1970) 1,098.

Stanley Falls. *See* **Boyoma Falls.**

Stanley Pool. *See* **Pool Malebo.**

Stanleyville. *See* **Kisangani.**

Stanlow, Ches., **Eng.**; petrol refinery, oil storage docks, chemicals.

Stanovoi Mtns., range of mtns., **USSR**; extending from N. of R. Amur to nr. Sea of Okhotsk.

Stara Zagora, t., central **Bulgaria**; textiles, agr. processing; educational ctr.; p. (est. 1969) 106,468.

Stargard Szczecinski, t., N.W. **Poland** (since 1945); formerly in Pomerania; rly. junc.; metal, chemical, and food inds.; devastated in second world war; p. (1970) 44,500.

Start Point, C., nr. Dartmouth. Devon, **Eng.**

Stassfurt, t., Magdeburg, **E. Germany**; in gr. potash mng. region; chemicals, machin., metals; p. (est. 1970) 25,695.

Staten I., the most S. point N.Y. st. **USA**; shipyds.; linked with Brooklyn by Verrazano-Narrows bridge (opened 1964); residtl.

Staten I., off Tierra del Fuego, S. America; 72 km long.

States of the Church. *See* **Papal States.**

Stavanger, spt., cap. of Rogaland prov., S.W. Norway; comm. and industl. ctr.; fish curing and canning; oil refinery at Sola; cath., airport; p. (1968) 80,781.

Staveley, t., Derbys., **Eng.**; 5 km N.E. of Chesterfield; coal, iron, chemicals, concrete and iron pipes; p. (1971) 17,644.

Stellenbosch, t., Cape Prov., **S. Africa**; 40 km E. of Cape Town; univ.; wines, saw milling, brick and tile mkg.; p. (est. 1969) 29,900.

Stelvio Pass, between Italy and Switzerland; road pass, alt. 2,762 m.

Stendal, c., Magdeburg, **E. Germany**; impt. rly. junc.; sugar, metal and food inds.; cath.; Stendhal (Henri Beyle) took his name from the c.; p. (est. 1970) 36,478.

Stepney. *See* **Tower Hamlets.**

Sterlitamak, t., Bashkir ASSR, **RSFSR**; on S.W. flank of Ural mtns.; impt. oil refineries on "second Baku" oilfield; linked by pipeline to Togliatti; p. (1970) 185,000.

Stettin. *See* **Szczecin.**

Stettiner Haff, lagoon, **E. Germany and Poland**; separated from Baltic Sea by Is. Usedom and Wollin; receives R. Oder; 56 km long.

Stevenage, t., Herts., **Eng.**; 6 km S.E. of Hitchin; first new t. to be designated under the New Towns Act 1946; old t. known in Domesday as Stevenach; agr., lt. engin., school furniture, elec. gds., chemicals, aircraft parts; p. (est. 1974) 74,800.

Stevenston, burgh, Cunninghame, **Scot.**; explosives factory; p. (1971) 12,047.

Steventon, v., Hants. **Eng.**; birthplace of Jane Austen.

Stewart I., S. of S.I., **N.Z.**; a. 1,735 km²; rises to over 900 m; famous for oysters.

Stewarton, burgh, Kilmarnock and Loudoun, **Scot.**; woollens, carpets; p. (1971) 4,492.

Steyning, v., West Sussex, **Eng.**; on R. Adur, 6 km N. of Shoreham at entrance to gap through S. Downs; residtl.

Steyr, t., **Austria**; at confluence of Rs. Enns and Steyr; bicycles, lorries, machin.; p. (1961) 38,306.

Stilton, v., Cambs., **Eng.**; 10 km S.W. of Peterborough; famous for cheese.

Stirling, royal burgh, Stirling, **Scot.**; on R. Forth in gap between Campsie Fells and Ochil hills; cas., univ.; coal mng., engin., concrete, wool, rubber gds.; p. (1971) 29,776.

Stirlingshire, former co., central **Scot.**; on S. edge of Grampians; now forms l. gov. dist. within the Central Reg.; a. of l. gov. dist. 2,168 km²; p. (1971) 75,520.

Stockholm, c., cap. of **Sweden**; on Is. at outlet of L. Malar; called the "Queen of the Baltic" for the beauty of its surroundings; comm. ctr.; machin., textiles, leather, sugar, chemicals; univ. and many academic institutions; p. (est. 1969) 747,490 (c.), 1,306,762 (met. a.).

Stockport, t., Gtr. Manchester, **Eng.**; on R. Mersey, 8 km S.E. of Manchester; cotton, man-made fibres, engin.; p. (1971) 139,663.

Stocksbridge, t., South Yorks., **Eng.**; iron and steel; p. (1971) 13,400.

Stockton, t., Cal., **USA**; R. pt. on San Joaquin R.; agr. processing, farm implements; p. (1970) 102,663 (t.), 284,506 (met. a.).

Stockton-on-Tees, mkt. t., Cleveland, **Eng.**; 6 km W. of Middlesbrough; impt. iron and steel inds., plywood; first rly. for passenger traffic opened 1825 between Stockton and Darlington; 18th cent. town hall; racecourse.

Stoke Newington. *See* **Hackney.**

Stoke-on-Trent, c., Staffs., **Eng.**; at S.W. foot of the Pennines; formed in 1910 by union of the "five towns" of Arnold Bennett's novels, Hanley, Burslem, Tunstall, Longton, and Fenton (with Stoke-upon-Trent); ceramics, coal, iron and steel, engin., brick and tile wks., precast concrete, rubber gds.; p. (1971) 265,153.

Stolberg, t., N. Rhine-Westphalia, **W. Germany**; E. of Aachen; metals. glass, wood, chemicals; p. (est. 1969) 39,393.

Stolp. *See* **Slupsk.**

Stone, mkt. t., Staffs., **Eng.**; on R. Trent, 11 km S. of Stoke-on-Trent; footwear, tiles, porcelain, scientific glassware; p. (1971) 10,985.

Stonvehaven, t., burgh, Kincardine and Deeside, **Scot.**; fish. pt. on E cst., 22 km S. of Aberdeen, distilling, net mftg.; p. (1971) 4,730.

Stonehenge, prehistoric gr. of monumental stones, on Salisbury Plain, Wilts., **Eng.**; date of erection est. between 2100–1600 B.C.

Stornoway, spt., burgh, **Scot.**; on E. cst. of I. of Lewis, Outer Hebrides; ctr. Harris Tweed ind.; fishing ctr.; p. (1971) 5,152.

Stour, R., Kent, **Eng.**; flows past Canterbury to Pegwell Bay; 64 km long.

Stour, R., Somerset, Dorset, **Eng.**; trib. of R. Avon; 88 km long.

Stour, R., Suffolk and Essex, **Eng.**; flows E. to sea at Harwich; 67 km long.

Stour, R., Hereford and Worcs./West Midlands, **Eng.**; trib. of R. Severn; 32 km long.

Stourbridge, t., West Midlands, **Eng.**; on R. Stour, 14 km W. of Birmingham; brick and glass wks.; p. (1971) 54,331.

Stourport-on-Severn, mkt. t., Hereford and Worcs., **Eng.**; at confluence of Rs. Stour and Severn; carpets, iron and steel gds., porcelain, ceramics; old canal and R. pt.; p. (1971) 17,913.

Stowmarket, t., Suffolk, **Eng.**; on R. Gipping, 18 km N.W. of Ipswich; I.C.I. paint factory; p. (1971) 8,670.

Strabane, t., l. gov. dist., **N. Ireland**; agr. ctr., shirt mkg.; p. (1966) 8,813.

Straits Settlements, former Brit. crown col., Malay Peninsula; comprised Penang, Malacca, and Singapore, established 1867, dissolved 1946. *See* **Malaysia, West.**

Stralsund, spt., Rostock, **E. Germany**; opposite Rügen I.; grain tr., machin., metals, fish smoking, shipbldg.; p. (est. 1970) 71,551.

Strangford Lough, arm of sea, Down and Ards, **N. Ireland**; 29 km long, 10 km wide at entrance.

Stranraer, royal burgh, Wigtown, **Scot.**; at head of Loch Ryan; steamer service to Larne, N. Ireland; creameries, brewing, knitwear; cas.; mkt.; p. (1971) 9,853.

Strasbourg, c., cap. of Bas-Rhin dep., **E. France**; impt. pt. in Rhine valley on Ill R., 16 km S. of confluence with Rhine; terminus of Marne-Rhine and Rhône-Rhine canals; industl., comm. and cultural ctr. of economically impt. Alsace region; food processing and varied mnfs.; historic c., with many fine bldgs., inc. cath., univ., imperial palace; surrendered to Germany 1871, recovered 1919; meeting-place of European Parliament; p. (1968) 254,038 (c.), 334,668 (met. a.).

Stratford. *See* **Newham.**

Stratford-on-Avon, t., Warwicks., **Eng.**; on R. Avon; birthplace of Shakespeare; memorial theatre, library; many bldgs. ass. with Shakespeare; tourist ctr. in attractive setting; lt. inds.; p. (1971) 19,449.

Strathclyde Region, l. gov. reg., Central **Scot.**; industl. dist. formed around Glasgow, inc. ts. on Ayr and Lanarkshire coalfields; borders the F. of Clyde; a. 13,794 km²; p. (1971) 2,579,555.

Strathmore, lowland belt, central **Scot.**; flanked to N. by Scot. Highlands, to S. by Sidlaw and Ochil hills; drained by Rs. Earn, Tay, Isla, S. Esk; famous for cereals and small fruits; length 96 km, width 11–16 km.

Strathspey, valley of the Spey, **Scot.**; 112 km long.

Stratton and Bude, N. Cornwall, **Eng.**; 19 km S. of Hartland Point; resort; p. (1971) 5,629.

Straubing, t., Lower Bavaria, **W. Germany**; agr. mkt. ctr.; machin.; p. (est. 1969) 37,024.

Strawberry, R., Utah, **USA**; on E. slopes of Wasatch mtns. 128 km S.E. of Salt Lake City; dammed to supply irrigation water, led through tunnel under Wasatch mtns. to 259 km² cultivable land round L. Utah.

Street, t., Somerset, **Eng.**; at foot of Polden hills, 11 km S.W. of Wells; footwear, leather; p. (1971) 8,161.

Stretford, t., Gtr. Manchester, **Eng.**; borders Manchester Ship Canal; inc. Trafford Park industl. estate; residtl.; Lancashire co. cricket ground, Manchester United football ground at Old Trafford; p. (1971) 54,011.

Stromboli, I., Lipari Is., Tyrrhenian Sea, N. of Sicily, **Italy**; active volcano, alt. 927 m.

Stromness, burgh, Mainland, Orkney Is., **Scot.**; 21 km W. of Kirkwall; mkt., fish. pt.; p. (1971) 1,646.

Stronsay, Orkney Is., Scot.; p. (1971) 439.
Stroud, mkt. t., Gloucs., Eng.; on R. Frome, in Cotswolds; former ctr. of impt. cloth ind. in W. Eng.; woollens, dyes, plastics, engin.; p. (1971) 19,125.
Sturminster Newton, t., Dorset, Eng.; impt. cattle mkt. on Stour R.; creameries; p. (1971) 10,715 (dist.).
Sturt Desert, a. N.W. of S. Australia; named after Charles Sturt, explorer.
Stuttgart, c., cap. of Baden-Württemburg, W. Germany; on Neckar R.; cas., cath., rly. junc.; industl. and comm. ctr.; publishing, science-based inds.; oil refinery nearby; p. (est. 1969) 621,000.
Styria, prov., Austria; borders Yugoslavia on S.; mtnous. with forests and pastures; lignite and iron mng., inds. around cap. Graz; grain, wine, fruit, stock-rearing; tourism; p. (1971) 1,191,000.
Suakin, former pt., Sudan, N.E. Africa; on Red Sea; now used only for pilgrim traffic to Jeddah; replaced by Pt. Sudan; plans for new pt.
Suanhwa (Xuanhua), c., Hopeh prov., China; iron mng.; p. (1953) 114,000.
Subotica, t., Serbia, Yugoslavia; univ.; agr. ctr. with Hungarian culture; agr. processing; expanding industl. ctr.; p. (1971) 88,787.
Suceava, t., S. Bukovina, N.E. Romania; mkt. t. on Suceava R.; once the residence of Moldavian princes; p. (1968) 40,441.
Suchow (Suzhou), c., Kiangsu, China; at junc. of N. China plain and Yangtse R. basin; impt. rly. junc.; p. (est. 1970) 1,500,000.
Sucre, c., cap. of Chuquisaca dep. and *de jura* cap. of Bolivia (La Paz is *de facto* cap.); in valley of Andes at 2,600 m; agr. ctr., oil refining, 47,800.
Sucre, st., Venezuela; on Caribbean cst.; coffee and cacao; fishing impt.; fish canning at cap. Cumaná; a. 11,800 km²; p. (est. 1970) 493,840.
Sudan, The, rep., N.E. Africa; climatic transition from N. desert to rainy equatorial S.; mainly plateaux, dissected by Nile R. system; sporadic conflict between N. and S. (1955–1972); 3 southern provs. now form an autonomous reg.; long staple cotton, grown in irrigated areas, provides most valuable exp.; gum arabic from lge. forest areas; food processing; dams under construction on Atbara and Blue Nile Rs.; cap. Khartoum; a. 2,530,430 km²; p. (1970) 15,503,000.
Sudbury, t., Ont., Canada; nickel, copper mng.; refining; univ.; p. (1971) 89,898. (c.), 172,458 (met. a.).
Sudbury, t., Suffolk, Eng.; on R. Stour, 19 km N.W. of Colchester; p. (1971) 8,183.
Sudene, terr., N.E. Brazil; government sponsored economic development.
Sudetenland, region of ČSSR bordering Germany, until 1945 German-speaking; annexed by Hitler 1938, recovered by ČSSR 1945; named after Sudeten mtns.; contains 20 per cent of p. of ČSSR.
Sudeten Mtns. or Sudetes, mtn. range along border of ČSSR and Poland; separating Bohemia and Moravia from Silesia; mineral resources.
Suez, spt., Egypt; the anc. Arsinoë; at head of G. of Suez (arm of Red Sea) and S. entrance of Suez canal, which crosses the isthmus of Suez to the Mediterranean at Port Said; Port Tewfiq adjoining has quay and docks; declined during closure of canal 1967–75; oil refining, fertilisers; p. (est. 1970) 315,000.
Suez Canal, ship canal, Egypt; connects Mediterranean Sea (Pt. Said) with Red Sea (Suez) through Ls. Manzala, Timsah, and Bitter; length 162 km; closed after Arab-Israeli war of June 1967; but since cleared of unexploded weaponry; reopened 1975.
Suez, G., Red Sea; N.W. arm of Red Sea between Arabian desert and Sinai peninsula, Egypt; southern approach to Suez canal; length 304 km., width varies from 19–40 km.
Suffolk, non-met. co. E. Anglia, Eng.; bounded on E. by N. Sea, drowned coastline; rises to 90 m in E. Anglian Heights in W.; impt. agr. a., lge farms, mixed farming; inds. based on agr.; many expanded ts. in S.; formerly divided into 2 admin. parts; co. t. Ipswich; a. 3,800 km²; p. (1971) 537,000.
Suhl, admin. dist., E. Germany; inc. Thuringian Forest; expanding inds. based on local potash and iron ore; a. 3,877 km²; p. (est. 1970) 553,020.
Suhl, t., Suhl, E. Germany; once famous for armaments; motor-cycles; p. (est. 1970) 31,445.
Sui, Baluchistan, Pakistan; natural gas; pipeline to Karachi.
Suir, R., R.o.I.; flows E. to Waterford harbour; 136 km long.
Sukhumi, spt., Georgian SSR, USSR; agr. processing, saw milling; resort; p. (1970) 102,000.
Sukkur, t., Pakistan; major bridging point of R. Indus; 368 km N.E. of Karachi; dam for irrigation; thermal sta.; p. (est. 1969) 131,000.
Sulaimaniya, t., Iraq; in hill dist. nr. Iran border; p. (1965) 131,000 (met. a.).
Sula Is., I. gr. in Molucca Sea, E. of Sulawesi, Indonesia; little developed.
Sulawesi (Celebes), I., Indonesia; mtnous., lge. forests; copra, coffee, gold, nickel, copper, asphalt; ch. pts. Menado, Makasar; a. 189,484 km²; p. (est. 1970) 8,925,000.
Sullum Voe, Shetland Is., Scot.; oil terminal and receiving ctr. for N. Sea oil.
Sultanabad. *See* Arak.
Sulu Is., Philippines; archipelago between Borneo and the Philippines; inc. over 400 volcanic Is. and coral islets; a. 2,461 km²; under US control 1899–1940.
Sumatra, I., Indonesia; relatively underdeveloped; sparse p.; main development in Cultuurgebied, rubber, oil palm, sisal, tobacco; impt. oil deposits and new oil refineries; a. 473,607 km²; p. (1967) 18,300,000
Sumba or Sandalwood I., S. of Flores, Indonesia; horse-breeding; rice, maize, tobacco, timber, cinnamon; cap. Waingapu; a. 11,150 km²; p. (1961) 251,126.
Sumbawa, I., Indonesia; between Flores and Lombok; wet climate, sparse p.; a. (inc. nearby Is.) 13,572 km²; p. 314,843.
Sumgait, t., Azerbaydzhan SSR, USSR; on Caspian Sea; 40 km N.W. of Baku; metallurgical ind.; chemicals; p. (1970) 124,000.
Sumy, t., Ukrainian SSR, USSR; engin., chemicals, textiles, agr. processing; p. (1970) 159,000.
Sunbury-on-Thames, t., Surrey, Eng.; W. of London; residtl., water wks., gravel pits; petrol research establishment; p. (1971) 40,035.
Sunda Is., Indonesia; between S. China Sea and Indian Oc.; form two grs., Greater Sunda Is., inc. Java, Sumatra, Borneo, Sulawesi, Banka, and the Lesser Sunda Is. (renamed Nusa Tenggara 1954) inc. Bali, Lombok, Sumbawa, Timor.
Sundarbans, The, tract of forest and swamps, fringing the delta of the Ganges, India/Bangladesh; 130 km wide; rice grown in N.; tigers and crocodiles found in S.
Sunda Strait, between Java and Sumatra, Indonesia; 21 km wide, contains the volcanic I. of Krakatao.
Sunday I., lgst. of Kermadec Is., N.Z.; 32 km in circuit and with a p. of 10 is the only one of the Kermadec Is. that is inhabited; meteorological and radio sta. established on I.
Sundbyberg, t., Sweden; adjoins Stockholm; chemicals, paper; p. (1968) 28,661.
Sunderland, spt. Tyne and Wear, Eng.; at mouth of R. Wear; precision and aero-engin., clothing, glass, shipbldg.; p. (1971) 216,892.
Sundsvall, spt., Västernorrland, Sweden; on a wide bay of the Baltic nr. Hernösand; timber and wood-pulp inds.; p. (1968) 62,278.
Sungari, R., N.E. China; trib. of R. Amur; inc. the Nonni, length 1,840 km; used for hydro-electric power.
Sunnyvale, t., Cal., USA; ctr. of fruit-growing a.; lt. inds.; p. (1970) 95,408.
Superior, t., Wis., USA; at head of L. Superior; tr. in grain, timber, coal; shipbldg. and flour mills; oil refining; p. (1970) 32,237.
Superior, L., N. America; lgst. sheet of fresh water in the world; lies between Canada and USA; one of chain of gr. Ls. in St. Lawrence system; outlet to L. Huron by St. Mary's R., receives waters of St. Louis, Pigeon and Nipigon; impt. waterway; a. 82,880 km².
Surabaya, spt., Java, Indonesia; ch. naval base; handles nearly half Indonesia's tr.; shipbldg.

oil refining, food processing; p. (1971) 1,556,255.

Surakarta (Solo), Java, Indonesia; on Solo R.; tr. ctr. for agr. region; former sultan's palace; p. (1971) 414,285.

Surat, c., Gujarat, India; on R. Tapti: textile ctr.; notable as first English trading post 1612; p. (1971) 471,656 (c.), 493,001 (met. a.).

Surbiton, Gtr. London, Eng.; on R. Thames, inc. in Royal Borough of Kingston-upon-Thames; residtl.; lt. engin., bricks, tiles, elec. components.

Suresnes, t., Hauts-de-Seine dep., France; sub. of Paris; cars, chemicals; p. (1968) 41,263.

Surinam (Dutch Guiana), former self-gov. terr. of Neth.; indep. 1975; **S. America**; sub-tropical climate; p. concentrated on cst. where rice, sugar, and citrus fruits grown; main exp. bauxite (86 per cent of total exp.); cap. Paramaribo; a. 161,875 km²; p. (1967) 345,000.

Surinumu Dam, 48 km from Port Moresby, **Papua New Guinea**; part of hydroelectric scheme; opened 1963.

Surrey, non-met. co., **S. Eng.**; S. of R. Thames inc. part of N. Downs; serves as dormitory a. and recreational dist. for London; mkt. gardening, dairying; co. t. Guildford; a. 1,655 km²; p. (1971) 981,000.

Susa. *See* **Sousse.**

Susquehanna, R., N.Y., Penns., and Md., USA; flows to Chesapeake Bay through highly industl. a.; routeway W. from Philadelphia and Baltimore across Appalachian mtns.; not navigable; hydroelectric power; 675 km long.

Sussex. *See* **East Sussex, and West Sussex.**

Susten Pass, alpine road, alt. 2,225 m between Hasli Tal and Reuss valley, links Bernese Oberland with Gotthard road. Switzerland.

Sutherland, l. gov. dist., former co., **Highland Reg., Scot.**; stretches from Atl. Oc. to Moray F.; sparsely p. reg.; a. 3,152 km²; p. (1971) 11,865.

Sutlej, R., Pakistan; rises in the Himalayas and flows to the R. Indus; used for lge. scale irrigation; 1,600 km long.

Sutton, outer bor., **Greater London, Eng.**; inc. former bors. of Beddington and Wallington, Sutton and Cheam, and Carshalton; residtl.; p. (1971) 168,775.

Sutton Coldfield, t., West Midlands, Eng.; 10 km N.E. of Birmingham; residtl.; hardware, plastics; p. (1971) 83,130.

Sutton-in-Ashfield, t., Notts., Eng.; 5 km S.W. of Mansfield; lt. engin.; hosiery; coal-mng. dist.; p. (1971) 40,725.

Suva, c., cap. of Fiji Is.; on Viti Levu I.; fine harbour; exp. coconut prods., sugar; international airport; p. (1966) 54,157 (c.), 80,248 (met. a.).

Suwalki, t., N.E. Poland; nr. Lithuanian bdy.; timber, grain, woollens; p. (1970) 25,400.

Suwannee, R., Fla., and Ga., USA; flows to G. of Mexico; known as "Swanee River," 400 km long.

Svendborg, spt., Fyn, Denmark; exp. dairy prods.; textiles, machin.; p. (est. 1970) 23,149.

Sverdlovsk (Ekaterinburg), c., cap. of S. oblast, RSFSR; on R. Iset in E. foothills of Ural mtns.; on Trans-Siberian rly.; industl. expansion during second world war; heavy machin., metallurgical and chemical plants; univ.; p. (1970) 1,026,000 (c.); (1969) 1,028,000 (met. a.).

Svir, R., USSR; flows between L. Onega and L. Ladoga; hydroelectric power; navigable; 200 km long.

Svishtov (Sistova), t., N. Bulgaria; R. pt. on Danube in vine-growing dist., nr. Romanian bdr.; cath., univ.; p. (est. 1968), 22,456.

Swabia, historic region, mediaeval duchy, **Germany**; now forms part of Baden-Württemberg and Bavaria; contains Black Forest.

Swabian Alps, mtns., Baden-Württemberg, W. Germany; inc. the Swabian Jura range between valleys of Neckar and Danube.

Swadlincote, t., Derbys., Eng.; 5 km E. of Burton-on-Trent; potteries, engin., clothing, coal-mng. ctr.; p. (1971) 20,235.

Swaffham, mkt. t., Norfolk, Eng.; fruit canning; p. (1971) 4,270.

Swale, R., North Yorks., Eng.; joins R. Ure to form R. Ouse, 96 km long.

Swanage, mkt. t.. Dorset. Eng.; on bay, E. cst. I. of Purbeck; seaside resort; stone quarries; p. (1971) 8,550.

Swanland, region, W. Australia; consists of extreme S.W. corner of W. Australia; forests of Karri and Jarrah; vines, citrus and deciduous fruits, wheat; highest p. density in W. Australia; ch. ts. Perth, Fremantle, Bunbury.

Swanscombe, t., Kent, Eng.; 5 km W. of Gravesend; cement and paper mnfs.; p. (1971) 9,184.

Swansea, c., spt., West Glamorgan, Wales; on Swansea Bay; univ.; grew with exp. of coal; now imports minerals; copper and zinc refining; steel, aluminium, wire, plastics; p. (1971) 172,566.

Swatow (Shantou), c., spt., S.E. Kwangtung prov., China; at mouth of Han R.; mftg. and exp. tr.; sugar refineries; p. (est. 1970) 400,000.

Swaziland, indep. kingdom, **S. Africa**; within Brit. Commonwealth (1968), bordered by S. Africa on S., W., and N. and by Moçambique on E.; four north-south regions: high, middle, low veld and Lebombo escarpment; rainfall increases with alt.; agr. basis of economy and sugar impt. exp., but iron ore major exp.; asbestos mng., food processing inds.; cattle raising main internal activity; cap. Mbabane; a. 17,363 km²; p. (1970) 451,000.

Sweden, kingdom, Scandinavia, **N.W. Europe**; divided for admin. purposes into 24 cos.; cap. c. Stockholm; mtnous. in N. and S. with central lowland belt containing major agr. a. and lge. proportion of p.; sm. home mkt. makes for dependency on exps., especially of minerals; inc. high-grade iron ore from Kiruna and Malmberget, N. of Arctic circle; development of high-value science-based inds.; furniture, porcelain and glass mnfs. have international reputation; social democratic st. since 1932; remained neutral in second world war; highly advanced system of social security; a. 449,792 km²; p. (1970) 8,013,696.

Swidnica (Schweidnitz), t., Poland (since 1945); formerly in Lower Silesia; ctr. of agr. dist.; metals, elec. machin., leather, textiles; p. (1970) 47,500.

Swilly, Lough, N.E. Donegal, R.o.I.; arm of Atl. Oc. between Fanad Point and Dunaff Head; extends 40 km inland.

Swindon, t., Wilts., Eng.; in upper Thames Valley (Vale of White Horse), 43 km S.W. of Oxford; impt. rly. junc.; mkt. for local dist.; heavy engin., textiles, tobacco; expanded t.; p. (1971) 90,830.

Świnoujście (Swinemünde), spt., N.W. Poland (since 1945); formerly in Pomerania; on I. of Usedom (Uznam), Baltic Sea; spt. for Szezecin; spa and summer resort; fishing; p. (1971) 27,900.

Swinton, t., South Yorks., Eng.; in Don valley, 5 km N.E. of Rotherham; potteries, bricks and tiles; p. (1971) 14,897.

Swinton and Pendlebury, ts., Gtr. Manchester, Eng.; 8 km W. of Manchester; cotton spinning, coal, engin., accumulator mftg.; p. (1971) 40,124.

Switzerland, confederation, **central Europe**; landlocked mtnous. st. with major physical features dominated by Alpine mtn. system; divided into 25 cantons and half-cantons for purposes of govt.; 3 official languages: German (72 per cent), French (20 per cent), Italian (6 per cent) in addition to Romansch; like Norway, major natural resource is water power; industl. specialisation on precision engin., especially watch and clock mnfs.; agr. in valleys with impt. output of dairy prod., transhumance between mtn. pastures and valley bottoms; tourism provides valuable source of income; cap. Berne; a. 41,310 km²; p. (1970) 6,269,783.

Sydney, c., cap. of N.S.W., Australia; on shore of Pt. Jackson Bay; many beautiful bldgs. and parks, stretching S. to Botany Bay; lge. comm. and active inds.; magnificent bridge, harbour and docks; ch. pt. of Australia; 2 caths., univ., oil refining, consumer gds.; wool tr.; p. (1972) 61,940 (c.), 2,799,634 (met. a.).

Sydney, spt., Cape Breton I., Nova Scotia Canada; coal mng. and exp.; steel, chemicals; p. (1971) 32,459.

Syktyvkar, c., Komi ASSR, RSFSR; R. pt. on Vychegda R.; shipyds., sawmilling, engin.; cultural ctr. of Komi people; p. (1970) 125,000.

Sylhet, t., **Bangladesh**; on Surma R. in tea growing dist.; fertilisers; p. (1961) 37,740.

Syracuse, c., S.E. Sicily, **Italy**; old t. on Ortygia I., off E. cst., modern t. on mainland, connected by bridge; founded c. 734 B.C.; ctr. of anc. Greek culture; exp. olive oil, oranges, lemons, wine; chemicals at Priolo; many Greek and Roman remains; p. (1969) 104,862.

Syracuse, c., N.Y., **USA**; on Erie Barge canal; impt. industl. ctr. for chemicals, electronics, machin.; formerly salt-producing ctr.; univ.; p. (1970) 192,529 (c.), 629,190 (met. a.).

Syr Dar'ya, one of main Rs. of central Asia; formed in Ferghana Valley in Uzbek SSR, **USSR**, flows through Tadzhik SSR and Kazakh SSR to Aral Sea; not navigable but used for irrigation and hydroelectric power; 2,400 km long.

Syria (Syrian Arab Rep.), S.W. **Asia**; on E. cst. Mediterranean; much of a. mtnous. and semi-desert; climate hot, but cold winters in highland interior; c. 70 per cent p. engaged in agr. which provides 30 per cent nat. income; mainly pastoral, but grains, fruit and cotton grown in well watered Euphrates R. valley and along cst.; oil exp. since 1968; textiles, food processing in Aleppo and cap. Damascus; a. 184,434 km²; p. (1970) 6,294,000.

Syriam, t., **Burma**; nr. Rangoon; main oil refining ctr. of cty.

Syros or **Syra**, I., one of Cyclades, Aegean Sea, S. **Greece**; heath-covered; most populous of Cyclades; ch. t. Hermoupolis; p. c. 33,000.

Syzran, c., **RSFSR**; impt. R. pt. on Volga nr. confluence with Syzran R.; rly. ctr.; engin., oil refining; p. (1970) 174,000.

Szazhalombatta, t., **Hungary**; on Danube, 24 km S. of Budapest; lgst. oil refinery in rep.; oil supplied through Druzhba pipeline.

Szczecin (Stettin), c., N.W. **Poland** (since 1945); formerly cap. of Prussian prov. of Pomerania; impt. spt. at mouth of R. Oder; deep-sea fishing base; shipbldg., metallurgy, engin., chemicals, technical univ.; p. (1970) 337,200.

Szczecin, prov., **Poland**; borders Baltic Sea; drained by R. Oder; mainly agr.; a. 31,339 km² p. (1970) 897,000.

Szechwan (Sichuan), prov., S.W. **China**; mostly occupied by Yangtse R., known as Red basin because of colour of its sandstone; fertile a. with mild climate; rice, tea, citrus fruit, tobacco, sugar-cane; lge. coal reserves; exp. tung oil; silk-producing a.; most populous prov.; cap. Chengtu; a. 568,997 km²; p. (est. 1968) 70,000,000.

Szeged, t., **Hungary**; nr. confluence of Rs. Tisza and Maros; anc. R. pt. destroyed by floods 1879, since rebuilt; univ.; tr. in cereals, paprika; textiles; p. (est. 1969) 117,000.

Szekesfehérvár, t., **Hungary**; nr. Budapest; mkt. t., with aluminium and metal inds., food processing; known since Roman times; once cap. of Hungarian kings; p. (1968) 68,000.

Szeping (Siping), c., Kirin prov., **China**; agr. distributing ctr.; cement; p. (est. 1970) 180,000.

Szolnok, t., **Hungary**; pt. on R. Tisa, E. of Budapest; route ctr.; machin., paper, cellulose, chemicals; p. (1968) 59,000.

Szombathely, t., W. **Hungary**; rly. ctr.; agr. machin., textiles, shoes; birthplace of St. Martin of Tours (c. A.D. 316); p. (1968) 60,000.

T

Tabasco, coastal st., **Mexico**; on Bay of Campeche; low-lying; rapid development with drainage of swamps; cash crops of cacao, coffee, sugar, tobacco; major petroleum deposits aiding industl. development; cap. Villa Hermosa; a. 25,335 km²; p. (1969) 691,000.

Table Bay, inlet of Atl., cst. of C. of Good Hope, **S. Africa**; site of Cape Town.

Table Mountain, Cape Prov., **S. Africa**; nr. Cape Town; alt. 1,082 m.

Tabor, t., **ČSSR**; S. of Prague, on R. Luznice; rly. junc.; textiles, tobacco; p. (1961) 20,142.

Tabora, t., central **Tanzania**; E. Africa; at junc. of rlys. from Dar es Salaam and L. Victoria; p. (1967) 21,012.

Tabriz, c., **Iran**; cap. of Azerbaijan; metal inds., carpets, leather, soap; famous blue mosque; univ.; p. (est. 1971) 475,600.

Tachira, st., **Venezuela**; mtnous. inland st. bordering Colombia; coffee; cap. San Cristobal; a. 11,100 km²; p. (est. 1970) 525,840.

Tacna, t., cap. of Tacna prov., **Peru**; in fertile valley of mtnous. region; agr. t.; p. (est. 1969) 30,500.

Tacna, prov., **Peru**; mtnous. and arid, some irrigated valleys; transferred from Chile by treaty 1929; cap. T.; subject to earthquakes; a. 12,769 km²; p. (est. 1969) 90,600

Tacoma, spt., Wash., **USA**; on Puget Sound; shipping, fishing; grew with Alaskan and Pac. tr.; port inds. and agr. processing; p. (1960) 147,970 (t.); (1968) 400,800 (met. a.).

Tacuarembo, dep., **Uruguay**; N. of Rio Negro R., which provides hydroelectricity; mainly agr.; cap. T.; a. 15,812 km²; p. (est. 1969) 80,600.

Tadmor. *See* **Palmyra**.

Tadoussac, t., Quebec, **Canada**; on R. Saguenay, where it enters St. Lawrence R.; tourist ctr.; oldest settlement in Canada 1599; p. (1966) 1,059.

Tadzhik (Tadzhikistan) **SSR**, constituent rep., **USSR**; borders China and Afghanistan; mainly mtnous., inc. Pamirs and Turkestan and part of highly cultivated Ferghana Valley; cattle breeding; cotton main cash crop; impt. oil and hydroelec. power resources; cap. Dushanbe; a. 144,263 km²; p. (1970) 2,900,000.

Taegu, c., **S. Korea**; textiles, agr. processing; p. (1966) 845,073.

Taejon, t., **S. Korea**; S. of Seoul; fish, petroleum, p. (1966) 315,094.

Taff, R., Powys, South and Mid Glamorgan, **Wales**; rises in Brecon Beacons, flows S.E. across coalfield to Bristol Channel at Cardiff; 64 km long.

Tafilalet, Morocco, N. Africa; oasis of the Sahara, E. of Atlas; dates.

Tagab, c., **Afghanistan**; in Panjshir R. valley N.W. of Kābul; p. (est. 1971) 102,028.

Taganrog, c., **RSFSR**; spt. on Sea of Azov; iron and steel, engin.; site of fortress founded by Peter the Great 1698; birthplace of Chekhov; p. (1970) 254,000.

Tagliamento, R., N.E. **Italy**; rises in Carnic Alps, flows W. into Adriatic Sea; 160 km long.

Tagus, R., **Spain** and **Portugal**; rises in E. Spain and flows across the Meseta to Atl. Oc. at Lisbon where there is a magnificent new bridge; its estuary forms one of the finest harbours in Europe.

Tahiti, ch. I., Society Is., **Fr. Polynesia**; contains Papeete, main admin. ctr. of Fr. Oceania; fertile alluvial belt; exp. copra, phosphates, vanilla; tourism; a. 1,041 km²; p. (1967) 61,519.

Taichow (Taizhou), c., Kiangsu prov., **China**; rice ctr.; p. (est. 1970) 275,000.

Taichung, t., **Taiwan**; agr. mkt., food processing; p. (est. 1970) 448,140.

Taif, t., Hejaz, **Saudi Arabia**; 80 km E. of Mecca; 1,800 m a.s.l.; summer resort; p. (est. 1963) 54,000.

Tai Hu, L., Kiangsu, **China**; focus of intensive system of small canals and waterways, 96 km N. of Shanghai; a. c. 260 km².

Taimyr Peninsula, N. cst., Siberia, **USSR**; terminates with C. Chelyuskin; occupies most of Taimyr National Area, inhabited by nomadic Samoyeds; p. (1970) 38,000.

Tainan, t., S.W. cst. of **Taiwan**; former cap.; univ.; p. (est. 1970) 474,835.

Taipei, c., cap. of **Taiwan**; on cst. plain in N. Taiwan; nucleus of major industl. a.; major transport ctr., international airpt.; 2 univs.; p. (est. 1970) 1,769,568.

Taiwan (Formosa), I., off cst. of S.E. **China**; beautiful I. with intensive agr.; most densely populated cty. in the world; part of Japan 1895–1945; returned to China 1945; occupied by Nationalist government (Chiang Kai-Shek) since 1949; growing political isolation; cap. Taipei; a. 35,975 km²; p. (1971) 14,833,012.

Taiyüan, c., cap. of Shansi prov., **N. China**; on Fen R.; walled c.; univ.; ctr. of rapid industl. development; integrated iron and steel plant; chemicals, textiles; p. (est. 1970) 2,725,000.

Taiz, t., **Yemen Arab Rep.**; in fertile valley; former cap.; p. (est. 1970) 48,000.

Takamatsu, t., **Japan**; N. cst. Shikoku; ferry terminal; univ.; tourism; p. (est. 1971) 280,000.

Takaoka, t., Honshu, **Japan**; ctr. of rice tr.; lacquer wk.; cars; p. (est. 1971) 162,000.

Takasaki, t., Honshu, **Japan**; radiation chemistry research ctr.; textiles; p. (est. 1971) 200,000.

Taklamakan, desert, W. **China**; basin of inland drainage; home of the Turko people; surrounded by a ring of oases.

Takoradi. *See* **Sekondi-Takoradi**.

Talara, t., N. **Peru**; on C. Pariñas; spt.; ctr. of petroleum refining; p. (est. 1969) 38,200.

Talaud I., **Indonesia**; N.E. of Sulawesi; copra; underdeveloped; a. 1,279 km².

Talavera, t., Toledo prov., central **Spain**; on Tagus R.; ceramics; scene of battle 1809; p. (1970) 45,327.

Talca, prov., **Chile**; predominantly agr.; various irrigated crops; livestock; cap. T.; a. 9,637 km²; p. (1961) 226,052.

Talca, t., cap. of Talca prov., **Chile**; S. of Santiago; lge. mftg. ctr.; matches, footwear, paper, and flour mills, foundries; p. (1966) 72,000.

Talcahuano, spt., **Chile**, nr. Concepción; naval sta.; steel plant at Huachipato; fish processing, oil refining; p. (est. 1970) 115,568.

Talien. *See* **Luta**.

Tallahassee, t., **Fla.**, **USA**; univ.; timber-based inds.; p. (1970) 71,763 (t.), 102,530 (met. a.).

Tallinn, spt., cap. of Estonian SSR, **USSR**; on G. of Finland; diverse inds. inc. radio equipment; mediaeval architecture; p. (1970) 363,000.

Tamale, t., cap. of Kaduna st., **Ghana**, W. **Africa**; admin. ctr.; cotton milling, sheanut processing; p. (1970) 81,612.

Tamar, R., Tasmania, **Australia**; formed at confluence of N. Esk and S. Esk at Launceston, flows into Bass Strait nr. Georgetown.

Tamar, R., Devon and Cornwall, **Eng.**; flows S. to Plymouth Sound; 72 km long.

Tamatave, t., **Malagasy Rep.**; ch. spt. on Indian Oc.; exp. graphite, rice, chromite ore; car assembly, oil refining; p. (est. 1970) 56,910.

Tamaulipas, st., **Mexico**; on G. of Mexico, S. of Texas; petroleum is main resource; fishing along lagoon cst.; cotton, livestock; cap. Ciudad Victoria; a. 79,593 km²; p. (1969) 1,487,000.

Tambov, c., cap. of Tambov oblast, **RSFSR**; on Tsna R.; regional ctr. serving agr. dist.; engin.; p. (1970) 229,000.

Tamil Nadu (formerly **Madras**) st., **India**; on S.E. cst. of peninsula; home of Tamils; crossed by R. Cauvery; dry crops; ch. ts. Madras, Madura; a. 130,357 km²; p. (1971) 41,103,125.

Tampa, c., **Fla.**, **USA**; popular winter resort, cigar factories, phosphates, electronics; fruit growing and canning; p. (1970) 274,359 (c.), 999,613 (met. a.).

Tampere (**Tammerfors**), t., S. **Finland**; on rly. between Helsinki and Vaasa; textiles, leather, paper, based on local hydroelec. power; cath.; p. (est. 1968) 151,278 (t.), 211,995 (met. a.).

Tampico, spt., **Mexico**; on R. Panuco, 14 km from G. of Mexico; exp. petroleum; oil refining, fish processing, chemicals; tourism; p. (1970) 179,584 (c.), 270,414 (met. a.).

Tamworth, t., **Staffs.**, **Eng.**; on R. Tame, 8 km S.E. of Lichfield; anc. cas.; lt. engin.; expanded t.; p. (1971) 40,254.

Tana, lge. freshwater L., N.W. **Ethiopia**, nr. Gondar; source of Blue Nile, surrounded by marsh, papyrus swamp.

Tana, R., **Kenya**; rises nr. Mt. Kenya and flows to Indian Oc.; impt. elephant habitat in valley; 800 km long.

Tanana, R. and R. pt., **Alaska**, **USA**; valley used for agr. and forestry; length of R. 760 km.

Tananarive, t., cap. of **Malagasy Rep.**; ctr. of commerce and communications; airpt.; lge. meat preserving factories, plastics, radios, car assembly, shoes, knitted gds., rice mills; univ.; p. (est. 1971) 347,466 (c.), 377,600 (met. a.).

Tandil, t., **Argentina**; resort; granite quarried in surrounding hills; p. (1960) 70,000.

Tanga, spt., **Tanzania**, E. **Africa**; on plateau overlooking Tanga Bay; rly. terminus; new plywood plant; p. (1967) 61,058.

Tanganyika, gr. L., E. Central **Africa**; lies in Gt. Rift Valley; c. 672 km long, 24–32 km wide; lgst. L. in Africa and except for L. Baykal deepest L. in world; *c.* 823 m a.s.l.; discovered by Burton and Speke 1858, explored by Livingstone and Stanley 1871.

Tangier, free pt., **Morocco**, N. **Africa**; on Strait of Gibraltar; no longer internationalised zone but integral part of kingdom of Morocco; summer cap.; shipyard; cigarettes, fishing; p. (1971) 185,850.

Tangshan, c., Hopeh prov., **China**; impt. industl. ctr.; steel, machin.; textiles, cement, oil refining; devastated by a series of earthquakes (1976); p. (est. 1970) 1,200,000.

Tanimbar Is., **Indonesia**; gr. of Is. in Banda Sea, S. Moluccas; forests, swamps; maize, rice, coconuts, sago; p. (est. 1965) 50,000.

Tanta, t., Lower **Egypt**; 55 m. N. of Cairo; impt. rly. junc.; religious fairs; cotton processing; univ. proposed; p. (est. 1970) 253,600.

Tanzania, rep., E. cst. **Africa**; inc. Is. of Zanzibar and Pemba, united since 1964; narrow coastal plain rises to inland plateau (Mt. Kilimanjaro, 5,895 m, hgst. peak in Africa); climate varies with alt., tropical in Zanzibar, temperate inland; predominantly subsistence agr., maize, millet, groundnuts, livestock; comm. crops inc. sisal, sugar, cotton, coffee; cloves on Is., especially Pemba; food processing, textile inds.; 5-year planning system to assist economic development; cap. Dar es Salaam; new cap. planned at Dodoma; a. 939,706 km²; p. (est. 1969) 12,926,000.

Taormino, resort, E. Sicily, **Italy**; 230 m above sea at foot of Mt. Etna; magnificent scenery and anc. ruins.

Tapachula, c., Chiapas st., S. **Mexico**; on Pac. cst. lowlands; comm. ctr. for agr. dist.; p. (1970) 108,464.

Tapti, R., W. **India**; flows W. to G. of Cambay from Betul dist., Madhya Pradesh; 720 km long.

Tarai, marshy, jungle tract at foot of Himalayas, **India**, **Nepal**; barrier to economic development of Nepal, now much modified and reduced in area by human occupation.

Taranaki, prov., N.I., **N.Z.**; impt. stock rearing and dairying a.; offshore oil and gas fields; a. 9,713 km²; p. (1971) 100,668.

Taranto, t., Lecce, **Italy**; on G. of Taranto, inlet of Ionian Sea; maritime arsenal with gr. comm. and industl. interests; strong cas.; steel wks.; cement; oil refinery; famous for its oyster and mussel fisheries; p. (1969) 219,484.

Tarapacá, prov., N. **Chile**; hot, arid desert; nitrate deposits; a. 55,270 km²; p. (1970) 174,730.

Tarascon, t., Bouches-du-Rhône dep., **France**; connected by bridges with Beaucaire on opposite bank of R. Rhône; old cas. famous festival; p. (1968) 10,857.

Tarwera Mtn., volcanic peak, N.I., **N.Z.**; 305 m; in Hot Springs dist.; eruption 1866 destroyed L. Rotomahana (water later returned to form bigger and deeper L.).

Tarbat Ness, promontory, N. side of Moray Firth, Ross and Cromarty, **Scot.**

Tarbes, t., cap. of Hautes-Pyrénées dep., **France**; on R. Adour; cath.; p. (1968) 59,432.

Taree, t., N.S.W., **Australia**; dairying, agr., fishing, timber and fibre-boards; p. (1972) 11,914.

Targul-Mures, c., **Romania**; on R. Mures; ch. t. of Magyar aut. region in Transylvania; old fort, Gothic Calvinist cath.; agr. tr. and processing; p. (1968) 92,104.

Tarifa, t., **Spain**; on Gilbraltar Strait; most S. point of mainland of Europe; fish tr., cereals, oranges, wines; p. (1970) 15,833.

Tarija, prov., **Bolivia**; part of Gran Chaco rising to W.; extensive agr. and forests; cap. T.; a. 64,196 km²; p. (est. 1969) 201,800.

Tarija, t., cap. of T. prov., **Bolivia**; alt. 1,906 m; cath., univ.; mkt. t.; p. (1967) 26,787.

Tarim Basin, depression, Sinkiang, **China**; desert with oases; crossed by Silk Road; anc. civilisation; state farms for wheat, millet, maize, cotton.

Tarn, dep., S. **France**; watered by Tarn and its tribs.; between Central Massif and basin of Aquitaine; mainly agr.; cap. Albi; a. 5,781 km²; p. (1968) 332,011.

Tarn, R., **France**; trib. of R. Garonne; rocky gorge 50 km long in its upper course; 376 km long.

Tarn-et-Garonne, dep., W. France; alluvial plain formed by Rs. Tarn, Garonne and Aveyron; mainly agr.; cap. Montauban; a. 3,730 km²; p. (1968) 183,572.
Tarnow, t., Poland; E. of Kraków; industl. ctr.; lge. nitrogen factory; synthetic fibres, metallurgy; cath.; p. (1970) 85,500.
Tarpon Springs, t., Fla., **USA**; pt.; main source of sponges in USA.
Tarragona, prov., Spain; on Mediterranean; vineyards and agr.; cap. Tarragona; a. 6,283 km²; p. (1970) 431,961.
Tarragona, spt., cap. of T. prov., Spain; at mouth of R. Francoli; exp. agr. prod. of Ebro valley; cath.; many Roman remains, inc. aqueduct; liqueur; p. (1967) 64,192.
Tarrasa, t., Barcelona, **Spain**; textile ctr.; p. est. (1967) 127,814.
Tarsus, anc. c., S. Turkey; nr. Adana; orange and citrus groves; ruined Roman temple; birthplace of St. Paul; exp. cotton, wool, hides; p. (1965) 57,035.
Tartary or Tatary, region, **Central Asia**; now divided into Chinese or E. Turkestan, and W. Turkestan, USSR.
Tartu, c., Estonian SSR, **USSR**; pt. on Emayygi R.; rly. junc.; famous univ. founded 1632; agr. machin., tobacco processing; p. (est. 1969) 87,000.
Tashkent, c., cap. of Uzbek SSR, **USSR**; cultural, industl. and scientific ctr. of central Asia; on Trans-Caspian rly. in fertile Ferghana valley; univ.; diverse inds.; terminus of gas pipeline; p. (1970) 1,385,000.
Tasman Bay, lge inlet, S.I., **N.Z.**; penetrates N. cst., between Separation Point and D'Urville I.; enclosed by mtns., sheltered, fertile, coastal fringe; ch. ts. Nelson, Motueka.
Tasman Glacier, S.I., **N.Z.**; one of the lgst. in the world.
Tasmania (formerly Van Diemen's Land), I., st., **Australia**; plateau with fertile valleys; temperate climate; forest and grasslands, grain, fruit, cattle-raising; aluminium, copper, zinc, lead, tin, silver; electro-metallurgical inds.; cap. Hobart; a. 67,897 km²; p. (1972) 389,874.
Tasman Sea, Australia; part of Pac. Oc. between Australia and Tasmania.
Tatabánya, t., N. **Hungary**; lignite mng. ctr.; aluminium refining, chemicals; p. (1968) 63,000.
Tatar ASSR, USSR; in middle Volga valley; wooded steppeland; extensive oil deposits and natural gas fields; cap. Kazan; a. 67,988 km²; p. (1970) 3,131,000.
Tatra Mtns., highest mtn. gr. of W. Carpathians, on border of ČSSR and Poland; highest peak Gerlach in Slovakia, 2,664 m; mountaineering and winter sports.
Tatung (Datong), c., Shansi prov., **China**; impt. coalfield; steam and diesel locomotives; p. (est. 1970) 300,000.
Taubaté, t., São Paulo st., **Brazil**; industl. ctr.; p. (est. 1968) 92,972.
Taunton, co. t., Somerset, **Eng.**; on R. Tone at W. end of Vale of Taunton; old cas.; clothing tr., engin. plastics; p. (1971) 37,373.
Taunton, t., Mass., **USA**; cotton, iron foundries, machin., plastics; p. (1970) 43,756.
Taunus, mtn. range, Hesse, W. Germany; between Rs. Lahn and Rhine and Main; forests, vineyards, and spas.
Taupo, L., N.I., N.Z.; lgst. L. in N.Z.; geysers, hot springs in vicinity; 40 km by 27 km.
Tauranga, t., N.I., N.Z.; spt. on Bay of Plenty; tourism; fishing; p. (1971) 28,126.
Taurus Mtns., range, S. Turkey; rise to over 3,660 m.
Tavastehus. *See* Hämeenlinna.
Tavistock, mkt. t., Devon, **Eng.**; on R. Tavy; anc. stannary t.; Drake born nearby; p. (1971) 24,310 (dist.).
Tavoy, t., Burma; on Tenasserim cst.; exp. tin to Singapore; p. c. 40,000.
Taw, R., Devon, Eng.; flows from Dartmoor to Barnstaple Bay; 80 km long.
Taxco, t., **Mexico**; alt. 1,700 m; gold- and silver-mng.; tourist ctr.; anc. Aztec t.; p. (1970) 64,368.
Taxila, ruined c., Pakistan; nr. Rawalpindi; anc. seat of learning; ruins of Buddhist univ.; heavy machin. wks. projected.
Tay, R., Scot.; flows S.E. from Loch Tay in Perth and Kinross, to Firth of Tay; longest R. in Scot., 188 km; salmon fisheries.
Tay, Firth of, lge. inlet, E. cst. Scot.; extends inland almost to Perth.
Tayeh, t., Hupeh, China; lies to S. of Yangtze R., 67 km S.E. of Wuhan; impt. iron-ore deposits; supplies Hwangshih; iron and steel inds., heavy engin.
Tayport, burgh, North East Fife, **Scot.**; at entrance to Firth of Tay; opposite Broughty Ferry; linen, jute; p. (1971) 2,897.
Tayside, l. gov. reg., Scot.; inc. former cos. of Perth and Angus bordering the Highlands; a. 7,500 km²; p. (1971) 395,285.
Tbilisi (Tiflis), c., Georgian SSR, **USSR**; route ctr. on Kura R.; major admin., economic and cultural ctr. of Transcaucasia; machin., textiles, tanneries, furniture, food processing; power from hydroelectric power stas.; anc. tr. ctr.; some mediaeval fragments in c. ctr.; p. (1970) 889,000.
Tczew (Dirschau), t., Gdansk prov., **N. Poland**; pt. on Vistula; rly. junc.; agr. implements; p. (1970) 40,800.
Team Valley, Tyne and Wear, **Eng.**; impt. trading estate has been developed here.
Tebessa, t., N.E. Algeria; in Atlas mtns., at 851 m; mkt.; carpets; phosphate deposits nearby; p. (1966) 40,521.
Teddington, S.W. sub. of London, **Eng.**; inc. in Greater London outer bor. of Richmond-upon-Thames; Nat. Physical Laboratory.
Tees, R., N. Eng.; rises on Cross Fell, Cumbria, flows E. to N. Sea between Hartlepool and Redcar; heavy inds. in lower section; 112 km long.
Teesport, oil refinery, between Redcar and Middlesbrough, Cleveland, **Eng.**
Teesside, dist., Cleveland, **Eng.**; inc. Middlesbrough, Redcar, Thornaby-on-Tees, Stockton-on-Tees, Billingham, and Eston; p. (1971) 395,477.
Tegal, spt., Java, **Indonesia**; textiles, sugar refining; lge. dam nearby; p. (1971) 105,752.
Tegucigalpa, c., cap. of **Honduras**; on R. Choluteca at 976 m; inter-ocean highway connects with Caribbean and Pac. Oc.; former ctr. of silver mng.; inc. Comayagüela, the modern part of c., where the nat. univ. is situated; p. (est. 1970) 232,276.
Tehran (Teheran), c., cap. of Iran, 112 km S. of Caspian Sea; mftg. and comm. ctr.; modern bldgs.; gas pipeline to USSR; international airpt.; univ.; car assembly, textiles, chemicals, glass; new oil refiniery; p. (est. 1971) 3,639,000.
Tehuantepec, Isthmus of, separates G. of Mexico from Pac. Oc. at narrowest point of Mexico; width 200 km.
Teifi, R., S. Wales; rises in Cambrian mtns., flows S.W. to Cardigan Bay; 150 km long.
Teign, R., Devon, Eng.; flows to sea at pt. of Teignmouth from Dartmoor; picturesque estuary; 48 km long.
Teignmouth, t., Devon, **Eng.**; at mouth of R. Teign, 21 km S. of Exeter; resort; revival of pt. with ball clay exp.; p. (1971) 12,554.
Tekirdag, t., Turkey; on Sea of Marmara, W. of Istanbul; former Greek settlement; p. (1965) 26,964.
Tel Aviv-Jaffa, c., **Israel**; on Mediterranean; lgst. c. of cty.; financial and cultural ctr.; univ.; founded by Zionists 1909; p. (1972) 362,200.
Telemark, co., Norway; borders Skagerrak; mtnous., lake-covered, much forested; hydroelectric power forms basis for electrochemical inds.; a. 15,118 km²; p. (est. 1972) 157,553.
Telford, new t. (1963), Shropshire, **Eng.**; 32 km W. of Wolverhampton; p. (est. 1974) 94,200.
Tellicherry, t., spt., Kerala, India; exp. pepper; lge. college; furniture; p. (1961) 44,763.
Telok Betong, spt., Sumatra, Indonesia; exp. pepper, agr. products; p. (1971) 198,986.
Tema, pt. (opened 1962), nr. Accra, **Ghana**; deepwater harbour, oil refinery, aluminium smelter; impt. industl. development.
Teme, R., on border of Wales and Hereford and Worcs., **Eng.**; trib. of R. Severn; 112 km long.
Temir-Tau, c., Kazakh SSR, USSR; on Nura R.; industl. ctr.; iron, steel, synthetic rubber, soda; lge. thermal power sta.; p. (1970) 167,000.
Templemore, mkt. t., U.D., Tipperary, **R.o.I.**; on R. Suir; p. (1966) 2,031.
Temuco, c., cap. of Cautin prov., **Chile**; cath.;

tr. in cereals, apples, timber; Araucanian Indian mkt.; p. (est. 1970) 104,372.

Tenali, t., Andhra Pradesh, **India**; nr. Guntur in Krishna delta; p. (1971) 102,937.

Tenasserim, div., lower **Burma**; on Thailand border; extends along Isthmus of Kra; tin and rubber; a. 92,945 km²; p. (est. 1969) 1,856,000.

Tenby, mkt. t. Dyfed, **Wales**; on W. side of Carmarthen Bay, Bristol Channel; seaside resort; walled cas. t.; p. (1971) 4,985.

Tenerife, I., Canary Is.; volcanic landscapes and mild climate attract tourists; mkt. gardening; cap. Santa Cruz; a. 2,025 km²; p. (1970) 500,381.

Tennessee, R., Tenn., Ky., **USA**; lgst. and most impt. branch of Ohio R.; its valley once liable to flooding, now controlled by dams, and land improved by the Tenn. Valley Authority; 1,251 km long.

Tennessee, st., **USA**; rises to Appalachians in E., crossed by Tennessee R. and tribs.; a. of heavy rainfall and severe soil erosion necessitated the Tenn. Valley Authority scheme of conservation, dam bldg., and afforestation; cheap hydroelectric power attracting new inds., many reservoirs attract tourists; cap. Nashville; a. 109,412 km²; p. (1970) 3,838,777.

Tenterden, mkt. t., Kent, **Eng.**; 13 km N. of Rye; church with famous 42 m tower; p. (1971) 5,922.

Teófilo Otoni, t., Minas Gerais, **Brazil**; semiprecious stone polishing; p. (est. 1968) 134,476.

Tepic, c., cap. of Nayarit st., **Mexico**; comm. ctr. for agr. dist.; nr. Sanguaney volcano; p. (1970) 111,344.

Teplice, wat. pl., **ČSSR**; N.W. of Prague; textile and hardware inds.; mineral springs; p. (1967) 52,000.

Teramo, c., cap. of T. prov., **Italy**; 24 km from Adriatic; route and agr. ctr.; cath.; textiles; the anc. Interamnium; p. (1969) 47,083.

Terek, R., N. Caucasia, **RSFSR**; flows to Caspian Sea; used for irrigation and hydroelectric power in lower course; 592 km long.

Teresina, t., cap. of Piauí st., **Brazil**; comm. ctr.; lt. inds.; p. (1970) 181,071.

Terezópolis, t., Rio de Janeiro, **Brazil**; health resort; textiles; p. (est. 1968) 69,636.

Ternate I., Moluccas Is., **Indonesia**; volcanic, wooded; p. 33,000.

Terneuzen, t., **Neth.**; on W. Schelde R.; pipeline to be constructed to carry ethylene from Pernis; p. (1967) 20,029.

Terni, t., Perugia, **Italy**; among the Apennines; iron and steelwks., arms factory; cath.; p. (1969) 106,062.

Ternopol (Tarnopol), t., Ukrainian SSR, **USSR**; E. of Lvov; rly. junc., mkt.; agr. machin., food inds.; p. (1970) 85,000.

Terre Adélie, name given to Fr. terr. and I. in Antarctic; est. a. 414,400 km².

Terre Haute, t., Ind., **USA**; coal, natural gas, flour, paper, glass, foundries; p. (1970) 69,247 (t.), 172,710 (met. a.).

Terreón, t., Coahuila, **Mexico**; ctr. of comm. agr.; oil pipeline connects to Chihuahua; thermo-elec. plant; p. (1969) 243,234.

Teruel, t., cap. of Teruel prov., **Spain**; on R. Turia; walled t., cath.; p. (1970) 21,638.

Tete, t., central **Moçambique**; on R. Zambesi; ctr. of coalfield; iron ore, graphite, radioactive materials.

Tetovo, t., Macedonia, **Yugoslavia**; chemicals, electro-metallurgy, textiles.

Tettenhall, West Midlands, **Eng.**; N.W. of Wolverhampton.

Tetuan, ch. spt., **Morocco**, N. Africa; walled t., former cap. of Spanish Morocco; p. (1971) 137,080 (t.), 273,050 (met. a.).

Teviot, R., Roxburgh, **Scot.**; trib. of R. Tweed; 59 km long.

Tewkesbury, mkt. t., Gloucs., **Eng.**; on R. Avon, close to confluence with R. Severn; milling, lt. engin.; Norman abbey; p. (1971) 8,742.

Texarkana, t., Texas and Ark., **USA**; bdy. passes down middle of main street; timber and cotton region; total p. (1970) 52,179.

Texas, st., S.W. **USA**; second lgst. st. by a.; borders Mexico; dry plains in W., humid cst. in E.; problems of soil erosion yet leading agr. st.; leading producer of petroleum and natural gas; cap. Austin; a. 692,408 km²; p. (1970) 10,989,123.

Texas City, spt., Texas, **USA**; petroleum, chemicals; p. (1970) 38,908.

Texel, one of the W. Frisian Is., **Neth.**; scene of several naval battles; p. (1967) 11,003.

Thailand (Siam), kingdom, S.E. Asia; 4 main regions; parallel N.–S. hill ranges (2,400 m) and valleys in N. producing teak; rice growing, fertile plain of Chao Phraya R. in ctr.; thinly populated E. plateau, drained by Mekong; S. coastal strip on G. of Siam; monsoon climate; predominantly agr., accounting for over 80 per cent p. and 30 per cent nat. income; lgst. world exporter of rice; forestry, fisheries, mng., especially tin, wolfram; oil exploration; industl. development based on processing of Thai raw materials; cap. Bangkok; a. 519,083 km²; p. (est. 1969) 34,738,000.

Thal Desert, **Pakistan**; W. of Punjab; now irrigated for wheat and cotton.

Thame, mkt. t., Oxford, **Eng.**; on R. Thame, 11 km S.W. of Aylesbury; p. (1971) 5,940.

Thames, R., **Eng.**; rises in Cotswold hills and flows past Oxford, Reading, Windsor, and London to the Nore; tribs. inc. Windrush, Cherwell, Thame, Kennet, Colne, Lea, and Roding; estuary impt. industl. a. with many oil refineries; flood barrier to be built at Silvertown in Woolwich; 336 km long.

Thameshaven, lge. oil refinery, Essex, **Eng.**; on N. cst. of Thames estuary 13 km below Tilbury.

Thana, t., Maharashtra, **India**; textiles, chemicals, matches; p. (1971) 170,675 (t.), 207,352 (met. a.).

Thanet, I. of, lge. promontory, N.E. extremity of Kent, **Eng.**; formed by bifurcation of R. Stour; contains Margate, Ramsgate, and Broadstairs.

Thanjavur, t., Tamil Nadu, **India**; silks, carpets, jewellery, inlaid metals; impt. Brahman ctr.; p. (1971) 140,547.

Thar Desert, on bdy. of **India** and **Pakistan**; covers slopes between N.W. Deccan and R. Indus; barren, lack of Rs. or level land prevents irrigation; crossed by caravan routes.

Thebes, c., of Boeotia, in anc. **Greece**; Mycenaean site; destroyed by Alexander the Great 335 B.C.; modern c. of Thivai occupies site.

Thebes, c. of anc. **Egypt**; on banks of Nile; site now partly occupied by vs. Karnak and Luxor; archeological discoveries in Valley of the Kings 1922, inc. tomb of Tutankhamun.

Theddlethorpe, v., Lincs., **Eng.**; proposed N. Sea gas terminal.

Theiss. *See* **Tisa.**

Thermopylae, celebrated pass between Mt. Oeta and the sea, N.E. **Greece**; heroic battle between Spartans and Persians 480 B.C.

Thessaloniki, c., **Greece**; spt. at head of G. of T.; with fiscal free zone; second c. of Greece; impt. route and industl. ctr.; univ.; p. (1971) 339,496.

Thessaly, prov., central **Greece**; fertile plain drained by R. Pinios; mainly agr.; a. 13,489 km²; p. (1971) 659,243.

Thetford, t., Norfolk, **Eng.**; on Little Ouse; industl. estate for London overspill; fruit and vegetable canning, pulp mftg., engin.; p. (1971) 13,706.

Thetford Mines, t., Quebec, **Canada**; asbestos mng. ctr.; p. (1966) 21,614.

Thienen (Tirlemont), t., Brabant prov., **Belgium**; ctr. of Belgian beet-sugar refining; captured by Marlborough 1705; p. (est. 1969) 22,584.

Thiès, t., **Senegal**, W. Africa; rly. ctr. and wkshps.; aluminium, phosphate quarrying; p. (est. 1970) 91,000.

Thimbu, t., **Bhutan**; hydroelectric plant; 176 km road link to Phuntsholing (Sikkim) 1968.

Thionville, t., Moselle dep., N. **France**; in Lorraine ironfield conurb.; metallurgical and chemical inds.; p. (1968) 37,079 (c.), 136,474 (met. a.).

Thira (Santorine), volcanic I., Cyclades, **Greece**; wine prods.; max. alt. 567 m; a. 75 km²; p. *c.* 10,000.

Thirlmere, L., Cumbria, **Eng.**; 5 km long; furnishes part of water supply of Manchester.

Thirsk, mkt. t., North Yorks., **Eng.**; in wide gap between Pennines and Cleveland hills, 11 km S.E. of Northallerton; racecourse; p. (1971) 14,383 (dist.).

Thompson, R., B.C., **Canada**; trib. of R. Fraser; forms impt. routeway through Rocky mtns.; 448 km long.

Thonburi, c., **Thailand**; on R. Menam opposite Bangkok; second c. of T.; former cap.; "Temple of Dawn"; lt. inds.; p. (1968) 540,300.

Thorez, (Chistyakovo), Ukrainian SSR, **USSR**; coalmng.; p. (est. 1967) 95,000 (c.), 300,000 (met. a.).

Thornaby-on-Tees. *See* Teesside.

Thornbury, mkt. t., Avon, **Eng.**; 16 km N. of Bristol; aircraft mftg.; expanded t.; p. (1971) 42,992 (dist.).

Thornton Cleveleys, t., Lancs., **Eng.**; 6 km N.E. of Blackpool; resort; p. (1971) 26,869.

Thörshavn, c., cap. of **Faroe Is.**; on Stromo I.; fish. pt.; anc. fortress; lighthouse; p. (1966) 9,738.

Thousand Isles, gr. of over 1,500 Is. in St. Lawrence R. which extend up-river for *c.* 48 km from Brockville to Gananoque, at junc. of L. Ont. and St. Lawrence R.; partly in N.Y. st. and partly in Canada.

Thrace, anc. name of terr. in S.E. Europe, part of which has been added to **Greece**; successively under Macedonian, Roman, Byzantine, and Turkish rule, before passing to Greece; tobacco; a. 8,586 km^2; p. of dep. (1971) 329,297.

Thule, N.W. **Greenland**; 1,600 km from N. Pole; American air base and site of ballistic missile early warning sta.; spt. open 2–3 months per annum.

Thumba, Kerala, **India**; space science and technological ctr.

Thun, L., Berne can., **Switzerland**; occupies valleys of R. Aare where it leaves Alpine region; separated from L. Brienz by deltaic neck of land on which is Interlaken; a. 98 km^2.

Thun, t., Berne, **Switzerland**; on N.W. end of L. Thun; cas. on hill above t.; tourism; p. (1969) 36,000.

Thunder Bay, t., **Canada**; formed from Port Arthur and Port William; pt. on N.W. cst. of L. Superior; grain exp. ctr.; p. (1971) 106,000 (t.), 111,492 (met. a.).

Thurgau, can., N.E. **Switzerland**; on L. Constance, bordered by R. Rhine; prosperous agr. a.; inds. ass. with textiles; cap. Frauenfeld; a. 1,005 km^2; p. (1969) 187,000.

Thuringia, former st., **E. Germany**; bordered by Bavaria, Saxony-Anhalt, Lower Saxony, and Hesse; drained by Rs. Saale and Werra; crossed by Thüringer Wald and extending to Harz mtns.; fertile arable agr. a.; now comprises dists. of Erfurt, Suhl and Gera.

Thuringian Forest or Thüringer Wald, forested range of hills, **E. Germany**; rising to 982 m in Beerberg; famous for romantic scenery and legends; resorts.

Thurles, mkt. t., Tipperary, **R.o.I.**; on R. Suir; agr. processing; cath., cas.; p. (1966) 6,743.

Thurrock, t., Essex, **Eng.**; on Thames, nr. Tilbury; oil refining, metal refining, cement, paper board; p. (1971) 124,682.

Thurso, burgh, Caithness, **Scot.**; nr. Dounreay; anc. stronghold of Vikings; p. (1971) 9,087.

Tiaret, t., W. **Algeria**; N. Africa; in strategic pass; walled; agr. mkt.; cereals, wool, cattle; p. (1966) 37,059.

Tiber, R., **Italy**; flows from Apennines to Mediterranean, passing through Rome; 352 km long.

Tiberias, t., **Israel**; on Sea of Galilee (L. Tiberias); agr. ctr.; health resort with medicinal springs; p. (est. 1970) 23,900.

Tibesti, mtns., on bdy. between **Libya** and **Chad**, Equatorial Africa; barren in spite of slight rainfall; mainly above 1,800 m, max. alt. 3,401 m.

Tibet, aut. region, **China**; lofty plateau, called "the roof of the world," its lowest plains being 3,660 m a.s.l.; semi-desert; network of roads being built, inc. one across Himalayas to Katmandu; pastoral agr., sheep; arable agr. in R. valleys, especially Tsangpo valley, wheat, barley, fruit, vegetables; tr. of wool, musk, gold, skins, drugs traditionally carried by yaks which can stand intense cold; salt, alluvial gold, radioactive ores; cap. Lhasa; a. 1,217,308 km^2; p. (est. 1968) 1,400,000.

Ticino, R., **Switzerland** and **Italy**; trib. of Po; forms S. approach to St. Gotthard Pass; irrigation in lower course; length 240 km.

Ticino, can., **Switzerland**; on S. slopes of central Alps, bordering Italy; contains parts of Ls. Maggiore and Lugano; mainly pastoral agr., but wine, corn, tobacco in valleys; industl. a. in S. based on hydroelectric power, chemicals, metallurgy; many tourist resorts, inc. Locarno, Lugano; cap. Bellinzona; a. 2,813 km^2; p. (1969) 242,000.

Tickhill, t., South Yorks., **Eng.**; cas.; p. (1971) 3,257.

Ticonderoga, v., N.E. N.Y., **USA**; resort between Ls. George and Champlain; L. George falls provide hydroelectric power for paper mill; local graphite used in pencil ind.; p. (1970) 3,268.

Tideswell, t., Derbys., **Eng.**; tourist ctr.; limestone quarrying in a.; lge. 14th cent. church known as "cath. of the Peak." p. c. 1,500.

Tidore I., Moluccas, **Indonesia**; volcanic; densely populated; coffee, tobacco, spices, fruit; a. 78 km^2; p. (est. 1969) 70,000.

Tien Shan (= Celestial Mtns.), mtn. chain, central Asia, along **China–USSR** border; highest peak 7,320 m; source of Syr-Dar'ya, Chu, Ili and many other Rs.

Tientsin (Tianjing), c., Hopeh prov., **China** 112 km S.E. of Peking; impt. pt. using poor harbour on Hai R.; industl. ctr., textiles elec. instruments, steel rolling mills, machine tools, chemicals, tobacco, food processing; p. (est. 1970) 4,280,000.

Tierra del Fuego, archipelago, southernmost part of **S. America**; separated from Patagonia by Strait of Magellan; divided politically between Chile and Argentina; timber, pastoral agr., sheep; oilfield at Rio Grande; mng.; a. *c.* 47,900 km^2.

Tigre, st., **Ethiopia**; formerly an independent kingdom; cap. Adua.

Tigris, R., S.W. **Asia**; rises in Taurus mtns., S. Turkey, flows through Iraq where it is joined by the Euphrates and proceeds to Persian G.; comm. routeway; dam projected 56 km N. of Mosul; many of the earliest cs. located in valley; 1,840 km long.

Tijuana, t., Baja Cal. st., **Mexico**; resort catering for Americans; casinos, race-tracks, bull-fights; p. (1970) 277,306 (t.), 327,400 (met. a.).

Tiksi, t., **USSR**; Arctic spt., at mouth of Lena R.; local coal deposits; linked by air and R. to Yakutsk.

Tilburg, c., N. Brabant, **Neth.**; nr. Breda; woollens, textiles, tobacco, leather; p. (est. 1969) 151,897 (c.), 201,253 (met. a.).

Tilbury, pt., Essex, **Eng.**; on N. bank of R. Thames 32 km E. of London; within Port of London; major container terminal; p. (1961) 18,387.

Tillicoultry, burgh, Clackmannan, **Scot.**; on Devon R.; woollen and worsted fabrics, paper; p. (1971) 4,026.

Tilsit. *See* Sovetsk.

Timaru, t., S.I., **N.Z.**; E. cst. spt., exp. frozen foods; fishing; regional ctr. for S. Canterbury; p. (1971) 28,327.

Timbuktu, Mali, W. **Africa**; nr. Niger R. on border of Sahara; salt tr., handicraft inds.; flourished as comm. mart and Moslem ctr. 14th–16th cent.; p. (1967) 9,000.

Timisoara, c., W. **Romania**; comm., industl. and educational ctr.; univ., 2 caths., cas.; once a frontier fortress; p. (est. 1969) 189,264.

Timmins, t., Ont., **Canada**; gold mng. declining; vast deposits of copper, zinc, silver, discovered 1964; timber inds., brewing; p. (1966) 29,303.

Timok Basin, Serbia, **Yugoslavia**; industl. region; coal mng., copper smelting, chemicals, glass, food processing; arable agr., vines.

Timor, lgst. of Lesser Sunda Is., **E. Indies**; divided politically until 1975 into W. Timor part of Indonesia and Port. Timor; now both part of Indonesia; a. 33,748 km^2; p. (est. 1970) 3,085,541.

Timor Sea, that part of the Indian Oc. N.W. of W. Australia, and S. of Timor I.

Timsah, L., **Egypt**; sm. L. midway along Suez Canal; formerly used for recreational purposes by Brit. garrison in Canal zone.

Tinogasta, t., Catamarca prov., **Argentina**; in E. foothills of Andes, 192 km N.W. of Catamarca; impt. copper mines.

Tintagel, v., Cornwall, **Eng.**; ruined Norman cas.; reputed birthplace of King Arthur; tourism.

Tintern, v., Gwent, **Wales**; Cistercian abbey.

Tinto, R., Huelva prov., **S.W. Spain**; in Andalusia; flows W. to Atl. Oc.; gives its name to Rio Tinto copper mng. region which it crosses; 104 km long.

Tipperary, inland co., Munster, **R.o.I.**; drained by Rs. Suir and Shannon; mtnous., Knockmealdown and Galty mtns.; fertile Golden Vale in S.W.; dairying, sugar-beet; divided into N. and S. Ridings; p. (1966) 53,832 (N.R.), 68,946 (S.R.).

Tipperary, t., **Tipperary**, **R.o.I.**; 46 km S.E. Limerick; dairy processing; p. (1966) 4,507.

Tipton. *See* **Dudley**.

Tiranë, t., cap. of **Albania**; rapid growth since becoming cap. 1920; many new inds.; agr. processing, engin., clothing, glass; univ.; airport; p. (1967) 169,300.

Tiraspol, c., S.E. Moldavian SSR, **USSR**; on R. Dniester; agr. processing ctr.; heat and power sta. recently constructed; p. (1970) 106,000.

Tiree, I., Inner Hebrides, **Scot.**; off cst. of Mull; 22 km long, up to 10 km wide; sm. freshwater lochs and prehistoric forts; p. (1971) 1,019 (inc. Coll).

Tiruchirapalli (Trichinopoly), c., Tamil Nadu, S.E. **India**; on R. Cauvery; rly. ctr.; textiles, cigars, goldsmithery; p. (1971) 307,400 (c.), 464,624 (met. a.).

Tirunelveli (Tinnevelly), c., Tamil Nadu, S.E. **India**; agr. tr. ctr. with sugar refinery; p. (1971) 108,498 (c.), 266,688 (met. a.).

Tiruppur, t., Tamil Nadu, **India**; nr. Coimbatore; p. (1971) 113,302 (t.), 151,127 (met. a.).

Tisa (Tisza), R., **E. Europe**; rises in E. Carpathians, W. Ukraine, flows across Hungary into Yugoslavia where it joins the Danube 72 km below Novi Sad; ch. tribs. Koros and Mures; length *c.* 960 km; navigable in part.

Titicaca, L., **S. America**; between two ranges of Andes, on borders of Bolivia and Peru; 3,812 m a.s.l.; highest lge. L. in world; max. depth 300 m; crossed by steamers; fishing; a. *c.* 8,300 km².

Titograd (Podgorica), t., cap. of Montenegro, S. **Yugoslavia**; nr. Albanian frontier; anc. t. but now mainly modern with growing industl. activity; agr. processing, aluminium smelting; airport; p. (1971) 54,509.

Titov Veles, t., central Macedonia, **Yugoslavia**; on R. Vardar, and main rly. to Belgrade; recent industl. growth; textiles; p. (est. 1965) 31,000.

Tiverton, mkt. t., Devon, **Eng.**; 22 km N. Exeter; once famous for lace; textiles, engin.; p. (1971) 15,548.

Tivoli, the anc. Tibur, nr. Rome, **Italy**; on Aniene R., magnificent situation; hydroelec. power; resort; remains of Hadrian's villa; p. (est. 1968) 40,501.

Tjirebon (Cheribon), spt., Java, **Indonesia**; on N. cst. 192 km E. of Djakarta; rice, tea, coffee tr.; ctr. of irrigation scheme; oil refining; p. (1971) 178,529.

Tlaxcala, smallest st., **Mexico**; on Mesa Central; dense p.; mainly agr.; cap. T.; a. 4,027 km²; p. (1969) 454,000.

Tlemcen, t., cap. of T. dep., N.W. **Algeria**; picturesque mediaeval t.; agr. ctr. in fertile region; textiles, furniture, handicrafts; p. (1967) 80,000.

Tobago, southernmost I., Windward Is., **W.I.**; volcanic, forested, picturesque, irregular topography; resorts utilising pleasant climate; exp. coconuts, copra, cacao, limes; ch. t. Scarborough; seeks internal self-gov.; a. 300 km²; p. (1970) 39,280. *See* **Trinidad and Tobago**.

Tobata. *See* **Kitakyushu**.

Tobermory, burgh, Argyll and Bute, **Scot.**; on I. of Mull at N. entrance to Sound of Mull; fish. pt., resort; p. (1971) 641.

Tobol, R., W. Siberia, **RSFSR**; trib. of R. Irtysh; navigable in lower course; 800 km long.

Tobolsk, t., W. Siberia, **RSFSR**; R. pt. on Irtysh R.; shipbldg., sawmilling, fishing; p. (est. 1967) 47,000.

Tobruk, spt., **Libya**, N. Africa; on cst. 352 km E. of Benghazi; exp. oil, served by pipeline from Libyan oilfields; p. (est. 1970) 28,000.

Tocantins, R., central **Brazil**; rises in Goiás prov., flows N. across plateau of Brazil through Pará estuary to Atl. Oc.; navigation interrupted by rapids 320 km above Pará; ch. trib. Araguaya R.; 2,560 km long.

Toce, R., N. **Italy**; rises in Lepontine Alps, flows S. and S.E. into L. Maggiore; valley used by trunk rly. from Milan to Berne as S. approach to Simplon Tunnel; 86 km long.

Tocopilla, spt., **Chile**; exp. nitrate, copper ore, sulphates, iodine; p. (est. 1966) 23,140.

Todmorden, mkt. t., West Yorks., **Eng.**; nr. source of R. Calder, 10 km N.E. of Rochdale; cottons, machin.; p. (1971) 15,150.

Togliatti (Tol'yatti), c., **RSFSR**; on R. Volga 56 km W.N.W. of Kuybyshev; engin., motor wks., natural gas pipeline to Moscow; chemicals; p. (1970) 251,000.

Togo, Rep. of, **W. Africa**; narrow strip between Ghana (W.) and Benin (E.); N. and S. lowlands separated by mtns. (1,000 m); climate hot and humid, but drier savannah conditions in N.; coffee on slopes of central mtns., cacao, copra in S., maize in N.; phosphate mng., major iron ore deposits in N. now form ch. exp.; developing food-processing inds.; cap. Lomé; a. 54,960 km²; p. (1970) 1,956,000.

Tokaido, **Japan**, one of gr. feudal highways, along S. cst. Honshu, now forms main line of modern communications network.

Tokaimura, v., Ibaraki, **Japan**; nuclear reactor and lge. nuclear power sta.

Tokaj, t., **Hungary**; at confluence of Bodrog and Tisa Rs.; nearby slopes of Hegyalja produce Tokay wine; p. (1960) 5,031.

Tokat, t., cap. of T. prov., **Turkey**; copper refining, leather mnfs.; p. (1965) 38,006.

Tokelau or **Union Isles**, gr. of 3 coral atolls, S. Pac., N. of W. Samoa, belonging to **N.Z.**; Fakaofo, Nukunono and Atafu; natives are Polynesians; subsistence economy; copra; a. 10 km²; p. (1970) 1,687.

Tokoroa, co. t., N.I., **N.Z.**; kraft paper, pulp, and sawn timber; p. (1971) 15,174.

Tokushima, t., Shikoku, **Japan**; spt. on E. cst.; mkt. ctr., cotton mnfs.; p. (est. 1971) 236,000.

Tokyo, c., cap. of **Japan**; spt. with deepened harbour handling mainly S. coastal tr.; major industl. ctr. with diverse mnfs. and major problems of pollution; built on marshy site with much expensive reclamation from sea; planned decentralisation of p. and economic activity in progress; with Osaka-Kobe-Kyoto conurbs. (480 km long ribbon development) spoken of as Tokaido (*q.v.*) megalopolis; major educational ctr. with many univs.; p. (est. 1971) 8,841,000 (c.); 11,403,744 (met. a.).

Tolbukhin, t., N.E. **Bulgaria**; comm. and agr. ctr. of Dobruja; food-processing, textiles, furniture, agr. machin.; formerly Dobrich, renamed in honour of Russian soldier who took it from Germans 1944; p. (est. 1968) 61,440.

Toledo, prov., **Spain**; mtnous.; agr., vineyards, stock-raising; a. 15,346 km²; p. (1970) 468,925.

Toledo, anc. c., cap. of T. prov., **Spain**; in New Castile; on hill above Tagus R.; Gothic, Moorish, and Castillian architecture; picturesque narrow streets; Alcázar citadel; associated with El Greco; sword-mkg. still flourishes; sm. arms; tourism; p. (1970) 44,382.

Toledo, c., Ohio, **USA**; rly. ctr. and L. pt. with natural harbour on Maumee R.; exp. mnfs., oil, coal, agr. prod.; imports iron ore; glass-mkg., shipbldg., car components and many varied mnfs.; p. (1970) 379,104 (c.), 685,455 (met. a.).

Tolentino, t., in the Marches, central **Italy**; on R. Chienti; mediaeval walls and houses; cath.; sm. handicraft inds.; spa and tourist ctr.; p. (est. 1968) 16,372.

Tolosa, t., Guipúzcoa prov., **Spain**; in the Basque cty.; mediaeval bldgs., and armour; paper mills; p. (1970) 18766.

Tolpuddle, v., Dorset, **Eng.**; 11 km N.E. of Dorchester; famous for "Tolpuddle martyrs," agr. labourers condemned to transportation for trying to form a trade union (1834).

Toluca, c., cap. of Mexico st., central **Mexico**; stands at 2,672 m; brewing, flour, cottons, pottery; especially noted for basket weaving; p. (1970) 223,104 (c.), 322,557 (met. a.).

Tom, R., Siberia, **RSFSR**; flows through Kuznetsk Basin and joins R. Ob; 704 km long.

Tomaszow Mazowieki, t., Lodz prov., central **Poland**; industl. t. on Pilica R., surrounded by forests; textile ind., artificial silk; p. (1970) 54,900.

Tombigbee, R., Miss., **USA**; flows S. to join

Alabama R. to form Mobile and Tensaw Rs.; navigable, partially canalised; length 654 km.

Tomsk, c., cap. of marshy T. oblast, **RSFSR**; one of few lge. ts. in N. Siberia; major pt. on R. Tom; rly. junc. on Trans-Siberian rly.; educational ctr.; univ., cath.; engin., chemicals; p. (1970) 339,000.

Tonawanda, t., N.Y. st., **USA**; on Niagara R. at terminus of Erie Barge Canal; steel, plastics, chemicals; power from Niagara Falls, adjacent to N. Tonawanda; p. (1970) 21,898.

Tonbridge, t., Kent, **Eng.**; on R. Medway; food processing; lt. inds., inc. cricket balls; Norman cas. gatehouse; public school; p. (1971) 31,006.

Tone, R., Honshu, Japan; flows E. across Kanto Plain to Pac. Oc., N. of Tokyo; longest R. in Japan.

Tonga, I. gr., S. Pac. **Oc.**; Polynesian kingdom, gained independence 1970; 158 coral and volcanic Is.; 50 per cent. p. on Tongatabu I.; exp. copra. bananas; fishing; oil discovered 1969; airport; cap. Nuku'alofa; a. 699 km^2; p. (1969) 83,630.

Tongariro, volcanic peak, N.I., **N.Z.**; nat. park in ctr. of volcanic dist.; crater L. at summit; alt. 1,970 m.

Tongeren (Tongres), t., Limburg prov., N.E. **Belgium**; mkt. ctr. for fertile Hesbaye region; historic bldgs.; p. (est. 1969) 17,224.

Tonkin, region, N. Vietnam; mtns. in N. and W., alluvial plain in E. around delta of Red R., containing most p. and lge. cs.; fertile agr.; ch. t. Hanoi; ch. pt. Haiphong; a. 104,973 km^2.

Tonle Sap, L., **Cambodia**; major comm. fishing a.; L. acts as natural reservoir to control floods of Mekong R.

Tönsberg, c., Vestfold prov., S.E. **Norway**; one of oldest Norwegian cs., on Skagerrak at entrance to Oslo fjord; ctr. of whaling fleet; oil mills; p. (est. 1970) 11,260.

Toowoomba, t., Queensland, **Australia**; rly. ctr. and mkt. t. for wheat, pastoral and dairy dist.; food processing, iron foundry using local coal; p. (1972) 57,543.

Topeka, c., cap. of Kansas st., **USA**; on Kansas R.; impt. tr. ctr. in rich agr. region; food processing, rly. ctr. and engin.; p. (1970) 123,043.

Torbay, former C.B., S. Devon, **Eng.**; formed by amalgamation of Torquay, Paignton, and Brixham; located around Tor Bay; tourism; p. (1971) 108,888.

Torcello, I., with anc. Byzantine cath., on lagoon nr. Venice, **Italy**.

Torgau, t., **E. Germany**; R. pt. on Elbe; industl. ctr.; American and Soviet armies met here 1945; p. (est. 1970) 21,688.

Torne, R., N. Europe; rises in Sweden, drains L. Tornetrask and flows S.W. to G. of Bothnia, forming Finno-Swedish bdy.; rich in salmon; 512 km long.

Toronto, c., cap. of Ont. prov., **Canada**; major Gt. Ls. pt., on L. Ont.; spacious harbour; exp. lge. quantities of wheat; comm., financial, industl. and educational ctr.; many varied mnfs., univ.; notable bldgs., parks; a. 622 km^2; p. (1971) 698,634 (c.), 2,609,638 (met. a.).

Torpoint, t., Cornwall, **Eng.**; on Plymouth Sound; p. (1971) 4,782.

Torquay, t., S. Devon, **Eng.**; incorporated in Torbay; on N. side of Tor Bay; seaside resort with all-year season.

Torre Annunziata, Campania, **Italy**; at foot of Vesuvius; spt., spa, bathing resort on Bay of Naples; arms factory, pasta mnf.; p. (est. 1968) 63,070.

Torre del Greco, t., Campania, **Italy**; spt. and resort on Bay of Naples at foot of Vesuvius; coral fishing; pasta mnf.; p. (est. 1968) 91,439.

Torremolinos, cst. resort, **Spain**; S. of Malaga.

Torrens, L., S. **Australia**; 208 km long, 32 km wide; varies from brackish lake to salt marsh.

Torreón, c., Coahuila, N. **Mexico**; developed rapidly after growth of cotton in surrounding Laguna dist.; cotton mills, rubber, smelting, food processing; rly. connection with ts. in S. Mexico; p. (1970) 257,045.

Torres Strait, between C. York, Queensland, **Australia**, and **New Guinea**; 144 km wide, dangerous navigation.

Torridge, R., Devon, **Eng.**; flows from Hartland dist. to a confluence with the Taw at Bideford Bay; 85 km long.

Torrington. *See* **Great Torrington**.

Tortona, t., Piedmont, N. **Italy**; on Scrivia R.; textiles, metallurgy, engin., wines; cath.; the Roman Dertona; p. c. (est. 1968) 28,577.

Tortosa, c., Tarragona prov., N.E. **Spain**; pt. on Ebro R., 35 km from mouth; food processing, soap, pottery; cath.; impt. Moorish t.; p. (1970) 46,376.

Tororo, t., **Uganda**; lge. chemical wks., cement, fertilisers.

Tortuga or **Ile de la Tortue**, I., Caribbean Sea; off N. cst. Haiti; provides shelter from N.E. tr. winds for Port-de-Paix; private development to convert I. into free pt. with tax incentives for inds.; scenic attractions being tapped to develop tourist tr.; airport under construction; subsistence agr. fishing; a. *c.* 65 km^2.

Torun (Ger. **Thorn**), c., Bydgoszcz prov., **Poland**; rly. junc., pt. on Vistula; industl. ctr.; chemicals, elec. gds., clothing, metallurgy, engin., food processing; univ. bears name of Copernicus who was born here; p. (1970) 129,200.

Tory I., off N.W. cst., Donegal, **R.o.I.**; lighthouse; fishing; p. *c.* 200.

Totnes, t., Devon, **Eng.**; on R. Dart, 10 km N.W. of Dartmouth; mediaeval t.; agr. mkt., food processing; p. (1971) 5,771.

Tottenham. *See* **Haringey**.

Tottington, t., Gtr. Manchester, **Eng.**; textiles; p. (1971) 9,740.

Tottori, t., Honshu, **Japan**; spt. on Sea of Japan, exp. lumber, raw silk, fruit; industl. ctr.; p. (est. 1971) 114,000.

Touggourt or **Tuggurt**, t., S. **Algeria**; on edge of Sahara; rly. terminus; dates; p. (1961) 26,000.

Toul, t., Meurthe-et-Moselle dep., N.E. **France**; in Lorraine, on Moselle R.; agr. ctr.; p. (1968) 14,780.

Toulon, c., Var dep., S.W. **France**; reinstated as cap. of Var dep. (1974); on Mediterranean cst.; base of Fr. navy; fine natural harbour; comm. pt. and industl. ctr.; many fine bldgs.; Port-Cros Nat. Park nearby; p. (1968) 174,746 (c.), 340,021 (met. a.).

Toulouse, c., cap. of Haute-Garonne dep., S. **France**; in Languedoc on Garonne R. and Canal du Midi, commanding route through Gate of Carcassonne; industl. and agr. tr. ctr.; food processing, varied mnfs.; many fine bldgs., notably mediaeval univ., basilica, Gothic cath.; p. (1968) 370,796 (c.), 439,764 (met. a.).

Touraine, region and former prov. of **France**, of which Tours was the cap.; now occupied by Indre-et-Loire dep. and part of Vienne dep.; known as the "garden of France."

Tourcoing, c., Nord dep., **N. France**; 16 km N.E. of Lille; with twin t. of Roubaix forms major wool textile ctr.; p. (1967) 99,369.

Tournai, c., Hainaut prov., W. **Belgium**; on R. Scheldt, nr. Mons; historic c.; famous cath.; textiles, carpet mftg., ctr. of cement ind.; p. (1968) 33,518.

Tours, c., cap. of Indre-et-Loire dep., **France**; in Touraine, on R. Loire; tourist ctr. for the châteaux of the Loire; route ctr.; agr. inds.; printing, engin.; Gothic cath.; p. (1968) 128,120 (c.), 201,556 (met. a.).

Towcester, mkt. t., Northants., **Eng.**; 14 km S.W. of Northampton; "Eatanswill" of *Pickwick Papers*; p. (1971) 20,998 (dist.).

Tower Hamlets, inner bor., E. London, **Eng.**; inc. former bors. of Bethnal Green, Stepney and Poplar; undergoing rapid economic and social change as p. and inds. are decentralised; site of lge. a. of London Docks with allied dockland inds.; clothing, brewing; p. (1971) 164,948.

Tow Law, t., Durham, **Eng.**; in Wear Dale, 16 km N.W. of Bishop Auckland; p. (1971) 2,547.

Townsville, spt., Queensland, **Australia**; on E. cst.; exp. prods. of rich dairying pastoral, and mng. terr.; copper-refining; p. (1972) 68,442.

Towton, v., North Yorks. **Eng.**; nearby Towton field, scene of bloodiest battle of Wars of the Roses 1461: Lancastrians under Henry VI defeated by Yorkists under Edward IV.

Towy, R., S. Wales; flows S.W. of Carmarthen Bay; 104 km long.

Toyama, c., Honshu, **Japan**; on Etchu plain to E. of Noto peninsula; regional admin. and comm. ctr.; patent medicines, aluminium smelting, machin.; p. (est. 1971) 275,000.

Toyohashi, t., Honshu, **Japan**; food processing, textiles; p. (est. 1971) 265,000.
Trabzon or **Trebizond**, spt., **Turkey**; on Black Sea; exp. tobacco, food prods., carpets; once a gr. tr. ctr. on caravan route between Persia and Europe; founded 8th cent. B.C. by Greek colonists.
Trafalgar, C., S.W. cst., Cadiz, **Spain**; Nelson's famous victory 1805.
Trail, t., B.C., **Canada**; lgst. metallurgical smelter in Commonwealth, using local non-ferrous metals; chemicals; p. (1971) 10,843.
Tralee, mkt. t., spt., Kerry, **R.o.I.**; on R. Lee; exp. grain, butter; p. (1966) 11,211.
Tranent, burgh, E. Lothian, **Scot.**; 16 km E. of Edinburgh; p. (1971) 6,281.
Trani, spt., N. Apulia, **Italy**; on Adriatic; mkt. t. for fertile coastal a.; fishing food processing; cath., cas.; p. (est. 1968) 41,530.
Transbaykal, region, Siberia, **RSFSR**; E. of L. Baykal; mineral wealth; ch. t., Chita.
Transcaucasia, region between the Black Sea and the Caspian Sea, **USSR**; comprising the constituent reps. of Georgia, Armenia, and Azerbaydzhan; ch. t., Tbilisi.
Transkei, indep. Bantu Terr. (1976), **S. Africa**; not recognised by UN as designed to consolidate apartheid; mainly agr., maize and livestock; heavily dependent on S. Africa; p. mainly employed in mines in Transvaal and Orange Free State; cap. Umtata; a. 42,849 km²; p. (1970) 1,751,327.
Transvaal, prov., **Rep. of S. Africa**; high veld plateau (900–1,200 m) with Kruger Nat. Park in N.E.; hot summers, temperate winters; livestock on grasslands, grains, citrus fruits and temperate crops on irrigated land; lge. mineral wealth, especially gold in Witwatersrand; diamonds, uranium, platinum; inds. in ch. cs., Johannesburg and cap. Pretoria; a. 286,066 km²; p. (1970) 6,385,762.
Transylvania, historic region and prov., central **Romania**; high plateau surrounded by Carpathians; forested; mineral wealth not yet fully realised; arable agr. in valleys; ch. ts., Cluj, Brasov.
Transylvanian Alps, range of mtns., **Romania**; continuation of Carpathians.
Trapani, t., cap. of T. prov., W. Sicily, **Italy**; spt. on promontory, sheltering natural harbour; exp. wine, pasta, tuna fish caught locally; p. (1969) 76,679.
Traralgon, t., Victoria, **Australia**; lignite mng. nearby; p. (1972) 14,624.
Trasimeno, L., Umbria, central **Italy**; occupies lge. extinct volcanic crater; drained S. to R. Tiber; a. *c.* 155 km².
Trás-os-Montes e Alto-Douro, prov., N. **Portugal**; high, bleak plateau, cultivated valleys; climate cold except in S.; port wine cty. of Douro R.; remote, sparsely populated; a. 11,834 km²; p. (1960) 667,054.
Trawsfynydd, Gwynedd, **Wales**; within N. Wales Nat. Park; nuclear power sta.
Trebizond. *See* Trabzon.
Tredegar, t., Gwent, **Wales**; in narrow valley 5 km W. of Ebbw Vale; engin.; home of Aneurin Bevan; p. (1971) 17,976.
Treforest, t., Mid Glamorgan, **Wales**; on R. Taff; lge. trading estate established in 1930s to alleviate unemployment in primary inds. of S. Wales; aircraft accessories, electronics, chemical, pharmaceutical, rayon, metal wks.
Trelleborg, spt., S. **Sweden**; on Baltic Sea; most impt. rubber factory in cty.; p. (est. 1970) 36,021.
Tremadoc Bay, N. **Wales**; N. part of Cardigan Bay formed by Lleyn penin., Gwynedd.
Trengganu, st., **Malaysia**; N.E. Malaya; rice, rubber, coconuts; tin, iron; cap. Kuala Trengganu; a. 13,080 km²; p. (1967) 378,738.
Trent, R., **Eng.**; rises in N. Staffs, flows round S. Pennines and joins the Ouse to form estuary of the Humber; many power stas. along its banks; polluted waterway, especially between Humber and Nottingham; 240 km long.
Trentino-Alto Adige, aut. region, N.E. **Italy**, between Austrian and Swiss Frontiers and L. Garda; embraces provs. Trento and Bolzano; cap. Trento; formerly called Venetia Tridentina; a. 13,598 km²; p. (1969) 839,625.
Trento, t., cap. of Trento prov. and ch. t. of Trentino-Alto Adige, N. **Italy**; on R. Adige and route to Brenner Pass; chemicals, cement, elec. engin.; picturesque t.; cath.; p. (1969) 89,410.
Trenton, c., cap. N.J. st., **USA**; on Delaware R.; transport and industl. ctr.; noted for its wire-rope and pottery inds., established mid-19th cent.; crockery, machin., metal and rubber gds.; p. (1970) 102,211 (c.), 299,919 (met. a.).
Tres Arroyos, t., E. **Argentina**; agr. and livestock ctr.; p. (1960) 40,000.
Trèves. *See* Trier.
Treviso, c., cap. of T. prov., Venetia, N.E. **Italy**; on R. Sile; agr. ctr. on fertile Venetian plain; silk mills, paper, furniture, fertilisers, pottery; p. (1969) 89,267.
Trichinopoly. *See* **Tiruchirapalli.**
Trichur, t., Kerala, **India**; comm. and educational ctr.; p. (1961) 73,038.
Trier (**Trèves**), c., Rhineland–Palatinate, **W. Germany**; on R. Moselle; Roman origin, (Augusta Trevorum, the Rome of the North), cath., Porta Nigra; ctr. of Moselle wine reg.; textiles, leather goods; birthplace of Marx; p. (est. 1969) 104,100.
Trieste, spt., cap. of T. prov., Friuli-Venezia Giulia, N.E. **Italy**; shipbldg., fishing, oil refining; pipeline to Schwechat, nr. Vienna; cath., cas., Roman antiquities; univ.; p. (1969) 278,370.
Trieste Free Territory, former free st. on the Adriatic; constituted by Peace Treaty with Italy, 1947, as compromise between conflicting Yugoslav and Italian claims; a. 743 km²; Zone A handed over to Italy, Zone B to Yugoslavia, 1954. Yugoslav/Italian agreement 1975 settled border dispute and established free industl. zone on both sides of border in region of Sezana-Fernetti.
Trikkala, t., cap. of T. dep., W. Thessaly, N. **Greece**; mkt. t. for pastoral prods.; damaged by earthquake 1954; p. (1971) 38,150.
Trim, co. t., U.D., Meath, **R.o.I.**; mkt. t. on R. Boyne; anc. seat of Irish Parliament; p. (1966) 1,467.
Trincomalee, t., N.E. cst. **Sri Lanka**; excellent natural harbour; formerly a British naval base; p. (est. 1968) 39,000.
Tring, mkt. t., Herts., **Eng.**; in gap through Chiltern hills, 14 km N.W. of Hemel Hempstead p. (1971) 9,155.
Trinidad, t., cap. of Beni dep., **Bolivia**; exp. beef by air, but development hampered by isolation; p. (est. 1969) 17,360.
Trinidad, I., **W.I.**; N. of Venezuela; climate warm and humid; oil, natural gas, asphalt, sugar, rum, coconut oil, molasses, citrus fruits; tourism; cap. Port of Spain; a. 4,828 km²; p. (est. 1970) 1,010,000. *See* Trinidad and Tobago.
Trinidad, t., central **Cuba**; picturesque old t. of colonial period, declared a national monument; p. (est. 1967) 57,840.
Trinidad and Tobago, indep. sov. st. within Commonwealth (1962), rep. (1976), **W.I.**; main exps. crude oil and petroleum prods. which with natural asphalt represent over 20 per cent national income; oil refining; tropical crops and food processing; sugar, molasses, rum, fruits, textiles; cap. and major spt. Port of Spain; internal self-gov. sought by Tobago; a. 5,128 km²; p. (est. 1970) 1,044,000.
Trinity, R., Texas, **USA**; flows S.E. to Galveston Bay; used for reservoirs; valley contains lge. p. and much economic activity; 800 km long.
Trino, Piedmont, N. **Italy**; 18 km S.S.W. of Vercelli; nuclear power sta.
Tripoli, c., **Lebanon**; spt. on Mediterranean; admin. ctr. for N. Lebanon; terminus of oil pipeline from Iraq; oil refining; exp. agr. prods.; p. (est. 1964) 127,611.
Tripoli, c., joint cap. of **Libya** (with Benghazi), on Mediterranean; stands on edge of palm-oasis, site of anc. Oea; tourist, comm. and mnf. ctr.; gd. harbour; p. (est. 1968) 247,365.
Tripura, new st. (1972), **India**; N.E. Ganges delta, bordering Assam and Bangladesh; cap. Agartala; rice, jute, cotton, sugar-cane; a. 10,360 km²; p. (est. 1971) 1,556,822.
Tristan da Cunha, sm. gr. S Is., **S. Atl. Oc.**; dependency of Brit. col. (t. Helena; ch. I. Tristan; evacuated 1961 volcanic eruption) but resettled 1963; a. 117 km²; p. (1970) 280.
Trivandrum, c., cap. of Kerala st., S.W. **India**; pt. on Arabian Sea; textiles, coconut processing; univ.; p. (1971) 409,672.

Trnava, c., W. Slovakia, **ČSSR**; mkt. t. in fertile agr. region on Váh R.; food processing, steel wks.; cath., monasteries, called " little Rome "; p. (1967) 36,000.

Trnovo or Tirnovo, c., **Bulgaria**; on Jantra R.; food processing, textiles, leather; anc. cap. of Bulgaria; p. (est. 1970) 42,344.

Trogir, t., S. Croatia, **Yugoslavia**; sm. pt. and seaside resort, partly sited on I. of Čiovo; mediaeval bldgs., inc. cath., palaces; p. c. 20,000.

Trois Rivières, t., Quebec, **Canada**; industl. ctr. on St. Lawrence R.; noted for newsprint; hydroelectric power from St. Maurice R.; p. (1966) 57,540.

Trojmiasto (Tri-City), **Poland**; name given to the three municipalities of Gdansk, Gdynia, and Sopot, a loosely-knit conurb.

Trollhättan, t., S.W. **Sweden**; on Göta R., nr. T. falls which generate power for metallurgical and chemical inds.; car and aircraft components; p. (1968) 40,803.

Trombay, I., off Bombay, **India**; oil refining; atomic reactor; zirconium metal produced; fertilisers.

Troms, co., N. **Norway**; deep fjords, offshore Is.; fishing, livestock, boat-bldg.; cap. Tromsö; a. 25,916 km²; p. (est. 1972) 138,085.

Tromsö, t., cap. of Troms prov., N. **Norway**; spt. on sm. I. of T. in Norwegian Sea; arctic fishing, sealing; fish processing; p. (1968) 36,340.

Trondheim, c., spt., **Norway**; on W. cst. on S. side of T. fjord; shipbldg., engin.; exp. timber and wood-pulp, butter, fish, copper; anc. cath., burial place of early Norwegian kings and place of coronation of recent sovereigns; p. (est. 1969) 124,870.

Troon, burgh, Kyle and Carrick, **Scot.**; on F. of Clyde, 10 km N. of Ayr; gd. harbour and graving docks; shipbldg., hosiery; seawater distillation research ctr. project; resort; p. (1971) 11,318.

Troppau. *See* **Opava**.

Trossachs, Stirling, **Scot.**; picturesque wooded glen; tourist resort.

Troste, nr. Llanelly, **Wales**; steel strip mill, tin plate.

Trouville, t., Calvados dep., N. **France**; popular seaside resort and fishing pt. on Normandy cst.; p. (1968) 6,577.

Trowbridge, mkt. t., Wilts., **Eng.**; cloth wks., bacon curing, dairying, engin.; p. (1971) 19,245.

Troy, c., N.Y., **USA**; at confluence of Rs. Hudson and Mohawk; gr. shirt-mftg. ctr.; p. (1970) 62,918.

Troyes, c., cap. of Aube dep., N.E. **France**; on R. Seine; once cap. of Champagne; hosiery, textile machin., food processing; magnificent cath.; site of mediaeval fairs which standardised Troy weight; p. (1968) 74,898 (c.), 114,209 (met. a.).

Trucial States. *See* **United Arab Emirates**.

Trujillo, c., N.W. **Peru**; comm. and mkt. ctr. for irrigated agr. region, on Moche R., in foothills of Andes; sugar, cocaine; univ., cath.; p. (est. 1970) 156,200.

Trujillo, t., cap. of T. st., W. **Venezuela**; on Transandean highway at 805 m; agr. mkt. for region producing coffee, cacao, tobacco, maize; p. (est. 1970) 27,107.

Truro, t., Nova Scotia, **Canada**; on Salmon R.; hosiery, lumber mills, printing, metallurgy, machin.; p. (1971) 12,968.

Truro, c., Cornwall, **Eng.**; at confluence of Rs. Kenwyn and Allen; mkt. t. and sm. pt.; admin. ctr. of Cornwall; cath.; p. (1971) 14,830.

Tsaidam, depression, Chinghai prov., **China**; a. of salt marsh and Ls.; rich deposits of oil; st. farms for intensive animal husbandry.

Tsamkong (Zhanjiang), c., Kwantung prov., **China**; spt. on Luichow peninsula; cotton milling, leather mnfs.; p. (1953) 166,000.

Tsangpo, R., Tibet, **China**; one of the headstreams of the R. Brahmaputra; 1,350 km long.

Tschenstokov. *See* **Czestochowa**.

Tselinograd, c., Kazakh SSR, **USSR**; cap. Virgin Lands terr.; on Ishim R., nr. Karaganda coalfield; chemicals, agr. machin.; p. (1970) 180,000.

Tsinan (Jinan), c., cap. of Shantung prov., **China**; on S. bank of Hwang-ho, 160 km from G. of Chihli; agr. ctr.; mnfs. glass, textiles, precious stones, trucks; p. (est. 1970) 1,500,000.

Tsinghai. *See* **Chinghai**.

Tsinling Shan, mtn. range, central **China**; rises to over 1,830 m; watershed between Hwang-ho and Yangtze R. basins; impt. climatic divide between temperate N. China and tropical S. China.

Tsingtao (Qingdao), c., Shantung prov., **China**; spt. with excellent harbour at head of Kiaochow Bay; exp. soya beans, groundnuts; mnfs. locomotives, cement, textiles, machin., chemicals; p. (est. 1970) 1,900,000.

Tsitsihar (Qiqihar), c., Heilungkiang prov., N. **China**; on Vladivostok portion of Trans-Siberian rly.; food processing and tr., chemicals; potential oilfield; p. (est. 1970) 1,500,000.

Tskhinvali, c., N. Georgian SSR, **USSR**; elec. prods., lumber mills, fruit canning; p. (1970) 30,000.

Tsu, t., Honshu, **Japan**; textiles; p. (est. 1971) 127,000.

Tsugaru Strait, **Japan**; separates Is. Hokkaido and Honshu; links Sea of Japan with Pac. Oc.; 72 km long, 24–32 km wide.

Tsuruga, spt., **Japan**; on W. cst. Honshu; rayon textiles, cotton, atomic power plant; p. (1970) 56,445.

Tuam, mkt. t., R.D., Galway, **R.o.I.**; sugar refining; p. (1961) 25,676 (R.D.); (1966) 3,621 (t.).

Tuamotu, coral archipelago, **Fr. Polynesia**, S. Pac. Oc.; pearl fisheries; p. of gr. (est. 1967) 6,148.

Tuapse, c., S. Krasnodar terr., **RSFSR**; at foot of Caucasus on Black Sea; major petroleum pt. at W. end of pipeline from Baku and Makhachkala; oil refineries; p. (est. 1967) 49,000.

Tubarao, t., Santa Catarina st., S. **Brazil**; on E. cst., 280 km N.W. of Pôrto Alegre; coal mines; p. (est. 1968) 59,210.

Tübingen, t., Baden-Württemberg, **W. Germany**; on R. Neckar; 15th cent. univ., cas.; mediaeval c. ctr.; birthplace of Hölderlin, p. (est. 1969) 55,795.

Tubuai, archipelago, **Fr. Polynesia**, S. Pac. Oc.; a. 163 km²; p. (est. 1967) 5,053.

Tucson, c., S.E. Arizona, **USA**; mkt. and distribution ctr. on Santa Cruz R.; cultural ctr. and winter resort based on Spanish heritage and warm dry climate; food processing, missile components; p. (1970) 258,303 (c.), 344,904 (met. a.).

Tucumán. *See* **San Miguel de Tucumán**.

Tudela, t., Navarre, N. **Spain**; mkt. ctr. for fertile fruit-growing dist. and I. of La Majana in Ebro R.; fine cath., Roman bridge; p. (1970) 20,942.

Tula, c., cap. of T. oblast, **RSFSR**; mnf. ctr. in Moscow industl. region; local iron and lignite mng.; Yasnaya Polyana, home of Tolstoy, nearby; p. (1970) 462,000.

Tulare, L., S. Cal., **USA**; ctr. of inland drainage 64 km S. of Fresno; streams feeding it used for irrigation; in drought years L. dries up completely; a. 233 km².

Tullamore, mkt. t., U.D., Offaly, **R.o.I.**; on Grand Canal; farming, distilling, brewing; p. (1966) 6,650.

Tulle, t., cap. of Corrèze dep., **France**; firearms, textiles; p. (1968) 21,324.

Tulsa, c., Okla., **USA**; impt. oil ctr., based on lge. local deposits; machin., aeroplanes; well laid out with many parks; p. (1970) 327,956 (c.), 471,743 (met. a.).

Tumaco, t., S.W. **Colombia**; spt. on Pac. Oc., on sm. I. off cst.; exp. agr. prods.; climate hot and humid; p. (est. 1968) 80,279.

Tummel, R., Perth and Kinross, **Scot.**; trib. of R. Tay; used by Perth to Inverness rly. as S. approach to Drumochter Pass; hydroelec. scheme nr. Pitlochry; 88 km long.

Tunbridge Wells (officially Royal Tunbridge Wells), t., Kent, **Eng.**; on border of East Sussex; chalybeate waters; attractive 17th cent. promenade known as " The Pantiles "; p. (1971) 44,506.

Tunghwa, c., S.W. Kirin, **China**; rly. junc.; soyabean processing; local iron and coal reserves; p. (est. 1970) 275,000.

Tung Ting Hu, lge. L., Hunan, **China**; on S. margin of Yangtze R. plain; receives waters of Yuan and Siang Rs., drains N. to Yangtze R.; surrounded by flat, intensively cultivated land; rice, sugar, mulberry; size varies with season; max. (in late summer) 6,500 km².

Tunguska, Upper, Stony and Lower, Rs., Siberia, **USSR**; all rise in Sayan mtns. nr. L. Baykal and flow N.W. through forested cty. into R. Yenisey.

Tunguska Basin, coalfield between Yenisey and Lena Rs., **RSFSR**; main ts., Norilsk, Igarka, Yeniseysk.

Tunis, c., cap. of **Tunisia**, N. Africa; spt. on inlet of Mediterranean; exp. raw materials; base for fishing fleets; univ., notable mosques; tourist ctr.; ruins of anc. Carthage to N.E.; p. (1966) 468,997 (c.), 647,640 (met. a.).

Tunisia, indep. st., N. Africa; bounded by Algeria on W., by Libya on E., indented Mediterranean cst.; Atlas mtns. penetrate into N.; temperate cst. climate, hot and dry in S. desert; agr. and mng. basis of economy; wheat, olive oil, wine, fruits, limited to wetter coastal areas and irrigated valleys; phosphates around Ghafsa; iron ore and lead in N.W.; steelwks. at Menzel Bourguiba; chemical and paper inds. based on local phosphates; cap. Tunis; a. 164,108 km²; p. (1966) 4,533,351.

Tunja, c., cap. of Boyacá dep., **Colombia**; route and agr. tr. ctr.; p. (est. 1972) 55,600.

Turda, t., Transylvania, **Romania**; local salt mines and quarrying aid chemical and ceramic inds.; p. (est. 1970) 50,113.

Turfan, depression, E. Sinkiang prov., **China**; on S. slopes of Tien Shan mtns.; desert a. irrigated by wells and canals for animal husbandry, fruit, cotton, grain; 275 m below sea level; ch. t. Turfan; archaeological finds.

Turgutlu (Kassaba), t., Manisa prov., **Turkey**; 48 km E.N.E. of Izmir; lignite, cotton, melons; p. (1965) 35,079.

Turin or Torino, c., cap. of T. prov., N. **Italy**; on R. Po at confluence with the Dora Riparia; former cap. of Piedmont and kingdom of Sardinia; univ., cath., many historic monuments; headquarters of Italian motor ind.; clothing, machin., furniture, chemicals; oil refinery nearby; p. (1969) 1,177,039.

Turkestan E., terr. included in Sinkiang, **China**; separated from W. or former Russian Turkestan by Pamir plateau; mainly desert.

Turkestan W., terr. of **USSR**; inc. Turkmen SSR, Uzbek SSR, Tadzhik SSR, Kirghiz SSR, and part of Kazakh SSR.

Turkey, rep., S.W. **Asia**; occupies mtnous. Anatolian penin.; equable climate on coastal margins, continental severity in interior; economy predominantly agr. but hampered by poor land resources; grain grown on Anatolian plateau and a Mediterranean variety of crops around cst.; noted for tobacco; industl. development based on mng. resources and oil in S.E.; cap. Ankara; a. 780,579 km²; p. (1970) 35,666,549.

Turkmen (Turkmenistan), SSR, constituent rep., **USSR**; borders on Afghanistan, Iran, and the Caspian Sea; much of a. in Kara-Kum desert; agr. based on irrigation; fruit, cotton, wool; sulphates, petroleum; p. concentrated in oases and industl. ctrs. of cap. Ashkhabad, Mary, Chadzhou, along Trans-Caspian rly; a. 491,072 km²; p. (1970) 2,158,000.

Turks and Caicos, Is., Caribbean Sea, **W.I.**; about 30 sm. Is., geographically S.E. continuation of Bahamas; dry climate, poor limestone soil; exp. salt, crawfish; cap. Gran Turk; a. 430 km²; p. (est. 1970) 5,675.

Turku (Åbo), spt., S.W. **Finland**; on Baltic Sea; ctr. of fertile agr. a.; exp. agr. prods.; industl. ctr.; shipbldg., steel, machin., textiles; Finnish and Swedish univs.; p. (1968) 149,078 (c.); (1967) 194,464 (met. a.).

Turnhout, t., N.E. **Belgium**, nr. Antwerp, on Campine canal; textiles, lace, printing; p. (1968) 37,803.

Turnu Severin, c., S.W. **Romania**; R. pt. on Danube below Iron Gate cataracts; grain, salt, petroleum tr., shipbldg.; p. (1968) 46,010.

Turriff, burgh, Banff and Buchan, **Scot.**; nr. R. Deveron; mkt. t.; engin.; p. (1971) 2,858.

Turton, t., Lancs., **Eng.**; 6 km N. of Bolton; p. (1971) 21,500.

Tuscaloosa, c., Ala., **USA**; on Black Warrior R.; rly. and industl. ctr. based on local coal, iron, cotton, timber; univ.; p. (1970) 61,933 (c.), 110,915 (met. a.).

Tuscany, region, central **Italy**; inc. provs. Arezzo, Firenze, Livorno, Siena, Grosseto, Lucca, Pisa, Massa and Carrara, Pistoia; mainly mtnous., drained by Arno R. system; wines, olive oil, cereals; iron ore from Elba, marble from Apuan Alps around Carrara; pt. at Livorno (Leghorn); cap. Firenze (Florence); a. 22,989 km²; p. (est. 1968) 3,434,618.

Tuticorin, t., Tamil Nadu, S.E. **India**; on G. of Manaar; fertiliser plant; declining cotton and tea pt.; p. (1971) 153,310 (t.), 181,913 (met. a.).

Tuttlingen, t., Baden-Württemberg, **W. Germany**; on R. Danube; surgical instruments; footwear; p. (est. 1969) 26,436.

Tuva ASSR, **RSFSR**; bounded by Siberia and Mongolia; mtn. basin, forested; timber inds., coal mng., asbestos, pastoral agr.; cap. Kyzyl; a. c. 165,800 km²; p. (1970) 231,000.

Tuvalu Is., formerly Ellice Is., until 1975 part of Gilbert and Ellice Is., W. Pac. Oc.; p. mainly Polynesian; coconut cultivation in high temps.; exp. copra; a. 25 km²; p. (est. 1975) 7,000.

Tuxtla Gutiérrez, c., cap. of Chiapas st., **Mexico**; in fertile valley at 450 m.; ctr. for sisal, tobacco, coffee, cattle; on Inter-American Highway; Mayan ruins nearby; p. (1969) 41,000.

Tuy Hoa, t., **S. Vietnam**; fertilisers, tyres, sugar mill.

Tuz, L., **Turkey**; salt L.; a. 1,619 km² in winter much reduced in summer.

Tuzla, t., Bosnia Hercegovina, **Yugoslavia**; salt, lignite, coal; hydroelectric power in a.; agr. mkt. ctr.; textiles; p. (1971) 53,825.

Tweed, R., S.E. **Scot.**; rises in Tweeddale, and reaches sea at Berwick; salmon fisheries; length 155 km.

Twelve Pins, star-shaped mtn. range, Galway, **R.o.I.**; Benbaum, 730 m.

Twickenham. *See* **Richmond-upon-Thames**.

Tychy, t., Katowice prov., **Poland**; on edge of Upper Silesian industl. a.; surrounded by forest; brewing; p. (1970) 71,400.

Tyldesley, t., Gtr. Manchester, **Eng.**; 6 km S. of Bolton; p. (1971) 21,163.

Tyler, c., Texas, **USA**; oil ctr. on E. Texan field; agr. ctr. for local mkt. gardening; famous for rose growing; p. (1970) 57,700.

Tyne, R., Tyne and Wear, Durham and Northumberland, **Eng.**; formed by confluence of N. Tyne and S. Tyne at Hexham; flows E. to sea at Tynemouth and S. Shields; valley gives easy route across mtns. from Newcastle to Carlisle; lower course forms harbour (with shipbldg. and other wks.) from Newcastle to Tynemouth; road tunnel between Wallsend and Jarrow; 128 km long.

Tynemouth, t., Tyne and Wear, **Eng.**; fishing pt. on N. bank of Tyne R.; shipbldg., engin.; ruined priory and cas.; residtl., resort; p. (1971) 68,861.

Tyne and Wear, met co., N.E. **Eng.**; mainly industl. a. around lower T. and W. Rs.; inc. Newcastle-upon-Tyne, Tynemouth, Gateshead, South Shields and Sunderland; traditionally ass. with shipbldg. and coal-mng., but inds. incr. diversified; p. (1971) 1,209,000.

Tyre (Sur), **Lebanon**; anc. Phoenician c. and spt., founded c. 15th cent. B.C.; now sm. comm. t., tr. in cotton, tobacco; p. 12,000.

Tyrol, Alpine region, **Europe**; falls within Austria and Italy, linked by Brenner Pass; embraces highest peaks of Austrian Alps, culminating in Ortler Spitz; two-fifths forest, timber inds.; mtn. pasture; tourism; Austrian prov. of Tyrol; cap. Innsbruck; a. 12,650 km²; p. (1971) 539,000.

Tyrone, former co., **N. Ireland**; now replaced by Strabane, Omagh, Dungannon and Cookstown l. gov. dists.

Tyrrhenian Sea, part of Mediterranean between Italy and Corsica, Sardinia and Sicily.

Tyumen, c., **RSFSR**; one of oldest Siberian ts., rly. ctr. on Trans-Siberian rly., R. pt. on Tura R.; many heavy inds.; ctr. of oil and natural gas region; p. (1970) 269,000.

Tywyn, mkt. t., Gwynedd, **Wales**; on cst. of Cardigan Bay, 5 km N.W. of Aberdovey; p. (1971) 3,818.

Tzekung (Zigong), c., Szechwan, **China**; petroleum, natural gas, salt wks.; p. (est. 1970) 350,000.

Tzepo (Zibo), c., Shantung, **China**; formed by merging 1950 coal mng. ts. of Tzechwan and Poshan and 1954 addition of Changchow; p. (1957) 806,000.

U

Ubangi, major R., **Central Africa**; trib. of R. Zaïre; rises on bdr. of Central African Rep. and Zaïre, flows W. and S. to join Zaïre R. at Irebu; partially navigable; 2,240 km long.

Ube, spt., S. Honshu, **Japan**; coal mng. and industl. ctr.; machin., synthetic petroleum; p. (est. 1971) 154,000.

Ubeda, t., Jaén prov., **Spain**; on plateau between Guadalquivir and Guadalimar; food processing, olive oil, soap; p. (1970) 30,186.

Uberaba, t., Minas Gerais, **Brazil**; ctr. of cattle rearing and arable agr. region; sugar milling, mnfs. lime; p. (1970) 108,576.

Ucayali, R., **Peru**; headstream of R. Amazon; over 2,240 km long, navigable for 1,600 km.

Uckfield, mkt. t., East Sussex, **Eng.**; 13 km N.E. of Lewes; a. ctr. of former Sussex iron ind.; p. (1971) 54,518 (dist.).

Udaipur, c., Rajasthan, N.W. **India**; in picturesque valley at 760 m a.s.l.; cap. of former princely st. of U.; maharajah's palace; p. (1971) 161,278.

Uddevalla, spt., S. **Sweden**; N. Göteborg; shipyds., prefab. houses, timber, granite quarrying, textiles; p. (1968) 36,480.

Udi, t., S. **Nigeria**, W. **Africa**; 160 km N. of Pt. Harcourt; impt. mng. ctr. on Enugu coalfield; linked by rail to Kaduna and Pt. Harcourt.

Udine, c., cap. of U. prov., Friuli-Venezia Giulia, N.E. **Italy**; between Alps and G. of Venice; route and industl. ctr. in agr. region; textiles, chemicals, engin., leather, woodwork; cath., many attractive bldgs., piazzas; severe earthquakes (1976); p. (1969) 96,694.

Udmurt ASSR, RSFSR; part of Urals industl. a.; two-fifths forested, timber inds.; arable agr., flax; steel inds. at cap. Izhevsk, Votkinsk, Sarapul; p. (1970) 1,417,000.

Udokan Khrebet, mtns., **RSFSR**; world's lgst. reserve of copper.

Ufa, c., cap. of Bashkir ASSR, **RSFSR**; in Urals industl. a., at confluence of Rs. Belaya and Ufa; machin., oil refineries, sawmills; p. (1970) 773,000.

Uganda, rep., E. **Africa**; equatorial cty., climate modified by alt.; forms part of E. African plateau (1,200 m); well-developed economy; coffee, tea, tobacco, cotton for exp.; developing pastoral economy, fishing on L. Victoria; copper at Kilembe, tin; hydroelectric power from Owen Falls, second project at Kabelega Falls; savannah areas contain abundant wildlife in Nat. Parks and Game Reserves; cap. Kampala; a. 235,887 km²; p. (est. 1970) 9,764,000.

Uist, N. and S., Is., Outer Hebrides, N.W. **Scot.**; indented csts.; N. Uist boggy in E., hilly in W.; S. Uist smaller but mtnous.; crofting, fishing; p. (1971) 1,726 (N.), 3,872 (S.).

Uitenhage, t., Cape prov., **S. Africa**; fruit, wool, rly. wks., tyres, car assembly, textiles; summer resort; p. (1970) 69,048.

Ujiji, t., in sm. terr. same name (a. 2,383 km²) on E. shore L. Tanganyika, **Tanzania**; where Stanley found Livingstone 1871; p. *c.* 14,000.

Ujiyamada. *See* **Ise.**

Ujjain, t., Madhya Pradesh, **India**; sacred c. and formerly cap. of Malwa; univ.; p. (1971) 203,278 (t.), 208,561 (met. a.).

Ujpest, industl. sub., Budapest, **Hungary**; elec. engin., leather, shoes, textiles, furniture, pharmaceuticals; p. 76,000.

Ujung Pandang (Makasar), c., Sulawesi, **Indonesia**; in dist. of rich volcanic soils; major spt. and airpt., entrepot tr.; p. (1971) 434,766.

Ukhta t., **RSFSR**; ctr of natural gas field in Pechora Basin; p. (est. 1969) 57,000.

Ukrainian SSR, constituent rep., **USSR**; in Eastern Europe; of dominating importance in Soviet economy; drained by Rs. Dnieper Dniester, S. Bug, Donets; Pripet Marshes in N., wooded steppes in ctr., fertile black-earth a in S.; major wheat-growing a. of Europe; highly mineralised, many industl. raw materials and ctrs. of metallurgical and heavy inds.; cap. Kiev; a. 582,750 km²; p. (1970) 47,126,000.

Ulan Bator, c., cap. of Mongolian People's Rep.; in stock-raising region; industl. ctr. of cty.; woollen gds., saddles, knitwear; new indust, ctr. at Darkhan nearby; rly. link to China and USSR; contains one-quarter of p. of rep.; p. (1966) 250,000.

Ulan-Ude (Verkhneudinsk), t., Siberia, **RSFSR**; major route and mnf. ctr.; pt. on R. Ude, junc. on Trans-Siberian rly., linked by rail to Peking; engin., textiles, glass, leather; p. (1970) 254,000.

Ullapool, v., Ross and Cromarty, **Scot.**; sm. fish. pt. (herring landings), on L. Broom, 72 km N.W. of Inverness; attractive mtn. and cst. scenery in a.

Ullswater, L. Cumbria, **Eng.**; 13 km long; supplies water to Manchester; attractive tourist a.

Ulm, c., Baden-Württemberg, **W. Germany**; route ctr. at limit of barge navigation on Danube, although navigable limits being extended by canalisation; food-processing, metal gds., textiles, cement; p. (est. 1969) 91,852.

Ulsan, t., **South Korea**; oil refining, fertilisers; p. (1966) 112,858.

Ulster. *See* **Northern Ireland.**

Ulúa-Chamelhcón, R. basin, N. cst. **Honduras**; major banana region of Central American cst.

Ulva, I., Argyll and Bute, **Scot.**; off W. cst. of Mull; 8 km long.

Ulverston, mkt. t., Cumbria, **Eng.**; nr. Morecambe Bay; antibiotics, elec. gds., tanning; p. (1971) 11,888.

Ul'yanovsk (Simbirsk), c., cap. of U. oblast, **RSFSR**; industl. ctr. of middle Volga region; birthplace of Lenin whose real name was Ulyanov; p. (1970) 351,000.

Uman, c., Ukrainian SSR, **USSR**; at confluence of Kamenka and Umanka Rs.; rly. junc.; agr.-processing; p. (est. 1969) 64,000.

Umanak, t., W. **Greenland**; hunting and fishing base on arm of Baffin Sea; marble mng.; p. (est. 1968) 2,348.

Umbria, region, central **Italy**; comprising provs. of Perugia and Terni, crossed by Apennines and upper Tiber; agr. mainstay of economy; inds. based on hydroelectric power at Terni; chemicals; developing tourist tr.; cap. Perugia; a. 8,472 km²; p. (1969) 783,048.

Ume, R., **Sweden**; flows S.E. to the G. of Bothnia; length 400 km.

Umeå, c., cap. of Västerbotten prov., N.E. **Sweden**; on G. of Bothnia at mouth of Ume R.; cultural ctr.; woodpulp; p. (1968) 51,952.

Umm-al-Quaywayn, emirate, member of **United Arab Emirates**; p. (est. 1968) 8,000.

Umm Qasr, t., **Kuwait**; on Iraq border; new deepwater port planned.

Umtali, t., **Rhodesia**; comm. ctr. for rich agr. a.; oil refinery at Feruka; pipeline to Beira; p. (1968) 53,500.

Umtata, t., Cape Prov., **S. Africa**; admin. ctr. for Transkei terrs.; cath.; p. (est. 1967) 17,200.

Uncia, t., Oruro dep., **Bolivia**; alt. 3,900 m in E. Cordillera of Andes, 96 km S.E. of Oruro; site of impt. Patino tin mines.

Ungava Bay, arm of Hudson Strait, projecting into Labrador, N.E. **Canada**; minerals abundant, recent exploitation of impt. medium and low-grade iron deposits.

Union of South Africa. *See* **South Africa, Rep. of.**

Union of Soviet Socialist Republics (USSR), E. **Europe**, N. **Asia**; major world economic and political power; ctr. of European communist bloc; extends over 9,600 km W.–E., 4,800 km N.–S.; continental climate with marked regional variations; comprises 1 fed. rep. and 14 constituent reps.; centrally planned economy emphasising development of heavy inds. at major sources of natural resources, and development of new resources in E.; timber inds. and textiles impt. with more recent developments in consumer inds.; lge.-scale, mechanised agr. with planned prod. reflecting regional variations in physical conditions; transport emphasis on rlys. to open up remote E. regions, but more recent road bldg. programme; 27 major pts. inc. Leningrad, Arkhangelsk, Riga, Murmansk, Odessa, Baku, Vladivostok; cap. Moscow; a. 22,272,290 km²; p. (1976) 255,500,000.

United Arab Emirates (Trucial Sts.), indep. sov. st. on Persian G., S.W. **Asia**; formed (1971) from Trucial Sts. (Abū Dhabi, Ajmān, Dubai, Al Fujayrah, Ra's al Khaymah, Shārjah, Umm-al-Quaywayn) after withdrawal of Brit. forces and termination of special defence treaty (1820–

1971); p. immigration from Middle and Far East as oil-based economic growth proceeds, esp. in Abu Dhabi; a. 82,880 km²; p. (est. 1970) 130,000 (mainly nomadic).

United Kingdom, cty., N.W. **Europe**; separated from continent of Europe by English Channel; consists of Gr. Britain (Eng., Wales, Scot.) and N. Ireland; a. 244,022 km²; p. (est 1973). 55,930,000.

United States of America, fed. rep., **N. America**; world's major economic power and one of the 3 political "super powers"; variety of climatic and physical conditions (*see* **N. America**); economically self-supporting, but imports petroleum, coffee, machin., textiles; extremely diversified mnfs.; consists of 50 sts. and Dist. of Columbia, co-extensive with cap. of Washington; outlying dependencies inc. Puerto Rico, U.S. Virgin Is., Panama Canal Zone, Guam, American Samoa, Trust Terr. of the Pac. Is.; a. 9,363,169 km²; p. (est. 1974) 211,910,000.

Unst, I., Shetlands, **Scot.**; most N. of gr.; length 20 km; p. (1971) 1,127.

Unterwalden, can., **Switzerland**; divided into Obwalden and Nidwalden; dairying, fruit and livestock; cap. Stans; a. 767 km²; p. (1969) 50,600.

Upernavik, t., W. **Greenland**; on sm. I. in Baffin Bay; sealing and whaling base; meteorological sta.; p. (est. 1968) 1,930.

Upper Austria, prov., **Austria**; borders on W. Germany and ČSSR; hilly and forested; drained by Danube R. system; inc. Salzkammergut resort a.; agr., forestry; inds. centred on Linz (cap.), Steyr and Wels; a. 11,979 km²; p. (est. 1968) 1,201,600.

Upper Hutt, c., N.I., **N.Z.**; p. (1971) 20,003.

Upper Volta (Voltaic Rep.), **W. Africa**; landlocked st.; hot dry climate, humid in S.; wooded savannah; agr. basis of economy; most of p. farmers and nomadic herdsmen; permanent agr. in irrigated R. valleys and oases, sorghum, millet, maize, yams, beans; inds. based on local handicrafts; economy hampered by landlocked location; one of poorest economies in world; rly. outlet to sea via Abidjan (Ivory Cst.); cap. Ouagadougou; a. 274,123 km²; p. (est. 1970) 5,437,000.

Uppingham, mkt. t., Leics., **Eng.**; 16th cent. school; p. (1971) 6,576 (dist.).

Uppsala, c., cap. of U. prov., **Sweden**; on R. Sala, 72 km from Stockholm; historic ctr. of anc. Sweden; cultural ctr., famous univ. (Linnaeus taught there); cath.; lt. inds.; p. (1968) 97,172.

Ur, anc. Chaldean c. **Iraq**; 208 km W.N.W. of Basra; ruins; flourished about 3,000 B.C.

Ural, R., **RSFSR**; flows S.W. and S. to Caspian Sea; used for domestic and industl. water supply; navigable; 2,400 km long.

Ural Mts., **USSR**; mtn. system, forms bdy. between Europe and Asia and separates Russian plain from W. Siberian lowlands; extends N.–S. for 2,400 km; highest peaks Narodnaya and Telpos-Iz; rich mineral resources have given rise to huge ctrs. of heavy ind., inc. Sverdlovsk, Chelyabinsk, Magnetogorsk.

Uralsk, N.W., Kasakh SSR, **USSR**; on R. Ural; grain-trading and cattle-mart ctr.; flour, leather, woollens, iron-ware; p. (1970) 134,000.

Uranium City, N. Saskatchewan, **Canada**; nr. N. shore of L. Athabasca, ctr. of Beaverlodge uranium-mng. a.; founded 1951; p. (1960) 3,349.

Urawa, t., Honshu, **Japan**; sub. of Tokyo; p. (est. 1971) 281,000.

Urbino, t., in the Marches, central **Italy**; agr. mkt. and route ctr.; picturesque tourist ctr.; cath., univ., palace; p. (est. 1968) 16,720.

Ure, R., North Yorks., **Eng.**; flows E. and S.E. to the Swale to form the Ouse; upper part of valley known as Wensleydale; 80 km long.

Urfa, t., **Turkey**; nr. Syrian bdr.; handicrafts, local agr. tr.; p. (1967) 72,873.

Urgench, t., cap. of Khorezm oblast, W. Uzbek SSR, **USSR**; pt. on Amu Dar'ya R. in Khiva oasis; cotton, food-processing; p. (est. 1967) 65,000.

Uri, can., **Switzerland**; S. of L. of Lucerne; forest and mtns.; traversed by St. Gotthard rly. and R. Reuss; sparse p., German speaking; cap. Altdorf; a. 1,075 km²; p. (1969) 34,000.

Urmia, L., nr. Tabriz, N.W. **Iran**; 136 km by 48 km; salt and shallow; no outlet.

Urmston, Gtr. Manchester, **Eng.**; residtl. sub. of Manchester; inc. part of Trafford Park industl. estate; p. (1971) 44,523.

Uruapan, t., Michoacán, W. **Mexico**; mkt. ctr. for semi-tropical mtnous. a.; famous handicrafts; parks, gardens; p. (1970) 104,475.

Urubamba, R., **Peru**; rises in E. Cordillera of Andes; forms one of headstreams of R. Amazon; length 560 km.

Urubupunga, t., **Brazil**; new. t. for 10,000, at site of hydroelectric power sta.

Uruguaiana, t., **Brazil**; on R. Uruguay; cattle ctr.; jerked beef, soap, candles; p. (est. 1968) 74,581.

Uruguay, rep., **S. America**; smallest of S. American reps.; situated on N. bank of Rio de la Plata estuary; low hills in N.; temperate climate; 60 per cent land a. devoted to livestock rearing, especially cattle, sheep, based on extensive natural grasslands; arable land in S., grains; ch. t. Montevideo, cap. and main ctr. of inds.; food processing, leather, metallurgy, textiles, rubber; a. 186,925 km²; p. (est. 1970) 2,886,000.

Uruguay, R., **S. America**; rises in S. Brazil, flows 1,360 km to Rio de la Plata; forms bdy. between Argentina and Uruguay and part of bdy. between Argentina and Brazil.

Urumchi (Wulumuchi), c., cap. of Sinkiang prov., N.W. **China**; admin., comm. and industl. ctr.; iron and steel, cement, textiles, nitrogenous fertilisers, agr. machin.; local coal, tin, silver mng.; p. (est. 1970) 500,000.

Usak, t., **Turkey**; connected by rail with Izmir; noted for pile carpet-weaving; p. (1965) 38,815.

Usambara, mtns., N.E. **Tanzania**; scene of early European settlement (1902); lumber, tea, coffee produced on slopes; max. alt. 2,560 m.

Usedom (Uznam), I., Baltic Sea; off mouth of R. Oder; since 1945 E. part belongs to **Poland**, W. (the larger part) to **E. Germany**; a. 445 km²; p. 45,000.

Ushant, I., off cst. of Finistère, **France**; at entrance to English Channel; it was off Ushant that Lord Howe gained his gr. naval victory on the "glorious first of June" 1794; lighthouse, fishing; p. 2,000.

Ushuaia, t., **Argentina**; most S. t. in world; sheep farming, timber, furs; freezing plant; p. 6,000.

Usk, mkt. t., Gwent, **Wales**; 13th cent. cas.; p. (1971) 2,028.

Usk, R., Gwent, S. **Wales**; flows S. past Newport to Bristol Channel; picturesque, gd. fishing; 91 km long.

Usküdar (Scutari), t., **Turkey**; on Bosporus, opposite Istanbul; mkt. ctr.; new bridge to European side of Bosporus; Crimean memorial cemetery for Brit. troops; Muslim cemeteries; p. (1965) 133,883.

Uspallata Pass, 3,800 m high over Andes between Mendoza, **Argentina**, and Santiago, **Chile**; monument "Christ of the Andes" marks international bdy. settlement; used by Mendoza–Valparaiso rly.

Ussuri, R., rises in Maritime prov. of **RSFSR**, flows *c.* 800 km to R. Amur; final 480 km forms Sino-Soviet bdy.

Ussuriysk (Voroshilov), t., **RSFSR**; 112 km N. of Vladivostok; rly. junc. of Trans-Siberian and Chinese Eastern rlys.; engin., agr. prod.; p. (1970) 128,000.

Ustica, I., Palermo, **Italy**; basalt; agr., fishing, handicrafts; a. 8 km²; p. *c.* 1,200.

Usti-nad-Labem (Aussig), c., Bohemia, **ČSSR**; R. pt. on Elbe; route and industl. ctr.; chemicals, textiles, machin.; p. (1967) 73,000.

Ust Kamenogorsk, c., Kazakh SSR, **USSR**; on Irtysh R.; mng. ctr.; food processing, clothing, furniture; hydroelectric power sta. nearby; p. (1970) 230,000.

Usumbura. *See* **Bujumbura**.

Utah, st., **USA**; Rocky mtns. in E.; forms part of Gr. Basin in W.; Gr. Salt L. in N.W.; dry continental climate; poor agr. conditions, soil erosion; copper, gold; tourism; Nat. Parks; cap. Salt L. City; a. 219,932 km²; p. (1970) 1,060,631.

Utica, c., N.Y., **USA**; on Mohawk R. and Barge Canal; in rich dairying region; textiles, electronics, tools, firearms; p. (1970) 90,802 (c.), 335,809 (met. a.).

Utrecht, c., **Neth.**; on Old Rhine (Oude Rijn); univ., cath.; chemical and cigar factories; printing, machin., woollens, silks, velvets; major transport and financial ctr.; picturesque; p. (est. 1969) 277,647 (c.), 451,646 (met. a.).
Utrecht, prov., **Neth.**; between Gelderland and N. and S. Holland; fertile agr., cattle rearing, horticulture; a. 1,362 km²; p. (1968) 768,715.
Utrera, t., **Spain**; S.E. of Seville; in irrigated valley; food processing; p. (1970) 35,775.
Utsunomiya, t., Honshu, **Japan**; ctr. for Nikko Nat. Park; p. (est. 1971) 308,000.
Uttar Pradesh, st., **India**; Himalayas on N. bdy., drained by Ganges and Jumna; irrigation; wheat, rice, millet, barley, maize, cotton, sugar, oil-seeds; ch. ts. Allahabad, Lucknow (cap.), Varanasi, Kanpur, Agra, Meerut; a. 293,732 km²; p. (1971) 88,299,453; (p. increasing by 2 million a year).
Uttoxeter, t., Staffs., **Eng.**; on R. Dove; machin., biscuit mftg.; expanded t.; p. (1971) 9,034.
Uusikaupunki (Swed. Nystad), spt., Abo-Bjorneborg, S.W. **Finland**; on G. of Bothnia; p. (1966) 5,074.
Uxbridge. *See* **Hillingdon**.
Uzbek (Uzbekistan) SSR, constituent rep., **USSR**; crossed by Rs. Amu Dar'ya and Syr Dar'ya; contains part of fertile Ferghana Valley; intensive farming based on irrigation; rice, cotton, fruits, silk, cattle, sheep; ch. cs. Tashkent (cap.), Samarkand; alluvial gold deposits and bauxite in Kizil-Kum desert; a. 412,250 km²; p. (1970) 11,963,000.
Uzhgorod, c., Ukrainian SSR, **USSR**; economic and cultural ctr.; friendship pipeline from Kuybyshev; univ.; p. (est. 1967) 61,000.

V

Vaal, R., **S. Africa**; rises in Drakensberg mtns., flows between the Transvaal and Orange Free State to join the Orange R. nr. Kimberley. V. dam irrigates lge. a. of Witwatersrand; 896 km long.
Vaasa, c., cap. of Vaasa prov., W. **Finland**; pt. on G. of Bothnia; exp. timber and timber prods.; agr. ctr.; food processing, textiles, timber inds.; p. (1968) 48,679.
Vác, t., **Hungary**; on R. Danube; comm. ctr.; summer resort for Budapest; cath.; p. (1966) 28,700.
Vadso, cap. of Finnmark prov., N.E. **Norway**; ice-free Arctic pt. on N. side of Varangar fjord; whaling and fishing base; p. (est. 1970) 5,625.
Vaduz, mkt. t., cap. of **Liechtenstein**; nr. Rhine; cotton inds.; sm. tourist resort; p. (1970) 3,921.
Vaigach, sm. I., between Novaya Zemlya and mainland of **USSR**; geological extension of Urals; low-lying reindeer pasture; seal fishing.
Valais, can., **Switzerland**; in upper valley of R. Rhône; surrounded by mtns., forested on slopes; vines and cereals in valleys; ch. resort Zermatt, cap. Sion; a. 5,234 km²; p. (1967) 193,000.
Valdai Hills, morainic ridges between Leningrad and Moscow, **RSFSR**; rise to *c.* 348 m and form ch. watershed of E. European Rs., Volga, Dvina and Dniester.
Val d'Aosta, aut. region, N.W. **Italy**; high Alpine cty., borders France and Switzerland; cap. Aosta; agr., hydroelectric power; winter resorts; a. 3,263 km²; p. (1969) 108,848.
Valdecañas, **Spain**; 192 km S.W. Madrid; dam and power sta.
Val-de-Marne, dep., S.E. of Paris **France**; cap. Créteil; a. 243 km²; p. (1968) 1,121,340.
Valdez, t., Alaska, **USA**; ice-free pt., fishing; terminal of oil pipeline from North Slope; p. (1970) 1,005.
Valdivia, c., cap. of V. prov., S. **Chile**; on R. Calle-calle nr. the sea (pt. Corral); damaged by earthquake and tidal wave 1960; univ.; metal, wood and leather gds.; paper, flour, brewing; p. (est. 1966) 80,035.
Val d'Oise, dep., N.W. of Paris, **France**; cap. Pontoise; a. 1,248 km²; p. (1968) 693,269.
Valdosta, t., Ga., **USA**; rly. and tr. ctr. for region producing tobacco, cotton, timber; p. (1970) 32,303.
Valence, t., cap. of Drôme dep., S.E. **France**; on R. Rhône; silks., hosiery, vineyards; agr. mkt.; p. (1968) 64,134.
Valencia, region, E. **Spain**; on Mediterranean; comprises provs. of Alicante, Castellón de la Plana and Valencia; mtnous., with densely populated, fertile coastal plain; irrigation makes a. a major producer of Mediterranean fruit and crops; a. 23,305 km²; p. (1970) 1,767,327.
Valencia, c., cap. of V. prov., E. **Spain**; pt. on Mediterranean at mouth of R. Turia; one of most impt. agr. ts. of cty., and active industl. and comm. ctr.; univ., cath.; resort; p. (est. 1969) 498,159.
Valencia, c., N. **Venezuela**; nr. L. Valencia; ctr. of agr. a., sugar-cane, cotton; leading industl. t.; cattle mart; cotton mills, meat packing; cath.; p. (est. 1970) 224,800.
Valenciennes, c., Nord dep., N. **France**; in Hainaut cty. on R. Escaut (Scheldt); metallurgical and chemical inds.; once famous for hand-made lace; birthplace of Froissart and Watteau; p. (1968) 46,626 (c.), 223,629 (met. a.)
Valentia, I., S.W. Kerry, **R.o.I.**; in Dingle Bay; agr., fishing; 10 km by 3 km.
Valladolid, c., cap. of V. prov., **Spain**; on R. Pisuerga (trib. of Douro); grain tr.; route, industl. and comm. ctr.; food processing, textiles; cath., univ.; p. (est. 1969) 177,797.
Valle del General, upland, S.W. **Costa Rica**; pioneer subsistence agr., maize, tropical fruit, cattle; improving transport.
Vallejo, t., Cal., **USA**; at mouth of Napa R., on San Pablo Bay; pt. and processing ctr. for farm prod.; naval shipyard; p. (1970) 67,905 (t.), 241,332 (met. a.).
Vallenar, t., Atacama prov., **Chile**; agr. ctr.; dried fruit, wines; iron ore nearby; p. (1960) 30,793.
Valletta, c., cap. of **Malta**; ch. spt. on rocky penin. of Mt. Scebarras, E. cst.; formerly impt. British naval base; badly damaged in second world war; cath., univ.; p. (est. 1969) 15,512.
Valli di Comacchio, lagoon a., N.E. **Italy**; ctr. of an impt. eel industry; a. 259 km².
Valona. *See* **Vlonë**.
Valparaiso, c., central **Chile**; leading pt. on Pac. cst. of S. America; attractive c. with backdrop of steep hills; mftg., comm. and industl. ctr. of rep. with textile mills, sugar refineries, paint, shoe and chemical factories; univ.; p. (est. 1970) 292,847.
Valtellina, fertile valley, **Italy**; in Lombard Alps above L. Como; impt. for vine cultivation; hydroelectric power resources; tourism.
Van, c., cap. of Van prov., S.E. **Turkey**; stands at 1,726 m on shore of salty L. Van; tr. ctr. of wheat-growing a.; new Turkish-Iranian rail link; p. (1965) 31,010.
Vancouver, c., B.C., **Canada**; Pac. cst. spt. with excellent natural harbour; international airport and terminus of transcontinental rly.; timber inds., shipbldg., fishing, oil and sugar refining; exp. prod. from these inds.; attractive hilly location and mild climate make c. a major tourist ctr.; univ.; p. (1971) 422,278 (c.), 1,071,081 (met. a.).
Vancouver, I., B.C., **Canada**; off W. cst.; mtnous., forested; woodpulp, paper; indented cst. provides many natural harbours; fishing; cap. Victoria; a. 33,797 km²; p. (1961) 290,835.
Vancouver, t., Wash., **USA**; spt. on Columbia R. opposite Portland (Ore.); exp. grain, timber; food processing; p. (1970) 42,493.
Vandellos, Tarragona, **Spain**; nuclear power sta.
Vanderbijlpark, t., Transvaal, **S. Africa**; on Vaal R.; ctr. for steel wks.; p. (1970) 78,745.
Vänern, lge. L. **Sweden**; W.N.W. of L. Vättern, with which it is connected by canal (and thence with the Baltic); a. 5,566 km².
Vänersborg, L. pt., **Sweden**; on tongue of land between R. Göta and the Vasobotten (southernmost bay of L. Vänern); footwear, wood and sulphite pulp; p. (est. 1970) 20,280.
Vannes, t., cap. of Morbihan dep., N.W. **France**; sm. pt. on S. cst. Brittany; tr. in agr. and fish; cath.; dates from Roman times; p. (1968) 40,724.
Var, dep., S.E. **France**; in Provence, on Mediterranean; mainly agr. with some inds. at Draguignan and Toulon (cap. since 1974); bauxite at Brignoles; rapid growth of p.; inc.

many coastal resorts; a. 6,042 km²; p. (1968) 555,926.

Varanasi (Benares), c., Uttar Pradesh, India; famous holy c. on Ganges, 640 km N.W. of Calcutta; place of annual pilgrimage; univ.; handicrafts, brasses, brocades, embroideries, now debased; p. (1971) 466,696 (c.), 467,487 (met. a.).

Varanger Fjord, inlet of Arctic Oc. into Finnmark, Norway; iron mng. on S. shore.

Vardar, R., flows through Yugoslav and Greek Macedonia into Aegean Sea nr. Salonika; inc. V. agr. region; hydroelectric power; routeway; 448 km long.

Varde, t., W. Jutland, Denmark; agr. and route ctr.; food processing; steelwks.; p. (1960) 9,577.

Vardö, t., Finnmark prov., N.E. Norway; sm. ice-free pt. on Vardoy I. with fish and oil interests; p. c. 3,500.

Vares, t., Bosnia, Yugoslavia; iron mng.; developing mnfs.

Varese, t., Lombardy, Italy; in Alpine foothills; resort and industl. ctr.; engin., furniture, paper, textiles, wines; p. (1969) 81,620.

Värmland, prov., Sweden; agr., iron mng. and processing, timber inds.; cap. Karlstad; a. 19,236 km²; p. (est. 1970) 284,930.

Varna, t., Bulgaria; spt. on Black Sea; industl. ctr. of heavy inds.; summer resorts on cst. nearby; p. (est. 1969) 212,642.

Varnsdorf, t., CSSR; rly. junc. on German bdr.; impt. textile ctr.; p (est. 1968) 13,912.

Västerås, c., cap. of Västmanland prov., Sweden; on L. Mälar; impt. elec. and metallurgical inds.; power sta.; impt. mediaeval c., cath., cas.; p. (est. 1969) 113,389.

Västerbotten, prov., Sweden; forested; timber inds.; cap. Umeå; a. 59,153 km²; p. (est. 1970) 233,971.

Västernorrland, prov., Sweden; forests and timber inds.; cap. Harnosand; a. 25.706 km²; p. (est. 1970) 274,104.

Västervik, t., Kalmar prov., Sweden; on Baltic cst.; engin., wire, nails, chemicals, paper; p. (est. 1970) 23,830.

Västmanland, prov., Sweden; N. of L. Mälar; mkt. gardening in S.; iron and silver mng. in N.; iron and steel inds.; cap. Västerås; a. 6,762 km²; p. (est. 1970) 260,869.

Vasto, t., Abruzzi e Molise, Italy; agr. ctr. on steep-sided vine-producing plateau; sm. Adriatic fishing pt.; p. (est. 1968) 24,474.

Vatican City, indep. sov. Papal st., Italy; forms an enclave in Rome; inc. Papal residence, St. Peter's cath.; a. 44 ha; p. (est. 1971) 648.

Vatna Jökull, mtn., Iceland; elevated snowfield; active volcano; alt. 2,120 m.

Vättern, L., Sweden; 40 km S.E. L. Vänern; a. 1,898 km².

Vaucluse, dep. S.E. France; in Provence; cap. Avignon; a. 3,577 km²; p. (1968) 353,966.

Vand, can., W. Switzerland; N. of L. Geneva; forests and vineyards; cap. Lausanne; a. 3,209 km²; p. (1969) 509,000.

Växjö, t., S. Sweden; engin., timber wks., hosiery; p. (1968) 32,886.

Vejle, spt., Jutland, Denmark; admin. ctr. V. prov.; industl.; p. (est. 1970) 31,763.

Velbert, t., N. Rhine-Westphalia, W. Germany; N.W. of Wuppertal; metal ind. locks and keys; p. (est. 1969) 27,307.

Vélez Málaga, t., Málaga prov., S. Spain; famous for wine, raisins, sugar, olive oil; Moorish cas.; p. (1970) 42,454.

Veliki Ustyug, t., RSFSR; R. pt. on Sukhona R.; shipyards, mftg.; p. (est. 1967) 35,000.

Velletri, t., central Italy; at foot of Alban hills overlooking Pontine marshes; noted for its wine; Garibaldi routed Neapolitans here 1849; (est. 1968) 37,469.

Vellore, t., Tamil Nadu, India; agr. mkt. t.; scene of Sepoy mutiny 1806; p. (1971) 139,082 (t.), 178,554 (met. a.).

Velsen, t., N. Holland prov., Neth; nr. entrance to N. Sea Canal, inc. IJmuiden iron and steel wks.; lge. paper mill; p. (1968) 67,864.

Veluwe, dist., Gelderland, Neth.; between Arnhem and IJselmeer; low hills of glacial sands and sand-dunes; heathland and pinewoods; relatively low p. density.

Venda Territory, Bantu homeland, Transvaal, S. Africa; p. (1970) 265,129.

Vendée, dep., W. France; on Bay of Biscay; fish. pts., beach resorts, agr. pasturage, vineyards; cap. La Roche-sur-Yon; a. 6,972 km²; p. (1968) 421,250.

Vendôme, t., Loir-et-Cher dep., France; on R. Loire; leather gds., cottons; mediaeval cas.; p. (1968) 16,728.

Venetia (Veneto), region, N.E. Italy; between the Alps and the Adriatic; embraces provs. Vicenza, Verona, Venice, Udine, Treviso, Padua, Belluno, and Rovigo; mtnous. in N., inc. Dolomite Alps; fertile plain of Po R. in S.; intensive arable agr.; ch. c. Venice; a. 18,384 km²; p. (1969) 4,088,285.

Venezia Giulia. *See* Friuli-Venezia Giulia.

Venezuela, fed. rep., N. cst. S. America; wealth derived from long-established but currently stagnant oil ind.; tropical climate, with temperate uplands, tropical forests and tall grass savannah lands (llanos); most economically advanced a. around cap. Carácas and oilfield a. of L. Maracaibo; counter pole of development based on hydroelectric power resources and iron ore in Caroni R. region; growing steel inds., lge. agr. areas economically neglected and socially deprived; coffee from highlands main comm. agr. crop and exp. a. 912,050 km²; p. (est. 1971) 10,778,071.

Venice (Venezia), c., cap. of V. prov. and ch. c. of Venetia, N.E. Italy; built on gr. of islets within lagoon in G. of V., at head of Adriatic; splendid architecture, rich in art treasures and historic associations; extensive canal network, inc. Grand Canal, intensive use leading to erosion of bldgs.; gradually sinking into Adriatic, lge.-scale projects to preserve c.; industl. zone on landward side in subs. of Porto Marghera and Mestre; craft and heavy inds.; p. (1969) 367,631.

Venlo, t., Neth.; on R. Maas; agr. mkt. and rly. junc.; chemicals, optical instruments, electric lamps; p. (1967) 60,773.

Ventimiglia, t., Liguria, N.W. Italy; on Mediterranean cst. nr. Fr. border; cath.; flower mkt.; tourism; p. (est. 1969) 25,564.

Ventnor, t., I. of Wight, Eng.; on S. cst. 18 km S. of Ryde; mild climate, tourist and health resort; p. (1971) 6,910.

Veracruz, st., E. Mexico; narrow coastal plain rising to Sierra Madre Oriental; contains volcano Orizaba; recent agr. improvements; growth of petroleum inds.; cap. Jalapa; a. 71,836 km²; p. (1969) 3,629,000.

Veracruz, c., V. st., E. Mexico; spt. on G. of Mexico; comm. and industl. ctr. of oil region; nr. site where Cortés landed 1519; p. (1970) 214,072.

Vercelli, c., cap. of V. prov. N. Italy; in Piedmont, on Sesia R.; rice mkt. for lge. irrigated plain textiles, machin., aircraft parts; p. (1969) 56,386.

Verde, Cape, most W. part of Africa; site of Dakar, cap. of Senegal.

Verdun, t., Quebec, Canada; sub. of Montreal; p. (1966) 76,832.

Verdun, t., Meuse dep., N.E. France; in Lorraine, on R. Meuse; strategic ctr. with varied mnfs.; 12th cent. cath.; scene of famous battle 1916; p. (1968) 24,716.

Vereeniging, c., Transvaal prov., S. Africa; on Vaal R.; coal, iron and steel, bricks; Treaty of Vereeniging 1902 ended Boer War; p. (1970) 169,553.

Verkhneudinsk. *See* Ulan-Ude.

Verkhoyansk, t., Yakutsk ASSR, RSFSR; in N.E. Siberia; coldest permanently inhabited place in world; mean Jan. temp. of —59°F.; ctr. of fur trapping a.; p. c. 2,000.

Vermont, st., New England, USA; adjoining Quebec prov., Canada; traversed by the Green mtns.; farming, dairying, stock-raising, lumbering, quarrying, machine tool and textile mftg.; cap. Montpelier; famous for autumn colours; a. 24,887 km²; p. (1970) 437,744.

Verona, c., cap. of V. prov., N.E. Italy; on R. Adige; commands route from central Europe to Brenner pass and from Venice to Milan; cath. and notable monuments; active agr. tr. and inds., printing; p. (1969) 258,559.

Versailles, c., cap. of Yvelines dep., N. France; S.W. sub. of Paris; famous royal palace; mkt. gardening, distilleries; Treaty of Versailles 1919; p. (1968) 94,915.

Verviers, t., **Belgium**; nr. Liége; ctr. of textile ind. in Ardennes; p. (1968) 35,335.
Vestmannaeyjar or **Westman Is.**, archipelago, S.W. **Iceland**; impt. cod fishing ind. based on Heimaey I.
Vesuvius, famous active volcano, S. **Italy**; on shore of Bay of Naples; alt. *c.* 1,186 m; its eruption in A.D. 79 destroyed Pompeii and Herculaneum, and frequent eruptions have since been recorded; observatory founded 1844; funicular rly. from base of mtn. to rim of crater since 1880.
Veszprem, c., **Hungary**; in fruit-growing dist., 96 km S. of Budapest; cath., univ. for chemical ind.; p. (1968) 32,000.
Vevey, t., Vaud can., **Switzerland**; on N. shore of L. Geneva; beautiful situation; chocolate, watches; resort; p. (1970) 17,957.
Viareggio, beach resort, Tuscany, **Italy**; on Tyrrhenian Sea, nr. Pisa; monument to Shelley; p. (est. 1968) 54,549.
Viborg, t., Jutland, **Denmark**; admin. ctr. V. prov.; comm. and route ctr.; anc. cath.; textiles, machin., food processing; p. (est. 1970) 25,468.
Vicenza, c., cap. of V. prov., N.E. **Italy**; in Venetia; mkt. ctr. for surrounding fertile agr. plain; textiles, iron and steel; many examples of Palladian architecture; p. (1969) 112,734.
Vichy, t., Allier dep., **France**; on Allier R.; famous spa; hot mineral springs; lge. exp. of V. water; seat of Pétain govt. during German occupation 1940–3; p. (1968) 33,898.
Vicksburg, t., Miss., **USA**; R. pt., on bluffs of Mississippi at junc. of Yazoo canal; shipping and mftg. ctr. in cotton and timber region; prominent in American Civil War; Confederate surrender 1863; p. (1970) 25,478.
Victoria, st., **Australia**; traversed by Gt. Dividing Range; temperate climate, modified by alt.; smallest and most densely populated st. of mainland; major industl. a.; wool, grain, dairy prod., fruit; gold, coal, tin mng., natural gas off E. cst.; cap. Melbourne; a. 227,516 km²; p. (1972) 3,496,161.
Victoria, c., cap. of B.C., **Canada**; spt. on Vancouver I.; fishing and fish-processing; sawmills, chemicals, cement; beautiful scenery; tourist ctr.; p.(1971) 60,897 (c.), 193,512 (met.a.)
Victoria, main pt. and harbour between Hong Kong I. and Kowloon; built on reclaimed land; admin. ctr. of Hong Kong; p. (1971) 521,612.
Victoria, t., cap. of Labuan I., Sabah, **Malaysia**; fine harbour; p. 3,213.
Victoria, t., cap. of **Seychelles, Ind. Oc.**; harbour on lgst. and most impt. I. of Mahé.
Victoria, t., S. Texas, **USA**; comm. ctr. in prosperous agr. a.; local oilfields; p. (1970) 41,349.
Victoria Falls (Mosi-oa-Toenja), on R. Zambesi, **Zambia**; discovered by Livingstone 1855; falls are 1,674 m wide and broken by islands and rocks.
Victoria, Lake, lgst. L. of **Africa**; bordered by Kenya, Uganda, Tanzania; in depression of Gt. Rift Valley, at alt. 999 m, a. *c.* 67,340 km²; discharges into Victoria Nile; impt. fisheries; discovered by Speke 1858.
Victoria Land, region, **Antactica**; discovered by Ross in 1841.
Victoria Nile, R., **Uganda**; E. Africa; name of R. Nile from its source at L. Victoria until it enters L. Mobuto Seso.
Viedma, t., cap. of Rio Negro terr. of **Argentine** Patagonia; p. (1960) 7,000.
Vienna (Wien), c., cap. of **Austria**; R. pt. on branch of Danube; surrounded by Wiener Wald (Vienna forest) and Carpathian foothills; major industl., comm. and transport ctr.; many fine bldgs., inc. univ., cath., Rathaus, parliament bldgs., magnificent Prater park; influential ctr. of music, cultural and scientific ctr.; home of Haydn, Mozart, Beethoven, Schubert, Mahler, Brahms, and Freud; p. (est. 1969) 1,644,976.
Vienne, dep., W. **France**; drained by R. Vienne; mainly agr. dist.; cap. Poitiers; a. 7,021 km²; p. (1968) 340,256.
Vienne, t., Isère, **France**; nr. Grenoble, on R. Rhône; textiles, metallurgical inds.; Roman remains; overshadowed by Lyons 27 km to N.; p. (1968) 30,276.
Vienne, R., **France**; trib. of the Loire; rises in Massif Central; 354 km long.
Vientiane, admin. cap., **Laos**; pt. and comm. ctr. on Mekong R.; p. (est. 1966) 132,253 (c.); (est. 1962) 162,297 (met. a.).
Viersen, t., N. Rhine–Westphalia, **W. Germany**; S.W. of Krefeld; textiles, machin., furniture, paper ind.; p. (est. 1969) 42,576.
Vierzon, t., Cher dep., **France**; on R. Cher; bricks, tiles, porcelain from local sands, clay; agr. machin.; p. (1968) 34,421.
Vietnam, Democratic Rep. of, S.E. Asia; comprises regions of Cochinchina and Tonkin in former French Indo-China; from 1954–1976 two separate countries, N. and S. Vietnam, based on two rivers, Song-koi and Mekong respectively, and separated by the high Annamite chain of mtns.; long period of civil war resulted in reunification; intensive agr. based on rice cultivation now largely collectivised; monsoon climate and river irrigation aid high yields; coffee, tea, rubber, sugar, main comm. crops but much devastation as result of war; minerals mainly concentrated in the N. with impt. anthracite deposit at Quang-Yen; industl. devel. also mainly in N. around Hanoi and ch. pt. Haiphong; hill tribes practising subsistence agr. inhabit the intervening Annamite mtns.; a. 335,724 km²; p. (est. 1969) 39,207,000.
Viet-Tri, t., N. **Vietnam**; 128 km N.W. of Hanoi; chemicals, paper mill, sugar refining.
Vigevano, t., Lombardy **Italy**; on R. Ticino; impt. agr. and industl. ctr.; footwear, plastics, textiles; cath.; p. (est. 1968) 66,443.
Vigo, spt., **Spain**; transatlantic pt. on V. Bay; processing of imports; oil refining; p. (est. 1967) 186,461.
Vijayanagar, ruined c., S.E. **India**; once cap. c. of Hindu empire in S. Deccan; 96 km in circumference; destroyed by Moslem forces at battle of Talikota 1565.
Vijayavada, t., Andhra Pradesh, **India**; rly. junc., comm. ctr.; irrigation dam, Kistna R.; p. (1971) 317,258 (t.), 344,607 (met. a.).
Vila Real de Santo António, pt., Faro, **Portugal**; on W. bank of Guadiana R.; exp. copper ore, fish, fruit; p. c. 6,000.
Villach, t., Carinthia, S. **Austria**; at junc. of Gail and Drava Rs.; impt. route ctr.; tourism; p. (1961) 32,971.
Villahermosa, c., cap. of Tabasco, S.E. **Mexico**; agr. mkt., sugar processing; rich local petroleum deposits; p. (1969) 52,000.
Villa María, t., **Argentina**; rly. junc.; ctr. of grain, timber, dairying dist.; p. (1960) 50,000.
Villarrica, t., S.E. **Paraguay**; agr. tr. ctr. for cattle, tobacco, fruit; wines, yerba-maté grown in surrounding a.; p. (est. 1970) 38,052.
Villavicencio, t., E. **Colombia**; in foothills of Andes; comm. ctr. for the *llanos*; cattle tr.; p. (est. 1968) 80,675.
Villaviciosa, t., Oviedo prov., N.W. **Spain**; major fishing pt. on Bay of Biscay; p. (1970) 17,213.
Villeurbanne, t., Rhône dep., **France**; sub. of Lyons; metallurgy, chemicals, leather, textiles; p. (1968) 119,879.
Vilna (Lith. Vilnius, Pol. Wilno), c., cap. of Lithuanian SSR, **USSR**; on Vilija R. (trib. of Niemen); cultural ctr., cath., univ., historic bldgs.; held by Poland 1920–39; lt. inds., food processing; p. (1970) 372,000.
Vilyui, R., Yakut ASSR, **RSFSR**; flows E. from Siberian uplands into Lena R.; R. basin impt. agr. and mng. a.; fishing; 2,400 km long.
Vimy, t., Pas-de-Calais dep., N. **France**; nearby Vimy Ridge, site of Allied victory led by Canadians 1915; p. (1968) 3,272.
Viña del Mar, seaside t., central **Chile**, nr. Valparaiso; fashionable S. American resort; oil and sugar refining, textiles; p. (est. 1970) 153,085.
Vincennes, t., Val-de-Marne dep., **France**; sub. of Paris; famous cas. and Bois; industl. and residtl.; p. (1968) 49,297.
Vindhya Hills, mtn. range, central **India**; separating the Deccan from the Ganges basin; *c.* 640 km long.
Vinnitsa, t., Ukrainian SSR, **USSR**; on R. Bug, 192 km S.W. of Kiev; agr. mkt. t.; engin., chemicals, textiles; p. (1970) 211,000.
Virginia, st., **USA**; one of original 13 sts.; wide Atl. coastal plain rising inland to Blue Ridge; famous for high quality "Virginia Leaf"

tobacco; industl. ts. of Norfolk, Richmond, Portsmouth and Newport News; cap. Richmond; a. 105,711 km²; p. (1970) 4,543,249.
Virgin Is. (Brit.), W.I.; gr. of Is. E. of Greater Antilles; most impt. Tortola, Virgin Gorda, Anegada; water scarcity, semi-subsistence agr. economy; livestock, fish, fruit, vegetables; a. 153 km²; p. (1970) 10,500.
Virgin Is. (USA), W.I.; external terr. of USA E. of Greater Antilles, 64 km E. of Puerto Rico; 3 main Is., St. Thomas, St. John, St. Croix; bought from Denmark 1917; favourite tourist a. in Caribbean; cap. Charlotte Amalie on St. Thomas; livestock, sugar; rum distilling; a. 344 km²; p. (est. 1969) 63,200.
Vis (Lissa), I., off Dalmatian cst., Adriatic, **Yugoslavia**; fish-canning ctr.; a. 91 km²; anc. remains; resort; sea battle 1866 between Italian and Austrian ironclads; p. 3,000.
Visby, old spt., **Sweden**; on Gotland I. in Baltic Sea; rich in historic interest; resort; p. (est. 1970) 19,319.
Vishakhapatnam, spt., Andhra Pradesh, **India**; deepwater harbour on Bay of Bengal; exp. manganese and oilseeds from Madhya Pradesh; shipbldg.; p. (1971) 352,504 (t.), 363,467 (met. a.).
Vistula, R., Poland; rises in Beskids range of Carpathians, flows through Poland past Krakow to Baltic Sea nr. Gdansk; forms major link in E. European waterway system; coal and timber transport; 1,056 km long.
Vitebsk, c., Belorussiyan SSR, **USSR**; R. pt. on W. Dvina and impt. rly. junc., in agr. region; textiles, machine tools, food processing; p. (1970) 231,000.
Viterbo, c., cap. of V. prov., **Italy**; N. of Rome; agr. ctr., food-processing; 12th cent. cath. and historic bldgs.; p. (1969) 53,110.
Vitim, R., E. Siberia, **RSFSR**; flows to R. Lena; navigable for 5 months of year; coal and grain tr.; 1,400 km long.
Vitória, spt., Espírito Santo, **Brazil**; exp. coffee, cocoa, fruit, iron ore; sugar refining, shoes, textiles, cement; p. (1970) 121,978.
Vitoria, c., cap. of Alava prov., **Spain**; in Basque cty.; stands on hill at 534 m; furniture mnf.; defeat of Fr. by Wellington 1813; p. (est. 1968) 126,098.
Vitry-le-François, t., Marne dep., N.E. **France**; on Marne R.; industl., textiles, earthenware; agr. mkt. for Champagne Pouilleuse; p. (1968) 16,879.
Vitry-sur-Seine, S.E. sub., Paris, **France**; flower growing on sand and gravel terraces of Seine R., acreage being reduced by competition from housing and inds.; p. (1968) 77,846.
Vittoria, t., Sicily, **Italy**; mkt. for wine; p. (est. 1968) 46,938.
Vittorio Veneto, t., **Italy**; N. of Venice; resort; textiles; p. (est. 1968) 29,697.
Vizcaya, Basque prov., N. **Spain**; on Bay of Biscay; iron mng.; iron and steel inds.; dense p.; cap. Bilbao; a. 2,165 km²; p. (1960) 1,043,310.
Vlaardingen, t., S. Holland prov., **Neth.**; 8 km W. of Rotterdam, on Nieuwe Maas; leading fish. pt.; p. (1968) 78,654.
Vladimir, c., cap. of V. oblast, **RSFSR**; between Gorki and Moscow, on trib. of Oka R.; founded 12th cent.; caths., historic bldgs.; machine tools, agr. machin., textiles; p. (1970) 234,000.
Vladimir-Volynski, c., N.W. Ukrainian SSR, **USSR**; one of oldest Ukrainian settlements, founded 9th cent.; agr. mkt. ctr.; p. (est. 1967) 23,000.
Vladivostok, c., spt., **RSFSR**; ch. pt. and naval base on Pac.; terminus of Trans-Siberian rly. and airline from Moscow; ch. cultural ctr. of Far East; shipyards, fisheries, oil refining, engin., chemicals; economic development in hinterland hindered by distance from major ctrs. of p. and ind.; p. (1970) 442,000.
Vlieland, Friesian I., at entrance to IJsselmeer, **Neth.**; resort, nature reserve.
Vlissingen or **Flushing**, spt., Zeeland prov., S.W. **Neth.**; on Walcheren I.; shipyards, oil refining, fishing; resort; birthplace of Admiral de Ruyter; p. (1967) 38,564.
Vlonë, spt., S.W. **Albania**; on Strait of Otranto, Adriatic Sea; salt; oil pipeline connects from Kucovë nr. Berat; p. (1967) 50,000.
Vltava or **Moldau, R.**, Bohemia, **ČSSR**; rises in Sumava mtns. (Bohemian Forest) and flows to R. Elbe below Prague; used for hydroelectric power; *c.* 416 km long.
Voghera, t., Lombardy, **Italy**; rly. junc. and agr. mkt.; textiles, machin. engin.; cas., cath.; p. (est. 1968) 39,841.
Voi, t., **Kenya**, E. Africa; 144 km N.W. of Mombasa on rly. to Nairobi; branch connection with Tanzania rly. system allows agr. prod. from Arusha and Moshi dists. to pass through Mombasa as alternative to Tanga.
Voiron, t., Isère dep., **France**; on Morge R., 24 km N.W. of Grenoble; textiles, paper; p. (1968) 19,038.
Vojvodina, aut. prov., N. Serbia, **Yugoslavia**; impt. and fertile agr. dist. crossed by Danube R.; intensive agr., prosperous and dense p.; fruit, vegetables, livestock, food processing; ch. c. Novi Sad; a. 22,489 km²; p. (1971) 1,950,268.
Volcano Is., Japan; 3 volcanic Is. in Pac. Oc., S. of Japan, admin. by USA until 1968, now Japanese.
Volga, R., USSR; rises in Valdai hills, flows in serpentine course to Caspian at Astrakhan in wide delta; ch. tribs., Oka, Sura, Vetluga, Kama, Samara; major waterway linked to Baltic Sea, Azov, and Black Seas, and to Moscow; hydroelectric developments reducing sturgeon in Caspian Sea and caviar prod. declining; longest R. in Europe, 3,720 km.
Volga Baltic Waterway (Mariinsk Waterway), **RSFSR**; inland deepwater navigation network linking Black Sea and Caspian Sea in S. with Baltic Sea and White Sea in N.
Volgograd (Stalingrad), c., **RSFSR**; R. pt. on Volga and major rly. ctr.; exp. raw materials, fish; industl. ctr. for steel, engin., chemicals, oil refining; hydroelectric power sta.; fierce siege and successful defence 1942 turning point of second world war; p. (1970) 818,000.
Volhynia, historic region, Ukrainian SSR, **USSR**; on Polish frontier; rich agr. lowland; coal mng. at Novovodinsk; cap. Lutsk.
Volkhov, R., RSFSR; flows from L. Ilmen to L. Ladoga; navigable; hydroelectric power sta. and aluminium smelting plant at Volkhov (Leningrad oblast); 208 km long.
Volklingen, t., Saarland, **W. Germany**; on Saar R., 13 km W. of Saarbrücken; coal mng., iron and steel; p. (est. 1969) 40,128.
Vologda, c., **RSFSR**; R. and rly. junc. on upper Sukhona R.; in dairying a.; engin., textiles, sawmilling, paper, dairy inds.; cath., historic bldgs.; p. (1970) 178,000.
Volos, spt., **Greece**; at head of G. of V.; impt. transport, industl., comm. ctr.; exp. agr. prods.; car mnfs.; p. (1971) 51,340.
Volsk, c., **RSFSR**; R. pt. on Volga R.; cement, tanneries, metallurgy, food processing; p. (est. 1969) 71,000.
Volta (White Volta), major R., **W. Africa**; drains extensive terr. in Niger bend, flows S. through Ghana to delta on Guinea cst., 112 km E. of Accra; main means of communication but rapids make through navigation impossible; Volta R. project for industrialisation of Ghana: dam and power plant at Akosombo, aluminium smelter at Tema; 1,520 km long. *See also* **Black Volta**.
Volta Redonda, t., Rio de Janeiro, **Brazil**; state-owned steel plant; p. (1970) 120,645.
Volterra, hill t., Tuscany, **Italy**; Etruscan and mediaeval walls; alabaster, salt; p. (est. 1968) 16,558.
Volzhsky, t., **RSFSR**; new industl. t. on Volga R.; aluminium smelting, chemicals; p. (1970) 142,000.
Voorburg, t., **Neth.**; industl. ctr. E. of the Hague; p. (1968) 46,703.
Vorarlberg, prov., **Austria**; forestry, dairying, tourism; inds. based on hydroelectric power; textiles; cap. Bregenz; a. 2,600 km²; p. (1971) 274,000.
Vorkuta, ctr. of Pechora coal basin, **RSFSR**; beyond Arctic circle, which supplies entire European N. RSFSR; p. (est. 1967) 65,000.
Voronezh, c., **RSFSR**; R. pt. on Voronezh R. nr. junc. with Don; impt. comm. ctr. in fertile agr. dist.; machin., rubber, oil refining, food processing; nuclear power sta.; univ., cath.; p. (1970) 660,000.
Voroshilovgrad. *See* **Lugansk**.
Voroshilovsk. *See* **Kommunarsk**.

Vosges, dep., **E. France**; on Franco-German frontier; dairying, vineyards, stone quarrying, textiles; cap. Epinal; a. 5,970 km²; p. (1968) 388,201.

Vosges, highlands, **E. France**; structurally similar to Black Forest, from which they are separated by Rhine rift valley; forested slopes, vineyards; source of Meurthe, Moselle, Sarve, Ill, and Saône Rs.; highest summit Ballon de Guebwiller, 1,425 m.

Voskresensk, t., **RSFSR**; S.E. Moscow; lignite, chemicals, fertilisers; p. (est. 1969) 61,000.

Votkinsk, t., **RSFSR**; 61 km N.E. of Izhevsk; lge. engin. plant; hydroelectric power sta.; birthplace of Tchaikovsky; p. (est. 1969) 73,000.

Vranja, t., **Yugoslavia**; flax and hemp culture and mnf.; developing industl. ctr. based on handicrafts; p. (est. 1965) 19,000.

Vratsa, t., **Bulgaria**; on R. Vratcanska; jewellery, wine, silk, tanning; p. (est. 1968) 45,232.

Vrsac, t., **Yugoslavia**; milling, wine, brandy; p. (1961) 31,620.

Vulcano, I., Lipari gr., **Italy**; off N.E. cst. Sicily; active volcano; gave its name as generic title for this type of mtn.

Vyatka, R., **RSFSR**; rises in foothills of Urals flows past Kirov into Kama R.; timber transport, fishing; c. 1,360 km long.

Vyborg (Viipuri), c., **RSFSR**; spt. on G. of Finland, occupies strategic site on Karelian Isthmus, N.W. of Leningrad; Finnish until 1945; exp. timber; shipyards, engin., food processing; p. (est. 1969) 65,000.

Vychegda, R., **RSFSR**; rises in Urals, flows W. to N. Dvina R.; timber transport; 1,120 km long.

Vyrnwy, L., reservoir, Powys, **Wales**; with dam 360 m long supplies water for Liverpool; a. 454 ha.

Vyshni-Volochek, t., **RSFSR**; 118 km N.W. of Kalinin; flour milling, textiles, glass inds. p. (est. 1969) 73,000.

W

Waal, R., **Neth.**; S. arm of R. Rhine.

Waco, c., Texas, **USA**; in Brazos valley; route ctr., airport; regional cultural ctr.; univ.; textiles, leather; p. (1970) 92,600 (c.), 142,772 (met. a.).

Waddenzee, stretch of shallow water between W. Frisian Is. and **Neth.** mainland.

Wadebridge, spt., Cornwall **Eng.**; at head of Camel estuary, 10 km N.W. of Bodmin; agr. mkt.; p. (1971) 17,799 (dist.).

Wadi Halfa, t., **Sudan**; on R. Nile at second cataract; rly. terminus of Sudan rlys.; inundated by Aswan L.; new t. Khashm el Girba for inhabitants.

Wad Medani, t., cap. of Blue Nile prov., **Sudan**; ctr. of cotton growing dist.; p. (est. 1969) 71,030.

Wagadugu. *See* **Ouagadougou.**

Wagga Wagga, t., N.S.W., **Australia**; on R. Murrumbidgee; ctr. of agr. and pastoral dist.; p. (1972) 27,636.

Wahiawa, t., Oahu I., **Hawaii**; pineapples; p. (1970) 37,329.

Waikaremoana, L., N.I., **N.Z.**; hydroelectric power.

Waikato, R., N.I., **N.Z.**; rises in L. Taupo and flows N.W. into Tasman Sea; coalfields, hydroelec. power stas.; 422 km long.

Wainuiomata, co. t., on Wainuiomata R., N.I., **N.Z.**; p. (1971) 16,670.

Wairakei, t., N.I., **N.Z.**; on L. Taupo; health resort; geothermal power sta.

Waitaki, t., Otago, S.I., **N.Z.**; Benmore hydroelectric power plant; p. (1971) 9,420.

Wakamatsu. *See* Kitakyushu.

Wakatipu, L. Otago, S.I., **N.Z.**; 83 km long, 5 km wide, 360 m deep, 320 m a.s.l.

Wakayama, spt., Honshu, **Japan**; textiles; new iron and steel plant; p. (est. 1971) 372,000.

Wakefield, c., West Yorks., **Eng.**; on R. Calder; 13 km S. of Leeds; cath.; ctr. of coal-mng. a.; woollen and worsted gds., chemicals, engin.; p. (1971) 59,650.

Wakefield, t., Va., **USA**; on Potomac R., nr. Fredericksburg; birthplace of George Washington.

Wake I., coral atoll, **Pac. Oc.**; between Marianas and Hawaii; comm. and naval base on route to Far East, belonging to USA.

Walachia, region, S. **Romania**; wide plain bounded by Transylvanian Alps and separated from Yugoslavia by Danube; rich agr. a., "the bread-basket of Romania"; Ploiesti oilfields; inds. nr. ch. c. Bucharest; a. 76,563 km²; p. c. 7,500,000.

Walbrzych (Waldenburg), c., S.W. Poland (since 1945); formerly in Lower Silesia; industl. and mng. ctr. at 427 m; porcelain, machin., engin.; p. (1970) 125,000.

Walchensee, Lake, Bavaria, **W. Germany**; a. 16 km²; hydroelectric power sta.

Walcheren, I., Zeeland prov., S.W. **Neth.**; in N. Sea at entrance to Scheldt estuary; mainly agr.; ch. ts., Vlissingen, Middelburg; flooded 1944 to stop German advance; tourism.

Waldenburg. *See* Walbrzych.

Wales, principality, **Great Britain**; mostly mtnous.; Cambrian mtns. rise to 1,085 m at Snowdon; contrast between N. and Central Wales (pastoral farming, forestry, water supply, tourism, rural depopulation) and S. Wales (coalfield, metal-based inds., lge. ts.); cap. Cardiff; a. 20,761 km²; p. (1971) 2,723,596 (26 per cent Welsh speaking).

Wallasey, t., adjoining Birkenhead, Merseyside, **Eng.**; residtl., seaside resort (New Brighton); p. (1971) 97,061.

Wallensee, L., **Switzerland**; 18 km long.

Wallingford, t. Oxon., **Eng.**; on R. Thames, to N. of its gap between Chilterns and Lambourn Downs; p. (1971) 6,184.

Wallis and Futuna Is., gr. of coral Is., **S. Pac. Oc.**; overseas terr. of France; copra; a. 275 km²; p. (est. 1969) 8,546 (mostly Polynesians).

Wallsend, t., Tyne and Wear, **Eng.**; on N. bank of Tyne, 6 km below Newcastle; Tyne tunnel links with Jarrow; shipbldg., engin., iron, plywood; at end of Hadrian's Wall; p. (1971) 45,793.

Walmer, t., Kent, **Eng.**; 3 km S. of Deal; holiday resort; cas., residence of Warden of Cinque Ports.

Walney, I., off cost. of Cumbria, **Eng.**; opposite Barrow.

Walsall, t., West Midlands, **Eng.**; 8 km E. of Wolverhampton; leather and iron gds., engin., steel tubes; p. (1971) 184,606.

Walsingham, v., Norfolk, **Eng.**; many old bldgs., priory ruins, abbey; mediaeval pilgrimage ctr.; p. (1971) 17,416 (dist.).

Walsum, t., N. Rhine-Westphalia, **W. Germany**; at confluence of Rhine and Emscher canal; R. pt. for Oberhausen steelwks.; p. (est. 1969) 48,262.

Waltham, c., Mass., **USA**; nr. Boston; science-based inds.; univ.; p. (1970) 61,582.

Waltham Abbey (Waltham Holy Cross), t., Essex, **Eng.**; 21 km N.E. London, on edge of Epping Forest; glasshouses (tomatoes); Norman nave of abbey part of parish church; p. (1971) 14,585.

Waltham Forest, outer bor., E. London, **Eng.**; incorporating former bors. of Chingford, Leyton, Walthamstow; industl. and residtl.; p. (1971) 233,528.

Walthamstow. *See* Waltham Forest.

Walton and Weybridge, ts., former U.D., Surrey, **Eng.**; on R. Thames, 27 km S.W. of London; engin., aircraft; p. (1971) 51,004.

Walton-le-Dale, t., N.E. Lancs., **Eng.**; on R. Ribble, 3 km E. of Preston; mkt. gardening, cottons, timber; p. (1971) 26,841.

Walvis Bay, spt., **South-West Africa**; on Walvis Bay, Atl. Oc.; fishing, fish processing; p. (est. 1965) 17,877.

Wandsworth, inner bor., S.W. London, **Eng.**; inc. Battersea; on R. Wandle at influx into Thames; oil mills, metal wks., paper, brewing; p. (1971) 298,931.

Wanganui, t., N.I., **N.Z.**; pt. on R. Wanganui; tr. ctr. for wool, grain, meat, dairy prod.; agr. processing, steel-pipes, fertilisers; iron ore deposits; p. (1971) 35,794.

Wanganui, R., N.I., **N.Z.**; famous for its beauty; 256 km long.

Wangaratta, t., Victoria, **Australia**; 232 km from Melbourne; agr. dist.; nylon and woollen wks.; p. (1972) 15,535.

Wankie, t., **Rhodesia**; site of coal-mng. ind.; 344 km N.W. of Bulawayo; p. (est. 1970) 21,000.

Wanne-Eickel, t., N. Rhine-Westphalia, W. Germany; pt. on Rhine-Herne canal; coal-mng. ctr. of Ruhr; p. (est. 1969) 100,300.

Wansbeck, R., Northumberland, Eng.; flows E. from Pennines into N. Sea 5 km N. of Blyth; 37 km long.

Wanstead and Woodford. *See* Redbridge.

Wantage, mkt. t., Oxon., Eng.; in Vale of the White Horse; birthplace of King Alfred; p. (1971) 8,007.

Wapping, Thames-side dist., London, Eng.; contains London docks and warehouses; inds. based on imports.

Warangal, t., Andhra Pradesh, India; textiles, carpets; p. (1971) 207,520.

Ware, mkt. t., Herts., Eng.; on R. Lea; 3 km N.E. of Hertford; malting, bricks; p. (1971) 14,666.

Wareham, mkt. t., Dorset, Eng.; on R. Frome, on N. of I. of Purbeck, 13 km S.W. of Poole; agr. machin., pipes; p. (1971) 4,379.

Warley, t. and dist., West Midlands, Eng.; inc. Smethwick, Oldbury and Rowley Regis; varied inds.; p. of dist. (1971) 163,388.

Warminster, t., Wilts., Eng.; on Wylye watershed at edge of Salisbury Plain: agr. mkt., gloves; p. (1971) 13,593.

Warmley, Avon, Eng.; expanded t.; p. (1971) 24,213 (dist.).

Warnemünde, spt., E. Germany; ferry pt. for rail traffic between Berlin and Copenhagen; shipbldg.; outport for Rostock; resort.

Warragamba Dam, 64 km W. Sydney, N.S.W., Australia; 137 m high, opened 1960.

Warrego, R., Queensland, N.S.W., Australia; trib. of R. Darling; 640 km long.

Warren, t., Ohio, USA; on Mahoning R.; iron and steel mftg.; p. (1970) 63,494.

Warrenpoint, spt., Newry and Mourne, N. Ireland; at head of Carlingford Lough; holiday resort; p. (1966) 3,579.

Warrington, t., Cheshire, Eng.; on R. Mersey and Manchester Ship Canal; metal inds. (wire-drawing), chemicals, brewing, paper; to be expanded as new c. (to take people from Manchester) with p. (1991) 205,000; p. (1971) 68,262; (est. 1974) 133,000 (new c.).

Warrnambool, t., spt., Victoria, Australia; mkt., timber, plastics, engin.; p. (1972) 18,663.

Warsak Dam, Pakistan; on Kabul R., 24 km N. of Peshawar, nr. Khyber Pass; hydro-electric power and irrigation.

Warsaw (Warszawa), c., cap. of Poland; on R. Vistula; devastated in second world war; facsimile rebuilding based on Canaletto's paintings; cath., univ.; rly, ctr.; iron, steel, engin., textiles, chemicals; p. (1970) 1,308,000.

Warsop, t., Notts., Eng.; 6 km N.E. of Mansfield; limestone, gravel; p. (1971) 13,036.

Warta, R., Poland; trib. of R. Oder; connected to R. Vistula by canal; 720 km long.

Warwick, t., Queensland Australia; sawmilling, agr. processing; p. (1966) 10,087.

Warwick, co. t., Warwicks., Eng.; on R. Avon, 13 km S.W. of Coventry; cas.; agr. implements, brewing, malting; p. (1971) 18,289.

Warwick, c., R.I., USA; on Narragansett Bay; textile ctr.; p. (1970) 83,694.

Warwickshire, non-met. co., W. Midlands, Eng.; undulating, drained by tribs. of Rs. Severn and Trent, crossed by Cotswolds to S.; sm. coalfield to N.; much of industl. N. now inc. in West Midlands met. co.; a. 1,981 km²; p. (1971) 456,000.

Wassatch Mtns., range of Rocky mtns., Utah and Idaho, USA; alt. 3,600 m.

Wash, The, bay, N. Sea between Lincs. and Norfolk, Eng.; 35 km long, 24 km wide; partly reclaimed to form the Fens; proposed barrage to aid further reclamation and water storage.

Washington, t., Tyne and Wear, Eng.; 8 km S.E. of Gateshead; coal, iron and steel, stone quarrying, chemicals; new t. 1964; p. (est. 1974) 39,000.

Washington, c., cap. of USA; in Dist. of Columbia on Potomac R.; c. planned as national seat of Government; White House, Capitol, 5 univs.; over half p. Negro; p. (1970) 764,169 (c.), 2,835,737 (met. a.).

Washington, st., USA; in extreme N.W., stretching from Pac. Oc. into Rocky mtns.; over half a. forested; Colombia R. and tribs. provide hydroelectric power; timber, fishing, tourism; cap. Olympia; a. 176,617 km²; p. (1970) 3,352,892.

Wast Water, L. Dist., deepest L. in Eng.; 5 km long, 79 m deep.

Watchet, t., Somerset, Eng.; sm. pt. on cst. of Bristol Channel; paper mkg., fishing; p. (1971) 2,892.

Watenstedt-Salzgitter. *See* Salzgitter.

Waterbury, c., Conn., USA; on Naugatuck R.; ctr. of brass ind. and metal gds.; p. (1970) 106,431 (c), 206,625 (met. a.).

Waterford, co., Munster, R.o.I.; mtnous. co. in S.E.; mainly agr., dairying, pigs; fishing; co. t. Waterford; a. 1,867 km²; p. (1966) 72,986.

Waterford, co. t., spt., Waterford, R.o.I.; on R. Suir; cath.; brewing, fishing, glass mnfs.; p. (1966) 29,642.

Waterloo, t., Brabant prov., Belgium, nr. Brussels; battle nearby 1815; p. (est. 1969) 16,924.

Waterloo, t., Ont., Canada; industl. sub. of Kitchener; p. (1971) 37,245.

Waterloo, c., Iowa, USA; on Cedar R.; agr. prod. and tools; p. (1970) 75,994 (c.), 132,533 (met. a.).

Waters of Merom (L. Hula), Upper Galilee Israel; extensive drainage completed 1957; a. 14 km².

Waterton Glacier International Peace Park, Albert and Mont., Canada and USA; glacial and lake scenery; a. 596 km².

Watertown, t., Mass., USA; on Charles R.; textiles, clothing; p. (1970) 39,309.

Watertown, t., N.Y., USA; on Black R.; engin., paper; p. (1960) 33,306.

Watford, t., Herts., Eng.; on R. Colne, 26 km N.W. of London; mkt.; varied inds., inc. lt. and elec. engin., paper, printing; p. (1971) 78,117.

Wath, t., South Yorks., Eng.; 6 km N. of Rotherham; coal, quarrying; p. (1971) 15,002.

Watlington, t., Oxford, Eng.; at N. foot of Chiltern hills, 8 km S.W. of Princes Risborough; mkt. hall; nearby cas.

Wattenscheid, t., N. Rhine-Westphalia, W. Germany; E. of Essen; coal, metals, footwear; p. (est. 1969) 80,527.

Waukegan, c., Ill., USA; on L. Michigan; summer resort; steel, brass, motors, sugar refining; p. (est. 1969) 65,000.

Wauwatosa, t., Wis., USA; sub. of Milwaukee; metals, concrete, chemicals; p. (est. 1969) 58,000.

Waveney, R., Norfolk and Suffolk, Eng.; 80 km long.

Wayatinah, hydroelectric commission v., Tasmania, Australia; dam, lagoon and power sta. at confluence of Rs. Nive and Derwent.

Wazirabad (Balkh), t., Afghanistan; anc. Bactra, cap of Bactria, called the "mother of cities", destroyed by Genghiz Khan 1221; textile plant projected; p. c. 13,000.

Weald, The, wooded and pastoral tracts S.E. Eng.; extending from Folkestone, Kent, through Surrey, Hants., and Sussex to the sea at Beachy Head; former a. of iron working; name derived from German *Wald* = forest.

Wear, R., Durham/Tyne and Wear, Eng.; rises in Pennines, flows through Durham to N. Sea at Sunderland; 96 km long.

Weaver, R., Cheshire, Eng.; industl. trib. of R. Mersey; 72 km long.

Weddell Sea, arm of S. Atl. Oc., Antarctica; whaling and sealing.

Wednesbury, t., West Midlands, Eng.; metal inds., iron and steel.

Wednesfield, t., West Midlands, Eng.; metal tubes, materials handling engin.; expanded t.

Wei, R., Shensi prov., W. China; rises in highlands of Kansu, flows E. between highlands of Shansi and Tsinling Shan to join Yellow R. nr. Tungkwan; valley contains very fertile loess soils; formed cradle of Chinese civilisation; c. 800 km long.

Weiden, t., Bavaria, W. Germany; porcelain, glass, textiles; p. (est. 1969) 43,081.

Weifang, c., Shantung prov., China; coal-mng.ctr.; tobacco processing; p. (est. 1970) 260,000.

Weihai, spt., Shantung prov., China; naval base; fishing; vegetable-oil processing, textiles; p. 222,000.

Weimar, t., Erfurt, E. Germany; on R. Ilm; ctr. of music and culture in 19th cent., associated with Goethe, Schiller, Nietzsche, Liszt, Herder;

scene of establishment of German rep. 1919; elec. and metal inds., textiles, musical instruments, glass; p. (est. 1970) 63,689.

Weipa, Queensland, Australia; new t., pt., and alumina plant; bauxite nearby at Aurukin.

Weirton, t., W. Va., **USA**; on R. Ohio; steel, tinplate; p. (est. 1969) 29,000.

Weissenfels, t., Halle, **E. Germany**; on R. Saale, in lignite mng. a.; footwear, paper, metals; p. (est. 1970) 46,120.

Weisshorn, mtn. peak, **Switzerland**; alt. 4,505 m.

Wejherowo, t., Gdansk, **Poland**; on R. Reda; mediaeval stronghold; palace; p. (1970) 33,700.

Welkom, t., O.F.S., **S. Africa**; ctr. of O.F.S. goldfields; p. (1970) 131,767 (met. a.).

Welland, t., Ont., **Canada**; on Welland Canal; farm machin., steel tubing, castings, rope; p. (1971) 44,222.

Welland, R., Northants. and Lincs., **Eng.**; rises in Northampton heights and flows N.E. into the Wash; 112 km long.

Welland Ship Canal, Ont., **Canada**; connects Ls. Erie and Ont.; 43 km long; 2-lane waterway, 1963.

Wellingborough, t., Northants., **Eng.**; on R. Nene, 14 km N.E. of Northampton; mkt.; footwear; expanded t.; p. (1971) 37,589.

Wellington, mkt. t., Salop, **Eng.**; brewing, sugar refining, timber, toys; name derived from "Watling Town" (stood on Watling Street); with Dawley and Oakengates forms new t. of Telford; p. (1971) 17,154.

Wellington, mkt. t., Somerset, **Eng.**; 10 km S.W. Taunton, anc. woollen ind. still survives; dairy prod.; p. (1971) 9,434.

Wellington, c., spt., N.I., cap. of **N.Z.**; univ.; impt. exp. ctr. for dairy prod., wool, meat; new inds. developing in Hutt valley with vehicle assembly, rubber, oil refineries; p., (1971) 135,515 (c.); (est. 1970) 179,300 (met. a.).

Wellington, prov., N.I., **N.Z.**; mtnous., pastoral and dairy farming; a. 28,153 km²; p. (1971) 552,640.

Wells, cath. t., Somerset, **Eng.**; on S. flank of Mendip hills; cath., bishop's palace; paper mftg.; tourism; p. (1971) 8,586.

Wells-next-the-Sea, t., Norfolk, **Eng.**; anc. pt. on N. cst. of E. Anglia, 22 km W. of Sheringham; whelks, cockles and mussels; p. (1971) 2,342.

Wels, t., **Upper Austria**; on Traun R.; mkt. for agr. a.; foodstuffs, textiles; cas.; p. (1961) 41,060.

Welshpool, mkt. t., Powys, **Wales**; on R. Severn; lt. inds. based on agr., hosiery; nearby is Powys cas.; p. (1971) 6,705.

Welwyn Garden City, t., Herts., **Eng.**; 34 km N. of London; founded by Sir Ebenezer Howard (1920) as first satellite t. of London; new t. 1948; pharmaceuticals, plastics, radio, and electronics, lt. inds.; p. (est. 1974) 40,000.

Wembley, former M.B., Middx., **Eng.**; now inc. in Brent outer bor. Greater London; lt. inds., sports ctr.; British Empire Exhibition 1924–5.

Wenchow (Wenzhou), c., spt., Chekiang prov., **China**; pt. on estuary of Wu R., E. China Sea; textiles, fishing, coastal tr.; exp. wood, tea, agr. prod.; p. (est. 1970) 250,000.

Wenlock Edge, narrow ridge, Salop, **Eng.**; extends 29 km S.W. from Much Wenlock to Craven Arms; limestone; moorland, mainly above 290 m.

Wensleydale, North Yorks., **Eng.**; valley in N. Pennines drained E. by R. Ure; cattle reared for fattening on lowland farms; some dairying (cheese); length 56 km.

Wernigerode, t., Magdeburg, **E. Germany**; on N. slopes of Harz mtns.; mediaeval cas.; glass, wood, metal inds.; tourism; p. (est. 1970). 32,662.

Wesel, t., N. Rhine-Westphalia, **W. Germany**; R. pt. at confluence of Rs. Lippe and Rhine, Ruhr conurb.; rebuilt since destruction in second world war; p. (est. 1969) 33,952.

Weser, R., **W. Germany**; formed by confluence of Fulda and Werra Rs. at Münden; flows N. to N. Sea at Bremerhaven; linked by Mittelland canal to Rhine, Ems, and Elbe; navigable for entire length of 330 m.

Wesermünde. *See* Bremerhaven.

Wessex, anc. kingdom, S. **Eng.**; inc. Berks., Hants., Wilts., Dorset, Somerset and Devon.

West Allis, t., Wis., **USA**; mng. machin., castings; heavy vehicles; p. (1970) 71,649.

West Bengal, st., N.E. **India**; W., mainly Hindu section of former presidency of B. (Muslim E.B. now Bangladesh); on Ganges delta and flood plain; humid sub-tropical climate; very dense p.; rice, jute; ch. c. Calcutta; a. 87,617 km²; p. (1971) 44,440,095.

West Bridgford, t., Notts., **Eng.**; at junc. of Grantham canal with R. Trent; residtl. sub. of Nottingham; p. (1971) 28,496.

West Bromwich, t., West Midlands, **Eng.**; on R. Thame, 8 km N.W. of Birmingham; heavy engin. and allied inds., chemicals, springs, oil refining; p. (1971) 166,626.

Western Australia, st. of the **Australian Commonwealth**; lgst. st., nearly a third of continent with only 8 per cent of p. concentrated in S.W. around st. cap. of Perth in fertile Mediterranean-like a.; diversity of relief, Hammersley range in N.W., Kimberley range in N.E., Gibson desert in interior; rich but irregularly distributed mineral deposits; intensive agr. in S.W., wheat and sheep in interior; a. 2,527,633 km²; p. (1972) 1,027,372.

Western Desert, **Egypt**; part of Libyan Desert; inc. Qattara depression; coastal road from Cairo to Tripoli; scene of fighting second world war.

Western Pacific High Commission Territories, inc. Solomon Is. and Gilbert and Tuvalu Is.

West Port Bay, Vic., **Australia**; major heavy industl. a. close to Melbourne, rapidly growing.

Western Sahara (**Spanish Sahara**), N.W. African cst.; comprising Rio de Oro and Sagui el Hamra; desert; rich phosphate mines at Bou Craa connected to El Aaiun pt. by rly.; upon decolonisation terr. split between Morocco and Mauritania (1976) but declared Saharan Arab Democratic Rep. by Algerians; a. 265,993 km²; p. largely nomadic (1967) 48,607.

Western Samoa, indep. sov. st., **S. Pac. Oc.**; member of Commonwealth (1970); gained independence from N.Z. 1962; consists of 2 lge Is. (Savai'i, Upolu) and 7 sm. Is.; 70 per cent p. in agr.; c. 30 per cent a. devoted to bananas; exp. bananas, copra, cacao beans; ch. spt. Apia on Upolu I.; a. 2,841 km²; p. (1966) 131,379.

Westerwald, plateau of old volcanic rocks, **W. Germany**; ending in steep slope E. of R. Rhine; fertile soil; pastureland or deciduous woodland; sm. quantities of iron ore in Siegerland.

West Glamorgan, co. S. **Wales**; borders Bristol Channel; inc. Gower Penin. and lge. industl. ts. of Swansea, Neath and Port Talbot; impt. metal refining and engin. inds.; a. 816 km²; p. (1971) 371,867.

West Ham, former C.B., Essex, **Eng.**; sub. to E. of London; bordered by Rs. Thames and Lea; now inc. in Newham bor., Greater London; residtl.; extensive docks, rubber, soap, jute wks., engin., smelting, chemicals.

West Hartford, t., Conn., **USA**; residtl. sub. of Hartford; metal gds., ctr. for dairying, tobacco-growing dist.; p. (1970) 68,031.

West Indies or Antilles, I. grs., **Atl. Oc.**; extend between csts. of Fla. and Venezuela, separating Caribbean Sea and G. of Mexico from Atl.; inc. Cuba, Haiti, Dominican Rep., Bahamas, Barbados, Jamaica, Leeward Is., Trinidad and Tobago, Windward Is., Guadeloupe, Martinique, Curaçao, Puerto Rico, Virgin Is.; mostly volcanic and coral Is.; former colonial terrs. developed for plantation agr. worked by W. African slaves; most of indigenous Indians killed.

West Irian (**Irian Jaya**), prov., **Indonesia**; formerly West New Guinea and Dutch col.; came under Indonesian admin. 1963; inaugurated as prov., 1969; primitive agr. of rice, poultry, cocoa; few oil deposits; cap. Djajapura; a. (inc. Ternate) 412,784 km²; p. (est. 1970) 957,000.

West Lothian, l. gov. dist., former co., Lothian Reg., **Scot.**; industl. dist. in Central Lowlands close to Edinburgh; a. 417 km²; p. (1971) 112,510.

Westmeath, co., Leinster, **R.o.I.**; low-lying, drained by R. Shannon, many Ls.; dairying; co. to Mullingar; ch. t. Athlone; a. 1,834 km²; p. (1966) 52,849.

West Mersea, t., Essex, **Eng.**; on Mersea I.; p. (1971) 4,131.

West Midlands, met. co., **Eng.**; mainly industl. a. centred around Birmingham and the S. Staffs. coalfield (Black Country) and Coventry and the Warwicks. coalfield; many forms of engin. and light inds. inc. vehicle mftg.; p. (1971) 2,790,000.

Westminster, City of, inner bor., London, **Eng.**; on N. bank of R. Thames; W. of City of London; incorporates former bors. of Paddington and St. Marylebone; contains Houses of Parliament, Westminster Abbey, Government offices, Royal Palaces (Buckingham Palace and St. James's); p. (1971) 225,632.

Westmorland, former co., **Eng.**; now part of Cumbria non-met. co.

Weston-super-Mare, t., Avon, **Eng.**; on Bristol Channel, 32 km S.W. of Bristol; holiday resort; expanded t.; p. (1971) 50,794.

West Orange, t., N.J., **USA**; elec. equipment; home of T. A. Edison; p. (1970) 43,715.

West Pakistan. *See* Pakistan.

West Palm Beach, Fla., **USA**; domestic hardware; spt.; tourism; p. (1970) 56,865 (t.), 345,553 (met. a.).

Westphalia. *See* **North Rhine–Westphalia.**

West Point, military sta., N.Y., **USA**; on Hudson R.; military academy.

Westport, spt., S.I., **N.Z.**; on R. Buller; coastal shipping; coal; nearby iron fields; p. (1971) 5,008.

Westport, spt., U.D., Mayo, **R.o.I.**; on Clew Bay; fishing; mkt.; p. (1966) 2,927.

Westray, I., Orkney Is., **Scot.**; 16 km long; p. (1971) 841.

West Sussex, non-met. co., S.E. **Eng.**; crossed by E.–W. chalk ridge of S. Downs and forested Weald; diverse agr.; dormitory, retirement and tourist ts. on cst. inc. Bognor Regis and Worthing; Crawley new t. in N.; a. 2,015 km^2; p. (1971) 610,000.

West Virginia, st., **USA**; inc. Allegheny plateau; impt. mng. st. for coal; fruit farming; many industl. ts.; cap. Charleston; a. 62,629 km^2; p. (1970) 1,701,913.

Westward Ho!, v., N. Devon, **Eng.**; named after Kingsley's novel.

West Yorkshire, met co., **Eng.**; industl. and mainly built-up a. E. of Pennines; traditionally ass. with woollen textile mftg.; inc. major ctrs. of Bradford and Leeds; p. (1971) 2,053,000.

Wetar I., **Indonesia**; N. of Timor I.; mtns.; underdeveloped; sparse p.; a. 31,080 km^2.

Wetherby, t., West Yorks., **Eng.**; on R. Wharfe; mkt., malting, brewing; p. (1971) 30,581 (dist.).

Wethersfield, t., Conn., **USA**; oldest settlement (1634) in st.; aircraft parts. agr. implements; p. (1970) 26,662.

Wetterhorn, mtn., **Switzerland**; alt. 3,710 m.

Wetzlar, t., Hesse, **W. Germany**; on R. Lahn; metallurgical and optical inds.; p. (est. 1969) 36,871.

Wexford, coastal co., Leinster, S.E. **R.o.I.**; mixed farming, fishing; cap. Wexford; a. 2,334 km^2; p. (1966) 83,355.

Wexford, t., cap. of Wexford; Leinster, S.E. **R.o.I.**; on R. Slaney; agr. processing; outport at Rosslare; p. (1966) 11,533.

Wey, R., Hants., Surrey, **Eng.**; rises in W. Weald, flows N. into R. Thames nr. Weybridge; cuts impt. gap through N. Downs at Guildford; length 56 km.

Weybridge. *See* **Walton and Weybridge.**

Weymouth and Melcombe Regis, t., Dorset, **Eng.**; on Weymouth Bay, 13 km S. of Dorchester; torpedo and boatbldg., bricks, tiles, engin.; holiday resort; p. (1971) 42,322.

Whaley Bridge, t., Derbys., **Eng.**; textile bleaching and finishing; p. (1971) 5,232.

Whangarei, c., N.I., **N.Z.**; deep harbour; oil refining; natural gas pipelines from Kapuni; fertilisers, sheet glass; p. (1971) 30,749.

Wharfe, R., West and North Yorks., **Eng.**; trib. of R. Ouse; 96 km long.

Wheeling, c., W. Va., **USA**; pt. on Ohio R.; comm. and mftg. ctr. in coal and natural gas a.; iron, steel, and metal plants; p. (1970) 46,854 (c.), 180,724 (met. a.).

Whickham, t., Tyne and Wear, **Eng.**; nr. Gateshead; chemicals, paper; p. (1971) 28,704.

Whiston, t., Merseyside, **Eng.**; nr. Prescott; coal mng.; p. (1971) 85,558 (dist.).

Whitburn, burgh, W. Lothian, **Scot.**; 32 km S.W. of Edinburgh; coal, limestone; p. (1971) 10,176.

Whitby, t., North Yorks., **Eng.**; at mouth of R. Esk, 27 km N.W. of Scarborough; anc. spt. and fishing t.; residtl. and coastal resort; abbey; famous for jet ornaments; potash to be mined nearby; p. (1971) 12,171.

Whitchurch, t., Salop, **Eng.**; 21 km S.W. of Crewe; structural steel, dairy prods.

White, R., Ark. and Mo., **USA**; trib. of Mississippi; hydroelectric power resources; 1,104 km long.

Whiteadder, R., Berwick, **Scot.**; trib. of R. Tweed; 54 km long.

Whitefield, t., Gtr. Manchester, **Eng.**; engin., textiles, confectionery; p. (1971) 21,814.

Whitehaven, spt., Cumbria, **Eng.**; on Solway F. 5 km N. of St. Bees Head; coal, methane gas, cement, chemicals; p. (1971) 26,720.

Whitehead, t., Carrickfergus, **N. Ireland**; at entrance to Belfast Lough; seaside resort; p. (1966) 2,740.

Whitehorse, t., cap. of Yukon terr., **Canada**; ctr. coal and copper mng., hunting and fur trapping; once a gold "boom town"; H.Q. Royal Canadian Mounted Police; end of Alaska highway linking Edmonton, Alberta; p. (1966) 4,771.

White Mtns., part. of Appalachian system, N.H., **USA**; highest summit Mt. Washington, 1,918 m; resort a.

White Nile (Bahr-el-Abiad), R., **Sudan**; N.E. Africa; strictly, name applied to stretch of R. Nile between L. No and Khartoum; 800 km long.

White Plains, t., N.Y., **USA**; on Bronx R.; residtl ; battle 1776; p. (1970) 50,346.

White Russia. *See* **Belorussiyan SSR.**

White Sea or G. of Arkangelsk, inlet of Barents Sea, **USSR**; frozen for 6 months of year; connected to Baltic Sea by new deep-water canal; impt. fisheries.

Whithorn, sm. burgh, Wigtown, **Scot.**; 14 km S. of Wigtown; ruined priory; p. (1971) 988.

Whitley Bay, t., Northumberland, **Eng.**; 5 km N. of Tynemouth; seaside resort; plastics; p. (1971) 37,775.

Whitstable, spt., Kent, **Eng.**; on Thames estuary 10 km N. of Canterbury; hoilday resort, oysters; p. (1971) 25,404.

Whittlesey, t., Cambs., **Eng.**; in the Fens, 13 km W. of March; bricks, mkt. gardening; p. (1971) 10,451.

Whitworth, t., S.E. Lancs., **Eng.**; textiles; p. (1971) 7,417.

Whyalla, t., spt., **S. Australia**; steel and shipbldg. inds.; ironstone, pig-iron, steel from Iron Knob; p. (1972) 32,085.

Wichita, c., Kan., **USA**; in Arkansas valley; rly. wks., oil refineries and equipment, meat-packing ctr. in agr. and stock-raising region; univs.; p. (1970) 274,448 (c.), 385,994 (met. a.).

Wichita Falls, c., Texas, **USA**; oil refining, ctr. in agr. and ranching a.; p. (1970) 94,976 (c.) 124,238 (met. a.).

Wick, spt., sm. burgh, Caithness, **Scot.**; on E. cst., 22 km S. of John O'Groats; airport to Orkneys and Shetlands; herring fishing ctr.; p. (1971) 7,617.

Wicklow, costal co., Leinster, **R.o.I.**; crossed by Wicklow mtns.; pastoral agr. and tourism; cap. Wicklow; a. 2,033 km^2; p. (1966) 60,281.

Wickow, t., cap. of Wicklow, Leinster, **R.o.I.**; on S.E. cst., 56 km S. of Dublin; mkt.; sm. seaside resort; p. (1966) 3,340.

Wicklow, mtns., Wicklow, **R.o.I.**; highest summit, Lugnaquillia, 927 m.

Widecombe, v., Devon, **Eng.**; Dartmoor tourist ctr.; famous through ballad "Widecombe Fair."

Widnes, t., Cheshire, **Eng.**; on R. Mersey 19 km E. of Liverpool; impt. chemical inds.; expanded t.; p. (1971) 56,709.

Wiener Neustadt, t., Lower **Austria**; rly. and industl. ctr.; heavy machin.; founded 1192; anc. bldgs., cas., cath.; educational ctr.; p. (1961) 38,845.

Wieringermeer Polder, reclaimed a., N. Holland, **Neth.**; N.W. of IJsselmeer; reclaimed in 1930; a. 202 km^2.

Wiesbaden, c., cap. of Hesse, **W. Germany**; on Rhine, at S. foot of the Taunus; famous spa.; cas.; ctr. for Rhine wines; chemicals, metal gds.; p. (est. 1969) 259,900.

Wigan, t., Gtr. Manchester, **Eng.**; 26 km N.E. of Liverpool; engin., chemicals, cement, food processing, paper; former coal-mng. ctr.; p. (1971) 81,258.

Wight, I. of, non-met. co., **Eng.**; English Channel, separated from Hampshire by Spithead and the Solent; crossed by chalk hills, terminating in the Needles; popular holiday resort; ch. ts., Newport, Ryde, Cowes; a. 381 km^2; p. (1971) 109,284.

Wigston, t., Leics., **Eng.**; 6 km S. of Leicester; engin., hosiery; p. (1971) 30,230.

Wigtown, l. gov. dist., former co., Dumfries and Galloway Reg., **Scot.**; along N. cst. of Solway F.; impt. dairying reg.; a. 1,712 km^2; p. (1971) 29,970.

Wigtown, sm. burgh, Wigtown, **Scot.**; on W. Bay, Solway F.; shares admin. with Newton Stewart; p. (1971) 1,118.

Wilhelmshaven, c., Lower Saxony, **W. Germany**; on inlet of N. Sea, 64 km N.W. of Bremen; ch. German naval base until 1945; industl. ctr. with heavy machin., elec. equipment, textiles, furniture; oil pipeline; p. (est. 1969) 102,700.

Wilkes-Barre, c., Penns., **USA**; on Susquehanna R.; industl. ctr. in rich anthracite mng. a.; p. (1970) 57,946 (c.), 124,238 (met. a.).

Wilkes Land, Antarctica; featureless plateau, alt. 2,900 m; immense glaciers; U.S. base taken over by Australia 1959.

Willamette, R., Ore., **USA**; rises in Cascade mtns., flows N. into Columbia R. below Portland; valley gives rich agr. land, wheat, root-crops, dairy prod., hard and soft fruits; ch. ts. Eugene, Salem, Oregon City, Portland; used for hydroelectric power; 480 km long.

Willemstad, pt., cap. of **Neth. Antilles**; on Curaçao I.; oil refining; tourism; p. (1964) 59,586.

Willenhall, t., West Midlands, **Eng.**; locks and keys, drop forgings.

Willesden, former M.B., Middx., **Eng.**; now inc. in Brent outer bor., Greater London impt. rly. junc., residtl. and indstl.

Williamsburg, c., Va., **USA**; between James and York Rs.; historic t., settled 1632; rebuilt in 1920s to original plan; in Colonial Nat. Historical Park; p. (1970) 9,069.

Williamsport, t., Penns., **USA**; on Susquehanna R.; rly. ctr., timber, machin.; summer resort; p. (1970) 37,918.

Williamstown, spt., sub. of Melbourne, Victoria, **Australia**; at mouth of Yarra R.; naval dockyards, shipbldg., railway wks.; p. (1966) 30,449.

Willington. *See* **Crook and Willington**.

Wilmington, t., spt., Del., **USA**; on Delaware R.; shipbldg., machin., iron- and steel-wks.; chemicals; leather, cork, rubber gds.; p. (1970) 79,978 (t.), 498,977 (met. a.).;

Wilmington, spt., N.C., **USA**; exp. cotton, tobacco, timber, fertilizers; shipbldg., textiles, chemicals; p. (1970) 45,067 (t.), 103,556 (met. a.).

Wilmslow, t., Cheshire, **Eng.**; on R. Bollen, 10 km S.W. of Stockport; residtl.; p. (1971) 28,982.

Wilton, t., Wilts., **Eng.**; on R. Wylye, 5 km W. of Salisbury; agr. mkt., carpets, felt; anc. cap. of Wessex; many old bldgs.; p. (1971) 3,815.

Wilton, industl. estate, Cleveland, **Eng.**; on S. side of Tees estuary; heavy organic- and petro-chemicals; nylon polymer plant.

Wiltshire, non-met. co., **Eng.**; crossed by chalk downland and Salisbury Plain; barley, wheat, dairying, pigs; co. t. Salisbury; a. 3,484 km^2; p. (1971) 486,048.

Wimbledon, dist., London, **Eng.**; lge. open common; site of international tennis tournament; part of London Bor. of Merton.

Wimborne Minster, mkt. t., Dorset, **Eng.**; on R. Stour; Roman site and home of Saxon kings; Badbury Rings earthworks nearby; p. (1971) 5,000.

Winchcomb, t., Gloucs., **Eng.**; nr. Cheltenham; old mills; pottery, paper; nearby cas.

Winchelsea, anc. t., East Sussex, **Eng.**; 3 km S.W. of Rye; once impt. walled spt. and Cinque port, now 3 km inland.

Winchester, cath. c., Hants., **Eng.**; on R. Itchen, 19 km N. of Southampton; anc. Anglo-Saxon cap.; meeting place of parliaments until time of Henry VII; magnificent cath., famous public school; p. (1971) 31,041.

Windermere, t., Cumbria, **Eng.**; on E. shore of L.; tourist ctr.; p. (1971) 8,063.

Windermere, lgst. English L., in Cumbria; outlet to Morecambe Bay; supplies water to Manchester; 16 km long, 1·6 km wide.

Windhoek, t., cap. of **South-West Africa**; in hills at 1,700 m; comm. ctr., agr. processing; tr. in karakul (Persian lamb); p. (1970) 61,260.

Windrush, R., Oxford, Gloucs., **Eng.**; trib. of R. Thames.

Windscale, Cumbria, **Eng.**; nuclear reactors for defence purposes and prod. of elec. for national grid.

Windsor, c., pt., Ont., **Canada**; on Detroit R., linked to Detroit, USA, by tunnel, bridge and ferry; ctr. for car mftg., salt wks., chemicals, paints; univ.; p. (1971) 199,784 (c.), 255,167 (met. a.).

Windsor, New, t., Berks., **Eng.**; on R. Thames 32 km W. of London; famous royal cas. (founded by William the Conqueror) and park, St. George's Chapel and the Royal Mausoleum; p. (1971) 30,065.

Windward Is., W.I., extend S. from Leeward Is.; consist of Fr. Martinique and former Brit. cols. of Grenada, St. Vincent, St. Lucia and Dominica with their dependencies (the Grenadines divided between Grenada and St. Vincent) which attained associated statehood 1967 ; sm. limited resources, economically depressed; volcanic.

Windward Passage, channel, 96 km wide, between Cuba and Haiti.

Winnebago, L., Wis., **USA**; 43 km long; lgst. L. in Wis.

Winnipeg, c., cap. of Manitoba, **Canada**; at junc. of Red and Assiniboine Rs.; cath., univ.; rly. ctr.; ch. world wheat mkt.; meat packing and food processing; lgst. garment mnf. ctr. in cty.; oil refining; p. (1971) 243,208 (c.), 534,685 (met. a.).

Winnipeg, L., Manitoba, **Canada**; 64 km N. of Winnipeg; 416 km long, 49–96 km wide; contains several lge. Is. (Reindeer, 181 km^2; Big I., 155 km^2;) used for hydroelectric power.

Winnipegosis, L., Manitoba and Saskatchewan, **Canada**; a. (exclusive of Is.) 5,180 km^2; 80 km W. of L. Winnipeg, into which it drains.

Winsford, t., Cheshire, **Eng.**; on R. Weaver; 6 km S. of Northwich; ctr. of salt inds., chemicals; expanded t.; p. (1971) 24,791.

Winston-Salem, t., N.C., **USA**; formed 1913 from union of 2 adjacent ts.; tobacco ctr.; p. (1970) 133,820.

Winterswijk, t., Gelderland, **Neth.**; textiles; p. (1968) 26,073.

Winterthur, t., Zurich, **Switzerland**; on Eulach R.; rly. ctr., locomotives, machines, cottons; p. (est. 1969) 94,200 (t.), 104,600 (met. a.).

Wiri, t., **N.Z.**; 24 km S. of Auckland; aluminium fabricating mill.

Wirksworth, t., Derbys., **Eng.**; in Pennines, 8 km S. of Matlock; limestone, fluorspar wks.; ctr. of Derbys. former lead-mng.; p. (1971) 5,151.

Wirral, penin., Merseyside, **Eng.**; between estuaries of Dee and Mersey; residtl.; p. (1971) 26,834.

Wisbech, t., Cambs., **Eng.**; on R. Nene, 18 km from its mouth in the Wash; mkt. gardening, fruit growing and canning, agr. implements; p. (1971) 17,002.

Wisconsin, st., **USA**; bounded by Gt. Ls.; low-lying; leading dairying st.; industl. ts. around Gt. Ls.; cap. Madison; ch. t. Milwaukee; a. 145,439 km^2. p. 1970 4,366,766.

Wisconsin, R., Wis., **USA**; trib. of R. Mississippi; used for hydroelectric power; 960 km long.

Wishaw. *See* **Motherwell**.

Wismar, spt., Rostock, **E. Germany**; on Baltic Sea, N. of Schwerin; oil pt. and industl. ctr. with shipyards and food processing inds.; p. (est. 1970) 56,057.

Witbank, t., Transvaal, **S. Africa**; leading coal-mng. dist. with power sta. and carbide and cyanide factories; p. (1970) 50,581.

Witham, t., Essex, **Eng.**; 14 km N.E. of Chelmsford; ctr. of mkt. gardening a.; expanded t.; p. (1971) 17,306.

Witham, R., Leics. and Lincs., **Eng.**; flows into the Wash; cuts impressive gap through Lincoln Edge at Lincoln; 128 km long.

Withernsea, t., Humberside, **Eng.**; on E. cst. 24 km E. of Hull; holiday resort; fishing; p. (1971) 5,976.

Withnell, t., Lancs., **Eng.**; at N. foot of Rossendale Fells, 5 km S.W. of Blackburn; textiles, stone, paper; p. (1971) 3,217.

Witney, t., Oxford, **Eng.**; on R. Windrush, 16 km W. of Oxford; woollens, blankets, gloves; p. (1971) 12,535.

Witten, t., N. Rhine-Westphalia, **W. Germany**; on R. Ruhr; glass, machin., metals, chemicals, optical inds.; p. (est. 1969) 97,472.

Wittenberg, t., Halle, **E. Germany**; on R. Elbe; ctr. of Reformation and burial place of Luther (Schlosskirche); cas.; machin., textiles; p. (est. 1970) 47,151.

Wittenberge, t., Schwerin, **E. Germany**; on R. Elbe; rly. junc., repair wkshps., machin.; p. (est. 1970) 33,028.

Witwatersrand, dist., Transvaal, **S. Africa**; gold-mng. dist. producing over quarter of world's gold.

Wivenhoe, t., Essex, **Eng.**; on R. Colne; boatbldg., oysters, lt. inds.; p. (1971) 5,310.

Wloclawek, t., pt., N. **Poland**; on R. Vistula; impt. paper mnfs., ceramics; p. (1970) 77,200.

Woburn, t., Beds., **Eng.**; 8 km N.E. of Leighton Buzzard; Woburn Abbey (seat of Dukes of Bedford).

Woking, t., Surrey, **Eng.**; 6 km N. of Guildford; residtl.; p. (1971) 75,771.

Wokingham, mkt. t., Berks., **Eng.**; 8 km S.E. of Reading; agr. tr. and machin., bricks; p. (1971) 21,051.

Wolds, The, chalk downland, Lincs., Humberside, **Eng.**; extend S. to E. Anglian heights; traditional pastoral agr. changing to extensive arable farming; 72 km long.

Wolfenbüttel, t., Lower Saxony, **W. Germany**; on R. Oker, 11 km S. of Brunswick; noted for ducal library, founded 17th cent., of which Leibnitz and Lessing were librarians; p. (est. 1969) 40,902.

Wolf Rock, isolated rock with lighthouse, at approach to English Channel from Bay of Biscay; 14 km S.W. of Lands End, Cornwall.

Wolsburg, t., Lower Saxony, **W. Germany**; on R. Aller, N.E. of Brunswick; Volkswagen wks.; p. (est. 1969) 88,024.

Wolin, I., Baltic Sea; off mouth of R. Oder, **Poland**; Nat. Park; fishing, tourism; a. 344 km^2; p. (est. 1966) 2,867.

Wollongong, Greater, t., N.S.W., **Australia**; coal mng., iron and steel wks., fertilisers, chemicals, bricks; inc. Port Kembla (*q.v.*); p. (1972) 160,902 (c.), 198,768 (met. a.).

Wolsingham, t., Durham, **Eng.**; on R. Wear; impt. steel wks.

Wolverhampton, t., West Midlands, **Eng.**; heavy and lt. engin., boilers, rayon, elec. engin. and apparatus, iron wks., aircraft and motor components, hollow-ware, tools, strongrooms and safes, paints; p. (1971) 268,874.

Wolverton, t., Bucks., **Eng.**; on R. Ouse, 24 km S.W. of Bedford; rly.-carriage wks.; p. (1971) 13,819.

Wombwell, t., South Yorks., **Eng.**; at E. foot of Pennines, 11 km N. of Sheffield; coal mng., bricks; p. (1971) 17,933.

Wonsan, spt., **N. Korea**; on Sea of Japan; major pt. and rly. ctr.; Japanese naval base in second world war; oil refining; p. (est. 1967) 300,000.

Woodbridge, t., Suffolk, **Eng.**; on R. Deben; engin., brush mkg.; p. (1971) 7,272.

Wood Green, former M.B., Middx., **Eng.**; now inc. in Haringey outer bor., Greater London.

Woodhall Spa, t., Lincs., **Eng.**; 6 km S.W. of Horncastle; former spa, bromoiodine springs; resort; p. (1971) 2,232.

Woodstock, t., Ont., **Canada**; on R. Thames; ctr. of agr. dist.; lt. mnfs. based on hydro-electric power; p. (1971) 25,559.

Woodstock, t., Oxford, **Eng.**; on Glyme R., 11 km N.W. of Oxford; glove mnfs.; Blenheim Palace; p. (1971) 1,940.

Wookey Hole, cave, Mendip Hills, Somerset, **Eng.**; at foot of limestone hills, 3 km N.W. of Wells; R. Axe emerges from the cave.

Woolwich, dist. former met. bor., London, **Eng.**; on either side of R. Thames; impt. Tudor dockyard, now closed; now part of Greenwich and Newham bors.

Woomera, S. **Australia**; *c.* 432 km N.W. of Adelaide; base for joint U.K.-Australian guided-weapon testing range extending N.W. across the continent; established 1947.

Woonsocket, t., R.I., **USA**; on Blackstone R.; textiles, rubber gds.; p. (1970) 46,820.

Worcester, Hereford and Worcs., **Eng.**; on R. Severn, 38 km N. of Gloucester; cath.; machin. porcelain, glove mkg.; birthplace of Elgar; p. (1971) 73,445.

Worcester, t., Cape Prov., **S. Africa**; viticultural and industl. ctr.; Goudini spa nearby; p. (1970) 175,140 (c.), 342,529 (met. a.).

Worcester, c., Mass., **USA**; univ.; cultural ctr.; machine tools, elec. engin.; p. (1970) 176,572.

Worcestershire, former Midland co., **Eng.**; now part of Hereford and Worcs. non-met. co. and West Midlands met. co.

Workington, t., Cumbria, **Eng.**; sm. spt. on Solway F. at mouth of Derwent R., first Bessemer steel plant, now heavily dependent upon iron and steel wks. (soon to close); industl. diversification on nearby industl. estates, inc. bus wks.; p. (1971) 28,414.

Worksop, t., Notts., **Eng.**; 24 km S.E. of Sheffield; coal-mng. dist.; brewing, knitwear, glass, flour; p. (1971) 36,034.

Worms, t., Rhineland-Palatinate, **W. Germany**; on left bank of Rhine; historic ctr.; famous imperial diet 1521 when Luther refused to retract; scene of *Nibelungenlied*; ctr. for Liebfraumilch wines; chemical, textile, leather and metal inds.; p. (est. 1969) 77,642.

Worms Head, promontory, on West Glamorgan cst., Gower peninsula, **Wales**.

Worsborough, t., South Yorks., **Eng.**; ctr. of coal-mng. dist.; p. (1971) 15,433.

Worsley, t., Gtr. Manchester, **Eng.**; ctr. of coal-mng. dist.; p. (1971) 49,573.

Worthing, t., West Sussex, **Eng.**; on S. cst., 16 km W. of Brighton; holiday resort, retirement ctr. in mkt. gardening dist.; p. (1971) 88,210.

Woy Woy, t., N.S.W., **Australia**; resort and commuter t. for Sydney; clothing; p. (1966) 16,264.

Wrangel I., Arctic Oc., off Khabarovsk terr., **RSFSR**; weather sta.

Wrath, C., N.W. Sutherland, **Scot.**

Wrekin, hill, Salop., **Eng.**; alt. 403 m.

Wrexham, t., Clwyd, **Wales**; 18 km S.W. Chester; tyres, synthetic fibres, clothing; p. (1971) 38,955.

Wroclaw (Breslau), c., Silesia, **Poland**; on R. Oder; impt. route ctr. and R. pt.; univ., cath.; rapid industl. development; ctr. of electronics inds.; p. (1970) 523,000.

Wroclaw (Breslau), prov., Lower Silesia, **Poland**; until 1945 part of Germany; heavy inds. based on local minerals; cap. Wroclaw; a. 24,740 km^2; p. (1970) 1,937,000.

Wroxeter, v., Salop, **Eng.**; on R. Severn, 8 km S.E. Shrewsbury; site of Roman c. of Uriconium.

Wuchang. *See* **Wuhan.**

Wuchow (Wuzhou), R. pt., Kwangsi prov., **China**; on R. Si; tr. ctr.; exp. tung oil, hides; p. (est. 1970) 150,000.

Wuhan, c., Hupeh prov., **China**; formed by union of Hankow, Hanyang, and Wuchang; major metropolis on R. Yangtze; integrated iron and steel wks., machine tools, walking tractors, textiles, shipbldg.; univ.; p. (est. 1970) 4,250,000.

Wuhu, c., Anhwei prov., **China**; former treaty pt. on R. Yangtze; textiles; p. (est. 1970) 300,000.

Wupper, R., **W. Germany**; trib. of Rhine; industl. concentration along middle course; 64 km long.

Wuppertal, t., N. Rhine-Westphalia, **W. Germany**; formed by amalgamation of Barmen and Elberfeld; textiles, rubber gds., paper, metals, pharmaceuticals; p. (est. 1969) 413,000.

Württemberg-Hohenzollern, former st., **W. Germany**; since 1952 part of Baden-Württemberg.

Würzburg, c., Bavaria, **W. Germany**; on R. Main; univ., cath.; historic bldgs., engin., chemicals, printing; p. (est. 1969) 120,100.

Wurzen, t., Leipzig, **E. Germany**; on R. Mulde; cath., cas.; machin., furniture, leather, foodstuffs; p. (est. 1970) 24,164.

Wusih (Wuxi), c., Kiangsu prov., **China**; on N. shore of Tai L., 120 km W. of Shanghai; univ.; industl. ctr. with cotton mills, chemical wks.; former treaty pt.; p. (est. 1970) 900,000.

Wutungkiao (Wutongqiao), c., Szechwan prov., **China**; 24 km S.E. of Loshan; p. (1953) 199,000.
Wyandotte, t., Mich., **USA**; on Detroit R.; salt deposits; chemical ind.; p. (1970) 41,061.
Wye, R., Bucks., **Eng.**; rises in Chiltern hills above High Wycombe, flows S.E. to R. Thames at Cookham.
Wye, R., Derbys., **Eng.**; trib. of R. Derwent; 32 km long.
Wye, R., **Eng.** and **Wales**; rises in Plynlimmon, flows S.E. into R. Severn at Chepstow; forms deeply incised valley at Symond's Yat; 208 km long.
Wye, t., Kent, **Eng.**; nr. Ashford; impt. agr. college (Univ. of London).
Wylfa Head, Anglesey, Gwynedd, **N. Wales**; nuclear power sta.
Wymondham, t., Norfolk, **Eng.**; 14 km S.W. of Norwich; mkt.; Benedictine abbey founded 1107; p. (1971) 8,510.
Wyoming, st., **USA**; inc. areas of Rocky mtns. and great plains; Yellowstone Nat. Park; scant rainfall; irrigation; cattle and sheep ranching; petroleum; sparse p.; cap. Cheyenne; a. 253,597 km²; p. (1970) 332,416.
Wyre, R., Lancs., **Eng.**; rises in Pennines, flows W. into Lancaster Bay at Fleetwood; 45 km long.

X

Xanthi, t., Thrace, **Greece**; on R. Mesta; ctr. of tobacco-growing a.; p. (1971) 25,341.
Xanthus, ruined c., **Turkey**; on R. Xanthus; destroyed 43 B.C.; tourism.
Xauen, t., **Morocco**, N. Africa; holy t. founded 15th cent.; p. (1960) 13,712.
Xingu, R., **Brazil**; trib. of Amazon; navigable in its lower course; 1,920 km long.

Y

Yablonovy, mtn. range, Siberia, **RSFSR**; E. of L. Baykal; highest peak, Sokhondo, 2,510 m; crossed by Trans-Siberian rly.
Yaila Mtns., Ukrainian SSR, **USSR**; form S.E. margin of Crimea penin., extend from Sevastopol to Kerch; form marked climate barrier between Black Sea littoral (Soviet Riviera) and N. part.
Yakima, t., Wash., **USA**; agr. ctr. of irrigated valley, noted for fruit; food processing; p. (1970) 45,588.
Yakima, R., Wash., **USA**; trib. of Columbia R.; used for irrigation; 333 km long.
Yakut ASSR, aut. rep., **RSFSR**; borders Arctic Oc.; home of Yakuts; tundra and forest region, isolated; fur trapping, diamond and gold mng., state farms; a. 3,963,355 km²; p. (1970) 664,000.
Yakutsk, t., cap. of Yakut ASSR, **RSFSR**; pt. on Lena R.; univ.; airport; p. (1970) 108,000.
Yallahs Valley, **Jamaica**; severe soil erosion; govt. improvement scheme of afforestation and new crops; a. 181 km².
Yallourn, t., Victoria, **Australia**; ctr. of lignite mng. a.; p. (1972) 20,764 inc. Moe.
Yalta, spt., Ukrainian SSR, **USSR**; sub-tropical resort on Black Sea, sheltered by Yaila mtns.; conference between Churchill, Roosevelt, and Stalin 1945; p. (est. 1969) 57,000.
Yalu, R., forms bdy. between N.E. China, and N. Korea; flows into Yellow Sea; used for hydroelectric power.
Yamagata, t., Honshu, **Japan**; ctr. of rice-growing a.; cas.; p. (est. 1971) 207,000.
Yamaguchi, t., cap. of Y. prov., S.W. Honshu, **Japan**; cas.; comm. ctr., chemicals; p. (est. 1971) 103,000.
Yamal-Nenets National Okrug, **RSFSR**; inc. Yamal penin.; permafrost; hunting, fishing; cap. Salekhard; lge. natural gas finds; a. 670,810 km²; p. (1970) 80,000.
Yambol, t., **Bulgaria**; on R. Tunja; ruined mosque; agr. tr.; recent inds. inc. canning, farm machin., textiles, ceramics; p. (est. 1968) 67,941.
Yamethin, dist., **Upper Burma**; teak forests, rice; ch. t. Yamethin; site of irrigation project; p. 9,291.
Yana, R., Siberia, **USSR**; flows into Arctic Sea; navigable; 1,600 km long.
Yangchow (Yangzhou), c., Kiangsu prov., **China**; on Grand Canal; agr. mkt. ctr., historic bldgs.; p. (est. 1970) 210,000.
Yangchuan (Yangqan), c., Shansi prov., **China**; ironworking ctr.; p. (1953) 177,000.
Yangi-yer, t., Uzbek SSR, **USSR**; founded 1957 as ctr. for new irrigated cotton lands of E. Uzbekistan.
Yangtze River, **China**; rises in plateau of Tibet, flows E. to E. China Sea, Pac. Oc., nr. Shanghai; traverses "Red Basin" of Szechwan, a deep gorge above Ichang, and finally a broad, level plain; many lge. cs. on its banks, Chungking, Ichang, Wuhan, Nanking, Chinkiang; navigable by ocean-going vessels 2,880 km to Ichang; total length 5,600 km.
Yaoundé, t., cap. of **Cameroon Rep.**, **W. Africa**; lt. inds. inc. beer, cigarettes, textiles; p. (est. 1969) 165,810 (met. a.).
Yap, I., Carolines, **Pac. Oc.**; US Atrusteeship; a. 205 km²; cable sta.; p. (1968) 6,761.
Yapura, R., **Brazil** and **Colombia**, S. America; trib. of R. Amazon; navigable for 960 km; length 2,400 km.
Yaracuy, st., **Venezuela**; crossed by Y. valley impt. agr. a. for bananas, coffee, sugar, tobacco; crossed by Pan-American Highway; cap. San Felipe; a. 7,099 km²; p. (est. 1970) 222,041.
Yare, R., Norfolk, **Eng.**; flows E. to N. Sea at Gorleston; forms part of Norfolk Broads navigable waterways; 80 km long.
Yarkand (Soche), c., Sinkiang prov., **China**; tr. ctr. in Y. oasis; tr. in wheat, rice, beans, fruit carpets, textiles; p. (est.) 60,000.
Yarkand, R., Sinkiang prov., **China**; trib. of Tarim R.; 800 km long.
Yarmouth, spt., Nova Scotia, **Canada**; fisheries; p. (1971) 8,291.
Yarmouth, par., I. of Wight, **Eng.**; on N.W. cst. 13 km W. of Newport; holiday resort, yachting.
Yarmouth, Great, pt., Norfolk, **Eng.**; at mouth of R. Yare; holiday resort; fish and food processing plants; base for N. Sea gas; p. (1971) 50,152.
Yaroslavl, c., cap. of Y. oblast, **RSFSR**; on upper Volga in Moscow industl. region; founded 1010; comm. and industl. ctr.; mnfs. inc. textiles, motor vehicles, synthetic rubber, agr. machin.; Volkov theatre, 12th cent. monastery, churches; p. (1970) 517,000.
Yasan, N., **Bulgaria**; lge. refinery and petrochemicals complex.
Yatsushiro, t., Kyushu, **Japan**; p. (est. 1971) 103,000.
Yawata. *See* **Kitakyushu**.
Yazd, c., Isfahan prov., **Iran**; in desert a. at 1,190 m; fine silks, carpets; p. (1967) 280,442 (met. a.).
Yazoo, dist., Miss., **USA**; flood plain of R. Mississippi and R. Yazoo; very fertile alluvial soil, but subject to disastrous floods; one of ch. cotton-growing dists. in USA.
Yegoryevsk, t., **RSFSR**; 115 km S.E. of Moscow; lge textile ind.; phosphorite deposits; p. (est. 1969) 65,000.
Yeletz, t., **RSFSR**; on R. Sosna; grain and cattle tr.; cultural ctr.; rly. junc.; p. (1970) 101,000.
Yell, I., Shetlands, **Scot.**; 27 km long; covered in peat moorland; p. (1971) 1,143.
Yellowhead Pass, B.C., Alberta, **Canada**; most N. and lowest of main passes across Rocky mtns.; carries Canadian Nat. rly. on route from Edmonton to Vancouver and Prince Rupert; summit alt. 1,130 m.
Yellowknife, t., N.W. Terr., **Canada**; on N. shore of Gr. Slave L.; ctr. of impt. gold-mng. dist.; linked by air to Edmonton, Alberta; p. (1966) 3,741.
Yellow R. *See* **Hwang-ho**.
Yellow Sea. *See* **Hwang-hai**.
Yellowstone, L., Wyo., **USA**; 32 km long, 24 km wide; alt. 2,360 m; in Y. Nat. Park.
Yellowstone National Park, N.W. Wyo., **USA**; volcanic scenery, geysers; a. 8,956 km².
Yemen Arab Republic (N. Yemen), S.W. Arabian penin.; climate hot and humid in semi-desert cst. strip; summer rainfall inland on high plateau; land slopes down in E. to desert of

Rub'al Khali; agr. basis of economy; irrigated, terraced, fertile land in highlands; millet, maize, sorghum, oats, fruits; Mocha coffee main exp.; expanding cotton a. in Tihama cst. a.; ch. spt. Hodeida; cap. Sana'a; proposed union with S. Yemen; a. 194,250 km²; p. (est. 1970) 5,728,000.

Yemen, People's Democratic Rep. of (S. Yemen), S.W. **Arabia**; comprises strategic pt. of Aden and much desert terr.; independence proclaimed 1967 when Brit. troops withdrawn; hot, dry climate; Brit. withdrawal, decline of tourism and closure of Suez Canal resulted in economic decline; subsistence agr., little comm. exploitation of rich fishing grounds; oil refinery at Aden; cap. Madinat ash Sha'b (N.W. of Aden); proposed union with N. Yemen; a. 290,274 km²; p. (est. 1970) 1,500,000.

Yenangyaung, t., R. pt., **Burma**; on left bank of R. Irrawaddy, 448 km N. of Rangoon; ctr. of Burma oilfields.

Yenisey, R., Siberia, **RSFSR**; rises in Sayan mtns., flows N. into Arctic Oc.; ch. tribs., Angara, Stony Tunguska, Lower Tunguska; hydroelectric power sta. at Krasnoyarsk; linked to Ob R. by canal; middle course navigable; 5,280 km long.

Yentai. *See* **Chefoo.**

Yeo or Ivel, R., Dorset, Somerset, **Eng.**; trib. of R. Parrett; 38 km long.

Yeovil, mkt. t., Somerset, **Eng.**; on R. Yeo; glove mnf., aero-engin., agr. machin., dairy processing; p. (1971) 25,492.

Yerevan or Erivan, c., cap. of Armenian SSR, **USSR**; on Zanga R. in deep valley of Caucasus mtns.; founded 8th cent. B.C.; major science-based, industl. ctr.; p. (1970) 767,000.

Yes Tor, second highest summit, Dartmoor, Devon, **Eng.**; 618 m.

Yevpatoriya or Eupatoria, spt., Crimea, on Black Sea, **USSR**; popular resort; children's sanatoria; chemicals, leather, locks, dried fish; new pt. being built; p. (est. 1969) 75,000.

Yezd. *See* **Yazd.**

Yiewsley and West Drayton, former. U.D., Middx., **Eng.**; now inc. in Hillingdon outer bor. Greater London; varied lt. inds.

Yinchwan, t., cap. of Ningsia aut. region, **China**; on Hwang-ho; ctr. of fertile agr. a.; new lt. inds.; p. (est. 1958) 91,000.

Yingkow (Ying-k'ou), c., Liaoning prov., N.E. **China**; 32 km upstream from mouth of Liao R.; soyabean prods.; p. (est. 1970) 215,000.

Yokkaichi, c., spt., S. Honshu, **Japan**; on Ise Bay, 37 km S. of Nagoya; textiles, petrochemicals, synthetic rubber, porcelain; p. (est. 1971) 231,000.

Yokohama, leading spt., Honshu, **Japan**; on W. shore of Tokyo Bay; steel, chemicals, cars, oil refining, shipyards; univs.; with Tokyo and Kawasaki forms conurb. of Keihin; p. (est. 1971) 2,342,000.

Yokosuka, spt., Honshu, **Japan**; S. of Tokyo; holiday resort; thermal power sta.; p. (est. 1971) 359,000.

Yonkers, c., N.Y., **USA**; on E. bank of Hudson R.; residtl.; lt. inds., textiles; p. (1970) 204,370; part of N.Y. met. a.

Yonne, dep., **France**; in S.E. of Paris basin, inc. Champagne, Burgundy, Orléanais; drained by R. Yonne; cap. Auxerre; agr., Chablis wines; a. 7,495 km²; p. (1968) 283,376.

Yonne, R., **France**; major trib. of R. Seine; 288 km long.

York, c., co. t., North Yorks., **Eng.**; on R. Ouse; in central position in Vale of York; anc. part of c. enclosed by walls; minster, cas., univ.; chocolate, confectionery, rly. wkshps.; p. (1971) 104,513.

York, c., Penn., **USA**; ctr. of fertile agr. region; varied inds., inc. agr. tools, machin., textiles metal gds.; p. (1970) 50,008 (c.), 326,482 (met. a.).

York, C., Queensland, **Australia**; most N. point on mainland of Australia.

York, Vale of, broad lowland, North Yorks., **Eng.**; between Pennines and N. Yorks. Moors and Yorks. Wolds; drained to Humber by R. Ouse and tribs.; glacial and alluvial soils have required draining; crop farming, wheat, barley, root-crops, associated with fattening of beef cattle; settlement mainly marginal; ch. t. York; length 96 km, width from 16 km in N. to 48 km in S.

Yorke, penin., S. **Australia**; separates Spencer G. and G. of St. Vincent; 160 km long, 48 km wide.

Yorkshire, former co., **Eng.**; formerly divided into 3 separate admin. parts (Ridings) N., E., and W.; now split into 3 non-met. cos., **Cleveland, North Yorks.,** and **Humberside** and 2 met. cos. **West Yorks.** and **South Yorks.**

Yorkshire Moors, hills North Yorks. and Cleveland, **Eng.**; inc. N. Yorks. Moors, Cleveland hills and Hambleton hills; bounded to N. by Tees valley, S. by vale of Pickering, W. by Swale valley. E. by sea; composed of oolitic limestone; gd. sheep pastures; impt. iron-ore deposits worked in Cleveland hills; max. alt. 454 m.

Yorkshire Wolds, hills, Humberside, **Eng.**; extend N.E. from Humber and terminate in Flamborough Head; chalk; gd. sheep pasture; average alt. 180 m.

Yorktown, v., Va., **USA**; scene of surrender by Lord Cornwallis to Washington 1781.

Yosemite National Park, Cal., **USA**; in Sierra Nevada; contains Yosemite creek and canyon with three famous cataracts.

Yoshkar-Ola, t., Mari ASSR, **RSFSR**; 128 km N.W. of Kazan; cultural ctr.; wood processing, food inds.; p. (1970) 166,000.

Youghal, spt., U.D., Cork, **R.o.I.**; on estuary of the Blackwater; resort; p. (1966) 5,098.

Youngstown, c., Ohio, **USA**; on Mahoning R.; 91 km N.W. of Pittsburgh; ctr. of one of most impt. iron and steel dists. in USA; heavy engin.; univ.; p. (1970) 139,905 (c.), 533,080 (met. a.).

Yoyang, t., Hunan prov., **China**; at outlet of Tung Ting L. on bank of R. Yangtze; p. 4,800.

Ypres (Ieper), t., W. Flanders prov., N.W. **Belgium**; textiles and textile machin.; ctr. of cloth ind. in middle ages; scene of battles 1914–17; p. (1969) 18,447.

Ypsilanti, t., Mich., **USA**; on Huron R.; residtl., agr. mkt., mnfs.; univ.; p. (1970) 29,538.

Ystwyth, R., Dyfed, **Wales**; flows 40 km to join R. Rheidol at Aberystwyth.

Yuan, R., N.W. Hunan prov., **China**; flows into Tung Ting L. and Yangtze R.; rapids; 640 km long.

Yucatán, st., S.E. **Mexico**; limestone lowlands, poor soils; henequen (sisal hemp), chicle (resin from which chewing gum is made); cap. Mérida; a. 61,968 km²; p. (1969) 817,000.

Yugoslavia, Socialist Fed. Rep., S.E. **Europe**; comprises reps. of Serbia, Croatia, Macedonia, Montenegro, Slovenia, Bosnia, Hercegovina, and aut. regions of Kosovo and Vojvodina; long W. cst. on Adriatic Sea with well-developed limestone karstic topography; hilly interior; climate Mediterranean on cst., continental in interior; distinctive political development after second world war; refused to accept Soviet hegemony; well-developed links with W.; with major attempts to industrialise, based on energy, heavy and consumer inds. less p. engaged in agr.; economic decision-making increasingly freed from central control; developing tourist tr., especially with countries of W. Europe, based on climate and attractive Adriatic littoral, with many sm. Is.; cap. Belgrade; a. 255,698 km²; p. (1971) 21,500,000.

Yukon, R., **Canada** and Alaska, **USA**; flows N.W. and W. into Bering Strait; navigable for 1,920 km; 3,200 km long.

Yukon Territory, prov., N.W. **Canada**; mtnous. (Mt. Logan 6,050 m); gold, silver, lead, zinc; Alaska Highway links with B.C. and Alberta; ch. ts. Dawson, and Whitehorse (cap.); a. 536,327 km²; p. (1971) 18,388.

Yuma, t., Arizona, **USA**; at confluence of Rs. Gila and Colorado, nr. Mexican bdr.; ctr. of irrigated agr. region; p. (est. 1969) 29,000.

Yumen, c., N.W. Kansu prov., **China**; leading petroleum ctr.; drilling equipment, precision instruments; on Old Silk Road to Sinkiang; p. (est. 1970) 325,000.

Yunnan, prov., S. **China**; adjoins Burma; mtnous. a. of minority groups; rice, tobacco, tea, cotton; copper, tin; cap. Kunming; a. 420,466 km²; p. (est. 1968) 23,000,000.

Yuzhno-Sakhalinsk, t., **RSFSR**; at S. end of Sakhalin I.; paper, lt. inds.; p. (1970) 106,000.

Yvelines, new dep., **France**; W. of Paris; cap. Versailles; a. 2,271 km²; p. (1968) 853,386.

Yverdon, t., Vaud, **Switzerland**; typewriters; p. (1969) 20,700.

Z

Zaandam, t., **Neth.**; industl. dist.; rly. junc.; timber-based inds.; p. (1968) 58,312.

Zabrze, t., Upper Silesia, Katowice, **Poland**; impt. coal-mng. ctr. with associated heavy inds.; cultural ctr.; p. (1970) 197,200.

Zacapa, t., cap. of Z. prov., **Guatemala**; mkt. t. at rly. junc.; tobacco tr. and processing; sulphur springs; p. (1964) 30,187.

Zacatecas, st., **Mexico**; on central plateau at 2,100 m; dry, agr. dist.; sm. mng. ctrs.; a. 72,836 km²; p. (1969) 1,082,000.

Zacatecas, t., cap. of Z. st., **Mexico**; cath.; ctr. of silver mng., pottery, clothing; p. (1970) 56,829.

Zacatecoluca, t., **El Salvador**; cigar mkg., hand looms; coffee, cotton, sugar, vanilla in a.; p. (est. 1968) 15,776.

Zadar (Zara), t., **Yugoslavia**; spt. on Croatian cst. of Adriatic Sea; formerly Italian (1920–47); Roman remains; cath.; car ferry to Pesaro (Italy); tourism; p. (est. 1965) 31,000.

Zagan (Sagan), t., Zielona Gora, **W. Poland** (since 1945); on R. Bober; cas.; textiles, paper, lignite mines; p. (1970) 21,500.

Zagazig, t., **Egypt**; on Nile delta; tr. ctr. of fertile agr. a. producing cotton, grains; cotton mills; p. (est. 1970) 173,300.

Zagorsk, c., **RSFSR**; 70 km N.E. of Moscow; woodcarving, toy mkg.; site of famous Troitse-Sergiyeva Lavra monastery, converted into museum 1920; p. (est. 1967) 85,000.

Zagreb, c., **Yugoslavia**; cap. of Croatia; on Sava R.; cath., univ.; tr. fair; many inds., notably petrochemicals based on local petroleum reserves, elec. engin.; airport; second c. of rep.; p. (est. 1969) 565,000.

Zagros, mtns., **Iran**; inc. Iran's major oilfield; highest peak Zardesh Kuh, 4,551 m.

Zahedan, c., **Iran**; cap. of Sistan and Baluchistan prov.; airport; terminus of rly. from Pakistan; p. (1967) 79,257.

Zahle, t., **Lebanon**, S.W. Asia; on slopes of L. mtn.; p. (est. 1964) 57,589.

Zaïre, Rep. of, Central **Africa**; comprises eight provs. (caps. in brackets): Bas-Zaïre (Matadi), Bandundu (Bandundu), Equateur (Mbandaka), Haut-Zaïre (Kisangani), Kivu (Bukavu), Shaba (Lubumbashi), Kasai Oriental (Mbuji-Mayi), Kasai Occidental (Kananga); lies in vast basin of Zaïre R., mtns. on E. and S. borders; climate equatorial in N., tropical in S.; agr. exp. inc. palm oil, cotton, coffee, but economy based on mng., diamonds (Kasai), cobalt, non-ferrous metals (Shaba), major world producer of copper; radium deposits nr. Lubumbashi; extensive navigation on Zaïre R.; main pt. Matadi on estuary, linked by rail to cap. Kinshasa; a. 2,345,457 km²; p. (1971) 22,480,000.

Zaïre, gr. R. of **Equatorial Africa**; numerous tribs., drains 3,885,000 km²; navigable from sea to Matadi for ocean steamers, from Matadi to Pool Malebo interrupted by rapids and falls, again navigable to Boyoma Falls; proposed power project to be lgst. in Africa; estuary 11–16 km wide; *c.* 4,800 km long.

Zakinthos (Zante), Ionian I., **Greece**; cap. Zakinthos (Zante); devastated by earthquake 1953; currants, wine, olives; a. 717 km²; p. (1971) 30,156.

Zakinthos (Zante), t., Zakinthos I., **Greece**; spt. on E. cst.; agr. tr. and processing; p. (1971) 30,156.

Zakopane, t., **Poland**; in High Tatra mtns.; base for mountaineering and winter sports; health resort; tourism; p. (1970) 27,000.

Zalaegerszeg, t., **Hungary**; in Göcsej dist.; oil refining; mkt. t. for grain and livestock; p. (1968) 32,000.

Zambesi, R., S.E. **Africa**; flows E. to Moçambique Channel, Indian Oc.; forms frontier between Zambia and Rhodesia; inc. Victoria Falls and Kariba and Cabora Bassa dams; navigable but impeded by rapids; 3,520 km long.

Zambia, rep., **Central Africa**; member of Commonwealth; tropical climate, modified by alt.; plateau (1,200 m); subsistence agr.; livestock on uplands free from tsetse fly; mng. basis of economy, especially in copperbelt; exp. disrupted by Rhodesian U.D.I.; need to develop alternative routes to cst.; pipeline from Ndola to Dar-es-Salaam; construction of Tan-Zam rly. financed by Chinese aid; cap. Lusaka; a. 752,618 km²; p. (1969) 4,056,995.

Zamboanga, t., Mindanao, **Philippines**; spt. on Basilian Strait, exp. prod. timber; p. (est. 1968) 176,800 (met. a.).

Zamora, prov., **Spain**; borders Portugal; drained by R. Duero; cereals, wine, merino sheep; cap. Zamora; a. 10,559 km²; p. (1970) 251,934.

Zamora, t., cap. of Zamora prov., **Spain**; on R. Duero; cath.; agr. tr. and processing ctr.; developing mnfs.; p. (1970) 49,029.

Zamosc, t., Lublin, **Poland**; Renaissance planned t. in valley of Lubianka R.; industl., comm. and cultural ctr. for E. part of Lublin prov.; p. (1970) 34,700.

Zanesville, t., Ohio, **USA**; textiles, pottery, machin.; p. (1970) 33,045.

Zanjan, c., **Iran**; cap. of Gilan prov.; cotton, woollen gds.; p. (1966) 82,350 (c.); p. (1967) 461,588 (met. a.).

Zanzibar, terr., E. **Africa**; comprises Is. of Z. and Pemba; joined Tanganyika to form **Tanzania** (1964); major world source of cloves; coconut and coconut prod. major exp. and basis of processing inds.; cap. Zanzibar; a. 2,642 km²; p. (1969) 369,000.

Zanzibar, spt., Zanzibar I., **Tanzania**; on W. cst. 35 km from E. Africa; outlet for clove exp., extrepot tr.; former slave mkt.; p. (1967) 68,400.

Zaporozh'ye, t., Ukrainian SSR, **USSR**; on R. Dnieper, nr. dam and hydroelec. power sta.; metal inds. based on Donets coal and Krivoi Rog iron ore; p. (1970) 658,000.

Zaragoza, prov., **Spain**; largely barren plain suffering from climatic extremes; a. 17,122 km² cap. Z.; p. (1970) 760,186.

Zaragoza, cap. Z. prov., **Spain**; on R. Ebro; 2 caths., univ.; former cap. of Aragon; rly. junc.; comm. ctr.; p. (est. 1969) 387,529.

Zarate, t., Entre Rios, **Argentina**; paper wks., agr. ctr., meat packing; p. (1960) 52,000.

Zaria, c., **N. Nigeria**; founded 15th cent., old part surrounded by walls; univ., cotton ctr.; rly. ctr., p. (est. 1971) 200,850.

Zary (Sorau), t., Zielona Gora, **Poland** (since 1945); textiles; p. (1970) 28,400.

Zawiercie, t., **Poland**; industl. ctr.; coal, iron, textiles, glass; p. (1970) 39,400.

Zdunska Wola, t., **Poland**; nr. Lodz; textiles, engin.; p. (1970) 29,100.

Zealand. *See* **Sjaelland.**

Zeebrugge, spt., **Belgium**; 14 km N. of Bruges; exp. coal, chemicals; oil refining; linked by canal to Bruges.

Zeeland, prov., **Neth.**; a. covering part of Scheldt estuary and Is.; low-lying; dairying; cap. Middelburg; a. 1,787 km²; p. (1968) 298,457.

Zeist, t., Utrecht, **Neth.**; chemicals, toys; p. (1968) 55,950.

Zeitz, t., Halle, **E. Germany**; textiles, chemicals; p. (est. 1970) 46,736.

Zelenodolsk, t., **RSFSR**; on R. Volga, 40 km W. of Kazan; rly. junc.; sawmills; p. (est. 1969) 76,000.

Zelten, **Libya**, N. Africa; oilfield; 320 km S. of Benghazi; pipeline to Mersa al-Brega.

Zenica, t., **Yugoslavia**; lge. iron and steel wks.; ctr. of Z. basin; rly. junc.; p. (est. 1965) 54,000.

Zeravshan, R., Tadzhik SSR and Usbek SSR, **USSR**; flows for 736 km before evaporating in desert region N. of Chardzhou.

Zetland. *See* **Shetland.**

Zgierz, t., Lodz. prov., central **Poland**; nr. source of R. Bzura; textiles, chemicals, textile machin.; p. (1970) 42,800.

Zhdanov (Mariupol), spt., S.E. Ukrainian SSR, **USSR**; on Sea of Azov; metallurgical ctr., chemicals; fishing and fish-processing; p. (1970) 417,000.

Zhitomir, t., Ukrainian SSR, **USSR**; engin., clothing; route ctr.; p. (1970) 161,000.

Zielona Gora (Grünberg), c., **W. Poland** (since 1945); in valley surrounded by wooded hills; admin. and industl. ctr., cap. of Z.G. prov.;

textiles, food processing, machin.; viticulture; p. (1970) 73,200.
Zielona Gora, prov., **Poland**; borders E. Germany; glacial sands, wooded; brown coal deposits; cap. Z.G.; a. 14,514 km²; p. (1970) 882,000.
Ziguinchor, t., **Senegal**; pt. on R. Casamance; exp. groundnuts; p. (est. 1967) 46,333.
Zilina, t., **Slovakia, ČSSR**; on R. Vah; paper, fertilisers; p. (1967) 39,000.
Zimbabwe National Park, Rhodesia; site nr. Victoria, Mashonaland, of ruined t. built c. 15th cent. A.D. by a Bantu people; discovered 1868.
Zinder, t., **Niger, W. Africa**; terminus of trans-Saharan motor route; tr. ctr.; former cap.; second t. of Niger; p. (est. 1969) 32,905.
Zion National Park, Utah, USA; contains Z. canyon; a. 596 km².
Zipaquirá, t., **Colombia**; 48 km N. of Bogotá; salt mng., chemicals; cattle-rearing a.; p. (est. 1968) 28,812.
Zistersdorf, t., **Lower Austria**; recently developed oilfields.
Zittau, t., Dresden, **E. Germany**; on R. Mandau; woollens, linens, machin., cars, chemicals; p. (est. 1970) 43,087.
Zlatoust, t., S.W. **RSFSR**; in Ural mtns.; metallurgical ctr.; steel, chemicals, sawmilling; p. (1970) 181,000.
Zletovo, terr., N.E. Macedonia, **Yugoslavia**; oil shales, lead, zinc deposits.
Zlin. *See* **Gottwaldov**.
Znojmo or **Znaim**, t., **ČSSR**; anc. t., cas.; ctr. of fertile agr. dist.; p. (est. 1968) 25,732.
Zomba, t., former cap. of **Malawi**, 884 m a.s.l. on slopes of Zomba mtn., 67 km N.E. Blantyre; Malawi's univ. t.; p. (1966) 19,616.
Zonguldak, t., **Turkey**; spt. on Black Sea; coal-mng. a.; p. (1965) 60,865.
Zorita De Los Canos, Guadalajara, **Spain**; on R. Tagus; nuclear power plant.
Zrenjanin, t., Vojvodina, **Yugoslavia**; pt. on R. Begej; ctr. of agr. dist.; agr. processing; p. (1971) 59,580.
Zug, smallest can., **Switzerland**; drained by R. Reuss; contains part of L. Z.; dairying, fruit; cap. Z.; a. 241 km²; p. (1969) 66,700.
Zug, t., cap. of Zug can., **Switzerland**; on L. Z.; elec. engin., printing; p. (1969) 23,400.
Zugspitze, mtn., Bavarian Alps, on Bavarian-Austrian bdr.; highest peak in Germany, 2,965 m; connected by rack-and-pinion to Garmisch-Partenkirchen at foot.
Zuider Zee. *See* **IJsselmeer**.
Zulia, st., **Venezuela**; centred on L. Maracaibo, producing 70 per cent of Venezuelan oil; timber reserves; cap. Maracaibo; a. 63,902 km² p. (est. 1970) 1,342,994.
Zululand, Bantu homeland, Natal, **S. Africa**; sugar on coastal plain, livestock on interior plateau; cap. Eshowe; a. 27,006 km²; p. (1970) 2,106,774.
Zürich, c., cap. of Z. can, **Switzerland**; on L. Z. and R. Limmat; cath., univ.; leading world banking ctr.; inds. inc. textiles, paper; p. (est. 1969) 433,500 (c.), 671,500 (met. a.).
Zürich, can., **Switzerland**; forested and agr. a. stretching N. from L. Z.; inds. at cap. Z. and Winterthur; a. 1,728 km²; p. (1969) 1,100,000.
Zürich, L. Z., Switzerland; drained by R. Limmat; length 40 km.
Zutphen, t., Gelderland, **Neth.**; on R. Ijssel; textiles, paper; Sir Philip Sidney died here 1586; p. (1968) 27,290.
Zuetina, oil pt. (1968), **Libya**; pipeline links shore storage sta. with offshore berths.
Zweibrücken, t., Rhineland-Palatinate, **W. Germany**; nr. Saarbrücken; cas.; machin., footwear, textiles; p. (est. 1969) 32,914.
Zwickau, c., Karl-Marx-Stadt, **E. Germany**; on R. Mulde; cas.; coal, motors, machin., textiles; birthplace of Schumann; p. (est. 1969) 127,500.
Zwolle, t., Overijssel, **Neth.**; canal ctr.; cattle, mkt.; p. (1968) 73,253.
Zyrardow, t., **Poland**; nr. Warsaw; specialised textile ctr.; p. (1970) 33,200.
Zyryanovsk, t., Kazakh SSR, **USSR**; lead, zinc; p. (est. 1969) 56,090.

THE WORLD'S LARGEST CITIES

New York	(1971) 7,895,000 (c.), (1970) 11,572,000 (met. a.).
Tokyo	(est. 1971) 8,841,000 (c.), 11,403,744 (met. a.).
Shanghai	(est. 1971) 10,820,000.
Mexico City	(1970) 6,874,165 (c.), 8,589,630 (met. a.).
Buenos Aires	(1970) 2,972,453 (c.), 8,352,900 (met. a.).
Peking	(est. 1971) 7,570,000.
London	(1971) 4,234 (City of London), 7,379,014 (met. a.).
Moscow	(1970) 6,942,000 (c.), 7,061,000 (met. a.).
Los Angeles	(1970) 2,781,829 (c.), 6,974,103 (met. a.).
Chicago	(1970) 3,322,855 (c.), 6,892,509 (met. a.).
Bombay	(1971) 5,970,575.
Seoul	(est. 1971) 5,536,000.
Cairo	(est. 1974) 5,384,000.
São Paulo	(1970) 5,186,752.
Philadelphia	(1970) 1,927,863 (c.), 4,777,414 (met. a.).
Djakarta	(1971) 4,576,009.
Tientsin	(est. 1970) 4,280,000.
Rio de Janeiro	(1970) 4,252,009.
Detroit	(1970) 1,429,914 (c.), 4,163,517 (met. a.).
Delhi	(1971) 3,287,883 (c.), 3,647,023 (met. a.).

The cities shown above are ranked according to the size in terms of population of their metropolitan area.

SOME RECENT CHANGES IN PLACE NAMES

Country	Former name	New Name
Algeria	Algiers	El Djezair
	Oran	Ouahran
Belize	British Honduras	Belize
Benin	Dahomey	People's Rep. of Benin
Botswana	Gaberones	Gaborone
Cambodia	Khmer Republic	Democratic Cambodia
	Kompong Som	Sihanoukville
Canada	Port Arthur, Port William	Thunder Bay
Chad	Fort Lamy	Ndjamene
Equatorial Guinea	Fernando Po	Marcias Nguema
	Annobon	Pagalu Island
	Santa Isabel	Malabo
France	Basses-Alpes	Alpes-de-Haute-Provence
Gambia	Bathurst	Banjul
Guinea-Bissau	Portuguese Guinea	Guinea-Bissau
India	North-East Frontier Agency	Arunachal Pradesh
	Mysore	Karnataka
Indonesia	Makasar	Ujung Pandang
	Port Timor	E. Timor
Laos	Kingdom of Laos	People's Dem. Rep. of Laos
Malaysia	Port Swettenham	Port Kelang
Mocambique	Lourenço Marques	Maputo
Morocco	Casablanca	El-Dar-el-Beida
Nigeria	Mid West st.	Benin st.
	Northern st.	Kaduna st.
Oman	Muscat and Oman	Sultanate of Oman
Pakistan	East Pakistan	Bangladesh
Solomon Is.	Brit. Solomon Is.	Solomon Is.
Turkey	Imbroz I.	Gokceade I.
Uganda	Lake Edward	Lake Idi Amin Dada
	Murchison Falls	Kabelega Falls
United Kingdom	Conway	Conwy
	Portmadoc	Porthmadog
Vietnam	N. Vietnam, S. Vietnam	Vietnam
	Saigon	Ho Chi-Minh City
West Africa	Bight of Biafra	Bight of Bonny
W. Pacific High Commission	Gilbert and Ellice Is.	Gilbert Is.
	Ellice Is.	Tuvalu Is.
Western Sahara	Spanish Sahara	Western Sahara
Zaïre	Congolese Republic	Republic of Zaïre
	Congo River	Zaïre River
	Katanga	Shaba
	Lake Albert	Lake Mobutu Seso
Zambia	Stanley Falls	Boyoma Falls

METRIC CONVERSION TABLE

Kilometres		Miles	Square Kilometres		Square Miles
16·09	10	6·21	25·90	10	3·86
32·19	20	12·43	51·80	20	7·72
48·28	30	18·64	77·70	30	11·58
64·37	40	24·85	103·60	40	15·44
80·47	50	31·07	129·50	50	19·30
96·56	60	37·28	155·40	60	23·17
112·66	70	43·50	181·30	70	27·03
128·75	80	49·71	207·20	80	30·89
144·84	90	55·92	233·10	90	34·75
160·94	100	62·14	259·00	100	38·61

THE COMMONWEALTH

The British Commonwealth of Nations is a free association of independent member nations and their dependencies. The political status of the member nations listed below is clarified and given legal substance in the *Statute of Westminster* drawn up in 1931, before the Commonwealth was founded, by the United Kingdom, Canada, Australia and New Zealand.

I. MEMBERS OF THE COMMONWEALTH

Original date of membership	Country	Land area (km²)	Population[1]
1931	United Kingdom	244,022	55,347,000 (1971) C
	Canada	9,976,185	21,324,000 (1970)
	Australia, Commonwealth of	7,686,884	12,713,000 (1970)
	Antarctic Territory	6,044,086	—
	Christmas Island	161	3,361 (1970)
	Cocos (Keeling) Island	13	611 (1970)
	Norfolk Island	34	1,240 (1970)
	New Zealand	268,676	2,860,475 (1971) C
	Cook Islands	241	24,000 (1970)
	Island Territories (Niue, Tokelau)	502	6,871 (1970) C
	Ross Dependency	414,400	262 (1966) C
1947	India, Republic of	3,268,580	586,060,000 (1974) C
1948	Sri Lanka, Republic of	65,610	12,514,000 (1970)
1957	Ghana, Republic of	238,539	8,545,561 (1970) C
1960	Nigeria, Federal Republic of	923,773	66,174,000 (1970)
1961	Cyprus, Republic of	9,251	633,000 (1970)
	Sierra Leone, Republic of	72,326	2,500,000 (1970)
1962	Jamaica	11,424	1,861,300 (1970)
	Trinidad and Tobago, Republic of	5,128	1,044,000 (1970)
	Uganda, Republic of	235,887	9,764,000 (1970)
1963	Kenya, Republic of	582,646	10,898,000 (1970)
	Malaysia, Federation of	334,110	10,434,034 (1970) C
1964	Malawi, Republic of	117,614	4,530,000 (1970)
	Malta, Republic of	316	326,000 (1970)
	Tanzania, United Republic of	939,706	13,273,000 (1970)
	Zambia, Republic of	752,618	4,295,000 (1970)
1965	Gambia, Republic of	10,368	374,000 (1970)
	Singapore, Republic of	580	2,074,507 (1970)
1966	Barbados	429	238,141 (1970) C
	Botswana, Republic of	574,980	648,000 (1970)
	Guyana, Cooperative Republic of	214,970	721,098 (1970)
	Lesotho	30,344	1,043,000 (1970)
1968	Mauritius	2,038	834,000 (1970)
	Nauru (limited membership)	21	6,664 (1970)
	Swaziland	17,363	451,000 (1970)
1970	Fiji	18,272	513,000 (1970)
	Tonga	699	87,000 (1970)
	Western Samoa	2,841	143,000 (1970)
1972	Bangladesh, Republic of	142,776	65,000,000 (1970)
1973	Bahamas	11,406	168,838 (1970) C
1974	Grenada	344	104,000 (1970)
1975	Papua New Guinea	461,693	2,522,890 (1970)
1976	Seychelles, Republic of	430	52,000 (1970)

[1] Estimates: those countries with recent census figures, indicated by a C.

II. TERRITORIES FOR WHICH THE U.K. IS RESPONSIBLE AND WHICH ARE ADMINISTERED BY A DEPARTMENT WITHIN THE FOREIGN AND COMMONWEALTH OFFICE

(Some of the very small, or practically uninhabited islands, have been omitted)

Territory	Political Status	Land Area km²	Population[1]
Anguilla	Former W.I. Ass. St., under direct Brit. rule since July 1971	91	6,000 (1971)
Antigua	W.I. Ass. St.	440	65,000 (1970)
Bermuda	Colony (internal self-gov.)	54	52,700 (1970) C
British Antarctic Territory	Colony	1,222,500	—
Belize	Colony (internal self-gov.)	22,962	119,645 (1970) C
British Indian Ocean Territories	Colony	75	2,000 (1970)
British Virgin Islands	Colony (internal self-gov.)	153	10,500 (1970) C
Brunei	Protected St.	15,765	121,000 (1970)
Cayman Islands	Colony	259	10,652 (1970) C
Dominica	W.I. Ass. St.	751	70,300 (1970) C
Falkland Islands	Colony	12,173	2,000 (1970)
S. Georgia	Falkland Islands dependency	3,755	11
S. Sandwich Islands	Falkland Islands dependency	337	—
Gibraltar	City	6·5	28,964 (1970)
Hong Kong	Colony	1,031	3,950,802 (1971) C
Montserrat	Colony	101	12,302 (1970) C
New Hebrides	Anglo-French Condominium	14,763	86,084 (1971)
Pitcairn Islands	Colony	5	80 (1970)
Rhodesia	Colony (internal self-gov.)[2]	389,329	5,310,000 (1970)
St. Helena	Colony	122	5,000 (1970)
Ascension	St. Helena dependency	88	1,266 (1969)
Tristan da Cunha	St. Helena dependency	111	280 (1970)
St. Kitts-Nevis	W.I. Ass. St.	262	45,457 (1970)
St. Lucia	W.I. Ass. St.	616	101,100 (1970) C
St. Vincent	W.I. Ass. St.	389	96,000 (1970)
Turks & Caicos Islands	Colony	404	6,000 (1970)
W. Pac. High Commission Terrs.:			
Solomon Is.	Protectorate	29,875	160,998 (1970) C
Gilbert Is.	Colony	813	50,000(1975)
Tuvalu Is.		30	7,000 (1975)

[1] Estimates: those territories with recent census figures, indicated by a C.
[2] Illegal declaration of independence 11 November 1965.

LOCAL GOVERNMENT REORGANISATION IN THE UNITED KINGDOM

In the spirit of the reorganisation of local government, the maps (6–7) and gazetteer now incorporate only the newly created local government units. This means that the distinction between the *administrative* counties (*e.g.*, Lancashire), which included all land within the county boundaries but excluded the administratively separate county boroughs (*e.g.*, Bolton), and the *geographical* counties, which were made up of both administrative counties and the county boroughs, has been discontinued.

In making their proposals for local government reform the Redcliffe Maud Commission (*see* **Local Government, Section C, Part I**) considered that the division between administrative counties and county boroughs, originally instituted in 1888, created an entirely artificial barrier to the planning and provision of services for city regions (*see* **K2**). This consideration gave rise to the concept of unitary local authorities, but despite the subsequent amalgamation of boroughs and county districts and the creation of metropolitan counties the old two-tier system was preserved by the Local Government Act 1972.

The new local government structure resulting from these proposals means the disappearance of certain geographical counties (*e.g.*, Pembroke and Rutland), the appearance of completely new counties (*e.g.*, Avon and Gwynedd) and the modification of former counties (*e.g.*, Glamorgan and Yorkshire). Details of the changes are listed below.

Within the gazetteer the population figures for places now stripped of major administrative status (*e.g.*, the former County Borough of Manchester, which now becomes a metropolitan district within the new metropolitan county of Greater Manchester), relate to the former areas of the administrative units.

ENGLAND

Under the Local Government Act 1972, the English counties now number 45. They are divided into 6 metropolitan counties (met. co.) and 39 non-metropolitan counties (non-met. co.).

Metropolitan Counties

Greater Manchester
Merseyside
South Yorkshire
Tyne and Wear
West Midlands
West Yorkshire

Non-Metropolitan Counties

Avon
Bedfordshire
Berkshire
Buckinghamshire
Cambridgeshire
Cheshire
Cleveland
Cornwall
Cumbria
Derbyshire
Devon
Dorset
Durham
East Sussex
Essex
Gloucestershire
Hampshire
Hereford and Worcester
Hertfordshire
Humberside
Isle of Wight
Kent
Lancashire
Leicestershire
Lincolnshire
Norfolk
North Yorkshire
Northamptonshire
Northumberland
Nottinghamshire
Oxfordshire
Salop
Somerset
Staffordshire
Suffolk
Surrey
Warwickshire
West Sussex
Wiltshire

WALES

The distinction between metropolitan and non-metropolitan counties does not apply to Wales. The new Welsh counties created by the 1972 Act now number 8.

Clwyd
Dyfed
Gwent
Gwynedd
Mid Glamorgan
Powys
South Glamorgan
West Glamorgan

NORTHERN IRELAND

Under the Local Government (Boundaries) Act (Northern Ireland) 1971 the 6 counties and one county borough have been replaced by 26 local government districts (l. gov. dist.).

Antrim
Ards
Armagh
Ballymena
Ballymoney
Banbridge
Belfast
Carrickfergus
Castlereagh
Coleraine
Cookstown
Craigavon
Down
Dungannon
Fermanagh
Larne
Limavady
Lisburn
Londonderry
Magherafelt
Moyle
Newry and Mourne
Newtownabbey
North Down
Omagh
Strabane

SCOTLAND

Local government reorganisation in Scotland came fully into force in May 1975 (a year later than the local government reforms in England and Wales and Northern Ireland). The Scottish counties have disappeared and been replaced by nine Regions (Highland, Grampian, Tayside, Fife, Lothian, Central, Borders, Strathclyde, and Dumfries and Galloway) each sub-divided into districts, together with three Island Areas of Orkney, Shetland and the Western Isles. These changes are reflected in the current edition.

SOME ASPECTS OF THE SOCIAL STRUCTURE OF THE WORLD ECONOMY

The most fundamental characteristic of the world economy is the gross inequality in economic power and income which exists between different nations and groups of nations. *See* **Section G, Part III.**

One measure of this is shown in the following table. This compares the distribution of population and of income in the world and shows that a tiny proportion of the population receives an overwhelming proportion of its income. The wealth produced by the world's labour is being systematically concentrated into the hands of the powerful within advanced capitalist countries.

Table 1. World population and income distribution in mid–1972.

	% total world population	% total world GNP	GNP per capita (US $)
Underdeveloped countries	49·9	14·0	280
petroleum exporters	7·4	2·0	270
higher income	9·6	7·3	740
middle income	7·4	2·0	260
lower income	25·5	2·8	110
Advanced capitalist countries	17·9	67·0	3,670
Centrally planned economies	32·1	18·9	580

Source: International Bank for Reconstruction and Development (1974). *World Bank Atlas.* Washington.

Table 2 illustrates this concentration even further. It includes similar information for the ten largest countries of the world (by population), the United Kingdom and EEC.

Note: The countries shown in **Tables 2–6** are arranged in descending order of population.

Table 2. Population and income of several selected countries for mid–1972.

	% total world population	% total world GNP	GNP per capita (US $)
China	21·3	3·7	170
India	15·2	1·7	110
USSR	6·7	10·4	1,530
USA	5·6	32·3	5,590
Indonesia	3·3	0·3	90
Japan	2·9	6·8	2,320
Brazil	2·7	1·4	530
Bangladesh	2·0	0·1	70
Nigeria	1·9	0·2	130
Pakistan	1·8	0·2	130
UK	1·5	4·0	2,600
EEC	6·9	20·4	2,909

Source: As for **Table 1.**

The concentration of income and power as shown in the above tables is closely related to social welfare. It is impossible to obtain a complete world picture in this case as statistics for individual countries are not collected on a uniform basis and are not available at all for certain countries. The following tables, however, do produce an interesting picture.

Table 3. Indicators of health and welfare for 1970.

	Expectation of life at birth (years)	Infant mortality rate per thousand	Inhabitants per physician	Inhabitants per hospital bed
India	52·6	140·2	4,820	2,022
USSR	69·5	24·4	420	91
USA	70·6	19·8	634	127
Indonesia	47·0	137·0	26,069	1,388
Japan	72·2	13·1	890	79
Brazil	—	—	2,067	269
UK	71·9	18·5	806	105
Ethiopia	43·0	155·0	73,973	3,011
Colombia	59·8	80·6	2,161	446
Australia	70·8	17·9	777	84
Uganda	46·5	120·0	9,204	641
Iraq	51·6	104·0	3,266	517
Cuba	71·7	40·0	—	218

Source: United Nations (1975). *Compilation of development indicators for 1970.* Paris.

Table 4. Indicators of nutrition and education for 1970.

	Calorie consumption per capita per day	Protein consumption per capita per day	Literate as % of total p.	School enrolment as % age group 6–11
India	2,060	52·6	33·3	—
USSR	3,280	101·0	—	—
USA	3,270	97·3	99·0	99·1
Indonesia	1,920	42·8	56·6	52·4
Japan	2,470	76·2	99·3	100
Brazil	2,600	63·8	67·0	65·7
UK	3,140	90·2	99·5	99·9
Ethiopia	2,150	68·6	—	10·0
Colombia	2,250	50·8	73·4	57·0
Australia	3,050	101·0	99·5	102·4
Uganda	2,230	55·3	36·5	49·5
Iraq	2,250	62·4	28·8	53·6
Cuba	2,500	62·8	—	107·5

Source: As for Table 3.

Table 5. Mass media and communications for 1970.

	Passenger cars per 1,000 p.	Telephones per 100,000 p.	Televisions per 1,000 p.
India	1·1	217	0
USSR	—	4,531	143
USA	433·6	58,677	413
Indonesia	2·1	228	0·8
Japan	84·1	25,239	217
Brazil	24·4	2,102	64
UK	215·7	27,006	294
Ethiopia	1·5	185	0·3
Colombia	10·8	3,665	37
Australia	310·6	31,174	227
Uganda	3·0	306	1
Iraq	7·1	1,271	37
Cuba	8·4	3,133	71

Source: As for Table 3.

Table 6. Indicators of political performance for 1970.

	Voters as % of electorate	No. of political riots 1948–67	Defence expenditure as % of GNP (1972)
India	53·1	558	3·0
USSR	99·9	44	9·6 (est.)
USA	58·7	683	7·2
Indonesia	—	82	9·6 (est.)
Japan	71·1	159	0·9
Brazil	79·6	95	42·9
UK	77·1	82	4·6
Ethiopia	88·4	16	—
Colombia	36·9	125	—
Australia	95·7	3	3·6
Uganda	66·0	104	—
Iraq	—	97	8·8
Cuba	40·0	51	7·1 (est.)

Note: Egypt spends 20·2% of GNP on defence, Israel 18·2%, Jordan 17·4%, Syria 11·5% and Korea (North) 15·8%. Much of this money is spent on arms produced in the advanced countries and it provides a profitable outlet for their industries.

Sources: US Department of Commerce (1974). *Statistical abstract of the United States* 1974. Washington. D.C.
Taylor C. L. and M. C. Hudson (1972). *World Handbook of political and social indicators* 2nd ed., Yale University Press.

GENERAL INFORMATION

Some three thousand entries, including a number of scientific terms and explanations. Cross references direct the reader to fuller information elsewhere in the book. A list of Nobel prize winners and of symbols for correcting proofs will be found at the end of the section.

MEASUREMENTS ARE GIVEN IN METRIC UNITS

Abbreviations

mm	= millimetre	m^2	= square metre
cm	= centimetre	km^2	= square kilometre
m	= metre	ha	= hectare
km	= kilometre	m^3	= cubic metre
km/h	= kilometres per hour	s	= second
g	= gramme	min	= minute
kg	= kilogramme	h	= hour
tonne	= metric ton		

Equivalents

		Reciprocal
Length		
1 cm	= 0·394 in	2·540
1 m	= 1·094 yd	0·914
1 km	= 0·621 mile	1·609
Area		
1 m^2	= 1·196 yd^2	0·836
1 km^2	= 0·386 $mile^2$	2·590
1 hectare	= 2·471 acres	0·405
Volume		
1 m^3	= 1·308 yd^3	0·765
1 litre	= 0·220 gallon	4·546
Mass		
1 kg	= 2·205 lb	0·454
1 tonne	= 0·984 ton	1·016

Temperature

$C = (F - 32) \div 1{\cdot}8$
$F = (1{\cdot}8 \times C) + 32$

See also **Metric Equivalents, N8.**

GENERAL INFORMATION

A

Aard-vark (Dutch *aarde* = earth + *vark* = pig), a large nocturnal mammal found only in Africa. It feeds on termites and ants, whose nests it excavates with its enormous claws.

Abacus, a device for making arithmetical calculations, consisting of parallel bars on which are strung movable coloured beads. The earliest form of this instrument was used in Mesopotamia about 3000 B.C., and its use spread westwards throughout the Graeco–Roman world and eastwards to China. An efficient form of the abacus is still used today in parts of Asia.

Abdication. The term usually refers to the renunciation of the royal office by a reigning monarch. Both Edward II (1327) and Richard II (1399) were forced to abdicate, James II left the throne vacant without waiting for a formal deposition, and the abdication of Edward VIII was effected by the Declaration of Abdication Act, 1936. Since 1688 when Parliament declared James II to have abdicated by reason of desertion and subversion of the constitution, no British monarch can abdicate without the consent of Parliament.

Aberration, in astronomy, is the apparent displacement of a star due to the speed of the observer with the earth (see Parallax). In optics (i) spherical aberration is when there is blurring of the image and fringes of colour at its edges, due to failure of lens to bring light to a single focus; (ii) chromatic aberration is due to the refractive index of glass being different for light of different colours. For instance, violet light is bent more than red.

Abiogenesis, or spontaneous generation; the origination of living from non-living matter. The term is applied to such discredited ideas as that frogs could be generated spontaneously by the action of sunlight on mud, or maggots arise spontaneously in dead meat without any eggs from which the maggots hatch being present. Spallanzani (1729–99) upset the hypothesis of spontaneous generation; Pasteur dealt it a death-blow.

Abominable Snowman. See **Yeti.**

Aborigines, a term first applied to an ancient mythical people of central Italy, derives from the Latin *ab origine* = from the beginning. It now signifies the original inhabitants of any country, in particular the aboriginal tribes of Australia. In contrast to their highly complex social and religious customs, the material culture of Australian aborigines is very low and ill adapted to stand up to contact with European civilisation. Originally esimated at 300,000, their number has dropped in the last 200 years to some 80,000. They have no legal title to their ancient tribal lands, unlike the native people of the USA, Canada, and New Zealand.

Absolute Temperature, Absolute Zero. This is a refined notion requiring some study of thermodynamics for its full understanding. For setting up an absolute temperature scale one must first assign a numerical value to one fixed temperature. For this, the triple point of water has been chosen, *i.e.*, the temperature at which solid, liquid, and gaseous water are all in equilibrium. The triple point is defined to be 273·16 K where K is read for kelvin (after Lord Kelvin). This temperature is 0·01°C on the Celsius scale (*q.v.*) and is thus very close to the melting point of ice. Suppose the pressure and volume of a mass of gas are measured (i) at the triple point of water, giving $(pV)_{tr}$ as the product of the pressure and volume; and (ii) at any unknown temperature T K, giving (pV) as the product. Then the absolute temperature, T K, is defined by

$$T\,\mathrm{K} = 273{\cdot}16\,\frac{(pV)}{(pV)_{tr}}$$

It is to be understood that the gas pressure is very low. The nature of the gas is immaterial. More subtly, it can be shown that the temperature so defined is identical with that derived in a rather abstract way in the science of thermodynamics. The absolute scale is therefore also called the thermodynamic scale. Absolute temperatures can be obtained from Celsius temperatures by adding 273·15; thus the absolute temperature of melting ice is 273·15 K. Conversely, absolute zero is a temperature 273·15 K below the temperature of melting ice, *i.e.*, −273·15°C. Theory shows that absolute zero is unattainable, but it has been approached to within about 1 millionth of a degree. Within ten or so degrees of absolute zero, matter develops some remarkable properties. *See* **Kelvin, Cryogenics, Superconductor, Helium.**

Abstract Art, a term applied to 20th cent. plastic arts in which form and colour possess aesthetic value apart from the subject. Usually represented as a modern movement beginning with Cézanne. The idea is ancient, abstract design being found in the Neolithic period, in folk-art, and particularly in Moslem art (which forbids naturalistic representations especially of the human figure). Among those in the tradition are Kandinsky, Braque, Mondrian, Calder.

Acetic Acid, an organic acid produced when ordinary (ethyl) alcohol is fermented by the organism called *Acetobacter aceti*. The same oxidation process yields vinegar; this is a weak and crude solution of acetic acid obtained by trickling dilute alcoholic liquor over beechwood shavings at 35°C. The souring of wine is due to the same process. Acetic acid is used as a food preservative and flavouring material, and in the manufacture of cellulose acetate and white lead.

Acetylene, a compound of carbon and hydrogen prepared from calcium carbide and water. A very reactive gas, it is used industrially on a large scale to prepare acetaldehyde, chlorohydrocarbon solvents, and many intermediates for plastics manufacture. Burns in air with a highly luminous flame formerly used for lighting purposes, but is now widely used, with oxygen, in welding. For safe storage and transportation it is dissolved in acetone.

Acids, substances having a tendency to lose a positive ion (a proton). This general definition overcomes difficulties of earlier views which merely described their properties and asserted that they are chemically opposite to bases. As a whole acids contain ionisable hydrogen, replaceable by a metal, to form a salt. Inorganic acids are compounds of non-metals or metalloids, *e.g.*, sulphuric, phosphoric acid. Carboxylic acids contain the group –COOH. *See* **F22.**

Actinides, the fourteen metallic elements from thorium (no. 90) to lawrencium (no. 103). All known isotopes of these elements are radioactive and those with atomic number greater than 92 (uranium) have only been produced in significant quantities artificially. Plutonium (no. 94) is obtained from uranium during the course of nuclear reactor operation and the higher transuranic elements can be made from it by the successive capture of neutrons or nuclei of light atoms. The availability of only minute quantities of short-lived isotopes makes the determination of the physical and chemical properties of the higher actinides very difficult. *See* **Periodic Table, Section F.**

Advent, a period devoted to religious preparation for the coming celebration of the Nativity (Christmas). It includes the four Sundays immediately preceding the festival.

Advocatus Diaboli ("the devil's advocte"), a Roman Catholic functionary who presents opposing evidence in regard to the life of any deceased person it may be proposed to canonise.

Aerodynamics, the science of gases (especially air) in motion, particularly in relation to aircraft (aeronautics). The idea of imitating the birds by the use of wings is of ancient origin. Leonardo da Vinci first carried out experiments in a scientific manner. The invention of the balloon in 1783 and the researches of scientists and engineers in the 19th cent. ultimately led to the development of the aeroplane.

Aerolites, the name given to the class of meteorites composed chiefly of heavy silicates. The other two main classes are *siderolites* (nickel–iron and silicates) and *siderites* (nickel–iron).

Aerosol, a suspension of a liquid in a gas; for example, a fog is very small drops of water suspended in air. Formed by spraying the liquid in air, aerosols are used to disperse liquid over a wide area in crop spraying, air freshening and pest control. *See also* **Fluorocarbons.**

Afrikander, type of cattle bred in South Africa.

Afrikaner, an Afrikaans-speaking South African, usually of Dutch descent.

After-damp occurs in a mine after an explosion, causing suffocation. It is composed mainly of carbon dioxide and nitrogen and contains water vapour and carbon monoxide (produced by the burning, in a restricted supply of air, of fine coal dust).

Agape, a "love-feast" held by the early Christians in commemoration of the Lord's Supper. *See* **Methodism, Section J.**

Agaric, large fungi of the family *Agaricaceae*, which includes the mushroom and what are popularly called "toadstools," though the idea that these two lay terms sharply differentiate between edible and poisonous fungi is an incorrect one. Characteristic of the agarics is the presence of a cap or *pileus* (bearing underneath the spore-shedding gills) and a stalk or *stipe*.

Agate, a variety of chalcedony. Parallel bands of colour are often characteristic. Brazil, Uruguay, India, and the USA furnish the main supplies, and Scotland has a species of agate called Scotch pebble.

Agave, the American aloe or Century Plant which sometimes does not attain to flowering maturity under sixty or seventy years, and then dies. The flower spray may reach a height of 6 m and in its development the rush of sap is so great that the Mexicans collect for brewing the strong spirit called mescal. 1,000 litres of sap can be obtained from a single plant. Some species of agave yield sisal used for making cord and rope.

Aggression. After many years of consideration a definition of aggression was agreed at the United Nations in 1974. It is the use of armed force by a state against the sovereignty, territorial integrity, or political independence of another state, or in any other manner inconsistent with the Charter of the UN.

Air is a mixture of gases forming the atmosphere we breathe. Nitrogen, oxygen, and argon are always present in air; a typical sample of dry air might contain these gases in the following proportions (by volume): nitrogen, 78·06%; oxygen, 21%; argon, 0·94%. A small quantity of carbon dioxide is present, about 3 parts in 10,000 parts of air. This carbon dioxide is the source of carbon compounds built up by green plants in photosynthesis (**F28**); in the process carbon dioxide is absorbed from the air and oxygen returned, the reverse of the respiratory process of animals. Air also contains a quantity of water vapour, and traces of ammonia, nitrogen oxides, hydrogen, sulphur dioxide, hydrogen sulphide, ozone and of the rare gases helium, krypton, neon, and xenon. In a city smoke and dust particles may be as abundant as 100,000 particles per cc. A litre of air at 0°C and 700 mm pressure weighs 1·2932 g. *See also* **Atmosphere, Pollution.**

Air Glow is a much weaker atmospheric glow than the bright glows of the aurora polaris (*q.v.*) that are observed in the sky near polar latitudes. The night air glow does not depend strongly on geographical location. Some of the light from this glow comes from photochemical reactions occurring at altitudes of 64–80 km, some from much higher altitudes.

Alabaster, a soft crystalline form of sulphate of lime, or granulated gypsum, easily worked for statuary and other ornamental articles, and capable of being highly polished. Volterra, in Tuscany, yields the finest; that in highest ancient repute came from Alabastron in Egypt, near to the modern Antinoë.

Alb, white vestment reaching to the feet, worn by priests in religious ceremonies.

Albatross, a large sea-bird of almost pure white, black and white, or brown plumage. It nests in colonies on remote islands, but at other times rarely approaches land. Of the thirteen species, nine are found in the southern oceans, one in the tropics, and the three others in the North Pacific.

Albert Memorial, a large Gothic monument designed by Sir George Gilbert Scott, and embellished with sculptures by eminent artists. Erected in memory of Prince Albert in Kensington Gardens at a cost of £120,000.

Alcázar, the palace at Seville, famed for the beauty of its halls and gardens, in ancient days the residence of the Moorish kings.

Alchemy, the art or craft by which its practitioners sought the philosopher's stone, a substance believed to have the power of transmuting base metals into gold and silver and of prolonging human life indefinitely. Alchemy was practised for some hundreds of years B.C. in the Near East, Europe and Asia. Its hey-day was between about A.D. 800 and 1600 when rich and poor, distinguished and humble, religious and lay people could all be found seeking the philosopher's stone, also known as the elixir. The techniques used rudimentary chemistry and metallurgy and these sciences undoubtedly acquired some techniques and facts from the alchemists. The alchemical methods were, however, closely bound up with mystical thought which made much of the analogy between the transmutation of metals and the purification of man from sin. The alchemical writings are very obscure and allegorical—no doubt to preserve the secrets which the alchemists thought they had won. Though alchemists made many chemical experiments and observations, true chemistry finally emerged as its originators Boyle, Black, Priestley, Lavoisier and others put the science on a rational basis and rejected the mystical associations and motivations of alchemy as well as its reliance on the Aristotelian ideas that matter consisted of four elements—earth, air, fire and water. *See also* **Section J.**

Alcohols. A class of organic compounds of general formula R–OH, where R is an aliphatic radical. "Alcohol" is the name used for ethyl alcohol (ethanol); this is produced by distilling fermented liquors, and synthetically from ethylene, a product of petroleum cracking. Industrially ethyl alcohol is used in the manufacture of chloroform, ether, perfumes, etc. Diluted with wood alcohol or other denaturants ethyl alcohol is called "methylated spirits"; the denaturants are varied according to the industrial purposes for which it is required, the methylated spirits then being largely exempt from duty. Wood alcohol (methyl alcohol or methanol) can be obtained by distilling wood, or synthetically from water gas. *See* **F24(1).**

Alcoholic Strength. In Great Britain the standard is the proof gallon which is an imperial gallon of spirits containing 49·28 per cent. of alcohol by weight or 57·1 per cent. by volume at 60°F. In Europe the strength of spirits is usually measured by the Guy-Lussac hydrometer. In the USA, because of the smaller gallon, 1·37 US proof gallons = 1 British proof gallon. In Britain the alcoholic content of spirits and liqueurs appears on the bottle in degrees proof. Whisky for example, at 70° proof (or 30° under proof) contains 70/100 % 57·1 alcohol, or about 40 per cent. The alcoholic content of wines is not shown on the label. A new international system is to be introduced in Britain in 1980.

Aldehyde, the generic term for a class of chemical compounds of general formula R–CHO, where R is an organic radical. Except for formaldehyde, which is a gas, aldehydes are volatile liquids. They are produced by oxidation of primary alcohols. Most important aldehyde is formaldehyde used in making the plastics described as formaldehyde resins. Formalin (formaldehyde solution in water) is much used for preserving zoological specimens.

Alder, a river-side tree of the genus *Alnus*, including some 30 species and found in north temperate regions and the Andes. The only species native to Britain is *A. glutinosa*, which has been described as " guardian of river-banks " because of the way its roots bind together the sand and stones, and so slow down erosion. The wood is used for furniture and charcoal.

Aldine Editions are the beautiful books printed in Venice by the Renaissance printer Aldo Pio Manuzio and his family between 1490 and 1597. Italics were first introduced in these books.

Algae, flowerless plants living mostly in water. Seaweeds and the green pond scums are the best known algae. The green powder found on trees is a microscopic alga (*Protococcus*). *See* **F39(2)**.

Algebra, a branch of mathematics in which symbols are used in place of numbers. Sir Isaac Newton styled it the " universal arithmetic ". The Chinese were able to solve the quadratic equation before the Christian era but it was Al-Khowarizmi, an Arab mathematician of the early 9th cent., who introduced algebra to Europe.

Alhambra, the ancient palace of the Moorish kings at Granada in Spain, built in the 13th and 14th cent. Though part of the castle was turned into a modern palace under Charles V, the most beautiful parts of the interior are still preserved—the graceful halls and dwelling-rooms grouped round the Court of Alberca and the Court of Lions, with their fountains, arcades, and lovely gardens.

Aliphatic describes derivatives of hydrocarbons having chains of carbon atoms, as distinct from rings of carbon atoms as in benzene (*see* **Aromatic**). The gas butane is aliphatic.

Alkali, the general name given to a number of chemicals which are bases (*q.v.*). The term should be limited to the hydroxides of metals in the first and second group of the periodic table and of ammonia, *e.g.*, NaOH, KOH. They are used commercially in the manufacture of paper, glass, soap, and artificial silk. The word comes from the Arabic *al-kali* meaning calcined wood ashes. Alkalis are extremely soluble in water and neutralise acids to form salts and water.

Alkaloids, a large group of natural products which contain nitrogen; they are usually basic. Isolated from plants and animals, they include some hormones, vitamins, and drugs. Examples are nicotine, adrenalin, and cocaine. Many alkaloids are made synthetically for medicinal use, *e.g.*, morphine, quinine. Their function in plants is not well understood. *See* **Belladonna.**

Alligator, the crocodile of America, found in the lower Mississippi and adjacent lakes and marshes. There is also a Chinese species. Alligators have broader snouts than other crocodiles.

Allotropy. Depending on the temperature, pressure or method of preparation, an element may exist in one of several forms, each having different physical properties (crystal structure, electrical conductivity, melting point, etc.). This is known as allotropy and the different forms of the element are called allotropes. Many elements exhibit allotropy, *e.g.*, sulphur, phosphorus, oxygen, tin and carbon, the most well-known allotropes of carbon being diamond and graphite.

Alloys are combinations of metals made for their valuable special properties, *e.g.*, durability, strength, lightness, magnetism, rust-resistance, etc. Some well-known ones are brass (zinc + copper), coinage bronze (copper + zinc + tin), steels (iron + carbon + various other materials), soft solder (tin + lead), dental fillings (mercury + various ingredients).

All Saints' Day (Nov. 1) is common to both the English and Roman Catholic Churches, and is in commemoration of the saints generally, or such as have no special day set apart for them. Instituted by Pope Boniface IV, early in the 7th cent., this ecclesiastical festival was formerly called " All Hallows ".

All Souls' Day (Nov. 2) is a festival of the Roman Church, intended for the mitigation by prayer of the sufferings of souls in purgatory. The commemoration was enjoined by Abbot Odilo of Cluny during the 11th cent. upon the monastic order over which he presided, and was afterwards adopted generally throughout the Roman Communion.

Allspice, a flavouring obtained from a West Indian tree of the myrtle family, *Pimenta officinalis*. The essential oil of its unripe fruit is a powerful irritant, and the bruised berries are carminative.

Alluvium, river transported deposits of sand, mud and gravel which accumulate to form distinctive features such as levées, flood plains and deltas. The frequent renewal of alluvium by flooding causes riverine lands to be some of the most fertile. In Asia alluvial lands support high densities of population, *e.g.*, the Hwang-ho plains and the Ganges delta.

Almond, the fruit of the *Amygdalus communis*, originally indigenous to Persia, Asia Minor and N. Africa; now cultivated in Italy, Spain, France, the USA and Australia. It yields both bitter and sweet oil. Bitter almond oil is obtained by macerating and distilling the ripe seeds; it is used for flavouring and scenting purposes, its fragrant odour being due to the presence of benzaldehyde and hydrogen cyanide. When the seeds are pressed sweet almond oil results: this is used in perfumery, and also as a lubricant for very delicate machinery.

Almuce, a fur stole worn by certain canons.

Aloe, large plants of the lily family, with about 180 species found mainly in the S. African veldt and Karroo. The bitter purgative drug (aloes) is prepared by evaporating the plant's sap. *See* **Agave.**

Alpaca, a South American ruminant related to the llama whose long, fine wool is woven into a soft dress fabric known by the same name. Sir Titus Salt first manufactured alpaca cloth (1836). Saltaire, near Bradford, remains to evidence the success which for many years attended the enterprise.

Alpha Particle, or alpha-ray, fast-moving helium nucleus ejected by some radioactive atoms, *e.g.*, polonium. It is a combination of 2 neutrons and 2 protons. *See* **F11(1).**

Alphabet (so called from the first two letters of the Greek alphabet—alpha, beta) is the term applied to the collection of letters from which the words of a language are made up. It grew out of the knowledge that all words can be expressed by a limited number of sounds arranged in various combinations. The Phoenicians were the first to make use of an alphabetic script derived from an earlier Semitic alphabet (earliest known inscriptions *c.* 1500–950 B.C.) from which all other alphabets have sprung. The stages in the development of the alphabet were mnemonic (memory aids), pictorial (actual pictures), ideographic (symbols), and lastly phonetic. All the ideographic systems died out, with the exception of that of the Chinese.

Altimeter, an instrument used in aircraft to estimate altitude; its usual essential feature is an aneroid barometer which registers the decrease of pressure with height. Roughly 1 millibar corresponds to 9 m. To read an aircraft altimeter correct for its destination, the zero setting must be adjusted for difference of ground height and difference of surface pressure, especially when pressure is falling or when flying towards low pressure.

Altitude, an astronomical term used to signify the angular elevation of a heavenly body; this is measured with a quadrant or sextant. In aeronautics it is the height (in feet or metres) above sea-level.

Alto-Relievo, a term applied to sculptured designs which are depicted in prominent relief on a flat surface, technically signifying that the projections exceeds one-half the true proportions of the objects represented. Basso-relievo is carving kept lower than one-half such projection.

Alum is a compound salt used in various industrial processes, especially dyeing, its constituents being the sulphate of one univalent metal or radical (*e.g.*, potassium, sodium, ammonium, rubidium, caesium, silver, thallium) and the sulphate of a tervalent metal (*e.g.*, aluminium, iron, chromium, manganese), and water of crystallisation.

Alumina is the oxide of aluminium. Very valuable as a refractory material. The ruby is almost 100 per cent. alumina; so also are the emerald, oriental amethyst, etc. An hydrated aluminium oxide is bauxite, chief ore of aluminium from which the metal is extracted electrolytically.

Aluminium is a light metal which conducts electricity well. Its specific gravity at 20°C is 2·705. Melting point of alumium is 660·2°C. It is made commercially by electrolysing bauxite dissolved in cryolite (double fluoride of aluminium and sodium). Aluminium alloys because of their strength and lightness are being increasingly used for the construction of railway coaches, automobiles, aeroplanes, etc.

Amadavat, a popular cage bird of the weaver family, mainly crimson with white spots, so named because the first specimens came from Ahmadabad in India about 1700.

Amalgam is the term applied to any alloy of which mercury forms a part.

Amber, a brittle resinous substance; in origin, fossilised resin. Obtained mostly from the Baltic coasts, and used for ornaments, pipe mouth-pieces, etc.

Ambergris is a waxy substance produced in the intestines of the sperm whale, and generally found floating on the sea. It is a valuable perfumery material.

Amblyopsis, a species of fish, practically sightless, and with inoperative organs of hearing and feeling, that inhabit the Mammoth Cave of Kentucky. A remarkable illustration of the failure of senses not brought into use.

America's Cup. In 1851 the Royal Yacht Squadron put up for competition a silver cup that has become the most famous trophy in yachting. In that year the New York Y.C. sent the schooner *America* across the Atlantic to compete in a 53-mile (85 km) race round the Isle of Wight; it captured the trophy which now bears its name. None of the many challenges by yachtsmen from Great Britain, Canada, and latterly, Australia, has been successful, though America's *Resolute* was nearly beaten in 1920 by Sir Thomas Lipton's *Shamrock IV*, which won the first two races and was first to cross the line in the third race, only to lose on corrected time.

Amethyst, the violet variety of quartz, used as a precious stone, containing traces of manganese, titanium and iron. The finest coloured specimens come from Brazil and the Urals.

Amice, a linen vestment worn about the neck by Roman and many Anglican priests over the alb when officiating at Mass or Holy Eucharist. Formerly worn on the head by priests and pilgrims.

Amines, organic chemicals composed of carbon, hydrogen and nitrogen. They are derived from ammonia, which they resemble in smell and chemical characteristics. The smell of bad fish is due to the presence of amines. Important industrially as intermediates in a wide variety of products, for example, the synthesis of dyestuffs and man-made fibres such as nylon.

Amino acids, organic compounds containing an amine group and an acid group. They are the "building bricks" of proteins (*q.v.*). *See* **F27(1), 29.**

Ammeter, an instrument for measuring the current flowing in an electric circuit. A contraction of ampere-meter. *See* **Ampere.**

Ammonia, a colourless gaseous compound comprising three atoms of hydrogen to one of nitrogen. Formerly it was made by heating the horns and hoofs of deer, acquiring the name of spirits of hartshorn. The ammonia of commerce is now procured by coal decomposition in the course of gas-making and by direct synthesis. In the very important Haber process of ammonia production by fixation of atmospheric nitrogen, the nitrogen is made to combine with hydrogen and the ammonia so prepared is converted into nitric acid, ammonium nitrate or ammonium sulphate. The Haber process made Germany self-sufficient in nitrates in the first world war, and was afterwards exploited all over the world.

Ammonites, extinct animals related to the Nautilus. The chambered shell is coiled, usually in a plane spiral, and they are confined to Mesozoic rocks.

Ammonium, the basic radical of ammonium salts, Composed of one atom of nitrogen and four of hydrogen, it behaves chemically like an ion of a monovalent alkali metal. Ammonium chloride is known as "sal ammoniac". "Sal volatile" is ammonium carbonate.

Amnesty, an act of grace by which a ruler or governing power pardons political offenders.

Amorphous, a term used to indicate the absence of crystalline form in any body or substance.

Ampere, unit of electric current in the SI system of units; named after André Marie Ampère, who in the 1820s helped to lay the foundations of modern electromagnetism. Defined as that constant current which, if maintained in two parallel rectilinear conductors of infinite length, of negligible circular cross section, and placed at a distance of one metre apart in a vacuum, would produce between these conductors a force equal to 2×10^{-7} newton per metre length.

Amphibia. *See* **F33(2).**

Amphioxus *or* **Lancelet**, a primitive chordate (**F33(1)**), occuring in sand-banks around British shores and elsewhere.

Anabolism. *See* **Catabolism.**

Analysis is one of the major branches of modern pure mathematics and includes the theories of differentiation, integration. differential equations and analytic functions.

Anarchism. *See* **Section J.**

Anchor, an instrument used for keeping ships stationary. Great improvements have been introduced in recent years, stockless anchors being now chiefly used, consisting of a shank and a loose fluke. Lloyd's rules prescribe the number and weight of anchors which must be carried by merchant ships.

Anchorite is a religious person who retires into solitude to employ himself with holy thoughts. Among the early Christians, anchorites were numerous, but in the Western Church they have been few. Their reputation for wisdom and prescience was high, and kings and rulers in olden days would visit their cells for counsel. An anchorite or "ankret" was in mediaeval times a source of fame and profit to the monastic house within which he was voluntarily immured.

Anchovy, a fish of the herring family, distinguished by its large mouth and projecting snout, plentiful in the Mediterranean and much esteemed when cured.

Ancient Lights are rights of light enjoyed by a property owner over adjoining land. Such a right is obtained either by uninterrupted enjoyment for twenty years, or by written authority, and once legally established cannct be upset, no building being permissible that would seriously interfere with the privilege.

Anemometer, an instrument for measuring the strength of the wind. In the most widely used pattern the rotation, about a vertical axis, of a group of hemispherical or conical cups gives a measure of the total flow of air past the cups, various registering devices being employed. The Dines anemograph provides a continuous record of the variation in both velocity and direction; changes of pressure produced in a horizontal tube, kept pointing into the wind by a vane, cause a float, to which a pen is attached, to rise and fall in sympathy with the gusts and lulls. The recently devised hot-wire anemometer, depending upon the change of electrical resistance experienced by a heated wire when cooled, enables very gentle air currents to be investigated.

Aneroid is the kind of barometer which does not depend upon atmospheric support of a mercury (or other liquid) column. It consists of a metallic box, partially exhausted of air, with a corrugated lid which moves with atmospheric changes. A lever system magnifies the lid movements about 200 times and atmospheric pressure is read from a dial. The construction of the vacuum chamber provides automatic compensation for temperature changes. An aneroid barometer is the basic component of an altimeter.

Angelica, an aromatic plant of the Umbelliferae order, *Angelica officinalis*, valuable as a flavouring and possessing medicinal properties. In olden times supposed to protect against poison.

Angelus, a church bell rung in Roman Catholic countries, at morn, noon, and sunset, to remind the faithful to say their Angelic Salutation.

Angevin Dynasty includes the Plantagenet kings from Henry II to Richard II. The name was derived from Henry II's father, Geoffrey, Count of Anjou.

Angles, a northern tribe originally settled in Schleswig, who with the Saxons and Jutes invaded Britain in the 5th cent.

Angstrom, a unit of wavelength, named after the Swedish physicist A. J. Ångström (1814–74), equal to one hundred-millionth of a centimetre (10^{-8} cm). It is used to measure wavelengths of light, X-rays, etc.

Aniline, a simple aromatic compound related to benzene and ammonia. It is obtained from coal-tar. The name recalls the fact that it was first prepared by distilling indigo (*anil* is Portuguese for indigo). In 1856 W. H. Perkin (1838–1907) discovered the first aniline or coal-tar dye, mauve, and thus founded the modern dyestuff industry.

Animal Kingdom. *See* **F32.**

Anise, an umbelliferous plant (*Pimpinella anisum*) found in Egypt and the Levant, and valued for its fruit, aniseed, possessing certain medicinal properties and yielding an aromatic, volatile oil. Also used in cooking. The anise of the Bible is *Anethum graveolens, i.e.*, dill.

Annates were acknowledgments formerly paid to the popes by way of fee or tax in respect of ecclesiastical preferment, and consisted usually of a proportion of the income (" first-fruits ") of the office. Introduced into England in the 13th cent.; annexed to the Crown under Henry VIII; transferred to a perpetual fund for the benefit of the poorer clergy in 1704. *See* **Queen Anne's Bounty.**

" Annual Register ", a yearly record of political and literary events, founded by Edmund Burke (as editor) in 1759 and Robert Dorsley, the bookseller.

Annunciation, Feast of the (March 25), is a church festival commemorating the message of the incarnation of Christ brought by the angel Gabriel to the Virgin Mary, hence the title Lady Day.

Anointing is the pouring of consecrated oil upon the body as a mark of supreme honour. In England it is restricted chiefly to the ceremony of the monarch's coronation, and the spoon with which the soil is applied forms part of the English regalia. In the Roman Catholic Church anointing represents the sacrament of extreme unction.

Ant. There are about 6,000 species of ants, which belong to the same order (Hymenoptera) as the bees, wasps and ichneumon flies. They are social in habit, living in communities of varying size and development. There are three basic castes in ants—the females or *queens*, the *males*, and the *workers* (the last-named being neuter), although specialised forms of workers are sometimes found, *e.g.*, the *soldiers* of the harvesting ants. In the communities of those species of ants which evolved most recently there is a highly complex social life and well-developed division of labour. Some species of these ants make slaves of other species, stealing the cocoons before the adult forms emerge. Many ants " milk " greenflies, which they protect for their honey-like secretion, and most ants' nests contain many " guests ", such as beetles and silver fish. Some ants harvest grains of corn, and others, from S. America, live on fungi which they cultivate in underground " mushroom beds ".

Antarctic Exploration. In earlier centuries it was thought that a great continent must exist in the southern hemisphere, around the South Pole, to balance the known land masses in the north. Its supposed extent was greatly reduced in the 18th cent., particularly when Capt. Cook sailed for the first time south of the Antarctic Circle and reached the edge of the ice pack. A portion of the ice-covered continent—the coast of Graham Land—was first sighted by Lieut. Edward Bransfield in 1820. Explorers of several other nations sighted portions of the coast-line in other quarters, but the first extensive exploration was made by Capt. James Clarke Ross, who with the *Erebus* and *Terror* penetrated into the Ross Sea in 1841, and discovered the great Ross Ice Barrier in 78° South lat. Interest in the Antarctic did not revive until after 1890, when an international scheme of research was drawn up. A Norwegian, C. E. Borchgrevink, in 1898–1900, was the first to winter in the Antarctic and to travel on the ice barrier. The British share in this work was carried out by Capt. R. F. Scott's expedition in the *Discovery*, 1901–4. Scott's party sledged across the barrier to 82° 17′ South, then a record " farthest south ". A little later, Ernest Shackleton beat this by travelling to within 160 km of the South Pole. The Scottish polar explorer William Spiers Bruce led the Scottish national Antarctic Expedition of 1902 in the *Scotia* and discovered Coats Land and founded a meteorological observatory on the South Orkneys. In 1910 Scott organised his second expedition of the *Terra Nova*, and became engaged against his will in a " race for the Pole ", when, after his departure, the Norwegian Arctic explorer, Roald Amundsen, suddenly announced that he was sailing for the Antarctic. Amundsen set up his base at the eastern end of the Barrier, and, relying on dog teams for hauling his sledges, reached the Pole on 14 December 1911. Meanwhile Scott and his party, their start delayed by adverse weather, were marching southwards, man-hauling their sledges, for Scott was against the use of dogs. After an arduous journey they reached the Pole one month after Amundsen. The return was a struggle against the weather and increasing weakness, probably due to scurvy, until at last they perished within a few kilometres of their base. After the first world war the development of the whaling industry greatly stimulated further exploration. Outstanding expeditions included that of Admiral R. E. Byrd, 1929, when he flew over the South Pole; The British Graham Land expedition, 1934, which carried out the first extensive mapping of any part of the Antarctic continent; and the US Navy's Antarctic Expedition of 1940, when the whole continent was circumnavigated and great areas photographed from the air. In recent years valuable work has been done by the first International expedition, the Norwegian–British–Swedish Expedition to Queen Maud Land, and by the French in Adélie Land. The Falkland Island Dependencies Survey, set up during the war, has continued the scientific exploration of Graham Land. The Antarctic was the scene of high adventure during the International Geophysical Year (1957–58), when scientists from many countries participated in the explorations. The Commonwealth Trans-Antarctic Expedition set out from opposite sides of the continent and met at the South Pole, the UK party, led by Sir Vivian Fuchs, from the Falklands, and Sir Edmund Hillary and his party from New Zealand. The UK party accomplished the first crossing of the White Continent in 99 days. Their scientific work included the marking of seismic and complementary gravimetric studies at frequent intervals along the 3,540 km traverse. Since the Antarctic is becoming important for many reasons, in weather forecasting, in the whaling industry, and as a possible centre for world air routes, the tempo of exploration and research will become even faster in the future.

Anteaters, a small family (the Myrmecophagidae) of mammals from Central and South America. They feed on ants, termites and other insects which they gather with a long tongue covered with sticky saliva.

Antennae, paired feelers of insects and custaceans. In radio, the term " antenna " is equivalent to " aerial ".

Anthem, a choral composition, with or without instrumental accompaniment, usually sung after the third collect in the Church of England service. The words are from the Scriptures, and the composition may be for solo voices only, for full choir, or for both. Among the chief British composers of anthems are Tallis, Purcell, Croft, Boyce, Goss and Stainer.

Anthracite is a black coal with a brilliant lustre. It contains 92 per cent. and over of carbon and burns slowly, without smoke or flame. *See* **Coal.**

Anthropoid, meaning " resembling man ", a sub-order of the primate mammals including man and also the gibbon, chimpanzee, orang-utan, and gorilla.

Anthropology. *See* **Section F, Part V.**

Antibiotics, a collective name for any substance

derived from micro-organisms or fungi which is capable of destroying infections, *e.g.*, penicillin. *See* **Section P.**

Anticyclone, a region where barometric pressure is greater than that of its surroundings. Such a system is distinguished on weather charts by a pattern of isobars, usually circular or oval-shaped, enclosing the centre of high pressure where the air is calm. In the remaining areas light or moderately strong winds blow spirally outwards, in a clockwise direction in the Northern Hemisphere (and in the reverse direction in the Southern Hemisphere), in accordance with Buys Ballot's law (an observer with back to wind in Northern Hemisphere has lower pressure to left; in Southern to right). Over the British Isles anticyclonic weather is generally quiet and settled, being fair, warm, and sunny in summer and either very cold and often foggy or overcast and gloomy in winter. These systems move slowly and sometimes remain practically stationary for days at a time, that over Siberia being particularly well defined. Extensive belts of almost permanent anticyclones occur in latitutdes 30° N and 30° S. Persistent anticyclonic weather with easterly winds during the months December to March, 1962–3, brought the coldest and hardest winter to Britain since 1740 (taking the Midlands as representative).

Antimony. Metal element, symbol Sb. In group 5 of the periodic table. Exists in various forms, the stable form being a grey brittle metal with a layer structure. The other forms are non-conductors. On being burned, it gives off dense fumes of oxide of antimony. By itself it is not of special utility; but as an alloy for hardening other metals, it is much used. As an alloy with lead for type-metal, and with tin and copper or zinc for Britannia-metal, it is of great value. Most important antimony ore is stibnite (antimony sulphide).

Anti-Pope, one elected in opposition to one held to be canonically chosen; commonly applied to the popes Urban VI and Clement VII, who resided at Avignon during the Great Schism (1378–1417).

Anti-proton, the "negative proton", an atomic particle created in high energy collisions of nuclear particles. Its existence was confirmed in Oct. 1955. *See* **F14.**

Antisemitism. *See* **Section J.**

Antlers are the branched horns of deer, the branches being called tines. Antlers originate as outgrowths of the frontal bone, and are usually shed once a year. Except in the reindeer and caribou they are restricted to the male.

Apartheid. *See* **Section J.**

Ape, a term applied to the gorilla, chimpanzee, orang-utan and gibbon—the anthropoid apes.

Aphelion, the point in the orbit of a planet farthest from the sun; the opposite of perihelion. At aphelion the earth is $1{\cdot}52 \times 10^8$ km from the sun.

Aphids, green-flies or plant lice, a numerous species of destructive insects living on young shoots and foliage, some on roots. Reproduction is by parthenogenesis (virgin birth). *See* **T29**(2).

Apis, the sacred bull worshipped by the ancient Egyptians; also the scientific name for the bee.

Apocalyptic writings are those which deal with revelation and prophecy, more especially the Revelation of St. John.

Apocrypha (hidden writings), the books which were included in the Septuagint (Greek) and Vulgate (Latin) versions of the Old Testament but excluded from the sacred canon at the Reformation by the Protestants on the grounds that they were not originally written in Hebrew nor regarded as genuine by the Jews. The books include: 1 and 2 Esdras, Tobit, Judith, additions to Esther, Wisdom of Solomon, Ecclesiasticus, Baruch, Song of the Three Holy Children, History of Susannah, Bel and the Dragon, Prayer of Manasses, 1 and 2 Maccabees. The term is usually applied to the additions to the old Testament, but there are also numerous Christian writings of the same character. *The New English Bible* was published in 1970.

Apogee, that point in the orbit of a heavenly body which is farthest from the earth; used in relation to the sun, moon and artificial satellites. The sun's apogee corresponds to the earth's aphelion. *See* **Perigee.**

Apostasy is a revolt, by an individual or party, from one form of opinions or doctrine to another. Julian, the Roman Emperor (331–63), brought up as a Christian, became converted to paganism and on coming to the throne (361), proclaimed religious toleration. Hence his name, Julian the Apostate.

Apostles. The twelve apostles who were disciples of Jesus were: Simon Peter and Andrew (his brother), James and John (sons of Zebedee), Philip, Bartholomew Thomas, Matthew, James, Thaddaeus, Simon, and Judas Iscariot. After the Ascension Matthias was chosen to take the place of Judas. St. Paul is always referred to as the chief apostle, though he is not one of the twelve. St. Barnabas has also been called an apostle.

Apostles' Creed, applied to the most ancient of the Church's statements of its belief: "I believe in God the Father Almighty; and in Jesus Christ his only Son our Lord, who was born of the Holy Ghost and the Virgin Mary. . . ." A later version is used in the Church of England at morning and evening prayer.

Apostolic Fathers were the immediate disciples or followers of the Apostles, especially such as left writings behind. They included Barnabas, Clement of Rome, Ignatius of Antioch, Hermas, Papias of Hieropolis and Polycarp.

Appeasement Policy. The name of the policy during 1937 and 1938 of yielding to the demands of Hitler and Mussolini in the hope that a point would be reached when the dictators would co-operate in the maintenance of peace. The policy culminated in the Munich Agreement (which was the subject of much criticism) after a series of concessions including the recognition of the Italian conquest of Abyssinia and the German annexation of Austria. The policy was finally demonstrated as futile when Hitler seized Czechoslovakia in March 1939.

Appian Way, the oldest and finest of the Roman roads originally laid by Appius Claudius (312 B.C.) from Rome to Capua and thence to Brundisium (Brindisi).

Approved Schools were residential schools, subject to Home Office inspection, for the training of young persons under 17 who, because of disturbed behaviour as a result of unfavourable influences such as bad environment or parental neglect, were guilty of offences or in need of care and protection and had been sent to them by magistrates from juvenile or other courts. The approved school order was abolished by the Children and Young Persons Act 1969. Such young people may now be committed to the care of a local authority and accommodated in a system of community homes ranging from children's homes to borstal type institutions.

April, the fourth month of the year, from the Roman *Aprilis* derived from *aperire* "to open" —the period when the buds begin to open.

Apse is a semicircular recess, arched or dome-roofed, at the end of the choir, aisles, or nave of a church.

Aqueducts are conduits in which water flows or is conveyed from its source to the place where it is to be used. Most famous builders were the Romans and the oldest Roman aqueduct was the Aqua Appia, which dates from about 310 B.C. Among modern aqueducts may be mentioned that of Glasgow, which brings water to that city from Loch Katrine; that of Manchester, which taps Thirlmere; that of Liverpool, with Lake Vyrnwy in North Wales as its source, and the Fron Aqueduct, Powys, which carries water from the Elan Valley to Birmingham.

Arabian Nights Entertainment or Book of A Thousand and One Nights, a collection of fascinating tales of the Orient, of mixed Indian, Persian, Arabic, and Egyptian origination, and first made known in Europe by Antoine Galland's French translation (1704–17) from Arabian texts. The "master" tale tells how the princess Shahrazad so beguiles the king through the telling of the tales over one thousand and one nights that her life was spared. English translators include E. W. Lane (1840), Sir Richard Burton (1885–8), John Payne (1882–4).

Arabic Numerals. The modern system of numbering, 0, 1, 2, 3, 4, 5, 6, 7, 8, 9, in which the digits depend on their position for their value, is called the Arabic numerical notation. The method is, in fact, of Indian origin. By the 9th cent. Hindu science was available in Arabic, and the Persian mathematician Al-Kwarizimi (*c.* 830) in his *Arithmetic* used the so-called "Arabic" system of numbering. Gradually the method spread to Europe, taking the place of the Roman system which was useless for calculation. The West is indebted to the Arabs for the zero symbol, the lack of which had been a serious drawback to Greek mathematics. It made the invention of decimal fractions possible.

Aragonite, the unstable form of calcium carbonate found as a mineral in some young deposits. It crystallises in the orthorhombic system but tends to revert to calcite (*q.v.*).

Aramaic Languages, the Semitic dialects current in Mesopotamia and the regions extending south-west from the Euphrates to Palestine from about the 12th cent. B.C. until after the rise of Islam, when Aramaic was superseded by Arabic. Both Aramaic and Greek were spoken in Palestine during the time of Christ.

Archaeopteryx, a fossil bird providing a connecting link between reptiles and birds. It had feathers, jaws with teeth, no bill, reptilian bones and skull, a long tail, and it probably used its fore-limbs for gliding flight. The first specimen, found in 1861, in the Solenhofen limestone of Bavaria, is in London's Natural History Museum.

Archbishop, the chief of the bishops of an ecclesiastical province in the Greek, Roman, and Anglican churches. In the Church of England there are two archbishops, the Archbishop of Canterbury, called the Primate of *all* England, and the Archbishop of York, styled the Primate of England.

Archimedes' Principle. When a body is weighed in air and then in any fluid, the apparent loss in weight is equal to the weight of fluid displaced. This scientific fact was noted by the Syracusan philosopher Archimedes (287–212 B.C.) and is frequently used as a basis for density measurements.

Architecture, the art and science of building. The provision of shelter for mankind by the orderly arrangement of materials in a manner which expresses man's attitude to living. The forms which buildings take are the outcome of the function for which they are to be used, of the architect's aesthetic sensibility and of the structural method adopted. Until the last hundred years structural methods were limited to timber frames, and columns, lintels, load-bearing walls, arches, vaults, and domes in brick or stone. From these few basic elements have evolved the great variety of historic styles of building to be found throughout the world. To give but one example, the Greeks created those systems of decorated columns and beams, known as the Orders, which were adapted by the Romans, revived decoratively rather than structurally during the Renaissance and are still used in debased form on the more presumptuous type of modern building. In recent years, however, architecture has taken on a new meaning. Once confined to the rich, in the form of Church, State or Commerce, it is now, with the coming of democracy, recognised as an essential social service for all. This, and the development of new structural techniques and materials (steel, aluminium, sheet glass, reinforced concrete, plastics and plywoods, to name a few), have made the interest in historic styles, the mainstay of the older architect, of secondary importance. Modern architecture is the creation of buildings with the highest possible standards of functional performance in terms of efficient planning and structure, good artificial and natural lighting, adequate heating or cooling, and proper acoustic conditions consistent with the price the client can afford to pay. At the same time the architect's task is to design a structure and the spaces the structure delimits, internally and externally which are aesthetically stimulating and satisfying, and well related to the land and buildings around.

Arctic Exploration. Modern exploration of the Arctic begins in the 16th cent. when men sought to reach the East Indies by sailing through the Arctic to the Pacific Ocean. The North-east Passage, via the shores of northern Asia, was the first attempted. In 1553 and 1554 the English navigators Sir Richard Chancellor and Stephen Burrough sailed into the White Sea, but were prevented by storms and ice from advancing farther eastwards. The project was later revived by the Dutch; Barendts in 1594 discovered Spitsbergen, but also failed to get beyond Novaya Zemlya. It was not, in fact, until 1879 that the Swede, A. E. Nordenskiöld, in the *Vega*, succeeded in reaching the Pacific. The attempts to find a North-west Passage were more numerous and determined. In 1585 John Davis penetrated Davis Strait and coasted along Baffin Island. Hopes ran high when Henry Hudson discovered Hudson Bay in 1610, but a practicable passage continued to elude explorers. The problem was to find a navigable route through the maze of channels in the short summer season, and to avoid being frozen in with supplies exhausted. After the Napoleonic Wars the Admiralty sent out many naval expeditions which culminated in Sir John Franklin's expedition with the *Erebus* and *Terror* in 1845. The ships were beset by ice in Victoria Channel and, after Franklin's death, were abandoned by their crews, who perished from scurvy and starvation on their march southwards. To ascertain their fate, several further expeditions were despatched, and the crew of the *Investigator*, commanded by R. J. M'Clure, sailing eastwards from Bering Strait, were the first to make the Passage, though in doing so they were obliged to abandon their ship. It was thirty years before the Norwegian, Roald Amundsen, succeeded in sailing the *Gjoa* from east to west. In the meantime, the North Pole had become the goal of explorers. Nansen, in 1893, put the *Fram* into the ice-pack to drift across the Polar basin, and himself made an unsuccessful attempt on the Pole across the pack. This was eventually achieved by the American explorer Robert E. Peary, who after several expeditions in the North Greenland region, sledged to the Pole with Eskimo companions in 1909. The next phase was the employment of airships and aeroplanes in Arctic exploration. In 1926 Admiral Byrd made the first flight over the Pole, and in the same year Amundsen and Lincoln Ellsworth flew the airship *Norge* from Spitsbergen to Point Barrow, Alaska. Two years later, the *Italia*, commanded by the Italian, Nobile, was wrecked on a return flight from the Pole, and Amundsen lost his life in an attempt to rescue the survivors. With modern developments in aircraft and navigation, flights over the Polar basin are almost a routine matter. The first voyage under the North Pole was made in August 1958 by the American nuclear-powered submarine *Nautilus*.

Arenaceous Rocks, the rocks composed of grains of sand, chiefly sandstones; quartz is the most abundant mineral in these rocks.

Argillaceous Rocks are a sedimentary group, including the shales and clays.

Argon, chemical element symbol A. This was the first of the inert gases (*q.v.*) to be isolated from air by Rayleigh and Ramsay in 1894. Argon is used for filling gas-filled metal filament electric lamps. In gas discharge tube it gives a blue glow.

Arithmetic, the branch of mathematics that deals with numerical calculations as in counting, measuring, weighing. The early civilisations used simple arithmetic for commercial purposes, employing symbols and later letters of the alphabet as numerals. When Hindu-Arabic numerals replaced Roman numerals in the Middle Ages it meant a great step forward and led to rapid developments—the invention of logarithms, slide-rule, calculating machines.

Arithmetic Progression, a sequence of numbers in which the successor of each number is obtained by adding or subtracting a fixed number, for example 2, 5, 8, 11, . . . or 100, 95, 90, 85. . . .

Ark of the Covenant was the sacred chest of the Hebrews and symbolised God's presence. It was overlaid with gold inside and outside. It accompanied the Israelites into battle and was once captured by the Philistines. Eventually it found a resting-place in Solomon's Temple.

Armada, Spanish, the naval expedition fitted out

by Phillip II of Spain in 1588 against England, commanded by the Duke of Medina Sidonia. It comprised 129 ships, was manned by 8,000 sailors and carried 19,000 soldiers and more than 2,000 cannon. Against this formidable force Elizabeth had only 80 ships, manned by 9,000 sailors, under Lord Howard of Effingham, under whom served Drake, Hawkins and Frobisher. The British Fleet awaited the Armada off Plymouth, and at Tilbury there was a considerable defensive land force under the command of the Earl of Leicester. On 19 July the ships of the Armada were sighted off the Lizard, disposed in a crescent 11 km long from horn to horn. The excellent manoeuvring of the English, their fire-ships, and a gale from the N.W. combined so effectively to cripple the Spanish ships that the Armada was scattered in confusion, a very small remnant contriving to reach home via the North of Scotland. It was impossible to embark the army of Parma waiting in the Netherlands. Elizabeth had a medal struck bearing in Latin the inscription, "God blew and they were scattered".

Armadillo, a genus of animals related to the sloths and anteaters, belonging to South America, and carrying a hard bony covering over the back, under which one species (*Tolypeutes*) can completely conceal itself when attacked, rolling itself up like a hedgehog.

Armageddon, according to the Revelation of St. John, the great battle in which the last conflict between good and evil is to be fought.

Armillary Sphere, an early form of astronomical apparatus with a number of circles representing equator, meridian, ecliptic, etc. Used by Hipparchus and Ptolemy and up to the time of Tycho Brahe for determining the position of the stars.

Aromatic. A term used by chemists, originally to describe compounds like benzene, having a characteristic smell. It is a term which implies a collection of chemical characteristics, the salient features being a flat ring structure and a general similarity to benzene.

Arsenic, a metalloid element, symbol As, in group 5 of the periodic table usually met with as a constituent of other minerals sometimes by itself. Its compounds are very poisonous. Lead arsenate is a powerful insecticide used for spraying fruit trees. The more stable allotropic form (grey) has a layer structure, and conducts electricity.

Art Deco, the name given by modern collectors to the decorative style of the 1920s and 1930s; it is derived from the long official name of the Paris Exhibition of 1925, which was almost exclusively devoted to "les Arts Décoratifs". Art Deco runs parallel in time with Functionalism (*q.v.*) but unlike that austere and philosophical style, Art Deco is gay, elegant and even frivolous, being a creation of fashionable Paris. It is related superficially to Cubism, using squares, circles and triangles in interesting combinations for ornament. Another popular motif is the modern girl with her shingled head dancing the tango or drinking cocktails. The style is brash and worldly, but in its best expressions full of charm and vitality. Famous names within the style are the glassmaker Rene Lalique (1860–1945), the fashion designers Gabrielle Chanel and Elsa Schiaparelli, and the decorator and illustrator Erte (Roman de Tirtoff, b. 1892). Recently there has been a nostalgic revival of Art Deco, *e.g.*, in films like "Bonny and Clyde" (1967) or "The Great Gatsby" (1974) based on F. Scott Fitzgerald's novel (1925).

Artesian Wells take their name from Artois in France, where the first wells of this kind were constructed in 1126. They are to be found only when a water-bearing bed is sandwiched between two impervious beds. When a boring is made to the lower part of the bed, the pressure of water is sufficient to cause the water to overflow at the surface. Artesian wells were known to ancient Egypt and China, and have existed in the Sahara since the earliest times. The fountains in Trafalgar Square were once fed by artesian wells sunk through the London clay into the chalk about 250 m.

Articles. The *Six Articles* are those contained in an Act of Henry VIII, and were of Roman Catholic origin. The *Thirty-nine Articles* were drawn up for the English church at the Reformation. They are printed at the back of the Prayer Book. Candidates for holy orders in the Church of England are required to subscribe to them, though the form of assent has recently been modified.

Art Nouveau (German *Jugend Stil*) was prevalent in architecture and decoration in Europe and the USA *c.* 1885–1910. It was rooted in the thoughts of Ruskin and William Morris. In reaction against the impersonal uniformity of industrial products which were flooding the market, artists turned to Nature for their inspiration, choosing organically growing forms, flowers or animals, as motifs for decoration or even for shaping whole objects. Another favourite motif was Romantic Woman with long robes and flowing hair, as interpreted so beautifully by Aubrey Beardsley. The sharply undulating line with a whiplash rhythm is a recurring theme. Famous names are the glassmakers Emile Gallé in France and Louis Comfort Tiffany in New York, the English goldsmith Charles Robert Ashbee (1863–1942), Henry Van de Velde (1867–1942) in Belgium and Charles Rennie Mackintosh (1868–1928) in Scotland, both architects and interior decorators, and in pure architecture Antonio Gaudí of Barcelona (1852–1926) and Victor Horta of Brussels (1861–1946).

Arts and Crafts Movement, the English revival of decorative art which began about 1875 as a revolt against the existing vulgarity of internal decoration and furnishings and the pettiness of academic art. Inspired by William Morris and Burne-Jones together with Rossetti, it was strongly influenced by the former's mediaevalism, his hatred of industrialism, and his own version of socialism which included the regeneration of man by handicrafts. His firm of Morris & Co. produced wallpapers, tapestries, furniture, stained-glass windows, carpets and fabrics in a style totally different from that of contemporary Victorian decoration. Morris's Kelmscott Press did much to raise the standards of book design and printing. *See* **Art Nouveau.**

Arum, a genus of plants of the Araceae family, of which there is but one British species, the wake-robin or cuckoo-pint, sometimes also styled "Lords and Ladies".

Arundel Marbles, a collection of ancient Greek sculptures formed by Thomas Howard, Earl of Arundel in the 17th cent. and presented to Oxford University by his grandson, Henry Howard, who became Duke of Norfolk.

Aryans, nomadic peoples who made their way in successive waves from the Eurasian steppes to the Indus and the Nile during the first half of the 2nd millennium B.C. They crossed the Hindu Kush into N.W. India and settled in the valleys of the Indus and Ganges, where an earlier Indus civilisation had flourished, *c.* 3240–2750 B.C. Their religious ideas are reflected in the Veda (oldest Hindu scriptures, written down many centuries later in Vedic, parent language of Sanskrit). Those who made their way to Syria and Egypt founded the Hyksos empire (*c.* 1720–1550 B.C.). The Aryans introduced the horse-drawn chariot and spoke a language from which the great Indo-European family of languages is derived, with one group in India and Iran, and another in Europe. Because of the misuse of the term by the Nazis, Aryan is now referred to as proto-Indo-European.

Asafoetida, an acrid, strong-smelling gum resin exuded from the stem of an umbelliferous plant, *Ferula foetida*, found in Iran and Afghanistan. Formerly used medicinally to treat hysteria; still used in cooking in India, Iran and France.

Ascension Day, or Holy Thursday, is the 40th day after Easter.

Ascot Races are an annual fashionable function dating from 1711 and taking place on Ascot Heath, only 10 km from Windsor, in June. These races have always had royal patronage. The course is *c.* 3 km long.

Ash, a familiar deciduous tree of the genus *Fraxinus*, of over 60 species, native to North-temperate regions. The ash held an important place in Norse mythology, as it was supposed to support the heavens with its roots in Hell. The species native to Britain, and to Europe, is *F. excelsior*, a tall tree with compound leaves, greenish flowers, winged seeds, and black buds in winter. It is a valuable timber tree, tough and elastic, and largely used for wheels and handles. The rowan, or mountain ash, *Sorbus aucuparia*, with similar leaves and orange berries, belongs to a different family. *F. pendula* or weeping ash is a weeping strain which makes an ideal natural summer house.

Ashes, The, the symbol which distinguishes the winning cricket team in the Australian Test Matches. In 1882 the Australians won at the Oval by 7 runs. After the match the following epitaph appeared in the *Sporting Times*: "In affectionate remembrance of English Cricket which died at the Oval on 29 Aug. 1882, deeply lamented by a large circle of sorrowing friends and acquaintances. R.I.P. NB. The body will be cremated and the ashes taken to Australia." When the English Eleven went to Australia the same winter it was said that they had come to recover the "ashes". England won two out of three matches, and after the third match the ashes of what is now generally believed to have been a stump were presented in an urn to Ivo Bligh, later Lord Darnley. He bequeathed the urn to the M.C.C., and it now stands in the Memorial Gallery at Lord's.

Ash Wednesday, first day of Lent, the seventh Wednesday before Easter.

Assassination, treacherous murder for political ends, usually of a ruler or distinguished person. Among the most notable: Julius Caesar, 44 B.C.; Thomas Becket, 1170; David Rizzio, 1566; William the Silent, 1584; Henry IV of France, 1610; Jean Paul Marat, 1793; Abraham Lincoln, 1865; Alexander II of Russia, 1881; Archduke Francis Ferdinand of Austria, 1914; Dr. Dollfuss, 1934; King Alexander of Yugoslavia, 1934; Mahatma Gandhi, 1948; King Abdullah of Jordan, 1951; Liaquat Ali Khan, 1951; King Feisal of Iraq, 1958; Mr. Bandaranaike, 1959; President Kennedy, 1963; Malcolm X, 1965; Dr. Verwoerd, 1966; Dr. Martin Luther King, 1968; Senator Robert Kennedy, 1968; Mr. Tom Mboya, 1969; Dr. E. Mondlane of Moçambique, 1969; Dr. A. Cabal of Port. Guinea, 1973; King Faisal of Saudi Arabia, 1975.

Asteroids are minor planets most of whose orbits lie between those of Mars and Jupiter; they were unknown until the discovery of Ceres by Piazzi in 1801. More than a thousand have been named and many thousands are believed to exist. After 1891 they were identified by their paths on exposed photographic plates. Most of them have a diameter of well under 80 km. Ceres, with a diameter of *c.* 772 km, is the largest, then there are Pallas (*c.* 489 km), Juno 193 km), Vesta (386 km), Astraea, Adonis, Hermes, Hidalgo, Eros, Amor, Apollo, and the Trojan group which all take their names from Homer's *Iliad*—Achilles, Patroclus, Hector, Nestor, Priam, Agamemnon, Ulysses, Aeneas, Anchises, Troilus, Ajax, and Diomede. The asteroid Icarus (diameter *c.* 0·8 km) was within a few kilometres of the Earth on 14 June 1968.

Astrolabe, a mediaeval scientific instrument for taking altitudes, observing the sun by day and the stars by night, and used for telling the time and finding the latitude. Used by the ancient Greeks, later by the Arabs and Persians, and introduced into Europe by way of Spain in the 14th cent. Chaucer is said to have sent his son Lois, a ten-year-old student at Oxford, an astrolabe with a treatise on its use in 1391.

Astronomical unit, the mean distance from the centre of the earth to the centre of the sun, or half the major axis of the earth's elliptical orbit. It has been known for some 300 years that the earth–sun distance is roughly 93 million miles (150 million km), but over the past 60-odd years astronomers have attempted to determine it with ever-greater accuracy, using various methods of computation. Spencer Jones (1931) deduced a value of 93,004,000 miles (149,643,436 km); the American astronomer E. K. Rabe (1950) obtained a value of 92,914,800 miles (149,499,913 km); and data from the *Pioneer V* space probe gave a value of 92,925,100 miles (149,516,486 km). There are two basic ways of determining the unit: one is based on observations of the minor planet Eros, the other is the radar method, based on the time taken for a radio signal bounced off the planet Venus to return to earth. The earth–sun distance is a fundamental value in astronomy.

Astrology. *See* **Section J.**

Astronomy. The Pythagoreans believed the stars and planets moved with uniform circular velocity in crystalline spheres, centred round the earth (the "harmony of the spheres"). Hipparchus (190–120 B.C.) made the first star catalogue, discovered the precession of the equinoxes and introduced the idea of epicyclic motion. His planetary system, in the form it was presented by Ptolemy 200 years later, held until the Renaissance when Copernicus revived the heretical view first put forward by Aristarchus of Samos (310–230 B.C.) that the sun and not the earth was at the centre. Galileo, accurate observer and experimenter, went beyond Copernicus; helped by the contributions of Tycho Brahe, Giordano Bruno, Kepler and others, he was able to overthrow the Ptolemaic system of the heavenly spheres and Aristotelian philosophy and pave the way for Newton and modern astronomy. To Galileo we owe the conception of acceleration; to Newton the theory of universal gravitation; they showed that the same laws govern both celestial and terrestrial physics. Three landmarks in more recent times were the discovery of Uranus by Herschel in 1781 which extended the solar system as then recognised; the estimation by Hubble in 1924 of the distance of Andromeda, which showed that our Galaxy was just one of many; and Einstein's theory of relativity which improved on Newton's theory of the solar system by bringing gravitation into the domain of space-time. Today radio-telescopes and space probes are advancing astronomical knowledge and making it possible to explore regions beyond the scope of optical telescopes. The following have held the position of Astronomer Royal (period of office in brackets): John Flamsteed (1675–1719), Edmund Halley (1719–42), James Bradley (1742–62), Nathaniel Bliss (1762–65), Nevil Maskelyne (1765–1811), John Pond (1811–35), Sir George Airy (1835–81), Sir William Christie (1881–1910), Sir Frank Dyson (1910–33), Sir Harold Spencer Jones (1933–55), Sir Richard Woolley (1956–72), Sir Martin Ryle (1972–). *See* **F5–7,** *also* **Radio Astronomy.**

Astrophysics, a branch of astronomy concerned with the physical nature and constitution of celestial bodies. Developments in space research technology have contributed to the great advance in this branch of science.

Athanasian Creed, one of the three ancient creeds of the Christian Church, often referred to as the *Quicunque Vult*, is a statement of the doctrine of the Trinity and the Incarnation, and though named after St. Athanasius, the view is now widely held that it is the work of St. Ambrose (339–97).

Atmosphere is the gaseous envelope of the earth, and consists of a mixture of gases (*see* **Air**) and water vapour, the variability of the latter being of great importance meteorologically. The ozone layer, which absorbs ultra-violet radiation which would be lethal to plant life if it reached the ground is concentr ted at about 32 km above the earth but extends to about twice that height. The lower level of the atmosphere up to a height of about 11 km (10 km at the Poles and 16 km at the Equator) is known as the *troposphere*, and it is in this region that nearly all weather phenomena occur. This is the region of most interest to the forecaster studying temperature, humidity, wind-speed, and the movement of air masses. Temperature falls with height by about 1°C per 152 m in this layer. The *tropopause* is the boundary between the troposphere and the *stratosphere*. Temperature varies little in the lower levels of this region: it is mainly cloudless, and has no vertical currents. Strangely enough, the lowest temperatures of the atmosphere are to be found not at the Poles, but at about 18 km above the Equator, where a temperature as low as −80°C has been recorded! Temperatures begin to rise about 32 km from the earth's surface at about the same rate as they fall in the troposphere owing to the absorption of solar radiation by the concentration of ozone. The stratospheric air is extremely dry. Near the 100 km level a number of important atmospheric phenomena occur. Above this level the oxygen becomes predominantly monatomic in contrast to the normal diatomic form at lower altitudes. This is the *ionosphere* (*q.v.*). This layer acts as an electrical radio mirror which makes long-distance radio transmission possible. The region of the Van Allen belts (*q.v.*) above the earth is called the magnetosphere. The auroras are most frequently observed at altitudes between about 100 and 400 km but do extend at times far higher. Many aspects of the upper air can only be studied through space-research techniques. These include the composition and temperature of the charged particles in the ionosphere, the location of the electric currents in the ionosphere which produce the regular variations of the compass needle, as well as those which circulate during magnetic storms, the variation of the intensity of different radiations in the air-glow (*q.v.*) with height, the composition of the air at heights above 32 km, and so on. In addition, the pressures, density, temperatures, and wind distribution of the neutral atmosphere can be studied more directly, in much greater detail, and up to much greater altitudes than is possible if one is confined to the use of equipment on the ground. Instruments outside the atmosphere can make systematic observations on a world-wide basis of the atmospheric circulation, through observation of cloud cover and of the thermal radiation into space from the atmosphere. Such observations are of great importance for meteorology. *See also* **Ionosphere.**

Atmospherics are electrical impulses which are believed to originate in atmospheric electrical discharges such as lightning. They give rise to crashing background noises in the loudspeakers of radio sets, interfering with reception at distances of up to 6,400 km from the centre of the disturbance. The location of atmospherics with the aid of radio direction-finding methods gives warning of the approach of thunderstorms.

Atom. *See* **F9–14, F20.**

Atomic Pile, an apparatus containing a fissionable element and a moderator, such as heavy water or graphite, in which a self-sustaining fission process proceeds at a controllable rate. The first atomic pile, constructed on a squash court at Chicago, was operated for the first time on 2 December 1942, under the direction of Enrico Fermi. The pile contained 12,400 lb (5,580 kg) of uranium. *See* **Nuclear Reactors.**

Augsburg Confession, name given to the doctrine of faith of the Lutheran churches, drawn up by Melanchthon and endorsed by Luther for the Diet of Augsburg (1530).

August, named after the Emperor Augustus, because it was his "lucky" month.

Auks, duck-like sea-birds, black and white, with short, narrow wings, compact bodies, and legs set well back. Breed in colonies on rocky coasts of N. Europe (incl. British Isles) and spend most time in coastal waters. Migrate south in winter. The Auk family includes the Razorbill, Little Auk, Guillemot and Puffin. The Great Auk became extinct in the 19th cent. after ruthless hunting for the sake of its feathers.

Aurora polaris. This wonderful phenomenon of the night sky is a common sight in some high latitudes, north and south. It is visible less often in temperate latitudes, and only very seldom in the tropics. As seen in the northern hemisphere it is called the aurora borealis or northern lights, and in the south, the aurora australis or southern lights. The zone of maximum frequency surrounds the north magnetic pole and includes Greenland, northern Canada, and the north coast of Alaska. Auroral displays may take several forms, *e.g.*, a faint glow, a diffuse ribbon of light crossing the heavens, great folded waving curtains like draperies; the whole sky may be a grand panoply of light. Both the aurora and the magnetic storm associated with it are ascribed to the envelopment of the earth in a great cloud or stream of solar gas shot out from stormy areas on the sun (sunspots) that has travelled to the earth at a speed of over 1,600 km a second. The gas is mainly atomic hydrogen, but the atoms are broken up into their two parts, protons and electrons. These are both electrically charged. This renders them subject to the influence of the earth's magnetic field, which deflects many of them to the high latitudes where the aurora is most commonly seen. The aurora is a kind of light essentially different from that of the rainbow which is a partly subjective phenomenon. Each beholder sees his own rainbow, whose light is sunlight refracted and reflected by many raindrops. The raindrops that produce his rainbow depend on his position as well as on the direction of the sun. The aurora, on the contrary, is a light as objective as that of a candle, though produced differently. It is a self-luminescence of the air in particular regions of the atmosphere that lie far above the clouds. By simultaneous observation from stations 32 km or more apart it is possible to locate the position of the luminous air, *i.e.*, to determine the height of the aurora, its location in plan, and its form and volume.

Austerlitz, Battle of, was fought near Brünn, in Moravia, on 2 December 1805, when Napoleon defeated the Russians and Austrians under Kutuzon.

Auto-da-Fé, or Act of Faith, was the ceremony connected with the sentencing of heretics under the Inquisition of Spain and Portugal, the persons found guilty being imprisoned or burned alive. The ceremony took place in some public square, sometimes in the presence of the king and court.

Automation is a modern word used to designate the adoption of methods of automatic control either of manufacturing processes or of any business process involving a large mass of routine work. The word is used in broader and narrower senses. In its broadest sense it covers any form of mechanisation which largely replaces human labour by the work of automatic or semi-automatic machines, such as has been in progress continuously since the Industrial Revolution; but it is better kept to a narrower meaning, in which it is confined to the recent development of electronic or similar devices, involving feedback (automatic detection and correction of malfunction). Human labour is eliminated save for that needed for watching and maintaining the elaborate machines used. In this sense, automation has been spreading rapidly in advanced countries.

Autumn, the third season of the year, begins with the autumnal equinox, and ends with the winter solstice, but the term is generally understood as covering the period from mid-August to mid-November.

Auxins, "plant hormones", organic substances produced by plants to regulate growth. Synthetic auxins are now widely used, *e.g.*, for promotion of root formation in cuttings, differential weed control, prevention of premature dropping of fruit, in storage of potatoes and hard fruit, and to overcome frost damage to fruit buds.

Average is a single number designed to give a typical example of a set of numbers, *e.g.*, a cricketer's batting average for a season gives an idea of his typical score. There are several kinds of average and their uses are studied in the science of statistics (*q.v.*). A statement that "so and so is the average value" can be misleading if one does not know which average is meant. Three common averages are: the arithmetic average (or mean), the mode, and the median. The arithmetic average of n numbers is found by adding them together and dividing by n; this is a very common method of averaging. The mode of n numbers is the most frequently occurring number. The median is the middle number, *i.e.*, the number which is smaller than just as many of the other numbers as it exceeds. Of the numbers 1, 2, 2, 2, 2, 3, 4, 5, 6, 8, 9, the arithmetic means is 4, the mode is 2, the median is 3.

Avocet, a graceful wading bird related to the stilts, of black-and-white plumage, bluish legs, and slender upturned bill. There are four species. Avocets nest in colonies and there is one in the sanctuary on Havergate Island, Suffolk.

Avogadro's Hypothesis. This is a fundamental concept of chemistry. Equal volumes of all gases under the same conditions of temperature and pressure contain the same number of molecules. This law was instrumental in assigning the formulae of molecules. The hypothesis was put forward in 1811, but was not generally accepted until 1860. *See* **F21(2)**.

Aztecs, the name of a native and powerful race found in Mexico when the Spaniards first discovered that country, and with difficulty subdued.

B

Babiroussa, a ferocious, long-legged wild pig, native of Sulawesi, sometimes called the horned-hog, because of the long upper tusks in the male, which are developments of the canine teeth whch grow upwards, piercing the upper lip, and curving backwards, often broken in fighting.

Baboon, monkeys belonging to the African genus *Papio*. They are considered the lowest of the Old World (Catarrhine) monkeys, and walk on all fours. In the main terrestrial, but take to trees after food. The mandrill is closely related.

Babylonian Captivity, the period spent by the Jews in Babylon after Jerusalem was captured by Nebuchadnezzar, the Babylonian emperor, in 586 B.C. Traditionally the captivity lasted 70 years, but when Babylon was in turn taken by Cyrus in 538 B.C., the exiles were permitted to return to Jerusalem. The term is also applied in church history to the period 1309–78 when the papacy moved to Avignon, into the control of the French monarchy.

Bacteria. *See* **F39**.

Bacteriophage (Phage), literally "bacteria eater" *i.e.*, a virus which specifically infects bacteria. In common with viruses which attack animal or plant cells, isolated phages are inert, and can only reproduce by making use of the chemical apparatus of a more sophisticated host cell (in this case, a bacterium). However phages may be of two types, virulent or temperate. Virulent phages completely disrupt the normal functioning of the infected bacterium and adapt its reproductive mechanism to produce more phage. This eventually kills the bacterium and the newly assembled phages are released. Temperate phages on the other hand may enter into a remarkable symbiotic relationship with the bacterium, known as lysogeny. The phage genetic material is incorporated into that of the bacterium and is reproduced each time the still functioning bacterium subsequently divides. Furthermore the bacterium is immune from attack by potentially virulent phages of the same type. When such lysogenic bacteria die, phage particles may again be released. Phages carried in lysogenic bacteria are in a state known as prophage and it is often difficult to obtain pure, prophage-free strains of bacteria. Because of their relatively simple structure, phages have been extensively used in research on genetics and molecular biology.

Badger, a carnivorous mammal related to the weasel, of nocturnal and burrowing habits, inoffensive, subsisting chiefly on roots and insects, though sometimes mice, young rabbits and eggs form part of its diet. Badger-baiting was a favourite sport in Britain until it was prohibited in the middle of 19th cent. The badger does little harm and quite a lot of good; badger digging is to be condemned as a cruel sport. In Britain the badger is protected by an Act of Parliament passed in 1973, and the new Nature Conservancy Council may declare an area to be one of special protection for the species.

Bagpipe. Once popular all over Europe, this instrument is still played in Scotland, Ireland, Brittany and elsewhere. The bag acts as a reservoir of air and, when squeezed by the player's arm, forces air through the pipes. One of these, the Chanter pipe, provides the tune and is played by the fingers as in a flageolet. The remainder, the Drone pipes, give a continuous, unvarying note.

Bailey Bridge, invented by Sir Donald Bailey and first used in the N. African campaign 1942–3. Built up of prefabricated girders, it can be easily transported and erected.

Bailiwick, a feudal term denoting the limits of a bailiff's jurisdiction. The term has survived in the Channel Islands, where Jersey and Guernsey are Bailiwicks.

Balance of Power was the doctrine in British policy whereby European groups should be so balanced as to prevent the emergence of a dominating Power. Thus the balance was maintained between the Triple Alliance (Germany, Austria and Italy) and the Triple Entente (Great Britain, France and Russia) and preserved peace from 1871 to 1914. After the first world war there was tentative support of Germany's recovery to counterweight a possible French hegemony; but when Germany's power grew under Hitler culminating in the second world war, Britain, France and Russia again became allies. By the end of the war the old system of a balance of power centred upon Europe collapsed to give way to a thermonuclear balance of power between the super-Powers, the Soviet Union (Warsaw Pact) and the United States (Nato alliance). In the future there may be a world of five great powers—United States, Soviet Union, China, Western Europe, Japan.

Baldachin (It. *Baldachino*), a canopy usually supported by four pillars over throne, altar, or other sacred object. The name is also applied to the silken canopy used in processions and borne by the priest who carries the Host.

Balearic Crane, the crowned crane of the Balearic Islands and the North African mainland, distinguished by its yellowish, black-tipped occipital tuft and by its trumpet note.

Baleen *or* **"whalebone"** the name given to a series of horny plates growing from the roof of the mouth in those whales classified as Whalebone or Baleen Whales (Mystacoceti). There are 300–400 or so plates on each side, and their inner edges are frayed, the whole system constituting a filter for collecting minute organisms used for food. The Baleen Whales include the Right-Whales, the Pacific Grey-Whale and the Rorquals. *See* **Whales**.

Ballet is a combination of four arts; dancing, music, painting, and drama, each of which is ideally of equal importance. The movement of the individual dancers and the "orchestration" of the whole group is in the hands of the choreographer. The dancer's training follows certain basic rules but save in classical ballet there is considerable freedom of movement. Ballet as we know it today developed professionally at the Court of King Louis XIV of France, though it owes its origins to Italy and in the earliest times to Greece and Rome. Its movements were made up from the dances of courtiers, country folk and tumblers. Technique grew more complex as costume became modified, the body gaining complete freedom with the invention of tights. A succession of great dancers—French, Italian and latterly Russian left their imprint on the art. Contemporary ballet reflects the aesthetic of the Russian, Sergei Diaghilev. In England Dame Ninette de Valois has laid the foundation of a national ballet, at Sadler's Wells and Covent Garden, with a personality that reflects the national character. A Royal Charter was granted in 1957 setting up the Royal Ballet to co-ordinate the activities of the Sadler's Wells group.

Ballistics the science dealing with the motion of projectiles, especially shells, bombs and rockets. Great advances have been made in this science.

Balloon, the modern ballon consists of a bag of plastic material inflated with a gas lighter than air. The first ascent by man in a hot-air balloon was made on 21 November 1783, and in a hydrogen balloon on 1 December 1783. The most famous of the early scientific flights by manned balloons were those of the Englishmen Coxwell and Glaisher, in 1862, when a height of 11 km was reached. The first aerial crossing of the English Channel by Blanchard and Jeffries was made on 7 January 1785. Piccard's ascent to 16 km, in 1931, marked the conquest of the stratosphere. Four years later the American balloon *Explorer II*, inflated with nearly 112,000m^3 of helium, carried a team of scientists with their floating laboratory to an altitude of 23 km. In 1957 a pressurised balloon carrying an American doctor rose 31 km above the Earth. Captive kite-balloons were widely used in the war as defensive measures against air attack. Meteorologists send their instruments up in balloons to collect data about the upper atmosphere, and of recent years physicists have learned much about cosmic radiation from the study of photographic plates sent to the upper regions in balloons. Ballooning as a hobby is carried on by a number of enthusiasts.

Balsam, a big genus (140 species) of flowering plants. Many species are cultivated for their showy flowers, *e.g., Impatiens noli-me-tangere,* the yellow balsam or "touch-me-not", so called because the fruit explodes when touched, slinging out the seeds. Balsam fir is a conifer (*Abies balsamea*) from which Canada balsam gum is obtained.

Bamboo, a genus of strong grasses, some species growing to over 36 m in height; much used by oriental peoples for all kinds of purposes. The young shoots of some species are tender and esculent. *See* **T5(2).**

Banana (family *Musaceae*), a large herbaceous plant cultivated in moist regions of the tropics, and one of the most productive plants known. The main areas of commercial cultivation are in tropical America, the Canary Islands and West Africa. World production is estimated at 20 million tonnes, of which only 3 million are for trade.

Bandicoots, Australasian marsupial mammals, of the size of a large rat or rabbit. They are burrowing animals living largely on insects. The rabbit-eared bandicoot, restricted to Australia, has shrew-like snout, long ears like a rabbit, long crested tail, and a silky coat. The long-nosed bandicoot has a spiny coat and comes from E. Australia. The pig-footed bandicoot has two functional toes on the foot, like a pig.

Bank Rate, the rate at which the Bank of England is prepared to lend to the clearing banks. If raised it has the immediate effect of raising the rate of discount on Treasury Bills. Since October 1972 known as the Minimum Lending Rate. *See* **Section G.**

Bantu (native word = people), term loosely used for large family of Negro races of Southern Africa.

Baobab, a tropical African tree. The species *Adansonia digitata* is one of the largest trees known, though not the tallest; the trunk can reach 9 m in thickness. The fruit is woody, but its juice provides a cooling beverage. The bark yields a fibre used for making rope and cloth.

Barbary Ape, a large monkey belonging to the genus *Macaca.* It is the only monkey living in relative freedom in Europe, a small colony being found on the Rock of Gibraltar. It has no tail.

Barberry, a genus of berry-producing shrubs containing a hundred species. Several species are cultivated for their flowers and bright berries. Has an interesting pollination mechanism; the base of each stamen is sensitive to touch, and insects probing for nectar cause top of stamen to spring inwards, so dusting visitor's head with pollen which can then be carried to the next flower visited. The common barberry (*Berberis communis*) harbours one stage of the fungus that causes rust of wheat.

Barbican, a fortified entrance to a castle or city, with projecting towers. In the London area called Barbican there was formerly a barbican in front of the city gates.

Barbiturates. A group of drugs derived from a parent compound called barbituric acid: phenobarbitone is the best-known example. They induce sleep and are used in the manufacture of sleeping pills and sometimes as anaesthetics, but they have the disadvantage of being habit forming. *See also* **P23(2).**

Barbizon School, a school of mid-19th-cent. landscape painters whose main tenet was a return to nature with an exact rendering of peasant life and country scenery painted on the spot. It was named after the village of that name in the Forest of Fontainebleau, where its chief members—Millet, Theodore Rousseau, Daubigny and Diaz—made their home. Their practice of painting direct from nature, which was far from universal at that time, made them the precursors of **Impressionism** (*q.v.*).

Barcarolle, a Venetian gondolier's song applied to instrumental as well as vocal compositions.

Bard, among the ancient Celts a poet or minstrel whose mission was to sing of heroic deeds. He was supposed to have the gift of prophecy, and was exempt from taxes and military service.

Barilla, soda carbonate or soda ash obtained by burning certain salt-marsh plants (*e.g.,* the saltwort, *Salsola kali*). It used to be in great demand, until the product of the Leblanc and then the Solvay ammonia-soda process was made available by the chemical industry.

Barium, metal element, symbol Ba. In group 2 of the periodic table. The metal is soft and easily cut. It occurs as the sulphate and carbonate in nature. It was first prepared by Sir Humphry Davy in 1808, as an amalgam, by electrolysis of barium chloride. The pure metal was not isolated until 1901.

Barium meal. Barium sulphate is opaque to X-rays and before taking X-ray pictures of the alimentary canal radiologists give a "barium meal" to the patients so that the alimentary canal shows up more clearly.

Barnacles constitute a sub-class (*Cirripedia*) of the Crustacea. The barnacle fouling the bottom of ships is the Goose Barnacle, which has a long muscular stalk and a shell composed of five plates. The Acorn Barnacles, which cover rocks, breakwaters, etc., just below high-water mark are similarly constructed, but have no stalk. The manner of feeding of barnacles was vividly described by T. H. Huxley, who said the barnacle is "a crustacean fixed by its head kicking the food into its mouth with its legs". It was a naval surgeon, J. Vaughan Thompson, who discovered in 1830 that barnacles have a free-swimming larva (or nauplius). In the Middle Ages a curious myth grew up to the effect that the Barnacle changed into a sea-bird called, for that reason, the Barnacle Goose.

Barometer is an instrument for measuring atmospheric pressure, invented at Florence by Torricelli, pupil of Galileo, in 1644. The standard method consists of balancing the air column against a column of mercury, used on account of its high density. The mercury is contained in a long glass tube, closed at one end, and inverted in a cistern also containing mercury. The height of the mercury column, supporting the air column, is taken as the pressure at the time, and can be read off very accurately by means of a vernier scale. Present-day tendency is to express the readings in units of pressure instead of length, the millibar being adopted (1 mb = 1,000 dynes per sq. cm.; 1,000 mb ≡ 75 cm of mercury approx.). The standard instrument is correct for pressures at 0°C in Lat. 45°, so that corrections have to be applied for temperatures and latitudes other than these. Also a correction has to be made for reducing the pressure to mean sea level. *See* **Aneroid.**

Baron, title given in feudal England to a man who held his land directly from the king by military or other honourable service. The first baron created by letters patent was John Beauchamp de Holt, Baron of Kidderminster, in 1387. A baron is a member of the fifth and last grade of the peerage of the United Kingdom and is addressed as "Lord". Life peers and life peeresses rank with hereditary barons and baronesses according to the date of their creation. In Scotland the term baron is used of the possessor of a feudal fief, or the representative by descent of such a fief. The equivalent of the English baron, as a rank of the Scottish peerage, is Lord of Parliament.

Baronet, the lowest hereditary title, instituted by James I to provide funds for the colonisation of Ulster. The first baronet was Sir Nicholas Bacon. Since 1964 no recommendations for hereditary honours have been made.

Baroque, a term used for the art style of the period *c.* 1600–1720 which was the artistic accompaniment of the Jesuit counter-Reformation. Its most obvious characteristics are: (*a*) its emotional appeal and dramatic intensity both related to its deliberate intention as propaganda ("a good picture makes better religious propaganda than a sermon" said one of its exponents); (*b*) in architecture, a style which is heavily and sometimes almost grotesquely ornate, plentifully covered with voluptuous sculpture on which draperies float rather than hang, with twisted and spiral instead of plain or fluted columns, and unnecessary windows or recesses added for ornament rather than use; (c) its emphasis on the whole at the expense of the parts such that a building's sculpture merges into its architecture and both into its painting (Baroque paintings are as closely knit as a jigsaw puzzle so that one cannot isolate individual figures as would be possible in a Renaissance one). Baroque architecture owing to its origin is found mainly in the Catholic countries: Italy, France, Austria, Bavaria, *e.g.*, the Barberini Palace, Rome, designed by its greatest exponent Bernini and others; the Church of the Invalides, Paris. Baroque artists include Caravaggio, Guido Reni, Murillo and Rubens, the greatest Northern Baroque painter. The Baroque style merges gradually into **Rococo** (*q.v.*).

Barque, a small sailing vessel with three or four masts. A three-masted barque has fore- and mainmasts square-rigged, the mizzenmast fore- and aft-rigged.

Barrow is an ancient artificial mound of earth or stone raised over the site of a burial. In Britain barrows were built from 2500 B.C. until the late Saxon period, but the Egyptian are the earliest barrows known, the great pyramids being a spectacular development of the custom of ceremonial burial. Silbury Hill, south of Avebury, is the biggest artificial mound in Europe, 512 m in circuit at the base, 96 m at top, and 41 m high.

Bartholomew, Massacre of St., occurred in Paris on the night of 24 August 1572, when over two thousand Huguenots were massacred by order of the Catholic French Court.

Baryons, the group of heavier subatomic particles which includes the proton, neutron, lambda and omega-minus particles (and their corresponding anti-particles, called anti-baryons). Baryons interact by means of all the known forces of nature (strong, weak, electromagnetic and gravitational). However, in any closed system the total baryon number (*i.e.*, the number of baryons minus the number of anti-baryons) is constant. This means that the proton, being the lightest known baryon, must be stable against spontaneous decay. Unlike the lighter leptons (*q.v.*), baryons are now thought to have internal structure reflecting the fact that they are composed of quarks (*q.v.*). *See* **F14**.

Basalt Rocks are fine-grained, dark coloured, of igneous origin and occur either as lava flows as in Mull and Staffa, or as intrusive sheets, like the Edinburgh Castle Rock and Salisbury Crags. One of the most noted examples of columnar basalt is that of the Giant's Causeway in Ireland.

Basanite, a smooth black siliceous mineral, or flinty jasper; a crypto-crystalline quartz used as a touchstone for testing the purity of gold, etc., by means of the mark left after rubbing the metal with it. Sometimes styled the Lydian stone.

Base, a substance having a tendency to accept a proton (H^+). This is a wide definition and covers unconventional types of compounds. In aqueous solution bases dissolve with formation of hydroxyl ions, and will neutralise an acid to form a salt. In non-aqueous solvents, like liquid ammonia or hydrogen fluoride, compounds classically regarded as salts can be bases, *e.g.*, sodium fluoride is a base in hydrogen fluoride solution. *See* **F22**.

Basilisk, is a lizard of aquatic habits, with an elevated crest (which it can erect or depress at will) down the centre of its back.

Basques, people of N. Spain and S.W. France, oldest surviving racial group in Europe, who have preserved their ancient language which is unrelated to any other tongue.

Bas-Relief (" low relief "), a term used in sculpture to denote a class of sculptures the figures of which are only slightly raised from the surface of the stone or clay upon which the design is wrought.

Bastille, a castle or fortress in Paris, built in the 14th cent., and used as a state prison, especially for political offenders. Its bad repute as an instrument of despotism excited the hatred of the populace, who stormed and demolished it on 14 July 1789, at the beginning of the Revolution.

Bastinado, an oriental punishment, by beating with a pliable cane on the soles of the feet.

Bats. These mammals fly by means of a membrane stretched between each of the long fingers of the hand and between the fifth finger and the body. Another membrane stretches between the legs and the tail. Most British bats, including the pipistrelle, long-eared bats, noctules, belong to the family Vespertilionidae (with the exception of the horseshoe bats which belong to the family Rhinolophidae). These all feed on insects which they catch on the wing. The problem of how bats can detect their insect prey and avoid obstacles when flying in total darkness has interested zoologists for a very long time. The problem was solved with the advent of sensitive ultrasonic recording devices. Blindness does not affect this ability but deafness leaves bats comparatively helpless. One of the most interesting types of bat is the fishing bat (*Noctilio*) found in central America, which can detect fish by means of the ripples they make on the water surface, receiving echoes from such ripples. *See also* **Ultrasonics.**

Bath, Order of the, Britain's second oldest order of knighthood. Exclusive to men since its institution by Henry IV in 1399, women became eligible for admission to the order in 1971. The order has three grades: Knight Grand Cross (G.C.B.), Knight Commander (K.C.B.), and Companion (C.B.). Women members of the order are known as Dame Grand Cross, Dame Commander and Companion.

Battery, Electric, the common term for an electric cell but really meaning a combination of two or more cells. A cell is a device for converting stored chemical energy into electricity which can then be used for heat, light, traction, or any desired purpose. A *primary* cell will do this until the chemical action is completed and the cell is then useless. In a *secondary* cell, the chemical actions are reversible and the cell can be returned to its initial condition and used again. This is done by passing an electric current through—a process called recharging. A common primary cell is the Leclanché dry cell used in torches. This works by the action of sal-ammoniac on electrodes made of zinc and carbon. About a century after it came into common use it is still the chief source of power for portable equipment in armed forces. A common secondary cell is the lead and sulphuric acid accumulator used in cars. Many other types of cell are known and some are under development because the demands of space travel, medicine, warfare, etc., call for batteries of lighter weight, greater reliability, or special properties. *See* **Fuel Cell, Energy Conversion.**

Bauhaus, a German institution for the training of architects, artists and industrial designers founded in 1919 at Weimar by Walter Gropius, (d. 1969). It was closed by Hitler in 1933 and re-opened at Chicago. The Bauhaus doctrine held that there should be no separation between architecture and the fine and applied arts; that art, science and technology should co-operate to create " the compositely inseparable work of art, the great building ". Thus it was an organisation with a social purpose. The original institution, at the instigation of Gropius, included on its teaching staff not only architects and technicians but also such noted artists as Paul Klee and Wassily Kandinsky.

Bauxite, the chief ore of aluminium. Chemically it is aluminium oxide. Aluminium metal is made industrially by electrolysing purified bauxite dissolved in fused cryolite. Chief producing areas: Jamaica, Australia, Surinam, USSR, Guyana, France, Greece, Guinea, USA, Hungary, Yugoslavia.

Bayeux Tapestry, a famous tapestry representing the conquest of England by William the Conqueror. It is embroidered on a band of linen 70 m long and 51 cm wide in blue, green, red and yellow, divided into 72 scenes ranging over the whole story of the conquest. The accepted view is that the tapestry was commissioned for Bayeux Cathedral, but a new interpretation is that it is an Anglo–Norman secular work of art, much influenced by the contemporary *chansons de geste* (songs of deeds), executed by

English embroiderers for a Norman patron. A representation can be seen in the Victoria and Albert Museum in London.

Beagle, a small hound that tracks by scent, and formerly used for hare hunting.

Bears belong to the Ursidae family of the Carnivora. They are plantigrade mammals, walking (like man) on the soles of their feet. Found in most parts of the world except Australia. The common Brown Bear was once spread over the whole of Europe; it became extinct in England about the 11th cent.; 2–2·5 m in length, and stands 1 m or more at the shoulder. The Grizzly Bear of N. America is larger, and the coat is shorter and greyer. The Polar Bear is remarkable in having a white coat all the year round; it spends much time in water, and unlike the other bears it is entirely carnivorous. Bear-baiting was made illegal in England in 1835.

Beaufort Scale of wind force is used to specify numerically the strength of the wind. Since the introduction of anemometers to measure the actual velocity, equivalent values of the ranges in miles per hour at a standard height in the open have been assigned to the Beaufort numbers. *See* **Section N.**

Beaver, a genus of mammals of the Rodentia order, with short, scaly ears, webbed hind feet, and a long broad scaly tail. They grow up to 1·2 m long, and live in communities, constructing dams and lodges where they breed. Found in N. America, Russia, and Poland. Hunted mercilessly by trappers for its valuable pelt before protective laws were passed.

Bedlam (a corruption of Bethlehem) was a priory in Bishopsgate, afterwards converted into a hospital for lunatics. The asylum was transferred to St. George's Fields, Lambeth, in 1815. The term "bedlamite" came to be applied to any person behaving like a madman.

Beech, a deciduous tree belonging to the genus *Fagus* of some eight or nine species found in north temperate regions. The common beech, *F. sylvatica*, is believed to be native to Britain and is one of our finest trees, with massive trunk, long, pointed winter buds, and smooth, grey bark. There is little undergrowth under its dense shade. It is shorter lived than the oak, taking about 200 years to reach full size and then declining. The timber of beech has a variety of uses, *e.g.*, spoons, handles, tools, and chairs.

Bee-eater, name of a family of brilliantly coloured birds closely related to the rollers and kingfishers inhabiting the tropical and sub-tropical parts of Africa, Asia and Europe. The European species successfully nested in Britain for the first time in 1955 and a pair nested in Alderney in 1956. With their long curved beaks they catch insects on the wing, especially bees and butterflies, and lay their eggs in dark nest tunnels.

Beefeater. *See* **Yeomen of the Guard.**

Beeswax, the secretion of the bee, used for the formation of the cells or honey-comb of the hive; when melted it is what is commercially known as yellow wax, white wax being made by bleaching. Being impervious to water, it acts as a good resistant and is an article of much utility.

Beetles (Coleoptera) constitute one of the biggest orders of insects, numbering over 200,000 species. There are two pairs of wings; the hind pair are used for flight, while the front pair are hardened to form a pair of protective covers (elytra). Some beetles have lost the power of flight and then the elytra are joined together.

Bel and the Dragon is the title of certain supplementary chapters to the "Book of Daniel" of an apocryphal character. First appeared in the Septuagint, but the Jewish Church did not accept it as inspired. In 1546 the Council of Trent declared it to be canonical.

Bell, a hollow body of metal used for making sounds. Bells are usually made from bell-metal, an alloy of copper and tin. Small bells used for interior functions are often made of silver, gold or brass. Ordinary hand-bells are of brass. From the 7th cent. large bells have been used in England in cathedrals, churches and monasteries. The greatest bell in the world is the "King of Bells" in the Kremlin at Moscow which weighs about 198 tonnes, is 627 cm high and 691 cm in diameter. It was cast in 1733 but cracked in the furnace (the broken part weighed 11 tonnes) and is now preserved as a national treasure. Other large bells in Russia include the 171 tonne one at Krasnogvardersk, near Leningrad, and the one of 110 tonnes at Moscow. The Great Bell (Great Paul) at St. Paul's, cast in 1881, weighs nearly 17 tonnes and is the largest in the United Kingdom. Other gigantic bells are the Great Bell at Peking (53 tonnes); Nanking (22 tonnes); Cologne Cathedral (25 tonnes); Big Ben, Westminster (over 13 tonnes,; Great Peter, York Minster (10 tonnes). The Curfew Bell is rung in some parts of England to this day, notably at Ripon. The number of changes that can be rung on a peal of bells is the *factorial* of the number of bells. Thus four bells allow 24 and eight bells 40,320

Belladonna or **Deadly Nightshade** (*Atropa belladonna*) a well-known poisonous wild plant found in Southern Europe and Western Asia. The alkaloid atropine it contains is valuable in medicine, although a large dose is poisonous.

Bell, Book, and Candle. To curse by "bell book, and candle" was a form of excommunication in the Roman Church ending with the words: "Close the book, quench the candle, ring the bell".

Benedicite, the canticle in the Book of Common Prayer, known also as "The Song of the Three Holy Children".

Benedictines are monks and nuns of the Benedictine Order who live under the rule of St. Benedict—the monastic code whose influence on the religious and cultural life of the West has been so powerful. The rule is marked by an absence of extravagant asceticism. The greatest of the early Benedictines was Pope Gregory I (590–604) who sent St. Augustine of Canterbury to Anglo-Saxon England. Gregorian plainsong is named after him. *See also* **Monasticism, Section J.**

Benzene. An aromatic hydrocarbon obtained from coal tar and some petroleum fractions. It is a volatile inflammable liquid with a characteristic smell. The molecule consists of a flat ring of six carbon atoms, each bound to one hydrogen atom. Benzene is the parent member of many aromatic organic compounds and is widely used in industry to synthesise intermediates for fibres, dyestuffs, explosives and pharmaceutical chemicals.

Beryl, a mineral, of which the emerald is a grass-green variety. Composed of beryllium and aluminium silicates. The pure mineral is colourless; the colour of most beryl comes from traces of impurities, notably iron and chromium. Otherwise it is yellowish, greenish-yellow, or blue, and is found in veins which traverse granite or gneiss, or embedded in granite, and sometimes in alluvial soil formed from such rocks.

Beryllium. Metallic element, symbol Be. Very similar to aluminium, it is stronger than steel and only one-quarter its weight. It is not very abundant, its main source is the mineral, beryl. Copper containing 2 per cent. beryllium is used for making springs. Because of its special properties the metal is used as a component in spacecraft, missiles and nuclear reactors. This accounts for its recent development on a technical scale. The metal powder is toxic.

Bessemer Process, for making steel depends on the forcing of atmospheric air into molten pig iron to burn out the impurities. *See* **Steel.**

Betel, the leaf of an Indian climbing plant, of pungent, narcotic properties. It is destructive to the teeth, and reddens the gums and lips.

Bhang, the Indian name for the hemp plant *Cannabis sativa*, the leaves and seed-capsules of which are chewed or smoked. The potent drug which comes from flowers of the female plant is called hashish in Arabia and marihuana in the United States and Mexico. *See* **P23**(2).

Bible (Greek *biblion* = scroll of paper; pl. *biblia* = writings) includes the Hebrew sacred Scriptures (Old Testament) and those held sacred by the Christians (New Testament). The Old Testament—the prehistoric portion—consists of 39 books, and is divided into three parts: (1) the Law, (2) the Prophets, (3) Miscellaneous Writings. The Old Testament was written in Hebrew except for parts of Ezra and Daniel, which were in Aramaic. It was not until the 9th cent. A.D. that a complete Hebrew text was made, the so-called Massoretic text. Before that the main versions were the Alexandrian Greek translation (Septuagint) made in the 2nd cent. B.C. and St. Jerome's Latin Vulgate of the 4th cent. A.D. (It was Jerome who used the Latin word "testament" (formed from *testis* = a witness).) Portions were translated into the Anglo-Saxon in the 8th cent. and the Venerable Bede put the greater part of St. John's gospel into English, but it was not until 1535 that a complete printed English version appeared—the Coverdale Translation. The Authorised Version dates from 1611 in the reign of James I, and its beautiful phraseology has given it a lasting appeal. The Revised Version dates from 1885. *The New English Bible*, with the Apocrypha, was published in 1970. It is a new translation in plain English prose of the earliest Hebrew, Aramaic, and Greek manuscripts. The finding of the Dead Sea Scrolls (since 1947) has added to our knowledge of Scripture.

Biedermeier, style in interior decoration and the decorative arts developed from Empire (*q.v.*). It was created in Vienna *c.* 1815 and the name was derived from a fantasy figure in Viennese writing personifying all that which is sedate and bourgeois. Biedermeier furniture is less austere and grandiose than Empire's predecessors, more intimate and homely. A most important creation is the large circular table on a stem-like foot, which became the centre of family life, around which chairs could be grouped freely, not formally against walls as previously. In Vienna itself the style died out *c.* 1830, but in other Continental countries it survived well into the second half of the 19th cent. Its English equivalent is Early Victorian.

Billion, formerly in English usage a million million; now a thousand million, or 10^9, to conform with American and French usage.

Bill of Rights, or Declaration of Rights, was the document setting forth the conditions upon which the British throne was offered to William and Mary in 1688. This was accepted and ultimately became an Act of Parliament.

Binary Notation, for numbers, is a way of representing numbers using only two digits, 0 and 1. Electronic digital computers handle numbers in this form and many people these days are having to learn it. Many school children find it both easy and fascinating—as did the great philosopher and mathematician Leibniz. The ordinary, or decimal numbers, 0, 1, 2, 3, 4, 5, 6, 7, 8, 9, 10 are written in binary notation as follows: 0, 1, 10, 11, 100, 101, 110, 111, 1000, 1001, 1010. The reader might divine the rules from this. The point is that you "carry 1", *i.e.*, move the digit 1 a place to the left, when you reach 2. In decimal notation you move 1 a place left when you reach 10. In other words, instead of columns for units, tens, hundreds, thousands, etc., the columns are for units, twos, fours, eights, etc. In binary notation: "1 + = 0 with 1 to carry". Since every digit in binary notation is either 0 or 1 it requires one bit of information to specify a binary digit. *See* **Bit.**

Biological Clock. All living organisms undergo cyclical changes in activity of some sort. These are linked to the changes in their environment which are produced by the alternation of night and day, the phases of the moon and the tides, and the cycle of the seasons. These cycles of activity frequently persist if the organism is put into a constant environment in which there appear to be no external clues as to what time or what season it is. A squirrel, for example, wakes up at about the same time each evening even when it is put into constant darkness. It is usual to refer to these activity patterns as being driven by a biological clock inside the organism. But very little is known about how these biological clocks work.

Biological Warfare, is the use for warlike purposes of bacteria, viruses, fungi, or other biological agents. These can be used to spread distress, incapacity, disease or death among the enemy's people or livestock. One of the strange uses to which mankind puts its science is to make naturally infective organisms even more virulent for military use. This sort of research can be done in many countries; it is much cheaper and easier to hide than nuclear weapons development. Secret attack by biological agents is supposed to be easy and it may affect the populations without damaging buildings or bridges. In 1975 the Biological Weapons Convention, 1972, signed by Britain, the United States and Russia, came into force outlawing germ warfare. Any nation suspecting violation may lodge a complaint with the UN Security Council.

Biosphere, that part of the earth in which life exists—a very thin layer near the surface bounded by regions too hostile for life processes to occur. The upper limit is at about 9,000 m above sea level and the lower limit at about 10,000 m in the deep oceans. Ample supplies of solar energy, liquid water and places where liquid, solid and gas all meet seem to be requirements for a biosphere to exist and for all the biological cycles of water, oxygen, minerals, nitrogen, etc., to function. Whether biospheres exist elsewhere than on earth is a perennially interesting question.

Birch, a genus of deciduous trees including about 40 species and found only in northern regions. Birches native to Britain, and to Europe generally, are of two species—the silver birch, *Betula pendula*, with its graceful, drooping branches and triangular leaves, and the white birch, *Betula pubescens*, which has erect branches and soft oval leaves. Birch timber is an important plywood timber, the bark is used for tanning leather, and wintergreen oil comes from the bark of black birch, *Betula lenta*, a North American species. The birch is not a long-lived tree, few standing for more than a hundred years. The tallest recorded is at Woburn in Bedfordshire, 31 m high.

Birds, or Aves, are, next to mammals, the highest class of animal life. There are two kinds of modern birds—*Carinatae*, possessing keeled breast-bones and having power of flight; *Ratitae*, having raft-life breast-bones, and incapable of flight; and a sub-class of fossil birds, Archaeornithes, including *Archaeopteryx*. It is estimated that there are about 120 million land birds breeding in Great Britain, including 10 million each of the chaffinch and blackbird, 7 million each of the starling and robin and about 2 million sparrows.

The wheatear is usually the first of the migratory birds to return, often reaching Britain at the end of February and always before the middle of March; the sand martin is the first of the "early swallows" to return, followed by the house martin. The first cuckoo arrives about the middle of April, and the whinchat, garden warbler, and sedge warbler during the last week in April. The nightjar, spotted flycatcher, and red-backed shrike are not seen until the first week in May. The swift is among the last to return from Africa and the earliest to depart. Bird-nesting is illegal in Britain. *See also* **F33.**

Birds of Paradise, over 40 species of tropical birds inhabiting the dense forests of New Guinea and neighbouring islands. The male birds are remarkable for their brilliant plumage, long tail feathers, and ruffs on wings and neck, which are displayed to advantage during courtship. Related to the Bower Birds of Australia.

Biretta, a cour-cornered head-covering worn by ecclesiastics of the Roman Church and varying in colour according to the rank of the wearer. A cardinal's biretta is red, a bishop's purple, a priest's black.

Bise, a keen dry north wind prevalent in Switzerland and South France.

Bishop is a Christian ecclesiastic, a person consecrated for the spiritual government of an area, a diocese or province, to the spritual oversight of which he has been appointed (diocesan bishops), or to aid a bishop so appointed (suffragan bishops). In the Church of England there are forty-three diocesan bishops, all nominated by the Crown. Two, Canterbury and York, are archbishops having primacy in the respective provinces. The archbishops of Canterbury and York and the bishops of London, Durham and Winchester and twenty-one other diocesan bishops in the order of seniority are spiritual peers, and sit in the House of Lords. The (Disestablished) Church of Ireland has two archbishops and twelve bishops; the (Disestablished) Church of Wales an archbishop and five bishops and the Episcopal Church in Scotland seven bishops. *See also* **Cardinal.**

Bismuth, metallic element, symbol Bi, in group 5 of the periodic table. Like antimony, the stable form is a grey, brittle, layer structure; electrical conductor. It is readily fusible, melting at 264°C and boiling at about 1420°C. Wood's metal, an alloy with one of the lowest melting points (under 65°C, so that a spoon made of it will melt when placed in a cup of hot tea), contains four parts bismuth, two parts lead, one part tin, one part cadmium.

Bison, a genus of wild cattle, distinguished from the ox by its shorter, wider skull, beard under the chin, high forequarters, and, in winter, a great mane of woolly hair covering head and forequarters. There are two species, the European and the American bison, both now protected in game preserves.

Bit, formerly the word often referred to the metal piece in the mouth of a bridled horse, now more likely to be a technical expression in the mouth of a computer expert. A bit is a unit of information; it is the information that can be conveyed by indicating which of two possibilities obtains. Any object that can be either of two states can therefore store one bit of information. In a technical device, the two states could be the presence or the absence of a magnetic field, or of an electric voltage. Since all numbers can be represented in the binary system (*see* **Binary Notation**) by a row of digits which are *either* 0 *or* 1, it takes one bit of information to specify a binary digit. Bit is short for binary digit.

Bittern, a bird of the heron genus, with long, loose plumage on the front and sides of the neck. It is a solitary bird inhabiting marshes, but rare in Britain.

Bivalves, shell-fish whose shell consists of two hinged valves, lying one on each side of the body, such as mussels, oysters and cockles.

Blackbird, or Merle, a number of the Thrush family, a familiar song bird in Britain. Male is all-black with orange bill; female is mottled brown with brown bill; the young are spotted brown.

Blackcock and Greyhen (as the female is called) are closely related to the Capercaillies but smaller. They nest on the ground and prefer wooded country to open moors. Found in northern half of northern hemisphere. Polygamous, they perform excited courtship dances; the male is a handsome blue-black bird with white undertail, the female dark brown mottled.

Black Death, the plague which swept across Europe in the years 1348–50, beginning in the ports of Italy, brought in by merchant ships from Black Sea ports. It was the worst scourge man has ever known; at least a quarter of the European population was wiped out in the first epidemic of 1348. It reached England in the winter of that year. The disease was transmitted to man by fleas from black rats, though this was not known at the time, the specific organism being *Bacillus pestis.* The disease continued to ravage Europe in recurrent outbreaks up to the late 17th cent. The epidemic which raged in England in 1665 wiped out whole villages and one-tenth of London's population of 460,000. Samuel Pepys wrote a grim account of it in his *Diary. See also* **Labourers, English Statute of.**

Black Hole of Calcutta, the name given to the place where a captured British garrison was confined in 1756, during the struggle for India between the French and British. Into a noisome space, about 6 m square, 146 persons were driven and only 23 were found alive the next morning. The authenticity of the story has been called into question, but after sifting the evidence Professor H. H. Dodwell, in the *Cambridge History of the British Empire,* believes it to be substantially true.

Black Holes. *See* **Astronomy, Section F, Part I.**

Black-letter, the Old English or Gothic type first used in printing blocks.

Black Power. *See* **Section J.**

Black Woodpecker (*Dryocopus martius*), a black bird about the size of a rook, with slightly crested scarlet crown, found in parts of Europe.

Blenny, a group of marine fishes with spiny rays part of the fin running along the back. Several species are found around the British coast.

Blood Groups. *See* **Index to Section P.**

Bloody Assizes, the assizes conducted in 1685 by George Jeffreys, Lord Chief Justice, at which participants in the Duke of Monmouth's rebellion against King James II were tried. They were marked by relentless cruelty.

Bluebird, a migratory bird of North America deriving its name from its deep blue plumage. It is one of the few song birds of America, and familiar in the woods from early spring to November. In India and Malaya there is the Fairy Blue-bird; the male is black with shiny blue upper parts. Used as the symbol of happiness by Maeterlinck in his play *The Blue Bird.*

Blue Peter, a blue flag with a white square in the centre, is hoisted 24 hours before a ship leaves harbour (the letter P in the alphabet of the International Code of Signals).

Blue Ribbon, a term in general use to denote the highest honour or prize attainable in any field or competition. Thus the Derby is the blue ribbon of the turf. The expression is derived from the highest Order of Knighthood in the gift of the British Crown, the insignia of which is a garter of blue velvet.

Blue Stocking, a term used to describe a learned or literary woman, particularly if pedantic and undomesticated. It is said that the term derives from the Bas-Bleu club of Paris, which was attended by the literary savantes of the 17th cent. In England a similar literary club was formed about 1780, whose members were distinguished by their blue stockings.

" Blue " Sun, Moon, etc., a phenomenon caused by the scattering of sunlight by transparent particles suspended in the atmosphere, the effect being that blue light is transmitted and red light extinguished to direct vision. The dust from the Krakatoa eruption in 1883 and the drifting layer of smoke from the forest fires in Alberta, Canada, in September 1950 gave rise to " blue " moons and suns, phenomena sufficiently rare to be described as occurring " once in a blue moon ". In the cold climatic conditions of the Pamirs and the far north, vegetation is said to look " blue " on account of the rays of high calorific value (red, yellow, green) being absorbed, while only the blue and violet are transmitted. It was Tyndall who first explained the blue colour of the sky.

Boa, a term applied to a family of snakes of large size, some attaining a length of 9 m. They are not poisonous, but kill their prey by crushing —constriction—hence the name " boa constrictor ". They occur both in the Old World and the New, but are more abundant in the latter. Most Boas retain the eggs within the body until young are fully developed, whereas the Pythons almost all lay leather-shelled eggs.

Boar, or Wild Hog, an animal largely distributed over the forest regions of Europe, Asia, Africa and South America. It has a longer snout and shorter ears than its descendant the domestic hog, and is provided with tusks. Having to forage for itself, it is a more active and intelligent animal than the pig of the sty, and offers good sport to the hunter.

Boat, an open vessel, propelled by oars or sails, or both. The boats of a ship of war are the launch, barge, pinnace, yawl, cutters, jolly boat and gig; of a merchant vessel, the launch, skiff, jolly boat or yawl, stern boat, quarter-boat and captain's gig. Every ship is compelled to carry adequate, fully provisioned and equipped lifeboats.

Bode's Law, a numerical relationship formulated by Bode in 1772, which states that the relative mean distances of the planets from the sun are found by adding 4 to each of the terms 0, 3, 6, 12, 24, 48, 96. The actual mean distances (in millions of kilometres) are: Mercury, 57·9; Venus, 108·1; Earth, 149·4; Mars, 227·8; Jupiter, 777·6; Saturn, 1,425·5; Uranus, 2,868·5. The gap between Mars and Jupiter caused Bode to predict the existence of a planet there, which was later confirmed by the discovery of Ceres and other minor planets. The law breaks down however, for Neptune and Pluto.

Boer War lasted from 11 October 1899, when the

Boers invaded Natal, to 31 May 1902, when the Treaty of Vereeniging ended hostilities. At first the operations of the British troops in Cape Colony were unsuccessful and disastrous reverses were sustained. Lord Roberts was then sent out as Commander-in-Chief, with Lord Kitchener as Chief-of-Staff, and from February 1900, when Kimberley was relieved and Cronje was compelled to surrender and Ladysmith and Mafeking were relieved, the struggle was practically over.

Boiling-point is the temperature at which a liquid boils. At that point the pressure of the vapour is equal to the pressure of the atmosphere. Under increased pressure the b.p. rises and under less pressure, as on the top of a mountain, it is lower. At standard atmospheric pressure (760 mm of mercury) the b.p. of water is 100°C; alcohol 78·4°C; ether 35·6°C.

Books, Sizes of. *See* **Section N.**

Books, Classification of. All libraries are classified to facilitate reference, but the favourite system is the Dewey Decimal System, which divides the whole field of knowledge into ten Main Classes: General Works; Philosophy; Religion; Sociology; Philology; Natural Science; Useful Arts and Applied Science; Fine Arts; Literature; History (including geography and travel and biography). Each of these Main Classes is again subdivided into ten main divisions. As an example: the main class of Sociology receives the number 300. This range 300 to 400 (the next main class) is graduated into tens, and Economics is 330. The range 330 to 340 is again graduated, and the subject of Labour and Capital is 331. This process is carried on by decimals so that 331·2 deals with Remuneration for Work, 331·22 with Wage Scales, and 331·225 with Extra Pay.

Borax (Sodium Pyroborate) is a white, soluble, crystalline salt. It is widely and diversely used, *e.g.*, as a mild antiseptic, in glazing pottery, in soldering, in the making of pyrex glass, as a cleansing agent and sometimes as a food preservative. Borax occurs naturally in the salt lakes of Tibet, where it is called tincal, in California (Borax Lake, Death Valley), and elsewhere.

Bore. In physical geography, an almost vertical wall of water which passes upstream along certain estuaries. Its formation requires special conditions of river flow, incoming high tide, and shape of river channel. It can be spectacular and dangerous on some rivers. In Britain the best known is the Severn bore which can be over a metre high and move at 16–19 km/h. In some parts of Britain the bore is called an eagre.

Boron. A metalloid element, symbol B. There are two forms, one crystalline, the other amorphous. It is not very abundant in nature but occurs in concentrated deposits. It is best known in boric acid, which is used as a mild antiseptic (called boracic acid) and borax (*q.v.*). Boron compounds are essential to some plants, *e.g.*, beans. Used in the preparation of various special-purpose alloys, such as impact resistant steel. Compounds of boron and hydrogen are used as rocket fuels.

Borstal, an institution where young offenders between 15 and 21 on conviction may be sent for detention and reform. Emphasis is placed on vocational training in skilled trades. The Children and Young Persons Act 1969 makes provision for the minimum age to be raised to 17, if and when the Home Secretary makes an order to that effect. The first was opened in 1902 at the village of Borstal, near Rochester in Kent.

Boston Tea Party, an incident which occurred on 17 December 1773, on board some tea-ships in Boston Harbour. High taxation imposed by the British Parliament under George III had caused bitter feelings, and instigated by popular meetings, a party of citizens, disguised as Indians, boarded the tea-ships and threw the tea overboard. This incident was a prelude to the American War of Independence (1775–83).

Bounds Beating, an old Anglo-Saxon custom. The parish clergyman and officials go round the parish boundaries accompanied by boys who beat the boundary stones with long sticks of willow. The ceremony takes place on the Rogation days preceding Ascension Day.

Bourgeoisie, a term used by Marxists to indicate those who do not, like the proletariat, live by the sale of their labour. They include, on the one hand, industrialists and financiers or members of the liberal professions and, on the other, small artisans and shop-keepers who, although their standard of living may not be appreciably higher (and today is often lower) than that of the proletariat, are described as the "petty bourgeoisie". According to the Marxist view of history, the bourgeoisie arose with modern industrialism after it had overthrown the old feudal aristocracy and replaced it as ruling class.

Bow, an instrument for propelling arrows, and, in the days when it was a weapon of war, was usually made of yew or ash, and was about 2 m long, with an arrow *c.* 1 m long. It was the weapon with which Crécy, Poitiers and Agincourt were won. The cross-bow was Italian and was adopted in France, but did not become popular in Britain.

Bow Bells is the peal of the London church of St. Mary-le-Bow, Cheapside, within sound of which one must be born to be entitled to be called a "cockney". Bow Bells had not been heard since 1939, but they once again rang out over the City of London on 20 December 1961.

Bowdlerize, to expurgate a book. Derived from Thomas Bowdler (1754–1825), the editor of the Family Shakespeare, in which "those words and expressions are omitted which cannot with propriety be read aloud in a family". He treated Gibbon's *History of the Decline and Fall of the Roman Empire* in the same way, omitting "all passages of an irreligious and immoral tendency". Such prudery met with ridicule and hence the words "bowdlerism", "bowdlerist", etc.

Bower Bird, native to Australia and New Guinea and related to the Bird of Paradise, though often less striking in appearance. In the mating season the male builds a "bower" of sticks and grasses for courtship displays and as a playground. The Gardener Bower Bird of Papua makes a lawn in front of his bower and adorns it with bright coloured pebbles and flowers which are replaced as they wither. The female builds her nest away from the bower.

Boycott, a term used in connection with a person that the general body of people, or a party or society, refuse to have dealings with. Originally used when Captain Boycott (1832–97) was made the victim of a conspiracy by the Irish Land League which prevented him making any purchases or holding any social intercourse in his district. He had incurred the League's hostility by a number of evictions.

Brass, an exceedingly useful alloy of copper and zinc. Much brass is about two-thirds copper, but different proportions give different properties. It is harder than copper and easily worked. Brass in the Bible (Matt. x, 9) probably refers to bronze.

Breadfruit Tree (*Artocarpus altilis*), a native of the South Sea Islands; the fruits are a brownish green, about the size of a melon, and contain a white pulpy substance which is roasted before being eaten. The tree grows 12 m or more. Captain Bligh's ship *Bounty* was on a voyage to Jamaica carrying a cargo of 1,000 breadfruit trees when the mutiny occurred.

Breeder Reactor, a kind of nuclear reactor (*q.v.*) which besides producing energy by the fission process also produces ("breeds") more nuclear fuel at the same time. A typical reaction is: a neutron induces fission of a U-235 nucleus which breaks up into two medium-sized nuclei and some neutrons; one of the latter then enters a U-238 nucleus turning it into U-239 which then decays radioactively *via* neptunium into plutonium which is useful fuel. There are technical problems in breeder reactors which have delayed their practical use but the "breeding" principle is so valuable that experiments have gone on for many years in, *e.g.*, Scotland and Idaho, and breeder reactors will no doubt increase in importance the more the supply of natural nuclear fuel appears to become depleted. *See also* **Nuclear Reactors.**

Breviary (Lat. *breviarium* = abridgment), the short prayer-book of the Roman Catholic Church which gives the Divine Office, *i.e.*, the canonical hours or services. The directions for Mass are in the Missal. The modern Roman breviary is a reformed version of the 11th-cent. breviary and was produced by Pope Pius V. in 1568 in response to a decree of the Council of Trent. All Roman Catholic priests are required to recite the whole of the breviary services allotted for each day. *See also* **Matins.**

Bridges are structures for continuing a road, railway, or canal across a river, valley, ravine, or a road or railway at a lower level. From early times bridges were made of timber, stone, or brick, and it was not until the 19th cent. that wrought- and cast-iron were used. Today the materials mostly used are steel and reinforced concrete. Among the most famous of ancient bridges is that of S. Angelo at Rome, built by Hadrian as the Pons Aelius, A.D. 134. The Rialto bridge at Venice dates from 1588. The Ponte Santa Trinita at Florence, one of the finest Renaissance bridges and deemed the most beautiful in the world, was destroyed by German mines in 1944 but has now been reconstructed just as it was before. The first stone bridge across the Thames was begun in 1176. It had 19 arches and was lined with houses and stood until 1831 when it was replaced by the granite bridge designed by Sir John Rennie which stood until 1972. This has been replaced by a three-span concrete bridge with a six-lane carriageway and two footways. The first cast-iron bridge (recently repaired) was built by Abraham Darby at Coalbrookdale, Salop, in 1779. Telford's Menai suspension bridge (1825) has since been enlarged but the original design has been maintained. Another example of Britain's supremacy in constructional iron-work was Robert Stephenson's tubular bridge across the Menai Straits (1850), the prototype of all modern plate girder railway bridges. Other famous bridges are the Niagara (suspension), Forth railway bridge (cantilever), London Tower bridge (suspension), Tay railway bridge, Victoria Jubilee bridge across the St. Lawrence at Montreal (an open steel structure), Sydney Harbour bridge, Lower Zambesi bridge, Storstrom bridge in Denmark, Howrah bridge at Calcutta, Volta bridge of Ghana, Auckland Harbour bridge, Verrazano-Narrows bridge spanning New York's harbour from Brooklyn to Staten I., exceeding by 18 m the centre span of San Francisco's Golden Gate bridge, Rio-Niterói bridge in Brazil. Britain has undertaken in recent years the largest bridge building programme for over a century. The bridges include the road suspension bridge across the Firth of Forth, completed 1964, the Severn suspension bridge (from which the design principles for the new bridge across the Bosphorous were taken) and the Tay road bridge, both completed 1966, the Tinsley viaduct, near Sheffield, opened 1968. When the new Humber suspension bridge is completed (1977) it will be the world's longest single-span bridge (2·4 km with a main span of *c.* 1·6 km).

Bridleway. In English law (sec. 27(6) of the National Parks and Access to the Countryside Act 1949) a highway over which the public have the following, but no other, rights of way, that is to say, a right of way on foot and a right of way on horseback or leading a horse, with or without a right to drive animals of any description along the highway.

Britannia Metal, an alloy of tin, antimony and copper, harder than pure tin, corrosion-resistant, used for teapots, and jugs (often electroplated)

British Association for the Advancement of Science, The, was founded in 1831 by a group of British scientists under the leadership of Charles Babbage (1792–1871) to stimulate scientific inquiry and promote research in the interest of the nation. Its meetings are held annually in different cities of the United Kingdom. The 1977 meeting will be held at the University of Aston in Birmingham under the presidency of Sir Andrew Huxley.

British Museum, was created by an Act of Parliament in 1753, when the Sir Hans Sloane collection, which the British Government had acquired for £20,000, was added to the Cottonian Library and the Harleian Manuscripts. It was opened to the public in 1759 at Montagu House, Bloomsbury. The acquisition of the library of George III (known as the King's Library) in 1823 led to the construction of the present building with the new wing (1829), quadrangle (1852), domed reading room (1857), and later additions. The books and the reading room are now part of the British Library (*see* **Libraries**). The Natural History Department was transferred to South Kensington in the eighties. As a museum it is perhaps the most famous in the world, since it has many priceless collections of sculptures, antiquities, prints and drawings coins and medals. Its treasures include the Elgin Marbles (*q.v.*), the Rosetta Stone (*q.v.*), the Portland Vase (*q.v.*). *See also* **Libraries.**

British Rail (British Railways). The name under which the railways of Britain were unified on 1 January 1948. Instead of the former four main railway systems six regions were formed: London Midland region (former L.M.S.R.), Western (former G.W.R.), Southern (formerly S.R.), Eastern (southern area of former L.N.E.R.), N.E. region (N.E. of former L.N.E.R.), Scottish region (Scottish system of the former L.M.S.R. nad L.N.E.R.). Under the Transport Act 1962 the British Railways Board was set up to manage railway affairs. The most far-reaching change in the modernisation and re-equipment programme since 1955 has been the replacement of steam traction by electric and diesel locomotives. Under the chairmanship of Lord (then Dr.) Richard Beeching the British Railways Board planned a viable railway system by closing uneconomic branch lines, by developing new services on the liner train principle, and by utilising a more limited trunk route system. Under the Transport Act 1968 some railway passenger services are eligible for grants on social grounds, including urban railways and unprofitable rural services. High-speed inter-city passenger services now link the main centres of Gt. Britain and a new high-speed train, operating at a sustained speed of 200 km/h, came into service in 1976. The name was changed to British Rail in 1964.

British Standard Time, The British Standard Time Act of 1968 put Britain an hour ahead of Greenwich Mean Time (GMT) throughout the year for an experimental 3 years. This brought Britain into line with countries in Western Europe where Central European Time is observed. In 1970 Parliament called for the restoration of the previous position—BST in the summer months and GMT in the winter months—as from 31 October 1971.

Brocken-spectre or Glory. The series of coloured rings which an observer sees around the shadow of his own head (or an aeroplane in which he is travelling) as cast upon a bank of mist or thin cloud. This effect is produced by reflection and refraction of sunlight in minute water-droplets in the air just as in a rainbow.

Bromine. A non-metal element, symbol Br, member of the halogen family (*q.v.*). It is a red, evil-smelling liquid (Greek *bromos*, a stink). It is an abundant element. In the USA bromide is extracted from sea-water on a large scale. It unites readily with many other elements, the products being termed bromides. Its derivatives with organic compounds are used in synthetic chemistry. Bromoform is a liquid resembling chloroform. Bromides are used in medicine to calm excitement.

Bronze is primarily an alloy of copper and tin, and was one of the earliest alloys known, the Bronze Age in the evolution of tool-using man coming between the Stone Age and the Iron Age. Some modern bronzes contain zinc or lead also, and a trace of phosphorus is present in " phosphor-bronze ".

Bubble Chamber. An instrument used by physicists to reveal the tracks of fast fundamental particles (*e.g.*, those produced in large accelerating machines) in a form suitable for photography; closely related to the Wilson cloud chamber (*q.v.*), but the particles leave trails of small bubbles in a superheated liquid (often liquid hydrogen) instead of droplets of liquid in a supersaturated gas; invented in 1952 by the American physicist, Dr. D. Glaser, Nobel Prizeman, 1960, and developed by Prof.

L. W. Alvarez, Univ. of California, Nobel Prizeman, 1968.

Buckingham Palace, London residence of British sovereigns since 1837. Originally built for the Duke of Buckingham (1703); bought by George III in 1762 and remodelled by Nash 1825–36.

Buddhism. *See* **Section J.**

Buntings, name of a group of finches, seed-eating birds, usually found in open country. The Yellowhammer, Reed Bunting, Corn Bunting and Cirl Bunting are resident in Britain; the Snow Bunting (which breeds in small numbers in Scotland) and Lapland Bunting are regular winter visitors, and the Ortolan is among the rare visitors.

Butane, a colourless inflammable gas made of carbon and hydrogen; formula C_4H_{10}. Found in natural gas and made as a by-product of oil refining. Butane, like propane (*q.v.*), can easily be liquefied and moved safely in cans and tanks. It is thus useful as a " portable gas supply "; also used in internal combustion fuels.

Byzantine Art developed in the eastern part of the Roman empire after Constantine founded the city of Constantinople (A.D. 300). It has many sources—Greek, Syrian, Egyptian and Islamic—and reached its zenith in the reign of Justinian (527–65). The major art form was ecclesiastical architecture, the basic plan of which was Roman—either basilican (symmetrical about an axis) or centralised (symmetrical about a point). Arched construction was developed, and the dome became the most typical feature, although, unlike the Roman dome which was placed on a round apartment, the Byzantine dome was placed on a square one on independent pendentives. Frequently small domes were clustered round a large one as in the case of the great church of Santa Sophia (537), the climax of Byzantine architecture. Usually the churches were small and include those of SS. Sergius and Bacchus, Sta. Irene (in Constantinople), S. Vitale in Ravenna, and the much later and larger St. Mark's in Venice. Byzantine art also took the form of miniatures, enamels, jewels, and textiles, but mosaics, frescos, and icons (*q.v.*) are its greatest treasures.

C

Cacao, *Theobroma cacao,* is an evergreen tree, from 4–6 m high, growing abundantly in tropical America, West Africa, the West Indies, Sri Lanka, etc., yielding seeds, called cocoa beans, from which cocoa and chocolate are manufactured. The fruit is 17–25 cm long, hard and ridged; inside are the beans, covered with a reddish-brown skin, which are first fermented, then dried. The trees mature at five to eight years and produce two crops a year.

Cactus, a family of flowering plants numbering about a thousand species adapted to living in very dry situations. The stem is usually fleshy, being composed of succulent tissue, remarkably retentive of water; commonly equipped with sharp thorns which deter animals from eating them. The roots are generally very long, tapping soil water over large area; a " prickly pear " cactus may have roots covering a circular area 7 m or more in diameter. The leaves are commonly insignificant or absent, and the stem takes over the photosynthetic leaf function and becomes accordingly flattened to expose greater area to sunlight and air. In some kinds of cactus (*e.g., Echinocactus*) the stem is shaped almost like a sea-urchin.

Cadmium. A metallic element, symbol Cd, chemically similar to zinc and mercury. Used in alloys to lower the melting point, as in Wood's metal with bismuth and tin. Alloyed with copper to make electric cables. Like zinc, it is a protective metal and is used in electroplating. The cadmium-vapour lamp gives a characteristic frequency used in measuring wavelength.

Caesium, also spelt **Cesium,** is an alkali metal element, symbol Cs, in first group of the periodic table. It resembles rubidium and potassium and was discovered by Bunsen and Kirchhoff in 1860. It was the first element whose existence was discovered spectroscopically. The caesium atom consists of a heavy nucleus surrounded by 55 electrons, 54 of which are arranged in stable orbits, and one of which, known as the valency electron, is in a less stable orbit surrounding them. Used in the construction of photo-electric cells and as an accurate time standard (atomic clock).

Calcium, a silvery-white metallic element, symbol Ca. It melts at 810°C and is very reactive. It was discovered by Sir Humphry Davy in 1808, but not until 1898 was it obtained pure, by Moissan. Does not occur as metal in nature, but calcium compounds make up a large part of the earth's crust. Most important calcium sources are marble, limestone, chalk (all three are, chemically, calcium carbonate); dolomite, which is the double carbonate of calcium and magnesium; gypsum, a hydrated calcium sulphate; calcium phosphate and calcium fluoride. Igneous rocks contain much calcium silicate. Calcium compounds are essential to plants and are used in fertilisers. Animals require calcium and phosphorus for bone and teeth formation; deficiency is treated by administration of calcium phosphate. Strontium is chemically similar to calcium, and the radioactive strontium 90 from atomic " fall-out " is therefore easily assimilated by the body.

Calendar, a collection of tables showing the days and months of the year, astronomical recurrences, chronological references, etc. The Julian Calendar, with its leap year, introduced by Julius Caesar, fixed the average length of the year at 365¼ days, which was about 11 minutes too long (the earth completes its orbit in 365 days 5 hours 48 minutes 46 seconds of mean solar time). The cumulative error was rectified by the Gregorian Calendar, introduced in Italy in 1582, whereby century years do not count as leap years unless divisible by 400. This is the rule we now follow. England did not adopt the reformed calendar until 1752, when she found herself 11 days behind the Continent. The Gregorian Calendar did not come into use in Russia until 1918. Old Style and New Style dates are identified as " O.S." and " N.S.".

Calends, the first day of the month in the Roman calendar, when interest fell due, and proclamations as to the order of days were made.

Calorie. Unit of quantity of heat. The " small " or fundamental calorie is the amount of heat required to raise the temperature of 1 gram of water from 14·5 to 15·5°C. This is the gram-calorie used in physics and chemistry. The large Calorie (written with a capital C), commonly used in nutritional connotations, is equal to 1000 small calories and is called the kilogram-calorie.

Calvinism. *See* **Section J.**

Calypso, West Indian song in the form of a doggerel lampoon composed spontaneously and sung to a guitar.

Cambridge University had a sufficiently good teaching reputation to attract Oxford students in 1209, when lectures at their own university were suspended. In 1226 it had a Chancellor who was recognised by King and Pope. The first college to be founded was Peterhouse in 1284. The university was reorganised and granted a Charter of Incorporation by an act of Elizabeth in 1571. The colleges with their dates of foundation are Christ's (1505), Churchill (1960), Clare (1326), Clare Hall (1966), Corpus Christi (1352), Darwin (1964), Downing (1800), Emmanuel (1584), Fitzwilliam (1966), Gonville and Caius (1348), Jesus (1496), King's (1441), Magdalene (1542), Pembroke (1347), Peterhouse (1284), Queens' (1448), St. Catharine's (1473), St. Edmund's House (1896), St. John's (1511), Selwyn (1882), Sidney Sussex (1596), Trinity (1546), Trinity Hall (1350), Wolfson (1965). The women's colleges are: Girton (1869), Newnham (1871), New Hall (1954), Hughes Hall (formerly Cambridge T.C.) (1885), and Lucy Cavendish Collegiate Society (1965) (for women research students and other graduates). Women were admitted to degrees (though not allowed to sit for examination) in 1920, and to full membership of the University in 1948.

Camel, a large ruminant quadruped, inhabiting Asia and Africa, where it is largely used as a beast of burden. There are two species—the

Arabian camel or dromedary, with only one hump; and the Bactrian, or double-humped camel. There are no wild dromedaries, and the only wild bactrians occur in the Gobi Desert. The camel is able to go for long periods without water, not, as was formerly believed, because it stored water in its hump, but because of the unique mechanism of its physiology which enables it to conserve water at the expense of not sweating until 40°C is reached.

Campanile, or bell-tower, is separate from but usually adjoining its parent church. The most famous are in Italy. Giotto's tower at Florence, adjoining the cathedral of Santa Maria del Fiore, is architecturally the finest in the world. Others are at Cremona, the loftiest in Italy (110 m) and Pisa (the leaning tower). The magnificent pointed campanile of St. Mark's, Venice, which collapsed in 1902 and has since been rebuilt in its original form, was begun in 902.

Canal, an artificial watercourse used for navigation which changes its level by means of locks. The completion of the Bridgewater Canal in 1761 to take coal from Worsley to Manchester marked the beginning of canal building in industrial Britain. There are over 4,000 km of navigable inland waterways in Great Britain today, *c.* 3,200 km of which are under the control of the British Waterways Board set up by the Transport Act 1962. The English network is based on the four great estuaries, Mersey, Humber, Severn and Thames. Under the Transport Act 1968, the Board is enabled to maintain an extensive network of amenity waterways. A number of disused canals are being restored to navigation by the Board in conjunction with local authorities and voluntary societies.

Candela, unit of luminous intensity, symbol cd. An idea of the value which this unit represents may be gained from the fact that light obtained from a 40 W filament-type electric lamp or bulb is approximately the same as would be given by a point source of luminous intensity 30 cd. *See* **S.I. units, Section N.**

Candlemas, an English and Roman Church festival in celebration of the Purification of the Virgin Mary. The date is 2 February.

Canon, a term applied to signify a recognised rule for the guide of conduct in matters legal, ecclesiastical and artistic, or an authoritative ordinance: thus we have Canonical Scriptures, Canon Law, etc. A Canon is also a dignitary of the Church, usually a member of a cathedral chapter in the Anglican communion, or in the Roman Church a member of an order standing between regular monks and secular clergy.

Canonical Hours were seven in number in the Western Church; Matins and Lauds, before dawn; Prime, early morning service; Terce, 9 a.m.; Sext, noon; Nones 3 p.m.; Vespers, 4 p.m.; Compline, bed-time.

Canonisation, the entering of one of the faithful departed on the list of saints of the Roman Catholic Church. The rules governing canonisation were simplified by papal decree in 1969. The forty English martyrs, of whom Edmund Campion was one, executed between 1535 and 1679 and beatified long ago, were canonised in 1970. Beatification, by which a person is called blessed, is usually followed by canonisation, but not necessarily.

Canticles, the name given to the scriptural passages from the Bible sung by the congregation in the various Christian liturgies. They are the *Benedicite, Benedictus, Magnificat, Nunc Dimittis.*

Capercaillie, the largest of the grouse family, found in the Scottish highlands and the pine forests and mountainous regions of Northern and Central Europe and Asia.

Capet, the family name of the royal house of France, founded by Hugh Capet in 987, with its collateral branches. The main line of the dynasty came to an end in 1328 with the death of Charles IV when the throne passed to the related house of Valois. The direct Valois line ended in 1498 with the death of Charles VIII. The first of the Bourbon line was Henry IV whose descendants ruled France (except during the French Revolution and the Napoleonic era) until 1848.

Capitalism. *See* **Section J.**

Capuchins are members of a mendicant order of Franciscans, founded in the 16th cent. with the aim of restoring the primitive and stricter observance of the rule of St. Francis, so called from the capuce or pointed cowl worn by them.

Carat, a term used in assessing the value of gold and precious stones. In connection with gold, it represents the proportion of pure gold contained in any gold alloy, and for this purpose the metal is divided into 24 parts. Thus 24-carat indicates pure gold, and any lesser number of carats shows the proportion of gold contained in the alloy. The carat as a measure of weight is now obsolete, having been replaced by the *metric carat* of 0·2 grams.

Caravan, a band of travellers or traders journeying together for safety across the Eastern deserts, sometimes numbering many hundreds. There are several allusions to caravans in the Old Testament. The great caravan routes of this period from Egypt to Babylon and from Palestine to Yemen linked up with the Syrian ports and so with western sea commerce. Many wars have been fought in the past over their control.

Carbohydrates. *See* **F23** *and* **Diet, Section P.**

Carbon, a non-metallic chemical element which occurs in crystalline form as diamonds and graphite; amorphous forms of carbon include charcoal and soot, while coke consists mainly of elementary carbon. The biochemistry of plants and animals largely hinges upon carbon compounds. The study of carbon compounds is called Organic Chemistry. **Carbon 14.** A radioactive isotope of carbon, with a half-life *c.* 6,000 years, used in following the path of compounds and their assimilation in the body. Also used in determination of the age of carbon-containing materials such as trees, fossils and very old documents. *See* **F25** and **Radiocarbon Dating.**

Carbonari, members of a secret political society originated in Naples, and at one time very numerous. Their chief aim was to free Italy from foreign rule, and they exerted considerable influence in the various revolutionary movements in the first half of the 19th cent. Their name was adopted from the charcoal-burners (*carbonari*), and their passwords, signs, etc. were all in the phraseology of the fraternity.

Carbon dioxide. Commonest of the oxides of carbon. It is formed when carbon and its compounds are burnt with abundant supply of air, and when carbon compounds are oxidised in the respiration process of animals. The atmosphere contains carbon dioxide to the extent of about three parts in 10,000; this figure remains more or less constant because, while carbon dioxide is always being added by animal respiration and the burning of fuels, such as coal and oil by man, plants are constantly removing it in the process known as photosynthesis (**F28**) or carbon assimilation.

Carbon monoxide is a colourless gas with no taste or smell. It is formed when coal and coke are burnt with a restricted supply of air; the blue flame to be seen in a coke brazier, for instance, is the flame of carbon monoxide. This gas is very poisonous, forming with the haemoglobin of the blood a compound which is useless for respiration and cherry red in colour, which gives a visible symptom of poisoning by carbon monoxide. With nickel it forms a volatile compound, called nickel carbonyl, and this reaction is the basis of the Mond process for extracting nickel.

Cardinal, one of the chief dignitaries of the Roman Catholic Church who constitute the Pope's council, or Sacred College, and when the papal chair is vacant elect by secret ballot a Pope from among themselves. There are three orders: cardinal bishops, members of the Roman Curia (the central administration of the Church) and bishops of sees near Rome; cardinal deacons, also members of the Curia, holding titular bishoprics; and cardinal priests who exercise pastoral duties over sees removed from Rome, though some are members of the Curia. Their numbers were fixed by Pope Sixtus V in 1586 at 6, 14 and 50 respectively. Both Pope John XXIII and Pope Paul VI increased the number. In 1977 there were 137 cardinals, of whom no more than 120 are entitled to elect a new Pope. Their insignia was trimmed of embellishment by papal decree in 1969 with the abolition of the famous red hat (the galero) and the shoes with buckles. Cardinals must now retire at 80.

Cardinal Virtues, according to Plato these were justice, prudence, temperance, fortitude—*natural* virtues as distinct from the *theological* virtues of the Roman Catholic Church, faith, hope, charity. The phrase " seven cardinal virtues ", combining the two, figures in mediaeval literature. *See* **Sins, Seven Deadly.**

Carmelites, a body of mendicant friars taking their name from Mount Carmel, where the order was first established in the 12th cent. The original rule of the order required absolute poverty, abstinence from meat and a hermit life. The rigidity of the rule of the order was mitigated by Innocent IV. They wear a brown habit with white mantle, hence their name of White Friars. The order of Carmelite nuns was instituted in the 15th cent.

Carolingians, dynasty of Frankish rulers founded in the 7th cent. The family was at its height when represented by Charlemagne. It ruled, with interruptions, until 987 when the Capetian dynasty succeeded.

Carp, a well-known fresh-water fish, found in plenty in most European and Asiatic still waters; reaches a length of about 60 cm and under favourable conditions lives for about 40 years. Familiar British members of the family are the roach, rudd, dace, chub, gudgeon, tench, minnow, barbel, bream and bleak. The goldfish, popular in ornamental ponds, is the domesticated variety of a Far Eastern member of the carp family.

Carthusians, an order of monks founded in 1084 by St. Bruno at the Grande Chartreuse near Grenoble, and introduced into England about a century later. They built the Charterhouse (corruption of Chartreuse) in London in 1371. The chief characteristics of the order are a separate dwelling-house in the precincts of the charterhouse for each monk, and the general assembly in the Church twice in the day and once at night. They wear a white habit, with white scapular and hood. The liqueur *Chartreuse* was invented by the order and is still their secret. For many years they have derived large revenues from its sale. The order of Carthusian nuns was founded in the 12th cent.

Casein, the chief protein in milk and cheese. It is coagulated by the action of rennet or acid. An important class of plastics (" casein plastics ") are produced from it, and these plastics are converted into buttons,knitting-needles, etc. 36,000 litres of milk yield about 1 tonne of casein.

Cassowary, a genus of ostrich-like birds which, together with the emu, form a separate order found only in Australasia. All species are black, with brightly coloured necks, and with a horny crest on the head. Noted for fleetness.

Castor-oil Plant (*Ricinus communis*), an African shrub now cultivated in most tropical countries. It has broad palmate leaves and bears a spiny fruit containing seeds which when pressed yield the well-known oil.

Cat, the general name for all members of the class *Felidae* of the carnivorous order, from the lion down to the domestic cat. The latter is believed to be descended from the European and African wild cats. Egypt is credited with having been the first country in which the cat was domesticated. *See* **Section Z.**

Catabolism, Anabolism, are the terms used to describe the two types of metabolic pathway. Catabolic pathways are routes by which large organic molecules are broken up by enzymes into their simpler constituents *e.g.*, starch into glucose. The anabolic pathways are the routes by which complex molecules are synthesised from simple sub-units, *e.g.*, proteins from amino acids.

Catalyst. A substance which speeds up a chemical reaction without being changed itself. Various aluminium and titanium compounds are catalysts in the formation of polythene from ethylene. Palladium catalyses the reaction of hydrogen with oxygen (hence its use in gas lighters). Enzymes in the body hasten the breakdown of carbohydrates and proteins by catalytic action. *See* **F24(2).**

Cataracts are gigantic waterfalls. The most famous are those of Niagara in North America, the Orinoco in South America, the Victoria Falls on the Zambesi in Africa, the Falls of the Rhine at Schaffhausen, and the Cascade of Gavarni in the Pyrenees.

Catechism, an elementary book of principles in any science or art, but more particularly in religion, in the form of questions and answers. There is a great variety of these, including the Lutheran, prepared by Luther in 1529, Calvin's Geneva (in 1536), and the Anglican, in the Book of Common Prayer.

Caterpillar, the larva of a butterfly or moth, worm-like in its segmented body, with 3 pairs of jointed true legs, often curiously marked and coloured, and frequently more or less hairy.

Cathedral, the chief church of a diocese, so called from its containing a Bishop's seat, or episcopal chair. The town in which it is situated is a cathedral city. Some celebrated cathedrals are St. John Lateran of Rome, Notre Dame of Paris, the cathedrals of Cologne and Milan, St. Paul's in London, Canterbury Cathedral, York Minster, and the cathedrals of Durham, Bristol, Gloucester, Peterborough, Exeter. Liverpool, and Coventry (destroyed by bombs, now rebuilt).

Catholicism. *See* **Section J.**

Cat's eye, a kind of quartz, much valued as a gem, opalescent, and of various shades.

Cavalier, a name adopted during the troubles of the Civil War to designate the Royalist party; it is also used generally in reference to a knightly, gallant or imperious personage.

Caves, natural hollow places in the earth, frequently found in Carboniferous limestone areas. The underground caves are formed by the action of rainwater carrying carbon dioxide, a dilute acid which slowly attacks the limestone rocks. The main caves in the British Isles are in the Mendips, Derbyshire, Yorkshire, S. Wales and in County Clare. Many British inland caves are thought to have been formed at the end of the Ice Age when there was a rise in the water table. The floods of September 1968 moved masses of débris in some of the British caves, redistributing it in a major way; new routes were blocked and old passages reopened. The scientific study of caves is known as spelaeology.

Cedar, a dark-leaved, cone-bearing, horizontal-branched evergreen tree that grows to a considerable height and girth, the best known species in Britain being the Cedar of Lebanon, which was introduced in the 17th cent.

Celluloid, one of the first synthetic thermoplastic materials, discovered by Alexander Parkes in 1865 when he was attempting to produce synthetic horn. It is made by treating cellulose nitrate with camphor and alcohol. Photographic film is made of a similar, but less-inflammable material, formed by the use of cellulose acetate instead of the nitrate.

Cellulose, a carbohydrate, and a constituent of nearly all plants. Cellulose occurs in an almost pure state in the fibres of linen (flax), absorbent cotton, jute, and filter-paper (used in laboratories).

Celsius was an 18th cent. Swedish scientist (**B13**) after whom the modern Celsius temperature scale is named. Since 1954, °C stands for " degree Celsius " instead of " degree Centigrade " but this is only a change in name. Both symbols refer to the temperature scale which calls the melting point of ice 0°C and the boiling point of water at one atmosphere pressure 100°C. *See* **Absolute Temperature.**

Celts, an ancient race found late in the third millennium B.C. in S.W. Germany, united by a common language and culture, who spread westward into Spain, northward into Britain, eastward to the Black Sea, reaching Galicia in Asia Minor. The " La Tène " iron-age Celts invaded Britain *c.* 250 B.C. After Britain was conquered by the Romans and invaded by the Angles and Saxons there remained as areas of Celtic speech only Wales (Brythonic speakers), Ireland, Scotland, Isle of Man (Gaelic speakers). The late Celtic period in Britain produced a distinctive Christian art (*e.g.*, the Lindisfarne Gospel *c.* 700, and the Irish Book of Kells, dating from about the same time). Surviving Celtic languages are Welsh, Irish, Breton and Scots Gaelic; Cornish survived until the 18th cent. and Manx Gaelic is on the point of extinction.

Centrifuge, a machine which produces large accelerations by utilising the radial force caused by rotating a body about a fixed centre. Centrifuges have found extensive application in modern science. They can be used for the separation of one size of particle from another (for this use in biochemistry see **F20**) or in the training of astronauts where the accelerations occurring during rocket lift-off can be simulated in a centrifuge on the ground.

Ceramics, are substances in which a combination of one or more metals with oxygen confers special and valuable properties. These include hardness, and resistance to heat and chemicals. Ceramic comes from the Greek word for pottery, and pottery materials of mud and clay were probably the first man-made ceramics. Nowadays the range is enormous and growing; apart from all the pottery materials, there are firebricks, gems, glasses, concretes, nuclear reactor fuel elements, special materials for electronic devices, coloured pigments, electrical insulators, abrasives, and many other things. The scientific study of ceramics is part of materials science (*see* **Materials Science**). The need to design ceramic objects has inspired great art, and the production of ceramics is a major industry. *See also* **China Marks, Section D.**

Cerium, a scarce metallic element discovered by Berzelius in 1803. A mixture of cerium and thorium nitrates is used in the manufacture of gas mantles, which owe their incandescent property to the deposit of cerium and thorium oxide with which they are coated.

Chain reaction. *See* **F12(1).**

Chalcedony, a mixture of crystalline silica and amorphous hydrated silica, *i.e.*, of quartz and opal. It has a waxy lustre, and is much used by jewellers for necklaces, bracelets, etc. Commonly it is white or creamy. Its bright orange-red variety is called carnelian; its brown variety, sard. Chrysoprase, plasma, bloodstone are varieties which are respectively pale apple-green, dark leek-green, green with red spots.

Chalk, a white limestone, calcium carbonate, found in the Upper Cretaceous deposits (formed from the shells of minute marine organisms). As chalk is porous, few streams form on its surface and consequently it is eroded slowly, although generally speaking it is a soft rock. Its juxtaposition with soft impervious clay in some areas results in its forming steep ridges known as escarpments, *e.g.*, N. and S. Downs and Chilterns. In contrast to the dry upland surfaces of chalk, lower levels are frequently saturated with water which emerges as springs.

Chamberlain, Lord, the senior officer of The Royal Household who is responsible for all ceremonial within the palace (levées, courts, garden parties, entertainment of foreign royalties and heads of state) but not the coronation or state opening of parliament. He is also in charge of appointments to The Royal Household. His office as censor of plays was abolished in 1968.

Chamberlain, Lord Great, one of the great officers of state whose duties are now mainly ceremonial. He attends the monarch at the state opening of parliament and at the coronation and is custodian of the Palace of Westminster (Houses of Parliament). The office is hereditary, dating from Norman times, and is held for one reign in turn by the descendants of the De Veres, Earls of Oxford. The present Lord Great Chamberlain is the Marquess of Cholmondeley.

Chameleon, a family of lizards with numerous species. Their ability to change colour is well known, but exaggerated, and is due to the movement of pigment cells beneath the skin. They are slow in movement, arboreal, and mainly insectivorous. Found in Africa, India, Sri Lanka, Madagascar and Arabia.

Chamois, a species of antelope, native of Western Europe and Asia. About the size of a goat, it lives in mountainous regions, and possesses wonderful leaping power, so that it is very difficult to capture. Its flesh is much esteemed, and from its skin chamois leather is made, although today sheep and goat skins are usually substituted. The mating season is October–November and the fawns are born in May or June. Live to be 20–25 years old.

Channel Tunnel, a scheme to bore a tunnel through 32–48 km of chalk under the sea between Dover and Calais has been a subject for discussion ever since Albert Mathieu first conceived the idea as a practical possibility in 1802. In the 1830s proposals for a bridge were made. Investigations have been undertaken from time to time, but on each occasion military doubts or cost, reinforced by the insular feelings of the English, caused the governments of the day to withhold support. However, in 1964 the British and French governments decided in principle to go ahead with a rail tunnel to link the British and European railway systems. The tunnel would provide ferry train services for road vehicles in addition to through rail services and would run from Cheriton near Folkestone, and from Sangatte, near Calais. Because of changes in the economic situation the British Government in 1975 decided to withdraw from the scheme, but, as with excavations made last century, the plans will be preserved in case the project is revived.

Chapel Royal, the church dedicated to the use of the Sovereign and Court. There are, among others, chapels royal at St. James's Palace, Buckingham Palace, Windsor, Hampton Court, the Tower, and Holyrood. *See also* **E4(2).**

Characterology. *See* **Section J.**

Charcoal, a term applied to wood that has been subjected to a process of slow smothered combustion. More generally it refers to the carbonaceous remains of vegetable, animal, or combustible mineral substances submitted to a similar process. Charcoal from special woods (in particular buckthorn) is used in making gunpowder. Bone charcoal finds use in sugar refining, as it removes dark colouring matter present in the crude syrup.

Chasuble, a sleeveless vestment worn by ecclesiastics over the alb during the celebration of Mass. It is supposed to symbolise the seamless coat of Christ.

Cheese, an article of food made from the curd of milk, which is separated from the whey and pressed in moulds and gradually dried. There are about 500 varieties differing with method of preparation and quality of milk. They used to be made in the regions after which they are named but nowadays many of them are mass-produced, *e.g.*, Cheddar is made not only in all parts of Britain but in Canada, New Zealand, Australia, Holland and the USA. Cheeses may be divided into 3 main classes: (1) soft, *e.g.*, Camembert, Cambridge, l'Evêque; (2) blue-veined, *e.g.*, Stilton, Gorgonzola, Roquefort (made from ewe's milk), (3) hard-pressed, *e.g.*, Cheddar, Cheshire, Gruyère, Parmesan, Gouda.

Cheetah or " hunting leopard ", the large spotted cat of Africa and Southern Asia whose ability to run at 72 km/h for 450 m makes it the swiftest four-footed animal alive.

Chemical Warfare. This term is usually restricted to mean the use in war of anti-personnel gases, aerosols and smokes, although explosives, napalm, herbicides and defoliants are also chemical agents that are used in war. Anti-personnel chemical weapons may be classified as (*a*) vesicants (agents which produce skin blisters, *e.g.*, mustard gas); (*b*) lacrimators (*e.g.*, the original tear gas, CN, and its British-developed successor CS, now preferred for riot control); (*c*) sternutators (sneeze and vomiting agents, usually arsenic compounds, *e.g.*, Adamsite DM); (*d*) nerve gases (extremely lethal agents which incapacitate the nervous system, *e.g.*, the G-agents developed during the second world war and the more powerful V-agents developed subsequently); (*e*) lung irritants (*e.g.*, phosgene and chlorine). Most of these chemicals can be lethal at sufficiently high concentrations and for this reason it is doubtful whether there exists the " humane " chemical agent which instantly incapacitates but leaves no long-term side effects.

The first occasion when poison gas was used on a large scale was in the first world war: more than 100,000 fatalities resulted from the use of principally chlorine, phosgene and mustard gas. Worldwide revulsion at the hideous effects of chemical weapons and their potential as indiscriminate weapons of mass destruction resulted in the Geneva Protocol of 1925 which prohibited the use both of chemical and bacteriological weapons. It has now been ratified by over 90 nations including all the major powers (although Japan and America are only recent signatories). The Protocol has been generally well observed although notable violations have been by the Italians in Abyssinia (1935–6), the Japanese in China during the second world war and the Americans in South East Asia in the 1960s. It has however failed to prevent the continual development and stock-piling of lethal chemical agents by many nations, although recently there have been moves towards chemical weapons disarmament. *See also* **Biological Warfare.**

Chemistry is the science of the elements and their compounds. It is concerned with the laws of their combination and behaviour under various conditions. It had its rise in alchemy and has gradually developed into a science of vast magnitude and importance. Organic chemistry deals with the chemistry of the compounds of carbon; inorganic chemistry is concerned with the chemistry of the elements; physical chemistry is concerned with the study of chemical reactions and with the theories and laws of chemistry. *See* **F20–6.**

Chestnut, the fruit of trees of the genus *Castanea*, members of the family *Fagaceae*. C. *sativa* is the sweet or Spanish chestnut, C. *dentata* the American chestnut and C. *crenata* the Japanese chestnut. The nut is edible. The wood is used in carpentry and fencing. *See also* **Horse Chestnut.**

Chiaroscuro, a term used in painting to denote the disposition of light and shade. Rembrandt is unrivalled as a painter for his contrasts of light and shadows.

Chiltern Hundreds, three hundreds—Stoke, Burnham and Desborough—the stewardship of which is now a nominal office under the Chancellor of the Exchequer. Since about 1750 the nomination to it has been used as a method of enabling a member of Parliament to resign seat on the plea that he holds an office of honour and profit under the crown. An alternate symbolic post for an M.P. giving up his seat is the stewardship of the Manor of Northstead in Yorkshire which has been used in the same way since 1841.

Chimpanzee, a large anthropoid ape, a native of tropical Africa, of a dark brown colour, with arms reaching to the knee, and capable of walking upright. Its brain is about a third of the weight of the human brain, but is anatomically similar. The animal has considerable intelligence and powers of learning. A suitable subject for space flight experiments.

Chinchilla, a South American burrowing rodent. Grey in colour, and white underneath. It is greatly esteemed for its beautiful fur.

Chippendale Furniture was introduced in the reign of George I by Thomas Chippendale, a cabinet-maker from Yorkshire who migrated to London and set up for himself in St. Martin's Lane, Charing Cross. He was fonder of inventing designs for furniture than of making it, and in 1752 published a book of patterns; the London furniture-makers of the day soon began to model their work upon it. *See* **Section D.**

Chivalry an international brotherhood of knights formed primarily during the 13th cent. to fight against the infidels in the Crusades. For the French the major battle was against the Moslems in the Holy Land and North Africa, the Spaniards fought the same enemy in their own country, and the Germans were concerned with the heathen of Baltic lands, but Chaucer's "very perfect gentle knight" had fought in all these areas. One did not easily become a knight who had to be of noble birth and then pass through a period of probation, beginning as a boy page in the castle of some great lord, serving his elders and betters humbly while he was taught good manners, singing, playing musical instruments, and the composition of verse. Probably he learned Latin, but he certainly learned French, which was the international language of knights as Latin was of scholars. At fourteen he became a squire and learned to fight with sword, battle-axe and lance, and to endure conditions of hard living while carrying out his duties of waiting on his lord, looking after his horses, and in time accompanying him in battle. Only if he showed himself suitable was he finally knighted by a stroke of the hand or sword on the shoulder from the king or lord. Knighthood was an international order and had its special code of behaviour: to honour one's sworn word, to protect the weak, to respect women, and defend the Faith. To some extent it had a civilising effect on the conduct of war (*e.g.*, knights of opposing sides might slaughter each other in battle but feast together after), but, since war was regarded as the supreme form of sport, it cannot be said to have contributed to peace.

Chlorine, a gaseous element of the halogen family, first isolated in 1774 by Scheele by the action of manganese dioxide in hydrochloric acid. It unites easily with many other elements, the compounds resulting being termed chlorides. The gaseous element is greenish-yellow, with a pungent odour. It is a suffocating gas, injuring the lungs at a concentration as low as 1 part in 50,000, and was used during the first world war as a poison gas. Has a powerful bleaching action, usually being used in form of bleaching powder, made by combining lime and chlorine. Also a valuable disinfectant; used, for instance, in rendering water of swimming baths sterile.

Chloroform, a volatile colourless liquid, compounded of carbon, hydrogen, and chlorine. It is a powerful solvent, not naturally occurring but synthesised on a large scale. When the vapour is inhaled it produces unconsciousness and insensibility to pain. It owes its discovery to Liebig, and its first application for medical purposes to Sir James Young Simpson (**P5(2)**).

Chlorophyll, the green pigment contained in the leaves of plants, first discovered by P. J. Pelletier (1788–1829) and J. B. Caventou (1795–1877) in 1818. Enables the plant to absorb sunlight and so to build up sugar. The total synthesis of chlorophyll was reported in 1960 by Prof. R. B. Woodward. This is an outstanding achievement in the field of organic chemistry. *See* **Photosynthesis, F28, F41(1).**

Chouans, the name given to the band of peasants, mainly smugglers and dealers in contraband salt, who rose in revolt in the west of France in 1793 and joined the royalists of La Vendée. Balzac gives a picture of the people and the country in which they operated in his novel *Les Chouans*. They used the hoot of an owl as a signal—hence the name.

Chough, a member of the crow family, of glossy blue-green-black plumage, whose long curved bill and legs are coral red. It is used to be abundant on the cliffs of Cornwall, but its haunts are now restricted to the rocky outcrops of the western coasts and in the mountains near by. It nests in cleft rocks and caves. The Alpine chough with yellow bill inhabits the mountainous districts of Europe and Asia and is not found in Britain. It was found at *c.* 8,200 m on Everest.

Christmas means "mass of Christ" from the old English *Cristes maesse*, which is celebrated by the Western church on 25 December. The actual day on which Christ was born is not known and there is some uncertainty about the year. 25 December as the day of Nativity was not generally observed until the 5th cent. A.D., though, as the winter solstice, it had long been observed as a pagan festival of *sol invictus* (unconquered sun). The first Christmas card dates from about 1843 and the Christmas tree, of pagan origin, was introduced into England from Germany where it had been a tradition since the Middle Ages. Santa Claus is a corruption of Santa Nikolaus (St. Nicholas) patron saint of children, whose feast day properly falls on 6 December.

Chromium, a very hard, bluish-white metal element, symbol Cr, melting at a very high temperature (above 1,900°C). Its chief ore is chromite or chrome iron-ore (ferrous chromite). "Ferro-chrome" is produced by heating chromite and anthracite in an electric furnace, and chrome steels are prepared by adding the pre-calculated amount of ferro-chrome to melted steel. Best known chrome steel is stainless steel first made by Brearley in 1912 and since then developed greatly at Sheffield. A typical formula is 18 per cent. chromium,

8 per cent. nickel, 74 per cent. iron. Equally important are Stellite alloys, containing chromium, cobalt, tungsten (or molybdenum), which have made possible modern high-speed cutting tools. Dies used in manufacture of plastics are commonly of chrome steel. The elementary metal finds little use alone except in chromium-plating for motor cars, etc.

Chromosomes, the structures contained within the nucleus of every animal and plant cell by which genetic information is transmitted. The chromosome number in somatic (body) cells is constant for each species of plant and animal, *e.g.*, man (46), cat (38), mouse (40), honey bee (16), fruit fly *Drosophila* (8), potato (48). Chromosomes are long molecules composed of deoxyribonucleoproteins (*i.e.*, proteins and DNA). Human chromosomes have been the subject of much recent research since it has been found that certain disorders are associated with chromosomal aberration, e.g., in Mongolism an extra chromosome is present. *See also* **Genes, Cell Division, F30**(2).

Church Commissioners. The Church Commissioners were established in 1948 by the amalgamation of Queen Anne's Bounty (established 1704) and the Ecclesiastical Commissioners (established 1836) to administer Church revenues and to manage Church property generally. The Commissioners control funds with a book value of some £600 million (1976).

Church of England. *See* **Section J.**

Church of Scotland. *See* **Section J.**

Cid, The, a famous Spanish hero of the 11th cent. Don Rodrigo Diaz de Vivar, who, before he was twenty, led a Spanish force against the Moors, and drove them out of Spain. He is celebrated in poem, play and romance.

Cilia, minute hair-like projections on the surface of some cells, which beat together in wavelike movements like the wind over a corn-field. These movements can be used as a means of locomotion as in the aquatic organism paramecium. Cilia are also found on the outer layers of the human trachea where they waft particles upwards to the throat, thus protecting the lungs. *See* **F34, P13,** *also* **Flagella.**

Cinque Ports, a number of seaport towns on the coast of Kent and Sussex, originally five; Hastings, Romney, Hythe, Dover and Sandwich. Winchelsea and Rye were added later. These ports were required to furnish a certain number of ships, ready for service, and in return they were granted many privileges. The official residence of the Lord Warden is Walmer Castle, near Dover.

Cistercians, an order of monks and nuns taking their names from Cîteaux, near Dijon, where their first monastery was established in 1098. The order was noted for the severity of its rule. They were famous agriculturists. The habit is white, with a black cowl or hood.

Civil List is the annual sum payable to the Sovereign to maintain the Royal Household and to uphold the dignity of the Crown. The amount is granted by Parliament upon the recommendation of a Select Committee and has to be settled afresh in the first six months of a new reign. The Civil List of Queen Victoria was £385,000; Edward VII and George V, £470,000; Edward VIII and George VI, £410,000; Elizabeth II £475,000. In 1972 the Civil List allowance to the Queen was increased to £980,000, in 1975 to £1·4 million, in 1977 to £1·665 million. Other Civil List allowances (1977) are: the Queen Mother, £140,000; the Duke of Edinburgh, £85,000; Princess Anne, £45,000; Princess Margaret, £50,000. (Annual revisions are to be expected if inflation continues.) The Prince of Wales is entitled to tax-free revenue from the Duchy of Cornwall. Other resources available to the Queen include (1) the sums which Parliament votes to government departments each year, *e.g.*, upkeep of palaces (Dept. of the Environment) royal yacht Britannia and the royal flight (Min. of Defence); (2) privy purse (revenues of the Duchy of Lancaster: (3) personal fortune, the size of which is not disclosed. The Queen pays no direct taxes. 80–100 per cent. of the annuities received by other members of the Royal family are treated as tax-free expenses. The system under which annual payments are made by the Government to the Queen was changed by the Civil List Act 1975: payments are now included in the annual estimates in the same way as the expenditure of a government department, and subject to scrutiny in the House of Commons. The Civil List now provides only for the Sovereign, the consort of a Sovereign, their children, and the widows of those children.

Cleopatra's Needle on the Thames Embankment is of the time of Tuthmosis III (1500–1450 B.C.). The monolith had nothing to do with Cleopatra as it only came to Alexandria after her death. It was first erected at the Biblical On (Greek Heliopolis), sacred City of the Sun. It was presented to the British Government by Mehemet Ali in 1819, but not brought to this country until 1878. Weight *c.* 183 tonnes; height, 208 m.

Climate is a generalised representation of the day-to-day weather conditions throughout the year, the combination of all weathers thus determining the climate of a place. Averages and extremes of temperature, variation of humidity, duration of sunshine and cloud cover, amount of rainfall and frequency of snow, frost, gales, etc., are amongst the data normally investigated. The interiors of great land masses are characterised by large ranges of temperature and low rainfall (continental climate), while proximity to oceans has an ameliorating effect with increase in rainfall (oceanic climate). Presence of mountain ranges and lakes and configuration generally produce local modifications of climate, also apparent between the centre and the outlying suburbs of a city. Latitude introduces zones of climate, *e.g.*, tropical rain, subtropical steppe and desert, temperate rain and polar. The climate is always changing in greater or less degree. Every year, every decade, every century brings a somewhat different experience. The recent tendency between 1880 and 1940 for most parts of the world to become warmer has eased off and appears to have given way to a more prolonged cooling tendency.

Clock, a device for measuring the passage of time. The earliest timekeeper was the shadow-clock, a primitive form of sundial, used in Ancient Egypt about 1500 B.C. To find the time at night the water-clock or clepsydra was used. The sand-glass dates from the 15th cent. No one knows when the first mechanical clocks were invented, but it is known that a complicated mechanical clock driven by water and controlled by a weighbridge escapement was built in Peking in 1090. The Dover Clock in the Science Museum is not the earliest surviving clock in England, as was once believed, but early 17th cent. The Salisbury Cathedral clock dates from 1386 and that of Wells Cathedral from 1392. The pendulum clock was invented by the Dutch scientist Christiaan Huygens (1625–95). The first watches were made in Nuremberg shortly after 1500. The marine chronometer is a high-precision timepiece used at sea for giving Greenwich mean time. The quartz-crystal clocks are accurate to one thousandth of a second a day, and the improved atomic clock, developed at the British National Physical Laboratory, which makes use of the natural vibrations of the caesium atom, is said to be an almost absolute measure of time (accurate to 1 sec. in 300 years, *i.e.*, one part in 10^{10}).

Cloud Chamber, an apparatus invented by C. T. R. Wilson in which the tracks of atomic particles can be made visible. Just as the vapour trails tell of the track of an invisible aircraft high up in the air, so the vapour trails of an unseeable particle can tell of its behaviour. The rays under investigation pass through a chamber containing a gas, *e.g.*, air thoroughly cleansed of dust, supersaturated with water- or alcohol-vapour. As the particle passes through it forms a track of tiny water droplets which can be photographed. After a long and honourable history this wonderful instrument is now virtually obsolete. A later ingenious device for tracking fast fundamental particles is the Bubble chamber (*q.v.*).

Clouds are formed by the cooling of moist air, the type depending on the way the air cools and the height at which condensation occurs. There are three main classes: (1) high cloud (about 6,100 m)—cirrus (delicate and fibrous), cirrostratus (thin white veil), and cirrocumulus (delicately rippled) consisting of ice crystals; (2) medium cloud (above 2,100 m)—altostratus (dense, greyish veil) and altocumulus (broken flattened cloudlets)—chiefly water particles, often supercooled; (3) low cloud (from near ground to 2,100 m)—cumulus (fair weather, broken, dome-topped), cumulominbus (heavy, towering to great heights), stratocumulus (layer of globular masses or rolls), stratus (like fog but off the ground), nimbostratus (low, rainy cloud). The highest clouds of all, and the rarest, are the noctilucent, seen only on summer nights in high latitudes. They form at about 80 km above the earth and consist of ice-coated dust from meteors.

Clover, plants of the *Trifolium* genus, family *Leguminosae*, with about 250 species. These are "nitrogen fixing" plants and include red clover, white clover, alsike clover and crimson clover. They are of great importance in agriculture because in a good pasture they supply directly or indirectly most of the protein available to the animals. Seed of "wild white" clover has been accepted since about 1939 as the indispensable plant of good United Kingdom grassland, largely through the efforts of pioneers like D. A. Gilchrist (1859–1927).

Coal. Until recently the most important single fuel has been coal. It is a mineral of organic origin, formed from the remains of vegetation which over millions of years has changed to coal by the effects of heat and pressure from overlying rock or water. All coal contains moisture, inflammable volatiles, mineral impurities (some of which remain as coal ash after the coal is burnt), and fixed carbon (the coke that is left after the volatiles have been driven off). The relative proportions vary—from Anthracite, a hard coal containing the highest proportion of fixed carbon, to Lignite or brown coal which is little more than a hard peat. World reserves of bituminous coal have been estimated at $7{\cdot}5 \times 10^{12}$ tonnes. If one adds the reserves of brown coal and lignite, this figure is increased by about 15 per cent. The proportion of the reserves that could be economically recovered varies from country to country and estimates vary from 50 to 100 per cent of the reserves. The reserves are highly localised—over half being located in the Soviet Union. In the United Kingdom coal has formed the basis of past industrial prosperity. Peak output occurred in 1913 when 290 million tonnes were mined one third of which was exported. At the end of the second world war production had fallen to 186 million tonnes and was far below demand. In 1947 the British coal industry was brought under public ownership and all its assets were vested in the National Coal Board. During the next ten years great efforts were made to increase coal output but, quite suddenly in 1956, demand for coal fell as oil became a popular fuel and the problem was to cut back the coal industry without causing undue social problems. The fall in demand was accompanied by increasing productivity, both mines and miners having been cut in their numbers by over half. Coal accounts for about 38 per cent. of primary energy consumption in Britain. Production is *c.* 122 million tonnes per annum. Exploration to find new reserves (including offshore drillings) is progressing. Expansion of the industry is again planned as a result of the high cost of oil since 1973.

Coat of Arms, in heraldry, a device containing a family's armorial bearings. In mediaeval times an actual coat upon which such device was embroidered; knights wore it over their armour.

Cobalt, a white metal melting at 1490°C. Two main ores are *cobalt glance* (in which the element is combined with arsenic and sulphur) and *smaltite* (cobalt arsenide). The principal sources are Ontario and Zaïre. Various cobalt alloys are important, *e.g.*, stellite, ferrocobalt and carboloy. Its monoxide is an important colouring medium, and is used for colouring glass and porcelain-blue.

Cobra, hooded and very venomous snakes. The best known species are the Indian Cobra, the Egyptian Cobra, and the Black-necked Cobra. Their food consists chiefly of small rodents. The King Cobra is almost exclusively a snake-eater. "Spitting" Cobras (or Ringhals) of S. Africa are a related genus, capable of spitting their venom several yards.

Coca, a S. American shrub, *Erythroxylon coca*, also cultivated in Java. The leaves yield cocaine, classified as a dangerous drug; used medicinally as a local anaesthetic, especially on the eyes and in dentistry. When the natives chew the leaves they are enabled to withstand astonishing amounts of hunger and fatigue, as cocaine acts both as a mental stimulant and as an anaesthetic on the mucous lining of the stomach.

Cochineal *or* **Carmine**, a dyestuff consisting of the dried bodies of the female scale insect (*Dactylopius coccus*) which feeds on cacti. Of ancient origin, the dye was well known to the Aztecs, and was used widely in the Middle Ages. The famous scarlet tunics worn by the English during the Napoleonic wars owed their colour to carmine. Today it is almost entirely replaced by aniline dyes.

Cockatoo, a member of the parrot family, bearing a crest of feathers on the head, native to Australia and adjacent regions. Predominant colour is white tinged with yellow or scarlet while some species have dark plumage. The cockatoo of New Guinea is slaty black with pale red cheeks and can crack Kanary nuts which usually require a hammer to break them open.

Cockchafer (*Melolontha*), one of the most destructive of beetles, the larvae feeding on roots. It is about 2·5 cm in length, of a brownish colour, and emits a loud whirring sound when flying.

Cockle, the popular name of the bi-valve shellfish of the genus *Cardium*, found plentifully in sandy bays near low-water line.

Cockroach, inaccurately called the "black beetle"; a pest of bakeries and kitchens. In Britain two species are commonly found: the Common Cockroach (*Blatta orientalis*), resident since the time of Elizabeth I, dark brown, about 2·5 cm long, with the wing covers long in the male and short in the female; and the German Cockroach (*Blatta germanica*), now the most common, half the size, dark yellow, with both sexes fully winged. All species have long antennae and flattened, leathery, shiny bodies. They are nocturnal and omnivorous.

Coconut Palm (*Cocos nucifera*), a tropical tree, growing to a height of 30 m, with a slender, leaning trunk surmounted by giant feather-like leaves. One of the most important sources of food and raw material for people living in the tropics. The juice of the fruit, or coconut, is drunk; the kernel is eaten fresh or dried to form copra, which yields animal feeding stuffs and oil, used in the manufacture of soap, margarine, cosmetics, synthetic rubber, etc.; leaves are used for thatching; leaf stalks for canes, fence posts, needles, etc., and the trunk for houses and bridges. Main producing areas: Indonesia, Philippines, Malaysia, Sri Lanka and S. India.

Codes, a term used to designate a system of laws properly classified. The Code of Hammurabi, king of Babylon, *c.* 1751 B.C., had extensive influence over a long period. The Romans formulated several codes of historic importance including the Theodosian Code which summarised the Roman laws from the time of Constantine to 438 A.D. The final codification was made under order of the Emperor Justinian by his chief minister Tribonian and published in 529 with a new edition in 534. The most important of modern codes is the *Code Napoléon*, compiled between 1803 and 1810, and still in force. It has been used as an example for the codification of the laws of a number of countries from America to Japan. Under Frederick the Great the law of Prussia was codified. English law has never been codified, although the law on certain subjects has been gathered up into a single statute. The Law Commission Act, 1965, was passed to consolidate and codify the law wherever possible.

Codex, a manuscript volume of the Scriptures comprising the Sinaitic codex of the 4th cent., the Vatican codex of the same period, the Alexandrine codex of the 5th cent., and others. The British Museum, in 1933, purchased the *Codex Sinaiticus* from the Soviet Government for £100,000.

Coelacanth, the name of the sole survivor of a long evolutionary line of lobe-finned fish, with large armoured head, which lived some 350 million years ago (Middle Devonian). Fossil records ceased 70 million years ago (Cretaceous), and it was believed it had become extinct. In 1938, however, a living coelacanth (*Latimeria chalumnae*) was caught off the coast of S. Africa and another off Madagascar in 1952 which stimulated world-wide interest. Recent research shows that young *Latimeria* are born and not hatched.

Coffee, a shrub found originally in Arabia and Ethiopia, but now extensively grown in Brazil, Colombia, Ivory Coast, Uganda, Angola and Central America. It yields a seed or berry which after undergoing the necessary preparation, is ground and used in most countries as a breakfast beverage. The best coffee is the Mocha, an Arabian variety. The stimulating effect of coffee is due to the caffeine, which is also present in tea. The beverage was introduced into Europe in the 16th cent., and the first London coffee shop was opened in 1632.

Coke is the solid residue remaining when coal is carbonised and nearly all the volatile constituents have been driven off. Used as fuel, and as an agent for reducing metallic oxides to metals, *e.g.*, iron ore to iron, in the manufacture of steel.

Colorado Beetle, a serious pest of potato crops. Both adults and larvae feed on the foliage where the orange eggs are laid. The grub is reddish, with two rows of small black spots on each side. The adults are about 1·2 cm long with yellow and black striped wing cases. The beetle is avoided by birds because of its nasty taste, and is controlled by arsenical sprays.

Colosseum, the name of the Flavian amphitheatre at Rome, begun by Vespasian and finished by Titus A.D. 80. In general outline it still remains one of the most magnificent ruins in the world. In the arena of this great building the famous gladiatorial displays and mimic naval battles used to be given, and about 50,000 spectators could be accommodated.

Colossus is the name which the ancients gave to any statue of gigantic size. The Colossus at Rhodes, which was a bronze statue of the sun god, Helios, was the most famous, and reckoned among the seven wonders of the world. It stood over 30 m high at the mouth of the harbour. There is no truth in the legend that ships could pass between its legs. It fell in an earthquake in 224 B.C.

Coluga, also known as **"flying lemur", caguan** or **kubuk,** a remarkable mammal which may be regarded as an aberrant insectivore or an aberrant form of the earliest ancestor of the bats. It has nothing to do with lemurs. There are two genera, one inhabiting the Philippines and one inhabiting Malaya. They have a parachute-like membrane which covers them from the neck to the tip of the tail, by means of which they can glide from treetop to ground a distance of up to 64 m.

Column, in architecture, is an upright solid body serving as a support or decoration to a building. Columns consist of a pedestal, a shaft, and a capital, over which the supported entablature rises. They are named according to the styles of architecture of which they form part, being Doric, Tuscan, Ionic, Corinthian or Composite as the case may be.

Comets are celestial bodies which move about the solar system in elliptical or hyperbolic orbits. Usually these star-like bodies are accompanied by a long shining tail. The hyperbolic comets are seen once only, and do not reappear; the elliptical comets are periodic, and their recurrence can be calculated with accuracy. The head of a comet is believed to consist of small lumps of solid matter accompanied by dust particles and gases such as carbon dioxide and methane. It used to be thought that the tail was produced by the pressure of sunlight on the cometary material but a modern explanation is that it is produced by the combined action of the solar wind (a continuous stream of ionised hydrogen originating in the sun) and the interplanetary magnetic field. When they run parallel the effect is to produce a long streaming tail pointing away from the sun. Chief among the periodic comets is Edmund Halley's, the first to return as predicted in 1757. It reappears about every 76 years and is next due in 1985. The most spectacular comet of the 19th cent. was Donati's in 1858. Kohoutek's comet, discovered in 1973 by the Czech astronomer of that name, was the first comet to be studied from space (by the Russian Soyuz and the American Skylab).

Commons are the remnants of the mediaeval open fields round villages in which the villagers had rights in common, *e.g.*, (i) estover—the right of taking wood for house building or firewood; (ii) pasture—the right of grazing beasts; (iii) turbary—the right of digging turf; (iv) piscary—the right to fish. Many of these common lands were enclosed during the agrarian revolution which went on steadily in England from the 15th cent. onwards, and with their enclosure common rights vanished. A Royal Commission on Common Land described the commons in 1965 as the "last reservoir of uncommitted land" which provide, as far as the public is concerned, by far the largest part of the accessible open spaces of the country. Under the Commons Registration Act, 1965, it was the duty of County Councils and County Borough Councils to make a register of all common land and all town and village greens in their areas.

Commons, House of, the Lower House of the British Parliament. *See* **Section C, Part I.**

Commune of Paris has twice played a dramatic part in the history of France. In 1792 it was able, through its control of the administrative organisation of Paris, to override the National Assembly. In 1871, after the withdrawal of the Prussian troops, it tried to assert its authority. Public buildings were destroyed by members of the Commune and civil war raged during April and half May, but Government troops savagely suppressed the rising.

Communism. *See* **Section J.**

Compass *or* **Mariner's Compass.** It has been known since very early times that an iron needle, suspended freely to hang horizontally when not magnetised, comes to rest roughly along the geographical north-south line when magnetised. Further, it generally does not hang horizontally. This is the essential behaviour of the *compass*, a navigational instrument whose invention is obscure but which seems to have been known to the Chinese 4,500 years ago. That the behaviour of the compass shows the existence of a *magnetic field* associated with the Earth was first fully recognised by William Gilbert in 1600. Aircraft and ships now largely employ gyrostatic compasses which are not affected by electrical and magnetic disturbances. Sperry, Brown and Anschutz are three important types of gyroscopic compass

Composite Materials, or more simply composites, are materials which derive useful properties by combining the virtues of two or more components. Combining clay with straw to make tougher bricks is an ancient example in which fibres (straw) are embedded in a matrix or body (the clay). A modern example is fibreglass in which glass fibres are embedded in a plastic matrix. Nature also uses composites as in bamboo in which a lignin matrix binds together the fibres of cellulose to make a light strong structure. Composites may contain flakes or particles embedded in the matrix instead of fibres—it depends on the application. Although the idea is not new, composite technology has made rapid strides in the last few decades guided by scientific insight into the nature of solids and the origin of their strengths and weaknesses. The motivation has been that scientifically designed composites offer materials with exceptional strength/weight ratio, desirable magnetic properties and other technological advantages which meet the extreme demands of a variety of industries. For example, composite aluminium containing boron fibres or resin containing graphite fibres can have strength/weight ratios over twice that of high-strength solid aluminium. Composites of many kinds are now widespread in industrial use and are attracting much research and development.

Computer, a technical device for accepting an input of information, processing this information according to some prescribed programme of operations and supplying an output of processed information. Many types of operation can be performed on many types of information and computers are now indispensable in science, business, warfare, government and other activities. Early thinkers in this field were Pascal (17th cent.), Babbage (19th cent.) and Turing (1930s), but electronic computers as we know them appeared during the second world war and the first commercial machine was on sale in 1950. Computers are millions of times faster than human beings at computing; and the introduction of computers into an organisation does more than just speed up the calculations, it tends to transform the whole nature of the organisation. The possibilities for future developments seem enormous. Analogue computers and digital computers are two different kinds stemming from the difference between *measuring* and *counting*. Analogue types handle data that is repeated by physical quantities of continuously variable size such as voltages or lengths. These quantities can be made to vary like the quantities in a problem which the computer is set to solve; the problem is thus solved by analogy. A slide rule is a rudimentary analogue computer in which numbers are represented by lengths of rule. Digital computers handle actual numbers expressed in digits and the quantities in the problem are represented by discrete numbers. These can all be expressed in binary form and thus stored or handled in bits. *See* **Bit, Binary Notation.**

Conclave, an assembly of Roman Catholic cardinals met together to elect a pope. The last Conclave was held in the Vatican in June 1963 when Cardinal Montini, archbishop of Milan, was elected Pope Paul VI.

Concordat, an agreement or convention between the pope and a secular government regarding ecclesiastical matters. The Concordat of Worms in 1122 between Calixtus II and the Emperor Henry V was famous as deciding a long struggle in regard to investiture. In 1801, Napoleon concluded a concordat with Pius VII defining the restored relations between the head of the Church and the French Roman Catholics.

Condor, a large eagle of brilliant black plumage with a circlet of white feathers round its neck. It is a native of the Andes.

Confederation is a free association of sovereign states united for some common purpose. It is to be distinguished from a **Federation,** which is a union of states with one central government, each state relinquishing its sovereignty, though retaining some independence in internal affairs.

Coniferae are cone-bearing trees, including firs, pines, cedars, cypresses, junipers, yews, etc., and are widely distributed in temperate regions.

Conservatism. *See* **Section J.**

Constitution, the fundamental organic law or principles of government of a nation, state, society, or other organised body, embodied in written documents, or implied in the institutions and customs of the country or society. The government of the USA, unlike Great Britain, works upon a written Constitution. It was framed when the USA came into existence as a sovereign body, when the Constitution built a republic out of a federation of thirteen states, based on representative government. The constitution was adopted in 1789, and its strength has been tested by the fact that, substantially unchanged, it is now the groundwork for a federation which now comprises fifty states. *See* **Section C, Part I** for the **British Constitution.**

Continent, a word used in physical geography to denote the larger continuous land masses in contrast to the great oceans of the earth. They are: Eurasia (conventionally regarded as 2 continents, Europe and Asia), Africa, North America, South America, Australia and Antarctica. (Australiasia is Australia, New Zealand and adjacent islands. Oceania is Australasia and the many islands of the S.W. Pacific).

Continental Drift. The hypothesis of drifting continents is due to F. B. Taylor, an American geologist who published his theory in 1908, and to the Austrian meteorologist Alfred Wegener in 1910. The latter was impressed by the matching coasts of South America and Africa, which seemed to him to fit together like the pieces of a jigsaw puzzle. Since then many other people have taken up and developed the idea. According to Wegener, at one time there were two primary super-continents, Laurasia and Gondwanaland. The one in the northern hemisphere consisted of North America, Europe, and the northern part of Asia. Its southern counterpart included Antarctica, Australia, India, Africa and South America. These super-continents broke up, and their various bits moved apart. In particular, the southern hemisphere continents drifted radially northwards away from the south pole, and the two Americas shifted westwards from Europe and Africa. What would have been the leading edges of the land masses on this hypothesis, are now heavily buckled up into mountain belts, such as the Cordillera and the Alpine-Himalayan chain. The resistance afforded to drifting by the strong ocean floors may well have been the cause of such structures. Despite the wealth of geological facts which have a bearing on the problem of continental drift, none of these has been able to decide the issue in a conclusive manner. Further studies of rock magnetism (*q.v.*) and of fossil climates should ultimately establish the concept of continental drift on a firm basis. *See also* **Earth, F8.**

Conurbation, a term used in reference to an extensive and continuous area of urban land-use. Conurbations are frequently formed by the physical coalescence of several formerly free-standing towns. They may themselves coalesce to form a higher order of physical urbanisation, known as a megalopolis. The seven conurbations officially recognised in the UK are Greater London, W. Midlands, S. E. Lancashire, W. Yorkshire, Merseyside, Tyneside and Clydeside, of which the first five are said to form the English megalopolis. In common with other old and well-developed cities throughout the capitalist world, conurbations in Britain show a marked decline in population and employment.

Convention is an assembly of delegates, representatives, members of a party met to accomplish some specific civil, social, political, ecclesiastical or other important object.

Convocation, an assembly called together to deliberate ecclesiastical affairs. In the Church of England the provinces of Canterbury and York each have their convocation. The term is also applied to assemblies of the graduates of certain universities.

Coot. A very widely distributed bird of the rail family and a common resident of the British Isles. The adult is black with a conspicuous white bald shield on the forehead and a white bill. The juvenile is brownish grey with whitish breast and throat. The coot flies heavily, but swims well. It dives frequently and can remain submerged for a considerable time. It is pugnacious and in winter gregarious. The food is chiefly vegetable. The large nest is usually built among aquatic vegetation and the young are fed by both parents. Another species, the Crested Coot, occurs in S. Europe.

Copper, one of the most familiar of metals, symbol Cu, used in ancient times as an alloy with tin in producing bronze, and preceding iron as an industrial material. Copper ores are most abundant in the USA, Chile, Canada, Zambia, Zaïre. All copper compounds are poisonous.

Copyright. Under the Copyright Act, 1956, copyright subsists in every original literary, dramatic musical, and artistic work if the author is a British subject or a citizen of the Republic of Ireland or resident in the United Kingdom, or if the work is first published in the United Kingdom. The Act provides that, except in certain special cases, the author of the work shall be the first owner of the copyright, and there are no formalities, such as registration or payment of fees, to be accomplished. Copyright includes the right to reproduce the work in any material form, to perform the work in public, or, if the work is unpublished, to publish the work. The Act also protects sound recordings, films and television and sound broadcasts. Literary, dramatic, musical and artistic works which enjoy the protection of the Act are automatically protected in those countries which are parties to the Berne Copyright Convention or the Universal Copyright Convention. In general, copyright in literary, dramatic, musical and artistic works is vested in the author for the period of his lifetime and 50 years following, after which it passes into the public domain and becomes freely available to any who wish to make use of it. The Copyright Libraries, entitled to receive copies of books published in the United Kingdom are given under **Libraries**. The Berne Copyright Convention and the Universal Copyright Convention were revised at a diplomatic conference held in Paris in 1971. The effect of the revisions allows any national of a developing country to obtain, under certain conditions, a compulsory licence to translate and publish a copyright work for the purpose of teaching, scholarship and research, upon payment of compensation to the copyright owner of the original work. The Government Department responsible for matters in connection with copyright is the Industrial Property and Copyright Department, 25 Southampton Buildings, London, WC2A 1AY.

Coral, an order of small marine animals closely related to the sea-anemone, but differing from it in their ability to develop a limy skeleton. They multiply sexually and by budding. The structure of the coral secretions assumes a variety of forms, fan-like, tree-like, mushroom shape, and so forth. Red coral (the skeleton of *Corallium rubrum*) is mainly obtained from the Mediterranean. The coral reefs of the Pacific and Indian Oceans are often many miles in extent. Living corals occur only in warm seas at about 23°C.

Cordite, a smokeless explosive adopted for small arms and heavy artillery by the British Government in the naval and military services in 1889, and composed of 58 parts of nitro-glycerine, 37 of gun-cotton, and 5 of vaseline. It is a jelly or plastic dough, and used in the form of sticks. Invented by Sir Frederick Abel and Sir John Dewar 1889.

Cork, the bark of a species of oak, *Quercus suber*, grown largely in the South of Europe and North America. The cork tree is said to yield bark every six to ten years for 150 years, and grows to a height of from 6–12 m. Its lightness, impermeability, and elasticity enable it to be used for a variety of commercial purposes, especially for stoppers of bottles.

Cormorant, a large, long-billed water-bird which captures fish by diving. The common cormorant has bronze-black plumage with white cheeks and sides and is found around the sea coasts of most parts of the world, including the British Isles. It nests in colonies on sea cliffs and rocky ledges. The Shag or Green Cormorant is a smaller bird with green-black plumage and a crest.

Corncrake. *See* **Landrail.**

Corn Laws were statutes intended for the benefit of British agriculture, and restricted import and export of grain. From the 14th to the mid-19th cent. such laws were in force, and were often of a stringent nature. They became so oppressive and caused corn to reach so high a price that the poorer classes were plunged into distress. A powerful anti-corn law agitation was organised of which Cobden, Bright and Villiers were the leaders, and Sir Robert Peel, in 1846, at the time of the Irish potato famine, carried through free trade. The repeal of the Corn Laws marked an important phase in the transformation of an agricultural to an industrial Britain.

Corona or **Solar Corona**, the outer atmosphere of the sun. This glows by virtue of light emitted by the sun and scattered by electrons and dust particles at various heights in the sun's atmosphere and also by light emitted from ionised atoms in the corona itself. Corona light is much fainter than the bright disc of the sun and is invisible against the normal blue of the sky. During total solar eclipses, the corona can be seen by the human eye as a faint glow extending irregularly outwards a few solar diameters from the sun. The sun's atmosphere extends much further than this but is invisible to the eye at large distances from the sun. The corona gases are thought to be very hot (millions of degrees), and in complex violent motion and the gross structure of the corona is connected with the sunspot cycle.

Cortes, the name of the Parliamentary assemblies of Spain and Portugal.

Cosmic Rays, a form of radiation coming from outer space, of deep penetrating power and of great scientific interest. The rays are believed to consist chiefly of fast protons, with a few α-particles and other positive nuclei. By interacting with the gas of the atmosphere, these rays initiate a complex series of events, in the course of which other particles ("secondary radiations") are generated. The secondary rays contain virtually all the particles listed on **F14**; indeed, several particles were first discovered as secondary cosmic rays. Cosmic rays are investigated at and below sea-level, on mountains, in mines, in balloons, rockets and satellites. Origin still uncertain. *See* **F3**(2).

Cosmology is the science which studies the whole universe, its origin, its nature, its size, and evolution. At present it is a very active science partly because new techniques such as radio-astronomy are revealing more facts about distant parts of the universe and partly because of fruitful clashes between theoretical ideas. *See* **F3–7.**

Cotton, the name of a plant of several species bearing large yellow flowers with purple centres. These centres expand into pods, which at maturity burst and yield the white fibrous substance known as cotton. The raw cotton contains a large proportion of seeds which are removed by "ginning". Long before the Christian era, cotton had been grown and used with great skill in India to make fabrics. The industry was not introduced into England until the middle of the 17th cent. when Protestant refugees from Flanders came to settle in the wool textile districts of East Anglia and Lancashire. With improvements in machinery and expansion of overseas trade in the 18th and 19th cent., Lancashire became the centre of the world's cotton industry but since the second world war man-made fibres have taken the place of cotton. Chief producers: USA, USSR, China, India, Brazil, Mexico, Pakistan, Egypt, Turkey.

Coulomb, a unit of electric charge, named after the French naval engineer, Charles Augustin de Coulomb (1736–1806), equal to the quantity of electricity transferred in one second by a current of one ampere.

County. The word county was introduced after the Norman conquest as an equivalent of the old English "shire". Since the recent reorganisation of local government in the United Kingdom the distinction between *administrative* counties and *geographical* counties no longer exists. Certain geographical counties have disappeared (*e.g.*, Rutland and Pembroke), new counties have appeared (*e.g.*, Avon and Gwynedd), while former counties have been modified (*e.g.*, Glamorgan and Yorkshire). *See* **K186.**

Coup d'Etat, a violent change in the government of a state carried out by force or illegally. Examples are the overthrow of the French Republic in 1851 by Louis Napoleon, who then became Emperor, and more recently the military *coups* in the Middle East which brought about the abdication of Farouk of Egypt in 1952 and the assassination of Feisal of Iraq in 1958.

Court Leet, a court of record held annually before the steward of any particular manor or lordship; originally there was only one court for a manor, but in the time of Edward I it branched into two, the court baron and the court leet.

Coypu or **Nutria rat**, a large beaver-like rodent found in S. America; now wild in E. Anglia, where it is causing damage to dykes, reeds, and crops, having escaped from farms where it is bred for its fur.

Crane, a large, graceful wading-bird with elegant long legs and neck, greyish plumage, superficially resembling the heron and related to the bustard. They migrate in V or W formation and have trumpet-like voices. There are several species, found in all continents except S. America, including the Crowned Crane with golden coronet and the Demoiselle with tuft-like crest of white feathers. The Common Crane nested in East Anglia in mediaeval times but now comes only as a rare visitor from the Continent.

Credit is an advance of money or of goods or services in consideration of a promise of payment later. Trade credit is such an advance from trader to customer; bank credit is an advance of money by a bank to a client, whether a business firm or a private person, in consideration of an interest payment by the borrower.

Creed (Latin *credo* = I believe), a formal statement of belief. The three orthodox Christian creeds are the Apostles' Creed (a summary of their teaching), the Nicene Creed (drawn up by the Church Council at Nicaea in A.D. 325 to define its theological doctrines), and the Athanasian Creed (concerning the nature and divinity of Christ). *See also* under individual headings.

Cremation, the ancient custom, revived in modern times, of burning the dead. Cremation was first legalised in Great Britain in 1885 and the first crematorium opened at Woking in that year. Application for cremation must be accompanied by two medical certificates.

Cricket, a genus of insects of the grasshopper order which move by leaps. The male produces a chirping noise by rubbing its wing-covers together. Just as the males inherit the nerve machinery for emitting the song of the species, so the females receive and respond to that song and to no other.

Crimean War (1853–56). This war between Russia and the allied powers of Turkey, England, France and Sardinia, was connected with the Eastern Question (*q.v.*) and the desire of Russia for a port on the Mediterranean. Chief engagements were the Alma, Balaclava and Inkerman. Fighting virtually ceased with fall of Sevastopol in September 1855. Treaty of Paris signed 30 March 1856.

Crocodiles and their allies (alligators, caimans and gavials) are the largest of modern reptiles. They are well equipped for a predatory life in shallow waters, having powerful tails and strong jaws. Their eggs are laid on land, in sand or decomposing vegetation.

Crow, a family of birds including many well-known species such as the rook, raven, jackdaw, carrion crow, hooded crow, magpie, nutcracker, jaw and chough.

Crusades were military expeditions undertaken by some of the Christian nations of Europe with the object of ensuring the safety of pilgrims visiting the Holy Sepulchre and to retain in Christian hands the Holy Places. For two centuries nine crusades were undertaken: First, 1095–99, under Godfrey of Bouillon, which succeeded in capturing Jerusalem; Second, 1147–49, led by Louis VII of France, a dismal failure, which ended with the fall of Jerusalem; Third, 1189–92, in which Richard I of England took part, making a truce with Saladin; Fourth, 1202–4, led by French and Flemish nobles, a shameful expedition, resulting in the founding of a Latin empire in Constantinople; Fifth, 1217–21, led by John of Brienne; Sixth, 1228–29, under the Emperor Frederick II; Seventh, 1248–54, under St. Louis of France; Eighth, 1270, under the same leadership, but cut short by his death on an ill-judged expedition to Tunis; Ninth, 1271–72, led by Prince Edward of England, which accomplished nothing. Millions of lives and an enormous amount of treasure were sacrificed in these enterprises and Jerusalem remained in the possession of the "infidels". The chief material beneficiaries were the Italian maritime cities; the chief spiritual beneficiary was the pope; but in literature and the arts both Europe and the Levant benefited enormously from the bringing together of the different cultures.

Cryogenics (Greek roots: productive of cold) is the science dealing with the production of very low temperatures and the study of their physical and technological consequences. "Very low" is often taken to mean below about −150°C. The growth of cryogenics (essentially a 20th-cent. science) is connected with the discovery of how to liquefy all gases including even helium which resisted liquefaction until 1908. Scientifically, cryogenics is important partly because special phenomena (*e.g.*, superconductivity (*q.v.*)) appear at lower temperatures and partly because more can be learned about ordinary properties by studying them in the absence of heat. Technologically, cryogenics is becoming more and more significant, for example, liquefied gases are rocket propellants, superconductors make valuable magnets, tissue-freezing techniques (using very cold liquids) have been introduced into surgery. *See* **Absolute Temperature.**

Crystal, in everyday usage, a solid chemical substance bounded by plane surfaces which show a regular geometrical arrangement as, *e.g.*, quartz crystals, rock salt, snow flakes. In physics the term means any substance whose atoms are arranged in a regular three-dimensional array. This includes most solids, even those not particularly crystalline in appearance, *e.g.*, a lump of lead. *See also* **Glass** and **Liquid Crystals.**

Cubism, the name of a revolutionary movement in art created in the years 1907–9 by the two painters Picasso and Braque. Rejecting purely visual effects, they approached nature from an intellectual point of view. reducing it to mathematical orderliness. Its respectable grandparent was Cézanne who had once written: "you must see in nature the cylinder, the sphere, and the cone"—a concept which, together with the contemporary interest in Negro sculpture, moved the two founders of the movement to experiment with the reduction of natural forms to their basic geometrical shapes. In practice, this meant combining several views of the object all more or less superimposed in order to express the idea of the object rather than any one view of it. The name Cubism was derisive and the movement aroused the same opposition as Impressionism, Fauvism and the later Futurism. Picasso's *Young Ladies of Avignon* was the first Cubist painting and his "Head" (1909) the first Cubist sculpture. Three phases are recognised: (1) Cubism under the influence of Cézanne; (2) high or analytical Cubism (*c.* 1909–12) concentrating on the breaking-down of form to the exclusion of interest in colour; (3) synthetic Cubism (*c.* 1913) making use of *collage* in which pieces of pasted-on paper (illustrations, wallpaper, newspaper) and other materials were used in addition to paint. Amongst other early cubist painters were Metzinger, Gleizes, Gris and Léger.

Cuckoo, a well-known migratory bird which is found in Great Britain from April to July, hawk-like in shape, with a very characteristic note, uttered during the mating season only by the male. The hen has a soft bubbling call. It lays its eggs in the nests of other birds, *e.g.*, the meadow pipit and hedge sparrow, but only one egg in each nest. Feeds mainly on insects, particularly hairy caterpillars.

Cuneiform, (Latin = *wedge-shaped*), an ancient method of writing by impressing wedge-like strokes into tablets of damp clay which when dried and hardened formed a permanent script. Cuneiform writing developed from its original pictographic form into a phonetic writing and can be traced back to the non-Semitic Sumerians of ancient Mesopotamia, the earliest civilisation known to us. It passed to the Semitic Accadians of Babylonia in the 3rd millennium B.C. who adapted it to their own language. Decipherment by Sir Henry Rawlinson, 1835.

Curfew (Old Fr. *covre-feu* = cover fire), a regulation common throughout Europe in mediaeval times by which, at a fixed hour in the evening, the church bell was rung as a signal that fires were to be put out and the people were to go to bed. The custom originated in the fear of fire when buildings were built of timber. Nowadays a curfew is imposed by the military in areas where riots or disturbances are expected, compelling the civilian population to remain indoors after nightfall.

Curia, the central government of the Roman Catholic Church. By the reform which came into force on 1 January 1968, its twelve Sacred Congregations or "ministries" were reorganised and reduced to nine. The aim of the reform was to streamline the Curial offices so that the Church's machinery can cope with modern problems, so favouring the desires expressed by the Ecumenical Council convened by Pope John.

Curie, a measure of the rate at which radioactive material emits radiation. One curie is a disintegration rate of $3{\cdot}7 \times 10^{10}$ disintegrations per second.

Curlew, a wading-bird of which there are several species. It frequents marshy places, feeds on worms, insects, molluscs and berries and possesses a very long, down-curved bill.

Currency is the name given to the types of cash money—metal or paper—in use in an area (*e.g.* pound, sterling, dollar, franc). It also designates the actual coins or notes issued. Its amount is usually subject to regulation by the Government, or by a Central Bank acting on the Government's behalf. Britain changed over to a £-based decimal currency in February 1971. *See also* **Foreign Currencies, Section N.**

Cybernetics, the science concerned with the automatic control and communication processes in both animals and machines. Thus it is concerned with brain function, information theory, electronic computers, and automation.

Cyclone, a term usually applied to a tropical revolving storm. Cyclones often occur towards the end of the hot seasons and are mainly confined to tracks in the western areas of the oceans, being known as hurricanes (Caribbean and Pacific), cyclones (Indian Ocean) and typhoons (China Seas). The circulation of air in a cyclone is similar to that in the *depression* of temperate latitudes, but the region of low pressure is much more localised and the pressure gradients steeper. Winds of hurricane strength and torrential rain occur generally, although at the centre of the storm there is a small area, known as the "eye", where fair, calm weather prevails.

Cyclotron, a machine for accelerating charged particles such as protons to very high energies. Devised by E. O. Lawrence in California in 1930, it uses a magnetic field to make the particles traverse nearly circular paths and an electric field to give them an additional pulse of energy each time round. The accelerated particles impinge on targets, and the resulting events are a basic source of information for nuclear physicists. The cyclotron is obsolescent and has led to the development of other machines, *e.g.*, betatrons, synchrotrons. Britain has two major national high-energy machines; a 7 GeV proton synchrotron and a 5 GeV electron synchrotron. The European Organisation for Nuclear Research (CERN), to which Britain contributes through the Science Research Council (SRC), carries out research at higher energies.

D

Dactylopterus, a fish of the gurnard family, with wing-like pectoral fins; sometimes known as the flying fish, though that appellation is more generally given to *Exocaetus exiliens*.

Dadaism (French *Dada* = hobby-horse) was a hysterical and nihilistic precursor of **Surrealism** (*q.v.*) resulting from the shock produced by the first world war. Beginning in Zurich about 1915, it spread to other continental cities, such as Berlin and Paris, dying out in 1922. The movement was deliberately anti-art, destructive, and without meaning; it intended to scandalise by such tricks as "compositions" made out of anything that came to hand—buttons, bus tickets, pieces of wire, bits of tin, etc. Other excesses included incoherent poetry, Dada night-clubs, plays, and short-lived newspapers. Many Dadaist painters became Surrealists at a later stage, but where Surrealism is a deliberate attempt to present subconscious and dream-like images, Dadaism was sheer anarchism. Leading Dadaists were Hans Arp, Marcel Duchamp, André Breton, Kurt Schwitters and Max Ernst.

Daddy Longlegs, or **Crane-fly**, a slender long-legged fly of the family Tipulidae. The larvae which do damage to lawns and plants are called leather-jackets. The Americans call Harvestmen (*q.v.*) daddy longlegs.

Daguerreotype, the first practical photographic process, invented in Paris by M. Daguerre during the years 1824–39. The light-sensitive plate was prepared by bringing iodine in contact with a plate of silver. After exposure a positive image came by development of the plate in mercury vapour. Even for open-air scenes the first daguerreotypes involved exposure of 5–10 minutes. The picture came in one copy only and the process was therefore of limited use. The wet collodion process (1851) rendered the technique obsolete.

Dail Eireann, the name of the national parliament of the Irish Republic.

Damaskeening, the art of inlaying one metal upon another, largely practised in the East in mediaeval times, especially in the decoration of sword blades.

Dandies, the name given to a class of exquisites prominent in early Victorian days, and who attracted attention by excessive regard for dress. Their feminine counterparts were the dandizettes.

Danegeld, a tax imposed in England in Anglo-Saxon times to raise funds for resisting the Danes or to buy them off. Edward the Confessor abolished the tax, but it was revived by the Conqueror and subsequently retained, under another name, after the danger from the Danes was past. It is the basis of all taxation in this country. Domesday Book (*q.v.*) was originally drawn up for the purpose of teaching the State how to levy the tax.

Danelaw, the law enforced by the Danes in the kingdoms of Northumbria, East Anglia, and in the districts of the five (Danish) boroughs—lands grouped round Leicester, Nottingham, Derby, Stamford and Lincoln—which they occupied during the Viking invasions of the 9th and 10th cent. The country occupied was also called the Danelaw or Danelagh.

Darter, 1. Snakebirds, a genus of the pelican family, with long, pointed bill and serpent-like neck and resembling cormorants in appearance. There are 5 species. 2. Numerous species of small freshwater fish belonging to the Perch family, found in N. America.

Date Palm, *Phoenix dactylifera*, one of the oldest known food plants widely cultivated in N. Africa and W. Asia. It grows to 30 m and continues to bear for 2 or 3 centuries, its fruit being of great value as a food. From the leaves the Africans make roofs for their huts; ropes are made from the fibrous parts of the stalks; and the sap furnishes a stimulating beverage.

Dauphin, the title borne by the eldest sons of the Kings of France from 1349 to the Revolution of 1830.

Day is the most natural unit of time and may be defined as the period of rotation of the earth relative to any selected heavenly body. Relative to the sun it is called the *solar day*. Relative to a fixed star it is called the *sidereal day*. Owing to irregularities in the earth's movements, the time taken for the earth to rotate through 360° relative to the sun is variable, and so the *mean solar day* of 24 hours has been introduced, which is the average throughout the year. The *mean solar day* is our standard, used for purposes of the calendar, and astronomers use *sidereal* clocks to check mean solar time. In practice, for convenience, the sidereal day is determined by the earth's rotation relative to the vernal equinox or first point of Aries, and is equal to 23 hours 56 minutes and 4·091 seconds of mean solar time (*i.e.*, about 4 minutes shorter than a solar day). *See* **Time.**

DDT, (dichloro-dephenyl-trichloroethane). A very powerful insecticide which has had wide success in the control of diseases, such as malaria and typhus, which is carried by insects. Mosquito swamps are sprayed with DDT to kill the carriers. Because this toxic chemical breaks down very slowly it builds up in birds and animals and its use is now banned in Britain. Its detection in Antarctic wild life confirmed that DDT pollution was virtually world-wide.

Deacon, an ecclesiastical official, who assists in some of the smaller ministerial duties in church or chapel; in the Anglican Church he ranks below a priest.

Dead Languages are such as the ancient Greek and Roman tongues, which are no longer spoken but are preserved in literature.

Dead Sea Scrolls, a group of ancient Jewish documents, consisting of scrolls and fragments which have been recovered since 1947 in the vicinity of Qumran near the Dead Sea and which represent one of the most important finds ever made in the field of biblical archaeology and Christian origins. The scrolls, written in Hebrew or Aramaic, were found in caves, the first by chance by an Arab shepherd in 1947. These consisted of biblical texts older by a thousand years than the earliest Hebrew manuscript of the Old Testament (A.D. 895). Many fragments have since been discovered, comprising the whole of the Old Testament with the exception of Esther. In addition there are commentaries and other non-biblical writings, including one called "The War of the Sons of Light with the Sons of Darkness". The writing on the scrolls indicates that they were written over a period of two centuries, the greater proportion before the birth of Christ. A nearby ruin is believed to have been the home of a religious sect called the Essenes (**J18**), to whom the scrolls belonged. By the aid of the latest scientific techniques, including radiocarbon tests, the age of the scrolls is being accurately determined. An account of the scrolls and their implications is given in Edmund Wilson's *The Dead Sea Scrolls: 1947–1969*.

Dean, a Church of England dignitary, ranking below a bishop, and the head of the chapter of a cathedral. A rural Dean supervises a *deanery* or group of parishes. There are also Deans of Faculties in some universities, and at Oxford and Cambridge the *Dean* is in charge of chapel services and disciplinary arrangements.

Death Watch Beetle (*Xextobium rufovillosum*), a wood-boring beetle, larger than the common furniture beetle, found chiefly in the old oak beams of churches and other historic buildings. The grub bores from 4–12 years. The name "death watch" comes from the superstition that the ticking sound, made by the beetle striking its head against the wood, is a sign of approaching death. The death watch beetle in the roof of Westminster Hall was recently smoked out by means of an insecticide called gamma benzine hexachloride. *See also* **Furniture Beetle, Woodworm.**

Decalogue, name given to the Ten Commandments of the Old Testament. There are two versions of them, differing in detail: Exodus xx. 2–17 and Deuteronomy v. 6–21. They are of Hebrew origin and are recognised by Jews and Christians as the divine law given by God to Moses on Mt. Sinai. Most of them are prohibitions in contrast to the beatitudes (pronounced by Christ in the Sermon on the Mount) which are positive, *e.g.*, Blessed are the merciful.

December, the last month of the year in our calendar, and the tenth in the old Roman.

Deciduous Trees are such as shed their leaves at certain seasons as distinguished from evergreens or permanent foliaged trees or shrubs.

Declaration of Independence was an Act by which the American Congress, on 4 July 1776, declared the American colonies to be independent of Great Britain. "Independence Day" is a holiday in the United States.

Defender of the Faith (*Defensor Fidei*), a title conferred upon Henry VIII by Pope Leo X in 1521 for entering the lists against Luther with his pamphlet in defence of the Seven Sacraments. After Henry assumed headship of the Church of England the Pope withdrew the title but it was confirmed to him by Parliament in 1554 and has been used ever since by English monarchs.

Deflation is a policy designed to bring down costs by reducing the supply of means of payment. It is usually advocated as a remedy for inflation, and in this connection is often referred to as Disinflation. It usually results in a fall in employment. *See* **Section G.**

Dehydrate, to eliminate the water from a substance. The process of dehydration is now used in the food industry, as a result of wartime research, in making such things as dried egg and packet soups. Most vegetables contain over 90 per cent. of water, and much of this can be removed under vacuum at low temperatures without appreciably impairing the flavour. The lightness of the dehydrated products is an advantage when supplies have to be transported.

Deliquescence, the process of dissolving by the absorption of moisture from the atmosphere. For instance, chromic acid crystals on exposure to the air quickly deliquesce.

Delta, a triangular tract of land between diverging branches of a river at its mouth, and so called from its general resemblance to the Greek letter Δ *delta*. The best-known examples are the deltas of the Nile, the Ganges, the Niger and the Mississippi.

Deluge, a flood, commonly applied to the story of the Deluge in the Bible, in which Noah and the Ark figure. A similar tradition lingers in the mythologies of all ancient peoples.

Democratic Party, one of the two great American political parties, originated about 1787, advocating restrictions on the federal governments and in opposition to the federalists. It was in 1825 that a group who were in favour of high tariffs seceded, later to become the Republican Party. The Democratic Party was split again over slavery before the Civil War (1861–65), and in the main the southern states have been supporters of the Democrats. The economic depression helped the Democrats to power in 1932 (*see* **New Deal**) and they held office until 1953 when Eisenhower became President. In 1960 Kennedy narrowly won the Presidency and in 1964 Lyndon Johnson swept in with a landslide victory over the Republican candidate. In 1968 and 1972 the Democratic candidates were beaten by Nixon. In 1976 Jimmy Carter defeated Gerald Ford who had become President after the resignation of Nixon in 1974. The symbol of the party is a donkey, invented, like the Rebublican's elephant, by the cartoonist Thomas Nast.

Dendrite, a stone or mineral on or in which tree-like tracery appears, the result of the action of the hydrous oxide of manganese.

Density, a measure of the mass per unit volume of a material, usually expressed in grams per cubic centimetre. *Specific gravity* is the ratio of the density of a material at the temperature under consideration to that of water at the temperature of its maximum density (4°C). In grams per cubic centimetre the density of gold is 19·3, silver 10·5, lead 11·3, water 0·99997, air 0·00129.

Depreciation of a currency is a fall in its relative value in terms of gold or of other currencies. The term is most often used to indicate a fall in the value of one country's money in relation to others. *See* **Section G.**

Depression, a region where barometric pressure is lower than that of its surroundings. These areas of low pressure are usually less extensive than anticyclones (*q.v.*) and may vary from hundreds to thousands of kilometres in diameter. The winds, often of gale force where the depression is deep, blow round the system in an anticlockwise direction in the Northern Hemisphere (in the reverse direction in the Southern Hemisphere). Well above the earth's surface the winds blow along rather than down the pressure gradient but near the surface, friction causes the winds to blow slightly (*c.* 15°) across the isobars. The depression exists only as long as more air diverges out of its upper parts than converges into its lower parts. The majority of depressions which cross the British Isles travel from the Atlantic, sometimes in series or families, at rates from a few kilometres to a thousand kilometres a day, bringing their generally unsettled weather with them.

Desalinisation, the process of removing minerals, chiefly salt, from sea or brackish water to provide pure water for drinking or industry. Small-scale desalinisation by distillation has been practised for many years on ships and small islands. By the 1960s, many large-scale distillation plants were in operation, many of them in hot dry countries as in the Middle East. Kuwait, for example, used oil revenues to buy desalinisation plant and powers the plant with natural gas. As water for large population centres becomes more precious and desalinisation techniques more efficient, the process may be more and more used though it is expensive in capital outlay and in the cost of heating required to distil the water. Methods other than distillation are under investigation but not as yet much used. Some useful by-products can be extracted from the salt.

Deserts, vast, barren, stone or sandy wastes where there is almost no rainfall and little or no vegetation. These regions are found in the interior of the continents Africa, Asia and America between 20° and 30° north and south of the equator. Europe is the only continent without deserts. The most famous are the Sahara, the largest in the world, the Gobi desert of central Asia, the Kalahari desert of south-west Africa and the great Australian desert. The marginal extension of deserts (desertification) is a topic of considerable debate. The increasing size of deserts is thought to result from either climatic change or the interference by man.

Detention Centres in Britain are for young people (boys and girls) over 14 but under 21 who have been found guilty of an offence for which an adult could be sent to prison. Controlled by the Home Office.

Determinism and Free-will. *See* **Section J.**

Deuterium or "heavy hydrogen". The second isotope of hydrogen; the third is called tritium. Deuterium atoms have in their nuclei a neutron as well as a proton; tritium nuclei have two neutrons and one proton. In ordinary hydrogen gas about one out of every 5,000 atoms is a deuterium atom. Deuterium was discovered in 1932 by Professor Harold Urey. The oxide of deuterium corresponding to water is called "heavy water". The nucleus of the deuterium atom is called a deuteron. An anti-deuteron consisting of an anti-proton and an anti-neutron was produced at Brookhaven in 1965, the first compound anti-nucleus ever to be produced.

Devaluation is a definite, official downward valuation of a country's currency in terms of its exchange value with other currencies. The £ was devalued in 1949, when an official exchange rate of £1 = $2.8 was established, and again in 1967, to a rate of £1 = $2.4. Since 1972 there has been greater flexibility in exchange rates and national currencies have been allowed to "float". *See* **Section G, Part IV.**

Devonian System in geology refers to the strata between the Silurian and the Carboniferous Formations. It includes the Old Red Sandstone Formation. The fauna of the Devonian include the group of fishes known as the Rhipidistra (on the evolutionary route towards the amphibians), Actinistia (coelacanth), and the Dipnoi or lung fishes. *See* **F45.**

Dew, moisture deposited by condensation of water vapour on exposed objects especially during calm, cloudless nights. The loss of heat from the ground after sunset, by radiation, causes the layer of atmosphere close to the surface to be chilled below the temperature, known as the dew-point, at which the air is saturated with vapour. Part of the vapour condensed may be transpired from blades of grass and foliage of plants.

Dew Pond is a shallow artificial pond which is on high ground and rarely dries up, even during prolonged droughts, despite being used by cattle and sheep as a drinking source. The name arose from the belief that dew deposits at night provided the moisture for replenishment. Drainage of rain-water and mist condensed on neighbouring trees and shrubs are probably more important factors.

Dialectical Materialism. *See* **Section J.**

Diamond, a mineral, one of the two crystalline forms of the element carbon (the other is graphite), the hardest known substance, used as a gem and in industry. India was the first country to mine diamonds (the Koh-i-noor, which means "mountain of light", known since 1304, came from Golconda near Hyderabad and came into British possession when the Punjab was annexed in 1849). The celebrated diamond mines of South Africa were discovered in the 1870s. Other important diamond producing countries are Zaïre, USSR, Congo, Ghana, Sierra Leone, Namibia, Angola, Tanzania. The world's biggest diamond is the 3,106-carat Cullinan, discovered near Pretoria, South Africa, in 1905. Diamonds can be made artificially by subjecting carbon to very high temperatures and pressures; many industrial diamonds are made this way. Antwerp is the main diamond centre of the world, London the main marketing centre, Amsterdam the main diamond cutting centre.

Diatoms. One-celled algae, common in fresh and salt water. Distinctive feature is the siliceous wall which is in two halves, one fitting over the other like the lid of a box. These walls are often very finely and beautifully sculptured. The diatoms constitute a class of the plant kingdom known as the Bacillariophyta. *Diatom ooze* is a deep-sea deposit made up of diatom shells. *Diatomite* or *diatomaceous earth* is the mineral form that such diatom oozes assume (sometimes known as kieselguhr which mixed with nitroglycerine yields dynamite).

Diesel Engine, an engine in which the liquid fuel is introduced into a compressed or partially compressed charge of air, and which does not need an extraneous source of ignition. The modern oil engine has been evolved mainly from the principles enunciated by Herbert Akroyd-Stuart in his patent of 1890 and, like the steam and other inventions, represents the improvements achieved by many men, including those by Rudolf Diesel of Germany, in respect of high compression pressures and greater fuel economy.

Diet, in German history, an assembly of dignitaries or delegates called together to debate upon and decide important political or ecclesiastical questions. The most famous imperial Diets were those held at Worms (1521), Speyer (1529), and Augsburg (1530), all of which dealt with matters of religious conflict arising from the Reformation.

Diffusion is the process of mixing which occurs when two liquids or gases are in contact. It is most rapid between gases, and, as laid down by Graham's law, "the rates of diffusion of different gases are in the inverse proportion to the square roots of their relative densities". Diffusion arises through the continual movement of molecules. Even in solids diffusion can occur. If a block of gold and a block of silver are welded together, after some time particles of gold are found in the silver, and *vice versa*.

Dimensions in common speech are the magnitudes of length, breadth and thickness giving, the size of an object, thus a line has only one dimension: length; a plane surface two: length and breadth; and a solid three: length, breadth and thickness. In mathematics, hypothetical objects with any number of dimensions are considered. In physics and mechanics, dimensions are numbers which relate the units in which any quantity is measured to the so-called fundamental units. The latter are usually but not necessarily those of length, mass and time. "Dimensional analysis" is an important technique of scientific reasoning.

Dimorphism, the quality of assuming two distinct forms. For instance, carbon, which is graphite in one form, is the diamond in another.

Dinosaur, the name given to a group of extinct reptiles of the Mesozoic period, some of which were of immense size—much larger than crocodiles. *See* **Diplodocus.**

Dip Needle. Instrument for measuring the *dip* or inclination of the earth's magnetic field.

Diplodocus, one of the best known of the extinct mammoth dinosaurs. Fossil remains have been discovered in the Jurassic rocks of the United States. Some reached a length of over 24 m.

Dipnoi *or* **Lung Fishes.** These have the air bladder adapted to function as a lung, and they can remain alive when the stream or marsh in which they live dries up. Species of lung fish occur in Australia, Africa and S. America.

Diptera, an order of insects. Their main characteristic is that they are two-winged, and the common house-fly is the best-known example. There are at least 50,000 species of these insects, including gnats, blow-flies, mosquitoes, tsetses.

Diptych was a folding two-leaved tablet of wood, ivory, or metal, with polished inner surfaces, utilised for writing with the style by the ancient Greeks and Romans. The same term was applied to the tablets on which the names of the persons to be commemorated were inscribed in the early Church. In art any pair of pictures hinged together is styled a diptych. *See also* **Triptych.**

Discus, a circular piece of metal or stone about 30 cm in diameter, used in athletic contests by the ancient Greeks and Romans. Throwing the discus was a very favourite game, which was deemed worthy of celebration in Myron's famous *Discobolus* (*c.* 460 B.C.–450 B.C.), the best copy of which is in Rome.

Disk, an astronomical term denoting the seemingly flat surface of celestial bodies as seen by the eye.

Distillation, a process used to separate liquids of different boiling points. This is effected by placing the mixture in a distillation apparatus and heating. The liquid with the lower boiling point distils over first, the vapour being condensed and collected, forming the first *fraction.* With continued heating the second liquid reaches its boiling point, distils over and the mixture is said to be *fractionated.* Mixtures of liquids with close very high boiling points require more elaborate apparatus. Fractional distillation is a common process in the chemical industry, particularly in the refining of petroleum.

DNA (Deoxyribonucleic acid), a polymer molecule in the form of a double-strand helix containing many thousands of sub-units. Contains the genetic information coded in sequences of sub-units called bases. The Nobel Prize for medicine was awarded in 1962 for the discovery of the structure of DNA; that for 1968 for interpreting the genetic code and its function in protein synthesis. *See* **Nucleic Acids.**

Docks are enclosed water spaces where ships rest while being loaded or unloaded, repaired, or waiting for cargo. There are three main types: the wet dock in which water is maintained at the level of high tide so that vessels remain afloat while loading and unloading; the tidal dock, with open entrance to permit free ebb and flow of tide (*e.g.*, Glasgow, Southampton (which has double tides)); and the dry dock, or graving dock, for overhauling and repairing vessels, so constructed that, after a ship has been docked, the water can be drawn off (*e.g.*, Southampton, Tilbury). The floating dock is a type of dry dock. The Port of London Authority operates four main groups of docks. With the closing of some of the older up-river docks, down-river docks, notably at Tilbury, have been extensively developed. Technological advances in the handling of cargo, *e.g.*, containers (sealed boxes of cargo), have led to modernisation of the docks and labour practices.

Dodo, an extinct bird, giant and flightless, which lived on the island of Mauritius up until 250 years ago. Another species, the white dodo, lived on Réunion. Some reached exceptional sizes. By the end of the 17th cent. Mauritius, Rodriguez, and Réunion had all been colonised, and the dodo along with many other birds vanished forever because of their inability to stand up to man and the animals imported into the islands.

Dog-days, a period of 40 days (3 July–11 August) when Sirius rises and sets with the sun. The ancient superstition, which can be traced back in Greek literature to Hesiod (8th cent. B.C.), was that this star exercised direct influence over the canine race.

Doge, the chief magistrate in the former republics of Venice (697–1797) and Genoa (1339–1797, 1802–5).

Dogfish, a large family of small sharks, seldom more than 1 m in length. The flesh is sold as "rock salmon". The eggs are contained in horny cases called "mermaid's purses". The commonest of the British dogfishes are the spur-dogs.

Doldrums, a nautical term applied to those areas of the Atlantic and Pacific within a few degrees of the Equator towards which the trade winds blow and where the weather is calm, hot and sultry. Pressure is low and the air often rises to produce heavy tropical rainfall and squalls, rendering navigation difficult.

Dolomite, a name applied to a limestone containing appreciable magnesium; also the mineral dolomite, a double carbonate of magnesium and calcium.

Dolphin, a mammal of the whale order, from 2–2·4 m long, with a long, sharp snout, and of an active disposition. They abound in most seas and swim in shoals. A few species live in large rivers (Ganges and Amazon). They can cruise for long periods at around 15 knots and produce bursts of speed in the region of 20 knots, the water apparently flowing smoothly past their bodies. Dolphins are some of the most intelligent of mammals and are currently the subject of scientific experiments in communication. Name also for the fish, dorado.

Domesday Book is the famous register of the lands of England framed by order of William the Conqueror. According to Stowe, the name was derived from *Domus dei*, the name of the place where the book was deposited in Winchester Cathedral; though by others it is connected with doom in the sense of judgment. Its compilation was determined upon in 1084, in order that William might compute what he considered to be due to him in the way of tax from his subjects. William sent into each county commissioners to make survey. They were to inquire the name of each place, the possessor, how many hides of land were in the manor, how many ploughs were in demesne, how many homagers, villeins, cottars, serving men, free tenants, and tenants in soccage; how much wood, meadow, and pasture; the number of mills and fish ponds; what had been added to or taken away from the place; what was the gross value at the time of Edward the Confessor. So minute was the survey that the Saxon chronicler of the time reports "there was not a single hide, nor one vintage of land, nor even, it is shame to tell, though it seemed no shame to do, an ox, nor a cow, nor a swine was left that was not set down". The record, which did not take in Northumberland, Cumberland, Durham and parts of Lancashire and Westmorland, was completed on 15 November 1085, and was comprised in two volumes—one a large folio, sometimes called the Little Domesday, which deals with Essex, Norfolk and Suffolk, the other a quarto, sometimes called the Great Domesday. The first is written on 384 double pages of vellum in one and the same hand, and in a small but plain character, each page having a double column. The quarto is written on 450 pages of vellum, but in a single column and in a large, fair character. The original is preserved in the Public Record Office. *See also* **Danegeld.**

Dominicans, an order of mendicant preaching friars founded by St. Dominic in Languedoc in 1215 and confirmed by the Pope in 1216. The rule of the order was rigorous. The dress was a white habit and scapular with a long black mantle. This gave them the name of Black Friars. Their official name is Friars Preachers.

Donjon, the keep, or inner tower of a castle, and the strongest and most secure portion of the structure. This was the last refuge of the garrison, and there was usually a prison on the lower floor, hence the name *dungeon.*

Don Juan, the legendary hero of many famous works, supposedly based on the life and character of the unscrupulous gallant Don Juan Tenorio of 14th-cent. Seville. The first dramatisation of the legend and the most famous is Tirso de Molina's *El Burlador de Sevilla.* Don Juan was also the subject of Molière's *Le Festin de Pierre*, Mozart's *Don Giovanni*, Byron's *Don Juan*, and José Zorilla's *Don Juan Tenorio.* The latter is played on All Saints' Day throughout Spanish-speaking countries.

Don Quixote, the "night of the doleful countenance", the hero and title of Cervantes' classic novel of 16th-cent. Spain. Don Quijote de la Mancha, a gentle country gentleman of lofty but unpractical ideals, having read many chivalric romances, believes he is called upon to redress the wrongs of the world. Mounted on his nag Rosinante and accompanied by his companion Sancho Panza, a hard-headed and practical peasant, he sets out on his journeys of knight-errantry.

Dormouse, a family of small, squirrel-like rodents widely distributed throughout Europe and Asia, and living mainly on fruit and nuts. It is of nocturnal habits and sleeps through the winter.

Dot, a French term indicating the property which a wife brings to her husband on marriage and is usually settled on the woman, being her separate property, though the income from it may go towards the general household expenses.

Dotterel, a handsome bird of the plover family found in northern Europe and Siberia. Nests in the Cairngorms, the Grampians and E. Ross. Very tame.

Doukhobors. *See* **Section J.**

Drachm (or **Drachma**), an ancient Greek silver coin and weight. One drachma was equivalent to six obols. The word has survived as the name of a weight: Avoirdupois, one-sixteenth part of an ounce; Apothecaries' Weight, one-eighth part of an ounce.

Drag. Term used in mechanics for resistance offered by a fluid to the passage of a body moving through it. When speed of sound is reached drag increases abruptly. The lift/drag ratio gives the aeroplane designer his measure of aerodynamic efficiency.

Dragon, a fabulous monster common to folk-lore in most countries; generally represented as a winged reptile with fiery eyes and breath of flame. A dragon guarded the garden of the Hesperides; in the New Testament there is mention of the " dragon, that old serpent, which is the devil "; St. George, England's patron saint, is supposed to have overcome the dragon; mediaeval legend abounds in dragons; in heraldry the dragon has also a conspicuous place; and in China it was the imperial emblem.

Dragonet, the name of the fish of the *Callionymus* genus, beautifully coloured, and about 30 cm in length. They are common on the British coast and in the Mediterranean.

Dragon Fly, the common name of a well-known order of insects having two pairs of membraneous wings, and often of very brilliant colours. They are swift of flight and may be seen hovering over sheets of water in the sunshine all through the summer. Their chief food is mosquitoes.

Dragon's Blood, a dark-red resinous substance obtained from the fruit of a Malay palm, and possessing medicinal virtues. In a special technique used for making line blocks in printing, dragon's blood is used.

Drawbridge, a bridge that can be lifted up so that no passage can be made across it. It was a usual feature of a fortified castle in the Middle Ages, and was raised or lowered by chains and levers. It spanned the fosse, and on the approach of an attacking party was raised and formed a special barricade to the gate. Modern drawbridges are such as are raised to allow of the passage of boats up and down a river or estuary. The Tower Bridge is a famous London bridge of this type.

Drongo. The King Crow or Indian Black Drongo is frequently seen in India perched on branches or telegraph wires, darting suddenly to catch insects and to attack crows and hawks. Other members of the family are found in Asia, Africa and Australia. Its plumage is black with steel-blue gloss.

Drosophila or Fruit Fly. More has been learnt by geneticists from breeding experiments with this insect than with any other.

Dross, the name generally applied to the refuse of molten metal, composed of slag, scales and cinders.

Drought occurs when there has been an absence of rain for a long period or a marked deficiency of precipitation over a much longer period in a climatic zone where precipitation is ordinarily adequate for vegetation or agriculture, river flow and water supplies. It is different from aridity which refers to the extreme dryness of desert or arid regions where rainless periods characterise the climatology. Hitherto in the British Isles " an absolute drought " was defined as " a period of at least 15 consecutive days without measurable rainfall ", but arbitrary definitions of this type are not now normally used. In the British Isles droughts occur from time to time but very long rainless spells at a place are rather rare. The longest recorded spell in the British Isles with no measurable daily rainfall lasted 61 days at Liss (Hants) from 16 March to 15 May 1893. Over the country as a whole the 12-month period beginning 1 May 1975 was the driest such period since records began, with less than 60 per cent. of normal precipitation in parts of the Midlands and S.W. England.

Druidism. *See* **Section J.**

Drupe is the scientific term for stone fruit. The stone forms the inner part (endocarp) of the fruit, and encloses a seed or kernel which is liberated after the fleshy part (pericarp) has rotted.

Dry-rot, the term was first used about 1775 to describe the fungal decay of timber in buildings. Creosote distilled from coal tar is the standard material for preservation of timber, and pentachlorophenol and copper naphthenate are two compounds now extensively used. Dry wood always escapes dry-rot. Chief fungi causing dry-rot are *Merulius* and *Poria*.

Duck, water bird smaller than the related goose and swan, which together form the family Antidae. Duck refers to the female, drake to the male. The duck family falls into two separate groups: the river or freshwater (surface feeding) ducks, such as the mallard, pintail, wigeon, shoveler, mandarin, teal, garganey; and the sea (diving) ducks, such as the goldeneye, pochard, scoter, eider, and the fish-eating mergansers or " sawbills ". The ancestor of all domestic breeds, with the exception of the muscovy, is the mallard.

Duckbill, *Ornithorhynchus anatinus*, also duck-billed platypus, a fur-covered, egg-laying, nest-building mammal inhabiting Australia and Tasmania. It has webbed feet and a muzzle like a duck's bill and is about 50 cm long.

Ductility is a property possessed by most metals which renders them capable of being stretched without breaking. Gold is the most, and lead the least ductile of metals, the order being gold, silver, platinum, iron, copper, palladium, aluminium, zinc, tin, lead. In animated nature the spider and the silkworm produce secretions of notable ductility.

Dugong. A marine mammal, belonging to the order Sirenia (sea-cows). Inhabits Red Sea and Indian Ocean; also found as far East as the Philippines and Australia. Lives on seaweed. Related to the Manatee.

Duke, the highest rank in the British peerage next to that of a royal prince. Edward, the Black Prince, eldest son of Edward III, who died before his father, was the first English duke, being created Duke of Cornwall in 1337. Since then all Princes of Wales have held that title.

Dukeries, a range of English woodland and park country, mainly in Nottinghamshire, comprising the adjacent demesnes of several English dukes and nobles. The Dukeries include Sherwood Forest and the estates of Welbeck Abbey, Clumber Park, Worksop Manor and Thoresby Hall.

Dunes. Sand dunes are elliptical or crescent-shaped mounds of loose sand produced by wind action. The dune has a gentle slope on windward side; a steep slope on the leeward side.

Dunlin, very common small wading-bird of the Sandpiper family nesting in Britain. Its range extends to other areas where it also breeds.

Dunmow Flitch, a custom which originated in the parish of Little Dunmow, Essex, in the reign of Henry III, which was that the husband who was prepared to swear before the prior, convent, and townsfolk of Dunmow that he had not repented of marriage or quarrelled with his wife for a year and a day, should be rewarded with the gift of a flitch of bacon. The custom has frequently been revived.

Dunnock (*Prunella modularis*), a small bird of rich brown and dark grey plumage common in gardens and hedgerows. Sings a cheerful song all the year round. Called hedge-sparrow in southern England. Another member of the same family, the larger Alpine Accentor (*Prunella collaris*), is found on rocky mountain slopes of Europe and Asia.

Duodecimo, a sheet of paper folded into twelve leaves, written " 12mo ".

Durbar, a term used in India from the Persian word *darbár* meaning " court " or " audience ". It may be either a council for administering affairs of state, or a purely ceremonial gathering. The word was applied to great ceremonial gatherings like Lord Lytton's durbar for the proclamation of the Queen-Empress in 1877 and the Delhi durbar of 1911.

Dust, solid particles of matter floating in the atmosphere, produced chiefly by volcanic eruptions, sand-storms in desert regions, and industrial and domestic smoke. When the island of Krakatoa erupted in 1883, more than 4 km^3 of dust was thrown into the air and carried three times round the earth by the explosive wave. The particles in dust-storms are much finer than those in sand-storms and are swept up to far greater hights. The local whirlwinds which form over loose dry soils are termed dust-devils.

Dyke. A wall-like intrusion of igneous rock

which cuts across the bedding or other layered structure of the country rock; the word also signifies in alternative usage, a sea-wall and an open drain.

Dynamite, a powerful explosive whose chief element is nitro-glycerine. It was discovered by Nobel in 1867, who absorbed nitro-glycerine in kieselguhr; has a disruptive force of about eight times that of gunpowder.

Dynamo. Machine for transforming mechanical energy into electrical energy. Depends on principle of electromagnetic induction whereby a current is produced in a conductor (*e.g.*, copper wire) traversing a magnetic field. The two essential parts of a dynamo are the conductors or *armature* and the *field magnets.*

Dynasty, a succession of monarchs of the same family, as the Carlovingian dynasty, the Bourbon dynasty, the Plantagenet dynasty, etc.

E

Eagle, large bird of prey with huge hooked bill, related to the buzzard, kite, hawk, harrier, falcon and vulture, together forming the family Falconidae. There are many species to be found throughout the world, the Golden, Imperial, Tawny, Spotted and Lesser Spotted being found in Europe. The Golden Eagle, a magnificent-looking bird, nests in the Scottish Highlands, and the White-tailed Sea Eagle, which used to breed in Britain, is now only an occasional visitor. The eagle has been the symbol of royal power since the earliest times, and the American or Bald Eagle is the emblem of the United States.

Earl, a British title of nobility of the third rank, duke and marquis coming first and second. The title dates from Saxon times, and until 1337 ranked highest in our peerage.

Earl-Marshal, in England ranks as the eighth of the great officers of state, is head of the College of Arms, attends the sovereign in opening and closing the session of Parliament, arranges state processions (especially coronations) and assists in introducing newly created peers in the House of Lords. The office is hereditary in the family of the Dukes of Norfolk.

Earth, our habitable globe, is the third of the planets of the solar system in order from the sun and on an average throughout the year takes 24 hours to turn completely round relative to the sun, the whole earth revolving round the sun in a slightly elliptical orbit once in a year of 365·2564 days. The mean distance of the earth from the sun is 93,004,000 miles (149,643,436 km). The shape of the earth is that of an oblate spheroid, its equatorial and polar axes measuring 12,756 km and 12,715 km respectively. Recent earth satellite studies have shown that it is even more pear-shaped than used to be thought with the north polar region having a definite stem and the south polar region a marked depression. Why this should be is not known. The crust consists of an outer layer of surface soil of varying thickness, beneath which there is a mass of hard rock several miles deep, the percentage (by weight) of the principal elements present being oxygen 47, silicon 28, aluminium 8, sodium and potassium 5, iron 4·5, calcium 3·5, magnesium 2·2, titanium 0·5, hydrogen 0·2, carbon 0·2, phosphorus and sulphur 0·2. Mass of the earth is estimated to be nearly 6,000 million million million tonnes. Two-thirds of the earth's surface is covered with water. It has only one satellite, the moon. The earth receives more light from the sun in 13 seconds than it does from the moon in one year. Weather changes are independent of the moon. A recent estimate of the age of the earth is 4,600 million years. Recent discoveries suggest that the earth is embedded in the atmosphere of the sun and that some of the heat that reaches us from the sun gets here by direct conduction through interplanetary space. *See* **F8–9.**

Earthquake, a sudden violent disturbance of the earth's crust; the region of the surface immediately above the " focus ", or source where the earthquake originates, is termed the " epicentre ". On account of their destructive power earthquakes have attracted attention from the earliest times, but accurate study dates only from the last century and the development of a world-wide network of recording stations from the present one. The majority of severe earthquakes result from fractures, usually along existing faults, in underlying rock strata subjected to great strains, the shearing movement sometimes extending to the surface. These dislocations set up vibrations which are propagated as waves throughout the bulk of the earth or round the crust. Frequently the main shock is followed by a series of smaller aftershocks. Minor local earthquakes may be attributed to the effects of volcanic activity, but most of the larger ones originate in non-volcanic regions along well-marked lines of weakness in the earth's crust. Generally the ground is felt to tremble, undergoing oscillations which may gradually or suddenly increase to a maximum and accompanied by sounds. Where there is movement of the sea-bed a tsunami (*q.v.*) may result. One of the greatest of historic times was that which destroyed and flooded Lisbon in 1755. Among the notable shocks of the present century rank those of San Francisco (1906), Messina, Italy (1908), China (1920), Japan (1923), Napier, New Zealand (1931), N.E. Assam (1950), Ionian Is. (1953), Agadir, Morocco (1960), Chile (1960), Iran (1962), Yugoslavia (1963), Alaska (1964), E. Turkey (1966), W. Sicily (1968), Peru (1970), 1976 was a year of major earthquakes, severe in China. *See also* **Richter Scale** *and* **F9(1).**

Earthworm, of which there are several species, has a cylindrical body, tapering at both ends, and segmented into rings. It moves by contraction of its rings, aided by retractive bristles; is eyeless, but has a mouth, gullet and stomach. Earthworms exist in immense numbers, and perform an important part in the scheme of nature by loosening the soil and rendering it more amenable to tillage. They also form a valuable food for birds and many mammals, and are unequalled as bait for certain kinds of fish.

Earwig, a genus of insects possessing two pairs of wings and anal forceps. It is nocturnal, lives on vegetable matter, and hides by day under stones or in flowers, *e.g.*, dahlias. The old belief that it deliberately creeps into people's ears is altogether unfounded. *See* **T30(2).**

Easter, the annual Christian festival in commemoration of the resurrection of Christ, the English name being derived from Eostre, goddess of Spring. The date cannot fall earlier than 22 March nor later than 25 April. Many disputes arose among the early Christians as to the proper time to celebrate this day which governs all other movable feasts. It was eventually ruled at the Council of Nicaea in 325 that Easter Day should be the first Sunday after the full moon following the vernal equinox. If this happens to be a Sunday, then Easter Day is the Sunday after. It should be remembered, however, that this moon is a hypothetical moon of the ecclesiastical calendar, quite imaginary, and generally one or two days later than the real moon we see in the heavens. In fact the reverend fathers at Nicaea did us a bad turn in having anything to do with the moon but then they had no Astronomer Royal to advise them of the complications. *See also* **Section N.**

Eastern Question, a term formerly applied to the problems arising from the instability of the Mohammedan power of Turkey and its relations with the other nations of Europe. Later connected with other problems of the Near East, such as the possession of Constantinople and the position of the Balkan states.

East India Company was incorporated by Elizabeth in 1600. In 1613 the Company set up a factory at Surat, India, and in 1662 Bombay came under the Company's influence and developed into an important trading port. Dupleix wanted to establish French power in India and a struggle for supremacy took place. Clive gained the victory for England and thenceforward British dominion in India remained undisputed except by native princes. In 1772 Warren Hastings was appointed the first Governor-General and in 1784 Pitt's India Act established a Board of Control for the India Company. A great increase of trade resulted, and this rule continued down to 1858, when, as a result of the mutiny, the Crown assumed the sovereignty. With the passing of the Indian Independence Act of 1947, British dominion ended and India was handed back to the Indians.

Eau-de-Cologne, a popular distilled perfume first manufactured at Cologne in the 18th cent. by Johann Maria Farina, an Italian, and since made in large quantities in Cologne and elsewhere.

Ebony, a name applied to various hard black woods, the best of which are grown in Mauritius and Sri Lanka. There are also Indian and American varieties. Only the inner portions, the heartwood, of the trees are of the necessary hardness and blackness. Ebony is largely used in ornamental cabinet work, for piano keys, canes, etc.

Ecce Homo (" Behold the Man! "), used in reference to the pictures and sculptures representing Christ crowned with thorns.

Ecclesiastical Courts, courts for administering ecclesiastical law and maintaining the discipline of the Church of England. Introduced by the Normans. Originally they had jurisdiction over both clergy and laity.

Eclipse, the partial or complete obscuring of one heavenly body by another. An eclipse of the sun occurs when the moon, which is 1/400th of the diameter of the sun and about 1/390th as far away, obscures some portion of the sun as seen by an observer on the earth. A total eclipse occurs when the whole of the sun's disc is covered by the moon. Astronomers travel many thousands of miles to observe the outer layers of the sun and its corona, which is only possible when the light from the sun is totally obscured by the moon during the few minutes of an eclipse. The total solar eclipse of 7 March 1970, as seen from Mexico, was watched by millions on their television screens. Total solar eclipses have occurred over parts of the British Isles in the years 1424, 1433, 1598, 1652, 1715, 1724, 1927, 1954 (visible from the Shetland Is.), and the next will be seen only from near Land's End on 11 August 1999. *See also* **N11**.

Ecliptic is the sun's apparent path in the sky: the great circle described by the sun from west to east in the course of a year. The sun is exactly on the equator on approx. 21 March, and 23 September, and the points where the celestial equator and ecliptic intersect on these days are called the *equinoctial points*. On approx. 21 June and 22 December the sun reaches its greatest and least midday elevation and its greatest distance north and south of the equator, and the points on the ecliptic on these days are called the *solstices* (*see* **Seasons, Section N**). These four points are equidistant from each other by 90°. The equinoctial points are not fixed. The angle of inclination of the ecliptic to the equator is called the obliquity of the ecliptic which is also variable, being influenced by the gravitational action of the other planets on the earth. At present the angle is 23½°.

Ecology, a term first described by the German biologist Haeckel in the 19th cent., is the study of the inter-relationships between living organisms and their environment. **Autecology** is the study of the environmental relationships of *individual* plants and species. **Synecology** is the study of plant and animal *communities* living together as groups and the relationship of these to their environment. Since 1935 the ecosystem has been the major unit of study in synecology. *See also* **F41–5**.

Ecumenical Council, a general council of the Christian Church summoned when important questions of Church doctrine and policy are to be decided. The early councils were predominantly Greek and convoked by the emperor. Those summoned by the pope when they meet at the Lateran Palace in Rome are called Lateran Councils; others have met at Constance, Florence, Trent and the Vatican. Their decisions are not binding on the rest of Christendom. Only 21 Ecumenical Councils have been held in the history of Christendom. The first was held at Nicaea in 325 when the mystery of the Trinity was defined. The 21st (known as the 2nd Vatican Council), convened by Pope John, opened in October 1962 in St. Peter's, Rome, and ended in December 1965. Two of the principal themes were the reunion of all Christians with the Church of Rome and the Church's place in the modern world. At the last session of the Council the Pope announced his decision to establish for the first time an international synod of bishops in Rome for consultation and collaboration in the government of the Roman Church. This Senate of Bishops will provide the balancing factor alongside the Curia, which represents the Papacy and not the episcopacy.

Edda, the name given to two important collections of early Icelandic literature—*the Elder or Poetic Edda*, poems handed down from the 9th and 10th cent., probably Norwegian in origin, and the *Younger* or *Prose Edda* of Snorri Sturluson compiled about 1230. They treat of mythical and religious legends of an early Scandinavian civilisation.

Eddystone Lighthouse, 21 km south of Plymouth, is one of the most isolated in the world. The tower is 51 m high, and its light can be seen for 28 km. The present structure is the fourth that has occupied this dangerous position. The first was of wood, completed by Winstanley in 1698, but it was destroyed by storm in 1703. In 1708 a second and stronger lighthouse was built by Rudyerd. This lasted until 1755, when it was destroyed by fire. Smeaton built the third lighthouse of granite and this withstood storm and tempest for over a hundred years, 1759–1881. The present lighthouse, also of granite, was built 1879–81 on a nearby rock by Sir James Douglass.

Eels, edible fishes of the order Apodes, with snakelike body covered with minute scales embedded in the skin. The common or freshwater eel *Anguilla anguilla* is found in the Atlantic coastal areas of N. America and Europe and in the Mediterranean, and breeds S.E. of Bermuda. The electric eel of S. America is a variety of great interest, being able to cause electric shocks.

Egghead, a term used derogatively to describe the more intelligent and thoughtful people. Frequently applied in USA to the late Adlai Stevenson, who is said to have responded with the appeal: " Eggheads of the world Unite. You have nothing to lose but your brains."

Egret, a slender, graceful bird of the heron family, of pure white plumage, famed for its beautiful silky plumes (aigrettes), which appear in the breeding season, and for which it was ruthlessly hunted and would have geen exterminated had not international action been taken to protect it. The Little Egret with black bill, black legs, and yellow feet breeds in Mediterranean lands.

Eider, a large diving duck, found along the rocky coasts of northern latitudes, well known for the beautifully warm soft down, called " eider down ", which the female bird plucks from her breast to line her nest. In Norway and Iceland the haunts of the eider are preserved and the birds protected by law on account of the much prized " eider down ", which is collected from the nests just before the breeding season. " Eider down " is so elastic that a kilogramme of it will fill an ordinary bed covering.

Eiffel Tower, built by the French engineer Alexandre Gustave Eiffel (1832–1923) for the Paris Exhibition of 1889. The tower which is made of iron is 300 m high and weighs about 7,000 tonnes.

Eisteddfod (a sitting) was originally a congress of Welsh bards and minstrels, and dates from before the 12th cent. These assemblies, discontinued for a long period, were resumed in 1819, and have been held yearly since, each lasting three or four days. Their object is to foster the Welsh patriotic spirit; they are devoted to orations and competitions in poetry, singing and harp-playing, prizes being awarded to the successful contestants.

Eland, largest species of antelope, native of Africa; large pointed horns, stands 1·5 m high at the withers, and weighs several hundred kg.

Elder, small trees of the *Sambucus* genus, with pinnate leaves, and clusters of white flowers and, later, small purplish-black berries. The black elder, the best known, is common in most parts of Europe, and thrives in Britain. A wine is made from its berries.

El Dorado, a " golden land ", was an idea much

favoured in the days of the early Spanish explorers. It was believed that somewhere on the South American continent there was a country abounding in gold and precious stones. Many expeditions were fitted out to discover it. Sir Walter Raleigh also went forth on this illusive quest. The term is still used in regard to any place of rich promise.

Electret, a piece of solid matter which retains a permanent electric polarisation analogous to the magnetic polarisation of a permanent magnet. There are various recipes for making them; carnauba wax is a common constituent.

Electricity. *See* **F18**, *also* **Energy Conversion.**

Electric Light is produced in several ways, commonly by causing a tungsten wire to heat up to incandescence by passing a current through it. Current may also be forced through ionised gases, causing them to glow. Such discharges include neon lights, sodium and mercury-vapour street-lamps, and various intense electric arcs used for technical purposes. In fluorescent lights an electric discharge causes ultra-violet (invisible) light, which then excites luminosity in certain chemical substances called luminescent materials. Other forms of electric lighting are being investigated.

Electric Telegraph may be said to date from 1836, when Sir Charles Wheatstone and his co-inventor Cooke introduced their Single-Needle instrument, which was soon followed by the Double-Needle apparatus. Morse, in 1837, invented his famous recording instrument. The first electric cable was between Dover and France, and was laid in 1850. The first Atlantic cable was laid in 1858, and the second in 1866. It was in 1899 that the first Marconi wireless telegraph messages were sent between England and France.

Electroencephalograph, an instrument which records the minute voltages produced by the electrical activity of the brain by means of electrodes taped to the scalp. The record of brain waves, known as EEG, shows that there is a general cycle of activity in the brain that underlies both sleep and wakefulness. *See* **Q5(2).**

Electrolysis is the condition established when an electric current passes through a conducting substance, between electrodes, resulting in decomposition and separation into constituents. Water thus becomes decomposed into hydrogen and oxygen.

Electromagnetic waves. *See* **F13.**

Electrometer, an instrument for measuring differences of electrical potential. The moving part, perhaps a needle, is affected by electrostatic forces and no current flows through the instrument. High sensitivity can be obtained.

Electron. *See* **F10, 14.**

Electronic Music, music composed of electronically generated sound, recorded on tape and played through loudspeakers. Modern technical developments mean that in theory, and to a large extent in practice, a composer can generate and record *any* sequence of sounds he likes, varying at will pitch, intensity, reverberation, rhythm, intervals and all other audible qualities. Such limitless freedom of choice imposes on him severe problems of selection, notation and intellectual and artistic organisation. Though widely composed and performed, *i.e.*, played through loudspeakers or broadcast, electronic music as an art form must still be regarded as experimental and controversial, though its use as incidental or "atmospheric" music in radio and television is well established. Among the well-known composers are Babbitt, Berio, Koenig and Stockhausen.

Electron Microscope. A microscope in which beams of electrons are focused by magnetic lenses in a manner analogous to the focusing of light beams in the ordinary optical microscope. Modern electron microscopes have very high resolving power and can magnify up to 1,500,000 times, making it possible to explore the cell and the virus. A development of the electron microscope is the scanning electron microscope (stereoscan), developed at Cambridge, which can examine an essentially thick object, giving a very large depth of focus. *See* **F27(2).**

Electronvolt, unit of energy used in nuclear physics. It is the amount of energy required to move one electronic charge through a potential difference of one volt. It is very small—$1{\cdot}6 \times 10^{19}$ joules—and therefore suited to atomic physics. 1 MeV = a million electronvolts; 1 GeV = a thousand million electronvolts; these larger units are used in high energy physics.

Electronics. The science which deals with the behaviour and control of free electrons. It started with the discovery of the electron by Sir J. J. Thomson in 1897. The practical applications, constituting electronic engineering, have given us radio, radar, photo-electric cells, cathode-ray oscillographs, electron microscopes, television. Nowadays electronics uses devices like transistors such that the electrons move inside solid matter instead of *in vacuo.* This is sometimes referred to as "solid state electronics". *See also* **Microelectronics.**

Electrophorus, a simple device for producing static electricity, consisting of a smooth disc of resin or ebonite mounted on a metal base and with a metal cover carrying an insulated handle. The disc is first electrified (negatively) by rubbing it with a dry catskin or flannel and the cover replaced, the upper surface receiving a positive charge and the lower a negative. On lifting off the cover, after having touched it with the finger, the negative charge leaks away to earth and the positive charge is isolated on the cover. The action may be repeated a number of times before it is necessary to replenish the original charge on the disc. Of historical interest only.

Elementary Particle, one of the basic constituents of the material universe. The idea that matter consists of tiny particles goes back to classical times but the modern concept of the atom grew out of the chemistry and physics of the 19th cent. With the discovery of the electron in 1897 and the rise of nuclear physics in the 20th cent., the chemical atom was understood to be a structure built of even more fundamental particles—the electron, the proton and the neutron. In the last few decades, many more particles have been discovered, especially in the study of cosmic rays and by the use of large accelerating machines like those at CERN (Geneva) and Brookhaven National Laboratory (Long Island, New York). Among the later discoveries are the neutrino, the positron, the antiproton, the muon, the pion. These differ in electric charge and mass and other intrinsic properties and many have only a very short lifetime before they change into something else. Whether there is a small number of really elementary particles out of which all the others can be constructed is an unanswered question at the frontier of contemporary physics. *See* **Quarks** and **F13–14.**

Elements. In chemistry, substances which cannot be separated into two or more simpler chemical substances. 91 elements are found naturally on the earth, one is observed spectroscopically in the stars, and a further twelve have been made artificially. Between them these elements can appear in some 1,200 different isotopes, of which 317 occur in Nature. (There are 274 stable isotopes among 81 stable elements.) *See* **F6, 20,** *also* **end Section F.**

Elephant, a proboscidian mammal of which only two species survive—the Asiatic, in India, and the African elephant. No other animals possess a trunk. Both males and females have large ivory tusks, of considerable commercial value. The Indian elephant is usually about 2·7 m high and weighs about 3 tonnes; African elephants are larger, weigh about 6 tonnes, and are usually much fiercer. Several fossil elephants of still larger bulk have been discovered, including the mammoth and the mastodon. The Indian elephant is domesticated and used as a beast of burden, and may live 70 years.

Eleusinian Mysteries, festivals common throughout ancient Greece, agricultural in their symbolism.

Elgin Marbles, a collection of ancient Greek sculptures and architectural fragments got together by the 7th Earl of Elgin and brought to England between 1802 and 1812. These celebrated treasures had originally formed part of the Parthenon at Athens, and were probably carved by pupils of the sculptor Phidias. Lord Elgin expended over £70,000 upon them, and they were purchased for £35,000 for the British Museum, where they can now be seen displayed.

Elk, the largest animal of the deer family, possessing enormous antlers, and standing, when mature, about 2 m high. The American moose is of the same family.

Elm, a stately, wide-spreading tree having some 20 species spread over north-temperate regions, several of which are native and peculiar to Britain. The grandest of the field elms is the English elm, *Ulmus procera*, which may reach a height of *c.* 42 m and a girth of 8 m. The wych elm, *U. glabra*, or Scots elm, is a valuable hardwood and used in boat-building. The fungus that causes Dutch elm disease is carried from tree to tree by a bark beetle. The fungus came from infected veneer logs from central Europe. Ironically the disease was named after the Dutch workers who discovered its cause!

Elzevir, the name of a celebrated family of Dutch printers, who produced editions of Latin, French and German classics, which were highly valued for their beauty of type and accuracy of printing. They flourished in the 17th cent.

Ember-days are set apart for fasting and prayer in the Western Church, at the periods appointed for ordination, viz., the Wednesday, Friday and Saturday after the first Sunday in Lent, Whit-Sunday, 14 September (Holy Cross Day), and 13 December (St. Lucia's Day); of very ancient origin.

Embossing, the art of stamping in relief letters or designs upon pliant substances.

Emerald. The rich green variety of beryl (beryllium aluminium silicate). The colour is due to the presence of chromium oxide.

Empire, the style created in France during the reign of Napoleon in architecture and all the arts. It is austerely classical, making much use of columns, pediments and the like in buildings as well as furniture, with eagles and sphinxes, reminiscent of Napoleon's campaigns, as ornaments. The style is heavy, grandiose and with a strong element of the heroic. A typical monument is the *Arc de Triomphe* in Paris (begun 1806), almost a repetition of a Roman model. In painting Jacques Louis David interpreted the style with heroic subjects taken from classical mythology or from Napoleon's career. The style was transmitted to the rest of Europe, remaining magnificent and rich at all the Bonaparte courts. In bourgeois surroundings in Germany and Scandinavia it became simple and domesticated but retained its essence of classical dignity.

Encaenia, a festival commemorating a dedication; at Oxford University the annual commemoration of benefactors, accompanied by the conferring of honorary degrees, is held in June.

Encyclical Letters, a term used in reference to letters addressed by the Pope to his bishops upon matters of doctrine or discipline.

Encyclopaedists, a term first applied to the eminent writers who collaborated in the French *Encyclopédie* (1751–65). They included Diderot, D'Alembert, Voltaire, Helvetius; their writings generally were sceptical as to religion, destructive as to politics, and had great influence in popularising the social ideas which afterwards resulted in the French Revolution.

Energy. One of the most fundamental concepts of science. A body in motion possesses *kinetic energy* as a result of the *work* done by the forces creating the motion. But a force which does work to stretch a spring does not create motion. Instead, the work is stored up in the spring and is one example of *potential energy*. A raised body also possesses potential energy which turns into kinetic when the body falls. The *heat energy* contained in a body is the sum of the kinetic and potential energy of the constituent atoms which are vibrating all the time. Heat and motion are obtainable from electrical, magnetic, chemical, atomic, and other sources, and physicists therefore define corresponding forms of energy. The vital point is that all forms of energy are transferable into one another *without loss or gain*. This is the Law of Conservation of Energy. It is one of the most fundamental laws of science, and its general validity is the reason why energy is an important idea. Since Einstein, it has been recognised that mass also is interchangeable with energy. *See* **F15**, *also* **Nuclear Energy.**

Energy Conversion. For practical purposes it is frequently necessary to change energy from one into another of its many forms; indeed almost every activity does this in one way or another. The primary sources of energy are the sun, uranium and other elements from which nuclear energy can be drawn, and the tides. The sun is not much used *directly* because its heat is intermittent and not very intense, but solar cookers and refrigerators have been invented and solar batteries (*q.v.*) are used in spacecraft. The sun can be used *indirectly* because it has produced, *via* living processes, fossil fuels like coal and oil and still continues to generate winds, rain and rivers and hence hydroelectric and wind power. Commonly both fossil fuels and the energy of river or tidal waters are converted into electricity. Windmill type electricity generators are also quite common. The bulk of electricity production is a two-stage process: first fossil or nuclear fuel is used to create heat (*see* **Nuclear Reactors**); then the heat is used to raise steam and drive generators. Efforts are being made to convert heat into electricity more directly, *e.g.*, by using thermoelectric or thermionic effects (*q.v.*), but these have not been used for large-scale production. Once electrical energy is available, factories can make chemical batteries in great numbers and these can then be used as portable energy sources, as can petrol and other refined forms of fossil fuel. *See* **Battery, Fuel Cell, Solar Battery.**

Engraving is the art of cutting or otherwise forming designs of pictures on wood, stone, or metal surfaces for reproduction by some method of printing. Wood-engraving was the earliest in the field, dating from the 15th cent. Later, engraving on steel and copper plates was introduced, and mezzotint, lithography, stipple, aquatint, etc. Most modern methods of reproduction are based on photography.

Ensilage, a method of storing and preserving fodder, vegetables, etc., in pits dug in the ground and excluded from air or light. The system was practised in ancient Rome and revived in England in the 19th cent.

Entablature, that portion of a building which surmounts the columns and extends to the roof of the tympana of the pediments; it comprises the architrave, the frieze and the cornice.

Entomology is the study of insects. *See* **Insects.**

Entrepreneur. An entrepreneur or undertaker is a firm which brings together the factors of production needed for producing goods or services, undertaking the risks and uncertainties involved—though it may transfer some of them by insurance or by other methods. The entrepreneur may be either an individual or a company or corporation, private or public.

Enzymes. Organic catalysts which accelerate chemical processes occurring in living organisms. There are a large number present in the cell, and most have a high degree of specificity. Enzyme mechanisms are the key to basic biological processes. *See* **F25(1), 30(1).**

Epaulette, a shoulder badge fringed with cord, worn by English army officers until 1855; now confined to naval officers, and varying in form and richness according to rank of wearer.

Ephemoptera or **May-flies**, an order of insects. In the larval condition they exist from two to three years aquatically, but no sooner do they arrive at maturity than their lives are burried to a close. They rise up in pyramids on warm summer nights, take no food, propagate and perish. The Latin name expresses the fact that the adults have an ephemeral existence.

Epiphany, a church festival celebrated on January 6, Twelfth Day.

Equator, the imaginary great circle of the earth, every point of which is 90 degrees from the earth's poles, and dividing the northern from the southern hemisphere. It is from this circle that the latitude of places north and south is reckoned. The celestial equator is the circle in which the plane of the earth's equator meets the celestial sphere (the imaginary sphere, in which the observer is at the centre, used for representing the apparent positions of the heavenly bodies).

Equinox, the time when the sun crosses the plane of the earth's equator, making day and night of equal length.

Eras are distinctive periods of time associated with some remarkable historical event or personage. *The Christian era* is computed according to a 6th-cent. reckoning to begin with Jesus's birth, A.D. 1. The date is placed some years too late. Scholars now believe that Jesus was born *c.* 6 B.C. The *Jewish era* dates from 3761 B.C.; the *Julian era* from the alteration of the calendar by Julius Caesar 45 B.C.; the *Mohammedan era* from the date of the *Hejira*, or the flight of Mohammed from Mecca to Medina, which is A.D. 622, 16 July, in the Gregorian Calendar.

Erbium, belongs to the group of rare-earth metals discovered by Mosander in 1842.

Erg, the unit of work and energy in the centimetre-gram-second system; the energy involved when a force of 1 dyne moves its point of application through a distance of 1 cm.

Ernie, the name given to the " electronic random number indicator equipment ", the electronic machine which selected the prizewinning numbers in the first Premium Bond draw held June 1–2, 1957.

Eros. This asteroid is 24–32 km in diameter. It comes closer to the earth than any other member of the solar system with the exception of the moon and several very small asteroids. Determination of solar parallax based on observations of Eros in 1930–31 yielded until then the most accurate estimate of the distance of the sun from the earth (149,643,436 km). *See* **Astronomical unit.**

Erse, a term used by Lowland Scottish, and English writers for the Gaelic language spoken in the Highlands of Scotland. Sometimes erroneously applied to Irish, the Gaelic language as spoken in Ireland and revived as an official language in recent times. Dr. Johnson, Sir Walter Scott, and other writers used " Erse " to signify Scottish Gaelic. The language of the Scottish Lowlands (that used by Robert Burns) is related to the English language and not to Gaelic and is variously termed Scots, Braid Scots, the Doric, the Scottish vernacular, and fashionably of late, Lallans.

Escurial or **Escorial,** Spanish monastery built in the mountains near Madrid by Philip II to commemorate the victory over the French at Saint-Quentin (1557). A palace was added later and it also includes a church, library and royal mausoleum. Built in granite in sombre style, it is one of the finest buildings in Europe.

Esperanto, an artificial international language created by L. Zamenhof of Warsaw and first published in 1887. It does not seek to replace national languages but to serve as a second language for international communication. It is based on the internationality of many words in the principal modern languages, and is entirely phonetic in spelling and pronunciation.

Estates of the Realm in Great Britain are the Lords Spiritual, the Lords Temporal and the Commons. They are the great classes invested with distinct political powers, and whose concurrence is necessary to legislation.

Esters. Organic chemicals formed by combining an alcohol with an acid. They have a pleasant smell, and occur naturally in plants as the scent of flowers. Manufactured for use in the perfumery industry, and as flavourings in food. Some esters are used as solvents, notably amyl-acetate (" pear drops ") in quick-drying paints. The polymeric fibre " Terylene " consists of chains of molecules containing many ester groups, formed by reacting an alcohol having two alcoholic (OH) groups with an acid having two acid (COOH) groups.

Etching, a technical method for producing graphic work and works of art. A plate, traditionally of copper, is covered with wax; the design or picture desired is drawn with a sharp implement which penetrates the wax. When the plate is exposed to the action of an acid this will etch into the copper where the lines have been drawn. The wax is then removed, ink is applied to the plate with its engraving, and the design or picture can be printed on to paper in many copies. Rembrandt, Goya and others made great and original works of art in the technique, but it was also widely used for reproductive purposes before the invention of photography. Hogarth painted his famous pictures in oil and reproduced them graphically to give them a wider circulation.

Ether, in chemistry, is a volatile inflammable liquid composed of carbon, hydrogen and oxygen. It is a valuable anaesthetic obtained by heating alcohol with sulphuric acid. In physics, in the 19th cent., all space was supposed to be filled with a substance called ether, the chief property of which was to carry light waves, *i.e.*, light was supposed to be waves in this all-pervading medium known as the ether. Speculation and experiment concerned with the ether were very fruitful in advancing physics. Ultimately the attempts by Michelson and Morley to detect the motion of the earth through the ether were unsuccessful in this respect but profoundly successful in stimulating the theory of relativity. The ether concept has now been abandoned. *See also* **F15(1).**

Ethylene. A gas compounded of carbon and hydrogen, it is related to acetylene and ethane. Industrially it is obtained as a by-product in petroleum refining. It has wide uses as a starting material in the industrial manufacture of intermediates, especially alcohol. Its most important application is in the production of polythene (poly-ethylene). *See* **Catalyst.**

Etruscans, people believed to have come from Asia Minor who colonised Italy about 900 B.C., settled in what is now Tuscancy and part of Umbria, reached the height of their civilisation about 500 B.C., and were ultimately absorbed by the Romans. They were skilled technicians in bronze, silver and goldwork, and excelled in the art of granular decoration.

Eucalyptus. This genus includes 300 species of evergreen, leathery-leaved trees native to Australia. The oils yielded by different species vary a great deal in their scent and other properties and are chiefly used in pharmacy and perfumery; about 30 species produce oils suitable for medicinal purposes. Various species produce timber.

Euro-dollar Market. An international financial market, located mainly in Britain and Europe, for lending and borrowing dollars, *i.e.*, titles to dollar deposits in United States banks. *See* **Section G, Part IV.**

Europium, element discovered by Demarcay in 1906. A member of the rare-earth metal group.

Evaporation is the process by which a solid or liquid is resolved into vapour by heat. The opposite process is condensation. Wherever a liquid or solid surface is exposed, evaporation takes place into the space above. If the vapour is continually removed the solid or liquid vanishes into vapour; the higher the temperature the quicker the process. If the vapour is confined, then it collects, getting more concentrated until as many atoms of vapour are condensing as are evaporating. The vapour is then said to be saturated. Evaporation of water from sea, soil, plants, skin, etc., is continuously in progress, so it is a process of fundamental importance to meteorology, botany, physiology, industry, not to speak of human comfort and homely activities such as laundering.

Everest Expeditions. For many years after Mt. Everest had been shown to be the highest mountain in the world, political conditions in Nepal, lying south of the summit, and in Tibet, to the north, prevented mountaineers from attempting an ascent. At last in 1921 the Tibetan authorities gave permission, and the first expedition, organised, as were all subsequent British expeditions, by a joint committee of the Royal Geographical Society and the Alpine Club, and led by Col. C. K. Howard-Bury, was sent out. This was primarily a reconnaissance; besides mapping the northern flanks, it found a practicable route up the mountain. By 1939, six further expeditions had climbed on the northern face. Some were baulked by bad weather, others by problems previously little known, such as the effect of high altitudes on the human body and spirit. Nevertheless, notable climbs were accomplished. In 1924, for example, Col. E. F. Norton reached 8,589 m, and it was on this expedition that G. L. Mallory and Andrew Irvine were seen going well at about the same height. They never returned, however, and what disaster befell them is not known. After the war, political conditions again closed the Tibet route: permission was eventually obtained from the Nepalese Government to make the attempt from the south. In 1951 a reconnaissance expedition under Eric Shipton reached the ice-fall at the exit of the Western Cwm (a high valley lying south-west of the massif), and reported favourably on the prospects for an ascent. The first attempt from this side was made the following year by a Swiss expedition led by Dr. E. Wyss-Dunant, two members of which made an attempt on the summit, but were stopped at approx. 8,601 m by the intense cold and the very strong winds. When the British 1953 Expedition led by Col. John Hunt (now Lord Hunt), was being organised, stress was laid on three main points; proper acclimatisation of the climbers; use of oxygen for the final stages; and the establishment of very high altitude camps, so that the final assault parties would set out fresh and unencumbered. Great attention was also paid to recent developments in diet, clothing and equipment. In all these matters the 1953 expedition was able to draw on the accumulated experience of their predecessors. By the end of April, a base camp had been established below the ice-fall, and with the aid of thirty-four Sherpa porters supplies had been carried up into the Western Cwm. The next critical stage was the ascent of the steep head of the cwm, the Lhotse face, with the threat of avalanches always present. By most strenuous efforts, a camp was established on the South Col (7,869 m) on 21 May. From this camp on 26 May, T. D. Bourdillon and R. C. Evans climbed the South Peak of Everest (8,760 m), then the highest altitude ever attained. On 28 May Edmund Hillary and the Sherpa leader, Tenzing Norkey, spent the night at the highest camp (8,510 m) and on the following day, 29 May, climbed to the South Summit, negotiated the difficult final ridge, and reached the summit of Everest—the climax of a long, arduous and stirring endeavour.

Evolution, in the words of Sir Julian Huxley (d. 1975), "a natural process of irreversible change which generates novelty, variety and increase of organisation". The theory, as laid down by Darwin, is that all existing species, genera and classes of animals and plants have developed from a few simple forms by processes of change and selection. Up to the time of Darwin a large part of the civilised world believed that life had been created suddenly at the beginning of the world which God had created, according to Archbishop Usher, on 22 October 4004 B.C. The evidence of the rocks, however, has given a more convincing theory of creation, and by studying the fossils preserved in the various layers of the earth's crust the past history of the earth's life has been pieced together. Darwin has been called the Newton of biology. *See* **F46–8.**

Exchequer, which derives its name from the checkered tablecloth on which accounts were calculated in early Norman times, is a term connected with the revenues of the Crown. In former times it had jurisdiction in all revenue matters. The term Exchequer is now applied to the Governmental department which deals with the public revenues, the working head of which is the Chancellor of the Exchequer.

Existentialism. *See* **Section J.**

Exploration. Modern exploration began in the second half of the 15th cent. with the voyages of the great Portuguese and Spanish discoverers. They were followed by sailors of other European nations, who profited from their developments in navigation and from their charts, and in less than one hundred years the coast-lines of much of the Americas, Africa and south-west Asia had been revealed and the globe circumnavigated. The motives of these early explorers were mixed: they were seeking adventure, trade, plunder, national power and the conversion of the heathen. Few if any were directly interested in advancing scientific knowledge. But from the reports of their voyages and travels, scholars at home compiled descriptions of the strange new world which stimulated their successors to undertake more systematic enquiries. One of the earliest English expeditions to be despatched for scientific research was that of William Dampier on the *Roebuck*, which was sent out by the Admiralty in 1699 to examine the coasts of North-west Australia. In the 18th cent. British explorers were at work mainly in the Pacific Ocean, with the object of breaking the Spanish monopoly of trade. Capt. James Cook sailed thither in 1769 to observe first the transit of Venus at Tahiti, and then to search for the alleged great southern continent. On this voyage he discovered and charted much of the coasts of New Zealand and the east coast of Australia. On his second voyage he was the first to sail across the Antarctic Circle, and he showed that the southern continent was much smaller than had been supposed. By 1800 the general outlines of the continents, except for Antarctica were known, and explorers in the 19th cent. were largely engaged in opening up the interiors. In Africa British explorers solved two problems which had puzzled men for centuries: Mungo Park and Richard Lander established the true course of the River Niger, and Sir Richard Burton, J. H. Speke, Sir Samuel Baker and others revealed the true sources of the Nile. The greatest African explorer of that age was undoubtedly David Livingstone, the missionary, who in three great journeys explored the Zambesi and the region of the Great Lakes, spreading the Gospel, fighting the slave trade, and opening up the interior to settlement and trade. In North America Alexander Mackenzie was the first to cross the main breadth of the continent from sea to sea. In Asia motives were also mixed; men like Charles Doughty, who explored in Arabia, and Sir Francis Younghusband, who journeyed from China to India across the Gobi and the Himalaya, were impelled by a love of adventure and the quest for knowledge, but political considerations were often involved. In recent years, with the main features of the world's surface known, exploration has become more intensive. Teams of scientists go out to study restricted areas in detail. An Antarctic expedition can contribute to our knowledge of world weather, or by biological research into the life history of whales, can help to improve our food supplies. Similarly, expeditions in Africa can help to check the loss of valuable agricultural land through soil erosion, or to develop areas of settlement by schemes for irrigation and power. And there are still great areas to be adequately mapped. All these problems are inter-related, and in solving them the modern explorer can call on many improved techniques and instruments—the aeroplane, the aerial camera, tracked motor vehicles, radio, in fact all the resources of modern science. But the human element is still vital, and for those with the old explorers' spirit there will always be problems left to solve.

Explosives, substances which burn violently to produce gases in such volume that an explosion is induced. Gunpowder was the first explosive to be used; Roger Bacon's powder, consisting of charcoal, sulphur and saltpetre, was the only effective explosive until the 19th cent., but it was difficult to control. Nitroglycerine (glyceryl trinitrate) was first compounded in 1847 by adding glycerine to a mixture of sulphuric acid and nitric acid. In 1866 Alfred Nobel discovered how to make dynamite by absorbing nitroglycerine in the fine sand kieselguhr. Cordite was the joint invention of Sir Frederick Abel and Sir James Dewar (1889). It came into general use as a propellant. High explosives, providing bursting charge for shells and bombs, include TNT (trinitrotoluene), picric acid, cyclonite (RDX) and many others. Slurry explosives can be pumped on to the site and therefore offer advantages in transportation and safety; they are also waterproof. Chemical explosives have been eclipsed by nuclear explosives which have developed from the first atom bomb (dropped on Hiroshima 6 August 1945) to the 100-megaton hydrogen bomb.

Expressionism, a modern art movement confined primarily to the non-Latin countries of Europe which sought to give expression to intimate and personal emotions by means of distortions of line and colour and simplified style which carried a greater impact in terms of feeling. Broadly speaking, this has been characteristic of northern art in general. (*See* **Gothic.**) The term is usually used of the modern movement which influenced the Post-impressionists and subsequent movements in France. Tired of the naturalism of the Impressionists, such artists as van Gogh, Gauguin, Matisse and Rouault together with the Fauvists (*q.v.*) made use of simple outlines and strong colours. Apart from Toulouse-Lautrec, the principal Expressionists were Norwegian, like Munch, or German, like the painters of *Die Brücke* and *Der Blaue Reiter* groups. Individual artists were Ensor, Kokoschka, Nolde, Rouault and Soutine.

F

Fabian Society. *See* **Section J.**

Fables are fictitious narratives intended to enforce some moral precept, and may be either in prose or verse, and deal with personified animals and objects or with human beings. Aesop in ancient times and Hans Christian Andersen and the Brothers Grimm (in many of their stories) in later days, have given fables. Mention must also be made of La Fontaine's and Krylov's fables.

Fairs were established in mediaeval times as a means of bringing traders and customers together at stated periods, and formed the chief means of distribution. The great English fairs of early times were those of Winchester and Stourbridge near Cambridge. Traders from the Netherlands and the Baltic gathered there with the great merchants of London, and goods of every kind, wholesale and retail, were sold. One of the biggest trade fairs was at Nijni-Novgorod, founded in the 17th cent.; other big continental fairs were those of Leipzig (founded in the 12th cent.), Lyons and Prague. Expositions of advanced industrial products are today popular, *e.g.* Expo 67 held in Montreal.

Fairy Rings are the circles caused in grassland by certain fungi. The circles expand outwards as the fungus spreads, the fruiting bodies being at the periphery. Farther inward where the fungi are decaying the grass grows more strongly, fertilised by the nitrogen released from the rotting fungi. In olden times these rings were held to be the scene of fairy dances.

Falcon, name given to diurnal birds of prey which belong to the same family, *Falconidae*, as the hawk, eagle, buzzard, kite and harrier. They are swift of wing and feed on birds and small mammals. These birds have long, pointed wings, strong, hooked and notched bill, long, curved claws, and an eye of great power. They are found all over the world. Those that breed in Britain are the Kestrel (the most common), Hobby (one of the swiftest of European birds), Merlin and Peregrine, a swift and magnificent bird with slate-grey back, blackish crown, black "moustache" and whitish breast. Other members of the family are the Gyr Falcon from northern latitudes, Iceland and Greenland, which is a winter visitor to Britain, the Lanner, Saker, Eleonora's falcon, Red-footed falcon and the Lesser Kestrel. The Gyr Falcon and the Peregrine were used in the sport of falconry in olden times. Because of its fearlessness and larger size, the female bird was used. When the quarry was sighted, the bird was unhooded, set free, and after mounting high into the air would dart swiftly down to strike the prey. The heron was the usual victim.

Fall-out. Radioactive material produced by nuclear explosions which may cause bodily and genetic damage. (1) *Local fall-out*, due to the return to earth of larger particles, occurs locally, and within a few hours after the explosion; (2) *Tropospheric fall-out*, due to particles which remain in the troposphere and come down within a month or so, possibly all over the world, but within the altitude in which the explosion occurred; (3) *Stratospheric fall-out*, which comes from fragments taken up into the stratosphere and then deposited, in the course of many years, uniformly all over the globe. The two radioactive materials which have given rise to the greatest concern for the health of the individual are strontium-90 and iodine-131. Both these materials are liable to become concentrated in certain parts of the human body, strontium-90 in bone and iodine-131 in the thyroid gland. Radiation exposure may produce genetic effects, that is effects which may show up in succeeding generations. An extensive survey was carried out by scientists of the US Atomic Energy Commission on the islands of the Bikini atoll, site of some 23 nuclear tests, 1946–58. Their records, published in 1969, revealed that the intensity of radioactivity underneath the point of explosion was still exceedingly high. Most of the radiation remaining was due to the radioactive isotope caesium-137. The variation in intensity from one place to another seemed to be correlated with the variations of vegetation: where there was little vegetation weathering had been rapid. (The nuclear test ban treaty, 1963, applies to all nuclear tests except those held underground.)

Fantail, a variety of the domestic pigeon; also a genus of Australian birds of the *Muscicapidae* family. A small New Zealand bird is called a fantail.

Fan Tracery, a complicated style of roof-vaulting, elaborately moulded, in which the lines of the curves in the masonry or other material employed diverge equally in every direction. It is characteristic of the late Perpendicular period of Gothic architecture, and may be seen in St. George's Chapel at Windsor and the Chapel of Henry VII at Westminster Abbey.

Farmer-General, the name given to the financiers who in the days of the old French monarchy farmed certain taxes, contracting to pay the Government a fixed sum yearly, on condition that the specified taxes were collected and appropriated by themselves. The revolution of 1789 swept Farmers-General away.

Fascism. *See* **Section J.**

Fata Morgana, the name given to a curious mirage often observed over the Straits of Messina, attributed to the magic of the fairy Morgana, half-sister of King Arthur, who was fabled to live in Calabria.

Fathers of the Church were early writers who laid the foundations of Christian ritual and doctrine. The earliest were the Apostolic Fathers (*q.v.*). The Four Fathers of the Latin Church were St. Ambrose, St. Jerome, St. Augustine and St. Gregory the Great. The Four Fathers of the Greek Church were St. Basil, St. Gregory Nazianzen, St. John Chrysostom and St. Athanasius.

Fathom, a nautical measure, the six-foot stretch (1·8 m) of a man's arms. Replaced by the metre on British Admiralty charts, but continued on yachtsmen's coastal charts.

Fatigue, a condition leading to breakage when a solid component, *e.g.*, an axle, is subjected to a large number of fluctuating repetitive stresses. Fatigue is the cause of most failures in service of metal engineering components though fatigue is not confined to metallic materials alone. Fatigue failures result from the *repetition*, not simply from the *size* of the stresses; indeed, fatigue breakage can result from stresses much lower than the material could stand if the load were applied steadily. Fatigue causes minute cracks, usually at the surface, which grow and spread. Early detection is difficult and fatigue, discovered by the railway engineers of the 19th cent., remains a severe engineering problem.

Fats are important foodstuffs. In physiology they constitute a valuable form of reserve food. They contain carbon, hydrogen and oxygen; chemically they are described as esters of glycerol (glycerine). Commonest fats are stearin, palmitin and olein, esters formed by the combination of glycerol with stearic, palmitic and oleic acid respectively. Fats are converted into soap by alkali; this process (saponification) also releases glycerol.

Fault, a term designating a breakage coupled with displacement of geological strata. *See* **F9(1).**

Fauvism (French *Fauve* = wild beast), a term used, at first contemptuously, to describe the work of a group of French painters who first exhibited at the Salon d'Automne in Paris in 1905. The most prominent among them was Henri Matisse. Forms are freely distorted and colours are selected and applied for their emotive power with no necessary reference to the "real" colour of the object in question. Other famous *Fauves* were Derain, Vlaminck and Rouault. By 1908 the group had lost its cohesion and its members went their separate ways.

February, the second month of the year, contains in ordinary years 28 days, but in leap years 29 days. When first introduced into the Roman calendar by Numa *c.* 700 B.C. it was made the last month of the year, preceding January, but in 452 B.C. the position of the two months was changed, February following January.

Federation. *See under* **Confederation.**

Félibrige, a movement founded in 1854 to revive the ancient glories of Provence, initiated by the French poet Frédéric Mistral.

Felspar, the name given to a group of minerals, silicates of aluminium with some calcium and sodium, or potassium, which make up probably more than half of the earth's crust. It is formed in granite and other rocks, both igneous and metamorphic.

Fenestella, the niche set apart on the south side of the altar for the piscina in Roman Catholic churches.

Fermentation, the action of chemical ferments or *enzymes* in bringing about chemical changes in the materials of living animals and plants, *e.g.*, the breaking-down of sugar by yeast into alcohol.

Ferret, a domesticated polecat. It is about half the size of a cat and is bred in captivity to hunt rats and rabbits. It has a long sinuous body and short legs which enable it to enter rabbit and rat holes and chase the quarry out to guns or into nets. Such ferreting is a popular country sport. *See* **Z17.**

Ferrites are compounds containing iron, oxygen, and one or two of a certain range of other possible metallic elements. Ferrites have recently become very important technically, because, unlike ordinary magnetic materials, they combine strong magnetism with electrical insulating properties. Ferrite-rod aerials are now common in portable radios, and ferrite devices are used in radar. *See* **F20(1).**

Feudalism. *See* **Section J.**

Fieldfare, the largest member of the thrush family, a regular winter visitor to Britain from Scandinavia. It is brown in colour with a lighter spotted breast and a grey head.

Field-Marshal, the highest ranking title in the British army, and only bestowed on royal personages and generals who have attained great distinction. The first British Field-Marshal was created in 1736, when John, Duke of Argyll, had the title conferred upon him by George II.

Fifth Column. When Franco, the Spanish dictator, revolted against the Spanish Republic in 1936 and attacked Madrid with four armies, he declared that a group of fascists within the city was assisting the besiegers. The term is used to describe a body of spies behind a fighting front.

Fighting-Fish, small pugnacious Siamese fish with long caudal and ventral fins. They are kept in glass globes in Siam, and when brought into contact will fight to the death, these encounters being the occasion of much gambling.

Filibuster, a name first given to pirates and buccaneers in the 17th cent. who took possession of small islands or lonely coast lands, and there maintained themselves apart from any governing authority. In later times the term was used to specify men taking part in expeditions whose object was to appropriate tracts of country, and settle upon them in disregard of international law. The most notable expeditions of this kind in modern times were those of Narcisco Lopez against Cuba in 1850–51, and of William Walker against Nicaragua, between 1855 and 1860. Both leaders were captured and executed. The term is also used to express the right of a minority in the United States Senate for unlimited debate, which is used on occasions to delay legislation.

Finches, a large family of small birds belonging to the Passerine or perching order of birds. There are about 200 species, including greenfinch, hawfinch, chaffinch, goldfinch, siskin, bullfinch, crossbill, linnet, twite and buntings.

Fir, a cone-bearing tree with small evergreen leaves and of considerable use as timber. There are two types: the Silver Firs and the Douglas Firs numbering about 25 species. All these firs attain to a considerable height, and all yield turpentine or other resinous material.

Fire-damp. *See* **Methane.**

Fire-Fly, a small winged insect of the *Eleteridae* family, is able to throw out a strong phosphorescent light in the dark. There are some remarkable specimens in tropical countries.

Fire of London, of 1666, extended from East to West, from the Tower to the Temple church, and northward to Holborn Bridge. It broke out in a baker's shop in Pudding Lane, and lasted four days, and destroyed 87 churches, including St. Paul's Cathedral, and many public buildings, among them the Royal Exchange, the Custom House and the Guildhall. In the ruins were involved 13,200 houses and 400 streets. About 100,000 people were made homeless yet in about 10 years all the houses had been rebuilt. The plague had not disappeared from London when the fire occurred.

Firkin, a former measure of capacity, the fourth part of a barrel, now only used in reference to a small cask or tub for butter, lard, tallow, etc.

Fischer-Tropsch Process. A process for making synthetic petrol from carbon monoxide and hydrogen. The synthesis is accelerated by cobalt-thoria and nickel-thoria catalysts.

Fish Louse. Parasitic crustacea found on marine and fresh-water fishes and whales.

Fission, Nuclear. A nuclear reaction in which the nucleus of an atom (*e.g.*, uranium 235, plutonium) captures a neutron, and the unstable nucleus so produced breaks into two nearly equal fragments and throws out several neutrons as well. In biology the term fission is applied to reproduction by fragmentation of a single-cell organism, as in amoeba. *See* **F12(1).**

Flagella, single hair-like projections found on many micro-organisms. Their sole function is, by complicated motion, to move the organism about. They are longer and less versatile than cilia (*q.v.*).

Flag Officer, a British naval officer who enjoys the right of carrying a flag at the mast-head of his ship, and is of the rank of Admiral, Vice-Admiral or Rear-Admiral.

Flagship, the ship that flies the Admiral's flag, and from which all orders proceed.

Flamingo, a strangely beautiful, extremely slender wading bird of white and rose-pink plumage with long, slender legs and neck and a long, down-curved bill with which it rakes the mud and obtains its food of worms and molluscs. The wings are bright crimson, bordered with black, and a flock in flight is a picture of singular beauty. There is a large and famous colony in the Camargue, S.E. France.

Flash-Point. This is found by heating an oil in a special cup and taking the temperature at which sufficient vapour is produced to ignite when a small flame is applied. It is an index of the inflammability of oils.

Flea. Fleas are small parasitic insects belonging to the order *Aphaniptera* (so called because these creatures have no wings). They obtain their food by sucking blood from their host. They are laterally compressed, which immediately distinguishes them from lice. The human flea (*Pulex irritans*) is able to jump vertically a distance of over 18 cm.

Fleet Prison, a noted debtors' prison that stood in Farringdon Street, London, where the Congregational Memorial Hall now stands, taking its name from the Fleet Ditch. Notorious for the cruelties inflicted on prisoners. It was pulled down in 1846.

Fleet Street, a famous thoroughfare in London, now the centre of journalism and newspaperdom, though it was long celebrated for its taverns where the literary coteries of the day were wont to meet. It takes its name from the Fleet stream which used to run from Hampstead through Holborn to the Thames at Blackfriars.

Flemings, the people of Flanders, whose ancestors of mediaeval times excelled in the textile arts; England owes its early eminence as a manufacturing nation to the migration of numbers of Flemings to this country in the 16th and 17th cent. *See also* **Walloons.**

Fleur de Lis, the former national emblem of France, the flower of the lily. It was superseded by the Tricolour in 1789, but is still adhered to by the supporters of the old French royalties.

Flint, consists of granular chalcedony with some opaline silica, and occurs as nodules and bands in the Chalk. It is hard and has a conchoidal fracture, so enabling it to be used in making cutting implements in prehistoric times. Before the invention of lucifer matches, it was used along with steel for striking lights.

Flint implements are objects found in the younger geological strata, and constituting evidence of the condition and life of the period. They include knives, clubs, arrow-heads, scrapers, etc., used as weapons, tools and possibly as surgical instruments and in religious ceremonies. Similar to prehistoric specimens are the flint and obsidian implements of some of the primitive peoples of today. Ritual weapons and sacrificial knives continued to be made of stone long after the introduction of metals for practical purposes.

Flounder, one of the most familiar of the smaller flat fishes common round the British coasts, and seldom attaining a weight of over 1·3 kg.

Fluoridation, the process of adding the element fluorine, in the form of suitable compounds, to something deficient in it. Commonly met with as a proposal to add fluorides (fluorine compounds) to drinking water to combat dental decay, especially in children. Some toothpastes are fluoridated and fluoride can also be taken as tablets and in other ways. In 1976 a working party of the Royal College of Physicians recommended that water supplies should be fluoridated when the natural fluoride level is below 1 mg/litre. This recommendation drew on many investigations throughout the world giving evidence for the effectiveness of fluoride in the prevention of decay without harmful side-effects. There is, however, a body of opinion unconvinced by this and opposed to adding fluoride to drinking water, one argument being that to take or not to take fluoride should be a personal decision.

Fluorine, a chemical element, member of the halogen family, symbol F, it is found in combination with calcium in fluorspar, and occurs in minute quantities in certain other minerals. Discovered by Scheele in 1771, it was first obtained by Moissan in 1886. A pale yellow gas, it is very reactive and combines with most elements except oxygen. Its acid, hydrogen fluoride, etches glass, the fluorine combining with the silicon to form volatile silicon fluoride. Organic fluorine compounds have found use as very stable polymers which resist a wide variety of chemical actions.

Fluorescent Lamp. *See* **Electric Light** and **Ultra-Violet Rays.**

Fluorocarbons are hydrocarbons in which some or all of the hydrogen atoms have been replaced by atoms of chlorine or fluorine. They are non-toxic, non-flammable and chemically inert gases or low boiling point liquids. These properties make them very suitable for use as refrigerants, and propellants in fire-extinguishers and aerosols. The most widely used fluorocarbons are the chlorofluoromethanes (CCl_2F_2, CCl_3F and $CHClF_2$). In 1974 it was first suggested that the vast release of fluorocarbons into the atmosphere due to the greatly increased use of aerosols could cause a significant depletion of the protective ozone (*q.v.*) layer in the upper atmosphere. The mechanism for this involves the decomposition of fluorocarbons at high altitudes as a result of intense solar irradiation. The chlorine atoms so released can then catalyse the conversion of ozone into ordinary molecular oxygen. The degree of ozone depletion that will result is a matter of considerable current controversy. Similarly, opinions differ as to the detrimental effect ozone depletion might have on the incidence of skin cancer and on the climate.

Fluorspar, a mineral; chemically calcium fluoride. Can be colourless, green or yellow, but is most commonly purple. Blue fluorspar under the name of Derbyshire "blue John" has been used for ornamental purposes.

Fly, the popular name for a large number of insects with one pair of wings and a proboscis terminating in a sucker through which fluid substances can be drawn up. The best-known species are the common house-fly, the bluebottle and the blow-fly. In the larval form flies are maggots, and feed upon decaying substances, animal flesh, etc. Flies are able to walk upon ceilings or upright surfaces by having suckers at the soles of their feet. *See* **Diptera.**

Flycatcher, name of a large family of small birds, the Muscicapidae. They are insect feeders, catch their food in the air, and are distributed over most countries of the world. The spotted and the pied nest in Britain, which they visit from April to September.

Flying Fish are frequently to be seen in southern waters, and are capable of gliding considerable distances without touching the water. To build up speed for its "take-off" the fish swims rapidly, to break the surface at 24–32 km/h. Maximum air speed is about 64 km/h.

Flying Fox, a member of the bat family, but of much larger size, and confined to the tropical and sub-tropical Old World. Like the bats, it is nocturnal, but it feeds entirely on fruits.

Flying Lemur. *See* **Colugo.**

Flying Lizard, or *Draco*, an Asiatic lizard, possessing wing-like projections from each side, which enable it to make flying leaps through the air, though not sufficient for continuous flight.

Flying Saucers, the name given to certain saucer-like shapes which have on occasion been seen travelling through the atmosphere. For some time speculation was rife, especially in America, but it is now believed that when not hallucinations, meteorological or cosmic-ray balloons, they are nothing more than atmospheric phenomena like mirages or mock suns caused by unusual atmospheric conditions. Described by Dr. Menzel, astrophysics professor at Harvard, "as real as rainbows are real, and no more dangerous". It has been suggested that the study of some of the people who report the sighting of unidentified flying objects (UFOs) would be more rewarding than the investigation of what they saw! *See also* **Section J.**

Flying Squirrel, rodents of which there are several species in Europe, Asia and America. It possesses a parachute-like fold of skin by means of which it projects itself through the air. In appearance they are much like ordinary squirrels, to which they are related. The African flying squirrels belong to a different family.

Fog is caused by the presence of particles of condensed water vapour or smoke in the surface layers of the atmosphere, the term being applied meteorologically when the resulting obscurity is such as to render objects invisible at distances of up to 1 km. Fogs are frequently formed when the air near the ground is cooled below its dew-point temperature by radiation on a still, cloudless night; by flowing over a relatively cold land or water mass; or by mixing with a colder air stream. An accumulation of smoke over a large city may cause a high fog cutting off the daylight and producing gloom. *See* **Pollution** *and also* **Aerosol.**

Foliation, a geological term applied to rocks whose component minerals are arranged in parallel layers as the result of strong metamorphic action.

Folio, a printing term for a sheet of paper folded once, a half sheet constituting a leaf.

Folklore concerns itself with the mental and spiritual life of the people—both civilised and primitive—as expressed in the traditional beliefs, customs, institutions and sayings that have been handed down from generation to generation by word of mouth and with the observation, recording and interpretation of such traditions. (The word *folklore* itself was first suggested and used—as two words *Folk Lore*—by W. J. Thoms in the *Athenaeum* of 22 August 1846, and was at once absorbed into the English language.) Traditional lore of the kind included in the term folklore takes many forms and ranges from omens of good and bad luck (spilling the salt, breaking a mirror, dropping an umbrella, etc.) and the wearing of amulets or the possession of talismans (such as the horseshoe) as protection against misfortune, to elaborate ceremonial dances such as the Abbots Bromley Horn Dance, the Hobby horses of Padstow and Minehead, the Northern sword-dances and the Christmas mummers' plays. Especially important are the beliefs and customs associated with birth, babyhood, marriage and death such being occasions when the individuals concerned require special protection or when unusual happenings can be used for foretelling their future. The child born on a Sunday will be the luckiest; rocking on an empty cradle will ensure the speedy arrival of a new baby; throwing an old shoe after a newly-married couple brings them luck; the bride should be carried over the threshold of the new home; on the sea-coast, death is believed to take place at the ebb-tide; the bees must be told of the death of the master of the house, or they will leave the hive. Another very large section of the subject deals with the traditional sayings and practices associated with particular days and seasons of the year—calendar customs, as they are called. The eating of pancakes on Shrove Tuesday; Mother Sunday customs and the simnel cake; Good Friday as the right day for planting potatoes, but emphatically the wrong day for washing clothes or cutting one's finger-nails; the necessity of wearing something new on Easter Sunday; the children's maypole dances and May garlands; midsummer fires; All Hallowe'en as the most favourable occasion for divining the future—especially in respect of marriage—and for games and sports such as apple-bobbing; the numerous practices accompanying the harvest. All these are examples of calendar customs; their full story would occupy several volumes. Folklorists are interested in all such oral tradition because they think that to a large extent it represents what folk have mentally stored up from the past and transmitted to their descendants throughout the centuries, and because therefore it is able to assist other historic methods—ethnographical linguistic, archaeological, etc.—in the elucidation of the early story of man. In those countries with a great diversity of peoples in all stages of culture, a knowledge of folklore and what it can teach of the mind of man is of great importance to administrators. The Folk-Lore Society was founded in 1878, and that part of the subject represented by song and dance has now its own organisation in the English Folk Dance and Song Society.

Footpath. In English law a highway over which the public have a right of way on foot only, other than such a highway at the side of a public road.

Force, as a term in physics, signifies an influence or exertion which, when made to act upon a body, tends to move it if at rest, or to affect or stop its progress if it be already in motion. In the c.g.s. system, the unit of force is the dyne; in the foot-pound-second system, the poundal; in the SI system, the newton.

Formaldehyde Chemically it lies between methyl alcohol and formic acid; oxidation of methyl alcohol yields formaldehyde, and oxidation of formaldehyde produces formic acid. It is used as a disinfectant, in silvering mirrors, and in the manufacture of phenol-formaldehyde plastics (of which bakelite is the best-known example). Solutions of formaldehyde in water, formalin, are used to preserve biological specimens.

Forme, a body of letterpress type, composed and secured for printing from; or a stereotype or electrotype. The former is used more for newspaper formes and the latter in good book work.

Formic Acid can be obtained from a colourless fluid secreted by ants and other insects and plants. It is a strong irritant. Commercially it is obtained from sodium formate, which is synthesised by the absorption of carbon monoxide in caustic soda. It is used in the electroplating, tanning and textile industries.

Fossils. Remains of animals and plants, or direct evidence of their presence, preserved in rocks. They include petrified skeletons and shells, leaf imprints, footprints, etc.

Four Freedoms, a phrase coined by President Roosevelt in January 1941, embodying what should be the goal of the Allies. They were (1) Freedom of speech and expression; (2) Freedom of every person to worship God in his own way; (3) Freedom from want; (4) Freedom from fear.

Fox, carnivorous animal of the canine family, found in considerable numbers in most parts of the world. The common fox *Vulpes vulpes* of Europe is a burrowing animal of nocturnal habits, living upon birds, rabbits and domestic poultry, in the capture of which it displays much cunning. The fox in Britain is preserved from extinction chiefly for hunting purposes. Among other notable species are the Arctic fox and the red fox of North America, of which the valuable silver fox, coveted for its fur, is a variety.

Fox-Shark, *or* **Thresher Shark,** a large species of shark common in the Atlantic and in the Mediterranean. It is very destructive to small fish, but although it attains a length of 4·5 m it is not dangerous to man.

Franciscans. *See* **Friars.**

Franco-German War (1870–71) was opened by a declaration of war by Napoleon III, but the Germans who were better prepared than the French, won victory after victory. In September Napoleon and the whole French army were made prisoners at Sedan, a republic was then proclaimed, and Paris sustained a four months' siege. In the end France ceded Alsace and part of Lorraine to Germany, who claimed a war indemnity of over £20 million.

Francolin, a genus of birds closely related to the common partridge, belonging to Africa. It includes the spur-legged partridge, and the black partridge which ranges from Cyprus to Assam.

Frankincense is of two kinds, one being used as incense in certain religious services and obtained from olibanum, an Eastern shrub, the other is a resinous exudation derived from firs and pines, and largely used in pharmacy.

Franklin, the name given in feudal times to a country landowner who was independent of the territorial lord, and performed many of the minor functions of local government, such as serving as magistrate.

Fresco, a painting executed upon plaster walls or ceilings, a technique which has remained unchanged since it was practised by the great Renaissance artists.

Freshwater Shrimp, a small crustacean abounding in British streams, and feeding on dead fish or other decomposing matter. Although of shrimp-like form it is not closely related to salt-water shrimps. Its generic name is *Gammarus.*

Friars, members of certain mendicant orders of the Roman Catholic Church. The four chief orders are the Franciscans or Grey Friars, the Dominicans or Black Friars, the Carmelites or White Friars and the Augustinians (Austin Friars).

Friday, the 6th day of the week, named after Frigga, the wife of Odin. It is the Mohammedan Sabbath, a general abstinence day of the Roman Catholic Church, and according to popular superstition, an unlucky day.

Friends, The Society of. *See* **Quakers, Section J.**

Frigate-Bird, a web-footed bird widely distributed over tropical latitudes, and deriving its name from its great expanse of wing and forked tail, resembling the shape of a swift vessel. It feeds on flying fish mostly, being unable to dive and also steals from other birds. A frigate-bird was found dying on the Hebridean island of Tiree in July 1953: only twice previously had one been recorded in Europe—the first on the German coast in 1792, and the second on the coast of France in 1902.

Frog, a familiar amphibian, breathing through gills in the earlier (tadpole) part of its existence, and through lungs later. It remains three months in the tadpole stage. The frog hibernates underwater in the mud during the winter.

Frost occurs when the temperature falls to, or below, 0°C, which is freezing point. Hoar frost is applied to the needles or feather-like crystals of ice deposited on the ground, in the same manner as dew. Glazed frost is the clear icy coating which may be formed as a result of rain falling on objects whose temperatures are below the freezing point. These layers of ice, often rendering roads impassable for traffic, damaging overhead power and communication systems and endangering aircraft, can also be caused by condensation from warm, damp winds coming into contact with very cold air and freezing surfaces.

Froth-Hopper *or* **Frog-Hopper.** A family of bugs

(belonging to the insect order *Hemiptera*) which in the larval stage surround themselves with a protective mass of froth ("cuckoo spit"). These insects, which suck the sap of plants, bear a faint resemblance to frogs, and the adults possess great leaping powers.

Fuel Cells. A recent development is a type of battery into which the active chemicals are fed from external fuel tanks. This is the *fuel cell*, which is being developed in a number of versions in several countries. One was demonstrated in action when in 1959 Bacon of Cambridge University used his fuel cell to drive a fork-lift truck and a welding machine. The Bacon fuel cell consists of two electrodes of porous nickel dipping into a solution of caustic potash in water. One electrode is supplied with hydrogen gas from an outside cylinder and the other with oxygen. These gases, forming layers on the nickel, are the active chemicals. The oxygen combines with water to make two negatively charged ions, each consisting of an oxygen and a hydrogen atom joined together (a hydroxyl ion). The hydroxyl ions travel through the solution to the hydrogen electrode, where they combine with hydrogen to form neutral water. Their negative charge (one electron per ion involved) has now arrived at the hydrogen electrode and is ready to flow back to the other electrode through any outside circuit that is provided. This flow constitutes the useful electric current, and it has been provided at the expense of creating water out of the original hydrogen and oxygen. The water can be removed in the form of steam. What is the advantage of all this? In the first place the fuel gases are easy to make and to store in cylinders. Supplying a new gas cylinder is easier and quicker than recharging an ordinary accumulator. Furthermore, a fuel cell is lighter for a given power than an accumulator; satellite designers have found them useful. The fuel cell is not damaged by heavy overloading, and this is valuable for application to vehicle driving. Fuel-cell-driven buses could combine the advantages of diesel buses and trolleybuses. Fuel cells are still in the development stage. It is not certain how they will compete with combustion engines or, in the oil-less future, with improved ordinary batteries.

Fulani, a non-Negro people of Hamitic stock widely distributed in N.W. Africa, chiefly in Nigeria. There are two main branches: the dark-skinned Fulani, settled farmers and city dwellers, Moslem in religion, and the light-coloured Bororo'en who are semi-nomadic herdsmen. The Fulani are different from any tribe in W. Africa though they resemble in some ways the Masai of E. Africa. The Fulani conquered the Hausa states at the beginning of the 19th cent. which passed under British suzerainty after 1903. Sokoto, built in 1810, was capital of the Fulani empire.

Fuller's Earth, a special kind of clay or marl possessing highly absorbent qualities, originally used in the "fulling"—that is, cleansing and felting—of cloth. Now used in clarifying oils. Deposits in America and in south of England.

Function. In mathematics, one quantity y is said to be a function of another quantity x, written $y = f(x)$, if a change in x results in some corresponding change in y. Thus $\sin x$ or $\log x$ are functions of x. If y depends not only on x but on several other quantities as well, y is called a function of many variables.

Functionalism, in architecture, a movement originated by Le Corbusier, Swiss-born French architect and town-planner, who applied the austere principles of the Purist movement in painting to his own art. From about 1924 he designed in concrete, steel and glass, buildings in which every part had a significance in terms of function on the theory that objects created to carry out their particular function to perfection cannot help being beautiful. "A house is a machine for living in." The style was in vogue between the two wars, and although its severity became somewhat modified, it is still the basis of most modern architecture.

Fungi, a class of simple plants, which reproduce from spores and lack the green colouring matter *chlorophyll*. It includes moulds, rusts, mildews, smuts, mushrooms, etc. Potato blight is a fungus disease which caused the failure of the potato crop in Ireland in 1846. 50,000 different fungi are known. *See also* **F39(2)**, **P8(1)**.

Furniture Beetle (*Anobium punctatum*). The common furniture beetle is responsible for 80 per cent of all woodworm damage and is the great pest of the comparatively modern house, causing damage in the main to softwood roofing and flooring timbers. Adults are 3 mm long. The grub tunnels for about 33 months. *See also* **Woodworm, Death Watch Beetle.**

Futurism, the only important modern art movement to arise outside France, initiated by Marinetti, an Italian writer and mountebank friend of Mussolini at a later period. Its origin took the form of a manifesto published in Paris in 1909 in which Marinetti glorified violence, war and the machine age. In its aggression it favoured the growth of fascism. One of the distinctive features of Futurist art was the use of the principle of "simultaneity" in which the same figure (*e.g.*, a woman descending a flight of stairs) is represented in successive positions like film "stills" superimposed on each other. In spite of two further manifestoes it was not until 1911 that the first examples of Futurist painting and sculpture appeared by the artists Severini, Balla and Boccioni. Apart from the principle of simultaneity, Futurism derived from Cubist and Post-impressionist techniques. The movement faded out early in first world war.

G

Gabardine, a long, loose, coarse, over-garment, worn by men of the common class in the Middle Ages, and prescribed by law as the distinctive garment of the Jews. The name is now given to a closely woven cloth of wool and cotton used to make raincoats.

Gabbro, a kind of igneous rock, often very coarse-grained, containing a good deal of plagioclase felspar, and monoclinic pyroxene; it may occasionally also include biotite, magnetite, ilmenite and hornblende. A gabbro containing nickel at Sudbury in Canada is one of the richest sources known of that metal.

Gadfly, a widely distributed family of flies with only one pair of wings, including the horse fly. The females are very voracious, being able to bite through the skin and suck the blood of animals. The males are harmless.

Gadolinium. An element belonging to the rare-earths metals discovered in 1886 by Marignac. It is strongly magnetic.

Gaelic, relating to the Gaels and their language, a term now applied only to the Celtic people inhabiting the Highlands of Scotland, but formerly also to the Celts of Ireland and the Isle of Man.

Galago, "Bush Babies", related to the lemur, native to Africa, large-eyed, in keeping with its nocturnal characteristics.

Galaxy *or* **Milky Way Galaxy** is the huge disk-shaped cloud of gas and stars (some 100,000 million, one of which is the sun) that is turning in space like a great wheel, with a diameter of about 100,000 light years. The Milky Way (that part of the heavens in Milton's words "powdered with stars") is really only a small part of this disk, and every star in the galaxy is moving round the centre under the gravitational control of the whole. The sun and planets lie near the edge of the disk, and it takes them about 250 million years to travel once round. The number of stars that can be seen with the unaided eye is about 3,000, and they all belong to the Milky Way Galaxy, as do most of the stars that can be seen with anything but the greatest telescopes. With the large modern optical and radar telescopes many other systems, similar in size and weight to our galaxy, have been discovered, scattered more or less uniformly through space, and the universe is said to include at least 10,000 million such galaxies. *See also* **F3–6.**

Gale, a high wind now technically defined as one of at least Beaufort force 8. Between thirty and forty gales a year occur on the north and west coasts of the British Isles and only about half of this number in the south-east. At St.

Ann's Head, Dyfed, the anemometer registered a gust of 113 mile/h (182 km/h) on 18 Jan. 1945, which is a record for these islands. Gusts exceeding 113 km/h are rarely experienced in London. Gale warnings are issued for specified areas by the Meteorological Office, the warnings taking the form of radio broadcasts and the hoisting of storm signals at certain points on the coast. *See* **Beaufort Wind Scale, Section N.**

Gall, abnormal vegetable growths caused by insects, mites, bacteria, or fungi, found on all parts of the plant. Oak-apples, Robin's pincushion (on wild rose), "witches' brooms" (on trees) are examples. Some are useful commercially, *e.g.*, oak apples yield tannic acid and the black oak gall is used in America as animal food.

Galleon, the name given to the old three-decked Spanish treasure vessels employed in conveying the precious minerals from the American colonies to Spain. The term is often applied to any large, especially stately, sailing vessel.

Galley, an oar-propelled sea-boat used by the ancient Greeks and Romans for transport purposes, manned by slaves. Boats of a similar class were used by the French down to the middle of the 18th cent., and manned by convicts.

Gallic Acid, obtained from gall nuts, sumach, tea, coffee, and the seeds of the mango, is used in the manufacture of inks and as an astringent in medicine. It was discovered by C. W. Scheele (1742–86), a Swedish chemist.

Gallium, a white metal, symbol Ga, related to aluminium, but which can be cut with a knife. It was discovered spectroscopically by L. de Boisbaudran in 1875. Long before Mendeleyev had predicted that an element with its properties would be found to fill the then existing gap in the Periodic Table; this gap came immediately below aluminium, so he suggested the name "eka aluminium" for it.

Gallup Poll, a system, introduced by Dr. Gallup of the United States, for testing public opinion on topical subjects by taking a test poll on questions framed to elicit opinions.

Galvanised Iron is iron coated with zinc. The name comes from the fact that such a coat protective against rust could be deposited electrolytically. Electrodeposition is sometimes used, but the cheaper and more common process depends on dipping the iron in a bath of molten zinc.

Gamboge, a resinous gum obtained from the sap of *Garcinia morella*, a tree native to Thailand, Cambodia and Sri Lanka, and used as a yellow pigment in paints and also as a purgative.

Game is the term applied to wild animals which are protected from indiscriminate slaughter by Game Laws. In the United Kingdom game comprehends deer, hares, pheasants, partridges, grouse, black game, moor game, woodcocks, bustards and certain other birds and animals of the chase. Game can only be killed (with few exceptions) by persons holding game licences. Occupiers of land and one other person authorised by them in each case are allowed to kill hares and rabbits on their land without licence. Game cannot be sold except by a person holding a proper licence. There is a "close time" prescribed for the different classes of game; for instance, the selling or exposing for sale of any hare or leveret during March, April, May, June or July is prohibited by law. Grouse cannot be shot between 11 December and 11 August; partridges between 2 February and 31 August; pheasants between 2 February and 30 September; and black game between 11 December and 10 August. In regard to foxes, stags and otters, custom and not Parliament prescribes a certain law which sportsmen rigidly adhere to. Game reserves are legally protected areas where natural vegetation and wild life are allowed to remain unmolested by sportsmen or those who might destroy for economic ends.

Gaming, *or* **Gambling**—*i.e.*, staking money on the chances of a game—differs from betting in that it depends upon the result of a trial of skill or a turn of chance. The Betting and Gaming Act of 1959, passed by the Macmillan administration, replaced all the old laws on gaming, which went back to an Act of 1541 entitled "An Acte for Mayntenance of Artyllarie and debarringe of unlauful games", under which some games were unlawful if played for money in any circumstances. Roulette and any game of dice were among such games. Under the 1959 Act any game was lawful, subject to certain conditions. Since then the Betting, Gaming and Lotteries Act, 1963, and the Gaming Act, 1968, have been passed, to deal with unlawful gaming and to prevent the exploitation of gaming by commercial interests. The playing of bingo is now restricted to clubs licensed for bingo only. The Gaming Board in its evidence to the Royal Commission on Gambling (1976) recommended a new Gambling Authority or Commission to ensure that any legalised gambling is not penetrated by criminals.

Gammexane, a powerful insecticide, used particularly to kill the tsetse fly and mosquito.

Gangue. Useless minerals associated with metallic ores.

Gannet, a fish-eating bird which dives on its prey from a great height, swallowing it under water; is found in large numbers off the coast of Scotland, and has breeding stations in the Hebrides, St. Kilda, Ailsa Craig, the Bass Rock, Grassholme Island and on Ortac and Les Etacs (rocks off Alderney). It is a bird of white plumage, black tips to long narrow wings and wedge-shaped tail, and weighs about 3 kg. The gannet breeds in colonies on ledges of steep, rocky, island cliffs. Related to the cormorants, pelicans and frigate-birds.

Garden Cities in England were founded by Ebenezer Howard (1850–1928), and his ideas were put forward in his book *Tomorrow—A Peaceful Path to Real Reform* (later re-issued as *Garden Cities of Tomorrow*). New towns should be so placed and planned as to get the best of town and country life, an adaptation of the model villages of certain industrial philanthropists such as Salt, Richardson, Cadbury, Leverhulme and others. The Garden City Association (later the Town and Country Planning Association) was formed in 1899, and the first garden city was begun at Letchworth in 1903 and successfully established. Welwyn Garden City was also Howard's foundation, established in 1919.

Gardener-Bird, a bird possessing many of the characteristics of the bower-bird, and found only in Papua–New Guinea. *See also* **Bower Bird.**

Gargantua, the giant hero of Rabelais' satire, of immense eating and drinking capacity, symbolical of an antagonistic ideal of the greed of the Church.

Gargoyle, a projecting spout for carrying off water from the roof gutter of a building. Gargoyles are only found in old structures, modern water-pipe systems having rendered them unnecessary. In Gothic architecture they were turned to architectural account and made to take all kinds of grotesque forms—grinning goblins, hideous monsters, dragons and so forth.

Garlic, a bulbous plant of the same genus as the onion and the leek, and a favourite condiment among the people of Southern Europe. It possesses a very strong odour and pungent taste and its culinary use is agelong.

Garnet, a group of minerals; chemically they are orthosilicates of the metals calcium, magnesium, titanium, iron, aluminium. Garnets can be coloured yellow, brown, black, green or red; the blood-red garnet is an important gemstone.

Garrotte, a method of strangulation used as capital punishment in Spain, and consisting of a collar which is compressed by a screw that causes death by piercing the spinal marrow. Garrotting was also applied to a system of highway robbery common in England in 1862–63, the assailants seizing their victims from behind, and by a sudden compression of the windpipe disabling them until the robbery was completed.

Garter. The Most Noble Order of the Garter was founded (*c.* 1348) by King Edward III, and is the premier order of knighthood in Great Britain. The traditional story associating the garter and the motto with the Countess of Salisbury, who it was said dropped her garter while dancing with the King, who remarked "honi soit qui mal y pense" cannot be accepted. The order was originally limited to the

Sovereign and 25 knights, but the number has been extended, and it may now be bestowed on royal personages and leading representatives of the British peerage. The insignia of the order are the garter of dark-blue velvet with the motto in letters of gold, the mantle of dark-blue velvet lined with white silk, the surcoat and hood, and the gold-and-enamel collar. The garter is worn on the left leg below the knee and by women as a sash over the left shoulder. *See* **Knighthood.**

Gas is an elastic fluid substance, the molecules of which are in constant rapid motion, and exerting pressure. The technique whereby gases are liquefied depends on increasing pressure and diminishing temperature. Each gas has a critical point; unless the temperature is brought down to this point no amount of pressure will bring about liquefaction. Last gas to be liquefied was helium (1908) which boils at −209°C. *See* **F17**(1).

Gas from coal was first used as an illuminating agent by William Murdoch towards the end of the 18th cent. in Birmingham, and about 1807 was introduced in London, one side of Pall Mall being lighted with it. It became widely used as an illuminant, and for space heating and cooking. In the U.K. increasing attention has been paid to the use of a primary fuel—natural gas—instead of producing gas from coal or oil. *See* **Gas, Natural.**

Gas, Natural, natural mixture of gases often present with deposits of petroleum, found issuing from the ground in many parts of the world—in the oilfields of Venezuela and the Caucasus, in China, Saudi-Arabia, but chiefly in North America. Its chief component is methane. Large industrial centres have made use of this gas since the latter part of the 19th cent., but much of this valuable fuel still goes to waste. Pipelines have been constructed to deliver the gas to where it is wanted. Britain began to ship liquid methane from the Saharan oilfield in 1964. Some of the world's largest natural gas fields have recently been discovered in the North Sea and are being actively exploited. Domestic gas appliances have to be modified if the natural product is substituted for ordinary town gas because the burning characteristics are different. Oil production from the North Sea fields began in 1975 and the main single source of gas in the U.K. is now natural gas.

Gas Turbine. In this kind of engine mechanical movement is produced by a jet of gas impinging on a turbine wheel; used in aeroplanes, locomotives and ships. These engines are mechanically simple compared with internal combustion engines, and require less maintenance.

Gauge, a standard dimension or measurement applied in various branches of construction. Thus the standard railway gauge is 4 ft 8½ in (143·5 cm) in the UK, USA and most European countries. The Soviet Union uses the narrow gauge of 5 ft (152 cm). Narrow railway gauges of different standards are in use on very steep inclines in various countries. Other standard gauges are fixed in building and gun-boring.

Gauls were inhabitants of ancient Gaul, the country which comprised what is now France, Belgium and parts of the Netherlands, Switzerland and Germany.

Gault, a stratum of blue clay between the Lower Greensand and the Chalk. A typical section of the Gault can be seen at Folkestone.

Gauss, a unit of magnetic induction in the c.g.s. system, named after the great German mathematician and astronomer, K. F. Gauss.

Gavelkind, an old English custom of land tenure in Kent and other places in England, whereby on the death, intestate, of a property owner his property is divided equally among his children and not according to the law of primogeniture. Abolished by the Law of Property Act, 1922, and the Administration of Estates Act, 1925.

Gazelles, a group of small, graceful antelopes which live in the drier regions of Africa and Asia. They can run very fast: speeds of over 64 km/h have been recorded.

Geiger Counter, an electrical device, invented by Geiger, which can detect individual atomic particles, *e.g.*, electrons, protons, etc. It often consists of a tube of gas at a few cm Hg pressure, fitted with two electrodes—a cylinder and an axial wire. A high voltage is kept across the electrodes, and the passage of a charged particle through the gas releases ions which permit a momentary discharge between the electrodes. Electronic circuits register this discharge as a "count". Geiger counters are used to detect and measure radioactivity and cosmic rays both for technical and research purposes.

Gelatine, a transparent, tasteless, organic substance obtained from animal membranes, bones, tendons, etc., by boiling in water. It is of various kinds, according to the substance used in making it. Isinglass, the purest form of it, is made from air-bladders and other membranes of fish, while the coarser kind—glue—is made from hoofs, skin, hides, etc. Its constituents are carbon, hydrogen, oxygen and nitrogen. Gelatine is applied to an immense variety of purposes, from the making of food jellies to photographic materials.

Gemsbok, a large South African antelope of the open dry plains, sandy coloured with black and white markings on its face, and with long straight horns.

General, a military title next in rank to that of Field-Marshal, the highest officer in the army. Ranking below full General are Lieutenant-General, Major-General and Brigadier.

Generation, a time-measure reckoned at about 30 years when children are ready to replace parents; also the body of persons existing at the same time or period. According to a U.N. report in 1958 "one can no longer think of generations in traditional terms. Interests and activities are today changing so fast that sets of young people not more than seven or eight years apart in age may be as far apart in their thinking and behaviour as two generations once were." The generation gap is now even less years apart.

Generation, Spontaneous. *See* **Abiogenesis.**

Genes, the elementary units of heredity. They exist as highly differentiated regions arranged along the length of the chromosomes which the nuclei of cells carry. A chromosome may carry hundreds or even thousands of genes, each with its own particular structure and specific properties. The position of a particular gene on a chromosome is called its locus. The material of the gene is DNA (*q.v.*). *See* **Cell Division, F30**(2).

Genesis, the first book of the Pentateuch, compiled in the 5th cent. B.C. from earlier documents, which carries the scriptural narrative from the creation to the death of Joseph. Sometimes there is disagreement, as in the story of the creation, Gen. i and ii. Gen. i reflects the views of the ancient Greek scientist Thales (*c.* 640–546 B.C.) and may be said to be the first scientific account of the creation of the world. The conditions described around the figures of Abraham, Isaac, Jacob and Joseph have a genuine historical basis.

Genetic Code. The elucidation of the structure of DNA (*q.v.*) for which Crick, Wilkins and Watson were jointly awarded the 1962 Nobel Prize for medicine, revealed the code or chemical dictionary out of which messages serving as blueprints for living structures can be made. *See* **Protein synthesis, F29**(2).

Genetic Engineering is the name given to the introduction of human choice and design criteria into the construction and combination of genes. This refers not to breeding by selection, a traditional process, but to the biochemical alteration of the actual DNA in cells (*see* **Section F, Part IV**) so as to produce novel self-reproducing organisms. Such manipulations became possible when techniques were recently discovered for severing and rejoining DNA molecules and inserting sections into them. Many people regard this development as fraught with enormous significance. Like nuclear power, it can lead to good, to evil, and to accidental hazards, not all of which can be foreseen. Thus when biologists realised they could create new lifeforms, *e.g.*, bacteria, with novel genes, they appreciated that, as well as medically beneficial strains, new virulent forms might by accident be produced and escape into the world. Ultimately, not imminently, men may be able to design the genes of higher animals and even of man himself and thus consciously influence biological evolution.

Many scientists have been brought by these possibilities up against an old problem: is science going too far too fast?

Geneva Convention, an agreement made by the European Powers at Geneva in 1864, establishing humane regulations regarding the treatment of the sick and wounded in war and the status of those who minister to them. All persons, hospitals, hospital ships are required to display the Geneva cross—a red cross on a white ground. A second conference held at Geneva in 1868 drew up a supplementary agreement. An important result of this Convention was the establishment of the Red Cross Society in 1870.

Genocide is an international crime, defined by the General Assembly of the United Nations in 1948 as " acts committed with intent to destroy, in whole or in part a national, ethnic, racial or religious group as such ". The UN Convention came into force in 1951.

Genus, a term applied in biology to designate a group of similar species. A group of similar genera is called a family.

Geodesy, the science of calculating the configuration and extent of the earth's surface, and determining exact geographical positions and directions, with variations of gravity, etc. Land-surveying is a branch of geodesy.

Geography, a science concerned with the spatial organisation of natural features and life and man-made artifacts upon and immediately above the surface of the earth. It is increasingly concerned with the processes by which such patterns are generated and this concern is leading to both a greater degree of specialisation within the subject and to the merging of its constituent parts with related disciplines of economics, sociology, political science, geology, biology and meteorology.

Geology, the science which deals with the condition and structure of the earth, and the evidence afforded of ancient forms of life. The geological strata are classified in the following categories: *Primary* or *Palaeozoic* (the oldest fossil-bearing rocks including the Cambrian, Ordovician, Silurian, Devonian, Carboniferous, Permian); *Secondary* or *Mesozoic* (Triassic, Jurassic, Cretaceous); *Tertiary* or *Cainozoic* (Eocene, Oligocene, Miocene, Pliocene, Pleistocene); *Post tertiary* (most recent rocks). *See* **F45.**

Geometrical Progression is a term used to indicate a succession of numbers which increase or decrease at an equal ratio—as 3, 9, 27; or 64, 16, 4.

Geometry is the branch of mathematics which demonstrates the properties of figures, and the distances of points of space from each other by means of deductions. It is a science of reason from fundamental axioms, and was perfected by Euclid about 300 B.C. The books of Euclid contain a full elucidation of the science, though supplemented in modern times by Descartes, Newton and Carnot. Of recent years non-Euclidean geometry has been developed.

Geophysics, the branches of physics which are concerned with the earth and its atmosphere. Meteorology, geomagnetism, aurora and airglow, ionosphere, solar activity, cosmic rays, glaciology, oceanography, seismology, nuclear radiation in the atmosphere, rockets and satellites—all these are geophysical subjects. The object of the International Geophysical Year, 1957–58, was to investigate the physical phenomena occurring on and around the earth by means of carefully co-ordinated observations made simultaneously all over the globe.

Geothermal Energy. Some of the heavy elements within the earth's crust are radioactive and this gives rise to a temperature rise towards the centre of the earth. The practical exploitation of this geothermal energy comes about when there are hot springs or geysers. It is believed that these are caused by rainwater slowly percolating down to the hot rocks and blowing out as steam. The homes of people living in Reykjavik are heated by geothermal steam and there are a number of small power stations in various parts of the world. Although the costs in the few cases where geothermal power has actually been exploited are remarkably low, the expense of drilling, etc., required when attempting to exploit the heat in the rocks where surface manifestations do not occur, is likely to limit the use of this source of power.

Geothermal Heating. The earth's interior is hot and in certain localities, often adjacent to volcanic or earthquake-prone regions, reservoirs of hot water or steam exist at accessible depths. Natural hot geysers occur in many such places and people, *e.g.*, the ancient Romans and present-day Japanese, use natural hot water for bathing, cooking and laundry. Occasionally the subterranean reserves permit large-scale power generation by drilling for hot steam and passing it into turbines to produce electricity. Pioneering work on this was done at Lardarello in Italy which can produce hundreds of megawatts. Other sites are in New Zealand, California, Japan and Iceland. There are possibilities in South-West England.

Germanium. A grey, hard, brittle chemical element, symbol Ge, chemically related to silicon and tin. Discovered by Winkler in 1886. Its richest ore is germanite containing 6% of the metal. Coal is also a relatively rich source. Since 1948 it has assumed great importance as a semi-conducting material for making transsistors (*q.v.*). Because of this it has been so intensively studied that more is known about its physical properties than about those of any other element.

Gesta Romanorum (Latin = deeds of the Romans), a mediaeval collection of Latin stories of unknown authorship which circulated widely in Europe during the Middle Ages. First printed in the 15th cent. The stories were used by Chaucer, Shakespeare and other writers who found many romantic incidents and legends which they were able to turn to good account.

Gestation, the carrying of young in animals during pregnancy, varies considerably in its length. In the case of an elephant, the period is 21 months; a camel, 12 months; a cow, 9 months; a cat, 8 weeks; a horse, 48 weeks; a dog, 9 weeks; and a pig, 16 weeks. Hens " sit " for 21 days; geese, 30; swans, 42; turkeys, 28; pigeons, 18.

Geysers, hot springs of volcanic origination and action, are remarkable for the fact that they throw out huge streams of boiling water instead of lava as in the case of a volcano. The most famous geysers are those of Iceland, which number over a hundred, the principal one having an opening of 21 m in diameter and discharging a column of water to a height of 61 m. There are also geysers in the Yellowstone region of America, and some in New Zealand.

Ghost-Moth or **Ghost Swift**, an interesting nocturnal insect (*Hepialus humuli*), common in England, possessing in the male a white collar and known for its habit of hovering with a pendulum-like action in the twilight over a particular spot where the female is concealed.

Gibbon, the name of a long-armed ape mainly inhabiting S.E. Asia. It is without tail, and possesses the power of very rapid movement among the trees of the forests.

Gin, a well-known spirit distilled from malt or barley and flavoured with the juniper berry. The principal varieties are the English and American, known as " Gin " or " Dry Gin ", and the Dutch, referred to as " jenever " or " Hollandse jenever ". In Germany and Austria it is called " Schnapps ". The word " Gin " is an abbreviation of " Geneva ", both being primarily derived from the French genièvre (juniper).

Giraffe, the tallest of existing animals, reaching a height of from 5–6 m when full grown. Its sloping back and elongated neck seem to be the natural evolution of an animal that has to feed on the branches of trees. It is a native of Africa, is of a light fawn colour marked with darker spots and has a prehensile tongue.

Giralda, a beautiful and remarkable example of Arabian art, erected in 1195 at Seville, still in existence.

Glaciers form in the higher Alpine ranges, and are immense consolidated masses of snow, which are gradually impelled by their force down the mountain-sides until they reach a point where the temperature causes them to melt, and they run off in streams. From such glaciers the five great rivers, the Rhine, the Po, the Rhône, the Inn and the Adige, have their source. The longest of the Swiss glaciers is the Gross Aletsch, which sometimes extends over 16 km. Some of the glaciers of the Himalayas are four times as long. The Muir in Alaska is of enormous magnitude, and that of Justeldals Brae in Norway is the largest in Europe.

Gladiators were professional athletes and combatants in ancient Rome, contesting with each other or with wild beasts. At first they were drawn from the slave and prisoner classes exclusively, but so much were the successful gladiators held in esteem that men came to make a profession of athletics, and gladiatorial training schools were established. When a gladiator was vanquished without being killed in combat, it was left with the spectators to decide his fate, death being voted by holding the hands out with the thumb turned inward, and life by putting forth the hands with the thumb extended. Gladiatorial shows were the chief public displays in Rome from the 3rd to the 4th cent. A.D.

Glass is an amorphous, man-made substance, fluid when hot, solid, though fragile, when cooled. It is made of sand mixed with an alkaline flux, usually soda or potash. While hot, glass can be formed into almost any shape by moulding, blowing or, since the early 19th cent., by machine pressing. Unrefined glass normally has a greenish tinge, due to the iron content of most sands, but it is transparent or at least translucent. To make truly colourless glass is a difficult and expensive process, and such glass resembling the natural mineral, rock crystal, is given the name crystal. Glass can be tinted by the addition of various metallic oxides, cobalt producing blue, manganese mauve, etc. Because it is at once solid and transparent, glass is the perfect material for windows for which it has been used since Roman times. And since it can be made cheaply and is easy to clean, it has been used for containers in homes, shops and pharmacies, again since Roman days. Glass can also be made into things of beauty, by the use of coloured glass and by cutting, engraving, painting and gilding. The earliest vessels of glass so far found come from Egypt and date back to *c.* 1500 B.C. With the invention of glass-blowing in the 1st cent. A.D., the use of glass spread throughout the Roman empire. Many varieties were made, including superb art glass like the Portland vase (*q.v.*). The Arabs were great glassmakers from the 7th to 15th cent. During the Renaissance the Venetians created luxurious art glass, rich in colour and often manipulated into fantastic forms. Bohemia's 17th-cent. glass is wonderfully engraved with pictures and cut into glittering facets. During the 1670s in England George Ravenscroft invented a new, heavy, water-clear crystal, with an addition of lead as the magic ingredient, and English lead glass is still the basis for all modern crystals.

Glass-Snake, genus, *Ophisaurus*, of legless lizards with long fragile tails capable of re-generation when broken. Six species are known; in S.E. Europe, S.W. Asia, Indo-China and N. America. Attains a length of about 60 cm; main colouring, green, with black and yellow markings.

Glauconite. A green mineral, chemically a hydrated silicate of potassium and iron. Commonly found in marine sands (hence these rocks are known as "greensands") and sandstones.

Glaucus is a curious genus of sea slugs often called the Sea Lizard belonging to the molluscs. It is without shell and has a soft body, with horny mouth and four tentacles. It is a native of the Atlantic, and is not more than 30 cm in length.

Glee, an unaccompanied piece for three or more voices. Glee-singing was popular in England during the 18th and early 19th cent. and glee-clubs are still in existence.

Globigerina, an oceanic unicellular animalcule with a perforated shell, and occurring in certain parts of the Atlantic in such vast numbers as to form a bed of chalk ooze with their empty shells.

Glockenspiel, an instrument composed of metal bars each of which is tuned to a note. The bars are struck by hand-hammers and give forth chiming sounds.

Glow-worm, a beetle, possessing the power (much stronger in the female than the male) of emitting phosphorescent light from the hind end of the body. The female is wingless.

Glucinium. *See* **Beryllium.**

Glucose, Dextrose *or* **Grape Sugar** is a carbohydrate (*q.v.*). It is produced by hydrolysis from cane sugar, dextrine, starch, cellulose, etc., by the action of reagents. It also occurs in many plants, fruits and honey. For brewing purposes glucose is prepared by the conversion of starch by sulphuric acid. Malt also converts starch into glucose.

Glutton *or* **Wolverine**, the biggest animal of the weasel family, inhabits the northernmost parts of Europe and America. In build it resembles the bear, and is rather larger than a badger. Its fur is of a brown-black hue, but coarse.

Glycerine *or* **Glycerol**, occurs in natural fats combined with fatty acids, and is obtained by decomposing those substances with alkalies or by superheated steam. It is colourless and oily and sweet, and is put to a variety of commercial uses, being widely utilised for medicaments, for lubricating purposes, and in the manufacture of nitro-glycerine.

Glycols. Organic compounds containing two alcohol groups. Ethylene glycol is the most widely known example; it is used as an anti-freeze in motor-car radiators on account of its property of greatly reducing the freezing point of water. Also used in the manufacture of "Terylene". *See* **Esters.**

Glyptodon, an extinct species of gigantic armadillo, fossil remains of which have been discovered in S. America. It was some 2·7 m long, carried a huge tortoise-like shell and had fluted teeth.

Gneiss, a metamorphic rock usually containing quartz, felspar and mica. It is banded, the light-coloured minerals being concentrated apart from the dark minerals.

Gnosticism. *See* **Section J.**

Gnu or Wildebeest, a large antelope from Africa south of the Sahara, distinguished by its excessively short thick neck and large head with a pronounced roman nose. There are two species: the white-tailed gnu is almost extinct, the brindled gnu is still common and migrates in large herds.

Goat-Moth (*Cossus cossus*), a large moth of the *Cossidae* family, common in Britain, evil-smelling and very destructive in the larval stage to trees of the poplar and willow genus, into the wood of which the caterpillar bores during its three years' period of development.

Goats are horned ruminant quadrupeds, indigenous to the Eastern Hemisphere, but now domesticated in all parts of the world. Though related to the sheep, they are a much hardier and more active animal. The male has a tuft of hair under the chin. Many species, including those of Cashmere and Angora, are valuable for their hair, which is used for fine textile fabrics. The milk of the goat is nutritive, and goat-skins are in good demand for leather for gloves, shoes, etc.

God and Man. *See* **Section J.**

God and Magog, two legendary City of London giants, supposed to be the offspring of certain wicked daughters of the Emperor Diocletian and a band of demons. They were brought captive to London and made to serve as prisoners at the Palace of Brute, which stood on the site of Guildhall. Effigies of the giants have stood in Guildhall since the time of Henry V. They were destroyed in the Great Fire of 1666, replaced in 1672 and used to be carried through the streets of London in the Lord Mayor's Show. The present figures, newly carved in lime wood by Mr. David Evans, replaced those carved in 1708 by Richard Saunders, which were destroyed in an air raid during the last war.

Gold. Metallic element, symbol Au (Latin *Aurum*) related to silver and copper, the coinage metals. The greatest amount of gold is obtained by treating gold-bearing quartz by the cyanide process. The gold is dissolved out by cyanide solution, which is then run into long boxes filled with zinc shavings when the gold is precipitated as a black slime. This is melted with an oxidising agent which removes the zinc.

Gold-Beaters' Skin is the outside membrane of the large intestine of the ox, specially prepared and used by gold-beaters for placing between the leaves of gold while they beat them. This membrane is of great tenacity, and gets beaten to such extreme thinness that it is used to put on cuts and bruises.

Gold Standard. Under the gold-standard system which was widely prevalent up to 1914, each gold-standard country fixed the value of its currency in terms of a weight of gold of a certain fineness and was, broadly speaking, ready to exchange its currency freely for gold, which could then be exported without restriction. This involved keeping a gold reserve big enough to meet all likely demands and also to serve as a backing for the issue of notes. The gold standard had to be given up during the first world war; and though it was in substance restored in Great Britain in 1925 (when Churchill was Chancellor), the restoration was never complete, as the gold reserve remained too small for complete freedom to export to be practicable. Sterling had to be devalued in the financial crisis of 1931 (which brought about the fall of the Labour Government) and Great Britain was forced off the gold standard. Imbalance in payments between countries is financed by transfers of gold or foreign exchange. Such reserves are known as international liquidity. *See* **Section G, Part IV.**

Goldeneye, a species of wild duck, widely distributed over Arctic regions. It is a passage-migrant and winter-visitor to the British Isles. Has nested in Cheshire. Distinguished by a large white spot in front of each eye on a dark ground.

Golden Dawn. *See* **Section J.**

Golden Number, the number of any year in the metonic cycle of 19 years, deriving its name from the fact that in the old calendars it was always printed in gold. It is found by adding 1 to the number of the year A.D. and dividing by 19, the remainder being the Golden Number; or, if no remainder, the Golden Number is 19. The only use to which the Golden Number is put now is in making ecclesiastical calculations for determining movable feasts.

Goldsmiths Company, one of the richest London City Companies; the official assayers of gold and silver, invested with the power of "hall-marking" the quality of objects made from these metals. First charter granted in 1327.

Gondola, the old regulation black boats so common on the canals of Venice, propelled by a gondolier with one oar who stands at the stern, his passengers being accommodated in a covered space in the centre.

Gonfalon, the pennon affixed to a lance, spear or standard, consisting usually of two or three streamers and made to turn like a weather-cock.

Good and Evil. *See* **Section J.**

Gophers. Rodent mammals. The pocket gophers are stout-bodied burrowers common in the USA. The slender burrowing gophers, also called "ground squirrels", occur in central and western USA. The sisel or suslik is a related European species. They are a great pest among grain crops.

Gordon Riots of 1780 were an anti-popery agitation fomented by Lord George Gordon. Called also "No-Popery Riots".

Gorilla, the largest of the anthropoid apes, found in the forests of Equatorial Africa, and at maturity standing from 1·2–1·5 m high.

Goshawk (*Accipter gentilis*), a diurnal bird of prey, fearless and extremely agile; loves wooded country and is very destructive of poultry and game-birds. It resembles the peregrine falcon in appearance, but has shorter, rounded wings. This bird was a great favourite of falconers in mediaeval times.

Gospels are those portions of the New Testament which deal with the life, death, resurrection and teachings of Christ. They are the gospels of Matthew, Mark, Luke and John, all compiled in the later part of the 1st cent. The first three are called the *synoptic gospels* because of their general unity of narrative. Mark was the first to be written and John the last, and it is to Mark that one should turn for the most reliable source of knowledge of the life of Jesus. The word *gospel* comes from two Anglo-Saxon words *gode* (good) and *spell* (tidings), a translation of the Greek *euangelion* = evangel, evangelist.

Gothic, the predominant style of architecture in northern Europe from 12th–15th cent. Its most striking characteristic is the extensive use of the pointed arch, but this is really a mere external reflection of the important structural invention of the 12th cent., that of the rib vault, whereby the whole pressure of the stone vaulting is supported on slim ribs which cross each other at a rising centre. On the outside of the building, the pressure from the vaults is caught up and supported by flying buttresses. A complete Gothic construction gives a marvellous effect of airy lightness, also of something striving upwards, towards the heavens, and this is further accentuated when the churches are crowned by lofty towers and spires. The vital structural elements of Gothic architecture were first put into use in the abbey church of St. Denis in Paris *c.* 1140. The style was further developed in a glorious sequence of cathedrals in northern France: Nôtre Dame in Paris, Rheims, Amiens, Beauvais and others. When, as in Chartres, the windows are filled with stained glass of glowing colours and the doorways flanked with magnificently carved life-size figures of saints and apostles, the whole effect is one of unsurpassed solemnity and grandeur. From France the style spread to other lands in each of which it developed its own characteristics; thus the English churches tended to have massive towers and delicate spires and, as at Salisbury, were often set in open grounds surrounded by lawns; Flemish and Dutch churches were sometimes built of brick as were those in north Germany and Scandinavia; in Spain the Flamboyant style was followed. The main Gothic cathedral in Italy, that of Milan, although begun in 1386 was not completed until the early 19th cent. Late English Gothic is seen, for example, at King's College Chapel, Cambridge, Henry's Chapel at Westminster and St. George's Chapel at Windsor (all *c.* 1500). Gothic is also found in secular buildings, *e.g.* Little Wenham Hall in Suffolk, the castle at Ghent, the town halls of Louvain and Middelburg and the streets of Gothic houses in Bruges still in use today. Virtually Gothic as a style (excluding the "Gothic revival" of 19th cent. England) ended at the close of the 15th cent. Gothic art is best seen in the illuminated manuscripts of the 13th and 14th cent. and in the church sculpture. Its characteristic is a complete departure from the cool, perfectionist realism of classical times with distortion to produce emotional effects. The human figures are not ideal forms but recognisable as people we might meet in the street; yet there was also the element of wild imagination, intricate design and a wealth of feeling which might be grotesque, humorous, macabre, or even obscene. Gothic style also found expression in the decorative arts, retaining its architectural character even in small-scale works like caskets, chalices and the like in metalwork and ivory.

Goths. A Teutonic people who originally came from southern Sweden (Gotland) and by the 3rd cent. were settled in the region north of the Black Sea. They began to encroach on the Roman Empire and early in the 4th cent. split into two divisions: the "wise" Goths or Visigoths between the Danube and the Dniester (referred to as the West Goths), and the "bright" Goths or Ostrogoths in southern Russia on the Dnieper (referred to as the East Goths). The Ostrogoths were conquered by the Huns *c.* 370, while the Visigoths under Alaric devastated Greece and sacked Rome in 410. Eventually the Visigoths spread to France and Spain and their last king Roderick fell in battle against the Moors in 711. The Ostrogoths regained their independence on the death of Attila in 453 and under their king Theodoric the Great conquered Italy in 493. They lost their identity after Justinian regained Italy, 525–552.

Gourd Family *or* **Cucurbitaceae.** This family of about 650 species of flowering plants includes the gourds, pumpkins, cantaloupes, cucumber, gherkin, water-melon and squashes. Most abundant in the tropics, the cucurbits are mainly climbing annuals with very rapid growth. The bath-room loofah is the skeleton of one cucurbit fruit, *Luffa cylindrica.* The squirting cucumber is another member of the family.

Governor. A device attached to an engine, turbine, compressor, etc., which automatically controls the engine's speed in accordance with power demand. Most governors depend upon the centrifugal action of two or more balls which are thrown outwards as their speed of rotation increases and actuate a throttle valve or cut-off. The centrifugal governor was invented by Thomas Mead, patented by him in 1787 and used on windmills. Watt adapted it to the steam engine.

Grail, Legend of the Holy, a tale of Celtic origin which became part of Arthurian legend and the subject of many mediaeval quest-romances. According to the Christian version the grail was the cup which Christ used at the Last Supper, brought to England by St. Joseph of Arimathea.

Grand Prix, the " French Derby " was established by Napoleon III, in 1863. It is the chief French race and is an international competition of three-year-olds.

Granite is a coarsely crystalline igneous rock consisting of quartz and alkali felspars plus mica or hornblende. It is a much used ornamental and building stone; it forms the high ground of Dartmoor and Bodmin Moor.

Graphite *or* **Plumbago,** commonly called blacklead, is a form of carbon occurring in foliated masses in marble, schist, etc. It is soft, will make black marks on paper or other plain surfaces, and is mainly used for lead pencils. It is also a valuable lubricant. Pure graphite has found a new use with the construction of atomic piles. Important deposits occur in Siberia, Sri Lanka, Malagasy, Canada and USA.

Graptolites, fossil animals confined to Cambrian, Ordovician and Silurian strata. Once classified as hydrazoa but now considered more likely to be hemichordates.

Grasshopper. There are many species of these leaping insects which are related to the locusts and crickets. Most are vegetarians; some eat flies and caterpillars also. The chirping sound they make is made by scraping the hind legs against the wings; in some species a noise is produced by rubbing the wings together.

Gravitation. One of the four types of force known to physics. The others are electromagnetic forces and two types of nuclear force (**F15**(2)). Gravitational forces are an attraction that one piece of matter has for another; they dominate astronomical phenomena, but inside the atom they are negligible compared with the other three types of force. Einstein's General Theory of Relativity is the only theory at present extant which attempts to interpret gravitational forces in terms of more fundamental concepts. *See* **F13, 15**(2).

Graylag, the ordinary wild grey goose of Europe, the species from which domestic geese are derived; frequents fens and marshes; breeds in Iceland, Scandinavia and Scotland; distinguished by pinkish legs and feet and lack of black markings on bill.

Grebe, a diving bird of beautiful plumage found over a great part of the world on lakes and oceans. The two species familiar in Great Britain are the Dabchick or Little Grebe and the large and handsome Great Crested Grebe, which has a feathery tuft, lost in the autumn, on each side of the head. Grebes have remarkable courtship displays. The breast feathers are of a downy softness and silver lustre, for which they were formerly much hunted.

Greek Art. *See* **Hellenic Art.**

Greek Fire, a combustible supposed to have been composed of sulphur, nitre, naphtha and asphalt, used with destructive effect by the Greeks of the Eastern Empire in their wars.

Greek Kalends, equivalent to never, as only the Romans, not the Greeks, had kalends.

Green Revolution. The " green revolution " is principally due to the American agricultural expert, Dr. Norman Borlaug, who worked in Mexico on the development of new improved strains of wheat, rice, maize and other cereals. The application of new plant varieties transformed the agricultural prospects of India, Pakistan, Sri Lanka, Mexico, the Philippines and other underdeveloped countries; food importers turned into exporters. However of late the inequity in the distribution of fertilisers has affected the grain production of these countries. For his pioneering work Dr. Borlaug was awarded the 1970 Nobel peace prize. *See* **Section G, Part III.**

Greenwich Mean Time. The first Nautical Almanac, for the use of navigators and astronomers, was published by the Astronomer Royal in 1767. It was based on the meridian at Greenwich, with longitude measured east and west of 0°. A master clock, which still exists, was built at Greenwich Observatory in 1852 to control the railway station clocks and Greenwich Mean Time, or Railway Time as it was sometimes called, prevailed. In 1884 Greenwich was chosen as the prime meridian of the world and GMT became known as Universal Time. *See also* **British Standard Time.**

Gregorian Calendar. *See* **Calendar.**

Gresham's Law states that if good money, *i.e.*, money with the higher intrinsic value, and bad money are in circulation together, the bad money will tend to drive out the good money from circulation. For instance, the good money is more likely to be melted down or demanded in payment by foreign creditors.

Gretna Green, a celebrated village in Annandale and Eskdale, just over the border from England, where runaway marriages were performed from 1754 to 1856, though only completely stopped during present century.

Griffin, in ancient mythology, a winged creature with an eagle's head and the body of a lion, found in ancient sculptures of Persia and Assyria. Its origin is traced to the Hittites.

Grilse, a young salmon that has only been once to the sea.

Grimm's Law, formulated by Jacob Grimm, an eminent German philologist, lays down a principle of consonantal change in the Germanic languages. For instance, Lat. *pater*, Eng. *father*, Ger. *Vater*; Lat. *frater*, Eng. *brother*, Ger. *Bruder*; Lat. *decem*, Eng. *ten*, Ger. *zehn*.

Grogram (French = *gros grain*) a kind of rough fabric made of wool and some other fibre such as silk, mohair or cotton, formerly much used for commoner kinds of wearing apparel.

Grotto, a natural or artificial cave. Among the most famous are the blue grotto of Capri and the stalactite grotto of Antiparos (Cyclades, Aegean).

Ground Wave, that part of the energy emitted by a radio transmitter which travels along the ground; as opposed to the sky wave which is reflected back to earth by the ionosphere. With the lower radio-frequencies, the ground wave can be picked up over several thousand miles; in the broadcasting band, over a hundred or so miles; it is virtually useless at high frequencies.

Grouse, game bird of the northern latitudes where some 20 species occur. They are stout, compact, ground-dwelling birds, protectively plumaged (the willow grouse turns white in winter), the male usually being larger and more brightly coloured than the female. The red grouse of the British moorlands has been introduced into Belgium and W. Germany. Of the same family are the blackcock, ptarmigan, capercaillie, American prairie-hen and the common partridge. Grouse shooting begins in Britain on Aug. 12.

Guanaco, a large species of llama, common to South America, and utilised as a beast of burden.

Guano, the excrement of sea-birds, found in large quantities on the rocky islands of the western coasts of South America and Nauru Is. It forms a useful fertilising agent, being rich in phosphate and ammonia, and first came into use in 1841, since which time Peruvian guano has been a recognised article of commerce. Beds of guano from 15–18 m in thickness are not uncommon. Fish guano and bat guano from caves in South America and the Bahamas are also used as fertilisers.

Gudgeon, a small fresh-water fish of the carp family with 2 small barbels on the upper lip.

Guelph and Ghibelline, italianised forms of the German words " Welf " and " Waiblingen ", the names of two rival princely families whose conflicts made much of the history of Germany and Italy during the Middle Ages. The feuds between these two factions continued in Italy during the campaigns of Emperor Frederick I, and later developed into the fierce struggles of the 13th cent. between emperor and pope. In Italy the Ghibellines supported the side of the German emperors and the Guelphs the cause of the pope. The present Royal Family of England and other Northern monarchies are descended by different routes from the Guelph George I, Duke of Brunswick-Lüneburg of the House of Hanover.

Guildhall, the place of assembly of the members of a guild, and at one time, when guilds were in full strength, was practically the Town Hall. The London Guildhall is today the hall of meeting for the City of London Corporation.

Guilds for the fostering and protection of various trades have existed in England since Anglo-Saxon times, and from the 12th to the 16th cent. exercised great influence and enjoyed many privileges. There were trades' guilds and craftsmen's guilds, and in all large cities and towns there was a guild hall. Their successes in the Middle Ages led to many monopolistic abuses, and in the end it became necessary to free the country from their restrictive power. The City Guilds (Livery Companies of the City of London) derive their name from the distinctive dress assumed by their members in the 14th cent. There are 84 Guilds in existence.

Guild Socialism. *See* **Section J.**

Guillemot, a genus of sea-birds of the auk family, common in Northern Europe, two species—the Common Guillemot and the Black Guillemot—being natives of our own sea coasts, nesting on the cliffs. Brünnich's Guillemot, an Arctic species, is a rare straggler in the British Isles.

Guinea, an English gold coin of the value of twenty-one shillings, current from 1663 to 1817, and deriving its name from the first guinea coinage having been struck from gold obtained on the coast of Guinea.

Guinea-Pig, a rodent of the cavy family about 25 cm in length and with a tail so short that it does not project outside the body. It makes an excellent pet, though easily frightened. Its ancestors were species of the wild cavy of S. America said to have been domesticated by the Incas of Peru. *See* **Z20–22.**

Gules, a heraldic term, denoting a rose of red tincture, indicated by vertical lines drawn or engraved without colour.

Gulf Stream is confined entirely to the western side of the N. Atlantic and is the warm-water current flowing through the Straits of Florida from the Gulf of Mexico parallel to the American coast up as far as Cape Hatteras. From there it continues north-eastwards as a slower, broader, cooler (yet even so, relatively warm) drift of water, merging with the North Atlantic Drift and losing its identity about 40° N. Lat., 60° W. Long. It is a common error to attribute the warmth of the British Isles and Western Europe generally to the Gulf Stream but this has no influence whatever except in so far as it feeds the North Atlantic Drift. Both the Gulf Stream and the North Atlantic Drift owe their movement to the direction of the prevailing winds, and it is the south-westerly airstream coming from warmer regions and passing over the surface waters of the Atlantic Drift that brings the warmth inland to influence the climate of Western Europe.

Gull. An extremely well-known, long-winged seabird with rather short legs and webbed feet. In almost all adults the body and tail are white whilst the back and most of the wings are grey or black. In the majority of cases the plumage of juveniles is partly or entirely dusky. Gulls are omnivorous, and are very useful as scavengers. They follow ships and quickly seize upon any refuse which may be thrown overboard. There are 44 species, which vary in size from moderately small to large. With certain exceptions, such as the Kittiwake in the North Atlantic, they are not found very far from land. They are sociable and mostly breed in colonies on cliff-ledges, on islands, beaches and sandhills and among vegetation in swamps, sometimes a long way from the sea. The nest is usually substantial, and the eggs generally number from two to three. Of the 29 species breeding in the northern hemisphere, 14 occur in the British Isles. The pure white Ivory Gull is the most northerly of birds. Sabine's and the Swallow-tailed Gull have forked tails. Ross's Gull has a black ring round the neck and one species, Franklin's Gull, migrates from the North, where it breeds, to pass the winter in the Southern hemisphere.

Gums are glutinous compounds obtained from vegetable sources, soluble in cold or hot water, but not in alcohol. There are innumerable varieties. Gum Arabic is exuded from a species of acacia grown in Senegal, the Sudan, Arabia, India and other countries, and is a valuable commercial product, used in dyeing, ink-making, as a mucilage, and in medicine. India-rubber is an elastic gum. Gums are also made from starch, potatoes, wheat, etc., from seeds, bark, roots and weeds. Many so-called gums are resins.

Gun-Cotton, a powerful explosive manufactured by subjecting a prepared cotton to the prolonged action of a mixture of three parts sulphuric acid and one part of nitric acid. It burns without explosion on ignition, but by percussion explodes with a force five times greater than gunpowder does.

Gunpowder, also called "black powder", the oldest of explosive mixtures, consists of saltpetre, sulphur and charcoal, intimately mixed, the proportions being varied for different intended uses.

Gunpowder Plot was a conspiracy by a desperate band of Roman Catholics in the reign of James I to avenge the harsh treatment to which Catholics were subjected. Barrels of gunpowder were secreted in the vaults underneath the Houses of Parliament, and it was proposed to fire these when the King and his Ministers assembled on 5 November 1605. The plot was betrayed and Guy Fawkes and his co-conspirators were arrested and executed. The date serves to perpetuate the ancient custom of burning the effigy of Fawkes, a custom in which young people are the most enthusiastic participants, with bonfires, fireworks, etc.

Gurnard, a sea-fish, with large, bony head and diminutive body, of which there are some forty species. They are plentiful in British waters.

Gymnasium, originally the name given in ancient Greece to the public places where Greek youth used to exercise and receive instruction. Plato, Aristotle and other great teachers lectured there. The Greek institution was never very popular with the Romans, and it was not until the 18th and 19th cent. that the cult of combining physical with intellectual activity again found a place in educational systems. In Germany the name was applied to the classical grammar school; in this country and America to the halls where gymnastics were practised.

Gypsies, a nomadic race, believed to be of Indian origin; their language, Romany, is related to the languages of N.W. India. The Rom are spread over many parts of the world, but are most common in Europe where they appeared towards the end of the Middle Ages. The English name *gypsy* comes from the Spanish *gitano* = Egyptian; other European names are *Zigeuner* (Ger.), *zingaro* (It.), *fzigany* (Magyar), all resembling the Persian *zingar* = a saddler. Their history has been one of persecution. Hitler treated them like the Jews. In Britain since the war they have been kept increasingly on the move, but in 1968 Parliament passed a Bill to make the provision of sites a duty of local authorities. However, it is likely at the present rate of building to be many years before the 4,500 gypsy households have a site. Economic pressure has largely removed their traditional crafts of tinkering, basket-making, peg-making. The majority now deal in scrap-iron.

Gypsum, a whitish mineral consisting of hydrated sulphate of calcium. The finest gypsum is alabaster. When heated gypsum is converted into the powder called Plaster of Paris; the water it loses can be taken up when the plaster is wetted, and the reconversion of Plaster of Paris into gypsum accounts for the way in which the former sets hard. The name "Plaster of Paris" came from the location of important gypsum quarries in the Montmartre district of Paris. It was found after the flood disasters of January 1953 that gypsum could undo the effect of sea-water. By spreading it for the rain to wash into the soil, thousands of acres of farmland in Holland and Britain were made productive again.

Gyroscope is a symmetrical rapidly rotating object, typically wheel-like, which because of its mass and rotation possesses a lot of the dynamical property known as angular momentum. Basic dynamical laws tell us that angular momentum is conserved and a consequence of this is that the axis of rotation tends to stay pointing in the same direction. Disturbing influences make a gyroscope's motion complicated but the general effect of the presence of a gyroscope attached to any body is to help to stabilise the body's motion. This is made use of in reducing the rocking of ships and in compasses and control systems in aircraft, torpedoes and missiles.

H

Habeas Corpus, the name given to a writ ordering the body of a person under restraint or imprisonment to be brought into court for full inquiry into the legality of the restraint to be made. The first Habeas Corpus Act was passed in 1679, though nominally such a right had existed from Magna Carta, but some of the more despotic kings had disregarded it. In times of public peril the privilege of *habeas corpus* is sometimes temporarily suspended, many instances occurring in the history of Ireland and during the first and second world wars.

Haber Process, the important industrial process for synthesising ammonia from atmospheric nitrogen. Nitrogen and hydrogen are made to combine at high pressure (200 atmospheres or upwards) in an electric arc.

Haddock, one of the best-known fishes abounding in northern seas and averaging about 1·8 kg in weight. Related to the cod. Largely used for curing, and sold as " finnan haddies ".

Hade of veins, a mining term indicating the particular inclination that any vein, seam or strata may have from the perpendicular; thus, in Weardale the veins mainly " hade " to the north.

Hadrian's Wall. *See* **Roman walls.**

Haematite, ferric oxide, one of the principal iron ores, containing about 70% of the metal. It is usually found in kidney-shaped masses, and is specular, red or brown, in thin fragments but greyish in bulk.

Haemocyanin, the respiratory pigment of crustaceans and molluscs. It functions like haemoglobin, from which it differs in containing copper instead of iron and being blue when oxidised instead of red. *See* **F36(2).**

Haemoglobin, the pigment containing iron which gives red blood corpuscles their colour. It is a respiratory pigment, having the property of picking up oxygen when the blood passes through the lungs to produce the compound known as oxyhaemoglobin. In other parts of the body the oxyhaemoglobin breaks down, liberating oxygen, which is used in the oxidation process (respiration) that the body tissues carry on. *See* **F36(2).**

Hafiz, besides being the pseudonym of a famous Persian poet, is a title conferred upon any Mohammedan who has committed the whole of the Koran to memory.

Hafnium, a metallic element discovered by Coster and Hevesy in 1922 and important in the atomic-energy field. It occurs in most zirconium minerals to the extent of about 5 per cent.

Hagiology, a branch of literature that is wholly given up to the history of the saints, and the setting forth of the stories and legends associated with their names.

Hail, hard, roughly spherical balls of ice, consisting of white cores covered by layers of both transparent and opaque ice, frequently falling during thunderstorms. They usually do not exceed 2·5 cm in size, but hailstones as large as tennis balls have been observed. The general theory of a hailstone is that near the top of a cumulonimbus cloud a raindrop becomes frozen, grows in size by condensation and through collisions with snow particles, and eventually becomes so weighty as to overcome the ascending air currents in the cloud. Falling, it first encounters supercooled water drops, immediately freezing on it, increasing the white core, and then at lower levels ordinary water drops, freezing more slowly, producing a layer of clear ice. Before the hailstone arrives at the ground gusts and lulls may transport it several times up and down both regions, adding alternate coatings of soft white and hard clear ice.

Hake, a fish of the cod family, found in large numbers in the seas of Europe, but not in high favour for the table with fastidious feeders.

Halcyon, a term associated in olden times with the kingfisher and days of soothing calm, " halcyon days " being a frequently used expression. The legend was that the kingfisher laid its eggs on the surface of the sea at the time of the winter solstice when the sea was unruffled. Halcyon is the Greek for kingfisher.

Halibut, one of the largest of the flat fishes, averaging when full grown from 1·2–1·8 m in length, and highly esteemed for the table. Specimens of still larger size occasionally occur. It is plentifully distributed. Its two eyes are on the right side of the head.

Hallmark. A mark or group of marks, impressed by an assay office on gold or silver articles (and on platinum since 1974) guaranteeing the standard of fineness of the precious metal used in them. These marks, which have been applied to silver made in London since the beginning of the 14th cent. and perhaps earlier, make it possible to establish the year and place of assay as also the name of the maker. English pieces of silver usually have not less than four marks, viz., (1) town mark; (2) maker's mark; (3) date letter; (4) sterling mark.

The town mark is rarely changed; in London a crowned leopard's head was used from the earliest days until 1820 with only minor modifications, except for the period 1697–1720 when a lion's head erased was substituted; since 1820 the crown has been omitted.

Until the late 17th cent. a symbol was often used as a maker's mark, from 1696 to 1720 the first two letters of the maker's surname, and subsequently the maker's initials. Owing to the destruction of the earlier mark plates at Goldsmiths' Hall no maker's name prior to the late 17th cent. can be identified with certainty.

The London date letter is changed at the end of May each year, so each letter covers seven months of one year and five months of the following. The London date cycle has usually consisted of twenty letters: the alphabet of each cycle is of different style, and the letters are enclosed in shields of different shape.

The sterling mark, the lion passant, was introduced in 1544 and continued in use until 1697, when the higher Britannia standard was introduced in order to discourage the practice current amongst goldsmiths of melting down coin of the realm to make plate. The leopard's head crowned and the lion passant were then replaced by a figure of Britannia and a lion's head erased. Though the regulation imposing the higher standard was withdrawn in 1720, a small amount of Britannia standard silver continued to be made and still is made.

From 1784 until 1890 a plate tax was levied on all silver assayed in Great Britain and an additional duty mark, the sovereign's head, was used during this period. A Jubilee mark bearing the head of George V and of Queen Mary was used in between the years 1933 and 1935, and in 1953 a coronation mark with the head of Queen Elizabeth was introduced.

The tables of hallmarks in **Section D** give the London date letter cycles from 1598 to 1955. The form of town mark and sterling mark used during each cycle is given at the head of each column. Where a major alteration took place in either of these marks during a date-letter cycle, the alternative forms are also shown. The date of the change can be established by reference to the notes above. At the bottom of each page the marks used by the major provincial, Scottish and Irish assay offices are shown. Owing to lack of space, the complete date-letter cycles are not shown, but two examples only from the 17th, 18th or 19th cent. Where a provincial assay office was established in the 17th cent. or earlier, the marks of one year in the 17th and 18th cent. respectively are shown, where the office was not established until the 18th cent., the marks of one year in the 18th and 19th cent. are given.

Under the Hallmarking Act 1973 the hallmarking of platinum is now compulsory; the hallmark symbol is an orb surmounted by a cross and encompassed by a pentagon; assay offices London and Birmingham.

Halloween (31 October), the eve of All Saints' Day, a time associated, especially in Scotland, with certain pleasing superstitions attractively set forth in Burns's famous poem "Hallowe'en". It is the night when young men and maidens are supposed, by observing certain rites, to have their future wives and husbands disclosed to them.

Hallucinogen, a drug which acts upon the brain to create sensory illusions or hallucinations with a variety of emotional effects. One of the most widely studied is LSD (*q.v.*) which will produce symptoms very similar to those found in some mental disorders.

Halo, a luminous circle usually of 22° radius, surrounding sun or moon, produced by the refraction and reflection of light by ice crystals of high cirrus cloud. It is a very common occurrence, in the British Isles almost one day in three. The inner side is red and the outer a whitish-yellow colour. "Mock suns", *i.e.*, patches of light at the same elevation as the sun are much rarer occurrences, sometimes being of great beauty and brilliance. Halo is the Greek for threshing-floor. *See* **Coronae.**

Halogens, the group name for the four non-metallic elements fluorine, chlorine, bromine and iodine. The term "halogen" means "salt-producer".

Halteres, the modified hind-wings of the two-winged flies or *Diptera* (*e.g.*, the house-fly). The equilibrium in flight of these insects depends on the halteres, which are commonly called "balancers".

Hampton Court Conference, presided over at Hampton Court Palace by James I in 1604 and which brought about his authorised translation of the Bible, had an important bearing on the religious differences of the time. James refused to grant tolerations to the Puritans. This sowed the seeds of civil war. Following the conference three hundred English Puritan clergy were ejected from their livings.

Hanaper Office, a former Chancery office, deriving its name from the fact that its writs and papers were kept in a hanaper (hamper). The Chancellor's officer thus came to be known as the Hanaper. The Comptrollers of the Hanaper were abolished in England in 1842.

Hand, a measure of 4 in (10 cm), the average size of the palm; used in reckoning height of horses.

Handfasting, an informal marriage custom once prevalent in Scotland, whereby a man and woman bound themselves to cohabit for a year and a day, and at the end of that period either confirmed their contract by a regular marriage or separated.

Hansard, the title given to the official reports of Parliamentary debates, so named after Luke Hansard who in 1774 became partner in a firm of printers to the House of Commons. His son T. C. Hansard was first the printer and then the publisher of an unofficial series of parliamentary debates inaugurated by William Cobbett in 1803. In 1909 production was taken over by H.M. Stationery Office and today's volumes contain full, substantially verbatim, reports of what is said in both Houses of Parliament.

Hanseatic League was a confederation of North German towns established about 1241 for purposes of mutual protection in carrying on international commerce. The League became so powerful that it was able to dominate the foreign trade of Norway, Sweden, Denmark, and even to some extent of London. A branch was established in London and had its guild hall in Cannon Street for hundreds of years. The League existed down to the middle of the 17th cent. Hamburg, Lübeck and Bremen are the only cities which, as free ports, still by commercial courtesy retain the name of Hanse towns. *Hansa* is Old High German for Association or Merchants' Guild.

Hapsburg (*Ger.* **Habsburg**), the ruling house of Austria, 1282–1918; held title of Holy Roman Emperor, 1438–1806, except for 1740–5. The aggrandisement of the Hapsburg family was mainly brought about by a series of fortunate marriages. In 1521 when the Hapsburg power was at its zenith, Charles V divided his dominions into two branches—Austrian Hapsburg and Spanish Hapsburg. The Hapsburg Danubian Monarchy dates from 1526 when the Hungarian and Bohemian crowns were united with the Austrian patrimony of the Hapsburg. The triple union lasted 400 years. The murder of the heir to the Hapsburg thrones, Francis Ferdinand, at Sarajevo in 1914, provoked the outbreak of the first world war. Francis Joseph's great-nephew, Charles, abdicated in 1918. (Prof. C. A. Macartney's authoritative work, *The Habsburg Empire, 1790–1918*, was published in 1969.)

Hara-kiri, the custom of suicide, as formerly practised in Japan, when in disgrace.

Hardware, the electrical, electronic magnetic and mechanical parts of a computer or data-processing system. *See* **Software.**

Hare, a rabbit-like animal with longer ears and legs. There are many kinds of hare distributed over the northern hemisphere and in Africa south to the Cape. They do not burrow as do rabbits but rely on camouflage, speed and mobility for safety. *See* **Game.**

Harleian MSS. comprise some thousands of volumes of MSS. and documents, collected by the first Earl of Oxford (1661–1724) and his son Edward. After the death of the latter, his widow handed the MSS. over to the nation for £10,000, and they are deposited in the British Museum.

Harlequin, the buffoon of ancient Italian comedy. As adapted to the British stage, however, harlequin is a pantomime character only, in love with Columbine, appearing in parti-coloured garments and carrying a wand, by which he exercises a magic influence in thwarting the fantastic tricks of the clown and pantaloon.

Harmattan, a dry wind which may blow between January and May across the Sahara to the Gulf of Guinea. Although affording relief from the tropical heat, vegetation withers because of its extreme dryness and much irritation is caused by the clouds of fine dust which it carries.

Harmonic Motion, regular periodic motion of the kind exemplified by a ball bobbing up and down at the end of a spring, and by the piston in a steam engine. It may be simple (simple harmonic motion) or composed of two or more simple harmonic motions. In simple harmonic motion the acceleration is proportional to the distance of the moving body from its original rest position.

Harp-seal, the ordinary Greenland seal, with a dark harp-shaped marking on its back, hence its name. It abounds in Newfoundland waters and further northward towards the Arctic.

Harpy Eagle, a large bird of prey named from the winged monsters of Greek mythology, inhabiting the forest regions of Central and South America. There are eight species, one with handsome grey plumage and large crest which attacks and kills animals much larger than itself, and was called by the Aztecs "winged wolf".

Harrier, a bird of prey of the falcon family; of the various species distributed over the world, three breed in Britain: the moorland Hen harrier, the Marsh harrier and Montagu's harrier. They are large birds with long tails, long legs, long wings and gliding flight. They nest on the ground and eat small mammals, frogs, lizards and small birds.

Hartebeest, common African antelope of a grey-brown colour, with ringed and knotted horns bending backward and tapering to sharp points; gregarious, of large size. There are several species.

Harvest Bug, a very small insect, of a dark red colour, which appears in large numbers in the fields in autumn, and is peculiarly irritating to animals and man by the tenacity with which it attaches itself to the skin and burrows underneath. Probably the larvae of spinning mites (Trombidoids). In the USA they are called "chiggers".

Harvest Moon, the full moon that occurs nearest to the autumn equinox, in September. It rises for several nights running about the same time, and yields an unusually brilliant series of moonlight nights.

Harvestmen are, like spiders, members of the arachnid class but belong to the distinctly different order of Phalangida. They are common in the countryside in autumn and have small oval bodies and eight long slender legs which besides being mere organs of locomotion also act as sense organs. Known as "daddy longlegs" in America.

Hashish, an Arabic word for the narcotic substance prepared from the hemp plant (*Cannabis sativa*). It is known by a variety of names, *e.g.*, bhang in India and marijuana in America.

Hatchment, in heraldry, is a square board, in vertical diagonal position, placed outside a house or on the tomb at the death of a member of a family and so arranged that it indicates the sex and condition of the deceased.

Hawfinch, a well-known European bird of the finch family, having a variegated plumage, a sturdy bill and black-and-white tail. In England it is found in the Midland and Eastern counties, and locally in Scotland.

Hawk. This name is applied to almost any diurnal bird of prey other than eagle, falcon or vulture, but in its strict sense applies only to the *Accipiter* genus—the small Sparrow Hawk and the larger Goshawk, round-winged, long-tailed birds with barred under-parts. They prey upon small birds captured in flight and small mammals.

Hawk-moths, large species of moths, thick of body and strong of wing, which fly with rapid swooping motion, hence the name. There are numerous handsome species in Britain.

Hearth-Money was a tax laid on hearths (in all houses paying the church and poor rates). Charles II introduced it in 1662, and it was repealed in the reign of William and Mary.

Heat, after prolonged controversy over whether or not heat is a "substance" (formerly called "caloric"), it was established in the 19th cent. that heat is a form of energy; it is in fact the combined kinetic and potential energy of the atoms of which a body is composed. Heat can be turned into other forms of energy, *e.g.*, a red hot body loses heat by radiating it in the form of electromagnetic waves ("radiant heat"—chiefly infra-red rays). Heat may also be transferred from one place to another by conduction and, in fluids, by convection. All three processes occur when a glowing fire heats a room. A unit quantity of heat is the calorie, which is the amount of heat sufficient to raise the temperature of 1 g of water by 1°C. In general, adding heat to a body raises its temperature. The number of calories required per gram of material to raise the temperature 1°C is called the *specific heat* of the material. However, adding heat may not raise the temperature but may instead cause a change of state, *e.g.*, from solid to liquid (melting) or liquid to gas (evaporation). The amount of heat required to melt 1 gram of a solid is called the latent heat of melting. Similarly, there is a latent heat of evaporation. Strictly speaking, the specific and latent heats of a substance depend on how much its pressure and volume are allowed to vary during the measurements. Water has a high specific heat, and this makes the oceans a vast heat reservoir, a factor of great meteorological significance. The science of heat is called thermodynamics, and is of great importance in physics and chemistry. *See* **F17**.

Heat Pump, essentially a refrigerator working in reverse, *i.e.*, a device which warms up one place, say, a house by releasing into it heat transferred from another place, say, the air or earth outside the house. The idea is attributed to Lord Kelvin (1852) and later Haldane used a heat pump to heat his house in Scotland. In summer, a house could be cooled by operating the device in reverse. As in a domestic refrigerator, the heat is transferred by a suitable fluid whose circulation has to be driven by an external supply of energy, *e.g.*, by running a mechanical compressor. With good design and favourable conditions, the energy required to run the heat pump is considerably less than would be required to produce the same warming effect directly. Since the 1930s heat pumps have been produced commercially for domestic and industrial use but, as always, careful consideration is needed to decide whether in a particular application they are cheaper to run than alternative methods of heating.

Heath, flowering plants of the *Ericaceae* family. Heaths are widely distributed over uncultivated spaces of Europe and Africa. In Britain they are represented by heather (of which there are several species) and ling (*Calluna vulgaris*), which cover thousands of acres of moorland. Some of the African or Cape heaths are very beautiful and much prized by florists. One species of heath (*Erica arborea*) which grows in S. Europe and N. Africa has close-grained woody rootstock used for making briar pipes. In N. Europe acid heathlands, dominated by heather and ling, form one of the most wide-spread vegetation areas created by man through the destruction of former oak forests, grazing and burning. *See* **Erica, T7**(2).

Heat Wave is a spell of very hot weather, due chiefly in the British Isles to a warm southerly current of air caused by the presence of an anticyclone over western or central Europe at the same time as a depression is stationary over the Atlantic. High humidity increases the discomfort.

Hegira, an Arab term signifying departure or flight, and used in reference to Mohammed's departure from Mecca for Medina, A.D. 622, from which date the Mohammedan era is reckoned.

Helicopter, heavier-than-air aircraft which obtains its lift from blades rotating above the fuselage in windmill-fashion. The first successful helicopters were the Focke-Wulf 61, a German machine (1936), and the VS-300, designed by Igor Sikorsky, flown in 1937. Helicopters can hover, and rise and descend vertically, in addition to being capable of horizontal flight.

Heliotrope, a favourite sweet-scented flowering plant, common in tropical and sub-tropical countries; the Peruvian heliotrope is the "cherry pie" of our summer garden borders. *See* **T9**(1).

Helium, a gaseous element first discovered by means of the spectroscope in the sun's atmosphere. This discovery, made in 1868 by the astronomer Sir Norman Lockyer, was followed in 1895 by Sir William Ramsay's proof that the element existed on earth. He found it in the uranium ore, clevite. Later it was established that helium is formed by the radioactive decay of many elements which emit α-particles (nuclei of helium atoms) and is contained in all radioactive minerals. The largest source of helium is natural gas, the richest in helium being the gas from certain wells in Utah, USA. Next to hydrogen, helium is the lightest gas known, has a lifting power equal to 92% of hydrogen and the advantage that it is inert and non-inflammable. It is used for inflating airships. Ordinary air contains 1 part in 200,000 of helium. It was the last gaseous element to be liquefied, this being achieved by Onnes in 1908 in Leyden. Liquid helium has many remarkable properties only imperfectly understood. As well as being scientifically fascinating it is indispensable in cryogenics (*q.v.*) as a medium for cooling other substances to temperatures near absolute zero. Hydrogen fusion in the "H bomb" produces helium.

Hellebore, a plant of the *Ranunculaceae* (buttercup) family. The best-known British examples are the green and stinking varieties. There is also a garden kind which flowers in December called the Christmas Rose. Hellebore yields a bitter substance which forms a drastic purgative, but is now little used. *See* **T9**(1).

Hellenic Art. The art of ancient Greece may be roughly divided into three periods: the prehistoric period (*c.* 1500–1000 B.C.) of the bronze age Mycenaeans; the archaic period (*c.* 600–500 B.C.); and the classical period (*c.* 500–300 B.C.). Of the first period centred on Mycenae in Peloponnesus but extending to the coasts of Asia and the city of Troy we can mention only the massive stone gateways and the shaft graves of Mycenae, where the archaeologist Schliemann discovered painted vases, gold cups, bronze swords and ornaments of what had once been a great, if primitive, civilisation. During the archaic period sculpture was the principal form of art expression. The magnificent male and female figures are reminiscent of Egyptian art, but are distinctive in liveliness of facial expression. The vase-paintings of this period became more elaborate, depicting scenes from mythology or ceremonial events. Typical of classical Greek art is the representation of the beautiful and healthy human body deliberately posed and often carrying out heroic or athletic acts. The vast majority of these statues are known to us only through Roman copies. The *Hermes* of Praxiteles (born *c.* 385 B.C.) is possibly the only existing statue which can be assigned with any degree of certainty to an individual artist. Almost the whole of the Greek genius in architecture was expended on temples which are all basically similar in design—a rectangle with a low-pitched gabled roof resting on side walls. The three orders Doric, Corinthian and Ionic mainly referred to the type of column used, but naturally the whole building was influenced thereby. Some of the main buildings are on the Acropolis, a hill outside Athens, on which stand the Parthenon (from the outer frieze of which the Elgin marbles (*q.v.*), now mostly in the British Museum, were taken), the Erechtheum, famous for its Porch of Maidens, and the gateway known as the Propylaea with its broad flight of marble steps. Apart from that on vases, no Greek painting has come down to us, although Greek painters existed and were noted in their time. All we have are copies in mosaic and fresco made by the Romans, at Naples and Pompeii. Of Greek literature in prose, verse and the drama little can be said here. To the early period (*i.e.*, the archaic age) belong Homer's *Iliad* and *Odyssey*, Hesiod's long poem *Work and Days* and Sappho's love poems, and Pindar's Odes. The period of Pericles in the 5th cent. B.C. produced more great literature than any comparable period in history: the philosophical writings of Plato and Aristotle, the tragedies of Aeschylus, Euripides and Sophocles, the comedies of Aristophanes—all these are still part of the European tradition, and together with Greek architecture played a major part in the Renaissance (*see* **Section J**).

Hellenistic Art, the art of the period of Greek civilisation which began with the conquests of Alexander the Great (356–323 B.C.) and lasted until his former empire (which encompassed most of the Middle East and part of North Africa) was conquered by the Romans in 146 B.C. Culturally it was an important period because it spread Greek culture far beyond its original boundaries—even as far as the north of India, and its centres spread from Athens to the cities of Alexandria in Egypt, Antioch in Syria and Pergamum in Asia Minor. But equally Eastern culture spread to the West: democracy was replaced by absolute monarchy, cosmopolitanism took the place of the Greek tendency to believe that all who were not Greeks were barbarians, and mystical philosophies took the place of Greek rationalism. This was a sensuous, secular, pleasure-loving, rootless society and these tendencies were reflected in its art. Hellenistic sculpture was sensual, effeminate and violently emotional, yet it depicted individuals and not always noble or beautiful ones. (Classical Greek sculpture was idealistic, showed types rather than individuals and appealed to the intellect rather than the emotions.) Some of the best examples came from the school at Pergamum and later from the island of Rhodes, and the titles themselves speak of their nature: *The Dying Gaul, Gaul Slaying his Wife and Himself*, and the famous *Laocoön* (representing Laocoön and his two sons being crushed by two enormous serpents). All these date from about 240 to 50 B.C.—for the culture did not immediately end with the Roman conquest. The enormous frieze of the altar of the temple in Pergamum depicts a battle between gods and giants with tremendous realism and brutal violence far removed from the serene art of classical times. Portrait sculpture is typical of Hellenistic art, where it may almost be said to have been invented, since such ventures in the past had been idealistic rather than realistic. The great Hellenistic cities were geometrically planned and fine public buildings made their appearance in which the slender and graceful Ionic or the ornate Corinthian columns took the place of the more austere and heavy classical ones. Alexandria was celebrated for its vast libraries and was the centre of a brilliant intellectual life (the Septuagint or Greek translation of the Bible was prepared here). Here too worked the mathematicians Euclid and Archimedes, the physicians Erasistratus and Herophilus, and the geographer Pytheas. But Hellenistic literature was a pale reflection of the glories of the past and we mention only the comedies of Menander and the pastoral verse of Theocritus of Syracuse.

Hemiptera, the order of insects to which belong the true bugs. Their wing structure is in most species incomplete, hence the term hemiptera. This order includes the familiar water insects, the water boatman and water skater, also the aphids, cicadas, leaf hoppers, scale insects. *See* **T29(2)**.

Hemlock, a plant of the *Umbelliferae* family, growing in all parts of Britain, and containing a strong alkaloid poison. Used medicinally, this alkaline substance is of considerable service, being a powerful sedative. According to Pliny, hemlock was the poison used by the Athenians in putting criminals to death.

Hemp (*Cannabis sativa*), name of a plant native to Asia, now cultivated widely for the valuable fibre contained in the stalk or in some species in the leaves. Hemp fibre has been replaced by cotton for textiles and by jute for sacks and is now chiefly used for cordage and twine. It contains a resinous substance from which the narcotic hashish is made. The seed yields a valuable oil. The term hemp is also used for other fibre plants, including manila hemp from the Philippines, sunn hemp from India, sisal from W. and E. Africa and phorium from New Zealand.

Henbane, a plant found in Britain and other parts of Europe and Northern Asia. It belongs to the potato family *Solanaceae*, grows mostly on waste ground and bears yellow-brown flowers veined with purple. The leaves yield a poisonous alkaloid substance which, medicinally prepared and administered, is of great use. Tincture of henbane is often preferred to laudanum.

Heptarchy, a word derived from the Greek *hepta*, seven, and denoting the seven kingdoms (*archai*) into which Anglo-Saxon England was divided before 900. The seven were Kent, Essex, Sussex, Wessex, Mercia, East Anglia and Northumbria.

Heracleum, a plant of the *Umbelliferae* family, common in southern and central Europe, though only one species, the cow parsnip, grows in England. It has a bitter root, and from the juice of the stem an intoxicating liquor is occasionally prepared.

Herald, an officer of state empowered to make formal proclamations and deliver messages from the sovereign or other high personage whom he serves. In the developments which took place in armorial bearings, the herald was the functionary charged with the duty of their proper depiction.

Heraldry, the knowledge of armorial bearings, was mainly the outcome of the love of outward distinction which prevailed in mediaeval times. "Heraldry," says Stubbs, "became a handmaid of chivalry, and the marshalling of badges, crests, coat-armour, pennons, helmets and other devices of distinction grew into an important branch of knowledge." The *shield*, or *escutcheon*, is the ground upon which armorial signs are traced, the colour of the shield being called the *tincture*, the signs recorded the *charges*. There are seven *tinctures*—*or* (gold), *argent* (silver), *gules* (red), *azure* (blue), *vert* (green), *purpure* (purple) and *sable* (black). The *charges* are classed as "Honourable" and "Subordinate" ordinaries, comprising lines and geometrical forms; and "Common" ordinaries, which latter includes all representations of natural objects. There is also a system of external signs, such as crowns, coronets, mitres, helmets, mantlings, wreaths and crests, each having its distinctive significance. For other distinguishing marks see **Hatchments, Quartering, Rampant.**

Heralds' College or **College of Arms,** was incorporated by Richard III in 1483. Its head is the Earl Marshal (an office hereditary in the family of the Dukes of Norfolk), and there are three Kings of Arms, six Heralds and four Pursuivants. The business transacted is wholly connected with the tracing of genealogies and the granting of armorial bearings. In Scotland the Heraldic functions are performed by the Lord Lyon King of Arms.

Herbarium, a systematically classified collection of preserved plants. One of the largest in the world is at the Royal Botanic Gardens at Kew.

Heredity is the study of the transmission of physical and mental characteristics from one generation to another. Gregor Mendel (1822–84), a great experimenter in the field of inheritance, established the principle embodied in Mendel's law in his work published in 1866. The ideas which he then put forward were forgotten until the early years of this century, but today they form the basis of the modern study of genetics. Genes are the units of heredity; they are contained in the chromosomes of the cell nucleus. In human cells there are 46 chromosomes—22 pairs of characteristic shape, and a 23rd (the sex chromosomes) similar in women and dissimilar in men, which unite in the process of fertilisation. An individual can only develop, even under the most favourable surroundings, as far as his inherited characteristics, *i.e.*, his genes will allow him to do so. It is in the development of personality that the interplay between heredity and environment becomes most apparent. *See* **The Evolution of Organisms, Section F, Part IV,** *also* **Q27.**

Hermaphrodite, animals or plants possessing both male and female reproductive organs, *e.g.*, snail, earthworms, most flowering plants.

Hermit Crab, a decapod, with a soft asymmetrical body which it protects by thrusting it into an empty gastropod shell, *e.g.*, whelk, which it carries about, only abandoning it when necessary for a larger one. Found in all seas, many live in commensal relationship with sea anemones etc.

Heron, a large wading bird with long curved neck and pointed bill, is a member of the *Ardeidae* family, of which there are many species. Egrets and bitterns are included as herons. Herons are to be met with in marsh lands and near rivers and lakes, where they feed on fish and frogs. They nest in trees in large numbers, these colonies being called heronries. The common heron is native to England, and other species from the Continent are frequent visitors.

Herring, a common sea-fish, related to the sardine and pilchard, abounding in northern seas and found mainly in Scottish waters. The fishing season proper lasts from May to October, the enormous shoals being followed as they move from place to place. The spawning season is about the end of August. One female herring may produce 20 to 50 thousand eggs, which sink to the sea-bed, where they develop.

Hibernation, the dormant condition in which numerous mammals, reptiles, amphibians, insects, plants, etc., pass the winter. The rate of metabolism slows down, and the body temperature drops to that of the surroundings. Work on these low temperatures and their physiological effect has led to improved surgical techniques. Animals of the torrid regions pass through an analogous period (aestivation) during the hot season, when the sources of food are dried up.

Hickory, several species of American tree of the walnut family, remarkable for its very hard, solid, heavy white wood, and bearing an edible, four-lobed nut.

Hieratic Art, a type of art (typified by the major part of the art of ancient Egypt) which is (*a*) exclusively religious and (*b*) conventionally based on earlier forms and traditions.

Hieroglyphics are the earliest form of pictured symbolic expressions, and are supposed to have been introduced by the ancient Egyptians. They consist of rude depictions of animals, plants, signs and objects, and in their later examples express, in abridged form, ideas and records from which significant historical information has been gleaned. The deciphering of Egyptian hieroglyphics long formed an ardent study, but gradually the key to the riddle was discovered, and most of the ancient records can now be understood. Besides the Egyptian there are also Hittite, Minoan and Mayan hieroglyphic scripts. *See* **Rosetta Stone.**

Hi-Fi means high fidelity and refers to gramophones, tape recorders and similar apparatus which will *faithfully* reproduce sounds. It is not too difficult these days to amplify electrical signals without distorting them much; it is more difficult to turn electrical impulses into exactly equivalent sound waves (with a loudspeaker, for example) or *vice versa* (with a microphone or gramophone pick-up). Pick-up and loudspeaker are therefore often the weak links in domestic hi-fi and faults in their design, deficiencies in the electronic amplifiers, imperfect gramophone motors can all contribute to audible results ranging from the tolerable to the execrable. Almost perfect sound reproduction is however available to enthusiasts possessing a suitable combination of discrimination, know-how and financial resources. There are periodical magazines which provide guidance.

Hindi, the official language of India.

Hinduism. *See* **Section J.**

Hindustani, the spoken form of Hindi (written in Devanagari script) and Urdu (written in Arabic characters).

Hippogriff, a fabulous animal like a horse in body, but with the head, wings and front legs and claws of an eagle. The monster frequently appears in the romances of the Middle Ages.

Hippopotamus or " river-horse ", the largest living representative of the hog family, widely distributed over Africa, where it lives in herds. It is of immense bulk, attaining a length of 3·6 m and a weight of 4 tonnes and stands about 1·5 m high. Its skin is hairless and about 5 cm thick, and it has a pair of tusks often weighing as much as 2·7 kg. It spends most of its time in the water, and lives entirely on vegetation, both aquatic and terrestrial. The pigmy hippopotamus, which occurs in forests and swamps in W. Africa, is only half the size.

Histology is the study of the structure of plant and animal tissues. These mainly consist of groups of cells with similar functions, *e.g.*, muscle, brain tissue.

Hittites, an ancient race (often mentioned in the Old Testament) who inhabited Cappadocia (region of Eastern Asia Minor) from the third to the first millennium B.C. Excavations have revealed that they attained a high level of civilisation round about 1350 B.C. The Hittites were rivals of Egypt, disputing with the Pharaohs the mastery of the Middle East. They were the first to smelt iron successfully.

Hobby, a bird of the falcon family, 30–35 cm long. Local breeding visitor to England and Wales, April–September; irregular visitor to Scotland and Ireland. They winter in Africa.

Hog, the common name of animals of the Suina family, including the wild boar, pig and sow. The wild boar, *Sus scrofa*, is the common ancestor. The skin of the hog is covered with bristles, the snout truncated and each foot has four hoofed toes. Hogs are omnivorous feeders and eat almost anything that is given them.

Hogmanay, the Scottish New Year's Eve festival and a national holiday of the country. The custom of demanding Hogmanay bread is still upheld in many parts of Scotland.

Hogshead, a cask of varying capacity, also a specific measure. In the old English measure a hogshead was 63 old gallons of wine (= $52\frac{1}{2}$ imperial gallons = 238·6 litres). Of beer 54 old gallons make a hogshead.

Holly, a hardy evergreen shrub, largely grown in England. Its bright dark green prickly curved leaves and clusters of red berries are familiar in all parts of the country, and used as house decoration between Christmas Eve and Twelfth Night, probably a relic from Roman and Teutonic customs. Its wood is white and hard, valued for carved work, while its bark yields a gummy substance which is converted into bird-lime.

Hologram, a photographic record, taken under special optical conditions, of light reflected from a scene or object. The hologram is typically a piece of film. However it is nothing like a photographic negative of the ordinary kind;

for one thing it will show an unintelligible pattern of light and dark patches. Nevertheless if it is illuminated (again under special optical conditions) the light coming through it will form a *three dimensional* image of the original object. Another radical difference between a hologram and an ordinary film is that if the hologram is cut up, each fragment can be used to construct the entire image. Holography, as a method of recording and reproducing photographic information, was conceived by Gabor in 1947 but was only fully realised in practice after the invention of the laser (*q.v.*), which made available powerful sources of coherent light. The use of laser light is one of the "special conditions" referred to above. Technical applications are being explored in many laboratories. Gabor received the 1971 Nobel prize for his discovery and invention.

Holy Alliance, an alliance ostensibly for conserving religion, justice and peace in Europe, but used for repressing popular tendencies towards constitutional government. Formed by Alexander I of Russia, Francis I of Austria and Frederick William III of Prussia, at Paris on 26 September 1815. Subsequently joined by all the sovereigns of Europe, except the Pope and the King of England. It ended after the 1830 revolution in France.

Holy Coat of Treves, a garment preserved in the Cathedral of Trèves and said to have been worn by Christ. It was brought from Jerusalem by the Empress Helena in the fourth century.

Holy Rood, an annual Roman Catholic festival held on 14 September to celebrate the Elevation of the Cross in commemoration of its re-erection in Jerusalem by the Emperor Heraclius in 628 after retaking it from the Persians. Also included in the Church of England calendar.

Holyrood, the ancient royal palace at Edinburgh, dating from the 15th cent., and inhabited by many Scottish sovereigns, notably Mary Stuart, the rooms occupied by her (including the one in which Rizzio was murdered) being still shown. It is now known as Holyrood House and is still used as a royal residence.

Holy Roman Empire, the title which the German Empire received in 962 when Pope John XII crowned Otto I at Rome. It endured until 1806 when Francis II became Emperor of Austria.

Holy Water, water blessed by a priest and kept in small fonts at the entrance to Roman Catholic churches, and used by worshippers going in, and out, or by priests in sprinkling.

Holy Week is the week preceding Easter Sunday, and includes the days of the Sufferings of Christ, ending on Good Friday.

Homoeopathy. *See* **Section J.**

Honey, the sweet syrup formed by bees from the nectar of flowers, the sucrose in the nectar being converted into a mixture of the simple sugars, glucose and fructose. Hybla, an ancient town of Sicily, on the southern slope of Mt. Etna, was famous for its honey.

> "For your words, they rob the Hybla bees
> And leave them honeyless." (*Julius Caesar*).

Honey-eater, an Australian bird (of which there are many species) provided with a long curved bill and tufted tongue. It lives by sucking the "nectar" from the flowers which abound in rural parts of Australia and New Zealand.

Hookah, an Oriental pipe for tobacco smoking, the smoke being drawn through the water of a goblet (commonly a coconut shell) by means of a long flexible tube.

Hoopoe, a remarkably handsome bird with vivid black and white-barred wings and tail and black-tipped crest which opens like a fan. Ranges over Europe, Asia and Africa. It has bred in England and Wales and occurs in the British Isles in small numbers at all seasons. Other species are confined to Africa, Madagascar and India.

Hops, the female "cones" of the hop plant used in brewing; their essential oils give beer an aromatic flavour, and their tannin and resin act as a preservative as well as accounting for the bitter taste desired. The hop is a perennial climber belonging to the mulberry family. The male and female organs are on separate plants; as only the female flower-heads are commercially useful, female plants predominate in a hop garden, only a very few male plants being grown so that the female flowers can be fertilised.

Horizon, the limit of vision, the apparent line where sea and sky, or land and sky meet. This is termed the visible horizon. An ordinary person at the height of 1·5 m can see for 4·8 km, at 6 m 9·6 km, at 15 m 14·8 km and at 305 m 67·5 km. The figures are approximate.

Hormone, a chemical substance which is released by one part of the body and produces a response in other parts after having been carried there by the bloodstream or some other transport system. Prolactin, for example, is a hormone produced by the pituitary gland of nursing mothers and serves to stimulate and maintain the milk supply.

Horn *or* **French Horn,** a brass instrument of the trumpet family (*i.e.*, played by three valves) whose tube is very thin and long (Horn in F = 12 ft). In consequence the tube is curled in a complicated manner. Owing to the sweet tone it is capable of producing, the Horn sometimes plays as part of the wood-wind.

Hornbill, large bird found in Africa and oriental regions. Some species have a casque or a horny growth above the very powerful beak. It feeds on fruits. When the female has laid her eggs in the hollow of a tree, the male bird stops up the entrance, and keeps her imprisoned until the hatching is completed and the young ones are able to fly. There are about 45 species.

Hornblende, the commonest member of the amphibole group of minerals, a silicate of calcium, magnesium, iron and aluminium, of a dark green colour. It is a constituent of numerous rocks, including diorite, syenite and hornblende schist.

Horned Viper, any of a number of species of African viper which have scales over each eye resembling horns. Their bite is usually very poisonous. The significance of the horns is not known.

Hornet, a general name for many of the bigger wasps. It usually nests in hollow trees, and despite its rather fiercesome appearance does not sting unless unduly provoked.

Horology, the science of time-measurement, including the construction and management of clocks, watches, etc. Instruments of this kind are not known to have existed before the 12th cent. and until the introduction of the pendulum in the 17th cent., clocks were ill-regulated and inaccurate. The time-recording mechanisms of the present day include (*a*) the *clock*, which shows the hours and minutes by hands, and strikes the hours, and sometimes quarters; (*b*) the *timepiece*, which is not generally a fixture and shows the time, but does not strike; (*c*) the *watch*, which is a pocket time-keeper; (*d*) the *chronometer*, which indicates the minutest portions of time; (*e*) electric timepieces, mains electric clocks; (*f*) the highly accurate quartz-crystal and atomic clocks used for astronomical purposes. *See* **Clocks.**

Horse Chestnut, one of the large forest trees, with ample branches, and full foliage, and much esteemed for parks and ornamental grounds. The flowers, which appear in May, are white tinged with red and yellow. The tree is native to the mountainous regions of northern Greece. *See also* **Chestnut.**

Horse Guards, the building in Whitehall which until 1872 was the headquarters of the Commander-in-Chief of the British Army. The archway is still sentinelled by mounted guards.

Horse Latitudes, the latitudes of the sub-tropical high pressure systems, between the trade winds and the prevailing westerlies, characterised by light variable winds and low humidity.

Hospitallers, Knights, were of the order of St. John of Jerusalem, at first devoted to the aid of the sick, but afterwards military monks, who became prominent figures in the Crusades of the 12th cent. They adopted the Benedictine black habit with the eight-pointed cross worn by the modern St. John's Ambulance Brigade. In 1309 they took Rhodes, but were expelled by the Ottomans in 1522. In 1530 the emperor Charles V gave them the island of Malta, which, as Knights of Malta, they held until 1798, when they were dislodged by Napoleon. The Knights still survive as a sovereign order, with headquarters in Rome. *See* **Templars** and **Teutonic Order.**

Hottentots, name given to certain African natives by Dutch settlers in the 17th cent. They used to occupy the greater part of Cape Colony and though driven out a number still survive in S.W. Africa. Appear to be related to the Bushmen, though their culture is more advanced. In addition to herding, they practise some farming and know how to smelt iron.

Hounds are dogs that were originally bred and trained for hunting, such as the greyhound, foxhound, bloodhound, wolfhound, deerhound, beagle, harrier, etc., but now often kept also as domestic dogs. The greyhound, deerhound and wolfhound hunt by sight, the others, with the bloodhound first in order, track by scent.

House Flies are world-wide and prolific. Their eggs are hatched within 24 hours of being laid, and full maturity is attained in a month. They feed mainly on decayed animal and vegetable matter.

Hovercraft, or air cushion vehicle, is a craft which is lifted on a pad of air underneath it. This pad or cushion must be at a pressure higher than that of the atmosphere and it is made by sucking in air above the craft and ejecting it in a downward stream all round the lower edge. The stream is guided by a flexible skirt and the high pressure air pad is contained partly by the skirt and partly by the air stream itself which forms a continuous air curtain all round the vehicle. Hovercraft are being intensively developed and there are variations in the basic scheme just described and also in the means of propulsion which can be by air or water jets or propellers. Hovercraft were devised by Cockerell in the 1950s and a full-scale example appeared before the British public in June 1959. Craft of over 100 tonnes are made commercially and much bigger ones conceived. The air pad support means that hovercraft can move over land, water or marsh. Cross-Channel hovercraft were introduced in 1966.

Howler Monkey, a genus of South American monkey noted for a laryngeal conformation which enables it to emit a loud reverberant noise something between a yell and a howl, as the name suggests.

Huanuco-bark, a medicinal bark, brought from the Peruvian town of that name, and derived from the *Cinchona micrantha* tree. *See* **Cinchona.**

Huguenots, a name applied to the French Protestant communities of the 16th and 17th cent. Henry of Navarre, by the Edict of Nantes in 1598, granted them religious freedom, but more than a quarter of a century before—24 August 1572—thousands had been put to death in the massacre of St. Bartholomew. The revocation of the Edict of Nantes by Louis XIV in 1685 drove thousands into exile in England, Holland, Germany and America.

Humanism. *See* **Section J.**

Humble-bee or **Bumble-bee,** the common name of the insects of the genus *bombus*, of the Hymenoptera order. They live in small communities comprising males, females and drones, their habitations being underground. They do not have one queen bee only like the hive bee, but several females occupy the same nest, and these alone live through the winter, breeding and forming new colonies in the spring. Their sting does not have a barb like the honey bee's.

Humidity, the state of the atmosphere with respect to the water-vapour it contains. "Absolute humidity" is defined as the density of the vapour present, while "relative humidity", more frequently employed indicates the degree of saturation, *i.e.*, the ratio of the actual vapour pressure to the saturation vapour pressure at the particular temperature, expressed as a percentage.

Humming Birds are so called because of the humming noise made by the vibration of their wings in flying. They are of radiant plumage, and are among the smallest birds. The smallest bird in the world is the Fairy or Princess Helen's humming bird of Cuba, whose body is only 5·7 cm long. There are from four to five hundred species, and they are confined wholly to North and South America, being most numerous in the tropical latitudes. They have long, slender bills and tubular tongues which reach down into flowers to suck up the nectar on which they feed.

Hummum, the original name for what is now called the Turkish Bath in this country. One of the first of these baths to be established in London was the Hummums in Covent Garden.

Hundred, the ancient divisional name given to a portion of a county for administration or military purposes. It is supposed to imply the territory occupied by a hundred families; or the space of a hundred hides of land, or the capacity of providing 100 soldiers. Each hundred had its hundred court, with powers similar to those of a manor court, but this was abolished in 1867 by County Court Act.

Hundred Days, the interval of time between Napoleon Bonaparte's entry into Paris after his escape from Elba and his departure after his abdication, extending from 20 March 1815 to 28 June. During this period occurred the battle of Waterloo, 18 June.

Hundred Years' War, a term applied to the almost incessant contest between England and France, lasting from 1338 to 1453, including such famous battles as Crécy, Poitiers and Agincourt, and engaging successively Edward III, Henry V and Henry VI, among English kings.

Huns, a fierce Asiatic race which swept over eastern Europe in the 4th cent. Under Attila about the middle of the 5th cent. they obtained control of a large portion of central and eastern Europe, forcing even Rome to pay tribute. Their defeat at Châlons-sur-Marne in 451 by a mixed army of Romans, Goths and Teutonic tribes, and the death of Attila in 453, terminated their empire.

Hurdy-Gurdy, an Italian rustic so-called musical stringed instrument of the lute order, the sounds of which are produced by the action of a rosined wheel turned by the left hand, the notes being made by the fingering of the right hand.

Hussites. *See* **Section J.**

Hurricane. *See* **Cyclone** *and* **Wind.**

Hydra, an aquatic animal of simple structure, whose body is in the form of a cylindrical tube, with a disc-shaped base by which it attaches itself to any shifting substance. Its mouth is surrounded by tentacles by which it catches its food. The Hydra has the power of reproducing lost parts.

Hydrates are compounds containing water of crystallisation.

Hydraulic Ram, a form of automatic pump, used to raise water to a height by the action of its own falling velocity.

Hydraulics, the science of applied hydrodynamics, or water-machine engineering, ranging from pumps to marine engines.

Hydrocarbons are compounds of carbon and hydrogen. They include the *paraffins*, which are saturated compounds (*e.g.*, methane); the ethylene, acetylene and other series which are unsaturated; compounds with ring structures, *e.g.*, benzene, naphthalene and anthracene. Petroleum is composed almost entirely of hydrocarbons. *See* **F23.**

Hydrochloric Acid, a solution of hydrogen chloride gas in water, and resulting in considerable quantities as a by-product of the soda-ash or salt-cake manufacture. Its solution forms the common hydrochloric or muriatic acid of commerce. It is present to the extent of nearly half a per cent. in the digestive juice secreted by the stomach.

Hydrocyanic Acid, cyanide of hydrogen or prussic acid; very poisonous, and of the odour of bitter almonds. It is formed by the action of acids on sodium or potassium cyanide. Used to kill wasps (and in the gas chamber in the USA). It is a very important chemical on account of the reactions of its derivatives in many synthetic fields. Discovered by Scheele in 1782.

Hydroelectric Schemes. The sun's energy has been indirectly exploited in the past by harnessing the energy of the winds and rain. The climate is due, essentially, to differential heating of the earth. The resulting convection currents in the air (the motion of which is complicated by the rotation of the earth) give rise to winds. Moisture is collected from the sea and deposited high up on mountains as rain. Some of the gravitational energy may be collected as hydropower. Simple windmills or waterwheels are so undependable that they have not been used to any extent since the beginning of the Industrial Revolution. However, the modern form of the waterwheel—the hydroelectric generation plant—is extensively used in mountainous countries and about a third of the world's electricity is produced by this means. The essential requirements for a modern hydroelectric scheme are a river with a sufficient flow of water to provide the required power, a large "head" of water so that a cheap, compact turbine can be used and a dam so that water can be stored until it is required. In some cases a hydroelectric scheme is made economic by being associated with an irrigation or drainage scheme. Such multi-purpose schemes are especially important in India and Pakistan, where most hydro projects are of this type. Other well-known examples include the Snowy Mountains scheme in Australia and the Aswan High Dam in Egypt. Although over 90 per cent of the electricity in certain individual countries, notably Norway, Sweden, Portugal, Switzerland and Uganda is produced from hydroelectric schemes, only a relatively small fraction of the total potential has been exploited. This fraction varies from about a third in Western Europe to a quarter in the United States to a very small fraction in Alaska, Canada, Africa and the hinterland of Asia.

Hydrofluoric Acid is obtained by distillation of fluorspar with sulphuric acid, and is a compound of fluorine and hydrogen. Its action is highly corrosive; a valuable agent in etching on glass, and a rapid decomposer of animal matter.

Hydrogen, symbol H, the simplest element, atomic number (*q.v.*) of 1, colourless, and the lightest of all substances. Cavendish in 1766 was the first to recognise that it was an element. It is 14·4 times as light as air, and is found in a free state in volcanic regions. It can be obtained by the action of metals on acids, and forms an explosive mixture with air, burning with oxygen to form water. Commercially it is used to produce the very hot flame of the oxy-hydrogen blowpipe for cutting metals; to fill balloons and airships; to harden certain oils and render them suitable for margarine- and soap-production. The gas can be liquefied, and the presence of the isotope deuterium was detected by Urey in 1931 in the residue of the evaporated liquid. The third isotope, tritium, is very rare. *See also* **Deuterium, Tritium** *and* **F22, F23.**

Hydrography, the science of water measurement, as applied to seas, rivers, lakes, currents, rocks, reefs, etc., and embracing the whole art of navigation.

Hydrometer, an instrument for measuring the specific gravity of liquids, especially for ascertaining the strength of spiritous liquors and solutions. It is usually in the form of a glass bulb, to the lower end of which a smaller bulb, containing mercury, is attached, which forces the instrument to sink into the liquid which it is to test. The larger bulb has a scale fixed to it, and the indication on this scale of the sinking point shows the specific gravity. There are many varieties: Twaddell's—a pear-shaped bulb containing mercury: Beaumé's, of similar construction, but applicable to liquids both heavier and lighter than water: Sykes', largely employed for determining the strength of alcohol: and Nicholson's, used for taking the specific gravities of solids.

Hydropathy, the method of treating disease with water, either by bathing or drinking. Natural springs of special chemical and therapeutic properties, such as sulphur springs, and other mineral sources, have been used since prehistoric times for this purpose. It is probably one of the most ancient methods of cure. Recently the beneficial effects of pure water treatment have been advocated. Hydropathic establishments have been set up in many health resorts.

Hydroponics, or soilless growth, is the craft and science of growing plants in liquid nutrients instead of soil. Originally a laboratory technique, hydroponics has become since the 1930s a practical method of vegetable, fruit and flower production on both small and large scale. Basically, the growing plants have their roots in troughs of nutrient solution, either in or out of doors. Advantages include: much higher crop yields; the close control of weeds and diseases; quicker growth; and, very important, the possibilities of growing food in places where ordinary agriculture would be impracticable, *e.g.*, deserts and stony land, city roofs, in houses and in remote situations like Antarctic expeditions. Hydroponics is widely practised and contributes usefully to agriculture and horticulture in many countries, including the USA, Britain, India and France. Its value in space-ships and planetary colonies has often been pointed out by technological prophets.

Hydrostatics, the science of the pressure and equilibrium of liquids that are non-elastic.

Hydrozoa are a class of water animals of the *Coelenterata phylum* to which Hydra (*q.v.*) belongs. In one order of the Hydrozoa, free-swimming colonies showing marked division of labour between the individual units occur; this order includes the Portuguese man-of-war.

Hyena, a nocturnal carnivore with powerful jaws. The striped hyenas inhabit N. Africa and S.W. India. The brown hyenas with long shaggy hair are natives of S. Africa. The spotted, or laughing hyena, noted for the peculiar cry from which its name is derived, is also confined to Africa.

Hygrometer, an instrument for measuring the amount of water vapour in the atmosphere. A simple form of hygrometer, known as the wet-and-dry bulb, consists of two vertical thermometers affixed to a frame. One bulb is exposed to the air, and the other is covered with muslin which dips into a water-bath to keep it moist. If the air is saturated, it takes up no moisture from the wet bulb and the two thermometers read the same. If the air is not saturated, evaporation takes place from the wet bulb, latent heat is absorbed from the air and the temperature of the wet bulb is lower than that of the dry bulb. Relative humidity and dew-point of the air can then be derived from suitable tables. Hygrometers depending upon the expansion of human hair and gold-beater's skin and the deposition of dew on a polished surface, when cooled sufficiently, are also in general use. *See* **Humidity.**

Hymenoptera, the order of insects to which bees, wasps, hornets, ants and sawflies belong. They have a well-defined waist, two pairs of membranous wings coupled together, mouth parts modified for biting or sucking; the females possess an ovipositor used for depositing eggs and is sometimes modified for stinging. There are about 70,000 species in this order and many live in highly organised communities. *See also* **Ichneumon Fly.**

Hyperbola. A curve described by certain comets that go round the sun and never return.

Hypsometer, an instrument formerly used by mountaineers to find the height above sea-level by indirectly measuring the atmospheric pressure by determining the boiling point of water at the particular height. Based on the fact that as pressure decreases with height so the boiling point is lowered. Superseded by the aneroid barometer.

I

Ibex, wild goats of several species found in the mountain regions of Europe, Asia and Africa. The male has exceedingly large curved ridged horns. The species that lives in the Alps is called the Steinbock or bouquetin.

Ibis, belongs to a family of birds related to the stork. The sacred ibis of ancient Egypt is now extinct in Egypt but is found in the lakes and swamps of the Sudan near the Upper Nile. It has white and black plumage and a long curved beak. Other species are found elsewhere, the Glossy Ibis (black plumage glossed with purple and green) occasionally visiting England.

Ibo (properly **Igbo**), a large tribe of S.E. Nigeria, numbering between 5 and 6 million. After the end of British rule they were active in their struggle for national independence and under their leader, Ojukwu, embarked upon the secessionist state of Biafra and the unsuccessful civil war against Federal forces. The Hausa and the Yoruba are the other main Nigerian groups.

Ice is frozen water. It is a colourless, crystalline and brittle solid. Being only 92% as dense as water, it floats on the latter; the expansion which occurs as water changes into ice causes the fracture of water-pipes, though the fracture only becomes obvious when the ice melts and leaks out through the crack. The temperature at which ice forms is 0°C, 32°F. Ice can be melted by pressure, and the ease and smoothness with which one is able to skate on ice depends on this phenomenon.

Ice Ages. Periods during which the continents were partly or largely covered by ice-sheets and glaciers. The present-day ice-sheets of Greenland and Antarctica are relics of the most recent ice age (one of the eight major ones during the past 700,000 years), which began in the Pleistocene and ended about 10,000 years ago. During this last great glaciation ice sheets covered the northern part of Europe, Asia and North America. There is strong evidence that periodic changes in the earth's orbit around the sun caused the ice ages. The earth is now in one of its warm periods though there are signs that a moderate cooling trend has begun. *See also* **Climate.**

Icebergs are detached masses of glacier which subside into the sea and float as wind or current may take them. About one-ninth of an iceberg is above sea-level. The North Atlantic is the chief home of icebergs, which reach the ocean from the ice-clad plateaux of Greenland. Some of these floating masses of ice are of enormous proportions, and constitute in the spring and early summer seasons a great menace to the safety of ships, as was disastrously shown in the *Titanic* catastrophe of 1912. For some years past these menaces to N. Atlantic shipping have been kept under close observation by vessels specially detailed for this work.

Ice-breaker, a special heavy bow-plated ship for forcing a way through ice and used especially at ports of the Baltic Sea and the Great Lakes region of Canada which freeze during the winter months. The Soviet atomic ice-breaker *Lenin*, the first of its kind in the world, launched in December 1957, was designed to cut a channel through ice of any thickness. Her icebreaking performance allowed the sea-route to the north of Siberia to be kept open throughout the year.

Icelandic Literature, the old Norse literature, centred about Iceland, which includes numerous works of poetry, mythology and history of interest and importance. Much of this literature is in the saga form. *See also* **Edda.**

Iceland Moss, a kind of lichen (*Cetrario islandica*) which grows in great quantities in the mountain regions of Iceland and other Northern countries. It possesses certain nutritive qualities and is of some value in medicine.

Iceland Spar, a colourless form of calcite (calcium carbonate), frequently found in association with metallic ores; it has the power to produce strong double refraction of light so that two images are seen of an object viewed through a piece of Iceland spar. It was formerly used in optical apparatus for producing polarised light.

Iceni, an ancient British race who in early times lived in Norfolk and other parts of Eastern England. Their most famous ruler was Queen Boadicea, who led her people against the Romans in A.D. 61.

Ice Plant, also called "dew plant" and "diamond plant". A South African mesembryanthemum commonly grown in British gardens. Introduced in 1690.

Ice Saints, St. Mamertus, St. Pancras and St. Servatius, so called because of the legendary cold on these Saints' Days, namely, 11–13 May.

Ichneumon, the Egyptian mongoose, popularly known as "Pharaoh's Rat". It is of great use in checking the multiplication of reptiles. It is frequently domesticated.

Ichneumon Fly, a numerous group of parasitic hymenopterous insects abounding in many lands, and all having the peculiarity of depositing their eggs in the bodies of other insects. It destroys swarms of caterpillars, which become the unwilling hosts of its progeny.

Ichthyology, the natural history of fishes.

Ichthyosaurus was a gigantic marine reptile of the Mesozoic age. The fossils are mostly found in the lias formation. Some were over 9 m.

Icon, an image of a sacred personage used in the home or in churches for devotional purposes by Christians of the Eastern Orthodox faith. Icons can be painted on wood, perhaps with the figures picked out against a golden background, or they can be cast in bronze, in the form of a crucifix, diptych (*q.v.*) or triptych (*q.v.*), with details in coloured enamels. Subjects are taken from the life of Christ or of the Saints. In churches several icons are sometimes placed together on a screen (the iconostasis, which divides the altar and sanctuary from the main body of the church). The earliest preserved icons date from the 12th cent. Icons were venerated in Russia until the Revolution and remain, still in their archaic stylised form of mediaeval origin, a characteristic feature of the Orthodox Church to this day.

Ides, in the ancient Roman Calendar, the 15th of March, May, July, October, and the 13th of all other months; always the eighth day after the Nones.

Idiom, an expression characteristic of a country, district, dialect or language, which usually gives strength and force to a phrase or sentence. The idioms of a language are its distinctive marks, and the best writers are the most idiomatic.

Idris, a famous giant belonging to the myths of Wales, commemorated by a chair of rock on the top of the Cader Idris mountain in Gwynedd.

Igneous Rocks are such as have been molten under conditions of great heat at some stage in their history: *e.g.*, granite, basalt. *See* **F8**(2).

Ignis Fatuus *or* **"Will-o'-the-wisp",** a phosphorescent light which may often be seen on summer and autumn evenings hovering over marshy ground or graveyards. Its nature is hardly understood, though it is generally believed to be the result of the spontaneous combustion of the gases from decaying organic matter. In olden times when marshy grounds were more common than now, this "dancing light" was very frequently visible and was regarded with superstition.

Iguana, large South American lizards, with a long tail, a scaly back and head, a thick fleshy tongue and a prominent dew-lap in the throat. Specimens of the different species average 1·2–1·5 m in length, and they live mostly in trees, though they are equally at home on land or in the water. The flesh of some species is good eating, as are also the eggs.

Iguanodon, a genus of extinct dinosaurs, whose fossils are found in the Jurassic and Cretaceous rocks. Iguanodons were 4·5–7·6 m long, and walked on their hind legs, the front legs being small and adapted for grasping the branches of trees on the leaves of which they fed.

Ilex, mentioned by classical authors, the holm- or holly-oak, which flourishes round the Mediterranean. To botanists Ilex is the genus to which the holly and maté plant belong. *See* **T9**(2).

Iliad, the great epic poem of ancient Greece attributed to Homer (*c.* 700 B.C.). It consists of ancient folk tale and saga, welded into an artistic unity, having as plot the carrying off of Helen by Paris to Troy and the subsequent siege of Troy.

Illuminated MSS. of great value and beauty of decoration exist in most public museums and in many private collections, some of them being of great antiquity, especially those of ancient Egypt executed on papyri. Greek and Latin specimens are also numerous, and the British Museum contains fine examples of all these kinds and also an extensive collection of mediaeval English MSS.

Illuminati. *See* **Section J.**

Ilmenite, a mineral widespread in igneous rocks: chemically it is an oxide of iron and titanium. Rich deposits have recently been found in the Allard Lake area of Quebec; the Travancore sands are also a source of ilmenite.

Immortality. *See* **Section J.**

Immortelles are wreaths, crosses or other designs made from what are called everlasting flowers, which are obtained from certain plants of the Composite order, and retain their colours and compactness for a long time. Immortelles are largely used as mementoes for decorating graves, especially in France.

Impeachment, a special arraignment, usually before Parliament or other high tribunal, of a person charged with some offence against the State. The custom in England was for the impeachment to be made in the House of Commons, and the trial to be before the House of Lords. The first instance occurred in 1376 when Lord Latimer was impeached. With present parliamentary procedure, impeachment is no longer necessary, since the Cabinet is responsible for the individual actions of its ministers, who, acting as a team, must carry the Commons with them, or resign, when it falls to the Leader of the Opposition to form a new Cabinet. Other famous impeachments were those of the Lord High Chancellor Francis Bacon (1621), Earl of Strafford and Archbishop Laud (1640), Warren Hastings (1788), the last being that of Lord Melville (1805). Under the constitution of the United States public officials may be impeached by the House of Representatives and tried by the Senate. A famous case was that of President Andrew Johnson who was saved from impeachment in 1868 by one vote. Had President Nixon not resigned in 1974 he would have been impeached for the affair of the tapes and his abuse of executive privilege.

Imperialism. *See* **Section J.**

Impressionism, the most important and influential movement in 19th cent. European painting. It gained its name, at first contemptuously, in 1874 from a picture painted by Claude Monet and named by the artist *Impression: soleil levant*, which showed the play of light on water with the observer looking straight into the rising sun. Although intended to be the ultimate form of naturalism the inspiration of the school had been the scientific study of light with an attempt to render the play of light on the surface of objects. Feeling that putting a line around a form was bound to cause it to look unnatural, they used bright colours corresponding to the spectrum and unmixed on the palette, and noted that an object of any given colour casts a shadow tinged with the complementary one (*e.g.*, red-green, yellow-blue). Hence bright sunlight was represented in clear yellows and orange with violet shadows. The first Impressionist exhibition held in Paris in 1874 aroused derision with its paintings by Monet, Renoir, Sisley, Pissaro, Cézanne and Degas among others. Impressionism subsequently led to the entirely artistic and anti-naturalist movement of Post-impressionism. Cézanne, who felt that he wanted to produce "something solid and durable, like the art of the museums" was only dubiously impressionist, as were also Degas and Renoir. Of course, in the wider sense of the word (*i.e.*, the recording of an ephemeral impression of a scene), Whistler, Turner and even Rembrandt usedthe technique.

Impressment, the forced seizure of persons for military service resorted to by many countries before the establishment of conscription. Press gangs forcibly recruited men for British warships especially during the Napoleonic wars, but such measures were abandoned after about 1850.

Imprimatur, originally an official licence to print and an important formula in the early days of printing. The term is now used in the wider significance of authority, or endorsement.

Incas, an Indian people who inhabited ancient Peru, founded a great empire and reached a high level of civilisation; overthrown by the Spaniards in 1533.

Incense, an aromatic resinous substance which, under combustion, exhales a pungent odour, and is used, mixed with certain fragment perfumes, in the celebration of Mass in Roman Catholic churches. Olibanum or frankincense is ordinarily the leading ingredient.

Incisors, the sharp-edged cutting teeth at the front of mammalian jaws. Rodents have long, sharp incisor teeth. Elephant tusks are modified incisors.

Independence Day, commemorates the adoption of the Declaration of Independence on 4 July 1776. 4 July is celebrated as a holiday in the USA.

Index. The name given to a list of books, prepared by papal authority, which are declared to be dangerous to faith and morals, and therefore forbidden to Roman Catholics, called the *Index librorum prohibitorum.* One of the reforms of the Vatican Council was the closing in 1966 of the Curia office which judged writings for the Church's Index of forbidden books, though the Index itself still remains. The Pope ordered that nothing should be placed on the Index until the author had been given a chance of explaining his views. The first Index was issued by Pope Pius IV, in 1559.

Indian Mutiny. This turning-point in the history of modern India occurred in 1857–58. The ostensible cause was the serving out to the native troops of cartridges greased with animal fat, for contact with this was forbidden both by the Hindu and Mohammedan faiths. A rebellious feeling, however, had long been developing, and when the Sepoys at Meerut in May 1857 refused to obey the English officers, overpowered and put them to death, the mutiny spread like wildfire. The rebels took Delhi and Lucknow, and for many months terrible massacres and atrocities were committed; men, women and children were slain in thousands. Order was re-established in the autumn of 1858 when the governing power was transferred from the East India Company to the Crown.

Indicators, substances which by a marked change in colour are used to indicate the course of a chemical reaction. Litmus paper, for instance, is red with acids and blue with alkalis. In biological work some radioactive substances are used as tracer elements.

Indigo, the substance obtained from the plant *Indigofera tinctoria*, a native of S. Asia, India being the chief producing country. The colouring matter is the result of the decomposition and fermentation of a glucoside contained in the plant. This is afterwards dried and becomes the caked indigo of commerce. Natural indigo has been eclipsed by artificial indigo, a coal-tar dye which came into commercial production at the end of the last century, which is cheaper and more uniform in quality.

Indium, a scarce lead-coloured metal, symbol In, found in zinc blende in Saxony and certain other ores. This element was discovered in 1863 by Reich and Richter. It is an important material in the manufacture of transistors.

Indulgence. In the Roman Catholic Church the remission granted by ecclesiastical authority to a repentant sinner of the temporal punishment still due after the guilt of sin has been forgiven by God. The indiscriminate sale of Indulgences by Tetzel and other Papal agents in the 16th cent. was one of the grievances which led to the Reformation (*see* **Section J**); the Council of Trent made such traffic unlawful.

Indulgence, Declaration of, was the proclamation by which James II suspended the penal laws against Roman Catholics and Dissenters. It was issued in 1688, but the clergy as a body refused to obey, and the trial of the Seven Bishops and their acquittal by a jury followed. An invitation was thereupon sent to William of Orange to become King.

Industrialisation is simply a name for industrial development. It is customarily used in particular to designate the course of events in a hitherto underdeveloped country which is seeking to increase its wealth and productivity by the introduction of more advanced techniques and by the establishment of industries previously not carried on within it. The word usually covers not only the development of modern industrial production but also the provision of electric power-stations, irrigation works and transport and other developments designed to improve production in any field by methods involving large capital investments. The outstanding example in our time of rapid industrialisation has been the Soviet Union, which, unable to get the capital from abroad, had to carry it through by ruthless restriction of the people's consuming power so as to achieve an unprecedentedly high ratio of investment to total production. Industrialisation has in practice meant a high concentration on the expansion of the basic heavy industries and of power supply, coupled with much slower development of the industries supplying consumers' goods and of agricultural production; but there is no reason why this should always be the case. It may well be that in most underdeveloped countries development can but be devoted largely to the industries making consumers' goods and to measures designed to increase agricultural production and productivity.

Industrial Revolution. The name, first given by Engels in 1844, to describe the radical changes that took place in Britain during *c.* 1730–1850 to transform a mainly agricultural country into one predominantly industrial. It began with the mechanisation of the textile industry (Hargreave's spinning jenny, 1764, Arkwright's water-frame, 1769, Crompton's mule, 1770, and Watt's steam-engine, 1785), with subsequent major developments in mining, transport and industrial organisation. It was based on Britain's rich mineral resources, particularly coal and iron ore. With the use of the steam-engine as power, industry became concentrated round the coalfields and the great new industrial towns developed—Birmingham, Manchester, Newcastle and Glasgow. Britain became supreme in constructional ironwork (Telford, George and Robert Stephenson). Canals, bridges, railways and ships were built, and great advances were made in the practical application of scientific principles. Aided by colonial exploitation Britain became the most prosperous country in the world. The new industrial capitalists began to replace the country squires as ruling class. But the great accumulation of wealth at one pole of society was matched at the other by poverty and misery, for child labour, long working hours, low wages and slums were features of the industrial revolution in its infancy. As with all great technological developments, the industrial revolution produced related changes in all fields of social life—in politics, art, religon, literature and morals, and with the rise of democracy, social reforms.

Inertia, a term used in mechanics for the property of matter by which it offers resistance to a change in its state of rest or in its state or direction of motion.

Inertial Navigation, an automatic method of dead-reckoning which at present finds its chief application in guided missiles, submarines and aircraft. Navigation by this means is carried out with reference to inertial space (*i.e.*, space which is stationary with respect to the fixed stars) and not to the surface of the earth as in normal navigation (latitude and longitude). This is done by means of high-accuracy gyroscopes combined with highly sensitive accelerometers in an apparatus known as the Ship's Inertial Navigation System. The American nuclear-powered submarine *Nautilus* pioneered the new north-west passage under the polar ice pack by this method of dead-reckoning in August 1958.

Inflorescence, a flowering shoot. Many arrangements of the flowers are possible and there are many kinds of inflorescence; *e.g.*, the spike, catkin, umbel, capitulum (in composites).

Inflation. *See* **Section G.**

Infra-red Rays *or* **Radiation.** This is the range of rays which come between the visible red rays and the ultra-short Hertzian radiation. The wave-lengths involved range from about 0·00076 millimetre (7,600 Angstrom units) to 0·4 millimetre. Infra-red rays penetrate haze; hence landscapes obscured by haze or cloud can be photographed using plates sensitive to infra-red. Many substances strongly absorb these rays and thereby become hot; this happens in toasting bread. Many industries use infra-red lamps for drying paints and lacquers. Very important to chemists, as a tool in the investigation of the structure of compounds, since various groups of elements absorb infra-red radiation at a characteristic frequency.

Infula, a sacred fillet, of woollen material, worn on the forehead by priests, magistrates and rulers in Roman times, also by persons fleeing for protection to sanctuary. Later, each of the two lappets of a bishop's mitre.

Ingoldsby Legends, a series of whimsical metrical tales full of droll humour written by the Rev. R. H. Barham, and first published in *Bentley's Miscellany* in 1837. The best known is the *Jackdaw of Rheims.*

Ink, a liquid pigment ordinarily made from an infusion of nut-galls, copperas and gum arabic. Shumac is substituted for nut-galls for inferior inks. An acid is sometimes added to prevent oxidation, and for the blue-black inks a small quantity of solution of indigo serves for colouring. Copying ink contains glycerine or sugar, which keeps the ink moist. Lampblack used to be the leading ingredient in printer's ink but now new methods of manufacturing have been developed. Marking ink is composed of a solution of nitrate of silver, gum, ammonia and carbonate of soda. For red, blue and other coloured inks, colouring solutions are used, for example, Prussian blue. The earliest examples of ink writing (on wooden tablets) ever found in Britain were recovered from the well of a Roman villa (3rd cent. A.D.) during excavations in 1954 at Chew Stoke, Somerset.

Ink Sac, a glandular organ found in squids and other cephalopods which contains an inky solution. When roused the animal discharges the contents of the ink sac into the water, to make a cloud through which its enemies cannot see. The pigment, sepia, comes from the ink sac of the cuttlefish.

Innocents' Day, a festival day in Roman, Greek and Anglican Churches in commemoration of the killing of the children of Bethlehem by Herod, 28 December.

Inns of Court, the four bodies in London which enjoy the privilege of calling candidates to the bar after they have studied for a certain number of terms and passed certain examinations. The Inns are: the Inner Temple, the Middle Temple, Lincoln's Inn and Gray's Inn.

Inquisition, a Roman Catholic ecclesiastical court which became a formidable weapon of the Church in the 13th cent. under Pope Innocent III in dealing with charges of heresy. It was effectively set up in the various Catholic countries of the Continent, obtaining its fullest and most sweeping organisation in Spain in the days of Ferdinand and Isabella, when Torquemada was made Grand Inquisitor, and used its powers with terrible severity. *See* **Auto-da-fé.** In the 18th cent. its influence began to wane, and the jurisdiction of the Congregation of the Holy Office at Rome was limited to the suppression of heretical literature (*see* **Index**).

Insectivorous Plants, plants which trap insects with special mechanisms. Plant enzymes or bacteria digest the prey, providing the plants with nitrogen usually scarce in the soil in which they grow. The most common British species are the Sun-dew and the Bladderwort.

Insects. This huge class of invertebrate animals (*see* **Arthropods (F33)**) includes about 100,000 species. Insects are ubiquitous except in the sea, only a very few species being adapted to marine existence. Characteristic features are: the body is divided into three parts, head, thorax and abdomen: the head carries a pair of antennae, the thorax three pairs of legs and usually two pairs of wings. The most primitive insects constituting the sub-class *Apterygota* are wingless. The other sub-class, *Pterygota*, is divided into the *Exopterygota* (*Hemimetabola*), which have a simple metamorphosis, *e.g.*, cockroach, and the *Endopterygota* (*Holometabola*), with a complex metamorphosis, *e.g.*, butterfly, bee. Although many are parasitic on man, animals and plants, innumerable animals and some plants use them as food, and many flowering plants are dependent on a variety of insects for pollination leading to the development of seeds and fruits. *See* **F33(1), 38(2), T28(1).**

Insignia, marks or badges of office or honour, such as stars, ribbons, crosses, medallions or other designating objects, worn by members of special Orders or holders of prominent offices.

Instinct.—*See* **F38(1).**

Institut de France was formed in 1795, and after various modifications was in 1832 organised on its present basis. Its five academies are—the Académie Française, Académie des Inscriptions et Belles-Lettres, Académie des Sciences, Académie des Beaux-Arts, Académie des Sciences morales et politiques. It is restricted to 40 members.

Instruments, Musical. Musical instruments may be classified in a number of ways, but in general they fall into one of the three main classes, String, Wind and Percussion, according to how the sound is produced. **Stringed Instruments** are those which produce the sound by the vibration of a string: (*a*) by plucking, as in Harp, Lyre, Psaltery, Zither, Lute, Guitar, Balalaika, Ukelele, Harpsichord; (*b*) by friction (bowed), as in Crwth, Rebec, Viol, Violin, Marine Trumpet, Hurdy-Gurdy; (*c*) by striking (hammered), as in Dulcimer, Pianoforte, Clavichord; (*d*) by wind (blown), as in the Aeolian Harp. **Wind Instruments** are those in which the air in the instruments is set in vibration: (*a*) by blowing into a tube (flue-voiced), as in Recorder, Pandean Pipe, Flute, Organ; (*b*) by means of reeds (reed-voiced), as in Oboe, Clarinet, Saxophone, Bagpipe, Cor Anglais, Bassoon, Organ reed-stops; (*c*) those in which the sound is produced by the vibration of the player's lips against the mouthpiece (lip-voiced), as in Bugle, Horn, Trumpet, Tuba, Trombone, Saxhorn, Flügelhorn, Cornet. In a modern orchestra these are known as the *Brass*: instruments of the flute, oboe and clarinet families as the *Woodwinds*. Then there are the **Percussion Instruments,** which include the Drums, Cymbals, Tambourines, Castenets.

Insulator, a substance that will not conduct electric current. Many solids, liquids and gases are important insulators—rubber, cotton, silk, plastics, porcelain, glass, air, oil. If the applied voltage is too high, all insulators will "break down", *i.e.*, conduct electricity perhaps with resulting breakage, puncture or charring. Thermal insulators will not conduct heat; they are usually the same kinds of substance as electrical insulators.

Insulin is a hormone which controls the supply of sugar from the blood to muscles. The breakdown of sugar provides energy. In diabetes there is a lack of insulin, causing a build-up of blood sugar which can be released by the injection of insulin. It is secreted by the islet tissue of the pancreas, from which it was isolated in 1922 by Banting and Best. Dr. F. Sanger of Cambridge won the 1958 Nobel Prize in Chemistry for isolating and identifying its amino acid components. Prof. Dorothy Hodgkin and her team at the Dept. of Molecular Biophysics at Oxford have recently succeeded in determining the structure of insulin, a task which would not have been possible without the electronic computer. The discovery may lead to a better use of insulin.

Intelligence. Intelligence has been variously defined as the innate potential of a person to learn and understand; to make appropriate judgments; to see the relationships between things; to profit from experience; or to meet adequately new problems and conditions in life. There are many lines of evidence to show that intellectual capacity is closely related to heredity and influenced by environmental factors. The idea of intelligence testing was first devised by the French psychologist Binet at the beginning of this century. He was asked by the French government to invent a test which would weed out backward children in state schools, and thus save public money and avoid holding back the work of the class by teaching children who were incapable of learning at a given standard. Briefly, a series of problems are given to a large number of children and it is thus found out which series can be solved by the average child of a given age-group; if a child of 7 can only pass the tests suitable to the average child of 6, then his mental age is 6. The intelligence quotient or I.Q. is discovered by dividing his mental age by his chronological age and multiplying by 100. A gifted child can usually be spotted at an early age. Although I.Q. tests are the standard method of estimating intelligence, they are not universally accepted as a criterion; a teacher's general judgement may be the best assessment. High intelligence may be inherited, but fail to develop to the full because facilities for education are not available. Recent research suggests that the growth of the brain may be permanently affected by undernutrition at the time of its fastest growth (the last weeks before birth, and, to a lesser extent, the first weeks after birth). At this vulnerable period even quite minor deprivation can affect the rate and ultimate extent of growth of the brain. This has significance not only for the severely under-nourished babies in the poor parts of the world, but for babies of low birth weight in our own communities. *See also* **Q28.**

Interest is the payment made for the use of borrowed money over time. The rate of interest is the rate per cent per annum charged for such loans. There are many such rates, varying with the plenty or scarcity on borrowable money, with the length of time for which the loans are made, and with the degree of risk, if any, that the loans will not be duly repaid. Short-term loans are usually cheaper than long-term: the lowest rates are usually for "call money" repayable immediately on demand. These are used principally in short-term financial transactions, such as bill discounting. Bank loans, though usually made for fairly short terms, command higher rates. Long-term loans are made chiefly to public authorities, or as bonds or debentures to business concerns. The rates obtained vary with the demand and the supply of such accommodation.

Interferon, the name given to a substance discovered in 1957 by Drs. Isaacs and Lindenmann at the National Institute for Medical Research. It is produced by the interaction of viruses with living cells and has the important property of inhibiting virus reproduction. Its development may lead to a new approach to the therapy of viral diseases.

International Date Line, a line along the 180° meridian marking the difference in time between E. and W. For the westward-bound traveller crossing the line the date would be put forward one day, for the eastward-bound, back one day. To avoid difference of date in adjacent land areas, the line deviates from the 180° meridian where this crosses land.

Introit, the psalm sung by the choir as the priest approaches the altar to celebrate the Eucharist.

Invention of the Cross, a Roman Catholic festival held on 3 May, to celebrate the finding of the alleged True Cross at Calvary by the Empress St. Helena in 326. Also included in the Church of England calendar. *See* **Holy Rood.**

Iodine, a non-metal element, symbol I, member of the halogen family (*q.v.*), a substance formerly exclusively obtained from the ribbon-wrack seaweeds. These were burnt and the ashes (kelp) extracted with water. After concentrating the iodides, these were distilled with manganese dioxide and sulphuric acid to yield iodine vapour which was condensed in stoneware bottles. Nearly all iodine now in use is derived from the iodine salt present in Chile saltpetre (natural sodium nitrate). Iodine is used in photography, as an antiseptic solution in alcohol or potassium iodide (tincture of iodine), and in medicine. Discovered by Courtois in 1812.

Ionosphere, a succession of ionised layers of the earth's atmosphere lying above the stratosphere. In this region free electrically charged particles —electrons and positive ions—occur in sufficient concentration to affect substantially the propagation of radio waves through the region. It extends upwards from a height of 100 km, being most concentrated at an altitude of *c.* 300 km. The behaviour of the upper atmosphere is strongly influenced by the sun. A great deal of new information about the ionosphere above an altitude of *c.* 250 km (the topside ionosphere) has been obtained by the use of instruments carried in satellites. Normally the aurorae (*q.v.*) occur at heights between 100 and 400 km. *See also* **Atmosphere.**

Ions, electrically charged atoms, or groups of atoms. Atoms of the metals lose electrons to become positively charged ions, *e.g.*, the sodium ion (Na^+) has one electron less than the atom. The non-metal ions are negatively charged, *e.g.*, the chloride ion (Cl^-) has one electron more than the atom. Similarly, a group like the sulphate ion (SO_4^{2-}) has more electrons than the constituent atoms. Thus, the hydrogen atom without its electron is a hydrogen ion or *proton* and the helium atom without its two electrons is a helium ion or *alpha-particle*. When an electric force is applied to certain solutions, the ions into which molecules of the dissolved substance are broken up are attracted to the oppositely charged electrodes, their movements constituting an electric current through the solution. In the same way gases, including air, conduct electricity by virtue of free ions (*see* **F12(2)**). Combustion, radioactivity and ultra-violet and cosmic radiations produce ionisation. *See* **F20(2)**.

Ipecacuanha, a flowering plant of the Brazilian forests. Various alkaloids are isolated from ipecacuanha, one is emetine, which is used in medicine to cause vomiting and so remove poisons from the stomach. Another is used as an expectorant in cough mixtures.

Iridium, a white and very hard metal, symbol Ir, discovered by Tennant in 1804. It occurs naturally as an alloy with platinum or osmium; tips for fountain-pen nibs have been made from the former native alloy. The former standard metre was composed of platinum–iridium alloy (*see* **Metre**) as are parts of scientific apparatus and surgical tools that must be non-corrodible.

Iris, the typical genus of the botanical order *Iridacae*, with tuberous rhizomes and sword-shaped leaves, many of the family having beautiful flowers. About 100 species of Iris are recorded from the northern temperate zone, the most common species wild in Britain being the yellow flag. Orris root, used in perfumery, comes from another iris species. *See* **T9**.

Iron is a metallic element, symbol Fe (Latin *ferrum*), occurring widely in nature in such ores as haematite, loadstone (magnetic iron oxide), spathic ore and iron pyrites. It is extracted by a process known as smelting, with coke and limestone in a furnace. Its many uses are familiar, the most important being in the manufacture of cast- and wrought-iron products and of steels, which are alloys mainly of iron with added carbon and various metals. Iron rust is formed by the action of oxygen and water, and is a coating of iron oxide. *See* **Smelting**.

Ironclads, ships of war cased in iron or steel plates of sufficient thickness to resist projectiles. They were first introduced (1858) in the French Navy, and in 1860 the first British ironclad, the *Warrior*, was launched.

Iron Curtain. In a speech at Fulton, USA, on 5 March 1946, Sir Winston Churchill used this phrase to describe the dividing line behind which, he said, lie all the capitals of the ancient States of Central and Eastern Europe—Warsaw, Berlin, Prague, Vienna, Budapest, Belgrade, Bucharest and Sofia. These famous cities and the populations around them, said Sir Winston, lie in the Soviet sphere and are subject "to a very high and increasing measure of control from Moscow". The phrase is said to have had dining rather than diplomatic origins. The practice of carving at a sideboard behind a screen (an iron curtain) was called dining *à la Russe*.

Ironsides were Cromwell's special troopers, so called because of their solidity and firmness in battle.

Irrational Number, a number such as the square root of two, or pi, which cannot be expressed as the ratio of two whole numbers. *See* **Rational Number**, and *Pi*.

Irredentists, a political party organised in Italy about 1878 with the object of incorporating within Italy neighbouring regions. Also a person, group or party advocating policies for the restoration to their country of territory formerly belonging to it but later lost.

Irrigation, an artificial method of providing water for the growth of plants on lands where the natural supply of water is deficient. For many hundreds of years techniques of irrigation have been slow and primitive (*e.g.*, tanks, inundation canals and the Archimedes screw) and consequent inefficiencies include large water losses by evaporation and seepage, and the watering of only a small area. New developments in perennial irrigation, using barrages, large reservoirs and pumping stations, permit vast tracts of land to be irrigated. Yet these are not without their problems as witnessed after the construction of the Aswan High Dam on the Nile where complex problems of delta erosion and dam lake silting ensued. Irrigation also serves the purpose of supplying *warmth* in winter; *e.g.*, in the English water-meadows, and in the more highly developed Italian *marcite* and winter-meadows where the water is mostly applied in winter when there is plenty of rain. There are several other functions of irrigation; *e.g.*, washing out of excess salts and the renewing of fertility by the addition of alluvium.

Isinglass, a gelatinous substance manufactured from the swim bladders of certain fish; used to preserve eggs, to keep beer free from sediment and to make a glue.

Islam. *See* **Section J**.

Isobars are the lines drawn on charts linking together points of equal barometric pressure.

Isochasms, lines connecting places at which there is an equal probability of seeing an aurora, taking the average over a number of years, based on the auroral catalogue of Fritz.

Isomers are chemical compounds having the same composition but different structural arrangements, and consequently different physical and chemical properties. For example, ethyl alcohol and methyl ether are isomers, since the molecules of both are built up of two atoms of carbon, six of hydrogen and one of oxygen, *viz.*, C_2H_6O; ethyl alcohol, C_2H_5OH; and methyl ether, CH_3OCH_3.

Isotherms are lines drawn on charts through points of equal temperature.

Isotopes. When one talks of an element, say, uranium or lead, the name of the element is a generic name for a collection of uranium species and lead species. The different species are called isotopes. For any particular element, the number and arrangement of electrons around the nucleus are the same in all the isotopes, so all the isotopes have the same chemical properties. Soddy has described isotopes as "elements, the atoms of which have similar outsides but different insides". For example, in the nucleus of the uranium isotopes, U 235, U 238 and U 239, there are respectively 143, 146 and 147 neutrons, but all have 92 protons. The isotopes have different at om i weights, in this instance respectively 235, 238 and 239. But all have the same chemical properties. *See* **F10(2)**.

Ivory, the dentine substance of which the tusks of the elephant, hippopotamus, walrus, etc., are composed. The tusks of the African elephant sometimes weigh as much as 45 kg, and reach a length of 2·4–2·7 m.

Ivory Gull, a small, beautifully shaped sea-bird with striking all-white plumage and black legs which breeds on the rocky shores of the Arctic, being found farther north than any other bird; it occasionally wanders south in the winter.

J

Jabiru, the Brazilian name for the giant stork of South America.

Jacamar, from *Jacameri*, the Brazilian name for a smallish bird with long, sharply pointed bill and brilliant plumage which inhabits the tropical regions of South America east of the Andes. These birds are seen sitting motionless on trees, darting off at intervals, like flycatchers, to catch insects on the wing.

Jacanas, small water birds with immensely long toes which enable them to walk on water lily leaves. They are sometimes called "lily-trotters" and are found in tropical Africa and America. They live in swamps and feed on seeds and insects. Sometimes brilliantly coloured.

Jack, a small schooner-rigged vessel, used in the Newfoundland fisheries; a pike; an oscillating lever; a device used in roasting meat.

Jackal, *Canis aureus*, a small wild dog related to the wolf and resembling a fox. The Common Jackal is found in S.E. Europe, India and Sri Lanka; other species inhabit Africa and Egypt. The jackal is a well-known scavenger. It hunts singly or in pairs, unlike the wolf, which usually hunts in packs.

Jackdaw, one of the smaller members of the Crow family. This European bird is typically black with grey collar. It is easily tamed, makes an amusing pet and delights in making off with and taking to its nest bright objects, such as silverware.

Jacobins, a French revolutionary club or party, formed in 1789, and accustomed to meet at a Jacobin convent, hence the name. It became a controlling force in the Revolution, especially in the movement which led to the Terror. Robespierre was its chief spokesman.

Jacobites, adherents of the Stuart cause after the abdication of James II. First James himself, then his son (the Old Pretender), and later his grandson (the Young Pretender) tried to fan the flame of rebellion in Scotland and Ireland, but after the defeat at Culloden in 1746 the cause was lost. Also the name of the monophysite heretics of Syria, so named after their leader Jacobus Baradaeus in the 6th cent. A.D.

Jade, an exquisite kind of hardstone, ranging in colour from a whitish green to a deep mauvish brown. It can be translucent or opaque and sometimes it is veined. Jade is the common name for two minerals—the rarer *jadeite* (found in Burma, Tibet and China), a sodium-aluminium silicate, and *nephrite* (found in New Zealand, China, Turkestan and Siberia), a calcium-magnesium silicate. The presence of small quantities of other chemicals accounts for the wide range of shades. In China jade has for centuries been looked upon with great veneration, magical powers have been ascribed to it, and it has been fashioned into ritual objects, also into miniature sculptures of animals or even whole landscapes, charming to look at and incredibly skilfully made. The Chinese word for jade is *yü*, used as a symbol for all that is noble, beautiful and pure.

Jaguar, a South American carnivorous animal resembling the leopard, but larger and more powerful. It preys on other animals but rarely attacks man.

Jainism. *See* **Section J.**

Janeite, a devotee of Jane Austen and her writings.

Janissaries, an élite band of Ottoman foot soldiers who acted as the Sultan's bodyguard. They were conscripts, raised by the "tribute of children" from conquered Christian countries, mainly Serbia and Albania. First recruited under Murad I (14th cent.). They were not allowed to marry. They gained great power under the Ottoman Empire. In 1826 the Sultan Mahmud II had them massacred.

January, the first month of the year, named after Janus, the two-faced god of the Romans. It was the *Wolf monath* and *Aefter Yule* of the Saxons.

Jasmine, a graceful climber belonging to the olive family with odoriferous blossom, originally a Persian plant, but now acclimatised in many varieties in almost all parts of the world. Two species of jasmine (the common jasmine and the Spanish jasmine) yield oils used in perfumery. *See* **T9–10.**

Jasper, a precious stone of the chalcedony variety, opaque, and coloured red, brown, yellow and sometimes green. It was greatly esteemed by the ancients, the Bible having numerous allusions to it.

Jay, a gaily-coloured bird of the Crow family, of many species—the Blue jay of N. America, the Canada jay, sometimes called "whisky jack", the Siberian jay and the British jay, fawn-coloured with black and whitish crest and bright blue feathers in the wings. It lives in woods and like the magpie, takes the eggs and young of small nesting birds.

Jazz, a rhythmical syncopated music characterised by a strong element of improvisation in the performance, probably originating among the Negro population of the Southern States of the USA. It became popular during the first world war and, in a commercialised form, has held the popular field ever since. Modern dance music and popular songs are based on the jazz idiom, which has also had a profound effect upon contemporary music of a more serious kind.

Jean, a stout kind of twilled cotton cloth much worn in olden times, and resembling fustian. Blue *jeans*, adopted by American city youngsters from farmworkers, are now the fashion elsewhere and worn not only as overalls by workmen but by both sexes in leisure time.

Jelly-fish. The jelly-fishes, which have gelatinous, translucent bodies fringed at the margin with delicate tentacles, constitute the coelenterate order *Scyphozoa*. The mouth, with a squarish opening, is seen on the underside, and there are four horseshoe-shaped sex organs.

Jerboa, small jumping mammals of the Rodent order. These mice-like animals have long tufted tails and very long hind legs, the front legs not being used for locomotion.

Jeremiad, any utterance or writing in which sorrow or complaint is the chief characteristic, so named as recalling the style of the "Lamentations of Jeremiah", in the Old Testament.

Jerusalem Chamber, a room in Westminster Abbey, deriving its name from the circumstance of its having originally been decorated with a view of Jerusalem. Henry IV died in this chamber, and the Committee for the Revision of the Bible met there in 1870 and later.

Jesuits, members of the Roman Catholic teaching order founded by Ignatius Loyola in 1534. A long and vigorous course of study is prescribed before they are admitted into the privileges of full membership. They are required to take the vows of voluntary poverty, perfect chastity, perfect obedience and complete submission to the Pope. The Society played an important part in politics.

Jet, a deep black fossil substance admitting of a high polish and much used for jewellery, ornaments and trimming. It is a form of lignite, the most important British deposit being found near Whitby, where jet manufacture has been an established industry for a long period.

Jet Engine, an aeroplane engine which derives its thrust from the high velocity of the gases it ejects. The essential units in a jet engine are a rotary compressor and a gas turbine, the latter driving the compressor. The first reliable, high-performance jet propulsion engine for aircraft was invented by Air Commodore Sir Frank Whittle.

Jet Stream, a meteorological term coined in 1946 to describe the relatively narrow belt of strong winds (160–320 km/h) at levels in the atmosphere from 5–11 km. These winds are important in forecasting weather, and can be a valuable aid to aircraft. From the ground, where there may be little wind, the jet stream can sometimes be seen as high cirrus cloud moving across the sky at high speed.

Jew's Harp. The name is believed to be a corruption of "jaws harp". This instrument consists of a metal frame with a central tongue of spring steel. The frame is pressed against the teeth, and the tongue of the harp is twanged with the finger, the mouth acting as a resonating chamber. By altering the shape of the mouth the resonant frequency and therefore the note can be varied.

Jockey Club, the governing body that, although possessing no legal status, frames rules and laws by which horse-racing and turf matters generally are regulated. The club-house is at Newmarket.

John Bull, the typical figure of an Englishman, bluff, big and burly. Arbuthnot's *History of John Bull* is supposed to have originated the character.

John Dory, a fish found in most temperate seas and common in British waters. It is of a golden-yellow colour (*jaune doré*), has a high dorsal fin with long filaments projecting from the spines, very protractile jaws and is much valued as a table fish. According to legend the dark spot on each side of its body is the thumbprint of St. Peter who took a coin from the fish's mouth (Matt. XVII 24–7).

John o' Groat's House, W. of Duncansby Head, Caithness, popularly named as the northernmost point of Scotland. According to legend the house, which has now disappeared, was built in octagonal form by a Dutchman Jan de Groot who came to live there in the 16th cent. The site is marked and an inn was erected near it in 1876.

Jongleurs were minstrels and jesters who wandered from town to town singing songs, playing musical instruments, dancing and giving entertainments in mediaeval France and Norman England. Jongleurs were low-born in contrast to the Troubadours, who were often of the nobility.

Joule, a unit of energy in the SI system of units,

defined as the work done when the point of application of a force of one newton is displaced through a distance of one metre in the direction of the force. Named after J. P. Joule (1818–89). The relationship between mechanical energy and heat energy is called the mechanical equivalent of heat and was found by Joule to be 778 ft lbf in lb °F units, or $4{\cdot}18 \times 10^7$ ergs in gram °C units. *See* **F17**.

Judaism. *See* **Section J.**

Julian Calendar, named after Julius Caesar, who in 46 B.C., finding the Roman year 90 days in advance of the real time, was the first to adopt the calculation of time by the solar year, the average length being fixed at 365¼ days. There was still an overplus of a few minutes every year, and this was rectified by the Gregorian Calendar, introduced in Italy in 1582 and adopted in England in 1752, from which date what is called the " New Style " begins.

July, the seventh month of the year, named after Julius Caesar. It was the *Maed monath* (Mead-month) of the Saxons.

June, the sixth month of the year, containing 30 days and deriving its name from Juno. It was the *Sear* (Dry) *monath* of the Saxons.

Jungle-Fowl, birds related to the peacocks and peacock-pheasants. At least four species are known from the jungles of India, Sri Lanka and Java. The domestic chicken has been derived from the Red Jungle-Fowl (*Gallus gallus*).

Junkers, name of the ruling class of Prussia, military in spirit, who were the party of reaction and defenders of the landed interests. Supported Bismarck prior to the Franco-Prussian war and helped bring Hitler to power.

Jupiter, the largest and, after Venus, the brightest of the planets, 1.312 times the volume of the Earth but only 317 times its mass. It circles the sun in 11·86 years and its mean period of rotation is 9 h 50 min. Hydrogen, methane and ammonia have been detected in its atmosphere. Striking features are the coloured bands and the Great Red Spot of Jupiter's atmosphere. In 1610 Galileo made history by discovering the four major satellites of Jupiter, which he named Medicean planets after his patron Cosimo Medici; these are visible with good field-glasses. There are nine other Jovian moons. *Pioneer* 10 passed *c.* 130,000 km above the planet's surface in December 1973. *Pioneer* 11, travelling at *c.* 172,000 km/h, reached the planet in December 1974, before speeding on to Saturn which it will not reach until September 1979. It came within *c.* 43,000 km of the Jovian surface, beaming back close-up pictures and successfully passing through a belt of high-energy particles. It was thought there might be a radiation hazard (electrons and protons from the solar wind are trapped by Jupiter's magnetosphere) but it seems the spacecraft followed a path swept clean by Jupiter's moons which prevented radiation damage. *See* **F7**.

Jurassic Formation, a series of rocks (the evidences of which are most marked in the Jura Mountains) coming between the Cretaceous and Triassic groups and including the Oolite and the Lias. It is a formation rich in fauna, abounding in echinoids, lamellibranchs, ammonites and belemnites; large reptiles, marine and land, are common, as are the plants called cyads. In Britain the Jurassic outcrop extends from the Dorset coast to the Yorkshire moors and includes the Cotswolds. *See* **F45**.

Jury, a body of private citizens chosen and sworn to hear and pass verdict upon evidence brought forward at a trial, inquest or inquiry. The origin of the English jury is obscure but it is thought to have been introduced by the Normans. The jurors are the sole judges of the true facts upon the evidence laid before them. Under the Criminal Justice Act of 1967 their verdicts in criminal courts in England and Wales no longer have to be unanimous but may be by a majority of 10 to 2. The age limit has recently been reduced from 21 to 18 and raised from 60 to 65. In Scotland 45 jurors are summoned in criminal cases, of whom 15 are chosen by ballot, and majority verdicts are accepted: not guilty, not proven and guilty.

Jute, the name given to the fibre of a plant grown largely in Bangladesh in the Ganges delta and used for the manufacture of coarse cloths, cordage and sacks. Calcutta is the biggest jute-manufacturing centre of the world, as Dundee was in the 19th cent.

Jutes, a Low German race who in the 5th cent. invaded the south-eastern part of England, establishing themselves in Kent and making Canterbury their capital.

Juvenile Courts. This is a special kind of Magistrates' Court to deal with accused persons under the age of seventeen. The Magistrates chosen are specially qualified for the work, and where possible a woman is appointed as one of the magistrates who constitute the Court. The Court is held in private away from the ordinary court room. The object of the Juvenile Court is to introduce into the trial a plan to reform the offender by providing for the care and protection which he may need, by removal from undesirable surroundings, and by subsequent education or training. In these objectives the Court has the co-operation of social workers, including Probation Officers (*q.v.*). Radical changes in methods of preventing and treating juvenile delinquency are contained in the Children and Young Persons Act, 1969, the result of the findings of two White Papers, 1965 and 1968. They emphasise the necessity of helping and supporting the child as far as possible in his own family and community, with resort to formal procedures only where he is exposed to moral danger, or control is necessary in the interest of society or of the child. The minimum age for prosecution will be raised from 10 to 12 when the Government is satisfied that " local authorities and other services have the necessary capacity to cope with this change ". Children who are below prosecutable age will be dealt with by social casework or by care proceedings. Although the Act places restrictions on the prosecution of 14 to 17 year-olds, so that prosecution would be restricted to categories of offences to be prescribed and only if action by other means were inadequate, these provisions will be phased into operation.

K

Kakapo, the Maori name for the New Zealand owl-parrot, a peculiar and interesting species, possessing wings but not able to use them for flight (though it can glide); of sap-green plumage, nocturnal in its habits and nesting in burrows. Still to be found in the larger forest areas of the South I.

Kangaroo, pouched (marsupial) mammals of Australia and adjacent islands. There are over 20 species, the smaller ones being known as " wallabies ". Kangaroos leap in a succession of springy bounds 3–6 m long, the forefeet not touching the ground. They can reach a height of over 2 m and a weight of 90 kg. First seen by white men when Capt. Cook's expedition visited Australia in 1770. Related genera include the tree kangaroos, rat kangaroos and the Tasmanian Jerboa kangaroo.

Kaolin or **China Clay** is an essential ingredient in hard-paste porcelain (*q.v.*). It results from the decomposition of felspar, and is widely found in China, Japan and the USA. The richest deposits in Europe are in Cornwall, near Limoges in France, and in Czechoslovakia.

Karst, geological formations typical of limestone regions in which the drainage is by underground channels. Rain water carries part of the limestone away in solution, leaving the surface dry and barren and pitted with innumerable hollows. The name comes from the Karst (Slav *Kras*) region of N.W. Yugoslavia where the rocks are massive pure limestone; the barren plateau is characterised by fissures, caves and subterranean rivers.

Kauri Pine, a large coniferous tree yielding a fine copal resin which ranges from Malay to New Zealand. The New Zealand Kauri, *Agathis australis*, is found only in the N. Island. Some of the best Kaurigum comes from fossilised pines and is dug out of the soil far from any living trees.

Kelvin. Lord Kelvin, an important 19th-cent.

physicist, gave his name to the kelvin, symbol K, a measure of temperature on the absolute scale. The Kelvin scale is a development of the scale invented by Celsius (*q.v.*) for everyday use, long known as the "centigrade" scale; the degree interval on both scales is the same. The conversion formula for the absolute or Kelvin scale is K = C + 273·15. *See* **Absolute Temperature.**

Kestrel, the most common British falcon, well known for its habit of hovering for minutes at a time with vibrating wings and then swooping down to attack mice and insects. The male has spotted chestnut-brown back, greyish head and tail, which has a broad black band near tip.

Ketones. A class of organic compounds, related to aldehydes, of general formula R_2CO (where R is an organic radical). The simpler ketones, especially acetone, are widely used as solvents for lacquers, synthetic rubber and polymers, such as cellulose acetate and perspex. More complex ketones occur in nature, and some are used in the perfumery industry, muscone (from the musk deer (*q.v.*)) is an example.

Kew Gardens, officially known as the Royal Botanic Gardens, are among the most celebrated gardens in the world. They were started in 1759 by Princess Augusta of Saxe-Gotha, widow of Frederick, Prince of Wales, and mother of George III. They remained private property until 1841, when control passed to the Commissioners of Woods and Forests. They now cover 121 hectares and are administered by the Min. of Agriculture, Fisheries and Food. Since 1841 the gardens have been open to the public, and form one of the most attractive resorts near London.

Keys, House of, is the Manx representative assembly. *See* **Tynwald.**

Keystone, the stone which occupies the centre and highest point of an arch and is usually the last to be inserted.

Khaki, a clay-coloured cloth adopted for uniforms in the British Army in the time of the war with the Boers, and used in the first and second world wars. First used by Indian regiments.

Kilderkin, once a common liquid measure in England, representing 18 gallons or 82 litres.

Kilogramme, unit of mass, defined as the mass of the international prototype kilogramme of platinum-iridium kept at the International Bureau of Weights and Measures at Sèvres. A remeasurement of Avogadro's Number (**F21(2)**) may lead to an atomic standard of mass (the second and the metre are already defined in atomic terms), but this will depend on the precision with which atoms can be counted.

Kilowatt. Unit of power, equal to one thousand watts. *See* **Watt.**

Kinetic Art denotes works of art which actually move or give the illusion of so doing. An early exponent of kinetic art was the American sculptor Alexander Calder (1898–1976) when he launched his famous "mobiles" in the early 1950s. Since then, constructions which rotate, jump, blink with lights, etc. have been made by many artists and the genre is being further elaborated upon today. Kinetic painters give a visual illusion of movement to their pictures by the use of particular colour contrasts or by a skilful play with spirals, squares, etc. in black and white, sometimes with colours blended in. An interesting exponent of the style is the English artist Bridget Riley (b. 1931).

Kinetic Energy, the energy (*q.v.*) possessed by a particle or body in virtue of its motion. If the motion is destroyed, *e.g.*, by the impact of the body with an obstacle, the kinetic energy vanishes, being turned into some other form of energy such as heat and sound. If the body has mass m and speed v its kinetic energy (leaving out corrections due to relativity) is $\frac{1}{2}mv^2$.

King Crab, remarkable arthropods now classified separately from both Arachnids and Crustacea which they resemble, inhabiting the sea coasts of America, Japan, India and Malay Peninsula, carrying a shield-shaped shell, and having a long pointed spine projecting from the posterior. The body comprises three separate sections articulated together. These crabs—in America known commonly as the horseshoe crab because of their shape—are from 45–60 cm in length. Fossil king-crabs are found as far back as the Silurian. There are about six living species.

Kingfisher, a well-known family of brilliant-plumaged birds, found in all continents, comprising some 250 species and sub-species. The British kingfisher, *Aceldo atthis*, haunts the rivers and streams, and is one of the most beautiful of native birds, having iridescent blue-green, white and rich chestnut in its plumage and bright-red feet. All kingfishers have long, dagger-shaped bills. In the Malayan region, New Guinea, the Moluccas and Australia the varieties are very numerous. The quaint *Laughing Jackass* of Australia is among the largest of the kingfisher family. The European kingfisher is the bird of the Greek legend of the Halcyon.

King-of-Arms, the name of the chief officials of the Heralds' College. There are several in England —the principal being those of the Garter, Norroy and Ulster, Clarenceux. *See* **Heralds' College.**

Kiosk, a word of Russian or Turkish origin meaning a small open pavilion of light construction much used in Eastern countries as a place of shade and rest. Similar structures are common in the streets of Paris as news and advertisement stands, and in London as telephone offices.

Kirimon (*Kiri no go Mon*) and **Kikumon** (*Kiki no go Mon*), the two Japanese imperial crests, the first a design of leaves, stems and flowers of the Paulownia plant, and the other representing the sixteen-petalled chrysanthemum.

Kite, name of several birds of prey, widely distributed, related to the hawks and eagles, graceful in flight, and distinguished by their long wings and deeply forked tails. The red kite, light chestnut brown, once the most familiar bird of prey in Britain, seen scavenging the streets of London, is now the rarest, and found only in Wales. The Egyptian kite and the pariah kite of India, notorious for their daring thefts, are closely related to the black kite, a smaller European species, with less forked tail and blackish-brown plumage.

Kittiwake, a beautiful white and pearl-grey gull with black legs, dark eyes and greenish-yellow bill. Its range is wide, and includes the British Isles, where it is a local resident. The flight of this only truly oceanic gull, which except in the breeding-season is generally found offshore, is graceful, swift and buoyant. A triangular black patch, noticeable on the ends of the wings when open, is characteristic of the species, as is the call kitti-wake, from which the bird derives its name. It nests in colonies on the ledges of caves and steep cliffs.

Kiwi, flightless, stoutly-built birds of New Zealand, now very rare and carefully protected by the Government. They are little larger than a domestic hen, and lay astonishingly large eggs for their size. Incubation and care of chicks fall to the male bird. They have rudimentary wings concealed by the plumage, and the feathers are hair-like. They are nocturnal in habit.

Knighthood is a degree of honour or title common in Europe since the Middle Ages, and was at first exclusively a military order. In Great Britain the four main orders of knighthood are those of the Garter, the Bath, the Thistle and St. Patrick; in addition to which there are several other orders, such as the Order of St. Michael and St. George, the Star of India, etc. There are also Knights Bachelors such as are not associated with any special order. The title is not hereditary, and therefore ranks below that of a baronet, though both are entitled to the prefix "Sir".

Knot, a nautical measure of speed (1 sea mile per hour), and formerly measured by a log-line, divided by knots at equal distances $\frac{1}{120}$ of a geographical mile. The number of knots travelled by the ship in half a minute corresponded to the numbers of sea miles it travelled per hour. A sea mile is equal to about $1\frac{1}{8}$ of a statute mile or 1·9 km. Also, a grey and white wading bird, usually a winter visitor to Britain found in flocks on the coast.

Knout, a whip of many thongs, often fatal in its effects, formerly used in Russia for flogging criminals.

Koala, the Australian arboreal marsupial mammal

that looks like a toy teddy-bear, with ashy-grey fur, bushy ears and rudimentary tail. It feeds on the leaves and shoots of certain eucalyptus trees, and is not more than 60 cm in length.

Kohl, a powder prepared from antimony or burnt almond shells, and in common use by the women of the East for darkening the eyelids.

Koto, a musical instrument in general use in Japan consisting of a series of 13 silken strings stretched across a curved wooden surface, and played with the fingers. Each string is 1·5 m long, and has a separate bridge so fixed as to give the vibration necessary for the note it has to produce. It is a sort of horizontal harp, and in the hands of an expert player is capable of giving forth excellent music.

Kremlin, the citadel or walled city within a Russian city which during the Middle Ages served as an administrative and religious centre and offered protection. That of Moscow, now the headquarters of the Russian government, contains the cathedral where the Tsars were crowned, an imperial palace and the " King of Bells " (*see* **Bells**). Its walls which are topped with towers were built in the 15th cent.

Krypton, one of the rare gases, symbol Kr, occurring in the air to the extent of 1 part in 20 million. It was discovered in 1898 by Ramsay and Travers. It is used in gas-filled electric lamps.

Kusti, the sacred cord or girdle of the Parsees, consisting of 72 threads—the number of the chapters of the *Yasna*—and two branches, each branch containing six knots, together standing for the 12 months of the year.

Kyrie Eleison (" Lord, have mercy "), the name of a common form of prayer in the Anglican, Roman Catholic and Greek Churches; also applied to the English Church responses after the recital of the commandments.

Kyrle Society, named after Pope's " Man of Ross ", John Kyrle, founded by Miss Miranda and Miss Octavia Hill in 1875, and having for its object, the decoration of workmen's clubs, hospitals, etc. and the promotion among the poor of a taste for literature, music and outdoor recreation.

L

Labarum, the standard of Constantine the Great, adopted after his conversion to Christianity, marked with his seal and represented upon the coinage.

Labourers, English Statute of, was passed 1350–51, with the object of compelling labourers to accept a certain rate of wages and not leave their employers' service, the Plague having rendered labourers so scarce that they were in great demand and had been insisting on higher pay. These enactments were bitterly opposed and led to the " Peasants' Revolt ", headed by Wat Tyler.

Labradorite, a felspar rich in calcium and of a pearly lustre on cleavage, found in masses in igneous rocks, the best samples of which come from Labrador.

Labyrinth, or **Maze**, a combination of roads and passages so constructed as to render it difficult for anyone ignorant of the clue to trace the way to the central part. The Egyptian labyrinth near Lake Moeris had 3,000 rooms, half of them subterranean and the remainder above ground. The labyrinth in Crete, according to Greek myth, was built by Daedalus to house the Minotaur. There was one at Lemnos, renowned for its stalactite columns; and another at Clusium constructed by Porsenna, King of Etruria, about 520 B.C. The labyrinth in which Fair Rosamond was concealed was at Woodstock. Hampton Court maze dates from the 16th cent.

Labyrinthodonts, gigantic fossil amphibians which get their name from the curious labyrinthine structure of their teeth, probably an evolutionary link between fishes and reptiles. They occur in the Carboniferous, Permian and Triassic formations, and remains have been found in Britain and other parts of Europe. Their heads were long, and their footprints, by which they were discovered, closely resemble the prints of the human hand.

Lac, a resinous matter deposited on the branches of a number of tropical trees by the females of the lac insect, the exudation including eggs and a viscous covering. At the gathering time the twigs are broken off and dried in the sun, when the insects die, and the lac that remains is termed *stick-lac*. From this, by the removal of extraneous accretions and dissolving, *seed-lac* is produced. *Shell-lac* is seed-lac after it has been melted and otherwise prepared, and this is the best known of the lacs, being used in printing and the manufacture of varnishes and sealing-wax, and for other commercial purposes.

Lace, a delicate fabric of linen, silk or cotton threads, made by hand or machinery, and worked in various ornamental designs. The kinds of lace are many, deriving their distinctive names either from the method employed in production or from the place where any special variety was originally made. The best-known makes are pillow or bobbin-lace, woven and plaited by hand; needle-point lace, worked by the needle over a traced design; and machine lace, which practically dates from Heathcote's invention of the early part of the 19th cent. Some of the most famed laces are the following: *Alençon*, a needle-point lace; *Brussels*, a very fine kind, with needle-point sprigs and flowers; *Chantilly*, a silk variety with flowers and openwork; *Cluny*, a netlace with darned stitch; *Honiton*, a delicate kind with dainty sprigs and figures; *Mechlin*, generally made in one piece and very varied in design; and *Valenciennes*, or bobbin lace, of great durability, the pattern and ground of which are made at the same time, being one of the best and most costly of laces, now manufactured mainly in Belgium. Nottingham is famous for its lace.

Lace-Wings, insects with frail, transparent and much-veined wings whose grubs eat large numbers of insect pests such as aphids. The eggs are borne at the ends of threads attached to plants.

Ladybird, the common name of a large family of beetles—the *Coccinellidae*. The insect is usually of a red or yellow colour with small black or coloured spots. Ladybirds are of good service to the gardener because their larvae feed on aphids. There are about 2,000 species.

Lady-Day, the day of the festival of the Annunciation of the Virgin Mary, 25 March. One of the four English quarter days.

Lake Dwelling, the name given to certain prehistoric habitations which were thought to have stood on platforms over lakes, like villages in certain Pacific islands. Recent excavations at the Lake of Burgäschi in Switzerland show that the prehistoric Swiss pile dwellings probably stood on the shores of lakes, not on platforms over the water. Also found at Mere and Glastonbury, Somerset.

Lakes are bodies of water collected in depressions of the earth's surface. The most notable lakes are the Great Lake series of North America, including Superior, Michigan, Huron, Erie and Ontario, all discharging into the St. Lawrence River. Africa has an enormous area of lakes, including the Mobutu Seso and the Victoria, forming the sources of the White Nile. Smaller lakes are numerous in other countries—Switzerland, Germany, Italy, England, Ireland, Scotland, all having their lake regions, where the scenery is invariably beautiful and romantic. The Kariba Dam (Rhodesia–Zambia border) and the Nasser (Egypt) are the largest man-made lakes in the world.

Lake School, the name given, at first in ridicule, to a distinguished trio of poets—Wordsworth, Coleridge and Southey—who made their homes in the English Lake District.

Lamellibranchs (Pelecypods), the class of aquatic, bi-valve molluscs to which the oysters, cockles, mussels, clams and scallops belong. In these animals the body, which is compressed laterally, is enclosed in two hinged shells held together by muscular action. The gills are thin plates hence the name " lamellibranch ". *See* **F33**(1), **38**(2).

Lamination, stratification on a very fine scale, as in shades.

Lammas Day is one of the oldest of the Church festivals, probably derived from the loaf-mass (*hlafmaesse*) of the Anglo-Saxons. It occurs on 1 August. In the olden times it was the day when loaves were given in place of first-fruit offerings.

Lammergeyer, the bearded vulture of alpine regions, resembling an eagle in appearance. It has a white head with black tufts at base of the bill, and its general plumage is dark brown, nearly black. It is found in the remote mountain ranges from southern Spain and parts of Africa to China, and is becoming scarce.

Lampblack, a carboniferous pigment obtained from flame-smoke, and now produced in specially constructed furnaces in which bodies rich in carbon, such as tar, resin, petroleum, etc., are burned. The smoke or soot resulting is collected from the sides of the furnace, and forms lampblack. It finds use in making printer's ink, black paint, etc. Being a very pure form of carbon, it is also utilised in the manufacture of dynamo brushes and arc-lamp carbons.

Lamprey. Eel-like fish having no scales, bones, paired fins or jaws. They attach themselves by their mouths to fish whose blood they suck. Together with the hagfishes, the lampreys are placed in a special class—the Cyclostomes. There are three British lampreys.

"Lancet", the name of a noted English medical journal, established in 1823 by Dr. Wakley.

Land Crab, a family of crabs (*Gecarcinidae*) which live mainly on land, though migrating to the sea to deposit their eggs.

Land League, an association formed in 1879, with Parnell as president, for compelling a reduction in the rents of land, and a reconstruction of the land laws in Ireland, and in case of non-compliance refusing to pay rent. For a time this League exercised great political influence and was an important aid to the Home Rule agitation.

Landrail, popularly known as the Corncrake, was a regular summer visitor to Britain two generations ago, but no longer. Its harsh and piercing note was a familiar sound in English cornfields. It is decreasing almost everywhere.

Landslip, a sudden downward sliding under gravity of large masses of rock, soil, etc.; often set off by earthquake shock or saturation of a particular stratum with water. Many serious landslides have occurred from time to time. In 1618, an earthfall happened at Plurs, on Lake Como, involving the destruction of many buildings and the loss of numerous lives. In 1806 a portion of Rossberg mountain in Switzerland slipped from its position, and falling into the valley below buried many villages and hamlets and over 800 people. A chalk cliff 30–45 m high and 1·2 km long fell at Lyme Regis, in Dorsetshire, in 1839, doing great damage. Over 200 people were killed by a landslip in Naini Tal, in India, in 1880; and at Quebec, in 1889, a rocky eminence called Cape Diamond gave way, many buildings being destroyed and lives lost. Notable landslips in recent times have occurred at Amalfi (Italy) in 1924, at Murchiston (New Zealand) in 1929, at Aberfan (Wales) in 1966 and near St. Gervais (France) in 1970.

Langue d'oc and Langue d'oïl, the two principal mediaeval French dialects, *oc* and *oïl* being their respective words for the affirmative particle (modern French *oui*). *Langue d'oc*, spoken south of the Loire, was the language of the troubadours. Provençal, one of its dialects had a literary revival in the 19th cent. under the influence of the poet Frédéric Mistral. *Langue d'oïl* was spoken in northern France, and it was the dialect of the Paris region which developed into modern French.

Lantern Fly, bugs belonging to the family *Fulgoridae* in which the head is drawn out to form a lantern-like structure. In no instance is the "lantern" luminous, though naturalists used to think it was.

Lanthanides, the fourteen metallic elements following lanthanum in the Periodic Table, *i.e.*, the elements cerium (no. 58) to lutetium (no. 71). They are also known as the rare-earth metals, though they are in fact all more terrestrially abundant than, for instance, mercury or arsenic (with the exception of the unstable radioactive element promethium, no. 61). The lanthanide atoms are distinguished by having an incomplete inner electron sub-shell (the 4f level), this feature giving them interesting magnetic properties. For instance, gadolinium, holmium and dysprosium are ferromagnetic (*see* **F19**) at low temperatures. Chemically, the lanthanides behave similarly, being highly reactive metals usually forming trivalent salts. *See* **Periodic Table, Section F.**

Lapis Lazuli, an azure-blue mineral, being a silicate of aluminium and sodium. The pigment ultramarine is made by grinding it, though artificial ultramarine has largely superseded it. The mineral (also called *lazurite*) has been used as a gemstone since ancient times.

Lapwing *or* **Green Plover,** familiar British bird on moors and marshlands with iridescent greenish-black plumage, white underparts and black crest. Often called "peewit" from its cry. Protected under Protection of Birds Act, 1967.

Larboard is the old nautical term indicating the left-hand side of a ship, and changed by Admiralty order to "port" in 1844. Starboard is the right-hand side.

Larch, a familiar coniferous tree in the mountain regions of northern Europe, and though not native to Britain, the Common Larch is successfully cultivated in various parts of the kingdom. It is one of the best of all turpentine-yielding trees, and the bark is valued for tanning. The larch is an unusual conifer in being deciduous.

Lark, a family of song birds (*Alaudidae*) of many species, some of which—notably the skylark—are famed for their habit of soaring into the air, singing all the while. They build their nests on the ground in the open country and, except for the black lark of Russia, have streaked brown plumage. The skylark and woodlark are the best known British species, while the crested lark and shore lark are among the occasional visitors. Africa has the greatest number of larks; America has only one species, the horned lark.

Larkspur, the common name of the genus *Delphinium*, a favourite flower introduced into British gardens from Switzerland in 1573. The common larkspur is *D. consolida*.

Larva, the undeveloped form of any animal which, before maturity, undergoes metamorphosis, usually different from the adult in structure and habits.

Laser. A remarkable kind of light source that was discovered in 1960. With the laser it is possible to probe the behaviour of matter under the influence of enormous energy densities, range and survey vast distances to microscopic accuracy and send millions of telephone and television messages between any two points that can see each other with telescopes. Laser light, in contrast to natural light, is coherent and can be expressed as a regular progression of waves carrying energy along a particular path. Thus the essential difference is that laser light is an orderly sort of wave motion in contrast to ordinary light which is inherently unsteady and therefore an inefficient carrier of information in time. The name *maser*, which is the microwave parent of the laser, derives from the expression "*m*icrowave *a*mplification by the *s*timulated *e*mission of *r*adiation". Upon application to light wavelengths the microwave part of the name lost its meaning and the term maser became generally descriptive of any device in which stimulated emission dominates.

Laser Fusion is a method by which it has been proposed that thermonuclear reactions may be controlled and exploited as a source of energy (*see* **Nuclear Fusion**). The idea is to irradiate a millimetre-sized pellet of a mixture of frozen deuterium and tritium with a short ($\sim 10^{-9}$ s) but very intense pulse of energy in the form of laser light. This has the effect of both compressing the pellet by a factor of at least a thousand and heating it to about 10^8 °C. Under these conditions, thermonuclear reactions (principally $^2D + ^3T \rightarrow ^4He + ^1n$) proceed sufficiently fast that a net output of energy is obtained before the pellet explosively separates. Formidable technical problems need to be solved before laser fusion can become a practical proposition. These include the development of efficient high-powered lasers and the design of a suitable reactor that can withstand up to 100 micro-hydrogen bomb explosions per second. It is still not clear whether this method of controlling nuclear fusion is more practical than the more conventional approach involving the magnetic confinement of plasmas.

Latent Heat is the quantity of heat required to convert 1 gram of a substance from one form into another. For example, when a solid changes into a liquid or a liquid into a gas, the addition of heat to bring about the change produces no rise in temperature, the energy being absorbed in the form of latent heat. An equal amount is released when the process is reversed. The latent heat of fusion of ice is about 79·6 calories per gram, that of the vaporisation of water about 539 calories per gram.

Lateran Councils were the religious conventions held in the Lateran basilica at Rome for deciding important questions of Church doctrine. The most brilliant was that of 1215, which pronounced in favour of a Crusade. *See* **Ecumenical Councils.**

Lateran Treaty, 1929, between Italy and the Vatican established the Vatican City as an independent sovereign state.

Laterite refers to any tropical soil or soil horizon rich in hydrated ferric and aluminium oxides which harden when exposed to the atmosphere. It is difficult to cultivate and is commonly used for bricks and road metal. Laterite buildings have been known to withstand weathering for many centuries and a number of fine examples are found in India and S.E. Asia.

Latin America. The Spanish-speaking, Portuguese-speaking and French-speaking countries of N. America, S. America, Central America and the W. Indies. *See* **Section K.**

Latitude of a point on the earth's surface is its angular distance from the equator, measured on the surface of the earth in degrees, minutes and seconds. Thus the equator is 0° Lat. and the poles 90° Lat. (N. or S.). First determined by Hipparchus of Nicaea about 160 B.C. Latitude introduces zones of climate, *e.g.*, tropical rain, subtropical steppe and desert, temperate rain and polar.

Laughing Gas. *See* **Nitrous oxide.**

Launce *or* **Sand Eel,** a family of eel-like sea fishes found in large numbers on the coasts of North America and Europe. There are two species common to British waters. These fishes are of a bright silvery hue, and live much in the sand underneath the water. They are prized as human food and as bait.

Laurentian Shield refers to the Pre-Cambrian rocks in the region of the Upper Lakes of Canada, nearly 5 million sq km in extent. Of enormous importance to Canada on account of the mineral wealth, forests yielding valuable timber and wood-pulp, and water-power.

Lava, the molten rock which is erupted from a volcanic vent or fissure. Also the same material which has cooled and solidified.

Lawn, very fine sun-bleached linen, in olden time called " cloth of Rheims ".

Lead, a soft malleable metal, symbol Pb (Latin *plumbum*), occurring in numerous ores, which are easily smelted. Its most important source is the mineral galena which consists chiefly of lead sulphide; rarely is it found free. Lead is largely used in plumbing on account of its pliability, and in nuclear reactors as a shield against radiation because of its very high density. As an alloy element it combines in the formation of type metal, stereo metal, shot metal, pewter and many other compounds. Oxides of lead are used in some types of glass and in the manufacture of paints (red lead). All lead compounds are poisonous. Leading producers of lead are the United States (Missouri), Australia (Broken Hill) and the Soviet Union.

Leaf Miners, insect larvae which tunnel between the upper and lower skins of leaves. Most leaf miners are caterpillars of tiny moths; some sawfly larvae have the same habit.

Leagues, or combinations of kings, countries, communities, have been frequent since the kings of Canaan united against the Israelites. Among the most famous leagues may be mentioned the Holy or Catholic League, which prevented the accession of Henry IV of France until he became a Roman Catholic; and the League of Augsburg against Louis XIV of France in 1686.

League of Nations, was founded on 10 January 1920, with the object of promoting international peace and security. The original members were the signatories to the Peace Treaties at Versailles, and membership grew to fifty-three as new nations and ex-enemy States were admitted. Two notable absentees were the United States and Soviet Russia, the latter not being represented until 1934. Germany was a member from 1926 to 1933. The League had an Assembly which met at Geneva every year and a Council which met five or six times a year. The Permanent Court of International Justice sits at The Hague. The final Assembly of the League was held at Geneva between 8 and 18 April 1946. Its place has been taken by the United Nations. The International Labour Organisation, set up by the League of Nations, met on 20 April 1944, at Philadelphia and resumed its old quarters at Geneva under the new organisation in 1946.

Leap Year *or* **Bissextile,** was fixed by Julius Caesar, 45 B.C., the addition of one day in every four years bringing the measure of the calendar year even with the astronomical year with three minutes per year over. The Gregorian Calendar corrected this by dropping leap year at the centuries not divisible by 400. For instance, 1700, 1800 and 1900 were not leap years.

Learning. *See* **F38(1), Q16–20.**

Leather was made in ancient Egypt, Greece and Rome, and has through succeeding centuries played an important part in the service of man. It consists of the dressed hides or skins of animals after the process of tanning has been gone through. Untanned skins are known as pelts. Leather is classed either according to the skins from which it is made or the system of preparation employed. The best-known kinds are morocco, kid, Russian, chamois, Cordovan, grained, patent, russet, tan, calf, Hungarian.

Leech, an aquatic blood-sucking worm, mostly found in fresh-water ponds. Each end of the body is provided with a sucker, but that at the head end has jaws and teeth. The medicinal leech has three jaws. The leech attaches itself with avidity to animal bodies and sucks until glutted. Its saliva contains an anti-coagulant.

Leeward, a nautical term, meaning the sheltered side of a vessel—that is, the opposite side to that from which the wind is blowing.

Legion, a body of Roman troops, varying in numbers at different periods. A legion was divided into 10 cohorts, and every cohort into three maniples. Three legions composed the Roman army of occupation in Britain.

Legion of Honour, the French order for distinguished services, military or civil, was instituted by Napoleon I in 1802, and confirmed and modified under later rules. There are five grades—Grands Croix, Grands Officiers, Commandeurs, Officiers and Chevaliers.

Legume, the fruit typical of the pea, bean family, or *Leguminosae.*

Lemming, small light-brown rodents with dark spots, abounding in Scandinavian countries and in Siberia, about 12 cm long, with a short stump of a tail. The migrations of the lemming are famous, probably caused by overbreeding when food is plentiful. So insistent is the urge to keep moving that these animals will march on into the sea in their thousands and be drowned.

Lemur, almost the most primitive member of the primate order of mammals (to which man, apes and monkeys also belong). They are noted for having strong pliant toes enabling them to use their feet as hands, and also well-developed thumbs on the hands. They have long squirrel-like tails, fox-shaped heads and large staring eyes. True lemurs are confined to the Malagasy Rep.; closely related are the " bush-babies " of S. Africa.

Lend-Lease. During the earlier phases of the second world war the bulk of British investments in the USA had to be either sold or pledged to Americans in payment for dollar supplies. After the United States entered the war this drain was stopped by the Lease-Lend arrangement, under which Great Britain met the costs of American consumption in Great Britain, while the United States paid for British supplies from America. This arrangement was abruptly terminated on the ending of hostilities; and Great Britain and other belligerent countries found themselves without means of paying in dollars for indispensable American supplies, including the foodstuffs, materials and capital goods needed for economic reconstruction. In these circumstances Great Britain negotiated with the United States and also with Canada a large loan, which was used for buying dollar supplies and played an important part in helping the West European economies to maintain themselves and feed their peoples while they were carrying through the earlier stages of post-war reconstruction. These loans involved large charges for interest and amortisation in future years, but proved far too small to meet the dollar deficit for more than a short period. In face of this situation the United States launched the Marshall Plan (*q.v.*).

Lenses, pieces of transparent material designed to focus an image of an illuminated object. Usually of glass, but plastic lenses are common, and quartz, etc. are used for special purposes. The surfaces of the simplest lenses are parts of spheres. Lenses which are thickest, or thinnest, at the centre are called convex and concave respectively. Lenses of complex shape are often used in microscopes, etc. Electron lenses are arrangements of electric or magnetic fields which focus beams of electrons, *e.g.*, on to television screens.

Lent, the forty days' period of fasting that precedes Easter.

Lepidoptera, the order of insects with scaly wings and bodies, to which the 90,000 butterflies and moths belong.

Leptons. A group of particles which include electrons, neutrinos and muons. All are much lighter than protons or any of the baryons. *See* **F14.**

Lepus, the constellation of the Hare, situated under the Orion group, and one of the constellations with which the ancients were familiar.

Lettres de Cachet, sealed letters which the kings of France issued to their agents to secure the imprisonment of distrusted or disliked persons without trial. Abolished in 1789.

Levée, a State reception held by the Sovereign or his representative and attended by men only.

Lewis, a contrivance for stone-lifting, the principle of which was known to the ancient Romans; it consists of two dovetail tenons of iron or other metal, expanded by an intervening key in a dovetail-shaped mortice in the stone, and shackled by a ringed bolt to the hoisting chain.

Leyden Jar, the earliest form of electrical condenser. Its invention is usually credited to Muschenbroeck of Leyden (1745). It consisted of a jar coated inside and out with tinfoil for about two-thirds of its height and having its inner coating connected with the top by a brass knob and chain. The jar was charged by connecting it to an electrostatic machine.

Lias, a geological term referring to the lower section of the Jurassic group, and mainly comprising shales and limestones.

Liberalism. *See* **Section J.**

Libraries, before the invention of printing, were few, and collected together at enormous cost. At Nineveh remains of libraries, consisting of tablets of baked clay, have been discovered. There were two libraries at Alexandria containing a vast collection of rolls or volumes, founded by Ptolemy I Soter (367–283 B.C.) and established by Ptolemy II Philadelphus (309–246 B.C.). Among the great libraries of later times may be mentioned the Vatican Library at Rome, moved to its present premises in 1588; the Royal Library in Paris which later became the Bibliothèque Nationale; The Astor Library, New York; and in England, the Bodleian Library, Oxford, and the British Library (see below). Since 1850 public libraries have been established in all the chief cities and towns of the kingdom. The first lending library was opened in Edinburgh in 1726. In most villages there is a "county library centre" to which collections of books are sent by the County Library. In Great Britain there are 24,000 centres of this kind in village clubs, halls, shops, schools and even homes. In some counties there is a library van or the bibliobus, as it has been called by a French writer. This travelling library tours on a pre-arranged time-table so that everyone knows exactly when it will arrive. The British Library in London, the National Library of Scotland, in Edinburgh, that of Wales in Aberystwyth, the Bodleian Library of Oxford and the Cambridge University Library comprise the "copyright" libraries, entitled to receive a copy of each new book and journal published in Britain. The British Library Act 1972 brought together into a single organisation (a) the former British Museum Library (the books remaining in the Museum) and the Science Reference Library in Holborn and Bayswater, the whole now being known as the British Library, Reference Division; (b) the former National Lending Library for Science and Technology and its arts and humanities counterpart, the National Central Library, together now known as the British Library, Lending Division, and located at Boston Spa, Yorkshire. Reference Division will eventually be re-housed in a single new building in London, due for completion in the early 1980s. Lending Division, which has an international reputation for rapid postal lending of journals and photocopies to institutions and libraries throughout the world, will remain in Yorkshire.

Libretto (It. booklet), the literary text of an opera or oratorio. Usually the composer and the librettist collaborate in the writing of an opera, but several composers (*e.g.*, Wagner) wrote their own librettos. Boito, librettist to Verdi for *Otello* and *Falstaff*, himself composed two operas, *Mefistofele* and *Nerone*. Most famous of Italian opera librettists was the poet and dramatist Metastasio (1698–1782). His librettos were set to music by many composers, including Gluck, Handel, Mozart, Rossini.

Licence is a permission given to do some act, which without such permission, it would be unlawful to do. Licences are required for keeping dogs, for operating a television receiving set, for driving a motor vehicle, for killing game, for setting up as a bookmaker, for selling beer, wines and spirits, tobacco, etc. and for importing certain items such as arms, ammunition, radioactive materials, animals, plants, drugs and explosives. The licence on a private motor car is £50 a year.

Lichens. In every lichen, two plants are associated, one being an alga and the other a fungus. The fungus derives its food from the alga; probably the alga gains too from the association, being protected against desiccation by the fungus (an example of symbiosis). Lichens are the first plants to colonise bare rocks.

Life-Boat was invented by three men, Lionel Lukin who converted a coble into a boat for saving life in 1785; William Wouldhave, who discovered how to make a boat right herself if she capsized, and Henry Greathead, who built a life-boat, partly from Wouldhave's model, in 1789. This boat was stationed at South Shields, which was the first permanent life-boat station to be established. It was not until 1851 that the first life-boat able to self-right was built, and a motor was first installed in a life-boat in 1904. Modern motor life-boats have engines of from twin-18 h.p. to twin-80 h.p., with a speed of nearly 10 knots. All coastal life-boats in this country are maintained by the Royal National Lifeboat Institution founded by Sir William Hillary in 1824. It is supported entirely by voluntary contributions.

Light, a particular kind of electromagnetic disturbance capable of travelling through space, and some kinds of matter, and of affecting our eyes to cause vision. Its finite speed was first demonstrated by O. Römer, using observations of the eclipses of Jupiter's satellites in 1675. In 1860 Maxwell showed that light waves are electromagnetic. Since Einstein's theory of relativity (1905) it has been generally realised that the speed of light is a fundamental natural constant. Visible light with wavelengths between about 4 and 6×10^{-5} cm is only a small part of the electromagnetic spectrum. Subtle modern methods give the speed of light as $2{\cdot}997925 \times 10^{8}$ m/s (about 186,282 miles per sec).

Light Year. A measure of astronomical distance, equal to the distance light travels in the course of a year. A light year is thus $5{\cdot}88 \times 10^{12}$ miles ($9{\cdot}463 \times 10^{12}$ km). *See also* **F3**(2).

Lighthouses, to warn ships of dangerous places and indicate coasts, points, harbours, etc., have existed since the building of the Pharos, a tower of white marble 183 m high, built by Ptolemy II Philadelphus at Alexandria about 280 B.C. In early lighthouses the lights were simple fires. The most famous and one of the earliest British lighthouses is the Eddystone (*q.v.*). Dungeness lighthouse, opened in 1960, is very modern in design, capable of automatic operation and the first of its kind to incorporate the xenon electric arc lamp as a source of illumination. The electric fog signal consists of sixty loud-speaker units built into the tower just below the lantern, giving a honeycomb effect. The lighthouses of England and Wales, the Channel Islands and Gibraltar are under the control of Trinity House; Commissioners of Northern Lighthouses control those of Scotland; and the Commissioners of Irish Lights control the coasts of Ireland. Particulars of lights in all parts of the world are published for the guidance of navigation in the *Admiralty Lists of Lights*, compiled annually by the British Admiralty.

Lightning, the flash of a discharge of electricity between two clouds, or between a cloud and the earth, when the strength of the electric fields becomes so great as to break down the resistance of the intervening air. With "forked" lightning the actual path, often branched, is visible, while with "sheet" lightning the flash is hidden by the clouds which themselves are illuminated. "Ball" lightning or fireballs is the name given to the luminous balls which have been seen floating in the air during a thunderstorm. The Boys camera has provided much information regarding the sequence of events in a lightning discharge. It is found that a flash consists of a number of separate strokes, usually four or five, and that the discharge of electricity to earth begins with a faintly luminous "leader" moving downwards and branching at intervals. As the ground is approached a much brighter luminosity travels back along the conducting channels, lighting up the several branches. The multiple strokes which follow in fractions of a second have the same "return" nature and are rarely branched. Lightning flashes to earth damage structures, cause loss of life and endanger overhead power systems, often interrupting electricity supply. Such storms generally affect radio transmissions and present hazards to aircraft. Thunderclouds may develop energy far exceeding the capacity of our largest power generating stations.

Lightning Conductor, a metal rod, the upper part of which is of copper with a conical point, the lower portion being iron, which extends into the earth. Its effect is to gather to itself the surrounding electricity and discharge it into the earth, thus preventing its falling upon the protected building. In ships, lightning conductors are fixed to the masts and carried down through the ship's keel-sheathing. Benjamin Franklin was the first to realise the possibilities of lightning protection and, in 1752, carried out his famous experiment of drawing electricity from thunder-clouds, with the aid of a sharp-pointed conductor fixed to a kite.

Lillibulero, an old marching song composed by Purcell. With words by Wharton, it is said to have "sung James II out of three kingdoms". Used by the B.B.C. during the second world war as a station identification signal preceding news bulletins, and still in use to announce the Overseas Service programmes in English.

Lily Family (Liliaceae), one of the largest families of flowering plants, with 200 genera and 2,500 species. It includes the true lilies (*Lilium*), tulips and hyacinths. Vegetables belonging to the family are the onion and asparagus.

Limes, trees of the genus *Tilia*, including some 30 species spread over north temperate regions. The word is a corruption of "linden". Limes native to Britain are the small-leaved *T. cordata* and the broad-leaved *T. platyphyllos*. The hybrid *T. vulgaris* was introduced into Britain from the Continent during the 17th cent. and is frequently seen in streets and parks. Lime-wood was used by Grinling Gibbons for his fruit, flower and bird decorations.

Limestones, sedimentary rocks composed wholly or largely of calcium carbonate and formed by two main processes, (1) organic (skeletal remains of organisms), *e.g.*, chalk (*q.v.*) and (2) chemical (precipitation of calcium carbonate), *e.g.*, oolite (*q.v.*). Marble is limestone that will polish after cutting.

Linen, a textile fabric manufactured from flax fibre, known to the ancient Egyptians, and first manufactured in England under Henry III by Flemish weavers. The greatest linen-manufacturing region in the world is Northern Ireland (largely yarns and the lighter types of fabrics); Scotland produces coarse linens and canvas as well as household linens.

Ling, a sea-fish common on the coasts of Britain, and abounding in more northern waters. It averages from *c.* 1 m in length, and is a voracious feeder, living chiefly on small fish. Ling is also the name applied to *Calluna vulgaris*, the plant commonly called "heather".

Linseed, the seed of the flax plant, containing, apart from its fibrous substance, certain oily and nitrogenous matter of considerable commercial value. This yields linseed oil, and some of the residue is used to make cattle food.

Lion, the most impressive of the Cat family. It is chiefly found in open bush country in Africa, being comparatively rare in Asia. Its large square head, its flowing mane (in the males only) and its tufted tail distinguish it. From tip to tip it can reach a length of 3 m; a weight of 225 kg.

Lion and Unicorn, the supporting figures of the royal arms of Great Britain, date from the union of Scotland with England (1603) at the accession of James I (James VI of Scotland), the lion representing England and the unicorn Scotland.

Liqueurs are essences combined with alcoholic liquid, and are of many kinds, named according to their flavourings or place of production, and include Maraschino, Chartreuse, Curaçao, Benedictine, Noyau, Kümmel, etc.

Liquid, the name given to matter in such state that it takes its shape from the containing vessel. The volume it occupies is independent of the container, however. *See* **F17, 18.**

Liquid Crystals form a special class of substance and are true liquids in that they flow easily and can be poured. However, unlike ordinary liquids, liquid crystals have their molecules arranged with geometrical regularity in one or two dimensions, so that they have a certain internal structure similar to that of solid crystals. They are fairly complicated chemicals with somewhat elongated molecules. Liquid crystals are of interest to biologists as well as to chemists and physicists, and not just because they account for the iridescence of beetles. Some body fluids are in fact liquid crystals. There are also technological applications because of their unique electrical and optical properties. They are receiving increasing attention for these reasons. *See also* **Crystals.**

Litanies were first used in church processions in the 5th cent. The first English litany was commanded to be recited in the Reformed churches by Henry VIII in 1544.

Lithium, a soft metallic element, symbol Li, similar to sodium. It is very reactive and is stored under paraffin oil. It is the lightest metal element.

Lithography, the art of drawing on stone and printing therefrom, was discovered by Alois Senefelder about 1796, and was introduced into England a few years later. Many improvements in the art have been made, especially in chrome-lithography and photo-lithography.

Litre, a metric measure, was abolished in 1964 as a scientific unit of volume, but remains as a special name for the cubic decimetre and as an everyday unit, *e.g.*, a litre of petrol.

Liturgy, the name given to the Church ritual, though strictly applying only to the portion used in the celebration of the Eucharist or Lord's Supper. The Anglican liturgy is laid down in the Book of Common Prayer (1662). Temporary powers granted by Parliament in

1965 to the Church to make changes in the form of worship were made permanent in 1974.

Liverworts (Hepatics), a class of simple green plants related to the mosses. There is no differentiation into stem and leaves. Liverworts are most common in damp situations, such as the banks of ditches.

Lizard, the name given to a diversified order of reptiles, of which there are about 1,600 species. Included among the lizards are the geckos, chameleons, glass snakes, skinks and blind worms.

Llama, mammals related to the camels, from which they differ in small size, absence of humps, and more woolly coat. The domestic llama of S. America is used as a beast of burden, also providing wool, meat and milk. *See also* **Alpaca, Guanaco.**

Loadstone *or* **Lodestone**, an oxide of iron, found chiefly in Sweden and Norway. Its scientific name is magnetite. It has the power of attracting pieces of iron and served as the first magnets used in compasses. One of the class of non-metallic magnetic materials nowadays known as " ferrites " (*q.v.*).

Lobby Correspondents are political correspondents of newspapers who do not report the actual proceedings of Parliament—this is done by Parliamentary Correspondents—but interpret political news and events.

Lobsters are marine crustacean animals existing in large numbers in the northern seas of Europe and America and in fair proportion on some parts of the British coasts, especially in the neighbourhood of the Channel Islands.

Locarno, Treaty of, 1925, whereby Germany, France and Belgium undertook to maintain their present frontiers and to abstain from the use of force against each other. Hitler broke the pact by re-occupying the Rhineland, the demilitarisation of which had been recognised by Germany.

Locust, insects of the grasshopper family, but much more powerful. They are inhabitants of hot countries, and often make their appearance in untold millions, like clouds, devastating all the vegetation that comes within their course. The locust-tree (*Ceratonia siliqua*) is supposed to have furnished food to St. John the Baptist in the wilderness, and its " beans " have accordingly been styled " St. John's Bread ".

Loess, a deposit of silt or marl laid down by wind action. The biggest loess deposits are in Asia, the source of the dust of which they are composed probably being the deserts of Central Asia. Large deposits in Europe are thought to have originated from the edge of ice sheets during the Ice Age.

Logarithms, a system of calculation invented by John Napier in 1614, and developed by Henry Briggs a few years later. Thus if a number is expressed as the power of another number, *i.e.*, if $a = b^n$, then n is said to be the logarithm of a to base b, written $\log_b a$. Common logs are to base 10 and Napierian to base 2·7182818 . . ., expressed as e. Their use represents a great saving of time.

Logical Positivism. *See* **Section J.**

Lollards. *See* **Section J.**

Lombards, a German people, originating on the Elbe, who settled in Italy in the 6th cent., occupying northern and central regions, and establishing a kingdom with Pavia as capital. They were conquered by Charlemagne in 774, but left their name to the region of Lombardy. Lombard Street, London, takes its name from the Lombard merchants and bankers who came to settle there in the 12th cent.

London Clay, geological stratum which occupies much of the London Basin and part of the Hampshire Basin. It represents the lower stratum of the Eocene. Outside the metropolis, brickfields utilise the clay for brickmaking. Water held down in the Chalk by this impervious stratum is tapped by a number of artesian wells in London. The tunnels of the Capital's underground railways run through the London Clay.

London University comprises nearly one-third of the academic activity of the United Kingdom, and is recognised as one of the great universities of the world. Originated in the foundation of a non-sectarian college in Gower Street in 1828. Among the chief colleges are: University, Kings, Imperial College of Science and Technology, London School of Economics, School of Oriental and African Studies, Queen Mary, Birkbeck, Royal Holloway, Bedford, Westfield and Queen Elizabeth College. London University was the first to throw open all degrees to women (1878).

Long Distance Routes. The National Parks and Access to the Countryside Act 1949 provided for the establishment in England and Wales of Long Distance Footpaths and Bridleways. The following have been approved: Pennine Way (a magnificent hill walk of 250 miles (402 km) from Edale in Derbyshire along the Pennines over the Cheviots to the Scottish border); Pembrokeshire Coast Path, Dyfed; Offa's Dyke Path (168 miles (270 km) along the marches of Wales); South Downs Way (Beachy Head to Salisbury); South-West Peninsula Coast Path (North Cornwall, South Cornwall, South Devon, Somerset and North Devon, Dorset); Yorkshire Coast and North York Moors. The Pennine Way (the first long-distance footpath), the South Downs Way (the first long-distance bridleway), Offa's Dyke (one of the most important remaining earthworks of its kind in northwestern Europe), and the Yorkshire Wolds Way have been opened. *See also* **National Parks.**

Longitude of a point on the earth's surface is the angle which the meridian through the poles and that point makes with some standard meridian. The meridian through Greenwich is usually accepted as the standard meridian and the longitude is measured east or west of that line. As the earth revolves through 360° in 24 h, 15° longitude represent 1 hour's difference in apparent time.

Long Parliament (1640–60), marked the end of Charles I's 11-year attempt to govern without Parliament. It carried through what has come to be called " the English Revolution " and was the parliament of the civil war (1642–49).

Lord Lieutenant is the Queen's representative in the county, and his office is now largely ceremonial. On his recommendation the magistrates or Justices of the Peace are appointed by the Lord Chancellor. The office was created in 1549 to take over the military duties of the sheriff.

Lords, House of, the Upper House of the British Parliament composed of Lords Spiritual and Lords Temporal. The former consist of the two Archbishops and twenty-four English Bishops and the latter of Peers and Peeresses. The right of the Lords to veto Bills passed by the Commons is restricted by the Parliament Acts of 1911 and 1949. The Lord Chancellor presides over the House of Lords. Under the Peerage Act 1963 a peerage may be disclaimed for life. *See* **Section C, Part I.**

Louse, parasitic insect found on the skin of birds and mammals. The bird or biting lice belong to the order *Mallophaga*; the true or sucking lice to the order *Anoplura*. Two species of lice parasitise man, and one of these, the body louse, is a carrier of typhus.

Louvre, one of the old royal palaces of Paris, was built in its present form partly by Francis I and added to by later monarchs, Louis XIV completing the edifice. Napoleon I turned it into a museum and enriched it with the plunder of many foreign art galleries. The great extension to the Louvre building begun by Napoleon I was completed under Napoleon III in 1857. Much injury was done to the building during the Commune of 1871. Amongst other famous treasures it houses the Venus de Milo and Leonardo da Vinci's masterpiece, *La Gioconda*.

LSD (d-lysergic acid diethylamide). This hallucinogenic drug has achieved wide notoriety because of its use by certain people to give themselves abnormal mental experiences. Doctors have frequently warned against the dangers of its use. It is active in extremely small quantities and a dose as small as a fifty-millionth part of a gram can cause marked disturbances of the mental function in man. LSD has been used in the study of mental disease because it produces symptoms very similar to mental disorders such as schizophrenia.

Luddites, a combination of workmen formed in

1811, in a period of great distress, with the object of destroying the new textile machinery then being largely adopted, which they regarded as the cause of their troubles. Their first outbreak was at Nottingham, and was stated to have been started by a young apprentice named Ned Ludd. Afterwards, serious Luddite riots occurred in various parts of the country, especially in West Yorkshire, where many people were killed, mills were destroyed and numbers of rioters were tried and executed. Charlotte Brontë used the period in her novel, *Shirley*.

Lunatic Fringe, term used by Theodore Roosevelt to characterise adherents of reform movements who refuse to recognise difficulty of practical administration and insist upon immediate fulfilment of an extreme programme.

Lutecium, element of the rare-earth metal group discovered in 1907 by Urbain.

Lutheranism. *See* **Section J.**

Lynx, cats of sturdy build, with tufted ears and spotted fur, inhabiting many parts of the world, including Northern and Central Europe. They commit serious ravages among sheep and goats and are very fierce.

Lyon King of Arms, the President of the Scottish Lyon Court, and head of the heraldic organisation for Scotland.

Lyre-Bird, a remarkable family of Australian birds, the males of which possess a beautiful lyre-shaped tail. The bird is not more than 38 cm long, but its tail, displayed during its remarkable courtship dance, is 58 cm in length. There are two species: the Superb and Albert's Lyrebird.

M

Macaque. A family of monkeys which include the Barbary ape (specimens of which live on Gibraltar), the Rhesus macaque (the organ grinder's monkey and the one used for experimental work in the investigation of disease), the Bonnet monkey of southern India and Sri Lanka, the Crab-eating and the Pig-tailed monkeys of south-eastern Asia.

Macaw, a genus of large parrots with brilliant scarlet and sky-blue plumage, with interminglings of green. Native to South and Central America.

McCarthyism, the term given to the wave of anti-Communist hysteria, associated with the name of Senator McCarthy (1908–57), whose campaign of vilification resulted in the loss of careers and livelihood of many innocent Americans.

Mace, originally a weapon of offence, now an ensign of authority borne before officers of state and other dignitaries. In the House of Commons the mace is handed to an official of the Crown by the Sergeant-at-Arms at the close of a parliamentary session.

Mach Number. Unit of flight speed. The ratio of speed of flight to speed of sound under same conditions of pressure and density. Speed of sound at sea-level is 762 mile/h (1,226 km/h), so flight speed of 381 mile/h (613 km/h) is equivalent to a Mach Number of ½. At supersonic speeds the Mach Number is greater than 1; subsonic speeds, less than 1.

Mackerel, a familiar sea-fish existing in large numbers in the northern waters of both hemispheres. In May and June immense shoals are to be found round the British coasts.

Macromolecules are very large molecules about 10,000 times or more as heavy as ordinary small molecules like hydrogen. Most are built up from a large number of simple sub-units, *i.e.*, are polymers (*q.v.*). The term macromolecule is often used in biology, *e.g.*, starch and cellulose are biological macromolecules, both built from glucose sub-units. Other important ones are proteins and nucleic acids. The properties of macromolecules depend on the sub-units of which they are composed.

Madder, one of the most important of dye-stuffs, largely used in producing Turkey-red dye, but now superseded by synthetic alizarin. Natural madder is the root of the *Rubia tinctorum*.

Maelstrom, a great whirlpool. The most famous is that off the coast of Norway, between the islands of Moskenës and Mosken, of the Lofoten group, the power of which has been much exaggerated.

Mafia. A term which is connected with Italo-American organised crime. Historically, remoteness from the central government of Italy encouraged the growth in Sicily in the 19th cent. of *mafiosi*, key-men who gained power through fear and violence. Contemporary police records give details of *mafia* behaviour in defending their authority. Emigration of vast numbers of southern Italians to the United States led to a new type of urban *mafioso* who became connected with gangsterism and vice. Sometimes called the *Cosa Nostra*, the organisation has infiltrated city governments and is reputed to be in control of drug smuggling and other illegal operations. In Italy neo-fascist groups have made use of the *mafia* in acts of terrorism, especially in the north. An Italian parliamentary commission of inquiry into *mafia* activities set up in 1962 took twelve years to report. No legislation has as yet followed its recommendations.

Magellan, Clouds of, the name given to a pair of small galaxies, satellite systems of our own galaxy, visible only from the southern hemisphere. On account of their relative nearness to the earth (186,000 light-years), they are receiving much attention from astronomers.

Magenta, a blue-red aniline dye discovered in 1859 by Sir W. H. Perkin, and named after the great battle of that year between the French and Austrians.

Magic. *See* **Section J.**

Magistrates *or* **Justices of the Peace** preside over petty sessional and juvenile courts and are appointed by the Lord Chancellor on the recommendation of the Lord Lieutenant of the County. Most J.P.s are laymen and are unpaid. In certain big towns a legally-qualified, paid, full-time magistrate is appointed, known as a stipendiary magistrate. In London stipendiaries are known as Metropolitan Stipendiary Magistrates. J.P.s are no longer appointed over the age of 60 and they must retire when they reach 70. By the Justices of the Peace Act, 1968, *ex officio* J.P.s are abolished, except for the Lord Mayor and aldermen of the City of London.

Magma, molten rock material rich in volatile constituents prior to its eruption at the surface. On eruption and loss of volatiles it becomes lava.

Magna Carta was sealed by King John at Runnymede on 15 June 1215, in obedience to the insistent demands of the barons, and has been confirmed many times by later monarchs. It was not a revolutionary document. It laid down what the barons took to be the recognised and fundamental principles for the government of the realm and bound king and barons alike to maintain them. Its main provisions were that no man should be punished without fair trial, that ancient liberties generally should be preserved, and that no demands should be made by an overlord to his vassal (other than those recognised) without the sanction of the great council of the realm.

Magnesium, a metallic element, symbol Mg, first isolated in 1808 by Sir Humphry Davy, who prepared it by electrolysing the chloride. Its chief ores are magnesite and dolomite. Industrially it is obtained by electrolysis. Many important light alloys contain magnesium. The metal burns with a very bright light, and for this reason it is used in photographers' flash bulbs and also in firework manufacture.

Magnetic Storms, large irregular disturbances superimposed upon the normal magnetic field of the earth. They may occur at any time, but are most frequent during equinoctial months and in years of sunspot maxima. World-wide in extent, magnetic storms are most pronounced in the polar regions, being due apparently to intense electric currents located in the upper atmosphere near to the zones of greatest auroral frequency. One theory attributes the high ionisation of these belts to solar radiation. Magnetic storms cause radio fade-outs and interfere with telegraphic communication.

Magnetism, originally the name given to the quality of attraction for iron possessed by lodestone (*q.v.*). Now known to be a phenomenon inseparably connected with electricity (**F18**). Strong magnetic attraction is possessed by a comparatively small class of substances; iron, nickel and cobalt are the most common elements, but there are several less well known, *e.g.*, gadolinium. Many alloys have valuable magnetic properties which make possible numberless technical devices. New magnetic substances are always being developed (*see* **Ferrite**). The earth acts like a huge magnet with its axis inclined at about 11° to the axis of rotation, the magnetic poles being on the Boothia Peninsula (North Canada) and South Victoria Land (Antarctica). The magnetic field at the surface consists of the regular field of a magnetised sphere with an irregular field superimposed upon it. Variation in the magnetic forces occurs from place to place and from time to time, and maps showing the distribution over the globe of points of the same declination (*i.e.*, the angle which the magnetic meridian makes with the geographical one) are of the utmost importance in navigation. In the south-east of the British Isles, at present, a magnetic needle points 9° and in the north-west 14° west of true north. Little is known regarding the origin of the main (regular) field of the earth, but it is believed that the irregularities are due to the presence of intense electric currents in the upper atmospheres and local magnetisation of rock strata. In 1967 the discovery was claimed of isolated magnetic poles, *i.e.*, north and south magnetic poles existing separately, just as positive and negative electrical charges exist separately. If this is confirmed it will probably rank as one of the most important experimental results of the 20th cent., because of its significance for the theory of electromagnetism and fundamental particles.

Magnetohydro-dynamics. A current-carrying wire always experiences a force if it is in a magnetic field. This is the well-known electrodynamic force, and electric motors work because of it. If the current is carried in a fluid, *e.g.*, a liquid metal or a plasma, these forces cause bodily movements of the fluid, which are in general very difficult to calculate. The forces are then called *magnetohydro-dynamic forces*. Now magnetic fields are themselves produced by electric currents; so a current flowing in a fluid produces a magnetic field, which then reacts on the fluid itself by means of the magnetohydrodynamic forces. In the Harwell machine Zeta, used in studying the technical problems of thermonuclear reactions, this effect acts so as to constrict the electric discharge on to the axis of the tube and thus keeps it away from the walls. This action is assisted by an extra magnetic field produced by a separate current flowing in metallic conductors outside the tube. Thus the hot plasma is contained by magnetohydro-dynamic forces and not at all by the material tube wall. In practical devices of the future magnetic forces may have to sustain plasma pressure of 60 atmospheres—a pressure for which a thick steel wall would normally be used! *See also* **Plasma Physics**.

Magnificat, the hymn of the Virgin Mary, given in Luke 1, 46 beginning in the Vulgate with the words "Magnificat anima mea Dominum" ("My soul doth magnify the Lord"), and used in the services of all Christian Churches.

Magnitude in astronomy is a measure of the apparent brightness of a star, which is inversely proportional to the square of its distance. A low number indicates a bright star, and a high one a faint star. The *absolute magnitude* is a measure of *real* brightness, *i.e.*, the brightness a star would have at a standard distance away of 32·6 light years. The distance can be calculated if the apparent and absolute magnitudes are known.

Magnolia, species of the family *Magnoliaceae* comprising many beautiful trees, and shrubs with large and fragrant flowers, and chiefly native to North America and Asia. Introduced in 1688. *See* **T10**.

Magpie, a well-known bird of the crow family, of glossy black and white plumage, famed for its mischievous propensities.

Magyars, the Hungarian race who came to eastern Europe from S.W. Asia and settled in Hungary in the 10th cent. Their language belongs to the Finno-Ugrian group.

Mahdi, an Arab leader of great influence, invested with powers akin to those of a Messiah in the Mohammedan mind. The title was taken by Mohammed Ahmed, who overran the Egyptian Sudan, and in 1885 captured Khartoum.

Maidenhair Tree *or* **Ginkgo.** This tree takes its name from the shape of its leaves, which resemble those of the maidenhair fern. Widely cultivated in China and Japan. It is the only survivor of an order of gymnosperms which flourished in Mesozoic times. Botanically interesting because the male gametes are motile.

Malmaison, château at Rueil-Malmaison, a western suburb of Paris. It derives its name from having been inhabited in the 11th cent. by the Norman brigand Odon, and afterwards, according to the tradition, by evil spirits, exorcised by the monks of St. Denis. It was the residence of Napoleon and of the Empress Josephine after her divorce. She died there in 1814 as the result of a chill caught while showing the Russian Emperor round the grounds. In 1900 it was given to the nation.

Malmsey, a strong, sweet wine originally made in Greece, but now also in Spain, Madeira and the Azores; known also as Malvoisie.

Maltose, a sugar formed in cereal grains during germination. It is produced by hydrolysis of starch, and further hydrolysis converts the maltose into glucose.

Mamluks, commonly known as Mameluks, were originally—in the 13th cent.—a bodyguard of Turkish and Circassian slaves in the service of the Sultan of Egypt, and attained such influence that in 1250 they were strong enough to appoint one of their own body to the throne of Egypt. After that a succession of Mamluk Sultans reigned down to 1517. Then the Turks annexed Egypt, and the Mamluks were taken into the service of the Beys. They again came to the front after Nepoleon's conquest of Egypt, and for a time resumed governmental sway; but in 1811 they were decoyed into the citadel of Cairo and massacred by order of Mehemet Ali.

Mammoth, extinct elephants of gigantic size. In 1799 the first perfectly preserved specimen was found in Siberia in a block of ice. It was in prehistoric times an inhabitant of Britain and other parts of Europe, as well as of Asia and America.

Mammoth Cave of Kentucky, one of the largest known limestone caverns in the world, with subterranean passages at different levels, lakes and rivers (the Echo R. flows 110 m below the surface); stalactites and stalagmites abound.

Manatee, an aquatic mammal of the sea cow (Sirenia) order of mammals, averaging when full grown from 3–3·6 m in length, with shovel-shaped tail, and forelimbs and nails which almost give the appearance of arms and hands. In spite of their ungainly aspect, these creatures are believed to have given rise to the legend of mermaids.

Manchus, the original nomadic race inhabiting northern Manchuria who invaded China early in the 17th cent. A Manchu dynasty occupied the imperial throne of China from 1644 to 1911.

Mandarin, the name given to a powerful Chinese official, civil or military, under the old régime, whose rank was shown by the wearing of a button on the cap. Mandarin is the major language of N. China.

Mandible, the lower jaw in human anatomy. The two parts of a bird's beak are known as the upper and lower mandible. The term is also used for biting jaws in arthropods.

Manganese, a metallic element, symbol Mn, discovered by Scheele in 1774. It is silver-white, not very hard (it forms a hard alloy with carbon), brittle, and tarnishes when exposed to air. Its chief ore is pyrolusite (manganese dioxide). Steels containing manganese are very tough, and used for making machine parts.

Maniple, eucharistic vestment worn over left arm.

Manna, a tree of the ash genus, *Fraxinus ornus*, growing in the South of Europe and in the East and exuding a sweet substance which is gathered, boiled and eaten.

Manometer, instrument used to measure gas

pressure. Usually a U-tube containing water or mercury, one end open to the atmosphere, the other to the gas whose pressure is to be measured. More sensitive for small pressures than the Bourdon gauge.

Manors were estates originally granted in Anglo-Saxon times as rewards for knightly service, and included the privilege of a special court with jurisdiction, criminal and civil, within the manorial territory. *See* **Court-Leet.**

Mansion House, the official residence of the Lord Mayor of London, stands opposite to the Bank of England, and was erected in 1739–53 from the designs of George Dance.

Mantis. Large insects belonging to the same order as the locusts and grasshoppers. The manner in which the forelegs are held, as though in suppliance, has gained for these insects the common name of "praying mantis". They are distributed throughout the warmer countries of the world.

Manx, the Celtic dialect (Manx Gaelic) of the Isle of Man, now on the point of extinction.

Maoism. *See* **Section J.**

Maoris, the race found in New Zealand at the time of its discovery by Captain Cook in 1769. They are believed to have migrated from Polynesia about 1350. Up to 1871 they were frequently in arms against the European settlers but their high intelligence and stamina enabled them to adapt themselves and the New Zealand laws have encouraged equal citizenship. They number 223,300 (1971). Today in New Zealand a pure Maori is a rarity.

Maple, trees native to the northern hemisphere. There are over 100 species. The sycamore is the best-known species growing in Britain. The sugar maple abounds in Canada and the eastern parts of the United States. The sugar is tapped by boring holes in the tree in February and March, and the juice that escapes is collected and evaporated. The maple-leaf is the Canadian national emblem.

Maquis, name of the dense scrub in Mediterranean France and Corsica, providing good cover for bandits and outlaws. The French resistance movement adopted the name Maquis during the German Occupation, 1940–45.

Marble is limestone in its hardest and most crystalline form. There are many varieties—33 were used in the building of the Paris Opera House—but white is the purest and rarest. White marble was used by the ancient Greeks for their temples and statues. Among the famous marbles of Italy are the Carrara and Siena marbles, which were used by Renaissance sculptors. Devonshire and Derbyshire yield some beautiful marbles and Connemara furnishes a serpentine-marble.

March, the third month of the year, and the first of the old Roman Calendar. It was named after the god Mars, and was the *Hlyd* (storm) *monath* of the Anglo-Saxons.

Mardi Gras, the last day of the Carnival in France, Shrove Tuesday.

Marionettes are puppets moved by strings. They originated in the *Fantoccini* of the 15th cent. which had such a vogue in Italy and elsewhere on the Continent. The English *Punch and Judy* is a version of Punchinello.

Marlinspike, a pointed iron tool used by sailors to splice wire. The instrument used when rope splicing is called a fid.

Marmoset, small monkeys confined to the New World. Very squirrel-like in appearance, with long bushy tails, and thick woolly fur, they are pretty little animals and the smallest of all monkeys. There are claws, not nails, on their digits, the big toe excepted.

Marprelate Tracts, seditious pamphlets written with great maliciousness by a group of Elizabethan puritans about 1586, and intended to discredit the episcopacy, caused a great sensation in their time and led to the execution of their supposed author, John Penry.

Marquess *or* **Marquis**, the title next in precedence to that of duke. The first English marquess was Rovery de Vere, Earl of Oxford, who received the honour from Richard II, in 1385.

Marquetry, a kind of inlaying in which thin layers of coloured woods are wrought into a design, and mainly used in ornamental floors.

Mars, the fourth nearest planet to the sun (*see* **F7**). There used to be much speculation among scientists about certain dark lines which some observers had seen on the surface of the planet; photographs gave no support to the theory of an artificially constructed network of canals, but it seemed possible they represented areas covered by some simple form of vegetation of the lichenous type. However, the *Mariner* probes have increased our knowledge and raised new questions. *Mariner 9* carried out an extensive study of Mars in 1971/2 covering 85 per cent of the surface in great detail. Important new findings showed that water had played an active rôle in the planet's evolution and that it was not, as scientists had concluded from the *Mariner 6* and *Mariner 7* probes, a dead and featureless planet, but one with its own distinctive character. Photographs revealed four major geological regions: volcanic; equatorial plateau marked by deep canyons, with evidence of water erosion; large cratered terrain like the moon (photographed by the 1969 probes); and a polar region with terrace-like formations and deep grooves. The 1976 *Viking* mission found no organic compounds in the soil analysed but scientists have not ruled out the possibility of life still existing on the planet. The Soviet Union has also sent spaceships to Mars to pioneer new techniques of planetary exploration. Mars has two small moons—Phobos and Deimos.

Marseillaise, the French national hymn, written and composed by Rouget de L'Isle, a French engineer officer, who was inspired to write it in 1792 to encourage the Strasburg conscripts. It immediately became popular, and received its name from the fact that it was sung by the Marseillaise troops while marching into Paris.

Marshalsea, a former prison in Southwark, London, closed 1849. It existed as early as Edward III's time and was used as a jail for royal servants convicted of offences. In its later days it became a debtors' prison. Dickens described it in *Little Dorrit.*

Marsh Gas. *See* **Methane.**

Marsh Tortoise, an amphibious animal of the order *Chelonia*, spread over many countries and inhabiting ponds and small rivers. There are 42 species, and they are all carnivorous.

Marston Moor, near York, was the scene of the famous battle between Prince Rupert and Cromwell on 2 July 1644. Cromwell's victory was the turning-point in the Civil War.

Marsupials, members of the order of pouched mammals. Except for the opossums of America, all marsupials occur in Australasia and include the kangaroos, wallabies and wombats.

Martello Towers, circular forts erected on the coasts of England and Jersey early in the 19th cent. as defences against the threatened Napoleonic invasion. So called from the circular fort at Mortella (Corsica), which resisted an English fleet in 1794.

Marten, carnivorous animals of the weasel family; one species (the Pine Marten) was once common in Britain. Most famous for their fur are the Siberian Sable and the American Marten.

Martial Law is a term loosely employed to indicate the suspension of the administration of normal civil law and its replacement by military authority when this is rendered desirable by such circumstances as war or rebellion.

Martin, a well-known bird-visitor to Britain. It belongs to the swallow family, and the two species that spend their summers here are the house-martin, which makes its nest of mud under the eaves of houses, and the sand martin, which builds in sandy banks.

Martinmas *or* **St. Martin's Day**, falls on 11 November, and is one of the Scottish quarter days. St. Martin was a popular Saint with our ancestors and Martinmas was a busy time for the mediaeval housewife. It was the date when "Martlemas Beef" was dried in the chimney, and enough bacon and mutton cured to last until the spring, because, owing to the scarcity of winter fodder, fresh meat could seldom be obtained. This diet of dried meat without vegetables caused scurvy. St. Martin (c. 316–400) was regarded as the patron saint of drinking and jovial meetings, as well as of reformed drunkards. The spell of fine weather sometimes occurring at Martinmas is called St. Martin's Summer.

Martyrs. People who suffer death in testimony to their faith. Stephen (Acts 6; 7) was the first Christian martyr in 39. The first English martyr was St. Alban, 286, and in Tudor times many eminent churchmen went to the stake. The Smithfield martyrs' memorial church used to be St. Peter's, St. John Street, Clerkenwell. When that church was demolished the memorial moved to the Church of St. James, Clerkenwell Green.

Marxism. *See* **Section J.**

Mason and Dixon Line, boundary line between Pennsylvania and Maryland, for long a source of dispute, drawn up by two English surveyors, Charles Mason and Jeremiah Dixon, between 1763 and 1767. It came to designate the boundary dividing the slave states from the free states of America, and is still used in distinguishing the "North" from the "South".

Masques were light dramatic compositions set to music and performed on special occasions. One of the best-known examples is Milton's "Comus", which was given at Ludlow Castle in 1634.

Mass, the service in the Roman Catholic Church in which are enacted and enshrined Christ's words and actions at the Last Supper. It is high or low, *i.e.*, performed with full choral service, or merely by the rehearsal of prayers without singing. Mass was first celebrated in Latin in the 4th cent., and was introduced into England in the 7th cent. The use of a vernacular language was sanctioned by the Second Vatican Council (1965).

Mass Spectrograph, an instrument for separating isotopes. It works by sorting electrified particles according to their masses; the particles stream through a magnetic and possibly an electric field, and the lightest particles undergo the greatest deflection.

Massorah, a collection of criticisms on the Hebrew text of the Scriptures, and rules for its correct interpretation.

Mast, a long round piece of timber or tubular steel or iron, standing upright in a vessel, and supporting the yards, sails and rigging in general. The earliest ships had only one mast, carrying a simple sail. The number increased until there were 4 or 5, or even more. Above the lower mast of a sailing-ship comes the topmast, and above that, the topgallantmast and royalmast. The position of each mast is indicated by a prefix, as foremast, foretopmast, foretopgallantmast, foreroyalmast, mainmast, maintopmast, etc. The foremast is in the fore of the ship, the mainmast in the centre and the mizzen nearest the stern. In large vessels nowadays the mast does not extend to the keel, as it formerly did, but is usually stopped at the second deck.

Master of the Revels was an important Court official upon whom devolved the arrangement of Court festivities. The office is at least as old as the time of Edward III. By 1737 it seems to have died.

Master of the Rolls, one of the English judges, formerly a judge of Chancery, but since 1881 a judge of the Court of Appeal only. In addition he has charge of the rolls or records of Chancery and ranks next to the Lord Chancellor and Lord Chief Justice.

Mastodon, an extinct order of quadruped closely resembling the elephant in structure, but larger.

Materials Science is a blend of science and technology; it is the use of scientific research methods to study and improve materials for practical use. The deeper understanding so obtained enables scientists to design new substances with hitherto unknown combinations of properties that are useful in engineering, aircraft, nuclear power, surgery, etc. Materials science institutes or university departments will usually contain an assortment of chemists, physicists, metallurgists, ceramicists, engineers and others because materials science brings to bear on materials a great many specialised techniques. The scientific study of materials is bringing continual improvement in metals, ceramics, plastics, fibres and many valuable combinations of these.

Mathematics is a body of knowledge expressed in a language of symbols. *Pure* mathematics studies the propositions that can be deduced in this language by applying definite rules of reasoning to sets of axioms. In *Applied* mathematics, the mathematical language is used, often with great effect, to discuss problems of the real world, such as mechanics, statistics and science generally. In range, subtlety, complexity and depth mathematics is unsurpassed among the intellectual disciplines and its study has attracted some of the most brilliant men in history.

Matins, the first of the canonical hours or services of the day in the Roman Catholic Church and Morning Prayer in the Anglican Church. The daily service in the Roman breviary (*q.v.*) consists of eight offices or "hours", fixed by canon, for prayer and devotion. Formerly, Matins was recited or sung at midnight, Lauds at sunrise, Prime at 6 a.m., Terce at 9 a.m., Sext at midday, Nones at 3 p.m., Vespers at sunset and Compline before retiring for the night. Lauds are now commonly joined to Matins.

Matrix, a rectangular array of numbers considered as a single mathematical object. There are special rules for multiplying and adding matrices and they are often used in mathematics, physics and elsewhere to simplify calculations and as a notational device.

Mau-Mau, a secret, anti-European, terrorist movement which agitated the Kikuyu tribe of Kenya during the years 1953–57. Mau-mau was a symptom of native insecurity and discontent; emergency powers were lifted in November 1959, and large-scale reforms were instituted. Kenya attained independence in December 1963 with Mr. Jomo Kenyatta as Prime Minister.

Maundy Thursday, the day before Good Friday, commemorates the Last Supper. "Maundy" derives from Christ's command (mandatum) to his disciples on that day to love one another. It was the custom in the monasteries for the monks to wash the feet of the poor on this day, and for many centuries the sovereigns of England, through their almoners, have distributed money, food and clothing to "as many old men and as many old women as the Sovereign is years of age". The Royal Maundy ceremony is still observed, maundy coins being struck from standard silver.

Mausoleum, a special place of sepulture, generally for the reception of the remains of members of a royal or other family of distinction. The name is derived from the tomb of King Mausolus at Halicarnassus, erected 352 B.C., and forming one of the seven wonders of the ancient world. Another mausoleum of antiquity is that of Hadrian in Rome.

Mauve, a colouring matter produced from lichens by Dr. Stenhouse in 1848, but in 1856 obtained from aniline by William Perkin (1838–1907), who gave it the name Mauveen. This was the first synthetic organic dyestuff ever to be produced, which led to the building up of the great synthetic dyestuffs industry (which Germany dominated before the first world war).

May, the fifth month of the year, but the third of the ancient Roman calendar. Supposed to be named after Maia, the mother of Mercury, to whom sacrifices were offered on the first day of this month. In England in former days May Day was made the occasion of many festivities, including the crowning of the May Queen, dancing round the Maypole, etc.

"Mayflower", the name of the ship which in 1620 conveyed the Pilgrim Fathers, 101 in number, from England to America. *See* **Pilgrim Fathers.**

May Fly. *See* **Ephemoptera.**

Mazarin Bible, an edition of the Latin Vulgate, acknowledged as the masterpiece of the Gutenberg press (1456). It was the first book completely printed from movable types. It is called the Mazarin Bible because the first copy to capture the attention of scholars was found in the library of Cardinal Mazarin, in Paris. Sometimes called the Gutenberg or the 42-line Bible.

Mean. In statistics and mathematics generally understood to be the arithmetic mean. The geometric mean between two quantities is the square root of their product. *See* **Average.**

Mechanical Equivalent of Heat. *See* **Joule.**

Medals, as decorations for military service, were first issued in this country by Charles I, who ordered medals for gallantry to be distributed to certain soldiers in 1643. Medals were also issued to officers and men who were victorious against the Dutch fleet in 1653. After Lord Howe's victory in 1794 a naval medal was instituted. Medals were also struck for the victory of Waterloo, and since that time special medals have been issued in connection with all our wars. The Victoria Cross, a special reward for personal gallantry in the Navy, Army and Air Force, was instituted in 1856. The George Cross for gallantry instituted in 1940 ranks next to the Victoria Cross. The Military Cross was instituted in 1914.

Meerschaum, a white or yellow-white earthy mineral, found in beds in Asia Minor, Greece, and other places, is a silicate of magnesium allied with water. Its chief use is in making pipe-bowls.

Megalith, a prehistoric monument, consisting of a large single stone or a group of such stones, in a circle as at Stonehenge or in burial chambers as at New Grange, Ireland. Megalithic monuments have been constructed by different peoples in different parts of the world since the third millennium B.C.

Meiosis, a special type of cell division by which the gametes or sex cells are generated, resulting in the sperm or ovum receiving only half the number of chromosomes found in a somatic cell. *See* **Mitosis.**

Mendelian Law. The first statistical rules of inheritance, determining the ratio of variation of characteristics in the offspring of differing individuals, and the classification of characters discontinuously inherited, were first formulated by the Austrian monk Gregor Mendel. The results of his most important experiments in the crossing of peas were published in 1866, and showed that when two races are crossed, the resultant hybrids will exhibit the dominant features of one parent, but the offspring of the second generation will show those of both grandparents. *See* **Section F, Part IV.**

Mendicant Friars, certain religious orders which spread over Europe in the 13th cent., and comprised the Franciscans, Dominicans, Augustines and Carmelites. Originally they depended entirely on alms.

Mercator's Projection, a method of indicating meridians and parallels of latitudes on maps, introduced by Mercator in the 16th cent., and still universally used in navigators' charts.

Mercury, one of the smaller planets and the nearest to the sun, being $57{\cdot}9 \times 10^6$ km distant. It has no satellite. *See* **F7.**

Mercury *or* **Quicksilver,** symbol Hg (Latin *hydrargyrum*) is one of the oldest-known metals, whose chief ore is the sulphide, cinnabar, found in certain parts of Spain, China, Japan, Mexico and South America. It is liquid at ordinary temperature and is used in the construction of barometers and thermometers. Alloys of mercury are called amalgams. It is also of great value in medicine. The metal is used in the mercury-vapour (or "sunlight") lamp, since the vapour gives a bright yellow-white glow in an electric discharge.

Mercy-killing, taking the life of a person suffering from a painful and incurable disease. The killer is often actuated by a good *motive*—the desire to relieve hopeless suffering; but the *intention* is to kill, and the act, in English law, is therefore a crime. (It is not necessary for the prosecution to prove any motive.)

Meridian, an imaginary circle extending through the North and South Poles and any given place. When the sun is at its midday height at any place it is "on the meridian"; hence the terms ante-meridian (a.m.) and post-meridian (p.m.). *See also* **Greenwich Mean Time.**

Merino Sheep were imported into England from Spain in 1788 and had great influence in improving native breeds, especially in regard to the quality of the wool.

Merit, Order of, founded by King Edward VII in 1902 as a special distinction for eminent men and women without conferring a knighthood upon them. The Order has twenty-four British companions in addition to foreign honorary members limited in number, as the choice of members is, by the Sovereign's pleasure. Lord Kelvin was the founder companion. Dr. Sarvepalli Radhakrishnan (1963) was an honorary member. Florence Nightingale (1907), Professor Dorothy Hodgkin (1965) and Dame Veronica Wedgwood (1969) are the only women to have received this coveted decoration.

Merovingians, the name given to the family that ruled over France from about 500 to 750. Clovis was first of the line and Childeric the last.

Mesons (from Greek *meso* = middle), a family of unstable particles of mass between that of an electron and that of a proton. Some are positive, some negative, some neutral. No stable meson is known, the longest-lived particle having a lifetime of only two-millionths of a second. The first of these particles was discovered in cosmic radiation in 1937 and called the mu-meson or *muon*. In 1947 a heavier type was discovered called the pi-meson or *pion* which behaved like the meson predicted on theoretical grounds by Yukawa in 1935. The pion is connected with the theory of nuclear forces. *See also* **F13, 14.**

Mesozoic. The geological era which includes the Triassic, Jurassic and Cretaceous rocks. *See* **F45.**

Metabolism, the general term for the physical and chemical processes occurring within a living organism. *See* **F26.**

Metalloid, an element which has properties intermediate between those of a metal and a non-metal. Arsenic is a metalloid.

Metamorphic Rocks are such geological deposits as have undergone alterations of structure and mineral reorganisation. The most active agents in producing these metamorphic changes are heat, water and pressure. *See* **F8(2).**

Metamorphosis, period of development from egg to adult, during which the animals have different forms, as found, *e.g.*, in the life histories of frog and butterfly.

Meteorites. The word meteor originally signified any natural phenomenon, but in modern usage meteors are small bodies coming from inter-planetary space which become luminous by friction on enterng the earth's atmosphere. Popularly called "shooting stars". Larger meteors are known as fireballs. Some of these reach the ground. The object which has been a meteor in flight then becomes a meteorite. In some meteorites iron and nickel are the chief metals (siderites), others are like rock (aerolites). The iron meteorites are more common amongst those which have been preserved, but falls of rock-like meteorites occur more frequently. At L'Aigle in France in 1803 from 2000 to 3000 meteorite stones fell; this fall is famous because it convinced scientists that meteorites really came from outside our atmosphere. (The largest meteorite stone actually known to have fallen to earth is one which descended in Emmott County, Iowa, in 1870, weighing 197 kg.) A meteorite weighing no less than 37 tonnes found in Greenland is now in New York. On 30 June 1908, an enormous object fell in Siberia in a sparsely-inhabited region. A hot blast destroyed all trees within a radius of about 8–16 km, the explosion waves being recorded by barographs as far distant as London, Washington and Batavia. For the next few nights there was in Europe in the northern sky brilliant illumination due to sunlight falling on clouds of dust at a great height in the atmosphere. Whether this dust had accompanied the object in its journey through space like the tail of a comet or whether the dust had come from Siberia is unknown. (Many Russian astronomers now believe this Siberian meteorite, as it is commonly called, was the nucleus of a small comet.) When the place where the object fell was visited in 1927 some 200 craters were found, but no considerable meteorite has been recovered. Meteorites are possibly débris from the disintegration of a body in the solar system.

Meteorology, the science of the atmosphere considered as a heat engine. Deals with weather, climate, optical phenomena, atmospheric electricity, physical processes such as radiation and precipitation, the dynamics and structure of cyclones, anticyclones, etc. Wide application to problems of aviation, agriculture, commerce and shipping. Meteorological observing stations are in operation all over the world, and on the simultaneous or synoptic reports of their instrument readings and estimates of pressure, temperature, humidity, speed and direction of wind, rain, character and amount of cloud, visibility, etc., forecasts, gale, snow and frost warnings are based. Instruments carried by earth satellites (*e.g.*, *Tiros*, *Nimbus*) outside the atmosphere can make systematic observations on a world-wide basis of the atmospheric circulation, through observation of cloud cover and of the thermal radiation into space from the atmosphere. Such observations together with the use of computers are of great importance for weather analysis and forecasting. The main communications centre for the UK is at the headquarters of the Meteorological Office at Bracknell, Berkshire, where the collection, editing and re-transmission of weather messages continue according to strict schedules day and night throughout the year.

Methane. The simplest hydrocarbon, compounded of one carbon atom and four hydrogen atoms. This gas occurs over marshes and swamps, where it is liberated in the decay of vegetable matter. It is the main constituent of natural gas, and also occurs in coal-mines, where it is called "fire-damp" because of the explosive character of its mixture with air. Formerly this natural gas was removed from the coal seams and ran to waste; now in many countries (including Britain) it is being used for commercial purposes.

Methodism. *See* **Section J.**

Methylated Spirit, a mixture of 90 parts by volume ethyl alcohol, 9½ parts wood naphtha (methyl alcohol), ½ part crude pyridine, together with small amounts of petroleum oil and methyl violet dye. Industrial methylated spirit consists of a mixture of 95 parts by volume ethyl alcohol and 5 parts wood naphtha. It is used as a solvent and a fuel.

Metre, the rhythmical pattern of Verse. *See* **English Verse, Section M.**

Metre, unit of length in the metric system; since 1960 the wavelength of the orange-red light of krypton 86 has been adopted as the basis of the international unit of length. Before that (since 1889) the platinum–iridium bar kept at Sèvres was the international prototype metre.

Metric System, the system of weights and measures based on the gramme and the metre, smaller and larger units being decimals and multiples of the primary units respectively. A decimal currency was adopted in France in 1795 and the metric system of weights and measures in 1799. (In that year the quadrant of the earth was surveyed and the standard metre adopted). Nevertheless the change was accepted slowly, and as late as 1837 the French Government had to pass a law forbidding the use of the old measures. Since then the metric system has been adopted in most of the continental countries and is used universally in scientific work. Although there have been many attempts to get the system adopted in Britain, it was not until 1965 that the Government encouraged the adoption of the metric system of weights and measures. The changeover to decimal coinage was made in 1971; the system of weights and measures in industry is now mainly metric. *See* **N7** for **SI** units.

Mezzotint, a technical method for producing graphic work and works of art. A copper plate is made rough by close cross-hatching, so that a print from it produces an even black. When parts of the cross-hatching are scraped away, these areas will come out white when printed. By skilful use of his tools, the artist or technician can produce pictures finely graded from black to white and with a velvety black as background. The principles of the method were known and practised, for instance, by Rembrandt, but mezzotint became most popular for the reproduction of famous paintings from the end of the 18th cent.

Mica. The mica of commerce is a nearly transparent mineral, which has great heat-resisting power, and can be split into thin plates. The most important micas are muscovite (potassium mica), the commoner variety, phlogopite (magnesium mica) and biotite, the magnesium and iron mica.

Michael, St., and George, St., an order of knighthood originally founded for the Ionian Isles and Malta in 1818, and reorganised in 1869, so as to admit Crown servants connected with the Colonies. The Earl of Derby, Earl Russell and Earl Grey were the first of the new knights.

Michaelmas Day, the festival day of St. Michael and All Angels, 29 September, one of the English quarter days.

Microbe, a term proposed by Sédillot in 1878 to denote any microscopic organism, vegetable or animal, or found on the borderland between the two great natural kingdoms. The term is commonly used, but not by scientists.

Microelectronics, a rapidly developing technology of the 1960s which reduces entire electronic circuits to minute size and embeds them in tiny chips of solid material. These are then called integrated circuits. A circuit consisting of, say, a dozen transistors and fifty resistors can be built into a small piece of semiconductor (*q.v.*) measuring not more than a couple of millimetres in any direction. Hundreds of these circuits can be made simultaneously in penny-size wafers of silicon about one-hundredth of an inch thick. There are great advantages in cheapness, reliability, robustness and speed of electronic performance. The small size is in itself an advantage in space vehicles and medical instruments. Applications to missile control systems, computers and communications equipment are no doubt only the first fruits of this new achievement of the current technological revolution.

Micrometer, an instrument for measuring minute distances; usually attached to the eye-pieces of a microscope or telescope, and consisting of two very fine hairs or wires stretched across the field of view, one fixed, the other movable. It was invented by William Gascoigne in the 17th cent. and improved by later inventors. Sir Joseph Whitworth made one in 1858 to measure the millionth part of an inch.

Micro-organisms, the collective term applied to several types of organism, the most important of which are fungi, viruses, bacteria and protozoa. It is a classification of convenience in biological studies. These organisms are generally simple in their environmental requirements (*e.g.*, have simple nutritional needs) and in cellular organisation. This makes them very suitable for modern biological research. Much of the information on the nature of the genetic code (**F31**) was obtained from experiments on these organisms.

Microphone, device for converting the acoustic energy of sound waves into waves of electrical energy, used in sound amplifying systems. Developed independently by Edison (1877) and Hughes (1878).

Microscope, invented about 1590 by Janssen, and improved by Galileo, Fontana and others, is an instrument which by a lens system magnifies minute objects. Microscopes are simple, compound and binocular. *See also* **Electron Microscope.**

Middle Ages (*c.* A.D. 400–1500), usually considered to be the period between the decline and fall of the Western Roman Empire and the fall of Constantinople to the Turks (*see* **A4-7**). The period covers (*a*) an earlier part ending with the 12th cent. (sometimes called the Dark Ages) when science was dead, when theology was the main preoccupation, and when the language of the learned West was Latin; and (*b*) a later age of Arabian influence when alchemy and astrology (at that time indistinguishable from astronomy) were central interests, technology was advancing, and Greek learning was transmitted by Arab scholars. Characteristic features of the mediaeval scene were monasticism (**Sec. J**), the Crusades (*q.v.*), Gothic art (*q.v.*), feudalism (**Sec. J**), and the supremacy of Islam in the field of learning. The period came to an end with the general decline of Christendom and the ushering in of the Renaissance (**Sec. J**). The term "Middle Ages" was coined by the 17th-cent. German historian Christoph Keller.

Midrash, name given to the homiletical interpretation of some of the Hebrew Scriptures in which allegory and legendary illustration were freely used. Compiled by Jewish rabbis from *c.* A.D. 200.

Millenary Petition was presented to James I in 1603, on behalf of nearly 1000 Puritan Ministers against certain of the rites and ceremonies of the Church of England. The Hampton Court Conference was the outcome of this petition.

Millennium, a period of a thousand years. The term is specifically used of the period of a thousand years during which, according to Rev. xx. 1–5, Christ will reign in person on earth. The Millenarians are a sect that interprets the " Millennium " as beginning with the commencement of the 6001st year from the Creation, which, according to Archbishop Ussher (1581–1650), was in 4004 B.C.

Millipede. Arthropods (**F33**) allied to the centipedes, from which they differ in having two pairs of legs to each body segment (except the first three) instead of one pair. Worm-like in shape but with a pair of antennae on the head, they can do much harm to garden plants. *See* **T29(1).**

Millstone-Grit, a series of grits and sandstones of deltaic origin underlying the coal measures of the Carboniferous system and attaining in England a thickness in parts of 1,525 m. It is from this rock that millstones have been made from time immemorial.

Mimicry, protective similarity of an animal to another animal or to inanimate objects. Examples of the former are the hover flies, which mimic wasps and bees; of the latter, leaf insects, stick insects and caterpillars that look like dead twigs.

Mink. Semi-aquatic mammals closely related to polecats. There is one American species and one European. The fur, which varies light to dark brown, is soft and thick, and is among the most valuable of commercial furs. They now live in the wild in the British Isles.

Minnesingers were minstrel poets of Germany who, during the 12th and 13th cent., composed and sang verses of heroism and love. They were of knightly rank, the counterpart of the French troubadours. *See* **E3(2).**

Minnow, a small fresh-water fish of the carp family, abounding in all the waters of Europe; it has a mottled back and silvery belly, and forms a popular bait for trout.

Minstrels were originally specially appointed instrumentalists and singers—pipers, harpers and gleemen—engaged by barons and manorial lords to amuse their tenants. Later, minstrels assumed nomadic habits, made their way into the houses of the great and were generally welcome. By Elizabeth's time, however, they were too numerous, and were classed as " rogues and vagabonds ", along with actors.

Miracle Plays, popular in England in the 15th cent., were usually religious in character, representing some of the dramatic incidents of the Bible. Staging of plays was one of the many activities of the Guilds of those days. *See* **Section M, Part VI.**

Mirage, an optical illusion caused by unequal temperatures in different layers of the atmosphere near the earth's surface. These temperature variations alter the refracting power of the air and cause light rays to be curved, making the air act as a huge distorting lens. This can happen at sea, in deserts and elsewhere and various types of mirage are known. A common kind in deserts curves light from the sky so that it appears to come from the ground, deceiving the observer into thinking that the sky is reflected in a lake of water. Inverted images of hills, trees, etc. also look as if reflected in the non-existent lake.

Mishna, the first part of the Talmud, setting forth the " Oral Law " of the Jews.

Missal, the name of the mass-book of the Roman Church compiled 492–96 by Pope Gelasius I, and revised by Gregory I, 590–604. The present Roman Missal was sanctioned by the Council of Trent 1546–63. In the Anglican Communion the Book of Common Prayer superseded the Missal in 1549.

Mistle Thrush receives its name from its partiality to the mistletoe-berry. Larger than the song-thrush, with spotted breast rather than speckled.

Mistletoe, a parasitic evergreen with white berries used as a decoration at Christmas-time. The familiar mistletoe of Europe is the *Viscum album*, which grows on the boughs of lime, willow, apple, poplar, maple, ash, hawthorn, but seldom on oak-trees. It was sacred to the Druids, and in Norse mythology it was a mistletoe dart that killed the god Baldur.

Mistral, a cold, dry, northerly wind peculiar to the French coast of the Mediterranean.

Mitosis, cell division whereby each daughter cell receives the same number of chromosomes as the parent cell. When the gametes (sex cells) are formed a special type of division occurs (meiosis) in which the number of chromosomes is halved. *See* **F30(2).**

Mitre, the twofold pointed head-dress of bishops and certain abbots of the Western Church and occasionally of other ecclesiastics.

Moa, the name for several species of ostrich-like extinct birds related to the New Zealand kiwi. The largest species, *Diornis maximus*, stood 2·6 m high, the smallest, *Anomalopteryx parva*, was nearer the size of a turkey. This wingless bird became extinct several centuries ago because of hunting by the Maoris from whom the name comes.

Moabite Stone, a stone of the 9th cent. B.C. containing the earliest known inscription in Phoenician characters, and discovered in the highlands of Moab in 1868. It is now in the Louvre, Paris. It records the campaign between Moab and Israel, a differing account of which is given in the Old Testament.

Moderator, a material used to slow down neutrons in an atomic pile. Examples of moderators are pure graphite and heavy water. *See* **Nuclear Reactors.**

Mohole Project, a scheme to bore through the earth's crust to take samples of the mantle rocks beneath. Drilling trials, led by an American team of geophysicists, began in 1961 near the island of Guadalupe off the Mexican coast in the Pacific. The project, however, was cancelled in 1966 on account of the escalating cost. Russian geophysicists started on a similar experiment, boring through land rocks where the digging is much deeper and higher temperatures are met with. The name " Anti-Cosmos " was given to the project. The boundary between the earth's crustal and mantle rocks is known as the Mohorovičić Discontinuity, or, more simply, as the Moho. The technology of deep sea drilling came from this project. *See* **F8(1).**

Molasses, sugar-cane juice in its uncrystallised form after boiling. The crystallised part is the raw sugar. Used to make rum.

Mole, a small burrowing animal with long, sensitive nose, about the size of a small rat, with short legs and forefeet armed with strong claws for digging in the earth. Their subterranean dwellings are of curiously ingenious construction, and they do not often leave them except to make raids on mice, frogs, snails, etc. The earth-worm, however, is the mole's chief item of food. Not to be confused with the vole which has a blunt nose.

Mole, or gram molecular weight. *See* **F21(8).**

Molecular Biology, a rapidly expanding branch of science mainly concerned with cell structure and function at a molecular level, in particular with genes and enzymes and the interaction between the two. Recent work in Britain has led to the unravelling of the structure of DNA, the hereditary substance of the genes, and has played a major part in uncovering the molecular mechanism of the transfer of hereditary information and the nature of the genetic code. Crystallisation of the first enzyme (urease) took place in 1929; the gene as a definite chemical entity was discovered in 1943. *See* **F26–32.**

Molecule. A group of atoms held together by chemical forces. *See* **F12(2), 20,** *also* **Macromolecule.**

Molybdenum, symbol Mo, a fairly hard white metal with properties resembling those of chromium. Its commonest ore is the sulphide, molybdenite. The chief use of the metals is in the manufacture of alloy steels.

Monasticism. *See* **Section J.**

Monazite, a cerium mineral containing some thorium. Occurs as grains, often as sand (" monazite sands "), derived from granites. Deposits occur in India (Travancore), Russia, Norway, Malagasy Rep., S. Africa, Brazil, USA.

Monday, the second day of the week, called by the Anglo-Saxons *Monandaeg* (moon-day).

Mongoose, species of mammals related to the civets, feeding on vermin and reptiles. These animals, which have long tails and short legs, occur in Africa and Asia (especially India). The biggest mongoose is the Egyptian ichneumon, and this has been introduced into the W. Indies because of its ability to kill large poisonous snakes.

Monitor, a family of lizards most resembling dragons. There are about 30 species widely distributed over the tropical parts of Asia, Australia and Africa.

Monroe Doctrine, a principle of American policy declining any European intervention in political affairs of the American continent, outlined by President Monroe in 1823. At the same time interference was disclaimed with existing European colonies in the Western Hemisphere. The American Civil War hampered the application of the doctrine for some time, but afterwards the United States firmly insisted on it. The Doctrine is not international law, but a national policy of the USA.

Monsoons, regular persistent winds which blow at certain seasons in middle latitudes, mainly in South and East Asia. Their occurrence is related to the great changes of pressure which take place between summer and winter over the land mass. In India the south-west monsoon (June–October) is moisture-laden from its long passage over the sea and in the higher regions, especially, there is heavy rainfall. Sudden reversal of the wind results in the cold north-east monsoon (October–March) which is dry on account of the shelter afforded by the mountain ranges to the north. Frequently the term "monsoon" is applied to denote the associated rainfall without reference to the actual winds.

Monstrance, an ornamental transparent receptacle in which the Sacred Host is carried in procession or exposed for adoration.

Month, the 12th part of the calendar year. A lunar month is the interval of new moon to new moon or full moon to full moon; mean length, 29 days, 12 hours, 44 minutes, 2·87 seconds. A sidereal month represents the time of the moon's revolution from a given star back to the same again, 27 days, 7 hours, 43 minutes, 11·5 seconds. In English law, since 1926, a month, unless otherwise expressed, means a calendar month.

Monument of London, a 202 ft (61·6 m) column, overlooking Billingsgate, designed by Wren and erected (1671–77) to mark the starting-point of the Great Fire of London (1666). The original inscription upon it ascribed the fire to "the treachery and malice of the popish faction", which stood until 1831, when the words were erased as objectionable. The black marble staircase has 345 steps (311 to the balcony).

Moon, the earth's satellite, 3,475 km in diameter and 384,321 km distant from the earth. It rotates in the same time as it revolves round the earth (27 days 7 hours 43 minutes), so that the same face is always presented to the earth. The lunar surface is pockmarked by innumerable collisions with solid particles of all sizes. Unlike the earth, it is unprotected by any atmosphere and for aeons of time it has been exposed to every kind of cosmic influence, including the parching effect of solar radiation. All moonlight derives from the sun but on the whole it is a pretty poor reflector. The exploration of the moon by means of rockets began in 1959 when the Russian *Luna* 2 crashlanded on the plains of the *Mare Imbrium.* 1969 will be remembered as the year of the U.S. *Apollo* triumphs when man first set foot on the moon. The samples of lunar rock and dust brought back to earth by the *Apollo* astronauts and the Soviet *Luna* unmanned automatic stations are being studied by lunar scientists. Samples date back further than any found on Earth as yet. The most famous, known as the Genesis Rock, is 4,100 million years old. The exploration of the moon at close range by means of spacecraft was made possible only by parallel developments in several branches of technology—rocket propulsion, long-range radio and television transmission, electronic computer control.

Moorhen, a widely distributed bird of the rail family, a common resident in the British Isles. The adult is blackish with white under tail-coverts, a white line on the flanks and a yellow-tipped bill. The frontal shield and the base of the bill are vermilion. It bobs its head, flirts its tail and dives well. The nest is usually placed close to the water's edge or on an overhanging branch. In feeding the young the parents are sometimes helped by their offspring of a previous brood of the season. In N. America the bird is known as the Florida Gallinule.

Moors, the name given to the Moslems who live in N.W. Africa and to those who once lived in Spain. In 711 Moorish Arabs invaded Spain and spread beyond the Pyrenees into France, where they were driven back by the end of the century. Spain, however, remained virtually under Moorish domination until the 11th cent., and during that period was the most civilised and prosperous part of Western Europe. In the arts and sciences the impact of Moorish culture was profound and lasting. Examples of the brilliant splendour of Moorish architecture are still to be seen in Toledo, Córdoba, Seville and Granada. During the long struggle for the Christian reconquest thousands were killed and expelled, and in 1492 Granada, their last remaining kingdom, was forced to surrender. They were virtually exterminated by the Inquisition, and the last were expelled in 1609.

Moose, the largest members of the deer family. The N. American Moose stands 1·6–2 m high, and has huge palmate antlers. There is another New World species, occurring in Alaska. The European species is known as the elk.

Morse Alphabet, a system of dots and dashes, intended to be used in combination with the indicator in telegraphy; but usually read by sound, the receiving operator writing down the words in the system as transmitted. This system of signals was invented by the American inventor and artist Samuel Finley Breese Morse (1791–1872) of Charlestown, Massachusetts.

Mosaic, art of arranging small pieces of coloured glass, marble, or other materials in such a fashion as to produce a decorative pattern. Some of the best examples of Byzantine mosaics are to be seen at Ravenna, Rome, Venice and Sicily.

Mosque, a Mohammedan church, the greatest being that of Santa Sophia at Istanbul, now converted into a museum of Byzantine art.

Mosquito, small two-winged flies with long legs and slender body. Their larvae are aquatic. The females of some species are blood-suckers, and thus come to transmit the blood parasites which cause malaria and yellow fever, for example. *See* **DDT** *and* **Gammexane.**

Mosses. With liverworts, mosses comprise an important group of relatively simple non-vascular land plants, the bryophytes (**F39**). In the main they are small plants, the largest between 30–70 cm high, having been recorded in the Southern Hemisphere. Mosses rarely occur singly, but usually form cushions or small colonies on moist soil, bark, wood, rock or walls. The genus *sphagnum* known as "peat" or "bog moss" is of commercial value in horticulture. In Lancashire and Cheshire lowland moors in which sphagnum is common are known as "mosses". Reindeer moss is a lichen and Spanish moss a seed plant.

Moths, of the insect order, *Lepidoptera*, differing from butterflies which have clubbed antennae, in having feathery, sometimes thin, pointed antennae, rarely clubbed. Most are nocturnal, and the pupae are usually brown and enclosed in a cocoon unlike those of the butterfly, which are usually naked. *See also* **Lepidoptera.**

Motion, Laws of. According to Newton: (1) A body continues in its state of rest or uniform motion in a straight line except in so far as it is compelled by external forces to change that state. (2) Rate of change of momentum is proportional to the applied force, and takes place in the direction in which the force acts. (3) To every action there is an equal and opposite reaction. These laws are the basis of almost all engineering and everyday mechanics. Corrections to them have been made by relativity and the quantum theory. *See* **F15, 16.**

Mule, a cross between a male ass and a horse mare; a hinny is a cross between an ass mare and a horse stallion. Also the name of the spinning machine invented by Crompton in 1779 which combined the principle of Hargreaves' spinning jenny with the machine invented by Arkwright.

Mullions, the vertical bars dividing the lights in a window, forming a highly decorative feature in the Tudor period of English Gothic architecture. The cross-beam or horizontal bar of wood or stone in a mullioned window is styled a transom. *See* Windows.

Munich Agreement. In September 1938 Mr. Neville Chamberlain and M. Daladier, British and French Premiers, reached agreement with Hitler at Munich for the dismemberment of Czechoslovakia, primarily for the benefit of Germany. Czechoslovakia itself was not consulted, nor Russia who with Britain and France had jointly pledged themselves to uphold the independence of Czechoslovakia. Hitler had been threatening that country for some time, but every concession had been met by further demands. After three visits to Germany, during which Hitler raised his demands, the British and French statesmen gave way. Mr. Chamberlain declared on return that he had secured " Peace in our Time ". The Agreement was the subject of much controversy. Hitler seized Czechoslovakia in March 1939.

Muscles. *See* **F34**(1).

Musk Deer, a small deer of the Himalayas, standing about 51 cm high. It is grey in colour, slightly brindled, and carries a small pouch in the abdominal region, containing what is commercially known as musk, an article which is of great value in the manufacture of various perfumes. The active constituent of musk, muscone, is now made synthetically. The species was becoming rare on account of its slaughter for its musk.

Mutton Bird, an Australian name of controversial origin for a shearwater or petrel, *e.g.*, the Short-tailed and Sooty Shearwaters and the Great-winged, Kermadec, and White-headed Petrels. The young are taken by hand from their burrows for human food.

Myrrh, a resinous substance obtained from a tree of the natural order *Amyridaceae*, growing plentifully in Ethiopia and Arabia. Its use for embalming, medical and aromatic purposes may be traced back to the most remote times.

Mysteries, Greek, secret mystic ceremonies of the ancient Greeks, religious drama accompanied by dancing, the most well known being the Eleusinian and Orphic ceremonies.

Mystery Plays were mediaeval religious dramas performed at great ecclesiastical festivals, particularly in France and Bavaria, staging the Nativity, Passion and Resurrection. *See* **Section M, Part VI.**

N

Nadir, one of the two poles of the horizon, the other being the zenith. The nadir is the pole vertically below the observer's feet.

Nahum, one of the books of the Minor Prophets of the Old Testament. It is a prophecy of doom on the approaching sack of Nineveh which fell in 612 B.C. to the Medes and Babylonians.

Nantes, Edict of, was a decree promulgated by Henry IV of France in 1598, giving full freedom of worship to the Protestants of the country. It was the revocation of this edict in 1685 by Louis XIV that drove hundreds of thousands of French Huguenots to this country.

Naphtha, a liquid combustible believed to have been one of the ingredients of " Greek fire ". Naphtha is a light, highly inflammable oil obtained by distilling petroleum, shale oil, or coal tar. The petroleum naphtha consists of a mixture of paraffins; that from shale contains olefines as well as paraffins. Coal-tar naphtha contains xylol.

Naphthalene is an aromatic hydrocarbon; it is obtained from coal tar, and its derivatives are much used in the manufacture of colours for dyers and printers. " Moth balls " are made of naphthalene.

Narcotic, a medical dictionary definition is that a narcotic is a drug that produces stupor, complete insanity or sleep. In terms of drug addiction, a narcotic has been defined as altering and distorting the user's perception of himself and of the external world, being taken primarily for that purpose. *See* **P22–24**.

Nardus, a genus of coarse grasses, growing on bleak upland heaths and hill slopes. *Nardus stricta*, known as " mat-weed ", is a British species.

Narghile, an oriental tobacco pipe so constructed that smoke passes through water and up a long flexible tube before reaching lips of the smoker.

Narrative Art, a type of art popular during the late 19th cent. based on the principle: " every picture tells a story "—*e.g.*, such paintings as the little Royalist boy surrounded by his anxious family and confronted across a table by the Roundheads bearing the title: " When did you last see your father? " The term, although often applied derisively, suitably describes many works of considerable artistic merit: *e.g.*, Hogarth's *Marriage à la Mode*, his series of eight engravings entitled *A Rake's Progress*, the Bayeux Tapestry, and many Babylonian and Egyptian friezes.

Naseby, Battle of, was fought on 14 June 1645, between the Royalists under the command of Prince Rupert and the King, and the Parliamentarians under Fairfax and Cromwell. It resulted in a complete defeat for Charles.

National Anthem, a musical composition with words, officially adopted for ceremonial use as an expression of patriotism and loyalty to a national cause. The national anthem of the United Kingdom, " God save the King (Queen) ", probably dates from late-17th cent. to mid-18th cent. It was sung in 1745, the year of the landing of the Young Pretender. It had no one composer and was probably a recasting of folk-tunes and plainsong. Resemblances can be traced in pieces by Purcell and John Bull.

National Assembly, the name taken by the body responsible for the opening stages of the French Revolution and subsequently by other sovereign bodies in France and elsewhere.

National Covenant, an oath and declaration subscribed to by the Scottish Presbyterians in 1638 to maintain their religion against Charles I's episcopalianising designs.

National Gallery, established in 1824 at Pall Mall, London, with the Angerstein Collection of 38 pictures, purchased for £60,000 as a nucleus. The existing building which was opened in 1838 has been enlarged several times. The National Gallery at Millbank, the Tate Gallery, was given to the nation by Sir Henry Tate in 1897.

Nationalisation is the taking over by the State of the ownership and operation of an industry or service—*e.g.*, coal-mining, railway, transport, gas and electricity. Where this is done without revolution, compensation is usually paid to the previous owners at what is regarded as a fair market price; the compensation is sometimes paid in cash, but more often in fixed-interest-bearing bonds issued either by the State or by the administration of the nationalised service, which is usually a publicly appointed Board or Corporation acting, with greater or lesser autonomy, under the direction of a Minister responsible to Parliament. In some cases the State becomes a partner with private investors in the ownership of a particular enterprise, *e.g.*, oil companies, such as the former Anglo-Iranian and some recent French examples. Nationalisation is usually brought about by a separate Act of Parliament relating to each industry or service taken over. These Acts, in Great Britain, include provision for joint consultation at all levels between the administering boards and the workers employed and their Trade Unions. When, as in the Soviet Union, nationalisation occurs as an outcome of social revolution no compensation is paid to the dispossessed owners.

National Parks. Under the National Parks Act 1949 a National Parks Commission was set up to create National Parks in England and Wales. Ten have been established: Peak District, Lake District, Snowdonia, Yorkshire Dales, Exmoor, Brecon Beacons, Dartmoor, Pembrokeshire Coast, North York Moors and Northumberland. They cover an area of some 13,618

km^2, or 9 per cent of the total area of England and Wales. It is not intended to change the character of these territories but to control their development so as to harmonise with the two dominant principles: (*a*) that the characteristic beauty of the landscape within the Park area shall be preserved and (*b*) that the visiting public shall have ample access and facilities for recreation and enjoyment. The establishment of a new national park has been proposed for mid-Wales. The Commission also has power to designate areas in England and Wales outside the national parks as "areas of outstanding natural beauty". Thirty-three areas had been designated by 1977: Gower, Quantock Hills, Lleyn, Surrey Hills, Dorset, Northumberland Coast, Cannock Chase, Shropshire Hills, Malvern Hills, Cornwall, N. Devon, S. Devon, E. Devon, E. Hampshire, Isle of Wight, Forest of Bowland, Chichester Harbour, Solway Coast, Chilterns, Sussex Downs, Cotswolds, Anglesey, South Hampshire Coast, Kent Downs, Norfolk Coast, Dedham Vale, Suffolk Coast and Heaths, Wye Valley, Arnside and Silverdale, Lincolnshire Wolds, Mendip Hills, North Wessex Downs, Isles of Scilly. Under the Countryside Act, 1968, the National Parks Commission has been reconstituted as the Countryside Commission. *See also* **Long Distance Routes.**

National Physical Laboratory, situated at Teddington, is one of the world's largest and best-equipped laboratories. It conducts research in its three main groups: Measurement, Materials and Engineering Sciences, and maintains British primary standards and physical units. First established in 1900 and managed by the Royal Society, it is now one of the industrial research establishments under the control of the Dept. of Industry.

National Portrait Gallery, established in 1856, and now located in a building in St. Martin's Lane adjoining the National Gallery. Contains portraits of eminent people in British history and a valuable collection of medals and autographs.

National Trust, founded in 1895. "A non-profit-making organisation incorporated by Act of Parliament for the purposes of promoting the permanent preservation of lands and buildings of historic interest or natural beauty for the benefit and access of the people." As a consequence of gifts of public-spirited individuals the Trust now owns many hectares of magnificent scenery and property, including mediaeval castles, bird sanctuaries, ancient monuments, birthplaces and homes of famous men, and classic examples of domestic architecture, preserved for the enjoyment of present and future generations. Since 1946 lands and houses of interest to the nation may be given to the National Trust in lieu of death duties.

Nativity. There are three nativity festivals of the Christian Church: Christmas, 25 December, festival of birth of Christ; the birthday of the Virgin Mary (8 September); and of St. John the Baptist (24 June).

Natterjack, a curious warty, prominent-eyed, brown toad (*Bufo calamita*), having a bright yellow line down the middle of its back. It utters a muttering sort of croak, hence its name.

Natural Law. *See* **Section J.**

Naturalism in painting has been defined as "a direct and spontaneous approach to nature"—to landscape primarily. Constable, Turner and Boudin were among the great naturalist painters of the 19th cent. *See* **Section I** for naturalism in drama.

Natural Numbers, the counting numbers 1, 2, 3, 4, 5, . . .

"Nautical Almanac", published under the authority of the Admiralty, is always issued four years in advance, and contains information specially prepared for the use of navigators and astronomers. It first appeared in 1767.

Nautilus, a term now applied only to the pearly-shelled nautilus, the sole surviving example of the four-gilled section of the *Cephalopoda.* Its fossil relatives are called Ammonites. The spiral shell is divided into a number of compartments, the animal living in the last and largest chamber. There are three or four species, all living in tropical seas. The Paper Nautilus is not related to the Pearly Nautilus, belonging to the same order as the octopus.

Nave is the body or main open portion of a cathedral or church, and extends from the chief entrance to the choir, or chancel, and is usually flanked by aisles. A nave, in mechanics, indicates the "hub" or central part of a wheel.

Nazism. *See* **Section J.**

Neanderthal, the name of the valley lying between Düsseldorf and Wuppertal, where in a limestone cave a now famous skull of a very early species of prehistoric man was discovered in 1856. Fossils of Neanderthal man have been found over a wide area, and from archaeological evidence he began to disappear from Europe during the last Ice Age, about 40,000 B.C.

Necromancy, "the black art", was in olden times much believed in, and supposed to be an occult power by which its practitioners could converse with the spirits of the dead and learn the future.

Nekton, term used to differentiate actively swimming aquatic organisms (*e.g.*, fishes) from the "drifters" or plankton.

Nelson Column, in Trafalgar Square, London, designed by Mr. William Railton, was chosen from among a number of designs—temples, obelisks and various sculptural groups—sent in as a result of a competition held in 1839. The erection of the column was begun in 1840. Twenty-six years later the lions designed by Landseer were set up at the foot of the completed column. The statue of Nelson himself was made by E. H. Bailey and the bronze reliefs at the base executed by Carew, Woodington, Ternouth and Watson, representing the Battles of the Nile, St. Vincent, Copenhagen and Trafalgar. Height 52 m, executed in Portland stone instead of granite, as originally planned, at a cost of £46,000.

Néné or Hawaiian Goose. At the Severn Wildfowl Trust at Slimbridge Sir Peter Scott saved this bird from extinction.

Neo-Classical Style, term applied to the revival of classical logic and order after the extravagances of Rococo (*q.v.*), beginning in France in the mid-18th cent. and finding expression in architecture and the decorative arts. The style retains some of the daintiness of Rococo, furniture is on a small scale, often gilt, and silks and porcelain favour pastel shades. Straight lines take the place of the wild curvatures of Rococo and classical details like festoons and urn forms are used in many contexts and materials. Its English version is closely associated with the name of the architect Robert Adam whose light and graceful adaptations of Greek and Roman forms were introduced into English country houses. In France the style is sometimes called *Style Louis XVI*, though its dates, *c.* 1750–*c.* 1790, do not exactly coincide with the reign of that monarch. Eventually the Neo-Classical style merges into Empire (*q.v.*).

Neodymium, an element belonging to the rare earth metal group. Discovered by Welsbach in 1885.

Neo-Impressionism, a development of Impressionism (*q.v.*) by Seurat and Signac during the 1880s who devised the method of painting known as *pointillism* (the application of pure colours in minute touches to form a composite whole, based on a knowledge of the laws of colour and optics). One of the best-known examples of this technique is Seurat's *Sunday Afternoon on the Grand Jatte.*

Neon, inert gas present in air to the extent of about 1 part in 65,000. The crimson glow produced when an electric discharge passes through the gas is familiar in advertising signs.

Neoprene, generic name for a class of synthetic rubbers made from acetylene.

Nepotism, the bestowal of patronage by reason of relationship rather than of merit. It had its origin in the custom of certain Popes to enrich their families out of the offices of the Church.

Neptune. Apart from Pluto this is the most distant of the planets, estimated to be about $4{,}496 \times 10^6$ km from the sun, and taking about 165 years to revolve around it. Discovered by the German astronomer Galle on 23 September 1846, after its existence had been predicted by Leverrier and Adams. *See* **F7.**

Neptunium, element 93, one of the four new elements discovered during the progress of the atomic bomb project in the second world war.

Neptunium is formed when a neutron enters a nucleus of Uranium 238, and it decays radioactively to yield plutonium.

Neutrino, a neutral particle which carries energy and spin and although possessing little or no mass plays an important part in the interaction of other fundamental particles. The discovery that there are in fact two distinct neutrinos, each with its counterpart, was discovered in 1962 as a result of an experiment made with the 30,000 million-electronvolt proton accelerator at Brookhaven. *See* **F14**.

Neutron, a neutral particle present in all atomic nuclei except the hydrogen nucleus which is a single proton. In the development of nuclear science and technology the neutron has played a most important role and neutrons produce the radioisotopes now widely used in medicine, agriculture and industry. Neutrons and protons are termed nucleons. *See* **F10, 14.**

New Deal. The measures taken by President Roosevelt in USA in 1933 to overcome the great economic crisis which broke out at the end of 1929 and to restore the social security threatened by it. The measures were drawn up by a group of experts called a Brains Trust and they provided for recovery by a programme of public works, including large-scale construction of houses and large-scale assistance to farmers. Loans were granted and authorities formed to stimulate activities which reduced the workless from 17 millions to between 7 and 10 millions. Unemployment relief was regulated and enlarged; and social insurance (which for decades had been a subject of dispute, being held to be contrary to American principles of self-help) was introduced. Many of the changes have become a permanent part of American legislation though some laws were repealed by the US Supreme Court as being unconstitutional.

Newgate Prison was situated at the western end of Newgate Street, opposite the Old Bailey, at the site of one of the old London city gates. There is a record of a prison upon this spot in the 13th cent. Later a new one was built by the executors of Richard Whittington, but this was destroyed by the Great Fire in 1666. Still another new prison on this site was erected between 1778 and 1780. In the Gordon Riots of the latter year it was destroyed by fire and re-erected. It was not used as a prison after 1880 and was demolished in 1902–3.

News Letters were an early form of newspaper, popular in the time of Charles II. They consisted of items of news and gossip collected at the various coffee-houses and other places of public resort. They often included blank pages on which readers wrote their private letters.

Newspapers. The first news-books to be published at regular intervals in Britain appeared in 1662 with news of what was going on abroad translated from German and Italian news-sheets. Licence to print was obtained from the Star Chamber, which until its abolition in 1641 allowed only the printing of foreign news. With the lifting of the ban on domestic news the Press became free. In the reign of Queen Anne English newspapers employed writers of great intellectual power and versatility. Despite the newspaper tax introduced in 1712, the number of newspapers published in London in 1776 had increased to 53, though the standard of writing was below that of earlier times. The development of the Press was greatly assisted in the 19th cent. by the abolition of the "taxes on knowledge", by the introduction of the cheap postal system and by improvements in printing, distribution, collection of news and advertising. The *London Gazette*, founded in 1665 (and still appearing twice weekly as the official organ of the Government), is the oldest newspaper living. *The Times*, known throughout the world, began as the *Daily Universal Register* in 1785, and adopted its present title in 1788. The *Manchester Guardian* (renamed *Guardian* in 1959), once a provincial but now a national newspaper with a world-wide reputation, began as a weekly in 1821, and became a daily in 1855. The *Scotsman*, founded as a weekly in 1817 and established as a daily in 1855, and the *Glasgow Herald*, which began as the *Glasgow Advertiser* in 1783, are the leading Scottish newspapers. The London Press, which is national, publishes 10 daily, 2 evening and 7 Sunday newspapers.

Newt, amphibians of lizard shape and mottled markings. There are three British species, the largest being the Great-Crested Newt (*Triturus cristatus*), which attains a length of 15 cm.

Newton, the unit of force in the SI system of units. Under its influence a body with a mass of 1 kilogramme will accelerate at a rate of 1 metre per second each second.

Newton's Rings. Concentric circular rings, due to the phenomenon of interference, which are seen around the point of contact of a slightly convex lens with a flat plate of glass.

New Towns. Under the New Town Act 1946 and subsequent Acts 33 new towns have now been designated in Britain; 23 are in England and Wales, six in Scotland and four in Northern Ireland. They are: Basildon, Bracknell, Crawley, Harlow, Hatfield, Hemel Hempstead, Milton Keynes, Northampton, Peterborough, Stevenage and Welwyn (to relieve housing problems in the Greater London area); Aycliffe, Corby, Cwmbran, Peterlee and Washington (to serve the special needs of their areas); Newtown (to help stem rural depopulation in mid-Wales); Runcorn and Skelmersdale (to meet the overspill needs of Liverpool and north Merseyside); Telford and Redditch (to take population from Birmingham); Warrington (expanded to take people from Liverpool and Manchester); Central Lancashire New Town (new regional city based on existing towns of Preston, Leyland and Chorley). The six Scottish new towns are Cumbernauld, East Kilbride, Glenrothes, Irvine and Livingston. In Northern Ireland Craigavon is being developed as a new city; Antrim and Ballymena are becoming centres of economic growth; Londonderry and the surrounding district have been designated as an area of special development. The population of the new towns in Great Britain is about 1·7 million. The expansion of large existing towns like Northampton, Peterborough and Warrington means that they are becoming regional centres. A major reversal in Government policy was announced in 1976: development resources in future to be directed towards inner-city areas to halt decline and to slow the growth of new and expanding towns.

New Year's Day, 1 January. The first New Year's festival of which we have record is that constituted by Numa 713 B.C., and dedicated to Janus.

Nibelungenlied, the German epic of the early 13th cent. comprising numerous mythical poems or sagas of which several English translations exist. Wagner's *The Ring of the Nibelungs* was based largely on Norse legends and on the Nibelungenlied.

Nicene Creed, a summary of the principles of Christian faith, first issued in 325 by the Council of Nicaea (summoned by the emperor Constantine the Great) for the purpose of thwarting the Arian heresy and asserting the godhead of Christ. Date of Easter fixed at Council of Nicaea.

Nickel, silver-coloured metal, symbol Ni, fairly soft though harder than iron. Chief source of the metal is the nickel sulphide in iron–copper pyrites deposits in Ontario. Chief uses are: in electroplating, in coins, as an element in alloy steels. A novel method of making pure nickel (by treating the metal with carbon monoxide and heating the resulting liquid, nickel carbonyl) was developed in 1890 by Mond. This discovery led to many technical advances in industrial chemistry, one of which is the production of catalysts for a variety of processes.

Night Heron, a stocky, short-legged heron of black and white plumage, red eyes and yellowish legs, crepuscular except in breeding season, and an occasional visitor to Britain.

Nightingale, a familiar singing bird which visits the southern counties of England every summer, and is sometimes found as far north as Yorkshire. It is a shy, brown bird, not often seen, but the song of the male, usually heard in the late evening or at early morn, is of remarkable sweetness and variety. After its wooing period is over its song ceases.

Nightjar, nocturnal, insectivorous bird, owl-like in appearance, with mottled brown plumage of "dead leaf" pattern, and a churring song. It is a common breeding visitor to the British Isles, April to September, and lays its eggs on bare ground.

Niobium is a metal element, symbol Nb, related to vanadium. Technical development has been slow because of its rare occurrence, although niobium is now used in ferrous alloys to increase resistance to corrosion and produce steel which can be used at high temperatures.

Nitre *or* **Saltpetre,** is now mostly manufactured by the double decomposition of sodium nitrate and potassium chloride. Its chief use is the manufacture of gunpowder and fireworks. It has been manufactured in England since 1625.

Nitrogen, a non-combustible gaseous element, symbol N, devoid of taste or smell, and constituting nearly four-fifths of the atmospheric air. Nitrogen compounds are essential to plants and animals, and are used in fertilisers.

Nitro-Glycerine, an explosive yellow fluid produced by mixing small quantities of glycerine with a combination of one part of nitric acid and two parts of sulphuric acid. By itself it is a dangerously explosive substance to handle. In 1867, Nobel produced dynamite, a safe explosive made by absorbing nitro-glycerine in kieselguhr.

Nitrous Oxide, a compound of nitrogen and oxygen possessing mild anaesthetic power. Termed "laughing gas" on account of its exhilarating effect. It is still used in dentistry, and for minor operations and has proved useful in a new technique for finding leaks in water mains.

Nobel Prizes. The Nobel Foundation was established at the beginning of the century to give effect to the wishes expressed by Alfred Nobel in his Will. By the terms of the Will the judges are the Swedish Academy of Science, the Caroline Medico-Surgical Institute, the Swedish Academy and five members of the Norwegian Storting. The award of a Nobel Prize is accepted as the highest form of international recognition in the field in which it is given: physics, chemistry, medicine, literature, peace and, since 1969, economics. *See* end of Section.

Nones were dates of the Roman calendar which fell on the 5th of each month, excepting March, May, July and October, when they fell on the 7th.

Norman Architecture is English Romanesque (*q.v.*), which flourished from the time of the Norman Conquest and was gradually superseded through a transition period (*c.* 1175–1200) by the introduction of the pointed arch characteristic of the Early English (first Gothic style). Typical of Norman churches are the round arches, thick walls, massive cylindrical columns, with throughout the basic pattern of the square and the circle. Some churches (*e.g.*, the Temple church in London or the chapel at Ludlow Castle) are wholly circular. Roofs in the early days were flat and towers, usually placed at the "crossing", were square but occasionally round; the spires of all these towers have perished, but it seems likely that they were squat and pyramidal.

North-East Passage, from the North Atlantic to Bering Strait has been rapidly developed by the USSR in recent years as a northern sea route to render accessible vast areas of northern Siberia. Attempts to find a north-east passage were made by Englishmen and Dutchmen in the 16th cent. but they were always defeated by the ice, for the sea is completely frozen for some 4,800 km for 9 months of the year. A Swede succeeded in sailing from Europe to Japan via the Arctic in the late 19th cent. *See also* **Arctic Exploration.**

North-West Passage, from the Atlantic to the Pacific through the Arctic Seas, has been the dream of navigators for centuries. Attempts to find it were made in the 16th and early 17th cent. by John and Sebastian Cabot, Frobisher, Gilbert, Davis, Hudson and Baffin. Two centuries later Ross, Parry, Franklin and others made the attempt; but it was not until 1903–5 that Amundsen, discoverer of the South Pole, made the complete voyage in the *Gjoa.* The Canadian icebreaker *Labrador* was the first deep-draft vessel to traverse the North-West Passage (1954) and the US tanker *Manhattan* was the first commercial vessel to do so (1969).

Notre Dame, the famous Paris cathedral, was founded in 1163, and is one of the finest specimens of Gothic architecture in Europe. The best descriptions of the buildings are to be found in Victor Hugo's *Hunchback of Notre Dame.*

November, the 9th month of the year originally, but from *c.* 700 B.C., when Numa added January and February, it became the 11th month.

Nuclear Energy. Atomic nuclei consist of protons and neutrons joined in various proportions (**F10**). The heaviest naturally occurring nucleus contains 238 particles (92 protons, 146 neutrons) and is uranium 238 (U^{238}); the lightest is hydrogen, which consists of 1 proton. Neutrons and protons attract one another by very strong forces which are not at all well understood; they are called *nuclear forces.* Consequently it requires energy to be supplied if a nucleus is to be pulled apart into its constituent particles. The energy is required to overcome the attractions of the nuclear forces. Conversely, when the particles rush together to form a nucleus energy is released in the form of heat or radiation. The energy released when protons and neutrons coalesce to form a nucleus is called *Binding Energy.* The binding energy of a nucleus divided by the number of particles involved is called the binding energy per particle, which we will call B. It is very difficult to overestimate the importance of B to the human race. B varies from nucleus to nucleus, and the exact form of its variation is only roughly understood at the present time. But the most significant thing is that B is greatest for elements of medium atomic weight and lowest at the heavy (uranium) and light (hydrogen) ends of the periodic table. This means that if middleweight nuclei can be formed either from heavy ones or from light ones, B increases and *energy is released in either case.*

Nuclear Fission. *See* **F12(1).**

Nuclear Fusion. If light nuclei are hurled at high speeds into intimate contact they sometimes coalesce and release binding energy (*see* **Nuclear Energy**). This has been studied in laboratories where powerful and energy-consuming machines accelerate small numbers of particles for purely experimental purposes. If useful amounts of energy are to be gained these fusion reactions will have to occur on a bigger scale in an apparatus from which the resulting heat can be extracted in a controlled way. The one "useful" fusion device so far made is the thermonuclear bomb ("H-bomb"). Thermonuclear is the important word. If a suitable gas can be raised to a very high temperature the nuclei are stripped of their electrons and all particles move with very high speeds. The gas is then called a plasma. High enough temperatures will make speeds great enough for fusion reactions to occur and nuclear energy to be released. This is a thermonuclear reaction. For example, in deuterium gas, at temperatures over a million degrees Centigrade, the deuterium nuclei (*i.e.*, heavy hydrogen nuclei consisting of 1 proton joined to 1 neutron) interact to produce helium nuclei. To obtain a net gain in energy from this process, the temperature must be raised to about 300 million degrees C and maintained long enough; otherwise the energy released is less than that required to heat the fuel and to make up for heat losses. Many attempts to study the staggering technical problems are being made, and fusion research is very active in Britain, the USA and the Soviet Union. Nuclear fusion for the generating of electricity has the advantage over nuclear fission of producing no dangerous radioactive waste.

Nuclear Power Stations. Britain generates about 11 per cent of her electricity for public supply in nuclear power stations. The Atomic Energy Authority has three main stations which produce electricity for the national grid: the AGR station at Windscale, Cumbria, the experimental fast breeder station at Dounreay, Caithness, and the Steam Generating Heavy Water Moderated Reactor (SGHWR) at Winfrith, Dorset. The nine nuclear power stations operated by the electricity authorities are at Berkeley, Gloucs. (1962), Bradwell, Essex (1962), Hunterston "A", Scotland (1964), Hinkley Point "A", Somerset (1965), Trawsfyndd, Wales (1966), Dungeness "A", Kent (1966), Sizewell, Suffolk (1966), Oldbury, Avon (1968), Wylfa, Anglesey (1970). They have all been developed from the classic Calder Hall type, burning natural uranium inserted in a graphite moderator and cooled by carbon dioxide gas. They are called Magnox stations because the fuel elements of natural uranium rods are encased in magnesium alloy cans. A second nuclear power programme is based on the AGR at Windscale, and include the reactors now under construction at Dungeness "B", Hinkley Point "B", Hunterston "B", Seaton Carew and Heysham. Further stations are planned at Sizewell and Portskewett (Gwent). For the third stage of the nuclear power programme in the 1980s the steam-generating heavy-water reactor (SGHWR) had been chosen (Sizewell "B" and Torness, Lothian), though at the time of writing (Feb. 1977) no final decision had been made by the Government.

Nuclear Reactors are pieces of apparatus designed to permit nuclear chain reactions to occur under controlled conditions. (Uncontrolled chain reactions are dangerous, *e.g.* atomic bombs.) The success of a reactor depends on the neutrons reaching the U^{235} nuclei to produce more fissions and not being wasted in irrelevant processes or simply escaping through the wall of the apparatus (neutrons are quite difficult to contain). The neutrons leaving the scene of fission are rapidly moving, and they stand more chance of causing another fission if they are slowed down. Consequently a material other than the uranium has to be present to facilitate this, and it is called a moderator. A useful moderator is pure graphite. Thus a reactor may consist of alternate blocks of uranium and graphite. If the reactor is too small so many neutrons escape that there are not enough to keep the chain reaction going. The reactor must therefore be greater than a certain *critical size.* In order to intensify or damp down the chain reaction, it is arranged for pieces of neutron-absorbing material, such as cadmium, to be inserted or withdrawn as required. While the chain reaction is proceeding countless numbers of fissions are occurring, each one liberating energy which turns into heat. The temperature therefore increases, and to prevent a catastrophic rise, cooling has to be provided. The reactor therefore has cooling pipes through which a fluid coolant is pumped. The coolant carries the heat away and, in a reactor designed to produce electrical power, the heat is taken to steam-raising boilers and the high-pressure steam is led to turbines which drive the electric generators. What has been briefly described is the type of reactor first used for serious power production at Calder Hall (1956). This is a graphite-moderated, gas-cooled reactor using as fuel natural uranium (*i.e.*, fissile U^{235} greatly diluted with U^{238}). Other thermal types of nuclear reactor are the advanced gas-cooled reactor (AGR), the high temperature reactor (HTR), the steam-generating heavy-water (SGHWR) and the light-water reactor (LWR). It is also possible to make reactors work without slowing the neutrons with a moderator; these are called *fast reactors.* The design of the prototype fast reactor (PFR) at Dounreay is based on experience gained with the Dounreay experimental fast breeder reactor (closed 1977) which was the first to produce electricity on a commercial scale (1962) and achieved the highest power output of any of its type in the world. These fast reactors can produce new nuclear fuel in the course of their operation and therefore offer great economies; but they are more difficult to develop than thermal reactors. The fuel is made from the mixed oxides of plutonium and uranium. The Government has still to make a crucial decision whether and when to go ahead with a commercial fast breeder reactor.

Environmental considerations are likely to be increasingly topical. Most of the products of the fission process are of necessity radioactive isotopes: they could be gaseous, like krypton, xenon and tritium or solid like strontium, caesium, zirconium and ruthenium. There are also present the new radioactive elements plutonium, curium, actinium, etc. Further, in both the nuclear reactor and in the plant which is used to chemically treat and reprocess the nuclear fuel, radioactivity will be induced in associated structural materials, to varying degrees. In this latter case, unlike the former, the radioactive waste with which one is left can to a great extent be selected and is largely overshadowed in importance by the wastes arising from the fission and breeding processes. Even if the whole of the UK electrical power was produced by nuclear means, the volumes of such wastes would be relatively small and need in principle tens of acres of storage area. Much of the activity would decay in a decade, a great deal more in a century, but that associated with the elements bred from uranium, would be present for thousands of years: Pu^{239} has a half-life of 25,000 years. Segregation of the various types of activity is feasible; their incorporation into physically and chemically stable form has received a great deal of study so that storage, readily monitored even for many generations, seems entirely possible. The radioactive properties of these wastes can only be changed by nuclear reactions. Bombardment with neutrons or other highly energetic particles can bring about such reactions so that forms of "nuclear incineration" are feasible but are not yet fully explored.

Nucleic Acids. Living matter is built up of cells each of which has a nucleus surrounded by cytoplasm. Cell nuclei are composed chiefly of substances called nucleoproteins, which consist of a protein attached to a nucleic acid (this original name is still used, although nucleic acids are found in the cytoplasm as well as the nucleus). Nucleic acids are complex organic structures made up of chains of compounds called nucleotides (**F29(1)**). Nucleotide molecules have a sugar group attached to a nitrogenous base and a phosphate group. Only two sugar groups are found in the nucleotides, ribose, giving rise to ribonucleic acids (R.N.A.s, found mainly in the cytoplasm) and deoxyribose, which forms deoxyribonucleic acids (D.N.A.s, found mainly in cell nuclei). Seven different nitrogenous bases have been isolated, so that a number of different nucleotides are possible. A repeating, regular pattern of nucleotides is linked by the phosphate groups, forming nucleic acids. The functions of nucleic acids are of fundamental importance. They are concerned in the process of transmission of inherited qualities in reproduction and in building up body proteins. *See* **F28(2)**.

Nuremberg Trial. On 21 November 1945, an International Military Tribunal, consisting of one American, one British, one Russian and one French member, began the trial of twenty-four Nazi leaders. There were four counts: the conspiracy of Nazism; wars of aggression; war crimes; and crimes against humanity. Twelve were condemned to hanging of whom ten were hanged on 16 October 1946. Goering committed suicide; Bormann is now presumed dead; Papen, Schacht and Fritsche were acquitted. The rest received varying terms of imprisonment.

Nuthatch, name of a number of tree-creeping birds, plump, with short tail, bluish-grey plumage and black stripe under eye. Nest in holes and wedge nuts in bark of trees, hammering them to get a kernel. There are three European species, one, *Sitta europaea*, resident in England.

Nylon, a generic term for any long-chain synthetic polymeric amide which has recurring amide groups as an integral part of the main polymer chain, and which is capable of being formed into a filament in which the structural elements are orientated in the direction of the axis. The first nylon of commercial interest was made in 1935, and the world's first nylon factory—in the United States—began production in 1940.

O

Oak, a tree of the genus *Quercus*, including some 300 species distributed over the northern hemisphere and into the tropics. Two species are native to Britain, where the oak is the commonest tree (1 in 3)—*Q. petraea*, more common in the west and north on shallower, lighter soils, and *Q. robur*, more common in the south on deeper, heavier soils. Oak timber is much prized for its strength and durability, and from the time of the Spanish Armada to Nelson's day was in great demand for naval construction. It has always been used for building, flooring, furniture and cabinet work. The oak is attacked by many insects, the round nut-like oak galls, or oak-apples, being produced by the sting of certain minute gall wasps.

"Oaks," a famous race for three-year-old fillies run at Epsom two days after the "Derby".

Obelisk, a tapering monolithic column, square at the base and pyramidal at the top, regarded by the ancient Egyptians as a sacred stone and usually found at the entrance to the sun temples. Many were transported from Egypt and set up at various times: there is one in the Place de la Concorde in Paris, and one on the Thames Embankment in London—Cleopatra's Needle—originally erected at Heliopolis, centre of the sun-cult, by Tuthmosis III *c.* 1500 B.C.

Observatories. *See* **Astronomy** *and* **Telescopes.**

Occam's Razor. *See* **Section J, Q8(1).**

Ocean, comprises the great body of water which covers seven-tenths of the surface of the earth, and has an average depth of 3·2 km. The principal oceans are the Pacific, Atlantic, Indian and Arctic. The greatest ocean depth is in the Pacific, in the Mindanao Deep, 37,782 ft (11,524 m). *See* **F8(2)** *and* **Oceanography.**

Ocean Currents are well-defined streams running over certain portions of the ocean and caused mainly by wind-friction, slope of the sea surface and differences in density of the water, all movements being influenced by the deflective forces due to the earth's rotation. The climatic importance of the great ocean currents is that they constitute one of the means whereby heat is transferred from lower to higher latitudes.

Oceanography is the scientific study of the world ocean, *i.e.*, the single connected body of water that covers 70·8 per cent of the earth's surface. Modern oceanography dates from the voyage of *HMS Challenger* (1872–6) during which wide-ranging observations of the ocean were made, for the first time going well beyond what was directly required to assist shipping. Since then oceanography has matured into a highly technical and interdisciplinary science which may be roughly divided into: biological oceanography (the study of marine organisms and marine ecology); chemical oceanography (concerned with the composition of sea-water); physical oceanography (the study of ocean currents, tides and waves and the role played by the oceans in climate and weather); and geological oceanography (concerned with the formation, composition and evolution of the ocean basins). Oceanographic knowledge is essential to allow exploitation of the enormous food, mineral and energy resources of the ocean with the minimum damage to the ocean environment. However, close international co-operation (through such bodies as the Law of the Sea Conference) will also be necessary in order to avoid such hazards as overfishing and marine pollution. By 1980 it is estimated that one third of the world's oil and gas will come from offshore wells and recently vast deposits of metal-rich nodules have been located on the ocean floor. As important future sources of energy, both tidal and wave power have the attractions of being non-polluting and renewable.

Ocelot, the most common wild cat of S. America. It is about 1·2 m in length, including tail, and of a grey or tawny colour and spotted. Closely related to the Leopard cats.

Octane Number, the index of the knock-rating of petrol. It is based on the arbitrary scale in which iso-octane (which does not cause "knocking") has a value of 100, and normal heptane (which is prone to "knocking") has a value of 0. A good fuel for modern cars must have an octane number greater than 80.

Octarch, the kings of the English heptarchy, Hengist (455) being the first, and Egbert (800) the last.

October, the 10th month, but the 8th in the old Roman calendar. It was held sacred to Mars.

Octopus, a genus of marine molluscs with eight tentacles that bear suckers.

Odyssey, Homer's epic setting forth the incidents of the wanderings of Odysseus on his way back to Ithaca after the Siege of Troy.

Oersted, a unit of magnetic-field intensity in the c.g.s. system.

Offa's Dyke, largest remaining earthwork in Britain, supposed to have been built by Offa (A.D. 757–96) as a defensive boundary line between the English settlers and the dispossessed Welsh of Gwynedd, Powys and Gwent. *See also* **Long Distance Routes.**

Ohm's Law, propounded by G. S. Ohm in 1826, is expressed in the equation: electromotive force (in volts) = current (in amperes) × resistance (in ohms). The ohm is the unit of electrical resistance in the metre-kilogram-second system.

Oil. The great expansion in energy demand over recent years has been met to a large extent by petroleum oil. This contains a wide range of hydrocarbon molecules of varying complexity. The various components are separated from each other by making use of their different boiling points. Crude oil is heated in the base of a fractionating tower; the various components condense at different temperatures in trays at different levels of the tower. The fraction of a given composition can be increased by "cracking" or breaking down the heavier hydrocarbons into lighter ones. The total world reserves of petroleum oil are still uncertain since large parts of the world are still not fully prospected. The cutback and the rise in the price of Middle Eastern oil following the 1973 Arab–Israeli war unleashed a worldwide energy crisis which affected the economies of consumer countries. The United Kingdom can look forward to producing all her oil needs by 1980 from North Sea wells.

Okapi, nocturnal ruminant mammal, smaller than the giraffe, chestnut brown in colour with zebra-striped legs, native to the African Congo.

Olbers' Comet was discovered in 1815 by Olbers the German astronomer. Olbers also discovered the asteroids Pallas and Vesta (1802–07).

Old Red Sandstone, the continental rocks formed during the Devonian. *See* **F45.**

Olefines, a series of hydrocarbons, in which the hydrogen atoms are double the number of carbon. The first member of the series is ethylene.

Oléron Laws or Judgments, were a code of maritime laws, introduced into England in the reign of Richard I in the 12th cent. Oléron is an island off the west coast of France, opposite the mouth of the Charente.

Olive. This small tree, whose fruit yields olive oil is a native of the eastern Mediterranean countries, but has been introduced into cultivation elsewhere. The green unripe fruit is pickled in brine for table olives.

Olympiads were periods of four years which elapsed between each celebration of the Olympic games, held at Olympia in honour of Zeus. These festivals included competitions in literature, art, drama, rhetoric, music and gymnastics, and they were continued, with intervals, from 776 B.C. to A.D. 394. Athletic revivals have taken place at Athens 1896, Paris 1900, St. Louis 1904, London 1908, Stockholm 1912, Antwerp 1920, Paris 1924, Amsterdam 1928, Los Angeles 1932, Berlin 1936, London 1948, Helsinki 1952, Melbourne 1956, Rome 1960, Tokyo 1964, Mexico City 1968, Munich 1972, Montreal 1976. It is planned to hold the Games in 1980 in Moscow.

Onomasticians are scientists who study the fascinating subject of names—names of places and names of people—to find out their origins. They tell us, for example, that Cambridge is an Anglo-Norman corruption of *Grantabrycg* = bridge over the Granta; that Harrow-on-the-Hill was an early Anglo-Saxon settlement—"heathen temple on the hill"; that we owe the ridings of Yorkshire to the Vikings (Old Norse *thrithungr* = third part); that in Scotland *-ton* and *-toun* indicate not a town but a hamlet or village. Onomasticians are also concerned with the international standardisation of place names.

Onyx or Sardonyx, a variety of chalcedony built up of different-coloured layers, which are parallel and straight (not curved as in agate).

Oolite, a geological term for the Jurassic oolitic

limestones existing through a long stretch of country extending from Yorkshire to Dorsetshire. It abounds in fossils of molluscs and reptiles. The term " oolite " derives from the fact that these rocks are made of egg-shaped particles of calcium carbonate.

Opal, a mineral consisting of hydrous silica, occurring in numerous varieties and colours. Opals have been prized as gems since at least 400 B.C. but the secret of their unique internal " fire " or opalescence has only recently been learned. It is a result of the diffraction of light by a regular array of tiny silica spheres, about 100 nm in diameter, of which gem opals are now known to be composed. Opal miners are called gougers. Chief source—the Andanooka and Coober Pedy fields of South Australia.

Opera. *See* Section E.

Opium was known to the ancients, and used by them as a medicine. It is obtained from the poppy (*Papaver somniferum*), the unripe " head " or seed capsule of that flower yielding a juice which when dried becomes the opium of commerce. The poppy is cultivated in India, Iran, Turkey, Macedonia and China for the sake of this juice, which yields various alkaloids, such as morphine, narcotine, codeine, etc. These days the drug is rarely used medicinally. *See also* P22(2).

Opossum, marsupial mammals found in the more southerly of the United States, South America and Australasia. They are arboreal except for the water-oppossum, which eats fish.

Optics, the branch of physics which investigates the nature and properties of light and the phenomena of colour. Burning lenses were known to the ancient Greeks and Ptolemy wrote a treatise on optics A.D. 150. Lenses as visual aids were known in ancient China but eyeglasses were not in use until the 13th cent. Spectacles were in more general use after the invention of printing in the 15th cent. The camera obscura was invented in the 16th cent. and the telescope and microscope at the beginning of the 17th cent.

Oracles were in ancient times supposed to be words spoken by the gods, and it was the custom on important occasions to consult them about the future. The Greeks had the Oracles of Zeus at Dodona, and Apollo at Delphi, while the Romans consulted the Oracles of Mars, Fortune and others.

Orange, a fruit growing in most sub-tropical climates and in universal demand. It is grown on an evergreen tree that attains a height of about 6 m at maturity.

Orang-utan one of the largest of the anthropoid apes, found only in the swampy forests of Borneo and Sumatra. When full-grown it stands over 1·2 m in height and weighs about 67 kg.

Orchestra, a group of instruments and instrumentalists whose playing is under the direction of a conductor. The composition of a typical symphony orchestra is as follows: STRINGS: 1st Violin (16), 2nd Violin (16), Viola (12), Violoncello (12), Double Bass (8). WOODWIND: Flute (3–4), Piccolo (1), Oboe(3), Cor Anglais (1), Bass Oboe (1), Clarinet (3), Bass Clarinet (1), Bassoon (3), Contra-bassoon (1). BRASS: Horn (6), Trumpet (5), Trombone (3–4), Tuba (2). PERCUSSION: Timpani (3–6), Side Drum (1), Bass Drum (1), Cymbals (1), Harp (2).

Orders in Council are issued by the sovereign on the advice of a few selected members of the Privy Council. They must not seriously alter the law of the land. Another class of Orders in Council are issued by authority of an Act of Parliament for the carrying out of its provisions.

Ordination, the ceremony of installing ministers or clergymen in clerical offices, has existed from the earliest times. In the Anglican and Roman Catholic Churches the rites of Ordination are performed by bishops; among Nonconformists the power of ordination rests with the governing bodies of the different Churches.

Organ is a musical wind instrument of ancient origin whose tones are produced by the vibrations of air in pipes of varying length. Basically, an organ consists of a number of pipes grouped in rows or ranks according to their special tone-character. The air is fed by bellows or, in modern organs, by a rotary fan, electrically driven. Each rank is controlled by a slider, and the knob that controls the slider is called a stop. The organist pulls out the stops to give the tones he wants, the other pipes being kept out of action by the slider. When a particular note on the keyboard is depressed the player may hear, by pulling out the appropriate stop, not only the normal pitch but the note in several octaves. A stop of which the notes are of normal pitch is called an 8-foot stop, a 16-foot stop would give an octave lower, a 4-foot stop an octave higher and a 2-foot stop two octaves higher. The hand keyboard is called a manual, and the foot keyboard the pedal board. The basic tone of an organ is its diapason tone, and is normally of 8-foot length and pitch. Most large organs have four manual keyboards and one pedal board. The most important manual is the great organ which comprises the majority of basic stops. The next in importance is the swell organ, so called because the pipes are enclosed in a box fitted with movable shutters operated by a swell-pedal. The effect provides a controlled crescendo or diminuendo. The tone of a typical English swell has a reedy character. The third manual controls the choir organ—a collection of stops suitable for vocal accompaniment. The fourth manual controls the solo organ—a group of stops which, singly or in combination, may provide a solo melody which the remainder of the organ accompanies. The pedal keyboard controls most of the bass stops. In some very large organs there is a fifth manual controlling the echo organ. This is a small group of stops usually set high in the roof of the building to give the effect of distant music. Most church organs have two or three manuals. Modern cinema organs may have some normal stops but rely chiefly on a number of effects unknown to the straight organ.

Organic Chemistry. The chemistry of compounds containing carbon and usually associated with living organisms. *See* F24–5.

Oriel Window is a window projected from the front of a building, rectangular, triangular, or pentagonal. The ordinary bay window and bow window are varieties of Oriel. When an Oriel window does not reach to the ground it usually rests upon moulded sills supported by corbels.

Oriflamme, the name of the original banner of the abbey of St. Denis, and adopted by Louis VI as his standard. It remained the national emblem of France for three centuries. The flag was of red silk, the outer edge being cut in the form of flames.

Original Sin, according to Christian doctrine the corruption that is born with us, as a result of Adam's fall.

Orioles, brilliantly coloured birds, members of the passerine family *Oriolidae*, found in the tropical regions of Asia, Africa and Australia. The golden oriole, perhaps the most beautiful of them all, with brilliant yellow plumage, black wings and tail, winters in Africa, visits England and is known to have nested here.

Orion, a famous constellation of the heavens, comprising nearly a hundred stars, all visible to the naked eye. It contains three stars of the second magnitude in a line, and these are called " Orion's Belt ".

Ormer, a shellfish (*Haliotis tuberculata*) which occurs in the Channel Islands and on parts of the French coast. It is considered a great delicacy.

Ornithology, the scientific study of birds.

Ornithorhynchus. *See* Duckbill.

Orogeny, large-scale earth movements, including faulting and folding and sometimes igneous activity, which produce a linear belt of mountains, *e.g.*, the Alpine orogeny in Europe which produced the Alps.

Orphism. *See* Section J.

Orphrey, the name of an ornamental border of gold and silver embroidered on ecclesiastical vestments.

Orrery, an instrument used in the 18th and early 19th cent. which showed the motions of the planets round the sun and the satellites round their primaries. The first orrery made was named after Charles Boyle, Earl of Orrery.

Orthodox Eastern Church. *See* Section J.

Osborne House, near Cowes, in the Isle of Wight. Queen Victoria's favourite winter-residence, and where she died. It was given to the nation by Edward VII, and is now a convalescent home.

Osier, a species of willow growing in damp soils and yielding branches utilised in basket-making.

Osmium, a very hard, bluish-white metal, symbol Os, of the platinum group and one of the heaviest of known metals. It is obtained from certain sands of South America, California, Australia and Russia. The alloy of osmium and iridium (osmiridium) provides long-wearing tips for gold fountain-pen nibs.

Osmosis, the process by which absorption of liquids through semi-permeable membranes takes place. A solution exerts osmotic pressure (O.P.) or suction in proportion to concentration but also depending on kind of dissolved substance. The roots of the higher plants are covered with fine root-hairs, within the cell-walls of which the sap is normally of a higher concentration than the dissolved matter in the surrounding soil. The root-hairs, therefore, draw into themselves these weaker salt-solutions. (The explanation of water and salt exchanges is complicated by the selective ability of some cells (*e.g.*, roots) to accept or reject particular dissolved substances along with the water. The absorption of salts by a plant is selective, each plant selecting through the semi-permeable membranes of its root-hairs those substances which are most suited to itself.)

Osprey (*Pandion haliaetus*), a large and magnificent bird of prey, dark brown above and nearly white below. The head is whitish with a dark band from eye to nape. To the British Isles it is a rare passage migrant. In 1959, thanks to the energy and vigilance of the Royal Society for the Protection of Birds, a pair nested in a Scots pine in Inverness-shire and reared three young. Since then more young ospreys have been safely fledged in this sanctuary. The food consists almost entirely of fish, which the bird seizes with its talons. The so-called osprey plumes do not come from this bird but from the egret.

Ostrich, the largest living bird, related to the rhea, emu and extinct moa, now found only on the sandy plains of Africa and parts of S.W. Asia. The male has beautiful white plumes on wings and tail. The wings are useless in flight, but the birds have a fleetness of foot exceeding that of the swiftest horse. An ostrich's egg weighs 1·3 kg.

Otary, any seal which has external ears (as opposed to the *true seals* which lack them). The eared seals make up the family *Otariidae*, which includes the Sea-Lion and the Fur-seal of the N. Pacific.

Otter, an aquatic carnivorous mammal widely distributed over Europe, and at one time very common in England and Wales. The otter averages about 60 cm in length, exclusive of tail, has web-feet and is a very expert swimmer. Otters are harmless and their hunting is a cruel and senseless blood sport.

Ounce or **Snow Leopard,** a very beautiful pale spotted cat from the Himalayas about the size of a labrador retriever but with a long furry tail.

Outcrop. Where a bed of rock appears at the surface of the ground, there is an outcrop of the particular rock. Outcrop coal is surface coal; the mining of such coal is called open-cast mining.

Oviparous, a zoological term referring to animals which lay eggs to be hatched outside the body of the parent.

Ovipositor, the organ by means of which female insects lay their eggs.

Owls, nocturnal birds of prey, distributed over the greater part of the world. Their forward-looking eyes, embedded in rings of feathers, give them a characteristic "owl-like" appearance, and their plumage, usually a mottled blend of browns and greys, is so soft that their flight is almost noiseless. Owls live on small mammals, reptiles, birds, insects and fish, and are very valuable birds to the farmer. British owls include the barn owl (screech owl), short-eared owl, long-eared owl, tawny owl, little owl. Snowy owls have recently nested in the Shetland Is.

Ox, the popular name of the mammals included in the genus *Bos*. They are hollow-horned ruminants and hoofed quadrupeds, and include the various classes of domestic cattle as well as the different wild species. The adult male is called a bull, the female a cow and the young a calf. The best-known breeds of domesticated cattle are the Durham or Shorthorn, the Angus, the Jersey, Ayrshire, Suffolk and Hereford.

Oxalic Acid, an organic acid obtained from numerous plants, such as sorrel and rhubarb and produced artificially for commercial purposes from sawdust, treated with caustic potash or caustic soda. It combines with metals to form oxalates; used in the manufacture of ink.

Oxford Clay, a geological formation consisting of a bed of blue clay *c.* 200 m thick, and forming the lower portion of the Upper Jurassic. It makes good bricks.

Oxford Movement. *See* **Tractarianism, Section J.**

Oxford University. The early history of the university is obscure. There was a school at Oxford as early as 1115 and it is known that Robert Pullen, a theologian from Paris, lectured there in 1133. Allusions to Oxford as the most celebrated centre of learning in England occurred in a work of Gerald of Wales in 1184–5. The earliest colleges to be founded were University College (1249), Balliol (about 1263), Merton (1264). In 1571 the university was reorganised and granted a Charter of Incorporation by an Act of Elizabeth. Other colleges and halls with their dates of foundation are: All Souls (1438), Brasenose (1509), Christ Church (1546), Corpus Christi (1517), Exeter (1314), Hertford (1874), Jesus (1571), Keble (1868), Linacre (1962), Lincoln (1427), Magdalen (1458), New College (1379), Nuffield (1937), Oriel (1326), Pembroke (1624), Queen's (1340), St. Anthony's (1950), St. Catherine's (1962), St. Cross (1965), St. Edmund Hall (1270), St.John's (1555), St. Peter's (1929), Trinity (1554), Wadham (1612), Wolfson (1965), Worcester (1714), Campion Hall (1962), St. Benet's Hall (1964), Mansfield (1886), Regent's Park (1958), Greyfriars Hall (1953). The women's colleges are:—Lady Margaret Hall (1878), Somerville (1879), St. Hugh's (1886), St. Hilda's (1893), St. Anne's (1952). Women were not admitted to degrees (though allowed to sit for examination) till 1920.

Oxygen is the most abundant of all terrestrial elements, symbol O. In combination, this gaseous element forms about 46% of the earth's crust; one-fifth of the atmosphere; eight-ninths by weight of all water. Discovered independently by Scheele (*c.* 1773) and Priestley (1774). It is colouress, tasteless and odourless, and forms the chief life-supporting element of animal and vegetable life.

Oyster, a bivalve mollusc, of the genus Ostrea, having very numerous species and abounding in nearly all seas. The shell is rough and irregular. Oysters are exceedingly prolific, spawning in May and June. In England and Scotland deep-sea oysters are not allowed to be sold between 15 June and 4 August, and other kinds between 14 May and 4 August. In Ireland, no oysters may be taken between 1 May and 1 September, except in certain waters. The Whitstable oyster beds have existed since pre-Roman times; "clocks" are dead oysters.

Oystercatcher, a wading bird with black-and-white plumage and long, orange bill, inhabiting estuaries and sea-shores. Feeds on mussels, shell fish, etc., but not oysters.

Ozone, a modified form of oxygen, containing three atoms of oxygen per molecule instead of two. It is prepared by passing oxygen through a silent electric discharge. When present in air to the extent of 1 part in 4 million parts of air it kills bacteria, and has been used for this purpose in ventilating systems, *e.g.*, that of underground railways. It is present in extremely small quantities in the lower atmosphere but is comparatively plentiful at heights of about 32 km. The belief widely held that seaside air is particularly rich in ozone is untrue. As ozone absorbs ultra-violet light of certain wavelengths spectroscopic methods, involving the analysis of sunlight, are chiefly used in ozone determinations. *See also* **Atmosphere.**

P

Paca, a genus of large rodents found in Central and South America, and resembling the guinea-pig. It is of nocturnal habits, has streaked and spotted fur and lives on fruits and plants.

Pacific Ocean. The first European to recognise the Pacific as distinct from the Atlantic was the Spanish explorer, Vasco Nuñez de Balboa, who discovered its eastern shore from a peak in Panama in 1513. The first European to sail upon it was Magellan, who entered it by the strait that bears his name in 1520. Sir Francis Drake was the first Englishman to sail upon it in 1577. The world's greatest known ocean depth is in the Mindanao Trench, off the Philippines, 37,782 ft (11,524 m).

Pagan, a person who does not worship God; a heathen. The word is derived from the Latin *paganus* (a countryman or uncultivated person). In the Middle Ages the term was used largely to describe Mohammedans (Moors, Saracens, etc.).

Pagoda, the name given in China, India and other Asiatic countries to a high pyramidal tower, usually, but not necessarily, connected with a temple.

Palaeontology, the science which is devoted to the investigation of fossils: animal (palaeozoology) and plants (palaeobotany). By studying the markings and fossils of living things in the stratified rocks, palaeontologists have been able to establish with astonishing accuracy a record of the evolution of life through geological time. The geologist at the same time with the evidence of the fossils has been able to work out the order and the age of the rocks. *See also* **F45.**

Palatinate, a term formerly applied to two German electorates or provinces, the Upper and Lower Palatinates. Now provinces of Bavaria.

Pale, the name given to the part of Ireland colonised by the English and comprising portions of the counties of Louth, Dublin, Meath and Kildare. The Anglo-Norman rulers were styled " Lords of the Pale ".

Palimpsests are ancient MSS. or parchments which have been partly effaced and used for fresh writings. Many valuable MSS. were thus lost, but sometimes the second writing has been washed out, enabling the original writings to be deciphered. Among such restorations are a dialogue of Cicero's, a portion of a book of Livy, etc.

Palladium, a scarce metallic element, symbol Pd, similar to platinum, with which it is usually found. It is an expensive metal, with desirable properties as a catalyst in reactions involving hydrogen, since it has a remarkable capacity for absorbing this gas; for example, coal gas and air will inflame in the presence of palladium at room temperature. It forms a silver-white alloy with gold, and this is used in some kinds of jewellery. It is used in expensive watches to make non-magnetic springs.

Pallium, a vestmental ornamentation of white wool presented by the Pope to archbishops on their appointment, and the sign of Papal confirmation.

Palm, a large straight-trunked plant or tree common to tropical countries, and usually fruit yielding, such as dates, coconuts, etc. Many commodities useful to man are obtained from plants of the Palm family (*Palmaceae*).

Palm Sunday, the Sunday before Easter, upon which occasion it is customary to carry palms to the churches in some countries, in commemoration of Christ's entry into Jerusalem for the Feast of the Passover, when the people went forth to greet Him with palm branches.

Panama Canal. In 1903 the United States signed a treaty with Panama (which had previously seceded from Colombia) which gave the United States rights in perpetuity over a 16 km-wide strip of land extending across the isthmus for the purposes of building and running the canal. The canal connects the Atlantic and Pacific Oceans, is just over 80 kilometres long (with sea approaches) and the depth varies from 12 to 26 m. It is constructed above sea-level, with locks, and has been available for commercial shipping since 3 August 1914. In 1976 it seemed that the canal might well become a cause of contention between America and the Panama Republic.

Panda, *or* **Cat-Bear**, is related to the Raccoon. There are two kinds, the Red or True Panda, resembling a large domestic cat, which lives in the eastern Himalayas and S.W. China, and the Giant Panda, which is more lke a bear in appearance and inhabits the mountains of western China. Both frequent the dense bamboo forests of those regions.

Pangolin, the scientific name of the " scaly anteater ", a toothless mammal, found in W. Africa and S.E. Asia. It has a long extensible tongue which it uses in catching ants and termites, its chief food. When attacked the pangolin rolls itself into a ball, and its scales assume the form of sharp spikes. Pangolins have an Order of their own—the Pholidota, the scale-bearers.

Pantagruel, the leading character in one of the satires of Rabelais.

Pantheon, the famous temple in Rome, originally consecrated to the gods, built by Agrippa in 27 B.C. and rebuilt in the 2nd cent. by Hadrian. Its splendid dome and portico make it one of the most interesting architectural monuments of ancient days. Since the 7th cent. it has been used as a Christian church.

Panther, another name for the leopard, *Panthera pardus*, related to the lion, carnivorous, active climber, found in India, and other parts of Asia, also in Africa.

Papal Infallibility. *See* **Section J.**

Paper has been known in one form or another from very early times. The papyrus reeds of the Nile swamps served the ancient Egyptians for sheets upon which to inscribe their records. The Chinese and Japanese, centuries later, were using something more akin to modern paper in substance, an Asiatic paper-mulberry, yielding a smooth fibrous material, being utilised. With the spread of learning in Western Europe the necessity of a readier medium made itself felt and paper began to be manufactured from pulped rags and other substances. The first known English paper-mill was Sele mill near Stevenage, built about 1490, which produced the paper for an edition of Chaucer in 1498. Other mills were set up under Elizabeth, using linen and cotton as raw material. Other papermaking staples were later introduced, such as surat, esparto grass and wood-pulp. The chief raw material in the world paper industry is wood-pulp, the main exporters being the timber-growing countries of Canada, Sweden and Finland. Canada is the world's chief producer of newsprint and supplies a large proportion of US requirements.

Papyrus, the earliest known paper made in Egypt at a very remote period from a large species of reed, *Cyperus papyrus*. This plant is to be found all over tropical Africa, especially in the " sudd " region of the White Nile.

Parachute, the umbrella-shaped safety device used in emergency by the crew and passengers of aircraft. The first parachute descent from a great height was made in 1797 by André Garnerin who dropped 915 m from a balloon. Rate of descent for a parachute jump is about 5 m/s.

Paraclete (the Holy Ghost, or Comforter), the name used in the English translations of St. John's Gospel, and adopted by Abelard to designate the convent in Champagne founded by him, and of which Héloïse became the abbess.

Paradise, a Persian word used by the translators of the Old Testament to designate the Garden of Eden, and since meaning any place of happiness.

Paraffin, a mixture of hydrocarbons of higher boiling point than petrol. Paraffin was first obtained by distillation of coal, the process being discovered about 1830. About 1848, Mr. James Young procured it from mineral oil, and Irish peat also yielded it. The main source of paraffin supply today is crude petroleum. Used in the manufacture of candles, for waterproofing and numerous other purposes.

Parakeets, various small parrots of vivid plumage native to Australia, Polynesia, Asia and Africa. One of the loveliest of the parakeets is the budgerigar of Australia.

Parallax, the change in direction of a body caused by a change in position of the observer. If the parallax is measured (in degrees of angle) and the distance between the two observation points is known the distance of the observed body can be calculated. The distance of heavenly bodies has been found this way. The first stellar distances were so obtained in 1838 by Henderson, Struve and Bessel. Stellar distances are so great that even when the two observations are made at opposite points of the earth's orbit round the sun the parallax is always less than 1·0″ of arc. *See* **Aberration.**

Parameter, a number which is fixed for the application of a theory to one particular situation but may be different for other situations. For example, in a theory of motion near the surface of a planet the acceleration due to gravity may be regarded as a parameter constant for a particular planet but differing from planet to planet. The word is often used in a similar way in discussions of economic affairs.

Parchment, made chiefly from the skins of animals, usually of goats and sheep, was employed in olden times before printing was invented and superseded papyrus as writing material. Vegetable parchment, invented by W. E. Gaine in 1853, though not equal in strength and durability to skin parchment, is about five times stronger than ordinary paper. Vellum is parchment made from the skins of young calves or lambs.

Paris University, of which the Sorbonne forms a part was founded in the 12th cent. and is one of the greatest educational institutions of Europe.

Parliament, is the name given to the supreme legislature of the United Kingdom. It consists of the Queen, the Lords spiritual and temporal and the Commons. It meets in two houses: the House of Lords (the Upper or Second Chamber) and the House of Commons. It derives from the Anglo-Saxon *Witans* (*see* **Witan**). The Statute of Westminster (1275) first uses "parlement" of the Great Council in England, which comes from the French word meaning discourse. *See* **Central Government, Section C, Part I.**

Parliamentary Correspondents sit in the Press Gallery of the House of Commons and describe its proceedings for the news media either by impressions or a summary of the debate.

Parquetry, the name of a style of flooring consisting of small rectangular wooden blocks laid down according to geometrical pattern.

Parrot, the popular name of a widely distributed family of tropical birds, including the African grey parrot, the green parrot of South America —both familiar cage pets in this country—and the various parakeets, cockatoos, macaws, lories, etc. Many of these birds possess a remarkable gift of imitating sound, especially that of the human voice. *See* **Section Z.**

Parsec, unit of distance used by astronomers for expressing distances between stars; equivalent to about three and a quarter light-years.

Parthenogenesis. The development of animals from unfertilised eggs. The drones of the honey bee are parthenogenetic, and the phenomenon is also common among aphids.

Parthenon, the famous Temple of Athena on the Acropolis at Athens, was built under the rule of Pericles between 447 B.C. and 432 B.C. It was made wholly of marble without mortar. The famous sculptured friezes, known as the Elgin Marbles, are now in the British Museum.

Partridge, a well-known British game-bird. Close time: 2 February to 31 August. Two species are common in Britain.

Passeriformes, the order of perching birds which includes about half the known species.

Passport is an official document issued to a person by his own government, certifying to his citizenship and permitting him to travel abroad. Passports to British subjects are granted by the Foreign Office, authorise bearer to leave the country and guarantee him the state's protection. Passports (1977) cost £10—and are issued for a period of 10 years. Children over 16 years of age require separate passports. Parents of children under 16 who require passports should make application on form (B). A simplified form of travel document (British visitor's passport) is issued for British subjects wishing to pay short visits to certain foreign countries for a fee of £5—valid for 12 months. For those making frequent visits abroad a 94-page passport was issued in 1973, which now costs £20.

Patricians, the aristocracy of ancient Rome.

Paul's Cathedral, St., is the third cathedral church to be built on the site. It was preceded by a Norman building which was practically destroyed by the Great Fire in 1666. This followed a Saxon church which was burnt in 1086. The present building was designed by Sir Christopher Wren. The foundation stone was laid in 1675 and the structure was completed in 1710. It cost a little under £748,000. Its central feature is the dome, crowned by its cupola and lantern with the golden ball and cross. It escaped serious damage during the air raids of the second world war, but many of the surrounding buildings were laid waste.

***p*C Value,** introduced by Dr. C. L. Whittles in 1935 as a measure of salinity of aqueous solutions (soil extract, irrigation water, etc.); defined as the negative logarithm of specific electrical conductivity in reciprocal ohms. Alone or joined with *pH* (below) is useful as an index of osmotic pressure (*see* **Osmosis**) and related hindrance to plant growth resulting from excess of fertiliser or soil salts. If manuring is balanced, growth is best about *pC* 3.3. *See* **F22(2).**

Peacock, a bird of large size and beautiful plumage, its characteristic feature being a tail of brilliant "eyed" feathers, which it can erect and spread out, the males possessing resplendent feathering to a much greater extent than the females. It is related to the pheasant; one species is found wild in the forests of India, and another inhabits Burma and the Malayan regions, in Africa there is the Congo Peacock.

Peanut, Ground Nut *or* **Monkey Nut.** A member of the pea family native to S. America, but now cultivated in many parts of the world. After pollination, the flower stalk bends down and buries the pod containing the peas ("nuts") in the ground. The oil from these "nuts" can be used for margarine manufacture.

Pearl is produced by certain shelled molluscs, chiefly the oyster. The inner surface of the shells of the pearl oyster yield "mother-of-pearl", and distinct pearls are believed to be morbid secretions, caused by some external irritation. Many fine pearls are found in the actual body of the oyster. The Persian Gulf, Sri Lanka, the north-west coast of Western Australia, many Pacific islands and the Gulf of Mexico are among the most productive pearl-fishing grounds. In ancient times Britain was renowned for its pearl fisheries, the pearls being obtained from a species of fresh-water mussel. Western Australia has produced a 40-grain pearl, the finest the world has seen. The largest pearl ever found was the "Beresford-Hope Pearl", which weighed 1,800 grains, over six times as much as the oyster that produced it.

Peat, decayed vegetable matter found mostly in marshy positions, and common in Ireland and Scotland. Peat is coal in its first stage of development; burnt for fuel in many cottage homes.

Peccary, a pig-like animal native to the Americas. There are two species: the collared peccary and the white-lipped peccary, the latter being a vicious and dangerous animal.

Pelican, a genus of bird with long depressed bill pouched underneath, thus able to hold fish in reserve. It has immense wings and webbed feet. Eight species.

Pemmican, venison or other meat, sliced, dried, pounded and made into cakes, used by explorers and others when out of reach of fresh meat.

Penguin, a genus of flightless, fish-eating sea-birds of the southern hemisphere. They are stout-bodied, short-necked and of small, moderate or large size. The Emperor and King Penguins make no nest but protect and incubate the single egg by carrying it in the down feathers between the feet and the body. Other species brood in the usual way and may lay as many as three eggs. Penguins use their flippers for swimming under water. All 17 species are bluish-grey or blackish above and white below. They are very sociable and breed in colonies.

Penicillin. An antibiotic drug produced by the mould *Penicillium notatum*, and discovered by Sir Alexander Fleming in 1928. It is one of the most effective chemotherapeutic agents known

The mould produces a number of penicillins, all of which are effective antibiotics. *See* **P4(1), 9(1).**

Peninsular War lasted from 1808 to 1814. Fought in Spain and Portugal (the Iberian peninsula) by the British, Spanish and Portuguese forces, chiefly under Wellington, against the French. The latter were defeated.

Pentagon, government office in Washington (the largest in the world), housing many thousands of military and civilian workers in the War Department of the United States (Army, Navy and Air Force).

Pentateuch, the first five books of the Old Testament—Genesis, Exodus, Leviticus, Numbers and Deuteronomy. Referred to in the Gospel of Mark as " the book of Moses ".

Pepys Diary, by Samuel Pepys, was first published in 1825. It gives a picture of the social life of the period 1 January 1660 to 31 May 1669. He bequeathed the manuscript, together with his library, to Magdalene College, Cambridge.

Perch, a well-known family of fresh-water fish, with dark striped sides. The common perch of British rivers and lakes falls an easy prey to the angler because of its voracity.

Perfumes are essences or odours obtained from floral and other substances. The chief flower perfumes are those obtained from rose, jasmine, orange flower, violet and acacia. Heliotrope perfume is largely obtained from vanilla and almonds. Among the aromatic herbs which yield attractive perfumes are the rosemary, thyme, geranium, lavender, etc., while orange peel, citron peel, musk, sandalwood, patchouli and other vegetable products are largely drawn upon. In recent times chemistry has been called into play in aid of the perfumer, and many of the popular perfumes of today are chemically prepared in simulation of the scents of the flowers or other natural substances the names of which they bear. *See* **Musk Deer.**

Perigee, the smallest distance of the earth from any of the heavenly bodies; opposite of apogee (*q.v.*).

Perihelion. That point in a planet's orbit when it is nearest to the sun; opposite of aphelion. The earth is at perihelion ($1{\cdot}47 \times 10^8$ km) in mid-winter, about 3 January.

Peripatus, an animal which stands as a link between the annelid worms and the arthropods. Wormlike with short unjointed legs it breathes by a system of air tubes like those in insects. Certain other points of internal structure point to a relationship with annelid worms. There are some fifty species, the best known being the S. African *Peripatus capensis.*

Perjury, the offence of giving false evidence. The ancient Romans threw the perjurer from the Tarpeian Rock, and after the Empire was Christianised, those who swore falsely upon the Gospel had their tongues cut out. The usual punishment in England from the 16th to the 19th cent. was the pillory, fine and imprisonment.

Permian Formation, a group of rocks lying between the Trias and the Carboniferous strata. It has three subdivisions, Upper, Middle and Lower Permian. *See* **F45.**

Per Procurationem signature means that the subject of the correspondence has been put into the writer's care by his principal for him to use his personal judgment in the matter, and that he is authorised to sign on behalf of his principal. Normally contracted to *per pro* or *p.p.*

Peruke, the name given to the wigs worn by men in the latter half of the 18th cent. The custom of wearing wigs was gradually superseded by powdering the natural hair. Wigs are still worn by the Speaker of the House of Commons, judges and barristers.

Petrel, the name given to a member of a large, widely-distributed family of sea-birds of great diversity of size and colouring and distinguished by tube-like external nostrils. They usually skim low over the waves, and some, for this reason, are known as shearwaters. The storm petrel or Mother Carey's chicken occasionally patters along the surface, and is often called Little Peter—a reference to St. Peter walking on the water. Except when breeding, petrels are always at sea. They mostly nest in holes and crevices on islands and lay one egg, which is invariably white. The storm petrel, Leach's petrel, Manx shearwater and the fulmar petrel are resident in the British Isles. *See also* **Mutton Bird.**

Petroleum. *See* **Oil.**

Pewter, alloy of tin and lead formerly used for making household utensils and ornaments.

***pH* Value.** Introduced in 1909 by the Danish chemist Sørensen to indicate hydrogen-ion concentration on the basis of electrical conductivity and a view of ionisation since discarded; is now taken as a logarithmic scale of acidity or alkalinity of aqueous solutions: acidity 0–7, neutrality at 7·0, alkalinity 7–14. The *pH* of blood is about 7·6 (faintly alkaline). *See* **F22.**

Phalanger, pouched marsupial mammals. They are arboreal and superficially resemble squirrels. There are two genera of flying phalangers or flying squirrels, which have a remarkable membrane along each side of the body enabling the animals to glide through the air. The members of the phalanger family are confined to the Australasian and oriental regions.

Phalangid, a member of the arachnid family Phalangida: popularly known as " harvesters ".

Phalanx, a name applied by the ancient Greeks to a body of pike-men drawn up in close array, with overlapping shields, and eight, ten or more rows deep. The Macedonians stood sixteen rows deep. As many as 500 men could be in the front row.

Pharisees and Sadducees, two ancient Jewish sects. *See* **Judaism, Section J.**

Pharmacopoeia, an official publication containing information on the recognised drugs used in medicine. Each country has its own pharmacopoeia. The British Pharmacopoeia (B.P.) is published under the direction of the General Medical Council. The Pharmaceutical Society issues the British Pharmaceutical Codex (B.P.C.); there is also an International Pharmacopoeia (2 vols.) which is issued by the World Health Organisation.

Pharos, the name of the first lighthouse, built by Ptolemy II about 280 B.C., on the Isle of Pharos, at the entrance to the harbour of Alexandria. It was 183 m high, and one of the " seven wonders ".

Pheasant, game birds related to the partridges, quails, peacocks, chickens and turkeys, distinguished by their brilliant plumage and long tapering tail. First found by the Greeks in Georgia where the River Phasis flows through to the Black Sea. Close time: 2 February to 30 September.

Phillippics, the oration delivered by Demosthenes, 352–341 B.C., against Philip of Macedon—remarkable for their acrimonious invective. The word was also used for Cicero's speeches against Antony. In modern use, any impassioned invective.

Philosopher's Stone. *See* **Alchemy.**

Phosphorus is a non-metal element, symbol P. Most familiar as a waxy, yellow solid which is spontaneously inflammable in air. It has chemical similarities to arsenic, like which it is very poisonous. It was discovered by Brandt in urine in 1669. It is found in most animal and vegetable tissues. It is an essential element of all plants and of the bones of animals. In combination with various metals it forms different phosphates, which are largely utilised as manures. The chief commercial use of phosphorus is in the preparation of matches.

Photoelectric Cell, a device which gives a useful electrical response to light falling on it. There are several kinds depending on the different effects which light may have on a suitably chosen solid (usually a semiconductor), viz., the emission of electrons from the surface (" photoemissive cell "); change in electrical resistance (" photoconducting cell "); generation of electric current from a specially designed sensitive structure (" barrier layer " or " photovoltaic cell ", " solar battery "). Different cells respond differently to lights of various wavelength and must be chosen for each application. *See also* **Solar Battery.**

Photogrammetry, the science of measurement from photographs taken from an aircraft. Aerial photography has many uses and is of great value to military intelligence and for mapmaking.

Photon. When light behaves like a stream of discrete particles and not like waves, the particles are called photons. *See* **F13(1), 14.**

Photosynthesis. *See* **F28, F41(1).**

Phrenology. *See* **Section J.**

Phylloxera, a genus of plant-lice related to the aphids, which attacks the grape vine. Many vineyards of France, in common with the rest of Europe, were replanted with native vines grafted on immune stocks from California in 1879 after being ravaged by the insect (which came from America). Curiously enough, the remedy also came from America, the vine stocks there being immune to *phylloxera*.

Pi is the unique number denoted by the Greek letter π and obtained by dividing the length of the circumference of any circle by its diameter. Its value is approximately 3·14159.

Picts, inhabitants of Scotland in pre-Roman times, are held by some historians to be a branch of the old Celtic race, by others to have been of Scythian origin. They occupied the north eastern portion of Scotland, and were subdued by the Scots in Argyll in the 9th cent., Kenneth MacAlpin becoming king of a united kingdom of the Picts and Scots—the kingdom of Alban.

Pike, a familiar fresh-water fish abundant in the temperate regions of both hemispheres. It forms good sport for the angler in rivers and lakes, and sometimes attains a weight of from 9–13 kg. It is extremely voracious, is covered with small scales and has a ferocious-looking head.

Pilchard, a fish of the herring family, but with smaller scales and more rounded body. It appears off the Cornish coasts in vast shoals every summer.

Pilgrimage, the undertaking of a journey to a distant place or shrine to satisfy a religious vow or secure spiritual benefit, was resorted to in early Christian times. The first recorded pilgrimage is that of the Empress Helena to Jerusalem in 326. In the Middle Ages pilgrimages became common, and were undertaken by monarchs and people of rank in all Christian countries. Moslems have been making pilgrimages to Mecca since the death of the Prophet, such duty being enjoined by the Koran. Among the great centres of Christian pilgrimages are Jerusalem, Rome, the tomb of Becket at Canterbury and the holy places of Lourdes and La Salette in France.

Pilgrimage of Grace (1536), the rising in Lincolnshire and Yorkshire in the reign of Henry VIII against religious innovations and the dissolution of the smaller monasteries, which overlapped with discontents caused by taxation, rising prices, enclosures and land speculation. The insurrection was followed by many executions.

Pilgrim Fathers, the 101 English Puritans, who, after living some years in exile in Holland, to escape persecution in their own country, set sail for America in the *Mayflower*, 6 September 1620, landing at Plymouth, Mass., 4 December. They founded the settlement of Plymouth, and are regarded as the pioneers of American colonisation although 13 years earlier a small Virginian colony had been established.

"Pilgrim's Progress", Bunyan's famous allegory, written in Bedford gaol. The first part was issued in 1678. It is the greatest work of its kind. *See* **Section M, Part VI.**

Pillory, a wooden instrument of punishment in use in England until 1837. It consisted of a pair of movable boards with holes through which the culprit's head and hands were put, and was usually erected on a scaffold. While a person was undergoing this punishment the mob generally pelted him with stones and rubbish, sometimes to his serious injury. People convicted of forgery, perjury or libel were often condemned to the pillory, but from 1816 to 1837 the only offence for which it could be inflicted was perjury.

Pine, a conifer of the genus *Pinus*, which flourishes all over the northern hemisphere and includes 80–90 species, which afford valuable timber and yield turpentine and tar. The Scots Pine, *Pinus silvestris*, with its blue-green, short needles, set in pairs, and its rosy-orange branches, is native to Britain, as it is to the whole of Europe. It provides the red and yellow deal in everyday use.

Pitcairn Islanders were originally the mutineers of the *Bounty*. They took possession of the island in 1790, and it was not until 1814 that their whereabouts was ascertained, accidentally, by a passing ship. The mutineers, under their leader, Adams, had settled down to a communal existence, married Tahitian women and increased so in numbers that in the course of years they were too many for the island to support, and in 1856 they were removed by the British Government to Norfolk Island. A small number returned to Pitcairn.

Pitchblende *or* **Uraninite,** a relatively scarce mineral. It is nearly all uranium oxide, but lead, thorium, etc., are also present. Pitchblende from Joachimstal in Czechoslovakia was the material in which radium was discovered by the Curies. Other major sources are the Great Lakes region of Canada and Zaïre.

Placebo, medical treatment that the therapist uses deliberately although he knows it is without any specific effect on the condition being treated. There may be various medical reasons for using placebos, *e.g.*, for the beneficial psychological effect on people who like to feel something is being done for them; for differentiating during clinical trials of a new treatment between those persons given the real thing and a control or comparison group of persons given a placebo or inactive imitation.

Plainsong, a style of musical composition sung in unison (all voices singing the same tune without harmony), familiar in the Western Church from very early times and still performed, principally in the Roman Catholic Church. Though restrained and contemplative in spirit, it is capable of expressing deep emotion. *See* **E3(2).**

Planetarium, a complex optical system which projects into the interior of a dome a replica of all the phenomena of the sky that can be seen by the naked eye, *e.g.*, sun, moon, planets, stars, comets, meteors, aurora, eclipses and clouds. There is a planetarium in the Marylebone Road, London, and another (opened in 1966) at Armagh Observatory, N. Ireland.

Planets, the name given to such celestial bodies as revolve round the sun in elliptical orbits. The name was first used by the Greeks to indicate their difference from the fixed stars. There are nine planets, Mercury, Venus, Earth, Mars, Jupiter, Saturn, Uranus, Neptune, Pluto. Only Saturn and Uranus are ringed. Many important questions can be answered by means of probes sent to the neighbourhood of the planets. These include the measurement of the magnetic field, if any, of the planets, the study of their atmospheres, much of which can be done without actually penetrating to the surface. With instruments landed gently on the surface it is possible to investigate surface conditions and composition by many methods. Even without a soft-landing information on these questions can be obtained by photography and subsequent transmission of the picture back to earth by some form of television scanning. The US Mars probe *Mariner IV* transmitted pictures of the Martian surface in 1965 when it was at its closest approach to the planet, the Russian *Venus IV* in 1967 made a soft-landing on Venus, and the US *Pioneer 11* came within 43,400 km of Jupiter in December 1974. *See* under their names and **F7.**

Plankton, a word which first came into biological use in 1886 to describe the usually microscopic plants and animals floating, swimming and drifting in the surface waters of the sea. To be distinguished from *nekton* (swimming animals like fishes and squids) and *benthos* (plants and animals living on the sea bottom, like fixed algae, sponges, oysters, crabs, etc.). Of great economic importance, providing food for fish and whales.

Plantagenets, the kings who reigned in England between 1154 and 1485 and included the Houses of Lancaster and York. More correctly they are styled Angevins, from Anjou, of which Geoffrey, father of Henry II, was Count, and whose badge was a sprig of broom (*Planta genista*).

Plasma Physics is the physics of wholly ionised gases, *i.e.*, gases in which the atoms initially present have lost practically the whole of the electrons that usually surround their nuclei, so that the gas consists of a mixture of two components, positively charged ions and negatively charged electrons. The physical properties of a *plasma* are very different from those of an unionised gas. In particular, a plasma has a high electrical conductivity and can carry large currents. *See also* **Nuclear Fusion.**

Plastics, a broad term covering those substances which become plastic when subjected to increased temperatures or pressures. The Plastics Industry is based on synthetic organic examples of this group. There are two classes of plastics: the *thermoplastic,* which become plastic every time they are heated (*e.g.* cellulosic plastics) and *thermosetting,* which undergo chemical change when heated, so that once set they cannot be rendered plastic again (*e.g.* Bakelite). Plastics are composed of long-chained molecules, *e.g.*, polyethylene.

Plate Tectonics, the contemporary and by now well-developed theory of the movements of the earth's crust. The view is that the surface of the Earth consists of about a dozen rigid plates, some larger than continents, some much smaller, all in ceaseless motion relative to one another. Their separation and approach and their friction and collision are closely related to the evolution of mountain ranges, oceans and rift valleys and to phenomena like earthquakes and volcanoes. *See* **F9.**

Platinum, a metal element, symbol Pt. It is a scarce white metal generally allied with iridium, osmium, ruthenium and palladium. It can only be melted in an oxyhydrogen or electric furnace, but can be rolled out into a film-like sheet, or drawn out to the finest wire; being resistant to acids it is termed a noble metal.

Platonic Solids, five regular solid figures known to the ancient world. They are: the tetrahedron (4 triangular faces), cube (6 square faces), octahedron (8 triangular faces), dodecahedron (12 five-sided faces), icosahedron (20 triangular faces). All the faces and angles of each solid are identical.

Pleiades, famous cluster of stars in the constellation of Taurus. Of the seven principal stars in the group, one is rather faint, and many myths have sprung up about this "lost pleiad".

Pleistocene, the geological period that succeeded the Pliocene. During the Pleistocene, also known as the *Great Ice Age,* there were four cold periods, when the ice sheets covered northern Europe and N. America, separated by warm periods when the glaciers drew back into the mountains. From recent studies based on rock magnetic measurements the transition to Pleistocene took place about 1,850,000 years ago.

Pliocene, the geological period preceding the Pleistocene, and the last major division of the Tertiary strata. It began about fifteen million years ago. *See* **F45.**

Plough Monday, the first Monday after the Epiphany, when in olden times the rustic population returned to work after the Christmas festivities.

Plover, wading birds, widely distributed over marshy places of Europe. Several species occur in Britain, including the Golden-plover, which breeds on the moors of Devon, Somerset, Wales, N.E. Yorkshire and Scotland, and the Ringed plover, Kentish plover and Dotterel.

Pluto, the last planet to be discovered; existence established by C. W. Tombaugh at the Flagstaff Observatory in Arizona in January 1930 from reckonings made by P. Lowell in 1914. It is the most distant of all the known planets; diameter about 6,000 km. Mean distance from the sun estimated at $5{,}900 \times 10^6$ km. *See* **F7.**

Plutonium, a chemical element, symbol Pu, capable of nuclear fission in the same way as Uranium 235. Not until after it had been synthesised in atomic piles during the second world war was it shown to occur in infinitesimally small traces in nature. Its synthesis in the atomic pile depends on the capture by Uranium 238 nuclei of neutrons; immediate product of this reaction is the element neptunium, but this undergoes rapid radioactive disintegration to plutonium. Because of its explosive power and poisonous character, an American scientist once remarked: "If ever there was an element which deserved a name associated with hell, it is plutonium."

Poet Laureate is the poet attached to the royal household, an office officially established in 1668, though its origins go back to the early Middle Ages, when minstrels were employed at the courts of English kings. Chaucer, Skelton and Spenser, though not court poets, were all unofficial poets laureate. Ben Jonson has been called the first "official laureate" (1616), but the office was not officially recognised until 1668, when Dryden was formally granted the office. It is customary for the poet laureate to write verse in celebration of events of national importance. Sir John Betjeman succeeded Cecil Day-Lewis as poet laureate in 1972.

Pogrom. Russian word meaning "destruction". First used to describe the Tsarist attacks on the Jews in 1881 in Russia. In 1938 Hitler ordered a general pogrom in Germany: all synagogues were destroyed and nearly all Jewish shops and homes, Jewish hospitals and children's homes suffered. During the subsequent war Jews of central Europe were systematically exterminated in cold blood by the Nazis.

Poitiers, Battle of, was fought on 19 September 1356, during the Hundred Years' War, when Edward the Black Prince gained a complete victory over John, King of France, who was taken prisoner and brought to London.

Polecat, an animal of a dark-brown colour, about 46 cm in length, exclusive of tail; the ears and face-markings are white or light brown. It is carnivorous and belongs to the weasel family. Like the skunk, it emits an offensive odour.

Pole-Star is of the second magnitude, and the last in the tail of the Little Bear constellation. Being near the North pole of the heavens—never more than about one degree from due north—it always remains visible in the Northern hemisphere; hence its use as a guide to seamen.

Police, a regular force established for the preservation of law and order and the prevention and detection of crime. The powers they have vary from country to country and with the type of government; the more civilised and democratic the state, the less police intervention. England, compared with countries abroad, was slow to develop a police force, and it was not until 1829 that Sir Robert Peel's Metropolitan Police Act established a regular force for the metropolis, later legislation establishing county and borough forces maintained by local police authorities throughout England and Wales. Up to that time police duties were discharged by individual constables and watchmen appointed by local areas in England and Wales. The police service in Great Britain today is organised in a number of forces (43 in England and Wales and 6 regional and 2 combined forces in Scotland). Strength *c.* 110,000. In Northern Ireland there is a single force (the Royal Ulster Constabulary). In England and Wales the forces are defined according to area of responsibility:

1. County forces, under a police committee consisting of local councillors and magistrates.
2. Combined forces, covering more than one county, also under a police committee consisting of local councillors and magistrates and representatives from each constituent area.
3. The Metropolitan Police Force, covering an area within a 15-mile (24-km) radius of Charing Cross, but excluding the City of London, under the control of the Home Secretary. Strength *c.* 21,000.
4. The City of London force operating in the area of the city, under the Court of Common Council.

In Scotland the police authority is the regional or island council. Police ranks are: chief constable, assistant chief constable, chief superintendent, superintendent, chief inspector, inspector, sergeant and constable. In the Metropolitan Police area the chief officer is the Commissioner of Police of the Metropolis. Central authority rests with the Home Secretary in England and Wales and the Secretary of State for Scotland in Scotland. In the present troubles in Northern Ireland responsibility for law and order is retained at Westminster.

Pollution of the atmosphere is due chiefly to the

incomplete combustion of fuels, especially coal, large particles of soot being deposited fairly quickly close to their place of origin and smaller particles (including smoke) remaining suspended in the air for a long time. Invisible air pollutants include sulphur dioxide from power stations and home heating, and carbon monoxide from cars. The introduction of more efficient furnaces, the washing of flue gases and the introduction of smokeless zones have assisted in the abatement of smoke and other forms of pollution. Atomic weapon tests add to the load of pollution in the atmosphere (*see* **Fall-out**). "Smog" (smoke-laden fog) which reduces visibility to zero and affects the respiratory organs, is liable to occur when the air near the earth is cooled below the dew-point temperature by radiation on a still, cloudless night when an accumulation of smoke over a large city cuts off daylight and produces gloom, and absence of wind or vertical currents prevents the lower layers of the air from getting away. Such conditions are associated with the smoke-laden atmosphere of large industrial towns during a winter anticyclone. During the great London smog of 1952 there were 2,000 deaths over and above those expected for the time of year. Since the Clean Air Act of 1956 pollution by smoke and sulphur dioxide has continued to diminish in London, winter sunshine has increased by 70 per cent. and fish now live in the Thames. In 1969 a special Secretaryship of State was created to deal with a wide range of functions relating to the physical environment in which people live and work, including pollution (air, waters in rivers and around coasts, noise, pesticides harmful to food and wildlife). In his 1969 Reith lectures Dr. Fraser Darling said "most pollution comes from getting rid of waste at the least possible cost". *See also* **Pollution, Section F, Part V.**

Polonium, a radioactive element, symbol Po, discovered by Madame Curie in 1898, and named after her native land of Poland.

Poltergeist. *See* **Section J.**

Polymerisation is the linking together of small molecules to make a large long-chain molecule. The general name for polymers of ethylene is Polythene, a wax-like plastic solid which because of its special qualities is used in a variety of ways today.

Polytheism. *See* **God and Man, Section J.**

Pomology, the science of fruit-growing.

Pontifex, the title assigned in ancient Rome to members of the college of pontifices. "Pontifex maximus" was the official head of Roman religion. It was as "pontifex maximus" that Julius Caesar revised the calendar in 46 B.C., and when after the rise of Christianity the popes took over the title the revision fell to them.

Pope, The, the head of the Roman Catholic Church, recognised by that Church as the lawful successor of St. Peter. He is elected by the body of Cardinals. Since 1870, when the King of Italy deposed the holder from temporal power, no pope had left the Vatican between appointment and death until 1929, when peace was made between the Church and State in Italy and compensation was paid to the Holy See for the loss of temporal power. Cardinal Montini, Archbishop of Milan, was elected Pope Paul VI in 1963 on the death of Pope John XXIII.

Porcelain. The word is thought to be derived from the Italian *porcellana*, indicating the texture of a piglet. The majority of porcelain made on the continent was of "hard-paste", or true porcelain, similar to that discovered by the Chinese as early as the T'ang Dynasty (A.D. 618–907). It was composed of *kaolin* (china-clay) and *petuntse* (china-stone) which when fired in a kiln at a temperature of *c.* 1300°C became an extremely hard and translucent material. The recipe of "hard-paste" porcelain remained a secret of the Chinese until 1709, when it was re-discovered in Europe by Johann Böttger of the Meissen factory (popularly known as Dresden). Aided by disloyal Meissen workmen, factories were later established at Vienna, Venice and in many parts of Germany. Plymouth and Bristol were the only English factories to produce this type of porcelain, from 1768 to 1781. Elsewhere, both in England and France, the material manufactured was known as "soft-paste" or artificial porcelain which was made by blending varying white-firing clays with the ingredients of glass. The French factory of Sèvres began to make some hard-paste porcelain by 1768 and by the 19th cent. such porcelain was the only type being made throughout the whole of the continent. In England Josiah Spode is credited with the introduction of "bone-china" about 1794. This hybrid-paste was quickly adopted by many other factories and today remains the most popular type of English porcelain. *See* **Pottery and Porcelain Marks, Section D.**

Porcupine, a rodent whose back is covered with long, sharp, black and white spikes, which form a powerful means of defence. There are two families of porcupines; one is confined to the Old World and the other contains the American porcupines.

Porphyry, a form of crystalline rock of many varieties that in ancient Egypt was quarried and used for the decorative portions of buildings and vessels. The term is applied generally to the eruptive rocks in which large well-formed crystals of one mineral are set in a matrix of other minerals.

Porpoise, a highly intelligent marine mammal of the dolphin and whale family, and a common inhabitant of northern seas. Porpoises travel in shoals, their progression being marked by constant leapings and plungings. Their average length is from 1·2–1·5 m. There are several species, nearly all being confined to northern oceans.

Port, a special kind of red Portuguese wine, taking its name from Oporto. It was little known in England until the Methuen Treaty of 1703, when it was permitted to be imported at a low duty.

Portcullis, a strong, movable timber or iron grating let into the wall of the gateway to a feudal castle, and capable of being lowered or raised at will. It formed an effective protection against attack in the days before firearms.

Portland Vase, one of the most renowned specimens of ancient art, long in the possession of the Portland family. In 1810 it was loaned to the British Museum. Here it was shattered in 1845 by a stone from a maniac's hand, but has been skilfully restored. It is said to have been found in the 17th cent. in an ancient tomb near Rome. It was purchased from the Barberini family in 1770 by Sir Wm. Hamilton, subsequently sold to the Duchess of Portland. The vase, which is actually a two-handled urn, stands about 25 cm high, is of transparent dark blue glass, ornamented with figures cut in relief in overlaid white opaque glass. It was purchased by the British Museum in 1945. *See also* **Glass.**

Portreeve in olden times was an official appointed to superintend a port or harbour, and before the name of mayor was used the chief magistrate of London was styled the Portreeve.

Positivism. *See* **Section J.**

Positron, the "positive electron", an atomic particle having the same mass but an electric charge equal but opposite to that of an electron. It was discovered in 1932. *See also* **F14.**

Post-Impressionism, a term introduced by Roger Fry to describe the exhibition of paintings sponsored by himself in London (1910–11) officially entitled "Manet and the Post-Impressionists". The exhibition included paintings by Manet, Cézanne, Gauguin, Van Gogh, Seurat, Signac, works by Matisse, Rouault and the *Fauves* (*q.v.*), and sculpture by Maillol. In a second exhibition, held in 1912, Picasso and the Cubists were also represented. The term therefore refers to the movement in modern art which reacted against the transient naturalism of the Impressionists by concerning itself primarily with colour, form and solidity. Most artists today would include Cézanne, Van Gogh and Gauguin as the main Post-Impressionists and maintain that it prepared the way for Fauvism, Cubism and Expressionism.

Potassium, a metal, symbol K (German *Kalium*). It is similar to sodium, like which it reacts violently with water. It was discovered by Sir Humphry Davy in 1807, and now generally obtained by the electrolysis of fused potassium hydroxide or chloride/fluoride mixture. Its principal minerals are carnallite and kainite and it is relatively common in rocks, accounting for about 2½% of the earth's crust. An essential element for healthy plant growth; the ashes of plants are relatively rich in potassium.

Potsdam Agreement was signed by Truman, Stalin and Attlee in August 1945. By this Agreement a Council of Foreign Ministers was established, representing the five principal Powers: China, France, Soviet Russia, the United Kingdom and United States of America, with the task of drawing up the peace treaties for submission to the United Nations. It laid down, *inter alia*, that German militarism and Hitlerism should be destroyed; that industrial power should be so reduced that Germany would never again be in a position to wage aggressive war; that surplus equipment should be destroyed or transferred to replace wrecked plant in allied territories; that Germany should be treated as an economic whole; and that local self-government should be restored on democratic lines as rapidly as was consistent with military security. The Potsdam Agreement became a dead letter with the creation of a communist régime in the Russian zone of Germany, and marked the beginning of the "cold war".

Prado Gallery, the great public picture collection of Madrid, containing a superb collection of paintings by Velasquez, Murillo, Raphael, Titian, Dürer, Van Dyck, Rubens and Goya.

Pragmatism. *See* **Section J.**

Prefect, chief magistrates in ancient Rome. The title is now applied to the chiefs of administration of the departments of France.

Pre-Raphaelite Brotherhood was the name given to their school of thought by three British artists, Dante Gabriel Rossetti, J. E. Millais and W. Holman Hunt, who in 1848 revolted against the academic art of their time and advocated a return to the style of the Italian painters prior to Raphael—the simple naturalism of the Primitives, such as Botticelli, Fra Angelico and Filippo Lippi. Thus they avoided the use of heavy shadows and painted on a white ground in bright colours—a technique which aroused the ire of those used to the dark and murky canvases of the contemporary romantic artists. Although they held these principles in common the three members of the "P.R.B.", as it was popularly called, were really quite different in other respects. Thus Rossetti (who for some reason is always thought of as the typical Pre-Raphaelite) produced works of a highly romanticised mediaevalism which, apart from certain aspects of technique, bear not the slightest resemblance to the sentimental naturalism of Millais or the much more dramatic realism of Holman Hunt (*e.g.*, in *The Scapegoat*). The Brotherhood was later joined by a number of lesser artists, but its works are not commonly accepted with enthusiasm today when the general feeling is that they are sentimental and religiose rather than the product of deeply-felt emotions. Ruskin in his writings defended their work but the movement came to an end in 1853.

Presbyterianism. *See* **Section J.**

Press-Gang, a body of sailors employed to impress men into naval service, frequently resorted to in England, especially during the war with France in the early 19th cent. Press gangs were not used after about 1850.

Primitive Art. The word "primitive" has a number of different meanings: (1) the art of prehistoric communities (*e.g.*, the famous animal cave-drawings of the Aurignacians, *c.* 25,000 B.C., at Altamira in Spain); (2) the art of modern primitive communities (*e.g.*, Bushman rock-paintings); (3) child art; (4) peasant art which springs from a spontaneous desire to impart beauty to objects of daily use and shows a tendency towards abstraction. Peasant art has many features in common the world over, the woodcarving of the Norsemen being almost indistinguishable from that of the Maoris; (5) the modern school of primitive painting in which naïveté of presentation is either the aim of a highly sophisticated mind (*e.g.*, the self-taught French painter Le Douanier Rousseau (d. 1910)), or arises naturally from a simple one (the American "grandma" Moses (d. 1961) who began to paint in her seventies).

Printing by movable types was first used in Europe in 1454 by Johann Gutenberg, a citizen of Mainz. The invention is also claimed for Laurens Koster of Haarlem. It was introduced into England by Caxton, who set up a printing press in Westminster in 1476. Gothic characters were first used, being superseded by Roman letters in 1518. In 1798 Earl Stanhope replaced the wood printing press by one of iron. In 1814 Friedrich Koenig applied the principle of steam power to the press. Mr. John Walter, of *The Times* newspaper, was the first to use the steam press. Improvements were introduced by Applegarth and Cowper in 1828 and great strides were made in 1858 when the Hoe machine was put on the market. Then came the Walter press in 1866 which printed on continuous rolls of paper from curved stereotyped plates. The Monotype machine casts single letters and the Linotype whole lines. The term letterpress is used for all printing methods using plates where the characters stand in *relief*. The other main printing methods are *intaglio* and *planographic*.

The Privy Council is the Sovereign's own council, consisting of about 300 persons who have reached eminence in some branch of public affairs (Cabinet ministers must be Privy Counsellors), on whose advice and through which the Sovereign exercises his or her statutory and a number of prerogative powers. From it have sprung many organs of the constitution and many of our government departments have grown from committees of the Privy Council. For example the Judiciary or courts of justice have grown from the Sovereign's Council sitting as a Court of Justice, and today the Judicial Committee of the Privy Council is a body of distinguished lawyers acting as a Court of Appeal from courts of the Commonwealth.

Probation Officers are attached to particular Courts, sometimes a Magistrates' or a higher court. Sometimes an offender is not sentenced to punishment, but is released "on probation", that is on the condition that he behaves well and follows directions given by the Court or by a probation officer. Such an officer is a trained man (or woman) who advises, assists and befriends people who are placed under his supervision by a court of law. The probation officer, by his assessment of the social background of the offender, can advise the court upon the wisdom of putting the offender on probation. The probation officer by his understanding can so befriend an offender as to provide a basis for his rehabilitation. He undertakes the "after care" of those released from prison or Borstal. A juvenile offender, or in need of care, may be made subject to supervision by a probation officer or local authority. *See also* **Juvenile Courts.**

Productivity. Physical productivity is the output of products during a time unit, *e.g.*, so many products per man hour, or day, or year. Total productivity is the sum of all the units of product created during the given time. Labour productivity is the part of the total that is attributed to labour as a factor of production. Productivity of capital is the element attributed to capital as a factor. Productivity of land is the element attributed to the natural powers of the soil, as distinct from what is contributed by the application to it of capital or labour. The term productivity is also used to refer not to the quantity of output, but to its money value.

Propane, a colourless inflammable gas made of carbon and hydrogen; formula C_3H_8. It is easily liquefied and transported liquid in cylinders and tanks. In this form it is familiar as a "portable gas supply" for domestic and industrial uses. It is sometimes mixed with butane (*q.v.*) for this purpose. Propane occurs in natural gas and is a by-product of oil refining.

Proteins are the main chemical substances of living matter: they are a part of every living cell and are found in all animals and plants. All proteins are basically constructed of carbon, hydrogen, oxygen and nitrogen, and some contain sulphur, phosphorus (nucleoproteins) and iron (haemoglobin). Proteins are built up of very long chains of amino-acids connected by amide linkages (the synthetic polymers such as "nylon" and casein plastics (from milk) are built up of the same linkages). The structure of protein molecules allows a variety of function. Enzymes, which bring about chemical reactions in living cells, are proteins having specific properties. *See* F27(1), *also* **Diet, Section P.**

Proton, a basic constituent of the atomic nucleus, positively charged, having a mass about 1836 times that of the electron. It is a positive hydrogen ion. *See* **F10(2), 14.**

Prout's hypothesis. The English chemist William Prout (1785–1850) advanced the idea that all atoms are made of hydrogen, and their weights are exact multiples of the weight of a hydrogen atom. With the modification that neutrons as well as protons occur in the nucleus, Prout's belief, though rejected for many years, has been substantially vindicated.

Provost, a Scottish official similar in rank to an English mayor. The Provosts of Edinburgh, Glasgow, Aberdeen, Perth and Dundee are styled Lords Provost. The title of provost is also given to the heads of certain colleges.

Prud'hommes (Prudent Men), **Councils of,** were French trade tribunals, of masters and workmen, formed to decide on disputes. Originally a mediaeval institution, they were revived by Napoleon in 1806, and were carried on by the Third Republic.

Psalms, Book of, for many years attributed to David, but present-day scholars are of opinion that the psalms were written by a series of authors at different times and for different purposes, and that few, if any, were written by David. The Holy Scriptures contain 150.

Psychedelism. *See* **Section J.**

Psychic Research. *See* **Section J.**

Psychoanalysis. *See* **Section J.**

Ptarmigan, birds of the grouse family, one species of which inhabits the Scottish Highlands. In the winter the bird assumes a white plumage.

Ptomaines, amino acids produced during the putrefaction of proteins of animal origin. Not a cause of food poisoning, as was once generally supposed, which is almost invariably due to certain specific bacteria.

Publicans, under the Roman Empire, were people who farmed the public taxes. It is this class of officials that is alluded to in the " publicans and sinners " phrase in the New Testament.

Public Corporations, statutory bodies which operate major industries and services in the public interest, *e.g.,* UK Atomic Energy Authority, Bank of England, B.B.C., Electricity Authorities, Gas Council, National Coal Board, British Steel Corporation, British Railways Board. They are accountable to Parliament but their staffs are not civil servants. The Post Office became a public corporation in 1969, responsible to the Minister of Posts and Telecommunications.

Public Schools. The Public Schools Act of 1864 named nine " public " schools: Eton, Harrow, Rugby, Winchester, Westminster, Shrewsbury, Charterhouse, St. Paul's and Merchant Taylors. Today the term embraces many more, and can be applied to all those schools which are financed by bodies other than the State and whose headmasters belong to the Headmasters' Conference as distinct from the Headmasters' Association. There are about 200 such schools in Britain, including among others: Bedford School (founded 1552); Bradfield College, Berks. (1850); Charterhouse, Godalming (1611); Cheltenham College (1841); Christ's Hospital, Horsham (1553); City of London (1442); Clifton College, Bristol (1862); Dulwich College (1619); Eton College (1440); Felsted, Dunmow, Essex (1564); Haileybury College (1862); Harrow (1571); King Edward's, Birmingham (1552); King's School, Canterbury (600); Malvern College (1865); Manchester Grammar School (1515); Marlborough College (1843); Merchant Taylors' (1561); Mill Hill (1807); Oundle (1556); Radley College, Abingdon (1847); Repton, Derbyshire (1557); Rugby School (1567); St. Albans (948); St. Paul's (1509); Sevenoaks School (1418); Sherborne (1550); Shrewsbury School (1552); Stonyhurst College (1593); Stowe School, Bucks (1923); Tonbridge (1553); Uppingham, Leics. (1584); Warwick (914); Wellington College (1859); Westminster (1560); Winchester College (1382). Public schools for girls include: Christ's Hospital, Hertford (1552), Cheltenham Ladies' College (founded by Miss Beale in 1853), North London Collegiate School (founded by Miss Buss in 1850), Roedean (1885), Wycombe Abbey (1806).

Pulsars, cosmic objects discovered in 1967 by the radio astronomy group at Cambridge; of great scientific interest because they are probably made of highly compressed matter. Unlike quasars (*q.v.*) they are near objects—all are contained in the Milky way. *See* **F5.**

Puma, mountain-lion or cougar, a large wild cat found throughout the Americas. It looks like a lean greyish lioness.

Pyramids of Egypt, on the west bank of the Nile, are vast stone or brick-built structures with inner chambers and subterranean entrances, built by the Pharaohs as royal tombs and dating from about 3000 B.C. The most celebrated are at Gizeh built during the 4th dynasty. The largest, originally 147 m high, is called the Great Pyramid, one of the seven wonders of the world, built by the Pharaoh Khufu, better known as Cheops, and there he was buried. 100,000 men, according to Herodotus, being employed for 20 years upon it. Chephren, successor of Cheops, erected the second pyramid, and the third was built by Mycerinus, a son of Cheops. The pyramid at Meidum built by King Snefru, founder of the 4th dynasty, is the most imposing of all. American and Egyptian scientists are cooperating in a project to X-ray (by means of cosmic rays) the interior of the Pyramid of Chephren.

Pythons, large snakes, non-poisonous and destroying their prey by crushing it. Some species may reach 9 m in length, and prey upon deer and other small mammals. Found in Asia, Africa and Australia. They lay eggs.

Q

Quadrant, an astronomical instrument for measuring altitudes, superseded for navigational purposes in modern times by the sextant. It consists of a graduated arc of 90° with a movable radius for measuring angles on it.

Quai d'Orsay. An embankment in Paris where the French Foreign Office is situated.

Quail, an edible bird of the partridge family, of which only one species, the Common Quail, is found in England. It is not more than 20 cm long. It is found in most of the warmer regions of the world. In England and Wales the Quail is covered by the Wild Bird Protection Acts.

Quair, an old name for a pamphlet or little book.

Quantum Theory. The rapid development of quantum theory has been almost entirely due to the experimental and theoretical study of the interactions between electromagnetic radiation and matter. One of the first steps was taken when it was discovered that the electrons emitted from metals due to the action of ultraviolet radiation have an energy which is not related to the intensity of the incident radiation, but is dependent on its wavelength. Einstein showed in 1905 that this could only be explained on the basis that energy is transferred between radiation and matter in finite amounts, or *quanta,* which are inversely proportional to wavelength. *See* **F13(1).**

Quarks are hypothetical subnuclear particles recently postulated by theoretical physicists concerned with the so-called elementary particles. There may be three kinds, possibly more, all carrying electrical charges which are fractions of those carried by familiar particles like electrons and protons. This and other special properties of quarks make them suitable for explaining the existence of the large number of other particles referred to on **F13, 14.** The physical existence of quarks may be demonstrated by experiment at any time and if this happens it will be an exciting triumph for speculative theoretical physics. *See also* **F13.**

Quartering, in heraldry, is the disposition of various escutcheons or coats of arms in their proper " quarters " of the family shield, in such order as indicates the alliances with other families.

Quartermaster, a military officer charged with the provisioning and superintendence of soldiers in camp or barracks, and holding the equivalent rank to a lieutenant. The Quartermaster-General is an officer who presides over the provisioning department of the whole army. A Quartermaster in the Navy is a petty officer responsible to the Officer of the Watch; at sea for the correct steering of the ship and in harbour for the running of the ship's routine.

Quarto, a sheet of paper folded twice to make four leaves, or eight pages; abbreviated to "4to".

Quartz is a common and usually colourless mineral, occurring both crystallised and massive. In the first form it is in hexagonal prisms, terminating in pyramids. When pure its specific gravity is 2·66. It is one of the constituents of granite, gneiss, etc. Among the quartz varieties are *rock crystal* (colourless), *smoky quartz* (yellow or brown), *amethyst* (purple), *rose quartz* (pink) and *milky quartz* (white). Quartz veins in metamorphic rocks may yield rich deposits of gold. Mining for gold in the rock is termed quartz-mining.

Quasars, or in preferred terminology, quasi-stellar radio-sources, form a new class of astronomical object, first identified in the period 1960 to 1962. They have enormous energy output, and are at vast distances. Many are strong sources of radio waves and fluctuate in intensity. Their nature and cosmological significance presented the major astronomical problem of the 1960s. In the view of Professor Philip Morrison, of the Massachusetts Institute of Technology, quasars are the condensed remains of entire galaxies, while pulsars (*q.v.*) seem to be the ashes of a star that has exploded. Both, he suggests, contain a core of highly concentrated magnetised material. *See* **F5**.

Queen Anne's Bounty, established by Queen Anne in 1704 for the augmentation of the maintenance of the poor clergy. Since 1 April 1948, Queen Anne's Bounty and the Ecclesiastical Commissioners ceased to exist and became embodied in the Church Commissioners for England.

Queen's (or **King's**) **Speech** is the speech prepared by the Government in consultation with the Queen and delivered by Her Majesty in person or by her deputy, at the opening or closing of a Parliamentary session.

Quicksilver. *See* **Mercury.**

Quinine, a vegetable alkaloid obtained from the bark of several trees of the *Cinchona* genus. It is colourless and extremely bitter. The drug, sulphate of quinine, is one of the most valuable medicines, forming a powerful tonic. It is antiperiodic, antipyretic and antineuralgic. In cases of malaria it is the most efficacious remedy of natural origin known.

Quirinal, one of the seven hills of Rome.

Quisling, term which came into use during the second world war to denote traitor, collaborator or fifth-columnist. After Vidkun Quisling, who became head of the puppet government after the German invasion of Norway in 1940.

Quorum, the number of members of any body or company necessary to be present at any meeting or commission before business can be transacted. The House of Commons needs a quorum of 40, the Lords a quorum of 3.

R

Rabbi, a Jewish term applied to specially ordained officials who pronounce upon questions of legal form and ritual, and also generally accorded to any Jewish scholar of eminence.

Raccoon, plantigrade carnivorous mammals common to the American continent. There are several species. The common Raccoon (*Procyon lotor*) is about 60 cm long, with a bushy ringed tail and sharp snout. Its skin is valuable.

Race. In the old text-books anthropologists were much concerned with the differences between the various races of Man; they described the Black Man (Negro), the Yellow Man (Mongol), the Red Man (American Indian), the Brown Man (Indian), and the White Man (European). Those who study Man from this point of view further subdivide each group into others. Thus White Man may be divided into Nordic, Alpine and Mediterranean; Black Man into Hamitic, Bushman and so on. Each of these groups tends to have physical traits which its members hold in common, although, of course, there are no *pure* racial types. All existing races have been fairly thoroughly mixed. What, in view of recent experience, is really important, is that races or even nations do not have psychological traits—at least not *innate* traits. Anthropology dismisses all theories of a superior race as unscientific: there is not the slightest evidence that one race differs in any way from another in its psychological potentialities; Jews, Irish Scots, Italians do differ (so do the inhabitants of Edinburgh and London): but their differences are due to their situation and not to anything inborn. *See* **Racism, Section J.**

Raceme, an inflorescence in which the main stem bears stalked flowers, *e.g.*, lupin, foxglove. The youngest flowers are at the tip of this axis.

Radar. The basic principle of radar is very similar to that of sight. We switch on a light in the dark, and we *see* an object because the light waves are reflected from it and return to our eye, which is able to detect them. Similarly, the radar station *sees* an object because the invisible radio waves sent out from the transmitter are reflected from it and return to the receiver, which is able to detect them. Thus radar is the use of radio signals that man broadcasts.

The utilisation of radio waves for the detection of reflecting surfaces began with the classical experiment of the late Sir Edward Appleton in 1925, which he conducted in order to demonstrate the existence of the Heaviside layer in the upper atmosphere. During the course of the last war developments took place which tremendously improved the methods and instruments used. As in the case of so many of the inventions primarily developed for the purpose of waging war, many useful applications have been found for radar in times of peace, and, in particular, it has proved of great service as an aid to aerial and marine navigation, and in meteorology and astronomy. Radar astronomy investigates the solar system with the echoes of signals sent out from the Earth.

Radiation, energy emitted in the form of a beam of rays or waves, *e.g.*, acoustic (sound) radiation from a loudspeaker, radiant heat from a fire, β-radiation from a radioactive substance. The radiation of electromagnetic waves from a body depends on its temperature, the amount of energy radiated per second being proportional to the fourth power of the absolute temperature. The hotter the body, the shorter the wavelengths of the radiation; thus the colour of a glowing body depends on its temperature. Of paramount importance to us is radiation from the sun. Amongst other radiations, the sun sends ultra-violet, visible and infra-red (heat) waves. The principal gases of the atmosphere are transparent to practically all of the solar and sky radiation and also that which the earth re-transmits to space. Carbon dioxide and water vapour, however, strongly absorb certain types, the latter, as clouds, playing an important rôle in regulating the temperature of the globe. The cooling of the ground on a clear night is a result of the outgoing long-wave radiation exceeding that coming down from the sky; at sunrise cooling ceases as the incoming radiation becomes sufficient to compensate for the loss of heat.

Radiation, Cosmic. *See* **F3**(2).

Radio. The theory of electromagnetic waves—of which the radio wave is one—was originated by the British physicist James Clerk Maxwell (**F12**). He showed that both electrical and optical phenomena in space are essentially similar in character, and that the waves if short in wavelength are those of light, and if of longer wavelength those of radio waves. Heinrich Hertz made many useful discoveries about the waves themselves, and about their behaviour under differing conditions, and also about the apparatus for producing them. Marconi developed the use of radio waves as a practical means of communication.

Radio methods are vital for the transmission of observed data from space vehicles back to earth, a process known as "telemetering". This is done by converting the observations into electrical pulses which actuate a suitable radio transmitter so that it radiates a signal, in coded form, which can be received at a ground station and decoded. The transmission of such a signal can also be remotely controlled by means of signals from the earth. Photographic and television techniques may also be employed for obtaining the desired information and sending it back to earth, as in the case of the Russian picture of the reverse side of the moon and the American pictures of the lunar surface. The information may be stored within the spacecraft for a time, and then, upon receipt of a particular radio signal from the earth transmitted by the spacecraft at a time convenient for its reception. Soviet scientists, by a special technique, were able in the case of their *Venus IV* probe (October 1967) to parachute an instrumented canister from the spacecraft so that it could descend slowly to the surface of the planet—a feat described by Sir Bernard Lovell, who was recording the enterprise at Jodrell Bank, as "an experiment of classic elegance". *See also* Radio Astronomy, Telemetry.

Radioactivity is the spontaneous transformation of atomic nuclei, accompanied by the emission of ionising radiations. It was discovered in 1896 by Becquerel, who noticed that salts containing uranium sent off radiations which, like X-rays, can blacken a photographic plate. Two years later Marie and Pierre Curie discovered several new chemical elements which possessed the same property, but many times more intense than uranium, the most important of these was radium. Shortly afterwards it was established, mainly by Rutherford, that three types of radiations called α-, β- and γ-rays, are emitted from radioactive substances. It was also Rutherford who, jointly with Soddy, deduced that the emission of the radiations is associated with the spontaneous disintegration of atoms which result in the transformation of one radioactive substance into another. A series of such transformations ends when a stable element is produced. All of the heavy radioactive elements can be arranged in three radioactive series, called, the uranium, thorium and actinium series. Initially, radioactivity was thought to be a property confined only to a few elements occurring in nature. In 1934, however, Irene and Frederick Joliot-Curie discovered that ordinary elements can be transformed into radioactive forms by subjecting them to bombardment with α-particles. Following this, it was found that beams of other fast particles produced in accelerators can also render ordinary substances radioactive. Nowadays it is known that radioactivity is a general property of matter; any chemical element can be produced in one or more radioactive forms, or isotopes. *See* **F11**.

Radio Astronomy. The science of radio astronomy makes use of radio apparatus and techniques for the observation of events occurring in far distant parts of the universe, and, in so doing, is able to enlarge upon the observational field of optical astronomy in a remarkable way. By means of radio telescopes it is possible to observe parts of the universe so far distant that the radio waves received have taken thousands of millions of years to travel from their source to the earth, and thus to observe happenings which may have occurred near the beginning of the history of the universe. Thus radio astronomy works with signals that are broadcast by objects in space.

There are two main types of radio telescope. The first, known as the interferometer, uses aerials spaced at large distances so as to cover a wide tract of ground. This has a high "resolution" but suffers from the disadvantage that it can "observe" only a very limited area of the sky overhead, as the earth turns upon its axis. The second, and "steerable", type, is that of the radio telescope at Jodrell Bank, Cheshire, which consists of an enormous concave metal bowl, with the radio aerials at its centre. This, though it has a lower "resolution", can be directed or "steered" on to any part of the sky which is above the horizon, and so can undertake a much more comprehensive observational programme. It can be used either to receive radio waves coming from desired sources or to transmit them and then pick up the echo from, for example, the moon or a planet, as in radar.

One source of radio waves which can be detected by radio telescopes is our own sun, whose behaviour under "quiet" and "abnormal" conditions can be observed in this way. Some of the planets also appear to emit radio waves from parts of their surface. But much more remarkable are the waves which are received from quasars (*q.v.*).

Radiocarbon Dating is a method of dating the origin of organic materials or objects by observing their radioactivity. It is of great importance to archaeology because it enables prehistoric dates back to about 50,000 B.C. to be established for animal and vegetable remains. It works because cosmic rays (*q.v.*) entering the atmosphere create neutrons which convert nitrogen in the air to radioactive carbon. This forms radioactive carbon dioxide and gets incorporated into animals and vegetables throughout the world along with ordinary carbon dioxide in a definite ratio, approximately 1 radio carbon atom to $0{\cdot}8 \times 10^{13}$ ordinary carbon atoms. When the tissue dies it stops interchanging its carbon with the atmosphere, *e.g.*, by breathing, and the radioactive carbon in it gradually turns into nitrogen emitting a β-particle (*see* **F11(1)**). The radiocarbon content decreases by about 1% in 88 years. By measuring the proportion of radioactive carbon left in, say, dead wood, and comparing it with living wood, the age of the dead sample can be calculated. This needs careful laboratory experiments. It is now believed that the proportion of radioactive carbon in the atmosphere varied from time to time in the past because changes in the earth's magnetic field affected the cosmic rays. This has to be allowed for in calculating the radiocarbon date. One use of radiocarbon dating has been to trace the spread of agriculture through the world from its origin in the Near East *c.* 7000 B.C. *See also* Tree-rings.

Radiosonde, a weather station in miniature carried aloft by a free balloon to heights normally in the neighbourhood of 16 km. Signals representative of values of atmospheric pressure, temperature and humidity are transmitted simultaneously by radio to ground receiving apparatus. The position of the balloon at any instant can be determined by radar, enabling the speed and direction of the upper winds to be deduced.

Radium, a radioactive metal, symbol Ra, discovered by Marie and Pierre Curie in 1898. Atomic weight 226. The Radium Institute, founded and equipped by Lord Iveagh and Sir Ernest Cassel, was opened in 1911 for the treatment of patients and research into the effect of radium on the human system. Radiotherapy (use of X-rays from radium) is used in the treatment of cancer.

Radon, a radioactive gaseous element, symbol Rn, formed by radioactive decay of radium. Its discovery completed the series of elements known as the inert (or rare) gases.

Rail, a well-known genus of the *Rallidae* family, including the Water Rail, the Moorhen, Corncrake and Coot, resident in the British Isles.

Rain. When moist air rises into lower temperatures and becomes saturated, condensation takes place on the numerous hygroscopic particles present in the atmosphere. If the temperature is above freezing a cloud of small droplets is formed. These droplets may then grow larger by coalescing with each other as they pass through the cloud until their weight is great enough to make them fall to the earth as rain. In clouds which extend above freezing level, snow and rain both form from the preferential growth of ice crystals at the expense of liquid water droplets. If the resultant ice particle melts as it falls to earth, it gives rain: if not it gives snow.

Rainbow, a beautiful colour effect visible to an observer with back to the sun and facing a rain shower, caused by the refraction and reflection of sunlight in minute water-droplets in the air. From high in the air it would be possible to see a rainbow as a complete circle, but from the ground the most that can be seen is a semicircle when the sun is just on the horizon; the higher the sun is, the smaller the arc of the rainbow. When conditions are suitable two bows are seen, the secondary with the colours of the spectrum reversed. The colours of the rainbow are seven: red, orange, yellow, green, blue, indigo and violet—the colours of the spectrum. *See also* **Aurora.**

Raingauge, an instrument consisting of a deep metal funnel whose stem dips into a graduated glass jar from which the depth of the rain water collected can be read. Continuous records of rainfall are provided by self-registering instruments.

Rain Making is a facility long desired by mankind especially in the drought-ridden regions, and attempted throughout history by numerous non-scientific means. Since the second world war it has been proved that clouds can sometimes be made to rain or snow by dropping into them from an aeroplane very cold particles of solid carbon dioxide or by burning a solution containing silver iodide. This makes the moisture of the cloud form tiny ice crystals which grow big and finally fall out of the cloud. The process is quite complicated and not fully understood. The practical exploitation is somewhat chancy at present, but experiments have been made in many countries and the United States has a considerable programme of study. As well as scientific there are commercial and legal problems; premature commercial exploitation has resulted in disillusionment in some cases.

Rambouillet, a royal French château (14th cent. rebuilt 18th cent.), near Paris, and the official summer residence of the President of the French Republic. Also the name of the famous literary salon of the Marquise de Rambouillet (1588–1665).

Rampant, in heraldry, is a term applied to the figure of an animal with forelegs elevated, the dexter uppermost. When the animal is shown side-faced it is *rampant displayed*, when full-face, *rampant guardant*; when looking back *rampant reguardant*; and when in sitting position *rampant sejant.*

Rape, a cruciferous plant yielding coleseed or rapeseed, extensively grown in all parts of Europe and India. Rape oil is made from the seeds and as oilcake is a valuable animal feeding-stuff.

Rare Gases (also called **Inert Gases**). These are a group of elements which are chemically inert, comprising helium, neon, argon, krypton, xenon and radon. Cavendish in 1785 noticed that there was in air some gas which was not oxygen, nitrogen or carbon dioxide, but it was not until 1894 that the first of the rare gases was found by Rayleigh and Ramsay. This they called argon (inert). After the discovery of helium in 1895 Kayser, Rayleigh and Travers soon isolated the other gases except radon, which was later detected as a radioactive decay product of radium. Some of these inert gases are used to fill electric-light bulbs, and helium is used in balloons, since it is very light.

Rat, a well-known group of rodent embracing many species. The *brown rat* appeared in Europe early in the 18th cent., coming from the East and entering by way of Russia; now it is widespread and met with in Britain and all parts of the Continent. The *black rat*, which was the common rat before the arrival of the brown species, is a smaller animal and now comparatively scarce. There are numerous other kinds, all of them gross feeders, and existing in such numbers in many places as to constitute a pest. *See* **Section Z.**

Rational Number, a number which can be expressed as a ratio of two whole numbers. Examples are 2, ½, 0·3, −8. *See* **Irrational Number.**

Rationalism. *See* **Section J.**

Rattlesnake, venomous snakes which obtain their name from the possession of a rattle in the end of their tail, consisting of horny pieces so arranged that when vibrated they make a rattling sound. They are only found in N. and S. America.

Raven, a black-plumaged bird of the crow family, with raucous voice and massive bill. Occurs in many parts of Europe, Asia and America. Ravens are easily domesticated and form interesting pets. Dickens had one which he described in *Barnaby Rudge.*

Ray, fish with a very flat body and broad and fleshy pectoral fins, related to the sharks. There are about 140 species. In Britain they are generally called *skate.*

Razorbill, a sea-bird of the auk family, having a high, furrowed bill and black-and-white plumage. It inhabits rocky cliffs during the breeding season, and at other times is mostly out on the open sea.

Realism is a vague term. As a movement in art it can be said to have started with Gustave Courbet in the mid-19th cent. in his revolt against the classicism of Ingres and the romanticism of Delacroix. He was a man of strong radical views, and like Zola, Balzac and Flaubert in literature, turned to the actuality of everyday life, recording it with frankness and vigour. Some young English painters, notably Bratby, of the "kitchen sink" school, practise what some describe as social realism. In another sense, realism is an attitude concerned with interpreting the essential nature of the subject, revealing truths hidden by the accidentals of ordinary visual appearance. Thus form becomes more significant than content. Beginning with Cézanne and Van Gogh this trend passes on to Cubist and Abstract painting. *See also* **Section J** (philosophy), and **Section I** (dramatic term).

Record Office, in Chancery Lane, London, the place where the Public Records of England are preserved, including Domesday Book, the various Rolls of Charters and important historical documents.

Rectifier, an electrical device which will allow electric current to flow in one direction only and can therefore be used for turning alternating current into direct current. Since electricity is usually supplied in alternating form and frequently needed in direct form, rectifiers are of very common use both in industry and the home, for example in radio and television and for battery chargers. Rectifying properties are possessed by a number of different devices, one of which is a thermionic diode (*see* **Valve**). Very large valves filled with mercury vapour are often used for rectifying heavy currents for industrial purposes. Many other rectifiers use semiconductors in close contact with metals or with other semiconductors because such junctions have the property of passing electric current easily only in one direction.

Recusants, people who refused to attend the Anglican Church or to acknowledge the ecclesiastical supremacy of the Crown in the 16th and 17th cent.

Recycling, the process of sorting and re-using waste products. By no means a new idea, and already much used in industry and by the whole community in war-time, recycling assumes prominence when materials are scarce and prices high. There is much evidence from several countries that the public responds well to properly organised schemes for the collection, sorting and re-use of paper, plastic, glass, metals and other waste products common in industrialised countries. *See also* **Section F, Part VI.**

Redstart, a small bird of the Thrush family of handsome plumage and striking song. Two species visit Great Britain: the Common Redstart, with bright chestnut rump and tail, white forehead and black cheeks, favours wooded country, and the Black Redstart, with black breast and throat, chestnut tail and white wing bars, prefers rocky ground or bombed buildings, and breeds in S. England.

Redwing, a bird of the Thrush family which finds its way to this country for the winter. Resembles the song thrush, but distinguished by smaller size, buffish-white eye-stripe, chestnut flanks and underwings. It has bred in Scotland and on Fair Isle.

Redwood *or* **Sequoia.** This genus of coniferous tree comprises two species of Redwoods occurring in N.W. America. Specimens of one species, the Giant Redwood, reach a height of over 90 m and a thickness of 11 m. The age of the largest, the General Sherman tree, is put at 3,500 years.

Referendum and Initiative, two methods by which the wishes of electors may be expressed with regard to proposed legislation. It is developed to the highest extent in Switzerland. In a *Referendum* some specific matter is referred to the electors. The *Initiative* is the means by which electors can compel their representatives to consider a specific issue. Gen. de Gaulle made use of the referendum in seeking the consent of the French nation for his policies. The British Labour Government held a referendum in June 1975, asking voters whether they felt the nation should remain in or withdraw from the European Economic Community. An Act of Parliament was required to authorise the referendum (which was something new in British constitutional history), and a further Act would have been necessary if the majority had been in favour of withdrawal. The result was for continued membership.

Reformation. *See* **Section J.**

Reform Bills. The principal Bills have been passed for the reform of the Parliamentary franchise. The first was the great Reform Bill of 1832, introduced by Lord John Russell and enacted under the Whig administration of Lord Grey. In addition to a sweeping redistribution of seats, this Act greatly extended the franchise but still left many people without the right to vote. The second Bill, passed by Disraeli in 1867, by giving the vote to workers in towns, established household suffrage. A third Bill, passed in 1884 under a Gladstone ministry, removed the distinction between borough and county franchises, enfranchised agricultural workers, and thus gave the vote to all men over 21. Women had to wait until 1918 to get the vote at the age of 30. The Representation of the People (Equal Franchise) Act, 1928, gave them the right to be registered as Parliamentary electors at the age of 21, thus making England into a true democracy. The Representation of the People Act, 1948, abolished the representation of the universities and the separate representation of the City of London and the business-premises vote. The Representation of the People Act, 1969, reduced the minimum voting age from 21 to 18 at both parliamentary and local government elections.

Refraction. The change of direction which light rays undergo when passing from one medium to another. The phenomenon is due to the fact that in different media light (and other forms of radiation) has different speeds.

Refractory, a substance capable of standing high temperatures and therefore useful for making furnaces and allied apparatus. Some insulating refractories are fire-clay, alumina, porcelain, carborundum, graphite and silica. Some refractory metals are platinum, molybdenum, tungsten, tantalum and the alloys nichrome, chromel, alumel.

Regency Style is the English version of the French Empire (*q.v.*) and approximately covers the period of the regency of Prince George, later George IV, from 1810 to 1820. It is somewhat less austere than the French style, and contains elements of the fantastic and exotic absent from Empire. The most famous monument of Regency style is the Royal Pavilion at Brighton, built for the Prince Regent by John Nash. (Regency style should not be confused with the *Régence* style in France, fashionable during the regency period between the death of Louis XIV in 1715 and the ascent to the throne of Louis XV in 1723. Here the English equivalent is Queen Anne style.)

Reindeer, a genus of deer horned in both sexes, occurring only in northerly regions. It has an average height of 1·3 m, is very fleet of foot and the Laplanders utilise it for draught purposes and for food.

Relativity. The laws of relativity have been substantially proved and have revolutionised our ideas as to the nature of space, time, matter and energy and forced us to think along new lines. In 1949 a new theory by Einstein was announced which sets forth in a series of equations the laws governing both gravitation and electromagnetism, which is said to bridge the gap that separates the universe of the stars and galaxies and the universe of the atom. At present the one is explained by relativity, and the other rests on the quantum theory. *See* **F15.**

Relief in sculpture is of three kinds—high relief (*alto-relievo*), in which the figures stand out to the extent of one-half of their natural proportions, low-relief (*basso-relievo*) when the figures project but slightly; and middle-relief (*mezzo-relievo*), when the projection is intermediate.

Renaissance. *See* **Section J.**

Republican Party of the United States was born by the fusion in 1854 of the group who called themselves National Republicans, having split from the Democrats over tariffs in 1825, and the northern Democrats, both of them being opposed to slavery. It came to power when Abraham Lincoln was elected President in 1860 and won 14 of the 18 presidential elections held between 1860 and 1932. It was defeated in 1932 largely as a result of the economic depression and reached its lowest ebb in the years of Roosevelt's New Deal (*q.v.*). The Party went on being defeated every four years until Eisenhower's victory in 1952. Nixon narrowly failed to defeat Kennedy in 1960 and Goldwater was decisively beaten by Lyndon Johnson in 1964. In 1968 and again in 1972 Nixon was successful in winning the Presidency. His fall from power in the aftermath of Watergate made 1974 a bad year for the Republican Party. The symbol of the Party is an elephant, the invention of Thomas Nast, a cartoonist, in 1874.

Requiem. Properly a mass for the dead, the term is extended to cover musical settings by Palestrina, Mozart, Verdi and others.

Reredos, the ornamental screen at the back of the altar or communion table. It is often of a highly decorative character and is an architectural feature in many churches in Spain. Other examples are to be found in the following cathedrals in England: Southwark, St. Albans, Winchester, Durham and Liverpool.

Resins, natural resins are vegetable compounds largely employed in the industrial arts. They comprise india-rubber, amber, mastic, copal, etc. "Synthetic resins" is a term sometimes used as a synonym for "plastics".

Reuter, an international news agency, organised since 1941 as a trust and owned by the newspapers of Britain, Australia and New Zealand, founded by Baron J. de Reuter in 1849.

Rhea, a large flightless bird, the "ostrich" of S. America, distinguished from the ostrich proper by smaller size, longer beak, larger wings, no tail and 3 toes instead of 2. There are 2 species.

Rheology, the science of flow. *See* **F17**(2).

Rhesus Factor. *See* **Index to Section P.**

Rhinoceros, a large almost hairless animal related to the horse. Two kinds in Africa and several others in Asia. They have a horn, sometimes two, over the snout composed of modified hair. Most are leaf eaters but the largest species, the white rhino of South Africa, is a grazer. Rhinoceroses have been much hunted for their horns, which are reputed to have curative and aphrodisiac properties.

Rhodium, a metallic element, symbol Rh, discovered by Wollaston in 1804. It is found in platinum ores in small amounts, generally less than 2 per cent. With platinum it gives a very hard and durable alloy. It is also used, instead of silver, in putting the reflecting layer on a mirror.

Ribbon Fish *or* **Oarfish,** a deep-sea fish, deriving its name from its ribbon-like shape. Though fairly long, it is only a few centimetres thick. The ribbon fish is rarely met with because of its habitat, and most of what is known about it has been learnt from specimens occasionally cast ashore during storms.

Rice, a grain-yielding grass, of which thousands of strains are known today, extensively cultivated in China, India and certain parts of America, and forming the main food of the peoples of China, Japan, India and S.E. Asia. Some 95 per cent. of the world's rice is produced and consumed in the Orient. The grain with the husk is known as "paddy". Arrack, an alcoholic liquor, is made from fermented rice seeds.

Richter Scale, a series of numbers used to record the relative magnitude of earthquakes. Devised by F. Richter of the California Institute of Technology. An earthquake is given a number on the scale by measuring the amplitude of earth movements, *i.e.*, the size of the to and fro motion in an earthquake wave, with a special instrument called a seismometer. The reading is corrected by calculation to allow for the distance of the instrument from the earthquake and the corrected results by observers at different places agree quite well. The scale is logarithmic, *i.e.*, earthquakes differing by one unit on the Richter scale are a factor 10 different in amplitude. An earthquake allotted zero on the scale would give a reading of 10^{-6} m on a standard seismometer 100 km from the centre of the earthquake. Smaller disturbances would have negative values on the scale. The largest known earthquakes had Richter values between +8 and +9, *i.e.*, they had 10^{+8} to 10^{+9} bigger amplitudes than earthquakes of magnitude zero. It is a widespread misconception that the scale has an upper limit of 10; there are no upper or lower limits to the scale.

Rime, a crystalline deposit of ice formed on objects exposed to wet fog at the same time as frost.

Rinderpest *or* **Cattle Plague,** is a highly contagious disease affecting cattle, sheep and other ruminants. In Europe the disease has been eradicated, but it was formerly very widespread and caused great loss of life among cattle. The disease is caused by a filtrable virus, and is attended by fever and congestion of the mucous membranes.

Ring Dove *or* **Wood Pigeon,** a blue-grey bird, distinguished from other pigeons by larger size (41 cm), white wing-bar, glossy green-and-purple neck and white half-collar. It is very common in Britain.

Rituale, the book of rites used in the Roman Catholic Church for the administration of certain sacraments and other church ceremonies. Like the Roman breviary, it dates in its present form from the Council of Trent.

RNA (Ribonucleic Acid). *See* **Nucleic Acids.**

Roaring Forties, name applied to the prevailing westerly winds over the oceans in the temperate latitudes of the Southern Hemisphere. Because unimpeded by large land areas the winds are more regular and stronger than the westerlies in the Northern Hemisphere.

Robin (or **Redbreast**). A small bird with olive-brown upper parts and orange-red forehead, throat and breast; both sexes look alike. The young are speckled, lacking the red breast. Its wide European distribution includes the British Isles, where it is the national bird. It also occurs in N. Africa and W. Asia. The nest is placed in a great variety of situations including holes in banks, trees and walls; in sheds, amongst ivy and sometimes in old tins. Nesting-boxes are readily adopted, but care should be taken to ensure that the entrance-hole is small enough to exclude starlings. Robins are pugnacious and defend their territories with vigour. Their attractive appearance, trustful disposition, engaging ways and sweet song make them extremely popular. The name robin is also applied to a number of very different birds, one of which, the American Robin, occasionally wanders to Europe.

Rock Dove, the grey pigeon *Columba livia* of Europe and Asia, ancestor of the domestic pigeons as Darwin was the first to show.

Rockets for use in war were first studied by Sir William Congreve early in the 19th cent., and proved very destructive in siege operations. They were invented by the Chinese as long ago as the 11th cent. The Germans devised the huge V2 rocket, carrying a ton of explosive, which was used near the end of the war to bombard London. Rockets are propelled by the burning of fuel (*e.g.*, oxygen or nitric acid), the exhaust, being ejected at high velocity, thrusts the rocket forward. For the study of the properties of the atmosphere vertical sounding rockets are used. Rocket flight in outer space was first presented as practicable by the Russian rocket expert, K. E. Tsiolkovsky, in 1903. The provision of sufficient launching velocity involves the use of rocket motors with adequate thrust. To launch a satellite into an orbit circulating within a few hundred kilometres of the surface a velocity of 29,000 km/h must be imparted. This may be done by using a multi-stage launching system. When the first-stage motor has burned out it drops off, so that, when the second-stage motor ignites, it does not have to support the weight of the first-stage, and so on. If the launching velocity is increased to 40,000 km/h the vehicle will not return to the neighbourhood of the earth but pass out of the range of the earth's gravitational pull completely. Unless the launching velocity reaches 161,000 km/h it will not escape from the sun and will become an artificial planet. *See also* **Space Research.**

Rock Magnetism. The study of naturally occurring magnetism in rocks is a subject which has gained considerable importance in recent years. There are two principal reasons for this. One is that this so-called "fossilised magnetism" may be able to tell us more about the past history of the earth's magnetic field. The other is that after many years of heated dispute between geologists rock magnetism promises to settle once and for all the controversy as to whether or not the continents have changed their relative positions in past times (continental drift theory (*q.v.*)). This branch of geophysical research, in addition to its academic interest, may well have important economic consequences. It might, for instance, become possible to locate mineral deposits once accumulated under special conditions at certain latitudes but now drifted to other places. Salt and similar deposits formed by the continuous evaporation of solutions in hot countries are one example; oil may well be another. There has been a *steady* change in rock magnetisation direction with geological time. It is now known with some accuracy that the most recent reversal took place 700,000 years ago. It has been found that the older the rock, the farther removed is its fossil magnetisation from the present field.

Rococo, an architectural style which was, in effect, the final stage of **Baroque** (*q.v.*). The name first came into use about 1830 to describe the period 1720–70 and means "shell-shaped" (French *Rocaille*), since the shell was a favourite motif in Rococo ornamentation. At about the beginning of the 18th cent. the heavy older type of Baroque began to show even less restraint than had characterised it in the past; it became still less utilitarian, and showed a kind of playful lighthearted vitality which manifested itself in a wealth of ornamental invention. Baroque was flamboyant and robust, Rococo dainty, graceful and smiling. Its ornaments are frequently asymmetrical, and in this Rococo is unique among the historical styles of Europe. In architecture Rococo is naturally found in those areas where the Baroque had flourished, *i.e.*, Munich, Prague, Vienna and Dresden. In painting, the best expressions of Rococo are to be seen in the works of the French painters Watteau (d. 1721), Boucher (d. 1770), a favourite of Mme de Pompadour, and famous as a decorator of boudoirs, and Fragonard (d. 1806). (As in the case of Baroque, it was typical of Rococo that the sculpture, painting and the decorative arts of a building all expressed the same spirit.)

Roe, popular name given to organs in fish which produce eggs and sperms. "Hard roe" is that of the female and consists of eggs; that of the male is the soft roe or milt.

Roe Deer (*Capreolus capreolus*) deer native to Europe and found in England and Scotland but not Ireland. "Roebuck" is the name of the male adult.

Roller, a tropical Old World bird of the *Coraciidae* family, related to the hoopoe, kingfisher and bee-eater, of strikingly brilliant blue, chestnut, greenish-blue plumage. There are fifteen species, one of which breeds in the far north and visits the British Isles on its migrations to and from its winter quarters in Africa.

Romanesque Architecture, prevailed throughout Europe from the mid-10th to the 13th cent., and implies an art which developed from that of the Romans. Notable in Romanesque style were the rounded arch and masonry vaulting. Romanesque led to the graceful and more complex Gothic (*q.v.*). The Italians never regarded Gothic highly and Romanesque churches, generally based on the basilican plan (oblong with double colonnades and a semi-circular apse at the end), continued to be built there until the beginning of the 15th cent. Some of the best examples can be seen at Pisa (11th cent.), Florence (San Miniato, 1013), Lucca (12th cent.) and Milan (the 12th cent. San Ambrogio, most famous of all). In Germany Romanesque architecture flourished longer than in France or England; the most famous churches are in the valley of the Rhine, at Cologne (completely destroyed during the second world war), Mainz and Speyer. In France Romanesque churches are found in Burgundy, Provence and Normandy. For English Romanesque *see* **Norman Architecture.**

Roman Roads, highways constructed by the Romans. They were of great durability. The best known British roads were Ermine Street (London, Lincoln, York), Fosse Way (Lincoln through Leicester, Cirencester, Bath, Exeter), Watling Street (London to Salop).

Romanticism, a term for a movement in the arts—whether in music, painting, sculpture or literature—which seeks to give expression to the artist's feelings about his subject rather than to be concerned with form or reality. The romantic view is that art is nature seen through a temperament; the realist view is that art is a slice of life. In painting Delacroix (1798–1863) is the romantic artist par excellence with his uncontrolled expression of the passions and love of the exotic. In literature the Romantic movement reached its finest form in the works of Goethe, Schiller and Heine; in the poetry of Byron, Keats, Wordsworth, Shelley and Blake; and in the writings of Victor Hugo. Since Romanticism is partly a matter of temperament in the artist just as Classicism is, it may be found at all times and places, although whether or not it becomes predominant depends on contemporary taste. Cubism, for example, with its attention to form is classical, whereas Surrealism with its attention to content is romantic. *See also* **Romantic Movement, Section J.**

Roman Walls were built as frontier barriers under the Emperors Hadrian (76–138) and Antoninus Pius (86–161). Hadrian's works, linking Wallsend-on-Tyne with Bowness-on-Solway, comprised a twenty-foot stone wall, ditches, turrets, "milecastles", fortresses and a double earthen mound, or "Vallum". Impressive ruins are still visible at Chesters and Housesteads. Antoninus Pius, Hadrian's successor, made a further advance, but the turf wall which he built between Forth and Clyde was soon abandoned. Septimius Severus (146–211) restored Hadrian's wall after the assassination of Commodus and the subsequent civil wars. It was finally abandoned between 380 and 390. Archaeologists from Lancaster University have recently excavated the Roman fort at Ravenglass (Roman Glannaventa) on the Cumbrian coast and believe it to have been built as an extension to Hadrian's wall.

Rood Screen, an ornamental partition, separating the choir from the nave in a church, and supporting a crucifix or rood.

Rook, a member of the crow family, abounding in most parts of the British Isles and found in Europe, Asia and N. Africa. It has been introduced into New Zealand. Rooks usually nest in colonies in tall trees. They are highly intelligent birds, and their ways have long been the subject of much careful study.

Rosary, a circular chain of beads, used by Catholics when reciting a particular form of sustained prayer. Each bead represents an entire prayer, and the combined prayers constitute the Rosary.

Roses, Wars of the (1455–85), between the rival houses of York and Lancaster, for the possession of the English crown, began in the reign of Henry VI and ended with the death of Richard III on Bosworth Field. The emblem or badge of the Lancastrians was the red rose and of the Yorkists the white rose. All rivalry between The Roses ended by the marriage of Henry VII, the Lancastrian, with the Princess Elizabeth, daughter of Edward IV, the Yorkist.

Rosetta Stone, discovered in 1799 by the French at Rosetta in Egypt, and deposited in the British Museum. It is a piece of black basalt about 91 cm long, and contains a decree of the Egyptian priests of Ptolemy V Epiphanes (205–181 B.C.) in (1) hieroglyphics, (2) demotic and (3) Greek characters. It was by means of the three different inscriptions on the same stone that hieroglyphic writing was first able to be deciphered.

Rotten Row, a corruption of *route de roi* (king's drive), the famous riding resort in Hyde Park.

Rouge et Noir, a well-known gambling card game played on a table divided into two sections and marked with two black and two red lozenges. Any number of players can take part, and the money is staked on the red or black spaces. The cards are dealt out, first to Noir, until the pips aggregate more than 30; then in like manner to the Rouge, and the packet coming nearest to 31 wins the stakes.

Roulette, a gambling game played on a table carrying a revolving wheel divided into 37 compartments. Each compartment bears a number, 0 (zero) and 1 to 36. The numbers are mixed and do not follow any particular order. Of these 37 numbers 18 are black and 18 are red, whereas zero is green. The players stake their money on any compartment, colour or combination of numbers they please. The wheel is whirled round and a ball is set rolling in the opposite direction, dropping finally into one of the compartments, thus deciding the winning number and colour.

Roundhead. In the reign of Charles I and later, a Puritan or member of the Parliamentary party who wore his hair cut short. It was originally a term of derision applied by the Royalists, who usually wore ringlets.

Round Towers, high circular towers with conical roof and massive masonry walls, built during the early Middle Ages (*c.* 10th cent.). It is believed that they served as refugees and lookouts. These buildings are numerous in Ireland, and three remain in Scotland, including that at Brechin which is attached to the church.

Royal Academy of Arts was founded in London in 1768, under the patronage of George III. The early exhibitions of the Academy were held first in Pall Mall, and after in Somerset House, where the exhibitions continued to be held until 1836, when the National Gallery being built, the Academy moved its quarters to that building. In 1869 the present Royal Academy at Burlington House was opened. The Academy numbers (1976) 64 R.A.s and 20 A.R.A.s. List of presidents: Sir Joshua Reynolds (1768), Benjamin West (1792), James Wyatt (1805), B. West (1806), Sir Thomas Lawrence (1820), Sir M. A. Shee (1830), Sir C. Eastlake (1850), Sir F. Grant (1866), Lord Leighton (1878), Sir J. E. Millais (1896), Sir E. J. Poynter (1896), Sir Aston Webb (1919), Sir F. Dicksee (1924), Sir William Llewellyn (1928), Sir E. Lutyens (1938), Sir A. J. Munnings (1944), Sir Gerald F. Kelly (1949), Sir A. E. Richardson (1954), Sir Charles Wheeler (1956), Sir Thomas Monnington (1966) and Sir Hugh Casson (1976). The Academy holds an exhibition of pictures, statuary and architectural designs every summer.

Royal Hospital, Chelsea, built by Wren, was opened in 1694 as an institution for invalid soldiers.

Royal Institution, established 1799, and incorporated by Royal Charter in 1800 for "the promotion, extension and diffusion of Science and of Useful Knowledge". It was in the building of the Institution that Faraday conducted his experiments. Today it has extensive research laboratories. Famous also for its Christmas lectures designed for a juvenile audience. Director, Prof Sir G. Porter, F.R.S.

Royal Society was founded in 1660 and incorporated by Royal Charter in 1662. Viscount Brouncker being named the first president. Its *Philosophical Transactions* date from 1665. Among those who served as president of the Royal Society are Sir Christopher Wren, Pepys, Sir Isaac Newton, Sir Joseph Banks, Sir Humphry Davy, Prof. T. H. Huxley, Lord Rayleigh, Sir Archibald Geikie, Sir J. J. Thomson, O.M., Prof. Sir C. S. Sherrington, O.M., G.B.E., Lord Rutherford, O.M., Sir William Henry Bragg, O.M., Sir Henry Dale, O.M., Sir Robert Robinson, O.M., Lord Adrian, O.M., Sir Cyril Hinshelwood, O.M., Lord Florey, O.M., Lord Blackett O.M. (1965), Sir Alan Hodgkin, O.M. (1970), Lord Todd (1975).

Rubber, produced from the juice of certain trees and shrubs of tropical countries, is in such extensive demand now for tyres and other purposes that rubber plantations have been established in almost every part of the world where rubber can be grown, particularly in Indonesia and Malaysia. The Amazon is the original source of all present-day rubber. In recent years great advances have been made in the production of synthetic rubber.

Rubicon, a small river falling into the Adriatic, and forming one of the Italian boundaries, the crossing of which anciently involved decisive action and constituted a declaration of war. Thus the phrase "crossing the Rubicon", denoting an act from which there is no withdrawal.

Rubidium, a metallic element, symbol Rb, most closely resembling potassium. It is silver-white and very soft, and was discovered in 1861 by Bunsen and Kirchhoff, using the spectroscope. It is rare, occurring in small amounts in the mica called lepidolite and in potash salts of the Strassfurt deposits in Germany.

Rubrics are instructions in regard to the ceremonies of the Church, appearing in red in the Prayer Book.

Ruby is a deep red variety of Corundum (aluminium oxide); one of the most valued of precious stones. Burma yields some of the finest, and rubies of inferior colour are found in Thailand, Sri Lanka, South Africa and Brazil.

Rudd, a fresh-water fish of wide distribution, plentiful in the rivers of Britain, and found in most other parts of Europe, also in Asia Minor. It is of a reddish-gold colour, with a greenish-blue beard.

Ruff, a bird related to the common sandpiper, at one time common in the Fen districts. The males have a ruff of feathers round the neck in the breeding season. The female is the Reeve.

Ruffe *or* **Pope,** a small fresh-water fish common in most parts of central Europe, and similar in appearance to the ordinary perch. It is found in British rivers.

"Rule, Britannia!" the national sea-song of England, was written by James Thomson (1700–48), the author of the "Seasons", and set to music by Dr. Arne about 1740. The poet's words were "Britannia, rule the waves!" but it is usually rendered "Britannia rules the waves."

Rum, an ardent spirit distilled from molasses, and containing from 40 to 50 per cent. of alcohol. It is chiefly manufactured in the West Indies, and derives its special flavour from a volatile oil.

Ruminants, animals that chew the cud, being provided with a compartmented stomach, enabling them to swallow food, and later to bring it back to the mouth for mastication; *e.g.*, sheep, goats, oxen, etc. While in the rumen, or storage compartment, some digestion of food, especially cellulose, takes place by bacterial action.

Runcible spoon, a kind of fork used for pickles having three broad prongs. The word was used by Edward Lear about 1870 as a nonsense word and may be derived from *Rouncival* meaning large or huge from the bones said to have been dug up at *Roncesvalles* where Roland fell. Rouncival peas are the large peas called "marrowfats".

Runes, certain characters of an alphabet found in inscriptions in the Germanic languages, found cut into buildings and implements of stone or wood in many parts of northern Europe, including Britain. The runic alphabet originally had 24 letters. Scholars agree that some of the runes derive from Greek and others from Latin.

Ruskin College, the first residential college for working people, founded at Oxford in 1899 by Mr. Walter Vrooman, an American.

Rusts, parasitic fungi, some common species of which have reddish spores which in a mass have a rusty appearance. A well-known species is the Wheat Rust (*Puccinia graminis*), which has an alternative host in the barberry.

Ruthenium, a greyish-white metallic element, symbol Ru, discovered by Claus in 1845. It is harder and more brittle than platinum, in whose ores it occurs.

Rutile, mineral titanium dioxide. It is found in many igneous rocks, and in gneisses and schists. Its commonest colour is reddish-brown.

S

Sabaoth, a Hebrew word, meaning an army or host, and applied sometimes to the Supreme Being, *e.g.*, "the Lord of Hosts" (Rom. ix. 29).

Sabbath and Sunday. Sunday, or the Lord's Day, is the first day of the week in the Christian year. It was substituted for the Jewish Sabbath in the 1st cent. A.D. as the Christian day of worship in commemoration of the Resurrection. The Sabbath, in the Jewish system, was the last day of the week (Saturday in the Christian calendar), designated as the day of religious rest in the fourth commandment of the Decalogue. It was the Puritans at the time of the Reformation who applied the term Sabbath to the Christian Sunday and the two terms have been used indiscriminately ever since.

Sabbatical Year was instituted by the Jews in ancient times for the purpose of giving the soil a rest from cultivation. This was every seventh year. In universities a sabbatical year is a year of absence from duty for the purpose of study and travel, granted to professors at certain intervals.

Sable, a furred mammal of the weasel family mainly inhabiting Siberia. It is bright brown in colour, and has a long, bushy tail. American sable is a marten.

Saccharin, a white crystalline solid manufactured from toluene, 550 times as sweet as cane sugar. It is used as a sweetening agent; as a substitute for sugar when sugar is forbidden, as in certain diseases, or when there is a shortage. It has no value as a food.

Safety Lamp, as used in coal mines, was invented by Sir Humphry Davy in 1816. The flame is enclosed in a cage of fine-meshed wire which allows air to enter and promote burning, but conducts away the heat generated in combustion so that no product of combustion escapes at a temperature high enough to ignite explosive gases in the mine.

Sainfoin, a widely cultivated forage plant, especially adapted for sheep. It is of strong, leafy growth and bears bright red flowers. It belongs to the same family of flowering plants as peas and beans.

St. Elmo's Fire, a glowing brush-like discharge of electricity which takes place from sharp-pointed objects on mountains or the masts of ships exposed to the intense electric fields of thunder-clouds.

Saints' Days. In the liturgy of the Roman Catholic church a saint is commemorated and his intercession sought on a special day (saint's day), usually the anniversary of his death. Pope Paul decreed that from 1 January 1970 the following saints were to be dropped from the calendar: Christopher, Catherine of Alexandria, Alexis, Pudenzia, Susan, Margaret, Viviana, Eustace, Martina, Venantius and Domitilla. Many others, including our own Saint George, and Nicholas (Santa Claus) have been demoted though they may be venerated locally. There are now only 153 saints' days in addition to those in honour of the Apostles, Saint Joseph and the Virgin Mary. The festival of All Saints is on 1 November.

Salamanders are amphibia superficially resembling lizards, from which they differ in having a moist skin and no scales.

Salic Law was probably instituted in France in the 5th cent. for the purpose of excluding females from inheriting the Crown. The Bourbons introduced the same law into Spain, but this was abolished by decree in 1830 to enable Isabella II to succeed.

Salmon, a fish notable for its habit of returning from the sea to spawn in the river where it was itself hatched. Their origin can be inferred from the chemical composition of certain blood proteins. Salmon from the two sides of the Atlantic migrate to communal feeding grounds off Greenland.

Saltpetre. *See* Nitre.

Salvarsan, the organic arsenical compound arsphenamine, which Ehrlich discovered was able to kill inside the human body the spirochaete germ that causes syphilis. Also known as "606". It has been superseded by neosalvarsan.

Salvation Army. *See* Section J.

San Andreas Fault, is the dividing line between the North American plate and the North Pacific Ocean plate where "plate" means one of the rigid sections of the earth's crust as conceived in the theory of plate tectonics (*q.v.*). The fault runs roughly north-west—south-east in California passing near San Francisco. The Pacific Ocean bed and the North American continent are sliding past each other along this fault at about 5 cm per year. As at all plate-to-plate boundaries—another is the Western Pacific coast – the San Andreas fault is the scene of great earthquake activity. Between 1934 and 1970 there were over 7,000 earthquakes severer than magnitude 4 on Richter scale (*q.v.*) in and near southern California. Because of large population centres, the activity of the San Andreas region is studied with great care and some apprehension about a repeat of the San Francisco earthquake of 1906 which caused displacements of up to 6·4 m along the San Andreas Fault. *See also* **F9**.

Sanctuaries were places where offenders against the law were free from arrest, and previous to 1697, when sanctuaries were suppressed, several parts of London were treated as sanctuaries. The chief of these refuge localities was in Whitefriars. There were others in the Minories, Mitre Court, the Savoy, Wesminster and the Mint. Other sanctuaries were at Beverley and at St. Burian's in Cornwall.

Sanderling, small wading bird of sandpiper family; breeds in tundra regions of far north, and is seen on sandy beaches of Britain as a winter visitor. Conspicuous white wing stripe and, like Curlew, Sandpiper, Knot, Dunlin and other members of sandpiper family, has marked change of plumage between winter and summer.

Sandpiper, small- to medium-sized wading birds of several species whose migratory powers are so great that they are found in most parts of the world. They include the Common Sandpiper, a bird about 18 cm long, greenish-brown head and back, white under-parts; beak long and slender. Purple, Wood and Curlew-Sandpipers.

Sans-culottes (French = without knee breeches), a term applied by the French aristocrats to the revolutionary leaders during the French Revolution who wore long trousers instead of knee breeches.

Sanskrit is the language of ancient India, spoken by the Brahmins, and existing in early Oriental literature. It was the language of literature and government and is now confined to temples and places of learning. Its relationship to the modern Indian languages is rather like that of Latin and Greek to modern European languages.

Saponin. The term is a generic one applied to a range of organic compounds which produce frothy, soapy solutions. Saponins are extracted from the soapwort root, horse chestnut seeds, etc. Saponin is the basis of the "foam" used for fire fighting; it can be used like soap to make insecticides and fungicides adhere to the leaves of plants. Also used as detergents.

Sapphic Verse, a form of verse said to have been invented by Sappho, the lyric poetess of Lesbos, who flourished about 600 B.C.

Sapphire, a valuable deep blue variety of Corundum (aluminium oxide) found mostly in India, Sri Lanka and Northern Italy. Synthetic sapphire is often used for gramophone styli.

Saracen, the name given in classic times to the Arab tribes of Syria and adjacent territories. In the Middle Ages the current designation among the Christians for their Muslim enemies.

Sarcophagus, the name given to a stone coffin, such as was used by the ancient Egyptians, Greeks and Romans, for receiving the remains of their famous dead. These sarcophagi were often decorated with rich carvings and sculptures.

Sardonyx. *See* **Onyx**.

Sassanides were a dynasty of Persian rulers descended from Artaxerxes from 226 to 625.

Satellites are small planets revolving round the larger ones. The moon is the earth's only satellite. Jupiter has thirteen; Saturn, ten; Uranus, five; Mars, two; and Neptune, two. Earth satellite research since 1957 has yielded important scientific data.

Satin-Bird, one of the bower birds of Australia; the male is silky blue-black and the female greyish green. *See* **Bower bird**.

Satrap, the name given in ancient times to a Persian Governor of a Province.

Saturday, the seventh day of the week (the Jewish Sabbath), derived its name from Saturn, or, as some hold, is called after the Saxon idol, Saterne, which was worshipped on this day.

Saturn, a planet, the sixth from the sun, from which it is distant about 1427 × 10^6 km, and around which it makes a revolution in about twenty-nine and a half years. It is about 120,000 km in diameter, or nine times as large as the earth, and rotates on its axis in ten and a quarter hours. It is surrounded by a series of rings composed of myriads of tiny satellites. It has at least ten small satellites. *See* **F7**.

Saturnalia, festivals held in ancient Rome in honour of the god Saturnus. They were made the scene of boisterous festivities, and were continued for several days at the end of December.

Sawfish, a large marine ray found in tropical America and Guinea, whose snout often attains the length of a metre or so, and is provided with saw-like teeth. This "saw" is swung from side to side among a shoal of fish which form the food of this ray.

Sawfly. These insects are considered to be the most primitive members of the order (*Hymenoptera*) to which the bees and wasps belong. In appearance they resemble somewhat the latter, but there is no waist separating thorax and abdomen. The ovipositor is never used as a sting; usually it is saw-like so that the female can use it to make incisions into tissues of plants where the eggs are laid. The larvae look like caterpillars of butterflies and moths. One of the commonest species occurs on gooseberry bushes.

Saxons, a Teutonic race originally inhabiting what is now Holstein. By the 7th cent. they had, with the Angles and Jutes, conquered and colonised most of England.

Scald, the name of the Norse poets, who were similar to the bards of Wales. They had to celebrate the achievements of their warriors and leaders.

Scallop, marine bivalve molluscs of the genus *Pecten*, which is widely distributed. The scalloped edge to the shell results from a pattern of radiating grooves. Related to the oyster.

Scandium, a metal element, symbol Sc. It was discovered in 1879 by Nilson, and occurs in small quantities in certain rarer minerals such as wolframite.

Scapular, a vestment hanging from the shoulder to the knees, worn by members of certain Roman Catholic orders. The name is also given to two small pieces of cloth worn over the shoulders by lay members of the Church in honour of the Virgin.

Scarabaeidae, a family of beetles (Scarabs) widely distributed through Africa and Asia and the inner parts of Europe. It is to this genus that the "Sacred Beetle" of the Egyptians belongs, and numerous representations of it are found on ancient monuments.

Sceptre, the staff or rod used since ancient times to symbolise supreme authority. The sceptre used for the coronation of Queen Elizabeth II is the one made for Charles II. It is about 90 cm long and tipped with a jewelled cross.

Schism, an ecclesiastical term for division in a church. The Great Schism was the separation of the Greek Church from the Latin, finally established in 1054. The Western Schism was the division in the Roman Catholic Church from 1378 to 1417, when there were two lines of popes, one at Rome and one at Avignon, which arose over the election of Urban VI and Clement VII to the papacy and was more a matter of persons and politics than a question of faith.

Schist, the geological name of certain metamorphic rocks composed for the most part of minerals with thin plate-like crystals (*e.g.*, mica) so that the layers of a schist are closely parallel. Quartz occurs in schists, and where it preponderates the term "quartz schist" is applied.

Scientific Units. The International Bureau of Weights and Measures at Sèvres near Paris, is the custodian of accurate scientific measurement in terms of internationally agreed units.

Methods of measurement are continually being improved and measurements of new kinds coming into use. In defining units certain principles have evolved which can be expressed as a statement of priorities:

(i) units should be so defined that measurements made in one laboratory should be reproducible in another with as much consistency as possible;

(ii) units of all kinds should, so far as practical, form an interrelated system based on as few fundamental units as possible;

(iii) the fundamental units adopted should have a natural basis, independent of particular man-made objects such as metal bars or weights. An invariable universal natural standard was achieved for the metre in 1958 when it was defined in terms of the wavelength of a line in the spectrum of krypton–86. *See* **S.I. Units.**

Schoolmen, the great scholastic philosophers of the Middle Ages who devoted themselves to the study and exposition of questions of religious inquiry, and attempted to reconcile the teaching of the Church with that of Aristotle. The chief Schoolmen were Archbishop Anselm, Albertus Magnus, Thomas Aquinas, Peter Lombard, Duns Scotus. *See also* **Section J.**

Scorpion. The scorpions constitute an order of the arthropods. Distinctive features are the pair of powerful claws at the head and a "sting" at the tail, which curves over the back in attack or defence so that it points forwards. The poison injected by the sting is potent, causing instant death in spiders, centipedes, etc., and acute discomfort to humans. The idea that a cornered scorpion can sting itself to death is a myth; scorpions are immune to their own poison.

Scorpion Fly. The scorpion fly, of which there are less than 500 species, constitute a separate order of insects, the *Mecoptera.* They have 2 pairs of membranous wings, and gain their popular name because in some species the end of the abdomen is turned up, though it does not function as a sting.

Scree *or* **Talus**, the mass of loose, angular rock fragments which accumulate towards the bottom of hill-sides and mountain-sides. These fragments have been detached by weathering processes, in particular frost action.

Scythians, nomadic conquerors and skilled horsemen of ancient times (9th–3rd cent. B.C.) who inhabited much of Southern Europe and Asiatic Russia.

Sea Anemones *or* **Actinaria**, an order of marine animals of the coelenterate class *Anthozia.* They form a large and varied group of about 1,100 species and occur in many beautiful colours, flower-like in form.

Sea Butterfly, marine molluscs which propel themselves by two "wings", or side expansions of the foot. They constitute the order called *Pteropoda.*

Sea Cow. *See* **Manatee.**

Sea Cucumbers *or* **Holothurians.** These animals constitute the class of echinoderms called *Holothuroidea.* They are elongated and wormlike, with a ring of about twenty tentacles round the mouth. There are about 500 species.

Sea Eagle, a genus of flesh-eating birds related to the true eagles, kites and other birds of prey. Examples are the Bald Eagle, emblem of the USA, White-tailed Eagle (Grey Sea Eagle), and Steller's Sea Eagle of the Pacific coast of Asia. Last known in Britain in 1911.

Sea Elephant *or* **Elephant Seal**, a curious genus of seal, the males of which possess a proboscis of *c.* 30 cm in length that suggests an elephant's trunk. They are found on the coast of California and in certain parts of the Southern Ocean; their blubber has a commercial value.

Sea Gravimeter, an instrument to determine the density of the earth's crust beneath the oceans of the world. Designed by Dr. A. Graf of Munich and Dr. J. Lamar Worzel of Columbia University, it can detect changes of one-millionth of the value of gravity at the earth's surface and was used in the oceanographical research programme of the IGY.

Sea Hare, a genus of molluscs (*Aplysia*), so-called because of resemblance to a crouching hare. The shell is thin curved plate largely sunk in the animal's body. They have four tentacles, occur in Britain in the laminaria or ribbon wrack zone, and discharge a purple fluid when molested.

Sea Horse, a sea-fish (*Hippocampus*), very numerous in the tropics and comprising some twenty species. Their bodies are ringed and they have prehensile tails. Their heads are horse-shaped, and they swim in a vertical position.

Sea Lily. A class of echinoderms, the sea lilies may be roughly described as "stalked starfishes". There are about 400 living species, and several thousand extinct species are known. Otherwise called Crinoids.

Sea Mouse, a genus of marine worms called *Aphrodite*, oval in shape, 20–23 cm long, iridescent, covered with fine bristles.

Sea Squirts *or* **Tunicates.** These animals are placed in the sub-phylum called *Urochorda*; found growing in rounded, jelly-like masses on rocks near low-water level. They get their name through the water jets they discharge.

Sea Urchin, species forming the class *Echinoidae.* The body is globular and covered with spines which may be used for both defence and locomotion. The main organs of locomotion are, however, the tube feet, as in starfishes. Much has been learnt of recent years by marine biologists from experiments with the purple sea-urchin *Arbacia.*

Seasons comprise the four natural divisions of the year, and are due to the inclinations of the earth's axis to the plane of the eliptic. *See* **Section N.**

Secondary Sexual Characters, characters of animals which are distinctive of sex, but have no direct connection with the reproductive process. Examples are: the mane of the lion and the antlers of some deer.

Secretary Bird, so called because of the quill-like plumes about its ears, is a bird of prey related to the eagles and vultures; common in Africa, and of considerable service as an exterminator of snakes. It is a large bird about 1·2 m in height.

Sedimentary Rocks. *See* **F8**(2).

Seismology, the branch of geophysics devoted to the study of earthquakes and other earth movements. The instruments used for the registration of earth tremors are termed seismographs and consist in principle of a pendulum system, the supporting framework following the ground movement and the bob remaining at rest, thus setting up a relative movement between two parts. In order to record the displacements completely, at one station, three seismographs are necessary to show the two horizontal and the vertical components of the motion. Apart from detection and study of waves from earthquakes sensitive seismographs are now widely used in geophysical prospecting, particularly in the search for possible oilfields.

Selenuim, a non-metalic element, symbol Se; related to sulphur it is a dark red colour, and solid, found associated with sulphur, iron, pyrites, etc., though only in small quantities. It is a semiconductor (*q.v.*) and its special electrical properties have led to its use in photoelectric cells and rectifiers. Selenium is widely used in the chemical industry as a catalyst (*q.v.*) in producing aromatic hydrocarbons from less useful hydrocarbons. Also used in making some types of glass.

Semiconductors, substances with numerous special and useful electrical properties a few of which are:

(i) they conduct electricity much better than do insulators, but much less well than metals (hence their name);

(ii) their power to conduct depends strongly on their temperature—which makes them useful for temperature sensitive devices;

(iii) they are sensitive to light—hence their use in photoelectric cells and solar batteries;

(iv) when in contact with metals, or with other suitable semiconductors, they form a boundary layer which conducts electricity much better one way than the other—this is the basis of many rectifiers some of which, called crystal diodes, are an important component in radios and electronic devices;

(v) their electrical properties can be greatly influenced by putting in minute amounts of impurity, this enables semiconductor devices, especially transistors, to be made with carefully selected properties.

Semiconductors were known to Faraday, but the semiconductor age really arrived with the invention of the transistor (*q.v.*) in 1947. The ubiquitous transistor is only one of very many semiconductor devices which perform a variety of functions in technical apparatus of all kinds. Semiconductors used in technology are usually small crystals, frequently of germanium or silicon, and their robustness and small power consumption often make them superior to other devices, such as thermionic valves, which they often replace. Other semiconducting materials are cadmium sulphide, selenium, lead telluride, indium antimonide. *See also* **F19.**

Senate, the higher governing Assembly of a Legislature. The word, applied primarily to the Roman council, is also used to denote the upper chamber in the legislatures of France, the United States, and other countries. In certain universities the governing body is also called the Senate.

Sensitive Plant. A species of Mimosa (*Mimosa pudica*), whose leaves are extremely sensitive to touch, shaking and burning.

Sepia, the " ink " of the cuttlefish. *See* **Ink Sac.**

September, the ninth month of the year, and the seventh of the old Roman calendar; hence the name, from Septimus. The designation was several times changed by the Emperors, but none of the new names survived for long.

Septuagesima Sunday, the third Sunday before Lent.

Septuagint, the Greek translation of the Old Testament made by Alexandrian Jews between 250 B.C. and 100 B.C. from Hebrew texts now lost. There are many differences between the Septuagint and the Massoretic version (A.D. 900), and therefore it is of great value for textual criticism. The symbol for the Septuagint is LXX.

Serfs, the name given to the slaves formerly existing in Russia, who answered to the condition of the feudal " villeins " of England. They were attached to the soil and were transferred with it in all sales or leases. Serfdom existed in Prussia until 1807 and in Russia until 1861.

Serpentine, a mineral: chemically a hydrous silicate of magnesium. Green serpentine is used as an ornament stone. Fibrous serpentine is called asbestos.

Serval, a collie-dog-sized cat, long-limbed and spotted, from Africa. Preys on a variety of animals, from lizards to small antelope. Black servals occur mainly in mountainous regions.

Set, both in everyday speech (as in tea set, chess set) and in mathematics, a set is a collection of things. The members of the set can be specified by listing them or by describing the properties necessary for membership of the set, *e.g.*, the set of ginger-haired boxers. Set theory is a very important branch of mathematics founded by a great mathematician, Georg Cantor (1845–1918). Its development has influenced many other branches of mathematics. Perhaps one reflection of its fundamental nature is to be found in the fact that many schoolchildren, even of tender age, are now learning set theory and confounding parents who did not hear of it at school when they were there.

Settlement, Act of, passed in 1701, assigned the Crown to the House of Hanover in case of Anne's death without children. The decision represented the determination of the squires and the Anglican Church never again to trust themselves to a Roman Catholic king.

Seven Champions of Christendom, as set forth in mediaeval literature, were St. George of England, St. Andrew of Scotland, St. Patrick of Ireland, St. David of Wales, St. James of Spain, St. Denis of France, and St. Anthony of Italy.

Seven Churches of Asia, referred to in the Revelation of St. John, were those of Ephesus, founded by St. Paul in 57, Smyrna, Pergamos, Thyatira, Sardis, Philadelphia (Lydia) and Laodicea (Phrygia), all in W. Asia Minor.

Seven Wonders of the World were: 1, the Pyramids of Egypt; 2, the tomb of Mausolus, King of Caria (hence the word mausoleum); 3, the Temple of Diana at Ephesus; 4, the Walls and Hanging Gardens of Babylon; 5, the Colossus at Rhodes; 6, the Ivory and Gold Statue of Jupiter Olympus; and 7, the Pharos, or Watch Tower, built at Alexandria by Ptolemy Philadelphus, King of Egypt.

Seven Years War was waged by Frederick the Great and England against Austria, France, and Russia, from 1756 to 1763. It resulted in the secession of Silesia to Prussia, of Canada to England, and in the strengthening of our Indian Empire.

Severn Barrage, a barrier across the River Severn estuary proposed with a view to extracting useful electrical energy from tidal power. Essentially the idea is to let the tidal water flow into a reservoir upstream from the barrage and then to flow seaward under gravity through specially designed hydroelectric generators situated on the barrage. Tidal power has been harnessed in a French project and there is little doubt that the Severn scheme is technically feasible. However, environmental, economic and social factors enter the matter and are influencing consideration of its overall desirability. *See also* **Tidal Power.**

Sexagesima Sunday is the 2nd Sunday before Lent.

Sextant, an instrument which has superseded the quadrant as a measurer of angles between distant objects. It is of special importance in navigation and surveying, and contains 60 degrees described on a graduated arc. A small telescope is attached and there are also a couple of mirrors which reflect the distant objects so as to enable them to be accurately observed. The invention is attributed to John Hadley, and to Thomas Godfrey independently, about 1730. Even today it is still the best instrument for telling where you are at sea.

Shad, a marine fish belonging to the same genus as the herring. It is found along the Atlantic Coast of the USA, and ascends rivers to spawn.

Shagreen, shark's skin: also untanned leather of peculiar grain made from skins of wild asses, camels and horses.

Shalloon, a kind of cloth manufactured from wool and worsted, and used chiefly for women's dresses and coat linings. It gets its name from the fact that it was originally made at Châlons-sur Marne. It was called " chalouns " by Chaucer and " shalloons " by Swift.

Shamrock, the three-leaved clover-like plant native to Ireland and its national emblem.

Shark, a large and powerful ocean fish, comprising many species, very widely distributed, but most numerous in tropical seas. They have formidable teeth and are the most carnivorous of all fishes. They usually attain a large size, the whale-shark being often of a length of 15 m. Commercially the shark yields shagreen from its skin, the fins are made into gelatine, and an oil is obtained from the liver.

Sheep, a well-known family of ruminants of great utility as wool-producers, and for food. From the earliest times sheep have been a source of wealth to England. So much were they valued in the 15th and 16th cent., that their exportation was frequently prohibited. Sheep are classified under (1) longwools; (2) shortwools; and (3) mountain breeds. Most of the longwools carry Leicester blood in their ancestry and the shortwooled Down breeds carry the blood of the Southdown. The Southdown produced the present Suffolk, one of the most popular breeds. Cheviot is an important mountain breed. Of the foreign breeds the most valued are the Merino sheep of Spain, which yield a fine long wool. Australia, USSR, China, New Zealand, India, Argentina, South Africa, Turkey, Iran, UK are the chief wool-producing countries in the world.

Shelduck, a handsome genus of surface-feeding ducks, one of which, the common shelduck, is an inhabitant of this country. It is a beautiful white-and-chestnut plumaged bird with dark-green head and neck and red bill. Another species, the ruddy shelduck, appears in Britain only occasionally.

Shellac. This resin is the secretion of the lac

insect (*Coccus lacca*), which occurs in forests of Assam and Thailand. It is used for making varnish and in the manufacture of gramophone records. *See also* **Lac.**

Sherardizing. Process for coating steel or iron parts with zinc to prevent corrosion; this is done by heating the parts in a closed rotating drum containing zinc dust.

Shilling has been an English coin from Saxon times, but it was not of the value of 12 pence until after the Conquest. It is interchangeable with the 5 new pence decimal piece which came into circulation in 1968.

Ships have existed from prehistoric times. There is mention of one that sailed from Egypt to Greece in 1485 B.C., and in 786 B.C. the Tyrians built a double-decked vessel. No double-decked ship was known in England, however, before the *Royal Harry* was built by Henry VII, and it was not until the 17th cent. that ship-building was carried on in this country as a prominent industry.

Ship-worm. *See* **Teredo.**

Shoddy, the name given to a kind of cloth mainly composed of woollen or worsted rags, torn up and re-fabricated by powerful machinery. It was first made at Batley in Yorkshire about 1813, and became a very important industry employing many thousands of people at Batley and the neighbouring town of Dewsbury.

Shot, the name given to solid projectiles fired from guns. In the time of Henry V stone shot was used, later leaden shot, then iron shot, and finally steel shot, introduced by Sir Joseph Whitworth.

Shrike, a large and varied family of birds of hawk-like behaviour found in all continents except S. America. The Red-backed Shrike, which winters in Africa, is a breeding visitor to England and Wales. It is commonly called the "Butcher Bird" from the way it impales its prey (small birds and insects) on thorn-twigs. The other species on the British list are the Great Grey Shrike, the Lesser Grey Shrike, the Woodchat Shrike, and the Masked Shrike.

Shrove Tuesday, the day before the first day of Lent, receiving its name from the old custom of shriving, or making confession, on that day. In England the day has always been associated with the making of pancakes.

Sicilian Vespers, the term applied to the terrible massacre of French people in Sicily in 1282. The French under Charles of Anjou were then in occupation of the island and had been guilty of many cruelties. It began at Palermo on Easter Monday at the hour of vespers and resulted in the expulsion of the French king and the introduction of Spanish rule.

Silence, Tower of, or *dakhma*, a tower about 8 m high, built by the Parsees for their dead. The corpse is taken inside by professional corpse-bearers and left to be consumed by vultures. Parsees do not burn or bury their dead, and the *dakhma* is to protect the living and the elements from defilement.

Silicon, an important non-metallic element, symbol Si, it is related to carbon. Next to oxygen, it is the most abundant constituent of the earth's crust (27% by weight). It occurs in many rocks, and its oxide occurs in many forms (*e.g.* quartz, sand, flint, agate, chalcedony, opal, etc.). Principally used as a semi-conducting material for making transistors and similar devices.

Silicones are synthetic organic derivatives of silicon which because of their high resistance to heat and moisture have special uses, *e.g.*, lubricants, heat-resistant resins and lacquers, and water-repellent finishes. Silicones are compounds in which the molecules consist of chains of atoms of silicon and oxygen alternately. Silicones were developed in the United States from discoveries first made by Prof. F. S. Kipping at Nottingham University. Manufacture began in Britain in 1950, and in the form of fluids, resins, rubbers and greases they find wide use in industry. The largest plant in Europe is in Glamorgan.

Silk, the name given to a soft glossy fabric manufactured from the fine thread produced by the silkworm. It was known to, and highly prized by the ancients, being at one time paid for, weight for weight, with gold. The manufacture of silk was carried on in Sicily in the 12th cent., later spreading to Italy, Spain and France, where Lyons has been the great centre of production from 1450 to this day. It was not manufactured in England before 1604; but when certain French refugees established themselves at Spitalfields in 1688, the industry was developed and became of importance. In the 18th cent. the Lombes of Derby achieved great success in this industry. Japan, China, Italy, Korea and the Soviet Union are the chief silk-producing countries.

Silkworm, the larva of a species of moth, *Bombyx mori*. It is native to China, and has been cultivated with success in India, Iran, Turkey and Italy. The silkworm of commerce feeds on mulberry leaves and produces a cocoon of silk varying in colour from white to orange. The cocoon is the silken habitation constructed by the worm for its entrance upon the pupal condition, and to obtain the silk the pupa is killed by immersion in hot-water.

Sill, a sheet-like mass of igneous rock which has been intruded parallel with the stratification of the country rock, cf. a dyke.

Silurian. This geological period is one of the major subdivisions of the Palaeozoic era. Its beginning is estimated at 440 million years ago, and the period lasted about 40 million years. Maximum thickness of the Silurian strata in Britain measures 4,575 m. *See* **F45.**

Silver, a white precious metal, symbol Ag (Latin *argentum*) found in a free state, also in certain combinations, and in a variety of ores. The chief silver-producing regions are the Andes and Cordilleras. Peru, Bolivia and Mexico have yielded vast supplies of the metal since the 16th century, and Colorado and Nevada in the United States have also been very prolific in silver yield. In England standard silver (that used for coinage) formerly contained 92½ per cent. fine silver and 7½ per cent. alloy, but when the price rose to 89½*d.* per oz and the coins became worth more than face value, the Coinage Act of 1920 was passed, reducing the fineness to half. To provide silver bullion for industry and for a fund towards the redemption of our silver debt to America, it was decided in 1946 to replace the United Kingdom silver coinage by one made of cupro-nickel (75 per cent. copper, 25 per cent. nickel). Maundy money, however, is of the original silver standard. Silver chloride and bromide are light-sensitive compounds and are used in photography.

Simony, the offence of trading in church offices, has been contrary to English law since the time of Edward VI. Elizabeth also promulgated laws against simony. In 1879 a Royal Commission reported on the law and existing practice as to the sale, exchange and resignation of benefices. The position is now controlled by the Benefices Act 1898, the Amendment Measure 1923, and the Benefices Rules 1926.

Sinn Fein (*Irish* = ourselves alone), Irish nationalistic movement founded in 1905 which developed into a mass republican party and triumphed in the establishment of the Irish Free State. An extremist group has survived which represents politically the outlawed IRA. In Northern Ireland *Sinn Fein* was legalized in 1974.

Sins, The Seven Deadly or Capital Sins are pride, avarice, lust, anger, gluttony, envy, sloth.

Sirius, the dog-star, so called because of its situation in the mouth of the Dog (Canis Major): it is the brightest of all the fixed stars, and is also one of the nearest to us.

Sirocco, a warm, southerly, often dust-laden, wind blowing across Mediterranean lands from the Sahara, in advance of an eastward-moving depression over the Mediterranean.

Siskin, a small bird of the finch family, common in Northern regions, nesting in Britain. The common Siskin has a yellow-green colour and is a lively, swift-flying bird with a stout bill.

Sistine Chapel, the chapel of the Pope in the Vatican, renowned for its frescoes by Michelangelo.

S.I. Units (Système International d'Unités) form an internationally recognised system of metric units for scientific and technical quantities. The basic units of length, time, mass, electric current, temperature and luminous intensity are, respectively the metre, second, kilogramme, ampre, kelvin (*see* **Absolute Temperature**) and candela. The S.I. was recommended for general adoption by a number of international organisations such as the General Conference on Weights and Measures (1960). Many countries have made or are making the S.I. the only legally recognised set of units. Gt. Britain's intention to " go metric " has brought widespread use of S.I. units in its train. These units command the widespread though not absolutely unanimous support of industrialists, technologists, and scientists. Many have urged that their adoption will be a triumph of commonsense and end the confusing multiplicity of units on the world scene. *See* **Section N.**

Six Articles, The Statute of the, was passed in 1539 for compelling adhesion to the chief doctrines of Roman Catholic faith: transubstantiation, communion in one kind only for the laity, vows of chastity, celibacy of the clergy, private masses and auricular confession; those who refused to subscribe to the Articles were treated as heretics. The Act was repealed in 1547.

Skink. The skinks constitute a large family of lizards with large smooth scales, under each of which is a bony plate. The largest species, found in Australia, is about 61 cm long. Some skinks have adopted a burrowing habit and degeneration of the limbs is associated with this. The Common Skink is a small species c. 12 cm long, living in deserts of N. Africa.

Skua, falcon-like marine birds related to the gulls found throughout the world. Known as " Robber Birds " because they steal not only the young and eggs of other birds (including penguins) but also their food, which they force them to disgorge in mid-air. The Arctic Skua breeds as far south as Scotland. The Great Skua breeds in both Antarctica and Arctica. Other species are the Pomarine, the Long-tailed, and McCormick's Skua.

Skunk, a North American mammal of the weasel family, with short legs and long bushy tail. All fifteen species are black and white, some being striped and the rest spotted. It secretes and ejects at will a foul-smeling fluid.

Sky. The blue colour of the sky on a summer's day is the result of the scattering of light waves by particles of dust and vapour in the earth's atmosphere. Blue light having almost the smallest wavelength in the visible spectrum (0·00004 cm) is scattered laterally about 10 times as much as the red (0·00007 cm).

Skyscraper. Owing to lack of ground space, increasing cost of land, and growth of modern cities, buildings are being made higher than broader; hence the name. The structures are constructed of steel framework usually clothed in concrete or reinforced concrete. The first modern skyscraper of steel skeletal construction was the Home Insurance Building in Chicago, designed (1883) by William Le Baron. The New York skyscapers include the World Trade Center building (110 stories), Empire State building (102 stories), Chrysler (77 stories), Rockefeller Center (70 stories), and 60 Wall Tower (67 stories). The tallest building in Britain when it is completed in 1978 will be the National Westminster Bank tower, dominating the city skyline (183 m), topping the Post Office radio tower by 6 m.

Slate, fine-grained clayey rocks which have undergone metamorphism. They cleave easily, and it is this property of cleavage which makes them a valuable source of roofing material. Important quarries producing mainly green slate are in the Coniston–Ambleside area of the Lake District.

Slavery. In its earlier forms, as in the times of ancient Greece and Rome, in the feudal ages, when vassalage and villeinage existed, and in the serfdom of Russia and other northern nations, slavery was attended by many inhumanities and evils; but perhaps in the negro slavery system which prevailed in the British colonies for upwards of 200 years and in certain parts of the United States up to 1865, it attained its highest point of cruelty. In 1883 the Act of Emancipation was passed, emancipating all slaves in British territories, though slavery continued to be tolerated in northern Nigeria, Sierre Leone and in the Anglo-Egyptian Sudan long after that date. Even today slavery and forced labour are still prevalent in some parts of the world.

Slide Rule, an instrument which consists of two logarithmic scales sliding alongside each other. By its use multiplication, division, extraction of roots, etc., are speedily carried out.

Sloth, a curious family of mammals, only found in Central and South America. They dwell almost entirely in the trees, proceeding from branch to branch with their bodies hanging downwards, their weight being supported by their large hook-like claws. They eat foliage.

Slow-Worm, a species of lizard found in Britain which lacks legs. Silver with longitudinal brown stripes, it lives almost entirely on slugs.

Smelting. The process of heating an ore with a reducing agent to convert ore into metal, and with a flux to convert rocky impurities into a slag that will float on top of the molten metal. Slag and metal can then be tapped separately. An example is iron smelting; the reducing agent is coke, and limestone is added as the flux; the smelting is carried out in a blast furnace.

Snake. The snakes constitute the important reptilian order *Ophidia.* Snakes have a scaly, cylindrical, limbless body, lidless eyes, forked tongue, and the upper and lower jaws joined by an elastic ligament. All snakes have teeth used for seizing prey, and the poisonous varieties are furnished with poison fangs in the upper jaw. These fangs are hollow modified teeth and the venom passes into them from a special gland situated behind the angle of the mouth. Some 2,500 species of snakes are known, divided into 13 families. There are 3 British species—the grass-snake, smooth-snake, and adder.

Snipe, a wading bird, long-legged, with long, slender, straight bill, brown plumage, and zig-zag flight. The Common Snipe breeds locally throughout Britain; the Great Snipe and small Jack Snipe are occasional visitors. The close season is February 1 to August 11.

Snow. When water vapour condenses at high levels at a temperature below freezing (sublimation), a cloud of ice particles if formed. If these frozen droplets are small, they fall slowly and gradually assume a feathery crystalline structure, reaching the earth as snowflakes if the temperature remains below freezing.

Socialism. *See* **Section J.**

Soda, carbonate of sodium, is now mainly obtained by certain processes of manufacture from common salt. It was formerly obtained from the ashes of plants. Bicarbonate of sodium is the primary product in the Solvay or Ammonia-soda method for commercial manufacture of soda; it is also formed when carbon dioxide is passed into strong soda solution. The bicarbonate is used in medicine and in the preparation of baking powder.

Sodium, a metallic element, symbol Na (Latin *Natrium*), first obtained by Sir Humphry Davy in 1807 from caustic soda by means of the electric battery. Its chloride is *common salt*; the deposits of salt (*e.g.*, in Cheshire and at Stassfurt) have come into existence through the drying up of inland seas. Salt occurs in sea-water to the extent of about 3 per cent.; the Dead Sea contains about 22 per cent. The blood of animals is maintained at a level of about 0.6% sodium chloride. That there is sodium in the sun's atmosphere was confirmed in 1859 by Kirchhoff from his spectroscopic observations. Liquid sodium metal has properties which make it suitable as a coolant in some nuclear reactors; a technique of handling this very reactive liquid has had to be developed.

Soil Erosion occurs when the soil is removed from an area at a faster rate than soil formation. This situation usually occurs as a result of man's interference with the natural balance of the environment by the removal of natural vegetation, overgrazing or by poor farming techniques. Soil thus exposed is then removed by the wind (as in the Dust Bowl in the 1930s) or by rain in the form of gully or sheet erosion (as in the Tennessee Valley, USA). Methods introduced to stop soil erosion include contour ploughing, afforestation and dry farming techniques.

Software, the internal programmes and operating procedures of a computer as opposed to its hardware. This includes system software designed to make the computer usable as well as programmes intended for particular applications such as commercial or scientific calculations. *See* **Hardware.**

Solar Battery, one of the innumerable devices made possible by the development of semiconducting materials, notably germanium and silicon. This device creates an electric current from light falling on it. The current can be put to use or stored in storage batteries. The energy of the current is derived from the sunlight, and the solar battery is thus an *energy converting* apparatus. Solar batteries have provided power for the instruments in satellites.

Solar Wind, a continuous stream of electrically charged particles blowing outwards from the sun, supplemented from time to time by intense outbursts from particular regions of the sun's surface. These streams of protons and electrons on encountering the earth's magnetic field distort it and cause magnetic storms and aurorae.

Soldering is a means of joining together two pieces of material, usually metals, by melting a third metal (the solder) into the joint. The solder solidifies in the pores of the other metals and holds them together. The materials to be joined are not themselves melted so the technique requires less heat than welding. Solders are alloys; there are many kinds depending on the materials to be joined and the strength of joint desired. *See* **Welding.**

Solstice, an astronomical term indicating the point at which the sun is most distant from the equator. *See* **Seasons, Section N.**

Soundings at sea, to determine depth at any point, have been taken in all seas, and with considerable accuracy. A deep reading was that of the *Challenger* expedition in 1873, near St. Thomas's in the North Atlantic, when 3,875 fathoms (7,091 m) were sounded. In 1851 H.M.S. *Challenger* recorded the then maximum ocean depth in the Marianas Trench (W. Pacific) by echo-sounding as between 5,882 and 5,950 fathoms (10,764 and 10,870 m). Another deep was located in the S. Pacific in 1952–53 of 5,814 fathoms (10,640 m) in the Tonga Trench, 290 km S. of Tonga Tabu. Since then even greater depths have been recorded, in the Marianas Trench and the Mindanao Deep. *See* **Pacific Ocean.**

Southern Cross, popular name of *Crux*, a constellation of the Southern hemisphere, consisting of four bright stars in the form of a Latin cross. It has been called the pole-star of the south and is indispensable to seafarers.

South Sea Bubble, the name given to a series of financial projects which began with the formation of the South Sea Company in 1711 and ended nine years later in disaster after a mania of speculation. The idea behind the parent scheme was that the state should sell certain trading monopolies in the South seas in return for a sum of money to pay off the National Debt (which stood at £51,300,000 in 1719 when the scheme started). The idea fascinated the public, fabulous profits being dreamt of, and the price of the stock rose out of all proportion to the earnings of the Company. Many dishonest speculative ventures sprang up in imitation with the inevitable result that thousands were ruined. All classes had joined in the gamble and a Committee of Secrecy set up by the House of Commons in December 1720 to investigate the affairs of the Company proved that there had been fraud and corruption on a large scale in the affairs of the Company. Sir Robert Walpole who had been an opponent of the scheme from the outset dealt with the crisis.

Space Flight. The Soviet Union was the first country to launch a man into space and bring him safely back to earth. This epoch-making event took place on 12 April 1961, when Yuri Gagarin, tragically killed in an air crash in 1968, circled the earth in a spaceship weighing about 4,826 kg. It was launched by rocket in an elliptical orbit with greatest height 300 km and least 175 km. The inclination of the orbit to the equator was 65° 4′, and the period of revolution was 89 min. 6s. Since then, the Russian *Vostok* cosmonauts Titov (17 orbits), Nikolayev (64 orbits), Popovich (48 orbits), Bykovsky (81 orbits), Tereshkova, the first woman space traveller (48 orbits), the *Voskhod* cosmonauts Komarov, Feoktistov and Yegorov (16 orbits), Belyaev and Leonov (17 orbits), the American *Mercury* astronauts Glenn (3 orbits), Carpenter (3 orbits), Schirra (6 orbits), Cooper (22 orbits), the *Gemini* astronauts Grissom and Young (3 orbits), McDivitt and White (62 orbits), Cooper and Conrad (120 orbits), Borman and Lovell (206 orbits), Schirra and Stafford (15 orbits), Armstrong and Scott (6·6 orbits), Stafford and Cernan (44 orbits), Young and Collins (43 orbits), Conrad and Gordon (44 orbits), Lovell and Aldrin (60 orbits) were among the first to complete successful missions in space. Leonov was the first to perform the extra-vehicular (EVA) experiment (1965), *i.e.*, to leave an orbiting spaceship and float freely in space. Russia was the first to achieve an automatic docking (link-up) between two unmanned spacecraft in orbital flight (October 1967), and of two manned spacecraft (January 1969.) The American *Apollo* mission was accomplished when Armstrong and Aldrin became the first men to set foot on the moon. This milestone in manned space flight took place on 20 July 1969. A joint Soviet-American project culminated in a *Soyuz-Apollo* link-up 225 km up on 17 July 1975. The Russian cosmonauts were Leonov and Kubasov, the American astronauts Stafford, Brand and Slayton. *See also* **Sputniks, Space Research.**

Space Research. By space research we mean scientific research work which can only be carried to otherwise inaccessible observing locations by rocket propulsion. Such propulsion does not rely on the presence of an atmosphere to provide oxygen so that it is capable in principle of conveying objects to unlimited distances. The subject of space research is, therefore, one which is concerned with scientific applications in various fields of a single highly specialised and powerful technique. It is not a single discipline, but can provide data of great importance for many such as the physics of the earth, the sun, moon and other bodies of the solar system, astronomy, geodesy and the study of gravitation. The prospect of investigating the biological conditions on different planets such as Mars and Venus is also opened, as well as that of experimental biological studies under conditions of zero gravity. Although the results of many aspects of space research are vital for those concerned with the practical realisation of manned travel in space, space research is largely a branch of pure science, independent of any applications which may stem from it. The major technical problems involved in space research are:

(*a*) Launching of the instrument-containing vehicle with the necessary velocity.

(*b*) Guidance and control of the vehicle so it pursues the desired path.

(*c*) Tracking the vehicle to determine its actual path and the position on the path at any time.

(*d*) Transmission of the data, recorded by the instruments, back to the earth.

(*e*) Satisfactory operation of scientific instruments in the environment within the vehicle.

(*f*) Provision of adequate power supplies to operate the equipment within the vehicle for sufficiently long periods.

It is important to distinguish three distinct types of vehicle—the vertical sounding rocket, the artificial earth satellite, and the deep space probe. The track of a vertical sounding rocket is mainly vertical, and the whole path to the highest point and back is traversed in a few minutes only. An earth satellite circulates in an orbit round the earth in the same way as does our natural satellite, the moon. If it approaches the earth at any point within 160 km of the surface the air resistance causes the path to spiral in so rapidly that the vehicle is eventually burnt up by air friction within the dense atmosphere after an orbital life of a few months only. It follows that artificial satellite vehicles are only useful as instrument containers if the distance of closest approach (the perigee distance) is not much less than 160 km. For the study of the properties of the atmosphere at lower altitudes down to the limit (32 km) attainable by balloons, vertical sounding rockets must be used. It is a great advantage for work at higher altitudes to use satellites, as it is then possible to make systematic observations for months at a time from a great number of positions relative to the earth. The successful space flights achieved by manned satellites also suggest that it should not be long before manned observatories become practicable. Deep space probes include vehicles which pass out to great distances from the earth and may leave the neighbourhood of the earth for ever to become artificial planets. Such probes may pass close to, or soft-land on, the moon or planets or may merely pursue paths well out into interplanetary space.

Spanish Civil War, 1936 to 1939. The war commenced by a revolt by the Fascist General Franco against the Republic which had succeeded the Monarchy in 1931. Germany and Italy aided the rebels who besieged Madrid for over 2 years. An International Brigade was formed to help the Republic, but the Spanish Government was faced by the greater part of the Army, and very effective assistance from Italy and Germany. Those powers seized the opportunity to have a curtain-raiser to the world conflict which they intended to precipitate. After a total loss of a million men the Fascists overpowered the Republic.

Sparrow, name given to finch-like birds found in most parts of the world, of which the House Sparrow *Passer domesticus*, is the most familiar of British birds. Also native to Britain is the rural Tree Sparrow, distinguished from the male House Sparrow by its chestnut crown. Other European species are the Italian, Spanish and Rock Sparrows.

Specific Gravity, defined as the ratio of the mass of a particular volume of a substance to the mass of an equal volume of water at 4°C. *See* **Hydrometer.**

Spectroscopy. Newton's arrangement with the prism was the first spectroscope; its function was to separate out the colour components of a source of light. Two hundred years elapsed before this apparatus was developed into a precise scientific instrument, capable of measuring both the wavelength and intensity of each colour component. In this form it is called a spectrometer. All atoms and molecules have well defined characteristic spectra which can be used to recognise them. In order to produce emission spectra it is necessary to energise the material under investigation by some means, such as by heating in a flame. The resulting radiation then consists largely of sharp bright lines, characteristic of the material. Absorption spectra are produced by interposing the experimental material between a white light source and the spectrometer. Then dark lines are seen, corresponding to absorptions of energy, in exactly the same places as the bright lines are observed in the emission spectra. Spectroscopic techniques have now been developed to such an extent that accurate measurements of wavelength and intensity are possible not only in the visible region, but over almost the whole of the electromagnetic spectrum. Not only does spectroscopy play an important rôle in probing the structure of matter, but it can be applied in the field of astronomy. The use of radio wave spectroscopy has led to the discovery of several new types of stellar object, and this data is now producing a complete reappraisal of our understanding of the universe.

Sphinx, in Greek mythology, a winged creature with a woman's head and a lion's body. The sphinx of ancient Egypt represented the pharaoh in a divine form.

Spiritualism. *See* **Section J.**

Spirituals, negro melodies with religious inspiration and which are still spontaneously created, but have also passed into art-music.

Sponge. *See* **Porifera, F33(1).**

Spoonbill, a long-legged, marsh bird, closely related to the ibis and stork, remarkable for its snow-white plumage and broad, flat, spoon-shaped bill. The European species has not bred in England since the beginning of the 17th cent., but is still a regular summer visitor from the Netherlands, where it nests in colonies in reed-beds and islets.

Sputniks, the name of the Russian earth satellites first launched during the period of the International Geophysical Year. *Sputnik I*, launched 4 October 1957, became the first man-made earth satellite. *Sputnik II*, launched a month later carried a dog as passenger. *Sputnik III*, launched in May 1958, and weighing well over 2 tonnes, became the first fully-equipped laboratory to operate in space. The father of space travel with rockets was a Russian—Konstantin Eduardovich Tsiolkovsky—the centenary of whose birth practically coincided with the launching of the first earth satellite.

Squirting Cucumber, *Ecballium elatarium*, so named from the fact that when ripe it breaks from the stalk and ejects its seeds and juice from the hole made by the breakage.

Stainless Steel. The development of stainless steel for cutlery manufacture, etc., began with the discovery of Harry Brearsley in 1912 that steel containing 12 per cent. of chromium is rust-proof.

Stalactites are deposits of calcium carbonate formed on the roofs and sides of limestone caves, and in tunnels, under bridges, and other places where the carbonic acid of rain-water percolates through and partly dissolves the limestone, resulting in the growth of icicle-like forms that often assume groupings. The water that drops from these may deposit further calcium carbonate, which accumulates and hardens into a series of sharp mounds or hillocks called stalagmites.

Standard Deviation. In statistics it is often desirable to compare the variability or "spread" of different sets of data. For example, two kinds of light bulb could have the same average life but one kind could be more uniform or consistent than the other. The standard deviation is one of the commonest measures of spread. It is found as follows. If x is one of the data and $\bar{x}$ is the mean of all the x's, then $x - \bar{x}$ is called the deviation. Every deviation is now squared and the average squared deviation calculated. The standard deviation is then the square root of the average squared deviation. The lifetimes of the more uniform kind of light bulb would have a smaller standard deviation than those of the more erratic one.

Starch is an organic compound occurring in granules in nearly all green plants, and especially in the seeds of dicotyledonous and cereal plants, potatoes, etc. In its pure form starch is a tasteless, odourless white powder, and is a carbohydrate consisting of carbon, hydrogen, and oxygen.

Star Chamber, an ancient tribunal of state in existence in 1487 and possibly earlier, charged with the duty of trying offences against the government, unfettered by the ordinary rules of law. It was in effect a Privy Council entrusted with judicial functions. Under Charles I the Star Chamber was used by the King and his party to persecute opponents; and in 1641 a Bill carried in both Houses abolished it.

Starling (*Sturnus vulagris*), a well-known European bird now common in many parts of the world. It has handsome iridescent blackish plumage and nests in holes and crevices. Flocks of starlings are often seen wheeling in the air; thousands roost on buildings in the heart of London. Other European species are the Spotless and Rose-coloured starlings. The latter sometimes wanders to the British Isles.

States-General, national assembly in which the chief estates of the realm were represented as separate bodies. The name, though not the institution, has survived in the Netherlands, where the two houses of parliament are known as states-general. In France the states-general consisted of three orders, clergy, nobility and commons. Philip IV first summoned it in 1302 to support him in his quarrel with Pope Boniface VIII. While absolute monarchy was establishing itself it met rarely, and not at all from 1614 until 1789, when it was convoked as a last resort by Louis XVI. But when it met it declared itself the National Assembly which marked the beginning of the revolution.

Statistics is a science that deals with the collection of numerical facts and the evaluation of their significance. The word is also used to refer to the facts themselves as in "trade statistics". This important science gives precise meanings to words like "average" and to statements like "this set of data is significantly different from that". In a world in which more and more information is becoming available in numerical form (I.Q.s, examination results, tax yields, health records, road accidents, etc.) the proper—as opposed to the misleading—use of statistics cannot be over-emphasised. Many young people can now study statistics at school and college, and governments and industries employ many statisticians. *See* Average.

Statute of Westminster 1931. An Act of parliament which gave a basis of equality to the British Dominions. The Dominions as well as the United Kingdom were defined by the Balfour Memorandum of 1926 as "autonomous communities within the British Empire, equal in status, in no way subordinate one to another in any aspect of their domestic or external affairs, though united by a common allegiance to the Crown, and freely associated as members of the British Commonwealth of Nations". The Statute was the sequel. The Dominions are sovereign States governed solely by their own Parliaments and Governments. *See* K184.

Steam Engine, a machine whereby steam becomes the active agent of the working of machinery, and of very wide application. The leading types of steam engine are: (*a*) condensing, or low-pressure engines, where the steam is generated by a boiler; (*b*) non-condensing, in which the cylinder exhausts its steam into the open air. Engines of the latter type are used where portable engines are required.

Steam-hammer, invented (1839) by the Scottish engineer James Nasmyth. Consists basically of a vertical steam cylinder atop two legs with piston-rod passing through cylinder base and attached to a tup (hammer) of from 100 kg to 15 tonnes which rests on an anvil. The tup slides in V grooves on inside of legs. Length of stroke and therefore weight of blow can be accurately controlled from a light tap to a massive punch. It made possible the forging in one piece of multi-throw crankshafts for marine engines, etc. and the mass production of high-class axles and wheels, con rods and buffers, etc. for locomotives and rolling stock.

Stearin is the portion of fatty matters and oils which remains solid at an ordinary temperature, and is a compound of stearic acid with glycerine. It is largely used in the manufacture of candles. With caustic soda stearin forms a soap (sodium stearate), which is present in most commercial soaps which contain sodium palmitate and oleate in addition.

Steel, an alloy of iron and carbon, with varying proportions of other minerals. The famous blades of Damascus and steels of Toledo were made by the cementation and crucible method. The metal produced by the "Bessemer process" (*q.v.*) is of the highest value for structural purposes, rails, etc. In recent years the technique known as continuous casting has been developed which bypasses some major steps in the conventional process of steel-making.

Stereophonic Broadcasting. A person having normal hearing is able to determine the direction from which a sound reaches him by virtue of the fact that he has two ears, and, therefore, the sound will reach one of them a fraction of a second before it reaches the other. This difference in arrival time allows the brain to calculate direction. It will, therefore, be apparent that if the same person listens to, say, an orchestral concert in a large hall he will be able to determine—even with his eyes shut—the approximate position of a particular instrument with respect to the rest of the orchestra. If, however, he listens at home to a broadcast of the same concert, then, due to the fact that he hears the music after it has been picked up by a single microphone located at one point and radiated over a single-channel transmission system, he will be unable to allocate a definite position to any instrument. The aim of stereophonic broadcasting or sound reproduction, therefore, is to restore the listener's ability to locate the position in space of the various sources of sound and to follow movement. To do this it is necessary to use two microphones in the studio—to simulate the two human ears—and to transmit their outputs, through two similar, but separate, chains of equipment, to two radio receivers and their two loudspeakers, which must be placed some distance apart, in the listener's home. The fundamental work on two-channel stereophony was done by the late A. D. Blumlein of E.M.I. Ltd., his original patent being dated 1931.

Stereotype, a metal cast taken from movable type which has been set up in the ordinary way. The first to introduce the process in practical form in this country was William Ged, of Edinburgh, who made stereotype plates in 1730. An impression of the type matter is first taken by means of a mould of prepared plaster of Paris or moistened sheets of specially prepared paper, and when molten stereo metal is poured upon the mould and allowed to cool and harden, the stereo plate is formed, and can be printed from as a solid block for some time.

Steroids. A class of structurally related compounds, based on a system of condensed rings of carbon and hydrogen, which are widely distributed in animals and plants. Included in the steroid family are sterols, found in all animal cells, vitamin D, sex hormones, bile acids and cortisone, a drug used in the treatment of rheumatic fever.

Stickleback, a family of small spiny-finned fish widely distributed in both fresh and salt water. Male constructs roofed nest held together by sticky secretion from glands near kidneys. Several females deposit eggs therein which he jealously guards until after young are hatched.

Stirrup, a loop of metal U-shaped strap suspended from the sides of the saddle, used for mounting and to support the horesman's foot. Some authorities allege their use as far back as the early Iron Age, and it is generally believed that they were used in battle in A.D. 378, when the Gothic cavalry defeated the legionaries of the Emperor Valens at Adrianople. Stirrups relieved the tension of the rider's knees and so enabled him to be armed from top to toe.

Stoat, a slender, carnivorous mammal with short legs, related to the weasels. The stoat is distinguished from the latter by its longer tail, which has a black tip. The black tip is retained even in the winter when the animal turns white, the fur then being known as "ermine". It is found in northern latitudes, and is abundant in Arctic America.

Stoma (pl. stomata), microscopic pores on the surfaces of leaves through which gaseous exchanges take place and water is lost. It has been estimated that a single maize plant bears 200 million stomata, usually closed at night.

Stone-Flies, comprise the order of insects called *Plecoptera*, which includes some 700 species, of which about thirty occur in Britain. The wings are membranous, and two long, thread-like feelers protrude at the tail end. The larvae are aquatic.

Stonehenge, a remarkable collection of Bronze Age monuments arranged in two circles, 104 m in diameter, standing on Salisbury Plain, Wiltshire. Modern archaeological research dates origin back to between 2100 and 1600 B.C. There is some evidence to suggest that the monument may have been built for astronomical purposes, providing a method of keeping a calendar for predicting the seasons and foretelling eclipses of sun and moon.

Stork, a family of heron-like birds with long bills, freely distributed over Europe, Asia, Africa and S. America. The White Stork is an occasional visitor to England, and, more rarely, the Black Stork: these are the only two European storks.

Stratosphere, a layer of the earth's atmosphere, which begins 10–11 km above the earth. The attraction of the stratosphere as a medium for air travel rests upon the absence of storms; indeed weather phenomena as commonly understood do not occur, there being no vertical temperature gradient in the stratosphere and no convection currents.

Stratum (pl. strata), a bed or layer of rock.

Strontium. This silver-white metallic element was discovered by Hope and Klaproth in 1793, and isolated by Sir Humphry Davy in 1808. The chief strontium minerals are celestite (sulphate) and strontianite (carbonate). Compounds of strontium give a brilliant colour to fireworks and signal flares. Radioactive isotopes of strontium (strontium-90) are formed as fission products in nuclear explosions and tend to collect in bone on account of the chemical similarity of strontium and calcium (*q.v.*). This genetic hazard is a cause of great alarm. *See* **Fall-out.**

Sturgeon, a large fish found in northern seas and rivers with five rows of bony plates along the back and sides and pointed mouth with four barbels. Caviare is prepared from sturgeon ova. The rights of the Crown to certain wild creatures, including sturgeon, caught off the coasts of Britain and held since the time of Edward II, were abolished in 1970.

Sublimation, when a solid substance is heated and turns into vapour without passing through the liquid stage and then condenses as a solid on a cold surface, it is said to "sublime" and the process is called "sublimation". Iodine behaves in this way, and sublimation is used as a method of purifying it.

Submarine, the first submarine, the *Nautilus*, was designed by Robert Fulton and tried out in the river Seine and in the sea off Brest in 1801. The idea was too revolutionary to find acceptance and it was not until electricity for under-water propulsion became available that the submarine underwent extensive development. Britain became interested about 1900 and the Germans developed it and made it into an instrument of warfare. The first voyage under the North Pole was made in 1958 by the American nuclear-powered submarine *Nautilus* (*q.v.*). The Royal Navy's nuclear submarine fleet includes 4 Polaris vessels—HMS *Resolution* (1968), *Renown* (1969), *Repulse* (1969), *Revenge* (1970), each armed with 16 missiles with thermonuclear warheads—and the 8 nuclear-powered Fleet submarines—*Dreadnought, Valiant, Warspite, Churchill, Conqueror, Swiftsure, Sovereign* and *Courageous*. Britain's nuclear strategic force is assigned to NATO.

Suez Canal, connecting the Mediterranean and the Red Sea, was built by the French engineer Ferdinand de Lesseps and opened in 1869. An Egyptian company, *Canal Maritime de Suez*, was formed in 1866 with a capital of 200 million francs. The British Government acquired 176,602 shares out of a total of 400,000 for £4 million (value 31 March 1956, £28,982,544). Under the Convention of 1888 all nations were granted freedom of navigation without discrimination in peace or war. The right was recognised by Egypt in the Anglo-Egyptian Agreement of 1954, under which Britain agreed to give up the Suez base. The Suez Canal Company was nationalised by the Egyptian Government without warning on 28 July 1956, since it has been widened and deepened and the average time of transit reduced. The waterway which had been barred to Israeli ships since the creation of the state of Israel in 1948, and to all shipping since the Middle East war of 1967, was reopened in 1975. Israeli civilian cargo ships are allowed through.

Suffragette, member of the Women's Suffrage Movement who in the early part of this century agitated to obtain the parliamentary vote. The movement ended in 1918, when women of 30 were given the vote. In 1928 a Bill was passed which granted equal suffrage to men and women. The leaders of the Women's Suffrage Movement were Mrs. Pankhurst and her two daughters, Sylvia and Dame Christabel, Mrs. Fawcett, Annie Kenney and others.

Sugar, to the chemist the term is a generic one covering a group of carbohydrates, including cane sugar (sucrose), glucose, fructose, and maltose. In ordinary parlance sugar means sucrose, which is obtained from the sugar cane, sugar beet or sugar maple.

Sulphur, an elementary, brittle, crystalline solid, symbol S, abounding in the vicinity of volcanoes. It is yellow in colour. It occurs in combination with other elements, as sulphates and sulphides, and allied with oxygen, hydrogen, chlorine, etc., is of great commercial utility. Used in its pure state it constitutes the inflammable element in gunpowder; it is also used for matches and for making sulphuric acid.

Sulphuric Acid, a compound of great commercial importance, used in a variety of manufactures, and composed of sulphur, oxygen and hydrogen. Extremely corrosive.

Sun, one of the millions of stars in the universe, the centre of the solar system, estimated to have a mean distance from the earth of 93 million miles ($149{\cdot}6 \times 10^6$ km), a diameter of 865,000 miles ($1{\cdot}39 \times 10^6$ km), and a volume a million times that of the earth. The gravitational force on the sun is almost 28 times that of the earth, *i.e.*, a body would weigh 28 times its weight on earth. It rotates on its axis from east to west, though not as a solid, the solar equator turning once in about 25½ days and the poles in about 34 days. Large spots are observed on the sun which form and disappear at irregular intervals. The area of the disc covered by the spots, however, reaches a maximum roughly every 11 years, when the sun's heat seems rather greater than usual and magnetic storms more frequent (sunspot cycle). Spectrum analysis shows that the sun is composed of many elements found in the earth. Its surface temperature is about 6,000°C. Observations made in 1964–65 (Year of the Quiet Sun) complemented those obtained during the International Geophysical Year 1957–58, when the sun was remarkably active. The earth is in the outer atmosphere of the sun and subject to its winds and storms. The apparently inexhaustible heat of the sun, which has maintained life on the earth for millions of years, is derived from the destruction of matter, involved in the transmutation of hydrogen nuclei into helium nuclei, in which process about four million tonnes of matter are destroyed every second. At this rate of conversion the sun will go on radiating for 30,000 million years. The Soviet space rocket *Lunik I*, fired on 2 January 1959, became the first artificial planet of the sun. *See also* **F7.**

Superconductor, a metal in a state in which its electrical resistance has entirely vanished so that electric currents can flow indefinitely without generating heat or decreasing in strength. The superconducting state of metals was first discovered in mercury by Onnes in Leiden in 1911. There are many magnetic and thermal properties associated with superconductivity and the phenomenon as a whole has proved to be of great scientific interest; it resisted explanation till about 1957. In the meantime many metals and alloys were found to show the property but only at very low temperatures—below *c.*−260°C. There is a growing number of practical applications, *e.g.*, coils of superconducting wire (kept very cold by liquid helium) can be made to carry enough electric current to produce strong magnetic fields. Such fields are very constant and do not require the large supply of electrical power that ordinary electromagnets need.

Supersonic Speed, a speed greater than the speed of sound (in air at sea-level sound waves travel at about 1223 km/h). When a body travels at a speed which is greater than the speed at which disturbances themselves can travel, a mechanism exists for the generation of waves of enhanced intensity. Thus aircraft travelling at supersonic speeds produce shock waves in the air somewhat analogous to the bow waves of fast-moving ships. These shock waves are regions of intensely disturbed air which produce the sonic boom effect so distressing to people living near supersonic routes. *Supersonic* is not to be confused with *ultrasonic* (*q.v.*).

Surface Tension. The surfaces of fluids behave in some respects as though they were covered by a stretched elastic membrane. This property is called "surface tension". The action of detergents may be attributed in part to a reduction in the surface tension of water, allowing it to wet the surface of dirty articles.

Surrealism. The aim of the Surrealist school of painting and sculpture is to overcome the barriers between conscious and unconscious mind, the real and unreal worlds of waking and dreaming. As such it has a long and respectable ancestry, although the term was not in use until 1922 when it was picked by André Breton from Guillaume Apollinaire who had used it in connection with certain works by Chagall. However, Bosch in the 15th cent., Fuseli and Goya in the 18th, and many other purveyors of the weird and fantastic were the forerunners of modern Surrealism. The modern movement has broadly speaking taken two different directions: the first was towards complete fantasy and absurdity which took the form of "found objects"—*e.g.* a bird-cage filled with sugar-cubes and a thermometer, a bottle-dryer, a bicycle wheel, or abstract works with strange and apparently irrelevant titles such as Paul Klee's *Twittering Machine*; the second towards highly detailed and realistic paintings of objects placed in strange juxtapositions—*e.g.*, Salvador Dali's trees with limp watches drooping over their branches or Georgio de Chirico's deserted and classical-looking streets with long arcaded perspectives and a lone statue or a bunch of bananas in the foreground. On the whole Surrealism has spent its initial force and become almost respectable; its idea of strange juxtapositions, now widely commercialised, finds a place in advertisement illustrations and in the more sophisticated forms of window-dressing.

Swans, large, graceful birds which together with the ducks and geese form the family Anatidae. There are three European species with white plumage; the Mute Swan distinguished by its orange bill with black knob (less prominent in female), a familiar sight on the rivers and ornamental lakes of this country. Two wild swans are winter visitors here, the Whooper and Bewick's Swan. The "pen" (female) and "cob" (male) mate for life and the young swans are called "cygnets."

Swan-upping. The annual marking of the Thames swans which takes place during the third week of July. This ancient ceremony dates back to the 15th cent. when all the Thames swans were declared to be Royal birds owned by the Crown. Two city guilds—the Vintners' and Dyers' Companies—own one third of the 600 swans now on the Thames. This privilege was granted to them by King Edward IV in return for money grants. Vintners' birds are marked with a nick on each side of the bill, the Dyers' with a nick on the right side only. The Queen's birds are unmarked.

Sweet Potato. This plant (*Ipomoea batatas*), which is a climbing perennial belonging to the convolvulus family, has thick roots that are rich in starch, and are eaten like potatoes. A native of the W. Indies and Central America, new varieties of sweet potato have been bred which stand cooler climates and can be grown as far north as Cape Cod. The sweet potato of New Zealand is called the Kumara.

Swift, a bird so-called from the extreme speed of its flight, resembling a swallow but related to the humming-bird. It has long, scythe-like wings, sooty-black plumage and greyish-white chin. There are several species inhabiting most parts of the world, particularly the tropics. The British breeding bird is among the latest to return from Africa and the earliest to go. Swifts are the only birds to use saliva for their nests. One oriental species builds its nest entirely from saliva.

Sword, hand weapon of metal used in open combat, characterised by a longish blade. During the Middle Ages the most famous blades were those made by the Arabs at Damascus and those made at Toledo.

Symbiosis. When two organisms live together and both derive mutual benefit from the association, the partnership is known as symbiosis. An example is the symbiosis of an alga and a fungus in lichens; another is the ordinary pea plant and the bacteria which live in the nodules on the pea's roots.

Synapse is the point of association between one nerve cell and another. The nervous impulse travelling along one nerve has to be transmitted to the next across a minute gap. This is the synaptic gap. The mode of transmission is chemical though it was at first thought to be electrical. The impulse arriving at the synapse releases a chemical transmitter which diffuses across the gap and stimulates an impulse in the adjacent nerve cell. *See* Q5(2).

Syndicalism. *See* Section J.

Synod, an assembly of the clergy of a particular church, state, province, or diocese. The Synod of Whitby (664) settled the dispute between the Celtic and the Roman churches in the matter of Easter in favour of the Roman system of reckoning.

Synoptic Charts. These are meteorological charts used in forecasting on which weather conditions at a network of stations, at a standard hour of observation, are recorded, using symbols of the international weather code. Surface weather maps have been drawn regularly for more than a hundred years and the modern advance is the drawing of other maps showing conditions in the upper air. The plotting is done quickly by computer.

Synoptists. The writers of the first three Gospels whose narratives in the main agree, though Matthew and Luke add material not found in Mark (written first); all three differ from John's Gospel.

T

Tabard, a cloak or outer garment worn in mediaeval days by the peasantry. The name was also applied to a garment worn by knights over their armour.

Tailor-Bird, name of a small group of warblers, familiar in India and China, and remarkable for their habit of sewing leaves together to enclose their nests. The bill is used as needle, vegetable fibre as thread, and a knot is tied to prevent it slipping.

Taiping Rebellion, 1850–64, most famous of China's many peasant uprisings. It took place in Hunan (the province where Mao Tse-tung was born) and was savagely suppressed with the help of foreign powers.

Taj Mahal, the white marble mausoleum built at Agra by Shah Jehan in memory of his favourite wife who died 1629. Over 20,000 men were occupied for over 20 years in its erection.

Takahe or Notornis, large New Zealand bird of the rail family which for many years was believed to be extinct. Small colony found in 1948 in remote valley of mountainous part of the S. Island. The bird is strictly protected.

Take-over Bid describes an offer made to all the shareholders of a company to purchase their shares at a named price and conditional upon acceptance by the holders of a named proportion of the total share issue. If accepted the purchaser thus gains control of the company.

Tallage, in Norman times, were taxes levied by the Crown upon lands of the royal demesnes. The levying of tallage was taken away by a statute of 1340 which required the consent of Parliament for all direct taxes.

Tally Office, in the Exchequer, was the department of the Government in which tallies were kept, representing the acknowledgment of moneys paid or lent; in 1834 the Houses of Parliament were burnt down through the overheating of a stove with discarded Exchequer tallies.

Tambourine, a light, small, single-headed drum with loose metal discs let into the side of the hoop so that they jingle when the tambourine is shaken. An older name for it is the timbrel.

Tammany, an organisation founded in New York (c. 1786) and formed from a benevolent society named after an Indian chief. It came to exert a powerful influence over political movements in that city. The leaders of the organisation used their power when their party was successful at the polls to appoint their nominees to every prominent office, and exacted bribes for concessions and privileges, and generally Tammany rule has meant wholesale corruption. Of this there was ample evidence in the disclosures of the Tweed and other Tammany frauds, and in the fact that the "Boss" usually contrived to make himself wealthy.

Tannins are chemical substances obtained from a variety of plants and trees, from oak-bark, and from galls. They are used in the leather trade, the tanning process making the skins resistant to decay.

Tantalum, a scarce bluish metallic element, symbol Ta, discovered by Ekeberg in 1802. Chemically related to vanadium and niobium, it is usually associated with the latter in nature. For several purposes it can be used in place of platinum, and it finds application in the making of surgical instruments. Tantalum is very hard, and resistant to acids (other than hydrofluoric acid); it is used in alloys.

Taoism. *See* **Section J.**

Tapestry, a fabric largely used in former times for wall decoration and hangings. It was known to the ancient Greeks, but in its modern form came into prominence in the 15th and 16th cent., when it was manufactured in a marked degree of excellence by the weavers of Flanders, especially those of Arras. The manufacture was introduced into England early in the 17th cent., and was attended by considerable success. At the present day the term is applied to worsted cloths for furniture coverings, and there are also various kinds of tapestry carpets now made. The most famous tapestries of olden times were the Aubusson Tapestry and the Savonnerie. The Gobelin Tapestry factory, originated in Paris in the reign of Francis I, is still a national establishment. *See also* **Bayeux Tapestry.**

Tapirs. The tapirs constitute a family close to the horse family and the rhinoceros in the Ungulate order. They have four toes on the front feet and three on the hind. The snout is drawn out into a short trunk. The largest tapir is the Malayan tapir, which stands 1 m at the shoulder. Four species occur in Central and S. America.

Tar is a dark viscid product obtained from the destructive distillation of wood, coal, peat, etc. Wood tar is acid owing to the presence of acetic acid ("pyroligneous acid"). The highest proportion of coal tar goes into road making. Distillation of coal tar yields many valuable compounds, including benzene, phenol (carbolic acid), naphthalene and creosote; the final residue after distillation is pitch. Based on the chemical manipulation of compounds from coal tar is the preparation of many perfumes, food essences, drugs, antiseptics and plastics.

Tarpeian Rock at Rome received its name from the tradition that Tarpeia, the daughter of the Governor of the Citadel who betrayed the fortress to the Sabines, was crushed to death by their shields and buried beneath the rock. From this height persons guilty of treason were hurled to death.

Tartaric Acid is prepared from tartar (potassium hydrogen tartrate) deposited in wine vats during fermentation. "Cream of tartar" is purified potassium hydrogen tartrate, which is incorporated in baking powder. Tartaric acid is also used in the manufacture of effervescent salts.

Tate Gallery, named after its founder, Sir Henry Tate, at Millbank, S.W., was opened in 1897; Sir Henry Tate bore the cost of the building (£80,000) and also contributed the nucleus of the present collection. "The Turner Wing", the gift of Sir Joseph Duveen, was added in 1910. The collection is thoroughly representative of British art and has been extended several times to include modern foreign art.

Tay Bridge spans the Tay at Dundee, opened for rail traffic on 20 June 1887. A previous bridge, completed in 1877, was blown down on 28 December 1879, as a train was passing over it. A new bridge was opened on 18 August 1966 for road traffic, 2,244 m in length, the longest road bridge in Britain.

Tea was introduced into England about the middle of the 17th cent., when it was a great luxury, and fetched from £6 to £10 a pound. It is an Asiatic plant, native properly to China, Japan and India. Up to about 1885 most of the tea imported into this country came from China; the bulk now comes from India and Sri Lanka.

Teal, the smallest of the European ducks and next to the Mallard the commonest British species. It is a handsome bird and a very swift flier, but not as swift as the Garganey or Summer Teal.

Telecommunications. The sending of messages over a distance. The term is generally applied to the sending of messages by telegraph, telephone, radio, television or radar. The first submarine telegraph cable between England and France was laid in 1850 and, following Hertz's investigations into electric waves, Marconi's invention led to Britain being linked with Europe by wireless telegraphy in 1899. The first permanently successful telegraph cable across the Atlantic was laid in 1866. The first telephone service between London and Paris was opened in 1891. The electro-magnetic telephone was invented by Alexander Graham Bell, a Scottish-born American, in 1876. The first submarine telephone cable to span the Atlantic was laid in 1956 connecting Britain with Canada and the United States, and many submarine telephone cables have since been laid, including the Commonwealth cable system completed in 1967. The spectacular advances in space research depended on the new tools of work provided by parallel developments in telecommunications, *e.g.*, long-range radio and television transmission, electronic computer control. The performance of *Telstar* in July 1962 and of *Early Bird* in April 1965 showed that intercontinental communication by satellites in space was practical. *See also* **Radar, Radio, Television.**

Telemetry, measurement at remote distances by means of a radio-link from the object (missile or satellite) to the ground. The third Russian sputnik, for instance, carried apparatus for measuring, among other things, the pressure and composition of the atmosphere, and the intensity of different kinds of radiation from the sun. Its radio transmitter, powered by solar-energy batteries, sent out the information in coded form by means of uninterrupted signals at 20·005 megacycles with a duration of 150–300 milli-seconds. Radio telemetry from inside the body is being increasingly used in medical and biological research; miniature radio transmitters can be swallowed or implanted in man or animal to detect physiological conditions.

Telepathy and Clairvoyance. *See* **Section J.**

Teleprinter, a telegraph transmitter with a typewriter keyboard, by which characters of a message are transmitted electrically in combinations of 5 units, being recorded similarly by the receiving instrument, which then translates the matter mechanically into printed characters. The telex or public teleprinter service provides direct person-to-person transmission of written messages.

Telescope, an optical instrument for viewing objects at a distance, "the astronomer's intelligencer". Lippershey is credited with construction of the first in 1608; Galileo constructed several from 1609 and Newton was the first to construct a reflecting telescope. The ordinary telescope consists of an object-glass and an eye-lens, with two intermediates to bring the object into an erect position. A lens brings it near to us, and the magnifier enlarges it for inspection. A refracting telescope gathers the rays together near the eye-piece and is necessarily limited as to size, but the reflecting telescope collects the rays on a larger mirror, and these are thrown back to the eye-piece. The world's largest reflectors are at Mount Semirodriki, Caucasus (600 cm), Mount Palomar, California (508 cm), Mount Wilson, California (254 cm), the McDonald Observatory at Mount Locke, Texas (208 cm), and the Victoria B.C. Observatory (183 cm). The *Hale* 508 cm telescope at Mount Palomar has revealed objects never before photographed; it is able to probe space and photograph remote galaxies out to a limiting distance of 2,000 million light years. The *Schmidt* telescope at Mount Palomar has been used to make a huge photographic map of the universe. There are plans to move the 249 cm *Isaac Newton* telescope at the Royal Observatory at Herstmonceux, Sussex, to the Canary I. of La Palma. The giant steerable radio telescope built by Manchester University at Jodrell Bank, Cheshire, has a 76 m reflector with a beam width of 12 minutes of arc. Early in its career it tracked the Russian earth satellites and the American lunar probes. Another instrument of radio astronomy is the interferometer which consists of spaced aerials. Recently the technique of linking radio telescopes on different continents has been developed for fine observation. *See also* **F3, Astronomy.**

Television, or the transmission of images of moving objects by radio. To understand the problems of television it is necessary to consider the action of the human eye. Basically the eye consists of a lens which projects an image of the scene before it upon the retina, a light-sensitive screen at the back of the eye. The retina is made up of several millions of tiny light-sensitive elements, each quite separate and distinct from its neighbours, and each separately connected to the brain by an individual fibre in the optic nerve. Thus the eye is a very complex organ, and it is able to pick out numbers of tiny details from a scene and convey each detail separately and simultaneously to the brain. It does not send a blend of different points of light and shade in the same way that the ear sends a blend of different sounds; if it did the brain would receive a completely unintelligible blur. From this it is clear that a television system which transmitted a mixture of detail would be useless; it must transmit all the details in a scene separately, yet almost simultaneously, and re-assemble them at such a speed that the eye cannot observe the building-up process. A means of doing this was provided by Nipkow in 1884, when he invented his famous scanning disc, and later Weiller invented the mirror drum for the same purpose. Such mechanical devices as these held the field for many years and in 1923 Baird in this country and Jenkins in America were both using them for the experiments which, in 1925, led to the successful transmission of shadows and simple outlines. It was not until 1926, however, that the first practical demonstration of television, as we understand it, took place when Baird transmitted by radio moving pictures of living human faces over a short distance. The B.B.C. began television broadcasts in 1930; the I.T.A. in 1955. The first television exchange across the Atlantic was made in July 1962 by way of the *Telstar* satellite.

Tellurium, a relatively scarce element, symbol Te, discovered in 1782 by Reichenstein. Chemically it behaves rather like sulphur; its salts are known as tellurides. It occurs chiefly combined with metals in ores of gold, silver, copper and lead. It is a semiconductor and some of its compounds (also semiconductors) are coming into use in technical devices.

Templars were soldier knights organised in the 12th cent. for the purpose of protecting pilgrims in their journeyings to and from Jerusalem, and obtained their name from having had granted to them by Baldwin II a temple for their accommodation. At first they were non-military, and wore neither crests nor helmets, but a long wide mantle and a red cross on the left shoulder. They were established in England about 1180. During the crusades they rendered valuable service, showing great bravery and devotion. In the 12th cent. they founded numerous religious houses in various parts of Europe and became possessed of considerable wealth. It was this that caused their downfall. Kings and Popes alike grew jealous of their influence, and they were subjected to much persecution, and Pope Clement V abolished the Order in 1312. Edward II in 1308 seized all the property of the English Templars. The English possessions of the Order were transferred to the Hospitallers of St. John, afterwards called the Knights of Malta. *See also* **Hospitallers, Knights, Teutonic Order.**

Temple, a building dedicated to the worship of a deity or deities. Those built by the ancient Greeks at Olympia, Athens and Delphi were the most famous. The Temple of Diana at Ephesus was another. The Temple of Solomon at Jerusalem was destroyed and rebuilt several times; Herod's Temple was destroyed by the Romans in A.D. 70.

Temple Bar, an historic gateway (designed by Sir Christopher Wren in 1672) that until 1877 stood at the junction of the Strand and Fleet Street, London, dividing the City from Westminster. It was re-erected at the entrance to Theobald's Park, near Cheshunt, Herts., in 1888.

Terbium, an element, symbol Tb, discovered in 1842 by Mosander, belonging to the group of rare-earth metals.

Teredo, the scientific name of the ship-worm, a peculiar bivalve mollusc, which lodges itself when young on the bottoms of wooden ships and bores its way inwards, causing much injury.

Termites, also known as *White Ants*, though they are not related to the true ants and are placed in an entirely different insect order (*Isoptera*). They abound in the tropics and also occur in temperate countries, though only two species are common in Europe. There is no British species. They live in colonies and their nests take the form of mounds of earth and wood, cemented together with saliva, and up to 6 m in height. Five separate castes are recognised, three of them being capable of reproduction, and the other two are sterile.

Tern. This slender, gull-like bird has long pointed wings, a deeply-forked tail, pale grey and white plumage, black cap, and is a very graceful flier. There are several species, some of which are summer migrants to Britain. The Arctic tern winters in the Antarctic, returning to find a nesting place in the spring.

Terrapin, a kind of fresh-water tortoise. There are several species widely distributed in the Northern Hemisphere.

Tertiary Rocks, in geology the rocks formed during the Caenozoic era comprising the Eocene, Oligocene, Miocene and Pliocene periods. *See* **F45.**

Teutonic Order, of German military knights, was founded in the Holy Land at the end of the 12th cent. for succouring the wounded of the Christian army before Acre. They were dispersed in the 15th cent. but the Order continued to exist until 1809, when Napoleon I confiscated its properties. In 1840 the order was resuscitated in Austria as a semi-religious knighthood. *See also* **Hospitallers, Knights, Templars.**

Textured Vegetable Protein, often referred to as TVP, is an edible protein material given a fibrous texture in the course of its manufacture from agricultural products. Nutritionally the material resembles meat and the extent to which it also resembles meat in succulence, flavour, feel in the mouth, suitability for chewing, etc. depends on the sophistication of the manufacturing technique and on the skill of the cook. The common starting material is the soya bean which is rich in protein and oil. The latter is removed, also for use in the food industry, and the residue is further processed to concentrate the protein and to remove unwanted flavours. A paste of suitable consistency is then forced under pressure through small holes and solidified as fibres. Bound together with a suitable binder and appropriately flavoured, these fibres form a lump of protein substance analagous to meat. TVP is widely produced, available commercially and used domestically and in the catering industry. Meat products containing it must show it in the list of ingredients.

Thallium, a blue-grey metallic element, symbol Tl, discovered by Crookes in 1861. It is obtained from the flue dust resulting from the burning of pyrites for sulphuric acid manufacture.

Thanksgiving Day, a national holiday in the United States, observed on the fourth Thursday in November: instituted by the Pilgrim Fathers in 1621 to celebrate their first successful harvest.

Theodolite. The instrument used by surveyors for measuring angles in the horizontal and vertical planes; also used in meteorology for following balloons to measure the speed and direction of wind.

Therm. The charges for gas for lighting and heating (formerly reckoned at per cubic foot) are now based on the calorific, or heat, value of the gas, and the unit used is termed a therm. The therm is 100,000 British thermal units.

Thermionic Emission is the departure of charged particles from matter under the influence of heat. The higher the temperature the greater the flow of escaping particles. The most common example is the emission of electrons from red-hot electrodes—this is the basic phenomenon made use of in thermionic valves (*see* **Valve**). If the hot electrode (the cathode) is enclosed in an evacuated or gas-filled bulb, the emitted electrons can be collected at another electrode (the anode) and will flow through an external circuit back to the emitter. Thus an electric current has been generated by heat.

Thermodynamics, a term first applied by Joule to designate that branch of physical science which treats of the relations of heat to work. What is called the first law of thermodynamics is thus stated by Clerk Maxwell: " When work is transformed into heat, or heat into work, the quantity of work is mechanically equivalent to the quantity of heat." In one of its many formulations, the second law asserts that " the heat tends to flow from a body of hotter temperature to one that is colder, and will not naturally flow in any other way". *See* **F17(1).**

Thermo-electric Devices. If two wires of different materials are formed into a loop and if the two joins are kept at different temperatures a current flows in the loop. This was discovered by Seebeck in 1822, and the device is called a thermocouple. The electric current could in principle be made to drive some useful machine, and the energy comes from the heat that is absorbed by the thermocouple—if one part of the thermocouple is not hotter than the others it will not work. It has long been realised that this is a device that converts heat directly into electricity without raising steam and driving dynamos as in a power-station. However, until recently nobody has used thermocouples for much besides temperature measurement, for which they are exceedingly useful. The new development is the manufacture of semiconductors (*q.v.*); for the thermoelectric effects of these new materials are much greater than those of metals. A material much studied in this connection is a compound of bismuth and tellurium, bismuth telluride. It now seems practicable to generate useful electricity from suitably designed thermocouples. For example, the USSR produces a thermoelectric device which uses the heat from the chimney of a domestic oil-lamp to produce enough electricity to work a radio. Presumably this is very useful in remote parts with no electricity supply. But the possibilities do not stop there. Indeed, an eminent Russian authority has stated that thermocouples could produce electricity direct from the warmth of sunlight on a scale and at a cost comparable with conventional fuel-burning power-stations. Even if solar energy cannot be so used, it might be possible to use the heat of nuclear reactors, but this means that the thermoelectric devices would have to stand up to very heavy radioactivity and still work. It is not surprising, however, that many firms are showing great interest in thermoelectricity these days.

Thermometer, an instrument by which the temperature of bodies is ascertained. The most familiar kind of thermometer consists of a glass tube with a very small bore, containing, in general, mercury or alcohol. This expands or contracts with variation in the temperature, and the length of the thread of mercury or alcohol gives the temperature reading on a scale graduated in degrees. Various forms of thermometer are used for particular purposes. *See* **Thermometer Comparisons, Section N.**

Thermonuclear Reactions. *See* **Nuclear Fusion.**

Thirty-nine Articles. *See* **Articles.**

Thistle, Order of. *See* **Knighthood.**

Thorium, a scarce, dark grey, metal element, symbol Th, discovered by Berzelius in 1828. All substances containing thorium are radioactive. Chief source of thorium is monazite sand, big deposits of which occur in Travancore (India), Brazil and the USA. Considered important as a potential source of atomic energy since the discovery that it can be transmuted into U^{233}, which is capable of fission like U^{235}.

Thrush, a large family of song-birds of the *Passeriform* order, distributed all over the world. The British species include the robin, redstart, nightingale, song-thrush (or mavis), blackbird, mistle-thrush, ring-ouzel of the mountains and large numbers of migrant fieldfares and redwings from northern Europe are winter visitors.

Thunder, the sound heard after the occurrence of a lightning flash. It is due to vibrations of the air along the path of the flash, which are set up by the sudden heating (and expansion) followed by the rapid cooling (and contraction) to which the air is subjected. It is unusual for thunder to be heard more than 16 km away, the distance being estimated roughly by allowing 1 km for every 3 seconds which elapse between seeing the flash and hearing the thunder. Continued rolling of thunder results from the zig-zag nature of the flash and the multiple strokes of which it is composed, variations in the energy developed along the path, and echo effects. Thunderstorms are caused by powerful rising currents of air within towering cumulonimbus clouds and are most frequent during the afternoons and evenings of sunny summer days.

Thursday, the 5th day of the week, named after Thor, the Scandinavian deity. To the ancient Romans Thursday was *dies Jovis*, or Jupiter's day.

Tidal Power. The principle of exploiting the energy of the tides is similar to hydro-power since it involves the harnessing of falling water. A barrage across a bay or estuary is filled during flow tide and closed during ebb tide creating a difference in level. When the water is allowed to fall towards the lower side of the barrage it operates a turbine which drives a generator. More sophisticated schemes would incorporate pumped storage facilities. An essential requirement is a large tidal range in order to get a sufficient head of water. Although a 240MW scheme has recently been completed on the River Rance in France, it is believed that the economics of tidal power are generally insufficiently favourable for the method to be widely used. *See also* **Hydroelectric Schemes and Severn Barrage.**

Tides, the periodical rise and fall of the waters of the ocean and its arms, are due to the gravitational effect of the moon and sun. Newton was the first to give a general explanation of the phenomenon of the tides. He supposed the ocean to cover the whole earth and to assume at each instant a figure of equilibrium, under the combined gravitational influence of earth, sun and moon, thus making and controlling the tides. At most places there are two tides a day, and the times of high- and low-water vary according to the positions of the sun and moon relative to the earth. When earth, moon and sun are in line (at full moon and new moon) the gravitational pull is greatest and we get "spring" tides. When sun and moon are at right angles (first and third quarters of the moon's phases) we get the smaller "neap" tides.

Tiers Etat, the lowest of the three estates of the realm as reckoned in France—nobility, clergy and commons (*tiers état*)—prior to the Revolution.

Tiger, a powerful carnivorous animal of the cat family, which occurs in India and certain other parts of Asia. Its skin is of a tawny yellow, relieved by black stripings of great beauty of formation. Some tigers attain a length of from 3 to 3·6 m.

Time. The measurement of time has become of increasing importance to man with the advance of civilisation. It was at first almost inevitably based on the succession of night and day, the waxing and the waning of the moon, and on the changing seasons of the year, and the astronomical observation of these three periodic effects has served as the basis of time measurement until recent years. The precision of the observations has continually increased, and clocks have been developed for dividing the day into smaller units. The clocks were adjusted so as to keep in step with the rotation of the earth on its axis, but during recent years an atomic standard of time has been developed, and clocks are now adjusted so as to keep in step with the natural period of an atomic vibration. *See* **Clocks, Greenwich Mean Time, British Standard Time.**

Tin is a white, metal element, symbol Sn (Latin *Stannum*), whose commonest ore is cassiterite (tin oxide), which occurs in Malaya, Indonesia, Bolivia, Zaïre, Nigeria and Cornwall. It protects iron from rusting, and the tin coating on tinplate is applied by dipping the thin steel sheet in molten tin or by electrolysis. Tin alloys of importance include solder, bronze, pewter and Britannia metal.

Tit *or* **Titmouse,** a small insectivorous bird of the woodlands and forests, bright of plumage and very active and agile, often seen hanging upside down searching for food. There are over fifty species, eight of which occur in Britain: the Great and Blue Tits, familiar in gardens and countryside, the Cole Tit, Marsh Tit, Willow Tit, Bearded Tit, Long-tailed or "Bottle" Tit and the Scottish Crested Tit.

Titanium, a scarce metal, symbol Ti, difficult to extract from ores, found in association with oxygen in rutile, anatase and brookite, as well as with certain magnetic iron ores. It combines with nitrogen at a high temperature. Discovered by the Rev. William Gregor in 1791. Titanium alloys, being very resistant to stress and corrosion, and combining strength with lightness, are finding wide application not only in marine and chemical engineering but in the building of aircraft, rockets, and the nuclear-energy field. Titanium dioxide is now widely used in making paints.

Tithes, an ecclesiastical tax consisting of a tenth part of the annual produce known to the ancient Jews, and first imposed by Christian authorities in the 4th cent., although not made compulsory in England before the 9th cent. Tithes derived from land are termed " praedial ", those derived from cattle being styled " mixed ", while others are personal. After the passing of the Tithes' Commutation Act of 1836, tithes were gradually converted into rent charges, and today the old form of tithes exists only to a small degree. Consult Tithe Act of 1936.

TNT (Trinitrotoluene). A high explosive formed by the action of a mixture of nitric and sulphuric acids on toluene. Not highly sensitive to shock, it can be used in shells without danger, and is exploded by a time, or detonator, fuse. Apart from wartime applications, it is used in blasting in quarries and mines.

Toad, an amphibian, differing from the frog in having a dry, warty skin, a heavier, squat build and shorter limbs. It has a similar metamorphosis, is largely nocturnal, and will wander far from water after the breeding season. Two toads occur in Britain, the Common Toad and the Natterjack. The latter can be identified by the narrow light stripe running down the middle of the back.

Tobacco is made from the leaves of various narcotic plants of the *Nicotiana* family, which contain a volatile oil and an alkaloid called nicotine. Tobacco is largely grown in America, India, Japan, Turkey, Greece, Canada, Italy, Indonesia, Bulgaria, Philippines, France, Congo, China, Rhodesia, Zambia, S. Africa, S. America and other countries of a warm climate. It undergoes various processes of preparation. The leaves are first dried, then cut into small pieces, moistened and compressed, and in this form it is known as cut or " shag " tobacco; when moistened with syrup or treacle and pressed into cakes, it is Cavendish; when twisted into string form, it is " twist " or " pig-tail ". For cigars the midribs of the dry leaves are removed, and what is left is moistened and rolled into cylindrical shape. For snuff, the tobacco leaves are moistened and allowed to ferment, then dried, powdered and scented. *See* Section P (**Respiratory System**) for the connection between tobacco-smoking and lung cancer.

Tolls. Payments for privileges of passage were first exacted in respect of ships passing up rivers, tolls being demanded on the Elbe in 1109. Tolls for land passage are said to have originated in England in 1269, toll-bars being erected at certain distances on the high-roads in the 17th cent., where toll had to be paid for all vehicles passing to and fro. After about 1825 they began to disappear, but still linger on some country roads and bridges. Tolls on London river bridges ceased in 1878–79.

Tonic Sol-Fa, a system of musical notation in which monosyllables are substituted for notes. Thus the major diatonic scale is represented by Doh, Ray, Me, Fah, Soh, La, Te, Doh. The system was invented by a Miss Glover of Norwich in about 1840 and has proved of great assistance in the teaching of music in schools.

Tonsure, the shaven part of the head of a Roman Catholic ecclesiastic, dates from the 5th or 6th cent. In the Roman Catholic Churches only a circle, or a crown, is shaved, while in the Greek Church shaving is forbidden.

Topaz, a transparent mineral gem, being a silicate and fluoride of aluminium and generally found in granite rocks. Its colour is yellow, but it also occurs in pink and blue shades. The best kinds come from Brazil.

Topiary, the art of clipping and trimming trees, shrubs, etc., into ornamental shapes. In Britain this art goes back before Elizabethan times when gardens were formal and the shapes simple and symmetrical. By the end of Queen Anne's reign topiary had become much more elaborate, and all kinds of fanciful shapes were produced. Pliny in his *Letters* tells how box hedges were clipped into different shapes in Roman times.

Topology is a branch of mathematics which studies geometrical objects from the point of view of their general shape rather than their precise measurements. For example, from the point of view of topology a ring doughnut and a picture frame have the same shape because they both have one single hole through them. Topology is used, for example, to deduce geometrical facts about an irregularly shaped object such as the Earth from the geometry of a regular object such as a perfect sphere of the same general shape. In its more formal aspects topology is an important tool in other parts of mathematics.

Tornado, a violent whirlwind, characterised by a black, funnel-shaped cloud hanging from heavy cumulonimbus and travelling at speeds up to 60 km/h. Tornadoes vary in diameter from less than a metre to a kilometre and occur frequently in the Mississippi region of the USA, where it has been estimated that the circling winds of the vortex may reach a velocity of 600 km/h. In West Africa the term is applied to thundery squalls.

Tortoises and Turtles, are cold-blooded reptiles, four-footed and encased in a strong shell protection, the shells of some species being of beautifully horny substance and design, once in much demand for combs, spectacle frames and ornamental work. It is the custom to designate the land species as tortoises and the aquatic kinds as turtles. The green turtle, so called because its fat has a green tinge, is in great demand for soup. Together the tortoises and turtles make up the reptilian order called *Chelonia*, the biggest representatives of which are the giant land tortoises of the Galapagos Islands, reaching a weight of 225 kg and living a century. Some of these giant tortoises are even said to have reached 200 or 300 years of age.

Toucan, a South and Central American family of brilliantly coloured birds, remarkable for their huge bills. Toucans live on fruit, are of arboreal habits, and nest in holes. There are about 37 species.

Touchstone, a kind of jasper called by the ancients " Lydian stone ", of economic value in testing the quality of metal alloys, especially gold alloys. The testing process is very simple. The alloy is drawn across the broken surface of the Touchstone, and from the nature of the mark or streak it makes the quality of the alloy can be ascertained.

Tourmaline, a mineral occurring in different colours in prismatic crystals. It is a well-known example of a pyro-electric crystal, *i.e.*, one that has a permanent electric polarisation. A double silicate of aluminium and boron, it occurs in Cornwall, Devon, S. America and Asia.

Tournaments were equestrian contests between military knights and others armed with lances, and frequent in the Middle Ages. The Normans introduced them to England.

Tower of London was built as a fortress by William the Conqueror. It was a royal palace in the Middle Ages and later used as a garrison and prison. Many distinguished prisoners were executed there, or on the neighbouring Tower Hill, including Anne Boleyn, Catherine Howard, Lady Jane Grey, the 2nd Earl of Essex, and the Duke of Monmouth. The Chapel Royal of St. Peter and Vincula in the Tower was built in 1105 and took its present shape in the reign of Henry VIII. The Crown Jewels are kept at the Tower, and in the Armoury a fine collection of armour is preserved. The attendant staff are called Yeomen Warders of the Tower. Their style of dress is of the Tudor period.

Trade-Mark, a mark used in relation to goods for the purpose of indicating a connection in the course of trade between the goods and some person having the right, either as a proprietor or registered user, to use the mark. Trade-marks can be registered, the registration holding good for 7 years and being renewable thereafter indefinitely for periods of 14 years. Infringement of a registered trade-mark renders the infringer liable to damages.

Trade Winds form part of the circulation of air round the great permanent anticyclones of the tropics and blow inwards from north-east (Northern Hemisphere) and south-east (Southern Hemisphere) towards the equatorial region of low pressure. Atlantic trades are more regular than those of the Pacific. The belts may extend over 2,400 km of latitude and, together with the Doldrums, move north and south in sympathy with the seasonal changes in the sun's declination, the average annual range being about 5 degrees of latitude.

Trafalgar, Battle of, was fought off Cape Trafalgar on 21 October 1805, between the British under Nelson and the French and Spanish under Villeneuve and Gravina. It was a complete victory for the British, but Nelson was killed.

Trafalgar Square. The site has often been referred to as the finest in Europe. It was conceived originally as a square by John Nash (1752–1835) when the project was considered of linking Whitehall with Bloomsbury and the British Museum. It was to be named after the new monarch as King William the Fourth's Square but on the suggestion of George Ledwell Taylor (a property owner near the site) alteration to the more popular name Trafalgar Square was agreed to by the King. On the north side the National Gallery was planned by Nash and erected by William Wilkins on the place of the Royal Mews—a work of William Kent a century before. The lay-out was the idea of Charles Barry but he did not approve the erection of the Nelson column (which see). His idea was for the square to have a grand flight of steps from the north side with sculptural figures of Wellington and Nelson but the Commons decided otherwise and the column as designed by William Railton was begun in 1840. The two fountains by Barry were supplanted in 1948 by ones designed (1938) by Sir Edwin Lutyens. Executed in Portland stone they are flanked by some bronze sculptures. In the same year memorial busts of Lords Jellicoe and Beatty were placed by the north wall.

Transept, the portion of a church which extends across the interior between the nave and the choir.

Transistor. An electronic device consisting of a small piece of semiconducting solid (usually germanium or silicon) to which contact is made at appropriate places by three wires. The three parts resemble in function (not construction or behaviour) the cathode, anode, and grid of a thermionic valve, and transistors can perform many of the operations that valves have hitherto been used for in radio, television, etc. They possess several advantages over valves since there is no need for evacuated glass bulbs nor for a heated emitter to give off electrons. This leads to much greater compactness and economy as well as to a much longer life. Nevertheless, there are certain limitations to their use, and they are not yet suitable as substitutes for valves in all cases. The device was invented by the Americans Bardeen, Brattain and Shockley in 1948.

Transubstantiation. *See* **Section J.**

Treasure-Trove, a legal term applying to treasure (coin, bullion, gold or silver articles) found hidden in the earth or other place, for which no owner can be discovered. The treasure legally belongs to the Crown, but it is the practice to return to the finder all articles not required for national museums and to reward him with the full market value of such as may be retained. It is the duty of the finder to report to the Coroner for the district in which the find is made who holds an inquest to find whether the discovery be treasure-trove or no. In England concealment is a criminal offence. *See also* **Wreck.**

Tree Frog, occurs most commonly in America and Australasia. The common European tree frog is a brilliant green animal, the adhesive discs at the tips of its fingers and toes enabling it to cling to trees, etc., with ease.

Tree Rings as Natural Calendar. The approximate relationship between radiocarbon dating (*q.v.*) and true calendar age for the past 7,000 years has been established from measurements on tree-rings. Because one tree-ring is formed annually and its thickness is characteristic of the climatic conditions during its growth, it is possible, by comparing distinctive groups of rings, to date a series of trees. By using the long-lived Bristle Cone pines, tree-rings dating back to 5000 B.C. have been obtained. It has been found that the radiocarbon age around, say, 3000 B.C. is too young by *c.* 600 years and because of short-term fluctuations near, say, 2000 B.C., a particular radiocarbon age can correspond to more than one true calendar age. These corrections are far less than those proved necessary after the publication of the first radiocarbon dates. Tree-rings (based on the measurement of deuterium in wood) can also show the pattern of temperature fluctuations over hundreds of years and thus make it possible to trace climatic changes before written records began.

Tree Shrew, an arboreal insectivorous mammal of Asia belonging to the family *Tupaiidae.* Tree shrews are related to the shrews, though in appearance they resemble squirrels except for their sharply pointed snout. They occur in Borneo, Thailand, China and Malaya. Some zoologists classify them as primitive primates.

Trent, Council of, the longest and one of the most important in the history of the Roman Catholic Church, was convened to combat the doctrines of Martin Luther. It first sat in 1545, the last sitting being in 1563. At this Council the general policy, principles and dogmas of the Roman Catholic Church were authoritatively settled.

Triassic *or* **Trias,** the earliest geological period in the Mesozoic era, which began some 225 million years ago. Triassic formations 7,600 m thick occur in the Alps. Modern insects were appearing, and also small reptile-like mammals. Other important Triassic animals were: dinosaurs, ichthyosaurs (marine reptiles), and pterosaurs (flying reptiles). *See* **F45.**

Tribunes, name assigned to officers of different descriptions in ancient Rome. The original tribunes were the commanders of contingents of cavalry and infantry. The most important tribunes were the tribunes of the plebs, first elected in 494 B.C. as the outcome of the struggle between the patrician and the plebeian orders. They held the power of veto and their persons were sacred.

Trichoptera. This is the insect order comprising the Caddis-flies. These are moth-like insects having hairs on the wings. They are usually found fluttering weakly near water. The larvae are aquatic and are remarkable for the cases (caddis cases) which they build out of sticks, small stones, sand grains, and shells.

Tricolour, the flag of the French Republic since 1789, consisting of three nearly equal vertical bands of blue, white and red (ratio 90 : 99 : 111).

Trilobites, extinct marine arthropods, most abundant in the Cambrian and Ordovician systems. Their appearance may be roughly described as resembling that of a woodlouse, and like that animal the trilobites were capable of rolling their bodies up into a ball.

Trinity. The Christian doctrine that God exists in three persons, all co-equal, and indivisible, of the same substance—God the Father, God the Son (who became incarnate as Jesus), begotten of the Father, and God the Holy Ghost, proceeding from Father and Son. The system denying the Trinity is Unitarianism. *See* **Section J.**

Trinity House, on Tower Hill, London, was incorporated in 1514 as an association for piloting ships, and has ever since been entrusted with various matters connected with the regulation of British navigation. Since 1854 the lighthouses of the country have been under its supervision. The acting Elder Brethren act as Nautical Assessors in Marine causes which are tried by the High Court of Justice.

Trireme, an ancient vessel with three rows of oars of great effectuality in early naval warfare. Mentioned by Thucydides. It was a long, narrow vessel propelled by 170 rowers. The Romans copied it from the Greeks.

Tritium, a radioactive isotope of hydrogen which has three times the weight of the ordinary hydrogen atom. It is produced by bombarding an isotope of lithium with neutrons and has a half-life of 12¼ years, decaying with the emission of β-particles (electrons).

Triumvirate, a term used to denote a coalition of three persons in the exercise of supreme authority. The first Roman triumvirate was that of Pompey, Julius Caesar, and Crassus, 60 B.C.; the second was that of Mark Antony, Octavus and Lepidus, 43 B.C.

Tropic-Bird, a long-tailed sea bird, of which there are 3 species (the Red-billed, the White-tailed, and the Red-tailed), frequenting the tropical regions of the Atlantic, Pacific and Indian oceans. They are commonly called Bo'sun Birds.

Troposphere. The atmospheric layer which extends from the earth's surface to the stratosphere. As a general rule the temperature in the troposphere falls as altitude increases. *See* **Atmosphere.**

Troubadours, lyric poets who flourished from the 11th to the end of the 13th cent., chiefly in Provence and the north of Italy. They were often knightly amateurs, and cultivated a lyrical poetry intricate in metre and rhyme and usually of a romantic amatory strain. They did much to cultivate the romantic sentiment in days when society was somewhat barbaric and helped considerably in the formation of those unwritten codes of honour which served to mitigate the rudeness of mediaeval days. *See also* **Jongleurs.**

Trouvère *or* **Trouveur**, mediaeval poet of northern France, whose compositions were of a more elaborate character—epics, romances, fables, and chansons de geste—than those of the troubadour of the south. Flourished between the 11th and 14th cent.

Truffles are subterranean edible fungi much esteemed for seasoning purposes. There are many species, and they are found in considerable quantities in France and Italy, less commonly in Britain. They are often met with under beach or oak trees, and prefer calcareous soils, but there are no positive indications on the surface to show where they are, and they are not to be cultivated. Hogs, and sometimes dogs, are used to scent them out, the former, by reason of their rooting propensities, being the most successful in the work.

Tsetse, an African dipterous fly belonging to the same family as the house-fly. It is a serious economic pest as it transmits the protozoon causing African sleeping sickness when it pierces human skin in order to suck blood, which forms its food. *See* **Gammexane.**

Tsunami, a seismic sea wave originating from any one of several submarine geological phenomena such as volcanic explosions, landslides or earth movements. Tsunamis are extremely long wavelength waves which travel in the open ocean at speeds up to 640 km/h. In deep water their height is only barely perceptible, but on reaching shallow coastal water they may attain heights of up to 30 m and can cause devastation to low-lying areas. The Pacific Ocean, whose rim is a seismically active area, is particularly susceptible to tsunamis. Following the damage caused by a tsunami which struck the volcanic islands of Hawaii on 1 April 1946, an early-warning system has been in operation. Tsunamis are often incorrectly referred to as tidal waves.

Tuatara or *Sphenodon punctatum*, a primitive lizard found in New Zealand. It has a rudimentary third eye on the top of the head; this is called the pineal eye and corresponds to tissue which in mammals forms the pineal gland.

Tube Foot, the characteristic organ of locomotion of starfishes and kindred animals. They are arranged in pairs along the underside of the arms, and their sucker-like ends can grip a surface very tightly. The action of the suckers depends on hydraulic pressure.

Tudor Period extends from 1485 to 1603. The first Tudor sovereign was Henry VII, descended from Owen Tudor; then followed Henry VIII, Edward VI, Mary and Elizabeth, the last of the line.

Tuesday, the third day of the week, named from the Saxon deity Tuisto, Tiw or Tuesco. To the Romans it was the day of Mars.

Tuileries, a French royal and imperial palace dating from 1564. It was attacked by insurgents during the outbreaks of 1792, 1830 and 1848, and was burned down during the Commune of Paris in 1871.

Tumulus, a mound of earth raised over the bodies of the dead. The mound of Marathon, enclosing the bodies of the Athenians who were killed in the famous battle with the Persians, is a celebrated tumulus. Such mounds were commonly raised over the tombs of the distinguished dead in ancient times, and sometimes enclosed heavy structures of masonry. The Roman " barrows " were tumuli. Evidences of such mounds are frequent in prehistoric remains.

Tuna *or* **Tunny**, a large marine fish belonging to the mackerel family, frequenting the warm waters of the Atlantic, Pacific and Mediterranean. Tuna fisheries are an important industry.

Tundra, the vast treeless plains lying in northern N. America and northern USSR where long severe winters and permanently frozen subsoils (permafrost) have resulted in specially adapted plant communities. The summer thaw and impervious permafrost cause waterlogging of lowland areas and marsh plants occur on these sites. In summer the ground cover of lichens and mosses with some flowering plants is distinctive. Stunted willows and birches occur in certain sites.

Tungsten, a hard, brittle metal, symbol W (it was formerly called wolfram), silver to grey in colour. Its chief ores are wolframite (iron and manganese tungstate) and scheelite (calcium tungstate). Tungsten is alloyed in steel for the manufacture of cutting tools; also in the non-ferrous alloy stellite (*q.v.*). Electric lamp filaments are made from tungsten. Tungsten carbide is one of the hardest substances known and is used for tipping tools.

Turbines propelled by steam provide power for the propulsion of many ships, and on land steam turbines are a principal source of power, being used in large central electricity stations, for instance, to convert heat energy into electrical energy. Gas turbines have recently come into use in aeroplanes, and gas-turbine railway locomotives are being developed. The first gas-turbine ship had its trials in 1947, just half a century after the first steam-turbine ship.

Turbot, a large flat fish, highly valued as food. It often attains from 13 to 18 kg in weight. Its flesh is white and firm. It is confined to European waters, and is caught by line or trawl.

Turkey, a fowl of American origin, brought to Europe from America soon after the discovery of that country. It was a domesticated bird in England in the first half of the 16th cent.

Turpentine, an oily substance obtained from coniferous trees, mostly pines and firs. It is widely used especially in making paints and varnishes, and also has medicinal properties.

Turquoise, formerly called Turkey-Stone, is a blue or greenish-blue precious stone, the earliest and best specimens of which came from Persia. It is composed of a phosphate of aluminium, with small proportions of copper and iron. India, Tibet, and Silesia yield turquoises, and a variety is found in New Mexico and Nevada. It derives its name from the fact that the first specimens were imported through Turkey.

Turtle Dove, a summer visitor from Africa to southern England. It is a small, slender bird with reddish-brown upper parts, pinkish throat, black tail with white edges, and a repeated purring note.

Tweed. A rough-surfaced fabric of the twilled type, usually all-wool, though cheaper kinds may include cotton. Of a soft, open, flexible texture, it may have a check, twill or herring-bone pattern. Harris, Lewis, Bannockburn and Donegal tweeds are well known. " Tweeds " is said to have been written in error by a clerk for " twill ".

Twelfth Night is the eve of the feast of the Epiphany, and in olden times was made the occasion of many festivities. It was the most popular festival next to Christmas, but is now little observed.

Twilight is the light which is reflected from the upper portion of the earth's atmosphere when the sun is below the horizon (before sunrise or after sunset). The term is most usually understood to refer, however, to the evening light; the morning light we call dawn. The twilight varies in duration in different countries, according to the position of the sun. In tropical countries it is short; in the extreme north it continues through the night.

Tyburn, a former small tributary of the Thames, which gave its name to the district where now stands the Marble Arch, Hyde Park. Here public executions formerly took place.

Tycoon, the title by which the commander-in-chief of the Japanese army (virtually the ruler of Japan) was formerly described by foreigners. (In Japanese *taikun* means great lord or prince.) The term is now applied, usually in a derogatory sense, to an influential business magnate.

Tympanum is, in architectural phraseology, the triangular space at the back of a pediment, or, indeed, any space in a similar position, as over window or between the lintel and the arch of a doorway. In ecclesiastical edifices the tympanum is often adorned with sculpture.

Tynwald, the title given to the Parliament of the Isle of Man, which includes the Governor and Council (the Upper House), and the House of Keys, the representative assembly. This practically constitutes Home Rule, the Acts passed by the Tynwald simply requiring the assent of the Sovereign.

U

Uhlan, a light cavalry soldier armed with lance, pistol, and sabre and employed chiefly as skirmisher or scout. Marshal Saxe had a corps of them in the French Army; and in the Franco-German war of 1870 the Prussian Uhlans won fame.

Ultramarine, a sky-blue pigment obtained from *Lapis lazuli*, a stone found in Tibet, Iran, Siberia and some other countries. A cheaper ultramarine is now produced by grinding and heating a mixture of clay, sulphur, carbonate of soda and resin.

Ultrasonics, sound waves of frequency so high as to be inaudible to humans, *i.e.* about 20,000 Hz and upwards (Hz is SI unit for cycle per sec.). Ultrasonic waves are commonly produced by causing a solid object to vibrate with a suitably high frequency and to impart its vibrations to the air or other fluid. The object may be a quartz or other crystal in which vibrations are excited electrically, or a nickel component which is magnetically energised. There are numerous technical applications, *e.g.* submarine echo sounding, flaw detection in castings, drilling glass and ceramics, emulsification. Ultrasonic waves are an important tool of research in physics. Bats produce very loud sounds when they are flying, but at ultrasonic frequencies (20,000 to 100,000 Hz), so that we cannot ourselves hear them.

Ultra-Violet Rays. These are invisible electromagnetic rays whose wavelengths are less than 3900 Å. (Angstrom = one hundred-millionth of a centimetre.) The sun's radiation is rich in ultra-violet light, but much of it never reaches the earth, being absorbed by molecules of atmospheric gases (in particular, ozone) as well as by soot and smoke particles. One beneficial effect of ultra-violet light on human beings is that it brings about synthesis of vitamin-D from certain fatty substances (called sterols) in the skin. The wavelengths which effect this vitamin synthesis also cause sun tan and sun burn. Ultra-violet lamps (which are mercury-vapour discharge lamps) are also used for sterilising the air inside buildings, their rays being lethal to bacteria. Many substances fluoresce under ultra-violet light; for instance, zinc silicate glows green, while cadmium borate throws out red light. This phenomenon is applied practically in fluorescent lamps, the light of requisite hue being secured by judicious mixture of the fluorescent materials which coat the lamp. *See* **Electric Light.**

Umbra, the full shadow of the earth or moon during an eclipse; the half shadow is called penumbra.

Unciae. The Romans took over the Egyptian cubit and divided it into 16 digits as well as into 12 parts called *unciae*, the *uncia* being the origin of the inch.

Underdeveloped Countries are those in which economic structure and development are held back, or, as some would have it, countries which are underdeveloped in the transitive sense of the word. The causes of the condition of underdevelopment are complex but two opposing sets of theories dominate discussion. On the one hand there are those theories that attribute underdevelopment to the internal characteristics of the underdeveloped countries themselves. This is the doctrine of original underdevelopment as it implies that such countries are responsible for their own underdevelopment. On the other hand there are the theories that ascribe underdevelopment directly to the distortions of economic structure and the exploitation involved in the relations between the developed and underdeveloped countries. The expansion of capitalism from its birthplace in Western Europe has created a world-wide production system and market (*i.e.*, a world economy from which no country is completely isolated) structured and determined by the imperatives of capital accumulation in the developed countries. This view implies that the state and process of underdevelopment in one part of the world is inevitable as long as there is development in another. Development and underdevelopment are then mutually interdependent. *See also* **Sections G, Part III and F, Part V.**

Unicorn, a fabulous single-horned animal. In heraldry its form is horse-like, with the tail of a lion and pointed single horn growing out of the forehead. In the Middle Ages the unicorn was a symbol of virginity.

Union of Great Britain and Ireland was proposed in the Irish Parliament in January 1799 after the 1798 Rebellion and came into force on 1 January 1801. The troubled history of Ireland, associated with the question of self-government, nationalism, land and religion, culminated in the Easter revolution of 1916. A treaty giving the 26 southern counties independence in 1921, as the Irish Free State, was followed by a period of internal dissension. In 1937 a new constitution was enacted in Eire in which no reference was made to the Crown. This, however, left in force the External Relations Act of 1936 and with its repeal in 1948, Eire separated itself from the British Crown and thus severed the last constitutional link with the Commonwealth, and became an independent Republic.

Union, Treaty of, was the treaty by which Scotland became formally united to England, the two countries being incorporated as the United Kingdom of Great Britain, the same Parliament to represent both, Scotland electing sixteen peers and forty-five members of the House of Commons. Uniformity of coins, weights, and measures was provided for, Scottish trade laws and customs were assimilated to those of England, and as regards religion and the practices of the law, Scotland was to continue as before. This Act was ratified on 1 May 1707.

Universe in astronomy means not only the star system (of which the sun and planets are a small part) but all the countless star systems or nebulae which may be separated from each other by millions of light-years. *See* **F3–7.**

Universities are institutions of higher education whose principal objects are the increase of knowledge over a wide field through original thought and research and its extension by the teaching of students. Such societies existed in the ancient world, notably in Greece and India, but the origin of the University as we know it today lies in mediaeval Europe, the word *universitas* being a contraction of the Latin term for corporations of teachers and students organised for the promotion of higher learning. The earliest bodies to become recognised under this description were at Bologna and Paris in the first half of the 12th cent.; Oxford was founded by an early migration of scholars from Paris, and Cambridge began with a further migration from Oxford. Other Universities sprang up all over Europe, including three in Scotland—St. Andrews (1412), Glasgow (1451) and Aberdeen (1494)—which were followed by Edinburgh in 1582. These six bodies remained the only Universities in Great Britain until the foundation in 1826–29 of University and King's Colleges in London (resulting in the establishment of the University of London in 1836) and of the University of Durham in 1832. There are (1977) thirty-three Universities in England: Aston, Bath, Birmingham, Bradford, Bristol, Brunel, Cambridge, The City, Durham, East Anglia, Essex, Exeter, Hull, Keele, Kent, Lancaster, Leeds, Leicester, Liverpool, London, Loughborough, Manchester, Newcastle, Nottingham, Oxford, Reading, Salford, Sheffield, Southampton, Surrey, Sussex, Warwick and York. Other institutions where the work is of university standard are the University of Manchester Institute of Science and Technology; the Manchester Business School; the London Graduate School of Business Studies; Cranfield Institute of Technology; and the Royal College of Art. Formed from colleges of technology, art and design, commerce and other institutions, thirty polytechnics have been established in England and Wales as centres of higher education. Wales has one University (The University of Wales with colleges at Aberystwyth, Bangor, Cardiff and Swansea) in addition to the Welsh National School of Medicine, the Institute of Science and Technology, and St. David's, Lampeter. Scotland now has eight: Aberdeen, Dundee (1967), Edinburgh, Glasgow, Heriot-Watt (1966), St. Andrews, Stirling (1967), and Strathclyde (1964), Britain's first technological University. Northern Ireland has two: Queen's University, Belfast and the New University of Ulster at Coleraine. The Open University received its charter in 1969; it provides degree and other courses together with radio and television programmes and began its broadcasts in January 1971. The Republic of Ireland has the University of Dublin (Trinity College, Dublin), and the National University of Ireland with colleges at Dublin, Cork and Galway. The early important foundations in the British Empire were: New Brunswick (1785), McGill (1821), Toronto (1827), Queen's (1841), Laval (1852) in Canada; Sydney (1850), Melbourne (1853) in Australia; Otago (1869), Canterbury (1873), Auckland (1882) in New Zealand; Bombay, Calcutta and Madras (1857) in India; and the University of the Punjab (1882) in the present Pakistan. Since the war a number of Commonwealth Universities have been established. In the USA the development of higher education has left the Universities less sharply defined than in Europe and the Commonwealth, among the best known being Harvard (1636), Yale (1701), Princeton (1746), Columbia (1754), Cornell (1865), California (Berkeley), Massachusetts Institute of Technology. In 1973 the United Nations University was established with headquarters in Tokyo. In Britain, Universities receive aid from the State mainly in the form of direct grants from the Treasury made on the advice of the University Grants Committee. But they are self-governing institutions free from State control. In recent years students have increased their contributions to the formulation of university policy.

Uranium, a metal, symbol U, discovered by Klaproth in 1789 in pitchblende. It is a white metal which tarnishes readily in air. Great developments have followed the discovery that the nucleus of the uranium isotope U^{235} undergoes fission, and uranium minerals have become very important since it was found that atomic energy could be released controllably by taking advantage of fission. Before atomic energy work began to take the major part of the world's output of uranium minerals, the chief users of uranium compounds were the ceramics and textile industries. *See also* **Nuclear Reactors, Nuclear Fission, F12(1).**

Uranus. This planet was discovered by Herschel in 1781. Its diameter is *c.* 51,800 km and its mean distance from the sun is $2{,}869{\cdot}6 \times 10^6$ km. It has five small satellites and a ring of moonlets (first seen 1977). *See* **F7.**

Urea, the final product in mammals of the breakdown of nitrogenous waste, *e.g.*, excess amino-acids. It is very soluble in water and is excreted in urine. In 1828 Wohler synthesised urea from inorganic matter. This was the first laboratory synthesis of an organic substance and refuted the idea that living creatures or life force are necessary to create such substances.

Ursa Major and Ursa Minor ("Greater Bear" and "Lesser Bear"), two celebrated constellations, each of seven stars, in the northern celestial hemisphere, familiar since ancient times. Ursa Major has also been called "the Plough", "Charles's (Charlemagne's) Wain" or "the Wagon". The "Pointers" in this group of bright stars point to the brightest star in Ursa Minor, the Pole Star. Called the Big Dipper and the Little Dipper in the USA.

Utopias. *See* **Section J.**

V

Valency. A term used by chemists to describe the combining ability of an element with respect to hydrogen. Thus oxygen, which forms water, H_2O, with hydrogen is said to have a valency of two, nitrogen (forms ammonia, NH_3) three, and carbon (forms methane, CH_4) four. Chlorine forms hydrogen chloride, HCl, and is said to be monovalent. This empirical approach cannot account for valency in such compounds as carbon monoxide, CO, which appears to require both elements to have the same valency. With the discovery of the electron it was realised that the concept of valency and chemical bonds is intimately concerned with the electronic structure of atoms, and theories have been advanced to explain why the same element can have different valencies in different compounds. Iron, for example, can have a valency of two ($FeCl_2$, ferrous chloride) or three ($FeCl_3$, ferric chloride). *See* **F20(2)** and **Table of Elements** (*see* **F2**).

Valentine's Day, (14 February), is a festival in celebration of St. Valentine, one of the Christian martyrs of the 3rd cent. A sweetheart or Valentine is chosen on that day and letters or tokens sent secretly to the object of affection.

Valhalla, in Scandinavian mythology, is the special Paradise to which the souls of warriors slain in battle were transported.

Valkyries, the chosen handmaidens of Odin, appointed to serve at the Valhalla banquets. Their most important office, however, according to the Norse mythology, was to ride through the air at a time of battle and point out the heroes who were to fall. It is one of these Valkyries who is made the heroine of Wagner's opera "Die Walküre".

Valve, an electronic device consisting of two or more metal plates (electrodes) usually enclosed in an evacuated glass bulb. One of the electrodes is heated causing electrons to be emitted. If a positive voltage is applied to the other electrode, the electrons will move towards it and the valve must conduct electricity. The current will only flow in one direction as the electrons are emitted only from one electrode. A valve with two electrodes is called a diode, but by putting in one or more intermediate electrodes the flow of current can be sensitively controlled and the valves are then called triodes, pentodes, etc., according to the total number of electrodes in them. Valves have found extensive applications in amplifiers, rectifiers oscillators and many electronic devices, but are now being superseded by transistors in many applications where it is advantageous to have greater reliability, smaller power consumption and smaller size.

Vampire *or* **Werewolf,** according to ancient superstition, was a spectre in human form which rose from its grave in the night-time and preyed upon the living as they slept, sucking their blood and then returning to the grave.

Vampire-Bats, blood-eating bats of tropical America. They puncture the skin with their incisor teeth, leaving a wound that bleeds profusely. The blood is lapped up by the bat, not sucked.

Vanadium, a scarce metallic element, symbol V, whose chief ores are carnotite and patronite.

Some iron ores contain it. Most of the vanadium commercially produced finds its way into vanadium steels, which are used for tools and parts of vehicles, being hard, tough and very resistant to shocks. The oxide is used as a catalyst in industry, especially in making sulphuric acid.

Van Allen Belts. One of the most remarkable discoveries made during the IGY, 1957–58, was that the earth is surrounded by a great belt of radiation. Evidence came from *Sputnik II* (which carried the dog Laika) and from the American satellites, *Explorers I* and *III*. The American scientist, J. A. van Allen, was able to explain the puzzling data collected from these satellites. Subsequent observations with deep space-probes showed that there are in fact two zones of high intensity particle radiation surrounding the earth, one concentrated at a distance of about 1,600 km, the other at about 24,000 km. A close relation exists between the shapes of the zones and the earth's magnetic field. Recent evidence suggests that Jupiter also is surrounded by a dense belt of trapped energetic particles.

Varnish is of two leading kinds: spirit varnish, made from resinous substances dissolved in spirit; and oil varnish, in which the dissolving agent is linseed oil and turpentine.

Vatican, the Papal residence at Rome, a famous palace on the hill adjacent to St. Peter's. Its museum is a rich treasure-house of literary and artistic objects. Works of Michelangelo glorify the Sistine Chapel.

Vauxhall Gardens, a famous London pleasure resort from the early part of the 18th to the middle of the 19th cent. It was here that many great singers appeared, where the earliest balloon ascents were made, and where there were fine displays of fireworks.

Venus, the brightest of all the planets, whose orbit lies between that of Mercury and the earth, second in order from the sun (*see* **F7**). It can approach the earth to within 40 million km. In common with all the other planets it moves around the sun in the same direction as the earth, but is the only one that rotates about its axis in the opposite direction. The planet takes just under 225 earth days to complete an orbit round the sun. In 1967 Russia succeeded in soft-landing an instrumented canister from their *Venus 4* research spacecraft. Measurements gave a picture of a very hostile environment—high surface temperature, a very high atmospheric pressure, and an atmosphere of almost pure carbon dioxide, findings very close to those obtained by later probes. *Venus 5* and *Venus 6* made twin landings in May 1969 and sent back data on the planet's mysterious veil of white clouds. *Venus 9* and *Venus 10* which made twin landings in 1975 gave data of importance to the study of Venusian geology. The pictures taken appeared to suggest volcanic activity. *See* **F7**.

Venus Fly-trap, a well-known insectivorous plant (*Dionaea muscipula*) occurring in Carolina in damp mossy places. It is related to the Sundew. The leaf is the organ that catches the insects. The leaf blade is in two halves, hinged along the centre line. Each half bears three sensitive hairs called " trigger hairs ". When an insect touches a trigger, the two halves of the leaf clap together, trapping the insect between them, when it is digested by a secretion (digestive enzymes) from the leaf, which afterwards absorbs the soluble products.

Vernalization. Seeds which, after being exposed to a low temperature, produce plants that flower earlier than usual are said to have been " vernalized ". This technique of seed treatment devised by Lysenko is called vernalization. It is claimed to have been widely used in Russia to obtain cereal crops in places where climatic conditions are favourable for only a short season.

Versailles, Treaty of. The Peace Treaty, 1919, ending the first world war. The first half was devoted to the organisation of the League of Nations. Among the territorial changes Germany ceded Alsace-Lorraine to France, Posen and the Corridor to Poland. Germany undertook to disarm, to abolish universal military service, to keep only a small army of 100,000 and a small navy. Her colonies were to be shared out among the Allies under League Mandates. Reparations were to be paid, but were gradually reduced and entirely ceased in 1932. Hitler took unilateral action against the Treaty especially in regard to rearmament and the annexation of Austria. Hitler's attempt to change the eastern frontiers was the immediate cause of the second world war.

Victoria and Albert Museum, in Kensington, London, was begun in 1852 as the Museum of Ornamental Art at Marlborough House. The present building was completed in 1909. It has the following departments: Architecture and Sculpture, Conservation, Ceramics, Paintings, Prints and Drawings, Oriental, Library, Metalwork, Museum Services (inc. Information and Slide Loan Service), Textiles, Furniture and Woodwork, Education (into which the old Circulation Dept. has been absorbed), Theatre Museum. The V. & A. also administers the Wellington Museum (Apsley House, Piccadilly), Ham House (Richmond, Surrey), Osterley Park House (Middx). The Bethnal Green Museum (The Museum of Childhood) is a branch of the V. & A., opened 1872.

Victoria Cross, an order of merit for conspicuous valour, awarded to members of the Army, Navy and Air Force, was established in 1856.

Vienna Congress, sat at Vienna from September 1814 to June 1815, and settled the delimination of the territories of the various European nations after the defeat of Napoleon. The Treaty of Vienna which resulted gave Sri Lanka, Mauritius, Cape Colony, Heligoland, Malta and part of Guyana to England; France was not permitted to hold more territory than she had possessed at the outbreak of the Revolution in 1789; Austria took Northern Italy; Russia part of Poland; and Prussia, part of Saxony and the Rhenish province. Except for one or two changes the clauses of the treaty were maintained for over forty years.

Vikings. Scandinavian pirates who from the 8th to the 10th cent. were the terror of northern waters. Sometimes the Viking raids reached south to the Mediterranean and east to the White Sea. Their leader Rurik founded the first Russian kingdom of Novgorod in A.D. 862. The Icelandic Vikings under Eric the Red discovered Greenland in A.D. 982 and a warm period in world climate allowed many to settle there. Their expeditions took them to Labrador and Newfoundland. The Vikings excelled in shipbuilding, were fine sailors and splendid craftsmen.

Vinegar. This condiment and preservative is a weak solution of acetic acid (3–9%) formed by the oxidation of ethyl alcohol by the action of bacteria on alcoholic liquor (wine, beer, cider, fermented fruit juices, or malted cereals). Wine vinegar is usually red; malt vinegar is brown. The name vinegar is derived from the Latin *vinum aigre*, bad wine. *See also* **Acetic Acid.**

Vinyl Plastics are polymers made from derivatives of ethylene, examples are polyvinyl chloride (PVC), which is used in making plastic pipes and kitchen utensils, among other things; polyvinyl acetate used in the paint industry and in bonding laminated articles like plywood; and polystyrene (poly vinyl benzene) used in making electrical fittings and for lenses.

Viper, a family of poisonous snakes in which the venom-conducting fangs hinge forward when the snake bites. One species is found in Britain, the common viper or adder.

Virus. *See* **P7, F26(2).**

Visibility is defined by the distance at which the farthest of a series of objects, specially selected to show against the skyline or in good contrast with their background, can be distinguished. Visibility depends chiefly upon the concentration of water or dust particles suspended in the air. Instruments are available to measure the obscurity of the atmosphere more directly, including that at night. A large lapse rate of temperature and a strong wind are favourable to good visibility; a small lapse rate, calm or light wind favourable to bad visibility. Fog is when the visibility is less than 1,000 m; mist or haze when it is between 1,000 and 2,000 m. *See* **Pollution.**

Viscount, a title of rank coming between that of Earl and Baron. The title originally stood for deputy-earl. The first English Viscount was Viscount Beaumont, created in 1440.

Vitamins, name of a group of organic substances found in relatively minute amounts in certain foodstuffs, essential for growth and the maintenance of normal bodily structure and function. The Hungarian biochemist Szent-Györgyi, who first isolated vitamin C or ascorbic acid, defined the vitamin as "a substance that makes you ill if you don't eat it!" *See* **F27(1).**

Volcanoes are vents through which magma reaches the surface as lava flows, or as the solid products, *e.g.*, ashes and bombs, of explosive eruption. The vent may be cylindrical or it may be a long fissure. The former type usually builds up cones, *e.g.*, Vesuvius. Notable active volcanoes are Etna, Vesuvius and Stromboli, in Italy; Hekla in Iceland; and Mont Pelée in Martinique. The last-named was in violent eruption in 1902, when the chief town of St. Pierre was completely destroyed. Volcanic eruptions are sometimes linked with brilliant sunset phenomena, *e.g.*, the Indonesian island of Krakatoa (1883), whose atmospheric and tidal effects were recorded all over the world, and Agung on the island of Bali (1963), which had been dormant for 120 years. A new fissure volcano (Surtsey) developed off the coast of Iceland in 1963. The 1971 eruption of Etna was a serious one, though minor compared with that of 1669.

Vole, a small rodent with blunt nose, round face and short tail. Three kinds occur in Britain: the field, the bank and the water vole.

Volt, the electromotive force unit, named after Alessandro Volta (1745–1827), and defined in terms of the coulomb, the second and the joule.

Vraic, a name for seaweed in the Channel Islands, where it is extensively used as a manure.

Vulgate, a term used to designate the Latin version of the Scriptures sanctioned by the Council of Trent. The work of St. Jerome in the late 4th cent. A.D. and still the official Bible of the Roman Catholic Church.

Vulture, a famous bird of prey of two distinctive groups; that of the Old World, whose nostrils are separated by a bony partition, and the New World vulture, which has no such division. Vultures feed on carrion and are the great scavengers of tropical regions. The European species are the Egyptian vulture, Griffon vulture, Black vulture and Bearded vulture. Vultures have no feathers on the head and neck.

W

Wading Birds, *Charadriiformes*, an order of migratory, long-legged, long-billed birds, frequenting marshes and shallow waters. They include the plovers, avocets, stilts, oystercatchers, curlews, phalaropes, godwits, dunlins, sandpipers, redshanks, greenshanks, snipe, woodcocks, the pratincole of the Mediterranean and the sun bittern of tropical America. Many species breed in Britain.

Wagtails, familiar long-tailed small birds, the most common British species being the Pied or Water (with sub-species White) Grey and the Yellow (sub-species Blue). Wagtails nest in holes and are active of habit.

Walloons, name given to the French-speaking population of the southern provinces of Belgium, in contrast to the Flemings or Dutch-speaking population of the northern provinces. The Walloon areas contain the mining and heavy industries of the country; the Flemish regions are more agricultural. Walloons number *c.* 3 million, Flemings *c.* 5 million. The *Mouvement Populaire Wallon* desires an autonomous Wallonia within the Belgian state.

Walpurgis Night, the night before 1 May, when witches and creatures of evil are supposed to have liberty to roam. Named after St. Walpurgis, an English nun, who went on a mission to Germany in the 8th cent.

Walrus, a very large marine mammal, related to the seals having in the upper jaw two large curved tusks, which average in length from 38 to 60 cm. It lives on bi-valve molluscs, and inhabits the Arctic seas. An adult walrus can exceed 4 m in length and weigh over a tonne.

Wankel Engine or **Rotary Engine,** is an internal combustion engine invented by Felix Wankel in the 1930s and greatly developed since by large automobile firms in several countries. The ordinary internal combustion engine has to convert reciprocating motion of the pistons into rotatory motion. In the Wankel engine the explosion of the fuel and air mixture drives a moving part (the rotor) directly into rotatory motion, and the rotor itself opens and closes the fuel inlet and exhaust ports. The three spaces between the triangular rotor and its specially shaped housing act successively as intake, compression, explosion and exhaust chambers as the rotor revolves. There are no valves and far fewer moving parts than in an ordinary piston engine. The Wankel engine is claimed to have many advantages in that it is smaller and lighter for a given horse-power, relatively simple, quieter and freer from vibration, and could contribute to pollution control. There are cars now on sale with the Wankel engine and continuous research and development will no doubt test in practice the claim of some protagonists that this engine is the agent of a technological revolution in the automobile.

Wapentake, the ancient name given in the northern counties to territorial divisions corresponding to the Hundreds of southern counties.

Warblers, a family of small, lively song-birds closely related to the flycatchers and thrushes. Represented in Britain by about 36 species, including the chiffchaff, one of the earliest spring visitors, willow-wren, wood-warbler, blackcap, garden-warbler, whitethroats, sedge and grasshopper-warbler.

Water is the simplest compound of hydrogen and oxygen. It is formed when an electric spark is passed through a mixture of the gases, and is a product of combustion of all hydrogen-containing compounds, *e.g.*, petrol, coal, coal gas and wood. Water is essential to living matter, and is the medium which carries food to animals and plants. Salts in hard water may be removed by distillation of the water or by a process known as ion-exchange (water softening). Pure water freezes at 0°C and boils at 100°C and is used as a standard of temperature on this scale. It has a maximum density at 4°C. Heating water above 100°C converts it into steam, which is used under pressure to convert heat energy into useful work, as in electrical power stations and steam engines. Water gas is a mixture mainly of carbon monoxide and hydrogen formed by blowing steam and oxygen through red-hot coke: it is used as a fuel. Water is one of the very few compounds which freezes from the surface down rather than from the bulk of the liquid up. This property has important consequences on the preservation of life in rivers and lakes when they are frozen over. *See also* **F23.**

Water Hyacinth (*Eichhornia crassipes*), a beautiful aquatic plant native to Brazil which has spread to other favourable equatorial regions of the world causing havoc on account of its abnormal rate of reproduction away from its natural environment. In recent years it has invaded the Nile and the Zaire, forming vast floating carpets which block the channels, clog the paddles of river craft and de-oxygenate the water, killing the fish. It is being held in check by spraying with the herbicide 2,4-D.

Waterloo, Battle of, was fought on 18 June 1815. The Allies (British, German and Dutch) under Wellington and Blücher defeated the French under Napoleon. This ended Napoleon's career.

Waterloo Bridge, crossing the Thames, was built by Rennie, and opened in 1817. It had nine arches, each 120 ft (36 m) span, was built of granite, and had a length (including approaches) of 2,456 ft (749 m). The present bridge, completed in 1942, and formally opened 10 December 1945, is a fine example of reinforced concrete construction. (Architect, Sir Giles Gilbert-Scott.)

Water-Spider, an interesting little animal which spins a sac of silk on a water-plant, which it uses as a sort of diving bell. Into this bell it introduces bubbles of air, one at a time; thus the spider is enabled to remain below the surface a considerable time.

Waterspout, whirling tornado-like cloud, occurring at sea. It begins as a cone of cloud tapering slowly downwards, the sea surface becoming disturbed; on reaching the centre of the cloud of spray the spout takes on the appearance of a column of water. A number of these vortices may form fairly close together at about the same time, their duration ranging up to 30 minutes.

Watling Street, the name of the old Roman road which ran from the Channel ports by way of London to Salop. *See also* **Roman Roads.**

Watt. A unit of electrical power equivalent to 1 joule of work per second, named after James Watt (1736–1819). *See* **N7.**

Wax, the name applied to certain substances or mixtures which are solids having little crystalline form and may be regarded as solidified oils. They are used for various purposes, such as the making of wax candles, bleaching and making artificial flowers and anatomical models, also in pharmacy for blending in the composition of plasters, ointment, etc. The best-known natural wax is beeswax, and there are others, such as spermaceti, obtained from the sperm whale, and Chinese wax, which is a cerotyl cerotate.

Waxbill, a small Oriental and African bird of the *Estrildidae* family, with wax-like bill and beautifully variegated plumage. The Java sparrow, and the Blue-breasted waxbill are attractive, and often find their way into cages.

Wayz-Goose, the name given to a festive gathering of people employed in printing and other works, so called from the fact that in earlier times a goose was the principal dish of the feast.

Weasel. A carnivore mammal found in Britain, smallest member of the group including the Stoat, Polecat, and Pine-marten, about 20 cm long. Its fur is reddish on the upper side of the animal, white on the under side; it may all turn white in winter with the exception of the tail.

Weather is generally accepted as being the current state of the atmosphere, particularly as regards its pressure and temperature, wind, cloud and precipitation. Many other features such as fog, sunshine duration, humidity, pressure tendency, may be added to the list, all items of which are routinely observed by specially instrumented stations usually sponsored by the national meteorological services. Day-to-day changes in the weather as experienced by the individual are due to the passage of circulation systems, many of which bring clearly recognisable areas of "good" (*i.e.*, calm and sunny) weather as frequently occurs in anticyclones and "bad" (*i.e.*, cold, windy, cloudy and rainy) weather. Clearly, the weather in any place at any time is primarily determined by the frequency and intensity of synoptic-scale weather circulation systems (*c.* 3,000 km across). Local weather (over areas of *c.* 100 km) may be heavily influenced by topography, *e.g.*, valley fogs, frost hollows, etc.

Weather Lore. Before instruments were invented to measure atmospheric conditions, man relied on his own observation of wind and sky, behaviour of birds and animals, and came to associate certain phenomena with types of weather. Many popular weather rhymes have survived the centuries, and as long as forecasting is confined to the next 24 hours there is perhaps something to be said for them, particularly those dealing with the winds. What is very unlikely is that next year's summer can be predicted from this year's winter, or that one month's weather is related to that of another. The study of past records reveals too many exceptions for such predictions to be of much use in forecasting.

Weaver Bird, the popular name for a large group of finch-like birds belonging to the family *Ploceidae*, found principally in Africa but also in Southern Asia, Australia, and Europe and remarkable for their habit of building nests formed of blades of grass dexterously interwoven and suspended from the boughs of trees.

Weaving has been practised since before any times of which we have record. The Egyptians credit the invention to Isis, the Grecians to Minerva. The main principle of the weaving loom is the same to-day as it was thousands of years ago; a warp extends lengthwise through the loom, the threads being held in separate regular order by being passed through a reed or "slay", while the weft is crossed through alternating threads of the warp by means of a shuttle which holds the weft. Thus the fabric is built up. Weaving was done by hand up to the early part of the 19th cent., when Cartwright's steam-power loom was introduced. The Jacquard loom for weaving figured designs dates from 1801.

Wedding Anniversaries are: first, Cotton; second, Paper; third, Leather; fourth, Fruit and Flower; fifth, Wooden; sixth, Sugar; seventh, Woollen; eighth, Salt; ninth, Copper; tenth, Tin; twelfth, Silk and Fine Linen; fifteenth, Crystal; twentieth, China; twenty-fifth, Silver; thirtieth, Pearl; thirty-fifth, Coral; fortieth, Ruby; fiftieth, Golden; sixtieth, Diamond; sixty-fifth, Blue Sapphire; seventieth, Platinum.

Wednesday, the 4th day of the week, derived its name from Woden or Odin, the Norse god of war.

Weights and Measures. *See* **Section N.**

Welding is a means of joining together two pieces of material, often metals, by heating the joint until the substances melt locally, run together, and then solidify. The heating can be by burning gas (*e.g.*, oxy-acetylene welding) or electric current (electric arc welding). Techniques exist for welding anything from hair-like wires to massive steel plates. *See* **Soldering.**

Werewolf, a man or woman, who according to mediaeval belief, could be turned by witchcraft or magic into a wolf, eat human flesh or drink human blood and turn into himself again. This belief was widely held in Europe, and similar superstitions prevail among most primitive peoples, *e.g.*, the "leopard man" of certain African tribes. Lycanthropy (from Gr. = wolf-man) is a form of madness in which the patient imagines himself a beast. *See* **Section J.**

Westminster Abbey stands on the site of an old church and Benedictine foundation of the 7th cent. It was rebuilt under Edward the Confessor, and again under Henry III, and important additions were made by Edward II, Edward III, Richard II, Richard III and Henry VII, the latter erecting the beautiful eastern chapel in the perpendicular style which bears his name. The western towers and front were rebuilt by Wren in the 18th cent. It contains tombs of many sovereigns, of the Unknown Warrior, and many other illustrious men are commemorated by monuments.

Westminster Cathedral, seat of the Roman Catholic Archbishop of Westminster. It was designed by J. F. Bentley and built between 1895 and 1910. It is of red brick, in early Christian Byzantine style with a domed campanile, 283 ft (86 m) high, and a decorative interior.

Westminster Hall, adjoining the Houses of Parliament, was built as a Banqueting Hall by William Rufus, and many courtly festivals were held there in succeeding centuries. King John established the Law Courts there. It now forms a gigantic hallway, leading to the Houses of Parliament. Charles I, Sir Thomas More, and Warren Hastings were tried there.

Whale, a completely aquatic mammal; the fore-limbs are modified to form fin-like paddles and there is virtually no external trace of the hind-limbs. There are two major groups of whales—the *Toothed Whales*, including the Sperm-whale (Cachalot), Dolphin, Killer-whales and Porpoises; and the *Whalebone Whales*. In the latter a series of whalebone plates grow down from the roof of the mouth, and, being frayed at their edges into a hairy fringe, together constitute a filtering mechanism. The animal takes in sea water containing minute organisms on which it feeds; the mouth is then closed and the tongue raised when the water is forced out through the filter, on which is left the food. As the tongue is lowered, the whalebone plates straighten up, flicking the food on to the tongue, which transfers it to the gut. Most whale oil is obtained from the thick layer of fat under the skin (blubber), but in the Sperm-whale there is a large reserve of oil in the head. The oil is used for making candles, margarine and soap. Ambergris used in perfumery comes from the intestine of whales.

The number of whales that may be killed in a season is limited by International Convention. The two main whaling nations are Japan and the Soviet Union.

Whimbrel, a bird of the Curlew family, more common in Scotland than in England.

Whinchat, a small migratory bird, a breeding visitor to Britain (April to October); bright brown plumage, with prominent eye stripe.

Whiskers in physics and material science (*q.v.*) are tiny rods of crystal, thinner than human hair and perhaps 1 cm long. Their importance lies in the fact that such crystals are free from the defects described on **F18**. They are also free from surface cracks and steps. This means they are immensely strong because failures of strength in ordinary solids are due to imperfections and cracks of one kind or another. Large numbers of whiskers of strong solids like graphite, silicon, or silicon carbide embedded in a matrix of softer matter such as plastic or metal would make a very strong new material. Many laboratories are developing such substances.

Whisky, an ardent spirit distilled from malt or other grain, and containing a large percentage of alcohol. It has a greater consumption than any other spirit, and is of many kinds, Scotch and Irish whiskies being chiefly consumed in this country, and being of pot still or patent still production, or a blend of the two. Whisky is the most heavily taxed product: in 1661 a duty of 4*d*. a gallon was imposed; today (1977) the duty on Scotch and Irish whiskies is £27·09 per proof gallon. American whiskies are mostly distilled from corn (maize), or rye. *See* **Alcohol.**

White Elephant, a term in common use to designate a gift that causes the recipient more trouble or cost than it is worth; derived from an old-time custom of the Kings of Thailand who presented a white elephant to a courtier whom it was desired to ruin.

Whitehall Palace, built within sight of Westminster by Hubert de Burgh, Earl of Kent, round about 1240, was the residence of the Archbishops of York until Wolsey presented it to Henry VIII in 1530. From then until 1697, when it was burned down, it continued to be the favourite town residence of royalty, and to the Stuarts especially it was a great centre of court festivities. In those days, with its grounds, it extended from the Strand to the river. The only portion of Whitehall Palace now standing is the Banqueting Hall built by Inigo Jones, on a scaffold projected from the front of which Charles I was beheaded. A block of new government buildings has recently been built on part of the site of the old Palace.

White House, the official residence at Washington of the President of the United States.

Whitsuntide, the festival celebrating the descent of the Holy Ghost and occurring seven weeks after Easter.

Whydah Bird, the widow-bird of Equatorial Africa. The Paradise Whydah is remarkable for the long tail and handsome black-and-scarlet plumage of the male during mating season.

Widow Bird, certain species of African weaver birds with predominantly black plumage. In the breeding season the male birds are strikingly beautiful, with scarlet and buff markings and long tail feathers. They are social parasites and trick other birds into rearing their young.

Wigeon, a surface-feeding duck of northern Europe, known in Britain more as a winter visitor than a nesting bird. It feeds in flocks in the muddy estuaries and has a characteristic "whee-oo" call.

Willow, a water-side-loving tree of the genus *Salix*, to which the osiers belong. The best cricket-bat blades are made from a white willow, *S. alba* var. *caerulea*, a fine tree with bluish-green leaves, mostly found in Essex. Willow is also used for polo balls. Weeping willow, *S. babylonica*, is native to China and is the willow seen on Old China willow-pattern plates.

Wind, air set in motion by special atmospheric conditions, is of various degrees, from a slight rustling breeze to a hurricane. Winds are *constant*, as in trade winds or anti-trade winds; *periodic*, as in monsoons and other wind-visitations occurring according to influences of season; *cyclonic* and *anti-cyclonic*, when their motion is spiral: *whirlwinds*, *hurricanes*, and *tornados*, when high temperature and great density induce extreme agitation. Ordinarily, a wind is named from the point of the compass from which it blows, or it may be expressed in degrees from true north. The *sirocco*, the *mistral*, and the *simoom* are local forms of winds of great velocity. A *blizzard* is a biting blast of icy temperature. *See also* **Beaufort Scale, Section N.**

Windmills were in use in the East in ancient times, but were not much seen in Europe before the 13th cent. Wind sawmills were invented by a Dutchman in the 17th cent., and one was erected near the Strand in London in 1633. Great improvements have been made in these mills, especially in the United States, where, by the application of the windshaft principle, much space is saved and the mills can be used for pumping, grinding and other purposes.

Windows (Old Norse *vindauga* = wind-eye), an opening in a wall of a building to admit light and air, and to afford a view of what is outside. In northern Europe windows, as the derivation of the word implies, were first used for ventilation and glass was not used in private houses before the end of the 12th cent. In early Gothic (12th cent.) windows were still small and narrow, with rounded heads. In Early English (13th cent.) they became longer and the heads pointed. In the Decorated period (14th cent.) windows were mullioned (divided by slender bars into panes) and the pointed heads often traceried. In Tudor times when the Renaissance had found its way to England, windows were larger and the bay-window (projecting from the wall) and the oriel window (*q.v.*) were much in vogue; in the late 18th cent. curved bays (called bow-windows) became fashionable. Sash windows (invented by the English) with wooden frames and divided into equal rectangular panes were used in Queen Anne and Georgian houses. Their design was influenced by a passion for symmetry; they were very efficient ventilators. The French window reaches to the floor and has double casements opening as doors. A Dormer window is a vertical window set on the sloping side of a roof. One of the main features of modern architecture is the large area devoted to windows, a development made possible by improved heating systems. Windows are now mass-produced in stock sizes and patterns.

Windsor Castle, the famous British royal residence on the banks of the Thames, as it now stands, was mainly built by Henry III, though a royal residence had existed there from the time of the Conqueror. Additions were made by Henry VIII, Elizabeth and Charles II. Windsor Park and Forest comprise over 5,200 ha.

Wine, the fermented juice of the freshly-gathered grape. There are innumerable varieties, each obtaining its distinctive character from the species of wine producing the grape, the locality of the vineyard, method of cultivation, etc. Wines are of three main kinds: *sparkling*, as in champagne, due to their having been bottled before fermentation is complete; *beverage*, when the must has been fermented out before bottling. Such wines include the famous red and white wines of Burgundy, Bordeaux and the Rhone valley and the white wines of the Rhine, Moselle and Loire valleys. Wines are *fortified* by the addition of alcohol either after fermentation is complete (*e.g.*, Sherry) or during fermentation (*e.g.*, Port). The principal wine-producing countries are: France, Italy, Algeria, Spain, Portugal, Rumania, Argentine, Yugoslavia, USSR, Greece, W. Germany, Hungary.

Witan *or* **Witenagemot**, the name given to the king's council of "wise men" in Anglo-Saxon times, composed of the archbishops, bishops, abbots of the greater abbeys, earldormen and influential thanes.

Witchcraft. *See* **Section J.**

Woad, a plant (*Isastis tinctoria*) that in olden days was largely used in England for the blue dye obtained from the leaves. It is a biennial plant belonging to the same family (*Cruciferae*) as the wallflower.

Wolves, well-known carnivorous animals still found in many parts of Europe, but not existing in Britain since the middle of the 17th cent. They usually hunt in packs.

Women's Liberation Movement. *See* **Section J.**

Woodcock, a wading bird, valued for its flesh. It is a member of the snipe family, and breeds in Britain. The parent bird is able to carry its young between its thigh and body when flying to and from the feeding spots. It is one of the birds protected by the Game Laws.

Woodpecker, a familiar tree-climbing, insectivorous bird of conspicuous plumage, of which four species are found in Britain, the green woodpecker or yaffle (because of its harsh cry), the great spotted, the lesser spotted, and the wryneck. They build in the hollows of trees. Yaffle has a long sticky tongue for licking up ground insects, especially ants. The great and lesser woodpeckers obtain insects by digging into tree trunks with strong, chisel-like bills, spearing the insects with a sharp tongue. The metallic drumming sound made by the birds in spring is thought to be caused by their beaks hammering away at some hard resounding substance.

Wood's Metal, an alloy with a very low melting point (65°C, which is under 150°F) so that a spoon made of it will melt when used to stir a cup of tea. Contains bismuth 4 parts, lead 2 parts, tin 1 part, cadmium 1 part. Its use as a heat exchanger has now been largely superseded by silicone oils, which have a wider temperature range.

Woodworm. Four beetles are mainly responsible for woodworm damage: common furniture beetle (*Anobium punctatum*), powder post beetle (*Lyctus brunneus*), death watch beetle (*Xestobium rufovillosum*), and house longhorn beetle (*Hylotrupes bajulus*). Particular attention should be paid to wood in damp, dark and out-of-the-way places, and the backs and underneaths of furniture. The most frequent cause of woodworm damage is the common furniture beetle (*q.v.*).

Wool is a fibre, made up of very long protein molecules. It has been largely grown and used in the manufacture of cloth in England since before the Roman invasion. It is grown on the backs of sheep, and is of various kinds, according to the breed of sheep from which it is derived. Wool differs from hair in that it has a wavy, serrated fibre, its curl being a notable characteristic, whereas hair has a smooth surface comparatively free from serratures. Long wools are mostly used for the manufacture of worsted goods, and short wools for woollen cloths, though the improvements in machinery in recent years have enabled manufacturers to utilise short wools to a great extent for dress fabrics as well as for woollens. The finest wools are obtained from the fleece of the Spanish merino sheep. Australia, USSR, New Zealand, Argentina and South Africa are the greatest wool-producing countries.

Woolsack, the name given to the seat occupied by the Lord Chancellor in the House of Lords. It is a large square bag of wool, without back or arms, covered with red cloth. At the time when it was first used, in the reign of Edward III, wool was the great staple commodity of the country and, it is said, chosen for the seat of judges as a constant reminder of the main source of the national wealth. The lord Chancellor is said to be "appointed to the woolsack".

World Population. According to United Nations sources world population in mid-1975 was 3,967 million, an increase of 77 million in one year. More than half the total live in Asia (56·9 per cent). Different countries are at different stages in a demographic transition from the stability provided by a combintion of high birth rate and high death rate to that provided by a combination of low birth rate and low death rate. Their recent population history and current trent of growth, the age-structure of their population, and consequently their population potential for the near future are all widely different. Most rapid growth is in Africa with rates of over 3 per cent in some countries. In most European countries the rate is less than 1 per cent. A baby girl born in Norway may expect to live the longest (77·6 years) and a baby boy in Sweden (72·11 years), but a baby born in some African countries may not live to reach 40 years. It is estimated that about one in 25 of all human beings who have ever lived are alive today. *See also* **Section G Part III** and **Population, Section F, Part V.**

Wreck, the name given to trove found under water, usually from a maritime wreck. Finds must be brought to the notice of the Official Receiver of Wrecks, an officer of H.M. Customs and Excise.

Wren, a family of small passerine birds possessing upturned tails and most abundant in South America. The British species is an interesting singing bird with a suprisingly loud note for its size.

X

Xenon a rare gaseous element, symbol Xe, occurring in minute quantities in the atmosphere, discovered by Sir William Ramsay and M. W. Travers in 1898. *See* **Rare Gases.**

X-Rays were discovered in 1895 by Professor Röntgen, of Wurzburg, while experimenting with a Crookes vacuum tube, when the fact was accidentally revealed that a photographic plate, contained in a dark box and exposed to its rays, was affected. To the X-rays the box was transparent. X-ray photographs are now commonly taken to obtain information about objects enclosed within solid bodies; they enable bullets and any solid bodies of metal, as well as bones, etc., in the body to be perfectly located and investigated. The discovery has proved of great advantage in surgical operations. X-rays are used to determine the structure of matter; the atoms in a substance may be located and their relative positions determined by photographing reflections of the X-rays by the specimen. *See* **F11 (1).**

Xylem, the woody tissue of higher plants whose function is to conduct water and mineral salts upwards, and to provide mechanical support.

Y

Yacht, a light vessel now much used for pleasure trips and racing. The first yachting club was the Cork Harbour Club, started about 1720; and in 1812 the Royal Yacht Squadron was founded at Cowes. The Royal Thames Yacht Club dates from 1823. The most famous international yachting trophy is *The America's Cup* (*q.v.*).

Yak, a curious, long-haired ox, found in Tibet, used as a beast of burden, and also kept for milk and meat.

Yard, a standard measure of 36 in, the word being derived from the Saxon gyrd, or rod. The yard and pound are now defined by reference to the metre and the kilogramme: yard = 0·9144 of a metre; pound = 0·45359237 of a kilogramme. By international agreement the metre is defined by reference to the wavelength of krypton-86 light.

Yellowhammer, a common British bird of the bunting family, of lemon-yellow and brown plumage. Nests on or near the ground.

Yeomen of the Guard are a body of Foot Guards established in the reign of Henry VII for the protection of the Royal Person. Yeomen are now about 100 in number, and their duties consist in being present on ceremonial State occasions, the yearly distribution of Maundy Money, and the searching of the vaults of the Houses of Parliament on Guy Fawkes' day. "Beefeater" is the nickname of both Yeomen of the Guard and Yeomen Warders of the Tower, and they both wear the style of dress of the Tudor period, but with one distinction, the Yeomen of the Guard wear a cross belt, the Warders do not.

Yeti, opinions differ as to whether this is a mythical inhabitant of the Himalayas, a primitive primate or bear. Evidence to date is inconclusive.

Yoga. *See* **Section J.**

York Minster, one of the oldest and finest of English cathedrals, is 160 m long, its nave is 73 m broad, and the central tower is 66 m high. The present edifice, in parts, dates back to the 12th cent., but a church stood on the site in the 7th cent. In 1829 it was set on fire by a lunatic named Jonathan Martin, and the destruction that then took place cost £60,000 to restore.

Ytterbium, a chemical element discovered by Urbain in 1907; one of the group of rare earth metals.

Yttrium, a chemical element discovered by Mosander in 1842. It is found in a few rare minerals such as gadolinite, xenotine, fergusonite and euxenite. One of the group of rare-earth metals.

Z

Zamboni Pile, a dry galvanic battery, which can provide small amounts of high-voltage current over a very long time. At Oxford a couple of Zamboni piles have kept a bell ringing for over a hundred years. These piles in the second world war were perfected and produced in quantity, being the most convenient source of current for infra-red signalling devices.

Zebra, an African quadruped of whitish-grey colour, with regular black stripings, perhaps the most beautiful member of the Equine family. Rather larger than an ass and smaller than the horse, it has a tufted tail, is of light build, wild and fleet of foot. The Zebra may be threatened with extinction—already the fate of the Quagga species—because of its slaughter by man for its beautiful skin.

Zen Buddhism. *See* **Section J.**

Zenith, the highest point in the heavens above an observer's head, the opposite pole to the nadir.

Zero, the cypher signifying nothing. The West is indebted to the Arabs for it, who probably got it from the Hindus and passed it to European mathematicians towards the end of the Middle Ages. The zero has also been found in Babylonian cuneiform. The Greeks had no such symbol, which hindered the development of their mathematics. The use of zero led to the invention of decimal fractions and to the later developments in astronomy, physics and chemistry. For absolute zero on the temperature scale *see* **Absolute Temperature.**

Zinc, a familiar metallic element, symbol Zn, known to the ancients, and used by them in the making of brass. It occurs as the sulphide, carbonate, etc. The ores of zinc are crushed, roasted and reduced with coal. In combination with copper it constitutes the familiar alloy called brass, and zinc itself is much used for roofing and other protective purposes. Zinc ores are mined in Canada, the USA, Mexico, Poland, Australia, Russia, Italy, Spain and many other parts of the world. Zinc smelting is carried on in most industrial countries, including Great Britain.

Zionism. *See* **Section J.**

Zirconium, metallic element, symbol Zr, was discovered by Klaproth in the sand of the rivers of Sri Lanka in 1789. The crystalline metal is white, soft and ductile; in its amorphous condition it is a blue-black powder. Zirconium is used in atomic reactors as containers for fuel elements, since it does not absorb neutrons.

Zodiac, an imaginary zone or belt of the sky enclosing the circuit over which the principal planets travel. It is divided into 12 equal spaces of 30 degrees each, comprising respectively the 12 signs of the zodiac—Aries, Taurus, Gemini, Cancer, Leo, Virgo, Libra, Scorpio, Sagittarius, Capricornus, Aquarius and Pisces. The idea of the zodiac originated with the Babylonians about 2000 B.C. and passed by way of the Greeks to the Western world.

Zodiacal Light, a faint cone of light occasionally seen stretching along the zodiac from the western horizon after evening twilight or the eastern horizon before morning twilight. It is believed to be due to the scattering of the sun's light by dust particles in orbit round the sun and extending beyond the earth. Recent observations at the high altitude station at Chacaltaya in the Andes suggest that the dust is travelling round the sun in regular planetary orbits.

Zonda, a warm moist wind in Argentina of great velocity blowing from the north or northwest, and, like the Sirocco in Southern Europe, causes much discomfort. It happens when a depression is moving across the pampas, bringing with it a mass of air from the humid tropics. It is followed by a refreshing wind from the south east.

Zoological Gardens of London were opened in 1828, and belong to the Zoological Society of London. They contain one of the largest and most varied collections of living animals in the world. The Society maintains an open-air zoo at Whipsnade, on the edge of Dunstable Downs; this was opened in 1931.

Zoology, the branch of science concerned with animal life, embracing many aspects such as anatomy, behaviour, classification, distribution and ecology. *See* **Section F, Part IV.**

Zoroastrianism, *See* **Section J.**

NOBEL PRIZE WINNERS (1901–1976)

YEAR.	PHYSICS.	CHEMISTRY.	PHYSIOLOGY AND MEDICINE.	LITERATURE.	PEACE.
1901	W. C. Röntgen (G).	J. H. van't Hoff (D).	E. v. Behring (G).	R. F. A. Sully Prudhomme (F).	H. Dunant (Sw), F. Passy (F).
1902	H. A. Lorentz (D), P. Zeeman (D).	E. Fischer (G).	R. Ross (B).	T. Mommsen (G).	E. Ducommun (Sw), A. Gobat (Sw).
1903	H. Becquerel (F), P. Curie (F), Marie Curie (F).	S. Arrhenius (S).	N. R. Finsen (Da).	B. Björnson (N).	Sir W. R. Cremer (B).
1904	Lord J. W. S. Rayleigh (B).	W. Ramsay (B).	I. P. Pavlov (R).	F. Mistral (F), J. Echegaray (Sp).	Institut de Droit International.
1905	P. Lenard (G).	A. v. Bayer (G).	R. Koch (G).	H. Sienkiewicz (P).	Bertha von Suttner (Au).
1906	J. J. Thomson (B).	H. Moissan (F).	C. Golgi (I), S. R. y Cajal (Sp).	G. Carducci (I).	T. Roosevelt (A).
1907	A. A. Michelson (A).	E. Buchner (G).	C. I. A. Laveran (F).	Rudyard Kipling (B).	E. T. Moneta (I), L. Renault (F).
1908	G. Lippmann (F).	E. Rutherford (B).	P. Ehrich (G), E. Metchnikoff (R).	R. Eucken (G).	K. P. Arnoldson (S), F. Bajer (Da).
1909	F. Braun (G), G. Marconi (I).	W. Ostwald (G).	T. Kocher (Sw).	S. Lagerlöf (S).	A. M. F. Beernaert (Be), Baron d'Estournelles de Constant de Rebecque (F).
1910	J. D. van der Waals (D).	O. Wallach (G).	A. Kossel (G).	P. Heyse (G).	The Bureau International Permanent de la Paix, Berne.
1911	W. Wien (G).	Marie Curie (F).	A. Gullstrand (S).	M. Maeterlinck (Be).	T. M. C. Asser (D), A. H. Fried (Au).
1912	G. Dalén (S).	V. Grignard (F), P. Sabatier (F).	A. Carrel (A).	G. Hauptmann (G).	E. Root (A).
1913	H. Kamerlingh Onnes (D).	A. Werner (Sw).	C. Richet (F).	R. Tagore (In).	H. la Fontaine (Be).
1914	M. v. Laue (G).	T. W. Richards (A).	R. Bárány (Au.).	—	—
1915	W. H. Bragg (B), W. L. Bragg (B).	R. Willstaetter (G).	—	R. Roland (F).	—
1916	—	—	—	V. von Heidenstam (S).	—
1917	C. G. Barkla (B).	—	—	K. Gjellerup (Da), H. Pontoppidan (Da).	Comité International de la Croix-Rouge, Geneva.
1918	M. Planck (G).	F. Haber (G).	—	—	—
1919	J. Stark (G).	—	J. Bordet (Be).	C. Spitteler (Sw).	W. Wilson (A).
1920	C. E. Guillaume (F).	W. Nernst (G).	A. Krogh (Da).	K. Hamsun (N).	L. Bourgeois (F).
1921	A. Einstein (G).	F. Soddy (B).	—	A. France (F).	K. H. Branting (S), C. L. Lange (N).
1922	N. Bohr (Da).	F. W. Aston (B).	A. Hill (B), O. Meyerhof (G).	J. Benavente y Martinez (Sp).	F. Nansen (N).
1923	R. A. Millikan (A).	F. Pregl (Au).	F. G. Banting (C), J. R. Macleod (C).	W. B. Yeats (Ir).	—
1924	M. Siegbahn (S).	—	W. E. Einthoven (D).	W. Reymont (P).	—
1925	J. Franck (G), G. Hertz (G).	R. Zsigmondy (G).	—	G. B. Shaw (B).	Sir A. Chamberlain (B), C. G. Dawes (A).
1926	J. Perrin (F).	T. Svedberg (S).	J. Fibiger (Da).	G. Deledda (I).	A. Briand (F), G. Stresemann (G).
1927	A. H. Compton (A), C. T. R. Wilson (B).	H. Wieland (G).	J. Wagner-Jauregg (Au).	H. Bergson (F).	F. Buisson (F), L. Quidde (G).
1928	O. W. Richardson (B).	A. Windans (G).	C. Nicolle (F).	S. Undset (N).	—

1929	L. de Broglie (F).	H. v. Euler-Chelpin (S), A. Harden (B).	C. Eijkman (D), F. G. Hopkins (B).	T. Mann (G).	F. B. Kellogg (A).
1930	C. V. Raman (In).	H. Fischer (G).	K. Landsteiner (Au).	S. Lewis (A).	L. O. J. Söderblom (S).
1931	—	F. Bergius (G), K. Bosch (G).	O. Warburg (G).	E. A. Karlfeldt (S).	Jane Addams (A), N. M. Butler (A).
1932	W. Heisenberg (G).	I. Langmuir (A).	C. S. Sherrington (B), E. D. Adrian (B).	J. Galsworthy (B).	—
1933	P. A. M. Dirac (B), E. Schroedinger (Au).	—	T. H. Morgan (A).	I. A. Bunin (R).	Sir Norman Angell (B).
1934	—	H. C. Urey (A).	G. Minot (A), W. Murphy (A), G. Whipple (A).	L. Pirandello (I).	Arthur Henderson (B).
1935	J. Chadwick (B).	F. Joliot (F), I. Joliot-Curie (F).	H. Spemann (G).	—	C. von Ossietzky (G).
1936	V. F. Hess (Au), C. D. Anderson (A).	P. Debye (D).	Sir H. H. Dale (B), O. Loewi (G).	E. O'Neill (A).	C. de S. Lamas (Ar).
1937	C. J. Davisson (A), G. F. Thomson (B).	W. N. Haworth (B), P. Karrer (Sw).	A. v. Szent-Dyörgyi (H).	R. Martin du Gard (F).	Viscount Cecil of Chelwood (B).
1938	E. Fermi (I).	R. Kuhn (G).	C. Heymans (Be).	Pearl S. Buck (A).	Office International Nansen pour les Réfugiés.
1939	E. O. Lawrence (A).	A. F. Butenandt (G), L. Ruzicka (Sw).	G. Domagk (G).	F. E. Sillanpää (Fi).	—
1940–42	—	—	—	—	—
1943	O. Stern (A).	G. Hevsey (H).	H. Dam (Da), E. A. Doisy (A).	—	—
1944	I. I. Rabi (A).	O. Hahn (G).	E. J. Erlanger (A), H. S. Gasser (A).	J. V. Jensen (Da).	Comité International de la Croix-Rouge, Geneva.
1945	W. Pauli (Au.).	A. Virtanen (Fi).	Sir A. Fleming (B), Sir H. Florey (B), E. B. Chain (B).	G. Mistral (Ch).	Cordell Hull (A).
1946	P. W. Bridgman (A).	J. B. Sumner (A), J. H. Northrop (A), W. M. Stanley (A).	H. J. Muller (A).	H. Hesse (Sw).	Emily G. Balch (A), J. R. Mott (A).
1947	Sir Edward Appleton (B).	Sir Robert Robinson (B).	B. A. Houssay (Ar), C. F. Cori (A), G. T. Cori (A).	André Gide (F).	American and British Quaker Organisations.
1948	P. M. S. Blackett (B).	A. Tiselius (S).	P. Müller (Sw).	T. S. Eliot (B).	—
1949	H. Yukawa (J).	W. F. Giauque (A).	W. R. Hess (Sw), A. E. Moniz (Po).	W. Faulkner (A).	Lord Boyd-Orr (B).
1950	Cecil F. Powell (B).	Otto Diels (G), K. Alder (G).	E. C. Kendall (A), P. S. Hench (A), R. Reichstein (Sw).	Lord Russell (B).	Ralph Bunche (A).
1951	Sir J. Cockcroft (B), E. T. S. Walton (Ir.)	E. M. MacMillan (A), G. T. Seaborg (A).	M. Theiler (A).	P. Lagerkvist (S).	Léon Jouhaux (F).
1952	E. Purcell (A), F. Bloch (A).	A. J. P. Martin (B), R. L. M. Synge (B).	S. Waksman (A).	F. Mauriac (F).	A. Schweitzer (F).
1953	F. Zernike (D).	H. Staudinger (G).	H. A. Krebs (B), F. A. Lipmann (A).	Sir W. S. Churchill (B).	Gen. G. Marshall (A).
1954	M. Born (B), W. Bothe (G).	L. Pauling (A).	J. F. Enders (A), F. C. Robins (A), T. H. Weller (A).	E. Hemingway (A).	U.N. High Commission for Refugees,
1955	W. E. Lamb (A), P. Kusch (A).	Vicent du Vigneaud (A).	Hugo Theorell (S).	Halldor Laxness (Ic).	—
1956	W. Shockley (A), J. Bardeen (A), W. H. Brattain (A).	Sir Cyril Hinshelwood (B), N. Semenov (R).	A. F. Cournaud (A), D. W. Richards (A), W. Forssmann (G).	J. Ramón Jiménez (Sp.)	—

Year.	Physics.	Chemistry.	Physiology and Medicine.	Literature.	Peace.
1957	T. D. Lee (Chi), C. N. Yang (Chi).	Lord Todd (B).	D. Bovet (I).	A. Camus (F).	L. B. Pearson (C).
1958	P. A. Cerenkov (R), I. M. Frank (R), I. Tamm (R).	F. Sanger (B).	G. W. Beadle (A), E. Tatum (A), J. Lederberg (A).	B. Pasternak (R).	Father George Pire (Be).
1959	E. Segré (A). O. Chamberlain (A).	J. Heyrovsky (Cz).	S. Ochoa (A), A. Kornberg (A).	S. Quasimodo (I).	P. J. Noel-Baker (B).
1960	D. A. Glaser (A).	W. F. Libby (A).	P. B. Medawar (B), Sir M. Burnet (Aus).	A. St. Léger (F).	A. Luthuli (S.A.).
1961	R. Hofstadter (A), R. Mossbauer (G),	M. Calvin (A).	G. von Bekesy (H).	L. Andric (Y).	D. Hammarskjöld (S).
1962	L. Davidovich Landau (R).	M. F. Perutz (B), J. C. Kendrew (B).	F. H. C. Crick (B), M. H. F. Wilkins (B), J. D. Watson (A).	J. Steinbeck (A).	L. Pauling (A).
1963	Maria Goeppert-Mayer (A), J. H. D. Jensen (G), E. P. Wigner (A).	K. Ziegler (G), G. Natta (I).	A. L. Hodgkin (B), A. F. Huxley (B), Sir J. Eccles (B).	G. Seferis (Gr).	International Red Cross Committee and the International League of Red Cross Societies.
1964	C. H. Townes (A), N. G. Basov (R), A. M. Prokhorov (R).	Dorothy Hodgkin (B).	K. E. Bloch (A), F. Lynen (G).	Jean-Paul Sartre (F).	Martin Luther King (A).
1965	S. Tomonaga (J), J. Schwinger (A), P. Feynman (A).	A. B. Woodward (A).	F. Jacob (F), A. Lwoff (F), J. Monod (F).	M. Sholokhov (R).	UNICEF
1966	A. Kastler (F).	R. S. Mulliken (A).	F. P. Rous (A), C. A. Huggins (A).	S. Y. Agnon (Is), Nelly Sachs (Sw).	No award
1967	H. A. Bethe (A).	R. G. W. Norrish (B), G. Porter (B), M. Eigen (G).	R. Granit (S), H. K. Hartline (A), G. Wald (A).	M. A. Asturias (Gu).	No award
1968	L. W. Alvarez (A).	L. Onsager (A).	M. Nirenberg (A), H. G. Khorana (A), R. Holley (A).	Y. Kawabata (J).	R. Cassn (F).
1969	M. Gell-Mann (A).	D. H. R. Barton (B), O. Hassel (N).	M. Dellbrück (A), A. D. Hershey (A), S. E. Luria (A).	S. Beckett (Ir).	The International Labour Organisation
1970	L. E. Néel (F), H. Alfvén (Sw).	L. F. Leloir (Ar).	Sir Bernard Katz (B), U. von Euler (S), J. Axelrod (A).	A. Solzhenitsyn (R).	N. E. Borlang (A).
1971	D. Gabor (B).	G. Herzberg (C).	E. W. Sutherland (A).	P. Neruda (Ch).	W. Brandt (G).
1972	J. Bardeen (A), L. N. Cooper (A), J. R. Schrieffer (A).	C. B. Anfinsen (A), S. Moore (A), W. H. Stein (A).	R. Porter (B), G. Edelman (A).	Heinrich Böll (G).	No award
1973	B. Josephson (B).	E. O. Fischer (G).	N. Tinbergen (D).	P. White (Aus).	H. Kissinger (A).
	L. Esaki (J).	G. Wilkinson (B).	K. von Frisch (Au).		Le Duc Tho (NV).
	I. Giaever (A).		K. Lorenz (Au).		

Note: The first Nobel Prize in the Economic Sciences was awarded in 1969 jointly to J. Tinbergen (D), and R. Frisch (N); 1970: P. A. Samuelson; 1971: S. Kuznets (A); 1972: Sir J. Hicks (B), K. Arrow (A); 1973: W. Leontief (A).

Year.	Physics.	Chemistry.	Medicine.	Literature.	Economics.	Peace.
1974	Sir Martin Ryle (B). A. Hewish (B).	P. J. Flory (A).	A. Claude (Be), C. de Duve (Be), G. E. Palade (A).	E. Johnson (S), H. Martinson (S).	G. Myrdal (S), F. von Hayek (B).	S. MacBride (Ir), E. Sato (J).
1975	J. Rainwater (A), A. Bohr (Da), B. Mottelson (Da).	J. Warcup (Aus), V. Prelog (Sw).	D. Baltimore (A), R. Dulbecco (A), H. M. Temin (A).	E. Montale (I).	L. V. Kantorovich (R), T. C. Koopmans (A)	A. D. Sakharov (R).
1976	B. Richter (A), S. Ting (A).	W. N. Lipscomb (A).	B. S. Blumberg (A), D. C. Gajdusek (A).	S. Bellow (A).	M. Friedman (A).	Reserved for 1977.

A = American
Ar = Argentine
Au = Austrian
Aus = Australian
B = British
Be = Belgian
C = Canadian
Ch = Chilean
Chi = Chinese
Cz = Czech
D = Dutch
Da = Danish
F = French
Fi = Finnish
G = German
Gr = Greek
Gu = Guatemalan
H = Hungarian
I = Italian
Ic = Icelandic
In = Indian
Ir = Irish
Is = Israeli
J = Japanese
N = Norwegian
NV = North Vietnamese
P = Polish
Po = Portuguese
R = Russian
S = Swedish
S.A. = South African
Sp = Spanish
Sw = Swiss
Y = Yugoslav

Marginal mark	Meaning	Corresponding mark in text
δ/	Delete (take out)	Cross through
δ (enclosed in close-up marks)	Delete and close-up	Above and below letters to be taken out
stet	Leave as printed (when words have been crossed out by mistake)	. . . . Under letters or words to remain
caps	Change to capital letters	≡ Under letters or words to be altered
s.c.	Change to small capitals	= Under letters or words to be altered
caps & s.c.	Use capital letters for initial letters and small capitals for rest of words	≡ Under initial letters and = under the rest of the words
l.c.	Change from capitals to lower case	Encircle letters to be altered
bold	Change to bold type	~~~ Under letters or words to be altered
ital.	Change to italics	—— Under letters or words to be altered
rom.	Change to roman type	Encircle words to be altered
w.f.	(Wrong fount.) Replace by letter of correct fount	Encircle letter to be altered
ϑ	Invert type	Encircle letter to be altered
×	Replace by similar but undamaged character	Encircle letter to be altered
⅄	Insert (or substitute) superior figure or sign	⋌ (Or encircle letters or signs to be altered)
⅄	Insert (or substitute) inferior figure or sign	⋌ (Or encircle letters or signs to be altered)
⁀‿	Close-up—delete space between letters	⁀‿ Linking words or letters
#	Insert space	⋀
eq.#	Make spacing equal	L Between words
less#	Reduce space	L Between words
trs.	Transpose	⌴⌐ Between letters or words, numbered when necessary
centre	Place in centre of line	Indicate position with ⌐ ¬
⌐	Move to the left	⌐
¬	Move to the right	¬
n.p.	Begin a new paragraph	[Before first word of new paragraph
run on	No fresh paragraph here	⟶ Between paragraphs
spell out	The abbreviation or figure to be spelt out in full	Encircle words or figures to be altered
⋌	(Caret mark.) Insert matter indicated in margin	⋌
‘⅄ ’⅄	Insert single quotation marks	⋌ ⋌
“⅄ ”⅄	Insert double quotation marks	⋌ ⋌

LITERARY COMPANION

This section discusses the modern novel and suggests ways of approaching the poetry of the current century. It contains a guide to versification and to our figures of speech.

TABLE OF CONTENTS

I. THE CONTEMPORARY NOVEL

This section discusses novels written in English and published since 1945. It consists of two parts: I. Introduction; II. Directory of Novelists.

Most of us read novels because they "take us out of ourselves". Sometimes we are just seeking relaxation and enjoyment, at others we hope that the book will leave us with a feeling of having lived more intensely, that it will make us more aware of life's possibilities and help us better to understand its meaning.

If we pick up a modern novel that seems incoherent or even to consist of little more than detailed descriptions of objects, we may well be tempted to abandon it; but, although of course novels exist which not only seem, but indeed are incoherent rubbish, many only appear so because we do not know how to read them. If we can learn to, we may find them some of the most rewarding of all novels.

Perhaps the author's technique is unfamiliar to us. Perhaps our disappointment and difficulty stem from the fact we have misunderstood his intention. If we are accustomed to novelists who, like Jane Austen, describe their characters' emotions, we may at first be confused by Joyce's technique in *Portrait of the Artist*, which involves not the description but the poetic evocation of feeling. Bellow's fine comedy *Herzog* will seem trivial if we are expecting it to be a symbolic tragedy on the lines of Melville's *Moby Dick*. In a novel of ideas, such as Vonnegut's *Player Piano* or Orwell's *1984*, there is no place for the kind of realistic description and subtle characterisation that we find in James's *Wings of a Dove* or George Eliot's *Middlemarch*.

Wide and attentive reading makes it easier for us to appreciate an author's techniques and to understand his intention, but we must also remember that every worthwhile novel is an individual work of art, creating its own rules. However strange the book at first may seem, we should, therefore, try to suspend judgment until we have read, and perhaps even re-read, it carefully and receptively.

The second part of this article reviews some of the most interesting and talented novels of the last three decades and suggests ways of approaching them; but the contemporary novel developed from, and in some respects in reaction to, European and American novels of the nineteenth and early twentieth centuries. Our first section therefore summarises important characteristics of these earlier novels and suggests some of the ways in which new ideas and attitudes seem to have affected the work of our contemporary writers.

INTRODUCTION.

The Mid-Nineteenth Century.

(a) English and American Novels.

At this time English novelists were members of a comparatively secure and stable society which possessed generally accepted social and moral standards, and the theme of almost all their writing is the interaction of the individual and the community. Novelists such as George Eliot, Dickens, Thackeray, and Trollope depict characters who progress towards self-knowledge as they learn to discriminate between the genuine and the false, the good and the evil in the people and institutions with which they are brought into contact. Since these writers were as much concerned with the presentation of society as of individuals, most of their work contains naturalistic descriptions of the life and manners of their day and, although the main characters of the Victorian novel are the focal points of its action, as Douglas Hewitt has remarked, they are not central to it in the way that the hero of a tragedy is central, the action is not "orientated towards them."

Most English novels of this period are comparatively loose and episodic in form. They usually present a chronological story told by an omniscient narrator, who reports the characters' actions and feelings, commenting upon them and judging them against standards the reader is assumed to share. Quite often the narrator addresses the reader directly and it is common for him or her to introduce general remarks on social and intellectual questions.

A notable exception to this general pattern is *Wuthering Heights*. In both its techniques and its view of life Emily Brontë's novel has more in common with mid-nineteenth-century American fiction than with the work of her compatriots and is unique among the English novels of its day in its disregard of society and of social and moral conventions.

American novelists, such as Twain, Hawthorne and Melville, were interested in the presentation of individuals rather than of society. This was natural in a country inhabited by pioneers and exiles, and their descendants, who had no common culture. Like the heroes of tragedies, the main characters of mid-nineteenth-century American novels are central to their action, isolated pioneers and exiles who create their own worlds.

American novelists used chronological narrative, but they generally wrote in the first person and their techniques were in other ways different from those of most of their English contemporaries and characterised by the use of allegory and symbolism.

In both countries novelists wrote for a middle-class public and, like their readers, they saw fiction as a mode of entertainment and, or, instruction. However, in France other ideas were being born which were to affect both the form and content of twentieth-century English and American fiction and lead many writers to think of novels as primarily works of art.

(b) French Novels.

Gautier and Aestheticism.

As early as 1825 Gautier had said that a writer must concern himself only with perfecting the style and form of his work and that this was impossible if he considered "the needs of society", "civilization", or "progress". Later, he wrote, "A beautiful form is a beautiful idea", implying that a novelist could treat any subject, no matter how sordid or painful, so long as he embodied it in a beautiful work of art.

Flaubert and Realism.

Flaubert, a leading member of the Realist school, felt that novelists must strive to be impersonal, adapting their style to their subject-matter, for only thus could they write "realistically". He believed that it helped novelists to be objective if they based their work on scientific documentation and said, "It is necessary to discuss the human soul with the [same] impersonality that one uses in [the study of] physical sciences." To the public, who were shocked by Flaubert's unconventional subject-matter, "realistic" became a term signifying moral disapproval.

"Realistic" is now used of (i) novels of working-class life, such as Sillitoe's *Saturday Night and Sunday Morning* (*see* **Neo-Realism, M8**); (ii) any frank treatment of the physical aspects of life, or of painful or sordid subjects, as in Mailer's *The Naked and the Dead*. Our use of the term has been influenced by Marxist theory and by the writing of the Naturalists.

Zola and Naturalism.

Zola and his followers called themselves Naturalists because, although they agreed with Flaubert that novelists should aim at objectivity, they wanted to produce "slices of life" rather than "works of art". Zola was stimulated by new scientific ideas and particularly interested in the effects of heredity and environment upon character. He inclined to the theory that character is largely determined by environment and wrote of the former in terms of the latter. Fascinated by the sordid side of nineteenth-century life, he tended to concentrate on it to the exclusion of all else and stimulated interest in the portrayal of moral degradation, brutality, and squalor. In England the National Vigilance Society waged a vigorous, and unsuccessful, campaign against the publication of translations of such "corrupt literature"!

1880–1910.

This period introduced some of the most popular kinds of modern novel: inspired by the work of the Frenchman Verne, H. G. Wells began to write Science Fiction; W. Le Queux's *Guilty Bonds*, 1890, introduced the Spy Thriller, a genre brilliantly exploited by Conrad in *The Secret Agent*, 1907, and Conan Doyle developed the Detective Story.

The work of the French Naturalists was influential throughout this period, but, although it helped to widen the scope of the novel it found few close adherents among English or American writers who were, and are, more interested in those idiosyncratic aspects of personality disregarded by the Naturalists. The influence of Gautier and, particularly, Flaubert was more important and was first apparent in the work of James and Conrad, both of whom saw themselves as artists, rather than teachers or entertainers. They have been called the first Modern English Novelists.

(a) Henry James (1843–1916).

James admired the work of Gautier and was much impressed by Flaubert's theory of fiction. Like Flaubert, he strove towards an objective, detailed presentation of character and constantly sought to depict the nuances of feeling more delicately and precisely and to give his novels greater aesthetic unity. Many twentieth-century writers call James "The Master", for the scrupulous care with which he revised and polished the style of his novels and short-stories established an ideal of literary craftsmanship. The artistry and poetic sensitivity of his writing have had a marked effect upon the work of writers such as Elizabeth Bowen and Hartley. James began the process of combining the social novel of the European tradition with the more poetic American novel, a process to be carried much farther by Conrad in *Nostromo*.

(b) Joseph Conrad (1857–1926).

Conrad spent his youth in France and was well read in French literature. The sense of insecurity which permeates his writing is one of the first signs in English fiction of the break-up of the social and moral stability of the nineteenth century. This change appeared earlier on the Continent than in England and it is perhaps significant that Conrad was of Polish birth and always spoke French better than English, but his sense of insecurity was doubtless intensified by the hazards of his early naval career in the days of sailing-ships.

Like the novels of present-day writers such as Beckett, Lowry, and White, Conrad's books are essentially poetic and can be read on a number of different levels. They are as realistic as nineteenth-century French novels, but their every detail bears a significant relation to the plight of their central characters, and in his masterpiece, *Nostromo*, Conrad showed that a novel of great poetic intensity could yet encompass the life of a whole society.

James had been unable to banish the intrusive presence of the author from his novels; Conrad managed to: at times by using a narrator who is deeply involved in the action, at others by reviving an eighteenth-century technique of telling the story from shifting points of view. At the same time he abandoned chronological narrative for a shifting time sequence, which reinforces his themes by intensifying a feeling of insecurity. Narrative of this kind has been used with similar effect by a number of modern novelists, including Beckett, Bellow, and Naipaul, and, although the use of the shifting time sequence, which marks one of the most obvious differences between nineteenth- and twentieth-century fiction, has been influenced by the writing of Proust and Joyce and by new ideas in theoretical physics and psychology, Conrad was the first modern novelist to use this kind of narrative.

The Early Twentieth Century.

"On or about December 1910 human nature changed", said Virginia Woolf. She probably chose that date because it marked the opening of the first London exhibition of the paintings of the post-impressionists. The work of these artists expressed a new vision of reality which was characteristic of the intellectual and cultural revolution sweeping Western society in the early decades of the century. The stimulus of this new Renaissance was reflected not only in painting, but in the music of Stravinsky, the dance of the Diaghilev Ballet, the poetry of Pound and Eliot and the novels of Proust, Joyce, and Virginia Woolf herself. The sense of exhilaration felt at this time is vividly suggested in Leonard Woolf's autobiographical work *Beginning Again*.

The stability and formality of nineteenth-century life, which had already been undermined by the ideas of Darwin and Huxley, the growing literacy of the working-classes, and the accelerating technological revolution, was now shattered by the combined impact of psychological theories, the ideas of social anthropologists such as Sir James Frazer and the work of physicists like Planck, Einstein, and Rutherford (*see* **F10–13**). As a result, novelists could no longer assume that readers' attitudes and values would resemble their own and were obliged to reconsider the nature of the relationship between art and life. The exploration of this relationship becomes one of the major themes of twentieth-century fiction, and after the First World War it is accompanied by an increasing sense of the isolation and insecurity of the individual's life and the inadequacy of words as vehicles for communicating experience.

For most writers the nineteenth-century European novel now seemed inadequate to express the complex and fluid nature of consciousness revealed by psychologists, and narrative consisting of a simple chronological progression of events was felt to give a misleading impression of our experience of time. Novelists were therefore compelled to search for new techniques, and were encouraged to do so by the example of experiments already taking place in art and music and by the example of the French Symbolist poets.

(a) The Influence of Psychological Theories.

The interest in the nature of perception revealed in the work of impressionist and post-impressionist painters had been growing since the turn of the century and was stimulated by the writings of the American William James and the Frenchman Henri Bergson.

In 1890, James, the brother of novelist Henry James, had published *Principles of Psychology*, in which he compared consciousness with a "river or a stream," implying that it carries within it submerged and floating memories and receives a fluid series of impressions of the exterior world.

The term "stream of consciousness", derived from James's theory, was later applied to a new literary technique evolved by Joyce.

In *Matter and Memory* (1894), Bergson had suggested that perception is controlled by memory and said that our view of the world changes at every moment, "as though by a turn of a kaleidoscope," suggesting that perception involves an involuntary, creative readjustment of elements of past experience. This idea was to have a profound effect upon the work of Proust, to whom Bergson was related by marriage.

The writings of Freud, which began to be published in English in 1913, drew further attention to details of human experience, stimulating the growing interest in the subconscious mind, in dreams and the symbolic transformation of experience, and combining with the influence of the Symbolist writers and the music of Wagner to give new impetus to the use of symbolism in fiction.

The influence of Freudian theory also extended the novel's potential subject-matter in two most important ways.

By emphasising the frail barrier between rational and irrational behaviour Freud made possible an imaginative discussion of neurosis and insanity, which had been regarded as shameful in the nineteenth century. The results of this more sympathetic attitude can be seen in the novels of writers such as Faulkner, Bellow, and White, while novels like Doris Lessing's *Briefing for a Descent into Hell* (1971) and Jennifer Dawson's *The Ha-Ha* (1961), an imaginative study of a schizophrenic, are inconceivable as the work of any pre-Freudian writer.

Perhaps the most influential of all Freud's theories was his suggestion that our attitudes and behaviour are determined primarily by sexual needs and experience. Nineteenth-century novelists had been extremely reserved in their treatment of sexual life and although eighteenth-century writers had been uninhibited they had regarded erotic experience either as merely incidental to their characters' lives, or as a subject for ribald comedy and satire. Freudian theories have encouraged modern novelists to treat sexual experience more freely than it was in the nineteenth century and more imaginatively and seriously than it had been by earlier writers. Indeed it is now unusual for a novelist to treat sex humorously!

Freud's ideas on infantile sexuality also aroused enormous interest in childhood experience and relationships between parents and children, particularly in the ways that these might later affect the adult. Novelists whose work reflects this interest include Ivy Compton-Burnett, Hartley, Styron, and Wilson.

It is interesting to note that, despite the influence of Freud and later psychologists, and writers such as Kinsey, it is only within the last decade that English public opinion has allowed novelists to treat erotic love and sexual deviation as frankly as eighteenth-century writers could. An important date in the restriction of censorship came in 1960, when Penguin Books won their case for the publication of an unexpurgated edition of Lawrence's *Lady Chatterley's Lover*.

(b) The Influence of the Symbolists. *See also* **M32.**

The work and ideas of the writers associated with this school, which arose in France in the last decades of the nineteenth century, and included the poets Rimbaud and Mallarmé, have had a far-reaching effect upon modern fiction.

The Symbolists' technical experiments in using verbal association, deliberate ambiguities of phrase and syntax, multiple analogies and esoteric allusion, in poetry, and interior monologue in fiction, suggested means by which modern novelists might attempt to express the subtleties of individual consciousness and to create new forms of novel. The Symbolists' feeling that artists are gifted with a mystical apprehension of Reality, and their consequent belief that, in order to express this apprehension, art should possess the evocative, lyrical qualities of music, not only helped novelists like Proust and Joyce to evolve new forms for the novel, but has had a less happy influence on some other writers, encouraging them to indulge in vague metaphysical musings. Two gifted novelists whose work seems to have suffered in this way are the Austrian Hermann Broch and a writer from Guyana, Wilson Harris, both of whose novels are at times highly evocative, but too often seem to degenerate into meaningless verbiage. (However, the eminent critic George Steiner suggests in *Language and Silence* that Broch's *Death of Virgil* (1945) is one of the greatest novels of the century, comparable only with Joyce's *Ulysses*. Its theme is similar to that of T. S. Eliot's *Four Quartets*, and, like Eliot's poem, it is constructed in the form of four "movements", each based on the "key" of one of the elements, earth, air, fire, and water).

The Symbolists' dream of producing a "universal poem", an epic myth on the scale of Goethe's *Faust*, has been reflected in the work of many modern novelists, notably in Joyce's *Ulysses* and *Finnegans Wake*, the German Thomas Mann's *Joseph and His Brothers*, Broch's *Death of Virgil* and, more recently, in the novels of Beckett, Golding, Lowry, Styron, and White.

(c) The Influence of Russian Literature.

A subsidiary, but nevertheless important influence upon the novel has come from the writing of the great nineteenth-century Russian authors. Turgenev has been available in English since the 1890s. Tolstoy, Dostoyevsky, and Chekhov began to be translated just before the First World War. Their writing heightened novelists' interest in conveying a more spiritual reality and the work of Turgenev and Chekhov particularly encouraged writers who were moving towards a more lyrical treatment of style and form, while the novels of Dostoyevsky stimulated the interest aroused by Freud in the imaginative presentation of mentally handicapped, neurotic, psychotic, and psychopathic characters. American and English novelists' attitudes to the work of these and other Russian authors can be studied in the anthology *Russian Literature and Modern English Fiction*, edited, D. Davie.

(d) Innovators of Literary Techniques.

Marcel Proust (1871–1922).

In his huge novel *À la recherche du temps perdu* (1913–27) Proust evokes the kaleidoscopic patterns of involuntary memory as they float through his narrator's mind. His work has therefore been called a *roman fleuve*—a river novel. Its plot seems non-existent, but the novel is in fact constructed with the greatest artistry and, just as the Symbolist poets used evocative images with a multiplicity of associations, so Proust introduces the characters and events of his narrative, presenting them from different viewpoints and investing them with new significance each time they are recalled. A translation of *À la recherche du temps perdu* is now published in paperback by Chatto and Windus.

James Joyce (1882–1941).

Joyce, an Irishman, spent most of his life on the Continent and although his work, like that of all great artists, was highly individual, it owed much to the stimulus of the ideas of Flaubert and the work of the Symbolists. Like Flaubert, Joyce believed that a novel should be objective and rooted in experience of everyday life, and by developing the Symbolists' techniques he achieved an hitherto unparalleled impression of objectivity in his portrayal of character.

Joyce's name is particularly associated with the "stream of consciousness" technique, which he evolved from the Symbolist writer Dujardin's "interior monologue", in order to be able to express the mind's activity—not only the way we receive passive impressions of the exterior world and associate them with past experience, the subconscious distortion and imaginative control exercised by the mind, but also how our sensibility and imagination are involved in an active "dialogue" with the world as we apprehend it. Joyce's use of this technique therefore varies considerably, according to the kind of character he is presenting, and since he attempts to express non-verbal experience, as well as verbal thought, his sentences often have a poetic rather than a discursive logic. Stimulated by Joyce's example, later novelists, including Faulkner and Lowry, have evolved their own poetic forms of the stream of consciousness technique, but most later writers have preferred to use a less poetic version, more akin to the interior monologue, expressing the stream of thought, rather than of consciousness. A contemporary novelist who uses interior monologue in this way is Bellow.

It has been suggested that Joyce, having created a new kind of novel, himself used it in every possible way. In *Portrait of the Artist* (1916) he covered the childhood and adolescence of a writer. *Ulysses* (1922) shows a day in the life of Dublin through the eyes of three people and, at the same time, creates a universal image of man's experience of life. In *Finnegans Wake* (1939) Joyce attempted to express the history of the world by evoking the dreams of a Dublin publican, but, despite its occasional brilliance, *Finnegans Wake* is largely inaccessible to readers who have not spent years studying it. Joyce has, therefore, a twofold significance for later writers: he evolved a new kind of novel and, although he wrote with such skill that others have often despaired of emulating him, his achievements have encouraged novelists to experiment, while *Finnegans Wake* has provided a classic warning of the dangers of indulging in esoteric mythmaking.

(e) Heirs of the Victorian Tradition.

D. H. Lawrence (1885–1930). *See also* **Section I.**

Lawrence had a vivid appreciation of the beauty of the natural world and emphasised the importance of the instinctual, as opposed to the intellectual, life. He felt that it was only through basic human experience, particularly through the experience of unselfish erotic love, that we could attain the peaceful self-unity that comes from an apprehension of the sacramental quality of life.

Although he abhorred didactic literature, Lawrence was, therefore, a man with a message, the "flag-bearer of intuition in its interminable struggle against logic and reason"—a true heir of the Romantic movement (*see* Section J). Lawrence's attitude to the novel was thus akin to that of Victorian writers and the form of his work has much in common with theirs, although, unlike most Victorians, he made deliberate use of poetic symbolism, which, as Walter Allen has said, "enabled him to render the felt quality of the immediate, instinctive self as it had never been before."

Although no later novelist has equalled Lawrence in the tender poetic expression of unselfish erotic love, his ideas have been widely influential. Doris Lessing is among those later novelists whose work, like Lawrence's, has emphasised the unhappiness and sterility of selfish relationships, and the American writer Baldwin also reflects his influence.

E. M. Forster (1879–1970).

Like Lawrence, Forster was a moralist, primarily interested in relationships between people and used techniques and a novel form that have much in common with those of the Victorians. A much more sophisticated novelist than Lawrence, Forster was, superficially, a writer of social comedy in the tradition of Jane Austen, but he was always aware of the numinous quality of life, and expressed it in his novels through complex symbols. His books explore individuals' attempts to "connect" with each other across "the divisions of daily life" in a mutual quest for truth. These themes, which are stated, rather than successfully conveyed in symbolic terms in his early novels, find poetic expression in his masterpiece, *A Passage to India* (1924).

Forster preferred that his early novel, *Maurice*, written 1913–14, should not appear in his lifetime. He wrote no others after *A Passage to India*, because, he said, "I had been accustomed to write about the old-fashioned world with its homes and its family life and its comparative peace. All that went, and though I can think about the new world I cannot write about it."

The "new world" is the theme of Kafka and Huxley.

(f) Important Novelists of the 1930s.

Franz Kafka (1883–1924).

A Czech by birth, Kafka wrote in German. His novels first became known to the English-speaking world on the appearance of a translation of *The Castle* in 1930. It was followed in 1935 by *The Trial*. These haunting parables of a man's nightmare life in a world where everything appears contingent, now seem prophetic, and their influence is apparent in works like Rex Warner's *The Aerodrome* (1941), Orwell's *1984*, Ellison's *The Invisible Man*, and the novels of Beckett. Surrealist techniques, giving an effect of confusion between the world of consciousness and that of dream, had been used before Kafka, but he gave them fresh significance.

His tragic short story, *Metamorphosis*, which tells of a man who wakes one day to find himself transformed into a huge insect, brought new dimensions to serious science fiction.

Aldous Huxley (1894–1963).

Huxley was unique among the novelists of the inter-war years. He declared that nothing deserved to be taken seriously save the suffering men inflict upon themselves by their own crimes and follies, and he criticised both the traditional "social" novel of personal relationships and the more poetic individualism of Joyce, Virginia Woolf, *et al.*, as reflecting conventional values that create suffering and help to perpetuate misery. Although Huxley's highly intelligent satires are very different in style from those of any other twentieth-century writer, his themes look forward to those of some of the more important post-war novelists.

John Dos Passos (1896–1970).

Dos Passos was a member of the group of Radical American novelists which also included Farrell and Steinbeck, all of whom were influenced by the work of the Naturalists. In his trilogy *U.S.A.* (1930–36), which is a panorama of American life between 1910 and 1927, Dos Passos developed the collage techniques he had evolved in *Manhattan Transfer* (1925). The trilogy is composed of short sections: some are written in interior monologue, others consist of extracts from newspaper headlines and articles and snatches of popular song, others are biographies of leading American personalities, written in a kind of "free verse" and yet others consist of extracts from the lives of fictional characters. *U.S.A.* does not form an imaginative whole and has nothing of the power of Proust's and Joyce's novels, but Dos Passos' technical experiments have exerted considerable influence, not only on a number of later American novelists, particularly Mailer, but also on French writers such as Sartre.

Recent Developments.

(a) Le Nouveau Roman.

Some critics consider the most exciting recent developments in the novel's form have been made in France by the heterogeneous group of writers whose work is given the title of *le nouveau roman*. Most of their novels are published by Éditions de Minuit, of which Alain Robbe-Grillet, one of their leaders, is a director, and are available in English translation from Calder and Boyars.

Apart from Robbe-Grillet, the most notable of these novelists include Claude Simon Michel Butor and Nathalie Sarraute. Some of their theories about fiction are to be found in Robbe-Grillet's *For a New Novel*, Butor's *The Inventory* and Sarraute's *The Age Of Suspicion*. Interested readers should also refer to *Writing Degree Zero*, *Mythologies* and *S/Z*, by the influential critic and linguistic philosopher Roland Barthes.

Although the writers of the *nouveau roman* have individual styles, all seek to present a character's state of mind over a brief period of time, while introducing incidental details of his past experience. Their techniques involve the inconsequential repetition of key images and phrases in ever differing combinations and contexts. Such aims may seem new to the French literary scene but they are familiar to English readers of the eighteenth-century Lawrence Sterne (*v.* his *Tristram Shandy*, 1760–7). The techniques of the *nouveau roman*, derived from the Symbolists, Joyce and Proust, are not really new either and, although skilfully deployed, often mask the trivial content of works which have nothing of the power of Samuel Beckett's fables (*qq.v.*), their immediate inspiration.

The only English novelist closely associated with this French group is Christine Brooke-Rose (*q.v.*). The experimental writer B. S. Johnson has expressed similar aims to those of authors of the *nouveau roman*, but his novels are very different from theirs.

(b) Novels from the Commonwealth.

Since 1945 the language of the English novel has been invigorated by the work of talented African and West Indian writers. Drawing upon a long tradition of oral story-telling these novelists are particularly skilful in their treatment of narrative and dialogue. The importance of their work was recognised in 1965 by the institution of the Jock Campbell–New Statesman prize, awarded triennially to an African or Caribbean novelist writing in English. The first two prizes went to the leading Nigerian writers Chinua Achebe and Wole Soyinka (*qq.v.*). The third was won by Shiva Naipaul, younger brother of the outstanding V. S. Naipaul from Trinidad (*qq.v.*)

There are various guides to the work of the new African novelists. Charles K. Larson's *The Emergence of African Fiction*, 1972, is particularly recommended. Heinemann Educational publish a very good, inexpensive series of editions of African writing.

Novelists from other areas of the Commonwealth have also made their mark. Nadine Gordimer, Dan Jacobson and Doris Lessing (*qq.v.*), Southern African writers of European stock, have given new impetus to the English novel's traditional interest in the interaction of society and the individual. A more idiosyncratic genius is that of the Australian Patrick White (*q.v.*). Some consider his *Tree of Man* and *Voss* to be among the finest modern novels in any language.

Indian writers have made a smaller impression, partly because their work has, with few important exceptions, seemed more conventional and less vigorous, partly because the work of some of the leading Indian novelists writing in English can be difficult to obtain. However, most libraries can offer some examples of R. K. Narayan's classic comedies (*q.v.*) and *bona fide* students may be able to borrow the work of other important writers such as Mulk Raj Anand and Raj Rao (*qq.v.*) from the London library of the Indian High Commission. Two critical guides are worth consulting: K. R. Srinavasa Iyengar's *Indian Writing in English*, 1962, and Margaret E. Derrett's *Modern Indian Novel in English*, 1966.

(c) Neo-Realism.

In the late 1950s and early '60s there was an upsurge of realistic writing in England. The early "kitchen sink" dramas of Osborne and Wesker (*see* Section I) were complemented by novels such as Keith Waterhouse's *There is a Happy Land*, 1957 (P) and *Billy Liar*, 1959 (P); Allan Sillitoe's *Saturday Night and Sunday Morning*, 1958 (P) and his fine *nouvelle The Loneliness of the Long-Distance Runner*, 1959; David Storey's *This Sporting Life*, 1960 and Stan Barstow's *A Kind of Loving*, 1960.

Most earlier novels of working-class life, such as Arthur Morrison's *The Hole in the Wall*, 1902, and Walter Greenwood's classic of the '30s *Love on the Dole*, had been primarily concerned to reveal the suffering of the poor. This new group of young writers, though very aware of its hardships, sought rather to present objective realistic images of working life as seen from the inside. The most interesting member of the group is David Storey (*q.v.*). At the moment a new reaction against neo-realistic writing is affecting the novel as well as the theatre, but two new younger writers, Melvyn Bragg and Philip Callow have produced promising work.

(d) Documentary and Brechtian Novels.

The "theatre of fact" (*see* I5), which attempted to present objective documentary plays on political subjects such as the Oppenheimer case, was followed towards the end of the '60s by a new kind of "documentary" novel when Mailer published his *Armies of the Night*, 1968 (*q.v.*), a factual account of the 1967 Peace March on the Pentagon in which Mailer participated. In the novel he is himself humorously described in the third person. This book and Mailer's subsequent *Miami and the Siege of Chicago* and *Of a Fire on the Moon* (*qq.v.*) differ from plays of the "theatre of fact" in using a comic tone as the vehicle of their implied criticism of the American authorities. Brian Moore's *The Revolution Script*, 1972 is more sombre. Its subject is the Quebec Separatist Movement's kidnapping of James Cross and Pierre Laporte.

Another dramatic influence, that of Brechtian epic theatre (*see* I28), would seem to lie behind John Berger's *G.*, 1972 (*q.v.*), in which the narrator assumes the pose of a completely detached observer calmly presenting his characters, now pausing to refer to contemporary social and political questions, now introducing lyrical passages of first-person narrative in which the protagonist "speaks" to the "audience", now discussing matters of literary techniques.

The influence of Brecht's "alienation" methods may also have affected the narrative approach of John Fowles in his *French Lieutenant's Woman*, 1969 (*q.v.*), and possibly had some influence on the form of Alan Burns's satire *Dreamerika!* 1972.

Unlike the Victorian "omniscient" author, the modern Brechtian novelist makes no pretence of complete knowledge of his characters. He presents what a privileged observer may see of their actions and deduce of their thought and feelings.

Conclusions.

In general during the twentieth century the novel has gained in dramatic and poetic intensity but its vision of the world has become restricted to that of one or a few characters. It thus resembles the nineteenth-century American novel more closely than that of Victorian England. The reason for this may be partly a result of the interest in individual experience aroused by psychology, but seems more particularly a reflection of modern life. The diverse nature of our urbanised society makes it virtually impossible to write a modern *Middlemarch*, and in a world possessing few generally accepted moral or social standards men are likely to feel more akin to the pioneers and exiles of nineteenth-century America. But nineteenth-century Americans were supported by a strong religious or humanist faith, which we have generally lost. A great deal of modern art, not only fiction, expresses feelings of isolation, bewilderment and suffering, themes which find their supreme expression in modern literature in the tragi-comic novels and plays of Beckett. But some fine novelists, such as Bellow, have a more positive vision.

Many writers continue to use and adapt the techniques developed by Proust and Joyce in the early part of the century but others are combining a poetic use of symbols with a comparatively straightforward, realistic narrative, more akin to that of Lawrence and Forster. It is interesting that, except for Kingsley Amis, Graham Greene and the French Robbe-Grillet, no contemporary novelist of any stature has chosen to exploit the highly popular form of the detective novel, while the vigorous school of science fiction writers has produced no work of outstanding literary merit since the 1930s.

II. DIRECTORY OF NOVELISTS.

In this part we discuss the work of some of the more important novelists who have published since 1945. It is inevitably selective. A more detailed treatment of the twentieth-century American and English novel may be found in Walter Allen's *Tradition and Dream* (P). The revised edition of Anthony Burgess's *The Novel Now* has some useful bibliographies and helpful studies of individual authors are available in Oliver and Boyd's paperbacked series *Writers and Their Critics*.

Dates quoted are those of the first publication.

Paperback editions are referred to thus: C: Calder and Boyars. Co: Corgi. F: Faber and Faber. Fo: Fontana. FS: Four Square. M: Mayflower. P: Penguin. Pa: Panther. S: Signet Books.

Chinua Achebe (b. 1930).

Achebe, the Nigerian author of four most elegantly-written novels, was awarded the first *New Statesman* prize for African and Caribbean writers in 1965.

Things Fall Apart, 1958; *No Longer at Ease*, 1960; *Arrow of God*, 1964.

These novels are all concerned with the impact of Western society upon Ibo culture in earlier years of the century. Achebe shows a vivid appreciation of the value and dignity of the Ibo's traditional ways of life, but his overriding theme is the need for men to have flexible, receptive minds. The hero of each of these novels comes to a tragic end because he cannot adapt to the demands of a new and unforeseen situation.

The three books are characterised by the grace and dignity of their language and are very different in tone from Achebe's latest novel.

A Man of People. 1966.

This is a fiercely ironic study of the career of Chief Nanga, leading demagogue in a newly independent African state. It has been suggested that the portrait of Nanga is modelled from Nkrumah. Although Achebe presents Nanga as an unscrupulous opportunist he also stresses the attractive qualities of his character and suggests that he is, ultimately, a victim of circumstances. It is interesting to compare this novel with Gordimer's *A Guest of Honour* and Naipaul's *Mimic Men* (*qq.v.*).

Kingsley Amis (b. 1922).

Amis made his name with *Lucky Jim*, 1954 (P), which was later filmed with Ian Carmichael giving an hilarious performance in the title role of a young lecturer in rebellion against the "phoneyness" of middle-class values in his provincial university.

Together with John Wain, whose *Hurry on Down* had appeared a few months earlier, Amis articulated the feelings of the post-war generation of graduates, many of them from the lower-middle and working classes, the beneficiaries of the 1944 Education Act. They scorned the pretentions of an upper-middle-class "Establishment" while envying its confidence and jealous of its power. "Lucky Jim" became something of a folk hero and Amis was spoken of as if he had inaugurated the cult of the Angry Young Man. His name was for a time associated with those of Braine, Barstow and Sillitoe who, in novels like *Room at the Top*, *A Kind of Loving* and *Saturday Night and Sunday Morning* portrayed other young men rebelling against the provincial society in which they found themselves; but Amis never had much in common with such neo-realist novelists (*see* M8), and as time has passed his difference from them has become ever more apparent. He is primarily a writer of farcical satire, with a lively talent for mimicry and a beautifully lucid style.

Amis has now some dozen novels to his credit, of which the most interesting, apart from *Lucky Jim* are *The Anti-Death League*, 1966 (P), a parody of the spy thriller, and *Girl 20*, 1971 (Pa), his best novel, which satirises those middle-aged men who strenuously attempt to preserve a youthful veneer by aping the latest adolescent fashion and having affaires with very young women.

A writer of great natural gifts Amis is always entertaining but has yet to publish a really outstanding novel.

Mulk Raj Anand (b. 1905).

Mulk Raj Anand is one of the most important Indian novelists writing in English. Much of his work is published in Bombay, but can sometimes be obtained from libraries. His novels include *The Private Life of an Indian Prince*, 1953; *The Old Woman and the Cow*, 1960; *Death of a Hero*, 1963, and *Morning Face*, 1968.

James Baldwin (b. 1924).

Baldwin emphasises the harsh brutality of contemporary life, particularly for the Black American.

Go Tell It on the Mountain. 1954. Co.

The novel covers two days in the lives of a Black American family who belong to a strict fundamentalist sect, The Fire Baptised. The members of this fellowship identify themselves with the Israelites in captivity. Baldwin shows how this is a reaction to the harshness of their lives and compassionately reveals the mixture of genuine and deluded religious experience among the sect's members. The language of the novel is permeated by echoes of the Authorised Version of the Bible.

Giovanni's Room. 1956. Co.

This is a tragic story of a young American who fears his homosexual predilections and hideously ruins the lives of his Italian lover and of his own fiancée.

Another Country. 1962. Co.

The novel is centred on the lives of a mixed racial group of Greenwich Village artists and intellectuals. The brutality of New York life is reflected in the crude and obscene language the characters use so casually. At the end of the novel five of its central figures are, as the title suggests, on the verge of a new, though not necessarily easy, life, after their difficult and often bitter quest for love and self-knowledge.

Tell Me How Long the Train's Been Gone. 1968. Co.

A star Negro actor looks back on a life dominated by fear and concludes that, for the majority of Black Americans, violence offers the only road to freedom. This is a disappointing novel when compared with Baldwin's earlier ones, for it is less objective and therefore less powerful than they. It is, nevertheless, an important expression of the growing bitterness of Black Americans and constitutes a vehement denunciation of the behaviour of the White community.

In each of these novels Baldwin uses a mixture of straightforward narrative and "flash-back" techniques.

Samuel Beckett (b. 1906). *See also* **Section I.**

Since about 1945 Beckett, who now lives in Paris, has written in French then recreated his work in English. In the following notes, dates refer to the first publication of a novel. Where its first English edition came later this date is given in brackets.

Beckett's work first reached a wide public with the production of his play *En attendant Godot* (*Waiting for Godot*) in 1953, but he began as a satiric poet and novelist and has become one of the greatest novelists of the age. In 1969 he received the Nobel Prize for Literature.

The compelling force of his work derives from the courageous honesty and poetic power with which it expresses contemporary uncertainties about the meaning and purpose of life, together with the experience of confronting these uncertainties with a mingled sense of helplessness, fear and fluctuating resolution. He is a supreme exponent of the themes of isolation, bewilderment and suffering that are to be found in the work of so many contemporary writers and of artists such as Francis Bacon.

In his search for a form which would truthfully "accommodate the mess" of modern life Beckett has made use of various philosophical and religious ideas. Their symbolic power and poetic shape are important to his work. Their content offers few keys to it. Similarly, some of Beckett's images are inspired by Dante and a knowledge of the Italian poet helps us to appreciate Beckett, but to read his novels as religious allegories would be to oversimplify. For example, Belacqua, the hero of his first book, *More Pricks Than Kicks*, 1934 (C), derives from the sluggish Belacqua of the *Purgatorio* (canto iv, 97–135). Knowing that he will be refused entry to the "cleansing pain" beyond the gate of Mt. Purgatory until he has redeemed his mis-spent past, Dante's Belacqua sits idly in the shadows with his head between his knees. Beckett's heroes often speak of him and in their rare moments of tranquillity always copy Belacqua's pose. However, they only do so because it recalls the time of their greatest happiness, the first months of life—as an embryo. In Beckett's novels birth is the supreme evil. To be born means to sign one's "life warrant" into a cruel world of fear, irrational hope and compulsive need. Dante's Belacqua will eventually move towards Paradise. Beckett's heroes wonder, "Might not even the Beatific vision become boring in the long run?" They prefer "rotting in peace"

In the 1930s Beckett published a collection of stories, *More Pricks Than Kicks*, and a picaresque satire, *Murphy*, 1938 (C). These offer a helpful introduction to his subsequent writing. Allusions to them appear in the later work and its themes of pursuit and quest are adumbrated in these first books, whose protagonists, learned eccentric "layabouts" foreshadow the tramps and outcasts of Beckett's later novels and plays.

In the post-war novels life is reduced to its barest essentials. Even memory and imagination flicker and die. The wheel comes full circle and man returns to the helpless state of the embryo. There remains only waiting for an end, but no end is assured. The novels' circular forms suggest only a new beginning. The religious expectation of a rebirth has here become fraught with menace.

Watt. 1953. C.

A rather prolix transitional work, the last novel Beckett has completed in English, was composed between 1942 and '44 when he was in hiding as a member of the French Resistance. Its tone is comic and its style recalls Sterne's *Tristram Shandy.*

Sam, a patient in a psychiatric hospital, tells the story of his fellow inmate Watt, formerly servant to the mysterious Mr. Knott. Watt's purpose in becoming Knott's servant and his resulting discoveries are expressed in terms of a religious quest.

The Nouvelles, written *c.* 1945, published 1946–55 (1954–67).

Beckett's first work in French consisted of four *nouvelles* and a draft novel, *Mercier and Camier* (see below).

Three of the nouvelles form a short trilogy. They are *The End*, *The Calmative* and *The Expelled.* These stories underwent several revisions and were published in their final forms in the French *Nouvelles et Textes pour rien* (1955) and the English *No's Knife* (1967). They seem in some ways to have been a trial outline of the form which Beckett brought to perfection in his later *Molloy Trilogy* and give most poignant expression to his recurrent theme of exile. Like the abandoned Jesus, to whom he is often compared, Beckett's tramp-like hero is "despised and rejected of men, a man of sorrows and acquainted with grief", a "crucified bastard". Through him Beckett expresses a biting criticism of our society's hypocritical cruelty towards its outcasts.

Beckett has said that the three stories can be read as tales of the three phases of existence—prime (*The Expelled*), death (*The End*) and limbo (*The Calmative*). Each story seems to be told by the same, anonymous speaker who, like the narrator of the *Molloy Trilogy*, recounts stories of his past.

In *The End* the speaker is ejected from a "charitable institution", eventually finds lodging in a cellar, but then expelled by a new landlord he wanders, ever more wretched, until his life slowly dwindles away.

The dead narrator of *The Calmative* tells himself a tranquillising story so as to avoid listening to the sound of his body decaying. The time of the tale's action is uncertain, possibly it represents the present, possibly the future, and with characteristic glee the speaker here contemplates his readers' confusion! In his story he wanders, as if in a dream, through the streets of his home town seeking people to talk to.

In *The Expelled* he goes on to speak of the prime of his life, when "they" ejected him from his childhood home. Hiring a cab he spent the day seeking lodgings and, unsuccessful, eventually accepted the cab driver's offer of a night's shelter in a stable, before resuming his quest.

First Love, written *c.* 1945, published 1970 (1973).

A fourth nouvelle, *First Love*, seems to concern the same speaker as the previous three stories. Again he is ejected from his childhood home. This time he makes his way to a canal bench and there encounters the prostitute Lulu, who seduces him. As winter approaches he abandons the bench for a deserted cattle shed, but unable to forget the woman, now called Anna, seeks her again. She provides him with a room and cares for him, but on the night of their child's birth he runs away, pursued by the cries of her agonising labour, which for ever haunt him.

It would seem that Beckett may have delayed publication of this story because it is extraneous to his first trilogy and yet, if considered as an independent work, it seems very slight.

Mercier and Camier written *c.* 1945, published 1974 (1975).

In this draft novel a pair of Irish tramps, resembling the Gogo and Didi of Beckett's play *Waiting for Godot* (**I16**), are engaged in a fruitless circuitous quest. Although its themes resemble those of Beckett's tragedies the tone of the book is more like that of his earlier comic satires.

The Trilogy: ***Molloy*, 1951 (1955), C; *Malone Dies*, 1951 (1956), C & P: *The Unnamable*, 1953 (1958), C.**

A first-person narrative as compelling as the Ancient Mariner's, Beckett's finest novel is painful, yet constantly enlivened by bizarre comedy and wry humour. Its first volume, *Molloy*, is divided into halves. In the first, the bedridden Molloy, a disreputable old Irish writer, recounts the vicissitudes of his search for his mother. In the second half the tyrant Youdi sends a messenger, Gaber, to a conventionally respectable French smallholder, Moran, ordering him to go and find Molloy. Moran doubts Youdi's existence but fears to disobey After many adventures he comes upon Molloy but does not recognise him, so at last returns home, believing he has failed in his mission. However, he has gradually come to resemble Molloy and at the end of the book is in the state Molloy was in at its beginning.

The form of this tale may derive from Jungian psychological theories of the quest for the mother and the invasion of the personality by its subconscious " shadow ". It would be unwise to attribute any particular religious significance to Youdi and Gaber but their names have religious overtones: Youdi, a French colloquialism for *Jew*, is derived from the Arabic *Yahudi* and recalls the Old Testament *Yaweh*; Gaber suggests *Gabriel*.

In the second book, *Malone Dies*, the story is told by the all but helpless Malone, who says that Molloy and Moran were characters he invented. Awaiting death he " tells stories " about other personifications of himself in order to pass the time. It would seem that he dies between the end of this book and the beginning of the next.

The harrowing *The Unnamable* discovers the hero in a formless limbo continuing an ever more frenzied quest for identity, recalling all his past " selves ", including Murphy, Watt, Molloy and Moran, before deciding that the embryonic Worm most nearly approximates to the true self whose essence yet eludes him.

The circular form of each volume of the trilogy symbolises the hero's endless, repetitive journey. A possible interpretation of the whole is suggested by Beckett's early essay on Proust, where he says, " the individual is a succession of individuals ", life, " a succession of habits ", broken only by " periods of transition . . . when for a moment the boredom of living is replaced by the suffering of being."

Texts For Nothing, 1955 (1974).

After finishing *The Unnamable* Beckett was uncertain how to proceed. He began to resolve his dilemma in the experimental *Textes pour rien* (*Texts For Nothing*), thirteen short pieces of lyric prose resembling contemporary French experimental poetry. Their name derives from the musical term *mesure pour rien* (a bar's rest). Opening and closing with the same words—on the same note—they are essentially compositions in word music and sound beautiful, particularly in French, but little meaning can be ascribed to them: they mean " nothing ".

From an Abandoned Work written 1955. Published 1967 in *No's Knife*.

An unfinished novel, Beckett's most recent attempt at work in English, was probably put aside because he felt a dramatic form would be more suitable for his material. The novel bears resemblances to his subsequent play, *Krapp's Last Tape* (*see* **I16**). In both an old man recalls his youth and looks forward to " a long unbroken time without before or after . . . life and death all nothing. "

From an Unabandoned Work, 1960, was the title given to an extract from Beckett's next novel, *How It Is*.

How It Is. 1961 (1964). C.

Expressing an experience akin to the power of nightmare delirium in its pain and horror, an anonymous " mouthpiece " who seems in the throes of a mortal illness, speaks of his life. Naked and dumb [*sic*], in pitch darkness he crawls through mud with a sack of tinned fish hanging from his neck. His only other possession is a tin opener. He refers to " dreams ", apparently connected with a previous life " above " in the light, but then says these are only " visions " seen in the mud. Suddenly he bumps into another man, Pim whom he tortures with the tin opener until Pim speaks. Now the " mouthpiece " has a name, Bom. After a while the pair are separated. In anguished solitude Bom, posing the idea of life as a circle of torturers and victims, awaits his own torturer; then, suddenly, he dismisses the whole story as rubbish. There is no one and never has been anyone but himself—spreadeagled, as on the cross, alone in the mud in the dark.

Bom's grim determination and sardonic self-mockery form the only positive aspect of this dreadful recital, which may have been inspired by cantos vi and vii of the *Inferno*, where Dante pictures the damned crawling through mud. Kermode suggests parallels with symbols of other mediaeval allegories: Bom's sack recalls symbols of the soul, the burden and support of the body; Pim suggests an image of Christ, the tortured Word Incarnate.

The novel is divided into three equal parts, " before Pim with Pim after Pim ", and is written in short passages of ritualistic prose punctuated only by Bom's panting for breath. Fletcher has shown that, in the original French, the language echoes the patterns of uneducated speech. The novel is again circular in form and its closing words repeat the opening ones. The effect of this horrifying symbolic repetition is heightened in the original version for, when spoken, the words *comment c'est* (how it is) are indistinguishable from *commencez* (begin).

The Residua.

Beckett has published no full-length work since 1961 and seems again to be searching for a new way forward. He describes his recent work as *Residua* and has explained that the title has a twofold significance: these pieces are all that remain of more extended writings; they are also residual to " the whole body of previous work ". Any reader unfamiliar with this previous work would probably find the *Residua* baffling, and, as usual with Beckett's works, our appreciation is enhanced if we read each in the order of its composition.

In *Since " How It Is "*, a helpful analysis of the later pieces, B. H. Finney says that Beckett has told him the *Residua* were written in the following order, *Imagination Dead Imagine*, *Enough*, *The Lost Ones*, *Ping*, *Lessness*. However, they were published: *Imagination Dead Imagine*, 1965, *Enough*, 1966 (1967 in *No's Knife*), *Ping*, 1966 (1967 in *Encounter* XXVII, 2 and in *No's Knife*), *Lessness*, 1969 (1970, *The New Statesman*, 1 May) and *The Lost Ones* 1970 (1972).

Like the *Texts for Nothing*, *Enough*, *Ping* and *Lessness* are concentrated prose poems. The other two *Residua*, discussed below, are short novels.

Imagination Dead Imagine. 1965. C.

In striking contrast to *How It Is*, a work of plangent lyric beauty presents a scene of clinical whiteness, but Beckett's themes remain those of loss and anguish.

As imagination dies life becomes a fluctuating vision of a tiny white rotunda. Here a naked couple lie curled side by side, motionless except when shaken by the rotunda's intermittent trembling. The vision fades for the last time and the novel ends on a reverberating cry of fear and anguish.

The significance of the rotunda and its tiny figures, described with mathematical precision, remains elusive, paradoxically suggesting both embryonic life and mankind on the verge of extinction. The novel's linear form and dramatic ending are unusual in Beckett's work.

The Lost Ones. 1970 (1972).

Although published later, all but the final paragraph of this novel was written in 1966.

A brief ritualistic work of mythical power, originally entitled *Le Dépeupleur*, it was inspired by a line from Lamartine's *Méditations Poetiques*: "Un seul être vous manque et tout est dépeuplé." (You lose a single human being and the world is empty.) The words, which appear in the first *Méditation, L'Isôlement*, express Lamartine's sense of blank indifference to a world which his solitude has rendered utterly meaningless. Beckett's novel is not intended to illustrate Lamartine's line. It rather offers a comment on it. In Beckett's world such an indifference is highly to be prized, but his characters seldom achieve it. Instead they are condemned to a repetitive search for meaning and purpose where none, it seems exists.

Unlike the other post-war novels this concerns a large group of people, the two hundred naked Lost Ones, prisoners in a gloomy cylinder suggestive of a concentration camp.

Two figures are distinguished from the throng. They are both among the vanquished. The first, a woman with red hair, the second a white-haired mother clasping a baby to her breast. Because of the unusual fixity of her pose, the red-haired woman is used by the others as a point of orientation, since they have no other means of determining their whereabouts in the cylinder. She may be intended to recall the Scarlet Woman, a Protestant symbol of the Catholic church. The archetypal figure of the mother and child has more general religious associations but here, as elsewhere in Beckett's writing, an image of the continuing renewal of life is filled with tragic import.

Saul Bellow (b. 1915).

Bellow is a leading American novelist and short story writer. Like Beckett's, his characters engage in purgatorial quests, but whereas Beckett's seek answers to the questions, "Who am I? What is truth?" Bellow's ask rather, "What makes a good life?" For the heroes of Beckett's tragic fables death is both sought as a release from their quest and feared lest the apparent release it offers prove an illusion. For Bellow it is death which above all else gives meaning to life, and only when his heroes face the physical reality of death, which they fear, do they begin to accept that death of the self which will enable them to combine individual freedom with social responsibility. Thus, while Beckett's characters become increasingly isolated in a sterile world, Bellow's move towards escaping from self-absorption into an awareness that the significance of life is to be found "in the ranks with other people" and in selfless love for them. Only in *The Victim*, 1947 (P), *Mr. Sammler's Planet*, 1969 (P), and *Humboldt's Gift*, 1975, does Bellow show any of his heroes attempting to put this into practice.

Bellow's ethical and social concern, a product of his heritage as the son of Russian Jewish emigrés, links him with the great nineteenth-century European novelists. He feels that although earlier writers' answers to the question of what makes a good life may be inadequate for us who live in an urban, technological society, the question nevertheless remains and he considers that most modern novelists evade it, retreating into ivory towers and concentrating upon the production of formally perfect works of art.

Despite his emphasis upon the importance of a novel's content, Bellow has always striven to improve the style and form of his work. This led him to abandon the "Flaubertian standard" he had adopted for his first two novels, when he discovered it was an inadequate vehicle for his own—very different—experience. The form of the transitional *Adventures of Augie March*, 1953 (P), is shapeless and Bellow's style in this book and in *Henderson the Rain King*, 1959 (P), is sometimes undisciplined, but his later novels *Herzog*, 1964 (P), *Mr. Sammler's Planet* and *Humboldt's Gift* are very carefully and skilfully constructed and at its best his writing is vigorously exuberant and often wildly funny.

Bellow is keenly aware of the ugliness and suffering of life, which he vividly portrays in his novels, yet the overall effect of his work is one of hopeful optimism, in contrast to the anguish and wryly stoical endurance of Beckett. In 1976 he was awarded the Nobel prize.

John Berger (b. 1926).

Berger, an art critic, essayist and Marxist humanist, had already published three interesting naturalistic novels when his fine *G.* appeared in 1972. They were *A Painter of Our Time*, 1958; *The Foot of Clive*, 1962; *Corker's Freedom*, 1964 P.

G. 1972. P.

This novel, for which Berger received the Booker prize, is arguably the best to have been published in 1972.

G., the hero of this Brechtian epic set at the turn of the century, is the illegitimate son of an Anglo-American heiress and a prosperous Livornese merchant. Deprived of affection as a child he becomes a promiscuous man, seeking to reveal his own true nature and to discover that of the woman of the moment through the intimacy of the sexual act. Berger has the gift of creating vivid word pictures and the most moving part of his novel is the early section on G.'s childhood. This stimulating book combines detached observation with intense impressionism, interposed by factual references to history and politics and discussions of literary, social and moral problems, in a manner unlike that of any other contemporary novel but akin to the style of Brecht's dramas.

Elizabeth Bowen (1899–1973).

A stylistic artist in the tradition of James, Elizabeth Bowen is famed for the beauty of her descriptive writing and for her sensitive analyses of feeling. Her finest novels are *To the North*, 1932, *The House in Paris*, 1935, *The Death of the Heart*, 1938 (P).

Of her later novels, the best seems *The Heat of the Day*, 1949 (P), a love story set in war-time London; but her last book, *Eva Trout*, 1969, was awarded the James Tait Black Memorial prize for the best novel of 1969.

Christine Brooke-Rose (b. 1916).

The writing of Christine Brooke-Rose, a lecturer at the free university of Valenciennes, is associated with that of the French authors of the *nouveau roman* and she has translated the work of Robbe-Grillet, one of their leaders.

Herself the author of eight novels, she now disowns the first five, which are traditional in style and form, acknowledging only her recent, experimental work, the novels *Out*, *Such*, *Between* and the short stories *Go When You See the Green Man Walking*, 1970.

She has a poetic gift for creating precise visual images and a comedian's joy in the ambiguity of words, which she delights to place in novel and unexpected juxtapositions, using a stream-of-consciousness technique which relies on the repetition of key images and symbols in various forms and contexts.

Ivy Compton-Burnett (1884–1969).

Dame Ivy Compton-Burnett was a highly conscious artist, who knew her limits and never exceeded them. Apart from an early rejected work, *Dolores*, she published eighteen novels, the first, *Pastors and Masters* in 1925, the last, *The Mighty and Their Fall*, in 1963. Her nineteenth novel, *The Last and the First* was published posthumously, in 1971. Written mainly in dialogue, each of her books deals with the claustrophobic life of a well-to-do middle-class household at the turn of the century. Dame Ivy's themes are those of Greek tragedy; her formal, decorous language is reminiscent of Jane Austen. The combination can be disconcerting.

Margaret Drabble (b. 1939).

Margaret Drabble had already published five novels and won two important literary prizes when her first major work, *The Needle's Eye*, appeared in 1972. Its reviewers compared her with George Eliot, another writer in whom moral sensibility was allied with acute intelligence. Like the nineteenth-century novelist, and like her own older contemporaries Doris Lessing and Iris Murdoch (*qq.v.*), Margaret Drabble charts her characters' growing self-knowledge and moral education at the hands of society. She explores the conflicts of reason and emotion, of duty and desire, in the dilemmas of everyday life. She is less concerned with blacks and whites of moral absolutes than with difficulties of distinguishing the various shades of grey, and her novels are much warmer and less melodramatic than Iris Murdoch's, where characters are deployed in symbolic moral fables, but they lack the passion of Doris Lessing's concern with the demands of moral absolutes in extreme situations. They are ratiocinative rather than poetic and have little of the visual immediacy which the work of Iris Murdoch and Doris Lessing shares with the greater Victorians'.

Margaret Drabble's first three novels, *A Summer Bird-Cage*, 1962, *The Garrick Year*, 1964, and *The Millstone*, 1965 (all P), are in many ways alike. Each is a first-person narrative and although the speakers are given different names and face rather different problems they speak in the same voice and are all, like Margaret Drabble herself, highly intelligent, well-educated young women from professional families.

With *Jerusalem the Golden*, 1967 (P), Margaret Drabble began to widen her range, presenting a more varied cast in greater depth and adopting a more indirect narrative until in her most recent novel, *Realms of Gold*, 1975, she has so far distanced herself from the narrative as to address the reader directly with comments on the problems of authorship. This change in narrative technique has been marked by the emergence of a more genial tone than was evident in the earlier books, but from first to last the novels are dominated by a single, highly idiosyncratic voice, brisk, colloquial and gossipy. Since it also pervades the dialogue—all the characters speaking in the same manner and tone—it can at times become monotonous. Whereas in the novels of Ivy Compton-Burnett (*q.v.*) such a mannerism is a cultivated asset, here it sometimes seems rather a weakness.

At present Margaret Drabble is a writer of great potential rather than of great achievement, but her work, particularly her last two novels, *The Needle's Eye*, 1972 (P), and *Realms of Gold* is generally both interesting and enjoyable.

Lawrence Durrell (b. 1912).

Durrell's shorter novels are *The Black Book*, *White Eagles Over Serbia*, and *The Dark Labyrinth*. His longer, baroque fantasies have had a mixed reception. Their most appreciative critic is G. S. Fraser.

The Alexandria Quartet—*Justine*, 1956, *Balthazar*, 1958, *Mountolive*, 1958, *Clea*, 1960 (all F).

Some find the Quartet a most enjoyable novel, for others it is all but unreadable. Its form, says Durrell, is based on the relativity proposition, the first three volumes, which give differing aspects and views of the characters' lives and motives, having a "spatial" relationship, the fourth, which continues the narrative more or less chronologically, representing time. The novel's construction thus resembles that of Faulkner's *The Sound and the Fury*, and has much in common too with works like Cary's Gulley Jimpson trilogy.

Durrell's apparent theme is erotic love, but his underlying interest is the relationship between art and life. He suggests life is significant only when interpreted by art. This attitude, rather than the form of his work, differentiates it from novels like Faulkner's and Cary's.

Durrell's volumes contain splendid passages, but too often in the novel as a whole his sensuous language seems merely florid and pretentious, his characters but flimsy inhabitants of a decadent fairyland.

Tunc. 1968. F. *Nunquam*. F. 1970.

These two volumes comprise a single novel. Their titles are derived from a line from Petronius's *Satyricon*, "Aut tunc, aut nunquam"—"Then or never." The theme of the work seems to be the individual's struggle for a sense of freedom in a world dominated by international commerce, but, although Durrell's theme is serious, his treatment of it seems not only bizarre but frivolous as he chronicles the career of his protagonist, Charlock, an inventor who is taken captive by the all-powerful international firm of Merlin and eventually becomes its head.

Some passages in *Tunc* describing Athens and Constantinople recall the better parts of *The Alexandria Quartet*, but in *Nunquam* there is a loss of momentum. This second volume is mainly concerned with the creation of a life-like dummy representing the dead film star Iolanthe, with whom Julian, the impotent head of Merlin, falls desperately in love, and dies as he tries to prevent "her" from committing "suicide" by jumping from the gallery of St. Paul's Cathedral.

Ralph Ellison (b. 1914).

***The Invisible Man*. 1952. P.**

Ellison is an American Negro and former musician. This, his only novel, is poetic in its complex symbolism and compelling language, and in the intensity of its feeling.

We learn from the prologue that Ellison's hero is not only "invisible," but an "underground man", living in a cellar. He has affinities with the narrator of Dostoyevsky's *Notes from the Underground*. The novel also recalls Kafka. Like Kafka's, Ellison's hero is anonymous, and his vividly recounted experiences have the quality of bewildering dreams, at times of nightmare. He tells of his life from the night he received a scholarship to the State Negro College, to the night of a terrifying Harlem race riot, when, fleeing from supporters of a deranged Black nationalist, Ras the Destroyer, he took refuge in the cellar.

One of the novel's central episodes is that in a paint factory hospital, where the hero is subjected to torturous experiments. Among other things, the episode signifies the way in which all the "scientists" he encounters exploit those in their power, attempting to force all life into rigid sterile patterns. "Life", he says, "is to be lived, not controlled." A free society is loving and infinitely various.

The hero realises the "scientists"—politicians, demagogues, and confidence men—are unaware of the limitations of their vision and cannot see they are destroying themselves as well as their dupes and victims. Images of blindness recur throughout the novel. The narrator calls himself "invisible" because he has come to feel people who look at him see only projections of their own imaginations. He realises he has been equally blind. One of the novel's themes is his gradual enlightenment as he learns to understand himself and others better—to see "reality".

J. G. Farrell (b. 1935).

Although born in Liverpool, Farrell was brought up in Ireland. Before going to Oxford he taught in a Dublin prep school and worked as a labourer in the Canadian Arctic. He lived for some years in France—the scene of his first novel—and has since travelled in Mexico, Morocco and India.

His early novels, which were favourably reviewed, are *A Man from Elsewhere*, *The Lung* and *A Girl in the Head*. Recently, Farrell has been working on a set of three novels covering "watersheds" in the history of the British Empire. Two have appeared, *Troubles*, which is set in Ireland during 1919–20, and *The Siege of Krishnapur*, whose action takes place in 1857, at the time of the Indian Mutiny. The third volume will concern life in Singapore in 1941.

Each of these novels is self-contained and they are designed to be read in any order, but Farrell said, "each will bear some relation, possibly subterranean, to the other two."

In choosing the form of the historical novel he has been prompted by a desire to show the past as reflected in the present, the present as reflected by the past, and so to encourage us to think again about ourselves and our society, the ideas and prejudices by which they are motivated.

At the same time, Farrell seeks to write a captivating story, which will "lead the reader into a new experience." Giving Kafka as an example, he says that the best novelists do this "with extraordinary ease. To read them is like undergoing an hallucination." Both *Troubles* and *The Siege of Krishnapur* have this kind of intense imaginative power to make us see the world in a new light.

Both are in some respects very sad books, but both are also extraordinarily comic. Farrell has a rare gift for surprising his reader, sometimes with a shock of horror, more often with a shock of astonished amusement. One of the funniest episodes in modern fiction is his account of how during the heat of the sepoys' attack on beleaguered Krishnapur, the compound's padre pursues a young civilian, Fleury, who had once mildly objected to God's being described as "the designer of the universe." Dodging the enemy fire and frantically trying to help re-load the only canon, Fleury cannot pause to draw a breath before up pops the parson with another question! Here, as always in these novels, Farrell convinces us that this is the kind of way in which people both did and do behave.

William Faulkner (1897–1965).

The American Faulkner received the Nobel Prize for Literature in 1950. Although his last novel was published only three years before his death, most of his best work appeared between 1929 and 1936: *The Sound and the Fury*, *As I Lay Dying*, *Light in August* (all P), *Absalom, Absalom!* Together with the comic *The Hamlet*, 1940, these novels are his finest achievement.

Faulkner's post-war novels can be divided into three groups: (1) those which are simply enjoyable stories: *The Town*, 1957, *The Mansion*, 1959, which together with *The Hamlet* form the Snopes trilogy, and *The Reivers*, 1962 (P); (2) *The Intruder in the Dust*, 1948 (P), which is too overtly didactic to be a successful novel, though of great interest to anyone concerned by the racial problems of the South; (3) two ritualistic novels: *Requiem for a Nun*, 1951 (P), and *A Fable*, 1954; the latter, set in France in early 1918, is constructed on an elaborate series of parallels with the events of Holy Week.

Faulkner's work is concerned almost exclusively with the Southern States and set in the mythological Yoknapatawpha County, Mississippi. A Southerner by birth, he is soaked in the history and legendary folklore of Mississippi. Although many of his most memorable characters are bizarre, tragic figures, subnormal poor-Whites, murderers, or other outcasts of society, his work reflects not only the grimness, the callousness and brutality of the South, but also the proud individualism, courage, humour, and vitality of its people. Thus one reads Faulkner with pleasure, despite the difficulties presented by his style.

These difficulties are at times inherent in his subject, as at the beginning of *The Sound and the Fury*, which is told from the viewpoint of a moron; in the touching episode in *The Hamlet*, when the idiot Ike Snopes steals a cow he loves; in the evocation of Charles Mallison's nightmare (*Intruder in the Dust*). Sometimes, however, Faulkner seems needlessly obscure; he indulges in turgid rhetoric; his sentences are often three or four pages long, sparsely punctuated and containing innumerable parentheses, and parentheses within parentheses. The effect of such clumsy syntax is utterly bewildering, and one sympathises with the exasperated critic who declared Faulkner a "genius without talent." Such criticism, however, ignores the comic aspect of Faulkner's work, his gift for racy, demotic humour.

John Fowles (b. 1926).

Once a schoolmaster, Fowles became a full-time writer in 1963. He has published three novels, including the prize-winning *French Lieutenant's Woman*. A helpful introduction to his novels and to the artistic attitudes determining their forms is to be found in *The Aristos*, rev. ed., 1968 (Pan). In this controversial book Fowles sets forth his personal philosophy. In reading it we must always bear in mind his prefactory remark that he does not "expect agreement". "By stating baldly what I believe I hope to force you to state baldly to yourself what *you* believe." We must also remember that although we may profoundly disagree with Fowles's ideas on some matters we need to understand his point of view if we are to appreciate his novels.

In *The Aristos* Fowles distinguishes an intellectual and moral Élite from an unthinking, conformist Mass. This division does not correspond with any between "upper" and "lower" social classes, but cuts right across them. He also feels that class distinctions are in any case wrong and that the gifted Élite should not be thought of as in any way superior to the rest. They are simply more fortunate and have commensurate responsibilities towards their fellow men.

Fowles adds that the division between the Few and the Many is present not only in mankind as a whole but also in every person, for there exists in all of us a fruitful tension between individuality and pressure to conform with the social mores of our class and group. He sees a similar tension existing between "art" and "science"—the "two great manners of apprehending and enjoying existence". Each of Fowles's three novels may be understood as an exploration of such tensions.

Fowles is highly critical of the modern emphasis on the importance of self-expression and of our tendency to equate genius with the ability to develop a distinctive artistic style and technique. He pertinently remarks that the genius, a rare bird, may discover a new technique, but does so as a result of having something new to say. To concentrate on style and form at the expense of content is to produce lifeless art. "What will finally matter . . . will be skill in expressing one's meaning with *styles*, not just one style carefully selected and developed to signal one's individuality rather than to satisfy the requirements of the subject matter." As a novelist Fowles has therefore used various forms and techniques.

The Collector. 1963. Pan.

A psychological thriller, later filmed, explores the way the relationship between the sexes and that between the Few and the Many is damaged by feelings of contempt and envy arising from invidious social distinctions. A subsidiary theme is the way ignorance and fear distort the relationship between art and science.

Fowles presents only two characters. The isolated clerk, Fred Clegg, butt of his workmates at the Town Hall, has been brought up by a loveless aunt. He divides his free time between collecting butterflies and day-dreaming "respectfully" about the pretty Miranda Grey, to whom he has never spoken. Miranda, a doctor's daughter, wins a scholarship to the Slade. Fred wins the pools, buys an isolated cottage and kidnaps Miranda so that she may learn to love him.

The first half of the story is told by the whining, self-righteous, yet pitifully envious and insecure Fred. There follows Miranda's bewildered, partly sympathetic, partly contemptuous, increasingly frightened diary of their relationship. Fred concludes the tale.

The Magus. 1966. Pan.

Here the main theme is age-old—the education of a young man as he finds himself torn between love for two women. Nicholas Urfe, the narrator, is a typical, conventionally unconventional public-schoolmaster, who fancies himself as something of a Don Juan. When his affair with the pretty air-hostess Alison shows signs of becoming serious, Nicholas runs off to a job on a Greek island. There he meets a puzzling millionaire, Conchis, and is subjected to a series of trials organised by this self-appointed Magus and his talented assistants, who include the beautiful Julie, alias Lily.

The conflict caused by class distinction plays some part in the relationship between the young people, but is subordinate to the theme of the Élite's responsibility towards the Many. The Élite are here represented by Conchis and his friends, who also exemplify the union of art and science.

The book is something of a *roman à thèse.* Fowles organises his complicated narrative very skilfully, but invention and interest flag in the second half and the revelation of the rôle of Conchis and his helpers, and their subsequent disappearance after a bizarre ritualistic ceremony, is unconvincing.

The chief interest of the novel lies in the contrast it presents to the stark simplicity of *The Collector* and the complex realism of *The French Lieutenant's Woman.*

The French Lieutenant's Woman. 1969. Pan.

This novel, a popular success in both Britain and America, won the W. H. Smith Literary Award in 1970. Set in Lyme Regis, Exeter and London in the 1860s, it offers a much more subtle and complex exploration of Fowles's chosen themes.

Its form is based on that of the traditional Victorian novel, with indirect narrative, references to social, religious and political events and comments on the characters' behaviour and motives from the point of view of an omniscient observer conversing with his readers. However, Fowles, parodying Thackeray the "puppet-master", disclaims omniscience, often says he does not understand a character's motives, sometimes that he does not know exactly what happened next and gives his story two, equally plausible, endings. The effect, which is to make one constantly aware that one is reading an invented story, may owe something to Brechtian dramatic theory. (*See* M8 and I9).

In essence the plot is a simple one. Charles Smithson, a disciple of Darwin and heir to a baronet, is engaged to the pretty Ernestina, cosseted only child of a wealthy tradesman. Visiting Ernestina while she is on holiday with her aunt, Charles meets and falls passionately in love with the penurious Sarah, an orphaned ex-governess, whose reputation has been ruined by her innocent infatuation for a shipwrecked French Lieutenant.

We are shown Charles, Ernestina and Sarah each engaged in a struggle to realise their individuality, in the best sense, rather than to obey the dictates of convention. Charles's is the most fully drawn character, but all three are splendidly convincing.

A sub-plot concerns the complementary love story of Charles's man Sam, and Mary, Ernestina's maid.

William Golding (b. 1911).

Golding has said that he aims to write "total myths", illuminating contemporary life. A novelist of extraordinary technical virtuosity, he is essentially a religious—though not a specifically Christian—writer, expressing a poetic vision of the tragedy of men who have lost their faith and "seem unable to move without killing each other". However, Golding's vision is far from negative, for he suggests that it is possible to regain freedom and that state of grace in "which everything that lives is holy", and all his novels except *Pincher Martin* express the wonder and beauty of life as well as its horror. His most recent work, a collection of three *nouvelles* entitled *The Scorpion God* (P), suggests that an anguished loss of faith is inevitable at times when a comparatively simple form of religion is developing into a more sophisticated one.

Lord of the Flies. 1954. F. P.

Golding rewrites *Coral Island* in "realistic" terms, as an allegory of the Fall and an image of twentieth-century society that makes and drops atomic bombs.

The Inheritors. 1955. F.

This astonishing *tour de force* shows the advent of *Homo sapiens*, mainly through the eyes of the Neanderthal Lok. The measure of Golding's skill is not simply his brilliant evocation of the largely non-verbal world of Neanderthal Man, but his avoidance of sentimentality. He shows the inevitability of *Homo sapiens*' supremacy, and the tragedy in which it involves him, as well as Lok.

Pincher Martin. 1956. F. P.

This novel chronicles the struggles of a drowned sailor against God's overwhelming love. Made, like all men, in God's image, Martin is named Christopher. Alive he chose to "pinch" everything he could; dead, he refuses abnegation of himself, and therefore continues to exist, in a self-made Hell, on a rock he creates from the memory of a decaying tooth. Martin's struggles for "survival" are heroic, ghastly, futile.

Free Fall. 1959. F. P.

Sammy Mountjoy retraces his life, to discover when he lost his innocent delight in life and its beauty, and how he regained this. Containing fine passages, the novel is marred by the fact that Sammy interprets the significance of events, instead of the interpretation being left to us.

The Spire. 1964. F.

The narrative of this, Golding's masterpiece, centres on the building of the spire of Barchester (Salisbury) Cathedral. The cathedral symbolises three aspects of life: man suffering, crucified; man praying; erotic man.

Jocelyn, the Dean, believing himself divinely appointed to build the spire, presses for its completion with ruthless disregard of the suffering and death he causes. His motives are in fact mixed and largely unconscious. Gradually he recognises his hubris and the mixed motives behind his obsession, realising his wicked folly. Admitting on his deathbed he knows nothing about God, Jocelyn is granted a vision of His glory and the wonder of creation, as he gazes at the transfigured spire.

The Pyramid. 1967. F.

Set in Stillbourne, a small Wiltshire town, the novel is superficially a tragi-comedy of provincial life (its central episode is very funny) but on a deeper level *The Pyramid* is a searching exposure of materialism.

The novel's central images are musical ones. Various tastes in, and ways of performing, music signify various kinds of love and modes of life. The title suggests the social pyramid on which the townsfolk wish to rise, and also a metronome, to whose rhythm, that of a selfish, class-ridden society, they choose to move like robots.

Nadine Gordimer (b. 1923).

The work of this South African writer is banned in her own country. She has published six novels, three of them very short, and five collections of stories, the most recent being *Livingstone's Companions*, 1972.

Her earlier work suggested that the short story and *nouvelle* were her true *métiers*. Her crisp vignettes of the dilemmas of South Africa compelled admiration, but in her first long novel, *A World of Strangers*, 1958, her handling of character was less assured.

Although Miss Gordimer has been labelled a "political" novelist, like English Victorian writers she is concerned with the inter-relation of the individual and society. Politics are important in her writing in so far as they play an important part in social and individual life in Africa. In her last short novel, *The Late Bourgeois World*, 1965, one of her themes was the dilemma of a white liberal who supports majority rule in South Africa and is yet too considerate to give uncritical support to every revolutionary scheme. She showed how this attitude affected her heroine's personal and social life, but her novel was equally concerned with the heroine's adjustment to the violent death of her husband, a neurotic, compulsive revolutionary from whom she had long been separated. Here, as in all her work, personal, political and social themes are inextricably entwined.

Miss Gordimer's recent work has included two full-length novels, *A Guest of Honour*, 1971 (P), and *The Collector*, 1974. Of these, the first is incomparably the better book, a brilliant study of an ex-colonial civil servant who returns to a newly-independent African state at its president's invitation. Here, as in the later book, the underlying theme is the opposition of creative adaptability and destructive rigidity. The two novels may, indeed, be read as presenting the obverse and reverse of the same coin, for their heroes are opposed in character, though both come to tragic ends.

Graham Greene (b. 1904).

Greene's best work is *The Power and the Glory*, 1940 (P). Apart from the books he calls "entertainments", of which the latest is *Travels with My Aunt*, 1969, Greene has published six novels since the War. They are: *The Heart of the Matter*, 1948, *The End of the Affair*, 1951, *The Quiet American*, 1955 (all P), *A Burnt-out Case*, 1961, *The Comedians*, 1966 (P). All have settings of topical interest: war-time London, the Congo, Vietnam, Haiti, South America.

While Greene's work has been influenced by the thriller and the film, his literary master is Conrad and, although Greene's novels often seem rather superficial and, at times, he appears unable to treat his characters objectively, he nevertheless tells a good story and is skilled at evoking the discomfort and squalor of life in the tropics. In his first two post-war novels he failed to achieve artistic resolution between his religious beliefs and his feeling that life is a sordid struggle against impossible odds, but *The Quiet American* and *The Comedians*, which have no overtly religious themes, are more successful.

The Honorary Consul. 1973.

Greene's latest novel is a typical example of his better work and combines an exciting, up-to-the-minute melodrama with an exploration of fundamentally religious feeling. Its setting is a small town on the Argentine–Paraguayan border, its subject the kidnapping of an Honorary British Consul by left-wing revolutionaries who hope to exhange him for their imprisioned comrades.

The main characters present types familiar from Greene's earlier work. His central figures are two men of British nationality but South American upbringing, Charlie Fortnum, the Honorary Consul, and his friend Dr. Plarr.

As his title suggests, Fortnum's official standing is more nominal than actual. A seedy, elderly drunkard, kind and sentimental, he has fallen helplessly in love with a young girl from the local brothel and married her, knowing that since he cannot live long, his pension will assure her financial security for the rest of her life.

Plarr, a rootless cynic, divides his time between treating poverty-stricken peasants and having casual affairs with rich married women. Although chary of any sort of commitment, he allows himself to become involved with Fortnum's kidnappers, who include two of his former schoolfriends. In this Plarr is motivated partly by the revolutionaries' promise to ask for the release of his own father, inprisoned some twenty years before as an associate of Paraguayan rebels. But he also wants to protect the kidnappers from the results of their own incompetence and to save not only Fortnum's life, but theirs. In the attempt to do so Plarr himself is killed.

The revolutionaries are led by an unfrocked married priest, Father Rivas. His feeling for the poor had led him to reject the institutionalised Church whose officials live in luxury, hob-nobbing with dictators while telling their undernourished and poverty-stricken flock to "sell all you have and give to the poor." Rivas realises the comfort of religion helps the suffering peasant but he himself retains only a half-hopeful half-sceptical belief in God: "I do not forget my old claptrap . . . but I have never yet seen any sign that He interferes in our world or our politics."

Whereas in books like *The Heart of the Matter* and *The End of the Affair* religious themes are obtrusive and overtly didactic, in *The Honorary Consul* Greene fully incorporates them into the fabric of his novel. He is able to do so partly because he has chosen a setting where the question of the relationship of Church and State is of vital topical importance. We therefore feel that it is entirely appropriate that Rivas and his friends should be concerned with it. At the same time, the intractability of the problems faced by all liberals in South American dictatorships makes Rivas's ambivalent attitude to the Church relevant and meaningful.

Moreover, although the novel is thus, and appropriately, concerned with contemporary feelings about specifically Christian problems, it is equally an exploration of the secular virtue of *máchismo*—self-respect—and, at a deeper level gives expression to two general themes: of the necessity for self-sacrificial commitment to those weaker than ourselves and of man's need for some awareness of an all-absorbing, parental love.

L. P. Hartley (1895–1972).

Hartley is a professional novelist and craftsman in the tradition of James and Hawthorne, the latter his acknowledged master. Like Hawthorne's, Hartley's themes are moral, illuminated by skilful use of symbolism. In his best novels his style is humorous and gently ironical, but in others he lapses into sentimental melodrama.

Hartley seems at his happiest when writing of children and adolescents: a recurrent figure in his work is the delicate, overprotected, hypersensitive, and introspective boy, as in *Eustace and Hilda*, 1947, *The Go-Between*, 1953, *The Brickfield*, 1964. (The heroes of *The Boat*, 1950 (Co), *The Betrayal*, 1966, and *My Sisters' Keeper*, 1970, are older, less successful versions of the same figure.) Hartley is skilled in evoking the atmosphere and scene of his characters' environment, particularly when this is Oxford, Venice or East Anglia in the earlier years of the century.

The Will and the Way, 1973, was the last of his eighteen novels, but his best work is earlier, the *Eustace and Hilda trilogy*, *The Go-Between* and *A Perfect Woman*.

Ernest Hemingway (1898–1961).

This controversial American was awarded the Nobel Prize for Literature in 1954. Hemingway's language and syntax are of extreme, at times monotonous, simplicity. He writes best of physical activities like hunting and fishing. The theme of all his writing is personal honour and courage, but he tends to romanticise violence and suffering. His finest work is his earliest, the short stories *In Our Time*, 1924, and the novel *A Farewell to Arms*, 1929 (P). Hemingway's last novel *The Old Man and the Sea*, 1952, the story of an old man's struggle to catch and land an enormous fish, has immediate appeal, but on subsequent readings its language seems contrived and precious.

Originally entitled *The Sea in Being*, *The Old Man and the Sea* was planned as one of four volumes set in the Caribbean. Hemingway intended eventually to weld them into a single novel. Two of the other books he called *The Sea When Young* and *The Sea When Absent*. The other, unnamed one, he considered complete and intended to publish it in 1951, but this plan fell through. Now given the posthumous titles *Bimini*, *Cuba* and *At Sea* these volumes, which have been subjected to the editorial cutting of Mrs. Hemingway and C. J. Schribner Jr., have been collected and published as *The Islands in the Stream*, 1970.

Susan Hill (b. 1942).

By the time she graduated from London University Susan Hill was the author of two novels: *The Enclosure*, 1961, written when she was sixteen, and an undergraduate work, *Do Me a Favour*, which flopped and is now unobtainable. She spent five years as a literary critic of the *Coventry Evening Telegraph* before returning to novel-writing with *Gentleman and Ladies*, 1968, and has since published six other novels including *A Change for the Better*, 1969: *I'm the King of the Castle*, 1970 (P)—which won the Somerset Maugham award; *Strange Meeting*, 1971 (P); *The Bird of Night*, 1972—which won the Whitbread prize and was short-listed for the Booker award. In 1972 she won the John Llewellyn Rhys Memorial Prize for a volume of short stories, *The Albatross*, (P), which contains some of her best work.

R. Prawer Jhabvala (b. 1927).

Born in Germany to Polish parents, Mrs. Prawer Jhabvala accompanied them to England in 1939. In 1951 she married an Indian architect and now lives in Delhi, and it is Delhi which provides the setting for most of her novels and short stories.

Her early works, gentle comedies of Hindu family life, were traditional in form, making no great demands upon their readers, but offering agreeable, light-hearted entertainment. These include the novels *To Whom She Will*, 1955; *The Nature of Passion* 1956; *Esmond in India*, 1958; *The Householder*, 1960; *Get Ready for Battle*, 1962.

Recently Mrs. Jhabvala has turned from the presentation of Indians to the presentation of Europeans in India. At the same time, her experience as a script-writer for James Ivory's films, including the famous *Shakespeare Wallah* and recent *Autobiography of a Princess*, has led to modifications in her style. Her latest novel, which won the Booker Prize for 1975 is *Heat and Dust*. It traces two young Englishwomen's experience of India. The first, Olivia, in 1923, married Douglas, a stick of a civil servant and scandalised Anglo-India by abandoning him within a year for a scallywag Indian princeling. The second girl, Douglas's grand-daughter by his second wife, goes out to India to try to reconstruct the story of this family adventuress. Their stories are presented alternately, so that each offers comments upon and insights into the other's experience and character.

Doris Lessing (b. 1919).

Doris Lessing has published poems, short stories, plays and other books, including *Particularly Cats*, and *In Search of the English*, but, she is probably best known for her novels.

Doris Lessing was born in Iran, but her British parents soon moved to Rhodesia, where her mother, who had enjoyed Iranian social life, "found herself sitting in the middle of the bush in a thatched hut, with her visiting cards and her piano and her curtains from Liberty's"—a prototype of her daughter's Mrs. Quest in *The Children of Violence*, a sequence comprising: *Martha Quest*, 1952; *A Proper Marriage*, 1954; *A Ripple from the Storm*, 1958; *Landlocked*, 1965; *The Four-Gated City*, 1969 (all Pa).

At the age of eighteen, Doris Lessing went to Salisbury to work as a telephone operator. There she says, she had "the kind of compulsive good time described in *Martha Quest*."

In 1949 she came to England carrying the manuscript of her first novel, *The Grass is Singing*, 1950 (P), which was quickly published and outstandingly successful. Her subsequent work has revealed a writer who combines an almost Victorian quality of "high seriousness" with an extremely flexible, creative approach to the form of the novel.

In varying ways, and usually with a remarkable degree of objective sympathy, her fiction is concerned to explore how people are affected by belonging to minority groups, and how society reacts to such minorities. At first she was particularly concerned with the position of white Africans, of those with left-wing sympathies in conservative societies and with women who resent that ours is still mainly a man's world—a theme of Mrs. Lessing's work long before the days of Women's Lib! In *The Four-Gated City* and most particularly in *Briefing for a Descent into Hell*, 1971, she explores the situation of those deemed insane, as they struggle towards a fuller knowledge of themselves. Allied with this last theme is a prophetic sense of mankind's imminent destiny as one of struggling through a painful time of anarchy and deprivation.

While very responsive to the issues and pre-occupations of our time, which play an important part in all her novels, Mrs. Lessing's chief concern is to explore and express their significance in the lives of individuals. Thus, although one might wish to dispute the validity of some of the ideas she expresses, she almost invariably succeeds in inducing that willing suspension of disbelief which is the acid test of art.

Her early novels were naturalistic and conventional in form but from the time of *The Golden Notebook*, 1962 (P), she has when appropriate used more experimental forms and techniques. Some of her more recent work, particularly the appendix of *The Four-Gated City* and most of *Memoirs of a Survivor*, 1974, is akin to science fiction.

Her best work to date, and arguably one of the finest of all post-war novels is *The Summer Before the Dark*, 1973 (P), which presents the individual's experience of growing old and going down into "the dark" in a context of the world where natural resources also seem fast to be running out.

Malcolm Lowry (1909–57).

While many novelists' work is to some degree autobiographical, Lowry's writing seems to have been inspired by a sense that the events of his own life formed significant patterns. Some knowledge of these events facilitates understanding of the versions of his unfinished novels which have recently been published by his wife. The best available guides to his life and work are *The Selected Letters of Malcolm Lowry*, edited by H. Breit and M. B. Lowry, and D. Day's *Malcolm Lowry*, 1974.

Born in Birkenhead, Lowry, who once described himself as "a conservative Christian Anarchist at heart", early rejected the ideals of his prosperous father and, inspired by reading Conrad, he ran away to sea, working as bosun's boy on a tramp steamer to the Far East. Later, while at Cambridge, he spent a long vacation as fireman on a Norwegian ship. These experiences inspired a talented undergraduate novel *Ultramarine*, 1933, and for the rest of his life Lowry remained fascinated by the sea. He became a great admirer of the work of Herman Melville.

Lowry's career, dogged by misfortune and suffering, culminated in an early death as the result of a tragic accident. His reputation derives from the one complete work of his maturity, the magnificent *Under the Volcano*. He left a mass of unfinished writing. The published versions of this work are uneven in quality, at times approaching the concentrated poetic style of *Under the Volcano*, at others lush and mawkish.

Lowry conceived his novels as parts of a modern *Divine Comedy* to be called *The Voyage That Never Ends*. This was originally planned as a trilogy, with *Under the Volcano* as the first volume.

Under the Volcano. 1947. P

"Man cannot live without love" is the main theme of a splendid novel set in Mexico and giving poetic expression to the age-old dilemmas of man's relationship to God and to his fellow human-beings.

In a portrait of the tortured world of addiction, remarkable in its objectivity, Lowry presents the alcoholic Firmin, a former British consul, as a tragic hero in the tradition of Marlowe's Faustus.

The novel has an exciting story and Lowry expresses his themes not only through subtle allusive images but also through the events of the narrative, the lives and feelings of the characters and vivid descriptions of Mexico and its people.

The action takes place in 1938 on the Day of the Dead—all Souls' Day—the occasion of a great fiesta, and links the tragedies of Firmin and his wife, Yvonne, to the world tragedies of war and man's inhumanity to man.

On the morning of the Day of the Dead, which is to be his Day of Reckoning, Firmin staggers round his neglected garden, a symbol both of his ruined marriage and of the mutilated world. Here, he stumbles on a broken notice-board bearing the words,

"Do you like this garden?
Why is it yours?
We evict those who destroy!"

These words, which are repeated at the end of the book, recall two of its central images, Eden, signifying the beauty man discovers in Nature and the beauty he creates in loving human relationships, and Hell, signifying the agony he suffers and causes others when he rejects love. Lowry suggests that man, a splendid and noble creature, must nevertheless struggle constantly to control sado-masochistic impulses, and can restrain them only when he loves others and is able to accept their love.

Lowry's own critical analysis of the book is to be found in his letter to Jonathan Cape, dated 2 January 1946.

Mary McCarthy (b. 1912).

The American journalist and critic Mary McCarthy has published seven satirical novels on the lives of American artists and intellectuals: *The Company She Keeps*, 1942 (P); *The Oasis*, 1949 (S); *A Source of Embarrassment*, 1950; *The Groves of Academe*, 1952 (S); *A Charmed Life*, 1955 (P); *The Group*, 1962 (P); *The Birds of America*, 1971. Like Simone de Beauvoir and Doris Lessing, Miss McCarthy is particularly interested in the rôle of the educated woman in twentieth-century society. Parts of her novels are very amusing, but in general they seem too cerebral and anaemic.

Norman Mailer (b. 1923).

Mailer, an American, is a journalist and film-director and the author of one book of verse as well as six novels. He sees life as a battlefield between the forces of good and evil and the motive behind the sensationalism of much of his later work seems to be a desire to shock readers into an awareness of the nature of American society, which he feels is obscene and life-denying. Mailer suggests that the majority of Americans are either becoming cogs in the machines of a brutal, totalitarian "technology land," or taking selfish refuge in drugs and nihilism, instead of accepting the dangers of living adventurously and trying to establish creative relationships. Readers interested in Mailer's social philosophy should refer to *Advertisements for Myself*, 1959; *The Presidential Papers*, 1963; *Cannibals and Christians*, 1966.

The Naked and the Dead. 1948. Pa.

Many critics feel this novel constitutes Mailer's most successful expression of his view of the human condition. He regards it as "the work of a young engineer." Its subject is the American troops' capture of a Pacific island from the Japanese, but its interest lies in Mailer's treatment of the power structure within the American force, which is presented as a microcosm of society. The mass of the troops, represented by the soldiers of one platoon, are shown as the all but helpless victims of the men of power—the fascist General Cummings and the Platoon Sergeant, Croft. Between the two groups stands the ineffectual liberal, Lieutenant Hearn.

Mailer paints a remorseless picture of the agony of the ordinary soldier's life and of the absurdity of the war, and is very successful in his treatment of the characters of Cummings and Croft. The weakness of the book lies in his characterisation of the lower ranks. These soldiers are obviously intended to represent a cross-section of American society, but, although using techniques derived from Dos Passos, Mailer gives a biographical sketch of each man in the platoon, none of them is clearly differentiated from the others.

Barbary Shore. 1951.

In this turgid allegory of the Cold War, the amnesiac Lovett finds himself involved in a contest between two secret agents, McLeod and Hollingsworth, for the affections of McLeod's wife, the promiscuous Guinevere.

The Deer Park. 1955. Co.

Mailer planned this novel as the first of eight, whose themes were to cover the whole of American life. This was the only one to be finished. Its theme is pleasure and its title comes from D'Angerville's *Vie privée de Louis XV*, which refers to "the Deer Park, that gorge of innocence and virtue in which were engulfed so many victims . . .". Mailer's Deer Park is Desert D'Or, a fictional pleasure resort near Hollywood.

An American Dream. 1965. M.

Both the title and the wild improbability of this novel's action suggest that Mailer intends it to be read as an allegory, showing the narrator, Rojack, resisting the suicidal lure of nihilism presented by the moon and then escaping from the evil forces of American society, personified in his wife, her father, and her maid. The sexual relationships between the characters would thus have symbolic importance.

The novel has its comic moments, but its style is generally sensational and its language often highly obscene.

Why Are We in Vietnam? 1967. Pa.

D.J., an eighteen-year-old Texan, accompanying his parents at a dinner party shortly before leaving to fight in Vietnam, remembers a hunting trip he and his friend and his father took to Alaska two years before.

This scatalogical novel suggests, with a measure of success, the confused and distorted values of a society whose motto is "Go out and kill." The book is divided into alternating sections of breathless narrative and hysterical commentary, progressing at a speed which leaves the reader feeling rather stunned, but the chief impression is of the relish and gusto with which Mailer wrote the novel.

The Armies of the Night. 1968. P.

Mailer's finest work since *The Naked and the Dead*, this is an absorbing and at times highly comic reconstruction of the events of the Peace March on the Pentagon in October 1967. It is written in two sections. In the first the protagonist is Mailer himself, described objectively in the third person. In the second part we are helped to understand the motives and feelings of other marchers and the fears of the police and troops who confronted them. The book is notable for its objectivity and humour.

Miami and the Siege of Chicago. 1968. P.

A second documentary novel tells the story of the American Republican and Democratic party conventions in 1968.

Of a Fire on the Moon. 1970.

In a confessed pot-boiler, his third documentary novel, Mailer writes of the moonflight of *Apollo 11*.

Bernard Malamud (b. 1917).

Like Bellow (*q.v.*), with whom his name is often coupled, Malamud is a Jewish American. Both writers have a gift for wry comedy, but whereas Bellow is essentially an optimist Malamud takes a more sombre view of life. His heroes are born losers, presented with detached affection. Malamud's particular talent lies in the creation of ironic comedy offering a poetic image of an archetypal dilemma—that of the sacrificial victim.

The Natural. 1952. P.

The theme of the Arthurian regeneration myth is here expressed through the story of a baseball player, Roy Hobbs. A simple country bumpkin, Roy is a "natural" star, convinced of his own genius. His sole aim in life is to win recognition as "the greatest". Noticed by an old talent-spotter, Roy sets out to Chicago for a trial as a professional, but on the way he meets the beautiful Harriet, who has already shot two star athletes with the pistol she hides in her hat box! Luring him to her hotel room she now shoots Roy, wounding him in the stomach.

After many years of wandering in the wilderness, he is given another chance and joins the Knights, a professional team managed by the old Pop Fisher. The Knights are in the doldrums due to the selfishness of their leading player, Bump. Rivalry between Bump and Roy, who challenges his supremacy, results in Bump's death. Now Roy, armed with his precious bat "Wonderboy", revives the fortunes of the team, only to be struck down at the height of his triumph by the treachery of Bump's former mistress, whom the financial wizard, Judge, has encouraged to play on Roy's vanity.

Malamud cleverly reproduces the jargon of the baseball world and his inarticulate hero is sympathetically presented, but at times the realistic story is distorted to fit the demands of its theme and the result is a strained artifice.

The Assistant. 1957. P.

Here Malamud found a much more fruitful subject, the quiet tragedy of Morris Bober, an unsuccessful Jewish grocer and, of his Gentile assistant, Frank Alpine. For the sake of Bober and of the latter's daughter, Helen, Alpine, who has made many "false starts" in life, gives up what may well be his last hope of achieving material success. The novel is written with beautiful restraint and Chekhovian irony.

A New Life. 1961. FS. P.

Levin, a reformed drunkard, obtains an English post at a small state college, but eventually sacrifices his hard-won chance of an academic career for the sake of the woman he has loved.

The novel is set in the early 1950s, the period of McCarthyism. Malamud criticises the hysteria pervading American life at this time, exemplified in the academic and social atmosphere of Cascadia College, where Levin, a man of liberal principles, becomes the scapegoat of his colleagues' fears and prejudices.

A New Life is less concentrated than *The Assistant*. It contains elements of picaresque comedy and is at times very amusing indeed.

The Fixer. 1966. P.

Yakov Bok is, like Levin, a victim of hysterical feelings of national insecurity. A Jewish odd-job-man—a fixer—he leaves the Pale Settlement for Kiev, hoping to begin a new, more fruitful life, but is arrested on a trumped-up charge and endures three terrible years' imprisonment awaiting trial.

The inspiration of the novel was the case of Mendel Beiliss, a Kiev labourer arrested in 1911, and falsely charged with the ritual murder of a Christian child. Malamud says the novel is intended to stand "rather as a myth than an isolated case-study." But it lacks the compelling force of myth.

Pictures of Fidelman. 1969. P.

Parts of this book were published in slightly different forms in Malamud's collections of short stories *The Magic Barrel*, 1958 (P) and *Idiots First*, 1963 (P). It is an episodic work containing six "pictures" on the career of a would-be artist, Arthur Fidelman, who goes to Italy to study the work of Giotto, but soon abandons this project in order to make further attempts to discover where his own talent as an artist lies.

This is an uneven work, but enjoyable for its humour, which is derived as much from Malamud's style as from the ludicrous situations in which he places Fidelman. The best "pictures" are those entitled *The Last Mohican* and *Portraits of the Artist*. The latter contains an hilarious account of Fidelman as a sculptor of holes.

The Tenants. 1971.

In a condemned New York tenement, Lesser, a Jewish novelist, struggles to finish his third book, the masterpiece on which he has already spent ten years. He ignores the pleas of his old landlord, who begs him to move so that the building may be demolished and its site profitably developed. Unfortunately Lesser cannot turn an equally deaf ear to the claims of a fellow writer, Willie Spearmint, alias Bill Spear, a would-be Shakespearian genius, whom he discovers "squatting" in an adjoining flat.

Ex-gaol-bird and dope peddlar, Willie has become a member of the fanatic Black Soul Brothers, a group particularly hostile to Jews, who they see as exemplifying White exploitation of the Blacks. Lesser is fool enough to agree to read and criticise Willie's book. Even more disastrously, he falls in love with Willie's neglected mistress.

The novel is at once a highly comic portrayal of the writer's obsessive struggle with his material and a horrifying vision of the internecine relationship between sections of the Coloured and Jewish communities.

Iris Murdoch (b. 1919).

Iris Murdoch is by profession a university don, a specialist in moral philosophy. Her collection of papers, *The Sovereignty of Good* (Routledge & Kegan Paul 1970), offers helpful insights to the student of her novels. In this book she questions the validity of that contemporary philosophy which depicts morality simply as a " matter of thinking clearly and then proceeding to outward dealings with other people," a philosophy whose ideal man " aims at being a ' realist ' and regards sincerity as perhaps the only virtue." She remarks that this man is familiar to us as " lurking behind much that is written nowadays on the subject . . . of politics ", and as " the hero of almost every contemporary novel."

To this Kantian view of morality as a matter of clear thought and rational expediency, Miss Murdoch opposes the Platonic ideal of morality as a matter of clear vision and disinterested love, of moral endeavour as the movement towards emergence from the dark cave of self-interest and self-absorbtion. Her novels may be seen as attempts to express this philosophy in artistic forms.

In one of her most recent, *An Accidental Man*, 1971, most of the action is concerned with the dilemmas facing two contrasted men, the young Anglo-American, Ludwig, and the middle-aged Austin. Ludwig refuses to fight in Vietnam and has destroyed his draft card. If he returns to America he will be imprisoned and lose all chance of an academic career. He feels assured of a successful future if he remains in England, where he has been offered an Oxford lectureship and become engaged to the pretty heiress Gracie Tisbourne. Common sense and expediency suggest he remain, but eventually, after he has been helped by Sir Matthew Gibson Grey (Austin's elder brother) to see clearly the moral issues involved in his problem, Ludwig decides to go home. Austin, the " accidental man", is a self-absorbed hysteric, who has morally destroyed himself through jealous hatred of the successful Matthew, and literally destroys other people; he runs down and kills a child—and tries to persuade Matthew to take the blame; indirectly he causes the deaths by drowning of both of his own wives, and falsely convinces himself that both women have been Matthew's mistresses. Only when he symbolically destroys Matthew, by smashing his treasured collection of jades and seducing the woman whom Matthew has always loved and is at last to marry, does Austin achieve a sense of satisfaction with life.

Matthew himself is a kind of Prospero figure and the novel ends with an allusion to Prospero's speech from Act V Sc. I of *The Tempest*, " All our revels now are ended," and with echoes of the mad Ophelia's words, quoted by T. S. Eliot at the end of *The Game of Chess* in *The Waste Land*.

As we have seen, Miss Murdoch dislikes the ethos of much contemporary fiction. Her own experiments with the novel bear some relation to Eliot's experiments in drama (*see* I19). Eliot sought by means of poetic rituals, to give expression to the ultimate themes of man's search for truth and the conflict between good and evil. From the time of *The Cocktail Party* he sought to embody these rituals within the conventions of the well-made play. Miss Murdoch, whose themes are not dissimilar, has tried to combine ritualistic actions with the conventions of popular fiction.

All her earlier novels have symbolic moments of vivid poetic intensity and beauty, such as the evocations of Rainborough's feelings as he gazes at a snail, in *The Flight From the Enchanter*, 1956 (P); of Dora's releasing a butterfly, in *The Bell*, 1958 (P); of fog-bound east London in *Time of the Angels*, 1966 (P). In her more recent books, however, the use of such symbols degenerates into mannerism, as in the description of Morgan pursuing a pigeon through the tunnels of Piccadilly Circus Underground Station in *A Fairly Honourable Defeat*, 1970, and, in *An Accidental Man*, the owl, symbolising wisdom, which attacks first Austin's landlady then Austin himself—he kills it with a brick!

With few exceptions, most notably the splendidly drawn Bruno of *Bruno's Dream*, 1969, Miss Murdoch's characters tend to be stereotyped, puppets manipulated in the service of her themes. Her use of names can be self-consciously literary. In *The Unicorn*, 1963 (P), the action takes place at Gaze Castle, while two " child wives " Dora, in *The Bell* and Dorina in *The Accidental Man* derive from David Copperfield's Dora.

Miss Murdoch continues to experiment with new techniques. The greater part of the bizarre *A Fairly Honourable Defeat* was written as dialogue. This was unsuccessful, for the characters lacked individual voices, so the narrative was extremely difficult to follow. However, the experiment bore fruit in *An Accidental Man*, where the vacuity of the Tisbournes' circle is comically expressed in chapters of characterless, inconsequential gossip. The rest of this novel is divided between chapters of conventional narrative and others, following the eighteenth century fashion, composed of letters.

Despite their sophisticated veneer, few of Miss Murdoch's novels rise far above the level of undemanding entertainment. Her first tale, *Under the Net*, 1955 (P), an amusing existentialist fantasy owing much to Beckett's *Murphy*, seems her most satisfying work to date. A sympathetic study of the earlier of her seventeen novels has been published by A. S. Byatt under the title *Degrees of Freedom*.

Vladimir Nabokov (b. 1899).

A Russian by birth, Nabokov came to England during the Revolution, subsequently lived in Germany and France and emigrated to America in 1940.

Translations of his early novels are now becoming available. Those he has written in English include *Lolita*, 1955 (Co), *Pnin*, 1957, (P), *Pale Fire*, 1962 (Co), *Ada*, 1969 (P), *Transparent Things*, 1973. The first of these gained notoriety among the ill-informed who imagined it was pornographic. Nothing could be further from the truth.

Nabokov is a learned writer. His humour, wit, and above all his masterly use of language, make his novels a constant source of delight.

Shiva Naipaul (b. 1945).

The younger brother of V. S. Naipaul (*q.v.*) was born in Trinidad of Indian parents. Educated at Oxford he now lives in England.

The Naipaul brothers' childhood was spent in a " very large and sprawling Hindu clan " of which their family was an impoverished branch. This early experience is reflected in both Shiva's *Fireflies* and his brother's *Biswas*.

***Fireflies*. 1970. P.**

This extraordinarily accomplished first novel won the 1971 *New Statesman* prize. It is a vividly comic yet sad chronicle of the decay of the Khoja clan, acknowledged leaders of Trinidad's Hindu community by virtue of their " deliberate backwardness and eccentricities ". The story centres on the fortunes of the Lutchman family, an undistinguished branch of the clan.

The novel's traditional form and leisured, naturalistic style are both appropriate to its theme and also necessary to its understanding, since Naipaul writes for readers unfamiliar with Hindu life in the West Indies.

The Chip-Chip Gatherers. 1973.

Chip-chip are tiny flavourless molluscs. Although a pailful will provide only a mouthful of food, people in some coastal villages of Trinidad are so poor that they live on them. Such chip-chip gatherers aptly symbolise the society of Naipaul's second prize-winning novel.

The main action of the book concerns members of two families from the Settlement, an Indian shanty town. Most of the inhabitants find the struggle to scrape a bare subsistence takes all their energy, but two adolescents seek wider horizons.

The gentle Bholai dreams of becoming a lawyer and a happy family man, but lacking the necessary ruthlessness to achieve his aim, he succeeds only in becoming a grocer, despised by his wife and mocked by his children as he slaves to give his graceless son the education of which he was himself deprived.

From the first Bholai's friend Ramsaran rejects all thought of happiness and with " singleminded determination and harshness " seeks money and the power that money gives. Mysteriously he manages to save enough to start a transport business which he then runs and expands by lending money at exorbitant rates. He destroys his wife and reduces his son, Wilbert, to a hopeless cipher, but is himself destroyed by the predatory Sushila.

A beautiful woman who had run away from the Settlement and become a prostitute, Sushila seeks greater security as Ramsaran's mistress, only to be brought face to face with the realisation that as her beauty fades she is doomed.

Stark though its vision be the novel glints with humour and positive notes are suggested by Bholai's dignity and self-sacrifice—which enables his graceless son to go to England as a medical student—while, as Ramsaran bitterly observes, most people in the Settlement are happy enough, despite their grinding poverty.

V. S. Naipaul (b. 1932).

This most distinguished Caribbean writer came to Oxford at the age of eighteen and has since lived in England, travelling widely abroad.

The heroes of all his novels are men who seek freedom to give their lives order and significance and so, although his early work has a Caribbean setting, its themes are of world-wide interest. Naipaul began as a writer of comedy and all his novels have comic elements, but his work has become increasingly sombre in tone as it has increased in complexity and the conventional structure of his early novels has been replaced by more subtle and sophisticated forms.

In an interview published in *The Times Literary Supplement* of 30 July 1971, Naipaul spoke of how his work had been affected by the circumstances of his life, which have impressed upon him a sense of the insecurity of the individual. He believes the impression of security which he discerns in English society derives from the fact we have in some respects become an impotent colony of America. Naipaul remarks that the Colonial lives in an apparently secure, closed world. All important decisions are made by other people. Politicians in such countries have no effective power and can easily seem absurd—a view reflected in *The Mystic Masseur*, 1957 (P), and *The Suffrage of Elvira*, 1958 (P), but Naipaul's later *Mimic Men*, 1967 (P), emphasises the sadness, insecurity and brevity of the Colonial politician's career. He is soon overthrown and exiled, becoming a stateless man. *In A Free State*, 1971, develops the theme adumbrated in *Mimic Men*, that, in pursuing the power and freedom to govern our own lives, we pursue a mirage. Even as we seem to gain our end, we are brought face to face with the tyranny of our inner selves. Naipaul regarded this novel " as a rather final statement " of his themes of insecurity and the pursuit of freedom but his recent *Guerillas*, 1975, is concerned with similar problems.

R. K. Narayan (b. 1907).

Born in Madras, Narayan was educated there and at the Maharaja's College in Mysore, the south Indian city in which he now lives.

His first novel, *Swami and Friends*, 1935, which was highly praised by Graham Greene, introduced the imaginary town of Malgudi, which has since provided the setting of over two hundred short stories and nine more novels, including *The English Teacher*, 1945; *Mr. Sampath*, 1949; *The Financial Expert*, 1952; *Waiting for the Mahatma*, 1955; *The Guide*, 1958; *The Man-Eater of Malgudi*, 1962; *The Sweet-Vendor*, 1967.

Narayan is a master of classic English prose and his novels, at once sad yet delightfully humorous, offer an inimitable picture of the contradictions of Indian life. His best-known work is probably *The Guide*, for which he was awarded India's highest literary honour, the National Prize of the Indian Literary Academy.

George Orwell (1903–50).

Orwell's post-war novels express feelings apparent in his earlier journalism.

Animal Farm. 1945. P.

The theme of this satirical fable is the futility of popular revolutions. Led by the pigs, the animals of Manor Farm evict their brutal owners. However, one of the pigs, Napoleon, gains absolute power, establishing a police state. The animals are worse off than before.

1984. 1949. P.

This grim nightmare, which Orwell wished to call *1948*—his publisher dissuaded him—develops the ideas of *Animal Farm* in a vision of a totalitarian world whose rulers exploit psychological and technological discoveries to retain and consolidate power.

As a novel it is less successful than *Animal Farm*. It has not the latter's occasional humour, and the presentation of its villain, O'Brien, is unconvincing. Raymond Williams's *Culture and Society* (P) sympathetically relates the novel to Orwell's paradoxical feelings about socialism.

Anthony Powell (b. 1905).

Powell published five novels in the 1930s, when the elegance of his style and the fact that he took a comic view of the upper middle-class and Bohemian worlds led to his comparison with Waugh; but his novels were never marred by the snobbishness or cruelty which so often spoils Waugh's writing.

His sixth and most important work, *A Dance to the Music of Time*, 1951–75, comprises twelve volumes arranged in four trilogies. Most of the books are available in paperback either from Penguin or Fontana.

This novel's central image, to which its title alludes, is that of time as a formal dance in which people appear and reappear unexpectedly and with surprising companions. The action covers the period from 1914 to the present day, proceeding more or less chronologically, though the first book opens in the early 1920s and the hero-narrator's memories of his childhood during the First War occupy the second volume.

For the most part, like Powell's earlier work, it is set in the millieu of the upper middle-class and Bohemian artistic circles, between which its narrator, Jenkins, moves. An intelligent thoughtful man, he has an insatiable curiosity about human motivation, particularly how we are influenced by the thirst for power and love of adventure. Vividly aware of the danger of forming stereotyped ideas about other people, he feels that "all human beings . . . seen at close range are equally extraordinary."

The novel has often been compared with Proust's *À la recherche du temps perdus*, but Powell himself does not feel he has been at all influenced by Proust and despite the superficial similarities between their novels they really have little in common.

Each volume of Powell's work concerns not only a particular historical period but its action also centres on the doings of a single individual, supported by a large cast of vividly differentiated characters. Of these the most striking is undoubtedly the grotesque Widmerpool, who is, with some justice, often spoken of as the novel's hero.

It is too soon for us to judge this huge novel at the moment, but its penultimate trilogy, concerning Jenkin's war experiences stands out above the rest. It is at once more concentrated and more vivid; but the work as a whole is extremely enjoyable and often highly comic, presenting a most interesting contrast to Snow's similarly long, but rather portentous, *Strangers and Brothers* (q.v.).

Raja Rao (b. 1909).

Considered one of the most important Indian novelists writing in English, Rao published his first book *Kanthapura*, a story of village life, in 1938. His subsequent work consists of *The Cow of the Barracades*, 1947, a book of nine short stories, and two novels, *The Serpent and the Rope*, 1960, and *The Cat and Shakespeare*, 1965, complex works whose themes concern the interplay of illusion and reality in man's experience. The second book is the more optimistic in tone.

C. P. Snow (b. 1905).

Strangers and Brothers—11 vols. 1940–70. P.

In the course of this sequence the narrator, Lewis Eliot, rises from humble beginnings to success at the Bar, at Cambridge, and in the Administrative Civil Service. While this is clearly not an autobiographical work, the course of Snow's own career as a scientist, don, and civil servant has followed a similar pattern.

The volumes follow no strict chronology and only two, *A Time of Hope* and *Homecomings*, are concerned directly with Eliot's personal life. The other books of the sequence are each centred on the life of one of Eliot's friends or acquaintances. The best of them all is *The Masters*, where an account of the election of the Master of a Cambridge college becomes an image of political life. The other volumes have a less perfect form and vary in quality, but all are of documentary interest.

The New Men deals with the making of the first atomic bomb and the painful decisions in which scientists were involved at that time. A central figure in *Corridors of Power* is a Cabinet minister who supports the Campaign for Nuclear Disarmament. *The Sleep of Reason*, inspired by the Moors' Murder case, is more concerned with younger members of society and their rebellion against rational values and materialistic standards.

Snow is unlikely to be numbered among the greatest writers of our century, but his novels are workmanlike and readable. Their greatest strength and also their greatest weakness, derives from Snow's detached, unprejudiced observation of people's behaviour. We feel that, like his protagonist, Eliot, he prefers some men to others, but rarely judges any of them. At times, however, this bland detachment seems too cold-blooded, as if people were little more than interesting laboratory specimens.

Wole Soyinka (b. 1934). *See also* Section I.

A member of the Yoruba people of Western Nigeria, Soyinka has been a fierce critic of the Federal military government and during the Nigerian civil war he was imprisoned as a security risk.

His early work includes poetry, plays and an outstandingly powerful and original novel, *The Interpreters*, for which he won the second Jock-Campbell-*New Statesman* prize.

While in prison Soyinka covertly continued to write on tiny scraps of paper and since his release he has published a mass of poems, plays and polemical prose as well as a second novel, *Season of Anomy*.

The Interpreters. 1965. Fo.

In this original, highly enjoyable novel, Soyinka writes about a group of young Nigerian artists and intellectuals. The narrative is arranged in "solo" and "choral" sections, now reflecting the experience of individuals, now that of the group. The work has two main themes, which are expressed through complex symbols. The first is the characters' struggle to discover and express the relationship between their traditional culture and contemporary Nigerian society. The second is the need for a fearless commitment to the search for truth. Soyinka includes some highly comic episodes and sketches of dishonest and selfish people. Particularly memorable are an encounter with a German reporter, who likes to pretend he is American, a party given by the Oguazors, an ignorant, snobbish Nigerian don and his wife, and the ridiculous behaviour of Faseyi, who accuses his charming wife of behaving like "a bush-girl from a London slum". Soyinka takes a poet's delight in vivid and inventive use of words and is particularly skilful in his treatment of comic dialogue.

Season of Anomy. 1973.

A less complex novel, set in a fictitious African state, is an allegory of life during a period of corruption and terror. The action centres on Ofeyi's search for his girlfriend Iriyise, who has been kidnapped by officials of Cross State—the country's dominant region, although ultimate power is in the hands of the vicious international Cartel.

Ofeyi seeks to combat the Cartel's power by the peaceful means of education and example, but another young man, the revolutionary Dentist, believes that the forces of oppression can only be defeated by violence. The novel's conclusion suggests that both methods can play their part. While it is Ofeyi who discovers Iriyise's whereabouts, it is Dentist who effects her rescue.

Muriel Spark (b. 1918).

Although Muriel Spark had previously edited poetry magazines and published critical works, her literary career really began in 1951, when she gained first prize in a short story competition organised by the Sunday *Observer*. This success was followed in 1957 by the publication of the first of her ten *nouvelles*, *The Comforters* (P). A full-length novel, *The Mandelbaum Gate* (P) appeared in 1965, but, finding it "boring" and "too long", Mrs. Spark "decided never again to write a long book." Most of her work seems not only short but slight.

Her *nouvelles* can be divided into two groups. The first comprises *The Comforters*, 1957; *Robinson*, 1958; *Memento Mori*, 1959; *The Ballad of Peckham Rye*, 1960; *The Bachelors*, 1960; *The Prime of Miss Jean Brodie*, 1961; *The Girls of Slender Means*, 1963 (all P). These may all be enjoyed for their economy of language and precise vignettes of the absurd and grotesque aspects of life. The books are strange mixtures of comedy of manners and surrealist fantasy. In the later *The Public Image*, 1969, *The Driver's Seat*, 1970 (both P), *Not to Disturb*, 1971, and *The Hothouse By the East River*, 1973, surrealism gives way to whimsical melodrama and gothic "horror."

Some critics discern in Mrs. Spark's writing images of the world as God's novel. Certainly, the relation between the creator and his creation, between the novelist and his fiction, is a recurrent theme of her work, but she more often presents the agent as demonic than divine and her writing is preoccupied with violence and violent death, subjects she sometimes treats with naïve callousness.

The early *Memento Mori* remains her most satisfying book. It chronicles the reactions of a group of elderly people to mysterious telephone calls saying, "remember you must die." Only in this book and, to a lesser extent, in *The Prime of Miss Jean Brodie* does Mrs. Spark seem to show any imaginative sympathy for human weakness. However, her work, like that of many other contemporary writers, has had a mixed reception. One of its most consistent admirers is Professor Frank Kermode. His reviews of Mrs. Spark's books may be found in back numbers of *The Listener*.

David Storey (b. 1933). *See also* **Section I.**

Storey, the most gifted of the group of neo-realistic novelists who emerged during the late '50s and early '60s, has drawn upon his experience of the conflicts engendered in working-class children given opportunities denied to their parents.

Trained as an artist, Storey, himself the son of a miner, has worked not only as a rugby footballer but as a showground-tent erector, as a teacher, and is now a highly successful dramatist, as well as the author of six novels: *This Sporting Life*, 1960; *Flight into Camden*, 1960 (P); *Radcliffe*, 1963 (P); *Pasmore*, 1972 (P); *A Temporary Life*, 1973; *Saville*, 1976. The last won the Booker prize. Storey's novels show less versatility than his plays but nevertheless have much of interest to offer.

Although they are generally realistic in style and combine vivid scene-painting with first-rate dialogue, Storey's chief concern is to depict the inner lives of his characters and in his novels, as in his play *In Celebration* (*q.v.*), he seeks particularly to explore the ways in which the unthinking emotional force of working people, although it may give them an inner resilience, can also blind them to others' needs, and may make them cruelly destructive of both others and themselves.

William Styron (b. 1925).

A native of Virginia, one of the former slave states, Styron is particularly concerned with the theme of slavery as an emotional or spiritual condition. He implies that it is responsible for the immaturity, brutality, and ugliness of much American life and suggests that it stems primarily from the Americans' heritage of militant, repressive, and self-righteous Puritanism.

Styron's weakness is his tendency to illustrate rather than to explore his novels' themes and many of his characters are too cerebrally conceived, yet even in *Set This House on Fire*, his least successful work, Styron remains an impressive novelist. The architecture of his books, three of which are very long, is most skilful and all his work is illumined by a poetic gift for capturing the atmosphere of an event or scene and embodying fleeting visual impressions in vivid, precise images.

Lie Down in Darkness. 1948. Co.

The events of this novel take place on the day of Peyton Loftis's funeral, but most of the book consists of long flashbacks through which we learn about the lives of Peyton and her unhappy parents and come to understand why she committed suicide.

Styron implies that the Loftises' story is symbolic of life in the southern States and that the latter is itself a paradigm of American life in general. However, the novel does not sustain the weight of this interpretation, for although the characters arouse our pity they never attain the stature of representative tragic figures that such a theme demands. Nevertheless, this is a remarkable novel to have been produced by a writer of twenty-three. Its strength comes from Styron's gift for presenting individual scenes, illustrated in the novel's brilliant opening paragraphs and in episodes such as the account of Peyton,s wedding.

The Long March. 1952. P.

The narrative of this very short book gives an account of the relationships between two Marines, recalled for service during the Korean war, with which they have no sympathy, and their Colonel, a regular officer, whose avoidance of any sign of emotion has earned him the sobriquet of Old Rocky. Here Styron writes of the slavery of military life and the corruption and brutality it engenders, but his underlying theme is the dilemma of liberals, who "born into a generation of conformists" are thus "trapped in a predicament which personal insurrection could, if anything, only make worse", and yet to acquiesce in it would be to become, "like cannibals, hardly men at all." The passion with which Styron expresses this dilemma makes *The Long March* his masterpiece.

Set This House on Fire. 1960

Themes from the previous books are here combined with a sweeping condemnation of the "moral and spiritual anarchy" of contemporary American life, but the novel remains essentially a *roman à thèse* and of the three main characters only Kinsolving, a drunken artist and ex-soldier, becomes more than a blueprint, and even so the parallels Styron suggests between him and Oedipus seem grotesquely inappropriate. Nevertheless, the novel is well worth reading for its incidental poetry. It contains brilliant evocations of the beauty of the Italian countryside and of rural Virginia, the hideousness of American cities and the languor of New York on a Spring Sunday.

The Confessions of Nat Turner. 1967.

This is an imaginative reconstruction of the life of the leader of an abortive slave rebellion. The story is told in the first person as Nat, awaiting trial, looks back over the events of his life and explains why he decided to murder his White masters. Nat himself is not a fully convincing figure, but minor characters are, and Styron is particularly successful in his portrayal of the liberal Judge Cobb, whose predicament recalls that of the marines in *The Long March.*

John Updike (b. 1932).

Updike, a novelist and short story writer from Pennsylvania, has a genuine and congenial talent for recreating the atmosphere and daily life of rural New England. His early ambition was to be a painter and he retains an artist's eye for precise visual detail, but, unlike Jane Austen, another "miniaturist" of country life, Updike seems to lack a sense of his own limitations as a novelist. He sometimes spoils his work by decorating it with superfluous symbols and fails when he ventures outside the rural American scene which is the source of his inspiration.

Updike has so far published seven novels: *The Poorhouse Fair*, 1958; *Rabbit Run*, 1960; *The Centaur*, 1963; *Of the Farm*, 1965; *Couples*, 1968; *Bech: A Book*, 1970; *Rabbit Redux*, 1972 (all P).

Evelyn Waugh (1902–66)

Waugh seems unlikely to be regarded by future generations as anything other than a minor, though talented, novelist, but he was an eccentric on the grandest scale and this has assured a continuing public interest in his writing, an interest recently stimulated by the modish revival of inter-war fashions, by the publication of a number of memoirs by Waugh's friends, of Ricks' biography and of Waugh's own *Diary*.

His literary style is always elegant and many of his pre-war satires and fantasies skilfully catch the flavour of the period. Though often marred by cruelty and distasteful snobbery, they are also often highly entertaining. After 1945—the period with which this article is concerned—Waugh published nine more novels. Noteworthy among these are *The Ordeal of Gilbert Pinfold*

(1957) and the trilogy *Men at Arms*, *Officers and Gentlemen* and *Unconditional Surrender* (1955–61).

Both of these are based on Waugh's own life, the first describing a nightmare period of schizoid hallucinations while crossing the Atlantic, the trilogy concerned with his experiences during the Second World War.

Revised and re-issued as one book, *The Sword of Honour*, in 1965, the trilogy has some claims to be regarded as Waugh's finest work.

The first two volumes offer convincing, and sometines very amusing, satire on administrative incompetence. The second is more interesting for its protagonist, hitherto a cardboard figure, is brought to life, and in a moving encounter with a refugee woman is forced to admit that he became a soldier in order to evade his own personal problems. He and others like him were as responsible as "the enemy" for the horrors of the War.

Patrick White (b. 1912).

White, the winner of the Nobel Prize for Literature in 1973, is unique among Australian novelists for the range of his cultural experience and understanding, which encompasses not only that of his own country and of Britain but also parts of Western and Central Europe.

After an early childhood in Australia, at the age of thirteen he was sent to England to be educated or, as he himself has put it, "ironed out", at Cheltenham College. However, on leaving school he at once returned to Australia and worked as a jackaroo—a lowly apprentice and general factotum—on remote sheep stations. Some idea of his life at this time may be gleaned from Chapter 2 of *The Vivisector*, where an account of the hero's visit to a sheep station of the period includes a sketch of young Col Forster, jackaroo and would-be novelist—"The trouble is I haven't yet experienced enough." We may suppose that this reflects White's own feeling at the time. Certainly he was already writing novels, although none were published.

After two or three years' sheep farming, he returned to England, taking a degree in modern languages at Kings College, Cambridge. He then made his home in London but also travelled, both on the Continent and in the United States. During the War, as an intelligence officer in the R.A.F., he went further afield, to Egypt, Palestine and Greece.

Finding post-war England "an actual and spiritual graveyard", White decided to "seek the stimulus of time remembered", and so returned to Australia. Together with a friend, he set up house in a, then rural, suburb of Sydney and the two young men supported themselves by market-gardening, breeding dogs and goats and selling milk.

White had apparently finished his sixth novel when he returned home. He had also written a number of plays and short stories and published a collection of verse, *The Ploughman and Other Poems*. However, much of this early work was unpublished, more has never been reprinted. For most readers without access to specialised Australian libraries White's earliest available work is, therefore, his fifth novel *The Living and the Dead*, 1941 (P), and a play, *The Ham Funeral*, written in 1947 (*Four Plays*, 1965).

The Living and the Dead is an uneven book but already displays the extraordinary fusion of visionary intensity with brilliant social comedy and satire which characterises all White's later work and springs from his perception of life's essential ambivalence.

All his novels emphasise the dual nature of reality, as both good and evil. While insight brings his characters intense joy it also involves them in great suffering, since it demands recognition and acceptance of evil in both others and themselves. Yet the overall effect of all the books except *The Solid Mandala* is positive and joyful.

In so far as it resembles any other novelists' White's work seems more akin to that of German writers, particularly Thomas Mann and Hermann Broch, than it does to any British novelist's. That is not to imply that Mann or Broch influenced him. White himself says that in his early novels he was indebted to James Joyce: "I think anyone who started writing seriously then was influenced by Joyce" and "I suppose I was influenced by Lawrence", but he believes that music and painting have had a greater effect than any writing on his work as a whole. "They have helped me to express myself, I feel . . . I'd much rather have been a painter or a composer than a writer."

It would seem he feels that while it is difficult to express one's vision truthfully through the medium of paint or music it is almost impossible to do so in words. The problem of how to communicate is a recurrent theme of his earlier post-war novels, in which even the most educated of his protagonists find it all but impossible to articulate their experiences of joy and suffering. Empathetic communion is their most reliable form of communication, although many of them try also to express their visions through painting, music or dance.

The post-war novels all present characters who are struggling for insight into the true nature of life, seeking to distinguish the "white radiance of eternity" from the multicoloured images we impose upon it. The novels often seem harshly critical of conventional Christianity, but they express an essentially religious vision and the characters' quest for the immanent and mysteriously transcendent "God above [the] God" of Christian convention reminds one of the work of the existentialist Tillich, particularly in his *Courage to Be* (Fo).

White may be said to fuse insights which other men have seen primarily in terms of either theology or of the psychology of perception. Some critics suggest that he does little more than give rhetorical grandeur to expressions of the pathetic fallacy, but a careful reading shows that he is concerned rather with an experience of the natural world, which we in a sense "create", since our vision of it is a reflection of ourselves, and yet at its most intense, the vision has a religious quality and changes us, stripping away the masks of everyday life, penetrating and releasing our essential selves.

White's visionary characters are thus stripped and seared by life. To others they may appear as "The Burnt Ones"—*'Oi kaimenoi*, the poor unfortunates—but they are more likely to see themselves as "stroked by God", tried in the furnace of his love. Their acquaintances usually feel they are at best eccentric. They may seem subnormal or insane and they are generally avoided, frequently feared and attacked by other people, to whom their honesty and essential innocence, their refusal, or inability, to adopt the masks of social convention, present an intolerable challenge. In many cases the characters' "eccentricity" is emphasised by physical deformity, in essence a reflection of society's judgment of them. At the same time, by placing them on the fringe of society, if not quite outside its pale, their strangeness, whether the result of an unfortunate physical or mental abnormality, artistic talent or racial difference, frees the characters from social conventions and impels them to pursue their quests for truth and understanding: "honesty of purpose . . . is something that gets overlaid by civilization, in houses by gable and portico, in man by the social hypocrisies."

In expressing his themes White deploys poetic images and symbols, including, among a host of others, such age-old figures as the Explorer, the Scapegoat and the Wise Simpleton. At the same time, each novel's pattern is determined, at least in part, by archetypal images such as those of the Journey and the Creation and Fall, but White also exploits pictorial and musical forms. *Riders in the*

Chariot, in particular, draws upon images of religious art, including the Pieta and the Deposition from the Cross, while the shape of the whole novel resembles that of an early Renaissance narrative painting. *The Tree of Man* is given a symphonic musical design and it is probable that forms analogous to other musical patterns will be discerned in White's work by readers who share something of his wide knowledge of this art.

While he uses the resonance of poetic, visual and musical images to give his novels depth, intensity and formal beauty, White embodies these images and symbols in highly individual characters and precisely realised social settings. Except for *The Solid Mandala*, each of his novels has a large cast and he presents a wide variety of social types, from inarticulate bush farmers and talented Aborigines to butterfly socialites and highly cultured central European Jews. The settings of the novels are equally varied, moving between rural and desert Australia, France, Germany, Greece and the American prairies; but White's most characteristic setting is suburban Sydney, immortalised in his creation Sarsaparilla, the scene of *The Solid Mandala* and the main part of *Riders in the Chariot* as well as appearing in most of his other novels, various short stories and the play *Season at Sarsaparilla*.

White uses this fictional suburb to exemplify his vision of the pretentions of so-called "civilised" life, which, he suggests we use to deflect and cushion us from the demands of reality. Such a life is presented variously as comic, sterile, hypocritical, cowardly, possessive and destructive. Its visual manifestations are pretentious and usually hideous. Above all, White suggests, such a life is at once cruel and pitiful. Those who suffer at the hands of the "civilised" will be destroyed if they cannot learn to love and forgive their tormentors.

The blindness and pretentions of this world are caught in moments of scintillating comedy and satire: "Uncle . . . was under the impression that foreigners only understood what was shouted at them . . ." A flute is "'A peculiar and not very suitable instrument for a young girl,' Mrs. Bonner was compelled to observe. 'If difference is desired—and there are some who are averse to the piano—there is always the harp.'" "Mrs. Goodman had never encouraged religion, as she herself was God."

In general, White's style makes challenging demands upon his readers. He takes a poet's delight in the metaphorical ambiguities of words and is a master of ironic bathos and the witty epigram. His work is uneven and, particularly in *Riders in the Chariot* and *The Eye of the Storm*, his style from time to time seems rather emptily rhetorical. Nonetheless, White is one of the most rewarding, if also one of the most demanding of contemporary writers. Each of his novels is extraordinarily complex and to attempt to give some idea of their nature in such a short article is to afford them at best summary justice.

The Aunt's Story. 1948. P.

A beautifully organised novel sparkling with comedy is said to be White's own favourite. It tells the story of Theodora Goodman, a spinster of independent means. As her name suggests, she has been given a special gift by God. It is a capacity for insight. Her sense of the dual nature of all life is also suggested by her name, as well as by her rather masculine physique.

The novel is divided into three unequal sections. In the first a family gathering after the death of Theodora's mother leads naturally into a recapitulation of the daughter's life up to this time. Its central experience has been the ungainly, sensitive girl's love for her father and for their home Meroë, a golden house set in a rose garden among volcanic hills.

In this childhood Eden, Theodora cannot distinguish between good and evil "in the sum total of the garden." Her first intimation of darkness comes when her father tells her of the original Meroë, "a dark place in the black country of Ethiopia", whose truth she at first wishes to deny, but in time it becomes a "dim and accepted apprehension lying quietly at the back of her mind. She was free to love the first," although there come "many bitter days" when her mother's cruelty "hardens and blackens the roselight."

The central part of the novel, *Jardin exotique*, expresses the "fragmentation of maturity". Travelling in Europe Theodora comes to the *Hôtel du Midi*, a half-way house significant of her own middle-age and of the central period of her spiritual journey as well as being literally half-way between her Australian birth-place and the American prairies where she is to end her days.

The hotel houses a huddle of exotic refugees, Jewish, White Russian, Greek and American-Italian, who foregather in the frigid spiky cactus garden. Here Theodora experiences in herself the breakdown of European culture and a psychological disintegration. In terms of the novel this is necessary. Through her intuitive sharing of her fellow guests' lives she comes to recognise the complexity of her own nature, and, by implication, of all life, "a state of interminable being, hope and despair devouring and disgorging endlessly . . . 'How beautiful it all is,' said Theodora Goodman."

When the hotel goes up in flames Theodora begins her journey home, but literally and metaphorically "goes west".

A brief coda finds her in the American prairies. Here she is overcome with a sense of her own frailty and incongruity, feeling, "there is finally no safeguard against the violence of personality". She forms "a black note" in the golden landscape. But, the intuition that "there is sometimes little to choose between the reality of illusion and the illusion of reality" leads to a sense of having returned to the perfection of her childhood home and she is placidly content to accept the "illusion" other people have of her "reality" as deranged.

Counterpointed images of gold and black form a *leitmotif* beautifully enhancing the novel's theme, while associated references to Ethiopia take up an image earlier suggested by the title of White's unpublished play, *Return to Abyssinia*, which is about an adolescent's loss of innocence. The image reappears in *The Riders in the Chariot*, where Mary Hare lives in a house named *Xanadu*, recalling Coleridge's poem *Khubla Khan*, with its vision of the "Abyssinian maid". To his collection of short stories White was later to give the associated title *Burnt Ones*—"Ethiopian" is thought to signify "burnt one", and in Classical times Abyssinia was thought of as a land of fire.

Such images of burning are of particular importance in White's earlier post-war novels and vividly embody his sense that visionary insight is associated with searing, refining experience.

The Tree of Man. 1955. P.

A compelling and highly entertaining novel opens towards the end of the last century with the young Stan Parker clearing the bush to make himself a farm. It follows his story, and that of his wife Amy and their two children until the middle 1930s when the smallholding is beginning to be swallowed up in the expansion of suburban Sydney.

On one level the novel is an Australian epic, but it is also concerned to express the "mystery and poetry" of the lives of ordinary inarticulate people. Stan and Amy are strongly contrasted. Both seek illumination, but while he tries to see more clearly and is content to accept life as it is, she wants to possess life and is much more gradual in coming to recognise her own frailty. Part of the novel's distinction comes from the compassion with which White traces her decline into cross-grained old age.

The book's style is initially challenging, with idiosyncratic punctuation and many verbless sentences, which reflect the characters' inarticulate, sensuous apprehension of a life which affords little time for reading. The whole is woven into a symphonic pattern, based on the rhythms of the four seasons and the cycle of the agricultural year, expressing the underlying theme of man's creation, fall, exile and salvation.

Voss. 1957. P.

White's most perfect novel in a formal sense, *Voss* is an historical tale inspired by the life of the German explorer Ludwig Leichhardt who in 1848 set out to cross the Australian continent from east to west and disappeared with all his party.

Two main characters are presented although, as in the previous novels, there is a large and diverse array of subsidiary figures. Laura Trevelyan, a highly intelligent young woman, stifled by the inanities of her comfortable middle-class home, meets the German Voss, who hopes her uncle will support him in an attempt to cross the great Australian desert. The two young people, who are both seeking to explore the realms of the spirit, feel a mutual sympathy, which continues throughout the novel in experiences of intense telepathetic communion.

Voss's trials in the desert are thus set against Laura's more commonplace, but in a sense equally demanding, struggles to achieve a humble, disinterested love for the people whom her lively intelligence makes her at first more inclined to scorn. Both the social world of Laura's suburb and the desert experiences of Voss and his party are brought vividly before the reader's imagination in a brilliant fusion of comedy of manners and poetic tragedy.

The Riders in the Chariot. 1961. P.

In the opening chapter of *Ezekiel* the prophet tells of his vision of four creatures riding, enfolded in a fiery whirlwind, driven by the spirit over earth and sky, heralding the voice of God. In the novel, this image is associated with the Classical legend of the horse-drawn chariot of Apollo and becomes the unifying symbol, expressing a vision shared by four characters.

The first " rider " is Miss Mary Hare, " a small freckled thing ". Even the discreet postmistress, who refuses to say that she is unusual, "cannot deny that Miss Hare is *different*." Miss Hare lives alone in the decaying splendour of Xanadu, a mansion built by her father and now set amid a tangled wilderness of shrub and tree on the outskirts of Sarsaparilla. A visionary, with an intense sensuous appreciation of the world, she is also an epileptic and probably of subnormal intelligence though this may result from her rudimentary education. A cruel childhood has made it very difficult for her to love other people.

Her complement is kindly Mrs. Godbold, whose life is a ceaseless round of caring for others. A naturally good, motherly woman, a laundress who supports her violent drunken husband and a host of children, placid, capable, above all loving, Mrs. Godbold has the resilient strength to endure all life's blows.

The other two " riders in the chariot " similarly complement each other. Dubbo, an Aborigini painter of genius lives in a shack among the Sydney slums. He meets Himmelfarb, a highly cultivated and scholarly Jewish refugee, at the engineering factory where Dubbo sweeps the floor and Himmelfarb has a menial job on the production line.

While Ezekiel speaks of " four creatures " he also refers to the " four faces " of each and we may see White's four riders as embodying the four aspects of the Jungian mandala: Miss Hare the sensitive, Mrs. Godbold the feeling, Dubbo the intuitive, Himmelfarb the thoughtful.

Towards the end of the book it becomes apparent that they are also to be understood as embodying some (by no means all) aspects of the Gospel figures Mary Magdalene, Mary the mother of Jesus, the apostle John and Jesus himself.

These mystical, psychological and religious images are unobtrusively deployed to give extra dimensions to characters who are clearly defined and wholly convincing individuals in their own right.

The novel is divided into seven parts. The first two are concerned primarily with the lives of Miss Hare and Himmelfarb. A brief third part continues the narrative, but is chiefly taken up with painting the background of life in Sarsaparilla. Mrs. Godbold is the central figure of the fourth part, Dubbo of the fifth. In the sixth the four riders come together in a tragic climax and a short final section celebrates a resurgence of creative love. Two of the main characters have died, a third has disappeared. Xanadu is destroyed, but there remains Mrs. Godbold's hut, " in which she continued to live " amid her burgeoning family.

Here, as elsewhere in his novels, White suggests that love which " bears all things, believes all things, hopes all things, endures all things " always survives. In one sense his book may be read as an illustration to *1 Corinthians* 13.

The setting of the story moves between the splendours of Edwardian Xanadu, the horrors of Nazi Germany, Mrs. Godbold's childhood home in the Cambridgeshire fens, and Sydney, with its slums, its discreet middle-class suburbs and sprawling fringe, in Sarsaparilla, where the book's main action takes place.

Critical reception of *The Riders in the Chariot* and novels which follow it has been curious. In each case the initial reaction was that the novel, although extraordinarily exciting, is inferior to White's best work. As time passes however, these later novels seem to move up into the critics' pantheon. Probably, like other major artists, White is often somewhat ahead of his time!

The Solid Mandala. 1966. P.

The mandala image implicit in *The Riders in the Chariot* now comes to the fore and governs both the form and nature of a book whose veneer is deceptively simple.

White presents two contrasted twin brothers, Waldo and Arthur Brown. Waldo's appearance reflects his mind, which is neat, small and dark. Clumsy, blond Arthur's childlike spontaneity and unselfconsciousness make some people treat him as a simpleton, but he is both thoughtful and perceptive. His attitude to Waldo, who hates and despises him, covertly attempting to engineer his death, is one of protective love—at once maternal and paternal in its nature. As Arthur himself comes to feel, in some ways he exemplifies the hermaphroditic Adam, but the brothers' lives are interdependent, inextricably entwined, like the threads of colour in one of the " solid mandala " marbles which Arthur treasures as symbols of life's essential form.

The story is again set in Sarsaparilla, but this time White deals with a very limited section of society, although he gives his work a more general significance by its imagery, by the incorporation of literary and musical references and by allusions to the European background of the twins' parents and of Arthur's Jewish friends.

The book opens and closes with brief encounters between the brothers' neighbours, Mrs. Poulter and Mrs. Dan, who place the old men's lives in perspective. Otherwise the twins are described from their own points of view, although ironically and in the third person. As he would consider only fitting, Waldo's story is presented first, followed by Arthur's much shorter one, which, characteristically, nevertheless gives much more information about the family's history and presents incidents previously seen from Waldo's viewpoint in a very different, and generally happier, light.

Initially the book may seem unbalanced, for it is cunningly arranged to give us lifelike shocks of such force that we can hardly credit what we read. The first section offers plenty of hints of Arthur's sanity and kindly perceptiveness, but Waldo's contempt for him is so strong and so pervasive that we are apt to think of Arthur as virtually a moron, and so cannot at first accept the validity of the novel's second part, which presents him in such a startlingly different light.

The Vivisector. **1970. P.**

The narrative concerns the life and career of a highly successful painter, Hurtle Duffield. The son of a laundress and her penurious scrap-dealing husband, Duffield is sold to the Courtneys, a gentle landowner and his frigidly neurotic butterfly of a wife. Their own child, Rhoda, is a stunted hunchback.

The novel's title has a multiple significance. Driven by sado-masochistic impulses, Mrs. Courtney is a fanatic anti-vivisectionist, but her treatment of Rhoda, whom she forces to lie splayed upon a backboard, prefigures the model of a tortured dog Duffield notices in the window of the National League Against Vivisection. Mrs. Courtney's treatment of Duffield himself is equally unfeeling, if more subtly cruel, and as a result, although he is later hailed as a painter of genius, he is in fact the " vivisector " of his subjects.

Only towards the end of his life does Duffield attain a truly creative vision. This happens partly as a result of his reunion with Rhoda, who loves him, more especially because he responds to the love of an adolescent girl, and most particularly because a cerebral haemmorrhage brings him a moment of intense insight into the world's beauty. Being thus "stroked by God", an experience comparable with that which earlier novels express in terms of lightning and fire, changes Duffield's attitude to other people, for whom he now begins to feel a sympathetic, if rather ironic, friendship. It is exemplified in his relationship with a humble and kindly homosexual grocer, whom he had formerly used in one of his paintings as a symbol of destructive hatred.

A most convincing " portrait of the artist " and his compulsive search for ways to express the truth of his vision, is set amid a diversity of vividly drawn minor characters as the action moves between the Sydney slums and suburbs, remote sheep stations, Brittany, London and the Greek islands.

The Eye of the Storm. **1973.**

A charming and beautiful society woman, who is also a cruelly possessive and frigid mother, plays a minor part in several of White's novels. Here she takes the centre of the stage and is presented with ironic sympathy.

Bedridden and only intermittently conscious after a severe stroke, Elizabeth Hunter lies, cared for by three nurses and a housekeeper, while her elderly solicitor and man of affairs, Arnold Wybrd is always at her beck and call. It is typical of White's irony that Arnold is in another sense the solicited victim of a single affair, having once, early in his career, fallen prey to Mrs. Hunter's beauty.

She has been a spoilt and possessive charmer all her life, and remains one to the end, but now she has become conscious of her failings and regrets them, while seeking to acknowledge her attendants' care in the only way now left to her, by giving them presents and good—though caustically expressed—advice. Above all, she drives them to face the truth about themselves.

In her bedroom, where the tumult of everyday life is suspended, others therefore enter the " eye of the storm ", where their weaknesses are revealed and accepted, just as Elizabeth Hunter had once literally entered such a storm centre.

Until the age of seventy, she was almost completely selfish and self-absorbed, though also greatly loved. The fortuitous experience of being alone on an island during a cyclone then brought an overwhelming realisation of her own weakness and insignificance. It also made her recognise that she was probably " responsible for the worst in people ", particularly her own awful children. In the peace at the storm's centre, when the " myth " of herself as a kind of goddess has been exploded, she sees she is in fact a " flaw " in the world's beauty, and while acknowledging this moral ugliness, turns outward for the first time in her life to contemplate the external beauty which enfolds and accepts her as a part of itself.

Now again at the " eye of the storm ", between her incapacitating stroke and the coming of death, she drifts between consciousness of the present and memories of the past, acknowledging her many cruelties and thankfully re-living the happy months she spent nursing her dying husband, the single truly disinterested act of her life.

The two elderly children who have come post-haste from Europe, offer a vivid contrast. Neither can bear to stay for more than a few moments in their mother's bedroom, where they are confronted by their weaknesses.

Sir Basil is a failed Shakespearean actor who fancies himself as Lear and never stops playing a part, while his sister Dorothy, the frigid, deserted wife of a French prince, takes refuge from the world behind her title and self-congratulatory reflections on her housekeeping and dress-sense. Unhappy and self-absorbed they are corroded by hatred and fear of their mother, who understands them only too well, and on whom they shamelessly sponge. They want her to die quickly, so that they can divide her money, and meanwhile plan the economy of hustling her into an old people's home.

Almost equally important to the novel are Mrs. Hunter's attendants, Sisters de Santis and Manhood, who, while being fully realised as humanly muddled individuals, also embody the qualities of serene goodness and creative sensuality which the Hunters so conspicuously lack.

The power of the novel comes not only from the skill with which White organises and presents his themes through a large and varied cast, but also from his choice of the central character and her predicament. Except in *The Tree of Man* his heroes and heroines have been people who, by character or circumstances, are unusual. There is little unusual about Elizabeth Hunter's brilliantly realised character and, apart from the fact that she can afford private nursing, her circumstances are commonplace.

A Fringe of Leaves. **1976.**

Like the earlier *Voss*, White's latest book takes its subject from a legendary episode in Australian history, the story of Eliza Fraser, shipwrecked in 1836 off the Queensland coast, when her husband's ship foundered on the Great Barrier Reef. Captured by aborigines, she eventually escaped and reached Moreton Bay in a boat manned by convicts. White draws not only upon the factual story but the legend which has grown up round it.

White makes his heroine, Ellen, a kindly Cornish farm girl married above her station to a hypochondriac gentleman, Roxburgh. The first half of the book is chiefly concerned with their relationship and its stultifying effect on Ellen, who accompanies her husband on a trip to Australia to visit his settler brother.

On the return voyage their ship runs aground. Roxburgh is killed and Ellen abducted by natives, who use her as a mixture of slave and goddess. Stripped of all pretentions as of her clothes, she must face the reality that life is at once glorious and shockingly brutal, not the tame and bloodless affair that she has been taught to think of as civilised.

Angus Wilson (b. 1913).

In *The Wild Garden*, a collection of lectures about his literary career, Wilson says that, as a young man, he had no thought of becoming a writer. In some ways his upbringing was unusual. The youngest child by thirteen years of his middle-class parents, as a boy Wilson was spoilt, lonely and precocious, "learning about the nature of the world from [the] unhappy, pseudo-sophisticated declassé adults" who frequented the shabby-genteel hotels and boarding houses in which his parents lived. When he was fifteen his mother died and he became the "sole companion" of his raffish, elderly father, a compulsive gambler for whom he felt an "over close, intense affection". Wilson was later to portray the old man in various guises, most directly in "A Story of Historical Interest".

After graduating from Oxford Wilson took a post as a cataloguer in the British Museum's library. The work was intensely frustrating, but his emotions and intellect were otherwise engaged, in his relationship with his father and in the coterie political activities he shared with left-wing intellectual friends. Not until this "somewhat cosy" world was shattered by his father's death and the onset of war was Wilson forced to come to terms with adult life. There followed a long period of intense anxiety and depression. Emerging from this he began to write, producing his first story suddenly and "in intense excitement" one November Sunday in 1946. On subsequent weekends he wrote several more of the tales which were to appear in *The Wrong Set*, 1949 (P).

In this and his next collection, *Such Darling Dodos*, 1950 (P), Wilson portrays a deracinated middle-class which has failed to adapt to the sudden changes of the post-war world. The stories contain much lively social satire, but they also adumbrate themes which were to become more prominent in Wilson's later novels, themes relating to the dangers of immaturity and cherished illusions, to the need for honest self-realisation.

Until 1955 Wilson continued to work at the British Museum, now as deputy to the Superintendent of the Reading Room. During a month's holiday he wrote his first novel, *Hemlock and After*, 1953 (P) and later turned his hand to a play, *The Mulberry Bush*, which the English Stage Company chose to open its repertory at the Royal Court Theatre in 1956. Wilson found that he needed more time to work on this play than a holiday would afford, so he resigned from the Civil Service.

The adventurousness he showed in thus abandoning financial security is paralleled in his writing by a courageous readiness to experiment. He is no radical innovator, such as Beckett, but each of his novels shows him taking a new step, extending both his subject matter and his command of techniques.

His courage was particularly evident in *Hemlock and After* where he became the first contemporary British novelist to write frankly of homosexuality, a topic he has always treated as a normal aspect of human behaviour and as such amenable to sympathetic, comic or satiric treatment, depending on the nature of the character. This may seem unremarkable in today's climate, but few other novelists have written of homosexuality so objectively, and to publish such work in the early fifties, when *Hemlock and After* appeared, required no little courage, especially from a novelist at the beginning of his career. One recalls that Forster's *Maurice* (*q.v.*) was only published posthumously.

Wilson, who has written studies of Zola and Dickens, and is now a visiting professor of English at the University of East Anglia, is in some ways a very literary writer. Allusions to Dickens's novels are particularly common in his work. He is apt, for example, to speak of a character's "Quilpish humour", and in his latest book it is the memory of an incident from *Little Dorrit* that spurs the heroine to action during an Indian riot.

Like Dickens, Wilson has a taste for the grotesque and a delight in histrionics. *Hemlock and After*, *Anglo-Saxon Attitudes*, 1956 (P), and *No Laughing Matter*, 1968 (P), are all conceived in dramatic terms and prefaced with cast lists, while even Wilson's most reflective novels, *The Middle Age of Mrs. Eliot*, 1958 (P), and *Late Call*, 1964 (P), from time to time exploit his histrionic talent.

Wilson himself believes that a gift for impressionistic mimicry is his "principal natural asset as a writer." Allied with his dramatic sense it enables him to create episodes of high comedy, but at times it can result in a certain posturing vulgarity for, although Wilson always treats his main characters sympathetically—if with a certain comic detachment—he cannot always resist the temptation to score off his minor figures. This trait is particularly noticeable in his early work and again in his most recent novel, *As If By Magic*, 1973 (P).

A more serious weakness is Wilson's deployment of his mimetic gifts in the creation of vivid illusions of ugliness and cruelty, which he makes almost more painful to read about than they would be to witness, for the predominant feeling expressed in such passages is not revulsion but fascinated relish. Passages of this kind comprise so large a part of many of his books that much of his work is only tolerable in small doses. Critics such as Walter Allen have therefore considered Wilson more successful as a writer of short stories than as a novelist. However his two novels *The Middle Age of Mrs. Eliot* and *Late Call* are only rarely marred in this way and, despite such faults, Wilson is always a writer of immense vitality and ingenuity.

Like Jane Austen, whose work he greatly admires, he is a novelist with sharp eyes and ears for the foibles and follies of mankind and a gift for placing his characters in a precise, immediately recognisable social setting. He was the first novelist to observe and record the changing social climate of the post-war world and its strong contrast to the milieu of the thirties.

His early prose style was much influenced by Jane Austen, as a glance at the opening paragraphs of *Hemlock and After* will show, but a preoccupation with narrative technique and a desire to give his work a more "resonant", poetic quality has led him greatly to modify his style, and in his recent work he acknowledges a debt to Virginia Woolf, a writer he earlier had found unsympathetic.

Wilson has now developed a highly sophisticated command of narrative and his later novels demand close, attentive reading, but he is yet far from achieving his avowed aim, which is to marry a "sense of a transcendent evil and good to the fully felt social novel that the English have constructed in their great tradition."

A definite sense of values emerges from his novels. All suggest the importance of an honest and clear-sighted appraisal of one's actions and motives. They also emphasise the damage we do to others by refusing to face and, as far as possible to remedy, our shortcomings, and Wilson is particularly critical of the evils of acting from motives of pure expediency. But only in his presentation of ugliness and cruelty is there any sense of passionate feeling and, as we have noticed, the feeling is usually ambivalent. As this intense awareness of evil is not matched by any correspondingly vivid or numinous apprehension of goodness, most of Wilson's novels have a certain nightmarish imbalance. Except in *Late Call* and *The Middle Age of Mrs. Eliot* his world is not so much that of "the fully felt social novel" as of *Grand Guignol* and while his initial courage in presenting homosexual characters is wholly admirable, homosexuality seems to be given a disproportionate emphasis in his work as a whole.

II. HOW TO ENJOY A POEM

References are to the *New Oxford Book of English Verse*, 1972.

Many people who enjoy listening to music and looking at pictures and sculpture find it difficult to appreciate poetry and a few suggestions as to how we may approach a poem may be helpful. Perhaps the first thing to bear in mind is that just as we cannot fully appreciate an unfamiliar piece of music at a first hearing, nor the subtle interplay of form line and colour in a picture with a single hasty glance, so it is equally impossible to savour the full richness of a poem in the course of one or two quick readings. A writer was once looking round an exhibition of modern paintings, fascinated by their unusual colours but utterly at a loss as to their significance and inclined foolishly to criticise what he could not understand. Sitting down to rest his aching feet, he gazed at the painting in front of him. Suddenly, as if he had put on a new pair of spectacles, the picture came into focus. It still seemed mysterious, but though he still could not fully understand it the writer now began to enjoy it. In a similar way, we can "walk around" and gaze at a poem for a long time feeling more a sense of bewildered fascination than pleasure, then, suddenly, we find a clue to the poet's vision. But how shall we seek it?

When we first meet a poem it is often helpful to read it aloud, for the poet makes use of the sound and rhythmical patterns of words and although the printed poem may seem flat as does a music score to the uninitiated, when heard it comes alive.

Then we must remember that a poet normally uses words not only literally but also figuratively and loves to speak of one thing as if it were another. When Keats describes the pleasure he has found in books he talks of them as if they were countries and he a traveller:

"Much have I travell'd in the realms of gold
And many goodly states and kingdoms seen;"
(OBEV 562).

Another important point is suggested by Peter Porter's *Sanitized Sonnet 4*, which begins,

"Much have I travelled in the realms of gold
for which I thank the Paddington and
Westminster Public Libraries:"
(*The Last Of England*, p. 41).

A poem, even a contemporary poem, is an histori cal object. It has been affected by the poetry which preceded it—Porter expects us to recognise his quotation from Keats and to appreciate the new perspective in which he places it. A poet may write within, or in reaction from a particular convention: in Elizabethan and Jacobean times it was a poetic fashion to speak of women as gardens, or as if their faces shone like the sun, (OBEV 158, 164, 178, 255). A poem may be inspired by particular events and people, as are Yeats's *Easter 1916* and Dryden's *Absolom and Achitophel* (OBEV 767 and 365–366) and our enjoyment may be enhanced if we know to what and whom the writer refers. A poem always grows out of the experience of a single individual at a particular point in time. We are therefore helped to enjoy it if we know when and by whom it was written and can place it in its historical perspective.

In *The Business of Criticism* Helen Gardner quotes the case of the student who said that the poem beginning

"At the round earth's imagined corners
Blow your trumpets, angels,"
(OBEV 200)

was written by a very simple man. She points out that it is indeed true that no contemporary educated Christian would use such images and we may fail to enjoy the striking originality and sophistication of the way they are employed to express a simple faith unless we know that they were conceived by a writer of the early seventeenth century and unless we have some idea of the ways in which men of that day lived, thought and wrote. We will enjoy the poem even more if we know something of the life and other work of its creator, John Donne. We can never learn too much about a poem, but always we come back to the work itself, for it exists not only as an historical object and the product of a particular mind and vision, but also in its own right, as an enduring work of art.

Making out the "Meaning".

Remembering always that the poet normally speaks in images and that the images he uses may be influenced by the particular conventions of his day, we need to give close attention to his words if we are to appreciate their full significance. I. A. Richards in *Practical Criticism* formulated certain principles which may aid one in making out the "meaning". He distinguished four kinds of "meaning": the "plain sense" of the poem, the "feeling", the "tone" and the "intention". The "plain sense" is arrived at simply by following the words, and incidentally the punctuation, in an attempt to find out what the poet actually says. Readers do not always do this. Another aspect of the "meaning" is the poet's "feeling" for his subject—does he, for instance, express awe, tenderness, anger, amusement? Then, is his "tone" towards the reader confidential, appealing or didactic? Finally, Richards speaks of the "intention" of the poem, the whole aim that the writer is trying to pursue.

Distinguishing Subject and Theme.

Another illuminating way of looking at a poem is to distinguish between its subject and its theme, for they are seldom identical. A poet loves to transpose his experience into another setting, and below his surface narrative or description we usually find a second "meaning", the theme, which is the core of the poem. Often there are many themes subtly interwoven. In *Resolution and Independence* (OBEV 484), Wordsworth writes of a spring morning walk, but the themes of his poem are many, one being his fear of failure, poverty and ignominious death. Shelley addressed an ode to the West Wind (OBEV 549) and here one of the main themes is a plea for poetic inspiration.

The Formal Aspects of the Poem.

Other pointers to its meaning are to be found in the formal patterns of the poem, the metre and literary form in which it is cast (*see* Part IV), the kind of imagery or figures of speech (Part V). Just as all roses have a certain fundamental similarity so do all examples of, say a sonnet. With a sonnet, as with a rose, we can enjoy its beauty without ever knowing its species, but we better understand and relish the peculiar beauties of the example before us if we can recognise it for what it is.

Study of Shakespeare's Sonnet 73 (OBEV 143).

That time of year thou mayst in me behold
When yellow leaves, or none, or few, do hang
Upon those boughs which shake against the cold,
Bare ruined choirs, where late the sweet birds sang.
In me thou seest the twilight of such day
As after sunset fadeth in the west;
Which by and by black night doth take away,
Death's second self, that seals up all in rest.
In me thou seest the glowing of such fire,
That on the ashes of his youth doth lie,
As the death-bed whereon it must expire,
Consumed with that which it was nourished by.

This thou perceiv'st, which makes thy love more strong,
To love that well which thou must leave ere long.

Kinds of Meaning.—Searching for the plain "sense", we find here three clearly defined images, the first of very late autumn,

"When yellow leaves, or none, or few, do hang
Upon those boughs which shake against the cold".

Then follows an image of twilight, the brief phase after the sunset has faded and before the fall of night. The third image is of a dying fire, glowing amid its ashes. All these, says Shakespeare, "thou mayst in me behold". All three, then, suggest that phase in man's life that follows the prime, the decline towards death. The "feeling" of these first twelve lines is sombre and foreboding, and in its "tone" the poem speaks to one alone—"thou mayst behold," "thou seest". Then when we reach the concluding couplet we perceive the "intention" of the poem. It is a love poem,

"This thou perceiv'st, which makes thy love more strong,
To love that well which thou must leave ere long."

Subject and Theme.—We can also approach the poem trying to distinguish "subject and theme". Then we perceive more clearly the theme of the imminence of death, which gradually develops and gathers momentum. For instance, the trees are called "bare ruined choirs" where the birds no longer sing, and this suggests a ruined empty abode from which the voice has flown, the spirit departed. Then the "black night" which succeeds twilight is "Death's second self", and the fire lies on the ashes "As the death-bed, whereon it must expire".

The very colours of the poem are suggestive. A picture is painted in sombre greys and black, lit up by a dull glow soon to be engulfed in darkness, the yellow leaves on the bough, the sunset fading into twilight, the fire dying on the ashes. It is like the chiaroscuro of a Rembrandt painting.

Formal Pattern.—If we now attend to the formal patterns of the poem we find how exquisitely they match the sense. The poem is a sonnet (*see* **M64**), that is a brief lyric poem of only fourteen lines, expressing feeling in a taut and concentrated way. There is no room for digression; every word counts.

As we expect from a Shakespearean sonnet we find the rhyme scheme ABAB CDCD EFEF GG. This indicates that the poem will naturally take the design of three quatrains and a concluding couplet. Then how exquisitely and precisely each image is contained within the brief compass of its quatrain, and how apt are the metaphors in which the images are expressed.

If we now turn to another "autumnal" poem we may be helped towards appreciating the variety of ways in which a poet can use familiar material to express a personal vision.

"**October Dawn**

October is marigold, and yet
A glass half full of wine left out

To the dark heaven all night, by dawn
Has dreamed a premonition

Of ice across its eye as if
The ice-age had begun its heave.

The lawn overtrodden and strewn
From the night before, and the whistling green

Shrubbery are doomed. Ice
Has got its spearhead into place.

First a skin, delicately here
Restraining a ripple from the air;

Soon plate and rivet on pond and brook;
Then tons of chain and massive lock

To hold rivers. Then, sound by sight
Will Mammoth and Sabre-tooth celebrate

Reunion while a fist of cold
Squeezes the fire at the core of the world,

Squeezes the fire at the core of the heart.
And now it is about to start."

Ted Hughes, *The Hawk in the Rain* (Faber, 1957).

Kinds of Meaning.—The title serves as an initial guide—the poem is about the dawn of an October day. The first three stanzas form a single sentence. It opens with a striking evocation of autumnal warmth and colour—"October is marigold"—but ends with a suggestion of the awakening of a great ice-age: the half-empty glass of wine has "dreamed a premonition of ice . . . as if/The ice-age had begun its heave." We notice that the wine glass is gradually personified and that the vague foreboding of its "dream" remains with it now that morning has come, it has a "premonition of ice across its eye"—a glazed look. The image of the wine glass combines with the images of stanza four to suggest the morning after a lively party which has continued late into the night. The poem tells us all this is doomed. "Ice has got its spearhead into place". We notice the warlike associations of "spearhead" and that it is a primitive weapon, but poised for the kill. There follows a description of the way the ice overpowers and imprisons first "a ripple", next "pond", next "brook" and then even "rivers"; then comes a startling image of the great ice-age monsters, the mammoth and sabre-tooth tiger, celebrating a "reunion" while a cold fist "Squeezes the fire at the core of the world"—as if the cruel power of the ice were penetrating even to earth's molten centre.

The "feeling" changes from one of relaxed warmth through a growing sense of menace to one of fear. The "tone" is impersonal and prophetic, quite different from Shakespeare's. Hughes is speaking of a process which may affect everyone. In his poem, as in Shakespeare's, the "intention" becomes clear only in the final couplet. It suggests that Hughes is writing not simply of the way winter encroaches upon the warmth of October, but expressing a terrible sense of the imminence of a nightmare state of psychological and spiritual winter, one in which ruthless primitive forces unite to destroy one's very life. This is the theme of the poem

Subject and Theme.—Subject and theme thus distinguished, the significance of the poem's images becomes clearer. We notice how the aural imagery of the first six lines is used to amplify the theme. At first the vowels are long and open, the consonants predominantly soft, but the sharp penultimate syllable of premon*it*ion introduces a series of menacing hissing sounds in lines five and six. Then, as in Shakespeare, we find an image of music—"whistling" shrubbery—implying cheerful, light-hearted gaiety. The phrase may suggest a shrubbery full of whistling birds—the dawn chorus—it may also suggest cheerful guests at the party—Hughes is unspecific, perhaps because he wants us to think of both. We also notice that the sound of the word whi*st*ling here contradicts its cheerful connotations, for it subtly echoes the menacing hisses of the earlier lines.

Hughes tells us that the shrubbery is "green" to emphasise that it is full of life—green is a traditional symbol of fertility. Later he uses other symbols of life and vitality—water and fire. All will be conquered by the "ice".

Beneath the main theme we may distinguish a subsidiary one, that of the approach of old age and death. Then we perceive that the glass of wine also symbolises life. It is spoken of as now half full—we begin to age, at first almost imperceptibly, in our prime, when we have drunk only half of life's glass.

Formal Patterns.—Turning to the poem's form, we notice that it is written in octosyllabic couplets (**M60**), but that the rhyme scheme, metre and sentence patterns have been adapted so as to match and reinforce the poem's themes. We expect couplets to rhyme. These ones suggest a rhyme, sometimes almost do rhyme, yet continually frustrate our expectation and so increase the sense of unease, until in the last stanza they meet with a clinching finality all the more powerful for having been so long delayed:

"Squeezes the fire at the core of the heart,
And now it is about to start."

Further Suggestions: The Poems in Their Settings.—There is yet much to discover about these two poems. We will find that each time we return to them we become aware of some fresh aspect of their significance. New insights will be given if we study the poems' settings.

J. W. Lever in *The Elizabethan Love Sonnet* shows how Shakespeare took a hackneyed convention of his day and gave it new vigour. The sonnet we have read is addressed not to the poet's real or supposed mistress, as were other Elizabethan love sonnets, but is one of a series celebrating the affection between the ageing Shakespeare and his younger patron. Modern recognition of homosexuality may lead us to assume their relationship was sexual, but in Elizabethan times homosexuality was a mortal sin and when we learn more of the relation of a Rennaissance poet to his patron and of the Rennaissance ideal of Platonic friendship between educated men, we understand Shakespeare's poem differently. Further light is shed on its significance by other sonnets in the series.

The condensed elliptical style of Hughes's *October Dawn* is characteristic of twentieth-century verse. If the mode is unfamiliar to us our understanding of the poem will be enhanced by reading other modern poetry and "learning the language". We can extend our acquaintance with Hughes's poetry and learn to recognise and savour the individuality of his vigorous, sensuous style. If we read other English "nature poems" we shall be better able to appreciate and enjoy the originality of his vision.

III. TWENTIETH-CENTURY POETRY

This section does not profess to be a full account of the poetry of the current century, as that would not be possible within the present compass. The aim is rather to touch upon some aspects of the poetry and to suggest ways of approaching it.

I. INTRODUCTION.

The Poem as an Art Form expressive of Feeling.

There is no short cut to the enjoyment of poetry. The only approach is an attentive reading, poem by poem, remembering always that the poet is attempting to express personal *feeling* through a pattern of words, in which their order, their associations, and their verbal music are all of the utmost significance.

Coleridge described poetry as a more than usual feeling with more than usual order, and the reader may like to turn to the paragraph on the function of dramatic art (**I3**) where reference is made to Susanne Langer's thesis that art gives form to our feeling response to life. By this is meant not only emotion as distinct from reason, but the whole gamut of our response to life as human beings—what it *feels* like to use the senses, to have emosions, even what it feels like to think.

Such feeling response cannot adequately be conveyed by logical discourse. How often we hear the phrases "I mean", "You know", from speakers who implicitly acknowledge that they are incapable of "expressing the inexpressible" through the medium of prose discourse and must rely on the sensitivity of their hearer to interpret their feeling. The artist's task is to translate the inarticulate cry into significant images, patterns and forms which convey their import with precision and beauty.

It is perhaps easier for us to see how the painter, the sculptor, or the musician can do this, and how, like Henry Moore, they may resolutely refuse to say what their work "means", for to limit it to "meaning" is to divert attention from its unique value, its numinous feeling quality. But the poet in his subtle and difficult art must use as his material words and grammatical structures which themselves have meaning from which they cannot be divorced. Although possible meanings of individual phrases must be established, the modern literary critic eschews any attempt to state what the poem as a whole "means". He attempts rather to "explicate" the poem, to unfold its hidden implications, to make clear its significance as a whole. We must remember first and foremost that a poet normally uses words not literally, but with a figurative meaning. He loves to speak of one thing as if it were another. The best approach is first to read the poem as a whole and then re-read it with particular attention for the special import of the individual figures of speech.

Special Difficulties of Twentieth-Century Poetry.

Poetry of the current century presents the reader with special difficulties. Hitherto, however strange or elaborate the imagery, in most poems prosaic statements and a rational framework could be discerned, but from about 1910 even these were often discarded, so that an even greater receptivity is demanded of the reader.

Drastic Social Changes in the Era between the Wars.

For a fuller understanding of modern poetry we should return to the vital period between the wars, when the masters, Yeats and Eliot, were developing new insights and techniques and setting standards which have not since been equalled.

Inevitably the poetry of the time reflected contemporary changes in society. The Georgian Books of Verse, 1911–22, illustrate how the familiar rural tradition was becoming outworn and it was now to be maintained by only a few poets, Hardy being the most distinguished and influential. For England was fast becoming a predominantly urban society and the imagery of the countryside, inevitably used by Shakespeare, Wordsworth, and Keats, was becoming no longer relevant, sometimes incomprehensible to the town-dweller.

In France, fifty years earlier, Baudelaire (1821–67) had drawn inspiration from the city, both in his preoccupations and in his imagery. In England it was the genius and originality of Ezra

Pound (1885–1972) and T. S. Eliot (1888–1965), with their highly original experiments in theme and style, who now gave direction to a new kind of poetry, urban, sophisticated, and cosmopolitan.

Other social factors had their influence. The horror and futility of the First World War, the Communist revolution, the economic slump, the decline in religious faith, the discoveries of Freud, all contributed to the collapse of the old stable sureties and left poets profoundly shaken and searching for new values and effective modes of expression.

Pound, Eliot, and W. B. Yeats (1865–1939) all repudiated the current bourgeois values of wealth and worldly success, which with the rapid growth of industry, commerce and advertising were becoming ever more deeply entrenched. Stigmatised by Matthew Arnold in *Culture and Anarchy* as " Philistine " in 1869, they are the corrosives of art and cause the poet to feel out of sympathy with society.

Pound and Eliot, and later William Empson (b. 1906) consciously directed their poetry to a select minority. Intellectual and satirical, it makes no appeal to facile emotion. The familiar metres and rhymes have been discarded. The elliptical syntax, the complex organisation of the imagery, the erudite references to other cultures, all make demands. A phrase like Pound's " His true Penelope was Flaubert " is not immediately clear. Such poetry is not intended to be lapped up by a complacent bourgeoisie.

Another aspect of the new style was indifference to accepted canons of " respectability ", in subject and in diction, a candour about sex (encouraged by the work of Freud), and the use of vernacular and slang, which in the Sixties sometimes degenerated into scurrility.

Aesthetic influences.

(a) *The development of the romantic aesthetic*

One of the prime causes of the change in poetic method is not social but aesthetic, the clarification and evolution of the Romantic concept of poetry.

In *Romantic Image*, Frank Kermode has pointed out that from the time of Coleridge there has been a growing conviction in writers such as Keats, Blake, Pater, and Yeats that the artist, in whom the powers of imagination are allied with a passionate sensibility, has a special quality of apprehension and expresses his intuitions in a unique way. The work of art, according to this theory, is original, essentially whole in itself, an " aesthetic monad " and resists analysis into form and content. Without ulterior purpose or utility, its only *raison d'être* is " to be." The image, Coleridge insisted, is essentially " vital ", not mechanistic but organic, and it has itself been presented by organic images, notably that of the tree and the dancer.

(b) *The French Symbolists*

In his *Axel's Castle*, 1931, Edmund Wilson discussed the aims of the French Symbolists and their stimulus to English writers, including Yeats and Eliot.

The Symbolist leader, Stephane Mallarmé, attempted to create a new idiom for poetry. Supremely disinterested, a " saint of literature ", he wrote little himself, but at his modest weekly receptions he gently expounded his influential views to such visitors as Whistler, Degas, Laforgue, Valéry, Claudel, Gide, Wilde, George Moore, Yeats, and Debussy.

Influenced by Poe, Mallarmé cultivated in his poetry a suggestive indefiniteness, blurring the distinctions between the actual world and that of dream and reverie. Debussy's well-known translation into music of his *L'Après-midi d'un Faune* wonderfully conveys his evocative and amorphous imagery.

Like Poe, the Symbolists were much concerned to reproduce in their poetry the flow of music and they were much influenced by Wagner. They came even to discard the classical Alexandrine and to develop *vers libre*. In the cult of indefiniteness they would, like Poe, confuse the perceptions of the senses. Poe, for instance, " hears " the oncoming of darkness.

What was the purpose of these experiments in poetic language? The Symbolists were so much preoccupied with the unique quality of individual experience, and with the complex and evanescent nature of consciousness, that they eschewed anything so commonplace as a description or statement as a falsification of experience and endeavoured, instead, to express unique and transitory feelings by suggestive images and symbols fastidiously chosen and patterned with exquisite care. The time-honoured rational framework of poetry was being scrapped so that it was becoming irrelevant to speak of the " meaning " of a poem.

(c) *The problem of objective validity in symbolist art*

The symbolism was not of the commonly accepted kind, such as the dove with the olive branch. Each poet deployed a highly idiosyncratic symbolism peculiar to himself in order to express his own intensely personal feelings. Such symbols were, says Wilson, really " metaphors detached from their subjects ". Inevitably such poetry is not easy to interpret. An example easily available in English is Valéry's *Le Cimitière Marin*, translated by Day Lewis as " The Graveyard by the Sea ".

The basic problem for the Symbolist poet is to find an imagery both true to his own unique experience and also in some way significant and communicable. That is the supreme test.

It is fascinating to see how English poets, such as Yeats, Eliot, and Sitwell, stimulated by the French experiments, tackle this problem and give objective validity to an intensely subjective vision.

II. SOME INDIVIDUAL POETS.

1. The Masters of the Decade between the Wars.

W. B. Yeats (1865–1939).

References are to the *Collected Poems* (Macmillan).

Yeats's influence is exerted not by the limp romantic Celtic twilight verses between 1889 and 1904 but by the complex, sinewy poems appearing between 1910 and 1939. Although in traditional verse forms they establish Yeats as a great master of the modern symbolic image.

Brought up by a father of sceptical mind, Yeats had sought from early youth for some significance to life in " heterodox mysticism ", such as theosophy and the Kabbala, and above all in Blake. Their highly developed systems of symbols stimulated his innate sensitiveness to this intuitive form of insight and expression and encouraged him to develop his gift for waiting on images as they arose from the deeper regions of his mind. Arthur Symons, whose *The Symbolist Movement in Literature* was published in 1899, introduced him to the work of Mallarmé and other French Symbolists, and confirmed him in his poetic approach which he now realised was part of a European movement.

To give objective validity to highly subjective images he used several techniques. Following Shelley's example, he would repeat the same symbol throughout the body of his work, so that one poem illuminates another. The symbol thus seen in perspective reveals new facets of its significance, sometimes even contradictory aspects.

For example, in early poems the rose signifies not only love and, in its Rosicrucian form, a mystic union, but also Ireland, beauty both sensuous and intellectual, and the beauty of Maud Gonne, with whom Yeats remained hopelessly in love.

A ruined Norman tower which Yeats had converted into a dwelling recurs from 1919 in many poems. Its basic significance is the artist's isolation, but it also suggests Milton's Platonist, Shelley's "visionary prince", Samuel Palmer's "lonely light", and Yeats's own Anglo-Irish heritage. He was greatly concerned to give the symbol solidity and firm outline and stresses the tower's emblematic "winding, gyring, spiring treadmill of a stair" and the "grey stone fireplace with an open hearth" and the "fire of turf" of simple hospitality.

He juxtaposed exalted symbols with the singularly down-to-earth motifs which he deployed with increasing frequency. The indignity of age is "a sort of battered kettle at the heel," or "a tattered coat upon a stick" until in his emblematic protagonist, "Crazy Jane," he presents the ultimate in physical destitution inspired by poetic frenzy.

Yeats also relied on archetypal images from the "Great Memory," to which we respond unconsciously. In *The Two Trees* (p. 54), he follows Blake in his use of the image of the tree, which develops from the Kabbala and the Biblical Tree of Life. To Yeats it came to embody the organic nature both of all life and of the imagination, or reality intuitively perceived by the artist as whole and vital. Yeats, like Blake, contrasted this imaginative vision with the abstractions of the discursive intellect and his most perfect expression of the work of art as an organic and indissoluble unit occurs at the climax of *Among School Children*. Here in a passage of multiple import he marries the image of the tree to that of the dance.

"O chestnut-tree, great-rooted blossomer,
Are you the leaf, the blossom or the bole?
O body swayed to music, O brightening glance,
How can we know the dancer from the dance?"

Yeats's poetry was also supported by a framework of mythology, whether of Gaelic legend, Greek mythology, as in *Leda and the Swan*, or, as in much of his more mature work, that of his own private system, which he expounded in his prose *A Vision*, 1926. For instance, he saw history as opposing cycles of 2000 years, each cycle being a reversal of the previous one. He represented this diagramatically by opposing "gyres", his gyre being the spiral traced on a cone.

But Yeats's finest poems, even when the meaning depends on his private hinterland, are still valid and intelligible in themselves. *The Second Coming* affects us through the singular clarity and force of the metaphors and the controlled energy of the rhythm:

". . . somewhere in sands of the desert
A shape with lion body and the head of a man,
A gaze blank and pitiless as the sun,
Is moving its slow thighs, while all about it
Reel shadows of the indignant desert birds.
The darkness drops again; but now I know
That twenty centuries of stony sleep
Were vexed to nightmare by a rocking cradle,
And what rough beast, its hour come round at last,
Slouches towards Bethlehem to be born?"

Yeats is the poet of paradox and often quoted Blake, "Without contraries there is no progression." His own life was one of manifold tensions, especially between contemplation and his active participation in Irish politics and art. (He was Production Manager of the Abbey Theatre and was made a Senator.)

A dominant theme is the dichotomy between sensuous living and the creation of immortal works of art, the latter symbolised by Byzantium in two splendid poems. Here he rejects the "sensual music" of "whatever is begotten, born, and dies" or "the fury and the mire of human veins" for "monuments of unageing intellect," symbolised by Byzantium, with its gold mosaic, the starlit or the moonlit dome and the golden singing bird, a miracle, "in glory of changeless metal," (pp. 217, 280).

Yet in the contemporary *Dialogue of Self and Soul*, p. 265, the poet opts for life, however sordid.

"I am content to live it all again
And yet again, if it be life to pitch
Into the frog-spawn of a blind man's ditch."

Paradoxically the splendour of Yeats is the unresolved conflict. In poem after poem he passionately faces his dilemmas, personal, political, artistic, metaphysical, never to rest in a complacent final solution but forging instead enigmatic and arresting images of universal experience.

T. S. Eliot (1888–1965).

The poems referred to are contained in *Collected Poems 1909–1962* (Faber).

Eliot, by some years the youngest child of his American parents, grew up in the town of St. Louis, on the Mississippi River. The family also had a house on the New England coast, at Cape Anne. Here, the young Eliot spent his summer holidays. Many of his most vivid lines and images derive from memories of these childhood scenes. It is through the dingy backstreets of St. Louis that Prufrock makes his way to the drawing room where the local bourgoisie talk vapidly of Michelangelo. The river of *Dry Salvages*, whose rhythm was "present in the nursery bedroom" is the Mississippi and the Dry Salvages themselves, rocks off the coast of Cape Anne. But we do not need to have seen the Mississippi to feel the force of the river which pulsates through the lines of *Dry Salvages*, nor to have seen "the ragged rock in the restless waters" to appreciate its significance as an image of abiding agony. Similarly, although Eliot was scholarly and exceptionally well-read, familiar with several languages, it is not essential that we share his scholarship in order to enjoy his poetry, any more than we need to share Milton's or Pope's knowledge of the Classics before enjoying their work, but our appreciation is greatly enhanced by some knowledge of the sources of their inspiration. Eliot draws particularly upon his reading of Dante, Shakespeare, Jacobean literature and the anthropological work of J. S. Fraser and Jessie Weston. The interested reader will find other suggestions to pursue in B. S. Southam's *A Student's Guide to the Selected Poems of T. S. Eliot.*

In Eliot's poems unity is achieved not by a framework of narrative or sensory description or even a logical sequence of thought, but by imaginative association where several layers of thought and feeling are fused. Like Milton, he is a poet who needs to be read aloud, for much of the import of his verse is expressed through its infinitely varied music.

Eliot gives his intensely subjective vision general significance by appealing not only or primarily to the literary experience of the educated, but to the general experience of twentieth-century man; to a sense of the futility and horror of the city's "strained time-ridden faces" in streets where "men and bits of paper" are "whirled by the cold wind", images counterpointed by others of delicate beauty, evoking life's rare and unaccountable moments of ecstasy and insight.

"Whisper of running streams and winter lighting
The wild thyme unseen and the wild strawberry".

There were two decisive influences upon Eliot's poetic development. The first was his discovery of the French Symbolist poets, to which he was led in 1908 by his reading of Symond's *The Symbolist Movement in Literature*. The other was his meeting with Ezra Pound in 1914. Pound not only helped him to find publishers for his work, but provided the stimulus of a discerning, critical audience.

Eliot's first book of poems, *Prufrock and Other Observations* appeared in 1917. The title poem offers a good introduction both to Eliot's allusive, kaleidoscopic style and to themes and attitudes which reappear in his later work. Although *The Love Song of J. Alfred Prufrock* is a dramatic monologue owing something to Browning, it offers no clear discursive framework to guide the reader, who is required to respond to shifting scenes and moods which cohere by force of the feelings inherent in them.

The poem's title suggests something at once conventional and rather comic, while the prefatory quotation from Dante's *L'Inferno* leads us towards the poem's profounder implications. The character of Prufrock's city and of his own life is established immediately through a startling image of suspended animation—

"... the evening is spread out against the sky
Like a patient etherised upon a table".

The correlation between the exterior scene and Prufrock's interior state is made more explicit as he and "you"—possibly the reader, possibly a young woman—make their way through a maze of sordid streets

"... that follow like a tedious argument
Of insidious intent
To lead you to an overwhelming question ..."

a question which is at once the proposal of marriage Prufrock dare not utter and a question of the very significance of his life and that of the social circle in which he moves.

Images of loneliness, futility, sensual attraction and suspended animation appear throughout the poem. The city is shrouded in fog and yellow smoke, at once sensual as a cat and yet stifling, suggestive of Baudelaire's Unreal City. "Lonely men in shirt sleeves" lean out of windows at dusk. The afternoon and evening sleep "smoothed by long fingers".

Prufrock attends a party, feeling at once nervously self-conscious, ready to run away, "I have seen the eternal Footman hold my coat, and snicker," and yet also complacent, "My necktie rich and modest, but asserted by a simple pin". He imagines himself as a modish gallant, the cynosure of all eyes, but wryly admits, "I am no Prince Hamlet". Nor is he a John the Baptist, fearlessly expressing a vital message, but a Lazarus who has not experienced the miracle of resurrection and who therefore cannot "tell you all". He has heard the bewitching song of the mermaids, "But I do not think that they will sing to me." He can only envisage himself walking, in "white flannel trousers" upon the margin of the vital sea of life and love. Drifting into a dream of sensuous bliss "we" are suddenly woken by the deadly voice of his everyday world and "drown."

The same loneliness and sense not only of failure but of there being nothing worth succeeding in, is expressed in *Gerontion* which Eliot considered publishing as a "prelude" or preface to *The Waste Land.* This meditation on approaching death is inconclusive.

"I would meet you upon this honestly",

but if the speaker is not sure what death means he is even less sure of the meaning or value of human life. The references to "windy spaces" (line 15) and

"Gull against the wind, in the windy straits"

suggest Claudio's speech on the terrifying prospect of existence after life has ended, in *Measure for Measure.* The quotation at the head of *Gerontion* comes from the Duke's speech in that play when he tries to steel Claudio's nerve for his coming execution by proving that life is not worth having. Eliot's Old Man seems to agree, but the Duke's Christian assurance, for he is disguised as a friar, evokes no response in him for Christ, the Word, cannot communicate through the swaddling darkness. Whatever the crucifixion may have once meant has been adulterated beyond recognition and there is nothing to replace it.

The *Waste Land*, published in 1922, established Eliot as a major figure on the contemporary scene. Some reviewers thought it a literary hoax because of the elaborate use of allusion and quotation in several languages as well as the lack of any formal structure. But Sir Robert Birley has said how exciting he and his contemporaries found the poem, "no other ... written in my lifetime has made so great and immediate an impact ... here was someone who could give expression to our own deep, but hardly understood, doubts and uncertainties and do this in language of unforgettable beauty." Eliot himself dismissed his poem as simply "the relief of a personal and wholly insignificant grouse against life." The recent publication of the original manuscripts of *The Waste Land* together with the comments of Pound and of Eliot's first wife, Vivien, and his own alterations to the drafts, give fascinating insight into the way this "piece of rhetorical grumbling" was pruned of its purely personal elements and the private vision transformed to express "the plight of a whole generation."

The poem impresses one with a sense of disillusion and anti-climax. The old pre-war Edwardian world has been destroyed, perhaps it was never very satisfactory, but there seems to be nothing to replace it. The theme is repeated at intervals throughout, in different ways; sometimes as a dead land where the sun beats, a place where the cisterns are empty, the wells exhausted, an empty chapel with dry bones. The crowds on London Bridge walking through the fog are dead, for each is locked within himself. The modern Cleopatra seated in her burnished chair is surrounded by erotic symbols, but the romantic suggestion of the gold Cupidon is disturbed by *synthetic* perfume and destroyed by recollection of the rape of Philomel. This "Cleopatra's" life is pointless and unreal; she can only look forward to a game of chess. At the other end of the social scale there is the prostitution of personal relationship to the level of having a "good time" and instead of new life, abortion. "The nymphs are departed" indeed.

But at the end there is perhaps some hope in

"The awful daring of a moment's surrender
Which an age of prudence can never retract".

In 1927 Eliot became an Anglican. His poems, *Ash Wednesday, Journey of the Magi, A Song for Simeon,* reflect his new belief and his gift for using allusion is directed towards Christian sources. Thus in *Ash Wednesday* single lines from well-known prayers and responses from the Ave Maria and The Reproaches of the Catholic Good Friday service are used technically in the same way that the repeated and echoed phrases in earlier poems are used to give unity; and as the phrases that Eliot uses are ones that are frequently repeated in the liturgy of the church, the poem provides, for some readers, a kind of ceremony, but this peculiarly Christian imagery excludes others. The generally accessible and most successful parts of the poem are not direct expressions of Christian experience but haunting, dreamlike images,

"Lady, three white leopards sat under a juniper tree
In the cool of the day"

and the expression of general human desire such as that for absolution and a tranquil mind,

"Teach us to care and not to care
Teach us to sit still".

Eliot's major work after this is *Four Quartets,* where he is concerned with the philosopher poet's experience of time, language and salvation. Helen Gardner has remarked how, whereas *Ash Wednesday* moves from personal experience to "the ageless prayer of the church," in *Four Quartets* the non-Christian and Christian experiences "suddenly touch ... we see that what the poet has been speaking of is what Christians speak of in another language." These poems, unlike *Ash Wednesday,* give *generally* meaningful expression to human experience.

Four Quartets are full of paradoxes and though a progression of thought may be traced in the four, each Quartet may be read as a unity in itself. The mood of the second Quartet, *East Coker,* is sombre and the fear of nothingness, the dissatisfaction with the "shabby equipment" of contemporary language recalls parts of *The Waste*

Land; but the fourth, *Little Gidding*, named after the home of a seventeenth-century community of Anglican mystics, is more hopeful

" All manner of thing shall be well."

Considerable time needs to be spent on these poems if the complexity of the thought is to be appreciated, but the pattern of the verses, the delicate manipulation of the metre may be enjoyed by the reader who is prepared to listen carefully.

2. Edith Sitwell (1887–1964).

In *The Scarlet Tree* Sir Osbert Sitwell vividly describes his sister's early background. She was saturated in English poetry, read Baudelaire at the age of seventeen and her governess, Helen Rootham, translator of Rimbaud, became her life-long friend.

Sitwell interprets her early verses in *Façade*, 1922, as " abstract patterns in sound " written in reaction against " rhythmical flaccidity " and " verbal deadness." She experimented indefatigably with the effect on rhythm and speed of subtle and elaborate patterns of rhyme, assonance and dissonance, successfully capturing dance rhythms. Some verses were set to music by Walton and accompany the well-known ballet.

Like the French Symbolist writer de l' Isle Adam (author of *Axel*) Sitwell also deliberately juxtaposed words that " clash in a protesting combination ". She adopted the synaesthesia practised by Poe and the French Symbolists, transferring the language of one sensation to indicate the experiences of another, as when morning light appears as " creaking " or " whining ". In later poems we find such phrases as " the dust brays ", or " purple perfumes of the polar Sun ", repeated from Rootham's Rimbaud.

Elegant and mannered, the butterfly verses of *Façade* lack inner significance yet they gave Sitwell the expertise to express intense feeling in her later poetry.

Gold Coast Customs, 1929, is the counterpart of Eliot's *Waste Land*. Both express the poet's revulsion from modern society by finding an objective parallel in primitive ritual. Sitwell, writing during the Depression, was most dismayed by the heartlessness of the city, which she images through the bygone Customs in Ashantee, where once at the death of an important person hundreds of the poor were butchered that their blood might lave his bones. This " Reeling appalling/Cannibal mart " symbolises the contemporary sacrifice of the poor demanded by the spiritually dead, epitomised by Lady Bamburger, " smart plague-cart ", massively indifferent to the destitution of the slums, where driven by " Want, a cruel rat gnawing there " the pathetic prostitutes, " The calico dummies/Flap and meet ".

The ghastly Customs, the desolate slums violently alternate and reflect each other in the kaleidoscope of nightmare, relentlessly maintained by the rhythm of savage drum beat and fevered pulse.

Although the metre and repetitive phrasing have an obsessive monotony, the impact of the poem which foretells " the sick thick smoke from London burning," is unforgettable.

In *Street Songs*, 1942, Sitwell was in command of images of arresting clarity. Two poems on the Raids are incidentally a clear vindication of Symbolist technique for both are extended " metaphors detached from their subjects ".

In the ironic *Lullaby* of despair the Pterodactyl, " the steel bird " which " fouls its nest ", has devastated the earth and only the Baboon is left to mother the surviving child.

Still Falls the Rain boldly uses the superbly simple image of rain, heavy reiteration, and a thudding, tolling rhythm, stressing the dark monosyllables:

" Still falls the Rain—
Dark as the world of man, black as our loss—
Blind as the nineteen hundred and forty nails
Upon the Cross."

It is a poem of profound and universal compassion for man and beast and also of religious faith, for the Rain is also Christ's blood shed in suffering, love and illumination.

In later publications Sitwell develops the long ode written from the vantage of the poet-seer matured by suffering. Like Yeats she was now giving her work coherence by playing variations on key symbols. Some images appear strained but the most effective are drawn from familiar sources, as the Bible, history, myth and mankind's most primitive experiences—of sun, earth, beasts, grain, fruit, metals, and of cold and warmth, always emblematic for her of evil and good. On these she sets her idiomatic stamp.

She constantly opposes two kinds of gold. In *Harvest* she celebrates the warm gold of the " laughing heat of the Sun " and " the ripe-bearded fire/Of wheat," reflecting divine energy and love. In *The Song of the Cold*, 1945, she laments the lust for the cold, destructive metal that possesses Dives and " the saints of Mammon," who " ache with the cold/From the polar wastes of the heart", the cold of hell.

Deeply shaken by Hiroshima, Sitwell wrote *The Shadow of Cain*, 1947. The theme of the title poem is fission and envisages Mankind's migration into the Cold, from Cain's first murder up to Hiroshima, when " the Primal Matter/Was broken," and " to the murdered Sun a totem pole arose of dust in memory of Man." The crisis stirs an obscure prescience of impending calamity, of a profound fission between the two aspects of Man: Lazarus embodiment of gold corn and human suffering and Dives of money and defilement. But the two golds fight and finally unite in a new resolution and hope.

This visionary poem is sometimes declamatory and the bleak *Dirge for the New Sunrise*, with its terse antitheses, is more immediate and moving.

After *The Shadow of Cain*, " haunted ever by the shadow that fell on Hiroshima," she yet continued to write poems that are " hymns of praise to the glory of Life."

3. Some Poets of the Thirties.

Wystan Hugh Auden (1907–73).

Auden was educated in a small public school, Gresham's, and later went to Oxford. Here he met Stephen Spender, Louis MacNeice, and others who formed temporarily a group of " political " poets most of whom were involved in the Spanish Civil War.

His first book of poems appeared in 1930 and was well received. After the publication of *The Ascent of F6*, a play which he wrote in collaboration with Christopher Isherwood, he was expected to become a major figure in English poetry. However, later books of verse were less well reviewed and in the mid-thirties the *Scrutiny* critics complained of his triviality, irresponsibility, and lack of maturity. Between 1939 and 1972 he made his home in America and Austria. As Eliot took out British citizenship Auden took out American, and, again, like Eliot, he accepted Christianity though perhaps in a less orthodox form.

Auden's interest in politics and the violence of political struggle is reflected in much of the imagery he uses as well as more directly in such different poems as *The Shield of Achilles* and *Alsono to Ferdinand*. *Let History be my Judge* is an early example of his political verse. Russia's forced collectivisation policy is the event which roused the feeling expressed here, but it is not directly referred to so that, if it were not for the date, the reader would not necessarily associate the poem with that particular policy, but with the harsh repression of any uprising or with the invasion of a weak country: the tragedy of the imposition of impersonal policy on the ignorant and defenceless is suggested and the callous self-justification of the powerful, ironically revealed. A later poem, *The Unknown Citizen*, satirises the omnipresence of the bureaucratic state and possibly the twentieth-century obsession with statistics. It begins with particular people, as in the dramatic monologues and some of the elegies, or poems for Auden's friends. In his less successful poems he tends to be either too clever (like Gratiano's in *The Merchant of Venice*, his reasons are like " two grains of wheat hid in two bushels of chaff ") or too anxious for effect. In the same way his dry humour and use of anti-climax is very effective at times, but sometimes the very ease with which he seems to do it betrays him and the joke becomes irritating.

Apart from anthologies, in some of which he is fairly well represented, the Penguin edition, which is the poet's own selection of verse, makes a good introduction to his work. There are two collected editions, *Collected Shorter Poems, 1927–1957* and *Collected Longer Poems* (both Faber). Otherwise his large production of verse is to be found in about ten small editions (all Faber). A recording of the poet's reading of his own poems has been made by Caedmon and is well worth listening to.

Stephen Spender (b. 1909).

Collected Poems 1928–1953; *The Generous Days*, 1971 (Faber).

Spender's first poems, up to 1933, are mainly concerned with or derived from the ideas of Marxism and Freud. There are stormy calls

" Oh, comrades, let not those who follow after
—The beautiful generation that will spring from our sides
Let them not wonder after the failure of banks
The failure of cathedrals, the declared insanity of our rulers,
We lacked the Spring-like resource of the tiger— "

but what the comrades are to do is not clear. One does not expect a political manifesto in a poem, but the vagueness of the sentiment of " equal like the shine from the snow " is irritating. It is difficult to take the optimism of such a poem as *The Funeral* seriously, yet if it is meant to be ironic the wit needs clarifying. Spender's early impact and placing in literature doubtless derived from his political and psychological idiom, but the poems which have stood the test of time are those which are more personal, *e.g.*, *My parents kept me from children who were rough*, which strike a more convincing note.

From 1936 onwards his poems are often about war, first the Spanish Civil War and then the Second World War. He is moved by the fate of the ordinary civilian, particularly the young who became involved in battles they do not understand. The defencelessness of the young soldier is poignantly conveyed and in poems such as *Ultima Ratio Regum* he links the greed of society, particularly the middle classes, with the slaughter of the innocent.

The belief in socialism and the brotherhood of man, rather glibly expressed in the earlier poems, is still present, but the tone of poems from this later period is compassionate. Spender rejects the easy, outright condemnation of either war or the enemy and refuses to glorify war by celebrating heroism. In fact there are no easy answers to the questions proposed in these exploratory poems. In the introduction to his collected volume Spender speaks of them as being " malleable " and possibly this unfinished sense is both their weakness and strength.

After a gap of over twenty years, Spender published *The Generous Days*. This slim collection of lyrics is preoccupied with the brevity of life, the inevitable approach of death and with the vital power of memory to elude the passage of time. Most of the poems are autobiographical and conventional in form. Their overall tone is one of plangent nostalgia, a note struck in the opening ballad (*see* **M51**), *If It Were Not*, whose theme is the way death clarifies and enhances our vision of life. Two of the subsequent poems are notably different from the rest. In *One More New Botched Beginning*, Spender recalls vivid incidents of the past—a walk with a friend; watching his little son gazing at some hens, " absorbed in their wire netted world " and finally an Oxford scene of himself and the poets Louis MacNeice and Bernard Spencer showing each other their verses. These friends are dead and the poet's son now a grown man who has forgotten watching the hens, yet the scenes still live in the memory as a vital part of the poet's present life. Spender's realisation of this common experience has freshness and charm. The " new beginning " comes in the book's final poem, *Art Student*. Here the subject is the contemporary artist's rejection of art in favour of primitive sensationalism: " all we can do now " is " send people back/To the real thing—the stinking corpse." In his oblique, ironic assertion of the validity of aesthetic values Spender's book flares into life. He himself feels this poem marks a new start in his work, a movement away from short, predominantly autobiographical lyrics towards the possibility of longer poems and more general themes.

C. Day Lewis (1904–72).

Collected Poems 1954 (Cape) and various short, later volumes.

Of this group of poets, C. Day Lewis is probably the most prolific. He began to publish in 1925 and was associated with Auden and Spender up to the outbreak of the Second World War. His early poems show Auden's influence—the use of colloquialism, the experiment with verse form and the concern with politics. How alien this type of verse was from his own vein may be seen from the symphonic poem *A Time to Dance*, 1935, where, in one section, he parodies the Apocalypse to describe the division of society into the exploiters and the exploited:

" I saw . . .
The director placing explosives under the infant's cradle, the editor keeping a nursery for snakes:
The scientist madly driving against traffic lights, the artist studying his acne in a pocket mirror: "

Later he imitates the rhythm of popular songs.

As his expectation of a Marxist solution faded and involvement in politics lessened, due at least in part to the Spanish Civil War and then the World War, he developed a quieter tone and used the more traditional verse forms. His work is generally polished, if not particularly vigorous. His translation of Virgil's *Aeneid* in 1952 was generally well received and in addition he has written several books of criticism, as well as detective stories under the pseudonym Nicholas Blake.

Louis MacNeice (1907–63).

The Collected Poems of Louis MacNeice, edited E. R. Dodds, 1967 (Faber).

Louis MacNeice was born in the same year as Auden, published his first book of poems in 1929 and continued writing fairly steadily until 1963. He was actively interested in politics of an idealist, left-wing type and was influenced by the contemporary interest in psychology. In 1937 he joined with Auden in publishing *Letters from Iceland*, but after Auden's departure for America in 1939 the partnership, if so it may be called, dissipated itself. MacNeice continued his work as a lecturer in classics and also wrote several radio scripts for the B.B.C., including the verse drama, *The Dark Tower*.

His longest non-dramatic poem is *Autumn Journal*, which covers events from August to December 1938. Apart from its obvious historical interest—he clearly records his impressions of and fears about the political events of that period —it is an unusually convincing poem. It has an authenticity as of Pepys's diary, but it is pervaded by a philosophical tone which brings details into focus. The verse flows smoothly most of the time, but the metre is not intrusive; in fact as an example of the "art to hide art" it is of its kind hardly bettered.

Observation of significant detail, personal reflection on the political situation as it affects society as a whole, reminiscence and a private transitory reaction are skilfully interwoven. For instance, he has spent most of the night anxiously assessing the possibilities of war breaking out and at six o'clock hears various sounds of people going to work—

"And I notice feathers sprouting from the rotten
Silk of my black
Double eiderdown which was a wedding
Present eight years back.
And the linen which I lie on came from Ireland
In the easy days
. . . .
. . . and I wonder what the morning
Papers will say,
And decide to go quickly to sleep for the morning
already
Is with us, the day is to-day."

Humour, often directed at himself, gives his poetry a sharpness which it might otherwise lack since he seldom seems driven by an overpowering inspiration. His use of colloquialisms and cliché is less frequent than Auden's and, possibly because of this, more effective. The opening to his tribute to his friend in *The Casualty* is a good example of this, and the rest of the poem illustrates MacNeice's gift for characterisation, for expressing admiration and regret without sentimentality.

In spite of disappointments and disillusionments MacNeice remained liberal in outlook, and sympathetic to many views (see, for example, *Bottleneck* and *The Conscript*). He may not be a major poet but he has integrity and a respect of poetry, reflected in his skilful handling of metre, which makes him an honest poet rather than a brilliant dilettante.

4. Dylan Thomas (1914–53).

Collected Poems, 1952 (Dent).

In many ways his poetry could hardly be more different from that of the previous group. Dylan Thomas, as a poet at least, was hardly touched by social concerns, and was uncommitted politically. His poems do not exhibit the intellectual force which Auden and Eliot's do. If these last-mentioned poets derived their inspiration from metaphysical poets like Donne, then Dylan Thomas may be said to derive his from poets such as Southwell or the visionary Blake.

The theme of much of his poetry is the oneness of all creation, the unity of experience: the human is intermingled with the divine, flesh and spirit are indivisible, and the world we inhabit is not essentially different from us.

"The force that through the green fuse drives
the flower
Drives my green age; that blasts the roots of
trees
Is my destroyer."

Death is incipient in birth and so in love—

"The word flowed up, translating to the heart
First characters of birth and death."

Sometimes death is accepted as in *And death shall have no dominion* and in *A Refusal to Mourn*; at other times Thomas seeks to defy death by protest:

"Do not go gentle into that good night
Old age should burn and rave at close of day."

The condensed language, particularly the use of verbal nouns and adjectives, reflects, sometimes not very clearly, this sense of the unity of creation.

His use of language though much imitated, remains recognisably his own. He uses cosmic symbols: sun, heaven, stars, sea, fire, and wind; images such as womb, bird, blood, and tomb; colours: green, gold, red, blue, and black. Much of the verse—that is when it is not overloaded with images—evokes kaleidoscopic pictures and the rhythmic metrical pattern is generally strong, which is possibly why he was in his own lifetime a popular poet. He draws too a great deal on biblical symbols and this coupled with the use of formal sound patterns, assonance, rhyme, and alliteration gives his verse an incantatory sound which is quite impressive. Finally he has resuscitated the "transferred epithet technique."

At his best he has produced moving but unsentimental celebrations of childhood, *Fern Hill*, *Poem in October*, *Over Sir John Hill*; some religious poems, for example, the unusual pattern poem *Vision and Prayer* and some "occasional" poems.

Very good recordings of Thomas's readings of his poems have been made by the Caedmon group.

5. The "Movement" Poets.

Robert Conquest's anthology *New Lines*, 1956 (Macmillan), marks the next stage—sometimes called the "Movement"—in English poetry. In his introduction Conquest remarks that groups of poets typical of their decade were "presented to public fire by anthologies which took up definite positions." His anthology was prepared in the belief that "a genuine and healthy poetry of the new period has established itself." The main objections he makes to criticism published from the beginning of the Second World War is that it encouraged poets "to produce diffuse and sentimental verbiage or hollow technical pirouettes." The poets he chose, apart from being contemporary, have in common only the acceptance that "poetry is written by and for the whole man, intellect, emotions, senses and all," and on the technical side a "refusal to abandon rational structure and comprehensible language." However, in their reaction against the undisciplined expression of emotion, the Movement poets tend to go to the opposite extreme. Their writing is highly intelligent and often witty, but generally seems more cerebral than truly imaginative, lacking the inspiration of passionate feeling. The wry self-mockery and hopelessness of much of Larkin's verse is typical of the work of the Movement as a whole, but some younger poets, notably Gunn and Hughes, who were early associated with the group, have gone on in another, more vigorous direction.

Philip Larkin (b. 1922).

The North Ship, 1945; *The Less Deceived*, 1955; *The Whitsun Weddings*, 1964 (all Faber).

Like Dylan Thomas, Larkin recalls his childhood, but he refuses to romanticise it. In *I Remember, I Remember*, he speaks of Coventry where he was born as a place where his childhood was "unspent" and he lists the crises commonly associated with precocious youth which did not occur. So far the poem is mildly ironic, but its end is disturbing:

"'You look as if you wished the place in Hell,'
My friend said, 'judging from your face.' 'Oh
well,
I suppose it's not the place's fault,' I said.

'Nothing, like something, happens anywhere.'"

The sense of emptiness, of opportunities untaken, of flatness, is a theme of much of Larkin's verse, *e.g.*, *Work*, *Departures*, *Triple Time*, but the self-mockery and irony give the work a pointedness which most elegaic verse lacks; when he reflects on the past he is neither nostalgic nor resentful. A conversational tone is used to attract attention, but the language is a "*selection* of the language really used by men"; he does not indulge in the vague slipshod phrasing of what passes for the conversation of "ordinary people." A good example of his style is *Church Going*, a reflection on the future of churches when they "fall completely out of use," which raises the whole question of belief (in values neither immediate nor material).

Thom Gunn (b. 1929).

Fighting Terms, 1954; *The Sense of Movement*, 1957; *My Sad Captains*, 1961; *Touch*, 1967; *Moly*, 1971 (Faber); *Jack Straw's Castle*, 1976.

At first glance Gunn's poetry seems as contemporary as the morning paper. Titles such as *On the Move*, subtitled *Man you gotta Go*, *Black Jackets*, *Elvis Presley*, suggest, rightly, that his poetry is rooted in the present, but not in such a way that it will be incomprehensible when the present has become the past. He is concerned with violence in the classical world in *The Wound* and *Helen's Rape*, in the sixteenth century in *A Mirror for Poets*, and in the twentieth century in *Claus von Stauffenberg*, in personal relationships as well as public, but it is not an unthinking surrender to mere excitement or admiration of brutality, but a recognition of its necessity:

" In this society the boundaries met
Of living, danger, death, leaving no space
Between, . . .
. . . Yet at this point they found
Arcadia, a fruitful permanent land."
(*A Mirror for Poets*).

In *Saint Martin and the Beggar*, Martin, the saint of man, must learn to fight before he can " grow " and then without hesitating he halves his cloak to cover the beggar. He is justified because his action was natural. The tragedy of modern man lies in his inability to marry instinct, intention, and action:

" One joins the movement in a valueless world,
. . . .
At worst, one is in motion; and at best,
Reaching no absolute, in which to rest,
One is always nearer by not keeping still."
(*On the Move*).

Ted Hughes (b. 1930).

The Hawk in the Rain, 1957; *Lupercal*, 1960; *Wodwo*, 1967; *Crow*, 1970 (Faber). There is also a small book of *Selections* from Hughes and Gunn (Faber).

There is some similarity between the early poetry of Hughes and Gunn. Both worked in America; both developed a concise style to mirror the toughness of their attitude to experience, their refusal to make the rough places smooth.

This said, the differences become more apparent as their individuality becomes clearer. Hughes uses animals, in whom the primitive instinctual drives are more evident than in man, to symbolise human dilemmas, but his animals are far from being ciphers. In *Pike*, for instance, the pike exists in its own right and, since Hughes did collect animals in his boyhood, the incident

" Suddenly there were two. Finally one

With a sag belly and the grin it was born with "

is probably true. But the recollected " nightmare " at the end of the poem goes beyond a boy's terror. The pond he fished, the eye, the dream darkness are symbolic both of the violence which lay in his own subconscious and that of the human race. The human being too is potentially a killer from the egg.

In other poems Hughes is searching for an identity. In *An Otter*, the otter

" Gallops along land he no longer belongs to;
Re-enters the water by melting."

At one level we have the hunt which loses and then finally catches the otter, but at another level there is the self, " attendant and withdrawn," the individual who " does not take root ".

In *Wodwo* Hughes moves away from naturalistic animal imagery. His Ghost Crabs are the creatures of a nightmare and in *Crow* the protagonist is a mythical figure, the pitiful but Satanic embodiment of the poet's increasingly grim vision.

In *Poetry In The Making*, originally a series of school broadcasts, Hughes gives fascinating accounts of his methods of composition and of the geneses of some of his early poems.

6. English Poetry in the 1960s.

Now the vogue for the " Liverpool sound " in pop music became a vogue for the " Liverpool sound " in pop verse. The voice of the Barrow Poet, and many another itinerant bard, was raised in the pubs and cellars of the metropolis and the day of the Poetry and Jazz Festival came upon us in the time of the Children of Albion (see the Penguin anthology of the same name, subtitled *Poetry of the Underground in Britain*, 1969).

Day Lewis became Poet Laureate and Graves, Blunden and Fuller followed Auden as the Oxford Professor of Poetry, but more people listened to reviewer and critic Alvarez as he proclaimed the eclipse of Larkin and the " genteel " Movement (*q.v.*) and extolled the greatness of the American Confessional school (*q.v.*). However, when *The Review*, a leading poetry quarterly, recently asked some thirty-five American and British poets, critics and editors what they had found encouraging about the poetry of the last decade, the name most often referred to was Larkin's *Whitsun Weddings* and while the speakers clearly admired the work of Lowell and Plath they seemed equally impressed by that of two relatively unknown British poets, Geoffrey Hill and Peter Porter.

Geoffrey Hill (b. 1932).

For the Unfallen, 1959; *King Log*, 1968; *Mercian Hymns*, 1971. (André Deutsch).

Our understanding and appreciation of Hill's strikingly original poetry depends to some extent upon a knowledge of the Bible, of Classical and Celtic myth and of mediaeval history, but more upon a relish for the ironic ambiguities of words and a delight in sensuous imagery and verbal music, for, like Yeats and Eliot's, Hill's poetry captures our attention with its vivid word play and musical power. At first we may feel that we can glimpse only a shadow of the significance of poems like his *Funeral Hymns*, but gradually, as their images sink into our subconscious minds, their import becomes clearer, though often still tantalisingly ambiguous and elusive.

Hill's first book, *For the Unfallen* is now out of print, but most of its poems can be found either in *Penguin Modern Poets 8* or in *The New Poetry*, a Penguin anthology edited by A. Alvarez.

Even in this early work Hill's mastery of form and language strikes one immediately. He adapts and develops traditional metres, verse forms and rhyme schemes into new pattern and renews outworn metaphors, as if by a sleight of hand, sometimes altering their form, as when he writes of " the mouthy cave ", at others placing them in a context where their meaning becomes reverberatingly ambiguous, as in *The Guardians*. Here he speaks of the young who have been caught in a thunderstorm while sailing. The old watch and then " Quietly they wade the disturbed shore;/Gather the dead as the first dead scrape home."

As these brief examples also show, Hill has a vivid command of pictorial detail and verbal irony. His approach is usually oblique, as in the later poem, *September Song*, an elegy subtitled *born 19.6.32—departed 24.9.42*. It begins,

"Undesirable you may have been, untouchable
you were not. Not forgotten
or passed over at the proper time."

Hill's measured tone is so deceptively calm, his imagery so condensed that the full impact of his words is delayed, and thereby intensified as gradually we become aware of the multiple significance of " undesirable ", " untouchable ", " Not forgotten ", " passed over ", " proper time ", of the menace conveyed in the transition from the conditional to the indicative voice, of the clinching effect of the antithesis, enhanced by the run-on line and the counterpointed pattern of major and minor stresses, suddenly broken by the abrupt caesura following " not ".

Here, as elsewhere, Hill's work is profoundly disquieting in its effect. He writes of innocence and corruption, violence and sacrifice, suffering and abnegation of responsibility, suggesting that in these matters man is as he always has been, that past and present are one. Within the general moral concern in each book we may distinguish a particular underlying theme: In *For the*

Unfallen it is "moral virtue", in *King Log*, "matters of power and commandment."

The opening poems of *King Log* explore this theme in terms of the Classical age, of mediaeval Catholicism, sixteenth-century humanism, nineteenth-century Calvinism, twentieth-century Nazism and existentialism. The sense of the indivisibility of past and present which permeates the poems is most obvious in the opening *Ovid in the Third Reich*, more obliquely expressed in the splendid *Funeral Hymns*, a set of eight unrhymed sonnets inspired by the Wars of the Roses.

The second part of *King Log* places Hill's theme in a new perspective through a series of moving poems of rejected love, *The Songbook of Sebastian Arrurruz*. Arrurruz is an imaginary Spanish poet, his name intended to recall both St. Sebastian—martyred with arrows—and the word arrowroot, suggesting that the arrows of love which pierce the poet are centred in his own person. Arrurruz's songs are addressed to the wife who has deserted him, but even while yearning for her he acknowledges her freedom and independence.

The underlying theme of Hill's third book, *Mercian Hymns* unites the concern of the earlier volumes in an exploration of private and public morality. In this modern "epic" the myth-making quality already apparent in *Funeral Hymns* and *The Songbook*, becomes more noticeable. Hill's hero is Offa, an eighth-century king of Mercia, here conceived of as the "presiding genius of the West Midlands, his dominion enduring" to the present day. Elements from primitive legend are used to suggest an even longer timespan by associating Offa with the British fertility god, the horned Cernunnos. The thirty stanzas of the poem, rich in pictorial detail and subtle irony and humour, cover such varied topics as childhood, money, laws industry, war and death. Not the least remarkable aspect of this extraordinary poem is Hill's achievement in having created a completely new stanza form, inspired by the canticles of the early Christian church.

Peter Porter (b. 1929).

Once Bitten, Twice Bitten, 1961; *Poems Ancient and Modern*, 1964; *A Porter Folio*, 1969. (Scorpion Press); *The Last of England*, 1970; *Preaching to the Converted*, 1972; *After Martial*, 1972; *Living in a Calm Country*, 1975. (Oxford University Press).

An Australian, Porter came to England in 1951 for "the opportunites which a common language gives to seek a wider frame of reference." He began as a satirist, but feels he is now moving towards a different position, an opinion supported by the increasingly complex and individual elegiac tone of recent poems.

In *The Sadness of the Creatures* Porter speaks of himself as "an historical cat", saying, "I run on rails". Both the forms and themes of his poems reveal his concern with "the continuity of the living and the dead . . . the only reality I can find in England". He has experimented with free verse but also uses and skilfully adapts traditional metres and verse forms.

Initially he may seem, as Eliot said of Webster, to be "much possessed by death", but he is not pessimistic and "death" has a multiple significance for him. In *Who Gets the Pope's Nose* Porter speaks of death as "God's greatest miracle" because it brings relief from suffering; in *Fossil Gathering* it is the means by which our essential nature is revealed: "... every feeling thing ascends from slime/to selfhood and in dying finds a face." In *There Are Too Many of Us* Porter equates death with the oblivion which should quickly descend upon the trivia of life. He suggests that it is a necessary condition of progress and that if we arrogantly complain at its inevitability oblivion comes all the sooner, for writers as for other men:

"... we world eaters
Are eaten in our turn and if we shout
At the gods they send us the god of death
Who is immortal and who cannot read."

Evolution presents the related concept of death as the process which enables life to renew itself, and Porter here draws a vivid parallel between Resurrection, symbolised by the resurrection of the Jewish nation in the state of Israel, and evolution, symbolised by the continuous renewal of the body's tissues. In *Preaching to the Converted* the "converted" are imaged as dead, incapable of change, fixed for ever in the marble postures of memorials in the church of San Lorenzo, they have only "a *Grundrisse*" of the possibilities of life. (*Grundrisse:* a set of sketches, rough drafts; an outline syllabus; also, the title of a work by Marx.)

Porter's writing is often extremely witty and he has produced some very amusing and ingenious light verse, such as *Mort aux chats*. His work can present unusual initial difficulties because its imagery is often allusive rather than sensuous, fragmentary rather than sustained and many poems combine esoteric references with a casual throwaway style, lacking verbal music, but in recent poems such as *May 1945*, *Fossil Gathering*, and the more personal *At Whitchurch Canonicorum* the imagery is sustained and the tone has a lyrical intensity.

Notes to a Biographer, *Homily in the English Reading Room*, *John Marston Advises Anger* and the more esoteric *Widow's Story* resemble Auden in the ways they show past jostling present and juxtapose learned references to music, literature and painting with references to the ephemerae of modern life. Porter also resembles Auden in the way he uses industrial and urban imagery. His other master is Pope, but in his satiric writing he generally eschews the felicitous elegance and visual immediacy of Pope's verse and his satiric juxtapositions and antitheses therefore often lack the force which Pope's command. However, in his better satiric verse, Porter applies stylistic devices learned from Auden to the subject matter of Pope and the result is powerful and individual. *The Workers* presents the young lovers Valerie and Hugues, "a torturer's and a peasant's descendants / On the broad back of money". Porter wittily describes Valerie's eye make-up in terms of industrial processes and building maintenance:

"It takes a whole Black Country
and at least one new oxidizing process
to maintain the canals in her fallen eyelids".

The fragmented style of much of his satiric writing seems to derive from an attempt to express the distorted values and incoherence of a life in which death has become the "great unmentionable" and "novel" is so often spoken of as if it were synonymous with "valuable". Porter mocks the pretentions and ephemeral fashions of contemporary pundits and versifiers and in *There Are Too Many of Us*, alluding to the "great theologian" (possibly the seventeenth-century priest and poet John Donne, *see* his *Satyre III*) Porter suggests that no-one has the sole key to wisdom and that the valuable thing in life is not anything new but man's continuing search for truth, which involves

"... a tradition
Of mind going uphill and always
Getting steeper."

He contrasts the "lucky genius", who "refines his burden to one thing at a time" with "his passenger friends" who "are quacking in the beautiful incomprehensible languages" and ridiculously try to preserve everything on video tape—"nothing is allowed to die."

In *Elegy* he draws ironic contrasts between the advances of bureaucracy and the steady rhythms of the natural world, the discoveries of science and continuous indignity and suffering:

"... the trees perform their ritual
leaf-shedding in the month of the setting-up
of a Ministry of Technology. A world of lasers
has millions who must be blanket bathed,
and a species of rat-like marsupial
is officially declared extinct—
the Ars Nova sound is a special
test of high-fidelity equipment."

Porter has spoken of the indelible impression of suffering he bears as a result of childhood experiences of the Depression in Brisbane and the loss of his mother, who died when he was nine. His awareness of the pain of mankind and of our inhumanity towards other people and creatures finds most powerful expression in works such as *The Sins of the Fathers, Story from Time of Disturbance*. However, some of Porter's finest writing is to be found in a handful of recent lyrical and elegiac poems. Here his gift for creating vivid precise images is used more freely and extensively and while many of his earlier poems had weak endings, as if he were afraid of being thought sententious, he now has the confidence to end boldly, as in *Thomas Hardy at Westbourne Park Villas*:

" Here, rather than in death-filled Dorset,
I see him,
The watchful conspirator against the gods
Come to the capital of light on his own grim
Journey into darkness; the dazzle would tell
Him these were the worst of possible odds—
ordinary gestures of time working on faces
the watermark of hell. "

Porter has said that his aim is now to " go back deeper into English poetry . . . and at the same time to put out feelers towards the European imagination "—a process already begun in his recent collections *The Last of England* and *Preaching to the Converted*. His latest book, *After Martial*, is a fine set of verses based on Martial's epigrams.

7. A Note on Twentieth-Century American Poetry.

The American Pound and the Anglo-American Eliot were cosmopolitan writers, as much, if not more at home in Europe as in America. Their poetry may, sometimes does, refer to specific scenes and places, but in general *Hugh Selwyn Mauberly, The Pisan Cantos, The Waste Land* and *Four Quartets* express a vision of twentieth-century man seen by poets highly cultivated and steeped in the history of civilisation.

By contrast, most American poets of our time, though often equally learned, have been self-consciously American, deliberately concentrating their attention on the immediate national, or even provincial, setting in which they find themselves.

One reason for this emphasis stems from the ideas of the Imagists, including Pound, who said that the writer should strive to create poems composed of vivid, concentrated and highly evocative images. Americans like William Carlos Williams (1883–1963) felt that one could best do this by focusing one's attention on the immediate environment.

At the same time they were eager to find ways of expressing the specifically American experience of life, which had hitherto found few outlets in poetry. This was especially important to Williams, who felt that the American spirit was being stifled by the dead weight of English literary forms. He said, " everything we do is tied up with words ", but, although many Americans " no longer speak English ", when writing they still used the for them stultifying syntax and " the prose or poetical rhythms which bind us to our pet indolences and mediaevalisms." American poets, he said, must break through the " deadness of copied forms which keep shouting above everything that wants to get said today, drowning out one man with the accumulated weight of a thousand voices of the past."

For Williams the writer to whom to turn for inspiration was the nineteenth-century Whitman. His derided free verse (*see* **M49**) suggested the possibility of new literary forms, within which the Imagist techniques could be deployed.

Two of the other pioneers of twentieth-century American poetry were more influenced by the Symbolists' emphasis on the music of poetry (*see* **M32**) than they were by Whitman. In her search for a freer and more musical verse form Marianne Moore (b. 1887) developed syllabic metre (*see* **M46**), while Wallace Stevens (1879–1955), one of the greatest poets of our century, used Symbolist techniques to bring new and sparkling life to traditional verse forms. In an age when most writers spurned the iambic pentameter and blank verse as museum pieces Stevens shows them still vigorously adaptable and tuneful.

None of these writers saw the development of new techniques as an end in itself, but as the necessary means for expressing a new vision of life. They shared a high concept of the poet's role which many English writers would now regard as misguided. Auden said that nothing he had written had saved anyone from the concentration camps or gas chambers. These American writers of a slightly older generation felt more optimistic. They shared a radical humanism which led them to rejoice in life's beauty and man's creative power as well as to recognise the cruelty of the world. They saw poetry as replacing religion and offering a new, illuminating vision of life in all its joy and sorrow.

Stevens said that poetry must be " abstract "—that is abstracted, separated from the old visions of life, including those offered by religion—it must present new and original insights. It must also give pleasure, not by encouraging the reader to indulge in fantasies but by offering him truthful images of reality in beautiful and illuminating forms. Poetry must also change, that is give the reader new insights into life, not confirm him in his old ones. These are the recurrent themes of Stevens's poetry and find their most complete expression in his great work *Notes Toward a Supreme Fiction*.

Stevens's attitude to poetry was shared by Moore and Williams, but Williams was a less speculative, more prophetic writer. He sought not only to offer a clear vision, but to arouse man's hatred for the brutal, life-denying materialism of industrial America, exemplified in the suburb of Paterson, where he worked as a medical practitioner. This radical strain has been taken up by many later American writers inspired by Williams's poem *Paterson*.

Anyone interested in the development of twentieth-century poetry should read the work of Pound, Williams, Moore and Stevens. They are all highly enjoyable as well as influential writers. Paperback editions of their poems are easily available and selections from their theoretical prose can be found in J. Scully's *Modern Poets on Modern Poetry*.

8. The Beat Poets.

The name " Beat Generation " (*see* **J7**) was applied to a group who were radical critics of American life under the complacent Eisenhower administration, which seemed to them to ignore the ugliness and cruelty of life in the industrial areas' " concrete jungles ". The distinctive protest of the Beats involved a rejection of all middle-class ideas of respectability. They practised communal living, often in considerable poverty, and had a relaxed attitude towards employment, sex and drugs. They were generally anarchic pacifists, but uninterested in politics as such.

Their attitudes find formal expression in Kerouac's novel *On the Road*, 1951, Burroughs's *Junkie*, 1953 and *The Naked Lunch*, 1959, and in the poetry of, among others, Laurence Ferlinghetti (b. 1928), Gregory Corso (b. 1930) and Allen Ginsberg (*q.v.*). A selection of their poems can be found in *Penguin Modern Poets 5*.

The journalist John Clellan Holmes defined the word " Beat " as " involving a sort of nakedness of soul, a feeling of being reduced to the bedrock of consciousness." Such " nakedness " is a distinguishing mark of Beat verse, which may be thought of as an extreme form of confessional poetry (*q.v.*). Its principles, in so far as they have been formulated by the leading Beat poet Ginsberg, take the Symbolist preoccupation with the expression of the unique, individual consciousness to its logical, egocentric conclusion. On the other hand, believing that art falsifies the truth of experience, the Beats in principle reject that fastidious care with which the Symbolist sought to formulate their experience. For the Beats, the beauty of a poem's form is not the result of artistry or talent, but is determined by the writer's character: a good, honest man will produce a good, honest poem, a rascal will compose bad verse! However, like most poets, in practice, the Beats sometimes break their own rules. The best of their work is far from artless, though its forms are often as unusual as its content is unconventional.

Allen Ginsberg (b. 1926).

Howl and Other Poems, 1956; *Kaddish and Other Poems*, 1961; *Reality Sandwiches*, 1963; *Planet News*, 1968; *Ankor Watt*, 1968; *The Fall of America, poems of these states 1965–71*, 1972. City Lights Books.

Ginsberg was brought up in Paterson, New Jersey, where his family was known to W. C. Williams and Williams, whose work Ginsberg is said to admire, wrote a warm introduction to the younger poet's first book, *Howl and Other Poems*. Like Williams, Ginsberg is a writer in the prophetic tradition of Whitman, Shelley and Blake. He was also early impressed by the writing of the eighteenth-century visionary Christopher Smart, but it was to Whitman in particular that he was indebted for the free verse techniques (*see* **M49**) which he used for many of his most impressive early poems.

It is important we should bear in mind that most of Ginsberg's work is intended to be read aloud—performed or chanted—to a sizeable audience, not quietly brooded over in solitude, although the power of such poems as "Kaddish" is clear even to the silent reader. Ginsberg himself has a charismatic personality, a theatrical flair, shrewd intelligence and a lively and amiable sense of humour, all of which add to the captivating power of his performances.

His finest work is contained in the two early collections, *Howl* and *Kaddish*. The famous—or notorious—"Howl" is a vatic lament for the way Ginsberg's talented contemporaries have, he feels, been destroyed by the inhumanity of American life. It is written in long, free verse canticles, the first sixteen pages comprising a single sentence, listing the ways in which "the best minds of my generation" have been driven to suicidal despair. It expresses a horrifying, if at times hysterical, vision of urban America.

"Sunflower Sutra", in the same volume, is a more concentrated and powerful piece of writing, in which a skeletal grey sunflower, growing in a filthy railway siding by a San Fransisco dock, becomes a symbol of man's courageous will to survive even in the harshest surroundings. The poem vividly exemplifies Ginsberg's talent for creating precise and original pictorial images, such as that of the sunflower itself, with its

"corolla of bleary spikes pushed down and broken like a battered
crown . . .
. . . sunrays obliterated on its hairy head
like a dried wire spiderweb . . ."

"America", another poem in Ginsberg's first collection, is more self-absorbed but concludes with a flash of characteristic humour as the poet speaks of a "Reds-under-the-bed" scare:

"The Russia wants to eat us alive. The Russia's power mad. She
wants to take our cars from out our garages.
. . . Her make us all work sixteen hours
a day. Help.
America this is quite serious.
America this is the impression I get from looking in the television
set.
America is this correct?
I'd better get right down to the job.
It's true I don't want to join the Army or turn lathes in precision
parts factories, I'm nearsighted and psychopathic anyway.
America I'm putting my queer shoulder to the wheel."

In his later work, such as a poem addressed to the singer Bob Dylan, Ginsberg sometimes verges on the sentimental, but his earlier "Kaddish", a lament for his unhappy mother, and "Aunt Rose", are at once tender and objective poems, creating memorable images of these two elderly women.

In 1965, Ginsberg, who had earlier known a transcendental experience of identity with "Supreme Reality" realised that he must stop living on the memory of past visions, "which is not the actual awareness of *now*." His later work therefore takes the form of diffuse verse "diaries", "chronicle tape recorded scribed by hand or sung condensed, the flux of car train air plane dream consciousness . . ." These verses lack the power of his early poems, although they contain still vivid images and flashes of humour.

9. The Black Mountain Group.

The most important poets generally referred to under this title are Charles Olson (*q.v.*), Robert Duncan (b. 1919) and Robert Creeley (b. 1926). Associated names include those of Denise Levertov (b. 1923), Ed Dorn (b. 1929) and Gary Snyder (b. 1930).

All these poets taught or studied at Black Mountain College in North Carolina, an experimental adult education centre founded during the Depression. Until its closure in 1956 it was the focal point for many who were discontented with accepted academic ideas and methods. It attracted a galaxy of talent, including the philosopher Dewey, the artist De Kooning and the musician John Cage.

Charles Olson (b. 1910).

Projective Verse, 1950 (in J. Scully, ed., *Modern Poets on Modern Poetry*, Fontana Bks., 1966); *The Maximus Poems*, 1960, *Maximus IV, V, VI*, 1968, both Cape Goliard Press.

Olson is the most influential of the poets associated with Black Mountain College. He has published a number of verse collections, including *In Cold Hell, in Thicket*, 1953, and *The Distances*, 1961, but his most important works are the two volumes of Maximus poems and the essay *Projective Verse*.

In this essay, Olson sought to define his concept of a poem. He speaks of it in terms of physics as a "high energy construct", imagining the poet's experience as a generator which charges the battery, or poem, whose energy is then projected to another person when he plugs into it by reading or listening to the poem.

In order to construct an efficient poetic battery the writer must think of his work in terms of its energy field. Its form should be determined solely by its content. However, Olson also says, somewhat paradoxically, that the writer must consider how "to shape the energies so that the form is accomplished" and suggests that the solution to this problem can be found in the dictum "in any given poem, always one perception must MOVE, INSTANTER, ON ANOTHER!"

The writer should avoid similes and descriptive passages, which dissipate a poem's energy, and, in so far as formal considerations enter his mind, he should concentrate not on rhyme or metre, sense or sound, so much as on the syllables, which are the "figures of the dance" and the line which is its "threshing floor" (*see also* **M46**). The line's length is determined by the poet's sense of breathing. Pauses are indicated not only by line endings, where they should be as long as "it takes the eye . . . to pick up the next line", they are also suggested by spacing: "space as long as the phrase before it . . . means that space to be held, by the breath, an equal length of time." Very light pauses are indicated by a diagonal line / rather than a comma, which has undesirable grammatical connotations. Varying amounts of indentation suggest the proper juxtaposition of the images.

Olson wrote his essay in the year that he composed the first of his Maximus poems and his ideas are helpful in understanding how these should be read, for, as the reader will quickly discern, they are best read aloud.

At his finest, as in the opening and closing poems of the sequence, Olson is a writer of considerable lyric power but in some poems, particularly those like " Later Tyrian Business " in the second volume, an elaborate and self-conscious typography confuses the reader and detracts from the poems' significance.

The subject of the Maximus sequence is the city of Gloucester, Massachusetts, and the treatment is heavily influenced by W. C. Williams's *Paterson*. The predominant theme, as in Williams's poem, is the way the region's inhabitants and its natural resources have from the time of the first settlers been corrupted and destroyed by capitalism and " pejorocracy ". By " pejorocracy ", a term coined by Pound, we are to understand a materialistic form of power based on the denial of life's essential meaning and purpose.

As in *Paterson*, passages of verse are divided by extracts from prose documents, letters and account books, etc., but the matter is generally less varied and less well chosen than that in Williams's poem. It depends heavily upon lists of long-dead settlers' names, precise accounts of their ownership of land, the relative positions and sizes of their fields, and so on. Such a plethora of antiquarian detail might possibly be meaningful to one thoroughly versed in the documents themselves and in the local history and geography of Gloucester, but a much more rigorous selection would have concentrated the poems' energies and enhanced their significance. As it is, the work as a whole seems prolix, and self-indulgent, although it also contains powerful and beautiful passages which it would be a great pity to miss.

10. The " Confessional " Poets.

The term " confessional poetry " seems to have been used first by reviewers of Lowell's *Life Studies*, poems which arose from their author's suffering a mental breakdown. It has since been applied to the work of Sylvia Plath and Anne Sexton, which also derives from the immediate experience of mental illness and, like *Life Studies*, expresses feelings of guilt, bitterness and isolation, the material of the confessional or the psychoanalyst's couch.

The label " confessional " is also used in a more general, though allied sense, to denote work in which the poet makes an uninhibited confession of hatred, addiction, lust or similar experience, about which, usually, most of us are reticent.

In " confessional " writing the poet's need to objectify his experience, in order to give it artistic validity, presents itself in an acute form. Its resolution demands the rare courage and technical virtuosity that Eliot displayed in *The Waste Land* and Lowell approaches, in a very different way, in *Near the Ocean*.

Robert Lowell (b. 1917). *See also* Section I.

Poems 1938–1949, 1950; *The Mills of the Kavanaughs*, 1951; *Life Studies*, 1959; *Imitations* 1961; *For The Union Dead*, 1964; *Near the Ocean*, 1967; *Notebook*, 1970; *History*, 1973; *For Lizzie and Harriet*, 1973; *The Dolphin*, 1973. (Faber).

In an interview, published in J. Scully's *Modern Poets on Modern Poetry*, Lowell records how he was early drawn to the work of Latin, Elizabethan and Jacobean poets. His own mature writing reflects the continuing influence of these early mentors, with whom he shares an anguished sense of the fragility and transience of beauty and a revulsion from the brutal, vicious materialism of the society in which he lives.

His first important work, *The Quaker Graveyard in Nantucket*, 1945, is an elegy for a cousin drowned while serving in the navy during the Second World War. The poem presents this cousin as continuing the brutal tradition of the Quaker whalers of Nantucket, and links him with Ahab, the tragic, deranged hero of Melville's *Moby Dick*. The vigour of the poem's language, the musical skill with which Lowell evokes the sounds and atmosphere of the bleak Nantucket coast and the force of his revulsion from the whalers' obscene cruelty are immediately impressive. As Hugh B. Staples has noted in his valuable reference book, *Robert Lowell—the First Twenty Years*, a central theme of the poem is " human evolution, considered as a part of God's plan." Here, as in much of his later work, Lowell shows the aggressive individualism of men bringing a return to primitive violence. The gentle, pastoral stanza VI presents the ideal, the figure of the Virgin, who, " Expressionless, expresses God." However, this stanza lacks the force of the others. The affirmation of faith in the poem's concluding line is similarly less convincing than Lowell's expression of revulsion from the Quakers' primitive lust for power and wealth.

The poem's images have multiple significance. The whale, " IS, the whited monster," is at once a symbol of Being Itself, of the vengeful Jehovah and of *I*esu *S*aviour. It is the victim of the sailors' greed and also the agent of their death and damnation, a whited sepulchre, an image of their corrupt faith. The sea is the god Poseidon, " the earth shaker ", and also the primitive source of life and life itself, " hurt " and " fouled " by man.

These and allied images take on new significance in Lowell's later poems, where they replace the Catholic symbols of his early work, as he strives to achieve a more flexible, resonant style, which will give objective validity to his vision. In his mature work the sea and water continue to symbolise life, particularly the life of the spirit. Fish at times represent the primitive violence man has loosed upon the world, but the fish is also an image of vitality struggling against " the stone and bone-crushing waterfall." Monsters become " grunting " " yellow dinosaur steamshovels ", possessive " dragons " and the Gorgon, a fearsome, yet beautiful and pitiful, " tyrant " and " tyrannicide."

Lowell's use of such images is linked with his frequent evocations of the language and imagery of the Bible, particularly the Old Testament and the Apocalyptic books beloved of the New England Puritans. He applies such language and imagery to the life-denying creeds of the Puritans themselves and to all those who seek to dominate their fellows, driving in " stakes " to " command/the infinite " and creating " God the Logos " in their own image, a tyrant with " bloody hands ". Lowell combines such Biblical allusions with references to Classical myths—particularly that of Perseus and Medusa—to give his work wider significance and fuller perspectives. He uses American place names with religious and historical associations, Mount Sion, Concord, Carthage, and writes of contemporary life in terms of that of Ancient Israel and Rome, as in the following passage, where the insistent rhythm, the punctuation and feminine rhymes accentuate the image of the clumsy military machines irrevocably lurching toward their shattering end:

" Hammering military splendor,
top-heavy Goliath in full armor—
little redemption in the mass
liquidations of their brass,
elephant and phalanx moving
with the times and still improving,
when that kingdom hit the crash:
a thousand foreskins stacked like trash . . ."

(*Waking Early Sunday Morning*).

In his early verse Lowell imitated the metrical forms of Elizabethan and Jacobean poetry. His middle period was a time of experiment: the dramatic monologues of *The Mills of the Kavanaughs* are written in more colloquial run-on couplets similar to those of Browning; *Life Studies* and *For the Union Dead* contain a number of poems in free verse. His volume, *Near the Ocean*, marks Lowell's return to stricter metrical forms, using a stanza based on four couplets, which he now deploys with the deceptive skill of a master. His earlier experiments with style and metre and the experience he has gained by writing plays and by recreating poems from Latin and other languages for the volume *Imitations*, now enable him to write with vigorous simplicity and haunting beauty:

"Lost in the Near Eastern dreck,
the tyrant and tyrannicide
lie like the bridegroom and the bride;
the battering ram, abandoned, prone,
beside the apeman's phallic stone."
(*Near the Ocean*).

Although the autobiographical poems of *Life Studies* have been among the most widely noted of Lowell's work, some later volumes seem of more lasting importance. They express a complex, tragic vision of life in a "black classic" world of "lost connections". We are all "tyrants". Mussolini was "one of us." Caligula is our "namesake" and "tyrannicide" itself a most arrogant form of tyranny, bringing widespread suffering and destruction:

"I have seen the Gorgon.
The erotic terror
of her helpless, big bosomed body
lay like slop.
Wall-eyed, staring the despot to stone,
her severed head swung
like a lantern in the victor's hand."
(*Florence*).

"Pity the monsters!" "Pity the planet, all joy gone/from this sweet volcanic cone."

Lowell's later poems express the anguish of our almost impossible quest for "asylum, peace". "We are like a lot of wild/spiders crying together/but without tears." Innocence, goodness and beauty, life itself, are as fragile as "the orange and black/oriole's swinging nest!" In *For the Union Dead* he suggests we can survive only by having the "angry wrenlike vigilance" which chooses death rather than "savage servility" or the security of "a Mosler safe, the 'Rock of Ages'/that survived the blast." The ultimate test is whether we dare become "alive enough" to "die".

Like Yeats, Lowell has come to feel that we experience innocent joy only in the creation and contemplation of art. Exploring the frightening "corners of the woodshed", he creates from its "lumber" poems that give "darkness some control", evoking joy even while they "sing" "despair."

His four most recent collections, beginning with *Notebook*, present various stages in the composition of three sets of poems written in a fairly loose sonnet form.

The 1970, English, edition of *Notebook* differs from the first, American, one of 1969. About a hundred of the poems were modified and nearly a hundred new ones added. They were arranged according to no discernible method. Lowell said their disposition was "intuitive . . . not a pile or a sequence of related material." However, in his three subsequent volumes, the poems of the 1970 *Notebook* were further modified, in some cases drastically, and re-arranged to form three sequences.

The first, *History*, is a chronological series about people and events from Biblical and Classical times to the present day. It contains a number of new poems and also new versions of some from Lowell's earlier collections, *Near the Ocean*, *Imitations* and *Life Studies*, as well as from *Notebook*.

For Lizzie and Harriet includes a little new work but most of it is derived from *Notebook* and forms a sequence concerning Lowell's relationship with his former wife, Elizabeth, and his daughter, Harriet.

The Dolphin celebrates Lowell's third marriage. Most of the poems in this book are new.

The three volumes contain many beautiful passages and throw an interesting sidelight on Lowell's methods of composition but the majority of the poems still seem rather unfinished. This may be because we have to accustom ourselves to Lowell's new development of the sonnet form.

Sylvia Plath (1932–63).

The Colossus, 1960; *Ariel*, 1965; *Crossing the Water*; *Winter Trees*, 1971. (Faber).

Sylvia Plath was an American of German ancestry. At the age of nine she suffered a traumatic shock with the death of her beloved father, a professor of biology at the University of Boston. Her adult attempts to come to terms with this overwhelming loss inspired some of her most powerful poems.

After a brilliant academic career in America and England, Plath married the English poet Ted Hughes (*q.v.*). The accounts of her premature death which were published recently by A. Alvarez have been disputed by Plath's husband and sister-in-law and, in any case, offer no new insights into her poetry.

The Colossus was the only one of Plath's books of poems to be published in her lifetime. The rest of her work has not appeared in the order of its composition. The poems of *Crossing the Water* predate those in *Winter Trees* and *Ariel*.

Plath spoke dismissively of the poems in *The Colossus*, which, unlike her subsequent ones, were not written to be read aloud and are rather monotonous in tone, although technically highly accomplished. The most important influence upon her writing was the publication of Lowell's *Life Studies* (*q.v.*). She admired these poems for the bold way they dealt with painful personal experience and she proceeded to emulate Lowell's achievement, but her work remains wholly individual in style and tone.

Like all poets, she has power to make us see the world as if for the first time, to enhance our awareness of life. She writes of poppies "wrinkly and clear red, like the skin of a mouth," and bells that "soberly bong out their names." Her world has the clarity of a primitive painting, but the poems of *Ariel* make almost intolerably painful reading, for they express the heightened vision and self-mockery, the frangible control of utter hopelessness. Their images are often grotesque and full of menace:

"Dawn gilds the farmers like pigs,
Swaying slightly in their thick suits,

White towers of Smithfield ahead."
(*Totem*).

The moon far from being a symbol of serene agape is a face

"White as a knuckle and terribly upset.
It drags the sea after it like a dark crime; it is quiet

With the O-gape of complete despair."
(*The Moon and the Yew Tree*).

Plath's world is starkly coloured in red, black, white and the yellow of decay. She combines these images with allied symbols of energy, death and living death: blood, the yew, moonlight, the winding-sheet and the pupa. Her poems are haunted by a black father-figure, the Nazi "panzer man" of *Daddy*. The power with which she expresses her anguished vision derives partly from the simplicity of her metres and verse forms, which often have the insistent quality of nursery rhyme.

Poems like *Daddy* and the allied *Lady Lazarus* are unlikely to be forgotten, but in future others, such as the title poem of *Ariel* and *The Arrival of the Bee Box*, *Sting*, and *Elm* may be valued more highly. Our judgment is distorted by Plath's recent death and the knowledge that the harrowing poems of *Ariel* were the prelude to her suicide.

Anne Sexton (b. 1928).

Anne Sexton began writing in 1957. *Selected Poems*, 1964, *Love Poems*, 1969, and *Transformations*, 1972, have been published in England by the Oxford University Press, *The Book of Folly*, 1973, by Chatto & Windus. She acknowledges a debt to Lowell and deals with the same kind of subject as Sylvia Plath.

John Berryman (1914–72).

Homage to Mistress Bradstreet, 1956; *77 Dream Songs*, 1964; *Berryman's Sonnets*, 1967; *His Toy, His Dream, His Rest*, 1969; *Love and Fame*, 1971; *Delusions, Etc.*, 1972. (Faber).

Berryman was the most distinguished of those poets to whom the label "confessional" applied in its more general sense. Technically he was most inventive and ingenious and his work expressed enormous vitality, but some critics have found it undisciplined and pretentious and it is indeed true that only in *Homage to Mistress Bradstreet* did Berryman achieve objective expression of his themes.

His earliest work includes the poems published in 1967 under the title *Berryman's Sonnets*. This sequence, written during the 1940s, deals with an unhappy love affair.

Berryman began as a disciple of Yeats. Later, before gradually finding his own voice, he was influenced by the colloquial style of Auden. His earlier experiments found fruition in the extraordinary *Homage to Mistress Bradstreet*, which the eminent American critic Edmund Wilson considers to be the finest long poem since Eliot's *The Waste Land*. It is interesting that Berryman made a conscious effort to produce a work wholly unlike Eliot's masterpiece, and gave his poem a narrative framework and composed it in regular, though unusual, metrical stanzas. The form of these stanzas was inspired by the one Yeats evolved for his *In Memory of Major Robert Gregory*. Berryman uses an iambic metre (*see* **M47**) and the eight lines of his stanza have respectively five, six, three, four, five, five, three and six feet. The first and last lines rhyme and the fifth and sixth form an heroic couplet (*see* **M48**).

The poem's theme is the frustrations of the creative writer in an hostile, life-denying environment. This is expressed through a recreation of the life and personality of the Puritan immigrant Anne Bradstreet, who is sometimes called the first American poet.

The work is divided into five sections. The brief opening prologue, or "exordium" and closing "coda" are spoken by the modern poet. The second and fourth sections are monologues by Anne Bradstreet, while in the third the two speakers engage in broken dialogue. The overall effect is of a conversation between two aspects of the same personality.

Berryman brilliantly evokes the harshness of the Puritan settlers' "barbarous" life; the rigour of its winters, "white air lashing high"; the "ruinous heat" of its summers. These exterior conditions are paralleled by the Puritans' "chapped souls" and "starched minds"; by rheumatic fever and religious fanaticism. Against these physical and spiritual limitations Mistress Bradstreet struggles to be true to her own, kindly, creative vision.

In *77 Dream Songs* and *His Toy, His Dream, His Rest* Berryman develops the techniques he used in the earlier work to present multiple facets of a protagonist called Henry, "a white American in early middle age, who has suffered an irrevocable loss." These two books form a single work of three hundred and eighty-five lyrics. Together they present a kind of open-ended *Odyssey* of contemporary American life. They are often very amusing, often intensely irritating and their allusions to American society sometimes make them difficult for the English reader to follow, but they are compulsive reading and individual Songs, the painful 29 and 53 and the grotesque 91, for example, remain fixed in our minds.

In the anecdotal *Love and Fame*, Berryman writes in his own person, composing brief lyrics on the subject of his life and loves and his pursuit of fame. The style is loose, rambling and self-absorbed, yet there are flashes of his characteristic and engaging humour here and in the lyrics and elegies, interposed with anguished prayers, which make up Berryman's last volume, *Delusions, Etc.*.

11. Conclusion.

Readers who are spurred by their study of the poets discussed here and wish to explore further will discover much to enjoy in the work of writers to whom space precludes more than reference: Wilfred Owen, Robert Graves, Edwin Muir, R. S. Thomas, Peter Redgrove, Christopher Middleton, David Wright; the Americans Robert Frost, Theodore Roethke, Elizabeth Bishop and George Oppen. Penguin Books publish various useful anthologies. An excellent new paperback series is *Corgi Modern Poets in Focus*.

IV. ENGLISH VERSE PATTERNS

The patterns of its verse point and enhance a poem's significance. Some knowledge of the principles on which they are based can therefore help us towards a fuller enjoyment and appreciation of poetry.

The following account casts its net wide, covering verse designs as far apart in time as the Anglo-Saxon and the most up-to-date American forms. It is fully illustrated with quotations and with references to the numbered poems of *The New Oxford Book of English Verse* (OBEV) and *The Oxford Book of Twentieth Century English Verse* (OBTCV).

I. INTRODUCTION—SOME DEFINITIONS.

Verse and Prose.

The distinction between verse and prose has become blurred in our century, but we may safely say that in all verse the words are arranged so as to fall into more or less regular musical and, or, visual patterns, whereas in prose they are not. For example, if we listen carefully to a spoken sentence, we notice that some syllables are emphasised. The conventional way of indicating this in writing is by placing an acute accent over the vowel of the stressed syllables. Unstressed syllables may be marked x as in the following sentences:

× × / / × × × / × × /
It is some sort of a solution, after all.

× / × / × / × ×
It is a part solution after all.

We may observe that in the first sentence the stressed and unstressed syllables fall haphazardly, while in the second they form a pattern. The first, unpatterned sentence is deemed prose, the second, patterned one, verse.

The designs of verse are almost infinitely variable and although, as it stands, alone, the unpatterned sentence is not verse, it could be incorporated into a poem and so become an element in its design. Poets are constantly modifying existing verse forms and sometimes invent entirely new ones, aural and visual.

While some reference will be made to the visual designs, this article will be chiefly concerned with the aural patterns of verse, which have been, and still are, exploited by most poets. Visual patterns, where not entirely arbitrary or whimsical, are either dependent on the musical ones or are individually determined by the poem's theme, which they are designed to reflect and enhance. They are therefore less susceptible to illustration and discussion within the compass of a short general article.

Metre.

Metre and Rhythm.

The word *metre* means a measure or rhythmical pattern. Verse originated in song, chant and invocation and its basic patterns are rhythmical. They may be founded on patterns of accent (stress), of single syllables, of cadences or lines.

Different Kinds of Metre.

Accentual verse: is written in accentual metre, a rhythmic pattern of accents or stresses.

Syllabic verse: is written in *syllabic metre*, a rhythmic pattern of syllables alone.

Accentual-syllabic or Metrical verse: is written in either *Iambic, Trochaic Dactyllic, Anapaestic, Amphibrach* or *Choriambic* metre. These metres, whose names are derived from those of Classical verse, will be further described. They are composed of regularly patterned groups of stressed and unstressed syllables, hence the name accentual-syllabic.

Quantitative Metrical verse: is usually written in one or other of six metres, also given the names *Iambic, Trochaic*, etc., quoted above. They are regularly patterned groups of long and short syllables and are the metres of Classical Greek and Latin verse. They are seldom used in English.

Free verse or *vers libre:* so called because it has no particular metre and is based on loosely patterned rhythms determined by the cadences of the speaking voice.

The Foot.

In some poetry the verse line is divided into groups of stressed and unstressed syllables, analogous to the bars in music. Such groups are known as feet. The line

" When you/shall see/me in/the toils/of Time" /
[OBTCV 2]

contains five feet, each comprising two syllables, unstressed followed by stressed.

The Caesura.

A long pause occurring at or about the middle of a line and usually indicated by a pause in the sense, *e.g.*,

" Hearing one saga,//we enact the next "
[OBTCV 493]

The Verse and the Stanza.

Some poems are divided into groups of lines, often called verses. Strictly speaking, *verse* is another name for the single line. A group of lines or verse is properly called a *stanza*. Generally the stanzas of a poem are uniform, but sometimes they are varied, as in Milton's " Lycidas "
[OBEV 304].

Rhyme.

Another formal pattern is created by the use of rhyme which can be at once visual and aural, though some kinds of rhyme appeal only to the eye, others chiefly to the ear. Rhymed words normally occur at the ends of lines.

In true rhyme the last stressed vowels and the letters following them are the same, while the letters preceding the stressed vowels are different. *e.g.*, cage/page; pleasure/treasure.

Alliteration.

The repetition of the same initial consonant, as in

" Full fathom five thy father lies "
[OBEV 130].

In some verse, most notably Anglo-Saxon narrative verse, alliteration is used instead of rhyme, but the two can be, and often are, combined.

Assonance.

A similarity between vowel sounds, *e.g.*, feet/creep; skin/swim.

Assonance is sometimes used instead of rhyme and occurs frequently in early folk poetry and informal verse.

II. DIFFERENT KINDS OF VERSE.

Accentual Verse.

Here the poet organises his verse according to a given number of stressed syllables in each line. The number of unstressed syllables varies.

Anglo-Saxon Verse.

This was written in an accentual metre in which each half-line contained two heavy stresses, the halves being linked by the alliteration of three of the stressed words. This kind of metrical form survived in such West Midland narrative poems of the fourteenth-century as Langland's " Piers Ploughman " and the anonymous " Sir Gawayne and the Grene Knight ", from which the following example is taken:

/ / /
" There passes non bi that place so proude in his
/
armes
/ /
That he ne dynges hym to deth with dynte of
/
his honde:"

Nineteenth-Century Romantic Verse.

Coleridge experimented with accentual metre and for his " Christabel " chose a line of four stressed syllables and between three and eight unstressed ones:

× × × / × /
A snake's small eye blinks dull and sly
× × / × / × / × × /
And the lady's eyes they shrank in her head
/ / × × × / ×
Each shrunk up to a serpent's eye."

Sir Walter Scott, acknowledging a debt to Coleridge, chose a similar metre for " The Lay of the Last Minstrel ".

Sprung Rhythm.

For his sonnets, Gerard Manley Hopkins devised an accentual metre which he called *sprung rhythm* and described in the preface to his *Collected Poems* (1918).

The basis of sprung rhythm, which follows the natural rhythms of speech, is a line of usually five or six feet. Each foot contains between one and four syllables and extra unstressed syllables may be added for " particular effects " and at the beginning or end of a line. The first syllable of each foot is stressed:

/ × / × × × /
" Gener/ations have/trod, have/trod;
× / × / × / / /
And/all is/seared with/trade;/bleared,/smeared/
/ /
with/toil;
× / / × × ×
And/wears/man's/smudge and shares man's/
/ × /
smell: the/soil/
/ / × × ×× /
Is/bare/now,/nor can foot/feel, being/shod. "
[OBEV 724]

Modern Accentual Metres.

Pound and Eliot are the modern masters of accentual metres. Examples of Pound's treatment may be found in " The River Merchant's Wife " and " Hugh Selwyn Mauberly " (OBEV 812–13). Pound's occasional division of a line, placing the second part below and to the right of the first, so as to introduce a marked " rest ", is a practice much imitated by modern American writers of free verse (*q.v.*), and their followers. In this example Pound divides a line of six stresses:

" What thou lovest well remains
the rest is dross ".
[OBEV 814]

In poems such as " The Waste Land " [OBEV 828] and " Four Quartets " Eliot chose a basic metre of, say, four stresses, for one part of his poem, *e.g.*, the opening of " The Waste Land ", and another, of, say, six stresses, for a different section. Within each section, moreover, he constantly modulated his pattern to reflect changes in the tone from one verse paragraph to another and even within each paragraph introduced occasional modifications and half-lines, the result being a metrical form of great subtlety and beauty. The following are typical examples of Eliot's use of regular and modified accentual metres:

Regular:

" Time present and time past
Are both perhaps present in time future
And time future contained in time past.
If all time is eternally present
All time is unredeemable."
" Burnt Norton ".

Modified:

" The river sweats
Oil and tar
The barges drift
With the turning tide
Red sails
Wide
To leeward, swing on the heavy spar "
[OBEV 828]

Syllabic Verse.

Writers of syllabic verse vary widely in their aims and practice. The reader is therefore referred to two issues of the magazine *Agenda*, Vol. 10 No. 4 and Vol. 11 No. 1 (double issue 1973) and Vol. 11 Nos. 2 & 3 (double issue 1974). These contain various leading British and American poets' accounts of their own understanding of syllabics. Roy Fuller's lecture " An Artifice of Versification " (*Oxford Lectures on Poetry*, 1971) is also helpful.

Basic Syllabics.

English syllabic verse was pioneered independently, but at roughly the same time, during the First World War, by the British Elizabeth Daryush and the American Marianne Moore. Its basis is a given number of syllables to the line, disregarding the number and arrangement of stresses. In the following example the lines have each six syllables:

" you've seen a strawberry
that's had a struggle; yet
was, where the fragments met,"
Marianne Moore: " Nevertheless ".

These lines also illustrate the common practice in syllabic verse of beginning all lines in lower case, which is felt to be less artificial than the conventional use of upper case.

Syllabic metre is natural to verse in French, but in a language such as English, where many words have feminine endings (*i.e.*, end on an unstressed syllable), it is difficult to use syllabic metres artfully.

The writer has to consider the following points:

Elision:

In spoken English some unstressed vowels are naturally elided, *e.g.*, the final " e " of learned. The poet must decide whether or not to count such elided syllables. Practice varies.

Poets such as Auden choose to make a nominal elision of certain syllables when writing but include them when the line is read aloud. Auden followed the Latin practice of eliding contiguous vowels separated by the letters " h " or " w " when counting syllables. Thus, " how elevating " would count as four syllables but be pronounced as five.

Line endings:

An obvious problem is that the strictly metrical line may end on an unimportant word, on an unstressed syllable or even in the middle of a word such as " happy " leaving the second syllable, " py ", to be carried over. Thus the line may seem boneless. Further, although on the page there is a difference between, say, three lines each of six syllables and two lines each of nine, there may be no audible difference. Poets have tackled these problems in various ways.

The first is by virtually ignoring them, usually with unhappy result. Some writers say that the reader should not pause automatically at the ends of lines, but only where the punctuation indicates a pause. This is measurement by cadence rather than by syllable and such verse is often really chopped-up free verse (*q.v.*).

Skilful practitioners such as Moore, Daryush and Auden treat the problems as a challenge and shape their verses by apt use of end-stopped lines, by carefully placing important words at the line's end and by employing rhyme. Auden used all three devices in his poem " In Memory of Sigmund Freud ", which is written in quatrains (*q.v.*) of 11, 11, 8 and 10 syllables:

" For one who lived among enemies so long;
If often he was wrong and at times absurd
To us he is no more a person
Now but a whole climate of opinion."

Accentual-Syllabic or Metrical Verse.

The traditional verse of English poetry is based on regular patterns of stressed and syllables grouped into feet.

English metrical verse uses several kinds of feet, some of two syllables, or disyllabic, some of three syllables or trisyllabic, and occasionally a foot of four syllables.

Disyllabic feet are of four kinds:

The Iamb, consisting of an unstressed syllable followed by a stressed, *e.g.* " return ".

The Trochee, consisting of a stressed syllable followed by an unstressed, *e.g.*, " river ".

The Spondee, consisting of two stressed syllables, *e.g.*, " door mat ".

The Pyrrhic, consisting of two unstressed syllables, *e.g.*, in the phrase " into town ", " into " is a pyrrhic.

Trisyllabic feet are of four kinds:

The Anapaest, consisting of two unstressed syllables followed by a stressed, *e.g.* " as you wish ".

The Dactyl, consisting of a stressed syllable followed by two unstressed, *e.g.*, " archery ".

The Amphibrach, very rarely used, consisting of a stressed syllable between two unstressed, *e.g.*, " delighted ".

The Tribrach, still more rare, consisting of three unstressed syllables, *e.g.*, last three syllables of " incommunicable ".

A four-syllabled foot is very occasionally found:

The Choriambus, which may be thought of as a trochee followed by an iamb, *e.g.*, " Toll for the brave ".

Different Kinds of Metrical Line.

Based on the different kinds of feet are the different kinds of English metre, which may be compared with the "time" in music.

Disyllabic metres may be either iambic or trochaic, for it is impossible to speak at any length using only pyrrhic or spondees, and the most common trisyllabic metres are anapaestic or dactyllic. Examples of different kinds of metrical line follow.

Iambic Line.

"I stróve with nóne, for nóne was wórth my strife."
[OBEV 521]

Trochaic Line.

"Hóme art góne, and tá'en thy wáges."
[OBEV 127]

Anapaestic Line.

"With a héy, and a hó, and a héy noninó,"
[OBEV 122]

Dactylic Lines.

"Wit with his wántonness
Tásteth death's bitterness;"
[OBEV 85]

Amphibrach Lines.

"Most friendship is feígning, most lóving mere fólly.
Then héigh-ho! the hólly!
This life is most jólly." [OBEV 121]

Choriambic Line.

"Kéntish Sir Býng stóod for his King."

Variations in Metre.

Satisfying poetry is rarely entirely regular. Mechanical regularity is soon wearisome to the ear and is a characteristic doggerel. The poet satisfies our love of rhythm in a more interesting and subtle way by introducing all kinds of variations and inversions, while at the same time maintaining the throb of the basic metre. An account of the chief variations follows.

Elision.

Elision, as explained above, is the suppression of pronunciation of a vowel or a syllable.
In the anapaestic line,

"The Assýrîan came dówn like a wólf on the fóld."

the second foot appears to have four syllables, but in fact the "i" of "Assyrîan" is elided or dropped before the "a" as shown by the caret mark ˆ. The elision of "i," which is pronounced "y" and known as "consonantal y" is especially common, and occurs in such words as "familiar", "opinion". Elision is often shown by the use of the apostrophe as in "heav'n". In "heav'n" we see one of the many conventional elisions of poetry, like "'tis", "'twas", "did'st", "o'er", "'gainst" and many more.

Substitution.

Substitution is the use of a foot different from that of the metre in which the poem is written. In the following examples we can see the effect on iambic verse of some common substitutions.

(i) *Of a Trochee.*

"Stiffen the sinews, súmmon úp the blóod,"
Shakespeare, "Henry V."

Here the initial trochee gives force and emphasis.

(ii) *Of a Spondee.*

"Rócks, cáves, lákes, féns, bógs, déns, and shádes of déath."

In this extraordinary line of Milton's the spondees slow down and weight the verse.

(iii) *Of a Pyrrhic.*

"They flŷ forgótten as a dréam"

Here the pyrrhic in the third foot gives lightness to the line.

(iv) *Of a Dactyl.*

"Shrieking his bálefull nóte, which éver dráve"
[OBEV 58]

When a dactyl replaces an iamb it is usually in the first foot as in this typical instance from Spenser where the dactyl gives emphasis and variety to the line.

(v) *Of Anapaests.*

"And the cóming wind did róar more lóud,
And the sáils did sigh like sédge;"
[OBEV 509]

The initial anapaests in these two lines from "The Ancient Mariner" give an effect of hurry and speed.

Additional Syllable.

An additional syllable may be added to either the beginning or end of a line.

(i) *Feminine Ending.*

A feminine ending is an extra unstressed syllable that is added after the final stressed syllable of a line, giving a gentle falling inflexion. It is often used in blank verse and is a marked characteristic of Shakespeare's later plays, *e.g.*,

"Be not afear'd; the isle is full of noises,
Sounds and sweet airs, that give delight, and hurt not."

(ii) *Anacrusis.*

Anacrusis is the use of an extra syllable before the first regular foot of the line.

Dropped Syllable.

It sometimes appears that a line is a syllable, or syllables, short, until we realise that a suspense or pause occupies the time that would have been taken by the missing syllable. The dropped syllable can be indicated by the caret mark ˆ. The following technical terms are used for lines that are short of syllables.

(i) *Catalectic Line.*

This leaves off in the middle of the last foot as in the trochaic line

"Éver lét the fáncy róam,"

or the dactylic line,

"Rings on her fingers and bélls on her tóes,"

The catalectic line is common in trochaic and dactylic verse, for it is in keeping with the tendency of English verse to end on a stressed syllable.

(ii) *Acephalous Line.*

This omits the first syllable of the line, as in the anapaestic line,

"That hóst with their bánners at súnset were séen."

Iambic Metres.

The metre most natural to the English language is undoubtedly the iambic.

With Iambic Pentameter as Basis.

The iambic pentameter of five stresses and ten syllables, also called the iambic decasyllabic line, is more used than any other, and is the basis of the following forms.

(i) *Blank Verse.* Blank verse, consisting of unrhymed iambic pentameters, is the metre of Shakespeare's plays, Milton's "Paradise Lost", Wordsworth's "Prelude", and Tennyson's

"Idylls of the King". In the hands of such masters it is a most flexible instrument especially when diversified with the eleven-syllabled line with a feminine ending. Shakespeare used the metre with increasing freedom, though it must be remembered that some apparent variations are due to the different pronunciation of Elizabethan times.

The following lines of blank verse occur in Wordsworth's "Prelude", Book III. He is describing his rooms in St. John's College, Cambridge.

"And from my pillow, looking forth by light
Of moon or favouring stars, I could behold
The antechapel where the statue stood
Of Newton with his prism and silent face,
The marble index of a mind for ever
Voyaging through strange seas of Thought, alone."

(ii) *Heroic Couplet.* The heroic couplet, consisting of iambic pentameters rhyming in pairs, was in Elizabethan times called "riding rhyme", possibly because it is the metre of The Prologue of Chaucer's "Canterbury Tales", and of many of the tales themselves. It became the most fashionable metre of the eighteenth century when it was used by Pope, Goldsmith, and Johnson. Keats later employed it in "Lamia."

The *Closed Couplet* was, in the heyday of the couplet's vogue, considered the most polished and correct. Here the sentence form exactly coincides with the couplet and the rhyme has a clinching effect, *e.g.*,

"True ease in writing comes from art, not chance
As they move easiest who have learned to dance."

Pope was the supreme master of the closed couplet, and eschewed variations such as enjambment, or the Alexandrine.

Enjambment is a variation used by poets before Pope's time and revived by the Romantic poets. In enjambment the sentence flows over from one line or couplet to the next, and the click of the rhyme is submerged, *e.g.*, Keats' description of Lamia in her serpent form with skin of "dazzling hue".

"And full of silver moons, that, as she breathed
Dissolv'd or brighter shone, or interwreathed
Their lustres with the gloomier tapestries."
Keats, "Lamia".

The Alexandrine, another variation, is a line of six iambic feet. Dryden made frequent use of the Alexandrine but Pope parodied it in the brilliant line that serves as a mnemonic:

"A needless Alexandrine ends the song,
That, like a wounded snake, drags its slow length along."

The triplet, another variation, consists of three lines rhyming together. The third line is frequently an Alexandrine.

Other Iambic Metres.

Many of our iambic verse forms use a shorter or longer line than the pentameter.

(i) *The Octosyllabic Couplet.* The octosyllabic couplet consists of lines of four stresses and eight syllables, and the lines rhyme in pairs. English poets like Marvell have used this metre effectively, *e.g.*, "The Garden" [OBEV 338, *see also* OBEV 337, 370]. It is the metre of Masefield's "Everlasting Mercy" and "Reynard the Fox".

(ii) *Double Iambic Metre.* When we are accustomed to hearing verse we come to realise that stresses are not always of equal weight. It is possible to distinguish in these "fourteeners" of Masefield a major stress, marked ″ and a minor stress marked ′.

"Oh sőme are fónd of Spănish wine, and sőme are fónd of Frĕnch,
And sőme'll swállow tăy and stúff fit őnly fór a wĕnch."
Masefield's "Captain Stratton's Fancy."

The lines have in fact four major stresses, and between the major stresses intervene three syllables, of which the middle has a minor stress. It is this alternation in the weight of the stress which gives its characteristic swing to such a poem as Chesterton's "The Rolling English Road" [OBEV 796].

Trochaic Metres.

Pure Trochaic Metre.

English poets seldom use a pure trochaic metre, partly because the continual feminine ending that it involves is not pleasing to the English ear. A few very short lyrics in this metre can be found, as Browne's Song "For her gait, if she be walking", but the only poem of any length is Longfellow's "Hiawatha", and the metre of this *tour de force* tends to sound monotonous. It consists of unrhymed lines, each of four stresses, *e.g.*,

"Líke a yéllow léaf in áutumn
Líke a yéllow wáter-lily."

Modified Trochaic Metre.

Ever since the Middle Ages our poets have contrived to combine the advantages of a trochaic metre and of a masculine ending by the simple expedient of shortening the last foot of the line to a stressed monosyllable. This catalectic, or shortened, trochaic line is found both in couplets and in stanza forms. *The seven-syllabled trochaic couplet, also called the trochaic tetrameter*, consists of these catalectic, or shortened, lines rhyming in pairs, and is a gay, tripping measure, as in some passages of Milton's "L'Allegro".

"Háste thee nýmph and bríng with thée
Jést and yóuthful jóllity."

In "Locksley Hall" Tennyson uses a fifteen-syllabled couplet, the last foot being catalectic, while a sixteen-syllabled trochaic line is used by E. A. Poe in his "Raven". Here each line is divided into halves by the caesura and the halves also rhyme:

"Ah, distinctly I remember, it was the bleak December."

Lyrics in modified trochaic metre are often found. Herrick uses the seven-syllabled lines rhyming in pairs in "Cherry Ripe", Wither in "A Lover's Resolution" [OBEV 245]. Edmund Blunden, in "Forefathers" [OBEV 843], uses it in a stanza rhyming ABABCC. George Herbert in his lyric "Discipline" [OBEV 276] brilliantly combines five- and three-syllabled lines rhyming ABAB, *e.g.*

"Thrów awáy Thy ród,
Thrów awáy Thy wráth;
Ó my Gód,
Táke the géntle páth."

Further Variations in Modified Trochaic Metre.

The modified trochaic line is especially subject to further variation.

(*a*) It is often combined with a pure trochaic line, *e.g.*, in Hunt's poem "Jenny Kiss'd Me" [OBEV 600] where the catalectic and the complete trochaic line alternate regularly.

(*b*) It often has an extra unstressed syllable preceding it (anacrusis), as in the second of these lines from Keats' poem "Fancy".

"Ín a dárk conspíracý
To | bánish Éven fróm her sky."

The line that results might well be taken for iambic, and there are some passages in English poetry, such as lines in Milton's "L'Allegro", which can be described either as irregular trochaic or irregular iambic lines! It depends on what the hearer judges to be the *basic* stress.

Double Trochaic Metre.

Corresponding to double iambic metre there is a double trochaic metre. W. S. Gilbert effectively uses it in many of his patter songs, as in "Ferdinando and Elvira", *e.g.*,

"Thén we lĕt off páper crăckers, eách of which
contáined a mŏtto,
Ánd she lĭstened whíle I rĕad them, till her
mŏther tóld her nŏt to."

These lines, like those in double iambic metre, have four major stresses (marked ´), and between the major stresses three syllables, of which the middle carries a minor stress.

A modified double trochaic metre, where the last foot is shortened to a stressed monosyllable, can be recognised in Tennyson's "Locksley Hall", or in Lewis Carroll's verses in "Alice in Wonderland":

"'Will you wălk a líttle făster?' sáid a whĭting
tó a snăil."

Trisyllabic Metres Generally.

Because of the irregularities incident to verse in anapaests, dactyls, and amphibrachs, it is not easy to distinguish one trisyllabic metre from another. Swinburne, the past master of trisyllabic metres, often passes with great freedom from anapaestic to dactylic lines within the same stanza.

Anapaestic Metres.

Anapaestic metre is used only in short poems, and often conveys a sense of speed and urgency. The chief variation is the omission of one or two of the unstressed syllables at the beginning of a line. Some of the best-known examples of anapaestic verse are Byron's "Sennacherib", Flecker's "The War Song of the Saracens", and Lewis Carroll's parodies, "'Tis the voice of the lobster", and "You are old, Father William", from *Alice in Wonderland.*

Dactylic Metres.

Pure Dactylic Metre.

Like pure trochaic metre, pure dactylic metre has a feminine ending to the line, which makes rhyming difficult and does not satisfy the English ear. Very few serious poems keep consistently to a pure dactylic verse, and Robert Graves' "In the Wilderness" is most unusual in this respect, *e.g.*,

"Christ of His géntleness
Thírsting and húngering
Wálked in the wílderness."

Modified Dactylic Metre.

Normally dactylic metre is modified in that a catalectic line is frequently used, where the final foot is shortened to a trochee or a stressed monosyllable, as in Hood's "Bridge of Sighs", the most remarkable dactylic poem in the language, *e.g.*,

"Óne more Unfórtunate
Wéary of bréath
Ráshly impórtunate,
Góne to her déath!"

Shakespeare also uses the catalectic line in the refrain to "Where the bee sucks" [OBEV 131]—

"Mérrily mérrily shăll I live nów
Ŭnder the blóssom that hángs on the bóugh."

It is interesting to note how the catalectic dactylic line of the refrain is matched by the catalectic trochaic line of the verse.

Amphibrach Metres.

Pure Amphibrach Metre.

The amphibrach metre is extremely rare in English, although it occurs occasionally in a few lines, or a refrain, like that to "Blow, blow thou Winter Wind" [OBEV 121]. Laurence Binyon's "Bablock Hythe" is one of the few poems to use amphibrachs continuously, *e.g.*,

"Till súnset was rímming
The Wést with pale flúshes;
Behínd the black rúshes
The lást light was dímming."

Modified Amphibrach metre.

The pure amphibrach line can be used alternating with a catalectic line, shorn of its last syllable, as in Goldsmith's drinking song in "She Stoops to Conquer", Act I, Scene 2, *e.g.*

"Let schóol-masters púzzle their bráin
With grámmar and nónsense and léarning."

Choriambic Metres.

There are few poems in pure choriambic metre. Ruskin's quatrain "Trust Thou thy Love" is one of the few examples, *e.g.*,

"Trúst thou thy Lóve; if she be próud, ís she not
swéet?"

Choriambic effects are often obtained incidentally especially in blank verse, when the first foot of a line is a trochee.

Lionel Johnson frequently achieves the same kind of effect in lyric verses by substituting a choriamb for two iambs, as in the poem "By the Statue of King Charles" [OBEV 757], *e.g.*,

"Cómely and cálm, he rides
Hárd by his ówn Whitehall:"

Quantitative Verse.

Since the Renaissance poets such as Spenser, Coleridge, and Tennyson have from time to time endeavoured to reproduce in English verse the complicated quantitative measures of Greek and Latin verse. The difficulty, if not impossibility, of putting the stress on the long vowel in English has for the most part rendered such experiments interesting only to the scholar.

It should always be remembered that the technical names, such as iamb and trochee, although borrowed from the classics, have in English verse a quite different meaning, referring never to quantity but always to stress.

Free Verse or *Vers Libre.*

The prosody of free verse is extremely complicated. The following note offers only a very general guide.

The free verse or *vers libre* of English and American poetry has two sources, the poems of Walt Whitman and of the French Symbolists, particularly as interpreted by Pound. It is a verse designed in the cadences and breath groups of the speaking voice and given shape by a cunning use of four rhetorical devices: repetition, parallelism —balancing one phrase or line against another, enjambment—run-on lines, and pauses.

Repetition and Parallelism.

These devices are characteristic of much ancient poetry and may be familar to the reader from the Old Testament Psalms, which are written in free verse:

"He giveth snow like wool: he scattereth the
hoar-frost
like ashes.
He casteth forth his ice like morsels: who
can stand before his cold?"

Psalm 147.

Whitman's verse recalls such translation of ancient Hebrew poetry in its deployment of rhetorical lists and repetitions, balancing one statement against another:

"Pleas'd with the native and pleas'd with the foreign, pleas'd with the new and old,
Pleas'd with the homely woman as well as the handsome,
Pleas'd with the quakeress as she puts off her bonnet and talks melodiously"
Whitman: "Song of Myself".

In "Howl" and "Kaddish" Allen Ginsberg makes similar use of parallelism and repetition.

D. H. Lawrence in "Snake" [OBEV 810] and "Kangaroo" [OBTCV 184] shows how such free verse is modified for contemplative and narrative poems, in which the parallels and repetitions are more subtlely deployed:

"He reached down from a fissure in the earth-wall in the gloom
And trailed his yellow-brown slackness soft-bellied down, over the edge of the stone trough
And rested his throat upon the stone bottom,
And where the water had dripped from the tap, in a small clearness,
He sipped with his straight mouth,
Softly drank through his straight gums, into his slack long body
Silently."
[OBEV 812]

Enjambment and Pause.

We will have noticed that the lines from Lawrence's poem owe much of their effectiveness to his adroit arrangement of pauses and of run-on lines. Other writers of free verse make particular use of these two devices, and poets like George Oppen create verses in which a complex musical pattern of pauses, or rests, is indicated by the very spacing of the words:

. . . . . Who
so poor the words

would   with and   take on substantial

meaning   handholds   footholds

to dig in one's heels   sliding

hands and heels beyond the residential
lots   the plots   it is a poem

which may be sung
may well be sung
"The Winds of Downhill".

Other writers, while making some use of such spacing, or of dashes, to indicate the rests, have developed Pound's device of breaking up the lines and placing one part below and to the right of another:

This was I,
a sparrow.
I did my best;
farewell.
W. C. Williams: "The Sparrow".

III. THE DIFFERENT KINDS OF RHYME

The most familiar division of rhyme is into masculine, feminine, and triple rhyme, but we also distinguish broken and Leonine rhyme.

Masculine, Male or Single Rhyme.

The final syllable is stressed, *e.g.*, "cage/page", "joy/boy".

Feminine, Female or Two-syllable Rhyme.

The syllable before the last is stressed, and the final syllable unstressed, *e.g.*, "pleasure/treasure", "bending/lending".

Triple, Tumbling or Three-syllabled Rhyme.

The antepenultimate syllable is stressed. Triple rhyme is normally found in light or comic verse, like that of W. S. Gilbert. This punning "Epitaph on a Dentist" employs it:

"Stranger! Approach this spot with gravity!
John Brown is filling his last cavity."

In "The Bridge of Sighs" Hood dares to use it in a serious poem with such rhymes as "scrútiny/mútiny".

Broken Rhyme.

Broken rhyme, where more than one word is needed to complete the rhyme, is occasionally used, *e.g.*, "estate/their gate".

Leonine Rhyme.

Although rhyme normally occurs at the end of the line, we also find verse where the first half of the line rhymes with the second. This device, known as Leonine rhyme, is frequently used in Coleridge's "Ancient Mariner" [OBEV 509], *e.g.*,

"The ice did split, with a thunder-fit;"

Poetic Licence in Rhyme.

The difficulty of rhyming in English is considerable, for many words have not a single rhyming word, some have only one, others very few. Certain licences are therefore allowed to the poet in the following ways:

Eye Rhyme or Printer's Rhyme.

Here words rhyme only to the eye, as "love/move". Keats in "Meg Merrilies" uses "rushes/bushes".

Identical Rhyme.

Here the same syllable or word is used twice so that the line rhymes with itself, *e.g.*, "universe/this verse" [OBEV 549]. The use of rhyming words spelt differently but pronounced identically is also a poetic licence, *e.g.*, "wright, write right".

Cockney Rhyme.

Keats' use of Cockney rhymes has been much criticised, *e.g.*, "mourn/torn", "faces/vases" "briar/attire". There is still considerable difference between regional pronunciation of English, and many eminent poets have availed themselves of a Southern pronunciation in rhyming "dawn/morn", although in some districts the "r" of "mourn" would be sounded.

Perversion of Rhyme.

Modern poets, following Wilfred Owen, have sometimes used a deliberate perversion of rhyme, which should not be confused with assonance. Wilfred Owen opens his bitter poem "A Terre" with the following stanza:

"Sit on the bed. I'm blind and three parts shell.
Be careful; can't shake hands now; never shall.
Both arms have mutinied against me,—brutes.
My fingers fidget like ten idle brats."

The deliberate falsity of rhymes like "shall/shell," and "brutes/brats" conveys Owen's horror at the disintegration and collapse of the First World War.

The Recording of Rhyme Schemes.

The conventional way of noting rhyme schemes is to call the first series *a*, the second *b*, and so on. Normally each new series is indented, *e.g.*,

"Joyful, joyful! *a*
 When virginity *b*
Seeks all coyful *a*
 Man's affinity. *b*
  Fate all flowery, *c*
  Bright and bowery *c*
  Is her dowery! *c*
Joyful, joyful." *a*

W. S. Gilbert, "Yeomen of the Guard."

IV. STANZA FORMS

Two-Line Stanzas.

Couplets.

These are rhymed. Regular couplets are also closed, that is, the sense does not run over from one stanza to another.

In "The Knight and the Lady" [OBEV 20] Sir William Cornish uses a stanza of irregular octosyllabic iambic couplets, while Auden's "Roman Wall Blues" is an example of couplets written in an irregular accentual metre:

"Over the heather the wet wind blows
 I've lice in my tunic and a cold in my nose."

Distiches.

These are unrhymed, but again the regular form is closed. John Wain's "Brooklyn Heights" [OBTCV 518] is an example of a poem written in distiches with an accentual metre of five stresses.

Three-Line Stanzas or Tercets.

There are various forms of which the most common are:

Triplets.

A three-line stanza with a single rhyme, AAA, BBB, etc., as in Robert Graves's "Sick Love" [OBEV 839] Roy Fuller's "The Statue" [OBEV 872].

Terza Rima.

The classic form, as used by Dante in the "Divine Comedy", has stanzas of three iambic pentameters linked by rhyme: ABA, BCB, CDC, etc., the concluding stanza having an extra line which rhymes with its middle one, *e.g.*, DEDE. A recent example of the form is Matthew Mitchell's "Printing Jenny" [OBTCV 533]. In "Ode to the West Wind" [OBEV 549] Shelley uses a modified *terza rima* in which the concluding stanza is a couplet. An interesting modification of the form is used by Auden in "If I Could Tell You" and "Miranda's Song". Each is a poem of six stanzas, the last a quatrain ending in a couplet. Only two rhymes are used throughout, ABA, the last stanzas rhyming ABAA.

In Italian the rhymes used in *terza rima* are feminine. English poets have generally preferred to use masculine rhymes.

Tercets with Short Third Lines.

These may be arranged in pairs, as in Herbert's "The British Church", where the rhyme scheme is AAB, CCB, etc., resembling the sestet of a sonnet (*q.v.*) with a strong median pause.

Unrhymed Tercets.

An example is Ted Hughes's "Thistles" [OBTCV 550] composed of four unrhymed tercets in free verse.

Four-Line Stanzas or Quatrains.

A great many variations are possible. The most common forms include:

The Ballad Stanza.

There are two main forms:

Strict ballad form.

It consists of stanzas of four iambic lines, the first and third having four feet, the second and fourth containing three. The rhyme scheme is ABCB. Ballads such as "Sir Patrick Spens" [OBEV 357] and "The Wife of Usher's Well" [OBEV 360] are in this form. Coleridge's "Ancient Mariner" [OBEV 509] shows how flexibly the ballad stanza can be used.

Less strict ballad form.

Octosyllabic iambic stanzas with a rhyme scheme of either ABCB or ABAB. Many ancient ballads, such as "Thomas the Rhymer" [OBEV 355] are of this type.

The Envelope or "In Memoriam" Stanza.

Used by Tennyson for his poem "In Memoriam" [OBEV 604–11] the stanza resembles that of the less strict ballad form in having four iambic lines, each of four feet, but its rhyme scheme is ABBA.

Hymns.

Most English hymns are written in short iambic lines, and English hymnology refers to them according to the number of syllables in their lines.

Common measure.

8686 rhyming ABAB, *e.g.*, "O for a thousand tongues to sing" (*Songs of Praise* 595).

Long measure.

8888 rhyming ABAB, *e.g.*, "When I survey the wondrous cross" (*Songs of Praise* 133).

Short measure.

6686 rhyming ABCB, *e.g.*, "Blest are the pure in heart" (*Songs of Praise* 455).

The Elegiac Stanza or Heroic Quatrain.

It consists of four iambic pentameters rhyming ABAB. The form is best known from Gray's "Elegy" [OBEV 429].

The "Jabberwocky" Stanza.

Used by Lewis Carroll for his nonsense verses "Jabberwocky" [OBEV 681] the stanza consists of four iambic lines, the first three of four feet, the final line of three. The rhyme scheme is ABAB.

The "Omar Khayyam" Stanza

Named from its use by Edward Fitzgerald in translating the "Rubaiyát" [OBEV 594], the stanza has four iambic pentameters rhyming AABA.

Sapphics.

A quatrain based on the form used by the Greek poetess Sappho in her surviving ode. The first three lines are each of five feet: a trochee, a spondee, a dactyl, a trochee, a spondee. English writers generally prefer the following variation: dactyl, spondee, trochee, trochee, trochee.

The fourth line of the stanza contains but two feet. The Classic form is dactyl and spondee. In English Sapphics the line may be of a dactyl and trochee.

Isaac Watts's "The Day of Judgement" [OBEV 392] illustrates the form:

"When the fierce North-wind with his airy forces
 Rears up the Baltic to a foaming fury;
 And the red lightning with a storm of hail comes
  Rushing down;"

Another example is Sir Henry Newbolt's famous "He Fell Among Thieves" [OBTCV 52].

Other Forms.

Another particularly interesting form is the stanza used by George Herbert in "Virtue" [OBEV 271] and by Sir Richard Fanshawe in "Ode on His Majesty's Proclamation" [OBEV 297]. It consists of three lines each of four iambics, followed by a line of two feet, again iambic. The rhyme scheme is ABAB.

Five-Line Stanzas or Quintains.

Although the quintain has been used by many poets in a variety of ways no particular form has become established. The quintain's lines often vary in length, as in this example from Hardy's "Old Furniture" [OBTCV 17]:

" I know not how it may be with others
Who sit amid relics of householdry
That date from the days of their mothers' mothers,
But well I know how it is with me
Continually."

Other interesting examples are the stanzas of Shakespeare's song "Who is Sylvia", Shelley's "Ode to a Skylark" [OBEV 550] Hugh MacDiarmid's "Cattle Show" [OBTCV 254] and Dylan Thomas's "The force . . ." [OBTCV 439].

Six-Line Stanzas or Sestets.

Again there are many examples and no definitive forms. A popular rhyme scheme is ABABCC giving the effect of a quatrain followed by a couplet. This is used with a stanza of six iambic pentameters in Marvell's "The Fair Singer" [OBEV 340] and Betjeman in "The Metropolitan Railway" [OBTCV 350]. Herbert's poem "Love" uses a more striking stanza:

" Love bade me welcome; yet my soul drew back
Guilty of dust and sin.
But quick-eyed Love, observing me grow slack
From my first entrance in,
Drew nearer to me, sweetly questioning,
If I lacked anything."
[OBEV 277]

Another interesting form is that used by Auden for his menacing chorus "We are the Town" [OBTCV 379].

Seven-Line Stanzas.

The only established form is

Rhyme Royal.

A stanza of seven iambic pentameters rhyming ABABBCC, this was used by Chaucer in "Troilus and Criseyde" [OBEV 7 & 8] and by Shakespeare in "Lucrece" [OBEV 115].

Eight-Line Stanzas or Octaves.

Ottava Rima

A stanza of eight iambic pentameters rhyming ABABABCC, it was used by Byron in "Don Juan" [OBEV 543], by Keats in "Isabella" and Auden in "Letter to Lord Byron".

Other Octaves.

Many other forms exist in various combinations of metres and rhyme schemes, but none have become well known. Examples of interest include Fletcher's "Away Delights" [OBEV 223] Marvell's "The Picture of Little T. C. . . ." [OBEV 341], Hardy's "Voices from Things Growing in a Country Churchyard" [OBTCV 31] and John Berryman's "Homage to Mistress Bradstreet".

The Nine-Line Stanza.

The Spenserian Stanza.

A stanza of eight iambic pentameters followed by an Alexandrine has a rhyme scheme of ABABBCBCC. It was invented by Spenser for his "Fairie Queene" [OBEV 58–63] and used by Byron in "Childe Harold" [OBEV 536–7], Shelley in "Adonais" [OBEV 552] and Burns in "The Cottar's Saturday Night".

Other Stanza Forms.

Stanzas of ten and more lines are used in many variations. Notable ones include those in Tennyson's "Mariana" [OBEV 595], Gray's "Ode on a Distant Prospect of Eton College" [OBEV 426], and Donne's in "The Anniversary" [OBEV 195].

The Diagrammatic Stanza.

Some poets have delighted to create stanzas whose very appearance echoes their theme, as in Herbert's "Easter Wings":

" Lord, Who createdst man in wealth and store,
Though foolishly he lost the same,
Decaying more and more,
Till he became
Most poore:
With Thee
O let me rise
As larks, harmoniously,
And sing this day Thy victories:
Then shall the fall further the flight in me."

The second half of the poem repeats this pattern so that the whole has the shape of two pairs of wings. In the present century Dylan Thomas succeeded in creating an even more complex structure in his extraordinary "Vision and Prayer".

V. OTHER METRICAL FORMS

The Sonnet.

A sonnet has fourteen iambic pentameters. Perfected in Italy by Petrarch, who died in 1374, it was introduced into England in the sixteenth century. There are two chief types of sonnet.

The Petrarchan, or Italian, sonnet has an "octave" of eight lines, rhyming ABBAABBA, followed by a "sestet" of six lines, where some variety of rhyme schemes is found. The strictest Petrarchan sonnets have either two "tercets" of three lines each, with rhymes CDECDE, or else three pairs of lines rhyming CDCDCD.

An example of sestet rhyming CDECDE is Milton's "On His Blindness" [OBEV 305].

Examples of sestets CDCDCD are Wordsworth's "Upon Westminster Bridge" [OBEV 486] and Keats' "On First Looking into Chapman's Homer" [OBEV 562].

Not all of these examples observe the natural pause between octave and sestet which is characteristic of the strict Italian form, and many of our finest sonnets depart from the original rhyme scheme in both octave and sestet.

A lesser-known Petrarchan sonnet by Keats:

" To one, who has been long in city pent,
'Tis very sweet to look into the fair
And open face of heaven,—to breathe a prayer
Full in the smile of the blue firmament.
Who is more happy, when, with heart's content
Fatigued he sinks into some pleasant lair
Of wavy grass, and reads a debonair
And gentle tale of love and languishment?
Returning home at evening with an ear
Catching the notes of Philomel,—an eye
Watching the sailing cloudlet's bright career,
He mourns that day so soon has glided by:
E'en like the passage of an angel's tear
That falls through the clear ether silently."

The Elizabethan or Shakespearean sonnet consists of three quatrains with the rhymes ABAB/CDCD/EFEF/ concluded by a couplet rhyming GG. The couplet often clinches the thought.

Examples are Shakespeare's sonnets [OBEV 134–153], and Keats' last sonnet [OBEV 571].

The Limerick.

The limerick may be defined as a single anapaestic stanza, having the first two lines of three feet, the next two lines of two feet and a concluding line of three feet, with the rhyme scheme AABBA.

The origin of the limerick is uncertain, but it became popular after the appearance in 1846 of Edward Lear's "Book of Nonsense". Lear's limericks differ from the contemporary type in that his final line is normally a repetition, adding nothing to the sense and repeating one of the previous rhyme words.

Most of our modern limericks are passed on by word of mouth, but some that concisely express some intellectual attitudes have appeared in print as the following, on "Determinism"—

"There wás a young mán who said 'Damn!
It appéars to me nów that I ám
Just a béing that móves
In predéstinate gróoves,
Not a táxi or bús, but a trám.'"

The Clerihew.

The clerihew is an amusing quatrain, so called after its inventor Edmund Clerihew Bentley. It disdains regular metre and depends on the simple rhyme scheme AABB. The distinctive characteristic of the clerihew is that it is concerned with some eminent person, who is named in the first line and then described in a wilfully fanciful way, the matter being dictated by the exigencies of the rhyme, as in Bentley's clerihew on J. S. Mill.

John Stuart Mill,
By a mighty effort of will,
Overcame his natural bonhomie
And wrote 'Principles of Political Economy'.

Metrical Forms of French Origin.

It became fashionable during the last years of the nineteenth century for poets to imitate certain verse forms which had long been practised in France, some of them from the time of the troubadours.

Chaucer and Gower had in the fourteenth century used some of these forms, later English poets had occasionally experimented with some of them, and Swinburne, Austin Dobson, Edmund Gosse, and others did much to adapt and naturalise them, although their intricate rhyming patterns are so very difficult to construct in a language so short of rhymes as English. The most popular were the triolet, villanelle, rondeau, ballade, and sestina.

Characteristic of the Anglicised versions are:

1. Freedom as regards metre and length of line.
2. Complicated and exacting rhyme schemes, which permit of no such poetic licence as identical rhyme.
3. A refrain line which recurs in certain stereotyped positions without any alteration of sound, although there may be significant alteration of meaning. Only the sestina is without a refrain.

The Triolet.

A triolet is a single stanza of eight short lines. The first line is repeated as the fourth, and the first and second appear again as seventh and eighth. Only two rhymes are used, the scheme being ABAAABAB.

The triolet was re-introduced into England by Bridges in 1873. Austin Dobson's "A Kiss" is a good example of the form.

"Rose kissed me today.
Will she kiss me tomorrow?
Let it be as it may,
Rose kissed me today,
But the pleasure gives way
To a savour of sorrow;—
Rose kissed me today,—
Will she kiss me tomorrow?"

The Villanelle.

The villanelle has five stanzas, each of three lines, followed by one stanza of four lines. It has a refrain which consists of the first and third lines of the first stanza. These lines alternately form the last lines of the four middle stanzas, and reappear as a concluding couplet to the poem. Only two rhymes are employed throughout. Stanzas one to five rhyme ABA and stanza six ABBAA.

Austin Dobson wrote several villanelles including the well-known "On a Nankin Plate", and W. E. Henley's poem called "Villanelle" is a good example of the form. A modern example is:

A villanelle by Dylan Thomas:

Do not go gentle into that good night

"Do not go gentle into that good night,
Old age should burn and rave at close of day;
Rage, rage against the dying of the light.

Though wise men at their end know dark is right,
Because their words had forked no lightning they
Do not go gentle into that good night.

Good men, the last wave by, crying how bright
Their frail deeds might have danced in a green bay,
Rage, rage against the dying of the light.

Wild men who caught and sang the sun in flight,
And learn, too late, they grieved it on its way,
Do not go gentle into that good night.

Grave men, near death, who see with blinding sight
Blind eyes could blaze like meteors and be gay
Rage, rage against the dying of the light.

And you, my father, there on the sad height,
Curse, bless, me now with your fierce tears, I pray.
Do not go gentle into that good night,
Rage, rage against the dying of the light."
[OBEV 882]

The Rondeau.

A rondeau is a short and compact verse form. It has thirteen lines, usually of eight syllables, which use only two rhymes, and in addition a refrain, usually of four syllables, which introduces a third rhyme. This refrain consists of the first half of the opening line and is twice repeated, thus giving the rondeau fifteen lines all told. The rondeau is divided into three stanzas with the following rhyme scheme: AABBA: AAB + refrain C; AABBA + refrain C.

Austin Dobson wrote many rondeaus to this exacting plan, including the ingenious "You bid me try":

"You bid me try, Blue-Eyes, to write
A Rondeau. What!—forthwith?—to-night?
Reflect. Some skill I have, 'tis true:—
But thirteen lines!—and rhymed on two!
"Refrain", as well. Ah, hapless plight!

Still, there are five lines,—ranged aright.
These Gallic bonds, I feared, would fright
My easy Muse. They did, till you—
You bid me try!

That makes them eight. The port's in sight:—
'Tis all because your eyes are bright!
Now just a pair to end in 'oo'—
When maids command, what can't we do.
Behold!—the RONDEAU, tasteful, light.
You bid me try!"

The Roundel.

The roundel is a variation of the rondeau. Swinburne in his "Century of Roundels" wrote a hundred, and his pattern is usually followed. It consists of nine full lines, plus the refrain (consisting of the opening half of the first line), which is twice repeated, giving eleven lines all told. Only two rhymes are u.ed throughout. The roundel is divided into three stanzas with the following rhyme scheme: ABA + refrain B; BAB; ABA + refrain B.

A Roundel by Swinburne.

The Roundel.

" A Roundel is wrought as a ring or a starbright sphere,
With craft of delight and with cunning of sound unsought
That the heart of the hearer may smile if to please his ear
A roundel is wrought.

Its jewel of music is carven of all or of aught—
Love, laughter, or mourning – rememberance of rapture of fear—
The fancy may fashion to hand in the ear of thought.

As a bird's quick song runs round, and the hearts in us hear—
Pause answers to pause, and again the same strain caught,
So moves the device whence, round as a pearl or tear,
A roundel is wrought."

The Rondel.

The rondel is a form of verse similar to the rondeau. The modern English version consists of fourteen lines all told. Only two rhymes are used, and the initial two lines are repeated as lines 7 and 8 and again as lines 13 and 14. The rondel is frequently arranged in three stanzas with a rhyme scheme as follows: ABBA; ABAB; ABBAAB.

The rondel was revived in the nineteenth century by Bridges, Dobson, Gosse, and Henley, and Dobson's " Love comes back to his vacant dwelling " is one of the best known.

The Ballade.

There are several kinds of ballade, but the most popular modern form consists of three eight-lined stanzas followed by an envoy of four lines. Each of the stanzas and the envoy end with a refrain. The rhymes of the eight-lined stanzas are ABABBCBC and of the envoy BCBC.

Austin Dobson wrote several ballades of this kind, the best known being, " This was the Pompadour's fan ", and " And where are the galleons of Spain? "

Chaucer's " Balade ", " Hyd, Absolon, thy gilte tresses clere," is of an earlier seven-lined type without an envoy.

A ballade by Austin Dobson:

The Ballad of the Thrush.

" Across the noisy street
I hear him careless throw
One warning utterance sweet;
This faint at first, and low
The full notes closer grow;
Hark! What a torrent gush!
They pour, they overflow—
Sing on, sing on, O Thrush!

What trick, what dream's deceit
Has fooled his fancy so
To scorn of dust and heat?
I, prisoned here below,
Feel the fresh breezes blow,
And see, thro' flag and rush,
Cool water sliding slow—
Sing on, sing on, O Thrush!

Sing on. What though thou beat
On that dull bar thy foe!
Somewhere the green boughs meet
Beyond the roofs a-row;
Somewhere the blue skies show,
Somewhere no black walls crush
Poor hearts with hopeless woe—
Sing on, sing on, O Thrush!

Envoy.

Bird, though they come we know,
The empty cage, the hush;
Still, ere the brief day go
Sing on, sing on, O Thrush! "

The Chant Royal.

The chant royal is a longer form of ballade. It has five stanzas of eleven lines and an envoy of five lines.

The rhyme scheme is ABABCCDDEDE, and the envoy has rhyme DDEDE.

The Sestina.

The sestina has six stanzas, each of six lines. The end words to the lines of the first stanza are repeated as end words in the other five stanzas, but in a different and stereotyped order. The poem concludes with an envoy.

The first sestina published in English was in Spenser's " Sheppeardes Calender " (1579). Swinburne wrote many, including " I saw my soul at rest upon a day ".

Metrical Forms of Japanese Origin.

The Haiku.

A poem of three syllabic lines, unrhymed. The first and third lines are of five syllables, the middle one has seven. It creates a vivid pictorial image expressing an imaginative or spiritual insight. The following gives some idea of the form:

Morning's white light, a
new beginning heralded
by a plump black bird.

As Japanese is a language without stresses its poetic forms are impossible to reproduce exactly in English. Most poets therefore concentrate on trying to capture the quality and spirit of the form rather than its exact structure. Pound's " Fan Piece for her Imperial Lord " is an example:

" O fan of white silk,
clear as frost on the grass-blade,
You also are laid aside ."

The Tanka.

A poem similar in kind to the Haiku contains five lines. The first and third contain five syllables each, the remainder seven.

VI. CONCLUSION.

The foregoing account is no more than a description of our verse forms. It in no way implies that verse is written according to rules.

We have only to look at Shakespeare's lyrics [OBEV 117–133] to realise how brilliantly free and inventive the poet can be in devising new and delightful patterns of verse—many of them so subtle as to be very difficult to define. All that the students and critics can do is to follow in the poet's wake, endeavouring to understand and elucidate the forms that the maker has created.

V. FIGURES OF SPEECH

We constantly use figurative language without realising it. When we say that we are "browned off", "fed up", "at the end of our tether", we do not expect to be taken literally. We are in fact employing metaphors.

An understanding of metaphors and other figurative expressions enables us to use our language with greater confidence and effectiveness. It also helps us to understand more fully what others have written. Especially is it valuable when we read a good novel, play, or poem, for to the creative writer figurative language is as natural as the air he breathes.

The following guide to our figures of speech is arranged alphabetically for ease of reference.

Alliteration. A kind of repetition. Two or more words in close succession beginning with the same letter, or sound, usually a consonant. Up to the fourteenth century much English verse was written according to an alliterative principle, as in this modernised quotation from "Piers Plowman":

"I had *w*andered me *w*eary so *w*eary I rested me
On a *b*road *b*ank by a merry-sounding *b*urn."

A strong tendency to alliteration still survives in our poetry. Shakespeare ridicules it in the mechanical's play in "A Midsummer Night's Dream" (Act V, Scene 1) in such lines as—

"Whereat, with blade, with bloody blameful blade,
He bravely broach'd his boiling bloody breast."

Anti-climax. See Bathos.

Antithesis. A figure of speech where ideas are so set out that they are in sharp contrast to each other, *e.g.*,

"Better to reign in hell, than serve in heav'n."
Milton.

"To err is human, to forgive, divine."
Pope.

Apostrophe. A figure of speech where the speaker or writer suddenly breaks off and directly addresses some other person who may be present either in the flesh or only in the imagination. Often it is not a person but a thing, abstraction, or personification that is addressed, as in Milton's famous apostrophe, "Hail, holy light" in "Paradise Lost" Book III, line 1. Apostrophe can be used with comic effect, *e.g.*,

"She turns, O guardian angels stop her
From doing anything improper."

(This couplet is also, incidentally, an example of bathos.)

Assonance. (1) Assonance is correspondence of vowel sounds. For instance, in the opening lines of the "fairy song" in "A Midsummer Night's Dream" (Act II, Scene 2) there is a play on only three vowels, and this repetition helps towards the effect of a magic charm, *e.g.*,

"Philomel with melody, Sing"

In Tennyson's poem "Break, break, break" the repetition of the "o" sound in the second line is like an outcry of grief, *e.g.*,

"On the cold grey stones, *O* Sea!"

(2) Assonance is sometimes used instead of rhyme, especially in early folk poetry. Here there is correspondence of one word with another in the accented vowel and any vowels which follow, but not in the consonants, *e.g.*, in "King Estmere", "Spain" is rhymed with "same" and "barone" with "home".

Bathos or Anti-climax. A figure of speech that consists of a sudden and ludicrous descent from lofty to trivial things. In "The Rape of the Lock" Pope wittily used bathos to satirise the frivolity of the woman of fashion, who lacking all sense of proper feeling, casts the same "screams of horror", and "shrieks to pitying heav'n".

"When *husbands*, or when *lapdogs* breathe their last."

The careless writer may fall to bathos which is unintentionally comic in its effect. The word "bathos" in Greek means "depth".

Climax. A figure of speech where ideas are set out in such a way that each rises above its predecessor in scale. In Greek the word "climax" means a ladder. One of the finest examples is in Shakespeare's "The Tempest" (Act IV, Scene 1) when Prospero says,

"And, like the baseless fabric of this vision,
The cloud-capp'd towers, the gorgeous palaces,
The solemn temples, the great globe itself,
Yea, all which it inherit, shall dissolve."

Epigram. A concise and pointed saying, effective by its wit and ingenuity. It often uses antithesis. S. T. Coleridge's definition of this form is in itself an epigram, *e.g.*,

"What is an epigram? a dwarfish whole:
Its body brevity, and wit its soul."

Euphemism. A figure of speech where a harsh or distressing expression is replaced by one that is gentler, if less accurate. Thus we may call a lie a "flight of fancy", or a "terminological inexactitude". There is a striking instance of euphemism in "Macbeth" (Act I, Scene 5), when Lady Macbeth, planning the murder of her guest, Duncan, says, "He that's coming must be provided for."

Hypallage or "Transferred Epithet." A figure of speech where an adjective, or adverb, is separated from the word to which it belongs grammatically, and is transferred to some other word in the sentence, its unusual position giving it a kind of emphasis. The word "obsequious" is thus transferred in the sentence "A lacquey presented an obsequious cup of coffee".

Hyperbole. A figure of speech where there is a deliberate use of exaggeration for the sake of effect as in the phrase "tons of money". Lady Macbeth uses hyperbole when she says, "Here's the smell of blood still; all the perfumes of Arabia will not sweeten this little hand" (Act V, Scene 1).

Writers of advertisements, blurbs and film trailers frequently indulge in hyperbole.

Innuendo. A figure of speech where something is hinted at, or suggested, but not openly stated. Dickens uses innuendo to suggest Scrooge's stinginess by saying, "Darkness was cheap, and Scrooge liked it".

Irony. (1) A figure of speech where the speaker says one thing but intends the opposite to be understood. Shylock uses the word "courtesies" ironically when he says,

"Fair sir, you spit on me on Wednesday last;
You spurn'd me such a day; another time
You call'd me dog; and for these courtesies
I'll lend you thus much moneys."
"Merchant of Venice" (Act I, Scene 3).

The use of irony can clearly be seen in Shakespeare's "Julius Cæsar" in Antony's well-known speech to the citizens. They gradually realise that when Antony repeats that Brutus and the rest are "honourable men", he is speaking ironically, and intends the opposite. When they fully perceive this they cry, "They were traitors . . . villains, murderers.". ("Julius Cæsar," Act III, Scene 2.)

(2) *Dramatic irony* is the use of words which have a second inner significance that is not realised by some of the actors in a scene. For instance, in Sheridan's "School for Scandal," Act IV, Scene 3, Sir Peter admires Joseph Surface's useful screen, and Surface replies, "Oh yes, I find great use in that screen." He and the audience know, but Sir Peter does not, that at that very moment the screen is concealing Sir Peter's own wife who had rashly visited Joseph.

It is helpful to remember that in Greek the word "irony" means "dissimulation."

Litotes. A figure of speech which is really a special kind of understatement (or Meiosis). Instead of making a positive statement (*e.g.*, "This is a difficult task") we might use Litotes, and say "This is no easy task", thus expressing a positive by the negative of its opposite.

Malapropism. An amusing inaccuracy in vocabulary. Words that have an accidental similarity in sound may become confused in the speaker's mind and the wrong word may come uppermost. Thus Mrs. Malaprop complains that the disobedience of her niece gives her, not "hysterics" but "hydrostatics." It is not surprising that Mrs. Malaprop, of Sheridan's "The Rivals", has given her name to this kind of verbal confusion, though many before her time, including humble folk in Shakespeare's plays, have uttered malapropism. Bottom, in "A Midsummer Night's Dream," says that in the wood they "may rehearse more obscenely" when he means "obscurely".

Meiosis. A figure of speech where a deliberate understatement is made for the sake of effect. English people are especially fond of Meiosis and often use it colloquially, in such an expression as "He made a very 'decent' contribution", meaning a very "generous" contribution. The full meaning of what we intend is often conveyed by the tone of voice, *e.g.*,

"This is *some* war."

Metaphor. It is helpful to think of the figure of speech, metaphor, as a condensed simile. In metaphor one thing is not merely *compared* to another, as in simile but is boldly spoken of as if it actually *were* that other. Thus Bacon, in the following metaphor, does not say books are *like* food, but speaks of them as if they actually *were* food, *e.g.*, "Some books are to be tasted, others to be swallowed, and some few to be chewed and digested."

Metaphor is usually defined as the transfer of a name, or descriptive term, to some object to which it is not properly applicable, thus making an implicit comparison. Shakespeare uses nautical terms to describe our human situation when Brutus says.

"There is a tide in the affairs of men which, taken at the flood, leads on to fortune" ("Julius Cæsar," Act IV, Scene 3).

In *Mixed Metaphor* two or more inconsistent metaphors are used of the same object, as when, speaking of a suspicion, someone said, "I smell a rat; I see it in the air; but I will nip it in the bud."

Metonymy. A figure of speech where a person or thing is not named directly, but by some associated thing. Instead of saying, "The prisoner addressed the magistrate", we might use metonymy and say, "The prisoner addressed the bench". Similarly, "a speech from the Lord Chancellor" is sometimes called "a speech from the Woolsack".

Onomatopœia. The use of words which imitate or echo the sounds they suggest, *e.g.*,

"Seas half-frozen slushed the deck with slime."
Masefield.

Oxymoron. A figure of speech where words that are usually contradictory are combined in one expression, *e.g.*, "bitter-sweet".

"I know this is a joyful trouble to you."
"Macbeth," Act II, Scene 3.

Paradox. A figure of speech where a statement is made that at first sight seems contradictory or absurd, *e.g.*,

"The rule of the road is a paradox quite:
If you keep to the left, you are sure to be right".

and

"The Child is father of the Man;"
Wordsworth.

Pathetic Fallacy. A figure of speech where it is assumed that things of nature have feelings like those of human beings, *e.g.*,

"And daffadillies fill their cups with tears".
Milton.

In Greek "pathos" means "feeling".

Personification. A figure of speech where some abstraction, or some inanimate thing is represented as a person, *e.g.*,

"Rule, Britannia".
James Thomson.

"But look the dawn in russet mantle clad
Walks o'er the dew of yon high eastern hill."
"Hamlet," Act I, Scene 1.

Personification is really a special kind of metaphor.

Pun. The use of words so as to convey a double meaning, as in Belloc's couplet

"When I am dead, I hope it may be said:
'His sins were scarlet, but his books were read'"

In the three puns that follow there is a suggestion of a banking transaction! "The Egyptians received a check on the bank of the Red Sea which was crossed by Moses." Puns, which were popular in the nineteenth century especially with Lamb and Hood, are now out of favour.

Simile. A figure of speech which makes a comparison pointing out a similarity between things otherwise unlike. It is usually introduced by "like" or "as", *e.g.*

"Men fear death as children fear to go in the dark."
Bacon.

"His own thought drove him like a goad."
Tennyson.

Spoonerism. An accidental transposition of the sound of two words, so called after Rev. W. A. Spooner, warden of New College, Oxford, *e.g.*,

"You have hissed all my mystery lectures" for "You have missed all my history lectures".

Synecdoche. A figure of speech where the name of a part is used for the whole, or the whole for the part, *e.g.*,

"A fleet of a hundred sail"

meaning of a hundred ships.

Synecdoche is really a special kind of Metonymy.

Transferred Epithet. See **Hypallage.**

VI. LITERARY FORMS

Allegory. A description or story which has a second and deeper significance below the surface. The characters are really personifications, usually representing some vice or virtue. Allegory flourished in the Middle Ages, but the best-known allegory in the world is Bunyan's "Pilgrim's Progress" (1678), which has been translated into over a hundred different languages and dialects. On the surface "The Pilgrim's Progress" is the story of a journey in which the hero encounters many difficulties but at last reaches his destination. Its inner meaning is the progress of the Christian soul through life on earth. Spenser's "Faerie Queene" (1589 and 1596) is a more subtle and complex allegory, capable of several interpretations, religious, ethical, and political. Allegory has been described as extended metaphor. *See* **M56.**

Autobiography. The story of a man's (or woman's) own life, written by himself. The autobiography is becoming increasingly popular, recent excellent examples being Stephen Spender's *World within World*, Richard Church's *Over the Bridge* and Laurie Lee's *Cider with Rosie*.

Ballad. There are two chief types of ballad:

1. A light song, often sentimental, as was the Victorian ballad, or a popular song, often of a personal kind, praising or attacking some notability.

2. A traditional poem, passed on by word of mouth. Many of our traditional ballads date from the 15th century. They tell some stirring tale, as do the many ballads about Robin Hood. Sometimes they record an actual occurrence, like the ballad "The Battle of Otterbourne", which tells of a Border skirmish, fought in 1388. Such ballads are enlivened by lively dialogue, and they use a special kind of stanza, which is described on **M51.**

Ballade. A short highly stylised poem, with a strict verse form. *See* **M54.**

Biography. A narrative telling the life story of some actual person, usually a well-known figure. The most famous biographer of classical times was Plutarch, who in the 1st century A.D. wrote his series of parallel "Lives" of twenty-three Greeks and twenty-three Romans. The English translation of this provided Shakespeare with some of the plots of his plays. Boswell's *Life of Samuel Johnson* (1791) is our best-known English biography.

Burlesque. The aim of burlesque is to make us laugh by ridiculing the work of some other writer. Sometimes it treats his serious subject in a mocking way. Sometimes it takes the form of an absurd imitation or caricature of his style. Some of our most successful burlesques are dramatic in form, like Sheridan's "The Critic", produced in 1779. This has a play within a play, called "A Tragedy Rehears'd", a brilliant burlesque of the sentimental, historical plays so popular in his time.

Chant Royal. A poem of a strictly formal kind. French in origin. *See* **M54.**

Clerihew. A single-stanza verse form, four lines long. *See* **M53.**

Comedy. A play which is happy and amusing in tone, but not necessarily light or superficial. A comedy always has a fortunate conclusion. Shakespeare's "Twelfth Night" and Oscar Wilde's "The Importance of being Earnest" are typical examples.

Drama. A play in verse or prose, where the story is unfolded and the characters represented through the actions and speeches of actors on a stage. It is essential to good drama that there should be some kind of dynamic action and some conflict between the characters. In comedy the conflict is usually open and external. "As You Like It" for instance, begins with a quarrel between Orlando and Oliver. But most of the world's finest tragedies reveal also an inner conflict in the soul of man. In "Hamlet" the hero is at odds with many people, including his mother, the king, Ophelia, Polonius, and Laertes but all these struggles are of secondary significance, compared with the conflict in his own mind. Even a play like "Waiting for Godot", which reduces incident and conflict to a minimum, must make some concession to the demand of the audience for the dynamic. Drama cannot be static. Occasionally poets have written dramas which they knew were not practicable for the stage. Shelley's lyrical dramas, "Prometheus Unbound" and "Hellas", are of this kind. *See* **Section I.**

Eclogue. In classical literature a brief poem, usually in the form of a dialogue between shepherds. It was a popular form in the time of the Renaissance; Spenser's "Shepheardes Calendar" (1579) consists of twelve eclogues, one for each month of the year.

Elegy. A lyric poem of lamentation for the dead. Gray's "Elegy in a Country Churchyard" (1750) is the best-known English elegy. It reflects in a general way on the "destiny obscure" of the humble folk who are buried in a quiet churchyard, probably that of Stoke Poges, but most elegies mourn the death of only one person. Such are Shelley's "Adonais" (1821), on the death of Keats, and Matthew Arnold's "Thyrsis" (1867), commemorating his friend Arthur Hugh Clough. Tennyson's "In Memoriam" (1850) is unusual, in that it is not a single elegy, but a series of elegiac poems, inspired by the poet's grief for the death in 1833 of his friend Arthur Hallam.

Epic. A very long narrative poem, usually consisting of several books. The epic tells of the splendid deeds of some hero of history or legend and is frequently concerned with war. Some of the world's greatest epics are the Greek "Iliad" and "Odyssey", ascribed to Homer, the Latin "Aeneid" of Virgil, the Hindu "Mahabharata", and Milton's "Paradise Lost", whose hero is God himself. The epic is distinguished by its sustained dignity of style.

Epilogue. *See* **Prologue.**

Essay. The word essay, derived from the French, means literally an "attempt" or "endeavour", and as a literary term it applies to a short prose composition which attempts to present the author's reflections on any subject he chooses. As a literary form the essay derives from the French "Essais" of Montaigne, first translated into English by Florio in 1603. Our first English essayist was Francis Bacon, who published between 1597 and 1625 three volumes of his essays, brief, pithy, and objective in character. In course of time the essay has become more subjective and personal, especially in the hands of Lamb, Hazlitt, and contemporary writers.

Extravaganza. A composition, musical or literary, which uses improbable and fantastic elements and incidents. A good example of narrative extravaganza is Thackeray's *Rose and the Ring* (1855), in which, for instance, Gruffanuff's husband, the footman, is, because of his rudeness, turned into a door-knocker. Extravaganzas are frequently dramatic in form, and most pantomimes may be regarded as such.

Fable. A very brief story designed to teach some lesson or moral. The characters of the story are often animals, birds, or insects, which converse like human beings. The most famous of all fables are those attributed to Aesop, and those of La Fontaine, the French writer of the 17th century.

Farce. A species of dramatic comedy whose whole aim is to excite laughter. It does not scruple to use improbable characters and incidents and absurd situations. "Charley's Aunt" is a typical farce.

Lampoon. A coarse satire (*q.v.*) attacking an individual. Lampoons are usually short. The word itself is derived from a French word meaning "drinking song."

Limerick. A single-stanza verse form, 5 lines long and with a formal metre and rhyme scheme. *See* M52.

Lyric. In ancient Greece a lyric was originally a poem meant to be sung to the accompaniment of the lyre, a stringed musical instrument rather like a small harp. Later the word was used for a poem with song-like qualities; short, usually divided into verses, and expressing the feelings of the poet. The lyric flourished in England in the Elizabethan age, as witnessed by the lovely lyrics scattered through Shakespeare's plays. Neglected in the 18th century, it became popular again with the Romantic poets of the 19th century. Odes, elegies, and sonnets are all species of lyrics.

Mask or Masque. A dramatic entertainment performed by amateurs and originating in the court masquerade. The action or plot of the masque is of the slightest and there is little concern with portrayal of character, for the masque gives pleasure by means of its verse, music, and dancing, and its elegant costume and scenery. It was very popular in the 16th and 17th centuries, and from 1605 Ben Jonson wrote many court masques, for which Inigo Jones designed original costumes and settings. Our best-known examples are Shakespeare's masque in Act IV of "The Tempest" and Milton's "Comus".

Melodrama. There are two meanings of the word melodrama.

1. In the early 19th century a melodrama meant a play, usually of a romantic and sensational kind, in which songs were inserted, and where an orchestra accompanied the action. The musical comedy of today might be regarded as its modern counterpart.

2. Today the word melodrama is used of an inferior kind of play, which deliberately excites the emotions by its sensational and violent happenings, but which has a happy ending. We should be careful to distinguish melodrama, which uses violence for its own sake, from serious plays, like "Hamlet" or "King Lear", where violent acts are only incidents necessary to a profound interpretation of human conduct.

Memoirs. The word is normally used of a record of events of which the author has some personal experience or special source of information.

Miracle Plays. Mediæval verse plays produced from the late 14th to 16th centuries by the town guilds and performed in the market-place, or other suitable open space. They consisted of a series of dramatised stories from the Bible or Lives of Saints. Each scene would be allotted to one of the guilds, which was then responsible for its production on a wheeled stage. As soon as the actors of one guild had completed their scene, their stage would be trundled off, sometimes to another rendezvous, and would itself be succeeded by another stage with its scene, until a whole cycle of episodes had been performed. Four great cycles of miracle plays are still extant, called after the towns where they were probably performed, York, Coventry, Chester, and Wakefield. The Wakefield cycle is often called the Towneley cycle. The plays have not only a strong religious sense but also a lively comic spirit. The Towneley cycle has some especially racy comic scenes. One popular incident shows the noisy quarrel that results when Noah's wife refuses to go into the ark.

Mock Heroic. A species of parody (*q.v.*), caricaturing some play or poem written in a lofty and high-flown style. "The Rehearsal" (1672), by Villiers, is typical. It is an absurd imitation ridiculing the artificial and high falutin' heroic plays which were then in vogue.

Monody. In Greek literature an ode sung by a single voice, like our solo in music. In English literature it signifies a poem of mourning for someone's death. The elegies "Lycidas", by Milton, and "Thyrsis", by Matthew Arnold, were both called monodies by their authors.

Monologue. Originally a scene where one person of the drama spoke alone. Today it usually means a dramatic composition for a single actor, such as the well-known Lancashire monologues presented by Stanley Holloway. The word is also sometimes used as meaning soliloquy.

Moralities or Morality Plays. Mediæval verse plays of an allegorical kind, which attempted to teach lessons of virtue, the persons of the drama usually being not real people, but personifications. Most Moralities date from the 15th century, the best known being "Everyman", which is Dutch in origin. The hero, Everyman, is summoned by Death, and vainly appeals for help to his friends, Fellowship, Kindred, Goods, Knowledge, Beauty, and Strength, but all fail him. Only his own

Good Deeds will consent to accompany him on his last journey.

Mysteries or Mystery Plays. Some modern writers use the term "Mystery play" instead of "Miracle play" (*q.v.*). It is really an alternative title. One critic tried to distinguish between "Mystery plays", as concerned with stories from the Gospels, and "Miracle plays", as concerned with the lives and deeds of Saints, but this distinction is not usually followed.

Novel. A lengthy prose fiction. It is traditionally a realistic story of people and events, but in the present century many novelists have sought rather to express the fluctuating patterns of the inner life of the mind, while the chief interest of the French "new novelists" is language itself.

Some consider Thomas Nashe's picaresque romance *The Unfortunate Traveller* (1594) to be the first English novel but Samuel Richardson is more usually thought to have invented this literary form. His *Pamela* (1740–41), the first realistic novel in English, won a European reputation. *See also* M4–28.

Ode. In classical literature an ode was a poem to be sung. In English literature it signifies a lyric poem, usually in rhyme, and is seldom longer than 150 lines. It is usually in the form of an address, and lofty in its feeling and style. The ode was popular with the romantic poets. Some of our best known are Shelley's "Ode to the West Wind", and Keats' "Ode to a Nightingale", "Ode on a Grecian Urn", and "To Autumn", all of them published in 1820.

Parable. A parable is an arresting simile or metaphor from nature or common life, which may be elaborated into a life-like story. It presents a situation which at a certain point implies some correspondence with ethical or religious principle. *See* C. H. Dodd's *The Parables of the Kingdom.*

Parody. A literary caricature, which mimics the themes and style of some other author in such a way as to make his faults seem absurd and laughable. J. C. Squire's *Tricks of the Trade* is an amusing collection of his skilful parodies of such writers as Byron, Wordsworth, and Masefield.

Pastoral. A pastoral poem, romance, or play is one in which the life of shepherds or of simple rustic folk is portrayed in an idealised way. Originating in Greek literature, the pastoral was revived at the time of the Renaissance. Spenser's "Shepheardes Calendar" consists of twelve pastoral eclogues. Shakespeare's "As You Like It" is a pastoral play, Milton's "Lycidas" is a pastoral elegy and his "Comus" a pastoral masque. There is usually in the pastoral a deeper meaning below the surface. A critic has said, "The shepherd's cloak was the acknowledged disguise of the lover, the poet, the courtier, the pastor of souls, the critic of contemporary life." In the pastoral form the charm of a simple setting and deeper significance are combined.

Prologue and Epilogue. Generally speaking, a prologue means a foreword, or preface, and an epilogue an appendix to a literary work, but the terms are often used more specifically when referring to a play. Here the prologue is a short speech in verse or prose spoken to the audience by one of the actors before the play begins, the epilogue a similar speech after its conclusion. The prologue endeavours to put the audience into a receptive state of mind, the epilogue to ask for a kind reception to the play. Shakespeare's "Romeo and Juliet" has a prologue, his "As You Like It" an epilogue, spoken by Rosalind, who says, "Good plays prove the better by the help of a good epilogue." In the 18th century it was customary for a leading actor to speak the prologue and for a leading actress to make a plea for the play in the epilogue.

Romance. The romance of the early Middle Ages was a fictitious tale in verse, telling the adventures of some hero of chivalry, the interest being in the incidents, sometimes of a supernatural kind, rather than in character. The most famous of these early romances is the French "Chanson de Roland" of the early 12th century. In the later Middle Ages a romance might be written in prose. In the 16th and 17th centuries a romance meant a tale in either prose or verse in which the scenes and incidents were remote from those of real life. Sir Philip Sidney's "Arcadia" (1590), written to entertain his sister, is of this type. Today the word romance is rather vaguely used of a tale of somewhat improbable events. Sir Henry Rider Haggard wrote several such romances, including *King Solomon's Mines* (1886) and *She* (1887).

Rondeau. A poem of a strictly formal kind, French in origin. *See* M53.

Rondel. A poem similar in form to the rondeau. *See* M54.

Roundel. A variation of the rondeau. *See* M53.

Saga. The word saga, which is of Norse origin and means story, is applied to the mediæval prose narratives of Iceland and Norway, especially those concerned with the traditions of Icelandic families and Norwegian kings. William Morris, in his "Earthly Paradise", gives in "The Lovers of Gudrun" a version of the Icelandic Laxdæla Saga.

Satire. A work in either verse or prose attacking folly and vice. Pope's "Dunciad", in verse-published between 1728 and 1743, ridicules contemporary authors and literary follies in a massive attack on dullness and literary hacks. Swift's *Gulliver's Travels* (1726), which on the surface is a series of prose tales of travel to imaginary countries, is actually a comprehensive satire. It begins, in the first book on "Lilliput", with incisive ridicule of the squabbles between English political parties and religious sects, and culminates, in the final book on the Houyhnhnms, in a devastating attack on all that is bestial in human nature. Samuel Butler's *Erewhon* (an anagram of Nowhere), published in 1872, also uses a prose travel tale in his satirical exposure of Victorian convention and hypocrisy. Although not precisely satires, many of Shaw's plays are satirical in spirit. "Arms and the Man" may be considered in one of its aspects as a satire on war.

Sestina. A poem of a strictly formal kind, French in origin. *See* M54.

Skit. A light satire, often in the form of parody.

Soliloquy. In a soliloquy a man talks to himself, or utters his thoughts aloud regardless of the presence of others who may hear him. The word is usually applied to such utterances by a character in a play. The most famous soliloquies in literature are those of Hamlet.

Sonnet. A lyric poem of fourteen lines, with an intricate rhyme scheme. *See* M52.

Squib. A brief, sharp satire (*q.v.*) attacking an individual.

Threnody. A term from the Greek, seldom used today. It means a song of mourning, especially a lament for the dead.

Tragedy. A play, or other literary work, which is preoccupied with the serious and unhappy aspects of life. It is sombre in tone and ends with misfortune. Shakespeare's "Macbeth" and Ibsen's "Ghosts" are typical tragedies.

Tragi-Comedy. The word is used in two different ways:

(*a*) It may denote a play (or very occasionally a story) which combines both tragic and comic elements Chekhov's "The Cherry Orchard" is a tragi-comedy of this type.

(*b*) It may also mean a play which is for the most part sombre in theme and tone, but which has a happy conclusion, like Shakespeare's "The Winter's Tale".

Trilogy. In Greek literature a series of three tragedies, like Aeschylus' trilogy, the "Oresteia," written when he was nearly seventy, in the 5th century B.C. In modern times the word trilogy is applied to any sequence of three literary works which are related to each other in subject and theme.

Triolet. A single-stanza verse form, eight lines long, and with a very formal pattern, French in origin. *See* M53.

Villanelle. A poem of a strictly formal kind, French in origin. *See* M53.

GENERAL COMPENDIUM

A collection of useful tables and data on a variety of unrelated subjects, including SI units, weights and measures, phases of the moon, sunrise and sunset, eclipses, colours of academical hoods, foreign phrases, abbreviations in common use and the rates of taxation introduced by the 1977 Budget.

TABLE OF CONTENTS

GENERAL COMPENDIUM

ENGLISH MONARCHS
(A.D. 827–1603)

Monarch	Accession	Died	Age	Reigned
I.—BEFORE THE CONQUEST.				
SAXONS AND DANES				
Egbert	827	839	—	12
Ethelwulf	839	858	—	19
Ethelbald	858	860	—	2
Ethelbert	858	865	—	7
Ethelred	865	871	—	6
Alfred the Great	871	899	50	28
Edward the Elder	899	924	54	25
Athelstan	924	939	45	15
Edmund	939	946	25	7
Eadred	946	955	32	9
Eadwig	955	959	18	3
Edgar	959	975	32	17
Edward the Martyr	975	978	17	3
Ethelred II ("the Unready")	978	1016	48	37
Edmund Ironside	1016	1016	27	Apr.–Nov.
Canute the Dane	1017	1035	40	18
Harold I	1035	1040	—	5
Hardicanute	1040	1042	24	2
Edward the Confessor	1042	1066	62	24
Harold II	1066	1066	44	Jan.–Oct.
II.—FROM THE CONQUEST TO THE PRESENT DAY.				
NORMANS				
William I	1066	1087	60	21
William II	1087	1100	43	13
Henry I	1100	1135	67	35
Stephen, Count of Blois	1135	1154	50	19
PLANTAGENETS				
Henry II	1154	1189	56	35
Richard I	1189	1199	42	10
John	1199	1216	50	17
Henry III	1216	1272	65	56
Edward I	1272	1307	68	35
Edward II	1307	dep. 1327	43	20
Edward III	1327	1377	65	50
Richard II	1377	dep. 1399	34	22
Henry IV (Lancaster)	1399	1413	47	13
Henry V (Lancaster)	1413	1422	34	9
Henry VI (Lancaster)	1422	dep. 1461	49	39
Edward IV (York)	1461	1483	41	22
Edward V (York)	1483	1483	13	Apr.–June
Richard III (York)	1483	1485	32	2
TUDORS				
Henry VII	1485	1509	53	24
Henry VIII	1509	1547	56	38
Edward VI	1547	1553	16	6
Jane	1553	1554	17	9 days
Mary I	1553	1558	43	5
Elizabeth I	1558	1603	69	44

BRITISH MONARCHS

(1603 to the Present day)

Monarch	Accession	Died	Age	Reigned
STUARTS				
James I (VI of Scotland)	1603	1625	59	22
Charles I	1625	beh. 1649	48	24
COMMONWEALTH DECLARED, MAY 19, 1649				
Oliver Cromwell, Lord Protector	1653–8	—	—	—
Richard Cromwell, Lord Protector	1658–9	—	—	—
STUARTS (RESTORATION)				
Charles II	1660	1685	55	25
James II (VII of Scotland)	1685	dep. 1688	68	3
Interregnum Dec. 11, 1688 to Feb. 13, 1689				
William III and Mary II	1689	1702 1694	51 33	13 6
Anne	1702	1714	49	12
HOUSE OF HANOVER				
George I	1714	1727	67	13
George II	1727	1760	77	33
George III	1760	1820	81	59
George IV	1820	1830	67	10
William IV	1830	1837	71	7
Victoria	1837	1901	81	63
HOUSE OF SAXE-COBURG				
Edward VII	1901	1910	68	9
HOUSE OF WINDSOR				
George V	1910	1936	70	25
Edward VIII	1936	Abd. 1936	—	325 days
George VI	1936	1952	56	15
Elizabeth II	1952			

SCOTTISH MONARCHS

(1057–1603)

Monarch		Accession	Died
Malcolm III (Canmore)	Son of Duncan I	1058	1093
Donald Ban	Brother of Malcolm Canmore	1093	—
Duncan II	Son of Malcolm Canmore, by first marriage	1094	1094
Donald Ban	Restored	1094	1097
Edgar	Son of Malcolm Canmore, by second marriage	1097	1107
Alexander I	Son of Malcolm Canmore	1107	1124
David I	Son of Malcolm Canmore	1124	1153
Malcolm IV (the Maiden)	Son of Henry, eldest son of David I	1153	1165
William I (the Lion)	Brother of Malcolm the Maiden	1165	1214
Alexander II	Son of William the Lion	1214	1249
Alexander III	Son of Alexander II, by second marriage	1249	1286
Margaret, Maid of Norway	Daughter of Eric II of Norway, granddaughter of Alexander III	1286	1290
John Baliol	Grandson of eldest daughter of David, Earl of Huntingdon, brother of William the Lion	1292	1296
Robert I (Bruce)	Great-grandson of 2nd daughter of David, Earl of Huntingdon, brother of William the Lion	1306	1329
David II	Son of Robert I, by second marriage	1329	1371
Robert II (Stewart)	Son of Marjorie, daughter of Robert I by first marriage, and Walter the Steward	1371	1390
Robert III	(John, Earl of Carrick) son of Robert II	1390	1406
James I	Son of Robert III	1406	1437
James II	Son of James I	1437	1460
James III	Eldest son of James II	1460	1488
James IV	Eldest son of James III	1488	1513
James V	Son of James IV	1513	1542
Mary	Daughter of James V, by second marriage	1542	1587
James VI (ascended the Throne of England 1603)	Son of Mary, by second marriage	1567	1625

BRITISH PRIME MINISTERS

	Party	Served
George I, 1714–27		
George II, 1727–60		
Sir Robert Walpole	Whig	1721–42
Earl of Wilmington	Whig	1742–3
Henry Pelham	Whig	1743–54
Duke of Newcastle	Whig	1754–6
Duke of Devonshire	Whig	1756–7
Duke of Newcastle	Whig	1757–60
George III, 1760–1820		
Duke of Newcastle	Whig	1760–2
Earl of Bute	Tory	1762–3
George Grenville	Whig	1763–5
Marquis of Rockingham	Whig	1766
Duke of Grafton	Whig	1766–9
Lord North	Tory	1770–82
Marquis of Rockingham	Whig	1782
Earl of Shelburne	Whig	1782–3
Duke of Portland	Coalition	1783
William Pitt	Tory	1783–1801
Viscount Sidmouth	Tory	1801–4
William Pitt	Tory	1804–6
Lord Grenville	Whig	1806–7
Duke of Portland	Tory	1807–9
Spencer Perceval (assassinated)	Tory	1809–12
George IV, 1820–30		
Earl of Liverpool	Tory	1812–27
George Canning	Tory	1827
Viscount Goderich	Tory	1827
Duke of Wellington	Tory	1827–30
William IV, 1830–7		
Earl Grey	Whig	1830–4
Viscount Melbourne	Whig	1834
Sir Robert Peel	Tory	1834–5
Viscount Melbourne	Whig	1835–7
Victoria, 1837–1901		
Viscount Melbourne	Whig	1837–41
Sir Robert Peel	Tory	1841–6
Lord John Russell	Whig	1846–52
Earl of Derby	Tory	1852
Earl of Aberdeen	Peelite	1852–5
Viscount Palmerston	Liberal	1855–8
Earl of Derby	Tory	1858–9
Viscount Palmerston	Liberal	1859–65
Earl Russell	Liberal	1865–6
Earl of Derby	Conservative	1866–8
B. Disraeli	Conservative	1868
W. E. Gladstone	Liberal	1868–74
B. Disraeli	Conservative	1874–80
W. E. Gladstone	Liberal	1880–5
Marquis of Salisbury	Conservative	1885–6
W. E. Gladstone	Liberal	1886
Marquis of Salisbury	Conservative	1886–92
W. E. Gladstone	Liberal	1892–4
Earl of Rosebery	Liberal	1894–5
Marquis of Salisbury	Conservative	1895–1901
Edward VII, 1901–10		
Marquis of Salisbury	Conservative	1901–2
A. J. Balfour	Conservative	1902–5
Sir H. Campbell-Bannerman	Liberal	1905–8
H. H. Asquith	Liberal	1908–10
George V, 1910–36		
H. H. Asquith	Liberal	1910–15
H. H. Asquith	Coalition	1915–16
D. Lloyd George	Coalition	1916–22
A. Bonar Law	Conservative	1922–3
S. Baldwin	Conservative	1923–4
J. R. MacDonald	Labour	1924
S. Baldwin	Conservative	1924–9
J. R. MacDonald	Labour	1929–31
J. R. MacDonald	National	1931–5
S. Baldwin	National	1935–6
Edward VIII, 1936		
George VI, 1936–52		
S. Baldwin	National	1936–7
N. Chamberlain	National	1937–39
N. Chamberlain	War Cabinet	1939
W. S. Churchill	War Cabinet	1940–45
W. S. Churchill	Caretaker	1945
C. R. Attlee	Labour	1945–51
Sir W. S. Churchill	Conservative	1951–2
Elizabeth II, 1952–		
Sir W. S. Churchill	Conservative	1952–5
Sir A. Eden	Conservative	1955–7
H. Macmillan	Conservative	1957–63
Sir A. Douglas-Home	Conservative	1963–4
H. Wilson	Labour	1964–70
E. Heath	Conservative	1970–4
H. Wilson	Labour	1974–6
J. Callaghan	Labour	1976–

PRESIDENTS OF THE UNITED STATES

The terms are for four years; only President F. D. Roosevelt has served more than two terms.

		Party	Served
1.	George Washington	Fed.	1789–97
2.	John Adams	Fed.	1797–1801
3.	Thomas Jefferson	Rep.	1801–9
4.	James Madison	Rep.	1809–17
5.	James Monroe	Rep.	1817–25
6.	John Quincey Adams	Rep.	1825–9
7.	Andrew Jackson	Dem.	1829–37
8.	Martin Van Buren	Dem.	1837–41
9.	William H. Harrison (died in office)	Whig	1841
10.	John Tyler	Whig	1841–5
11.	James K. Polk	Dem.	1845–9
12.	Zachary Taylor (died in office)	Whig	1849–50
13.	Millard Fillmore	Whig	1850–3
14.	Franklin Pierce	Dem.	1853–7
15.	James Buchanan	Dem.	1857–61
16.	Abraham Lincoln (assassinated)	Rep.	1861–5
17.	Andrew Johnson	Rep.	1865–9
18.	Ulysses S. Grant	Rep.	1869–77
19.	Rutherford B. Hayes	Rep.	1877–81
20.	James A. Garfield (assassinated)	Rep.	1881
21.	Chester A. Arthur	Rep.	1881–5
22.	Grover Cleveland	Dem.	1885–9
23.	Benjamin Harrison	Rep.	1889–93
24.	Grover Cleveland	Dem.	1893–7
25.	William McKinley (assassinated)	Rep.	1897–1901
26.	Theodore Roosevelt	Rep.	1901–9
27.	William Howard Taft	Rep.	1909–13
28.	Woodrow Wilson	Dem.	1913–21
29.	Warren G. Harding (died in office)	Rep.	1921–3
30.	Calvin Coolidge	Rep.	1923–9
31.	Herbert C. Hoover	Rep.	1929–33
32.	Franklin D. Roosevelt (died in office)	Dem.	1933–45
33.	Harry S. Truman	Dem.	1945–53
34.	Dwight D. Eisenhower	Rep.	1953–61
35.	John F. Kennedy (assassinated)	Dem.	1961–3
36.	Lyndon B. Johnson	Dem.	1963–69
37.	Richard M. Nixon (resigned)	Rep.	1969–74
38.	Gerald R. Ford	Rep.	1974–6
39.	James Carter	Dem.	1976–

WEIGHTS AND MEASURES

Many kinds of measure now in use in the United Kingdom are gradually being converted from Imperial units to SI units. SI is short for "Système International d'Unités" and it is a system of metric units now coming into international use through the agency of such bodies as the General Conference of the International Bureau of Weights and Measures and the International Organisation for Standardisation (ISO) in whose work Britain participates. Information about SI units is available in booklets published by the British Standards Institution, Sales Branch, 101–113 Pentonville Road, London, N.1.

For a transitional period of some years, Imperial and SI units will be in use simultaneously. Important parts of the two systems are given separately below. A selection of useful conversion factors is on N8.

Unit Symbols Used in the Tables

Unit	Symbol	Unit	Symbol
metre	m	kilogramme	kg
yard	yd	gramme	g
foot	ft	pound	lb
inch	in	ounce	oz
mile	mile	hundredweight	cwt
square metre	m^2	poundal	pdl
square inch	in^2	pound-force	lbf
square mile	$mile^2$	foot pound-force	ft lbf
cubic metre	m^3	calorie	cal
cubic inch	in^3	British thermal unit	Btu
litre	l	horsepower	hp
gallon	gal	tonne	t

I. IMPERIAL WEIGHTS AND MEASURES

Length.

1 nail	= 2¼ in
1 link	= 7·92 in
12 in	= 1 ft
3 ft	= 1 yd
22 yd	= 1 chain
10 chains	= 1 furlong
8 furlongs	= 1 mile = 1760 yd = 5280 ft

Area.

144 in^2	= 1 ft^2
9 ft^2	= 1 yd^2 = 1296 in^2
484 yd^2	= 1 square chain
1210 yd^2	= 1 rood
4 roods	= 1 acre = 4840 yd^2
640 acres	= 1 $mile^2$

Volume.

1728 in^3	= 1 ft^3
27 ft^3	= 1 yd^3

Capacity.

4 gills	= 1 pint
2 pints	= 1 quart
4 quarts	= 1 gallon
2 gallons	= 1 peck
4 pecks	= 1 bushel
8 bushels	= 1 quarter
36 bushels	= 1 chaldron

The gallon, as the capacity standard, is based upon the pound.

1 gal = 277·274 in^3

Weight (Avoirdupois).

1 dram	= 27·343 75 grains
16 drams	= 1 oz = 437·5 grains
16 oz	= 1 lb = 7000 grains
14 lb	= 1 stone
28 lb	= 1 quarter
4 quarters	= 1 cwt = 112 lb
20 cwt	= 1 ton = 2240 lb

Troy Weight.

1 pennyweight	= 24 grains
480 grains	= 1 ounce

The only unit of troy weight which is legal for use in trade in Britain is the ounce Troy, and weighings of precious metal are made in multiples and decimals of this unit.

The term *carat* is not a unit of weight for precious metals, but is used to denote the quality of gold plate, etc., and is a figure indicating the number of 24ths of pure gold in the alloy, *e.g.*, a 9 carat gold ring consists of nine parts of pure gold and fifteen parts of base metals.

Nautical Measures.

1 nautical mile = 6080 ft = 1853·18 m
1 knot = 1 nautical mile per hour = 1·151 mile/h

Note.—In future the international nautical mile of 1852 m will be used.

Note.—The British Pharmaceutical Code and the British National Formulary—the official works of medicinal reference—no longer contain the apothecaries' units of measurement since medicine is now measured in metric units. Prescriptions are in 5 millilitre (ml) units; medicine bottles are in six sizes from 50 to 500 ml.

II. SI UNITS

There are six base SI Units. They are:

Quantity	*Name of Unit*	*Symbol*
length	metre	m
mass	kilogramme	kg
time	second	s
electric current	ampere	A
temperature	kelvin	K
luminous intensity	candela	cd

Derived units are normally stated in terms of the base unit. Examples: the SI units of velocity and density are, respectively, the metre per second (m/s) and the kilogramme per cubic metre (kg/m^3). Some important derived units have well-established names of their own. They are:

Quantity	*Name of SI unit*	*Symbol*	*Expressed in terms of SI base-units or derived units*
frequency	hertz	Hz	1 Hz = 1/s
force	newton	N	1 N = 1 kg m/s^2
work, energy, quantity of heat	joule	J	1 J = 1 N m
power	watt	W	1 W = 1 J/s
quantity of electricity	coulomb	C	1 C = 1 A s
electric potential, potential difference, tension, electromotive force	volt	V	1 V = 1 W/A
electric capacitance	farad	F	1 F = 1 A s/V
electric resistance	ohm	Ω	1 Ω = 1 V/A
flux of magnetic induction, magnetic flux	weber	Wb	1 Wb = 1 V s
magnetic flux density, magnetic induction	tesla	T	1 T = 1 Wb/m^2
inductance	henry	H	1 H = 1 V s/A
luminous flux	lumen	lm	1 lm = 1 cd sr
illumination	lux	lx	= 1 lx 1 lm/m^2

There are special prefixes for forming multiples and sub-multiples of the SI units. These are:

Factor by which the unit is multiplied	*Prefix*	*Symbol*
10^{12}	tera	T
10^9	giga	G
10^6	mega	M
10^3	kilo	k
10^2	hecto	h
10	deca	da
10^{-1}	deci	d
10^{-2}	centi	c
10^{-3}	milli	m
10^{-6}	micro	μ
10^{-9}	nano	n
10^{-12}	pico	p
10^{-15}	femto	f
10^{-18}	atto	a

Examples: one thousandth of a metre is one millimetre (1 mm); one million volts is one megavolt (1 MV). These prefixes are *recommended* but other multiples and sub-multiples will be used when convenient, *e.g.*, the centimetre (cm), the cubic decimetre (dm^3).

The following is a selection of special points to note:

(i) The name litre now means 1 cubic decimetre or $10^{-3}m^3$ and is a measure of volume.

(ii) Days, hours, and minutes are still used to measure time, though some scientists may prefer to use kiloseconds, etc.

(iii) The SI unit of plane angle is the radian (rad), but degrees, minutes and seconds are still used as well. $1° = \frac{\pi}{180}$ rad; 1 rad = 57·295 78° = 57° 17′ 44·81″

(iv) A Celsius temperature, say 15 degrees, is written 15°C; note that 15C would mean 15 coulombs.

(v) The mole (mol) is important in science as a measure of "amount of substance" and may be adopted as a seventh basic SI unit. 1 mol is the amount of substance of a system which contains as many elementary units as there are carbon atoms in 0·012 kg of ^{12}C. The elementary unit must be specified and may be an atom, a molecule, an ion, an electron, etc., or a specified group of such particles.

(vi) The SI unit of area is the square metre (m^2) but the hectare (1 ha $=10^4m^2$) will be the normal unit for land measure where we have previously used the acre. The are (a) $= 10^2m^2$.

(vii) The SI unit of pressure is the newton per square metre (N/m^2), but in some technical fields, notably meteorology, the unit of pressure is the bar which approximates to normal atmospheric pressure; 1 bar = 10^5 N/m^2.

II. SELECTED METRIC EQUIVALENTS FOR IMPERIAL WEIGHTS AND MEASURES

Length.

1 in = 2·54 cm = 0·0254 m
12 in = 1 ft = 30·48 cm = 0·3048 m
3 ft = 1 yd = 0·9144 m
1760 yd = 1 mile = 1609·344 m

Area.

1 in^2 = $6·4516 \times 10^{-4}$m^2
144 in^2 = 1 ft^2 = 0·092 903 0 m^2
9 ft^2 = 1 yd^2 = 0·836 127 m^2
4840 yd^2 = 1 acre = 0·404 68
640 acres = 1 mile^2 = $2·589\ 99 \times 10^6$m^2

Volume.

1 in^3 = $1·638\ 71 \times 10^{-5}$m^3
1 ft^3 = 0·028 316 8 m^3
1 UK gal = 0·004 546 092 m^3

Velocity.

1 ft/s = 0·3048 m/s
1 mile/h = 0·447 04 m/s = $1·6093 \times 10^3$ m/h

Capacity.

1 pint = 0·568 *l* or 10^{-3}m^3
2 pints = 1 quart = 1·136 *l*
4 quarts = 1 gal = 4·546 *l*
8 gal = 1 bushel = 36·37 *l*
8 bushels = 1 quarter = $2·909 \times 10^2$

Weight.

1 oz = 28·35 g
16 oz = 1 lb = 0·453 592 37 kg
14 lb = 1 st = 6·350 kg
112 lb = 1 cwt = 50·80 kg

20 cwt (2240 lb) = 1 long ton = 1016 kg
2000 lb = 1 short ton = 907 kg

Note.—1 tonne (t) = 1000 kg

Density.

1 lb/in^3 = $2·767\ 99 \times 10^4$ kg/m^3
1 lb/ft^3 = 16·0185 kg/m^3
1 lb/UK gal = 99·7764 kg/m^3

Force.

1 pdl = 0·138 255 N
1 lbf = 4·448 22 N

Pressure.

1 lbf/in^2 = 6894·76 N/m^2

Energy (work, heat).

1 ft pdl = 0·042 140 1 J
1 ft lbf = 1·355 82 J
1 cal = 4·1868 J
1 Btu = 1055·06 J

Power.

1 hp = 745 700 W

Temperature.

1 Rankine degree = 1 Fahrenheit degree
= 5/9 Kelvin = 5/9 Celsius degree

(The Rankine scale of absolute temperature was developed from the Fahrenheit scale, exactly as the Kelvin scale was developed from the Celsius scale.)

Note.—Figures printed in bold type are exact. Unit symbols are the same in the singular and the plural and do not carry a full point (as a mark of an abbreviation).

THERMOMETER COMPARISONS

Celsius 100°	Fahrenheit 212°	Celsius 100°	Fahrenheit 212°
95	203	20	68
90	194	15·5	60
85	185	12·8	55
78·9	174	10	50
75	167	7·2	45
70	158	5	41
65	149	1·7	35
60	140	0	32
55	131	− 1·1	30
52·8	127	− 5	23
50	122	− 6·7	20
45	113	− 10	14
42·2	108	− 12·2	10
40	104	− 15	5
36·7	98	− 17·8	0
35	95	− 20	− 4
32·2	90	− 25	− 13
30	86	− 30	− 22
26·7	80	− 35	− 31
25	77	− 40	− 40

To reduce Fahrenheit to Celsius (centigrade), subtract 32 degrees and multiply by 5/9; to reduce Celsius to Fahrenheit, multiply by 9/5 and add 32 degrees.

An alternative method, perhaps easier to remember, is to add 40 to the given figure, multiply by 5/9 (°F to °C) or 9/5 (°C to °F) and subtract 40.

SIZES OF BOUND BOOKS

Standard sizes	Size of trimmed page	
	mm	in
Metric Crown 8vo .	186 × 123	$7\frac{5}{16} \times 4\frac{7}{8}$
Metric Crown 4to .	246 × 189	$9\frac{11}{16} \times 7\frac{7}{16}$
Metric Large Crown . 8vo	198 × 129	$7\frac{13}{16} \times 5\frac{1}{16}$
Metric Demy 8vo .	216 × 138	$8\frac{1}{2} \times 5\frac{7}{16}$
Metric Demy 4to .	276 × 219	$10\frac{7}{8} \times 8\frac{5}{8}$
A5	210 × 148	$8\frac{1}{4} \times 5\frac{13}{16}$
A4	297 × 210	$11\frac{5}{8} \times 8\frac{1}{4}$
Occasional sizes		
Metric Large Crown 4to	258 × 201	$10\frac{3}{16} \times 7\frac{15}{16}$
Medium 8vo . . .	222 × 144	$8\frac{3}{4} \times 5\frac{1}{16}$
Old Royal 8vo . .	246 × 156	$9\frac{11}{16} \times 6\frac{1}{4}$

NATIONAL CURRENCIES

Country	Currency
Albania	Lek
Argentine	Peso
Australia	Dollar
Austria	Schilling
Belgium/Lux.	Franc
Belize	Dollar
Bolivia	Peso Boliviano
Brazil	Cruzeiro
Bulgaria	Lev
Burma	Kyat
Canada	Dollar
Chile	Peso
China	Renminbi
Colombia	Peso
Costa Rica	Colón
Cuba	Peso
Czechoslovakia	Koruna
Denmark	Krone
Dominican Republic	Peso
Ecuador	Sucre
Egypt	Pound
El Salvador	Colón
Ethiopia	Dollar
Finland	Markka
France	Franc
Germany (E.)	Mark
Germany (Fed. Rep.)	D. Mark
Greece	Drachma
Guatemala	Quetzal
Guyana	Dollar
Haiti	Gourde
Honduras Rep.	Lempira
Hong Kong	Dollar
Iceland	Króna
India	Rupee
Indonesia	Rupiah
Iran	Rial
Iraq	Dinar
Israel	Pound
Italy	Lira
Jamaica	Dollar
Japan	Yen
Jordan	Dinar
Kenya	K. Shilling
Lebanon	Pound
Malaysia	Ringgit
Mexico	Peso
Morocco	Dirham
Netherlands	Guilder
New Zealand	Dollar
Nicaragua	Córdoba
Nigeria	Naira
Norway	Krone
Pakistan	Rupee
Panama	Balboa
Paraguay	Guaraní
Peru	Sol
Philippines	Peso
Poland	Zloty
Portugal	Escudo
Romania	Leu
South Africa	Rand
Spain	Peseta
Sri Lanka	Rupee
Sweden	Krona
Switzerland	Franc
Syria	Pound
Tanzania	T. Shilling
Thailand	Baht
Trinidad and Tobago	T.T. Dollar
Tunisia	Dinar
Turkey	Lira
United Arab Emirates	Dirham
United Kingdom	Pound
U.S.A.	Dollar
U.S.S.R.	Rouble
Uruguay	Peso
Venezuela	Bolivar
Yugoslavia	Dinar
Yemen Arab Rep.	Riyal
Yemen. South	Dinar
Zaïre	Zaïre
Zambia	Kwacha

ROMAN NUMERALS

I	1	LXX	70
II	2	LXXX	80
III	3	LXXXVIII	88
IV	4	XC	90
V	5	XCIX	99
VI	6	C	100
VII	7	CX	110
VIII	8	CXI	111
IX	9	CXC	190
X	10	CC	200
XI	11	CCXX	220
XII	12	CCC	300
XIII	13	CCCXX	320
XIV	14	CD	400
XV	15	D	500
XVI	16	DC	600
XVII	17	DCC	700
XVIII	18	DCCC	800
XIX	19	CM	900
XX	20	XM	990
XXX	30	M	1000
XL	40	MD	1500
L	50	MDCCC	1800
LV	55	MCMLXX	1970
LX	60	MM	2000

GREEK ALPHABET

Α	α	Alpha	Ν	ν	nu
Β	β	beta	Ξ	ξ	xi
Γ	γ	gamma	Ο	ο	omicron
Δ	δ	delta	Π	π	pi
Ε	ϵ	epsilon	Ρ	ρ	rho
Ζ	ζ	zeta	Σ	σ	sigma
Η	η	eta	Τ	τ	tau
Θ	θ	theta	Υ	υ	upsilon
Ι	ι	iota	Φ	φ	phi
Κ	κ	kappa	Χ	χ	chi
Λ	λ	lambda	Ψ	ψ	psi
Μ	μ	mu	Ω	ω	omega

RUSSIAN ALPHABET

А а	a	Р р	r
Б б	b	С с	s
В в	v	Т т	t
Г г	g	У у	u
Д д	d	Ф ф	f ph
Е е	e	Х х	kh [1]
Ж ж	zh	Ц ц	ts
З з	z	Ч ч	ch [2]
И и й	i	Ш ш	sh
К к	k	Щ щ	shch [3]
Л л	l	Ы ы	y [4]
М м	m	Э э	e [5]
Н н	n	Ю ю	yu [6]
О о	o	Я я	ya
П п	p	Ѳ ѳ	f

[1] as in "loch".
[2] as in "church".
[3] as in "Ashchurch".
[4] as in "bit".
[5] as in "epic".
[6] as in "you".

BANK AND PUBLIC HOLIDAYS

The number of public holidays in England and Wales comprise at present five bank holidays (New Year's Day, Easter Monday, Spring and Late Summer Holidays at the end of May and August respectively, and Boxing Day), with also two common law holidays (Good Friday and Christmas Day); in Scotland six bank holidays (New Year's Day, January 3, Good Friday, Spring and Late Summer Holidays at the beginning of May and August respectively, and Christmas Day); and in Northern Ireland six bank holidays (New Year's Day, St. Patrick's Day, Easter Monday, Spring Late Summer Holidays at the end of May and August respectively, and Boxing Day) plus two other public holidays (Easter Tuesday and the anniversary of the Battle of the Boyne).

1978 Bank Holidays in England and Wales—Jan. 2, Mar. 27, May 29, Aug. 28, Dec. 26
Northern Ireland—Jan. 2, Mar. 17, Mar. 27, May 29, Aug. 28, Dec. 26
Scotland—Jan. 2, Jan. 3, Mar. 24, May 1, Aug. 7, Dec. 25

Note: There are holidays in lieu of other public holidays which fall at weekends, with effect from Christmas Day and Boxing Day 1976, and New Year's Day, 1977.

THE SEASONS

	1977				1978			
		d	h	m		d	h	m
Vernal Equinox—Spring begins	Mar.	20	17	43	Mar.	20	23	34
Summer Solstice—Summer begins	June	21	12	14	June	21	18	10
Autumnal Equinox—Autumn begins	Sept.	23	03	30	Sept.	23	09	26
Winter Solstice—Winter begins	Dec.	21	23	24	Dec.	22	05	21

(All times are in GMT)

THE COUNTRY CODE

GUARD AGAINST THE RISK OF FIRE. Great damage is done every year to crops, plantations, woodlands, and heaths. A match or cigarette thrown away or a pipe carelessly knocked out, picnic fires not properly put out or lighted near dry crops, can quickly start a blaze.

FASTEN ALL GATES. If animals get out of a field they stray. As a result they may do serious damage to crops, suffer injury on the roads, or eat food that is harmful.

KEEP DOGS UNDER CONTROL. Animals are easily frightened, even by small, playful dogs. Stillbirths may be the result.

KEEP TO THE PATHS ACROSS FARM LAND. Crops are damaged by treading; flattened crops are difficult to harvest. Grass is a valuable crop.

AVOID DAMAGING FENCES, HEDGES, AND WALLS. If these are damaged, gaps will be caused. Where a man goes, an animal may follow.

LEAVE NO LITTER. Litter is not just unsightly, but often a danger as well. Broken glass and tins may injure animals and harm machinery.

SAFEGUARD WATER SUPPLIES. Countrymen often depend on wells and streams for water for themselves and for their animals.

PROTECT WILD LIFE, PLANTS, AND TREES. Wild animals should not be disturbed, plants uprooted, or trees treated roughly.

GO CAREFULLY ON COUNTRY ROADS. If there is no footpath, walkers are generally safer on the right, facing on-coming traffic. Care and patience are needed by motorists when passing farm animals.

RESPECT THE LIFE OF THE COUNTRYSIDE. Many of the machines and much of the business stock on which the farmer depends for his livelihood have to be kept in the open. Take care not to damage them.

THE BEAUFORT SCALE OF WIND FORCE

Beaufort number	*Wind*	*Effect on land*	*Speed*	
			mile/h	*Knots*
0	Calm	Smoke rises vertically	Less than 1	Less than 1
1	Light air	Direction shown by smoke but not by wind vanes	1–3	1–3
2	Light breeze	Wind felt on face; leaves rustle; wind vanes move	4–7	4–6
3	Gentle breeze	Leaves and twigs in motion; wind extends light flag	8–12	7–10
4	Moderate breeze	Raises dust, loose paper and moves small branches	13–18	11–16
5	Fresh breeze	Small trees in leaf begin to sway	19–24	17–21
6	Strong breeze	Large branches in motion; whistling in telegraph wires; difficulty with umbrellas	25–31	22–27
7	Moderate gale	Whole trees in motion; difficult to walk against wind	32–38	28–33
8	Fresh gale	Twigs break off trees; progress impeded	39–46	34–40
9	Strong gale	Slight structural damage occurs; chimney pots and slates blown off	47–54	41–47
10	Whole gale	Trees uprooted and considerable structural damage	55–63	48–56
11	Storm	Widespread damage, seldom experienced in England	64–75	57–65
12	Hurricane	Winds of this force only encountered in tropical revolving storms	Above 75	Above 65

SUNRISE AND SUNSET FOR LONDON, 1978

		Rise h m	Set h m			Rise h m	Set h m			Rise h m	Set h m
January	1	08 06	16 02	May	7	05 22	20 33	September	3	06 16	19 43
	8	08 05	16 09		14	05 11	20 44		10	06 27	19 28
	15	08 00	16 21		21	05 01	20 54		17	06 38	19 12
	22	07 53	16 32		28	04 53	21 03		24	06 49	18 55
	29	07 44	16 44	June	4	04 47	21 11	October	1	07 01	18 39
February	5	07 33	16 57		11	04 44	21 17		8	07 12	18 24
	12	07 21	17 10		18	04 43	21 21		15	07 24	18 08
	19	07 08	17 22		25	04 44	21 22		22	07 36	17 54
	26	06 53	17 35						29	06 48	16 40
March	5	06 38	17 47	July	2	04 48	21 21	November	5	07 01	16 27
	12	06 23	17 59		9	04 54	21 17		12	07 13	16 16
	19	07 07	19 11		16	05 02	21 11		19	07 25	16 07
	26	06 51	19 23		23	05 11	21 03		26	07 36	15 59
					30	05 21	20 52				
April	2	06 35	19 35					December	3	07 46	15 54
	9	06 19	19 47	August	6	05 31	20 41		10	07 55	15 52
	16	06 04	19 58		13	05 42	20 28		17	08 01	15 52
	23	05 49	20 10		20	05 53	20 14		24	08 05	15 55
	30	05 35	20 22		27	06 04	19 59		31	08 06	16 01

Note: These times are in GMT, except between 0200 on Mar. 19 and 0200 on Oct. 29, when the times are in BST. (1 hour in advance of GMT)

PHASES OF THE MOON, 1978

New Moon	d h m	First Quarter	d h m	Full Moon	d h m	Last Quarter	d h m
Dec.	10 17 33	Dec.	17 10 37	Dec.	25 12 49	Jan.	2 12 07
Jan.	9 04 00	Jan.	16 03 03	Jan.	24 07 55	Jan.	31 23 51
Feb.	7 14 54	Feb.	14 22 11	Feb.	23 01 26	Mar.	2 08 34
Mar.	9 02 36	Mar.	16 18 21	Mar.	24 16 20	Mar.	31 15 11
Apr.	7 15 15	Apr.	15 13 56	Apr.	23 04 11	Apr.	29 21 02
May	7 04 47	May	15 07 40	May	22 13 17	May	29 03 30
June	5 19 01	June	13 22 44	June	20 20 30	June	27 11 44
July	5 09 50	July	13 10 49	July	20 03 05	July	26 22 31
Aug.	4 01 01	Aug.	11 20 06	Aug.	18 10 14	Aug.	25 12 18
Sept.	2 16 09	Sept.	10 03 20	Sept.	16 19 01	Sept.	24 05 07
Oct.	2 06 41	Oct.	9 09 38	Oct.	16 06 09	Oct.	24 00 34
Oct.	31 20 06	Nov.	7 16 18	Nov.	14 20 00	Nov.	22 21 24
Nov.	30 08 19	Dec.	7 00 34	Dec.	14 12 31	Dec.	22 17 41
Dec.	29 19 36	Jan.	5 11 15	Jan.	13 07 09	Jan.	21 11 23

Note: All times are in GMT.

ECLIPSES 1978

1. A total eclipse of the Moon on March 24, visible from the extreme north-western part of North America, most of the Pacific Ocean, New Zealand, Australia, part of Antarctica, Asia, the Indian Ocean, Africa (except the extreme western part) and Europe (except the western part). The eclipse begins at 14h 33m and ends at 18h 12m. Totality lasts from 15h 37m to 17h 08m.

2. A partial eclipse of the Sun on April 7, visible from the southern part of South America, the southern part of the Atlantic Ocean, part of Antarctica and Southern Africa. The eclipse begins at 13h 02m and ends at 17h 04m. At the time of maximum eclipse 0.79 of the Sun's diameter is obscured.

3. A total eclipse of the Moon on September 16, visible from the western half of the Pacific Ocean, New Zealand, Australia, part of Antarctica, Asia, the Indian Ocean, Africa, Europe (including the British Isles), the eastern part of the Atlantic Ocean and the extreme north-eastern part of South America. The eclipse begins at 17h 20m and ends at 20h 48m. Totality lasts from 18h 24m to 19h 44m.

4. A partial eclipse of the Sun on October 2, visible from north-eastern Europe, the eastern half of the Arctic Ocean, Asia except the southern part and the north-western part of the Pacific Ocean. The eclipse begins at 04h 31m and ends at 08h 25m. At the time of maximum eclipse 0.69 of the Sun's diameter is obscured.

Source: H.M. Nautical Almanac Office, for the Science Research Council.

UNIVERSITY DEGREES—COLOURS OF HOODS

Aberdeen

M.A.	Black silk, lined with white silk.
M.Litt.	White silk, lined with violet silk.
D.Litt.	Scarlet cloth, lined with white silk.
Ph.D.	Scarlet cloth lined with black ribbed silk the ribs running horizontally.
B.Ed.	Black silk, lined with orange silk.
M.Ed.	White silk, lined with orange silk.
B.Sc.	Black silk, lined with green silk.
B.Sc.Agr.	Black silk, edged with green silk.
B.Sc.For.	Black silk, edged with waved green silk.
B.Sc.Eng.	Black silk edged with green silk and bordered inside, within the green edging, with white cloth (½″).
M.Sc.	White silk, lined with green silk.
D.Sc.	Scarlet cloth, lined with green silk.
B.D.	Black silk, lined with purple silk, and bordered inside with white silk (1″).
M.Th.	White silk, lined with purple silk.
D.D.	Scarlet cloth, lined with purple silk.
LL.B.	Black silk, lined with pale blue silk.
LL.D.	Scarlet cloth, lined with pale blue silk.
M.B., Ch.B.	Black silk, lined with crimson silk.
M.D.	Scarlet cloth, lined with crimson silk.
Ch.M.	White silk, lined with crimson silk.
D.Mus	Scarlet cloth, lined with light brown silk.
M.Mus.	White silk, lined with light brown silk.
B.Med.Bo.	Black silk, lined with crimson silk, and bordered inside with white cloth ½″ wide.

Note.—All the hoods of this University are of uniform pear shape of a cloth or silk foundation and lined or edged with the colour peculiar to the Faculty or Degree.

Aston (Birmingham)

B.Sc.	Black, faced with 3″ red silk interwoven with University crest.
M.Sc.	Like B.Sc. but fully lined.
M.Phil.	Like B.Sc. but in blue and fully lined.
Ph.D.	University red, faced as for B.Sc.
D.Sc.	Like Ph.D. but in gold and fully lined.

Bath

B.Sc. B.Pharm.	Old-gold lined light olive-green taffeta.
B.Arch.	Old-gold lined light olive-green taffeta with medium-crimson edging.
B.A.	Old-gold lined light olive-green taffeta with yellow edging.
B.Ed.	Old-gold lined light olive-green taffeta with orange edging.
M.Sc. M.Pharm.	Old-gold lined pale-blue taffeta.
M.Arch.	Old-gold lined pale-blue taffeta with medium-crimson edging.
M.A.	Old-gold lined pale-blue taffeta with yellow edging.
M.Ed.	Old-gold lined pale-blue taffeta with orange edging.
Ph.D.	Old-gold lined medium-crimson taffeta.
D.Sc.	Old-gold lined scarlet taffeta.
LL.D.	Old-gold lined scarlet taffeta with white edging.
D.Litt.	Old-gold lined scarlet taffeta with yellow edging.

Belfast, The Queen's University

B.A.	Black silk/stuff, rabbit-skin lining.
M.A.	Black silk, blue silk lining.
B.Ed.	Black silk, mauve silk lining.
M.Ed.	Red silk, mauve silk lining.
B.Mus.	Blue silk/stuff, white silk lining.
D.Lit.	Scarlet cloth, white silk lining.
D.Mus.	Scarlet cloth, blue silk lining.
B.Sc.	Black silk stuff, light green silk lining.
M.Sc.	Red silk, light green silk lining.
D.Sc.	Scarlet cloth, light green silk lining.
LL.B.	Black silk/stuff, pink silk lining.
LL.M.	Red silk, pink silk lining.
LL.D.	Scarlet cloth, pink silk lining.
B.Sc.(Econ.)	Black silk/stuff, light rose pink silk lining.
M.Sc.(Econ.)	Red silk, light rose pink silk lining.
D.Sc.(Econ.)	Scarlet cloth, light rose pink silk lining.
B.S.Sc.	Black silk/stuff, dark rose pink lining.
M.S.Sc.	Red silk, dark rose pink silk lining.
M.B.A.	Red silk, dark yellow silk lining.
M.B.B.Ch., B.A.O.	Black silk/stuff, scarlet silk lining.
B.D.S.	Black silk/stuff, dove-grey silk lining.
M.D.	Scarlet cloth, scarlet silk lining.
M.Ch.	Red silk, scarlet silk lining.
M.A.O.	Red silk, purple silk lining.
M.D.S.	Red silk, dove-grey silk lining.
B.Sc.(App. Sc. and Tech.	Black silk/stuff, dark green lining.
M.Sc.(App. Sc. and Tech.)	Red silk, dark green silk lining.
D.Sc.(App. Sc. and Tech.)	Scarlet cloth, dark green silk lining and facings.
B.Agr.	Black silk/stuff, light primrose silk lining.
M.Agr.	Red silk, light primrose silk lining.
B.D.	Black silk, white silk lining.
M.Th.	Red silk, white silk lining.
D.D.	Scarlet cloth, black silk lining.
Ph.D.	Scarlet cloth, violet silk lining.
B.L.S.	Black silk/stuff, dark blue silk lining.
M.L.S.	Red silk, dark blue silk lining.
B.Sc.(Food Science)	Black silk/stuff, dark primrose silk lining.
M.Sc.(Food Science)	Red silk, dark primrose silk lining.
B.Ed.	Black silk, mauve silk lining.

Note:—Bachelors' and Masters' hoods are of special simple shape; Doctors' of the full (Cambridge) shape. All hoods have blue watered-silk binding, except the B.A., which has fur edging.

Birmingham

B.Sc.	Black, edged with silver-grey watered silk.
M.Sc.	Black, lined with silver-grey watered silk.
D.Sc.	Scarlet, lined with silver-grey watered silk.
Ph.D.	Crimson, lined with silver-grey watered silk.
B.A.	Black, edged with electric-blue watered silk.
M.A.	Black, lined with electric-blue watered silk.
B.Ed.	Black, edged with primrose-yellow watered silk.
M.Ed.	Black, lined with primrose-yellow watered silk.
D.Litt.	Scarlet, lined with electric-blue watered silk.
Ph.D.	Crimson, lined with electric-blue watered silk.
B.Mus.	Black, edged with tangerine watered silk.
D.Mus.	Scarlet, lined with tangerine watered silk.
B.D.	Black, edged with cobalt-blue watered silk.
D.D.	Scarlet, lined with cobalt-blue watered silk.
M.B., Ch.B.	Black, edged with cardinal watered silk.
M.D.	Scarlet, lined with cardinal watered silk.
Ph.D.	Crimson, lined with cardinal watered silk.
B.D.S.	Black, edged with dark-red (Grenat) watered silk.
D.D.S.	Scarlet, lined with dark-red (Grenat) watered silk.
B.Com.	Black, edged with terracotta watered silk.
B.Soc.Sc.	Black, edged with terracotta watered silk and bound with grey silk at top edge.
M.Com.	Black, lined with terracotta watered silk.
M.Soc.Sc.	Black, lined with terracotta watered silk, edged with grey watered silk.
Ph.D.	Crimson, lined with terracotta watered silk.
D.Soc.Sc.	Scarlet, lined with terracotta watered silk and bound with grey silk at top edge.
LL.B.	Black, edged with bronze-green watered silk.
LL.M.	Black, lined with bronze-green watered silk.
M.Jur.	Black, lined with bronze-green watered silk, edged with grey watered silk.
Ph.D.	Crimson, lined with bronze-green watered silk.
LL.D.	Scarlet, lined with bronze-green watered silk.
B.Sc. B.Com.	Black, edged with silver-grey watered silk, bound with terracotta watered silk at top edge.
B.Phil.(Ed.)	Black, lined with primrose-yellow watered silk, bound with white silk at top edge.
B.Ed.	Black, edged with primrose-yellow watered silk.

Bradford

Bachelors (B.A., B.Sc., B.Tech.)	Black, edged 3″ saffron.
Masters	Black, edged and fully lined saffron.
Ph.D.	Scarlet, fully lined saffron.
Higher Doctorates:	
Technology	Scarlet, fully lined saffron, edged on inside 1½″ violet.
Science	Scarlet, fully lined saffron, edged on inside 1½″ blue.
Literature	Scarlet, fully lined saffron, edged on inside 1½″ white.

Bristol

B.Ed., B.A., M.A., M.Ed., M.Mus., LL.B., LL.M., LL.D., M.B., Ch.B., Ch.M., M.D., D.Mus., Ph.D., B.Sc., M.Sc., D.Sc., M.Litt., D.Litt., B.D.S., M.D.S., B.Arch., B.V.Sc.

All hoods are of the Cambridge pattern and made of University red stuff or silk. Bachelors' hoods are lined as far as the visible parts are concerned with silk of a lighter shade of University red. Hoods of Bachelors of Medicine and Surgery are fully lined with the lighter shade of University red, the lining bound at the edge with ¾″ white silk. Hoods of Bachelors of Law are fully lined with the lighter shade of University red, the lining bound at the edge with ¾″ violet silk. Masters' hoods are fully lined with white silk. Hoods of Doctors of Philosophy are fully lined with dark violet silk. Hoods of Doctors in particular faculties are fully lined with salmon-coloured silk.

Brunel Middlesex

Bachelor	Black, lined white and faced inside 1¼″ with Brunel blue velvet, reversed band showing blue in front.
Master	Brunel blue, lined silver and faced inside 2½″ with Brunel blue velvet.
Ph.D.	Mushroom, lined and edged Cardinal red, faced inside 3½″ with Brunel blue velvet.
D.Tech. and D.U.	Cardinal red, lined and edged gold and faced 4½″ with Brunel blue velvet.

Note:—Bachelors' hoods are of a special simple shape, Masters' and Doctors' of the Cambridge shape.

Cambridge

D.D.	Scarlet cloth lined with dove-coloured silk, that is silk of a turquoise-blue shot with rose-pink.
LL.D.	Scarlet cloth lined with light-cherry silk.
M.D.	Scarlet cloth lined with mid-cherry silk.
Sc.D.	Scarlet cloth lined with pink silk shot with light blue.
Litt.D.	Scarlet cloth lined with scarlet silk to match the cloth.
Mus.D.	Cream damask lined with dark-cherry satin.
B.D.	Black corded silk lined with black silk.
Ph.D.	Black corded silk lined with scarlet cloth.
M.Chir.	Black corded silk lined mid-cherry silk.
M.A.	Black corded silk lined with white silk.
LL.M.	Black corded silk lined light-cherry silk.
Mus.M.	Black corded silk lined dark-cherry satin.
M.Sc.	Black cloth lined pink silk shot light blue.
M.Litt.	Black cloth lined with scarlet silk.
B.Ed.	Black stuff, part-lined with blue silk and an edging of white fur, the tippet edged with white fur.
M.B.	Mid-cherry silk part-lined with white fur, the tippet edged with white fur.
B.Chir.	Mid-cherry silk part-lined with white fur but with no fur edging to the tippet.
B.A.	Black stuff, part-lined with white fur, the tippet edged with white fur (or black stuff, part-lined with white, the tippet edged with white).
LL.B.	Light-cherry silk part-lined with white fur, the tippet edged with white fur.
Mus.B.	Dark-cherry satin part-lined with white fur, the tippet edged with white fur.
Vet.M.B.	Mid-cherry silk part-lined white fur, with white fur edging (2″) to the tippet.

Note:—The neckband of the hood is of the outer colour, with no edging of the lining material. The corners of tippets are square. All hoods are of the full shape.

The City (London)

B.Sc.	Maroon cloth, lined gold taffeta, with discipline colour neckband.
M.Sc.	Maroon silk, lined and cape edged with gold taffeta, with discipline colour neckband.
M.Phil.	Maroon silk outside, edged with ½″ gold taffeta, with discipline colour neckband.
Ph.D.	Maroon cloth, lined half maroon and half gold taffeta, with discipline colour neckband.
D.Litt.	Cardinal red cloth, lined half maroon and half gold taffeta, with gold neckband.
D.Sc.	Cardinal red cloth, lined half maroon and half gold taffeta, with grey neckband.

Disciplines: Engineering Blue.
Science Grey.
Management, Social Science } Green.

Note:—Bachelors' hoods are of the simple shape, Masters and Doctors' of the full shape.

Dundee

M.D.	Stewart blue, cherry lining.
Ch.M.	Black, imperial purple lining.
M.B., Ch.B.	Black, cherry lining, white fur edging.
M.M.Sc.	Black, clover lining.
B.M.Sc.	Black, clover lining, white fur edging.
D.D.Sc.	Stewart blue, ruby lining.
M.D.S.	Black, ruby lining.
B.D.S.	Black, ruby lining, white fur edging.
D.Sc.	Stewart blue, buttercup-yellow lining.
M.Sc.	Black, buttercup-yellow lining.
B.Sc.	Black, buttercup-yellow lining, white fur edging.
LL.D.	Stewart blue, old-gold lining.
LL.M.	Black, old-gold lining.
LL.B.	Black, old-gold lining, white fur edging.
D.Sc. (Eng. & App. Sc.)	Stewart blue, powder-blue lining.
M.Sc. (Eng. & App. Sc.).	Black, powder-blue lining.
B.Sc. (Eng. & App. Sc.).	Black, powder-blue lining, white fur edging.
D.Litt.	Stewart blue, smalt-blue lining.
M.A. (Soc. Sc. & Letters)	Black, tartan-green lining.
M.A. (Soc. Admin.).	Black, chartreuse-green lining.
Ph.D.	Stewart blue, eggshell-blue lining.
B.Phil.	Black, eggshell-blue lining, white fur edging.
M.Ed.	Black, tuscan-yellow lining.
B.Ed.	Black, tuscan-yellow lining, white fur edging.
B.Arch.	Black, heliotrope lining, white fur edging.
B.Sc. (Arch.) or (Envl. Studs.) or (Town and Regl. Planning).	Black, gault-grey lining, white fur edging.

Note:—Hoods have a cowl without liripipe, the cape being oblong with rounded bottom corners. All are in silk ottoman.

Durham

B.A.	Black, trimmed white fur.
B.D.	Black, lined black.
D.D.	Scarlet, lined palatinate purple.
B.C.L.	Palatinate purple, bound white fur.
D.C.L. (awarded as an Honorary degree)	Scarlet, lined white.
B.Mus.	Palatinate purple, bound brocaded white silk 1″ wide.
M Mus.	Black, lined white brocade, bound palatinate purple.
D.Mus.	Brocaded white satin, lined palatinate purple.
Ph.D.	Scarlet, lined scarlet, bound palatinate purple 1″ wide.
B.Sc.	Palatinate purple, bound white fur, edged scarlet ½″ wide.
M.Sc.	Black, lined palatinate purple, bound scarlet ½″ wide.
D.Sc.	Palatinate purple, lined scarlet.
M.Litt.	Black, lined old gold.
D.Litt.	Scarlet, lined old gold.
B.Ed.	Black, edged palatinate purple, trimmed white fur.

M.Ed.	Black, lined white, edged palatinate 1″ wide.
M.Phil.	Black, lined scarlet, bound palatinate purple ½″ wide.

Note:—Palatinate purple silk, cloth, or cassimere is peculiar to this University; it is in fact a soft lilac shade.

East Anglia

B.A.	Blue with 6″ coral outside lining in one fold.
B.Sc.	Blue with 6″ spectrum-green outside lining in one fold.
B.Phil.	Blue with 6″ red outside lining in one fold.
M.A.	Blue with coral outside lining in folds.
M.Sc.	Blue with spectrum-green outside lining in folds.
M.Mus.	Blue with Beaton-pink outside lining in folds.
M.Phil.	Blue with red outside lining in folds.
Ph.D.	Guardsman red with facings same colour.
D.Litt.	Blue with coral outside lining, draped.
D.Mus.	Blue with Beaton-pink outside lining, draped.
D.Sc.	Blue with spectrum-green outside lining, draped.
D.C.L.	Blue with crocus outside lining, draped.

Edinburgh

B.Arch.	Black silk, lined with orange-brown silk, and edged with white fur.
B.Com.	Black silk, lined with pale primrose yellow silk, and edged with white fur.
B.D.	Black silk, lined with purple silk, and bordered with white fur.
B.D.S.	Black stuff, lined crimson silk bordered ivory poplin 3″ broad, edged white fur showing 3″ crimson silk at front of neckband.
B.Ed.	Black silk, lined with pale blue silk, and edged with white fur.
B.Litt.	Black silk, lined with royal blue silk shot with maize-colour, bordered with ivory poplin 3″ broad, edged with white fur showing 3″ royal blue silk.
B.Mus.	Scarlet silk, with white silk lining, and edged with white fur.
B.Sc.	Black silk, lined with green silk, and bordered with white fur.
B.Sc.(Med.Sc.).	As B.Sc.
B.Sc.(Soc.Sc.).	Black silk, lined with deep turquoise silk and edged with white fur.
B.V.M. & S.	Black silk, lined maroon silk bordered golden yellow 3″ broad, edged white fur.
Ch.M.	Black velvet, lined with golden silk.
D.D.	Black cloth, with appended cape, lined and faced with purple silk.
D.D.S.	Black silk, lined with crimson silk bordered with white silk 3″ broad.
D.Litt.	Black cloth, lined with royal blue silk shot with maize-colour.
D.Mus.	Rich scarlet cloth, lined with rich white corded silk.
D.Sc.	Black cloth, lined with green silk.
D.Sc.Soc.Sci.	Black cloth, lined with deep turquoise silk.
D.V.M. & S.	Black silk, lined with maroon silk bordered with golden yellow 3″ broad.
LL.B.	Black silk, lined with blue silk, and bordered with white fur.
LL.M.	Black silk. lined with blue silk.
LL.D.	Black cloth, with appended cape, lined and faced with blue silk.
M.A.	Black silk, lined with white silk.
M.A.(Religious Studs.)	Black silk, lined with white silk, bordered with purple 3″ broad.
M.Arch.	Black silk, lined with orange-brown silk.
M.B., Ch.B.	Black silk, lined with crimson silk bordered with white fur.
M.D.	Black silk, with appended cape, lined and faced with crimson silk.
M.Ed.	Black silk, lined with pale blue silk.
M.Litt.	Black silk, lined with royal blue silk shot with maize colour bordered with ivory poplin 3″ broad and showing 3″ of royal blue silk.
M.Mus.	Scarlet silk lined with white silk.
M.Phil.	Black silk, lined with silver silk, bordered with blue silk shot with brown 3″ broad.
M.Sc.	Black silk, lined white silk bordered green silk 3″ broad, showing 3″ green silk at front of neckband.
M.Theol.	Black silk, lined with purple silk bordered with ivory poplin 3″ broad and showing 3″ of purple silk at front of neckband.
Ph.D.	Black cloth, lined blue silk shot brown.

Essex

B.A.	Black, lined University red taffeta.
M.A. / M.Sc.	Black, lined University red, faced 1½″ inside with white.
M.Phil.	Black, lined University red, faced 3″ inside with white.
Ph.D.	University red, lined maroon taffeta.
Hon. Doctors	University red silk, lined and edged with white, faced with 2″ black ribbon on the inside ½″ from the edge.

Note:—Bachelor hood is of simple shape; other hoods are of full shape.

Exeter

B.A.	Dove grey cloth edged Faculty colour silk.
M.A.	Dove grey cloth lined Faculty colour silk.
D.Litt.	Scarlet superfine cloth lined dove grey cloth, edged with Faculty colour.
LL.B.	Dove grey cloth edged Faculty colour silk.
LL.M.	Dove grey cloth lined Faculty colour silk.
LL.D.	Scarlet superfine cloth lined dove grey, edged with Faculty colour.
B.Sc.	Dove grey cloth edged Faculty colour silk.
M.Sc.	Dove grey cloth lined Faculty colour silk.
D.Sc.	Scarlet superfine cloth lined dove grey, edged with Faculty colour.
B.A. (Social Studies).	Dove grey cloth edged Faculty colour silk.
M.A. (Social Studies).	Dove grey cloth lined Faculty colour silk.
Ph.D. (all Faculties).	Dove grey cloth lined with scarlet.
B.Phil.	Dove grey cloth edged Faculty colour silk, with thin white cord sewn to leading edge of hood, edging the Faculty colour.

The Faculty colours are:—

Arts	Kingfisher blue.
Education	Ultramarine blue.
Law	Purple.
Science and Applied Science	Turquoise blue.
Social Studies	Dark blue.

Note:—All bachelors have theological college style hoods unlined, all the seams show, and the hood proper is merely edged with the Faculty colour 2″ both inside and outside the cowl portion. All Doctors' hoods (incl. Ph.D.) are very heavy, being made of cloth and fully lined with cloth—no silk. All hoods are of the full (Cambridge) shape.

Glasgow

M.A.	Black, lined and edged purple silk (colour of bell heather, *Erica cinerea*).
M.Litt. / M.Phil.	Black, lined and edged white silk.
D.Litt.	Scarlet, lined purple silk.
B.Mus.	Black, lined azure blue silk, bordered scarlet cord.
D.Mus.	Black, lined azure blue silk.
B.Ed.	Black, lined blue silk (colour of bluebell of Scotland, *Campanula rotundifolia*), bordered scarlet cord.
M.Ed.	Black, lined and edged blue silk (colour of bluebell of Scotland, *Campanula rotundifolia*).
B.Arch.	Black, lined lime-coloured silk (colour of the lime flower, *Tilia europaea*), bordered scarlet cord.
B.D.	Black, lined light cherry silk, bordered scarlet cord.
M.Th.	Black, lined and edged light cherry silk.
D.D.	Scarlet, lined white silk.
B.L.	Black, bordered on inside venetian red silk.
LL.B.	Black, lined venetian red silk, bordered scarlet cord.
LL.M.	Black, lined and edged venetian red silk.
LL.D.	Scarlet, lined venetian red silk.
B.Acc.	Black, lined slate-grey silk, bordered scarlet cord.
M.Acc.	Black, lined and edged slate-grey silk.
M.B., Ch.B.	Black, lined scarlet silk, bordered scarlet cord.
Ch.M.	Black, lined and edged scarlet silk.
M.D.	Scarlet, lined scarlet silk.
B.D.S.	Black, lined emerald-green silk, bordered scarlet cord.
M.D.S.	Black, lined and edged emerald-green silk.
D.D.Sc.	Scarlet, lined emerald-green silk.
B.Sc.	Black, lined gold-coloured silk (colour of whin blossom, *Ulex europaeus*), bordered scarlet cord.
M.Sc.	Black, lined and edged gold-coloured silk.
D.Sc.	Scarlet, lined gold-coloured silk.
M.Eng.	Black, lined and edged gold-coloured silk.
B.V.M.S.	Black, lined terracotta silk, bordered scarlet cord.

M.V.M.	Black, lined and edged terracotta silk.
D.V.M. D.V.S.	Scarlet, lined terracotta silk.
Ph.D.	Black, lined and edged crimson silk.
M.Admin.	Black, lined and edged orange silk (colour of Slender St. John's Wort, *Hypericum pulchrum*).

Note:—All hoods are of the full shape. Bachelors who are also Masters may wear Bachelors' hoods of silk.

Heriot-Watt (Edinburgh)

Science	
B.Sc.	Black, lined light blue, edged 25 mm gold.
M.Sc.	Black, lined light blue.
Ph.D.	Magenta, lined white.
D.Sc.	Light blue, lined white.
Engineering	
B.Sc.	Black, lined dark blue, edged 25 mm gold.
M.Sc.	Black, lined dark blue.
M.Eng.	Black, lined dark blue, edged 25 mm white.
Ph.D.	Magenta, lined white.
D.Sc.	Dark blue, lined white.
Economic and Social Studies	
B.A.	Black, lined purple, edged 25 mm gold.
M.Litt.	Black, lined purple.
M.Admin.	Black, lined purple, edged 25 mm white.
Ph.D.	Magenta, lined white.
D.Litt.	Purple, lined white.
Environmental Studies	
B.Sc.	Black, lined red, edged 25 mm gold.
B.Arch.	Black, lined red, edged gold, 25 mm from edge.
B.A.	Black, lined red, edged gold, 50 mm from edge.
M.Sc.	Black, lined red.
Ph.D.	Magenta, lined white.
D.Sc./D.Litt.	Red, lined white.

Hull

B.A.
M.A.
D.Litt.
B.D.
D.D.
LL.B.
LL.M.
LL.D.
B.Mus.
M.Mus.
D.Mus.
B.Sc.
M.Sc.
D.Sc.
B.Sc.(Econ.)
M.Sc.(Econ.)
D.Sc.(Econ.)
B.Ed.
M.Ed.
B.Phil. (in faculties of Arts, Social Sciences, and Law)
Ph.D. (in all Faculties)

All hoods are lined throughout with the University silk, a turquoise blue taffeta. All Bachelors' hoods (other than B.D. and B.Phil.) are of black ribbed rayon, of the improved Oxford Burgon shape. The B.D. is of black superfine cloth of the same shape as the Doctors'. The Doctors' hoods are of the improved Oxford Doctors' shape with semi-circular cape. The Ph.D. is of claret coloured cloth and the D.Mus. of cream figured damask silk; all the other Doctors' hoods are of scarlet superfine cloth. The necks of all hoods are cut in one piece with a single central seam and no neck bands are let in. Edging of all hoods is forbidden except that Masters' hoods are ordered to be edged ″ with the lining silk (turquoise blue) round the cape portion only: all Masters' hoods are of the London shape, with well-rounded cape.

Keele

Bachelor of Arts, Bachelor of Social Science and Bachelor of Science	Black, faced inside with gold, top edge piped University red.
Bachelor of Education	Black, faced inside with silver, top edge piped University red.
Master	Black silk, lined University red and pipes gold.
Doctor of Philosophy	Gold cloth, lined University Red.
Doctor	Purple cloth, lined University red, piped gold.

Note:—All hoods are of the full shape.

Kent at Canterbury

Bachelors	Silver.
Masters	Gold.
Ph.D.	Cardinal red.
Higher Doctorates	Scarlet.
D.C.L.	Scarlet.

Faculty Colours:	Natural Sciences—Purple.
	Social Sciences—Grey.
	Humanities—Green.
	D.C.L.—Black.

Note:—All hoods are of the special University shape i.e., flat cape effect, with the faculty denoted by a centre "V" shape panel of velvet.

Lancaster

B.A.	Black, lined with grey taffeta with ½″ inside edging of red taffeta.
B.Ed.	Similar to the B.A. hood but with ½″ white ribbon sewn inside quarter of inch from red edging.
M.A.	Black, lined with red taffeta with 1½″ grey border.
M.Litt.	Black, lined with red taffeta with 1½″ blue taffeta border.
B.Sc.	Similar to the B.A. hood but with ½″ gold ribbon sewn inside quarter of inch from red edging.
M.Sc.	Black, lined with red taffeta with 1½″ gold taffeta border.
Ph.D.	Red, lined with red taffeta.
D.Litt.	Red, lined with blue taffeta.
D.Sc.	Red, lined with gold taffeta.
LL.D.	Red, lined with grey taffeta.
D.Mus.	Red, lined with red damask.

Note:—The B.A. hood is of the simple shape; all other hoods are of the full shape.

Leeds

B.A.	Dark green.
B.Mus.	Dark green with 1″ band white silk.
B.D.	Dark green with white lining and band, with 1″ scarlet laid on the white silk.
B.Com.	Light green lined dark green.
B.Ed.	Dark green with 1″ band light green.
LL.B.	Light green.
B.Sc.	Middle green.
M.B., Ch.B.	Dark green lined light green.
M.A.	Dark green with white lining.
M.Ed.	Dark green with white lining and band, with 1″ middle-green laid on the white silk.
M.Com.	Light green with white lining and band, with 1″ dark green laid on the white silk.
LL.M.	Light green with white lining.
M.Sc.	Middle green with white lining.
M.Phil.	Black stuff on silk lined with middle green with narrow binding of scarlet.
B.Ch.D.	Dark green lined middle green.
Ch.M.	Dark green with white lining, edged light green.
M.Ch.D.	Dark green lined with white, edged middle green.
Ph.D.	Green lined with green with narrow bindings of scarlet.
D.D.	Scarlet lined with dark green with white binding.
D.Mus.	Scarlet lined dark green with 1″ band white watered silk laid on the green 1″ from edge.
Doctors of Letters, Laws, Science and Medicine	Scarlet lined with green of the shade/shades appropriate to the faculty.

Note:—All hoods are of the single or Oxford pattern and hoods of Bachelors are lined.

Leicester

B.A.	Red, lined with silver grey.
B.Sc.	Red, lined with royal blue.
LL.B	Red, lined with black.
M.A.	Red, lined with silver grey.
M.Sc.	Red, lined with royal blue.
M.Ed.	Red, lined with tartan green.
Ph.D.	Red, lined with a watered taffeta of lighter shade.
D.Litt.	Silver grey, lined red.
D.Sc.	Royal blue, lined red.
LL.D.	Black, lined red.
B.Ed.	Red, lined tartan green.
D.Mus.	Cream brocade, lined red.

Liverpool

Arts	
B.A.	Black cloth, lined with apple-blossom silk, the colour of the Faculty, and bordered with white fur.

B.Ed.	Black cloth, lined with green silk and bordered with white fur.
B.Mus.	Blue silk bordered with white fur.
B.Phil.	Black cloth lined with yellow silk and bordered with white fur.
M.A.	Black silk or cloth, lined with apple-blossom silk.
M.Ed.	Black silk or cloth, lined with green silk.
D.Mus	Scarlet cloth, lined with blue silk.
Litt.D.	Scarlet cloth, lined with apple-blossom silk.
Science	
B.Sc.	Black cloth, lined with slate-blue silk, the colour of the Faculty and bordered with white fur.
M.Sc.	Black silk or cloth, lined with slate-blue silk.
D.Sc.	Scarlet cloth, lined with slate-blue silk.
Medicine	
M.B., Ch.B.	Black cloth, lined with lavender silk, the colour of the Faculty, and bordered with white fur.
Ch.M., M.Ch.Orth., M.Rad., M.Ch.Otol., M.Comm.H., M.Psy.Med.	Black silk or cloth, lined with lavender silk.
M.D.	Scarlet cloth, lined with lavender silk.
B.D.S.	Black cloth, lined with dark red silk, and bordered with white fur.
M.D.S.	Black silk or cloth, lined with dark red silk.
Law	
LL.B.	Black cloth, lined with bronze silk, the colour of the Faculty, and bordered with white fur.
LL.M.	Black silk or cloth, lined with bronze silk.
LL.D.	Scarlet cloth, lined with bronze silk.
Engineering Science	
B.Eng.	Black cloth, lined with orange silk, the colour of the Faculty, and bordered with white fur.
M.Eng.	Black silk or cloth, lined with orange silk.
D.Eng.	Scarlet cloth, lined with orange silk.
Veterinary Science	
B.V.Sc.	Black cloth, lined with grey silk, and bordered with white fur.
M.V.Sc.	Black silk or cloth, lined with grey silk.
D.V.Sc.	Scarlet cloth, lined with grey silk.
Social and Environmental Studies	
B.A.	Black cloth, lined with apple-blossom silk, the colour of the Faculty, and bordered with white fur.
B.Com.	Black cloth, lined with citron silk, and bordered with white fur.
B.Arch.	Black cloth, lined with white silk, edged with two narrow lines of black velvet, and bordered with white fur.
B.Phil.	Black cloth, lined with yellow silk and bordered with white fur.
M.A.	Black silk or cloth, lined with apple-blossom silk.
M.Arch.	Black silk or cloth, lined with white silk and edged with two narrow lines of black velvet.
M.T.D.	Black silk or cloth, lined with white silk and edged with one broad line of orange velvet.
M.C.D.	Black silk or cloth, lined with white silk, and edged with one broad line of black velvet.
M.B.A.	Black silk or cloth, lined with white silk and edged with one narrow line of gold ribbon.
M.Com.	Black silk or cloth, lined with citron silk.
M.Psychol.	Black silk or cloth, lined with purple silk.
Litt.D.	Scarlet cloth, lined with apple-blossom silk.
Doctor in Philosophy	
Ph.D.	Scarlet cloth or cord, lined with black silk, and trimmed with scarlet velvet.

London

	Faculty colour
Theology	
B.D., M.Th., D.D.	Sarum red
Arts	
B.A., M.A., D.Lit.	Russet-brown
Laws	
LL.B., LL.M., LL.D.	Blue
Music	
B.Mus., M.Mus., D.Mus.	White (watered silk)
Medicine	
M.B., B.S., M.S., M.D.	Violet
Medicine (Dental Surgery)	
B.D.S., M.D.S.	Olive green (corded
Medicine (Pharmacy)	
B.Pharm.	Old gold
Medicine (Veterinary)	
B.Vet.Med., D.Vet.Med.	Lilac
Science, Engineering and Economics	
B.Sc., M.Sc., D.Sc., B.Sc.(Eng.), M.Sc.(Eng.), D.Sc.(Eng.), B.Sc.(Econ.), M.Sc.(Econ.), D.Sc.(Econ.), B.Sc.(Est.Man.), M.Sc.(Est.Man.)	Gold
Education	
B.Ed., M.Ed.	Eau-de-nil green
Education (Humanities)	
B.Hum.	Pale pink.

Commerce, no longer awarded: Deep orange.

Note:—All London hoods are of identical shape (full shape with rounded cape). With the exception of B.Mus., for whom the hood is of light blue corded silk, Bachelors' hoods are of black silk or stuff faced and edged with silk of the faculty colour. Bachelors who are members of Convocation are entitled to wear hoods lined with silk and edged with silk of the faculty colour. With the exception of M.Mus., for whom the hood is of medium blue corded silk, Masters' hoods are of black corded silk, with a silk lining and edging of the faculty colour. For M.Phil. the lining is of claret colour with an edging of the colour of the faculty. Masters who are members of Convocation are entitled to wear hoods with a facing, 1½″ wide, of white silk. The Ph.D. hood is of claret-coloured cloth lined with silk of a lighter shade of claret, with an edging of the faculty colour about ⅛″ wide. Doctors' hoods are of scarlet cloth lined with silk of the faculty colour.

Loughborough

Bachelors	Purple, lined with grey, yellow or green-grey, according to degree.
Masters	Purple, lined with grey, yellow or green-grey, according to degree, with ½″ edging of degree colour.
Doctors of Philosophy	Purple, lined and edged 1″ all round with maroon taffeta.
Higher Doctors	Grey (Science), yellow (Technology), green-grey (Education), green (Arts), red (Library Studies), lined and edged all round with scarlet taffeta.

Degree Colours:
Science—Grey.
Technology—Yellow.
Education—Green-grey.
Arts—Green.
Library Studies—Red.

Manchester

B.A.	Black, pale blue and fur.
B.Arch., B.Ling., B.Pl., B.TP.	Black, pale blue edging.
M.A., M.A.(Urb. Des.), M.TP.	Black and pale blue.
D.Litt.	Gold and light gold.
B.A.(Econ.)	Black, orange and fur.
M.A.(Econ.), M.A.(E.C.S.)	Black and orange.
B.Ed.	Black, bluish-green and fur.
B.A. (in Education)	Black, pale blue, fur and bluish-green.
B.Sc. (in Education)	Black, salmon, fur and bluish-green
M.Ed.	Black and bluish-green.
M.Sc. (in Education)	Black and bluish-green, salmon edging.
LL.B.	Black, violet edging.
LL.M.	Black and violet.
LL.D.	Gold and light gold.
M.B., Ch.B.	Black, red edging.
B.Nurs.	Black, red and fur.
Ch.M.	Black and red.
M.Sc. (in Medicine)	Black and red, salmon edging.

M.D.	Gold and light gold.
B.D.S.	Black, fawn and fur.
M.D.S.	Black and fawn.
D.D.S.	Gold and light gold.
Mus.B.	Black and dark blue, light blue border.
Mus.D.	Gold and light gold.
B.Sc.	Black, salmon and fur.
M.Sc.	Black and salmon.
B.Sc. (in Technology)	Black, terracotta and fur.
M.Sc. (in Technology)	Black and terracotta.
D.Sc.	Gold and light gold.
B.D.	Black, heliotrope and fur.
B.A.(Theol.) B.A.(Relig Stud.) B.A. (in Theology)	Black, heliotrope edging and fur.
M.A.(Theol)	Black and heliotrope.
D.D.	Gold and light gold.
M.B.A. M.B.Sc.	Black and gold.
Ph.D.	Gold and light gold.

Note:—All hoods are of the simple shape, and are worn back-to-front with the tippet or liripipe outwards.

Newcastle upon Tyne

M.B., B.S.	Scarlet, Palatinate purple and white fur edging.
M.D.	Scarlet, scarlet and Palatinate purple.
M.S.	Rose and Palatinate purple.
D.Hy.	Scarlet, scarlet Palatinate purple and white.
D.Ch.	Scarlet, rose and Palatinate purple.
B.D.S.	Rose, ivory and white fur edging.
M.D.S.	Rose and ivory.
D.D.Sc.	Scarlet, rose and ivory white edging.
B.A.	Black, white fur, old gold edging.
B.Arch.	Same as B.A.
M.A.	Black and old gold.
B.Phil.	Same as M.A.
M.Phil.	Same as M.A.
M.F.A.	Same as M.A.
B.Ed.	Same as B.A.
M.Ed.	Same as M.A.
M.Litt.	Same as M.A.
D.Litt.	Scarlet, white and old gold edging.
M.Mus.	Same as M.A.
D.Mus.	Scarlet and white.
LL.B.	Maroon, Palatinate purple and white for edging.
LL.M.	Maroon and Palatinate purple.
LL.D.	Scarlet and maroon.
D.C.L.	Scarlet and white.
B.Sc.	Black, white fur, royal blue edging.
B.Sc.(Speech)	Same as B.Sc.
B.Med.Sci.	Same as B.Sc.
M.Sc.	Black and royal blue.
D.Sc.	Scarlet, white and royal blue edging.
Ph.D.	Scarlet and scarlet.

Nottingham

Arts	Faculty colour
B.A., B.Mus., B.Th., M.A., M.Th., M.Phil., Ph.D., D.Litt., D.D., D.Mus.	Cherry red
Law and Social Sciences	
B.A., B.Arch., LL.B., M.A., M.Phil., Ph.D., D.Litt., LL.D.	Maroon
Education	
B.Ed., M.Ed., M.Phil., Ph.D.	Lilac
Pure Science	
B.Sc., B.Pharm., M.Sc., M.Phil., Ph.D., D.Sc.	Royal blue
Agricultural Science	
B.Sc., M.Sc., M.Phil., Ph.D., D.Sc.	Green
Applied Science	
B.Sc., M.Sc., M.Phil., Ph.D., D.Sc.	Light navy blue
Medicine	
B.Med.Sci., B.M., B.S., M.Med.Sci., M.Phil., Ph.D., D.M., D.Sc.	Gold

Note:—All hoods of this University are of the Cambridge shape. The hoods of Bachelors other than Bachelors of Divinity, Bachelors of Medicine, Bachelors of Surgery and Bachelors of Architecture are of black stuff, lined with light blue silk to a depth of 3″. The lining is bound at the edges with a ribbon of the appropriate colour. In the case of Bachelors of Medicine, Bachelors of Surgery and Bachelors of Architecture the hood including the cape is bound with the appropriate colour. The hood of Bachelors of Divinity and of Masters is of black stuff or silk, lined throughout with light blue silk and bound at the edge with a ribbon of the appropriate colour. In the case of Masters of Philosophy the hood including the cape is bound with the appropriate colour. The hood of Doctors of Philosophy is of claret silk or cloth, lined throughout with light blue silk and bound at the edge with a ribbon of the appropriate colour. Hoods of Doctors other than Doctors of Philosophy are of scarlet silk or cloth, lined throughout with light blue silk and bound at the edge with a ribbon of the appropriate colour.

Oxford

B.Ed.	Black silk, lined beetle green taffeta.
B.A.	Black, half-lined and edged with white fur.
M.A.	Black silk, lined crimson or shot crimson silk.
B.D.	Black, lined fine ribbed black silk.
D.D.	Scarlet superfine cloth, lined fine ribbed black silk.
B.C.L.	Medium blue silk, half-lined and edged with white fur.
D.C.L.	Scarlet superfine cloth, lined crimson silk.
B.M., B.Ch.	Medium blue silk, half-lined and edged with white fur.
M.Ch.	Black silk, lined and edged with blue silk.
D.M.	Scarlet superfine cloth, lined crimson silk.
B.Mus.	Lilac silk, half-lined and edged white fur.
D.Mus.	Cream silk brocade, with apple-blossom embroidery, lined cherry crimson silk.
D.Litt. D.Sc.	Scarlet superfine cloth, lined with grey silk.
B.Litt.	Light blue, half-lined and edged white fur.
B.Sc.	Same as B.Litt.
M.Sc.	Light blue silk, lined and edged with neutral grey silk.
B.Phil.	Dark blue silk, lined with white silk.
D.Phil.	Scarlet superfine cloth, lined navy-blue silk.

Note:—The Oxford Bachelors' hoods (except B.D. & B.Phil.) and the M.A. hood are either of Burgon or Oxford shape. The M.Sc. hood is always of Burgon shape. The B.Phil. and M.Ch. hoods are always of Oxford shape. The B.D. and all Doctors' hoods are of the correct full apron shape. B.A., M.A., M.Ch., and B.D. hoods are of corded black silk: the other Bachelors' hoods are of corded or ribbed silk of the colour shown, lined or trimmed with white fur. When the Burgon shape is used the hood is half-lined and edged with fur, but for the Oxford shape only an edging of fur is used.

Reading

B.A.
LL.B.
B.Ed.
B.Mus.
M.A.
M.A. (Education)
M.Sc. (Education)
M.F.A.
B.Sc.
M.Sc.
M.Agr. Sc.
M.Agr. Eng.

All Reading hoods are lined with cream coloured silk. Bachelors' hoods are of dark blue lined with cream silk to a depth of 3″. All hoods are full shape. All Doctors' hoods are of scarlet superfine cloth fully lined with cream silk, of the full shape, except Ph.D., which is of crimson cloth lined with cream silk (maroon Russell-Cord is generally used).

M.Phil.
Ph.D.
D.Litt.
D.Sc.

St. Andrews

M.A.	Black silk with cherry silk lining.
B.D.	Violet silk or cloth bordered with white fur.
LL.D.	Pimento silk or cloth lined with ermine or white satin.
Mus.D.	Sky blue silk or cloth lined with ermine or white satin.
Ph.D.	Blue silk lined with white satin.
B.Sc.	Purple-lilac silk or cloth bordered with white fur.
M.Sc.	Black silk lined with purple-lilac silk or cloth.
D.Sc.	Purple-lilac silk or cloth lined with ermine or white satin.
B.Litt.	Saffron yellow silk bordered with white fur.
D.Litt.	Saffron yellow silk lined with ermine or white satin.
M.Litt.	Black silk lined with saffron yellow silk or cloth.
M.Theol.	Black silk lined with violet silk or cloth.
B.Phil.	Gold silk bordered with white fur.
D.D.	Violet silk or cloth lined with ermine or white satin.

Note:—All hoods of this University are of the full shape with well-rounded capes.

Salford

Bachelors	Light University blue corded silk, lined with gold satin and faced with 2″ of distinguishing colour inside.
Masters	Light University blue corded silk, the cape lined and edged with gold satin, and edged inside with 3″ of distinguishing colour.
Doctors of Philosophy	Light blue, lined and edged with scarlet satin.
Doctors (other than Doctors of Philosophy)	Dark blue, lined and edged all round with gold satin.

Note:—All the hoods are of the special full shape.

Sheffield

B.A.	(Arts) Green cloth, white fur, crushed strawberry.
B.Mus.	Green cloth, white fur, cream brocade.
B.Sc.	Green cloth, white fur, apricot.
M.B., Ch.B.	Green cloth, white fur, red.
B.Med.Sci.	Green cloth, white fur, cerise.
B.D.S.	Green cloth, white fur, pale rose-pink.
LL.B.	Green cloth, white fur, pale green.
B.Jur. } B.A. (Law) }	Green cloth, white fur, olive-green.
B.Eng.	Green cloth, white fur, purple.
B.Sc.Tech.	(Engineering and Materials Technology) Green cloth, white fur, lilac.
B.Met.	Green cloth, white fur, steel-grey.
B.A.	(Social Sciences) Green cloth, white fur, lemon-yellow.
B.A.(Econ.)	Green cloth, white fur, lemon-yellow.
B.A.	(Architectural Studies) Green cloth, white fur, old gold.
B.Ed.	Green cloth, white fur, pearl.
M.A.	(Arts) Green silk, crushed strawberry.
M.Sc.	(Pure Science) Green silk, apricot.
Ch.M.	Green silk, red.
M.Med.Sci.	Green silk, cerise.
M.D.S.	Green silk, pale rose-pink.
LL.M.	Green silk, pale green.
M.A.	(Law) Green silk, olive-green.
M.Eng.	Green silk, purple.
M.Sc.Tech.	(Engineering and Materials Technology) Green silk, lilac.
M.Met.	Green silk, steel-grey.
M.A.	(Social Sciences) Green silk, lemon-yellow.
M.A.(Econ.)	Green silk, lemon yellow.
M.A.	(Architectural Studies) Green silk, old gold.
M.A.	(Educational Studies) Green silk, pearl.
M.Sc.	(Educational Studies) Green silk, pearl.
M.Ed.	Green silk, pearl.
Ph.D.	Red silk, dark green.
Litt.D.	(Arts) Red silk, crushed strawberry.
D.Mus.	Red silk, cream brocade.
D.Sc.	(Pure Science) Red silk, apricot.
M.D.	Red silk, red.
LL.D.	Red silk, pale green.
D.Eng.	Red silk, purple.
D.Sc.Tech.	(Engineering and Material Technology. Red silk, lilac.
D.Met.	Red silk, steel-grey.
Litt.D.	(Social Sciences) Red silk lemon-yellow.
Litt.D.(Econ.)	Red silk, lemon-yellow.
Litt.D.	(Architectural Studies) Red silk, old gold.
Litt.D.	(Educational Studies) Red silk, pearl.
D.Sc.	(Educational Studies) Red silk, pearl.

Southampton

Degree colours:—

Arts and Letters	Mid-cerise
Music	Ivory
Science	Rich gold
Social Sciences	Light green
Education	White
Law	Blue (as the University silk)
Medicine and Surgery	Crimson
Philosophy	Claret

B.A., M.A., D.Litt., B.Mus., D.Mus., LL.B., LL.M., LL.D., B.Sc., M.Sc., D.Sc., B.Sc. (Social Sciences), M.Sc. (Social Sciences), D.Sc. (Social Sciences), B.Ed., B.M., M.S., D.M., M.Phil. (in all faculties), Ph.D. (in all faculties)

All hoods are fully lined with the University silk, a peacock blue. The neck portion is cut on the curve with a single central seam, no neckband is let in, and the neck is not edged. Bachelors, other than Bachelors of Music (who wear a blue hood), wear a black hood fully lined with the University silk and of the improved Oxford M.A. Burgon type. The hood proper is edged ⅜″ inside and out with the appropriate degree colour, except for Bachelor of Laws in which case the lining is turned over ⅜″ on the outside to form the edging. Masters, other than Masters of Surgery, wear a black hood fully lined with the University silk, of the London M.A. type. The hood proper is edged inside and out with the appropriate degree colour, except for Masters of Laws in which case the lining is turned over ⅜″ on the outside of the hood proper. Masters of Surgery wear a black hood fully lined with the University silk, of the Oxford Doctors' type. The hood proper is edged inside and out with crimson. Doctors of Philosophy wear a hood of claret-coloured cloth fully lined with the University silk and of the Oxford Doctors' type. Doctors (other than Doctors of Philosophy) wear a scarlet hood fully lined with the University silk of the Oxford Doctors' type.

Note:—The B.Sc. (Engineering) degree is no longer awarded, but graduates who took the B.Sc.(Eng.) degree may, if they wish, wear hoods with orange edging.

Stirling

D.Univ.	Malachite green lined powder blue.
B.A.	Black lined with dove grey.
B.Ed.	Black lined with bunting azure blue.
M.Sc.	Black lined with malachite green, edged with white ribbon and bordered with fur.
M.Litt.	Black lined with malachite green, edged with white ribbon and bordered with fur.
Ph.D.	Dove grey lined with malachite green.

Note:—The hoods for Bachelors, Masters and Ph.D. are of the Edinburgh shape.
The hood for D.Univ. is of the full shape.

Strathclyde

B.A.	Blue, lined white.
B.Sc.	Blue, lined gold.
B.Arch.	Blue, lined gold, bound with scarlet cord.
LL.B.	Blue, lined white, bound with scarlet cord.
B.Ed.	Blue, lined white, bound with gold cord.
M.A.	Blue, lined white, white edging.
M.B.A.	Blue, lined white, white edging bound with black cord.
M.Litt.	Blue, lined white, white edging bound with blue cord.
M.Sc.	Blue, lined gold, gold edging.
M.Arch.	Blue, lined gold, gold edging bound with scarlet cord.
LL.M.	Blue, lined white, white edging bound with scarlet cord.
Ph.D.	As for B.A., B.Sc., B.Arch, LL.B. (as appropriate).
D.Litt.	As for B.A.
D.Sc.	As for B.Sc., B.Arch. (as appropriate).
LL.D.	Blue, lined white, bound with scarlet cord.

Note:—All hoods are of saltire blue and of the full shape.

Surrey

B.Sc.	Black cloth, lined with rayon of Surrey blue.
B.Mus.	Black cloth, lined with rayon of Surrey blue, with white brocade band.
M.Sc.	Black cloth, lined with rayon of Surrey blue.
M.Phil.	Black cloth, lined with rayon of Surrey blue, with blue rayon damask edging.
Ph.D.	Cardinal red cloth.
D.Sc.	Gold rayon satin.

Note:—All the hoods of this University are fully lined with blue rayon damask and except for the B.Sc. hood, which is modified similar to simple Oxford, are all of uniform parabolic shape.

Sussex

B.A. B.Sc. B.Ed. LL.B.	Black cloth, lined with grey fur in squares.
M.A. M.Sc. M.S.W. (Master in Social Work) M.Ed.Psych.	Black alpaca lined with dove grey.
M.Phil. M.Phil. (Development Studies)	Black alpaca lined with dove grey with 1" scarlet band over lining set quarter inch from edge.
D.Phil.	For ordinary occasions, a hood of deep royal blue lined scarlet. No hood for special occasions.
LL.D. D.Litt. D.Sc.	As for Doctor of Philosophy.

Ulster (New University of Ulster)

B.A.	Black, lined University green, bound roy blue.
B.Sc.	Black, lined University green, bound Shannon green.
M.A.	Bordeaux, lined University green, bound royal blue.
M.Sc.	Bordeaux, lined University green, bound Shannon green.
M.Phil.	Bordeaux, lined University green, bound gold.
D.Sc.	Scarlet, lined University green, bound Shannon green.
D.Litt.	Scarlet, lined University green, bound royal blue.
D.Phil.	Scarlet, lined University green, bound gold.

Note:—All hoods are of the full shape and are silk-lined throughout.

Wales

B.A., B.Sc.(Econ.), B.Sc., B.Sc.(Tech.), B.Eng., B.Eng.(Tech.), B.Ed., B.Lib., LL.B., B.Mus., B.Pharm., B.Arch., B.N., B.D.S., M.B., B.Ch., B.D., M.A., M.Sc., M.Eng., M.Sc.(Econ.), M.Ed., M.Lib., LL.M., M.Mus., M.Th., M.Pharm., M.Sc.D., M.Ch.D., M.Ch., Ph.D., M.D., D.Ch.D., D., D.Sc., D.Sc.(Econ.), LL.D., D.Mus., D.D.

Bachelors' hoods are of the Oxford form, of black stuff or silk, except in the faculty of Music, in which they are dark blue silk. Except in the faculty of Medicine they are bordered with silk of the appropriate colour. In Medicine they are lined with silk of the appropriate colour and bordered with white (Medicine and Surgery) or purple (Dentistry). Masters' hoods are of the Cambridge form, of black silk, except in the faculty of Music, in which they are dark blue silk. They are lined with silk of the appropriate colour, the hood of a Master in Surgery being in addition bordered with white, and of a Master in Dental Surgery with purple. Doctors' hoods are of the Cambridge form, of scarlet cloth, except in the case of a Doctor of Philosophy, whose hood is of crimson cloth. They are lined with silk of the appropriate faculty colour, the hood of a Doctor in Medicine being in addition bordered with white.

Faculty colours:—

Arts—Mazarin blue shot with green.
Librarianship—Mazarin blue shot with green, edged with white.
Science—Bronze (yellow shot with black).
B.Sc.(Tech.)—Bronze, edged with white.
B.Eng.—Red shot with green.
B.Eng.(Tech.)—Red shot with green, edged with white.
Pharmacy—Shot silk of saxe blue.
Music—Pearl (a shot silk of three hues).
Law—Red shot with purple.
Theology—Mazarin blue shot with red.
Medicine—Green shot with black, edged with white.
Dentistry—Shot silk of saxe blue, edged with purple.
Nursing—Green shot with white, edged with red.
Architecture—Shot silk of scarlet red.
Economic and Social Studies—Red shot with yellow.
Education (B.Ed.)—Green shot with white

Warwick

B.A.	Black corded rayon fully lined and bound on the cowl and neckband with red taffeta.
B.Sc.	Black corded rayon fully lined and bound on the cowl and neck band with blue taffeta.
B.Ed.	Black corded rayon fully lined and bound on the cowl and neckband with green taffeta.
LL.B.	Black corded rayon fully lined and bound on the cowl and neckband with purple taffeta.
M.A.	Black corded rayon fully lined and bound with red taffeta.
M.Sc.	Black corded rayon fully lined and bound with blue taffeta.
M.Ed.	Black corded rayon fully lined and bound with green taffeta.
LL.M.	Black corded rayon fully lined and bound with purple taffeta.
M.Phil.	Black corded rayon fully lined and bound with red shot green taffeta.
Ph.D.	As Master's hood, but in maroon cloth full lined and bound with red shot green taffeta.
D.Litt.	As Master's hood, but in red cloth fully lined and bound with red taffeta.
D.Sc.	As Master's hood, but in red cloth fully lined and bound with blue taffeta.
LL.D.	As Master's hood, but in red cloth fully lined and bound with purple taffeta.

York

B.A.	Grey with white edging.
B.Phil.	Grey with red edging.
M.Phil.	Red with grey edging.
D.Phil.	Red with grey lining.
D.Univ.	Red silk with grey lining. (hon. degree)

Cranfield Institute of Technology (Bedford)

Doctor of Science	Neyron rose, lined with royal blue silk.
Doctor of Philosophy	Old gold cord, lined with neyron rose, neckband of neyron rose.
Master of Business Admin. Master of Science	Old gold cord, lined with royal blue, neckband of royal blue.

Note:—The hoods of Doctors of Science are of the full shape, those of Masters and Doctors of Philosophy of the simple shape.

Royal College of Art

Dr.(R.C.A.)	Vermilion cloth, trimmed with white fur.
M.A.(R.C.A.)	White silk, trimmed with white fur.

The Open University (Milton Keynes)

B.A.	Light blue, faced inside with 3" gold.
B.Phil.	Royal blue, faced inside with 3" gold.
M.Phil.	Light blue, full lined with gold and edged with narrow band of gold.
M.A.	Gold, fully lined with royal blue and edged with narrow band of royal blue.
Ph.D.	Royal blue, fully lined with gold and edged with 1" gold.
D.Sc.	Gold, fully lined with light blue.
D.Litt.	Gold, fully lined with royal blue.
D.Univ.	Royal blue, fully lined with light blue. The V-front to the hood is dark blue outside and light blue inside.

ABBREVIATIONS IN COMMON USE

A

a. = area; acre(s); are (100 sq. metres).
A.A. = Automobile Association; Alcoholics Anonymous.
AAA = Amateur Athletics Association.
A.A.I. = Associate of the Chartered Auctioneers' and Estate Agents' Institute.
A.A.L.P.A. = Associate of the Incorporated Society of Auctioneers and Landed Property Agents.
A. and M. = Ancient and Modern (Hymns).
A.B. = able-bodied seaman; *Artium Baccalaureus* (Bachelor of Arts).
A.B.A. = Amateur Boxing Association.
A.B.A.A. = Associate of the British Association of Accountants.
ABM = anti-ballistics missile defence system.
Abp. = Archbishop.
abr. = abridged.
ABRC = Advisory Board for Research Councils.
abs. = absolute.
a.c. (*or* A.C.) = alternating current.
A.C.A. = Associate of the Institute of Chartered Accountants.
A.C.C.A. = Associate of the Association of Certified Accountants.
A.C.I.S. = Associate of the Institute of Chartered Secretaries and Administrators.
ACT = Advisory Council on Technology.
ACTH = adreno-cortico-trophic hormone.
A.C.M.A. = Associate of the Institute of Cost and Management Accountants.
A.D. = *anno domini* (in the year of our Lord).
A.Dip. Art. Ed. = Advanced Diploma in Art Education.
A.Dip. Ed. = Advanced Diploma in Education.
A.D.C. = Aide-de-Camp.
Adm. = Admiral.
advt. (*or* adv.) = advertisement.
AEA = Atomic Energy Authority (UK).
AEC = Atomic Energy Commission (US).
AERE = Atomic Energy Research Establishment.
aet. (*or* aetat.) = *aetatis* (of age).
A.F.A.S. = Associate of the Faculty of Architects and Surveyors.
A.F.C. = Air Force Cross.
A.F.L. = American Federation of Labour.
A.F.M. = Air Force Medal.
AFRASEC = Afro-Asian Organisation for Economic Cooperation.
A.G. = Adjutant-General.
AGR = Advanced Gas-cooled Reactor.
A.H. = *anno Hegirae* (in the year of the Hegira).
A.I.A. = Associate of the Institute of Actuaries.
A.I.B. = Associate of the Institute of Bankers.
A.I.B.P. = Associate of the Institute of British Photographers.
A.I.C.E. = Associate of the Institution of Civil Engineers.
A.I.C.S. = Associate of the Institute of Chartered Shipbrokers.
AID = Agency for International Development (U.S.).
A.I.M.E. = Associate of the Institution of Mining Engineers.
A.I.Mech.E. = Associate of the Institution of Mechanical Engineers.
A.I.N.A. = Associate of the Institution of Naval Architects.
A.Inst.P. = Associate of the Institute of Physics.
A.I.Q.S. = Associate of the Institute of Quantity Surveyors.
A.L.A. = Associate of the Library Association.
A.L.S. = Associate of the Linnean Society.
alt. = altitude.
A.M. = *anno mundi* (in the year of the world); *Artium Magister* (Master of Arts); amplitude modulation.
a.m. = *ante meridiem* (before noon).
A.M.D.G. = *ad majorem Dei glorium* (to the greater glory of God).
amp. = ampere(s).
ANC = African National Congress.
anc. = ancient.
anhyd. = anhydrous.
anon. = anonymous.
ANZAC = Australian and New Zealand Army Corps.
ANZUS = Australian, New Zealand and U.S. Defence Pact (Pacific Security Treaty).
A.O.C. = Air Officer Commanding.
A.P. = Associated Press.
APT = Advanced Passenger Train.
aq. = aqueous.
A.R.A. = Associate of the Royal Academy.
A.R.A.D. = Associate of the Royal Academy of Dancing.
A.R.A.M. = Associate of the Royal Academy of Music.
A.R.B.S. = Associate of the Royal Society of British Sculptors.
ARC = Agricultural Research Council.
A.R.C.M. = Associate of the Royal College of Music.
arch. = archipelago.
A.R.C.O. = Associate of the Royal College of Organists.
A.R.C.Sc. = Associate of the Royal College of Science.
A.R.I.B.A. = Associate of the Royal Institute of British Architects.
A.R.I.C. = Associate of the Royal Institute of Chemistry.
A.R.I.C.S. = Associate of the Royal Institution of Chartered Surveyors.
A.R.P.S. = Associate of the Royal Photographic Society.
A.R.W.S. = Associate of the Royal Society of Painters in Water Colours.
A.S. (*or* AS) = Anglo-Saxon.
A.S.A. = Amateur Swimming Association.
ASDIC = Anti-submarine detector indicator.
ASEAN = Association of South-East Asian Nations (Indonesia, Malaysia, Philippines, Singapore, Thailand).
ASH = Action on Smoking and Health.
ASLIB = Association of Special Libraries and Information Bureaux.
ASPAC = Asian and Pacific Council.
A.T.C. = Air Training Corps.
A.T.D. = Art Teachers Diploma.
A.T.I.I. = Associate of the Taxation Institute Incorporated.
ATP = adenosine triphosphate.
atm. = atmospheric pressure.
at.wt. = atomic weight.
A.U.C. = *ab urbe condita* (from the founding of the City (Rome)), *or*, *anno urbis conditae* (in the year of the founding of the City).
av. = average.
AV = Authorized Version.
A.W.O.L. = Absent Without Leave.

B

b. = born; bowled.
B.A. = Bachelor of Arts.
B.A.A. = British Astronomical Association; British Airports Authority.
BAC = British Aircraft Corporation.
B.Acc. = Bachelor of Accountancy.
BAF = British Athletic Federation.
B.A.O. = Bachelor in the Art of Obstetrics.
BAOR = British Army of the Rhine.
B.Arch. = Bachelor of Architecture.
Bart. (*or* Bt.) = Baronet.
BAS = British Antarctic Survey.
B.B. = Boys' Brigade.
B.B.C. = British Broadcasting Corporation.
B.C. = before Christ; British Columbia.
B.Ch. (*or* Ch.B.) = Bachelor in Surgery.
B.C.L. = Bachelor in Civil Law.
B.Com. = Bachelor of Commerce.
B.D. = Bachelor in Divinity.
B.D.A. = British Dental Association.
Bde. = Brigade.
B.D.S. (*or* B.Ch.D.) = Bachelor in Dental Surgery.

B.Ed. = Bachelor of Education.
B.E.M. = British Empire Medal.
B.Eng. = Bachelor of Engineering.
BGC = British Gas Corporation.
BIM = British Institute of Management.
BIS = Bank for International Settlements.
BISRA = British Iron and Steel Research Association.
B.Litt. = Bachelor in Letters.
B.M. = Bachelor in Medicine; British Museum.
B.M.A. = British Medical Association.
B.M.C. = British Motor Corporation.
B.Mus. = Bachelor in Music.
B.N.C. = Brasenose College, Oxford.
BNOC = British National Oil Corporation.
bor. = borough.
b.p. = boiling point.
Bp. = Bishop.
B.Phil. = Bachelor of Philosophy.
Br. (*or* Brit.) = British.
Brit.Ass. = British Association for the Advancement of Science.
B.R. = British Railways; British Rail.
B.R.B. = British Rail Board.
B.R.C.S. = British Red Cross Society.
B.R.S. = British Road Services.
B.Sc. = Bachelor of Science.
BSC = British Steel Corporation.
B.S.I. = British Standards Institution.
BST = British summer time.
Bt. = Baronet; Brevet.
B.T.H.A. = British Travel and Holidays Association.
B.Th. = Bachelor in Theology.
Btu = British thermal unit.
B.V.M. = Blessed Virgin Mary.
B.V.M.S. = Bachelor in Veterinary Medicine and Surgery.
B.W.B. = British Waterways Board.

C

C. = Centigrade; Conservative.
c. = *circa* (about); centi- (10^{-2}).
C.A. = Chartered Accountant (Scottish Institute).
CAA = Civil Aviation Authority.
CARICOM = Caribbean Community and Common Market.
CABs = Citizens' Advice Bureaux.
Cal. = Calorie (nutritional kilogram-calorie).
cal. = calorie (gram-calorie used in physics and chemistry).
Cantab. = of Cambridge.
Cantuar. = of Canterbury.
cap. = capital letter; capitulum (chapter).
CAP = Common Agricultural Policy (Common Market).
CARD = Campaign Against Racial Discrimination.
CAS = Conciliation and Arbitration Service (took over some functions of former CIR 1974).
C.B. = Companion of the Order of the Bath.
C.B.E. = Commander of the Order of the British Empire.
CBI = Confederation of British Industry.
C.C. = County Council; County Councillor; Chamber of Commerce.
cc = cubic centimetre(s).
CCPR = Central Council of Physical Recreation.
C.D. = Civil Defence.
C.D.C. = Commonwealth Development Corporation.
C.D.S. = Chief of Defence Staff; Campaign for Democratic Socialism.
CDU = Christian Democratic Union (W. Ger.).
C.E. = Civil Engineer; Christian Era.
CEAO = West African Economic Community.
CEGB = Central Electricity Generating Board.
C.Eng. = Chartered Engineer.
CEI = Council of Engineering Institutions.
CENTO = Central Treaty Organisation.
centi = one-hundredth part (10^{-2}).
CERN = European Organisation for Nuclear Research.
CET = Central European Time; Common External Tariff (Common Market).
C.F. = Chaplain to the Forces.
cf. = *confer* (compare).
C.G.M. = Conspicuous Gallantry Medal.
C.G.S. = Chief of General Staff.
cgs = centimetre-gram-second.
CGT = Confédération Générale du Travail (French TUC).
C.H. = Companion of Honour.
Ch.Ch. = Christ Church.
Ch.M. = Master in Surgery.
C.I. = Lady of Imperial Order of the Crown of India; Channel Islands.
CIA = Central Intelligence Agency (US).
CID = Criminal Investigation Department.
C.I.E. = Companion of the Order of the Indian Empire.
Cie = Compagnie (Company).
c.i.f. = cost, insurance and freight.
C.-in-C. = Commander-in-Chief.
CIO = Congress of Industrial Organisations (US).
CIR = Commission on Industrial Relations (abolished 1974).
C.L. = Companion of Literature.
C.L.B. = Church Lads' Brigade.
cm = centimetre(s).
C.M.G. = Companion of the Order of St. Michael and St. George.
C.M.S. = Church Missionary Society.
CNAA = Council for National Academic Awards.
CND = Campaign for Nuclear Disarmament.
C.O. = Commanding Officer; Conscientious Objector.
Co. = County; Company.
c/o = care of.
C.O.D. = Cash on Delivery.
C. of E. = Church of England.
COI = Central Office of Information.
CoID = Council of Industrial Design.
COMECON = Council for Mutual Economic Assistance (East European).
Con. (*or* C.) = Conservative.
corr. = corrected.
COSPAR = Committee on Space Research.
CP = Communist Party.
CPAG = Child Poverty Action Group.
CPC = Communist Party of China.
C.P.R.E. = Council for the Protection of Rural England.
CPSU = Communist Party of the Soviet Union.
crit. = critical.
crystl. = crystalline.
C.S.C. = Conspicuous Service Cross; Commonwealth Scientific Committee.
C.S.E. = Certificate of Secondary Education.
C.S.I. = Companion of the Order of the Star of India.
CSP = Council on Scientific Policy.
CSU = Christian Social Union (W.Ger.).
C.T. = Civic Trust.
C.T.C. = Cyclists' Touring Club.
CTR = Controlled thermonuclear research.
cu. = cubic.
C.V.O. = Commander of the Royal Victorian Order.
cwt. = hundredweight.

D

d. = *denarius* (penny), *denarii* (pence); died; daughter.
D.A.R. = Daughters of the American Revolution.
dB = decibel(s).
D.B.E. = Dame Commander of Order of British Empire.
D.C. = District of Columbia.
d.c. (*or* D.C.) = direct current.
D.C.B. = Dame Commander of the Order of the Bath.
D.C.L. = Doctor in Civil Law.
D.C.M. = Distinguished Conduct Medal.
D.C.M.G. = Dame Commander, Order of St. Michael and St. George.
D.C.V.O. = Dame Commander of the Royal Victorian Order.
D.D. = Doctor in Divinity.
D.D.R. = German Democratic Republic (E. Ger.).
D.D.S. = Doctor in Dental Surgery.
DDT = Dichloro-diphenyl-trichloro-ethane.
DES = Department of Education and Science.
deca = ten times.
deci = one-tenth (10^{-1}).
del. = *delineavit* (he drew it).
D.ès L. = Docteur ès Lettres.
D.ès Sc. = Docteur ès Sciences.
D.F.C. = Distinguished Flying Cross.
D.F.M. = Distinguished Flying Medal.

D.G. = *dei gratie* (by the grace of God).
DIA = Design and Industries Association.
dil. = dilute.
Dip.Ed. = Diploma in Education.
Dip. H.E. = Diploma in Higher Education.
Dip.Tech. = Diploma in Technology.
DKP = Communist Party (W. Germany).
D.L. = Deputy-Lieutenant.
D.Lit. (*or* D. Litt) = Doctor of Literature.
D.M. = Doctor in Medicine (Oxford).
DM = Deutschemark.
D.Mus. = Doctor of Music.
DNA = deoxyribonucleic acid.
D.N.B. = Dictionary of National Biography.
do. = *ditto* (the same).
DoI = Department of Industry.
D.O.M. = *dominus optimo maximo* (To God, the best, the greatest).
D.P. = Displaced Person(s).
D.P.H. = Diploma in Public Health.
D.Phil. = Doctor of Philosophy.
D.P.M. = Diploma in Psychological Medicine.
Dr. = Doctor; debtor.
dr. = drachm.
D.Sc. = Doctor of Science.
D.S.C. = Distinguished Service Cross.
D.S.M. = Distinguished Service Medal.
D.S.O. = Companion of the Distinguished Service Order.
D.Th. = Doctor in Theology.
D.T.M. = Diploma in Tropical Medicine.
D.V. = *Deo volente* (God willing).
DVA = Dunkirk Veterans' Association.
dwt. = pennyweight.

E

EAAFRO = East African Agriculture and Forestry Research Organisation.
E. and O.E. = Errors and omissions excepted.
Ebor. = of York.
EBU = European Broadcasting Union.
EC = Electricity Council.
ECA = Economic Commission for Africa (UN).
ECAFE = Economic Commission for Asia and the Far East (UN).
ECE = Economic Commission for Europe (UN).
ECG = electro-cardiograph.
ECGD = Export Credits Guarantee Department.
ECLA = Economic Commission for Latin America (UN).
ECOSOC = Economic and Social Council (UN).
ECSC = European Coal and Steel Community.
ECTU = European Confederation of Trade Unions.
E.D. = Efficiency Decoration.
EEC = European Economic Community (Common Market).
EEG = electro-encephalogram.
EFTA = European Free Trade Association.
e.g. = *exempli gratio* (for example).
EMA = European Monetary Agreement.
EMBO = European Molecular Biology Organisation.
emf = electromotive force.
e.m.u. = electromagnetic unit.
ENEA = European Nuclear Energy Agency.
E.R. = Elizabetha Regina, *or* Edwardus Rex.
E.R.A. = Electrical Research Association.
ERNIE = electronic random number indicator equipment.
ERP = European Recovery Programme.
ESA = European Space Agency (incorporates former European Space Research Organisation (ESRO) and European Space Vehicle Launcher and Development Organisation (ELDO).
ESC = Economic and Social Council (UN).
et al. = *et alibi* (and elsewhere); *et alii* (and others).
etc. = *et cetera* (others; and so forth).
et seq. = *et sequens* (and the following).
et sqq. = *et sequentes, et sequentia* (and those following).
Euratom = European Atomic Energy Community.
ex lib. = *ex libris* (from the books of).

F

F. = Fahrenheit; Fellow.
f. = and the following page; ff. = and the following pages.
F.A. = Football Association.
F.A.L.P.A. = Fellow of the Incorporated Society of Auctioneers and Landed Property Agents.
F.A.N.Y. = First Aid Nursing Yeomanry.
FAO = Food and Agriculture Organisation (UN).
f.a.s. = free alongside.
F.B.A. = Fellow of the British Academy.
F.B.A.A. = Fellow of the British Association of Accountants.
FBI = Federal Bureau of Investigation (U.S.).
F.B.I.M. = Fellow of the British Institute of Management.
F.B.O.A. = Fellow of the British Optical Association.
F.B.S. = Fellow of the Botanical Society.
F.C.A. = Fellow of the Institute of Chartered Accountants.
F.C.C.A. = Fellow of the Association of Certified Accountants.
F.C.G.I. = Fellow of City and Guilds Institute.
F.C.I.A. = Fellow of Corporation of Insurance Agents.
F.C.I.B. = Fellow of Corporation of Insurance Brokers.
F.C.I.I. = Fellow of Chartered Insurance Institute.
F.C.I.S. = Fellow of the Institute of Chartered Secretaries and Administrators.
F.C.M.A. = Fellow of the Institute of Cost and Management Accountants.
F.D. = *Fidei Defensor* (Defender of the Faith).
FDP = Free Democratic Party (W. Ger.).
Fed. = Federation; Federal.
ff. = folios; and the following pages; fortissimo.
F.F.A.R.C.S. = Fellow of the Faculty of Anaesthetics, Royal College of Surgeons.
F.F.A.S. = Fellow of the Faculty of Architects and Surveyors.
FFI = Finance for Industry.
F.F.R. = Fellow of the Faculty of Radiologists.
F.G.S. = Fellow of the Geological Society.
F.H. = Fire Hydrant.
F.H.S. = Fellow of the Heraldry Society.
F.I.A. = Fellow of the Institute of Actuaries.
F.I.B. = Fellow of the Institute of Bankers.
F.I.B.P. = Fellow of the Institute of British Photographers.
F.I.C.S. = Fellow of the Chartered Institute of Shipbrokers.
F.I.E.E. = Fellow of the Institution of Electrical Engineers.
F. Inst.F. = Fellow of the Institute of Fuel.
F.Inst.P. = Fellow of the Institute of Physics.
F.Inst.Pet. = Fellow of the Institute of Petroleum.
F.I.Q.S. = Fellow of the Institute of Quantity Surveyors.
F.I.R.E. = Fellow of the Institute of Radio Engineers.
FIS = Family Income Supplement.
F.I.S. = Fellow of the Institute of Statisticians.
F.J.I. = Fellow of the Institute of Journalists.
fl. = *floruit* (flourished).
F.L.A. = Fellow of the Library Association.
F.L.S. = Fellow of the Linnaean Society.
FM = Frequency modulation.
FMC = Federal Maritime Commission (US).
F.N.S. = Fellow of the Newtonian Society.
F.O. = Foreign Office.
fo. = folio.
f.o.b. = free on board.
F.O.P. = Friendship Oil Pipeline (E.Europe).
f.p. = freezing point.
F.P.S. = Fellow of the Pharmaceutical Society.
F.Ph.S. = Fellow of the Philosophical Society.
F.R.A.D. = Fellow of the Royal Academy of Dancing.
F.R.A.I. = Fellow of the Royal Anthropological Institute.
F.R.A.M. = Fellow of the Royal Academy of Music.
F.R.A.S. = Fellow of the Royal Astronomical Society.
F.R.Ae.S. = Fellow of the Royal Aeronautical Society.
F.R.B.S. = Fellow of the Royal Society of British Sculptors.
F.R.C.M. = Fellow of the Royal College of Music.
F.R.C.O. = Fellow of the Royal College of Organists.
F.R.C.O.G. = Fellow of the Royal College of Obstetricians and Gynaecologists.
F.R.C.P. = Fellow of the Royal College of Physicians of London.

F.R.C.P.Ed. = Fellow of the Royal College of Physicians of Edinburgh.
F.R.C.S. = Fellow of the Royal College of Surgeons of England.
F.R.C.S.Ed. = Fellow of the Royal College of Surgeons of Edinburgh.
F.R.C.V.S. = Fellow of the Royal College of Veterinary Surgeons.
F.R.Econ.S. = Fellow of the Royal Economic Society.
F.R.F.P.S. = Fellow of the Royal Faculty of Physicians and Surgeons (Glas.).
F.R.G.S. = Fellow of the Royal Geographical Society.
F.R.H.S. = Fellow of the Royal Horticultural Society.
F.R.Hist.S. = Fellow of the Royal Historical Society.
F.R.I.B.A. = Fellow of the Royal Institute of British Architects.
F.R.I.C. = Fellow of the Royal Institute of Chemistry.
F.R.I.C.S. = Fellow of the Royal Institution of Chartered Surveyors.
F.R.M.S. = Fellow of the Royal Microscopical Society.
F.R.Met.S. = Fellow of the Royal Meteorological Society.
F.R.N.S. = Fellow of Royal Numismatic Society.
F.R.P.S. = Fellow of the Royal Photographic Society.
F.R.S. = Fellow of the Royal Society.
F.R.S.A. = Fellow of the Royal Society of Arts.
F.R.S.E. = Fellow of the Royal Society of Edinburgh.
F.R.S.L. = Fellow of the Royal Society of Literature.
FRTPI = Fellow of the Royal Town Planning Institute.
F.S.A. = Fellow of the Society of Antiquaries.
F.S.M.C. = Fellow of the Spectacle Makers Company.
F.S.S. = Fellow of the Royal Statistical Society.
F.T.I. = Fellow of the Textile Institute.
F.T.I.I. = Fellow of the Taxation Institute Incorporated.
F.Z.S. = Fellow of the Zoological Society.

G

g. = gram(s).
GATT = General Agreement on Tariffs and Trade.
G.B.E. = Knight (*or* Dame) Grand Cross of the Order of the British Empire.
G.C. = George Cross.
G.C.A. = Ground Control Approach.
G.C.E. = General Certificate of Education.
G.C.B. = Knight (or Dame) Grand Cross of the Order of the Bath.
G.C.I.E. = Knight Grand Commander of the Indian Empire.
G.C.M.G. = Knight (*or* Dame) Grand Cross of the Order of St. Michael and St. George.
G.C.S.I. = Knight Grand Commander of the Star of India.
G.C.V.O. = Knight (*or* Dame) Grand Cross of the Royal Victorian Order.
GDP = gross domestic product.
GDR = German Democratic Republic (E. Ger.).
Gen. = General; Genesis.
GeV = thousand million electron-volts.
G.H.Q. = General Headquarters.
G.I. = American soldier (from army term "Government Issue" applied to kit and equipment).
GLC = Greater London Council.
G.M. = George Medal.
G.M.C. = General Medical Council.
G.M.T. = Greenwich mean time.
GNP = gross national product.
G.O.C. = General Officer Commanding.
G.O.P. = Grand Old Party (US Republican Party).
G.P. = General Practitioner.
gr. = grain(s).
G.R.C.M. = Graduate of the Royal College of Music.
G.R.S.M. = Graduate of the Royal Schools of Music (Royal Academy and Royal College).
G.S.O. = General Staff Officer.
GTCs = Government Training Centres.
GYP = gross domestic income.

H

ha = hectare (100 ares).
H.E. = His Excellency; His Eminence: high explosive.
hecto = one hundred times (10^2).
H.H. = His (*or* Her) Highness.
hhd. = hogshead.
H.I.M. = His Imperial Majesty.
H.J.S. = *Hic jacet sepultus* (Here lies buried).
H.M. = His (*or* Her) Majesty.
H.M.A.S. = Her Majesty's Australian Ship.
H.M.I. = Her Majesty's Inspector.
H.M.L. = Her Majesty's Lieutenant.
H.M.S = Her Majesty's Ship; Her Majesty's Service.
H.M.S.O. = Her Majesty's Stationery Office.
H.N.C. = Higher National Certificate.
H. of C. = House of Commons.
H. of L. = House of Lords.
Hon. = Honourable; Honorary.
hp = horsepower.
H.P. = Hire purchase.
H.R. = House of Representatives (US).
H.R.H. = His (*or* Her) Royal Highness.
H.S.E. = *Hic sepultus est* (Here lies buried).
H.T. = high tension.
HTR = high-temperature reactor (type of nuclear power station).
H.V. = health visitor.
H.W.M. = high water mark.

I

IAAS = Incorporated Association of Architects and Surveyors.
IADB = Inter-American Development Bank.
IAEA = International Atomic Energy Agency (UN).
IATA = International Air Transport Association.
ib. (*or* ibid.) = *ibidem* (in the same place).
IBA = Independent Broadcasting Authority.
IBERLANT = Iberian Atlantic Command (NATO).
IBRD = International Bank for Reconstruction and Development (World Bank) (UN).
ICAO = International Civil Aviation Organisation (UN).
ICBM = Intercontinental ballistic missile.
ICEM = Intergovernmental Committee for European Migration.
ICFTU = International Confederation of Free Trade Unions.
ICI = Imperial Chemical Industries.
ICJ = International Court of Justice (UN).
ICRC = International Committee of the Red Cross.
ICSU International Council of Scientific Unions.
ICT = International Computers and Tabulators.
Id. = *idem* (the same).
IDA = International Development Association (UN).
IDC = Industrial Development Certificate system.
i.e. = *id est* (that is).
IEA = International Energy Agency.
IFC = International Finance Corporation (UN).
Ign. = *ignotus* (unknown).
IGY = International Geophysical Year (1957–8).
IHS = *Iesus Hominum Salvator* (Jesus Saviour of men)—repr. a Greek abbrev. of the word Jesus.
ILEA = Inner London Education Authority.
ILO = International Labour Organisation (UN).
I.L.S. = Instrument Landing System.
IMCO = Intergovernmental Maritime Consultative Organisation (UN).
IMF = International Monetary Fund (UN).
Inc. = Incorporated.
Incog. = *incognito* (unknown, unrecognised).
inf. = infinitive; *infra* (below).
in loc. (*in loco*) = in its place.
I.N.R.I. = *Iesus Nazarenus, Rex Iudaeorum* (Jesus of Nazareth, King of the Jews).
Inst. = Institute; Institution.
inst. = instant (the present month).

Interpol = International Criminal Police Commission (HQ in Paris).
Intelsat = International Telecommunications Satellite Consortium.
I.O.M. = Isle of Man.
I.O.W. = Isle of Wight.
IOU = I owe you.
I.P.F.A. = Institute of Public Finance and Accountancy.
IQ = intelligence quotient.
IQSY = International Years of the Quiet Sun.
I.R. = Inland Revenue.
I.R.A. = Irish Republican Army.
IRBM = Intermediate-range ballistic missile.
IRC = International Red Cross; Industrial Reorganisation Corporation (wound up 1970).
IRDA = Industrial Research and Development Authority.
I.S.O. = Imperial Service Order; International Standardisation Organisation.
I.T.A. = Independent Television Authority; Institute of Travel Agents; Industrial Transport Association; Invalid Tricycle Association.
I.T.O. = International Trade Organisation.
I.T.U. = International Telecommunication Union (UN).
ITV = Independent Television.
IWA = Inland Waterways Association.

J

J. = Judge; Jet (aircraft).
J.P. = Justice of the Peace.

K

K = Kelvin.
K. = Köchel numeration (of Mozart's works).
KANU = Kenya African National Union.
k = kilo = thousand.
K.B.E. = Knight Commander of the Order of the British Empire.
K.C. = King's Counsel.
kc. = kilocycle(s).
K.C.B. = Knight Commander of the Order of the Bath.
K.C.I.E. = Knight Commander of the Order of the Indian Empire.
K.C.M.G. = Knight Commander of the Order of St. Michael and St. George.
K.C.S.I. = Knight Commander of the Star of India.
K.C.V.O. = Knight Commander of the Royal Victorian Order.
K.G. = Knight of the Order of the Garter.
KGB = Soviet State Security Service.
kg = kilogram(s).
kilo = one thousand times (10^3).
KJV = King James Version.
K.K.K. = Ku Klux Klan.
km = kilometre(s).
k.o. = knock out (boxing).
K.P. = Knight of the Order of St. Patrick.
K.T. = Knight of the Order of the Thistle.
Kt. = knight.
kV = kilovolt(s).
kW = kilowatt(s).
kWh = kilowatt hour(s).

L

L. (*or* Lib.) = Liberal.
L.A. = Local Authority.
Lab. = Labour.
L.A.C. = London Athletic Club.
LAFTA = Latin American Free Trade Association.
LAMDA = London Academy of Music and Dramatic Art.
lat. = latitude.
lb = *libra* (pound), *librae* (pounds).
lbf = pound-force.
l.b.w. = leg before wicket.
l.c. = lower case (small letter(s)).
L.C.J. = Lord Chief Justice.
L.D.S. = Licentiate in Dental Surgery.
L.ès L. = Licencié ès Lettres.
L.F.B. = London Fire Brigade.
l.gov.dist. = local government district.
L.H.D. = *Litterarum Humaniorum Doctor* (Doctor of Humane Letters).
Lic.Med. = Licentiate in Medicine.
Lic.S. = Licentiate in Surgery.
Lit.Hum. = *Literae Humaniores* (Study of the Classics).
Litt.D. = *Litterarum Doctor* (Doctor of Letters; Doctor in Letters (Camb.)).
LL.B. = *Legum Baccalaureus* (Bachelor of Laws).
LL.D. = *Legum Doctor* (Doctor of Laws; Doctor in Law (Camb.)).
L.M. = Licentiate in Midwifery.
loc.cit. = *loco citato* (in the place sited).
log. = logarithm.
long. = longitude.
L.R.A.D. = Licentiate of the Royal Academy of Dancing.
L.R.A.M. = Licentiate of the Royal Academy of Music.
L.R.C.M. = Licentiate of the Royal College of Music.
L.R.C.P. = Licentiate of the Royal College of Physicians.
L.R.C.S. = Licentiate of the Royal College of Surgeons.
L.R.C.V.S. = Licentiate of the Royal College of Veterinary Surgeons.
L.S. = *loco sigilli* (place of the seal).
L.S.A. = Licentiate of the Society of Apothecaries.
L.s.d. = *Librae, solidi, denarii* (Pounds, shillings, pence).
LSD = Lysergic acid diethylamide.
L.S.E. = London School of Economics.
L.S.O. = London Symphony Orchestra.
L.T.A. = Lawn Tennis Association.
L.Th. = Licentiate in Theology.
Lt.-Gen. = Lieutenant-General.
L.W.M. = lower-water mark.
LXX = Septuagint.

M

M. = Member; Monsieur; mark (German coin); *meridies* (noon); mega (million times).
m = metre(s).
m. = married; masculine; million.
M.A. = Master of Arts.
MAOT = Member of the Association of Occupational Therapists.
M.A.O. = Master in the Art of Obstetrics.
max. = maximum.
M.B. = Bachelor in Medicine.
M.B.A. = Master of Business Administration.
M.B.E. = Member of the Order of the British Empire.
M.C. = Military Cross; Master of Ceremonies.
Mc = million cycles, *or* megacycle.
M.C.C. = Marylebone Cricket Club.
M.Ch. = Master in Surgery.
M.Ch.D. = Master in Dental Surgery.
M.Ch.Orth. = Master in Orthopaedic Surgery.
M.Com. = Master of Commerce.
M.C.S.P. = Member of the Chartered Society of Physiotherapy.
M.C.T. = Member of the College of Technologists.
M.D. = *Medicineae Doctor* (Doctor in Medicine).
M.D.S. = Master in Dental Surgery.
M.Ed. = Master of Education.
M.E. = Middle English.
mega = one million times (10^6).
met. co. = metropolitan county.
MeV = megaelectronvolt(s)
MFA = Movement of the Armed Forces (Portugal).
M.F.H. = Master of Foxhounds.
mg = milligram(s).
Mgr. = Monsignor.
MHD = magnetohydrodynamics.
micro = one-millionth part (10^{-6}).
M.I. = Military Intelligence.
M.I.C.E. = Member of the Institution of Civil Engineers.
M.I.Chem.E. = Member of the Institution of Chemical Engineers.
milli = one-thousandth part (10^{-3}).
M.I.M.A. = Member of the International Marine Association.

M.I.Mar.E. = Member of the Institute of Marine Engineers.
M.I.Mech.E. = Member of the Institution of Mechanical Engineers.
M.I.Min.E. = Member of the Institution of Mining Engineers.
min. = minimum.
M.I.N.A. = Member of the Institution of Naval Architects.
M.Inst.Met. = Member of the Institute of Metals.
Min. Plenip. = Minister Plenipotentiary.
M.I.Mun.E. = Member of the Institution of Municipal Engineers.
MIRV = multiple independent re-entry vehicle.
M.Inst.T. = Member of the Institute of Transport.
M.I.S. = Member of the Institute of Statisticians.
M.I.T. = Massachusetts Institute of Technology.
M.I.T.M.A. = Member of the Institute of Trade Mark Agents.
M.I.W.M. = Member of the Institution of Works Managers.
M.J.I. = Member of the Institute of Journalists.
MKS = metre-kilogram-second system.
MKSA = metre-kilogram-second-ampere (Giorgi) system.
Mlle = Mademoiselle.
MLR = Minimum Lending Rate.
MM. = Messieurs.
M.M. = Military Medal.
mm = millimetre(s).
Mme = Madame.
m.m.f. = magnetomotive force.
mmHg = millimetre(s) of mercury.
M.N. = Merchant Navy.
Mods. = Moderations (Oxford).
M.O.H. = Medical Officer of Health.
m.p. = melting point.
M.P. = Member of Parliament; Military Police.
m.p.h. = miles per hour.
M.Phil. = Master of Philosophy.
MPLA = Popular Movement for the Liberation of Angola.
M.P.S. = Member of the Pharmaceutical Society; Member of the Philological Society; Member of the Physical Society.
M.R. = Master of the Rolls.
M.R.A.S. = Member of the Royal Asiatic Society; Member of the Royal Academy of Science.
M.R.Ae.S. = Member of the Royal Aeronautical Society.
M.R.C. = Medical Research Council.
M.R.C.O.G. = Member of the Royal College of Obstetricians and Gynaecologists.
M.R.C.P. = Member of the Royal College of Physicians.
M.R.C.S. = Member of the Royal College of Surgeons.
M.R.C.V.S. = Member of the Royal College of Veterinary Surgeons.
M.R.I. = Member of the Royal Institution.
M.R. Inst. Nav. = Member of the Royal Institute of Navigation.
MRTPI = Member of the Royal Town Planning Institute.
M.S. = Master in Surgery.
Ms., Mss. = Manuscript, Manuscripts.
M.S.A. = Mutual Security Agency.
M.Sc. = Master of Science.
M.T.B. = Motor Torpedo Boat.
Mus.B. = *Musicae Baccalaureus* (Bachelor in Music).
Mus.D. = *Musicae Doctor* (Doctor in Music).
MV = million volts *or* megavolt.
M.V.O. = Member of the Royal Victorian Order.
MW = million watts *or* megawatt.

N

NAAFI = Navy, Army and Air Force Institutes.
N.A.B.M. = National Association of British Manufacturers.
NADGE = Nato Air Defence Ground Environment Organisation.
nano = one-thousand-millionth part (10^{-9}).
NASA = National Aeronautics and Space Administration (US).
NATO = North Atlantic Treaty Organisation.
NATSOPA = National Society of Operative Printers and Assistants.
N.B. = *nota bene* (note well).
NBS = National Bureau of Standards (US).
NCB = National Coal Board.
N.C.O. = Non-commissioned Officer.
N.C.U. = National Cyclists' Union.
n.d. = no date (of books).
N.D.D. = National Diploma in Design.
NEA = Nuclear Energy Agency (OECD).
NEB = National Enterprise Board; New English Bible.
NEDC = National Economic Development Council.
NEL = National Engineering Laboratory.
Nem.con. = *Nemine contradicente* (no one contradicting = unanimously).
Nem.diss. = *Nemine dissentiente* (no one dissenting = unanimously).
NERC = Natural Environment Research Council.
Net. (*or* Nett.) = free from, or not subject to, any deductions.
NHS = National Health Service.
NIBMR = no independence before majority rule.
NIRNS = National Institute for Research in Nuclear Science.
NLF = National Liberation Front (political arm of Vietcong in S. Vietnam).
NLL = National Lending Library for Science and Technology.
No. = *numero* (number).
non.seq. = *non sequitur* (it does not follow).
NPC = National Parks Commission; National Ports Council.
N.P. = Notary Public.
NPD = National Democratic Party (W. Ger.).
N.P.F.A. = National Playing Fields Association.
NPL = National Physical Laboratory.
N.R.A. = National Rifle Association.
NRDC = National Research Development Corporation.
N.S. = New Style in the calendar (in Gt. Britain since 1752).
N.S.P.C.C. = National Society for the Prevention of Cruelty to Children.
N.T. = New Testament; National Trust.
NUR = National Union of Railwaymen.
NUS = National Union of Students.
NUT = National Union of Teachers.
N.Y. = New York.
N.Z. = New Zealand.

O

OAPEC = Organisation of Arab Petroleum Exporting Countries.
OAS = Organisation of American States; Organisation de l'Armée Secrète (the clandestine army of the French colonists in Algeria).
OAU = Organisation of African Unity.
ob. = *obit* (died).
obs. = observed.
O.B.E. = Officer of the Order of the British Empire.
OBEV = Oxford Book of English Verse.
OCAM = Common African, Malagasy and Mauritanian Organisation.
OCAS = Organisation of Central American States.
OCTU = Officer Cadets' Training Unit.
ODECA = Organisation of Central American States.
OECD = Organisation for Economic Co-operation and Development.
O.E.D. = Oxford English Dictionary.
O.F.M. = *Ordo Fratrum Minorum* (Order of Friars Minor = Franciscan).
O.H.M.S. = On Her Majesty's Service.
O.M. = Member of the Order of Merit.
O.N.C. = Ordinary National Certificate.
O.P. = *Ordinis Praedicatorum* (Order of Preachers = Dominicans); opposite to prompter (stage term); out of print.
op. = *opus* (work).
op cit. = *opere citato* (in the work cited).
OPEC = Organisation of Petroleum Exporting Countries.
ORGEL = Organique et Eau Lourde (organic liquid and heavy water nuclear reactor).
O.S. = Old Style in calendar.
O.S.B. = *Ordo Sancti Benedicti* (Order of St. Benedict = Benedictines).
O.T. = Old Testament.
O.T.C. = Officers' Training Corps.
Oxon. = of Oxford.
oz. = ounce(s).

P

p = penny, pence (decimal system).
P.A. = Press Association.
PAYE = Pay as you earn (income tax scheme).
P.C. = Privy Councillor; Police Constable.
P.C.C. = People's Caretakers' Council (Nat. movement in Rhodesia).
p.c. = per cent.; postcard.
p.d. = potential difference.
pdl = poundal.
P.D.S.A. = People's Dispensary for Sick Animals.
P.E.N. = Poets, Playwrights, Essayists, Editors and Novelists (Club).
P.E.P. = Political and Economic Planning (Society).
per pro (*or* p.p.) = *per procurationem* (by proxy).
PFLP = Popular Front for the Liberation of Palestine.
Ph.D. = *Philosophiae Doctor* (Doctor of Philosophy).
pinx = *pinxit* (he painted).
P.L.A. = Port of London Authority.
PLO = Palestine Liberation Organisation.
PLP = Parliamentary Labour Party.
PLUTO = Pipe-line under the ocean.
P.M. = Prime Minister; Post master; *post meridiem* (afternoon); Polar Medal.
P.M.O. = Principal Medical Officer.
P.N.E.U. = Parents' National Education Union.
P.O. = Post Office; postal order; Petty Officer.
P. & O. = Peninsular and Oriental Steamship Co.
P.O.W. = prisoner of war.
pp. = pages.
P.P.C. = pour prendre congé (to take leave).
P.Q. = Parliamentary Question.
P.P.S. = Parliamentary Private Secretary.
P.R. = Proportional Representation.
P.R.A. = President of the Royal Academy.
P.R.B. = Pre-Raphaelite Brotherhood.
PRC = People's Republic of China.
Pro tem. = *pro tempore* (for the time being).
Prox = *proximo* (of the next month).
P.R.S. = President of the Royal Society.
P.S. = *post scriptum* (postscript).
Ps. = Psalm.
Pss. = Psalms.
P.S.W. = Psychiatric Social Worker.
P.T. = Physical Training.
Pte. = Private.
P.T.O. = please turn over.

Q

Q. = Queen.
Q = 10^{18} British Thermal Units ($1{\cdot}05 \times 10^{21}$ joules).
Q.B. = Queen's Bench.
Q.C. = Queen's Counsel.
Q.E.D. = *quod erat demonstrandum* (which was to be demonstrated).
Q.E.F. = *quod erat faciendum* (which was to be done).
Q.E.I. = *quod erat inveniendum* (which was to be found).
q.l. (*or* q.pl) = *quantum libet* (*or quantum placet*) (as much as one pleases).
Q.M. = Quartermaster.
Q.M.C. = Queen Mary College.
q.s. = *quantum sufficit* (a sufficient quantity).
Q.S. = Quarter Sessions.
QSEs = Qualified Scientists and Engineers (*i.e.*, skilled manpower).
QSSs = Quasars (quasi stellar radio sources).
Q.T. = quiet (slang).
Qto. = quarto (folded in four).
QTOL = Quiet Take-off and Landing.
q.v. = *quod vide* (which see).

R

R. = Réaumur; *Rex* (King); *Regina* (Queen); Right (stage direction).
R.A. = Rear Admiral; Royal Academy; Royal Academician; Research Association; Right Ascension (astron.).
R.A.C. = Royal Automobile Club.
RAE = Royal Aircraft Establishment.
R.Ae.S. = Royal Aeronautical Society.
R.A.F. = Royal Air Force.
R.A.M. = Royal Academy of Music.
R.A.O.C. = Royal Army Ordnance Corps.
R.C. = Red Cross; Roman Catholic.
RCD = Regional Co-operation for Development (Pakistan, Turkey, Iran).
R.D. = Rural Dean; Royal Naval Reserve Decoration; Refer to Drawer.
R.D.I. = Designer for Industry of the Royal Society of Arts.
R.E. = Royal Engineers.
Reg. Prof. = Regius Professor.
R.E.M.E. = Royal Electrical and Mechanical Engineers.
Rep. = Representative; Republican.
R.G.S. = Royal Geographical Society.
r.h. = relative humidity.
R.H.S. = Royal Humane Society; Royal Horticultural Society.
R.Hist.S. = Royal Historical Society.
R.I. = Royal Institution; Royal Institute of Painters in Water Colours; Rhode Island; Religious Instruction.
R.I.B.A. = Royal Institution of British Architects.
R.I.I.A. = Royal Institute of International Affairs (Chatham House, London).
R.I.P. = *requiescat in pace* (may he rest in peace).
R.M. = Royal Marines; Resident Magistrate.
R.M.C. = Royal Military College, Sandhurst.
r.m.s. = root mean square.
R.N. = Royal Navy.
RNA = ribonucleic acid.
R.N.L.I. = Royal National Lifeboat Institution.
Ro. = *recto* (on the right-hand page).
R.P. = Member of the Royal Society of Portrait Painters.
RRE = Royal Radar Establishment.
rpm = revolutions per minute.
R.S.A. = Royal Society of Arts; Royal Scottish Academician.
R.S.M. = Regimental Sergeant Major.
R.S.P.C.A. = Royal Society for the Prevention of Cruelty to Animals.
R.S.V.P. = *Répondez, s'il vous plaît* (An answer is requested).
R.S.S. = Registered Shoeing Smith.
R.S.W. = Royal Scottish Society of Painters in Water Colours.
Rt. Hon. = Right Honourable.
RTPI = Royal Town Planning Institute.
Rt. Rev. = Right Reverend (of a Bishop).
R.U. = Rugby Union.
RV = Revised Version.
R.W.S. = Royal Society of Painters in Water Colours.
R.Y.S. = Royal Yacht Squadron.

S

S. = *San, Santa, Santo,* or *São* (Saint); SS. = Saints.
s. = *solidus* (shilling), *solidi* (shillings).
S.A. = Salvation Army; Sex Appeal; South America; South Australia; South Africa; Société Anonyme (Limited).
SACEUR = Supreme Allied Commander Europe.
SACLANT = Supreme Allied Commander Atlantic.
SALT = Strategic Arms Limitation Talks.
Sarum = of Salisbury.
SAYE = Save as You Earn.
S.C. = qualified to admission to Staff College.
sc. = *scilicet* (namely).
Sc.D. = *Scientiae Doctor* (Doctor in Science).
S.C.F. = Senior Chaplain to the Forces.
S.C.M. = State Certified Midwife; Student Christian Movement.
SDLP = Social Democratic Labour Party (N. Ireland).
SEATO = South-East Asia Treaty Organisation.
SED = Socialist Unity Party (E. Ger.).
SET = selective employment tax.
S.G. = Solicitor-General; Scots Guards.
SGHWR = Steam Generating Heavy Water Reactor.
SHAPE = Supreme Headquarters Allied Powers in Europe.
SI = Système International d'Unités (International System of Units).
sic. = so written.

SINS = Ships Inertial Navigation System.
SOS = distress signal (wireless code signal, used especially by ships at sea).
s.p. = *sine prole* (without issue).
S.P.C.K. = Society for the Promotion of Christian Knowledge.
SPD = Social Democratic Party (W. Ger.).
sp. gr. = specific gravity.
sq. = square; *sequens* (the following).
sqq. = *sequentes, sequentia* (those following).
SRC = Science Research Council.
S.R.N. = State Registered Nurse.
SS. = Saints.
S.S. = Steamship.
S.S.C. = Solicitor before Supreme Court (Scotland).
SSRC = Social Science Research Council.
STADAN = Satellite Tracking and Data Acquisition Network.
STAR = Satellites for Telecommunications, Applications and Research (European consortium).
S.T.D. = *Sacrae Theologiae Doctor* (Doctor of Theology); Subscriber Trunk Dialling.
St. = Saint; Street.
Ste = *Sainte* (Saint, feminine).
Stet = Let it stand (printing term).
s.t.p. = standard temperature and pressure.
S.T.P. = *Sacrae Theologiae Professor* (Professor of Divinity, old form of D.D.)
s.v. = *sub verbo* (under the entry).

T

TAB = Technical Assistance Board (UN).
TAVR = Territorial and Army Volunteer Reserve.
T.B. = Tubercule bacillus (tuberculosis).
t.b. = torpedo boat.
T.C.D. = Trinity College, Dublin.
T.C.C.B. = Test and County Cricket Board.
T.D. = Territorial Decoration; Teachta Dála (Representative of the Dáil).
temp. = temperature.
T.F. = Territorial Force.
T.H. = Trinity House.
TNT = trinitrotoluene (high explosive).
Toc.H. = Talbot House.
tr. = transpose.
T.R.C. = Thames Rowing Club; Tithes Rent Charge.
T.T. = tubercular tested; teetotal.
TUC = Trades Union Congress.
TV = Television.
TVA = Tennessee Valley Authority.
TWA = Thames Water Autuority.
TWI = Training Within Industry for Supervisors.
T.Y.C. = Thames Yacht Club; Two-year Old (*or* Thousand Yards) Course.

U

U.A.M. = Afro-Malagasy Union.
U-boat = German submarine.
UCL = University College, London.
UCS = Upper Clyde Shipbuilders.
UDEAC = Central African Economic and Customs Union.
UDEAO = Customs Union of West African States.
UEAC = Union of Central African States.
UGC = University Grants Committee.
UHF = ultra-high frequency.
U.K. (*or* UK) = United Kingdom.
UKAEA = UK Atomic Energy Authority.
ult. = *ultimo* (of the last month).
UN *or* UNO = United Nations.
UNCTAD = United Nations Conference on Trade and Development.
UNDOF = UN Disengagement Observer Force.
UNDP = United Nations Development Programme.
UNEF = United Nations Emergency Force(s).
UNESCO = United Nations Education, Scientific, and Cultural Organisation.
UNICEF = United Nations Children's Fund.
UNIDO = United Nations Industrial Development Organisation.
UNRWA = United Nations Relief and Works Agency for Palestine Refugees.
UNTSO = UN Truce Supervision Organisation in the Middle East.
U.P. = United Press.
UPU = Universal Postal Union (UN).
U.S.A. (*or* USA) = United States of America.
USAEC = US Atomic Energy Commission.
U.S.P.G. = United Society for the Propagation of the Gospel.
USSR = Union of Soviet Socialist Republics (Russia).

V

V = volt(s).
v. = *vide* (see); *versus* (against).
V.A. = Vicar-Apostolic.
VAT = value added tax.
V. & A. = Victoria and Albert Museum, S. Kensington.
V.C. = Victoria Cross.
V.C.H. = Victoria County Histories.
V.D. = venereal disease; Volunteer Officers' Decoration.
v.d. = various dates.
V.E. Day = Victory in Europe Day, 8 May 1945.
Ven. = Venerable (of an Archdeacon).
verb. sap. = *verbum sapienti sat est* (a word to the wise is enough).
Very Rev. = Very Reverend (of a Dean or a Provost).
v.g. = very good.
v.h.c. = very highly commended.
V.H.F. = very high frequency.
V.I.P. = very important person.
viz. = *videlicet* (namely).
V.J. Day = Victory over Japan Day, 15 August 1945.
V.L. = Vice-Lieutenant (of a County).
V.M. = Virgin Mary.
V.M.H. = Victoria Medal of Honour (Royal Horticultural Society).
Vo. = *verso* (on the left-hand page).
V.P. = Vice-President.
V.R. = *Victoria Regina* (Queen Victoria).
v.r. = variant, *or* various reading.
V.S. = veterinary surgeon; vital statistics.
VTOL = vertical take-off and landing (aircraft).

W

W = watt(s).
Wasps = White Anglo-Saxon Protestants.
WCC = World Council of Churches.
W.E.A. = Workers' Educational Association.
WEU = Western European Union.
WFTU = World Federation of Trade Unions.
WHO = World Health Organisation (UN).
WMO = World Meteorological Organisation (UN).
W.O. = Warrant Officer.
W.R.A.C. = Women's Royal Army Corps.
W.R.A.F. = Women's Royal Air Force.
W.R.N.S. = Women's Royal Naval Service.
W.R.V.S. = Women's Royal Voluntary Service.
W.S. = Writer to the Signet.

Y

yd = yard(s).
Y.M.C.A. = Young Men's Christian Association.
Y.W.C.A. = Young Women's Christian Association.

Z

ZANU = Zimbabwe African National Union (Nat. movement in Rhodesia).
ZAPU = Zimbabwe African People's Union (Nat. movement in Rhodesia).
ZIPA = Zimbabwe People's Army.

FOREIGN PHRASES

Fr., French. Gr., Greek. Ger., German. It., Italian. L., Latin. Sp., Spanish.

à bas (Fr.), down, down with.
ab extra (L.), from without.
ab incunabilis (L.), from the cradle.
ab initio (L.), from the beginning.
ab intra (L.), from within.
à bon chat, bon rat (Fr.), to a good cat, a good rat; well attacked and defended; tit for tat; a Rowland for an Oliver.
à bon marché (Fr.), cheap, a good bargain.
à bras ouverts (Fr.), with open arms.
absente reo (L.), the accused being absent.
absit invidia (L.), let there be no ill-will; envy apart.
ab uno disce omnes (L.), from one specimen judge of all the rest; from a single instance infer the whole.
ab urbe conditâ (L.), from the building of the city; i.e., Rome.
a capite ad calcem (L.), from head to heel.
à chaque saint sa chandelle (Fr.), to each saint his candle; honour where honour is due.
à cheval (Fr.), on horseback.
à compte (Fr.), on account; in part payment.
à corps perdu (Fr.), with might and main.
à couvert (Fr.), under cover; protected; sheltered.
ad astra (L.), to the stars.
ad calendas Græcas (L.), at the Greek calends; *i.e.*, never, as the Greeks had no calends in their mode of reckoning.
à demi (Fr.), by halves; half-way.
a Deo et rege (L.), from God and the king.
ad hoc (L.), arranged for this purpose; special.
ad hominem (L.), to the man; to an individual's interests or passions; personal.
adhuc sub judice lis est (L.), the case has not yet been decided.
a die (L.), from that day.
ad infinitum (L.), to infinity
ad interim (L.), in the meantime.
ad libitum (L.), at pleasure.
ad modum (L.), after the manner of.
ad nauseam (L.), to disgust or satiety.
ad referendum (L.), for further consideration.
ad rem (L.), to the purpose; to the point.
ad valorem (L.), according to the value.
affaire d'amour (Fr.), a love affair.
affaire d'honneur (Fr.), an affair of honour; a duel.
affaire de cœur (Fr.), an affair of the heart.
a fortiori (L.), with stronger reason.
à gauche (Fr.), to the left.
à genoux (Fr.), on the knees.
à haute voix (Fr.), aloud.
à huis clos (Fr.), with closed doors; secretly.
à la belle étoile (Fr.), under the stars; in the open air.
à la bonne heure (Fr.), well timed; all right; very well; as you please.
à l'abri (Fr.), under shelter.
à la mode (Fr.), according to the custom or fashion.
à la Tartuffe (Fr.), like Tartuffe, the hero of a celebrated comedy by Molière; hypocritically.
al fresco (It.), in the open air; out-of-doors.
al più (It.), at most.
alter ego (L.), another self.
à merveille (Fr.), to a wonder; marvellously.
amor patriæ (L.), love of country.
amour-propre (Fr.), self-love; vanity.
ancien régime (Fr.), the ancient or former order of things.
anguis in herba (L.), a snake in the grass.
anno Christi (L.), in the year of Christ.
anno Domini (L.), in the year of our Lord.
anno mundi (L.), in the year of the world.
annus mirabilis (L.), year of wonders; wonderful year.
ante bellum (L.), before the war.
ante lucem (L.), before light.
ante meridiem (L.), before noon.
à outrance (Fr.), to the utmost; to extremities; without sparing.
à pied (Fr.), on foot.
à point (Fr.), to a point, just in time, exactly right.
a posse ad esse (L.), from possibility to reality.
ariston metron (Gr.), the middle course is the best; the golden mean.
arrière-pensée (Fr.), hidden thought; mental reservation.
au courant (Fr.), fully acquainted with.
audi alteram partem (L.), hear the other side.
au fait (Fr.), well acquainted with; expert.
au fond (Fr.), at bottom.
auf Wiedersehen! (Ger.), till we meet again.
au pis aller (Fr.), at the worst.
au revoir (Fr.), adieu till we meet again.
aut vincere aut mori (L.), either to conquer or to die; death or victory.
a verbis ad verbera (L.), from words to blows.
a vinculo matrimonii (L.), from the bond of matrimony.
à volonté (Fr.), at pleasure.
a vostra salute (It.), *à votre santé* (Fr.), *a vuestra salud* (Sp.), } to your health.
bas bleu (Fr.), a blue-stocking; a literary woman.
beau monde (Fr.), the world of fashion.
beaux esprits (Fr.), men of wit; gay spirits.
beaux yeux (Fr.), fine eyes; good looks.
ben trovato (It.), well or cleverly invented.
bête noire (Fr.), a black beast; a bugbear.
bon gré mal gré (Fr.), with good or ill grace; willing or unwilling.
bonhomie (Fr.), good-nature; artlessness.
bonne bouche (Fr.), a delicate or tasty morsel.
bon vivant (Fr.), a good liver; a gourmand.
brutum fulmen (L.), a harmless thunderbolt.
canaille (Fr.), rabble.
candida Pax (L.), white-robed Peace.
casus belli (L.), that which causes or justifies war.
causa sine qua non (L.), an indispensable cause or condition.
caveat emptor (L.), let the buyer beware (or look after his own interest).
cela va sans dire (Fr.), that goes without saying; needless to say.
ceteris paribus (L.), other things being equal.
chacun son goût (Fr.), every one to his taste.
cogito, ergo sum (L.), I think, therefore I exist.
comme il faut (Fr.), as it should be.
compos mentis (L.), sound of mind; quite sane.
compte rendu (Fr.), an account rendered; a report or statement drawn up.
conditio sine qua non (L.), a necessary condition.
conseil de famille (Fr.), a family consultation.
consensus facit legem (L.), consent makes the law.
consilio et animis (L.), by wisdom and courage.
consilio et prudentia (L.), by wisdom and prudence.
constantia et virtute (L.), by constancy and virtue.
contra bonos mores (L.), against good manners.
contretemps (Fr.), an unlucky accident; a hitch.
cordon bleu (Fr.), blue ribbon; a cook of the highest class.
cordon sanitaire (Fr.), a line of guards to prevent the spreading of contagion or pestilence.
corpus delicti (L.), the body or substance of a crime or offence.
corrigenda (L.), things to be corrected.
coup de grâce (Fr.), a finishing stroke.
coup d'état (Fr.), a sudden decisive blow in politics; a stroke of policy.
coup de soleil (Fr.), sunstroke.
credat Judæus Apella (L.), let Apella, the superstitious Jew, believe it (I won't); tell that to the marines.
cucullus non facit monachum (L.), the cowl does not make the friar.
cui bono? (L.), For whose advantage is it? to what end?
culpam pœna premit comes (L.), punishment follows hard upon crime.
cum grano salis (L.), with a grain of salt; with some allowance.
cum privilegio (L.), with privilege.
currente calamo (L.), with a fluent pen.
da locum melioribus (L.), give place to your betters.
damnant quod non intelligunt (L.), they condemn what they do not comprehend.
data et accepta (L.), expenditures and receipts.
de bon augure (Fr.), of good augury or omen.
de bonne grâce (Fr.), with good grace; willingly.

de die in diem (L.), from day to day.
de facto (L.), in point of fact; actual or actually.
dei gratia (L.), by God's grace.
de jure (L.), from the law; by right.
de mal en pis (Fr.), from bad to worse.
de novo (L.), anew.
deo volente (L.), God willing; by God's will.
de profundis (L.), out of the depths.
dernier ressort (Fr.), a last resource.
deus ex machina (L.), one who puts matters right at a critical moment; providential intervention.
dies non (L.), a day on which judges do not sit.
distingué (Fr.), distinguished; of genteel or elegant appearance.
dolce far niente (It.), sweet doing-nothing; sweet idleness.
double entente (Fr.), a double meaning; a play on words.
dramatis personæ (L.), characters of the drama or play.
dum spiro, spero (L.), while I breathe, I hope.
ecce homo! (L.), behold the man!
eheu! fugaces labuntur anni (L.), alas! the fleeting years glide by.
einmal ist keinmal (Ger.), just once doesn't count.
en avant (Fr.), forward.
en badinant (Fr.), in sport; in jest.
en déshabillé (Fr.), in undress.
en famille (Fr.), with one's family; in a domestic state.
enfant terrible (Fr.), a terrible child, or one that makes disconcerting remarks.
enfin (Fr.), in short; at last; finally.
en passant (Fr.), in passing; by the way.
en plein jour (Fr.), in broad day.
en rapport (Fr.), in harmony; in agreement; in relation.
en règle (Fr.), according to rules; in order.
entente cordiale (Fr.), cordial understanding, especially between two states.
entre nous (Fr.), between ourselves.
en vérité (Fr.), in truth; verily.
e pluribus unum (L.), one out of many; one composed of many.
esprit de corps (Fr.), the animating spirit of a collective body, as a regiment, learned profession or the like.
et sequentes, et sequentia (L.), and those that follow.
et tu, Brute! (L.), and thou also, Brutus!
ex animo (L.), heartily; sincerely.
ex capite (L.), from the head; from memory.
ex cathedra (L.), from the chair or seat of authority, with high authority.
exceptio probat regulam (L.), the exception proves the rule.
ex curia (L.), out of court.
ex dono (L.), by the gift.
exeunt omnes (L.), all go out or retire.
exit (L.), he goes out.
ex mero motu (L.), from his own impulse, from his own free will.
ex nihilo nihil fit (L.), out of nothing, nothing comes; nothing produces nothing.
ex officio (L.), in virtue of his office.
ex post facto (L.), after the deed is done; retrospective.
face à face (Fr.), face to face.
façon de parler (Fr.), manner of speaking.
faire bonne mine (Fr.), to put a good face upon the matter.
fait accompli (Fr.), a thing already done.
fama clamosa (L.), a current scandal; a prevailing report.
faute de mieux (Fr.), for want of better.
faux pas (Fr.), a false step; a slip in behaviour.
festina lente (L.), hasten slowly.
fiat justitia, ruat cœlum (L.), let justice be done though the heavens should fall.
fiat lux (L.), let there be light.
fide et amore (L.), by faith and love.
fide et fiduciâ (L.), by fidelity and confidence.
fide et fortitudine (L.), with faith and fortitude.
fidei defensor (L.), defender of the faith.
fide non armis (L.), by faith, not by arms.
fide, sed cui vide (L.), trust, but see whom.
fides et justitia (L.), fidelity and justice.
fides Punica (L.), Punic faith; treachery.
filius nullius (L.), a son of nobody; a bastard.
finis coronat opus (L.), the end crowns the work.
flagrante bello (L.), during hostilities.
flagrante delicto (L.), in the commission of the crime.
floreat (L.), let it flourish.
fons et origo (L.), the source and origin.
force majeure (Fr.), irresistible compulsion; war, strike, Act of God, etc.
forensis strepitus (L.), the clamour of the forum.
fortuna favet fortibus (L.), fortune favours the bold.
functus officio (L.), having performed one's office or duty; hence, out of office.
gaudeamus igitur (L.), so let us be joyful!
genius loci (L.), the genius or guardian spirit of a place.
gradu diverso, via una (L.), the same road by different steps.
grande parure, *grande toilette* (Fr.), full dress.
guerra al cuchillo (Sp.), war to the knife.
Hannibal ante portas (L.), Hannibal before the gates; the enemy close at hand.
hiatus valde deflendus (L.), a chasm or deficiency much to be regretted.
hic et nunc (L.), here and now.
hic et ubique (L.), here and everywhere.
hic jacet (L.), here lies.
hic labor, hoc opus est (L.), this is a labour, this is a toil.
hic sepultus (L.), here buried.
hoc genus omne (L.), all of this sort or class.
hoi polloi (Gr.), the many; the vulgar; the rabble.
hominis est errare (L.), to err is human.
homme de robe (Fr.), a man in civil office.
homme d'affaires (Fr.), a man of business.
homme d'esprit (Fr.), a man of wit or genius.
honi soit qui mal y pense (O. Fr.), evil to him who evil thinks.
honores mutant mores (L.), honours change men's manners or characters.
hors de combat (Fr.), out of condition to fight.
hors de propos (Fr.), not to the point or purpose.
hors-d'œuvre (Fr.), out of course; out of order.
ich dien (Ger.), I serve.
idée fixe (Fr.), a fixed idea.
id est (L.), that is.
il a le diable au corps (Fr.), the devil is in him.
Ilias malorum (L.), an Iliad of ills; a host of evils.
il penseroso (It.), the pensive man.
il sent le fagot (Fr.), he smells of the faggot; he is suspected of heresy.
imperium in imperio (L.), a state within a state; a government within another.
in actu (L.), in act or reality.
in articulo mortis (L.), at the point of death; in the last struggle.
in capite (L.), in chief.
in curia (L.), in court.
index expurgatorius, *index prohibitorius* (L.), a list of books prohibited to Roman Catholics.
in esse (L.), in being; in actuality.
in extenso (L.), at full length.
in extremis (L.), at the point of death.
in memoriam (L.), to the memory of; in memory.
in nubibus (L.), in the clouds.
in petto (It.), in (my) breast; to one's self.
in re (L.), in the matter of.
in sano sensu (L.), in a proper sense.
in situ (L.), in its original situation.
in vino veritas (L.), there is truth in wine; truth is told under the influence of intoxicants.
ipse dixit (L.), he himself said it; a dogmatic saying or assertion.
ipsissima verba (L.), the very words.
ipso facto (L.), in the fact itself.
ipso jure (L.), by the law itself.
jacta est alea (L.), the die is cast.
je ne sais quoi (Fr.), I know not what.
joci causa (L.), for the sake of a joke.
labor omnia vincit (L.), labour conquers everything.
l'allegro (It.), the merry man.
lapsus linguæ (L.), a slip of the tongue.
lares et penates (L.), household gods.
laus Deo (L.), praise to God.
le beau monde (Fr.), the fashionable world.
lector benevole (L.), kind or gentle reader.
le jeu n'en vaut pas la chandelle (Fr.), the game is not worth the candle; the object is not worth the trouble.
le mot de l'énigme (Fr.), the key to the mystery.
le point du jour (Fr.), daybreak.
lèse-majesté (Fr.), high-treason.
lettre de cachet (Fr.), a sealed letter containing private orders; a royal warrant.
lex loci (L.), the law or custom of the place.
lex non scripta (L.), unwritten law; common law.
lex scripta (L.), written law; statute law.
locum tenens (L.), a deputy.

lucri causa (L.), for the sake of gain.
magnum opus (L.), a great work.
mala fide (L.), with bad faith; treacherously.
mal à propos (Fr.), ill-timed; out of place.
malgré nous (Fr.), in spite of us.
malheur ne vient jamais seul (Fr.), misfortunes never come singly.
malum in se (L.), evil or an evil in itself.
mardi gras (Fr.), Shrove-Tuesday.
mariage de convenance (Fr.), marriage from motives of interest rather than of love.
mauvaise honte (Fr.), false modesty.
mauvais goût (Fr.), bad taste.
mea culpa (L.), my fault; by my fault.
me judice (L.), I being judge; in my opinion.
mens agitat molem (L.), mind moves matter.
mens legis (L.), the spirit of the law.
mens sana in corpore sano (L.), a sound mind in a sound body.
meo periculo (L.), at my own risk.
meo voto (L.), according to my wish.
mise en scène (Fr.), the getting up for the stage, or the putting on the stage.
modus operandi (L.), manner of working.
more suo (L.), in his own way.
motu proprio (L.), of his own accord.
multum in parvo (L.), much in little.
mutatis mutandis (L.), with suitable or necessary alteration.
nervus probandi (L.), the sinews of the argument.
nihil ad rem (L.), irrelevant.
nil desperandum (L.), there is no reason to despair.
noblesse oblige (Fr.), rank imposes obligations; much is expected from one in good position.
nolens volens (L.), willing or unwilling.
nom de guerre (Fr.), a false or assumed name.
non compos mentis (L.), not of sound mind.
non sequitur (L.), it does not follow.
nosce te ipsum (L.), know thyself.
nota bene (L.), mark well.
nudis verbis (L.), in plain words.
obiter dictum (L.), a thing said by the way.
omnia vincit amor (L.), love conquers all things.
ora pro nobis (L.), pray for us.
O tempora! O mores! (L.), O the times! O the manners (or morals)!
ouï-dire (Fr.), hearsay.
padrone (It.), a master; a landlord.
par excellence (Fr.), by way of eminence.
pari passu (L.), at an equal pace or rate of progress.
particeps criminis (L.), an accomplice in a crime.
pas de quoi (Fr. abbrev. Il n'y a pas de quoi), don't mention it.
passim (L.), everywhere; in all parts of the book, chapter, etc.
pâté de foie gras (Fr.), goose-liver pie.
pater patriæ (L.), father of his country.
patres conscripti (L.), the conscript fathers; Roman senatore.
pax vobiscum (L.), peace be with you.
per ardua ad astra (L.), through rough ways to the stars; through suffering to renown.
per capita (L.), by the head or poll.
per contra (It.), contrariwise.
per diem (L.), by the day; daily.
per se (L.), by itself; considered apart.
pied-à-terre (Fr.), a resting-place; a temporary lodging.
pis aller (Fr.), the worst or last shift.
plebs (L.), the common people.
poco a poco (It.), little by little. [called for.
poste restante (Fr.), to remain in the post-office till
prima facie (L.), at first view or consideration.
primus inter pares (L.), first among equals.
pro forma (L.), for the sake of form.
pro patria (L.), for our country.
pro tanto (L.), for so much; for as far as it goes.
pro tempore (L.), for the time being.
quid pro quo (L.), one thing for another; tit for tat; an equivalent.
qui m'aime, aime mon chien (Fr.), love me, love my dog. [sent.
qui tacet consentit (L.), he who is silent gives con-
quod erat demonstrandum (L.), which was to be proved or demonstrated.
quod erat faciendum (L.), which was to be done.
quod vide (L.), which see; refer to the word just mentioned.
quo jure? (L.), by what right? [tence.
raison d'être (Fr.), the reason for a thing's exis-
re (L.), in the matter or affair of.
reculer pour mieux sauter (Fr.), to draw back in order to make a better spring.
reductio ad adsurdum (L.), the reducing of a position to a logical absurdity.
requiescat in pace (L.), may he (or she) rest in peace.
respice finem (L.), look to the end.
respublica (L.), the commonwealth.
revenons à nos moutons (Fr.), let us return to our sheep; let us return to our subject.
re vera (L.), in truth.
sans peur et sans reproche (Fr.), without fear and without reproach.
sans rime ni raison (Fr.), without rhyme or reason.
sans souci (Fr.), without care.
sartor resartus (L.), the botcher repatched; the tailor patched or mended.
sauve qui peut (Fr.), let him save himself who can.
savoir-faire (Fr.), the knowing how to act; tact.
savoir-vivre (Fr.), good-breeding; refined manners.
semper idem (L.), always the same.
seriatim (L.), in a series; one by one.
sic passim (L.), so here and there throughout; so everywhere.
sicut ante (L.), as before.
sine die (L.), without a day being appointed.
sine mora (L.), without delay.
sine qua non (L.), without which, not; indispensable condition.
sotto voce (It.), in an undertone.
spirituel (Fr.), intellectual; witty.
stet (L.), let it stand; do not delete.
sub judice (L.), under consideration.
sub pœna (L.), under a penalty
sub rosa (L.), under the rose; privately.
sub voce (L.), under such or such a word.
sui generis (L.), of its own or of a peculiar kind.
summum bonum (L.), the chief good.
tableau vivant (Fr.), a living picture; the representation of some scene by a group of persons.
tant mieux (Fr.), so much the better.
tant pis (Fr.), so much the worse.
tempora mutantur, nos et mutamur in illis (L.), the times are changing and we with them.
tempus fugit (L.), time flies.
tête-à-tête (Fr.), together in private.
tiers état (Fr.), the third estate; the commons.
to kalon (Gr.), the beautiful; the chief good.
to prepon (Gr.), the becoming or proper.
tour de force (Fr.), a feat of strength or skill.
tout à fait (Fr.), wholly; entirely.
tout à l'heure (Fr.), instantly.
tout de suite (Fr.), immediately.
tu quoque (L.), thou also.
ubique (L.), everywhere.
ubi supra (L.), where above mentioned.
ultra licitum (L.), beyond what is allowable.
ultra vires (L.), beyond powers or rights conferred by law.
urbi et orbi (L.), to the city (Rome) and the world.
utile dulci (L.), the useful with the pleasant.
ut infra (L.), as below.
ut supra (L.), as above stated.
vade in pace (L.), go in peace.
variæ lectiones (L.), various readings.
variorum notæ (L.), the notes of various commentators.
vede et crede (L.), see and believe.
veni, vidi, vici (L.), I came, I saw, I conquered.
verbatim et literatim (L.), word for word and letter for letter.
verbum sat sapienti (L.), a word is enough for a wise man.
ver non semper viret (L.), spring is not always green.
vexata quæstio (L.), a disputed question.
via media (L.), a middle course.
via trita, via tuta (L.), the beaten path is the safe path.
vice versâ (L.), the terms of the case being reversed.
videlicet (L.), that is to say; namely.
vi et armis (L.), by force of arms; by main force; by violence.
vigilate et orate (L.), watch and pray.
vita brevis, ars longa (L.), life is short; art is long.
vivat regina! (L.), long live the queen!
vivat rex! (L.), long live the king!
viva voce (L.), by the living voice; orally.
voilà (Fr.), behold; there is; there are.
voilà tout (Fr.), that's all.
volo, non valeo (L.), I am willing, but unable.
vox populi, vox Dei (L.), the voice of the people is the voice of God.

TAXATION

INCOME TAX

In general, income tax is charged on all income which originates in the United Kingdom and on all income arising abroad of persons resident in the United Kingdom. The income tax year is from 6 April to the following 5 April. On 6 April 1973 a new unified system of personal tax replaced the old income tax and surtax. There is now no earned income relief, small income relief and age relief (personal allowances have been increased to allow for this) and no surtax (replaced by higher rates of income tax).

Tax liability. Income tax at the basic rate and higher rates (see below) is charged on your taxable income, i.e., that part which remains after all allowable deductions have been made.

In his 1977 April Budget the Chancellor announced that conditional upon a pay agreement being reached, the basic rate would be reduced from 35% to 33%.

		£
Single allowance and wife's earned income allowance		805
Married allowance		1,125
Additional personal allowance (certain people who have single-handed responsibility for children living with them)		420
Age allowance		
Single person over 65		1,080
Married couple (if one of them is over 65)		1,695
	first child	each of the others
Child allowances		
age under 11	196	170
11–16	231	207
over 16	261	235

(if receiving full-time instruction at university, college or school or being trained for not less than 2 years for a trade, etc.).

Note: child tax allowances are gradually being replaced by child benefits paid to mother (tax-free £52 for the first child, £78 for each of the others).

Dependent relative	
Single woman claimant	145
Others	100
(reduced by £1 for every £1 by which relative's income exceeds amount of basic National insurance retirement pension)	
Daughter's services (old or infirm tax-payer)	55
Housekeeper allowance	100
Blind person's allowance	180

Life insurance relief
amount of total premiums if less than £10
£10 if total premiums between £10 and £20
one-half allowable premiums if more than £20

Work abroad. If 30 days or more (continuously or not) are spent abroad for your employer in any one year, tax relief will be given on a quarter of that period's earnings.

It is still necessary to distinguish between earned and investment income because tax-payers with an investment income of between £1,500 and £2,000 (£2,000 and £2,500 for the over-65s) are surcharged by adding 10% to the rate of tax. Above £2,000 the surcharge is 15%.

Higher rates of tax

In his 1977 April Budget the Chancellor raised the tax-rate threshold for every income band, as follows:

%	1976–77 £	1977–78 £
Basic rate	1–5,000	1–6,000
40	5,001–5,500	6,001–7,000
45	5,501–6,500	7,001–8,000
50	6,501–7,500	8,001–9,000
55	7,501–8,500	9,001–10,000
60	8,501–10,000	10,001–12,000
65	10,001–12,000	12,001–14,000
70	12,001–15,000	14,001–16,000
75	15,001–20,000	16,001–21,000
83	over £20,000	over £21,000

CAPITAL TRANSFER TAX

Since the capital transfer tax (CTT) came into operation estate duty has been an unavoidable tax. The tax was approved by Parliament in March 1975 and applies to all gifts made since March 1974. It covers transmissions of personal wealth and is chargeable on the cumulative total of transfers made in a person's lifetime and on his death. All transfers of wealth between husband and wife are exempt (except where the recipient was not domiciled in the UK at the time of the gift or death). Gifts not exceeding £2,000 in any one year are not chargeable nor those made out of normal regular income. The tax is paid by the donor, and calculated not on the net value of the gift, but on the value of the gift plus the tax ("grossing-up"). Charitable gifts are exempt without limit unless made within one year of death or on death, when there is a maximum exemption of £100,000. A separate and lower rate scale applies to lifetime gifts (made more than three years before death) and to small businesses and farms.

Portion of value £'000.	Lifetime transfer rate. %	Death rate. %
0–15	—	—
15–20	5	10
20–25	7½	15
25–30	10	20
30–40	12½	25
40–50	15	30
50–60	17½	35
60–80	20	40
80–100	22½	45
100–120	27½	50
120–150	35	55
150–200	42½	
200–250	50	
250–300	55	
300–500	60	
150–500		60
500–1,000	65	65
1,000–2,000	70	70
2,000+	75	75

THE 1977 BUDGET

As a result of the changes announced by the Chancellor of the Exchequer on 29 March 1977, the following rates of taxation will come into force:

SINGLE PERSONS—INCOME ALL EARNED

Income	1976/77 Income Tax	Proposed change 1977/78 after initial changes only Income Tax	1977/78 after all changes Income Tax	Reduction in tax after all changes
£	£	£	£	£
1,000	92·75	68·25	64·35	28·40
1,500	267·75	243·25	229·35	38·40
2,000	442·75	418·25	394·35	48·40
2,500	617·75	593·25	559·35	58·40
3,000	792·75	768·25	724·35	68·40
3,500	967·75	943·25	889·35	78 40
4,000	1,142·75	1,118·25	1,054·35	88·40
4,500	1,317·75	1,293·25	1,219·35	98·40
5,000	1,492·75	1,468·25	1,384·35	108·40
6,000	1,856·00	1,818·25	1,714·35	141·65
7,000	2,294·25	2,178·00	2,058·00	236·25
8 000	2,782·50	2,587·75	2,467·75	314·75
9,000	3,320·75	3,047·50	2,927·50	393·25
10,000	3,909·00	3,557·25	3,437·25	471·75
15,000	7,235·50	6,636·50	6,516·50	719·00
20,000	10,948·75	10,296·25	10,176·25	772·50
25,000	15,039·95	14,301·85	14,181·85	858·10

MARRIED COUPLES—INCOME ALL EARNED

Income	1976/77 Income tax	Proposed change 1977/78 after initial changes only Income tax	1977/78 after all changes Income tax	Reduction in tax after all changes
£	£	£	£	£
1,200	40·25	0·00	0·00	0·00
1,500	145·25	96·25	90·75	54·50
2,000	320·25	271·25	255·75	64·50
2,500	495·25	446·25	420·75	74·50
3,000	670·25	621·25	585·75	84·50
3,500	845·25	796·25	750·75	94·50
4,000	1,020·25	971·25	915·75	104·50
4,500	1,195·25	1,146·25	1,080·75	114·50
5,000	1,370·25	1.321·25	1,245·75	124·50
6,000	1,720·25	1,671·25	1,575·75	144·50
7,000	2,136·75	2,021·25	1,905·75	231·00
8.000	2,607·50	2,410·00	2,290·00	317·50
9,000	3,128·25	2,848·75	2,728·75	399·50
10,000	3,699·00	3,337·50	3,217·50	481·50
15,000	6 990·50	6,353·75	6,233·75	756·75
20,000	10,686·25	9,861·25	9,861·25	825·00
25,000	14,749·45	13,953·25	13,833·25	916·20

MARRIED COUPLES WITH TWO CHILDREN NOT OVER 11—INCOME ALL EARNED

(Net income includes family allowance or child benefit, less income tax)

Income before child benefit	1976/77 Net income	Proposed change 1977/78 after initial changes only Net income	1977/78 after all changes Net income	Increases in net income after all changes
£	£	£	£	£
1.500	1,578·00	1,630·00	1,630·00	52·00
2,000	1,922·25	1,986·85	1,995·03	72·78
2,500	2,247·25	2,311·50	2,330·03	82·78
3,000	2,572·25	2,636·85	2.665·03	92·78
3,500	2,897·25	2,961·85	3,000·03	102·78
4,000	3,222·25	3,286·85	3,335·03	112·78
4,500	3,547·25	3,611·85	3,670·03	122·78
5,000	3,872·25	3,936·85	4,005·03	132·78
6,000	4.522·25	4,586·85	4,675·03	152·78
7,000	5,150·00	5,236·85	5,345·03	195·03
8,000	5,702·75	5,866·40	5,986·40	283·65
9,000	6,205·50	6,445·95	6,565·95	360·45
10,000	6,658·25	6,975·50	7,095·50	437·65
15,000	8,416·50	9,014·15	9,134·15	717·65
20,000	9,744·25	10,423·25	10,543·25	799·00
25,000	10,718·25	11,480·53	11,600·53	882·28

MEDICAL MATTERS

Here we give a brief summary of up-to-date medical knowledge, including some recent developments. It must not be allowed to replace your doctor, who should be consulted immediately if you are worried. An index ensures easy reference.

TABLE OF CONTENTS

MEDICAL MATTERS

PART I. INTRODUCTION.

(a) HOW TO USE THE SECTION.

Diseases do not exist in watertight compartments, but doctors arrange them according either to their cause or the area of the body affected. This plan has been followed here, and at the beginning of each part an account of the group of diseases under discussion is given. Unless you know enough already, you would be wise to read it.

Here is some advice about your attitude to disease in general, and your use of this section in particular.

First of all, and obviously, no book is a substitute for the doctor, and when you are ill you must see him. There are good and bad doctors, competent and incompetent ones, just as in any other profession or trade; so choose a doctor you can trust, *and then believe what he tells you and carry out his advice.* There is no use complaining about the whole medical profession just because you are dissatisfied with your own G.P. If you are, you should sign on with another.

Secondly, *never* believe what you hear from non-medical sources. Literally millions of people are made miserable every year by taking to heart nonsense told them by others, who may well be quite unaware of the harm they do, or even have the very best intentions. In any medical matter ask your doctor, and ignore your next-door neighbour's asked-for or unasked-for advice. Doctors are sometimes wrong, but they are much less likely to be wrong than someone without a medical education. Remember, too, that the statement that there is no cure for a disease does not necessarily mean that it is deadly: and it never means that nothing can be done to make it more tolerable. There is much more to modern doctoring than simply curing the curable.

Thirdly, don't try to diagnose your own trouble or decide what treatment you think you should have. This section will have failed completely in its intentions if it puts you in the position of a character described by an English humourist, who, from a medical dictionary, discovered that he had every disease listed in it with the solitary exception of housemaid's knee. Diseases which appear to the layman to have the "same" symptoms may be vastly different in seriousness: influenza and poliomyelitis, for example, may in the initial stages, appear very similar. So also may stomach ulcer and cancer of the stomach. No human being is infallible, but it is most important that you should go to the person who is best fitted to know—your doctor.

Lastly, you should not be misled into thinking that you can always tell the seriousness of a disease by the general appearance of the patient. Children, in particular, may have a high temperature, or even be delirious, on one day, and the next be out of bed and wanting to get back to school. On the other hand, many of the most dangerous fevers (as we shall see later) are accompanied by a low temperature and do not appear particularly dramatic in the initial stages. Thus a young woman who may be aware of nothing wrong but lack of energy and getting easily tired may be seriously ill with tuberculosis of the lungs.

The best rule is to seek medical advice either when you have suddenly become ill with symptoms you don't understand or (and this is equally important) if you have gradually been feeling less fit over a period of time. Perhaps, too, it is wise to call your doctor if you have been ill with *anything* for more than three days. You should *not* call in a specialist before seeing your G.P., as is so often done in America and on the Continent. Specialists are very clever, but are naturally prejudiced in favour of their own subject; for example, an eye specialist will be predisposed to think of your headache in terms of eyestrain, an ear, nose, and throat specialist in terms of sinus trouble, and a psychiatrist in terms of mother-in-law trouble. Therefore you should first have a check from your G.P., who knows a little of all these things and probably a great deal about you and your past history. He will then advise you about a specialist if necessary.

(b) NEW VIEWS ON MEDICINE.

(1) Body and Mind. In former times, or at least during the nineteenth century, the body was regarded as a sort of machine belonging to you in much the same way that you own your watch. You went to your doctor and, in effect, said: "Now what on earth are you going to do about my stomach?"—and you spoke as if, somehow, your stomach didn't have anything to do with the *real* you—it was just an awkward thing that happened to be annoying you. But we know now that this is not so—that your body *is* you, that it is a fort fighting against such enemies as poisons, parasites, germs, cancer, and injuries. The defences are seriously weakened by not enough of the right kind of food, insufficient sleep, or by anxiety. Your anxieties and worries can kill you just as surely as the other agents, and can prevent recovery or retard it when you are already ill.

A stomach ulcer therefore is not just something that is happening to you, you are happening to it. Your fears, your jealousies, your hatreds, your inability to get on in life, can be (in some cases) just as harmful as germs or poisons—in fact, they act by setting free glandular poisons in your blood-stream. Scientists have discovered a reaction which they call the "stress response," and we now know that stress can ultimately lead to sickness or death without any bodily injury at all. Thus, Dr. L. J. Saul, a leading American doctor, wrote: "Emotional stress in which there is no physical damage can produce responses which lead to actual damage and even to death." Rats in the laboratory can be killed through long exposure to fear caused by loud noises or other forms of shock without even being touched.

This stress factor is emphasised not because it is more important than the other enemies of the body or mind (it would be better to say body-mind), but because, as we shall see later, it does cause serious diseases, and, secondly, as mentioned already, it influences the process of recovery. A person who is afraid or has no hope is less likely to recover from pneumonia or another disease than one who is hopeful, who has peace of mind and confidence.

(2) New Views about Health. A great deal of nonsense has been talked about the healthy life; at one time we were told to take eighteen chews to each bite, to do deep breathing, to take plenty of exercise, to get lots of fresh air, to eat regularly (or to indulge in peculiar diets). But more recently eminent doctors have cast doubt on most of these fancies. Moderate exercise is necessary to health, but athletes who indulge in violent exercise have not always been noted for longevity. Fresh air is pleasant and stimulating, but, where actual breathing is concerned, it is no better than the air in most rooms. Certainly, one of the problems of our time is air pollution, but at present we are considering ordinary fresh air in comparison with the air indoors, and, in this case, the experts say there is little difference so far as health is concerned.

A balanced diet containing correct amounts of the basic food substances is essential, but there is no evidence that when, or at what intervals, you eat makes the slightest difference—unless you are a sufferer from stomach ulcer, in which case it is necessary that the intervals between meals should not be too long. The whole business of having meals at fixed intervals is nothing but a social convention, and in modern life obviously a matter of convenience. (*See* **Diet, P40**).

Sleep, too, is a necessity. But different people require vastly different amounts of sleep. Some manage on as little as three hours, others seem to believe that they need ten or more. The importance of the dream process is referred to in **Introduction to Psychology, Q15(1).**

In a number of studies of men and women who lived to a ripe old age it was found that the only factors in common between them were that they had a good balanced diet of healthy food, that they had contented minds, and that they were interested in something which gave them an aim in life. They also came of long-lived families—for living a long and healthy life depends partly upon heredity.

So the main rules of health are: (1) do not think too much about your health unless it gives you trouble; (2) have an interest in life and be prepared to sacrifice a lot for it (nothing useful has ever been done by those who are always "taking care" and being over-cautious); (3) eat a good balanced diet; (4) do not worry, and have a contented mind.

(3) New Drugs. A great surgeon, the first of the moderns, was Ambrose Paré, who died in 1590, and one of his best known sayings was: "I apply the dressing, but God heals the wound." He was quite right; for until about forty years ago, or even less, all the physician could do was to put the patient in as favourable a state as possible to enable his body to cure itself. That is to say, there were hardly any specific drugs—drugs that had a direct effect on the disease. There was quinine, discovered by the Spaniards in America, which was specific for malaria, and there were iron (specific for anæmia) and digitalis (specific for certain types of heart disease), but otherwise nothing until the nineteenth century, when Paul Ehrlich discovered salvarsan, which is specific for syphilis. Ehrlich died in 1914, having conceived the brilliant idea of drugs which he described as "magic bullets"—*i.e.*, drugs which, like bullets, would be aimed at the real cause of the disease. They would, that is to say, be specific.

Since then a large number of such drugs have been discovered. For example, the antibiotics, such as penicillin, discovered in 1928 by Fleming at St. Mary's Hospital, Paddington. Later, Florey and Chain in Oxford, helped in the war years by the vast resources of the American pharmaceutical industry, were able to make penicillin available to the public in sufficient quantities by new techniques of production. Penicillin is practically non-poisonous (although it is possible to become allergic to it, sometimes with serious results). It can kill some germs in a dilution of one part of penicillin to one hundred million parts of water; it is effective against streptococci, the cause of blood-poisoning, sepsis in wounds, and many other diseases; and also against the germs of anthrax, gonorrhœa, meningitis of some types, syphilis—a whole list of plagues which have troubled man for centuries. Blood-poisoning, whether from wounds or childbirth, used to be almost incurable—now the rate of cure is 80–90 per cent.; anthrax and gonorrhœa have an almost 100 per cent. rate of cure. In pneumonia the rate is about 90 per cent., and early syphilis can be cured in a week, instead of the previous two to three years.

But that was only the beginning. Other antibiotics—streptomycin, tetracycline, erythromycin, and many others—are helping to wipe out the terrible scourges of the human race, in particular, in the case of streptomycin, tuberculosis. The sulpha group of drugs—sulphadiazine, sulphadimidine, etc.—have also proved a great boon. Then there are the new drugs which have created a revolution in psychiatry—the tranquillisers which relieve anxiety, the drugs which clear up certain types of depression, and substances such as chlorpromazine which make it possible to nurse formerly violent patients in the wards of a general hospital. The antihistamine drugs help in allergies, anticoagulants are of value after heart attacks and levodopa mitigates some of the distressing features of Parkinson's Disease.

No drug, old or new, is completely safe—if we define "safe" as meaning having absolutely no potential for harm. The household aspirin, widely used in a variety of conditions for its analgesic (pain-relieving) and antipyretic (fever-reducing) qualities, can cause bleeding from the stomach and small intestine (**P23**). Phenacetin, at one time a component of compound codeine tablets but now withdrawn, can—with prolonged use—damage the kidney. Chloramphenicol, a powerful antibiotic effective in typhoid fever, typhus and whooping cough, can damage the blood-forming cells of the bone marrow producing an agranulocytosis which can be fatal.

Clearly, in any one case, the doctor must weigh up the advantages and disadvantages of this or that drug before prescribing. Minor, self-limiting illnesses do not require potent, potentially toxic remedies. Chloramphenicol is rarely justified in whooping cough, but would never be withheld from a patient with typhoid fever.

Man is a unique species. A new chemical compound promising in animal experiments, for example, as an anti-inflammatory agent, apparently safe when given, say, to mice in a dose 100 times that required to produce that anti-inflammatory effect may, over a long period of time in man, not only have no effect but make his hair fall out or perhaps cause retention of urine. Nevertheless, some animal species do react like man, or vice versa, and it is possible to make reasonably accurate extrapolations from animals to man in terms of drug effect. It is also possible to estimate the toxicity of a drug for man from its toxicity in certain animal species but the ultimate test, both of the effectiveness and the toxicity of a new drug, comes only when it is given to man.

Thalidomide was unique. In every animal test used throughout the drug industry at that time—it was introduced in the late 1950s—it had a clean bill of health. It was chemically related to other drugs which had been in use for a long time. Overdosage with other sedatives such as the barbiturates was common at that time, although less so now. Overdosage with thalidomide was unlikely to prove fatal. It was marketed in Europe and in Britain as a "safe sedative". The tragic results that followed its ingestion by women in the early weeks of pregnancy are now well known. Babies were born with severe deformities of limbs, internal organs or both. That effect could not have been foretold from any animal tests then in use. Since that date new drugs have been subjected to rigorous testing in various animal species to check the effect on foetal development as a statutory requirement, along with the older tests for toxicity which had always been undertaken by reputable drug companies.

The thalidomide disaster of the early 1960s led directly to the setting up of regulatory drug agencies in most countries of the world. In Britain the introduction and clinical testing of new compounds is controlled by the Medicines and Environmental Health Division of the Department of Health and Social Security, statutory machinery set up by the Medicines Act 1968, which followed the purely voluntary scheme of control under what was known as the Dunlop Committee after Sir Derrick Dunlop, its first chairman.

The development and introduction of new drugs is now very strictly controlled. No new drug can be marketed in Britain without the Medicines Commission being satisfied about its efficacy and its safety. We would need space in this edition almost the size of the complete Medical Section to describe fully the workings of the Commission and the limitations that the requirements of the Medicines Act inevitably place on the development and introduction of new remedies. The time from the initial synthesis of a novel compound likely to be of value to its eventual appearance in the pharmacy on prescription is now eight to 10 years. The cost is measured in millions of pounds because, for each successful drug, there will have been many thousands of unsuccessful ones.

Briefly, no new drug or modification of an old one can be sold, whether or not on prescription, unless it has been granted a product licence by the Department of Health and Social Security through its Medicines and Environmental Health Division. Many stages have to be passed to acquire that licence, from the granting of certificates to allow the drug to be tested initially in a limited way in patients in a strictly controlled manner by investigators approved by the Commission, to permission for extension of those trials at a later date to include larger numbers of patients or more investigators, to perhaps a "monitored release"—that is, to enable its use in, say, hospitals only—to the final release on the granting of a full product licence. Thus, the Medicines Commission has control at all stages.

Furthermore, all the stages are dependent on production of evidence relating to the safety and efficacy of the drug, evidence which may take the drug company months, sometimes years, to produce and which, of course, must be acceptable to the Commission. Trials may be stopped at any time, for example, if evidence of side effects of an undesirable nature come to light during clinical testing, or when evidence from some other similar compound indicates a likely risk in the use of the drug in question. Of course, "acceptable" means that the strict criteria which have been laid down by the specialist committees appointed to deal with all the various aspects of drug development, such as toxicology, adverse reactions and so forth, have been met. Experts serve on these committees which meet regularly, but the day-to-day running of the Medicines Commission is in the hands of full-time medically qualified personnel as well as pharmacists, pharmacologists and toxicologists. In addition, outside consultant opinion can be sought.

As well as all these rigid controls on development and testing in the early stages, there is also a scheme of surveillance for untoward side effects. These are the action, or actions, of a drug apart from its main one. Take the well-known side effect of drowsiness which occurs with certain antihistamine drugs: the main action, the one for which the drug is prescribed, is the mitigation of the effects of allergy, such as urticaria. Drowsiness would be an unwanted effect if the patient is not incapacitated and is able to do his usual job. On the other hand, some antihistamines have an appetite-stimulating effect which could, of course, be a useful attribute in certain situations or even allow the drug to be used solely for that purpose, the anti-allergic effect then being incidental.

An adverse reaction is a type of side effect which by definition, is unwanted and potentially harmful. The intestinal bleeding associated with aspirin, or the depressive effects of some of the earlier drugs used to lower blood pressure, such as reserpine and methyldopa, are good examples. When new drugs first become licenced for marketing and are prescribed by doctors on a gradually increasing scale it is important that adverse reactions such as those are reported. Every doctor in the National Health Service, whether in general practice or in hospital, has access to a stock of special record cards on which he can record in a standard way the details of any untoward reaction occurring in his patient during the prescribing of a new or existing drug, and which he has good reason to believe is associated with the taking of that drug. These record cards are posted to the DHSS which has a special unit to deal with them. A doctor noticing, for example, that one of his patients developed, say, double vision during treatment with a new antidepressant could not assume in the absence of other firm evidence that the two events were necessarily connected. However, if 100 cards are received by the DHSS reporting the same kind of event, there is good circumstantial evidence that those events are likely to be connected with drug administration. This adverse reaction reporting system, although voluntary, is working well and is an effective "early warning system" for drug toxicity.

We have come a long way since thalidomide, but have had to steer between the Scylla of stifling innovation in drug research by excessive control of development and the Charybdis of the free-for-all, profit-motivated bonanzas of the pre-thalidomide era. No system can be perfect, and it is fair to say that had it been necessary, for example, for aspirin, penicillin and streptomycin to be put through the system as we have set it up now they would probably never have reached the market and thence the patient.

(4) New Methods in Surgery. Only a few years before the Second World War many surgeons were saying that surgery had reached its extreme limits. It was impossible, they believed, to improve on the delicate techniques then reached. But events have proved them wrong. Operations on the heart, for example, which would have been inconceivable a short time ago are now carried out daily—the heart can be opened and defects of the all-important valves made good. "Blue babies" or adults with a heart disease which might have led to their death in a few years are now cured by surgery, and it is possible during such operations to cut off all the blood from the heart by deflecting it through tubes to an artificial heart outside the body—a machine which pumps the blood round the body whilst the real heart is at rest.

Then there are the intravenous anaesthetics, such as Pentothal, which are injected instead of breathed through a mask, as were ether and chloroform or ethyl chloride. Pentothal is much safer, and avoids the unpleasant after-effects of vomiting and nausea, which usually followed the old type of anaesthetic. Most curious of all, anaesthetists use the poison curare, used by South American Indians to poison their arrow-heads. Curare produces paralysis, but in small doses merely gives the degree of muscle relaxation which is so important to the surgeon when he is operating.

Lastly, we might mention the new techniques of plastic surgery. Thus large areas of skin which have been destroyed by severe burns can be replaced by shaving off thin layers from another part of the body. These do not need to cover completely the whole damaged area: small pieces are scattered over the wound and gradually grow together. Corneal disease (the cornea is the clear part of the eye, and when it becomes opaque the patient cannot see) is treated by removing the diseased part and replacing it by a cornea removed from a dead body, or sometimes from an eye which has had to be removed from a live patient for other reasons. There are, in fact, "cornea banks" where corneas are kept in refrigeration for future use, just as there are "blood banks" for use in blood transfusions. Other advances in surgery will be described elsewhere in the section.

(5) New Approaches in Social Medicine. Medicine has passed through many phases from the time when disease was regarded as a punishment from the gods or a sign of devil possession to the present era, when increasingly there is a tendency to look on society as the patient. Indeed, one commonly hears doctors and sociologists nowadays talking about "the sick society."

The early primitive stage came to an end—at least in one part of the world—when in Greece, five centuries before Christ, Hippocrates and others began to teach that all diseases were due to natural causes. But after the first ray of hope the outlook began to deteriorate when, during the Middle and Dark Ages (that is, from the fall of the Roman Empire right up to the fifteenth century), there was a return to the belief in devil possession and supernatural causes.

Eighteenth-century medicine in Europe was materialistic, regarding the body as a machine. It was founded upon a sort of pseudo-science—although, of course, there were always individual exceptions, physicians such as Sydenham in England, who, avoiding all theories, based their work on observation of the patient. This mechanistic approach persisted right through the nineteenth century, but medicine became more and more truly scientific, and the century saw the most rapid advances in the field ever known until our own times: the discovery of germs by Pasteur, of antiseptics to combat them by Lister, of vaccination by Jenner and anæsthetics by the American Wells and the Scot Simpson. The use of the microscope by Virchow, who was a German, brought great advances in the understanding of disease and Ehrlich, another German, conceived, as we have already seen, the idea of "magic bullets" which would attack the germs at the root of a disease without harming the patient. But one of the greatest of all these great men is perhaps the least known. His name was Edwin Chadwick.

From the earliest period of recorded history human communities had been constantly ravaged by great plagues which swept over their lands year after year, killing untold millions. The Black Death of 1348–9 wiped out almost half the population of Europe. But, even in the first quarter of the nineteenth century in London, tens of thousands died from typhus, typhoid, and smallpox—and not only these, for periodically cholera would be brought into the country by travellers from abroad.

In the face of these terrible visitations the individual physician was helpless. He could not treat each one of the many sick even had he known how, and Chadwick's claim to fame rests on the fact that he was the first man to think in terms of *social* control of diseases, by so dealing with their causes that they were prevented from arising at all. In order to wipe out typhoid and cholera, he argued, we must ensure clean water supplies; for these diseases are caused by germs carried in polluted water. In order to attack typhus and plague, one must get rid of the lice which carry the germs of typhus and the rat-fleas which carry the germs of plague (including, of course, the rats, which, in turn, carry the fleas).

Chadwick was born in a Lancashire farmhouse where the children were washed every day all over, and he ruthlessly drove an obsession with cleanliness into the heads of his countrymen until, later in the century, it was possible for the German philosopher Treitschke to tell his class in Berlin: "The English think soap is civilisation." Although this remark was meant cynically, there is little doubt that soap, if it is not civilisation in itself, has played a greater part in making civilisation possible than many more elaborate remedies. A population riddled with chronic infectious illness has neither the time nor the energy to apply to the arts or sciences, and soap did a great deal to reduce infection.

One of the first Public Health measures was introduced by Chadwick and others when they brought in legislation to purify the water supply of London. Previously, the citizens had used water from the Thames (they still do, but only after it has been filtered and sterilised at the waterworks!), and from filthy, refuse-laden ponds and springs. Later, Chadwick helped to found the Poor Law Commission, and produced a Report in 1842, the principal suggestions of which were: a municipal water supply for all towns; scientific drainage both in town and country; and an independent health service with large powers for dealing with those who endangered the lives of others by polluting water or causing nuisances. He also proposed a national service for interment of the dead; for in those days bodies often remained for days in the overcrowded homes of the poor without burial.

What has the twentieth century contributed to the concept of social health? Well, of course, there has been a great deal of legislation along the lines initiated by Chadwick to control disease, and a great many other measures have been introduced concerned with the idea of positive health—not merely preventing bad health, but trying to bring about the highest possible state of good health. Orange juice, milk, and good meals for schoolchildren have brought about a transformation in child health which has become apparent to the least observant. And the National Health Service is in the direct line of descent from early nineteenth-century legislation.

But in future years it is probable that the main achievement of the twentieth century will prove to be its extension of the term "social health" to cover every aspect of community life, not only in such subjects as bodily health and its control of social means, but also such problems as mental illness, crime, delinquency, drug addiction, and so on. What we are now asking ourselves is: how far are these problems produced by society itself, and if this is the case, how far can we go in preventing them by social means?

Community medicine takes the view that these problems can never be dealt with solely by moralising and retribution, but only by dispassionately analysing causes and dealing with them. In this century we have developed a social conscience. Not always, it is true, a very well-informed social conscience, but at least this is a good beginning. There are organisations for dealing scientifically with delinquency, for dealing with problem children, for spreading knowledge about cancer in order to show people that it can be successfully treated if taken in time. We can well say with John Donne, who died in 1631, that "no man is an island . . . every man's death diminisheth me; for I am involved in mankind." This is the attitude of twentieth-century community medicine.

Summary. Perhaps we can sum up our progress in the past hundred and forty years more dramatically in terms of hard facts.

Before the 1840s a surgical operation was never undertaken except under the gravest circumstances. There were no anæsthetics and no antiseptics, and the operation was carried out by a surgeon in a filthy tail-coat, stained with the congealed blood of countless operations (indeed the surgeons of that time took pride in the dirty condition of their coats as showing how much experience they had previously had). Germs and the part they play in producing disease were unknown, and Paul Ehrlich had not yet been born, so there were no "magic bullets" to attack syphilis, or sera for diphtheria and other diseases. The mentally ill were simply locked up with little treatment and subjected to such indignities as the strait-jacket and the padded cell; now they are given treatment which becomes more effective each year, the padded cell and strait-jacket have gone, and in very few hospitals are the ward doors locked. *See also* **Part III.**

Only fifty years ago you would very likely have died if you had developed pneumonia, "childbed fever" after the birth of a child, meningitis, dysentery, typhoid, or tuberculosis. With such infections as blood-poisoning you would have had practically no chance at all. Today, the sulpha drugs and the antibiotics have changed all that. Syphilis and gonorrhœa were lifelong tragedies both to the patient and his family, but now they, too, can be conquered.

The National Health Service has brought the possibility of good treatment equally to all, and other bodies—some of them privately run—deal with alcoholism and neurosis, with rehabilitation of the mentally and physically ill, with spastics, birth control, and marriage guidance. It is up to us to see that all these facilities are used to the full by all who need them.

PART II. DISEASES ARRANGED ACCORDING EITHER TO THEIR CAUSE OR THE AREA OF THE BODY AFFECTED.

THE INFECTIOUS DISEASES. INTRODUCTION.

INFECTIOUS diseases are those which are caused by an invasion of the body by organisms from outside (the word "organism" simply means other living things, and we are using this word because, as will be seen later, it is not only what are known as "germs" which can cause infection). We know, too, that what is generally typical about this group is: (*a*) that the disease can be passed on from one person to another, and (*b*) that it is usually accompanied by a raised temperature or fever. Now (*a*), of course, is always true, because the definition of an infectious disease is one that can be passed on to others, but (*b*) is not always true, because a few infections produce little or no temperature, and also because it is possible to have a raised temperature (again in only a few cases) without any infection. For example, certain types of brain injury, tumour, or hæmorrhage can produce a raised—or lowered—temperature, and so can the injection of some foreign substance such as milk into the muscles. This is known as "protein shock," and was at one time used in the treatment of certain illnesses. Finally, solutions of dead germs, such as the anti-typhoid vaccine given to protect troops during the War, may lead when injected to very high temperatures. But, by and large, we are entitled to suppose that the patient with a raised temperature is probably suffering from an infection.

Types of Infection.

As we have seen, it is not only germs which cause infections—so from now on we shall give germs their proper name of "bacteria." Here is a list of the chief offenders which are liable to attack our bodies: bacteria, spirochætes, viruses, fungi, amœbæ, worms and other parasites. Of these, bacteria and viruses are by far the most important, but let us look at them all more closely.

Bacteria are tiny living things which can be seen only under a fairly powerful microscope. Some are grouped like bunches of grapes (staphylococci) or in strings or chains (streptococci). They are given these names because "staphylos" is the Greek word for a bunch of grapes, and "streptos" means a chain. Yet others are comma-shaped (such as the cholera vibrio), or shaped like a drumstick—a rod with a small knob at the end (the tetanus bacillus, which causes lockjaw)

It would be a mistake to think that all bacteria are harmful; for without some species we could not survive for long. Bacteriologists divide them according to their behaviour in the human body into three groups: saprophytic, parasitic or pathogenic, and symbiotic. The *saprophytic* organisms are the bacteria normally found in the skin, mouth, and intestines; they do us neither harm nor good. The *parasitic*, or as they are more usually called, pathogenic (*i.e.*, disease-producing) organisms, are the harmful ones with which we are naturally more concerned. Lastly, there are the *symbiotic* organisms, which, whilst taking something from the body, give something in return. For example, cattle would not be able to digest the cellulose of the grass they eat were it not for helpful bacteria in the lower parts of the intestines, and there are certain bacteria in the large intestine of man which produce vitamins.

Bacteria have two peculiar characteristics: each reproduces by splitting into two separate individuals as often as every twenty minutes in favourable circumstances like an open wound. If no bacterium were destroyed, one individual could produce a mass of bacteria larger than the whole world in a matter of a few weeks (since each of the offspring also divides into two, which in turn divide again—the progression goes: one gives birth to two, these two to four, the four to eight, eight to sixteen, sixteen to thirty-two, and so on—you will see, if you work it out, that in a short period the figure becomes astronomical). Fortunately, many bacteria have accidents, so for the present the world is safe! The other curious thing about bacteria is that, barring accidents, they are potentially immortal. Under ideal conditions in which no bacteria were killed, none would die; for a bacterium there is no death from old age, no corpse except when it is actively destroyed. It simply goes on dividing, dividing, and subdividing for ever.

How, then, are bacteria destroyed? Briefly, the answer is that most are destroyed by the natural defences of the body of whatever host they are preying on; others are destroyed by antiseptics and the new drugs; and many are destroyed when they are excreted from the body in the sputum or through the bowels and land in places where they are dried up and cannot survive—although some bacteria in such circumstances can form what are called "spores," rather like the seed of plants, so making it possible for them to survive in a state of suspended animation for months on end until picked up accidentally by another unfortunate host. Finally, bacteria, in addition to all these possibilities, face another danger: they may themselves develop disease. This disease is caused by even more minute organisms known as bacteriophages (viruses which affect bacteria), discovered by F. W. Twort in 1915. Attack by bacteriophage causes whole groups of bacteria (known as "colonies") to disintegrate and become harmless.

Although bacteriophage has been used in the treatment of some diseases in human beings, this method has now been largely given up, since the new drugs are infinitely more effective.

Spirochaetes. Spirochætes, like bacteria, are minute organisms, but differ in being shaped somewhat like a corkscrew and in being able to move (which many bacteria cannot do). Their progress is produced by a sideways wriggling motion. The two main diseases caused by spirochætes are syphilis and spirochætal jaundice. Spirochætal jaundice is carried by rats, and is common in those who work in mines. It is now rare in Britain, but still occurs in Japan, Egypt, and Malaya; the infection is passed through the skin where the excreta of infected rats mingles with water on damp ground in the mine where miners kneel. Infection may also occur through eating infected food.

Viruses. Unlike bacteria, viruses are too small to be seen under an ordinary microscope. They can, however, be photographed in some cases under an electron microscope, which uses a magnetic field instead of a glass lens and a stream of electrons in place of a beam of light. Viruses cause such diseases as typhus, measles, mumps, poliomyelitis, smallpox, and chickenpox—not to mention such plant and animal diseases as tobacco mosaic disease and foot-and-mouth disease, which often have serious economic consequences. Other virus diseases are psittacosis (an infection of parrots and similar birds which can be transmitted to Man), swine fever in pigs, influenza in Man, and myxomatosis in rabbits. They also cause, it is believed, the common cold.

The main characteristics of viruses are, first, that they can only grow in living cells—unlike bacteria, which readily grow in the laboratory on plates containing a jelly made from meat broth, gelatin, milk, and other delicacies. The scientist, therefore, must keep them in portions of living tissue kept alive outside the body. Secondly, they are so small that they pass through the pores of the finest filter. Thirdly, a first attack usually produces immunity for life. Second attacks of the common virus diseases mentioned above are very rare; but unfortunately, this rule does not apply to influenza or the common cold. Fourthly, there is reason to believe that viruses represent an extraordinary intermediate stage between the living and non-living; they can, for instance, be produced in crystalline form and yet are just as dangerous when "thawed out." Lastly, the virus diseases have proved for the most part to be little affected by the new antibiotics and other drugs, although vaccination in smallpox and the injection of sera from infected patients in other infections may give immunity for longer or shorter periods.

The two great practical problems that doctors face with viruses are: (i) many viruses are unknown because of the difficulty of growing them outside the body in suitable tissue culture. They cannot therefore be conveniently identified in specimens from the patient, as bacteria can; and (ii) they are unaffected by antibiotics like penicillin. It has been a great step forward to grow viruses artificially in tissue culture, in which they are identified indirectly by the effects they have on the cultured *cells*. But since we do not know exactly how to grow some viruses (like those of infective hepatitis) they have still not been seen.

When we recover from a viral illness like chickenpox, we probably do so by producing virus-killing substances inside our own cells. Scientists are currently searching for these substances in case they can be used, like penicillin, to cure viral disease.

Fungi. Some infections are caused by fungi—that is to say organisms belonging to the same group as moulds, mushrooms, and toadstools. Penicillin and some other antibiotics are produced from moulds, so, as in the case of bacteria, some fungi are helpful; they even help to destroy each other, as bacteria do. For example actinomyces, which can cause infection of the jaw and other tissues, is destroyed by penicillin.

Most fungal infections are trivial and limited to the skin. But, although trivial, they can be unsightly and uncomfortable. Ringworm of the scalp, dhobie itch—an infection of the groin spread by infected underclothing—and so-called "athlete's foot" are caused by a fungus.

Amœbæ. Amœbæ are small, single-cell organisms, the largest of which (a harmless type found in stagnant ponds in Britain and elsewhere) is just visible to the naked eye. It is about the size of the head of a pin. Amœbæ move, in the species which are capable of moving, by pushing forward a part of the cell in the appropriate direction and causing the rest to flow into the advancing portion. Like bacteria, they reproduce by dividing into halves, each of which becomes a new amœba.

The main human disease caused by amœbæ is amœbic dysentery (not to be confused with bacillary dysentery).

Parasites. These may live on the skin like lice (which can carry typhus) or fleas (carriers of plague), or the parasites of scabies which burrow into the skin, or they may live part of their time in the blood or other tissues, like malaria. They often have complicated life-cycles involving other hosts (like mosquitoes) at certain stages of development.

Worms. Worms are intestinal parasites, but the only common types found in Britain are threadworms, the tiny thread-like worms which cause irritability and itching in the skin of children, less often in adults; round-worms, somewhat resembling the ordinary garden earthworm, which seldom lead to symptoms; and tapeworms, which may reach a length of 3 or even 6 m. Many parasitic worms (like parasites elsewhere) lead a double life—they spend part of their life in the human intestine and the other part in the muscles of another animal. The tapeworm, for example, whilst in the human intestine, lays eggs which pass out of the body in the excreta, and are then swallowed by pigs, especially in those parts of the world where human excreta are used as manure in the fields. In the pig, the eggs form cysts in the muscles—meat infected in this way is known as "measly pork"—and when, in turn, the meat is eaten by man, the process in the intestine begins all over again.

Less common types, from our point of view, are the Russian tape-worm (which, as befits a Russian, grows to nearly 9 m!); this type is spread by caviare or undercooked infected fish. The small, leaf-shaped liver fluke lays eggs which are passed into canals or pools in tropical countries in the urine of infected people, hatch out and enter a water snail, and finally leave the snail in the form of small parasites which pierce the skin of bathers, whence they pass to the liver and subsequently the bladder and rectum. This is a serious condition, as is also filariasis (another tropical disease), for which, unlike bilharzia—caused by the liver fluke—no cure is known. The tropical disease known as loa-loa is caused by a variety of filaria.

How the Infection is Spread.

Infection is spread in many ways, some of which have already been mentioned. In the common fevers found in Europe and elsewhere one of the most frequent ways is by *droplet infection*—that is to say, by minute drops carrying the germs which are coughed or sneezed into the air by someone already suffering from the disease. Such droplets can be projected into the air for 3m or more, and when breathed in by someone within range infection may result. Next commonest mode of spread is perhaps by *infected food, water*, and the dirty hands of those who prepare food: cholera, dysentery, food-poisoning, and typhoid are spread in this way. Spread by *direct contact* is found in the venereal diseases (usually, but not always, spread by sexual intercourse with someone who already has the disease), and, of course, lice, fleas, and other parasites, including the scabies mite, are spread by contact with the infested individual—or sometimes with his clothes or bed linen. Spread through an *intermediary host*, whether it be lice, fleas, or mosquitoes carrying infection, or the various means adopted by worms, has already been described above, so no more need be said. Lastly, the infection may result from *bacteria already within the body*; for example, the bacillus coli which lives in the large intestine is there harmless, but if it gets into the bladder or the ureters (the tubes leading from kidney to bladder) a quite unpleasant result may follow in the form of cystitis or pyelitis.

How the Body Deals with Infection.

The body has many mechanisms of defence against intruders, but suffice it to say here that there are two main ones. First, substances known as antibodies and antitoxins are produced in the blood—the antitoxins to neutralise the poisons produced by the invaders, the antibodies to render them helpless, for example, by causing them to clump together so that they can more easily be dealt with by the second defence mechanism. This second mechanism is provided by the white cells in the blood, some of which (the phagocytes) act like amœbæ and swallow up and destroy the germs. Antibodies and antitoxins can be transferred from one individual to another and are used in medicine both to prevent infection and to cure it. This is known as immunisation, and can be active or passive. Active immunisation is produced by injecting either a solution of dead bacteria, as in the case of anti-typhoid injections, or by injecting live, but weakened, strains of the organism, as in the case of smallpox vaccination. In both cases the body is stimulated to produce its own immune substances. Passive immunisation is used either for people who have been in recent contact with infection or who are already ill, and in this case the antitoxins produced in another person who has had the illness are injected in the form of serum—*i.e.*, the liquid part of the blood without the blood cells. All these natural defences are inefficient in the ill, the underfed, the very young, and the very old.

The mechanisms of the response of the body to infection is the broad field of study of the immunologist.

Antiseptics.

The earliest antiseptic was carbolic acid, used by Lister in his operating-theatre in the form of a fine spray directed throughout the operation on the wound, or sometimes in the form of steam from a kettle containing a solution of carbolic. But carbolic is dangerous, and since Lister's time many more useful antiseptics have been discovered. Acriflavine, thymol, and other old favourites have been discarded too. The various forms of carbolic are still used to disinfect drains, but, to tell the truth, the use of antiseptics nowadays is very limited. In surgery the *antiseptic* method has given way to the *aseptic* method—instead of fighting sepsis we see to it that no possibility of sepsis is present before operating: all instruments, the surgeons' and nurses' hands, the skin, are sterilised—the instruments by boiling, the dressings by dry heat, the hands by soap and water, and almost the only antiseptic used is to clean the patient's skin in the area to be operated on.

Antiseptics are used as first-aid treatment for cuts and wounds, but should be applied only once as a general rule—that is, when the wound is first received. The trouble with antiseptics is that as well as killing germs they also kill the surrounding tissues, which antibiotics never do.

Antiseptic sprays to purify the air of a room or to destroy germs lurking in the dust on the sick-room floor—or any other floor—are practically useless. To quote the *British Medical Journal*: "There is no good scientific evidence that any of the chemical air-disinfectants can control the spread of infection in places such as schools, offices, or cinemas. Nor is there good evidence that any substantial effect on the spread of illness can be obtained by disinfection of dust."

Neither is there any good reason to believe that mouth-washes and gargles have any effect other than making the mouth feel fresher and (temporarily) removing mouth odour—by covering it up with the scent of the antiseptic. Mouth-washes are in contact with the bacteria for far too short a time to have any damaging result, and, in the case of tonsillitis and other diseases, all the important bacteria are hidden far out of any danger from gargles.

Antibiotics.

The antibiotics—penicillin, streptomycin, erythromycin, terramycin, aureomycin, and many others—have already been dealt with, and only two important practical points need to be mentioned. These are that although most of such drugs are entirely safe under ordinary conditions, it is extremely dangerous for the layman to use them without medical guidance. If, for example, people get into the undesirable habit of sucking penicillin lozenges for sore throat and keep on doing this every time the sore throat returns, they may become sensitised to penicillin so that, when they become really ill—say, with pneumonia—the serious illness no longer responds to the drug. Or the same habit may make them allergic or hypersensitive to penicillin, and an injection given later may have serious and even fatal results.

Doctors no longer use the lozenges anyway, because of this danger and another one which is that excessive use of antibiotics may kill not only the dangerous bacteria, but also the ones which are helpful to the body. When this happens, other types of organism which are not affected by antibiotics will multiply in the absence of the bacteria which normally keep them under control. Thus terramycin or aureomycin, by killing useful germs in the large intestine, may cause vitamin B deficiency, and when the non-sensitive organisms have their natural enemies removed they may step in and multiply, causing inflammation of the mouth, diarrhoea, and occasionally a fatal bowel infection.

General Treatment of Fevers.

Fevers are ordinarily heralded in by a rise in temperature which is noticeable either by a flushed face or by alternate sensations of heat and cold. A patient with a high temperature may have shivering attacks known as "rigors." Tell the doctor.

A high temperature does not necessarily (especially in a child) mean that the trouble is serious but the lay person should always treat it as such and certainly call a doctor if the patient is a child or an elderly person.

Even the trained physician finds it difficult to tell one fever from another in the early days; for most of the common fevers begin in more or less the same way. It is only when a rash or some other more definite sign becomes evident that a certain diagnosis can be made, and these may not show themselves until the patient has been feeling "run-down" and fevered for some days. Incidentally, although a clinical thermometer is a very useful thing when properly used, many a doctor must feel that, in unskilled hands, it is a menace. The "fussy" type of mother who is constantly taking her child's temperature whenever it looks in the slightest degree different from usual (probably it is simply feeling justifiably bored with its parents), not only causes anxiety to herself but also gives the habit of anxiety to her child. The child is made to feel that the world is a dangerous place, full of germs and all sorts of causes for fear—as indeed it is, but one needs a sense of proportion, and other dangers which we think much less about are at least as frightening and twice as deadly as most germs. Whatever you do, don't get the thermometer habit; your child, so far as fevers are concerned, is a good deal tougher than you.

Briefly, then, the way to treat a fever in the early stages before the doctor comes, and before one knows exactly what is wrong, is as follows:

(1) Put the patient to bed.

(2) Give little, and easily digested, food; if the patient wants none, give none.

(3) Give plenty to drink—the proprietary preparations containing lemonade and glucose are excellent, but water, weak tea with sugar, or home-made lemonade with squeezed-out lemon juice and sugar, whichever the patient likes best, are at least as good.

(4) Aspirin is useful to relieve headache or other pains and will reduce fever for two or three hours. But it will cure nothing. The patient will be more comfortable, but his illness will not be cured by aspirin except in certain very special cases. Soluble aspirin is best. Do not have special children's aspirins in the house. They are often nicely flavoured, the children are tempted to eat them like sweets, and there have been serious cases of poisoning. For small children, use suitably small quantities of ordinary adult soluble aspirin, having checked the dose with your doctor. Other methods of cooling seriously fevered patients such as bathing, tepid sponging, etc., are strictly for the doctor to prescribe. A patient as hot as that should be in a doctor's hands anyway.

THE INFECTIOUS FEVERS.

The remarks made above apply to the management of *any* fever, and we are now going to discuss particular infectious diseases, beginning with the common childhood fevers, then passing on to less common ones, tropical diseases, and worm and parasitic infestations.

The common infectious fevers are caused by bacteria or viruses, and it is useful to know the meaning of the following terms: *incubation period* is the time which elapses between being infected and developing symptoms; *prodromal period* is the time which elapses between the end of the incubation period and the appearance of a rash; *quarantine period*, the maximum time during which a person who has been in contact with the infection may develop the disease—it is usually two days more than the incubation period; *isolation period*, the time a patient is supposed to be isolated.

Views regarding the common infectious fevers have changed a good deal in recent years. Disinfection of rooms is now regarded as almost useless, and more cases are treated at home.

Quarantine in the case of the common fevers is thought by a good many doctors to be a waste of time, since all it can do is to postpone infection from early childhood to early adult life, when it is likely to be more serious. For it is a characteristic of these fevers that they affect the adult much more violently than they do the child. However, on this, and all other points, you will have to be guided by the opinion of your family doctor.

Virus Diseases.

First, we shall take the common virus diseases, measles, chickenpox, and rubella or German measles, then the other virus diseases, mumps, infective hepatitis, viral pneumonia, and some less common conditions which do not always produce a typical rash as in the case of the first three.

In nearly all of these fevers there is a long incubation period, and one infection gives immunity for life.

Measles. The incubation period is 10–11 days. The first sign is the appearance of symptoms rather like a severe cold. The eyes become red, and exposure to light is unpleasant, the nose runs, the throat becomes inflamed, and a dry, harsh cough develops. There may be headache and the temperature rises to 39°C or more. Usually the patient is a child, and especially typical is the development of so-called Koplik's spots, which are small, bluish-white, raised spots seen on the inside of the cheek at the back of the mouth. The rash begins on the fourth day of the prodomal period, *i.e.*, 14 days after the initial infection. It shows on the forehead and behind the ears, spreading within a day downwards over the whole body; in another two days it starts to disappear, but often leaves behind a sort of brownish staining which may last for one to two weeks.

Measles can be serious, especially in very young children because of its complications, such as bronchopneumonia and infection of the ear, which can now be treated with antibiotics. These drugs have no effect on the measles virus, but only on the secondarily invading bacteria which have invaded the lungs and ear during the illness. The illness can be attenuated or lessened by injection of antibodies (gamma globulin) from an immune adult, and this is often worth while in the very young. Effective vaccination is now available.

Rubella or German Measles. Incubation period 14–19 days. A mild fever, similar to measles except that the rash is usually the first sign that anything is wrong, and the temperature is rarely above 38°C. The eyes may be pink, and there are enlarged glands at the back of the neck. The rash disappears completely in thirty-six hours. There are no complications.

German measles, in itself, is harmless, but if a woman gets the disease in the early months of pregnancy malformations in the child may appear at birth. Vaccination is advised if a girl has not contracted the disease by the time she reaches puberty. There is no special treatment, except the general rules for fevers given above.

Chickenpox. Incubation period 14–15 days, but may be more variable. In children chickenpox is a mild fever which begins with the appearance of tiny blisters on the chest and back. These later spread outwards to the legs, arms and face, and cause itching. Treatment is the general one for fevers already described. Calamine lotion or dusting powder will be helpful for the irritation, and the child's nails should be cut short to prevent scratching and infection of the spots. Whereas children are usually little bothered by chickenpox, young adults may be much more drastically affected—a temperature of 40°C is not uncommon, and then there may be severe headache.

Mumps. Incubation period 17–18 days. Everyone knows the typical appearance of the patient with mumps—the swelling in the salivary glands in front of the ears which makes the face look full. This causes pain later on, and it may be difficult to open the mouth. Temperature is not usually high (about 38°C). Although uncomfortable, mumps is rarely dangerous, but orchitis—swelling of the testicles—is sometimes a complication. Fluid diet should be given if eating is painful, with mouth-washes, and rest in bed.

Infective Hepatitis. "Hepatitis" means inflammation of the liver, and infective hepatitis, which is much the commonest cause of jaundice in young adults, is a viral infection of the liver. The main symptoms are fever, followed by jaundice, which is first noticed in the whites of the eyes as yellow staining, then in the skin. The urine becomes coloured also, and this is most easily noticed if, on shaking in a bottle, the froth shows coloration. If the froth remains white, no jaundice is present. Treatment is a matter for the doctor, but great care should be taken both by the patient and those in contact with him, to wash the hands thoroughly after urinating or defæcating, after handling utensils from the sickroom, and both before and after eating; for the disease is very infectious.

Viral Pneumonia. Pneumonia is usually caused by bacteria, and when we speak of pneumonia, that is the type we ordinarily refer to. Viral pneumonia is known by doctors as "pneumonitis," and is believed to be closely related to influenza. There is no specific treatment so far, and since diagnosis is a specialist matter, little more need be said except that the symptoms in general resemble those of ordinary pneumonia. Psittacosis, another virus disease, can also lead to pneumonia, and although there is no specific treatment for virus infections of the lungs, it is always worth while trying the antibiotics or sulpha drugs in view of the possibility that the lung condition may be caused by a secondary invasion by bacteria.

Influenza. While serious epidemics of influenza take the form of a very dramatic and often fatal disease—for example, the epidemic of "Spanish 'flu" which followed the First World War killed more people than the actual fighting—the milder type more usually seen is difficult to distinguish from the common cold. In fact, many people who complain of "a dose of the 'flu" are suffering from simple colds.

However, a sudden onset, aching in the muscles of the back and legs, and redness of the eyes, would suggest influenza, and especially typical is the depression and weakness which follow influenza but not a cold. The measures suggested above for the general treatment of fever should be applied; but the depression and weakness which follow influenza may need special treatment by the doctor.

Colds. Although everyone thinks he, or she, knows what a "cold" is, the issue is not so simple; for the symptoms of fever, running nose, and a run-down, "headachy" feeling are found in many illnesses. They may be observed, as we have seen, in the early stages of measles before the arrival of the rash, or in a number of other fevers, such as whooping cough. Mild attacks of influenza (see above) may resemble the common cold, and blocking of the nose with discharge and fever may be due to sinusitis—although here there is usually pain above, between, or below the eyes. Colds can be caused by any one of thirty different viruses known as "rhinoviruses" as well as by others which cause influenza, or infect glands (adenoviruses). This is why a single cold does not confer immunity on the sufferer. It is probable that you will not catch a cold from the same virus, at least for the rest of the year, but there are all those others waiting to infect you with other colds in buses, tubes, and other crowded places. Like all infections, do not forget that the best way to avoid them is to keep generally well, and in a good nutritional state. Do not spend money on injections or other vaccines. They do not work, probably because of the multiplicity of viruses involved. It is unlikely that adding vitamins or mineral supplements to normal diet will do any good at all provided you are eating sensibly. The vogue for prophylactic or therapeutic treatment of colds with massive doses of vitamin C has recently received much attention from scientists attempting, with little success, to prove the effect by controlled clinical trial and to find a rational basis for its use.

Poliomyelitis

Polio, or infantile paralysis as it used to be known, is caused by a virus which has a particular affinity for the nerve cells of the spinal cord and which results in paralysis of those muscles under the control of the particular group of cells infected. Rarely, the infection is widespread in the nerve tissue causing paralysis of muscles of swallowing and respiration as well as those of the trunk and limbs. The usual pattern is for a single muscle group to be affected, for example, the muscles controlling the movements of the arm at the shoulder. Such paralysis may be transient with complete recovery, partial with some residual weakness, or total, leaving a "flail limb" which is wasted and powerless.

At one time in this country epidemics of poliomyelitis were common, mainly affecting children and young adults. There is no doubt that mild forms of the disease were always occurring in very young children, forms never diagnosed as such but conferring a natural immunity in later life.

In common with other infections, poliomyelitis begins with a mild or moderate pyrexia, with a sore throat, headache, nausea and perhaps actual vomiting, some five to 10 days after contact with the virus. There may be rigidity of the neck muscles. Paralysis, if it occurs, will become apparent about the second or third day of illness. This stage may last two or three weeks, by which time the temperature will have subsided and the paralysis started to improve. There is no specific treatment and medical care is confined to symptomatic relief. Difficulty with swallowing and breathing calls for special nursing measures. In severe cases, artificial means of maintaining respiration may have to be continued for months, or for the rest of the patient's life. Many severely paralysed polio victims of the post-war epidemics —the self-styled "responauts"—depend for their lives on artificial respirators ("iron lungs").

With the development of the oral vaccine early in the 1960s, and its introduction into the immunisation schedule in this country, the disease has now virtually disappeared from Great Britain.

Smallpox. Smallpox was once common in Western Europe, and, as late as the early nineteenth century, was not unknown in Britain. Now, since the introduction of vaccination, it is comparatively rare in industrialised countries, although minor epidemics have occurred here recently. Jenner, who introduced vaccination, noted that dairy-maids who had suffered from the mild disease known as "cow-pox," contracted from the udders of infected cows, and transmitted to the hand of the dairy-maid, did not develop smallpox. In fact, cow-pox is a mild form of smallpox modified by transmission through cattle. Vaccination should be carried out at the age of three months, and repeated at the ages of seven, fourteen, and twenty-one years—also at any time when an epidemic occurs, or when travelling to any part of the world where smallpox is prevalent, or where immigration laws stipulate that it must be done. Many countries insist on an international certificate of recent vaccination before landing. Your family doctor will make out the certificate (he is entitled to charge you for it) and your local Community Health Office will countersign it. Smallpox is one of the diseases which can very readily be spread from countries where it is prevalent because of the great increase in numbers of people travelling about the world by air.

Smallpox attacks people of all ages and is carried by excreta and droplet infection, but particularly by the dried scales on the skins of convalescent patients; it is now most common in the tropics.

Smallpox is similar in many ways to chickenpox. Typical cases are easy for the qualified doctor to distinguish from one another, but one of the difficulties of vaccination (as with Typhoid, and other artificially conferred immunities) is that the typical signs are often modified. Differential diagnosis is a job for the expert, and if your own doctor is in any doubt, he will consult with the local health authorities. The disease begins with shivering, headache, and backache, and the temperature is raised to 39°–40°C. On the third day a rash appears, which turns into small blisters on the sixth day, and the blisters become filled with pus by the ninth day. On the twelfth day they burst and form crusts. Unlike chickenpox, in which the rash starts in the middle of the body and works towards the outer parts, smallpox produces a rash which begins in the scalp, forehead, wrists, and feet and then moves towards the middle.

Smallpox is a serious disease, and the result depends largely upon whether the patient has been vaccinated within seven years of the attack. Contacts should be vaccinated and kept under observation for sixteen days; the patient must be isolated until all the scabs have separated and the skin healed.

Glandular Fever. This is sometimes called infective mononucleosis, since one of its features is an increase in certain mononuclear white cells and an alteration in their appearance. Another feature is an apparent infectivity. Beyond this the disease is a great mystery, and although it is probably caused by a virus, it may even be related to other (malignant) diseases of white cells. This one, however, is not dangerous although it often causes a lot of trouble by dragging on for many weeks. The main symptoms are fever, enlargement of lymph glands and sore throat. The patient feels very debilitated and often very depressed. Diagnosis is often very difficult, but there is a blood test known as the "Paul-Bunnell" test which is almost specific for the disease. The patient is usually presented as a case known to doctors as "P.U.O.," meaning Pyrexia (fever) of Unknown Origin. He has often been treated with several antibiotics, one after another, without effect, because the causal agent is not affected by those drugs. He is only very mildly infective, and it is unusual to insist on isolation or quarantine.

Typhus. This disease used to be known as "jail fever," because it was frequent in prisons; but overcrowding, poverty, and bad hygienic surroundings anywhere are suitable conditions for epidemics of typhus. Improved conditions in industrialised countries have made it unusual, since typhus is carried from one person to another by infected body lice. It is due to the organism *Rickettsia prowazekii*, which displays both bacterial and viral characteristics.

Typhus comes on suddenly with a rise in temperature to about 39°C, but within four days it may be as high as 42°C. There may, or may not, be a rash at this time, and in the second week, when the temperature is at its highest, there is delirium, weakness, and a feeble pulse. The typical typhus rash appears about the fifth day as reddish blotches on the chest, abdomen, and wrists.

Typhus is, needless to say, very serious but responds to modern antibiotics. Preventive measures are directed towards eradicating lice.

Rabies. Finally, we shall deal very briefly with a number of less common virus diseases, beginning, as is appropriate, with *hydrophobia or rabies*, since it was in this infection that the great French scientist Louis Pasteur (1822–95) showed the possibility of prevention by vaccination. Unlike Jenner, with his ready-made cowpox virus, which we have seen to be the virus of smallpox weakened by natural passage through cows, Pasteur had to weaken the rabies virus by passing it through rabbits. The rabbits were infected, and after death the spinal cord was dried and powdered, a solution passed through another rabbit, and so on until the virus was sufficiently weakened.

Rabies is spread by the bite of infected animals, usually dogs, cats, or wolves, who are driven mad by the disease; in Trinidad, however, it has been spread by vampire bats. Those who are bitten usually show no symptoms for six weeks or more.

but sooner or later convulsions and delirium arise, which within four to five days are fatal.

There is no cure once the symptoms have developed, but Pasteur's serum, if given soon after the bite, prevents illness in the majority of cases—the sooner after the bite, the better the outlook. Dogs should be muzzled in areas where the disease is common, but quarantining imported dogs has made the infection almost unknown here.

Psittacosis. This is another virus disease which is of interest mainly in that it is spread by birds of the parrot group, such as parrots, lovebirds, macaws, and the rest. It occasionally occurs here in people who have been in contact with birds of this type, and is serious both to the bird and its owner. Quarantine regulations greatly reduced the risk of infection in Britain. They were lifted a few years ago but concern over recent outbreaks, not only of psittacosis but a number of economically important diseases such as fowl pest, led to their reintroduction in 1976.

The symptoms of psittacosis are fever, cough, and bronchitis. The disease is especially dangerous to old people, but it responds to the same antibiotics as typhus.

Sandfly Fever, or phlebotomus fever, *Dengue*, or breakbone fever, and *Trench Fever* are all somewhat similar conditions in that they resemble influenza and are rarely fatal. They are all due to viruses, spread in the first case by sandflies in tropical climates; in the second by mosquitoes in tropical climates; and in the third by lice in temperate climates. They are all typical "soldiers' diseases"; the first two were common in the Middle East and Far East during the last War, the third during the First World War in France.

Yellow Fever. Of all the virus diseases, seven can now be prevented, or largely prevented, by vaccination—smallpox, measles, German measles, rabies, poliomyelitis, if started early enough), influenza and yellow fever. Yellow fever is carried by a mosquito known as Stegomyia, common in South and Central America and in African ports. For its spread, it therefore needs: a hot climate, the stegomyia mosquito, and an infected person.

In 1898 the United States was at war with Spain in Central America, where yellow fever was a serious problem. Following this war the United States, by this time acutely aware of this terrible disease, asked a Dr. G. E. Waring to deal with it in Havana, where it was rife. But Waring died of yellow fever, as had many millions before him, without knowing its cause, and it was left to Walter Reed, who died in 1902, to prove the connection between the mosquito and yellow fever. By a vigorous war on the mosquito, the disease has been eradicated from Havana and the West Indian islands, and Reed's discovery made possible the building of the Panama Canal.

In yellow fever there is a sudden high temperature, aching of limbs and head, jaundice, and black vomit; the pulse-rate falls as the fever rises. Previous vaccination seems to be preventive if undertaken in time.

Conclusion.

All these virus diseases have this in common: that for many there is no specific cure, although some (see above) can be prevented by vaccination, or by the social control of the creatures carrying the virus. Some of the larger viruses (psittacosis) are destroyed by certain antibiotics. There is usually a long incubation period. Finally the question will sometimes arise of protecting some people from German measles or measles with gamma globulin containing another person's antibodies to the disease. This may be considered for measles in very young patients or to protect the foetus in pregnant mothers in contact with German measles.

Bacterial Diseases.

Bacterial diseases differ from virus infections in a number of respects: their incubation period tends to be shorter; having the disease once does not often confer lifelong protection; and unlike virus diseases, most bacterial diseases respond to one of the antibiotics or sulphonamides. In many cases it is possible to inoculate against the disease to prevent it occurring, as we have seen is possible with only a few of the virus diseases.

Scarlet Fever and Other Streptococcal Infections. In the days, not so long ago, before the arrival of chemotherapy (sulphonamides) and antibiotics, streptococci were very much feared and even caused a high mortality, particularly in such susceptible groups as children, and mothers and babies in maternity hospitals. They are still taken very seriously in the latter and rightly so, although one wonders how much of the mystique is simply a hangover from the days, fifty years ago, when many mothers died from "childbed fever." All signs of infection, such as fever, during the puerperium (the period following childbirth) must be promptly dealt with by a doctor, and only occasionally now is there real cause for anxiety provided treatment is prompt and rigorous.

Scarlet fever is much less common and very much less serious an illness than it used to be, partly because of the effective treatments available today, but also because of a definite but unexplained reduction in its severity. Perhaps the streptococcus has changed, and certainly the improved physical condition of people who are now much better fed and housed than they were, has helped to ward off the terrors of this disease as of so many other infections. The classical picture of signs and symptoms is now so rarely seen that it will not be further described.

The importance of streptococcal infections has shifted from the initial infection, such as a sore throat, to some serious conditions which occasionally arise as a result of some form of delayed sensitivity to the bacteria. Acute rheumatism or rheumatic fever (not to be confused with ordinary aches and pains nor with rheumatoid arthritis) occasionally arise in people who have had a sore throat a few weeks before. Since the streptococcus is not the direct cause of the damage which may consequently occur in the heart or kidney, the antibiotics are no answer except sometimes to keep off further streptococcal invasions.

Diphtheria. This used to be an extremely serious disease, but immunisation has made it almost unknown; it is important, therefore, that all children should be immunised. There are many modern and up-to-date doctors who have qualified since the war who have never seen a case because it has become so rare, and in spite of the propaganda of certain ill-informed people, this saving of children's lives is entirely the result of nationwide inoculation during the war and since. The following description is of historic interest only, and will remain so if a high level of inoculation is kept up by parents.

In a typical case of diphtheria the incubation period is about three days; the patient is a child who becomes ill and pale-looking (*i.e.*, the onset is not sudden, as in many fevers, but insidious); the temperature is only slightly raised to, perhaps, 37° or 38°C, and although there may be no complaint of sore throat, examination will reveal inflammation with—and this is typical of diphtheria —a grey membrane spread over the tonsils, the palate, and the back of the mouth generally. The diphtheria germ does not spread within the body. It stays at the place where it entered (in this case the throat) and sends its toxins throughout the body.

Even after the acute phase is over the patient must not be allowed to walk, because the diphtheria toxin is particularly poisonous to the heart. The ordinary rule is at least one or two months in bed.

Diphtheria also occurs in the larynx—in pre-inoculation days many children choked to death with this form of the infection; in the nose; and, although this is not generally known, wounds can be infected. The so-called "Desert sores" of the North African campaign seem to have been caused by diphtheria-like organisms.

Diphtheria may lead to paralysis of the throat, with difficulty in speaking or swallowing, and paralysis of the eyes or limbs; these are due to neuritis caused by the influence of the toxin on the nerves.

Whooping Cough. For many years whooping cough has been regarded merely as a bother to the patient and a nuisance to others, as, in fact, a trivial disease. Unfortunately, this is not so: because statistics show that it caused more deaths than polio, diphtheria, scarlet fever, and measles put together.

Whooping cough begins in a child as an ordinary cold with cough and slight fever, and this stage lasts for a week or ten days. Then the "paroxysmal stage" begins as a series of coughs following in rapid succession, during which time the patient is unable to breathe. The "whoop" is caused by the noisy indrawing of breath when the fit stops. The face may become blue and congested. Bronchitis is usually present, and bronchopneumonia may result as a complication, so inoculation of all children before the disease has a chance to strike them is most important.

Once whooping cough has begun, there is no specific treatment, although modern drugs can reduce the frequency of the fits of coughing. The antibiotic chloramphenicol has been used for this disease, but the general opinion is that it is ordinarily of little benefit. Chinese physicians once described whooping cough as the "hundred-days cough," and the cough may, indeed, continue for at least a hundred days.

Food Poisoning Diseases.

Strictly speaking there is no such thing as "food poisoning" if one is thinking of "poisoning" in terms of anything apart from germs. But not so long ago it used to be thought that decomposition of food in itself produced poisons known as "ptomaines" which were deadly to those who swallowed them. All food poisoning is caused by infection of food with bacteria and by no other cause—unless of course, we are thinking of the kind of poisoning which is the concern of the lawyer rather than the medical man.

Here we are considering those diseases which are commonly spread by contaminated food or drink. The classification is not scientific, but then no scientific classification has as yet been devised. First, we shall deal with typhoid, paratyphoid, and dysentery—uncommon here in Britain, although Sonné dysentery is fairly frequent. Then there is gastro-enteritis (which means irritation of the stomach and intestines), which is caused by staphylococci and the germs of the salmonella group, and lastly, botulism, which is rare.

Typhoid and Paratyphoid. These diseases are spread by infected water, food, or hands—especially uncooked food, such as milk, salads, oysters, and shellfish. Flies, too, play some part in spreading the disease. Some people are "carriers" and carry and excrete the germs without being themselves affected; for example, "Typhoid Mary," a carrier in the United States in the early years of this century, spent a large part of her life in custody as a public danger, although she did not show any symptoms of typhoid. Nevertheless, this woman caused a great deal of illness in others in her chosen profession of cook.

The influence of Chadwick's propaganda for pure water supplies is shown by the fact that deaths from typhoid, still 332 per 1,000,000 in 1870, fell to 198 per 1,000,000 at the beginning of this century. In the 1920s the death-rate was only 25 per 1,000,000, and now it is even less.

Typhoid fever begins like most fevers with headache, raised temperature, and general feeling of unwellness. This stage lasts about a week, and then the rash appears in the form of rose-red spots on the front of the chest and abdomen and on the back. In the second week there is great weakness, sometimes diarrhœa, flatulence, and mental dullness, together with dry and cracked lips and tongue. The third week is the week, in hopeful cases, of gradual decrease in temperature and other symptoms, and the fourth week is the week of convalescence.

Complications are perforation of the intestine (which needs surgical treatment), delirium, and bronchitis.

Paratyphoid fever is a milder form of typhoid (there are two forms, A and B); ordinarily it can be diagnosed only by scientific tests. The main thing is to inoculate contacts with T.A.B. vaccine and to protect food supplies; treatment is with chloramphenicol.

Dysentery. Dysentery may be caused *either* by a bacterium or an amœba; the first type is known as bacillary dysentery, the latter as amœbic dysentery (which is dealt with under tropical diseases). Infection is spread in much the same way as in typhoid. There is high fever, abdominal pain, and diarrhœa, at first consisting of fæcal matter, then blood and mucus. In severe cases the death-rate used to be over 20 per cent.

Various bacilli cause dysentery. The common tropical types are the Shiga and Flexner groups, but in this country most epidemics are due to the milder Sonné group.

However, in all these infections sulphaguanidine, ampicillin or tetracycline bring rapid relief but care must be taken to avoid infection of other people.

Diarrhœa and Vomiting. Leaving out typhoid and paratyphoid fevers and dysentery, there is a group of infections known as "D. & V."—diarrhœa and vomiting. In Britain D. & V. is mostly due to:

(1) Salmonella infection.
(2) Staphylococcal infections.
(3) Other bacteria, ordinarily harmless, such as bacillus coli, when present in sufficient numbers.

Salmonella Infections are the most serious of this group; they affect the small intestine and produce vomiting, severe abdominal pain, and diarrhœa. These symptoms occur about one day after eating infected food and usually clear up within about two weeks, but occasionally death results. Salmonella bacteria are most likely to be found in meat, egg powder, vegetables, and ducks' eggs, but staphylococci are liable to grow in milk products, such as ice-cream and cream buns. Food poisoning from staphylococci is seldom severe, and recovery takes place in about a week. Nevertheless, it is extremely infectious, and causes a great deal of lost time in industry and temporary illness in institutions; for it is in such situations that it is most likely to occur.

Staphylococcal Food Poisoning has greatly increased in recent years, so it is important to know what circumstances are likely to cause it. The reason for its increase has nothing to do, as many people suppose, with the greater use of canned foods, but it has much to do with the greater use of communal feeding and canteen meals. It is *possible* for bacterial toxins in infected food to bring about illness even when the canning process has killed the bacteria, but it is certainly extremely rare. Canned foods, in fact, are much safer than so-called "fresh" foods in this respect—except when they have been opened, left about, and then re-heated. The same applies to the re-heating of any kind of food.

The real enemy is the canteen worker with a boil, a discharging nose, dirty hands, or a septic finger. Occasionally food may be infected in the larder by rats or mice, but the sort of canteen or restaurant where this can happen has little to commend it. Frankly, these infections are caused by dirty or stupid people who do not realise that their sore finger or boil can become someone else's diarrhœa and vomiting. Where children are concerned, the outlook is potentially more serious, and in the early part of this century the Summer-time "procession of baby coffins" was all too familiar. Infection is much more common in artificially fed babies or in older children who eat infected ice-cream. However trivial the condition may seem, diarrhœa and vomiting with fever in a child should never be ignored. Those in charge of canteens or restaurants must ensure that staff is supervised, that anyone with a septic infection is put off duty, and that all know about washing after visiting the lavatory and absolute cleanliness.

Bacilli normally present in the intestine, such

as bacillus coli, can cause infections if absorbed in large amounts, or if of a different strain from those in the patient's intestine. They are not usually serious.

Botulism. Now uncommon, this is the disease which used to be known as " ptomaine poisoning " on the theory that it was caused by poisons produced by bad food apart from germs. In the 1920s a party of picnickers at Loch Maree in the Scottish Highlands developed botulism and a number died, with the result that the disease attracted much public attention. Botulism is caused by a germ, the bacillus botulinus, which is peculiar in that, like tetanus, its poison attacks the nervous system rather than the intestines, resulting in fits, double vision, paralysis beginning in the face and spreading downwards, and difficulty in swallowing. It is found in tinned fruits or vegetables containing the toxin even when the germ has been killed, but, as we have already seen, the toxin comes from the bacilli, not from decomposition of food as such (in fact, food does not decompose in the absence of germs). Death is common in botulism, but an antitoxin is now available which, if used in time, can cure the disease.

Tuberculosis. No disease causes more public concern, and no disease is more difficult to describe, than tuberculosis; for, like the streptococcus or the staphylococcus, the tubercle germ can attack many different parts of the body and manifest itself in many ways. Furthermore, it is a widely spread disease, infecting not only humans but also cattle, birds and reptiles. But here we shall be concerned with those types common to Man—the human and bovine (*i.e.*, the type occurring in cattle which can be spread to man by infected milk).

The tubercle bacillus is particularly hardy, so that when coughed or spat out on the ground it continues to be infectious for a long time. Infection is therefore caused by: (*a*) drinking infected milk; (*b*) droplet infection through having germs coughed in the face; (*c*) breathing in infected dust. In other words, tuberculosis is caused by absorption through either the lungs or the intestines; the former is common in adults, the latter in children.

But there is a good deal more to the problem than this; we know, for example, that over 90 per cent. of people in industrial countries have been infected with T.B. in early life and have conquered the infection. So the question arises: what conditions predispose to T.B.—why do some people get over the early infection and others not? There are two answers to this question: one is certain—that those who are impoverished and do not get enough food are liable to T.B.; the second is not so certain—that mental stress plays some part. Yet there is reasonably good evidence that such stress as a broken love-affair can cause lowered resistance to breakdown so that when germs are encountered infection will occur.

In children, lung tuberculosis is not common, but tuberculosis of the bones and glands is, as is also infection in the abdomen, the kidney or spine, and, worst of all, tuberculous meningitis. These are often of the bovine type from infected milk. Ordinarily, T.B. in children is less serious than adult infections; but tuberculous meningitis used to be almost invariably fatal until streptomycin was discovered.

Adult tuberculosis usually occurs in the lungs or the pleura—the thin membrane surrounding the lungs. In younger people military tuberculosis, which is a form of T.B. blood-poisoning or septicæmia, is a very serious condition, and the infection spreads throughout the whole body in a few weeks.

Lung infection begins gradually in someone who has previously felt unwell. There may be cough, and later blood-stained sputum (although blood which is coughed up does not necessarily prove that T.B. is present). Whatever means of treatment is used, the struggle between disease and patient is likely to be fairly long, but the outlook is now good. The closure of the Swiss sanatoria is due partly to modern disbelief that air in one place is better than that in another, but mainly to improved treatment.

Prevention depends on legal action ensuring tuberculosis-free herds of cattle; on control of spread of the disease by those " open " cases who carry germs in their sputum; on the use of vaccination in childhood with B.C.G. vaccine (which you can ask your doctor about).

Many methods are used in treatment: new drugs, such as streptomycin, isoniazid, and P.A.S., lung surgery, rest, and so on. At any rate, tuberculosis is being got under control, but anyone who is worried can get a free X-ray at the nearest Mass Radiography Centre. There are skin tests to show whether there is susceptibility to T.B.

Septicæmia. Commonly known as "blood-poisoning," is one of those diseases of which textbooks prior to the Second World war used to say: " death usually occurs."

Blood-poisoning occurs generally by spread from some septic area such as a wound (or even a small prick), after childbirth, or any place where certain germs have got admission to the body. The most usual germ is the streptococcus, although the pneumococcus—which ordinarily causes pneumonia—and the staphylococcus may also cause septicæmia.

Fever comes on suddenly and rises rapidly with headaches, sweating, and shivering. The patient is obviously very ill, and later there is wasting and delirium. The white blood cells increase in number. Septicæmia sometimes occurs without any apparent local infection in those who are weak and debilitated.

Pyoemia is a type of septicæmia which leads to the formation of numerous abscesses throughout the body. Its symptoms are the same as described above, except that the causative germ is usually the staphylococcus, and abscesses are found which may need surgical treatment.

However, in both conditions the state of affairs has been revolutionised by the use of the sulpha drugs and antibiotics; cure is now the rule rather than the exception.

Septicæmia should be suspected when any small wound or cut is followed by high temperature and the symptoms described above.

The word " *Toxœmia* " is used when the germs stay in their original position and produce symptoms by spreading their toxins throughout the body. Tetanus, diphtheria, and some kinds of childbirth infection come into this category; the symptoms may vary from mild disturbance to severe illness.

Meningitis means inflammation of the meninges, the covering which, like a layer of plastic, lies over the brain and spinal cord, just as the pleura covers the lungs and the peritoneum covers internal organs in the abdomen. (Hence inflammation of the pleura is known as pleurisy, and inflammation of the peritoneum as peritonitis.)

Various germs may cause meningitis, for example, the bacillus of tuberculosis, the pneumococcus, which ordinarily causes pneumonia, and the streptococcus or staphylococcus, but ordinarily the word refers to *Cerebrospinal Meningitis* or " spotted fever " caused by the meningococcus and occurring at times as an epidemic. It is commonest in the years from infancy to the early twenties, and begins suddenly with headache, vomiting, and fever. The temperature rises quickly, and pain develops in the back and legs; on the second or third day a rash appears on the body, and particularly on the inside of the thighs. Later there is stiffness of the neck, the head may be drawn back, vomiting persists, and the headache can be so severe as to cause the patient to scream with pain.

Fortunately, this type of meningitis (and most of the others) respond to treatment with antibiotics or the sulpha drugs, so the risks are very much less than formerly.

Pneumococcal Meningitis is an unusual conplication of pneumonia, and the septic types (*streptococcal or staphylococcal*) arise either following an infected fracture of the skull or from infection of the ear or mastoid.

Tuberculous Meningitis has already been mentioned; originally always fatal, it is now treatable with streptomycin.

All these diseases are very much a matter for

specialist and hospital treatment, but it is worth while mentioning *benign lymphocytic meningitis*, in which, although all the symptoms of meningitis are present, recovery without specific treatment is invariable. Meningitis, which was during the First World War and after what polio is to us now, is no longer common, and when taken in time is easily treated.

Tetanus is usually known as "lockjaw" because there may be difficulty in opening the mouth, although this is simply part of a spasm of all the muscles of the body. The tetanus bacillus is found in rich soil—hence the disease is less common in desert areas—and tetanus resembles rabies in that: (*a*) it enters at a wound; (*b*) it affects the nervous system; (*c*) it results in fits and ultimately death.

However, active immunisation with T.T. (tetanus toxoid) has resulted in the disease becoming uncommon, and even when developed, treatment with antitoxin, anæsthetics, and curare may lead to cure.

The bacillus is anærobic (*i.e.*, does not use oxygen) and is most likely to occur in such situations as when a man digging manure or working in his garden sticks a fork through his foot, or, in war-time, when he is wounded in soil contaminated with manure.

Undulant fever, also known as Malta fever or abortus fever, falls into two types: melitensis, which infects goats, and abortus, cattle and pigs. Man gets the disease by reason of close contact with or drinking the milk of infected animals. (The name abortus is given because abortion is produced in cattle and sows.)

In Undulant Fever, as one would suppose, the fever goes up and down for two to three weeks; it may then go down and rise again, persisting for many months. The disease may occur in Britain, but modern drugs are on the whole successful in dealing with it. A striking feature of the disease is the combination of a high temperature with an appearance of relative well-being.

Another disease carried by mammals is *Glanders* or *Farcy*, spread by horses. In glanders there is discharge from the nose and sometimes pneumonia. Occasionally the disease is fatal. In farcy abscesses form, usually along the lymph vessels. Both conditions are very contagious, and treatment is a matter for a specialist; infected horses should be destroyed.

Cholera. Cholera could be classified under the head of food-poisoning, because it is mainly spread by infected water (however, like typhoid, it can also be spread by flies, infected food, and carriers); it could also be classified as a tropical disease, since, although it used to be found in Europe, it is now mainly rife in India.

Also like typhoid, cholera is caused by a bacillus, and can be prevented by early inoculation and care over food supplies—boiling water and milk, washing uncooked foods in chlorinated water, and keeping flies away.

The fever begins in the usual way with a short incubation period, followed by abdominal pain, severe vomiting, and diarrhœa. Later with the loss of fluid from the body there may be cramps in the muscles, diarrhœa increases, and the motions become of the typical "rice-water" type —*i.e.*, there is no solid matter, and the appearance is that of water to which a little milk has been added. This stage is followed by collapse, with low pulse and cold hands and feet. Death, if adequate treatment is not available, results in about 70 per cent. of cases.

Anthrax. The bacillus of anthrax, like that of tuberculosis, can exist outside the body for long periods, and, like that of tetanus, then takes the form of spores or seed-like bodies. It is spread by infected cattle and horses, which get the disease from eating grass containing spores.

In human beings the form the disease takes depends on where the germ alights; sometimes it comes from infected shaving-brushes, when it causes a large sore, like a boil, on the face, known as "malignant pustule"; sometimes it develops in those who inhale the dust from infected hides or wool (hence the name "wool-sorters' disease," which is a form of bronchitis with blood-stained sputum); lastly it may arise through eating infected meat, when the result is intestinal anthrax.

In all cases the outlook is serious. Death is common, preceded by a high temperature, skin symptoms in the first instance, lung symptoms in the second, and food-poisoning symptoms in the third. Penicillin or tetracycline may be effective.

Diseases Caused by Fungi.

There are only two important groups of disease caused by fungus: the serious *actinomycosis* and the relatively harmless, if unpleasant, *ringworm*. Ringworm or tinea will be dealt with later; it affects the hair, the body, the groin (dhobie itch, already referred to), and the feet (athlete's foot). Actinomycosis is spread by a fungus in barley and grasses which may reach the human mouth, settle around bad teeth, and thence pass to the lungs, the bone of the jaw, and even to the intestines or brain. Fortunately, this unpleasant fungus, which was once difficult to eradicate, has proved susceptible to penicillin.

The Venereal Diseases.

The venereal diseases are those caused—or at least that is what the name means—by the goddess of love, Venus. Venus, of course, causes a great deal of trouble, but venereal disease is not necessarily the worst she can do. Venereal disease is spread by sexual intercourse with an infected person.

Gonorrhoea is the result of an infection by the gonococcus (*Neisseria gonorrhoea*) and ordinarily comes on after an incubation period of three to seven days. However, babies can get an infection of the eyes, known as ophthalmia, from their mother if she is infected, and gonorrhoea in young children is often the result of being in contact with infected towels or clothes. The disease in adults is evident when there is a thick, creamy discharge from the sexual organs and sometimes pain on passing water; in infants ophthalmia is prevented by the use of silver nitrate eye-drops at birth. Gonorrhoea is fairly easily cured by the use of sulpha drugs or penicillin; but unfortunately venereal disease is increasing in recent years and drug-resistant forms are becoming more common.

Syphilis is a serious venereal disease caused by a spirochete (*Treponema pallidum*). Stories about lavatory seats are simply stories, although it is occasionally possible to get syphilis by other than sexual means: for example, it has happened that a man playing football has been infected through his hand being grazed by the teeth of someone with syphilis. But this is very unusual, although kissing can spread the disease. Children, too, can be born with syphilis (the so-called congenital syphilis).

Adult syphilis begins with a sore, known as a hard chancre, at the point where the spirochete of syphilis has entered; this may be on the lips, through kissing; on the sexual organs, through intercourse; and very rarely, as explained above, elsewhere. In a short time the chancre disappears and all may seem to be well, but this primary stage is followed by a secondary stage with sore throat, a rash, headache, and enlargement of glands. This, if left alone, also clears up, but is followed by the tertiary stage, in which a chronic infection develops in some part of the body which, presumably, is most susceptible in the particular individual. Thus there may be chronic syphilis of the skin, the bones, the heart, liver, or nervous system.

In the nervous system, the commonest forms are the two diseases of *tabes dorsalis*, in which the spinal cord is infected, and G.P.I. (general paralysis of the insane), in which the brain and mind are affected. These will be discussed under Nervous Diseases.

In congenital syphilis the pregnant mother gives her child syphilis. Such infants are often stillborn or premature, they look wizened, like little old men, and amongst other symptoms are eye disease, "snuffles," a flattened nose, and when the adult teeth appear the front ones may be notched at the biting surface.

The treatment, of course, is very much a matter for a specialist, but diagnosis is usually made through the Wassermann blood test. It was for syphilis that Ehrlich produced his "magic bullet"—an arsenical drug, known as salvarsan, which could attack the organism selectively without harming the body and was the first of the modern specific drugs. Present-day treatment is with penicillin. G.P.I., was once treated with malarial therapy with some success. Penicillin alone is often adequate.

It is important to understand about venereal disease in general: (1) that it happens to many people who are no worse than anyone else; (2) that many patients believe themselves to have V.D. when, in fact, they have not; (3) that the best thing to do is to see your doctor as soon as possible—he is not concerned with your morals, and the sooner you go, the sooner you will get well; (4) every sore in the sexual area need not be V.D. There are other diseases which may be contracted as venereal infections.

Chancroid produces small septic ulcers around the sex organs, with swelling of the local glands in the groin, which may suppurate. It is caused by a bacillus, and can usually be cleared up by sulpha drugs within a week. Scabies and lice often pass from one body to another during sexual intercourse, but are not usually thought of as venereal in origin, although in many cases they are.

Tropical Diseases.

Nothing is more difficult than to define the term "tropical diseases." One might define them as the diseases which occur in tropical climates—but then measles occurs there too; and if they are defined as those diseases which are found *only* in the tropics, the solution is no easier, since leprosy, cholera, smallpox, and typhus are usually listed as tropical diseases, yet were found in this country until fairly recently—and the odd case still is.

But what a story could be told about the conquest of those infections which were—and many still are—the scourge of humanity! One day when generals and dictators are forgotten we shall remember that great international army of physicians and bacteriologists who have saved millions of lives and infinitely reduced human suffering: Koch and Ehrlich of Germany, Pasteur and Roux of France, Ross and Jenner of Britain, Reed of America, Noguchi of Japan, and many others. We shall remember how the Jesuit priests brought quinine from Peru to Europe in 1638, the first drug to save people from malaria; how in tropical heat Ronald Ross (1857–1932) peered for hours through his microscope to discover the connection between malaria and the mosquito until the sweat running from his brow rusted the instrument; how Major Walter Reed's work in Havana (1851–1902) made possible the building of the Panama Canal, and think, too, of the American soldiers who died in helping him to find the cause of yellow fever. In mentioning Jenner once more, we should recall Lady Mary Montagu (1689–1762), who brought the practice of vaccination to England from Turkey—or, rather, the practice of "variolation," which meant inoculating with the pus from smallpox cases. This was, of course, a dangerous practice, but the idea was there. Noguchi, one of the great bacteriologists of the nineteenth century, was the son of a poor peasant. He often had to steal to get enough bread even to keep alive, but was later to help in our understanding of syphilis and many tropical diseases.

Yet there is still much to do. Take, for example, the case of Egypt, one of the world's poorest countries, supporting with the help of water from the Nile about 24 million people. But if the river gives food and drink it does other things; for it carries the disease of bilharzia, which kills thousands of peasants yearly. In the villages of Egypt as many as 90–100 per cent. of the population suffer from this terrible disease. The infantile mortality rate is the second highest in the world—29·5 per cent.—seven times higher than that of Holland; the average expectation of life amongst the lower classes is thirty-one years, of the upper classes fifty to sixty years. The country is ridden with bilharzia, ankylostomiasis, malaria, plague, amoebic dysentery, typhus, tuberculosis, and pellagra. Blindness, due to trachoma and other diseases, affects tens of thousands. Such a situation cannot be treated simply by pouring drugs into the country; what is necessary is social control, to enforce purification of the water supplies, the use of insecticides to kill the disease-bearing pests, and removal of the causes of extreme poverty (tuberculosis and vitamin deficiencies which are common in Egypt are diseases of malnutrition).

Relapsing Fever, common in India and Africa, may be louse- or tick-borne; the germ is a spirochæte, similar to that of syphilis, but the disease is non-venereal. Relapsing fever gets its name from the fact that the temperature remains high (39°–41°C) for about a week, returns to normal for a week, and rises again. There may be three to five relapses of this sort. Penicillin is effective; lice or ticks must be eradicated.

Epidemic Jaundice (also known as Weil's disease or—if you prefer it—ictero-hæmorrhagica spirochætosis), is also caused by a spirochæte, and spread by rats. Now it is rarely found in Europe, although it occurred in the trenches during the First World War, in men working in sewers, and in the women who worked in the fish market of Aberdeen, which at one time was rat-infested. It is rarely fatal, but leads to high fever and jaundice. Penicillin in high dosage or tetracycline may help.

Yaws is also a spirochætal disease, common in the tropics and particularly in children. It is unpleasant, but not serious, and tends to clear up in a year or so. There are raspberry-like growths on the skin, which disappear with the drugs used in syphilis (although the condition is non-venereal). The Wassermann reaction, positive in syphilis, is also positive in yaws.

Leprosy. Whereas syphilis, relapsing fever, epidemic jaundice, and yaws are caused by spirochætes, leprosy is caused by a bacillus resembling the bacillus of tuberculosis. Leprosy, in fact, should not be included here at all, for it is non-spirochætal, and not necessarily a tropical infection. Apart from the difficulty of classification, many popular beliefs about the disease are untrue. It is *not* the oldest disease afflicting man; *not* a disease confined to tropical countries; it is *not* very catching; *not* hereditary, *not* incurable; in leprosy the fingers and toes do *not* drop off; it is *not* a divine punishment for wrongdoing. So there are many misunderstandings about this disease, and placing it in the wrong part of the medical section is probably the least.

Leprosy is a serious disease not because of disfiguring light-coloured skin patches and lumps, but because it destroys peripheral nerves. Leprosy may disappear spontaneously, or it may progress until the face is lion-like and the hands and feet wasted and ulcerated. The disease rarely kills, but it is the world's greatest crippler.

Leprosy was once fairly common in colder Western countries, though its extent was exaggerated. The great majority of the 15 million people who suffer from leprosy live in tropical countries, but it still exists in Iceland, Japan, Korea and some of the southern states of the United States. Prolonged and intimate contact with an "open" case is said to be the main mode of infection, but only one infected husband in twenty passes leprosy to his wife.

The sulphone drugs have revolutionised the treatment of leprosy. Given early diagnosis and adequate treatment, the great majority of sufferers could be cured. Established deformity (such as claw hand, drop foot, paralysed eyelids) can be mitigated by reconstructive surgery, although lost sensation cannot be restored.

In the past, only Christian missions were concerned with the plight of the leprosy sufferer. Now, non-sectarian voluntary agencies, Governments and the World Health Organisation have joined in the fight against the disease. Enough is known to control the disease, but not enough is being done, as only one victim in five is at present getting treatment.

Plague is another disease caused by bacteria, common in Europe at one time, but now largely restricted to Asia. Nevertheless, it caused millions of deaths in Europe during the years 1348–49 and 1665 and was the "Black Death," which, indeed, changed the course of history. Interested readers may read Hans Zinnser's *Rats, Lice, and History* about this aspect of the disease. Plague is carried by the bite of the rat flea, but, once people become infected, spread may occur from one to the other by droplet infection—*i.e.*, by coughing and sneezing. After an incubation period of two to ten days, fever develops, rather like severe influenza, and in a day or two the glands in the groin begin to swell, followed perhaps by swelling of the glands elsewhere. This is the usual type of plague, but it is also possible to get disease of the lungs from droplet infection and blood-poisoning from infection of the blood-stream. Both the latter types are almost invariably fatal, and even the glandular type (bubonic plague) has a mortality of about 80 per cent. The vaccine has given place to streptomycin and sulpha drugs which are also used on contacts.

Although we have little space to discuss the subject of plagues and epidemics in general, it is worth noting that serious epidemics have almost always followed wars, revolutions, and economic and political collapse. Thus the Black Death followed the break-up of the Roman Empire, and, in the fourteenth century, accompanied the end of mediæval civilisation. The Napoleonic wars were followed by other epidemics, and the wars of the 1830s in Europe were followed by influenza. In the most widespread outburst of influenza after the First World War, more people were killed by the disease than in all the fighting of four years. It is a reflection on the peculiar mentality of Man that this devastating epidemic, which affected almost the whole world, occupies little space in his history books—we still, with few exceptions, regard history as the doings of kings, queens, and generals. Yet, in 1918, 20 million men, and women, and children died from influenza, and no cure has, as yet, been found! Later we shall see that many millions of people die yearly from starvation or vitamin deficiencies But these facts—the real facts of life—we rarely hear about.

Protozoal Diseases.

Nearly all the diseases caused by protozoa are tropical diseases, although one of the best-known protozoans is the harmless amœba found in British ponds. Protozoal diseases are caused by these organisms, large in comparison with bacteria which are really one-celled plants. Viruses are neither animals nor plants, are much smaller than the other two groups, and have some distinctive characteristics described elsewhere.

The only important diseases caused by protozoa are sleeping sickness or trypanosomiasis, malaria, and amœbic dysentery (as contrasted with bacillary dysentery), another disease, leishmaniasis—also known by the numerous names of kala-azar, dum-dum fever, and, in milder form, Delhi boil, Oriental sore, or Bagdad sore—will also be mentioned briefly. These infections are few, but important in their influence on Man; for, as Dr. Clark-Kennedy has pointed out, malaria until recently was responsible for one-fifth of all human sickness, sleeping sickness not so long ago caused a large part of Central Africa to be uninhabitable, and in some areas of the tropics there are probably more people with, than without, amœbic dysentery.

Malaria. The word, of course, means "bad air," just as "influenza" means "influence"—in Italian *influenza di freddo*—the influence of cold. Human beings have a natural tendency to suppose that, when two events occur together, then one must be caused by the other. Yet, although malaria and "bad air" may often go together, and influenza and cold, it does not follow that bad air (whatever that may be) causes malaria nor that cold causes influenza. In fact, the anopheles mosquito carries the amœba of malaria, and the mosquito prefers climates which some people might describe as "bad," but it is the amœba, not the air, which causes the disease. Anyhow, the unfortunate mosquito might well use the phrase honoured by many generations of schoolmasters: "It hurts me more than it hurts you!" For the mosquito, too, is sick, and passes on its sickness to the person it bites.

There are several types of plasmodium—which is the scientific name for this amœba—producing attacks of fever varying in severity and frequency: benign tertian, quartan, and malignant quartan. Entering the body from the mosquito bite, the parasites penetrate the blood cells, multiply there, and finally burst into the blood stream. When this happens the temperature rises, and then they return to the cells to carry out once more the same procedure. Depending on the type, the attacks of fever may be at intervals of three or four days, severe or milder. When someone with malaria is bitten by a mosquito the infection can be transmitted to the next person it meets, but malaria is not infectious from one person to another directly. Quinine, of course, is the time-honoured remedy, but many other drugs are now available: mepacrine, primaquine, chloraquine and some sulpha drugs. The drug must be taken long enough for the infection to die out, otherwise relapses can occur even after leaving a malarial country (but it is only fair to say that, just as some people continue to give themselves the title of "Major" when they have left the Army, so others long in Britain continue to describe attacks of cold or 'flu as "my old malaria again," when, to say the least of it, they are exaggerating).

Important as are the drugs used in the treatment of malaria, even more so is the control of the parasite-bearing mosquito. The eggs of mosquitoes hatch in water, and there the young or larval forms can be attacked by pouring oil on the surface of pools so that they are unable to breathe, or by introducing small fish which have a partiality for them. Adult mosquitoes can be killed by insecticides or kept away by repellent creams or nets over beds. Prophylaxis with anti-malarials before entering and while living in known malarial zones is important.

Blackwater Fever is a sequel to malaria in tropical Africa and some parts of India. Rather illogically, it is described as "Blackwater," although the urine is red and the skin is yellow but the result is due to breaking down of the red blood cells by some malarial toxin. Possibly too much quinine may help in producing the illness. Treatment is to give plenty of fluids and no quinine or any other anti-malarial drugs in the early stages. The death-rate is about 25 per cent.

Trypanosomiasis or sleeping sickness—not to be confused with *sleepy* sickness—is essentially an African disease (although also found in tropical America) spread by the tsetse fly. Its cause is the type of protozoan known as a trypanosome, almond-shaped with vibrating membranes at the sides which enable it to move through the blood-stream, rather like a flat fish in the water.

There are three stages of the disease: first, the stage of fever with enlarged glands and a rapid pulse, which may continue off and on for three years; secondly, the stage of trembling hands, legs, and tongue, vacant expression, and slow and stumbling speech; thirdly, and lastly, the stage of low temperature, apathy, wasting of the muscles, and possibly death.

Treatment is with arsenical drugs—such as tryparsamide or Bayer 205—which give good results in early cases. Preventive measures in infected areas include the destruction of tsetse flies by insecticide, the cutting down of forests near rivers which are inhabited by tsetse flies, and some authorities have suggested the shooting of big game which may form a "reservoir" of the parasites, whence tsetse flies can carry them to human beings. For similar reasons infected people should not be allowed to move to non-infected areas.

Amœbic Dysentery, also known as *Amœbiasis*, is caused by the *Entamœba histolytica*, an amœba whose cysts are found in food, water, or spread by infected fingers or flies. There is mild fever and diarrhœa which contains blood. The disease may become chronic, and can cause abscesses, usually in the liver but sometimes in the lungs. Amœbiasis is treated with chloroquine or nitroimidazoles.

Leishmaniasis, kala-azar, or dum-dum fever, is another amœbic disease, probably spread in this instance by the bite of sandflies. It is also known as tropical splenomegaly—enlargement of the spleen in ordinary language—since infection results in enlargement of the spleen and liver, low, irregular fever, and death within a year or so. A milder form, affecting the skin, is known as Delhi boil, Oriental sore, or Baghdad sore, does not lead to kala-azar, and is fairly readily cured. The cure for both conditions is to give injections of antimony compounds which reduce the death-rate from kala-azar from 80 per cent. to about 5 per cent.

Diseases Caused by Parasitic Worms.

Many types of worms infest human beings and other animals. They are interesting for such reasons as their size (which may range from the almost invisible to 9 m or more), their life histories, and their serious or trivial consequences on their hosts. We shall mention only a few groups here, and mainly the ones likely to be met with in Europe—the tapeworms, the roundworms, and the threadworms—although some tropical types will be described briefly.

Tapeworms, as we have seen earlier, like many other types of intestinal worm, lead a double life. What usually happens is that the worm breeds in the human intestine, the eggs pass out in the fæces, and are then swallowed by animals eating contaminated material. In the animal the eggs hatch out into larvæ—primitive forms which penetrate the muscle, forming cysts—and Man is infected in turn by eating its meat. Thus *Tœnia solium* gets into the flesh of pigs, which, if imperfectly cooked (measly pork), causes infestation of the intestine in Man. It reaches a length of about 3 m. *Tœnia saginata*, which reaches a length of about 6 m, is spread in imperfectly cooked beef, and in Baltic countries *Dibothriocephalus latus* gets into the human intestine from caviare or undercooked fish. It reaches the awesome length of 9 m.

Now all the worms we have mentioned so far are found in the human intestine, and the cysts, which are much more dangerous and unpleasant, in the animal's muscles. But in some worms the reverse happens, with the adult in the animal's intestines and the cysts in Man. Thus in Australia the dog tapeworm (*Tœnia echinococcus*) produces cysts in both sheep and Man. This is known as hydatid disease, and may remain unsuspected until cysts in the lungs, liver, or elsewhere become infected or rupture. *Trichinella spiralis* is similar in action, being found in the intestines of pigs and getting into the muscles or other organs of Man. The main difference is that this worm migrates from the pig's intestines into its muscles, whence it reaches Man in undercooked pork meat or sausages. The muscular cysts cause swellings and sometimes pain. There are changes in the blood, swelling of the face and leg in the early stages, and fever. A minor epidemic occurred in England in 1941. *Tœnia echinococcus* and *Trichinella spiralis* are small—not more than 0·5 cm in length—but are more serious in their consequences than the large worms. Treatment is very difficult, and ordinarily all that can be done is to deal with individual cysts when they make themselves apparent.

The large tapeworms, *Tœnia solium* and *saginata* and *Dibothriocephalus latus*, produce varying symptoms or none at all. Usually they are not discovered until some segments of the worm are excreted, but there may be mild indigestion, excessive hunger, and occasionally anæmia. However, when the worm is discovered the patient, not unnaturally is likely to become anxious and uncomfortable at the thought of "having" a tapeworm; these symptoms are caused by the worry rather than the worm.

Treatment is, of course, a matter for a doctor, who now has a number of very effective drugs to choose from. One has to make sure that the head of the worm has been removed, otherwise it will continue to grow.

Roundworms are similar both in appearance and size to ordinary earth-worms and the eggs reach Man, not from an animal, but from the contaminated fingers of someone else who handles food. They give rise to no symptoms, and are noticed only when discharged in the fæces or occasionally vomited up. Piperazine is an effective treatment.

Threadworms, as the name suggests, are like small 0·5–1 cm long pieces of white thread. They are very common in children, and live mainly in the cæcum—*i.e.*, the part of the large intestine near the appendix. The males, which are the smaller ones, remain there, but the females pass down towards the rectum at night-time and lay their eggs in the area around the anus. Infection is by contaminated hands handling food—especially uncooked food—and water. Threadworms are not serious, and cause few symptoms other than itching around the anus and between the legs, but heavily infected children may show symptoms of anæmia. The nervousness often shown by such children is usually the result of the irritation produced by the worms in the anal region. Infection is not common in adults, and in children tends to disappear at puberty.

Treatment is, in theory, simple; for the worms are easily destroyed by a number of drugs, such as piperazine. Ointment is applied to the itching area, and the child should be prevented from scratching. However, since the eggs may lie about the house for some time, reinfection often happens, especially if there are several small children in the home who may pass the disease from one to another.

The idea that intestinal worms in general are likely to cause loss of weight by absorbing food eaten by the patient is largely mistaken: for, although it is true that they do live on this food, the amount taken is certainly not enough to be significant.

Tropical Worms. Bilharzia has been mentioned before in connection with its frequency in Egypt, although it is also found in other parts of Africa, Arabia, and Iraq. There are two main types: one infecting the bladder (*Schistosomum hæmatobium*), the other the rectum (*Schistosomum mansoni*). Bilharzia is more correctly known as schistosomiasis.

The parasite's fantastic life-history begins when a man bathes in infected water, and the small swimming forms known as cercariæ pierce and enter his skin—or they may enter the body by drinking infected water. From the skin they pass to the portal vein below the liver, remain there six weeks until they become adult and then swim against the blood-stream down to the pelvis, where the female lays eggs which have a sharp spine. The eggs penetrate into the bladder or rectum—depending on the type of fluke—and pass out in the fæces or urine. If they enter water they hatch out into small moving forms which seek out a water-snail, develop further in its body, and leave it in the form of cercariæ ready to find a new human victim. The female fluke is slender and round, about 2·5 cm in length, the male, flat and leaf-shaped, is about 2 cm long, and, as we have seen, their grisly courting takes place in the portal vein, whence the impregnated female passes to the bladder (hæmatobium) or rectum (mansoni) to lay her eggs.

Infection results in raised temperature and, in the urinary type, blood in the urine; in the intestinal type blood is found in the fæces, and there are symptoms resembling dysentery—*e.g.*, diarrhœa. Treatment in both cases is with antimony tartrate or niridazole. Needless to say, attempts should be made at prevention by telling people to avoid infected canals (usually easier said than done), and by periodically cutting off the water supply to the canals to kill the snails.

Hookworm Disease, or ankylostomiasis, is found in many parts of the world, especially in miners who work on damp ground. The tiny worm enters the body usually through the feet, passes through the blood-stream to the lungs, eats through into one of the bronchial tubes, climbs the windpipe, and passes down the œsophagus into the stomach to end up in the duodenum. It causes anæmia, can be fairly readily cured, but is occasionally fatal.

Elephantiasis. Some types of parasitic worm are spread by insects. Thus in *Filiarisis* mosquitoes inject by their bites the infantile forms of a tiny worm which enters the lymphatic channels; there the blockade they cause leads to the swelling of the legs and the lower part of the body, known as elephantiasis.

PHYSICAL INJURIES.

INTRODUCTION.

In this section we shall inevitably discuss much that could be described as Principles of First Aid. You cannot learn First Aid from a book, even if you read one of the excellent first aid manuals, like those published by the St. John Ambulance Association. The only way is to join one of their many classes of practical and theoretical instruction which are held in all parts of this country and many others. There is much to be said for many more people receiving instruction, to judge by the level of general ignorance and ineffectiveness to be witnessed at most road accidents before the ambulance comes.

The most difficult thing to learn is what *not* to do. When a patient is knocked down in the road, people instinctively seem to want to drag him immediately to his feet, or otherwise pull him on to the pavement away from the traffic. Someone will have entered the nearest shop and be emerging with a chair so that the casualty can sit down. Before long a hot strong sweet cup of tea has arrived, and this or some other beverage is being poured into him. All this is instinctive, and all of it is wrong. Do *not* move the patient until you are sure he has no fracture which will be further aggravated by movement. To take an extreme case, a fractured spine clumsily moved may result in permanent widespread paralysis. Guard your patient from the traffic but only move him when you are certain it is safe to do so. If he has any injury which is likely to require a general anaesthetic on arrival in hospital (and this applies to most fractures) do not give anything at all by mouth. No anaesthetic can be given to a patient who has eaten or drunk anything in the previous three hours, in case he vomits while unconscious and dies of obstruction of his airway. Keep your patient warm (do *not* warm him up artificially) keep his head low, and unless he is bleeding severely or has stopped breathing, do nothing but protect him from the ministrations of the uninstructed until the ambulance comes.

Injuries to the Head and Back.

The head contains the brain, an organ with a number of inconvenient properties from the point of view of injury. Its very great importance is matched by its very great vulnerability as a tissue. Its consistency is that of stiff junket. It is quite incapable of repair once damaged and cannot heal by growing new parts in the way that skin and bone can. So it has to be totally enclosed by protective bone which means it cannot swell without compressing itself dangerously within its box—and this not infrequently happens after injury. Furthermore, any bleeding into the interior of the skull can only occur at the expense of compressing the brain, since the brain box is already fully occupied by the brain. There is a story in first aid known as "Concussion and Compression." It begins with a knock-out blow to the head and this is known as concussion. The patient struck a hard enough blow to the head will lose consciousness, if only for a short time, due to the brain being shaken up. Even slight knocks would do this if the brain were not cushioned by a thin layer of cerebrospinal fluid. Most concussed patients quickly regain consciousness, and for the great majority that is the end of the affair except for a sore head and a headache for a few days. Unfortunately for a minority, even though there may have been no fracture, the blow that knocked them out will also have damaged a small blood vessel on the surface of the brain. These patients may be indistinguishable from the luckier ones at first. They may have regained consciousness and will be just as anxious to go home. They will often be quite lucid for some hours. Surgeons call this the "lucid interval." However, when more than a certain amount of blood has accumulated in the head, and the brain is sufficiently compressed by it the patient loses consciousness slowly, for a second time, and from this phase of "compression" he will not recover unless something is done. The lucid interval can last some hours. Brain surgeons can relieve the compression and save the life of the patient only if they have him in their care when it occurs. This is why *all* cases of head injury who have once lost consciousness (concussion), for however short a period of time, and however lucid they may subsequently appear, *all* must be seen by a doctor and, if thought necessary, observed overnight in hospital, in case they are bleeding and proceeding to compression. There is no way of saving these avoidable fatalities other than by treating all cases of concussion seriously. Fractured skull is potentially even more serious, because the blow will have been harder and, the brain is therefore more seriously at risk.

The spinal cord can be regarded as an extension of the brain which runs down the middle of the spinal bones of the vertebral column. It has the same delicate consistency, and the same inability to recover from injury as the brain. Injury is usually the result of a fracture-dislocation of the spine. The consequences of injury are due to a permanent interruption of its two main functions. All movements of the voluntary muscles are only possible if they are connected by nerves to the brain. Except for muscles in the head, all these "motor" nerves run in the spinal cord. The nerve pathways leave the skull through a large hole in its base and run down in the spinal cord to the required level. They then emerge between the spinal bones and travel in bundles to reach the muscles. Motor nerves for the arm leave the cord between the vertebrae of the neck. Those for the leg leave the cord in the lumbar region in the small of the back. If the nerve supply is damaged in any part of its course, the muscles being supplied become paralysed and are unable to move. It follows that if the spinal cord is damaged, all muscles below the point of damage have been cut off from the brain, and will be paralysed, and this will be permanent because the cord cannot be repaired. Damage to the nerve pathway *after* it has left the cord can often be repaired. Permanent paralysis is only one of the consequences of cord damage, since there is another whole series of nerves running in the cord which carry sensations from all parts of the body to the brain. Therefore there will be loss of sensation as well as paralysis below the point of injury.

It is emphasised that fracture of the spinal bones can occur without damage to the cord taking place. It is when these bones move one over the other, or "dislocate," that permanent cord damage occurs. It is therefore extremely important that cases of back injury be moved very carefully indeed in order to avoid such a disaster, and special ways of moving such patients are taught in First Aid classes.

Haemorrhage and Shock.

Every part of the body must have a blood supply, or else it will die. It is possible to stop the blood supply to a leg, for example, by fastening a wide rubber bandage tightly around the top of the thigh. This so-called "constrictive bandage" is still mentioned in First Aid books as a desperate means of controlling haemorrhage in a limb. It should hardly ever be used, because by stopping all circulation of blood, the entire limb will die in the course of time. Besides, most haemorrhage can be stemmed by direct pressure on the bleeding point. The tissues of the leg, such as its muscle and skin and bone will begin to die in a little more than half an hour after cutting off the blood supply. The brain, however, will begin to suffer within three *seconds* of its blood supply being cut off, and will die in about three minutes. Thus it can be seen that some parts of the body are more susceptible than others to a failure of the blood supply and the brain suffers earliest of all. Since the brain is where most of the vital functions of the body are controlled, it follows that a shortage of blood to the brain is likely to lead to a "depression of the vital functions"—a state of affairs known to First Aiders as "shock."

Shock occurs in a number of conditions, but is always due to a failure of the supply of blood to the vital functions of the brain for one reason or another. Its usual causes are:

(1) haemorrhage, when there is a general shortage, but the brain feels it most;

(2) severe burns, in which much fluid is lost from the blood as will be seen later; and

(3) certain medical conditions causing acute heart failure in which there is a failure to pump blood to the brain because the pump has failed.

The treatment for shock consists basically of restoring the blood supply to the brain, and where it is caused by loss of blood or other fluid, the treatment is transfusion. Finally, it must be emphasised that treatment is always urgent, since the brain cannot function for long without its blood supply, and once damaged by the shortage, can never be repaired. No attempt is made here to describe such treatment completely, but the most important things are to keep the head low so as to reduce the work the heart must do to drive blood to the brain; and to avoid artificial heating of the body by hot water bottles, etc., which only diverts blood away from the brain where it is needed, into the skin where it is not.

The treatment of severe haemorrhage is to stop the bleeding, usually by firm, direct pressure, and then to remember above all things that even though the bleeding has stopped, there may be a dangerous state of shock from which the patient could die. This can only be prevented by restoring the circulation to the brain, usually by transfusion; so, having stopped the bleeding drive him fast to hospital for the second part of the treatment which may be as necessary to save his life as the first.

There is great confusion over the use of the word "shock." In the lay mind it is a shake-up of the nervous system caused by a fright, or some bad news, or the sight of something nasty in the woodshed. Even in the medical mind it is sometimes confused and some of the First Aid books confuse it still further. Too frequently they give the treatment as "loosen all tight clothing from neck, chest, and waist; reassure the casualty and ensure a good supply of air." All this, together with grandmother's hot strong sweet tea is perfectly good enough if the patient is only "shaken-up" by a fright or a fall, but it will be dangerously negligent and time-wasting if he is suffering from true shock due to a failure of blood supply to the brain.

Fainting is a special case which can be prevented by keeping the head low in those who feel faint. It is usually self-curing due to the patient automatically falling into a position in which the head is low. If the faint, however, is due to severe blood loss, this is the same as shock in our proper meaning of the word and must be treated accordingly.

Haemorrhage can therefore be a difficult problem. It is even more so when it is internal. This may be in *medical* cases such as in occasional cases of peptic ulceration in which the blood will be vomited and also passed in the stool. Or it may be *surgical*, in the sense of being caused by injury to internal organs. The blood may emerge from one or other of the various orifices of the body, or it may be entirely concealed within the body. Rupture of internal abdominal organs such as the spleen, kidney and liver can occur with surprisingly little to show in the way of external injury. A fractured thigh bone can pierce the main artery of the leg and cause lethal internal haemorrhage without a drop of blood being visible. In all these cases diagnosis is urgent, followed by emergency blood transfusion if the brain, and hence the patient's life, is to be saved.

Means of detecting the presence of severe haemorrhage without seeing any blood are taught in First Aid Classes as the Signs of Haemorrhage. They are in fact manifestations of the reactions of the body in its attempts to save the failing brain, and are therefore the same as the signs of shock. The main ones are a rapid, feeble pulse, getting more rapid and more feeble as time goes on in a desperate attempt to get the remaining blood to the brain; skin pallor caused by constriction of blood vessels near the surface so that the blood which remains is shunted to the brain away from the less vulnerable skin; and finally, just before death, restlessness and air hunger.

A word of warning about the First Aid treatment of shock due to heart attack (coronary thrombosis). These patients must be transported at complete rest, but many of them react very badly to being made to lie down, since they have great difficulty in breathing in this position Transport them relaxed, in a sitting position, supported by a large comfortable back rest.

It cannot be too strongly emphasised that with haemorrhage and shock, as with so many First Aid emergencies, the importance of protecting the brain is paramount.

Asphyxia.

The previous section was concerned with maintaining an adequate supply of blood to the brain. This is needed in order to supply the brain's only possible fuel—glucose—and the oxygen with which to burn it. Many different circumstances can conspire to reduce the oxygen content of the blood, and the result in each case is asphyxia. Normally, air is taken into the lungs through the air passages and brought into contact with all the circulating blood. It diffuses from the lungs into the blood, where it enters into a special relationship with the pigment of the red cells—haemoglobin. At the same time, the waste gas carbon dioxide enters the lungs from the blood and is breathed out. The revitalised blood is passed through the heart to build up sufficient pressure to drive it into all the tissues of the body, and in particular into the brain. A special system in the brain—the respiratory centre—controls the complicated machinery of respiration and is itself, of course, kept alive by the products of the very mechanism it controls. This mechanism consists of all the muscles of respiration—those which lift the ribs, the diaphragm and many other so-called accessory muscles. They all have to be finely co-ordinated by means of nerve impulses which begin in the brain, pass down the spinal cord and out to the muscles. Information of many kinds comes along sensory nerve pathways to the respiratory centre so that breathing can be automatically adjusted to the changing needs of the moment. In order that life may continue there must be:

(1) a functioning breathing mechanism to revitalise the blood; and

(2) a circulation to carry the revitalised blood to the brain and other tissues.

In many cases when breathing stops and unconsciousness supervenes as brain function is depressed, the heart will go on beating for some time longer. The aim of First Aid is to restore the breathing by artificial respiration *before the heart stops*. Once the heart stops—and it eventually does so abruptly and without warning—the brain is dead within the usual few minutes unless *both* the heart and the breathing are restarted; and this is a very much more difficult proposition than artificial respiration alone.

For these reasons, a patient whose breathing has stopped must have it started again without any delay. Here, as in the case of severe haemorrhage, it is no use telephoning the doctor or even putting the patient in an ambulance. The First Aider must act himself, because he is on the spot and the only one in a position to save life. Both actions require elementary First Aid training, and even school children can accomplish them if they have been well taught.

Asphyxia is the name given to a failure of the oxygen supply to the brain and is due to a breakdown in some part of the complicated breathing mechanism outlined above. One of its chief causes is a blockage of the airway by (*a*) solids or (*b*) liquids. Any foreign body of the right shape and size will block the airway, as also will the tongue in the unconscious patient. Remember how much more easily the child's airway can become blocked because it is so much smaller. Blockage by a liquid, is of course, drowning. Remember that if a patient drowns in the entire ocean, it is only about half a cupful which is doing him any harm—as it only takes this amount to fill the airway. The same goes for the amount of tea, or vomit, required to kill an unconscious patient if it gets down the " wrong way "—as it will unless someone prevents it.

Another very common cause of asphyxia is carbon monoxide poisoning. Carbon monoxide is a lethal component of car exhaust fumes, incompletely burning and badly ventilated fires and stoves, and domestic coal gas. One of the inconvenient properties of haemoglobin is that it combines with carbon monoxide very much more eagerly than with oxygen. Prolonged contact with even a very slightly contaminated atmosphere can build up a concentration of carbon monoxide in the blood which will prevent the blood from carrying sufficient oxygen—and this is in fact how it kills. It takes a very short time for this to happen if the atmosphere is heavily contaminated. Remember the danger of even a very slight leak of the gas either in the kitchen, or into a car from a faulty exhaust pipe or silencer. Many elderly people die of coal gas poisoning every day because their sense of smell is poor and they do not detect the leak.

Other causes of asphyxia are lack of oxygen in the atmosphere, as occurs at high altitudes; crushing of the chest so that the ribs cannot move; paralysis of the muscles of breathing by interference with their nerve supply, usually in First Aid, as a result of a broken neck and consequent damage to the spinal cord (poliomyelitis can occasionally produce the same effect by attacking the nerves just before they leave the spine); and depressing the respiratory centre in the brain, most commonly nowadays by barbiturate poisoning.

The only really effective method of artificial respiration, which all members of any civilised community should be able to carry out, can be learned in half an hour at a good First Aid class. This is the direct, mouth-to-mouth method, sometimes dramatised by journalists as the " kiss of life." The method is taught with the aid of models and cannot be satisfactorily learned by only reading about it.

In discussing asphyxia, we have again had to consider the particularly vulnerable situation of the brain.

Fractures.

Broken bones are not the most serious possible consequences of injuries causing fractures. It is usually more to be feared that further damage will be done by the broken ends of the bones to tissues and organs in the neighbourhood of the fracture. The First Aid treatment of immobilising the part before transporting the casualty is designed to avoid this.

Six types of fracture are commonly taught, but some of them may co-exist in the same injury and the division is only for descriptive purposes. In addition there are two special fractures of the skull.

A " simple " or " closed " fracture is where only the bone is broken, without damage to surrounding tissues and without a wound. A " compound " or " open " fracture is one in which air, and hence germs, can get at the broken bone. This may be through a wound, in whose depths lies the broken bone; or the bone may have been pushed out through the skin; or a bullet track may lead down to the fracture. All these are examples of compound fracture and the great danger is that the bone will become infected. Even now that infections are less feared than before the days of antibiotics, it is still a grave matter for bone to get infected. However the antibiotic is given, we rely on the blood supply to carry it into the infected tissue, and bone has only a very small blood supply. If the infection is not successfully treated it can smoulder for a long time and become a " chronic osteomyelitis " which might ultimately necessitate amputation of the limb—and all because the original fracture was compound or open.

A " complicated " fracture is one in which the broken ends of the bone have damaged some important organ or tissue in the region. For example, a complicated fracture of the ribs is one in which the lung tissue, close behind the inner surface of the rib, has been pierced, and the patient will be coughing up small amounts of bright red, frothy blood. A " comminuted " fracture is one where the bone is broken into several pieces, and an " impacted " fracture is one in which the broken ends have been driven into each other and are firmly impacted. Finally a " greenstick " fracture occurs sometimes in children because their bones are not brittle and do not always break clean across. They partly break like a green stick.

" Depressed " fracture of the skull is where the vault of the skull has been struck and dinted. Many problems arise, since the brain is inevitably compressed and no dressing of the accompanying wound should be allowed to press on the brain. The dangers of infection here are not only to the broken bone, but to the meninges covering the brain, causing meningitis.

Fractured base of skull often passes through that part of the base through which the internal ear channel runs. Thus it frequently results in blood, or cerebrospinal fluid, or a mixture of both, emerging from the ear. The gravity of this fracture lies in the severity of the impact necessary to produce it, which will probably have also caused great destruction of delicate brain tissue. The outlook is usually very poor.

Remember that most casualties with fractures will require a general anaesthetic on arrival in hospital so that their fracture can be set in plaster or otherwise treated. Avoid giving them things by mouth such as drinks, which will mean a three-hour wait before anaesthetic can be administered.

Burns and Scalds.

The severity of a burn or scald depends largely on its surface area. If a patient dies of a burn, the cause of death is either infection or shock, the latter being due to fluid loss from the surface. Both hazards depend on surface area, since the bigger the surface the more germs are able to enter, and the more fluid can be lost.

It follows that the small burn on the hand or arm is seldom a threat to life, however deep the injury; and we shall therefore confine our attention to the larger burns of the whole surface of the limb or trunk.

Smaller bodies have a relatively larger surface area, and so a burn of the surface of a child's limb or trunk represents an even greater risk from fluid loss than a corresponding burn in the adult. Everyone has seen the fluid form in the blister of an ordinary small burn. It comes from the fluid part or "plasma" of the blood stream and the loss into such a blister may amount to a thimbleful. This will not hurt anyone. But the loss of similar fluid from the surface of a large burn may amount to many pints. The resultant shock will be partly due to this fluid loss from the blood stream resulting in a reduction in blood supply to the brain. Thus shock from burns has common features with shock from haemorrhage, and it is treated similarly, by transfusion. This time it is not a transfusion of blood but of plasma or some plasma substitute. In practice it is not only water that has been lost but a number of important chemicals dissolved in it as well, so that transfusion solutions have to contain sufficient of each individual substance to restore the deficit.

The arrangements for replacing the lost materials are complex and urgent; every bit as urgent as after a haemorrhage and for the same reason. The brain cannot be left too long in need. In general, the First Aid treatment of burns of large surface area is to keep them clean with a dry dressing and get the patient very quickly to hospital. Life-saving treatment by transfusion cannot start until arrival there. The only permissible delay is in the case of burns caused by corrosive chemicals which must be thoroughly washed off before transport, so that they do not continue to burn the patient on the way.

Unconsciousness.

It is not sufficiently appreciated that the dangers of being unconscious can often far outweigh the dangers from the cause of the unconsciousness. For example it is known that as many as half the deaths from head injuries are due to the airway becoming obstructed and not to the injury itself. The most important thing in managing the unconscious patient from any cause is to preserve an airway. Particularly if the patient is lying on his back it is likely to get blocked:

(*a*) by his own tongue as the lower jaw sags backwards;

(*b*) by his dentures (so remove them);

(*c*) by vomit; and

(*d*) by anything anyone may be tempted to give him by mouth.

Nothing whatever should be given by mouth in any circumstances to the unconscious patient, since he cannot swallow and it will inevitably go into his lungs.

Many of these dangers can be very much reduced by not having him on his back. Place him instead in the semi-prone position: half on his side, half on his front, with the upper leg drawn up to prevent him from rolling about. In this position the head will be inclined downwards. The jaw will tend to sag forwards and the tongue with it, away from the back of the throat. Any vomit will also come forwards. If the tongue does get in the way of the breathing the airway can usually be cleared by bending the head backwards as far as it will go and pushing the whole lower jaw forwards, by pushing from behind the angle of the jaw on both sides.

DRUG ABUSE AND DRUG DEPENDENCE.

This section of earlier editions of *Pears* was simply called "Addiction." This word is still much used, but is gradually being replaced by the terms in the present title, because ideas about the nature of the problem and methods of dealing with it are changing. Addiction is a word that conjures up rather 19th century ideas in the minds of readers: opium dens, inscrutable orientals, Sherlock Holmes injecting himself with cocaine—basically a phenomenon of foreign origin, rather frightening if its implications were not literary rather than factual, and not of great significance in Great Britain.

Drug Abuse.

It is now realised by doctors, research scientists, social workers, and the police—if still not by society as a whole—that the truth is quite different. The *abuse* of drugs in this country is at present of large proportions, increasing rapidly and showing no signs of diminishing. It is responsible each year for thousands of deaths by suicide and by accidental overdosage; for an enormous but virtually unmeasurable amount of private suffering; and for the loss to society, in terms of reduced working efficiency, of millions of man-hours every year. It has nothing to do with opium smoking which was never in any case more than the eccentricity of the few. Opium is virtually unused in medicine these days and the amount of smuggling, always small, is now negligible. The problems today arise chiefly from the misuse of drugs given by doctors for their effects on the central nervous system—the pain-killers, sleeping pills, "stimulants," and "tranquillisers."

Drugs and Medicines.

To the doctor, any substance is a drug that can be introduced into the body from outside, and that is capable of producing some detectable effect. Most such substances have a beneficial use. They are "medicines," and as such are given by doctors in suitable cases. Others, for example, nicotine (in cigarettes), alcohol (in beer, wine, or spirits), and carbon monoxide (in coal gas), are of doubtful benefit and of certain harm and are used by doctors, if at all, only under certain very special and usually experimental conditions.

Medicines may be classified under four main headings. First, there are those like quinine, or penicillin and other so-called antibiotics, that actually cure diseases by eradicating the organism (bacteria or other parasites) that cause disturbance of normal bodily function. Second, drugs such as insulin or the steroids overcome in the unhealthy the lack of some necessary substance a healthy body manufactures for itself: they must usually continue to be given for life. Third are the drugs which relieve the signs of disease—for example, there are many new drugs that lower the blood pressure or increase the output of urine—without being able to put right the disturbed basic situation which is the cause of the trouble. Fourth are drugs to relieve the patient's symptoms—which make him feel better, less breathless, take away his pain, help him to sleep, and so on—although we seldom know why they are able to do this. Indeed, in many cases we suspect that they are acting mainly as a token of help from doctor to patient, and so encouraging his body to fight a more successful battle on its own behalf.

There is no doubt that the genuine advances in beneficial drugs during the last thirty years have been enormous; but the very successes of the penicillins, tetracyclines, antimalarials, hormones, and so on have bred in the public and in the medical profession itself an attitude of uncritical wonder. There have been relatively few drugs in the first and second categories mentioned above: and in the field of mental health, the importance of which is now so rightly emphasised, there are virtually none. Yet drugs which act upon the brain are often received as if they were curative although they may pose fresh problems rather than solve the old. Thus, although there are many drugs which act upon the mind, few do this in any fundamental sense: they relieve pain and anxiety, bring sleep and lessening of stress, and may allow the patient to recuperate himself during the relief they provide. But often this deeper change does not occur—sometimes because the doctor has not clearly seen his part in helping to bring it about—and then the symptomatic relief may come to be sought for its own sake. *See also* **Treatment of Mental Illness, Part III.**

Dangers of Long-term Medication with Drugs acting on the Brain.

1. *Toxic effects.* Drugs which act upon the nervous system, like any others, have characteristic toxic or unwanted effects of their own (incidentally, these may become apparent rapidly; even, on rare occasions, after only a single dose). Such effects may have little or nothing to do with the desired effects for which they are being prescribed and taken. For example, it has only come to be realised quite recently that aspirin is liable to cause bleeding, which is occasionally serious, from the lining of the stomach in a large proportion of people who take aspirin regularly; or that phenacetin, another substance very frequently present in analgesics (*i.e.*, pain relievers) that can be bought from chemists without prescription, may lead (after prolonged use) to kidney damage. Some drugs may cause rashes and other allergic reactions in susceptible subjects; and jaundice, fainting, tremors, and motor disorders are known to occur in some patients taking a variety of other drugs.

2. "*Rebound.*" The body works in such a way, over a variety of its activities, that it tends to return to a "neutral" position after it has departed from this for any reason. For example, over-eating tends to be followed by a lessening of appetite, at least for a time; the runner makes up for his air-deficit during the race by breathing more deeply thereafter; and if, at rest, you breathe for a time more rapidly and deeply than you need, this period will be followed by one in which you breathe *less* often than usual until the balance is restored. These illustrations—and there are others—have nothing to do with drugs: but in a similar way, it seems that if a continued pain, or an unpleasant emotional state such as anxiety or depression is changed into its opposite, or removed altogether by the use of a drug, the prior state may return with increased force when the drug is no longer taken. The "rebound" phenomenon, naturally, encourages the patient to take another dose, and so on.

3. *Habit formation.* This alternation of mood-changed-by-drug with the disturbed mood itself leads to the habit of taking the drug. The patient comes to rely upon it and to take it anyway, even before the unpleasant state has returned. At this stage he is said to be "habituated": he has a psychological need for the drug, and later may become disturbed at the possibility that it will not be available when he needs it. This might not matter so greatly, if it were not that continued use of drugs in this way has physical consequences as well.

4. *Tolerance and habituation.* The body also tends to restore its own balance when drugs are given, too. It "learns" surprisingly quickly how to deal with substances with which it has never before been confronted, so that it eliminates subsequent doses more and more quickly and completely. Thus the effect of each successive dose is smaller and lasts for progressively shorter periods of time. To counter this, the patient tends to increase the dose: and the vicious circle continues. At this point he has become physically dependent upon the drug: and he may suffer physically—sometimes so severely that he dies—if supplies are not continued.

As he increases the dose in this way, so his tolerance of its effects increases, to such an extent that after prolonged use he may be taking doses of a drug that are five or ten times greater than those which will kill somebody not dependent upon them in this way. It sometimes happens that a patient develops a renewed craving at some point after a course of treatment, in which the dose of drug has been reduced without removing the underlying cause of his dependence. He may then obtain and use the dose he habitually took before treatment, not knowing that his body will have lost its tolerance of such doses. That dose is now as high for him as for any other person and so may be lethal. There has been a number of deaths for this reason.

Factors in the Causation of Dependence.

The risk of becoming dependent upon a drug is governed by three main factors: the drug itself, the personality of the individual who takes it, and the circumstances in which it is taken. Most adults have taken alcohol at one time or another, unless it is against their code to do so; yet *relatively* few are dependent upon it (relatively few, but many too many: more than half a million in the United Kingdom alone). Many of us have had morphine or some other strong analgesic for medical reasons, without becoming dependent upon it (whatever so-called addicts say, it is extremely rare for anyone to become dependent on an opiate because he was introduced to it in a medical setting). On the other hand, if we start to take such a drug "for kicks"—as more and more people, particularly teen-agers and young adults are doing—it is extremely probable that we shall become dependent upon it, and sooner rather than later at that. It is also probable that each one of us would become dependent, were he obliged to take it regularly, for long enough, and in sufficient dosage. Thus, although there are personalities—psychopathic, immature, or unstable—that are more prone than others to become dependent if they are exposed to the drug, there are also drugs that are more likely than others to cause such dependence no matter to whom they are given. The extent of the dependence will vary: with some, it is never physiological but remains psychological (but not the less real or disturbing for that). Also, the rate at which dependence develops may vary; and the picture presented by the dependent subject—the extent to which his normal life is impaired, or to which he becomes dangerous to himself or others—varies as well. In a very much oversimplified way, some of these relationships will now be summarised for certain substances.

Heroin, morphine and cocaine are usually injected. Barbiturates (sleeping pills) and amphetamines ("Benzedrine") are tablets or capsules, and marihuana ("reefers," hashish) is smoked in cigarettes. Heroin and cocaine are now usually taken together. Combinations of drugs often act differently from their individual constituents and patients dependent upon them are even more difficult to treat. Barbiturate and amphetamine, also, are often mixed (as in "purple hearts"). There is considerable *psychological* dependence on heroin, morphine, cocaine, and amphetamine, but much less with marihuana. *Physiological* dependence is great with heroin and morphine, less with barbiturates, alcohol, and amphetamine in that order, and virtually nil with cocaine and marihuana. Personality plays a greater part in initiating dependence on alcohol, marihuana, and barbiturates than with the others. Heroin, cocaine, and morphine are the cause of more antisocial tendencies in dependent people than alcohol, barbiturates, and amphetamine. The chief danger of marihuana (mere possession of which is illegal) seems to be that the search for it will lead the searcher into localities where his risk of exposure to even more dangerous influences is greatly increased. It is thus sometimes argued that if it were legal to consume marihuana, the number of young people who yearly become dependent upon the other more dangerous drugs would in fact decrease. There is as yet no evidence for or against this proposition. The number of drug dependent people in U.K. is rising fast for heroin and cocaine. This number is very large for alcohol, and is increasing in the case of barbiturates and marihuana. Very few people are dependent on morphine, and the number is not growing.

Treatment.

Exhortations, imprisonment, and other moralistic or legalistic approaches are useless. Treatment of any person dependent upon a drug is a matter for a qualified psychotherapist. It is liable to be time-consuming and frustrating for patient and doctor, and it is frequently unsuccessful. At present, there are too few specialists or centres where treatment can be obtained, although it is to be hoped that this situation will change as the problem is increasingly seen by our society to be of exceptional gravity.

When there is little or no chance of cure, prevention is certainly the best treatment. Drugs should only be taken on the prescription of a doctor: and the patient should remind him from time to time, if this be necessary, that he would like to dispense with his drugs as soon as the doctor thinks it possible. It should also be remembered that there is often no need to reach for the aspirin (or any other drug that anyone can buy from the chemist without prescription) at the first sign of a headache—or to reach for it at all to help one sleep or relax, for which purpose such drugs are in any case pharmacologically useless. A wait for ten minutes is good discipline, and will frequently resolve the problem to an extent that makes a drug unnecessary.

DISEASES OF THE BLOOD.

INTRODUCTION.

There are about five litres of blood in the adult human body. Its main function is to transport nutrient materials to all the various tissues and to carry waste products of tissue activity to organs such as the lungs, kidneys, and liver for disposal. It also helps to maintain a constant chemical environment for the body cells, some of which would be very disturbed in their function if the correct balance of organic and inorganic chemicals were not maintained. The blood also serves a protective function in fighting disease, either with certain of the white cells, or by means of immune antibodies dissolved and carried in the plasma.

A little more than half the volume of blood is the fluid plasma, in which are dissolved all the nutrient materials, organic and inorganic chemicals, hormones and large quantities of protein. The remainder consists of red cells, white cells, and some particles which are not really cells, called platelets. In every cubic millimetre of whole blood, or in every droplet the size of a pin head, there are about 5 million red cells, between 5,000 and 10,000 white cells, and 200,000 platelets as well as half a cubic millilitre of plasma. The red cells suffer a great deal of wear and tear as they are hurled round the circulation, and they only survive for three or four months. There is a red cell factory in the bone marrow which replaces them at exactly the rate they are destroyed, and you have made very many millions of new ones while you have been reading this single paragraph. The function of the red cells is to carry the oxygen from the lungs to the tissues, and to play an important part in carrying the waste gas, carbon dioxide, in the reverse direction. A shortage of red cells, and hence of their oxygen-carrying pigment, hæmoglobin, is called anæmia; an excess is called polycythæmia.

There are five kinds of white cells or leucocytes: neutrophils (or polymorphonuclear leucocytes), oesinophils, basophils, lymphocytes, and monocytes. The first three are quite actively motile, like amœbæ, and are capable of ingesting bacteria and other particles by "phagocytosis." There is a great increase in the number of neutrophils (a leucocytosis) during bacterial infections and other inflammatory conditions like appendicitis. Eosinophils are found in larger numbers than usual in allergic conditions like asthma, and in infestations by worms and other parasites, but we do not know why this should be. Lymphocytes are concerned with the manufacture of antibodies. In some infections, particularly tuberculosis and viral infections, there are fewer white cells than usual (leucopenia). Pus consists of the dissolved remnants of inflamed tissue and many dead neutrophils which have become casualties in the battle against infection. It also contains surviving bacteria, and as such is a source of further infection.

Platelets are curious particles, smaller than any of the cells. They are little pieces broken off certain special bone-marrow cells which produce them. They have a role in the stemming of blood loss after injury, partly because they are sticky and adhere to one another and to broken blood vessels and help to plug the open ends of damaged vessels; and partly because they contain a great deal of a substance (thrombokinase) which is necessary to the clotting mechanism of the blood.

Hæmatology, as the study of blood and its diseases is called, is a very complicated subject and only a brief general account will be given here. Diagnosis is usually made by taking small samples of blood (or of the bone marrow where blood cells are made), counting the numbers of the different cells and examining their appearance under the microscope. We shall briefly consider the main diseases involving red cells, white cells, and platelets.

Red Cell Diseases.

These are of two main groups leading to a shortage of red cells (anæmia), or an excess (polycythæmia). The former is much the more common and there are many different kinds. In all of them the shortage of red cells results in a depletion of the capacity of the blood to carry oxygen. This means that the heart must work harder to send more blood than usual to the tissues, and even so the tissues will often go short. The patient will be persistently tired and listless, and if the anæmia is severe the action of the brain and heart will be seriously impeded, even leading to fainting, cardiac pain, and breathlessness on exertion. All these symptoms, however, can be caused by many other conditions. The only way to be sure they are due to anæmia is by a proper examination of the blood, and even this will not lead to the truth if the picture has been spoilt by the patient taking iron tonics and other remedies of his own accord. Therefore do not dose yourself with tonics, in case you really have anæmia. You may make it impossible to arrive at a proper diagnosis later.

Hæmorrhagic Anæmia. Anæmia, a shortage of red cells, may be due to a variety of causes, singly or in combination. One very obvious cause is loss of blood, or hæmorrhage. Following the sudden loss of a half-litre of blood or more, the red-cell-producing bone marrow "factory" will step up its production; but even if it is adequately supplied with all the raw materials such as iron, it may well take many weeks to build up the numbers to normal. A very severe degree of hæmorrhagic anæmia is usually treated by blood transfusion. Milder degrees can be treated by taking extra iron, often over a long period of time. The supply of iron for making new red-cell pigment is nearly always the bottle-neck which limits production. Hæmorrhagic anæmia can commonly occur, however, without a sudden severe hæmorrhage. From what has been said about the constant replacement of red cells as they wear out, it must be obvious that even if there is only a slight failure to keep pace with the numbers lost, several months of such a failure can eventually deplete the numbers to the level of very severe anæmia. This situation is common when small amounts of blood are being continuously or repeatedly lost, and here again it is a shortage of dietary iron which is the usual cause of the failure to replace the lost red cells. Normal menstrual loss in women and girls whose diet is on the border-line of iron deficiency is a common cause of progressive tiredness and lack of energy. Where the menstrual flow is heavier than usual, or where it is frankly excessive in older women due to the various common gynæcological disorders, serious anæmia is surprisingly common. During pregnancy a great deal of iron is lost by the mother to the baby, and this, together with the inevitable blood loss at delivery, often makes for a very tired mother indeed, just at the time when there is an enormous amount of work to be done to manufacture milk and attend to all the extra household tasks of baby care. For these reasons it is almost routinely advisable to build up stocks of iron throughout the pregnancy by remembering to take the pills provided. Men as well as women can lose small amounts of blood continuously in later life from gastro-intestinal conditions such as piles, ulcers, and tropical infestations such as hookworm; and here again the anæmia may be just as severe in the long run as that which inevitably follows a sudden, massive hæmorrhage. One extra word of warning. Do not assume because you are pale that you are anæmic. Pallor is a very poor guide, because it is dependent on so many other things, like the blood vessels in your skin, and its thickness and translucency. Nothing but a blood test (which is so easy for your doctor to do) can really tell you if you are anæmic. And if your anæmia is due to a blood-losing condition, then that too must be treated. So do not be tempted to treat yourself, and never delay seeing your doctor about any excessive or unexplained bleeding, from any source.

Hæmolytic Anæmia occurs when for any reason, there are more blood cells than usual being destroyed in the body. This may be because the cells are abnormally fragile, or because normal cells have been attacked by something to which you are allergic, or rarely because you have become sensitive to your own red cells. Sometimes unborn babies have severe hæmolytic anæmia, due to an incompatability of blood group (Rh factor) between the mother and the baby, and the same sort of thing happens if incompatible blood is given by mistake in blood transfusion. Up to a point, in mild hæmolytic anæmia, the bone marrow can keep pace with the increased loss of cells, but beyond this point anæmia develops. After incompatible blood transfusions a very dangerous situation results from the effects of the destruction of red cells and the liberation of their products into the blood. One form of jaundice is often produced in hæmolytic anæmia, the patient becoming yellow because of the breakdown products of red cells circulating in excess as bile pigments. These latter are normally always present to a small extent due to the normal, comparatively small, rate of destruction of effete red cells

Aplastic Anæmia is the term given to anæmia due to a virtually total failure of the bone marrow red-cell factory. Sometimes this occurs for no obvious reason. It is sometimes due to a heavy dose of radioactivity or X-rays knocking out the cells of the "factory." It may even be due to cancer cells growing in the bone marrow cavity and not leaving sufficient room for the red marrow cells. It is fortunate that aplastic anæmia is very rare, because it can only be treated by blood transfusions every few weeks for the rest of the patient's life. Very occasionally there have been exceptions to this rule, when the patient's marrow has re-awakened for no apparent reason and suddenly begins to make red cells again.

Pernicious Anæmia. This is a fairly uncommon anæmia, which has a very interesting story. The processes by which red cells are manufactured are many and complex, and depend, like so many other bodily activities, on the supply of a vitamin containing cobalt, called vitamin B_{12}. This is nearly always present in more than adequate quantities in the diet, but in order for it to be absorbed from the intestine, there must also be a substance called "intrinsic factor" which is normally made by the lining of the stomach. People with pernicious anæmia have suffered a degeneration of the lining of their stomachs, probably because, for some reason, they have become "sensitive" to this part of their own tissue. This kind of civil war within the body is known as an "auto-immune" disease, and is comparable in type with some forms of hæmolytic anæmia. In other words they destroy their own stomach lining, fail to produce "intrinsic factor," and as a result fail to absorb vitamin B_{12} into the body. Faced with a failure in the supply of this essential substance, the bone marrow produces too few red cells, and the few that are produced are deformed, much too large, and very fragile. In addition to its role in blood formation, vitamin B_{12} is essential to the normal functioning of the spinal cord, and in long-standing cases of untreated pernicious anæmia, there is often a resulting neurological disability.

The cure for pernicious anæmia was discovered about forty years ago, and is a triumph for the scientific investigation of the causes of disease. While treating anæmic dogs, an American scientist named Minot discovered that eating raw liver in large quantities produced a tremendous improvement. Patients with pernicious anæmia were then made to eat vast quantities of raw liver—about one or two pounds a day—and were found to get better, whereas previously they had inevitably died. Raw liver is, of course, very unpleasant to eat, and after a few years it was found possible to prepare crude extracts for injection. Injection had the great advantage that no absorption difficulties arose, and much less liver could be used. Biochemists then began the enormous task of trying to find which of the thousands of substances in liver was the vital factor, and after many years of painstaking chemical fractionation of liver and trying out the various fractions as a cure for the disease, vitamin B_{12} was discovered. The pure substance is one of the most powerful substances known, being active in amounts as small as millionths of a gram. Nowadays pernicious anæmia is treated by small occasional injections of the vitamin, whose other name is cyanocobalamin.

Polycythæmia. Too many red cells per cubic millilitre of blood can be found without there being an increase of the total number of red cells in the body. This occurs in dehydration, when there is a loss of plasma without a comparable loss of cells, and is called hæmo-concentration. Alternatively, the bone marrow can manufacture more cells than usual as a response to living for long periods at high altitudes. The beneficial result can be that the blood can carry normal amounts of oxygen, even though the supply (in the rarefied air) is reduced. Finally there is a red cell disease, analagous to leukæmia (*q.v.*) in which the bone marrow factory gets out of control and produces too many cells with no beneficial results. The number in the blood can be double the normal and the blood becomes so thick that the heart has difficulty pumping it round the body. This disease (*polycythæmia rubra vera*) used to be treated by repeatedly bleeding the patient to reduce the numbers. It is now treated very successfully with carefully judged amounts of radioactive phosphorus or certain other "antimitotic" chemicals which reduce the rate of multiplication of bone marrow cells. Care has to be taken not to knock them out altogether, in which case aplastic anæmia or agranulocytosis (*q.v.*) could result.

White Cell Diseases.

These are fortunately much rarer than diseases involving red cells, and are usually much more to be feared.

Agranulocytosis. In this condition the number of those white cells which are responsible for phagocytosis of bacteria falls precipitously. The result is that one of the main bodily defences against infection fails, and the patient may die from an overwhelming invasion of germs and the accompanying high fever. The usual cause is abnormal sensitivity to certain drugs, often those which are in widespread use and only give trouble in the occasional case. One example among hundreds is the antibiotic chloramphenicol which specifically kills typhoid bacteria and is used for that purpose. It is believed that about one case in 60,000 becomes sensitive to it and agranulocytosis often fatally follows. The fact that almost any drug *can* do this to some people and yet be quite safe for the majority, is one good reason not to dose yourself unnecessarily with over-the-counter medicines.

Leukæmia. This is a cancer of the white cells, in which the normal rate of production of any of the white cells gets out of control, leading to a pile-up of abnormal cells at the site of production (bone marrow, lymph nodes, and spleen) or in the blood, or both. In spite of an increase in their numbers, their abnormality renders them unable to combat infection; sepsis and fever result. It is known that this kind of cancer can be caused by the effects of ionizing radiation on the white-cell factory, and it is certain at least in animals, that viruses can also be responsible. Survivors from the atomic explosions in Japan have subsequently suffered from leukæmia far more commonly than the rest of us, as have doctors, nurses, and patients who have been over-exposed to X-rays. At the time of writing, leukæmia is still a uniformly fatal disease, although patients may sometimes survive many years. Their remaining time can nearly always be made more comfortable by various forms of treatment, and one day a cure will be found by the research workers devoting their time to its study. It is difficult not to get very impatient with the slow rate of progress of these studies, particularly when caring for children and young people whose lives are inevitably ended by the disease. The solution, however, as with other forms of cancer, probably depends on the understanding of the nature of life itself, and as long as biological research remains short of the relatively small amounts of money required to tackle these problems at reasonable speed, we have no right to be impatient, except with our elected leaders who spend far more than is needed on less important things.

Hodgkin's Disease, Lymphosarcoma, and Reticulosarcoma. These are cancerous diseases in many ways similar to leukæmia, in which the cancer process involves cells of the so-called reticulo-endothelial system. Such cells are principally in lymph nodes (which used to be called lymph glands) and the spleen. Hodgkin's disease is named after one of the more illustrious pathologists at Guy's Hospital who first described it nearly a hundred years ago, and whose early specimens of affected lymph nodes are still preserved there; is an even greater puzzle than leukæmia. There are all grades of severity, and although many patients die within six months, many survive much longer, even for twenty years in some cases.

Hæmorrhagic or Bleeding Diseases.

Whenever blood vessels are damaged by injury, there is a remarkable series of mechanisms which automatically come into operation to stem the flow of blood. There is a constriction of all the smaller vessels in the locality. Platelets stick together and release substances which help the vessels to stay constricted as well as others necessary to blood clotting, and yet others which help to bind the clot tightly together. Later, materials appear to prevent too much clotting, and eventually the clot is removed altogether as healing proceeds. There are some very complicated diseases of this blood-conserving mechanism which can lead to abnormal bleeding, sometimes beneath the skin to produce bruising or even smaller leaks; sometimes leading to a greater loss of blood, particularly following a wound. In some kinds of *purpura* (bleeding tendency) the blood vessels are the cause of the trouble, having become fragile and leaky for a number of reasons. This happens in old age (*senile purpura*), in scurvy, or vitamin C deficiency, as an occasional accompaniment to infective diseases, or as an immunological effect on the lining of blood vessels when the patient becomes sensitised to certain substances (*Schönlein-Henoch* or *anaphylactoid purpura*). The latter often follows a streptococcal sore throat, just as rheumatic fever and acute nephritis do; and as well as the purpura there may be joint pains and nephritis. Just as almost any drug or chemical will cause agranulocytosis in some people, so it can also cause anaphylactoid purpura.

Purpura may also be due to a lack of platelets, known as thrombocytopenia (a shortage of thrombocytes or platelets). This can happen if the bone marrow factory is depressed, since this is where platelets too are made. It is therefore a common accompaniment of leukæmia or aplastic anæmia. Or there can be increased destruction of platelets in some diseases of the spleen. Platelets normally last eight to ten days, but their life-span can be shortened in heart failure, and following massive transfusions, or often for no apparent reason ("idiopathic" thrombocytopenia), when removal of the spleen can sometimes help.

Finally, defects of the *clotting mechanism* will lead to a bleeding tendency, and since the mechanism itself is very complex, so is the variety of things which can upset it. The liver provides the blood with many of the substances required for clotting, so it is not surprising that a clotting defect commonly accompanies liver disease. One necessary substance for blood clotting is called "antihæmophilic factor" and is missing from people who have inherited the disease *hæmophilia.* These unfortunate people may die of hæmorrhage from quite small cuts or minor surgical procedures like tooth-extraction, and although it is possible to prepare antihæmophilic factor, it is not yet possible to give continuous, life-long treatment with it. A new drug, aminocaproic acid, which prevents natural clots from dissolving, is now used to enable dental treatment, with the saving of much fresh blood transfusion which was formerly necessary.

DISEASES OF THE HEART AND BLOOD-VESSELS.

INTRODUCTION.

The heart consists of about 350g of muscle which makes up the walls of its four chambers. Anatomically the human heart closely resembles the sheep's hearts to be found in a butcher's shop. Indeed it would be an instructive exercise to dissect one of these in the order described below, since there is no other way of properly appreciating what the chambers, valves, etc., are really like. There are two quite separate pumps in the heart—one on the owner's right (or on your *left* if you are looking at the front of someone else), and one on his left. The right heart collects spent, deoxygenated, "venous" blood which returns there from the whole of the body, and gives it the comparatively small push required to drive it through the adjacent lungs. The left heart collects the revitalised, oxygenated "arterial" blood as it trickles away from the lungs, and gives it the enormous push required to build up the arterial blood-pressure, so that it can be forced through all the tissues of the body. As may be expected, the right heart chambers have much thinner walls than the left, since their muscle has much less work to do. This will help you get your bearings with the sheep's heart. The tip, or apex, is the lowest part. The thick-feeling side is the left, the thin the right; and the great vessels are at the top.

The upper chamber on the right, or right atrium, has two large openings into it through which all the spent blood arrives from the upper and lower great veins (the superior and inferior venae cavae).

Cut open the thin wall of the right atrium with scissors between these two holes to lay open the interior of the chamber, noting the "auricle" or "dog's ear" that forms a small cul-de-sac. The whole chamber is sometimes, inaccurately, called the auricle. You should be able to push a finger downwards into the lower chamber—the right ventricle—through a communicating hole guarded by the three thin cusps of the *tricuspid valve*. These will not obstruct your finger, since they are designed to permit blood flow in the same direction. When the atrium is full of blood, it squeezes its contents through the tricuspid valve into the right ventricle; and when, a split second later, the ventricle is full and contracts, the three cusps come together to prevent the blood from flowing backwards into the atrium again. Instead the spent blood is driven onwards through the *pulmonary valve* (in the upper part of the right ventricle), through the pulmonary artery, to be delivered to the lungs. The pulmonary valve has three very well-defined cusps which prevent blood from coming back into the ventricle as it relaxes to receive more blood from the atrium before the next contraction or beat. It is possible to pass a blade of the scissors from the opened-out right atrium, through the tricuspid valve towards the tip of the heart, and cut along the right border of the heart through the thickness of the ventricular muscle. Then cut upwards again, passing the scissors blade through the pulmonary valve and open up the *pulmonary artery*. If you have done this successfully you will have followed the path taken by the spent blood through the right heart to the lungs. Notice the thick round bands of muscle lining the ventricle, and notice too that you have not entered the left heart, which has no connection with the right except in some congenital malformations (see later). The same dissection can now be made of the left heart. Open up the *left atrium*, noting its "dog's ear" or "auricle," pass the scissors down into the *left ventricle* through the two rather flimsy cusps of the *mitral valve*. Notice how much thicker is the muscle of the left ventricle, and cut upwards through the three well-formed cusps of the *aortic valve* into the main artery of the body—the *aorta*. The aorta as it leaves the left heart is distinguishable from the pulmonary artery as it leaves the right, partly by the extreme toughness of the aortic wall (it has to withstand so much more blood-pressure); and partly by the entrances or orifices of the two small branches given off by the aorta, just beyond the valve cusps, which go to supply the heart muscle itself with blood. These are the *coronary arteries* which are so necessary for the heart's own survival.

The amount of blood pumped in unit time, or the *cardiac output*, can be varied a great deal, according to the needs of the moment. This is accomplished by altering both the heart rate and the stroke volume, the amount expelled per beat. Every minute, the healthy adult man at rest shifts about 5 l of blood through the heart—an amount equivalent to all the blood he possesses. When exercise is taken, or in response to anxiety or fear, this is stepped up many times, so that the muscles can receive a greatly augmented supply of the materials required for action. The controlling mechanisms which allow these changes to be made automatically are partly organised in the brain by the so-called *cardiac centre*; and partly by local mechanical and chemical stimuli to the heart muscle itself. The cardiac centre is continuously receiving information through nerves about the physical and chemical state of the circulation, and also from the mind; which is partly how certain emotions make the heart beat faster. All the information is integrated, and a cardiac output continuously arranged which is appropriate for current demands.

Cardiac Neurosis. In ordinary circumstances at rest, most healthy people are not conscious of their heart-beat. However, there are many perfectly healthy people whose hearts slip in an extra beat occasionally. Sometimes their owners are aware of this, and become unnecessarily alarmed. Their fear causes palpitations (a pounding of the heart) and the tension mounts. An undue anxiety about the tricks played by a healthy heart sometimes leads people to interpret minor pains in the chest, or even indigestion, as grave symptoms of heart disease, and the consequent anxiety leads to still worse symptoms. If you are one of these worried people, take your worries to your doctor, and let him decide for you whether there is anything wrong. A hundred to one there isn't, and then you will have to find something else to worry about, or better still give up the habit altogether. Many people secretly worry about heart disease and high blood-pressure for years, when very often they are worrying unnecessarily. Even if there is cause for worry, so much can be done for these conditions (as it can for cancer) provided medical advice is taken early in the course of the disease. Remember, too, that the slight feeling of giddiness when you get up suddenly from having been lying down, is often experienced by most normal people; but if you get frightened by it you will begin to breathe more quickly and deeply: and this in itself will make you feel even more faint—and so on.

Heart Failure. When the cardiac output of blood is too little for the requirements of the body, a state of *circulatory failure* has arisen, and when this is due primarily to the heart itself being at fault, it is more properly called *heart failure*. As will be seen, heart failure is not a disease, but the common result of a large number of different diseases. The signs and symptoms produced are caused by two sorts of process: (*a*) tissues of the body have too little blood flow through them and are therefore undersupplied; (*b*) blood accumulates and stagnates in tissues, causing congestion, since the failing heart cannot move forward the amount of blood presented to it in the great veins. Often the left or right side of the heart fails disproportionately. In *left heart failure* the lungs are congested because they are the territory from which the left heart is failing to move blood. The patient has great difficulty with his breathing, and in advanced cases may not be able to breathe when he lies down, because the lungs become so congested and waterlogged. In *right heart failure* the main veins are congested and other parts of the body become swollen with excess tissue fluid, mainly in the lower parts such as the legs and ankles. This swelling with fluid is called œdema, and in heart failure is only partly due to the mechanics of the failing heart. It is mainly due to a poorly understood retention of sodium in the body, a situation in which excess water is also retained. Whatever the type of heart failure, it is always likely to be a changing condition, since the amount of failure will depend as much on the demands being made as on the state of the heart. For instance, in mild cases at rest when the required cardiac output is small, there may be no signs or symptoms. These may only appear on exertion. Heart failure will be referred to again later under the various conditions which cause it.

Treatment of heart failure is quite logical. It is aimed at correcting the imbalance between supply and demand of blood, and at the removal of the accumulated excess fluid. We can therefore (*a*) reduce the body's demand for blood; (*b*) increase the supply or cardiac output; and (*c*) promote the excretion of sodium and fluid. Demand for blood is reduced by rest, both physical and mental, and by reduction of weight, since obesity (being overweight) is an additional demand on the cardiovascular system. The cardiac output can be increased by administering a "tonic" to the heart muscle in the form of *digitalis*, which is a powerful heart stimulant derived from foxglove leaf. Fluid (and hence salt) accumulation can be helped by restricting the intake of salt and by giving drugs which promote its excretion by the kidneys (diuretics). Very occasionally, very large accumulations of fluid in the legs, abdomen, or thorax, are tapped and drained physically, with needles. These remarks on treatment, as elsewhere in the Medical Section, are of course very general and must not encourage anyone to treat himself for such a potentially serious condition as heart failure. Even such a simple measure as doing without salt can be practised quite unnecessarily by many people for years, simply as a result of reading a paragraph like the above. The most they accomplish is to make their food taste horribly dull. If you need to reduce salt intake you should be in your doctor's care, and so please let him decide.

Congenital Heart Disease. It has been estimated that of all the babies born who survive at least one month, there will be about one in every two hundred with some form of congenital heart disease; that is to say that the heart will have failed to develop properly in embryonic life. In some cases this is associated with a virus disease of the mother (commonly rubella, or German measles) or with certain drugs taken by the mother (e.g. thalidomide) at a time, very early in pregnancy, when organs are assuming their adult shape. Parents should see to it that their daughters get German measles before they grow up; and drugs of all kinds should be avoided where possible during early pregnancy. In most cases of congenital heart disease, however, there is no known cause, and it seems that the manner of formation of the embryonic heart is so delicate that it can be thrown out of gear very easily, perhaps even by chance. Scores of different types of defect occur, singly and in combination. Any of the valves may be anatomically defective—either failing to close properly (*incompetence*) or being too tight (*stenosis*); the great vessels (pulmonary artery and aorta) may be switched round, or *transposed*, so that they emerge from the wrong ventricle; there may be defects in the wall (*septum*) which separates the atria or the ventricles on each side (*septal defect*, or " hole in the heart "); or there may be a persistence of the vessel which in the fœtus normally by-passes the lungs by joining the pulmonary artery to the aorta (*patent ductus arteriosus*). This vessel normally closes at the time of birth when the first breaths are taken, and subsequently disappears, so that the whole output of the heart is then sent round the lungs. Detecting congenital heart disease early is one of the purposes of routine post-natal check-up examinations of the baby. Exact diagnosis requires very complicated techniques, and sometimes the structural defect can be corrected by surgery, with almost miraculous results.

Rheumatic Heart Disease. Acute rheumatic fever is not to be confused with other forms of rheumatism. Many tissues of the body (particularly the heart) are attacked, as well as the joints, and the trouble is due to a sensitivity which has developed to certain bacteria (*hæmolytic streptococci*) which have probably caused a sore throat about three weeks before the onset of the disease. Why acute rheumatism only rarely follows streptococcal sore throat is poorly understood, but this is no consolation to the one per cent or so of the population whose hearts bear its scars. During the acute phase of the illness which usually occurs before the age of fifteen, inflammatory damage occurs to the valves, the heart muscle, and the sac in which the heart lives, the *pericardium*. So there is a *valvulitis* or *endocarditis*, a *myocarditis* and a *pericarditis*. There may be acute heart failure at this stage if the heart is severely affected. The better-known results of rheumatic heart disease, however, are caused in the ensuing years by scarring of the healed valves. The valves are thickened and deformed. They may have lost their elasticity and stretch, so that they do not close properly (*incompetence*); or they may contract and tighten (*stenosis*). In both cases the heart chamber situated next to the affected valve has to work progressively harder, either because it gets no rest in between beats (in *incompetence*); or it has to force the blood through too narrow a hole (in *stenosis*). The end result is some variety of heart failure (**P27**). Although there are other causes of valvular heart disease which will now be mentioned, rheumatic fever is much the commonest, and much valve trouble can be blamed on rheumatic fever even when the patient has no recollection of ever having suffered from it. The other, much rarer, causes may be syphilis, congenital valvular anomaly, healed bacterial endocarditis, atherosclerosis, and mechanical injury.

The most commonly affected valve is the mitral, usually causing *mitral stenosis*, in which the opening between the left atrium and left ventricle will sometimes only admit one finger-tip instead of three fingers as it should. In time the left atrium becomes much enlarged as it overworks to force blood through this narrow orifice. Later still a back pressure develops in the lungs causing congestion and breathlessness; and even later the right ventricle is strained as it tries to force blood into the already congested lung. This is a classic example of the march of trouble backwards from the site of the damaged valve involving first the chamber " behind " it (the left atrium), then the territory " behind " that (the lungs), then the pulmonary arteries taking blood to the lungs, and finally the right ventricle trying to send blood to the pulmonary artery. This steady march of events is usually very slow, and can commonly take twenty years or longer from the initial attack of acute rheumatism to the severer symptoms of advanced mitral stenosis. Treatment is both medical and surgical. The heart failure is treated medically as already described. These days surgical reopening of the valve is almost commonplace, either by inserting a finger through the left auricle and breaking down the constriction, or by opening up the heart and re-shaping the valve under direct vision. The latter involves the additional problem of by-passing the heart by the use of some sort of external pump and poses additional problems, even though from other points of view it is obviously more convenient. As always with major surgical procedures much of the problem is in selecting the patients who will benefit from the operation and in whom it is feasible. Quite often there are other valves involved, mainly the aortic or tricuspid or both, and the hydrostatic or " plumbing " problems can be extremely complex. With luck, however, combined with good judgement and good surgery, the lives of incapacitated patients can be transformed by mitral, and other valvular, surgery. Recently a great deal of progress has been made in designing new " ball-in-basket " valves of man-made materials to replace damaged natural valves. The *aortic valve* is stenosed or narrowed by other degenerative processes besides rheumatism. *Tricuspid stenosis* is nearly always rheumatic in origin.

Coronary Heart Disease. This is the term used whenever the blood supply to the heart muscle (through the coronary arteries) is reduced to such an extent that the heart muscle suffers from a lack of supplies. It has a number of causes, but the only really common one is partial obstruction of the coronary arteries by a condition known as *atheroma* or *atherosclerosis*, and sometimes inaccurately called *arteriosclerosis*. This arterial disease is described later (**P30**). It takes the form of swellings or lumps on the lining of the artery which, if they become large enough to interfere seriously with the flow of blood, produce a blood starvation or *ischaemia* of the tissue being supplied. Obviously, the smaller the artery, the more easily will a lump of given size impede the flow. Equally obviously, the greater the demand for blood, as in exercise, the more blood " starvation " there will be. There are two degrees of coronary artery disease: one in which the blood flow is reduced to the point where the increased demands of hard work cannot be met, and this results in *angina pectoris* due to *coronary insufficiency*; the other is when the coronary artery becomes completely blocked, preventing the flow of blood altogether, usually by a *thrombus* or clot of blood, and this is *coronary thrombosis*.

Angina Pectoris. Whenever activity is increased in any muscle, the demands for oxygen and nutriments from the blood-stream increase, and as these are used up there is an increased production of waste products known as metabolites. To meet these demands for a greater supply and a more efficient waste-disposal, the blood flow through the exercising muscle must always be increased. If sufficient increase does not occur, not only will there be a shortage of supplies, but there will also be a pile-up of metabolites in the muscle which cannot be carried away. It is mainly because of these latter that pain is caused in ischæmic, or blood-starved muscle, and pain is one of the chief symptoms when heart muscle becomes ischæmic. One important mechanism for increasing blood flow normally to exercising muscle is by automatically dilating the vessels concerned. Diseased vessels, such as coronary arteries when they are affected by atheroma, are not so easily dilated, although certain drugs which are powerful dilators of arterioles can accomplish a great deal, albeit temporarily. The measures taken to relieve the pain and blood-starvation of angina are two-fold. The patient can reduce the demands of the heart by a few minutes' rest, and a drug (usually nitroglycerin) can be taken to dilate the coronary vessels of supply. Another obvious long-term way to reduce demands is for the overweight patient to eat less, and reduce the load of extra body weight on his circulation. It is very frustrating, to say the least, that such an incapacitating and often lethal condition should be caused by the narrowing or blockage of only 5 or 8 cm of narrow piping about 3·5 mm wide. It is now possible to treat some forms of coronary artery disease by surgical means.

Heart Attack or *Coronary Thrombosis.* It should readily be understood from the above description that heart attacks will vary in their severity according to the amount of heart muscle deprived of blood; and this in turn will depend on where in the coronary artery the obstruction occurs. Most usually it is the left ventricular muscle which is cut off from supplies and dies, either in part or in all of its thickness. Since it is the left ventricle which does most of the work of pumping blood to the body, serious heart failure (P27) is to be expected. If too much muscle is killed, the heart will simply stop, and the patient will suddenly die. It is much more usual, however, for enough muscle to be left for survival, albeit with a greatly reduced cardiac efficiency. A heart attack is usually accompanied by severe pain, similar to the pain of angina but more severe, and unrelieved by rest or by the patient's usual drugs. Very occasionally the event occurs apparently without pain, or with so little that it is ignored. These so-called "silent" coronary attacks can make diagnosis extremely difficult. Since the doctor depends very considerably with heart attacks on an exact, spontaneous description of symptoms for his diagnosis, no description will be given here. There are many over-anxious people who will read these words and could be misled into an unspontaneous description of their own symptoms, and this could make the task of treating them such a problem that they could even be mis-diagnosed as a result. If you have the smallest worry that your chest pain is due to your heart, take your anxiety to your doctor without delay. He will almost certainly be able to reassure you; and if it happens to be your heart after all, you will have taken the first sensible step towards proper treatment. Dangerous as heart attacks are, they are by no means the death warrant that many lay people think, any more than cancer is. The treatment for a true heart attack is urgent and prolonged. Patients must be at complete rest and their pain relieved quickly. The area of heart muscle they have lost must be allowed to heal with a good, firm scar, and this can take three months of rest often in hospital.

You can help to avoid a heart attack by not smoking, avoiding obesity and living a physically active life. Avoid sudden exercise, however, when you are not in training. Surgeons are getting better at replacing diseased coronary arteries with pieces of vein from elsewhere.

Blood-pressure. The blood is normally under great pressure in the arterial system, since it is this which forces it into all the tissues of the body. It is therefore no more meaningful to say you have "blood-pressure" than to say you have a temperature. You would be very badly off without. Blood-pressure which is too high, however, can give rise to problems, though not always. It is another of those conditions like angina and cancer, which engender much anxiety among people even when they do not suffer from them. For this reason doctors are often unwilling to disclose a patient's blood-pressure and because of this they unjustifiably earn a reputation for unreasonable secrecy. They are themselves to blame for the general public anxiety as the following true story shows. Twenty years ago a lady in her fifties wished to accompany her husband to a post abroad which was to last four years. All arrangements had been made—the husband resigned his previous job, sold the house, etc.—when it was discovered at a routine medical examination that she had a high blood-pressure, and she was very solemnly advised by the rather elderly doctor not to go. There was great consternation and emotional upheaval, not least because of the inconvenience involved. Eventually she was allowed to go at her own risk. The husband's job lasted eight years instead of four, during which the lady was in no way inconvenienced by her blood-pressure; except that she worried interminably about it. On returning home to retire she began to think she had angina, and elaborate hospital investigation revealed that, as might be expected, her arteries were not as young as they used to be. She was undoubtedly suffering from mild angina, but not as badly as she thought. The opportunity then arose, in her late sixties, to go abroad yet again, and this she did, living a quite strenuous life, and one which she enjoyed. At the time of writing she has returned home, and, twenty years later, at the age of seventy-three is running a home very actively, still with very little inconvenience from her blood-pressure. There is no doubt that it has been very high all this time, and it is also certain that she will die one day, although it may well not be of her blood-pressure. How much better it would have been for her not to have been told it was high twenty years ago and to have avoided all these years of anxiety. It is not being suggested here that high blood-pressure is a trivial condition, but that it is for doctors to worry about rather than patients! If you ever find out your own blood-pressure, never try to work out for yourself what the figures mean. It is much too complicated. Finally, it should be mentioned that high blood-pressure may occasionally be associated with, or "secondary to," certain kidney diseases (*nephritis*) including a strange condition known as *toxaemia of pregnancy*, which lasts only as long as the pregnancy, provided great care is taken. Most high blood-pressure is, however, "primary", and without any known association or cause.

Low Blood-pressure. Some people seem normally to have surprisingly low blood-pressure all the time. There is nothing whatever wrong with this; indeed it may even be beneficial. At least they are unlikely ever to suffer the effects of high blood-pressure. The sudden low blood-pressure of circulatory failure or shock (P27) is another matter and must be urgently treated.

Irregularities of the Heart-beat. How quickly or how slowly the heart beats is largely under the control of the cardiac centre in the brain and the level of certain hormones in the blood. The *regularity* of the beat, however, is controlled by the so-called pace-maker in the wall of the right atrium, and by the way impulses from the pacemaker travel through specialised conducting heart cells (the bundle of His and its branches) to the ventricles. When any part of this elaborate mechanism is upset, either by altering the biochemical or electrical conditions of these specialised tissues, or by killing some of them off by deprivation of blood supply in the course of a heart attack, disordered rhythm can result. Increase (*tachycardia*) or decrease (*bradycardia*) in rate is nearly always a normal response to exercise, or anxiety. Very occasional irregularity, such as the mis-timing of an occasional beat is also quite normal in some people, although many are alarmed by it. Persistent irregularity, however, is abnormal. Its true nature can usually be elucidated by making an electrical record of the heart-beat—an electro-cardiogram. The commonest causes are varieties of coronary artery diseases or rheumatic heart disease.

Pericarditis. The heart beats inside a bag or sac. At every beat its outer surface slides against the lining of the sac, lubricated by a small amount of fluid. This is the pericardial sac, the *pericardium* being strictly the lubricated membrane which lines the sac and which also covers the outer surface of the heart. Sometimes inflammation occurs—*pericarditis*—and the sliding surfaces become roughened and even separated by a fluid effusion. Very occasionally, so much fluid accumulates that the heart's action is seriously impeded. Pericarditis may be due to infection or to rheumatic fever, and it usually overlies the area of damaged muscle after a heart attack. This illustrates something which people rarely appreciate—that inflammation is not by any means always due to infection by bacteria. The last two varieties of pericarditis are quite free from germs (sterile).

Myocarditis. A term loosely applied to disorders affecting the heart muscle. There are lots of very rare causes. The really common ones are due to acute or chronic rheumatic causes or to coronary artery disease, both of which are described above.

Endocarditis or inflammation of the lining of the heart is a term loosely applied to any disorder of the valves or heart lining. All varieties of rheumatic valvular disease (P28) are included. Bacterial endocarditis in its several forms usually involves valves already damaged by rheumatic disease. It is a complication which is still much to be feared, though somewhat less so now that antibiotic drugs are available.

Atheroma or Atherosclerosis. This is the condition referred to above in which lumps arise on the lining of arterial blood-vessels. Although it is therefore a disease of the arteries, its importance lies in the way blood flow is held up, either by the lumps themselves, or by thrombosis ultimately blocking the narrowed portion of the pipework. The effects on the body are therefore those of depriving the tissues of blood. It is an astonishing fact that in England and America, more people die of the consequences of atheroma than of any other single disease, including all forms of cancer put together. Furthermore, cancer is mainly a disease of old age, whereas many of the effects of atheroma on men occur in early middle age. If narrowing of the artery is going to do significant harm it is easy to see that it will be of more consequence in those parts of the body where small-bore vessels are supplying tissues whose functions are necessary for life. Exactly such a situation exists in the heart and in the brain. An additional factor is that the arrangement of the blood supply in these tissues is such that any particular area has only one vessel leading to it. This is unusual among the tissues generally, where several alternative, or " collateral " vessels usually supply an area, and where others can take over if one becomes obstructed. We have, therefore, a situation in which perhaps the most important tissues —the heart and the brain—run the greatest risk of deprivation, and this leads to angina and coronary thrombosis on the one hand, and cerebral thrombosis and hæmorrhage (" stroke illness ") on the other, accounting jointly for about one death in every five. In addition, the effects of atheromatous narrowing are often felt in the legs, where the blood supply to the muscles is inadequate for exercise, leading to intermittent pain comparable with that in the heart in similar circumstances. This is called *intermittent claudication*, or intermittent closing of the leg arteries. In its most severe forms, it leads to the need for amputation, although in most cases early treatment can avoid this. It is small wonder that there is intensive research into the causes of atheroma, as with cancer, but it is probably true to say that we still know rather more about cancer. A lot of attention has been given to the amounts of certain fats in the circulating blood, particularly cholesterol. This fat is found in larger amounts in the blood of sufferers from atheroma, and is also found in the arterial lumps themselves. Efforts have therefore been made to reduce blood cholesterol by modifications of the diet, but it has been extremely difficult to prove that this has done any good. Many other factors are known to contribute to atheroma, and hence to heart attacks and strokes, some of which can be reduced and others not. Such factors are age, obesity, high blood-pressure, and smoking cigarettes. People who lead an active life, like bus conductors, seem to have less trouble than others who are less active, like bus drivers. Sudden severe exercise, however, is bad if you are not used to it. It is better, and life saving, to take regular, moderate exercise. Women have less atheroma than men, until the menopause when they begin to catch up, so that hormones have something to do with it. Serious starvation, such as occurred in the German-occupied territories of Holland and Scandinavia and in the concentration camps conferred one benefit—a freedom from atheroma, but obviously we cannot all starve, and the puzzle remains. Like many of the more important outstanding medical puzzles, there is no single factor responsible, and this is what makes it difficult to solve. *See also* " Preventive Medicine " P III.

Aortic Disease. The aorta, the main artery of the body, running from the left ventricle down through the chest and abdomen, also suffers from atheroma, but is too wide (about 2·5 cm across) to become obstructed. However, weaknesses occur in the thickness of its wall, sometimes due to syphilis but nowadays much more usually due to atheroma, which results in a ballooning out of a part of the vessel, rather like you sometimes see in an old bicycle inner tube. In days gone by these *aneurysms*, as the dilations are called, reached an enormous size, and would wear away the breastbone and ribs, to appear as large pulsating masses on the chest. Now that advanced syphilis is less common, atheromatous aneurysm, with a predilection for the abdominal aorta, is the one most commonly seen; and these days it is treated by replacement of the diseased portion of vessel. *Dissecting aneurysms* of the aorta are another variety in which the blood, under high pressure, somehow finds its way in between the layers of the aortic wall and then suddenly rips up and down the whole length of the vessel, separating (or dissecting) one layer from another in its path. Sometimes it tracks back towards the heart and suddenly fills the pericardium with blood to stop the heart's action altogether.

Embolism. This term refers to any foreign object travelling in the circulation and becoming impacted when it reaches a vessel too small for it to pass through. It may be a thrombus (P31), a collection of cancer cells, a group of bacteria, a chunk of infected pus from an abscess, a collection of fat droplets or even a bubble of air. If it originates in a vein it travels to the right heart and to the lungs. If it comes from the left heart or an artery, it will impact in any part of the arterial tree. Reasonably enough an arterial embolus will commonly end up in those parts of the body with the richest blood supply, like the brain, the kidneys, the liver or the bone marrow. A thrombotic embolus will cause death of the tissue in the area previously supplied by the blocked vessel, a condition known as *infarction*. Perhaps the commonest source of thrombotic embolism is the lining of the heart chambers where a thrombus has occurred at the site of muscle damaged by a heart attack. Massive pulmonary (lung) embolism is usually the result of thrombosis of the leg veins in people kept immobile following surgery or childbirth. That is why postoperative patients are got out of bed for a while as soon as the first day after the operation. The cells of a cancer embolus usually die; but if they survive, a new cancer deposit begins to grow where the embolus impacts, and this is one of the ways cancer may spread. An infected embolus may infect the vessel wall when it impacts, producing a weakness which may give way. Air embolism, if enough insoluble gas enters the circulation, can kill by making so much froth in the heart chambers as to impede the normal pumping action. If bubbles pass the lungs and enter the brain, all sorts of neurological disorders like scores of tiny strokes arise. The same sort of thing happens all over the body in the " *bends* " or " *caisson* " *disease*, in which the blood literally boils. It is due to a too rapid return to normal pressure from regions of high pressure at great depths or from pressurised chambers. Fat embolism sometimes occurs after fractures due to marrow fat entering damaged veins and being carried away to the lungs.

Thrombosis. This is not quite the same as clotting. It is the mass which arises when platelets adhere to the lining of blood-vessels or heart chambers. Blood clot accumulates among layers of deposited platelets and the thrombus therefore has structure, unlike pure blood clot. Thrombosis usually occurs when the lining of the vessel or chamber is damaged by atheroma or inflammation, or when the circulation becomes very stagnant. One danger is that it will become dislodged and travel as an embolus during the first week or ten days of its existence. After this time it is usually firmly incorporated into the vessel walls by cells which migrate into it from the surrounding tissue. The other danger is, of course, that the tissue previously supplied by the blocked vessel will die before a collateral circulation can be established. As previously explained, this is called infarction. All the technical terms in this section are used elsewhere and can be looked up.

Varicose Veins. When veins become swollen they also often become tortuous (wriggly), and particularly on the surface of the leg look very unsightly. They are, however, a sign of a sluggish circulation, and are often due to disease in small valves within the veins which normally prevent the blood from pooling backwards, down towards the feet. They are often a normal maternal accompaniment of pregnancy and disappear after the child is born. If allowed to persist, the sluggish circulation allows the formation of unpleasant ulcers, mainly in elderly people. Treatment is according to severity. In the early stages they are helped by supportive stockings. Later, often as an out-patient, the sufferer may have to have them removed or obliterated by a surgeon.

Raynaud's Disease. This is a strange condition in which the finger tips and in severe cases all the fingers or the whole hand respond in an exaggerated way to cold. The vessels supplying the hand are constricted and the fingers go white as the blood drains from them. Then the capillaries dilate and become distended and filled with blood. But owing to stagnation it is venous and blue, and the fingers are therefore blue. Now we have all experienced this in very cold weather, but sufferers from Raynaud's disease, nearly always women, respond even to very slight cold, like putting their hands into cold water. Even emotional stress will start the process off. In very severe cases the fingers will be so deprived of blood for so long, that sores will develop and fingers can even be lost, but this is very rare, and can be avoided by an operation to cut the nerves which supply the circular muscle of the vessels concerned. In most cases it is sufficient to avoid getting the hands cold.

Frostbite. Strictly speaking, this is literally a freezing of the tissues. Although their freezing point might be expected to be close to that of water, it usually only occurs at temperatures below −13° C. The patient may feel a pricking feeling at first, and feel an area of firmer, pale skin on the cheeks, nose, ears, fingers. or toes. If these parts are numb with cold, the onset of frostbite may not be felt, and will often only be noticed by others. In countries where extreme cold is prevalent, it is usual for complete strangers to stop each other in the street and point it out when they see it. It is important not to rub the affected part, but contrary to popular belief it must be warmed as *rapidly* as possible. Fingers should be immersed in water as hot as the normal hand can bear (43° C). Many First Aid books still quite wrongly teach that return to warmth must be gradual.

DISEASES OF THE RESPIRATORY SYSTEM.

INTRODUCTION.

When air is drawn in during the process of breathing, it is brought into very close contact with the blood passing through the lungs. In this way the air we breathe in, which contains 20 per cent oxygen, is confronted with "spent" blood returning from the tissues which contains much less, and oxygen therefore diffuses into the blood from the air. At the same time, the waste gas, carbon dioxide, passes by diffusion in the reverse direction from the blood into the air, because there is much more carbon dioxide in the returning "spent" blood than the tiny amount in the air we breathe. The blood is therefore continually circulating through the lungs and exchanging carbon dioxide for oxygen from the air we breathe in. When we breathe out, we disperse the carbon dioxide into the atmosphere.

When the air enters the nose or mouth, it passes into the windpipe or *trachea*, through the vocal cords in the pharynx. The trachea is held open all the time by rings of cartilage and is lined by a mucus-secreting membrane covered by millions of tiny "hairs" or cilia. These continuously waft a sheet of sticky mucus upwards, which traps any dust or other small particles we may have inhaled, until a collection of this material in the pharynx stimulates us to cough and expel the phlegm, usually to be swallowed. At its lower end, the trachea or windpipe divides into two, the right and left main *bronchus*. Each main bronchial tube enters a lung, one on each side, and proceeds to divide repeatedly within the lung until the air is being carried by more and more smaller and ever smaller tubes called *bronchioles*. There are many millions of these on each side, and each one ends in a collection of very small balloon-like structures —the air sacs or *alveoli*. If you were to cut across a lung and examine the cut surface in a good light, you would see that it is a spongy tissue, with many millions of tiny holes, each one just visible to the naked eye. These are the air sacs. In their walls run the blood capillaries, each one of which is a branch of the vessels carrying "spent" blood from the right side of the heart. At this stage, the blood is only separated from the air in the sacs by the walls of the capillaries and of the air sacs themselves. Both structures are extremely thin, making for easy diffusion of the gases between blood and air.

The action of breathing is accomplished by two muscular mechanisms. One is by the muscles which move the ribs, and the other by the diaphragm, a sheet of muscle which runs across the body, separating the chest cavity from the abdominal cavity. These muscles are all actuated by nerves, just as all other muscles are. Those running to the muscles of breathing are organised by a mechanism in the brain known as the *respiratory centre*. It is this centre—one of the so-called vital centres of the brain—which receives information from many different sources, and translates it into instructions for the breathing mechanism. Thus, when you run for a bus, you will automatically breathe more deeply and more quickly because the respiratory centre has been informed about all the extra carbon dioxide in your blood which has been produced by the exercising leg muscles. Even the conscious instructions involved when you blow a trumpet, inflate a balloon, or during speaking, all pass first to the respiratory centre. It is the death of the cells of this and other vital centres of the brain that is the ultimate cause of death in everyone who dies.

Bronchitis may be acute or chronic. It is an inflammation of the lining mucous membrane of the larger air passages or bronchi, and results in much more secretion than the amount normally produced, mixed with some pus. The acute form is often caused by viruses, with "secondary" infection from bacteria. It may sometimes be caused by irritant gases, like the sulphur dioxide in smog. The chronic, or long-standing form of bronchitis is often associated with *emphysema*, in which the small air sacs of the lung architecture are destroyed or distorted, leaving larger spaces than normal, often surrounded by fibrous scar tissue. Such an arrangement makes the normal gaseous exchange difficult between air and blood. While the exact cause of chronic bronchitis is difficult to discover, because it is such a mixture of causes, it is mainly associated with older age groups, particularly men, in damp foggy climates like ours in Britain, with polluted town air and especially with smoking. Smoking also makes any existing bronchitis much worse. Bronchitis can cause even more trouble than lung cancer, since instead of dying in a short time, the bronchitic lives for many years in chronic sickness. About 30,000 people die of bronchitis each year. It isn't smart to smoke. Patients cough, and produce varying amounts of sputum, or phlegm. They often wheeze like asthmatics. This may go on for many years before the right side of the heart begins to fail (P27). Gradually, during this time, the chest tends to become barrel-shaped. Treatment consists of getting the patient to stop smoking or otherwise contaminating his lungs, preventing infection, particularly during winter months, with germ-killing antibiotics, and breathing exercises. The outlook for chronic bronchitis and emphysema is nevertheless not good, although many patients continue with their disease for many years, provided they take constant care to obey instructions and stop smoking.

Bronchial Asthma is a condition in which the finer air passages become constricted due to an allergic response. In addition, an increased secretion tends to obstruct them and the patient wheezes. In many cases it can be shown that he is allergic to a particular component of dust, or, less commonly , a foodstuff. This is the same sort of thing as occurs in the upper respiratory passages in hay fever, but the effect is on a different, lower part of the respiratory system. Many other cases are due to respiratory infection of some sort, probably combined with an allergy to the bacteria causing it. A predisposition to asthma is often inherited. Once a patient has become asthmatic, his attacks will be triggered off by such additional things as emotional stress, changes in temperature (particularly sudden cold), irritating fumes or smoke, and physical exertion. These are secondary factors, and although much of the treatment is concerned with them, it is unlikely that any of them is a sole cause of the condition. Treatment is directed at the relief of the breathing difficulty and of the wheezing, as well as the control of the causative factors. Many useful drugs are available to dilate the contracted air passages and reduce the obstructing secretions. Asthma in children often gets better as the patient grows up. Asthma is another condition made much worse by smoking. Patients should avoid extremes of cold and humidity particularly out-door exertion in cold, damp weather. They should also avoid exposure to respiratory infection.

A tiny living mite about 0·3 millimetres long exists in large numbers in nearly all mattress and floor dust. This is the cause of much asthma, and in such cases it is often very helpful to vacuum-clean mattresses and floors frequently.

Bronchiectasis. In this condition the bronchial air passages are abnormally and permanently dilated, and the normal structure of the walls destroyed. It is thought to be caused by obstructions of the tubes which lead to dilatation of the parts beyond. Secretions accumulate, and since they cannot easily drain away, they become infected. The infection helps to complete the process of destruction of structures in the bronchial wall. The patient has a chronic cough which often produces large quantities of purulent sputum, and there are often recurrent episodes of pneumonia. Diagnosis is made by a special X-ray examination—a bronchogram—in which a material, opaque to X-rays, is dropped into the air passages. This shows up the dilated and distorted tubes. In some cases, where the disease is localised to one part of the lung, it is often a good idea to cut out that portion, and this is particularly true in young people. Vigorous physiotheraphy, involving drainage of the lungs by placing the patient in a suitable posture, together with antibiotic drugs for the infection, are other forms of treatment.

Cystic Fibrosis is an inborn disease which affects chiefly the lungs and the digestive system. It is sometimes called *Fibrocystic disease of the Pancreas*, and sometimes "Mucoviscidosis" Until it was medically recognised twenty-five years ago, children affected usually died from pneumonia in the first year of life. This, of course, was before antibiotics were available for the treatment of infections. Today, cystic fibrosis is known to be the commonest genetically determined disorder affecting children in Britain. One child in 2,000 receives one of the abnormal genes from each parent. Such a child therefore has a double dose of the harmful gene, and will have the disease from birth. One person in 25 of the general population carries only one of these abnormal genes, and such an individual will not have the disease, but will be a carrier of the abnormal gene. If such a seemingly normal carrier marries another carrier, there is a one in four chance of each of their children being affected. The children, therefore, who actually develop cystic fibrosis, have inherited the disease *equally* from both parents, who are carriers, but are themselves unaffected by the disease. Although much has been learned about cystic fibrosis in the past twenty-five years, there remain many unsolved problems, and we still cannot define precisely the biochemical fault which causes it. The prospects for survival into reasonably healthy adult life are steadily improving, but they depend upon early diagnosis and careful management through childhood. In cystic fibrosis most of the damage is caused by the excessive viscidity, or stickiness, of the mucus which is produced in the breathing tubes as a lubricant, and also in the ducts of the pancreatic gland which provides enzymes to help digestion. Being thick and sticky, instead of thin and slimy as in the normal, this mucus tends to block the passages instead of keeping them clear. The pancreatic cells are permanently destroyed. The gland cannot secrete pancreatic enzymes, and the food, especially protein and fat, is not properly absorbed. This deficiency can be compensated fairly well by giving pancreatic extract by mouth with every meal, and by dietary care.

The major clinical problem is in the lungs. The lung passages normally have a thin coating of mucus which is propelled steadily upwards, and is completely renewed in less than one hour. It moves more suddenly on coughing. In cystic fibrosis this upward movement is slowed down and interrupted. There is difficulty in keeping the passages clear, especially when infection with bacteria or viruses greatly increases the amount of mucus. This results in intermittent blocking of the air passages, difficulty in breathing, incomplete use of the lungs, and persistent local pockets of infection. If such infectious processes are not controlled, areas of lung will be destroyed, chronic infection will persist, and multiple lung cavities will develop. These predispose to further infection, interfering with the natural development of the lung—a process not normally complete until halfway through childhood—thus adding to the respiratory problems which the child will face in later life. Unless a correct diagnosis is made, and proper treatment instituted before the first serious lung infection has occurred, the resulting lung damage may well be permanent.

Pneumonia. This is an infection of the lung tissue, rather than of the air passages. The lung is the only internal organ which is directly exposed to the air, and since there are germs of all kinds in the air, it is a source of surprise that pneumonia is not a much more common event in all of us. The answer lies, as with all infections, in the fact that it is not simply (or even mainly) bacteria which cause disease, but our own lack of resistance to them. If we allow germs to thrive and multiply by being unhealthy or run down or undernourished, infective disease will occur. If we are fit, the entry of those same harmful germs into the body causes us no inconvenience, unless we are very young, or very old, or unless the invasion of germs is abnormally overwhelming. This helps to explain why pneumonia is so often quoted as a cause of death. In most cases it is merely a terminal event occurring in the elderly sick, whose normal resistance is so far reduced by their illness that they succumb to an invasion which they would normally not notice. There are two main kinds of pneumonia, and in both the air sacs become filled with inflammatory secretions, making the normally porous lung tissue as solid as liver. In *lobar pneumonia*, a whole segment (or lobe) of the lung becomes solid. In *bronchopneumonia*, areas of lung tissue surrounding the smaller bronchioles become consolidated, leaving normal porous lung tissue in between. Bronchopneumonia is the one which occurs in the rather stagnant lungs of people who are already ill or bedridden. Both forms respond to treatment with the appropriate antibiotics, provided any underlying debility does not interfere with the patient's own resistance. In the terminal bronchopneumonia of fatal illness, it is sometimes considered kinder not to treat the additional pneumonia. *Pleurisy* is a natural complication, and before the days of antibiotic drugs *lung abscess* was very much feared. Another form of pneumonia—*virus pneumonia*—is referred to on **P10(2)**.

Pneumoconiosis. This is a term which refers to a large group of different diseases, all of which are caused by breathing in some form of dust over a very long period of time. It is therefore an occupational hazard of certain trades. We have already mentioned the mechanisms of mucus secretion in the air passages which normally trap small particles from the air, and prevent them reaching the lung. However, in some occupations there is so much dust breathed in over the months and years that these normal barriers are defeated. About a quarter of the earth's crust consists of silicon, in quartz, flint, or sand. *Silicosis* occurs in people who have worked for many years in trades like mining, stone crushing, sandblasting, or metal grinding, who are often breathing silicon dust in high concentration. When the particles arrive in the air sacs, they set up an irritant chemical reaction which produces nodules of scar tissue. Silicosis for some reason predisposes to tuberculosis (**P14(1)**). Emphysema also occurs and there is a general impairment of respiratory function. Coalminer's pneumoconiosis is similar to silicosis but not identical with it. It is more prevalent in some coalfields than others, owing to the different composition of the dust to which these unfortunate men are daily exposed. It is hoped that modern mining methods will help to reduce this dread disease. Asbestos is a complex silicate of magnesium, calcium, and iron. *Asbestosis* is caused by inhaling its fine fibres. *Berylliosis* is caused by compounds of beryllium, used in the manufacture of fluorescent lamps. *Farmers lung* is a pneumoconiosis caused by inhaling hay and grain dust, and is similar to *bagassosis* and *byssinosis* caused by sugar cane and cotton dust respectively. The newest pneumoconiosis to be reported is *mushroom worker's lung*, caused by something in the compost in which mushrooms are commercially grown.

Pulmonary Embolism. This catastrophic, yet quite common condition has already been briefly referred to (**P30**(2)). It is a cause of tragic, sudden death in people who have had operations or have given birth to babies some days previously, or who have been bedridden for any other cause. The first event is that the blood in the veins of the legs becomes stagnant, due to the lack of exercise; and together with the tendency to clot which often follows surgery or childbirth, the whole length of a leg vein may be obstructed for twelve inches or more by an elongated clot of blood. This does little harm to the circulation of the leg, since there are plenty of other veins for returning blood to the heart. The danger is that the clot will become dislodged and be swept upwards towards the heart by the flow of returning blood. When this happens it is carried by way of the right auricle and ventricle into the pulmonary vessels which normally carry spent blood to the lungs. Here, for the first time, it enters vessels which are getting smaller as they divide, and it then impacts in the main pulmonary artery. The patient, who may have been recovering very well, suddenly collapses and not unusually dies there and then. At autopsy a long coiled-up mass of clot is found obstructing the pulmonary vessels. It often can be seen to form a cast of the leg vein and even bears the marks of the small venous valves which are present at its site of origin. With the dramatic advances being made in chest surgery, it is now sometimes possible in selected cases to operate to remove the clot. Success clearly depends on the patient's surviving long enough to be taken to the operating theatre for the major operation of *pulmonary embolectomy*. Three quarters of all cases of pulmonary embolism die within two hours, and therefore the best hope would be to prevent the occurrence altogether. This is not at present possible, but clotting in leg veins can be discouraged by early exercise following surgery and childbirth. Patients often resent having to get up the next day because it is so uncomfortable. Herein, however, lies their best hope of avoiding pulmonary embolism.

Hæmoptysis. This means coughing up blood or blood-stained material. It must be distinguished from *hæmatemesis*, in which the blood is vomited from the stomach. It must always be taken seriously because of the underlying lung disease which may be present. No one who coughs up blood, in however small a quantity, should neglect to inform their doctor so that its source can be determined. Hæmoptysis occurs in a variety of lung disease, some of which is not serious but much of which must be treated immediately if it is not to become so. This is a suitable place to repeat our general rule that you should see your doctor without delay if you have any unexplained bleeding from any part of the body, however well you feel. And this includes hæmoptysis. *See also* "Preventive Medicine" **Part III**.

Fat Embolism. Liquid fat sometimes enters the bloodstream following extensive crush injuries to soft tissue and bone. It splits up into millions of small globules which are carried to the lungs, and impact in small blood vessels there, producing obstruction of the lung circulation and consequent difficulties in breathing.

Lung Cancer. This is one of the commonest, nastiest and most incurable forms of cancer which can occur. It is also probably the easiest to prevent. In 1969, 29,768 people died of lung cancer in Great Britain, all but 5,000 of them men. Every year the toll goes up. There has been no reasonable doubt for several years now that it is associated with cigarette smoking, and the evidence is overwhelming. However, in spite of this certain knowledge, smoking continues to increase, and every year there are more and more people dying unpleasantly of lung cancer. It seems that nothing the health authorities can do is able to stop it. Intensive campaigns of public advertising of the dangers, and well organised instruction in schools have so far made no impression whatever on the smoking habits even of people who accept the evidence. The only group of people who are known to have stopped smoking are British doctors, very many of whom have given it up, and it is easy to show that giving it up has saved them from the disease. Their colleagues who have not done so have continued to die. Undoubtedly a large factor contributing to the failure of anti-smoking propaganda is the enormous expenditure by the tobacco manufacturers on very clever advertising, amounting to many millions of pounds each year. Moreover they spend a pitiful fraction of this amount on their own research into the harmful effects of their own product, which has so far discovered nothing which was not already known by research doctors many years ago. Another problem is that it takes a number of years to get cancer. It is not like an infectious disease which is caught a few days after exposure to the bacteria concerned. It may be fifteen or twenty years before the cancer begins, and many smokers are apparently unwilling to look so far ahead. Furthermore, not everyone who smokes dies this way; and so a smoker can gamble with his life and hope it will not be him. The present writer once had to perform a series of post-mortem examinations on people who died of lung cancer, and this helped him to stop smoking completely, having smoked more than twenty cigarettes a day for several years. Not everyone can have this incentive. The main encouragement to smoke probably comes from other people. Schoolboys are easily impressed when their teachers and parents stop smoking. They are not likely to fear the habit when these same people smoke openly. The smoking doctor is also a powerful stimulus to people to carry on smoking.

Lung cancer grows in the wall of a main bronchial air passage. If it grows inwards it can obstruct the air way, choking that part of the lung it is supplying with air. This causes collapse and infection of the lung and may lead to *lung abscess.* The patient will then cough up blood-stained infected and purulent material. Such a case is comparatively lucky, since the disease declares itself early by producing symptoms. In others, the lump may grow outwards into the surrounding lung and produce no symptoms at all in the early stages. Indeed, it may spread to other parts of the body, like brain or bone or liver before causing any trouble to the patient. If this happens he may go to his doctor because of fits, changes of personality, or fracture, only to discover that the origin of the trouble is in the lung.

The chances of cure are negligible, although much can be done to relieve the pain and suffering of the last stages of the illness. Not more than one in twenty cases is alive two years after it is first diagnosed. Surgery, by removing the lung, and irradiation of the growth are the standard palliative treatment. It is not the practice of the Medical Section to alarm the reader unnecessarily, but if only a few are induced to stop giving themselves such a horrible disease, then writing in this way will have been justified. *See also* **Treatment of Cancer, Part III.**

Secondary Cancer of the Lung. In nearly all forms of cancer, the big problem is that it spreads to other parts of the body. If this were not so it could be eradicated by surgical removal more often than it is. One common way in which it spreads from any part of the body is by entering the bloodstream and being carried as clumps of living cancer cells to distant parts. When these come to rest in smaller blood vessels, they begin to grow and colonise the new environment. Such new colonies are called *secondary deposits* or *metastases.* It so happens that all veins (except portal veins of the liver) lead to the right heart and thence directly to the lungs, and for this reason the lungs are a very common site of *secondary* cancer, which may have begun in the bowel, or breast, or indeed anywhere else in the body. Other common sites of secondary, blood-borne cancer are the brain, liver, bone marrow, and kidney, since all of them have an abundant blood supply, and there is therefore a high chance of the travelling cells arriving there. Secondary cancer of the lung usually consists of several lumps scattered throughout the lung. Lung cancer itself is usually only one growth. One of the main reasons for the success of early diagnosis is that treatment may be possible before blood-borne and other means of spread have occurred. Unfortunately, in the case of primary cancer of the lung, even early diagnosis is of little avail, but in many other common cancers permanent cure is possible if treatment is begun early enough.

Pleurisy. The chest is lined by one layer of a thin membrane called the *pleura.* The lungs are covered and enclosed by a second, continuous layer of this same membrane. When the lungs move during respiration, the pleura covering the lungs rubs against the pleura lining the chest, lubricated by a very thin layer of pleural fluid separating the two pleura. Whenever the pleural surface becomes inflamed, this is known as *pleurisy.* It is nearly always due to inflammatory disease of the adjoining lung, and is therefore not strictly a disease in its own right. For example, pneumonia, tuberculosis, lung cancer, or a lung infarct (**P30(2)**) will produce a pleurisy if the area of diseased lung adjoins the lung surface. Sometimes the area of inflamed inner pleura will tend to stick to its outer layer or rub painfully against it, producing a sharp pain when the patient breathes. Sometimes a large effusion of fluid is produced which separates the two layers and collapses the lung by occupying space in the chest which the lung should be occupying. This latter is more usual in tuberculosis or cancer.

The lung can be collapsed by the entry of anything between the normally adjacent layers of pleura. For example, air can be introduced, either deliberately to rest the lung in tuberculosis, or by accidental penetrating wounds of the chest wall, or by accidental rupture of the emphysematous lung (*q.v.*). This condition is called *pneumothorax* or "air in the chest." Bleeding into the cavity between the pleura is called *haemothorax.*

DISEASES OF THE DIGESTIVE TRACT AND LARGE INTESTINE.

INTRODUCTION.

The digestive tract consists of the mouth, pharynx, œsophagus (or gullet), stomach, small intestine, large intestine (or colon), rectum, and anus. The small intestine is very long, and is subdivided into the duodenum, jejunum, and ileum. It ends at the junction of the ileum with the cæcum, where there is a small blind side-tube, the appendix. The cæcum leads into the colon. The whole tract has two main mechanical functions and two main biochemical ones. Mechanically, food has to be chewed in the mouth and further minced up by muscular squeezing, mainly by the stomach. It has also to be propelled along by an orderly series of squeezing movements known as *peristalsis.* While it is still in the digestive tract, food has to be digested. That is to say, it has to be broken down chemically into suitable materials for absorption into the system, and secondly, it has to be absorbed across the wall of the intestine into the blood stream, itself a highly complex biochemical process. The blood stream it now enters is a special part of the circulation, the "portal" system, which travels directly to the liver without first passing to the heart. In the liver the broken-down foods are processed and issued in their new form into the general, or "systemic" circulation, by which they are finally carried to all the tissues of the body.

As the food passes along the digestive tract (or as it is sometimes called, the alimentary canal), it is mixed with various secretions which are either made in the wall of the tract, or by organs outside the wall connected to the main pathway by small tubes. Examples of the latter are bile, manufactured by the liver and sent into the duodenum through the bile ducts. Also pancreatic juice comes from the pancreas down the pancreatic ducts, also into the duodenum. These secretions are either digestive juices concerned with splitting up the foodstuffs so that they can be absorbed, or they have a lubricant function so that the gut contents slide along easily under the influence of peristalsis. Roughly speaking, it may be said that digestive juices give place to lubricant secretions at the junction between the small and large intestine.

The constituents of the diet are dealt with in a later section. The principle classes with whose digestion we are now concerned are carbohydrates, proteins, and fats.

Carbohydrates are sugars and starches. There are many sugars, which may exist alone, in pairs, or with lots of them stuck together. Alone they are such things as glucose or fructose. Common table sugar is a substance called sucrose, formed by sticking one glucose molecule to one fructose molecule. Starch is lots of glucose molecules all stuck together. Digestion of carbohydrates consists of splitting up sugars and starch into single sugars like glucose, since only single sugars can be absorbed into the system. The splitting is done by digestive *enzymes* which are found in the juices secreted into the digestive tract. Sugar-splitters are found in the saliva of the mouth, in the pancreatic juice of the duodenum, and in the duodenum's own juice from its own wall. On the face of it, you might think it would be better to eat glucose which needs no digestion and can be absorbed in this form, than to eat starch which has first to be split; and so a lot of money has been made out of a gullible public by the sale of glucose drinks and powder. In fact digesting starch is no problem whatever, even for the sick, who can obtain their carbohydrate energy just as easily (and much more cheaply) from potatoes as from expensive glucose. The end result of eating both is the same. The starch-splitting enzyme in saliva is mixed with the food as it is chewed, and it is therefore probably a good idea to chew it well. However, even if the food is bolted it does not seem to matter very much. People without teeth (neither their own nor dentures) seem to digest their carbohydrate quite well, presumably by means of their pancreatic juice at a later stage.

Proteins, which are found in meat, cheese, and eggs, have very large molecules consisting of lots of small ones strung together. Unlike starch, in which all the component glucose molecules are identical, the amino acids of which proteins are composed come in many different types. They all contain nitrogen, and there are about twenty-seven varieties. One protein differs from another in the proportions of the mixture and the order in which they are stuck together. Only single amino acids can be absorbed from the food, and so protein digestion again consists of splitting the material down into its building bricks. There is a strong protein splitting enzyme in the gastric (or stomach) juice called pepsin, whose job it is to split the long amino-acid chains into shorter chains. Several other protein-splitters in the duodenal and pancreatic juice contrive to break the smaller chains into individual amino acids which are then absorbed and sent to the liver for processing.

Fats mainly consist of glycerol to which are attached three fatty acid molecules for each molecule of glycerol. An enzyme in pancreatic juice splits the fatty acids off the glycerol, but would have some difficulty penetrating the globules of fat without the help of bile. One of the constituents of bile (bile salts) has detergent properties like washing-up powder and breaks the fat globules up into a very fine suspension so that the enzyme can get at the fat. Some fat particles of this size can even be absorbed as such, without preliminary splitting.

The processes by which all these enzymic secretions are produced are very finely controlled. They are very expensive to make in terms of energy and raw materials, and so it would be very wasteful to produce them all the time, even when there was no food to digest. And so the body has some very well designed automatic arrangements for sampling the foods as they are eaten and passed on, which ensure that exactly the right kind of juice is waiting in every part of the digestive tract for whatever food arrives. As soon as the food is digested the supply of enzymes is automatically switched off, so that there is very little waste of precious materials. It is, of course, beyond the scope of this account to describe the control mechanisms. Suffice it to say that they are operated partly by nerve reflexes which signal the imminent arrival of food, and partly by special hormones produced in various parts of the gut wall. The best secretion is affected even by psychological factors, so that pleasant company and surroundings, attractive appearance of the food, and an eager anticipation of it all make for good digestion and good health. These psychological factors are all capable of proper scientific investigation and proof. The poor health of those who habitually and irregularly bolt unpalatable food is probably due to such factors as these. So is the failure of appetite in the depressed, the anxious adult, or the scolded child.

Nearly all the digestion which has been described occurs in the stomach and upper part of the small intestine (the duodenum, jejunum, and upper ileum). Almost all absorption of the products of digestion occurs in the small intestine which is long and intricately folded to give it a large surface area for this purpose. The colon, or large intestine, is adapted for conserving water, by removing it from the residual waste material. This has then to be eliminated, and being rather dry its passage has to be lubricated by suitable secretions of mucus.

Constipation. Here, perhaps we had better mention the morbid question of constipation, about which so many people are obsessed and hold such pronounced views. First of all, what is it? For some people it is entirely normal only to pass motions about once or twice a week. For others the normal frequency is once or twice a day. What is abnormal? The answer is that the only thing worth worrying about is any pronounced change of bowel habit, particularly in middle-aged and older people. By a change is meant a change from that individual person's normal routine. Such a pronounced change—either in the direction of constipation or diarrhœa—is worth consulting your doctor about if it persists for more than a week or two. Otherwise, forget your bowels and leave them to work naturally as they know best. Many believe that constipation is the root of all evil, that it causes a mysterious condition known to them (although, alas, not to doctors) as "auto-intoxication." Sedulously fostered by the manufacturers of patent medicines, their beliefs range from the notion that headaches, spotty skin, muddy skin, and tiredness are caused by constipation, to the more extreme idea that the whole system is being poisoned and that, if the bowels do not work, the individual will shortly die. Of course, all this is the merest rubbish; for, as Professor Samson Wright, whose *Applied Physiology* is one of the most famous of medical text-books, has pointed out, there is no such thing as absorption of poisonous products from the bowel. There is no such thing as "auto-intoxication." "The symptoms of constipation," he writes, "are largely due to distension and mechanical irritation of the rectum." It has been shown that an enema removes these symptoms *immediately*, which would not be the case if they were due to poisons in the blood, and exactly the same symptoms can be produced by packing the rectum with cotton-wool. Wright mentions the case of a man who went for just over a year without a bowel motion, and at the end of that time, although his abdomen was distended and he felt some discomfort, he was not noticeably ill. Needless to say, telling these facts to the purgative addict will only make him annoyed, but it is as well to note that if no known diseases are due to constipation (although constipation may be a symptom of another disease), the regular use of purgatives *can* cause disease.

Constipation should be treated first by diet containing plenty of roughage—bran and oatmeal are excellent—plenty of stewed and fresh fruits, and at least 1½ litres of fluid should be taken daily. Failing that, one of the best things to take is a proprietary product prepared from senna pods. Never to be taken regularly are liquid paraffin, castor oil, preparations of aloes, Epsom salts, and all the other dreadful stuff that people swill down.

Œsophagus.

The œsophagus, or gullet, is more than a simple tube for taking the food from the mouth to the stomach. It is normally closed except when swallowing, and the act of swallowing is very complicated. When the material to be swallowed arrives in the back of the throat there is an automatic mechanism which opens the top end of the œsophagus to receive it, and from then onwards everything happens automatically. The next portion of the tube opens and the top closes strongly, so that the food (or drink) is propelled forcibly down the next segment. Then the part below this relaxes and the material is squeezed further downwards and so on until it arrives in the stomach. This squeezing (or milking) action is akin to the action known as peristalsis which propels contents in other parts of the gut. Thus when you see someone swallowing a glass of beer very quickly in warm weather, it is not going "down the hatch" under the influence of gravity, however much it may look like it. It is perfectly possible to swallow the same, or any other liquid, standing on your head. Getting into that position is the only difficult part. Sometimes this complicated swallowing mechanism gets out of order, leading to difficulties of swallowing, or *dysphagia*. Another disorder known as *hiatus hernia* occurs at the lower end of the œsophagus as it meets the stomach. At this point the œsophagus has to pass through the diaphragm, the sheet of muscle which separates the chest from the abdomen. The muscular fibres of the diaphragm are normally arranged in a ring around the œsophagus. These help to keep the lower end shut, so that the acid contents of the stomach do not regurgitate upwards, causing inflammation (*oesophagitis*) or heartburn. A hiatus hernia is when muscle fibres get slack, and the upper end of the stomach can even slide upwards into the chest. People with hiatus hernia get heartburn after meals, and particularly when they bend down or lie down. Except for very severe forms, which need surgical repair, the treatment is to eat less at a time, reduce the acidity with a suitable antacid and reduce weight, so that the weight of the abdomen does not press upwards so much. The other disease of the œsophagus, quite unrelated to the above, is *cancer of the oesophagus*, the cause of which is still unknown in most cases. When cancer occurs in the wall of any tube, it will often encircle the tube and gradually narrow the way through. This is what happens in the œsophagus, leading to difficulty in swallowing, particularly solids. It is a condition, usually, of rather elderly men, although it is sometimes associated with a special form of severe anæmia in women. Treatment is in some way to keep the passage open, either by transplanting a new tube, or more usually, by removing the constricted piece and joining up the remainder.

The Stomach and Duodenum.

By far the commonest diseases of the stomach and duodenum are *gastric ulcer* and *duodenal ulcer*. They are actually the same condition in two different sites and are often classed together as *peptic ulcer* or *acid-peptic disease*. The ulcers, which are rather like sores on the lining of the stomach or duodenum, may be "acute" or "chronic." Acute ulcers tend to be small and there are often several of them. Chronic ulcers are usually single. They may be small, or they may be several centimetres across. Chronic ulcers smoulder for months and even years, like a sore which will not heal, and a great deal of scar tissue forms in their depths. Thus they may in time erode their way right through the wall of the stomach, destroying all its layers, and begin to eat into surrounding structures like the pancreas or liver. The fact that they do not perforate more frequently is due to all the fibrous scar tissue which is formed during the slow eroding process. Healing of such a destructive ulcer is nevertheless common, and the great problem is how to help the natural healing process to win against the ulcer's tendency to erode. Better still would be to discover the cause, and prevent it happening in the first place. This extremely common affliction is confined to the human species and has been known since the earliest times. It does not vary very much with diet or with social class. Although occurring at all ages, it usually begins between the ages of twenty and forty, and is most commonly found in men between forty-five and fifty-five. Gastric ulcer is four times, and duodenal ulcer ten times more common in men than in women. It is always due to an inability of the lining to stand up to the normal digestive activity of the stomach contents. These are normally acid and contain a powerful enzyme for digesting proteins. Again it is perhaps more surprising that we all do not digest our own stomachs, rather than that some unfortunate people do digest small areas slowly. In certain abnormal conditions when the stomach stops making acid, ulcers always heal. However, some ulcers occur without excessive secretion of acid and many heal without the acid being neutralised with antacids. All this points to the main trouble being in the response of the lining to acid rather than to the acid itself. Nevertheless, the most effective treatment at present known involves regulating gastric secretion, and particularly its acidity. It is also known that peptic ulcers are more common in people whose occupations involve administrative and professional responsibility, competitive effort and nervous tension, long periods of anxiety or frustration. Presumably the higher nervous system influences these events by the same nerves, which normally help to control secretion.

The main symptom of peptic ulcer is pain, and this usually responds well to proper doses of antacids. Many different varieties are available and a lot of money is made from selling them. When indigestion persists for longer than a few days it is always better to see your doctor so that a proper diagnosis can be made and the best remedies begun. Many other causes exist for similar pains, and you should not try to make the diagnosis yourself. It may be necessary to analyse your gastric secretions in the hospital laboratory. Almost certainly you will have a special X-ray examination, and since the stomach cannot easily be seen on a normal X-ray, they will have to show it up by making you drink a white material containing barium. This will be seen as a silhouette of the stomach and duodenal contents. Searching for an ulcer this way is a highly skilled matter and is performed by doctors specially trained in radiology.

Until recently, no drugs capable of influencing the course of peptic ulcer in any significant manner were available and the physician had to rely on general measures, such as rest, diet and the administration of antacids to relieve pain and discomfort; episodes of acute haemorrhage were not uncommon and required surgical intervention if life were threatened.

However, recent advances in our knowledge of gastric and duodenal pathology have led to the development of at least two therapeutic agents of which the newest, *cimetidine*, is highly effective. Developments in fibre-optic technology have contributed greatly to progress in peptic ulcer treatment. The gastro-enterologist can now pass a *flexible* instrument, the *gastroduodenal endoscope* (the gastroscope is a *rigid* tube), under mild sedation through the patient's gullet and into the stomach and duodenum and view the lesions directly. Once an ulcer is diagnosed, the time has come to stop treating yourself with antacids from the chemist's counter, and to take the ones your doctor decides are best. Smoking should be stopped by ulcer patients (as, indeed, by everyone else, but that is another matter) because it inhibits healing. Alcohol tends to increase acid secretion and should be avoided. It is also *extremely important* to avoid taking any form of aspirin, even in quite small amounts, since this can lead to very serious bleeding from the ulcer. The ulcer patient should be warned that hundreds of proprietary preparations contain aspirin and all of them are dangerous for him. Search for the formula in small print on the label before taking any remedy, looking particularly for acetyl salicylic acid—the correct name for aspirin. Even some widely sold "hang-over" remedies which are sold for "upset-stomach" contain large quantities of aspirin. Some of the patients with "upset stomach" are, of course, ulcer patients, and some even die of haemorrhage following the ingestion of aspirin.

The main complications of peptic ulcer are bleeding, perforation, and a narrowing of the pylorus, or lower part, known as *pyloric stenosis*. Bleeding is caused by the eroding ulcer eating away at one of the many blood vessels in the stomach or duodenal wall. It leads to the passing of "altered" blood in the stool (*melaena*), or to the vomiting of blood (*hæmatemesis*). When the initial bleeding occurs, the patient may feel suddenly faint, and a little later will notice the black, tarry colour of his stool. This is sometimes confused with a similiar colour when the patient is taking iron. Peptic ulcer is not the only cause of this very serious hæmorrhage, which constitutes a hospital emergency whatever its cause. The treatment, like that of every large hæmorrhage, is blood transfusion which must be continued until the bleeding stops, or until the patient is sufficiently fit for surgery, should that be deemed necessary. Perforation is perhaps the most serious complication of peptic ulcer, leading to the spilling of stomach contents within the abdominal cavity. Treatment is invariably surgical, either the closure of the perforation or the partial removal of the stomach.

Surgical removal of part of the stomach is often the only way to treat a peptic ulcer which has had its chance to heal in other ways. It is tempting for the patient to "have it out and done with," but the time for surgery is a matter of fine judgment. So many ulcers heal by medical means if you give them a chance, and operations are for those which persistently refuse, or which become complicated.

Stomach Cancer. The stomach is a fairly common site for primary cancer. There is no known reason for this, and it is particularly important to stress that we know of no connection whatever between the peptic ulcers which have just been discussed and cancer. Stomach cancer used to be the commonest cancer of men, but the current rise of lung cancer has pushed it into second place. There are some strange geographical differences in its distribution. For example, it is much commoner in Japan and Scandinavia than in England or the U.S.A. It is difficult to see any reason for this in dietary habits. In Wales it causes three times as many deaths as in South-East England. All this is very puzzling, as is so much of our information about cancer generally. One of the main problems with stomach cancer is that it often causes the patient no inconvenience and thus produces no symptoms of note until the disease is far advanced and it is difficult to do much. Treatment is by surgical removal of the growth, and even in the most advanced cases a great deal can often be done to make the patient more comfortable.

The Small Intestine.

The small intestine runs from the stomach to the cæcum and comprises the duodenum, jejunum, and ileum in that order. On a more cheerful note it may be remarked that it is very rarely the site of cancer. Its main problems arise in connection with defects in absorption mechanisms, with obstructions, and with a strange inflammatory condition known as *regional enteritis.* Most obstructions are due not to blockages of the tube, but to failures of peristaltic propulsion, the process which is briefly described above under "œsophagus." Such a failure is called *ileus.* When peristalsis stops for any reason, the result is severe dehydration and loss of important chemicals like sodium and chloride from the body. This is because about 9 litres of fluid enter the small intestine each day in the form of digestive juices, and all of this has to be pushed onwards to be reabsorbed into the system at lower levels. If peristalsis fails, this bulk of fluid remains in the small intestine, or is vomited. In both cases it is lost to the body itself, leading to serious dehydration and illness. Treatment is by very careful replacement by transfusion of the fluid and the chemicals lost, and by removal of the trapped fluid within the intestine through a tube threaded down through the mouth.

Regional enteritis or *ileitis* is sometimes known as *Crohn's disease.* It is a very mysterious condition in which the normally supple wall of the small intestine becomes inflamed and gradually replaced by thick fibrous scar tissue, so that it looks and feels like a thick garden hose. Loops of inflamed gut stick together, and channels open between them, and if the disease progresses a mass of adherent, thickened intestine results to which everything in the neighbourhood also adheres. However, for some unknown reason some cases do not progress downhill in this way and get better spontaneously. Surgical treatment is necessary for the majority, however, particularly those with advanced disease leading to complications such as obstruction or perforation. Sometimes an early case can be resolved by cutting out the length of affected gut, although recurrences are unfortunately common.

Appendicitis. This must be one of the best-known surgical diseases of the intestinal tract. The appendix is a narrow, blind-ended side tube attached to the cæcum near the end of the small intestine. Appendicitis is when it becomes obstructed, or infected, or both. From its position it is almost predictable that it will get obstructed sooner or later by pieces of fæcal matter which pass its entrance and which are normally infected. The surprising thing is that it does not happen more often. Once this has occurred, however, a closed abscess forms, and as the abscess distends the appendix, it first weakens its wall, making it gangrenous, and then bursts into the abdominal cavity causing *peritonitis* (see later). It would be useless and misleading to describe the symptoms of acute appendicitis in detail, since it is difficult even for experienced doctors to distinguish them from those of several other conditions. Suffice it to say that any severe, persisting pain in the abdomen, whether continuous or intermittent, whether associated with diarrhœa or not, should lead the sufferer to a doctor for a quick diagnosis. Germ-killing antibiotics are useless against appendicitis, and any laxative is extremely dangerous as it may cause an acutely inflamed appendix to perforate.

The Large Intestine or Colon.

The two main serious diseases of the colon are ulcerative colitis and cancer in its various forms. *Ulcerative colitis* is yet another mysterious disease in which severe ulceration of the lining of the colon gives rise most frequently to diarrhoea with the passage of blood and mucus. In fact it can be like dysentery, and it has often been considered to be due to some form of infection. Unfortunately no particular germ can routinely be found in these cases, and the situation is endlessly confused by the presence in the normal bowel of lots of different germs anyway. Nevertheless the ulcerated lining of the bowel certainly does get infected by the germs normally present, and this makes the disease worse. Therefore germ-killing antibiotics are often helpful in alleviating symptoms and can lead to an earlier settling down of the condition, although not to a cure. It has long been known that certain kinds of psychological upset are often associated, but here again the disease is so unpleasant for the sufferer that he is to be forgiven some despondency as a result of, rather than as a cause of, his troubles. It is also suspected that ulcerative colitis may be an auto-immune disease; that is it may represent rejection by the patient of his own colonic lining in a manner somewhat comparable to the tissue rejection which often follows organ transplantation. Some of the more alarming complications are perforation through the wall of the ulcerated bowel, and sometimes massive hæmorrhage occurs. The mainstay of medical treatment is the drug *sulphasalazine* together with dietary measures and the occasional use of other drugs to minimise symptoms. Surgery maybe required to relieve obstruction, deal with perforation, remove chronically affected parts of the bowel. etc.

Cancer of the Colon and Rectum. This is another very common form of cancer, which can often be completely cured by surgical removal of the growth provided it is caught in the early stages before it has spread. The commonest symptom is a change in bowel habit, either towards constipation or, more often, towards diarrhœa, in the second half of life. There may be rectal bleeding, or the passage of mucus, and there may be abdominal pain. We cannot too often repeat that any such change of bowel habit, or any unexplained bleeding from any site should lead the patient promptly to his doctor.

Diverticulitis. Some people have small pockets or sacs in the wall of the colon known as diverticula. A minority of these sometimes get inflamed, and this is *diverticulitis.* Occasionally perforation occurs.

Hernia or Rupture. This is a condition in which abdominal contents, usually a loop of intestine, protrude forwards through the muscular wall of the abdomen. The wall consists of a sheet of muscle fibres running in several directions. They normally become tense when we cough, or strain, or in getting up from a recumbent position. There are places in the groin on each side where there is a way through the muscle for the spermatic cord in the male. In many men a weakness can arise at this point, and if it persists, the way through may enlarge and allow loops of bowel to emerge from behind the muscle sheet to appear as a lump under the skin of the groin. On relaxation the lump can be made to disappear by pushing the contents back the way they came; and they will re-emerge when the patient strains. This is an extremely common complaint in men, and it should be treated by an operation in which the muscle wall is repaired. Some men, however, neglect to have their rupture treated until one day it proceeds to "strangulate." This is the term used when the muscle tightens around the neck of the protruding loop of bowel, cutting off its blood supply. From then onwards the loop becomes gangrenous and the intestine is obstructed by having a part of itself nipped outside the abdominal wall. The patient is in severe pain, vomits continously, and quickly is liable to get into such a poor condition that surgical relief is difficult. It is therefore a surgical emergency, and it would have been better to have had the relatively simple repair operation earlier and at leisure. Hernia in the region of the groin is of two types: *inguinal hernia* and *femoral hernia*, the difference between them being technical and of no consequence to the patient. They nearly always occur in men. Other types of hernia less frequently occur in both sexes. *Incisional hernia* is when the muscle wall has been weakened at the site of an old abdominal operation and has failed to heal properly. *Umbilical hernia* occurs owing to the natural weakness of the abdominal wall at the navel, and is so common in babies as to be almost normal. When a baby cries and thereby puts a strain on his abdominal wall, a lump often appears in the region of the navel, and this can be very alarming for the parents. They should of course show it to their doctor who will nearly always be able to reassure them. It is self-healing without operation in the majority of cases.

Peritonitis. The cavity of the abdomen in which the intestines and other organs lie is called the peritoneal cavity, and it is lined by a thin membrane called the peritoneum. When this becomes inflamed the condition is a serious one and is called *peritonitis*. Inflammation may be bacterial, as occurs following a burst appendix and the spillage of bacteria and pus in the cavity. It may be a sterile peritonitis as often follows perforation of a peptic ulcer, when the inflammation is caused by the acid contents of the stomach. It is always very dangerous, probably because of the large surface area afforded by the peritoneum for the absorption of inflammatory toxins.

Hæmorrhoids are simply varicose veins in the rectal and anal regions. They are very common, and are caused probably in about equal degrees by inherited weakness of the veins, strain such as heavy lifting, and constipation (this is one of the very few conditions in which constipation may do some damage, due to the mechanical pressure of hardened fæces in the rectum on the veins). Pregnant women are liable to develop hæmorrhoids or "*piles*," as they are commonly called, owing to the pressure of the baby's head in the pelvis. Hæmorrhoids may be external or internal, the former being in the anal region below the sphincter, the latter in the rectum; the two usually go together. There may be no symptoms, but the veins are liable to bleed, to get thrombosed (*i.e.*, a clot forms within) or to become infected. When clotting or infection occurs the piles enlarge and tend to be pushed out through the anus during defæcation, when they form extremely painful external swellings. Treatment in simple cases may be by the use of suppositories—cones of a firm grease containing suitable medicaments which are inserted in the rectum—in other cases the veins may be injected, as with varicose veins of the leg, in order to close them, but when there is much bleeding, thrombosis, infection, or interference with bowel movements they should be removed surgically.

DISEASES OF THE LIVER.

The liver is the largest organ and has such a wide variety of known functions (to say nothing of the unknown) that it is also one of the most complicated. Nearly all of its functions are biochemical, and it is often called the laboratory of the body. Medical students, when asked to enumerate the functions of the liver, usually stick at about twenty-five, nearly all of them to do with general metabolism: that is the biochemical processing of substances taking part in structure or as body fuel. For example, the liver makes proteins from the amino-acids absorbed from the gut, and breaks down amino-acids and manufactures a waste product (urea) from them. It stores carbohydrates as glycogen, and conducts many of the processes necessary to turn carbohydrates into energy. It manufactures prothrombin with the help of vitamin K, and this is essential for blood clotting. It makes bile and secretes it into the gall bladder and bile ducts (*see later*). The three main constituents of bile (cholesterol, bile pigment or bilirubin, and bile acids) all have to be processed, or metabolised, in the liver during the production of bile. Vitamin B_{12} and iron is also stored and dealt with there, and these are involved in preventing various forms of anæmia (*q.v.*); and in addition to all these things the liver is the place where harmful substances, both from within the body and from outside it, are dealt with and rendered harmless. This last function of "detoxication" is often accomplished by making the offending molecules suitable for rapid excretion by the kidneys, or by altering their chemical shape to make them harmless.

Nearly all of these very different things are done by one single type of cell: the liver cell, and it is one of the remarkable features of the design that this cell can be so versatile. There also have to be some very efficient transport systems in the liver, in addition to the usual blood supply and venous drainage possessed by all other tissues.

One of these is the "portal venous system." Whenever a substance is absorbed across the gut wall from any part of the intestine into the interior of the body it enters the special draining blood vessels of the portal system, which are arranged throughout the length of the digestive tract. All these veins eventually unite in the main portal vein which enters the liver. Everything absorbed from the gut is therefore taken first to the liver to be processed. After this the products are carried away from the liver in the ordinary veins to the heart, and are distributed to the rest of the body by the arterial system. The liver has arteries of its own by which it receives oxygen and nutriment like any other tissue. The fourth transport system collects the bile as it is formed within the liver and delivers it to the gall bladder and bile ducts, which eventually drain it into the duodenum.

Portal Hypertension means high blood pressure in the portal venous system, and is the usual accompaniment to *cirrhosis* (*see later*). When the terminations of the portal veins in the liver are strangled and obstructed by cirrhotic disease, this tends to blow them up, or dilate them with with blood. There is a natural escape route for the portal blood where the lower end of the œsophagus or gullet joins the upper end of the stomach. At this place some of the portal veins draining the stomach are connected with the ordinary veins draining the œsophagus so that when pressure rises in the portal system, blood tends to be diverted into these connecting veins, and they in turn become dilated, or varicose. Trouble begins when these dilated connecting veins, which bulge inwards into the œsophagus, are damaged by food particles passing across them and bleed severely into the stomach. The patient vomits large quantities of blood (*hæmatemesis*) or passes tarry altered blood in the stool (*melaena*). The other main cause of these is the bleeding which occasionally accompanies peptic ulcer (*q.v.*).

A second complication of portal hypertension (and hence of cirrhosis) is *ascites*, in which large amounts of a lymph-like fluid accumulate in the abdominal cavity. The fluid contains a great deal of precious protein and salt which is lost to the body economy. Ascites also sometimes accompanies cancerous deposits in the abdomen.

Jaundice means being yellow because there is too much yellow bile pigment circulating in the blood, and there are three main possible causes for this. The term "yellow jaundice," like "gastric stomach" is therefore unnecessarily redundant: there is no other kind.

Bile pigment comes from broken-down red blood cells, which normally come to the end of their time after existing for about 120 days. The breakdown products of red cells can always be found in the blood of normal people, but there is normally insufficient colour to show. Abnormal amounts of colour build up quite logically in any of the following three circumstances:

(1) If too many red cells are being destroyed and even the normal liver cannot deal with the amount of bile pigment produced, it piles up in the blood, and *hæmolytic jaundice* is the result. The expression simply means jaundice due to (abnormally large) red-cell destruction.

(2) If the liver cells are themselves sick and unable to cope even with the normal amounts of pigment from normal red-cell destruction. Here too the pigment will pile up and cause *hepatocellular jaundice*, or liver-cell jaundice.

(3) If the bile ducts carrying bile away from the liver are blocked, then bile will pile up behind the blockage and re-enter the blood stream, causing *obstructive jaundice*. In this case the rate of red-cell breakdown is normal, and the liver cells are normal: at least for a time.

It is enormously important for the treatment of jaundice for the doctor to diagnose its type correctly, since the treatment varies from surgical relief of obstruction to the medical treatment of viral infection or of excess red-cell destruction.

The so-called differential diagnosis of jaundice is often exceptionally difficult, and sometimes requires some very sophisticated laboratory tests and X-rays. At other times it is extremely easy and is obvious from a cursory glance at the urine and the stool. In any case all jaundice is a highly technical matter for the doctor who must be consulted early.

There is a special jaundice of newborn babies which resembles hæmolytic jaundice and can occasionally have serious consequences for the developing brain (*kernicterus*) if it is allowed to become too severe. When this is threatened, steps are taken to reduce the level of circulating bile pigment by replacement of the baby's blood or by other means.

The commonest cause of hepatocellular jaundice is infective or viral hepatitis. Obstructive jaundice is usually due either to blockage by gallstones (*q.v.*) or by a lump pressing on the bile ducts from an adjacent cancer. This can often be quite satisfactorily relieved by surgery.

Infective Hepatitis. There is a group of disorders affecting the liver which are caused by viruses. The incubation period is often very long, and the sickness and other debility caused is often quite severe and prolonged. One variety, known as serum sickness, is now much less common than a few years ago. It used to be transmitted by using the same needle for injections into several different people, or from transfusing contaminated blood. A greater awareness of the problem, and the use of disposable needles and syringes has cut down the incidence.

Cirrhosis. There are many different kinds of cirrhosis, the commonest of which has already been mentioned under *portal hypertension* above. In all cases, liver cells are slowly poisoned and are killed off over a long period of time. In response to this, the surviving liver cells undergo cell division, trying to make good the numbers lost, and at the same time fibrous scar tissue replaces the damaged tissue throughout the organ. The result is a hard, knobbly liver. The many "knobs" are spherical areas of regenerated new cells, and they are separated by thickened bands of scar tissue. All of this destroys the normal architecture and leads to the portal hypertension and ascites mentioned above. In some countries (*e.g.*, France and the United States) excessive alcohol is the main cause of the original liver damage which starts it all off. In others (*e.g.*, Bantu South Africa) it seems to be nutritional starvation of the liver. In England much less than half the cases are due to alcohol, and many are thought to be due to a previous episode of infective hepatitis (*q.v.*), but this is not certain. Infective hepatitis is quite common but cirrhosis is comparatively rare. So that the great majority of people do not progress from one to the other. One day soon the treatment for advanced cirrhosis will be to replace the liver by transplantation, but there are still many problems to overcome before this can become routine.

Cancer of the Liver. Cancer of the liver is quite common, but it is nearly always cancer which has spread in the blood stream from other parts of the body. The liver is a favourite site for such secondary deposits, since it has a large blood supply and will receive a generous helping of anything being carried. It is also a very "fertile soil" for the cancer seedlings to grow in. Primary cancer of the liver is uncommon, and only occurs in a few cases of pre-existing cirrhosis.

Gallstones. These are "stones" formed by some of the major constituents of bile coming out of solution and forming solid bodies. They are very common, and often cause no trouble at all. When they do, it is usually a colicky intermittent severe pain. This is due to the muscular walls of the bile passages contracting in an effort to expel an obstructing stone into the duodenum. The second common trouble arising from gallstones is obstructive jaundice, described above. It is small consolation to gallstone sufferers that the stones are often very pretty, often being composed of beautiful cholesterol crystals coloured by varying shades of bile. If they contain calcium they will be visible on an X-ray. Otherwise they are not seen. Stones often occur in conjunction with inflammation of the gall bladder, known as *cholecystitis*. The treatment for gallstones is to remove them surgically together with the gall bladder if they are causing persistent symptoms. Ways of avoiding surgery by dissolving them in substances taken by mouth are under investigation.

The Pancreas.

This is a soft, elongated gland lying behind the stomach; it is about 12·5 cm long and 5 cm wide. Within its tissues lies the duct, which, when it leaves the pancreas, passes into the duodenum near the point of entry of the bile-duct. This duct transmits the juices containing enzymes which aid in the digestion in the small intestine. The pancreas, however, has two main functions: not only does it manufacture these important digestive juices, but in certain specialised areas, known as the islets of Langerhans, it manufactures insulin, the hormone which makes it possible for the body to utilise sugar. *Diabetes mellitus* or ordinary diabetes is a chronic disorder usually caused by a deficient secretion of insulin. The unused sugar accumulates in the blood and acts as a poison, which, in extreme cases, sends the patient into coma and may—indeed, in former times, usually did—result in death. The treatment of diabetes was revolutionised by the discovery of the hormone insulin by Banting and Best in 1921. On the whole, diabetes is more severe in young people than in the elderly, but with correct treatment it is possible for all cases to lead a perfectly normal life except for dietary restrictions and insulin injections. Not to be confused with *Diabetes insipidus* (**P43(2)**).

DIET.

When considering diet, and the effect it has on our health and well-being, there is more to it than just the things we eat. We must also know about what our body does with the food, and it would be unscientific not to acknowledge the effects of our psychological make-up and our nutritional beliefs on what we eat, what we do with it, and how well (or ill) we feel as a result.

For example, a deep-rooted conviction that brown eggs or free-range poultry are better for us than white eggs or intensively reared birds is entirely unsupported by any evidence. However, if we believe such a thing sufficiently, we will not only eat the "better" ones, but we will feel happier and more secure afterwards, and this is likely to make us healthier. Food fads can occasionally be dangerous, as when extreme vegetarians become ill through lack of certain vitamins (*e.g.* B_1) which are present only in the foods they exclude. But this is so rare, even among strict vegetarians, that such danger can virtually be ignored. On the whole (and vegetarianism is probably a good example of this) food faddism often leads to a sense of health and well-being in the believer, and should not be attacked by the rest of us for that. It is an accepted fact that personal misfortune, even when it is severe, is more easily withstood by those with strong religious conviction than by others. In the same way, a firm attachment to a theory of what is good for you can produce a feeling of well-being and genuine good health, when another person on exactly the same food intake will not feel so fit. These factors—religious belief, food faddism, or the bedside manner of a kind or persuasive doctor—are commonly dismissed by free-thinking people because they are not "true" or "real." All three, however, can materially affect our health just as can a shock, a personal tragedy or being in love. The trouble starts, and the magic ceases to work, when adherents declaim their beliefs as *ex cathedra* truths and expect the rest of us to swallow them as wholly (or holy) as they do.

Thus there are genuine *facts* about food, and fallacies too; and as well as these there is a no-man's-land between in which one man's fact is another man's fallacy (see also **Part III**).

The basic constituents of any diet are protein, fats, carbohydrates, water, vitamins, minerals, salts, and indigestible roughage. All are chemicals whose structure and function are reasonably well understood. Even the mystical differences between fine table wines, so beloved of the connoisseur and gourmet, are reasonably well understood in chemical terms. Perhaps that is a pity.

Much nonsense is talked, especially by nutritionists, about minimal daily requirements. In general terms, however, requirements can be described in terms of how many calories there are in the total intake of proteins, fats, and carbohydrates per day, and how these are distributed between the three classes of food. The other substances mentioned above are only required in trace or small amounts except for water; and roughage is only required as a mechanical stimulus to bowel movement.

During the process of digestion (described on **P34–5**) all proteins are split into their constituent amino acids; all carbohydrates are split into their constituent simple sugars and most fats are converted into fatty acids and glycerol. At this stage, and not until this stage, all these simpler building bricks derived from the three classes of food are absorbed into the body proper, and taken to the liver and other tissues. Here they are "metabolised." That is to say they are either burned as fuel for the various processes of the body; or they are built up again into proteins, fats, and carbohydrates of the special kinds the body needs. They will either be used to rebuild structures suffering ordinary wear and tear or they will be stored. Many of them will be converted into a different class from the one they came from when they entered the body. For example, excess carbohydrate is converted into fat; or if there is a shortage of carbohydrate, some will be made out of the protein amino-acids which would normally have been used for tissue growth and repair. Thus it is only a generalisation to say that dietary carbohydrates are fuel and proteins are for building bodily structure. The body can convert one into the other, and spoil the calculation.

There is a great deal of confusion in people's minds about *energy*, and that is why the word *fuel* has been used above in connection with carbohydrates. The lay person uses energy as a term meaning something which allows us to leap about, running and jumping and skipping and dancing, and which keeps us from getting tired and run down. Thus, the food industry tells us, we need potatoes or breakfast cereals for these activities or for a hard day's work. This is a deliberate commercial confidence trick, and the scientist is largely to blame. He originally handed out the word energy to an eager food industry and an unsuspecting public, forgetting to explain that he meant it in the strictly scientific sense of fuel for bodily processes. It simply is not true that more potatoes, or more cornflakes will make you more active. Indeed the reverse is the case, and after a certain point they will only be converted into fat and reduce your activity. The nutritionist measures energy as calories, which are units of heat, and it is certainly true that you must eat enough of these each day if you wish to remain alive, let alone active.

All the three main classes of food provide calories, and in an ordinary well-balanced diet about 15% are provided by protein. Carbohydrates produce most of the remainder. Each gram of fat contains about twice the calories of a similar quantity of carbohydrate. We simply eat less fat than carbohydrate, because fat has a "high satiety value." It takes away the appetite for more. Proteins are mostly found in meat, fish, eggs, cheese, and milk. However, there is quite a lot of protein in many predominantly starchy foods like bread, and such grains as wheat, rice, and corn. Carbohydrates are mainly found in bread, potatoes, sugar, pastry, sweets, and so forth. That is one of the words which fortunately seems to be used by both scientists and laymen in much the same sense.

Some substances are absolutely essential to the body if life is to continue, even if they are only needed in trace amounts. These are substances which the body's own factories (like the liver) cannot make for themselves, even if they are provided with the correct ingredients.

One group of such substances are the *vitamins*. Some of these are found in predominantly fatty foods (milk, butter, cheese and so on) and are known as the fat-soluble vitamins—Vitamins A, D, E and K; the others are water-soluble—the Vitamin B group and Vitamin C. All have now been chemically identified, are manufactured and can be bought over a pharmacist's counter. The myth has grown up that if a little is good for one then a lot more will be better and there are a great many vitamin enthusiasts who consume vast quantities of such manufactured products in the belief that by doing so they will induce extra vitality and energy. Unless your diet is unbalanced in some way (a vegan diet may be grossly deficient in Vitamin B12) you will not need extra vitamins—with certain reservations, *see* **Part III**.

Thankfully, most people buy food because they like it, not because it does them good; and provided they have normal dietary tastes they will usually get a perfectly adequate selection of the things we have spoken of as necessary for good health. The main danger in England is to have a surfeit and become overweight. In addition there are certain times of life when conscious attention should be paid to what is necessary. For example babies and nursing mothers have special dietary needs and will hear about them from their Health Visitor or from their Welfare Clinic or Doctor. Elderly people living alone are also prone to dietary deficiencies for reasons ranging from poverty to loss of appetite or inability to look after themselves properly.

Recent surveys have revealed some interesting facts about people's attitude to food and their knowledge of it. For example, half the people asked knew that meat was a source of protein, a third mentioned eggs and a fifth cheese, fish, and milk. But practically no one knew there was protein in bread. Yet in England about a fifth of our daily protein intake comes from bread, and nearly a third from cereals as a whole. Fish is well known as a source of protein, but did you know that on average we only obtain 4% of our daily protein from fish—less than we get from potatoes (5%)? No one seems to know that potatoes are an important source of vitamin C, although fruit and vegetables are well-known sources. Calcium is recognised in milk, but most people forget its presence in cheese. Most people are very confused about iron. Why does everyone think it is mainly in green vegetables, when these are really such a poor source? For our daily requirement of iron we would each have to eat 1 kg. spring greens or peas; or 2 kg. of sprouts! In fact meat provides one of our best sources, and one-fifth of our daily needs is contained in bread.

Since most of the people who read *Pears* live in England let us return finally to our commonest nutritional disease, or our commonest form of malnutrition in these islands: obesity. Call it " being overweight " if you like, but acknowledge that it means being fat. Being fat is not only unattractive and unsightly but it is dangerous to health and carries a high mortality. Ask any life insurance company how they view your chances if you are overweight and you will find they are as worried about it as if you had high blood pressure, or smoke heavily. It is a particularly important cause of heart disease. However, it is very important to know exactly what we mean by fatness. Many girls who are not at all fat think they are, and this leads them to diet unnecessarily. On the other hand there are people who do not appreciate they are overweight. Here is a table which shows what your weight should be according to your height.

If you are overweight according to these tables you need to slim, and the question is how? Answer: by will-power. There is no other satisfactory method than to decide to eat less, and to eat as little carbohydrate as possible. For the time being eat as much meat, fruit, green vegetables, and as much fat as you like, but no sugar, starch, sweets, cakes, pastry, or biscuits, and no eating between meals. And cut down on beer and other alcoholic drinks. In case you are tempted to eat " slimming " foods, be aware that there is no such thing. There is nothing you can eat which will cause you to lose weight, in spite of what the advertisement says. In special cases doctors will prescribe tablets to suppress appetite, but they are too dangerous for general use without supervision, and they do not work as well as will-power. At the same time take more exercise. Walk to work. If you make a real and genuine effort for three months without success, you should ask your doctor for advice. Almost certainly you will have to admit you have not really tried. Good luck! (*see also* Part III).

NUTRITIONAL DISORDERS.

Nutritional Deficiency and Malnutrition.—Until quite recently a consideration of malnutrition would have merely led to an account of how too

DESIRABLE WEIGHTS FOR MEN AND WOMEN ACCORDING TO HEIGHT AND FRAME, AGES 25 AND OVER

Men Height (in shoes 2·5 cm heels)	Weight in kilograms (in indoor clothing)		
	Small frame	Medium frame	Large frame
157	51–54·5	53·5–59	57–64
160	52–56	55–60·5	59–65·5
162	53·5–57	56–62	60–67
165	55–59	58–63	61–69
167	56–60·5	59–65	63–71
170	58–62	61–67	64.5–73
172	60–64	63–69	67–75·5
175	62–66	64·5–71	68·5–77
177	63·5–68	66–72·5	70·5–79
180	65·5–70	68–75	72–81
183	67–72	70–77	74–83·5
185	69–73·5	72–79·5	76–86
188	71–76	73·5–82	78·5–88
190	72·5–77·5	76–84	81–90·5
193	74·5–79·5	78–86	82·5–93

Women Height (in shoes 5 cm heels)	Small frame	Medium frame	Large frame
147	42–44·5	43·5–48·5	47–54
150	43–46	44·5–50	48–55·5
152	43·5–47	46–51	49·5–57
155	45–48·5	47–53	51–58
157	46–50	48·5–54	52–59·5
160	48–51	50–55·5	53·5–61
162	49–53	51–57	55–63
165	50·5–54	53–59	57–64·5
167	52–56	54·5–61	59–66
170	53·5–58	56–63	60·5–68
172	55·5–59·5	58–65	62–70
175	57–61	60–67	64–72
177	59–63·5	62–68·5	66–74
180	61–65·5	63·5–70·5	68–76
183	63–67	65·5–72	69·5–78·5

little food, or a deficiency of certain articles in the diet, produced deficiency diseases at the time of the restriction. For example lack of vitamins of various kinds gives rise to such diseases as rickets, scurvy, beri-beri, and pellagra; and an overall shortage of food to general starvation. These may be considered the immediate or concurrent effects of a poor diet. Modern nutritionists, however, are beginning to be concerned with two more kinds of nutritional disorders; and although the study of both kinds is in its infancy, both will be introduced in this account.

The first deals with the effects of comparatively small amounts of harmful constituents in our diet, introduced either voluntarily or involuntarily, and consumed for a long period of time; and the second with the lasting effects on our adult well-being of nutritional deficiencies in early life even though they have long since been corrected.

When viewed in this light, one or other of these three kinds of nutritional disorder may at this moment be affecting almost every individual in every part of the world, " privileged " or " underprivileged." Let us first define some terms.

Undernutrition, strictly speaking, means a state of affairs in which the quality of the diet is perfectly good. There is the correct balance of the various dietary constituents and all the necessary components are present: but there is simply too little of it. Many hundreds of millions of people throughout the underprivileged world are suffering and dying from this kind of undernutrition, and the simplicity of the problem must be appreciated: they simply need more food of the kind they are at present getting, and which can often be produced locally.

Malnutrition means an imbalance of the various constituents: a relative lack or excess of one or more of them. It usually leads to conditions which are, from the point of view of medical treatment, much more difficult to deal with. And therefore doctors often class them as " more serious."

The diseases of malnutrition range from the widespread protein deficiencies in other parts of the underprivileged world to *obesity* in our own better-off industrial countries, which is usually due to excess carbohydrate. Make no mistake about it: obesity (or being overweight) is a widespread disease of nutritional imbalance, and it kills. It is the commonest form of malnutrition in (for example) England and America today, and is a consequence of the sophistication of our diet in modern times. Between one-fifth and one-tenth of the population of the United States is more than 20% overweight, and to be 10% or 15% overweight is almost the rule nowadays in people over thirty. There are high authorities in the world of nutritional science who attribute all this overfed malnutrition to the consumption of refined sugar, or sucrose. They say it is not only the amount of refined sugar we put in our tea or on our breakfast cereals, but also the amount in sweet cakes, biscuits, drinks, chocolates and sweets, and so forth. For some people it adds up to a phenomenal quantity each day. According to this school of thought we are not so much suffering from a surfeit of carbohydrates or starches, but from this single sugar, sucrose. It is interesting to reflect on the recent banning of the artificial sweetener, cyclamate, by many governments. This substance, having been used extensively throughout the world as an apparently harmless non-fattening substitute for sugar, was suddenly banned in America because in very large doses (equivalent to the amount taken in hundreds of cups of coffee per day for a long time) it was found to produce cancer in rats. It has never been shown to do humans any harm, whereas the effects of sugar in producing an overweight population, thereby indirectly kill tens of thousands of British people each year. This is a fascinating example of the difficulties confronting our legislators in making balanced judgments when deciding to ban a foodstuff, a drug, or an artificial fertiliser.

Much the most widespread form of malnutrition, however, is a variety protein-lack which is part of a collection of nutritional diseases known as *Protein-Calorie Deficiency*. In very large underprivileged areas of the world, the childhood population receives such an inadequate diet that children live continuously on the brink of nutritional disaster. It only requires a small extra restriction or stress to topple them over into one of the clinical conditions to be described. At this stage they cease to be merely hungry. They become nutritionally ill. Sometimes the force which produces the disaster is a community catastrophe like a famine, an earthquake, or a war. Sometimes it is a family catastrophe like the loss of a lactating mother or a parental delinquency. Parents abandon young children as often in Africa as anywhere else. Sometimes the clinical nutritional disease is unmasked by a common childhood illness like measles, or gastro-enteritis which the well-fed child would have overcome. The starved child reveals his malnutrition instead and frequently dies. When the precipitating cause of the " epidemic " of malnutrition is a war or other national calamity, our newspapers and television screens carry distressing pictures of thin skeletal, pot-bellied children, and the conscience of a few is touched. It is insufficiently realised that these scenes can be witnessed anywhere in the continents of Africa and Asia, and in large parts of Central and South America any day of the week in normal times. The war has not been the cause, but is only the precipitating factor which has revealed the chronic malnutrition in more children than would normally exhibit it openly.

Protein-Calorie Deficiency is a collection of different kinds of childhood malnutrition. Some are due predominantly to deficiency of protein and are collectively called Kwashiorkor, a West African word meaning " red-haired boy " (see below). Others are mainly due to a severe deficiency of overall foodstuffs and are called *Marasmus*. But in any real-life situation the severe *mal*nutrition of Kwashiorkor exists side-by-side with all gradations between itself and the severe *under*nutrition of Marasmus, so that many intermediate forms of " marasmic kwashiorkor " are described. In kwashiorkor the child is typically listless, apathetic, whining, with a reddish discoloration of the hair, a peeling, scaly skin, and with much extra fluid in his tissues causing œdema. He is so listless as not even to be hungry. In marasmus the child is ravenously hungry. He is extremely thin and " starved " looking and is quite a different picture.

There is good reason to believe that even when protein-calorie deficiency is successfully treated, there will always be some lasting restriction of mental function, particularly if the malnutrition occurred as early as the first year of life. This is especially true in situations of appalling poverty in towns, where thousands of babies are not breast-fed because their mothers are at work. Many of them die. Some of them are no heavier than their birth weight at one year of age. Breast feeding in an underprivileged community is an essential insurance for childhood health and survival.

Two new avenues of nutritional inquiry were mentioned at the beginning of this section. The impact of very long continued intake of refined sugar over many years on our bodily health is an example of one of them. Scientists and others are also becoming alarmed at the effects of modern food additives when taken, even in small amounts, over a long period. These additives include colouring matter, decolourising chemicals, taste " enhancers," and so forth, which are present in everyone's diet in a " civilised community." We are as unable to avoid a constant dosage with them as if they had been added to our water supply. It is, however, difficult to strike a balanced attitude. It is one thing to suspect that these additives are harmful and quite another to prove it. Naturally if any of them are shown to produce harm in animals given reasonable quantities they are invariably withdrawn. But in practice it is extremely difficult for animal experiments to mimic the conditions of human intake, especially as the human life span involves eating the substance concerned in small quantities for several decades. Thus it is easy to postulate the harmful effects of monosodium glutamate (a very common taste enhancer) but practically impossible to prove the question either way. It is not sufficient to condemn " chemicals." All natural foods consist of chemicals, and so do we. *See also* **Part III**.

The other new topic in nutrition is more soundly based on animal experiment. It has been repeatedly found that if animals do not grow quickly enough at certain early periods of life, they not only become small, but they remain smaller than they should be even when they are subsequently given as much as they like to eat. This is true of all animals and birds so far studied. For example, if rats are suckled in large families it is found that they are smaller by the time they are weaned (3 weeks of age) than those suckled in small families. The interesting thing is that if they are then given as much as they want to eat for the rest of their lives, the small animals from the larger families never catch up to the others. Whereas if their growth is not restricted until later in their " childhood," full " catch-up " is possible soon after normal diet is resumed. In other words there is a critical time in early life when growth can be permanently affected. At the moment it is difficult to know whether the same is true of humans and, if so, when is our period of vulnerability. There is some suggestion that the corresponding critical period in humans is during the last part of gestation in the uterus, and the first year or so of postnatal life. This new idea may turn out to be very important for world nutrition. Since there will not be enough food for all the children all the time, it may become important to concentrate our aid to underprivileged countries on certain sections of the population only. It may be a good idea to see that pregnant mothers and small babies are specially fed. In this way we may be able to put off the periods of inevitable malnutrition until a time of life when it is recoverable. Such a plan would also go a long way to safeguarding the development of the brain which also occurs mostly at the same early time of life.

We shall now describe some of the better-known nutritional deficiencies, bearing in mind that vitamin deficiencies are virtually unknown in the better-off countries. No one in England need spend money buying vitamins, as has been emphasised in the preceding section. Vitamin deficiency can still occur, however, in elderly people living alone and not having a well-balanced diet. It also occurs for similar reasons in alcoholics, vagrants, etc., and very occasionally in small children.

Beri-beri is a group of diseases usually confined to the Far East where a diet of polished rice results in a poor intake of vitamin B_1 (thiamine). In one form there is œdema (*q.v.*); in another the peripheral nerves are affected leading to tingling and numbness. A similar condition is occasionally seen in alcoholics and diabetics. Treatment is with thiamine, and with other vitamins too, since most sufferers are going short of more than one.

Pellagra is found among maize-eating populations and is due to a deficiency of several vitamins including niacin, another member of the B group of vitamins. There is dermatitis on exposed skin, and soreness of the mouth and tongue, with gastro-enteritis.

Scurvy is due to vitamin C deficiency. In children bone growth is affected. At all ages there is bleeding into the skin (bruising), impaired wound healing, mental depression, and anæmia. Most fresh fruit and vegetables contain vitamin C and a diet containing these prevents the disease.

Vitamin A deficiency is commonly found in children in some underprivileged countries. It causes permanent blindness, with thickening opacity and dryness of the whites of the eyes leading to ulceration of the eye. Beyond a certain stage, therefore, a child's sight cannot be saved. The only real hope is prevention, with an adequate diet.

Rickets, another disease of early childhood, is caused by deficiency of vitamin D. Bones are not properly calcified, and their softness leads to deformities of the legs and many other bones. Vitamin D can either be eaten in the diet or produced under the skin under the influence of sunlight. Therefore rickets commonly occurs when both the diet and the sunlight are inadequate. It was once very common in industrial England, and is still to be seen very occasionally there and in impoverished urban communities in the United States.

DISEASES OF THE ENDOCRINE GLANDS.

Glands are structures or organs which manufacture secretions (except for *lymph glands* which are not glands at all and should be called *lymph nodes*). The secretions are of two main kinds. The first are passed down tubes, or ducts, or are secreted directly into the hollow organs, and act locally. Good examples are the salivary glands which make saliva and pass it down ducts into the mouth for digestion of its contents and lubrication. These are *exocrine glands*. The second kind have no ducts, and secrete their product straight into the blood stream. This secretion is called a *hormone* and it is carried to all parts of the body by the blood where it acts at a distance on some remote part. These are the *endocrine glands* or *ductless glands*, and a number of them will be discussed in this section.

The first hormone, or "chemical messenger," was discovered by the British physiologist Starling in 1904, but the effects of removing some of the endocrine glands were known centuries before when removal of the male testes (castration) was practised to procure a form of manpower safe for the harem, to salvage a good male alto voice for the church choir, or to convert a rooster into a more eatable capon.

Anterior Pituitary.—Many of the endocrine glands do not act as separate autonomous organs in spite of their great differences. They are organised into a well-disciplined band by a "master-gland" called the anterior pituitary. Somebody once called it the "conductor of the endocrine orchestra" and the phrase is still repeated *ad nauseam* in students' examination papers. The pituitary, consisting of its two parts, anterior and posterior, is not much bigger than a pea and it sits right in the middle of the skull, centrally beneath the brain and joined to the brain by a short stalk. This astonishing tiny nodule of tissue produces at least eight important hormones.

One of these is *growth hormone*, which is necessary for normal growth, and also has an influence on insulin. An excess causes *gigantism* and *acromegaly*, often coinciding with diabetes, and too little results in a form of dwarfism. Three others, known as *gonadotrophic hormones* regulate the cyclical and other activities of the reproductive organs and lactating breast. Another, *thyrotrophic hormone*, regulates thyroid activity, *Adrenocorticotrophic hormone*, or *ACTH*, as its name implies, looks after the activities of another important endocrine gland, the adrenal cortex. And there are several others.

Hypopituitarism, including *Simmonds' disease* and *Sheehan's disease*, results from destruction of the anterior pituitary. It is extremely rare, and is usually associated with difficult childbirth involving very severe bleeding. There are disturbances of all the functions mentioned above, particularly thyroid and adrenal failure (*q.v.*) with upset sexual function. Treatment is by replacing the lost hormones.

Hyperpituitarism, including *gigantism* and *acromegaly*, results from over-activity of the anterior pituitary, and is usually due to a tumour or overgrowth of the gland. In acromegaly the growth hormone is produced in excess over a long period of time in an adult. This results in overgrowth of all the organs except the brain, and it is characteristic to find enlarged extremities—feet, hands, and jaw. In gigantism the same has occurred during childhood before the bones have stopped growing and the result is a person who may be 2 m tall or more.

Posterior Pituitary. The posterior part of the gland is really a quite separate gland. The main hormone it produces is concerned with the excretion of urine by the kidney (antidiuretic hormone). Deficiency of the hormone results in *Diabetes Insipidus*, not to be confused with *Diabetes Mellitus* or "sugar diabetes." In diabetes insipidus, the patient produces enormous quantities of dilute urine. He consequently has a prodigious thirst and consumes astonishing quantities of fluids. Treatment is by replacing the missing hormone.

Thyroid. The thyroid gland in the neck secretes an iodine-containing hormone called thyroxine. Excess of it causes *hyperthyroidism*, *thyrotoxicosis*, or *Graves' disease*. Lack of it produces *cretinism* in the growing child or *myxoedema* in the adult. Thyroxine is concerned with the metabolic rate of cells throughout the body, or the rate at which they work, as well as with the proper growth of developing tissues, especially the brain. Too much thyroxine as in thyrotoxicosis leads to over-activity, warm sweatiness in an over-excitable patient whose pulse is rapid and who is eating ravenously to try to replace the wasted energy. In spite of his appetite he is very thin, and he often has bulging eyes for a reason not understood. Treatment is by drugs which neutralise the thyroxine or by cutting out some of the gland. A *cretin* is a child usually born with insufficient thyroid. He is destined to grow poorly, and to mental subnormality of a permanent and distressing kind. If the condition is diagnosed soon after birth treatment with thyroxine can avert most of the trouble. In myxoedema, thyroxine is deficient in an adult. They become slow in all their bodily processes, the hair thins and their flesh is puffy with a dry, wrinkled skin. Treatment is by thyroid replacement. *Goitre* simply means enlargement of the gland. It may be accompanied by overactivity or underactivity, or with little functional change. One variety (Derbyshire neck) occurs in areas short of iodine in the soil and drinking water.

Adrenal Cortex. The adrenal or suprarenal glands sit, as the name implies, one on top of each kidney. There are two distinct parts: the cortex or outside which secretes steroid hormones, and the *adrenal medulla*, or core, which secretes adrenalin. There are many different steroid hormones in the adrenal cortical secretion, which look after such divers matters as sodium and potassium balance, sexual function, the reaction of the body to stress, and the regulation of sugar levels. *Addison's disease* (not to be confused with Addisonian anæmia) results from adrenal cortical insufficiency, and is often due to destruction of the gland by tuberculosis. There is weariness, malaise, pigmentation of skin creases and mucous membranes. They are short of sodium and have excess potassium. Treatment is with cortisone (replacement of the missing hormone) and by extra salt by mouth for the lack of sodium. *Cushing's* disease is due to excessive adrenal cortical function, and sometimes also occurs in patients treated with cortisone for other purposes. They have a striking redistribution of fat in the face, neck, and trunk, with stretch marks similar to those acquired by most women during pregnancy. The facial obesity makes them "moon-faced," and female patients may suffer masculinisation with deepening of the voice and hirsutism.

Testis. The male testes, as well as producing sperm are also endocrine glands producing steroid hormones known as androgens. They are mainly concerned with maintaining secondary sex characteristics. At the time of puberty the controlling secretions from the anterior pituitary begin to appear and androgens are produced. There is a whole range of rare disorders, resulting in everything from precocious puberty to delayed puberty. It should be born in mind that the normal time of puberty can vary by several years from one boy to another.

Ovary. The human ovary has two functions: to produce ova, or eggs; and to produce two hormones, oestrogen and progesterone. These functions begin at puberty, one of whose features in the female is the onset of menstruation, or menarche. Just as in boys, the timing of normal puberty is very variable, but on the average, girls achieve puberty before boys. As social conditions improve, the age of menarche is getting younger generation by generation. All the secondary sex characteristics are under the control of the ovarian hormones which are released in response to the appropriate anterior pituitary hormones. The changes which occur in the womb and elsewhere in the intervals between menstrual periods and the periods themselves are controlled by a cyclical or rhythmic secretion, first of oestrogen and then of progesterone, by the ovary. This cycle is upset by pregnancy to allow the development of the embryo. It can also be upset by taking certain combinations of the two hormones by mouth. These can prevent the formation of ova, and are a popular form of contraception. In late middle age, the ovaries lose their function, the menstrual cycles cease to occur, and reproductive life is at an end. This is called the *menopause* or "change of life," and is sometimes accompanied for a time by distressing symptoms due to a temporary imbalance between oestrogen and progesterone. Many sexual functions, however, continue well after the menopause into old age, and these can include a continuing libido or sexual desire.

Parathyroid. Four tiny parathyroid glands are buried behind the thyroid gland and are responsible for regulating the body calcium and phosphate. They are therefore particularly important for the building and maintenance of bones and teeth. Since a proper calcium level in the blood is necessary for muscle (including heart muscle) contraction, and for correct functioning of nerves, disorders of the parathyroids can give rise to muscular spasms as well as loss of bone calcium. The latter can result in fragility and fractures. Overactivity of the glands leads to too much calcium and the formation of stones especially in the kidney.

Pineal. We end this section with a mystery gland. Like the pituitary it is small—about the size of a pea—and sits well back at the base of the brain. It was endowed in ancient times with metaphysical properties all of which remain speculative. In fish and lizards and certain lower vertebrates it is a kind of third eye, and receives light. In higher mammals, like ourselves, it is so far from any source of light that it could scarcely do so. It can be removed without harm. Indeed it normally becomes calcified and inactive about the time of puberty, and its position seen on X-rays of the skull can be a good guide to whether the brain is being pushed to one side by an abnormal mass.

DISEASES OF THE URINARY SYSTEM.

Everyone knows what kidneys look like—in fact, the term "kidney-shaped" is used to describe other objects. Within the kidneys the blood-vessels carrying waste materials subdivide and finally end up in little coils or glomeruli through which waste products are filtered into the other system, the system of tubes which, beginning as tiny cups around the glomeruli, become larger and larger until they join the ureter passing out at the root of the kidney, the hilum, a point at which both the veins and tubes enter and leave. The kidneys, of course, lie one on each side in the loins, so that if one puts one's hands on the hips and then slides them farther back they will cover the area over the left and right kidney. The ureters pass down on each side to the bladder, which is the storage tank of the products excreted by the kidneys, and lies in the mid-line down low in the abdomen; it is somewhat pear-shaped, and at its base in men there lies the prostate gland—a gland which apparently has few functions but can be a nuisance. Its only known function is that it adds something to the semen from the testes without which the semen would be sterile. Then, from the base of the bladder a single tube, the urethra, passes to the outside. One can, in fact, visualise the urinary system as a capital Y, in which the two upper limbs are the ureters, the place where they meet is the bladder, and the single limb at the foot is the urethra. Clearly, then, there may be diseases of the kidneys, of the ureters, of the bladder, of the prostate gland, or of the urethra.

The amount of urine may be increased or diminished. It is *increased* in the following conditions: after drinking excess of fluids; after taking drugs (known as *diuretics*) which are given to increase the flow; in diabetes of both types—mellitus and insipidus; in some types of chronic kidney disease; and finally, in emotional states of excitement. It is *decreased* in the following conditions: acute nephritis; any disease in which fluid is being lost in other ways, such as diarrhœa or sweating in fevers; when the fluid intake is small; and when both ureters are blocked by stones. Passing a great deal of urine is known as *polyuria*, passing very little as *oligouria*, passing frequent small amounts is simply called *frequency*. Normally, the urine is acid, but in infections of the bladder it may become alkaline owing to decomposition by bacteria. Abnormal substances, or normal substances in abnormal quantities, may occur in the urine and give the doctor an indication of what is wrong. In fact, urine analysis is a very important part of medical diagnosis. Thus urea is a normal content of urine which is increased in fevers, wasting diseases, or diabetes; the amount of urea is to some extent a measure of the degree of tissue breakdown. Uric acid is found in small quantities in normal urine, but the amount is increased in fevers and after an attack of gout (uric acid is important in the causation of gout, but has nothing at all to do with rheumatism in general, so one may disregard the advertisements in the popular Press showing unpleasant pictures of joints with sharp crystals of uric acid which are alleged to cause the pain of rheumatic disease). Oxalates are not ordinarily found in urine, but, since they occur in such foods as rhubarb and strawberries, and some people are unable to deal with them, such individuals may develop stones or have pain on passing urine after eating oxalate-containing fruits.

Two very important substances which ought not to be in normal urine are albumen and sugar. Albumen is a protein, and its presence in the urine indicates that the filters of the kidney are leaking—they are allowing protein to pass out which ought to remain in the body. Albumen is easily tested for, and its presence may indicate kidney disease or nephritis as it is usually called by doctors. On the other hand, small amounts of albumen occur in fevers and in nervous conditions—*functional albuminuria*. Sugar, too, should not be present, but its presence does not necessarily indicate diabetes; for small amounts may occur in nervous conditions or in some people after taking large quantities of carbohydrate.

Blood in the urine may give it an appearance which varies from bright red to a dark, smoky colour. It is found in many diseases: acute nephritis, stone, tumours, poisoning by certain drugs, infections such as bilharzia or malaria, papilloma (*i.e.*, non-malignant tumour of the bladder), after injury, in high blood-pressure, scurvy, and blood diseases. Sometimes it occurs for no known reason at all.

It will be remembered (or if it is not, you can look it up on **P28 (1)**) that streptococcal infection of the throat may cause in some people disease of the valves in the heart or endocarditis. In such cases, although the germ is found in the throat, it is not found in the heart or indeed anywhere else in the body. *Acute nephritis* occurs in the same circumstances, with the sole difference that the kidneys instead of the heart are affected. The disease appears to be an allergic reaction to the toxins of the streptococcus. The patient, often a child, has a sore throat (and even this may be absent or fail to be noticed) or sometimes the infection may arise in other sites: after scarlet fever, erysipelas, burns, and disease of the ear. A few days later there is headache, vomiting, pain in the loins, slight rise in temperature, and especially typical is *dropsy* or œdema. This begins in the face, first around the eyelids, and then affects the ankles; later it may become more general and affect the rest of the body. Blood and albumen are found in the urine, and the blood-pressure is slightly raised. The outlook is usually good if the kidneys are rested by reducing the amount of protein taken in and also the amounts of salt and water. When this is done, the inflammation soon goes and no permanent harm results. In other cases, however, if treatment is inadequate or the condition severe, the symptoms may go, but the albumen found in the urine persists. This means that permanent damage has been done, and although there may be nothing else to show for many years, *chronic nephritis* develops. In this case, the blood-pressure continues to rise, and since the filters of the kidneys no longer work efficiently, urea, the principal waste-product of the body to be excreted in the urine, is retained in the blood and only small amounts escape from the system. Hence chronic nephritis sooner or later leads to heart failure or hæmorrhage in the brain from the rising blood-pressure, or to the form of poisoning known as *uræmia* which results from the retention of urea in the blood. Uræmia may come on suddenly or gradually, but ends in progressive coma, drowsiness, and unconsciousness. There may be convulsions similar to those of epilepsy, high fever, and difficulty in breathing to complicate the picture.

Another type of nephritis which seems to have nothing at all to do with streptococcal infections, and the cause of which is completely unknown, is *nephrosis*. Developing in early adult life, its onset is insidious, and the patient first shows signs of œdema in his white and puffy face and the swelling of his legs. (It should be said here that if you have swelling of the ankles or elsewhere, you would be foolish to jump to conclusions; for such swelling is common in many diseases—in heart disease, in allergic conditions, in neurotic illness, and even just from hot weather.) When the urine is examined in a case of nephrosis it is found to be full of albumen and, as in chronic nephritis, the blood urea starts to rise. The end-results of nephrosis are the same as those of chronic nephritis and depend upon the damage originally done.

The modern diuretics of the thiazide group help to control the œdema and, provided enough healthy tissue remains, remove both the fluid and the waste-products.

In recent years there have been considerable advances in the development of the artificial kidney. Once only used within hospital, artificial kidneys or dialysers as they are known, can now be used in patients' own homes, thus obviating in some cases long journeys to hospital twice a week for treatment. Dialysis is a relatively temporary measure; renal transplants now offer real hope to many sufferers although there are far more suitable recipients than there are potential donors.

Pyelitis is an infection of the pelvis of the kidney, that is to say, of the part where the ureter leaves the kidney. It is usually caused by the bacillus coli, which is normally present in the body, or by the streptococcus. These germs may reach the ureter through the blood-stream or may pass upwards from the bladder. Obstruction anywhere in the urinary tract which causes the urine to stagnate is liable to cause pyelitis. Symptoms come on suddenly, with high fever, pain in the loin (the infection is usually on one side only, and is commoner in women), and pain in the abdomen. When urine is passed there is a burning sensation, and it is passed frequently and in small amounts. On examination, the urine is found to be highly acid and full of bacillus coli or whatever the causative germ may be. Pyelitis is fairly readily treated by the antibiotics or sulpha drugs. Plenty of fluids should be given and the urine made alkaline by administration of alkalis.

Cystitis means inflammation of the bladder, either acute or chronic, and its causes are much the same as in the case of pyelitis. There is pain over the lower abdomen, frequency, and sometimes slight fever. The treatment is as for pyelitis. *Urethritis* is an inflammation of the urethra, with burning pain on passing water and frequency. The most serious cause (although it can usually be easily dealt with now) is gonorrhœa. But non-specific urethritis is common, and in this case various germs or none may bring about pain and frequency; there is often a large neurotic element. Urethritis should be regarded as probably due to gonorrhœa, which has already been discussed elsewhere, when there is a thick, creamy discharge from the penis or discharge in women following sexual intercourse with an infected person.

Kidney stones or Renal calculi sometimes form, and, as in the case of gall-stones, what causes them is not certain. They may be caused by disorders of metabolism—that is, in the inability of the body to deal with calcium, proteins, uric acid, and other products; or by vitamin deficiency, obstruction in the urinary tract, and urinary infections. But when a stone or stones are formed various events may occur: thus it may remain in the kidney and cause no symptoms; or it may cause repeated attacks of pain, infection, and blood in the urine (hæmaturia); or it may completely block the passage of urine from the kidney to such a degree that it degenerates and becomes useless; or, lastly, it may pass into the ureter, and when this occurs very severe pain, known as *renal colic*, will occur. A stone passing down the ureter into the bladder may become stuck in the urethra, although this is uncommon, since a stone small enough to get down the ureters is likely to be capable of manœuvring through the rest of the tract. In fact, about 80–90 per cent. of stones are passed spontaneously. Stones not passed spontaneously may have to be removed by operation, but whether this is undertaken or not depends on various factors, such as the general health of the patient, the amount of trouble caused by the stone, and the health of the other kidney —for it is dangerous to operate on one kidney unless one is sure that the other is functioning efficiently.

If a stone blocks the passage of urine on one side for any length of time *hydronephrosis* may result, in which the part where the ureter enters the kidney swells with the retained urine. Ultimately much of the kidney may be destroyed by the back-pressure. The same effect may be produced by kinking of the ureter or anything else which causes obstruction. Sometimes children are born with hydronephrosis, and when the dilation is due to kinking of the tube the condition may be intermittent, with attacks of renal colic during which only small amounts of urine are passed; this is followed with relief and the passage of large quantities.

Tumours and Cysts. The kidney may also be the site of tumours and cysts which produce pain in the loins, sometimes a lump over the kidney which can be felt, and blood in the urine. Cancer of the bladder is a serious condition in which the bladder may have to be removed, so the urinary flow has then to be directed elsewhere. Either the ureters are brought out on to the skin surface, a procedure known as *cutaneous ureterostomy*, or they are implanted in the large bowel, so that the urine flows out with the fæces. This is described as *uretero-colostomy*.

There may also be benign tumours of the bladder or *papillomas*, which are soft and bleed easily; a great deal of blood is passed, but there is usually little or no pain. In this, and similar, diseases of the bladder examination of the inside of the organ is carried out by means of a cystoscope, a thin tube which is passed up the urethra and has a small electric light at the end which enables the surgeon to see what is going on. Instruments may also be passed through the tube, and simple papillomas can be cauterised. Similar instruments are used in the examination of the stomach (gastroscope) and the bronchial tubes (bronchoscope). When some obstruction in the outlet of the bladder or in the urethra occurs the bladder, of course, fills with urine, which cannot be passed, and very painful dilation occurs. In this case an attempt may be made to pass a catheter, a thin rubber tube, into the bladder to relieve the tension, or if this fails a *suprapubic cystotomy* is performed—an incision is made in the abdomen over the bladder and a tube inserted into it, through which the urine escapes. This is ordinarily a temporary expedient, and later when the patient's health has improved an attempt will be made to remove the cause of obstruction. The most common cause of such obstruction is *enlargement of the prostate gland* at the base of the bladder, which surrounds this area and the beginning of the ureter. About 40 per cent. of men over sixty have some degree of obstruction due to this cause, and about 20 per cent. of these require operation. The gland is about the size of a walnut, and, as we have seen, its function is to supply part of the fluid which makes up the semen, the male sex secretion. Enlargement of the prostate may be benign or malignant, and, although nobody knows just why, such benign enlargement tends to occur in most men in later life. There may be no symptoms, but characteristically there is frequency during the day and the need to get up at night to pass water. The flow of urine being impeded by constriction of the urethra, the passage is less forceful than normal, and there is a tendency for dribbling to occur. If the obstruction is severe and not relieved the back-pressure may be transmitted to the ureters and kidneys, resulting finally in kidney failure and uræmia. The prostate, except in cases of very mild enlargement, has to be removed either through the abdomen or through the perineum (the part of the body lying between the sex organs and the anus). Sometimes, in less serious cases, it is possible without an incision to cut away the obstructing part by an electrocautery inserted, as is a cystoscope, through the urethra. Prostatectomy was once a serious operation, all the more so because the patient was usually elderly and not in good condition, but new techniques and the use of antibiotics have greatly improved the outlook.

Cancer oj the Prostate is always serious, but if discovered in time it can be operated on successfully. The gland, of course, has to be completely removed; in inoperable cases, or in patients unfit to stand operation, the tumour may be treated by means of female sex hormones, which cause it to shrink and may prolong life by some years.

DISEASES OF THE NERVOUS SYSTEM.

The nervous system consists of the Central Nervous System and the Peripheral Nervous System. The brain and spinal cord make up the former. The latter consists of the nerve fibres by which the Central Nervous System is connected to all parts of the body. Human beings have a more complicated brain than any other animal species, but it is only its complexity which makes it different from the brains of other mammals like rats and pigs and cows. We do not have the largest brains, since whales, for example, have much larger ones. Ours is not even the largest for the size of the body. Mice and dolphins and several other creatures have relatively larger brains when compared with body weight. Furthermore the cells and materials of which our brain is composed are virtually identical with those in other mammals, and its living properties are also the same.

Before describing some of the diseases of the nervous system it will be helpful to say a little about how it is made and how it works. Each human brain probably contains about ten thousand million (10,000,000,000) nerve cells and perhaps four or five times this number of supporting "glial" cells. Each nerve cell has many long thin branching projections, called dendrites, rather like the branches of a tree, leading to many thousands of "twigs" for each single nerve cell. At the end of each "twig" there is a special structure called a *synapse* by which contact is made with other nerve cells. It is through these connections that very large numbers of nerve cells give information (or send impulses) to each other so that they can be co-ordinated. As well as these dendritic branches, each nerve cell gives off one large trunk called the *axon*, down which final messages are sent as the result of all the information it receives from its dendrites. Some axons are many feet long. Some end in another synapse, by which the outgoing message is passed to yet another nerve cell. Some axons, those of the peripheral nerves, end directly on organs like muscles or glands, instructing them and making them work.

Messages are passed along dendrites and axons as electrical impulses. These are generated in the nerve cell " body." They are modified according to information received from other nerve cells and propagated down the axon. It is this superficial resemblance to a series of electrical cables which has given rise to comparisons of the brain with a telephone system or a computer, and as long as it is realised how infinitely more complicated each brain is than any known computer, the comparison is not a bad one. However, the brain generates its own electric power from the fuel brought in its own blood supply; and no spare parts or spare cables are available if the originals should get damaged, except in peripheral nerves. Furthermore the contact of one nerve cell with another through a synapse is not an electrical contact, and neither is the contact between a nerve and the muscle or other organ it is controlling. In both cases the connection is chemical. Thus when an electrical impulse arrives at the end of the nerve fibre, a chemical is released into the gap between it and the next nerve or organ, and it is this chemical which carries the stimulus forward. There is also an arrangement to neutralise the chemical transmitter when the impulse has been transmitted. So the resemblance to a telephone exchange or computer can sometimes be misleading.

Many of the nerve axons which transmit electrical impulses are clothed in fatty *myelin sheaths*, a little like the plastic insulation around an electric wire. Here again the resemblance is only partial, since the myelin sheaths are interrupted at regular intervals and these gaps in the insulation play an important role in transmitting the impulse. One of the important functions of the non-nervous *glial* cells of the brain is to manufacture and maintain the myelin sheaths.

Most of the functions of the brain are quite unknown, and even the ones we know about are very poorly understood. It is assumed to be the organ of higher mental function, of the mind and intellect; but there is surprisingly little evidence for this, and no one has any idea what physical structures or mechanisms subserve these functions. The brain is known to control all bodily functions by means of *motor* and other nerves which carry impulses from the brain outwards to all parts of the body. Sometimes these are under our voluntary control; mostly they are involuntary, reflex or automatic. Reflex actions are the result of impulses passed inwards from the body towards the brain by means of sensory nerves. Information arriving in the brain about the various sensations like heat, pain, touch, position, the need for saliva or gastric juice or even the thought or smell of food, are acted on in the various " centres " in the brain. These send out instructions down the " motor " or " secretary " nerves which instruct the muscles or glands to take appropriate action. Thus a *reflex* has a " sensory ending " which appreciates some sort of sensation. This is converted into an electrical impulse which is sent towards the brain or spinal cord along a sensory or " afferent " nerve. The impulse arrives at a " centre " in the central nervous system which co-ordinates all the relevant information and issues instructions. These travel as impulses outwards, along " efferent " nerves towards " effector " organs like muscles or glands, and an appropriate action occurs automatically. The pathway from sensory ending to effector organ is called a *reflex arc*. Many reflex activities are partly under voluntary control, although mainly automatic. If you touch something hot you will automatically withdraw your hand. But if it is a hot china cup which has cost you a lot of money, you are capable of overriding the tendency to drop it, at least for a time. Breathing is automatic, but it can also be controlled, again at least for a time.

Clearly the brain is a very delicately organised piece of machinery, and its cells are extremely specialised for their job. Achieving this kind of specialised perfection brings many difficulties, however, and the brain cells have become highly dependent on the proper functioning of the other body systems, especially the blood circulation, the respiratory system, and the systems regulating the detailed nutrient composition of the blood. Failure of these systems, even for a very short time, can damage the nerve cells. Nearly all death, from whatever original cause, is produced this way, by an ultimate interference with nerve cell function.

We have already mentioned that the brain and spinal cord are unable to repair or replace any components which get damaged. The vulnerability of the brain is even more obvious when it is realised how easily damage and destruction can occur. For example, unless a rich supply of oxygen and glucose is continuously arriving in the blood stream, brain cells will cease to function in a few seconds and will die in a few minutes, and they can never be replaced. This is in marked contrast to other tissues of the body. The leg, for example, may carry on for over half an hour without any blood at all because the muscle and other cells can find other ways of surviving. Thus the brain can be permanently damaged if the blood contains insufficient oxygen (through asphyxia), insufficient glucose, or if the blood supply is blocked or if the blood pressure falls. All these are likely to happen to any of us at any time, and so there are elaborate mechanisms trying to prevent them occurring. Most of the subject of physiology is concerned with the mechanisms designed to protect the brain, and most of us ultimately die because they eventually fail. One of the clever features of the body design is that all the mechanisms which protect the brain from a supply failure are controlled by the brain itself. Thus the brain has itself been made to control the heart beat and the breathing and the many other systems which are needed for its own survival.

In all that follows concerning disease of the nervous system it will be seen that the effects of neurological disease on the patient are the direct result of something going wrong with one of the structures or mechanisms we have described.

Diagnostic Techniques in Neurology. The doctor has many ways of testing the nervous system, most of which test its various functions as outlined in the introduction. Thus tests of sensation, muscular movement and reflexes of all kinds as well as the special functions of taste, smell, vision, hearing, speech and intellect play a part. A great deal can be learned about the brain by *arteriography.* In this test a radio opaque substance is put into the arteries supplying the brain, and an X-ray picture taken immediately afterwards shows up all the blood vessels. *Ventriculography* is an X-ray examination after gas has been introduced into the brain cavities or ventricles which are normally filled with *cerebrospinal fluid*; *myelography* is an X-ray of the spinal cord after a radio-opaque substance has been injected into the space between the spinal cord and the bony vertebral canal which houses it.

The development of the EMI Scanner, a relatively new concept in diagnostic radiology, has now made most of those "invasive" diagnostic techniques unnecessary. The equipment needed is expensive and is presently only available at a very few centres. Sometimes *radioactive isotopes* are put into the blood stream and carried into the brain where they can be detected from outside the skull by counters. *Electroencephalography* measures the electrical waves generated by the brain by placing electrodes on the scalp. *Electromyography* does the same for muscles.

Consciousness and Unconsciousness (*Coma*). Everyone knows what consciousness is until he tries to define it. Full consciousness is generally taken to imply not only wakefulness but the total complement of human mental faculties. In clinical medicine, however, something less than this is usually meant. For example a demented person, or one whose memory is lost (*amnesia*), or one whose powers of speech are lost (*aphasia*) may still be "conscious." There is really a continuous gradation between full consciousness and coma, passing through drowsiness and even "stupor" in which condition a patient can be aroused from coma but sinks back into it when left alone. Many different things can cause coma ranging from swelling of the brain, compressing it in its rigid box of bone, to disorders in other body systems resulting in a failure to provide for the brain's needs. Examples of the first are bleeding within the brain or *brain tumours*, both of which occupy space and can only do so by producing compression. In the second category are asphyxia preventing oxygen from reaching the brain, lack of glucose in the blood, circulatory failure in which there is insufficient blood, or insufficient blood pressure. Fainting is a comparatively minor example.

Sleep and Insomnia. Nobody knows what causes sleep, why it is necessary, and how it helps. It is quite different from coma or even stupor, since as much oxygen and glucose is necessary asleep as awake. Insomnia is experienced by everyone at some time, and for some reason is very distressing if it persists. There are three forms: failing to get to sleep, intermittent wakefulness, and awaking early. Nearly all insomniacs sleep more than they think. They should eat light evening meals and avoid stimulants like tea and coffee after mid-day. Elderly people should realise they need less sleep. Being cold or having a full bladder can be a cause. Or simply not being tired. Sedative drugs are a last resort, but they can be useful in "breaking the habit" of wakefulness. Obviously there may be psychological factors such as anxiety and excitement. *Narcolepsy*, or a true inability to keep awake is comparatively rare. Both narcolepsy and insomnia are really extreme examples of what all normal people suffer from occasionally.

Headache is man's most common pain. Here again we must distinguish between the very common varieties of comparatively trivial significance and the rare ones due to serious causes. Some headaches are due to continuous tightness in muscles of the scalp, and are often "nervous" or psychological in origin. Others result from nose blockage and congestion, sinus problems, eye strain, toothache, etc. Migraine is a special kind and will be described below. Very occasionally indeed headache is due to serious disease like brain tumour. Most headache results from "living it up" or being "run down," or both. The headache of alcoholic hangover is probably due to dehydration. It can often be avoided by consuming a great quantity of water (a half litre or so, before going to bed, but few people are prepared to do this in the circumstances. Be careful when using aspirin, which is a useful remedy for headache, since it is very dangerous for people with stomach complaints like gastritis or gastric or duodenal ulcer. Occasionally aspirin makes the stomach bleed, and this can be so severe as to kill. A safer pain killer is paracetamol. Be particularly careful in treating "hang-over" headaches by patent fizzy remedies. They are very effective, but often contain large quantities of aspirin described in small print by its proper name as acetyl salicylic acid.

Migraine. This is a very special variety of "sick headache" and requires special treatment under medical supervision. It has many different forms, but usually there is a definite sequence of events. An attack often starts with some alteration of vision. The patient has shimmering blind spots or other visual disorders. This is followed by a well localised severe headache which may end in nausea or vomiting. The whole thing is caused by a poorly understood disorder of the blood vessels. There are special drugs, mostly derivatives of ergot, which are effective, especially if used when the first signs of an attack appear. Although there is a direct physical cause for an attack, it is also certain that some of the trouble is psychological tenseness. People with migraine are often rather anxious, striving and perfectionist people. Also it has been noticed that attacks are much less frequent when the necessary pills are being carried available for use. However, as with all other conditions which are partly " psychological " in origin they are none the less distressing for the patient. It simply means that the treatment is also partly psychological in encouraging him to come to terms with his problems.

Menière's Disease is one of the conditions in which the organ of balance in the middle ear is affected, giving rise to *vertigo*, a form of giddiness. It usually begins in middle life in the same sort of person who sometimes has migraine. There is buzzing in the ears and some intermittent loss of hearing as well as vertigo. During an attack the patient may be unable to walk because of his loss of balance, and nausea and vomiting are common. Treatment is by special drugs, and occasionally an operation on the ear is necessary.

Epilepsy is a symptom, not a disease, which is common at all ages but especially children. It has been attributed to St. Paul, Julius Caesar, Napoleon, and (with more justice perhaps) to Dostoyevsky. Many varieties of attack occur often in the same patient, the commonest and best known being the *grand mal* or major seizure. In this the patient falls down unconscious and rigid and the jaw is clenched, so that there is danger of the tongue being bitten. This so-called tonic phase is followed, within a minute or so, by a clonic phase in which the limbs contract rhythmically. The attack ends with the patient going limp and gradually recovering consciousness, a process which may take up to an hour. Occasionally the patient has a brief warning, most often an indescribable feeling in the stomach. There are two common forms of minor seizure, one occurring mainly in children and the other more often in adults. The common minor attacks in children are often called *petit mal* or *absence*, which well describes the instantaneous and brief loss of consciousness often unaccompanied by any change in posture. Recovery is equally instantaneous. On the other hand, in the other forms of epilepsy which arise from various parts of the brain, but especially from the lobe under the temporal region, there is often a warning similar to that which may precede a major seizure. In these cases the patient shows only confusion, no definite loss of posture, but automatic activity such as fumbling with buttons, muttering, and grimacing. Following these attacks there may be a quite prolonged period of confusion in which the patient may wander away and occasionally may be violent. Criminal acts are very rarely carried out in this state.

A large number of people have had one or two fits in their lives, particularly at times of physical or psychological stress. " Fever " or " Febrile " convulsions (often called teething fits in the past) are extremely common in young children and are often thought of as something different from epilepsy since the attacks rarely continue in later years. This form of epilepsy and some cases of *petit mal* are the only forms in which hereditary factors are important in the causation, and these are the least serious forms of epilepsy. They are very rarely associated with serious physical or psychological disturbances. Most other forms of epilepsy are due to a scar or other area of brain damage. It is a proportion of these cases which develop the psychological disturbances that are occasionally very serious.

Not every patient who has had one or two fits need necessarily take regular anticonvulsant drugs; that is drugs which damp down the abnormal excessive activity of the brain that leads to the attacks. Many drugs are available of which the most important are phenobarbitone, phenytoin and clonazepam. The succinimides and troxidones are effective only against minor seizures. The choice is a matter of skilled medical judgment. Epileptics often find it difficult to get work because of the reluctance of employers to take on someone who may be more prone to accidents and whose fits may distress other workers. Obviously there are some jobs which epileptics should not do because of the danger involved (from, for example, moving machinery), and they should not drive a car. A few cases are so severe that work is almost impossible, but employers have a duty whenever possible to employ these people whose mental health may suffer greatly if they are made to feel outcasts and who ordinarily are as efficient, or even more so, as the next man. It is also hoped that employees will become less prejudiced about epilepsy as the general public become less ignorant about medical matters. In this way epileptics will come to be accepted in all those kinds of employment for which they are well suited. If some of the famous men who have suffered from this disease had had to rely on the charity of some employers today the world would have been much the poorer, although possibly we could have managed without the generals.

Congenital Malformations. The proper shape of the brain and spinal cord is achieved quite early in development by about the thirteenth week after conception. During this time very slight changes in the fœtal environment can produce disastrous malformations. The drug thalidomide, for example, operated on other body systems while they were passing through this phase of construction. Some viruses can do the same thing. Most malformations are without known cause, but it is certain that something went wrong at this very early stage, and it only needs a very minor interference with the normal process to do the permanent damage. At about this time the bones of the spine are beginning to enclose, or form a roof over the developing spinal cord. Sometimes they fail to complete the process, resulting in *spina bifida*. If the coverings of the cord protrude through the defect, this is a *meningocele*, and if the cord itself protrudes it is a *meningomyelocele*. The whole protrusion may be covered with skin. but if it is not, the cord soon becomes infected. The effect on the patient is variable, according to the amount of damage to the nerve fibres in the cord, and there are varying degrees of paralysis and loss of sensation below the area involved together with loss of bowel and bladder control. Much help is often obtained from surgical repair, but many cases remain in a distressing condition always, and the only really useful attack on the problem is research to find the cause and prevent it happening. The same is true of the *malformations of the brain*. In one of these, hydrocephaly, the narrow channel is blocked which transmits the cerebrospinal fluid from the chambers within the brain where it is secreted to the outer coverings to be taken back into the blood stream. Blockage of the channel (or aqueduct) results in distension of the brain by fluid, enlargement of the head, and mental retardation. Sometimes a by-pass valve can be inserted to restore normal fluid circulation with very gratifying results. This aqueduct can also be blocked by later disease (meningitis) or injury with the same result. Sometimes the brain fails to form altogether (*anencephaly*), and the child fortunately does not survive after birth.

Cerebral Palsy is a term covering many varieties of *spastic child*. It is thought to be due to brain damage at birth or in early infancy, and is depressingly common. Although a great deal can be done for the spastic (they are often of normal intelligence) the only satisfactory approach is prevention and this means expensive research into its causes. Donations, encouragement, and offers of practical help, please, to the Spastics Society 12 Park Crescent, London W.1.

Motor Neurone Disease. This is a group of distressing diseases usually occurring in people over 40, in whom the parts of the brain and spinal cord degenerate which look after muscular movement. The group includes *Amyotrophic Lateral Sclerosis, Progressive Muscular Atrophy, Progressive Bulbar Palsy*, and *Primary Lateral Sclerosis*. The results are paralysis or weakness with wasting of the muscles of the body, including those concerned with arms, legs, breathing, speaking, etc. Nothing whatever is known of the cause, and the only treatment is that designed to alleviate the results of the disease. It is uncommon, but this is little comfort to the sufferer.

Parkinson's Disease, paralysis agitans, or the "shaking palsy" is a common condition which begins in later life over the age of 50. It has three classical features: shaking (or tremor), muscular rigidity and loss of those automatic reflexes which look after bodily posture. This results in a stooping shuffling gait. Later there is a mask-like loss of facial expression with diminished eye blinking. It is a progressive disease, but it progresses so slowly that 10 or 20 years may elapse between its onset and incapacity. A good deal can now be done to help these patients with drugs, the most recent of which at the time of writing is levodopa. Occasionally patients have benefited from surgical destruction of small areas of diseased brain. It is important to remember that many elderly people have some tremor of the head or hands called *Senile Tremor*, and this is *not* Parkinson's Disease. It is merely one of the features of achieving advanced seniority as a citizen. The Parkinson's Disease Society, of 81 Queen's Road London SW19 8NR, looks after patient welfare, supports research and publishes a regular newsletter.

Chorea. This is a group of diseases in which there is involuntary muscle movement, weakness, and emotional instability. There will be clumsiness, awkward gait, twitching of limbs, face, hands, trunk, or tongue. They include *Acute Chorea or St. Vitus' Dance* occurring in children from 5 to 15, *Hereditary or Huntington's Chorea* occurring in a well-defined genetic pattern and beginning later, between 35 and 50. *Tics* or habit spasms are not part of these diseases but are often of psychological origin. They are usually eye blinking, head shaking, shoulder shrugging, or any other sudden gesture of limbs or face.

Stroke Illness or Cerebrovascular Diseases. Strokes are due to diseases of the brain's blood vessels which either burst or get blocked. The same blood-vessel disorders cause heart attacks by blocking the coronary arteries supplying the heart. Strokes and heart attacks together kill more people than any other single cause including cancer. They account for one death in every five. Perhaps less is known of the cause of this disease than is known about cancer, and much more research is needed to find out if it is to be prevented. The cause of the commonest cancer (of the lung) is now known and it can be prevented by stopping smoking. Perhaps the prevention of strokes and heart attacks will mean an equally difficult abstinence from all those foods which make us fat. At least it is known that being overweight leads to death from these causes, just as smoking may lead to death from lung cancer.

If any artery supplying blood to any part of the brain is blocked, the territory supplied will die; and the bodily functions for which that part of the brain is responsible will cease. The process is called *infarction* of the brain, the dead area being an *infarct*. The blockage is usually due to thrombosis (*see* **P31**) of the blood within a vessel, a *thrombus* being a rather complicated clot with a structure of its own. The underlying cause is the arterial disease, atheroma (*see* **P30**) together with stagnation of the circulation. About one blockage in ten is due to a small piece of a much larger thrombus in the heart chambers being flung into the blood stream and impacting in the distant vessel in the brain. This is *cerebral embolism* (*see* **P30**). If the area of dead or infarcted brain is not too large the patient will recover from his unconsciousness, but will be left with permanent loss of function (paralysis, etc.) related to that part of the brain.

When a blood vessel supplying the brain bursts, this causes *cerebral haemorrhage* or apoplexy. The vessel may be on the surface (*subarachnoid haemorrhage*) or in the depths of the tissue (*intracerebral haemorrhage*). Strokes tend to occur in older people, because the associated arterial disease is a product of age and high blood pressure. Occasionally a subarachnoid haemorrhage occurs in a younger person with an unsuspected malformation of the arteries of the base of the brain known as a *berry aneurysm*. This is a small berry-sized blown-out balloon due to a defect in the wall of the vessel. Berry aneurysms can often be treated surgically. Intracerebral haemorrhage carries a very poor outlook, however, since much brain tissue is often destroyed by the escaping blood, especially the deep tissues responsible for the vital functions. Haemorrhage within the brain cavity can also be caused by injury (*see concussion and compression*, **P19**).

Inflammatory Diseases of the Nervous System. The membranes covering the brain are called the meninges. Inflammation of these, nearly always by blood-born infection or infection following injury, is called *meningitis*. Cerebrospinal or spotted fever which used to be common and very much feared was only one variety caused by a germ called "meningococcus." It is now rare. Almost any other germ may cause meningitis, and when the germ is susceptible to one of the antibiotics it is usually treatable. It will usually be necessary to identify the germ by taking a sample of cerebrospinal fluid from a convenient space around the spinal cord in the lower back. When the disease is caused by the tubercle bacillus (*tuberculous meningitis*) the problem is more difficult because the patient is often not so obviously ill until the later, less treatable stages. *Cerebral abscess*, or abscess of the brain is very serious because it occupies space in the closed box of the skull and compresses the brain, as well as being a destructive process. It may arise due to an infected piece of tissue or pus being carried to the brain in the blood stream from a distant site in the lungs or heart. When the brain or cord tissue is itself inflamed it is called *encephalitis* (brain) or *myelitis* (cord) or *encephalo-myelitis* (both). These conditions are comparatively uncommon and are often due to infection with viruses rather than bacteria. Some have no known cause, possibly because many viruses are difficult to identify.

Multiple Sclerosis or *Disseminated Sclerosis* or the "creeping paralysis" as it used to be called, is the most important of the "*Demyelinating diseases*," in which the myelin sheaths wrapped around the nerve fibres disintegrate. This only occurs in small areas, or plaques. It is as if drops of acid have been placed at random throughout the brain and spinal cord and have dissolved away the insulating sheaths over (new) penny sized areas, leaving the wiring (the nerve fibres) running through as before. But this small loss of insulation is enough to spoil the carefully graded electrical impulses; and thus the bodily function subseved by those fibres is lost. So there are apparently random losses of sensation, movement, bowel or bladder control, speech, etc., according to which collection of nerve sheaths happen to have been attacked. Thus it is that no two cases are alike and many are difficult to diagnose. Many have even been labelled malingerers in the early stages, so bizarre are the signs and symptoms. The disease is not a killer. It smoulders on year after year, often beginning in the late teenager and getting steadily more incapacitating over many decades. No one can predict how quickly it will deteriorate, and in some cases many years will go by before yet another episode of more myelin sheath destruction. Neurology has more than its share of completely mysterious diseases. This is perhaps the most mysterious, and it is not very uncommon. The many years of disability in each individual case make it at least as disabling as far commoner diseases which run a much shorter course. There is no more enhumbling disease for the medical scientist, but the faith must remain that, with more and more research this crippling condition too can be prevented. Diagnosis, at present difficult in the early stages of the disease, may be made easier following the recent (1976) development of a test which can be carried out on a blood sample and which depends on a white cell "rosetting" phenomenon around added measles-infected cells from tissue cultures. The Multiple Sclerosis Society, 4 Tachbrook St., London S.W.I. looks after patient welfare, supports research and is very deserving of your donations. As in all other crippling conditions there are countless ways in which you can help the victims at no great expense. Visit them. Help with their shopping and other day-to-day needs. Take them out. And even write to your member of parliament demanding a better deal for the disabled who are still, in spite of recent legislation, among the most down trodden and deserving of our neighbours.

Brain Tumours. The brain is no exception to the rule that any cell in any tissue of the body can suddenly begin to disobey the body's rules regarding its growth and multiplication. A totally unknown mechanism governs how many cells of a certain type there ought to be and calls a halt to cell multiplication when this number is reached. Every now and then one of them turns a blind eye and goes on dividing, and the result is a tumour, or lump, of anarchic cells which obey no rules. Tumours are commonest in cells which normally go on dividing throughout life, in order to replace those lost by wear and tear. Examples are the cells lining the air passages in the lung, or the alimentary tract in the stomach or large bowel. Fortunately for the brain there is little cell division once it has grown. Nerve cells cannot divide at all in adult life, and the supporting glial cells only do so in response to injury. Therefore primary brain tumours are much less common than those elsewhere. Also many brain tumours like many of those elsewhere, are benign or "innocent" tumours. They are not cancerous, and need only be removed for the patient to be completely cured. The brain, however, is at two major disadvantages compared with other tissues when it comes to tumours. One is that all tumours as they grow take up space, and space in the skull is already fully occupied. Thus even an innocent tumour can compress the brain within its rigid box of bone and become most dangerous until it is removed. The second disadvantage is due to the very large blood supply of the brain. Cancer in other parts of the body spreads partly by sending small pieces of itself to other tissues by way of the blood stream, and those tissues like liver, lung, kidney, and brain which have a big blood supply naturally receive more than their share of other tissues' tumour. These secondary deposits, or *metastases*, cause compression and other trouble in the brain much more frequently than the brain's own primary tumours. Indeed convulsions or other signs of brain disorder may be the first indication that there is a primary tumour in the lung or breast or elsewhere.

Head Injuries are dealt with in the section on Physical Injuries (**P19**), where a great deal of space is given to the effects of most First Aid emergencies on the proper functioning of the brain and spinal cord.

Diseases of Peripheral Nerves. Compared with the nerves of the central nervous system (brain and spinal cord), the peripheral nerves are comparatively rarely affected by disease. They have some similarities of structure with central nerve fibres in that their fibres are often covered with myelin sheaths and are arranged in bundles. A special feature, however, is that they are enclosed by connective tissue sheaths and it is probably these which allow a peripheral nerve to grow again, or regenerate, after it has been cut or damaged. Central nerve fibres are unable to do this. After *injury of a peripheral nerve* the part away from the centre is cut off from its parent cell body and it dies. All function, whether motor or sensory, is lost. But in the course of many months the central surviving part grows into the connective tissue sheaths which act like tubes to guide the new nerve to its destination. Provided the cut ends are close enough together and correctly aligned, and provided enough fibres reach their correct destination, good functional recovery is possible.

A disorder of a peripheral nerve is called a *neuropathy* and means nothing more than that. There are many kinds. One of the most distressing is *trigeminal neuralgia*, again fortunately rare. The trigeminal or fifth cranial nerve has a motor and sensory territory on the face. In this condition there are paroxysmal episodes of extremely severe pain which may resist all treatment except destruction of the nerve itself with consequent facial paralysis and loss of sensation. At the other more trivial extreme are the occasions when a leg "goes to sleep" or gets "pins and needles" after crossing it and pressing on a nerve for too long. *Bell's Palsy* is sudden loss of function of the seventh cranial nerve and there is again paralysis on one side of the face which usually recovers in time. Some bacterial diseases especially leprosy, invade the nerves themselves. Chronic alcoholism may affect the nerves, as may diabetes, probably by interfering with the nutrition of the nerve cell. So may exposure to arsenic or lead or an unpleasant nerve poison which may contaminate cooking oil known as TOCP, or triorthocresylphosphate.

Muscular Dystrophies. These are a series of diseases of muscle in which there is progressive wasting and weakness of muscle, the causes of which are entirely unknown. They are divided up according to the age of onset and the muscles involved. *Duchenne's muscular dystrophy* occurs in the first decade of life. It affects most of the muscles eventually, including the heart muscle and those concerned with breathing, and so the outlook is not good. Other forms are inherited.

Myasthenia Gravis. This is a strange disorder of the mechanism which transmits instructions from nerve to muscle at the "neuromuscular junction." There is extreme weakness of muscles after they have been used, resembling in some respects the weakness following the administration of curare, or "arrow poison." It is often associated with disorders of the thymus gland. The drug neostigmine reverses the neuromuscular disorder and removal of the thymus is also sometimes effective.

MENTAL DISEASES.

Psychosis.

Mental diseases are divided into psychoses (*i.e.*, insanity) and neuroses (*i.e.*, what is ordinarily known as "nerves"). Psychoses, in their turn, are divided into organic and functional—those due to physical disease and those in which no physical cause has been discovered. In point of fact, the distinction into organic and functional is rather meaningless; for if we accept the modern view of psychosomatic medicine which regards the body and mind as a single unit it is clear that organic disease brings out psychological defects which were already there and that functional disease must, in the final analysis, be the result of physico-chemical causes, even if this is brought about by mental stress.

Organic disease results from poisoning of the nervous system by such poisons as alcohol, carbon monoxide, or lead; vitamin deficiencies, as in pellagra; infections such as syphilis; and degeneration of the brain, either primary or as a result of poor blood supply. In all cases its main symptoms are confusion, signs of other disease, and loss of memory. Alcohol leads to various conditions: in *delirium tremens* heavy bouts of drinking end in delirium ("D.T.s"), confusion, hallucination—although not necessarily of pink elephants or rats. It is a serious disease, but the outlook is much improved since it was discovered that injections of concentrated vitamins B and C can help. In more chronic cases *Korsakov's syndrome* manifests itself in the form of mental deterioration and memory defects. There can be little doubt that previously existing mental instability is a predisposing factor in these conditions. The same may be said of *general paralysis of the insane* or G.P.I., and in this case the immediate cause is syphilitic infection of the nervous system. Nevertheless, of all the patients with chronic syphilis, only a small number get syphilis of the nervous system. G.P.I. is typically associated with the usual symptoms of organic disease and delusions of grandeur; for example, a man with this disease may go out and buy several expensive cars in one day. However, it is not uncommon to find G.P.I. associated with severe depression—again the picture depends on the previous personality. The association of the above symptoms with a positive Wasserman test —which proves the presence of the spirochæte in the blood—indicates neurosyphilis. When the lower centres of the nervous system are affected the disease is known as *tabes dorsalis*, in which there is difficulty in passing urine, limb pains, inability to stand when the eyes are closed, and finally difficulty in walking. The patient becomes paralysed and ultimately bedridden. Treatment is with penicillin.

People age at varying rates, so that some are hale and hearty at eighty or ninety whereas others are old at sixty or seventy. They present the typical picture of old age: "second childishness and mere oblivion, sans eyes, sans teeth, sans everything." When this condition, which is caused by degenerative changes in the brain or by defective blood-supply resulting from arterio-sclerosis, is pronounced we speak of *senile psychosis*. There is mental confusion, forgetfulness, and delusions, in which the previous personality defects which we all have are accentuated. Such patients may have to be put under special care, but the process is largely irreversible.

The functional psychoses are two in number: schizophrenia and manic-depressive insanity. In *schizophrenia*, which, when it occurs in early adult life, is known (or used to be known) as *dementia præcox*, the symptoms are bizarre. There are delusions and hallucinations, so that the patient often believes himself to be persecuted and hears voices which say objectionable things to him. Sometimes the schizophrenic is wildly excited, and in other cases he goes into a state of stupor which is described as a catatonic state. Although the disease is described as functional, recent discoveries seem to suggest that there is some derangement of the blood chemistry. Treatment by insulin and the new tranquilising drugs has revolutionised the outlook in this admittedly serious disease. Indeed, some cases of psychosis are more easily treated than neurotic patients, since the former respond to physical methods, whereas the latter may require fairly prolonged psychotherapy (psychological treatment) and are less responsive to drugs.

In cases which do not respond to other methods, the brain operation known as *leucotomy* may be performed. Leucotomy is also performed to alleviate intractable pain, as in incurable cancer, but some of the ataraxic drugs (tranquilisers) are probably equally useful for this purpose. Leucotomy involves the severing of the connecting nerve fibres between certain areas of the brain, and the results are often favourable, but in fact the operation should be performed only in cases where the outlook is otherwise very poor; chronic severe neuroses, frequent attacks of manic depressive psychosis, severe chronic depression, and schizophrenia which has not responded to other forms of treatment. The operation reduces anxiety, fear, aggressiveness, and agitation, but may result in the less-desirable symptoms of apathy, impaired judgment, lack of self-control, and loss of initiative.

Schizophrenia developing in later life is likely to be less dramatic in origin, and the delusions tend to be more systematised—that is, they take a persistent form, which does not change from day to day. This type of the disease is known as *paraphrenia*. In those beyond middle age the rare but dangerous condition described as *paranoia* may develop in which there are no hallucinations and the only symptom is a completely systematised collection of persecutory delusions, which on recital may sound entirely convincing even to the ordinary doctor. Such people are dangerous precisely because they are so plausible, and they fill the ranks of the litigious, the trouble-makers, and the political and religious eccentrics. One such patient known to the writer spent his life in a mental hospital from which he had parole, employing this to form a society propagating highly eccentric sexual and political beliefs. It says little for the intelligence of the general population that his meetings were invariably crowded out (although, of course, when one reads of the people who apparently believe that the various fictitious families on radio or television really exist, one need not be surprised at such examples of communal dottiness, even if one may despair of democracy).

Manic-depressive insanity is characterised by mood swings in which the emotions alternate between wild elation without obvious cause and equally causeless depression. However, the picture is not quite as simple as this; for phases of mania or excitement may occur without depression obviously following, or there may be a single attack of depression with no manic phases. The disease may be absolutely incapacitating, or there may be periods of relative normality; typically, then, manic-depressive insanity is a disease of alternating moods. The depression responds to electroconvulsive therapy or E.C.T., but mania is less responsive to treatment. However, it ordinarily remits of itself. Sometimes in middle age *involutional depression* occurs, and this in the vast majority of cases is cured by E.C.T. As in the case of schizophrenia drugs are increasingly used for depression. *See also* **Part III.**

Neurosis.

The main neuroses are anxiety neurosis, hysteria, and obsessional neurosis. *Anxiety neurosis* is an illness in which the main symptom (as the name implies) is anxiety. There is fear which rationally the patient knows to be groundless; there may be anxiety attacks, in which the heart pounds, the patient feels he is going mad, is unable to sleep, and worries "for no reason at all." In hysteria, anxiety is largely absent, but there may be apparently physical symptoms ranging from paralysis of the limbs to blindness, deafness, inability to write, and lapses of memory (the so-called hysterical fugues or loss of memory). Typical of *hysteria* is the fact that the patient is less worried by his symptoms than would be expected from their apparent seriousness; this is what the early psychiatrists described as "la belle indifférence." The reason for the indifference is simple—it is that the paralysed individual *wants* to be paralysed, the blind *want* to be blind, the deaf to be deaf (there are none so blind—or deaf—as those who don't want to see, or hear), and the person who doesn't want to write conveniently finds that he cannot.

Generally speaking, neurotic people are suffering from a failure to face up to reality. They are not physically ill and are largely the end result of a faulty upbringing. It is wrong to suppose that the only bad families are those in which the children are ill-treated; much the worst ones are those in which children are spoilt, the parents possessive, and the wrong kind of love is dispensed. Neuroses are the result of a conflict between primitive desires and what the individual has been brought up to believe he should be. For example, before an examination a student may develop a nervous breakdown because he fears failure when he has been brought up to expect success. The excuse, of course, is "overwork"—an entirely non-existent condition. With his breakdown he solves his problem, he avoids the fear of failing and preserves his self-respect: he has been ill. Similarly, the soldier with "shell shock" (another non-existent condition) has a conflict between his sense of duty and his fear of death, which again is solved by becoming ill. Or, to take a final example, a woman feels the duty to look after her ageing mother. But she also wants to get married. So she unconsciously develops a neurosis which says, in effect, "I should like to do my duty in looking after my mother, but unfortunately I am unable to." There is an unconscious rebellion on the part of the mind.

Neurosis, in effect, is not a disease—it is a self-inflicted injury, a form of maladaptation to life. The neurotic, no matter how much he suffers, does not want to get well; he has found some way of getting along, even if a foolish way, and he intends to keep it. Often his symptoms are the sort of excuse that say: "If only I wasn't ill what wouldn't I be able to do!" The neurotic is a person who is different and is afraid to be himself; his problem is a conflict between being "ordinary," "like other people," and being what he was supposed to be.

Obsessional Neurosis is a more severe type of neurotic illness; for although in anxiety neurosis we find such symptoms as phobias—irrational fears of open spaces, closed spaces, animals, and so on obsessional states are characterised by compulsive feelings that certain acts must be performed or certain thoughts thought. In a mild form we all have obsessions: we feel that we must walk on the spaces between paving-stones, that we must touch lamp-posts, and so on. But when this type of compulsion gets to the stage when we must go back several times to make sure the lights have been put out, when we feel the need to wash our hands every few minutes, become obsessed with numbers on cars or dates on coins, then it becomes a nuisance and requires treatment. The obsessional neurotic is a person who feels that life must be controlled; he is "a creature who moves in predestinate grooves—he's not even a bus but a tram." His symptoms are an attempt to devise self-imposed rules which will control the unconscious desires of which he is so afraid.

All that remains to be said is that many of these conditions are treatable or, if not treatable so far as cure is concerned, they can at least be relieved. The world is full of people who are "different"; there are those who are different in the right way, who should take satisfaction from their achievements, and those who are different in the wrong way, who should seek expert advice.

Lastly, although not truly appropriate to this section, we include brief notes on neurasthenia psychopathic personality, and masturbation.

Neurasthenia is an entirely imaginary condition allegedly due to exhaustion of the nervous system. Since no such condition exists, we need not bother with it. Neuroses cannot be treated by feeding the nerves (which are perfectly normal). They can be helped by such things as sedatives, but not cured. *Neurosis has nothing at all to do with disease of the physical nerves, so nerve tonics do not exist, and anyone who asserts that they do is a humbug.*

Psychopathic Personality is the term given to anyone who has different standards of behaviour from those generally accepted by society. Some of these unfortunates may be *inadequate*, that is to say, although perfectly intelligent, unable to earn their own living. Others are the *creative* people, who, as in the case of Van Gogh, did many eccentric things but also many productive things—Van Gogh was gifted, or cursed, with an intense sensitivity. Lastly, there are those who have what others regard as peculiar sexual habits. Of the first two classes nothing more need be said, and all that is necessary is to mention certain of the so-called sexual perversions. (When we say so-called the implication is not that none of these forms of behaviour is perverse but that some of them are carried out by otherwise quite ordinary people.) *Sadism* and *Masochism* refer to, in the first place, pleasure in inflicting pain and, in the second, to receiving pain. The pleasure is sexual, and it is incorrect to talk of cruelty in itself as sadism. Sadism is named after the Marquis de Sade, who suffered from this perversion, although he certainly did much less harm in his small way than numerous politicians or generals of our time, and masochism is named after the Austrian novelist Sacher-Masoch, who wrote books which, although unpleasant, were not notably more so than certain Sunday newspapers of today.

Masturbation is sexual self-stimulation. Needless to say, it produces no more *physical* harm than ordinary sexual intercourse—that is to say, none at all, although some people have the strange belief that every act of intercourse weakens the body and it has even been believed that each act shortens life by a specific length of time. This is rather illogical in view of the fact that most of the famous rakes have been noted for their longevity! Masturbation is almost universal in infancy, adolescence, or even in later life when other outlets are not available. It need only be a matter of concern: (*a*) when it is chosen in preference to normal sexual activity, or (*b*) when it is compulsive and excessive, since then it is a sign, not of sexual desire, but of severe underlying anxiety.

DISEASES OF THE SKIN.

The skin in the course of development before birth is particularly closely associated with the nervous system. It is therefore not surprising that so many skin diseases are influenced by emotional states. Other causes of skin disease are infections, glandular disorders, vitamin deficiencies, and the numerous conditions for which no cause has been discovered, but which presumably are due to metabolic disorders.

One of the commonest skin symptoms is *itching or pruritus.* It may accompany many different general diseases, for example diabetes and jaundice. It may also be troublesome during the menopause (the change of life in women), in old age, or in nervous conditions. Sedatives and sex hormones sometimes help the itching during the menopause, and there are ointments which may be useful.

Itching in the region of the anus and genital organs is relatively common. It may be caused by worms, by irritating vaginal discharge, or by sugar in the urine, as in diabetes. The alteration in the normal bacteria of the bowel which follows treatment with various antibiotics also often causes anal pruritus and soreness. In many cases however the itching has some psychological cause. In treatment it is important to avoid ointments and creams which contain a local anæsthetic, because these substances can cause severe allergic reactions if used for longer than a few days, and may thus make the condition much worse. Treatment with a local corticosteroid application is more effective and safer.

Parasites, such as the *scabies* mite or *lice* can cause severe and persistent itching. The scabies mite is very small, and since it burrows under the skin surface, is unlikely to be seen; it is the cause of itching most commonly between the fingers and on the front of the wrists. The itching is worst when the body becomes heated, as in bed. Treatment consists of painting the body from head to foot with benzyl benzoate application, followed the next day by a hot bath. Since scabies is contracted through close personal contact with an infested person it is often desirable for several or all members of a family to be treated at the same time, even though only one of them may be affected. Lice are specialists, one type of which affects the scalp, another the body, and a third the genital area. Head lice are destroyed by lethane, body lice by insecticides and genital (pubic) lice by shaving off hair and washing. Obviously, the clothes, especially in the case of body lice, should be disinfested, by using a hot iron particularly over the seams, which lice (for some inexplicable reason) seem to favour. Apart from the discomfort they cause, lice are dangerous as potential carriers of typhus fever.

Baldness, or Alopecia. is a very common condition, as is manifested by the extraordinary number of preparations advertised as curing it. When many preparations are offered for the treatment of one condition it is a fair judgment to assume that none of them is likely to be effective. There are, in fact, two types of baldness; one, which is much the commoner, is hereditary, and cannot be influenced in the slightest by any treatment, the other, *alopecia areata*, is caused by nervous stress, and would recover in most cases by itself, whether one used a solution of soot and water or the most expensive "hair food." There is no such thing as a hair food, any more than there is such a thing as a nerve food, and although it is probable that hair hygiene may delay baldness, it certainly cannot prevent it. All hair tonics and "foods" are useless, and their uselessness is only equalled by their costliness. Those who have lost their hair and find it growing again after using some alleged tonic are people who have had *alopecia areata* and whose hair would have grown back anyhow. In women the hair often thins out soon after a pregnancy, but a few months later it usually returns to normal.

Seborrhœa is a condition in which there is overactivity of the sebaceous glands. The most usual form it takes is *dandruff*. However, it takes other forms, and those who have dandruff may also have rashes on the face, shoulders, and chest. In these areas there is a patchy, greasy, and often itchy, rash which does not clear up until the primary condition in the scalp is dealt with. The scalp should be washed with one of the modern sulphur-containing shampoos at least twice a week, and the affected parts on the face and chest can be dealt with by the use of a sulphur lotion (*not* on any account by greasy ointments). Seborrhœa is not in itself difficult to treat, but, since the condition depends on over-secretion of sebum, the skin lubricant, treatment may have to be persisted in during the years of early adulthood, when it is most active.

Erythema Intertrigo is, quite simply, the sort of irritation which occurs usually from excessive sweating under the armpits, between the legs, and under the breasts in women. All that need be done is to wash frequently and to dust the affected areas after washing with powder. This is the condition which, in the tropics, is known as "prickly heat" and elswhere as a "sweat rash." In some people *hyperidrosis* or *excessive sweating* is a problem, especially when the sweating is accompanied with body odour—the sort of thing that, according to the advertisements "even your best friends won't tell you." There is little need for anyone in these days to suffer in this way: for the cosmetic firms have produced many highly efficient deodorants which not only control odour but also control the amount of sweating. Chlorophyll, which has been much advertised as removing odours, is effective when applied directly to surfaces which give off an unpleasant smell. It is however ineffective when taken by mouth, and does not prevent body odours. Stale sweat smells bad because it is decomposed by bacteria, and this type of body odour can be largely prevented by preparations containing harmless antiseptic and anti-perspirants.

Erysipelas is an infection of the skin caused by the hæmolytic streptococcus. It begins as a red, raised area anywhere on the body where the germs have been able to enter through a small crack or cut in the skin. The red area advances and spreads over the body until the disease is got under control. Erysipelas is very infectious, and those who look after the patient should wash their hands throughly after contact. At one time the disease used to spread as an epidemic throughout the hospital wards, but this is very rare nowadays. Treatment is, of course, a matter for the doctor.

Chilblains are common in cold weather, especially in those with poor circulation. Ordinarily they occur in the toes and fingers, but may appear on the nose and ears. The part affected becomes swollen, dusky, and there is pain and itching, sometimes leading to ulceration. Protection of the body, especially the hands and feet, from cold is the best and the only really effective way of preventing chilblains. Warm lined gloves and footwear, and arm stockings or trousers should be worn outdoors. Adequate heating of rooms is essential: a temperature between 18° and 21° C is recommended. Most tablets, medicines, ointments, or creams for chilblains are useless. A skin affection caused by heat is rather grandiosely described as *erythema ab igne*, and is frequently seen on the legs of ladies addicted to roasting their legs before the fire. It takes the form of red patches on the front of the legs and can be removed only by avoiding the cause.

Dermatitis means "inflammation of the skin," and therefore the word could be, strictly speaking, applied to any skin disease. In fact the term is used almost interchangeably with the term *eczema*. There are three main types of dermatitis or eczema. The first, *primary irritant dermatitis* results from injury of the skin by some powerful chemical, such as strong alkali or turpentine. The second, *contact dermatitis* is due to sensitisation of the skin to some substance which is normally liable to cause this type of allergic sensitivity; examples are nickel (in jewellery and suspender buckles), epoxy resins, rubber additives, primulas and chrysanthemums, and even ingredients of cosmetics. Contact dermatitis may continue for a long time, even after the patient is no longer in contact with the offending material. The third type is often called *constitutional eczema*. Although the skin is apt to react adversely to various irritants and sensitisers the major part is played by the personality, and there is often a history of eczema, hay fever or asthma in the family. Treatment is more difficult, but local corticosteroids and tar, sedatives and psychological treatment can be of great help. Infantile eczema also belongs in this category, but in most patients it disappears as the child grows up.

Impetigo is an infectious skin disease caused primarily by the streptococcus, but later often infected with staphylococci. It usually occurs on the face, and takes the form of blisters filled with pus on a red base; when the blisters burst their place is taken by yellow crusts. Impetigo is very infectious and easily spread by the fingers, dirty towels, or cloths; therefore, one of the first necessities is to prevent infection of others or reinfection of oneself by avoiding scratching and using a different towel each day, which must on no account be used by anyone else. Treatment is simple with an antibacterial ointment, so the main issue is prevention of contamination.

Sycosis or "Barber's Rash" occurs in men, and is similarly treated.

Urticaria or *Nettlerash* is a familiar skin disease in which itching weals appear on the skin, usually for no obvious reason. It is not infectious, and can be caused by nervous stress, certain drugs, allergy to some foods, or even exposure of the skin to cold. In some people it is possible to write on the skin with a fingernail: the "writing" appears in the form of weals. This is known as *dermographism*; it occurs in many normal persons as well as in many patients with urticaria. The antihistamine drugs are the most useful in the treatment of urticaria. Urticarial swelling of the tongue or throat requires urgent medical attention.

Acne, or "*Blackheads*," is a condition found on the face and shoulders; its appearance is so familiar that no description is necessary. Acne is one of those conditions which is the end result of many factors. There is, first, a greasy skin, the result of glandular upset (which is why the disease usually occurs in adolescence); secondly, there is infection of the skin; and thirdly, there is blockage of the sebaceous ducts, which ordinarily allow the grease from the skin to pass out on to the surface. Since the condition starts with excess secretion of grease, ointments should never be used, and probably the best applications are drying lotions containing some sulphur preparation which inhibits secretion of grease. The face should be frequently washed, and it is possible now to obtain detergent solutions which are both antiseptic and prevent grease formation. In severe cases ultraviolet ray treatment may be necessary.

Rosacea. As has already been implied elsewhere, although the wages of sin may be extremely unpleasant, the wages of extreme virtue may be no less troublesome. Thus *rosacea*, in which the nose and cheeks become red and greasy and the skin coarsened, occurs alike in chronic alcoholics and elderly ladies with no vices other than a preference for strong tea. Both cases are associated with indigestion, since, regrettable as it may seem, strong tea and alcohol are about equally liable to cause the gastritis which may be at the root of this complaint. However, in many patients the chronic flushing is caused in other ways and psychological factors are important.

Lichen Planus is one of the numerous skin diseases which seem to be due to nervous states of tension. It may occur on any part of the body, but is most common on the front of the forearms and legs. The rash takes the form of nodules which are lilac in colour and have a dent on the top; when these disappear a stain is left behind. There is severe itching. Treatment is a matter for a doctor, as it also is in the case of *psoriasis*, a very common disease of largely unknown origin, which is extremely resistant to treatment. It tends to run in families. It takes the form of slightly raised papules, usually on the elbows and knees; typically the papules are covered with dry, silvery-looking scales. Apart from the rash, the patient is usually in perfectly good health and there is no itching. Many drugs have been used in psoriasis, notably chrysarobin, and while it is not difficult to cause the rash (which may occur anywhere on the body) to disappear in one area or even in all areas for a time it has a strong tendency to return.

Warts, or *Verrucae* are familiar enough. They are caused by a virus, and are, theoretically at least, contagious (although having removed many warts, the writer has never found them contagious). Most frequently they are found on the hands, but may occur elsewhere. Treatment is best carried out by a doctor, who will use a cautery, a caustic carbon dioxide frozen into " snow." A curious feature of the common wart is that it can sometimes be caused to disappear by suggestion, which is presumably why so many old wives charms are not necessarily without effect. Different altogether from the common wart is the *plantar wart*, which occurs on the soles of the feet and often causes a good deal of discomfort. It is best dealt with by a chiropodist or in bad cases by a skin specialist since it is highly infectious.

Icthyosis is a disorder of skin formation with which some unfortunate people are born. The oil and sweat-producing glands do not function well and the skin is dry and scaly like the skin of a fish. It is, however, possible to help the condition, which does not affect the general health, by frequent alkaline baths to wash off the scales, and the subsequent use of lanolin to replace the lacking oil. Large doses of vitamin A seem to help in some cases, and there have been reports in the medical Press of cases being helped by hypnosis; this, however, is very much a matter for speculation.

Cancer, Rodent Ulcer, and Cysts. Cancer of the skin occurs mostly in old people, and takes the form of what is described as an *epithelioma.* It is most common on the face or hands, and usually appears as a nodule which breaks down and produces an ulcer. The glands may later be affected, but such cancers can almost invariably be cured unless a considerable time has elapsed during which they have been neglected. *Rodent ulcer* is a form of ulcer which appears on the inner corner of the eye or the side of the nose in old people. It does not spread over the body, but acts by eating into the tissues in the area where it has started. X-ray or operation is necessary, but the outlook is good. *Cysts* on the skin are due to blockage of the sebaceous glands. They may become very large, and are best removed, as they may become infected. They do not turn into cancer, and there is no such thing as " male " and " female " cysts. It does sometimes happen that *moles*, especially of the bluish-black type, may become malignant, so it is perhaps best to have them removed surgically when they exist. *All moles which change in appearance or size should be at once referred to a doctor.*

Skin Grafts.

These are a very complex subject which can be only briefly discussed here. They are used basically for a number of conditions in which large areas of skin have been removed from the body, as in burns or serious accidents. In other cases, as in plastic surgery, grafts may be used to make a new nose, eyelids, and so on. The following are the main types:

Pinch Grafts are small, circular pieces of skin cut from some other part of the body. (The former method of using grafts from another person has been given up almost completely, since such grafts—except in the case of identical twins—never " take.") The small pieces are laid on the area without skin and gradually grow together. *Split-thickness grafts* are grafts removed from another part of the body by an instrument known as a dermatome, which cuts sections about 10 by 20 cm. containing part of the deep layers of the skin.

In *Full-thickness Grafts*, on the other hand, the whole thickness of the skin is removed from elsewhere and applied to an area which has to bear friction or heavy weights, such as the hand or the foot. Lastly, and this is largely used in plastic surgery, there is the *Pedicle graft*, which, unfortunately, although it is certainly the most exciting type, is rather difficult to describe. Briefly, if one, for example, wants to make a new nose, one cuts an area of skin and underlying fat about 5 cm wide and 12·5–15 cm long in the abdomen. One end, however, remains attached so that it gets adequate blood-supply. The problem is how to get this tissue to the nose, and this is done by a complicated process of leap-frog. First, the free end of the graft is attached to the forearm, whilst its " root " remains in the original site, and when it begins to grow and get its blood-supply from the arm, the original " root " is cut. So we now have a " sausage " of tissue attached to the arm. The arm is then lifted to the face and kept firmly in position there until the new free part becomes attached. It is then detached from the arm, modelled to the correct shape, and grows where the nose used to be!

DISEASES OF THE JOINTS.

Rheumatism is a word most doctors wish did not exist. This is partly because they do not understand it, but mainly because it is a condition which strictly does not exist: which is small comfort to the many millions of people who are more or less totally incapacitated by it. The truth is it is used for a hotch-potch of very real diseases, in all of which there is pain and stiffness of what is called the musculo-skeletal system, *i.e.*, the muscles and the joints. It may mainly involve the joints, in which case it should have been called arthritis; or it may involve other structures near the joints like tendons, muscles and fibrous tissue. Joints may either suffer from inflammation or degeneration or both, and the trouble may be acute or chronic or both; so it is easy to see what a mix-up the subject becomes, especially when we must include the joints of the spine as well as the limbs, feet and hands.

A good deal of arthritis used to be due to various germs, but these types are much less common now that the infections causing them have become rarer or better treated. They used to include gonorrhoea, tuberculosis, septic joints, syphilis, brucellosis, typhoid fever, dysentery and so on. The importance of *Rheumatic fever*, which is a reaction to an infection (streptococcal sore throat) rather than being actually caused by the streptococcus, is not because it involves the joints. This arthritis quickly clears up, but there may also be disease of the heart which may be serious and has been described on P28.

Rheumatoid arthritis is a completely different condition in which there is non-infective inflammation of connective tissues throughout the body. In the joints, the normally smooth, lubricated synovial membrane lining the joint cavity becomes scarred, leading to distortion, especially of smaller joints like those of the hand. Another characteristic feature is its capacity to vary in severity from time to time, with a strong tendency to unexplainable periods when it gets better or worse. This makes it extremely difficult to know whether any form of treatment is being useful, since any response may have occurred in any case. As in all diseases which behave like this, especially those in which medical men are also baffled, there are almost as many theories and treatments as there are doctors. It has never been satisfactorily shown to be caused by infection, faulty nutrition, " glands, " emotions, personality disturbance, nor is it convincingly inherited. The best current theory links it with an increased sensitivity reaction, perhaps to the body's own tissues, known as " autoimmunity. " From the patient's point of view there is swelling and deformity of the joints with tenderness on pressure and pain on movement. Treatment involves a lengthy and complicated regime of rest, relief of pain with aspirin, exercises and the application of heat, with attention to general physical and mental health. At some stage adrenal corticosteroids (cortisone and its derivatives) are often tried, but although these can give great relief they have to be very carefully used to avoid very unpleasant side-effects.

Osteoarthritis is another completely different

condition closely related to the normal processes of aging. Therefore it occurs in older people than those with rheumatoid arthritis, and tends to be in larger, weight-bearing joints of the spine, hips and knees rather than in the hand; although the end joint of the fingers is commonly affected. Hard wear and tear, especially that caused by overweight, or injury may be the beginning of it. It is *not* due to diet, and dieting has no part in treatment except in those who need to slim. Physiotherapy, including heat, is helpful. It is not such a relentless condition as rheumatoid arthritis and patients should be reassured about this.

Fibrositis and other vague forms of "rheumatism" are very often manifestations of psychological problems. This does not make them any less real, but it directs treatment towards the mental state rather than to the joints and muscles.

EYES, EARS, NOSE AND THROAT.

Diseases of the *eyes* are very specialised and only very general information can be given here. The most common is inflammation of the conjunctiva causing redness and usually due to infection or some irritant substance or dust. If it persists and leads to hard crusts of yellow pus on waking in the morning, get it seen by a doctor for treatment probably with antibiotics. First-aiders are usually instructed how to remove small particles of grit from under the lids. It is important that these should not scratch the front of the eye—your window on the world—as this may lead to scarring and poor vision. So, above all, do not rub them in. Also, if you are fishing one out of someone else's eye, see it before removing it. Do not have a general sweep round in vague hopes of finding it. If in any doubts, obtain skilled help. Remember the eyes are part of the brain: the only visible part. Perhaps this is why people's eyes are so revealing.

Conditions such as glaucoma, cataract and disorders of vision are beyond the scope of this section.

Foreign bodies in the ears and nose are a constant minor problem with children. In these cases, whether they be peas, beads or peanuts, do *not* attempt to fish them out. They are doing no harm where they are, provided the child can be prevented from fiddling with them. Get him to a doctor who knows far better than you do about the delicate structures of the ear drum or the internal nose just behind the object, and has the proper gadget to get it out.

Sore throats are a nuisance we all have to put up with from time to time. If they last more than a few days they should be treated professionally. Persistent or recurrent sore throats are often due to over-eager treatment with antibiotics not allowing the body to learn how to fight the germs itself. Never prescribe antibiotics for yourself, especially in lozenge form, and only expect your doctor to give them when other measures have failed.

Tonsils and their inflammation may be a problem. It is comparatively rarely that they should be removed, yet every year hundreds of thousands of innocent children are subjected to this ritual cruelty to satisfy the misconceptions of their parents and the greed (or ignorance) of 'some surgeons. Of course there are many children who benefit so much from having tonsils out that the operation (which has real dangers) is worth doing. But please allow your doctor to decide if it is necessary, and do not pressurise him into recommending it. (The same is true of *circumcision*, for which there are no hygenic, and practically no medical indications. If your reasons for inflicting this cruel assault on your little boy are religious or emotional, then please admit it: but do not pretend it is "necessary" or even medically helpful.)

DISEASES OF WOMEN.

The *internal sexual organs* of a woman, like the urinary system, can best be described as shaped like a capital Y. At the tips of the arms of the Y are the female sex glands, the ovaries: the two arms running downwards are the Fallopian tubes: the point where the arms meet is the womb or uterus: the single leg of the Y is the vagina. These are the *primary sexual organs* of a woman and they undergo regular cyclical changes in response to the control exercised over them by the pituitary gland, situated in the base of the skull. This control is mediated by chemical messengers (hormones) secreted into the circulation. The ovaries also secrete hormones, œstrogen, and progesterone, and a delicate hormonal balance is maintained between the pituitary gland and the ovaries. Each month an egg cell (ovum) matures and is released from the ovary, usually midway between two menstrual periods: the ovum is wafted along the Fallopian tubes by waves of contraction and if fertilised embeds in the lining of the uterus which has been conditioned to nourish it by the ovarian hormones. If it is not fertilised the ovum escapes from the uterus, altered hormone levels then cause the lining of the uterus to be shed (this is menstruation), usually about 14 days after ovulation. After menstruation a new cycle begins; another ovum matures and a fresh lining grows in the uterus. These cyclical changes recur from puberty to the menopause. Menstruation does not occur during pregnancy, of which a missed period is often the first sign. However, women do miss periods even though they are not pregnant, and this usually means that some minor and temporary change has occurred in the hormone balance. If three consecutive periods are missed it is wise to consult a doctor.

The *breasts* are called *secondary sexual organs* and are also under the influence of the ovarian hormones. Two conditions which need treatment are *mastitis* and *cancer of the breast*, both of which are characterised by lumps within the breast tissue. Mastitis may be uncomfortable but is not dangerous and can be treated medically, whereas cancer is more serious. The distinction between mastitis and cancer can only be made by a doctor and any woman who discovers a lump in her breast must seek medical aid *at once*.

Abscesses also occur in the breast, nearly always when the mother is feeding her child. Here again, a lump appears, the breast becomes red and very tender, and the woman may be feverish. Treatment with antibiotics is sometimes successful, especially if the mother consults her doctor quickly, otherwise treatment is by a small operation.

The Ovaries. The two commonest diseases of the ovaries are cysts and disorders arising from hormonal imbalance. The symptoms of ovarian disease are usually abdominal or low back pains, and heavy and painful loss during the periods, which may become irregular. These signs should be taken as a warning to consult a doctor.

The Fallopian Tubes. Infection of the Fallopian tubes is called salpingitis. The membrane lining the tubes is continuous with the lining of the uterus, hence an infection is rarely confined to a circumscribed area in either the tubes or the uterus, and pelvic inflammatory disease is a better name for this condition. Pelvic inflammatory disease often follows an abortion, or childbirth where part of the afterbirth (placenta) has been retained, or can spread from an infection in a nearby organ, for example the appendix. Infection is sometimes conveyed by the blood from another septic source in the body. The gonococcus is another cause of infection. The disease is characterised by pain and tenderness in the lower part of the abdomen, accompanied by fever, general malaise and frequently (but not invariably) a vaginal discharge. The treatment of pelvic inflammatory disease is usually medical and is the same irrespective of the primary site of infection. Before the introduction of antibiotics the disease often became chronic and the Fallopian tubes were frequently blocked by a cicatrising scar, a cause of subsequent sterility.

The Uterus. This is a hollow muscular organ and both its musculature and its lining membrane can be the site of disease. *Fibroids* are non-malignant muscular tumours which develop in many women. The main symptom is a heavy menstrual loss and surgical removal of the uterus (hysterectomy) is often necessary. This is a major operation, but modern anæsthesia and operative techniques minimise the discomfort. Hysterectomy does not impair sexual pleasure, but no more babies can be conceived. Infection of the lining of the uterus is usually part of a generalised pelvic inflammatory disease (*see* Fallopian tubes).

Cancer of the Uterus and Cervical Smears. The uterus is pear-shaped and consists of a body and neck. The wide end is uppermost (the body) and the narrow neck (cervix) projects into the top of the vagina. Cancer of the cervix is commonest in middle-aged women who have married young and have had a large family; cancer of the body of the uterus usually occurs after the menopause and is more common in nulliparous women. The of the uterus usually occurs after the menopause and is most common in childless women. The symptoms are variable and it is sufficient to emphasise that any woman who has unexpected bleeding, especially after intercourse, whether her periods have stopped or not, *must* see her doctor at once. The treatment depends on individual circumstances, but is usually by operation. It is now possible to detect cancer of the cervix long before symptoms develop and at a stage when the disease can be eradicated by a relatively small operation. This early detection has been made possible by the development of exfoliative cytology. Cells taken from the cervix (without discomfort to the woman) are examined under a microscope. This test is popularly known as the "cancer test" or "cervical smear." A cervical smear is often taken as part of the routine gynæcological examination by consultants, general practitioners, and family planning doctors, and is also being included in some population screening programmes. It is a big step forward in preventive medicine and may ultimately solve the problem of cancer of the cervix. Every woman between the ages of 25 and 60 should seize any chance to have this test done.

Prolapse means a sagging down of the uterus into the vagina and the cervix may even appear at the outside. It is a result of frequent childbirth and laxness of the ligaments which support the uterus: weakness of the vaginal walls often occurs at the same time. The symptoms of uterine prolapse are low back pain and a heavy dragging feeling in the lower abdomen: these are often overshadowed by the distressingly embarrassing incontinence which results from lax vaginal walls. The stress of only a sneeze, a cough, or a giggle often causes the involuntary escape of urine. The cure is operative and very rewarding.

Dysmenorrhœa or pain with the periods, is very common and most women experience this symptom at some time or another. Very often a girl's first periods are troublefree, but dysmenorrhœa develops after a year or two: this suggests that a psychological element is involved. Dysmenorrhœa is a symptom which has many varying causes, and the sensible thing to do, if pain is troublesome, is to see a doctor.

Amenorrhœa means stopping of the periods in a young woman. It may signify pregnancy or glandular disease or it can be purely psychological.

Abortion, or its more acceptable name, miscarriage, describes the spontaneous or induced termination of a pregnancy before the fœtus (baby) is able to survive. A baby cannot live unless it is born after the twenty-eighth week of pregnancy, though many infants born at this time die. The two main symptoms of abortion are bleeding and abdominal pain. Any bleeding occurring during pregnancy ought to be reported at once. Pain starts in the back and lower abdomen and is usually spasmodic in character, and like colic it works up to a peak and then temporarily passes off. Any pregnant woman with pain and bleeding should go to bed at once and send for her doctor. When doctors are convinced that a pregnancy should be terminated then an abortion by safe surgical means may be performed in hospital.

CONTRACEPTION.

If a couple intends to practise birth control expert advice should be obtained from their family doctor or family planning clinic. The matter of whether or not a baby is born is too important to leave to chance. The method chosen must be effective as well as acceptable to the couple concerned, and the extent of the choice only emphasises the fact that the ideal contraceptive which is best for every couple at all times has yet to be discovered. The only method which is 100 per cent. reliable is abstinence. If the male seed (sperm) fertilises the female seed (ovum) then pregnancy results. Contraception is only effective if this union is prevented. A couple can achieve a measure of contraception without the help of pills or appliances if the husband practises *coitus interruptus* or they rely on the wife's "safe period." *Coitus interruptus* (when the man withdraws before emission occurs) is a thoroughly unreliable method which often leads to psychological difficulties in both partners. The "rhythm" or "safe period" method relies on estimating the time of ovulation and abstaining from intercourse during this time. This is at best unreliable, though its effectiveness can be improved by keeping careful records of the body temperature on waking each morning as the temperature rises once ovulation has occurred. The interpretation of these temperature records needs care and couples who must rely on this method can obtain expert advice from, for example, The Catholic Marriage Advisory Council, or a family planning clinic. *Barrier methods* prevent the sperms from reaching the ovum and can be used by the man (sheath or condom) or woman (cap or diaphragm): the reliability of the barrier is greatly increased if it is used in conjunction with a spermicidal cream, jelly, or pessary. A great many women have found that the *oral contraceptive pill* is ideal for their needs: it is the most æsthetic means of contraception and offers the most complete protection against pregnancy. Oral contraceptive pills contain chemical substances (œstrogen and progestagen) which replace the hormones normally released from the ovary while an ovum is developing. Ovulation does not occur, and without an ovum there can be no pregnancy. Pills must be taken strictly as directed as the dose is the lowest that will provide effective contraception and missing a tablet may result in pregnancy. Side effects sometimes occur (for example, nausea, breast discomfort, headaches,) but usually decrease after a few cycles of medication. Newspaper reports of the deaths of young women taking the pill have caused widespread concern. These tragedies have followed blockage of a blood vessel (by thrombosis or embolism) and have been carefully investigated, and the conclusions are that the number of such deaths is small and does not differ from the number which would probably have occurred in any case. No satisfactory pill for a man has yet been developed. In the newest method of contraception a small plastic *intra-uterine device* (loop, bow, or coil) is inserted into the womb. Once inserted it can be forgotten: a tremendous advantage to many different peoples and societies. It is not as effective as the pill but is more satisfactory than barrier methods. This intra-uterine device is not suitable for all women and is usually not recommended to women who have borne no children or who have very heavy periods. However, careful selection of suitable women has resulted in a high proportion of satisfied users. The search for the ideal contraceptive continues.

Vasectomy (a form of sterilisation) may now be performed under the health service on a husband in the interests of the health of either husband or wife.

PART III. SPECIAL TOPICS.

THE TREATMENT OF CANCER.

It is only in recent years that cancer has come to be talked about relatively freely in the social setting or over the radio and on television. This is probably because we do not now accept the diagnosis as necessarily a pronouncement of doom. Great advances have been made, both in the early recognition and early treatment of the disease, and there is now a greater public awareness in many civilised communities of the need to seek medical advice at the first signs of possible mischief. Public health campaigns to promote such an awareness are slowly penetrating the protective barriers which have arisen from centuries of ignorance and fear.

What is *cancer*? Everyone knows that it is derived from the Latin word meaning crab; it would seem that the ancients, noting the apparent many-legged appearance of some superficial skin tumours, used the word *canker* for such growths and that around the early part of the seventeenth century this became *cancer*. The word is still used by laymen and doctors alike to describe disease which can appear in virtually any organ of the body, but which has the single characteristic—malignancy. This term is used in the opposite sense to benign. Tumours—simply, lumps—are classified as benign or malignant; malignant tumours are cancers, benign tumours are not. Malignant disease used to be synonymous with fatal disease. It is true that in the 1970s cancer remains in general unconquered, but its essential *malignancy* has been assailed on three fronts—surgery, radiotherapy (X-rays) and chemotherapy (drugs). Thus, many types of cancer are now eminently *curable*—if discovered early and treated early.

Early discovery means early diagnosis. Early diagnosis means early education about the nature of cancer and the importance to the individual and the community of taking notice of warning signs and symptoms. It means education too in the area of prevention, of the conscious avoidance of coming into contact with carcinogens (cancer-provoking agents) in the things we handle, the food we eat and the air we breathe.

A general definition of cancer is that it is a disorder of cell growth. The cancerous cell is one which has revolted as it were, against the system of orderly behaviour, in terms of function, growth and multiplication, and of good relationships with its neighbours. This characteristic may have been inherited or thrust upon it by viral invasion, or the action of a noxious chemical or of radiation; whatever the trigger factor or factors, this acquired disorder can be transmitted not only to its immediate neighbours but, by blood or lymphatic spread, to cells in other parts of the body. In broad terms, the affected cells at the site of the cancerous lesion lose their capacity for orderly behaviour and regular growth and multiplication, and gain an altogether foreign capacity for disorderly behaviour, irregular growth and excessive multiplication. Normal cells at the site may be transformed into cancer cells, or themselves be invaded and destroyed by cancer cells. This local *invasiveness* of such growths is one aspect of the cancerous character; distant spread, known as *metastasis*, the seeding of secondary growths away from the main one, is another. Some growths invade only locally, some invade little locally but disseminate broadly, and there are shades in between.

It must be appreciated that there are as many types of cancer as there are kinds of body tissue—lung, liver, skin, bone, intestine, blood cells and so on—but, in general, the character of the types is the same. Cancers developing in an easily accessible part, such as the skin, are readily treatable because of that accessibility. Skin tumours, with one—fortunately very rare—exception, hardly ever metastasise either, so local removal brings cure. The majority of skin tumours are therefore eminently curable—by surgery, radiotherapy or by locally applied drugs. Where spread does occur it may only be to the nearest and equally accessible glands which drain the lymph from the area and, again, excision of the glands will effect a cure.

Most skin cancers are not only curable, but preventable. Research in this area has advanced well because experiments with suspected local irritants on animal skins are so readily and simply carried out. Thus, a number of skin carcinogens have been identified and precautions taken by industry and in the home to avoid contact. The one potential carcinogen that none of us can avoid is sunlight. There is a direct correlation between the amount of sunshine falling in any one area and the incidence of skin cancer in its population. The fair skinned are more at risk than the darker, the outdoor worker than the indoor one. The lower lip, with its thin epithelium facing upwards to the light, is a common site of cancer in, for example, a sunny climate such as Queensland enjoys. Other forms of electromagnetic radiation can also cause skin cancer—as the early pioneers of diagnostic radiology found to their cost. But with our knowledge in this field, with the development of skin barrier creams and powerful, locally applied anticancer agents, skin cancer is controllable and is no threat to life. When deaths have occurred they have usually been the result of neglect.

The commonest cancers in Great Britain are those arising in internal organs—lung, stomach, colon, rectum—and in those specialised external organs, such as the female breast. (The male breast is not immune, although cancer in that site is relatively uncommon). The three commonest sites in this country are lung in men, breast in women and stomach in either sex, but predominantly in men.

Lung cancer heads the list of killers; the tragedy is that this disease is very largely, if not entirely *preventable*.

Lung Cancer.

Strictly speaking, these cancers usually arise from the bronchial tubes—or, rather from the cells lining those tubes, the cells which first meet the challenge of the inhaled carcinogen and the site of continued irritation from the retained secretions of chronic bronchitis. However, it is convenient to refer to " lung cancer " rather than the more accurate term " bronchial carcinoma ". The facts about this disease are probably already too well-known for repetition here. It is a major cause of death in most civilised countries of the world it affects men more than women, smokers far more than non-smokers or ex-smokers, and may affect anyone from the age of 20 onwards. Sadly, " early " diagnosis is already too late and our only real hope at present for the conquest of this disease lies in the one word—prevention. Even at the " early " stage when a suspicious shadow has been discovered on routine chest X-ray, treatment has to be drastic—excision, radiotherapy, chemotherapy or all three. Nevertheless, some patients do very well after such essenially destructive therapy, although lung cancer, in common with other internal growths such as those of the stomach, kidney and so on, can—and does—tend to spread to distant sites. Secondary growths all too easily become established in organs such as the liver and in bone, or in nervous tissue such as the brain.

Unquestionably, radical changes in our smoking habits could almost eliminate lung cancer from this and many other countries throughout the world. Cigarette smoking is a major causal factor. Between 1952 and 1961—the 10 years following the publication of the Royal College of Physicians' report which first drew public attention to the known facts linking smoking with lung cancer—British doctors drastically changed their smoking habits. That was not a random observation but a carefully documented piece of epidemiological research based on questionnaires filled up by a large number of doctors whose answers thereon formed the basis of the conclusions that were drawn from them.

Access to the Registrar General's returns on causes of death provided the vital link between answers and outcome; it was known who among the doctors had died during the years of the survey and, more importantly, from what they had died. It emerged that the incidence of deaths from lung cancer in this group fell *pari passu* with changes in smoking habits. If smoking among the general population had declined as much as it had among the doctors the 4 lung cancer deaths out of every 10 cancer deaths in men would have fallen to 2 by now.

Not all patients who contract this form of cancer are smokers. The majority are, but it is one of the curious facts about this disease that non-smokers are not immune. This is probably not the reason why the man-in-the-street finds it difficult to accept the evidence of the causal link between smoking and cancer; it is more likely to be because the interval between "cause and effect" is so long. If 20 cigarettes a day produced the disease in six months, not only would we have realised the connection much sooner but all the expensive health propaganda and education directed towards encouraging people to give up the habit would have been totally unnecessary. But the interval is more like 15 or 20 years, or even longer—and to the young smoker that is a lifetime and "you've got to die of something one day".

Alimentary Tract Cancers.

The other common cancers are of the alimentary tract and its associated organs. No area is immune, from the tongue to the rectum and anus. The stomach, large bowel and rectum are the commonest sites; all are diagnosable early and most are treatable by surgery, radiotherapy, cytotoxic drugs or a combination of all three. Again as in lung cancer, the danger is metastatic spread and the earlier the diagnosis is made the better the chance the patient will have.

Prevention is more difficult as the precipitating factors are not known with any certainty. The high incidence of gastric cancer in Japan and Finland may be related to the high consumption of smoked foods. Colonic cancers are more common in people with a condition known as diverticulosis of the bowel. This may be symptomless and discovered only on routine examination or radiography for some other related condition; in that situation, the awareness of the proneness of the patient to malignant change will lead to regular examination and monitoring of possible changes which might lead to malignancy.

The outlook for cancers of the alimentary tract has improved considerably in recent years. Surgical removal of the diseased portion with reconnection of the healthy ends ("anastomosis") either at that time or later offers the best hope of cure. Advances have been made in the development of new radiological techniques for more intimate examination of bowel wall changes and of fibre optics which enable examination of portions of the alimentary tract by direct vision hitherto quite out of reach of the gastroenterologist's eye.

Organs arising from the alimentary tract—liver, gall bladder and pancreas—are also possible cancer sites. Although primary cancer of the liver is relatively uncommon, secondary growths at that site from bowel or other types of cancer are not infrequent. The finding of such secondary growths in the liver is always of serious import. The pancreas is not an uncommon site of cancer, and again treatment is necessarily surgical. Primary gall bladder cancer is rare.

Genito-urinary System Cancers.

Again, any part of the genito-urinary system—kidney, bladder, uterine body or neck (cervix), ovary, testicle, external genitalia—may develop cancer. Success of treatment, as with all cancers, depends so much on early diagnosis. The once-yearly collection of small surface scrapings from the uterine cervix (the cervical smear) provides a useful insurance against later trouble as the pre-cancerous changes are detectable on microscopy and provide a clue to further investigation. This usually means the removal of a small portion of that part of the neck of the womb that protrudes into the vagina for further, more detailed microscopic examination. If the pre-neoplastic change is confirmed (neoplastic = new growth, that is, cancer) then a decision may be taken to go ahead with more radical treatment—surgery, radiotherapy or both.

Methods of Treatment.

In general, once cancer has been diagnosed, many factors must be taken into account before treatment is started: the age and sex of the patient, the site of the disease, the extent of any spread, the degree of malignancy and an assessment of the immediate threat to nearby vital organs and, indeed, to life. As has been indicated, there are three main courses of treatment open to the surgeon or physician under whose care the patient will be.

The first of these is still surgery—that is, the removal of the affected tissue and any associated lymph glands which may have already become affected, or which are in the direct path of spread by that course. Very often, of course, this means removal of an entire organ. Fortunately, many of our vital organs are paired and the loss of one is but a temporary setback. Mutilation in some degree is inevitable, but the price for a good chance of life is not usually regarded as excessive. The loss of a breast, an ovary, a testicle or even a kidney would be a small price to pay in such circumstances. The loss of limbs, or of a complete lung are more crippling and some patients may not be prepared to pay the price. *Surgery* is thus our first line of attack.

Next in importance and effectiveness is *radiotherapy*—the destruction of tissues or small organs (such as the thyroid gland) affected with cancer, by means of X-rays. Some cancers are readily treatable with radiotherapy alone, and it is the treatment of choice when for anatomical reasons surgery is next to impossible. Some areas of the brain, for example, are difficult or impossible for the surgeon to reach; modern techniques with X-rays, or with radiation from artificially-produced sources of a special type of radiation (radioactive isotopes) have made such hitherto untreatable tumours readily accessible and often curable. A refinement of this technique consists of implanting small radioactive "seeds" in the centre of growths where the circumscribed area of tissue destruction can be accurately assessed in such a manner as to perform as precise an excision of tumour tissue as a surgeon could have done had he been able to reach it with his scalpel. Physicists work closely with doctors in this sort of work because the precise mapping of the destructive potential of the isotope used is as vital to the technique as is the equally precise placing of the material which is usually done under X-ray control.

Once a tumour has been destroyed in this way, the debris is dealt with by the scavenger cells of the body tissues in the same way as a small piece of necrotic muscle from, say, an area of ischaemic necrosis (that is, an "infarct" arising as the result of a heart attack) is gradually "cleaned up" leaving a healthy scar.

The third arm of attack in the battle for the conquest of cancer is *drugs*. The concept of Ehrlich's "magic bullet" (*see* Introduction, P4) is still with us. Chemical agents are being developed which have a special affinity for cancer cells, rather like selective weedkillers used by the gardener. Drugs given by mouth, by injection into skin, subcutaneous tissue or muscle or, better, by venepuncture are carried to virtually every cell in the body by the bloodstream. Provided that no harm is done while the drug is in transit, this is the only way to ensure that the agent actually reaches the cancer cells. Obviously, the more vascular—that is, the more well supplied with blood—the tumour is, the better will be the concentration of cytotoxic agent. In situations in which vascularity is not prominent there may be problems with that type of treatment.

One of the more recent and intriguing developments has been of drugs which appear specifically to sensitise tumour cells to the effects of therapeutic radiation. The net result of this is to increase the effectiveness of treatment and reduce the likelihood of damage to surrounding tissues. This work is in its early stages but shows great promise.

Summary.

Cancer is less of a dreaded word than it used to be; health education campaigns and both radio and television publicity of medical programmes on the subject are slowly—very slowly—teaching that symptom awareness, early advice and early treatment give the greatest chance of real cure. Cure to the doctors at present means a further five or 10 years of life; to the patient, a return to a normal lifespan expectancy.

Almost every year that passes sees some advance—in early detection, improved surgical techniques or better drugs. Until all the causes of cancer are clearly laid before us—and no one can even hazard a guess about how much more research has to be done—we must rely on education aimed, first, at the importance of recognising early warning signs and of avoidance of known cancer-associated factors such as smoking cigarettes and, secondly, tackling the fear that the thought of malignant disease engenders. This latter is so engrained in our make-up that its eradication might seem impossible. Nevertheless, if the fear were removed, the inhibition on seeking medical advice early for warning symptoms or signs would vanish at a stroke, for it is fear of learning the truth that holds us back.

Although, in spite of a huge worldwide research effort, the true nature of the cancerous process remains largely ill-understood we are at least aware of many areas in which the removal of precipitating factors in the environment can reduce the risk. We have come a long way since the recognition of the connection between chimney-sweeps and scrotal cancer, dye-workers and bladder cancer. Early recognition and early treatment in themselves have vastly improved the outlook; refinements in surgical, radiological and chemotherapeutic techniques have enormously improved the chances of successful treatment in individual cases. Nevertheless with our increasing knowledge of predisposing factors and the very slowly growing public awareness of the importance of avoiding what might be termed personal carcinogen content, our best hope for the future still lies in prevention.

THE TREATMENT OF MENTAL ILLNESS.

Naturally occurring substances, or materials derived from them, such as alcohol, tobacco, opium, cannabis, caffeine and mescaline, have been used for centuries—and, indeed, still are—to calm or excite the mind. However, it is only in the last 140 years that uses have been found for *synthetic* chemical compounds such as chloral hydrate, a hypnotic. This was first used in the early nineteenth century.

Barbituric acid was the mother of a whole family of barbiturates and superseded alcohol in the latter half of the same century. Phenobarbitone, the oldest member of that family, soon found wide acceptance in the treatment of many conditions. For 50 years or so, with the exception of the introduction of amphetamines just after the first world war, there was little advance in the development of drugs like these which could affect the mind, the so-called psychotropic agents—or just psychotropics for short. This word comes from the Greek *psyche*, meaning the soul, and *tropos*, meaning movement. Then came chlorpromazine, the first major tranquilliser. This compound, one of a series of synthetic antihistamine-like chemicals being screened for *sedative* activity by the drug firm of May and Baker, was introduced as Largactil in 1953 and unquestionably revolutionised the management of patients in mental institutions. The chemists, in fact were looking at antihistamines—which were drugs used to control symptoms of allergy—because it had been noticed that one of their side effects was drowsiness and, as yet, there was still a need for better sleep-producing agents than the barbiturates which, by then, were being abused on a large scale.

But, with chlorpromazine, much more than simple sedation was produced. In the right dose and in the right patient, behavioural problems such as those associated with, for example, schizophrenia, were so modified as very often to transform a patient's way of life.

To guide the reader, if we can, through the psychotropic jungle that drug companies appear to have created since the Largactil breakthrough something has to be said about mental illness itself. Like cancer, discussed earlier (**P57-9**), insanity was once an almost taboo word and asylums places one knew about vaguely but hardly ever discussed. Changing the name to "mental hospital" and, more recently, integrating mental patients in blocks within general hospitals and calling them "psychiatric units" has helped to make psychiatric illness more respectable, but as yet it remains ill-understood by the man in the street.

In general, doctors may have to deal with two main categories of mental upset in its broadest sense: the neuroses and the psychoses. Nearly all of us have mental ups and downs, but these are normal variations in what may be termed the state of arousal. It is only when the ups or the downs last over long, or reach abnormal heights or depths, or are accompanied by physical signs of stress that they have to be considered abnormal and the person to be in need of medical help in some form or another.

The neuroses comprise that group of mental upsets which include anxiety states depression, hysteria, phobias and obsessions. The first point to make is that all such reactions should be considered normal if the precipitating factor is identifiable and reasonable as a cause; for example, the depression following bereavement and grief. When the condition persists after removal of the precipitating factor, or is considered to have been present for more than a reasonable time, then it is abnormal. The neurotic is aware, or can be made aware of the nature of his illness.

The psychoses comprise that group of mental upsets which affect the personality to a greater or lesser extent. These include principally, schizophrenia and manic-depressive illness. It must also be remembered that some physical diseases can affect the brain either temporarily or permanently. Delirium may accompany high fever or acute alcoholic intoxication or more severe damage may result from syphilis or arteriosclerosis of cerebral blood vessels. For a more detailed discussion of this see the section on mental diseases (**P50–2**).

There are two conflicting views about drug treatment of mental diseases. On the one hand, it is argued that until the many conditions that the doctor is called on to treat are better understood, it is both reasonable and ethical to use drugs to control symptoms and make the patient more manageable and feel better. That we do not yet know precisely how some of the drugs work is neither here nor there. Aspirin has been used as an analgesic for 75 years and we are still more or less ignorant of its mode of action. On the other hand it is argued that the use of drugs in mental illness is a positive barrier to understanding and must, in the long run, inhibit research into the cause and nature of the diseases encompassed by that term. The extreme protagonist of this view is Szasz who argues that in some ways the very concept of mental disease is a myth invented and perpetuated by those doctors who claim to be able to cure it. Somewhere between these two extremes is the view that the rational use of drugs, whose action in pharmacological terms is well understood in many cases—for example, some antidepressants—at least buys time for the patient, makes life more tolerable for him and his relatives and may ultimately advance, not hinder, understanding of the underlying disorder. Undoubtedly, the use of drugs in psychiatric practice has radically changed not only the management of these diseases in our mental hospitals since the early 1950s and improved the outlook in some chronic psychoses, but has also kept down mental hospital admissions.

What are these psychotropic medicines that have proliferated more than any other class of drug? In the current MIMS (Monthly Index of Medical Specialties), a reference catalogue of proprietary drugs, the psychotherapeutic section comprises over 200 entries. By comparison, the antibiotic section covers a little over 100. The 200 compounds can be divided into six principal groups: antidepressants, anxiolytics, hypnotic sedatives, neuroleptics, psychostimulants and psychodysleptics. Some of these categories need further explanation and description, but before this can be done it is necessary for the reader to know something of the chemical nature of brain and nerve function.

Just as insulin released into the blood stream from specialised cells in the pancreas is necessary for the proper utilisation of food sugar, so are a number of chemicals involved in the normal functioning of nervous tissue which, of course, includes brain. The first of these was isolated in the 1920s—acetylcholine. Since then a number of other neurotransmitters—for that is what they are called—have been discovered, such as adrenaline, noradrenaline, dopamine and serotonin. The study of the effect of substances on mood is known as psychopharmacology. Research in this area revolves around finding means of interfering chemically with neurotransmitter function. The means of such modification are diverse. It is possible, for example, to increase or inhibit production, block effects on target organs or to accelerate the natural breakdown or natural synthesis of these substances. Chlorpromazine, mentioned earlier (it was the father of modern psychotropics), antagonises the effects of dopamine which, in schizophrenia, may be produced to excess in certain areas of the brain. Clearly, in Parkinson's disease, which we know now is associated with lowered dopamine levels in the brain, a drug such as chlorpromazine would exacerbate the symptoms, having the opposite effect to levodopa. There are many other examples—too many—to include here.

Antidepressants.

As the name implies, drugs in this category elevate mood. They are sometimes referred to as thymoleptics or psychic energisers. Paradoxically, some act by sedation: for example, depression accompanied by an underlying anxiety may be relieved if the anxiety component is modified by sedation. The common observation is of "the cup that cheers". Alcohol will lessen the anxiety component and thus, by allowing elevation of mood, appear to lift the patient's depression.

Antidepressant drugs comprise:

(1) the tricyclics, such as amitriptyline, imipramine and others;

(2) the monoamine oxidase inhibitors (MAOI), such as iproniazid and isocarboxazid, which were developed following the observation that patients on isoniazid, an antituberculous drug, began to feel "on top of the world" long before the antituberculous effect could have got into its stride;

(3) an assorted group of drugs including the metal lithium. This group is of considerable value in the prophylaxis and treatment of manic-depressive psychosis and depression per se.

Anxiolytics.

This term simply means "anxiety dissolving". The group comprises some of the most widely used drugs, the anxiolytic sedatives and minor tranquillisers. We do not as yet know the precise action of any of them—but then, as has been pointed out, neither do we of aspirin. Typical examples are diazepam, chlordiazepoxide, meprobamate and—the oldest of all—alcohol.

Hypnotic Sedatives

These are really super-tranquillisers—drugs which, in very small doses, induce mild euphoria and hence are abused (*see* P22). But in the usual doses they are sleep-inducing agents, or "sleeping pills". This group includes the barbiturates such as phenobarbitone and amylobarbitone, and a whole series of non-barbiturate hypnotics, such as chloral hydrate (1832), glutethimide, nitrazepam and, again, alcohol.

Neuroleptics.

This literally means "nerve seizing". The group comprises the major tranquillisers and antipsychotic drugs developed since chlorpromazine. There are many of these, some given only by injection at weekly or monthly intervals, but all are potent and effective and in a class of their own, in the sense that strict medical supervision is necessary with their use. It is members of this group that have really changed the face of medicine in mental hospitals. It is hoped that our experience with these drugs will sooner or later lead to a clearer understanding of the aberrant biochemistry of the important psychoses such as schizophrenia.

Psychodysleptics.

Literally, "soul releasing", the psychodysleptics comprise a small, highly potent group of compounds of use primarily to researchers and include lysergide (LSD), mescaline and other hallucinogenic drugs.

Psychostimulants.

This is a self-explanatory word. This group includes caffeine and nicotine, as taken socially in coffee and from cigarettes, and amphetamine. The last-named, and others of its class are abused and medical use is now virtually nil.

Conclusion.

With this really quite extensive range of powerful weapons in his armamentarium, the drug oriented psychiatrist can not only manage more patients than his Freudian counterpart of 50 years ago, but treat more of them out of mental institutions and in their own social or work environment. After the introduction of chlorpromazine there was a fall in the number of mental hospital and psychiatric inpatients in England and Wales from a little over 150,000 in 1954 to less than 105,000 in 1972, although during that time the number of patients consulting their family doctor for psychological problems more than doubled. Furthermore, the introduction of safer hypnotic sedatives has been associated with a fall in the incidence of suicide by self-poisoning—the commonest method of suicide used in Great Britain. There are, of course, many other factors to be considered when discussing the causes of a falling suicide rate, and the introduction of safer drugs may not be as important as, say, the greater use of the effective antidepressants and social factors such as self-help groups like the Samaritans. The purists will say, with some justification, that the enormous developments in psychopharmacology have done little or nothing to advance our understanding of mental illness and that we are no nearer to determining and eradicating the causes of schizophrenia or manic-depressive psychosis than before the drugs appeared on the scene. But there is no doubt at all that the majority of patients with minor, chronic neuroses are now able, with the help of, for example, the minor tranquillisers, to cope more readily with their disablement, and their families with them.

More importantly perhaps, from the community point of view, many patients with the more serious psychoses can now be made more manageable and often treated without admission to mental hospitals or to the psychiatric units of general hospitals. There is no doubt that although we think we live in more enlightened times, admission to, and treatment in a mental hospital is still thought a stigma by many. Some employers still regard a history of psychiatric inpatient treatment, if not an actual bar to employment, at least a sufficient indication for moving a job application to the bottom of the pile. However, each day brings more evidence that attitudes of that kind are disappearing from our society.

PREVENTIVE MEDICINE.

"Look to your health; and if you have it, praise God, and value it next to a good conscience: for health is the second blessing that we mortals are capable of: a blessing that money cannot buy.'
("The Compleat Angler"—Izaak Walton)

Prevention is better than cure; an apple a day keeps the doctor away; the Chinese pay their doctors while they remain well. It goes without saying that keeping good health is better than falling ill, even if the best treatment is available. But money cannot buy good health, so how can it be achieved?

We cannot of course choose our parents or have much say in the way we are nourished and brought up in infancy. Nor can we do a great deal about our environment. But if one is born of " healthy stock " and survives the many hazards of infancy then keeping healthy in childhood and adult life is not too difficult. The main rules have already been mentioned (P4)—(1) do not think too much about your health unless it gives you trouble, (2) have an interest in life, (3) eat a balanced diet and (4) do not worry. This article will deal generally with the first of those precepts.

What is meant by not thinking *too much* about health is simply that the introspective, over-anxious, am-I-all-right attitude to body function is counter-productive. Obsession with bowel function is a common example of an over-anxious attitude to health; fear of constipation leads to self-medication with over-the-counter laxatives and daily, weekly or monthly ritual purges. Self-medication is no bad thing in itself—pharmacists all over the country are happy and competent to give advice on the home treatment of simple ailments and probably save the National Health Service a great deal of money—but very often simply changing a dietary habit or a particular mode of life gives better results.

How to Keep Well.

" Do not worry overmuch about health unless it gives you trouble." This is really a plea for less daily introspection on bodily functions—*e.g.*, studying the tongue, feeling the pulse, counting the respiration after a run up the stairs and keeping a diary of bowel movements and so on. There are three simple rules for ordinary people like us (we exclude those who have to maintain peak condition for athletic reasons) and these are summed up as :— Get enough (a) exercise, (b) food and (c) sleep.

What constitutes " enough "? As far as exercise is concerned that means simply using your locomotive powers whenever you can; for food, not overeating nor undereating—just watching your weight; and, for sleep, no slavish following of a golden eight-hour rule but getting sufficient to " recharge the batteries ". Let us look at each of these in turn.

(a) *Exercise*. Many people work in sedentary occupations and require to make an effort to exercise flabby bodies. There is no need to run round the block in a track suit every night. A walk of a mile or two, to and from the place of work each day; using the stairs instead of the lift; playing games at the weekend or walking or cycling or swimming—these are all that matter.

(b) *Food*. Many people eat and drink far too much. There is no need to buy expensive books of food tables to work out how many calories you're getting. If you are an adult and finished growing but steadily putting on weight, you are probably eating or drinking too much. " Middle-age spread " is almost an expected norm—but should not be and does not have to occur (see weight tables, P41). Obesity, even mild obesity, shortens life span and it is certainly the commonest form of *malnutrition* in this country today.

(c) *Sleep*. Sleep is a widely variable necessity. Some regularly manage happily and keep fit on anything from three to six hours a day; others may need ten. It is largely a matter of habit and there is no harm in the occasional use of sleep *inducers* (*not* hypnotics, such as barbiturates, your doctor will advise you) to restore a habit interfered with by anxiety about business or domestic matters.

How to Avoid Infection.

In recent years vaccination against *influenza* has become widely available and many industrial concerns offer free " shots " to their employees in the autumn. When the particular strain of virus likely to arise in a winter epidemic can be determined in advance and the appropriate vaccine produced then such schemes are undoubtedly useful. Frequently, however, vaccines are only prepared from the commoner strains of influenza virus and give no protection against new mutant strains which emerge yearly with uncanny regularity. Nevertheless, partial protection may be better than none at all. If you are a sufferer from chronic bronchitis or any other condition in which a bout of influenza would be an especial threat to your wellbeing you are entitled to such anti-flu vaccination on the National Health Service.

For the traveller to certain countries inoculation against *yellow feveir* and *cholera* is available. There is no preventve inoculation against rabies. Prevention is not confined to inoculation or vaccination; *drugs* are used to protect against malaria, for example, and such prophylactic therapy is available to travellers working or holidaying in malarial zones. The rapid expansion of air travel since the last war has in effect brought tropical diseases within reach of all. It is possible to contract malaria on holiday or on a business trip and be back in the UK before symptoms appear. Our doctors have to be alert to such possibilities.

The other way to avoid infection is of course to keep away from potential hazards such as the crowded train or cinema when influenza is about, and behave to others as you would they behaved towards you—we have forgotten the war-time advice—" Coughs and sneezes spread diseases—trap the germs in your handkerchief". Much has been written and spoken about avoiding the common cold and almost everyone has his or her favourite way to ward off an impending attack, from the traditional hot whisky and lemon through the mustard bath to the relatively modern idea of soaking the tissues in large doses of ascorbic acid. While Vitamin C still has its devotees (foremost among them the Nobel Prize winner Linus Pauling) the consensus of informed opinion is that after some fifteen years of clinical research we have failed to prove the efficacy of ascorbic acid either as a preventer of cold or as a modifier of its symptoms.

Environmental Medicine.

So far we have considered preventive medicine for the individual; *public* health is the concern of specialists in social medicine, whose quiet work behind the scenes makes a significant contribution to the health of the community as a whole. Identification of potential sources of infection, *e.g.*, contaminated water supplies, food, defective drainage and the like, has traditionally been the concern of Medical Officers of Health since Snow stopped people taking water from the Broad Street pump in London in 1854. Certain infective diseases are statutorily notifiable, *tuberculosis* for example, and it has only been through the vigilance of the Public Health services together with the development of successful anti-tuberculous drugs that the disease has been virtually eliminated from this country. Immigration on a large scale has posed a new threat but outbreaks have been small, sporadic and controlled.

Health Education.

This raises the question of how much the government should rely on health education and persuasive propaganda and how much on legislation in the areas of controversy—*e.g.*, fluoridation of water in the prevention of dental decay. An Inquiry by a nine-membered Committee of the Houses of Parliament, headed by Mrs Renee Short, is currently in progress into that very question and in the next edition some discussion of her Committee's findings should be possible. From evidence in four main areas before the Committee already—nutrition, exercise, smoking and alcohol—it is apparent that as a nation we are not greatly concerned with such issues as the value or otherwise of substituting vegetable for animal fats in the diet, the wisdom of " jogging ", the necessity to restrict, if not entirely ban, cigarette sales and the devastating effects of over-consumption of alcohol. The Americans have radically changed their dietary fat pattern and the Finnish Government subsidises margarine, not butter. It has been suggested that too often we ourselves subsidise the wrong foods—*e.g.*, sugar

—and one way to bring about indirect changes in food patterns is by switching subsidies from those foods known to contribute to obesity, dental caries and coronary heart disease to less risk-associated foods.

We have in England a Health Education Council which strives to disseminate its propaganda on a budget of £1 million (1976). This is chickenfeed in comparison with the N.H.S. £300 million bill for therapeutic purposes. Many people believe that the arguments for diverting the country's resources from *treatment* of disease to prevention are manifold and overwhelming, yet we lag behind in that sphere.

Early Diagnosis.

Lastly, almost as good as complete prevention—and we must face the fact that having the right forebears, eating the right food, developing in the right environment and taking all the inoculations offered will still not prevent the onset of cancer, cardiovascular disease, neurological disorders and the infirmities associated with aging—is *early diagnosis*. To know the danger signs and act on them is half the battle, particularly with cancer. The danger here is that listing all the warning signs will engender mass hypochondriasis and send many healthy people scurrying to their doctors. Therefore the list is limited to a few, most of which will be obvious to anyone who takes more than a cursory interest in his bodily and mental wellbeing.

First of the warning signs is *pain*. Many people will put up with great discomfort before seeking medical advice. Of equal importance is *bleeding* from any unusual site. The coughing up of blood does not necessarily mean tuberculosis or lung cancer, nor the vomiting of blood or its passing through the rectum necessarily mean cancer of the alimentary tract—a check costs nothing but time; it is imperative to locate the site of the bleeding. Less obvious to the layman in their importance as early signs of disease are *changes* in bodily functions such as appetite and associated functions of the digestive tract. *Loss of appetite*—in the absence of an obvious cause like a dietary indiscretion, anxiety and so on—whether or not accompanied by loss of weight, persistent discomfort after food, recurrent indigestion or any change in bowel habit, are all signs not to be ignored. Weight does not have to be monitored daily or weekly and a change in the fit of one's clothes is often the only pointer to a significant loss or gain which can then be checked on the scales. Only the obsessional weight watcher uses the bathroom scales daily.

Then there are a number of seeming trivia which merit medical advice. The little spot or sore on the back of the hand or the face (common sites for skin cancer) that refuses to heal up, the "smoker's cough" that persists after giving up smoking, the piles that seem to be giving more trouble, the stairs that seem to be getting steeper (or your breath getting shorter when you climb them), the swollen ankles at the end of the day, the cold that won't clear up—all may be heralds of largely treatable diseases provided advice is sought in time. Don't get too introspective, but do treat persisting symptoms such as the brief few mentioned above with serious respect. No doctor will feel his time wasted if his patients present him with any of the symptoms we have listed. Simple investigations *e.g.*, a blood test, an electrocardiogram or a chest X-ray, are often all that are needed to reassure a patient that he is not developing a serious disease and, even if he is, then because early diagnosis has been made the chances of successful treatment are thereby greatly increased.

HEALTH FOODS AND FADS.

The Concise Oxford Dictionary defines a fad as a "pet notion or rule of action, craze, piece of fancied enlightenment". Pet notions about foods, particularly "health foods", are common and may achieve a cult status—such as in some societies the Zen Macrobiotic diets. Nutrition is a relatively young science and its exponents are not among the best of communicators; messages from their researches are seldom heard and, if they are, cannot always readily be disentangled from the publicity given them by unscientifically trained journalists who ride dietary hobby-horses for the supposed benefit of a predominantly female readership.

The amount of dietary misinformation propagated in that way has never been quantified except in the USA. A National Survey in 1972 revealed, for example, that 75 per cent of the population believed that extra vitamins gave them more "pep and energy", 66 per cent believed that a *daily* bowel motion was essential to health and 20 per cent believed that arthritis and cancer were attributable to vitamin and mineral deficiencies.

It is likely that the British are not all that different in their beliefs and it is the purpose of this Special Topic article to highlight some of the more glaring items of nutrition misinformation prevalent today. The subject will be considered under three heads:—

(a) Vitamins
(b) Additives
(c) Diets

In an article of this size the topic can only be partially covered; the interested reader is referred to the bibliography at the end.

Vitamins.

In many ways the word *vitamin* is unfortunate, implying as it does that "vitality", in the sense of pep and energy, must result from the consumption thereof. If we had stuck to Hopkins' term "accessory food factors", the popular misconception that vitamins are energy-producing agents might never have arisen. Vitamins are *vital* only in the sense that they are essential to life and must be taken in small quantities in the diet because of our inability to make them for ourselves, as can plants and bacteria.

The average, adequate and mixed diet contains enough of each of the vitamins (*see* **P40**) to maintain health. Extra are needed only by the malnourished or undernourished by way of replacement or by those with an *increased* requirement over and above that provided in the diet, such as the pregnant, the elderly and perhaps the chronically sick. Claims have been made, even by eminent scientists, that extra large doses of certain of the vitamins—all of which can now be synthesised in pure forms—have properties not necessarily related to their normal physiological functions. Vitamin C is a good example. An average daily intake of between 10 and 50 mg is sufficient to prevent the deficiency disease scurvy. We now know that one of the functions of this vitamin (which is only a vitamin for man, the primates, the guinea-pig and one or two minor biological curiosities) is to maintain the integrity of one of the basic "cement" substances that hold cells in place—collagen. When collagen is of poor quality or insufficient in quantity one of the results is a loosening of teeth and bleeding of gums or into the skin. It is claimed that doses far in excess of the daily requirement for health—*e.g*, 1 to 10 g—are effective in reducing the incidence and severity of the common cold. However in spite of many attempts it has never been conclusively proved in controlled clinical trials that Vitamin C has such an effect. Fortunately it is harmless because the belief in its anti-cold property is well ensconced in some countries, notably in the USA and Britain, and vast quantities will continue to be bought over the counters of pharmacies and, in Europe, supermarkets, for many years.

Therapeutic claims are made, too, for each of the other vitamins but are backed by no reliable scientific data. For example, thiamine (vitamin B1) is promoted for *nervous debility*—an unjustified extrapolation from the known fact that the neuropathy of beri-beri responds (as does the disease itself of course) to replacement of that "missing" vitamin. Similarly, because it can be shown that vitamin E is a factor required for rat fertility it has been recommended for almost every human reproductive disorder from impotence to habitual abortion. The claims for vitamin A as an anti-sunburn agent and for vitamin D as a treatment for chilblains are equally without any scientific foundation.

Vitamin faddism is common, but probably harmless. There is no reliable evidence to show that extra large doses of vitamins contribute in any way to more " positive health ".

Additives.

Substances added to food for human consumption during or after processing or preparation are either to replace nutrients lost or reduced in concentration during preparation (*e.g.*, vitamin B1 to white flour) or to improve the texture, appearance or keeping properties (*e.g.*, vitamin C in bacon and sausages). In general there is no discussion about the replacement of lost nutrients although the protagonists of " natural " and " synthetic " vitamins still vie one with the other. Milling of wheat to produce the whitest of white flour (overwhelmingly preferred to any other colour) gives a virtually pure starch product with little or no vitamin or mineral content because those nutrients are lost in the process. Wholemeal flour is the complete (or almost complete) ground wheat grain and is nutritionally perfect in respect of its " natural " vitamins, mineral, fat and protein content. White flour is obtained by discarding some 30 per cent of the grain in milling and, by law, requires fortification with vitamin B1, iron and calcium before it can be sold for baking. White bread is of almost the same nutritional standard as wholemeal bread. Additionally, wholemeal bread has a much higher fibre (roughage) content. Fibre is indigestible—*i.e.*, not absorbed and utilised by the body as a nutrient is—but nevertheless it plays a part in the whole digestive process. There is epidemiological evidence linking low-fibre diets with a number of gastro-intestinal diseases, not the least of which is constipation. A greater consumption of wholemeal bread in the UK—indeed in all developed countries—would dramatically curtail the sale of bulk laxatives (*i.e.*, laxatives depending on the peristalsis-stimulating action of fibre) over the pharmacy counter.

The question therefore " Which is better—white or brown bread? " can be considered by saying that apart from the different fibre content (there are many other sources of dietary fibre anyway), it is merely a matter of taste. The addition of vitamins to breakfast cereal is not a statutory requirement but at the discretion of the manufacturer. Such additives, largely used as sales points, but probably also compensating for losses in processing, must be declared on the packet. The only other example of a statutory vitamin additive is that of vitamins A and D to margarine to bring it into line with butter. In fact, although the Vitamin A content is then the same, the Vitamin D content of margarine is about six times that of butter.

But what of the additives used to improve or preserve foodstuff? Here we are on more controversial ground. There is a very large range of substances used by the food industry, from relatively simple chemical compounds like magnesium carbonate to help the free-flowing quality of table salt and ascorbic acid (vitamin C) which is used in baking bread, to chemically complex natural substances like the plant pigments known as carotenoids which are used purely for colouring soft drinks and sweetmeats. But the manufacturer cannot add anything he chooses; he is restricted to a list of permitted substances which is revised from time to time by an expert governmental committee.

There are of course a very large number of additives which are themselves cooked or processed natural foods—*e.g.*, dried starch pastes which are incorporated in packet soups to provide the thickening, emulsifiers such as glyceryl monostearate and alginates (from seaweeds) which are important ingredients of ice-cream.

Anti-additive faddism is common and is the *raison d'être* of the health food stores. However, there is no reliable evidence that the controlled use of additives by the food industry as briefly outlined above is in any way a threat to health.

Special Diets.

Most of us have dietary likes and dislikes; taste is as individual as personality. A certain amount of faddism or fussiness is socially acceptable in a society with such a wide variety of food to choose from. Nutritionally, only five varieties of foodstuff (plus, of course, water) are required—*protein*, *carbohydrate*, *fat*, *vitamins* and *minerals* (*see* P40). Free-ranging man, left to himself, gets a pretty well-balanced diet; the plain English " meat and two veg " with a milk or fruit dessert as the main meal, with breakfast cereal and eggs at one end of the day and a sandwich and coffee or tea at the other, provides all that is necessary. Protein does not have to be meat protein; vegetable, dairy or nut sources are just as good. One's only carbohydrate source is usually vegetable but again, fat does not have to be animal fat (indeed there is much evidence to show that vegetable sources are preferable). Vitamins and minerals are amply provided for in a mixed diet as described above but may be taken as synthetic supplements. There are no differences between vitamins as they occur in nature (*e.g.*, vitamin B1 and vitamin E in cereal grains) and those synthesised by the chemical and pharmaceutical industries. The chemical structure of all vitamins is known and mammalian tissues utilise synthetic and " natural " vitamins with an equal facility.

Summary.

Food faddism is common but largely harmless. However, extreme forms of faddism which are propagated by nutritional quacks may acquire a cult status and be harmful to their adherents if appropriate proportions of the five basic nutrients are significantly altered.

Further reading:—

(i) Manual of Nutrition (8th edition), Ministry of Agriculture, Fisheries and Food, HMSO, London 1976.
(ii) Food for Man, by Aykroyd, W. R., Pergamon Press 1964.
(iii) Food—Facts and Fallacies, by Cameron, A. G., Faber & Faber, London 1971.
(iv) Nutrition Reviews, Supplement No. 1, 1974 (Volume 32), " Nutrition Misinformation and Food Faddism ", Nutrition Foundation, Washington DC. USA.

PART IV. INDEX AND GLOSSARY

Abortion. The termination of pregnancy, from whatever cause, before the child is capable of independent existence, 56 (1).

Abortus fever. An infectious disease known as undulant fever, 15 (1).

Abrasion. Any injury which rubs off the surface skin.

Acidity. *See under* **Peptic ulcer, 36 (1).**

Acne, 53 (2).

Acromegaly. A state of excessive growth of the body caused by overaction of the pituitary gland in the base of the brain, 43 (2).

Actinomycosis, 15 (2).

Acute chorea or St. Vitus' dance, 49 (1).

Acute nephritis, 45 (1).

Addiction to drugs. *See* **Drug abuse, 22.**

Addison's disease, 43 (2).

Adenoids, 32 (1).

Adrenal cortex, 43 (2).

Adrenocorticotrophic hormone (ACTH), 43 (1).

Agranulocytosis, 26 (1).

Allergy. Abnormal sensitivity to any substance which does not affect normal people.

Alopecia, 52 (2).

Amenorrhœa, 56 (1).

Amnesia, 47 (2).

Amœbæ, 8 (1).

Amœbic dysentery, 17 (1).

Amphetamine, 23 (2).

Amyotrophic lateral sclerosis, 48 (2).

Anæmias, 24–25.

Anæsthetic. Any drug used by surgeons to remove pain during an operation.

Anencephaly, 48 (2).

Aneurism, 30 (2).

Angina pectoris, 28 (2).

Ankylosis. Partial or complete fixation of a joint as after some types of arthritis. In other cases deliberately produced by surgery.

Ankylostomiasis, 19 (1).

Anorexia. Loss of appetite.

Anterior pituitary, 43 (1).

Anthrax, 15 (1).

Antibiotics are drugs which act directly against the organism causing the illness by interfering with its growth or some other aspect of its living mechanisms. Of all drugs which are used against bacteria, antibiotics do least harm to the patient's own tissues; some do have unwanted side-effect, but many have none at all. *See* 4, 9, 22.

Antigens and antibodies, 8 (2).

Antihistamine drugs, 4 (2), **5 (1).**

Antiseptics, 8 (2).

Anxiety neurosis, 51 (2).

Aortic diseases, 30 (2).

Aphasia, 47 (2).

Aplastic anæmia, 25 (1).

Appendicitis, 37 (1).

Arteriography, 47 (1).

Arthritis, 54 (2).

Artificial respiration (kiss of life), 21 (1).

Ascites, 39 (1).

Asphyxia, 20 (2).

Aspirin and "upset stomach", 23 (1), 36 (2); *see also* **Headache.**

Asthma, 32 (1).

Atheroma or Atherosclerosis, 30 (1).

Athlete's foot, 8 (1), 15 (2).

Backache. A symptom which may be caused by many different diseases—sometimes disease of the vertebræ themselves, sometimes strain of the ligaments, and sometimes inflammation or spasm of the surrounding muscles. "Lumbago" is usually due to inflammation of the muscles in the small of the back. Backache from purely local causes may be treated temporarily by applying heat in the form of a kaolin poultice or a rubber hot-water bottle and taking two aspirin tablets a day. On the other hand, many cases of backache are due to disease elsewhere. The most important thing is to find out the cause, and therefore a doctor should be consulted.

Bacteria, 7 (1). Bacterial diseases, 12–15.

Bacteriophage, 7 (2).

Baldness, 52 (2).

Barber's rash, 53 (2).

Barbiturates, 23 (2).

Bell's palsy, 50 (1).

Benzedrine. The proprietary name of a drug known as amphetamine. *See* **23 (2).**

Beri-beri, 42 (2).

Berry aneurysm, 49 (2).

Bilharzia, 18 (2), 16 (1).

Birth control, 56.

Blackwater fever, 17 (2).

Bladder. *See under* **Urinary diseases, 44 (2).**

Bleeding diseases, 26 (1).

Blood, function of the, 24.

Blood, diseases of the, 24.

Blood Groups. Human blood plasma contains factors which clump, or agglutinate, the red cells of some other people's blood. The main blood groups are called A, B, AB, and O. The plasma of group A blood contains an anti-B factor and *vice versa,* so that people of groups A and B cannot accept each other's blood. Group AB contains neither anti-A not anti-B factor and people with this group can therefore receive transfusions from both but can give to neither. Group O contains both anti-A and anti-B, and can therefore receive blood only from group O but can donate blood to all groups. It is important that transfused cells should not be agglutinated by the factors in the recipient's plasma. Apart from the so-called ABO system, there are several other blood groupings, one of which is mentioned under **Rhesus Factor.**

Blood poisoning (septicæmia), 14 (2).

Blood-pressure, 29.

Blood-vessels, diseases of the, 30.

Blue babies, 5 (2).

Botulism, 14 (1).

Brain. *See under* **Nervous system, 46, Physical injuries, 19.**

Brain tumour, 50 (1).

Breasts, 55 (2).

Bronchial asthma, 32 (1).

Bronchial carcinoma, 57 (2).

Bronchiectasis, 32 (1).

Bronchitis, 31(2).

Bruises and abrasions, 19 (2).

Burns and scalds, 21 (2).

Cachexia. Extreme wasting due to disease.

Cæsarean operation. When the abdomen has to be opened to remove the child, named after Julius Cæsar, who is said to have been born in this way.

Caisson disease, 30 (2).

Cancer of the breast, 55 (2), 57 (2).

Cancer of the cervix, 56 (1).

Cancer of the colon, 37 (2), 58 (1).

Cancer of the lung, 33 (2), 34 (1), 57 (2).

AN INTRODUCTION TO PSYCHOLOGY

This section is concerned with the science and study of the human mind, a territory rich in mystery, a glimpse of which we catch through the enigma of memory, and in the misty drama of our dreams. It represents a unique guide to one of the most exciting experimental sciences of today.

TABLE OF CONTENTS

AN INTRODUCTION TO PSYCHOLOGY

The purpose of this section is to provide a general introduction to the young but expanding science of psychology. The topic itself is of course enormously broad and can only be summarised at best. However, it is hoped it will serve to give some idea of the fascinating material that psychologists study and also of their occasionally remarkable, and always interesting findings. The section also aims to dispel some of the illusions that have surrounded the subject and to define its boundaries to the extent that the reader will not only begin to understand what psychology is, but also what it isn't!

I. INTRODUCTION.

What is a Psychologist?

The popular image of a psychologist is a fairly well-defined one—he is a man who treats mental illnesses in the way that a doctor treats physical ones. His principal equipment, apart from a well-furnished "consulting room," is a leather couch for patients to lie on, a well-stocked library, and a cabinet of mysterious drugs of one kind or another to send them off to sleep. He is particularly interested in the dreams of his clients and may use some form of hypnosis to study their "repressed" thoughts and secret emotions. He is probably very wealthy, because of the enormous fees he charges, and may speak with a central European accent.

Silly though the above description may sound, it is nevertheless unfortunately true that it corresponds pretty closely to the kind of picture that most people have of a psychologist and of the kind of work he does. Remote though this description is from the truth—at least as far as the vast majority of psychologists is concerned—the average person can be forgiven for having it firmly lodged in his mind, for in literally hundreds of movies, TV and radio plays, books and novels this is the picture that has been painted. One of the first tasks of this section will be to attempt to straighten out some of these misconceptions so that a clearer idea of the nature of psychology can be given. While the mysterious and, unfortunately, rather glamorous aspect of psychology that concerns itself with mental illness and its treatment is certainly one facet of the topic, there is a good deal more to it than that. Furthermore, the part of psychology which deals not with the abnormal but with the strictly *normal* brain is the area which has best repaid scientific study and, as we hope to show, which has uncovered the most exciting raw material.

This section, therefore, begins with a clarification of the role of the psychologist, and follows with a brief introduction to his principal fields of study—the brain and human behaviour. After this we take in turn the four main areas of study which assist him in his quest for an understanding of human nature. These are Perception, Learning and Memory, Motivation, and finally Personality and Thinking.

One of the main sources of confusion in people's minds arises from puzzlement over the distinction between four commonly used words which, while differing in meaning in important respects, are almost invariably lumped together as one. These are (1) Psychiatry, (2) Psychoanalysis, (3) Psychotherapy, and (4) Psychology. The words do look and sound rather similar but it is not difficult, once the right definitions have been given, to sort the four clearly out in one's mind. Let's take psychiatry first.

(1) **Psychiatry** is the art of *treating* mental diseases or illnesses by medical means and it is a specialist branch of medicine, entered through the medical profession and taught at hospitals or universities. A psychiatrist therefore is quite invariably a doctor of medicine with ordinary medical degrees but with a postgraduate training in mental illness and its treatment. No one may call himself a psychiatrist unless so qualified, and no one may prescribe drugs or surgery in treating mentally sick individuals unless he is medically qualified. There is an important point of issue here, for in England, and many other countries, people not trained as psychiatrists may nevertheless diagnose and treat mental illnesses—provided that they do not use drugs or surgery to do so.

(2) **Psychoanalysis** is a particular form of examination or diagnosis of an individual's mental state based on the theories of the mind and personality advanced by Sigmund Freud and his colleagues or followers, and the reader may like to turn to the entry on the subject in **Section J.** An interesting feature of psychoanalysis is that, unlike psychiatry, it may be practised without medical or academic qualifications on the part of the analyst. A special training analysis at a recognised institute is normally undertaken by the would-be practitioner, however this is not normally made available to individuals unqualified in medicine or psychology.

(3) **Psychotherapy** is the practice of treating mental diseases or illnesses by more or less *any* means. Thus, strictly speaking, both the psychiatrist and the psychoanalyst are psychotherapists—as are any other individuals using reputable methods who offer therapy for the mind. Once again notice that this implies that one may call oneself a psychotherapist irrespective of whether one has medical or academic qualifications, and it is a word that tends to be adopted, with impunity, by a good many "quacks" and charlatans who can of course do fearful damage in this tricky area.

(4) **Psychology** is literally the study of the mind (or soul) but its area has broadened somewhat in the last century as we have learned that one cannot consider the mind as totally isolated from the body, and it now includes the study of human personality and behaviour. Psychologists also study the behaviour and brain of animals wherever such studies throw light on human behaviour. It is important to realise that psychologists are first and foremost trained as scientists rather than as medical experts and do not necessarily take much interest in abnormalities of the brain and mental processes. Those who do, tend to take postgraduate training in what is known as "clinical psychology," and may add to their knowledge by undergoing training in psychoanalysis.

It is obvious that there is a good deal of overlap between these four aspects of the topic and in the following section we shall be entering the territory of psychiatry and psychoanalysis to some extent, but mainly concerning ourselves with psychology—the science and study of the human mind, personality, and behaviour.

1. The Brain.

From the moment of our birth and emergence from the security of the womb our body is controlled and dominated by a single but complex organ, a library, switchboard, signal-box, computer, and many other things all rolled into one—the brain (*see* **F37**(2), **P46**). Very properly encased in a hard shell of bone and equipped with instruments for detecting food or danger at a distance—eyes, ears, etc.—the brain matures slowly, unlike other bodily organs, reaching its peak of efficiency and potential approximately 18 years after birth. From then onwards, slowly and almost immeasurably at first but with remorseless steadiness, it slides into decline. Its proper functioning determines the "normality" of the behaviour of the individual and the part he can play in society, its efficiency determines to some extent his intelligence and his ability to compete, its storage capacity and information retrieval system, his potential to learn and remember. In addition its computing power determines his creativity and is the primary function which distinguishes between the mature human being and the other animals on earth. No organ or complex of organs is guarded and shielded so carefully.

The brain is the main focus of interest for the psychologist, for there can be little doubt that the key to the understanding of human personality and behaviour lies locked up within it. Its complexity of course is daunting, but thanks to physiological and anatomical studies it is possible to get at least a general idea of what's going on. In the first place the brain acts as the principal co-ordinator of messages coming in from the various sense organs, and then as the dispatch point for the appropriate responses. This co-ordinating centre is easily best developed in man, and is present in most of the "higher" animals. Simpler creatures, however, such as amoeba and certain tiny worms, get along without any important co-ordinator of nervous impulses and respond diffusely to changes in the environment—moving vaguely away from things that "annoy" or damage them and towards food or other "pleasant" things. Such animals are literally the slaves of their environment, incapable of setting up goals to achieve and with no facility for computing the consequences of any action. One important branch of the evolutionary tree shows a steady trend towards increasing brain size and, with it, freedom from this slavery.

In the second place the brain acts as the storehouse of information which the senses have gathered at some time in the individual's life. To us it may seem "obvious" that we have a memory—a device for looking at things that took place in the past—and indeed it is hard to imagine ourselves without one. However, a large number of creatures get by with only the most limited of memory systems, and some with none at all. Clearly a good deal must depend upon how long an animal is to live. If its life-span is to be brief, then it need not set aside much room to store information from its past. If it is to live for many years, survive in a changing and generally rather dangerous environment, and learn by its mistakes and its previous achievements, then this ability to refer back to the past is obviously essential. In human beings mechanisms of learning and memory are of vital importance and we will devote a good deal of this section to discussing the way in which psychologists study these.

The third primary function of the brain is to provide the computing and decision-making processes which dictate so much of human and higher animal behaviour. It is also, in the case of man, the centre of consciousness and at the same time that elusive faculty we call personality.

2. How Does the Brain Divide up its Functions?

Nowadays we rather take for granted that important things such as thinking, remembering, etc., are mediated through the brain and it comes as something of a shock to recall that early philosophers located the majority of such processes in the heart or the stomach! Even today, a good deal of controversy exists over exactly which part of the brain does what and, as we shall see when we discuss the contradictory experimental evidence later, there is even a suggestion that certain processes are dealt with by the brain *as a whole* rather than by some specific part. However, the picture is reasonably clear.

In the first place the brain is composed of a vast number of cells—the building blocks of all living systems—which in this case have become highly specialised and stretched out, rather like telephone lines. These are known as nerve or neural cells or, yet again, as neurones. They act as communication units, receiving electrical signals from other parts of the body. Comparative anatomists are able to trace the routes of whole chains of cells starting at, say, the finger tips and finishing up in a particular slab of the brain where such tactile messages are gathered and interpreted. On the whole messages from the eyes tend to finish up in the back of the brain, or occipital lobes; messages from the ears, nose, etc., on the side, or temporal lobes. In the front exists a large chunk of nervous tissue with a rather mysterious function inasmuch as it seems to be more directly related to the personality and mood of its owner than to any of his senses. In addition there are parts of the brain concerned more with output than input—the so-called motor areas which dispatch the signals commanding various parts of the body to move. Finally there are the parts principally involved in the storage of information, memory, etc.

All these areas we have been talking about up till now are known as the cerebral cortex and they are located on the outer surface of the brain itself—*i.e.*, right up against the inside of the skull. You should by now have gathered that the cortex deals largely with psychological factors closely tied up with consciousness and awareness—seeing, hearing, thinking, remembering, etc. This ties in rather nicely with its alternative name, the neocortex (or new tissue), for in evolutionary terms this part of the brain is "new." In general, the closer that an animal species approximates to man, the greater the proportion of its brain is assigned to neocortex, and the more the particular animal is capable of independent, deliberate and purposeful activity.

Tucked in beneath the cerebral cortex, growing out of the spinal cord, are the so-called lower centres—the old brain. Here in a number of specialised blocks are located the control centres which deal with the most automatic (but no less important) bodily functions such as cardiac activity, respiration, temperature, etc., and which it is unnecessary or inconvenient to keep under conscious control. Damage or injury to these centres is generally very serious, whereas damage to the outer layer of the brain, even when extensive, can have surprisingly little effect on the individual's way of life.

To sum up, we note that the brain is divided into two major functional areas in evolutionary terms—the old and the new. The former largely deals with the vital automatic processes, and the latter with the receiving and interpreting of sensory input and the decision-making processes which guide our interaction with the outside world. Clearly this is an enormously simplified picture (specific aspects of this topic are dealt with in greater detail later) and the brain and central nervous system (CNS) is complicated almost beyond description, with much of its mechanics and rules of operation still poorly understood. How then can one set out to study it properly and unravel its secrets?

3. Methods of Studying the Brain.

Psychologists and physiologists favour many approaches to finding out how the brain works, and while it won't be possible to look at them all in this section it will be worthwhile spending a bit of time on some of the most important lines of attack. These can be classed under the headings (1) comparative anatomy, (2) surgical tissue destruction, (3) electro-encephalography, (4) microelectrode recording, (5) biochemical analysis, (6) behavioural research, and (7) introspection. Some of these are really only possible with animals as the experimental subjects, and others are more suited for research on human beings.

(1) *Comparative Anatomy.*

This is perhaps the most obvious and logical method of all, but it has one serious and insurmountable drawback. Suppose that one wanted to find out how a motor-car engine worked and that one had no prior knowledge of its operation but knew what one looked like from the outside. Failing instruction booklets or advice from motor mechanics, the best method might seem to be to get hold of a complete engine and take it apart to examine its components. Given enough skill one might even be able to put it back together again. The chances are that with a relatively simple device, such as an automobile engine, an intelligent person would begin to see the principles of operation. However, until he had actually watched it at work and studied the effect of, say, depressing the accelerator or pulling out the choke, his comprehension of the device might be limited and he could well come to some funny conclusions about its function and operating habits. This approach is essentially that of the comparative anatomist who sets out to study the brain by examining a dead specimen, peering at it through a microscope, cutting out bits here and there and hoping to work out what each section contributes to the whole. Unfortunately, whereas the average motor-car engine probably contains a maximum of about 1,000 discrete and separate components, some of which are rather large and "obvious," the brain contains a conservative minimum of about *a thousand million* neurones or nerve cells and no large and obvious "moving parts" to give the anatomist useful clues. It is little wonder therefore that while students of the brain adopting post mortem dissection have, in the course of the last few centuries, acquired a pretty clear picture of the way in which the brain is laid out—an anatomical atlas so to speak—most of the principles of cerebral operation are still more or less unknown. One of the great drawbacks of this system, as you will probably have guessed, is the fact that anatomical dissection and analysis can only be done in the dead animal.

(2) *Surgical Tissue Destruction.*

To return to our rather inexact analogy with the motor-car engine, let us assume that our investigator finds himself with a working, running engine to play with. Let us also assume that he has already made himself pretty familiar with the anatomy of the "dead" engine and has perhaps formed some hypotheses as to what certain parts of it do. For example, he might have a suspicion that the carburettor and the sparking plugs were particularly important, or that a key to the complete device working was that the pistons should move up and down in the cylinders. One of the first things he might do would be to systematically remove what he considered to be important parts of the engine and note how its performance was effected. Using this technique of selective removal he might soon begin to confirm or reject his hunches and a gradual comprehension of the function and capabilities of the engine would build up in his mind. He might find that whereas the removal of one sparking plug did not stop the engine, it would lower its pulling power. Removal of the carburettor in toto would be calamitous, while twiddling with it might have unpredictable effects, making it run better or worse. On the other hand, filing bits off the iron cylinder block would make no difference whatsoever. Once again the psychophysiologist is faced with something immensely more complex when he studies the brain, but there is nevertheless obviously something to be gained by adopting a similar procedure with the working or living system. The systematic removal or destruction of parts of cerebral tissue has, in fact, been one of the most rewarding approaches adopted by brain scientists, though there are naturally severe limitations to the technique. In the first place such surgery cannot be performed on human beings, except where it is a necessary feature of therapeutic brain surgery (*e.g.*, as when removing a brain tumour) and can only be justified in living animals in the interest of serious and clearly defined scientific research. (Despite the assumptions of anti-vivisectionists, no reputable scientist enjoys performing experimental surgery on living animals and these are always conducted in such a way as to cause the creature as little distress and suffering as possible.) In the second place, the very act of surgery itself probably introduces side-effects which serve to complicate the picture. However, this technique, when skilfully used, has led to some informative experiments.

(3) *Electroencephalography.*

As we have said earlier, the principal building blocks of the brain are the neurones, specialised cells devoted to the transmission of information from one part of the body to the other. This transmission is effected by a change in the electrical potential of the cell along its long stem. The main bodies of cells tend to be pressed up against one another and when a change in potential occurs in one, this tends to trigger off a similar response in a neighbouring cell at a junction point known as a *synapse*. Incidentally, the long stems of the cells (which may be a yard or more in length in certain parts of the body) are covered by an insulating sheath which prevents the electrical "message" leaking out en route and which makes them strangely similar to the kind of electrical wires and cables we use in telecommunications. With a thousand million cells jammed up together in the head, all of them propagating electrical signals in one way or another, it should not surprise anyone to learn that sensitive recording devices can be used to get a picture of the overall electrical activity going on in the brain. Studies of this type (electroencephalography, or EEG for short) couldn't begin until suitable recording machines had been developed and thus, although scientists had been pretty confident that the brain was a potent source of electrical energy since the middle of the 19th cent., it wasn't until the 1920s that anyone was able to get a readable picture of this. The pioneers in this technique were the physiologists Berger and Adrian, who attached little electrodes to the outside of the human scalp and by hooking these up to amplifiers and then to special recording pens were able to get a kind of plot of the electrical activity going on within. To their surprise what emerged was not just a meaningless hodge-podge of electrical "noise" but rather a series of precise and elegant rhythms, the frequency and amplitude of these depending upon the part of the brain where the electrodes were applied, and also—most excitingly—on the individual's mental state at the time of the recording. As time has passed and recording technology has advanced, an immense amount of data has been gathered on these so-called brain waves, and while it is true to say that the high hopes of the pioneers who believed that they were about to unravel the brain's mysteries almost overnight with this technique have not been realised, the EEG has proved its worth in more ways than one. In medicine, for example, certain disruptions of the "normal" brain wave pattern can give clear indications to the expert of the presence of epilepsy or determine the site of otherwise totally inaccessible brain tumours. The EEG can also be enormously useful in evaluating the effectiveness and mode of operation of new drugs and is helping in our understanding of the nature of sleep—the EEG of a sleeping person differs significantly from that of a waking one. Curiously one of the most promising-looking of the many rhythms which the brain emits—and one of the first discovered by the English scientist Adrian, the so-called alpha rhythm, has turned out to be one of the most disappointing. The alpha rhythm, which is generally picked up by electrodes attached to the back of the head (over the occipital or visual cortex), is a beautifully neat and stable wave of about 14 cycles per second frequency. It is present when the individual is relaxed and has his eyes closed. Opening the eyes and looking around, or alternatively keeping them closed and doing a bit of mental arithmetic, causes the rhythm to disappear, and the hypothesis was soon advanced that alpha was a reliable index of the rather abstract mental state known as "attention." Unfortunately for this convenient idea, on further study it was found that the rhythm did not always behave as it should, sometimes doing exactly the opposite to what was expected of it. Furthermore about one in ten otherwise normal individuals show no alpha rhythm at all. The picture has been complicated even further by the publication in 1973 of a book *The Origin of the Alpha Rhythm*. In this the author, Dr. Olof Lippold of University College, London, advances the argument that alpha rhythm in fact reflects physiological tremor of the eye muscles, and therefore has very little to do with internal cerebral states. The presence of abundant alpha in the EEG, Lippold argues, is more likely to be evidence of poor vision than any special capacity to control one's attention. It's fair to say that Lippold's views are still highly controversial, but it should equally be clear that the simple view that brain waves denote complex internal processes is by no means established. All these drawbacks aside the EEG is still one of the best ways of getting some kind of index as to what is going on inside the head of a human or animal, without resorting to surgery or interfering seriously with normal thought processes.

(4) *Microelectrode Recording.*

For all practical purposes the record obtained by the EEG is a gross, overall view of the brain at work. The waves and rhythms encountered must, at the least, represent the sum of the activity of literally hundreds of thousands of neural cells, presumably firing more or less in synchrony. Going back once more to the motor-car analogy, the EEG could be likened to a garage mechanic listening with a stethoscope to the pulsing of an engine when running at high speed. Changes of speed, adjustments in carburation of timing, etc., would give characteristically different running sounds, but little if anything could be deduced about the state of activity of an individual component unless it were a very large one. Much the same limitations, only on a gigantic scale, surround the use of the EEG as a device for measuring specific aspects of brain activity. Quite recently, however, an interesting technological development has occurred which allows a more precise and delicate analysis of cortical cell firing to be undertaken—in fact to allow even the output from a single neural cell to be monitored. This technique involves the use of what are known as microelectrodes, tiny slivers of metal, thousandths of an inch in diameter, which when in contact with an electrical source—in this instance the body of a nerve cell or neurone—transmit a pulse of electricity to an amplifier and recording apparatus. We shall discuss the remarkable findings which have come from experiments of this kind later in the section on "Perception." Microelectrode techniques, incidentally, can on occasions be used with human subjects. In such cases, naturally the opportunity arises when an individual is undergoing brain surgery for, say, the removal of a cerebral tumour. In these circumstances, with the patient's permission, the surgeon may perform experiments to study single cell responses with results which have been of great interest.

(5) *Biochemical Analysis.*

Scientists have recently shown increasing interest in the microstructure of cerebral tissue, not just the neural cell but in its basic constituents—in other words at the molecular level. Clearly there is not much hope or point in trying to record the behaviour of molecules by electrode recording or even by microscopic visual analysis, so some other method must be found if one is concerned with this level of analysis at all. This is where the psychologist teams with the biochemist—an example of the kind of interdisciplinary approach which is becoming common in brain research. As with much of the chemical analysis performed in other fields, scientists discover the nature of the substance they are examining by observing its behaviour when mixed with other chemicals or compounds. Crudely speaking, one mixes the unknown substance with some known chemical and simply watches what happens, the reaction which follows giving clues as to the nature of the chemical under study. Now in the case of the brain or the constituents of neurones, it is obvious that one is dealing with more than one single substance so the first problem is how to separate the constituents in order to study them individually. To achieve this biochemists use a number of techniques such as chemical separation simple heating, and even whirling the material round at great speeds in centrifuges. The biochemical approach to brain research is a bit too complicated to deal with in detail here, but in the view of many it is one of the most promising avenues in this field.

(6) *Behavioural Research.*

Psychologists are interested not merely in the structure of the brain of humans and animals but also of course in their behaviour. By behaviour one means the way in which the individual interacts with its environment and its reasons for doing so. A study of what, when, and how a creature does something can tell one a good deal about the rules that govern behaviour. The way in which a bird builds its nest, a cat rears its kittens, a dog threatens another dog, frequently follow set patterns and presumably have something to do with the way in which at least a part of its brain is organised. Careful study of such behavioural patterns even allows one to make certain predictions about what an animal will do next in a given set of circumstances—and once one is able to predict accurately one has generally discovered something important. Studying animals (or people) " in the wild " is easier said than done and tends to be frustrating because of their tendency. to do unpredictable things and their general disinclination to perform to order. Furthermore the range of behaviour that one can study by such methods is limited to the so-called " instinctive " actions which are frequently simple in function and execution. The alternative is to confine the animal in a laboratory and observe its reactions to an experimentally controlled environment. In this way one can study its learning and memory processes, its sensory mechanisms, its intelligence and capacity to "reason," its behaviour under conditions of stress, its preference for various foods, etc., etc. Behavioural research of this kind has turned out to be almost the most important method employed by psychologists in their attempt to understand the brain.

(7) *Introspection.*

The oldest and perhaps most obvious method of studying the brain was simply to think about it! This was the method adopted by early philosophers who believed that if one was sufficiently logical and intelligent one could work out the solution to practically anything. Unfortunately, while the brain, mind, etc., might seem to be an ideal subject for its own thought processes, this method of analysis—known as introspection—just doesn't seem to work in the way that it should. The principal problem is that much of the brain's activities are exceedingly rapid and automatic, as anyone can demonstrate for themselves. For example, turn your head and look at an object on the wall. It will be " perceived " and recognised apparently instantaneously. Even if you can detect a faint lag between the act or inspection and the act of *perception*, it is quite impossible to describe the steps or stages in the process. Much the same applies to other important mental faculties. One cannot, merely by thinking about it, say how one actually *learns* something, or how one calls an item up from memory. It was realising the relative hopelessness of this quest which led philosophers interested in the brain to convert themselves, in the middle part of the 19th cent., into psychologists and adopt an experimental rather than an intellectual approach to the problem. However, it should be equally clear (though many psychologists seem to have forgotten this) that there is a whole world of material which does not seem to make itself available to any of the experimental approaches (1–6) which we have described above. The study of language itself is a good example, being part of our mental life and thus of great interest. Similarly certain features of abnormal psychology ranging from the bizarre thought processes of schizophrenics to the near-mystical states of mind reported by artists and poets, or the distortions of perception and personality induced by the hallucinogenic drugs, are central to the topic of psychology and are clearly only approached in the first instance through some measure of introspection. What too of the raw material of psychoanalysis and the rich glimpse of the interior of our minds granted us through our dreams? These are merely a few examples to highlight a single point that—when studying the brain we should not ignore the mind's power to look in on itself.

This concludes our condensed survey of some of the principal methods used by psychologists and their colleagues in attempting to get to grips with their exciting and challenging field. The reader may have been surprised by a number of things, one of which must surely be how very much wider is the territory covered by psychology than is commonly believed.

4. What do Psychologists Study?

We now come to examine the main areas making up the subject matter of psychology. There are all kinds of ways of breaking this material down and as the topic is so immense (and enlarging quite rapidly) one or two important aspects will have to be left aside. We shall only refer in passing, for example, to the important sub-sections of Child Psychology, Industrial Psychology, and Ergonomics, for these need to be treated separately if they are to be properly understood. Furthermore, much of the material inherent in Sociology will have to be passed over for similar reasons. The reader will also notice some overlap between the various headings which merely confirms what one ought to suspect—that in studying human beings or living animals, it is really impossible to segment the approach completely. A person is an entity and something more than the sum of his various parts.

For the purposes of this Introduction we will consider Psychology as constituting principally the study of four major factors—

(1) Perception, which includes the study of the way information is gathered by the brain and how it is interpreted;

(2) Learning and Memory, which deals with the way the information is stored once it has been gathered and, subsequently, how it is retrieved when wanted;

(3) Motivation, which includes the vital topic of why a human or animal interacts with its environment and why it does one thing rather than another; and

(4) Personality and Thinking, which tackles the abstruse problems concerned with consciousness, self-awareness, and, naturally, disorders of both.

Anyone reading this Introduction seriously will find that in acquiring his first formal background in Psychology he will also have to think at times like a physiologist, a philosopher, an anthropologist, and a good experimental scientist, all rolled into one. This will turn out to be less complicated than one might imagine.

II. PERCEPTION.

(a) Information Gathering and Information Decoding.

The topic of perception itself breaks down into two significantly different headings and it is very important to comprehend the distinction between the two before going any further. These are the processes of *information gathering* and *information decoding*. If these words seem a bit bothersome, they need not be. Information has a meaning in science rather broader than details of train times or facts from history, and it really deals with the influence of one object, person, or thing, on another. For example, when you look at the sun or a bright light, photons from the luminous object strike the retina or sensitive layer at the back of the eye. As the result of this the retina changes its state slightly and in due course passes signals back to the brain. Now the interaction between the sun and the retina, odd though it may seem at first, constitutes an exchange of information, and when the message finally reaches the brain and the sun is recognised for what it is, the information has flowed all the way from sun to brain. If this appears to be an odd use of the word "information," then this is probably because one has tended to think that information can only be conveyed through words or numbers and "meaningful" conversations. The more one considers this limited point of view, however, the less reasonable it seems. If one looks at a painting, which contains neither numbers nor words, but a picture of, say, a ship at sea, then most people will agree that it is conveying information (the artist originating it whenever he painted the picture). In fact we can use this analogy to add that the painting itself can be looked upon as a kind of information store since the artist who set the whole process going could easily be dead and gone, and yet his message continues to be conveyed. If one no longer feels it inappropriate to talk of the sun as an emmitter of information to the eye, then we have made a major advance and can move on into the meat of this sub-section. It is really important to get some grasp of the scientific use of words like information and information storage for they will pop up time and time again and one can make nothing of modern psychology without them. Incidentally, when we spoke of the retina sending signals up to the brain where the sun was "recognised," it should be remembered that what reaches the brain is not a kind of miniature sun but rather a pattern of impulses which need to be interpreted. This interpretation we call information decoding and it is the second important factor in perception which we will come to shortly. But first, how is the information received and gathered?

(b) The Five Senses.

Simple creatures, such as amoeba, react in a vague, generalised way to objects in their environment. The reason for this is that they have no specialised equipment to allow them to detect what is taking place, or about to take place, around them, and no computing centre capable of selecting alternative modes of behaviour. As we ascend the evolutionary scale from jellyfish to worms and up through reptiles, mammals, birds, etc., we note increasing specialisation of the body's cells, the development of devices capable of scanning the external environment and increasingly complex co-ordinating nervous centres (brains). By the time we reach Man and other advanced animals, the individual is not merely reacting to his environment but consciously aware of its flux, able to predict many of its changes before they can effect his body physically, and frequently manipulating it significantly to suit his own ends. This immense versatility is dependent upon information from the environment being fed into the nervous system for processing, and the devices which the body has developed to gather this information are known as the senses—vision, hearing, touch, taste, and smell—roughly in order of importance. Without these senses, the interface between the central nervous system and the world outside, a living creature is nothing more than a helpless vegetable, incapable of survival. For this reason if we are to get anywhere with understanding the operation of the brain we will need to know a fair bit about the sense organs that feed it. We shall spend most time on the two most important—vision and audition.

(c) The Eye.

Perhaps the most useful information from the brain's point of view would be that which concerns the detection of food or a mate at a distance or, of course, the presence of danger in the form of a predator. Consequently, the most vital and remarkably developed of our sense organs are our eyes, which are geared to detecting radiation over a frequency range which we call "light." For those who like this kind of detail, the actual spectrum detected by the eye covers light frequencies whose wavelengths range from about 380 nm to about 720 nm (1 nm = 10^{-9}m). All this means is that the distance from peak to peak of the waves which constitute the light is a very small amount indeed—far less than a thousandth of a millimetre in fact. Note, however, that not only can the eye detect the 380 nm and the 720 nm waves quite easily but it can also discriminate between them and a whole lot of other wavelengths in between as well. In fact we call the 380 nm waves "violet," the 720 nm "red," those of about 500 nm "green," etc. Remember the minute wavelengths involved and you will appreciate that whichever part of the eye handles this kind of information must be very sensitive indeed. This fabulous bit of equipment, one of the most remarkable of all biological systems, is called the retina.

The Retina.

Situated in a layer at the back of the eye the retina is a kind of screen on to which rays of light are focused by the lens after having passed through a window at the front, which is called the cornea. The question now arises as to how the retina detects the light rays and how it then signals the relevant information on to the brain. There are two ways of answering this question, one very complicated and reasonably accurate, the other quite simple and slightly less accurate. We'll choose the simpler and lose a bit of accuracy without worrying too much.

The principle employed is that of energy absorption. The retina is a densely packed mass of neural cells whose speciality is that they contain light-sensitive substances known as "pigments." These substances change their state rapidly when the photons from a light source strike them, and this change, which is really a high-speed chemical reaction, acts as the trigger which "fires" the cell. This in turn sends a pulse of electrical activity up the neurone's long stem in the direction of the brain. After it has fired, the cell then requires a brief period to recover its normal state and for the minute portion of bleached pigment to regenerate, during which time (known as the refractory period) it will not fire again. Multiply all this by one hundred million, which is the approximate number of cells in the retina, and you will get some idea of the frenzied activity contributing to the process of vision. To complicate matters there are at least two major types of visual receptors, the cones and the rods. To go into their infrastructure in detail is really the province of physiology, but it is necessary to know something about their prime function which is that the cones tend to handle the higher levels of luminance met in daytime and also mediate colour vision, while the rods, which are far more sensitive, tend to come into life in the dusk or dark. The shift from cone to rod vision, which, like most of the body's basic functions, is entirely automatic, is something we all experience regularly in our daily life. Walk out of the sun into a dark room and for a moment one is "blinded." Walk out of a dark room into the sun and again one is "blinded." Actually all that is happening is that the visual system is having to shift from one set of receptors to another and when the change is extreme and rapid, the lag in the switchover is dramatically apparent.

Colour Vision.

Psychologists have known for a long time that the cones, which tend to be packed in the centre or "more useful" part of the retina, have something to do with colour vision, but just how they do this job has been a matter of much debate and argument. One of the most likely bets would seem to be that particular types of cone are equipped with particular types of pigment, one sensitive to light in the "red" range, another to light in the "yellow," another in the "blue," etc. But how many types of cone would one need, therefore, to get the kind of colour vision we enjoy? Would one have a separate type for each subtle shade of hue for example? When thinking such things out scientists always try to see first if they can get by with the smallest possible number of hypothetical elements, and only bring in extra mechanisms when they are absolutely stumped—a principle known as "Occam's razor" and one universally revered in science and philosophy. With this in mind and with a bit of ingenuity, the general view at the moment is that three separate types of colour receptor are all that are needed to account for human colour vision; this is known as the trichromatic theory which is all we need to know about it for the purposes of this article. But just to show how complicated things are, and yet how interesting for this very reason, we will pause to look at some experiments in human colour vision which show that no matter how neat and simple an explanation is in psychology, there is always a joker hiding in the pack.

Some Experiments in Colour Vision.

To understand these experiments, which were performed by a Swiss psychologist, Dr. Ivo Kohler, we need to know a little bit about the phenomena known as after-images. This information will come in handy again a little later on when we talk about after-images in a slightly different context. You may have observed that if you look at a bright light for longer than a second or two, when you close your eyes you see a continuing image of the object which may persist for quite a while and exhibit a nice range of rather bright colour changes. If you haven't observed this, then you can experiment yourself by just fixing with one eye on the filament of an electric light bulb—not too close to the eye. Count five slowly as you do so, then close your eyes and observe. (Don't do this with the sun, by the way, as it could be dangerous.) Now the important point at this stage is the changes in colour you will see taking place, which are generally believed to occur because the bright light has slightly overbleached the retinal pigments and they are taking longer than usual to recover. In the process of recovering they continue to send signals to the brain, which interprets this information as if there was still a light source present and thus the bulb filament is "seen" long after it has really gone. The colour changes themselves are probably due to the fact that some pigments regenerate a bit more quickly than others and thus a sequence of colours is perceived. All this involves lights of greater than average intensity and the question is whether one could get "after-images" with low intensity objects looked at for a long time. The answer is yes, and for anyone who hasn't noticed this before, another simple experiment can be tried. Take a book with a brightish colour binding—say red. Fix on it with one eye, trying to keep your head and eye as still as possible and hold it for about one minute. Now, turn the head away from the book and look at a blank, light wall or other flat surface. What one will see is a rather amorphous image of the book, but coloured green, which will linger for about half a minute before it fades away. This is another version of the first trick, with the after-image being due to the bleaching of the red pigment, and to various other changes that follow in its wake. Now the after-image, as we have noted, soon fades away and no doubt this has something to do with the intensity of the original stimulus. But what would happen if, instead of merely exposing oneself to the colour for a minute or two, one extended the time period to an hour, or a day, or a week, or even longer? This is exactly the question that Kohler set out to answer. To get over the problem of how one could possibly go on looking at something for hours or days on end, he decided on the simple expedient of wearing tinted spectacles and going about his business as usual. For the first experiment, using pink spectacles, he made a number of interesting discoveries. Number one was that although for the first few hours in his experiment the world took on a rosy hue, before the first day was over things were nearly back to normal. After a few days there was no longer any suggestion of a more than normal amount of pink about and his vision appeared to be unaffected—even though, of course, all light was being filtered through the red lenses and thus inevitably tinted. Discovery number two came when he finally took the lenses off to find the whole world tinged with green—the so-called complementary colour of red—a tint which remained for days! His next experiment, apart from doing the whole thing over again with a different set of colours—blue lenses providing a yellow world, green a red one, etc.—was to wear spectacles with one lens red and the other green. This time the position was more complicated. If he closed his right eye, which had the red filter in front of it, then he saw green through the other lens and vice versa. With both eyes open, however, the two colours would "mix" in his brain and the world appeared through a kind of bluey haze. At this point you might care to try to predict what the scientist found when, after a few weeks of this and after all the colour had washed out, he finally removed the spectacles. In the first place, if he looked at the world through both eyes he saw the complementary to blue (which is yellow) but if he looked through either of his eyes singly he saw the world tinted with the appropriate complementary colour, red or green. Once again the new tints took some time to disperse. All this of course, while exceedingly interesting, could still be reasonably explained on the theory of pigments bleaching away due to long exposure and taking some time to regenerate. Unfortunately for this simple idea, but fortunately for people who like problems, Kohler's next experiment produced a surprise result. For this he had the ingenious idea of segmenting his spectacles so that the right half of each lens was tinted red, the left half green. The position now was that if the wearer looked to the *right* with *both* eyes he saw a red-tinted world, if to the *left* a green-tinted one. Looking straight ahead produced a muddling fusion of both colours. In due course, as one might predict, all spurious colours washed out wherever one was looking. Now came the surprise. On removal of the spectacles Kohler found that when he looked ahead he saw the complementary "fused" colour, but when he looked to the right he saw the complementary of red, which was green. When he looked to the left he saw the complementary of green, which was red. To work out why this was surprising one must think about what was happening in the retina. In the early experiments, with the whole of the right visual field tinted red, say, the persisting perception of the green after-image was felt to be due to some changes in the pigmentation of the cells in the retina. But clearly this will not do in the final experiment, for in this case the same areas of retina seem to be doing two different things. After the glasses had been removed, when the subject gazed to the right he saw a green field and one might assume that this was because the pigment had been changed by overstimulation. But how could this account for the fact that when the subject turned his eyes to the left there was a change of perceived colour to red? Clearly the pigment itself couldn't have changed in that time, nor could it change back when the eyes reverted to the left. Obviously, quite contrary to what one might expect, the colour changes were dependent, in this case, not on the state of the retina but rather on the direction of gaze!

No one has satisfactorily explained Kohler's intriguing results to date, but they do suggest one important point which one is always in danger of neglecting in psychology—that a living organism is not just a collection of parts acting independently of each other. In the drastic situation of wearing tinted lenses for days, or even weeks, changes were evidently taking place not just in the retina of the eye, but also in higher centres of the brain.

More About the Rods and Cones.

Returning briefly to the retina and its constituent cells we might just take a closer look at the rods which, you will recall, come largely into play in conditions of poor luminance.

The extraordinary sensitivity of the rods is the most interesting thing about them. Unlike the cones, which need the brightness of daylight to do them justice, one single rod will be triggered into action by light whose energy is as low as 100 aJ (1 aJ = 10^{-18} J), and if that is a value which has no meaning one can get a graphic idea of this sensitivity when one learns that in total blackness the eye could detect the light of a single candle five miles away! Put another way, the amount of kinetic energy used in lifting a pea only two cm would, if converted to light energy, be enough to give a brief sensation of light to every person that has ever lived on earth! The clustering of cones in the centre of the retina, the fovea, has been mentioned and the rods consequently tend to be scattered around in the periphery. You can detect this geographical distribution yourself by noticing that whereas in daytime your vision is much better directly in front of you, in very dim light you will be able to see objects on the edge of your visual field rather better. You might also care to note how the periphery of the retina, populated largely by rods and devoid of cones, is remarkably insensitive to colour. Offhand one gets the impression that the whole of one's visual field is richly endowed with colour, but this is far from true. A simple experiment will demonstrate this. Fix, with one eye closed, on a predetermined spot—a mark on a piece of paper will do. Then, slowly bring into your field of vision from the side a small piece of coloured paper drawing it closer and closer to the central spot. Now if you can manage to keep your eye really still and maintain fixation despite the tendency to peek at the incoming paper, you will be surprised how far in the latter will have to be before you can detect its colour with certainty. Try the experiment again with another colour and note that it may be recognised earlier or later. In this way it is possible to plot a simple map of one's own retina, defining the boundaries of the colour sensitive areas and nicely illustrating the division of retinal receptors into two distinct types with different jobs to do—the rods and the cones.

(d) Perception as a Dynamic Process.

Everything we have said in this particular section has reinforced the idea that creatures with complex brains are something far more than automata responding blindly to changes in the environment. Information fed in through the eyes, etc., is processed in some way by the brain, or "decoded," as we put it earlier. In fact it is this business of decoding and the possible mechanisms which help to achieve it that interest psychologists more than the raw details as to how the senses actually gather the information in the first place. Nevertheless until relatively recently there was a school of thought in psychology that made desperate attempts to deny, or at least reduce, the role of a central integrating process, implying that animal and human behaviour could ultimately be reduced to a great mass of stimulus-response networks, triggering each other into action in a totally mechanical fashion. This "Behaviourist" school, as it was known, had more impact on theories of learning and we shall look at it more closely when we come to the appropriate section, but it also influenced the thinking of psychologists interested in perception. The trouble with this point of view is that it is so obviously inadequate to explain the rich material of perceptual experience. One has only to think of the visual illusions that are experienced when information "correctly" relayed from the eye is "misunderstood" or incorrectly "decoded" in the brain itself. Clearly it is enormously interesting that all human beings fall prey to illusions, for it suggests that some common mechanism exists which is causing them.

The Gestalt Approach to Perception.

Among the first people to take this up as a general principle and use it as a frontal assault on the Behaviourist view was the so-called "Gestalt school" of psychology, founded in the early part of the century by three talented psychologists, Kurt Koffka, Wolfgang Kohler and Max Wertheimer. In point of fact they looked more closely at other common features or anomalies of perception than at visual illusions, for they believed that the introspective and experimental analysis of human perceptual experience allowed one to deduce the "laws of perceptual organisation" and that these laws must throw light on the fundamental operating procedures of the brain itself. A simple introduction to Gestalt theory is given in Section J so we will confine ourselves here to looking at a few of their more important ideas, most of which are still valid in modern psychology. The first was their insightful statement that in perception *the whole is something more than the sum of its parts.* This principle is nicely illustrated by the fact that a series of dots drawn fairly close together in the shape of a ring are perceived as having a very definite " form "—*i.e.*, that of a circle—despite the fact that all one has actually put on a paper is a collection of dots. Dots are all that are perceived by the retina, and the signals passed up to the brain can only be those arising as the result of the dot stimuli. Look at such a picture, however, and one sees a circle. But where does this come from? From the brain say the Gestalt psychologists, pointing out that the whole (*i.e.* the perception of the circle) is something over and above the sum of its parts (*i.e.* a collection of points or dots). The same thing can be applied to lines, or practically any other shape, and can even apply in the auditory sense (a " tune " is something over and above a collection of separate notes played in sequence).

Gestalt Laws of Perceptual Organisation.

The Gestalt school argued that this was clear evidence for the existence of dynamic forces in the brain whose function was to mould or *structure* the information as it was fed in by the senses. Further examples of this structuring could be seen in other types of visual phenomena, and Koffka and his colleagues formulated a number of " laws of perceptual organisation " which they held were universal and also, probably, innate or " built into " the brain at birth. These laws are a bit too involved for us to discuss in detail but one or two are worth mentioning because the reader can conduct simple experiments for himself. The first, known as " Continuity," is a rather obvious one and similar to the example of a dotted circle that we had earlier. This states that a collection of dots arranged so that they form a " continuous " line, whether straight or curved, would tend to be perceived *as a unit.* In other words, structuring forces within the brain tend to act upon such dots causing them to be perceptually linked despite the fact that they have no true continuity in the physical sense. The age-old perception of the constellations in the sky, formed out of near random stellar patterns, is a good example of the law of " Continuity " in action. Another important law is that of " Similarity." To observe this in operation, scribble on a sheet of paper about twenty small crosses at random. Now, among these crosses again scribble down about 10 small circles. Look at the composite picture and you will probably note that the circles, more or less wherever they are, tend to stand out in isolation from the crosses—the law of " Similarity " in operation. Obvious? Maybe—but why *should* similar things stand out against a dissimilar background? Obviously some important factor in perception must be at work. Yet one more Gestalt " law," that of " Closure," is worth mentioning because its operation is easy to observe experimentally. Koffka and his colleagues believed that the perceptual organising system tended to dislike incomplete or partial figures and where possible would " close " them. This was particularly true, they argued, with neat, simple figures such as circles, triangles, etc. To illustrate this, draw a small neat circle on a piece of paper but leave a small gap in it, say about a tenth of its circumference. Now close your eyes and open them very briefly to give yourself a fleeting glimpse of the figure you have drawn. The chances are that what you will see is a circle—without the gap. Try this on someone else who doesn't know that there is a gap present and it will work even better. Now one might reasonably argue that one has missed the gap because one didn't have time to see it, but that's really no explanation as to why one should see a *complete* circle. The Gestalt argument is that in such fleeting glimpses, the law of Closure within the brain overrides the rather feeble information about the gap that comes up from the retina and the result is the gap just never gets perceived. The effect, incidentally, works for longer looks at patterns viewed in dim light.

A good deal of controversy surrounded the Gestalt approach to perception, much of which has died down in recent years as the Gestalt point of view has gradually fallen out of favour. One of the most controversial facets of the theory was the belief that the so-called laws were innate, or present at birth. In other words if one could somehow question a new-born baby and get a sensible answer out of it we would find that it too had its perceptions modified according to the Gestalt laws of Continuity, Closure, etc. And this brings us to the very interesting question of just what it is that babies can see at birth—if anything.

(e) Learning to See.

Anyone who has spent any time with very young babies will realise that their powers of perception are at best poorly developed. The mother may feel greatly flattered at being " recognised " with a smile, but the harsh facts are that a young baby will produce a charming smile for practically anything—even an absolutely horrific mask—that's placed in front of it. The psychologist William James (brother of the novelist Henry James) actually stated that the world of the newborn baby was a " buzzing, booming confusion "—in other words a mass of sensory data rushing up to the brain with nothing up there to interpret it. This is probably close to the truth—at least as far as human babies are concerned, for there is very good evidence that babies do not come into the world equipped with the ability to perceive the environment in the orderly, clear-cut way that adults do. Incidentally, this is not due to any deficiency in their visual system for the new-born's eyes are physiologically mature with at least the *potential* for detailed colour and pattern vision. What seems to be happening is that in the first few months, perhaps years of life, young humans literally have to *learn to perceive*, as the brain gradually acquires the power to integrate the information sent up by the senses, into a meaningful picture of the environment. There can be no better illustration of the vital distinction psychologists draw between vision (or audition for that matter) and the act of *perception.* One concerns itself with input, the other with its interpretation. Now with animals it is a different story—somewhat. Among the primates, chimpanzees, monkeys, etc., perception at birth is better than with humans but still pretty uncertain and the lower down the animal kingdom (this is called the phylogenetic scale) one goes, in general, the better the creature is equipped at its birth to perceive the environment. Look at it another way and say that the simpler the creature and the less well equipped with cerebral cortex, the more wiring or circuitry is built into it and carried over to every member of the species. This of course is what is meant by instinct—an inherited behaviour pattern or function of some kind which appears in every member of a species at birth. *See also* F38(1)

Instincts are very useful in one sense since the creature endowed with them doesn't have to learn the instinctive task and can perform it at birth (suckling is one of the few human instinctive reflexes). On the debit side, however, is the fact that one can't *unlearn* the instincts either, so that the more of them one has, the more likely they are to get one into trouble if one is a creature likely to change its environment in any radical way. Think, for example, how powerless human beings would be if they were subject to an instinctive desire to hibernate for six months at the onset of each winter. Clearly instincts are good for creatures with limited cerebral capacity, but a big handicap if one wants to respond in a flexible way to the world around one. The big question now is, does the ability to perceive develop as a natural consequence of the maturing brain, or is it dependent upon practice and experience?

Some Investigations.

If one takes kittens and brings them up in total darkness for, say, a month, on being subjected to the light they seem to have normal perception—pretty well equivalent to that of kittens normally brought up. However, if one extends the rearing-in-the-dark for a much longer period, say a year, then the young cat never seems to achieve normal vision on its introduction to a lighted world. Post mortem examination of the brain reveals that certain parts of the visual system seem to have failed to develop in the normal way. Evidently there is a critical period, which when exceeded without visual experience, stultifies the brain so that normal perception can never be achieved. But what of humans? This may seem an impossible question to answer for how could one conduct the necessary experiment—*i.e.*, deprive new-born babies of light for up to a year—without outraging all moral and ethical values? In fact, by an odd and fortunate twist, the necessary data has come to us without the need to perform an impossible experiment. In the 1930s new techniques of surgery allowed the performance for the first time of an operation to graft the human cornea. This, you will recall, is the transparent window on the front of the eye which can, with age or disease, become clouded and opaque. Occasionally the cornea may be opaque at birth with the result that the individual can never achieve the perception of patterns or shapes. Because some light is getting through the milky window, however, he may be able to tell the difference between, say, periods of light and dark. Prior to the 1930s people afflicted with clouded corneas were consigned to a life of effective blindness—the more tragic because in all essentials they were frequently equipped with perfectly operating retinae, optic nerve, etc. With the development of corneal transplant surgery the picture dramatically changed and, while the operation is now usually performed at a relatively early age, there was an initial group of people in middle-age waiting to be treated who had *never had normal vision*. Realising that this provided a unique opportunity for an interesting observational study, the German psychologist Von Senden arranged to follow the progress of the patients with new corneas and record their reactions to the sight of objects which they had hitherto only heard described. Von Senden was set for some surprises—but nothing like the ones that he got. In the first place the newly-sighted patients, far from gazing round in wonder at the marvels of the visual world, were apparently totally incapable of making any sense out of it! This was not, incidentally, a mere failure to recognise subtle differences such as exist between people but a totally inability to tell the difference between most common, everyday objects. Showing the patients large simple drawings, such as a triangle and a square, naming them and then switching their relative position would totally confuse the patients. In order to tell the difference they would have to laboriously trace the outlines of each figure, carefully counting the corners. Notice that they could *see* the outlines, corners, etc.—their eyes were functioning properly—but they were unable to perceive the pattern. Their brains were simply not equipped to recognise shapes and, like young babies, they had to learn the whole process slowly and laboriously. Von Senden's second surprise came when he found that few of the patients seemed to find, at least in the early stages, the gift of sight at all welcome. Some, in fact, literally begged the doctors in the hospital to replace the bandages over their eyes! As with young babies, their visual world was indeed one of " buzzing, booming confusion " and it took some getting used to. There's a happy ending to Von Senden's story. All patients in due course acquired the ability to perceive, slowly at first but with increasing speed and confidence.

The moral of all this is clear, and once again emphasises all the points we have been trying to make about perception. The brain is a device designed to integrate information fed into it by its senses. In due course this integration becomes almost automatic, but this is reached only after a long period of training, which in humans occupies the greater part of infancy and early childhood. How much is actually " built into " human brains at birth in the field of perception? Probably very little, if Von Senden's work is accepted without reservation. Unfortunately there's some curious contradictory work to muddle the issue (as usual) and it concerns experiments with young babies performed by the psychologist J. J. Gibson. His strategy was to take infants and get them to crawl towards what he termed a " visual cliff." This consisted of a sheet of strong glass placed across a kind of trench or ditch in the laboratory, the bottom of which was lined with a chequer pattern. The children were tempted to cross the trench to come to their mother, this of course involving their venturing out over the glass sheet. Adults might naturally hesitate slightly, pondering perhaps the strength of the glass and the depth of the pit below it. Young babies would of course know nothing of the fragile nature of glass so should not be worried by that. Nor, if they were not equipped with proper pattern recognition mechanisms, should they be able to appreciate the " depth " of the pit or the nature of the visual " cliff " they would have to cross. Gibson found, however, that all children showed exceptional caution when reaching the " cliff " point, and many could not be tempted into apparently empty space. Common sense? Perhaps, but either they have the perceptual mechanism or they don't, and in this case it looks as though the perception of depth, and even some kind of appreciation of the gradients involved in the cliff were at least present in the babies capable of crawling. Does this contradict the work of Von Senden? Not necessarily—perhaps certain vital things (such as the ability to recognise a steep slope) are " instinctive " in humans, while matters such as the perception of patterns like faces, triangles, squares, etc., need to be learned.

(f) The Building Blocks of Perception.

To this point we have been considering (i) how the information is fed into the brain; and (ii) the evidence for the fact that dynamic integrating forces act on this information to mould it in specialised ways. We must now try to consider how this processing might take place. In other words what actually happens inside the brain when a particular pattern or shape is recognised?

Investigation of Individual Nerve Cells.

To get some insight into this we need to take a closer look at one of the latest techniques for studying the brain which we referred to earlier and which is known as microelectrode recording. The principle here is to insert an exceptionally fine electrode into the cortex of an anaesthetised animal, endeavour to place it against the body of a single neural cell and then, via a suitable amplifying system, record the pattern of electrical activity given off by the cell. This technique, which was developed in the 1950s, represents a significant advance over that of electroencephalography (the recording of brain waves from outside the head) inasmuch as instead of being faced with a rather vague pool of electrical activity, possibly coming from numerous cerebral sources, one is able to study the responses of what must surely be the brain's fundamental unit, the neural cell. Studied in this way the activity of a single cell is very interesting. Firstly cells appear to have no period of total inactivity—whether the creature is sleeping or waking and whether stimulated or not, single cells keep up a steady, periodic burst of firing at an average frequency of one burst every few seconds. This has acquired the name of " spontaneous activity," which is another way for saying that psychologists and physiologists don't know what causes it. In the normal, living brain therefore, even when the creature is in a totally relaxed state, millions of cells are bursting periodically into action, a continuous background of electrical noise. This presumably signals the presence of life itself for only with the death of the individual do the brain's cells cease their restless firing. When the animal is stimulated in some way, by light, noise, heat, cold, etc., then measurable changes take place. If the stimulus is visual, cells in the visual cortex of the brain burst into life, while those in areas subserving other senses remain at their spontaneous level. Introduce auditory stimuli, or mixtures of other stimuli and cells perk up in the appropriate areas of the brain. All this is very much as one might expect, backing up our knowledge that different sections of the cortex handle different tasks. But can one focus down rather more sharply? What happens if one studies the behaviour of cells within only one area of the cortex when different stimuli mediated by the same sense are fed in?

This experiment was first performed by the American physiologists, Hubel and Wiesel, with remarkable results. First, they located a cell in the visual cortex of the cat and began to record the output from it when the cat was shown a variety of visual patterns. At first the cell merely exhibited the normal background firing, but when the cat was shown a luminous vertical line, the cell suddenly burst into frenzied life. In the meanwhile other cells in different parts of the visual cortex continued with only background firing. When the vertical bar was slowly rotated so that it was tilted on to the diagonal, the first cell gradually relapsed into background firing but in the meanwhile, another cell began to increase its firing rate. This too "switched off" when the bar was rotated again to a new angle, while yet another cell sprang to life. In this way Hubel and Wiesel, in a memorable series of experiments in the 50s and 60s, began to systematically plot the cat's visual cortex, noting over and over again the fact that individual cells seemed to be specially "labelled" to respond only to specific stimuli. The same applied to cells in the auditory cortex and even—though these were much harder to track down—in other sensory areas. In homely terms what the two Americans had done was to isolate the building blocks of perception, the terminal points in the brain where information being fed in was categorised or classified and where the amazing process of pattern recognition was actually taking place. Similar experiments were soon being performed with a variety of animal species, and also with a range of ages from the infant animal to the totally mature. Here again evidence seemed to imply that with animals higher up the phylogenetic scale, these "perceptual units" tended to be learnt rather than built in, for they were rarely present in the very young animal or the mature animal which had been experimentally deprived of normal environment.

Recent Experiments on the Human Perceptual System.

All this tells one a good deal about the animal brain, but can one make the bald assumption that a recognition system of this kind exists in humans as well? Microelectrode recording with living humans is probably out, except in certain rare surgical cases, so one might expect this to remain an academic question for all time. However, by one of those happy chances which favour scientists from time to time, some recent experiments performed in England suggest that the human perceptual system *does* work along lines similar to that of the animals. These experiments involve a technique which has the rather daunting name of the "stabilised retinal image," but which is a good deal simpler than it sounds at first.

To see the significance of this one needs first to appreciate the relationship between movements of the eyes and the image projected on to the retina. Looking directly at a pattern of some kind, as we have learnt, leads to an image being focused on the retina at the back of the eye, much as an image is projected on to the film at the back of a camera. Now, suppose that the pattern, instead of remaining stationary, moves across the visual field, then clearly the image moves correspondingly across the retina. Conversely, if the object remains fixed, but one moves one's eyes, then the image is again displaced across the retina. Well, what happens if the object remains absolutely stationary and one keeps one's eyes fixed carefully on it? Does the projected image then lock solidly on to the retina? The answer is actually, no, but for no reason more peculiar than that it happens to be physically impossible to keep one's eyes absolutely still. No matter how hard one tries, the eyes continue to move in a fine, trembling motion, barely detectable without specialised instruments. Inevitably the image of any object in the visual field trembles rapidly on the retina at the same time. This might seem to make vision rather imprecise and blurry, but for reasons we haven't the space to go into, this tremor actually serves to *improve* vision—in particular the kind of super-detailed vision which allows us to see minute specks or very fine lines such as spiders' cobwebs. For some time psychologists have been curious about what would happen to vision if these fine eye movements did not exist, but since they are quite involuntary and automatic the task seemed pretty hopeless. Then someone—the physicist R. W. Ditchburn—had the bright idea of tackling the problem from a different viewpoint. He simply wore a contact lens (which of course acts like a new outer layer to the eye) with a short stalk sticking out of the front of it. On the end of this stalk he fastened a little photograph and a lens to focus the image sharply on the retina. By this trick he had effectively cut out the effect of all movement made by the eye, great or small, because wherever the eye moved now, so the contact lens followed it, and the stalk and photograph followed it too. If you think for a moment you will realise that this means that the projected image of the pattern remains in one position on the retina—the stabilised retinal image. (If you find this difficult to visualise, try sketching the system on a bit of paper—eye, contact lens, stalk, pattern, and of course image on the retina. The logic will immediately be apparent.)

With this system Ditchburn made two very interesting observations. Firstly, the "stabilised" pattern disappeared, thus suggesting that the fine eye movements were essential to visual perception. Secondly, he reported that when a pattern disappeared it frequently did so *in part*, rather than washing out as a whole as one would rather expect. Furthermore, the parts that came and went tended to be neat, even sections of the pattern. For example, a cross would alternate between the vertical and horizontal bars, a triangle would break up into one or other of its three sides, etc. A number of experiments have since been performed with human subjects using this ingenious and unusual apparatus, with results which suggest to psychologists that they are dealing with the same kind of perceptual units Hubel and Wiesel found in the cat. The tendency of the lines to appear and disappear as units when viewed as stabilised images seems to imply that basic "line units" are also present in the human brain—the building blocks of perception again.

It so happens that these fascinating fragmentation effects can be observed by a simple experimental method which does not involve wearing specially fitted contact lenses. You will recall that we spoke earlier of after-images, which are temporary changes in the state of the retina caused by a bright light and these are, of course, perfectly stabilised images since they are part of the retina itself. To observe them oneself the best trick is to sit in a rather dark room and stare at the window-frame against the bright sky outside. Do this, keeping one eye closed and the other as still as you can manage, for about thirty seconds. Then close both eyes and *keep them closed*. After a second or so you will see a vivid after-image of the cross-pieces of the window frame and you will note that the vertical and horizontal bars of which it is composed come and go independently of each other. This is something far more than a trick incidentally—as you do it you will be watching your own brain at work processing the pattern locked on to the retina.

We have spent a good deal of time on vision and visual perception because (*a*) it is easily the most important of the sensory channels, and (*b*) because it is the area of perception best charted by psychologists and physiologists. We will now take a less detailed look at the other senses.

(g) The Ear.

The eyes, as we have learnt, are equipped to detect visual radiations within a fantastically fine range of wavelength—less than a thousandth of a millimetre. From the brain's point of view this takes care of a good slab of some of the most important sources of energy and radiation within the universe, but a brain equipped only with eyes would be "blind" to a good deal of important information. Therefore we find a complete set of specialised receptors handling other areas of interest, of which by far the most important are the ears. These are tuned to pick up waves and vibrations too, but of air waves rather than light, and in an entirely different range. The absolute spectrum to which the human ear responds is between about 20 and 15,000 Hz (1 Hz = s^{-1}), with a peak sensitivity between about 1,000 and 6,000 Hz. All sounds we can hear, therefore, consist ultimately of vibrations of the air occurring within this frequency range, and in the case of human speech we are dealing with a complex pattern of such vibrations. The ear's method of detecting these and translating them into an electrical code is ingenious and enormously efficient.

Auditory Perception.

The process begins with the outer ears (the flaps of skin on the side of your head!) which serve to catch sound waves coming from the most important direction, which in the case of human beings is in front of them. The importance of these directional indicators is considerable and you can note how strikingly you can change your own auditory perception by flexing the ears with your hand, or cupping your hands so that the "directional indicators" point backwards. Once channelled into the innards of the system, the sound waves are forced down an ever-narrowing tube where they come up against something called the tympanic membrane which is better known as the eardrum. Popular belief seems to be that the auditory process stops here, but from what you have learnt already you can work out that there will need to be much more than this. The translation of the physical vibration of the eardrum into electrical signals will have to take place. In fact the vibrating drum itself sets into motion a beautiful percussive machine in miniature, three tiny and elegant bones known as the hammer, anvil, and stirrup, which carry the message deeper into the ear where they come up against yet another "drum." This is the gateway to a spiral tube called the cochlea, which is filled with a densely packed fluid, and the walls of which are lined with hundreds of thousands of tiny hairs. As the last of the bones in the tiny percussive link beats up against the fluid inside the cochlea, it sets up a series of rapid shock waves which in turn induce complex patterns and rhythms of movement in the hairs linking the cochlear wall—rather like the shifting waves of motion that the sea induces in forests of seaweeds, only on a faster time-scale. These hairs are themselves hooked up to auditory nerve cells and in some way, at present uncertain to psychologists and physiologists, specific movements of the hairs tend to activate specific cells, the end product being that a series of complex but significantly different patterns of electrical activity make their way up the brain. Here the auditory centres get down to the business of interpreting these electrical signals into "meaningful" sounds.

Thinking of the immense sensitivity of the hairs in the cochlear fluid, it may have occurred to you that it ought to be possible to set them in motion by almost any kind of external vibration—and thus hear without vibrating air waves having moved into the ear. This is quite true. Sound waves can be transmitted through other media than air, including bone, and thus even if the ears are blocked one can hear certain sounds remarkably well. Try it for yourself and you will note that the quality of your hearing changes markedly—your own voice, for example, will sound deeper and barely less loud, yet if you whisper you will not hear yourself at all. The reason for this is that with ears blocked, the sound is being propagated to the cochlea by bone conduction and this acts as a filter, cutting out the high-frequency components almost totally but letting in the lower notes without too much trouble. This is why earplugs are disappointingly ineffective.

This is probably enough about the ear which, if the truth is known, is rather less well understood by psychologists than the eye. Only one major point might be briefly touched on. Why do we have two ears rather than, say, one large one on the top of our head? The answer is that a binaural system allows us to locate sounds rather better; slight differences in the time it takes for sounds to reach each ear (as when one ear is slightly closer to a sound source) cause fractional delays in the arrival of the respective signals to the brain—enough for the magnificent computer there to deduce the sound source's rough location.

(h) Smell, Taste, and Touch.

Olfaction.

Of the remaining three senses, only one is concerned with detecting objects at a distance after the fashion of vision and audition. This is olfaction or, as we generally call it, the sense of smell. Olfaction is particularly interesting because it is concerned with the detection of chemical substances in the air, rather than with wave or vibration analysis. Animals of all kinds make much use of their ability to recognise the chemical changes taking place in plants, other animals, etc., which serve to indicate "good" (*i.e.* necessary for survival) or "bad" (*i.e.* dangerous) objects. These may range from the sweet smell of edible fruit, the characteristic odour of a mate in a sexually receptive state, or the nauseous smell of rotting flesh, riddled with dangerous bacteria. Unlike vision and audition, the olfactory sense mechanism is relatively simple in form, consisting of two small patches of cells situated rather high up in the nasal passages and not in the main line of breathing. This accounts for the animal habit of sniffing to detect smells better, the sniff being a method of pushing air up into the rather inaccessible smell receptors. As with pretty well everything else in the body the olfactory receptors are specialised nerve cells, immune of course to light or air vibration, but incredibly quick to react to a wide range of air-borne molecules. The presence of particular molecules on a receptor causes a chemical change to take place in the cell, this in turn inducing an electrical signal to pass up the olfactory nerve. Psychologists have not spent too much time on this sense for it seems to be of relatively low importance to modern man, but have pondered the interesting question as to just how many different kinds of smells human beings can detect. You might try to think about this for yourself and before you say hundreds, you should realise that most smells, like most colours, are probably mixtures of a relatively small number of primaries. There is, as it happens, no definite agreement as there is on the seven colours of the visual spectrum, but an early classification by the psychologist Findley in 1924 has probably not been bettered. His "smell prism" listed six primaries which you may like to compare with your own choice. Each smell is identified with a substance which Findley thought was a typical generator of the odour. (1) fragrant (oil of jasmine), (2) etherial (oil of lemon), (3) resinous (turpentine), (4) spicy (cinnamon), (5) putrid (hydrogen sulphide or rotten eggs) and (6) burned (oil of tar).

Taste.

We now move from the distance senses to the so-called "proprioceptors" which is the name psychologists give to the senses concerned with the detection of things actually in contact with the body. Although it is not classed in this way the logical one to look at next is taste, which has much more in common with smell than most people imagine. Taste in itself is a rather feeble sense, mediated by a number of chemically sensitive receptors on the back and sides of the tongue, and the relative overemphasis of its importance is due to the fact that when people talk about great subtleties of taste they are generally talking about great subtleties of smell, for the latter is vital in any gastronomic treat. The simplest test of this is to sample some particularly good tasting substance, savour its flavour and then hold one's nose. The reduction in taste is dramatic, and one can soon realise how a bad head cold can have such drastic effects on the enjoyment of food and drink. One other remarkable feature of the sense of taste is how quickly it adapts out—a drink which tastes sweet or sour at the first taste, slips into bland neutrality before the glass is emptied. This is another experiment the reader can surprise himself with, particularly if he holds his nose while drinking, thus eliminating the vital smell component. The classification of tastes is somewhat easier it seems than that of smell, with most psychologists settling for four primaries, with which you will probably find yourself agreeing—sour, salt, sweet, and bitter. Anyway the plain fact is that the gustatory sense is a very limited tool in mankind's sensory workshop and poses few experimental questions.

Touch and Sensitivity to Pain.

The remaining sense, that of touch, includes under its heading a good deal of sub-senses such as the detection of pressure, heat, cold, and the highly enigmatic pain. Pressure, heat, and cold are fairly well-understood, probably being mediated by a number of different types of specialised cells embedded in the skin. Much controversy surrounds the number of different types of receptors involved and the matter is complicated by the fact that no one has positively identified a "pain" receptor—*i.e.* one which fires only when a potentially dangerous stimulus contacts the body. An early view held that pain was simply the signal the brain received when any kind of stimulus was excessive, but for a number of reasons this will not do. There are also some peculiar factors such as the observation that it is not all that easy for a person, without any other cues, to tell the difference between hot and cold objects. Immersing a finger in icy cold water and in very hot water briefly provokes a generally unpleasant sensation, but it is hard to tell with the eyes closed and without prior knowledge which end of the temperature spectrum is being experienced. Pain itself, the scourge of mankind (and yet his saviour in cases where it keeps him out of danger) is an incredibly mysterious phenomenon and we will not be able to say much about it here except to point out that much of its operation is determined by processes going on in the brain rather than in peripheral parts of the body. Human sensitivity to pain also varies enormously. Among certain rather neurotic people intense pain may be felt at relatively minor physical afflictions, while other people may bear (or learn to bear?) what would generally be accounted as gross physical discomfort with equanimity. The action of pain-killing or analgesic drugs is also very poorly understood. Some recent exciting studies by the physiologist, P. D. Wall, suggest however that we may be on the edge of a major advance in our understanding of pain. He has shown that in certain cases of otherwise intractable pain—following, say, serious limb injury—great relief can be achieved by the electrical stimulation of certain "inhibiting nerves" *in the site of the wound itself*. This is not counter irritation but somehow bringing into action a "damping" or inhibiting system which in the area of the wound had ceased to function properly. In extraordinary experiments patients have been taught literally to switch off their pain by stimulating these inhibitory nerves with a small electrical device at the side of their bed. Other experiments along these lines are presently taking place in various parts of the world, and brain scientists are watching their outcome with the greatest interest.

(i) Are there any Other Senses?

If we take pleasure and pain as separate senses, which might seem reasonable, then even forgetting about all other possible sub-divisions of sensory detection the traditional five senses are not enough. Most psychologists, however, are content with the traditional categorisation. One important area not particularly well covered by the present human sensory range is that of high energy radiation beyond the ultra-violet. It so happens that until quite recently few living things came much into contact with radiation of this kind—the odd cosmic particles bursting through the earth's envelope of air, while dangerous, are too rare to be worth developing special receptors for. Within the past century, however, man has begun to work regularly with high-energy radiation sources and has suffered a good deal as a consequence. X-rays, for example, were grossly misused in the early days after their discovery, and similarly numerous deaths have been caused by the misapplication of nuclear fission devices. The problem is simply that although the radiation is doing our body mortal harm, we expose ourselves to it because we are not equipped with "radiation detectors" to warn us. Once the pain arising from tissue damage arrives—it may take decades for the damage to become apparent—it is too late to do anything about the original stimulus. This apparent digression is merely to remind one of the tremendous role the senses play in our lives, and how brief our span of life in this dangerous universe would be without them. But what of other senses? A frequently used term is that of the "sixth sense" and many people believe that humans and animals are equipped with some other major sense which allows the creature either to detect some danger at a vast distance—way beyond the range of vision or audition—or alternatively to allow one mind to communicate with another mind. We discuss this problem briefly in the section on Ideas and Beliefs, but it also has a place here since many people believe that the study of extra-sensory perception is a legitimate branch of modern psychology. The first argument against the idea of ESP (you may not feel it is particularly convincing) is that no one has been able to detect any mechanism in any part of the brain which could possibly be transmitting or receiving the messages conveyed by the sixth sense. Believers in ESP reply (*a*) that one might be discovered at any time, and (*b*) that perhaps no transmitter or receiver is necessary anyhow. The first point is of course irrefutable, but the second raises a different question and suggests that whatever mind-to-mind contact is, it cannot be looked on in the way we have been attempting to look at either sensation or its necessary complement, perception. There is an even more cogent argument, however, which the vast majority of psychologists today adopt—that there is simply no experimental evidence for the existence of telepathy anyhow. In this case it is quite unnecessary to start looking for mechanisms to mediate it. In experiments conducted to sort out the ESP controversy, psychologists *have* found that people are very much better at gathering information from each other without the use of speech than had hitherto been realised. Tiny changes in facial expression, nervous movements, shifts of eyes, even long periods of unusual silence can all serve to give the trained observer important clues as to what is going on in another person's head. Fortune tellers, detectives, and expert card players have known this for years and are only too aware that they are getting their information by clever and insightful use of their normal senses, but rely on other people's ignorance of just how good these mechanisms really are.

(j) Sensory Deprivation.

Any individual, human or animal, born without a reasonably complete complement of senses would almost certainly be doomed to an early death or a life of relying on other humans for assistance. A few startling souls, such as the late Helen Keller, fought their way out of the solitude of total blindness and deafness to lead full and useful lives, but these are golden exceptions to a fairly inflexible rule. Miss Keller in her autobiography tells of her gradually emerging realisation that the universe consisted of "other things" outside herself and states that it was only through an understanding of this that she began to form the concept of herself as an individual personality. This serves to reinforce the point of view stressed by modern psychology that the individual is a mesh between himself and his environment. True personality has no reality without constant and evolving interplay with the external world. But what would be the effect on the normal personality of inducing enforced perceptual isolation?

In the early 1950s, as scientists began to see that man would soon be able to make voyages into space, the psychologists began to ponder how well human beings could stand up to the physical and psychological isolation of a space capsule. Man is gregarious, naturally at ease among his fellows, and tends to become eccentric and unbalanced when separated from other humans for any length of time. What, they asked, would be the effect of the extended and rather dramatic isolation imposed on the astronauts of the future? To test this a number of experiments were set up in which people were isolated in sealed chambers under conditions of greatly reduced sensory input for lengthy periods. Initial studies seemed to show that the experience was unexpectedly unpleasant, and, sensing that they were on to something significant, psychologists at McGill University in Montreal, where the pioneering work was done, decided to tighten up their experimental situation. Students were hired at the relatively princely sum (for students) of a dollar an hour and told that they could spend as many hours in isolation as they pleased. They were then placed in stuffed clothing rather like divers' suits, and lowered into chambers of water maintained at body temperature. The helmets of their suits were lightproof and the chamber was sealed and covered to be soundproof. The outcome of all this was that even if the student made a body movement he would feel no apparent response as his body, encased in the bulky clothing, would merely float around in the unresisting water. External vision and sound being eliminated, and with ears plugged to prevent him hearing his own breathing, the subject was in a state of almost total sensory deprivation. His only link with the outside world was a "panic button," which he could press to alert the experimenters if for some reason he wanted to terminate the experiment. What did the psychologists expect? That most students would like nothing better than to do nothing for weeks on end and get paid a solid wage for doing so? The results surprised everyone. Most subjects had had more than enough after only a few hours, and only one stuck it out for more than a day and he suffered a neurotic hangover for his pains. For human beings, total isolation from sensory input is evidently one of the most unpleasant experiences imaginable.

The experiments caused a surge of controversy and a good deal of speculation as to what the results implied. The students' principal objection was that they became oppressed with vivid and bizarre hallucinations, both visual and auditory, apparently comparable in strength and unpleasantness to the hallucinations reported by alcoholics suffering from *delirium tremens* or (more fashionable today) the worst excesses of an LSD trip. These vanished as soon as the subject was removed from the chamber and apparently did not occur again. The first hypothesis advanced was interesting—that living things have a hunger or need for sensory input, comparable, but of greater strength, to the need for food. Furthermore, when the sensory appetite was not assuaged, the brain began in desperation to create its own sensory material, hence the hallucinations. This hypothesis was unchallenged at first, but an alternative point of view has recently been put forward based on the recent discoveries in the field of sleep and dream research. Many psychologists now believe that humans need to dream and that one of the principal functions of sleep is to allow our brains to undergo a kind of sort-out of the programmes which control the central computer. In this view the hallucinations occurring during sensory deprivation would really be an example of the individual dreaming *while he was awake*, the subject's brain having been fooled into "thinking" that it was asleep by the sharp reduction in sensory input which had occurred. For various reasons the human brain carefully keeps the important process of dreaming separate from the waking state and there is some suggestion that to fully experience our dreams would be a psychologically intolerable experience. If this is correct then the McGill experiments and their successors show not a need for sensory input with consequent hallucinations to feed the sensory appetite, but rather the effects of allowing waking human beings a glimpse of the "inner space" of their minds. Similarly, incidentally, one can look upon both the LSD trip and the alcoholic hallucinations as examples of the same process occurring—except that the tripper has stimulated his dreaming mechanism into action through the drug, while in the case of the alcoholic, his excessive intake of alcohol has led to an inhibition of the normal dream process which bursts into activity when he is awake. Whatever the explanation for the strange experiences of the isolated students, there is no doubt that the human being is not psychologically equipped to face up to total loss of sensory inflow for any sustained period. The adventures of the astronaut have in fact taken place in relatively richly-endowed sensory environments and so the expected problems have not arisen. But what of space voyages lasting for months, or even years?

(k) The Problem of Attention.

We have now really finished with the senses and perception as such, but before moving on to our section on Learning and Information storage, we need to think a little bit about the problems which are posed by the great influx of information to the brain, how it sets about coping with this and how it assigns priorities to the multitude of signals it is faced with. This involves the process which we know as Attention. To get some idea of the task facing the brain, let us take up another simple analogy, even if it isn't 100 per cent accurate to the purist's eye.

The brain can be likened to a complex communications centre, sorting vital information, rather like an air traffic control at an international airport. Information floods in from various sources, with the controller paying attention to the scene through the windows, to radio calls, to messages coming by teleprinter and by hand, etc. One way to sort out the muddle might be to assign one mode of messages to one controller, the second to another, etc., but the problem of co-ordination remains. At some stage the senior controller must select which set of signals he is to work on, switching when appropriate to other sets, and issuing instructions to the aircraft waiting to take off and land. Now there are two ways in which he might select the information. The first would be to cut off the unwanted signals at his desk by refusing to allow the stimuli to reach him, a strategy which might lead to a jam of information such as messengers, bits of paper, telephones off the hook, etc., cluttering up the control room. A second strategy would be to staunch the flow of information in the unwanted channels closer to their source, in this case at the point where they first come into the control tower. Real air traffic centres, fortunately, never get into the kind of muddle we are implying here, and nor, in most cases, does the brain. But which of the above strategies is the closest to that adopted by the brain in attending to one particular set out of a vast pool of competitive information? Until about 10 years ago psychologists tended to favour the idea that the first of the two systems was in operation with every sensory stimulus making its way to the brain to contribute to some great tangle in need of constant sorting out. Confusion and uncertainty under stress were considered to be an example of the tangle getting momentarily too complicated.

This view has now been largely rejected thanks to some brilliant experiments by the outstanding young Mexican psychologist, Raul Hernandez-Peon, who was later tragically killed in a car crash. Hernandez-Peon's experiment, which many people consider to be the first big breakthrough in the psychological study of attention, was performed first on that most useful of laboratory animals, the cat, but later repeated on other creatures. The first stage was to implant a microelectrode into the cat's brain, specifically in an area known as the cochlear nucleus. You will recall the word cochlea from our section on audition, as being the seat of the translation of the incoming sound waves into electrical signals. Now the cochlear nucleus is the first major junction box at which auditory signals meet before beginning their ascent to the brain. Prior to this there is only the network of neurones springing directly from the tiny hairs in the cochlea itself. By attaching the electrode to an amplifier and looking at the output on a TV screen, the experimenter could watch the electrical impulses from the ear as they passed through the big nucleus. The ticking of a metronome, for example, could be seen as a regular beat in time with the tick. Hernandez-Peon then set about trying to attract the cat's attention away from the metronome and did so by showing it a mouse. The cat, as predicted, gazed interestingly at the mouse whereupon—the electrical signal indicating the still-ticking metronome vanished from the TV screen! This is odder than one thinks at first. Remember that the electrode was planted in the nucleus in the region of the ear, and yet the electrical signals were no longer passing this point. If the metronome was still ticking, then its sound waves should still be activating the ear and should still be trying to send their impulses up the auditory nerve. Clearly then, a gate was being closed not in the brain but right down at the level of the ear—the message to close it, however presumably being sent down from the brain. How could this gate-shutting message get down to the ear? Evidently there must be neural fibres which send their messages downwards from brain to receptor and not just in the other direction as had hitherto been believed. These corticifugal fibres, as they are called, are now believed to run to other sensory areas, including to the retina in animals and humans, and while they are very difficult to track down by anatomical analysis they are thought to serve a very important function. The facts of the case seem to be that Hernandez-Peon had discovered one of the basic mechanisms of attention, the ability of a creature to filter relevant from irrelevant information. Thanks to his work it now looks as though the brain prevents itself from having to face a muddle of conflicting information by cutting off the unwanted signals actually at the level of the receptor, thus preventing a press of confusing and irrelevant information from flooding in. Once attention shifts again, then the appropriate gates are opened and information flows as before. If this tells us something about the selective filtering of important as against useless information, does it also say something about the way a mother will be undisturbed in the night by the flight of a jet plane and yet wake to her child's slightest cry? Perhaps this is an area which mothers know more about than psychologists ever will.

III. LEARNING AND MEMORY.

(a) How is the Information Stored?

Earlier we discussed the specialist use of the word information that psychologists and other scientists employ and remarked how important it is for an understanding of current work on the brain that one rids oneself of the idea that information can only be conveyed in the form of spoken or written messages. We now need to consider the general problem of the *storage* of information, a concept fundamental to the interesting topics of learning and memory. Most people can readily accept the idea that a book is a store of verbal information as, in a different way, is a gramophone record. In reality in neither case are words actually stored. In books the information is held in the form of coded marks, called printing which need to be decoded by the reader before he can understand the original message. Similarly in the case of the gramophone record the information, which might be the sound of a pop star singing, is coded into the form of a series of ridges on a plastic, the decoding being done by a needle plus amplifying equipment, speakers, etc. Using devices like books, films, and records, information can be held in store for very considerable periods of time, the original message sitting around more or less indefinitely until someone gets down to decoding it. Messages written on the walls of prehistoric caves by our dim and distant ancestors are still passing their information across today, and even the fossils we find in Cambrian rock formations are messages of a kind, though the senders did not consciously originate the signals. In essence then a message consists of an information source, some kind of transmitting medium and a receiver. There may also be a delay built in—storage—in which case some kind of encoding and decoding process will be added to get the message in and out of store. All this preamble leads us now to the point where, having in the previous section considered the information gathering and decoding processes in the brain, we can now consider its role as a storage device. Unlike books and records, which operate on fairly simple lines, the brain chooses immensely complicated and still rather mysterious techniques to do its job.

First, perhaps we should clear up a small point which otherwise will cause confusion—the fact that psychologists distinguish clearly between the two processes, learning and memory. In fact the distinction is simple, particularly in the light of the principles we have just been considering. Learning is the process of feeding information into store, and memory (or remembering) the process of extracting it once again. The next question is the really big one—in the case of the brain just how is this done?

Returning momentarily to gramophone records and books we can see that the process of information storage implies that the incoming signal has changed the state of the storage device, book, record, or whatever, in some way, either by covering it with marks, ridges, or, in the case of magnetic tape, altering the electrical properties of its surface. Something similar must happen in the brain. Information flows up from the receptors, is processed or interpreted by the perceptual mechanism, and then, depending upon circumstances, fed into some store where it is held until required. What kind of changes could be taking place in the neural circuitry of the brain to constitute the laying down of a memory? Psychologists have been divided on this question for decades, and there are three fairly separate competitive approaches. Without giving too much away we shall probably end up feeling that the true explanation will turn out to be some kind of mixture of all three. The three main suggestions can be summarised as (1) the neurological, (2) the biochemical, and (3) the electrical.

The first suggests that as information is fed in, causing certain patterns of brains cells to be activated, minor changes take place on the structure of these cells, modifying them in a rather gross, physical way. This would be similar in a sense to the changes that take place in the surface of a gramophone record when it is first made. The second argues that such gross changes are unlikely and that the storage must take the form of modification of the biochemical or even molecular structure of the brain, changes taking place *within* rather than on the surface of individual cells. The third view advances the hypothesis that since the brain is a mass of electrical energy, and electricity is the basis of neural activity, then the psychologist should look for changes in the electrical patterns of the brain as an index of the fact that something has been stored. We will look at each point of view in greater detail shortly, but first it will be useful to study the experimental evidence.

(b) Early Studies of Learning.

Experimental psychology started in the latter part of the 19th cent. largely as the result of pioneering work of the German physiologist and psychologist Wilhelm Wundt. No one today gets greatly excited at Wundt's experiments nor at his writings, but he was one of the first people in the world to realise that one could actually subject the raw material of mental activity to the experimental method and in this way he is memorable. Wundt concentrated on perception and similar topics and also conducted the first studies of reaction time—the delays humans make between being given the signal to start a task and actually beginning it. He had little to say about the matter of learning and memory, leaving it to a successor, Hermann Ebbinghaus, to get the ball rolling in this area.

Ebbinghaus's experiments were beautifully simple. He took human beings into his laboratory and set out to teach them lists of words, plotting the success rate (number of words in a sequence remembered) against the number of repetitions that had been given. This may all seem frightfully obvious, particularly when we say that Ebbinghaus found that the more repetitions, the better the list of words were learned. This is exactly what one would expect now, a century later, but at that time things weren't so clear cut. Furthermore, Ebbinghaus showed that when you plotted the rate of learning on a graph, a very characteristic curve emerged, common to all his normal subjects, which indicated a gentle improvement in learning with the first few repetitions of the list, followed in due course by a sharply accelerating rise which in turn tapered off. Finally a point came when the list was either completely learned, or no further improvement was made. The important factor was that while there were individual differences in the final level of achievement, and also in the time taken before the main surge of learning took place, the shape of the curve was very similar for all subjects. In other words, while there were significant differences in the ability of subjects to learn his word lists, the nature of the learning process seemed to be interestingly similar. Ebbinghaus's findings are as valid today as they were then and his learning curve fits rather well to the overall pattern of animal learning as well.

In his quest for objectivity he produced another interesting idea. It seemed to him that if one were to compare the performance of two different people in a learning task, one couldn't deduce much about their respective talents by examining the slope of the learning curve unless one knew something about their previous experience with the subject matter. For example, one person might, because of his job or something, simply have been more frequently exposed to the material featured and this would give him a built-in advantage which confused the issue. How about using foreign languages? Again Ebbinghaus felt that to get absolutely pure learning curves one would have to be certain that the subjects had not received prior exposure to the languages in question, a task almost impossible in principle. This led to his invention of a curious tool in the psychologist's workbox, the nonsense syllable, which is still used today as the standard material for many tests of learning ability. It consists ot a word with a meaningful sound and look to it, but which is almost complete nonsense inasmuch as it has no obvious meaningful association. ZAT, BOK, FID, BIJ, HAB are a few examples of this strange vocabulary. Ebbinghaus-type experiments are, as you can believe, immensely boring to perform and subjects today normally have to be paid in order to persuade them to take part! However, his realisation that human learning processes could be brought into a real, if rather dull, laboratory setting was a big step forward. Furthermore he had realised the necessity of separating out performance in one task from the background of past experience, an idea which has had far-reaching consequences on the design of all psychological experiments since and which even touches on the important question of the interplay between heredity and environment which we shall look at in the final section.

(c) Learning Experiments with Animals.

The use of nonsense syllables gets over the problem of past experience in one limited area of experimental psychology only, and if one really wants to know something about the formation of the learning process from scratch then one either has to start with very young babies, or use laboratory animals. One psychologist went so far as to read aloud lengthy passages of Greek prose to his infant son at an age when the baby couldn't even understand English. Years later the psychologist gave his son, by now a young man, a number of passages of Greek prose to learn, among which were the sections the baby had previously heard. The outcome was that the sections to which the child had been exposed as a baby were found to be significantly easier than the fresh material. This odd and very tedious experiment has never been repeated, though it is generally rejected by psychologists today as having been imperfectly controlled. For example, who can say for certain what the young man had or had not learnt in the period between the two phases of the experiment? It nevertheless remains as one of a few heroic efforts to use young babies as subjects in learning experiments and it also highlights some of the great difficulties involved.

By the turn of the century more and more psychologists were beginning to follow the lead given by their physiological cousins in bringing animals into the research laboratory. One of the first and most important figures to do so was the American Edward Thorndike, who began to look at the behaviour of specially bred white rats in laboratory learning experiments. Now with humans the problem of how to get the subject to do what one wants him to—learn nonsense syllables or whatever—is met by simply speaking to him about it. With animals this won't work, so Thorndike decided that they would have to be rewarded in some way if they were to learn anything. Reward can be any one of a lot of things, and for an animal it can be getting out of a situation it doesn't like, such as some kind of maze or puzzle box in which a number of specific moves have to be made in sequence before it can get out. Thorndike found that most animals make strenuous and fairly determined efforts to get out of boxes, mazes, etc., and can follow a fairly elaborate sequence of moves in order to reach their goal. Rats, for example, will learn to press a series of levers in the right order if they will open the door to a box, and they will gradually get better and better with practice. Similarly, when placed in a complicated maze, provided they are rewarded with food or escape at the end, they will soon find their way round it. The crucial point here seemed to be the reward, and while pet owners have known for centuries that a piece of sugar presented at the proper time will make a pet do tricks, it is really not clear why it should. To say that it is because the animal "wants the sugar" is no explanation as to why this trick should be learnt rather than some other pattern of behaviour. But Thorndike found without doubt that an animal would learn a maze or similar task far better if it were rewarded in some way at the completion of the task, and he too couldn't see just why, in physiological terms, the neural events which made up the correct performance of the task should be "built in" simply because the animal was rewarded, while incorrect patterns of behaviour were rejected. Ebbinghaus had come to the conclusion that successful learning was a function of the number of times the task was repeated. Thorndike argued that while practice helped to make perfect, it needed something else as well—*i.e.* the successful completion of the act. How would one measure success? Well, getting out of a maze or finding sugar at the other end would presumably count, and Thorndike described this principle as the "Law of Effect," believing that he had discovered two factors necessary for learning to be successful (for the information to be placed into the store), one being *frequency*, the other being *effect*. Psychologists at the time carefully sidestepped the niggling question of how *effect* (something happening at the end of a sequence) could work back in time to establish the sequence in memory by arguing that the reward or reinforcement did not itself cause the sequence to be stored in the memory system. It simply made that sequence more likely to be called up on some future occasion. But, replied the critics, wouldn't that imply that all sequences were stored with both right and wrong behaviour lodged equally firmly in memory? This question is still being hotly debated today, and we will shortly be taking a look at the evidence concerning what is and isn't learnt in an experimental situation. But first a word about one of the most important concepts not only in modern psychology, but also in 20th cent. science—the conditioned reflex.

(d) Pavlov and the Conditioned Reflex.

The great Russian physiologist Pavlov reached the peak of his scientific genius in the early years following the Communist revolution in Russia, where his very physical approach to psychological phenomena found favour with his country's leaders. The reasons were ideological. To many it seemed that Pavlov could explain all behaviour in purely mechanistic terms and thus do away with mystical, metaphysical, and, to Communist thinking, totally out-of-date views of Man's nature. Pavlov, it was felt, was at last exorcising the Ghost out of the Machine. His findings in fact sent ripples across the world, and the face of psychology was changed by them—notably in injecting into it the realisation that a good psychologist must think like a physiologist at least as often as he thinks like a philosopher. On the other hand, his naïvely simple view of the machinery of mind and brain was bound sooner or later to be exposed as only partially adequate, missing many of the richly complicated facets of human behaviour which must be faced up to and not denied. What was Pavlov really saying? At rock bottom his ideas revolved around the notion of the conditioned reflex arc, a concept that all wishing to understand modern psychology must get clear in their minds sooner or later.

The experiments in question were exceedingly simple inasmuch as they confined an animal to a rather limited environment and studied its behaviour in the most fundamental kind of learning situation. Pavlov, who was enormously interested in gastric and salivary secretion, had noticed that some of the animals in his laboratory would respond to the presence of food with copious flows of saliva, while others would not. Some would even respond excitedly when a particular food pan appeared while others again would not. He reasoned that these differences were in some way a function of the particular animal's past experience and set out to study this in detail. Firstly, he devised a method of measuring saliva flow, which would normally be copious when an animal was presented with its food bowl. He then introduced, just prior to the presentation of the food, a buzzer, bell, light, or some other similar stimulus. Initially the preliminary stimulus would yield no salivary response, but after a while, provided that the pairing of the presentations was kept up, the first traces of saliva would begin to appear upon the sound of the bell. If this were reliably followed by food, soon the saliva would appear in full flood to bell alone. Failure to offer up the food, however, if persistent, would lead to a gradual falling off in the amount of saliva until it ultimately dwindled away. Pavlov declared that this must imply that a probably instinctive reflex—salivating to food—had become linked in neural terms with a stimulus which had at first been totally irrelevant, the sounding of a bell. The more frequently the two events were linked and the more closely they were associated in time, the stronger the new reflex arc would be. Lack of association between bell and food would lead to the extinction of the reflex arc. The fact that extinction was not total could be nicely shown by introducing the food again, whereupon things would come rapidly back to normal with the bell producing copious flows of saliva once more. Today this seems a fairly trivial observation, but at the time Pavlov, his co-workers, and psychologists all over the world became immensely excited about the conditioned reflex. The reason was that there seemed to be no reason in principle why the whole of an animal's behavioural responses had not been acquired in just this simple way with the same argument applying with equal force to humans. At the root of all behaviour lay a simple physiological principle. By employing this properly, all living things could have their behaviour patterns moulded in whatever direction was felt to be appropriate, all psychological malfunctions could be corrected, education made simple, the wild beast tamed, the workings of the brain fully described and comprehended. This, for a brief period, was the golden goal (if one likes to think of it in that way) of the new science of psychology—to see man for what he really was; a complex mass of inherited and conditioned reflex arcs.

If Pavlov and his followers in Russia clung to this dream for decades longer than did less politically committed scientists in other parts of the world, then this is understandable. One of the goals of scientific endeavour is simplification and an explanation of human behaviour in terms of stimulus–response units would certainly meet part of that goal. But on the other hand part of the goal of science is also objectivity—even at the risk of complicating explanations—and before long it became obvious that the animal in the experimental Pavlovian set up was *not* behaving as a complicated automaton. For example, it is possible to condition an animal to lift its foot to avoid an electric shock if a bell reliably signals the imminence of the shock. Now place the animal on its side, ring the bell and—will the animal lift its foot? Yes—but not before getting up to the standing position first. But if the animal is blindly responding to the firing of a neuro-muscular reflex arc, why does it not simply raise its foot while lying down? And how does the standing up act become incorporated into the reflex sequence without prior training? Such experiments were simply discounted at first as being too inconvenient for the theory, but as time went on the immense oversimplification of the stimulus – response theory of behaviour became obvious. But not before a major movement sprang up in the United States which attempted to make dynamic and imaginative use of Pavlov's findings in an attempt at an all-embracing psychological theory. We now turn to look at this, the so-called Behaviourist School.

(e) The Rise of Behaviourism.

Sometime before Pavlov's ideas began to have impact in the West, a spontaneous movement had been developing among psychologists to reject the traditional methods of introspection in experimental research. The interplay of conscious thought and mental activity was felt inevitably to confuse the issue, and workers were urged wherever possible to make objective rather than subjective judgments. One of the hardest advocates of this line was J. B. Watson, who even went so far as to argue that introspective studies of consciousness, etc., were not merely misleading, but positively useless. In principle, Watson proposed, it should be possible to give a total explanation of the subject matter of psychology—whether human or animal—in descriptive, mechanical terms concerning the outward manifestations of behaviour. This implied ultimately taking such extreme points of view as declaring thinking to be merely "sub-verbal speaking," better described in terms of minor twitches of the throat, mouth, and tongue muscles than in patterns of electrical activity in the higher centres of the brain. All that was needed to give the Behaviourist school impetus was Pavlov's discovery of the conditioned reflex, and when this was published it was eagerly incorporated as the prop of Watson's argument. To Watson and his colleagues the only realistic and profitable way to look at human and animal behaviour was in terms of a strictly mechanistic model, the conditioned reflex arcs serving as the vital links in the creature's chain of activity. Now many people might agree that an animal in a highly restricted laboratory situation, trained to salivate to bells, raise its paw to avoid an electric shock, etc., might well be coming as close to a biological machine as one could imagine, but was this a really adequate way of describing its behaviour "in the wild"? Critics of Behaviourism were quick to point out certain peculiarities that they felt could not be handled by Watson's simple system. Take a dog, for example, and face it with a series of doors, behind one of which is to be found food, sometimes one door, sometimes another. Now train the dog to respond to a light switched on briefly as signalling food. Now indicate the door which has food by switching on a light above it, and the dog will soon learn to trot up reliably to the appropriate door. What has happened? Easy say the Behaviourists—the dog has been conditioned to approach a light for food, and the reflex carries over to a light above a door. The dog is not really responding to the door, but to the light which sets the appropriate reflex arc in motion, just as pushing a button can cause a car to start. But what, the critics argued, about the fact that the light is switched on for only a few seconds, and yet even after it is off the dog still moves towards the door? Watson replied that the light caused the animal to look towards the door and it immediately adopted a particular posture, setting its musculature up so that it would set off in the appropriate direction, no longer needing the light for a guide. This might seem fair enough, but for the fact that if, just as the animal is about to set off for the door, you hold it, refusing to allow it to move, it still "shows interest" in the door. Furthermore, if you let go in five minutes time, the chances are that the animal will set off to the correct door—a bit long one would have thought for the reflex arc to have been maintained in suspended animation. Was it not simpler, Watson's critics replied, to face up to the fact that the animal was using the light as a signal and was holding the door in some mental form as a kind of goal to which it could make a delayed response if necessary? So adamant were the Behaviourists that all behaviour could be explained in terms of sequences of conditioned muscular movements that they strove to argue that even during the delay the animal was still maintaining a muscular posture—rather in the way that a hunting dog freezes to point to prey. Furthermore, Watson produced what he believed to be irrefutable evidence for the dominance of the muscular activity, even on a task as complex as learning to run a maze. In this rather cruel-sounding experiment he trained a whole lot of rats to find their way through a rather detailed maze. He then preceded to eliminate by surgery all normal sensory equipment—eyes, ears, smell, etc., leaving only the kinaesthetic, or touch, sense. These grossly deprived animals nevertheless still managed to find their way through the maze, allowing him to conclude that in line with the conditioned-reflex notion, the animals were relying predominantly on a chain of muscle reflexes. For a brief period this dramatic experiment seemed to clinch the Behaviourist case. But then came a counter-experiment, even more drastic. A psychologist called Lashley repeated Watson's experiment, but this time also removed the sense of touch by spinal surgery. The wretched creatures even now managed to stagger through the maze—though they were certainly no longer equipped with proper muscular responses. Lashley, correctly, felt this dealt with the ultra-simple Behaviourist argument and that somehow or other the animals must be retaining some kind of general directional sense, a sort of "notion" as to where the exit lay. At about this time more attacks on Behaviourism came from a rival point of view—the Gestalt school. Watson himself shortly afterwards became involved in a sensational divorce case which forced him, in those less permissive times, to resign from academic life. He ended his brilliant career in, of all things, the advertising profession.

(f) Gestalt Psychologists and Learning.

With its emphasis on such ideas as "the whole is something more than the sum of its parts" and its insistence on the idea that the brain has dynamic organising powers which serve to modify input and intervene between stimulus and response, the Gestalt point of view was clearly about as far removed from the naïve Behaviourist viewpoint as was possible. One of the principal allies of the Gestaltists in its early days was K. S. Lashley, referred to above, a brilliant experimentalist with an eye for the essentials of the problem. Throughout his long research life he remained open-minded about various schools of psychology and unconvinced on the various rival theories concerning the physiological basis of memory. He was, however, quick to see the basic weaknesses in the various brain models that fellow psychologists were always confidently erecting, and the first to feel the sharpness of his attack were the Behaviourists. Lashley swiftly realised that the attractive simplicity of the Pavlov/Watson argument was that the basic unit in learning consisted of a fundamentally simple physiological system, a neural reflex arc. In ordinary terms this could be looked on as a chain of cells connecting from, say, the retina through the higher centres of the brain (where the chain would be forged) down to the muscle or set of muscles which constituted motor output. In other words, a light would strike the retina, a number of cells would fire. These in turn would excite cortical cells which had, by prior conditioning, become linked into a reflex arc. Finally these would, quite mechanically, induce the appropriate muscular response. The memory itself constituted the connecting cells in the cortex, and this memory had been established by the learning or conditioning process. Lashley then realised that a memory unit, or an engram as he named it, must be represented by a particular set of cells in a particular part of the brain. In principle, therefore, one should be able to discover these sets of cells and find out what kind of memory is located in what part of the brain.

Lashley's technique was again that of surgical destruction of tissue and using this he performed one of the most remarkable experiments in the history of modern psychology and physiology. His findings created a shock of disbelief and controversy, and their full implications are still not fully understood today—about 50 years after he performed the experiment. Taking a large number of rats, he trained them until they were highly familiar with a complicated maze. He then proceeded to remove from each rat a small portion of cortical tissue, taking a different area but an equivalent amount from each rat. In due course he had removed from his collection of rats the equivalent of one complete brain, though no individual animal had had more than 5 per cent of its cortical tissue destroyed. He then took another set of rats, trained them in the maze, and again removed the equivalent of a brain, but this time taking 10 per cent from each rat. With a further sample he went through the procedure again, but removed a quarter of each rat's brain, and in his final group he had a limited number of animals, each of which had had half its cortex removed. See if you can work out what he found. Remember that if the memory or engram consisted of a series of linked cells then one might expect that these would be found in one relatively small segment of the brain. Interrupting the chain at any point should presumably destroy or grossly handicap memory. Now from the simple behaviourist point of view, most people would have to predict that one or two rats whose hunk of cortex removed had featured the conditioned reflexes involving the maze, would be completely clueless when placed in it. The engram would have been removed. This would then tell the experimenter, as Lashley had hoped, which part of the brain dealt with such tasks as maze learning. Other animals, who had not lost their maze engram would show no detriment in their performance of this task. To his amazement, and to everyone else's for that matter, Lashley found that his first group of rats, each of whom had lost about 5 per cent of cortical tissue, were apparently totally unaffected by the surgery, running the maze just as well as they did before! The rat with bigger chunks of tissue removed were slightly more affected, but even those with only half a brain left were still able to run the maze fairly competently. The loss of memory seemed to be somewhat proportional to the amount of tissue removed, but *not in any way to the area removed*! In other words, the mysterious engram did not seem to be located in any single spot, and Lashley was forced to conclude that it looked as though learning and memory were a function of the whole brain rather than just part of it.

As could be imagined, these findings were not well received by the conditioned reflex advocates and numerous attempts made to repeat them merely served to support these first findings. They were received enthusiastically by the Gestalt psychologists, who saw them as another example of their argument that the brain must be considered as an integrated whole and not as simply a bundle of conditioned reflexes.

The next strong—perhaps the strongest—anti-Behaviourist argument came from one of the Gestalt school founders, Wolfgang Kohler. His findings were disclosed in his important book, *The Mentality of Apes*, which can be bought in paperback and which everyone interested in psychology should read. Kohler, who was one of those clever scientists who manage to find themselves work in exotic parts of the world, conducted his critical experiments at the Primate Research Station in the Canary Islands. Here he watched with great interest the considerable learning skills of the higher apes, such as chimpanzees, and quickly arrived at the conclusion that conditioned reflex theory was not adequate to explain the scope of their intellectual behaviour. His most famous observation concerned the never-to-be-forgotten chimpanzee, Sultan. Kohler had noticed that chimpanzees will play about with sticks and similar devices in their cage, which they seem to use as toys. He then began to wonder whether the monkeys could ever be induced to use them as tools, so after placing potential implements inside Sultan's cage he then put a banana on the other side of the bars just outside its reach. After a bit of fruitless stretching the ape took one of the sticks and pulled the banana in. Now this in itself is a remarkable achievement, and if the ape had actually "worked out" the solution then it would have been suggestive of very much higher thought processes in the animal than had hitherto been believed possible. However, it could be reasonably argued that the chimpanzee had seen some other person or animal using the stick as a tool and was therefore merely imitating, an action which could, with a bit of latitude, be thought of in behaviouristic terms. Kohler's next step put paid to that point of view. He placed in the cage several sticks of various lengths which could be fitted together to form a longer one, and, taking care not to show this technique to the monkey, again set a banana outside the bars but out of reach of any one single stick. After scratching round fruitlessly with various sticks and making aggrieved noises, Sultan began to play rather aimlessly with the sticks, occasionally fitting them together by chance. Suddenly Kohler, who was watching, saw the chimpanzee fit two sticks together, stare at them for a moment and then, as if making a decision, walk rapidly to the side of the cage and with this new long pole pull the banana in. The moment of comprehension when the ape "realised" what he could do Kohler wittily termed the "ah-ha reflex," a phrase which sums up beautifully a sensation we all understand and which was totally unaccounted for by the Pavlovian approach to the problem.

(g) Later Developments in Learning Theory.

You may have the feeling that Behaviourism, conditioned reflex theory, and its attendant experimental studies are more or less worthless and a hindrance rather than a help to the development of modern psychology. This is far from the truth. The point is that despite its vigorous self-confidence and contempt for "introspective" approaches to psychology, Behaviourism really only falls down through its pretentions to providing a *complete* theory of mind and brain. The Behaviourist experiments still work, and there is undoubtedly such a thing as the conditioned reflex, though one has next to no idea, from the physiological point of view, how it is laid down. Throughout the 1930s and beyond, psychologists supporting the Behaviourist position performed thousands of ingenious and often highly imaginative experiments to back up their ideas, these always being subject to counter-attack from the opposition, most of whom were followers of the Gestalt school. For years arguments raged over Kohler's "insight" study with the chimpanzees, and became even hotter when experiments claiming to demonstrate "insight" in lesser creatures, such as rats, were performed. Gradually, under intense pressure, the Behaviourist hard-line softened, the pretence that animals were no more than bundles of totally automatic reflexes was quietly abandoned. Once this occurred, and the Behaviourist method was put to work studying the functioning of living systems, then experimental psychology was set for a boom. One of the most significant features of the conditioned-reflex method, as exemplified by Pavlov's original experiments, was its usefulness for examining the nature of animal perception. Offhand one might wonder how it could be possible to tell what an animal sees, or more exactly, how fine is its capacity for perceptual discrimination. How could one find out whether a rat could tell the difference between a triangle and a square and between one colour and another? One can ask humans, but rats . . .? In the case of colours, what one could do would be to train the creature to respond to a red light, and then gradually alter its hue in the direction of another colour, say blue. If, before one had made much of a change in hue, the animal was ceasing to respond then one would know that it was detecting the change of hue. As for shape perception, the problem is even easier. In the very early days Pavlov conditioned his dogs to respond positively (*i.e.*, with saliva) to a circle, and negatively (*i.e.*, raising paw to avoid shock) when a rather angular ellipse was shown to it. Then he gradually made the circle more and more like an ellipse, and the ellipse more and more like a circle. Up to a point he got clear-cut appropriate responses, until the pattern lay somewhere in between. At this point the dog, poor creature, had a nervous breakdown, which wasn't too nice for it, but which told Pavlov a lot about its sensory and perceptual processes. While on these slightly macabre topics it might be worth mentioning that today dogs and rats have largely been supplanted for behaviouristic studies by a rather quaint choice of animal—the pigeon. The fact is that pigeons have been found to have quite remarkable powers of sensory discrimination and will peck away at buttons to get food or avoid electric shocks for hours on end. So good is the pigeon at telling the difference between patterns that it was even once proposed for a fantastic rôle in modern warfare—not its traditional job of carrying messages from spies but, believe it or not, as the control centre for a flying bomb! In the early days of guided missiles the kind of electrical equipment available was too bulky, cumbersome and unreliable to be easily put into flying bombs. This was particularly true about the equipment necessary to allow the bomb to select the correct target at the other end. One bright psychologist argued that the pigeon would be an inexpensive, compact, and reliable "pilot" for a flying bomb. The device, complete with pigeon in a little cabin, could be launched off on course and when the bird spotted the target (say an enemy battleship) which it had been previously trained to recognise, it would peck at the appropriate button and that would be that! So far as one can tell the idea was never implemented, which is probably a good thing for us humans—to say nothing of the pigeons. The idea might be described as one of the less fruitful to come from Pavlov's original idea and serves to remind us that psychology, just as any other science, can be properly or improperly used, depending upon circumstances and the individuals involved. But let us now return to the basic question—what is the actual nature of the learning process or the memory trace?

(h) The Nature of the Engram.

Earlier we said that there were three broad approaches to the problem of the memory trace, the neurological, the electrical, and the biochemical.

(1) *The Neurological.*

This is probably the kind of model that Pavlov would put forward today if he were alive. To understand it, remember that the conditioned reflex is essentially a chain of cells running from sense organ to motor-output (finger, paw, eye-blink, whatever). The cells of course were there in the first place, built into the animal from birth. It is the connections between cells, the links in the chain that are forged in the learning process. Fine, but how *are* the connections formed? Why one chain rather than another? A number of attempts have been made to solve this one, perhaps the most ingenious in recent years coming from the Canadian psychologist D. O. Hebb, an architect incidentally of the sensory deprivation experiments, and one of the first psychologists to be elected as a Fellow of the Royal Society. Hebb had been impressed by the discovery that nerve cells were frequently adorned with tiny bumps or knobs which tended to cluster at the points where the cell made contact with other cells—the *synapse*. There was even some suggestion from microscopic studies that these synaptic knobs tended to become larger and more profuse in the brains of more mature animals. Suppose, Hebb argued, that when a nerve cell was fired, it made contact with another via a synaptic knob and thus triggered the second cell into action. Suppose also that each time a synapse was bridged via a contact knob, this knob grew a little, as though through exercise, and thus made better contact. This, as time went on, would significantly raise the likelihood of a nervous impulse crossing at this point. If one can imagine the process repeated with a whole series of cells, then one can see that repeated firings would also increase the likelihood of particular chains of cells being activated, thus wearing a kind of path through the nervous system down which the neural impulse would "prefer" to travel. This Hebb suggested, could be the basis of the conditioned reflex—simply a connection made progressively easier each time the route was travelled.

Hebb's theory attracted a good deal of attention when it was first published over 20 years ago, first because it seemed to fit the known physiological facts (such as they were) and second because it seemed to get over one of the awful difficulties facing any neurological theory of learning—the experiments of Lashley. Recapping briefly, these showed that the memory trace or engram for a particular task was not located in any one small section of the brain. Now Hebb's synaptic knob model implied that the initial path followed by a nervous impulse might be pretty random throughout the cortex, wandering here and there until, with repeated firings, it became established. This would quite possibly be a rather straggly chain and not necessarily the shortest distance between two points. Add to this the fact that the acquisition of a complex habit, such as learning a maze, would obviously depend upon thousands, possibly hundreds of thousands, of these neural links being established, and one can begin to see that Lashley's experimental results no longer seem to fly in the face of reason. Removal of any single chunk of cortical tissue would simply serve to remove a more or less random selection of the neural chains serving as the maze-memory. The more one took out, the worse the memory of the maze would be, but no single piece removed would ever eliminate the whole of the memory! To many people Hebb's theory, crude though it might be, fairly tackles the apparent paradox of Lashley's results. Others are not so sure. Its main default, the intervening years have shown, is that his nice ideas about the growth of synaptic knobs and their significance as contact points between cells are probably no longer valid. Today their function, and even their existence in the form that Hebb discussed, is questioned by many physiologists. Furthermore, for various reasons, there has been a strong shift towards the point of view that whatever form the learning process takes it is unlikely to involve changes in neural tissue—at least of such magnitude. To many psychologists and their colleagues, changes in the molecular structure of the cell must be involved. Before considering the evidence for this hypothesis, we need to examine briefly the Gestalt psychologists' attempt to account for learning and memory.

(2) *Electrical Field Theory.*

We have been talking of the Gestalt psychologists without pointing out an interesting fact—that the two principal founders were first trained as physicists! Jumping the broad gap between physics and psychology might seem a bit much, but Wolfgang Kohler was one who did it, and in doing so he injected into his theorising some of the ideas basic to his native topic. In the main this involved the concepts of electrical field theory. Without going into this in boring detail, it so happens that an electrical source, either in the form of a battery, a current flowing down a wire or whatever, spouts electrons in its immediate neighbourhood and these constitute an electromagnetic field. As the name implies, the most striking example of such a field is to be seen in the ordinary common-or-garden magnet, and the structure of the field can be observed by placing the magnet in a large mass of iron filings. Now Kohler and his friends argued that the brain was a potent source of electromagnetic energy and ought, therefore, to create a field within and around its tissue. The field would be powerful enough to modify incoming electrical input from the senses and to some extent impose its own pattern on it. Hence the Gestalt "laws" of perceptual organisation. This would be a two-way process, however, for sensory input, no matter how feeble, would impose at least minor changes on the structure of the cerebral field. Such changes, the Gestaltists argued, would constitute the basis of learning. It was a bold, if somewhat implausible point of view, and was treated as a serious alternative to the Pavlovian conditioned reflex ideas for at least a period. It had one or two gross defects, however, which even the Gestalt psychologists found worrying. In the first place, no kind of recording device seemed able to pick up any signs of permanent or semi-permanent electrical fields surrounding the brain. The EEG seemed to be a rhythmic picture of electrical change within, rather than of a static, powerful field highly resistant to change. Secondly, there is the odd data from electro-shock therapy. This much-maligned method of treating highly-depressed psychiatric patients relies on jolting the brain with a powerful electric shock, a not particularly pleasant process which nevertheless generally brings a notable remission in patients' symptoms. The point here is not to argue the pros and cons of ECT, as it is called, but to indicate that such tremendous shocks should be enough to seriously disturb any electrical fields, no matter how well-established, with presumably drastic effects on memory. In fact, long-term memory is totally unaffected by ECT, though, as the Gestalt supporters were quick to point out, there is short-term amnesia for events immediately preceding the electric shock. Thirdly, and finally, as it happens, there is the clinching experimental work of Lashley—not his tissue-removal experiment, but yet another in the catalogue of his remarkable repertoire. Lashley's procedure was as follows. He first taught a large number of rats a particular maze. Then he inserted in their cortex very fine sheets of gold leaf—a notorious destroyer of electrical fields. He then ran the rats through the same maze again, and found no evidence of any detriment in their performance. He also taught other rats the maze after they had had the gold leaf implanted, and found that they learnt it with no undue difficulty. After this work the Gestalt battle cry never seemed so loud or so convincing again. It is doubtful, actually, whether they ever really believed the electrical field theory, but it was a nice idea while it lasted.

(3) *The Biochemical Argument: Some Fresh Surprises.*

The memory capacity of the human brain is absolutely enormous. It has been calculated that it is quite capable of storing all the information ever fed into it—in other words there is no need for anything ever to be thrown out of store to make room for fresh material. The real problem in this case is not finding enough room to pump in information, but in finding a sufficiently efficient system to pull it out rapidly. Not only do psychologists believe that the brain has this almost limitless storage capacity, but they also have some evidence that all the information fed in, no matter how trivial, actually *is* stored! Some of the most exciting evidence to back up this belief has come from studies made during human brain surgery. These studies are a trifle gruesome and the squeamish might like to jump a paragraph or two here.

For a particular type of surgery—such as the excision of a brain tumour—it is necessary to remove a portion of the cranium and for various reasons it is advisable to perform the entire operation with the patient fully conscious. This is not so horrific as all that, for the brain itself has no pain-detecting cells and the initial opening can be made with a local anaesthetic. One or two scientifically-minded surgeons, notably Dr. Wilder Penfield, have taken the opportunity presented by this surgical requirement to perform certain experiments which have turned out to be of immense interest. With the patient's permission and co-operation, Penfield stimulated selected exposed portions of their cortex with tiny electric currents. Moving round from sensory area to sensory area he found that his tiny electrical stimuli provoked characteristic sensations from the patients. In the visual areas they might "see" lights, colours, etc., in the auditory areas "hear" sounds, and in the temporal lobes, get impressions of smells, taste, etc. Stranger still, Penfield found that certain parts of the so-called association areas of cortex, when stimulated, led to the patient recalling specific memories, often of apparently forgotten items. One woman got a vivid impression of herself in a kitchen of a former home and hearing the voice of her mother, long since dead. Others reported equally specific memories, sometimes with fragments of speech or conversation attached, quite often of items which the patients reported they "hadn't thought of for years." One possible implication for this exciting work is, as we have said, that *all* information that has ever been put into the brain is stored as memory just in case it should ever be needed again. If this is so, then to most psychologists the idea that the memory trace is laid down in the form of major structural changes in the cell body (such as with synaptic knobs) is no longer tenable. There simply aren't enough cells to cope. But suppose that the engram is laid down *within* the cell, at sub-microscopic level in the form of, perhaps, the rearrangement of the specialised molecular structure. Since no one has ever got a really good look at a molecule, either in the nervous system or out of it, this might seem to be a bit of optimistic guesswork, but there is in fact some strange evidence to back the idea up. To consider this we must acquaint ourselves with one of the lowliest creatures capable of learning—the little flatworm, planaria. There is a good deal of argument about how far down the animal kingdom some form of learning can take place. Some workers even claim to have demonstrated memory mechanism in tiny single-celled creatures such as amoeba or its hairy cousin, paramecia, but you can be sure that any information stored was of the simplest and most rudimentary kind. It is when we get to the simplest form of worms, and planaria is one of these, that something closer to memory in the real sense can be clearly demonstrated. Typical of the kind of task which planaria manage, albeit with a good deal of intellectual effort, is to turn right rather than left at a little junction in order to get food or avoid an electric shock. They can also be conditioned to wince to a light being switched on when this is always followed by an electric shock—rather like Pavlov's dogs. Now planaria has the most rudimentary, almost non-existent central nervous system. It has a front end, shaped rather like an arrow with tiny light-sensitive organs in it, and which is clearly its head. It also has a back end which the charitable would call a tail. The question now is—in what part of the tiny body are memories laid down? The head would seem to be the most likely bet, though you might feel it would be hard to tell for sure. At this point the psychologist makes use of another of planaria's interesting features—its ability to regenerate tissue with ease. Take a knife and slice off planaria's tail and both ends swim away, one rather more efficiently than the other. Now in due course the head section will produce a new tail and—rather fantastically—the tail will produce a new head! Planaria can do other odd things too. Cut down the centre of its head without actually removing any tissue and in due course the two half-heads will regenerate into two full heads, producing a peculiar but rather neat looking creature. If one makes several flaps, instead of just two, you end up with lots and lots of heads on one body and get a very odd-looking planaria indeed. All this is very interesting, but the exercise has more point than this. In the first case, ask yourself a question; suppose you teach planaria a little maze and then slice the head into two. Now, of the regenerating heads, which has got the "memory" of the maze stored in it? Left; right; both; neither? Actually, the answer is both, and this should give some clue as to the answer to the next question. Cut a maze-trained planaria in half (head and tail) and let the respective sections develop again into a full creature. One would certainly expect that the head part plus its new tail would be able to perform its little task without much trouble, but what about the tail with its new head? The answer is that this too can "run" the maze. If this seems to be contradicting everything we've said about learning and the brain in general up to now, then in a way it is. We must remember that planaria is an exceedingly simple creature with no CNS to speak of and no nerve cells of the kind found in higher animals. The engram, wherever it is, is certainly not formed by the development of synaptic knobs or by the modification of complex electrical fields. Furthermore, as it is evidently stored in tail as well as head section, then it must presumably be laid down in most, if not necessarily all, of the animal's body cells. This is the point where the biochemists step in and argue that it is not the outside but rather the interior structure of the cell that is modified through learning. Odd indeed, but there is odder yet to come. Researchers got a collection of planaria and taught them a particular task—turning right in a simple maze and then took an equivalent number of planaria with no experience of this kind. They then collected the first group and whirled them round in a mixing bowl until all that was left was a homogeneous planaria soup, and repeated the process with the other, untrained group. They now fed the two kinds of soup (planaria will eat more or less anything that's hanging round) to different groups of totally untrained planaria and subsequently trained these in the original right-turn task. This produced an extraordinary result. The planaria who had been fed the soup consisting of trained planaria seemed to learn the maze task significantly quicker than those who had been fed the untrained soup! You will know enough about experimental psychology by now to realise that these results caused immense controversy, and a series of experiments were immediately launched by workers who had found the first result incredible. The controversy, incidentally, still rages as many of the attempts to repeat the experiments have not worked, but the original protagonists still maintain the validity of their results. It is not hard to see why the critics get so hot under the collar, for the implications of the findings, if valid, will throw into question just about every theoretical approach to learning to date. Since the planaria were thoroughly mashed up, no neural connections or even any formal kind of organisation within the system would remain to carry the maze information across to the cannibal planaria. Furthermore, one would have thought that the digestive processes of the cannibals would have completed the process of destruction. How then could the original maze habit, or traces of it, be possibly preserved and carried over? No one on either side of the argument has been able to offer up any convincing explanation, except that if the results are valid, then the maze habit, in the case of planaria at any rate, must be stored right down at molecular level—in other words at such a microscopic level that any mixing and digestion could have little or no effect on it. But even if the planaria results *are* valid, would the same thing necessarily apply to humans? Not necessarily, but if a process works for one living system it could in principle work for another, and we must remember our conclusion that the brain's enormous memory store suggests that modification of the neurone itself would be at too gross a level. It may well be that we shall find the brain puts down information in more than one way. There is reasonable evidence, for example, that many animals and humans are equipped with two kinds of memory store—a short-term, and possibly highly unstable one, and a long-term, more or less perpetual system. Information fed into our brains might go initially to the short-term store where it is filtered for relevance or general usefulness. If unwanted for some reason it might be eliminated, but if wanted, passed on to the longer-term system. Perhaps the short-term memory (the kind that allows you to "momentarily" remember a new telephone number) is electrical and the long-term biochemical, neurological or both. At this moment psychologists and physiologists across the world are concentrating on these exciting problems and perhaps, within the next few years, we shall have some new answers and, quite certainly, some fresh surprises.

(i) Unsolved Problems.

This section has attempted to raise some of the issues confronting psychologists in their attempt to solve one of the main mysteries of the brain—how information is stored and processed within it. Although a fair bit has been learned in the past decades, it has really served to show that the problem is much more complicated than the earlier workers ever imagined. Furthermore, you will have noticed that precious little has been said about how the information is extracted, for the very good reason that precious little is known about this. Curiously some interesting clues are beginning to come from the study of computers, man's own specially-created slave brains. These are already capable of storing quite immense quantities of information, and engineers have been working steadily at improving methods of storing information and of getting it out in a hurry. In recent years the computer engineers and the psychologists have been tending to get together and pool their ideas—with some interesting results. To more and more scientists it has become increasingly obvious that the study of the brain is real ground for interdisciplinary contact, and that contributions to its study can come equally from psychologists, physiologists, physicists, engineers, mathematicians, educationalists, and so on. The highly successful Brain Research Association, for example, is composed of scientists from practically every discipline, with psychologists and physiologists, who are traditionally the kingpins in brain science, making up no more than 25 per cent of its ranks. Perhaps the really big problems in brain research will only come from multi-disciplinary teams of this kind. But this is something of a digression and we must now pass on from learning and memory to the lesser, but no less interesting problem of motivation.

IV. MOTIVATION.

(1) Why Does an Animal Do One Thing Rather Than Another?

This question aptly sums up the problem of animal and human motivation, an important facet of modern psychological research. As is always the case with psychology, perhaps more so than with other fields of science, what initially seem to be straightforward questions, designed to elicit straightforward answers, become steadily more complicated on close inspection. The odd, almost philosophical difficulties surrounding motivation are a good example. Why *does* an animal do one thing rather than another? Because it wants to, is the stock reply—a reply which actually doesn't get anywhere at all. To say that the reason for doing something is because the doer *likes it* is no explanation, merely renaming the problem so that it comes up in a different guise. It so happens that we tend to like doing the things we do, though of course this doesn't always apply. We certainly like to eat, but do we eat principally because we like it or because the food is essential to our survival? Perhaps the key is tied up here somewhere, and the rock-bottom cause for all animal and human behaviour lies in the need to keep the individual creature alive. Well, that will certainly do for food and water, but it clearly doesn't work for other common activities, such as sex. In the long term the survival of all living things depends upon sexual activity but animals certainly don't understand this and humans only found out the link between the sexual act and conception a millennium or so ago. And anyone who believes that people indulge in sex solely to allow the human species to survive is very naive indeed. Now the situation gets even more complicated. It seems as if we make love because we like it, with the long-term result being that the species survives. But what can be the link, in physiological terms, between liking something and it " doing us good "? And just to complicate matters even more, supposing that we accept this link, how do we explain other common patterns of human behaviour? Why do some people like going to football matches or art galleries? Why don't they go there to eat the footballers or the paintings, and how is the survival of the human species helped by such practices anyway? Having muddled the issue thoroughly—or, rather, showed it up in its true light—we can now go on to see how psychologists have set to work to try to unravel it. They have not got very far, but they have got somewhere.

(2) The Mechanical Tortoise.

The first people to face up to the problems raised above were the Behaviourists. In their gallant attempt to explain human and animal behaviour in mechanistic terms they realised that they would have to account for the tendency of animals to set out to do things rather than simply engage in random, diffuse activity, and they thought this could be fairly simply handled. They were most anxious, of course, to avoid explaining different types of behaviour in terms of different goals—to suggest that an animal had got a goal in mind was to imply that it had a mind and furthermore some kind of " picture of the future " in it. To begin with they took the simplest possible form of mechanical analogy. Imagine a clockwork mouse, which when wound up runs across the floor. What caused it to do so? The clockwork and the energy tied up in the spring, of course, with its direction determined by such matters as the orientation of its wheels, the angle of the floor, etc. Anyone saying that the toy crossed the floor because it wanted to would be being silly. Similarly, the Behaviourists stated, one should be able to avoid the same kind of inference when observing the movements of a real mouse. If the response is that the real mouse can do a good deal more than just run across a floor—can squeak, change direction, avoid cats and eat cheese—then the reply in essence is that one could build a mechanical mouse to do that as well, provided one had the time and ingenuity. The more complicated and versatile the mechanical mouse the harder it would become to tell the difference between the two, and when one had two apparently identical mice, would one still talk about one " wanting " to cross a floor and the other doing it purely automatically? Was there an important difference anyway? Critics of Behaviourism argued that indeed there was a difference. The " real " mouse ate the cheese because it satisfied a need for the food, whereas the mechanical mouse, no matter how many bogus sounds of enjoyment it made as it munched the food, was merely going through an essentially meaningless mechanical process. This is a dangerous argument, for suppose that one decided to power the artificial mouse not by clockwork but by the combustion of cheese and made it so that it would stop when its inner store of cheese ran out . . . one would now have an artificial mouse with a " need " for cheese as great as that of its biological counterpart. If this seems an unlikely step to take, consider the case of Grey Walter's mechanical tortoise. In an effort to replicate some of the conditions of behaviour, the great English psychologist, Dr. Grey Walter of the Burden Neurological Institute, constructed a tortoise which exhibited some of the paramount properties of living creatures. His tortoise—a shell on wheels with no pretentions to looking like an animal—was powered by storage batteries which drove a motor allowing it to run around on the floor. Its movements were far from aimless, for it was also equipped with photocells in its head capable of detecting areas of light or dark. A series of simple switches inside were arranged so that when the tortoise's batteries were fully charged, the device would move towards dark areas of a room, finding its way underneath chairs and tables, carefully working its way round books, human feet, etc., placed in its way. With batteries low, a different switching arrangement would come into operation and the device would now tend to avoid dark areas and seek out light ones—in particular the light inside its " hutch " where a battery charge was conveniently situated. Once inside the hutch Grey Walter's tortoise would connect up to the battery charger, later emerging " replenished " to set out for dark places again! Here the Behaviourist argument emerges most strongly. It is not, of course, that Grey Walter had manufactured a living thing—no one is making that claim—but rather a matter of whether the tortoise's tendency to seek out its battery for recharging, etc., constituted a need in the same sense as does the real mouse's need for cheese. This is a big question which you will probably have to think out for yourself. In the meanwhile let's see how the Behaviourists attempted to translate animal behaviour into similar terms.

(3) Drives and Needs.

The Behaviourist position can be summed up as an attempt at describing animal behaviour in the simplest possible way, and to do this they evolved the concept of "Drive." A drive is described as something which causes an animal to perform a particular act, and the ideal position, from the behaviouristic viewpoint, would be to find that all animal activity could be explained in terms of a limited number of drives. To begin with things looked simple and promising, for it appeared as if a drive could be thought of as something that promoted bodily well-being. For example, when an animal is short of food it is running out of power. This causes a sensation known as "hunger" which signals a bodily "need" and this in turn sets in motion a chain of activity which culminates in eating. When the food has been ingested, the need is satisfied, the hunger vanishes and the drive is reduced. The same argument applies to thirst and, with a bit of modification, to sex. In the latter case if an animal does not engage in sexual activity for a given period of time certain substances build up in the body, the hormonal system becomes unbalanced, etc., and a need builds up in the body, which gives rise to a drive. This in turn pushes the creature towards sexual activity with a suitable mate. Carry this on just a bit more and include a "need" to escape painful situations and you've practically got the whole of animal behaviour sewn up. What's more it is sewn up in a very convincing way because the needs and drives are not vague and ambiguous, but relate directly to vital bodily processes which if not operating properly will cause the animal's death. All animal behaviour could be explained in terms of a drive to (i) reduce hunger, (ii) reduce thirst, (iii) reduce pain, and (iv) achieve sex. To those who didn't want to talk about "achievement," which seemed to imply that an animal was actually setting out to do something, then the final one could be rephrased (iv) to reduce sexual tension. An animal in a state of need would be activated by some or all of these drives and would continue to "behave" until all drives were reduced. Protagonists of this delightfully simple point of view even showed how learning theory could benefit from drive-reduction ideas; a pattern of behaviour or conditioned reflex would be established, they claimed, if at its conclusion a drive was reduced. If no drive-reduction took place, then the behaviour pattern would not be learned. In the 'thirties and 'forties a number of mathematically inclined psychologists even attempted to express this in the form of sets of equations which looked enormously impressive on paper but which, alas, bore little relationship in practice to the way living animals actually behaved. For example, people soon realised that a bit of a problem emerged for an animal if all its drives were set at maximum, as it were, and all the appropriate drive-reducing stimuli were at hand. Take a rat, severely deprived of food and water, and place it in a cage with both available. What is it going to do first, eat or drink? Presumably it will be pushed in the direction suggested by the strongest drive. Using this as an idea it was decided that it ought to be possible to rank animal drives in order of strength by a simple test. Place a rat deprived of either food, water, or sexual activity in a box facing the necessary drive-reduction stimulus across an electrified grid. Now, how strong an electric shock is the rat prepared to put up with in order to fulfil its need? Experimenters found that thirst was the most effective stimulus, food next, and sex third. This was all fine until they found that rats satiated in all three modes would still occasionally cross the grid even when there was nothing on the other side! Now what kind of drive could be operating here? Furthermore, they found that an animal, again supplied with plenty of food, water, etc., would still run through a complicated maze and learn it pretty well, despite the lack of drive-reduction at the other end! Before long the theorists found themselves rather glumly proposing "exploration" or curiosity-reducing drives to account for the well-known fact that animals like to roam about all over the place. This, naturally, allows one to have a completely comprehensive theory of behaviour and learning in drive-reduction terms, but with the penalty of converting a simple, fairly sharply defined theory, tied closely to describable bodily requirements, into a complicated, diffuse, and far less convincing one. If any activity not explained in terms of the original drives can now be accounted for in terms of a reduction of an exploratory drive, then one has an "explanation" of the behaviour. But to many people's minds it is no better than those around before the whole concept of drives and needs was introduced. Similarly, there was a certain neatness and utility to the idea that a pattern of behaviour could be learned if at its conclusion a drive such as hunger or thirst was reduced. This neatness vanishes when we are told that an animal has learnt something else because its curiosity was satisfied, or the opposite, that it was not learnt because its curiosity drive was *not* reduced! Clearly the root of all these difficulties lies in the refusal of many psychologists to admit that a creature or a person does something or learns something because it likes it. Fair enough. We have already pointed out how subjective is the idea of an animal doing something because it "wants to," and the job of the psychologist is to try to define behaviour objectively rather than subjectively. What was clearly needed was some definable describable physiological process which could correspond to "pleasure," and until this was found psychologists could proceed no further in the field of motivation. In 1954 experiments were published which gave them the green light.

(4) The Pleasure Centre.

The arrival of microelectrode recording techniques allowed numerous experimental studies of the animal and even, occasionally, the human brain in action to be made. In a prolonged assault on the inner intricacies of the cerebral cortex and lower control centres psychologists and physiologists began the elaborate job of mapping the brain, defining as rigidly as they could which areas were devoted to what function. In many cases the areas they stimulated seemed to be "silent," *i.e.*, provoking no obvious response from the animal. Others however were more dramatically active. In 1956 the American James Olds and the Englishman Peter Milner were studying the responses of rats with electrodes implanted in what is known as the septal area of the brain, a spot beneath a body known as the corpus callosum. Animals stimulated with low voltage electric currents in this area seemed to behave in an odd way—almost as if they were enjoying the experience. For many years it had been known that stimulating the area known as the hypothalamus could produce symptoms of rage in animals, the creatures responding as though angered or threatened, the "sham rage" switching off immediately the electric stimulus ceased. Similarly areas had been found which when stimulated would cause dozy, apparently sleepy behaviour. Now here was something very different and Olds and Milner began to suspect that they had hit on something akin to a "pleasure" centre. To test this they designed a weird electrical circuit, surely one of the oddest ever to be seen in a laboratory. From the electrode in the rat's septal region a wire ran to the battery providing the electrical stimulus. In the rat's cage they placed a lever, and connected this to the battery in such a way that when the lever was pressed the battery emitted a single pulse, thus allowing the rat—if it wanted to—to stimulate this particular area of the brain. Although they had half suspected that the rats might occasionally give themselves a jolt in this "pleasure area," no one had anticipated the extent of the rats' involvement. All animals, once they had discovered the trick of pushing the lever, went into a sustained surge of lever pressing, keeping the activity up for literally hours on end. In fact there was some suggestion that they might have kept it up for ever, had not physical exhaustion sooner or later intervened. Given the choice of alternative levers providing food, water, or the chance to stimulate their septal regions, all rats reliably chose the latter, even those who had been substantially deprived of opportunities to eat or drink for some time. The lack of apparent satiation of the effect was one of the really odd things about the discovery. No human or animal appetite has ever been found which cannot be satisfied, if only for short periods. Only where some severe pathology is involved, such as with a disease or brain tumour, do the normal appetites remain unquenched. But here was something quite different—an appetite which seemed to have boundless depths and which outrode any of the other paramount needs of the animal. It was for this reason that Olds and Milner hypothesised that they had hit on the centre in the brain which mediates the sensation which we humans know of as "pleasure." How surprising is it that some such centre exists? Not very. When we do something we like, be it eating, drinking, or even going to a football match, then the feeling of pleasure that we get must be matched by some parallel process in the brain, and it could well be that this is located in some convenient but specific centre. Olds and Milner, incidentally, found that their animals would very swiftly learn a task if they were rewarded by a session on the pleasure centre, and here perhaps another important point emerges. There has always been some evidence, though the matter is by no means settled, that learning was somehow improved if following the performance of the desired task, a "reward" such as food, drink, sex, etc., was given. The big question is, what kind of signal is given to the memory system to denote when something is to be permanently laid down? Olds and Milner appeared to have provided one possible answer, and one that would have greatly satisfied Pavlov, Watson, and their immediate successors, the reinforcing stimulus—the message that declares that something will be learnt—is a message that has passed through the pleasure centre. The validity of this idea is still uncertain, but it has the merit of answering an age-old question in reasonably simple fashion, and also of helping us towards the solution of an even more venerable philosophical one—the nature of pleasure itself.

(5) Emotion.

This is one of the most misunderstood words in the psychologist's vocabulary and is a source of endless confusion. The trouble is it means so many things to so many different people. To the psychologist, however, it has a fairly specific meaning and we must try to get some idea of what this is. Only by doing so can we avoid falling into such traps as to say, "Animals cannot feel emotions," or "Computers can never think because they have no emotions." First let's attempt to nail the word "emotion" to the wall and try to analyse it. When we talk of people being emotional, what exactly do we mean? That they tend to weep a lot, get easily angered? Sorrow and anger are emotions, that is clear. But is not love an emotion too? Do we mean that emotional people tend to fall in love a good deal? Or do we mean that their love is deeper than others—or perhaps shallower? Already some confusion is creeping in. Let's ask now how we know that someone is emotional, or in an emotional state. The answer is probably that they exhibit a characteristic behaviour pattern which allows us to judge. If they wave their fists, go red in the face and shout, then we might infer that they were angry. Of course they could be acting and merely pretending to be angry, in which case what is the dividing line between the real and the simulated emotion? The answer would seem to be that the latter was not accompanied by an internal *feeling* of a special kind, and this now tells us that there are at least two sides to emotion—subjective psychological state and an external, physiological one. In fact, psychologists find it convenient to consider three aspects. The first is the *behavioural—i.e.* the kind of activity in which the angry or otherwise emotional person engages. This is generally easily detected and is of the waving-arms-around variety. The second is the *physiological*, which consists of considerably more discrete behavioural signs, not always obvious to the observer but which may be detected by suitably sensitive instruments. The third is the *psychological* or introspective, and this refers to the "state of mind" of the individual when he is angry or whatever. This of course cannot be directly sensed by other individuals who rely on the angry person reporting to them "how he feels." How are these linked together, and what function do they serve?

(a) *The Behavioural.*

If you fire a pistol behind someone's back they exhibit a very characteristic response, the most common feature of which is that they jump some distance into the air. This may seem desperately obvious, but actually there is a good deal more to the response than that. High speed photography shows that all human beings respond to sudden loud noises by a highly predictable behavioural sequence, of which the jump is just one part, and which bears the name "the startle pattern." It includes a marked hunching of the shoulders, closing the eyes, baring the teeth, and raising the hands in the direction of the face. It doesn't take long to see that these actions, which occur reliably in all human beings, are not random and pointless but serve to help the individual respond rapidly to a dangerous situation. The jump is an alerting response, the eyes are closed to protect them, the hands raised in defence or perhaps to strike, the teeth bared possibly as a threatening or warning sign. Similarly, at a more common emotional level, the waving fists and loud voice of an angry man equip him to some extent for battle. And what of the tears and the cowering posture of a thoroughly frightened individual? Well, these in some way suggest to the aggressor that the battle is over and are signals to him to stop fighting. Men, being natural fighters, tend to do little in the way of crying and will generally scrap on until they are physically incapable of continuing. Women, on the other hand, who are not particularly strong or well-equipped to fight, tend to slip into weeping and submission rather easily, hence the well-known fact that tears are a woman's strongest weapon against a man. (This submissive pattern of behaviour fails dismally of course when the aggressor is a carnivore such as a tiger, when the one submitting is eaten, tears and all.) The very obvious facial expressions made by people in various emotional states led the great Charles Darwin to the view that the type of face made was a good index of what emotion the individual was in the grips of. To test this idea, psychologists took photographs of the facial expressions of people in various emotional states and then asked other people to try to name them. The results were poor, with few people doing better than chance. The only expression reliably recognised and correctly assigned to an emotion was a smile, and even this was occasionally confused with other emotional states such as pain, or even fear. The same experiment performed with movies yielded somewhat better results, and when sound was added results were again improved. The clinching thing, however, seems to be the setting in which the behaviour takes place, for people become very accurate at judging emotions when they see the surroundings in which the other people are behaving. Clearly the external signs of emotion, despite their immediate and rather obvious manifestations, are an unreliable guide to what is going on inside the individual's head. The same argument, incidentally, applies to animals, though somewhat less forcefully. Most animals give pretty explicit signs when they are angry or when they are afraid. One can even detect something suspiciously like guilt in the general pattern of behaviour of a dog which has done something it shouldn't. But can one really talk of a dog "feeling guilty"? If not—why not? Whatever answer you give will be quite as valid as any given by a psychologist.

(b) *The Physiological.*

The signs and signals we talked about above were all gross, obvious, and yet, as we pointed out, somewhat unreliable. To a large part they seem to be the outward manifestation of an internal process which at the same time serve a useful purpose, as when the startle pattern alerts the individual into a posture suitable for defensive or aggressive action. But what are the finer, physiological manifestations of emotion? These must obviously involve changes in the state of bodily and cerebral activity. Psychologists have pinned down no fewer than 11 distinct facets of human and animal behaviour which give a clear index of changes in emotional states. To give some idea of the complexity of emotional behaviour we will look at each of these briefly.

(1) The first, and perhaps the most obvious, is heart-rate. The heart's job is to pump blood around the body and the blood provides the vital organ supply to the brain. The more intense the activity, the more oxygen is consumed and the more the blood needs to be circulated. It should be no surprise therefore to anyone to learn that as activity is stepped up, so heart-rate increases and vice versa. Furthermore, heart-rate tends to accelerate just prior to some important or exciting piece of activity, or even on merely thinking about it, and this means that we have here one index of emotional state. A device known as the electrocardiogram (EKG) can give a very precise picture of heart fluctuations and represents one objective way of plotting this information.

(2) We have already implied another measure, respiration. This increases more or less alongside heart-rate, and is a pretty good index of most emotions. Irregularities of breathing, including variations in the depth of breaths, are a particularly good index of nervousness as most people know and all this can be detected by a suitable instrument

(3) More or less hand-in-hand with the above come changes in local blood pressure and volume, the facial accompaniments of which—blanching or blushing—are only too obvious. These can be measured by a device known as the pleythsmograph, which is merely a version of the kind of device a doctor uses to measure your blood pressure in a routine medical examination.

(4) A somewhat harder emotional symptom to measure, but very characteristic of most emotional states, is muscle tension and its associate, tremor. In anger, rage, and other aggressive states muscles become tensed to be ready for rapid action and if this is carried too far we get trembling of the limbs—a familiar accompaniment of great nervousness or fright.

All the above are easily discernible indices, amenable to instrumentation but not depending upon it. The remaining manifestations are harder to detect, though just as valuable once one has caught them. Beginning with the most obvious we have:

(5) The pilomotor response, which is a hangover from the days when our ancestors had a good deal more hair than we do today, and which can be seen when a cat's fur fluffs out in rage or fear. In humans today we call it goose-pimples and it is often a precursor to the feeling of full-blooded fear.

(6) Even harder to measure is salivary secretion which is the kind of response Pavlov studied with his dogs. In anxiety or fear the saliva flow tends to be inhibited and we find ourselves with "dry mouths."

(7) An index of emotion which is particularly obvious to the individual is the change in gastrointestinal motility. Movements of the stomach and intestine are brought to a brief but definite halt in strong emotional states with a complementary, and often rather dramatic, surge back to action shortly afterwards. There are plenty of homely and slightly vulgar expressions to describe the consequences of this.

(8) There has been a recent rise of interest in the pupillary response as an index of certain types of emotion. The pupil of the eye tends to dilate in moments of anger or pain with slight dilation occurring during periods of "interest" in something. This has led some clever psychologists who work in the advertising profession to use this as an index of the relative effectiveness of different types of advertisement. All the subjects have to do is look at the subject matter while a recording camera photographs the pupils of their eyes from a distance!

(9) Because the endocrine or glandular system is active in emotional states the chemical constitution of the blood changes markedly as the hormones flow within it, but this index, while potentially useful, is of course abnormally hard to measure directly.

(10) Next we come to the so-called galvanic skin response (GSR) which is in fact nothing more than the electrical resistance of the skin. For various reasons, not properly understood, the resistance of the skin to an electrical current changes with most emotional states, tending to decrease as a function of the intensity of the emotion. This can be detected with a suitable instrument and meter and is perhaps particularly interesting because it is an automatic response which the individual is not consciously aware of. Connect someone up to a GSR meter, tell him that you are going to stick a pin in him and the needle will swing wildly. It is a very effective demonstration of an entirely involuntary response and is generally one of the first experiments that fledgling psychologists perform on each other in their laboratory classes.

(11) Finally there is the EEG, which we referred to earlier on (*see* **Q5**). The electrical activity of the brain does change with varying degrees of bodily activity, though what these changes mean is a matter for skilled interpretation.

(c) *The Psychological.*

You will have noticed that many of the above indices—stomach motility, muscle tension, etc.—have definite physical accompaniments which are only too obvious to the individual experiencing the emotion and it should not be too surprising in the light of all this that an emotional state markedly alters our physical and psychological feelings and sensations. But is this all there is to emotion? Can the age-old human passions of love and hate be reduced to permutations of salivary secretion, blood pressure, pilomotor response and electro-cortical activity? Put so baldly of course the answer is no. Love demands a partner, a setting, a trigger and some temporal span—as does hate. In humans these require the active participation of the complex computer we call the brain, and a background of education, social activity, and some awareness of goals other than the immediate. Nevertheless, the intense physiological and psychological changes which envelop us when we are in love, or when we fight in passion, contribute the better part of the powerful sensations we feel. But which of the three faces of emotion, the behavioural, the physiological, or the psychological is the real or most significant one?

The answer is that no single one predominates for emotion is a complex of all three. When the object of our emotion, be it love, hate, or whatever, is first encountered then mind and body combine to set the individual up for the optimum pattern of responses. This involves some permutation of physical change which, naturally, is reflected in psychological changes of mood. These in turn provoke outward changes on a larger scale which may involve combat or the ritual of love. If this description seems to debase the concept of human emotional response then this is a pity for there is no reason why it should. The powerful forces that thrust men into the numerous passions of the world would have no meaning were they not accompanied by potent changes in bodily state. The artistry that springs from these passions is no fraction diminished because we can identify the physiological and psychological changes that accompany and, to some extent, determine them.

It will have occurred to you that in this section on motivation we have drifted closer and closer to another of the critical areas that psychologists study—the nature of human personality. Psychologists know far less about this area than they would like to, but their century of scientific activity (a small span compared with the history of the more traditional sciences, such as physics) has begun to pay off. In the next and final section we will take a look at what they have done, or have tried to do, in this most fascinating of areas.

V. PERSONALITY AND THINKING.

(1) What Constitutes a Person?

To many people this is the most important single question in psychology and indeed, perhaps, in the combined fields of science and philosophy. What is it that makes up that unique blend of psychological and physiological factors we call "personality"? The answer is, predictably, complicated and before we can even begin to consider it we must attempt to define the problems in the field. In the first place let's consider the most venerable and apparently simplest answer—a person is that thing in the head that thinks, feels, is aware of itself as an individual entity, and which controls a brain and body. This is the answer which probably fits best with the non-technical philosophy of the man-in-the-street and which matches also with a long-standing traditional view fostered by the majority of systems of religious belief. Put another way, it states that human beings are composed of essentially two parts. One of these is physical and consists of the body and its control centre, the brain. The second is non-physical, and is called the mind, soul, spirit, or some similar name. This is a separate entity which controls the body through its brain and while involved in this way must obey the laws of the physical world. It may, however, survive the death of its body (one of the most widespread of religious views of personality) and occasionally, as with telepathy, precognition, etc., may step outside to contact other similar minds in other parts of the world or even take a peek into the future. As we have said, this is an exceedingly widespread view of the nature of personality and it will be the one held by many who read this article. This is now the point where you could ask whether this view is acceptable to psychologists, and that is a fair and proper question. It requires, however, two separate answers. In the first place some psychologists, though certainly not the majority, accept this or some very similar view, but on an entirely personal plane. When they think as scientists, however, most are inclined to disagree with it. Nothing that has been uncovered in the history of experimental psychology, with the possible exception of the very dubious evidence for telepathy, suggests that the human personality is a separate entity to be considered in isolation from brain and body. Psychologists who choose to believe otherwise frankly admit that they do so on the basis of faith or hunch, and argue that even though the scientific facts appear to contradict their beliefs at the moment, perhaps in due course experimental psychology will uncover fresh new material to change the whole picture.

Does "Mind" Exist?

An increasing number of psychologists and brain scientists today take a hard-line on the "spiritual" view of personality, but does this mean that mind does not exist, as the Behaviourists strove so hard to prove? Certainly not. There is clearly a whole range of rich psychological activity which cannot be explained simply in terms of bundles of conditioned reflexes and the like. What seems to have happened in fact is that as animals have evolved via the remorseless processes of evolution, so more and more "power" has been given to the cerebral control centres. At some stage in the evolutionary ladder—it is very hard to say exactly where—the brain ceased to be a purely automatic device and some glimmerings of what we call consciousness began to appear. In the early stages, this probably merely took the form of a "switch" in the brain which allowed the creature to select from one or two alternative modes of action. This capacity would imply some system within the brain capable of making a "comparison" of the two modes and thus of "standing back from itself." Increase the complexity of the brain and its capacity to select, predict, and determine and you will see that the evolution of a higher control centre capable of "inspecting" ongoing activity will emerge. Thus could the thing we know of as consciousness develop. Incidentally, if you feel that such an abstracting, self-inspecting system could not be conceived in purely mechanical terms then you are wrong, for the latest developments in computer technology have been devoted to achieving this. But before getting caught up in arguments about whether computers could "think" (we'll tackle this briefly later on) let us just summarise the current approach to the problem that most psychologists accept today. Mind is a phenomenon which has arisen almost inevitably as brain complexity and power have increased, and its function is to select alternative activities and compute the consequences. Just as human bodies and brains differ in countless ways, so human minds, subtly moulded over the years from infancy to adulthood, differ too. The result is that the world is populated with a large number of human beings, united as a species, but each one an individual entity, compounded of body, brain, and mind. All three are equally real, equally important—and equally helpless without each other's company. Let us now take a look at the principal forces which serve to mould these individual entities we call people, and some of the essential ways in which they differ.

(2) Interplay of Heredity and Environment.

People and animals differ in a large number of ways, and are alike in others. We share certain features—upright posture, well-developed brains, etc.—with other primates, such as chimpanzees. We also share certain features—binocular vision, mammalian reproduction techniques, etc.—with white rats. We even have a limited amount in common—respiratory systems depending upon oxygen, need to ingest some kind of food, etc.—with creatures as lowly as the earwig, but nothing with cabbages or oak trees, except perhaps a dependence upon sunlight. Now what is it that determines these similarities and differences? The answer is summed up in the word heredity. Creatures of particular species mate with each other and hand on to their offspring, via the genes and chromosomes, the physical characteristics of the species (*see* **F31**). They may even hand on certain predetermined patterns of behaviour, which we have earlier referred to as instinct (*see also* **F38**). Broadly speaking, the lower down the phylogenetic scale, the more behavioural information is carried over via the genes, and the less flexible is the creature's ultimate behaviour pattern. Earwigs, for example, come into the world fully equipped to go about their simple business on this planet. They present almost identical faces to the world around them, and taking it all in all they change little from birth to death. Earwigs are largely the product of heredity, the principal forces which mould them lying in the genes of their parents and the incredible long history of their species stretching back for hundreds of millions of years. At the other end of the continuum we have human beings whose physical characteristics and a very limited number of behaviour patterns are inherited, but whose "personalities" and individualities (unlike the earwigs) change significantly throughout the span of their lives. These changes are the consequence of the impact of the environment on the flexible human brain, a flexibility which allows human beings to respond swiftly and intelligently to the changing hazards and opportunities of the world. It should be clear, therefore, that the basic differences that so obviously exist between the personalities of different people, reflect the experiences that each individual has had in his or her lifetime. See a newborn child and search for signs of its personality. You will look for a long time to no avail. But watch a child grow from infancy to adolescence and you will see the personality slowly building and emerging—more or less hand-in-hand with the young person's growing awareness of his own individuality, his strengths and his weaknesses.

Twin Studies.

Striking evidence of the immense influence that the environment has on us comes from the famous studies of identical twins performed in America by Newman in the 1930s. There is a bit of confusion in most people's minds about what actually are " identical " twins as opposed to the ordinary, born-on-the-same-day variety. In the case of the latter—known as fraternal twins—what has happened to produce the happy event is that during conception two of the eggs in the mother have been fertilised and thus two babies are born. Without going into too much detail this means that two quite separate creatures develop, each being equipped with the random genetic mix that follows the meeting of the father's sperm with the mother's egg. The children, when born, may be of different sex, different colour hair eyes, etc., and are likely to be no more alike than would be brothers or sisters born in different years or even decades. Each, therefore, begins with a different hereditary pattern, as determined by the genes. With identical twins a curious fluke occurs. By some process, *after* conception and *after* gene mixing has taken place, the fertilised egg splits, amoeba fashion, and two babies begin to develop—but both have identical gene patterns and thus, up to the moment of birth, can be looked upon as totally identical human beings. This weird identity is, as we all know, frequently carried on throughout the twins' lifetime, even though it is generally noticeable that the similarities become less marked with age. Now to return to Newman's experiment. Nineteen pairs of identical twins were found (a good deal of research was needed) who had for one reason or another been reared apart from an early age and had grown up in different environments. Newman found that while the adult twins maintained a striking physical resemblance, the personalities of the pairs seemed in many cases to have moved apart. In one case, the first of the pair had been successful in worldly terms, had acquired a college education, and was happily married with a stable family, while the second had been less fortunate and was leading a rather unsatisfactory life in an unskilled job in a working-class neighbourhood. Twin " A " seemed optimistic, good-humoured, and more dominant a personality, while twin " B " was morose, lethargic, and lacking in self-confidence. Similar observations were in general noted with other twins, particularly in cases where one of the pair had been reared in a more stable and economically more satisfactory environment. No better illustration of the relative influence of heredity and environment on human personality can be found than in studies of this kind. But is it only physical characteristics that are genetically determined? Is none of the psychological make-up of the individual " built-in " to him at birth? We can answer this by saying that twin-studies have shown that while personality is certainly modified by the environment, there is a good deal of evidence that intelligence is relatively untouched by normal environmental differences. Newman and his colleagues, for example, found that there was a higher correlation between the IQ test scores of *identical twins reared apart* than there was between *fraternal twins reared together*—a finding which suggests that intelligence may be largely inherited. The great British psychologist, Sir Cyril Burt, also produced what seemed to be striking evidence of the inheritability of intelligence with studies made of schoolchildren in the 1930s and the 1940s. In 1976, however, Burt's work came under severe and unexpected criticism, and this led to a reopening of the whole question of the relative importance of genetic as opposed to cultural factors in determining intelligence. Part of the problem, of course, is that there is often confusion over the meaning of the word " intelligence," and for this reason it is perhaps worth looking closer at it.

(3) Intelligence and IQ Testing.

Psychologists have spent a good deal of time arguing about what exactly is meant by intelligence and it is not worth covering this battle-scarred ground again. One definition which makes a good deal of sense is " versatility of adjustment " which is another way of talking about the kind of flexible response to the environment which is so characteristic of humans. This of course means that we can talk of animals having some degree of intelligence, and most psychologists nowadays would agree that this makes sense. The only problem arises if one considers intelligence to be inextricably tied up with consciousness, thought, language, etc., which of course it is not. Certainly the ability to communicate in linguistic terms and to think in abstract modes are signs of a highly intelligent creature, but some degree of intelligence may be present without those traits. Probably one could even talk of intelligence being present in any animal that could modify its behaviour in response to the environment and repeat this behavioural response at some later date. This means, as you will have gathered, that intelligence is present in any creature that can learn, including our little friend planaria. It is of course a *very* limited form of intelligence and planaria would not come out with much of an IQ (intelligence quotient) if submitted to human IQ tests. The structure of these tests, incidentally, becomes comprehensible if one sees them as measures of human flexibility rather than of knowledge. The standard IQ test, which forms the basis of the much-reviled 11-plus exam, is an attempt at getting some idea of an individual's general flexibility rather than how much information is actually crammed into his head. Without getting involved in the educational argument here, the point is that a test of the child's inherent capability is more likely to give some index of his fitness for higher education than is a test of his knowledge, and this is what the IQ test attempts to sort out. Hence the relative uselessness of " cramming " to prepare for the 11-plus and the surprise results it sometimes produces. You may think you see a bit of a contradiction here. On the one hand we have said that intelligence, whatever it is, seems to be built in the individual and is something to do with his basic brain power. In this case why are new-born babies not fully intelligent at birth? The paradox is solved by saying that the peak of intelligence is not reached until the brain is fully mature (at about 18 years of age in homo sapiens) after which it begins to decline remorselessly with increasing age. Thus you will find that scores on IQ tests are " weighted " according to age. For very young children considerable allowance is made for age and their " raw " score is upgraded according to a standard scale. So too is the score for older people who inevitably score lower in IQ tests than do 18-year olds. Thus we find that a university professor aged 60 would produce a far lower raw score than a young student of equivalent intelligence—even though the venerable professor's head contains far more knowledge! If this seems odd, remember that it is the individual's potential and general flexibility that the tests are all about and not the depth of his fund of knowledge. The IQ test itself is a rather arbitrary affair and was arrived at in the first place by a group of psychologists selecting a bunch of questions which they felt best tested this rather elusive faculty of flexibility. They then arrived at a scoring system which achieved the result that if you tested a large number of people, drawn randomly from the population, their average score would equal 100. In fact this is exactly what an IQ of 100 means—it is the average score of the population at large. This has led to the sarcastic observation of one psychologist that intelligence was " that faculty that is measured by intelligence tests "! This is a witticism with some truth in it, but nevertheless the IQ has a practical value, notably as a sorter out of the bright from the dull in a situation where environmental or social backgrounds might have intervened to cloud the issue. The 11-plus is one such example, as is the fact that the IQ test taken prior to university entrance is the best-known predictor of success in final degree examinations—at least in the USA. On the other hand, as you may have suspected, social and cultural factors can influence IQ scores, thus suggesting that they are not as pure as might have been hoped. Tests conducted on white and black children in America in the 1930s, for example, showed a marked difference in IQ between the two racial groups—the whites coming out pretty clearly ahead. This was greedily seized on by racialists as demonstrating the innate superiority of the white children until it was pointed out that the selection of the two samples was faulty, the black children had been drawn from rural parts of the south while the whites came from the urban north. When a repeat experiment was performed, drawing the whites from the rustic south and the blacks from the northern cities, exactly the reverse finding emerged, killing one age-old notion and at the same time highlighting the fact that IQ tests were vulnerable to social and cultural factors. Incidentally, for those who like to pursue racial arguments, it is interesting to note that the highest IQ ever recorded by standard tests, a shattering 200, was scored by—a young Negro girl. When considering the world as a whole, however, the fact remains that humans are very heavily divided from each other by a barrier potentially more difficult to surmount than those of race, class, or creed—intelligence. Furthermore the gulf is one that is particularly difficult to bridge because of lack of incentive on either side. A highly intelligent person generally finds the company of a rather dull person quite unacceptable, and the reverse is also true. Also, the differences between high and low IQs are likely to become more apparent in the coming decades as the old barriers of class, etc., which used to mask intelligence, dissolve. From this important aspect of human personality we now move on to consider the nature of one of the processes most characteristic of human brains—thought.

(4) Thinking.

We have suggested that personality is an amalgam of the various faculties which are associated with cerebral activity, and that variations in personality reflect variations in the individual's environmental history. Any creature with a reasonably flexible set of responses to its environment can therefore be said to have some rudimentary personality, and many of us can detect this in our domestic pets. If this seems a peculiar notion then this is only because we have erroneously tended to think of personality as being a solely human trait, rather in the way that people dismiss animals in general as having no intelligence. But what is it that does distinguish us from other animals—do we differ merely in terms of the capacity and computing power of our brains? Probably the answer is yes, though it has to be recognised that the gulf is pretty wide. Yet if one looks at the cerebral equipment of, say, a chimpanzee one gets the feeling that there shouldn't be all *that* difference! Furthermore, if one comes closer to home and looks at some of our ancestors such as Neanderthal or Cro-Magnon Man, it is hard to account for the differences between their primitive lives and ours today. Certainly we exist 100,000 years later in time and it would be a bit pathetic if we hadn't progressed since then. But the same argument surely should apply to chimpanzees who do not seem to have developed much in the same period, and the whole thing seems even odder when we learn that the now extinct Neanderthal Man had a cranial capacity (brain size) greater than that of modern man. One might explain the vast difference between Man and his rivals on the ground that he was the possessor of an immortal soul or divine spirit. Leaving this rather unsatisfactory explanation aside, let us try to find some other approach. The key lies in the capacity of humans for abstract thought—taking a step back in their minds and "introspecting." With this marvellous facility comes a natural talent to convert the results of these introspections into a code and communicate them to other members of the species. The communicating code is what we call language, and the introspective process, with or without a linguistic component, is known as thinking. Thinking of a kind probably comes in a good deal lower down, at the level where individual animals make "decisions," such as when a dog, faced with a fence blocking it from its food ultimately gives up trying to climb over it and simply walks round it! Kohler's chimpanzee Sultan was certainly indulging in something pretty close to thought when he fitted two sticks together to reach a banana. Nevertheless, there is rather good evidence that the development of a spoken language, such as only humans have, is the trigger which allows a kind of detached, abstract processing to go on and which has allowed us to build up an immense cultural heritage over the past 10,000 years.

(a) *Thought and Language.*

How much is thought tied in with speech? You will remember that Watson liked to call thought "sub-verbal speech" and there is some truth in this. Open your mouth and think the word "bubble." You will probably notice a kind of catch in your throat—which shows how the two processes are tied together. On the other hand, think of some visual scene—say a polar bear sitting on an iceberg. Most people can conjure up a pretty reasonable mental picture of scenes like this without too much trouble and certainly without saying vocally or sub-vocally, either the word bear or iceberg! Incidentally, if you *can't* get a mental image of this kind, don't worry, for about a third of the world's population can't either. This facility for producing "pictures in the mind" has puzzled psychologists for a century—in particular those who can't manage the images themselves, who are inclined to be a bit sceptical about the whole thing. Twist the topic round and consider the case of visual illusions and other perceptual anomalies. For example, take the kind where two lines, objectively the same, look to be of different length. No matter how much measuring with a ruler and how much you tell yourself that the lines are similar, your erroneous percept remains. Here perception and thought are *not* inextricably tied, which disposes of any lingering arguments that thinking was merely a consequence of visual, auditory, or some other input. Incidentally, the link between thought and language is suddenly coming under close study again, almost 50 years after Watson had originally tried to explain one in terms of the other. This arises from the young sub-science known as psycholinguistics, the founder of which is the American mathematician, Noam Chomsky. His thesis, rather seriously over-simplified, is that the structure of language can be used to give us a valuable key to the inner logic of the brain's operation. We can never hope to know directly how the inner mechanics of the brain work, he says, so we must look to find them reflected in some more directly observable process. Chomsky and his followers argue that in addition to its "surface" grammar (the kind of grammar we learn at school) all human languages have a deeper set of rules, closely tied in with the programmes which handle the deepest and most fundamental thought processes. Look closely at language, state and define the logic of the "deep grammar" and you have taken a peek at the brain's deepest secrets. It is an interesting idea, shared by many scientists who hold that similar clues can come from a study of dreams, but it suggests that the problem of defining thinking is even harder than we at first imagined.

(b) *Can a Machine Think?*

Yet another approach comes from computer scientists, who, concerned with devising computers capable of communicating in linguistic terms with human beings, have been taking a close look at these problems. From one of the pioneers of computer science, the late British Alan Turing, came a penetrating analysis of the philosophical problems of thought which reopens the discussion again from an entirely fresh angle. He did this by posing the question "Can a machine think?" Turing pointed out in their opinion, they were seldom able to give a really good reason for it. Typical responses, when they were asked why a machine couldn't think, included, "because you can never get more out a machine than you put into it," "because machines have no souls," and "because only people can think." None of these arguments is valid. In the first place, it is only partly true to say that you can get no more out of a machine than you put in it, and in any case what has that to do with thinking? The second and third points are equally dubious. However, Turing realised that people had a built-in inclination to assume that thinking was a property of humans only, and as a computer engineer who hoped ultimately to see "thinking computers" developed, he was anxious to correct this impression. To do so he rephrased the question this way: that the almost universal response to this question was "No," but while people felt pretty confident "Supposing that you continually built ever more clever computers, how would you know whether one had begun to think or not?" Pointing out that the only evidence we have about whether humans can think (apart from taking their word for it) is the nature of the conversation they have with us, he suggested that one would base one's decision on how well the computer was able to communicate and discourse. Assuming that the fact that the computer was a large metal object with glowing lights, reams of paper tape, etc., would bias people in their judgment of whether it was thinking or not, he proposed that the decision should be based on a simple game. Take one very clever computer which you have reason to suppose may be capable of thought and place it in a room "A." Now take a person in a room "B," and a third in a room "C." Connect up computer "A" and person "B" to person "C" by wires connected to teletypes (special typewriters which allow one to feed information into computers and allow them to respond). Person "C" doesn't know who is on the end of either teletype, "B" or the computer, but he proceeds to try to find out by asking them questions through their respective teletypes. Now if the computer was really dim it would soon give itself away by its dim answers, but if it was really clever it might easily fool "C" into thinking it was the person "B." One important rule of the game, incidentally, is that both "B" and the computer were attempting to fool "C," the object being not to be identified correctly as either human or machine. Now, said Turing, if the point comes where "C" cannot reliably and certainly decide which of his two communicators is which, then to all intents and purposes the computer "A" must be said to be capable of thought! This is really a brilliant approach to the problem even if it seems to be a bit obscure at first. What Turing was really saying was that the *real* evidence that thinking is taking place is evidenced by what the individual, be it human, animal, or computer, actually does, and not what it looks like.

Before leaving this enigmatic topic, consider two recent developments in this area:

(1) In at least two centres in the United States psychologists are engaged in dramatic and apparently successful attempts at "conversational" communication with chimpanzees. The husband and wife team of the Gardners at the State University in Reno, Nevada, have taught a chimpanzee to communicate using American sign language—a series of gestures with hand and arm. Their animals apparently are able to converse in sentences at about the level of communication of a three-year-old human child. Another researcher, David Premack at the University of California, has been teaching his chimpanzees to understand the meaning of special plastic symbols or "words." Using these the monkeys form sentences by placing the symbols on a magnetised blackboard, and have built up a substantial working vocabulary. They have even got to the stage of understanding and creating sentences featuring the conditional, for example "pick up the red cup *if* blue light is on," etc. Some of Premack's brightest animals are actually using a specially modified typewriter to generate their messages.

(2) Many psychologists and computer scientists believe that a breakthrough in the field of artificial intelligence—the creation of a robot or computer capable of "reason"—is imminent. Developments in this field, which have been painfully slow since the first major computers were constructed in the 1940s, have been accelerating in the 1970s. To take just one example—computers can now be programmed to play really good games of chess and can beat top-ranking club players—if not world masters yet. A game played between a Russian and an American computer for the computer chess championship of the world in Stockholm in 1974 was described as "startling" by one chess expert who watched it. The Russian computer won incidentally. The distinguished philosopher and statistician, Professor I. J. Good, himself an outstanding chess player, has evolved the concept of what he calls the "ultra-intelligent machine" (UIM). This he defines as a computer capable of performing every intellectual function at least as well as a human being. Professor Good now believes that the first UIM will be with us before the turn of the century and possibly even in the 1980s. UIMs, he points out, have one special advantage over human beings—there is no theoretical upper limit to their intelligence. He believes furthermore that one of the first tasks that scientists will give to the UIMs to perform will be to set about finding ways of making themselves even more intelligent. Incidentally, in 1976 an American computer program produced a solution to a famous mathematical puzzle, known as the "Four colour problem." Without going into details of this problem, the main point is that it had never been solved by any human brain, although mathematicians had been working on it for decades. In fact, no one was even certain whether or not it could be solved. Now a computer has done so—perhaps the first really major problem of this kind in which computer brains have shown themselves to be significantly superior to our own.

(5) The World of Inner Space.

We have constantly indicated that psychology is the study of behaviour—the activities of living creatures which respond to a meaningful non-random way to the vagaries of their environment. The key to understanding these patterns of behaviour is of course the brain, and within the brain itself the programmes which control and determine its actions. One important point which all who study the brain swiftly come to realise, and one which this section has attempted to emphasise, is that no living system can be considered as a mechanical assembly of different parts. Each, whether earwig, cat, or human being, is a complex, integrated system functioning as a unit. The further up the phylogenetic scale one rises, the more complex the system and the more sophisticated and elegant its mechanics. At the human level with mental activities and consciousness emerging as super-control systems, the study of psychology reaches its most fascinating point. Here too, it must be admitted, as a science it has made least headway. There are probably good reasons for this, some related to the intrinsically complicated nature of the mind, others to the attitude of the psychologists themselves. The early pioneering work of Wundt, Ebbinghaus, and others seemed to be setting psychology on course as a science in its own right. The work of Pavlov, immensely important and relevant as it was, served to weaken psychology as a discipline and shift its bias drastically in the direction of physiology. Psychologists themselves ceased to think like psychologists and instead attempted to convert themselves into second-hand physiologists, part-time mathematicians, and indifferent clinicians. This trend, which gathered strength in the 1930s, has persisted until quite recently when a growing disenchantment with the relatively meagre results stemming from the millions of behaviouristic experiments involving pigeons, monkeys, and rats has led to an inevitable swing of the pendulum. More now than at any time in this century is the principal creature for psychological study acknowledged to be man himself. Freud's fabulous and enduring insight—that the mind itself has two vitally important parts, the conscious and the unconscious, each integrated and yet strangely autonomous—is being treated with ever greater respect and understanding today. The realisation that human beings are controlled not merely by their conscious thoughts, wishes, and desires but also by dynamic forces of great power which are *not* under conscious control and barely available to linguistic analysis, is at last becoming a part of even the layman's view of mental life. The tip of the iceberg above the sea, as Freud pointed out, is that part of the mind which is under conscious control. Below the sea, massively enigmatic, lies the great bulk of the unconscious, the repository of the programmes which largely determine the behaviour of man. This is the zone, rich in mystery, which must ultimately be plotted by psychology and its researchers. This is the territory, glimpses of which we catch through the enigma of memory, the hallucinations of dementia, and in the misty drama of our dreams. The controversial English author J. G. Ballard has christened this territory "inner space," in contrast with the vast reaches of outer space that the first human astronauts are today beginning to explore.

VI. EXTRA-SENSORY PERCEPTION (ESP)

Man is a tiny animal, living on a minute planet in a vast and incomprehensible universe—a universe which gives up its secrets reluctantly and which, paradoxically, seems to be getting more incomprehensible and mysterious the more we learn about it. Man himself is also more or less a total enigma. We know that he is an animal, obeying all the usual laws of biology, including those of birth, growth, ageing and death. We also suspect that he is, in some indefinable way, something *more* than an animal. He has conscious thoughts and feelings, emotions, an inner rational life, a written language and other faculties, which he appears to share with none of the other life forms on his planet. But beyond that we know very little, and therefore find it extremely hard to define his true place in nature. In fact, at the risk of slightly oversimplifying things, one could say that there are only two very broad, mutually exclusive, views of man—one cannot really call them theories—and that the world is divided up into those that hold one view and those that hold the other.

The first, the physicalistic view, states that man is a totally material being, composed of atoms and molecules and not much else, and no different in principle from other material facets of the universe—animals, plants and even inanimate things such as rocks and ponds. The second view, the spiritual view if you like, holds that man is essentially *different* from all other things in the universe because he is really made up of two basic components—one a physical body controlled by a physical, material brain, the other a psychic or spiritual entity which, for the want of a better word, one might call a mind or soul. Mind and body are different in their nature according to this view, and while they interact at various levels, the body is temporary, destructible and must obey the laws of the material universe. The mind, soul or spirit on the other hand is permanent, indestructible and may—at times—disregard basic physicalistic laws. Now which of these two views you hold depends largely on whether you are at heart a materialist, or are more of a religious frame of mind. But, personal belief aside, how can one decide which of the two is most likely to be correct?

Materialists argue that human beings, while marvellously complicated biological systems, nevertheless behave in an essentially mechanistic way, and that no examination of the brain or nervous system has ever revealed anything that suggests the presence of a soul or spirit. Furthermore, they argue that when brains and bodies die, all evidence of the existence of the "minds" that were once associated with them vanishes too. Non-materialists, however, argue that while the above facts seem to be correct there are occasional flashes of evidence which suggest that some part of man—his mind—can on occasions escape the shackles of the body and—if only briefly—transcend the boundaries of space and time. These flashes of evidence, glimpses of a non-materialistic aspect of the universe, go under the general heading of "extra-sensory perception" (ESP for short), and they have puzzled and intrigued scientists and philosophers for a very long time. Actually, while the word ESP is bandied around a lot and often assumed to mean any kind of supernatural experience, it has a fairly precise meaning to those scientists (they are known as parapsychologists) who study it. In studying it they draw on two main sources—(1) anecdotal evidence, and (2) laboratory experiments. At its face value the former is very impressive—people have been recounting tales of amazing things that have happened to them (dreams about the future which come true, telepathic experiences, etc) as far back as history extends. Some of these experiences are exceedingly strange and make fascinating reading, but to show how unsatisfying they really are let's first take a homely example. Consider the following, rather familiar type of experience: You are just thinking of a friend whom you haven't thought of for some time when the telephone rings; it is your friend, who states that he had suddenly "felt the urge to call you."

Now most people having an experience of this kind are considerably affected by it and, feeling that it can hardly be dismissed as coincidence, put it down to what seems to them to be a more reasonable alternative—mind-to-mind contact or "telepathy." The trouble is that this alternative explanation is only more "reasonable" when one is absolutely certain that there is such a thing as telepathy in the first place. There is a safe and good rule in science known as Occam's Razor, which says that if two explanations have to be chosen to explain some phenomenon, one should choose the simplest of the two, *provided that it fits the facts*. And calling the experience of the telephone call above "telepathy" is not actually the simplest of the two possibilities when one knows nothing at all about telepathy, and isn't even sure that it exists at all. Therefore, until telepathy is demonstrated scientifically—which really means in controlled, laboratory experiments—one has to try to find explanations of a "normal" kind to explain phenomena of this kind. Of course, some people might argue that thinking of a friend that you haven't thought of for years at the very *instant* that he picks up the phone to call you is so unlikely that it is scarcely a normal explanation. But exactly how unlikely *is* it? Certainly it's very unlikely that it will happen to *you*, but that it will happen on occasions to someone in a big country with a large population is nowhere near so unlikely. In fact one American mathematician who had just such an experience was so amazed by it that he set out to work out the odds against it happening by chance. He came to the amazing conclusion that in a country like the United States, with a population of 200 million, it would happen by chance to *hundreds of people every single day!* And, needless to say, these people would be so impressed that they would be sure to tell all their friends about it, thus spreading the news about their amazing "telepathic experience." This particular story makes two important points—firstly that anecdotal material is often less impressive and significant than it first seems, and secondly that before one can decide whether an event is "likely or unlikely," one has to have some kind of numerical value as to how frequently one would expect it to occur by chance. And this is where the laboratory experiments come in.

The first serious work looking into telepathy and other such phenomena in scientific laboratories was probably that done by Dr. J. B. Rhine, who founded a "parapsychology laboratory" at Duke University in North Carolina in the 1930s. Rhine believed that the anecdotal material had built up to such an extent that there was clearly something there worth studying, but that if it was worth studying it should be done under laboratory conditions. In this way the problem of the vagueness of the anecdotal material could be overcome and, perhaps even more important, if he did discover something significant, other scientists would know exactly how and what had been done, and—most important of all from a scientific point of view—could then set up their own independent investigations.

Rhine soon decided that the supposed paranormal powers of the mind were not simply confined to mind-to-mind contact, or telepathy, and he identified four powers or faculties, coining the phrase extra-sensory perception as a blanket term for all of them. They were, in turn, (1) telepathy, (2) clairvoyance, (3) precognition and (4) psychokinesis.

Of these, the first has already been discussed and hardly needs any explanation or comment, other than to say that it implies that information is transmitted from one brain or mind to another brain or mind *without the use of the known senses*. This in turn seems to imply that physiologists probing about in the brain might some day expect to find some organ which serves to transmit the telepathic signals, and another which acts as a receiver. Any transmitter or receiver, incidentally, would have to be pretty powerful or sensitive, as the anecdotal evidence often suggests that people can be in telepathic contact with each other over huge distances.

Clairvoyance, the second supposed faculty, is more troublesome from all points of view. When used scientifically, incidentally, the word does not imply fairground tricks or Spiritualist mediumship, but refers to the supposed power of the mind to know something at a distance without the use of the normal senses, and *without receiving information from any other mind—e.g.* telepathically. For example, if someone claims they can find a lost object or read a page of a closed book, then they are claiming clairvoyant powers because the information is not known by any other mind or brain. Clairvoyance, if it were shown to exist, would, as we've indicated, be far more troublesome to science than telepathy because it is so hard to see how it could take place. With telepathy one has at least the transmitter-receiver possibility —after all we know that information can be sent quickly and invisibly from point to point through radio and TV. But in the case of clairvoyance one simply cannot imagine any mechanism, biological or otherwise, capable of reading the pages of a closed book or of hunting around finding a lost object.

The third faculty of mind which anecdotal evidence suggests might exist, and which Rhine therefore also hoped to prove in a laboratory setting, was psychokinesis—more popularly known as " mind-over-matter." Here it is supposed that by some mental effort, conscious or unconscious, the mind can reach out and move or otherwise affect objects at a distance. However unlikely this may seem, most people evidently have some kind of vague belief that they have powers of this kind. To give just one common example, notice the way in which people attempt to " will " dice to fall the way they want them to. Here again psychokinesis (generally abbreviated to PK) poses real problems for physiology and psychology—assuming that it occurs. What kind of mechanism could possibly exist in the brain with the power to move solid objects at a distance or, even more peculiarly, inside sealed containers?

As for the fourth faculty, precognition, this is even more staggering and, if demonstrated, would throw the whole of conventional science into a spin. Here the suggestion is that the mind can sometimes glimpse events taking place in the future—as when one dreams about a forthcoming disaster, the accidental death of a friend or, on a more cheerful level, the winner of the Grand National. The problem is that classical physics is based on certain assumptions about the way in which the universe behaves, and one of these is that a cause must always precede an effect, and that time therefore always flows in one specific direction. Admittedly the notion of time itself is a rather uncertain one, but no theory of physics in current use allows one to understand how the mind could conceivably have knowledge of an event *which has not yet taken place!*

But, despite these objections, Rhine's argument —and a point of view adopted by most other scientists seriously interested in studying ESP— was that however unlikely these phenomena might be, and however inadequate our present theories are to explain or understand them, if they exist then that's all there is to it. If the facts are such that the theories don't encompass them, then the theories must be modified accordingly. It is with this background that parapsychologists set out to turn anecdote into fact and trap the hidden powers of man's mind in the laboratory.

Their first step was to find a way of quantifying the phenomena—of measuring it numerically. The necessity for this will become obvious if one recalls the case of the telephone call from the long forgotten friend. This, at first thought, might seem to be " obviously " telepathy but, by the time one has done some sums on the total number of telephone calls received, the total number of one's friends, the total number of people on the telephone, etc., etc., one realises that it is a relatively *likely* rather than a paranormal event. Rhine therefore decided that all his experiments must be quantifiable, and with this in mind he developed a special pack of cards—the now quite famous Zener cards. Zener cards are in fact shaped like regular playing cards, but instead of the usual pictures and numbers, they each have one of five boldly marked symbols—a star, a plus sign, a triangle, a circle or a set of wavy lines. A standard Zener pack contains 25 cards in all—five of each of the above symbols. Now the point is that in doing ESP tests with these cards, one starts off with the important base of knowing exactly how many a person will guess right by chance. In fact, in the average run through of a pack of 25, one will get just five right simply by guessing. Clearly, sometimes one will get more right and sometimes less, but the most likely number to get right will be five, and in all cases it is possible to deduce mathematically the odds against getting a particular number correct. Now if the person generally gets five right, but occasionally gets six or seven, sometimes three or four, and now and again a much higher number—say nine or ten—at the end of the experiment one can total up the number of guesses, look at how many of them were correct and perform a simple statistical test to determine whether the hits were more frequent than they should have been. If they were, then one could run the experiment a few more times and if the above-chance scoring continues, then one might be faced with the possibility that the guesser was somehow getting information about the test cards—possibly by telepathy. The Zener cards, by the way, were also useful in testing clairvoyance—here the guesser would try to call out the sequence of a shuffled pack of cards whose order was not known to anyone until *after the experiment was over.* Equally, they could be used in precognition experiments, simply by inviting the guesser first to call out a sequence of cards and then *a few minutes later shuffling the pack,* counting them out and comparing the guesses against the final sequence. In the case of psychokinesis, rather obviously, cards are not particularly suitable and Rhine set up experiments involving dice rolled out by a machine on to a table—the task of the subject being to try to influence the dice to come up with a particular number face upwards.

As it happens, the first results coming out of Duke University laboratory were sensational and seemed to suggest beyond all reasonable doubt that some form of ESP existed. Time and time again the card guessing tests came up with significantly " above chance " results, and it really did seem as though some information was passing from the mind of the person dealing out the cards to the individual attempting to guess them. So remarkable were the results, in fact, that scientists in other laboratories in other parts of the world rushed to repeat Rhine's experiments, realising that establishing extra-sensory perception would be one of the most important developments in the history of science, with quite profound philosophical implications about the spiritual as opposed to the materialistic view of man. Unfortunately, the positive results simply failed to show in other laboratories—time and time again other experimenters repeated the Duke studies, obtaining only chance results. Rhine defended his position by generating yet more positive results, and in response his critics suggested that his successes might have been due to the fact that his experimental procedures were not rigid enough. For example, in early experiments, the guesser was only separated from the person handling the cards by a screen, and of course it has long been known that people can unconsciously give a lot of information away by minute body movements, whispering, etc., or even by deliberate cheating in order to " help the experiments along." To meet this objection the Duke group tightened up its experiments, separating the participants in ESP tests at least by solid walls, and in some cases by placing them in different buildings. They still claimed some above chance results, but very many fewer than before.

Slowly the world of science began to divide into two camps—a small but measurable minority who claimed that ESP had been demonstrated scientifically and that it was time for the fact to be faced, and a majority who felt that the topic was probably a red herring, and on the whole a waste of scientific brains and energy. Curiously, and perhaps significantly, the research groups with a pro-ESP attitude continued to produce pro-ESP results, while repeat studies in neutral or anti-ESP laboratories tended to show no evidence—a situation which prevails to the present day and which complicates the issue whenever the topic is discussed. At the heart of the problem is the fact that now and again, in apparently carefully controlled experiments, scientists come up with results suggesting telepathy, clairvoyance, etc, but that in the main these results are not repeatable in other laboratories. Because of this a basic scientific principle—that before a phenomenon is accepted into the mainframe of scientific knowledge, it must be reproducible in suitably equipped laboratories —is not met. This principle of repeatability is a quite fundamental one and is designed, among other things, to insure that research and scientific theory is not held back by having to accept every statement or premise put forward by misguided scientists or simple crackpots. If a phenomenon is a real one, it should be demonstrable to all and not just a chosen few. The strongest argument that the parapsychologists can offer to explain the non-repeatability is based on the assumption (which they claim is backed by some definite evidence) that ESP phenomena are sensitive to the attitude of mind of people taking part in ESP experiments; if they are positively disposed they somehow help the phenomena along, if sceptical or hyper-critical they damp it down. Intuitively this argument makes a kind of sense—if telepathy is real, then why should it not be "blocked" by sceptical minds or by unhelpful or aggressive attitudes? But the argument also has a terrible weakness from a scientific point of view—it allows the glib "explanation" or excuse whenever experiments fail that someone with a sceptical mind must have been present. Of course, on the other side of the coin, sceptics cannot choose to deny absolutely the evidence generated from time to time within parapsychology laboratories—it may be a great weakness that the results are not replicable, but how can one explain the positive results which *have* occurred?

If one can eliminate poor controls, incorrect statistical tests and other such variables, there doesn't seem to be much left unless one brings into the field the taboo topic of fakery and fraud. Traditionally scientists are disinclined to accuse each other of cheating—this also is a glib and unsavoury way of denying facts that one doesn't want to accept. Rhine himself once argued that when his opponents began to accuse him of cheating he would know that his battle was won—in other words, the sceptics would be implicitly acknowledging that they had no other explanation for his results. In fact, acusations of cheating and falsifying data were occasionally made, but never formed a substantial part of the case against ESP, until a few years ago when a major scandal broke out in Rhine's own laboratory.

The director of research at that laboratory (Rhine had retired some time previously) was actually caught falsifying data in a major series of experiments, altering it so that it indicated ESP results where none was in fact being obtained. Perhaps it was a healthy sign that his own scientific colleagues were the ones to catch him out, and also that he immediately resigned after admitting the fraud. But the fact remains that the incident put an enormously powerful weapon in the hands of the sceptics who can now argue, with justification, that even respected scientists can be guilty of fraud and deception in their eagerness to prove the case for ESP. Since this particular scandal, incidentally, strong suspicion has fallen on the work of the British investigator, the late Dr. S. G. Soal, whom it is now believed may have faked the results of one of his experiments—a study at one time believed to provide incontrovertible evidence for precognition.

The question now arises as to what is the status of ESP research today, and where is it likely to move in the future? In sum, it seems that contrary to the bright hopes of the pioneer parapsychologists, research in this area has moved forward very slowly, if at all, and the world of science is no more convinced of the reality of extra-sensory phenomena than it was when the Duke Laboratory opened its doors forty years ago. Worse, there is certainly a growing feeling among many scientists that if the phenomena did exist, some hard evidence really ought to have been forthcoming after so many years of diligent research. Of course, none of this disproves telepathy, clairvoyance, precognition or psychokinesis—it merely suggests that there is little scientific ground for assuming that they exist. Equally, the failure of scientific studies in this field will do nothing to shake the belief of millions of people that man is something more than a chunk of matter in a solidly materialistic universe, and that from time to time he is capable of demonstrating his spiritual nature through extra-sensory or paranormal powers. But one thing is quite certain—we don't know enough about the universe to say that ESP could or could *not* exist. No doubt one day we shall know for sure, but until that time the scientific view must remain—not proven.

VII. A QUICK GUIDE TO THE BRAIN

In anatomical terms, the brain is the collection of nervous tissue contained inside the skull; in functional terms, it is the principal organ of the central nervous system which receives, processes and stores information from the outside world, and utilises this information to control other parts of the nervous system and the organism as a whole. The brain is the most elaborate and complicated organ in the body—in fact it would be more accurate to describe it as a set of organs, all interdependent to some degree—and any attempt at describing it has to err on the side of oversimplification. In addition, there is no absolute agreement among anatomists as to how to break it down into separate parts or units, with some workers concentrating on the physical appearance of different parts, while others lean towards the functional roles of different segments. The problem is even further compounded because, despite intensive study lasting over a period of a century, the precise function of some parts of the brain is still not properly understood. One common descriptive approach, however, divides the brain into three main units which, starting from the one closest to the spinal cord, are (1) hindbrain, (2) midbrain and (3) forebrain.

1. *The Hindbrain.* This is a cluster of structures comprising the medulla, the pons and the cerebellum. The medulla is really a kind of extension of the spinal cord and contains a mass of fibres and nuclei which serve to control the most basic of automatic bodily functions, such as respiration and blood circulation. Just behind it is the cerebellum, sometimes called the "little brain" which is heavily involved in motor co-ordination while above it is the pons which, as its Latin name implies, acts as a bridge between the two halves of the cerebellum. The hindbrain is in many ways an evolutionary primitive structure.

2. *The Midbrain.* This is a small structure, directly above the pons and buried deep inside the mass of the brain. It contains a number of substructures, including the corpora quadragemina and the tegmentum, and its principal role appears to be the control of eye movements and the vestibular system.

3. *The Forebrain.* Whereas almost all vertebrates share rather similar structuring of the so-called lower centres—the mid- and hindbrains—the forebrain is enormously enlarged and developed in the higher animals, in particular the mammals. Anatomically the forebrain is divided into the diencephalon—consisting of the thalamus and the hypothalamus—and the telencephalon, which includes the limbic system, the basal ganglia and, most significant of all in primates, the cerebral cortex. The cortex, which is in fact a convoluted layer of neurones covering the surface of the entire telencephalon, plays an important role in sensory and motor functions, though as one ascends the phylogenetic scale a greater and greater proportion of it is given over to integrative and associative functions.

To confuse matters somewhat, a large part of the forebrain and midbrain is also known collectively as the cerebrum which is itself divided into the right and left hemispheres, connected at the base by the corpus callosum. The chasm separating the hemispheres, which is the most striking single feature of the brain when seen from above, is known as the interhemispherical fissure, while other deep folds include the central and lateral fissures. These fissures tend to be useful to the neurologist in marking out the various lobes of the cerebrum—frontal, temporal, parietal, etc. and they also tend to constitute boundary lines separating out functionally different areas of the cortex—e.g. those parts concerned with receiving sensory information and those concerned with associative or integratory processes.

Without resorting to elaborate drawings, or even to some practical anatomy itself, there is little point in going into greater detail on the structure of the brain, though it is worth emphasising again that many of its functions are still extremely poorly understood. It is still not entirely clear, for example, just why the cerebrum is divided up into two hemispheres, nor why local damage may sometimes have negligible, sometimes drastic effects. The mechanism of information storage within the brain—learning and memory—is almost totally mysterious, and little is known about the relationship between cortical activity and the " higher faculties " of reasoning, imagery and consciousness. To some extent the brain appears rather more mysterious now than it did half a century ago, and we will probably do well to prepare ourselves for things to get even more puzzling before any major advances in understanding it occur.

SPORTING RECORDS

Association Football, Athletics, Badminton, Baseball, Bowls, Cricket, Golf, Gymnastics, Hockey, Horse Racing, Lawn Tennis, Motor Racing, Rifle Shooting, Rowing and Sculling, Rugby League, Rugby Union, Speedway, Squash Rackets, Swimming, Table Tennis.

ASSOCIATION FOOTBALL

FOOTBALL LEAGUE CHAMPIONS

1950–1	Tottenham H	1961–2	Ipswich T	1972–3	Liverpool
1951–2	Manchester U	1962–3	Everton	1973–4	Leeds U
1952–3	Arsenal	1963–4	Liverpool	1974–5	Derby C
1953–4	Wolverhampton W	1964–5	Manchester U	1975–6	Liverpool
1954–5	Chelsea	1965–6	Liverpool	1976–7	Liverpool
1955–6	Manchester U	1966–7	Manchester U		
1956–7	Manchester U	1967–8	Manchester C		
1957–8	Wolverhampton W	1968–9	Leeds U		
1958–9	Wolverhampton W	1969–70	Everton		
1959–60	Burnley	1970–1	Arsenal		
1960–1	Tottenham H	1971–2	Derby C		

FOOTBALL ASSOCIATION CHALLENGE CUP WINNERS

1950–1	Newcastle U	1961–2	Tottenham H	1972–3	Sunderland
1951–2	Newcastle U	1962–3	Manchester U	1973–4	Liverpool
1952–3	Blackpool	1963–4	West Ham U	1974–5	West Ham U
1953–4	West Bromwich A	1964–5	Liverpool	1975–6	Southampton
1954–5	Newcastle U	1965–6	Everton	1976–7	Manchester U
1955–6	Manchester C	1966–7	Tottenham H		
1956–7	Aston Villa	1967–8	West Bromwich A		
1957–8	Bolton W	1968–9	Manchester C		
1958–9	Nottingham F	1969–70	Chelsea		
1959–60	Wolverhampton W	1970–1	Arsenal		
1960–1	Tottenham H	1971–2	Leeds U		

FOOTBALL LEAGUE CUP WINNERS

1960–1	Aston V	1967–8	Leeds U	1974–5	Aston V
1961–2	Norwich C	1968–9	Swindon T	1975–6	Manchester C
1962–3	Birmingham C	1969–70	Manchester C	1976–7	Aston V
1963–4	Leicester C	1970–1	Tottenham H		
1964–5	Chelsea	1971–2	Stoke C		
1965–6	West Bromwich A	1972–3	Tottenham H		
1966–7	Queen's Park R	1973–4	Wolverhampton W		

SCOTTISH LEAGUE CHAMPIONS

1950–1	Hibernian	1961–2	Dundee	1972–3	Celtic
1951–2	Hibernian	1962–3	Rangers	1973–4	Celtic
1952–3	Rangers	1963–4	Rangers	1974–5	Rangers
1953–4	Celtic	1964–5	Kilmarnock	1975–6	Rangers
1954–5	Aberdeen	1965–6	Celtic	1976–7	Celtic
1955–6	Rangers	1966–7	Celtic		
1956–7	Rangers	1967–8	Celtic		
1957–8	Hearts	1968–9	Celtic		
1958–9	Rangers	1969–70	Celtic		
1959–60	Hearts	1970–1	Celtic		
1960–1	Rangers	1971–2	Celtic		

SCOTTISH FOOTBALL ASSOCIATION CUP WINNERS

1950–1	Celtic	1961–2	Rangers	1972–3	Rangers
1951–2	Motherwell	1962–3	Rangers	1973–4	Celtic
1952–3	Rangers	1963–4	Rangers	1974–5	Celtic
1953–4	Celtic	1964–5	Celtic	1975–6	Rangers
1954–5	Clyde	1965–6	Rangers	1976–7	Celtic
1955–6	Hearts	1966–7	Celtic		
1956–7	Falkirk	1967–8	Dunfermline A		
1957–8	Clyde	1968–9	Celtic		
1958–9	St Mirren	1969–70	Aberdeen		
1959–60	Rangers	1970–1	Celtic		
1960–1	Dunfermline A	1971–2	Celtic		

SCOTTISH LEAGUE CUP WINNERS

1950–1	Motherwell	1961–2	Rangers	1972–3	Hibernian
1951–2	Dundee	1962–3	Hearts	1973–4	Dundee
1952–3	Dundee	1963–4	Rangers	1974–5	Celtic
1953–4	East Fife	1964–5	Rangers	1975–6	Rangers
1954–5	Hearts	1965–6	Celtic	1976–7	Aberdeen
1955–6	Aberdeen	1966–7	Celtic		
1956–7	Celtic	1967–8	Celtic		
1957–8	Celtic	1968–9	Celtic		
1958–9	Hearts	1969–70	Celtic		
1959–60	Hearts	1970–1	Rangers		
1960–1	Rangers	1971–2	Partick T		

BRITISH CHAMPIONSHIP

(80 Seasons since 1884)

	Champions	Joint Champions	Runners-up
England	29	20	24
Scotland	24	17	24
Wales	7	5	12
Ireland	1	5	9

WORLD CUP WINNERS

1930	Uruguay	1962	Brazil
1934	Italy	1966	England
1938	Italy	1970	Brazil
1950	Uruguay	1974	W Germany
1954	W Germany		
1958	Brazil		

EUROPEAN CUP WINNERS

1955–6	Real Madrid	1964–5	Inter Milan	1973–4	Bayern Munich
1956–7	Real Madrid	1965–6	Real Madrid	1974–5	Bayern Munich
1957–8	Real Madrid	1966–7	Glasgow C	1975–6	Bayern Munich
1958–9	Real Madrid	1967–8	Manchester U	1976–7	Liverpool
1959–60	Real Madrid	1968–9	A C Milan		
1960–1	Benfica	1969–70	Feyenoord		
1961–2	Benfica	1970–1	Ajax		
1962–3	A C Milan	1971–2	Ajax		
1963–4	Inter Milan	1972–3	Ajax		

EUROPEAN NATIONAL CUP WINNERS' CUP

1961	Florentina	1968	A C Milan	1975	Dynamo Kiev
1962	Atletico Madrid	1969	Sl Bratislava	1976	Anderlecht
1963	Tottenham H	1970	Manchester C	1977	Hamburg SV
1964	Sporting Lisbon	1971	Chelsea		
1965	West Ham U	1972	Glasgow R		
1966	Borussia Dortmund	1973	A C Milan		
1967	Bayern Munich	1974	Magdeburg		

UEFA CUP WINNERS

1958	Barcelona	1967	Dynamo Zagreb	1975	Borussia Moenchengladbach
1960	Barcelona	1968	Leeds U	1976	Liverpool
1961	A S Roma	1969	Newcastle U	1977	Juventus
1962	Valencia	1970	Arsenal		
1963	Valencia	1971	Leeds U		
1964	Real Zaragossa	1972	Tottenham H		
1965	Ferencvaros	1973	Liverpool		
1966	Barcelona	1974	Feyenoord		

EUROPEAN NATIONS COMPETITION

1960	USSR	1972	W Germany
1964	Spain	1976	Czechoslovakia
1968	Italy		

ATHLETICS

1976 OLYMPIC GAMES (MONTREAL)

Men

100 metres H Crawford Trinidad 10·06s
200 metres D Quarrie Jamaica 20·23s
400 metres A Juantorena Cuba 44·26s
800 metres A Juantorena Cuba 1 min 43·50s
1,500 metres J Walker N Zealand 3 min 39·17s
5,000 metres L Viren Finland 13 min 24·76s
10,000 metres L Viren Finland 27 min 40·38s
Marathon W Cierpinski E Ger 2h 9 min 55·00s
4 × 100 metres relay US 38·33s
4 × 400 metres relay US 2 min 58·65s
110 metres hurdles G Drut France 13·30s
400 metres hurdles E Moses US 47·64s
3,000 metres steeplechase A Garderud Sweden 8 min 8·02s
20 kilometres walk D Bautista Mexico 1h 24 min 40·60s
High jump J Wszola Poland 2·25m
Long jump A Robinson US 8·35m
Triple jump V Saneyev USSR 17·29m
Pole vault T Slusarski Poland 5·50m
Putting the shot U Beyer E Ger 21·05m
Throwing the discus M Wilkins US 67·50m
Throwing the javelin M Nemeth Hungary 94·58m
Throwing the hammer Y Sedyh USSR 77·52m
Decathlon B Jenner US 8,618 pts

Women

100 metres A Richter W Ger 11·08s
200 metres B Eckert E Ger 22·37s
400 metres I Szewinska Poland 49·29s
800 metres T Kazankina USSR 1 min 54·94s
1,500 metres T Kazankina USSR 4 min 5·48s
4 × 100 metres relay E Ger 42·56s
4 × 400 metres relay E Ger 3 min 19·23s
100 metres hurdles J Schaller E Ger 12·77s
High jump R Ackerman E Ger 1·93m
Long jump A Voigt E Ger 6·72m
Putting the shot I Christova Bulgaria 21·16m
Throwing the discus E Schlaak E Ger 69·00m
Throwing the javelin R Fuchs E Ger 65·94m
Pentathlon S Siegl E Ger 4,745 pts

OLYMPIC RECORDS

Men

100 metres 9·95s J Hines US 1968 Mex C
200 metres 19·80s T Smith US 1968 Mex C
400 metres 43·86s L Evans US 1968 Mex C
800 metres 1 min 43·50s A Juantorena Cuba 1976 Mont
1,500 metres 3 min 34·9s K Keino Kenya 1968 Mex C
5,000 metres 13 min 20·34s B Foster GB 1976 Mont
10,000 metres 27 min 38·4s L Viren Finland 1972 Mun
Marathon 2h 9 min 55s W Cierpinski E Ger 1976 Mont
4 × 100 metres relay 38·19s US 1972 Mun
4 × 400 metres relay 2 min 56·1s US 1968 Mex C
110 metres hurdles 13·24s R Milburn US 1972 Mun
400 metres hurdles 47·64s E Moses US 1976 Mont
3,000 metres steeplechase 8 min 8·02s A Garderud Sweden 1976 Mont
20 kilometres walk 1h 24 min 40·6s D Bautista Mexico 1976 Mont
50 kilometres walk 3h 56 min 11·6s B Kannenberg W Ger 1972 Mun
High jump 2·24m R Fosbury US 1968 Mex C
Long jump 8·90m R Beamon US 1968 Mex C
Triple jump 17·29m V Saneyev USSR 1976 Mont
Pole vault 5·50m W Nordwig E Ger 1972 Mun
Putting the shot 21·32m A Barisnikov USSR 1976 Mont
Throwing the discus 68·28m M Wilkins US 1976 Mont
Throwing the javelin 94·58m M Nemeth Hungary 1976 Mont
Throwing the hammer 77·52m Y Sedyh USSR 1976 Mont
Decathlon 8,618 pts B Jenner US 1976 Mont

Women

100 metres 11·01s A Richter W Ger 1976 Mont
200 metres 22·37s B Eckert E Ger 1976 Mont
400 metres 49·29s I Szewinska Poland 1976 Mont
800 metres 1 min 54·94s T Kazankina USSR 1976 Mont
1,500 metres 4 min 1·4s L Bragina USSR 1972 Mun
4 × 100 metres relay 42·56s E Ger 1976 Mont
4 × 400 metres relay 3 min 19·23s E Ger 1976 Mont
100 metres hurdles 12·59s A Ehrhardt E Ger 1972 Mun
High jump 1·93m R Ackerman E Ger 1976 Mont
Long jump 6·82m V Viscopoleanu Romania 1968 Mex C
Putting the shot 21·16m I Christova Bulgaria 1976 Mont
Throwing the discus 69·00m E Schlaak E Ger 1976 Mont
Throwing the javelin 65·94m R Fuchs E Ger 1976 Mont
Pentathlon 4,801 pts M Peters GB 1972 Mun

1974 EUROPEAN CHAMPIONSHIPS (ROME)

Men

100 metres V Borzov USSR 10·27s
200 metres P Mennea Italy 20·6s
400 metres K Honz W Ger 45·04s
800 metres L Susanj Yugoslavia 1 min 44·1s
1,500 metres K-P Justus E Ger 3 min 40·6s
5,000 metres B Foster UK 13 min 17·2s
10,000 metres M Kuschmann E Ger 28 min 25·8s
Marathon I Thompson UK 2h 13 min 18·8s
4 × 100 metres relay France 38·69s
4 × 400 metres relay UK 3 min 3·3s
110 metres hurdles G Drut France 13·4s
400 metres hurdles A Pascoe UK 48·82s
3,000 metres steeplechase B Malinowski Poland 8 min 15s
20 kilometres walk V Golubnichiy USSR 1h 29 min 30s
50 kilometres walk C Hohne E Ger 3h 59 min 5·6s
High jump J Torring Denmark 7ft 4½in
Long jump V Podluzhniy USSR 26ft 7¾in
Triple jump V Saneyev USSR 56ft 6¼in
Pole vault V Kishkun USSR 17ft 6½in
Putting the shot H Briesenick E Ger 67ft 3¼in
Throwing the discus P Kahma Finland 208ft 9in
Throwing the javelin H Siitonen Finland 293ft 11in
Throwing the hammer A Spiridonov USSR 243ft 5in
Decathlon R Skowronek Poland 8,207 pts

Women

100 metres I Szewinska Poland 11·13s
200 metres I Szewinska Poland 22·51s
400 metres R Salin Finland 50·14s
800 metres L Tomova Bulgaria 1 min 58·1s
1,500 metres G Hoffmeister E Ger 4 min 2·3s
3,000 metres N Holmen Finland 8 min 55·2s
4 × 100 metres relay E Ger 42·51s
4 × 400 metres relay E Ger 3 min 25·2s
100 metres hurdles A Ehrhardt E Ger 12·66s
High jump R Witschas E Ger 6ft 4¾in
Long jump I Bruzsenyak Hungary 21ft 10in
Putting the shot N Chizhova USSR 68ft 2½in
Throwing the discus F Melnik USSR 226ft 4in
Throwing the javelin R Fuchs E Ger 220ft 6in
Pentathlon N Tkachenko USSR 4,776 pts

1974 COMMONWEALTH GAMES (CHRISTCHURCH NZ)

Men

100 metres D Quarrie Jamaica 10·4s
200 metres D Quarrie Jamaica 20·7s
400 metres C Asati Kenya 46·00s
800 metres J Kipkurgat Kenya 1 min 43·9s
1,500 metres F Bayi Tanzania 3 min 32·2s
5,000 metres B Jipcho Kenya 13 min 14·4s
10,000 metres R Tayler NZ 27 min 47·4s
Marathon I Thompson Eng 2h 9 min 12s
4 × 100 metres relay Aus 39·3s
4 × 400 metres relay Kenya 3 min 4·4s
110 metres hurdles F Kimaiyo Kenya 13·7s
400 metres hurdles A Pascoe Eng 48·8s
3,000 metres steeplechase B Jipcho Kenya 8 min 20·8s
20 miles walk J Warhurst Eng 2h 35 min 23s
High jump G Windeyer Aus 7ft 1in
Long jump A Lerwill Eng 26ft 0½in
Triple jump J Owusu Ghana 54ft 1¾in
Pole vault D Baird Aus 16ft 6¾in
Putting the shot G Capes Eng 68ft 0½in
Throwing the discus R Tait NZ 206 ft 11in
Throwing the javelin C Clover Eng 278ft 7in
Throwing the hammer I Chipchase Eng 228ft 2in
Decathlon M Bull NI 7,417 pts

Women

100 metres R Boyle Aus 11·3s
200 metres R Boyle Aus 22·5s
400 metres V Saunders Can 51·7s
800 metres C Rendina Aus 2 min 1·1s
1 500 metres G Reiser Can 4 min 7·8s
4 × 100 metres relay Aus 43·5s
4 × 400 metres relay Eng 3 min 29·2s
100 metres hurdles J Vernon Eng 13·5s
High jump B Lawton Eng 6ft 0½in
Long jump M Oshikoya Nigeria 21ft 2¼in
Putting the shot J Haist Can 52ft 10¾in
Throwing the discus J Haist Can 182ft 2in
Throwing the javelin P Rivers Aus 182ft 0in

BADMINTON

ALL ENGLAND CHAMPIONSHIPS

Men's singles

1950–2	W P Soon (Malaya)
1953–4	E B Choong (Malaya)
1955	W P Soon (Malaya)
1956–7	E B Choong (Malaya)
1958	E Kops (Denmark)
1959	T J Hok (Indonesia)
1960–3	E Kops (Denmark)
1964	K A Nielsen (Denmark)
1965	E Kops (Denmark)
1966	T A Huang (Malaya)
1967	E Kops (Denmark)
1968–74	R Hartono (Indonesia)
1975	S Pri (Denmark)
1976	R Hartono (Indonesia)
1977	F Delfs (Denmark)

Women's singles

1950	T Ahm (Denmark)
1951	A S Jacobsen (Denmark)
1952	T Ahm (Denmark)
1953	M Ussing (Denmark)
1954	J Devlin (US)
1955–6	M Varner (US)
1957–8	J Devlin (US)
1959	H M Ward (GB)
1960	J Devlin (US)
1961–4	G C K Hashman (US)
1965	U H Smith (GB)
1966–7	G C K Hashman (US)
1968	E Twedberg (Sweden)
1969	H Yuki (Japan)
1970	E Takenaka (Japan)
1971	E Twedberg (Sweden)
1972	N Nakayama (Japan)
1973	M Beck (GB)
1974	H Yuki (Japan)
1975	H Yuki (Japan)
1976	G Gilks (GB)
1977	H Yuki (Japan)

BASEBALL (US)

WORLD SERIES WINNERS

1958	New York Yankees
1959	Los Angeles Dodgers
1960	Pittsburgh Pirates
1961	New York Yankees
1962	New York Yankees
1963	Lost Angeles Dodgers
1964	St Louis Cardinals
1965	Los Angeles Dodgers
1966	Baltimore Orioles
1967	St Louis Cardinals
1968	Detroit Tigers
1969	New York Mets
1970	Baltimore Orioles
1971	Pittsburgh Pirates
1972	Oakland Athletics
1973	Oakland Athletics
1974	Oakland Athletics
1975	Cincinnati Reds
1976	Cincinnati Reds

BOWLS

EBA NATIONAL CHAMPIONSHIPS
Single-handed

1960	D J Bryant
1961	P A Line
1962	C Mercer
1963	C S Graham
1964	P A Line
1965	R E Lewis
1966	D J Bryant
1967	W C Irish
1968	N R Groves
1969	J Davidson
1970	H Kershaw
1971	D J Bryant
1972	D J Bryant
1973	D J Bryant
1974	W C Irish
1975	D J Bryan
1976	A O'Connell

CRICKET

TEST MATCHES

England v. Australia
(first played 1876)
Won: England 71 Australia 88 Drawn: 66

England v. South Africa
(first played 1888)
Won: England 46 South Africa 18 Drawn: 38

England v. West Indies
(first played 1928)
Won: England 19 West Indies 22 Drawn: 27

England v. New Zealand
(first played 1929)
Won: England 22 New Zealand 0 Drawn: 23

England v. India
(first played 1932)
Won: England 25 India 7 Drawn: 21

England v. Pakistan
(first played 1954)
Won: England 9 Pakistan 1 Drawn: 17

COUNTY CHAMPIONSHIP

1950	Lancashire Surrey
1951	Warwickshire
1952	Surrey
1953	Surrey
1954	Surrey
1955	Surrey
1956	Surrey
1957	Surrey
1958	Surrey
1959	Yorkshire
1960	Yorkshire
1961	Hampshire
1962	Yorkshire
1963	Yorkshire
1964	Worcestershire
1965	Worcestershire
1966	Yorkshire
1967	Yorkshire
1968	Yorkshire
1969	Glamorgan
1970	Kent
1971	Surrey
1972	Warwickshire
1973	Hampshire
1974	Worcestershire
1975	Leicestershire
1976	Middlesex

GILLETTE CUP

1963	Sussex
1964	Sussex
1965	Yorkshire
1966	Warwickshire
1967	Kent
1968	Warwickshire
1969	Yorkshire
1970	Lancashire
1971	Lancashire
1972	Lancashire
1973	Gloucestershire
1974	Kent
1975	Lancashire
1976	Northamptonshire

JOHN PLAYER LEAGUE

1969 Lancashire
1970 Lancashire
1971 Worcestershire
1972 Kent
1973 Kent
1974 Leicestershire
1975 Hampshire
1976 Kent

BENSON & HEDGES CUP

1972 Leicestershire
1973 Kent
1974 Surrey
1975 Leicestershire
1976 Kent

GOLF

OPEN CHAMPIONSHIP

1950 A D Locke (SA)
1951 M Faulkner (GB)
1952 A D Locke (SA)
1953 B Hogan (US)
1954 P W Thomson (Aus)
1955 P W Thomson (Aus)
1956 P W Thomson (Aus)
1957 A D Locke (SA)
1958 P W Thomson (Aus)
1959 G J Player (SA)
1960 K D G Nagle (Aus)
1961 A Palmer (US)
1962 A Palmer (US)
1963 R J Charles (NZ)
1964 A Lema (US)
1965 P W Thomson (Aus)
1966 J Nicklaus (US)
1967 R de Vicenzo (Arg)
1968 G J Player (SA)
1969 A Jacklin (GB)
1970 J Nicklaus (US)
1971 L Trevino (US)
1972 L Trevino (US)
1973 T Weiskopf (US)
1974 G J Player (SA)
1975 T Watson (US)
1976 J Miller (US)

GYMNASTICS

1976 OLYMPIC GAMES (MONTREAL)

Men

Combined exercises N Andrianov (USSR)
Combined exercises (team) (Japan)
Floor exercises N Andrianov (USSR)
Horizontal bar M Tsukahara (Japan)
Parallel bars S Kato (Japan)
Horse vault N Andrianov (USSR)
Pommelled horse Z Magyar (Hungary)
Rings N Andrianov (USSR)

Women

Beam N Comaneci (Romania)
Combined exercises N Comaneci (Romania)
Combined exercises (team) (USSR)
Floor exercises N Kim (USSR)
Asymmetric bars N Comaneci (Romania)
Horse vault N Kim (USSR)

HOCKEY

OLYMPIC CHAMPIONS

1908 England
1920 Gt Britain
1928 India
1932 India
1936 India
1948 India
1952 India
1956 India
1960 Pakistan
1964 India
1968 Pakistan
1972 W Germany
1976 New Zealand

HORSE RACING

THE DERBY

	Horse	Jockey	Owner
1950	Galcador	W Johnstone	M Boussac
1951	Arctic Prince	C Spares	Mr J McGrath
1952	Tulyar	C Smirke	The Aga Khan
1953	Pinza	G Richards	Sir V Sassoon
1954	Never Say Die	L Piggott	Mr R S Clark
1955	Phil Drake	F Palmer	Mme Volterra
1956	Lavandin	W Johnstone	M Wertheimer
1957	Crepello	L Piggott	Sir V Sassoon
1958	Hard Ridden	C Smirke	Sir V Sassoon
1959	Parthia	W H Carr	Sir H de Trafford
1960	St Paddy	L Piggott	Sir V Sassoon
1961	Psidium	R Poincelet	Mrs Arpad Plesch
1962	Larkspur	N Sellwood	Mr R Guest
1963	Relko	Y Saint-Martin	M F Dupré
1964	Santa Claus	A Breasley	Mr J Ismay
1965	Sea Bird II	T P Glennon	Mr M J Ternynck
1966	Charlottown	A Breasley	Lady Z Wernher
1967	Royal Palace	G Moore	Mr H J Joel
1968	Sir Ivor	L Piggott	Mr R R Guest
1969	Blakeney	E Johnson	Mr A Budgett
1970	Nijinsky	L Piggott	Mr C W Engelhard
1971	Mill Reef	G Lewis	Mr P Mellon
1972	Roberto	L Piggott	Mr J Galbreath
1973	Morston	E Hide	Mr A Budgett
1974	Snow Knight	B Taylor	Mrs N Philips
1975	Grundy	P Eddery	Dr C Vittadini
1976	Empery	L Piggott	Mr B Hunt
1977	The Minstrel	L Piggott	Mr R Sangster

THE GRAND NATIONAL

	Horse	Jockey	Owner
1950	Freebooter	J Power	Mrs L Brotherton
1951	Nickel Coin	J A Bullock	Mr J Royle
1952	Teal	A P Thompson	Mr H Lane
1953	Early Mist	B Marshall	Mr J H Griffin
1954	Royal Tan	B Marshall	Mr J H Griffin
1955	Quare Times	P Taffe	Mrs W H E Welman
1956	ESB	D Dick	Mrs L Carver
1957	Sundew	F Winter	Mrs G Kohn
1958	Mr What	A Freeman	Mr D Coughlan
1959	Oxo	M Scudamore	Mr J E Bigg
1960	Merryman II	G Scott	Miss W H S Wallace
1961	Nicolaus Silver	H Beasley	Mr C Vaughan
1962	Kilmore	F Winter	Mr N Cohen
1963	Ayala	P Buckley	Mr P B Raymond
1964	Team Spirit	G W Robinson	Mr J Goodman
1965	Jay Trump	C Smith	Mrs M Stephenson
1966	Anglo	T Norman	Mr S Levy
1967	Foinavon	J Buckingham	Mr C P T Watkins
1968	Red Alligator	B Fletcher	Mr J Manners
1969	Highland Wedding	E Harty	Mr T H McKay, jnr
1970	Gay Trip	P Taaffe	Mr A Chambers
1971	Specify	J Cook	Mr F W Pontin
1972	Well to Do	G Thorner	Capt T Forster
1973	Red Rum	B Fletcher	Mr N Le Mare
1974	Red Rum	B Fletcher	Mr N Le Mare
1975	L'Escargot	T Carberry	Mr R Guest
1976	Rag Trade	J Burke	Mr P Raymond
1977	Red Rum	T Stack	Mr N Le Mare

LAWN TENNIS

DAVIS CUP

1950	Australia	1960	Australia	1970	USA
1951	Australia	1961	Australia	1971	USA
1952	Australia	1962	Australia	1972	USA
1953	Australia	1963	USA	1973	Australia
1954	USA	1964	Australia	1974	South Africa
1955	Australia	1965	Australia	1975	Sweden
1956	Australia	1966	Australia	1976	Italy
1957	Australia	1967	Australia		
1958	USA	1968	USA		
1959	Australia	1969	USA		

WIMBLEDON CHAMPIONSHIPS

Men's Singles

1950 J E Patty (US)
1951 R Savitt (US)
1952 F A Sedgman (Aus)
1953 E V Seixas (US)
1954 J Drobny (Egypt)
1955 M A Trabert (US)
1956 L A Hoad (Aus)
1957 L A Hoad (Aus)
1958 A J Cooper (Aus)
1959 A Olmedo (Peru)
1960 N A Fraser (Aus)
1961 R Laver (Aus)
1962 R Laver (Aus)
1963 C R McKinley (US)
1964 R Emerson (Aus)
1965 R Emerson (Aus)
1966 M Santana (Spain)
1967 J D Newcombe (Aus)
1968 R Laver (Aus)
1969 R Laver (Aus)
1970 J D Newcombe (Aus)
1971 J D Newcombe (Aus)
1972 S R Smith (US)
1973 J Kodes (Czech)
1974 J Connors (US)
1975 A R Ashe (US)
1976 B Borg (Sweden)

Women's Singles

1950 A L Brough (US)
1951 D J Hart (US)
1952 M Connolly (US)
1953 M Connolly (US)
1954 M Connolly (US)
1955 L Brough (US)
1956 S J Fry (US)
1957 A Gibson (US)
1958 A Gibson (US)
1959 M E Bueno (Braz)
1960 M E Bueno (Braz)
1961 A Mortimer (GB)
1962 J R Susman (US)
1963 M Smith (Aus)
1964 M E Bueno (Braz)
1965 M Smith (Aus)
1966 B-J King (US)
1967 B-J King (US)
1968 B-J King (US)
1969 A Jones (GB)
1970 M Court (Aus)
1971 E F Goolagong (Aus)
1972 B-J King (US)
1973 B-J King (US)
1974 C Evert (US)
1975 B-J King (US)
1976 C Evert (US)

Men's Doubles

1950 J E Bromwich & A K Quist
1951 K McGregor & F A Sedgman
1952 K McGregor & F A Sedgman
1953 L A Hoad & K R Rosewall
1954 R N Hartwig & M G Rose
1955 R N Hartwig & L A Hoad
1956 L A Hoad & K R Rosewall
1957 G Mulloy & J E Patty
1958 S Davidson & U Schmidt
1959 R Emerson & N A Fraser
1960 R H Osuna & R D Ralston
1961 R Emerson & N A Fraser
1962 R A Hewitt & F S Stolle
1963 R H Osuna & A Palafox
1964 R A Hewitt & F S Stolle
1965 J D Newcombe & A D Roche
1966 K N Fletcher & J D Newcombe
1967 R A Hewitt & F D McMillan
1968 J D Newcombe & A D Roche
1969 J D Newcombe & A D Roche
1970 J D Newcombe & A D Roche
1971 R Emerson & R Laver
1972 R A Hewitt & F D McMillan
1973 J S Connors & I Nastase
1974 J D Newcombe & A D Roche
1975 V Gerulaitis & A Mayer
1976 B E Gottfried & R Ramirez

Women's Doubles

1950 A L Brough & W Dupont
1951 S J Fry & D J Hart
1952 S J Fry & D J Hart
1953 S J Fry & D J Hart
1954 A L Brough & W Dupont
1955 A Mortimer & J A Shilcock
1956 A Buxton & A Gibson
1957 A Gibson & D R Hard
1958 M E Bueno & A Gibson
1959 J Arth & D R Hard
1960 M E Bueno & D R Hard
1961 K Hantze & B-J Moffitt
1962 B-J Moffitt & J R Susman
1963 M E Bueno & D R Hard
1964 M Smith & L R Turner
1965 M E Bueno & B-J Moffitt
1966 M E Bueno & N Richey
1967 R Casals & B-J King
1968 R Casals & B-J King
1969 M Court & J A Tegart
1970 R Casals & B-J King
1971 R Casals & B-J King
1972 B-J King & B Stove
1973 R Casals & B-J King
1974 E Goolagong & P Michel
1975 A K Kiyomura & K Sawamatsu
1976 C Evert & M Navratilova

Mixed Doubles

1950 E W Sturgess & A L Brough
1951 F A Sedgman & D J Hart
1952 F A Sedgman & D J Hart
1953 E V Seixas & D J Hart
1954 E V Seixas & D J Hart
1955 E V Seixas & D J Hart
1956 E V Seixas & S J Fry
1957 M G Rose & D R Hard
1958 R N Howe & L Coghlan
1959 R Laver & D R Hard
1960 R Laver & D R Hard
1961 F Stolle & L R Turner
1962 N A Fraser & W Dupont
1963 K N Fletcher & M Smith
1964 F Stolle & L R Turner
1965 K N Fletcher & M Smith
1966 K N Fletcher & M Smith
1967 O K Davidson & B-J King
1968 K N Fletcher & M Court
1969 F Stolle & A Jones
1970 I Nastase & R Casals
1971 O K Davidson & B-J King
1972 I Nastase & R Casals
1973 O K Davidson & B-J King
1974 O K Davidson & B-J King
1975 M C Riessen & B M Court
1976 A D Roche & F Durr

MOTOR RACING

World Champion Drivers

1950	G Farina (It)
1951	J M Fangio (Arg)
1952	A Ascari (It)
1953	A Ascari (It)
1954	J M Fangio (Arg)
1955	J M Fangio (Arg)
1956	J M Fangio (Arg)
1957	J M Fangio (Arg)
1958	M Hawthorn (GB)
1959	J Brabham (Aus)
1960	J Brabham (Aus)
1961	P Hill (US)
1962	G Hill (GB)
1963	J Clark (GB)
1964	J Surtees (GB)
1965	J Clark (GB)
1966	J Brabham (Aus)
1967	D Hulme (NZ)
1968	G Hill (GB)
1969	J Stewart (GB)
1970	J Rindt (Austria)
1971	J Stewart (GB)
1972	E Fittipaldi (Braz)
1973	J Stewart (GB)
1974	E Fittipaldi (Braz)
1975	N Lauda (Austria)
1976	J Hunt (GB)

RIFLE SHOOTING

Queen's/King's Prize Winners

1950	R Greig
1951	G Boa
1952	A Kinnier-Wilson
1953	N McCaw
1954	G Twine
1955	L Fenwick
1956	G Twine
1957	J Love
1958	R Fulton
1959	I Mallabar
1960	G Westling
1961	N Beckett
1962	P Hall
1963	K Pilcher
1964	A Harris
1965	J Allen
1966	R Hampton
1967	J Powell
1968	A Parke
1969	F Little
1970	G F Arnold
1971	R M Stevens
1972	R P Rosling
1973	K M Pilcher
1974	F Harris
1975	C M Y Trotter
1976	W H Magnay

ROWING AND SCULLING

THE UNIVERSITY BOAT RACE

		min	s	lengths
1952	Oxford	20	23	canvas
1953	Cambridge	19	54	8
1954	Oxford	20	23	4½
1955	Cambridge	19	10	16
1956	Cambridge	18	36	1¼
1957	Cambridge	19	1	2
1958	Cambridge	18	15	3½
1959	Oxford	18	52	6
1960	Oxford	18	59	1
1961	Cambridge	19	22	4¼
1962	Cambridge	19	46	5
1963	Oxford	20	47	5
1964	Cambridge	19	18	6½
1965	Oxford	18	7	4
1966	Oxford	19	12	3¾
1967	Oxford	18	52	3¼
1968	Cambridge	18	22	3½
1969	Cambridge	18	4	4
1970	Cambridge	20	22	3
1971	Cambridge	17	58	10
1972	Cambridge	18	36	9½
1973	Cambridge	19	21	13
1974	Oxford	17	35	5½
1975	Cambridge	19	27	3¾
1976	Oxford	16	58*	6½
1977	Oxford	19	28	7

*Record time
Won: Cambridge 68 Oxford 54

1976 OLYMPIC GAMES WINNERS (MONTREAL)

Men

Single sculls P Karppinen Finland 7 min 29·03s
Double sculls Norway 7 min 13·20s
Coxless pairs E Ger 7 min 23·31s
Coxed pairs E Ger 7 min 58·99s
Coxless fours E Ger 6 min 37·42s
Coxed fours USSR 6 min 40·22s
Coxless quadruple sculls E Ger 6 min 18·65s
Eights E Ger 5 min 58·29s

Women

Single sculls C Scheiblich E Ger 4 min 5·56s
Double sculls Bulgaria 3 min 44·36s
Coxless pairs Bulgaria 4 min 1·22s
Coxed fours E Ger 3 min 45·08s
Coxed quadruple sculls E Ger 3 min 29·99s
Eights E Ger 3 min 33·32s

RUGBY LEAGUE

LEAGUE CHAMPIONS

1950–1	Workington T
1951–2	Wigan
1952–3	St Helens
1953–4	Warrington
1954–5	Warrington
1955–6	Hull
1956–7	Oldham
1957–8	Hull
1958–9	St Helens
1959–60	Wigan
1960–1	Leeds
1961–2	Huddersfield
1962–3	Swinton/Hunslet
1963–4	Swinton/Oldham
1964–5	Halifax
1965–6	St Helens
1966–7	Wakefield T
1967–8	Wakefield T
1968–9	Leeds
1969–70	St Helens
1970–1	St Helens
1971–2	Leeds
1972–3	Dewsbury
1973–4	Salford
1974–5	St Helens
1975–6	Salford
1976–7	St Helens

CHALLENGE CUP WINNERS

1950 Warrington
1951 Wigan
1952 Workington T
1953 Huddersfield
1954 Warrington
1955 Barrow
1956 St Helens
1957 Leeds
1958 Wigan
1959 Wigan
1960 Wakefield T
1961 St Helens
1962 Wakefield T
1963 Wakefield T
1964 Widnes
1965 Wigan
1966 St Helens
1967 Featherstone R
1968 Leeds
1969 Castleford
1970 Castleford
1971 Leigh
1972 St Helens
1973 Featherstone R
1974 Warrington
1975 Widnes
1976 St Helens
1977 Leeds

WORLD CUP WINNERS

1954 England
1957 Australia
1960 Great Britain
1968 Australia
1970 Australia
1972 Great Britain
1976 Australia

RUGBY UNION

COUNTY CHAMPIONS

1950 Cheshire
1951 E Midlands
1952 Middlesex
1953 Yorkshire
1954 Middlesex
1955 Lancashire
1956 Middlesex
1957 Devon
1958 Warwickshire
1959 Warwickshire
1960 Warwickshire
1961 Cheshire
1962 Warwickshire
1963 Warwickshire
1964 Warwickshire
1965 Warwickshire
1966 Middlesex
1967 Durham/Surrey
1968 Middlesex
1969 Lancashire
1970 Staffordshire
1971 Surrey
1972 Gloucestershire
1973 Lancashire
1974 Gloucestershire
1975 Gloucestershire
1976 Gloucestershire
1977 Lancashire

INTERNATIONAL CHAMPIONS

1950–1 Ireland
1951–2 Wales
1952–3 England
1953–4 England, France, Wales
1954–5 France, Wales
1955–6 Wales
1956–7 England
1957–8 England
1958–9 France
1959–60 England, France
1960–1 France
1961–2 France
1962–3 England
1963–4 Scotland, Wales
1964–5 Wales
1965–6 Wales
1966–7 France
1967–8 France
1968–9 Wales
1969–70 France, Wales
1970–1 Wales
1971–2 Wales
1972–3 England, France, Ireland, Scotland, Wales
1973–4 Ireland
1974–5 Wales
1975–6 Wales
1976–7 France

SPEEDWAY

WORLD CHAMPIONS

1950 F Williams (W)
1951 J Young (Aus)
1952 J Young (Aus)
1953 F Williams (W)
1954 R Moore (NZ)
1955 P Craven (E)
1956 O Fundin (Sw)
1957 B Briggs (NZ)
1958 B Briggs (NZ)
1959 R Moore (NZ)
1960 O Fundin (Sw)
1961 O Fundin (Sw)
1962 P Craven (E)
1963 O Fundin (Sw)
1964 B Briggs (NZ)
1965 B Knutsson (Sw)
1966 B Briggs (NZ)
1967 O Fundin (Sw)
1968 I Mauger (NZ)
1969 I Mauger (NZ)
1970 I Mauger (NZ)
1971 O Olsen (Nor)
1972 I Mauger (NZ)
1973 J Szczakiel (Pol)
1974 A Michanek (Sw)
1975 O Olsen (Denmark)
1976 P Collins (E)

SQUASH RACKETS

OPEN CHAMPIONSHIP

1950–5	Hashim Khan (Pak)
1956	Roshan Khan (Pak)
1957	Hashim Khan (Pak)
1958–61	Azam Khan (Pak)
1962	Mohibullah Khan (Pak)
1963–5	A F A Taleb (UAR)
1966–7	J P Barrington (Ire)
1968	G B Hunt (Aus)
1969–72	J P Barrington (Ire)
1973–4	G B Hunt (Aus)
1975	Q Zaman (Pak)
1976	G B Hunt (Aus)
1977	G B Hunt (Aus)

SWIMMING

1976 OLYMPIC GAMES WINNERS (MONTREAL)

Men

100 metres free-style J Montgomery US 49·99s
200 metres free-style B Furniss US 1 min 50·29s
400 metres free-style B Goodall US 3 min 51·93s
1,500 metres free-style B Goodall US 15 min 2·40s
100 metres back-stroke J Naber US 55·49s
200 metres back-stroke J Naber US 1 min 59·19s
100 metres breast-stroke J Hencken US 1 min 3·11s
200 metres breast-stroke D Wilkie GB 2 min 15·11s
100 metres butterfly M Vogel US 54·35s
200 metres butterfly M Bruner US 1 min 59·23s
400 metres medley R Strachan US 4 min 23·68s
4 × 100 metres medley relay US 3 min 42·22s
4 × 200 metres free-style relay US 7 min 23·22s
Highboard diving K Dibiasi Italy 600·51 pts
Springboard diving P Boggs US 619·05 pts
Water polo Hungary

Women

100 metres free-style K Ender E Ger 55·65s
200 metres free-style K Ender E Ger 1 min 59·26s
400 metres free-style P Thumer E Ger 4 min 9·89s
800 metres free-style P Thumer E Ger 8 min 37·14s
100 metres back-stroke U Richter E Ger 1 min 1·83s
200 metres back-stroke U Richter E Ger 2 min 13·43s
100 metres breast-stroke H Anke E Ger 1 min 11·16s
200 metres breast-stroke M Koshevaia USSR 2 min 33·35s
100 metres butterfly K Ender E Ger 1 min 0·13s
200 metres butterfly A Pollack E Ger 2 min 11·41s
400 metres medley U Tauber E Ger 4 min 42·77s
4 × 100 metres free-style relay US 3 min 44·82s
4 × 100 metres medley relay E Ger 4 min 7·95s
Highboard diving E Vaytsekhovskaia USSR 406·59 pts
Springboard diving J Chandler US 506·19 pts

TABLE TENNIS

WORLD CHAMPIONSHIP

Men

1950	R. Bergmann (Eng)
1951	J Leach (Eng)
1952	H Satoh (Japan)
1953	F Sido (Hungary)
1954	I Ogimura (Japan)
1955	T Tanaka (Japan)
1956	I Ogimura (Japan)
1957	T Tanaka (Japan)
1959	Jung Kuo-Tuan (China)
1961	Chuang Tse-Tung (China)
1963	Chuang Tse-Tung (China)
1965	Chuang Tse-Tung (China)
1967	N Hasegawa (Japan)
1969	S Itoh (Japan)
1971	S Bengtsson (Sweden)
1973	Hsi En-Ting (China)
1975	I Jonyer (Hungary)
1977	M Kohno (Japan)

Women

1950–5	A Rozeanu (Romania)
1956	T Okawa (Japan)
1957	F Eguchi (Japan)
1959	K Matsuzaki (Japan)
1961	Chiu Chung-Hui (China)
1963	K Matsuzaki (Japan)
1965	N Fukazu (Japan)
1967	S Morisawa (Japan)
1969	T Kowada (Japan)
1971	Lin Hui-Ching (China)
1973	Hu Yu-Lan (China)
1974	M Alexandra (Romania)
1975	Pak Yung Sun (Korea DPR)
1977	Pak Yung Sun (Korea DPR)

MODERN GARDENING

A guide for the gardener on all aspects of modern horticulture particularly in the control of pests and diseases and the eradication of weeds by the latest means.

TABLE OF CONTENTS

MODERN GARDENING

CULTIVATION OF FLOWERS.

Throughout this section the notes must be taken to refer to cultural conditions in the British Isles, although in many cases the information can be adopted to suit the necessity of readers living abroad. Undoubtedly, in many temperate parts of the world interest in gardening has increased enormously during the past decade or so, despite the fact that numbers of large gardens have ceased to exist and that few people can afford to pay for full-time help in their gardens. To counteract this, the all important labour-saving garden has come into its own; shrubby plants have replaced annual bedding schemes and large lawns put down instead of herbaceous borders or beds of particular plants.

In addition, the owner-gardener is anxious to avail himself of the excellent selection of modern tools; thus the conventional hoe is being replaced by the "Swoe" or the Wolf pattern of Dutch weeder, both of which are very easy to use, and digging can be done quickly—and with much less effort—by using a German digger called a "Terrex" spade. For grass mowing, the work is easily done with the wide range of motor mowers to suit every purpose.

For greenhouse work, smaller houses are being used and one, say, 12 ft. by 8 ft., can be run economically with a minimum winter temperature of 40° Fahrenheit by the introduction of trouble-free, thermostatic heaters or the turbo-heaters. At the moment, besides automatic heating, the prototypes for automatic ventilation and watering are making an appearance.

While advocating the use of such appliances, it must be pointed out that there are also to be found tools, sundries, and fertilisers of little value, and many of which have never been properly tested prior to being put on the market. It is, therefore, a good plan to discuss the comparative merits of any appliance or horticultural sundry with a competent horticulturist or to contact a public authority. In particular, many local horticultural societies have special trading facilities, and the merits of most garden things are generally known and discussed among members.

Throughout this Guide the vexed question of change in scientific name has been dealt with as liberally as possible and, whenever necessary, synonyms and cross references are given. In dealing with cultivar names, that is, varietal names like rose 'Peace,' reference is made as recommended in the *International Code of Nomenclature for Cultivated Plants* (1967). By so doing, the references are right up to date and further information on any particular plant or subject is easy to find. For the purpose, a few standard works of reference are given after each section. Normally, all the plants mentioned in the text are available through the usual trade channels.

After each plant listed there is a note on its propagation. Generally, this is the easiest or most efficient way of doing so, but it is not necessarily the only means. Details of the various methods employed are as follows:

Seed. Generally speaking, the early spring is the most suitable time for sowing seeds of trees and shrubs besides those of herbaceous plants and alpines. Where only a few plants are needed, the seed can be sown in pots and a suitable compost made up with 2 parts of soil, 1 part of peat, and 1 part of coarse sand. Before sowing, the pot should be stood up to its rim in water so that the soil is soaked. Then the seed can be sown thinly and covered with a light sprinkling of sifted compost.

For very fine seed, like begonias or azaleas, the seed must have only the merest "sugaring" of sand just sufficient to anchor it. When sown, the pots should be covered with a pane of glass (to prevent evaporation) and kept, if possible, in a warm greenhouse or frame. With this method of propagation it is important to remember that failure will result if the seed is sown too deeply, if the temperature is too low, or if the soil is too dry.

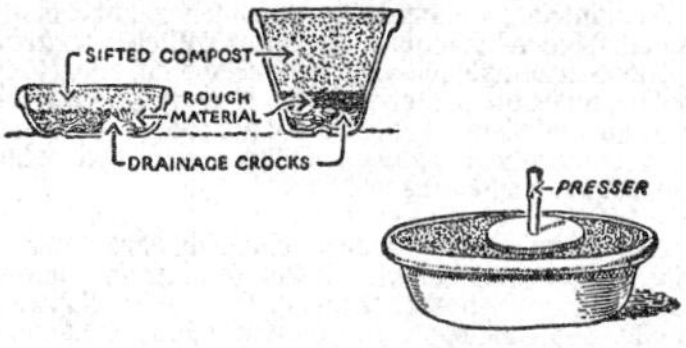

CORRECT PREPARATION OF SEED POTS AND PANS—Note provision for ample drainage and compost to rim of its container. After sowing, the containers are covered with a sheet of glass.

Cuttings. There are two main types of cutting: soft-wood cuttings made from fresh, green shoots in the spring and summer and hard-wood cuttings made of mature or semi-mature woody shoots in the autumn. A soft cutting is taken about 3 in. long, the lower leaves removed and a clean cut made through a node in the stem. These are then inserted in pots containing a light, sandy soil or a rooting medium such as horticultural vermiculite, well watered, and covered with a bell jar or plastic bag. Delphiniums, hydrangeas, and lupins are all propagated in this way.

Hard-wood cuttings are taken in the autumn and made from shoots about 8–12 in. long. These are inserted in a sandy soil out of doors or in a cold frame, and left to develop for a year. Black-currants, forsythia, and roses can be propagated by this means.

Layering. This is one of the easiest ways of propagating the majority of woody plants, and is used to increase stocks of plants like clematis, lilacs, and rhododendrons. Normally, layering is done in the autumn or spring when suitable branches are pegged down. On each of these the young shoots are, in turn, pegged down and tips turned upwards and tied in position. To encourage rooting, gritty sand and peat should be worked around each layer, and usually the young plant can be severed from the parent after about eighteen months.

Division. By this method it is easy to propagate the majority of herbaceous plants, some rock-garden plants, and a few shrubs. A few herbaceous plants, like delphinium and paeony, are slow to get established after moving, and here the method should not be employed. In any case, old plants should not be split up in a wholesale manner; instead, it is far better to select a few young healthy plants, divide these, and replant the best of the young shoots, in the autumn.

ALPHABETICAL LIST OF ORNAMENTAL PLANTS.

Abutilon.—The greenhouse species is often used in public parks for bedding schemes. *A. vitifolium*, with white, mauve, or blue flowers makes a fine wall shrub for warm gardens. If given full sun it will quickly reach 10–15 ft., but is sometimes short-lived. *Prop.*—Easily raised from seed sown in March in a warm greenhouse or frame.

Acer (Maple).—Hardy, ornamental trees; the Norway maple is often planted for its magnificent autumn colour and as a lawn tree. *A. palmatum* and vars. constitute the Japanese maples; all colour brilliantly in the autumn but do not grow freely unless given some shade and a light soil rich in humus. *Prop.*—Seed, layering, or budding.

Achillea (Yarrow).—Grey-leaved perennials for open border or, dwarf species, for rock garden. Valued as a cut flower, particularly *A. ptarmica* 'Perry's White,' with double, white flowers and *A. eupatorium* 'Gold Plate,' with large, flat, yellow flower heads. *A. millefolium* is a pernicious weed of turf (T34). *Prop.*—Division in autumn.

Acidanthera.—Scented, bulbous plant introduced from Abyssinia. It is not difficult to grow if the corms are planted in the spring and lifted in the autumn for storing in a frost-proof shed. It requires a sunny position and plenty of water in the summer. *Prop.*—Offsets removed when the old crop of bulbs is lifted.

Aconitum (Monkshood).—Blue-flowered perennial plants particularly useful for lightly shaded positions or full sun; flowers from May to July, height 3–5 ft.; roots poisonous. *Prop.*—Seed or division.

Adiantum.—*See* Ferns.

A WELL-GROWN AGAPANTHUS—In winter the pot should be kept in a cold greenhouse or some protected place; in summer afforded full sun.

Agapanthus.—A bulbous plant, native of South Africa, usually found in seaside gardens and sometimes grown in tubs; flowers blue, violet, or white. It needs winter protection in the form of a covering of bracken or straw and a light soil heavily enriched with manure. Worthy of wider cultivation. *Prop.*—Seed or division in March.

Ageratum.—Blue-flowered carpeting plant. *See* Annuals.

Allium (Flowering Onion).—A genus of nearly 300 species of bulbous plants widely distributed over the Northern Hemisphere. The foliage has the distinctive smell of garlic, but some species are grown for garden ornamentation; in particular *A. roseum*, valuable late-flowering rock plant for dry positions. *Prop.*—Offsets, taken from parent bulbs in the spring.

Alstroemeria aurantiaca (Peruvian Lily).—This tuberous-rooted, herbaceous plant is often grown for cutting. Flowers orange-red and height 2–3 ft.; of easy culture if afforded a sunny position and left undisturbed. For best results apply liquid manure or soot water when growth starts. *Prop.*—Seed or division.

Althaea (Hollyhock).—A truly delightful, old-world plant, but not often seen, as modern hybrids have given way to rust disease. Best grown in a rich, heavy loam. Mulch with manure of any sort and stake as necessary. *Prop.*—Seed in June, thin out, and transfer to flowering position in September. Although a perennial, in some localities the best results are obtained by treating it as a biennial and raising a small supply annually.

Alyssum.—Low-growing annuals and perennials for rock garden and sunny border. The perennial, *A. saxatile*, is deservedly popular by reason of its bright, spring flowers and value as a wall plant. The variety 'Citrinum' is bright yellow and 'Dudley Neville' biscuit-yellow. *Prop.*—Perennial sorts by cuttings in June.

Amaryllis belladonna.—Often this plant is confused with the greenhouse, bulbous plant, *Hippeastrum*. The true amaryllis is a half-hardy bulb for planting at the foot of a warm wall; it has white to pinkish-red flowers. When planting, cover neck of bulb with an inch of soil and leave undisturbed, as the plant resents moving and is slow to get established. Lack of flowering is generally due to planting too deep. Established clumps may be fed with hoof and horn meal at 2 oz. per sq. yd. in July. *Prop.*—Divide and replant clumps in early July.

Amelanchier canadensis.—A large shrub or small tree; valuable for its spring flowers and autumn colour. As it will grow almost anywhere in sun or shade, it makes a good plant for informal screening. *Prop.*—Seed or layers.

Amepelopsis.—*See* Parthenocissus.

Anchusa italica.—A blue-flowered perennial with fleshy roots, growing to a height of about 3 ft. Responds to feeding and needs a position in full sun. *Prop.*—Root cuttings in the spring; division in the autumn.

Anemone.—The tuberous-rooted section includes the 'Caen' and 'St. Brigid' strains. These are best grown in an open position in light, rich soil; plant in October, lift and store when foliage dies. The hardy, fibrous-rooted perennials are varieties of *A. hybrida* (syn. *japonica*) and constitute one of the most accommodating of perennials, being particularly useful for damp, shady positions. Worthy of wider attention from gardeners. *Prop.*—Perennial sorts by division in autumn.

Annuals.—These are plants which develop from seed, flower, fruit, and die within a year. Additionally, some perennials, like antirrhinums, may be treated as annuals for the convenience of their cultivation. Sunny borders may be planted solely with annuals, they may be interplanted with perennials, used for window boxes, or, occasionally, in the rock garden. All sorts do best in well-worked, light loam enriched each year with a dressing of fish meal at 3 oz. per sq. yd., ten days before sowing or planting.

In the division of the group Hardy Annuals may be sown in the open ground as soon as conditions permit during March or April where the plants are to flower. Wet or cold soils will give many failures, and fine seed should be covered only with the lightest sugaring of soil. Often surprising—but delightful—results may be obtained by sowing broadcast mixed seed of annuals specially offered by some trade houses.

To raise Half Hardy Annuals, seed may be sown in early March in a warm greenhouse and the seedlings pricked out into boxes. Subsequently, the plants are grown on in a cold frame, gradually hardened off, and then transferred to their flowering positions towards the end of May.

Anthemis tinctoria.—Hardy perennial with feathery, grey foliage and flowers in varying shades of yellow. Height 2–3 ft., needs full sun and good for cutting. *Prop.*—Division in the autumn. *Anthemis nobilis* is the chamomile sometimes unwisely used to make lawns.

Antirrhinum (Snapdragon).—The popular bedding plant requiring a good soil and position in full sun now largely in disfavour owing to rust disease; planting should be restricted to rust-resistant varieties. *See* **Annuals.**

Aphelandra squarrosa.—An evergreen, perennial plant introduced from Brazil. Often sold as a house plant, albeit a warm temperature and a high humidity are necessary for its cultivation. When grown indoors it is best discarded when the flowers fade and the foliage starts to wither, as it cannot be successfully grown on from year to year under normal conditions indoors.

Aquilegia.—The modern race of hybrids are the result of much interbreeding with wild forms to give a wide range of colours. Best when planted in light shade where soil is naturally moist. *Prop.*—Seed in late spring; transplant to flowering position for following year.

Arabis caucasica.—Once known as *A. albida*, this common rock plant is often used on dry walls. The double-flowered form is particularly good. *Prop.*—Cuttings in July; a fresh stock should be raised regularly, as the special forms tend to die out.

Araucaria (Monkey Puzzle).—This tree was introduced from Chile, where it forms large natural forests, and widely planted in Victorian days. Browning of foliage suggests lack of water in the summer or, occasionally, effects of very cold weather. It should be planted in a position protected from the prevailing wind. *Prop.*—Seed in a warm greenhouse.

Armeria maritima.—A hardy perennial with pink or red flowers in the spring; must be grown in full sun where the soil is dry. *Prop.*—Division after flowering.

Artemisia.—A genus of shrubs and perennials suitable for sunny borders or rockeries. *A. lactiflora* is among the best of the herbaceous species, having grey foliage and creamy-white flowers. *A. abrotanum* (lad's love) in the shrubby section has grey, fragrant foliage. *Prop.*—Herbaceous section by division; shrubs by cuttings in the early summer.

Arundinaria.—*See* **Bamboo.**

Aster (Michaelmas Daisy).—By careful breeding this plant has been improved out of all recognition, and many first-class varieties are available in the trade. Responsive to good cultivation, it is used for its colour late in season and properties as a cut flower, particularly *A. yunnanensis* 'Napsbury' and *A.* 'Barr's Pink.' A wide range of colours are available besides some fine, low-growing forms. In the border one pleasing combination can be made with *A.* 'Harrington's Pink' and *Scabious* 'Dinkie.' *Prop.*—The clumps should be split up *annually* in the spring, and only the plumpest pieces of outer root replanted.

Aster, China or Common.—*See* **Callistephus.**

Astilbe.—Allied to the *Spiraea* and useful for planting in moist, rich soils; flowers white, pink, and crimson; height 2 ft. *Prop.*—Division of clumps.

Aubrieta.—A name often misspelt. Throughout the country it is used as edging or for dry walls. Many lovely sorts available apart from the commonly found, pale-blue variety. It is a lime lover. *Prop.*—After flowering the plants should be severely trimmed and, as necessary, stock increased by division.

Aucuba japonica.—Much maligned and over-planted shrub, but one tolerant of neglect and sunless or smoky conditions. Interesting variants of the type, like 'Crotonifolia,' may be found in trade lists. *Prop.*—Cuttings rooted in the open in July.

Auricula.—Correctly known botanically as *Primula auricula*. Flowers of alpine auriculas are white or yellow, while in those of florists' auriculas are to be found some of the most delicate colourings among hardy plants Choice varieties are grown in pots under glass; others in moist, shady borders. *Prop.*—Seed or division in the spring.

Azalea.—*See* **Rhododendron.**

Bamboo.—The common name for the large group of woody grasses, reference to which is difficult owing to the confusion in their nomenclature. Often grown for screening and wind breaks, and is a favourite shelter for small birds; the best for home-grown canes are *Phyllostachys viridi-glaucescens* and *Sinarundinaria nitida*. An interesting account of bamboo growing is found in the *Jour. Roy. Hort. Soc.* (June 1957). Growth can be encouraged by feeding with sulphate of ammonia and mulching with leaf-mould in the spring. *Prop.*—Division of clumps in late spring; transplants must be kept watered until established.

Begonia.—A genus showing wide diversity of form and much horticultural value. Of particular interest is the tuberous-rooted section, of which many of the loveliest varieties have originated in the nurseries of Messrs. Blackmore and Landon at Bath. For bedding schemes, the tubers are started in boxes of rich soil under glass in late March and planted out 9 in. apart in June. During the summer feed with liquid manure of any sort and keep moist in dry periods. *Prop.*—Cuttings in early spring in a warm case.

Berberis.—An extensive genus of beautiful and easily grown shrubs, evergreen and deciduous; the former used mainly for beauty of flower, and the latter for autumn colouring and ornamental fruits. *B. stenophylla* makes a fine evergreen hedge; invaluable for preventing illicit entry by dogs and, even, unruly children. *B. aggregata* and *B. jamesiana* are among the best berrying kinds. Prune in the winter by removing old wood. *Prop.*—Seed in spring or layering in autumn.

Buddleia.—Deciduous shrubs of easy culture for sunny positions. Varieties of *B. davidii* available in range of colours from purple to white; best when pruned hard by cutting all previous year's growth back to main stems in February. The weeping species, *B. alternifolia*, often grown as a standard; good specimens at R.H.S. Gardens, Wisley. This sort must be pruned in the summer by cutting off the dead flowering stems. *Prop.*—Cuttings in July–August in cold frame.

Cactus.—In the main grown in cool greenhouses or as house plants and, if cultivated well, many will flower every year. As a general guide, plants should be watered fairly freely in the summer and little in the winter, but there are exceptions. A detailed account of growing these fascinating plants will be found in *The Cactus Grower's Guide*, by Vera Higgings (Latimer House), 1946.

Calceolaria.—Seed of the greenhouse biennials sown in June or July for flowering in the following year. Mixed seed provides a wide range of colour. *C. integrifolia* is a half-hardy perennial, raised by cuttings or seed, for greenhouse or bedding work.

Calendula (Marigold).—This common hardy annual is freely raised from seed sown in August. Of easy culture in any sort of soil, although it is worth getting seed of new varieties now available. *See* **Annuals.**

Callistephus.—The China asters are among the best half-hardy annuals for garden and indoor decoration, but good soil and full sun are necessary for best results. *See* **Annuals.**

Camellia japonica.—Hardy, evergreen shrub rightly beloved by connoisseurs and cultivated in gardens for many centuries. May be grown in cold greenhouses, woodland gardens, and against north- and west-facing walls; under all conditions camellias must have a moist, acid soil. Best varieties for outdoors are 'Althaeaflora' (dark red), 'Donckelarii' (red, white marbling), and 'C. M. Wilson' (pink). Of recent introduction is the desirable *C. williamsii* bred from *C. japonica* in part; often the subject of television and gardening notes. The dropping of buds is thought due to dryness at the roots at some time or sharp fluctuation in temperature. *Prop.*—Named varieties by cuttings under glass in early July. Otherwise plants easily raised from seeds if sown in the autumn immediately they are ripe, in acidic peat and kept moist.

Campsis grandiflora.—Sometimes found listed as *Bignonia* or *Tecoma*; choice deciduous climber for warm wall, large reddish-orange flowers in autumn. To encourage flowering growth, prune hard back to old growth in spring. *Prop.*—Cuttings in April struck in a warm case.

Canary Creeper.—*See* **Tropaeolum.**

Candytuft.—Hardy annual (*q.v.*) and perennials with white, crimson, blue, or purple flowers. The perennial—*Iberis sempervirens*—is a fine plant for a rock wall. *Prop.*—Seed or, perennials, from cuttings.

Carnation.—*See* **Dianthus.**

Centaurea (Cornflower).—The perennial species are valuable for cutting and border use, and may be found in such colours as pink, crimson, and yellow. *Prop.*—Lift and divide every third or fourth year. The hardy annual, *C. cyanus*, is often sold as a cut flower. *See* **Annuals.**

Chaenomeles speciosa.—This is the correct botanical name for japonica. The species commonly grown is a wide-spreading, rounded shrub, 6–10 ft. in height, and often used against walls. It is a plant of easy culture with best results being achieved by the annual spurring back of the current season's growth in the same way as an apple tree is pruned. All japonicas can be used for making jelly but, for this purpose, the best one is *Chaenomeles cathayensis*, a gaunt shrub about 10 ft. in height which bears fruit up to 8 oz. in weight. To obtain a crop within a reasonable time, two or three plants may be set in a group about 5 ft. apart. If growth or flowering is below par all japonicas should be fed with "Growmore" and mulched with compost.

Cheiranthus cheiri (Wallflower).—Among the finest displays of this biennial are those found each year in the public gardens of Southend-on-Sea, where it is used in conjunction with bulbs and forget-me-nots. *Prop.*—Seed sown thinly in rows in May and seedlings thinned or lined out and then transplanted in late autumn. The so-called Siberian wallflower, *Erysimun asperum*, which has bright orange flowers, is grown in the same way, but it is intolerant of wet soils. Both sorts are lime lovers, and on acid soils plants may receive treatment with 1 oz. of lime in a gallon of water.

Chimonanthus (Winter Sweet).—Hardy, winter-flowering shrub with heavily scented flowers. Although brought to this country from the Far East in the mid-eighteenth century its garden value is not widely appreciated. The large-flowered, yellow sort, *C. praecox*, is particularly fine, but like all the varieties, it is best grown against a sunny wall and where the soil tends to be poor. If growth is excessive and flowering poor, trim back young growth severely in March to encourage short, spur-like shoots. *Prop.*—Easily raised from seed or layers.

Christmas Rose.—*See* **Helleborus.**

Chrysanthemum.—Hardy annual sorts are available in a wide range of colours and give a fine display in the summer months. *See* **Annuals.** There are also a number of perennials such as the shafta daisy and the oxeye daisy for sunny, herbaceous borders; all do well in ordinary soil, but should be lifted and split up about every three years. The plant sold by florists in the autumn is the Japanese chrysanthemum. Many are hardy out-of-doors, but no plant is more responsive to good cultivation and normally is best left to the specialist grower. For ordinary garden work, the best sorts are the Korean and Otley types. Under a brief reference the interesting details of cultivation cannot be dealt with fairly, and reference to specialist books is recommended.

Clematis.—A hardy climber for walls, screens pergolas, and the like. Best kinds are to be found among named varieties in nurserymen's lists. A light, well-drained soil is necessary and if fed annually with a bucketful of manure or compost the plant will thrive for many years. Occasionally plants will be found on north walls, and if grown in full sun some light protection from the sun is desirable for the roots. Varieties which flower on the *current* season's growth, like *C. jackmanii*, should be pruned in late February to within a foot of the ground; other sorts should have sufficient old growth removed, after flowering, to keep them within bounds.

Sometimes the climber is killed by clematis wilt so premature death of young plants should not be automatically blamed on the supplier. Control is by spraying with a copper-containing fungicide. *Prop.*—Layering, by which means one shoot will often give three or four plants.

Convallaria majalis (Lily of the Valley).—Well-known perennial that will thrive in any damp, shady position. For best results lift every four or five years and mulch annually with old manure. *Prop.*—Division when foliage fades.

Coreopsis.—The hardy annuals are found in catalogues under "Callipsis," and all will thrive in ordinary soil. The flowers are mainly bright yellow, and many are good for cutting. *See* **Annuals.** Similarly, the perennials have the same predominant colour and are useful because of their long flowering season and abundance of flower. *Prop.*—Division.

Cornflower.—*See* **Centaurea.**

Cosmos.—Tall-growing, half-hardy annuals that are best grown in full sun in a dryish border. The large, daisy-like flowers can be had in a variety of colours, including white, yellow, pink, and crimson. *See* **Annuals.**

Cotoneaster.—Hardy evergreen and deciduous shrubs or small trees bearing scarlet or sometimes yellow berries in the autumn. All may be grown in ordinary or poor soil and planted in open or shady shrubberies and trailing species used against walls, over banks, or as ground cover. For shrubberies *C. lacteus* and *C.* 'Cornubia' with red berries and *C. rothchildianus* with yellow berries are among the best sorts; *C. conspicuus* 'Decora' is a strong grower for banks, while *C. horizontalis* is an excellent cover for any wall. Planting may be done in the autumn or spring, and no pruning, apart from occasional shaping, is required. *Prop.*—Seeds and layering.

Crataegus (Hawthorn).—There are many good varieties of our British hawthorn, *C. oxyacantha*, worthy of attention, particularly 'Coccinea' (crimson) and 'Paulii' (double, red). All will do well on poor soils, and no pruning is required. The common hawthorn makes a stout, impenetrable hedge planted 9 in. apart in a double row 9 in. asunder. *Prop.*—Common sort by seed; choice varieties by budding.

Crocus.—A hardy bulb of great beauty which was studied for many years by one of the best horticulturists of the twentieth century, the late E. A. Bowles. Does best in rich soil planted in bold groups around margins of beds or borders and naturalised in grass. When required, feed in early spring with bone meal at 2 oz. per sq. yd. *C. sieberi* and *C. tomasinianus* flower very early; the large-flowered, garden forms about three weeks later. *C. zonatus* flowers in the autumn and is often naturalised in grass. *Prop.*—Clumps may be lifted and divided about every five years, in July. The so-called autumn crocus is *Colchicum autumnale*. This bears large, lustrous leaves in the summer, followed by mauve or white flowers—of fleeting duration—in the autumn.

Crown Imperial.—*See* **Fritillaria.**

Cytisus (Broom).—Only does really well in dry, poor soils in full sun; choice, procumbent sorts like *C. kewensis*, used in rock gardens and tall ones in open shrubberies. Pruning is important; shoots should be shortened after flowering, but old wood must never be cut. *Prop.*—Seed and cuttings in August in a sandy soil.

Daffodil.—*See* Narcissus.

Dahlia.—The cultivation of this plant is a special study, and there are probably more garden varieties of it than any other plant. Ordinary soil enriched with manure and an open position is required. Tubers may be planted 3 in. deep in April or young plants in late May. During the summer feed with soot water and liquid manure. After the first frosts lift, dry, and then store tubers in peat or straw in frost-proof place. Many stocks of dahlia are affected by virus (T30), and purchasers should be careful to check source of supply.

Daphne.—Shrubby plants, giving some of the most richly scented of all flowers. In particular, there is *D. mezereum*, which requires a damp soil; failure with the shrub is due usually to root disturbance or virus disease (T31) *D. odora* is one of the evergreen, fragrant species. Some references have suggested that this lovely shrub is not hardy, but there is no evidence to support the supposition. *Prop.*—Seed or layering.

Delphinium.—Hardy annuals and perennials. The latter sorts have gained popularity enormously since the War, due in the main to the activities of the Delphinium Society but also to the introduction of many very fine new varieties. American hybrids, like the 'Pacific Strain,' are very large but tend to die out and, consequently, lack the true, perennial habit of European sorts, albeit some of these have been weakened by the introduction of poor lines. It is important therefore to select stocks of strong constitution. Delphiniums need a deep, rich soil and a sunny position protected from wind. Plant in autumn 3 ft. apart, feed in the summer with liquid soot water, and mulch with decayed compost or manure in the spring. When growth starts, thin out weak growths to leave not more than five stems per plant. In winter take steps against possible slug damage (T29), and on this point it is beneficial to protect crowns with a covering of ashes. *Prop.*—Cuttings in the spring or seed; division of clumps is a poor alternative.

The hardy annual sorts are the well-known larkspurs, which grow to a height of 18 in. to 2 ft. and may be found in a range of colours including pink, red, white, and shades of blue. *See* Annuals.

Deutzia.—Hardy deciduous shrubs thriving in any soil and valuable for their summer flowers of white or whitish-pink shade. To keep the plants vigorous, shoots should be shortened after flowering and old or weak wood cut out. *D. scabra* is of robust habit, reaching about 7 ft., and *D. elegantissima* 'Fasciculata' proves a graceful shrub some 5 ft. tall with clusters of about twenty flowers coloured rosy-pink and each nearly an inch across. *Prop.*—Cuttings made from firm young growths about 10 in. long in sandy soil out-of-doors.

Dianthus.—This name covers a wide range of annual, biennial, and perennial plants. At one time often grown for their fragrance, but to a large extent this has been lost with the introduction of wider ranges of colour. Border carnations and picotees grown out-of-doors need a limy, fairly rich soil in full sun. Plant in the autumn or spring and, as the buds appear, feed with soot water or liquid animal manure, if necessary. These groups are *not* of good perennial habit and should be propagated annually to ensure continuation of stock.

The common pink requires the same soil conditions, and should be propagated when the stock gets weak; good scented varieties should be sought, and include the 'Imperial Pinks,' 'Mrs. Simkins,' and 'White Ladies.' *Prop.*—The best method is by layering in July so that the new plants can be put in their flowering position by mid-September. The lower leaves are pulled off selected shoots and a slit passing through a joint is made in the stem. Each layer is then pegged down with a hair-pin, the pin being placed above the cut. The layers are then covered with an inch of sandy compost and well watered.

In this genus is the sweet william; although truly a perennial, it is generally grown as a biennial and, consequently, the plant is raised from seed in May out-of-doors. In gardens where it is prone to rust disease control is most difficult and it is not worth a place.

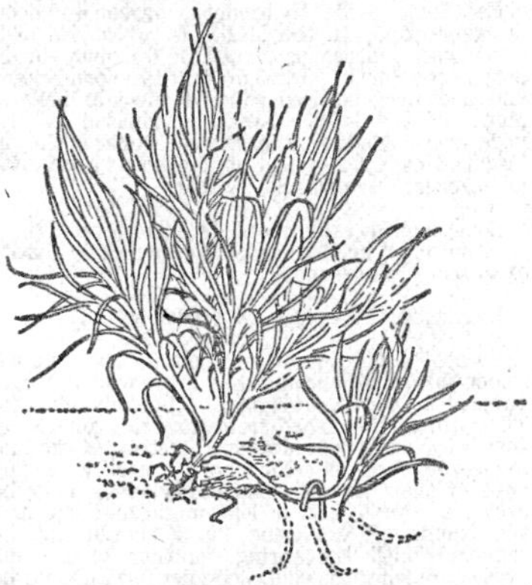

LAYERING CARNATIONS—This is a typical example of how many plants can be propagated. A strong, new growth is pegged down into sandy soil after a cut has been made in the stem, at the point of pegging. Once rooted the layer can be severed from the parent and transplanted a week or two later.

Digitalis.—The biennial sort generally found in gardens is the common foxglove, which is grown in light shade in fairly rich, moist soil. In the past many named forms have been offered in the trade, but undoubtedly the best one is *D.* 'Sutton's Excelsior.' *Prop.*—Seed sown in May out-of-doors.

Doronicum.—Hardy perennials with yellow flowers; warrants wider planting, as they are among the earliest perennials to bloom and will thrive in poor soil or in some shade. The best is *D. austriacum* flowering in March, height 9 in. *Prop.*—Division after flowering.

Echinops.—Name appropriately derived from *echinos*, a hedgehog, in reference to the spiny, long scales of the flowers. The plant does well in an open position, where the globular heads of steely-blue flowers can be seen to advantage. *Prop.*—Division in March, but best left undisturbed as long as possible, as it must be moved with care.

Elaeagnus.—Hardy deciduous and evergreen shrubs generally grown in rather dry positions as foliage plants. Of the evergreen sort, *E. pungens* 'Aureo-Variegata' has bright golden variegation, and is therefore valuable for indoor decoration during the winter. *Prop.*—Layering in late summer.

Erica.—The heathers are native plants to Britain, and many variants found in the wild have been introduced into gardens to good purpose. Indeed, heathers have become so popular that special Heather Gardens have been made, and two fine examples may be found in the Royal Gardens, Windsor where the planting is new and the Royal Horticultural Society's Gardens, Wisley. Here, different sorts reaching the dimensions of small trees, dwarf kinds, and many scores of interesting variants, to supply flower throughout the year, will be found.

The Scottish heather is, botanically, *Calluna vulgaris*, and, like all British heathers, it is intolerant of lime or chalk. Where alkaline conditions exist, planters can try *E. carnea*—a winter-flowering heather—or *E. darleyensis*, but the results are usually disappointing. When planting all heathers, clumps must be well firmed and afterwards kept moist; subsequently, mulch all types annually with peat. *Prop.*—Division and layering.

Erigeron.—Hardy perennial for sunny borders; daisy-like flowers freely develop and are good for cutting. *Prop.*—Division in the autumn.

Escallonia.—Slightly tender evergreen and deciduous shrubs. In the Midlands protection of a south wall is necessary; suitable for open shrubbery in the South. Ideal for maritime conditions, and here may be used to good effect as hedges. Many of the best varieties originated in the nursery of Messrs. The Slieve Donard Co. in County Down. *Prop.*—Cuttings under a glass jar in summer; layers in September.

Eschscholzia californica.—A hardy annual of easy culture; height 18 in., flowers mainly shades of orange. *See* **Annuals.**

Everlasting Flowers.—*See* **Helichrysum.**

Ferns.—A large number of plants are included under this name and, as they grow wild in many parts of the world, some need hothouse conditions. They are distinguished from flowering plants by their method of reproduction; instead of producing seeds, ferns develop spores, usually on the back of their leaves. The hardy kinds may be grown in equal parts of leaf-mould and soil, and the fronds of leaf-losing kinds should not be removed until the spring, as they offer some protection from the cold. Tender ferns should be repotted when new growth starts in the spring in a compost of equal parts soil, leaf-mould, and sand, using a pot just large enough for the purpose. During the growing season, in particular, keep the roots moist and plants free from a dry or smokey atmosphere. *Prop.*—Division of clumps when growth starts in the spring.

Forget-me-nots.—*See* **Myosotis.**

Forsythia.—Commonly found in many gardens, as it is of easy culture in any soil. Flowers bright yellow in early spring. To keep in good shape prune directly after flowering by cutting out old wood. *F. intermedia* 'Lynwood' is upright in growth and *F. suspensa* of weeping habit; both types make good wall plants for North aspects. *Prop.*—Cuttings in the autumn.

Foxglove.—*See* **Digitalis.**

Freesia.—Greenhouse bulbous plant and, if grown for scent, care must be taken to select fragrant varieties. Pot in the autumn in a fairly rich compost and keep as cold as possible until growth is seen. Then bring into a frost-free greenhouse and water freely. When flower stems appear, feed with liquid manure; after flowering, gradually dry-off until time for repotting. Failures almost invariably traced to premature forcing before root growth has been made or growing in excessively high temperature. *Prop.*—Offsets at potting time.

Fritillaria.—The one mainly used in gardens is *F. imperialis*, a handsome, spring-flowering bulb. To grow it *really* well, this species must be given a deep, rich soil and, contrary to some views, it is best lifted every year as soon as the foliage fades. If growth is poor or plants do not flower, feed when growth starts in the following spring with equal parts of bone meal and superphosphate at 3 oz. per sq. yd. *Prop.*—Offsets removed from parent bulb at lifting time. The old bulb should then be replanted at once and any offsets lined out in a nursery row.

Fuchsia.—Greenhouse and tender flowering shrubs. The outdoor sorts (of which *F. riccartonii* is the best) may be grown in light soil in full sun. In the spring prune all growth down to ground level; protect, if necessary, in winter with covering of cut bracken or dry straw. Greenhouse varieties are potted firmly before growth starts in the spring and, when buds burst, all the previous year's growth can be cut back hard. To encourage flowering, feed with a liquid manure, such as dried blood, and syringe foliage in hot weather. During the winter keep plants dry and house in a cool greenhouse. *Prop.*—Cuttings of new growth taken about 1 in. long and inserted in sand under a plastic cover in the spring.

Gaillardia.—Hardy annuals and perennials 18 in. to 3 ft. high which bear large, richly coloured flowers invaluable for cutting in mid- and late-summer. Unfortunately, on heavy soil the perennials are liable to die after flowering, and even on well-drained soils they cannot be considered long-lived plants. *Prop.*—Normally it is necessary to raise a fresh stock in alternate years; seed is sown in May in a cold frame and the young plants lined out in a reserve border prior to planting in the autumn.

Galanthus (Snowdrop).—Hardy bulbs well worth growing if given a moist, shady position where stock can be left undisturbed. Planting should be done in fairly bold clumps; bulbs are not expensive, and many variants, like double-flowered and tall-stemmed ones, are well worth a trial. *Prop.*—Lift and divide clumps in August.

Gentiana.—The gentians comprise some of the most fascinating of all rock-garden plants partly, perhaps, because some are difficult to manage. In particular, *G. acaulis*—which has true "gentian blue" flowers—is exacting in its requirements, and in many gardens flowering can never be induced. What controls flowering has not been discovered, and the plant can be grown well in acid or limy soils. On the other hand, *G. sino-ornata* must have an acid soil and is best in a position out of the direct sun. Beginners with the genus are advised to start with easily grown sorts, like *G. lagodechina* and *G. septemfida*. *Prop.*—Seed sown in cold frame in March or division in early spring.

Geranium.—The true geranium or cranesbill is a hardy floriferous perennial for rock garden or open border. In the latter case *G. ibericum* (blue flowers) and *G. sanguineum* 'Lancastriense' (rosy-pink flowers) are exceptionally good, and both do well in dry, sunny positions. The so-called "bedding" or "greenhouse" geranium is a pelargonium (*q.v.*). *Prop.*—Seed in March.

Gladiolus.—Dutch hybridists have done much work on this bulbous plant, and many new and lovely varieties are now available. The plant is responsive to good cultivation, and corms may be planted 4 in. deep and 6 in. apart during the spring in well-prepared ground. When the blooms fade remove the dead spikes of flower and lift the corms in September. After a month—and this point is important—pull off the old shrivelled corm and clean the new one. By doing this there is less likelihood of spores of diseases overwintering on the new stock. Finally, the corms should be stored in a dry, frost-free shed, and if given proper attention can be kept for a number of years. *Prop.*—Bulbils, removed when the corms are cleaned, can be sown in the spring in nursery rows and will flower within two years.

Godetia.—Hardy annual of easy culture and tolerant of poor soil conditions and even some shade. There are many varieties, mainly with bright flowers of rosy-pink and crimson. *See* **Annuals.**

Guernsey Lily.—*See* **Nerine.**

Gypsophila.—The favourite sort is *G. paniculata*, which is often grown for cutting, together with its double-flowered form, 'Bristol Fairy.' To do well gypsophila must be given a dryish soil which the roots can penetrate undisturbed; if growth is poor mulch in the spring with animal manure. *Prop.*—Generally done by seed in spring; special forms by grafting.

Hamamelis.—A lovely, but little grown, winter-flowering, heavily-scented shrub. The delicate, lemon-coloured flowers appear interminably from December to February. Although it flowers in its young stage, hamamelis is slow to get established and must be left free of root disturbance. The best sort is *H. mollis* introduced from China in 1879. *Prop.*—Usually by grafting; can be layered.

Heather.—*See* Erica.

Hedera.—Although ivy is seldom planted nowadays, there are a few evergreens to equal it for covering buildings. The large-leaved ivy with golden variegation, *H. colchica* 'Dentato-Variegata,' is invaluable for cold or shady walls. *Prop.*—Cuttings in August in shady border out-of-doors.

Helianthus.—The perennial sunflowers are tall, yellow-flowered plants of vigorous habit. They spread quickly and become a nuisance, and therefore clumps should be lifted and single, rooted pieces replanted every other year. The annual sunflower may reach a height of 10 ft. or so; seed is sown out-of-doors in April or seedlings raised under glass in the spring. When the flower bud appears, feed with soot water. The seed may be used as food for large birds like parrots.

Helichrysum.—Although this is a large group of plants, the most interesting is the half-hardy annual, *H. bracteatum*, the everlasting flower. When the flowers are fully developed they are cut with long stems and hung up to dry for winter decoration. *See* Annuals.

Heliotropium peruvianum (Cherry Pie).—Scented, shrubby plants used for greenhouse decoration or summer bedding. *H.* 'Sir Edward Fry' is among the scented varieties and *H.* 'Princess Marina' is the best dark-purple variety. For really good results, heliotropes need a rich soil and plenty of water in summer. *Prop.*—Cuttings 2–3 in. long in early autumn or spring, struck in sandy loam in a warm greenhouse.

Helleborus.—The Christmas rose, *H. niger*, should be planted out of the direct sun in a moist soil which has been liberally enriched with leaf-mould and old manure and here left free from root disturbance. Its large, white flowers appear irregularly from December to February with early flowering encouraged by protection with cloches. The Lenten rose, *H. orientalis*, flowers from February to April, and it is well worth searching nurserymen's lists for varieties with a wide range of colours. *Prop.*—Division of clumps in the spring, with each piece having four or five growth buds; the clumps should not be split into small pieces.

Hemerocallis.—Hardy perennial for moist border either open or slightly shaded. Mulch established clumps in the spring with compost or manure. Many new varieties are coming on the market as a result of introductions from America, where the plant is popular. *Prop.*—Division.

Hibiscus.—The evergreen, shrubby sorts with large exotic flowers are widely grown in the tropics and can be seen under glass in botanic gardens in Britain. *H. syriacus* is a deciduous, hardy species; little pruning is required, and in full sun it will reach 8–10 ft. Normally, it is a free-flowering plant of great beauty and, in cases where the flowers fail to develop, the stock is best replaced with good varieties, like 'Coeleste' (single, blue) and 'Woodbridge' (single, red). *Prop.*—Cuttings under glass; grafting.

Holly.—*See* Ilex.

Hollyhock.—*See* Althaea.

Honeysuckle.—*See* Lonicera.

House Leek.—*See* Sempervivum.

Hyacinth.—Bulbs generally used for bowl culture; often results are disappointing, but responsibility does not necessarily rest with the nurseryman, as poor cultivation is the most probable cause. Plant in September–early October (not later) in peat, loam, and sand, and keep as cool as possible until growth starts, when bowls may be brought into a warm room. Care must be taken with watering, as the bulbs must not dry out nor the compost allowed to become wet and soggy. After flowering, plant out-of-doors and lift annually in June for replanting in the autumn; for bowls a fresh stock is required every year. Failures are mostly due to late planting or faulty watering.

Hydrangea.—A favourite shrub introduced from the Far East. Of the many forms, the one offered by florists, *H. macrophylla*, is the most popular. This can be bought in a wide range of shades, from white and pink through to crimson and blue. The colour will depend on soil reaction; in alkaline or neutral soils *only* white and pink shades can be grown, and blue flowers will be found *only* on acid soil. The intensity of colour can be improved by adding lime in the first instance and flowers of sulphur in the second, but it is not possible to make an alkaline garden soil acid in reaction. Lack of flower is generally the result of buds being killed by cold weather. For this reason, hydrangeas are best not pruned until the late spring; then old flower-heads and any weak or unwanted growth can be cut out. During the summer the plants must not suffer from lack of water.

Among the many other sorts are *H. paniculata*, with large, cone-shaped panicles of flower and *H. petiolaris*. The latter plant is a vigorous climber, well suited to cover cold walls or for climbing over dead trees. *Prop.*—Cuttings in July–August in a cold frame.

Iberis (Candytuft).—The hardy annual sorts will thrive in any soil, and may be had in a range of colours. *See* Annuals. The perennial candytuft (*I. sempervirens*) is a good plant for a rock wall and has white flowers in early spring. *Prop.*—Seeds in spring and cuttings in summer.

Ilex.—The ornamental value of our native holly is rarely fully appreciated, bearing in mind that, on good varieties, the berries sometimes persist until March. The greenish flowers are sometimes bisexual, and sometimes male and female flowers are on *separate* plants. For this reason hollies should be planted in groups, and at least one plant of good berrying habit, like *I. aquifolium* 'Pyramidalis,' grown. Some varieties have yellow berries and gold or silver variegations on their leaves. *Prop.*—Seed; special forms by budding.

Iris.—This plant is divided into two main sections: those types which grow from bulbs and those which grow from fleshy rhizomes, with many subdivisions in each of them. Of the latter type, there are the commonly grown bearded flag irises, which, owing to their ease of cultivation and wide range of colours, are appropriately known as the poor man's orchid. Notwithstanding, these irises respond to good treatment, doing best in well-dug soil to which a little manure has been added and a dressing of rough chalk forked into the surface. The site should be in full sun for preference and one that never lies wet in winter. Planting or division of established clumps is done in July, setting the rhizome on the surface of the soil but firming the roots well. To maintain growth and flower, feed annually in the spring with equal parts of superphosphate and bone meal at 3–4 oz. per sq. yd. Iris gardens are not often found nowadays, but the fine example still maintained at Kew is well worth close inspection.

In the bulbous section the Siberian iris is a graceful plant with delicate foliage, though much smaller-flowered than the flags. They make a fine waterside planting or may be grown in the herbaceous border. The Japanese iris is another water lover, and this has delicate-coloured, clematis-like flowers. On the other hand, for dry, poor, stony soils in full sun the lovely, winter-flowering, Algerian iris, *I. unguicularis* (*stylosa*), is an ideal plant flowering as it does in December and January. This is a plant which must be left undisturbed after planting in June and if leafy growth is excessive the foliage can be cut back by half in August. Spanish, Dutch, and English types of bulbous iris are often used as cut flowers. These may be planted in ordinary garden soil in the autumn and left undisturbed until signs of deterioration are found.

Japonica.—Common misnomer of *Chaenomeles*. (*q.v.*).

Jasminum.—The yellow-flowered, sweetly scented winter jasmine blooms intermittently from November to February. It grows in any soil, and is best trained up a wall or grown on a trellis. Pruning consists of cutting out the flowering shoots as soon as the blossoms fade. The summer jasmine is a vigorous climbing plant with white, scented flowers. It needs a sunny position and should be well thinned after flowering. *Prop.*—Layering in summer.

Kalmia.—Hardy American shrubs with clusters of waxy, rose or pink blossoms in early summer. Although slow to get established and requiring a damp, acid soil, the plant is well worth growing. It constitutes a feature of the gardens of the National Trust at Sheffield Park, Sussex. *Prop.*—Seed or layering.

Kerria japonica.—A hardy shrub which will thrive in any garden but is best fed with manure to encourage strong growth. When the yellow flowers fade, the stock should be kept vigorous by cutting out old or weak growth. The plant is named after William Kerr, a young man despatched from Kew to collect plants in China. *Prop.*—Division in autumn.

Kniphofia (Red-hot Poker).—Although these plants are so commonly seen, their full value as late-flowering subjects is not often fully explored. There are a number of good varieties worth growing, such as 'Maid of Orleans' (white, 4 ft.), 'Mount Etna' (scarlet, 5 ft.), and 'Royal Standard' (gold and scarlet, 4 ft.). Of equal value is the dwarf variety with grass-like foliage, *K. nelsonii*. *Prop.*—Division in March; easily raised from seed if so desired.

Laburnum.—Handsome trees with long racemes of yellow flowers, the seeds of which are very poisonous. It is not advisable to remove branches, as wounds do not heal well or quickly, and once a specimen shows signs of deterioration it is best replaced with little delay. *Prop.*—Seed or grafting.

Larkspur.—*See* **Delphinium.**

Lathyrus (Sweet Pea).—For general garden decoration, seed may be sown in pots in a warm greenhouse in early February prior to transplanting out-of-doors in April. When heat is not available sowing can be done in the open in October, setting the seed 4–6 in. apart and 2 in. deep where the plants are to grow. In this case the rows are best protected by cloches. As the plants flower with great freedom and make strong growth, a rich, deep soil is required. During the summer water should be given freely and liquid animal manure or soot water applied weekly when flowering starts. When raised for exhibition, special cultural treatment is necessary. The cause of the condition referred to as bud drop is not known, but it is thought to be connected with low temperature and faulty root action.

There is also the hardy, perennial sweet pea, an old-world plant usually seen at its best in cottage gardens. This plant requires the same cultural conditions, except that the old stems are cut down in the autumn. Three or four different species are available, and all are easily raised from seed sown in the spring.

Lavandula.—The lavender is one of the best known of garden plants. It thrives in full sun in a light soil; old flower heads should be clipped off in the summer, but any cutting back into old growth must be left until the spring. The best garden form is *L. spica* 'Nana Atropurpurea'; it has a neat, dwarf habit, with deep purple flowers, and is available from leading nurserymen. *Prop.*—Cuttings out-of-doors in August–September.

Leucojum.—The spring snowflake flowers in February and is a charming plant for any damp, shady border. Although it has a large flower, it has never become as popular as the snowdrop, despite its ease of culture. It should be grown by everyone who values early spring flowers. *Prop.*—Lift clumps and replant after removing offsets in August.

Lilac.—*See* **Syringa.**

Lilium.—The lilies constitute a large genus of plants, some of easy culture, some demanding the most exacting of conditions. For a soil containing chalk two of the best lilies are *L. candidum*, the Madonna lily, and *L. regale*. The former is a feature of many gardens in South Wales, where bulbs are planted near the surface of the soil and the clumps eventually left to develop undisturbed. Only the easiest-grown lilies are suitable for the herbaceous border and, here, apart from the Madonna lily, the tiger and martagon lilies should be first choices for beginners in the cultivation of this genus. *Prop.*—Those referred to above may all be raised from seed sown out-of-doors (or in deep boxes in a cold frame) in the spring. In the following April line out into nursery rows prior to transplanting to flowering positions. Also propagated by offsets and bulbils.

Lily of the Valley.—*See* **Convallaria.**

Lobelia.—The bedding lobelias are perennial plants best raised as annuals (*q.v.*). They do well in a light soil, but should be firmed at planting time to prevent plants dying off during a hot spell. The handsome, tall-growing lobelias with scarlet flowers, like *L. fulgens* 'Huntsman,' may be used in herbaceous borders with great effect, but the roots must be lifted and overwintered in a cold frame. These sorts grow to a height of 2–3 ft. and will do well only on a wet, heavily manured soil.

Lonicera.—The honeysuckles make effective climbing plants if grown on the shady side of arches or tree stumps or against north or west walls. Care should be taken to train young growth before it becomes hard. Old shoots may be cut out each spring to keep the plant within bounds, although space must be available for free development. If growth and flowering is poor mulch the roots in the spring with old manure. *Prop.*—Easily done by layering in late summer.

Lupins.—There are two sorts of lupins, perennial and annual. The herbaceous perennials are among the most colourful of plants as a result of the famous 'Russell' strain being introduced. Of late years, however, the constitution of the plant has been weakened through, perhaps, breeding and virus diseases, and it should be taken for granted that most stocks have to be replaced every two years or even annually in some cases. The plant requires a rich soil and is best in ground free of lime. Conversely, in poor soil the tree lupin thrives and will reach a height of 7–9 ft.; plant in full sun and lightly prune into shape after flowering. *Prop.*—Both sorts are best raised from seed sown in May out-of-doors and transferred to flowering positions in October. The annual lupin may be obtained in a range of colours, and should be grown in full sun. *See* Annuals.

Magnolia.—Rightly said to be one of the most beautiful of all flowering plants. Contrary to popular belief, some kinds are of easy culture, flowering when young and suitable for small gardens. Of course, careful selection is necessary and for a specimen on a lawn *M.* 'Soulangeana' (large, white or white, purple-stained flowers) is ideal. *M. stellata* freely flowers in the young stage, and may be planted in an ordinary border if the soil is lime free. To encourage growth, mulch annually with peat or leaf mould, but never dig near the roots. The evergreen magnolia is often seen as a fine wall plant in old gardens. This is the only species which may be pruned, and long shoots can be cut back hard in April. There are a number of non-flowering strains of the evergreen one, and unsatisfactory plants are best destroyed, as flowering cannot be induced; in buying a replacement care is necessary in order to avoid *another* dud. *Prop.*—Seed sown as soon as it is ripe in October; layering.

Mahonia.—Hardy evergreen shrub of great merit if grown well. *M. aquifolium* is useful as ground cover, thriving in any soil and in shade if protected from cold winds. *M. japonica* has long racemes of lemon-scented flowers in winter; inferior sorts are often listed by nurserymen under this name. Of equal merit is *M.* 'Charity' which by reason of its flowering in November warrants a place in any garden if free from exposure to wind. Foliage sought after by flower arrangement groups. *Prop.*—Seed, suckers, layers, cuttings in August.

Mathiola.—The night-scented stock is a hardy annual with insignificant purplish flowers which open at dusk; grown primarily for its perfume. Conversely, the so-called Ten-Week stocks and a selection of these, the East Lothian stocks, have a wide range of colours. If sown in March they may be used for summer bedding or if sown in August overwintered in a sunny frame and grown as a biennial.

Brompton stocks flower earlier than the other sorts, and are grown as a biennial by sowing seed in June or early July and, after pricking out into boxes, are overwintered in a sunny frame. In mild districts, if the soil is well drained, stocks may be planted out-of-doors in the autumn, but a reserve should be kept for filling up gaps in the spring.

Meconopsis.—This genus includes the famous "blue poppy," introduced from the Himalayas. It is not a plant of easy culture, albeit large groups are grown in many woodland gardens where soil conditions permit. After flowering the plants generally die, although an occasional plant may persist. *Prop.*—Seed sown in March.

Michaelmas Daisy.—*See* **Aster.**

Montbretia.—This bulbous plant is of easy culture and has a long season of flowering. Many new varieties with large flowers are now available, and growth can be kept vigorous by lifting and dividing the clumps every three or four years. Plant in early spring 4 in. deep and 6 in. apart and in cold gardens protect clumps in winter with a covering of ashes.

Myosotis.—The forget-me-not is grown as a biennial by sowing seed in May and planting out in the autumn in conjunction with spring-flowering bulbs and wallflowers. Poor varieties freely establish themselves, and these should be destroyed before planting any of the really good sorts offered by seedsmen.

Narcissus.—This botanical name includes plants commonly known as "daffodil" and "narcissus." Although often grown, the wide garden value of these spring-flowering bulbs is not fully realised, as by careful selection of varieties a long season of flower can be obtained when they are grown in formal borders or naturalised. Thus, a season may be extended with 'Peeping Tom' and 'Covent Garden' (early) and 'Geranium' and 'Buttermilk' (late). The bulbs can be left undisturbed until flowering is affected by over-crowding; the clumps should then be lifted and be divided in the late summer. To maintain vigour, feed annually in February with 2 parts bone meal, 1 part hoof and horn meal, and 1 part sulphate of potash at 2–3 oz. per sq. yd. The chief troubles with narcissi are due to eelworm (T29) and the narcissus bulb fly (T28). For indoor work, plant in bowls in October and keep in cold place until growth is an inch high; failure is invariably due to premature forcing or faulty watering.

Nasturtium.—*See* **Tropaeolum.**

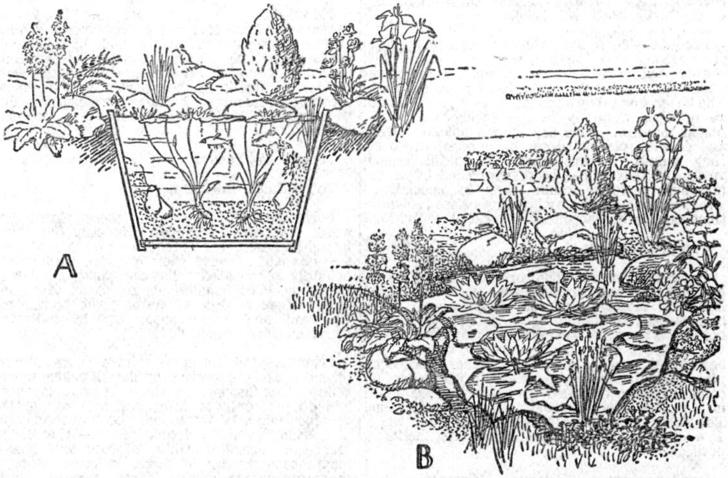

WATER LILIES IN TUBS—Drawing (A) shows a cross-section with correct percentage of water and soil together with water lilies and fish. Drawing (B) illustrates marginal planting with primulas, Japanese irises, and a dwarf coniferous tree.

Nepeta (Catmint).—In recent years this edging plant with silvery foliage and mauve flowers has become increasingly popular. When flowering in mid-summer there is no finer display of colour. It grows freely on any light, well-drained soil in full sun. The best sort is *N. faassenii*. *Prop.*—Division of clumps in March.

Nerine.—Lately this lovely bulbous plant has increased in popularity mainly through the varieties introduced from the late Lionel de Rothschild's garden at Exbury. The hardy sort *N. bowdenii* flowers in the autumn and should be planted at the foot of a warm wall in August or September and left undisturbed for many years. As the bulbs gradually multiply and work to the surface, a light dressing of sandy compost, to which has been added a little bone meal, can be applied. *Prop.*—Separation of bulbs in August.

Nicotiana (Tobacco Plant).—This half-hardy annual is grown mainly for its heavily scented flowers, which open in the evening. It is worth remembering that the white-flowered sorts are the best in this respect; scarlets and pinks are very much inferior. *See* **Annuals.** The tobacco of commerce is a different plant, namely, *N. tabacum.*

Nymphaea.—No branch of gardening is more fascinating than the water garden, and for it the chief plant must be the water lily. Basically, the main reason for failure is in the fact that in most pools the *average* depth of water is less than 18 in.; this means that the water is liable to be adversely affected by extremes of temperature. All nymphaeas should be grown in full sun and where the water is still; in streams it is necessary to utilise a little backwater out of the current. Water lilies are planted in May in large wicker baskets with a compost of three-quarters of loam and a quarter of peat; alternatively, planting sites can be built up with bricks to the desired height. If growth is poor, mould "Clay's Fertiliser" into the size of pigeons' eggs and drop one around each clump. To maintain a healthy condition in the water, fish should be introduced as soon as the plants are established. *Prop.*—Division of tuberous roots in late May.

Orchids.—In the main, this large group of plants needs greenhouse conditions and specialised knowledge. Their cultivation has attracted the attention of some of the greatest of horticulturists, and detailed references may be found in books like *Orchids, their Description and Cultivation*, by C. H. Curtis (Putnam), 1950.

Paeonia.—There are two sorts of paeony, the tree paeony and the herbaceous paeony. The former needs a sheltered, warm position and takes about three years to flower from planting time. The latter sort needs a moist, rich soil, and should be mulched annually in the spring with well-rotted manure; some are known not to flower, and as such plants cannot be induced to do so they should be destroyed. The old-fashioned variety of paeony has been superseded by many fine new varieties found listed by specialists. *Prop.*—Tree paeonies by layering or seed sown in the autumn; herbaceous sorts by seed or division.

Pansy.—*See* **Viola.**

Papaver (Poppy).—The oriental poppy is a hardy herbaceous perennial with striking flowers, intolerant of shade and root disturbance. As it blooms early, it should be set near the back of a border, as the large leaves look untidy later in the year. Apart from the commonly grown, red-flowered sort there are others in shades of crimson, pink, and lavender. *Prop.*—A wide range of colours can be obtained by sowing mixed seeds in May. This is a better method than division. The Shirley poppy is a hardy annual (*q.v.*), while *P. nudicale* is a biennial needing a warm, sheltered position.

Parthenocissus (Virginia Creeper).—This climber, with its brilliantly-coloured leaves, makes a fine sight in the autumn, and there is no better plant for covering brickwork or unsightly buildings with a south or west aspect. It has been suggested (mainly by builders) that the plant will damage stonework or cause dampness. There is little evidence to support these suppositions, and reasons for damage can usually be traced—often without difficulty—to other sources. The plant has had a number of names—*Ampelopsis veitchii* is one—but up-to-date nurserymen are listing it correctly as *P. tricuspidata*. *Prop.*—Cuttings out-of-doors in the late summer; layering.

Passiflora caerulea (Passion Flower).—A south wall in favoured gardens is needed to grow this plant. It is of vigorous habit and, once the framework of branches has been produced, it should be pruned annually in the early spring, by cutting back all the previous season's growth to 2–3 in. of the main stem. *Prop.*—Layering.

Pelargonium (Geranium).—So-called "bedding geraniums," such as 'Paul Crampel,' are really zonal pelargoniums. To maintain a stock, take cuttings in early August and insert in sandy soil around the edge of a pot and overwinter in a frost-free greenhouse. In the spring pot-up singly and use for bedding. Otherwise pot-on after two months and, if early buds are nipped off, plants can be adopted for late flowering indoors. Pelargoniums are easy to grow, but for best results a position in full sun is necessary, and cuttings should be rooted *before* the autumn so that overwintering constitutes no great difficulty.

Petunia.—Although really perennials, these plants, native of South America, are treated as annuals (*q.v.*). They are sun lovers and do best on light soils. Petunias make fine plants for sunny window boxes, and particularly happy combinations can be made by planting together varieties such as 'Violacea' (deep violet) and 'Cheerful' (pale pink) or 'Flaming Velvet' (crimson) and 'Cream Star' (pale cream). The violet-flowered sorts are faintly scented.

Philadelphus (Mock Orange).—Although some fine varieties of this shrub are available in the trade, it is not grown as widely as its merit deserves. As a scented shrub it has few equals, while it is tolerant of poor soil conditions and shade. Particularly good sorts worth searching for are 'Albatre' (double), 'Beauclerk' (single), and 'Sybille,' which, at 3 ft., is about half the height of the others. After flowering, prune annually by removing as much old flowering wood as possible. *Prop.*—Hard-wood cuttings out-of-doors in November.

Phlox.—A wide range of varieties of the border phlox are offered to make an impressive display late in the season. If grown on light soils some shade is desirable, as phloxes do well where only the soil is damp. For this reason, mulching should be done annually in the spring with compost or animal manure. Failures are usually due to eelworm (**T30**). *Prop.*—Seeds in autumn; division.

Poppy.—*See* **Papaver.**

Polyanthus.—*See* **Primula.**

Polygonum.—In the main these plants are weeds of gardens, although originally they were introduced from the Orient or ornamental purposes at a time when their invasive habits were not fully appreciated. The one woody climber in the genus, *P. baldschuanicum*, makes an admirable cover where a very vigorous plant is wanted. Rampant and unwanted species may be eradicated by hormone treatment (**T34**).

Primula.—Polyanthuses, primroses, greenhouse primulas, and the hardy primulas all belong in this genus. The first two are the most popular; both will do well only in damp soil and respond to generous manurial treatment; both are available in a wide range of colours. *Prop.*—The Blackmore and Langdon strains of seed will give a magnificent display of mixed colours. Sow in warm greenhouse in early March or cold frame in April; prick out into boxes and transfer to flowering positions in the autumn.

Prunus.—A large genus which includes the flowering peaches, Japanese cherries, and flowering almonds. All of them are best left to develop naturally and are not responsive to pruning or cutting back in any way. A few sorts are over-planted in gardens and as street trees (by Park Superintendents), but anybody wishing to be a little out of the ordinary would do well to see the wide range of some of these lovely trees flowering in April and May in our botanic gardens and many of the large gardens now under the jurisdiction of the National Trust. The selection offered by nurserymen is often strictly along conventional lines. Lack of flower in some seasons can often be traced to bird damage.

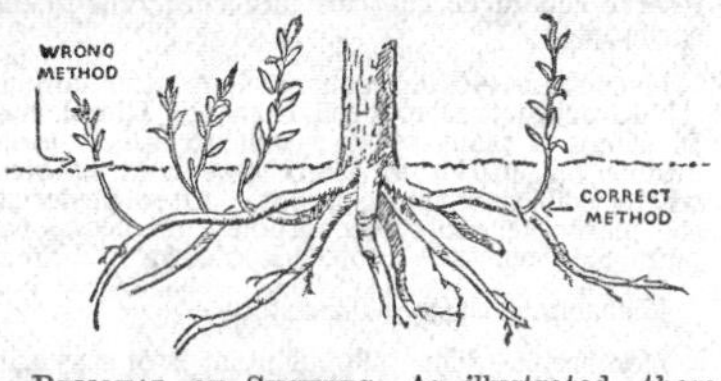

REMOVAL OF SUCKERS—As illustrated, these must be sawn off into the root or pulled off the root with a sharp tug and never so removed that dormant buds are left.

Red-hot Poker.—*See* **Kniphofia.**

Rhododendron.—Greenhouse and hardy, evergreen and deciduous shrubs, including *Azalea.* With something like ten thousand different sorts, it is impossible to deal with individual requirements. General cultivation; an acidic soil is essential, with adequate moisture in summer. If growth is poor on established plants, mulch liberally with animal manure. Beginners should plant from the accepted list of hardy garden hybrids. Since the turn of the century widely planted and fine examples are to be found, for instance, in many gardens of the National Trust. *Prop.*—Seed and layering.

Romneya.—Since its introduction from California in about 1850 the plant has proved a fascination to gardeners, as sometimes it fails completely or does exceedingly well. It apears to require a light soil and a sheltered position, preferably against a sunny wall, and there is no point in trying to grow a romneya on a heavy, wet soil. Usually the annual stems die off in the winter and may be cut down at ground level in the early spring; if persistent the stems can be cut back to sound growth. The new growth is susceptible to slug damage, and appropriate steps must be taken (T29). *Prop.*—Seed or suckers taken off in the spring.

Rosa (Rose).—Undoubtedly the rose is the most popular of all garden flowers, and it may be found in a multitude of forms. The dwarf roses for bedding may be grown on most soils, but are best on a rich, heavy loam. Planting is done from early November onwards when soil conditions permit and the first pruning carried out in the following spring, when the extent of any winter damage can be seen. Opinions differ sharply on pruning; a sound, general rule is to do the work in March and—unless there are special circumstances—to prune on the light side. Thus, for Hybrid Teas and the like, reduce strong stems by about one-third of their length, medium ones by a half, and weak ones to within two or three buds of the main stem.

Whatever sorts of soil roses are grown in, feeding is important, but, of course, it is particularly so on poor ones. It is in soils of *low* fertility that diseases such as rust and black spot are most prevalent and, in some measure, persistence of the disease is due to bad cultivation and lack of treatment with fertilisers. Regular dinocap sprays will control mildew provided the bushes are well mulched and watered. Captan or maneb should be used immediately after pruning and throughout the summer to control black spot, but thiram for rust control need not be used until the disease appears. Good manurial treatment including foliar feeding will help to *prevent* disease. For control of greenfly *see* Aphids, T29.

For a manurial programme, an application of 2 parts of superphosphate and 1 part of sulphate of potash should be applied at 3 oz. per sq. yd. after pruning. Following this, a surface mulch of animal manure, compost, peat, or leaf-mould or a mixture of all of them is given about 2–3 in. thick. Subsequently, if growth is poor, a dressing of nitro-chalk can be made at 1 oz. per sq. yd.

Where soil conditions are poor and disease prevalent, it is important to buy plants only from nurserymen who take special precautions to ensure that their customers have disease-free stock. Likewise, varieties of robust constitution are essential, and a selection list may include: *Hybrid Teas:* 'Ballet' (pink), 'Eden Rose' (magenta pink, 'King's Ransome' (yellow), 'Perfecta' (pink and white), 'Super Star' (coral orange) and 'Wendy Cussons' (rosy red). *Floribundas:* 'Circus' (bicolour yellow/scarlet), 'Dusky Maiden' (crimson), 'Iceberg' (white), 'Queen Elizabeth' (pink) and 'Spartan' (deep salmon).

In most of the modern hybrids scent is almost absent. The true rose perfume is found only in the Old Fashion or shrub roses and, normally, these are planted in a mixed shrub border. For the richest perfume varieties like 'Alba Celestial,' 'Mrs. John Laing' and 'Conrad F. Meyer' should be sought.

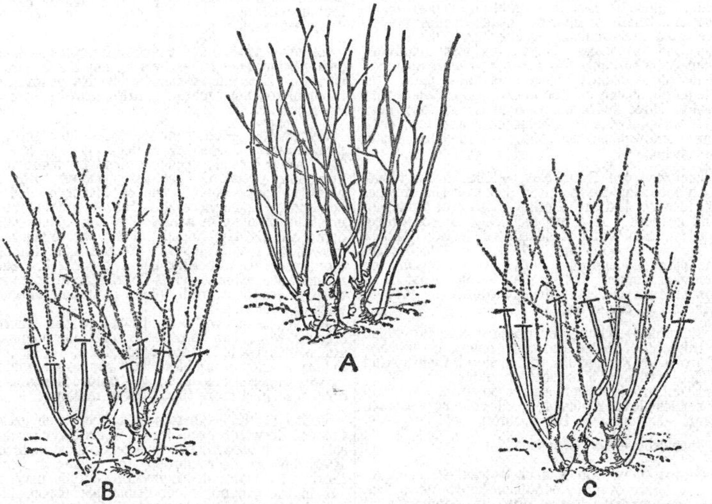

PRUNING ROSES—(A) A vigorous unpruned plant. (B) The same plant pruned for the production of exhibition blooms, (C) and pruned for garden decoration.

Salvia.—Annuals, perennials, and tender shrubs. The most popular one is the scarlet sort used for bedding. It requires careful attention, and seed should be sown in February in a temperature of 60° Fahrenheit and seedlings put into single pots when large enough. Gradually the young plants are hardened off and finally planted out in rich soil in a sunny bed.

Saxifraga.—A large genus of plants suitable for the rock garden and valued for their bright flowers in the spring. The encrusted saxifrages are cushion-forming plants requiring sharp, surface drainage and an open position out of the direct sun. The mossy saxifrages are mat-forming in growth and of easy culture. In time old clumps develop brown patches and then require splitting up and replanting in the spring.

Scabiosa.—The commonly grown perennial sort is *S. caucasica* and is invaluable as a cut flower. It is not at home on all soils, and only does really well in a deep, rich loam containing plenty of chalk. In addition, it must be grown in full sun and particular care taken against slugs. *Prop.*—Old plants divided in the spring and rooted pieces replanted in their flowering positions. A wide range of shades in white, blue, and purple can be had normally from sowing mixed seed in April.

Sedum.—The stonecrops make up a large group of hardy and tender plants, but comparatively few are of horticultural value. Notwithstanding, *Sedum spectabile* is to be found in most herbaceous borders, where its fine, flat heads of pink flowers are a feature for many weeks. It is beloved by bees and butterflies. *S. sieboldii* was introduced from Japan about 100 years ago and, although hardy, it is usually grown as a house plant. In the winter it can be stood out-of-doors, and every two or three years repotted in the spring; keep well watered during the summer and feed with liquid manure occasionally. *Prop.*—Division in the spring.

Sempervivum (House leek).—These hardy plants with succulent leaves often decorate the crevices of old walls and are regular features of trough or sink gardens. If given a light, poor soil and a position in full sun a fascinating collection of house leeks can be built up. The species which gives the plant its common name can be established easily on a sunny roof by planting in a mixture of cow manure and clay during the spring. *Prop.*—Division in the spring.

Skimmia.—A hardy evergreen 2–3 ft. tall which is tolerant of shade and some degree of dryness. If growth is poor water with a liquid manure and mulch with peat or leaf mould. Some forms bear only male flowers and to ensure a good crop of berries plant an hermaphrodite like *S. foremanii*. *Prop.*—Layering in the autumn.

Snowdrop.—*See* **Galanthus.**

Sorbus (Mountain Ash or Rowan)—This small tree, tolerant of many conditions and soils, is ideal for the garden. Regretfully its popularity is declining because with a change in their feeding habits birds take the showy autumn berries of most sorts before their beauty is seen. An exception is *Sorbus* ' Joseph Rock ', a Chinese species of recent introduction, which makes a tall, informal pyramid. The berries are amber yellow and the leaves have notable autumn colouring. Another good one is *S. aucuparia* 'Asplenifolia', the fern-leaved rowan. It has distinctive foliage and makes a fine small specimen tree.

Related are the white beams which do well in open or windy aspects. They are vigorous growers of medium dimensions and are good for screening purposes.

Once established rowans need no further attention but at planting time room should be left for them to develop fully.

Spiraea.—Hardy deciduous shrubs for open borders; tolerant of poor soil conditions. The commonly grown one is *Spiraea bumalda* (syn. *japonica*). After flowering, a percentage of the old wood should be removed together with any weak growth, and development of new shoots encouraged by mulching with compost or animal manure. *Prop.*—Cuttings rooted in sandy soil under a hand light in summer; suckers thinned out in winter.

Stocks.—*See* **Mathiola.**

Sunflower.—*See* **Helianthus.**

Sweet William.—*See* **Dianthus.**

Symphoricarpos (Snowberry).—Often found existing in deep shade and in competition with roots of overhanging trees, presumably as a result of the generalisation that the shrub is a shade lover. Certainly a useful one in this respect, but it is responsive to good treatment. Given an average soil and if growth is thinned annually in the early spring, then *S. albus* 'Laevigatus' is well worth having. Its large white fruits are untouched by birds and hang well into the winter, and are thus beloved by the floral decorator. *Prop.*—Suckers removed in the winter.

Syringa (Lilac).—The botanical name of *Syringa* is often erroneously applied to the Mock Orange, correctly named *Philadelphus* (*q.v.*). A wide selection of first-class varieties are available in nurserymen's lists. To obtain heavy crops of flowers nip off all dead flower-heads as the blossom fades, but do *not* cut back into the old stem, as this will prevent flowering. At the same time any branches causing overcrowding can be removed. Annually feed with " National Growmore " at 2 oz. per sq. yd. and on sandy soils mulch with any sort of manure or compost. *Prop.*—Layering in the autumn.

Tagetes (African and French Marigolds).—Half-hardy annuals of free-flowering habit and easiest culture. Best if fed generously with soot water or other nitrogenous manure during growing season. *See* **Annuals.**

Tropaeolum.—The common nasturtium and the flame flower (*T. speciosum*) belong to this genus. The former is easily grown from seed sown in May in a sunny position. The latter is a very difficult plant to grow outside the conditions which it demands. To be successful, this perennial climber must be planted in acid soil which is naturally damp and lightly shaded but yet where the new growth can reach full sun. Much disappointment often results from planting it in eastern England, for instance, after seeing it flourishing almost as a weed where the rainfall is high in Ireland and the west of Scotland.

In the genus will also be found the canary creeper, which can be used for screening purposes and will thrive in full sun or shade. Seed is sown in May in open ground and light supports supplied by way of pea sticks or strings; failure is normally due to nothing more than lack of moisture.

Tulipa (Tulip).—Thrives in a deep, rich loam, but will do well for one season in ordinary garden soil. When used for bedding, bulbs must be lifted after flowering, replanted in a trench, and thoroughly watered. Sometimes tulips may be left in the ground *if* conditions are favourable, and then the stock only needs lifting and replanting every three years. To check the incidence of tulip fire plant in late November or early December, covering the bulbs with 4–5 in. of soil and treat the ground with a fungicide like " Botrilex." Before doing so rake in a dressing of 2 oz. superphosphate and 1 oz. sulphate of potash per square yard. A national collection of wild tulips is being got together at Cambridge and grown there in the University Botanic Garden.

Viola.—This name embraces pansies, violas, and violets. Although the viola has not got the rich colours of the pansy (or its attractive markings), it has got a remarkably long season of flower, and for this reason it is invaluable as an edging plant or as ground cover for roses. *Prop.*—Both plants are easily raised from seed sown in a frame in the spring, pricked out, and then transferred to their flowering positions in late May. Alternatively, seed may be sown in July for planting out in October. Named varieties increased by cuttings in a frame in late summer.

Virginia creeper.—*See* **Parthenocissus.**

Wallflower.—*See* **Cheirianthus.**

Water Lily.—*See* **Nymphaea.**

Winter Sweet.—*See* **Chimonanthus.**

Wistaria.—One of the finest of all climbing plants for south or west walls or stout pergolas. Plants which do not flower, or only do so poorly, are probably seedlings and the true flowering habit cannot be induced; the only solution is to replace with a *grafted* plant of known flowering capacity from a reliable nurseryman. All young shoots not required for the extension of branches should be shortened to within 3 in. of the old stem in the autumn. Wistarias growing over trees do not require pruning. *Prop.*—Layer shoots of current season's growth in the autumn.

Zinnia.—Half-hardy annual, ideally grown on moist, deep loam liberally enriched with well-decayed manure. Mulch with manure after planting and apply liquid fertiliser as buds appear; plants must not suffer from lack of water. *See* Annuals.

Standard References.

Collins Guide to Roses, by Bertram Park (Collins), 1962.

A Gardener's Dictionary of Plant Names by A. W. Smith and W. T. Stearn (Cassell), 1972.

R.H.S. *Dictionary of Gardening,* edited by F. J. Chittenden (Oxford), 1956.

Sanders' *Encyclopaedia of Gardening,* revised by A. G. L. Hellyer (Collingridge), 1952

The Collingridge Encyclopaedia of Gardening, edited by Arthur Hellyer (Hamlyn), 1976.

MAKING A LAWN.

In almost every garden the most prominent feature is the lawn, and often a lot of work is put into making one without any great measure of success. Usually, the reason for failure may be found in faulty preparation of the soil or premature sowing, albeit the blame is often placed on bird damage or poor seed.

For anything like a reasonable turf, the site must be thoroughly dug and the content of organic matter increased by incorporating generous quantities of materials like peat, leaf-mould, compost, sewage sludge, and animal manure. A dressing of these ingredients can be applied in a layer 3–4 in. thick and buried in the bottom of the top spit of soil. As the ground is dug to incorporate the organic matter, roots of perennial weeds should be removed.

If the site is one on which water tends to lie or if the soil is heavy, then surface drainage should be sharpened by forking into the top 2 or 3 in. a liberal application of some coarse material such as builders' rubble, road grit, screened ashes, or coarse sand. In some cases this treatment will not be sufficient, and then the installation of land drains must be resorted to. This particular task is not as difficult as is sometimes imagined, but, before a start is made, it is always a good plan to discuss the matter with an experienced man.

After the initial work a fine tilth on the soil may be obtained by thoroughly raking and cross-raking and at the same time establishing a level surface. On this point, it should be remembered that good lawns can be made on undulating ground or on natural slopes, but the things to avoid are the shallow depressions where water will naturally tend to lie. Finally, ten to fourteen days before sowing the subsequent growth of grass can be encouraged by making an application of "National Growmore" at 2 oz. per sq. yd.

Sowing is best done in the late summer at a time when the soil is moist. For the purpose, a good mixture of seed should be obtained from a reliable seedsman, and it is worth paying a reasonable price for it, as, by and large, the coarsest and roughest grasses have the largest and heaviest seeds. Opinions differ on rates of sowing, but, with care and in a well-prepared soil, 1 oz. per sq. yd. is ample; heavier rates will give quicker results, but the density of seedlings in such cases often leads to the finer grasses being choked by the coarser ones.

After sowing, the ground should be lightly raked, but not rolled. At this stage the important point is to protect the seed bed from birds by the use of hazel sticks, strings of papers tied to stakes after they have been dipped in lime-wash, and strands of black cotton. Subsequently, annual weeds may appear in quantity; these are of no consequence, and they will be eliminated once the grass is cut regularly. Until a good turf is formed—usually about twelve months after sowing—it is not desirable (or probably necessary) to use hormone weed-killers. *See* T33.

Care of Established Lawns.

Most turf is never manured from year to year, and the soil may seriously lack plant foods. In the first place this can be corrected by making an application annually in the spring of "National Growmore" at 1 oz. per sq. yd. Following this, if growth is below par in the early part of the year an application of sulphate of ammonia can be made at the same rate. To avoid scorching or blackening of the foliage, each fertiliser can be mixed with equal parts of dry soil or sand as a carrier to ensure even distribution and, what is most important, each one should be applied only when the turf is wet and there is the prospect of rain to follow. Linked with this treatment, turf is always responsive to top dressings. A compost for the purpose can be made up with:

2 parts of loam;
1 part of sieved compost;
1 part of fine peat or leaf soil.

This may be used in the spring at 3–5 lb. per sq. yd. and if the soil is heavy 1–2 parts of gritty sand may be added.

With the introduction of new designs in motor mowers, most lawns are seriously overcut, and this has led to a sharp decline in the quality of the grass and the appearance of one or two pernicious weeds. Special turf, such as that found on a bowling green, may be shaved off to one-sixteenth of an inch, but if a utility lawn is cut below half to one inch then the quality of the grass will deteriorate. Of course, it is a good thing to occasionally cut the grass very short, but, conversely, if the blades of the mower are set as low as possible and left like it throughout the season nothing but harm can result. The reason for this hard fact is that when the turf is cut very close the grasses simply cannot develop and spread, and weeds will gradually establish themselves. Eventually the cultivator will be faced with the difficult problem of trying to deal with such plants as pearlwort, yarrow, and various mosses, all of which are resistant to hormones.

As for the vexed question of whether or not to remove the mowings, there is no doubt that the best turf is found where the mowings are collected up, although in very dry weather they can be left on the surface. If the clippings are not removed the surface of the turf tends to become choked with semi-decayed organic matter, and conditions are brought about which are inducive to the spread of moss.

Finally, it is worth noting that the finest turf is found on acidic—not alkaline—soils. For this reason, lime should not be applied as a general rule, for apart from helping the development of coarse grasses, it encourages the growth of clover. Of course, there are times when lime is necessary, but the occasions are rare and before it is used it is a good plan to test the soil by chemical means.

THE FRUIT GARDEN.

The guidance of an expert is probably more important in the growing of fruit than for most of the commoner vegetables and ornamentals. This is primarily because the majority of fruit trees and bushes are long-lived, and only in the case of strawberries can a change of site or variety be made easily and inexpensively.

Gardens which are low-lying are very prone to damage from spring frosts, and should not have too much space devoted to fruit, as returns may well prove unprofitable. Here, as with the selection of varieties, advice of a local expert is invaluable. Some varieties do better in certain localities and on certain soils than others, although personal preferences will naturally be met where possible. Varieties chosen should cover as long a season as is practicable so that the fruit can be used and enjoyed to the full.

Tree fruits are grown on a rootstock, and for apples and pears special dwarfing stocks make these a possibility for the small garden. It is therefore important to explain to the nurseryman what type of tree is required. As a general rule, however, the smaller gardens will gain by concentrating on currants, gooseberries, raspberries, and strawberries. Plums and cherries have no dwarfing stocks, and should be included only where sufficient room is available.

Apples.—Can be grown on most soils. Manure should not be used when planting, except in sandy and chalky gardens.

Plant between late October and early March, preferably before Christmas if soil and weather allow. Make the hole large enough to spread the roots evenly; firm thoroughly while filling in and plant level with the nursery soil mark already on the tree. Mulch around each tree with manure or compost, mainly to avoid drying out, and supplement with watering during the summer when necessary.

In the first year any flowers produced are best pinched out to encourage root and shoot development. For walls or fences use oblique cordons or espaliers; these are also useful for flanking paths and lawns. Plant cordons 2½ ft. apart with 6 ft. between rows, and espaliers 12–15 ft. apart. For larger areas use bush trees sited 12–15 ft. apart.

Manuring for cropping trees should be varied according to growth. Generally apply 1 oz. sulphate of ammonia (or nitro chalk on acid soils) in early March, repeating this in early April if trees are growing in grass. Give ½ oz. sulphate or potash in February and add 3 oz. of superphosphate every third year. The above rates are per square yard, and a complete fertiliser can be used in lieu if preferred.

Young bush trees should have main shoots reduced by half in early years to produce strong branches. Thereafter prune side shoots to three to six buds. For weak growers prune harder, and for strong growers prune less. It is wiser to leave a strong tree unpruned than to prune it too severely, the latter merely encouraging even stronger growth. A few varieties (*e.g.*, 'Bramley's Seedling,' 'Worcester Pearmain') fruit at shoot tips, and here a proportion of side shoots should be left unpruned.

At least two sorts should be planted to ensure satisfactory crops. Good combinations are 'Cox's Orange Pippin' with 'Laxton's Fortune' and 'Winston' with the cooker 'Lord Derby.' Seek expert advice on pairings if in doubt.

Very few varieties are self-fertile and *all* do best when cross-pollinated. If only one sort is to be grown then, for cooking, plant 'Lane's Prince Albert.' Alternatively 'Annie Elizabeth' can be selected but, while making a fine, large specimen tree it is too vigorous in many gardens. For dessert the best is 'Ellison's Orange' or 'Lord Lambourne.'

Some discerning housewives like apples which break down or fluff on cooking; in this case 'Emneth Early,' 'Lane's Prince Albert' or 'Monarch' may be planted. For those wanting one which stays firm on cooking 'Bramley's Seedling' may be chosen.

Blackberries.—In modern gardens, where space is limited, the best returns in fruit growing are often with the cultivated forms of blackberries and loganberries. Plant at least 10–12 ft. apart against fences and train on wires set 3 ft., 5 ft. and 6 ft. above soil level.

Cropping is dependent on manurial treatment as all are heavy feeders. When planting enrich the site with manure, compost or leafsoil; afterwards mulch the surface with one of them. Annually the ground should be topdressed with compost supplemented with a nitrogenous manure like sulphate of ammonia, chicken manure or dried blood. Also apply sulphate of potash at 1 oz. per sq. yard. Such treatment will show excellent results and, as a bonus, normally ensures a prize at any local Show. After planting, do not lack courage to cut back all growths to within a foot of ground level and keep the soil moist throughout the growing season.

Cherries.—Sweet cherries are unsuited to most gardens. The trees become too large, and *must* be planted in selected pairs to fruit satisfactorily, as all varieties are self-sterile. Large wall spaces are ideal for fan trees, as the fruit can then be protected from birds by the use of nets. Pinch side shoots on fans to four leaves in July; further pruning details being as for plums. Expert advice is essential to ensure that suitable varieties are grown together the factors involved being complicated. 'Early Rivers' with 'Bigarreau Schrecken' and 'Merton Heart' with 'Waterloo' are good combinations.

Currants, Black.—These are perhaps the most valuable of all hardy fruits, and bushes will give up to 10 lb. and more of currants with correct treatment. Plant from November to February, preferably autumn, at 5 ft. square on clean, heavily manured ground. In the following spring it is important to cut *all* the shoots to within 3 ins. of ground level in order to encourage strong new growth.

Poor results with this fruit are often due to keeping old or worn out bushes when the cropping life is past which, for blackcurrants is around 10 years. Another reason is the lack of feeding. Each spring bushes should be mulched with compost supplemented with a nitrogenous fertilizer like sulphate of ammonia at 1 oz per sq. yard and superphosphate at double this rate.

On established bushes prune preferably after fruiting or in winter, retaining strong young wood and cutting out older shoots, where possible from ground level. If necessary, alternate bushes can be cut down completely every other year to maintain vigour, as the bulk of the crop is always borne on young wood. Increase by 8-in. cuttings of one-year-old wood taken in late September from healthy bushes. Remove lower leaves and insert firmly with one bud above ground. Good varieties: 'Boskoop Giant,' 'Wellington XXX.'

Currants, Red and White.—One or two well-grown bushes are usually sufficient for the average household. Plant between November and March at a minimum of 5 ft. square on well-manured ground and mulch each spring. Supplement with fertilisers if necessary, potash being particularly important in the form of sulphate of potash at 1 oz. per sq. yd. in February. Can be grown as cordons or fans against walls or fences, on which the pinching of young side shoots to four leaves in mid-June is essential. Winter pruning of all types simply involves cutting side shoots to one bud and tip pruning branch leaders.

Propagate by 12-in. cuttings of young shoots in late September inserted to half their length with all buds removed except the top four. This enables the bush to be grown on a "leg." A permanent framework of branches is then developed, as, in contrast to the black currant, fruit is borne on spurs on the old wood. Good varieties: 'Laxton's No. 1,' 'White Grape.'

Damson.—*See* **Plums.**

Figs.—A warm south wall is usually essential, 'Brown Turkey' being one of the few reliable outdoor varieties. Plant in a brick or concrete trough (with drainage holes) about 2½ ft. wide, 5 ft. long, and 2½ ft. deep so that the root run is restricted. This will curb excessive growth (which otherwise is difficult to control) and encourage fruiting.

Plant in March for preference, to avoid frost injury to young shoots, and then train fan-wise. A rich soil is not essential. Figs visible as such in the autumn will never over-winter, and should be rubbed out. Those the size of a pea and less at the tips of short, well-ripened shoots, on the other hand, are the potential crop for the following year, and should be covered in severe weather to avoid frost damage. To encourage the formation of these embryo fruits pinch young shoots back to the fifth leaf in late August. Winter prune in March, removing any wood that is frosted, overcrowded, or worn out; growths should be spaced at about 1 ft. Apply a spring mulch and water freely when required to avoid premature fruit drop.

Gooseberries.—Need conditions and spacing very similar to red currants, but with rather more moisture to ensure ample new wood, as this bears fruit as well as the older wood. Apply sulphate of ammonia and sulphate of potash annually in late February or March at 1 oz. per sq. yd. of each in addition to mulching. Can also be grown as cordons, etc., as for red currants. Pruning is also similar, though not quite so severe, as the young wood is productive of fruit. Cuttings are more difficult to root, and for best results should be taken in mid-September, again as for red currants. Good varieties: 'Lancer,' 'Leveller,' 'Whinham's Industry.'

Grapes.—Outdoor vines should be grown against a warm south- or south-west-facing wall. With good cultivation, the grapes should then ripen successfully providing suitable varieties are chosen. In preparing the site ensure that it is well drained and break up the soil to a depth of about 2 ft. Add bone meal to the top few inches at 3–4 oz. per sq. yd. and incorporate mortar rubble, particularly on the heavier soils. Do not dig in any manure except on poor, light soils, but always apply some as a mulch after planting, repeating this every spring. On poor, hungry soils the importation of some fibrous loam is advisable where possible.

Plant in November or, failing this, before early March, with the stem about 6–9 in. away from the wall. Firm well and then wait a further two months before tying to any wires or stakes, in case of soil sinkage. Cut the vine back in winter to well-ripened wood and to just above a bud. The training of subsequent growth will then depend on the space available, single and double cordons being the most convenient. Unwanted shoots should be pinched at about 2 ft. in summer and leading shoots carefully tied in to wire or bamboo supports. The following winter (December) prune leading shoots back to well-ripened wood so as to leave 3–4 ft. of new growth. Then cut all laterals hard back to *one* bud. In spring reduce young side shoots to one at each bud, stop laterals at about 12 in., and pinch any sub-laterals that may develop to the first leaf. Do not allow any crop to develop, except perhaps one bunch if growth is adequate; others should be pinched off. As fruit develops, thinning should be done as required. Winter prune as before, and then in the third summer four or five bunches of grapes can be allowed if the vine is healthy, the crop then increasing annually. Shoots carrying bunches should be pinched to two leaves beyond the bunch. Winter pruning is repeated each year as already described. Sour top-soil should be carefully removed when necessary and replaced with good loam while the vine is dormant. Good varieties: 'Black Hamburgh' and 'Foster's Seedling.'

Loganberries.—A very popular hybrid berry which should be treated as for blackberries. A thornless form is now available. Suitable for a north wall.

Medlars.—A tree of spreading habit, the peculiar fruits of which are best used for jelly before they are fully ripened. Most soils are suitable, and no pruning is needed except to keep in shape.

Nectarines.—A fruit very closely allied to the peach but with a richer flavour and needing rather more warmth. The skin is smooth, as distinct from the hairiness of the peach. For full details see Peach.

Nuts.—The most important kinds grown are cobnuts, the closely related filberts, and walnuts, but none of these is cultivated to any great extent. The two former kinds flower very early in February, and are therefore predisposed to frost damage; similarly, the young shoots of walnuts are easily injured by spring frosts, and all are therefore inadvisable for frosty areas.

Cobnuts and filberts.—Highly developed forms of the ordinary hazel nut. The nut of a cob is only partially covered by the husk, whereas a filbert is completely enclosed by it, this being the essential difference between the two. Will grow on most soils, including the poorer ones, and spacing should be about 15 ft., choosing sites sheltered from the colder winds. Plant during the autumn. Prune established bushes in March, cutting back shoots that have borne nuts to two or three buds; strong young shoots are cut back to a catkin near their base, and the weaker ones are left untouched. In August any strong new side growths are "brutted"—that is, broken off—and left hanging until the March pruning. Gather the nuts as they fall and allow to dry. Then store in jars for Christmas use, packing salt and coconut fibre between each layer of nuts.

Walnuts.—Special, grafted varieties are now available which produce early crops compared with the unreliable seedling trees that used to be planted. Plant between October and March and water well in spring and summer. Do not prune, as walnuts bleed badly. Gather nuts in mid-July for pickling. For storing allow to drop naturally and remove outer husk immediately, scrubbing the shell clean and then drying thoroughly. The shells can be bleached if necessary before storing the nuts as for cobs above.

Peaches.—This fruit along with its close ally, the nectarine, is best grown against a warm south or south-west wall, but two varieties of peach, 'Peregrine' and more particularly 'Rochester,' will succeed as bushes in the open in southern England. The fan-trained peach is one of the most difficult trees to keep in order, as sufficient new shoots must be retained annually to replace old wood. This is essential, as it is only the previous year's shoots which bear fruit. Badly placed shoots are rubbed out when only an inch long, and the principle is to allow one young replacement shoot to develop near the base of each fruiting shoot, pruning back to the former and tying it in as soon as all fruit has been picked. Other shoots may be used to extend the fan where space allows or to replace any branches or parts of them which may have become worn out. Other unwanted shoots are bound to arise during each summer, and these are either removed immediately or pinched to three leaves and then removed when pruning in late summer. Those shoots retained are spaced at about 4 in. apart.

Most peaches are self-fertile, but hand-pollinating on sunny days can improve the set. Excessive feeding should be avoided, varying this according to each tree's performance, but as a general rule a surface mulch of well-rotted manure or compost should always be given each spring, together with sulphate of potash at $\frac{1}{2}$–1 oz. per sq. yd. Prick over and rake off top-soil and replace with good loam every few years. Never allow the sub-soil to dry out—this can quickly occur against warm walls—and water thoroughly when doing so to ensure an even distribution of moisture. On the other hand, drainage must be satisfactory to avoid waterlogging.

There are numerous other essential operations in the growing of trained peach trees (for example, fruit thinning), and it is impossible to deal with these adequately in brief notes. Would-be growers should therefore seek expert advice and obtain literature dealing specifically with the crop rather than risk disappointment. Good varieties for outside wall training include: *Peaches:* 'Peregrine,' 'Bellegarde.' *Nectarines:* 'Early Rivers,' 'Lord Napier.'

Pears.—The requirements for pears are similar to those for apples, but the necessity for adequate summer and autumn warmth rules out many varieties for northern areas. In these less-favoured localities enquire which varieties do succeed, and where possible make use of a warm, south-facing wall. Protection from wind is very important, particularly from the cold easterlies of spring. Many soil types grow pears satisfactorily, providing drainage is good and the trees are looked after. Plant as for apples. Fertiliser requirements are also similar once cropping commences, except that pears may require a little more nitrogen.

Pruning (winter) is comparatively simple, the spur pruning given for apples suiting all except a very few pears. Initial shaping is essential, cutting the stronger shoots selected to form branches by about half their length and keeping the centre of the tree open. For cordons and other restricted forms of tree, to which pears lend themselves particularly well, summer pruning is advisable. This involves shortening all young shoots more than 10 in. in length to about 5 in. from the base. Do this when the base of such shoots is hardening and turning brown in colour, usually late July–early August. Pruned shoots may then be further reduced in winter. Such summer treatment may also be given to trained apple trees with advantage during August.

Only a few pears are self-fertile and 'Conference' is the most reliable if only one tree can be planted. Good pollinating pairings include 'Laxton's Superb' with 'Doyenné du Comice' and 'Conference' with 'Williams' Bon Chrétien.' Early varieties should be picked a little before ripening and used quickly.

Plums.—This general term includes gages and damsons. Numerous varieties are easy to grow but are unsuited to small gardens because of the amount of space required. Unlike apples and pears, there are no dwarfing rootstocks, and a minimum spacing of 14 ft. should be allowed for, growing the trees as half standards, or fan-trained against a south or west wall. Flowering is during April, and frost damage can be serious in some seasons. Plant preferably in the autumn, and by early March at the latest, using no manure unless soil is distinctly poor. Young trees should be staked during their early years, and must not be allowed to rub against the support.

Pruning should be reduced to a minimum, as the spores of silver leaf disease gain entry through wounds such as pruning cuts and stake rubs. Shorten branch leaders on young trees just as buds are bursting, but on older trees prune only when branches become overcrowded. Do this between June and August, when the risk of silver leaf is at a minimum. Cut cleanly and coat the wounds thoroughly with a bituminous paint; treat broken branches similarly immediately they are noticed. Trees fruiting heavily should have the branches supported and the fruit thinned in late June. Side shoots on fans must be cut to four to five leaves in late June and reduced still further following picking if necessary. Feed cropping trees regularly to encourage new growth, by mulching the soil generously with manure, compost, or leaf mould in early spring. Some varieties are self-fertile, including 'Victoria,' 'Oullin's Golden Gage,' and 'Merryweather Damson.'

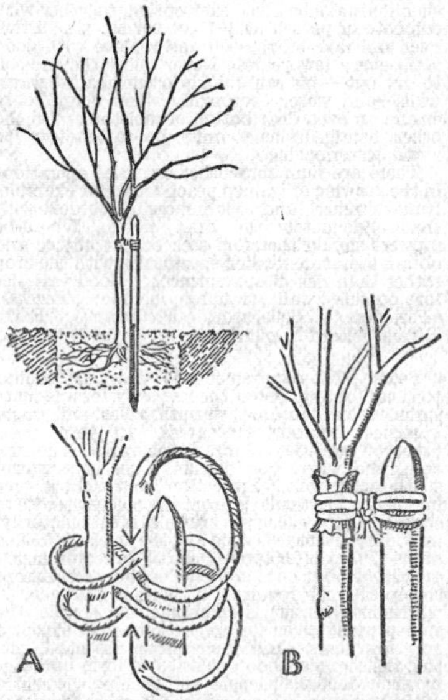

A WELL-PLANTED TREE, illustrating (A) a good method of tying and (B) sapling firmly secured with sacking around the trunk and held with stout cord.

Raspberries.—These are an ideal fruit for the small garden, but because of virus disease always buy certified canes from a fruit nursery. Plant between November and March on clean, well-manured ground, allowing 18 in. between canes and 6 ft. between rows. After planting prune each cane back to 12 in. Do *not* attempt to crop them in their first year, or the production of young canes for the following year's fruit will suffer.

A semi-shaded position will answer, but full sun is preferable for quality fruit. New canes should be looped with string to a post-and-wire fence and later tied individually to each wire when fully hardened. Space them at about 4 in. and remove any weak or diseased canes at ground level. In late February cut each cane to just above the top wire, which is usually 5–6 ft. high. This removes any damaged tips and may encourage fruiting over a longer length of cane. In the second summer a fair crop should result, and netting against birds is essential. Regular watering is imperative in dry weather, and spring and summer mulches of well-rotted manure or compost should always be applied. Supplement this in March with nitrogen and potash (fertilisers) if required, this depending on how well the ground was manured before planting. After fruiting cut out all old canes and tie in the new ones as already described. 'Malling Promise' and 'Lloyd George' are good varieties.

For autumn-fruiting varieties prune all canes to the ground in late February and tie in the best during the summer for cropping in September–October. 'September' is a good variety, and 'Lloyd George' can also be used.

Strawberries.—This is the one fruit that should be included in the vegetable garden. Fresh ground can then be used regularly for establishing new beds. Plants more than two years old are seldom profitable, and the best fruit is always picked from healthy one-year-olds planted the previous August or September. Runners put in later than early October should be deblossomed the following spring, the reward being a much heavier crop in the second year. This wastes ground, however, and early planting is preferable on all counts. Prepare the ground well in advance of planting and dig in plenty of well-rotted manure or compost or both, as this is the key to success.

Because of virus diseases order certified plants from a fruit nursery and burn any unhealthy ones in old beds before planting. Insert firmly with the base of the crown of each plant just at soil level and refirm after winter frosts; space at 20 in. in rows and 2 ft. 6 in. between rows (3 ft. if possible). A mulch of rotted manure or compost is beneficial each autumn, together with an application of sulphate of potash at 1 oz. per sq. yd. In the spring growth can be encouraged by feeling with "Maxicrop"; quick-acting *nitrogenous* fertilisers should normally be avoided.

During flowering cover the plants where possible to guard against frost damage reducing the crop. Keep the ground weed-free and remove runners regularly; a few plants should always be grown away from the main bed, deblossomed and kept purely for runner production, as this then helps to reduce the spread of virus. Ruthlessly burn any plant that remains stunted, including its runners, as this is usually a symptom of virus disease. When the young fruits are just forming spread clean straw underneath them to avoid splashing from the soil; it is a mistake to do this too early, as it increases the risk of frost damage. Net the fruit against birds and remove any rotting specimens when picking.

After fruiting remove and burn all old foliage, weeds, and straw, and feed as already described. Plant a percentage of new, vigorous runners each year on fresh ground, at the same time burning the old ones they are replacing. For flavour, the best variety is still 'Royal Sovereign' of which healthy stocks are available.

Alpine strawberries require similar treatment, preferably with a semi-shaded position, and should be raised from seed. Perpetual fruiting types continue fruiting on and off well into the autumn, and should be treated as for ordinary varieties. In all cases cloches can be used from late February onwards to obtain early fruit.

Standard References:

Tree Fruit Growing by Raymond Bush, revised by E. G. Gilbert. (Penguin) 1962.

The Fruit Garden Displayed (R.H.S.). Revised Ed. 1965 (£1·80, post free). Available from The Sec., Royal Hort. Soc., Vincent Sq., London, S.W.1.

THE VEGETABLE GARDEN.

The Small Plot.—For some years the trend in gardening has been decidedly towards growing ornamental plants; vegetables have been neglected. This has gone so far that in many instances the vegetable plot has been done away with altogether. As a result, throughout the summer housewives have faced the high cost of buying even such easily grown crops as lettuce or going without them when supplies are short. A further factor promoting a return to home gardening has been the information now available on the toxic properties of some chemicals used freely in commercial horticulture.

To avoid these problems, even a small piece of ground can be used to excellent purpose if first manured and dug over thoroughly. The ideal site is an open, sunny position, sheltered from cold winds with the soil a deep rich loam well supplied with humus; obviously few gardens have such a site but much can be done in most circumstances. Once the ground is ready a few sowings of radishes can be made and lettuce crops and a suitable succession. The land can be divided into four plots; one is used for the more or less permanent crops, such as asparagus, rhubarb, and globe artichokes, and the other three will provide a rotation. This is used to stop any group of vegetables being grown on the same land more than once in every three years, so preventing the carry-over of some pests and diseases and providing for a full use of the manures in the soil, as different groups of vegetables need more of some nutrients than others. It also allows the clearance of one section to enable winter digging and manuring to be carried out. On this freshly manured plot peas, beans, onions, leeks, and lettuces, all revelling in rich ground, should be grown. The next plot, manured for the *previous* crop, can be used for root crops—early potatoes, carrots, parsnips, and beet. A light dressing of artificial fertiliser such as "National Growmore" should be applied before sowing. On the third plot the green vegetables should be grown; a dressing of fertilisers is desirable, and lime should also be applied.

In the following season the root crops can be cropped throughout the summer. Other vegetables worthy of consideration are the sowing of spinach and onions grown from sets. Of course, in the small plot, priority should be given to providing a fresh supply of herbs like sage, thyme, chives, parsley and a clump or two of rhubarb.

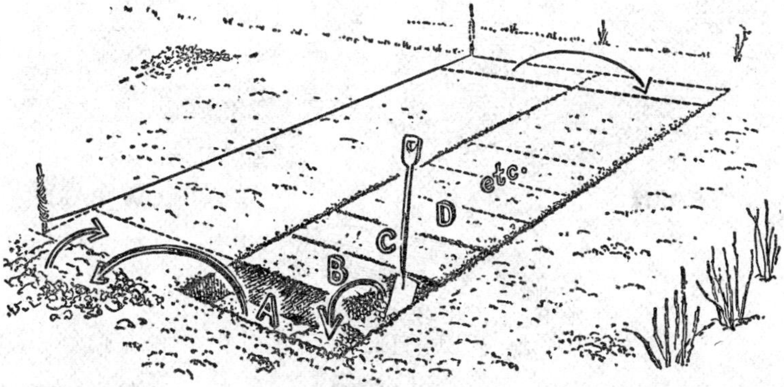

DOUBLE DIGGING—A sound cultural practice. A trench 2 ft. wide and the depth of a spade is taken out at A and placed as shown. The bottom of trench A is then forked up and filled in with soil from B and the process repeated with C and D, etc. In double digging the sub-soil is *always* left on the bottom and never brought to the surface.

General Cultivation.—On a new site soil preparation is important as all vegetables do best on ground in good heart. The land should be dug two spits deep ("double digging") and for this purpose the plot is divided into two longitudinally and a trench 2 ft. wide and 10 in. deep is dug out, as illustrated above. The sub-soil at the bottom of the trench is then broken up and manure or compost added (or turf if grassland is being dug). The next strip is then dealt with in a similar manner and the practice continued down the plot to the last trench which is finally filled in with the loose soil from the first trench. Double digging is not necessary every year and single digging carried out in a similar way without breaking up the second spit, or sometimes a light forking over is sufficient.

Clay soils can be lightened by adding heavy dressings of peat or compost and coarse materials like ashes and road grit. Sandy soils are also improved by addition of humus, in this case to conserve moisture. These soils are less fertile than clay ones but are easier to cultivate, are warmer, and crop earlier. In both cases the addition of lime is only desirable if the ground is too acid; most vegetables, it should be noted, do best on slightly acidic soils *not* alkaline ones. If any doubt exists then it is always best *not* to lime.

The lay-out with vegetables must be designed to provide a succession through the year and to utilise the full capacity of the ground by catch grown on the plot which was manured the previous year, and the brassicas grown on the land vacated by the root crops. The plot on which the brassicas were growing is double dug and manured ready for the peas, beans, and onions. A system of this type proves very satisfactory, but numerous variations can be devised, and it is really a matter for the gardener to decide his best method. The growing of maincrop potatoes will complicate the system, as a large area is usually required. They are better grown separately in another part of the vegetable garden.

Usually it is wise to have a small piece of ground available for a nursery bed. This should be of good, fine soil in which seeds can be sown to supply the main plot. In all cases seed should be sown very thinly to prevent the necessity for much pricking out, and a slug-killer is often a wise precaution to use before sowing. Sowing dates, as given, are mainly for growers in the South. In the North sowing dates in spring will be generally two weeks or more later and autumn operations the same amount earlier. Any gardener must adjust his work to suit local conditions of soil and climate, and this knowledge is only gained by experience of the particular area.

General cleanliness in the vegetable garden is at all times desirable; weeds and rubbish only harbour pests and diseases, and the hoe should be busy whenever possible. Waste material can be utilised in that essential of the modern garden—the compost heap. *See* Manures and Fertilisers for description.

Frames and Cloches.—The gardener is able to extend the season of many crops by protecting them under frames and cloches; this is particularly useful where spring or early autumn frosts are prevalent. The use of frames is limited, as they are in a fixed position, but nevertheless they are very useful for obtaining out-of-season salad crops, especially if they are heated by electricity or a hot bed.

Cloches have the advantage of mobility and can be used on a number of crops in succession. Essentially, each is a number of pieces of glass in a tent or barn shape held together by wire. Pattern, size, and height vary according to the crop to be covered and the manufacturer's design. A good cloche should be of simple design, rigid and capable of standing up to ordinary winds, easily transported, and well ventilated.

The low barn cloche is probably the most economical type. This is 23 in. wide and 13 in. high when erected, and will allow two rows of lettuce to be grown, with an intercrop of another vegetable. The large barn or barn cloche of similar design, but with 12-in. side is 19 in. high in the centre, enabling taller crops, *e.g.*, peas and dwarf beans, to be grown on, almost to maturity. The tomato cloche has sides 24 in. square and a basal width of 26 in. Many others of various shapes and sizes are offered; the amateur should buy to suit his own requirements. Other materials have been tried instead of glass with varying success. Plastic cloches are on the market, but their lightness entails very safe anchoring, and at the moment glass still seems to be the best material in most instances.

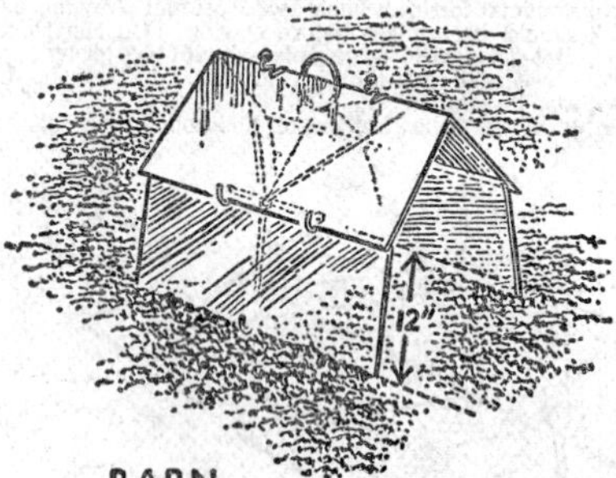

BARN

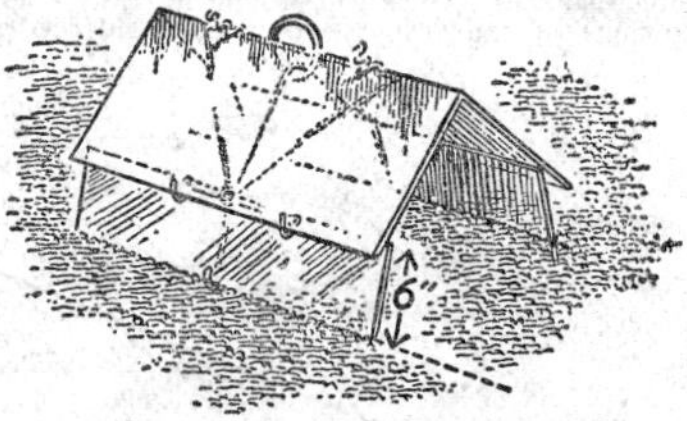

LOW BARN

PLASTIC

Types of Cloches—The most popular is the barn cloche; with 12-in. sides it will cover strawberries and peas and beans in their early stages. The low barn will accommodate three rows of lettuce in winter and cucumbers in the summer. Plastic cloches are growing in popularity, especially those patterns using toughened plastic, and have some decided advantages over glass ones.

Gardening under cloches obviously is a subject too large to be dealt with in a few sentences, and the reader would be well advised to refer to one of the books mentioned in the bibliography for fuller information. A few of the main points are mentioned here and also under the individual crops.

Cloche cultivation is an intensive method of production, and this means that the land must be well cultivated and manured to ensure good-quality crops at all times. About ten days before crops are sown or planted the cloches should be put in the position where they are to be used, to warm the soil. The crop is sometimes sown a month before the normal date, and this prewarming ensures that the soil can be cultivated to a good tilth, as well as giving the plants a good start. Watering is a problem that often bothers the amateur. Provided the soil is well watered at sowing time, there should be no need to decloche to water. Rain seeping under the cloches and a spray directed over them occasionally will provide enough for the crop in normal weather; on dry, sandy soils it may be necessary to spray over the cloches more often. A mulch of compost is also very useful to help retain water.

Dwarf varieties should be used for growing under cloches, although methods of raising the cloches another foot or so have been devised and are on the market, which allow the use of taller growing varieties. Many different vegetables can be helped to some extent in the early stages, besides those crops which can be grown entirely under cloches; the grower must decide what crops he needs and fit a rotation to cover as many crops as possible with the cloches available. This is mainly a matter of experience, but books on the subject will suggest many variations that can be tried. Intercropping with quick-maturing crops can also be practised. As instances, radish or mustard and cress can be cropped between two rows of lettuce, or a row of cos lettuce can be grown between two rows of cabbage lettuce.

It must be remembered that the glass of cloches will need cleaning from time to time; the crop still needs the maximum light available, although shading of certain crops may be necessary in hot sun.

Artichokes.—Two different plants are grown as artichokes. One, the Jerusalem artichoke (*Helianthus tuberosus*), is related to the sunflower and is grown for its tuberous roots, which are second in food value only to the potato. It will grow in poor soil, but amply repays good cultivation, and may be placed at the more exposed end of the vegetable plot as a windbreak and screen. Tubers should be planted during February or March, on well-manured ground in drills 4–6 in. deep, and 2 ft. 6 in. apart, with 15 in. between the tubers. Hoe frequently during the summer and cut the stalks down in early winter. The tubers may then be lifted and stored, or better dug as required, reserving a number for replanting the following February.

The other type, the globe artichoke (*Cynara scolymus*), is often grown as an ornamental plant, but is esteemed as a vegetable for its young, fleshy flower-heads, which must be cut before the scales begin to open, after which they become hard and unpalatable. A deep, rich, well-manured soil is required, and after planting in early spring in rows 4 ft. apart, with 2 ft. between the plants, a compost or manure mulch is beneficial. A good crop may be expected for five or six years provided an annual dressing of manure is applied. After this time they should be replaced by young suckers, planted in a fresh position. A covering of straw or bracken on the crowns is advisable during winter.

Asparagus.—This will grow on most types of soil provided that drainage is good and that plenty of organic matter is available. The site for the asparagus bed should be double dug in the autumn prior to planting, and a generous dressing of about half a barrow load of manure per square yard incorporated. Crowns up to three years old may be bought, but it is found that one-year-old crowns give the best results. Plants may be obtained cheaply by sowing seed in late March in drills 1½ in. deep and 18 in. apart and thinning the seedlings to 4 in. apart. It is thought that male plants produce more stalks of better quality than female plants, but at present no supplies of male crowns alone are available.

Planting may be on the single-row system or the wide-bed system. In the single-row system crowns are planted 18 in. apart in rows 4½ ft. apart; the wide-bed system consists of 5-ft. beds, with three rows of crowns 15 in. apart each way, and 2 ft. between each bed. Planting is best done during April and the plants are placed in a trench 8 in. deep and 1 ft. wide, with a slight ridge at the base, and covered with 3 in. of soil. The remaining soil is worked in during the summer. The roots should never be allowed to dry out.

The following March 2 oz. per sq. yd. of sulphate of ammonia should be applied; in subsequent years 3 oz. per sq. yd. of "National Growmore" applied at the same time, followed by 2 oz. per sq. yd. of sulphate of ammonia in June, after cutting, can be used. Salt, as a fertiliser, is not recommended nowadays. An annual dressing of manure or compost in November is desirable.

No cutting should be done for the first two years after planting and only a light cut taken in the third year. After this a six-to-eight-week season beginning in early May is usual. The spears should be cut when about 4 in. above soil level and severed about 2 or 3 in. below the soil, giving an overall length of 6–7 in. The fronds should be cut in October before the seeds drop, but not during the summer, as the plant is weakened. Weeds should be kept down, and in the autumn the plant may be earthed up.

Varieties: 'Connover's Colossal' and 'Kidner's Pedigree.'

Beans. Three types are commonly grown, as follows:

Broad Beans are the hardiest and can, in warm gardens, be sown during autumn to obtain an early crop. Little is gained by this as a rule, and sowing in well-manured ground in February, when the soil is frost free, with successional sowings during March and April, is generally better in most gardens. The soil is broken down, finely raked, and the seed sown 9 in. apart in drills 3 in. deep, with 18 in. between each row. If double rows are sown 10 in. should be left between the rows, and 2 ft. between each pair of rows. Staking may be necessary. Plants from sowings under glass or under cloches in January may be used to obtain an earlier crop; the cloches should be removed in March and a further crop sown, and recloched.

Black aphis was a serious pest, but is now easily checked by pinching out the young tips and applying malathion or lindane as soon as any are seen. The pods may be used before the beans are fully developed and sliced as are runner beans, but normally they are picked when the beans are well formed but not tough.

Varieties: 'Aquadulce' and 'Green Masterpiece.'

Dwarf Beans (which include French, Kidney, and Haricot Beans) may be either used as young pods in a similar manner to runner beans or ripened in the pod for winter use. A rich well-manured soil gives the best results, and seeds sown during the first week in May, 2 in. deep and 6 in. apart, in drills 18 in. apart, may be followed by a second sowing at the end of May. The young plants should be thinned out to 1 ft. apart and small twigs used to stake them. If sown earlier, frost damage may occur. Seeds may also be sown in the greenhouse and the seedlings transplanted, or sown under cloches in the last week in March, provided the soil has been prewarmed.

The plants, as long as the pods are picked over frequently, will continue to bear until the frosts; a little liquid manure will be beneficial during the summer. A late sowing in July, cloched in September, will continue the season into the autumn.

If required for winter use (Haricot varieties) certain plants should be left unpicked and the pods allowed to ripen on the plants. They should not be picked green; if unripe when frosts come, the plants should be pulled up and dried in a shed.

Varieties: 'The Prince' (Cloche), 'Masterpiece,' and 'Comtesse de Chambord' (Haricot).

Runner Beans are the most popular type, and can be grown in two ways: either without stakes, in which case the tips of main and side shoots are regularly pinched out to make a bushy, dwarf plant, a method often used by farmers, or staked, with cross poles, allowing the plants to climb to the tops of the poles before pinching. Seed is sown from early May (mid-April under cloches) until late June, depending on the danger of frost, usually in a double row with drills 15 in. apart, and with seeds 3 in. deep and 6 in. apart in the rows, alternate plants being removed later.

Staking should be done as soon as the first pair of leaves unfolds, and a surface mulch is then applied. If the beans are to be dwarfed the rows should be about 18 in. or 2 ft. apart, and pinching may be required about once a week. A good, well-manured soil is essential, and plenty of moisture is required. The flowers may fail to set in dry weather, and an evening spray of water is helpful in preventing this "running off." Harvesting should be carried out regularly while the pods are young, before the seeds swell; older pods are stringy and seldom worth eating.

Varieties: 'White Czar' (white-flowered, heavy cropper) and 'Streamline.'

Beetroot.—From mid-April onwards varieties of beet may be sown on soil that has not recently been manured but is in good heart; on freshly manured soils coarse, forked roots subject to cracking occur. If in poor condition a light dressing of a complete fertiliser should be given before sowing. Sow in drills 1 in. deep and 12 in. apart and make a first thinning to 4 in. apart when the first rough leaf appears, and a second later, leaving 9 in. between the plants. Transplanting is inadvisable. Early roots for summer pulling may be obtained from a sowing of a Globe type in mid-April, and the main sowing should be made during May or early June for the winter supply. A sowing under cloches in late February will provide roots for pulling in late May.

On a heavy soil the oval-rooted types are best, but on a lighter soil the long-rooted types may be used. A sowing in late July of the Globe type will provide beet for use at the end of winter. Salad beet from early sowings may be pulled as required; the main crop should be allowed to mature and is lifted in October before the roots become woody and tough. Any damaged roots should not be stored. Twist off the tops just above the roots, shake the soil from the roots, and store in boxes of sand or peat in a frost-free shed. If clamped outside, straw and a thick layer of soil should be used; if frost reaches them they are spoilt.

Varieties: globe—'Detroit Red,' 'Red Globe, and 'Crimson Globe'; oval—'Cobham Early'; long—'Cheltenham Green Top.'

Sugar beet is similar but is white, not red-fleshed, and is mainly a farm crop; if desired it may be grown in a similar manner. Care should be taken in hoeing all beet crops to avoid damage to the small surface roots which feed the swollen rootstock.

Borecole.—*See* **Kale.**

Brassica.—A generic name of vegetables usually known to gardeners as "greens." This group includes brussels sprouts, cabbages, cauliflowers, kale, turnips, kohl-rabi, broccoli, and couve tronchuda. As they are all related, similar soil and cultural treatment is needed, and many pests and diseases are common to them. Each is dealt with under a separate heading.

Broccoli.—*See* Cauliflower.

Brussels Sprouts.—Young plants from seed sown thinly in a nursery seed bed during mid-March can be transplanted during May or June. The soil should be firm, well drained, in good heart, and contain adequate lime, some manure preferably having been dug in during the winter; a supplementary dressing of 2 oz. superphosphate and 1 oz. of sulphate of potash per square yard is given before planting. The young plants should be set out 3 ft. apart both ways, planted firmly, and watered in thoroughly. Regular hoeing is necessary, and about a month after planting a little soil should be drawn round the stems.

If growth seems weak a top dressing of nitro-chalk should be given and this repeated in early September. As the lower leaves yellow, cut them off and gather the sprouts as they mature, picking from the bottom of the stem. Where space is available a succession of sowings from March to June can be made to lengthen the cropping period.

Club root, the worst disease of brassicas, is kept in check by only using well-limed, well-drained soil, and dipping the roots in 4% calomel before planting, and cabbage root fly, a frequent insect pest, by using lindane.

Varieties: early—'Cambridge No. 1'; mid-season—'Rous Lench' and 'Triumph' (dark foliage, distinct).

Cabbage.—Sowings in March and April for summer use, in May or June for winter use, and in late July or August for spring use will give a succession of cabbages all the year round. Seed is sown thinly in a nursery bed of well-firmed, limed soil, clear of weeds, in drills ¾ in. deep and 6 in. apart, and the seedlings dusted with lindane to check flea beetle attack (prevalent with all brassica seedlings). All cabbages are gross feeders, and a well-drained soil in good heart, with adequate lime, is required.

"Spring cabbage" should be sown during late July (north) and August (south). If sown too early the plants may "bolt" without making a heart. The young plants are set out in mid-September 18 in. apart and with 18 in. between the rows if for hearting, or 9 in. apart with 18 in. between the rows, in which case the alternate plants are cut for "spring greens." On a heavy soil ridging along the rows of plants keeps the soil round the roots drained and helps to prevent loosening by frosts. In cold districts cloches may be used with advantage to help plants through the winter. In early March a dressing of 1 oz. per sq. yd. of sulphate of ammonia or nitro-chalk is a good stimulant.

Seed of "summer" and "autumn cabbage" is sown in March and April and planted during late May and June, 18 in. to 2 ft. each way between the plants, depending on the variety. The plants should be thoroughly watered, both before and after transplanting. A top dressing of 1 oz. per sq. yd. nitro-chalk may be given if required.

"Winter cabbage," maturing from October to February from sowings during May and early June, are set out 2 ft. apart each way in July or early August, usually on ground which has been cropped with early potatoes or peas. No nitrogen fertiliser should be given late in the season, as soft growth, liable to frost damage, is encouraged. A balanced fertiliser, such as "National Growmore," may be used if needed. When the stalks of cabbage are left standing over winter a common practice is to cut across the tops to obtain bunches of leaves, for use as greens during early spring.

"Savoy cabbages" mature during winter and early spring from seed sown in May. Seedlings are transplanted in late July and early August on to land manured for the previous crop, to which a dressing of 2 oz. superphosphate and 1 oz. sulphate of potash per sq. yd. has been applied. The young plants should be set out 2 ft. apart each way; they are exceptionally hardy, and should be grown in every garden in case of a hard winter.

Varieties: Spring sowing—autumn cutting, 'Greyhound' (early). 'Winningstadt.' Autumn sowing—spring cutting, 'April,' 'Wheeler's Imperial.' Savoy 'Ormskirk Late Green.'

Red cabbage is slow to mature; plants from sowings in August are transplanted 6 in. each way in autumn and set out in early spring 18 in. each way. They are ready to cut in late summer.

Cardoon (Cynara cardunculus).—Closely related to the globe artichoke and grown for the blanched hearts. Seed is sown in trenches 18 in. wide and 1 ft. deep; 3 in. of manure is worked into the bottom soil and covered with 3 in. of fine soil. Three or four seeds are dibbled in every 18 in. and covered with a flower pot till visible, and then thinned out, leaving one strong seedling at each station. Protection from sun and late frosts is provided by twigs over the trench, and copious watering is given during the summer.

On a fine day in September the plants are blanched by tying the leaves together and covering with dry hay, 3 in. thick, kept in position by raffia, and earthed up in the same way as celery. Blanching is completed in about a month.

Carrots.—A light, well-drained soil, enriched with decayed organic matter, is suitable for carrots. No fresh manure should be given, but a light dressing of "National Growmore" fertiliser can be applied prior to sowing. The surface is left rough until sowing time and then broken down to a fine tilth. The first sowing is made in early April in drills ¾ in. deep and 12 in. apart, and a succession is obtained by sowing at intervals of a month until the end of July.

On heavy, unfavourable soils stump-rooted varieties are best grown, long-rooted varieties needing a light soil. Thin out the stump-rooted varieties to 4 in. apart and the longer varieties to 6 in. Thinnings should be removed and the soil pressed firmly back to minimise damage by carrot fly. The early sowings are pulled as required, but the later sowings for winter use should be lifted in October and stored in slightly damp sand in a frost-proof shed or clamped in the open.

Frames and cloches are sometimes used to obtain early and late carrots. Seed of a quick-growing variety, such as 'Amsterdam Forcing' or 'Early Nantes,' sown in late January under cloches or in frames will provide an early crop; the same varieties sown in frames or cloches in early August will provide young carrots for the autumn. Carrot fly is a bad pest, especially on light soils; the seedlings should be dusted in the rows with lindane when 2–4 in. high to prevent the flies from egg laying.

Varieties: globular—'Early Gem'; stump-rooted—'French Short Horn'; intermediate—'Amsterdam Forcing' and 'Early Nantes'; long—'St. Valery' and 'Long Red Surrey.'

Catch Crops.—A term used for quick-growing crops interplanted between rows of other crops. Radishes between rows of broad beans, and lettuce between celery rows provide examples. In this way the best use of a limited amount of land can be made.

Cauliflower.—Broccoli is for all practical purposes a hardy winter cauliflower. Seed is sown ¾ in. deep in a nursery bed from mid-April to mid-May, depending on the variety, and transplanted during June and July on to firm soil, well manured for the previous crop. The plants are set out 2 ft. apart each way; 2 oz. superphosphate and ¾ oz. of sulphate of potash per square yard may be hoed in before transplanting. No nitrogenous manure should be given late in the year.

Varieties: cauliflower—'Snowball' (summer), 'Majestic' (autumn). Broccoli—'Snow's Winter White' (winter), 'St. George' (early spring). Sprouting broccoli—'Nine Star Perennial' (a many-headed sort).

Sprouting broccoli is very hardy, has a more leafy head, and is cultivated in the same way. Purple- and green-sprouting sorts are grown also.

Summer cauliflowers require a soil which has been limed and manured during the winter; 1–2 oz. per sq. yd. of superphosphate should be given before transplanting. An early sowing in frames in February or March will provide plants for cropping in June. These should be hardened off and planted in March or April from 18 to 24 in. square, depending on the variety. Seed sown outdoors in April in drills ¾ in. deep will give plants for transplanting in May or June, for cropping from late July onwards. If growth is slow a dressing of 1 oz. per sq. yd. of sulphate of ammonia should be given. Leaves broken over the curds will help to prevent any damage from early frosts. Varieties given in previous paragraph.

Celeriac.—A plant allied to celery grown for its edible root, which resembles a turnip but has the flavour of celery; the stems are bitter to the taste and are not eaten. It is used in salads or boiled as other root crops.

Seed is sown in gentle heat in March and seedlings pricked out into seed-boxes, 2 in. apart each way. In June, after hardening off, the seedlings are planted out in shallow drills 18 in. apart, leaving 12 in. between each plant in the row. Water freely during the summer and remove side shoots as they appear. Lift the roots in October or November and store in a frost-free shed.

Celery.—Richly prepared ground is required. A trench 15 in. wide and 1 ft. deep is taken out and manure worked into the bottom of the trench. The soil is then returned to within 3 in. of the ground level. Seed should be sown in early March at about 60° Fahrenheit and the seedlings pricked out in deep boxes 3 in. each way and gradually hardened off. Celery seed is very fine, and care should be taken to cover it with only a fine layer of soil; if covered too deeply it may not germinate.

In late May or June set the plants out in staggered double rows 1 ft. apart, with 10 in. between the plants, and water them in. Frequent watering during the summer is required, and a light dressing of nitrate of soda will stimulate them if growth is poor. Before earthing up to blanch the plants, tie the stems loosely below the leaves and remove any suckers. Earthing up begins when the plants are about 15 in. high; the ground should be moist, and the first earthing should only be slight. The second and third earthings, at intervals of about three weeks, should be more generous, but should never reach higher than the base of the leaves, and no earth should fall into the heart. For exhibition purposes brown-paper collars may be tied round the stalks before earthing. The final earthing should cover all the stems right up to the leaves, and the soil should slope away neatly. In winter litter or bracken spread over the plants will help protect them from frost.

Celery fly is a serious pest, and the brown leaf-blisters should be pinched to kill the maggot inside and lindane applied two or three times at fortnightly intervals. Slugs are a serious pest and must be eradicated. This can be done easily with slug pellets or a liquid formulation of "Slugit." Leaf spot, a seed-borne disease, can be prevented by spraying with May & Baker's, "Bordeaux Mixture."

Varieties: white—'Solid White'; pink—'Clayworth Prize Pink'; red—'Standard Bearer' self-blanching—'Golden Self-Blanching.'

Chicory.—The young, blanched growths are used in winter salads. Seeds are sown in drills 1 ft. apart in May; the young seedlings are thinned to 8 in. apart and grown on until October or November, when they are lifted and the roots trimmed to 8 or 10 in. long. They are then planted in deep boxes in a moist, sandy soil 5 in. apart each way, leaving 1 in. above the soil surface, and the boxes put in a warm greenhouse or cellar.

No light must reach the crowns; one method sometimes used is to cover the crowns with 6 in. of sand. When the blanched growths show through they are about 6 in. high and ready for cutting.

Chives.—These are like small onions, and the leaves are used for flavouring salads and soups. They are easily grown in window boxes and town gardens. Bulbs can be planted in March 6 in. apart and divided when the clusters become too large.

Corn Salad or Lamb's Lettuce.—Occasionally grown for the leaves, which are used in early spring salads. Seed sown from August to October will provide plants for winter and spring use.

Couve Tronchuda.—A large brassica known as "Portugal cabbage," not generally suitable for smaller gardens. Seed is sown in March and the plants set out 2–3 ft. apart each way. The hearts may be cooked in the same way as cabbage.

Cress.—An annual growing rapidly from seed and used as a salad when only the seed leaves have developed. Seed sown as required, in boxes of light, moist soil and covered with brown paper until germination, when it is removed, will provide salad all the year round. The seed is merely pressed into the soil and the boxes kept moist. Cress may even be grown on damp flannel in a window.

Cucumber.—The cucumber of the shops is grown as a specialist crop under glass. Temperatures of 85° Fahrenheit or more may be required, and only occasionally are they grown by the amateur, although cloche and frame culture is now popular.

Ridge cucumbers, which are smaller and prickly outside, may be grown outdoors in summer. Plants from seed sown singly in pots under glass can be planted during late May on ridges of good, well-manured soil or, alternatively, sown on the ridges 1 in. deep at the same date. Water freely during the summer and cut the cucumbers while young to encourage further production.

If cloches are available greenhouse-raised cucumbers can be planted under them, in mid-April. Frame cucumbers are less hardy, but young plants raised under glass can be planted under cloches in early May.

Varieties: ridge—'King of the Ridge' and 'Stockwood Ridge'; frame—'Conqueror' and 'Telegraph.'

Endive.—Used in winter or autumn salads. Seed is sown during April in drills 18 in. apart and the seedlings thinned to 12–15 in. apart. Sowings in June and August will provide a succession. A rich soil and plenty of moisture are the main requirements; before eating blanching is necessary, as the leaves are very bitter. This is achieved by tying the leaves loosely together and covering the plants with inverted flower pots (with the holes blocked) to exclude the light; frost should be kept out by piling litter over the pots in winter. If cloches are used they can be coated inside with lime-wash to achieve the same effect. Alternatively, plants may be lifted in October and blanched in darkened frames.

Varieties: summer—'Green Curled'; winter—'Batavian Broad Leaved.'

Fennel.—A perennial culinary herb used in fish sauces and salads. Blanched stems may also be cooked in the same way as celery. Seed is sown in drills 2 ft. apart in rich soil and the seedlings thinned to 18 in.

French Beans.—*See* Dwarf Beans.

Garlic.—One or two "cloves" planted in February, 9 in. apart, will provide ample garlic for salads, as only a little is required. After growth is complete in summer the bulbs can be lifted, dried, and stored and some saved for replanting.

Haricot Beans.—*See* Dwarf Beans.

Herbs.—Many herbs are useful in small quantities for flavouring and garnishing, as well as being decorative. If possible, a separate herb garden should be made as a feature in the garden, or they may be used as edging plants. Perennial herbs, of which borage, caraway, chamomile, chives, fennel, garlic, horseradish, lavender, mint, pennyroyal, marjoram, rosemary, rue, sage, tansy, tarragon, and thymes are the main types grown, should be given a permanent position. Those grown as annuals—anise, basil, coriander, dill, parsley, purslane, and summer savory—can be used as "fill-ins" on the vegetable garden. Brick and cobble paths associate well with herbs, imparting something of the character of the gardens of bygone days, when herb gardens were considered one of the most important features.

Horseradish.—A deep-rooting perennial herb which appreciates a well-manured, moist soil. It is easily propagated from root cuttings and can become a nuisance, as pieces of root left in the soil will make a new plant; care should be taken to lift the complete root when digging it for use. Straight roots planted in spring with the crowns 6 in. below soil level and 1 ft. apart can be lifted for use in autumn; no further treatment is required, apart from keeping weeds in check. Some of the roots should be kept for planting the following spring.

Kale.—Very useful during a cold winter, when other green vegetables are scarce, because of its hardiness. Seed sown in April or May will provide young plants for transplanting 18 in. apart each way in July or early August, on to a site used for peas or early potatoes, in good heart. A catch crop of lettuce can usually be taken from between the rows. The variety 'Hungry Gap' is usually sown in rows 18 in. apart where it is to mature and thinned, leaving 18 in. between the plants. There are many varieties; which types are grown is a matter of personal preference.

Varieties: 'Cottager's' and 'Hungry Gap.'

Kidney Beans.—*See* **Dwarf Beans.**

Kohl Rabi.—A brassica with a swollen stem base, in flavour and appearance something between a turnip and a cabbage. Seeds sown in April in rows 1 ft. apart are thinned to 1 ft. apart in the rows, and the swollen stem harvested when about the size of a tennis ball. If left to grow it becomes coarse.

Lamb's Lettuce.—*See* **Corn Salad.**

Leeks.—A vegetable which repays planting on a well-manured soil. If they are to follow winter greens, then manure or compost should be dug in after the previous crop is cleared. Leeks may be sown from early March to April in lines 8 in. apart on a prepared seed bed, and the seedlings transplanted as land becomes available during June and July, when about 6 in. high. Thinning in the seed bed should be unnecessary provided the sowing has been correct. The seedlings are set out 9 in. apart in rows 15 in. apart; a hole is made with a dibber, and each seedling dropped in and watered thoroughly. No firming is needed, the watering should tighten the plants sufficiently. Alternatively, drills 4 in. deep and 15 in. apart can be drawn out with a hoe and the plants put in 9 in. apart in the drills.

Regular hoeing is required, and a feed of sulphate of ammonia (1 oz. per gallon of water) can be applied if in poor growth. In September a little earth should be drawn up around the roots, which should, by then, be almost full grown. Leeks are very hardy and can be left in the soil until required for use.

Varieties: 'Lyon' and 'Musselburgh.'

Lettuce.—Two main types are grown: cos lettuce, a summer crop with long, straight leaves that curl inwards naturally or are tied in so that the heart is more or less blanched; and cabbage lettuce, which are broad and spreading, with round cabbage-like hearts, and are grown to supply salad all the year round. Lettuce should be grown on ground manured during autumn or winter, dug and left rough till planting time, when it is broken down and raked to a fine tilth. This crop is a particularly valuable one for town gardens with restricted space. In these circumstances excellent returns can be had by raising seed indoors and pricking out the seedlings into small peat pots ("Root-o-Pots"). At this stage the plants can be grown on in a "Stewart" propagator which is simply a seed tray covered with a plastic hood, and finally planted out-of-doors in their pots. The practice can be repeated or small sowings made in the open and seedlings thinned to 9 in. apart. Quick, unchecked growth with plenty of moisture is essential; on poor soils peat can be forked into the surface and an application of liquid "Maxicrop" made during the growing season.

Varieties: wide selection available of all types; small, quick maturing sorts include 'Little Gem' ('Sugar Cos') and 'Continuity.'

Maize.—*See* **Sweet Corn.**

Marrows.—Pumpkins, gourds, bush, and trailing marrows all require similar treatment; plenty of sun and water and a rich soil, such as an old hotbed or compost heap, which will provide a porous medium of humus. Seed can be sown singly in pots under glass in March, or outdoors on the site in May. For cloches a bush variety must be used, and greenhouse-raised plants are cloched in mid-April. Plant four or five seeds in groups about 6 in. apart and 1 in. deep and finally thin to two plants 15 in. apart. Protection from late frosts may be necessary. Water copiously and hoe regularly. Cut marrows when about 12 in. long to encourage further fruits. Some can be left until they are full size and cut before the frosts, for storing in a dry, frost-proof place.

Varieties: bush—'Green Bush' and 'White Bush'; trailing—'Long Green Trailing.'

Melons.—Although usually a glasshouse crop, melons can be grown outdoors under cloches and in frames. Seed is sown under glass in April at 60° Fahrenheit, and seedlings can be set out 3 ft. apart in early May. The soil should be manured generously and the seedlings planted on a mound of compost mixed with soil. The plants must be stopped at the fourth or fifth leaf to encourage laterals. Two can be selected to grow on and, when 18 in. long, pinched out to obtain sub-laterals, which will bear the fruit. The female flowers may require pollinating, and on a sunny day a male flower or rabbit's tail can be used to transfer the pollen; as soon as the young fruits swell, remove all but two or three per plant and pinch back the laterals bearing fruit to two leaves from the melon. A feed of dried blood once a week, with plenty of watering (though not saturation!) will help the developing fruits. Light shading may be necessary.

Varieties: 'Dutch Net' and 'Tiger.'

Mint.—Easily grown from suckers in any soil. For winter use a few pieces can be planted in a frame. A number of varieties—'Apple Mint,' 'Peppermint,' and 'Spearmint'—can be grown besides common mint.

Mushrooms.—Growing mushrooms is really a specialist occupation. For the experimental amateur, beds of composted stable-manure are made up in a warm, damp cellar or disused air-raid shelter. Pieces of spawn are inserted when the temperature of the compost has dropped to about 70° Fahrenheit and the whole bed covered with an inch of inert sub-soil. The air temperature should be from 60° to 70° Fahrenheit, and in a few weeks mushrooms may appear. Full instructions will be given with the spawn, but it is advisable to consult a text-book dealing with the culture, as even for professional growers a crop is never certain.

Mustard.—Grown exactly in the same way as cress, but is ready two or three days earlier. If used together, mustard seed should be sown two or three days after cress. Again it is the seed leaves which are eaten.

Onions.—These respond well to good cultivation. The site is dug deeply in winter manure incorporated, and left rough until February, when it is broken down to a fine tilth and firmed well. Seed can be sown ½ in. deep in drills during August and planted in March for exhibition onions, but the usual practice is to sow seed in late February outdoors or under glass in January and transplant during April in rows 12 in. apart with 6 in. between the onions, taking care to keep the bases about ½ in. below the surface. If sown outdoors and thinned the thinnings may be used in salads. Autumn-sown onions are liable to bolt, but less liable to attack by onion fly than spring-sown plants.

Dressings of a balanced feed can be applied but not after July, and in August the tops are bent over to hasten ripening. The chief pest is onion fly, the larvae of which eat the roots of the seedlings. Control can be maintained by sprinkling the seed drills with Murphy's "Gamma-BHC Dust" or applying a 4-in. band of the dust along the rows at the loop stage.

In small gardens, onion sets are popular. These are small onions grown in the previous summer, stored and replanted the next spring. Plant the bulbils 6 in. apart, leaving only the necks exposed.

Varieties: spring sowing—'Bedfordshire Champion,' 'Best of All,' and 'White Silverskin' (pickling); autumn sowing—'Giant Zittau,' 'Sutton's Solidity,' and 'White Lisbon' (salad onions); sets—'Ebenezer' and 'Stuttgarter Reisen.'

Parsley.—Sow thinly in rows 8 in. apart during March and again in July for a succession of young foliage; thin to 4 in. between plants.

Parsnip.—Grow parsnips on ground manured for a previous crop; if given fresh manure splitting and forked roots occur. Dig the soil deeply, and at sowing time in March, work the soil to a fine tilth. On a soil unsuitable for deep-rooted crops special holes 10–12 in. apart, filled with sifted soil, may be prepared. If this method has to be used four or five seeds are sown per hole; normally drills 15 in. apart and 1 in. deep are made and four or five seeds sown every 9 in. The seedlings are thinned, leaving one at each station. Parsnips should be left in the ground until needed; litter over the rows will ease lifting in frosty weather.

Varieties: 'Evesham' and 'Student.'

Peas.—Dig the ground well in autumn and add a generous amount of manure or compost. Seed sowing begins at the end of February, and can be continued at three-weekly intervals until early July. Under cloches sowings in January and October will lengthen the season. Both early and late sowings should be of a quick-maturing variety. Seed is sown in drills 6–8 in. wide and 3 in. deep, with 2 ft. between drills; the seeds can be scattered thinly in the drill or spaced 3 in. apart in a treble row. Cover with 2 or 3 in. of soil and as soon as the peas are about 2 in. high stake with twigs.

Failures are often due to attacks by birds and field-mice. The former should be discouraged by netting and the latter by trapping. Pea-sticks will be necessary for the taller varieties which should have 3–4 ft. between the rows. With limited space only the dwarf quick-maturing varieties should be used. A summer mulch will keep the soil moist, and picking should be done regularly.

Varieties: 1½–2 ft.—'Kelvedon Wonder,' 'Kelvedon Triumph,' and 'Meteor' (cloches); 2½ ft.—'Onward'; 3½–4 ft.—'Gladstone.'

Potatoes.—In general, it is only economic for the amateur to produce an early crop; the main winter supply can be grown if room and labour are available. They should be grown on land well manured the previous season, dressed at planting time with a mixed fertiliser, such as "National Growmore," at a rate of 1½ lb. to a 30-yd. row. The soil should not contain too much lime, as the damage of scab disease is increased.

"Seed" tubers about the size of a large egg are best used, and these can be bought or saved from the previous season's crop. Large potatoes may be cut leaving about three eyes to each part. New stocks should be bought occasionally if the "seed" is home saved to obviate risk of virus. "Seed" should be put in trays during February in a frost-proof shed to sprout, and in early April the "first-earlies" can be planted.

Drills 2 ft. apart and 4–5 in. deep are taken out and the sprouting "seed" planted 12 in. apart in the rows. Maincrop varieties are planted in early May 15 in. apart. The young growths should be protected from frost by earthing up slightly, and a further earthing is done as the potatoes mature. This practice of earthing prevents the tubers near the surface from becoming green when exposed to light, keeps weeds down, and protects the tubers from spores of potato blight, which are washed into the gullies. If growth is poor sulphate of ammonia can be applied at a rate of ¼ lb. per 30-yd. row. Early varieties should mature in late July and later varieties in September and October; when the tops (haulm) turn yellow the crop can be lifted, dried for a few hours (too much light will turn them green), and stored in boxes in a frost-proof shed or clamps.

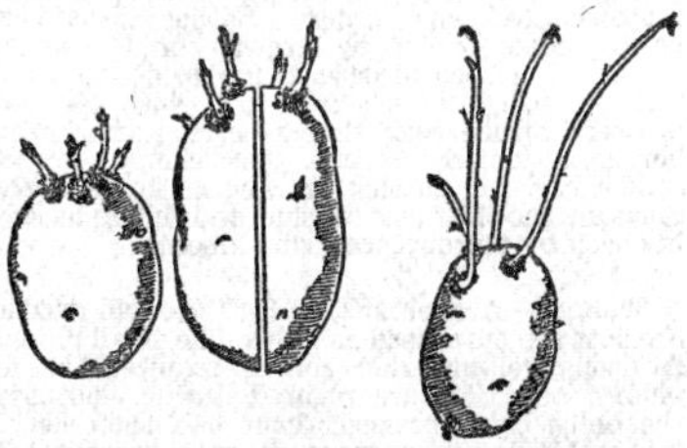

Seed Potatoes—Good seed is essential for first-rate crops. Illustration shows (*left*) a well-sprouted tuber, (*centre*) a large well-sprouted tuber suitable for cutting, and (*right*) a poor, badly sprouted tuber.

Potato blight is a common disease, and control by a spraying with maneb before the leaves touch in the rows is effective. Virus diseases, spread by greenfly, are checked by using "seed" from Scotland, where greenfly is less troublesome because of the lower temperatures. Colorado beetle should be watched for, and if found notified to the Ministry of Agriculture.

Varieties: Discerning growers will find the following well worth growing: 'Edzell Blue' (violet-coloured skin; excellent cooker), 'Pentland Dell' (white-fleshed; heavy cropper), 'Red Craigs Royal' (red-fleshed; heavy cropper), 'Ulster Chieftain' (white-fleshed, good early variety). Epicureans seeking a first-class potato should grow 'Maris Peer', a sort understandably gaining in popularity in Scotland, since its introduction. Another interesting sort is the Dutch-raised 'Record', a yellow-fleshed variety which has a trace of sweetness in its flavour.

Pumpkin.—*See* Melon.

Radish.—Although of the easiest culture, it is not grown as much as it should be due probably to the damage done by maggots of the cabbage root fly. This pest can be controlled by dusting the seed drills with Murphy's "Gamma-BHC Dust." Successional sowing can be made in the spring and again in early autumn if desired; summer-sown radish bolt, and are hot and tough.

Varieties: 'French Breakfast' (cylindrical) and 'Scarlet Globe' (round).

Rhubarb.—Before planting the ground should be generously manured and deeply dug. Crowns are planted in March, 3–4 ft. apart each way and mulched, but no rhubarb should be pulled until the following year, when a light pull can be taken. Remove any flowering shoots and give a dressing of sulphate of ammonia if growth is weak. Manure well each winter; if early supplies are needed, some of the crowns can be covered with inverted boxes or barrels and a packing of loose straw or bracken. An established, well-cultivated bed will continue almost indefinitely.

Sage.—A hardy shrub for the herb garden easily raised from cuttings. The leaves are harvested and dried in summer.

Salsify (Oyster Plant).—A winter root rather like a parsnip which requires similar growing conditions.

Savoy.—*See* **Cabbage.**

Scorzonera.—A winter root cultivated in the same way as salsify. It has a purplish root instead of the yellow-green one of salsify.

Sea-kale.—A perennial plant native to our sea-shores, which can be either grown from seed sown in March and left for two years to produce forcing crowns or from bought thongs, which are planted during March, 9 in. apart in groups of three, leaving 3 ft. between groups. During summer a manure mulch and nitrogenous fertiliser can be applied. When the tops die down in autumn the crowns are covered with boxes to force and blanch the new growths. Crowns can be covered in succession to keep a supply. Earlier sea-kale can be obtained by lifting crowns in November. These are planted in batches five or six to a pot, watered well, and a second pot, with the hole blocked, placed over them. In a warm green-house or similar position they should develop sufficiently for cutting in about three weeks. Slugs are the chief pest outside, and should be kept in check by a proprietary slug-killer.

Shallots.—A popular crop for the small garden. Shallots are purchased as bulbs, like small onions. A deep, well-manured soil is required, as for onions, and they are planted during February, the bulbs being pressed about half their length into soft soil, 6 in. apart in the rows, leaving 1 ft. between rows. In mid-July the little bunches of bulbs can be lifted. Leave them on the surface to dry for a few days and then store in a dry, frost-proof shed. Some, about the size of a shilling, should be kept for planting the following year.

Spinach.—Sowings in February to April on a well-manured soil will provide a succession during the summer. Sow in drills 1 in. deep and 12 in. apart and thin the young plants to 3 in., and then to 6 in., using the second thinning to eat.

When green vegetables are expensive, in winter, the perpetual or prickly spinach is particularly valuable. Sow in August and treat as for the summer variety.

If plants are crowded or suffer from dryness, mildew can be troublesome. Therefore thin seedlings early and water whenever necessary. On poor soils, moisture can be conserved by mulching the rows with peat. Should growth be slow feed with liquid "Maxicrop" and repeat, if required.

Varieties: 'America' and 'Giant Prickly.'

Sprouting Broccoli.—*See* **Cauliflower.**

Sugar Beet.—*See* **Beetroot.**

Swede.—*See* **Turnip.**

Sweet Corn (Maize).—Gardeners should distinguish between the types of maize used for poultry food and those which supply sweet corn for human consumption. It is wise to use cloches for growing sweet corn, as it is only half-hardy and resents transplanting. Seeds sown under cloches in mid-April in two drills 12 in. apart and 1½ in. deep should be placed 1 ft. apart in staggered positions in the rows. More robust varieties may need 15 in. from plant to plant. A soil well manured for the previous crop is best used, and a mulch can be given as soon as the plants are a few inches high. The first cobs should be ready by mid-July, and should be eaten when the cob is milky.

Variety recommended: 'John Innes Hybrid.'

Tomato.—A sunny, sheltered site is required, otherwise ripening outdoors in our climate is uncertain. Sow seeds under glass in late March and harden off the plants in a cold frame or buy plants for setting out in late May or early June. The soil should be thoroughly dug and some artificial manure applied before planting. Allow 18 in. between plants and 2½ ft. between rows, and put in a strong stake with each plant. Keep to a single stem, pinching out side shoots regularly. When four or five trusses are set pinch out the top of the main shoot.

Feed with a liquid manure during summer. Fruit which fails to ripen outdoors can be gathered and stored at about 50° Fahrenheit or the plants laid flat on the ground and covered with cloches, when the tomatoes should ripen. Under cloches plants can be planted out in mid-April instead of late May, gaining six weeks growing time, and the Cloches removed when they become too large.

Potato blight attacks tomatoes, and a spray of maneb during the first week in August and repeated after fourteen days will give a control.

Varieties: 'Market King' and 'Moneymaker'; some heavy-cropping sorts have little or no flavour and a thick skin.

Turnips.—Ground manured the previous season should be dug well and dressed with 2 oz. superphosphate per square yard. A good early variety can be sown during April in drills ¾ in. deep and 15 in. apart, followed by successional sowings at three-week intervals as required. The main crop for storage is sown in July and August, and seedlings should be thinned gradually to 10 in. apart. Use when about the size of tennis balls. A sowing can be made in September, left almost unthinned and the tops used as "greens" in spring. In autumn the storage crop is lifted and all undamaged roots put in sand in a shed or clamped. Flea beetle and turnip fly can be checked by lindane at the seedling stage.

Swedes are grown in a similar manner.

Varieties: turnips—'Early Milan' (summer) and 'Green Top Stone' (winter storage); swedes—'Purple Top.'

Standard References.

Cloche Cultivation by G. B. Walkden (Collingridge) 1955.

The Vegetable Garden Displayed (R.H.S.), 1969. Available from The Sec., Royal Hort. Soc., Vincent Sq., London, S.W.1. £1·80 (post free).

Vegetables for Garden and Exhibition, by S. M. Gault (Collingridge) 1956.

FERTILISERS AND ORGANIC MANURES.

The elements essential for healthy plant growth may be roughly grouped into classes—first, those required in some quantity, the major elements, nitrogen, potassium, and phosphorus; secondly, calcium, magnesium, and sulphur, which are required in lesser quantities; and thirdly, the trace elements, boron, manganese, iron, zinc, copper, and molybdenum, of which only minute quantities are needed. As well as the elements mentioned, others, such as silicon, aluminium, chlorine, nickel, and sodium, are often found on plant analysis, but the evidence that these are essential is inconclusive, though they may be beneficial to certain crops.

It is important to remember, when adding fertilisers to the soil, that different crops may require relatively more of one element than another, but a balance between all the elements is essential. As an instance, brassicas (the cabbage family) are gross nitrogen feeders, while root crops (*e.g.*, carrots) require far less nitrogen, and an excess may be harmful. A further point to notice is that although an element may be present in the soil the plant may be unable to absorb any because it is being kept in an insoluble state by excess of another element. An instance of this is the frequent yellow and sickly appearance of plants on very chalky soils due to lack of iron, which is present, but locked in an insoluble state by too much calcium.

The elements needed by the plant are in the form of various compounds, such as nitrates and phosphates, and may be applied as artificial fertilisers, which are manufactured, or as humus, which contains most of the foods required and also provides the essential soil micro-organisms or bacteria, without which the soil would be inert and no plants would grow. Bacteria break down the complicated animal and vegetable matter of which humus is composed to soluble compounds which plants can absorb. Humus can be supplied as farmyard and poultry manure, leaf mould, compost, sewage sludge, spent hops, and from animal by-products like hoof and horn, dried blood, meat and bone meal, and many others.

Nitrogen is mainly concerned with vegetative growth, encouraging leaf and stem formation. It is also contained in chlorophyll, the green colouring matter of the plant, and one of the symptoms of nitrogen starvation is a pale-green colour to the leaf, indicating a lack of chlorophyll. Most of the nitrogen compounds used are soluble, and it is a wise maxim to apply "little and often"; if given in large doses much is washed through the soil and wasted.

Nitrogenous fertiliser should not be given to any plant late in the season, as sappy growth, easily damaged by winter cold and frosts, is encouraged. Similarly, at no time should large quantities be given to any plant, as this results in an excess of leafy growth, which is very susceptible to disease and adverse conditions of drought and cold; also plants tend to be later flowering.

Sulphate of ammonia is the most used inorganic nitrogenous fertiliser, and is excellent for spring use on seed beds, lawns, and early crops, and it is contained in most fertiliser mixtures. It makes soils acid in reaction, and if both lime and nitrogen are required, nitro-chalk should be used instead. Other nitrogen fertilisers used are potassium nitrate, which has the advantage of supplying two major elements at once, and is very soluble, and nitrate of soda, often used on beet and mangolds. The latter chemical should not be applied in excess, as too much sodium has a bad effect on soil structure. These inorganic fertilisers are all soluble and quick acting.

As a general guide, 1 oz. of the fertiliser to a gallon of water, applied at 1 oz. per sq. yd., is a good summer dressing, given at intervals of two or three weeks. It should always be given after rain or watering, and should be applied to the soil and not to the foliage.

Among organic fertilisers containing a percentage of easily available nitrogen are dried blood, soot, and meat and fish meals. Slower to decompose, and so having a more lasting effect, are shoddy (wool waste) and hoof and horn.

Phosphorus is concerned in the plant with the production of young cells of the root and shoot, and also encourages flower and fruit production and early ripening. Most of the compounds are relatively insoluble (rendering absorption by the plant difficult), and so large amounts can be supplied without deleterious effects, especially on acid soils, where the availability is less than on alkaline soils.

Phosphorus is generally applied to the soil in the form of phosphates, and among these superphosphate of lime is quick acting, and is usually applied at 2–3 oz. per sq. yd. in spring and summer, when the need is greatest. More slow acting is basic slag, a by-product of the steel industry, sold as a fine black powder and containing, besides phosphates, many of the trace elements, as well as a considerable percentage of lime. This is good for application to acid, wet soils, but should not be applied to potatoes owing to the risk of scab disease with the increase in the content of lime. It should not be applied with sulphate of ammonia. Bonemeal is also slow acting and also contains some nitrogen. It is excellent for crops like tomatoes, and is also used extensively for ornamental and pot plants.

Potassium, the third major element, is essential for good flower colour and ripeness in fruits. Dessert apples, potatoes, cereals, and root crops all need potash in some quantity, and if excess nitrogen has been applied a dressing of potash may counterbalance the effect. Sulphate of potash is the main inorganic compound in use. Muriate of potash (potassium chloride), to which some crops are sensitive, is much less used; it should be applied as a winter dressing before the crop is sown to lose the impurities by weathering. Sulphate of potash is purer, and may be applied during the growing season at 1 oz. per sq. yd. on the vegetable plot, and is used in many proprietary fertiliser mixtures.

Wood ash contains variable quantities of potassium, and provided that the ash has not been washed by rain and the potassium leached out, is a useful addition to the soil; bracken, cut during June and July, when large amounts of potassium are present in the foliage, can be composted when green to provide a good supply of the element.

Elements Required in Lesser Quantity.—Calcium, although required in small quantities in the plant, has profound effects on the soil. Its main function in the plant is in the production of the cell walls, but in the soil it helps to bind light soils together and to make the structure of sticky clay soils finer and more workable. Also soils without calcium are acid and tend to lock up some elements in an insoluble form. Addition of calcium changes the acidity, making it slightly alkaline or neutral, and releases the locked elements.

Calcium is applied as some form or derivative of calcium carbonate, commonly known as lime, which can be obtained in various forms. Hydrated or slaked lime (calcium hydroxide) is commonly used on clay soils, and chalk or ground limestone on lighter soils. Calcium is gradually leached from the soil, and it is necessary to replace it, or the soil becomes too acid and many crops will fail to grow. A normal dressing of lime for a vegetable garden is about 4 oz. lime or ½ lb. chalk per square yard every two or three years, and is best applied in autumn as a surface dressing after digging. It should not be applied together with other fertilisers. The amount of lime will depend on the type of soil, but it must be remembered that most vegetables grow best on a slightly acid soil.

Gypsum, or calcium sulphate, is sometimes recommended to supply calcium, but its solubility is negligible, and it is preferable to chalk or limestone only on soils containing salt due to sea flooding. It was used to help reclaim districts of East Anglia flooded by sea-water during the storm surge of January 1953 by improving the soil structure. Sulphur, as sulphates, and magnesium, as an impurity in limestone, are usually present in sufficient quantiites for the plants' needs.

Trace Elements.—In the case of the trace elements most soils contain enough for the plant, but in certain circumstances deficiencies occur. Iron on very alkaline soils is insoluble and, as it is essential for the production of chlorophyll, deficiency results in the chlorosis of the leaves. It can be rectified by spraying the leaves with "Sequestrene"; likewise the lack of magnesium and manganese can be remedied where deficient on acidic soils.

Chlorosis in brassicas can be due to a deficiency of both manganese and magnesium. Boron deficiency, often occurring on light, calcareous soils, is responsible for brown heart of cauliflower and several other "diseases," mainly affecting the growing point. It can be rectified by applying borax to the soil at about 1 oz. per 15 sq. yd. Zinc and copper deficiencies are unusual in England, but lack of molybdenum has caused whiptail disease of cauliflower. Only minute quantities of the last three are required; more may be poisonous to plants and animals.

Organic Manures.—It should be noted that most of the deficiencies will not concern the amateur, especially if he keeps the ground in good heart with ample organic manure, which contains all the plant foods necessary. Well-rotted farmyard manure from cows and pigs is by far the best organic food, but is scarce now, good farmers returning it to their own land, and generally the material offered is low in nutrients. Poultry manure, which is rich in soluble nitrogen salts, is excellent either applied direct to the soil (not to the growing crop for fear of damage) or composted with straw.

There are many good substitutes for animal manure for use in generous quantities, *e.g.*, fallen leaves, seaweeds, spent hops from breweries and sawdust. With pine needles the latter is a useful inclusion in the compost heap and as a surface mulch helps to conserve soil moisture and suppress weeds. (Sawdust should not be used fresh but partially rotted.) With all these materials decomposition is speeded up by sprinkling with a nitrogenous fertiliser (*e.g.*, fish meal) at 2 oz. per sq. yd. The rough organic matter gradually breaks down to form humus, an essential ingredient for building up a rich soil structure which artificial fertilisers alone do not provide.

Among proprietary organic manures now available the seaweed-based "Maxicrop" has given good results on vegetables, flowers and lawns. Some others which mainly supply the necessary nitrogen to the soil are in the form of prepared sewage sludge which has been milled and dried. These may be bought locally at around 50p for 56 lb. Scottish gardeners are fortunate in having available a prepared by-product of the poultry industry known by the misleading name of "S.O.I.L.". In 1971 it was sold as cheap as 60p for 56 lb. and, like the others mentioned, can be used for a wide range of crops.

Compost Making.—The fertility of all soils is increased by the addition of humus. Texture too is improved, for on heavy clay drainage is sharpened and the soil lightened, while on poor sandy or chalky soils the water-holding capacity is increased.

Apart from buying humus-forming materials, like animal manure or peat, the compost heap is the most readily available source of plant food. The methods developed for making compost are numerous but all depend on three basic principles: (i) good aeration, (ii) plenty of moisture and (iii) a supply of nitrogen for the bacteria which bring about the decay of plant material.

A small compost heap can be had by making a loose-sided box about 4 ft. sq. with pieces of stout board 8 in. × 2 in., like that used by housebuilders. As the heap grows in height, so the boards can be put in place until the box is 4–5 ft. high. Use all vegetable refuse like weeds, straw, lawn mowings and kitchen waste. Contrary to some opinion, autumn leaves of all sorts can be used. Hawthorn and oak, being rich in plant food, are particularly valuable, while horse chestnut and London plane which have a thick leaf stem take longer to decompose.

When the heap is about 9 in. high it should be sprinkled with a nitrogenous fertiliser like fish meal at 2 oz. per sq. yd., watered and, if possible, covered with a layer of soil. Then the process is repeated by building up another layer. The addition of soil will keep the heap moist and is a means of introducing a population of earthworms. To keep the compost sweet, a sprinkling of lime may be applied on top of each layer of soil. There are a few proprietary compost makers on the market which are said to "accelerate" decomposition but compost made in the way described is a well proven method.

In a properly made heap grass mowings and weeds previously treated with hormone weedkillers can be used. The bulk of compost may be increased by adding a layer of newspaper for each one of plant material. (The papers must be torn up first and not applied too thickly otherwise the rate of decomposition is slowed down.)

If time permits, a completed heap can be turned over after a month or two, re-covered with soil and thoroughly watered. Otherwise it can be left until rotted and used as required, putting any unrotted material as a base for a new heap. The time taken for rotting will vary with the time of year and the vegetable material used, but, as a guide, a heap made in the early summer can be used in the winter.

General Fertiliser.—Many firms supply compound fertilisers containing given amounts of the main nutrients needed, in either liquid or powder form, and some are made up with quantities of nitrogen, potassium, and phosphorus suitable for specific crops like roses, tomatoes, and chrysanthemums. A general fertiliser which can be made up by the amateur is as follows:

7 parts by weight superphosphate.
5 parts by weight sulphate of ammonia.
2 parts by weight sulphate of potash.

A mixture of this sort may be applied at 2–3 oz. per sq. yd. for feeding shrubberies, herbaceous borders or ground where annuals are to be grown.

Green Manuring.—Another method of enriching the soil with organic matter is green manuring, which has been practised for some time by farmers and can no doubt be adapted to the gardener's purpose. Green manuring consists of planting a fast-growing catch-crop and ploughing the mature crop back into the soil. Legumes are especially good for this, as certain bacteria in their roots can "fix" the nitrogen in the air. Field peas, sown at 4–5 oz. per sq. yd. and Italian rye grass at 2 oz. per sq. yd are commonly used, while clover and annual lupins are also suitable.

If sown after an early crop on land needing organic matter the green manure may be dug in during late summer. Alternatively, if the land is not being cropped at all during the year two green-manure crops may be grown; an early sowing of field peas in April may be dug in during July, and a further sowing of field peas or Italian rye grass sown immediately after may be dug in following the first few frosts.

New chemicals often appear on the market at exorbitant prices and with fantastic claims as to their value as "soil conditioners" and the like. Contrary to this generalisation, in recent years a chemical known as "Gibberellin" has been used to increase the growth of certain plants. It is now available to the amateur, but should be used with care and mainly in a spirit of experimentation, as no conclusive proof of its efficacy has yet been put forward.

Standard References.

Fertilizers and Manures by Keith Paisley (Collingridge) 1960.
Seed and Potting Composts by Lawrence and Newell (Allen and Unwin).

GARDEN PESTS.

Every garden abounds in insects and other small creatures, but comparatively few species are pests which feed on plants. The great majority are quite harmless, while many are positively beneficial and help to keep the number of pests under control by catching and eating them. Every good gardener should make it his business to be able to differentiate between friend and foe. This is not always easy, but the speed of a creature's movements may often provide a clue. Fast-running, active creatures, such as the black ground-beetle or the centipede, are usually beneficial, while the slow-moving and sluggish ones, *e.g.*, wireworms, aphids and caterpillars, are usually pests. This is by no means an infallible rule, but it is handy to remember when in doubt.

The good gardener should also get to know the pests which are most prevalent in his district and which can be expected to crop up year after year. The first principle of good control measures is to act while an infestation is still in its early stages and before a great deal of damage is done. When one knows what to expect, steps can be taken to prevent an attack or to stop it developing to serious proportions.

Also, from the experience of past years one can often forecast whether a pest is likely to become numerous enough to make chemical treatment worthwhile. Remember, insecticides can become an expensive item, and there is little point in using them if the damage is negligible. In these circumstances insecticides may eventually increase the numbers of pests, since the treatment will also have killed off many of their natural enemies which had hitherto kept the pests under adequate control. In addition, good cultivation and general garden hygiene helps to reduce the numbers of pests.

The common pests of garden plants can be roughly divided into four main groups.

I. Root Pests.—These destroy the feeding mechanism of plants or tunnel into fleshy tap roots, tubers, and bulbs. Attacked plants make poor growth, and may eventually wilt and die.

Some insects are general root-feeders. These include (*a*) **Swift Moth Caterpillars**, soft, white caterpillars with reddish-brown heads; (*b*) **Chafer Grubs**, large, C-shaped, whitish grubs with chestnut-brown heads; (*c*) **Wireworms**, long, cylindrical, yellowish-brown grubs with a hard shiny skin; and (*d*) **Leatherjackets**, greyish-black grubs with a wrinkled, leathery skin. These are particularly prevalent in recently cultivated grassland or in gardens surrounded by fields, and will attack the roots of a wide range of plants. Chafer grubs, however, are particularly fond of the roots of shrubs, and wireworms will often tunnel in potato tubers and other fleshy roots, whereas leatherjackets prefer the roots of grasses, and may cause browning on large patches of lawn.

Badly infested ground should be dressed with lindane dust when cultivating, working the dust into the top 4 in. of soil. Where this is not possible, *i.e.*, on lawns or around established shrubs, the liquid form of the insecticide should be watered into the soil.

Cutworms are stout, fleshy caterpillars, varying in colour from greyish-brown to dingy green. They feed on roots during the day, but at night come to the surface and feed at the base of the stems of plants, causing them suddenly to collapse and wither. Brassicas and lettuce are commonly damaged in this way and the pests should be removed by hand and killed when the soil is cultivated.

Millepedes are hard-skinned, cylindrical creatures, brown or black, with numerous short, hair-like legs. They are slow-moving and curl up when disturbed. They should not be confused with the active, long-legged centipedes, which are beneficial. Millepedes commonly extend the damage made by other pests, such as slugs and wireworms. They also bore into the sown seeds of peas and beans. During the day they hide in dark, damp places, such as long vegetation or under stones and pieces of wood. Such hiding-places should be removed or dusted with lindane. Drills for pea and bean seed should also be dusted before covering.

Weevil Grubs, small, curved, white grubs, may infest the roots of pot plants and plants in rockeries. Such plants should be removed, the roots cleaned, and replanted in soil which has been dressed or mixed with lindane dust. Where it is not practicable to remove the plants they should be watered copiously with a liquid form of these insecticides and soil dressed properly at the earliest opportunity.

Slugs need no description. They vary greatly in colour. The most destructive are the underground keeled slugs, small, grey-black in colour, which tunnel in roots, tubers, and bulbs. There are also several foliage-feeding species which rasp holes in the top parts of plants. Slugs like wet conditions, and much can be done to control them by ensuring that the soil is well-drained and that long, tangled vegetation is removed.

Poison baits can be bought or made by mixing 1 oz. metaldehyde with 3 lb. bran (or bonemeal for keeled slugs). The bait is sprinkled over the infested ground or distributed in small heaps and protected from the rain. There is also available on the market a metaldehyde spray for dealing with the foliage-feeding types.

Cabbage Root Fly attacks brassicas and wallflowers. The small white maggot eats away the side roots and tunnels in the main root, causing the plant to wilt and collapse. The roots of young seedlings should be dipped in lindane before planting out. Alternatively, the plants can be given a drench of lindane within four days of planting out.

The maggots also tunnel in radishes and turnips, and this can be avoided by dusting the seed drills with lindane.

Carrot Fly.—The maggot of this fly tunnels in carrots and parsnips. Where the pest is serious it is best to delay sowing until the end of May. If possible, seeds should be sown in exposed. windy places, which are avoided by the egg-laying flies. Seedlings should be dusted or sprayed when 2–4 in. high with Murphy's "Lindex Garden Spray," an approved chemical.

Onion Fly maggots tunnel into the bulbs of onions, leeks, and shallots, causing the foliage to collapse. Dig out attacked plants carefully, ensuring that parts of them are not left in the soil, and burn them. To prevent attacks dust around the seedlings with lindane when they are at the "loop" stage, *i.e.*, about 1 in. high, and again ten days later.

Narcissus Bulb Flies are serious pests of narcissi and also snowdrops and other bulbous plants. The maggots burrow in the centre of the bulbs, causing them to rot. All soft bulbs should be burned and the remainder immersed for three hours in a solution of lindane containing a wetter. To prevent future attacks and a reinfestation, dust around the necks of growing bulbs with lindane at fortnightly intervals from the end of April until the end of June.

Insects which feed above ground include:

II. Sucking Pests pierce the tissues of plants with needle-like mouth parts and suck the sap. This devitalises the plant, checks growth, and causes wilting. Some species cause distortion of leaves and young shoots, and aphids, suckers, scale insects, and mealy bugs excrete a sugary fluid which disfigures the foliage, attracts ants, and allows the growth of sooty moulds.

Aphids, *i.e.*, blackfly, greenfly, etc., are serious pests which attack almost all plants and multiply rapidly in warm weather. They feed on the shoots and undersides of the leaves, and many species are responsible for the transmission of virus diseases. Infestations should be treated as early as possible. Malathion and nicotine both give excellent results if used properly and thoroughly to both the surface and undersides of the affected foliage. With the advent of these sprays the control of aphids on roses and broad beans, for example, is no longer a serious problem.

Tree fruits should be sprayed when the buds are bursting and again when the flower buds are still green. Currants should be treated at the "grape" stage, but lindane should not be used on this fruit. Tar oil, applied to deciduous woody plants while they are completely dormant, will kill the over-wintering stages of these and many other pests. It does not, however, give a good winter control for **Woolly Aphid** on apples. This pest is best controlled by spraying at the pink-bud stage with B.H.C. with a succinate spreader added. Small colonies on the bark can be eradicated by painting with 10% tar oil.

Some aphids feed underground on roots, particularly of lettuces, currants, and cacti. Where practicable, infested plants should be lifted and the roots cleaned and sprayed before replanting in clean soil. Otherwise water them copiously with malathion or lindane.

Scale Insects are often found in greenhouses, but also occur out-of-doors on trees and shrubs. Flat or dome-shaped, these creatures spend most of their lives immobile, and they do not at all resemble insects, or even appear to be alive. Again tar oil is useful for killing the overwintering stages on deciduous woody shrubs which are dormant. Plants which are in leaf should be sprayed with malathion or nicotine/white oil emulsion two or three times at fortnightly intervals. These substances are more effective if as much as possible of the scale is first removed by means of a sponge, brush, or scraper with water in which soft soap has been dissolved. **Mealy Bugs** are common pests of greenhouse plants, and should be given the same treatment as scale insects.

Capsid Bugs are very active insects which cause considerable damage to fruit trees and bushes and also to various ornamental plants, principally chrysanthemums and dahlias. They feed on the young leaves, causing distortion and raggedness, and on the buds, which later produce misshapen blooms. These insects, green or reddish in colour, can be controlled by spraying with lindane when the flower buds are still green as, for instance, on fruit trees. Herbaceous plants should be sprayed twice or three times at three-weekly intervals, starting when the plants are young and before the damage is seen. Less persistent insecticides which can be used in this case are malathion and nicotine.

Leafhoppers are small, yellowish-green insects like aphids but much more active. They feed on the undersides of the leaves of a variety of plants, causing them to become speckled with yellow. Roses are commonly attacked. The treatment given to capsids on herbaceous plants will control these also, the sprays being directed to the undersides of the leaves.

Whiteflies are serious pests in greenhouses, and also occur out-of-doors on rhododendrons and other evergreen shrubs The adults are like miniature moths with white wings, and the young are small, scale-like creatures, generally greenish in colour, which feed without movement on the undersides of the leaves. To control all whiteflies lindane or malathion should be used as a spray or smoke, two to three applications being given at fortnightly intervals.

Red Spider Mites are extremely small creatures, red or greenish in colour and just visible with the naked eye. They feed on the undersides of the leaves of many greenhouse and outdoor plants, including fruit, causing the leaves to turn sickly yellow. Control is difficult, the most effective materials being malathion, derris, summer ovicides, or azobenzene smoke. The directions on the labels of these products should be followed carefully.

III. Biting Insects have chewing and biting mouth parts which are used to cut away pieces of plants.

Caterpillars (the young stages of moths and butterflies) are the best-known pests in this group. They vary in size and colour according to the species, and most plants are liable to be attacked. These should be sprayed or dusted with derris as soon as the damage is noticed.

On apple and pear trees caterpillars can cause serious trouble and, in this case, treatment should take the form of a pre-blossom spray with trichlorphon.

The greatest problem with caterpillars arises with the well-known large and small white butterflies which in some seasons skeletonise the leaves. The worst damage is in the late summer when the infestation has built up to its highest point. Control is laborious; crush the egg clusters of the large butterfly and remove colonies of caterpillars by hand. As far as chemical control is concerned, this should be restricted to the use of derris up to within two weeks of picking. In recent years various other chemical controls have been suggested and applied on a large scale but their use is not now recommended unless specific approval has been granted. *See* T31.

Sawfly Caterpillars are very similar to those above, and commonly attack gooseberry and rose foliage. They can be controlled by spraying with malathion or derris.

Attacks by the **Apple Sawfly**, which burrows in young apples and forms ribbon-like scars on the skin, can be prevented by spraying with lindane seven days after 80% of the blossom has fallen.

Beetles and Weevils which feed on foliage are usually best controlled by spraying or dusting with derris. To kill the tiny **Flea-beetles** which eat small holes in the seedlings of brassicas and turnips, treat the plants at fourteen-day intervals until they reach the "rough-leaf" stage.

The golden-brown **Raspberry Beetle**, which feeds on the flowers and whose grub tunnels in the fruit, is best eradicated with derris applied ten days after full bloom and again ten days later. For other common pests in this group, *e.g.*, **Vine Weevil, Clay-coloured Weevil, Pea and Bean Weevil**, etc., apply the derris as soon as the damage is first seen

Earwigs feed at night on the foliage and flower petals of many plants. They hide by day inside flowers, in the folds of leaves, and in nooks and crannies on the ground, under flat stones, etc. These pests are killed by derris applied to the plants (but not to open flowers) and to their hiding-places.

Leaf Miners are very small grubs which tunnel between the upper and lower surfaces of leaves, forming pale blisters, as on lilac, holly, celery, etc., or long, twisting galleries, as on chrysanthemum, pea, and tomato. In small infestations the affected leaves should be picked off and burned. Otherwise spray with lindane as soon as the damage starts, giving three applications at fourteen-day intervals.

IV. Eelworms are microscopic pests which are invisible to the naked eye. They are able to live for very long periods without food and are extremely difficult to eradicate. The most common species are:

Stem and Bulb Eelworm, which infests narcissus, phlox, strawberry, hyacinth, onion, and other plants. Infested plants show distorted foliage and dwarfing and gradually deteriorate. They can only be sterilised by immersion in hot water kept at well-defined temperatures for one to three hours, but expert diagnosis and advice should be obtained before this or any other control is attempted. Infested ground must be kept clear of any host plants for at least three years to starve out the eelworms.

Chrysanthemum Eelworm causes the formation of yellowish blotches between the veins of chrysanthemum leaves, which later turn black and drop off. In severe infestations the blooms are undersized and malformed. Expert advice should be obtained before control measures are attempted.

Potato Root Eelworm is a serious and widespread pest of potatoes, causing the plants to become stunted and sickly, giving very poor yields. The pest can only be kept in check by crop rotation, potatoes being grown on the same ground only once in four years. This is difficult in small gardens, and where land becomes heavily infested the only remedy is to rest it from potatoes for at least five years.

The Purchase and Use of Insecticides.—To ensure that an insecticide will do what the maker claims, it is advisable only to buy brands which have been tested and approved by the Ministry of Agriculture. This can be ascertained from the Approval Mark (T31) on the label. Read the directions and following them carefully. Never apply insecticides to flowers in bloom, otherwise many valuable pollinating insects will be killed.

Standard References.

Encyclopaedia of Garden Pests and Diseases, by van Konynenburg and Lawfield (Collingridge), 1958.

Gardening Chemicals. Lists of insecticides, fungicides, herbicides, etc., listed under trade names. Available from The Sec., Royal Hort. Soc., Vincent Sq., London, S.W.1, 1967.

Horticultural Pests: Detection and Control, by G. Fox Wilson, revised by P. Becker (Crosby Lockwood), 1960.

DISEASES OF PLANTS.

Plant diseases are important because they can cause great loss not only in growing crops but also in the produce after it has been harvested and stored. The skill in growing crops is wasted if they are destroyed by disease, and many people know the wastage of potatoes through blight disease in winter stores and rotting of onions when they decay through neck rot disease. For these reasons the keen gardener must take notice of diseases and use the knowledge available to him in checking them wherever possible.

The most important point to remember about plant diseases is to recognise the first signs so that the remedy can be applied at once. In greenhouses this is of great importance because the atmosphere is warm and moist, and in such conditions diseases flourish. It must also be remembered that the same crop is often grown in the same soil in a greenhouse so that we get a build-up of disease, and this causes the well-known "soil sickness." This means that new soil must be brought in or the old soil enriched and also sterilised by steam or by chemicals. Even frames and propagating pits require periodic cleaning up by a disinfection treatment.

Unlike insect pests, the actual cause of a plant disease cannot be seen with the naked eye, and microscopic examination is required for its detection. The scientists who study diseases are called plant pathologists, and these are stationed

THE APPROVAL MARK—An officially approved crop-protection product shows on its label this design.

at universities and other institutes throughout the country, where they carry out research on various plant troubles and advise on suitable remedies for checking them. It is obviously necessary to understand the exact cause of a disease and how that cause operates before a means of checking the trouble can be devised. The advice can then be passed on to growers, farmers, and the gardening public.

The presence of disease in most cases can only be detected by the symptoms shown by the affected plant, which is called the "host" plant. The actual cause must then be determined by careful examination in the laboratory, which is done by the pathologist.

Plant diseases in general are divided into three classes as follows: 1. Fungus and Bacterial. 2. Virus. 3. Functional Disorders.

1. Fungus and Bacterial Diseases.—The first kind called fungus diseases are caused by the attack of fungus parasites; examples being the well-known club root of cabbages, potato scab, apple scab, and plum brown rot. These parasitic fungi are microscopic and composed of fine threads, but they attack plants and penetrate them either through wounds (insect bites, hail damage, pruning cuts) or directly through the surface cells (epidermis). The threads grow into the plant, killing the cells and absorbing their contents. There is usually some discoloration or even decay of the tissues around the point of infection, but it is possible for the plant to show distress in one part although the parasite is at work some distance away. Examples are silver leaf in plums and the honey fungus, which kills trees by attacking the roots.

The fungus spreads by means of spores which are equivalent to seeds in flowering plants but which are microscopic in size. These spores are produced on the surface of the plant in enormous numbers and are blown (wind), splashed (rain), or carried (insects, etc.) in all directions to alight on other healthy plants, where they germinate and spread the disease. This occurs in the growing season, but when winter approaches, the parasite forms tough, resting bodies of one kind or another, and these are resistant to extreme cold.

They overwinter in the soil or in the surface of tree bark, etc., so that in the following spring they can germinate and cause disease again. So we get the reappearance of such troubles as damping off in seedlings, scab in apples, brown rot in apples and plums, foot rot in peas, wart disease in potatoes, mildews on all kinds of plants, and so on. This question of soil contamination by overwintering spores is one of the most serious in the fight against plant disease.

The signs of fungus and bacterial diseases are varied, and may show as yellowing, silvering, brown spotting, or blackening of leaves (potato blight, rose black spot, celery leaf spot, antirrhinum rust), as stunting (cabbage wire stem), as pustules and cankers in stems (coral spot, apple canker), as gumming or dieback in branches (rose canker, plum dieback), as galls, warts, witches brooms, or other malformation (club root in cabbages, crown gall, leafy gall, peach leaf curl), as dry or soft rots of fruits, tubers, vegetable bulbs, and corms (gladiolus dry rot, potato dry rot, iris rhizome rot, celery heart rot), and many other abnormal conditions. Sometimes only a part of the plant is affected and can be removed, *e.g.*, branches showing attack by coral spot or one of the large bracket fungi seen on trees, these having gained entrance through a wound.

2. Virus Diseases.—This class of disease is becoming increasingly important as more is discovered about them, although research on them is a comparatively recent development. A virus disease is caused by infection with a virus, and the exact nature of this is not yet clearly understood, but it is so small that it cannot be seen with ordinary microscopes. Its detection is therefore not easy, but when the sap of a virus-diseased plant is injected into a healthy one it causes the disease.

In nature this spread is brought about by biting and sucking insects, which are referred to as Vectors. They transmit the virus by feeding on infected plants and then travelling to healthy ones, on which they feed and so spread the disease. Most viruses are transmitted by aphids (greenflies).

In the garden and nursery they can be carried from plant to plant by pruning knives or by the fingers in the process of trimming plants such as tomatoes, melons, and cucumbers or by the use of the knife in taking cuttings. In general, the virus does not kill a plant quickly but tends to cripple it and cause a slow deterioration. Infected plants cannot recover but remain, sometimes for years, as sources of infection on which insects feed and carry on the disease. So viruses may increase in lily stocks, strawberry beds, and raspberry plantations unless virus-infected plants are removed and aphids strictly suppressed.

The signs of virus disease are of different kinds, but the commonest are those of the type called mosaic, in which the leaves show a mottling with light-green or yellow patches scattered in irregular fashion on the darker green of the leaf. There may be also some reduction in the leaf blades. These symptoms can be seen in the mosaic of cucumber, vegetable marrow, lettuce, cabbage, turnip, tomato, delphinium, primula, dahlia, apple, raspberry, and many other common plants. In some, such as lilies, daffodils, and onions, the mosaic is more in the form of stripes down the leaf blades.

Another virus symptom is flower "breaking," where the normal colour of the petals is broken by streaks and spots of white, and this can be seen in tulip, wallflower, pansy, stocks, or carnations affected by the mosaic virus. Other viruses cause bronzing of the top leaves (as in tomato spotted wilt) or small light-coloured rings arranged in concentric circles (as in dahlia ring spot) or even reduction of leaves until they are tendril like (as in tomato fern leaf). Sometimes there is malformation or even proliferation, producing innumerable stunted shoots, as in blackberry dwarf disease.

The important point to note about these virus diseases is that every part of the plant is quickly infected, so that the sap is infectious to other plants of the same kind. The virus is present in all parts, and for this reason it is useless to propagate from a virus-infected plant. This means that all the scales and offsets from bulbs such as lilies and tulips, all the tubers from potatoes, and all cuttings from herbaceous plants which are taken from a virus-infected plant are useless, because they will carry the virus. They should be destroyed, and the only exception is where the plant is greatly valued, in which case seed can be taken from it before it is destroyed. In general, viruses do not travel in the seed, and only in one or two cases is seed infected, and this only in negligible quantity.

3. Functional Disorders.—This third class of disease is often called non-parasitic, because unlike the previous two kinds there is no parasite involved, and these troubles are therefore not infectious. They are due to faulty cultivation or unsuitable environment, in which soil conditions or climate affect the plants adversely. In this group we include cases of unsatisfactory growth due to waterlogging, drought, frost, high temperature, damage by fumes or atmospheric pollution, or even excess lime.

Perhaps the most important kinds of trouble in this class are the so called **Deficiency Diseases**, where the plants suffer from shortage of some important food. This may be one of the common food substances, such as nitrogen, potash, or phosphate, and details will be found under the section on manures and fertilisers (T26).

CONTROL OF DISEASES.

1 Garden Hygiene.—The control of plant diseases can be dealt with only briefly, but to begin with we must emphasise the value of good cultivation as an insurance against losses from disease. Robust plants are better able to stand up to disease than sickly ones, and everything in the way of proper drainage, soil aeration, proper spacing, sensible feeding, and so on, will help to keep the plants vigorous, and this is the first line of defence against diseases. Garden hygiene is important, weeds need to be kept down, wounds in trees and shrubs covered with a good paint against infection, new stocks examined carefully, seed bought only from reliable sources, diseased plants burnt, and dead material regularly removed from plants, especially in greenhouses.

2. Soil Sterilisation.—There are other precautions, among which the sterilisation of the soil in greenhouses by means of steam or chemicals is of some importance. Dazomet can be used outside but rotation of crops is a most useful system in helping to avoid disease. Disinfection of frames, propagating pits, and seed boxes by formalin or cresylic acid are other useful measures.

All these operations aim at destroying the resting spores of fungus parasites responsible for such diseases as tomato leaf mould, gladiolus dry rot, damping off in seedlings, root rots, and downy mildews of many kinds in young plants such as stocks, cheiranthus, cineraria, tomato, aster, and calceolaria when grown in boxes or pots.

3. Disease Resistant Plants.—The use of disease-resistant varieties of plants is very desirable, but there are not many kinds available, and often the resistant kind does not possess flowers or fruit of such fine quality or flavour as the more susceptible kind. The outstanding success of this kind is that of potatoes immune to the dreaded wart disease, and these can be grown safely in the most heavily infected land. There are antirrhinums resistant to rust disease, and there is resistance in some degree in the case of delphinium mildew, potato blight, tomato leaf mould, and some others. Research goes on to discover still more, because any such plants are always worth a trial.

4. Treatment of Seeds and Bulbs.—For seed-borne diseases seed treatments may be done with captan or thiram seed dressings, or even by immersion of the infected seed in warm water.

In some diseases, for example, tulip fire, we can protect the bulbs from the danger of infected soil by raking in a powder such as "Botrilex" when planting the bulbs, and a similar treatment is done with calomel dust against club root in beds intended for sowing brassica seeds.

5. Fungicides.—Even after all this, a disease may still appear in the crop, and more direct action must be taken. It is then necessary to protect the plants by means of a **Fungicide**. This is a chemical which is poisonous to fungus parasites but which will not harm the crop plant (host). Fungicides are used as wet sprays or in powder form as dusts, and they are sprayed or dusted all over the plants to protect them from infection by diseases.

The object of the treatment is to cover the plants with a film of the fungicide so as to protect the still healthy ones. To help the spray fluid to spread over and adhere to the foliage another substance, called a wetter, spreader, or sticker, is added to the spray, but sometimes this is already included by the manufacturer.

5. (*a*) Sprays.—Sprays are applied by means of machines called sprayers which vary from small, hand-syringe types giving a continuous jet of spray to those pumped up to a pressure and carried on the back (knapsack machines), and so on to the large machines driven by a petrol engine, which deliver the spray at a high pressure. It is necessary to have a suitable nozzle giving a fine mist-like cone of spray which settles on the foliage and is not wasted.

5. (*b*) Dusts.—Dusts are similar chemicals produced in such finely divided form that the powder can be blown over and on the foliage almost like a fog. This is best done after a shower of rain or after a heavy dew. The machines used are far more varied in design than spraying machines. There are small hand dusters worked either like a small pump or like a bellows, of which the "Acme" is a good example, and there are those which are carried on the back and worked as a double-bellows action or on the front of the body with a rotary-fan action. It is important in gardens to clean and dry the machines after use, and small sprayers may be best put upside down to drain for a time after use.

The substances used as sprays and dusts against plant diseases for many years have been copper and sulphur and their compounds. Perhaps the best known copper-containing spray is "Bordeaux Mixture," which is still a good spray, but which has been largely replaced by liquid copper available as "Murphy's Liquid Copper Fungicide" for such diseases as tomato blight, etc. Sulphur is used extensively as lime-sulphur against apple scab and as colloidal sulphur against the powdery mildew diseases. As dusts, copper is mixed with lime to give copper–lime dust and sulphur is used alone either as flowers of sulphur or green sulphur.

5. (*c*) The Newer Fungicides.—In recent years much research has been carried out in tests to see whether other chemicals have value as fungicides, and the search has been in the field of organic chemistry and among all kinds of these chemicals. Tests of this kind take a long time, but a few substances have already been picked out as showing special promise and we can mention captan which is so good against apple and pear scab, zineb against tomato leaf mould, onion mildew and tulip fire and dinocap against any of the powdery mildews such as American gooseberry mildew, strawberry mildew, vine mildew as well as the same diseases on ornamental roses, delphiniums, michaelmas daisies and other plants.

6. Control of Viruses.—The control of virus diseases is very different, because in this case the only spray treatments likely to be of use are those designed to keep down insects. The other necessary control measure is to remove and destroy the virus-infected plants, which are a danger as sources of infection.

This is best done when the plants are young, so

that any young marrows, cucumbers, dahlias, delphiniums, sweet peas, lupins, lilies, etc., which show virus symptoms as commonly revealed in mottling and stunted growth, are removed early on.

Propagation should be done carefully, so that young stock is not propagated from stocks of strawberries, raspberries, and all kinds of herbaceous perennials which show signs of virus infection.

7. Prevention of Functional Disorders.—In the case of Functional Disorders (non-parasitic diseases) it is not always easy to advise remedies. Where the soil conditions are faulty attention can be directed to improving drainage if necessary or counteracting dryness by digging in humus, irrigating, and general mulching. Dryness at the roots of tomatoes causes loss of fruit, and so does extreme dryness in the air of the greenhouse, but these should be adjusted fairly easily.

Hail damage can spoil many crops, but robust foliage may help a little to lessen the damage. Late frost damage to fruit in some areas can be lessened by various methods of cultivation and planting. The effects of drought can be aggravated by shortage of certain foods, especially potash, so that even here some attempt can be made to avoid loss. Excess liming may cause food shortages by causing the appearance, in the leaves, of a yellowish or even whitish colour, which is known as lime-induced chlorosis. The real reason may be lack of iron or manganese due to the excess lime in the soil, but recently very good results at counteracting this condition have been obtained by using the substance known as "Sequestrene."

Another method of treating these food shortages is to spray the young foliage in early summer with the required element in a very weak solution. They can even be included in sprays used for keeping down diseases or pests. It must not be forgotten that even the ordinary foods, such as nitrogen, potash, and phosphate, may sometimes be in short supply, and the effect can be seen by the trained plant pathologist. In these cases the effect may not always show clearly in the growing crop, but may appear long afterwards in the stored fruits and vegetables, which as a result deteriorate and break down long before they are required for use.

The present-day methods of cultivating large numbers of the same plant in one spot tend to increase the risk of large-scale disease attacks. Modern plants may be highly bred and selected for great purity of strain. Indeed, they have often been chosen for fine quality and flavour, with little regard to their ability to resist disease, so that the gardener must always be ready to give them the protection they may need.

Standard References.

Diseases of Vegetables, by Donald E. Green (Macmillan), 1946.

Directory of Garden Chemicals, Brit. Agrochemicals Ass., 93 Albert Embankment, London, SE1 7TU (price 50 p., post free), 1976.

Insecticide and Fungicide Handbook, Ed. Hubert Martin (Blackwell), 1968.

USES OF MODERN WEEDKILLERS.

The eradication of weeds by chemical means is one of the greatest advances of recent years albeit the value of herbicides is still unappreciated by most gardeners. With a planned programme, all cultivated ground and lawns can be kept free of weeds without hoeing or any other sort of manual cultivation.

Occasionally troubles have arisen in not following makers' instructions. Sometimes the damage has been most unfortunate, as the majority of herbicides are toxic, in varying degrees, to a wide range of plant life. In the main, controls are determined by circumstance, as typified in the following cases:

Asparagus Beds.—Annuals and top growth of perennial weeds can be controlled with cresylic acid in the autumn and before the asparagus appears in the spring. In beds free of perennials, a first-class control of weeds can be maintained with Simazine applied in the early spring.

Where annual and perennial grasses predominate, Dalapon or Diquat will give good control. As for bindweed, this may be eradicated by watering the foliage with 2,4-D in late July or August taking care to avoid contact with the asparagus stems and particularly the fern.

Fruit Garden.—Around fruit trees and bushes, grasses and perennial weeds can be controlled with diquat. This only kills the foliage but repeated applications during the growing season will clear the ground. Once free of perennials, annual weeds may be controlled effectively by an application of simazine each spring.

Garden Paths.—The introduction of new herbicides has made the control of weeds in garden paths an easy matter. For the purpose, mixtures of different herbicides are available in small packs under the names of "Kilweed" and "Super Weedex." As both contain simazine they remain active in the soil for a long period killing off germinating seedlings. For this reason, once paths have been cleared of weeds an annual application is all that is required to prevent a reinfestation.

Success is dependent on careful use as the herbicides must be distributed evenly, at the correct dosage in the spring and early summer. They are used in solution and application is made by a can with a fine rose or, better still, with a sprinkler bar attachment.

Lawns.—The majority of weeds in turf can be eradicated easily with formulations of 2,4-D or M.C.P.A. (*see* **Finding List**). In particular, daisies, dandelions, plantains, and most broad-leaved weeds are susceptible although it may be necessary to repeat the dose after 10 days. The best time to do the work is on a warm, fine day in the spring when the plants are growing actively and there is the prospect of fine weather to follow for twenty-four hours.

The action of the herbicides is rapid and grass may be cut after a couple of days, composting with mowings in the normal way. It appears that the hormones are not injurious to bacterial life in the soil and in a few weeks break down into harmless substances.

Where bulbs are naturalised in grass, steps to control weeds should not be taken until the foliage of the bulbs has died down and the bulbs are dormant. Thus, as a general rule, control measures are best applied throughout July.

To deal with weeds in turf where there arises the danger of the spray—or even a drift from it—touching cultivated plants nearby, as, for instance on grass paths in a rose garden then one of the plastic cans filled with a solution of hormone can be used to spot-treat weeds.

Some weeds are resistant to normal doses of hormones and need special treatment. These are mostly mat-forming plants of low-growing habit generally found in poor soils and which are not cut off by mowing. Typical examples include mosses of all sorts, yarrow, and yellow-flowered clover. Here, the main control must be in the use of lawn sand, a good mixture of which can be made up with:

2 parts by weight sulphate of ammonia.
1 part by weight sulphate of iron
13 parts by weight LIME-FREE sand.

Where moss is the most prevalent weed, to the mixture should be added sufficient superphosphate to give 1 oz. of it per sq. yd. for the area to be treated. Alternatively, patches of moss can be dusted with a formulation of mercurous chloride like "Mos-Tox." This will kill the weed but generous feeding should be given to prevent reinfestation.

Applications of lawn sand to weeds should be made when the turf is damp and there is the prospect of fine weather; if a period of drought follows an application, then water should be applied to avoid serious scorching. Repeat the treatment as necessary throughout the growing season.

Linked with this "spot" treatment, the growth of grass must be encouraged, as this will tend to smother low-growing weeds. Thus, in the early spring when the turf is wet, feed with a mixture of equal parts or superphosphate, sulphate of ammonia and dry soil at 2 oz. per sq. yd. over the whole area and repeat after a month, if desirable. In addition, do *not* shave off the grass by close cutting instead, the blades of the mower should be set reasonably high for a whole season.

Where fertility is low, clovers often predominate in turf. The Dutch clovers with white—or pink—flowers and a white-angled band towards the base of each leaflet, can be eradicated with Mecoprop. Afterwards the turf should be fed with nitrogenous fertilisers like soot and sulphate of ammonia, to discourage reinfestation. Other types of clover found in turf are species of *Trifolium*. Compared to the Dutch clover, these have a tight, bunched habit of growth and yellow flowers. All of them are resistant to hormones and, in addition to manurial treatment, should be treated with lawn sand.

Lakes.—It sometimes happens that aquatic plants with large floating leaves, such as water lilies, get out of hand. Here, control can be established by cutting off the foliage with a long-handled appliance like the "Corypu Water Scythe." The work should be done early in June and repeated as often as any fresh growth is seen.

Bulrushes are difficult to eliminate, but can be destroyed by digging out the roots when the level of the water permits. Dalapon has been found to give a control; applications should be made, with a wetting agent added, when the rushes reach maturity.

Ponds.—Problems of weed control in ornamental ponds are often not easy to solve. Where duckweed is prevalent this small floating plant can be eliminated by sweeping the surface of the water at regular intervals. If this practice is carried out thoroughly much of the vegetative growth will be eliminated, and the plant will not be able to form resting bodies whereby it overwinters. Once a control has been established, further spread of the plant can be prevented by introducing a few moorhens or ornamental ducks.

The most common of unwanted plants in pools is blanket weed. There is no single means of dealing with this plant, for its spread is governed, to a certain extent, by unbalanced plant and animal life in the water. With this fact in mind, water lilies should be established so that their foliage shades about 25 per cent of the water. In addition, a few oxygenating plants should be introduced from local ponds or streams and a supply of goldfish added. Blanket weed is usually found in pools where the water gets overheated in summer; for this reason, the average depth of garden ponds should be a minimum of 2 ft. and preferably a minimum of 3 ft.

Rose Beds.—A complete control of annual weeds among roses can be obtained with Simazine. Here, the salient point is to apply the herbicide immediately after pruning in March *before* any weed growth starts. Alternatively, Diquat can be used in April or early May and the application repeated as necessary.

Shrubberies.—With a shortage of labour, beds of shrubs are often weed infested. Perennials can be eradicated with Diquat and annuals controlled by this treatment as they appear. Alternatively, once the perennials are removed, the ground can be kept clear with Simazine used in the early spring.

Much to check weeds in shrubberies can be done by mulching the surface of the soil with heavy dressings of peat, fallen leaves, or sawdust; if the weeds push through the mulch, a second application should be made at once.

Vacant Ground.—On land free of crops all plants can be killed by watering the herbage with sodium chlorate at 1 lb. to a gallon of water. In some cases repetition may be necessary. When using this method it should be remembered that treated ground will remain toxic to plant life for a period of up to six months; if doubt exists about the persistence of the chlorate in the soil, then it is advisable to wait for the appearance of annual weeds before planting.

Apart from its persistence, sodium chlorate is prone to seep through soil and affect plants for some distance away. To avoid danger of fire from clothes being soaked in a solution of the chlorate and then dried, it is prudent to use a formulation with an additive to reduce the risk of fire. (*See* **Finding List.**) Where couch grass is predominant then the best control is to be obtained with Dalapon.

SPECIAL PROBLEMS OF WEED CONTROL.

Bindweed.—Probably the most ubiquitous of all garden weeds. Up to the present time the main control has been to carefully fork out the roots as new growth is seen; if this is done methodically the plant can be eliminated within a reasonable time.

Lately, chemicals have come to the fore, and bindweed may now be eliminated by watering or painting the foliage with a formulation of 2,4-D when the annual growth has nearly reached maturity. Thus, first applications can be applied in July and the treatment repeated, if necessary, to good effect. Where the weed is among cultivated plants, the herbicides must be applied with a paint brush or the foliage rubbed with a cloth damped in a solution. When doing this rubber gloves should be worn.

Blanket Weed.—*See* **Ponds.**

Bracken.—Horticulturally, control is not a big problem, and in limited areas it is easily dealt with by repeatedly cutting the aerial stems with a grass hook as the first fronds open. This practice will exhaust the underground food supply of the plant, and gradually it will die out. The young fronds are rich in plant food and, while still green and fresh, they should be composted. On large areas, spraying with "Asulox" offers a good control. The chemical can be ordered from any sundriesman but it is only available in gallon cans.

Couch Grass.—Where the soil is light and tends to be low in fertility, it is often found that this is a difficult plant to eradicate by cultural means. If the long, underground stems are forked out in the conventional manner and left on the surface to dry, the roots may be composted to advantage and a good control established. To prevent reinfestation, manures and fertilisers should be applied generously and the ground kept hoed regularly.

Chemically, couch grass can be killed easily by watering the foliage with Dalapon.

Ground Elder.—Without question this is one of the worst garden weeds and, whether or not the fact is pleasant or acceptable, it is indubitably a weed of neglected ground. In varying degrees it is resistant to hormone weed-killers of all sorts. On ground free of crops it may be reduced by an application of sodium chlorate, as explained in the paragraph **Vacant Ground.** The first treatment should be made as soon as growth starts in the spring and repeated if the desired effect is not abundantly clear. When ground elder is to be found among herbaceous plants the cultivated plants must be lifted out and the weed removed by repeated hand-forking.

In shrubberies reasonable control can be had by smothering the young growth in the spring with a thick dressing of peat, leaf mould, baled straw, or sawdust. If growth penetrates the surface dressing it will be found that the etiolated shoots are not difficult to remove by hand, or a second layer can be applied to complete the treatment.

Alternatively, the foliage of ground elder can be watered with Diquat and the treatment repeated once or twice during the growing season.

Horsetail.—This is sometimes erroneously called marestail and on poor, sandy soils it is often a common weed. Fortunately, recent experiments have proved that it can be easily controlled by spraying or painting the *mature* growths with a formulation of 2,4-D, taking care, of course, to keep the spray off cultivated plants near by. As the appearance of horsetail is symptomatic of low fertility, manurial treatment should be carried out on a generous scale. Where the weed is growing among cultivated crops, individual stems must be treated separately as recommended for bindweed.

Marestail.—*See* **Horsetail.**

Moss.—*See* **Lawns (T33 and T36).**

Nettles.—It is difficult to understand why the perennial nettle is so abundant as it is immediately responsive to applications of 2,4-D and 2,4,5-T made any time during the growing season. The annual nettle is usually proved a denizen of rich, light soils and may be eradicated with cresylic acid, Diquat or 2,4-D.

Oxalis.—Of all weeds this is probably the most difficult to destroy. It is easily identified by its large, trifoliolate leaves like that of clover. Unlike other weeds, oxalis cannot be efficiently removed by hand, as this disturbs the bulbils clustered around the base of the stem of mature plants. On ground free of crops, sodium chlorate can be applied in March (*see* **Vacant Ground**). Perhaps a second application may be necessary, but, even so, control may not be complete. Among shrubby plants, it may be possible to eradicate the weed by smothering, as suggested in the paragraph on ground elder.

The foliage can be killed with Diquat and, by repeated applications, this may constitute the best means of control.

Speedwell.—*See* **Veronica.**

Veronica.—This procumbent, blue-flowered weed of turf is sometimes known as speedwell. Until recently difficult to control. Now effectively eradicated with Ioxynil. (*See* **T36**).

Woody Plants.—With or without the addition of 2,4-D, these may be killed with 2,4,5-T. This hormone is particularly useful on bramble, gorse, ivy, and other unwanted shrubby plants. It is necessary to thoroughly saturate the foliage of deciduous trees, and the best results are obtainable when the leaves are fully mature but not starting to die off. In the case of ivy, the dormant shoots should be generously sprayed for the best results.

Yarrow.—A weed found in many lawns where its presence often signifies low fertility. Control is with lawn sand. *See* **Lawns (T33).**

Summary.—From these notes it will be seen that there are many aids for dealing with weeds. The salient point is to get the *right* method for *each* plant. Equally important is to check the reason why certain weeds grow profusely under some conditions. Very often this natural tendency can be counteracted as in the case of phosphatic fertilisers against moss and in the application of organic manures and chemical fertilizers where horsetail and yarrow are concerned.

Standard References.

Chemicals for the Gardener, H.M. Stationery Office, 1965.

List of Approved Products for Farmers and Growers (published annually), copies free from Ministry of Agriculture, Fisheries, and Food (Publications), Tolcarne Drive, Pinner, Middlesex.

Weed Control Handbook, issued by the British Weed Control Council (Blackwell), 1965.

HORTICULTURAL SOCIETIES.

There are many specialist societies in Britain. Detailed information on particular plants is normally available from them, and membership is open to all wishing to join. The most prominent societies are:

Alpine Garden Society
Sec. Michael Upward Lye End Link, St John's, Woking, Surrey.

Auricula and Primula Society, The National
Sec. D. Hadfield, 146 Queen's Rd., Cheadle, Cheshire.

Begonia Society, The National
Sec. F. J. Martin, 50 Woodlands Farm Road, Erdington, Birmingham 24.

Cactus and Succulent Society of Great Britain
Sec. R. H. I. Read, 5 Wilbury Avenue, Cheam, Surrey.

Camellia Society, The International
Sec. Roger Gray, 9, Hanover Avenue, North Epping 2121, New South Wales, Australia.

Carnation Society, The British National
Sec. Mrs. G. F. How, 56 Kingston Road, Romford, Essex.

Chrysanthemum Society, The National
Sec. S. G. Gosling, 65 St Margaret's Avenue, Whetstone, N.20.

Daffodil Society, The
Sec. D. J. Pearce, 1 Noak's Cross Cottages, Great Braxted, Witham, Essex.

Dahlia Society, The National
Sec. P. Damp, 26 Burns Road, Lillington, Leamington Spa, Warwickshire.

Delphinium Society, The
Sec. J. H. Seager, Birklands, Douglas Grove, Lower Bourne, Farnham, Essex.

Floral Arrangement Societies of Great Britain, National Association of
Sec. Mrs. F. C. Dobson, 21A Denbigh Street, London, S.W.1.

Fuchsia Society, The British
Sec. C. H. Leytham, 72 Ash Lane, Hale, Altringham, Cheshire.

Gladiolus Society, The British
Sec. Mrs. M. Rowley, 10 Sandbach Rd. Thurlwood, Stoke-on-Trent, Staffs.

Hardy Plant Society
Sec. Miss B. White, 10 St. Barnabas Rd. Emmer Green, Reading, Berks.

Heather Society, The
Sec. Mrs. C. I. MacLeod, Yew Trees, Horley Row, Horley, Surrey.

Iris Society, The British
Sec. Mrs. T. A. Blanco-White, 72 South Hill Park, London, N.W.3.

Northern Horticultural Society, The
Harlow Car Gardens, Harrogate.

Pansy and Viola Society, The North of England
Sec. R. Trippitt, 329 Whitehall Road, Wyke, Bradford, West Yorks.

Pelargonium and Geranium Society, The British
Sec. H. J. Wood, 129 Aylesford Avenue, Beckenham, Kent.

Pteridological Society, The British
Sec. J. W. Dyce, 46 Sedley Rise, Loughton, Essex.

Rose Society, The Royal National
Sec. L. G. Turner, Chiswell Green Lane, St. Albans, Herts.

Royal Horticultural Society
Sec. John Cowell, M.A., Royal Horticultural Society's Offices, Vincent Square, S.W.1.

Royal Caledonian Horticultural Society
Sec. John Turnbull, D.S.O., D.F.C., C.A., Royal Caledonian Horticultural Society, 7 Melville Crescent, Edinburgh 3.

Saintpaulia and Houseplant Society
Sec. Miss N. Tanburn, 82 Rossmore Court, Park Road, London, N.W.1.

Scottish Rock Garden Club
Sec. Mrs. I. Simpson, 48 St Alban's Road, Edinburgh.

Sweet Pea Society, The National
Sec. R. J. Huntley, 431 Wokingham Road, Earley, Reading, Berks.

Vegetable Society, The National
Sec. A. Scott, 8 Hazelwood Mansions, Rostrevor Road, London, S.W.6.

FINDING LIST FOR WEEDKILLERS

All the herbicides in this list are first-rate chemicals available in small packs suitable for use by amateur gardeners. Unless otherwise stated all the formulations have been approved by the Ministry of Agriculture. In case of difficulty in obtaining any of them, the manufacturers should be contacted.

The list may appear lengthy but the multipurpose herbicide is not a reality. The full value of chemical weed control is only obtained by using herbicides for their specific purposes; as such, they constitute an efficient and economic method of eradicating unwanted plants of all sorts.

Weedkillers for Use on Turf

Trade Names	Chemicals	Manufacturers	Type of action	Plants controlled	Notes and precautions
"Bugges 2, 4-D"	2, 4-D	Bugges Insecticides Ltd., Sittingbourne, Kent.	Hormone growth regulator translocated throughout the plant.	Many broad-leafed weeds and some perennial ones. Best hormone type for killing dandelions, daisies and plantains. With daisies, in particular, a second application is usually required.	Primarily for use on turf so at all times beware of drift which may kill plants growing nearby. Fine, warm weather, moist soil and active growth are conducive to the best results. Conversely, poor results are likely during cold weather or spells of drought. Light showers after spraying are unlikely to affect control but application should not be done in rainy weather. Some formulations are slower acting than others and some weeds show a resistance to treatment. Where necessary a second application can be applied after 10–14 days.
"Dicotox"		May and Baker Ltd., Dagenham, Essex.			
"Iotox"	Ioxynil and mecoprop	May and Baker Ltd.	Contact and translocated herbicide.	Veronicas (speedwells) primarily.	
"Bugges MCPA"	MCPA	Bugges Insecticides Ltd.	Hormone growth regulator translocated throughout the plant.	Many broad-leaved weeds and some perennial ones. Best hormone type for killing creeping buttercup. Repeat application after 14 days if necessary.	
"Clovotox"	Mecoprop	May and Baker Ltd.	Hormone growth regulator translocated throughout the plant.	White- and pink-flowered Dutch clover, chickweeds, field woodrush and pearlwort, a small moss-like plant found in many lawns.	
"pbi Calomel Dust"	Mercurous Chloride	Pan Britannica Industries Ltd. Britannica House, Waltham Cross, Herts.	Scorching of foliage and inhibition of development.	Mosses and fungi.	The use of this chloride should be confined to mosses and fungi. It offers a good control and may be used at any time but the best results are obtained in the late summer and autumn. It is of no manurial value.
"Mos-Tox"		May and Baker Ltd.			
Lawn sand	*See* **T33(2)**	Usually home made.	Scorching of annual growth.	Particularly mosses. Also weeds semi-resistant to hormones, like yellow-flowered clover and yarrow.	*See* **Lawns (T33(2))** for detailed information.
"Velves Lawn Sand"		Pan Britannica Industries Ltd.	Of herbicidal and manurial value.		
"Malachite Powder"	Malachite Green	Bugges Insecticides Ltd.	Inhibition of development.	Puff balls and *some* fairy ring fungi.	Apply in growing season. Not on List of Approved Chemicals.

Weedkillers for Garden Use

Trade names	Chemicals	Manufacturers	Type of action	Plants controlled	Notes and precautions
"Nova Soil Steriliser"	Cresylic Acid	The Murphy Chemical Co. Ltd., Wheathampsted, St. Albans, Herts.	Contact herbicide.	For destruction of growth of annual weeds and top growth of perennials.	Particularly valuable on asparagus beds and where annual weeds have to be controlled. Also used as a soil sterilant.
"Bugges Dalapon" "XL All Dalapon"	Dalapon	Bugges Insecticides Ltd. Synchemicals Ltd., Grange Walk, London, SE1 3EN.	Translocated throughout the plant, killing vegetation by movement from leaves to roots.	Annual grasses, couch grass, sedges, reeds and bulrushes.	Delay planting for 40 days after application. May be used, upon maker instructions, as a selective herbicide on asparagus, shrubberies, fruit gardens, etc.
"Weedol"	Diquat + paraquat	I.C.I. Plant Protection Division, Woolmead Walk, Farnham, Surrey.	Translocated throughout the plant but with scorching effect similar to contact herbicides.	Kills annual weeds and top growth of perennials. One of the few herbicides to give a good control of ground elder. Selective only by application, i.e. kills all foliage it contacts.	Undoubtedly one of the most valuable and interesting herbicides to be introduced. Inactivated upon contact with soil; no residual effects. Available in small packs. Can be stored from season to season.
"Gesal Weedex," "Path Weed Control"	Simazine	Airwick (U.K.) Ltd., Brook House, Church Street, Wimslow, Cheshire. The Boots Company Ltd., Nottingham.	Soil acting, killing seedling vegetation by uptake through roots.	Controls germinating seeds of many weeds over a long period.	Apply when ground is wet in early spring on asparagus, apples, pears (not plums), soft fruit, ornamental trees and shrubs including roses. Slow acting.
"Boots Bramble, Brushwood and Nettle Killer" "Kilnet"	2,4,5-T 2,4,5-T + 2,4-D	The Boots Company Ltd. May and Baker Ltd.	Hormone growth regulator translocated throughout the plant.	Special value in control of woody plants like brambles, brushwood and ivy. Also good against nettles.	Beware of drift.

Weedkillers for Use on Drives and Garden Paths: in addition to their use among cultivated plants, some herbicides can be used for weed control on garden paths.

"Kilweed" "Super Weedex"	Aminotriazole + MCPA and simazine Aminotriazole + simazine	Fisons Ltd., Agrochemical Div., Hauxton, Cambridge. Airwick (U.K.) Ltd.	Enters the plants through leaves and roots and is readily translocated.	All broad-leaved weeds found in paths. Gives lasting protection against seedling weeds.	In all cases of weed control on paths, apply carefully and thoroughly to ensure even distribution of the herbicide
"Pathclear"	Diquat + paraquat and simazine	I.C.I. Plant Protection Division.	Enters the plants through leaves and roots and is readily translocated.	All weeds of garden paths and seedling leaves.	Not on the List of Approved Chemicals.
"Double Strength Weedkiller"	Phenals	I.C.I. Plant Protection Division.	Contact with foliage but is not persistent.	Kills plant foliage but chief use is in dealing with moss.	Not on the List of Approved Chemicals.
"Gesal Weedex" "Path Weed Control"	Simazine	Airwick (U.K.) Ltd. The Boots Company Ltd.	Soil acting, killing seedling vegetation by uptake through the roots.	Once established weeds are eradicated will keep paths free of reinfestation.	Slow acting; persistent in the soil.

CARE OF INDOOR PLANTS

By definition a house plant is one which can be permanently grown for decoration indoors. Such plants should not be confused with orchids, crotons, hibiscus, and the like, for these are really greenhouse plants or denizens of Scandinavian or American houses, where heat and air conditions may be automatically controlled. Conversely, the average British home is often cold and draughty, and has a high temperature in the evening and a very low one at night. This is far from satisfactory, but, in view of the fact, the cultivator of house plants must choose subjects tolerant of existing conditions.

Cultural Conditions.—Ideally, the temperature should be kept as constant as possible and in cold weather plants grown in window-boxes are best moved nightly into the centre of the room to avoid damage by frost. Linked with temperature is the question of humidity, for plants respond well to a moist atmosphere. Here again the majority of rooms are ill-suited for growing plants. The condition can be improved, however, by sinking the pots in peat or wrapping them around with sphagnum moss. Alternatively, pots may be stood on a layer of gravel which can be kept damp without allowing water to seep through the bottom of the pot and thereby saturating the soil.

Other factors influence the health of plants indoors—gas fumes, for example, and draughts—so both must be avoided if possible. It will also be found that dust collects on the foliage, therefore plants with large leaves should be sponged regularly with soapy water. Others, with hairy leaves, like saintpaulia, may be gently sprayed, but the water must not be allowed to remain on the foliage, as it may lead to scorching or rotting.

Of all cultural practices, the most important is watering. Unfortunately, the right way and time to do this cannot be laid down emphatically, but as a general guide, plants may become *nearly* dry before watering and then be given a *thorough* soak by standing the pots up to their rims in a bucket of water. For all plants, rain-water is best; if tap water has to be used, it should reach the same temperature as that of the room before being applied.

Soils and Potting.—However well a plant has been grown, the turning point culturally is in its repotting, as from this juncture it either grows vigorously or soon declines. The important factor is to get the correct compost. This may vary slightly, but an all-round mixture can be made up of:

7 parts by loose bulk medium loam
3 parts by loose bulk granulated peat (or leaf soil)
2 parts by loose bulk coarse, gritty sand

This mixture is the basis of John Innes Potting Compost and, with fertilisers added, can be purchased in small quantities from horticultural sundriesmen. If fertilisers are not added, plants should be fed during the growing season at about fortnightly intervals (depending on the particular plant) with a dilute solution of liquid animal manure; alternatively, 2 oz. of the following mixture dissolved in a gallon of rain-water can be used:

5 parts by weight of sulphate of ammonia
7 parts by weight of superphosphate
2 parts by weight of sulphate of potash

Normally a plant will grow satisfactorily in the same soil for three or four years. After this annual growth may be poor, together with yellowing or dropping of the foliage. The plant is then in immediate need of repotting. To do this a large crock should be put into the bottom of the new pot—which should be generally a shade larger—followed by a little compost. Then the matted roots of the plant can be teased out with a pointed stick, put in the pot and more compost worked firmly around the roots.

Some plants, of which palms are an example prove intolerant of root damage, and repotting must be done with particular care, but, nevertheless, the compost must be made firm. When repotting is not absolutely necessary, the top inch of soil can be taken off annually and the pot top-dressed with fresh compost. Both repotting and top-dressing are best done before growth starts in the spring.

Propagation.—Many house plants are easy to propagate from cuttings or layered shoots. The former are taken off the parent plant at a joint in the stem by severing cleanly with a razor blade. After the lower leaves have been removed, the stems are inserted into a mixture of equal parts of sand and peat in a pot. A glass tumbler or specially-made, small, plastic tent is then placed over the top to avoid loss of moisture, and in a week or two rooting will have taken place.

As for layering, this can be done by bending a shoot into a pot of sandy soil and pegging it down at a joint. When the layer has rooted it can be severed from the parent.

Health of Plants.—Fortunately the number of pests and diseases affecting indoor plants is small, and the large majority of troubles are due to faulty cultivation. Occasionally aphids (green or black flies) may be found on young growth, and can be destroyed by carefully wiping affected leaves and shoots with water containing a little detergent, repeating the practice if necessary. On ivies, in particular, sometimes a brown, waxy scale can be found. Underneath the protective scale is a small insect which sucks the sap, and without difficulty these can be removed by hand.

Another insect occasionally seen is the mealy bug, an aphid which is surrounded by a prominent coating of a white, woolly substance; control in this case is to paint individuals with a dab of methylated spirits and to deal regularly with any reinfestation.

Basal rotting of flower stems and leaves, to be seen often on cyclamen and peperomias, is due to fungal infection, but this can be avoided by attention to correct watering and temperature. Similarly, premature yellowing of the foliage and leaf dropping is primarily a cultural trouble brought about by excessive cold, draughts, gas fumes, dryness, over-watering, perhaps over-feeding, or a combination of some of these factors.

SELECTION OF PLANTS FOR GROWING INDOORS.

For ease of reference the following list includes plants which can be grown as permanent features indoors and florists' plants like cyclamen and primulas. These latter sorts are normally purchased in bloom and discarded when flowering finishes.

Araucaria excelsa (Norfolk Island Pine).—Because of its likeness to a small fir tree, it is a plant to stand on its own. It is not difficult to grow if kept out of the full sun and the soil moist. One of the earliest plants adopted for growing indoors, but not often seen at present.

Azalea.—Varieties in a wide range of colours are sold in late autumn and early winter. The plants are imported from Belgium and forced by English nurserymen. Azaleas need generous watering, preferably by immersion, in order to soak the root ball thoroughly. After flowering plants may be stood out of doors in the summer and kept moist but normally do not flower freely again for two or three years.

Begonia.—An enormous genus of plants of world-wide distribution, many being suitable for indoor cultivation. The large-flowered sorts known as tuberous begonias are potted in the early spring and kept in a temperature of 65–70°F. Once the growth starts, water freely and feed fortnightly. After flowering gradually withhold water and then store the corms until the following spring. Bud drop and yellowing of the leaves is usually due to faulty watering or draughts.

Billbergia nutans.—This is a member of the pineapple family, the Bromeliads, having typically narrow, spiny-edged leaves. Nearly hardy and will flower in a warm room. Do not re-pot unless absolutely necessary, as the roots are best confined.

Campanula isophylla (Harebell).— A charming blue-flowered plant with a long flowering period. Easily grown in cool conditions, and its pendulous habit it useful for a basket. After flowering, remove dead flower-heads and trim straggly shoots. There is a good white form, *alba*.

Cacti.—Innumerable sorts are used as house plants. In the main, all should be grown in a sandy, gritty soil with sharp drainage; water may be given freely in the summer, but withheld in winter, except to prevent the soil drying out. Two cacti which will flower freely and are particularly worthy of cultivation are *Aporocactus flagelliformis*, the rat's tail cactus, and *Epiphyllum ackermanii*. Both are tolerant of poor conditions and neglect.

Mention should also be made of the old-fashioned Christmas cactus, *Schlumbergera bridgesii*, as a great favourite, but an infinitely more exciting one of a similar type is the rare *Rhipsalidopsis gaertneri* with bright red flowers. These two are both easy to grow if the soil is kept on the moist side.

Chlorophytum elatum.—This plant will tolerate a range of temperature and responds to occasional feeding in the summer. It is most attractive, with its green leaves striped with cream-coloured bands. A good plant for beginners.

Christmas or White Cherry.—*See* **Solanum capsicastrum.**

Cineraria.—Normally plants are bought in flower in the winter. They require cool conditions, good light, but not full sun, and care in watering. Numerous varieties have been raised with their daisy-like flowers ranging in colour from white to red and violet-blue. In nature the cineraria is a perennial, but the hybrids are not worth keeping once flowering is over.

Crassula.—Shrubby members of this genus make fine house plants, growing well in light soil in full sun. Particularly valuable are *C. lactea*—which has white flowers annually and large, succulent, spoon-shaped foliage—and *C. falcata*, a choice plant with red and yellow flowers.

Cyclamen.—Indisputably a really well-grown cyclamen is the hallmark of a good cultivator. When buying a plant choose one which has been grown slowly in cool conditions and therefore has stiff, self-supporting stems. Failures are usually due to faulty watering. Rules cannot be formulated for correct watering, but as a generalisation the pot should be filled to the brim about once a week (*see* **Health of Indoor Plants**).

When annual growth dies, water can be withheld to a large extent and the corm saved for another year. It must be remembered however that while corms can be grown on for 15–20 years the *best* results are always obtained in the first season.

Mr Allan G. Langdon, an expert in growing cyclamen, wrote an excellent account of the plant in the R.H.S. *Journal* (October 1948), pp. 322–7, which may be consulted at most public libraries.

Ferns.—Some will grow in rooms, but well-grown specimens of maidenhairs and the like need first-rate cultivation. Species of *Asplenium blechnum*, and *Nephrolepis* are worth trying. Compost is made up with equal parts of fibrous loam, peat, leafsoil and coarse sand.

Ficus.—Species like *F. elastica decora* with broad, leathery, shiny leaves are often seen as window decoration in large stores. Not easy to grow in some circumstances; leaf-drop and yellowing may be caused by fluctuations in temperature or draughts, and rain-water should be used when watering.

Gloxinia.—Although often used to good effect for house decoration, the best specimens are to be found in the moist atmosphere of warm greenhouses. When grown indoors keep the plants moist in a warm room but shaded from direct sun. To encourage a succession of flowers feed fortnightly with liquid manure.

Strange as it may seem, all of the lovely forms in a wide range of colours have been selected from a single Brazilian species.

Helxine soleirolii (Mind-your-own-business).—Appropriately named from its habit of thriving where it is not wanted. Makes a pleasant mass of thin, green trailing stems. Should be kept always on the wet side.

Indiarubber Plant.—*See* **Ficus.**

Ivy.—Ivies show an interesting range of colour, shape and size in their foliage and are to be found in many continental houses. Invaluable as climbing plants in warm rooms, the Canary Island ivy is worth trying. A related plant, raised in France, is *Fatshedera lizei*. All of these prefer a damp, leafy soil and the foliage should be sprayed occasionally.

Monstera deliciosa.—A striking plant with large deeply-cut leaves and long thick aerial roots, many of which do not reach the ground. Often seen as a prominent decorative feature of continental homes. Requires a leafy soil and generous watering. Spray or sponge foliage regularly and avoid fluctuation of temperature in its cultivation.

Nepeta hederacea variegata (Ground Ivy).—Creeping, hardy perennial native of Britain; variegated form makes an attractive addition to a hanging basket, having long stems and small kidney-shaped leaves. Correctly known botanically as *Glechoma*, not *Nepeta*. Good plant for beginners.

Palms.—Like the aspidistra, the palm is considered a relic of Victorianism, and on such slender evidence is condemned on many counts. Notwithstanding, palms of various sizes make good decorative plants. Care must be taken when re-potting, and for a number of years it is only necessary to top-dress provided that feeding is done in summer. To keep the foliage green, the leaves should be sponged regularly or, better still, the plant taken out of doors and vigorously sprayed with water from a hose.

Pelargonium (Geranium).—Ease of cultivation and beauty are found in this plant and its infinite varieties. Some of these, like 'Mrs Cox,' have multi-coloured leaves and are well worth hunting for in trade lists. During the summer feed generously and keep the stock vigorous by rooting cuttings annually in July–August.

Philodendron.—Mostly climbing plants with aerial roots and represented by a number of species from tropical America. Fairly tolerant of adverse conditions, but dislikes draughts and requires light shade, free watering and a rich open soil. *P. scandens*, with heart-shaped leaves, is typical of the climbing group; *P. bipinnatifidum*, with broad incised leaves, of the non-climbers.

Primula.—At Christmas time numerous varieties of primulas are offered for sale and make good presents, for with care they have a long season of flowering. Further, all are of easy culture and, if top dressed and fed can be grown on for a year or two.

The three species grown have their origin in China and varieties of one, *Primula obconica*, may cause a rash on those susceptible to it.

Saintpaulia (African violet).—A charming dwarf with hairy leaves and pretty single and double flowers in many colours. It is a difficult plant to grow well, as it thrives in a steady temperature of 65–70°F. and a wet atmosphere. Water from below. Rotting of leaves is due to excess of moisture, draughts, cold, or gas fumes.

Sansevieria trifasciata.—Perhaps unkindly but appropriately known as Mother-in-law's tongue. It has a distinctive appearance, with stiff, erect leaves striped with gold. Keep warm and fairly dry; do not over-pot; tough.

Saxifraga sarmentosa.—Of easy culture and hardy out of doors; should be afforded a cool position and kept moist. Reddish leaves and pink flowers make it most attractive.

Setcreasea purpurea.—Visitors returning from holiday in the Canary Isles or parts of the Mediterranean often slip a cutting of this plant in their luggage. The leaves are about 4 inches long and, like the fleshy stems, are coloured a striking shade of violet-purple. Over a long period there is a succession of purple-pink flowers if afforded a warm temperature. Pieces of stems root quickly, during the summer, in sandy soil.

Although now widely grown, it is interesting to note that this plant was found growing unnoticed in a window box at Tampico Airport, Mexico, than less 35 years ago.

Solanum capsicastrum.—Commonly known as Winter, Christmas or Jerusalem cherry, this plant is a native of Madeira and is grown for its brilliant scarlet berries. If grown in a cool temperature, watered freely, and fed with liquid manure occasionally it has a long season. But it is intolerant of gas fumes which quickly cause the leaves and berries to drop. The winter cherry can be grown from year to year, but it is best to replenish the stock annually.

Tolmiea menziesii.—Although of no distinctive beauty, the pick-a-back plant is often grown indoors as it is tolerant of the worst of conditions. Young plants develop on the hairy, oval leaves, hence its common name.

Probably it was introduced from British Columbia by the Scottish plant collector, Dr Archibald Menzies. The leaves of tolmiea root easily in water.

Tradescantia (Wandering Jew)—Tolerant of neglect this trailing plant with its deep green leaves and silver variegations makes a good house plant. It will grow in any soil but pots must be well drained to prevent sourness and subsequent dead patches appearing on the foliage.

To encourage deeper variegations on the leaves, the soil should be kept fairly dry.

Vines.—Two of these are particularly valuable as climbing plants; *Cissus antarctica*, kangaroo vine, is a native of Australia and *Rhoicissus rhomboidea*, a Natalese plant which does not appear to have been grown to any great extent in Britain until after the Second World War. Both climbers make an attractive addition to any collection of house plants. It must be remembered however that they need a cool atmosphere and will not flourish in hot, dry rooms. Occasionally the foliage should be sprayed with water or, better still, the plants stood out of doors in rainy weather.

Zebrina pendula.—Related closely to tradescantia; often their nomenclature is confused. Like its relative, zebrina is a difficult plant to kill. Its leaves have a pleasing metallic lustre with a shade of blood-purple beneath. When kept moist and grown in warm conditions it is very vigorous and the leaves are fleshy. To obtain its characteristic purple colouring the plant should be grown in a cool position in full sunlight and kept on the dry side.

Both this plant and the tradescantia are easily increased by inserting cuttings in a sandy compost or keeping them in a glass of water until roots develop.

DOUBLE CONVERSION TABLES
(approximate equivalents)

cm		inches	m		feet
2·5	1	0·4	0·3	1	3·3
5·1	2	0·8	0·6	2	6·6
8·0	3	1·2	0·9	3	9·9
10·2	4	1·6	1·2	4	13·1
12·7	5	2·0	1·5	5	16·4
15·2	6	2·4	1·8	6	19·7
17·8	7	2·8	2·1	7	23·0
20·3	8	3·1	2·4	8	26·3
22·9	9	3·5	2·7	9	29·5
25·4	10	3·9	3·0	10	32·8
27·9	11	4·3	3 3	11	36 3
30·5	12	4·7	3·6	12	39·6

oz/yd²	g/m²	oz	g
1	34	1	28·35
2	68	2	56·70
3	102	3	85·05

PETS AND PONIES

The most important factors in maintaining a pet in health and comfort are regular care and attention, cleanliness, wise feeding, and knowing what to do if it becomes ill or out of condition. This section has been compiled to give this guidance and contains suggestions for further reading.

TABLE OF CONTENTS

DOMESTIC PETS

By ALASTAIR N. WORDEN, M.A., Ph.D. (Cantab); D.Sc., D.Vet. Med. (London). (Chairman Huntingdon Research Centre; Co-ordinator of Environmental Studies, University College, Cambridge; Professor of Toxicology, University of Bath).
SARAH E. M. WORDEN
(Norwich City College).

Introduction.

This section attempts to deal not with all the many hundreds of species and varieties of animal that may be kept as pets, but mainly with those that are best suited to average homes in Great Britain. The maintenance of monkeys, squirrels, bats, mongooses, and snakes while quite feasible to those with experience and facilities, requires considerable time and—in some instances—expense. Those who contemplate such exotic pets should consult works of reference, study the methods adopted in zoological gardens, and discuss the matter with experts. Even in the case of the more common animals the information provided in the following pages is to be regarded only as a beginning, to be supplemented so far as possible by practical experience, discussions with more knowledgeable owners, and the study of more detailed writings.

Certain considerations are basic. Never keep a pet unless you are really interested in it and are prepared to give it due—and regular—care and attention. Do not keep a pet you cannot afford to maintain in health and comfort. Scrupulous attention to cleanliness is essential, and wise feeding is one of the most important factors in avoiding illness and loss of condition.

The choice of species is nowadays restricted—perhaps as well from the standpoint of animal welfare—on account of stringent import regulations. The Rabies (Importation of Dogs, Cats and Other Mammals) Order 1974 controls the landing in this country of all mammals of the orders Carnivora (dog and cat families, bears, racoons, mink, stoats, civets, mongooses, *etc.*) and Chiroptera (bats), and of certain members of the orders Dermoptera (gliding or "flying" lemurs), Edentata (sloths, armadillos, *etc.*), Hyracoidea (hyraxes or "conies"), Insectivora (moles, shrews, hedgehogs and other insect-eating mammals), Lagomorpha (hares and rabbits) and Marsupalia (opossums, kangaroos, wallabies bandicoots and other pouched mammals). Animals subject to control may only be landed at specified ports and airports, and must be moved as soon as practicable after landing to authorised quarantine premises—except vampire bats, which must be quarantined for life. Licences are not, however, required for animals coming from Northern Ireland, the Republic of Ireland, the Channel Islands and the Isle of Man provided that they have not been outside the British Isles within the previous 6 months. Animals landed illegally, or in breach of a licence, may be destroyed. There are other legislative measures that control the importation of monkeys, various kinds of birds and other animals, and these are unlikely to be relaxed.

Since the passing of the Veterinary Surgeons Act of 1948 it has been illegal for anyone but a veterinary surgeon (or whose name has been placed upon a special register) to practise the diagnosis and treatment of animal diseases. Not even a pharmacist may do so. Anyone may, of course, render "first aid" and an owner may—at his own risk—apply treatment. It is, of course, a wise precaution to seek veterinary advice for any ailing animal, and the sooner it is sought the more likely is it to prove beneficial. Nowadays, veterinary surgeons take a keen interest not only in diseases but also in animal husbandry and good practices and can prove of help to the owners of a vast variety of pets. There are, for example, branches of the B.V.A. such as the British Small Animals Veterinary Association and the British Veterinary Zoological Society. Their interests extend even to fish, and the current editor of *Fish Biology* is a veterinarian.

The maintenance of animals in or near the house is not free from medical hazard. There are various infections and parasites that can be passed from animals to man, and vice-versa. Rabies is not the only potential hazard from imported stock although one should heed the advice given by Dr. Ethelward Vella in a letter to the *Lancet* in December 1975: "It would be a great help to doctors if holidaymakers, before going abroad, were to learn not to befriend any animal whatsoever. If they do get bitten by a domestic animal such as a dog, the name and address of the owner should be taken, the vaccination status of the animal should be ascertained, and local medical assistance should be sought." In this country, any person bitten or scratched by an animal should seek medical advice promptly and, in all appropriate instances, request an anti-tetanus injection. The infection known as psittacosis in members of the parrot family, and as ornithosis in other birds—including pigeons—is quite easily transmitted to human beings through the inhalation of dust that contains faecal material from infected birds. Although the pneumonia that often results is usually susceptible to treatment, it can be severe and sometimes fatal. Other hazards of pet-keeping include asthma or allergic sensitivity, which may become progressively severe in susceptible persons. "Small furry animals" are regarded with suspicion by many clinicians who seek the cause of childhood asthma—and, of course, larger animals may also produce a dander that provokes severe reactions. "Bird fancier's lung" is usually regarded as an allergic alveolitis resulting from the inhalation of dust from pigeon lofts or bird cages. More mundane hazards include the simple contamination of food and water by animal excretion. Nor should it be forgotten that some species of animal can contract diseases from man.

Against such risks one has to balance the enjoyment, education and companionship to be derived from a healthy association with pets. Most children, and very many adults, benefit from an association with animals and from the responsibilities of maintaining them properly. There are some restrictions placed upon flat-dwellers and some other owners and tenants of urban properties, but it would be a sad day if some at least of the animals referred to in this section did not form part of the British home background.

There are many recommendations to follow regarding further reading. One of the authors was privileged to edit, in 1947, the first edition of the *Handbook on the Care and Management of Laboratory Animals* produced by the UFAW (the Universities' Federation for Animal Welfare). There have been several subsequent editions and the latest, edited by the UFAW staff is a mine of information, much of it applicable to pets as distinct from laboratory animals. It is published by Churchill Livingstone (London and Edinburgh). Still valuable, although written just before the second world war, is the work produced from the Zoological Society of London by Margaret Shaw and James Fisher (London: Dent), *Animals as Friends (and how to keep them)*, which deals with several species not included here. The late James Fisher, incidentally, shared with one of the present authors in the production of the first-ever section on **Domestic Pets** to appear in *Pears Cyclopaedia.*

DOGS

Description.

"Man's best friend" has been associated with man, in many parts of the world, for thousands of years. There has always been considerable scientific debate over the exact origin—or origins—of the domestic dog, and Darwin himself, over a century ago, reviewed the evidence then available for and against the polyphyletic origin of the different domesticated races and suggested that: "We shall probably never be able to ascertain their origin with certainty." The northern wolf, the coyote and Asiatic jackal have been among the several wild canids that are thought to have been the progenitors, and although most of the evidence favours the first of these, there are contrary thoughts. From whatever species the domestic dog may have been derived, it is highly probable that its ancestors were pack hunters and strictly monogamous. The fidelity of the dog fox and his excellent manners towards his vixen are models of male behaviour and constitute a problem for the fox breeder. Domesticity appears to have relaxed the dogs' attitude, and the dog breeder does not find himself faced with the same problems as the fox breeder in breaking the monogamous habit. Nevertheless, as the great animal behaviourist, Konrad Lorenz, has emphasised, male dogs behave with great chivalry towards bitches and puppies. He states that in the wolf this chivalrous self-control is extended to females of the same pack, whereas in certain breeds of dogs that he believes to be predominantly jackel in origin, it applies to every bitch even though she may be a complete stranger. He states that the Chow Chow holds an intermediate position, and that if the male lives with own breed it may behave loutishly towards strange bitches, though he has never known one that actually bit one.

There are more than 100 breeds of domesticated dog (*Canis familiaris*) and the weight range varies between a few kg for the toy breeds to 70 kg or more for St. Bernards and Wolfhounds. Pets should be selected carefully on the grounds of temperament and size, and may, of course, either be purebreds or crossbreds, the latter usually being described as mongrels, while the former are, of course, the only suitable animals for dog-breeding in the usual sense of that term.

Dog breeding and showing have become highly specialised during the present century, and average persons cannot be expected to take them up without adequate time, resources and knowledge. Any amateur who wishes to breed for profit should seek expert advice before attempting to do so.

The General Committee of the Kennel Club, 1 Clarges Street, London, W.1 (01-493-6651), maintains a breed register for each pure breed recognised by it. For the purposes of competition between dogs of different breeds, the grouping of breeds—see accompanying table—is held to define Sporting (Hounds, Gundogs and Terriers) and Non-Sporting (Utility, Working and Toys). Full details of registration, including some new regulations dating from 1 January 1976 that relate to the progeny of certain purebred dogs of different breeds within the same category, are available on application to the Kennel Club. Before an imported dog can be accepted for registration, the applicant must give the date of importation, the address of the quarantine station at which it had been detained, and the name and the address of the importer.

SPORTING BREEDS

Hound Group

Afghan Hounds	Dachshunds (Miniature Wire-Haired)
Basenjis	Deerhounds
Basset Hounds	Elkhounds
Bassets Griffons Vendeen	Finnish Spitz
Beagles	Foxhounds
Bloodhounds	Greyhounds
Borzois	Ibizan Hounds
Dachsbracke	Irish Wolfhounds
Dachshunds (Long-Haired)	Otterhounds
Dachshunds (Miniature Long-Haired)	Pharaoh Hounds
Dachshunds (Smooth-Haired)	Portuguese Warren Hounds
Dachshunds (Miniature Smooth-Haired)	Rhodesian Ridgebacks
Dachshunds (Wire-Haired)	Salukis
	Sloughis
	Swedish Foxhounds
	Swiss Laufhunds (Jura)
	Whippets

Gundog Group

English Setter	German Wirehaired Pointers
German Longhaired Pointers	Gordon Setters
German Shorthaired Pointers	Hungarian Vizslas
Italian Spinones	Irish Setters
Large Munsterlanders	Small Munsterlanders
Pointers	Spaniels (American Cocker)
Pointing Wirehaired Griffons	Spaniels (Clumber)
Retrievers (Chesapeake Bay)	Spaniels (Cocker)
Retrievers (Curly Coated)	Spaniels (English Springer)
Retrievers (Flat Coated)	Spaniels (Field)
Retrievers (Golden)	Spaniels (Irish Water)
Retrievers (Labrador)	Spaniels (Sussex)
	Spaniels (Welsh Springer)
	Weimaraners

Terrier Group

Airedale Terriers	Lakeland Terriers
Australian Terriers	Manchester Terriers
Bedlington Terriers	Norfolk Terriers
Border Terriers	Norwich Terriers
Bull Terriers	Scottish Terriers
Bull Terriers (Miniature)	Sealyham Terriers
Cairn Terriers	Skye Terriers
Dandie Dinmont Terriers	Soft-Coated Wheaten Terriers
Fox Terriers (Smooth)	Staffordshire Bull Terriers
Fox Terriers (Wire)	Welsh Terriers
Glen of Imaal Terriers	West Highland White Terriers
Irish Terriers	
Kerry Blue Terriers	

NON-SPORTING BREEDS

Utility Group

Boston Terriers	Lhasa Apsos
Bulldogs	Mexican Hairless
Canaan Dogs	Miniature Schnauzers
Chow Chows	Poodles (Standard)
Dalmations	Poodles (Miniature)
French Bulldogs	Poodles (Toy)
Giant Schnauzers	Schipperkes
Iceland Dogs	Schnauzers
Japanese Akitas	Shih Tzus
Keeshonds	Tibetan Spaniels
Leonbergers	Tibetan Terriers

Working Group

Alaskan Malamutes	Hungarian Kuvasz
Alsatians (German Shepherd Dogs)	Hungarian Pulis
Anatolian (Karabash) Dogs	Huskies
Australian Kelpies	Komondors
Bearded Collies	Maremma Sheepdogs
Beaucerons	Mastiffs
Belgian Shepherd Dogs (Groenendaels)	Newfoundlands
Belgian Shepherd Dogs (Malinois)	Norwegian Buhunds
Belgian Shepherd Dogs (Tervuerens)	Old English Sheepdogs
Bernese Mountain Dogs	Polish Sheepdogs
Bouviers Des Flandres	Portuguese Water Dogs
Boxers	Pyrenean Mountain Dogs
Briards	Rottweilers
Bullmastiffs	St. Bernards
Collies (Rough)	Samoyeds
Collies (Smooth)	Shetland Sheepdogs
Dobermanns	Siberian Huskies
Great Danes	Tibetan Mastiffs
	Welsh Corgis (Cardigan)
	Welsh Corgis (Pembroke)

Toy Group

Affenpinschers	Italian Greyhounds
Bichons Frises	Japanese Chin
Cavalier King Charles Spaniels	King Charles Spaniels
Chihuahuas (Long Coat)	Lowchen
Chihuahuas (Smooth Coat)	Maltese
Chinese Crested Dogs	Miniature Pinschers
English Toy terriers (Black and Tan)	Papillons
Griffons Bruxellois	Pekingese
	Pomeranians
	Pugs
	Silky Terriers
	Yorkshire Terriers

There are many valuable books upon the dog, among which may be cited *The Book of the Dog*, edited by Brian Vesey-FitzGerald (London: Nicholson & Watson), *Dogs in Britain* by Clifford

Hubbard (London: Macmillan), *Feeding Our Dogs* and *The Natural Method of Dog Training*, both by Dr. Leon Whitney (London: Macmillan, and Nicholas Vane, respectively), *The Genetics of the Dog* by Marca Burns (Technical Communications No. 9 of the Commonwealth Bureau of Animal Breeding and Genetics, Edinburgh) and *The Natural History of the Dog* by Richard and Alice T.-W.-Fiennes (London: Weidenfeld & Nicolson). There is also a chapter in the *UFAW Handbook*, already referred to, by Dr. Malcom Hime. Works on individual breeds are too numerous to mention, but there have been several excellent series of individual booklets, including, for example, those issued in the USA, by All-Pets Books of Fond du Lac, Wisconsin. Douglas and Carol Appleton provide much valuable information in their *Beagles and Beagling* (London: Kaye & Ward), which contains sections by Dr. Ralph Heywood on the abnormalities that are not uncommon in this—as in almost every other breed of long standing—and other veterinary matters. Those who wish to maintain a Husky or other sled dog should contact the Husky Club of Great Britain, the present secretary of which is Mrs. Stella Colling-Mudge. The editor of its publication, *The Sled Dog*, is Mrs. Janet Ward, 3 Turpins Close, Oaklands, Welwyn, Herts., AL6 0Q2 (048-871-5413).

There are important breed differences in the way in which young dogs become adapted to man. Thus, there is evidence that the Basenji has much greater shyness at 5 weeks compared with, say, the Cocker Spaniel, and that this difference is inherited on Mendelian lines, there probably being two genetic factors involved. Similar differences are often found to exist in respect of crouching, which appears to represent the " setting " that has survived in Cocker Spaniels since there has now been no selection against it. Modern setters are really pointers.

Some understanding of agonistic, sexual and territorial behaviour and of dominance relationships is of considerable importance not only for professional training, breeding and showing but also for successful maintenance of dogs as pets. When puppies are left together in groups, a tendency to fighting may be noticed from a very early age. It occurs during the play periods and appears to be a response to unusual roughness on the part of a particular member of the litter, when there will be a slight flare up of tempers, a bit of a fight, and then all will settle down again. So far as is possible, this tendency should be checked at an early age if it is intended to run dogs together subsequently. Real fighting comes later, and is usually linked with defence of owner or of territorial, or with sexual considerations. In household dogs, there may be evidence of real male aggressive behaviour as early as 4–5 months of age, before there is any sign of sexual activity. Fighting in the female usually starts at a later stage. At about 6–7 months of age, the first signs of sexual maturity will appear, and is manifested in the male by the typical lifting of the leg at urination and by some degree of interest in the odours outlining the animal's own territorial area.

Dominance orders are clearly manifest among dogs within litters or colonies maintained together, and in the animals of a neighbourhood. In some groups of dogs, there is real persecution of an individual by other members. In dog breeding and training, aggressiveness is usually regarded as valuable only if limited, although in the past some breeds were selected for their ability to fight. Dr. J. P. Scott, who with his colleagues has made many contributions to dog behaviour, states that all of the terriers are fighting breeds: they are easily excited and relatively insensitive to pain with tough skin on their necks and shoulders and strong jaws and teeth. On the other hand, many breeds are selected for the opposite kind of behaviour. Hounds work in packs to find game, and fighting is highly undesirable. Beagles—which make docile pets and are good animals for laboratory studies—get along peaceably together, and even strange adult males can be put in the same kennel with little more than some growling and barking.

To a domesticated dog, a human being is his pack leader, and Konrad Lorenz has suggested that the failure of the adult male wolf to accept this situation is basically the reason why it, with the exception sometimes of the wolf bitch, is usually impossible to train as a pet, even from an early age. Dominance is usually shown by the taking of the other dog by the scruff of its neck, and indeed the most effective means of punishment is to mimic this by shaking the animal by its scruff. Lorenz pointed out that since dogs, like monkeys, do not hit, but bite each other during their ranking order disputes, a blow is not really an adequate or intelligible form of chastisement. One can imitate the penal methods of the pack leader, and involve one's own personal feelings much less, by lifting the dog up by the neck and shaking him. Although this form of punishment seems to us to be much less severe than beating with a cane or whip, we must be very chary of using it, even on adult dogs, if we do not wish to intimidate them altogether.

Marking out of territory by urination is an inborn habit that has to be suppressed for satisfactory domesticated relationships in the average household, but will be revived at once if that territory is invaded by a strange dog. Lorenz considers it unfair to take one's dog to a household where another dog is kept, if only in regard of the housewife's feelings at the effects upon her soft furnishings.

Within the age range corresponding to the period of socialisation indicated in the paragraphs on training, the vast majority of puppies will, in appropriate circumstances, begin a form a strong attachment to an individual human being. This may persist or wane according to type, but there is often a phase of adolescent independence when the dog will become disobedient and defiant. Discipline must be persisted with during this period, and patience must also be shown and the animal will normally become more obedient again at the age of 18 months to 2 years.

Dogs are equipped with good senses of hearing and smell and their sound localisation has been shown to be about twice as accurate as that of a human. The capacity of the dog to detect an individual odour of human beings is quite remarkable. This individual odour is perceived by the dog even when it is mixed with the odour of another person or with other strongly smelling substances. In tracking experiments, dogs have been found able to distinguish even between the odours of identical human twin sisters. Sight is of much less importance, although it has been suggested that the Greyhound, Whippet, Borzoi, Saluki, Afghan, Irish Wolfhound, Scottish Deerhound and Dachshund all hunt by sight, and that the smallness of the optical angle suggests that the dog may have good binocular and stereoscopic vision. It is extremely difficult to detect blindness from simple observation in domestic or laboratory animals that know their quarters well.

With advancing age, hearing fails frequently, and the first sign of this may be an inability to detect the direction the sound is coming from, though it obviously can be heard. This may lead gradually or suddenly to total deafness. Such animals can be taught to respond to signs, but, of course, they become an increased responsibility as they have to be watched in relation to traffic and other hazards. Sight, on the whole, remains good as does the sense of smell.

All domestic dogs over six months of age must, of course, be licensed, the licences being available from Post Offices. Since the Control of Dogs Order of 1930, it has been obligatory for every domestic dog while in a highway or any place public resort to wear a collar with the name and address of the owner inscribed on the collar or on a plate or badge attached thereto. It is also within the power of Local Authorities to make regulations requiring that dogs of any class shall be kept under control between sunset and sunrise with a view to the prevention of worrying cattle—the expression " cattle " including not only cows but also horses, mules, asses, sheep, goats and swine. There are also many local regulations that request the use of leads in the street or other public places, so making it an offence to allow a dog to foul the pavement.

Accommodation.

Up till comparatively recently most dogs were kennelled down out of doors. This practice has its advantages, but today the majority of pet dogs are allowed more or less the run of the house. A warm sleeping-place, such as a box or basket, should be provided, and should contain removable bedding. Newspaper is an excellent non-conductor of heat. It is a very useful material to place at the bottom of a dog's box; and on two or three thicknesses may be placed a rug or blanket on which the animal may lie. It is astonishing the amount of grit and dust a dog can bring into a house on his limbs and the lower part of his body. His bedding will require frequent shaking out and renewal, and paper is easily changed. The box or basket in which the dog lies should be allowed a place free from draughts, and requires airing daily when the dog leaves its bed in the morning. Wood-wool makes excellent bedding in outhouses or where a special structure is provided by way of dog-kennel, but is inclined to be messy about the house, as a dog will draw portions of it about the room as he leaves his bed. If straw is used, it is best stuffed into a sack and made into a kind of mattress. An odd piece of linoleum forms an excellent foundation to the dog's sleeping-box or kennel; it does not strike cold to the skin, is a slow conductor of heat, and has the advantage of being easily kept clean, particularly during illness where there may be discharges and messes to be frequently cleaned up, until the animal can once more go out of doors.

Exercise.

Every dog should be exercised regularly, but there is no need to over-exercise, and the practice of allowing a dog (other than a large and athletic animal) to run behind a bicycle for mile after mile cannot be too strongly deprecated. Two or three fairly short walks a day are sufficient for a small terrier, always provided that there is a garden in which he can play on fine days and some open space where he can run freely for a short time. While still in the puppyhood stages, a dog should be trained to walk to heel and to beware of traffic. Even so, it is usually safer to put him on a lead in busy thoroughfares. One point which, to the annoyance of the public, many dog-owners fail to realise, is that their animals would show much less tendency to fight if allowed to investigate one another off the lead. A dog naturally feels aggressive if put on the lead immediately a rival hails in sight. There are, of course, certain dogs which attack others at sight; these are a public nuisance, and should never be allowed loose on the streets.

The practice of allowing a dog to take his own exercise is to be deprecated, especially in towns and suburbs. The animal will be tempted to sniff into dustbins, and, if a male, will tend to follow a bitch in season or to take part in the unsavoury "dog parties" which are so often to be seen. Furthermore, such an animal is usually responsible for the disgusting habit of fouling the pavements and gateways. In this connection, it should be emphasised that dogs may quite easily be trained to defaecate in the gutter, or on the grass verge, and so avoid contamination of the pavement or carriage-way. In some districts owners are liable to a fine if their dogs foul the pavement.

Training.

Patience combined with the gift of putting yourself in the dog's place is the chief requisite for successful education. It is most important to encourage regularity of habit, as an animal will obviously learn very much more quickly if his daily walks, meals, and grooming take place at fairly constant times. A quiet firmness is the ideal method, and a puppy should learn early that a command *is* a command, and must be obeyed. There is no need to shout and make an exhibition of oneself, or to race in circles after a disobedient puppy; if these things are done, the animal will never become so well trained as it otherwise would. Again, it is rather ridiculous to chastise a puppy *after* he has somewhat belatedly decided to come to heel: quite obviously, he will then be liable to think that he has done wrong in actually coming to heel. Whatever happens, it must never be that the dog becomes master; there is no more unbecoming sight than that of a person with a frankly disobedient dog, and if the animal be large and powerful it may prove a menace to its owner and to the public.

Puppies should be house-trained at an early stage. If care and thought are given to the matter, the animal will soon learn not to make messes in the house. However, it is very stupid to forget all about a puppy or dog for many hours, and then, out of sheer vexation, chastise it for having made a mess. If puppies are let out every two hours or so at first, they will soon learn not to make a mess. Encourage them for performing in the right place rather than scold them for doing so in the wrong one. Physical punishment should be administered only where strictly necessary, and then in a sensible fashion.

It is important to realise that the puppy has its own pattern of infant behaviour, that of sleep, feeding and play and to base training upon the subsequent normal developmental processes. During the first 1–2 weeks of life, sleep takes precedence and newly-born pups (and kittens) probably sleep for up to 90% of the time, wakening only to be fed and cleaned by the dam. Gradually the sleep periods will become slightly less and feeding periods rather more prolonged, and, by about the 3rd or 4th week of life, some slight evidence of a play pattern will be noted. Very shortly after the play pattern is noticed there is obvious sexual activity in that puppies at the age of 3–4 weeks will frequently make copulatory movements. This phase lasts only about two weeks and subsequently disappears until sexual maturity. The sucking instinct is very persistent indeed and, when puppies are 3–4 weeks old and the dam is leaving them for longer periods at a time, during the waking part of the time puppies will frequently suck the preputial orifice of other males in the litter.

Observation of puppies in the nest makes it clear that excretory activity follows a certain pattern. From the age of about 3–4 weeks, when some locomotor activity is possible, it will be noticed that immediately on waking puppies attempt to leave the sleeping area and immediately urinate. They will then feed and, having fed, will be cleaned by the dam and will then indulge in a play period. Midway through the play period it will be noted that one puppy after another suddenly becomes pensive and will again urinate and probably defaecate. Considerable use can be made of this pattern of behaviour in the house training of young puppies. Nearly all books on the training of puppies recommend that, in order to instil habits of cleanliness, puppies should be put out immediately after feeding. This would seem to be absolutely wrong. A puppy should be put out immediately after waking, should be allowed to empty the bladder, should then be brought in to feed and should be carefully watched during the subsequent play period and, immediately there is a cessation of play activity, it should be transferred to the place intended for toilet purposes, when it will probably relieve itself again. Persistence of this popular fallacy that a puppy should be clean after feeding is not based on observation of normal behaviour.

Over the first few weeks of life, sleep periods will gradually decrease and be replaced by longer and longer periods of activity. It is essential that during the immediate post-weaning period long periods of sleep should be allowed. Far too many people, on obtaining a new puppy, make no allowance for the enormous infant requirement of sleep.

Dr. Scott refers to the habit in puppies, from about 3 weeks of age, of tasting various odorous substances combined with mouthing of pieces of wood or pebbles, as well as the bodies of other puppies, and states that stronger reactions are given to raw meat and to the vomit of the mother, both of which are eaten without hesitation if the pup is hungry.

Dr. Scott and his colleagues have divided the developmental period in puppies into four periods, which vary from one individual to another within relatively narrow limits: viz. a neonatal period from birth until the eyes open; a transition period from then until the animal first appears to respond to sound, at about 20 days of age; a period of socialisation lasting until a final weaning at 7–10 weeks of age; and a juvenile period from then until the animal is first capable of mating behaviour proper—as opposed to the juvenile activities already mentioned—at any time from 6 months onwards. Until the end of the transition period the puppy cannot be made to develop conditioned reflexes or to indicate other evidence of learned responses. Electroencephalograms first indicate a difference between sleeping and waking waves at about 20 days of age and the adult form of electroencephalogram is attained between 7–8 weeks. Similar development appears to be the case in wolf puppies, which can readily be socialised to human beings if taken just before the eyes open, but which if taken a few weeks later have become extremely difficult to handle The majority of dog puppies raised under kennel conditions with but little human contact to 5 weeks of age will show fear reaction which, however, will gradually disappear within the next two weeks if the pups are handled regularly. Puppies taken from the litter at 3–4 weeks of age, and raised by hand, do not show fear reactions at 5 weeks, but those allowed to run wild without handling to about 12 weeks of age become increasingly timid and may be extremely difficult to catch. Such puppies can be trained, but will always be more timid and less responsive than those socialised earlier.

Grooming and Washing.

Whilst short-haired breeds need little or no attention to the coat, bar an occasional brisk rub down with a brush or rough towel (which incidentally puts a pleasant gloss on the smooth-haired breeds), yet with the long-haired breeds grooming should be carried out regularly, and if the habit is made a daily one it will not be forgotten so readily. Nearly all dogs love this procedure, and most dogs will actually ask for their daily groom by jumping on the table or bench on which it is carried out. Steel combs and brushes are sold by many shops, principally corn chandlers, though some store chemists also provide a suitable range of grooming kit for all breeds. There is a curious fetish current among many breeds that dogs should not be washed. There is no reason why, with a few simple precautions, a dog should not be washed whenever it is socially necessary. The first precaution is to use a soap that does not contain an excess of soda. The strong washing-up soaps, excellent as they are for certain purposes, are too irritant for a dog's skin. While some of the toilet soaps suitable for human use may be employed for dogs, the special dog soaps and shampoos are much better for the purpose. They are more suited to the dog's skin and coat and have better detergent properties. It is important not to have water that is too hot—as with a baby's bath, it should be possible to dip the point of one's elbow into the water and find that it gives a pleasantly warm sensation but is easily bearable, *i.e.*, it should not be above 35–38 °C. On emerging from a bath a dog will shake himself thoroughly, and then, if not curbed will roll on the floor or ground and speedily cover himself with dust or dirt! It is therefore necessary to give him a brisk rub down with old (but clean) towelling, whereupon he may be allowed to dry off in a warm place free from draughts or, in good weather, put on a lead and taken for a brisk walk. In the case of many of the long-coated breeds it is customary to have them trimmed at the beginning of summer, and this is a sensible precaution that may avoid a good deal of distress during hot weather. The smaller long-haired dogs in particular, such as Scottish Terriers, suffer unduly from the heat if their coats are grown too long.

Feeding.

Nowadays many domestic dogs are fed on canned or "dry" diets that are intended to be nutritionally complete. In the laboratory, the dry diets or "dog chows" do seem to be able to provide for long and active life over many years, although in the laboratory of one of the authors there is also a daily allowance—for Beagles and for the other relatively small breeds, *e.g.*, Scottish Terriers, Cocker Spaniels and Pembrokeshire Corgis used in the past—of ⅛ pint (*c.* 20 ml) of cow's milk, and vitamin tablets were also given while there was some doubt about the effective vitamin content of that kind of diet. It is important to distinguish between "complete" dry diets and dog biscuits, although the latter, as indicated below, many be safely incorporated in mixed diets. Canned foods have varied considerably in the past, but some are almost certainly capable of maintaining animals in health with few additions. In the authors' view it is probably best to give the household dog the advantage and variety that is possible, *i.e.* to use "complete dog" or canned foods on some days and so-called "scraps" on others. The following paragraphs discuss the subject in terms of suitable non-processed foodstuffs.

Meat, usually beef, is generally regarded as the staple article of the dog's diet. It must be pointed out, however, that although the dog is naturally a carnivore (flesh eater) ordinary meat (muscle or "flesh") is not a completely adequate diet, and lacks certain factors which the wild dog would find in the blood, bones, liver, and other organs of his prey. The ratio of calcium: phosphorus in lean meat is quite unsuitable for dogs, and indeed for all the carnivora kept in domestication or captivity, and a diet consisting solely of this has led to serious problems in Zoological gardens, where nowadays extra calcium is fed to balance the deficiency. Furthermore, it has been proved scientifically that dogs can thrive on a meatless diet. In spite of these reservations, however, meat must be regarded as an excellent article of food, and if properly supplemented will prove very satisfactory. In recommendations made in America, Dr. S. R. Speelman, of the US Department of Agriculture, suggested that meat (beef, lamb, mutton, or horseflesh, providing that the last was fed regularly and not spasmodically) or meat substitutes (fish, milk, eggs, *etc.*) should constitute ⅓ of the daily ration, and that the remainder should comprise approximately equal parts of cereal substances (bread, biscuits) and of vegetables (carrots, spinach, onion, beet, *etc.*). He pointed out that many dogs do not accept the vegetable material readily. On this basis, the approximate quantities of food required by adult dogs—expressed in metric terms—were calculated as follows:—

Weight of dog	*Total food/day*
500 g	60 g
5 kg	400 g
10 kg	750 g
20 kg	1 kg
35 kg	1.5 kg
50 kg	2 kg
70 kg	2.5 kg

(Weights of up to 5 kg would include the toy breeds, 10 kg would correspond to a Fox Terrier; Airedale Terriers and Retrievers would fall into the 25–35 kg class, and the larger weights would be those of the very big breeds, such as the St. Bernard.) The quantities given are, of course, an *approximation* and no more. Dogs which lead a very active life will require more, while those which take little exercise, or which tend to put on fat easily, will require less. Common sense is necessary, and great care must be taken not to over-feed or to under-nourish.

Meat is probably best fed raw, or lightly cooked, but many animals appear to have a preference (probably through habit) for well-cooked meat. In any event, the meat should not be "over-done," as there is substantial evidence that prolonged heating destroys much of the food value of the meat protein. *Fish* is an excellent substitute. There need be no anxiety about the greed with which a dog swallows lumps of meat and also neglects to masticate them. The teeth of the dog are for tearing meat, he is not concerned with biting his food up small; indeed, his salivary glands contain no digestive ferments, as is the case with some other animals.

Milk is almost essential during pregnancy and lactation and may well be included in normal dietaries. Whether or not *bones* should be fed is a matter which has been hotly debated, but for mature household dogs the evidence suggests that they are unnecessary. (The teeth of racing greyhounds, which receive a "sloppy" diet, are quite as good as those of the average household dog). Bone-feeding is responsible for much trouble, including constipation, actual impaction of the rectum, and lodgement of pieces of bone in the mouth or throat. The value of bones is, of course, that they contain large quantities of essential mineral substances, and for this reason the inclusion in the diet of bone-meal, or of steamed *bone-*

flour, or, preferably, a mineral supplement, is recommended. Only very small quantities of these substances are required.

Bread is an article of food which is often overlooked in the case of the dog, but there is no doubt that wholemeal bread is very suitable indeed, provided it is not fed to excess.

The answer to the question whether a dog requires vegetables is, in the main, no. From the Vitamin C standpoint they are quite unnecessary, since it has been shown that a dog manufactures this vitamin for itself, but the fact remains that many dogs, particularly of the toy variety, enjoy a few slices of banana or apple, and there is no harm in letting them pander to their taste. Vegetables do help, however, to provide roughage, and cooked (*not* raw) *potatoes* may be used in place of bread or biscuits. The dog—like many other animals—cannot digest raw starch properly. *Flaked maize* and *oatmeal* are other substitutes, but it must be remembered that the energy value of maize is high and that the dogs must never be overfed. *Dog biscuits* were long in disfavour with some professional people on account of their often having been made from agenised white flour, but now that this factor has been overcome, and the biscuits themselves are being improved in other ways, their use for the non-meat portion of the diet may be recommended.

Clean fresh *water* must be provided at all times.

In addition to the diets recommended above there are on the market several tinned dog food which claim to be complete, or almost complete diets for the dog. It must be said that many dogs (including those of the writer) have remained in excellent health when receiving one of these foods as a large part of the diet over long periods. There is, therefore, little that may be said against the widespread use of the better varieties of such products. Again, it is a matter for common sense; if an owner finds that his animal is thriving on such a diet, he is wise to continue to use it.

It is customary to give dogs two meals a day. There is no need to give more than two to healthy adults, for the dog's stomach is exceedingly capacious and adapted to long gaps between meals. Many dogs thrive on only one meal in twenty-four hours. Whatever plan is decided on, regularity should be adhered to, and a meal or meals given at the same times every day. Dogs require vitamins A and D and B complex. There are several ways of administering these, but the special commercial preparations, including the modern form of condition-powder tablet, are the most convenient.

The *pregnant* and *lactating bitch* require special consideration. The food requirements are very much increased in a bitch which is carrying puppies, especially towards the end of the period. Normally, appetite is not a complete guide to a dog's food requirements, but in pregnancy and lactation the bitch must not be allowed to go hungry. It is quite normal for a heavily pregnant bitch to require over one and a half times her normal amount of food, and in lactation her requirements will increase still further. Milk is a most excellent article of diet at this time; indeed, there is no better way (apart from commercial preparations) of replacing the milk which the bitch is giving to her own puppies.

Up to the age of three weeks or so, *puppies* need have mother's milk only, but at any time after this it is a sound policy to give them additional food, and so spare the mother and also render weaning (at from six to eight weeks) a *gradual* process. At first a little cow's milk or one of the commercial "dog-milk" preparations may be given, and gradually the puppies should be encouraged to eat solid food. Eggs (if they can be spared), wholemeal bread in milk, or even finely minced meat may be given, at first in very small amounts but later in larger quantities. If this process is carefully carried out, there will be far less trouble at and after weaning time. After weaning, puppies should receive five or six meals a day, and this number may be cut down gradually until two or three only are given to the fully grown dog. (The smaller breeds are fully grown at about a year.) *More* meat or meat substitutes and milk, and *less* cereal or vegetable matter, should be fed to the growing dog as compared with the adult. This fact is important, as the substances present in meat and milk are required for laying down the growing tissues. Nevertheless, the energy portion of the ration is important, and the cereal or vegetable should be nutritious and not fibrous. It is possible to rear puppies by hand from birth if the bitch for any reason should die. It requires great patience for the first two or three weeks, as naturally the puppies will require feeding once or twice during the night. Special milks for puppies are to be recommended. Cow's milk requires enriching with fat and sugar to approximate to the composition of bitch's milk. Feeding will have to be done at every two or three hours, and a very useful gadget is a fountain-pen filler attached to cyclo-valve tubing. Very small quantities are required for the first two or three days, and a level teaspoonful of milk is more than sufficient for the average terrier at first. Even with the best care in the world hand-fed puppies tend to be weaklings and do not grow as fast as those naturally fed. A foster bitch, if obtainable, is much to be preferred.

A summary by one of the authors on the feeding of dogs (and cats) is given in *Canine and Feline Nutritional Requirements*, edited by O. Graham-Jones (Oxford: Pergamon).

Breeding.

It is natural for adult dogs of both sexes to wish to breed, and in the case of the female especially it is an excellent thing if one can arrange for a suitable mating to take place. Bitches come "into season" or "on heat" (lay terms for oestrus) at approximately six-monthly intervals, but it is not advisable to breed from the first season which occurs usually at about eight to nine months of age, but over a wide range of age according to breed and other factors. The periods of season often occur between January and March and in early autumn, but there is no fixed rule. Each season lasts for three weeks. For the first seven days, approximately (pro-oestrus), a bitch does not permit mating, though during this time she is a source of strong attraction to all males in the neighbourhood. At about the seventh to the tenth day the blood-stained discharge, which ushers in the heat, stops; this is usually taken by the breeder as an indication that the bitch will stand to service. If possible, it is always better when puppies are wanted to allow mating to occur more than once. Under natural conditions a dog and bitch are usually strictly monogamous and mate for life, and during the period of oestrus will mate many times. A dog and bitch that are kept together all the time will probably behave naturally, but under domestication both dogs and bitches usually become promiscuous. Many bitches will in fact accept service from different males on different days, and the phenomenon of superfecundation, *i.e.*, the production of a litter that is fathered by *two* males, may occur. It is therefore wise to retain strict control of the bitch throughout the whole of the three weeks or so she is in season. At the end of season the bitch passes into a state of "metoestrus" if she has not conceived.

If a bitch conceives, she carries her puppies for a period of about nine weeks. There is, however, a normal variation of fifty-eight to seventy days, and puppies born before the fifty-eighth day sometimes live. The number of puppies born varies with breed; in the smaller terriers it is usually from four to six, but in Airedales and Alsatians the number may be eight to ten, and the larger breeds tend to have even more offspring at a time. Birth usually takes place fairly easily in the larger breeds, but there is often much difficulty in the case of the short-legged breeds, such as Scottish and Sealyham Terriers, Pekingese and Dachshunds. In some breeds, in fact, the problem is one that is giving serious concern to veterinary surgeons and breeders.

A short while before her puppies are due, a bitch will "make her bed." Owners are often amazed at the destruction of soft furnishings, or even of wall-paper, that a previously well-behaved bitch may carry out at this time; it is therefore by far the best to provide a suitable box (if the animal has not one already). A smooth flooring such as a strip of linoleum serves for the bitch to give birth to her puppies. Her instinct to tear up everything given to her for bedding may lead to suffocation of the puppies by pieces of bedding. Provided labour occurs in a warm room, it is sometimes better—according to the temperament of the bitch—to remove each puppy as it is born, placing a warm bottle underneath, and bring it back to the mother when the last birth has occurred. At this time the bitch should be watched carefully for any discharge from the vulva or for any evidence of straining. If either of these occurs without results, it is advisable to send for help as early as possible, especially in the case of the smaller breeds. Many hundreds of bitches are lost through neglect at this time, and usually because it was not suspected that anything was wrong. If the discharge becomes bloody, or green, help should be obtained *at once* if no puppy is delivered. Similarly, any great delay between births is a matter for concern. The afterbirth usually follows the puppy within a few minutes, but puppies are sometimes delivered in their foetal membranes, and in this case the latter should be gently but quickly removed. It is quite normal for the umbilical cord to remain attached to the puppy, but the bitch will normally break it by biting through it.

The mother will wash and attend to the newborn puppies, and after the last is born it is a good idea to burn all the mess and to provide clean newspaper, but do not worry or frighten the bitch more than is necessary. Puppies, like kittens, are born with their eyes closed, but open them after about nine days—there again being considerable variation.

The phenomenon of pseudopregnancy is common in bitches, and indeed to a minor degree it is probably present in most bitches following an oestrus without conception. In some bitches, however, presumably those with strong maternal drives, the changes in the ovary, may be accompanied by external signs of "phantom" or "ghost" pregnancy. These may include not only enlargement but actual functioning of the mammary glands, and the making of a "nest" by the bitch just as if her puppies were really due. The average duration of pseudopregnancy is usually given as about two months, and although variable, it is often sufficiently near to the correct time after oestrus that everyone suspects the bitch to be truly pregnant. The condition may be suppressed with the aid of modern drugs, but in some instances it is not realised that the condition is not real. In many cases only professional advice can solve the mystery, and radiographical examinations have often proved necessary to ascertain the truth, particularly in fat bitches of the heavier breeds. It might be well to note, at this point, that there is another condition of the older bitch that is known as *Pyometra*. This condition usually reveals itself at the same time as the ghost pregnancy (and is sometimes a pathological extension of it) but is accompanied by considerable disturbance of health, coupled in many instances with purulent discharge from the vagina. A bitch which is off-colour in the weeks following pregnancy, or which develops a discharge from the vulva (especially one which is dark in colour), may well be a pyometra subject. The disease is most serious, and often requires surgical intervention. As the best chance of success is to operate or otherwise deal with early, a veterinary surgeon should be consulted immediately.

Diseases and Injuries.

Since the days when one of the authors took a veterinary qualification, shortly before the second world war, there has been a tremendous advance in the understanding of disease in dogs. Except as indicated below, it is wise to seek prompt veterinary advice whenever a dog is "off colour". As in human beings, the pattern of disease may change quite markedly with the years, and there is always the risk of the emergence of new or modified strains of organism that can create havoc, especially among large kennels or packs.

Canine Distemper and "Para-distemper" (Including so-called "Hard-pad").

It has long been recognised that the commonest and most serious disease of dogs throughout the world is canine distemper. Dogs of all ages and breeds are susceptible, and no dog is free from the risk of infection unless it has recovered from the disease or has acquired an immunity for other reasons. The disease is caused primarily by a minute agent known as a filterable virus, which may be of varying type in that it will attack the body in different ways. Thus some strains of the virus are known as "neurotropic" because they show an affinity for the nervous system. Sometimes a dog will apparently recover from an attack of distemper, only to succumb later to "fits" or other nervous manifestations due to permanent damage to the central nervous system by the virus. Often, however, the virus is not fatal in itself, but will lower the dog's resistance and permit the entry or the activity of bacteria that may lead to pneumonia or other serious effects. These so-called "secondary invaders," as the bacteria are termed, may prove as harmful as the original virus. Indeed, once these bacteria have set to work it is too late to expect the best results from the use of serum, and whether or not the dog will live through will depend upon the severity of the attack, the dog's powers of resistance, and good nursing. It is therefore most important either to prevent the disease by vaccination or to be able to send for veterinary attention (and hence for an injection of serum) *immediately* an attack is suspected. Any puppy which is listless or off its food, or which may throw a fit, or which is obviously unwell with other symptoms (*e.g.*, cough or diarrhoea) may well be in the early stages of distemper, and it is *then* (not the next day) that help should be sought. Many thousands of puppies (and older dogs) that have been injected with serum in the early stages of the disease have become perfectly normal within forty-eight hours. On the other hand, the number of dogs that die in Great Britain alone from distemper and distemper-like infections must assume enormous proportions. Distemper is a highly infectious disease, and it is important that the owner of an infected animal should do his best to avoid contact with other dogs, ferrets, or mink. Ferrets and mink are very susceptible to canine distemper. On the other hand, human beings and cats are *not* susceptible to canine distemper, and the so-called distemper of cats is quite a distinct disease.

A highly satisfactory means of vaccinating puppies against distemper was worked out about 1926–30, and this—named the "Laidlaw–Dunkin" after its two inventors—has since afforded protection to thousands of animals. Modern vaccines are based on a virus which has been modified by growth on developing egg embryos; or, more recently, in tissue culture. Puppies should be vaccinated when they are 10–12 weeks; prior to this age the immunity induced by the vaccine may not develop satisfactorily. After vaccination the puppy requires some time, possibly 2 weeks, before an immunity is established. Sometimes vaccinated dogs suffer distemper or distemper-like signs due to "secondary invaders" causing disease on their own account: or because they were already infected when vaccinated. Variants of distemper, of which "hard pad" was an example, may also overwhelm a vaccinated dog's immunity, although this is uncommon with modern vaccines, since several distemper strains are used in their production. Hyperimmune serum, which is collected from animals previously hyperimmunised against distemper, is available and can immediately aid the dog suffering from distemper but its effect is short-lived (7–10 days).

Infectious Hepatitis or Rubarth's Disease.

Another virus disease of dogs (and foxes) is known as Rubarth's disease, after one of its discoverers, now known as infectious hepatitis. This disease has been recognised in Sweden ever since the 1930s, but in Great Britain only since the end of the second world war. The condition is extremely sudden in onset, and an infected dog may be found dead. Many cases are, however, mild, and in some instances only one or two out of a large group of dogs have been affected. The changes seen after death vary, but the findings in the liver cells are usually characteristic. Specific treatment is not yet established, as in the case of the distemper-like conditions, although the administration of antibiotics may prevent the effects of secondary infection. An effective vaccine is often combined with distemper vaccine. A dog is thereby protected against both these diseases. (It has recently been established that canine hepatitis is due to an adenovirus, and that while it predominantly attacks the liver it can—even in some vaccinated animals—sometimes spread by droplet infection. After causing relatively little trouble for nearly 20 years, fresh outbreaks became evident in the 1970s).

Canine Hysteria.

Called "fright disease" or "running fits" in the USA. this is an alarming but not necessarily serious condition (in that it can often be cured very readily) which appears to arise from a variety of exciting causes. The affected animal rushes around wildly, often screaming and howling, and obviously loses all sense of whereabouts or ability to recognise people. After a more severe attack (and there are all degrees up to a full epileptiform fit) the dog may appear quite exhausted but returns to normal. Sometimes there are many attacks in one day. The dog will not wilfully attack people during a bout of hysteria—at least that has been the experience of the writers—but is very difficult to control. Apart from ensuring that the dog does itself no grievous bodily harm, there is little that can be done until the attack has subsided. Then the animal should be kept as quiet as possible and given a tranquilliser

Hysteria may arise from an hereditary taint, derived from one or other parent. In certain circumstances, however, it may arise in apparently normal animals. There are several possible causes (including parasites), but a definite one is the bleaching agent—nitrogen trichloride or "agene" once employed in the manufacture of flour, and hence present in white bread and certain dog biscuits. Indeed, the clear demonstration that agene could set up hysteria in dogs, and subsequent scientific work, resulted in its abandonment as a bleaching agent in favour of other methods which have been found not to cause hysteria. There has since been an almost total reduction in the incidence of hysteria due to dietary factors.

Rabies.

Rabies is a fatal disease of dogs, and is also due to a "filterable virus." It is transmissible to the human being and to many other species, but has fortunately been absent from Great Britain for many years. Stringent precautions are taken to prevent its entry, and dogs which are brought into Great Britain must spend a long period in quarantine. A vaccine is available and people taking dogs to countries where rabies occurs should have their animals protected. Many countries insist on this procedure.

Tonsilitis.

Tonsilitis appears quite frequently in dogs, and seems in many cases to be part of a more generalised infection. It demands expert treatment, but although it may persist for a long time, it usually yields to treatment.

Nephritis.

Inflammation of the kidneys is unfortunately all too common in dogs, and in adult males in particular there is a high incidence of chronic kidney damage. One of the symptoms is a marked thirst. Sometimes this condition is a sequel to an infection known as *leptospirosis*, which calls for prompt veterinary treatment if death or permanent damage is not to follow. It is always worth while seeking professional advice for a dog that drinks excessively or has a somewhat characteristic type of bad breath. A vaccine which gives a good immunity against the two common forms of *leptospirosis* is available.

Anal Glands.

Anal glands which are found in the dog and in other carnivora, often give rise to trouble. Animals which "rub themselves along the ground" are not necessarily affected with "worms," but with impaction of these two little glands, which are situated one on each side of the anus. They secrete a peculiar dark-coloured, very offensive fluid, which sometimes is not discharged properly and causes the animal great discomfort. The glands in such cases should be relieved periodically. Those who do not mind this somewhat dirty task may perhaps learn how to do it themselves. Occasionally, segments of tapeworm are responsible for the impaction, but usually the trouble has nothing to do with worms. Whenever a dog pays considerable attention to his anus, this impaction should be suspected. Actual infection of the glands is also fairly common, and demands expert attention.

Diseases of the Ear.

Diseases of the ear, especially of the outer ear, are very common in dogs. The dog's outer ear is somewhat more complicated than is our own, and the drum is set more deeply. Hence it is easy for wax and dirt to accumulate, for various parasites to establish themselves, and for inflammatory conditions to result. The word "canker" (which has no precise scientific meaning) is sometimes applied by lay people to the more serious or chronic forms of inflammation of the outer ear canal. It is not difficult to diagnose "ear trouble," as the affected animal usually shakes its head or worries or scratches its ear and rubs it along the ground. The ears should be inspected regularly to see that there is no great accumulation of wax or dirt. Cotton-wool twisted on to the end of a match-stick or orange-stick is quite satisfactory for cleaning out the ear, providing care is taken. A dog which is continually worrying its ear, or which has ears which are obviously diseased, should not be neglected, as the sooner expert treatment is begun the more readily will the condition be cured. Even if the lining of the ear is greatly thickened through inflammatory reaction, and the lumen nearly occluded, it is still possible for a plastic operation to be performed. Many hundreds of such cases have been successfully treated in this way. A percentage of inflammatory conditions of the outer ear is associated with ear mange mites. In such an event treatment with modern anti-mange preparations should be carried out.

Deafness.

Deafness in certain white dogs (*e.g.*, in some Bull Terriers) appears to be hereditary, and is quite incurable. Old dogs often become deaf, and deafness has been produced experimentally in young puppies by feeding them on a deficient diet.

Diseases of the Eye.

Diseases of the eye are very common in dogs, and are often the result of injury. Except for minor discharges from the corners of their eyes (and in younger dogs especially it must be ascertained that these are not a symptom of distemper) any eye disease is sufficiently serious to merit professional advice. Boracic lotion is not suitable for the eyes of dogs. It is slightly irritant, and dogs are apt to scratch and make the eyes raw after application. Colloidal silver eye lotions and ointments are far more suitable pending the advice of a veterinary surgeon. In eye inflammation avoid sunlight and wind. For some days in the early stages of inflamed eyes, the light in the room should be subdued. Pekingese seem to be especially prone to eye disease, but the remarkably unwholesome appearance of some affected eyes in this breed is not necessarily evidence that recovery is unlikely. Steps should be taken to ensure that the dog does not inflict further injury on an already diseased eye. Cat scratches are a frequent source of inflammatory conditions of the dog's eye. Eyes must never be neglected, for the consequences are serious. Hereditary eye defects are well known in some breeds.

Skin Diseases.

Skin diseases are common in dogs, and may be contagious. Among the common contagious causes of skin disease are lice, mange mites and fleas. Lice and mange mites (except for demodex) are killed by modern insecticides although two applications at a 10–14 day interval are required to destroy the young stages which are within the insecticide-resistant eggs at the first dressing.

The flea actually on the dog is only one of four stages in the life cycle of the flea; the others are in the house or dog's bedding. Insecticides used for flea control should therefore be applied every week or 10 days during the summer to kill the young fleas as they hatch and infest the dog. The dog's bedding should be discarded or cleaned. The dog also suffers from other skin diseases caused by systemic disorders for which expert attention is required.

Diseases of the Teeth and Gums.

Diseases of the teeth and gums are very common in household dogs. A serious systemic disease, such as distemper, may leave the enamel of the teeth permanently pitted, hence "distemper teeth." More serious than this, however, is a form of pyorrhœa, which is really a disease of the gums rather than a primary disease of the teeth themselves. The margins of the gums become red and swollen, and may bleed easily. As the condition progresses the teeth may become loosened. Particles of food become lodged between the teeth or between teeth and gums, and add to the inflammation and to the smell of the breath.

This disease may, if unchecked, become very serious. In many cases extraction of one or more teeth is indicated, but unfortunately it is not always possible to do this. The condition demands expert attention.

Another common condition of dogs' teeth is the deposition around them of "tartar." This should be removed by scaling or by special use of dental forceps. Some breeders and others may themselves have learnt how to carry out these operations with the requisite skill and care, but they are not easy to the amateur, and it is essential that no harm be done to the animal's soft tissues by injudicious use of the instruments. Ordinary dog-owners are strongly advised to take their dogs to a veterinary surgeon in order to have the "tartar" removed.

Most puppies lose their first or "milk" teeth quite regularly between the ages of three and five months, but sometimes there is difficulty and the primary teeth are not shed properly. These cases should be treated by a veterinary surgeon before the permanent teeth are thrown out of their proper alignment.

One hears very much about "teething fits" in puppies, and while these occur, owners should be *very* careful to ensure that a "teething fit" is not a sign of distemper, which often starts with a fit. As puppies of this age are so susceptible to distemper, it is advisable to seek professional advice should any form of fit occur. It may save much time, money, and trouble, and even the animal's life.

Internal Parasites: "Worms."

It is probable that more nonsense has been talked and written about "worms" in dogs than about any other canine subject. According to some people, "worms" are the root of nearly all doggy evil, and so long as a dog is regularly "wormed" all will go well with him. These beliefs are frankly absurd. The real facts are very different, and are stated in as brief a fashion as possible in the following sentences. In this country dogs are infested by a species of "roundworm" (a creature which is a dirty-white colour and in shape somewhat resembles the common earthworm) and by several species of "tapeworm," which are also whitish but which are flat and are made up of many small segments joined to a little "head" which is attached to the lining of the gut. In spite of all that is said, tapeworms as such are rarely responsible for much harm to the dog, although they can, of course, prove debilitating and should be removed. They are a nuisance, and attempts to remove them should be made by administration of the appropriate drug. Occasionally, segments of worm are responsible for impaction of the ducts of the *anal glands* (see above).

The roundworms may be extremely serious in young puppies, in which they cause stunting, "pot-belly," harshness of coat and dangerous or fatal illness. Fortunately, modern anti-roundworm preparations are available for animals of this age. Once over the age of 4–8 months, dogs rarely suffer serious illness from roundworms, although these may cause occasional vomiting, or even diarrhoea, and some loss of coat and bodily condition. It is now known that puppies are infected before birth from their mother. It is therefore desirable to keep down the incidence of roundworms in the mother—and in dogs generally—and fortunately the modern preparations are—unlike some of the old-fashioned ones—safe in use and unlikely to cause digestive disturbances. From all that has been said above owners will realise the necessity of taking professional advice about young dogs which are ill, and any signs of "worms" in young puppies—either in the stools or by some obvious intestinal upset or bloated appearance of the belly—should be acted upon. One last word about this aspect of worms—do not assume that your adult dog has "tapeworms" unless you see some evidence in his stools. There are so many "signs of worms" that veterinary surgeons must at times get a little tired of being assured that "My dog has worms" because of some trivial habit connected with appetite.

There is, however, another side to the study of tapeworms, and one which is not generally realised. The tapeworm which is found in the dog represents one stage in the life-cycle. The eggs, which are present in the ripe segment passed by the dog, develop, not in the outside world, but in another animal altogether. Thus one of the commonest tapeworms in this country has an intermediate stage, as it is called, in the flea, and it is when the flea is eaten by the dog that this intermediate stage develops further to become a tapeworm. Another tapeworm has an intermediate stage which develops in the sheep, and a third has one which develops in the ox. There is a fourth tapeworm which has an intermediate stage which *may* develop in man, to set up serious diseases in certain cases. Children may become infected through handling the dog, and so picking up the eggs, which may then be eaten through putting the hands in the mouth. The dogs which are most likely to be infested are those which have the opportunity to eat freshly killed sheep and other food-animals. An ordinary household dog is not likely to be infested, and people should not worry unduly in this connection, provided they do not allow their dogs to stray into the wrong places. It is illegal to allow dogs to enter a slaughter-house, but unfortunately one often sees dogs in such places. The routine worming of dogs is justified if evidence of infection exists, and certainly in country areas where opportunities of tapeworm re-infection may be plentiful.

Tumours.

Tumours, including malignant tumours ("cancers") are relatively very common in the dog—almost as common as in the human subject. Space does not permit of a detailed account, but the following examples of growths may be mentioned: a proliferation of warts on the skin of puppies (usually disappear spontaneously); a true cancer of the tonsil in middle-aged and older dogs of both sexes; cancer of the mammary glands in bitches (both incurable); fatty growths of the vagina of bitches (amenable to operation).

Space does not allow of the discussion of other diseases, but it should be pointed out that dogs are susceptible to human and bovine forms of *tuberculosis*, especially the former. In a household which contains a tubercular person, the dog should be watched for any signs of illness, and the thought entertained that he might be responsible for the further spread of the disease. In the late 1960s, it was reported that a virus of the herpes group could cause the death of pups at 3–4 weeks of age. The infection is transmitted from dam to young *in utero*. For a discussion on ringworm see the appropriate heading in the section on the cat.

Accidents and Injuries.

In these days of swiftly moving motor transport, street accidents to dogs are extremely common. Many could be prevented by training the animal to walk to heel, by the use of a lead in busy thoroughfares, and by not allowing dogs to roam the streets unaccompanied—a thoroughly bad habit. Sometimes the victim escapes with a scare and a few bruises, and at others death is mercifully swift. In the vast majority of accidents, however, a more or less serious injury is incurred, and if the animal is unable to move, the police should be notified immediately. The dog is best left quiet, and it is not recommended that attempts be made to administer brandy or other supposed "stimulants" unless help is markedly delayed. Excessive haemorrhage may in some instances be prevented by common-sense application of principles learnt in first-aid courses.

One of the commonest accidents to dogs, especially to young dogs, is a fracture involving the head of the femur, or thigh-bone. Inability to put one of the hind legs to the ground, or to bear any weight on this limb, is an indication of such an injury. (This injury may occur also from falling off a chair or wall.) Professional help is, of course, required in such cases.

Cuts and Bruises.

Cuts and bruises, if not serious, may be treated at home as in the case of human beings. The indiscriminate use of tincture of iodine is not to be recommended, and spirit alone makes a more satisfactory dressing in most cases. Simple washing and removal of dirt are usually sufficient, combined, perhaps, with modern antiseptic ointments or other preparations. The dog (and also the cat) are very liable to sepsis, and it is best in such cases to send for proper assistance early, or there may be grave trouble. It is probable that in nature many of the flesh-eating animals end their lives as victims of the sepsis following wounds.

Injuries from cat-scratches are exceedingly common, as are bites from other dogs. These are serious, as they more readily result in septic places. The scratch or bite sometimes penetrates quite deeply, leaving a pocket which fills up with pus. This pus may spread under the skin to form sinuses. Never neglect such places.

Conclusion.

There are a few concluding remarks on the treatment of the diseases of the dog:—

(1) It is not correct that "water should be withheld from a sick dog." It is true that an animal which is using water only to vomit, or which is drinking excessively, should have its water intake restricted but it is wrong to deprive a dog altogether. It may be suffering from diabetes and should be taken to the vet for testing.

(2) There have been such wonderful advances in the field of veterinary anaesthetics that there is nowadays little to fear in this connection from operations to dogs and cats. The records over the past years at the Royal Veterinary College, London and at other centres have been most encouraging, and the anaesthetic risk is now small indeed.

(3) When a dog's life is a burden to him, it is unfair to keep him alive, and he should be put to sleep. It must be realised, however, that putting a dog to sleep is a very skilled task. It is made much easier if an owner will allow his veterinary surgeon to administer an anaesthetic and not allow the animal "to come round," and shooting is also straightforward and painless if *skilfully* carried out. There are no "magical ways" of destroying human or animal life, and an owner must not expect his veterinary surgeon to be able to bring about death merely by holding a pad to the dog's face. It is usually better that the task be carried out at a veterinary surgeon's own premises, where there is skilled assistance.

CATS

Description.

Many of the general remarks in the preceding section apply equally to cats, and will not be repeated unnecessarily in the following paragraphs.

The domestic cat (*Felis catus*) is one of the smallest members of the genus *Felis*, a group of predatory carnivorous mammals that includes lions and tigers. They have characteristic rounded skulls with small incisor teeth, prominent sharp canine teeth and large molars. They can climb, leap and move rapidly for short periods, and cheetahs are the fastest runners of all animals, but do not need or benefit from prolonged exercise. Indeed, a fully grown, healthy cat may be unable to follow the leisurely pace of a strolling human being for even half an hour without showing signs of exhaustion.

Dr. Patricia Scott, of the Royal Free Hospital School of Medicine, and perhaps the world's leading scientific authority on cats, has written a valuable chapter on them in the *UFAW Handbook*.

Most authorities subscribe to the view that the European domestic cat probably originated from crossing between 2 wild species, *Felis sylvestris* and *F. lybica*, and certainly it has been domesticated for thousands of years. (The wild cat of Scotland is a sub-species of *F. sylvestris*). The tabby markings of *F. catus* appear in 2 distinct forms: the first, "torquata" with narrow vertical stripes on the body, and the second, "catus" with 3 dorsal stripes running to the root of the tail and a looped or spiral arrangement of blotched stripes on the side.

Konrad Lorenz, whose observations have already been referred to, has provided beautiful descriptions of the play of kittens, which, in fact, provide evidence for the existence of inborn hunting behaviour. Kittens and other cats are attracted by almost any moving object. Since the majority of cats are neutered at an early age, while entire males indulge in sexual behaviour out of doors, the development of certain forms of adolescent behaviour are often absent or unseen in domestic pets.

Cats will defend their homes against neighbouring or intruding cats, and also possess a fairly large hunting territory which they will guard against trespassers. There may, of course, be partial overlap between neighbouring territories. Encounters between strange cats are enacted according to what seem to be fixed rules. The territory "owner" usually has the better of it. The superior cat attempts to smell the nose and anus of the intruder as the latter tries to explore the strange territory. Even quite young cats will attempt a thorough exploration of a new room. A true submissive attitude does not, however, appear to be usual in adult cats, which as solitary animals do not establish rigid social orders if several of them are kept together in a fairly large room. One or two "despots" and one or more "pariahs" may emerge but the rest of the crowd appears to be on equal footing.

The reaction of cats to dogs and to man has received considerable study. Most people look upon cats and dogs as sworn enemies, but the kitten does not seem to have any inborn understanding of the facial expressions of the dog. It would seem that cats, without previous experience do not understand the expressive movements of dogs, even though these are so similar to their own. Cats which are on friendly terms with dogs in the same house may display a trustfulness towards strange dogs with disastrous results. It is equally unusual, incidentally, for a cat-friendly dog to understand the threatening of a cat unless it has already learnt to do so from bitter experience.

Many cat owners are proud of the independence of their charges, and Lorenz has emphasised the dual role of the cat that hunts and fights out of doors but becomes a peaceful pet within. He said that, in spite of their well-defined private lives in the wild which often kept them from home for days on end, his most temperamental and virile cats were at the same time the most affectionate.

Some animal behaviourists say that cats, alone among mammals below the primates, are capable of true imitative behaviour, *i.e.*, can copy a novel or otherwise improbable act, or some act for which there is clearly no instructive tendency. Cats will spontaneously copy the begging of dogs at table and one of the authors, when young and with plenty of time to spare, succeeded in teaching young kittens to play "hide and seek" both ways, and even to learn to box one another.

Cat showing and pedigree breeding are not so extensive as comparable activities for dogs, but there exists a Governing Council of the Cat Fancy. The secretary is Mrs. W. Davis, Dovefields, Petworth Road, Witley, Surrey GU8 5QW and the receptor for all registration, transfers and export pedigrees is Mr. R. Loveys, 28 Brendon Road, Watchet, Somerset (Watchet 395). There are separate secretaries for the many different Cat Groups, and the Honorary Secretary of the National Cat Club is Mrs. Rosemary Gowdy, Porlock House, Haw Lane, Bledlow Ridge, Bucks. (024-027-463). The objects of the Council are to provide for the registration of cats and cat pedigrees, to classify cat breeds, to provide cat shows, to improve cat breeding, to protect the welfare of cats and the interests of cat owners generally, to exercise disciplinary powers and to concern itself with publications.

The accompanying table lists the different breeds by the numbers that have been registered by the Council.

There is an up-to-date book by Dr. R. Robinson, *Genetics for Cat Breeders* (Oxford: Pergamon). For those who wish to make a scientific study, further information can be found in the issues of *Carnivore Genetics Newsletter*, obtainable from P.O. Box 5, Newtownville, Massachusetts 02160, USA.

BREED NUMBERS

Long-Haired Cats

1	Black.
2	White (Blue Eyes).
2a	White (Orange Eyes).
2b	White (Odd Eyes).
3	Blue.
4	Red Self.
5	Cream.
6	Smoke.
6a	Blue Smoke.
7	Silver Tabby.
8	Brown Tabby.
9	Red Tabby
10	Chinchilla.
11	Tortoiseshell.
12	Tortoiseshell-and-White.
12a	Bi-Coloured.
13	Blue Cream.
13a	Any Other Colour.
13b/1	Seal Colourpoint.
13b/2	Blue Colourpoint.
13b/3	Chocolate Colourpoint.
13b/4	Lilac Colourpoint.
13b/5	Red Colourpoint.
13b/6	Tortie Colourpoint.
13b/7	Cream Colourpoint.
13b/8	Blue Cream Colourpoint.
13b/9	Chocolate Cream Colourpoint.
13b/10	Lilac Cream Colourpoint.
13c	Birman.
13d	Turkish.

Short-Haired Cats

14	White (Blue Eyes).
14a	White (Orange Eyes).
14b	White (Odd Eyes).
15	Black.
16	Blue British.
16a	Blue Russian.
17	Cream.
18	Silver Tabby.
19	Red Tabby.
20	Brown Tabby.
21	Tortoiseshell.
22	Tortoiseshell-and-White.
23	Abyssinian.
23a	Red Abyssinian.
23b	Cream Abyssinian.
23c	Blue Abyssinian.
23d	Chocolate Abyssinian.
23e	Lilac Abyssinian.
23x	A.O.C. Abyssinian.
24	Seal-Pointed Siamese.
24a	Blue-Pointed Siamese.
24b	Chocolate-Pointed Siamese.
24c	Lilac-Pointed Siamese.
25	Manx.
25a	Stumpies.
25b	Tailed.
26	Any Other Variety.
27	Brown Burmese.
27a	Blue Burmese.
27b	Chocolate Burmese.
27c	Lilac Burmese.
27d	Red Burmese.
27e	Tortie Burmese.
27f	Cream Burmese.
27g	Blue-Cream Burmese.
27h	Chocolate-Tortie Burmese.
27j	Lilac-Cream Burmese.
28	Blue Cream.
29	Havana.
29c	Foreign Lilac.
30	Spotted.
31	Bi-Coloured.
32	Tabby-Point Siamese.
32a	Red-Point Siamese.
32b	Tortie-Point Siamese.
32x	A.O.C. Siamese.
33	Cornish Rex.
33a	Devon Rex.
35	Foreign White.
32c	Cream Point.
34	Korat.
36	Smoke.

Although there are, as noted above, many varieties of cat, most people are content to accept an ordinary kitten, and for them the chief points to consider will be: (*a*) whether to have a long-haired or a short-haired animal, (*b*) whether to have a male or female, (*c*) whether or not to have the kitten "doctored" (*i.e.*, castrated or spayed). As a general rule, short-haired cats are probably more suitable for the average household, since their fur does not become shed so noticeably and they probably suffer less from "fur-balling." Nevertheless, many long-haired cats are so attractive that they will obviously be preferred, and there is no reason why they should not be chosen. Sex is a rather more important question, although, as may be seen in the section on management, it is possible to have both males and females "doctored." Male cats which are kept as entires are often a nuisance in that they make abominable smells in the house and spend much of their time in fighting. These characteristics are by no means invariable; but they are so common as to justify the castration of the majority of males. Siamese males in particular may be a liability. Females are generally credited with a greater attachment to the home (although they wander when "in season") and with being better mousers. The principal objection to females is that they seem to be bearing kittens almost continuously. In normal circumstances it is, of course, quite impossible to prevent cats from mating by keeping the female in confinement during her season, a practice which is frequently adopted in the case of the dog. For one thing, most people are never aware when their female cats are in season.

Whatever animal is chosen, it is essential to pick a healthy and preferably a fairly young—but *not* too young—kitten. It is best not to accept a kitten under about eight weeks of age.

For those who are prepared for additional responsibilities, Siamese cats make excellent and highly intelligent pets. Siamese kittens are born white, but gradually develop their even pale fawn colour, with cream on belly and chest and with "seal brown" mask, ears, legs, feet, and tail. The coat is very short, and the eyes are blue. There has long been a popular belief that Siamese cats are delicate creatures, but the present writers have seen healthy specimens, kept under ordinary household conditions, living to a mature age. It is not wise to keep a male Siamese as a household pet. The male is a fierce fighter, and is generally a worse offender in the house than the males of other breeds, and should therefore be castrated if it is to be kept as a pet.

Many people find Manx cats attractive. Instead of the normal large number of tail bones, they have but three, and hence appear almost tailless. One should beware against fraudulent amputation of the tail of ordinary cats, which are then described as "Manx."

Accommodation and Management.

The cat is an independent creature, so much so that one may say that to a large extent it manages its own affairs. This, however, is not true of all cats, and every reasonable attempt should be made to provide the cat with a comfortable and friendly home. Cats are highly intelligent, and if sufficient patience is exercised they will respond to a very great degree to human attention. Kittens should not be neglected, but should be talked to and played with just as are puppies. Many cats, especially young cats, make excellent playmates for children.

In order to prevent to a large extent their nocturnal wanderings, many cats of both sexes are castrated or spayed (the popular lay expression for this is "doctored"). In the male cat the testicles are removed by an operation which is almost always safe and simple if carried out skilfully. From three to four months is a good age at which to have this done. Female cats may also be "doctored." As the female glands or ovaries lie within the body cavity, this operation is a major one, but it is nevertheless quite a straightforward, though a more expensive, procedure, if conducted at the right age (about five months). Very many thousands of female cats have been so operated upon and the subsequent health of these cats has been excellent. Indeed, it has been said that a spayed female makes one of the best of all household cats.

Cats may choose to sleep in a variety of places, and will often lie on beds, chairs, mats, and other warm places. It is a sound policy to provide them with a box or basket, and to encourage them to use newspaper as a bedding. Most cats will take well to newspaper. The bed should be placed in a warm site—it is of little use putting it in a cold corner of a room and expecting the cat to lie in it.

Owing to the fact that, even in play, a cat's claws may inflict serious injury, dogs and cats do not always make the best of house companions. Nevertheless, the traditional enmity of cat and dog is often overcome, and if the two are brought up together they often make firm friends, sharing the same basket or hearth-rug and feeding together without serious consequences.

A cat normally attends to its own toilet, and everyone must be aware that a cat devotes long periods each day to cleaning and washing itself. Except in special cases, therefore, bathing is quite unnecessary, while in short-haired cats especially grooming, too, is superfluous (this does not apply to show-cats). For some reason (and sometimes, apparently, because an owner attempts to assist in the daily grooming) an occasional cat may cease to wash or care for itself. Such an animal is a dejected sight, and should be taken to a veterinary surgeon to have its matted fur cut or combed, and its dirt removed. Such animals (unless they completely re-acquire their self-respect) must be groomed regularly if they are to be kept at all.

All household cats are accustomed to take their own exercise, and it is advisable (except in any special circumstances) to allow them free access to and from the outer world. Do not shut your cat in the house for a long period and then blame it for making a mess. Cats are clean creatures; they normally dig small holes in which to defaecate or urinate, and subsequently cover the deposit with earth. If, therefore, they are for some reason debarred temporarily or permanently from access to a garden, they should be provided with a box or tray containing soil or cinders. Indeed, in many types of houses it is a good plan to encourage kittens to use such a device. (Note the corresponding remarks about puppies.)

It is generally stated that "cats never forget a blow," and for that reason it is recommended that cats are not chastised. It may be said that, if a cat (or dog) be brought up conscientiously and well, it should never, or very rarely, require such punishment. An animal which has been brought up properly seems to develop a fair sense of what is right and what is wrong.

For pedigree cats, or those kept in confinement for other reasons, see the relevant remarks in the section on breeding.

Feeding.

Cats are true carnivores, and wild or feral cats eat rodents, frogs, insects and occasionally birds, supplementing these by raids on human food-stores and waste-bins. Both large and small members of the cat family consume all their prey, *i.e.*, they eat the skin, bones and viscera as well as the lean meat or muscle, and thus obtain adequate supplies of all essential foods. The well-nourished adult cat is an occasional feeder, and usually has a considerable body reserve of fat and protein. It can generally withstand periods of fasting remarkably well, as has been shown by the survival of cats that have been accidentally shut in outhouses. Dr. Scott states that cats differ from rodents in that they will starve to death rather than eat a diet they dislike. The first criterion of satisfactory diet, therefore, must be that the animal will eat sufficient of it to supply enough calories for maintenance, growth and—in the case of breeding stock—reproduction. Cats can very easily be put off their food by anything which frightens them or which affects their general health, and some who are used to being fed by one person will refuse food offered by others.

The taste of food is very important: meat flavours—especially fresh, raw meat but also meat extracts—are appreciated, as are sweet-tasting foods such as milk powder, condensed milk or chocolate, while most cats like butter, margarine and other fats. For good acceptance of food, it must be fresh and free from bacterial decay, and this applies especially to fish. If food has been overcooked, or has been overheated in processing to above about 120°C, it is likely to be rejected.

At weaning, a kitten can be trained to like one particular food in preference to another or to eat a variety of foods, but once the cat's tastes have become fixed it may prove difficult to persuade it to eat a different diet.

The cat requires a greater proportion of protein to ensure satisfactory maintenance and growth than does the dog, and good diets for cats usually contain 12–14% or so of protein on a wet basis. Fat is a valuable source of energy, and especially when canned or dried foods are fed it is important to ensure an adequate intake of vitamin A. As was indicated in the section on dogs, the ratio of calcium to phosphorus is much too low in lean meat, and indeed calcium deficiency is by no means uncommon in cats. Iodine intake may also be low.

Weaned kittens require a total of about 100g of wet diet daily at first, and this should be about 200g at 10 weeks, while a cat feeding 4 kittens may eat up to 500g of meat a day. The fluid requirements of cats are usually met by giving liquid milk, but access to a clean water supply is always desirable. Fluid requirements are greatly increased during lactation.

Although most cats are capable of supplementing their diet by catching small rodents or birds, it is unwise to rely on this as a regular source of food. The idea that hungry cats make the best mousers is by no means always correct. Indeed, animals that are in poor condition are less likely to be successful hunters. Moreoever, while the riddance of pests is an excellent matter from the human point of view—and one of the reasons why the keeping of cats is economically justified—the "cruel" fashion in which most cats tackle their prey is repulsive to most of us.

It is therefore necessary and desirable to provide regular daily feeding. Kittens should receive several meals a day, but by the time they are six months old the number of daily feeds should be reduced to one or at most, two. Most cats (many Siamese are exceptions) are extremely fond of *milk*, especially if it is creamy, and the cat's love of *fish* is well known. Many *meats*, especially *rabbit meat*, are relished, and a diet high in "animal protein" is indeed the aim, always provided that it contains sufficient "dietary energy," and is balanced in the ways indicated above. It is significant that cat's milk has a higher content of fat and sugar than cow's milk, *i.e.*, it is a richer source of energy. Some of the proprietary bitch-milk substitutes are nearer to cat's milk in composition than is cow's milk.

Many hundreds of cats have been reared and bred successfully in experimental laboratories on a diet consisting, in the main, of one part of fish or meat and two parts of *cooked potatoes*. This is relatively inexpensive, and may be supplemented by milk and by some of the proprietary cat foods.

Cats are also extremely fond of liver. Some of the proprietary cat foods—the better ones of which are excellent—and vitamin tablets contain liver, which is a rich source of the vitamin B complex.

Within reason a healthy kitten should be fed to appetite, always provided good-quality foods are available. The amount should be restricted when they are adult, however, except for pregnant and lactating cats, which are sometimes referred to as "queens" as opposed to the male "toms."

Cats are, as noted above, fastidious eaters; they usually sniff and examine carefully any strange or doubtful food. At the same time they are often greedy, especially with relished food to which they are accustomed, but fortunately they can, like dogs vomit very readily. Here, incidentically, is one very good tip—an excellent emetic for both cat and dog is a small crystal of washing-soda, given as a pill. People are usually amazed at the way this simple device results in a dog's or a cat's bringing up undesirable food.

It is important not to overfeed cats, and it is almost equally important to prepare all food in a clean manner, and to make it as attractive as possible. Cats will greatly appreciate this care. While milk is an excellent food for kittens (see under breeding), and is relished by most adult cats, it must be supplemented by solid food.

As already indicated, clean fresh water should be provided at all times even if the cat appears to drink it but little.

Breeding.

Pedigree animals are normally confined, and their breeding is strictly controlled. Ordinary household cats are at the opposite extreme, and there is little that can be done to prevent their mating. The length and scope of this article does not permit of a discussion of controlled mating.

Scientifically, there is as yet a good deal to learn about the reproductive behaviour of the cat. As an American physiologist has succinctly put it in a description of the reproductive cycle of the female cat, "no two authors agree." In Northern Europe there are two main heat periods a year, in spring and early autumn, but some animals may appear in heat at any time from January to July, and those who keep female cats in confinement describe their charges as "calling" quite frequently if not mated. A cat which is "in season" or "on heat" is often observed to be behaving in a quite characteristic fashion, rolling about on the floor and making peculiar sounds. The periods of heat, which commence usually at about eight months of age, may last for several days, and during this time the female will make every attempt to find a mate.

Gestation lasts about nine weeks, as in the case of the bitch but here again there is a considerable variation. As most owners are quite unaware of the time at which their cats were mated, it is difficult to talk of "going overtime," but if there is any evidence of trouble during pregnancy, or at birth, veterinary advice should be obtained. As soon as a cat is obviously pregnant, her food allowance should be increased, and she should be allowed plenty of milk. It is highly important to increase her food and milk ration still further after the kittens are born, as lactation is a great drain on the mother.

Cats sometimes choose strange, out-of-the-way places in which to litter, and many healthy litters are born and reared out of doors. Rats are a source of danger, and will often destroy very young kittens during the mother's absence. For this and other reasons it is better in town and suburban areas to have the litter comfortably housed indoors. A wooden box containing newspaper is ideal, provided it is kept in a fairly warm place and out of the way of draughts. An average litter consists of three to six kittens, which are born blind, but which normally open their eyes after eight or nine days. There is no need to be alarmed if the eyes remain closed for a few days longer. Kittens which are born dead should be removed and buried or burnt. If the whole litter is born dead, the mother's food supply should be cut down considerably, and little milk given for a few days. If the mammary glands become inflamed, they may be bathed in a cold solution of alum. The glands normally return to their former size within a short space of time if they are not milked, but if there is persistent trouble veterinary advice should be sought.

While many pedigree owners wean kittens at four to five weeks of age, it is strongly advised that the household cat be allowed to continue to feed her family for a longer period, and eight weeks is not too long if the mother is still in good bodily condition. She *must*, however, be well fed and be allowed plenty of milk. As in the case of puppies, it is an excellent idea to provide the kittens with a little solid food as from a few weeks of age. It is very wrong to remove a kitten from its mother too early, and such an animal is often weakly, develops an intestinal infection, and dies as a miserable bedraggled creature. Moreoever, during the period following weaning the mother educates her offspring in the art of living, including mousing.

As many litters are unwanted, some people get rid of all the kittens as soon as possible after birth. Drowning is frequently practised, but it is not recommended as a merciful death. Indeed, a hard blow on the back of the head is more humane if given accurately. It is much better to take the kittens to a veterinary surgeon or clinic.

Diseases.

A normally healthy cat, which is unafraid, has an alert bearing and moves about readily with head held straight, showing interest in its surroundings. It is able to spring to the floor from a table or window sill with an easy controlled movement. Its skin is clean and free from blemishes and there is in most instances a thick bushy undercoat with either short or long silky guard hairs according to variety. Its eyes are shining, its teeth are white and free from tartar, and its tongue and gums are clean and pinkish. The ear holes are also clean. It grooms itself frequently and has a sleek appearance. On the back of a well-fed cat, the lumbar muscles form a firm bundle on either side, and the vertebrae should not be felt easily in the adult. A cat that remains in its box or resting place at mealtimes and that displays little interest in food, may not be well. Watery or purulent discharges from the eyes, discharges from the nose or ears, excessive salivation, vomiting and diarrhoea are all indications of possible infection, including that which may result from accidents or fighting.

The principal infectious diseases of cats are still in need of much scientific study. It is now clear, however, that there are at least two major cat plagues. Both have been given many names, and there is much confusion between them.

Feline Enteritis or Panleucopenia.

This is a highly infectious disease, due to a filterable virus. The symptoms include loss of appetite, sometimes accompanied by a rise in body temperature, followed by listlessness, usually vomiting, sometimes diarrhoea, and a marked tendency to show tenderness or pain on being handled. This tenderness or pain is due to a developing peritonitis. The poor animal may become seriously ill, with loss of water from the tissues or dehydration, prostrate and dead within 48 hours or less from the time of the first symptoms. The incubation period of the disease is believed to be from 4 to 8 days, or sometimes longer. There is a fall in the white-cell count of the blood, hence the term "panleucopenia." Some cats recover, the recovery rate in different outbreaks that have been studied ranging from 30 to 80 per cent., and recovered animals are probably immune to further attacks. Cats that are able to take a little food during the early stages of recovery have the best chance of recovery, but require careful nursing. There may be complications during the convalescent stage due to secondary bacterial infections or to vitamin deficiency, and a light nourishing diet, combined with vitamin preparations, is recommended. Fleas may transmit the disease to other cats, as may contact with infected materials. It has been shown that bedding and dirt trays from sick cats were infectious for other cats for up to 16 days. The disease is not transmissible to dogs or to human beings. There is nowadays a protective vaccine, and it is a wise precaution to have your pet vaccinated.

Feline Pneumonitis.

This disease is sometimes called "cat distemper"—as indeed is feline enteritis—but it has no connection with dog distemper, and is not transmissible to dogs or to human beings. Both mild and severe forms occur, and the incubation period varies from 5 to 8 days. The mild form may seem like a cold, and there is a weeping from the eyes and a varying degree of conjunctivitis. There is a thin, clear discharge from the nose, with a characteristic sneezing. Provided that the animals can be made to continue eating, and are kept in warm and dry but ventilated conditions, recovery may be rapid and not entail serious loss of condition. The eyes should be treated with a suitable preparation, such as silver vitellin. There may be secondary bacterial infection in cases that are neglected.

The severe form of the disease has similar, although more severe, commencing symptoms, but the nasal discharge becomes purulent and there is often profuse salivation, with much spreading of the long ropes of saliva. The cat is listless, dislikes strong light, and seems to resent being disturbed. It loses its appetite, and rapidly becomes thinner over a period of from 2 to 5 days or so. Breathing becomes laboured, and a bronchopneumonia develops. There may be a high death rate in young kittens, and pregnant females may abort. Recovery tends to be slow, and is often complicated by bacterial infection. Some of the modern antibiotics appear to be highly effective in the treatment of many cases of this disease, but they must, of course, be given under veterinary supervision.

Tuberculosis.

The cat, like the dog, can contract tuberculosis, but so far as is known only the bovine form has been known to infect it. The infection usually comes, of course, from milk, and the elimination of bovine tuberculosis from this country will stop the incidence of the disease in cats. The disease commences in the abdomen, but may spread to the lungs. There is general wasting.

Skin Diseases.

As in the case of the dog, skin disease in the cat is usually of parasitic origin, and fleas and mange mites are again the chief source of trouble in Great Britain. Cats do so much of their own toilet that the average household cat has probably a cleaner skin than its canine counterpart. When skin disease does develop, it is strongly advised that the animal be taken to a veterinary surgeon for appropriate treatment. As a rule cats greatly resent the interference which must accompany any attempt to bathe or dress an affected place, an for this reason it is usually unwise for an owner to attempt to do other than make an inspection. Very small patches of skin eruption may clear satisfactorily if the surrounding hair is clipped away with curved scissors, but generally speaking skin disease calls for professional attention. The cat flea has a similar life cycle to the dog flea.

Diseases of the Ear.

The outer ear of the cat is frequently affected, and in a great many cases a form of mange mite is responsible. The animal provides evidence of the trouble by scratching and shaking its ear and generally showing its discomfort. It will not always be possible, for an owner to make a thorough examination, as in many cases the cat objects, but if it is possible to look inside the ear it will be seen that there is a dirty and usually brownish mess of tissue, sometimes mixed with dried blood or pus. Not all cases are as bad as this, of course, but if a cat persistently worries its ear it should be taken to a veterinary surgeon. There are satisfactory dressings for this condition, and owners will be able to dress their cats if the latter are docile. Otherwise it is necessary to have the ears dressed by a veterinary surgeon or by one of his staff.

A cat's ear is frequently the site of a blood blister, or haematoma. This is usually the sequel to a blow, such as a slamming door, and shows itself as a large, tense swelling, which when opened by the surgeon proves to be an accumulation of serum usually tinged with blood. Some cases become infected at the time of injury, some after with the patient's rubbing. With the greatest surgical skill in the world one must expect a slight deformity, and the cat develops a puckered ear, much the same as the human boxer.

Disease of the Bladder.

The bladder is a common seat of disease in cats and is frequently affected through the blocking of the natural water-passage by small sand-like calculi. Naturally, male cats are more often affected, as the terminal end of the urinary tracts is wider and more dilatable in females. The urine is unable to escape, and the bladder becomes filled with a mixture of urine and the sandy calcular matter. The condition may be diagnosed quite readily, as the cat usually collapses, or partially collapses and one may easily feel the distended bladder through the walls of the abdomen (belly). It is necessary to send for professional help immediately, and, while no relief can be guaranteed it is often possible to relieve the condition by judicious manipulation. Owners should not attempt to do this themselves (unless help cannot be obtained), as they may easily burst the bladder. As the animal is usually in a state of collapse when the condition is discovered, it makes a bad risk for actual operation, and relief by *skilled* pressure is usually to be recommended.

Ringworm.

There are two common kinds of ringworm in the cat (a third, which may also infect the dog, is more rare; it is the trichophyton which is usually found on cattle). The first kind is acquired from rats and mice, and is most commonly to be found at the bases of the claws, from where it may spread to the ears and face. The individual lesions are circular and yellow in colour, and consist largely of a scabby material. This kind of ringworm is known as "favus."

The second type of ringworm (microsporon) is more important, because it is more readily transmissible to human beings. Whereas this form usually sets up circular scaly lesions in the dog, it often infects cats without there being much naked-eye evidence of its presence. Indeed, in the cat the condition is often unsuspected until the owner himself becomes infected and consults his doctor.

Ringworm should be treated or dealt with by a veterinary surgeon, who will also confirm or refute by special methods the presence of microsporon in cats.

Intestinal Parasites—"Worms."

The cat also is subject to both roundworms and tapeworms. The roundworm which parasitises cats in this country is similar to that of the dog (although a different species) and is also much more harmful to the young than to the adult animal. In kittens the symptoms are a general unthriftiness, staring coat, and in some cases diarrhæa and a "pot-bellied" appearance.

The commonest cat tapeworm in this country is one which passes its intermediate stage in the rat or mouse, or sometimes in other rodents. The tapeworm, which, as mentioned under the section on dogs, is dangerous to man, is sometimes found in the cat also.

Accidents and Injuries.

Despite their sagacity and alertness in many ways, cats seem curiously unable, in many instances, to acquire road-sense. They are dazed by a car's head-lights, while if a motorist sounds his horn they tend to stop still in their tracks.

Injuries from traps, *e.g.*, gin-traps, are very common, and it is probable that many thousands of cats annually are maimed in this fashion. Cats suffer injury from shooting, from stoning, and from blows with sticks. Since they are predatory animals, they have often to pay the penalty inflicted on them by wrathful people. Needless to say, cats which survive to return home usually require expert treatment.

Poisoning may be included under this heading. Although there are doubtless many deliberate attempts to poison marauding cats, alleged "poisoning" is often no more than a case of feline enteritis, and owners should not claim glibly that their cats have been poisoned until they have expert evidence to back their judgment.

Fur-balling, as it has been termed, may be mentioned here. Cats, especially the long-haired varieties, must often ingest hair during their toilet, and occasionally serious trouble (a stoppage of the bowels) is brought about by a mass of such hair which has collected in a part of the bowel. There is constipation, loss of condition, and often evidence of considerable pain. Such cats should be taken to a veterinary surgeon.

Bites and scratches are even more common in the cat than they are in the dog and subsequent sepsis is equally likely.

FERRETS

Description.

The ferret (*Mustela putorius furo*) is a carnivore of the mustelid group to which belong otters, weasels and mink. In their chapter in the *UFAW Handbook*, Doctors J. Hammond Jr. & F. C. Chesterman report that it has been domesticated for at least 2000 years and that it is generally held to be a form of the European polecat, with which it will interbreed, although some consider it to be a hybrid between the polecat and other species. As a domesticated animal it has been used principally for hunting rabbits and other prey, and has thus gained a reputation for ferocity which Dr. Hammond suggests is quite undeserved. One of the authors has employed ferrets for nutritional studies, and is well aware of the fact that they must be handled with care especially by strangers. They are most easily rendered completely docile so far as human beings are concerned, by handling them while still young, and in this respect they may be compared with the "finger-tamed" mink. Most tame ferrets have pink eyes and yellowish-white fur, but there are darker forms believed to have resulted from crossing in previous generations with wild polecats. Indeed, these darker forms are popularly termed "polecat ferrets." They are of two main kinds, the first having creamy under-fur and black guard hairs, and the second being a chocolate-brown colour, with brown upper-parts and black under-parts, and a few scattered light hairs on the face.

Ferrets are long creatures in relation to their body weight, and when fully grown may have a body 36 cm long or more and a tail of 13 cm. Some strains grow appreciably larger.

Accommodation.

Ferrets must have dry, clean accommodation in a room free from draughts but well ventilated. Wood is warmer than metal, but more difficult to clean, and is best lined with hard asbestos sheeting, which is resistant to water. The most suitable accommodation comprises a sleeping compartment of similar proportions to a small kennel, leading by a small doorway or "pop-hole" to a wire-netting exercising run, which should be as large as possible compatible with cleanliness. It is a good idea to have a means of closing the doorway so that the ferret or ferrets may be confined within the sleeping-compartment if necessary. Wood-wool makes an excellent bedding, but if difficult to obtain newspaper may be provided for the ferret to lie on. The floor of the run may have a false bottom or may be sprinkled with sawdust. It is imperative to keep the whole of the accommodation clean and dry, not only to avoid smell but also to prevent the ferrets from developing a very serious necrotic infection of the feet known as "foot-rot", see below.

Feeding.

Many ferrets are unfortunately not fed adequately. It must be appreciated that basically they are carnivorous animals, and that their food requirements are more similar to those of the dog and cat than those of rodents. Indeed, many of the general remarks made about the principles of feeding dogs and cats apply to ferrets also.

Most ferrets like bread-and-milk, and while this is an excellent article of diet, it is in itself inadequate. Up to about 125 g of raw meat (minced for younger animals) daily is an excellent basis, and this may be replaced by fish. Liver, especially raw liver, is an excellent source of many factors, and there is good reason to provide some at least weekly if it can be obtained. Failing this, it is advisable to add 1–2 per cent. of whole dry liver to the diet. Once ferrets are grown, one feeding daily—at a fixed time—is sufficient. The female (jill) should have ample supplies of milk just prior to the birth of her young and while she is suckling them.

Breeding.

In the northern hemisphere the female ferret usually comes into oestrus (season) in early March of the year following that in which it is born. If the jill does not conceive during this oestrus she will have a further oestral period in July or August. The desire of the jill to mate is very strong, and if not allowed to do so, some animals sometimes have been found to waste and pine. The act of mating is prefaced by very vigorous behaviour on the part of the male (hob), and anyone not appreciating the performance might think that he was out to kill his mate! The mating act itself is usually prolonged, and may take up to three hours. If left together the hob and jill will probably mate from two to four times during the course of a couple of days. As in the cat and rabbit, ovulation or the shedding of the egg from the ovary takes place as a result of mating, and not spontaneously. The period of gestation is forty-two days, and the numbers of young born usually varies from five to thirteen, the average litter being six to eight. Pseudo-pregnancy occurs if the jill is not mated, and may become outwardly obvious as in the case of certain bitches.

Males also have a seasonal rhythm, their capacity to fertilise being greatest from early March to August. Young hobs seem to be active about a month earlier than older ones. The length of daylight or, rather, the incrementation in light from day to day, has an important bearing on breeding capacity in both sexes, and by the use of artificial light it has proved possible to induce either oestrus or male activity at different times of the year.

The young are hairless and blind, and weigh on the average under 15 g at birth. Their eyes open at about four weeks, and they can then commence to eat small pieces of solid food to supplement their mother's milk. They may be weaned at from six to eight weeks.

Diseases.

Ferrets are extremely susceptible to the virus of *canine distemper*, which is capable of wiping out a whole colony. The disease is transmitted by contact or by droplet infection, with the incubation period of about 10 days. The usual first signs include a watery discharge from the eyes and nose and later there may be muscular tremors, twitching and convulsions. Routine vaccination is, of course, highly desirable. Ferrets are susceptible also to some of the strains of influenza virus that affect man, and cross-infection between staff and ferrets has been described in medical laboratories.

In the days when unpasteurised milk was widely used, ferrets sometimes contracted the bovine strain of *tuberculosis*. *Foot-rot* is a form of mange and should on no account be neglected, the feet becoming swollen, scabby and eventually clawless. *Mange* or "scabies" of the back and tail region should also be dealt with promptly, employing modern preparations. Ear mite (*Otodectes cyanotis*) may produce inflammation and irritation, with resultant scratching of the ears. Following any of these ectoparasitic conditions, the bedding should be burnt and quarters treated with a blow-lamp or treated with a hot, strong solution of washing soda and, of course, thoroughly washed and dried out before the animals are reinstated. *Abscesses* of the neck region are often encountered and should receive treatment if they do not clear up rapidly, as they are likely to spread, with dire consequences. Such abscesses may sometimes arise from perforations from fish bones in the diet. Abscesses of the groin region and of the scent glands are sometimes seen.

Many other diseases of the ferret have been described, and veterinary advice should be sought in the case of any sick animal.

RATS

Description.

Tame rats are domesticated varieties of the wild Norway or "brown" rat (*Rattus norvegicus*). Such rats are usually albinos or black-and-white, although other colours have been bred. The hooded varieties are those in which the head and foreparts are mainly black or chocolate and the remainder of the body, apart from small patches the same colours as the hood, is white. Tame rats differ materially from wild ones in disposition, and properly managed are extremely tractable. Healthy specimens accustomed to handling bite only when frightened, *e.g.* when a sudden movement is made in front of them. Males appear to live longer than females, but three years is a good age.

"Black" rats, *i.e.* the species (*Rattus rattus*) sometimes known as the ship or Alexandrine rat, have been bred in captivity, but tame strains are not generally available.

Housing.

Tame rats require a warm, even temperature 18–21 °C all the year round—and draughts or lowered temperature may precipitate lung disease or other disorders. It is best to have a complete spare set of boxes or cages, and to change to fresh quarters weekly except when the females have unweaned young with them. Empty cages should be cleaned and disinfected thoroughly before being used again. Provided the temperature conditions are suitable—and this is essential—metal cages of the types employed in scientific laboratories are best with wire-mesh false bottoms and trays containing sawdust to catch the droppings. Accommodation should be ample, and

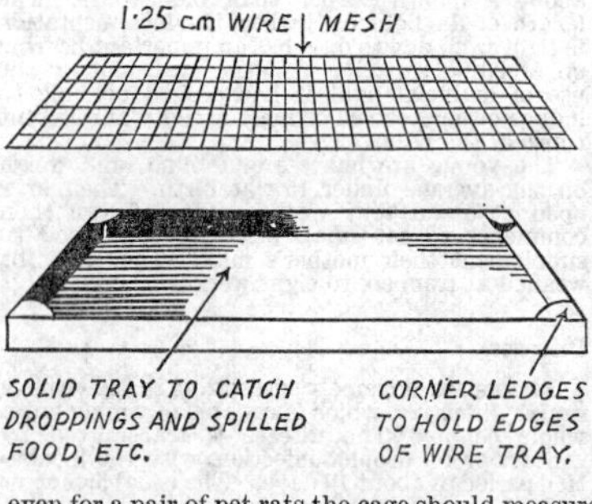

even for a pair of pet rats the cage should measure about 75 cm × 45 cm × 45 cm. If wooden boxes are employed it maybe desirable to line them with hard asbestos sheeting or galvanised metal to prevent damage from gnawing.

Small, dark "shelters" and exercising devices, *e.g.*, wheels or ladders, are appreciated by the rats, but must be kept clean. Wood-wool makes the best bedding.

Feeding.

Rats may take a wide variety of foods, including many of our own, and there are several successful ways of feeding them, including the provision of specially formulated "rat-cubes," of the same type as that described below for mice. A good daily diet is wholemeal bread, mixed creals (*e.g.*, oats, wheat, hempseed), with about 5 per cent. dried brewers' yeast and milk either fed separately or mixed with the rest of the food. Twice weekly each rat should be given up to 15 g or more of meat, liver, fish, or other "animal protein." A little fresh greenfood (even grass) is appreciated, and in winter especially some supplement containing vitamins A and D is desirable. Expectant and nursing mothers should have as much milk as they require. Never overfeed or allow uneaten food residues to remain in the cage. Fresh water (preferably in bulbs or bottles) should be available at all times. Far cleaner than open dishes are the special but simple type of water bulbs suspended on or in front of the cage or box so that the rat can drink from the rounded end of the spout. A simple substitute is a medicine "flat" bottle—or even a $\frac{1}{4}$- or $\frac{1}{2}$-pint milk-type bottle. This should be fitted with a cork—or, better, a rubber bung—pierced for a piece of

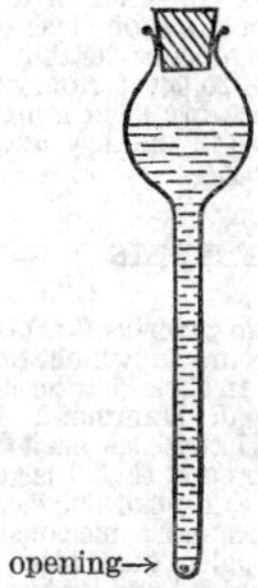

WATER BULB SUITABLE FOR USE WITH PET RODENTS

bent glass tubing. Provided that the free end of the glass tubing is not sharp, and is chosen so that the aperture is considerably smaller than that of the tube itself, the water will not run out unless sucked out by the rat. The spout should, of course, be within easy access of the rat, which will soon learn to drink from it.

Breeding.

Rats can breed at quite a young age (usually being capable of mating when fifty to sixty days old), but it is better to separate the sexes within a fortnight or so of weaning (weaning being usually at twenty-one days of age) and to mate at about 100 to 120 days of age onwards, the female rat has an oestrous cycle lasting just over four days. One male (buck) may be mated to one female (doe)—this is probably best in the case of pet rats—or with two or three females if preferred, but it is unwise to keep more than one adult male in the presence of females. The gestation period is twenty-one to twenty-two days or occasionally a few days longer. The number born varies considerably, but often it is best to try to rear only six to eight young. The young have their ears open at $2\frac{1}{2}$ to $3\frac{1}{2}$ days, cut their incisor teeth at eight to ten days, can find their way to their mother at about the same time, open their eyes at fourteen to seventeen days, and may leave the nest at twenty-one days. In the case of pet rats it is probably best to leave the young with the mother for up to a week or so longer. Breeding can occur all the year round, but takes place less readily in winter.

Handling.

Rats should not be "tailed," or the skin may slough off. Regular handling after weaning is excellent and promotes docility. The weight of the body should be supported.

Diseases.

Since many tame rats are derived from laboratory stocks or from breeders who provide laboratories, it is possible for pet animals to suffer from the same infections and parasites. Generally speaking, rats in domestic conditions are much less prone than are mice, provided that temperature conditions are suitable. The commonest infection is a form of *broncho-pneumonia*, carried by some of the animals and precipitated either by the introduction of additional stock or by conditions of cold. *Mange*, especially of the ear, and *infestation of lice* may occur, and should be dealt with promptly by means of modern insecticides.

Those who are interested in the diseases of the rat may follow the references of Dr. W. Lane-Petter in the chapter in the *UFAW Handbook.*

The most important principle in preventing disease in tame rats is to avoid contact with wild rodents and the use of food or bedding that may have been contaminated by wild rats or mice.

MICE

Description.

Tame mice are descended from the common wild or house mouse (*Mus musculus*), and it is believed that they may have been domesticated for over 3000 years. The wild house mouse exists in very many parts of the world, and is commonly found in places that are inhabited by man, including dwellings, warehouses, food stores and farms. It is quite often found in habitats apart from man where there is plentiful food and shelter. The fur of the wild mouse is agouti, lighter on the under surface, while the eyes are black and the skin is pigmented. Dr. W. Lane-Petter, in his comprehensive chapter in the *UFAW Handbook*, states that wild mice are somewhat variable in size but are likely to weigh 18–20 g by 4 weeks of age and may reach 30–40 g by six months or so, when they are fully mature. (Newborn mice weigh about 1 g). They are omniverous, daring to eat many things that are edible and many things that are not, although they begin tentatively with unfamiliar substances. They are capable of penetrating small holes, wall cavities and roof spaces, and are often able to travel considerable distances in pipes of only 2·5 cm diameter. They can also climb brick walls quite easily. Although they prefer warmth, they have been found able to survive and to breed at low temperatures, and during the second world war they showed themselves capable of breeding in refrigerated meat stores. The animals that did this successfully laid down a great deal of body fat, and had well-developed coats.

Tame mice are similar in size to wild mice, but they have been bred so extensively for scientific and other fancy purposes that there is now a very wide range of coat colours, while both large and small strains exist. Most laboratory, and many tame mice, are albinos.

Laboratory and tame mice are timid, gentle and easily handled. They tend to avoid strong light, and are more active by night than by day. They are gregarious creatures but most of them are determined escapers. Males of some strains tend to be pugnacious when mature, but females are usually docile and seldom fight except when they have young and are disturbed by strangers. Males that are kept in the same cage or box may attack each other fiercely, especially when the weaker cannot escape or seek refuge in bedding, and this is one of the situations in which the characteristic "mousey" odour of acetamide is given off. Provided that they remain healthy, mice may live up to 30 months or more and some to over 3 years.

Housing.

Although strains vary, most tame mice require a warm even temperature and the same general remarks concerning temperature range, bedding, and wooden or metal cages apply as in the case of rats. If a solid floor is used, this should be covered with clean sawdust, wood shavings, cellulose webbing, peat moss, treated wood chips or even sugar beet. It is a good plan to change to a clean cage regularly, except when the female (doe) is nursing her young. If the cage is large (as in the case of pet mice it should be, with a floor space of say 60 cm × 30 cm × 30 cm for a group of mice), inner nesting boxes should be provided—one for each doe if breeding is taking place, although two does will often share the same nest box. (In changing to fresh cages the nest box, with mother and young inside, may, of course, be moved over.) A "two-storey" cage, with a ladder or "staircase" to the upper part, is an attractive variation, although difficult to keep clean. Mice should be kept well out of reach of wild rodents, from which they may all too readily contract disease.

Feeding.

The wild house-mouse is, as already stated, omniverous, but its preferred foods appear to be cereals, seeds and many types of other substances that are capable of being stored. Mice, like most rodents, have a simple digestive tract, and it has been found that a female in full lactation may eat her own body weight of food and water in 24 hours. The easiest diets to feed are those of the kind employed in laboratories, and sold either as compressed or expanded pellets some 8–12 mm in diameter. Many are in use but all basically contain a large cereal element, sometimes of one kind and sometimes a mixture. Most of the protein is derived from fish meal, meat meal, dried milk or a combination of these. Fat is usually of vegetable origin but may include tallow. Yeast is often included, but there is usually a guaranteed supply of vitamins and minerals that have been added during manufacture in the form of a premix.

Needless to say, there is a considerable variation and the owner should be able to utilise pellets that appear to suit his stock. The pellets should be reasonably hard, especially if fed through a wire hopper, since mice will gnaw at them to the base and pull them through when small enough, then dropping them in the cage to go back for more, thus wasting partially eaten pellets. There should be a supply of pellets in the hopper at all times.

There are, of course, many other ways of feeding mice, and some owners rely upon such items as bread, biscuit and vegetables. Wholemeal bread is excellent if not allowed to become stale but it should not form the sole article of diet, and it is a good plan to feed it alternatively with a grain mixture made up of rolled oats and other cereal grains or mixed bird seed. Cheese is relished, but may smell if not fed carefully. Mice sometimes like the occasional pinch of marmalade, and it is not a bad idea to offer them fresh lettuce or other green food every week or so, always with care to remove eaten and soiled food. It is perhaps worth emphasising that cod-liver oil should not be fed in excess—½% of the total diet is quite sufficient to provide vitamins A and D—or it may prevent breeding and possibly have other harmful effects.

There should be a constant supply of fresh water preferably from bulbs or bottles as described for rats.

Breeding.

Young mice may be weaned at twenty-one days, although it is usually preferable to leave them with their mother for a further week. The age at which mice are capable of mating varies considerably from one strain or individual to another, and while the average is six to eight weeks, it may be much younger. It is therefore desirable to separate the males from the females at or shortly after weaning. Mice may be mated up at at two to three months of age, and the best arrangements are one male (buck) to one or two females. A pair of mice or a "bigamous trio" makes a successful combination. The oestrus cycle is similar to that of the rat, but its length appears to vary with coat colour, being longest in the brown mice and shortest in blacks and albinos. The gestation period is usually from eighteen to twenty days, but may be prolonged if the female was still suckling her previous litter when she conceived. There may be up to twelve or more young in a litter, but the average litter size is from five to seven. The second litter is usually the largest, and subsequent litters tend to decrease in numbers, so that the sixth is usually smaller than the first. Breeding may take place all the year round, although, as with rats, fertility is higher during the summer months.

Handling.

Any rapid or rough movement may frighten mice and cause them to bite through fear. Mice should be lifted by the tail—not too near the tip—and may be held in the palm of the hand, where they may be suitably restrained by keeping the tail between two fingers.

Diseases.

Mice are, unfortunately, prone to a considerable number of diseases, among them being the virus infections, ectromelia and infantile diarrhoea. Like other rodents, they are susceptible to *salmonellosis*, while susceptible also to what is probably another bacterial infection known as *Tyzzer's disease*.

The risks of diseases are greatly reduced if the mice are kept in suitable surroundings, with avoidance of contamination from other rodents including that from bedding. The quarters should not be accessible to wild house-mice, and it is a good practice to keep the house or building completely free from wild rodents and birds. Dr. Lane-Petter points out that anything that places an extra burden on the animal's metabolism is likely to predispose to disease, and that poor nutrition, overcrowding, lack of hygiene, inadequate ventilation, bad handling and exposure—direct or indirect—to mice suffering from disease will all favour an outbreak of disease in a colony. A large colony of high density offers a more favourable environment for the spread of infection than a smaller colony. Infrequent changes of bedding may also favour the development of disease as will poor general standards of cleanliness. Poor ventilation is another adverse factor.

The accurate diagnosis of important diseases of mice calls for expert opinion and even for special laboratory examinations. Most owners should, however, be able to recognise signs of ill-health or departure from normal, one of the commonest being loss of appetite. In young mice the coat should be smooth and glossy. As mice get older there may be loss of pigmentation (in coloured mice) or even loss of fur. A sick mouse usually sits hunched up and has a ruffled coat, while the eyes may be partially closed or have some discharge. A healthy mouse will usually catch on to suitable objects when held by its tail and is capable of pulling quite hard, whereas the pull of a sick mouse is much weaker. If one or more mice die it is best to destroy at once any cage-mates that appear seedy. As in the case of rats, external parasites should be dealt with promptly with the aid of modern insecticidal preparations.

GOLDEN HAMSTERS

Description.

There are at least 54 different species, varieties or sub-species of hamster, all being rodents of the family Cricetidae: the general description is that they are "mouse-like animals with thick-set bodies, short tails and cheek pouches." They are distributed throughout many parts of Europe, Africa and Asia as far east as China. Most of them appear to be active in the evening and early morning, and possibly throughout the night, and some species are known to hibernate in winter. There is an excellent chapter on hamsters in the *UFAW Handbook* by Dr. Michael Festing. Not a great deal is known about the habits of wild hamsters, but most of them are solitary territorial animals that live in extensive burrows in which they store food consisting of seeds and vegetable matter. This habit of hoarding food causes some of them to be classified as pests.

The common pet hamster is the Golden—sometimes referred to as the Syrian-Hamster (*Mesocricetus auratus*), a delightful little creature of which the full-grown female—females being larger than males—rarely exceeds 18 cm in length.

The history of the domestication of the golden hamster is quite remarkable, for prior to 1930 only museum specimens were known. In that year a mother and her twelve young were dug up in a field near Aleppo and were taken to the Hebrew University Jerusalem, and from that one family have been bred the hundreds of thousands of golden hamsters now employed as pets or as laboratory animals in many parts of the world. The species has taken well to captivity and, although capable of inflicting a nasty little bite if frightened or handled roughly, becomes docile and friendly when properly cared for. Characteristic features are the soft, smooth fur, the large black eyes, the "cheek pouches" in which food is stored and which may become enormously distended after a meal, the short, stumpy tail, and the extremely loose skin, inside which the hamster can turn round to a considerable degree.

Housing.

The same remarks about accommodation, environmental temperature, freedom from draughts, fittings, and other general considerations (including cleanliness) apply as in the case of rats and mice. For breeding purposes a dark inner chamber or nest-box is desirable. Several hamsters may be kept together, but the introduction of a stranger (or even the re-introduction of a former cage-mate that has been removed for some time) may lead to fighting.

Feeding.

Satisfactory diets include the following: (1) rat cubes, carrots, greenfood and milk; (2) cereal grains and/or wholemeal bread, carrots, greenfood and milk; (3) steamed Rangoon beans, wheat, maize meal bread, a little Marmite and milk. Care must be taken not to allow storage of excess food, which will deteriorate and cause a smell. Grass is a suitable source of greenfood during its growing season. Apples and other fruits are often relished. Water, preferably in bulbs or bottles as described for rats, should always be available.

Breeding.

Golden Hamsters attain puberty at from ten to fifteen weeks of age, or even younger, males being usually earlier. Generally speaking, it is best to defer breeding until after fifteen weeks of age. There is an oestrus cycle of about four days, and the gestation period is very short, averaging sixteen days, although sometimes up to nineteen days. Mating not followed by conception results in phantom or pseudopregnancy. Litter size varies from one to fifteen, but the average is six to seven. Not many females have more than four litters and although both sexes may live up to two years, breeding by the female is rare after nine months. The young are naked and blind at birth. Hair first appears at five days, and covers the whole body at eight days. The eyes open at about eleven days, and soon after this the young begin to take food for themselves and may be weaned at three to four weeks. Care must be taken that the female does not injure the male, and for safety's sake it is probably better to keep only one female and one male together and to remove the male before the young are born.

Handling.

Gentleness is essential, and sudden movements should be avoided. The tail is much too short to use, and the easiest way is to lift them by the loose skin over the back and shoulders. As already noted, they can twist easily within their skins, unless a substantial amount is taken in the hand. After picking up they may be allowed to sit on the palm of the hand.

Diseases.

Like most rodents, hamsters are susceptible to *Salmonella* infections but probably the most serious disease is known as "wet tail", a diarrhoea that is usually fatal and has been known in some cases, to destroy whole colonies. The exact cause has not been established with certainty, but the intestines of affected animals frequently contain large numbers of coliform bacteria, and Dr. Festing refers to the effective prophylactic use of neomycin sulphate. There are several spontaneous diseases which appear to be due to nutritional deficiencies, and in one large colony that was studied over a 15-year period there was a high incidence of cirrhosis of the liver.

CAVIES (GUINEA-PIGS)

Description.

Cavies or guinea-pigs (*Cavia porcellus*) are rodents descended from one of the several kinds of wild South American cavy, probably *Caviae cutleri*, still to be found in Peru. It used to be thought that the name "Guinea" was a corruption of Guiana, but the *O.E.D.* regards this as unlikely; more probably it relates to a former designation for an unknown distant country, or because the animal was thought to resemble the young of the river-pig (*Potomochoerus pictus*) of W. Africa. Detailed information is provided in the *UFAW Handbook* by Dr. J. Stuart Paterson, who had unrivalled knowledge of this species in health and disease. Three main varieties are recognised. The *English* is the commonest, is short-haired (3·8 cm) and may be self-coloured (*e.g.*, white, black, agouti, sandy, red, chocolate, cream) or a combination of either two or three colours, described as bicolour or tricolour respectively. The fancy recognises such descriptions as Himalayan or Dutch, which denote colourings similar to those of the relevant varieties of rabbit. The *Abyssinian* is also short-coated, but one that is rough and radiates as rosettes. The *Peruvian* is long-haired (15 cm).

Guinea-pigs, which are thought to have been domesticated by the Incas long before the advent of Europeans, are extremely tame, and are easily frightened; they should always be treated gently and quietly. The males (boars) tend to fight, and should be kept apart from one another, but they do not usually attack females (sows), nor is fighting between females common.

Cavies make safe and reliable pets which breed prolifically if allowed to do so. Many regard them as relatively unresponsive to human affection. They speedily distinguish their owners, or those who feed and tend them, from strangers, and greet the former with a characteristic chirruping noise, especially at feeding times! Their short legs and heavy bodies prevent them from climbing or jumping, and it is, therefore, possible to keep them in open pens or runs, but this is inadvisable in most cases, since they are helpless against a variety of would be predators.

In health, this is an alert animal, with a smooth, silky coat unsoiled by faeces or urine. The flesh should be firm, and the animal should not feel "light." There should not be any obvious discharge from the nose or ears, nor any evidence of slobbering or diarrhoea and breathing should be regular and quiet.

The life-span is variable, but the authors have maintained individuals for up to eight years. At birth the average weight of the English variety is about 90 g for males and 85 g for females although with single births, up to 150 g has been recorded, by weaning, body weight may average nearly 250 g, and maturity is attained by about five months when the average weight lies between 700 and 750 g. A further weight increase may take place until the animals are about fifteen months, by which time really heavy males may be 1000 g and females 850 g.

Housing.

This may be outside or inside, or a combination of both. For individual animals, the authors have found the most successful system to consist of a movable hutch with a floor—approximately 100 cm × 50 cm and covered, except over the sleeping area, by an impervious tray—raised (on legs or wheels) some six inches above the ground. The sides (approximately 40 cm at front, and 30 cm at back), back and roof (with a 5 cm overhang at the front) are made of solid wood and roofing-felt. The interior is divided, by a wooden partition, allowing free access from a smaller sleeping-quarter, with solid door, into a larger living area fronted by framed chicken wire. To the hutch is attached a run, comprising a frame with sides, top and end of strong, small-mesh, chicken wire. Such a hutch, with its run, may be kept outdoors, on grass, throughout a good deal of the year. Except on wet or inclement days, the guinea-pig may be allowed into its run for up to several hours, and be permitted to graze freely. These animals are good grazers and it is necessary, therefore, to move the hutch and run on to a new patch every 2–3 days or so. The floor of both the sleeping and living quarters should be covered with several layers of newspaper or other absorbant bedding which should be changed and destroyed at least weekly, and there should be abundant, additional bedding in the sleeping quarter, the best being shavings from seasoned soft wood, or woodwool which provides a cosy resting place. This too should be changed every few days. In severe weather, the hutch and, if space permits, the run may be kept in a shed or indoors.

There are several types of indoor housing including floor pens and cages. If there is any danger from cats, dogs or other predators, the pens should have a top of some kind. Peat moss may be used instead of newspaper to cover the floors. Some persons prefer to have two separate pens for each animal or group of animals, moving them from one to the other to permit of cleaning and resting between use. Cages or wooden boxes may have solid floors in which case they should be covered as indicated for outside hutches, or they should be fitted with wire-mesh bottoms. If the animals are to be bred, however, great care should be taken with wire bottoms for the new born can easily break their legs or strangle themselves. Dr. Paterson states that if losses are to be avoided, guinea-pigs must be brought up to live on wire so that they learn to walk on it without trouble, and if they have been reared on solid bottomed cages and transferred to wire-floor cages in later life, it is wise to keep the wire well covered with hay for the first week or two. The size of the wire is important: the rigid welded floor of 7·62 cm × 1·27 cm mesh is ordinarily satisfactory.

Feeding.

Guinea-pigs are vegetarians. Like human beings, apes and monkeys, they require a dietary source of vitamin C or ascorbic acid. A growing animal weighing 250 g requires 3 mg, a fully grown one at least 10 mg and pregnant females 20 mg daily to prevent the occurence of scurvy and to maintain natural resistance to disease. They also have a requirement for vitamins E and K, and for an unknown but apparently essential factor or factors in hay. Provided that these necessary vitamins are in adequate supply, a wide variety of diet has been found satisfactory. Unless ascorbic acid is provided in some other way, liberal amounts of fresh green food are essential throughout the year. As Dr. Paterson states, the term "green food" should not be taken too literally; certain roots are a valuable source of vitamin C during the winter months and sprouted green has been employed with success. All members of the cabbage and kale family are suitable, as are chicory and lucerne. Carrots are excellent but mangolds, although relished, have a relatively low vitamin C content. Dr. Paterson suggests that while the type of green food should not be suddenly changed he has found that guinea-pigs flourish well when different types of green food are offered in rotation on successive days. All green food should be given as fresh as possible and any spoiled material should be rejected. Soil should be washed off, and in frosty conditions, greens should be thoroughly thawed out before being fed. Even when the guinea-pig is in an outdoor run, additional fresh greens are necessary during the winter months.

Hay should be given *ad libitum*. Most suitable is fine meadow hay of good quality free from weeds and particularly from thistles, the spines of which may injure the mouth. If young, actively-growing stock are deprived of hay, illness and death may ensue, and in suckling females deprived of hay, there may be a severe and rapid dental overgrowth.

The rest of the food should comprise mash or pellets. The simplest mash consists of 2 parts crushed oats mixed with 1 part broad bran fed dry or slightly dampened. Another suitable mixture comprises bran and sugar beet pulp in the ratio of 2:1, the beet being soaked overnight, the surplus water drained off and the bran mixed to form a moist crumbly mass. Only the required amount of mash should be prepared at one time as it quickly goes sour. These simple mashes require the addition of protein concentrate and minerals in order to promote reproduction and good growth. Pelleted diets have been used for many years in laboratories and can be obtained from pet shops and corn chandlers. They are of several kinds and some even contain declared amounts of vitamin C. For pet animals, however it is probably wise always to provide fresh green food throughout the year. For breeding stock, a pelleted diet is advisable, and one known as Diet S.G.1, after Short & Gammage, comprises white fish meal (67% protein) 10; grass meal (18% protein) 20; finely ground oats 12; medium bran 18 and coarse bran 40. Pellets may be fed from small bowls or from specially constructed hoppers that permit free access and supplies that will last for several days. It is wise, however, not to leave such food unchanged for more than a few days at a time owing to the possibility of contamination by moulds. Although guinea-pigs normally derive moisture from fresh green food, and may appear to take little or no water for long periods, it is a mistake not to provide a fresh supply, either from bowls (washed and replenished regularly to prevent contamination) or from inverted bottles or from troughs fed with special drinking spouts (these lessen contamination but should still be kept clean and freshly supplied).

Diseases.

The most important and probably the most lethal of all guinea-pig diseases is *salmonellosis* or "paratyphoid." This is caused by organisms of the *Salmonella* group, usually *S. Typhimurium* and sometimes by *S. Enteritidis* or *S. dublin.* Infection takes place by mouth, usually from food or water being contaminated by wild rodents. Where guinea-pigs are kept in groups, it usually begins in one or two deaths, followed by the loss of almost all the colony. There is also a more chronic form in which the animals may survive for two weeks. The animals that recover may remain as "carriers" of the disease and are liable to infect guinea-pigs with which they are placed. Cold or other environmental variations, including faulty feeding, can help to set off an outbreak. There is, unfortunately, no completely successful treatment for this disease, attempts to immunise breeding stock have not, as yet, been successful.

Another disease is *Pseudotuberculosis* usually a chronic infection caused by *Pasteurella pseudotuberculosis* characterised by the development of cheese-like nodules particularly in the lymph nodes and internal organs. This, again, is usually acquired by eating material contaminated by wild rodents or rabbits. There are three forms of the disease. The first is an acute septicaemia, which is rapidly fatal The second, and by far the most common, is characterised by progressive emaciation ("going light") and death in 3–4 weeks. In the case of breeding stock, the young of infected animals may be congenitally affected or may become infected soon after birth. The third form is not usually fatal since the lesions are confined to the lymph nodes of the head and neck, and the danger lies in the risk that these lesions may burst externally and spread infection. It has been claimed that infection of breeding stock can be controlled but Dr. Paterson regards such claims as unconfirmed. In the case of large colonies, the disease may be controlled under veterinary supervision by making use of the fact that some of the enlarged glands can be palpated in the early stages, before the animals become infectious to others, with the weeding out of others that are affected.

Coccidiosis is common, but is usually much less of a threat than in the case of rabbits. It is developed in infected stocks through feeding inadequate diets, and provided that nutrition and hygiene are adequate, there is little serious trouble from this disease. In the case of larger colonies, control may be based upon the regular and adequate cleaning and sterilisation of cages, since the oocysts responsible take a minimum time of six days to sporulate and to become infectious.

Respiratory infections, due to a variety of organisms are usually uncommon except when there is overcrowding or when guinea-pigs are kept in draught, damp, poorly-ventilated or cold houses In the case of large colonies, it may be necessary to adopt fairly rigorous culling of affected animals.

Middle ear disease is not uncommon especially in large colonies, and is characterised by the tilting of the head to one side. This may become so severe that the animal is unable to walk in a straight line. In the case of individual animals veterinary attention should be sought promptly. With large colonies, prompt culling is usually necessary to prevent spread.

External parasites of the guinea-pig, including *lice*, which live on skin debris, cause the animals to scratch themselves, especially at the backs of the ears, and if infestation is heavy, the animals show loss of condition and a harsh coat. Aerial insecticidal vapours are said to be more effective than dusting powders.

Non-parasitic skin disorders may occur when the diet is too dry or is lacking in sufficient fresh green food of good quality and will clear up when this is put right.

RABBITS

Description.

Domesticated varieties of the wild European rabbit (*Oryctolagus cuniculus*) are now kept in many countries. The wild rabbit is believed to have been introduced into Great Britain in the 12th cent., and a full description of its biology is given in *The Rabbit* by Harry V. Thompson & Alastair N. Worden (London: Collins, New Naturalist "Special" Volume). Tame rabbits have been bred for centuries, and the breeds and strains produced differ appreciably in size, colour, and habits from the common wild form. Some breeds have been specially bred for table purposes, while others (*e.g.* the Angora, Sitka, and Argente de Champagne) have been developed for their fur. In addition, many varieties are produced for show purposes by the extensive rabbit "fancy". The small hardy Dutch rabbit (usually black and white) is one of the kinds suitable for beginners. Among well-known categories are the English, Japaneses, Himalayan, Belgian Hare (really a rabbit), Flemish Giant, Beveren, Blue Imperial, Polish, Havana, Lop, Half-Lop, Chinchilla and New Zealand White. The Copenhagen rabbit appears to be identical with the New Zealand White. The smaller breeds weigh only 2–3 kg when fully grown, whereas some specimens of some of the giant breeds attain a weight of 9 kg or more.

Rabbits and hares were formerly classified with the rodents, but are now placed in a separate Order of mammals, known as the Lagomorphs. Young rabbits (in contrast to leverets or young hares) are blind and helpless for some time after birth. Tame specimens may live for 4–5 years, individuals have lived for up to 13 years.

Housing.

Since rabbits are kept for commercial purposes, various systems have been devised, including the use of movable ark-huts, with covered runs, that can be moved regularly to fresh ground. If kept indoors rabbits do not need special heating, but freedom from draughts, damp, excessive cold and access by wild rodents is most desirable. A garage is regarded as an unsuitable place, owing to the susceptibility of rabbits to exhaust or engine fumes. One of the great difficulties of rabbit-keeping is coccidiosis, which is a serious disease in rabbits and hares. (European hares could never be bred successfully in captivity until means of overcoming coccidiosis were discovered.) With young rabbits especially (*i.e.*, those that have left the nest and are able to run about freely) it is a sound principle to move them to a clean floor or fresh ground every two days, so as to "break" the life-cycle of the coccidial parasite. One way of doing this is to have "back-to-back" cages or hutches, from one to the other of which the rabbits may be transferred easily. The empty cage or hutch may then be cleaned and disinfected thoroughly and allowed to dry out before the rabbits are returned to it. Wood-wool makes a suitable bedding material, although the female (doe) will pluck her own fur to line the nest when her litter is due to be born. Wire-mesh floors with a tray beneath are convenient, but if solid floors are used these should be sprinkled with fresh sawdust daily or every other day. Provided the standard of hygiene can be maintained, cages or hutches and their runs should be large. The absolute minimum is "1 sq. ft of floor space for each 1 lb weight of rabbit" *i.e.*, if there are two rabbits totalling 12 lb in weight there must be at least 12 sq. ft of floor space. In metric terms one can refer to approximately 200 cm^2 for each 500 gm of rabbit, this being a slightly more generous allowance but still on the low side.

Feeding.

The wild rabbit grazes at dusk and dawn, and it is preferable to feed tame rabbits twice daily, while pregnant or lactating does and young rabbits benefit from three meals a day. As in the case of guinea-pigs, the ratio may be thought of as consisting of two parts, a concentrate portion and a portion consisting of greenfood and other succulent material. The concentrate portion consists usually of a mixture of cereal grains or of some other form of mash. Successful mashes, of which there are many, include: (1) a mixture of 4 parts cereal grains and 1 part dairy cake; (2) equal parts of bran, weatings, flaked maize—or barley meal—and fish meal. This second is useful for breeding. If materials for the mash are in short supply they may in part be replaced by cooked potatoes. An average daily food allowance for a resting (non-breeding) adult of medium size would be: greenfood (grass, clover, weeds, lettuce, etc.) and/or roots 350–450 g; hay (good quality) 60–90 g; and concentrates (cereal grain or meal mash), 60 g. If cooked potatoes are used they should be fed at the rate of 4 parts to each 1 part of cereal that they replace. For a doe nursing her litter a suitable diet would comprise: greenfood to appetite, hay (good quality and preferably containing clover or other legume), 60–120 g; concentrates (preferably with fish meal or some other suitable source of "animal protein"), 120–180 g; and common salt at the level of up to 1% of the ration. A mineral mixture is preferable to salt alone. Excessive greenfood, especially in the form of cabbage and other Brassica plants, may cause polyuria, *i.e.*, the passage of excessive quantities of urine. No matter how much fresh greenfood rabbits may have available, a supply of fresh water should always be provided. The daily water requirement of the rabbit is quite high, and certain bad habits such as urine drinking or even cannibalism may result from an inadequate supply of water. Pots that cannot be overturned or, preferably, water bulbs or bottles as described for guinea-pigs, are the most suitable means of providing water.

Cubed diets, as described for guinea-pigs, are suitable for rabbits. Although the rabbit is capable of synthesising its own vitamin C, fresh greenfood is preferably fed in addition as a source of other nutrients, while the water requirement with diets of this kind is considerable.

Breeding.

The age of puberty varies with the breed, and also with the time of year at which the individual rabbit was born. Rabbits born in spring are usually capable of breeding at a younger age than those born in the autumn. In Great Britain the wild rabbit has a fairly sharply defined main breeding season, lasting from January to June, but some degree of "out-of-season" breeding may take place at almost all other times. Tame rabbits may not breed freely during the winter months, especially if environmental conditions are cold. Mating may take place as early as four months of age, and although this does not often result in pregnancy, it is accompanied by competition and fighting between individuals of the same sex. Males (bucks) and females should therefore be separated at weaning or at least before they are four months old. Fertile matings may occur at from about 5½ months of age onwards, but it is wise to defer breeding until later—say seven to eight months for most breeds. The female does not ovulate or shed her eggs from the ovary spontaneously as do most domestic mammals, but, like the cat and ferret, does so in response to the act of mating or some other strong stimulus. Even playing between two does may precipitate ovulation, in which case a so-called "phantom pregnancy" (pseudopregnancy) may result, the doe that has ovulated appearing pregnant and even developing lactating mammary glands. There is not therefore an obvious regularly recurring oestrus cycle as in the domestic rat, mouse, and guinea-pig, and in summer at least the doe may be ready to mate at almost any time. Observation suggests, however, that there are fluctuations in the desire to mate. The act of mating in rabbits sometimes causes alarm that all is not well to those that have not hitherto witnessed it, for the buck usually emits a peculiar cry and loses his balance to fall over sideways. It is usually best to separate the buck from the doe before the young are born. The gestation period is usually thirty to thirty-two days. In wild rabbits a high percentage of embryos die and are "resorbed," and are therefore never born. In some populations it appears that about two-thirds of all rabbits conceived (including about 60 per cent. of total litters) are lost before birth in this way. Losses from this cause are probably much less common in domesticated rabbits, especially when the standards of feeding and management are high. Litter size is variable, and depends in part on the breed or strain. In some strains mean litter sizes up to eight or nine have been obtained, but a mean of four or so is more common. Does that do not prepare the nest or rear their young properly should not be selected for further breeding. The doe with her new-born litter should not be disturbed unduly, or she may desert her young, which are blind and helpless at birth and are entirely dependent on her for at least three weeks, after which they begin to nibble food to supplement the milk that they receive from her. The eyes open at about fourteen days. Weaning should be carried out at between six and eight weeks of age, by which time the young should be able to fend for themselves completely.

Handling.

Rabbits should never be lifted by the ears alone. One good way of lifting them is to grip the ears firmly but gently with one hand and to place the other hand under the rump to take the weight of the rabbit's body. Alternatively, one hand may be placed flat under the rabbit's belly, but this requires more care, and may be a risky procedure with pregnant does. Another convenient way to handle rabbits, especially young ones, is to lift them by the loose skin over the shoulders. Rabbits can inflict quite nasty scratches with the nails of the hind feet. It is incidentally a good plan to examine the nails of all four feet and to trim them if they are too long. Care should be taken not to cut back as far as the "quick," *i.e.*, the bluish portion at the base of the nail that contains blood vessels.

Diseases.

In his chapter in the *UFAW Handbook*, Dr. C. E. Adams refers to a survey conducted on over 30,000 laboratory rabbits, which showed that in breeding colonies about one-fifth of all those that were born, died before they were fully mature, and that approximately half of these deaths occurred before weaning. Some 5% of bought-in rabbits also died. The most commonly reported diseases were intestinal ones and included enteritis, mucoid enteritis, impaction, scours and diarrhoea. Coccidiosis and respiratory diseases (snuffles and pneumonia) were also significant.

Coccidiosis is highly important in young animals. It may be either of the "hepatic type", affecting principally the liver, or the "intestinal type" affecting principally the gut. Even in the case of the hepatic type, however, the coccidial parasites are picked up by the mouth and after penetrating the intestinal walls make their way via the blood-stream to the liver. Hygienic measures are the best means of preventing the disease (see under Housing), but should it break out, prompt treatment with certain sulphonamides or other anti-coccidial drugs may prove effective. In certain rabbitries in which coccidiosis is a constant problem, protection has been obtained by feeding a dilute solution of one of the soluble sulphonamides in place of drinking-water. There are certain types of digestive disturbance that may resemble cocciosis, and one of these, the cause of which has not yet been established with certainty, is known as *mucoid enteritis*. Some such cases are probably variations of "*bloat*" ("the blows") a condition the cause of which is again not fully established, although there may in fact be several factors. A rabbit may, of course, "blow" after eating fermentative food but cases of "bloat" can occur independently of this, and some may be due to a virus.

Snuffles is characterised by a nasal discharge, and is not always associated with the same organism. In its milder forms it is not a severe disease, but with the more chronic forms the nasal discharge becomes marked and gives rise to a typical snuffling noise. Severe chronic cases become progressively worse and die of a terminal pneumonia. There is also a severe acute form in which the rabbit dies so rapidly that the condition is sometimes not recognised. Acute cases that are treated in time with certain sulphonamides may respond well but chronic snufflers are difficult to treat and go on spreading the infection, and hence are better destroyed. Correct environmental conditions are a great help in preventing this disease.

A chronic type of infection is known as *pseudo-tuberculosis*, which is usually acquired from eating material contaminated by wild rodents or by other infected rabbits. It is caused by quite a different organism from that of true tuberculosis, which is much rarer in rabbits. Clinical cases should be killed, and prevention lies in hygienic measures.

Infected wounds or skin abscesses may lead to a disease caused by the "necrosis bacillus" (*Fusiformis necrophorus*) and known sometimes as *necrobacillosis*. It is usually characterised by subcutaneous swellings distributed irregularly over the head and body. Although in the early stages the affected rabbit may remain in apparently good health, the spread of the disease is insidious and usually fatal, and in most instances it is kinder and safer to destroy a case before it progresses too far. There are, unfortunately, several other infectious conditions occurring in rabbits, but all call for expert help in diagnosis and treatment.

Among non-infectious conditions *pregnancy toxaemia* is not uncommon in does during the very late pregnancy, and usually proves fatal within two to three days. It is a "metabolic disorder" *i.e.*, it is associated with some functional derangement of the endocrine or ductless glands or with the inability to control properly the utilisation of its food. Faulty feeding is probably a contributory cause.

Ringworm is not common among external parasites but may be acquired from rodents. Affected rabbits that are to be treated must be isolated. *Ear mange* (known usually as *ear canker*) is common, and may be treated by strict attention to hygiene, with thorough disinfection of the hut or cage, and by dressing with a modern anti-mange preparation. *Body mange* is much less common but far more difficult to treat.

So-called "*bladder worms*," *i.e.*, the larval stages of two dog tapeworms (*Taenia pisiformis* and *Taenia serialis*) are quite common among internal parasites although rarely fatal. The feeding of grass or other greenstuff to which dogs have had access should be avoided, as well as the contamination of the drinking-water with dog faeces.

Myxomatosis has not died out completely in this country, and it is probably a wise precaution to vaccinate stock against it as recommended in suitable instances for all animal diseases. This, and other forms of prophylaxis and treatment should be carried out by, or with the advice of, a veterinary surgeon.

GERBILS

Description.

Gerbils, also known as jirds, sand rats and desert rats, are members of the sub-family *Gerbillinae* of the rodent family *Cricetidae*. There are some fourteen genera comprising some 50 species. The genera *Meriones* and *Gerbillus* are the most widely represented (about 14 and 10 species respectively). Virtually unknown in Britain until the mid-1960s, a few species have now been introduced from Asia, Africa and the Middle East, initially as laboratory animals.

Gerbils have now become immensely popular pets, both in schools and in the home, and provided one ensures that a docile species is acquired, one has perhaps the ideal pet mammal. They are virtually odourless, easy to handle and to breed, and pleasing to watch, both in appearance and antics.

Species differ widely in both size and disposition and hence one must take care when acquiring specimens. The Indian gerbil *Tatera indica* is, for example, large, aggressive and virtually untameable. Species recommended include *Gerbillus pyramidum*, *Meriones libycus* and *Meriones unguiculatus* (the Mongolian gerbil). The following advice applies to these species and particularly to the Mongolian gerbil—which is by far the most popular species available in Great Britain and hence the one most likely to be offered. There is a valuable chapter on this species by Dr. J. H. Marston in the *UFAW Handbook*.

Housing.

Gerbils appear to tolerate a wide range of temperature conditions. Petter has bred several species (though not *M. unguiculatus*) in outdoor conditions in Paris. There is no evidence to suggest that the Mongolian gerbil is less hardy, though indoor conditions are advised. Precautions against escape should be exercised since gerbils could become feral, and a pest.

Metal cages comprised largely of bars are recommended. Two-storey hamster cages are suitable and these enable one to watch the gerbils' complex and fascinating behaviour. Provide plenty of hay, straw or wood shavings and white paper. The animals shred material to make bedding and "nests." Since the animals are virtually odourless, as too are their urine and faeces, they need cleaning out less frequently than other rodents: once per two weeks suffices.

Either a pair of gerbils may be kept, or two males with two or three females. It is important, however, to introduce only young animals from separate litters into the same cage. Adults unused to one another are frequently hostile and aggressive.

Since the animals are burrowers in their natural state, they may be kept in a deep container, *e.g.*, a large aquarium, and supplied with a good depth of peat or a similar material. This method of housing, however, has the drawback that one sees little of the animals.

Pieces of wood provide a gnawing surface: very necessary for most rodents.

Feeding.

Virtually nothing is known of the gerbils' natural foods; still less their nutritional requirements. One must simply provide a range of foodstuffs from which the animals select what is adequate for their needs. Gerbils will take insects, spiders and meat, though they thrive on an entirely vegetarian diet.

Satisfactory foodstuffs include rodent pellets or a coarse seed mixture such as that sold for parrots or for wild birds. Sunflower seeds are taken with avidity as too is germinating grain (*i.e.*, soaked and allowed to grow for a few days to seedling stage). Pieces of raw fruit and vegetable are also consumed.

Water should be provided, though the animals drink little, particularly if vegetables are available.

Breeding.

As indicated under **Housing**, several adults may be run together.

Mating is rarely observed, though it is said to occur most usually in the late afternoon. Little is known about the breeding cycle.

The duration of pregnancy is about 25 days and the average litter number is about 6. Not infrequently the first litter is small in number and the young may be killed by the parents. Second and subsequent litters are usually reared successfully. Hair develops in 6–10 days and the eyes open at about 3 weeks. Varieties of gerbils have been reported since the late 1960s.

Handling.

Recently weaned specimens up to some 8 weeks of age require firm "cupping" in the hands since they are prone to jump with little regard for their own safety.

Regular handling over this age ensures a tame yet ever-inquisitive pet. Grasping by the base of the tail is usually necessary to enable one to remove the animal from a cage. Thereafter cupping is to be preferred.

Careless or over-enthusiastic handling of a timid individual sometimes produces a "fright reaction" where the animal lies trembling though otherwise almost inert for a minute or two. However, this soon passes.

Diseases.

Apart from the vulnerability of the first litter these animals are remarkably healthy. The result of fighting between adults from different cages is the only likely injury encountered apart from occasional skin infection around the nose and lips—possibly due to burrowing activity. This condition responds to a mild antiseptic cream.

Old animals may develop a condition where the eyeball tends to protrude. Neither cause nor cure has been investigated.

Any unwanted or infirm animal may be quickly and painlessly killed by the following procedure: put a little ether (diethyl ether) on a generous pad of cotton wool. Introduce this into a screw-cap jar, place the animal in, and fix the cap on firmly. Leave for 20 minutes.

HEDGEHOGS

Description.

The European hedgehog (*Erinaceus europaceus*), found throughout Great Britain, belongs to the Order Insectivora, of which moles and shrews are also members. Its diet is, however, by no means restricted to insects, although in nature a considerable portion is probably made up of small invertebrates. There is a good deal of prejudice against them as pets, owing to the fact that freshly caught specimens are usually infested with fleas or other external parasites. The spines of the hedgehog, being well-spaced, make the presence of external parasites more obvious than is the case in animals with a coat of close fur. The hedgehog's spines form its defence, and its capacity to roll up into a prickly ball at the threat of danger is well known. This defence reaction is unfortunately of no avail to it when the danger is an oncoming car or lorry, and thousands of hedgehogs die every year as a result of being killed by vehicles on the roads. Many other species of mammals wander on to the roads, but most attempt to flee when they sense the approach of a vehicle. The capacity to roll up is not secure defence even against animal enemies. There are some foxes, dogs, and cats that have learned to "uncurl" a hedgehog, and subsequently eat it.

Provided that care is taken, a hedgehog makes an excellent pet, especially if given a suitable enclosure in the garden. For a variable time during winter hedgehogs hibernate, and during this time they must not be disturbed. Should they emerge at any time however, food must be provided. Some specimens have lived for five years or more in captivity.

Accommodation.

The most satisfactory way to maintain a pet hedgehog is to provide it with a large "run" in part of the garden. If wire-netting is employed it should be sunk under the ground to a depth of several inches, or the hedgehog will burrow underneath and escape. The top of the run must be wired in, or alternatively there must be a "baffle board" or wire-frame (at least 23 cm wide) near the top of the sides to prevent escape that way, for hedgehogs can scale wire-netting—and some other types of fence—with ease. There should be a warm, dry box for shelter, containing wood-wool or other bedding material. A simple but suitable shelter may be made out of a soap-box, preferably lined with asbestos sheeting or some other material impervious to water. A shallow sunken bath in the enclosure may be of interest, for hedgehogs take well to water, but the edges should be such that the hedgehog can get out easily.

If it is decided to keep a hedgehog indoors, then the best accommodation is probably similar to that described for ferrets.

Feeding.

The simplest diet consists of milk, some bread, and minced lean meat. Cooked meat is preferred to raw, but raw liver should be given occasionally. Another satisfactory diet comprises meat offals, "root" vegetables (*e.g.*, carrot, potato, and swede), and wheaten wholemeal biscuit, steamed together until cooked, and then mixed and minced with a small proportion of raw liver. A small quantity (say 1–2 per cent.) of mineral mixture is also desirable, and milk should be given freely. Although hedgehogs appear to drink but little water, a fresh supply should always be provided.

Breeding.

During the breeding season marked changes occur in both males and females, and the structures associated with reproduction increase enormously in size from about March onwards. The female is capable of having two litters a year, the first in May or June and the second in August or September. The period of gestation has not been determined exactly, but is believed to be thirty-five days, possibly with variations of up to well over forty days. During the breeding season the males are very pugnacious towards each other if females are with them, and may do each other considerable damage. (The mixing of strange hedgehogs is often a difficult procedure anyway, for they often fight and inflict nasty bites on one another's feet.)

The litter size is usually four to six, and the young, which have "soft" spines, are suckled by their mother for nearly six weeks. The young can partake of some solid food at about three weeks, and there is some evidence that if left with their mother for longer than six weeks she may compete unfairly with them for food!

Diseases.

Hedgehogs in captivity are susceptible to *respiratory infections*, and can sometimes contract certain strains of *human influenza*. They are susceptible also to *Salmonellosis* (see under mice and guinea-pigs). Fleas and other external parasites have been mentioned; these often disappear spontaneously as the hedgehog begins to thrive in captivity, but if not they should be dealt with by modern methods. The nails of a hedgehog may need trimming.

LAND TORTOISES

Tortoises are popular pets, but although many have been kept with great success in Great Britain, the majority of those imported have never been looked after adequately, or have failed to thrive for other reasons.

Most land tortoises imported into Great Britain for sale through dealers have been:

(1) the Spur-thighed Mediterranean Land Tortoise (*Testudo graeca*), commonly known as the "Moroccan tortoise" and sometimes as the "Iberian" or "Algerian"; or

(2) Hermann's Tortoise (*Testudo hermanni*). The second is distributed in Southern France, Southern Italy, the larger islands of the Western Mediterranean, and parts of Yugoslavia, Albania, and Greece. There is a species found in Greece, the Margined Tortoise (*Testudo marginata*), but while adaptable to life in Great Britain, it is more difficult to acquire. The two common species differ in several ways, the "Moroccan tortoise" having a small bony spur on the back of the thigh. (The upper part of the shell is termed the carapace and the ventral portion the plastron.)

In selecting a tortoise one should ensure that the animal appears healthy. It should be active and withdraw quickly into its shell on being disturbed. Its legs should be firm and not limp, and there should be no abnormal discharge from the eyes or nostrils. The shell and limbs should be uninjured. Females are generally larger and have a shorter tail than the male. The shield above the tail is flat in the former and curved in the male. It is a good idea to obtain a pair or more of tortoises, but not more than can be looked after with care. On being purchased they should be washed in tepid water.

Many tortoises are given free range in gardens, but this is not advised with all, as they eat a wide variety of vegetables and young plants, and being wandering animals are liable to get lost if the garden is not completely fenced or walled. They should be provided with as large a "pen" or "run" as possible, the walls or wire-netting of which should be high enough to prevent their climbing over. The practice of tethering tortoises by a hole in the shell should be discouraged. They should always be provided with a box or shelter, the cheapest form being a wooden soap box turned on one side and with a sufficiently wide entrance, the wood being creosoted and covered with roofing felt. It can be lined with asbestos sheeting if desired, and have its floor covered with dry leaves or other bedding material. Some other shelter should also be provided in the run. The tortoises should be bathed during the hot weather. The occasional appliction of olive oil will keep the shell polished.

Land tortoises must be fed daily, and it is important to allow them to build up good reserves to enable them to hibernate through the winter successfully. Suitable foods include lettuce, young cabbage, peas, clover, dandelions, and a wide variety of green plants and ripe, sweet fruits. Generally bread and milk should be avoided. For young tortoises especially, it is recommended that once weekly or so the food should be sprinkled with powdered cuttlefish bone, or better still a small quantity of powdered calcium gluconate or cod-liver oil. Fresh water in a shallow tray, or even a saucer, should always be provided.

One of the most difficult problems in tortoise keeping is hibernation. Some persons avoid allowing their pets to hibernate by transferring them to a warm place, such as a heated greenhouse; if this is done they must be kept well fed and their place maintained at a summer temperature. It is imperative to do one thing or the other—the half-torpid tortoise that is neither hibernating nor kept at summer temperature will die. Moreoever, a tortoise that is allowed to hibernate must not be disturbed.

Signs of pending hibernation, including sluggishness and lowered appetite, are usually evident late in September or early in October. Tortoises living in the garden may commence to bury themselves. If this is allowed they must be well covered, else they may be killed by the ensuing frost. It is, though, more convenient and perhaps provides a greater chance of survival, due to the changeable winter conditions in Britain, to place the animal in a large box, which should be packed with straw, leaves, or hay. The box should be stored in a cool but frostproof place, such as out-building, cellar, or attic. It is important not to create conditions that will awaken the tortoise or tempt it to emerge before the following spring. Rats have been known to attack hibernating tortoises, and so precautions should be taken.

On emerging from hibernation the eyes and nostrils are somewhat sealed, and should be released by bathing with a 4 per cent. boric acid solution and warm water.

Recently imported female tortoises frequently lay eggs, but it is not a common occurrence for pairs to breed freely in Britain. During the early part of the summer the male is sometimes seen butting the shell of the female, this being a courtship action. If eggs are laid it is unlikely that they will be fertile, and less likely that they can be hatched. They have been hatched by placing them on damp sand and storing them in a warm place—a heated greenhouse or airing cupboard. The eggs should not be disturbed or "turned" once incubation has commenced.

Tortoise ticks are often present on freshly imported specimens, and may best be removed by damping the tick with paraffin or methylated spirits and then removing it gently with tweezers. Round worms are very numerous in tortoises, and should they be seen in the faecal matter the remainder may be eliminated by sprinkling up to one grain of powdered santonin on the food once a week for six weeks. Possibly, some of the newer, safe anthelmintic preparations containing piperazine derivatives may be equally effective. Eye infections are common, and are usually remedied by bathing the eye well with a 4 per cent. boric acid solution or warm cod-liver oil. Continuous discharge from the nose indicates lung infection, and as a primary measure the animal should be kept warm. Bleeding can be stopped by using Friar's Balsam, and care should be taken to prevent insects settling on open wounds.

WATER TORTOISES (TERRAPINS)

In Great Britain the tortoises that have become adapted to life in ponds and rivers are usually termed "terrapins," the name turtle being applied to marine forms. In the U.S.A. and Canada, however, not only the marine species but also terrapins and tortoises are all termed "turtles."

Several kinds of terrapin are available and capable of thriving in Great Britain. These include several American species, the European Pond Tortoise (*Emys orbicularis*), the Spanish Terrapin (*Clemmys leprosa*), the Caspian Terrapin (*Clemmys caspica*), and the Reeves' Terrapin (*Chinemys reevesii*), which hails from China and Japan.

The ideal place in which to keep terrapins is a garden pond within an enclosure. The pond should contain an "island" of dry ground on to which the animals can climb easily. The water should vary in depth, and at one point be at least 0·6 m deep. Provided that there is a suitable "island" the boundary walls of the pond can be upright to prevent escape. The final coat of cement should be smooth and mixed with a waterproofing agent. Shade should be available, not only on the island but also in some parts of the water. This may be provided by suitable plants.

Terrapins are almost entirely carnivorous, although the young of some species may take a little lettuce or other vegetable food. Suitable foods include *small* pieces of raw meat, raw liver (this should certainly be given from time to time), fish, and earthworms. Terrapins prefer to take their food in the water, and it is best to feed them individually if there are several, to ensure that each receives his proper share.

Water tortoises also hibernate. Some bury themselves in mud or sand at the bottom of their ponds, others will dig themselves into the earth in the island or banks of their pond, while others again may go to sleep in the box that, as in the case of land tortoises, should preferably be provided for them on part of their "land." Should they sleep at the bottom of the pond, it is as well to prevent freezing of the water. One means of doing this is to leave a log or logs floating on the surface. Moving these logs on cold mornings will help to break any ice formed and to prevent total freezing.

There is a valuable chapter on reptiles by Dr. D. J. Ball and Professor A. d'A. Bellair in the *UFAW Handbook*.

AQUARIUM FISH

There are two types of aquaria—the cold-water for fish from this and other temperate countries and the heated, for tropical varieties of fish. Apart from the fact that a suitable heating mechanism—usually electric, with thermostatic control—has to be maintained for tropical aquaria, the general principles governing the two types are much the same. There is a certain amount of additional initial expense in setting up a heated aquarium—the running costs are not high—but in some respects tropical fish are easier to maintain than many of the cold-water varieties.

It should be emphasised at the outset that those who want to keep fish should invest in a proper aquarium and not in a "goldfish bowl," unless the latter be very large in relation to the fish to be kept. Far too many fish suffer from overcrowding or from lack of sufficient water surface. In the case of cold freshwater fish such as carp and goldfish (which need quite different conditions from tropical fish) it has been calculated that every "1 inch of body" (*i.e.*, 2·5 cm) requires 1 sq ft (*i.e.*, 930 cm^2) of water surface in order to obtain sufficient oxygen for respiration. Thus a fish the body of which (*i.e.*, the length minus the tail fins) is 10 cm will require at least an area of 60 cm × 60 cm. Two such fish will require twice this area, and so on. In *The Right Way to Keep Pet Fish* by R. Dutta, it is pointed out that a goldfish should normally live for twenty-five years in a suitable pond, and grow to its full length of over 35 cm. There are few indoor aquaria capable of supporting many full-grown goldfish in adequate conditions, and indeed it is recommended that domestic varieties of goldfish such as shubunkins, fantails, veiltails, and orandas, which grow more slowly, are far better adapted to cold-water aquaria. Tropical fish of the varieties kept in aquaria are usually much smaller, differ in their oxygen requirements, and can be kept in more crowded conditions. Many have an average body length of only about 3 cm, and eighteen such fish may be maintained in a suitably heated tank with an area of water surface of 45 cm × 30 cm.

A beginner should not only read good books on the subject (including *Water Life* publications) *e.g.*, *Guide to Tropical Fish-keeping* by J. H. P. Brymer) but also consult experts and his local aquarist or dealer. There is a useful chapter by Dr. H. G. Vevers in the *UFAW Handbook*, while a symposia on *Diseases of Fish*, edited by the late Dr. Lionel Mawdesley-Thomas, was published for the Zoological Society of London by Academic Press. Whatever aquarium is chosen, the conditions should be correct *before* any fish are introduced. Should fish be suddenly acquired, before a proper aquarium has been fitted up for them, they should be kept in some temporary (but sufficiently capacious) quarters until the aquarium is ready.

The instructions for installing and fitting up an aquarium are usually supplied, and should be followed carefully. The sand that is usually placed on the bottom should be thoroughly washed, and is best put in a little at a time. Make sure that the inside of the aquarium is thoroughly clean before anything at all is put into it. Ornamental rocks may next be introduced, and great care should be taken to ensure that these are of the correct type, unlikely to harm the fish physically or chemically. Water is then added very gently indeed, and suitable plants set. In the case of large tanks the planting is best done when the tank is only partly filled with water, but in any event the plants themselves should be kept wet all the time, or they may quickly shrivel up. In the case of cold-water aquaria everything may now be left for a few days—preferably a week or more—to ensure that all is well, and to allow certain micro-organisms that help form the food of the fish to develop. In the case of heated aquaria it is necessary also to ensure that the thermostat is working correctly and that the temperature is remaining constant or within very narrow limits. Here again it is advisable to wait at least a week before introducing any fish. Should conditions " go wrong " before or after the fish are introduced, it is best to start filling the tank all over again.

Fish should not be overfed, although regular feeding is essential. Attention must be paid to the feeding instructions issued with prepared fish foods, and to details given by the supplier of " live " foods. Provided fish are neither overcrowded nor overfed, the amount of sediment that accumulates in the tank will not be excessive, but it should be siphoned away gently every month, or more often if necessary. Water lost by evaporation should be replaced, and in the case of heated tanks especially, it is most desirable that the added water be of the same temperature as that already in the tanks.

Certain species of water snail are often placed in aquaria to act as scavengers. It is necessary to ensure that, if snails are kept, they are of the right type, and it is important to consult experts on this matter.

Breeding is an interesting topic, there being both egg-laying and viviparous or " live-bearing " fish. The beginner is well advised to learn first how to keep fish in healthy condition in his aquarium before indulging in any planned breeding, and he should study the relevant information in books on the subject.

An aeration plant is often recommended on the grounds that it will increase the fish-carrying capacity of the aquarium. This is true up to a point, but overcrowding may bring other troubles besides those connected with lack of sufficient oxygen, and the golden rule is never to keep too many fish for the size of aquarium in question. Another factor to be remembered is that should the aerator break down it may leave the fish with less oxygen than their proper requirement. It has been recommended that an aerator is best thought of as a stand-by, to be employed only in emergencies, *e.g.*, when for some reason extra fish have to be added to a tank already holding all or almost all its proper capacity.

There are unfortunately many diseases of fish, and as yet scientific knowledge concerning many of them is far less detailed than it should be. It is clear, however, that environmental factors are responsible for many deaths or cases of unthriftiness, and among the factors concerned may be listed: overcrowding, overfeeding, the provision of a diet that is qualitatively inadequate, lack of " balance " in the aquarium leading to unsuitable conditions, dirt, too strong light, lead paint and noxious substances, that may somehow have come into contact with the water (*e.g.* from the hands of the person tending them) or been absorbed from the atmosphere. One must be careful of such things as disinfectants, soaps, petrol, etc. In the case of tropical fish the temperature of the water may be incorrect. Should fish troubles occur, therefore, it is as well to consider these various possibilities, although one should not hesitate to seek professional advice where there appears to be a case of infectious disease. An ailing fish should certainly be removed from the tank (assuming that there are other fish present) and given separate quarters of its own if such a course is feasible.

It is not intended to provide a description of the separate diseases, although it may be mentioned that such signs as the appearance of material resembling cotton-wool (actual fungal growths) and " rotting " of the tail or fins, are among those that should lead the owner to isolate affected fish and to seek help immediately.

No attempt is made here to describe any of the many different species and varieties of fish suitable for private aquaria. Some of the " points "

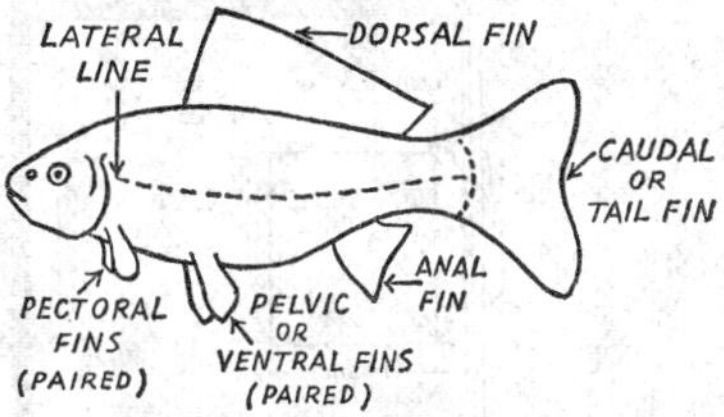

of a fish are shown in the accompanying illustration. Great care must be taken in mixing species, *e.g.*, " hard mouthed " and " soft mouthed " kinds should not be kept together. The temptation to put other species (*e.g.*, newts) with aquarium fish must likewise be avoided.

CAGE-BIRDS

Many species and varieties of birds are maintained successfully in captivity and there exists in Great Britain a general fancy that caters for a high proportion of the smaller adapted for cage or aviary life. The increase in the numbers of budgerigars after the end of the second world war was phenomenal, and by the peak year of 1957 it was estimated that there were over 6 million in the country, and that the corresponding figure for the USA, where the popular name for this species is " parakeet," exceeded 18 million.

There are various restrictions on the importation of certain types of cage bird but the following notes refer to species that have, generally speaking, been available from breeders or dealers.

The different types and sizes of birds have different requirements, and in the space available it is not possible to do more than cover the general principles and to deal briefly with the special characteristics of the management of the more easily maintained species. The beginner is advised to restrict his attention to one of the better-known species, *e.g.*, canaries or budgerigars, and not to attempt to maintain exotic varieties until he has acquired considerable experience.

Most species thrive best in aviaries, which may be indoor, outdoor, or of the combined " outdoor-indoor " type. An indoor aviary is usually all-wire and portable. The criticism of many such aviaries is that they tend to be high and narrow. whereas a fairly large floor-space is desirable. They should not be placed in cold or draughty places, nor too near a fire. If sited so as to receive much direct sunlight they must have adequate shelter. The wires must be close together, especially if smaller species are kept, a distance between them of about 10 mm being generally suitable. An outdoor aviary—suitable only for some species or at certain times in the case of others—should occupy a sunny position, although it too must include shade, and must be protected from winds. There ought in fact to be a sheltered portion, dry and well protected from the elements. The aviary must be strongly made and safe from all predators, including rats and mice. While it is often considered desirable to allow herbage to protrude through the wire-mesh floor, it is essential that the birds are never in close contact with wild rodents or their droppings. Most birds are highly susceptible to some forms of *Salmonellosis* (see under mice and guinea-pigs), and can contract them in this way. It is advisable also that the roof of the aviary is solid: corrugated asbestos sheeting, projecting well clear of the edges of the uprights so as to prevent water and other matter from entering the interior, is excellent. The droppings of wild birds may be a potent source of bacterial infection or of internal parasites. To prevent close contact otherwise with wild birds, the wire or wire-netting "walls" of the aviary may be double. If an "outdoor-indoor" aviary is employed, there is usually an indoor flight cage, separated from the external portion either by a very light hanging door of suitable size, through which the birds can easily push their way, or by a sliding partition that the owner can operate as required.

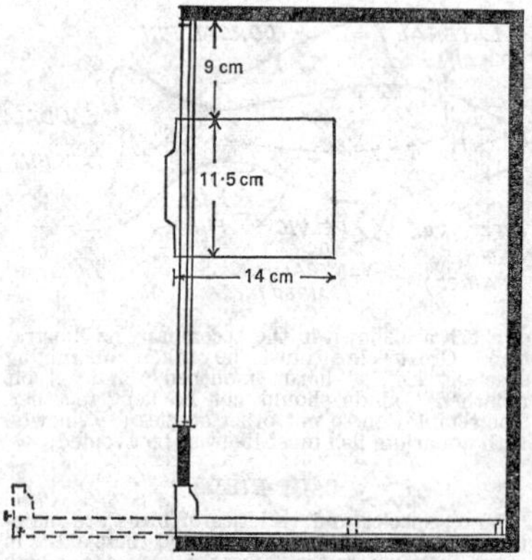

Section through Cage

If an aviary is out of the question, then a suitable cage should be purchased or constructed. The cage need not be ornate—indeed simplicity of design usually facilitates the highly important task of keeping everything clean—but it must be large enough. A cross-section through a breeding-cage suitable for canaries, and for many other species, is shown in the accompanying illustration. Such a cage should measure about 100 cm in length × 30 cm × 45 cm high. It is constructed of wood or some suitable sheeting except for the front, which consists of vertical wires with horizontal stays, and can be divided into two parts by means of a suitable partition containing a removable section made of wire. By this means the cock and hen canaries can be introduced into the separate sections and develop a courtship

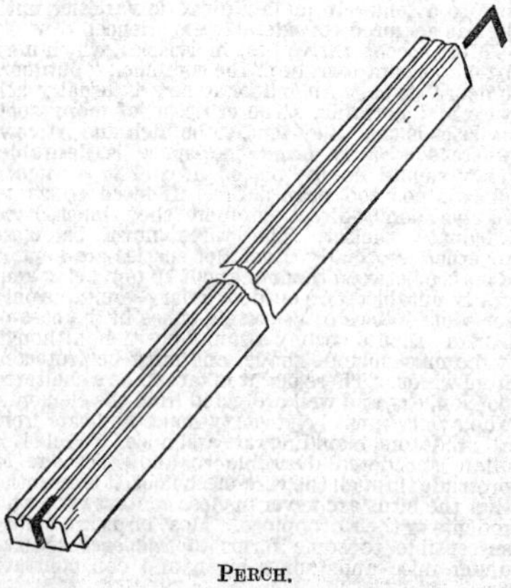
Perch.

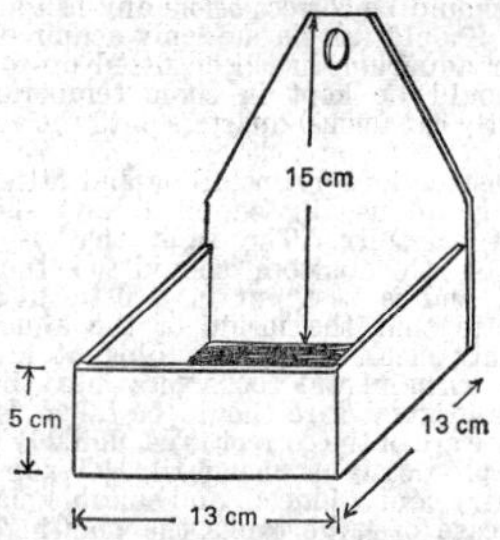

Nesting-box with Plain Wood Bottom.

before being allowed to be together for actual mating. The cross-section indicates the site and size of the removable portion of the partition, and it shows also the removable tray that is such an excellent fitting for almost any type of cage, and which greatly facilitates cleaning.

Whether an aviary or a cage is employed, it is essential to have proper fittings, including conveniently placed drinking-troughs, feeding-trays and bird-baths, and good perches. Much unnecessary discomfort is brought about through the use of unsuitable perches, or ones that are incorrectly situated or not sufficiently "firm." A suitable type of perch, of which there should be several in the cage or aviary, is shown in the accompanying illustration, and it should be of the appropriate dimensions for the size of bird. In the case of the larger canaries (Norwich and

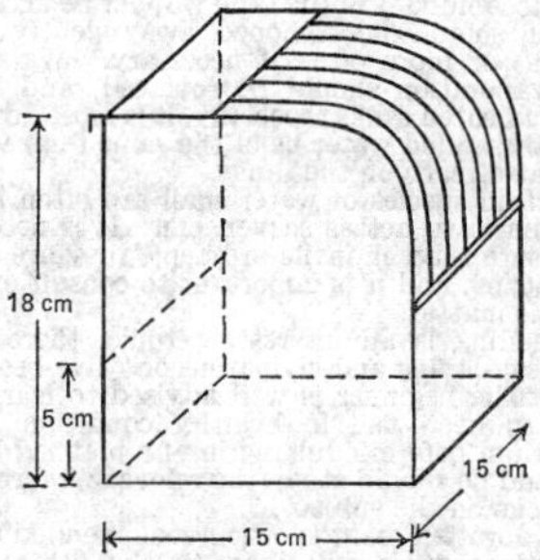

Bird Bath.

Yorkshire), *e.g.*, the sectional measurements should be 16 mm × 20 mm, whereas for a smaller canary (Border) they should be 13 mm × 20 mm. The type of perch shown is easy to clean and does not possess awkward corners in which parasites may be harboured. The dimensions of a nesting box a bird-bath, and a feeding-tray suitable for canaries are also given in the accompanying illustrations.

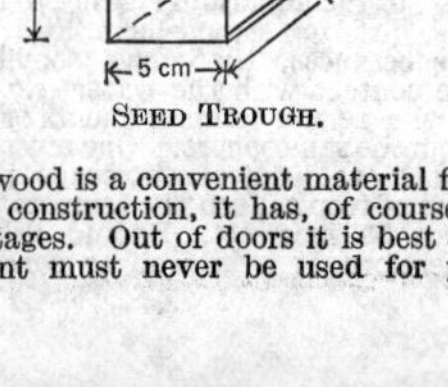

Seed Trough.

While wood is a convenient material for aviary and cage construction, it has, of course, several disadvantages. Out of doors it is best creosoted (lead paint must never be used for places in which birds or other small animals are kept), and indoors it is better lined with hard asbestos sheeting. Metal is suitable—provided that it does not rust or corrode and that the environmental conditions are warm enough.

In all cases a supply of clean, fresh water should be available. Strict cleanliness should be observed, and professional advice taken immediatey if a bird is not thriving.

Canaries (*Serinus cnarius*).

These are domesticated forms of the race of wild serin found in the Canary Islands, and may live up to twenty-five years. Many varieties are known, and although most individuals are " canary yellow," other colours have been developed by fanciers. Many books have been written about the canary, although there is still much to be learned concerning its feeding and diseases—as is indeed the case with almost all cage-birds. The system of feeding generally recommended is based upon a mixture of 2 or 3 parts of canary seed (which is rich in energy, and which is sometimes mixed with a little millet seed) to 1 part of summer rape seed, which is high in fat and protein. There seems to have been some difficulty in obtaining suitable rape seed in some areas since the war. The best is German summer rape or Rübsen rape. Other seeds are employed as substitutes, or for special purposes, *e.g.*, niger is usually added at breeding time, and linseed if there is any indication of premature or soft (out-of-season) moult. Good proprietary seed mixtures are available. A little greenfood should be provided twice weekly, and a piece of cuttlefish bone placed between the wires is a suitable source of calcium. Soft-bill food (containing boiled egg, dried egg yolk, dried flies, and ants' pupæ) is also recommended by many breeders, while others give chopped egg alone. Others again favour milk, especially for young birds.

Breeding is usually started late in March or early in April, but not unless the daily shade temperature is at least 10° C. The pairs should be selected earlier than this and transferred to breeding-cages, with the partition in position. By the middle of February the wire partition may be installed so that the two birds can see one another. A little niger seed is usually added to the diet, while finely ground oystershell or eggshell may be sprinkled on the floor. (Otherwise the floor may be covered with washed sand that is not too fine and is free from dust.) When the birds begin to feed one another through the wire they are ready for mating, and the partition may be removed. The nest-box can then be inserted and suitable nesting materials, *e.g.*, cow hair and moss, placed in the cage. The incubation period is thirteen to fourteen days. After the eggs are laid some owners prefer to separate the cock and the hen, but allow him to rejoin her after the young are all about eight to nine days old and have opened their eyes. If it is desired that all the chicks be hatched together then one can remove the first three eggs that are laid—usually one egg is laid daily—and keep them in a box at room temperature, substituting dummy eggs for them in the nest-box. On the afternoon of the third day of laying they are returned to the nest-box in place of the dummies.

When the young chicks are able to feed for themselves they should be provided with special food, such as egg and bread crumbs and a little cracked canary seed. If the cock bird interferes with them, or causes the hen to nelgect them, he must be returned to his own section. Usually, however, all goes well, and the hen will go to the nest again when the first chicks are almost sixteen days old. Some three or four broods may be raised in a season. There is a useful chapter on the canary by Dr. I. F. Keymer in the *UFAW Handbook*. Crosses between the canary and other birds, and indeed cross breeds in general, are dealt with by V. A. Carr in *Mule and Hybrid Birds* (London: Cage Birds).

Waxbills, Finches, and Other Seed-eaters.

The canary is of course a finch, but most of the other " foreign finches " are considered by dealers and writers together with other types of seed-eating birds. Well over 30 species of *Avadavats*, *Buntings*, *Mannikins*, *Cardinals*, *Whydahs*, *Weavers*, and *Finches* of various descriptions have been maintained successfully in captivity in Great Britain. One of the most popular is the *Zebra finch* (*Taeniopygia castanotis*), from Australia, which has bred so successfully in this country that supplies no longer depend upon fresh importations and which appears in several varieties. The native bird, and many of its descendants, are grey and white, with red beaks. The male bird has orange cheek-patches, and orange flanks with white markings. The throat has black barring on a white background, and indeed the characteristic markings of the male have been the subject of interesting behaviour studies. The female lacks these special markings. The species is hardy, and is capable of living in outdoor aviaries all the year round, so long as it has shelter from draughts or strong winds and adequate facilities for roosting. If provided with nest-boxes, the birds will attempt—often successfully—to breed all the year round, so to avoid overbreeding it is better to remove these boxes in winter. A mixture of millet and canary seed forms the basis of their diet, which should be supplemented with fresh greenfood, millet sprays, fine grit, and cuttlebone—and, of course, fresh water should be available. A useful introduction is *Zebra Finches* by C. H. Rogers (London: Iliffe). Another bird suitable for the relatively uninitiated bird-keeper is the *Bengalese* (a domestic variety of *Munia striata*). It seems that these birds are the result of careful breeding by the Japanese, and may be regarded as fertile hybrids. Three main forms, the Chocolate-and-White, the Fawn-and-White, and the White, have been developed. These birds will thrive in cages or in aviaries. As in the case of Zebra Finches, they will attempt to breed all the year round if provided with nest-boxes. Bengalese are sociable birds, sometimes known in the USA as Society Finches. They appear to require less additional food than most species, thriving on a mixture of canary and millet seed, together with grit, cuttlebone and an occasional millet spray or item of greenstuff.

For details of these birds, and of the many others from which a selection may be made, works of reference should be consulted. Three very useful books, all published by Cage Birds London, are *Foreign Bird Keeping*, by Edward J. Boosey, *Foreign Birds for Beginners*, by D. H. S. Risdon, and *Foreign Birds for Garden Aviaries*, by Alec Brooksbank.

Budgerigars.

The increase in the popularity of this bird has been phenomenal, although to those who have experience of other birds as pets the reasons are soon fairly obvious. Apart from the capacity to talk, shown by many birds—especially males kept alone and trained, there is a liveliness, almost a " cheekiness," and an apparent like of human companionship. The wild green budgerigar (*Melopsittacus undulatus*) exists in large numbers in the grassland and desert shrub regions of Australia. The usual colour is grass green—it is frequently known as the Grass Parakeet—with a yellow mask, with three black spots on either side. As a result of intensive breeding, a considerable number of colour varieties has been produced, and the genetics of colour are a constant source of interest to budgerigar breeders. A vast budgerigar " fancy " has been built up in the United Kingdom, the USA, and other countries, and World Budgerigar Congresses are held every few years. Budgerigars will thrive in outdoor aviaries all the year round, but the vast majority are kept as indoor pets in cages or small aviaries. The cages can be similar to those used for canaries and care should be taken that the perches are of the correct diameter. If nest-boxes are put up, and the environmental conditions are suitable, budgerigars suitably paired will breed at almost any time of the year. It is customary, however, to restrict breeding to the spring, summer, and early autumn. Overbreeding may lead to difficulties, including the production of " runners " or " French moult." The sexes may normally be distinguished, at any rate in mature individuals by the colour of the cere at the base of the beak, which is blue in males and brown in females. Males may lose their colour if not in good condition and for other reasons.

There are now many proprietary seeds mixtures, but some owners prefer to make up their own mixtures of millet (usually mixing small yellow and large white varieties) and canary seed. Millet sprays, fresh greenfood, good grit, and cuttlebone are all desirable, and it is important that the correct size and consistency of grit be chosen. Variety in "extras" to the basal seeds diet is probably important, for the captive bird has not the same opportunities as its wild ancestors for ranging widely for, possibly, important trace items of food. Breeding birds secrete a "milk," comparable with the crop milk of pigeons and some other birds, and this is of importance in the early feeding of the young.

Most healthy budgerigars seem to live to the age of 5–7 years or more, and considerably greater ages have been attained in captivity.

Such is the development of the budgerigar fancy that most equipment as well as food can be obtained ready for use. The playful habits of budgerigars have led to their being given table-tennis balls or a variety of small toys to play with, while some forms of food are supplied as budgerigar bells or otherwise in special shapes that seem to amuse the birds as they take the constituent seed from them.

The study of budgerigar diseases is in its infancy, but already some important facts have become realised. *French moult* is certainly reproducible by overbreeding, and may be linked with deficiencies in the ability of the parent birds to feed their young—or to hand over to them at the time of laying sufficient nutritional reserves to carry them through hatching and parental feeding until the time that they can fend for themselves. A deficiency in the "milk" has been shown in some cases, and may be generally true. Large chicks can be produced by killing off or removing all but a single member of the clutch, and allowing the parents to deal with it alone.

A mite infestation, due to *Cnemidocoptes pilae*, may give rise to *Scaly face*, *Scaly beak*, or *Scaly leg*, for which veterinary treatment is now available. Another condition, known as *Brown hypertrophy of the cere*, is characterised by thickening and darkening of the surface of the cere. In the early stages it is sometimes thought that the bird is changing its sex. There is no known successful treatment at the time of writing, and if the overgrowth is cut away it will only reform. These are various disturbances of the *digestive tract*, and some of these may be associated with inability to stand properly.

There are many treatises on the budgerigar, including the chapter in the *UFAW Handbook* by Dr. I. F. Keymer. Still a very useful work is *The Cult of the Budgerigar* by W. Watmough (London: Cage Birds) as is *Genetics for Budgerigar Breeders* by T. G. Taylor & Cyril Warmer (London: Iliffe).

Lovebirds and Parrotlets.

These birds are also members of the parrot family, and while they are unlikely to equal the budgerigar in popularity, they are nevertheless interesting birds that are being kept in increasing numbers as pets. Lovebirds, of the genus *Agapornis*, are African in origin, and some six species are commonly kept in captivity. Parrotlets derive from South America, the commonest species being the Guiana Parrotlet, *Forpus passerinus*. Both types of bird are relatively simple to maintain in aviaries or large cages, and their basal diet (which should be supplemented widely) is a mixture of millet and canary seed. They are hardy and vigorous creatures, many details of which are to be found in condensed form in *Guide to Lovebirds and Parrotlets* by E. N. T. Vane (Cage Birds). There are many works on the larger parrots, one that is still useful being *Parrots and Parrot-like Birds* by the Duke of Bedford with a section on diseases by David L. Coffin (Fond du Lac, Wisconsin All-Pets Books).

PONIES

Introduction.

As indicated for pets in general, it is necessary before acquiring any animal to consider carefully the time, expense and work involved: these factors are especially apt when contemplating the purchase of a child's riding pony. Doubtless every child, at some time or another, dreams of owning his or her own pony but it is not every family that can afford one in terms of space, time and cost.

Ponies are not machines to be ridden at one's whim: they require kindness, companionship and sensible treatment. Also one should never consider buying a pony without having acquired some background knowledge of equitation, saddlery and horsemastership. These skills can only be learnt by practical experience, and the best method is to enrol for a full course of instruction at a Riding School which has British Horse Society approved instructors. The address of the B.H.S. is 35 Belgrave Sq., London S.W.1 (01-235-6431). Horsemanship is a subject about which even the experts are still learning, but a valuable grounding for any child with a pony or with access to one is membership of the Pony Club which competently promotes better horsemanship for young people and which is associated with the B.H.S.

It is impossible in a few paragraphs to give a full outline of every aspect of horsemanship. The authors attempt only to cover the very basic management of a child's riding pony and leave the more expert matters, such as breaking-in, breeding and veterinary care, to be studied under the guidance of the appropriate professionals. Children wishing to keep ponies should, even after becoming competent riders, seek expert advice and read widely on the subject. An extremely valuable reference book to have is *The Manual of Horsemanship of the British Horse Society and The Pony Club* (London; The British Horse Society).

Description.

Ponies are, by definition horses who attain a height of not more than 15 hands (152 cm) at the highest point of the withers. (A "hand" is 4 inches, or approximately 10 cm). Larger children or young adults may require a horse, but a pony is suitable for a child in terms of size and temperament.

In the British Isles there are 9 breeds of native ponies which are renowned for their hardiness, sure-footedness and kind temperament: all are comprehensively described in *British Native Ponies* by Daphne Machin Goodall (London: Country Life). The 9 breeds are Connemara, Dales, Dartmoor, Exmoor, Fell, Highland, New Forest, Shetland and Welsh. These breeds of pure, or crosses between them, form the basis of the pony stock of this country and will be seen all over the British Isles, and in many other countries as well. The most usual colours are, depending on breed, black, brown, bay, chestnut, various greys, various roans, dun, piebald (black with white) and skewbald (any colour except black with white).

A pony at birth is a foal—either a colt (male) or a filly (female). After the age of 3, a filly is known as a mare and a colt, if left uncastrated, a stallion or entire. However, most colts—unless being kept for breeding purposes—will be castrated and are then called geldings. A gelding is considered more serene and manageable, and hence more suitable for riding.

Feeding and Accommodation.

The feeding of a pony will depend, to a great extent, on whether it is kept out at grass or in a stable, or by a combination of the two. The amount of food a pony requires will depend on the season of the year, the quality of the grass and the amount of work being undertaken.

For a pony kept at grass, there may be more than enough for it in rich pasture during the summer months, especially in some parts of the country, about which there will be local knowledge. Some ponies, especially those with a tendency to gain weight easily, may contract *laminitis* if grazing on lush grass, especially in May, is not restricted. This same pasture may have little or no feeding value from September through to April, again according to locality. A grass-kept pony requires, depending upon the quality of grass, a minimum of 1 acre, and 2 acres is more generous.

Preferably, a single pony should have up to 4 acres divided into sections. They are selective grazers, unlike cattle, and are best moved from one section to another periodically. This allows the grass to rest and is more economical in the long run. The land should be conserved by removing dung daily by barrow and shovel, or by harrowing periodically to spread the dung.

A very dry summer may make the grass bare and if the pony cannot be moved to better pasture, it will need supplementary feeding with hay.

During the winter months, extra feed will be needed. An average 13·2 hands high pony will need about 10 pounds (4·5 kg) of hay daily. Hay must be of good quality; mouldy or musty hay should never be fed. Sainfoin and meadow hay are probably the best two types for feeding. An average-sized pony will probably need two feeds of hay daily, fed either from the ground or from a hay-net tied high enough so that the pony cannot get his feet in it, even when it is empty. Hay-nets are economical methods of feeding as there is less wastage. It will take about 25 cwt (*c.* 1,275 kg) of hay to last the winter. If being worked daily, the pony will need about 3 pounds (*c.* 1·5 kg) of bruised or rolled oats and 1 pound (*c.* 0·5 kg) of bran mixed together, slightly dampened and fed in 2 feeds. For variety, boiled turnips, sliced carrots, beetroots, parsnips, mangels or swedes may be added. Manufactured horsecubes can also be incorporated into the feeds: these have proved very successful but must not, of course, be fed to excess.

Fresh, clean water should be available at all times and a mineral " salt lick " should be placed in the paddock or stable. A shelter should also be provided in the paddock, either by a thicket, coppice or high hedge on the north side, or a built shelter shed. Ponies are fairly resilient to the elements but a shelter is appreciated, particularly during the summer months in order to escape heat and flies. If the field is sectioned, the provision of water and shelter to cover all parts must be considered.

A stabled pony will require a loose box of about 10 feet (*c.* 3 m) × 12 feet (*c.* 4 m) with a door, in two parts, of about 4 feet (*c.* 1·25 m) in width. The floor must be non-slippery and impervious to moisture. Stable bricks are undoubtedly the best. Adequate ventilation is very important, and the stable should have a window, best when it opens inwards so that fresh air enters in an upwards direction and so goes over rather than on to the pony's back.

The floor needs to be covered with bedding—wheat straw, wood shavings or peat moss being the best—which will have to be " mucked out " each morning and " bedded-down " each evening.

A stabled pony will require more food—probably 3 feeds daily and a continual supply of water.

Food should be adjusted accordingly if the pony is kept by a combination of indoor and outdoor methods.

Grain foodstuffs must be stored in a dry, cool place, preferably in special bins with vermin-proof lids. Hay should be kept in a dry place, under cover.

General Management.

Ponies must be treated kindly, sensibly but firmly at all times. Shouting and sudden jerky movements of the arms will frighten them and should, therefore, be avoided. Always speak to a pony before approaching to handle it and before moving: this will warn and prepare it. Approach a pony at his shoulder, speak and then pat it on the neck or shoulder. Lead a pony from its near (left) side with one's right hand close to the bridle or head-collar and the left hand holding the slack of the rope. If a pony does not follow readily, persist patiently using the voice all the time: do not stare the pony in the eye or it will usually stop dead in its tracks. In order to turn a pony, push its head away rather than pull it towards one, as this will help it to remain better balanced and more co-ordinated.

A pony at grass should not be forgotten but visited daily, caught and checked over. When catching a pony, one should approach gently, offering a tit-bit in a feed-tin or bucket. If caught at feeding time, a pony soon associates the two and comes readily to its owner's call.

Grooming.

As well as improving the appearance and ensuring cleanliness, grooming helps to promote health and prevent disease. It is important that it should be carried out regularly, but not too frequently on a grass-kept pony as this may remove the insulating and waterproofing grease from the coat. A healthy pony should have a sleek, shiny coat indicative of good condition.

The basic grooming kit should consist of:

(i) a hoof pick for cleaning out the feet;
(ii) a dandy brush for removing caked mud and dust;
(iii) a body brush for removing dust and scurf from the coat and from the mane and tail;
(iv) a curry comb for cleaning the body brush;
(v) a water brush to use, slightly dampened, on the mane, tail and feet;
(vi) a stable sponge for cleaning the eyes, muzzle and dock and
(vii) a stable rubber to add a final polish.

The feet must be picked out daily—a stone left in the foot will probably lead to lameness—with a hoof pick and this should be done *downwards* from the heel towards the toe. This prevents any risk of the pick's penetrating the soft part of the " frog ", which is nature's anti-slipping device for ponies.

Shoeing.

" No foot—no horse " is a wise saying. Shoeing is necessary for ponies who are worked on roads or other hard surfaces which, without shoeing, would wear the wall of the foot away at a faster rate than it is replaced. The wall of the foot will grow whilst the shoes are on and so regular attention by a farrier or blacksmith is essential. Unshod ponies need their feet trimmed regularly, so that every pony should be seen by a farrier at least every 4–6 weeks or so. Shoeing is carried out either " hot " or " cold," and great care must be taken to ensure that the shoes fit correctly.

Saddlery.

The harness or " tack " for a pony should be well-fitting and clean. There are a great many items of saddlery available and the following are only the very basic ones:

Saddle
Girth
Stirrup irons
Stirrup leathers
Bridle
Headcollar and rope

Great care must be taken to ensure that a saddle does not pinch on the withers and that the girth is not likely to cause sores or " galls."

The " bit " of the bridle must be suitable for the pony's mouth, and most ponies can be ridden in a smooth-jointed snaffle.

All saddlery must be kept scrupulously clean, as this will improve appearance and keep the leather soft. Tack should be cleaned regularly, preferably every time it has been used. Leather should be cleaned with glycerine saddle soap, and metal washed, dried and then cleaned with metal polish (except the mouthpiece of the bit).

Saddlery should be stored in a dry place, the saddle itself put on a special purpose bracket and covered, and the bridle hung on a round or " half-moon " shaped hanger.

Saddlery is a vast and expert subject and an excellent book available is *Saddlery* by Captain E. Hartley Edwards (London: Country Life).

Diseases and Injuries.

These, almost without exception, call for prompt veterinary attention and any sign of lameness should not be neglected. A pony in good health is alert, has a shiny coat, quiet, regular breathing and a keen appetite. Any signs of it being " off-colour " should not be ignored. However, a useful reference book in which diseases and injuries are illustrated is the *TV Vet Horse Book* by " The TV Vet " (Ipswich: Farming Press).

INDEX

Each section has a letter and, where appropriate, the column is given in brackets after the page number, e.g., F8(1), G26(2).